This Edition To: BR
Forward Earlier
Edition To: TSD

2016

REDBOOKS™

REDBOOKS
Brands, Marketers, Agencies. Search Less. Find More.

Content Operations:
General Manager: Peter Valli
Operations Manager: Patricia M. Phillips
Content Analysts: Himanshu P. Goodluck, Sarah E. Cox

2016

REDBOOKS™

Advertisers Indexes

QUESTIONS ABOUT THIS PUBLICATION?

For CONTENT questions concerning this publication, please call:
The Content Operations Department at 800-908-5395, press 3

For CUSTOMER SERVICE ASSISTANCE concerning shipments, billing or other matters, please call:
The Customer Service Department at 800-908-5395, press 2

For SALES ASSISTANCE, please call:
The Sales Department at 800-908-5395, press 1

ISBN Number:
Vol. 1 978-1-9376-0622-0 (Business Classifications volume)
978-1-9376-0623-7 (Geographic volume)

Red Books LLC
Content Operations
330 Seventh Avenue, Floor 10
New York, NY 10001

www.redbooks.com

CONTENTS

How to Use the *Indexes* Edition vii

Product Categories by State 1
Brands and Products Index 151
S.I.C. Index 867
Personnel Index 1033
Alphabetical Compendium of N.A.I.C.S. Codes 1421
Numerical Compendium of N.A.I.C.S. Codes 1431
Alphabetical Compendium of S.I.C Codes 1441
Numerical Compendium of S.I.C Codes 1453

HOW TO USE THE *INDEXES EDITION*

REDBOOKS™ - Indexes edition provides a comprehensive overview of over 12,700 companies in the United States and Canada that spend at least $50,000 on national or regional advertising campaigns. (For the purpose of this book, a regional campaign is one in which a company uses media that broadcasts its message in two or more states.) Arranged in an easy to use two volume format, this directory provides several different ways for the user to locate detailed information on companies that advertise. The following guidelines are intended to help you find the data you need in the most logical way and to make that information work to your maximum benefit.

USING THE INDEXES VOLUME

The *Indexes* edition is designed to help you quickly and easily locate companies and individuals of particular importance with four easy-to-use indexes: the Product Categories by State Index, the Brands & Products Index, the S.I.C. Index and the Personnel Index.

Note Regarding Page References In each index, you will notice that there are two sets of page references for each listing. The first reference, in italic type, will direct you to the company's listing in the Business Classifications edition of the directory. The page reference in regular type, on the other hand, will highlight the company's entry in the Geographic edition.

Locating Entries Geographically Within Each Classification If you are interested in companies featured in a particular classification but you only want to find those within a specific geographic area, consult the **Product Categories by State Index**. This index arranges the companies found in each of the 56 classifications alphabetically by state and by city within each state. Canadian companies can be found at the end of each classification section. You can find such valuable data as the company's street address, zip code, and the page reference to its entry in volume one.

Apparel I - Women's, Children's & Infants' Wear

ALABAMA
RUSSELL CORP., ATHLETIC DIV., PO Box 272,
Alexander City, 35010, *pg. 27*, pg. 1
RUSSELL CORP., JERZEES DIV., Drawer 272,
Alexander City, 35010, *pg. 28*, pg. 1

CALIFORNIA
GUESS ?, INC., 1444 S Alameda, **Los Angeles**,
90021, *pg. 22*, pg. 88
LANZ, INC., 525 Brannan St, Ste 300, **San Francisco**,
94107, *pg. 24*, pg. 134

Locating a Company If You Know the Brand Name If you know the name of a product, but cannot identify its manufacturer, the **Brands and Products Index** will be particularly helpful. This index presents over 93,000 major trade names in common use by national advertisers. Each listing includes a brief description of the product, the manufacturer's name, and the page reference to the company's entry in volume one.

CUSTOM CLUB INTERNATIONAL—Apparel—PHILLIPS-
VAN HEUSEN CORPORATION, *pg. 41*, pg.1024
CUSTOM COLOR—Pencils—DIXON TICONDEROGA
COMPANY, *pg. 331*, pg. 272
CUSTOM CURL—Beauty Prods.—WINDMERE
DURABLE HOLDINGS, *pg. 414*, pg. 273
CUSTOM DESIGNS—Waterbed Linens—SPRINGS

INDUSTRIES, INC., *pg. 552*, pg. 1331
CUSTOM FIT SEATING—Ergonomic Seating—DOMORE
CORPORATION, *pg. 331*, pg. 484

Searching for Companies in a Given Line of Business If you need to identify companies that manufacture a certain type of product, the **S.I.C. Index** will simplify your search. This index groups all the companies in the book by areas of business. The index itself is arranged numerically by S.I.C. code, and then alphabetically by company. The S.I.C. Index is preceded by alphabetical and numerical compendiums. If you know the S.I.C. code of a company and need to know what the code represents, use the numerical compendium. On the other hand, if you know the product or service and do not know its corresponding S.I.C. code, start with the alphabetical compendium. (NEC in a category heading stands for "Not Elsewhere Classified.")

3715-TRUCK TRAILERS

CMI CORPORATION, *pg. 180*, pg. 1214
CRANE CARRIER COMPANY, *pg. 182*, pg. 1220
CSN, INC., *pg. 180*, pg. 1180
DORSEY TRAILERS, INC., *pg. 182*, pg. 310

Locating Executive Personnel If you are looking for a certain executive involved in a company's advertising or marketing operations, the **Personnel Index** is a useful reference tool. From the over 113,000 corporate personnel featured in the volume one listings, this index compiles over 50,000 advertising/marketing decision makers into one handy location. In addition to the individual's name, the index also provides their title, the name of their company along with its city and state, and the page number referencing you to the company's listing in volume one.

Lindahl, Carol A., Dir-Corp Commun—
Guidant Corp.-Cardiac Rhythm Mngmt. Grp., Saint Paul, MN,
pg. 1297, pg. 731
Linde, Ken, Dir-Sls—Phase Linear, Lincolnshire, IL,
pg. 519, pg. 276
Lindeke, Ronald C., Dir—Commun-Lockheed
Martin Skunk Works, Palmdale, CA,
pg. 241, pg. 111

OTHER WAYS TO FIND USEFUL INFORMATION

Finding Individual Companies If there is a particular company you need data about, you can consult the **Index of Companies** in volume one.

DANIEL, MANN, JOHNSON & MENDENHALL, pg. 84
DANIEL VALVE COMPANY, pg. 1405
DANIELS, INC., pg. 578
THE DANIS COMPANIES, pg. 1171

Note in the example above that company names beginning with a person's name are alphabetized according to the last name followed by the first name or initials.

Companies who wish to add or correct their listings can send information to:
Patricia Phillips, Operations Manager
Red Books LLC
330 Seventh Avenue, 10th Floor, New York, NY 10001
Tel: (646) 710-4465
E-mail: patricia.phillips@redbooks.com

In addition to keeping the information in our directories as up to date as possible, we are constantly trying to improve their design and add useful new features. Any comments or suggestions in this regard can be directed to the General Manager at the above address.

PRODUCT CATEGORIES BY STATE

Accessories, Jewelry & Watches

California

AMINCO INTERNATIONAL (USA) INC., 20571 Crescent Bay Dr, **Lake Forest,** CA 92630-8825, *pg.* 1, *pg.* 120
CHARISMA BRANDS, LLC, 23482 Peralta Dr Ste A, **Laguna Hills,** CA 92653, *pg.* 2, *pg.* 120
CHASE-DURER LTD., 9601 Wilshire Dr Ste 1118, **Beverly Hills,** CA 90210, *pg.* 3, *pg.* 46
CITIZEN WATCH CO. OF AMERICA, INC., 1000 W 190th St, **Torrance,** CA 90502, *pg.* 3, *pg.* 293
HARRY KOTLAR & CO., INC., 607 S Hill St Ste 710, **Los Angeles,** CA 90014, *pg.* 6, *pg.* 132
MONEX DEPOSIT COMPANY, 4910 Birch St, **Newport Beach,** CA 92660-8100, *pg.* 10, *pg.* 165
TACORI ENTERPRISES, 1736 Gardena Ave, **Glendale,** CA 91204, *pg.* 13, *pg.* 99

Colorado

ROYAL GOLD, INC., 1660 Wynkoop St Ste 1000, **Denver,** CO 80202-1115, *pg.* 11, *pg.* 323

Connecticut

BREITLING USA, 206 Danbury Rd, **Wilton,** CT 06897, *pg.* 2, *pg.* 385
TIMEX CORPORATION, 555 Christian Rd, **Middlebury,** CT 06762, *pg.* 14, *pg.* 355

Florida

BIRKS & MAYORS INC., 5870 N Hiatus Rd, **Tamarac,** FL 33321, *pg.* 1, *pg.* 470
FORWARD INDUSTRIES, INC., 477 S Rosemary Ave, Ste 217-219, **West Palm Beach,** FL 33401, *pg.* 5, *pg.* 478
MERCURY LUGGAGE/SEWARD TRUNK, 4843 Victor St, **Jacksonville,** FL 32207-7963, *pg.* 9, *pg.* 434
RICHLINE GROUP, INC., 6701 Nob Hill Rd, **Tamarac,** FL 33321, *pg.* 11, *pg.* 470
TRAVELPRO INTERNATIONAL, INC., 700 Banyan Trl, **Boca Raton,** FL 33431, *pg.* 14, *pg.* 413

Georgia

LAURA PEARCE, LTD., 2300 Peachtree Rd NW Ste A103, **Atlanta,** GA 30309, *pg.* 8, *pg.* 513

Illinois

MAUI JIM, INC., 1 Aloha Ln, **Peoria,** IL 61615-1871, *pg.* 9, *pg.* 651
ROGERS & HOLLANDS ENTERPRISES INC., 20821 Cicero Ave, **Matteson,** IL 60443-1201, *pg.* 11, *pg.* 631
WELLS LAMONT CORPORATION, 6640 W Touhy Ave, **Niles,** IL 60714-4516, *pg.* 15, *pg.* 638

Indiana

HERFF JONES, INC., 4501 W 62nd St, **Indianapolis,** IN 46268-2587, *pg.* 7, *pg.* 686
VERA BRADLEY, INC., 12420 Stonebridge Rd, **Roanoke,** IN 46783, *pg.* 15, *pg.* 697

Louisiana

STULLER, INC., 302 Rue Louis XIV, **Lafayette,** LA 70508, *pg.* 13, *pg.* 745

Maine

THE PORT CANVAS COMPANY, 39 Limerick Rd, **Kennebunkport,** ME 04046, *pg.* 11, *pg.* 750

Maryland

NIKAIA, INC., 7962 Old Georgetown Rd 3C, **Bethesda,** MD 20814, *pg.* 10, *pg.* 765

Massachusetts

BUXTON ACQUISITION CO., LLC, 245 Cadwell Dr, **Springfield,** MA 01104, *pg.* 2, *pg.* 845
CHELSEA CLOCK CO., INC., 101 2nd St, **Chelsea,** MA 02150, *pg.* 3, *pg.* 814
ELECTRIC TIME CO., INC., 97 W St, **Medfield,** MA 02052, *pg.* 4, *pg.* 832
HEARTS ON FIRE COMPANY, 99 Summer St, **Boston,** MA 02110, *pg.* 6, *pg.* 796
LONG'S JEWELERS LTD., 60A S Ave, **Burlington,** MA 01803, *pg.* 8, *pg.* 805
ROMAN RESEARCH, INC., 800 Franklin St, **Hanson,** MA 02341-1002, *pg.* 11, *pg.* 824
SAMSONITE CORPORATION, 575 W St Ste 110, **Mansfield,** MA 02048, *pg.* 11, *pg.* 830

Michigan

HOWARD MILLER COMPANY, 860 E Main Ave, **Zeeland,** MI 49464-1300, *pg.* 7, *pg.* 914

Minnesota

JOSTENS, INC., 5501 American Blvd W, **Minneapolis,** MN 55437, *pg.* 7, *pg.* 938

Missouri

HELZBERG'S DIAMOND SHOPS, INC., 1825 Swift Ave, **Kansas City,** MO 64116-3644, *pg.* 6, *pg.* 984

Nebraska

ELISA ILANA CUSTOM DESIGNS, 13132 Deven Port St, **Omaha,** NE 68154, *pg.* 4, *pg.* 1015

Nevada

UNIVERSAL WATCH CO., INC., 5016 Schuster St, **Las Vegas,** NV 89118, *pg.* 15, *pg.* 1030

New Jersey

BERGIO INTERNATIONAL, INC., 12 Daniel Rd E, **Fairfield,** NJ 07004, *pg.* 1, *pg.* 1065
BRAUNSCHWEIGER JEWELERS, 33 S St, **Morristown,** NJ 07960-4137, *pg.* 2, *pg.* 1088
CRYSTAL WORLD, INC., 89 Leuning St Unit A 2, **South Hackensack,** NJ 07606, *pg.* 4, *pg.* 1122
GEORGE GLOVE CO., INC., 301 Greenwood Ave, **Midland Park,** NJ 07432-1446, *pg.* 5, *pg.* 1084
HARTGERS DIAMONDS, LTD., 699 Wyckoff Ave, **Wyckoff,** NJ 07841, *pg.* 6, *pg.* 1134
MOVADO GROUP, INC., 650 From Rd Ste 375, **Paramus,** NJ 07652-3556, *pg.* 10, *pg.* 1101
OMEGA WATCH COMPANY, 1200 Harbor Blvd, **Weehawken,** NJ 07086, *pg.* 10, *pg.* 1131
SAFILO USA INC., 801 Jefferson Rd, **Parsippany,** NJ 07054, *pg.* 11, *pg.* 1106
SANTA FE LEATHER CORPORATION, 223 S Van Brunt St, **Englewood,** NJ 07631-4010, *pg.* 12, *pg.* 1059
SEIKO CORPORATION OF AMERICA, 1111 McArthur Blvd, **Mahwah,** NJ 07430-2038, *pg.* 12, *pg.* 1082
SWATCH GROUP USA, 1200 Harbor Blvd, **Weehawken,** NJ 07086, *pg.* 13, *pg.* 1131
TUMI, INC., 1001 Durham Ave, **South Plainfield,** NJ 07080, *pg.* 15, *pg.* 1123

New York

ARMITRON WATCH DIVISION, 6015 Little Neck Pkwy, **Little Neck,** NY 11362, *pg.* 1, *pg.* 1174
ASCH/GROSSBARDT, INC., 580 5th Ave Ste 918, **New York,** NY 10036, *pg.* 1, *pg.* 1197
AUDEMARS PIGUET (NORTH AMERICA), 40 E 57th St, **New York,** NY 10022, *pg.* 1, *pg.* 1198
BAUME & MERCIER, INC., 645 5th Ave Fl 6, **New York,** NY 10022-5346, *pg.* 1, *pg.* 1201
BRIGGS & RILEY TRAVELWARE, 400 Wireless Blvd, **Hauppauge,** NY 11788-3934, *pg.* 2, *pg.* 1164
BULGARI CORPORATION OF AMERICA, 625 Madison Ave, **New York,** NY 10022, *pg.* 2, *pg.* 1208
BULOVA CORPORATION, One Bulova Ave, **Woodside,** NY 11377-7826, *pg.* 2, *pg.* 1356
CARELLE LTD., 2 W 46th St Ste 709, **New York,** NY 10036, *pg.* 2, *pg.* 1209
CHRISTOPHER DESIGNS, INC., 50 W 47th St Ste 1507, **New York,** NY 10036, *pg.* 3, *pg.* 1212
COACH, INC., 516 W 34th St, **New York,** NY 10001-1311, *pg.* 3, *pg.* 1214
CROTON WATCH COMPANY & NATIONWIDE TIME, 250 W Nyack Rd, Ste 114, **West Nyack,** NY 10994, *pg.* 4, *pg.* 1350
DAVID BIRNBAUM/RARE 1 CORPORATION, 589 5th Ave Ste 710, **New York,** NY 10017, *pg.* 4, *pg.* 1221
DE HAGO, INC., 38 W 48th St Ste 600, **New York,** NY 10036, *pg.* 4, *pg.* 1222
THE ECHO DESIGN GROUP, INC., 10 E 40th St 16th Fl, **New York,** NY 10016, *pg.* 4, *pg.* 1226
EMPIRE DIAMOND CORPORATION, 350 5th Ave, **New York,** NY 10118, *pg.* 4, *pg.* 1227
EUGENE BIRO CORP., 581 5th Ave 3rd Fl, **New York,** NY 10017, *pg.* 5, *pg.* 1230
FOWNES BROTHERS & CO., INC., 16 E 34th St 5th Fl, **New York,** NY 10016-2203, *pg.* 5, *pg.* 1233
GENEVA WATCH GROUP, 47-14 32nd St, **Long Island City,** NY 11101, *pg.* 5, *pg.* 1174
GEVRIL USA, 9 Pine Crest Rd, **Valley Cottage,** NY 10989, *pg.* 6, *pg.* 1348
GORDON INDUSTRIES LTD., 1500 Plz Ave, **New Hyde Park,** NY 11040, *pg.* 6, *pg.* 1184
GUCCI AMERICA INC., 685 5th Ave, **New York,** NY 10022-4204, *pg.* 6, *pg.* 1237
HARRY WINSTON, INC., 718 5th Ave, **New York,** NY 10019, *pg.* 6, *pg.* 1238
HERMES OF PARIS, INC., 55 E 59th St #3, **New York,** NY 10022-1199, *pg.* 7, *pg.* 1240
JOHN HARDY USA, INC., 601 W 26th St 19th Fl, **New York,** NY 10001, *pg.* 7, *pg.* 1246
JUDITH RIPKA COMPANIES INC., 200 Madison Ave, **New York,** NY 10016-3902, *pg.* 7, *pg.* 1247
KARAT PLATINUM LLC, 15 Hoover St, **Inwood,** NY 11096, *pg.* 7, *pg.* 1168
KWIAT INC., 725 Madison Ave, # 14, **New York,** NY 10022, *pg.* 8, *pg.* 1249
LAZARE KAPLAN INTERNATIONAL, INC., 19 W 44th St, **New York,** NY 10036, *pg.* 8, *pg.* 1250
LOU MADDALONI JEWELERS INC., 1870 E Jericho Tpke, **Huntington,** NY 11743, *pg.* 8, *pg.* 1168
LUXOTTICA GROUP, 12 Harbor Park Dr, **Port Washington,** NY 11050-4625, *pg.* 8, *pg.* 1323
LVMH INC., 19 E 57th St 5th Fl, **New York,** NY 10022-2508, *pg.* 9, *pg.* 1254
MARTIN FLYER INC., 48 W 48th St, **New York,** NY 10036, *pg.* 9, *pg.* 1257
MELE COMPANIES, INC., 2007 Beechgrove Pl, **Utica,** NY 13501, *pg.* 9, *pg.* 1347
MICHAEL ANTHONY JEWELERS, INC., 115 S MacQuesten Pkwy, **Mount Vernon,** NY 10550-1724, *pg.* 10, *pg.* 1183
MIKIMOTO (AMERICA) CO. LTD., 730 5th Ave, **New York,**

First page reference indicates Business Class Edition
Second page reference indicates Geographic Edition

NY 10019-5429, *pg.* 10, *pg.* 1260

M.Z. BERGER & CO., INC., 29 76 Northern Blvd 4th Fl, **Long Island City,** NY 11101, *pg.* 10, *pg.* 1175

PARIS ACCESSORIES, INC., 1385 Broadway 21st Fl, **New York,** NY 10018, *pg.* 10, *pg.* 1276

PLATINUM GUILD INTERNATIONAL (USA) JEWELRY, INC., 500 5th Ave Ste 5120, **New York,** NY 10110, *pg.* 10, *pg.* 1282

ROLEX WATCH U.S.A., INC., 665 5th Ave, **New York,** NY 10022, *pg.* 11, *pg.* 1286

THE SARUT GROUP, 780 Humbolted St, **Brooklyn,** NY 11222, *pg.* 12, *pg.* 1146

SOLO, 400 Wireless Blvd, **Hauppauge,** NY 11788-3934, *pg.* 12, *pg.* 1165

SWANK, INC., 90 Park Ave, **New York,** NY 10016, *pg.* 13, *pg.* 1297

TANO, INC., 350 Lexington Ave, **Mount Kisco,** NY 10549-2725, *pg.* 13, *pg.* 1183

TIFFANY & CO., 200 5th Ave, **New York,** NY 10010, *pg.* 13, *pg.* 1299

TIFFANY & CO. INTERNATIONAL, 600 Madison, **New York,** NY 10022, *pg.* 14, *pg.* 1300

TOURNEAU INC., 3 E 54th St 3rd Fl, **New York,** NY 10022-3108, *pg.* 14, *pg.* 1303

VAN CLEEF & ARPELS, INC., 12 W 57th St, **New York,** NY 10019, *pg.* 15, *pg.* 1308

YURMAN DESIGN, INC., 24 Vestry St, **New York,** NY 10013, *pg.* 15, *pg.* 1316

North Carolina

CHARLES & COLVARD LTD, 300 Perimeter Park Ste A, **Morrisville,** NC 27560, *pg.* 3, *pg.* 1384

REEDS JEWELERS, INC., 2525 S 17th St, **Wilmington,** NC 28401-7705, *pg.* 11, *pg.* 1393

Ohio

LUXOTTICA RETAIL, 4000 Luxottica Pl, **Mason,** OH 45040, *pg.* 8, *pg.* 1460

PUPPYPAWS, INC., Fairhaven Rd, **Mayfield Heights,** OH 44124, *pg.* 11, *pg.* 1463

STERLING JEWELERS INC., 375 Ghent Rd, **Akron,** OH 44333-4601, *pg.* 13, *pg.* 1402

TOTES ISOTONER CORPORATION, 9655 International Blvd, **Cincinnati,** OH 45246, *pg.* 14, *pg.* 1426

Oklahoma

MCCUBBIN HOSIERY, INC., 815 Robert S Kerr Ave, **Oklahoma City,** OK 73106, *pg.* 9, *pg.* 1486

Pennsylvania

CRAIGER DRAKE DESIGNS, 1701 Walnut St, Fl 5, **Philadelphia,** PA 19103, *pg.* 4, *pg.* 1562

LAGOS INC., Rittenhouse Sq 1735 Walnut St, **Philadelphia,** PA 19103, *pg.* 8, *pg.* 1566

THE PENN COMPANIES, 10909 Dutton Rd, **Philadelphia,** PA 19154-3203, *pg.* 10, *pg.* 1568

Rhode Island

ALEX AND ANI, 2000 Chapel View Blvd, **Cranston,** RI 02920, *pg.* 1, *pg.* 1600

DANECRAFT INC., 1 Baker St, **Providence,** RI 02905-4417, *pg.* 4, *pg.* 1606

FGX INTERNATIONAL, INC., 500 George Washington Hwy, **Smithfield,** RI 02917, *pg.* 5, *pg.* 1608

IMPERIAL-DELTAH, INC., 795 Waterman Ave, **East Providence,** RI 02914-1713, *pg.* 7, *pg.* 1601

SWAROVSKI NORTH AMERICA LIMITED INC., 1 Kenney Dr, **Cranston,** RI 02920-4468, *pg.* 13, *pg.* 1600

UNCAS MANUFACTURING COMPANY, 150 Niantic Ave, **Providence,** RI 02907-3118, *pg.* 15, *pg.* 1608

W.R. COBB COMPANY, 800 Waterman Ave, **East Providence,** RI 02914, *pg.* 15, *pg.* 1601

Tennessee

JEWELRY TELEVISION, 9600 Parkside Dr, **Knoxville,** TN 37922, *pg.* 7, *pg.* 1637

Texas

BARRINGTON GROUP LTD., 2300 N Hasko Ave, **Dallas,** TX 75204, *pg.* 1, *pg.* 1676

DGSE COMPANIES, INC., 11311 Reeder Rd, **Dallas,** TX 75229, *pg.* 4, *pg.* 1680

FOSSIL GROUP, INC., 901 S. Central Expressway, **Richardson,** TX 75080, *pg.* 5, *pg.* 1735

HATCO, INC., 601 Marion Dr, **Garland,** TX 75042-7930, *pg.* 6, *pg.* 1698

SAMUELS JEWELERS, INC., 2914 Montopolis Dr Ste 200, **Austin,** TX 78741, *pg.* 12, *pg.* 1665

ZALE CORPORATION, 901 W Walnut Hill Ln, **Irving,** TX 75038-1003, *pg.* 16, *pg.* 1724

Washington

BAG BORROW OR STEAL, INC., 601 Union St Ste 3720, **Seattle,** WA 98101, *pg* 1, *pg.* 1833

BLUE NILE, INC., 411 1st Ave S Ste 700, **Seattle,** WA 98104-3847, *pg.* 2, *pg.* 1834

CENTURY 21 PROMOTIONS, INC., 2601 W Commodore Way, **Seattle,** WA 98199-1231, *pg.* 2, *pg.* 1834

SCREAMER INC., 4314 S 104th Pl, **Seattle,** WA 98178, *pg.* 12, *pg.* 1839

ZUMIEZ INC., 4001 204th St SW, **Lynnwood,** WA 98036, *pg.* 16, *pg.* 1822

Wisconsin

WIGWAM MILLS, INC., 3402 Crocker Ave, **Sheboygan,** WI 53081-6402, *pg.* 15, *pg.* 1894

First page reference indicates Business Class Edition
Second page reference indicates Geographic Edition

Apparel I-Women's, Children's & Infants' Wear

California

AMERICAN APPAREL, INC., 747 Warehouse St, **Los Angeles,** CA 90021-1106, *pg.* 18, *pg.* 126
ATHLETA, 2100 S McDowell Ave, **Petaluma,** CA 94954, *pg.* 19, *pg.* 181
BARCO UNIFORMS, INC., 350 W Rosecrans Ave, **Gardena,** CA 90248-1728, *pg.* 19, *pg.* 94
BCBG MAX AZRIA GROUP LLC, 2761 Fruitland Ave, **Vernon,** CA 90058, *pg.* 19, *pg.* 301
BEBE STORES, INC., 400 Valley Dr, **Brisbane,** CA 94005-1210, *pg.* 19, *pg.* 49
BLUE CANOE BODYWEAR, 390 A Lk Benbow Dr, **Garberville,** CA 95542, *pg.* 20, *pg.* 94
BRA SMYTH OF CALIFORNIA, INC., 100 N Winchester Blvd, **Santa Clara,** CA 95050, *pg.* 20, *pg.* 265
CHARLOTTE RUSSE, INC., 5910 Pacific Center Blvd, Ste 120, **San Diego,** CA 92121, *pg.* 21, *pg.* 201
CHEROKEE GLOBAL BRANDS, 5990 Sepulveda Blvd, Ste 600, **Sherman Oaks,** CA 91411, *pg.* 21, *pg.* 278
DRAPER'S & DAMON'S, INC., 9 Pasteur Ste 200, **Irvine,** CA 92618-3804, *pg.* 24, *pg.* 109
ERICA TANOV INC., 1627 San Pablo Ave, **Berkeley,** CA 94702, *pg.* 24, *pg.* 46
FOREVER 21, INC., 3880 N Mission Rd, **Los Angeles,** CA 90031, *pg.* 24, *pg.* 130
GUESS?, INC., 1444 S Alameda St, **Los Angeles,** CA 90021-2433, *pg.* 25, *pg.* 132
THE GYMBOREE CORPORATION, 2299 Kids Way, **Dixon,** CA 95620, *pg.* 25, *pg.* 77
JUSTFAB, INC., 800 Apollo St, **El Segundo,** CA 90245, *pg.* 27, *pg.* 80
KIYONNA CLOTHING, INC., 1440 S State College Blvd Units 5F & 5G, **Anaheim,** CA 92806, *pg.* 28, *pg.* 42
LUCKY BRAND DUNGAREES, INC., 5233 Alcoa Ave, **Vernon,** CA 90085, *pg.* 29, *pg.* 301
MICHAEL STARS, INC., 12955 Chadron Ave, **Hawthorne,** CA 90250, *pg.* 29, *pg.* 100
NYDJ APPAREL, LLC, 5401 S Soto St, **Vernon,** CA 90058, *pg.* 30, *pg.* 302
OTOMIX, INC., 747 Glasgow Ave, **Inglewood,** CA 90301, *pg.* 30, *pg.* 105
PATAGONIA, 259 W Santa Clara St, **Ventura,** CA 93001-2545, *pg.* 31, *pg.* 301
QUIKSILVER, INC., 15202 Graham St, **Huntington Beach,** CA 92649, *pg.* 31, *pg.* 104
SAN FRANCISCO MERCANTILE COMPANY, INC., 525 Brannan St Ste 410, **San Francisco,** CA 94107, *pg.* 32, *pg.* 227
ST. JOHN KNITS INTERNATIONAL, INC., 17622 Armstrong Ave, **Irvine,** CA 92614-5726, *pg.* 33, *pg.* 116
SUNRISE BRANDS, LLC, 801 S Figueroa St Ste 2500, **Los Angeles,** CA 90017, *pg.* 33, *pg.* 140
UJENA SWIMWEAR AND FASHIONS, 1931A Old Middlefield Way, **Mountain View,** CA 94043, *pg.* 34, *pg.* 163
UNIQUE VINTAGE, 2830 N Ontario St, **Burbank,** CA 91504, *pg.* 34, *pg.* 52
WEST COAST LEATHER, 290 Futter, **San Francisco,** CA 94108, *pg.* 35, *pg.* 233
THE WET SEAL, LLC, 26972 Burbank, **Foothill Ranch,** CA 92610-2506, *pg.* 35, *pg.* 88

Colorado

THE BOPPY COMPANY, LLC, 560 Golden Ridge Rd Ste 150, **Golden,** CO 80401, *pg.* 20, *pg.* 329
SMARTWOOL, 3495 Airport Cir, **Steamboat Springs,** CO 80487, *pg.* 32, *pg.* 335
SPORT HALEY, INC., 200 Union Blvd Ste 400, **Lakewood,** CO 80228, *pg.* 33, *pg.* 333

Connecticut

DOONEY & BOURKE, INC., 1 Regent St, **Norwalk,** CT 06855, *pg.* 24, *pg.* 361

Florida

ALGY TRIMMING COMPANY, 440 NE First Ave, **Hallandale,** FL 33008, *pg.* 17, *pg.* 429
BOSTON PROPER, INC., 6500 Park of Commerce Blvd, **Boca Raton,** FL 33487-8217, *pg.* 20, *pg.* 410
CHICO'S FAS, INC., 11215 Metro Pkwy, **Fort Myers,** FL 33966, *pg.* 21, *pg.* 427
SUPERIOR UNIFORM GROUP, INC., 10055 Seminole Blvd, **Seminole,** FL 33772, *pg.* 33, *pg.* 468

Georgia

CARTER'S, INC., Phipps Tower 3438 Peachtree Rd NE Ste 1800, **Atlanta,** GA 30326, *pg.* 21, *pg.* 491
CITI TRENDS INC., 104 Coleman Blvd, **Savannah,** GA 31408, *pg.* 22, *pg.* 539
OXFORD INDUSTRIES, INC., 999 Peachtree St NE, Ste 688, **Atlanta,** GA 30309, *pg.* 30, *pg.* 517
REGAL LAGER, INC., 1100 Cobb Pl Blvd, **Kennesaw,** GA 30144, *pg.* 32, *pg.* 534
RIVERSIDE MANUFACTURING COMPANY, 301 Riverside Dr, **Moultrie,** GA 31768-8603, *pg.* 32, *pg.* 536
SPANX INC., 3344 Peachtree Rd Ste 1700, **Atlanta,** GA 30326, *pg.* 32, *pg.* 520

Illinois

ALYCE PARIS, 7901 Caldwell Ave, **Morton Grove,** IL 60053, *pg.* 18, *pg.* 634

Kansas

PAYLESS SHOESOURCE, INC., 3231 SE 6th Ave, **Topeka,** KS 66607-2260, *pg.* 31, *pg.* 722

Massachusetts

BLAUER MANUFACTURING COMPANY, INC., 20 Aberdeen St, **Boston,** MA 02215, *pg.* 20, *pg.* 789
LADY GRACE STORES INC., 5 Commonwealth Ave Unit 1, **Woburn,** MA 01801, *pg.* 28, *pg.* 861
THE TALBOTS, INC., 1 Talbots Dr, **Hingham,** MA 02043, *pg.* 34, *pg.* 824

Michigan

BERMO ENTERPRISES INC., 12033 US 131, **Schoolcraft,** MI 49087-0426, *pg.* 20, *pg.* 906

Minnesota

CHRISTOPHER & BANKS CORPORATION, 2400 Xenium Ln N, **Plymouth,** MN 55441, *pg.* 22, *pg.* 953
JUNONIA LTD., 1355 Mendota Heights Rd Ste 290, **Mendota Heights,** MN 55120, *pg.* 27, *pg.* 929

Mississippi

LANDAU UNIFORMS INCORPORATED, 8410 W Sandidge Rd, **Olive Branch,** MS 38654, *pg.* 28, *pg.* 971

Missouri

BAKERS FOOTWEAR GROUP, INC., 2815 Scott Ave, **Saint Louis,** MO 63103-3032, *pg.* 19, *pg.* 992
KELLWOOD COMPANY, 600 Kellwood Pkwy, **Chesterfield,** MO 63017-5800, *pg.* 28, *pg.* 975
SCRUBS & BEYOND, 2132 Kratky Rd, **Saint Louis,** MO 63114, *pg.* 32, *pg.* 1003
WEISSMAN THEATRICAL SUPPLY, INC., 6750 Manchester Rd, **Saint Louis,** MO 63139, *pg.* 35, *pg.* 1004

Nevada

SPORTIF USA INC., 1415 Greg St Ste 101, **Sparks,** NV 89431, *pg.* 33, *pg.* 1032

New Jersey

A&E STORES, INC., 1000 Huyler St, **Teterboro,** NJ 07608, *pg.* 17, *pg.* 1124
ASCENA RETAIL GROUP, INC., 933 MacArthur Blvd, **Mahwah,** NJ 07430, *pg.* 18, *pg.* 1081
ATTITUDES IN DRESSING INC., 107 Trumbull St Bldg B8, **Elizabeth,** NJ 07206, *pg.* 19, *pg.* 1057
BARE NECESSITIES, INC., 90 Northfield Ave, **Edison,** NJ 08837-3807, *pg.* 19, *pg.* 1056
THE CHILDREN'S PLACE, INC., 500 Plaza Dr, **Secaucus,** NJ 07094, *pg.* 22, *pg.* 1119
MAYER/BERKSHIRE CORPORATION, 25 Edison Dr, **Wayne,** NJ 07470-4712, *pg.* 29, *pg.* 1129
SAFER PRINTS INC., 1875 McCarter Hwy, **Newark,** NJ 07104, *pg.* 32, *pg.* 1098

New York

3.1 PHILLIP LIM, 304 Hudson St 8th Fl N, **New York,** NY 10013, *pg.* 17, *pg.* 1185
AEROPOSTALE, INC., 112 W 34th St 22nd Fl, **New York,** NY 10120, *pg.* 17, *pg.* 1188
A.H. SCHREIBER CO., INC., 460 W 34th St, **New York,** NY 10001-2320, *pg.* 17, *pg.* 1188
AIDAN INDUSTRIES, INC., 275 W 39th St, **New York,** NY 10018, *pg.* 17, *pg.* 1188
ALLSTAR PRODUCTS GROUP LLC, 2 Skyline Dr, **Hawthorne,** NY 10532, *pg.* 17, *pg.* 1166
ALWAYS FOR ME INC., 740 Veterans Memorial Hwy Ste 303, **Hauppauge,** NY 11788, *pg.* 17, *pg.* 1163
ANN INC., 7 Times Sq, **New York,** NY 10036, *pg.* 18, *pg.* 1195
ANVIL HOLDINGS, INC., 521 5th Ave 9th Fl, **New York,** NY 10175, *pg.* 18, *pg.* 1195
BEN SHERMAN USA, 1071 Ave of the Americas 10th Fl, **New York,** NY 10018, *pg.* 19, *pg.* 1202
BENETTON U.S.A. CORPORATION, 601 Fifth Ave, **New York,** NY 10017-8260, *pg.* 19, *pg.* 1202
BURBERRY LIMITED, 444 Maddison Ave, **New York,** NY 10022, *pg.* 20, *pg.* 1208
CALVIN KLEIN, INC., 205 W 39th St, **New York,** NY 10018-3102, *pg.* 20, *pg.* 1209
CUPID FOUNDATIONS, INC., 475 Park Ave S, **New York,** NY 10016-3903, *pg.* 22, *pg.* 1220
DELIA'S, INC., 50 W 23rd St 10th Fl, **New York,** NY 10010, *pg.* 23, *pg.* 1222
DOLCE & GABBANA USA, INC., 148 Lafayette St, **New York,** NY 10013, *pg.* 23, *pg.* 1225
THE DONNA KARAN COMPANY LLC, 550 7th Ave, **New York,** NY 10018-3203, *pg.* 23, *pg.* 1225
D.V.F. STUDIOS, Studio Ln, **New York,** NY 10304, *pg.* 24, *pg.* 1226
EILEEN FISHER, INC., 2 Bridge St, **Irvington,** NY 10533-1527, *pg.* 24, *pg.* 1168
GARAN, INCORPORATED, 350 5th Ave, **New York,** NY 10118, *pg.* 24, *pg.* 1234
GILT GROUPE INC., 2 Park Ave 4th Fl, **New York,** NY 10016, *pg.* 24, *pg.* 1234
GIORGIO ARMANI CORPORATION, 114 5th Ave, **New York,** NY 10011-5604, *pg.* 25, *pg.* 1234
GLAMORISE FOUNDATIONS, INC., 135 Madison Ave, **New York,** NY 10016-6712, *pg.* 25, *pg.* 1235
HAMPSHIRE GROUP LIMITED, 114 W 41st St, **New York,** NY 10036, *pg.* 25, *pg.* 1237
HOUSE OF Z LLC, 13 17 Laight St, **New York,** NY 10013, *pg.* 26, *pg.* 1241
ICONIX BRAND GROUP, INC., 1450 Broadway, **New York,** NY 10018, *pg.* 26, *pg.* 1243
JACQUES MORET, INC., 1411 Broadway, **New York,** NY 10018, *pg.* 27, *pg.* 1245
JLM COUTURE, INC., 225 W 37th St 5th Fl, **New York,** NY 10018, *pg.* 27, *pg.* 1246
JORDACHE ENTERPRISES, INC., 1400 Broadway 15th Fl, **New York,** NY 10018, *pg.* 27, *pg.* 1246
KATE SPADE & COMPANY, 2 Park Ave, **New York,** NY 10016, *pg.* 27, *pg.* 1248
KATE SPADE LLC, 48 W 25th St, **New York,** NY 10010, *pg.* 28, *pg.* 1248
LOEHMANN'S HOLDINGS INC., 2500 Halsey St, **Bronx,** NY 10461, *pg.* 29, *pg.* 1144
LT APPAREL GROUP, 100 W 33rd St Ste 1012, **New York,** NY 10001-2914, *pg.* 29, *pg.* 1254
MICHAEL KORS (USA), INC., 11 W 42nd St, **New York,** NY 10036, *pg.* 29, *pg.* 1260
OLEG CASSINI, INC., Radio City Sta, **New York,** NY 10101, *pg.* 30, *pg.* 1274
OSCAR DE LA RENTA LTD., 11 W 42nd St 25th Fl, **New York,** NY 10036, *pg.* 30, *pg.* 1274

PRADA U.S.A. CORP., 610 W 52nd St, **New York,** NY 10019, *pg.* 31, *pg.* 1283
SEA ISLAND CLOTHIERS, LLC, 236-250 Greenpoint Ave Bldg 6 2nd Fl, **Brooklyn,** NY 11222, *pg.* 32, *pg.* 1146
SIONI APPAREL GROUP, 525 7th Ave Ste 806, **New York,** NY 10018, *pg.* 32, *pg.* 1292
THEORY, 38 Gansevoort St, **New York,** NY 10014, *pg.* 34, *pg.* 1299
TORY BURCH LLC, 11 W 19th St 7th Fl, **New York,** NY 10011, *pg.* 34, *pg.* 1302
VERA WANG BRIDAL HOUSE LTD., 225 W 39th St Fl 9, **New York,** NY 10018, *pg.* 34, *pg.* 1309
VERSACE USA, 200 Madison Ave Fl 21, **New York,** NY 10016, *pg.* 34, *pg.* 1310
WACOAL AMERICA INC., 136 Madison Ave, **New York,** NY 10016-6711, *pg.* 35, *pg.* 1312
WOODEN SHIPS OF HOBOKEN, 231 W 39th St Ste 711, **New York,** NY 10018, *pg.* 35, *pg.* 1315

North Carolina

THE CATO CORPORATION, 8100 Denmark Rd, **Charlotte,** NC 28273-5975, *pg.* 21, *pg.* 1364
HANESBRANDS INC., 1000 E Hanes Mill Rd, **Winston Salem,** NC 27105, *pg.* 26, *pg.* 1394
INDERA MILLS COMPANY, 350 W Maple St, **Yadkinville,** NC 27055, *pg.* 26, *pg.* 1396
KAYSER-ROTH CORPORATION, 102 Corporate Ctr Blvd, **Greensboro,** NC 27408, *pg.* 28, *pg.* 1374
NATIONAL WHOLESALE COMPANY INC., 400 National Blvd, **Lexington,** NC 27292, *pg.* 30, *pg.* 1381
PLAYTEX APPAREL, INC., 1000 E Haines Mill Rd, **Winston Salem,** NC 27105, *pg.* 31, *pg.* 1395
TANNER COMPANIES, LP, 537 Rock Rd, **Rutherfordton,** NC 28139-8125, *pg.* 34, *pg.* 1390
V.F. CORPORATION, 105 Corporate Center Blvd, **Greensboro,** NC 27408, *pg.* 34, *pg.* 1376

Ohio

EXPRESS, INC., 1 Express Dr, **Columbus,** OH 43230, *pg.* 24, *pg.* 1440
HERITAGE SPORTSWEAR, LLC, PO Box 760, **Hebron,** OH 43025, *pg.* 26, *pg.* 1455
OATEY SUPPLY CHAIN SERVICES, 4700 W 160th St, **Cleveland,** OH 44135, *pg.* 30, *pg.* 1433
TWEEN BRANDS INC., 8323 Walton Pkwy, **New Albany,** OH 43054, *pg.* 34, *pg.* 1467

Pennsylvania

ALFRED ANGELO, INC., 1301 Virginia Dr Ste 110, **Fort Washington,** PA 19034, *pg.* 17, *pg.* 1532
ANTHROPOLOGIE, INC., 5000 S Broad St Bldg 10, **Philadelphia,** PA 19112, *pg.* 18, *pg.* 1558
DAVID'S BRIDAL, INC., 1001 Washington St, **Conshohocken,** PA 19428-2356, *pg.* 23, *pg.* 1523
DEB SHOPS, INC., 9401 Blue Grass Rd, **Philadelphia,** PA 19114-2305, *pg.* 23, *pg.* 1563
DESTINATION MATERNITY CORPORATION, 456 N 5th St, **Philadelphia,** PA 19123-4007, *pg.* 23, *pg.* 1563
DOLFIN INTERNATIONAL CORPORATION, 4 Front St Plz, **Mohnton,** PA 19540-2007, *pg.* 23, *pg.* 1553
PERFORM GROUP, LLC, 333 E 7th Ave, **York,** PA 17404-2144, *pg.* 31, *pg.* 1597
RUE21, INC., 800 Commonwealth Dr Ste 100, **Warrendale,** PA 15086-7527, *pg.* 32, *pg.* 1591
SUGARTOWN WORLDWIDE INC., 800 3rd Ave, **King of Prussia,** PA 19406, *pg.* 33, *pg.* 1544

South Carolina

LAURA ASHLEY, INC., 7000 Regent Pkwy, **Fort Mill,** SC 29715-8313, *pg.* 29, *pg.* 1615

Texas

NEIMAN MARCUS, INC., 1618 Main St, **Dallas,** TX 75201, *pg.* 30, *pg.* 1684
STAGE STORES, INC., 10201 Main St, **Houston,** TX 77025, *pg.* 33, *pg.* 1715

Virginia

CHILDREN'S WEAR DIGEST INC., 3607 Mayland Ct, **Richmond,** VA 23233, *pg.* 22, *pg.* 1801
CUSTOMINK, LLC, 2910 District Ave, **Fairfax,** VA 22031, *pg.* 22, *pg.* 1780

Washington

AMERICAN LEGEND COOPERATIVE, PO Box 58308, **Seattle,** WA 98138, *pg.* 18, *pg.* 1833
HELLY-HANSEN (US), INC., 3703 I ST NW - #100, **Auburn,** WA 98001, *pg.* 26, *pg.* 1813
SUN PRECAUTIONS, INC., 2815 Wetmore Ave, **Everett,** WA 98201, *pg.* 33, *pg.* 1820

Wisconsin

BUYSEASONS, INC., 5915 S Moorland Rd, **New Berlin,** WI 53151, *pg.* 20, *pg.* 1883
FLORENCE EISEMAN COMPANY LLC, 342 N Water St 6th Fl, **Milwaukee,** WI 53202-5715, *pg.* 24, *pg.* 1874
JOCKEY INTERNATIONAL, INC., 2300 60th St, **Kenosha,** WI 53140, *pg.* 27, *pg.* 1861

First page reference indicates Business Class Edition
Second page reference indicates Geographic Edition

Apparel II-Men's & Boys' Wear

Arizona

SABAS BUNCH LIMITED PARTNERSHIP, 3270 N Colorado St Ste 101, **Chandler,** AZ 85225, *pg.* 47, *pg.* 12

California

DOCKERS BRAND, 1155 Battery St, **San Francisco,** CA 94111-1230, *pg.* 40, *pg.* 217
HOT TOPIC, INC., 18305 E San Jose Ave, **City of Industry,** CA 91748, *pg.* 42, *pg.* 67
LEVI STRAUSS & CO., 1155 Battery St, **San Francisco,** CA 94111-1230, *pg.* 43, *pg.* 220
LOST ARROW CORPORATION, 259 W Santa Clara St, **Ventura,** CA 93001, *pg.* 44, *pg.* 301
OLD NAVY, 2 Folsom St, **San Francisco,** CA 94105-1205, *pg.* 45, *pg.* 224
PVH NECKWEAR GROUP, 1735 S Santa Fe Ave, **Los Angeles,** CA 90021-2904, *pg.* 46, *pg.* 139
TRUE RELIGION BRAND JEANS, 1888 Rosecrans Ave, **Manhattan Beach,** CA 90266, *pg.* 49, *pg.* 143
THE WALKING COMPANY HOLDINGS, INC., 121 Gray Ave, **Santa Barbara,** CA 93101-1831, *pg.* 50, *pg.* 263

Connecticut

BOB'S STORES CORP., 160 Corp Ct, **Meriden,** CT 06450-8313, *pg.* 38, *pg.* 354
VINEYARD VINES LLC, 37 Brown House Rd, **Stamford,** CT 06902, *pg.* 50, *pg.* 379

Florida

PERRY ELLIS INTERNATIONAL, INC., 3000 NW 107th Ave, **Miami,** FL 33172-2133, *pg.* 45, *pg.* 445
VF IMAGEWEAR, 4408 W Linebaugh Ave, **Tampa,** FL 33624-5245, *pg.* 50, *pg.* 476

Georgia

ANGELICA CORPORATION, 1105 Lakewood Pkwy Ste 210, **Alpharetta,** GA 30009, *pg.* 38, *pg.* 483
REFRIGIWEAR, INC., 54 Breakstone Dr, **Dahlonega,** GA 30533-6698, *pg.* 47, *pg.* 529

Illinois

RANDA ACCESSORIES, LLC, 5600 N River Rd, Ste 500, **Rosemont,** IL 60018, *pg.* 47, *pg.* 657
TRUNK CLUB, 325 W Ohio St, **Chicago,** IL 60654, *pg.* 49, *pg.* 593

Indiana

HAT WORLD, INC., 7555 Woodland Dr, **Indianapolis,** IN 46278-1347, *pg.* 42, *pg.* 686

Kansas

KEY INDUSTRIES, INC., 400 Marble Rd, **Fort Scott,** KS 66701-8639, *pg.* 43, *pg.* 714
LEE JEANS, 9001 W 67th St, **Shawnee Mission,** KS 66202, *pg.* 43, *pg.* 721

Kentucky

FRUIT OF THE LOOM, INC., 1 Fruit of the Loom Dr, **Bowling Green,** KY 42103-9015, *pg.* 41, *pg.* 725

Maryland

JOS. A. BANK CLOTHIERS, INC., 500 Hanover Pike, **Hampstead,** MD 21074-2002, *pg.* 42, *pg.* 771
UNDER ARMOUR, INC., 1020 Hull St, **Baltimore,** MD 21230, *pg.* 49, *pg.* 759

Massachusetts

DESTINATION XL GROUP, INC., 555 Turnpike St, **Canton,** MA 02021, *pg.* 40, *pg.* 810
SOUTHWICK CLOTHING LLC, 20 Computer Dr, **Haverhill,** MA 01832, *pg.* 48, *pg.* 824
UNIFIRST CORPORATION, 68 Jonspin Rd, **Wilmington,** MA 01887-1090, *pg.* 50, *pg.* 860

Michigan

CARHARTT, INC., 5750 Mercury Dr, **Dearborn,** MI 48126-4234, *pg.* 39, *pg.* 875
KAZOO, INC., 4900 9th St, **Kalamazoo,** MI 49009, *pg.* 43, *pg.* 894

Minnesota

BEMIDJI WOOLEN MILLS, 301 Irvine Ave NW, **Bemidji,** MN 56601, *pg.* 38, *pg.* 916

Missouri

ELDER MANUFACTURING COMPANY, INC., 999 Executive Pkwy Ste 300, **Saint Louis,** MO 63141, *pg.* 40, *pg.* 996

New Hampshire

THE LIFE IS GOOD COMPANY, 15 Hudson Park Dr, **Hudson,** NH 03051, *pg.* 44, *pg.* 1034

New Jersey

DR. JAY'S INC., 17 S Middlesex Ave, **Monroe Township,** NJ 08831, *pg.* 40, *pg.* 1085
IZOD, 1001 Frontier Rd MS No 44, **Bridgewater,** NJ 08807, *pg.* 42, *pg.* 1046

New York

ALLESON OF ROCHESTER, INC., 2921 Brighton Henrietta Town Line Rd, **Rochester,** NY 14623, *pg.* 37, *pg.* 1333
BARNEYS NEW YORK, INC., 575 5th Ave, **New York,** NY 10017-2429, *pg.* 38, *pg.* 1201
BONOBOS, 45 W 25th St, 5th Fl, **New York,** NY 10010, *pg.* 39, *pg.* 1205
BROOKS BROTHERS GROUP, INC., 346 Madison Ave, **New York,** NY 10017, *pg.* 39, *pg.* 1208
COUNTESS MARA, INC., 120 W 45th St, **New York,** NY 10036, *pg.* 39, *pg.* 1219
G-III APPAREL GROUP, LTD., 512 7th Ave 35th Fl, **New York,** NY 10018 0832, *pg.* 41, *pg.* 1233
GTFM LLC, 350 5th Ave Ste 6617, **New York,** NY 10118-6617, *pg.* 41, *pg.* 1236
HICKEY-FREEMAN CO., INC., 1155 Clinton Ave N, **Rochester,** NY 14621, *pg.* 42, *pg.* 1336
HUGO BOSS FASHIONS INC., 601 W 26th St 8th Fl, **New York,** NY 10001, *pg.* 42, *pg.* 1242
I. SPIEWAK & SONS, INC., 469 7th Ave 10th Fl, **New York,** NY 10018-7605, *pg.* 42, *pg.* 1242
JHANE BARNES, INC., 140 W 57th St, **New York,** NY 10019, *pg.* 42, *pg.* 1246
NAUTICA APPAREL, INC., 40 W 57th St, **New York,** NY 10019-4001, *pg.* 45, *pg.* 1265
PVH CORP., 200 Madison Ave, **New York,** NY 10016-3903, *pg.* 46, *pg.* 1283
RAG & BONE, 425 W 13th St 3rd Fl, **New York,** NY 10014, *pg.* 46, *pg.* 1284
RALPH LAUREN CORPORATION, 650 Madison Ave, **New York,** NY 10022-1029, *pg.* 46, *pg.* 1284
RANDA CORP., 120 W 45th St Ste 3801, **New York,** NY 10036-4041, *pg.* 47, *pg.* 1285
ROYTEX, INC., 16 E 34th St Fl 17, **New York,** NY 10016-4328, *pg.* 47, *pg.* 1287
SEAN JOHN CLOTHING, INC., 1710 Broadway, **New York,** NY 10019, *pg.* 48, *pg.* 1290
TOMMY HILFIGER USA, 601 W 26th St Fl 17, **New York,** NY 10001, *pg.* 48, *pg.* 1302

North Carolina

CHAMPION ATHLETICWEAR INC., 1000 E Hanes Mill Rd, **Winston Salem,** NC 27105-1384, *pg.* 39, *pg.* 1394
GEM-DANDY, INC., 200 W Academy St, **Madison,** NC 27025, *pg.* 41, *pg.* 1382
PETER MILLAR, 4300 Emperor Blvd, Ste 100, **Durham,** NC 27703, *pg.* 46, *pg.* 1372
VF JEANSWEAR LIMITED PARTNERSHIP, 400 N Elm St, **Greensboro,** NC 27401-2143, *pg.* 50, *pg.* 1377

North Dakota

SCHEELS, 4550 15th Ave S, **Fargo,** ND 58103, *pg.* 47, *pg.* 1397

Ohio

ABERCROMBIE & FITCH CO., 6301 Fitch Path, **New Albany,** OH 43054-9269, *pg.* 37, *pg.* 1466
THE FECHHEIMER BROTHERS COMPANY, 4545 Malsbary Rd, **Cincinnati,** OH 45242-5624, *pg.* 41, *pg.* 1412
LEHIGH OUTFITTERS, LLC, 39 E Canal St, **Nelsonville,** OH 45764, *pg.* 43, *pg.* 1466

Pennsylvania

AMERICAN EAGLE OUTFITTERS, INC., 77 Hot Metal St, **Pittsburgh,** PA 15203, *pg.* 37, *pg.* 1572
ELBECO INCORPORATED, 4418 Pottsville Pike, **Reading,** PA 19605-1205, *pg.* 40, *pg.* 1584
FISHMAN & TOBIN, INC., 4000 Chemical Rd Ste 500, **Plymouth Meeting,** PA 19462, *pg.* 41, *pg.* 1582
PAUL FREDRICK MENSTYLE INC., 223 W Poplar St, **Fleetwood,** PA 19522, *pg.* 45, *pg.* 1532
TELEFLEX INCORPORATED, 155 S Limerick Rd, **Limerick,** PA 19468, *pg.* 48, *pg.* 1548

Rhode Island

HONEYWELL NORTH SAFETY PRODUCTS, 2000 Plainfield Pke, **Cranston,** RI 02921, *pg.* 42, *pg.* 1600

South Carolina

THE BEN SILVER CORPORATION, 149 King St, **Charleston,** SC 29401, *pg.* 38, *pg.* 1613
DELTA APPAREL, INC., 322 S Main St, **Greenville,** SC 29601, *pg.* 39, *pg.* 1617
HAMRICK INC., 742 Peachoid Rd, **Gaffney,** SC 29341-3440, *pg.* 41, *pg.* 1616

Tennessee

HARDWICK CLOTHES INC., 3800 Old Tasso Rd, **Cleveland,** TN 37312, *pg.* 42, *pg.* 1630

Texas

CAVENDER'S STORES LIMITED, 7820 S Broadway Ave, **Tyler,** TX 75703-5241, *pg.* 39, *pg.* 1748
HAGGAR CORPORATION, 11511 Luna Rd, **Dallas,** TX 75234-6022, *pg.* 41, *pg.* 1682
LUSKEY'S WESTERN STORES, INC., 3402 Catclaw Dr, **Abilene,** TX 79606, *pg.* 44, *pg.* 1657
THE MEN'S WEARHOUSE, INC., 6380 Rogerdale Rd, **Houston,** TX 77072-1624, *pg.* 44, *pg.* 1711
NEWFIELD EXPLORATION COMPANY, 4 Waterway Square Place Suite 100, **The Woodlands,** TX 77380, *pg.* 45, *pg.* 1747
TANDY LEATHER FACTORY, INC., 1900 SE Loop, **Fort Worth,** TX 76119-4337, *pg.* 48, *pg.* 1696
WILLIAMSON-DICKIE MANUFACTURING COMPANY, 509 W Vickery Blvd, **Fort Worth,** TX 76104, *pg.* 50, *pg.* 1696

Vermont

BEAU TIES LTD., 69 Industrial Ave, **Middlebury,** VT 05753-1129, *pg.* 38, *pg.* 1766

Washington

CUTTER & BUCK, INC., 701 N 34th St Ste 400, **Seattle,** WA 98103-3415, *pg.* 39, *pg.* 1835

EDDIE BAUER, INC., 10401 NE 8th St Ste 500, **Bellevue,** WA 98004, *pg.* 40, *pg.* 1814
EX OFFICIO, LLC, 4202 6th Ave S, **Seattle,** WA 98108, *pg.* 40, *pg.* 1835
SEATTLE PACIFIC INDUSTRIES, INC., 21216 72nd Ave S, **Kent,** WA 98032, *pg.* 48, *pg.* 1822
TOMMY BAHAMA, 428 Westlake Ave N Ste 388, **Seattle,** WA 98109, *pg.* 48, *pg.* 1842

Wisconsin

OSHKOSH B'GOSH, INC., 206 Spate st, **Oshkosh,** WI 54901-5008, *pg.* 45, *pg.* 1885
RIVER'S END TRADING COMPANY, 301 N Broome St 2nd Fl, **Madison,** WI 53703, *pg.* 47, *pg.* 1867

First page reference indicates Business Class Edition
Second page reference indicates Geographic Edition

Appliances

California

ANAHEIM MANUFACTURING COMPANY, 2680 Orbiter St, **Brea,** CA 92821-6265, *pg.* 51, *pg.* 48
BARBEQUES GALORE, INC., 2650 E Lindsay Privado Ste A, **Ontario,** CA 91761, *pg.* 51, *pg.* 173
BSH HOME APPLIANCES CORPORATION, 1901 Main St Ste 600, **Irvine,** CA 92614-0521, *pg.* 53, *pg.* 108
CAPITAL BRANDS, LLC, 11755 Wilshire Blvd, **Los Angeles,** CA 90025, *pg.* 53, *pg.* 127
DACOR, 14425 Clark Ave, **City of Industry,** CA 91745, *pg.* 54, *pg.* 67
PURCELL MURRAY COMPANY INC., 185 Park Ln, **Brisbane,** CA 94005, *pg.* 59, *pg.* 50

Connecticut

VEEDER-ROOT COMPANY, 125 Powder Forest Dr, **Simsbury,** CT 06070, *pg.* 61, *pg.* 371
WARING PRODUCTS, INC., 1 Cummings Point Rd, **Stamford,** CT 06902-7901, *pg.* 62, *pg.* 379

Florida

APSCO APPLIANCE CENTERS, 4520 E Bay Dr, **Clearwater,** FL 33764, *pg.* 51, *pg.* 415
JARDEN CONSUMER SOLUTIONS, 2381 NW Executive Ctr Dr, **Boca Raton,** FL 33431-7321, *pg.* 57, *pg.* 412
JESSUP'S APPLIANCES, 1210 E Venice Ave, **Venice,** FL 34285, *pg.* 58, *pg.* 477
VAPOR CORP., 3001 Griffin Rd, **Fort Lauderdale,** FL 33312-5649, *pg.* 61, *pg.* 427

Georgia

W.C. BRADLEY CO., 1017 Front Ave, **Columbus,** GA 31901-5260, *pg.* 62, *pg.* 528

Illinois

BERNINA OF AMERICA INC., 3702 Prairie Lake Ct, **Aurora,** IL 60504, *pg.* 51, *pg.* 554
BUNN-O-MATIC CORPORATION, 1400 Stevenson Dr, **Springfield,** IL 62703-4228, *pg.* 53, *pg.* 661
CORNELIUS INC., 500 Regency Dr, **Glendale Heights,** IL 60139-2285, *pg.* 54, *pg.* 614
CULLIGAN INTERNATIONAL COMPANY, 9399 W Higgins Rd Ste 1100, **Rosemont,** IL 60018, *pg.* 54, *pg.* 656
EDWARD DON & COMPANY, 9801 Adam Don Pkwy, **Woodridge,** IL 60517, *pg.* 54, *pg.* 672
FORTUNE BRANDS HOME & SECURITY, INC., 520 Lake Cook Rd, **Deerfield,** IL 60015-5611, *pg.* 55, *pg.* 600
THERMOS L.L.C., 475 N Martingale Rd Ste 1100, **Schaumburg,** IL 60173-2051, *pg.* 61, *pg.* 660
WEBER-STEPHEN PRODUCTS LLC, 200 E Daniels Rd, **Palatine,** IL 60067-6266, *pg.* 62, *pg.* 650
WORLD DRYER CORPORATION, 5700 McDermott Dr, **Berkeley,** IL 60163-1102, *pg.* 63, *pg.* 556

Indiana

ETS, LLC, 7445 Company Dr, **Indianapolis,** IN 46237-9296, *pg.* 54, *pg.* 685
HHGREGG, INC., 4151 E 96th St, **Indianapolis,** IN 46240-1442, *pg.* 56, *pg.* 686
IDI COMPOSITES INTERNATIONAL, 407 S 7th St, **Noblesville,** IN 46060, *pg.* 57, *pg.* 696
MONOSOL, LLC, 707 E 80th Pl Ste 301, **Merrillville,** IN 46410, *pg.* 59, *pg.* 694

Kentucky

GE CONSUMER & INDUSTRIAL, Appliance Park AP3-232, **Louisville,** KY 40225, *pg.* 55, *pg.* 733
GRINDMASTER CORPORATION, 4003 Collins Ln, **Louisville,** KY 40245-1643, *pg.* 56, *pg.* 734

Louisiana

FRYMASTER LLC, 8700 Line Ave, **Shreveport,** LA 71106, *pg.* 55, *pg.* 748

Massachusetts

BRAUN NORTH AMERICA, 1 Gillette Park, **Boston,** MA 02127-1028, *pg.* 52, *pg.* 792
KAZ, INC., 250 Turnpike Rd, **Southborough,** MA 01772, *pg.* 58, *pg.* 844
MAC-GRAY CORPORATION, 404 Wyman St Ste 400, **Waltham,** MA 02451, *pg.* 58, *pg.* 852
MERROW MACHINE COMPANY, 502 Bedford St, **Fall River,** MA 02720, *pg.* 58, *pg.* 819
MICROFLUIDICS INTERNATIONAL CORPORATION, 30 Ossipee Rd, **Newton,** MA 02464-9101, *pg.* 58, *pg.* 836
VITASOY USA INC., 1 New England Way, **Ayer,** MA 01432, *pg.* 62, *pg.* 784

Michigan

BISSELL HOMECARE, INC., 2345 Walker Ave NW, **Grand Rapids,** MI 49544-2516, *pg.* 52, *pg.* 887
WHIRLPOOL CORPORATION, 2000 N M-63, **Benton Harbor,** MI 49022-2692, *pg.* 62, *pg.* 872

Minnesota

APPLIANCE RECYCLING CENTERS OF AMERICA, INC., 7400 Excelsior Blvd, **Minneapolis,** MN 55426-4517, *pg.* 51, *pg.* 930
WARNER'S STELLIAN CO., INC., 550 Atwater Cir, **Saint Paul,** MN 55103-4401, *pg.* 62, *pg.* 964

Mississippi

VIKING RANGE CORPORATION, 111 W Frnt St, **Greenwood,** MS 38930-4442, *pg.* 61, *pg.* 968

Missouri

DUKE MANUFACTURING COMPANY, INC., 2224 N Tenth St, **Saint Louis,** MO 63102, *pg.* 54, *pg.* 995
THE SALVAJOR COMPANY, 4530 E 75th Ter, **Kansas City,** MO 64132-2081, *pg.* 60, *pg.* 986

Nevada

HAWS CORPORATION, 1455 Kleppe Ln, **Sparks,** NV 89431, *pg.* 56, *pg.* 1032

New Hampshire

STANDEX INTERNATIONAL CORPORATION, 11 Keewaydin Dr, **Salem,** NH 03079, *pg.* 60, *pg.* 1039

New Jersey

BROTHER INTERNATIONAL CORPORATION - USA, 100 Somerset Corporate Blvd, **Bridgewater,** NJ 08807-0911, *pg.* 53, *pg.* 1046
CONSEW, 400 Veterans Blvd, **Carlstadt,** NJ 07072-7201, *pg.* 53, *pg.* 1049
DE'LONGHI AMERICA INC., 2 Park Way & Rte 17 S, Ste 3A, **Saddle Brook,** NJ 07458, *pg.* 54, *pg.* 1118
FUJITSU GENERAL AMERICA, INC., 353 Route 46 W, **Fairfield,** NJ 07004, *pg.* 55, *pg.* 1065
JANOME AMERICA, INC., 10 Industrial Ave, **Mahwah,** NJ 07430, *pg.* 57, *pg.* 1081
JURA-CAPRESSO INC., 81 Ruckman Rd, **Closter,** NJ 07624, *pg.* 58, *pg.* 1052
MIELE INC., 9 Independence Way, **Princeton,** NJ 08540, *pg.* 59, *pg.* 1112
ROWENTA (USA), INC., 2121 Eden Rd, **Millville,** NJ 08332, *pg.* 60, *pg.* 1084
UNITED STATES COLD STORAGE, INC., 100 Dobbs Ln Ste 102, **Cherry Hill,** NJ 08034-1436, *pg.* 61, *pg.* 1051
VICTORY REFRIGERATION COMPANY LLC, 110 Woodcrest Rd, **Cherry Hill,** NJ 08003-3648, *pg.* 61, *pg.* 1051

New York

P.C. RICHARD & SON, 150 Price Pkwy, **Farmingdale,** NY 11735-1315, *pg.* 59, *pg.* 1159

North Carolina

ELECTROLUX HOME PRODUCTS NORTH AMERICA, 10200 David Taylor Dr, **Charlotte,** NC 28262, *pg.* 54, *pg.* 1366

Ohio

ADAMS MFG. CO., 9790 Midwest Ave, **Cleveland,** OH 44125-2425, *pg.* 51, *pg.* 1427
THE GENIE COMPANY, 22790 Lk Park Blvd, **Alliance,** OH 44601-3498, *pg.* 55, *pg.* 1403
GOLD MEDAL PRODUCTS CO., 10700 Medallion Dr, **Cincinnati,** OH 45241-4807, *pg.* 55, *pg.* 1414
HI-VAC CORPORATION, 117 Industry Rd, **Marietta,** OH 45750-9355, *pg.* 56, *pg.* 1458
HMI INDUSTRIES INC., 13325 Darice Pkwy Unit A, **Strongsville,** OH 44149, *pg.* 56, *pg.* 1475
LSI INDUSTRIES INC., 10000 Alliance Rd, **Cincinnati,** OH 45242-4706, *pg.* 58, *pg.* 1416
NSS ENTERPRISES, INC., 3115 Frenchmens Rd, **Toledo,** OH 43607-2918, *pg.* 59, *pg.* 1476
RANGE KLEEN MANUFACTURING INC., 4240 E Rd, **Lima,** OH 45807-1533, *pg.* 60, *pg.* 1458
TTI FLOOR CARE NORTH AMERICA, 7005 Cochran Rd, **Solon,** OH 44139, *pg.* 61, *pg.* 1473

South Carolina

BKI, 2812 Grandview Dr, **Simpsonville,** SC 29680, *pg.* 52, *pg.* 1621

Tennessee

FRANKE INC., 800 Aviation PW, **Smyrna,** TN 37167, *pg.* 55, *pg.* 1656
HUNTER FAN COMPANY, 7130 Goodlett Farm Pkwy Ste 400, **Cordova,** TN 38016, *pg.* 57, *pg.* 1631
ORECK CORPORATION, 565 Marriott Dr Ste 300, **Nashville,** TN 37214, *pg.* 59, *pg.* 1653

Texas

AERUS LLC, 5420 LBJ Fwy Ste 1010, **Dallas,** TX 75240, *pg.* 51, *pg.* 1673
BESTWAY, INC., 12400 Coit Rd Ste 950, **Dallas,** TX 75251, *pg.* 52, *pg.* 1676
BRAY INTERNATIONAL, INC., 13333 Westland E Blvd, **Houston,** TX 77041-1219, *pg.* 52, *pg.* 1702
NATERRA INTERNATIONAL INC., 13525 Denton Dr, **Dallas,** TX 75234, *pg.* 59, *pg.* 1684
SALADMASTER, 230 Westway Pl, **Arlington,** TX 76018, *pg.* 60, *pg.* 1659
STEAMATIC INC., 3333 Quorum Dr Ste 280, **Fort Worth,** TX 76137, *pg.* 60, *pg.* 1696

Virginia

HAMILTON BEACH BRANDS, INC., 4421 Waterfront Dr, **Glen Allen,** VA 23060-3375, *pg.* 56, *pg.* 1783

Wisconsin

ALLIANCE LAUNDRY HOLDINGS LLC, Shepard St, **Ripon,** WI 54971-0990, *pg.* 51, *pg.* 1890
IN-SINK-ERATOR, 4700 21st St, **Racine,** WI 53406-5031, *pg.* 57, *pg.* 1888
MANITOWOC ICE, INC., 2110 S 26th St, **Manitowoc,** WI 54220, *pg.* 58, *pg.* 1868
NOBLES MANUFACTURING, INC., 1105 E Pine St, **Saint Croix Falls,** WI 54024, *pg.* 59, *pg.* 1890
SPECTRUM BRANDS HOLDINGS, INC., 601 Rayovac Dr, **Madison,** WI 53711, *pg.* 60, *pg.* 1867
SUB ZERO WOLF, 4717 Hammersley Rd, **Madison,** WI 53711-2708, *pg.* 60, *pg.* 1867
VON SCHRADER COMPANY, 1600 Junction Ave, **Racine,** WI 53403-2568, *pg.* 62, *pg.* 1890

Architecture, Engineering & Construction

Alabama

ALABAMA METAL INDUSTRIES CORPORATION, 3245 Fayette Ave, **Birmingham,** AL 35208-4822, *pg.* 65, *pg.* 1
BRASFIELD & GORRIE, LLC, 3021 7th Ave S, **Birmingham,** AL 35233-2939, *pg.* 71, *pg.* 2
UNITED STATES PIPE & FOUNDRY COMPANY, INC., 2 Chase Corporate Dr, Ste 200, **Hoover,** AL 35244, *pg.* 117, *pg.* 5
VULCAN MATERIALS COMPANY, 1200 Urban Center Dr, **Birmingham,** AL 35242, *pg.* 119, *pg.* 4
WALTER ENERGY, INC., 3000 Riverchase Galleria Ste 1700, **Birmingham,** AL 35244-2378, *pg.* 120, *pg.* 4

Arizona

ACE ASPHALT OF ARIZONA, INC., 3030 S 7th St, **Phoenix,** AZ 85040, *pg.* 64, *pg.* 13
AMKOR TECHNOLOGY, INC., 2045 E Innovation Cir, **Tempe,** AZ 85284, *pg.* 67, *pg.* 25
ASARCO INCORPORATED, 8224 S 48th Ste 220, **Phoenix,** AZ 85044, *pg.* 69, *pg.* 15
CAVCO INDUSTRIES, INC., 1001 N Central Ave Ste 800, **Phoenix,** AZ 85004-1962, *pg.* 74, *pg.* 16
THE HUNT CORPORATION, 6720 N Scottsdale Rd Ste 300, **Scottsdale,** AZ 85253-4460, *pg.* 88, *pg.* 22
IVEDA SOLUTIONS, INC., 1201 S Alma School Ste 8500, **Mesa,** AZ 85210, *pg.* 88, *pg.* 13
MERITAGE HOMES CORPORATION, 17851 N 85th St Ste 300, **Scottsdale,** AZ 85255, *pg.* 97, *pg.* 23
ON SEMICONDUCTOR CORPORATION, 5005 E McDowell Rd, **Phoenix,** AZ 85008, *pg.* 101, *pg.* 18
REPUBLIC SERVICES, INC., 18500 N Allied Way, **Phoenix,** AZ 85054, *pg.* 107, *pg.* 19

Arkansas

ANTHONY FOREST PRODUCTS CO., INC., 309 N Washington Ave, **El Dorado,** AR 71730-5614, *pg.* 67, *pg.* 31
E.C. BARTON & COMPANY, 2929 Browns Ln, **Jonesboro,** AR 72401, *pg.* 80, *pg.* 33
NLC PRODUCTS INC., 3801 Woodland Hts Rd Ste 100, **Little Rock,** AR 72212, *pg.* 99, *pg.* 34
WHITE RIVER HARDWOODS-WOODWORKS, INC., 1197 Happy Hollow Rd, **Fayetteville,** AR 72701, *pg.* 121, *pg.* 31

California

AECOM, 999 Town & Country Rd, **Orange,** CA 92868-4713, *pg.* 64, *pg.* 173
AECOM TECHNOLOGY CORPORATION, 555 S Flower St Ste 3700, **Los Angeles,** CA 90071-2300, *pg.* 65, *pg.* 125
AQUATIC, 8101 E Kaiser Blvd Ste 200, **Anaheim,** CA 92808-2261, *pg.* 68, *pg.* 42
BORAL ROOFING, 7575 Irvine Ctr Dr Ste 100, **Irvine,** CA 92618-2930, *pg.* 71, *pg.* 107
BROOKFIELD HOMES, 12865 Pointe Del Mar Way Ste 200, **Del Mar,** CA 92014-3860, *pg.* 71, *pg.* 77
BROWN AND CALDWELL, 201 N Civic Dr, **Walnut Creek,** CA 94596-3864, *pg.* 72, *pg.* 303
CRATEX MANUFACTURING CO., INC., 328 Encinitas Blvd Ste 200, **Encinitas,** CA 92024, *pg.* 77, *pg.* 85
DPR CONSTRUCTION, INC., 1450 Veterans Blvd, **Redwood City,** CA 94063, *pg.* 79, *pg.* 189
EARLE M. JORGENSEN COMPANY, 10650 S Alameda St, **Lynwood,** CA 90262, *pg.* 80, *pg.* 142
FISHER DEVELOPMENT INC., 201 Spear St Ste 220, **San Francisco,** CA 94105, *pg.* 81, *pg.* 218
FISHER MANUFACTURING COMPANY, 1900 S O St, **Tulare,** CA 93274, *pg.* 81, *pg.* 297
FLEXTRONICS INTERNATIONAL LTD., 6201 America Ctr Dr, **San Jose,** CA 95002, *pg.* 81, *pg.* 245
GRANITE CONSTRUCTION INCORPORATED, 585 W Beach St, **Watsonville,** CA 95076, *pg.* 84, *pg.* 305
JACOBS ENGINEERING GROUP, INC., 1111 S Arroyo Pkwy, **Pasadena,** CA 91105, *pg.* 88, *pg.* 180
J.H. BAXTER & COMPANY, 1700 S El Camino Real Ste 407, **San Mateo,** CA 94402, *pg.* 89, *pg.* 255
KAISER ALUMINUM CORPORATION, 27422 Portola Pkwy Ste 200, **Foothill Ranch,** CA 92610-2831, *pg.* 90, *pg.* 86
KB HOME, 10990 Wilshire Blvd 7th Fl, **Los Angeles,** CA 90024, *pg.* 90, *pg.* 134
LAVI INDUSTRIES INC., 27810 Ave Hopkins, **Valencia,** CA 91355-1246, *pg.* 93, *pg.* 299
L.M. SCOFIELD COMPANY, 6533 Bandini Blvd, **Los Angeles,** CA 90040, *pg.* 94, *pg.* 134
M&G DURA-VENT, INC., 877 Cotting Ct, **Vacaville,** CA 95688, *pg.* 95, *pg.* 298
MURDOCK, INC., 125 Proctor Ave, **City of Industry,** CA 91746, *pg.* 98, *pg.* 67
NASSCO HOLDINGS INCORPORATED, 2798 Harbor Dr, **San Diego,** CA 92113, *pg.* 99, *pg.* 205
NATIONAL TECHNICAL SYSTEMS INC., 24007 Ventura Blvd Ste 200, **Calabasas,** CA 91302, *pg.* 99, *pg.* 56
NOV AMERON, 10681 Foothill Blvd Ste 450, **Rancho Cucamonga,** CA 91730, *pg.* 100, *pg.* 187
NUPLA CORPORATION, 11912 Sheldon St, **Sun Valley,** CA 91352-1509, *pg.* 101, *pg.* 281
PACIFIC COLUMNS, INC., 505 W Lambert Rd, **Brea,** CA 92821, *pg.* 103, *pg.* 49
PACIFIC NATIONAL GROUP INC., 2392 S Bateman Ave, **Irwindale,** CA 91010-3312, *pg.* 103, *pg.* 119
PARSONS CORPORATION, 100 W Walnut St, **Pasadena,** CA 91124-0001, *pg.* 103, *pg.* 180
SCS ENGINEERS, 3900 Kilroy Airport Way Ste 100, **Long Beach,** CA 90806-6816, *pg.* 109, *pg.* 124
SENSEGIZ INC., 425 2nd St Ste 100, **San Francisco,** CA 94107, *pg.* 110, *pg.* 227
SIERRA PACIFIC INDUSTRIES, 19794 Riverside Ave, **Anderson,** CA 96007-4908, *pg.* 110, *pg.* 43
SOLARCITY CORPORATION, 3055 Clearview Way, **San Mateo,** CA 94402, *pg.* 111, *pg.* 256
SOLUTIONS OFFICE INTERIORS, INC., 1702L Meridian Ave Ste 261, **San Jose,** CA 95125, *pg.* 112, *pg.* 250
SYAR INDUSTRIES, INC., 2301 Napa Vallejo Hwy, **Napa,** CA 94558-6242, *pg.* 114, *pg.* 163
TETRA TECH, INC., 3475 E Foothill Blvd, **Pasadena,** CA 91107-6024, *pg.* 115, *pg.* 181
VIKING DOOR & WINDOW, 2099 S 10th St, **San Jose,** CA 95112, *pg.* 119, *pg.* 251
WALKER & ZANGER, INC., 8901 Bradley Ave, **Sun Valley,** CA 91352, *pg.* 119, *pg.* 281
WATKINS MANUFACTURING CORPORATION, 1280 Park Ctr Dr, **Vista,** CA 92083-8314, *pg.* 120, *pg.* 303
WILLIAM LYON HOMES, 4695 Macarthur Ct, # 8, **Newport Beach,** CA 92660, *pg.* 122, *pg.* 166

Colorado

CH2M HILL COMPANIES, LTD., 9191 S Jamaica St, **Englewood,** CO 80112, *pg.* 75, *pg.* 325
COORSTEK, INC., 16000 Table Mountain Pkwy, **Golden,** CO 80403-1693, *pg.* 77, *pg.* 330
DIAMOND SPAS, INC., 4409 Coriolis Way, **Frederick,** CO 80504, *pg.* 79, *pg.* 329
D.R. HORTON/CONTINENTAL SERIES, 7600 E Orchard Rd Ste 350F, **Greenwood Village,** CO 80111-2556, *pg.* 79, *pg.* 330
ELCAR FENCE & SUPPLY CO., 2155 S Valentia St, **Denver,** CO 80231-3324, *pg.* 80, *pg.* 319
GREASE MONKEY INTERNATIONAL, INC., 7450 E Progress Pl, **Greenwood Village,** CO 80111-2108, *pg.* 84, *pg.* 331
JOHNS MANVILLE CORPORATION, 717 17th St, **Denver,** CO 80202, *pg.* 89, *pg.* 320
MWH GLOBAL, INC., 380 Interlocken Crescent Ste 200, **Broomfield,** CO 80021, *pg.* 98, *pg.* 312
WOODWARD, INC., 1000 E Drake Rd, **Fort Collins,** CO 80525, *pg.* 122, *pg.* 329

Connecticut

THE BILCO COMPANY, 37 Water St PO Box 1203, **West Haven,** CT 06516-3837, *pg.* 70, *pg.* 383
CO-EX CORP., 5 Alexander Dr, **Wallingford,** CT 06492-2429, *pg.* 76, *pg.* 382
E.L. WAGNER CO., INC., 750 Wordin Ave, **Bridgeport,** CT 06605-2423, *pg.* 80, *pg.* 339
EMCOR GROUP, INC., 301 Merritt Seven, **Norwalk,** CT 06851-1092, *pg.* 80, *pg.* 361
GENERAL CABLE CORPORATION, 1600 W Main St, **Willimantic,** CT 06226-1128, *pg.* 83, *pg.* 384
KEENEY MANUFACTURING COMPANY, 1170 Main St, **Newington,** CT 06111, *pg.* 90, *pg.* 360
OTIS ELEVATOR COMPANY, 10 Farm Springs Rd, **Farmington,** CT 06032, *pg.* 102, *pg.* 349
PANOLAM INDUSTRIES INTERNATIONAL, INC., 20 Progress Dr, **Shelton,** CT 06484-6216, *pg.* 103, *pg.* 370
SANFORD & HAWLEY, INC., 1790 Farmington Ave, **Unionville,** CT 06085-1209, *pg.* 109, *pg.* 381
STANLEY ACCESS TECHNOLOGIES, LLC, 65 Scott Swamp Rd, **Farmington,** CT 06032, *pg.* 112, *pg.* 349
SUNPORCH STRUCTURES INC., 495 Post Rd E, **Westport,** CT 06880-4400, *pg.* 113, *pg.* 384
ULBRICH STAINLESS STEEL & SPECIAL METALS, INC., 57 Dodge Ave, **North Haven,** CT 06473-1191, *pg.* 117, *pg.* 360

Delaware

SPEAKMAN COMPANY, 400 Anchor Mill Rd Twin Spans Business Park, **New Castle,** DE 19720, *pg.* 112, *pg.* 388
W.L. GORE & ASSOCIATES, INC., 555 Papermill Rd, **Newark,** DE 19711-7513, *pg.* 122, *pg.* 388

Florida

ALVAREZ HOMES, INC., 3617 Hudson Ln, **Tampa,** FL 33618, *pg.* 66, *pg.* 470
ARCS INVESTMENTS, LLC, 2244 Trade Ctr Way, **Naples,** FL 34109, *pg.* 68, *pg.* 450
THE GOLDFIELD CORPORATION, 1684 W Hibiscus Blvd, **Melbourne,** FL 32901-3073, *pg.* 84, *pg.* 439
JOHN CANNON HOMES INC., 6710 Professional Pkwy W, **Sarasota,** FL 34240-8444, *pg.* 89, *pg.* 466
KIMMINS CORP., 1501 E 2nd Ave, **Tampa,** FL 33605, *pg.* 91, *pg.* 473
MASTER HALCO, 9800 Reeves Rd, **Tampa,** FL 33619, *pg.* 96, *pg.* 474
MEADOW BURKE, 5110 Santa Fe Rd, **Tampa,** FL 33619, *pg.* 96, *pg.* 474
METALS USA, INC., 2400 E Commercial Blvd Ste 905, **Fort Lauderdale,** FL 33308, *pg.* 97, *pg.* 425
NAPLES LUMBER & SUPPLY INC., 3828 Radio Rd, **Naples,** FL 34104, *pg.* 99, *pg.* 451
PGT, INC., 1070 Technology Dr, **North Venice,** FL 34275, *pg.* 104, *pg.* 452
PYRAMID MOULDINGS, 300 S Magnolia Ave, **Green Cove Springs,** FL 32043, *pg.* 105, *pg.* 429
ROOFING BY CURRY, 6245 Clark Center Ave Ste J, **Sarasota,** FL 34238, *pg.* 108, *pg.* 467
SCAN DESIGN OF FLORIDA INC., 1153 Bennett Dr, **Longwood,** FL 32750, *pg.* 109, *pg.* 438
SOUTH FLORIDA DESIGN, 9990 Coconut Rd, Ste 330, **Bonita Springs,** FL 34135, *pg.* 112, *pg.* 413
TOPBUILD CORPORATION, 260 Jimmy Ann Dr, **Daytona Beach,** FL 32114, *pg.* 116, *pg.* 421
TRI-CITY ELECTRICAL CONTRACTORS, INC., 430 W Dr, **Altamonte Springs,** FL 32714, *pg.* 116, *pg.* 409
TRI COUNTY AIR CONDITIONING-HEATING, INC., 1080 Enterprise Ct, **Nokomis,** FL 34275, *pg.* 116, *pg.* 451
UNITED STATES AWNING COMPANY, 1935 18th St, **Sarasota,** FL 34234, *pg.* 117, *pg.* 467

Georgia

AGC GLASS NORTH AMERICA, INC., 11175 Cicero Dr Ste 400, **Alpharetta,** GA 30022, *pg.* 65, *pg.* 482
AXIALL CORPORATION, 115 Perimeter Ctr Pl Ste 460, **Atlanta,** GA 30346, *pg.* 69, *pg.* 491
BLUELINX HOLDINGS, INC., 4300 Wildwood Pkwy, **Atlanta,** GA 30339, *pg.* 70, *pg.* 491
BRAND ENERGY, INC., 1325 Cobb International Dr Ste A-1, **Kennesaw,** GA 30152, *pg.* 71, *pg.* 533
CHEROKEE BRICK & TILE COMPANY, 3250 Waterville Rd, **Macon,** GA 31206-1246, *pg.* 75, *pg.* 535
EIS, INC., 2018 Powers Ferry Rd Ste 500, **Atlanta,** GA 30339, *pg.* 80, *pg.* 504
HD SUPPLY, INC., 3100 Cumberland Blvd Ste 1480, **Atlanta,** GA 30339, *pg.* 86, *pg.* 509
HEERY INTERNATIONAL, INC., 999 Peachtree St NE, **Atlanta,** GA 30309-3953, *pg.* 86, *pg.* 510
KAWNEER COMPANY, INC., 555 Guthridge Ct, **Norcross,** GA 30092, *pg.* 90, *pg.* 537
MUELLER WATER PRODUCTS, INC., 1200 Albernathy Rd

First page reference indicates Business Class Edition
Second page reference indicates Geographic Edition

NE Ste 1200, **Atlanta,** GA 30328, *pg.* 98, *pg.* 515
NOVELIS INC., 3399 Peachtree Rd NE Lenox Bldg Ste 1500, **Atlanta,** GA 30326, *pg.* 100, *pg.* 516
OSMOSE, INC., 1016 Everee Inn Rd, **Griffin,** GA 30224-4733, *pg.* 102, *pg.* 533
QUIKRETE COMPANIES, 3490 Piedmont Rd NE Ste 1300, **Atlanta,** GA 30305-4811, *pg.* 106, *pg.* 519
TENSAR CORPORATION, 2500 Northwinds Pkwy, Ste 500, **Alpharetta,** GA 30009, *pg.* 114, *pg.* 485

Idaho

BMC SELECT, 720 Park Blvd Ste 200, **Boise,** ID 83712, *pg.* 71, *pg.* 546
MOUNTAIN WEST, LLC, 4212 S Hwy 191, **Rexburg,** ID 83440-4251, *pg.* 98, *pg.* 550
REDBUILT LLC, 200 E Mallard Dr, **Boise,** ID 83706, *pg.* 106, *pg.* 548

Illinois

A. M. CASTLE & CO., 1420 Kensington Rd Ste 220, **Oak Brook,** IL 60523, *pg.* 64, *pg.* 644
AMD INDUSTRIES, INC., 4620 W 19th St, **Cicero,** IL 60804-2502, *pg.* 66, *pg.* 598
ARCELORMITTAL STEEL USA INC., 1 S Dearborn, **Chicago,** IL 60603, *pg.* 68, *pg.* 564
BLACK BROTHERS COMPANY, 501 9th Ave, **Mendota,** IL 61342-1927, *pg.* 70, *pg.* 632
BODYCOTE THERMAL PROCESSING, 1975 N Ruby St, **Melrose Park,** IL 60160-1109, *pg.* 71, *pg.* 632
CENTRAL STEEL & WIRE COMPANY, 3000 W 51st St, **Chicago,** IL 60632-2122, *pg.* 74, *pg.* 569
THE CHAMBERLAIN GROUP, INC., 845 N Larch Ave, **Elmhurst,** IL 60126-1114, *pg.* 75, *pg.* 611
CLUNE CONSTRUCTION CO., 10 S La Salle St Ste 300, **Chicago,** IL 60603-1095, *pg.* 76, *pg.* 571
DEUBLIN COMPANY, 2050 Norman Dr W, **Waukegan,** IL 60085-6747, *pg.* 78, *pg.* 666
ELKAY MANUFACTURING COMPANY, 2222 Camden Ct, **Oak Brook,** IL 60523-4674, *pg.* 80, *pg.* 645
GERBER PLUMBING FIXTURES CORPORATION, 2500 Internationale Pkwy, **Woodridge,** IL 60517, *pg.* 84, *pg.* 672
GRAYCOR INC., 1 Graycor Dr, **Homewood,** IL 60430-4618, *pg.* 84, *pg.* 619
GREAT LAKES DREDGE & DOCK CORPORATION, 2122 York Rd, **Oak Brook,** IL 60523, *pg.* 84, *pg.* 645
THE HANDY/KENLIN GROUP, 29 E Hintz Rd, **Wheeling,** IL 60090, *pg.* 86, *pg.* 670
KEYSTONE STEEL & WIRE CO., 7000 SW Adams St, **Peoria,** IL 61641, *pg.* 91, *pg.* 651
KOMATSU AMERICA CORP., 1701 Golf Rd Ste 1-100, **Rolling Meadows,** IL 60008, *pg.* 92, *pg.* 655
LAFARGE NORTH AMERICA INC., 8700 W Bryn Mawr Ave Ste 300, **Chicago,** IL 60631, *pg.* 93, *pg.* 579
LIFTOMATIC MATERIAL HANDLING INC., 700 Dartmouth Ln, **Buffalo Grove,** IL 60089, *pg.* 94, *pg.* 560
MODERN TRACK MACHINERY, 1415 Davis Rd, **Elgin,** IL 60123-1321, *pg.* 98, *pg.* 610
MODERNFORGECOMPANIES, LLC, 13810 S Western Ave, **Blue Island,** IL 60406-3229, *pg.* 98, *pg.* 558
MYR GROUP INC., 1701 W Golf Rd Ste 1012, **Rolling Meadows,** IL 60008-4270, *pg.* 98, *pg.* 656
PETERSEN ALUMINUM CORPORATION, 1005 Tonne Rd, **Elk Grove Village,** IL 60007, *pg.* 104, *pg.* 611
PLIBRICO CO. LLC, 1010 N Hooker St, **Chicago,** IL 60622-4220, *pg.* 104, *pg.* 587
RAYNOR GARAGE DOORS, 1101 E River Rd, **Dixon,** IL 61021-3252, *pg.* 106, *pg.* 607
SILBRICO CORPORATION, 6300 River Rd, **Hodgkins,** IL 60525-4257, *pg.* 110, *pg.* 617
SIMPSON TECHNOLOGIES CORPORATION, 751 Shoreline Dr, **Aurora,** IL 60504-6194, *pg.* 111, *pg.* 555
USG CORPORATION, 550 W Adams St, **Chicago,** IL 60661-3676, *pg.* 118, *pg.* 594

Indiana

THE BLOOMFIELD MANUFACTURING CO., INC., 46 W Spring St, **Bloomfield,** IN 47424-1473, *pg.* 70, *pg.* 674
THE CYCLONE MFG. CO., 151 N Washington St, **Urbana,** IN 46990-9539, *pg.* 78, *pg.* 698
DELTA FAUCET COMPANY, 55 E 111th St, **Indianapolis,** IN 46280-1071, *pg.* 78, *pg.* 684
HUNT CONSTRUCTION GROUP, INC., 2450 S Tibbs Ave, **Indianapolis,** IN 46241, *pg.* 87, *pg.* 686
INTERNATIONAL REVOLVING DOORS, 2138 N Sixth Ave, **Evansville,** IN 47710-2814, *pg.* 88, *pg.* 679
JOSAM COMPANY, 525 W US Hwy 20, **Michigan City,** IN 46360, *pg.* 89, *pg.* 695
KITCHEN KOMPACT, INC., 911 E 11th St, **Jeffersonville,** IN 47131, *pg.* 91, *pg.* 692
KOCH ENTERPRISES, INC., 14 S 11th Ave, **Evansville,** IN 47712, *pg.* 91, *pg.* 679
LIBERTY HOMES, INC., 1101 Eisenhower Dr N, P.O. Box 35, **Goshen,** IN 46527, *pg.* 93, *pg.* 681
LINGENFELTER PERFORMANCE ENGINEERING, INC., 1557 Winchester Road, **Decatur,** IN 46733, *pg.* 94, *pg.* 677
MASTERBRAND CABINETS, INC., 1 MasterBrand Cabinets Dr, **Jasper,** IN 47546, *pg.* 96, *pg.* 692
MEG, 502 S Green St, **Cambridge City,** IN 47327, *pg.* 97, *pg.* 675
MODERNFOLD, INC., 215 W New Rd, **Greenfield,** IN 46140, *pg.* 98, *pg.* 681
SCHOTT NORTH AMERICA, INC., 2000 Chestnut St, PO Box 317, **Vincennes,** IN 47591-1760, *pg.* 109, *pg.* 698
SOMMER METALCRAFT CORPORATION, 315 Poston Dr, **Crawfordsville,** IN 47933, *pg.* 112, *pg.* 676
STEEL DYNAMICS, INC., 7575 W Jefferson Blvd, **Fort Wayne,** IN 46804, *pg.* 113, *pg.* 681

Iowa

CURRIES COMPANY, 1502 12th St NW, **Mason City,** IA 50401-5809, *pg.* 77, *pg.* 709
OWEN INDUSTRIES, INC., 501 Ave H, **Carter Lake,** IA 51510-1513, *pg.* 102, *pg.* 702
PELLA CORPORATION, 102 Main St, **Pella,** IA 50219-2147, *pg.* 104, *pg.* 711
THE WEITZ COMPANY, Capital Sq 400 Locust St Ste 300, **Des Moines,** IA 50309, *pg.* 121, *pg.* 707

Kansas

ARBOR MASTERS TREE SERVICE, 8250 Cole Pkwy, **Shawnee,** KS 66227, *pg.* 68, *pg.* 721
STAR LUMBER & SUPPLY COMPANY, INC., 325 S W St, **Wichita,** KS 67213-2105, *pg.* 113, *pg.* 724

Kentucky

FLORIDA TILE INDUSTRIES, INC., 998 Governors Ln, Ste 300, **Lexington,** KY 40513, *pg.* 82, *pg.* 730
GENERAL CABLE CORPORATION, 4 Tesseneer Dr, **Highland Heights,** KY 41076, *pg.* 83, *pg.* 729
TRUE HOME VALUE, INC., 5611 Fern Valley Rd PO Box 34749, **Louisville,** KY 40228-1055, *pg.* 117, *pg.* 738

Louisiana

H&E EQUIPMENT SERVICES, INC., 7500 Pecue Ln, **Baton Rouge,** LA 70809, *pg.* 85, *pg.* 742

Maine

WASCO PRODUCTS, INC., 22 Pioneer Ave, **Sanford,** ME 04073-3046, *pg.* 120, *pg.* 752

Maryland

ARCHITECTURAL ART MFG. INC., 6409 Rhode Island Ave, **Riverdale,** MD 20737, *pg.* 68, *pg.* 775
FISHER HOUSE FOUNDATION, INC., 111 Rockville Pke Ste 420, **Rockville,** MD 20850, *pg.* 81, *pg.* 776
JAMISON DOOR COMPANY, 55 JV Jamison Dr, **Hagerstown,** MD 21740, *pg.* 89, *pg.* 771
LAFARGE NORTH AMERICA INC., 300 E Joppa Rd Hampton Plz, **Towson,** MD 21286, *pg.* 93, *pg.* 779
MACCAFERRI, INC., 10303 Governor Ln Blvd, **Williamsport,** MD 21795, *pg.* 95, *pg.* 780
TSS, INC., 7226 Lee DeForest Dr Ste 203, **Columbia,** MD 21046, *pg.* 117, *pg.* 768

Massachusetts

AECOM, 250 Apollo Dr, **Chelmsford,** MA 01824-3627, *pg.* 64, *pg.* 812
BEACON ROOFING SUPPLY, INC., 1 Lakeland Park Dr, **Peabody,** MA 01960, *pg.* 70, *pg.* 840
CDM SMITH, 1 Cambridge Pl 50 Hampshire St, **Cambridge,** MA 02139, *pg.* 74, *pg.* 807
CIRCOR INTERNATIONAL, INC., 30 Corporate Dr, Ste 200, **Burlington,** MA 01803, *pg.* 76, *pg.* 805
GROSSMANS BARGAIN OUTLET, 90 Hawes Way, **Stoughton,** MA 02072, *pg.* 85, *pg.* 847
HARVEY INDUSTRIES, INC., 1400 Main St, **Waltham,** MA 02451-1601, *pg.* 86, *pg.* 851
HERITAGE HOMES INC., 456 S Hampton Rd, **Westfield,** MA 01085-1327, *pg.* 87, *pg.* 857
SUNSETTER PRODUCTS, LP, 184 Charles St, **Malden,** MA 02148, *pg.* 113, *pg.* 830
SYMMONS INDUSTRIES, INC., 31 Brooks Dr, **Braintree,** MA 02184-3804, *pg.* 114, *pg.* 803
TIAX LLC, 35 Hartwell Ave, **Lexington,** MA 02421, *pg.* 115, *pg.* 829
WALPOLE WOODWORKERS, INC., 767 E St, **Walpole,** MA 02081, *pg.* 120, *pg.* 849
W.R. GRACE & CO., 62 Whittemore Ave, **Cambridge,** MA 02140-1623, *pg.* 123, *pg.* 810

Michigan

CHAMPION ENTERPRISES HOLDINGS, LLC, 755 W Big Beaver Rd Ste 1000, **Troy,** MI 48084, *pg.* 75, *pg.* 910
CUNNINGHAM-LIMP COMPANY, 39300 W Twelve Mile Rd Ste 200, **Farmington Hills,** MI 48331-2997, *pg.* 77, *pg.* 885
FALCON WATERFREE TECHNOLOGIES, LLC, 4729 Division St # C, **Wayland,** MI 49348-9773, *pg.* 81, *pg.* 912
GENOVA PRODUCTS, INC., 7034 E Ct St, **Davison,** MI 48423, *pg.* 83, *pg.* 875
GUARDIAN INDUSTRIES CORP., 2300 Harmon Rd, **Auburn Hills,** MI 48326-1714, *pg.* 85, *pg.* 869
MASCO CORPORATION, 21001 Van Born Rd, **Taylor,** MI 48180-1340, *pg.* 96, *pg.* 909
MSX INTERNATIONAL, INC., 1950 Concept Dr, **Warren,** MI 48091, *pg.* 98, *pg.* 912
ODL INCORPORATED, 215 E Roosevelt Ave, **Zeeland,** MI 49464-1239, *pg.* 101, *pg.* 914
SPEEDRACK PRODUCTS GROUP, LTD., 7903 Venture Ave NW, **Sparta,** MI 49345-9309, *pg.* 112, *pg.* 908
UNISTRUT CORPORATION, 4205 Elizabeth, **Wayne,** MI 48184, *pg.* 117, *pg.* 913
UNIVERSAL FOREST PRODUCTS, INC., 2801 E Beltline Ave NE, **Grand Rapids,** MI 49525-9680, *pg.* 117, *pg.* 890
THE VIKING GROUP, 210 N Industrial Park Rd, **Hastings,** MI 49058-9706, *pg.* 119, *pg.* 891

Minnesota

ANDERSEN CORPORATION, 100 4th Ave N, **Bayport,** MN 55003-1096, *pg.* 67, *pg.* 916
APOGEE ENTERPRISES, INC., 4400 W 78th St Ste 520, **Minneapolis,** MN 55435, *pg.* 67, *pg.* 930
COLD SPRING GRANITE COMPANY, 17482 Granite W Rd, **Cold Spring,** MN 56320-2508, *pg.* 76, *pg.* 920
CRENLO, LLC, 1600 4th Ave NW, **Rochester,** MN 55901-2573, *pg.* 77, *pg.* 955
LESTER BUILDING SYSTEMS, LLC, 1111 Second Ave S, **Lester Prairie,** MN 55354, *pg.* 93, *pg.* 927
MET-CON CONSTRUCTION INC., 15760 Acorn Trl, **Faribault,** MN 55021, *pg.* 97, *pg.* 925
NORCRAFT HOLDINGS, LP, 3020 Denmark Ave Ste 100, **Eagan,** MN 55121-2417, *pg.* 100, *pg.* 921
OPUS CORPORATION, 10350 Bren Rd W, **Minnetonka,** MN 55343-9014, *pg.* 101, *pg.* 949

Mississippi

GULF STATES MANUFACTURERS, INC., 101 Airport Rd, **Starkville,** MS 39759-9682, *pg.* 85, *pg.* 971
SOUTHERN PIPE & SUPPLY CO., INC., 4330 Hwy 39 N, **Meridian,** MS 39301, *pg.* 112, *pg.* 970

Missouri

ARCH COAL, INC., One CityPlace Dr Ste 300, **Saint Louis,**

MO 63141, *pg.* 68, *pg.* 992
BUTLER MANUFACTURING COMPANY, 1540 Genessee St, **Kansas City,** MO 64102, *pg.* 72, *pg.* 981
HBE CORPORATION, 11330 Olive Blvd, **Saint Louis,** MO 63141-7149, *pg.* 86, *pg.* 998
HUTTIG BUILDING PRODUCTS, INC., 555 Maryville University Dr Ste 400, **Saint Louis,** MO 63141, *pg.* 88, *pg.* 998
INSITUFORM TECHNOLOGIES INC, 17988 Edison Ave, **Chesterfield,** MO 63005-1195, *pg.* 88, *pg.* 974
J.E. DUNN CONSTRUCTION GROUP, INC., 929 Holmes St, **Kansas City,** MO 64106, *pg.* 89, *pg.* 984
MCCARTHY BUILDING COMPANIES, INC., 1341 N Rock Hill Rd, **Saint Louis,** MO 63124, *pg.* 96, *pg.* 999
NEWGROUND RESOURCES, 15450 S Outr 40 Ste 300, **Chesterfield,** MO 63017-2062, *pg.* 99, *pg.* 975
PLY GEM SIDING GROUP, 2600 Grand Blvd Ste 900, **Kansas City,** MO 64108, *pg.* 105, *pg.* 986
STARRCO COMPANY INC., 11700 Fairgrove Indus Blvd, **Maryland Heights,** MO 63043-3436, *pg.* 113, *pg.* 988
SWARTWOUT DIVISION, 3900 Doctor Greaves Rd, **Grandview,** MO 64030-1134, *pg.* 114, *pg.* 978
TUBULAR STEEL INC., 1031 Executive Pkwy Dr, **Saint Louis,** MO 63141-6339, *pg.* 117, *pg.* 1004
UNIQUE TILE, 1364 N Kelly, **Nixa,** MO 65714, *pg.* 117, *pg.* 988
ZOLTEK COMPANIES, INC., 3101 McKelvey Rd, **Bridgeton,** MO 63044, *pg.* 123, *pg.* 974

Montana

ROCKY MOUNTAIN LOG HOMES, 1883 US Hwy 93 S, **Hamilton,** MT 59840, *pg.* 108, *pg.* 1008

Nebraska

LOZIER CORPORATION, 6336 Pershing Dr, **Omaha,** NE 68110, *pg.* 94, *pg.* 1016
PROCHASKA & ASSOCIATES, 11317 Chicago Cir, **Omaha,** NE 68154-2633, *pg.* 105, *pg.* 1017

Nevada

BLUE EARTH, INC., 2298 Horizon Ridge Pkwy Ste 205, **Henderson,** NV 89052, *pg.* 70, *pg.* 1021
FORTIFIBER CORPORATION, 300 Industrial Blvd, **Fernley,** NV 89451-9309, *pg.* 83, *pg.* 1021
MARNELL COMPANIES, 222 Via Marnell Way, **Las Vegas,** NV 89119, *pg.* 95, *pg.* 1028

New Hampshire

HITCHINER MANUFACTURING COMPANY INC., 594 Elm St, **Milford,** NH 03055, *pg.* 87, *pg.* 1037
R.P. WILLIAMS & SONS, INC., 400 Summer St, **Bristol,** NH 03222-3213, *pg.* 108, *pg.* 1033
WAKEFIELD-VETTE, 33 Bridge St, **Pelham,** NH 03076-3475, *pg.* 119, *pg.* 1038

New Jersey

AS AMERICA, INC., 1 Centennial Ave, **Piscataway,** NJ 08855-6820, *pg.* 68, *pg.* 1108
BUILDING MATERIALS CORPORATION OF AMERICA, 1361 Alps Rd, **Wayne,** NJ 07470-3700, *pg.* 72, *pg.* 1129
DELAIR GROUP, LLC, 8600 River Rd, **Delair,** NJ 08110-3328, *pg.* 78, *pg.* 1053
DENHOLTZ MANAGEMENT CORP., 14 Cliffwood Ave, **Matawan,** NJ 07047, *pg.* 78, *pg.* 1083
HILL INTERNATIONAL INC., 303 Lippincott Ctr, **Marlton,** NJ 08053-4160, *pg.* 87, *pg.* 1083
HOMASOTE COMPANY, 932 Lower Ferry Rd, **Trenton,** NJ 08628, *pg.* 87, *pg.* 1126
JARMEL KIZEL ARCHITECTS & ENGINEERS, INC., 42 Okner Pkwy, **Livingston,** NJ 07039, *pg.* 89, *pg.* 1079
LARKEN ASSOCIATES, 390 Amelo Rd Bldg 5 Ste 507, **Hillsborough,** NJ 08844, *pg.* 93, *pg.* 1073
MERCHANT & EVANS, INC., 308 Connecticut Dr, **Burlington,** NJ 08016, *pg.* 97, *pg.* 1048
METALICO INC., 186 N Ave E, **Cranford,** NJ 07016-2439, *pg.* 97, *pg.* 1053
NEWARK WIRE CLOTH CO., 160 Fornelius Ave, **Clifton,** NJ 07013, *pg.* 99, *pg.* 1052
POGGENPOHL U.S., INC., 350 Passaic Ave, **Fairfield,** NJ 07004, *pg.* 105, *pg.* 1065
SIKA CORPORATION, 201 Polito Ave, **Lyndhurst,** NJ 07071-3601, *pg.* 110, *pg.* 1080
SUBURBAN PROPANE PARTNERS, L.P., 1 Suburban Plz 240 Rte 10 W PO Box 206, **Whippany,** NJ 07981-0206, *pg.* 113, *pg.* 1132
SWEPCO TUBE CORPORATION, 1 Clifton Blvd, **Clifton,** NJ 07015, *pg.* 114, *pg.* 1052
TORCON, INC., 328 Newman Springs Rd, **Red Bank,** NJ 07701, *pg.* 116, *pg.* 1114
TRANE INC., 1 Centennial Ave, **Piscataway,** NJ 08855-6820, *pg.* 116, *pg.* 1109
THE WHITMAN COMPANIES, INC., 7 Pleasant Hill Rd, # 1, **Cranbury,** NJ 08512, *pg.* 121, *pg.* 1053

New York

ABM INDUSTRIES, INC., 551 Fifth Ave Ste 300, **New York,** NY 10176, *pg.* 64, *pg.* 1186
AECOM, 1 Penn Plz Ste 610, **New York,** NY 10119-0698, *pg.* 64, *pg.* 1187
ALCOA INC., 390 Park Ave, **New York,** NY 10022-4608, *pg.* 65, *pg.* 1188
BUFFALO WIRE WORKS CO., INC., 1165 Clinton St, **Buffalo,** NY 14206-2825, *pg.* 72, *pg.* 1147
COGENIC MECHANICAL, 405 Lyell Ave, **Rochester,** NY 14606, *pg.* 76, *pg.* 1333
CONSUMERS KITCHENS & BATHS, 717 Broadway Ave, **Holbrook,** NY 11741-4905, *pg.* 77, *pg.* 1167
DURASOL AWNINGS, INC., 445 Bellvale Rd, **Chester,** NY 10918, *pg.* 79, *pg.* 1153
FOUR SEASONS SUNROOM, 5005 Veterans Memorial Hwy, **Holbrook,** NY 11741-4506, *pg.* 83, *pg.* 1167
GASSER & SONS, INC., 440 Moreland Rd, **Commack,** NY 11725, *pg.* 83, *pg.* 1153
HANDY & HARMAN LTD., 1133 Westchester Ave Ste N222, **White Plains,** NY 10604, *pg.* 85, *pg.* 1352
METPAR CORP., 95 State St, **Westbury,** NY 11590-5006, *pg.* 97, *pg.* 1350
OSMOSE, INC., 980 Ellicott St, **Buffalo,** NY 14209-2323, *pg.* 102, *pg.* 1150
PARSONS & WHITTEMORE, INC., 4 Intl Dr Ste 5, **Rye Brook,** NY 10573, *pg.* 103, *pg.* 1339
PARSONS BRINCKERHOFF INC., 1 Penn Plz, **New York,** NY 10119-0002, *pg.* 103, *pg.* 1276
PENTAIR WATER POOL AND SPA, INC., 1351 Rte 55, **Lagrangeville,** NY 12540, *pg.* 104, *pg.* 1171
RIGIDIZED METALS CORP., 658 Ohio St, **Buffalo,** NY 14203-3122, *pg.* 108, *pg.* 1151
SCHLEGEL SYSTEMS, INC., 1555 Jefferson Rd, **Rochester,** NY 14623-3109, *pg.* 109, *pg.* 1337
SONO-TEK CORPORATION, 2012 Rte 9W, **Milton,** NY 12547, *pg.* 112, *pg.* 1182
STEBBINS ENGINEERING & MANUFACTURING COMPANY, 363 Eastern Blvd, **Watertown,** NY 13601-3140, *pg.* 113, *pg.* 1349
THEO KALOMIRAKIS THEATERS, 517 W 35th St Fl 7, **New York,** NY 10001, *pg.* 115, *pg.* 1298
UNADILLA SILO COMPANY INC., 18 Clifton St, **Unadilla,** NY 13849-3361, *pg.* 117, *pg.* 1346

North Carolina

GREGORY POOLE EQUIPMENT COMPANY INC., 4807 Beryl Rd PO Box 469, **Raleigh,** NC 27606-1406, *pg.* 85, *pg.* 1387
NUCOR CORPORATION, 1915 Rexford Rd, **Charlotte,** NC 28211, *pg.* 101, *pg.* 1368
PIKE ELECTRIC CORPORATION, 100 Pike Way, **Mount Airy,** NC 27030-8147, *pg.* 104, *pg.* 1385
POWERSECURE INTERNATIONAL, INC., 1609 Heritage Commerce Ct, **Wake Forest,** NC 27587, *pg.* 105, *pg.* 1392
RESCO PRODUCTS GREENSBORO, 3514 W Wendover Ave, **Greensboro,** NC 27407, *pg.* 107, *pg.* 1375
RSI HOME PRODUCTS, 350 N Generals Blvd, **Lincolnton,** NC 28092-3557, *pg.* 108, *pg.* 1381
STONECUTTER MILLS CORP., 230 Spindale St, **Spindale,** NC 28160, *pg.* 113, *pg.* 1391

Ohio

ALCOA WHEEL & FORGED PRODUCTS, 1600 Harvard Ave, **Cleveland,** OH 44105-3040, *pg.* 66, *pg.* 1427
ALERIS RECYCLING & SPECIFICATION ALLOYS AMERICAS, 25825 Science Park Dr Ste 400, **Beachwood,** OH 44122, *pg.* 66, *pg.* 1405
ASSOCIATED MATERIALS LLC, 3773 State Rd, **Cuyahoga Falls,** OH 44223, *pg.* 69, *pg.* 1445
THE AUSTIN COMPANY, 6095 Parkland Blvd, **Cleveland,** OH 44124, *pg.* 69, *pg.* 1428
BAKER CONCRETE CONSTRUCTION, INC., 900 N Garver Rd, **Monroe,** OH 45050-1241, *pg.* 69, *pg.* 1465
BURGESS & NIPLE, INC., 5085 Reed Rd, **Columbus,** OH 43220, *pg.* 72, *pg.* 1438
CLARK GRAVE VAULT COMPANY, 375 E 5th Ave, **Columbus,** OH 43201-2819, *pg.* 76, *pg.* 1438
CLOPAY BUILDING PRODUCTS COMPANY, 8585 Duke Blvd, **Mason,** OH 45040, *pg.* 76, *pg.* 1459
DOMINION HOMES, INC., 4900 Tuttle Crossing Blvd, **Dublin,** OH 43016, *pg.* 79, *pg.* 1449
THE D.S. BROWN COMPANY, 300 E Cherry St, **North Baltimore,** OH 45872-1227, *pg.* 79, *pg.* 1468
DUGAN & MEYERS CONSTRUCTION CO., INC., 11110 Kenwood Rd, **Cincinnati,** OH 45242-1818, *pg.* 79, *pg.* 1412
ELECTRIC EEL MANUFACTURING CO., INC., 501 W Leffel Ln, **Springfield,** OH 45506-3529, *pg.* 80, *pg.* 1473
ENERFAB, INC., 4955 Spring Grove Ave, **Cincinnati,** OH 45232-1925, *pg.* 81, *pg.* 1412
THE EUCLID CHEMICAL COMPANY, 19218 Redwood Rd, **Cleveland,** OH 44110, *pg.* 81, *pg.* 1430
GREAT LAKES WINDOW, INC., 30499 Tracy Rd, **Walbridge,** OH 43465-9777, *pg.* 85, *pg.* 1478
GREER STEEL COMPANY, 624 Blvd, **Dover,** OH 44622, *pg.* 85, *pg.* 1447
H-P PRODUCTS, INC., 512 W Gorgas St, **Louisville,** OH 44641-1332, *pg.* 85, *pg.* 1458
HARROP INDUSTRIES, INC., 3470 E 5th Ave, **Columbus,** OH 43219, *pg.* 86, *pg.* 1440
HICKMAN, WILLIAMS & COMPANY, Chiquita Ctr 250 E 5th St Ste 300, **Cincinnati,** OH 45202, *pg.* 87, *pg.* 1414
M/I HOMES, INC., 3 Easton Oval Ste 500, **Columbus,** OH 43219-6011, *pg.* 95, *pg.* 1441
MAINTENANCE, INC., 1051 W Liberty St, **Wooster,** OH 44691-0408, *pg.* 95, *pg.* 1482
MARLITE, INC., 202 Harger St, **Dover,** OH 44622, *pg.* 95, *pg.* 1448
NIXCO PLUMBING INC., 4281 State Rt 42, **Mason,** OH 45040, *pg.* 99, *pg.* 1461
NORANDEX/REYNOLDS DISTRIBUTION, INC., 300 Executive Pwy W Ste 100, **Hudson,** OH 44236, *pg.* 99, *pg.* 1455
OLYMPIC STEEL INC., 5096 Richmond Rd, **Cleveland,** OH 44146-1329, *pg.* 101, *pg.* 1433
OWENS CORNING, 1 Owens Corning Pkwy, **Toledo,** OH 43659-1000, *pg.* 102, *pg.* 1476
REVERE PRODUCTS, 4529 Industrial Pkwy, **Cleveland,** OH 44135-4541, *pg.* 107, *pg.* 1435
RICHARDS INDUSTRIES VALVE GROUP, 3170 Wasson Rd, **Cincinnati,** OH 45209, *pg.* 107, *pg.* 1425
ROBBINS, INC., 4777 Eastern Ave, **Cincinnati,** OH 45226-2338, *pg.* 108, *pg.* 1425
ROTO-ROOTER, INC., 255 E Fifth St Chemed Ctr Ste 2500, **Cincinnati,** OH 45202-4726, *pg.* 108, *pg.* 1425
ROUGH BROTHERS, INC., 5513 Vine St, **Cincinnati,** OH 45217-1003, *pg.* 108, *pg.* 1425
SAFELITE SOLUTIONS LLC, 2400 Farmers Dr, **Columbus,** OH 43235, *pg.* 109, *pg.* 1443
SAKRETE OF NORTH AMERICA, LLC, 5155 Fischer Ave, **Cincinnati,** OH 45217, *pg.* 109, *pg.* 1425
SCHUMACHER HOMES, INC., 2715 Wise Ave NW, **Canton,** OH 44708, *pg.* 109, *pg.* 1408
SUMMITVILLE TILES, INC., PO Box 73, **Summitville,** OH 43962-0073, *pg.* 113, *pg.* 1475
THERMA-TRU CORP., 1750 Indian Wood Cir, **Maumee,** OH 43537-4049, *pg.* 115, *pg.* 1462
TODCO, INC., 1332 Fairground Rd E, **Marion,** OH 43302, *pg.* 115, *pg.* 1459
TREMCO INCORPORATED, 3735 Green Rd, **Beachwood,** OH 44122, *pg.* 116, *pg.* 1405
WAXMAN INDUSTRIES, INC., 24460 Aurora Rd, **Bedford,** OH 44146-1728, *pg.* 120, *pg.* 1406
WAYNE-DALTON CORP., 1 Door Dr, **Mount Hope,** OH 44660, *pg.* 120, *pg.* 1465
W.J. RUSCOE COMPANY, 485 Kenmore Blvd, **Akron,** OH 44301-1013, *pg.* 122, *pg.* 1403
WORTHINGTON INDUSTRIES, INC., 200 Old Wilson Bridge

First page reference indicates Business Class Edition
Second page reference indicates Geographic Edition

Rd, **Columbus,** OH 43085, *pg.* 123, *pg.* 1444

Oklahoma

THE BOARDMAN INC., 1135 S McKinley Ave, **Oklahoma City,** OK 73108, *pg.* 71, *pg.* 1484
M-D BUILDING PRODUCTS, INC., 4041 N Santa Fe Ave, **Oklahoma City,** OK 73118, *pg.* 95, *pg.* 1486
STAR BUILDING SYSTEMS, 8600 S Interstate 35, **Oklahoma City,** OK 73149, *pg.* 112, *pg.* 1488

Oregon

OREPAC HOLDING COMPANY INC., 30170 SW Ore Pac Ave, **Wilsonville,** OR 97070-9794, *pg.* 102, *pg.* 1512
PRECISION CASTPARTS CORP., 4650 SW Macadam Ave Ste 440, **Portland,** OR 97239-4262, *pg.* 105, *pg.* 1506

Pennsylvania

ALLEGHENY TECHNOLOGIES INCORPORATED, 1000 Six PPG Pl 10 Fl, **Pittsburgh,** PA 15222-5479, *pg.* 66, *pg.* 1572
ATLAS MINERALS & CHEMICALS, INC., 1227 Vly Rd, **Mertztown,** PA 19539-8827, *pg.* 69, *pg.* 1552
BATEMAN BROTHERS LUMBER CO., INC., 89 S Sand Rd, **New Britain,** PA 18901-5122, *pg.* 70, *pg.* 1555
BENJAMIN OBDYKE, INC., 400 Babyllon Rd Ste A, **Horsham,** PA 19044-1232, *pg.* 70, *pg.* 1540
CARMEUSE NORTH AMERICA, 11 Stanwix St 21th Fl, **Pittsburgh,** PA 15222-1312, *pg.* 73, *pg.* 1574
CARPENTER TECHNOLOGY CORPORATION, P.O. Box 14662, **Reading,** PA 19610-1339, *pg.* 73, *pg.* 1584
CENTRIA ARCHITECTURAL SYSTEMS, 1005 Beaver Grade Rd, **Moon Township,** PA 15108, *pg.* 74, *pg.* 1554
CENTRIA, INC., 1005 Beaver Grade Rd, **Moon Township,** PA 15108-2964, *pg.* 74, *pg.* 1554
CERTAINTEED CORPORATION, 750 E Swedesford Rd, **Valley Forge,** PA 19482, *pg.* 74, *pg.* 1589
CLESTRA HAUSERMAN, INC., 259 Veterans Ln Ste 201, **Doylestown,** PA 18901, *pg.* 76, *pg.* 1526
CORNELL IRON WORKS, INC., 100 Elmwood Ave Crestwood Industrial Park, **Mountain Top,** PA 18707, *pg.* 77, *pg.* 1554
DCK WORLDWIDE, LLC, 1 PPG Place 27th Fl, **Pittsburgh,** PA 15222, *pg.* 78, *pg.* 1574
DIPCRAFT MANUFACTURING COMPANY, 111 W Braddock Ave, **Braddock,** PA 15104-1115, *pg.* 79, *pg.* 1518
THE FLINCHBAUGH CO., INC., 245 Beshore School Rd, **Manchester,** PA 17345, *pg.* 82, *pg.* 1551
GEOSPATIAL HOLDINGS, INC., 229 Howes Run Rd, **Sarver,** PA 16055, *pg.* 84, *pg.* 1585
GLEN-GERY CORPORATION, 1166 Spring St, **Wyomissing,** PA 19610-6001, *pg.* 84, *pg.* 1595
HARSCO CORPORATION, 350 Poplar Church Rd, **Camp Hill,** PA 17011, *pg.* 86, *pg.* 1519
HENDRICK MANUFACTURING COMPANY, 1 7th Ave, **Carbondale,** PA 18407-2203, *pg.* 86, *pg.* 1520
HENKELS & MCCOY, INC., 985 Jolly Rd, **Blue Bell,** PA 19422-1903, *pg.* 86, *pg.* 1517
INCLINATOR COMPANY OF AMERICA, 601 Gibson Blvd, **Harrisburg,** PA 17104, *pg.* 88, *pg.* 1536
THE KULJIAN CORPORATION, 3700 Market St No 2, **Philadelphia,** PA 19104-3169, *pg.* 92, *pg.* 1566
LEHIGH HANSON, INC., 7660 Imperial Way, **Allentown,** PA 18195-1016, *pg.* 93, *pg.* 1513
OVERLY MANUFACTURING COMPANY, 574 W Otterman St, **Greensburg,** PA 15601-2148, *pg.* 102, *pg.* 1534
PARISI INCORPORATED, 305 Pheasant Run, **Newtown,** PA 18940, *pg.* 103, *pg.* 1556
PENFLEX, INC., 105-B Industrial Dr, **Gilbertsville,** PA 19525, *pg.* 104, *pg.* 1534
P.J. DICK-TRUMBULL-LINDY, 225 North Shore Dr, **Pittsburgh,** PA 15212, *pg.* 104, *pg.* 1579
POTTERS INDUSTRIES, INC., 1200 W Swedesford Rd, **Berwyn,** PA 19312, *pg.* 105, *pg.* 1515
R.D. BITZER CO. INC., 776 American Dr, **Bensalem,** PA 19020-7342, *pg.* 106, *pg.* 1515
RESCO PRODUCTS, INC., 2 Penn Ctr W Ste 430, **Pittsburgh,** PA 15276, *pg.* 107, *pg.* 1581
SAE INTERNATIONAL, 400 Commonwealth Dr, **Warrendale,** PA 15096-0001, *pg.* 108, *pg.* 1591
SILBERLINE MANUFACTURING CO., INC., 130 Lincoln Dr, **Tamaqua,** PA 18252-0420, *pg.* 110, *pg.* 1588
SMOOTH-ON INC., 2000 Saint John St, **Easton,** PA 18042-6646, *pg.* 111, *pg.* 1528
SUPERIOR TUBE COMPANY INC., 3900 Germantown Pike, **Collegeville,** PA 19426-3112, *pg.* 113, *pg.* 1522
TENOVA, 100 Corp Ctr Dr, **Coraopolis,** PA 15108-3185, *pg.* 114, *pg.* 1525
THERMAL INDUSTRIES, INC., 3700 Haney Ct, **Murrysville,** PA 15668, *pg.* 115, *pg.* 1555
TOLL BROTHERS, INC., 250 Gibraltar Rd, **Horsham,** PA 19044-2323, *pg.* 115, *pg.* 1541
WERNER HOLDING CO., 93 Werner Rd, **Greenville,** PA 16125-9434, *pg.* 121, *pg.* 1534
WHEATLAND TUBE COMPANY, 1 Council Ave, **Wheatland,** PA 16161-0608, *pg.* 121, *pg.* 1594

Rhode Island

GILBANE BUILDING COMPANY, 7 Jackson Walkway, **Providence,** RI 02903-3623, *pg.* 84, *pg.* 1606
NORTEK, INC., 500 Exchange St, **Providence,** RI 02903, *pg.* 100, *pg.* 1607

South Carolina

ANDERSON HARDWOOD FLOORS, 384 Torrington Rd, **Clinton,** SC 29325-1155, *pg.* 67, *pg.* 1613
BURROUGHS & CHAPIN CO. INC., 611 Burroughs & Chapin Blvd Ste 100, **Myrtle Beach,** SC 29577, *pg.* 72, *pg.* 1621
GUARDIAN BUILDING PRODUCTS DISTRIBUTION, 979 Batesville Rd, **Greer,** SC 29651, *pg.* 85, *pg.* 1619
LEIGH FIBERS, INC., 1101 Syphrit Rd, **Wellford,** SC 29385-9460, *pg.* 93, *pg.* 1623
SOUTHERN LUMBER & MILLWORK CORP., 2031 King St Ext, **Charleston,** SC 29405-9419, *pg.* 112, *pg.* 1613
T&S BRASS & BRONZE WORKS, INC., 2 Saddleback Cove, **Travelers Rest,** SC 29690-2232, *pg.* 114, *pg.* 1623

South Dakota

LARSON MANUFACTURING COMPANY, 2333 Eastbrook Dr, **Brookings,** SD 57006-2838, *pg.* 93, *pg.* 1624
SHUR-CO, INC., 2309 Shurlock St, **Yankton,** SD 57078-1210, *pg.* 110, *pg.* 1626

Tennessee

ALLEN & HOSHALL, INC., 1661 Intl Dr Ste 100, **Memphis,** TN 38120-1440, *pg.* 66, *pg.* 1641
ASTEC INDUSTRIES, INC., 1725 Shepherd Rd, **Chattanooga,** TN 37421, *pg.* 69, *pg.* 1628
CROSSVILLE, INC., 346 Sweeney Dr, **Crossville,** TN 38555, *pg.* 77, *pg.* 1632
CUMMINGS INCORPORATED, 4560 Trousdale Dr, **Knoxville,** TN 37204, *pg.* 77, *pg.* 1636
I.C. THOMASSON ASSOCIATES, INC., 2950 Kraft Dr Ste 500, **Nashville,** TN 37204-0527, *pg.* 88, *pg.* 1651
KIRBY BUILDING SYSTEMS, INC., 124 Kirby Dr, **Portland,** TN 37148, *pg.* 91, *pg.* 1655
LENNOX HEARTH PRODUCTS, 1508 Elm Hill Pike, Ste 108, **Nashville,** TN 37210, *pg.* 93, *pg.* 1652
LOUISIANA-PACIFIC CORPORATION, 414 Union St Ste 2000, **Nashville,** TN 37219, *pg.* 94, *pg.* 1652
LUCITE INTERNATIONAL, INC., The Lucite Ctr 7275 Goodlett Farms Pkwy, **Cordova,** TN 38016, *pg.* 94, *pg.* 1631
SCHOTT GEMTRON CORPORATION, 615 Hwy 68, **Sweetwater,** TN 37874-1911, *pg.* 109, *pg.* 1656
VARCO PRUDEN BUILDINGS, INC., 3200 Players Club Cir, **Memphis,** TN 38125, *pg.* 118, *pg.* 1647

Texas

ALIMAK HEK INC, 12552 Old Galveston Rd Ste A-160, **Webster,** TX 77598, *pg.* 66, *pg.* 1749
AMERICAN HOMESTAR CORPORATION, 2450 S Shore Blvd Ste 300, **League City,** TX 77573-2997, *pg.* 67, *pg.* 1725
ATRIUM COMPANIES, INC., 3890 W NW Hwy Ste 500, **Dallas,** TX 75220, *pg.* 69, *pg.* 1676
THE BECK GROUP, 1807 Ross Ave Ste 500, **Dallas,** TX 75201-4691, *pg.* 70, *pg.* 1676
CANTEX INC., 2101 SE 1st St, **Mineral Wells,** TX 76067-5601, *pg.* 73, *pg.* 1727
CEMEX, INC., 202 Holmes Rd, **Houston,** TX 77045, *pg.* 74, *pg.* 1703
CHICAGO BRIDGE & IRON COMPANY, 2103 Research Forest Dr, **The Woodlands,** TX 77380-1123, *pg.* 75, *pg.* 1747
CHILDERS CARPORTS AND STRUCTURES, INC., 11711 Brittmoore Pk Dr, **Houston,** TX 77041-6923, *pg.* 76, *pg.* 1703
COMMERCIAL METALS COMPANY, 6565 MacArthur Blvd, **Irving,** TX 75039, *pg.* 76, *pg.* 1718
COSENTINO USA, 13124 Trinity Dr, **Stafford,** TX 77477, *pg.* 77, *pg.* 1745
DAL-TILE CORPORATION, 7834 C F Hawn Freeway PO Box 170130, **Dallas,** TX 75217-6529, *pg.* 78, *pg.* 1678
DALLAS MARKET CENTER COMPANY, 2100 N Stemmons Freeway 1000, **Dallas,** TX 75207, *pg.* 78, *pg.* 1678
DAVID WEEKLEY HOMES, LP, 1111 N Post Oak Rd, **Houston,** TX 77055-7211, *pg.* 78, *pg.* 1704
THE DWYER GROUP, INC., 1010 N University Parks Dr, **Waco,** TX 76707-3854, *pg.* 79, *pg.* 1748
ELGIN-BUTLER BRICK COMPANY, 1007 E 40th St, **Austin,** TX 78751-4805, *pg.* 80, *pg.* 1662
ENGLOBAL CORPORATION, Ste 400 654 N Sam Houston Pkwy E, **Houston,** TX 77060-5914, *pg.* 81, *pg.* 1705
FASTSIGNS INTERNATIONAL, INC., 2542 Highlander Way, **Carrollton,** TX 75006-2333, *pg.* 81, *pg.* 1669
FLOWSERVE CORPORATION, 5215 N O'Connor Blvd Ste 2300, **Irving,** TX 75039-5435, *pg.* 82, *pg.* 1719
FLUOR CORPORATION, 6700 Las Colinas Blvd, **Irving,** TX 75039, *pg.* 82, *pg.* 1719
GAF MATERIALS CORP., 14911 Quorum Dr Ste 600, **Dallas,** TX 75254, *pg.* 83, *pg.* 1681
HIRSCHFELD INDUSTRIES, INC., 112 W 29th St, **San Angelo,** TX 76903-2553, *pg.* 87, *pg.* 1739
HUNT BUILDING COMPANY LIMITED, 4401 N Mesa St, **El Paso,** TX 79902-1107, *pg.* 87, *pg.* 1692
INTEGRATED ELECTRICAL SERVICES, INC., 5433 Westheimer Rd, Ste 500, **Houston,** TX 77056, *pg.* 88, *pg.* 1708
KBR, INC., 601 Jefferson St Ste 9400, **Houston,** TX 77002, *pg.* 90, *pg.* 1709
KEYSTONE CONSOLIDATED INDUSTRIES, INC., 5430 LBJ Fwy Ste 1700, **Dallas,** TX 75240-2697, *pg.* 90, *pg.* 1683
LENNAR HOMES, INC., 550 Greens Pkwy Ste 111, **Houston,** TX 77067, *pg.* 93, *pg.* 1710
OVERHEAD DOOR CORPORATION, 2501 S State Hwy 121 Ste 200, **Lewisville,** TX 75067, *pg.* 102, *pg.* 1725
PRIMESOURCE BUILDING PRODUCTS, INC., 1321 Greenway Dr, **Irving,** TX 75038, *pg.* 105, *pg.* 1723
TANKNOLOGY INC, 11000 N Mopac Expy Ste 500, **Austin,** TX 78759, *pg.* 114, *pg.* 1666
TRINITY INDUSTRIES, INC., 2525 Stemmons Fwy, **Dallas,** TX 75207-2401, *pg.* 116, *pg.* 1690

Utah

DAW TECHNOLOGIES, INC., 1600 W 2200 S Ste 201, **Salt Lake City,** UT 84119, *pg.* 78, *pg.* 1756
MARTIN DOOR MANUFACTURING, INC., 2828 S 900 West, **Salt Lake City,** UT 84119-2420, *pg.* 96, *pg.* 1759

Vermont

ROCK OF AGES CORPORATION, 560 Graniteville Rd, **Graniteville,** VT 05654, *pg.* 108, *pg.* 1766

Virginia

BROOKFIELD HOMES CORPORATION, 8500 Executive Park Ave Ste 300, **Fairfax,** VA 22031, *pg.* 72, *pg.* 1779
E.V. WILLIAMS, INC., 925 S Military Hwy, **Virginia Beach,** VA 23464, *pg.* 81, *pg.* 1810
LUMBER LIQUIDATORS HOLDINGS, INC., 3000 John Deere Rd, **Toano,** VA 23168-9332, *pg.* 94, *pg.* 1808
MILLER AND SMITH HOMES, INC., 8401 Greensboro Dr Ste 300, **McLean,** VA 22102-3054, *pg.* 97, *pg.* 1794
NATIONWIDE HOMES, INC., 1100 Rives Rd, **Martinsville,** VA 24112, *pg.* 99, *pg.* 1788
THE REINFORCED EARTH COMPANY, 12001 Sunrise Valley Dr Ste 400, **Reston,** VA 20191, *pg.* 106, *pg.* 1799
SMITH-MIDLAND CORPORATION, 5119 Catlett Rd, **Midland,** VA 22728-0300, *pg.* 111, *pg.* 1795
TREX COMPANY, INC., 160 Exeter Dr, **Winchester,** VA 22603-8605, *pg.* 116, *pg.* 1812
VIRGINIA GLASS PRODUCTS CORPORATION, 347 Old Sand Rd, **Martinsville,** VA 24148, *pg.* 119, *pg.* 1788

W.M. JORDAN COMPANY INC., 11010 Jefferson Ave, **Newport News,** VA 23601, *pg.* 122, *pg.* 1796

Washington

HCS CORPORATION, 22626 85th Pl S, **Kent,** WA 98031-2469, *pg.* 86, *pg.* 1821
LINDAL CEDAR HOMES, INC., 4300 S 104th Pl, **Seattle,** WA 98178, *pg.* 94, *pg.* 1837
NORTHWEST PIPE COMPANY, 5721 SE Columbia Way Ste 200, **Vancouver,** WA 98661, *pg.* 100, *pg.* 1846
PLUM CREEK TIMBER COMPANY, INC., Ste 4300 999 3rd Ave, **Seattle,** WA 98104-4096, *pg.* 105, *pg.* 1838
SHANNON & WILSON, INC., 400 N 34th St Ste 100, **Seattle,** WA 98103-8600, *pg.* 110, *pg.* 1840
SIMPSON DOOR COMPANY, 400 Simpson Ave, **McCleary,** WA 98557, *pg.* 110, *pg.* 1823
SIMPSON LUMBER COMPANY, LLC, 917 E 11th St, **Tacoma,** WA 98421, *pg.* 110, *pg.* 1845
WEYERHAEUSER COMPANY, 33663 Weyerhaeuser Way S, **Federal Way,** WA 98063, *pg.* 121, *pg.* 1820

West Virginia

CENTURY ALUMINUM OF WEST VIRGINIA, INC., Century Rd, **Ravenswood,** WV 26164, *pg.* 74, *pg.* 1851
EAGLE MANUFACTURING COMPANY, 2400 Charles St, **Wellsburg,** WV 26070-1000, *pg.* 79, *pg.* 1851

Wisconsin

AMERICAN BUILDERS & CONTRACTORS SUPPLY CO., INC., 1 ABC Pkwy, **Beloit,** WI 53511-4466, *pg.* 66, *pg.* 1854
ATI LADISH FORGING, 5481 S Packard Ave, **Cudahy,** WI 53110, *pg.* 69, *pg.* 1856
BRADLEY CORPORATION, W 142 N 9101 Fountain Blvd, **Menomonee Falls,** WI 53051-2348, *pg.* 71, *pg.* 1870
CENTURY FENCE COMPANY, 1300 Hickory St, **Pewaukee,** WI 53072-5505, *pg.* 74, *pg.* 1886
CLEAVER-BROOKS, 11950 W Lk Park Dr, **Milwaukee,** WI 53201-0421, *pg.* 76, *pg.* 1874
FIBERESIN INDUSTRIES, INC., 37031 E Wisconsin Ave, **Oconomowoc,** WI 53066, *pg.* 81, *pg.* 1885
HUFCOR INCORPORATED, 2101 Kennedy Rd, **Janesville,** WI 53545-0824, *pg.* 87, *pg.* 1861
HURD WINDOWS & DOORS INC, 575 S Whelen Ave, **Medford,** WI 54451-1738, *pg.* 88, *pg.* 1869
JACK WALTERS & SONS CORP., 6600 Midland Ct, **Allenton,** WI 53002, *pg.* 88, *pg.* 1852
KOHLER CO., 444 Highland Dr, **Kohler,** WI 53044-1515, *pg.* 91, *pg.* 1862
LURIE GLASS COMPANY, 12000 W Wirth St, **Milwaukee,** WI 53222, *pg.* 95, *pg.* 1877
MICHELS CORPORATION, 817 W Main St, **Brownsville,** WI 53006, *pg.* 97, *pg.* 1855
NABCO ENTRANCES, INC., S 82 W 18717 Gemini Dr, **Muskego,** WI 53150-0906, *pg.* 99, *pg.* 1882
NEENAH ENTERPRISES, INC., 2121 Brooks Ave, **Neenah,** WI 54956, *pg.* 99, *pg.* 1883
NEENAH FOUNDRY COMPANY, 2121 Brooks St, **Neenah,** WI 54956, *pg.* 99, *pg.* 1883
P&H MINING EQUIPMENT, 4400 W National Ave, **Milwaukee,** WI 53214-3639, *pg.* 103, *pg.* 1879
REGAL BELOIT CORPORATION, 200 State St, **Beloit,** WI 53511-6254, *pg.* 106, *pg.* 1854
SAFWAY SERVICES, LLC, N19 W 24200 Riverwood Dr, **Waukesha,** WI 53188, *pg.* 109, *pg.* 1898
SAMUELS GROUP, INC., 311 Fiancial Way St 300, **Wausau,** WI 54401-1404, *pg.* 109, *pg.* 1898
SUPER SKY PRODUCTS, INC., 10301 N Enterprise Dr, **Mequon,** WI 53092-4639, *pg.* 113, *pg.* 1871
VINTAGE PARTS, 120 Corporate Dr, **Beaver Dam,** WI 53916-3116, *pg.* 119, *pg.* 1854
W.A. ROOSEVELT COMPANY, 2727 Commerce St, **La Crosse,** WI 54603-1760, *pg.* 119, *pg.* 1864
WAUSAU HOMES, INC., 10805 Bus Hwy 51, **Rothschild,** WI 54474, *pg.* 120, *pg.* 1890

Associations, Institutions, Unions, Etc.

Alabama

DUCTILE IRON PIPE RESEARCH ASSOCIATION, 1322 Riverhaven Pl, **Birmingham,** AL 35244, *pg.* 140, *pg.* 2
THE SOUTHERN POVERTY LAW CENTER, 403 Washington Ave, **Montgomery,** AL 36104-4344, *pg.* 157, *pg.* 7

Alaska

ALASKA SEAFOOD MARKETING INSTITUTE, 311 N Franklin St Ste 200, **Juneau,** AK 99801-1147, *pg.* 125, *pg.* 10

Arizona

INTEGRITY SOLUTIONS, 4150 N Drinkwater Blvd, Ste 150, **Scottsdale,** AZ 85251, *pg.* 145, *pg.* 22

California

THE ACADEMY OF SCIENCE FICTION, FANTASY & HORROR FILMS, 334 W 54th St, **Los Angeles,** CA 90037-3806, *pg.* 125, *pg.* 125
AMERICAN ASSOCIATION OF CRITICAL-CARE NURSES, 101 Columbia, **Aliso Viejo,** CA 92656-4109, *pg.* 126, *pg.* 40
AUTOMOBILE CLUB OF SOUTHERN CALIFORNIA, 2601 S Figueroa St, **Los Angeles,** CA 90007, *pg.* 134, *pg.* 126
BUTTE HUMANE SOCIETY, 2579 Fair St, **Chico,** CA 95928, *pg.* 135, *pg.* 65
CALIFORNIA AVOCADO COMMISSION, 12 Mauchly Ste L, **Irvine,** CA 92618, *pg.* 135, *pg.* 108
CALIFORNIA DRIED PLUM BOARD, 3840 Rosin Ct Ste 170, **Sacramento,** CA 95834-1699, *pg.* 135, *pg.* 195
CALIFORNIA FIG ADVISORY BOARD, 392 W Fallbrook Ave, Ste 105, **Fresno,** CA 93711, *pg.* 135, *pg.* 92
CALIFORNIA MANUFACTURED HOUSING INSTITUTE, 1945 Chicago Ave, Ste B North, **Riverside,** CA 92507, *pg.* 135, *pg.* 194
CALIFORNIA OLIVE COMMITTEE, 1903 N Fine Ave Ste 102, **Fresno,** CA 93727-1510, *pg.* 135, *pg.* 92
CALIFORNIA REDWOOD ASSOCIATION, 818 Grayson Rd, Ste 201, **Pleasant Hill,** CA 94523, *pg.* 135, *pg.* 182
CALIFORNIA STRAWBERRY COMMISSION, 180 Westridge Dr Ste 101, **Watsonville,** CA 95076, *pg.* 135, *pg.* 305
CALIFORNIA TABLE GRAPE COMMISSION, 392 W Fallbrook Ave Ste 101, **Fresno,** CA 93711-6150, *pg.* 135, *pg.* 93
DIRECTORS GUILD OF AMERICA, INC., 7920 W Sunset Blvd, **Los Angeles,** CA 90046-3300, *pg.* 139, *pg.* 129
DIVING EQUIPMENT & MARKETING ASSOCIATION, 3750 Convoy St Ste 310, **San Diego,** CA 92111-3741, *pg.* 139, *pg.* 202
ELECTRIC POWER RESEARCH INSTITUTE INC, 3420 Hillview Ave, **Palo Alto,** CA 94304, *pg.* 140, *pg.* 175
ENTERTAINMENT INDUSTRY FOUNDATION, 1201 W 5th St Ste T-700, **Los Angeles,** CA 90017, *pg.* 140, *pg.* 130
FULL GOSPEL BUSINESS MEN'S FELLOWSHIP INTERNATIONAL, 18101 Von Kaman Ave Ste 330, **Irvine,** CA 92612, *pg.* 141, *pg.* 110
GLAUCOMA RESEARCH FOUNDATION, 251 Post St Ste 600, **San Francisco,** CA 94108, *pg.* 142, *pg.* 219
INSURANCE BROKERS & AGENTS OF THE WEST, 7041 Koll Ctr Pkwy Ste 290, **Pleasanton,** CA 94566, *pg.* 144, *pg.* 183
MAKE-A-WISH FOUNDATION OF GREATER LOS ANGELES, 1875 Century Park E Ste 950, **Los Angeles,** CA 90067-2515, *pg.* 146, *pg.* 136
MORRIS CERULLO WORLD EVANGELISM, 3545 Aero Ct, **San Diego,** CA 92123-1710, *pg.* 147, *pg.* 205
THE NATIONAL ASSOCIATION FOR PET CONTAINER RESOURCES, PO Box 1327, **Sonoma,** CA 95476, *pg.* 147, *pg.* 279
NATIONAL BRAIN TUMOR SOCIETY, 22 Battery St Ste 612, **San Francisco,** CA 94111-5520, *pg.* 148, *pg.* 223
NATIONAL HOT ROD ASSOCIATION, 2035 Financial Way, **Glendora,** CA 91740, *pg.* 149, *pg.* 99
NATIONAL NOTARY ASSOCIATION, 9350 De Soto Ave, **Chatsworth,** CA 91311-4926, *pg.* 150, *pg.* 64
THE NORTH AMERICAN BLUEBERRY COUNCIL, 80 Iron Point Cir Ste 114, **Folsom,** CA 95630, *pg.* 152, *pg.* 86
RECORDING MUSICIANS ASSOCIATION LOS ANGELES, 817 Vine St Ste 209, **Los Angeles,** CA 90038-3715, *pg.* 154, *pg.* 139
SIERRA CLUB, 85 2nd St 2nd Fl, **San Francisco,** CA 94105, *pg.* 156, *pg.* 227
SPECIALTY EQUIPMENT MARKET ASSOCIATION, 1575 S Valley Vista Dr, **Diamond Bar,** CA 91765, *pg.* 157, *pg.* 77
SURFRIDER FOUNDATION, 942 Calle Negocio Ste 350, **San Clemente,** CA 92673, *pg.* 158, *pg.* 199
UNITED THROUGH READING, 11750 Sorrento Valley Rd Ste 100, **San Diego,** CA 92121, *pg.* 160, *pg.* 210
UNTIL THERE'S A CURE FOUNDATION, 560 Mtn Home Rd, **Redwood City,** CA 94062, *pg.* 160, *pg.* 192
WIKIMEDIA FOUNDATION INC., PO Box 78350, **San Francisco,** CA 94107-8350, *pg.* 161, *pg.* 234
WILDAID, 744 Montgomery St, Ste 300, **San Francisco,** CA 94111, *pg.* 161, *pg.* 234

Colorado

AMERICAN SHEEP INDUSTRY ASSOCIATION, INC., 9785 Maroon Cir Ste 360, **Englewood,** CO 80112, *pg.* 131, *pg.* 325
AMERICAN WATER WORKS ASSOCIATION, 6666 W Quincy Ave, **Denver,** CO 80235-3098, *pg.* 131, *pg.* 316
CATTLEMEN'S BEEF PROMOTION & RESEARCH BOARD, 9000 E Nichols Ave St 215, **Centennial,** CO 80112, *pg.* 136, *pg.* 314
DARE 2 SHARE MINISTRIES INTERNATIONAL, INC., PO Box 745323, **Arvada,** CO 80006-5323, *pg.* 138, *pg.* 310
NATIONAL CATTLEMEN'S BEEF ASSOCIATION, 9110 E Nichols Ave Ste 300, **Centennial,** CO 80112-3450, *pg.* 148, *pg.* 314
NATIONAL HONEY BOARD, 11409 Business Park Cir Ste 10, **Firestone,** CO 80504, *pg.* 149, *pg.* 328
NATIONAL POTATO PROMOTION BOARD, 4949 S Syracuse St, #400, **Denver,** CO 80237, *pg.* 150, *pg.* 322

Connecticut

AMERICAN RADIO RELAY LEAGUE, INC., 225 Main St, **Newington,** CT 06111-1400, *pg.* 130, *pg.* 359
FRIENDS OF ANIMALS, INC., 777 Post Rd Ste 205, **Darien,** CT 06820, *pg.* 141, *pg.* 345
GREATER NEW HAVEN ASSOCIATION OF REALTORS, 127 Washington Ave WLL, **North Haven,** CT 06473, *pg.* 142, *pg.* 360
SAVE THE CHILDREN FEDERATION, INC., 54 Wilton Rd, **Westport,** CT 06881-9948, *pg.* 156, *pg.* 384

Delaware

PRODUCE MARKETING ASSOCIATION, 1500 Casho Mill Rd, **Newark,** DE 19711, *pg.* 154, *pg.* 388

District of Columbia

AARP, 601 E St NW, **Washington,** DC 20049, *pg.* 124, *pg.* 393
AFTERSCHOOL ALLIANCE, 1616 H St NW Ste 820, **Washington,** DC 20006, *pg.* 125, *pg.* 393
ALEXANDER GRAHAM BELL ASSOCIATION FOR THE DEAF AND HARD OF HEARING, 3417 Volta Pl NW, **Washington,** DC 20007, *pg.* 126, *pg.* 393
THE ALS ASSOCIATION, 1275 K Street NW Ste 250, **Washington,** DC 20005, *pg.* 126, *pg.* 393
AMERICAN ASSOCIATION FOR THE ADVANCEMENT OF SCIENCE, 1200 New York Ave NW, **Washington,** DC 20005, *pg.* 126, *pg.* 394
THE AMERICAN BANKERS ASSOCIATION, 1120 Connecticut Ave NW, **Washington,** DC 20036-3902, *pg.* 126, *pg.* 394
THE AMERICAN CLEANING INSTITUTE, 1500 K St NW Ste 300, **Washington,** DC 20005, *pg.* 127, *pg.* 394
AMERICAN COUNCIL OF LIFE INSURERS, 101 Constitution Ave NW, **Washington,** DC 20001-2133, *pg.* 127, *pg.* 394
AMERICAN ENTERPRISE INSTITUTE FOR PUBLIC POLICY RESEARCH, 1150 17th St NW, **Washington,** DC 20036-4603, *pg.* 128, *pg.* 394
AMERICAN FEDERATION OF LABOR - CONGRESS OF INDUSTRIAL ORGANIZATIONS, 815 16th St NW, **Washington,** DC 20006-4101, *pg.* 128, *pg.* 394
AMERICAN FOREST & PAPER ASSOCIATION, 1111 19th St NW Ste 800, **Washington,** DC 20036-3603, *pg.* 128, *pg.* 394
AMERICAN FORESTS, 734 15th St NW Ste 800, **Washington,** DC 20005, *pg.* 128, *pg.* 394
AMERICAN IRON AND STEEL INSTITUTE, 25 Massachusetts Ave NW, Ste 800, **Washington,** DC 20001, *pg.* 129, *pg.* 394
AMERICAN LUNG ASSOCIATION, 1301 Pennsylvania Ave NW Ste 800, **Washington,** DC 20004, *pg.* 129, *pg.* 395
AMERICAN PLASTICS COUNCIL, 700 Second St NE, **Washington,** DC 20002, *pg.* 130, *pg.* 395
AMERICAN PUBLIC TRANSPORTATION ASSOCIATION, 1666 K St NW Ste 1100, **Washington,** DC 20006-1215, *pg.* 130, *pg.* 395
AMERICAN RED CROSS, 2025 E St NW, **Washington,** DC 20006, *pg.* 130, *pg.* 395
ASSOCIATION OF AMERICAN RAILROADS, 425 3rd St SW, **Washington,** DC 20024, *pg.* 133, *pg.* 396
BENTON FOUNDATION, 1250 Connecticut NW Ste 200, **Washington,** DC 20036, *pg.* 134, *pg.* 396
BUSINESS SOFTWARE ALLIANCE, INC., 20 F St NW, Ste 800, **Washington,** DC 20001, *pg.* 135, *pg.* 397
CITIZENS FOR GLOBAL SOLUTIONS, 420 7th St SE, **Washington,** DC 20003-2769, *pg.* 137, *pg.* 397
COMMUNICATIONS WORKERS OF AMERICA, 501 3rd St NW, **Washington,** DC 20001, *pg.* 137, *pg.* 397
CONSUMER HEALTHCARE PRODUCTS ASSOCIATION, 900 19th St NW Ste 700, **Washington,** DC 20006, *pg.* 138, *pg.* 397
DEFENDERS OF WILDLIFE, 1130 17th St NW, **Washington,** DC 20036, *pg.* 138, *pg.* 398
DEMOCRATIC NATIONAL COMMITTEE, 430 S Capitol St SE, **Washington,** DC 20003-4024, *pg.* 139, *pg.* 398
DIRECT SELLING ASSOCIATION, 1667 K St NW Ste 1100, **Washington,** DC 20006, *pg.* 139, *pg.* 398
DISTILLED SPIRITS COUNCIL OF THE UNITED STATES, INC., 1250 Eye St NW Ste 400, **Washington,** DC 20005-5977, *pg.* 139, *pg.* 398
FOUNDATION FOR BIOMEDICAL RESEARCH, 818 Connecticut Ave NW Ste 900, **Washington,** DC 20006-2702, *pg.* 141, *pg.* 399
GREENPEACE, 702 H St NW, **Washington,** DC 20001, *pg.* 142, *pg.* 400
HUMAN RIGHTS CAMPAIGN, 1640 Rhode Island Ave NW, **Washington,** DC 20036-3278, *pg.* 143, *pg.* 400
THE HUMANE SOCIETY OF THE UNITED STATES, 2100 L St NW, **Washington,** DC 20037, *pg.* 143, *pg.* 400
MELANOMA RESEARCH ALLIANCE, 1101 New York Ave NW Ste 620, **Washington,** DC 20005, *pg.* 146, *pg.* 401
NATIONAL COUNCIL ON PROBLEM GAMBLING, 730 11th St NW Ste 601, **Washington,** DC 20001, *pg.* 148, *pg.* 401
NATIONAL EDUCATION ASSOCIATION, 1201 16th St NW, **Washington,** DC 20036, *pg.* 148, *pg.* 401
NATIONAL FOOTBALL LEAGUE PLAYERS INCORPORATED, 1133 20th St NW, **Washington,** DC 20036, *pg.* 149, *pg.* 401
NATIONAL PARKS CONSERVATION ASSOCIATION, 777 6th St NW, **Washington,** DC 20001-3723, *pg.* 150, *pg.* 403
NATIONAL RESTAURANT ASSOCIATION, 1200 17th St NW, **Washington,** DC 20036, *pg.* 150, *pg.* 403
NATIONAL TRUST FOR HISTORIC PRESERVATION, 1785 Massachusetts Ave NW, **Washington,** DC 20036-2117, *pg.* 151, *pg.* 403
OUTDOOR ADVERTISING ASSOCIATION OF AMERICA, 1850 M St NW Ste 1040, **Washington,** DC 20036, *pg.* 152, *pg.* 403
PHARMACEUTICAL RESEARCH & MANUFACTURERS OF AMERICA, 950 F St NW Ste 300, **Washington,** DC 20004, *pg.* 153, *pg.* 404
SOCIETY OF CHEMICAL MNAUFACTURERS & AFFILIATES, INC., 1850 M St NW Ste 700, **Washington,** DC 20036-5810, *pg.* 156, *pg.* 404
THE SOCIETY OF THE PLASTICS INDUSTRY, INC., 1667 K St NW Ste 1000, **Washington,** DC 20006, *pg.* 157, *pg.* 404
SPECIAL OLYMPICS INTERNATIONAL, INC., 1133 19th St NW, **Washington,** DC 20036, *pg.* 157, *pg.* 405
THE SUGAR ASSOCIATION, INC., 1300 L St NW Ste 1001, **Washington,** DC 20005, *pg.* 157, *pg.* 405
TRAVEL INDUSTRY ASSOCIATION OF AMERICA, 1100 New York Ave NW Ste 450, **Washington,** DC 20005-3934, *pg.* 158, *pg.* 405
TRUTH INITIATIVE, 1724 Massachusetts Ave NW,

Washington, DC 20036, *pg.* 158, *pg.* 405
UNITED NEGRO COLLEGE FUND, INC., 1805 7th St NW, **Washington,** DC 20001, *pg.* 159, *pg.* 405
UNITED STATES TELECOM ASSOCIATION, 607 14th St NW Ste 400, **Washington,** DC 20005, *pg.* 159, *pg.* 407
WORLD WILDLIFE FUND, INC., 1250 24th St NW 6th Fl, **Washington,** DC 20037, *pg.* 162, *pg.* 408

Florida

CRUISE LINES INTERNATIONAL ASSOCIATION, INC., 910 SE 17th St Ste 400, **Fort Lauderdale,** FL 33316, *pg.* 138, *pg.* 424
FAMILY FIRST, 5211 W Lourel St, **Tampa,** FL 33607, *pg.* 140, *pg.* 472
FLORIDA AVOCADO ADMINISTRATIVE COMMITTEES, 18710 SW 288th St, **Homestead,** FL 33030-2309, *pg.* 140, *pg.* 431
FLORIDA FRUIT & VEGETABLE ASSOCIATION, 800 Trafalgar Ct Ste 200, **Maitland,** FL 32751-5219, *pg.* 140, *pg.* 438
FLORIDA HOSPITAL ASSOCIATION, 306 E College Ave, **Tallahassee,** FL 32301-1522, *pg.* 140, *pg.* 469
FLORIDA TOMATO COMMITTEE, 800 Trafalgar Ct Ste 300, **Maitland,** FL 32751, *pg.* 141, *pg.* 438
GOODWILL INDUSTRIES-SUNCOAST, INC., 10596 Gandy Blvd, **Saint Petersburg,** FL 33702, *pg.* 142, *pg.* 462
LEAGUE OF SOUTHEASTERN CREDIT UNIONS, 3773 Commonwealth Blvd, **Tallahassee,** FL 32303, *pg.* 145, *pg.* 469
METROPOLITAN MINISTRIES INC., 2002 N Florida Ave, **Tampa,** FL 33602-2204, *pg.* 146, *pg.* 474
NATIONAL WATERMELON PROMOTION BOARD, 3361 Rouse Rd Ste 150, **Orlando,** FL 32817, *pg.* 151, *pg.* 454
SAVE THE MANATEE CLUB, INC., 500 N Maitland Ave, **Maitland,** FL 32751, *pg.* 156, *pg.* 439
SEMINOLE TRIBE OF FLORIDA, INC., 6300 Stirling Rd, **Hollywood,** FL 33024-2153, *pg.* 156, *pg.* 431
SHERLOQ SOLUTIONS, PO Box 972, **Tampa,** FL 33601-0972, *pg.* 156, *pg.* 475
ST. PETERSBURG AREA CHAMBER OF COMMERCE, The Chamber Bldg 100 2nd Ave N Ste 150, **Saint Petersburg,** FL 33701, *pg.* 157, *pg.* 464
SUNCOAST WORKFORCE BOARD, INC., 3660 N Washington Blvd, **Sarasota,** FL 34234, *pg.* 158, *pg.* 467

Georgia

AMERICAN CANCER SOCIETY, INC., 250 William St NW, **Atlanta,** GA 30303, *pg.* 126, *pg.* 487
BOYS AND GIRLS CLUB OF AMERICA, 1275 Peachtree St NE, **Atlanta,** GA 30309-3506, *pg.* 134, *pg.* 491
THE DIAN FOSSEY GORILLA FUND INTERNATIONAL, 800 Cherokee Ave SE, **Atlanta,** GA 30315-1440, *pg.* 139, *pg.* 504
HABITAT FOR HUMANITY INTERNATIONAL, INC., 121 Habitat St, **Americus,** GA 31709-3423, *pg.* 143, *pg.* 486
HIRE HEROES USA, 1360 Union Hill Rd Bldg 2 Ste A, **Alpharetta,** GA 30004, *pg.* 143, *pg.* 484
NATIONAL PEANUT BOARD, Ste 210 2839 Paces Ferry Rd SE, **Atlanta,** GA 30339-5769, *pg.* 150, *pg.* 515
WELLSTAR HEALTH SYSTEM, INC., 805 Sandy Plains Rd, **Marietta,** GA 30066, *pg.* 161, *pg.* 536

Idaho

HEALTHWISE, INCORPORATED, 2601 N Bogus Basin Rd, **Boise,** ID 83702-0909, *pg.* 143, *pg.* 546
IDAHO POTATO COMMISSION, 661 S Rivershore Ln Ste 230, **Eagle,** ID 83616, *pg.* 144, *pg.* 549

Illinois

AMERICAN ARCHITECTURAL MANUFACTURERS ASSOCIATION, 1827 Walden Ofc Sq Ste 550, **Schaumburg,** IL 60173-4268, *pg.* 126, *pg.* 658
AMERICAN DAIRY ASSOCIATION, 10255 W Higgins Rd Ste 900, **Rosemont,** IL 60018-5616, *pg.* 127, *pg.* 656
THE AMERICAN DENTAL ASSOCIATION, 211 E Chicago Ave, **Chicago,** IL 60611, *pg.* 127, *pg.* 564
AMERICAN EGG BOARD, 1460 Renaissance Dr Ste 301, **Park Ridge,** IL 60068-1348, *pg.* 128, *pg.* 650
AMERICAN MEDICAL ASSOCIATION, 330 N Wabash Ave, **Chicago,** IL 60611, *pg.* 130, *pg.* 564
AMERICAN SOCIETY OF PLASTIC SURGEONS INC., 444 E Algonquin Rd, **Arlington Heights,** IL 60005, *pg.* 131, *pg.* 553
CHICAGO AUTOMOBILE TRADE ASSOCIATION, 18 W 200 Butterfield Rd, **Oakbrook Terrace,** IL 60181-4810, *pg.* 137, *pg.* 649
COIN LAUNDRY ASSOCIATION, 1S660 Midwest Rd Ste 205, **Oakbrook Terrace,** IL 60181, *pg.* 137, *pg.* 649
DAIRY MANAGEMENT, INC., 10255 W Higgins Rd Ste 900, **Rosemont,** IL 60018-5616, *pg.* 138, *pg.* 656
EDUCATIONAL ASSISTANCE LTD., PO Box 3021, **Glen Ellyn,** IL 60138-3021, *pg.* 140, *pg.* 613
INSTITUTE OF REAL ESTATE MANAGEMENT, 430 N Michigan Ave, **Chicago,** IL 60611-4011, *pg.* 144, *pg.* 578
INTERNATIONAL FELLOWSHIP OF CHRISTIANS & JEWS, INC., 30 N La Salle St Ste 2600, **Chicago,** IL 60602, *pg.* 145, *pg.* 579
ISSA, 3300 Dundee Rd, **Northbrook,** IL 60062, *pg.* 145, *pg.* 640
NATIONAL ASSOCIATION OF ORTHOPAEDIC NURSES, 330 N Wabash Ave, Ste 2000, **Chicago,** IL 60611, *pg.* 148, *pg.* 584
NATIONAL MARINE MANUFACTURERS ASSOCIATION, 231 S La Salle St, Ste 2050, **Chicago,** IL 60604, *pg.* 149, *pg.* 584
NATIONAL SPORTING GOODS ASSOCIATION, 1601 Feehanville Dr Ste 300, **Mount Prospect,** IL 60056-6042, *pg.* 151, *pg.* 634
NIGHTINGALE-CONANT CORPORATION, 1400 S Wolf Rd Bldg 300 Ste 103, **Wheeling,** IL 60090, *pg.* 152, *pg.* 670
PRECAST/PRESTRESSED CONCRETE INSTITUTE, 200 W Adams St #2100, **Chicago,** IL 60606-6938, *pg.* 154, *pg.* 587
QUALITY CHEKD DAIRIES, INC., 901 Warrenville Rd Ste 405, **Lisle,** IL 60532-4309, *pg.* 154, *pg.* 630
RONALD MCDONALD HOUSE CHARITIES, INC., One Kroc Dr, **Oak Brook,** IL 60523, *pg.* 155, *pg.* 648
ROTARY INTERNATIONAL, One Rotary Ctr 1560 Sherman Ave, **Evanston,** IL 60201, *pg.* 155, *pg.* 612

Indiana

INDIANA CROP IMPROVEMENT ASSOCIATION, INC., 7700 Stockwell Rd, **Lafayette,** IN 47909, *pg.* 144, *pg.* 693
NATIONAL FFA ORGANIZATION, 6060 FFA Dr, **Indianapolis,** IN 46278-1370, *pg.* 149, *pg.* 688
ROLLER SKATING ASSOCIATION INTERNATIONAL, 6905 Corporate Dr, **Indianapolis,** IN 46278-1927, *pg.* 155, *pg.* 689

Iowa

IOWA BEEF INDUSTRY COUNCIL, 2055 Ironwood Ct, **Ames,** IA 50014, *pg.* 145, *pg.* 701
NATIONAL PORK PRODUCERS COUNCIL, 10676 Justin Dr, **Urbandale,** IA 50322-3755, *pg.* 150, *pg.* 712

Kentucky

ANSWERS IN GENESIS, 2800 Bullittsburg Church Rd, **Petersburg,** KY 41080, *pg.* 132, *pg.* 740
ASPHALT INSTITUTE, 2696 Research Park Dr, **Lexington,** KY 40511-8480, *pg.* 133, *pg.* 729
INTERNATIONAL SPA ASSOCIATION, 2365 Harrodsburg Rd Ste A325, **Lexington,** KY 40504-4326, *pg.* 145, *pg.* 730

Louisiana

SOUTHERN FOREST PRODUCTS ASSOCIATION, 6660 Riverside Dr, Ste 212, **Kenner,** LA 70003, *pg.* 157, *pg.* 744

Maine

MAINE POTATO BOARD, 744 Main St Ste 1, **Presque Isle,** ME 04769, *pg.* 146, *pg.* 752

Maryland

ACCURACY IN MEDIA, INC., 4350 East West Hwy, Ste 555, **Bethesda,** MD 20814, *pg.* 125, *pg.* 761
THE ADHESIVE AND SEALANT COUNCIL, INC., 7101 Wiscosin Ave Ste 990, **Bethesda,** MD 20814, *pg.* 125, *pg.* 761
AMERICAN COLLEGE OF NURSE-MIDWIVES, 8403 Colesville Rd Ste 1550, **Silver Spring,** MD 20910-6374, *pg.* 127, *pg.* 777
THE AMERICAN GASTROENTEROLOGICAL ASSOCIATION, 4930 Del Ray Ave, **Bethesda,** MD 20814, *pg.* 128, *pg.* 761
AMERICAN PODIATRIC MEDICAL ASSOCIATION, 9312 Old Georgetown Rd, **Bethesda,** MD 20814, *pg.* 130, *pg.* 761
AMERICAN SOCIETY OF HEALTH-SYSTEM PHARMACISTS, 7272 Wisconsin Ave, **Bethesda,** MD 20814-4836, *pg.* 131, *pg.* 761
APACHE SOFTWARE FOUNDATION, 1901 Munsey Dr, **Forest Hill,** MD 21050-2747, *pg.* 132, *pg.* 769
THE ASCII GROUP, INC., 7101 Wisconsin Ave, Ste 1350, **Bethesda,** MD 20814, *pg.* 132, *pg.* 761
CATHOLIC RELIEF SERVICES, 228 W Lexington St, **Baltimore,** MD 21201-3443, *pg.* 136, *pg.* 756
EARTH SHARE, 7735 Old Georgetown Rd Ste 900, **Bethesda,** MD 20814, *pg.* 140, *pg.* 762
HOLISTIC LIFE FOUNDATION, INC., 2008 N Smallwood St, **Baltimore,** MD 21216, *pg.* 143, *pg.* 757
WESTAT INC., 1600 Research Blvd, **Rockville,** MD 20850, *pg.* 161, *pg.* 776

Massachusetts

NATIONAL FIRE PROTECTION ASSOCIATION, 1 Batterymarch Pk, **Quincy,** MA 02169-7454, *pg.* 149, *pg.* 842
NEW ENGLAND APPLE ASSOCIATION, 8 Elm St, **Hatfield,** MA 01038, *pg.* 151, *pg.* 824

Michigan

AMERICAN CONCRETE INSTITUTE, 38800 Country Club Dr, **Farmington Hills,** MI 48333-9094, *pg.* 127, *pg.* 885
CHERRY MARKETING INSTITUTE, 12800 Escanaba Dr, **Dewitt,** MI 48820-8680, *pg.* 136, *pg.* 884
DETROIT METRO CONVENTION & VISITORS BUREAU, 211 W Fort St Ste 1000, **Detroit,** MI 48226, *pg.* 139, *pg.* 880
FOCUS: HOPE, 1355 Oakman Blvd, **Detroit,** MI 48238-2849, *pg.* 141, *pg.* 881
MICHIGAN APPLE COMMITTEE, 13750 S Sedona Pkwy, **Lansing,** MI 48906, *pg.* 147, *pg.* 895
MICHIGAN ASSOCIATION OF INSURANCE AGENTS, 1141 Centennial Way, **Lansing,** MI 48917, *pg.* 147, *pg.* 895
MICHIGAN BLUEBERRY GROWERS ASSOCIATION, 04726 County Rd 215, **Grand Junction,** MI 49056-9218, *pg.* 147, *pg.* 886
MICHIGAN MILK PRODUCERS ASSOCIATION, 41310 Bridge St, **Novi,** MI 48376-3002, *pg.* 147, *pg.* 903
SOCIETY OF MANUFACTURING ENGINEERS, 1 SME Dr, **Dearborn,** MI 48128-2408, *pg.* 157, *pg.* 878
W.K. KELLOGG FOUNDATION, 1 Michigan Ave E, **Battle Creek,** MI 49017-4005, *pg.* 161, *pg.* 872

Minnesota

MINNESOTA GOLF ASSOCIATION, 6550 York Ave S Ste 211, **Edina,** MN 55435-2333, *pg.* 147, *pg.* 925
NATIONAL MARROW DONOR PROGRAM, INC., 3001 Broadway St Ste 500, **Minneapolis,** MN 55413-2195, *pg.* 150, *pg.* 941

Mississippi

THE CATFISH INSTITUTE, 6311 Ridgewood Rd, Ste W404, **Jackson,** MS 39211, *pg.* 136, *pg.* 969

Missouri

AMERICAN HEREFORD ASSOCIATION, 1501 Wyandotte St, **Kansas City,** MO 64108-1222, *pg.* 129, *pg.* 980
GOVERNMENT EMPLOYEES HOSPITAL ASSOCIATION, INC., 17306 E 24 Hwy, **Independence,** MO 64056, *pg.* 142, *pg.* 979

Nebraska

AMERICAN SHORTHORN ASSOCIATION, 8288 Hascall St, **Omaha,** NE 68124, *pg.* 131, *pg.* 1013

First page reference indicates Business Class Edition
Second page reference indicates Geographic Edition

OMAHA CONVENTION AND VISITORS BUREAU, 1001 Farnam, **Omaha,** NE 68102, *pg.* 152, *pg.* 1017

Nevada

LAS VEGAS INSTITUTE FOR ADVANCED DENTAL STUDIES, 9501 Hillwood Dr, **Las Vegas,** NV 89134, *pg.* 145, *pg.* 1027

New Jersey

CHARITY NAVIGATOR, 139 Harristown Rd Ste 101, **Glen Rock,** NJ 07452, *pg.* 136, *pg.* 1071
CHRISTOPHER & DANA REEVE FOUNDATION, 636 Morris Tpke Ste 3A, **Short Hills,** NJ 07078, *pg.* 137, *pg.* 1120
INSTITUTE OF ELECTRICAL AND ELECTRONICS ENGINEERS, INC., IEEE 445 Hose Ln, **Piscataway,** NJ 08854, *pg.* 144, *pg.* 1109
INSTITUTE OF MANAGEMENT ACCOUNTANTS, INC., 10 Paragon Dr, **Montvale,** NJ 07645-1718, *pg.* 144, *pg.* 1086
MARTS & LUNDY, INC., 1200 Wall St W, **Lyndhurst,** NJ 07071, *pg.* 146, *pg.* 1080
NEW JERSEY HOSPITAL ASSOCIATION, PO Box 1 760 Alexander Rd, **Princeton,** NJ 08540-0001, *pg.* 152, *pg.* 1112

New York

9/11 MEMORIAL, 1 Liberty Plaza 20th Fl, **New York,** NY 10006, *pg.* 124, *pg.* 1185
92ND STREET YOUNG MEN'S & YOUNG WOMEN'S HEBREW ASSOCIATION, 1395 Lexington Ave, **New York,** NY 10128, *pg.* 124, *pg.* 1185
THE ADVENTURE PROJECT, 320 7th Ave, **Brooklyn,** NY 11215, *pg.* 125, *pg.* 1145
THE ADVERTISING COUNCIL, INC., 815 2nd Ave Fl 9, **New York,** NY 10017-2303, *pg.* 125, *pg.* 1187
AIGA, THE PROFESSIONAL ASSOCIATION FOR DESIGN, 233 Broadway 17th Fl, **New York,** NY 10279, *pg.* 125, *pg.* 1188
AIRLINE PASSENGER EXPERIENCE ASSOCIATION, 355 Lexington Ave 15th Fl, **New York,** NY 10017-6603, *pg.* 125, *pg.* 1188
AMALGAMATED LITHOGRAPHERS OF AMERICA, 113 University Pl, **New York,** NY 10003-4527, *pg.* 126, *pg.* 1189
AMERICAN BUSINESS MEDIA, 675 3rd Ave 7th Fl, **New York,** NY 10017-5704, *pg.* 126, *pg.* 1190
AMERICAN INSTITUTE OF CERTIFIED PUBLIC ACCOUNTANTS INC., 1211 Ave of the Americas, **New York,** NY 10036-8775, *pg.* 129, *pg.* 1192
AMERICAN INSTITUTE OF CHEMICAL ENGINEERS, 3 Park Ave Fl 19, **New York,** NY 10016, *pg.* 129, *pg.* 1193
AMERICAN KENNEL CLUB, INC., 260 Madison Ave, **New York,** NY 10016-2401, *pg.* 129, *pg.* 1193
AMERICAN SOCIETY FOR THE PREVENTION OF CRUELTY TO ANIMALS, 424 E 92nd St, **New York,** NY 10128, *pg.* 131, *pg.* 1193
AMNESTY INTERNATIONAL USA, 5 Penn Plz 16th Fl, **New York,** NY 10001, *pg.* 131, *pg.* 1194
ANIMAL CARE & CONTROL OF NEW YORK CITY, INC., 11 Park Pl Ste 805, **New York,** NY 10007, *pg.* 132, *pg.* 1195
ASSOCIATION OF AMERICAN PUBLISHERS, INC., 71 5th Ave 2nd Fl, **New York,** NY 10003-3004, *pg.* 133, *pg.* 1197
ASSOCIATION OF AMERICAN UNIVERSITY PRESSES, 28 W 36th St Ste 602, **New York,** NY 10018, *pg.* 133, *pg.* 1197
THE ASSOCIATION OF MAGAZINE MEDIA, 810 7th Ave 24th Fl, **New York,** NY 10019, *pg.* 133, *pg.* 1197
ASSOCIATION OF NATIONAL ADVERTISERS, INC., 708 3rd Ave, **New York,** NY 10017, *pg.* 133, *pg.* 1197
AUTISM SPEAKS, INC., 1 E 33rd St, **New York,** NY 10016, *pg.* 133, *pg.* 1198
AVON FOUNDATION, 1345 Ave of the Americas, **New York,** NY 10105-0196, *pg.* 134, *pg.* 1198
THE BETTER BUSINESS BUREAU OF METROPOLITAN NEW YORK, 257 Park Ave S, **New York,** NY 10010-7384, *pg.* 134, *pg.* 1202
BREAST CANCER RESEARCH FOUNDATION, 60 E 56th St 8th Fl, **New York,** NY 10022, *pg.* 134, *pg.* 1206
THE CHILDREN'S HEALTH FUND, 215 W 125 St Ste 301, **New York,** NY 10027, *pg.* 137, *pg.* 1211
CMI MARKETING, INC., 401 Park Ave S, **New York,** NY 10016, *pg.* 137, *pg.* 1214
COLOMBIAN COFFEE FEDERATION, INC., 140 E 57th St, **New York,** NY 10022-2703, *pg.* 137, *pg.* 1216
COPPER DEVELOPMENT ASSOCIATION INC., 260 Madison Ave, Fl 17, **New York,** NY 10016, *pg.* 138, *pg.* 1218
COUNCIL ON FOREIGN RELATIONS, 58 E 68th St, **New York,** NY 10065, *pg.* 138, *pg.* 1219
THE DIRECT MARKETING ASSOCIATION INC., 1120 Ave of the Americas, **New York,** NY 10036-6700, *pg.* 139, *pg.* 1224
DOCTORS WITHOUT BORDERS USA, INC., 333 7th Ave 2nd Fl, **New York,** NY 10001, *pg.* 139, *pg.* 1225
ENVIRONMENTAL DEFENSE FUND, 257 Park Ave S, **New York,** NY 10010, *pg.* 140, *pg.* 1228
THE FORD FOUNDATION, 320 E 43rd St, **New York,** NY 10017, *pg.* 141, *pg.* 1232
FRENCH INSTITUTE ALLIANCE FRANCAISE, 22 E 60th St, **New York,** NY 10022, *pg.* 141, *pg.* 1233
FRESH AIR FUND, 633 3rd Ave 14th Fl, **New York,** NY 10017-8152, *pg.* 141, *pg.* 1233
GIRL SCOUTS OF THE UNITED STATES OF AMERICA, 420 5th Ave, **New York,** NY 10018-2729, *pg.* 142, *pg.* 1235
GLOBAL FOUNDATION FOR EATING DISORDERS, 611 Broadway Ste 838, **New York,** NY 10012, *pg.* 142, *pg.* 1235
INTERNATIONAL AIDS VACCINE INITIATIVE, 110 William St 27th Fl, **New York,** NY 10038-3901, *pg.* 145, *pg.* 1244
JUVENILE DIABETES RESEARCH FOUNDATION INTERNATIONAL, 26 Broadway, **New York,** NY 10004, *pg.* 145, *pg.* 1247
LENOX HILL NEIGHBORHOOD HOUSE, 331 E 70th St, **New York,** NY 10021, *pg.* 146, *pg.* 1251
THE LUSTGARTEN FOUNDATION, 1111 Stewart Ave, **Bethpage,** NY 11714, *pg.* 146, *pg.* 1142
MARCH OF DIMES BIRTH DEFECTS FOUNDATION, 1275 Mamaroneck Ave, **White Plains,** NY 10605, *pg.* 146, *pg.* 1354
MICHAEL J. FOX FOUNDATION FOR PARKINSON'S RESEARCH, Church St Sta PO Box 780, **New York,** NY 10008, *pg.* 147, *pg.* 1260
THE NATIONAL ASSOCIATION FOR FEMALE EXECUTIVES, 2 Park Ave, **New York,** NY 10016, *pg.* 147, *pg.* 1263
NATIONAL AUDUBON SOCIETY, 700 Broadway, **New York,** NY 10003-9536, *pg.* 148, *pg.* 1263
NATIONAL COFFEE ASSOCIATION OF USA, INC., 45 Broadway Ste 1140, **New York,** NY 10006-5113, *pg.* 148, *pg.* 1264
NATIONAL EATING DISORDERS ASSOCIATION, 165 W 46th St Ste 402, **New York,** NY 10036-2522, *pg.* 148, *pg.* 1264
NATIONAL KIDNEY FOUNDATION, INC., 30 E 33rd St 8th Fl, **New York,** NY 10016, *pg.* 149, *pg.* 1265
NEGOTIATION INSTITUTE, INC., 350 5th Ave Ste 5701, **New York,** NY 10118-7415, *pg.* 151, *pg.* 1268
NEW YORK APPLE ASSOCIATION, INC., 7645 Main St, **Fishers,** NY 14453-0350, *pg.* 152, *pg.* 1160
NEW YORK ROAD RUNNERS CLUB, INC., 9 E 89th St, **New York,** NY 10128, *pg.* 152, *pg.* 1269
NORTH SHORE ANIMAL LEAGUE, INC., 25 Davis Ave, **Port Washington,** NY 11050, *pg.* 152, *pg.* 1323
THE OVARIAN CANCER RESEARCH FUND, INC., 14 Pennsylvania Plz Ste 1400, **New York,** NY 10122, *pg.* 153, *pg.* 1275
THE PARTNERSHIP AT DRUGFREE.ORG, 352 Park Ave S, # 9, **New York,** NY 10010, *pg.* 153, *pg.* 1276
PATROLMAN'S BENEVOLENT ASSOCIATION OF THE CITY OF NEW YORK, INC., 40 Fulton St, **New York,** NY 10038-1850, *pg.* 153, *pg.* 1276
PLANNED PARENTHOOD FEDERATION OF AMERICA, INC., 434 W 33rd St, **New York,** NY 10001, *pg.* 154, *pg.* 1282
QSAC INC., 253 W 35th St 16th Fl, **New York,** NY 10001, *pg.* 154, *pg.* 1284
QUALITY SERVICES FOR THE AUTISM COMMUNITY, 253 W 35th St 14th Fl, **New York,** NY 10001, *pg.* 154, *pg.* 1284
THE ROCKEFELLER FOUNDATION, 420 5th Ave, **New York,** NY 10018, *pg.* 155, *pg.* 1286
TOY INDUSTRY ASSOCIATION, INC., 1115 Broadway Ste 400, **New York,** NY 10010-2803, *pg.* 158, *pg.* 1303
TRADE COMMISSION OF SPAIN, 405 Lexington Ave 44 Fl, **New York,** NY 10174-4499, *pg.* 158, *pg.* 1304
UNITE HERE, 275 7th Ave, **New York,** NY 10001-6708, *pg.* 159, *pg.* 1306
UNITED NATIONS CHILDREN'S FUND, 3 United Nations Plz, **New York,** NY 10017, *pg.* 159, *pg.* 1306
UNITED STATES TENNIS ASSOCIATION, 70 West Red Oak Lane, **White Plains,** NY 10604, *pg.* 160, *pg.* 1354
VIDEO ADVERTISING BUREAU, 830 3rd Ave 2nd Fl, **New York,** NY 10022, *pg.* 160, *pg.* 1311
THE WHAT TO EXPECT FOUNDATION, 211 W 80th St Lowr Level, **New York,** NY 10024, *pg.* 161, *pg.* 1314
WORD OF LIFE FELLOWSHIP, INC., PO Box 600, **Schroon Lake,** NY 12870, *pg.* 161, *pg.* 1341
WORLD GOLD COUNCIL, 510 Madison Ave, 9th Fl, **New York,** NY 10022, *pg.* 162, *pg.* 1315

Ohio

AMERICAN CONFERENCE OF GOVERNMENTAL INDUSTRIAL HYGIENISTS, 1330 Kemper Meadow Dr, **Cincinnati,** OH 45240, *pg.* 127, *pg.* 1409
AMERICAN HORT, 2133 Steward Ct, **Columbus,** OH 43215, *pg.* 129, *pg.* 1437
ASM INTERNATIONAL, 9639 Kinsman Rd, **Materials Park,** OH 44073-0002, *pg.* 132, *pg.* 1461
ATHLETES IN ACTION, 651 Taylor Dr, **Xenia,** OH 45385, *pg.* 133, *pg.* 1482
COALITION FOR A DRUG-FREE GREATER CINCINNATI, 2330 Victory Pkwy Ste 703, **Cincinnati,** OH 45206, *pg.* 137, *pg.* 1412
FORGING INDUSTRY ASSOCIATION, 1111 Superior Ave E Ste 615, **Cleveland,** OH 44114-2568, *pg.* 141, *pg.* 1431
PARENT PROJECT MUSCULAR DISTROPHY, 1012 N University Blvd, **Middletown,** OH 45042, *pg.* 153, *pg.* 1465
UPSPRING, PO Box 23300, **Cincinnati,** OH 45223-0300, *pg.* 160, *pg.* 1426

Oklahoma

THE DEAN A. MCGEE EYE INSTITUTE, 608 S L Young Blvd, **Oklahoma City,** OK 73104, *pg.* 138, *pg.* 1485

Oregon

OREGON BEEF COUNCIL, 1827 NE 44th Ave Ste 315, **Portland,** OR 97213-1467, *pg.* 152, *pg.* 1504
PEAR BUREAU NORTHWEST, 4382 SE International Way Ste A, **Milwaukie,** OR 97222, *pg.* 153, *pg.* 1500
WESTERN WOOD PRODUCTS ASSOCIATION, 1500 SW First Ave, Ste 870, **Portland,** OR 97201, *pg.* 161, *pg.* 1508

Pennsylvania

ALLIANCE OF CONFESSING EVANGELICALS, INC., 600 Eden Rd, **Lancaster,** PA 17601, *pg.* 126, *pg.* 1545
FRENCH-AMERICAN CHAMBER OF COMMERCE, 200 S Broad St, Ste 700, **Philadelphia,** PA 19102, *pg.* 141, *pg.* 1565
GODDARD SYSTEMS, INC., 1016 W 9th Ave, **King of Prussia,** PA 19406, *pg.* 142, *pg.* 1543
JAPAN AMERICA SOCIETY OF GREATER PHILADELPHIA, 200 S Broad St Ste 910, **Philadelphia,** PA 19102, *pg.* 145, *pg.* 1566
PENNSYLVANIA CHAMBER OF BUSINESS & INDUSTRY, 417 Walnut St, **Harrisburg,** PA 17101-1902, *pg.* 153, *pg.* 1537

Rhode Island

AMERICAN MATHEMATICAL SOCIETY, INC., 201 Charles St, **Providence,** RI 02904-2213, *pg.* 129, *pg.* 1605
PLAN USA, INC., 155 Plan Way, **Warwick,** RI 02886, *pg.* 154, *pg.* 1609
RHODE ISLAND COALITION AGAINST DOMESTIC VIOLENCE, 422 Post Rd, **Warwick,** RI 02888-1524, *pg.* 155, *pg.* 1609

Tennessee

COUNTRY MUSIC ASSOCIATION, 1 Music Cir S, **Nashville,** TN 37203-4312, *pg.* 138, *pg.* 1649
DUCKS UNLIMITED, INC., 1 Waterfowl Way, **Memphis,** TN 38120-2350, *pg.* 139, *pg.* 1642
EDISONLEARNING, INC., 900 S Gay St Ste 1000, **Knoxville,**

TN 37902, *pg.* 140, *pg.* 1636
NATIONAL COTTON COUNCIL OF AMERICA, 7193 Goodlett Farms Pkwy, **Cordova,** TN 38016, *pg.* 148, *pg.* 1631
OPTICIANS ASSOCIATION OF AMERICA, 3740 Canada Rd, **Lakeland,** TN 38002, *pg.* 152, *pg.* 1639
SAINT JUDE CHILDREN'S RESEARCH HOSPITAL INC., 262 Danny Thomas Pl, **Memphis,** TN 38105, *pg.* 155, *pg.* 1646

Texas

AMERICAN HEART ASSOCIATION INC., 7272 Greenville Ave, **Dallas,** TX 75231-5129, *pg.* 128, *pg.* 1673
AMERICAN QUARTER HORSE ASSOCIATION, 1600 Quarter Horse Dr, **Amarillo,** TX 79104, *pg.* 130, *pg.* 1658
AUTOMOTIVE SERVICE ASSOCIATION, 8190 Precinct Line Rd, Ste 100, **Colleyville,** TX 76034, *pg.* 134, *pg.* 1670
BOY SCOUTS OF AMERICA, 1325 W Walnut Hill Ln, **Irving,** TX 75038-3008, *pg.* 134, *pg.* 1717
BUSINESS BROKERS NETWORK, Palisades Central II, 2435 N Central Expy, Ste 925, **Richardson,** TX 75080, *pg.* 135, *pg.* 1735
THE GLADNEY CENTER FOR ADOPTION, 6300 John Ryan Dr, **Fort Worth,** TX 76132-4122, *pg.* 142, *pg.* 1695
HERITAGE GALLERIES & AUCTIONEER, 3500 Maple Ave 17th Fl, **Dallas,** TX 75219, *pg.* 143, *pg.* 1682
MEETING PROFESSIONALS INTERNATIONAL (MPI), 3030 LBJ Freeway Ste 1700, **Dallas,** TX 75234-2759, *pg.* 146, *pg.* 1683
MOTHERS AGAINST DRUNK DRIVING (MADD), 511 E John Carpenter Fwy Ste 700, **Irving,** TX 75062, *pg.* 147, *pg.* 1723
THE PLASTICS PIPE INSTITUTE, INC., 105 Decker Ct Ste 825, **Irving,** TX 75062, *pg.* 154, *pg.* 1723
THE PROFESSIONAL PUTTERS ASSOCIATION, 28 Sioux Trl, **Ransom Canyon,** TX 79366, *pg.* 154, *pg.* 1735
SUSAN G. KOMEN FOR THE CURE, 5005 LBJ Fwy Ste 250, **Dallas,** TX 75244, *pg.* 158, *pg.* 1688
TEXAS BEEF COUNCIL, 8708 N FM 620, **Austin,** TX 78726, *pg.* 158, *pg.* 1666
UNITED STATES BOWLING CONGRESS, 621 Six Flags Dr, **Arlington,** TX 76011, *pg.* 159, *pg.* 1660

Utah

MANAGEMENT & TRAINING CORPORATION, 500 N Market Pl Dr, **Centerville,** UT 84014-1708, *pg.* 146, *pg.* 1751

Vermont

HOLSTEIN ASSOCIATION USA, INC., 1 Holstein Pl, **Brattleboro,** VT 05301-3363, *pg.* 143, *pg.* 1764
VERMONT SKI AREAS ASSOCIATION, INC., 26 State St, **Montpelier,** VT 05602-2943, *pg.* 160, *pg.* 1767

Virginia

AEROSPACE INDUSTRIES ASSOCIATION, 1000 Wilson Blvd Ste 1700, **Arlington,** VA 22209-3928, *pg.* 125, *pg.* 1772
AMERICAN DIABETES ASSOCIATION, 1701 N Beauregard St, **Alexandria,** VA 22311-1717, *pg.* 127, *pg.* 1770
BOAT OWNERS ASSOCIATION OF THE UNITED STATES, 880 S Pickett St, **Alexandria,** VA 22304-4606, *pg.* 134, *pg.* 1770
BRICK INDUSTRY ASSOCIATION, 1850 Centenial Park Dr Ste 310, **Reston,** VA 20191, *pg.* 135, *pg.* 1798
CHILDFUND INTERNATIONAL, 2821 Emerywood Pkwy, **Richmond,** VA 23294-3726, *pg.* 137, *pg.* 1801
COMMON GROUND ALLIANCE, 1421 Prince St Ste 410, **Alexandria,** VA 22314, *pg.* 137, *pg.* 1770
FOODSERVICE & PACKAGING INSTITUTE, INC., 201 Park Washington Ct, **Falls Church,** VA 22046-2921, *pg.* 141, *pg.* 1781
HARDWOOD PLYWOOD & VENEER ASSOCATION, 1825 Michael Faraday Dr, **Reston,** VA 20190-5304, *pg.* 143, *pg.* 1798
INDEPENDENT INSURANCE AGENTS & BROKERS OF AMERICA, INC., 127 S Peyton St, **Alexandria,** VA 22314-2803, *pg.* 144, *pg.* 1770
THE INDEPENDENT LUBRICANT MANUFACTURERS ASSOCIATION, 400 N Columbus St, **Alexandria,** VA 22314, *pg.* 144, *pg.* 1770
INDUSTRIAL DESIGNERS SOCIETY OF AMERICA, 555 Grove St Ste 200, **Herndon,** VA 20170-4727, *pg.* 144, *pg.* 1785
NATIONAL ASSOCIATION OF CONVENIENCE STORES, 1600 Duke St, **Alexandria,** VA 22314, *pg.* 148, *pg.* 1771
NATIONAL COMMUNITY PHARMACISTS ASSOCIATION, 100 Daingerfield Rd, **Alexandria,** VA 22314-2833, *pg.* 148, *pg.* 1771
NATIONAL CONCRETE MASONRY ASSOCIATION, 13750 Sunrise Valley Dr, **Herndon,** VA 20171-4662, *pg.* 148, *pg.* 1785
NATIONAL ELECTRICAL MANUFACTURERS ASSOCIATION, 1300 N 17th St N Ste 1752, **Rosslyn,** VA 22209-3801, *pg.* 149, *pg.* 1806
NATIONAL OILHEAT RESEARCH ALLIANCE, 600 Cameron St Ste 206, **Alexandria,** VA 22314, *pg.* 150, *pg.* 1771
NATIONAL RIFLE ASSOCIATION, 11250 Waples Mill Rd, **Fairfax,** VA 22030-7400, *pg.* 151, *pg.* 1780
NATIONAL VENTURE CAPITAL ASSOCIATION, 1655 N Fort Myer Dr Ste 850, **Arlington,** VA 22209-3199, *pg.* 151, *pg.* 1774
NATSO, INC., 1737 King St Ste 200, **Alexandria,** VA 22314, *pg.* 151, *pg.* 1771
THE NATURE CONSERVANCY, 4245 N Fairfax Dr Ste 100, **Arlington,** VA 22203-1606, *pg.* 151, *pg.* 1774
PETA, 501 Front St, **Norfolk,** VA 23510, *pg.* 153, *pg.* 1797
PHILANTHROPEDIA, 427 Scotland Street, **Williamsburg,** VA 23185, *pg.* 153, *pg.* 1811
PLUMBING-HEATING-COOLING CONTRACTORS-NATIONAL ASSOCIATION, 180 S Washington St, **Falls Church,** VA 22046, *pg.* 154, *pg.* 1782
RECREATION VEHICLE INDUSTRY ASSOCIATION, 1896 Preston White Dr, **Reston,** VA 20191-4363, *pg.* 155, *pg.* 1799
THE SALVATION ARMY, 615 Slaters Ln, **Alexandria,** VA 22313, *pg.* 155, *pg.* 1771
SOCIETY OF AMERICAN FLORISTS, 1601 Duke St, **Alexandria,** VA 22314-3406, *pg.* 156, *pg.* 1771
THE SOCIETY OF AMERICAN MILITARY ENGINEERS, 607 Prince St, **Alexandria,** VA 22314-3117, *pg.* 156, *pg.* 1771
SPELNA, INC., 225 Industrial Ct, **Fredericksburg,** VA 22408-2420, *pg.* 157, *pg.* 1782
STEVIE AWARDS, INC., 10560 Main St Ste 215, **Fairfax,** VA 22030-7176, *pg.* 157, *pg.* 1780
UNITED WAY WORLDWIDE, 701 N Fairfax St, **Alexandria,** VA 22314, *pg.* 160, *pg.* 1772
U.S. DAIRY EXPORT COUNCIL, 2101 Wilson Blvd Ste 400, **Arlington,** VA 22201-3061, *pg.* 160, *pg.* 1775
USA RICE FEDERATION, 2101 Wilson Blvd, Ste 610, **Arlington,** VA 22201, *pg.* 160, *pg.* 1775
ZERO - THE PROJECT TO END PROSTATE CANCER, 515 King St, Ste 420, **Alexandria,** VA 22314, *pg.* 162, *pg.* 1772

Washington

APA-THE ENGINEERED WOOD ASSOCIATION, 7011 S 19th St, **Tacoma,** WA 98466-5333, *pg.* 132, *pg.* 1844
THE BILL AND MELINDA GATES FOUNDATION, 500 Fifth Ave N, **Seattle,** WA 98109, *pg.* 134, *pg.* 1833
INSPIRE YOUTH PROJECT, 417 23rd Ave S, **Seattle,** WA 98144, *pg.* 144, *pg.* 1836
PACIFIC NORTHWEST CANNED PEAR SERVICE, INC., 105 S 18th St, **Yakima,** WA 98901-2175, *pg.* 153, *pg.* 1847
WASHINGTON STATE APPLE COMMISSION, 2900 Euclid Ave, **Wenatchee,** WA 98801, *pg.* 160, *pg.* 1847
WASHINGTON STATE DAIRY PRODUCTS COMMISSION, 4201 198th St SW Ste 101, **Lynnwood,** WA 98036-6751, *pg.* 161, *pg.* 1822
WASHINGTON STATE FRUIT COMMISSION, 105 S 18th St Ste 205, **Yakima,** WA 98901-2176, *pg.* 161, *pg.* 1847

Wisconsin

CREDIT UNION NATIONAL ASSOCIATION, 5710 Mineral Point Rd, **Madison,** WI 53705-4454, *pg.* 138, *pg.* 1865
INTERNATIONAL DAIRY-DELI-BAKERY-ASSOCIATION, 636 Science Dr, **Madison,** WI 53711-1073, *pg.* 145, *pg.* 1866
WISCONSIN BEEF COUNCIL, INC., 632 Grand Canyon Dr, **Madison,** WI 53719-2904, *pg.* 161, *pg.* 1867
WISCONSIN MILK MARKETING BOARD, INC., 8418 Excelsior Dr, **Madison,** WI 53717, *pg.* 161, *pg.* 1868

Automobiles & Trucks

Alabama

CONFEDERATE MOTORS, INC., 2222 5th Ave S, **Birmingham,** AL 35222, *pg.* 168, *pg.* 2

Arizona

CARVANA LLC, 4020 East Indian School Rd, **Phoenix,** AZ 85018, *pg.* 168, *pg.* 16
DRIVETIME AUTOMOTIVE GROUP, INC., 4020 E Indian School Rd, **Phoenix,** AZ 85018, *pg.* 169, *pg.* 16
EARNHARDT HONDA, 10151 W Papago Freeway, **Avondale,** AZ 85323, *pg.* 169, *pg.* 12
EARNHARDT'S AUTO CENTERS, 7300 W Orchid Ln, **Chandler,** AZ 85226, *pg.* 169, *pg.* 12
SANDERSON FORD INC., 6400 N 51st Ave, **Glendale,** AZ 85301, *pg.* 190, *pg.* 13

Arkansas

AMERICA'S CAR-MART, INC., 802 Southeast Plaza Ave Ste 200, **Bentonville,** AR 72712, *pg.* 164, *pg.* 29

California

AMERICAN HONDA MOTOR CO., INC., 1919 Torrance Blvd, **Torrance,** CA 90501-2722, *pg.* 163, *pg.* 292
CANEPA DESIGN GROUP, 4900 Scotts Valley Dr, **Scotts Valley,** CA 95066-4208, *pg.* 167, *pg.* 278
COPART, INC., 4665 Business Center Dr, **Fairfield,** CA 94534, *pg.* 168, *pg.* 86
DESERT EUROPEAN MOTORCARS, LTD., 71387 Hwy 111, **Rancho Mirage,** CA 92270-4110, *pg.* 169, *pg.* 187
DOWNTOWN FORD SALES INC., 525 N 16th St, **Sacramento,** CA 95811, *pg.* 169, *pg.* 196
GALPIN MOTORS, INC., 15505 Roscoe Blvd, **North Hills,** CA 91343-6503, *pg.* 174, *pg.* 166
HYUNDAI MOTOR AMERICA, 10550 Talbert Ave, **Fountain Valley,** CA 92708-6031, *pg.* 179, *pg.* 89
KIA MOTORS AMERICA INC., 111 Peters Canyon Rd, **Irvine,** CA 92606, *pg.* 181, *pg.* 112
KUMHO TIRE USA, INC., 10299 6th St, **Rancho Cucamonga,** CA 91730, *pg.* 182, *pg.* 187
LEXUS DIVISION, 19001 S Western Ave, **Torrance,** CA 90501, *pg.* 182, *pg.* 294
MAITA ENTERPRISES INC., 2500 Auburn Blvd, **Sacramento,** CA 95821, *pg.* 183, *pg.* 196
MAZDA NORTH AMERICAN OPERATIONS, 7755 Irvine Ctr Dr, **Irvine,** CA 92618, *pg.* 183, *pg.* 113
MITSUBISHI MOTORS NORTH AMERICA, INC., 6400 Katella Ave, **Cypress,** CA 90630-5208, *pg.* 185, *pg.* 75
O'GARA COACH LA JOLLA, 7440 La Jolla Blvd, **La Jolla,** CA 92037, *pg.* 187, *pg.* 120
STRUT, LLC, 236 Calle Pintoresco, **San Clemente,** CA 92672, *pg.* 190, *pg.* 199
TESLA MOTORS, INC., 3500 Deer Creek Rd, **Palo Alto,** CA 94304, *pg.* 191, *pg.* 178
TOYOTA MOTOR SALES, U.S.A., INC., 19001 S Western Ave, **Torrance,** CA 90501-1106, *pg.* 193, *pg.* 296

Connecticut

CROWLEY AUTO GROUP, 223 Broad St Rte 72, **Bristol,** CT 06010, *pg.* 168, *pg.* 340

Florida

AUTONATION, INC., 200 SW 1st Ave, **Fort Lauderdale,** FL 33301, *pg.* 165, *pg.* 423
BRAMAN MOTORS, INC., 2901 Okeechobee Blvd, **West Palm Beach,** FL 33409, *pg.* 167, *pg.* 478
CHAMPION MOTORSPORT, 3101 Centerport Cir, **Pompano Beach,** FL 33064, *pg.* 168, *pg.* 459
THE COLLECTION, INC., 200 Bird Rd, **Coral Gables,** FL 33146, *pg.* 168, *pg.* 418
DAYTON ANDREWS FIVE STAR CHRYSLER PLYMOUTH JEEP, INC., 2388 Gulf to Bay Blvd, **Clearwater,** FL 33765-4103, *pg.* 169, *pg.* 415
DIMMITT LUXURY MOTORS, 25191 US Hwy 19 N, **Clearwater,** FL 33763, *pg.* 169, *pg.* 416
DRIVER'S MART, 1970 SR 436, **Winter Park,** FL 32792, *pg.* 169, *pg.* 480
FERMAN MOTOR CAR CO., INC., 1306 W Kennedy Blvd, **Tampa,** FL 33606-1849, *pg.* 171, *pg.* 473
GATOR FORD TRUCK SALES INC., 11780 Tampa Gateway Blvd, **Seffner,** FL 33584, *pg.* 174, *pg.* 467
GENERAL ENGINES COMPANY INC., 14893 Hwy 27, **Lake Wales,** FL 33859, *pg.* 174, *pg.* 437
HERTZ GLOBAL HOLDINGS, INC., 999 Vanderbilt Beach Rd 3rd Fl, **Naples,** FL 34108, *pg.* 179, *pg.* 450
JENKINS AUTO SALES OF FLORIDA, 4531 N Federal Hwy, **Pompano Beach,** FL 33064, *pg.* 180, *pg.* 459
JM FAMILY ENTERPRISES INC., 100 Jim Moran Blvd, **Deerfield Beach,** FL 33442-1702, *pg.* 180, *pg.* 421
LAZY DAYS R.V. CENTER, INC., 6130 Lazy Days Blvd, **Seffner,** FL 33584-2968, *pg.* 182, *pg.* 467
MIKE KASHTAN'S SUPERIOR AUTO SALES, 7290 Park Blvd, **Pinellas Park,** FL 33781, *pg.* 185, *pg.* 458
POTAMKIN AUTOMOTIVE, 6600 Cowpen Rd Ste 200, **Miami,** FL 33014-7618, *pg.* 189, *pg.* 445
REEVES IMPORT MOTORCARS INC., 11333 N Florida Ave, **Tampa,** FL 33617, *pg.* 189, *pg.* 475
SOUTHEAST TOYOTA DISTRIBUTORS, LLC, 100 Jim Moran Blvd, **Deerfield Beach,** FL 33442-1702, *pg.* 190, *pg.* 421
TOM BUSH REGENCY MOTORS INC., 9850 Atlantic Blvd, **Jacksonville,** FL 32225-6536, *pg.* 192, *pg.* 435

Georgia

ASBURY AUTOMOTIVE GROUP, INC., 2905 Premiere Pkwy NW Ste 300, **Duluth,** GA 30097, *pg.* 164, *pg.* 531
MERCEDES-BENZ USA, LLC, 303 Perimeter Ctr N, **Atlanta,** GA 30346, *pg.* 184, *pg.* 514
PORSCHE CARS NORTH AMERICA, INC., 980 Hammond Dr NE Ste 1000, **Atlanta,** GA 30328-8187, *pg.* 189, *pg.* 518
WORLD TOYOTA, 5800 Peachtree Industrial Blvd, **Atlanta,** GA 30341, *pg.* 195, *pg.* 524
YANMAR AMERICA CORPORATION, 101 International Parkway, **Adairsville,** GA 30103, *pg.* 196, *pg.* 482

Hawaii

SERVCO PACIFIC INC., 2850 Pukoloa St Ste 300, **Honolulu,** HI 96819, *pg.* 190, *pg.* 544

Illinois

ADELPHI ENTERPRISES L.P., 2000 Waukegan Rd, **Glenview,** IL 60025, *pg.* 163, *pg.* 614
INSURANCE AUTO AUCTIONS, INC., 2 Westbrook Corporate Ctr Ste 500, **Westchester,** IL 60154, *pg.* 180, *pg.* 669
JERRY BIGGERS CHEVROLET - ISUZU INC., 1385 E Chicago St, **Elgin,** IL 60120, *pg.* 180, *pg.* 610
NAPLETON SCHAUMBURG MOTORS, INC., 100 W Golf Rd, **Schaumburg,** IL 60195, *pg.* 185, *pg.* 659
NAVISTAR INTERNATIONAL CORPORATION, 2701 Navistar Dr, **Lisle,** IL 60532, *pg.* 186, *pg.* 630
NES RENTALS HOLDINGS, INC., 5440 N Cumberland, **Chicago,** IL 60656, *pg.* 186, *pg.* 584
NISSAN FORKLIFT CORPORATION, NORTH AMERICA, 240 N Prospect St, **Marengo,** IL 60152, *pg.* 186, *pg.* 631
O'BRIEN AUTOMOTIVE TEAM, 1111 O'Brien Dr, **Urbana,** IL 61801, *pg.* 187, *pg.* 663
SP PLUS CORPORATION, 200 E Randolph St Ste 7700, **Chicago,** IL 60601, *pg.* 190, *pg.* 590
STEVE FOLEY CADILLAC, 100 Skokie Blvd, **Northbrook,** IL 60062-1610, *pg.* 190, *pg.* 641

Indiana

AM GENERAL, LLC, 105 N Niles Ave, **South Bend,** IN 46617, *pg.* 163, *pg.* 697
KELLEY AUTOMOTIVE GROUP, 633 Ave of Autos, **Fort Wayne,** IN 46804, *pg.* 181, *pg.* 680
SUPREME INDUSTRIES, INC., 2581 E Kercher Rd, **Goshen,** IN 46528, *pg.* 191, *pg.* 681

Iowa

MIDWEST INDUSTRIES, INC., 122 E Hwy 175, **Ida Grove,** IA 51445, *pg.* 185, *pg.* 708

Kansas

THE CARLSON COMPANY INC., 6045 N Broadway St, **Wichita,** KS 67219-2013, *pg.* 167, *pg.* 722
CARSTAR, 4200 W 115th St, Ste 300, **Overland Park,** KS 66211, *pg.* 168, *pg.* 718
MECHANICAL PROTECTION PLAN, 8500 Shawnee Mission Pkwy Ste 200, **Merriam,** KS 66202-2960, *pg.* 184, *pg.* 717

Maine

DARLING'S INC., 96 Pkwy S Unit 1, **Brewer,** ME 04412, *pg.* 168, *pg.* 749

Maryland

AUTONATION, 501 Washington Blvd S 5, **Laurel,** MD 20707, *pg.* 165, *pg.* 773

Massachusetts

AMERICAN TOWER CORPORATION, 116 Huntington Ave, **Boston,** MA 02116, *pg.* 164, *pg.* 789

Michigan

BORGWARNER INC., 3850 Hamlin Rd, **Auburn Hills,** MI 48326-2872, *pg.* 167, *pg.* 867
DEAN ARBOUR CHEVROLET CADILLAC, 1859 N US Hwy, **East Tawas,** MI 48730, *pg.* 169, *pg.* 885
FCA US LLC, 800 Chrysler Dr, **Auburn Hills,** MI 48326, *pg.* 170, *pg.* 868
FORD MOTOR COMPANY, 1 American Rd, **Dearborn,** MI 48126, *pg.* 172, *pg.* 876
GARBER MANAGEMENT GROUP INC., 999 S Washington, **Saginaw,** MI 48601, *pg.* 174, *pg.* 906
GENERAL MOTORS COMPANY, 300 Renaissance Ctr, **Detroit,** MI 48265-3000, *pg.* 175, *pg.* 881
JEFFERSON CHEVROLET CO., 2130 E Jefferson Ave, **Detroit,** MI 48207, *pg.* 180, *pg.* 883
THE LINCOLN MOTOR COMPANY, 16800 Executive Plaza Dr 4th Fl, **Dearborn,** MI 48126, *pg.* 182, *pg.* 878
LOU LARICHE CHEVROLET INC., 40875 Plymouth Rd, **Plymouth,** MI 48170, *pg.* 183, *pg.* 904
MCINERNEY INC., 14100 W Eight Mile Rd, **Oak Park,** MI 48237-3045, *pg.* 184, *pg.* 903
PENSKE AUTOMOTIVE GROUP, INC., 2555 Telegraph Rd, **Bloomfield Hills,** MI 48302-0954, *pg.* 188, *pg.* 873
PENSKE CORPORATION, 2555 Telegraph Rd, **Bloomfield Hills,** MI 48302, *pg.* 188, *pg.* 873
RIVERSIDE FORD, 2625 Ludington St, **Escanaba,** MI 49829, *pg.* 189, *pg.* 885
TI AUTOMOTIVE LIMITED, 1272 Doris Rd, **Auburn Hills,** MI 48326, *pg.* 191, *pg.* 869

Minnesota

DAVE SYVERSON INC., 2310 E Main St, **Albert Lea,** MN 56007-0251, *pg.* 168, *pg.* 915
EVELAND'S INC., Hwy 371 N, **Backus,** MN 56435, *pg.* 169, *pg.* 916
FORKLIFTS OF MINNESOTA, INC., 2201 W 94th St, **Bloomington,** MN 55431, *pg.* 174, *pg.* 918

Missouri

BEUCKMAN FORD INC., 15675 Manchester Rd, **Ballwin,** MO 63011-2242, *pg.* 166, *pg.* 973
JOE MACHENS FORD INC., 1911 W Worley St, **Columbia,** MO 65203, *pg.* 180, *pg.* 976
XTRA LEASE LLC, 7911 Forsyth Blvd, Ste 600, **Saint Louis,** MO 63105, *pg.* 195, *pg.* 1005

New Jersey

A-1 LIMOUSINE INC., 2 Emmons Dr, **Princeton,** NJ 08540, *pg.* 163, *pg.* 1110
AVIS RENT A CAR SYSTEM, LLC, 6 Sylvan Way, **Parsippany,** NJ 07054, *pg.* 165, *pg.* 1102
BMW OF NORTH AMERICA, LLC, 300 Chestnut Ridge Rd,

Woodcliff Lake, NJ 07675, *pg.* 166, *pg.* 1133
FERRARI NORTH AMERICA, INC., 250 Sylvan Ave, **Englewood Cliffs,** NJ 07632-2500, *pg.* 171, *pg.* 1060
JAGUAR LAND ROVER NORTH AMERICA LLC, 555 MacArthur Blvd, **Mahwah,** NJ 07430, *pg.* 180, *pg.* 1081
JOYCE MOTORS CORP., 3166 State Rte 10, **Denville,** NJ 07834, *pg.* 181, *pg.* 1053
MASERATI NORTH AMERICA, INC., 250 Sylvan Ave, **Englewood Cliffs,** NJ 07632, *pg.* 183, *pg.* 1060
MITSUBISHI FUSO TRUCK OF AMERICA, INC., 2015 Ctr Square Rd, **Bridgeport,** NJ 08014, *pg.* 185, *pg.* 1045
SUBARU OF AMERICA, INC., 2235 Rte 70 W, **Cherry Hill,** NJ 08002, *pg.* 191, *pg.* 1050
TOWNE HYUNDAI, 3170 Rte 10 W, **Denville,** NJ 07834, *pg.* 192, *pg.* 1053
TOYOTA OF MORRISTOWN, 169 Ridgedale Ave, **Morristown,** NJ 07960, *pg.* 194, *pg.* 1089
VOLVO CARS OF NORTH AMERICA LLC, 1 Volvo Dr, **Rockleigh,** NJ 07647-2507, *pg.* 195, *pg.* 1117

New York

ALL STAR CARTS AND VEHICLES CORP., 1565D 5th Industrial Ct, **Bay Shore,** NY 11706, *pg.* 163, *pg.* 1141
CURRY ACURA, 685 Central Ave, **Scarsdale,** NY 10583, *pg.* 168, *pg.* 1340
MAGUIRE CHEVROLET-CADILLAC, 35 Cinema Dr, **Ithaca,** NY 14850, *pg.* 183, *pg.* 1170
THE MAJOR AUTOMOTIVE COMPANIES, INC., 43-40 Northern Blvd, **Long Island City,** NY 11101, *pg.* 183, *pg.* 1175
MITSUBISHI INTERNATIONAL CORPORATION, 655 3rd Ave, **New York,** NY 10017, *pg.* 185, *pg.* 1260
NEW COUNTRY MOTOR CAR GROUP INC., 358 Broadway Ste 403, **Saratoga Springs,** NY 12866, *pg.* 186, *pg.* 1340
PIAGGIO USA, INC., 140 E 45th St Ste 17C, **New York,** NY 10017, *pg.* 188, *pg.* 1282
TOYOTA MOTOR NORTH AMERICA, INC., 601 Lexington Ave, **New York,** NY 10022, *pg.* 192, *pg.* 1303

North Carolina

CARQUEST CORPORATION, 2635 E Millbrook Rd, **Raleigh,** NC 27604, *pg.* 168, *pg.* 1386
HACKNEY INTERNATIONAL, 911 W 5th St, **Washington,** NC 27889, *pg.* 178, *pg.* 1392
MACK TRUCKS, INC., 7900 National Svc Rd, **Greensboro,** NC 27409, *pg.* 183, *pg.* 1375
SONIC AUTOMOTIVE, INC., 4401 Colwick Rd, **Charlotte,** NC 28211-2311, *pg.* 190, *pg.* 1369
THOMAS BUILT BUSES, INC., 1408 Courtesy Rd, **High Point,** NC 27260-7248, *pg.* 191, *pg.* 1379
VOLVO TRUCKS NORTH AMERICA, INC., 7900 National Service Rd, **Greensboro,** NC 27409, *pg.* 195, *pg.* 1377

North Dakota

W.W. WALLWORK, INC., 900 35th St NW, **Fargo,** ND 58102-3089, *pg.* 195, *pg.* 1398

Ohio

AIRSTREAM, INC., 419 W Pike St PO Box 629, **Jackson Center,** OH 45334-9728, *pg.* 163, *pg.* 1456
AMP HOLDING INC., 4540 Alpine Rd, **Blue Ash,** OH 45242, *pg.* 164, *pg.* 1406
BEECHMONT AUTOMOTIVE GROUP, 8639 Beechmont Ave, **Cincinnati,** OH 45255-4709, *pg.* 166, *pg.* 1410
KIDRON, INC., 13442 Emerson Rd, **Kidron,** OH 44636, *pg.* 181, *pg.* 1457
MIKE ALBERT LEASING, INC., 10340 Evendale Dr, **Cincinnati,** OH 45241-2512, *pg.* 185, *pg.* 1417

Oklahoma

CRANE CARRIER COMPANY, 12536 E 52nd St, **Tulsa,** OK 74146, *pg.* 168, *pg.* 1489
DOLLAR THRIFTY AUTOMOTIVE GROUP, INC., 5330 E 31st St, **Tulsa,** OK 74153-0985, *pg.* 169, *pg.* 1489

Oregon

FREIGHTLINER TRUCKS, 4747 N Channel Ave, **Portland,** OR 97217-7613, *pg.* 174, *pg.* 1502
GUARANTY CHEVROLET-PONTIAC, 20 Hwy 99 S, **Junction City,** OR 97448-9714, *pg.* 177, *pg.* 1498
LITHIA MOTORS INC, 150 N Bartlett St, **Medford,** OR 97501, *pg.* 183, *pg.* 1499

Pennsylvania

PACIFICO ENTERPRISES, INC., 6701 Essington Ave, **Philadelphia,** PA 19153-3407, *pg.* 188, *pg.* 1568
PENSKE LOGISTICS, LLC, Route 10 Green Hills PO Box 563, **Reading,** PA 19603, *pg.* 188, *pg.* 1584
PENSKE TRUCK LEASING COMPANY, L.P., Rte 10 Green Hills, **Reading,** PA 19607, *pg.* 188, *pg.* 1585
REEDMAN TOLL AUTO WORLD, 1700 E Lincoln Hwy US Rte 1, **Langhorne,** PA 19047, *pg.* 189, *pg.* 1547
WOLFINGTON BODY COMPANY, INC., 30 N Pottstown Pke, **Exton,** PA 19341, *pg.* 195, *pg.* 1532

Puerto Rico

BELLA GROUP, PO Box 190816, **San Juan,** PR 00919-0816, *pg.* 166, *pg.* 1599

South Carolina

FAIRWAY FORD LINCOLN, 2323 Laurens Rd, **Greenville,** SC 29607-3246, *pg.* 170, *pg.* 1617

Tennessee

BUD DAVIS CADILLAC, INC., 5433 Poplar Ave, **Memphis,** TN 38119-3634, *pg.* 167, *pg.* 1641
HAROLD MATTHEWS NISSAN INC., 185 Hwy 76, **Clarksville,** TN 37043, *pg.* 178, *pg.* 1630
MILLER INDUSTRIES, INC., 8503 Hilltop Dr, **Ooltewah,** TN 37363, *pg.* 185, *pg.* 1655
NISSAN NORTH AMERICA, INC., One Nissan Way, **Franklin,** TN 37067, *pg.* 186, *pg.* 1633

Texas

ADVANTAGE BMW CLEAR LAKE, 400 Gulf Freeway, **League City,** TX 77573, *pg.* 163, *pg.* 1725
ADVANTAGE BMW MIDTOWN, 2101 San Jacinto, **Houston,** TX 77002, *pg.* 163, *pg.* 1699
ANCIRA ENTERPRISES INC., 6111 Bandera Rd, **San Antonio,** TX 78238-1643, *pg.* 164, *pg.* 1739
BMW OF EL PASO, 6318 Montana Ave, **El Paso,** TX 79925, *pg.* 166, *pg.* 1691
BRUCKNER TRUCK SALES, INC., 9471 Interstate 40 E, **Amarillo,** TX 79118, *pg.* 167, *pg.* 1659
GRAHAM MOTORS AND CONTROLS, PO Box 960607, **El Paso,** TX 79996, *pg.* 177, *pg.* 1692
GROUP 1 AUTOMOTIVE, INC., 800 Gessner Ste 500, **Houston,** TX 77024, *pg.* 177, *pg.* 1706
GULF STATES TOYOTA, INC., 1375 Enclave Pkwy, **Houston,** TX 77077, *pg.* 177, *pg.* 1707
JOHN EAGLE HONDA OF HOUSTON, 18787 NW Fwy, **Houston,** TX 77065, *pg.* 180, *pg.* 1709
KRUSE ENERGY & EQUIPMENT, 11611 County Rd 128 W, **Odessa,** TX 79765, *pg.* 182, *pg.* 1728
PETERBILT MOTORS CO., 1700 Woodbrook St, **Denton,** TX 76205-7864, *pg.* 188, *pg.* 1691
RANDALL REED'S PRESTIGE LINCOLN MERCURY, 3601 Shiloh Rd, **Garland,** TX 75041, *pg.* 189, *pg.* 1698
RELIABLE CHEVROLET, 800 N Central Expwy, **Richardson,** TX 75080-5204, *pg.* 189, *pg.* 1736
RUSH ENTERPRISES INC., 555 IH 35 S Ste 500, **New Braunfels,** TX 78130, *pg.* 189, *pg.* 1728
RUSSELL & SMITH FORD INC., 3440 S Loop W, **Houston,** TX 77025, *pg.* 190, *pg.* 1713
SEWELL AUTOMOTIVE COMPANIES, 3860 W NW Hwy Ste 100, **Dallas,** TX 75220, *pg.* 190, *pg.* 1686

Utah

GARFF ENTERPRISES INC., 405 S Main Ste 1200, **Salt Lake City,** UT 84111-3521, *pg.* 174, *pg.* 1758
LARRY H. MILLER GROUP OF COMPANIES, 9350 South 150 East Rte 1000, **Sandy,** UT 84070, *pg.* 182, *pg.* 1762

Virginia

AUDI OF AMERICA, INC., 2200 Ferdinand Porsche Dr, **Herndon,** VA 20171, *pg.* 164, *pg.* 1784
CARMAX, INC., 12800 Tuckahoe Creek Pkwy, **Richmond,** VA 23238-1115, *pg.* 167, *pg.* 1800
RICHMOND FORD, 4600 W Broad St, **Richmond,** VA 23230-3206, *pg.* 189, *pg.* 1803
VOLKSWAGEN GROUP OF AMERICA, INC., 2200 Ferdinand Porsche Dr, **Herndon,** VA 20171, *pg.* 194, *pg.* 1785

Washington

KENWORTH TRUCK CO., 10630 NE 38th Pl, **Kirkland,** WA 98033-7909, *pg.* 181, *pg.* 1822
KUNI ENTERPRISES INC., 203 Southeast Park Plz Dr Ste 290, **Vancouver,** WA 98684, *pg.* 182, *pg.* 1846
PACCAR INC., PACCAR Bldg 777 106th Ave NE, **Bellevue,** WA 98004-5027, *pg.* 187, *pg.* 1816

Wisconsin

BERGSTROM AUTOMOTIVE, 1 Neenah Ctr 7th Fl, **Neenah,** WI 54956, *pg.* 166, *pg.* 1883
BRICKNER MOTORS, INC., 16450 County Hwy A, **Marathon,** WI 54448-9599, *pg.* 167, *pg.* 1869
EWALD AUTOMOTIVE GROUP, LLC, 6319 S 108th St, **Franklin,** WI 53132, *pg.* 170, *pg.* 1858
HARLEY-DAVIDSON, INC., 3700 W Juneau Ave, **Milwaukee,** WI 53208, *pg.* 178, *pg.* 1874
HEISER AUTOMOTIVE GROUP INC., 1700 W Silverspring Dr, **Glendale,** WI 53209, *pg.* 179, *pg.* 1858
OSHKOSH CORPORATION, 2307 Oregon St, **Oshkosh,** WI 54902-7062, *pg.* 187, *pg.* 1885
PIERCE MANUFACTURING, INC., PO Box 2017, **Appleton,** WI 54912-2017, *pg.* 188, *pg.* 1852

Automotive Parts & Accessories

Alabama

MOTION INDUSTRIES, INC., 1605 Alton Rd, **Birmingham,** AL 35210-3770, *pg.* 213, *pg.* 3

Arkansas

CPI HOLDINGS, LLC, 2005 West Ave B, **Hope,** AR 71801-8882, *pg.* 203, *pg.* 32

California

AKH COMPANY, INC., 1160 N Anaheim Blvd, **Anaheim,** CA 92801, *pg.* 198, *pg.* 42
CLAUS ETTENSBERGER CORPORATION, 10349 Santa Monica Blvd, **West Los Angeles,** CA 90025, *pg.* 202, *pg.* 305
EDELBROCK CORPORATION, 2700 California St, **Torrance,** CA 90503-3907, *pg.* 204, *pg.* 293
IMPCO TECHNOLOGIES, INC., 3030 S Susan St, **Santa Ana,** CA 92704-6435, *pg.* 208, *pg.* 261
K&N ENGINEERING INC., 1455 Citrus St, **Riverside,** CA 92507, *pg.* 210, *pg.* 194
KRACO ENTERPRISES, LLC, 505 E Euclid Ave, **Compton,** CA 90222, *pg.* 210, *pg.* 68
LKQ CORP., 700 E Bonita Ave, **Pomona,** CA 91767, *pg.* 210, *pg.* 185
MOTORCAR PARTS OF AMERICA, INC., 2929 California St, **Torrance,** CA 90503-3914, *pg.* 213, *pg.* 295
OFF ROAD UNLIMITED CORP., 300 N Victory Blvd, **Burbank,** CA 91504, *pg.* 214, *pg.* 52
U.S. AUTO PARTS NETWORK, INC., 17150 S Margay Ave, **Carson,** CA 90746, *pg.* 221, *pg.* 64
WESTIN AUTOMOTIVE PRODUCTS, INC., 320 W Covina Blvd, **San Dimas,** CA 91773, *pg.* 222, *pg.* 211
ZAP, 501 4th St, **Santa Rosa,** CA 95401, *pg.* 222, *pg.* 277

Colorado

BESTOP, INC., 2100 W Midway Blvd, **Broomfield,** CO 80020-1626, *pg.* 200, *pg.* 312
BIG O TIRES, INC., 12650 E Briarwood Ave Ste 2D, **Centennial,** CO 80112, *pg.* 201, *pg.* 314
THE GATES CORPORATION, 1551 Wewatta St, **Denver,** CO 80202, *pg.* 205, *pg.* 319

Connecticut

ARMORED AUTOGROUP INC., 39 Old Ridgebury Rd, **Danbury,** CT 06810, *pg.* 199, *pg.* 342
AUTOSWAGE PRODUCTS, INC., 726 River Rd, **Shelton,** CT 06484-4848, *pg.* 200, *pg.* 369
BEAD INDUSTRIES INC., 11 Cascade Blvd, **Milford,** CT 06460, *pg.* 200, *pg.* 356
HONEYWELL CONSUMER PRODUCTS GROUP, 39 Old Ridgebury Rd, **Danbury,** CT 06810-5109, *pg.* 208, *pg.* 344
THULE, INC., 42 Silvermine Rd, **Seymour,** CT 06483-3907, *pg.* 218, *pg.* 369

Florida

ARCTIC FREEZE DISCOUNT AUTO & TRUCK REPAIR, 1198 East Bay Dr, **Largo,** FL 33770, *pg.* 199, *pg.* 437
MILE MARKER INTERNATIONAL INC., 2121 Blunt Rd, **Pompano Beach,** FL 33069, *pg.* 213, *pg.* 459
PURADYN FILTER TECHNOLOGIES, INC., 2017 High Ridge Rd, **Boynton Beach,** FL 33426, *pg.* 215, *pg.* 414
RENNTECH, INC., 1369 N Killian Dr, **Lake Park,** FL 33403, *pg.* 216, *pg.* 436
TIRE KINGDOM, INC., 823 Donald Ross Rd, **Juno Beach,** FL 33408-1605, *pg.* 219, *pg.* 436
TIRES PLUS TOTAL CAR CARE, 2021 Sunnydale Blvd, **Clearwater,** FL 33765-1202, *pg.* 219, *pg.* 417

Georgia

EXIDE TECHNOLOGIES, 13000 Deerfield Pkwy Bldg 200, **Alpharetta,** GA 30004-6118, *pg.* 204, *pg.* 483
GENUINE PARTS COMPANY, 2999 Circle 75 Pkwy, **Atlanta,** GA 30339-3050, *pg.* 206, *pg.* 506
LUND INTERNATIONAL, INC., 4325 Hamilton Mill Rd Ste 400, **Buford,** GA 30518, *pg.* 211, *pg.* 526
MIGHTY DISTRIBUTING SYSTEM OF AMERICA, 650 Engineering Dr, **Norcross,** GA 30092-2821, *pg.* 213, *pg.* 538
NATIONAL AUTOMOTIVE PARTS ASSOCIATION, 2999 Cir 75 Pkwy SE, **Atlanta,** GA 30339-3050, *pg.* 213, *pg.* 515

Illinois

AIRTEX PRODUCTS, 407 W Main St, **Fairfield,** IL 62837-1622, *pg.* 198, *pg.* 612
BURGESS-NORTON MANUFACTURING COMPANY, 737 Peyton St, **Geneva,** IL 60134-2150, *pg.* 202, *pg.* 613
CHICAGO-WILCOX MFG. COMPANY, INC., 16928 State St, **South Holland,** IL 60473, *pg.* 202, *pg.* 661
CUSTOM ACCESSORIES INC., 5900 Ami Dr, **Richmond,** IL 60071, *pg.* 203, *pg.* 653
GOLD EAGLE COMPANY, 4400 S Kildare Ave, **Chicago,** IL 60632-4356, *pg.* 206, *pg.* 575
HENDRICKSON INTERNATIONAL, 800 S Frontage Rd, **Woodridge,** IL 60517-4904, *pg.* 207, *pg.* 672
J.C. WHITNEY & CO., 761 Progress Pkwy, **La Salle,** IL 61301, *pg.* 209, *pg.* 621
MACNEIL AUTOMOTIVE PRODUCTS, LTD., 1 MacNeil Ct, **Bolingbrook,** IL 60440, *pg.* 211, *pg.* 559
MIDAS, INC., 1300 N Arlington, **Itasca,** IL 60143, *pg.* 212, *pg.* 620
MIDAS INTERNATIONAL, INC., 1300 N Arlington Hts Rd, **Itasca,** IL 60143-3174, *pg.* 212, *pg.* 620
MORAN INDUSTRIES, INC., 4444 147th St, **Midlothian,** IL 60445-2644, *pg.* 213, *pg.* 632
PLEWS/EDELMANN, 1550 Franklin Grove Rd, **Dixon,** IL 61021, *pg.* 215, *pg.* 607
SKF SEALING SOLUTIONS, 900 N State St, **Elgin,** IL 60123-2147, *pg.* 217, *pg.* 610
TITAN INTERNATIONAL, INC., 2701 Spruce St, **Quincy,** IL 62301-3473, *pg.* 219, *pg.* 653
TRIPPE MANUFACTURING COMPANY, 1111 W 35th St, **Chicago,** IL 60609-1404, *pg.* 220, *pg.* 592
TURTLE WAX, INC., 625 Willowbrook Ctr Pkwy, **Willowbrook,** IL 60527-7969, *pg.* 220, *pg.* 671
UNITY MANUFACTURING COMPANY, 1260 N Clybourn Ave, **Chicago,** IL 60610, *pg.* 221, *pg.* 594
U.S. TSUBAKI, INC., 301 E Marquardt Dr, **Wheeling,** IL 60090-6431, *pg.* 221, *pg.* 670
VAPOR BUS INTERNATIONAL, 1010 Johnson Dr, **Buffalo Grove,** IL 60089, *pg.* 221, *pg.* 560
WARNER ELECTRIC, INC., 449 Gardner St, **South Beloit,** IL 61080, *pg.* 221, *pg.* 661

Indiana

ALLISON TRANSMISSION, INC., One Allison Way, **Indianapolis,** IN 46222, *pg.* 198, *pg.* 682
GROTE INDUSTRIES, INC., 2600 Lanier Dr, **Madison,** IN 47250, *pg.* 206, *pg.* 693
JASPER ELECTRIC MOTORS, 733 W Division Rd, **Jasper,** IN 47546, *pg.* 209, *pg.* 691
JASPER ENGINE & TRANSMISSION EXCHANGE, 815 Wernsing Rd, **Jasper,** IN 47547, *pg.* 209, *pg.* 691
KYB AMERICA LLC, 850 N Graham Rd, Ste C, **Greenwood,** IN 46143, *pg.* 210, *pg.* 681
REGAL POWER TRANSMISSION SOLUTIONS, 909 Lafayette St, **Valparaiso,** IN 46383-4210, *pg.* 216, *pg.* 698
REMY INTERNATIONAL, INC., 600 Corporation Dr, **Pendleton,** IN 46064, *pg.* 216, *pg.* 696
ROLLS-ROYCE CORPORATION, 450 S Meridian St, **Indianapolis,** IN 46225-1103, *pg.* 216, *pg.* 689
ROTARY LIFT, 2700 Lanier Dr, **Madison,** IN 47250-1753, *pg.* 216, *pg.* 694
UNITED COMPONENTS, INC., 14601 Hwy 41 N, **Evansville,** IN 47725, *pg.* 220, *pg.* 679

Iowa

BEE LINE COMPANY, 2700 62nd St Ct, **Bettendorf,** IA 52722-5575, *pg.* 200, *pg.* 701

Kansas

BG PRODUCTS, INC., 740 S Wichita St, **Wichita,** KS 67213, *pg.* 200, *pg.* 722
CLORE AUTOMOTIVE LLC, 8735 Rosehill Rd Ste 220, **Lenexa,** KS 66215, *pg.* 202, *pg.* 716
LONG MOTOR CORPORATION, 14600 W 107th St, **Lenexa,** KS 66215, *pg.* 211, *pg.* 716

Louisiana

LONNIE MCCURRY'S FOUR WHEEL DRIVE CENTER, INC., 212 Stevenson St, **West Monroe,** LA 71292, *pg.* 211, *pg.* 748

Massachusetts

ALTRA HOLDINGS, INC., 300 Granite St Ste 201, **Braintree,** MA 02184, *pg.* 198, *pg.* 802
BOSTON GEAR, 300 Granite St, **Braintree,** MA 02184, *pg.* 201, *pg.* 802
COLE HERSEE COMPANY, 20 Old Colony Ave, **Boston,** MA 02127-2467, *pg.* 202, *pg.* 792
LOJACK CORPORATION, 40 Pequot Way, **Canton,** MA 02021, *pg.* 210, *pg.* 811

Michigan

AIR LIFT COMPANY, 2727 Snow Rd, **Lansing,** MI 48917-9595, *pg.* 198, *pg.* 895
AMERICAN AXLE & MANUFACTURING HOLDINGS, INC., 1 Dauch Dr, **Detroit,** MI 48211-1198, *pg.* 198, *pg.* 879
AUSCO PRODUCTS, INC., 2245 Pipestone Rd, **Benton Harbor,** MI 49022-2425, *pg.* 199, *pg.* 872
AUTOLIV NORTH AMERICA, AMERICAN TECHNICAL CENTER, 1320 Pacific Dr, **Auburn Hills,** MI 48326-1569, *pg.* 200, *pg.* 867
BELLE TIRE INC., 1000 Enterprise Dr, **Allen Park,** MI 48101, *pg.* 200, *pg.* 864
DELPHI AUTOMOTIVE LLP, 5725 Delphi Dr, **Troy,** MI 48098-2815, *pg.* 204, *pg.* 910
FEDERAL-MOGUL HOLDINGS CORPORATION, 27300 W 11 Mile Rd, **Southfield,** MI 48034, *pg.* 205, *pg.* 907
GENTEX CORPORATION, 600 N Centennial St, **Zeeland,** MI 49464-1318, *pg.* 206, *pg.* 913
GKN AUTOMOTIVE INC., 3300 University Dr, **Auburn Hills,** MI 48326-2362, *pg.* 206, *pg.* 869
HASTINGS MANUFACTURING COMPANY, LLC, 325 N Hanover St, **Hastings,** MI 49058-1527, *pg.* 207, *pg.* 891
IAV AUTOMOTIVE ENGINEERING INC., 15620 Technology Dr, **Northville,** MI 48168, *pg.* 208, *pg.* 902
KEY SAFETY SYSTEMS, INC., 7000 Nineteen Mile Rd, **Sterling Heights,** MI 48314, *pg.* 210, *pg* 908
MAHLE BEHR USA INC., TROY, 2700 Daley Dr, **Troy,** MI 48083, *pg.* 212, *pg.* 911
MAXION WHEELS, 39500 Orchard Hill Pl Ste 500, **Novi,** MI 48375, *pg.* 212, *pg.* 903
MERITOR, INC., 2135 W Maple Rd, **Troy,** MI 48084, *pg.* 212, *pg.* 911
ONSTAR CORPORATION, 400 Renaissance Ctr, **Detroit,** MI 48243, *pg.* 214, *pg.* 884
O'REILLY AUTO PARTS, 8080 Haggerty Rd, **Belleville,** MI 48111-1643, *pg.* 214, *pg.* 872
PERCEPTRON, INC., 47827 Halyard Dr, **Plymouth,** MI 48170-2461, *pg.* 215, *pg.* 904
RECARO NORTH AMERICA, INC., 3275 Lapeer Rd W, **Auburn Hills,** MI 48326, *pg.* 216, *pg.* 869
RIETER AUTOMOTIVE NORTH AMERICA, INC., 38555 Hills Tech Dr, **Farmington Hills,** MI 48331, *pg.* 216, *pg.* 886
SAF-HOLLAND INTERNATIONAL, INC., 1950 Industrial Blvd, **Muskegon,** MI 49442-6114, *pg.* 217, *pg.* 902
SPARTAN MOTORS, INC., 1541 Reynolds Rd, **Charlotte,** MI 48813, *pg.* 217, *pg.* 874
TOWER INTERNATIONAL, INC., 17672 Laurel Park Dr N Ste 400E, **Livonia,** MI 48152, *pg.* 219, *pg.* 897
TRICO PRODUCTS CORPORATION, 3255 W Hamlin Rd, **Rochester Hills,** MI 48309-3231, *pg.* 220, *pg.* 905
VALLEY TRUCK PARTS, INC., 1900 Chicago Dr, **Wyoming,** MI 49519, *pg.* 221, *pg.* 913
VISTEON CORPORATION, 1 Village Center Dr, **Van Buren Township,** MI 48111, *pg.* 221, *pg.* 912
ZF TRW, 12001 Tech Ctr Dr, **Livonia,** MI 48150, *pg.* 222, *pg.* 897

First page reference indicates Business Class Edition
Second page reference indicates Geographic Edition

ZIEBART INTERNATIONAL CORPORATION, 1290 E Maple Rd, **Troy,** MI 48083-2817, *pg.* 222, *pg.* 912

Minnesota

MICO, INCORPORATED, 1911 Lee Blvd, **North Mankato,** MN 56003-2507, *pg.* 212, *pg.* 951
THEXTON MANUFACTURING COMPANY, INC., 6539 Cecilia Cir, **Edina,** MN 55439-2719, *pg.* 218, *pg.* 925
ZERO-MAX, INC., 13200 6th Ave N, **Plymouth,** MN 55441, *pg.* 222, *pg.* 954

Missouri

CTP TRANSPORTATION PRODUCTS, 2601 West Butterfield Rd, **Springfield,** MO 65807, *pg.* 203, *pg.* 1006
DENT WIZARD INTERNATIONAL CORP., 4710 Earth City Expy, **Bridgeton,** MO 63044, *pg.* 204, *pg.* 973
HUNTER ENGINEERING COMPANY, 11250 Hunter Dr, **Bridgeton,** MO 63044-2306, *pg.* 208, *pg.* 973
HUTCHENS INDUSTRIES INC., 215 N Patterson Ave, **Springfield,** MO 65802, *pg.* 208, *pg.* 1006
O'REILLY AUTOMOTIVE, INC., 233 S Patterson Ave, **Springfield,** MO 65802-2210, *pg.* 214, *pg.* 1006
PARKHURST MANUFACTURING CO., INC., 18999 Hwy Y, **Sedalia,** MO 65301, *pg.* 214, *pg.* 1005

Nebraska

SPEEDWAY MOTORS INC., PO Box 81906, **Lincoln,** NE 68501, *pg.* 218, *pg.* 1012

New Hampshire

AUTOMOTIVE SUPPLY ASSOCIATES, INC., 129 Manchester St, **Concord,** NH 03301-5118, *pg.* 200, *pg.* 1033

New Jersey

AMERICAN VAN EQUIPMENT INC., 149 Leheigh Ave, **Lakewood,** NJ 08701, *pg.* 199, *pg.* 1078
MORGAN'S TIRE SERVICE, 813 Sunset Rd, **Burlington,** NJ 08016, *pg.* 213, *pg.* 1048
SOMERSET TIRE SERVICE, INC., 1 STS Dr Bldg #1, **Bridgewater,** NJ 08807, *pg.* 217, *pg.* 1047

New York

ALLOMATIC PRODUCTS COMPANY, 102 Jericho Tpke, **Floral Park,** NY 11001, *pg.* 198, *pg.* 1160
GARLOCK SEALING TECHNOLOGIES, 1666 Division St, **Palmyra,** NY 14522-9383, *pg.* 205, *pg.* 1320
GENERAL BEARING CORPORATION, 44 High St, **West Nyack,** NY 10994-2702, *pg.* 205, *pg.* 1350
HAHN AUTOMOTIVE WAREHOUSE, INC., 415 W Main St, **Rochester,** NY 14608-1944, *pg.* 206, *pg.* 1336
MONRO MUFFLER BRAKE, INC., 200 Holleder Pkwy, **Rochester,** NY 14615, *pg.* 213, *pg.* 1336
STANDARD MOTOR PRODUCTS, INC., 37-18 Northern Blvd, **Long Island City,** NY 11101, *pg.* 218, *pg.* 1176
UNIFRAX CORPORATION, 2351 Whirlpool St, **Niagara Falls,** NY 14305-2413, *pg.* 220, *pg.* 1317
VARTA MICROBATTERY, INC., 555 Theodore Fremd Ave, # 304, **Rye,** NY 10580, *pg.* 221, *pg.* 1339

North Carolina

AFFINIA GROUP INTERMEDIATE HOLDINGS INC., 1 Wix Way, **Gastonia,** NC 28053, *pg.* 197, *pg.* 1373
AFFINIA WIX FILTRATION PRODUCTS, 1 Wix Way, **Gastonia,** NC 28054, *pg.* 198, *pg.* 1373
AMERICAN TIRE DISTRIBUTORS HOLDINGS, INC., 12200 Herbert Wayne Ct Ste 150, **Huntersville,** NC 28078, *pg.* 199, *pg.* 1379
AP EXHAUST PRODUCTS, INC., 300 Dixie Trl, **Goldsboro,** NC 27530, *pg.* 199, *pg.* 1373
COLONY TIRE CORPORATION, 1415 N Broad St, **Edenton,** NC 27932-9613, *pg.* 203, *pg.* 1372
DUFF-NORTON, 9415 Pioneer Ave, **Charlotte,** NC 28273-6318, *pg.* 204, *pg.* 1365
INDIAN HEAD INDUSTRIES, INC., 8530 Cliff Cameron Dr, **Charlotte,** NC 28269-9786, *pg.* 208, *pg.* 1367
MAACO FRANCHISING, INC., 440 S Church St, Ste 700, **Charlotte,** NC 28202, *pg.* 211, *pg.* 1367
MEINEKE CAR CARE CENTERS, INC., 128 S Tryon St Ste 900, **Charlotte,** NC 28202, *pg.* 212, *pg.* 1367
RADIATOR SPECIALTY COMPANY, 600 Radiator Rd, **Indian Trail,** NC 28079-5225, *pg.* 215, *pg.* 1380
ROSTRA PRECISION CONTROLS, INC., 2519 Dana Dr, **Laurinburg,** NC 28352, *pg.* 216, *pg.* 1381
SPX CORPORATION, 13320 Ballantyne Corporate Pl, **Charlotte,** NC 28277, *pg.* 218, *pg.* 1369

Ohio

APPLIED INDUSTRIAL TECHNOLOGIES, INC., 1 Applied Plz, **Cleveland,** OH 44115, *pg.* 199, *pg.* 1428
COMMERCIAL VEHICLE GROUP, INC., 7800 Walton Pkwy, **New Albany,** OH 43054, *pg.* 203, *pg.* 1467
CORSA PERFORMANCE, 140 Blaze Industrial Pkwy, **Berea,** OH 44017, *pg.* 203, *pg.* 1406
DANA HOLDING CORPORATION, 3939 Technology Dr, **Maumee,** OH 43537, *pg.* 203, *pg.* 1461
HAMILTON CASTER & MFG. CO., 1637 Dixie Hwy, **Hamilton,** OH 45011-4087, *pg.* 206, *pg.* 1454
HBD INDUSTRIES, INC., 5200 Upper Metro Pl Ste 110, **Dublin,** OH 43017, *pg.* 207, *pg.* 1449
MR. GASKET INC., 10601 Memphis Ave Ste 12, **Brooklyn,** OH 44144-2043, *pg.* 213, *pg.* 1406
PILKINGTON NORTH AMERICA, INC., 811 Madison Ave, **Toledo,** OH 43604, *pg.* 215, *pg.* 1477
THE TIMKEN COMPANY, 1835 Dueber Ave SW, **Canton,** OH 44706-0932, *pg.* 218, *pg.* 1408
TRANSTAR INDUSTRIES, INC., 7350 Young Dr, **Walton Hills,** OH 44146-5357, *pg.* 219, *pg.* 1478
TUFFY ASSOCIATES CORPORATION, 7150 Granite Cir, **Toledo,** OH 43617, *pg.* 220, *pg.* 1477

Oregon

LES SCHWAB TIRE CENTERS OF OREGON, INC., 646 NW Madras Hwy PO Box 667, **Prineville,** OR 97754, *pg.* 210, *pg.* 1508
WARN INDUSTRIES, INC., 12900 SE Capps Rd, **Clackamas,** OR 97015-8903, *pg.* 221, *pg.* 1497
WILLIAMS CONTROLS, INC., 14100 SW 72nd Ave, **Portland,** OR 97224-8009, *pg.* 222, *pg.* 1508

Pennsylvania

AAMCO TRANSMISSIONS, INC., 201 Gibraltar Rd Ste 100, **Horsham,** PA 19044-2331, *pg.* 197, *pg.* 1540
DORMAN PRODUCTS, INC., 3400 E Walnut St, **Colmar,** PA 18915-9768, *pg.* 204, *pg.* 1522
KEYSTONE AUTOMOTIVE OPERATIONS, INC., 44 Tunkhannock Ave, **Exeter,** PA 18643, *pg.* 210, *pg.* 1531
LEE MYLES ASSOCIATES CORPORATION, 847 Fern Ave, **Reading,** PA 19607, *pg.* 210, *pg.* 1584
NEAPCO, INC., 740 Queen St, **Pottstown,** PA 19464-6014, *pg.* 214, *pg.* 1582
THE PEP BOYS - MANNY, MOE & JACK, 3111 W Allegheny Ave, **Philadelphia,** PA 19132-1116, *pg.* 215, *pg.* 1568
SKF USA, 20 Industrial Dr, **Hanover,** PA 17331-9582, *pg.* 217, *pg.* 1535
STANDARD BENT GLASS CORPORATION, 136 Lincoln Ave, **Butler,** PA 16029, *pg.* 218, *pg.* 1519
U.S. AXLE, INC., 275 Shoemaker Rd, **Pottstown,** PA 19464-6433, *pg.* 221, *pg.* 1582
WAIGLOBAL, 1101 Enterprise Dr, **Royersford,** PA 19468-4251, *pg.* 221, *pg.* 1585
WINNER INTERNATIONAL, LLC, 32 W State St, **Sharon,** PA 16146, *pg.* 222, *pg.* 1586

South Carolina

AMBAC INTERNATIONAL CORPORATION, 910 Spears Creek Ct, **Elgin,** SC 29045, *pg.* 198, *pg.* 1615

South Dakota

WORTHINGTON INDUSTRIES, 315 Airport Dr, **Watertown,** SD 57201-5606, *pg.* 222, *pg.* 1626

Tennessee

ADVANCED PLATING INC., 1425 Cowan Ct, **Nashville,** TN 37207, *pg.* 197, *pg.* 1648
AUTOZONE, INC., 123 S Front St, **Memphis,** TN 38103-3607, *pg.* 200, *pg.* 1641
BRIDGESTONE AMERICAS, INC., 535 Marriott Dr, PO Box 140990, **Nashville,** TN 37214-0990, *pg.* 201, *pg.* 1649
FREE SERVICE TIRE COMPANY, INC., 126 Buffalo St, **Johnson City,** TN 37604-5702, *pg.* 205, *pg.* 1635
HECKETHORN MANUFACTURING COMPANY, INC., 2005 Forrest St, **Dyersburg,** TN 38024-3683, *pg.* 207, *pg.* 1632
HEIL ENVIRONMENTAL INDUSTRIES, LTD., 2030 Hamilton Pl Blvd Ste 300, **Chattanooga,** TN 37421, *pg.* 207, *pg.* 1629
HENNESSY INDUSTRIES, INC., 1601 J P Hennessy Dr, **La Vergne,** TN 37086-3524, *pg.* 207, *pg.* 1639

Texas

FLEETPRIDE, INC., 8708 Technology Forest Pl Ste 125, **The Woodlands,** TX 77381, *pg.* 205, *pg.* 1747
INTERSTATE BATTERY SYSTEM OF AMERICA INC., 12770 Merit Dr Ste 400, **Dallas,** TX 75251-1296, *pg.* 208, *pg.* 1682
J.B. POINDEXTER & CO., INC., 600 Travis Ste 200, **Houston,** TX 77002-5218, *pg.* 209, *pg.* 1709
JIFFY LUBE INTERNATIONAL, INC., 910 Louisiana St, **Houston,** TX 77002, *pg.* 209, *pg.* 1709
SANDEN INTERNATIONAL (USA), INC., 601 S Sanden Blvd, **Wylie,** TX 75098, *pg.* 217, *pg.* 1750
SHELL LUBRICANTS, 700 Milam St, **Houston,** TX 77010, *pg.* 217, *pg.* 1714

Utah

STS TURBO, INC., 165 N 1330 W Ste A-4, **Orem,** UT 84057, *pg.* 218, *pg.* 1753

Virginia

ADVANCE AUTO PARTS, INC., 5008 Airport Rd, **Roanoke,** VA 24012, *pg.* 197, *pg.* 1805
CARFAX INC., 5860 Trinity Pkwy Ste 600, **Centreville,** VA 20120, *pg.* 202, *pg.* 1777
PRECISION AUTO CARE, INC., 748 Miller Dr SE Ste G-1, **Leesburg,** VA 20175, *pg.* 215, *pg.* 1787
ZENITH FUEL SYSTEMS LLC, 14570 Industrial Park Rd, **Bristol,** VA 24202-3706, *pg.* 222, *pg.* 1776

Washington

COMPETITION SPECIALTIES INC., 2402 W Vly Hwy N, **Auburn,** WA 98001, *pg.* 203, *pg.* 1813

Wisconsin

BRIGGS & STRATTON CORPORATION, 12301 W Wirth St, **Wauwatosa,** WI 53222-2110, *pg.* 201, *pg.* 1899
DANFOSS GRAHAM, 8800 W Bradley Rd, **Milwaukee,** WI 53224, *pg.* 203, *pg.* 1874
DOUGLAS DYNAMICS, INC., 7777 N 73rd St, **Milwaukee,** WI 53233, *pg.* 204, *pg.* 1874
JASON INDUSTRIES, INC., 411 E Wisconsin Ave Ste 2100, **Milwaukee,** WI 53202, *pg.* 208, *pg.* 1875
JOHNSON CONTROLS, INC., 5757 N Green Bay Ave, **Milwaukee,** WI 53209, *pg.* 209, *pg.* 1876
PENDA CORPORATION, 2344 W Wisconsin St PO Box 449, **Portage,** WI 53901, *pg.* 214, *pg.* 1887
SEATS INCORPORATED, 1515 Industrial St, **Reedsburg,** WI 53959, *pg.* 217, *pg.* 1890
TRICO MFG. CORP., 1235 Hickory St, **Pewaukee,** WI 53072-3999, *pg.* 219, *pg.* 1886
TWIN DISC, INCORPORATED, 1328 Racine St, **Racine,** WI 53403, *pg.* 220, *pg.* 1889
WELLS MANUFACTURING, L.P., 26 S Brooke St, **Fond Du Lac,** WI 54935-4007, *pg.* 222, *pg.* 1858

First page reference indicates Business Class Edition
Second page reference indicates Geographic Edition

Aviation & Aerospace

Alabama

CONTINENTAL MOTORS, 2039 S Broad St, **Mobile,** AL 36615, *pg.* 227, *pg.* 7
TELEDYNE BROWN ENGINEERING, INC., 300 Sparkman Dr Cummings Research Pk, **Huntsville,** AL 35805-1912, *pg.* 235, *pg.* 6

Arizona

THE BOEING COMPANY - HELICOPTER DIVISION, 5000 E McDowell Rd, **Mesa,** AZ 85215-9707, *pg.* 226, *pg.* 13
CUTTER AVIATION, INC., 2802 E Old Twr Rd, **Phoenix,** AZ 85034, *pg.* 227, *pg.* 16
HONEYWELL AEROSPACE, 1944 E Sky Harbor Cir N, **Phoenix,** AZ 85034-3442, *pg.* 228, *pg.* 16
HONEYWELL AEROSPACE ELECTRONIC SYSTEMS, 21111 N 19th Ave, **Phoenix,** AZ 85027-2708, *pg.* 228, *pg.* 17

California

AEROVIRONMENT, INC., 181 W Huntington Dr Ste 202, **Monrovia,** CA 91016, *pg.* 223, *pg.* 150
CIRCOR AEROSPACE, INC., 2301 Wardlow Cir, **Corona,** CA 92880, *pg.* 226, *pg.* 69
CLARY CORPORATION, 150 E Huntington Dr, **Monrovia,** CA 91016-4847, *pg.* 226, *pg.* 150
ROBINSON HELICOPTER COMPANY, 2901 Airport Dr, **Torrance,** CA 90505-6115, *pg.* 234, *pg.* 295
ROGERSON AIRCRAFT CORPORATION, 2201 Alton Pkwy, **Irvine,** CA 92606-5033, *pg.* 234, *pg.* 115
SPACEDEV INC., 13855 Stowe Dr, **Poway,** CA 92064-6800, *pg.* 234, *pg.* 186
WOODWARD HRT, 25200 W Rye Canyon Rd, **Santa Clarita,** CA 91355-1265, *pg.* 236, *pg.* 270
ZODIAC WATER & WASTE SYSTEMS, 1500 Glenn Curtiss St, **Carson,** CA 90746-4012, *pg.* 236, *pg.* 64

Colorado

NORGREN, INC., 5400 S Delaware St, **Littleton,** CO 80120-1663, *pg.* 231, *pg.* 333

Connecticut

CRANE CO., 100 First Stamford Pl, **Stamford,** CT 06902, *pg.* 227, *pg.* 373
FIRST AVIATION SERVICES INC., 15 Riverside Ave, **Westport,** CT 06880-4214, *pg.* 227, *pg.* 384
GE CAPITAL AVIATION SERVICES, 601 Merritt 7 Corporate Park, **Norwalk,** CT 06851, *pg.* 228, *pg.* 362
KAMAN CORPORATION, 1332 Blue Hills Ave, **Bloomfield,** CT 06002, *pg.* 229, *pg.* 338
PASSUR AEROSPACE, INC., 1 Landmark Sq, **Stamford,** CT 06901, *pg.* 233, *pg.* 376
PRATT & WHITNEY, 400 Main St, **East Hartford,** CT 06108-0968, *pg.* 233, *pg.* 345
UNITED TECHNOLOGIES CORPORATION, United Technologies Bldg 1 Financial Plz, **Hartford,** CT 06101, *pg.* 235, *pg.* 353

Florida

AERO CONTROLS, INC., 5415 NW 36th St, **Miami,** FL 33166, *pg.* 223, *pg.* 439
BE AEROSPACE, INC., 1400 Corporate Center Way, **Wellington,** FL 33414-2105, *pg.* 224, *pg.* 478
CAE USA, INC., 4908 Tampa W Blvd, **Tampa,** FL 33634-2411, *pg.* 226, *pg.* 472
EMBRAER AIRCRAFT HOLDING INC., 276 SW 34th St, **Fort Lauderdale,** FL 33315-3603, *pg.* 227, *pg.* 425
HEICO CORPORATION, 3000 Taft St, **Hollywood,** FL 33021-4441, *pg.* 228, *pg.* 431
LOCKHEED MARTIN SIMULATION, TRAINING & SUPPORT, 12506 Lake Underhill Rd, **Orlando,** FL 32825, *pg.* 231, *pg.* 454
PIPER AIRCRAFT, INC., 2926 Piper Dr, **Vero Beach,** FL 32960-1955, *pg.* 233, *pg.* 477
SIGNATURE FLIGHT SUPPORT CORP., 201 S Orange Ave Ste 1100-S, **Orlando,** FL 32801, *pg.* 234, *pg.* 456
SPIRIT AIRLINES, INC., 2800 Executive Way, **Miramar,** FL 33025, *pg.* 234, *pg.* 449
UNISON INDUSTRIES, LLC, 7575 Baymeadows Way, **Jacksonville,** FL 32256, *pg.* 235, *pg.* 435

Georgia

GULFSTREAM AEROSPACE CORPORATION, 500 Gulfstream Rd, **Savannah,** GA 31407-9643, *pg.* 228, *pg.* 540

Illinois

AAR CORP., 1 AAR Pl 1100 N Wood Dale Rd, **Wood Dale,** IL 60191, *pg.* 223, *pg.* 671
THE BOEING COMPANY, 100 N Riverside Plz, **Chicago,** IL 60606-1596, *pg.* 225, *pg.* 567

Iowa

ROCKWELL COLLINS, INC., 400 Collins Rd NE, **Cedar Rapids,** IA 52498, *pg.* 234, *pg.* 702

Kansas

CESSNA AIRCRAFT COMPANY, 1 Cessna Blvd, **Wichita,** KS 67215-1400, *pg.* 226, *pg.* 723
MCCAULEY PROPELLER SYSTEMS, 5800 E Pawnee St, **Wichita,** KS 67218-5541, *pg.* 231, *pg.* 724

Maryland

LOCKHEED MARTIN CORPORATION, 6801 Rockledge Dr, **Bethesda,** MD 20817-1877, *pg.* 229, *pg.* 762

Massachusetts

RAYTHEON COMPANY, 870 Winter St, **Waltham,** MA 02451-1449, *pg.* 233, *pg.* 854
TEXTRON SYSTEMS CORPORATION, 201 Lowell St, **Wilmington,** MA 01887-4113, *pg.* 235, *pg.* 860

Michigan

KAISER OPTICAL SYSTEMS, INC., 371 Parkland Plz, **Ann Arbor,** MI 48103, *pg.* 229, *pg.* 866
LEAR CORPORATION, 21557 Telegraph Rd, **Southfield,** MI 48034-4248, *pg.* 229, *pg.* 907
THERMOTRON INDUSTRIES, 291 Kollen Pk Dr, **Holland,** MI 49423, *pg.* 235, *pg.* 892

Minnesota

AERO SYSTEMS ENGINEERING INC., 358 E Fillmore Ave, **Saint Paul,** MN 55107-1289, *pg.* 223, *pg.* 959
CIRRUS DESIGN CORPORATION, 4515 Taylor Cir, **Duluth,** MN 55811, *pg.* 226, *pg.* 921
HONEYWELL SENSING & CONTROL, 1985 Douglas Dr N, **Golden Valley,** MN 55422, *pg.* 229, *pg.* 926

New Jersey

DASSAULT FALCON JET CORP., Teterboro Airport PO Box 2000, **South Hackensack,** NJ 07606-0620, *pg.* 227, *pg.* 1122

New Mexico

ONE AVIATION CORPORATION, 2503 Clark Carr Loop SE, **Albuquerque,** NM 87106, *pg.* 232, *pg.* 1135

New York

AIR INDUSTRIES GROUP, INC., 1479 N Clinton Ave, **Bay Shore,** NY 11706, *pg.* 223, *pg.* 1141
LORAL SPACE & COMMUNICATIONS INC., 888 Seventh Ave 40th Fl, **New York,** NY 10106, *pg.* 231, *pg.* 1252
MOOG INC., 300 Jamison Rd, **East Aurora,** NY 14052-0018, *pg.* 231, *pg.* 1156
PALL CORPORATION, 25 Harbor Park Dr, **Port Washington,** NY 11050, *pg.* 232, *pg.* 1323

North Carolina

HAECO AMERICAS, 623 Radar Rd, **Greensboro,** NC 27410-6221, *pg.* 228, *pg.* 1374
UTC AEROSPACE SYSTEMS, Four Coliseum Centre 2730 W Tyvola Rd, **Charlotte,** NC 28217-4578, *pg.* 236, *pg.* 1369

Ohio

ALLEN AIRCRAFT PRODUCTS, INC., 6168 Woodbine Rd, **Ravenna,** OH 44266-9665, *pg.* 223, *pg.* 1471
DAYTON INTERNATIONAL AIRPORT, 3600 Terminal Dr Ste 300, **Vandalia,** OH 45377-3313, *pg.* 227, *pg.* 1478
GE AVIATION, 1 Neumann Way, **Cincinnati,** OH 45215-1915, *pg.* 227, *pg.* 1413
SCHNELLER, INC., 6019 Powdermill Rd, **Kent,** OH 44240-7109, *pg.* 234, *pg.* 1456
TRIUMPH THERMAL SYSTEMS, INC., 200 Railroad St, **Forest,** OH 45843-9193, *pg.* 235, *pg.* 1454

Oklahoma

MINT TURBINES LLC, 2915 N State Hwy 99 PO Box 460, **Stroud,** OK 74079-0460, *pg.* 231, *pg.* 1488

Rhode Island

TEXTRON INC., 40 Westminster St, **Providence,** RI 02903, *pg.* 235, *pg.* 1607

Texas

AIRBUS HELICOPTERS, INC., 2701 N Forum Dr, **Grand Prairie,** TX 75052-7027, *pg.* 223, *pg.* 1698
AMERICAN AIRLINES GROUP INC., 4333 Amon Carter Blvd, **Fort Worth,** TX 76155-2605, *pg.* 224, *pg.* 1693
ATLANTIC AVIATION CORPORATION, 6504 International Pkwy Ste 2400, **Plano,** TX 75093-8236, *pg.* 224, *pg.* 1729
AVIALL, INC., 2750 Regent Blvd, **Dallas,** TX 75261-9048, *pg.* 224, *pg.* 1676
BELL HELICOPTER TEXTRON, INC., 600 E Hurst Blvd, **Fort Worth,** TX 76101, *pg.* 224, *pg.* 1693
ENGINE COMPONENTS, INC., 9503 Middlex Dr, **San Antonio,** TX 78217-5915, *pg.* 227, *pg.* 1740

Virginia

AEROJET ROCKETDYNE, 5731 Wellington Rd, **Gainesville,** VA 20155, *pg.* 223, *pg.* 1782
ATLANTIC AVIATION, 1501 Lee Hwy Ste 180, **Arlington,** VA 22209, *pg.* 224, *pg.* 1772
DIGITALGLOBE, 2325 Dulles Corner Blvd 10th Fl, **Herndon,** VA 20171, *pg.* 227, *pg.* 1785
GENERAL DYNAMICS CORPORATION, 2941 Fairview Park Dr Ste 100, **Falls Church,** VA 22042-4510, *pg.* 228, *pg.* 1781
NORTHROP GRUMMAN CORPORATION, 2980 Fairview Park Dr, **Falls Church,** VA 22042, *pg.* 231, *pg.* 1781

Wisconsin

ASTRONAUTICS CORPORATION OF AMERICA, 4115 N Teutonia Ave, **Milwaukee,** WI 53209, *pg.* 224, *pg.* 1873

First page reference indicates Business Class Edition
Second page reference indicates Geographic Edition

Beer, Ale & Soft Drinks

Arkansas

MOUNTAIN VALLEY SPRING COMPANY, 150 Central Ave, **Hot Springs National Park,** AR 71902, *pg.* 257, *pg.* 33

California

CRYSTAL GEYSER WATER COMPANY, 501 Washington St, **Calistoga,** CA 94515-1425, *pg.* 248, *pg.* 57
FIJI WATER, 11444 W Olympic Blvd Ste 210, **Los Angeles,** CA 90064, *pg.* 251, *pg.* 130
GREEN SPOT, INC., 100 S Cambridge Ave, **Claremont,** CA 91711-4842, *pg.* 251, *pg.* 68
KIRIN BREWERY OF AMERICA, LLC, 5230 Pacific Concourse Dr Ste 310, **Los Angeles,** CA 90045, *pg.* 253, *pg.* 134
MENDOCINO BREWING COMPANY, 1601 Airport Rd, **Ukiah,** CA 95482, *pg.* 254, *pg.* 298
MONSTER BEVERAGE CORPORATION, 1 Monster Way, **Corona,** CA 92879, *pg.* 257, *pg.* 69
NOR-CAL BEVERAGE CO., INC., 2286 Stone Blvd, **West Sacramento,** CA 95691-4050, *pg.* 258, *pg.* 305
PABST BREWING COMPANY, 10635 Santa Monica Blvd Ste 350, **Los Angeles,** CA 90025, *pg.* 258, *pg.* 137
REBBL INC., 530 Divisadero St, #308, **San Francisco,** CA 94117, *pg.* 264, *pg.* 225
RED BULL NORTH AMERICA, INC., 1740 Stewart St, **Santa Monica,** CA 90404-3596, *pg.* 264, *pg.* 275
REED'S, INC., 13000 S Spring St, **Los Angeles,** CA 90061-1634, *pg.* 264, *pg.* 139
SIERRA NEVADA BREWING CO., 1075 E 20th St, **Chico,** CA 95928, *pg.* 265, *pg.* 65
SUJA JUICE, 8380 Camino Santa Fe Ste 200, **San Diego,** CA 92121, *pg.* 265, *pg.* 210
VISAGE MOBILE, INC., 500 Sansome St Ste 300, **San Francisco,** CA 94111, *pg.* 266, *pg.* 232

Colorado

FLYING DOG BREWERY, 2401 Blake St, **Denver,** CO 80205, *pg.* 251, *pg.* 319
MOLSON COORS BREWING COMPANY, 1225 17th St Ste 3200, **Denver,** CO 80202, *pg.* 256, *pg.* 321
NEW BELGIUM BREWING COMPANY, INC., 500 Linden, **Fort Collins,** CO 80524, *pg.* 258, *pg.* 328

Connecticut

ARROWHEAD MOUNTAIN SPRING WATER COMPANY, 777 W Putnam Ave, **Greenwich,** CT 06830-5091, *pg.* 238, *pg.* 349
CRYSTAL ROCK HOLDINGS, INC., 1050 Buckingham St, **Watertown,** CT 06795, *pg.* 248, *pg.* 382
HARVEST HILL BEVERAGE COMPANY, 1 Highridge Park, **Stamford,** CT 06905, *pg.* 251, *pg.* 375
NESTLE WATERS NORTH AMERICA INC., 900 Long Ridge Rd Bldg 2, **Stamford,** CT 06902-1138, *pg.* 257, *pg.* 375
UNITED STATES BEVERAGE LLC, 700 Canal St, **Stamford,** CT 06902, *pg.* 266, *pg.* 379

Delaware

DOGFISH HEAD CRAFT BREWERY, INC., 6 Cannery Village Ctr Blvd, **Milton,** DE 19968, *pg.* 249, *pg.* 388
KRAFT FOODS GEVALIA, Holmparken Sq, PO Box 6276, **Dover,** DE 19905, *pg.* 253, *pg.* 387

Florida

CELSIUS HOLDINGS, INC., 2424 N Federal Hwy Ste 208, **Boca Raton,** FL 33431, *pg.* 239, *pg.* 411
NATIONAL BEVERAGE CORP., 8100 SW 10th St Ste 4000, **Fort Lauderdale,** FL 33324, *pg.* 257, *pg.* 425
NESTLE PROFESSIONAL BEVERAGES, 400 N Tampa St Ste 1500, **Tampa,** FL 33602-4793, *pg.* 257, *pg.* 474

Georgia

THE COCA-COLA COMPANY, 1 Coca Cola Plaza, **Atlanta,** GA 30313, *pg.* 240, *pg.* 493
COCA-COLA REFRESHMENTS USA, INC., 2500 Windy Ridge Pkwy, **Atlanta,** GA 30339-5677, *pg.* 247, *pg.* 500
DS WATERS OF AMERICA, INC., 5660 New Northside Dr Ste 500, **Atlanta,** GA 30328-5826, *pg.* 250, *pg.* 504
EMPIRE DISTRIBUTORS, INC., 3755 Atlanta Indus Pkwy, **Atlanta,** GA 30331, *pg.* 251, *pg.* 504
THE MONARCH BEVERAGE COMPANY, INC., 1123 Zonolite Rd Ste 10, **Atlanta,** GA 30306, *pg.* 257, *pg.* 514

Illinois

CROWN IMPORTS LLC, 1 S Dearborn St Ste 1700, **Chicago,** IL 60603, *pg.* 248, *pg.* 572
THE GATORADE COMPANY, 555 W Monroe St, **Chicago,** IL 60661-3605, *pg.* 251, *pg.* 574
MILLERCOORS LLC, 250 S Wacker Dr, **Chicago,** IL 60606-6301, *pg.* 255, *pg.* 582

Louisiana

ABITA BREWING COMPANY, 21084 Hwy 36, **Abita Springs,** LA 70433, *pg.* 237, *pg.* 741

Maryland

HONEST TEA, 4827 Bethesda Ave, **Bethesda,** MD 20814, *pg.* 253, *pg.* 762

Massachusetts

THE BOSTON BEER COMPANY, INC., One Design Center Pl Ste 850, **Boston,** MA 02210, *pg.* 239, *pg.* 790
PEPSI-COLA BOTTLING OF CENTRAL NEW ENGLAND, 90 Indus Dr, **Holden,** MA 01520, *pg.* 259, *pg.* 824
POLAR BEVERAGES, 1001 Southbridge St, **Worcester,** MA 01610-2218, *pg.* 264, *pg.* 862

Minnesota

SUMMIT BREWING CO., 910 Montreal Cir, **Saint Paul,** MN 55102, *pg.* 265, *pg.* 963

Missouri

ANHEUSER-BUSCH COMPANIES, LLC, 1 Busch Pl, **Saint Louis,** MO 63118-1849, *pg.* 237, *pg.* 991

Nevada

ROCKSTAR, INC., 101 Convention Center Dr Ste 777, **Las Vegas,** NV 89109, *pg.* 265, *pg.* 1029

New Jersey

BAI BRANDS, 1800 E State St Ste 153, **Hamilton,** NJ 08609, *pg.* 238, *pg.* 1073
CENTRAL EUROPEAN DISTRIBUTION CORPORATION, 3000 Atrium Way Ste 265, **Mount Laurel,** NJ 08054, *pg.* 240, *pg.* 1090
EIGHT O'CLOCK COFFEE, 155 Chestnut Rdg, **Montvale,** NJ 07645, *pg.* 250, *pg.* 1086
LEONARD KREUSCH, INC., 200 Legrand Ave, **Northvale,** NJ 07647-0910, *pg.* 254, *pg.* 1099

New York

ALL MARKET, INC., 38 W 21st St 11th Fl, **New York,** NY 10010, *pg.* 237, *pg.* 1189
THE BROOKLYN BREWERY, 79 N 11th St, **Brooklyn,** NY 11249, *pg.* 239, *pg.* 1145
CASTLE BRANDS INC., 122 E 42nd St Ste 4700, **New York,** NY 10168, *pg.* 239, *pg.* 1209
DIAGEO NORTH AMERICA INC., 530 5th Ave, **New York,** NY 10036, *pg.* 248, *pg.* 1223
HEINEKEN USA INC., 360 Hamilton Ave Ste 1103, **White Plains,** NY 10601-1811, *pg.* 252, *pg.* 1352
LABATT USA LLC, 50 Fountain Plaza Ste 900, **Buffalo,** NY 14202, *pg.* 254, *pg.* 1149
MYX BEVERAGES LLC, 424 W 33rd St Ste 520, **New York,** NY 10001, *pg.* 257, *pg.* 1263
PEPSI BEVERAGES COMPANY, 1 Pepsi Way, **Somers,** NY 10589-2212, *pg.* 258, *pg.* 1342
PEPSI-COLA NORTH AMERICA, 700 Anderson Hill Rd, **Purchase,** NY 10577, *pg.* 259, *pg.* 1327
PEPSICO, INC., 700 Anderson Hill Rd, **Purchase,** NY 10577-1401, *pg.* 259, *pg.* 1327
WHITE ROCK PRODUCTS CORP., 14107 20th Ave Ste 403, **Whitestone,** NY 11357-3055, *pg.* 266, *pg.* 1355

North Carolina

CAROLINA BEVERAGE CORPORATION, 1413 Jake Alexander Blvd S, **Salisbury,** NC 28146-8359, *pg.* 239, *pg.* 1390
COCA-COLA BOTTLING CO. CONSOLIDATED, 4100 Coca Cola Plz, **Charlotte,** NC 28211-3481, *pg.* 240, *pg.* 1365

Ohio

COUNTRY PURE FOODS, INC., 681 W Waterloo Rd, **Akron,** OH 44314-1587, *pg.* 247, *pg.* 1400
WARSTEINER IMPORTERS AGENCY, INC., 9359 Allen Rd, **West Chester,** OH 45069, *pg.* 266, *pg.* 1479

Oregon

CRAFT BREWERS ALLIANCE, INC, 929 N Russell St, **Portland,** OR 97227, *pg.* 247, *pg.* 1502
DESCHUTES BREWERY INC., 901 Southwest Simpson Ave, **Bend,** OR 97702, *pg.* 248, *pg.* 1496

Pennsylvania

D.G. YUENGLING & SON INCORPORATED, 500 Mahantongo St, **Pottsville,** PA 17901, *pg.* 248, *pg.* 1582
THE LION BREWERY, INC., 700 N Pennsylvania Ave, **Wilkes Barre,** PA 18705-2451, *pg.* 254, *pg.* 1594

Rhode Island

COASTAL EXTREME BREWING COMPANY, 293 JT Connell Rd, **Newport,** RI 02840, *pg.* 240, *pg.* 1602

Tennessee

DOUBLE-COLA CO.-USA, 537 Market St Ste 100, **Chattanooga,** TN 37402-1229, *pg.* 249, *pg.* 1629

Texas

DR PEPPER SNAPPLE GROUP, INC., 5301 Legacy Dr, **Plano,** TX 75024, *pg.* 250, *pg.* 1729
REPUBLIC NATIONAL DISTRIBUTING COMPANY, 8045 Northcourt Rd, **Houston,** TX 77040, *pg.* 264, *pg.* 1713

Washington

JONES SODA CO., 1000 1st Ave S # 100, **Seattle,** WA 98134-1206, *pg.* 253, *pg.* 1836
SEATTLE COFFEE COMPANY, 2401 Utah Ave S, **Seattle,** WA 98101-2078, *pg.* 265, *pg.* 1839
TALKINGRAIN BEVERAGE COMPANY, PO Box 549, **Preston,** WA 98050, *pg.* 266, *pg.* 1823

Wisconsin

CAPITAL BREWERY CO., INC., 7734 Ter Ave, **Middleton,** WI 53562-3163, *pg.* 239, *pg.* 1872
JACOB LEINENKUGEL BREWING CO., 1 Jefferson Ave, **Chippewa Falls,** WI 54729-1318, *pg.* 253, *pg.* 1856
KRIER FOODS, INC., 520 Wolf Rd, **Random Lake,** WI 53075, *pg.* 253, *pg.* 1890
MILLERCOORS, 3939 W Highland Blvd, **Milwaukee,** WI 53208-2816, *pg.* 254, *pg.* 1877
SPRECHER BREWING COMPANY, 701 W Glendale Ave, **Glendale,** WI 53209, *pg.* 265, *pg.* 1858

Broadcasting, Cable, Film & Video

Alabama

B.A.S.S., L.L.C., 3500 Blue Lake Cir Ste 330, **Birmingham,** AL 35243, *pg.* 270, *pg.* 1
ETERNAL WORLD TELEVISION NETWORK, INC., 5817 Old Leeds Rd, **Irondale,** AL 35210, *pg.* 286, *pg.* 6

Alaska

ALASKA COMMUNICATIONS SYSTEMS GROUP, INC., 600 Telephone Ave, **Anchorage,** AK 99503-6091, *pg.* 269, *pg.* 10

Arizona

KNXV-TV, 515 N 44th St, **Phoenix,** AZ 85008-6511, *pg.* 294, *pg.* 17
KTVK-TV, INC., 5555 N 7th Ave, **Phoenix,** AZ 85013-1701, *pg.* 295, *pg.* 17

Arkansas

WINDSTREAM CORPORATION, 4001 Rodney Parham Rd, **Little Rock,** AR 72212-2442, *pg.* 321, *pg.* 34

California

20TH CENTURY FOX FILM CORP., 10201 W Pico Blvd, **Los Angeles,** CA 90064, *pg.* 267, *pg.* 124
20TH CENTURY FOX HOME ENTERTAINMENT, INC., 2121 Ave of the Stars, **Los Angeles,** CA 90067, *pg.* 267, *pg.* 125
ABC CABLE NETWORKS GROUP, 500 S Buena Vista St, **Burbank,** CA 91521, *pg.* 268, *pg.* 51
ABC FAMILY CHANNEL, 500 S Buena Vista St, **Burbank,** CA 91521-9078, *pg.* 268, *pg.* 51
ACME COMMUNICATIONS, INC., 2101 E 4th St Ste 202, **Santa Ana,** CA 92705-3825, *pg.* 268, *pg.* 260
ALIEN TECHNOLOGY CORPORATION, 18220 Butterfield Blvd, **Morgan Hill,** CA 95037, *pg.* 269, *pg.* 152
BEACHBODY, LLC, 3301 Exhibition Blvd, **Santa Monica,** CA 90404, *pg.* 271, *pg.* 272
CBC (AMERICA) CORP., 21241 S Western Ave, Ste 160, **Torrance,** CA 90501, *pg.* 273, *pg.* 293
CHILDREN'S HOSPITAL LOS ANGELES, 4650 Sunset Blvd, **Los Angeles,** CA 90027, *pg.* 275, *pg.* 128
COLUMBIA TRISTAR MOTION PICTURE GROUP, 10202 W Washington Blvd, **Culver City,** CA 90232-3119, *pg.* 275, *pg.* 72
COMMUNITY TELEVISION OF SOUTHERN CALIFORNIA, 2900 W Alameda Ave, **Burbank,** CA 91505, *pg.* 279, *pg.* 51
CROWN MEDIA HOLDINGS INC., 12700 Ventura Blvd Ste 200, **Studio City,** CA 91604, *pg.* 280, *pg.* 281
CSR, 1390 Kifer Rd, **Sunnyvale,** CA 94086, *pg.* 280, *pg.* 284
DELUXE LABORATORIES, INC., 1377 N Serrano Ave, **Hollywood,** CA 90027, *pg.* 281, *pg.* 103
DIALOGIC INC., 926 Rock Ave, **San Jose,** CA 95131, *pg.* 281, *pg.* 243
DICK CLARK PRODUCTIONS, INC., 2900 Olympic Blvd, **Santa Monica,** CA 90404, *pg.* 281, *pg.* 273
DIRECTV GROUP HOLDINGS, LLC, 2230 E Imperial Hwy, **El Segundo,** CA 90245-0956, *pg.* 281, *pg.* 79
DOLBY LABORATORIES, INC., 100 Potrero Ave, **San Francisco,** CA 94103-4813, *pg.* 284, *pg.* 217
DREAMWORKS ANIMATION SKG, INC., 1000 Flower St, **Glendale,** CA 91201, *pg.* 284, *pg.* 96
EDUCATIONAL MEDIA FOUNDATION, 5700 W Oaks Blvd, **Rocklin,** CA 95765, *pg.* 284, *pg.* 194
ENTRAVISION COMMUNICATIONS CORPORATION, 2425 Olympic Blvd Ste 6000 W, **Santa Monica,** CA 90404-4056, *pg.* 285, *pg.* 273
EXTREME NETWORKS INC, 145 Rio Robles, **San Jose,** CA 95134, *pg.* 287, *pg.* 245
FOCUS FEATURES, 1540 2nd St #200, **Santa Monica,** CA 90401, *pg.* 287, *pg.* 273
FOX BROADCASTING COMPANY, 10201 W Pico Blvd, **Los Angeles,** CA 90064, *pg.* 287, *pg.* 130
FOX ENTERTAINMENT GROUP, INC., 10201 W Pico Blvd, **Los Angeles,** CA 90035-2606, *pg.* 288, *pg.* 131
FOX SPORTS NET, 10000 Santa Monica Blvd, **Los Angeles,** CA 90067, *pg.* 288, *pg.* 131
FOX TELEVISION STATIONS INC., 2044 Armacost Ave, **Los Angeles,** CA 90925, *pg.* 288, *pg.* 131
FX NETWORKS, LLC, 10201 W Pico Blvd, **Los Angeles,** CA 90067, *pg.* 288, *pg.* 131
G4 MEDIA, INC., 5750 Wilshire Blvd, 4th Floor, **Los Angeles,** CA 90036-7201, *pg.* 289, *pg.* 132
GUTHY-RENKER LLC, 3340 Ocean Park Blvd, **Santa Monica,** CA 90405, *pg.* 289, *pg.* 273
THE HALLMARK CHANNEL, 12700 Ventura Blvd Ste 200, **Studio City,** CA 91604, *pg.* 290, *pg.* 281
HERE MEDIA INC., 10990 Wilshire Blvd Penthouse, **Los Angeles,** CA 90024, *pg.* 290, *pg.* 132
IMAGINE ENTERTAINMENT, 9465 Wilshire Blvd 7th Fl, **Beverly Hills,** CA 90212, *pg.* 292, *pg.* 46
INTERSCOPE GEFFEN & A&M RECORDS, 2220 Colorado Ave, **Santa Monica,** CA 90404, *pg.* 293, *pg.* 274
ITERIS, INC., 1700 Carnegie Ave, **Santa Ana,** CA 92705, *pg.* 293, *pg.* 261
THE JIM HENSON COMPANY, 1416 N La Brea Ave, **Hollywood,** CA 90028, *pg.* 293, *pg.* 103
KCRA-TV, 3 Television Cir, **Sacramento,** CA 95814-0794, *pg.* 293, *pg.* 196
KGO TELEVISION, INC., 900 Frnt St, **San Francisco,** CA 94111-1427, *pg.* 294, *pg.* 220
KLOS-FM RADIO, LLC, 3321 S La Cienega Blvd, **Los Angeles,** CA 90016-3114, *pg.* 294, *pg.* 134
KPWR-FM, 2600 W Olive Ave Ste 800, **Burbank,** CA 91505-4553, *pg.* 294, *pg.* 52
KQED INC., 2601 Mariposa St, **San Francisco,** CA 94110-1426, *pg.* 294, *pg.* 220
KSCI-TV, 1990 S Bundy Dr Ste 850, **Los Angeles,** CA 90025-5245, *pg.* 295, *pg.* 134
LANTERN LANE ENTERTAINMENT LTD., PO Box 8187, **Calabasas,** CA 91372-8187, *pg.* 296, *pg.* 56
LIBERMAN BROADCASTING CORPORATION, 1845 Empire Ave, **Burbank,** CA 91504, *pg.* 296, *pg.* 52
LIONS GATE ENTERTAINMENT CORP., 2700 Colorado Ave Ste 200, **Santa Monica,** CA 90404, *pg.* 296, *pg.* 274
LUCASFILM, LTD., 1110 Gorgas PO Box 29901, **San Francisco,** CA 94129, *pg.* 297, *pg.* 222
MEGATRAX PRODUCTION MUSIC, INC., 7629 Fulton Ave, **North Hollywood,** CA 91605, *pg.* 297, *pg.* 167
METRO-GOLDWYN-MAYER INC., 245 N Beverly Dr, **Beverly Hills,** CA 90210-5317, *pg.* 298, *pg.* 47
MIRAMAX FILM CORP., Watergarden Complex Ste 2000, 1601 Cloverfield Blvd, **Santa Monica,** CA 90404, *pg.* 298, *pg.* 275
NEW DIMENSIONS WORLD BROADCASTING NETWORK, PO Box 569, **Ukiah,** CA 95482, *pg.* 302, *pg.* 298
NEW HORIZONS PICTURE CORP., 11600 San Vicente Blvd, **Los Angeles,** CA 90049-5102, *pg.* 302, *pg.* 137
NEXSTAR BROADCASTING, 5035 E McKinley Ave, **Fresno,** CA 93727, *pg.* 303, *pg.* 93
THE OUTDOOR CHANNEL, 43455 Business Park Dr, **Temecula,** CA 92590, *pg.* 303, *pg.* 291
PACKETVIDEO CORPORATION, 10350 Science Center Dr Ste 210, **San Diego,** CA 92121-1138, *pg.* 304, *pg.* 205
PARAMOUNT PICTURES CORPORATION, 5555 Melrose Ave, **Los Angeles,** CA 90038, *pg.* 304, *pg.* 138
PHOENIX PICTURES INC., 10203 Santa Monica Blvd Ste 400, **Los Angeles,** CA 90067-6439, *pg.* 304, *pg.* 138
PIXAR ANIMATION STUDIOS, 1200 Park Ave, **Emeryville,** CA 94608, *pg.* 304, *pg.* 85
POINT.360, INC., 2777 N Ontario St, **Burbank,** CA 91504, *pg.* 305, *pg.* 52
PROGRAM PARTNERS, INC., 818 Hampton Dr Ste 1, **Venice,** CA 90291, *pg.* 305, *pg.* 301
RELATIVITY MEDIA, LLC, 9242 Beverly Blvd, Ste 300, **Beverly Hills,** CA 90210, *pg.* 306, *pg.* 47
SALEM MEDIA GROUP, INC., 4880 Santa Rosa Rd Ste 300, **Camarillo,** CA 93012, *pg.* 307, *pg.* 57
SAMUEL GOLDWYN FILMS, 9570 W Pico Blvd Ste 400, **Los Angeles,** CA 90035-1216, *pg.* 307, *pg.* 140
SF GLOBAL SOURCING, 1000 Sansome St, **San Francisco,** CA 94111, *pg.* 307, *pg.* 227
SONAR ENTERTAINMENT, 2121 Ave of the Stars Ste 2150, **Los Angeles,** CA 90067, *pg.* 309, *pg.* 140
SONY PICTURES ENTERTAINMENT INC., 10202 Washington Blvd, **Culver City,** CA 90232-3119, *pg.* 309, *pg.* 72
SONY PICTURES HOME ENTERTAINMENT, 10202 W Washington Blvd, **Culver City,** CA 90232-3119, *pg.* 310, *pg.* 72
SONY PICTURES RELEASING CORPORATION, 10202 W Washington Blvd, **Culver City,** CA 90232-3119, *pg.* 310, *pg.* 72
TAPESTRY FILMS, 9328 Civic Center Dr, **Beverly Hills,** CA 90210, *pg.* 311, *pg.* 47
TECHNICOLOR, INC., 3233 Mission Oaks Blvd, **Camarillo,** CA 93012-5047, *pg.* 311, *pg.* 57
TIVO INC., 2160 Gold St, **San Jose,** CA 95002, *pg.* 313, *pg.* 251
TRINITY BROADCASTING NETWORK, PO Box A, **Santa Ana,** CA 92711, *pg.* 314, *pg.* 262
UNIVERSAL STUDIOS, INC., 100 Universal City Plz, **Universal City,** CA 91608-1002, *pg.* 315, *pg.* 298
WALDEN MEDIA, LLC, 1888 Century Park E 14th Fl, **Los Angeles,** CA 90067, *pg.* 317, *pg.* 141
THE WALT DISNEY COMPANY, 500 S Buena Vista St, **Burbank,** CA 91521-0001, *pg.* 317, *pg.* 52
WARNER BROS. ANIMATION INC., 4000 Warner Blvd, **Burbank,** CA 91522, *pg.* 319, *pg.* 54
WARNER BROS. ENTERTAINMENT INC., 4000 Warner Blvd, **Burbank,** CA 91522, *pg.* 319, *pg.* 54
WARNER HOME VIDEO INC., 4000 Warner Blvd, **Burbank,** CA 91522, *pg.* 319, *pg.* 55

Colorado

ASCENT CAPITAL GROUP, 5251 DTC Pkwy Ste1000, **Greenwood Village,** CO 80111, *pg.* 270, *pg.* 330
DISH NETWORK CORPORATION, 9601 S Meridian Blvd, **Englewood,** CO 80112, *pg.* 283, *pg.* 325
KCNC-TV, 1044 Lincoln St, **Denver,** CO 80203, *pg.* 293, *pg.* 320
NEW FRONTIER MEDIA, INC., 6000 Spine Rd # 100, **Boulder,** CO 80301-3323, *pg.* 302, *pg.* 311
PIKES PEAK TELEVISION INC., 399 S Eighth St, **Colorado Springs,** CO 80905-1803, *pg.* 304, *pg.* 315
ROOMLINX, INC., 1101 W 120th Ave Ste 200, **Broomfield,** CO 80021, *pg.* 307, *pg.* 313
STARZ ENTERTAINMENT, LLC, 8900 Liberty Cir, **Englewood,** CO 80112-7057, *pg.* 310, *pg.* 327

Connecticut

ARCHIE COMICS ENTERTAINMENT, LLC, 488 Main Ave, **Norwalk,** CT 06851, *pg.* 270, *pg.* 360
CHARTER COMMUNICATIONS, INC., 400 Atlantic St, **Stamford,** CT 06901, *pg.* 274, *pg.* 372
CONNECTICUT PUBLIC BROADCASTING CORP., 1049 Asylum Ave, **Hartford,** CT 06105, *pg.* 279, *pg.* 351
ESPN, INC., ESPN Plz 545 Middle St, **Bristol,** CT 06010-7454, *pg.* 285, *pg.* 340
HALL COMMUNICATIONS INC., 40 Cuprak Rd, **Norwich,** CT 06360, *pg.* 290, *pg.* 367
NBC SPORTS NETWORK, 3 Landmark Sq, **Stamford,** CT 06901, *pg.* 300, *pg.* 375
TOWNSQUARE MEDIA, INC., 240 Greenwich Ave, **Greenwich,** CT 06830, *pg.* 313, *pg.* 350

District of Columbia

BET HOLDINGS LLC, 1 BET Plz 1235 W St NE, **Washington,** DC 20018-1211, *pg.* 271, *pg.* 396
CABLE IN THE CLASSROOM, 25 Massachusetts Ave NW Ste 100, **Washington,** DC 20001, *pg.* 272, *pg.* 397
NATIONAL GEOGRAPHIC CHANNEL, 1145 17th St NW, **Washington,** DC 20036-4688, *pg.* 299, *pg.* 402
WMAL-AM RADIO, 4400 Jenifer St NW, **Washington,** DC 20015-2113, *pg.* 322, *pg.* 408
WRQX-FM RADIO, 4400 Jenifer St NW, **Washington,** DC 20015-2113, *pg.* 323, *pg.* 408

Florida

BEASLEY BROADCAST GROUP, INC., 3033 Riviera Dr Ste 200, **Naples,** FL 34103, *pg.* 271, *pg.* 450
BRIGHT HOUSE NETWORKS LLC, 700 Carillon Pkwy Ste 6, **Saint Petersburg,** FL 33716-1101, *pg.* 272, *pg.* 461
COMMUNITY TELEVISION FOUNDATION OF SOUTH FLORIDA, INC., 14901 NE 20th Ave, **Miami,** FL 33181, *pg.* 278, *pg.* 441
FLORIDA WEST COAST PUBLIC BROADCASTING, INC.,

1300 N Blvd, **Tampa,** FL 33607-5699, *pg.* 287, *pg.* 473
HSN, INC., 1 HSN Dr, **Saint Petersburg,** FL 33729, *pg.* 291, *pg.* 462
ION MEDIA NETWORKS, INC., 601 Clearwater Park Rd, **West Palm Beach,** FL 33401, *pg.* 293, *pg.* 479
MONAKER GROUP, INC., 2690 Weston Road Suite 200, **Weston,** FL 33331, *pg.* 298, *pg.* 479
MTI HOME VIDEO, 14216 SW 136th St, **Miami,** FL 33186, *pg.* 298, *pg.* 444
SPANISH BROADCASTING SYSTEM INC., 7007 NW 77th Ave., **Miami,** FL 33166, *pg.* 310, *pg.* 446
SUNBEAM TELEVISION CORP., 1401 79th St Causeway, **Miami,** FL 33141-4104, *pg.* 311, *pg.* 447
TELEMUNDO NETWORK INC., 2290 W 8th Ave, **Hialeah,** FL 33010-2017, *pg.* 311, *pg.* 430
WFOR-TV, 8900 NW 18th Ter, **Miami,** FL 33172, *pg.* 320, *pg.* 447
WMOR, 7201 E Hillsborough Ave, **Tampa,** FL 33610, *pg.* 322, *pg.* 476
WPEC-TV, 1100 Fairfield Dr, **West Palm Beach,** FL 33407, *pg.* 322, *pg.* 479
WTWC NBC 40, 8440 Dear Lk Rd, **Tallahassee,** FL 32312, *pg.* 323, *pg.* 470
WZVN TV ABC 7, 3719 Central Ave PO Box 7087 33911, **Fort Myers,** FL 33901, *pg.* 323, *pg.* 428

Georgia

CARMIKE CINEMAS, INC., Carmike Plz 1301 1st Ave, **Columbus,** GA 31901, *pg.* 273, *pg.* 528
THE CARTOON NETWORK, 1050 Techwood Dr NW, **Atlanta,** GA 30318-5604, *pg.* 273, *pg.* 492
COX COMMUNICATIONS, INC., 6205 B Peachtree Dunwoody Rd, **Atlanta,** GA 30319, *pg.* 279, *pg.* 501
COX MEDIA GROUP, 6205 Peachtree Dunwoody Rd, **Atlanta,** GA 30319-1464, *pg.* 280, *pg.* 502
CUMULUS BROADCASTING INC, 3280 Peachtree Rd NW Ste 2300, **Atlanta,** GA 30305, *pg.* 280, *pg.* 502
CUMULUS MEDIA INC., 3280 Peachtree Rd NW Ste 2300, **Atlanta,** GA 30305, *pg.* 280, *pg.* 503
CWK NETWORK, INC., 6849 Peachtree NE Ste 4-150, **Atlanta,** GA 30328, *pg.* 281, *pg.* 503
GRAY TELEVISION, INC., 4370 Peachtree Rd NE, **Atlanta,** GA 30319, *pg.* 289, *pg.* 509
HLN, 1 CNN Ctr Northwest Box 105366, **Atlanta,** GA 30303-2762, *pg.* 290, *pg.* 510
TURNER BROADCASTING SYSTEM, INC., 1 CNN Ctr, **Atlanta,** GA 30303-2762, *pg.* 314, *pg.* 521
THE WEATHER CHANNEL LLC, 300 Interstate N Pkwy SE, **Atlanta,** GA 30339-2403, *pg.* 320, *pg.* 523
WJBF-TV, 1336 Augusta W Pkwy, **Augusta,** GA 30909-6427, *pg.* 321, *pg.* 525

Hawaii

KHON-TV, 88 Piikoi St, **Honolulu,** HI 96814, *pg.* 294, *pg.* 544

Illinois

CHICAGOLAND TELEVISION NEWS, INC., 2501 W Bradley Pl, **Chicago,** IL 60618-4718, *pg.* 275, *pg.* 570
HARPO, INC., 110 N Carpenter St, **Chicago,** IL 60607-2104, *pg.* 290, *pg.* 576
NETWORK CHICAGO, 5400 N Saint Louis Ave, **Chicago,** IL 60625-4623, *pg.* 302, *pg.* 585
REDBOX AUTOMATED RETAIL, LLC, 1 Tower Ln Ste 1200, **Oakbrook Terrace,** IL 60181, *pg.* 306, *pg.* 649
U.S. MUSIC CORPORATION, 1000 Corporate Grove Dr, **Buffalo Grove,** IL 60089, *pg.* 315, *pg.* 560
WEIGEL BROADCASTING CO., 26 N Halsted St, **Chicago,** IL 60661, *pg.* 320, *pg.* 595
WHBF-TV, 231 18th St, **Rock Island,** IL 61201, *pg.* 321, *pg.* 654
WICD-TV, 250 S Country Fair Dr, **Champaign,** IL 61821-2920, *pg.* 321, *pg.* 562
WLS TELEVISION, INC., 190 N State St, **Chicago,** IL 60601-3302, *pg.* 322, *pg.* 596

Indiana

1070 WIBC, 40 Monument Cir Ste 400, **Indianapolis,** IN 46204, *pg.* 267, *pg.* 682
EMMIS COMMUNICATIONS CORPORATION, One Emmis Plaza 40 Monument Cir Ste 700, **Indianapolis,** IN 46204-3011, *pg.* 285, *pg.* 685
SARKES TARZIAN INC., 205 N College Ave 8th Fl, **Bloomington,** IN 47404, *pg.* 307, *pg.* 674
SOUTH CENTRAL COMMUNICATIONS CORPORATION, 20 NW 3rd St, **Evansville,** IN 47708, *pg.* 310, *pg.* 679
WTHI TV, 800 Ohio St, **Terre Haute,** IN 47808-1486, *pg.* 323, *pg.* 698

Iowa

KCRG TV STATION, 501 2nd Ave SE, **Cedar Rapids,** IA 52401, *pg.* 293, *pg.* 702
KWWL-TV, 500 4th St, **Waterloo,** IA 50703, *pg.* 295, *pg.* 712

Kansas

EAGLE COMMUNICATIONS INC., 2703 Hall St Ste 13, **Hays,** KS 67601, *pg.* 284, *pg.* 715

Louisiana

KTVE-TV, 200 Pavilion Rd, **West Monroe,** LA 71292, *pg.* 295, *pg.* 748
LOUISIANA PUBLIC BROADCASTING, 7733 Perkins Rd, **Baton Rouge,** LA 70810, *pg.* 296, *pg.* 742
LOUISIANA TELEVISION BROADCASTING CORPORATION, 1650 Highland Rd, **Baton Rouge,** LA 70802, *pg.* 296, *pg.* 742
WWL-TV, INC., 1024 N Rampart St, **New Orleans,** LA 70116-2406, *pg.* 323, *pg.* 747

Maine

DIVERSIFIED COMMUNICATIONS, 121 Free St, **Portland,** ME 04112-7437, *pg.* 284, *pg.* 751
MAINE PUBLIC BROADCASTING NETWORK, 1450 Lisbon St, **Lewiston,** ME 04240, *pg.* 297, *pg.* 751
WGME, INC., 1335 Washington Ave, **Portland,** ME 04103-3638, *pg.* 321, *pg.* 752

Maryland

ANIMAL PLANET, LLC, 1 Discovery Pl, **Silver Spring,** MD 20910-3354, *pg.* 270, *pg.* 777
DISCOVERY COMMUNICATIONS, INC., 1 Discovery Pl, **Silver Spring,** MD 20910, *pg.* 282, *pg.* 777
RADIO ONE, INC., 1010 Wayne Ave 14th Fl, **Silver Spring,** MD 20910, *pg.* 305, *pg.* 778
RLJ ENTERTAINMENT, INC., 8515 Georgia Ave Ste 650, **Silver Spring,** MD 20910-3495, *pg.* 306, *pg.* 778
SINCLAIR BROADCAST GROUP, INC., 10706 Beaver Dam Rd, **Hunt Valley,** MD 21030, *pg.* 308, *pg.* 773
SIQURA, 12920 Cloverleaf Center Dr, **Germantown,** MD 20874, *pg.* 308, *pg.* 771
TRAVEL CHANNEL LLC, 5425 Wisconsin Ave, **Chevy Chase,** MD 20815, *pg.* 313, *pg.* 766
WJZ-TV, 3725 Malden Ave, **Baltimore,** MD 21211, *pg.* 322, *pg.* 760
WMAR-TV, 6400 York Rd, **Baltimore,** MD 21212-2117, *pg.* 322, *pg.* 760

Massachusetts

AIRVANA, INC., 250 Apollo Dr, **Chelmsford,** MA 01824, *pg.* 268, *pg.* 812
NATIONAL AMUSEMENTS, INC., 846 University Ave, **Norwood,** MA 02062, *pg.* 299, *pg.* 840
ROUNDER RECORDS CORPORATION, 1 Rounder Rd, **Burlington,** MA 01803, *pg.* 307, *pg.* 807

Michigan

ANCHOR BAY ENTERTAINMENT, INC., 2401 W Big Beaver Ste 200, **Troy,** MI 48084-4501, *pg.* 270, *pg.* 910
DETROIT PUBLIC TV, Riley Broadcast Ctr 1 Clover Ct Wixom, **Detroit,** MI 48393, *pg.* 281, *pg.* 880
GOODRICH QUALITY THEATERS, 4417 Broadmoor Ave SE, **Grand Rapids,** MI 49512-5367, *pg.* 289, *pg.* 887
WJR-AM RADIO, 3011 W Grand Blvd Fisher Bldg Ste 800, **Detroit,** MI 48202, *pg.* 322, *pg.* 884
WWMT-TV, 590 W Maple St, **Kalamazoo,** MI 49008, *pg.* 323, *pg.* 895
WXYZ-TV, 20777 W 10 Mile Rd, **Southfield,** MI 48075, *pg.* 323, *pg.* 908

Minnesota

ALLIED VAUGHN INC., 7951 Computer Ave, **Minneapolis,** MN 55435, *pg.* 269, *pg.* 929
ALPHA VIDEO & AUDIO, INC., 7711 Computer Ave, **Edina,** MN 55435, *pg.* 269, *pg.* 924
HUBBARD BROADCASTING, INC., 3415 University Ave, **Saint Paul,** MN 55114-1019, *pg.* 291, *pg.* 961
KSTC-TV CHANNEL 45, 3415 University Ave W, **Saint Paul,** MN 55114-1019, *pg.* 295, *pg.* 962
KSTP-FM, LLC, 3415 University Ave, **Saint Paul,** MN 55114-1019, *pg.* 295, *pg.* 962
KSTP-TV, LLC, 3415 University Ave W, **Saint Paul,** MN 55114-2099, *pg.* 295, *pg.* 962
TWIN CITIES PUBLIC TELEVISION, INC., 172 E 4th St, **Saint Paul,** MN 55101, *pg.* 315, *pg.* 964
WDIO-TV, 10 Observation Rd, **Duluth,** MN 55811, *pg.* 320, *pg.* 921

Missouri

AVATAR STUDIOS, 2675 Scott Ave Ste G, **Saint Louis,** MO 63103, *pg.* 270, *pg.* 992
INTERNATIONAL LUTHERAN LAYMEN'S LEAGUE, 660 Mason Rdg Ctr Dr, **Saint Louis,** MO 63141-8557, *pg.* 293, *pg.* 998
KSHE-FM, 800 St Louis Union Sta, **Saint Louis,** MO 63103, *pg.* 295, *pg.* 999
KTVI-TV, 2250 Ball Dr, **Saint Louis,** MO 63146, *pg.* 295, *pg.* 999
LEARFIELD COMMUNICATIONS, INC., 505 Hobbs Rd, **Jefferson City,** MO 65109-6829, *pg.* 296, *pg.* 979
SWANK MOTION PICTURES INC., 1795 Watson Rd, **Saint Louis,** MO 63127, *pg.* 311, *pg.* 1004

Nebraska

BACK TO THE BIBLE, 6400 Cornhusker Hwy, **Lincoln,** NE 68507-3123, *pg.* 270, *pg.* 1011

New Jersey

CNBC, 900 Sylvan Ave, **Englewood Cliffs,** NJ 07632, *pg.* 275, *pg.* 1059
MILLENNIUM RADIO NEW JERSEY, 109 Walters Ave, **Trenton,** NJ 08638, *pg.* 298, *pg.* 1126
MLB NETWORK, One MLB Network Plz, **Secaucus,** NJ 07094, *pg.* 298, *pg.* 1120
NFL FILMS, INC., 1 NFL Plz, **Mount Laurel,** NJ 08054-1201, *pg.* 303, *pg.* 1090
PRESS COMMUNICATIONS, LLC, 1329 Campus Pkwy, **Neptune,** NJ 07753-6822, *pg.* 305, *pg.* 1090

New Mexico

KOB-TV, INC., 4 Broadcast Plz SW, **Albuquerque,** NM 87104-1000, *pg.* 294, *pg.* 1135
KRQE-TV, 13 Broadcast Plz W, **Albuquerque,** NM 87104-1056, *pg.* 294, *pg.* 1135
REELZCHANNEL LLC, 5650 University Blvd SE, **Albuquerque,** NM 87106, *pg.* 306, *pg.* 1135

New York

A&E TELEVISION NETWORKS, LLC, 235 E 45th St, **New York,** NY 10017, *pg.* 267, *pg.* 1185
ABC, INC., 77 W 66th St, **New York,** NY 10023-6201, *pg.* 268, *pg.* 1185
AL JAZEERA AMERICA, LLC, 311 W 34th St, **New York,** NY 10001-2418, *pg.* 269, *pg.* 1188
AMC NETWORKS INC., 11 Penn Plz, **New York,** NY 10001, *pg.* 269, *pg.* 1189
THE ASSOCIATED PRESS, INC., 450 W 33rd St, **New York,** NY 10001, *pg.* 270, *pg.* 1197
ATLANTIC RECORDS GROUP, 1290 Ave of the Americas, **New York,** NY 10104-0101, *pg.* 270, *pg.* 1198
BAD BOY WORLDWIDE ENTERTAINMENT GROUP, 1710 Broadway, **New York,** NY 10019, *pg.* 270, *pg.* 1199

First page reference indicates Business Class Edition
Second page reference indicates Geographic Edition

BBC WORLDWIDE AMERICA INC., 747 3rd Ave Fl 7, **New York,** NY 10017-2803, *pg.* 271, *pg.* 1201
BRAVO MEDIA LLC, 30 Rockefeller Plz, **New York,** NY 10112, *pg.* 271, *pg.* 1206
CABLEVISION SYSTEMS CORPORATION, 1111 Stewart Ave, **Bethpage,** NY 11714, *pg.* 272, *pg.* 1141
CAPTIVATE, 1350 Broadway Ste 2400, **New York,** NY 10018, *pg.* 272, *pg.* 1209
CBS BROADCASTING INC., 51 W 52nd St, **New York,** NY 10019, *pg.* 273, *pg.* 1210
CBS CORPORATION, 51 W 52 St, **New York,** NY 10019-6188, *pg.* 273, *pg.* 1210
CBS ENTERTAINMENT DIVISION, 51 W 52nd St, **New York,** NY 10019, *pg.* 274, *pg.* 1211
CBS SPORTS DIVISION, 51 W 52nd St, **New York,** NY 10019, *pg.* 274, *pg.* 1211
COMEDY PARTNERS, 345 Hudson, **New York,** NY 10014, *pg.* 278, *pg.* 1216
E1 ENTERTAINMENT U.S. LP, 22 Harbor Pk Dr, **Port Washington,** NY 11050, *pg.* 284, *pg.* 1323
EPIX, 1515 Broadway 43rd Fl, **New York,** NY 10036, *pg.* 285, *pg.* 1228
EPOCH FILMS INC., 180 Varick St, Ste 1206, **New York,** NY 10014, *pg.* 285, *pg.* 1228
ESQUIRE NETWORK, 1221 Ave of the Americas, **New York,** NY 10020, *pg.* 286, *pg.* 1229
FOOD NETWORK, 75 9th Ave, **New York,** NY 10011, *pg.* 287, *pg.* 1231
FREMANTLEMEDIA NORTH AMERICA INC., 28 E 28th St, **New York,** NY 10016, *pg.* 288, *pg.* 1233
FUSE NETWORKS LLC, 11 Penn Plz 17th Fl, **New York,** NY 10001, *pg.* 288, *pg.* 1233
GRANITE BROADCASTING CORPORATION, 767 3rd Ave 34th Fl, **New York,** NY 10017-2023, *pg.* 289, *pg.* 1236
THE HISTORY CHANNEL, 235 E 45th St, **New York,** NY 10017, *pg.* 290, *pg.* 1240
HOME BOX OFFICE, INC., 1100 Ave of the Americas, **New York,** NY 10036-6712, *pg.* 290, *pg.* 1240
IAC/INTERACTIVECORP, 555 W 18th St, **New York,** NY 10011, *pg.* 292, *pg.* 1242
INNER CITY BROADCASTING CORPORATION, 3 Pk Ave 41st Fl, **New York,** NY 10016, *pg.* 292, *pg.* 1243
JBI, INC., 20 Iroquois St, **Niagara Falls,** NY 14303, *pg.* 293, *pg.* 1317
KINO INTERNATIONAL CORP., 333 W 39th St, **New York,** NY 10018, *pg.* 294, *pg.* 1249
LIFETIME ENTERTAINMENT SERVICES LLC, 111 8th Ave, **New York,** NY 10011-7316, *pg.* 296, *pg.* 1251
MADISON SQUARE GARDEN NETWORK, 2 Pennsylvania Plz 14th fl, **New York,** NY 10121, *pg.* 297, *pg.* 1255
MEDIACOM LLC, 100 Crystal Run Rd, **Middletown,** NY 10941, *pg.* 297, *pg.* 1182
MTV NETWORKS COMPANY, 1515 Broadway, **New York,** NY 10036, *pg.* 298, *pg.* 1262
MTVN VIDEO HITS INC., 1515 Broadway, **New York,** NY 10036-8901, *pg.* 299, *pg.* 1263
NBC NEWS, 30 Rockefeller Plaza, **New York,** NY 10112, *pg.* 300, *pg.* 1265
NBC UNIVERSAL, INC., 30 Rockefeller Plz, **New York,** NY 10112, *pg.* 300, *pg.* 1266
NBC UNIVERSAL TELEVISION NETWORKS GROUP, 30 Rockefeller Plz, **New York,** NY 10112, *pg.* 302, *pg.* 1267
NEULION, INC., 1600 Old Country Rd, **Plainview,** NY 11803, *pg.* 302, *pg.* 1321
NICKELODEON DIRECT INC., 1515 Broadway, **New York,** NY 10036-8901, *pg.* 303, *pg.* 1271
NIELSEN MEDIA RESEARCH, INC., 770 Broadway, **New York,** NY 10003, *pg.* 303, *pg.* 1272
NY 1 NEWS, 75 9th Ave, **New York,** NY 10011-4276, *pg.* 303, *pg.* 1273
OXYGEN MEDIA LLC, 75 9th Ave, **New York,** NY 10011, *pg.* 303, *pg.* 1275
PAMAL BROADCASTING LTD., 6 Johnson Rd, **Latham,** NY 12110, *pg.* 304, *pg.* 1173
RUSH COMMUNICATIONS, INC., 512 7th Ave Ste 43-45, **New York,** NY 10018-4603, *pg.* 307, *pg.* 1287
SESAME WORKSHOP, 1 Lincoln Plz, **New York,** NY 10023-7129, *pg.* 307, *pg.* 1290
SHOWTIME NETWORKS INC., 1633 Brdwy, **New York,** NY 10019-6708, *pg.* 308, *pg.* 1291
SIRIUS XM HOLDINGS INC., 1221 Ave of the Americas 36th Fl, **New York,** NY 10020-1001, *pg.* 308, *pg.* 1292
SONY MUSIC ENTERTAINMENT, 550 Madison Ave, **New York,** NY 10022-3211, *pg.* 309, *pg.* 1294
SPIKE TV, 1515 Broadway 37th Fl, **New York,** NY 10036, *pg.* 310, *pg.* 1295
SUNRISE BROADCASTING OF NEW YORK, INC., 661 Little Britain Rd, **New Windsor,** NY 12553-6150, *pg.* 311, *pg.* 1184
SYFY, 30 Rockefeller Plz, **New York,** NY 10112, *pg.* 311, *pg.* 1297
TIME WARNER CABLE INC., 60 Columbus Cir, **New York,** NY 10023, *pg.* 312, *pg.* 1301
TIME WARNER INC., 1 Time Warner Ctr, **New York,** NY 10019, *pg.* 312, *pg.* 1302
TRANS WORLD ENTERTAINMENT CORPORATION, 38 Corporate Cir, **Albany,** NY 12203, *pg.* 313, *pg.* 1137
TRUTV, One Time Warner Ctr, **New York,** NY 10019-6038, *pg.* 314, *pg.* 1305
TWENTY-FIRST CENTURY FOX, INC., 1211 Ave of the Americas, **New York,** NY 10036, *pg.* 315, *pg.* 1305
UNIVERSAL MOTOWN RECORDS, 1755 Broadway, **New York,** NY 10019, *pg.* 315, *pg.* 1307
USA NETWORKS, 30 Rockefeller Plz 21st Fl, **New York,** NY 10112, *pg.* 315, *pg.* 1308
VIACOM INC., 1515 Broadway, **New York,** NY 10036-8901, *pg.* 316, *pg.* 1310
VIRGIL FILMS & ENTERTAINMENT, 304 Hudson St 7th Fl, **New York,** NY 10013, *pg.* 317, *pg.* 1311
WABC-TV INC., 7 Lincoln Sq, **New York,** NY 10023-5998, *pg.* 317, *pg.* 1312
WHAM-TV, 4225 W Henrietta Rd, **Rochester,** NY 14623, *pg.* 321, *pg.* 1338
WHEC-TV LLC, 191 E Ave, **Rochester,** NY 14604-2605, *pg.* 321, *pg.* 1338
WNET.ORG, 825 Eighth Ave, **New York,** NY 10019, *pg.* 322, *pg.* 1315
WNYT-TV, 715 N Pearl St, **Albany,** NY 12204-1819, *pg.* 322, *pg.* 1137
WPIX, INC., 220 E 42nd St, **New York,** NY 10017, *pg.* 322, *pg.* 1316
WPLJ RADIO, LLC, 2 Penn Plz 17th Fl, **New York,** NY 10121, *pg.* 322, *pg.* 1316
WRGB-TV, 1400 Balltown Rd, **Schenectady,** NY 12309-4301, *pg.* 323, *pg.* 1341
YANKEES ENTERTAINMENT & SPORTS NETWORK, LLC, 405 Lexington Ave 36th Fl, **New York,** NY 10174-3699, *pg.* 324, *pg.* 1316

North Carolina

CAPITOL BROADCASTING COMPANY, INC., 2619 Western Blvd, **Raleigh,** NC 27606, *pg.* 272, *pg.* 1386
COMMSCOPE, INC., 1100 CommScope Pl SE, **Hickory,** NC 28602, *pg.* 278, *pg.* 1378
CURTIS MEDIA GROUP, 3012 Highwoods Blvd Ste 200, **Raleigh,** NC 27604-1031, *pg.* 281, *pg.* 1387
EUE SCREEN GEMS LTD., 1223 N 23rd St, **Wilmington,** NC 28405, *pg.* 286, *pg.* 1393
TRANS WORLD RADIO INC., 300 Gregson Dr, **Cary,** NC 27511-6444, *pg.* 313, *pg.* 1361
WGBR-AM, 2581 US Hwy 70 W, **Goldsboro,** NC 27530-1934, *pg.* 321, *pg.* 1373
WQDR-FM, 3012 Highwoods Blvd, **Raleigh,** NC 27604-1037, *pg.* 323, *pg.* 1389
WTVD-TV INC., 411 Liberty St, **Durham,** NC 27701-3407, *pg.* 323, *pg.* 1372

Ohio

IDEASTREAM, 1375 Euclid Ave, **Cleveland,** OH 44134-1191, *pg.* 292, *pg.* 1431
WBNS TELEVISION, 770 Twin Rivers Dr, **Columbus,** OH 43215-1127, *pg.* 320, *pg.* 1444
WCPO-TV, 1720 Gilbert Ave, **Cincinnati,** OH 45202, *pg.* 320, *pg.* 1427
WEWS-TV, 3001 Euclid Ave, **Cleveland,** OH 44115-2516, *pg.* 320, *pg.* 1437
WTVG 13ABC, 4247 Dorr St, **Toledo,** OH 43607-2134, *pg.* 323, *pg.* 1477

Oklahoma

KFOR-TV, 444 E Britton Rd, **Oklahoma City,** OK 73114-7515, *pg.* 294, *pg.* 1486
KJRH, 3701 S Peoria Ave, **Tulsa,** OK 74105, *pg.* 294, *pg.* 1490

Oregon

KTVL-TV, 1440 Rossanley Dr, **Medford,** OR 97501, *pg.* 295, *pg.* 1499
RENTRAK CORPORATION, One Airport Ctr 7700 NE Ambassador Pl, **Portland,** OR 97220, *pg.* 306, *pg.* 1506
TALK RADIO NETWORK, PO Box 3755, **Central Point,** OR 97502, *pg.* 311, *pg.* 1497

Pennsylvania

ACCUWEATHER, INC., 385 Science Pk Rd, **State College,** PA 16803-2215, *pg.* 268, *pg.* 1587
AMERICAN URBAN RADIO NETWORKS, 960 Penn Ave Ste 200, **Pittsburgh,** PA 15222-3811, *pg.* 269, *pg.* 1573
COMCAST CABLE COMMUNICATIONS, INC., 1500 Market St, **Philadelphia,** PA 19102-2100, *pg.* 276, *pg.* 1560
COMCAST CORPORATION, 1 Comcast Ctr, **Philadelphia,** PA 19103-2838, *pg.* 276, *pg.* 1560
COMCAST SPECTACOR, L.P., 3601 S Broad St, **Philadelphia,** PA 19148-5250, *pg.* 278, *pg.* 1562
COMCAST SPORTSNET, 3601 S Broad St, **Philadelphia,** PA 19148, *pg.* 278, *pg.* 1562
PENNS WOODS BANCORP, INC., 300 Market St, **Williamsport,** PA 17701, *pg.* 304, *pg.* 1595
QVC INC, 1200 Wilson Dr, **West Chester,** PA 19380-4267, *pg.* 305, *pg.* 1593
RENDA BROADCASTING CORPORATION, 900 Parish St, **Pittsburgh,** PA 15220, *pg.* 306, *pg.* 1581
TIMES-SHAMROCK, INC., 149 Penn Ave Fl 5, **Scranton,** PA 18503, *pg.* 313, *pg.* 1586
TLA ENTERTAINMENT GROUP, INC., 234 Market St, **Philadelphia,** PA 19106, *pg.* 313, *pg.* 1571
WHYY INC., 150 N 6th St, **Philadelphia,** PA 19106-1521, *pg.* 321, *pg.* 1572
WPVI-TV INC., 4100 City Line Ave, **Philadelphia,** PA 19131-1610, *pg.* 323, *pg.* 1572

Rhode Island

MEDIA GENERAL, One West Exchange St Ste 5A, **Providence,** RI 02903, *pg.* 297, *pg.* 1607
WLNE-TV, 10 Orms St, **Providence,** RI 02904, *pg.* 322, *pg.* 1608

South Carolina

MOOD MEDIA, 3318 Lakemont Blvd, **Fort Mill,** SC 29708, *pg.* 298, *pg.* 1616
SOUTH CAROLINA EDUCATIONAL TELEVISION COMMISSION, 1101 George Rogers Blvd, **Columbia,** SC 29201, *pg.* 310, *pg.* 1614

South Dakota

MIDCONTINENT COMMUNICATIONS CO., 410 S Phillips Ave PO Box 5010, **Sioux Falls,** SD 57102, *pg.* 298, *pg.* 1625

Tennessee

BIG IDEA, INC., 230 Franklin Rd 2A, **Franklin,** TN 37064, *pg.* 271, *pg.* 1632
COUNTRY MUSIC TELEVISION, INC., 330 Commerce St, **Nashville,** TN 37201, *pg.* 279, *pg.* 1649
GRAND OLE OPRY, 2802 Opryland Dr, **Nashville,** TN 37214, *pg.* 289, *pg.* 1651
HOME & GARDEN TELEVISION, 9721 Sherrill Blvd, **Knoxville,** TN 37932, *pg.* 290, *pg.* 1637
INGRAM ENTERTAINMENT INC., 2 Ingram Blvd, **La Vergne,** TN 37089, *pg.* 292, *pg.* 1639
NEWSCHANNEL 5, 474 James Robertson Pkwy, **Nashville,** TN 37219-1212, *pg.* 303, *pg.* 1653
WTVC-TV, 4279 Benton Dr, **Chattanooga,** TN 37406-1244, *pg.* 323, *pg.* 1630

Texas

GANNETT CO., INC., 400 S Record St, **Dallas,** TX 75202-4841, *pg.* 289, *pg.* 1681
IHEARTMEDIA INC., 200 East Basse Rd, **San Antonio,** TX 78209, *pg.* 292, *pg.* 1741

First page reference indicates Business Class Edition
Second page reference indicates Geographic Edition

KENS-TV, 5400 Fredericksburg Rd, **San Antonio,** TX 78229, *pg.* 294, *pg.* 1741
KFDM-TV, 2955 Interstate 10 E, **Beaumont,** TX 77702, *pg.* 294, *pg.* 1668
KHOU-TV, INC., 1945 Allen Pkwy, **Houston,** TX 77019, *pg.* 294, *pg.* 1709
KTRK TELEVISION, INC., 3310 Bissonnet St, **Houston,** TX 77005-2114, *pg.* 295, *pg.* 1709
KTVT BROADCASTING COMPANY LP, 10111 N Central Expy, **Dallas,** TX 75231, *pg.* 295, *pg.* 1683
KVUE-TV, 3201 Steck Ave, **Austin,** TX 78757-8026, *pg.* 295, *pg.* 1663
NEXSTAR BROADCASTING GROUP, INC., 5215 N O'Connor Blvd Ste 1400, **Irving,** TX 75039, *pg.* 303, *pg.* 1723
WFAA-TV, 606 Young St, **Dallas,** TX 75202, *pg.* 320, *pg.* 1690
YOUTOO TECHNOLOGIES, 6565 N MacArthur Blvd Ste 400, **Irving,** TX 75039, *pg.* 324, *pg.* 1724

Utah

POWER MUSIC, INC., 380 North 200 West #105, **Bountiful,** UT 84010, *pg.* 305, *pg.* 1751
SUNDANCE INSTITUTE, 1825 Three Kings Dr, **Park City,** UT 84060, *pg.* 311, *pg.* 1754

Vermont

MOUNT MANSFIELD TELEVISION INC., 30 Joy Dr, **South Burlington,** VT 05403, *pg.* 298, *pg.* 1768

Virginia

THE CHRISTIAN BROADCASTING NETWORK INC., 977 Centerville Tpke, **Virginia Beach,** VA 23463-7701, *pg.* 275, *pg.* 1810
IRIDIUM COMMUNICATIONS INC., 1750 Tysons Blvd Ste 1400, **McLean,** VA 22102, *pg.* 293, *pg.* 1792
LANDMARK MEDIA ENTERPRISES LLC, 150 W Brambleton Ave, **Norfolk,** VA 23510-2075, *pg.* 295, *pg.* 1797
MACNEIL/LEHRER PRODUCTIONS, 2700 S Quincy St, **Arlington,** VA 22206, *pg.* 297, *pg.* 1774
MEDIA GENERAL, INC., 333 E Franklin St, **Richmond,** VA 23219-2213, *pg.* 297, *pg.* 1803
PUBLIC BROADCASTING SERVICE, 2100 Crystal Dr, **Arlington,** VA 22202-1649, *pg.* 305, *pg.* 1774
RCN TELECOM SERVICES, LLC., 196 Van Buren St Ste 300, **Herndon,** VA 20170-5337, *pg.* 306, *pg.* 1785
VERSTANDIG BROADCASTING, 1820 Heritage Cener Way, **Harrisonburg,** VA 22801, *pg.* 316, *pg.* 1784
WASHINGTON EDUCATIONAL TELECOMMUNICATIONS ASSOCIATION, 2775 S Quincy St, **Arlington,** VA 22206, *pg.* 320, *pg.* 1775
WJLA & TBD, 1100 Wilson Blvd, **Arlington,** VA 22209, *pg.* 322, *pg.* 1775
WVEC-TELEVISION, INC., 613 Woodis Ave, **Norfolk,** VA 23510-1017, *pg.* 323, *pg.* 1798

Washington

TWISTED SCHOLAR, INC., 3241 35th Ave SW, **Seattle,** WA 98126, *pg.* 315, *pg.* 1842
VULCAN PRODUCTIONS INC., 505 5th Ave S Ste 900, **Seattle,** WA 98104-3821, *pg.* 317, *pg.* 1842

West Virginia

WSAZ-TV, 645 5th Ave, **Huntington,** WV 25701, *pg.* 323, *pg.* 1850

Wisconsin

WISCONSIN EDUCATIONAL COMMUNICATIONS BOARD, 3319 W Beltline Hwy, **Madison,** WI 53713-2834, *pg.* 321, *pg.* 1868
WLUK-TV, 787 Lombardi Ave, **Green Bay,** WI 54304-3925, *pg.* 322, *pg.* 1860

Cleaning Agents

California

BLUE CROSS LABORATORIES, 20950 Ctr Point Pkwy, **Saugus,** CA 91350-2621, *pg.* 326, *pg.* 277
THE CLOROX COMPANY, 1221 Broadway, **Oakland,** CA 94612-1888, *pg.* 327, *pg.* 169
COPPER-BRITE, INC., 1482 E Valley Rd Ste 29, **Santa Barbara,** CA 93108-1200, *pg.* 329, *pg.* 263
CUSTOM CHEMICAL FORMULATORS, INC., 8707 Millergrove Dr, **Santa Fe Springs,** CA 90670, *pg.* 329, *pg.* 271
METHOD PRODUCTS INC., 637 Commercial St Ste 300, **San Francisco,** CA 94111, *pg.* 332, *pg.* 223
MOC PRODUCTS COMPANY, INC., 12306 Montague St, **Pacoima,** CA 91331, *pg.* 332, *pg.* 174
SUNSHINE MAKERS, INC., 15922 Pacific Coast Hwy, **Huntington Beach,** CA 92649-1806, *pg.* 336, *pg.* 105
WD-40 COMPANY, 1061 Cudahy Pl, **San Diego,** CA 92110-3929, *pg.* 337, *pg.* 210

Colorado

RIO TINTO BORAX, 8051 E Maplewood Ave Bldg 4, **Greenwood Village,** CO 80111, *pg.* 334, *pg.* 331
SCOTT'S LIQUID GOLD-INC., 4880 Havana St, **Denver,** CO 80239-2416, *pg.* 335, *pg.* 323

Connecticut

THE SUN PRODUCTS CORPORATION, 60 Danbury Rd, **Wilton,** CT 06897, *pg.* 336, *pg.* 385

Florida

COVE CLEANERS, INC., 1400 Fruitville Rd, **Sarasota,** FL 34236, *pg.* 329, *pg.* 465
COVERALL NORTH AMERICA, INC., 350 SW 12th Ave, **Deerfield Beach,** FL 33442, *pg.* 329, *pg.* 421
PULLMAN HOLT CORPORATION, 10702 N 46th St, **Tampa,** FL 33617, *pg.* 333, *pg.* 475
STARBRITE CORP., 4041 SW 47th Ave, **Fort Lauderdale,** FL 33314-4023, *pg.* 336, *pg.* 426

Georgia

ADCO, INC., 1909 W Oakridge Dr, **Albany,** GA 31707, *pg.* 325, *pg.* 482
AMERICO MANUFACTURING CO., INC., 6224 N Main St, **Acworth,** GA 30101-3330, *pg.* 325, *pg.* 482
PREMIUM FRANCHISE BRANDS LLC, 2520 Northwinds Pkwy, Ste 375, **Alpharetta,** GA 30009, *pg.* 333, *pg.* 485
PURAFIL, INC., 2654 Weaver Way, **Doraville,** GA 30340-1554, *pg.* 333, *pg.* 530
ZEP INC., 1310 Seaboard Industrial Blvd NW, **Atlanta,** GA 30318, *pg.* 338, *pg.* 524

Illinois

DURACLEAN INTERNATIONAL, INC., 220 Campus Dr, **Arlington Heights,** IL 60004-1498, *pg.* 329, *pg.* 553
EARTH FRIENDLY PRODUCTS, 111 S Rohlwing Rd, **Addison,** IL 60101, *pg.* 329, *pg.* 552
JELMAR COMPANY, 5550 Touhy Ave Ste 200, **Skokie,** IL 60077, *pg.* 331, *pg.* 660
THE LIBMAN COMPANY, 220 N Sheldon St, **Arcola,** IL 61910, *pg.* 331, *pg.* 553
MINUTEMAN INTERNATIONAL, INC., 14 th N 845 US Rd 20, **Pingree Grove,** IL 60140, *pg.* 332, *pg.* 652
WEIMAN PRODUCTS, LLC, 755 Tri State Pkwy, **Gurnee,** IL 60031, *pg.* 337, *pg.* 616

Kansas

THE FULLER BRUSH COMPANY, 1 Fuller Way, **Great Bend,** KS 67530, *pg.* 330, *pg.* 715

Massachusetts

CONNOISSEURS PRODUCTS CORPORATION, 17 Presidential Dr, **Woburn,** MA 01801, *pg.* 329, *pg.* 861

Michigan

AMWAY CORPORATION, 7575 Fulton St E, **Ada,** MI 49355-0001, *pg.* 326, *pg.* 864
ARMALY BRANDS, 1900 Easy St, **Walled Lake,** MI 48390, *pg.* 326, *pg.* 912
THETFORD CORPORATION, 7101 Jackson Rd, **Ann Arbor,** MI 48103, *pg.* 337, *pg.* 867

Minnesota

ECOLAB INC., Ecolab Ctr 370 N Wabasha St, **Saint Paul,** MN 55102, *pg.* 329, *pg.* 960
ECOLAB INC.-FOOD & BEVERAGE DIVISION, Ecolab Ctr 370 N Wabasha St, **Saint Paul,** MN 55102, *pg.* 330, *pg.* 960
NILFISK-ADVANCE, INC., 14600 21st Ave N, **Plymouth,** MN 55447-4648, *pg.* 332, *pg.* 953

Missouri

CRITZAS INDUSTRIES, INC., 4041 Park Ave, **Saint Louis,** MO 63110-2319, *pg.* 329, *pg.* 995
FAULTLESS STARCH/BON AMI COMPANY, 1025 W 8th St, **Kansas City,** MO 64101-1207, *pg.* 330, *pg.* 982
HILLYARD, INC., 302 N 4th St, **Saint Joseph,** MO 64501-1720, *pg.* 331, *pg.* 990

New Jersey

A.L. WILSON CHEMICAL CO., 1050 Harrison Ave, **Kearny,** NJ 07032-5941, *pg.* 325, *pg.* 1076
ARM & HAMMER CONSUMER PRODUCTS, 469 N Harrison St, **Princeton,** NJ 08540, *pg.* 326, *pg.* 1110
FINE ORGANICS CORPORATION, 420 Kuller Rd, **Clifton,** NJ 07015-2277, *pg.* 330, *pg.* 1052
PENETONE CORPORATION, 700 Gotham Pkwy, **Carlstadt,** NJ 07072, *pg.* 333, *pg.* 1050
SYSCO GUEST SUPPLY, LLC, 4301 US Hwy 1 PO Box 902, **Monmouth Junction,** NJ 08852-0902, *pg.* 336, *pg.* 1085

New York

ALCONOX, INC., 30 Glenn St Ste 309, **White Plains,** NY 10603-3252, *pg.* 325, *pg.* 1351
AMERICAN SPECIALTIES INC., 441 Saw Mill River Rd, **Yonkers,** NY 10701-4913, *pg.* 325, *pg.* 1356
AXEL PLASTICS RESEARCH LABORATORIES, INC., PO Box 770855, **Woodside,** NY 11377, *pg.* 326, *pg.* 1356
BRONDOW, INC., 68 Marbledale Rd, **Tuckahoe,** NY 10707-3420, *pg.* 327, *pg.* 1346
MAXONS RESTORATIONS, 280 Madison Ave, **New York,** NY 10016, *pg.* 332, *pg.* 1257
PURESAFE WATER SYSTEMS, INC., 25 Fairchild Ave Ste 250, **Plainview,** NY 11803, *pg.* 333, *pg.* 1322
ROCHESTER MIDLAND CORPORATION, 155 Paragon Dr, **Rochester,** NY 14624-1167, *pg.* 334, *pg.* 1337
WALTER G. LEGGE COMPANY, INC., 444 Central Ave, **Peekskill,** NY 10566-0591, *pg.* 337, *pg.* 1321

Ohio

CHEMED CORPORATION, 2600 Chemed Ctr 255 E 5th St, **Cincinnati,** OH 45202-4726, *pg.* 327, *pg.* 1410
GOJO INDUSTRIES, INC., 1 Gojo Plz Ste 500, **Akron,** OH 44311, *pg.* 330, *pg.* 1401
MARTIN FRANCHISES INC., 422 Wards Corner Rd, **Loveland,** OH 45140, *pg.* 332, *pg.* 1458
NILODOR, INC., 10966 Industrial Pkwy NW, **Bolivar,** OH 44612-8991, *pg.* 332, *pg.* 1406

Oregon

SWISHER HYGIENE INC., 14546 N Lombard, **Portland,** OR 97203, *pg.* 336, *pg.* 1507

Pennsylvania

CRC INDUSTRIES, INC., 885 Louis Dr, **Warminster,** PA 18974-0586, *pg.* 329, *pg.* 1590
JENNY PRODUCTS, INC., 850 N Pleasant Ave, **Somerset,** PA 15501, *pg.* 331, *pg.* 1586
SENORET CHEMICAL COMPANY, 69 N Locust St, **Lititz,** PA 17543, *pg.* 335, *pg.* 1548
SURCO PRODUCTS, INC., RIDC Indus Pk 292 Alpha Dr, **Pittsburgh,** PA 15238, *pg.* 336, *pg.* 1581

Tennessee

KYZEN CORPORATION, 430 Harding Industrial Dr, **Nashville,** TN 37211, *pg.* 331, *pg.* 1652
THE SERVICEMASTER COMPANY, LLC, 860 Ridge Lake Blvd, **Memphis,** TN 38120, *pg.* 335, *pg.* 1646
SERVPRO INDUSTRIES, INC., 801 Industrial Blvd, **Gallatin,** TN 37066, *pg.* 335, *pg.* 1635
THE TERMINIX INTERNATIONAL COMPANY LIMITED PARTNERSHIP, 860 Rdg Lk Blvd, **Memphis,** TN 38120-9421, *pg.* 337, *pg.* 1646
W.M. BARR & COMPANY, INC., 2105 Channel Ave, **Memphis,** TN 38113, *pg.* 338, *pg.* 1647

Texas

ALEN AMERICAS INC., 9326 Baythorn Dr, **Houston,** TX 77041, *pg.* 325, *pg.* 1699

Vermont

SEVENTH GENERATION, INC., 60 Lake St, **Burlington,** VT 54015-5218, *pg.* 335, *pg.* 1765

Washington

BI-O-KLEEN INDUSTRIES, INC., PO Box 820689, **Vancouver,** WA 98682, *pg.* 326, *pg.* 1845
EVERGREEN LABS, INC., 4 W Rees Ave, **Walla Walla,** WA 99362, *pg.* 330, *pg.* 1847

Wisconsin

S C JOHNSON & SON, INC., 1525 Howe St, **Racine,** WI 53403-2237, *pg.* 334, *pg.* 1889

Computers & Office Equipment, Supplies & Services

Alabama

ADTRAN, INC., 901 Explorer Blvd, **Huntsville,** AL 35806-2807, *pg.* 344, *pg.* 6
COMPUTER PROGRAMS & SYSTEMS, INC., 6600 Wall St, **Mobile,** AL 36695, *pg.* 378, *pg.* 7
HDI SOLUTIONS, INC., 1550 Pumphrey Ave, **Auburn,** AL 36832, *pg.* 403, *pg.* 1
MILTOPE GROUP, INC., 500 Richardson Rd S, **Hope Hull,** AL 36043, *pg.* 440, *pg.* 6
THE SSI GROUP, INC., 4721 Morrison Dr, **Mobile,** AL 36609-3350, *pg.* 473, *pg.* 7
SUNGARD EMPLOYEE BENEFIT SYSTEMS, 104 Inverness Ctr Pl, **Birmingham,** AL 35242, *pg.* 477, *pg.* 4

Arizona

ALANCO TECHNOLOGIES, INC., 7950 E Acoma Dr Ste 111, **Scottsdale,** AZ 85260, *pg.* 346, *pg.* 20
AMERICAN AUCTION COMPANY, 951 W Watkins St, **Phoenix,** AZ 85007, *pg.* 349, *pg.* 14
AVNET TECHNOLOGY SOLUTIONS, 8700 S Price Rd, **Tempe,** AZ 85284-2608, *pg.* 359, *pg.* 25
CALIBRUS, INC., 1225 W Washington St Ste 213, **Tempe,** AZ 85281, *pg.* 368, *pg.* 25
INSIGHT ENTERPRISES, INC., 6820 S Harl Ave, **Tempe,** AZ 85283-4318, *pg.* 415, *pg.* 26
JDA SOFTWARE GROUP, INC., 14400 N 87th St, **Scottsdale,** AZ 85260-3653, *pg.* 423, *pg.* 22
MICROAGE, INC., 8160 S Hardy Dr Ste 101, **Tempe,** AZ 85284, *pg.* 434, *pg.* 26
MUTOH AMERICA INC., 2602 S 47th St Ste 102, **Phoenix,** AZ 85034, *pg.* 443, *pg.* 18

Arkansas

ACXIOM CORPORATION, 601 E 3rd St, **Little Rock,** AR 72201, *pg.* 342, *pg.* 33
CELERIT CORPORATION, 216 Atkins Rd, **Little Rock,** AR 72211, *pg.* 371, *pg.* 33

California

3M, 639 N Rosemead Blvd, **Pasadena,** CA 91107, *pg.* 339, *pg.* 179
ACCELRYS, INC., 10188 Telesis Ct Ste 100, **San Diego,** CA 92121, *pg.* 340, *pg.* 199
ACER AMERICA CORPORATION, 333 W San Carlos Street Ste 1500, **San Jose,** CA 95110, *pg.* 341, *pg.* 235
ACTIAN CORPORATION, 500 Arguello St Ste 200, **Redwood City,** CA 94063, *pg.* 342, *pg.* 188
ACTIONTEC ELECTRONICS, INC., 760 N Mary Ave, **Sunnyvale,** CA 94085-2908, *pg.* 342, *pg.* 282
ACTUATE CORPORATION, 951 Mariners Island Blvd, Ste 600, **San Mateo,** CA 94404, *pg.* 342, *pg.* 253
ADOBE SYSTEMS INCORPORATED, 345 Park Ave, **San Jose,** CA 95110-2704, *pg.* 342, *pg.* 235
ADVENT SOFTWARE, INC., 600 Townsend St Ste 500, **San Francisco,** CA 94103, *pg.* 345, *pg.* 211
AKANA, 12100 Wilshire Blvd Ste 1800, **Los Angeles,** CA 90025, *pg.* 346, *pg.* 125
ALACRITECH, INC., 1995 N First St Ste 200, **San Jose,** CA 95112, *pg.* 346, *pg.* 237
ALPHABET INC., 1600 Ampitheatre Pkwy, **Mountain View,** CA 94043, *pg.* 347, *pg.* 153
ALTERA CORPORATION, 101 Innovation Dr, **San Jose,** CA 95134, *pg.* 348, *pg.* 237
ANTEC INCORPORATED, 47900 Fremont Blvd, **Fremont,** CA 94538, *pg.* 350, *pg.* 90
APPLE INC., 1 Infinite Loop, **Cupertino,** CA 95014-2083, *pg.* 350, *pg.* 73
ARCSOFT, INC., 46601 Fremont Blvd, **Fremont,** CA 94538, *pg.* 352, *pg.* 90
ARIBA, INC., 910 Hermosa Ct, **Sunnyvale,** CA 94085-4199, *pg.* 353, *pg.* 283
ARUBA NETWORKS, INC., 1344 Crossman Ave, **Sunnyvale,** CA 94089-1113, *pg.* 353, *pg.* 284
ASI CORPORATION, 48289 Fremont Blvd, **Fremont,** CA 94538-6522, *pg.* 354, *pg.* 90
ASPECT SOFTWARE, INC., 1310 Ridder Park Dr, **San Jose,** CA 95131-2313, *pg.* 354, *pg.* 238
ASPYRA, INC., 4360 Park Terrace Dr Ste 100, **Westlake Village,** CA 91361-4627, *pg.* 355, *pg.* 306
ASUSTEK COMPUTER INC, 800 Corporate Way, **Fremont,** CA 94539, *pg.* 355, *pg.* 90
@XI COMPUTER CORPORATION, 980 Calle Negocio, **San Clemente,** CA 92673, *pg.* 355, *pg.* 199
AUTODESK INC., 111 McInnis Pkwy, **San Rafael,** CA 94903-2773, *pg.* 356, *pg.* 257
AUTONOMY, INC., 1 Market Plz 19th Fl Spear Twr, **San Francisco,** CA 94105, *pg.* 358, *pg.* 212
AUTONOMY PLEASANTON, 5758 West Las Positas Blvd, **Pleasanton,** CA 94588, *pg.* 358, *pg.* 183
AVAGO TECHNOLOGIES, 1320 Ridder Park Dr, **San Jose,** CA 95131, *pg.* 358, *pg.* 238
BACKUPWORKS.COM INC., 26439 Rancho Pkwy S, Ste 105, **Lake Forest,** CA 92630, *pg.* 359, *pg.* 120
BARRACUDA NETWORKS, INC., 3175 Winchester Blvd, **Campbell,** CA 95008, *pg.* 360, *pg.* 58
BELKIN INTERNATIONAL, INC., 12045 E Waterfront Dr, **Playa Vista,** CA 90094, *pg.* 361, *pg.* 182
BLUE COAT SYSTEMS, INC., 420 N Mary Ave, **Sunnyvale,** CA 94085, *pg.* 362, *pg.* 284
BRADY/TISCOR, INC., 10815 Rancho Bernardo Rd Ste 205, **San Diego,** CA 92127, *pg.* 364, *pg.* 200
BRANDVIA ALLIANCE, INC., 2159 Bering Dr, **San Jose,** CA 95131, *pg.* 364, *pg.* 239
BROADCOM CORPORATION, 5300 California Ave, **Irvine,** CA 92617-3038, *pg.* 364, *pg.* 108
BROADVISION, INC., 1700 Seaport Blvd, Ste 210, **Redwood City,** CA 94063, *pg.* 365, *pg.* 189
BROCADE COMMUNICATIONS SYSTEMS, INC., 130 Holger Way, **San Jose,** CA 95134, *pg.* 365, *pg.* 239
BUGOPOLIS, INC., 409 Locust St, **Sausalito,** CA 94965, *pg.* 366, *pg.* 278
CADENCE DESIGN SYSTEMS, INC., 2655 Seely Ave Bldg 5, **San Jose,** CA 95134, *pg.* 367, *pg.* 239
CALLIDUS SOFTWARE INC., 6200 Stoneridge Mall Rd Ste 500, **Pleasanton,** CA 94588, *pg.* 368, *pg.* 183
CANDELIS, INC., 5010 Campus Dr, **Newport Beach,** CA 92660-2120, *pg.* 368, *pg.* 165
CASESTACK, INC., 2850 Ocean Pk Blvd Ste 100, **Santa Monica,** CA 90405, *pg.* 369, *pg.* 272
CAVIUM NETWORKS, INC., 2315 N 1st St, **San Jose,** CA 95131-1010, *pg.* 369, *pg.* 240
CBS INTERACTIVE, INC., 235 2nd St, **San Francisco,** CA 94105, *pg.* 369, *pg.* 215
CISCO SYSTEMS, INC., 170 W Tasman Dr, **San Jose,** CA 95134-1706, *pg.* 372, *pg.* 240
CITIZEN SYSTEMS AMERICA CORPORATION, 363 Van Ness Way Ste 404, **Torrance,** CA 90501-6282, *pg.* 375, *pg.* 293
CLOUDMARK, INC., 128 King St 2nd Fl, **San Francisco,** CA 94107, *pg.* 376, *pg.* 216
COLLECTORS UNIVERSE INC., 1921 E Alton Ave, **Santa Ana,** CA 92705, *pg.* 377, *pg.* 260
COMPUMED, INC., 5777 W Century Blvd Ste 360, **Los Angeles,** CA 90045, *pg.* 378, *pg.* 128
CONDUSIV TECHNOLOGIES, 7590 N Glenoaks Blvd, **Burbank,** CA 91504-1052, *pg.* 379, *pg.* 51
CONEXANT SYSTEMS, INC., 4000 MacArthur Blvd, **Newport Beach,** CA 92660-3095, *pg.* 379, *pg.* 165
CORSAIR COMPONENTS, INC., 46221 Landing Pkwy, **Fremont,** CA 94538, *pg.* 380, *pg.* 90
CURVATURE, 6500 Hollister Ave Ste 210, **Santa Barbara,** CA 93117-5554, *pg.* 381, *pg.* 263
CYBERSOURCE CORPORATION, PO Box 8999, **San Francisco,** CA 94128-8999, *pg.* 381, *pg.* 216
D-LINK SYSTEMS, INC., 17595 Mount Herrmann St, **Fountain Valley,** CA 92708, *pg.* 381, *pg.* 89
DAEGIS INC, 1420 Rocky Ridge Dr Ste 380, **Roseville,** CA 95661, *pg.* 381, *pg.* 195
DELL FORCE10 NETWORKS, INC., 350 Holger Way, **San Jose,** CA 95134-1362, *pg.* 383, *pg.* 243
DELL SOFTWARE, 5 Polaris Way, **Aliso Viejo,** CA 92656-5356, *pg.* 385, *pg.* 40
DETERMINE, INC., 2121 S El Camino Real, Fl 10, **San Mateo,** CA 94403, *pg.* 386, *pg.* 254
DRIVESAVERS DATA RECOVERY, INC., 400 Bel Marin Keys Blvd, **Novato,** CA 94949, *pg.* 388, *pg.* 168
DYNTEK, INC., 4440 Von Karman Ave Ste 200, **Newport Beach,** CA 92660, *pg.* 389, *pg.* 165
ECHELON CORPORATION, 550 Meridian Ave, **San Jose,** CA 95126, *pg.* 389, *pg.* 245
EDGEWAVE INC, 15333 Ave of Science, **San Diego,** CA 92128, *pg.* 390, *pg.* 202
EDUPOINT EDUCATIONAL SYSTEMS, LLC, 101 Pacifica Ste 240, **Irvine,** CA 92618-7343, *pg.* 390, *pg.* 109
ELECTRO RENT CORPORATION, 6060 Sepulveda Blvd, **Van Nuys,** CA 91411-2512, *pg.* 390, *pg.* 300
ELECTRONICS FOR IMAGING, INC., 303 Velocity Way, **Foster City,** CA 94404-4803, *pg.* 390, *pg.* 88
ELEKTA, 100 Methilda Pl, **Sunnyvale,** CA 94086, *pg.* 391, *pg.* 284
ELMA ELECTRONIC INC., 44350 Grimmer Blvd, **Fremont,** CA 94538, *pg.* 391, *pg.* 90
EMULEX CORPORATION, 3333 Susan St, **Costa Mesa,** CA 92626, *pg.* 392, *pg.* 70
ENERGY & POWER SOLUTIONS, INC., 150 Paularino Ave Ste A120, **Costa Mesa,** CA 92626, *pg.* 392, *pg.* 71
ENVIRONMENTAL SYSTEMS RESEARCH INSTITUTE INC., 380 New York St, **Redlands,** CA 92373-8118, *pg.* 393, *pg.* 188
EPICOR SOFTWARE CORPORATION, 18200 Von Karman Ave Ste 1000, **Irvine,** CA 92612, *pg.* 393, *pg.* 110
EPSON AMERICA INC., 3840 Kilroy Airport Way MS 4-30, **Long Beach,** CA 90806-2452, *pg.* 394, *pg.* 122
EQUINIX, INC., One Lagoon Dr 4th Fl, **Redwood City,** CA 94065, *pg.* 394, *pg.* 190
ESS TECHNOLOGY, INC., 48401 Fremont Blvd, **Fremont,** CA 94538-6581, *pg.* 395, *pg.* 90
EXAR CORPORATION, 48720 Kato Rd, **Fremont,** CA 94538, *pg.* 395, *pg.* 91
FIRST DATABANK, INC., 701 Gateway Blvd Ste 600, **San Francisco,** CA 94080, *pg.* 397, *pg.* 217
FUJITSU COMPUTER SYSTEMS CORPORATION, 1250 E Arques Ave, **Sunnyvale,** CA 94088-3470, *pg.* 398, *pg.* 285
FUTURESTEP, 1900 Ave Of The Stars Ste 2600, **Los Angeles,** CA 90067, *pg.* 399, *pg.* 131
GIGOPTIX, INC., 130 Baytech Dr, **San Jose,** CA 95134-2302, *pg.* 400, *pg.* 245
GLOBAL EPOINT INC., 339 S Cheryl Ln, **City of Industry,** CA 91789, *pg.* 400, *pg.* 67
HARMONIC, INC., 4300 N First St, **San Jose,** CA 95134, *pg.* 402, *pg.* 246
HEAT SOFTWARE, 490 N McCarthy Blvd, **Milpitas,** CA 95035, *pg.* 403, *pg.* 145
HEWLETT-PACKARD COMPANY, 3000 Hanover St, **Palo Alto,** CA 94304-1185, *pg.* 404, *pg.* 175
HGST, 3001 Daimler St, **Santa Ana,** CA 92705-5812, *pg.* 406, *pg.* 260
HITACHI DATA SYSTEMS CORPORATION, 750 Central Expy, **Santa Clara,** CA 95050-2627, *pg.* 407, *pg.* 265
HYNIX SEMICONDUCTOR AMERICA INC., 3101 N First St, **San Jose,** CA 95134, *pg.* 409, *pg.* 246
IDEO, INC., 150 Forest Ave, **Palo Alto,** CA 94301, *pg.* 411, *pg.* 178
IGATE CORPORATION, 6528 Kaiser Dr, **Fremont,** CA 94555, *pg.* 411, *pg.* 91
ILLUMINA, INC., 5200 Illumina Way, **San Diego,** CA 92121, *pg.* 412, *pg.* 203
IMAGEWARE SYSTEMS, INC., 10815 Rancho Bernardo Rd Ste 310, **San Diego,** CA 92127-2189, *pg.* 412, *pg.* 203
IMAGINATION TECHNOLOGIES, 955 E Arques Ave, **Sunnyvale,** CA 94085, *pg.* 412, *pg.* 285
IMATION NEXSAN SOLUTIONS, 1445 Lawrence Dr, **Thousand Oaks,** CA 91320, *pg.* 413, *pg.* 292
IMMERSION CORPORATION, 30 Rio Robles, **San Jose,** CA 95134-1806, *pg.* 413, *pg.* 246
IMPERVA, INC., 3400 Bridge Pkwy, Ste 200, **Redwood Shores,** CA 94065, *pg.* 413, *pg.* 193
INFORMATICA CORPORATION, 100 Cardinal Way, **Redwood City,** CA 94063-4755, *pg.* 414, *pg.* 190
INGRAM MICRO INC., 1600 E Saint Andrew Pl, **Santa Ana,** CA 92799-5125, *pg.* 415, *pg.* 261
INTELLICORP, INC., Ste 221 2900 Lakeside Dr, **Santa Clara,** CA 95054-2817, *pg.* 417, *pg.* 268
INTERLINK ELECTRONICS, INC., 546 Flynn Rd, **Camarillo,** CA 93012, *pg.* 417, *pg.* 57
INTERMETRO COMMUNICATIONS, INC., 2685 Park Center Dr Bldg A, **Simi Valley,** CA 93065, *pg.* 417, *pg.* 278
INTERPLAY ENTERTAINMENT CORP., 12301 Wilshire Blvd Ste 502, **Los Angeles,** CA 90025, *pg.* 420, *pg.* 133
IOGEAR, INC., 19641 Da Vinci, **Foothill Ranch,** CA 92610, *pg.* 421, *pg.* 86
ISLAND PACIFIC, 17310 Redhill Ave Ste 320, **Irvine,** CA 92614, *pg.* 422, *pg.* 111

First page reference indicates Business Class Edition
Second page reference indicates Geographic Edition

IXIA, 26601 W Agoura Rd, **Calabasas,** CA 91302, *pg.* 422, *pg.* 56
IXYS CORPORATION, 1590 Buckeye Dr, **Milpitas,** CA 95035, *pg.* 422, *pg.* 146
JAMS, THE RESOLUTION EXPERTS, 1920 Main St at Gillette Ave Ste 300, **Irvine,** CA 92614, *pg.* 423, *pg.* 111
KENSINGTON TECHNOLOGY GROUP, 333 Twin Dolphin Dr 6th Fl, **Redwood City,** CA 94065, *pg.* 424, *pg.* 191
KEYNOTE SYSTEMS INCORPORATED, 777 Mariners Island Blvd, **San Mateo,** CA 94404, *pg.* 425, *pg.* 255
KINGSTON TECHNOLOGY COMPANY, INC., 17600 Newhope St, **Fountain Valley,** CA 92708-4220, *pg.* 425, *pg.* 90
LABEL-AIRE, INC., 550 Burning Tree Rd, **Fullerton,** CA 92833-1400, *pg.* 426, *pg.* 93
LANDACORP, INC., 500 Orient St Ste 110, **Chico,** CA 95928-5672, *pg.* 426, *pg.* 65
LANGUAGE LINE SERVICES HOLDINGS, INC., 1 Lowr Ragsdale Dr Bldg 2, **Monterey,** CA 93940, *pg.* 426, *pg.* 151
LANTRONIX, INC., 167 Technology Dr, **Irvine,** CA 92618, *pg.* 426, *pg.* 112
LAPWORKS, INC., 7955 Layton St, **Rancho Cucamonga,** CA 91730, *pg.* 426, *pg.* 187
LYFT, 2300 Harrison St, **San Francisco,** CA 94143-1001, *pg.* 429, *pg.* 222
LYNX SOFTWARE TECHNOLOGIES, 855 Embedded Way, **San Jose,** CA 95138-1018, *pg.* 429, *pg.* 247
LYRIS, INC., 6401 Hollis St Ste 125, **Emeryville,** CA 94608, *pg.* 429, *pg.* 84
MAD CATZ INTERACTIVE INC., 7480 Mission Valley Rd Ste 101, **San Diego,** CA 92108, *pg.* 429, *pg.* 204
MAXXESS SYSTEMS, INC., 1515 S Manchester Ave, **Anaheim,** CA 92802-2907, *pg.* 431, *pg.* 43
MEGAPATH, INC., 555 Anton Blvd Ste 200, **Costa Mesa,** CA 92626, *pg.* 432, *pg.* 71
MELISSA DATA CORP., 22382 Avenida Empresa, **Rancho Santa Margarita,** CA 92688-2112, *pg.* 432, *pg.* 188
MERU NETWORKS, INC., 894 Ross Dr, **Sunnyvale,** CA 94089, *pg.* 434, *pg.* 286
MICRO 2000, INC., 600 N Central Ave, **Glendale,** CA 91203, *pg.* 434, *pg.* 96
MICROSEMI CORPORATION, 1 Enterprise, **Aliso Viejo,** CA 92656-2606, *pg.* 435, *pg.* 41
MITEK SYSTEMS, INC., 8911 Balboa Ave Ste B, **San Diego,** CA 92123-1507, *pg.* 440, *pg.* 204
MRV COMMUNICATIONS, INC., 20415 Nordhoff St, **Chatsworth,** CA 91311, *pg.* 441, *pg.* 64
MSC SOFTWARE CORPORATION, 2 MacArthur Pl, **Santa Ana,** CA 92707, *pg.* 441, *pg.* 262
NAGRA USA, 275 Sacramento St, **San Francisco,** CA 94111, *pg.* 443, *pg.* 223
NETAPP, INC., 495 E Java Dr, **Sunnyvale,** CA 94089, *pg.* 444, *pg.* 287
NETGEAR, INC., 350 E Plumeria Dr, **San Jose,** CA 95134, *pg.* 444, *pg.* 247
NETWORKFLEET, INC., 6363 Greenwich Dr Ste 200, **San Diego,** CA 92122, *pg.* 445, *pg.* 205
NEW HORIZONS WORLDWIDE, INC., 1900 S State College Blvd Ste 450, **Anaheim,** CA 92806, *pg.* 445, *pg.* 43
NEW RELIC, INC., 188 Spear St Ste 1200, **San Francisco,** CA 94105, *pg.* 445, *pg.* 224
NEXTEST SYSTEMS CORPORATION, 875 Embedded Way, **San Jose,** CA 95138, *pg.* 445, *pg.* 248
NIGHTINGALE, 10670 White Rock Rd Ste 300, **Rancho Cordova,** CA 95670-6018, *pg.* 446, *pg.* 186
NTI CORPORATION, 9999 Muirlands Blvd, **Irvine,** CA 92618, *pg.* 446, *pg.* 114
NVIDIA CORPORATION, 2701 San Tomas Expy, **Santa Clara,** CA 95050-2519, *pg.* 447, *pg.* 268
OBSIDIAN ENTERTAINMENT, INC., 8105 Irvine Ctr Dr, **Irvine,** CA 92681, *pg.* 448, *pg.* 114
OCZ STORAGE SOLUTIONS, 6373 San Ignacio Ave, **San Jose,** CA 95119, *pg.* 448, *pg.* 248
ON ASSIGNMENT, INC., 26745 Malibu Hills Rd, **Calabasas,** CA 91301, *pg.* 449, *pg.* 56
OPENTABLE, INC., 1 Montgomery St 7th Fl, **San Francisco,** CA 94104, *pg.* 450, *pg.* 224
ORACLE CORPORATION, 500 Oracle Pkwy, **Redwood City,** CA 94065, *pg.* 450, *pg.* 191
OVERLAND STORAGE, INC., 9112 Spectrum Center Blvd, **San Diego,** CA 92123, *pg.* 451, *pg.* 205
PALISADES MEDIA GROUP, INC., 1620 26th St Ste 200 S, **Santa Monica,** CA 90404-4013, *pg.* 452, *pg.* 275
PC MALL, INC., 2555 W 190th St, **Torrance,** CA 90504-6002, *pg.* 452, *pg.* 295
PEGASYSTEMS INC., 20400 Stevens Creek Blvd Ste 400, **Cupertino,** CA 95014, *pg.* 453, *pg.* 74
PENTEL OF AMERICA, LTD., 2715 Columbia St, **Torrance,** CA 90503, *pg.* 453, *pg.* 295
PHOENIX TECHNOLOGIES LTD., 915 Murphy Ranch Rd, **Milpitas,** CA 95035, *pg.* 454, *pg.* 147
PIVOTAL RESOURCES, INC., 1646 N California Blvd Ste 520, **Walnut Creek,** CA 94596, *pg.* 455, *pg.* 304
POLYWELL COMPUTERS, INC., 1461 San Mateo Ave, **South San Francisco,** CA 94080-6505, *pg.* 456, *pg.* 280
PRINTRONIX, INC., 15345 Barranca Pkwy, **Irvine,** CA 92618, *pg.* 456, *pg.* 115
PURPLE COMMUNICATIONS, INC., 595 Menlo Dr, **Rocklin,** CA 95765, *pg.* 457, *pg.* 194
QUALSTAR CORPORATION, 3990-B Heritage Oak Ct, **Simi Valley,** CA 93063-6711, *pg.* 458, *pg.* 279
QUANTUM CORPORATION, 1650 Technology Dr Ste 800, **San Jose,** CA 95110, *pg.* 458, *pg.* 250
RAINMAKER SYSTEMS INC., 900 E Hamilton Ave Ste 400, **Campbell,** CA 95008-0670, *pg.* 458, *pg.* 58
RAMBUS INC., 1050 Enterprise Way Ste 700, **Sunnyvale,** CA 94089, *pg.* 459, *pg.* 288
RAYTHEON, 6 Venture Ste 315, **Irvine,** CA 92618, *pg.* 459, *pg.* 115
RELAX TECHNOLOGY, INC., 3101 Whipple Rd, **Union City,** CA 94587, *pg.* 461, *pg.* 298
RESOURCES CONNECTION, INC., 17101 Armstrong Ave, **Irvine,** CA 92614, *pg.* 461, *pg.* 115
RF INDUSTRIES, LTD., 7610 Miramar Rd Bldg 6000, **San Diego,** CA 92126-4202, *pg.* 461, *pg.* 208
RICOH PRINTING SYSTEMS AMERICA, INC., 2635-A Park Center Dr, **Simi Valley,** CA 93065, *pg.* 462, *pg.* 279
ROBERT HALF INTERNATIONAL INC., 2884 Sand Hill Rd, **Menlo Park,** CA 94025-7072, *pg.* 462, *pg.* 145
ROCKET ALDON, 2200 Powell St Ste 900, **Emeryville,** CA 94608-1901, *pg.* 462, *pg.* 85
ROVI CORPORATION, 2830 De La Cruz Blvd, **Santa Clara,** CA 95050-2619, *pg.* 463, *pg.* 269
SABA SOFTWARE, INC., 2400 Bridge Pkwy, **Redwood City,** CA 94065, *pg.* 464, *pg.* 192
SAGE SOFTWARE, INC., 6561 Irvine Center Dr, **Irvine,** CA 92618-2118, *pg.* 464, *pg.* 116
SALSBURY INDUSTRIES, 1010 E 62nd St, **Los Angeles,** CA 90001-1598, *pg.* 464, *pg.* 139
SANDISK CORPORATION, 601 McCarthy Blvd, **Milpitas,** CA 95035-7932, *pg.* 465, *pg.* 147
SAP, 1 Sybase Dr, **Dublin,** CA 94568-7902, *pg.* 465, *pg.* 78
SELECTREMEDY, 3820 State St, **Santa Barbara,** CA 93105-2610, *pg.* 468, *pg.* 263
SERENA SOFTWARE, INC., 1900 Seaport Blvd 2nd Fl, **Redwood City,** CA 94063-5587, *pg.* 468, *pg.* 192
SHORETEL, INC., 960 Stewart Dr, **Sunnyvale,** CA 94085, *pg.* 469, *pg.* 288
SIGMA DESIGNS, INC., 1778 McCarthy Blvd, **Milpitas,** CA 95035, *pg.* 469, *pg.* 148
SILICON GRAPHICS INTERNATIONAL CORP, 900 N McCarthy Blvd, **Milpitas,** CA 95035, *pg.* 470, *pg.* 148
SIMULATIONS PLUS, INC., 42505 10th St W Ste 109, **Lancaster,** CA 93534-7059, *pg.* 470, *pg.* 121
SMITH MICRO SOFTWARE, INC., 51 Columbia Ste 200, **Aliso Viejo,** CA 92656-1456, *pg.* 471, *pg.* 41
SOCKET MOBILE, INC., 39700 Eureka Dr, **Newark,** CA 94560, *pg.* 471, *pg.* 164
SPARK NETWORKS, INC., 1150 Santa Monica Blvd Ste 600, **Los Angeles,** CA 90025, *pg.* 472, *pg.* 140
SPECTRUM GROUP INTERNATIONAL, INC., 1063 McGaw, **Irvine,** CA 92614, *pg.* 472, *pg.* 116
SPP PROCESS TECHNOLOGY SYSTEMS LIMITED-THERMAL DIVISION, 1150 Ringwood Ct, **San Jose,** CA 95131, *pg.* 472, *pg.* 250
SQUARE INC., 1455 Market St Ste 600, **San Francisco,** CA 94103, *pg.* 473, *pg.* 228
SUCCESSFACTORS, INC., 1 Tower Pl Ste 1100, **San Francisco,** CA 94080, *pg.* 477, *pg.* 228
SUPER MICRO COMPUTER, INC., 980 Rock Ave, **San Jose,** CA 95131, *pg.* 478, *pg.* 251
SYMANTEC CORPORATION, 350 Ellis St, **Mountain View,** CA 94043, *pg.* 478, *pg.* 161
SYNNEX CORPORATION, 44201 Nobel Dr, **Fremont,** CA 94538-3178, *pg.* 480, *pg.* 92
SYNOPSYS, INC., 700 E Middlefield Rd, **Mountain View,** CA 94043-4033, *pg.* 480, *pg.* 162
TARGUS GROUP INTERNATIONAL, INC., 1211 N Miller St, **Anaheim,** CA 92806-1933, *pg.* 482, *pg.* 43
THOMSON ELITE, 800 Corporate Pointe Ste 150, **Culver City,** CA 90230-7676, *pg.* 484, *pg.* 72
TIBCO SOFTWARE INC., 3303 Hillview Ave, **Palo Alto,** CA 94304, *pg.* 484, *pg.* 178
TIGERLOGIC CORPORATION, 2855 Michelle Dr Ste 190, **Irvine,** CA 92606, *pg.* 484, *pg.* 117
TRANSEND CORPORATION, 225 Emerson St, **Palo Alto,** CA 94301-1026, *pg.* 485, *pg.* 178
TROWBRIDGE ENTERPRISES, 2606 Chanticleer Ave, **Santa Cruz,** CA 95065, *pg.* 485, *pg.* 271
TROY GROUP INC., 940 S Coast Dr, Ste 260, **Costa Mesa,** CA 92626, *pg.* 485, *pg.* 71
VERIFONE SYSTEMS, INC., 2099 Gateway Pl Ste 600, **San Jose,** CA 95110, *pg.* 487, *pg.* 251
VERTICAL COMMUNICATIONS, INC., 3940 Freedom Circle, **Santa Clara,** CA 95054, *pg.* 488, *pg.* 270
VERTICALRESPONSE, INC., 50 Beale St 10th Fl, **San Francisco,** CA 94105-1813, *pg.* 489, *pg.* 230
VIASAT, INC., 6155 El Camino Real, **Carlsbad,** CA 92009-1602, *pg.* 489, *pg.* 62
VIEWSONIC CORPORATION, 381 Brea Cyn Rd, **Walnut,** CA 91789, *pg.* 489, *pg.* 303
VITRIA TECHNOLOGY, INC., 945 Stewart Dr, **Sunnyvale,** CA 94085, *pg.* 490, *pg.* 289
VMWARE, INC., 3401 Hillview Ave, **Palo Alto,** CA 94304, *pg.* 490, *pg.* 179
WARNER BROS. WORLDWIDE CONSUMER PRODUCTS, 4000 Warner Blvd, **Burbank,** CA 91522-0001, *pg.* 490, *pg.* 55
WEBEX COMMUNICATIONS, INC., 3979 Freedom Cir, **Santa Clara,** CA 95054, *pg.* 491, *pg.* 270
WEBSENSE, INC., 10240 Sorrento Valley Rd, **San Diego,** CA 92121, *pg.* 491, *pg.* 210
WESTERN DIGITAL CORPORATION, 3355 Michelson Dr Ste 100, **Irvine,** CA 92612, *pg.* 492, *pg.* 118
WHITE SKY, INC., 825 S Grant St Ste 250, **San Mateo,** CA 94402, *pg.* 492, *pg.* 256
WIND RIVER SYSTEMS, INC., 500 Wind River Way, **Alameda,** CA 94501-1171, *pg.* 493, *pg.* 38
WIS INTERNATIONAL, 9265 Sky Park Ct, **San Diego,** CA 92123-4375, *pg.* 493, *pg.* 211
XILINX, INC., 2100 Logic Dr, **San Jose,** CA 95154-3400, *pg.* 496, *pg.* 252
YASUTOMO & CO., 490 Eccles Ave, **South San Francisco,** CA 94080-1901, *pg.* 497, *pg.* 280
YOTTAMARK, 1400 Bridge Pkwy Ste 101, **Redwood City,** CA 94065, *pg.* 497, *pg.* 193
ZILOG INC., 6800 Santa Teresa Blvd, **San Jose,** CA 95119, *pg.* 497, *pg.* 252

Colorado

3T SYSTEMS, INC., 5990 Greenwood Plaza Blvd, Building 2 Ste 350, **Greenwood Village,** CO 80111, *pg.* 339, *pg.* 330
BROCADE CORPORATION, 4 Brocade Pkway, **Broomfield,** CO 80021-5059, *pg.* 365, *pg.* 312
CIBER, INC., 6363 S Fiddler's Green Cir Ste 1400, **Greenwood Village,** CO 80111, *pg.* 372, *pg.* 330
DOT HILL SYSTEMS CORP., 1351 S Sunset St, **Longmont,** CO 80501, *pg.* 388, *pg.* 333
EVOLVING SYSTEMS, INC., 9777 Pyramid Ct Ste 100, **Englewood,** CO 80112, *pg.* 395, *pg.* 326
FIRSTBANK DATA CORPORATION, 12345 W Colfax Ave, **Lakewood,** CO 80215-3742, *pg.* 397, *pg.* 333
HEALTHTRIO INC., 400 S. Colorado Blvd., Suite 540, **Denver,** CO 80246, *pg.* 403, *pg.* 320
INTRADO INC., 1601 Dry Creek Dr, **Longmont,** CO 80503, *pg.* 420, *pg.* 334
MICROSOFT CORP., 7595 Technology Way, Ste 400, **Denver,** CO 80237, *pg.* 440, *pg.* 321
OTTERBOX PRODUCTS LLC, 209 S. Meldrum St, **Fort Collins,** CO 80524, *pg.* 451, *pg.* 329
POSTNET INTERNATIONAL FRANCHISE CORPORATION, 1819 Wazee St, **Denver,** CO 80202, *pg.* 456, *pg.* 322
PRESILIENT, LLC, 12303 Airport Way Ste 250, **Broomfield,** CO 80021, *pg.* 456, *pg.* 313
QUARK, INC., 1225 17th St Ste 1200, **Denver,** CO 80202, *pg.* 458, *pg.* 322
RALLY SOFTWARE DEVELOPMENT CORP., 3333 Walnut St, **Boulder,** CO 80301-2515, *pg.* 459, *pg.* 311
ROGUE WAVE SOFTWARE, INC., 5500 Flatiron Pkwy Ste 200, **Boulder,** CO 80301, *pg.* 462, *pg.* 311
STAPLES, 1 Environmental Way, **Broomfield,** CO 80021-

3415, *pg.* 474, *pg.* 313
TANDBERG DATA, 2108 55th St, **Boulder,** CO 80301-2601, *pg.* 481, *pg.* 311
TRIZETTO CORPORATION, 9655 Maroon Cir, **Englewood,** CO 80112, *pg.* 485, *pg.* 327
TRUVEN HEALTH ANALYTICS, 6200 S Syracuse Way Ste 300, **Greenwood Village,** CO 80111-4740, *pg.* 486, *pg.* 331

Connecticut

BUTLER AMERICA, 2 Trap Falls Rd Ste 204, **Shelton,** CT 06484, *pg.* 366, *pg.* 370
COCC, 135 Darling Dr, **Avon,** CT 06001, *pg.* 376, *pg.* 337
CYBERRESEARCH INC., 25 Business Park Dr, **Branford,** CT 06405, *pg.* 381, *pg.* 339
DATAVIZ, INC., Merritt Corporate Woods 612 Wheelers Farms Rd, **Milford,** CT 06461, *pg.* 383, *pg.* 356
GENERAL DATACOMM INDUSTRIES, INC., 6 Rubber Ave, **Naugatuck,** CT 06770-4117, *pg.* 400, *pg.* 357
INFOGROUP, 200 Pemberwick Rd, **Greenwich,** CT 06831, *pg.* 414, *pg.* 350
IPSOS-ASI, INC., 301 Merit 7, **Norwalk,** CT 06851, *pg.* 421, *pg.* 363
MPHASE TECHNOLOGIES, INC., 587 Connecticut Ave, **Norwalk,** CT 06854-1711, *pg.* 441, *pg.* 363
MTM TECHNOLOGIES, INC., 1200 High Ridge Rd, **Stamford,** CT 06905, *pg.* 442, *pg.* 375
ORTRONICS/LEGRAND, 125 Eugene O'Neill Dr, **New London,** CT 06320-6417, *pg.* 451, *pg.* 359
PITNEY BOWES INC., 1 Elmcroft Rd, **Stamford,** CT 06926-0700, *pg.* 454, *pg.* 376
REED EXHIBITIONS USA, 383 Main Ave, **Norwalk,** CT 06851, *pg.* 460, *pg.* 364
SCAN-OPTICS, LLC, 169 Progress Dr, **Manchester,** CT 06042, *pg.* 467, *pg.* 354
SHEAFFER PEN CORPORATION, One BIC Way, **Shelton,** CT 06484-6299, *pg.* 469, *pg.* 371
SS&C TECHNOLOGIES HOLDINGS, INC., 80 Lamberton Rd, **Windsor,** CT 06095, *pg.* 473, *pg.* 386
TANGOE, INC., 35 Executive Blvd, **Orange,** CT 06477, *pg.* 481, *pg.* 368
TRANSACT TECHNOLOGIES INCORPORATED, 2319 Whitney Ave Ste 3B, **Hamden,** CT 06518-3534, *pg.* 484, *pg.* 351
XEROX CORPORATION, 45 Glover Ave, PO Box 4505, **Norwalk,** CT 06856-4505, *pg.* 494, *pg.* 365

Delaware

ACORN ENERGY, INC., 3903 Centerville Rd, **Wilmington,** DE 19807, *pg.* 341, *pg.* 389
CORPORATION SERVICE COMPANY, 2711 Centerville Rd Ste 400, **Wilmington,** DE 19808-1645, *pg.* 380, *pg.* 390

District of Columbia

APTIFY, 1850 K St NW 3rd Fl Ste350, **Washington,** DC 20006-1605, *pg.* 352, *pg.* 395
THE GALLUP ORGANIZATION, The Gallup Bldg 901 F St NW, **Washington,** DC 20004, *pg.* 399, *pg.* 399

Florida

ACI WORLDWIDE, Ste 300 3520 Kraft Rd, **Naples,** FL 34105, *pg.* 341, *pg.* 449
AESP, INC., 16295 NW 13th Ave Ste A, **Miami,** FL 33169, *pg.* 345, *pg.* 439
AIRSPAN NETWORKS INC., 777 Yamato Rd Ste 310, **Boca Raton,** FL 33431, *pg.* 346, *pg.* 410
ALIENWARE CORPORATION, 14591 SW 120th St, **Miami,** FL 33186, *pg.* 346, *pg.* 439
ALLEN SYSTEMS GROUP, INC., 1333 3rd Ave S, **Naples,** FL 34102-6400, *pg.* 346, *pg.* 449
AMERICA'S CALL CENTER, INC., 7901 Baymeadows Way Ste 14, **Jacksonville,** FL 32256, *pg.* 349, *pg.* 431
APPLIED GLOBAL TECHNOLOGIES, 1006 Pathfinder Way, **Rockledge,** FL 32955, *pg.* 352, *pg.* 460
BAE SYSTEMS PRODUCTS GROUP, 13386 International Pkwy, **Jacksonville,** FL 32218, *pg.* 359, *pg.* 432
CATALINA MARKETING CORPORATION, 200 Carillon Pkwy, **Saint Petersburg,** FL 33716, *pg.* 369, *pg.* 462
CITRIX SYSTEMS, INC., 851 W Cypress Creek Rd, **Fort Lauderdale,** FL 33309-6123, *pg.* 375, *pg.* 424
CSPI TECHNOLOGY SOLUTIONS, 1182 E Newport Center Dr, **Deerfield Beach,** FL 33442, *pg.* 381, *pg.* 421
DIRECT INSITE CORP., 500 E Broward Blvd, Ste 1550, **Fort Lauderdale,** FL 33394, *pg.* 387, *pg.* 425
DIXON TICONDEROGA COMPANY, 195 International Pkwy, **Heathrow,** FL 32746-5007, *pg.* 388, *pg.* 430
DON BELL SIGNS LLC, 365 Oak Pl, **Port Orange,** FL 32127-4388, *pg.* 388, *pg.* 460
EMS CONSULTING, 300 S Hyde Pk Ave Ste 201, **Tampa,** FL 33606-2293, *pg.* 392, *pg.* 472
EWS, 950 S Tamiami Trl Ste 210, **Sarasota,** FL 34236, *pg.* 395, *pg.* 466
FIDELITY INFORMATION SERVICES, INC., 601 Riverside Ave, **Jacksonville,** FL 32204, *pg.* 397, *pg.* 433
G4S SECURE SOLUTIONS USA, 1395 University Dr, **Jupiter,** FL 33458, *pg.* 399, *pg.* 436
GDT TEK, INC., 2816 E. Robinson St, **Orlando,** FL 32803, *pg.* 399, *pg.* 453
GE ENERGY, 1990 W NASA Blvd, **Melbourne,** FL 32904-2309, *pg.* 399, *pg.* 439
GLOBAL IMAGING SYSTEMS, INC., 3820 Northdale Blvd Ste 200A, **Tampa,** FL 33624-1856, *pg.* 400, *pg.* 473
GLOBAL RESPONSE CORPORATION, 777 S State Rd 7, **Margate,** FL 33068, *pg.* 400, *pg.* 439
INTCOMEX, INC., 3505 NW 107th Ave, **Miami,** FL 33178, *pg.* 416, *pg.* 443
INTERIM HEALTHCARE INC., 1601 Sawgrass Corporate Expy, **Sunrise,** FL 33323, *pg.* 417, *pg.* 469
INVESTMENT SEMINARS, INC., The Githler Ctr 1258 N Palm Ave, **Sarasota,** FL 34236, *pg.* 420, *pg.* 466
JABIL CIRCUIT, INC., 10560 Dr Martin Luther King Jr St N, **Saint Petersburg,** FL 33716, *pg.* 422, *pg.* 463
MASTEC, INC., 800 S Douglas Rd 12th Fl, **Coral Gables,** FL 33134, *pg.* 430, *pg.* 418
MHI GLOBAL, 8875 Hidden River Pkwy Ste 400, **Tampa,** FL 33637, *pg.* 434, *pg.* 474
MOREDIRECT, 1001 Yamato Rd Ste 200, **Boca Raton,** FL 33431-4403, *pg.* 441, *pg.* 412
MTS MEDICATION TECHNOLOGIES, INC., 2003 Gandy Blvd N, **Saint Petersburg,** FL 33702, *pg.* 442, *pg.* 463
NET TALK.COM, INC., 1080 NW 163rd Dr, **Miami Gardens,** FL 33169, *pg.* 444, *pg.* 448
OFFICE DEPOT, INC., 6600 N Military Tr, **Boca Raton,** FL 33496, *pg.* 448, *pg.* 412
ONSTREAM MEDIA CORPORATION, 1291 SW 29th Ave, **Pompano Beach,** FL 33069, *pg.* 449, *pg.* 459
OPUS INTERNATIONAL, INC., 1191 E Newport Center Dr PH-E, **Deerfield Beach,** FL 33442, *pg.* 450, *pg.* 421
SUMTOTAL SYSTEMS, INC., 2850 NW 43rd St, Ste #200, **Gainesville,** FL 32606, *pg.* 477, *pg.* 429
SUNGARD FINANCIAL SYSTEMS-RELIUS-JACKSONVILLE, 1660 Prudential Dr, **Jacksonville,** FL 32207-8197, *pg.* 477, *pg.* 435
SYKES ENTERPRISES, INCORPORATED, 400 N Ashley Dr Ste 2800, **Tampa,** FL 33602, *pg.* 478, *pg.* 475
SYNIVERSE HOLDINGS, INC., 8125 Highwoods Palm Way, **Tampa,** FL 33647, *pg.* 479, *pg.* 475
TECH DATA CORPORATION, 5350 Tech Data Dr, **Clearwater,** FL 33760-3122, *pg.* 482, *pg.* 416
THE ULTIMATE SOFTWARE GROUP, INC., 2000 Ultimate Way, **Weston,** FL 33326, *pg.* 486, *pg.* 479
VERITEQ, 220 Congress Park Dr Ste 200, **Delray Beach,** FL 33445, *pg.* 488, *pg.* 422

Georgia

ABB, 400 Perimeter Center Ter, Ste 500, **Atlanta,** GA 30346, *pg.* 340, *pg.* 486
AMERICAN SOFTWARE, INC., 470 E Paces Ferry Rd NE, **Atlanta,** GA 30305-3301, *pg.* 349, *pg.* 488
APPLIED SOFTWARE TECHNOLOGY, INC., 2801 Buford Hwy Druid Chase Ste 100, **Atlanta,** GA 30329, *pg.* 352, *pg.* 488
ARRIS GROUP, INC., 3871 Lakefield Dr, **Suwanee,** GA 30024-1292, *pg.* 353, *pg.* 541
BOTTOMLINE TECHNOLOGIES INC., 3015 Windward Plz Fairways 2, **Alpharetta,** GA 30005, *pg.* 363, *pg.* 483
COMPONENTSOURCE HOLDING CORPORATION, 3391 Town Point Dr NW Ste 350, **Kennesaw,** GA 30144, *pg.* 378, *pg.* 533
CONCURRENT COMPUTER CORPORATION, 4375 River Green Pkwy Ste 100, **Duluth,** GA 30096-8319, *pg.* 379, *pg.* 531
CRICKET WIRELESS LLC, 12735 Morris Rd Ste 300, **Alpharetta,** GA 30004, *pg.* 381, *pg.* 483
EASYLINK SERVICES INTERNATIONAL CORPORATION, 6025 The Corners Pkwy Ste 100, **Norcross,** GA 30092-3328, *pg.* 389, *pg.* 536
HEALTHPORT, INC., 120 Bluegrass Valley Pkwy, **Alpharetta,** GA 30005, *pg.* 403, *pg.* 484
INFOR, 13560 Morris Rd Ste 4100, **Alpharetta,** GA 30004, *pg.* 414, *pg.* 484
INTERNAP NETWORK SERVICES CORPORATION, 1 Ravinia Dr Ste 1300, **Atlanta,** GA 30346, *pg.* 417, *pg.* 513
LOGILITY, INC., 470 E Paces Ferry Rd NE, **Atlanta,** GA 30305, *pg.* 428, *pg.* 513
MANHATTAN ASSOCIATES, INC., 2300 Windy Ridge Pkwy Ste 1000, **Atlanta,** GA 30339, *pg.* 430, *pg.* 513
NCR CORPORATION, 3097 Satellite Blvd, **Duluth,** GA 30096, *pg.* 443, *pg.* 531
RICOH AMERICAS CORP., 5550-A Peachtree Pkwy Ste 150, **Norcross,** GA 30092, *pg.* 462, *pg.* 538
SED INTERNATIONAL HOLDINGS, INC., 2150 Cedars Rd Ste 200, **Lawrenceville,** GA 30043, *pg.* 468, *pg.* 534
TOTAL SYSTEM SERVICES, INC., 1 TSYS Way, **Columbus,** GA 31901, *pg.* 484, *pg.* 528
VERINT WITNESS ACTIONABLE SOLUTIONS, 300 Colonial Ctr Pkwy Ste 600, **Roswell,** GA 30076, *pg.* 488, *pg.* 539

Idaho

MICRON TECHNOLOGY, INC., 8000 S Federal Way, **Boise,** ID 83716-9632, *pg.* 435, *pg.* 547

Illinois

ACCO BRANDS CORPORATION, Four Corporate Dr, **Lake Zurich,** IL 60047, *pg.* 340, *pg.* 626
ACXIOM CORPORATION, 1501 Opus Pl, **Downers Grove,** IL 60515, *pg.* 342, *pg.* 607
AON HEWITT, 100 Half Day Rd, **Lincolnshire,** IL 60069, *pg.* 350, *pg.* 627
APPLIED SYSTEMS INC., 200 Applied Pkwy, **University Park,** IL 60484, *pg.* 352, *pg.* 663
BADGER AIR BRUSH COMPANY, 9128 W Belmont Ave, **Franklin Park,** IL 60131-2806, *pg.* 359, *pg.* 612
CARTRIDGE WORLD NORTH AMERICA, LLC., 3106 N U.S. Hwy 12 Ste A, **Spring Grove,** IL 60081, *pg.* 369, *pg.* 661
CDK GLOBAL, INC., 1950 Hassell Rd, **Hoffman Estates,** IL 60169, *pg.* 370, *pg.* 617
CDW CORPORATION, 200 N Milwaukee Ave, **Vernon Hills,** IL 60061, *pg.* 370, *pg.* 663
CHICAGO SHOW INC., 851 Asbury Dr, **Buffalo Grove,** IL 60089, *pg.* 371, *pg.* 560
FELLOWES, INC., 1789 Norwood Ave, **Itasca,** IL 60143-1059, *pg.* 397, *pg.* 620
FLEXERA SOFTWARE INC., 1000 E Woodfield Rd Ste 400, **Schaumburg,** IL 60173-5145, *pg.* 398, *pg.* 658
GENERAL EMPLOYMENT ENTERPRISES, INC., 184 Shuman Blvd Ste 420, **Naperville,** IL 60563, *pg.* 400, *pg.* 636
GLORY GLOBAL SOLUTIONS, 2441 Warrenville Rd Ste 100, **Lisle,** IL 60532, *pg.* 401, *pg.* 628
HERE, 425 W Randolph St, **Chicago,** IL 60606, *pg.* 404, *pg.* 576
INFOGIX INC., 1240 E Diehl Rd Ste 400, **Naperville,** IL 60563, *pg.* 414, *pg.* 636
INSIGHT ENTERPRISES, INC., 444 Scott Dr, **Bloomingdale,** IL 60108, *pg.* 415, *pg.* 557
INTERCALL, INC., 8420 Bryn Mawr Ste 400, **Chicago,** IL 60631, *pg.* 417, *pg.* 578
INX INTERNATIONAL INK CO., 150 N Martingale Rd Ste 700, **Schaumburg,** IL 60173, *pg.* 421, *pg.* 658
IRI GROUP, 150 N Clinton St, **Chicago,** IL 60661, *pg.* 421, *pg.* 579
LUXOR CORP., 2245 N Delaney Rd, **Waukegan,** IL 60087, *pg.* 428, *pg.* 666
MANROLAND INC., 800 E Oakhill Dr, **Westmont,** IL 60559, *pg.* 430, *pg.* 669
MARKETING INNOVATORS INTERNATIONAL, INC., 9701 W Higgins Rd, **Rosemont,** IL 60018, *pg.* 430, *pg.* 657
MICROSYSTEMS, 3025 Highland Pkwy Ste 450, **Downers Grove,** IL 60515, *pg.* 440, *pg.* 608
THE MILLARD GROUP, 7301 N Cicero Ave, **Lincolnwood,** IL 60712, *pg.* 440, *pg.* 628
NORTH AMERICAN CORP., 2101 Claire Ct, **Glenview,** IL 60025-7634, *pg.* 446, *pg.* 615

PCTEL, INC., 471 Brighton Dr, **Bloomingdale, IL** 60108, *pg.* 452, *pg.* 557
PERRYGRAF, 25 W 550 Geneva Rd, **Carol Stream, IL** 60118, *pg.* 454, *pg.* 561
PRESSTEK, INC., 201 W Oakton St, **Des Plaines, IL** 60018-1855, *pg.* 456, *pg.* 606
PROFESSIONAL EDUCATION INSTITUTE, 7020 High Grove Blvd, **Burr Ridge, IL** 60527, *pg.* 457, *pg.* 561
REPLOGLE GLOBES, INC., 2801 S 25th Ave, **Broadview, IL** 60155-4531, *pg.* 461, *pg.* 559
S. GRAHAM & ASSOCIATES, 737 N Michigan Ave, Ste 1050, **Chicago, IL** 60611, *pg.* 463, *pg.* 589
SAPORITO FINISHING COMPANY, 3119 South Austin Blvd, **Cicero, IL** 60804, *pg.* 466, *pg.* 598
SILVON SOFTWARE INC., 900 Oakmont Ln Ste 400, **Westmont, IL** 60559, *pg.* 470, *pg.* 669
TALK-A-PHONE CO., 7530 N Natchez Ave, **Niles, IL** 60714, *pg.* 481, *pg.* 638
TECHNOLOGY EXECUTIVES CLUB, LTD., 1580 S Milwaukee Ave Ste 305, **Libertyville, IL** 60048, *pg.* 482, *pg.* 627
TTC AMERIDIAL, LLC, 3945 N Neenah Ave, **Chicago, IL** 60634, *pg.* 486, *pg.* 593
VIDEOJET TECHNOLOGIES INC., 1500 Mittel Blvd, **Wood Dale, IL** 60191-1073, *pg.* 489, *pg.* 671
WEBER PACKAGING SOLUTIONS, INC., 711 W Algonquin Rd, **Arlington Heights, IL** 60005-4415, *pg.* 491, *pg.* 554
XENTRIS WIRELESS, LLC, 1250A Greenbriar Dr, **Addison,** IL 60101, *pg.* 494, *pg.* 552

Indiana

AMERICAN STATIONERY CO., INC., 100 N Park Ave, **Peru,** IN 46970-1701, *pg.* 349, *pg.* 696
CTI GROUP HOLDINGS INC., 333 N Alabama St Ste 240, **Indianapolis, IN** 46204-1767, *pg.* 381, *pg.* 684
HURCO COMPANIES, INC., 1 Technology Way, **Indianapolis, IN** 46268-0180, *pg.* 409, *pg.* 686
INGRAM MICRO MOBILITY, 501 Airtech Pkwy, **Plainfield, IN** 46168, *pg.* 415, *pg.* 697
INTERACTIVE INTELLIGENCE, INC., 7601 Interactive Way, **Indianapolis, IN** 46278, *pg.* 417, *pg.* 687
MATRIX INTEGRATION LLC, 417 Main St, **Jasper,** IN 47546, *pg.* 430, *pg.* 692

Iowa

CDS GLOBAL, INC., 1901 Bell Ave, **Des Moines,** IA 50315-1099, *pg.* 370, *pg.* 704
EAGLE POINT SOFTWARE CORPORATION, 4131 Westmark Dr, **Dubuque,** IA 52002-2627, *pg.* 389, *pg.* 707
ITAGROUP, INC., 4600 Westown Pkwy, **West Des Moines,** IA 50266-6719, *pg.* 422, *pg.* 713
THE VERNON COMPANY, 1 Promotional Pl, **Newton,** IA 50208, *pg.* 488, *pg.* 710
WORKIVA, 2900 University Blvd, **Ames,** IA 50010, *pg.* 493, *pg.* 701

Kansas

CARTESIAN, 7300 College Blvd Ste 302, **Overland Park,** KS 66210, *pg.* 369, *pg.* 718
MEDIWARE INFORMATION SYSTEMS, INC., 11711 W 79th St, **Lenexa,** KS 66214, *pg.* 431, *pg.* 716
NIC INC., 25501 W Valley Parkway Ste 300, **Olathe,** KS 66061, *pg.* 445, *pg.* 718

Kentucky

HEALTHWAREHOUSE.COM, INC., 7107 Industrial Rd, **Florence,** KY 41042-2979, *pg.* 403, *pg.* 728
LEXMARK INTERNATIONAL, INC., 740 W New Cir Rd, **Lexington,** KY 40550, *pg.* 427, *pg.* 730
POMEROY IT SOLUTIONS, INC., 1020 Petersburg Rd, **Hebron,** KY 41048-8222, *pg.* 456, *pg.* 728

Louisiana

BARRISTER GLOBAL SERVICES NETWORK, INC., 42548 Happywoods Dr, **Hammond,** LA 70401, *pg.* 360, *pg.* 744
GLOBALSTAR, INC., 300 Holiday Square Blvd, **Covington,** LA 70433, *pg.* 401, *pg.* 743

Maine

WRIGHT EXPRESS CORPORATION, 97 Darling Ave, **South Portland,** ME 04106, *pg.* 493, *pg.* 753

Maryland

AVF CONSULTING, INC., 1220-C E Joppa Rd Ste 514, **Baltimore,** MD 21286, *pg.* 358, *pg.* 755
BARCODING INC., 2220 Boston St, **Baltimore,** MD 21231, *pg.* 360, *pg.* 755
CISION, INC., 12051 Indian Creek Ct, **Beltsville,** MD 20705-1246, *pg.* 375, *pg.* 761
CONNECTUS SOFTWARE, 810 Cromwell Park Dr Ste D, **Hanover,** MD 21061, *pg.* 379, *pg.* 772
EA ENGINEERING, SCIENCE & TECHNOLOGY, INC., 11019 McCormick Rd Ste 400, **Hunt Valley,** MD 21031, *pg.* 389, *pg.* 772
FEI SYSTEMS, 7257 Pkwy Dr Ste 200, **Hanover,** MD 21076, *pg.* 397, *pg.* 772
GLOBAL LEARNING SYSTEMS LLC, 5300 Westview Dr Ste 405, **Frederick,** MD 21703, *pg.* 400, *pg.* 769
IBIQUITY DIGITAL CORPORATION, 6711 Columbia Gtwy Dr Ste 500, **Columbia,** MD 21046, *pg.* 409, *pg.* 767
INTEGRAL SYSTEMS, INC., 6721 Columbia Gateway Dr, **Columbia,** MD 21046, *pg.* 416, *pg.* 767
MICROS SYSTEMS, INC., 7031 Columbia Gateway Dr, **Columbia,** MD 21046-2289, *pg.* 435, *pg.* 768
NIELSEN AUDIO, 9705 Patuxent Woods Dr, **Columbia,** MD 21046-1572, *pg.* 446, *pg.* 768
RAND A TECHNOLOGY CORPORATION, 11201 Dolfield Blvd, Ste 112, **Owings Mills,** MD 21117, *pg.* 459, *pg.* 774
RAXCO SOFTWARE, INC., 6 Montgomery Vlg Ave Ste 500, **Gaithersburg,** MD 20879, *pg.* 459, *pg.* 770
RIVERBED PERFORMANCE MANAGEMENT, 7255 Woodmont Ave, **Bethesda,** MD 20814, *pg.* 462, *pg.* 765
TELECOMMUNICATION SYSTEMS INC., 275 West St, **Annapolis,** MD 21401, *pg.* 483, *pg.* 754
VIEW SYSTEMS, INC., 1550 Caton Center Dr Ste E, **Baltimore,** MD 21227, *pg.* 489, *pg.* 760

Massachusetts

3M TOUCH SYSTEMS, INC., 501 Griffin Brook Park Dr, **Methuen,** MA 01844-1873, *pg.* 339, *pg.* 833
ALPHA CTP SYSTEM, 554 Clark Rd, # 2, **Tewksbury,** MA 01876, *pg.* 347, *pg.* 848
ASPECT SOFTWARE, INC., 300 Apollo Dr, **Chelmsford,** MA 01824, *pg.* 354, *pg.* 813
ASPEN TECHNOLOGY, INC., 200 Wheeler Rd, **Burlington,** MA 01803, *pg.* 354, *pg.* 804
ATEX MEDIA COMMAND, INC., 1 Highwood Dr Ste 301, **Tewksbury,** MA 01876, *pg.* 355, *pg.* 848
AXEDA SYSTEMS INC., Unit 3 25 Forbes Blvd, **Foxboro,** MA 02035-2873, *pg.* 359, *pg.* 819
BARE BONES SOFTWARE, INC., 73 Princeton St Ste 206, **North Chelmsford,** MA 01863, *pg.* 360, *pg.* 838
THE BOSTON CONSULTING GROUP, INC., Exchange Pl 31 Fl, **Boston,** MA 02109, *pg.* 363, *pg.* 790
BRAINSTORM GROUP, INC., 386 W Main St, **Northborough,** MA 01532-2128, *pg.* 364, *pg.* 838
BRIDGELINE DIGITAL, INC., 10 6th Rd, **Woburn,** MA 01801, *pg.* 364, *pg.* 861
CAMBEX CORPORATION, 337 Turnpike Rd, **Southborough,** MA 01772, *pg.* 368, *pg.* 844
CARBONITE, INC., 334 Boylston St 3rd Fl, **Boston,** MA 02116, *pg.* 368, *pg.* 792
CLAVEL, LTD., 3 Crafts Rd, **Gloucester,** MA 01930-2135, *pg.* 376, *pg.* 823
CLEAN HARBORS, INC., 42 Longwater Dr, **Norwell,** MA 02061-9149, *pg.* 376, *pg.* 839
CONSTANT CONTACT, INC., Reservoir Pl 1601 Trapelo Rd Ste 329, **Waltham,** MA 02451, *pg.* 379, *pg.* 850
DASSAULT SYSTEMS ENOVIA, 175 Wyman St, **Waltham,** MA 02451, *pg.* 382, *pg.* 851
DATAWATCH CORPORATION, Quorum Office Park 271 Mill Rd, **Chelmsford,** MA 01824-4105, *pg.* 383, *pg.* 813
DIMENSIONAL INSIGHT, INC., 60 Mall Rd, **Burlington,** MA 01803, *pg.* 387, *pg.* 805
ECLINICALWORKS, LLC, Westborough Executive Pk 112 Turnpike Rd, **Westborough,** MA 01581, *pg.* 389, *pg.* 857
EDGEWATER TECHNOLOGY, INC., 200 Harvard Mill Sq Ste 210, **Wakefield,** MA 01880, *pg.* 389, *pg.* 848
EGENERA, INC., 80 Central St Ste 300, **Boxborough,** MA 01719-1245, *pg.* 390, *pg.* 802
EMC CORPORATION, 176 S St, **Hopkinton,** MA 01748, *pg.* 391, *pg.* 825
FOLEY HOAG LLP, Seaport World Trade Ctr W 155 Seaport Blvd, **Boston,** MA 02210-2600, *pg.* 398, *pg.* 794
THE FORUM CORPORATION, 265 Franklin St 4th Fl, **Boston,** MA 02110-3113, *pg.* 398, *pg.* 794
GLASSHOUSE TECHNOLOGIES, INC., 352 Turnpike Rd, Ste 200, **Southborough,** MA 01772, *pg.* 400, *pg.* 844
GROSSMAN MARKETING GROUP, 30 Cobble Hill Rd, **Somerville,** MA 02143, *pg.* 401, *pg.* 843
HUBSPOT, INC., 25 First St 2nd Fl, **Cambridge,** MA 02141, *pg.* 409, *pg.* 808
IGATE CORPORATION, 1 Broadway 13th fl, **Cambridge,** MA 02142, *pg.* 411, *pg.* 809
IMAKENEWS, INC., 460 Totten Pond Rd Ste 530, **Waltham,** MA 02451, *pg.* 413, *pg.* 851
INTEGRATED SOFTWARE DESIGN, INC., 171 Forbes Blvd, **Mansfield,** MA 02048, *pg.* 416, *pg.* 830
INTERVALZERO INC., 400 5th Ave, **Waltham,** MA 02451, *pg.* 420, *pg.* 851
IPSWITCH, INC., 10 Maguire Rd Ste 220, **Lexington,** MA 02421, *pg.* 421, *pg.* 828
IRON MOUNTAIN INCORPORATED, 745 Atlantic Ave, **Boston,** MA 02111-2735, *pg.* 421, *pg.* 796
JUNIPER NETWORKS, 1 Rogers St 6th Fl, **Cambridge,** MA 02142-1102, *pg.* 424, *pg.* 809
KOPIN CORPORATION, 200 John Hancock Rd, **Taunton,** MA 02780, *pg.* 425, *pg.* 847
KRONOS INCORPORATED, 297 Billerica Rd, **Chelmsford,** MA 01824, *pg.* 425, *pg.* 813
LAVASTORM ANALYTICS, 321 Summer St 5th Fl, **Boston,** MA 02210, *pg.* 427, *pg.* 797
LIONBRIDGE TECHNOLOGIES INC., 1050 Winter St, **Waltham,** MA 02451-1460, *pg.* 428, *pg.* 851
LOGMEIN, INC., 500 Unicorn Pk Dr, **Woburn,** MA 01801-3345, *pg.* 428, *pg.* 861
MEDICAL INFORMATION TECHNOLOGY, INC., Meditech Cir, **Westwood,** MA 02090, *pg.* 431, *pg.* 859
MERCURY COMPUTER SYSTEMS, INC., 201 Riverneck Rd, **Chelmsford,** MA 01824-2820, *pg.* 434, *pg.* 813
MTI SYSTEMS INC., 59 Interstate Dr, **West Springfield,** MA 01089, *pg.* 442, *pg.* 857
NOVELL INC., 404 Wyman St, Ste 390, **Waltham,** MA 02451, *pg.* 446, *pg.* 852
NTT DATA, 100 City Sq, **Boston,** MA 02129, *pg.* 447, *pg.* 799
NUANCE COMMUNICATIONS, INC., 1 Wayside Rd, **Burlington,** MA 01803, *pg.* 447, *pg.* 806
NUANCE DICTAPHONE HEALTHCARE SOLUTIONS, 1 Wayside Rd, **Burlington,** MA 01803, *pg.* 447, *pg.* 806
OMTOOL, LTD., 6 Riverside Dr, **Andover,** MA 01810, *pg.* 449, *pg.* 782
ONMOBILE LIVE, INC., 1 Monarch Dr Ste 203, **Littleton,** MA 01460, *pg.* 449, *pg.* 829
OPTUM CLINICAL SOLUTIONS, 100 Quannapowitt Pkwy Ste 405, **Wakefield,** MA 01880, *pg.* 450, *pg.* 848
PARAMETRIC TECHNOLOGY CORPORATION, 140 Kendrick St, **Needham,** MA 02494-2714, *pg.* 452, *pg.* 835
PEGASYSTEMS INC., 101 Main St, **Cambridge,** MA 02142-1590, *pg.* 453, *pg.* 809
PEOPLEFLUENT, 300 Fifth Ave, **Waltham,** MA 02451, *pg.* 453, *pg.* 853
PROGRESS SOFTWARE CORPORATION, 14 Oak Park Dr, **Bedford,** MA 01730-1414, *pg.* 457, *pg.* 786
QVIDIAN, 175 Cabot St Ste 210, **Lowell,** MA 01854, *pg.* 458, *pg.* 829
RAND WORLDWIDE, INC., 161 Worcester Rd Ste 401, **Framingham,** MA 01701, *pg.* 459, *pg.* 821
RSA SECURITY INC., 174 Middlesex Tpke, **Bedford,** MA 01730-1408, *pg.* 463, *pg.* 786
SMART SOFTWARE, INC., 4 Hill Rd, **Belmont,** MA 02478-4303, *pg.* 470, *pg.* 787
SOLIDWORKS CORPORATION, 300 Baker Ave, **Concord,** MA 01742, *pg.* 472, *pg.* 815
STANDARD DUPLICATING MACHINES CORPORATION, 10 Connector Rd, **Andover,** MA 01810-5927, *pg.* 473, *pg.* 783
STAPLES, INC., 500 Staples Dr, **Framingham,** MA 01702, *pg.* 474, *pg.* 821
STRATUS TECHNOLOGIES, INC., 111 Powdermill Rd, **Maynard,** MA 01754-3409, *pg.* 477, *pg.* 832
TECHTARGET, INC., 275 Grove St, **Newton,** MA 02466, *pg.* 482, *pg.* 837
THOMSON COMPUMARK, 500 Victory Rd, **North Quincy,**

MA 02171-3132, *pg.* 484, *pg.* 838
UGL SERVICES, 275 Grove St, **Auburndale,** MA 02466-2272, *pg.* 486, *pg.* 784
THE UNION GROUP, 649 Alden St, **Fall River,** MA 02722-3160, *pg.* 487, *pg.* 819
VIRTUSA CORPORATION, 2000 W Park Dr, **Westborough,** MA 01581, *pg.* 490, *pg.* 857
W.B. MASON COMPANY, 59 Centre St, **Brockton,** MA 02303, *pg.* 491, *pg.* 803

Michigan

BMC INDUSTRIAL EDUCATIONAL SERVICES, 2831 Maffett St, **Muskegon Heights,** MI 49444-2153, *pg.* 362, *pg.* 902
BULLSEYE TELECOM INC., 25925 Telegraph Rd Ste 210, **Southfield,** MI 48033-2527, *pg.* 366, *pg.* 906
COMPUWARE CORPORATION, 1 Campus Martius, **Detroit,** MI 48226, *pg.* 379, *pg.* 879
GREENVIEW DATA, INC., 8178 Jackson Rd, Ste A, **Ann Arbor,** MI 48103, *pg.* 401, *pg.* 866
HAWORTH, INC., 1 Haworth Ctr, **Holland,** MI 49423-9570, *pg.* 402, *pg.* 891
HTC GLOBAL SERVICES INC., 3270 W Big Beaver Rd, **Troy,** MI 48084-1840, *pg.* 409, *pg.* 911
KELLY SERVICES, INC., 999 W Big Beaver Rd, **Troy,** MI 48084-4782, *pg.* 424, *pg.* 911
LOWRY COMPUTER PRODUCTS, INC., 9420 Maltby Rd, **Brighton,** MI 48116, *pg.* 428, *pg.* 874
MARTIN UNIVERSAL DESIGN, INC., 4444 Lawton St, **Detroit,** MI 48208, *pg.* 430, *pg.* 884
PRECISION DATA PRODUCTS, INC., 5036 Falcon View Ave SE, **Kentwood,** MI 49512, *pg.* 456, *pg.* 895
STEELCASE INC., 901 44th St SE, **Grand Rapids,** MI 49508, *pg.* 475, *pg.* 889
STEFANINI TECHTEAM GLOBAL, INC., 27335 W 11 Mile Rd, **Southfield,** MI 48033, *pg.* 476, *pg.* 907
SUPPORTSAVE SOLUTIONS, INC., 801 W Big Beaver Ste 650, **Troy,** MI 48084, *pg.* 478, *pg.* 911
SYNTEL, INC., 525 E Big Beaver Rd Ste 300, **Troy,** MI 48083-1364, *pg.* 480, *pg.* 911
THOMSON REUTERS TAX & ACCOUNTING, 510 E Milham Ave, **Portage,** MI 49002, *pg.* 484, *pg.* 905

Minnesota

ANALYSTS INTERNATIONAL CORPORATION, 7700 France Ave South, **Minneapolis,** MN 55435-3000, *pg.* 350, *pg.* 930
CARLSON JPM STORE FIXTURES, 7147 Northland Dr, **Brooklyn Park,** MN 55428, *pg.* 369, *pg.* 919
CERIDIAN CORPORATION, 3311 E Old Shakopee Rd, **Minneapolis,** MN 55425, *pg.* 371, *pg.* 932
DATA LISTING SERVICE LLC, 11351 Rupp Dr, **Burnsville,** MN 55337, *pg.* 382, *pg.* 919
DATACARD CORPORATION, 11111 Bren Rd W, **Minnetonka,** MN 55343-9015, *pg.* 382, *pg.* 948
DATALINK CORPORATION, 10050 Crosstown Cir Ste 500, **Eden Prairie,** MN 55344, *pg.* 382, *pg.* 922
DELL STORAGE, 7625 Smetana Ln, **Eden Prairie,** MN 55344, *pg.* 386, *pg.* 922
DELPHAX TECHNOLOGIES INC., 6100 W 110th St, **Bloomington,** MN 55438-2664, *pg.* 386, *pg.* 917
DIGI INTERNATIONAL INC., 11001 Bren Rd E, **Minnetonka,** MN 55343-9605, *pg.* 387, *pg.* 948
EDMENTUM, INC., 5600 W 83rd St Ste 300 8200 Twr, **Bloomington,** MN 55437, *pg.* 390, *pg.* 917
ERGOTRON, INC., 1181 Trapp Rd, **Saint Paul,** MN 55121-1325, *pg.* 395, *pg.* 960
FASTENAL COMPANY, 2001 Theurer Blvd, **Winona,** MN 55987-1500, *pg.* 396, *pg.* 966
HALLMARK BUSINESS CONNECTIONS, 121 S 8th St Ste 700, **Minneapolis,** MN 55402-2841, *pg.* 402, *pg.* 937
HUTCHINSON TECHNOLOGY INC., 40 W Highland Park Dr NE, **Hutchinson,** MN 55350-9784, *pg.* 409, *pg.* 926
IMAGE SENSING SYSTEMS, INC., 1600 University Ave W Ste 500, **Saint Paul,** MN 55104-3828, *pg.* 412, *pg.* 961
IMATION CORP., 1 Imation Way, **Oakdale,** MN 55128, *pg.* 413, *pg.* 952
INFOR LAWSON, 380 Saint Peter St, **Saint Paul,** MN 55102-1302, *pg.* 414, *pg.* 961
INTERNATIONAL DECISION SYSTEMS, 1500 IDS Ctr 80th S 8th St, **Minneapolis,** MN 55402, *pg.* 419, *pg.* 938
LOFFLER BUSINESS SYSTEMS INC., 1101 E 78th St Ste 200, **Bloomington,** MN 55420, *pg.* 428, *pg.* 918
MARUDAS PRINT SERVICES & PROMOTIONAL PRODUCTS, INC., 20 Yorkton Ct, **Saint Paul,** MN 55117, *pg.* 430, *pg.* 962
MICROBOARDS TECHNOLOGY, LLC, 8150 Mallory Ct, **Chanhassen,** MN 55317-0846, *pg.* 434, *pg.* 920
MTS SYSTEMS CORPORATION, 14000 Technology Dr, **Eden Prairie,** MN 55344, *pg.* 442, *pg.* 923
MULTI-TECH SYSTEMS INC., 2205 Woodale Dr, **Mounds View,** MN 55112-4909, *pg.* 442, *pg.* 951
MULTIBAND CORPORATION, 9449 Science Ctr Dr, **Minneapolis,** MN 55428, *pg.* 442, *pg.* 940
NVE CORPORATION, 11409 Valley View Rd, **Eden Prairie,** MN 55344-3617, *pg.* 447, *pg.* 923
RANDSTAD USA, 651 Nicollet Mall Ste 313, **Minneapolis,** MN 55402, *pg.* 459, *pg.* 941
SCANTRON CORPORATION, 1313 Loan Oak Rd, **Eagan,** MN 55121, *pg.* 467, *pg.* 922
SMEAD MANUFACTURING COMPANY, 600 Smead Blvd, **Hastings,** MN 55033-2200, *pg.* 470, *pg.* 926
SPS COMMERCE, INC., 333 S Seventh St Ste 1000, **Minneapolis,** MN 55402, *pg.* 472, *pg.* 942
STRATASYS, INC., 7665 Commerce Way, **Eden Prairie,** MN 55344, *pg.* 476, *pg.* 923
VARITRONICS, LLC, 2355 Polaris Ln N, Ste 100, **Plymouth,** MN 55447, *pg.* 487, *pg.* 954

Missouri

AMDOCS INC., 1390 Timberlake Manor Pkwy, **Chesterfield,** MO 63017-6041, *pg.* 348, *pg.* 974
DIAGRAPH, 1 Missouri Research Pk Dr, **Saint Charles,** MO 63304-5685, *pg.* 387, *pg.* 989
DIRECTORY DISTRIBUTING ASSOCIATES, INC., 1602 Park 370 Ct, **Hazelwood,** MO 63042-3814, *pg.* 388, *pg.* 978
DST SYSTEMS, INC., 333 W 11th St, **Kansas City,** MO 64105-1773, *pg.* 388, *pg.* 982
ELEKTA, 13723 Riverport Dr Ste 100, **Maryland Heights,** MO 63043, *pg.* 391, *pg.* 987
EQUIFAX WORKFORCE SOLUTIONS, 11432 Lackland, **Saint Louis,** MO 63146, *pg.* 394, *pg.* 997
JACK HENRY & ASSOCIATES, INC., 663 W Hwy 60, **Monett,** MO 65708, *pg.* 422, *pg.* 988
MAGNA VISUAL, INC., 9400 Watson Rd, **Saint Louis,** MO 63126-1596, *pg.* 429, *pg.* 999
TENSION ENVELOPE CORPORATION, 819 E 19th St, **Kansas City,** MO 64108-1703, *pg.* 483, *pg.* 986
WORLD WIDE TECHNOLOGY HOLDING CO., INC., 60 Weldon Pkwy, **Maryland Heights,** MO 63043-3202, *pg.* 493, *pg.* 988

Montana

PRINTINGFORLESS.COM, INC., 100 PFL Way, **Livingston,** MT 59047, *pg.* 456, *pg.* 1009

Nebraska

ACCURATE COMMUNICATIONS, INC., 2215 Harney St, **Omaha,** NE 68131-3620, *pg.* 340, *pg.* 1013
ACI WORLDWIDE INC., 6060 Coventry Dr, **Elkhorn,** NE 68022, *pg.* 341, *pg.* 1010
NATIONAL RESEARCH CORPORATION, 1245 Q St, **Lincoln,** NE 68508-3636, *pg.* 443, *pg.* 1012
WEST CORPORATION, 11808 Miracle Hills Dr, **Omaha,** NE 68154, *pg.* 492, *pg.* 1019

Nevada

AHERN RENTALS, INC., 4241 S Arville St, **Las Vegas,** NV 89103, *pg.* 345, *pg.* 1022
ALLEGIANT TRAVEL COMPANY, 8360 S Durango Dr, **Las Vegas,** NV 89113, *pg.* 346, *pg.* 1022
IGT, 9295 Prototype Dr, **Reno,** NV 89521, *pg.* 412, *pg.* 1031
MILLER HEIMAN INC., 10509 Professional Cir Ste 100, **Reno,** NV 89521, *pg.* 440, *pg.* 1031
SCIENTIFIC GAMES CORPORATION, 6650 S El Camino Rd, **Las Vegas,** NV 89118, *pg.* 468, *pg.* 1029

New Hampshire

ACME STAPLE COMPANY, INC., 87 Hill Rd, **Franklin,** NH 03235, *pg.* 341, *pg.* 1034
AMBERWAVE INC, 13 Garabedian Dr, **Salem,** NH 03079, *pg.* 348, *pg.* 1039
ASA INTERNATIONAL LTD., 25 Manchester St, Ste 100, **Merrimack,** NH 03054, *pg.* 353, *pg.* 1036
DAHLE USA, 49 Vose Farm Rd, **Peterborough,** NH 03458-1792, *pg.* 382, *pg.* 1038
DELL, INC., 110 Spit Brook Rd, Bld ZKO2, **Nashua,** NH 03062, *pg.* 385, *pg.* 1037
EZENIA! INC., 45 Stiles Rd, Ste 210, **Salem,** NH 03079, *pg.* 396, *pg.* 1039
PC CONNECTION, INC., Rte 101 A 730 Milford Rd, **Merrimack,** NH 03054, *pg.* 452, *pg.* 1036
SKILLSOFT PLC, 107 Northeastern Blvd, **Nashua,** NH 03062, *pg.* 470, *pg.* 1037

New Jersey

123 STAFFING, INC., 475 Springfield Ave Ste 401, **Summit,** NJ 07901, *pg.* 339, *pg.* 1123
ACSIS, INC., 9 East Stow Rd Ste D, **Marlton,** NJ 08053, *pg.* 341, *pg.* 1083
AMANO CINCINNATI, INC., 140 Harrison Ave, **Roseland,** NJ 07068, *pg.* 348, *pg.* 1117
AMBER ROAD, INC., 1 Meadowlands Plz, **East Rutherford,** NJ 07073, *pg.* 348, *pg.* 1054
AMERICAN LIST COUNSEL, INC., 4300 US Hwy 1 CN 5219, **Princeton,** NJ 08543, *pg.* 349, *pg.* 1110
AMERICAN MARKING SYSTEMS, INC., 1015 Paulison Ave, **Clifton,** NJ 07011-3610, *pg.* 349, *pg.* 1051
AUDIOCODES USA, 27 World's Fair Dr, **Somerset,** NJ 08873, *pg.* 356, *pg.* 1121
AUTHENTIDATE HOLDING CORP., 300 Connell Dr 5th Fl, **Berkeley Heights,** NJ 07922, *pg.* 356, *pg.* 1044
AUTOMATIC DATA PROCESSING, INC., 1 ADP Blvd, **Roseland,** NJ 07068-1728, *pg.* 357, *pg.* 1117
CALIPER CORPORATION, 506 Carnegie Ctr Ste 300, **Princeton,** NJ 08540, *pg.* 368, *pg.* 1111
CAMO SOFTWARE, INC., 1 Woodbridge Ctr, **Woodbridge,** NJ 07095, *pg.* 368, *pg.* 1133
THE CASEY GROUP, 77 E Halsey Rd, **Parsippany,** NJ 07054-3704, *pg.* 369, *pg.* 1102
COGNIZANT TECHNOLOGY SOLUTIONS CORPORATION, Glenpointe Ctr W 500 Frank W Burr Blvd, **Teaneck,** NJ 07666-6804, *pg.* 377, *pg.* 1124
COMMENCE CORPORATION, 2 Industrial Way W, Ste 2, **Eatontown,** NJ 07724, *pg.* 377, *pg.* 1055
COMMVAULT SYSTEMS, INC., 1 CommVault Way, **Tinton Falls,** NJ 07724, *pg.* 377, *pg.* 1125
D.A. KOPP & ASSOCIATES, INC., 11-D Commerce Way, **Totowa,** NJ 07512-1154, *pg.* 381, *pg.* 1126
DATARAM CORPORATION, Route 571 PO Box 7258, **Princeton,** NJ 08543-7528, *pg.* 383, *pg.* 1111
EMTEC, INC., 11 Diamond Rd, **Springfield,** NJ 07081, *pg.* 392, *pg.* 1123
ERICSSON, 1 Ericsson Dr, **Piscataway,** NJ 08854-4157, *pg.* 395, *pg.* 1108
FRANKLIN ELECTRONIC PUBLISHERS, INC., 2 Manhattan Dr, **Burlington,** NJ 08016-4903, *pg.* 398, *pg.* 1048
GLOWPOINT, INC., 430 Mountain Ave Ste 301, **New Providence,** NJ 07974, *pg.* 401, *pg.* 1094
THE HIBBERT GROUP, 400 Pennington Ave, **Trenton,** NJ 08618, *pg.* 407, *pg.* 1126
HONEYWELL INTERNATIONAL INC., 101 Columbia Rd, **Morristown,** NJ 07962, *pg.* 407, *pg.* 1088
ICIMS, INC., 90 Matawan Rd, 5th Fl, **Matawan,** NJ 07747, *pg.* 411, *pg.* 1083
INFOCROSSING, INC., 2 Christie Heights St, **Leonia,** NJ 07605, *pg.* 414, *pg.* 1079
THE INTELLIGENCE GROUP, 1545 US Hwy 206 Ste 202, **Bedminster,** NJ 07921, *pg.* 417, *pg.* 1043
KEPNER-TREGOE, INC., Princeton Forrestal Village, 116 Village Blvd Ste 300, **Princeton,** NJ 08540, *pg.* 424, *pg.* 1112
KYOCERA DOCUMENT SOLUTIONS AMERICA, 225 Sand Rd, **Fairfield,** NJ 07004, *pg.* 426, *pg.* 1065
MAJESCO, 412 Mount Kemble Ave, Ste 110C, **Morristown,** NJ 07960, *pg.* 429, *pg.* 1089
MAJESCO ENTERTAINMENT COMPANY, 160 Raritan Ctr Pkwy, **Edison,** NJ 08837, *pg.* 429, *pg.* 1056
MFV EXPOSITIONS, LLC, 210 Rte 4 E Ste 204, **Paramus,** NJ 07652, *pg.* 434, *pg.* 1101
NER HOLDINGS INC., 307 S Delsea Dr, **Glassboro,** NJ 08028-2608, *pg.* 444, *pg.* 1071
OKI DATA AMERICAS, INC., 2000 Bishops Gate Blvd, **Mount Laurel,** NJ 08054-4620, *pg.* 449, *pg.* 1090

First page reference indicates Business Class Edition
Second page reference indicates Geographic Edition

OPEX CORPORATION, 305 Commerce Dr, **Moorestown,** NJ 08057-4215, *pg.* 450, *pg.* 1087
ORIEL STAT-A-MATRIX, INC., 1 Quality Pl, **Edison,** NJ 08820-1073, *pg.* 451, *pg.* 1057
PNY TECHNOLOGIES, INC., 299 Webro Rd, **Parsippany,** NJ 07054-0218, *pg.* 455, *pg.* 1105
RCM TECHNOLOGIES, INC., 2500 McClellan Ave Ste 350, **Pennsauken,** NJ 08109-4613, *pg.* 459, *pg.* 1108
RICOH AMERICAS CORPORATION, 5 Dedrick Pl, **West Caldwell,** NJ 07006-6304, *pg.* 461, *pg.* 1131
ROYAL CONSUMER INFORMATION PRODUCTS INC., 2 Riverview Dr 3rd Fl, **Somerset,** NJ 08873, *pg.* 463, *pg.* 1122
SOFTWARE HOUSE INTERNATIONAL, INC. (SHI), 290 Davidson Ave, # 101, **Somerset,** NJ 08873, *pg.* 471, *pg.* 1122
SYNCHRONOSS TECHNOLOGIES, INC., 750 Route 202 S Ste 600, **Bridgewater,** NJ 08807, *pg.* 479, *pg.* 1047
WAYSIDE TECHNOLOGY GROUP, INC., 1157 Shrewsbury Ave, **Shrewsbury,** NJ 07702-4321, *pg.* 491, *pg.* 1121

New Mexico

GE INTELLIGENT PLATFORMS, 7401 Snaproll NE, **Albuquerque,** NM 87109, *pg.* 400, *pg.* 1135

New York

ACNIELSEN CORPORATION, 770 Broadway, **New York, NY** 10003, *pg.* 341, *pg.* 1187
ADECCO USA, INC., 175 Broadhollow Rd, **Melville, NY** 11747-4902, *pg.* 342, *pg.* 1178
ADVERTISING CHECKING BUREAU INCORPORATED, 2 Pk Ave 18th Fl, **New York,** NY 10016-5675, *pg.* 345, *pg.* 1187
ADVERTISING DISTRIBUTORS OF AMERICA INC., 200 Trade Zone Dr, **Ronkonkoma,** NY 11779, *pg.* 345, *pg.* 1338
ALACRA, INC., 100 Broadway Ste 1101, **New York,** NY 10005-4512, *pg.* 346, *pg.* 1188
ALSTATE PROCESS SERVICE INC., 60 Burt Dr, **Deer Park,** NY 11729-5702, *pg.* 347, *pg.* 1155
APPNEXUS, 28 W 23rd St 4th Fl, **New York,** NY 10010, *pg.* 352, *pg.* 1196
ARCADE MARKETING, INC., 1700 Broadway Ste 2500, **New York,** NY 10019, *pg.* 352, *pg.* 1196
ARTNET WORLDWIDE CORPORATION, 233 Broadway, Fl 26, **New York,** NY 10279, *pg.* 353, *pg.* 1197
ATARI, INC., 417 5th Ave, **New York,** NY 10016-2204, *pg.* 355, *pg.* 1198
BAE SYSTEMS-COMMUNICATION, NAVIGATION, IDENTIFICATION & RECONNAISSANCE, 450 Pulaski Rd, **Greenlawn,** NY 11740-1606, *pg.* 359, *pg.* 1163
BROADVIEW NETWORKS, INC., 800 Westchester Ave Ste N501, **Rye Brook,** NY 10573, *pg.* 365, *pg.* 1339
CA TECHNOLOGIES, 1 CA Plz, **Islandia,** NY 11749-7000, *pg.* 366, *pg.* 1168
CALERO SOFTWARE, LLC, 1565 Jefferson Rd Ste 120, **Rochester,** NY 14623, *pg.* 368, *pg.* 1333
CAPGEMINI U.S., 623 5th Ave 33rd Fl, **New York,** NY 10022, *pg.* 368, *pg.* 1209
CHYRONHEGO, 5 Hub Dr, **Melville,** NY 11747, *pg.* 371, *pg.* 1179
THE COLAD GROUP, INC., 801 Exchange St, **Buffalo,** NY 14210-1434, *pg.* 377, *pg.* 1147
COMFORCE CORPORATION, 415 Crossways Park Dr, **Woodbury,** NY 11797-2061, *pg.* 377, *pg.* 1355
COMMAND SECURITY CORPORATION, Rte 55 Lexington Park, **Lagrangeville,** NY 12540, *pg.* 377, *pg.* 1171
COMMUNICATIONS SPECIALTIES, INC., 125 Comac St, **Ronkonkoma,** NY 11779, *pg.* 377, *pg.* 1338
COMPUTER TASK GROUP, INC., 800 Delaware Ave, **Buffalo,** NY 14209-2006, *pg.* 378, *pg.* 1147
COMTECH TELECOMMUNICATIONS CORP., 68 S Service Rd Ste 230, **Melville,** NY 11747-3833, *pg.* 379, *pg.* 1179
DOCUMENT SECURITY SYSTEMS, INC., 28 Main St E Ste 1525, **Rochester,** NY 14614, *pg.* 388, *pg.* 1333
DRI MARK PRODUCTS, INC., 15 Harbor Pk Dr, **Port Washington,** NY 11050-4604, *pg.* 388, *pg.* 1323
ELECTION SERVICES CORPORATION, 990 Stewart Ave Ste 500, **Garden City,** NY 11530-2925, *pg.* 390, *pg.* 1161
EMERALD EXPOSITIONS, 1133 Westchester Ave Ste N136, **White Plains,** NY 10604, *pg.* 392, *pg.* 1352
ENHERENT CORP., 6800 Jericho Tpke, Ste 116E, **Syosset,** NY 11791, *pg.* 393, *pg.* 1343
ESSELTE BUSINESS CORP, 48 S Service Rd Ste 400, **Melville,** NY 11747, *pg.* 395, *pg.* 1179
FALCONSTOR SOFTWARE, INC., 2 Huntingdon Quadrangle Ste 2S01, **Melville,** NY 11747-3800, *pg.* 396, *pg.* 1179
FRONTIER COMMUNICATIONS OF NEW YORK, INC., 180 S Clinton Ave Frontier Ctr, **Rochester,** NY 14646-0700, *pg.* 398, *pg.* 1335
GRAPHIC CONTROLS LLC, 400 Exchange St, **Buffalo,** NY 14204-2064, *pg.* 401, *pg.* 1148
GUARDSMARK, LLC, 10 Rockefeller Plz 12th Fl, **New York,** NY 10020, *pg.* 401, *pg.* 1237
GUIDELINE, INC., 625 Ave of the Americas, **New York,** NY 10011-2020, *pg.* 402, *pg.* 1237
H&S BUSINESS EXPRESS INC., One Blue Hill Plaza, 2nd Fl, **Pearl River,** NY 10965, *pg.* 402, *pg.* 1320
HAUPPAUGE DIGITAL, INC., 91 Cabot Ct, **Hauppauge,** NY 11788-3717, *pg.* 402, *pg.* 1164
INFORMATION BUILDERS INC., 2 Penn Plz, **New York,** NY 10121-0101, *pg.* 415, *pg.* 1243
INTERNATIONAL BUSINESS MACHINES CORPORATION, 1 New Orchard Rd, **Armonk,** NY 10504, *pg.* 418, *pg.* 1138
INTRALINKS INC., 150 E 42nd St 8th Fl, **New York,** NY 10017, *pg.* 420, *pg.* 1244
ITUS CORPORATION, 900 Walt Whitman Rd, **Melville,** NY 11747, *pg.* 422, *pg.* 1180
JACOBY & MEYERS LLP, 436 Robinson Ave, **Newburgh,** NY 12550-3341, *pg.* 423, *pg.* 1317
JUSTWORKS, INC., 29 E 19th St, 7th Fl, **New York,** NY 10003, *pg.* 424, *pg.* 1247
KROLL INC., 1166 6th Ave, **New York,** NY 10036, *pg.* 425, *pg.* 1249
MC2, 3 Alpine Ct, **Chestnut Ridge,** NY 10977, *pg.* 431, *pg.* 1153
MEADWESTVACO CORP. - OFFICE PRODUCTS GROUP, 101 ONeil Rd, **Sidney,** NY 13838-1055, *pg.* 431, *pg.* 1342
MEDIDATA SOLUTIONS, INC., 79 Fifth Ave 8th Fl, **New York,** NY 10003, *pg.* 431, *pg.* 1258
MOTOROLA ENTERPRISE MOBILITY, 1 Motorola Plz, **Holtsville,** NY 11742-1300, *pg.* 441, *pg.* 1167
NETSMART TECHNOLOGIES, INC., 3500 Sunrise Hwy Ste D-122, **Great River,** NY 11739, *pg.* 445, *pg.* 1163
OPENLINK FINANCIAL, INC., 1502 RXR Plz 8h Fl W Tower, **Uniondale,** NY 11556, *pg.* 449, *pg.* 1346
PAR TECHNOLOGY CORPORATION, PAR Technology Park 8383 Seneca Tpke, **New Hartford,** NY 13413-4991, *pg.* 452, *pg.* 1183
PERMISSION DATA, 451 Park Ave S 3rd Fl, **New York,** NY 10016, *pg.* 454, *pg.* 1278
PITNEY BOWES SOFTWARE INC., 1 Global View, **Troy,** NY 12180-8399, *pg.* 455, *pg.* 1346
RETURN PATH, INC., 304 Park Ave S 7th Fl, **New York,** NY 10010-4311, *pg.* 461, *pg.* 1285
RUSSELL REYNOLDS ASSOCIATES INC., 200 Park Ave 23rd Fl, **New York,** NY 10166-2399, *pg.* 463, *pg.* 1287
SENTRY GROUP, INC., 900 Linden Ave, **Rochester,** NY 14625-2700, *pg.* 468, *pg.* 1337
SIEMENS ENERGY, INC., 400 State St, **Schenectady,** NY 12301-1058, *pg.* 469, *pg.* 1341
SOTHEBY'S INC., 1334 York Ave, **New York,** NY 10021, *pg.* 472, *pg.* 1294
SOVRAN SELF STORAGE, INC., 6467 Main St, **Williamsville,** NY 14221, *pg.* 472, *pg.* 1355
THE STAPLEX COMPANY, INC., 777 5th Ave, **Brooklyn,** NY 11232, *pg.* 474, *pg.* 1146
SYSTEMAX, INC., 11 Harbor Park Dr, **Port Washington,** NY 11050-4650, *pg.* 481, *pg.* 1324
TAKE-TWO INTERACTIVE SOFTWARE, INC., 622 Broadway, **New York,** NY 10012-3230, *pg.* 481, *pg.* 1297
TELEBYTE, INC., 355 Marcus Blvd, **Hauppauge,** NY 11788, *pg.* 482, *pg.* 1165
THE TELX GROUP, INC., 1 State St 21st Fl, **New York,** NY 10004, *pg.* 483, *pg.* 1298
THINAIRE TRANSMEDIA NETWORK, LLC, 650 5th Ave 9th Fl, **New York,** NY 10104, *pg.* 483, *pg.* 1299
TRANSLATIONS.COM, 3 Park Ave, **New York,** NY 10016-5902, *pg.* 485, *pg.* 1304
ULTIMATE TECHNOLOGY CORPORATION, 100 Rawson Rd, **Victor,** NY 14564-1170, *pg.* 486, *pg.* 1349
VAN SON HOLLAND INK CORPORATION OF AMERICA, 185 Oval Dr, **Islandia,** NY 11749, *pg.* 487, *pg.* 1169
VERINT SYSTEMS INC., 330 S Service Rd, **Melville,** NY 11747, *pg.* 488, *pg.* 1182
VIATECH PUBLISHING SOLUTIONS, 1440 5th Ave, **Bay Shore,** NY 11706, *pg.* 489, *pg.* 1141
VOLT INFORMATION SCIENCES, INC., 1065 Ave 20th Fl, **New York,** NY 10022-6828, *pg.* 490, *pg.* 1312
WESTCON GROUP, INC., 520 White Plains Rd, 2 Fl, **Tarrytown,** NY 10591-5116, *pg.* 492, *pg.* 1345
ZOOM TECHNOLOGIES, INC., 1345 Ave of the Americas, **New York,** NY 10105, *pg.* 497, *pg.* 1317

North Carolina

BANDWIDTH.COM, INC., 900 Main Campus Dr, **Raleigh,** NC 27606, *pg.* 360, *pg.* 1386
CAROLINA WHOLESALE OFFICE MACHINE COMPANY, INC., 425 E Arrowhead Dr, **Charlotte,** NC 28213-6378, *pg.* 369, *pg.* 1364
CICERO INC., 8000 Regency Pkwy, **Cary,** NC 27518, *pg.* 372, *pg.* 1360
INDUSTRIAL DISTRIBUTION GROUP, INC., 2100 The Oaks Pkwy, **Belmont,** NC 28012, *pg.* 413, *pg.* 1358
LENOVO GROUP LTD, 1009 Think Pl, **Morrisville,** NC 27560, *pg.* 427, *pg.* 1384
NETWORK SYSTEMS INTERNATIONAL, INC., 3859 Battleground Ave Suite 301, **Greensboro,** NC 27401, *pg.* 445, *pg.* 1375
PROGRESS DATADIRECT, 3005 Carrington Mill Blvd Ste 400, **Morrisville,** NC 27560, *pg.* 457, *pg.* 1385
RED HAT, INC., 100 E Davie St, **Raleigh,** NC 27601, *pg.* 460, *pg.* 1388
SALES PERFORMANCE INTERNATIONAL, INC., 6201 Fairview Rd Ste 400, **Charlotte,** NC 28210, *pg.* 464, *pg.* 1368
SAS INSTITUTE INC., SAS Campus Dr, **Cary,** NC 27513-2414, *pg.* 466, *pg.* 1361
SCIQUEST, INC., 6501 Weston Pkwy Ste 200, **Cary,** NC 27513, *pg.* 468, *pg.* 1361
SYNACOR, INC., 16810 Kenton Dr Ste 240, **Huntersville,** NC 28078-4845, *pg.* 479, *pg.* 1380
WORKPLACE OPTIONS, 3020 Highwood Blvd, **Raleigh,** NC 27604, *pg.* 493, *pg.* 1389

Ohio

AUTOMATION MAILING AND SHIPPING SOLUTIONS, INC., 1138-58 W 9th St, **Cleveland,** OH 44113-1060, *pg.* 358, *pg.* 1428
BAE SYSTEMS MOBILITY & PROTECTION SYSTEMS, 9113 LeSaint Dr, **Fairfield,** OH 45014-5453, *pg.* 359, *pg.* 1452
BAUMFOLDER CORPORATION, 1660 Campbell Rd, **Sidney,** OH 45365, *pg.* 360, *pg.* 1472
CINCOM SYSTEMS, INC., 55 Merchant St, **Cincinnati,** OH 45246-3732, *pg.* 372, *pg.* 1411
CINTAS CORPORATION, 6800 Cintas Blvd, **Cincinnati,** OH 45262-5737, *pg.* 372, *pg.* 1411
CONVERGYS CORPORATION, 201 E 4th St, **Cincinnati,** OH 45202, *pg.* 379, *pg.* 1412
DATATRAK INTERNATIONAL, INC., 5900 Landerbrook Dr, Ste 170, **Mayfield Heights,** OH 44124, *pg.* 383, *pg.* 1462
DEE SIGN COMPANY, 6163 Allen Rd, **West Chester,** OH 45069-3855, *pg.* 383, *pg.* 1479
DIEBOLD, INCORPORATED, 5995 Mayfair Rd, **Canton,** OH 44720-1550, *pg.* 387, *pg.* 1407
HENKEL CONSUMER ADHESIVES, INC., 26235 First St, **Westlake,** OH 44145, *pg.* 403, *pg.* 1480
HYLAND SOFTWARE, INC., 28500 Clemens Rd, **Westlake,** OH 44145, *pg.* 409, *pg.* 1480
IBM, 4600 Lakehurst Ct, **Dublin,** OH 43016-3255, *pg.* 410, *pg.* 1449
JONES DAY, North Point Bldg 901 Lakeside Ave, **Cleveland,** OH 44114-1190, *pg.* 423, *pg.* 1431
MEADWESTVACO CONSUMER & OFFICE PRODUCTS, 4751 Hempstead Sta Dr, **Kettering,** OH 45429, *pg.* 431, *pg.* 1456
PUBCO CORPORATION, 3830 Kelley Ave, **Cleveland,** OH 44114, *pg.* 457, *pg.* 1434
THE REYNOLDS & REYNOLDS COMPANY, 1 Reynolds Way, **Kettering,** OH 45430, *pg.* 461, *pg.* 1457
THE STANDARD REGISTER COMPANY, 600 Albany St, **Dayton,** OH 45401, *pg.* 473, *pg.* 1446
TERADATA CORPORATION, 10000 Innovation Dr, **Dayton,** OH 45342, *pg.* 483, *pg.* 1447

Oklahoma

BHI ENERGY, 7633 E 63rd Pl Ste 400, **Tulsa,** OK 74133-1272, *pg.* 361, *pg.* 1489

Oregon

GEMSTONE SYSTEMS, INC., 1260 NW Waterhouse Ave Ste 200, **Beaverton,** OR 97006-5794, *pg.* 400, *pg.* 1492
MENTOR GRAPHICS CORPORATION, 8005 SW Boeckman Rd, **Wilsonville,** OR 97070-9733, *pg.* 432, *pg.* 1510
MILLER, NASH, WIENER, HAGER & CARLSEN, 111 SW Fifth Ave, **Portland,** OR 97204, *pg.* 440, *pg.* 1504
NUVIEW WEST, 855 SW Yates Dr Ste 201, **Bend,** OR 97702, *pg.* 447, *pg.* 1496
PLANAR SYSTEMS, INC., 1195 NW Compton Dr, **Beaverton,** OR 97006-1992, *pg.* 455, *pg.* 1495
RADISYS CORPORATION, 5445 NE Dawson Creek Dr, **Hillsboro,** OR 97124, *pg.* 458, *pg.* 1498
STRUCTURED COMMUNICATION SYSTEMS, INC., 12901 se 97 Ave Ste 400, **Clackamas,** OR 97015, *pg.* 477, *pg.* 1497
TRIPWIRE, INC., 101 SW Main St Ste 1500, **Portland,** OR 97204, *pg.* 485, *pg.* 1507

Pennsylvania

ALLIN CORPORATION, 381 Mansfield Ave, **Pittsburgh,** PA 15220, *pg.* 347, *pg.* 1572
ALTEC LANSING LLC, Rte 6 & 209, **Milford,** PA 18337-0277, *pg.* 348, *pg.* 1553
AMERICAN THERMOPLASTIC COMPANY, 106 Gamma Dr, **Pittsburgh,** PA 15238-2920, *pg.* 349, *pg.* 1573
ASTEA INTERNATIONAL INC., 240 Gibraltar Rd, **Horsham,** PA 19044-2306, *pg.* 355, *pg.* 1540
BENTLEY SYSTEMS, INC., 685 Stockton Dr, **Exton,** PA 19341-0678, *pg.* 361, *pg.* 1531
BLACK BOX CORPORATION, 1000 Park Dr, **Lawrence,** PA 15055-1018, *pg.* 361, *pg.* 1547
BRODART CO., 500 Arch St, **Williamsport,** PA 17701-7809, *pg.* 366, *pg.* 1594
CORBY INDUSTRIES, INC., 812 N Gilmore St, **Allentown,** PA 18109, *pg.* 380, *pg.* 1513
D&H DISTRIBUTING CO., INC., 2525 N 7th St, **Harrisburg,** PA 17110-2511, *pg.* 381, *pg.* 1536
DATALOGIC, 511 School House Rd, **Telford,** PA 18969-1148, *pg.* 382, *pg.* 1588
ESSINTIAL ENTERPRISE SOLUTIONS, One Sterling Place 100 Sterling Pkwy Ste 100, **Mechanicsburg,** PA 17050, *pg.* 395, *pg.* 1552
FIDELITY NATIONAL INFORMATION SERVICES, 2 W Liberty Ste 300, **Malvern,** PA 19355, *pg.* 397, *pg.* 1549
GREAT LAKES CASE & CABINET CO., INC., PO Box 551, **Edinboro,** PA 16412, *pg.* 401, *pg.* 1529
THE JUDGE GROUP, INC., 4 Falls Corp Ctr 300 Conshohocken State Rd, **West Conshohocken,** PA 19428-2949, *pg.* 424, *pg.* 1594
KNOLL, INC., 1235 Water St, **East Greenville,** PA 18041, *pg.* 425, *pg.* 1527
MANAGEMENT RECRUITERS INTERNATIONAL, INC., 1717 Arch St 36th Fl, **Philadelphia,** PA 19103, *pg.* 429, *pg.* 1567
MEDECISION, INC., 601 Lee Rd Chesterbrook Corporate Center, **Wayne,** PA 19087, *pg.* 431, *pg.* 1592
MEDSTAFF, INC., 3805 W Chester Pike Ste 200, **Newtown Square,** PA 19073, *pg.* 431, *pg.* 1556
MONROE SYSTEMS FOR BUSINESS, 2530-B Pearl Buck Rd, **Bristol,** PA 19007-6809, *pg.* 441, *pg.* 1518
MOORE PUSH PIN CO., 1300 E Mermaid Ln, **Wyndmoor,** PA 19038-7664, *pg.* 441, *pg.* 1595
QLIK TECHNOLOGIES INC., 150 N Radnor Chester Rd Ste E-220, **Radnor,** PA 19087, *pg.* 457, *pg.* 1583
RICHARDSON GROUP INC., 1818 Market St Ste 2800, **Philadelphia,** PA 19103, *pg.* 461, *pg.* 1570
RICOH AMERICA, 70 Valley Stream Pkwy, **Malvern,** PA 19355-1407, *pg.* 461, *pg.* 1550
SAFEGUARD SCIENTIFICS, INC., 435 Devon Park Dr Bldg 800, **Wayne,** PA 19087-1945, *pg.* 464, *pg.* 1592
SAP AMERICA, INC., 3999 W Chester Pke, **Newtown Square,** PA 19073, *pg.* 466, *pg.* 1557
SIEMENS MEDICAL SOLUTIONS USA, INC., 51 Valley Stream Pkwy, **Malvern,** PA 19355, *pg.* 469, *pg.* 1550
SUNGARD DATA SYSTEMS INC., 680 E Swedesford Rd, **Wayne,** PA 19087, *pg.* 477, *pg.* 1592
SYNYGY, INC., 2501 Seaport Dr Ste 100, **Chester,** PA 19013-2249, *pg.* 481, *pg.* 1521
TRANSCORE HOLDINGS INC., 8158 Adams Dr, **Hummelstown,** PA 17036, *pg.* 485, *pg.* 1541
UBICS, INC., 333 Technology Dr Ste 210, **Canonsburg,** PA 15317-9513, *pg.* 486, *pg.* 1520
UNISYS CORPORATION, 801 Lakeview Dr Ste 100, **Blue Bell,** PA 19422, *pg.* 487, *pg.* 1517
WIZZARD SPEECH LLC., 5001 Baum Blvd Ste 770, **Pittsburgh,** PA 15213, *pg.* 493, *pg.* 1582

Rhode Island

A. T. CROSS COMPANY, 1 Albion Rd, **Lincoln,** RI 02865-3703, *pg.* 339, *pg.* 1602
ELECTRO STANDARDS LABORATORIES INC., 36 W Indus Dr, **Cranston,** RI 02921-3403, *pg.* 390, *pg.* 1600
INTERNATIONAL GAME TECHNOLOGY, 10 Memorial Blvd, **Providence,** RI 02903, *pg.* 420, *pg.* 1606
SCHNEIDER ELECTRIC, 132 Fairgrounds Rd, **West Kingston,** RI 02892, *pg.* 467, *pg.* 1609

South Carolina

3D SYSTEMS CORPORATION, 333 Three D Systems Cir, **Rock Hill,** SC 29730, *pg.* 339, *pg.* 1621
BLACKBAUD, INC., 2000 Daniel Island Dr, **Charleston,** SC 29492, *pg.* 361, *pg.* 1613

Tennessee

DURA-LINE HOLDINGS, 11400 Parkside Dr Ste 300, **Knoxville,** TN 37934, *pg.* 389, *pg.* 1636
MMODAL INC., 9009 Carothers Pkwy, **Franklin,** TN 37067, *pg.* 441, *pg.* 1633
SITEL CORPORATION, 2 American Center 3102 W End Ave Ste 1000, **Nashville,** TN 37203-1324, *pg.* 470, *pg.* 1654
STINGER MEDICAL LLC, 1152 Park Ave, **Murfreesboro,** TN 37129-4912, *pg.* 476, *pg.* 1648
TEAM HEALTH, INC., 1900 Winston Rd Ste 300, **Knoxville,** TN 37919-3606, *pg.* 482, *pg.* 1639

Texas

ABILA, INC., 10800 Pecan Park Blvd Ste 400, **Austin,** TX 78750, *pg.* 340, *pg.* 1660
ALLIANCE DATA SYSTEMS CORPORATION, 7500 Dallas Pkwy Ste 700, **Plano,** TX 75024, *pg.* 347, *pg.* 1729
ALTEX ELECTRONICS, LTD., 11342 IH 35 N, **San Antonio,** TX 78233, *pg.* 348, *pg.* 1739
AMERICAN ELECTRIC TECHNOLOGIES, INC., 6410 Long Dr, **Houston,** TX 77087, *pg.* 349, *pg.* 1700
AMX CORPORATION, 3000 Research Dr, **Richardson,** TX 75082-3546, *pg.* 349, *pg.* 1735
ASURE SOFTWARE, INC., 110 Wild Basin Dr Ste 100, **Austin,** TX 78746, *pg.* 355, *pg.* 1660
BANCTEC, INC., 2701 E Grauwyler Rd, **Irving,** TX 75061-3414, *pg.* 360, *pg.* 1717
BMC SOFTWARE, INC., 2101 Citywest Blvd, **Houston,** TX 77042-2827, *pg.* 362, *pg.* 1701
BRANDMUSCLE, INC., 11149 Research Blvd Ste 400, **Austin,** TX 78759, *pg.* 364, *pg.* 1660
COMPUCOM SYSTEMS, INC., 7171 Forest Ln, **Dallas,** TX 75230-2306, *pg.* 378, *pg.* 1678
DAWSON GEOPHYSICAL COMPANY, 508 W Wall St Ste 800, **Midland,** TX 79701-5034, *pg.* 383, *pg.* 1727
DELL INC., 1 Dell Way, **Round Rock,** TX 78682-7000, *pg.* 383, *pg.* 1737
DOUGLAS-GUARDIAN SERVICES CORPORATION, 14800 St Marys Ln Ste 200, **Houston,** TX 77079-2936, *pg.* 388, *pg.* 1704
ECORA SOFTWARE CORPORATION, 6011 W Courtyard Dr Ste 300, **Austin,** TX 78730, *pg.* 389, *pg.* 1662
EF JOHNSON TECHNOLOGIES, INC., 1440 Corporate Dr, **Irving,** TX 75038, *pg.* 390, *pg.* 1718
ENNIS, INC., 2441 Presidential Pkwy, **Midlothian,** TX 76065, *pg.* 393, *pg.* 1727
ENTRUST, INC., One Lincoln Centre 5400 LBJ Fwy Ste 1340, **Dallas,** TX 75240, *pg.* 393, *pg.* 1680
FEDEX OFFICE & PRINT SERVICES, INC., 3 Galleria Tower 13155 Noel Rd Ste 1600, **Dallas,** TX 75240, *pg.* 396, *pg.* 1681
FREESCALE SEMICONDUCTOR, INC., 6501 William Cannon Dr W, **Austin,** TX 78735, *pg.* 398, *pg.* 1662
GAMESTOP CORP., 625 Westport Pkwy, **Grapevine,** TX 76051, *pg.* 399, *pg.* 1699
GLOBALSCAPE INC., 4500 Lockhill-Selma Ste 150, **San Antonio,** TX 78249, *pg.* 401, *pg.* 1740
HP ENTERPRISE SERVICES, LLC, 5400 Legacy Dr, **Plano,** TX 75024-3105, *pg.* 409, *pg.* 1731
IFCO SYSTEMS NORTH AMERICA, 13100 NW Freeway Ste 625, **Houston,** TX 77040, *pg.* 411, *pg.* 1708
IMPRESO, INC., 652 Southwestern Blvd, **Coppell,** TX 75019-4419, *pg.* 413, *pg.* 1671
INSIGHT ENTERPRISES, INC., 3480 Lotus Dr, **Plano,** TX 75075, *pg.* 416, *pg.* 1732
INSPERITY, INC., 19001 Crescent Springs Dr, **Kingwood,** TX 77339-3802, *pg.* 416, *pg.* 1725
INTERPHASE CORPORATION, 2901 N Dallas Pkwy Ste 200, **Plano,** TX 75093, *pg.* 420, *pg.* 1732
MANPOWER GROUP, 4400 Post Oak Pkwy Ste 1800, **Houston,** TX 77027-3421, *pg.* 430, *pg.* 1710
MULTIMEDIA GAMES INC., Bldg B Ste 400 206 Wild Basin Rd S, **Austin,** TX 78746, *pg.* 442, *pg.* 1664
MURATEC AMERICA, INC., 3301 E Plano Pkwy Ste 100, **Plano,** TX 75074, *pg.* 443, *pg.* 1733
NATIONAL INSTRUMENTS CORPORATION, 11500 N Mopac Expy Bldg B, **Austin,** TX 78759-3504, *pg.* 443, *pg.* 1664
NOVATION LLC, 125 E John Carpenter Freeway, **Irving,** TX 75062, *pg.* 446, *pg.* 1723
OMNITRACS, LLC, 717 N Harwood St, Ste 1300, **Dallas,** TX 75201, *pg.* 449, *pg.* 1685
OPENCONNECT SYSTEMS, INC., 2711 Lyndon B Johnson Fwy Ste 700, **Dallas,** TX 75234-7323, *pg.* 449, *pg.* 1685
OPENTEXT, 1301 S Mopac Expwy Ste 150, **Austin,** TX 78746, *pg.* 450, *pg.* 1665
PEGASUS SOLUTIONS, INC., 5430 Lyndon B Johnson Fwy, Ste 1100, **Dallas,** TX 75240, *pg.* 452, *pg.* 1685
PRESIDIO, 1955 Lakeway Dr, **Lewisville,** TX 75057, *pg.* 456, *pg.* 1725
RECURSION SOFTWARE, INC., 2591 N Dallas Pkwy Ste 200, **Frisco,** TX 75034, *pg.* 460, *pg.* 1697
SAFEGUARD BUSINESS SYSTEMS, INC., 8585 N Stemmons Fwy Ste 600N, **Dallas,** TX 75247, *pg.* 464, *pg.* 1686
SCALABLE SOFTWARE, INC., 421 E 6th St, Ste B, **Austin,** TX 78701, *pg.* 467, *pg.* 1665
SIEMENS PLM SOFTWARE, 5800 Granite Pkwy Ste 600, **Plano,** TX 75024, *pg.* 469, *pg.* 1734
SNELLING STAFFING SERVICES, 12801 N Central Expy Ste 600, **Dallas,** TX 75243-1726, *pg.* 471, *pg.* 1686
SOFTLAYER TECHNOLOGIES INC, 4849 Alpha Rd, **Dallas,** TX 75244, *pg.* 471, *pg.* 1686
SOLARWINDS, INC., 3711 S MoPac Expressway, **Austin,** TX 78746, *pg.* 471, *pg.* 1666
TELETOUCH COMMUNICATIONS, INC., 5718 Airport Freeway, **Fort Worth,** TX 76117, *pg.* 483, *pg.* 1696
TYLER TECHNOLOGIES, INC., 5949 Sherry Ln Ste 1400, **Dallas,** TX 75225-8010, *pg.* 486, *pg.* 1690
WARRANTECH CORPORATION, 2200 Hwy 121, **Bedford,** TX 76021, *pg.* 491, *pg.* 1668
XPLORE TECHNOLOGIES CORP., 14000 Summit Dr Ste 900, **Austin,** TX 78728, *pg.* 497, *pg.* 1667
ZILLIANT, INC., 3815 S Capital Texas Hwy Ste 300, **Austin,** TX 78704, *pg.* 497, *pg.* 1668
ZIX CORPORATION, 2711 N Haskell Ave Ste 2300, **Dallas,** TX 75204-2911, *pg.* 497, *pg.* 1691

Utah

ALLEN COMMUNICATION LEARNING SERVICES, INC., 175 W 200 S Ste 100, **Salt Lake City,** UT 84101, *pg.* 346, *pg.* 1755
AUTHORIZE.NET HOLDINGS, INC., 808 E Utah Valley Dr, **American Fork,** UT 84003, *pg.* 356, *pg.* 1751
CIMETRIX INCORPORATED, 6979 S High Tech Dr, **Salt Lake City,** UT 84047-3757, *pg.* 372, *pg.* 1756
EVANS & SUTHERLAND COMPUTER CORPORATION - DIGITAL THEATER DIVISION, 770 Komas Dr, **Salt Lake City,** UT 84108-1229, *pg.* 395, *pg.* 1757
INCONTACT, INC., 7730 S Union Park Ave Ste 500, **Midvale,** UT 84047, *pg.* 413, *pg.* 1752
INTEGRACORE, INC., 6077 W Wells Park Rd, **West Jordan,** UT 84081, *pg.* 416, *pg.* 1763
PARK CITY GROUP, INC., 299 S Main St, Ste 2370, **Salt Lake City,** UT 84111, *pg.* 452, *pg.* 1760
SIRSIDYNIX CORPORATION, 3300 N Ashton Blvd Ste 500, **Lehi,** UT 84043, *pg.* 470, *pg.* 1751
SUPPLEMENTAL HEALTH CARE SERVICES, INC., 1640 Redstone Ctr Dr Ste 200, **Park City,** UT 84098, *pg.* 478, *pg.* 1754

First page reference indicates Business Class Edition
Second page reference indicates Geographic Edition

SYMANTEC CORPORATION, 1359 N Research Way Bldg K, **Orem,** UT 84059, *pg.* 479, *pg.* 1753

Vermont

GE HEALTHCARE, 40 IDX Dr, **Burlington,** VT 05402, *pg.* 399, *pg.* 1765

Virginia

ANACOMP, INC., 3675 Concorde Parkway Suite 1500, **Chantilly,** VA 20151, *pg.* 350, *pg.* 1777

AT&T GOVERNMENT SOLUTIONS, 1900 Gallows Rd, **Vienna,** VA 22182-3865, *pg.* 355, *pg.* 1809

BOOZ ALLEN HAMILTON INC, 8283 Greensboro Dr, **McLean,** VA 22102-4904, *pg.* 363, *pg.* 1788

THE BRINK'S COMPANY, 1801 Bayberry Ct, **Richmond,** VA 23226-8100, *pg.* 364, *pg.* 1800

CACI INTERNATIONAL INC., 1100 N Glebe Rd, **Arlington,** VA 22201-4798, *pg.* 367, *pg.* 1773

CGI TECHNOLOGIES & SOLUTIONS INC., 1130 Random Hills, **Fairfax,** VA 22033, *pg.* 371, *pg.* 1779

COMPUTER SCIENCES CORPORATION, 3170 Fairview Park Dr, **Falls Church,** VA 22042, *pg.* 378, *pg.* 1780

DELTEK, INC., 2291 Wood Oak Dr, **Herndon,** VA 20171, *pg.* 386, *pg.* 1784

EMPLOYMENT ENTERPRISES INC., 10550 Linden Lake Plz Ste 200, **Manassas,** VA 20109-6495, *pg.* 392, *pg.* 1787

GLOBALLOGIC, INC., 1420 Spring Hill Rd Ste 155, **McLean,** VA 22102, *pg.* 400, *pg.* 1791

HEADSTRONG CORPORATION, One Fountain Sq 11911 Freedom Dr Ste 900, **Reston,** VA 20190, *pg.* 403, *pg.* 1798

INFERX CORPORATION, 46950 Jennings Farm Dr Ste 290, **Sterling,** VA 20164, *pg.* 414, *pg.* 1807

INTEGRATED SYSTEMS ANALYSTS, INC., Ste 600 2001 N Beauregard St, **Alexandria,** VA 22311-1722, *pg.* 416, *pg.* 1771

KNOWLOGY CORPORATION, 1934 Old Gallows Rd, 2nd Fl, **Vienna,** VA 22182, *pg.* 425, *pg.* 1809

MYBIZOFFICE, INC, 13454 Sunrise Vly Dr 5th Fl, **Herndon,** VA 20171, *pg.* 443, *pg.* 1785

PERCEPTIVE SOFTWARE, 20110 Ashbrook Pl Ste 150, **Ashburn,** VA 20147, *pg.* 453, *pg.* 1775

PROGRESSIVE NURSING STAFFERS INC., 5531 B Hempstead Way, **Springfield,** VA 22151, *pg.* 457, *pg.* 1807

ROSETTA STONE INC., 1919 N Lynn St 7th Floor, **Arlington,** VA 22209, *pg.* 462, *pg.* 1774

SAIC, INC., 1710 SAIC Dr, **McLean,** VA 22102, *pg.* 464, *pg.* 1794

SIGHTLINE SYSTEMS CORPORATION, 4035 Ridge Top Rd, Ste 510, **Fairfax,** VA 22030, *pg.* 469, *pg.* 1780

SOFTWARE AG, INC., 11700 Plaza America Dr Ste 700, **Reston,** VA 20191-5453, *pg.* 471, *pg.* 1799

SRA INTERNATIONAL, INC., 4300 Fair Lakes Ct, **Fairfax,** VA 22033-4232, *pg.* 473, *pg.* 1780

STEELCLOUD, INC., 20110 Ashbrook Place Ste 270, **Ashburn,** VA 20147, *pg.* 476, *pg.* 1776

TELOS CORPORATION, 19886 Ashburn Rd, **Ashburn,** VA 20147-2358, *pg.* 483, *pg.* 1776

UNIFIEDONLINE, INC., 4216 Leonard Dr, **Fairfax,** VA 22030, *pg.* 486, *pg.* 1780

VERISIGN, INC., 12061 Bluemont Way, **Reston,** VA 20190, *pg.* 488, *pg.* 1799

VERTICAL SEARCH WORKS INC., 1919 Gallows Rd Ste 1050, **Vienna,** VA 22182-3900, *pg.* 489, *pg.* 1809

XO COMMUNICATIONS, 13865 Sunrise Vly Rd, **Herndon,** VA 20171, *pg.* 497, *pg.* 1786

Washington

ALLSOP, INC., 4201 Meridian St, **Bellingham,** WA 98226, *pg.* 347, *pg.* 1817

ATTACHMATE CORPORATION, 705 5th Ave S, Ste 1100, **Seattle,** WA 98104, *pg.* 356, *pg.* 1833

BARRETT BUSINESS SERVICES, INC., 8100 NE Parkway Dr Ste 200, **Vancouver,** WA 98662, *pg.* 360, *pg.* 1845

BSQUARE CORPORATION, 110 110th Ave NE Ste 202, **Bellevue,** WA 98004-5840, *pg.* 366, *pg.* 1813

CORBIS CORPORATION, 710 2nd Ave Ste 200, **Seattle,** WA 98104, *pg.* 380, *pg.* 1834

CRAY INC., 901 Fifth Ave Suite 1000, **Seattle,** WA 98164, *pg.* 380, *pg.* 1834

DATA I/O CORPORATION, 6464 185th Ave NE Ste 101, **Redmond,** WA 98052-2545, *pg.* 382, *pg.* 1824

ENVISION, 901 5th Ave Ste 3300, **Seattle,** WA 98104, *pg.* 393, *pg.* 1835

F5 NETWORKS, INC., 401 Elliott Ave W, **Seattle,** WA 98119, *pg.* 396, *pg.* 1835

INTELIUS, INC., 500 108th Ave NE 25th Fl, **Bellevue,** WA 98004, *pg.* 416, *pg.* 1815

INTELLICHECK MOBILISA, INC., 191 Otto St, **Port Townsend,** WA 98368, *pg.* 416, *pg.* 1823

INTERMEDIA, 11201 SE 8th St Ste 200, **Bellevue,** WA 98004, *pg.* 417, *pg.* 1815

ITRON INC., 2111 N Molter Rd, **Liberty Lake,** WA 99019, *pg.* 422, *pg.* 1822

KEY TRONIC CORPORATION, N 4424 Sullivan Rd Lower Level, **Spokane,** WA 99216-1593, *pg.* 424, *pg.* 1844

LAPLINK SOFTWARE, INC., 600 108th Ave NE Ste 610, **Bellevue,** WA 98004-5125, *pg.* 426, *pg.* 1815

MICROSOFT CORPORATION, 1 Microsoft Way, **Redmond,** WA 98052-6399, *pg.* 435, *pg.* 1824

NETMOTION WIRELESS, INC., 701 N 34th St Ste 250, **Seattle,** WA 98103, *pg.* 445, *pg.* 1837

REALNETWORKS, INC., 2601 Elliott Ave Ste 1000, **Seattle,** WA 98121-3306, *pg.* 460, *pg.* 1839

TABLEAU SOFTWARE, INC., 837 N 34th St Ste 200, **Seattle,** WA 98103, *pg.* 481, *pg.* 1841

TRUEBLUE, INC., 1015 A St, **Tacoma,** WA 98402, *pg.* 485, *pg.* 1845

VALVE CORPORATION, PO Box 1688, **Bellevue,** WA 98009, *pg.* 487, *pg.* 1817

WATCHGUARD TECHNOLOGIES, INC., 505 5th Ave S Ste 500, **Seattle,** WA 98104-3892, *pg.* 491, *pg.* 1842

Wisconsin

ALTA RESOURCES CORPORATION, 120 N Commercial St, **Neenah,** WI 54956, *pg.* 347, *pg.* 1882

AMERICAN APPRAISAL ASSOCIATES, INC., 411 E Wisconsin Ave Ste 1900, **Milwaukee,** WI 53202-4466, *pg.* 349, *pg.* 1872

API HEALTHCARE CORP., 1550 Innovation Way, **Hartford,** WI 53027-8720, *pg.* 350, *pg.* 1860

ARI NETWORK SERVICES, INC., 10850 W Pk Pl Ste 1200, **Milwaukee,** WI 53224, *pg.* 353, *pg.* 1873

BATTERIES PLUS BULBS LLC, 925 Walnut Ridge Dr, **Hartland,** WI 53029, *pg.* 360, *pg.* 1860

BRADY CORPORATION, 6555 W Good Hope Rd, **Milwaukee,** WI 53223, *pg.* 363, *pg.* 1873

DEMCO INC., 4810 Forest Run Rd, **Madison,** WI 53704-7336, *pg.* 386, *pg.* 1865

ELECTRONIC TELE-COMMUNICATIONS, INC., 1915 MacArthur Rd, **Waukesha,** WI 53188-5702, *pg.* 390, *pg.* 1897

ESKER, INC., Ste 350 1212 Deming Way, **Madison,** WI 53717-1984, *pg.* 395, *pg.* 1865

FISERV, INC., 255 Fiserv Dr, **Brookfield,** WI 53045-5815, *pg.* 397, *pg.* 1855

INVINCIBLE OFFICE FURNITURE, 842 S 26th St, **Manitowoc,** WI 54220, *pg.* 420, *pg.* 1868

MANPOWER INC., 100 Manpower Place, **Milwaukee,** WI 53212, *pg.* 430, *pg.* 1877

PLEXUS CORP., 1 Plexus Way, **Neenah,** WI 54956, *pg.* 455, *pg.* 1883

PROFESSIONAL CONTROL CORPORATION, N11 4W 18770 Clinton Dr, **Germantown,** WI 53022-3118, *pg.* 456, *pg.* 1858

SCHOOL SPECIALTY, INC., W6316 Design Dr, **Greenville,** WI 54942-8404, *pg.* 467, *pg.* 1860

SONIC FOUNDRY, INC., 222 W Washington Ave Ste 775, **Madison,** WI 53703, *pg.* 472, *pg.* 1867

TAB PRODUCTS CO. LLC, 605 Fourth St, **Mayville,** WI 53050, *pg.* 481, *pg.* 1869

WESTERN STATES ENVELOPE & LABEL, 4480 N 132nd St, **Butler,** WI 53007-2099, *pg.* 492, *pg.* 1856

Cosmetics & Toiletries

Arizona

HENKEL CONSUMER GOODS, 7201 E Henkel Way, **Scottsdale,** AZ 85255, *pg.* 511, *pg.* 22
MASSAGE ENVY LIMITED, LLC, 14350 N 87th St Ste 200, **Scottsdale,** AZ 85260, *pg.* 516, *pg.* 23

Arkansas

AROMATIQUE INC., 3421 Hwy 25 N, **Heber Springs,** AR 72543, *pg.* 499, *pg.* 32

California

AMERICAN INTERNATIONAL INDUSTRIES COMPANY, 2220 Gaspar Ave, **Los Angeles,** CA 90040-1516, *pg.* 498, *pg.* 126
BARE ESCENTUALS, INC., 71 Stevenson St 22nd Flr, **San Francisco,** CA 94105, *pg.* 500, *pg.* 213
BENEFIT COSMETICS LLC, 685 Market St 7th Fl, **San Francisco,** CA 94105, *pg.* 501, *pg.* 213
THE COLOR FACTORY, INC., 8430 Tujunga Ave, **Sun Valley,** CA 91352-3108, *pg.* 505, *pg.* 281
CREATIVE NAIL DESIGN, INC., 1125 Joshua Way, **Vista,** CA 92081, *pg.* 506, *pg.* 302
DHC USA INC., 555 Montgomery St, Ste 1400, **San Francisco,** CA 94111, *pg.* 507, *pg.* 216
DOLLAR SHAVE CLUB, INC., PO Box 5688, **Santa Monica,** CA 90409-5688, *pg.* 507, *pg.* 273
THE ELTRON COMPANY, 3611 Cahuenga Blvd W, **Hollywood,** CA 90068, *pg.* 507, *pg.* 103
FANCL INTERNATIONAL, INC., 17138 Pullman St Ste 100, **Irvine,** CA 92614, *pg.* 509, *pg.* 110
JOHN PAUL MITCHELL SYSTEMS, 1888 Century Park E, Ste 1600, **Los Angeles,** CA 90067, *pg.* 512, *pg.* 133
KERSTIN FLORIAN, INC., 20492 Crescent Bay Dr Ste 100, **Lake Forest,** CA 92630, *pg.* 513, *pg.* 121
MARKWINS INTERNATIONAL CORP., 22067 Ferrero Pkwy, **City of Industry,** CA 91789, *pg.* 516, *pg.* 67
MERLE NORMAN COSMETICS, INC., 9130 Bellanca Ave, **Los Angeles,** CA 90045-4710, *pg.* 517, *pg.* 136
NEUTROGENA CORPORATION, 5760 W 96th St, **Los Angeles,** CA 90045, *pg.* 517, *pg.* 137
OPI PRODUCTS INC., 13034 Saticoy St, **North Hollywood,** CA 91605-3510, *pg.* 518, *pg.* 167
ORLY INTERNATIONAL, INC., 7710 Haskell Ave, **Los Angeles,** CA 91406, *pg.* 518, *pg.* 137
PLANET BEAUTY, 3199 Red Hill Ave Ste A, **Costa Mesa,** CA 92626, *pg.* 520, *pg.* 71
RODAN + FIELDS, LLC, 60 Spear St, Ste 600, **San Francisco,** CA 94105, *pg.* 522, *pg.* 225
SEPHORA USA INC, 525 Market St 11th Fl, **San Francisco,** CA 94105-2708, *pg.* 522, *pg.* 227
STEARNS PRODUCTS INC., 2130 Ward Ave, **Simi Valley,** CA 93063, *pg.* 523, *pg.* 279
STILA COSMETICS, 801 N Brand Blvd Ste 500, **Glendale,** CA 91203, *pg.* 523, *pg.* 99

Colorado

AMERICAN CREW, INC., 1515 Wazee St Ste 200, **Denver,** CO 80202-2705, *pg.* 498, *pg.* 316

Connecticut

BEIERSDORF NORTH AMERICA INC., Wilson Corp Ctr 187 Danbury Rd, **Wilton,** CT 06897, *pg.* 501, *pg.* 385
BIC CORPORATION, 1 BIC Way Ste 1, **Shelton,** CT 06484, *pg.* 501, *pg.* 369
BLYTH, INC., 1 E Weaver St, **Greenwich,** CT 06831, *pg.* 502, *pg.* 349
JOLEN CREME BLEACH CORP., 25 Walls Dr Ste 1, **Fairfield,** CT 06824, *pg.* 513, *pg.* 348
PARFUMS DE COEUR LTD., 6 High Ridge Pk, **Stamford,** CT 06905, *pg.* 519, *pg.* 376
THE W.E. BASSETT COMPANY, 100 Trap Falls Rd, **Shelton,** CT 06484, *pg.* 524, *pg.* 371
ZOTOS INTERNATIONAL, INC., 100 Tokeneke Rd, **Darien,** CT 06820-4825, *pg.* 524, *pg.* 345

District of Columbia

BLUEMERCURY, INC., 1010 Wisconsin Ave NW Ste 700, **Washington,** DC 20007, *pg.* 502, *pg.* 396

Florida

AUBREY ORGANICS INC., 5046 W Linebaugh Ave, **Tampa,** FL 33624, *pg.* 499, *pg.* 470
DS LABORATORIES, INC., 1680 Meridian Ave Ste 301, **Miami,** FL 33139, *pg.* 507, *pg.* 442
ELIZABETH ARDEN, INC., 2400 SW 145th Ave 2nd Fl, **Miramar,** FL 33027-4145, *pg.* 507, *pg.* 448
HAIR CLUB FOR MEN, LTD., INC., 1515 S Federal Hwy Ste 401, **Boca Raton,** FL 33432-7450, *pg.* 511, *pg.* 411
JAMES GRIFFITH SALON, 257 Tamiami Trl S, **Venice,** FL 34285, *pg.* 512, *pg.* 477
PARLUX FRAGRANCES, INC., 5900 N Andrews Ave Ste 500, **Fort Lauderdale,** FL 33309, *pg.* 519, *pg.* 426
PERFUMANIA, INC., 251 International Pkwy, **Sunrise,** FL 33325, *pg.* 520, *pg.* 469

Georgia

ALOETTE COSMETICS, INC., 3715 Northside Pkwy Bldg 200 Ste 200, **Atlanta,** GA 30327, *pg.* 498, *pg.* 487
GOODY PRODUCTS, INC., 3 Glenlake Pkwy, **Atlanta,** GA 30328, *pg.* 510, *pg.* 509

Illinois

BELL FLAVORS & FRAGRANCES, INC., 500 Academy Dr, **Northbrook,** IL 60062-2419, *pg.* 501, *pg.* 640
BLISTEX, INC., 1800 Swift Dr, **Oak Brook,** IL 60523-1574, *pg.* 502, *pg.* 644
FASHION FAIR COSMETICS, LLC, 820 S Michigan Ave, **Chicago,** IL 60605-2103, *pg.* 509, *pg.* 573
LUSTER PRODUCTS INC., 1104 W 43rd St, **Chicago,** IL 60609, *pg.* 515, *pg.* 581
MARILYN MIGLIN, L.P., 321 N Loomis St, **Chicago,** IL 60607, *pg.* 516, *pg.* 581
STA-RITE GINNIE LOU, INC., 245 E S 1st St, **Shelbyville,** IL 62565-2332, *pg.* 523, *pg.* 660
ULTA SALON, COSMETICS & FRAGRANCE, INC., 1000 Remington Blvd Ste 120, **Bolingbrook,** IL 60440, *pg.* 524, *pg.* 559
WAHL CLIPPER CORPORATION, 3001 N Locust St, **Sterling,** IL 61081, *pg.* 524, *pg.* 662

Indiana

ANNIE OAKLEY ENTERPRISES, INC., 300 Johnson St, **Ligonier,** IN 46767, *pg.* 499, *pg.* 693

Iowa

FRONTIER NATURAL PRODUCTS CO-OP, 3021 78th St, **Norway,** IA 52318, *pg.* 509, *pg.* 710

Kentucky

SUN TAN CITY, LLC, 445 E Market St, Ste 310, **Louisville,** KY 40202, *pg.* 523, *pg.* 738

Louisiana

PLANET BEACH FRANCHISING CORPORATION, 5145 Taravella Rd, **Marrero,** LA 70072, *pg.* 520, *pg.* 745

Maine

TOM'S OF MAINE, INC., 302 Lafayette Ctr, **Kennebunk,** ME 04043-0710, *pg.* 523, *pg.* 750

Maryland

COVER GIRL COSMETICS, 11050 York Rd, **Hunt Valley,** MD 21030-2005, *pg.* 506, *pg.* 772

Massachusetts

DESSANGE INTERNATIONAL, INC., 500 Cummings Ctr, Ste 1100, **Beverly,** MA 01915, *pg.* 506, *pg.* 787
THE GILLETTE COMPANY, 1 Gillette Park, **Boston,** MA 02127, *pg.* 509, *pg.* 795
INVERNESS CORPORATION, 49 Pearl St, **Attleboro,** MA 02703, *pg.* 512, *pg.* 783
LIVING PROOF, INC., 301 Binney St, 1st Fl, **Cambridge,** MA 02142, *pg.* 514, *pg.* 809

Michigan

RANIR LLC, 4701 E Paris Rd SE, **Grand Rapids,** MI 49512, *pg.* 520, *pg.* 888

Minnesota

AVEDA CORPORATION, 4000 Pheasant Ridge Dr NE, **Blaine,** MN 55449-7106, *pg.* 499, *pg.* 917
GREAT CLIPS, INC., 4400 W 78th St Ste 700, **Minneapolis,** MN 55435, *pg.* 510, *pg.* 937
REGIS CORPORATION, 7201 Metro Blvd, **Minneapolis,** MN 55439-2130, *pg.* 521, *pg.* 941
SUPERCUTS, INC., 7201 Metro Blvd, **Minneapolis,** MN 55439, *pg.* 523, *pg.* 942

Mississippi

J. STRICKLAND & COMPANY, 10420 Desoto Rd, **Olive Branch,** MS 38654-5301, *pg.* 512, *pg.* 970

Missouri

LUZIER PERSONALIZED COSMETICS, INC., 5601 E 135th St, **Grandview,** MO 64030, *pg.* 515, *pg.* 978

New Jersey

CCA INDUSTRIES, INC., 65 Challenger Rd, **Ridgefield Park,** NJ 07660, *pg.* 503, *pg.* 1114
CONAIR CORPORATION, 150 Milford Rd, **East Windsor,** NJ 08520, *pg.* 505, *pg.* 1055
E.T. BROWNE DRUG COMPANY, INC., 440 Sylvan Ave, **Englewood Cliffs,** NJ 07632, *pg.* 509, *pg.* 1060
FIRMENICH INCORPORATED, 250 Plainsboro Rd, **Plainsboro,** NJ 08536, *pg.* 509, *pg.* 1109
FRAGRANCE RESOURCES, INC., 620 Rte 3 W PO Box 4277, **Clifton,** NJ 07014, *pg.* 509, *pg.* 1052
LANMAN & KEMP-BARCLAY CO., INC., 25 Woodland Ave, **Westwood,** NJ 07675, *pg.* 514, *pg.* 1132
ROBERTET, INC., 125 Bauer Dr, **Oakland,** NJ 07436-3123, *pg.* 522, *pg.* 1100
TRI-K INDUSTRIES, INC., 151 Veterans Dr, **Northvale,** NJ 07647, *pg.* 523, *pg.* 1099
UNGERER & COMPANY, 4 Bridgewater Ln, **Lincoln Park,** NJ 07035-1439, *pg.* 524, *pg.* 1079

New Mexico

AROMALAND INC., 1326 Rufina Cir, **Santa Fe,** NM 87507, *pg.* 499, *pg.* 1135

New York

AMOREPACIFIC US, INC., 1385 Broadway Ste 1005, **New York,** NY 10018, *pg.* 498, *pg.* 1195
AT LAST NATURALS, INC., 401 Columbus Ave, **Valhalla,** NY 10595, *pg.* 499, *pg.* 1347
AVON PRODUCTS, INC., 777 Third Ave, **New York,** NY 10017-1307, *pg.* 500, *pg.* 1198
BLISSWORLD LLC, 75 Varick St, **New York,** NY 10013, *pg.* 501, *pg.* 1204
BORGHESE, INC., 3 E 54th St, Fl 20, **New York,** NY 10022, *pg.* 502, *pg.* 1205
CHANEL, INC., 9 W 57th St Fl 44, **New York,** NY 10019-2701, *pg.* 503, *pg.* 1211
CLINIQUE LABORATORIES LLC, 767 5th Ave, **New York,** NY 10153, *pg.* 503, *pg.* 1214
COLGATE-PALMOLIVE COMPANY, 300 Park Ave, **New York,** NY 10022-7499, *pg.* 504, *pg.* 1215
COTY, INC., 350 5th Ave 17th Fl, **New York,** NY 10018, *pg.* 506, *pg.* 1219

First page reference indicates Business Class Edition
Second page reference indicates Geographic Edition

THE ESTEE LAUDER COMPANIES INC., 767 5th Ave, **New York,** NY 10153-0023, *pg.* 508, *pg.* 1229
INSPIRED BEAUTY BRANDS, 330 7th Ave, **New York,** NY 10001, *pg.* 512, *pg.* 1244
INTER PARFUMS, INC., 551 5th Ave Ste 1500, **New York,** NY 10176, *pg.* 512, *pg.* 1244
INTERNATIONAL FLAVORS & FRAGRANCES INC., 521 W 57th St, **New York,** NY 10019-2901, *pg.* 512, *pg.* 1244
KOLMAR LABS GROUP, PO Box 1111, 20 W King St, **Port Jervis,** NY 12771, *pg.* 513, *pg.* 1322
L'OREAL USA, 575 5th Ave, **New York,** NY 10017-2422, *pg.* 514, *pg.* 1252
MAJESTIC DRUG COMPANY, INC., 4996 Main St, **South Fallsburg,** NY 12779, *pg.* 516, *pg.* 1343
MAYBELLINE LLC, 575 5th Ave, **New York,** NY 10017-2422, *pg.* 516, *pg.* 1257
NATUROPATHICA LTD., Red Horse Plz 74 Montauk Hwy Ste 1, **East Hampton,** NY 11937, *pg.* 517, *pg.* 1156
OUIDAD, 20 W 55th St, **New York,** NY 10019, *pg.* 519, *pg.* 1275
PARFUMS CHRISTIAN DIOR, INC, 19 E 57th St, **New York,** NY 10022-2508, *pg.* 519, *pg.* 1276
PERFUMANIA HOLDINGS, INC., 35 Sawgrass Dr Ste 2, **Bellport,** NY 11713, *pg.* 520, *pg.* 1141
PETER THOMAS ROTH LABS LLC, 460 Park Ave 16th Fl, **New York,** NY 10022-1829, *pg.* 520, *pg.* 1278
PRESTIGE BRANDS HOLDINGS, INC., 660 White Plains Rd, Ste 250, **Tarrytown,** NY 10591, *pg.* 520, *pg.* 1345
REDKEN LABORATORIES LLC, 565 5th Ave, **New York,** NY 10017, *pg.* 520, *pg.* 1285
REVLON CONSUMER PRODUCTS CORPORATION, One New York Plz, **New York,** NY 10004, *pg.* 521, *pg.* 1286
REVLON, INC., 1 New York Plz, **New York,** NY 10004, *pg.* 521, *pg.* 1286
SHISEIDO COSMETICS AMERICA OF SAC, 900 3rd Ave Fl 15, **New York,** NY 10022-4795, *pg.* 522, *pg.* 1291
TWEEZERMAN INTERNATIONAL, 2 Tri Harbor Ct, **Port Washington,** NY 11050, *pg.* 524, *pg.* 1324

North Carolina

BURT'S BEES INC., 210 W Pettigrew St, **Durham,** NC 27701, *pg.* 502, *pg.* 1370

Ohio

BATH & BODY WORKS, LLC, 7 Limited Pkwy E, **Reynoldsburg,** OH 43068-5300, *pg.* 500, *pg.* 1471
THE BONNE BELL COMPANY, 1006 Crocker Rd, **Westlake,** OH 44145, *pg.* 502, *pg.* 1480
KAO BRANDS CO. INC., 2535 Spring Grove Ave, **Cincinnati,** OH 45214-1773, *pg.* 513, *pg.* 1415
P&G-CLAIROL, INC., 1 Procter & Gamble Plz, **Cincinnati,** OH 45202, *pg.* 519, *pg.* 1418
VIDAL SASSOON CO., PO Box 599, **Cincinnati,** OH 45201-0599, *pg.* 524, *pg.* 1426

Pennsylvania

GLAXOSMITHKLINE CONSUMER HEALTHCARE, 1000 GSK Dr, **Moon Township,** PA 15108, *pg.* 510, *pg.* 1554
STRAIGHT ARROW PRODUCTS, INC., 2020 Highland Ave, **Bethlehem,** PA 18020, *pg.* 523, *pg.* 1517

Rhode Island

INSTANTRON CO., INC., 3712 Pawtucket Ave, **Riverside,** RI 02915-5105, *pg.* 512, *pg.* 1608

Texas

ACTIVE ORGANICS, INC., 1097 Yates St, **Lewisville,** TX 75057, *pg.* 498, *pg.* 1725
ADVANCED BEAUTY SYSTEMS INC., 5501 Lyndon B Johnson Fwy, Ste 900, **Dallas,** TX 75240, *pg.* 498, *pg.* 1672
BEAUTICONTROL COSMETICS, INC., 2121 Midway Rd, **Carrollton,** TX 75006-5039, *pg.* 501, *pg.* 1669
ER'GO CANDLES INC., 10830 Composite Dr, **Dallas,** TX 75220, *pg.* 508, *pg.* 1680
HELEN OF TROY L.P., 1 Helen of Troy Plz, **El Paso,** TX 79912-1148, *pg.* 511, *pg.* 1692
LADY PRIMROSE'S, INC., 3631 W Davis Ste C, **Dallas,** TX 75211-3145, *pg.* 513, *pg.* 1683
MARY KAY INC., 16251 Dallas Pkwy, **Addison,** TX 75001, *pg.* 516, *pg.* 1657
MARY KAY INC., 16251 Dallas Pkwy, **Addison,** TX 75001-6801, *pg.* 516, *pg.* 1657
PALM BEACH TAN, INC., 633 E State Hwy 121, Ste 500, **Coppell,** TX 75019, *pg.* 519, *pg.* 1671
SALLY BEAUTY HOLDINGS, INC., 3001 Colorado Blvd, **Denton,** TX 76210, *pg.* 522, *pg.* 1691
SPORT CLIPS, INC., 110 Briarwood Dr, **Georgetown,** TX 78628, *pg.* 523, *pg.* 1698
TONI & GUY USA, INC., 2311 Midway Rd, **Dallas,** TX 75006, *pg.* 523, *pg.* 1689

Utah

GREEN ENDEAVORS, INC., 59 W 100 S 2nd Fl, **Salt Lake City,** UT 84101, *pg.* 511, *pg.* 1758
NU SKIN ENTERPRISES, INC., 1 Nu Skin Plz 75 W Center St, **Provo,** UT 84601-4432, *pg.* 518, *pg.* 1755

Virginia

COLOR ME BEAUTIFUL, INC., 7000 Infantry Ridge Rd Ste 400, **Manassas,** VA 20109, *pg.* 505, *pg.* 1787
THE RATNER COMPANIES, 1577 Spring Hill Rd Ste 500, **Vienna,** VA 22182-2223, *pg.* 520, *pg.* 1809

Wisconsin

ANDIS COMPANY, 1800 Renaissance Blvd, **Sturtevant,** WI 53177-1743, *pg.* 498, *pg.* 1895
NORTHERN LABS, INC., 5800 W Dr, **Manitowoc,** WI 54220-4168, *pg.* 517, *pg.* 1869

Cultural & Recreational Entertainment

Alabama

ALABAMA SYMPHONY ORCHESTRA, 3621 6th Ave S, **Birmingham,** AL 35222, *pg.* 526, *pg.* 1
HUNTSVILLE SYMPHONY ORCHESTRA, Von Braun Ctr 700 Monroe St, **Huntsville,** AL 35801, *pg.* 553, *pg.* 6
MOBILE SYMPHONY, INC., 257 Dolphin, **Mobile,** AL 36652-3127, *pg.* 564, *pg.* 7

Alaska

ANCHORAGE SYMPHONY ORCHESTRA, 400 D St Ste 230, **Anchorage,** AK 99501, *pg.* 528, *pg.* 10
FAIRBANKS SYMPHONY ASSOCIATION, 234 Fine Arts Complex 312 Tanana Dr, **Fairbanks,** AK 99775, *pg.* 547, *pg.* 10
JUNEAU SYMPHONY, 522 W 10th St Basement, **Juneau,** AK 99801, *pg.* 555, *pg.* 11

Arizona

ARIZONA CARDINALS FOOTBALL CLUB, INC., 8701 S Hardy Dr, **Tempe,** AZ 85284, *pg.* 529, *pg.* 25
ARIZONA DIAMONDBACKS, 401 E Jefferson St, **Phoenix,** AZ 85004, *pg.* 529, *pg.* 14
COYOTES HOCKEY, LLC, 9400 W Maryland Ave, **Glendale,** AZ 85305, *pg.* 542, *pg.* 13
FENDER MUSICAL INSTRUMENTS CORPORATION, 17600 N Perimeter Drive Ste 100, **Scottsdale,** AZ 85250-2618, *pg.* 547, *pg.* 21
FLAGSTAFF SYMPHONY ASSOCIATION, 113 E Aspen Ave Ste A, **Flagstaff,** AZ 86001, *pg.* 548, *pg.* 12
PHOENIX SUNS, 201 E Jefferson St, **Phoenix,** AZ 85004-2412, *pg.* 576, *pg.* 19
PHOENIX SYMPHONY ASSOCIATION, 1 N 1st St Ste 200, **Phoenix,** AZ 85004, *pg.* 576, *pg.* 19
SYMPHONY OF THE SOUTHWEST, 56 S Ctr, **Mesa,** AZ 85211, *pg.* 586, *pg.* 13
TUCSON SYMPHONY ORCHESTRA, 2175 N 6th Ave, **Tucson,** AZ 85705-5606, *pg.* 589, *pg.* 27

Arkansas

OAKLAWN JOCKEY CLUB, INC., 2705 Central Ave, **Hot Springs,** AR 71902, *pg.* 571, *pg.* 32

California

24 HOUR FITNESS WORLDWIDE INC., 12647 Alcosta Blvd 5th Fl, **San Ramon,** CA 94583, *pg.* 526, *pg.* 258
3ALITY TECHNICA, 55 E Orange Grove Ave, **Burbank,** CA 91502, *pg.* 526, *pg.* 51
ACADEMY OF MOTION PICTURE ARTS & SCIENCES, 8949 Wilshire Blvd, **Beverly Hills,** CA 90211-1907, *pg.* 526, *pg.* 46
AMERICAN CONSERVATORY THEATRE, 30 Grant Ave FL 6, **San Francisco,** CA 94108, *pg.* 528, *pg.* 212
AMERICAN FILM INSTITUTE, 2021 N Western Ave, **Los Angeles,** CA 90027-1657, *pg.* 528, *pg.* 126
AMERICAN GOLF CORPORATION, 2951 28th St, **Santa Monica,** CA 90405-2961, *pg.* 528, *pg.* 272
ANAHEIM DUCKS HOCKEY CLUB, LLC, Honda Ctr 2695 E Katella Ave, **Anaheim,** CA 92806, *pg.* 528, *pg.* 42
ANGELS BASEBALL, L.P., 2000 Gene Autry Way, **Anaheim,** CA 92806-6100, *pg.* 529, *pg.* 42
ATOM FACTORY, 10351 W Washington Blvd, **Culver City,** CA 90232, *pg.* 531, *pg.* 71
AXL MUSICAL INSTRUMENTS CO., LTD., CORP., PO Box 808, **Millbrae,** CA 94030-9998, *pg.* 531, *pg.* 145
BAKERSFIELD SYMPHONY ORCHESTRA, 1328 34th St Ste A, **Bakersfield,** CA 93301, *pg.* 531, *pg.* 44
BERKELEY SYMPHONY ORCHESTRA, 1942 University Ave Ste 207, **Berkeley,** CA 94704, *pg.* 533, *pg.* 45
CALIFORNIA MUSICAL THEATRE CORPORATION, 1510 J St Ste 200, **Sacramento,** CA 95814, *pg.* 536, *pg.* 196
CALIFORNIA PHILHARMONIC ORCHESTRA, 1120 Huntington Dr, **San Marino,** CA 91108, *pg.* 536, *pg.* 253
CALIFORNIA SPORTS, INC., 555 N Nash St, **El Segundo,** CA 90245, *pg.* 536, *pg.* 78
CENTER THEATRE GROUP OF LOS ANGELES, INC., 601 W Temple St, **Los Angeles,** CA 90012, *pg.* 538, *pg.* 128
CHANEY ENTERTAINMENT, INC., PO Box 4550, **Palm Springs,** CA 92263, *pg.* 538, *pg.* 174
DEAN MARKLEY STRINGS, INC., 3350 Scott Blvd Ste 45, **Santa Clara,** CA 95054, *pg.* 543, *pg.* 265
EXODUS FILM GROUP, 1211 Electric Ave, **Venice,** CA 90291, *pg.* 546, *pg.* 301
FREMONT SYMPHONY ORCHESTRA, PO Box 104, **Fremont,** CA 94537, *pg.* 549, *pg.* 91
FUNRISE TOY CORP., 7811 Lemona Ave, **Van Nuys,** CA 94105, *pg.* 549, *pg.* 300
GAME SHOW PLACEMENTS LTD., 7011 Willoughby Ave, **Los Angeles,** CA 90038-2332, *pg.* 550, *pg.* 132
GOLDEN STATE WARRIORS, LLC, 1011 Broadway, **Oakland,** CA 94607-4019, *pg.* 550, *pg.* 171
GREAT AMERICA, 2401 Agnew Rd, **Santa Clara,** CA 95054, *pg.* 551, *pg.* 265
JACUZZI BRANDS CORPORATION, 14525 Montevista Ave, **Chino,** CA 91710, *pg.* 554, *pg.* 65
JAZZERCISE, INC., 2460 Impala Dr, **Carlsbad,** CA 92010, *pg.* 554, *pg.* 59
KNOTT'S BERRY FARM, 8039 Beach Blvd, **Buena Park,** CA 90620, *pg.* 556, *pg.* 50
LEGOLAND CALIFORNIA LLC, 1 Legoland Dr, **Carlsbad,** CA 92008, *pg.* 557, *pg.* 59
LIVE NATION ENTERTAINMENT, INC., 9348 Civic Center Dr, **Beverly Hills,** CA 90210, *pg.* 558, *pg.* 47
LONG BEACH SYMPHONY ORCHESTRA, 555 E Ocean Blvd Ste 106, **Long Beach,** CA 90802-5056, *pg.* 558, *pg.* 123
LOS ANGELES CLIPPERS, 1111 S Figueroa St Ste 1100, **Los Angeles,** CA 90015, *pg.* 558, *pg.* 135
LOS ANGELES COUNTY FAIR ASSOCIATION, 1101 W McKinley Ave, **Pomona,** CA 91768, *pg.* 559, *pg.* 185
LOS ANGELES DODGERS INC., 1000 Elysian Park Ave, **Los Angeles,** CA 90012-1199, *pg.* 559, *pg.* 135
LOS ANGELES KINGS HOCKEY CLUB L.P., 1111 S Figueroa St Ste 3100, **Los Angeles,** CA 90015, *pg.* 559, *pg.* 135
LOS ANGELES PHILHARMONIC ASSOCIATION, 111 S Grand Ave, **Los Angeles,** CA 90012, *pg.* 559, *pg.* 135
LOS ANGELES TURF CLUB, INCORPORATED, 285 W Huntington Dr, **Arcadia,** CA 91007, *pg.* 559, *pg.* 43
MEDIEVAL TIMES INC., 7662 Beach Blvd, **Buena Park,** CA 90620-1838, *pg.* 561, *pg.* 51
METROPOLITAN THEATRES CORPORATION, 8727 W Third St, **Los Angeles,** CA 90048-3843, *pg.* 562, *pg.* 136
MODESTO SYMPHONY ORCHESTRA, 911 13th St, **Modesto,** CA 95354, *pg.* 564, *pg.* 150
OAKLAND ATHLETICS LIMITED PARTNERSHIP, 7000 Coliseum Way, **Oakland,** CA 94621, *pg.* 571, *pg.* 172
THE OAKLAND RAIDERS, L.P., 1220 Harbor Bay Pkwy, **Alameda,** CA 94502-6501, *pg.* 571, *pg.* 38
PADI AMERICAS, 30151 Tomas St, **Rancho Santa Margarita,** CA 92688-2125, *pg.* 573, *pg.* 188
PADRES L.P., PETCO Park 100 Pk Blvd, **San Diego,** CA 92101, *pg.* 573, *pg.* 206
PARENTS TELEVISION COUNCIL, 707 Wilshire Blvd, Ste 2075, **Los Angeles,** CA 90017, *pg.* 574, *pg.* 138
PASADENA PLAYHOUSE, 39 S El Molino Ave, **Pasadena,** CA 91101, *pg.* 574, *pg.* 181
PASADENA SYMPHONY ASSOCIATION, 117 E Colorado Blvd Ste 200, **Pasadena,** CA 91105, *pg.* 574, *pg.* 181
PHILHARMONIA BAROQUE ORCHESTRA, 414 Mason St, Ste 606, **San Francisco,** CA 94102, *pg.* 575, *pg.* 225
READING INTERNATIONAL, INC., 6100 Center Dr Ste 900, **Los Angeles,** CA 90045, *pg.* 578, *pg.* 139
RESPAWN ENTERTAINMENT, PO Box 56507, **Sherman Oaks,** CA 91413, *pg.* 579, *pg.* 278
SACRAMENTO KINGS, Arco Arena 1 Sports Pkwy, **Sacramento,** CA 95834-2300, *pg.* 579, *pg.* 197
SACRAMENTO PHILHARMONIC ORCHESTRA, 1030 15th St Ste 200, **Sacramento,** CA 95814, *pg.* 579, *pg.* 197
SAN DIEGO CHARGERS FOOTBALL CO., 4020 Murphy Canyon Rd, **San Diego,** CA 92123, *pg.* 580, *pg.* 208
SAN DIEGO SOCIETY OF NATURAL HISTORY, 1788 El Prado, **San Diego,** CA 92101, *pg.* 580, *pg.* 208
SAN DIEGO SYMPHONY ORCHESTRA ASSOCIATION, 1245 7th Ave, **San Diego,** CA 92101, *pg.* 580, *pg.* 208
SAN FRANCISCO FORTY NINERS, LTD., 4949 Centennial Blvd, **Santa Clara,** CA 95054-1229, *pg.* 581, *pg.* 270
SAN FRANCISCO GIANTS BASEBALL CLUB, AT&T Park 24 Willie Mays Plz, **San Francisco,** CA 94107, *pg.* 581, *pg.* 226
SAN FRANCISCO SYMPHONY, 201 Van Ness Ave, **San Francisco,** CA 94102, *pg.* 581, *pg.* 227
SAN JOSE SHARKS, LLC, 525 W Santa Clara St, **San Jose,** CA 95113-1520, *pg.* 581, *pg.* 250
STUBHUB, INC., 199 Fremont St Ste 300, **San Francisco,** CA 94105, *pg.* 586, *pg.* 228
TAYLOR-LISTUG INC., 1980 Gillespie Way, **El Cajon,** CA 92020, *pg.* 587, *pg.* 78
THEATER & ARTS FOUNDATION, PO Box 12039, **La Jolla,** CA 92039, *pg.* 587, *pg.* 120
TIX CORPORATION, 12711 Ventura Blvd Ste 340, **Studio City,** CA 91604, *pg.* 588, *pg.* 281
UBISOFT INC., 625 Third St, **San Francisco,** CA 94107, *pg.* 589, *pg.* 229
YAMAHA CORPORATION OF AMERICA, 6600 Orangethorpe Ave, **Buena Park,** CA 90620, *pg.* 595, *pg.* 51
YOUNG CHANG NORTH AMERICA, 6000 Phyllis Dr, **Cypress,** CA 90630, *pg.* 595, *pg.* 77
ZOOLOGICAL SOCIETY OF SAN DIEGO, 2920 Zoo Dr, **San Diego,** CA 92101-1646, *pg.* 595, *pg.* 211

Colorado

BOULDER PHILHARMONIC ORCHESTRA, 2590 Walnut St, **Boulder,** CO 80302, *pg.* 534, *pg.* 310
THE CABLE CENTER, 2000 Buchtel Blvd, **Denver,** CO 80210, *pg.* 535, *pg.* 317
CENTURY CASINOS INC., 2860 S Circle Dr Ste 350, **Colorado Springs,** CO 80906, *pg.* 538, *pg.* 315
CHILDREN'S MUSEUM OF DENVER, INC., 2121 Children's Museum Dr, **Denver,** CO 80211, *pg.* 540, *pg.* 317
COLORADO AVALANCHE, LLC, Pepsi Ctr 1000 Chopper Cir, **Denver,** CO 80204, *pg.* 541, *pg.* 317
COLORADO ROCKIES BASEBALL CLUB, LTD., Coors Field 2001 Blake St, **Denver,** CO 80205-2000, *pg.* 542, *pg.* 317
COLORADO SYMPHONY ASSOCIATION INC., Boettcher Concert Hall Denver Performing Arts Complex 1000 14th St #15, **Denver,** CO 80202-2333, *pg.* 542, *pg.* 318
DENVER BRONCOS FOOTBALL CLUB, 13655 Broncos Pkwy, **Englewood,** CO 80112-4150, *pg.* 544, *pg.* 325
DENVER CENTER FOR THE PERFORMING ARTS INC., 1101 13th St, **Denver,** CO 80204-2154, *pg.* 544, *pg.* 318
THE DENVER NUGGETS LIMITED PARTNERSHIP, 1000 Chopper Cir, **Denver,** CO 80204-5809, *pg.* 544, *pg.* 319
LITTLETON SYMPHONY ORCHESTRA, 5894 S Datura, **Littleton,** CO 80120, *pg.* 558, *pg.* 333
NATIONAL CINEMEDIA, INC., 9110 E Nichols Ave Ste 200, **Centennial,** CO 80112-3405, *pg.* 567, *pg.* 314
TELLURIDE SKI & GOLF COMPANY LLP, 565 Mtn Vlg Blvd, **Telluride,** CO 81435-9521, *pg.* 587, *pg.* 336
UNITED STATES OLYMPIC COMMITTEE, One Olympic Plz, **Colorado Springs,** CO 80909-5766, *pg.* 589, *pg.* 315
VCG HOLDING CORP., 390 Union Blvd Ste 540, **Lakewood,** CO 80228, *pg.* 590, *pg.* 333
WOW! WORLD OF WONDER CHILDREN'S MUSEUM, 110 N Harrison Ave, **Lafayette,** CO 80026, *pg.* 595, *pg.* 332

Connecticut

FOXWOODS RESORT CASINO, 39 Norwich Westerly Rd, **Ledyard,** CT 06338, *pg.* 549, *pg.* 353
GREENWICH SYMPHONY ORCHESTRA INC., PO Box 35, **Greenwich,** CT 06836, *pg.* 551, *pg.* 350
HARTFORD SYMPHONY ORCHESTRA INC., 99 Pett St Ste 500, **Hartford,** CT 06103, *pg.* 551, *pg.* 352
KAMAN MUSIC CORPORATION, 55 Griffin Rd S, **Bloomfield,** CT 06002, *pg.* 555, *pg.* 339
MOHEGAN TRIBAL GAMING AUTHORITY, 1 Mohegan Sun Blvd, **Uncasville,** CT 06382-1355, *pg.* 564, *pg.* 381
NEW HAVEN SYMPHONY ORCHESTRA, 105 Court St Ste 302, **New Haven,** CT 06511, *pg.* 569, *pg.* 359
THE STAMFORD SYMPHONY ORCHESTRA, 263 Tresser Blvd, **Stamford,** CT 06901-3532, *pg.* 585, *pg.* 378
WORLD WRESTLING ENTERTAINMENT, INC., 1241 E Main St, **Stamford,** CT 06902-3521, *pg.* 595, *pg.* 380

Delaware

DELAWARE ART MUSEUM, 2301 Kentmere Pkwy, **Wilmington,** DE 19806, *pg.* 543, *pg.* 390
DELAWARE MUSEUM OF NATURAL HISTORY, 4840 Kennett Pike, **Wilmington,** DE 19807, *pg.* 543, *pg.* 390
DELAWARE SYMPHONY ASSOCIATION, 818 N Market St, **Wilmington,** DE 19801, *pg.* 544, *pg.* 390

First page reference indicates Business Class Edition
Second page reference indicates Geographic Edition

DOVER DOWNS GAMING & ENTERTAINMENT, INC., 1131 N DuPont Hwy, **Dover,** DE 19901, *pg.* 545, *pg.* 387
DOVER MOTORSPORTS, INC., 1131 N Dupont Hwy, **Dover,** DE 19901, *pg.* 545, *pg.* 387

District of Columbia

ARENA STAGE, 1101 6th St SW, **Washington,** DC 20024, *pg.* 529, *pg.* 395
FORD'S THEATRE SOCIETY INC., 511 10th St NW, **Washington,** DC 20004, *pg.* 549, *pg.* 399
JOHN F. KENNEDY CENTER FOR THE PERFORMING ARTS, 2700 F St NW, **Washington,** DC 20566, *pg.* 555, *pg.* 401
NATIONAL SYMPHONY ORCHESTRA, 2700 F St NW, **Washington,** DC 20566, *pg.* 568, *pg.* 403
THE NATIONAL THEATRE CORPORATION, 1321 Pennsylvania Ave, **Washington,** DC 20004, *pg.* 569, *pg.* 403
THE SHAKESPEARE THEATRE, INC., 516 8th St SE, **Washington,** DC 20003-2834, *pg.* 583, *pg.* 404
WASHINGTON NATIONALS, L.P., 1500 S Capitol St SE, **Washington,** DC 20003-1507, *pg.* 591, *pg.* 407
WASHINGTON WIZARDS, 601 F St NW, **Washington,** DC 20004-1605, *pg.* 591, *pg.* 408

Florida

ALACHUA COUNTY VISITORS & CONVENTION BUREAU, 30 E University Ave, **Gainesville,** FL 32601, *pg.* 527, *pg.* 428
AMALIE ARENA, 401 Channelside Dr, **Tampa,** FL 33602, *pg.* 527, *pg.* 470
THE AMERICAN STAGE COMPANY INC., 163 3rd St N, **Saint Petersburg,** FL 33701, *pg.* 528, *pg.* 461
ARCADIA ALL-FLORIDA CHAMPIONSHIP RODEO, 124 Heard St, **Arcadia,** FL 34266, *pg.* 529, *pg.* 409
THE ARMED FORCES MILITARY MUSEUM, 2050 34th Way N, **Largo,** FL 33771, *pg.* 530, *pg.* 438
ARTHUR MURRAY INTERNATIONAL, INC., 1077 Ponce De Leon Blvd, **Coral Gables,** FL 33134-3319, *pg.* 530, *pg.* 417
BARBARA B. MANN PERFORMING ARTS HALL, 8099 College Pkwy SW, **Fort Myers,** FL 33919, *pg.* 532, *pg.* 427
BATANGA, INC., 2121 Ponce De Leon Blvd, **Coral Gables,** FL 33134, *pg.* 533, *pg.* 418
BUCCANEERS LIMITED PARTNERSHIP, 1 Buccaneer Pl, **Tampa,** FL 33607, *pg.* 534, *pg.* 471
BUSCH GARDENS TAMPA BAY, 3605 E Bougainvillea Ave, **Tampa,** FL 33612-6433, *pg.* 535, *pg.* 472
CARMIKE CINEMAS, 3101 N Federal Hwy 6th Fl, **Fort Lauderdale,** FL 33306, *pg.* 537, *pg.* 423
CASINO PLAYERS, INC., 700 W Hillsboro Blvd Bldg 2 Ste 102, **Deerfield,** FL 33441, *pg.* 537, *pg.* 421
DAVID A. STRAZ JR. CENTER, 1010 N WC MacInnes Pl, **Tampa,** FL 33602, *pg.* 543, *pg.* 472
FELD ENTERTAINMENT, INC., 2001 US Hwy 3001, **Palmetto,** FL 34221, *pg.* 547, *pg.* 458
FLORIDA GAMING CORPORATION, 3500 NW 37th Ave, **Miami,** FL 33142-4923, *pg.* 548, *pg.* 442
FLORIDA HOLOCAUST MUSEUM, INC., 55 5th St S, **Saint Petersburg,** FL 33701, *pg.* 548, *pg.* 462
FLORIDA MARLINS, L.P., 501 Marlins Way, **Miami,** FL 33125, *pg.* 548, *pg.* 442
THE FLORIDA ORCHESTRA, 244 Second Ave N Stw 420, **Saint Petersburg,** FL 33701, *pg.* 548, *pg.* 462
FLORIDA PANTHERS HOCKEY CLUB, LTD., One Panther Pkwy, **Sunrise,** FL 33323-5315, *pg.* 548, *pg.* 469
FLORIDA STATE FAIR AUTHORITY, 4800 US Hwy 301 N, **Tampa,** FL 33610, *pg.* 549, *pg.* 473
GODWIN'S GATORLAND, INC., 14501 S Orange Blossom Trl, **Orlando,** FL 32837, *pg.* 550, *pg.* 453
GOLF CHANNEL, 7580 Golf Channel Dr, **Orlando,** FL 32819, *pg.* 551, *pg.* 454
INTERNATIONAL SPEEDWAY CORPORATION, 1 Daytona Blvd, **Daytona Beach,** FL 32114, *pg.* 553, *pg.* 420
JACKSONVILLE JAGUARS, LTD., 1 Everbank Fields Dr, **Jacksonville,** FL 32202, *pg.* 554, *pg.* 433
JACKSONVILLE SYMPHONY ASSOCIATION, 300 W Water St Ste 200, **Jacksonville,** FL 32202, *pg.* 554, *pg.* 434
LIGHTNING HOCKEY LP, 401 Channelside Dr, **Tampa,** FL 33602-5400, *pg.* 557, *pg.* 474
LOWRY PARK ZOOLOGICAL SOCIETY OF TAMPA INC., 1101 W Sligh Ave, **Tampa,** FL 33604, *pg.* 559, *pg.* 474
MARINELAND OF FLORIDA, 9600 Ocean Shore Blvd, **Saint Augustine,** FL 32080-8613, *pg.* 561, *pg.* 461
THE MENNELLO MUSEUM OF AMERICAN ART, 900 E Princeton St, **Orlando,** FL 32803, *pg.* 561, *pg.* 454
MIAMI CITY BALLET, INC., 2200 Liberty Ave, **Miami Beach,** FL 33139, *pg.* 562, *pg.* 448
MIAMI DOLPHINS, LTD., 7500 SW 30th St, **Davie,** FL 33314-1020, *pg.* 562, *pg.* 419
MIAMI HEAT LIMITED PARTNERSHIP, 601 Biscayne Blvd, **Miami,** FL 33132-1801, *pg.* 562, *pg.* 444
MOSI (MUSEUM OF SCIENCE & INDUSTRY), 4801 E Fowler Ave, **Tampa,** FL 33617, *pg.* 564, *pg.* 474
MOTE MARINE LABORATORY, INC., 1600 Ken Thompson Pkwy, **Sarasota,** FL 34236, *pg.* 564, *pg.* 466
MUSEUM OF DISCOVERY & SCIENCE, INC., 401 SW 2nd St, **Fort Lauderdale,** FL 33312, *pg.* 565, *pg.* 425
MUSEUM OF FINE ARTS OF ST. PETERSBURG FLORIDA INC., 255 Beach Dr NE, **Saint Petersburg,** FL 33701, *pg.* 565, *pg.* 463
NAPLES ZOO INC., 1590 Goodlette-Frank Rd, **Naples,** FL 34102, *pg.* 565, *pg.* 451
NATIONAL ASSOCIATION FOR STOCK CAR AUTO RACING, 1801 W International Speedway Blvd, **Daytona Beach,** FL 32114-1215, *pg.* 566, *pg.* 420
NATIONAL ASSOCIATION OF PROFESSIONAL BASEBALL LEAGUES, INC., 9550 16th St N, **Saint Petersburg,** FL 33716, *pg.* 566, *pg.* 463
THE OPIUM GROUP, 690 Lincoln Rd, **Miami Beach,** FL 33139, *pg.* 572, *pg.* 448
ORLANDO MAGIC, 8701 Maitland Summit Blvd, **Orlando,** FL 32810-5915, *pg.* 572, *pg.* 455
ORLANDO PHILHARMONIC ORCHESTRA INC., 812 E Rollins St Ste 300, **Orlando,** FL 32803, *pg.* 573, *pg.* 455
PALLADIUM THEATER, INC., 253 5th Ave N, **Saint Petersburg,** FL 33701, *pg.* 573, *pg.* 463
PGA TOUR, INC., 100 PGA Tour Blvd, **Ponte Vedra Beach,** FL 32082, *pg.* 574, *pg.* 460
SALVADOR DALI MUSEUM, 1 Dali Blvd, **Saint Petersburg,** FL 33701-3920, *pg.* 580, *pg.* 464
SARASOTA OPERA, 61 N Pineapple Ave, **Sarasota,** FL 34236, *pg.* 581, *pg.* 467
SEAWORLD ORLANDO, 7007 SeaWorld Dr, **Orlando,** FL 32821-8009, *pg.* 582, *pg.* 455
SEAWORLD PARKS & ENTERTAINMENT LLC, 9205 S Park Ctr Loop Ste 400, **Orlando,** FL 32819, *pg.* 582, *pg.* 456
SILVER SPRINGS, INC., 5656 E Silver Springs Blvd, **Silver Springs,** FL 34488, *pg.* 583, *pg.* 468
SOUTH FLORIDA MUSEUM, 201 10th St W, **Bradenton,** FL 34205, *pg.* 584, *pg.* 415
SOUTHWEST FLORIDA SYMPHONY, 8290 College Pkwy Ste 103, **Fort Myers,** FL 33919, *pg.* 584, *pg.* 428
ST. PETERSBURG MUSEUM OF HISTORY, 335 2nd Ave NE, **Saint Petersburg,** FL 33701, *pg.* 585, *pg.* 464
STAGES PRODUCTIONS, INC., 7906 Bayshore Dr, **Seminole,** FL 33776, *pg.* 585, *pg.* 468
TAMPA BAY RAYS BASEBALL, LTD., Tropicana Field 1 Tropicana Dr, **Saint Petersburg,** FL 33705, *pg.* 586, *pg.* 464
TAMPA BAY STORM, 401 Channelside Dr, **Tampa,** FL 33602-5400, *pg.* 587, *pg.* 476
ULTIMATE FITNESS GROUP, LLC, 1815 Cordova Rd, Ste 206, **Fort Lauderdale,** FL 33316, *pg.* 589, *pg.* 427
UNIVERSAL ORLANDO, 1000 Universal Studios Plz, **Orlando,** FL 32819-7601, *pg.* 590, *pg.* 456
WEEKI WACHEE SPRINGS, LLC, 6131 Commercial Way, **Weeki Wachee,** FL 34606-1121, *pg.* 591, *pg.* 478
WET 'N WILD, INC., 6200 International Dr, **Orlando,** FL 32819, *pg.* 592, *pg.* 457
WORLD GOLF HALL OF FAME, 1 World Golf Pl, **Saint Augustine,** FL 32092, *pg.* 595, *pg.* 461

Georgia

ALBANY SYMPHONY ORCHESTRA, 308 Flint Ave, **Albany,** GA 31701, *pg.* 527, *pg.* 482
ATLANTA FALCONS FOOTBALL CLUB, LLC, 4400 Falcon Pkwy, **Flowery Branch,** GA 30542-3176, *pg.* 530, *pg.* 532
ATLANTA MOTOR SPEEDWAY, INC., 1500 Tara Pl, **Hampton,** GA 30228-1884, *pg.* 530, *pg.* 533
ATLANTA NATIONAL LEAGUE BASEBALL CLUB, INC., 755 Hank Aaron Dr, **Atlanta,** GA 30315, *pg.* 530, *pg.* 490
ATLANTA SYMPHONY ORCHESTRA, 1280 Peachtree St NE, **Atlanta,** GA 30309-3552, *pg.* 531, *pg.* 490
AUGUSTA SYMPHONY INC., 1301 Greene St Ste 200, **Augusta,** GA 30901, *pg.* 531, *pg.* 524
COLLEGE FOOTBALL HALL OF FAME, 250 Marietta St NW, **Atlanta,** GA 30313, *pg.* 541, *pg.* 501
HAWKS BASKETBALL, INC., Centennial Tower 101 Marietta St NW Ste 1900, **Atlanta,** GA 30303, *pg.* 551, *pg.* 509
PREMIER EXHIBITIONS, INC., 3340 Peachtree Rd NE, Ste 900, **Atlanta,** GA 30326, *pg.* 577, *pg.* 518
SIX FLAGS OVER GEORGIA, INC., 275 Riverside Pkwy SW, **Austell,** GA 30168, *pg.* 583, *pg.* 525
WILD ADVENTURES, INC., 3766 Old Clyattville Rd, **Valdosta,** GA 31601, *pg.* 592, *pg.* 542
WOODRUFF ARTS CENTER, 1280 Peachtree St NE, **Atlanta,** GA 30309, *pg.* 595, *pg.* 524

Hawaii

POLYNESIAN CULTURAL CENTER, 55-220 Kam Hwy, **Laie,** HI 96762, *pg.* 577, *pg.* 545
TIHATI PRODUCTIONS LTD., INC., 3615 Harding Ave, Ste 507, **Honolulu,** HI 96816, *pg.* 587, *pg.* 545

Idaho

BOISE PHILHARMONIC ASSOCIATION, INC., 516 S 9th St, **Boise,** ID 83702, *pg.* 533, *pg.* 546
DISCOVERY CENTER OF IDAHO, 131 W Myrtle St, **Boise,** ID 83702, *pg.* 545, *pg.* 546

Illinois

THE ADLER PLANETARIUM & ASTRONOMY MUSEUM, 1300 S Lk Shore Dr, **Chicago,** IL 60605-2403, *pg.* 526, *pg.* 563
THE ART INSTITUTE OF CHICAGO, 111 S Michigan Ave, **Chicago,** IL 60603-6492, *pg.* 530, *pg.* 565
AWARE RECORDS, 624 Davis St 2nd Fl, **Evanston,** IL 60201, *pg.* 531, *pg.* 611
CASINO QUEEN, INC., 200 S Front St, **East Saint Louis,** IL 62201-1222, *pg.* 537, *pg.* 609
CHICAGO BEARS FOOTBALL CLUB, INC., Halas Hall 1000 Football Dr, **Lake Forest,** IL 60045, *pg.* 538, *pg.* 623
CHICAGO BLACKHAWK HOCKEY TEAM, INC., 1901 W Madison St, **Chicago,** IL 60612, *pg.* 538, *pg.* 569
CHICAGO NATIONAL LEAGUE BALL CLUB, LLC, 1060 W Addison St, **Chicago,** IL 60613-4397, *pg.* 539, *pg.* 569
CHICAGO PROFESSIONAL SPORTS LIMITED PARTNERSHIP, 1901 W Madison St, **Chicago,** IL 60612-2459, *pg.* 539, *pg.* 570
CHICAGO SYMPHONY ORCHESTRA, 220 S Michigan Ave, **Chicago,** IL 60604, *pg.* 539, *pg.* 570
CHICAGO THEATRE GROUP INC., 170 N Dearborn St, **Chicago,** IL 60601, *pg.* 539, *pg.* 570
CHICAGO WHITE SOX LTD., 333 W 35th St, **Chicago,** IL 60616-3651, *pg.* 539, *pg.* 570
CHICAGO ZOOLOGICAL SOCIETY, INC., 3300 Golf Rd, **Brookfield,** IL 60513-1060, *pg.* 539, *pg.* 559
EVANSTON SYMPHONY ORCHESTRA ASSOCIATION, PO Box 778, **Evanston,** IL 60204, *pg.* 546, *pg.* 611
FACETS MULTI-MEDIA, INC., 1517 W Fullerton Ave, **Chicago,** IL 60614-2096, *pg.* 547, *pg.* 573
THE FIELD MUSEUM, 1400 S Lk Shore Dr, **Chicago,** IL 60605-2496, *pg.* 548, *pg.* 573
ILLINOIS PHILHARMONIC ORCHESTRA, 377 Artists Walk, **Park Forest,** IL 60466, *pg.* 553, *pg.* 650
ILLINOIS SYMPHONY ORCHESTRA, 524 1/2 Capitol Ave, **Springfield,** IL 62701, *pg.* 553, *pg.* 662
JOHN G. SHEDD AQUARIUM, 1200 S Lk Shore Dr, **Chicago,** IL 60605, *pg.* 555, *pg.* 579
LAKE SHORE SYMPHONY ORCHESTRA, PO Box 57237, **Chicago,** IL 60657, *pg.* 556, *pg.* 580
LINCOLN PARK ZOO, 2001 N Clark St, **Chicago,** IL 60614, *pg.* 557, *pg.* 580
MAYWOOD PARK TROTTING ASSOCIATION, INC., 8600 W N Ave, **Maywood,** IL 60160, *pg.* 561, *pg.* 631
METROPOLITAN PIER & EXPOSITION AUTHORITY, 301 E Cermak Rd, **Chicago,** IL 60616, *pg.* 562, *pg.* 581
MUSEUM OF SCIENCE AND INDUSTRY, 57th St and Lk Shore Dr, **Chicago,** IL 60637, *pg.* 565, *pg.* 583
NORTHBROOK SYMPHONY ORCHESTRA INC., 899 Skokie Blvd Ste LL12, **Northbrook,** IL 60062, *pg.* 571, *pg.* 641
QUINCY SYMPHONY ORCHESTRA ASSOCIATION, 428 Maine St Ste 270, **Quincy,** IL 62301, *pg.* 578, *pg.* 653

ROCKFORD SYMPHONY ORCHESTRA, 711 N Main St, **Rockford,** IL 61103, pg. 579, pg. 655

WMS INDUSTRIES INC., 800 S Northpoint Blvd, **Waukegan,** IL 60085, pg. 593, pg. 666

Indiana

ANDERSON SYMPHONY ORCHESTRA, 1124 Meridian St, **Anderson,** IN 46016, pg. 528, pg. 673

CARMEL SYMPHONY ORCHESTRA, INC., 11 1st Ave NE, **Carmel,** IN 46032, pg. 536, pg. 675

COLUMBUS PRO MUSICA INC., 315 Franklin St, **Columbus,** IN 47201, pg. 542, pg. 676

CONN-SELMER, INC., 600 Industrial Pkwy, **Elkhart,** IN 46516-5414, pg. 542, pg. 677

EVANSVILLE PHILHARMONIC ORCHESTRA CORP., 530 Main St, **Evansville,** IN 47701, pg. 546, pg. 678

FORT WAYNE PHILHARMONIC ORCHESTRA, 4901 Fuller Dr, **Fort Wayne,** IN 46835, pg. 549, pg. 680

INDIANAPOLIS COLTS, INC., 7001 W 56th St, **Indianapolis,** IN 46254-9725, pg. 553, pg. 687

INDIANAPOLIS SYMPHONY ORCHESTRA, 32 E Washington St Ste 600, **Indianapolis,** IN 46204-2919, pg. 553, pg. 687

MADAME WALKER THEATRE CENTER, 617 Indiana Ave, **Indianapolis,** IN 46202, pg. 560, pg. 688

NATIONAL COLLEGIATE ATHLETIC ASSOCIATION, 1802 Alonzo Watford Sr Dr, **Indianapolis,** IN 46202, pg. 567, pg. 688

PACERS BASKETBALL, LLC, 125 S Pennsylvania St, **Indianapolis,** IN 46204-3610, pg. 573, pg. 689

Iowa

ADVENTURE LANDS OF AMERICA, INC., 305 34th Ave NW, **Altoona,** IA 50009, pg. 526, pg. 701

CEDAR RAPIDS SYMPHONY, 119 3rd Ave SE, **Cedar Rapids,** IA 52401, pg. 538, pg. 702

DES MOINES SYMPHONY ASSOCIATION, 1011 Locust St Ste 200, **Des Moines,** IA 50309, pg. 544, pg. 705

SIOUX CITY SYMPHONY ORCHESTRA, 520 Pierce St Ste 375, **Sioux City,** IA 51101, pg. 583, pg. 712

WATERLOO-CEDAR FALLS SYMPHONY ORCHESTRA, Gallagher-Bluedorn Performing Arts Ctr, **Cedar Falls,** IA 50614-0803, pg. 591, pg. 702

Kansas

AMC ENTERTAINMENT INC., One AMC Way 11500 Ash St, **Leawood,** KS 66211, pg. 527, pg. 716

CHANCE RIDES MANUFACTURING CO., 4219 Irving St, **Wichita,** KS 67209-2613, pg. 538, pg. 723

TITLE BOXING CLUB, 14711 W 112 St, **Lenexa,** KS 66215, pg. 588, pg. 717

WICHITA SYMPHONY SOCIETY INC., 225 W Douglas Ste 207, **Wichita,** KS 67202, pg. 592, pg. 724

Kentucky

CHURCHILL DOWNS, INC., 700 Central Ave, **Louisville,** KY 40208-1212, pg. 540, pg. 733

KENTUCKY DERBY FESTIVAL, INC., 1001 S 3rd St, **Louisville,** KY 40203, pg. 556, pg. 735

LEXINGTON PHILHARMONIC SOCIETY, 161 N Mill St, **Lexington,** KY 40507, pg. 557, pg. 730

LOUISVILLE ORCHESTRA, INC., 323 W Broadway Ste 700, **Louisville,** KY 40202, pg. 559, pg. 736

NATIONAL THOROUGHBRED RACING ASSOCIATION, 2525 Harrodsburg Rd Ste 400, **Lexington,** KY 40504-3359, pg. 569, pg. 730

NEWPORT AQUARIUM, One Aquarium Way, **Newport,** KY 41071, pg. 571, pg. 739

PADUCAH SYMPHONY ORCHESTRA, 760 Broadway St, **Paducah,** KY 42001, pg. 573, pg. 739

Louisiana

ACADIANA SYMPHONY ASSOCIATION, 412 Travis St, **Lafayette,** LA 70505, pg. 526, pg. 744

AUDUBON NATURE INSTITUTE, 6500 Magazine St, **New Orleans,** LA 70118, pg. 531, pg. 746

FAIR GROUNDS CORPORATION, 1751 Gentilly Blvd, **New Orleans,** LA 70119, pg. 547, pg. 747

HARRAH'S LOUISIANA DOWNS CASINO & RACETRACK, 8000 E Texas St, **Bossier City,** LA 71111, pg. 551, pg. 743

LOUISIANA PHILHARMONIC ORCHESTRA, 1010 Common St Ste 2120, **New Orleans,** LA 70112-2465, pg. 559, pg. 747

NEW ORLEANS PELICANS NBA LIMITED PARTNERSHIP, 1250 Poydras St 19th Fl, **New Orleans,** LA 70113, pg. 569, pg. 747

NEW ORLEANS SAINTS L.P., 5800 Airline Dr, **Metairie,** LA 70003-3876, pg. 569, pg. 745

SHREVEPORT SYMPHONY ORCHESTRA, 616 Jordan St, **Shreveport,** LA 71101, pg. 583, pg. 748

Maine

BANGOR SYMPHONY ORCHESTRA, 51A Main St, **Bangor,** ME 04402, pg. 532, pg. 749

PORTLAND SYMPHONY ORCHESTRA, 50 Monument Sq 2nd Fl, **Portland,** ME 04101, pg. 577, pg. 752

SUGARLOAF/USA, 5092 Access Rd, **Carrabassett Valley,** ME 04947-9799, pg. 586, pg. 749

SUNDAY RIVER SKIWAY CORP., 15 S Rdg Rd PO Box 450, **Bethel,** ME 04217-0450, pg. 586, pg. 749

Maryland

ANNAPOLIS SYMPHONY ORCHESTRA ASSOCIATION INC., 801 Chase St, **Annapolis,** MD 21401, pg. 529, pg. 754

BALTIMORE ORIOLES, L.P., 333 W Camden St, **Baltimore,** MD 21201, pg. 532, pg. 755

BALTIMORE RAVENS LIMITED PARTNERSHIP, 1101 Russell St, **Baltimore,** MD 21230, pg. 532, pg. 755

BALTIMORE SYMPHONY ORCHESTRA, 1212 Cathedral St, **Baltimore,** MD 21201, pg. 532, pg. 755

THE COLUMBIA ORCHESTRA, 8510 High Ridge Rd, **Ellicott City,** MD 21043-3308, pg. 542, pg. 769

MARYLAND SYMPHONY ORCHESTRA, 30 W Washington St, **Hagerstown,** MD 21740, pg. 561, pg. 771

MARYLAND ZOOLOGICAL SOCIETY, INC., Druid Hill Park, **Baltimore,** MD 21217, pg. 561, pg. 758

NATIONAL AQUARIUM IN BALTIMORE INC., 501 E Pratt St, **Baltimore,** MD 21202, pg. 565, pg. 758

NATIONAL PHILHARMONIC, 5301 Tuckerman Ln, **Bethesda,** MD 20852-3385, pg. 568, pg. 765

PAUL REED SMITH GUITARS, 380 Log Canoe Cir, **Stevensville,** MD 21666-2166, pg. 574, pg. 779

Massachusetts

AVEDIS ZILDJIAN COMPANY, 22 Longwater Dr, **Norwell,** MA 02061-1612, pg. 531, pg. 839

BOSTON BALLET INC., 19 Clarendon St, **Boston,** MA 02116, pg. 533, pg. 790

BOSTON CELTICS LIMITED PARTNERSHIP, 226 Causeway St, **Boston,** MA 02114, pg. 533, pg. 790

BOSTON PROFESSIONAL HOCKEY ASSOCIATION, INC., 100 Legends Way, **Boston,** MA 02114-1390, pg. 534, pg. 791

BOSTON RED SOX BASEBALL CLUB LIMITED PARTNERSHIP, 4 Yawkey Way Fenway Park, **Boston,** MA 02215, pg. 534, pg. 791

BOSTON SYMPHONY ORCHESTRA INC., 301 Massachusetts Ave, **Boston,** MA 02115, pg. 534, pg. 791

COMMONWEALTH ZOOLOGICAL CORP., 1 Franklin Pk Rd, **Boston,** MA 02121, pg. 542, pg. 793

DRAFTKINGS, INC., 225 Franklin St., 26th Fl, **Boston,** MA 02110, pg. 545, pg. 793

MASSACHUSETTS CONVENTION CENTER AUTHORITY, 415 Summer St, **Boston,** MA 02210-1719, pg. 561, pg. 798

NEW BOSTON GARDEN CORP., 100 Legends Way, **Boston,** MA 02114-1303, pg. 569, pg. 799

NEW ENGLAND PATRIOTS FOOTBALL CLUB, INC., 1 Patriot Pl, **Foxboro,** MA 02035, pg. 569, pg. 819

NORTH SHORE PHILHARMONIC ORCHESTRA, PO Box 461, **Danvers,** MA 01923-0761, pg. 571, pg. 816

STEINWAY MUSICAL INSTRUMENTS, INC., 800 South St Ste 305, **Waltham,** MA 02453-1480, pg. 586, pg. 854

Michigan

ANN ARBOR SYMPHONY ORCHESTRA, 220 E Huron St, **Ann Arbor,** MI 48104, pg. 529, pg. 865

DEARBORN SYMPHONY ORCHESTRA, PO Box 2063, **Dearborn,** MI 48123, pg. 543, pg. 876

THE DETROIT LIONS, INC., 222 Republic Dr, **Allen Park,** MI 48101, pg. 544, pg. 864

DETROIT PISTONS BASKETBALL COMPANY, 6 Championship Dr, **Auburn Hills,** MI 48326-1753, pg. 544, pg. 868

DETROIT RED WINGS, INC., Joe Louis Arena 600 Civic Ctr Dr, **Detroit,** MI 48226, pg. 544, pg. 880

DETROIT SYMPHONY ORCHESTRA, INC., 3711 Woodward Ave, **Detroit,** MI 48201, pg. 544, pg. 880

DETROIT TIGERS BASEBALL CLUB, INC., 2100 Woodward Ave, **Detroit,** MI 48201-3474, pg. 545, pg. 880

GENERAL SPORTS & ENTERTAINMENT, LLC, 400 Water St Ste 250, **Rochester,** MI 48307, pg. 550, pg. 905

GRAND RAPIDS SYMPHONY SOCIETY, 300 Ottawa Ave NW Ste 100, **Grand Rapids,** MI 49503, pg. 551, pg. 887

HENRY FORD MUSEUM AND GREENFIELD VILLAGE, 20900 Oakwood Blvd, **Dearborn,** MI 48124-5029, pg. 552, pg. 878

HOLLAND SYMPHONY ORCHESTRA, PO Box 2685, **Holland,** MI 49422-8084, pg. 552, pg. 892

KALAMAZOO SYMPHONY ORCHESTRA, 359 S Kalamazoo Mall Ste 100, **Kalamazoo,** MI 49007, pg. 555, pg. 894

LANSING SYMPHONY ORCHESTRA, 501 S Capitol Ave Ste 400, **Lansing,** MI 48933, pg. 557, pg. 895

MICHIGAN PHILHARMONIC, 774 N Sheldon Rd, **Plymouth,** MI 48170, pg. 562, pg. 904

MICHIGAN SCIENCE CENTER, 5020 John R St, **Detroit,** MI 48202, pg. 562, pg. 884

Minnesota

ANYTIME FITNESS, 12181 Margo Ave South, **Hastings,** MN 55033, pg. 529, pg. 926

CANTERBURY PARK HOLDING CORPORATION, 1100 Canterbury Rd, **Shakopee,** MN 55379-1867, pg. 536, pg. 964

DULUTH SUPERIOR SYMPHONY ORCHESTRA, 331 W Superior St Ste 100, **Duluth,** MN 55802, pg. 545, pg. 921

GUTHRIE THEATER FOUNDATION, 818 S Seconds St, **Minneapolis,** MN 55415, pg. 551, pg. 937

LIFT BRANDS, 2411 Galpin Ct, Ste 110, **Chanhassen,** MN 55317, pg. 557, pg. 920

MINNESOTA ORCHESTRA, 1111 Nicollet Mall, **Minneapolis,** MN 55403, pg. 563, pg. 940

MINNESOTA TIMBERWOLVES BASKETBALL LIMITED PARTNERSHIP, 600 1st Ave N, **Minneapolis,** MN 55403-1400, pg. 563, pg. 940

MINNESOTA TWINS, LLC, 1 Twins Way, **Minneapolis,** MN 55403, pg. 563, pg. 940

MINNESOTA VIKINGS FOOTBALL CLUB, INC., 9520 Viking Dr, **Eden Prairie,** MN 55344, pg. 563, pg. 923

MINNESOTA WILD HOCKEY CLUB, LP, 317 Washington St, **Saint Paul,** MN 55102-1609, pg. 563, pg. 962

THE SAINT PAUL CHAMBER ORCHESTRA, 3rd Fl The Hamm Bldg 408 Saint Peter St, **Saint Paul,** MN 55102-1497, pg. 580, pg. 963

SMSC ENTERPRISES, 2400 Mystic Lake Blvd, **Prior Lake,** MN 55372, pg. 584, pg. 954

WCCO-TV, 90 S 11th St, **Minneapolis,** MN 55403-2414, pg. 591, pg. 946

Mississippi

MISSISSIPPI MUSEUM OF ART, 380 S Lamar St, **Jackson,** MS 39201, pg. 563, pg. 969

MISSISSIPPI SYMPHONY ORCHESTRA, 201 E Pascagoula St, **Jackson,** MS 39201, pg. 564, pg. 969

Missouri

FOX ASSOCIATES, LLC, 527 N Grand Blvd, **Saint Louis,** MO 63103, pg. 549, pg. 997

HERSCHEND FAMILY ENTERTAINMENT CORP., 399 Silver Dollar City Pkwy, **Branson,** MO 65616-6172, pg. 552, pg. 973

ISLE OF CAPRI CASINOS, INC., 600 Emerson Rd Ste 300, **Saint Louis,** MO 63141, pg. 553, pg. 998

KANSAS CITY CHIEFS FOOTBALL CLUB, INC., 1 Arrowhead Dr, **Kansas City,** MO 64129-1651, pg. 555, pg. 984

KANSAS CITY ROYALS BASEBALL CORPORATION, 1

Royal Way, **Kansas City,** MO 64129, *pg.* 555, *pg.* 985
KANSAS CITY SYMPHONY, 1703 Wyandotte St Ste 200, **Kansas City,** MO 64108-1672, *pg.* 555, *pg.* 985
PEAK RESORTS, INC., 17409 Hidden Valley Dr, **Wildwood,** MO 63025-2213, *pg.* 574, *pg.* 1007
SAINT LOUIS CARDINALS, L.P., Busch Stadium 700 Clark St, **Saint Louis,** MO 63102-1722, *pg.* 580, *pg.* 1002
SAINT LOUIS RAMS FOOTBALL COMPANY, 1 Rams Way, **Saint Louis,** MO 63045-1523, *pg.* 580, *pg.* 1002
SIX FLAGS SAINT LOUIS LLC, 4900 6 Flags Rd, **Eureka,** MO 63025, *pg.* 584, *pg.* 977
SPRINGFIELD SYMPHONY ASSOCIATION, INC., 411 N Sherman Pkwy, **Springfield,** MO 65802, *pg.* 585, *pg.* 1007
ST. LOUIS BLUES HOCKEY CLUB, LLC, 1401 Clark Ave, **Saint Louis,** MO 63103-2700, *pg.* 585, *pg.* 1003
ST. LOUIS PHILHARMONIC ORCHESTRA, PO Box 220537, **Saint Louis,** MO 63122, *pg.* 585, *pg.* 1003
ST. LOUIS SYMPHONY ORCHESTRA, 718 N Grand Blvd, **Saint Louis,** MO 63103, *pg.* 585, *pg.* 1004
THEATER LEAGUE INC., 9140 Ward Pkwy, Ste 200, **Kansas City,** MO 64114, *pg.* 587, *pg.* 986

Montana

BILLINGS SYMPHONY SOCIETY INC., 2721 2nd Ave N Ste 350, **Billings,** MT 59101, *pg.* 533, *pg.* 1008
HELENA SYMPHONY SOCIETY INC., 2 N Last Chance Gulch, Ste 1, **Helena,** MT 59601, *pg.* 552, *pg.* 1008
KAMPGROUNDS OF AMERICA, INC., 550 N 31st St, **Billings,** MT 59101, *pg.* 555, *pg.* 1008

Nebraska

CABELA'S INCORPORATED, 1 Cabela Dr, **Sidney,** NE 69160-1001, *pg.* 535, *pg.* 1019
LINCOLN SYMPHONY ORCHESTRA, 233 S 13th St Ste 1702, **Lincoln,** NE 68508, *pg.* 557, *pg.* 1012
OMAHA COMMUNITY PLAYHOUSE, 6915 Cass St, **Omaha,** NE 68132, *pg.* 572, *pg.* 1017
OMAHA SYMPHONY ASSOCIATION, 1605 Howard St, **Omaha,** NE 68102-2705, *pg.* 572, *pg.* 1017
OMAHA ZOOLOGICAL SOCIETY, 3701 S 10th St, **Omaha,** NE 68107, *pg.* 572, *pg.* 1017
OPERA OMAHA INC., 1850 Farnam St, **Omaha,** NE 68102, *pg.* 572, *pg.* 1017

Nevada

AFFINITY GAMING LLC, 3755 Breakthrough Way, Ste 300, **Las Vegas,** NV 89135, *pg.* 526, *pg.* 1022
ALL-AMERICAN SPORTPARK, INC., 6730 Las Vegas Blvd S, **Las Vegas,** NV 89119-3311, *pg.* 527, *pg.* 1022
AMERICAN CASINO & ENTERTAINMENT PROPERTIES LLC, 2000 Las Vegas Blvd S, **Las Vegas,** NV 89104, *pg.* 527, *pg.* 1022
AMERISTAR CASINOS, INC., 3773 Howard Hughes Pkwy Ste 490 S, **Las Vegas,** NV 89109, *pg.* 528, *pg.* 1022
BALLY TECHNOLOGIES, INC., 6601 S Bermuda Rd, **Las Vegas,** NV 89119-3605, *pg.* 531, *pg.* 1022
ELDORADO RESORTS, INC., 100 W Liberty St Ste 1150, **Reno,** NV 89501, *pg.* 546, *pg.* 1031
GOLDEN NUGGET HOTEL, 129 E Fremont St, **Las Vegas,** NV 89101-5603, *pg.* 550, *pg.* 1024
THE MAJESTIC STAR CASINO, LLC, 301 Fremont St, **Las Vegas,** NV 89101, *pg.* 560, *pg.* 1027
THE MOB MUSEUM, 300 Stewart Ave, **Las Vegas,** NV 89101, *pg.* 564, *pg.* 1028
MONARCH CASINO & RESORT, INC., 3800 S Virginia St, **Reno,** NV 89502, *pg.* 564, *pg.* 1031
PINNACLE ENTERTAINMENT, INC., 8918 Spanish Ridge Ave, **Las Vegas,** NV 89148, *pg.* 576, *pg.* 1029
STATION CASINOS, INC., 1505 S Pavilion Center Dr, **Las Vegas,** NV 89135, *pg.* 585, *pg.* 1030
ZUFFA LLC, 2960 W Sahara Ave, **Las Vegas,** NV 89102, *pg.* 596, *pg.* 1030

New Hampshire

ATTITASH, Rte 302 PO Box 308, **Bartlett,** NH 03812-0308, *pg.* 531, *pg.* 1033
MOUNT CRANMORE SKI RESORT, INC., 1 Skimobile Rd, **North Conway,** NH 03860-5364, *pg.* 564, *pg.* 1038
THE NEW HAMPSHIRE PHILHARMONIC, 83 Hanover St, **Manchester,** NH 03101, *pg.* 569, *pg.* 1036

New Jersey

GARDEN STATE PHILHARMONIC, 1 College Dr Po BOX 2001, **Toms River,** NJ 08754, *pg.* 550, *pg.* 1125
LIBERTY SCIENCE CENTER, INC., 222 Jersey City Blvd, **Jersey City,** NJ 07305, *pg.* 557, *pg.* 1075
MAYO PERFORMING ARTS CENTER, 100 S St, **Morristown,** NJ 07960, *pg.* 561, *pg.* 1089
MORRIS MUSEUM INC., 6 Normandy Heights Rd, **Morristown,** NJ 07960, *pg.* 564, *pg.* 1089
NBA PROPERTIES, INC., 100 Plz Dr, **Secaucus,** NJ 07094-3766, *pg.* 569, *pg.* 1120
NEW JERSEY DEVILS LLC, Prudential Ctr 165 Mulberry St, **Newark,** NJ 07102, *pg.* 569, *pg.* 1097
THE NEW YORK GIANTS, Timex Performance Ctr 1925 Giant Dr, **East Rutherford,** NJ 07073, *pg.* 570, *pg.* 1055
NEW YORK JETS FOOTBALL CLUB, INC., 1 Jets Dr, **Florham Park,** NJ 07932, *pg.* 570, *pg.* 1067
PLAINFIELD SYMPHONY SOCIETY INC., PO Box 5093, **Plainfield,** NJ 07061, *pg.* 577, *pg.* 1109
PRINCETON SYMPHONY ORCHESTRA, PO Box 250, **Princeton,** NJ 08542, *pg.* 577, *pg.* 1112
THE STATE THEATRE, 11 Livingston Ave, **New Brunswick,** NJ 08901-1903, *pg.* 585, *pg.* 1094
SYMPHONY IN C, One Market St Ste 1C, **Camden,** NJ 08102, *pg.* 586, *pg.* 1049
TIGER SCHULMANN'S MIXED MARTIAL ARTS, 485 Boulevard, **Elmwood Park,** NJ 07407, *pg.* 587, *pg.* 1059

New Mexico

EXPLORA SCIENCE CENTER & CHILDREN'S MUSEUM OF ALBUQUERQUE, 1701 Mountain Rd NW, **Albuquerque,** NM 87104, *pg.* 546, *pg.* 1135

New York

AMERICAN SYMPHONY ORCHESTRA LEAGUE, 33 W 60th St 5th Fl, **New York,** NY 10023-7905, *pg.* 528, *pg.* 1194
BALLET THEATRE FOUNDATION, INC., 890 Broadway, **New York,** NY 10003, *pg.* 531, *pg.* 1200
BALLY TOTAL FITNESS HOLDINGS CORPORATION, 139 W 32nd St, **New York,** NY 10001, *pg.* 532, *pg.* 1200
BATAVIA DOWNS GAMING, 8315 Park Rd, **Batavia,** NY 14020, *pg.* 533, *pg.* 1140
BIG APPLE CIRCUS LTD., 1 Metrotech Ctr N Fl 3, **Brooklyn,** NY 11201-3873, *pg.* 533, *pg.* 1145
BLINK FITNESS, 386 Park Ave S, 11th Fl, **New York,** NY 10016, *pg.* 533, *pg.* 1204
BLUE MAN PRODUCTIONS, INC., 434 Lafayette St, Ste 300, **New York,** NY 10003, *pg.* 533, *pg.* 1205
BMG/MUSIC, 1540 Broadway, **New York,** NY 10036-4039, *pg.* 533, *pg.* 1205
BROOKLYN NETS, 15 MetroTech Center 11th Fl, **Brooklyn,** NY 11201, *pg.* 534, *pg.* 1145
BUFFALO BILLS, INC., 1 Bills Dr, **Orchard Park,** NY 14127-2237, *pg.* 535, *pg.* 1319
BUFFALO PHILHARMONIC ORCHESTRA SOCIETY INC., 499 Franklin St, **Buffalo,** NY 14202, *pg.* 535, *pg.* 1147
CAMPGROUP LLC, 3 New King St, **White Plains,** NY 10604, *pg.* 536, *pg.* 1351
CHARLES ATLAS, LTD., PO Box D, **New York,** NY 10159-1049, *pg.* 538, *pg.* 1211
THE CHILDREN'S MUSEUM AT SARATOGA, 69 Caroline St, **Saratoga Springs,** NY 12866, *pg.* 540, *pg.* 1340
DISNEY THEATRICAL PRODUCTIONS, 214 W 42nd St, **New York,** NY 10036, *pg.* 545, *pg.* 1224
EMPIRE STATE BUILDING COMPANY LLC, 60 E 42nd St 48th Fl, **New York,** NY 10165-0006, *pg.* 546, *pg.* 1227
EQUINOX FITNESS CLUBS, 895 Broadway, **New York,** NY 10003, *pg.* 546, *pg.* 1228
FANDUEL, INC., 19 Union Sq W, 9th Fl, **New York,** NY 10003, *pg.* 547, *pg.* 1231
FINGER LAKES RACING ASSOCIATION INC., 5857 Rte 96, **Farmington,** NY 14425, *pg.* 548, *pg.* 1160
GLENS FALLS SYMPHONY ORCHESTRA, INC., PO Box 2036, **Glens Falls,** NY 12801-2036, *pg.* 550, *pg.* 1162
GREENWICH VILLAGE ORCHESTRA, PO Box 910, **New York,** NY 10113, *pg.* 551, *pg.* 1236
HOCKEY WESTERN NEW YORK, LLC, HSBC Arena 1 Seymour Knox III Plz, **Buffalo,** NY 14203, *pg.* 552, *pg.* 1149
J&R MUSIC WORLD, 23 Pk Row, **New York,** NY 10038-2302, *pg.* 554, *pg.* 1245
THE KAUFMAN CENTER, 129 W 67th St, **New York,** NY 10023, *pg.* 556, *pg.* 1248
KORG USA, INC., 316 S Service Rd, **Melville,** NY 11747, *pg.* 556, *pg.* 1180
LINCOLN CENTER FOR THE PERFORMING ARTS, INC., 70 Lincoln Ctr Plz, **New York,** NY 10023, *pg.* 557, *pg.* 1251
LIVE NATION WORLDWIDE - TIMES SQUARE OFFICE, 220 W 42nd St, **New York,** NY 10036-7202, *pg.* 558, *pg.* 1252
LONG ISLAND CHILDREN'S MUSEUM, 11 Davis Ave, **Garden City,** NY 11530, *pg.* 558, *pg.* 1161
LONG ISLAND PHILHARMONIC, 1 Huntington Quadrangle, **Melville,** NY 11747, *pg.* 558, *pg.* 1180
MAJOR LEAGUE BASEBALL, 245 Park Ave, **New York,** NY 10167, *pg.* 560, *pg.* 1255
MAJOR LEAGUE SOCCER LLC, 420 5th Ave, **New York,** NY 10018, *pg.* 560, *pg.* 1256
THE METROPOLITAN MUSEUM OF ART, 1000 5th Ave, **New York,** NY 10028-0198, *pg.* 561, *pg.* 1259
THE METROPOLITAN OPERA, Lincoln Ctr, **New York,** NY 10023, *pg.* 561, *pg.* 1260
THE MUSEUM OF MODERN ART, 11 W 53rd St, **New York,** NY 10019, *pg.* 565, *pg.* 1263
NATIONAL BASEBALL HALL OF FAME & MUSEUM, INC., 25 Main St, **Cooperstown,** NY 13326, *pg.* 566, *pg.* 1154
NATIONAL BASKETBALL ASSOCIATION, Olympic Twr 645 5th Ave, **New York,** NY 10022, *pg.* 566, *pg.* 1264
NATIONAL FOOTBALL LEAGUE, 345 Park Ave, **New York,** NY 10154, *pg.* 567, *pg.* 1264
NATIONAL HOCKEY LEAGUE, 1185 Ave of the Americas 15th Fl, **New York,** NY 10036-1104, *pg.* 568, *pg.* 1265
NEW YORK CITY BALLET, 20 Lincoln Ctr Plz, **New York,** NY 10023, *pg.* 569, *pg.* 1268
NEW YORK CITY OPERA INC., 75 Broad St, Rm 510, **New York,** NY 10004, *pg.* 570, *pg.* 1268
NEW YORK HALL OF SCIENCE, 4701 11th St, **Corona,** NY 11368, *pg.* 570, *pg.* 1155
NEW YORK ISLANDERS HOCKEY CLUB, L.P., 1255 Hempstead Tpke, **Uniondale,** NY 11553, *pg.* 570, *pg.* 1346
NEW YORK KNICKERBOCKERS, Madison Sq Garden 2 Pennsylvania Plz, **New York,** NY 10121-0091, *pg.* 570, *pg.* 1268
NEW YORK RANGERS HOCKEY CLUB, 2 Pennsylvania Plz, **New York,** NY 10121, *pg.* 570, *pg.* 1269
NEW YORK YANKEES, Yankee Stadium 1 E 161st St & River Ave, **Bronx,** NY 10451, *pg.* 570, *pg.* 1144
OPERA AMERICA, 330 7th Ave, **New York,** NY 10001, *pg.* 572, *pg.* 1274
THE ORCHARD ENTERPRISES, INC., 23 E 4th St 3rd Fl, **New York,** NY 10003, *pg.* 572, *pg.* 1274
THE PALEY CENTER FOR MEDIA, 25 W 52nd St, **New York,** NY 10019, *pg.* 573, *pg.* 1275
PHILHARMONIC SYMPHONY SOCIETY OF NEW YORK INC., Avery Fisher Hall 10 Lincoln Ctr Plz, **New York,** NY 10023-6990, *pg.* 575, *pg.* 1282
PHILLIPS DE PURY & COMPANY, 450 W 15th St, **New York,** NY 10011, *pg.* 576, *pg.* 1282
THE PUBLIC THEATER, 425 Lafayette St, **New York,** NY 10003, *pg.* 578, *pg.* 1283
QUEENS SYMPHONY ORCHESTRA, 6530 Kissena Blvd, **Flushing,** NY 11367-1575, *pg.* 578, *pg.* 1160
ROCHESTER BROADWAY THEATRE LEAGUE, 885 E Main St, **Rochester,** NY 14605, *pg.* 579, *pg.* 1337
ROCHESTER PHILHARMONIC ORCHESTRA INC., 108 E Ave, **Rochester,** NY 14604, *pg.* 579, *pg.* 1337
ROUNDABOUT THEATRE COMPANY, 231 W 39th St, **New York,** NY 10018, *pg.* 579, *pg.* 1287
SARATOGA CASINO & RACEWAY, 342 Jefferson St, **Saratoga Springs,** NY 12866, *pg.* 581, *pg.* 1340
SARATOGA PERFORMING ARTS CENTER, INC., 108 Ave of the Pines, **Saratoga Springs,** NY 12866, *pg.* 581, *pg.* 1340
SCREENVISION CINEMA NETWORK LLC, 1411 Broadway, **New York,** NY 10018, *pg.* 581, *pg.* 1290
SENECA PARK ZOOLOGICAL SOCIETY, 2222 Saint Paul St, **Rochester,** NY 14621-1097, *pg.* 583, *pg.* 1337
THE SOUND SYMPHONY, 20 Nevinwood Pl, **Huntington Station,** NY 11746, *pg.* 584, *pg.* 1168
SPORTSNET NEW YORK, LLC, 75 Rockefeller Plz, **New York,** NY 10019, *pg.* 585, *pg.* 1295
STEINWAY & SONS, 1 Steinway Pl, **Long Island City,** NY 11105, *pg.* 586, *pg.* 1176

First page reference indicates Business Class Edition
Second page reference indicates Geographic Edition

STERLING METS, L.P., Citi Field 126th St & Roosevelt Ave, **Flushing,** NY 11368-1699, *pg.* 586, *pg.* 1160
THEATRE COMMUNICATIONS GROUP, INC., 520 8th Ave 24th Fl, **New York,** NY 10018-4156, *pg.* 587, *pg.* 1298
THEATRE FOR A NEW AUDIENCE, 154 Christopher St Ste 3D, **New York,** NY 10014, *pg.* 587, *pg.* 1298
THEATREWORKSUSA, 151 W 26th St FL 7, **New York,** NY 10001, *pg.* 587, *pg.* 1298
THE TOPPS COMPANY, INC., 1 Whitehall St, **New York,** NY 10004-2109, *pg.* 588, *pg.* 1302
TOWN SPORTS INTERNATIONAL HOLDINGS, INC., 5 Penn Plz 4th Fl, **New York,** NY 10001, *pg.* 589, *pg.* 1303
THE UTICA SYMPHONY ORCHESTRA, 261 Genesee St, **Utica,** NY 13501, *pg.* 590, *pg.* 1347
WARNER MUSIC GROUP CORP., 75 Rockefeller Plz, **New York,** NY 10019, *pg.* 590, *pg.* 1313
THE WEINSTEIN COMPANY, 99 Hudson St 4th Fl, **New York,** NY 10013, *pg.* 591, *pg.* 1314
WESTCHESTER PHILHARMONIC, 123 Main St Lbby Level, **White Plains,** NY 10601, *pg.* 592, *pg.* 1354
WILDLIFE CONSERVATION SOCIETY, Bronx Zoo 2300 Southern Blvd, **Bronx,** NY 10460, *pg.* 592, *pg.* 1145
WIND-UP RECORDS, 79 Madison Ave, **New York,** NY 10016, *pg.* 592, *pg.* 1314
WNBA ENTERPRISES, LLC, 645 5th Ave, **New York,** NY 10022-5910, *pg.* 594, *pg.* 1314
WQXR FM, 122 5th Ave, **New York,** NY 10011-5605, *pg.* 595, *pg.* 1316

North Carolina

ASHEVILLE SYMPHONY SOCIETY INC., PO Box 2852, **Asheville,** NC 28802, *pg.* 530, *pg.* 1358
CAROLINA HURRICANES HOCKEY CLUB, 1400 Edwards Mill Rd, **Raleigh,** NC 27607-3624, *pg.* 537, *pg.* 1386
CAROWINDS, 14523 Carowinds Blvd, **Charlotte,** NC 28273, *pg.* 537, *pg.* 1364
CHARLOTTE SYMPHONY ORCHESTRA, 301 S Tryon St Ste 1700, **Charlotte,** NC 28282, *pg.* 538, *pg.* 1365
NORTH CAROLINA SYMPHONY, 3700 Glenwood Ave, Ste 130, **Raleigh,** NC 27612, *pg.* 571, *pg.* 1388
OLD SALEM, INCORPORATED, 600 S Main St, **Winston Salem,** NC 27101, *pg.* 572, *pg.* 1395
PANTHERS FOOTBALL, LLC, 800 S Mint St, **Charlotte,** NC 28202, *pg.* 573, *pg.* 1368
SPEEDWAY MOTORSPORTS, INC., 5555 Concord Pkwy S, **Concord,** NC 28027, *pg.* 584, *pg.* 1370
WESTERN PIEDMONT SYMPHONY, 243 3rd Ave NE Ste 1-N, **Hickory,** NC 28601, *pg.* 592, *pg.* 1379
WILMINGTON SYMPHONY ORCHESTRA, 4608 Cedar Ave Ste 105, **Wilmington,** NC 28403, *pg.* 592, *pg.* 1393
WINSTON-SALEM SYMPHONY ASSOCIATION INC., 680 W 4th St Ste 101, **Winston Salem,** NC 27101, *pg.* 593, *pg.* 1396

Ohio

AKRON SYMPHONY ORCHESTRA, 92 N Main St, **Akron,** OH 44308, *pg.* 526, *pg.* 1400
ASHLAND SYMPHONY ORCHESTRA, 401 College Ave, **Ashland,** OH 44805, *pg.* 530, *pg.* 1403
CEDAR FAIR, L.P., 1 Cedar Point Dr, **Sandusky,** OH 44870-5259, *pg.* 537, *pg.* 1471
CEDAR POINT, 1 Cedar Point Dr, **Sandusky,** OH 44870-5259, *pg.* 537, *pg.* 1472
CINCINNATI ART MUSEUM, 953 Eden Park Dr, **Cincinnati,** OH 45202, *pg.* 540, *pg.* 1410
CINCINNATI BENGALS, INC., 1 Paul Brown Stadium, **Cincinnati,** OH 45202-3418, *pg.* 540, *pg.* 1410
CINCINNATI MUSEUM CENTER INC., 1301 Western Ave, **Cincinnati,** OH 45203-1130, *pg.* 540, *pg.* 1411
CINCINNATI SYMPHONY ORCHESTRA, 1241 Elm St, **Cincinnati,** OH 45202, *pg.* 540, *pg.* 1411
CLEVELAND BROWNS FOOTBALL COMPANY LLC, 76 Lou Groza Blvd, **Berea,** OH 44017-1238, *pg.* 541, *pg.* 1406
CLEVELAND CAVALIERS/QUICKEN LOANS ARENA, 1 Center Ct, **Cleveland,** OH 44115-4001, *pg.* 541, *pg.* 1429
CLEVELAND INDIANS BASEBALL COMPANY, INC., 2401 Ontario St, **Cleveland,** OH 44115, *pg.* 541, *pg.* 1429
COLUMBUS BLUE JACKETS, Nationwide Arena 200 W Nationwide Blvd 3rd Fl, **Columbus,** OH 43215, *pg.* 542, *pg.* 1439
DAYTON PHILHARMONIC ORCHESTRA ASSOCIATION, INC., 126 N Main St Ste 210, **Dayton,** OH 45402, *pg.* 543, *pg.* 1445
MUSICAL ARTS ASSOCIATION, 11001 Euclid Ave, **Cleveland,** OH 44106, *pg.* 565, *pg.* 1433
NATIONAL FOOTBALL MUSEUM, INC., 2121 George Halas Dr NW, **Canton,** OH 44708-2630, *pg.* 568, *pg.* 1408
PLAYHOUSE SQUARE FOUNDATION, 1501 Euclid Ave Ste 200, **Cleveland,** OH 44115, *pg.* 577, *pg.* 1434
PROMUSICA CHAMBER ORCHESTRA, 243 N 5th St Ste 202, **Columbus,** OH 43215, *pg.* 578, *pg.* 1443
REDS BASEBALL PARTNERS, LLC, Great American Ball Park 100 Main St, **Cincinnati,** OH 45202, *pg.* 578, *pg.* 1425
SPRINGFIELD SYMPHONY ORCHESTRA, 300 S Fountain Ave, **Springfield,** OH 45506, *pg.* 585, *pg.* 1473
TOLEDO SYMPHONY, 1838 Parkwood Ave Ste 310, **Toledo,** OH 43604, *pg.* 588, *pg.* 1477
WESTERVILLE SYMPHONY ORCHESTRA, 167 S State St, **Westerville,** OH 43086, *pg.* 592, *pg.* 1480
WILDWATER KINGDOM, 1100 Squires Rd, **Aurora,** OH 44202-8749, *pg.* 592, *pg.* 1404

Oklahoma

HOB-LOB LIMITED PARTNERSHIP, 7707 SW 44th St, **Oklahoma City,** OK 73179-4808, *pg.* 552, *pg.* 1486
OKLAHOMA CITY PHILHARMONIC ORCHESTRA SOCIETY, INC., 428 W California Ste 210, **Oklahoma City,** OK 73102, *pg.* 571, *pg.* 1487
OKLAHOMA CITY THUNDER, 2 Leadership Sq 211 N Robinson Ave Ste 300, **Oklahoma City,** OK 73102, *pg.* 571, *pg.* 1487
OKLAHOMA CITY ZOOLOGICAL PARK, 2101 NE 50th St, **Oklahoma City,** OK 73111-7106, *pg.* 572, *pg.* 1487

Oregon

PORTLAND TRAIL BLAZERS, 1 Center Ct Ste 200, **Portland,** OR 97227-2103, *pg.* 577, *pg.* 1505

Pennsylvania

ALLEN ORGAN COMPANY, 150 Locust St, **Macungie,** PA 18062-1165, *pg.* 527, *pg.* 1549
THE ANDY WARHOL MUSEUM, 117 Sandusky St, **Pittsburgh,** PA 15212-5890, *pg.* 529, *pg.* 1573
CHAMBER ORCHESTRA OF PHILADELPHIA, 1520 Locust St Ste 500, **Philadelphia,** PA 19102, *pg.* 538, *pg.* 1559
ERIE PHILHARMONIC, 609 Walnut St, **Erie,** PA 16502-1852, *pg.* 546, *pg.* 1530
THE FRANKLIN INSTITUTE, 222 N 20th St, **Philadelphia,** PA 19103-1115, *pg.* 549, *pg.* 1565
JOHNSTOWN SYMPHONY ORCHESTRA, 300 Market St, # 303, **Johnstown,** PA 15901, *pg.* 555, *pg.* 1542
LANCASTER SYMPHONY ORCHESTRA, 226 N Arch St, **Lancaster,** PA 17603, *pg.* 556, *pg.* 1546
MOTOR TREND AUTO SHOWS, LLC, 6375 Flank Dr, **Harrisburg,** PA 17112, *pg.* 564, *pg.* 1537
PENN NATIONAL GAMING, INC., Wyomissing Professional Ctr 825 Berkshire Blvd Ste 200, **Wyomissing,** PA 19610, *pg.* 574, *pg.* 1595
PHILADELPHIA 76ERS, L.P., 3601 S Broad St, **Philadelphia,** PA 19148, *pg.* 575, *pg.* 1568
PHILADELPHIA EAGLES FOOTBALL CLUB, INC., 1 Novacare Way, **Philadelphia,** PA 19145-5900, *pg.* 575, *pg.* 1569
PHILADELPHIA FLYERS, L.P., 3601 S Broad St, **Philadelphia,** PA 19148, *pg.* 575, *pg.* 1569
PHILADELPHIA MUSEUM OF ART, 26th Benjamin Franklin Pkwy, **Philadelphia,** PA 19130, *pg.* 575, *pg.* 1569
THE PHILADELPHIA ORCHESTRA ASSOCIATION, The Atlantic Bldg 260 S Broad St 16th Fl, **Philadelphia,** PA 19102, *pg.* 575, *pg.* 1569
PHILHARMONIC SOCIETY OF NORTHEASTERN PENNSYLVANIA, 195 Hanover St, **Wilkes Barre,** PA 18711, *pg.* 575, *pg.* 1594
THE PHILLIES, L.P., Citizens Bank Park 1 Citizens Bank Way, **Philadelphia,** PA 19148, *pg.* 575, *pg.* 1569
PITTSBURGH BASEBALL, INC., PNC Pk 115 Federal St, **Pittsburgh,** PA 15212, *pg.* 576, *pg.* 1578
PITTSBURGH PENGUINS LLC, 1001 5th Ave, **Pittsburgh,** PA 15219, *pg.* 577, *pg.* 1578
PITTSBURGH STEELERS SPORTS INC., 3400 S Water St, **Pittsburgh,** PA 15203, *pg.* 577, *pg.* 1578
PITTSBURGH SYMPHONY INC., 600 Penn Ave, **Pittsburgh,** PA 15222, *pg.* 577, *pg.* 1579
READING SYMPHONY ORCHESTRA ASSOCIATION, 147 N 5th St, **Reading,** PA 19601-3401, *pg.* 578, *pg.* 1585
THE SCIENCE CENTER, 3711 Market St Ste 800, **Philadelphia,** PA 19104, *pg.* 581, *pg.* 1570
WESTMORELAND SYMPHONY ORCHESTRA, Ste 1 951 Old Salem Rd, **Greensburg,** PA 15601-1386, *pg.* 592, *pg.* 1534
WILLIAMSPORT SYMPHONY ORCHESTRA, 220 W Fourth St, **Williamsport,** PA 17701-6102, *pg.* 592, *pg.* 1595
YORK SYMPHONY ORCHESTRA, 50 N George St, **York,** PA 17401-1214, *pg.* 595, *pg.* 1598

Rhode Island

NEWPORT ART MUSEUM, 76 Bellevue Ave, **Newport,** RI 02840, *pg.* 571, *pg.* 1603
PROVIDENCE PERFORMING ARTS CENTER, 220 Weybosset St, **Providence,** RI 02903, *pg.* 578, *pg.* 1607
RHODE ISLAND PHILHARMONIC ORCHESTRA INC., 667 Waterman Ave, **East Providence,** RI 02914, *pg.* 579, *pg.* 1601

South Carolina

MYRTLE BEACH AREA CONVENTION AND VISITORS BUREAU, 1200 North Oak Street, **Myrtle Beach,** SC 29578, *pg.* 565, *pg.* 1621
PURE BARRE, 100 Dunbar St, **Spartanburg,** SC 29306, *pg.* 578, *pg.* 1623
SOUTH CAROLINA PHILHARMONIC ASSOCIATION INC., 721 Lady St Ste B, **Columbia,** SC 29201, *pg.* 584, *pg.* 1615
SPOLETO FESTIVAL USA, 14 George St, **Charleston,** SC 29401, *pg.* 584, *pg.* 1613

South Dakota

SOUTH DAKOTA SYMPHONY ORCHESTRA, 301 S Main Ave 4th Fl, **Sioux Falls,** SD 57104-6311, *pg.* 584, *pg.* 1625

Tennessee

CHATTANOOGA SYMPHONY & OPERA ASSOCIATION, 701 Broad St, **Chattanooga,** TN 37402-1811, *pg.* 538, *pg.* 1628
GIBSON GUITAR CORP., 309 Plus Pk Blvd, **Nashville,** TN 37217, *pg.* 550, *pg.* 1650
JACKSON SYMPHONY ASSOCIATION INC., 1903 N Highland Ave, **Jackson,** TN 38301, *pg.* 554, *pg.* 1635
KNOXVILLE SYMPHONY SOCIETY INC., 100 Southgate St Ste 302, **Knoxville,** TN 37902, *pg.* 556, *pg.* 1637
MEMPHIS GRIZZLIES, 191 Beale St, **Memphis,** TN 38103-3715, *pg.* 561, *pg.* 1645
MEMPHIS SYMPHONY ORCHESTRA, 585 S Mendenhall Rd, **Memphis,** TN 38117, *pg.* 561, *pg.* 1645
NASHVILLE PREDATORS, LLC, 501 Broadway, **Nashville,** TN 37203-3932, *pg.* 565, *pg.* 1652
NASHVILLE SYMPHONY ASSOCIATION, 1 Symphony Pl, **Nashville,** TN 37201, *pg.* 565, *pg.* 1653
REGAL ENTERTAINMENT GROUP, 7132 Regal Ln, **Knoxville,** TN 37918, *pg.* 579, *pg.* 1638
TENNESSEE FOOTBALL, INC., Baptist Sports Park 460 Great Cir Rd, **Nashville,** TN 37228, *pg.* 587, *pg.* 1654

Texas

ABILENE PHILHARMONIC ASSOCIATION, 401 Cypress St, Ste 520, **Abilene,** TX 79601, *pg.* 526, *pg.* 1657
ALLEY THEATRE, 615 Texas Ave, **Houston,** TX 77002, *pg.* 527, *pg.* 1699
AUSTIN SYMPHONY ORCHESTRA, 1101 Red River, **Austin,** TX 78701, *pg.* 531, *pg.* 1660
CINEMARK HOLDINGS, INC., 3900 Dallas Pkwy Ste 500, **Plano,** TX 75093, *pg.* 540, *pg.* 1729
CURVES INTERNATIONAL INC., 100 Ritchie Rd, **Waco,** TX 76712, *pg.* 542, *pg.* 1748
DALLAS COWBOYS FOOTBALL CLUB, LTD., Cowboys Ctr 1 Cowboys Pkwy, **Irving,** TX 75063, *pg.* 543, *pg.* 1718
DALLAS MAVERICKS, The Pavilion 2909 Taylor St, **Dallas,** TX 75226, *pg.* 543, *pg.* 1678
THE DALLAS OPERA, 2403 Flora St, # 500, **Dallas,** TX

75201, *pg.* 543, *pg.* 1679
DALLAS STARS L.P., 2601 Ave Of The Stars, **Frisco,** TX 75034, *pg.* 543, *pg.* 1697
DALLAS SYMPHONY ASSOCIATION INC., 2301 Flora St, **Dallas,** TX 75201, *pg.* 543, *pg.* 1679
EAST TEXAS SYMPHONY ORCHESTRA, 522 S Broadway Ave Ste 101, **Tyler,** TX 75702-8111, *pg.* 545, *pg.* 1748
EL PASO SYMPHONY ORCHESTRA, PO Box 180, **El Paso,** TX 79942, *pg.* 546, *pg.* 1691
FIESTA TEXAS, INC., 17000 IH-10 W, **San Antonio,** TX 78257, *pg.* 548, *pg.* 1740
FORT WORTH SYMPHONY ASSOCIATION, 330 E 4th St Ste 200, **Fort Worth,** TX 76102, *pg.* 549, *pg.* 1694
GOLD'S GYM, 4001 Maple Ave Ste 200, **Dallas,** TX 75219, *pg.* 550, *pg.* 1681
HOUSTON ASTROS BASEBALL CLUB, 501 Crawford St Ste 400 PO Box 288, **Houston,** TX 77002-2113, *pg.* 552, *pg.* 1707
HOUSTON GRAND OPERA ASSOCIATION, 510 Preston, **Houston,** TX 77002, *pg.* 552, *pg.* 1707
HOUSTON ROCKETS, 1510 Polk St, **Houston,** TX 77002, *pg.* 552, *pg.* 1707
HOUSTON SYMPHONY SOCIETY, 615 Louisiana St Ste 102, **Houston,** TX 77002, *pg.* 552, *pg.* 1708
HOUSTON TEXANS, L.P., 2 Reliant Pk, **Houston,** TX 77054, *pg.* 553, *pg.* 1708
LAS COLINAS SYMPHONY ORCHESTRA ASSOCIATION INC., 4322 N Beltline Rd Ste B114, **Irving,** TX 75038, *pg.* 557, *pg.* 1722
LITTLEFIELD CORPORATION, 2501 N Lamar Blvd, **Austin,** TX 78705, *pg.* 558, *pg.* 1664
LUBBOCK SYMPHONY ORCHESTRA, 601 Ave K, **Lubbock,** TX 79401, *pg.* 560, *pg.* 1726
MASSAGE HEIGHTS CORPORATE, LLC, 13750 US Hwy 281 N, Ste 230, **San Antonio,** TX 78232, *pg.* 561, *pg.* 1741
THE MID-TEXAS SYMPHONY SOCIETY, PO Box 3216, **Seguin,** TX 78155, *pg.* 562, *pg.* 1745
RANGERS BASEBALL LLC, 1000 Ballpark Way Ste 400, **Arlington,** TX 76011-5170, *pg.* 578, *pg.* 1659
SAN ANTONIO SPURS LLC, 1 At AT&T Center Pkwy, **San Antonio,** TX 78219, *pg.* 580, *pg.* 1742
SEAWORLD TEXAS, 10500 SeaWorld Dr, **San Antonio,** TX 78251-3001, *pg.* 583, *pg.* 1742
SIX FLAGS ENTERTAINMENT CORPORATION, 924 Ave J East, **Grand Prairie,** TX 75050, *pg.* 583, *pg.* 1698
SIX FLAGS OVER TEXAS, INC., 2201 Road To Six Flags, **Arlington,** TX 76011-5157, *pg.* 583, *pg.* 1660
SIX FLAGS THEME PARKS INC., 924 E Ave J, **Grand Prairie,** TX 75050-2622, *pg.* 584, *pg.* 1699
TM STUDIOS, INC., 2002 Academy Ln Ste 110, **Dallas,** TX 75234, *pg.* 588, *pg.* 1689

Utah

CLEARPLAY, 2385 S 300 W, **Salt Lake City,** UT 84115, *pg.* 541, *pg.* 1756
DISCOVERY GATEWAY CHILDREN'S MUSEUM, 444 W 100 S, **Salt Lake City,** UT 84101, *pg.* 545, *pg.* 1757
JAZZ BASKETBALL INVESTORS, INC., 301 W S Temple, **Salt Lake City,** UT 84101-1216, *pg.* 554, *pg.* 1759
SALT LAKE BEES, 77 W 1300 S, **Salt Lake City,** UT 84115-5326, *pg.* 580, *pg.* 1760
THANKSGIVING POINT, 3003 N Thanksgiving Way, **Lehi,** UT 84043, *pg.* 587, *pg.* 1751
UTAH SYMPHONY & OPERA, Abavenel Hall 123 W S Temple, **Salt Lake City,** UT 84101-1496, *pg.* 590, *pg.* 1761

Vermont

MOUNT SNOW LTD., 39 Pisgah Rd, **West Dover,** VT 05356, *pg.* 564, *pg.* 1769
VERMONT SYMPHONY ORCHESTRA, 2 Church St Ste 19, **Burlington,** VT 05401-4457, *pg.* 590, *pg.* 1765

Virginia

ALEXANDRIA SYMPHONY ORCHESTRA, 2121 Eisenhower Ave Ste 608, **Alexandria,** VA 22314, *pg.* 527, *pg.* 1770
AMF BOWLING CENTERS, INC., 7313 Bell Creek Rd, **Mechanicsville,** VA 23111, *pg.* 528, *pg.* 1795
ANDREAS ENTERPRISES, INC., 2547 Halfway Rd, **Middleburg,** VA 20118, *pg.* 529, *pg.* 1795
BOWL AMERICA INCORPORATED, 6446 Edsall Rd, **Alexandria,** VA 22312, *pg.* 534, *pg.* 1770
COLONIAL WILLIAMSBURG FOUNDATION, 134 N Henry St, **Williamsburg,** VA 23187, *pg.* 541, *pg.* 1811
LYNCHBURG SYMPHONY ORCHESTRA, 621 Court St, **Lynchburg,** VA 24504, *pg.* 560, *pg.* 1787
RICHMOND PHILHARMONIC INC., 8100 Three Chopt Rd Ste 238, **Richmond,** VA 23229, *pg.* 579, *pg.* 1803
RICHMOND SYMPHONY, 612 E Grace St Ste 401, **Richmond,** VA 23219, *pg.* 579, *pg.* 1803
ROANOKE SYMPHONY SOCIETY, 541 Luck Ave SW Ste 200, **Roanoke,** VA 24016, *pg.* 579, *pg.* 1806
VIRGINIA LOTTERY, 2306-2308 W Mercury Blvd, **Hampton,** VA 23666, *pg.* 590, *pg.* 1783
VIRGINIA SYMPHONY ORCHESTRA, 150 Boush St, Ste 201, **Norfolk,** VA 23510, *pg.* 590, *pg.* 1797
WASHINGTON CAPITALS, 627 N Glebe Rd Ste 850, **Arlington,** VA 22203, *pg.* 591, *pg.* 1775
WASHINGTON FOOTBALL, INC., 21300 Redskin Park Dr, **Ashburn,** VA 20147, *pg.* 591, *pg.* 1776
WOLFTRAP FOUNDATION FOR THE PERFORMING ARTS, 1645 Trap Rd, **Vienna,** VA 22182, *pg.* 594, *pg.* 1809

Washington

THE BASEBALL CLUB OF SEATTLE, L.P., 1250 1st Ave S, **Seattle,** WA 98134-1216, *pg.* 532, *pg.* 1833
PLAYNETWORK, INC., 8727 148th Ave NE, **Redmond,** WA 98052, *pg.* 577, *pg.* 1829
RAINIER SYMPHONY, PO Box 58182, **Seattle,** WA 98138, *pg.* 578, *pg.* 1839
SEATTLE PHILHARMONIC ORCHESTRA, PO Box 177, **Seattle,** WA 98111, *pg.* 582, *pg.* 1839
SEATTLE SEAHAWKS, 12 Seahawks Way, **Renton,** WA 98056, *pg.* 582, *pg.* 1830
SEATTLE STORM, 3421 Thorn Dyke Ave W, **Seattle,** WA 98119-4153, *pg.* 582, *pg.* 1839
SEATTLE SYMPHONY ORCHESTRA, 200 University St, **Seattle,** WA 98111-3906, *pg.* 582, *pg.* 1840
SEATTLE THEATRE GROUP, 911 Pine St, **Seattle,** WA 98101, *pg.* 582, *pg.* 1840
SNOHOMISH COUNTY MUSIC PROJECT, 2710 Colby Ave, **Everett,** WA 98201-3511, *pg.* 584, *pg.* 1819
SPOKANE SYMPHONY ORCHESTRA, 1001 W Sprague Ave, **Spokane,** WA 99201, *pg.* 584, *pg.* 1844
WALLA WALLA SYMPHONY SOCIETY, PO Box 92, **Walla Walla,** WA 99362, *pg.* 590, *pg.* 1847

West Virginia

HUNTINGTON SYMPHONY ORCHESTRA, PO Box 2434, **Huntington,** WV 25725-2434, *pg.* 553, *pg.* 1850
WEST VIRGINIA SYMPHONY ORCHESTRA INC., 1 Clay Sq, **Charleston,** WV 25301, *pg.* 592, *pg.* 1849

Wisconsin

CENTRAL WISCONSIN SYMPHONY ORCHESTRA INC., 1128 Main St PO Box 65, **Stevens Point,** WI 54481, *pg.* 538, *pg.* 1895
FOX VALLEY SYMPHONY ASSOCIATION INC., 111 W College Ave Ste 550, **Appleton,** WI 54911-5706, *pg.* 549, *pg.* 1852
GREEN BAY PACKERS, INC., 1265 Lombardi Ave, **Green Bay,** WI 54304-3927, *pg.* 551, *pg.* 1859
KCS INTERNATIONAL, INC., 804 Pecor St, **Oconto,** WI 54153, *pg.* 556, *pg.* 1885
LA CROSSE SYMPHONY ORCHESTRA, INC., 3217 Commerce St, **La Crosse,** WI 54603, *pg.* 556, *pg.* 1864
MILWAUKEE BREWERS BASEBALL CLUB, INC., 1 Brewers Way, **Milwaukee,** WI 53214-3651, *pg.* 562, *pg.* 1878
MILWAUKEE BUCKS, INC., 1001 N 4th St, **Milwaukee,** WI 53203-1314, *pg.* 563, *pg.* 1878
MILWAUKEE SYMPHONY ORCHESTRA INC., 1101 N Market St Ste 100, **Milwaukee,** WI 53202, *pg.* 563, *pg.* 1878
TOMMY BARTLETT, INC., 560 Wisconsin Dells Pkwy, **Wisconsin Dells,** WI 53965, *pg.* 588, *pg.* 1899
WISCONSIN CHAMBER ORCHESTRA, 321 E Main St, **Madison,** WI 53703, *pg.* 593, *pg.* 1867

Wyoming

CHEYENNE SYMPHONY SOCIETY, INC., 1904 Thomes Ave, **Cheyenne,** WY 82001, *pg.* 538, *pg.* 1901

Education

Alabama

THE UNIVERSITY OF ALABAMA, 801 Campus Dr, **Tuscaloosa,** AL 35487, *pg.* 608, *pg.* 9

Arizona

APOLLO EDUCATION GROUP INC., 4025 S Riverpoint Pkwy, **Phoenix,** AZ 85040, *pg.* 597, *pg.* 14
ARIZONA STATE UNIVERSITY, 1151 South Forest Ave, **Tempe,** AZ 85281, *pg.* 597, *pg.* 25
GRAND CANYON EDUCATION, INC., 3300 W Camelback Rd, **Phoenix,** AZ 85017, *pg.* 602, *pg.* 16
NORTHERN ARIZONA UNIVERSITY, S San Francisco St, **Flagstaff,** AZ 86011, *pg.* 606, *pg.* 12
UNIVERSAL TECHNICAL INSTITUTE, INC., 16220 N Scottsdale Rd Ste 100, **Scottsdale,** AZ 85254-1825, *pg.* 608, *pg.* 24
THE UNIVERSITY OF PHOENIX, INC., 1625 W Fountainhead Pkwy, **Tempe,** AZ 85282-2371, *pg.* 610, *pg.* 27

Arkansas

UNIVERSITY OF ARKANSAS, 1125 West Maple, **Fayetteville,** AR 72701, *pg.* 608, *pg.* 31
UNIVERSITY OF ARKANSAS FOR MEDICAL SCIENCES, 4301 W Markham, **Little Rock,** AR 72205-7199, *pg.* 608, *pg.* 34

California

ACADEMY OF ART UNIVERSITY, 79 New Montgomery St., **San Francisco,** CA 94105, *pg.* 597, *pg.* 211
THE ACADEMY OF RADIO BROADCASTING, INC., 16052 Beach Blvd Ste 263, **Huntington Beach,** CA 92647-3819, *pg.* 597, *pg.* 104
ASHFORD UNIVERSITY, 8620 Spectrum Ctr Blvd, **San Diego,** CA 92123, *pg.* 598, *pg.* 200
BRIDGEPOINT EDUCATION, INC., 13500 Evening Creek Dr N Ste 600, **San Diego,** CA 92128, *pg.* 598, *pg.* 201
CHAPMAN UNIVERSITY, One University Dr, **Orange,** CA 92866, *pg.* 599, *pg.* 174
GOLDEN GATE UNIVERSITY, 536 Mission St, **San Francisco,** CA 94105-2921, *pg.* 602, *pg.* 219
GURNICK ACADEMY OF MEDICAL ARTS, Bay View Plz 2121 S El Camino Real Bldg C-200, **San Mateo,** CA 94403, *pg.* 602, *pg.* 255
LEXICON MARKETING CORPORATION, 640 S San Vicente Blvd, **Los Angeles,** CA 90048, *pg.* 604, *pg.* 134
NATIONAL UNIVERSITY, 11255 North Torrey Pines Rd, **La Jolla,** CA 92037, *pg.* 605, *pg.* 119
SCIENTIFIC LEARNING CORPORATION, 300 Frank H Ogawa Plz Ste 600, **Oakland,** CA 94612-2040, *pg.* 607, *pg.* 172
STANFORD UNIVERSITY, 450 Serra Mall, **Stanford,** CA 94305, *pg.* 607, *pg.* 280
UCLA, 405 Hilgard Ave, **Los Angeles,** CA 90095, *pg.* 608, *pg.* 141
WEST COAST UNIVERSITY, 151 Innovation Dr, **Irvine,** CA 92617-3040, *pg.* 610, *pg.* 118

Colorado

COLORADO STATE UNIVERSITY, 0150 Campus Delivery (301 Admin), **Fort Collins,** CO 80523-0150, *pg.* 599, *pg.* 328
COLORADO TECHNICAL UNIVERSITY, 4435 N Chestnut St, **Colorado Springs,** CO 80907-3812, *pg.* 599, *pg.* 315
UNIVERSITY OF COLORADO, 1800 Grant St, Ste 800, **Denver,** CO 80203, *pg.* 608, *pg.* 323
UNIVERSITY OF DENVER, 2199 S University Blvd, **Denver,** CO 80208, *pg.* 609, *pg.* 323
US CAREER INSTITUTE, 2001 Lowe St, **Fort Collins,** CO 80525, *pg.* 610, *pg.* 329

Connecticut

CORTINA LEARNING INTERNATIONAL, INC., 9 Hollyhock Rd, **Wilton,** CT 06897-4414, *pg.* 600, *pg.* 385
POST UNIVERSITY, 800 Country Club Rd, **Waterbury,** CT 06708, *pg.* 606, *pg.* 382
QUINNIPIAC UNIVERSITY, 275 Mount Carmel Ave, **Hamden,** CT 06518, *pg.* 607, *pg.* 351

Delaware

WILMINGTON UNIVERSITY, 320 N DuPont Hwy, **New Castle,** DE 19720, *pg.* 611, *pg.* 388

District of Columbia

AMERICAN UNIVERSITY, 4400 Massachusetts Ave NW, **Washington,** DC 20016-8001, *pg.* 597, *pg.* 395
THE GEORGE WASHINGTON UNIVERSITY, 2121 Eye St NW, **Washington,** DC 20052, *pg.* 602, *pg.* 400
GEORGETOWN UNIVERSITY, 3700 O St NW, **Washington,** DC 20057, *pg.* 602, *pg.* 400
STRAYER UNIVERSITY, 1133 15th St NW Ste 200, **Washington,** DC 20005-2746, *pg.* 607, *pg.* 405

Florida

EMBRY-RIDDLE AERONAUTICAL UNIVERSITY, 600 S Clyde Morris Blvd, **Daytona Beach,** FL 32114-3966, *pg.* 601, *pg.* 420
FLORIDA INSTITUTE OF TECHNOLOGY, 150 W University Blvd, **Melbourne,** FL 32901, *pg.* 601, *pg.* 439
KAPLAN, INC., 6301 Kaplan University Ave, **Fort Lauderdale,** FL 33309, *pg.* 603, *pg.* 425
KEISER UNIVERSITY, 2101 NW 117th Ave, **Miami,** FL 33172, *pg.* 603, *pg.* 443
OFFSHORE SAILING SCHOOL, LTD., INC., 16731 McGregor Blvd, **Fort Myers,** FL 33908, *pg.* 606, *pg.* 428
TIGRENT INC., 1612 E Cape Coral Pkwy, **Cape Coral,** FL 33904, *pg.* 608, *pg.* 415
TRINITY COLLEGE OF FLORIDA, 2430 Welbilt Blvd, **New Port Richey,** FL 34655, *pg.* 608, *pg.* 451
UNIVERSITY OF FLORIDA, 201 Criser Hall, **Gainesville,** FL 32611, *pg.* 609, *pg.* 429
UNIVERSITY OF MIAMI, 1252 Memorial Dr Ashe Bldg Ste 240, **Coral Gables,** FL 33124-4628, *pg.* 609, *pg.* 418

Georgia

EMORY UNIVERSITY, 201 Dowman Dr, **Atlanta,** GA 30322, *pg.* 601, *pg.* 504
GEORGIA INSTITUTE OF TECHNOLOGY, North Ave, **Atlanta,** GA 30332, *pg.* 602, *pg.* 506
GEORGIA SOUTHERN UNIVERSITY, 1332 Southern Dr, **Statesboro,** GA 30458, *pg.* 602, *pg.* 541
GEORGIA STATE UNIVERSITY, 33 Gilmer St SE, **Atlanta,** GA 30303, *pg.* 602, *pg.* 508
KENNESAW STATE UNIVERSITY, 1000 Chastain Rd, **Kennesaw,** GA 30144, *pg.* 603, *pg.* 534
MERCER UNIVERSITY, 1501 Mercer University Dr, **Macon,** GA 31207, *pg.* 604, *pg.* 535
PRIMROSE HOLDINGS INC., 3660 Cedarcrest Rd, **Acworth,** GA 30101, *pg.* 606, *pg.* 482
UNIVERSITY OF GEORGIA, The Administration Bldg, **Athens,** GA 30602, *pg.* 609, *pg.* 486

Illinois

AMERICAN SCHOOL OF CORRESPONDENCE, 2200 E 170th St, **Lansing,** IL 60438-1002, *pg.* 597, *pg.* 626
CAREER EDUCATION CORPORATION, 231 N Martingale Rd, **Schaumburg,** IL 60173, *pg.* 599, *pg.* 658
CHAMBERLAIN COLLEGE OF NURSING, LLC, 3005 Highland Pkwy, **Downers Grove,** IL 60515, *pg.* 599, *pg.* 607
DEPAUL UNIVERSITY, 1 E Jackson, **Chicago,** IL 60604, *pg.* 600, *pg.* 572
DEVRY EDUCATION GROUP INC., 3005 Highland Pkwy, **Downers Grove,** IL 60515, *pg.* 600, *pg.* 607
DEVRY UNIVERSITY INC., 1 Tower Ln Ste 1000, **Oakbrook Terrace,** IL 60181, *pg.* 600, *pg.* 649
THE JOHN MARSHALL LAW SCHOOL, 315 S Plymouth Ct, **Chicago,** IL 60604, *pg.* 603, *pg.* 579
LOYOLA UNIVERSITY CHICAGO SCHOOL OF LAW, 25 E Pearson St, **Chicago,** IL 60611, *pg.* 604, *pg.* 581
MOODY BIBLE INSTITUTE, 820 N La Salle Blvd, **Chicago,** IL 60610-3214, *pg.* 605, *pg.* 583
NORTHSHORE UNIVERSITY HEALTHSYSTEM, 1301 Central St, **Evanston,** IL 60201, *pg.* 606, *pg.* 612
NORTHWESTERN UNIVERSITY, 633 Clark St, **Evanston,** IL 60208-0001, *pg.* 606, *pg.* 612
SIEBEL INSTITUTE OF TECHNOLOGY, 1777 N Clybourn Ave Ste 2F, **Chicago,** IL 60614, *pg.* 607, *pg.* 590
THE UNIVERSITY OF CHICAGO, Edward H. Levi Hall, 5801 South Ellis Ave, **Chicago,** IL 60637, *pg.* 608, *pg.* 594
THE UNIVERSITY OF ILLINOIS COLLEGE OF LAW, 504 E Pennsylvania Ave, **Champaign,** IL 61820, *pg.* 609, *pg.* 562

Indiana

INDIANA WESLEYAN UNIVERSITY, 4201 S Washington St, **Marion,** IN 46953, *pg.* 602, *pg.* 694
ITT EDUCATIONAL SERVICES, INC., 13000 N Meridian St, **Carmel,** IN 46032-1404, *pg.* 603, *pg.* 675

Iowa

ACT INC., 500 A Ct Dr, **Iowa City,** IA 52243, *pg.* 597, *pg.* 708

Maryland

THE JOHNS HOPKINS UNIVERSITY, 3400 N Charles St, **Baltimore,** MD 21218, *pg.* 603, *pg.* 757
LAUREATE EDUCATION, INC., 650 S Exeter St, **Baltimore,** MD 21202, *pg.* 603, *pg.* 757
UNIVERSITY OF MARYLAND, College Park, **College Park,** MD 20742, *pg.* 609, *pg.* 767

Massachusetts

BABSON COLLEGE, 231 Forest Street, **Babson Park,** MA 02457, *pg.* 598, *pg.* 784
BENTLEY UNIVERSITY, 175 Forest St, **Waltham,** MA 02452, *pg.* 598, *pg.* 850
BOSTON COLLEGE, 140 Commonwealth Ave, **Chestnut Hill,** MA 02467, *pg.* 598, *pg.* 814
BOSTON UNIVERSITY, One Silber Way, **Boston,** MA 02215, *pg.* 598, *pg.* 791
BRIGHT HORIZONS FAMILY SOLUTIONS INC., 200 Talcott Ave S, **Watertown,** MA 02472, *pg.* 598, *pg.* 855
HARVARD UNIVERSITY, Massachusetts Hall, **Cambridge,** MA 02138, *pg.* 602, *pg.* 808
MASSACHUSETTS INSTITUTE OF TECHNOLOGY, 77 Massachusetts Ave, **Cambridge,** MA 02139-4307, *pg.* 604, *pg.* 809
NORTHEASTERN UNIVERSITY, 360 Huntington Ave, **Boston,** MA 02115-5005, *pg.* 605, *pg.* 799
UNIVERSITY OF MASSACHUSETTS, 300 Massachusetts Ave, **Amherst,** MA 01003, *pg.* 609, *pg.* 781

Michigan

LA PETITE ACADEMY, INC., 21333 Haggerty Rd Ste 300, **Novi,** MI 48375, *pg.* 603, *pg.* 903
LEARNING CARE GROUP INC., 21333 Haggerty Rd Ste 300, **Novi,** MI 48375, *pg.* 604, *pg.* 903
UNIVERSITY OF MICHIGAN, 500 S State St, **Ann Arbor,** MI 48109, *pg.* 609, *pg.* 867

Minnesota

CAPELLA EDUCATION COMPANY, 225 S 6th St 9th Fl, **Minneapolis,** MN 55402, *pg.* 599, *pg.* 931
GLOBE UNIVERSITY, 8089 Globe Dr, **Woodbury,** MN 55125, *pg.* 602, *pg.* 967
UNIVERSITY OF MINNESOTA, 100 Church St SE, **Minneapolis,** MN 55455, *pg.* 609, *pg.* 945
WALDEN UNIVERSITY, 100 Washington Ave S Ste 900, **Minneapolis,** MN 55401, *pg.* 610, *pg.* 946

Missouri

MISSOURI STATE UNIVERSITY, 901 S National Ave, **Springfield,** MO 65897, *pg.* 605, *pg.* 1006
WEBSTER UNIVERSITY, 470 E Lockwood Ave, **Saint Louis,** MO 63119, *pg.* 610, *pg.* 1004

First page reference indicates Business Class Edition
Second page reference indicates Geographic Edition

New Hampshire

SOUTHERN NEW HAMPSHIRE UNIVERSITY, 2500 N River Rd, **Manchester,** NH 03106, *pg.* 607, *pg.* 1036

New Jersey

BERLITZ INTERNATIONAL, INC., 400 Alexander Park, **Princeton,** NJ 08540-6306, *pg.* 598, *pg.* 1110
LINCOLN EDUCATIONAL SERVICES CORPORATION, 200 Executive Dr Ste 340, **West Orange,** NJ 07052, *pg.* 604, *pg.* 1131
PEOPLES EDUCATIONAL HOLDINGS INC., PO Box 513, **Saddle Brook,** NJ 07663, *pg.* 606, *pg.* 1118
ROWAN UNIVERSITY, 201 Mullica Hill Rd, **Glassboro,** NJ 08028, *pg.* 607, *pg.* 1071

New York

BRYANT & STRATTON COLLEGE, 465 Main St, Ste 400, **Buffalo,** NY 14203, *pg.* 599, *pg.* 1147
COLUMBIA UNIVERSITY, 2690 Broadway, **New York,** NY 10027-6902, *pg.* 600, *pg.* 1216
DALE CARNEGIE TRAINING, 780 3 Ave, **New York,** NY 10017, *pg.* 600, *pg.* 1221
EXCELSIOR COLLEGE, 7 Columbia Cir, **Albany,** NY 12203-5159, *pg.* 601, *pg.* 1137
FLIGHTSAFETY INTERNATIONAL, INC., Marine Air Terminal Laguardia Airport, **Flushing,** NY 11371, *pg.* 601, *pg.* 1160
HOFSTRA UNIVERSITY, 900 Fulton Ave, **Hempstead,** NY 11550, *pg.* 602, *pg.* 1166
THE JUILLIARD SCHOOL, 60 Lincoln Ctr Plz, **New York,** NY 10023-6500, *pg.* 603, *pg.* 1247
LEHMAN COLLEGE, 250 Bedford Park Blvd W, **Bronx,** NY 10468, *pg.* 604, *pg.* 1144
MARIST COLLEGE, 3399 N Rd, **Poughkeepsie,** NY 12601, *pg.* 604, *pg.* 1325
NEW YORK INSTITUTE OF TECHNOLOGY, Northern Blvd PO Box 8000, **Old Westbury,** NY 11568, *pg.* 605, *pg.* 1318
THE NEW YORK PUBLIC LIBRARY, 5th Ave & 42nd St, **New York,** NY 10018, *pg.* 605, *pg.* 1269
NEW YORK UNIVERSITY, 70 Washington Sq S, **New York,** NY 10012, *pg.* 605, *pg.* 1271
PRATT INSTITUTE, 200 Willoughby Ave, **Brooklyn,** NY 11205, *pg.* 606, *pg.* 1146
SUNY EMPIRE STATE COLLEGE, 2 Union Ave, **Saratoga Springs,** NY 12866, *pg.* 608, *pg.* 1340

North Carolina

DUKE UNIVERSITY, 2138 Campus Dr, **Durham,** NC 27708, *pg.* 600, *pg.* 1371
DUKE UNIVERSITY HEALTH SYSTEM, 2301 Erwin Rd, **Durham,** NC 27710, *pg.* 601, *pg.* 1371

Ohio

CIE DIRECT, 1776 E 17th St, **Cleveland,** OH 44114-3636, *pg.* 599, *pg.* 1429
CINCINNATI HILLS CHRISTIAN ACADEMY, 11525 Snider Rd, **Cincinnati,** OH 45249, *pg.* 599, *pg.* 1411
OHIO STATE UNIVERSITY, 281 W Lane Ave, **Columbus,** OH 43210, *pg.* 606, *pg.* 1443

Pennsylvania

BRODY COMMUNICATIONS, LTD., 115 West Ave Ste 114, **Jenkintown,** PA 19046, *pg.* 598, *pg.* 1542
DREXEL UNIVERSITY, 3141 Chestnut St, **Philadelphia,** PA 19104, *pg.* 600, *pg.* 1564
EDUCATION MANAGEMENT CORPORATION, 210 6th Ave, 33rd Fl, **Pittsburgh,** PA 15222, *pg.* 601, *pg.* 1575
NOBEL LEARNING COMMUNITIES, INC., 1615 West Chester Pike Ste 200, **West Chester,** PA 19382-6233, *pg.* 605, *pg.* 1593
PENN FOSTER EDUCATION GROUP, INC., 925 Oak St, **Scranton,** PA 18515-0999, *pg.* 606, *pg.* 1586
PENN STATE UNIVERSITY, Department of University Marketing, 312 Old Main, **University Park,** PA 16802, *pg.* 606, *pg.* 1589
TEMPLE UNIVERSITY, 1801 N. Broad St, **Philadelphia,** PA 19122, *pg.* 608, *pg.* 1571
UNIVERSITY OF PENNSYLVANIA, 3451 Walnut St, **Philadelphia,** PA 19104, *pg.* 609, *pg.* 1571
UNIVERSITY OF PITTSBURGH MEDICAL SCHOOL, 3550 Terrace St, **Pittsburgh,** PA 15260, *pg.* 610, *pg.* 1582
VILLANOVA UNIVERSITY, 800 E Lancaster Ave, **Villanova,** PA 19085, *pg.* 610, *pg.* 1589

Rhode Island

JOHNSON & WALES UNIVERSITY, 8 Abbott Park Pl, **Providence,** RI 02903, *pg.* 603, *pg.* 1606

South Dakota

BULLDOG MEDIA GROUP, 114 N Egan Ave, **Madison,** SD 57042, *pg.* 599, *pg.* 1624
NATIONAL AMERICAN UNIVERSITY, 5301 S Hwy 16 Ste 200, **Rapid City,** SD 57701, *pg.* 605, *pg.* 1624

Texas

CAMBIUM LEARNING GROUP, INC., 17855 Dallas Pkwy Ste 400, **Dallas,** TX 75287, *pg.* 599, *pg.* 1677
THE UNIVERSITY OF TEXAS SYSTEM, 601 Colorado St, **Austin,** TX 78701-2982, *pg.* 610, *pg.* 1667
VALE NATIONAL TRAINING CENTER INC., 2424 E Randol Mill Rd, **Arlington,** TX 76011, *pg.* 610, *pg.* 1660

Utah

WESTERN GOVERNORS UNIVERSITY, 4001 S 700 E Ste 700, **Salt Lake City,** UT 84107, *pg.* 610, *pg.* 1762

Virginia

ECPI UNIVERSITY, 5555 Greenwich Rd #300, **Virginia Beach,** VA 23462, *pg.* 601, *pg.* 1810
LEARNING TREE INTERNATIONAL, INC., 1805 Library St, **Reston,** VA 20190-5630, *pg.* 604, *pg.* 1799
SHENANDOAH UNIVERSITY, 1460 University Dr, **Winchester,** VA 22601, *pg.* 607, *pg.* 1812
STRAYER EDUCATION INC., 2303 Dulles Sta Blvd, **Herndon,** VA 20171, *pg.* 607, *pg.* 1785
THE UNIVERSITY OF VIRGINIA, 400 Ray C Hunt Dr 2nd Fl, **Charlottesville,** VA 22904, *pg.* 610, *pg.* 1778

West Virginia

AMERICAN PUBLIC EDUCATION, INC., 111 W Congress St, **Charles Town,** WV 25414, *pg.* 597, *pg.* 1849

Wisconsin

MILWAUKEE SCHOOL OF ENGINEERING, 1025 N Broadway, **Milwaukee,** WI 53202-3109, *pg.* 605, *pg.* 1878
RENAISSANCE LEARNING, INC., 2911 Peach St, **Wisconsin Rapids,** WI 54494-1905, *pg.* 607, *pg.* 1899

Electronics, Radio & Television

Alabama

MAYER ELECTRIC SUPPLY COMPANY INC., 3405 4th Ave S, **Birmingham,** AL 35222-2305, *pg.* 653, *pg.* 3
VULCAN, INC., 400 E Berry Ave, **Foley,** AL 36535-2833, *pg.* 687, *pg.* 5

Alaska

AT&T ALASCOM, 505 E Bluff Dr, **Anchorage,** AK 99501-1107, *pg.* 619, *pg.* 10

Arizona

AVNET ELECTRONICS MARKETING, 2211 S 47th St, **Phoenix,** AZ 85034, *pg.* 622, *pg.* 15
AVNET, INC., 2211 S 47th St, **Phoenix,** AZ 85034-6403, *pg.* 622, *pg.* 15
FIRST SOLAR, INC., 350 W Washington St Ste 600, **Tempe,** AZ 85281, *pg.* 639, *pg.* 26
IGO, INC., Ste 200 17800 N Perimeter Dr, **Scottsdale,** AZ 85255-5433, *pg.* 644, *pg.* 22
ROCKFORD CORPORATION, 600 S Rockford Dr, **Tempe,** AZ 85281, *pg.* 667, *pg.* 26
SION POWER CORPORATION, 9040 S Rita Rd 20900 E Zira RD, **Tucson,** AZ 85756, *pg.* 674, *pg.* 27
TASER INTERNATIONAL, INC., 17800 N 85th St, **Scottsdale,** AZ 85255-6311, *pg.* 677, *pg.* 24

California

ADVANCED MICRO DEVICES, INC., 1 AMD Pl, **Sunnyvale,** CA 94085-3905, *pg.* 613, *pg.* 282
AEROJET ROCKETDYNE INC, 2001 Aerojet Rd, **Rancho Cordova,** CA 95742, *pg.* 614, *pg.* 186
AGILENT TECHNOLOGIES, INC., 5301 Stevens Creek Blvd, **Santa Clara,** CA 95051, *pg.* 614, *pg.* 264
AL & ED'S CORPORATION, 6855 Havenhurst Hwy, **Van Nuys,** CA 91406, *pg.* 615, *pg.* 299
ALCATEL-LUCENT, 1701 Harbor Bay Pkwy Ste 1, **Alameda,** CA 94502, *pg.* 615, *pg.* 38
ALIPHCOM, INC., 99 Rhode Island St, **San Francisco,** CA 94103, *pg.* 616, *pg.* 212
ALPINE ELECTRONICS OF AMERICA, INC., 19145 Gramercy Pl, **Torrance,** CA 90501-1128, *pg.* 616, *pg.* 292
AMETEK PROGRAMMABLE POWER, INC., 9250 Brown Deer Rd, **San Diego,** CA 92121-2267, *pg.* 616, *pg.* 200
ANRITSU COMPANY, 490 Jarvis Dr, **Morgan Hill,** CA 95037-2809, *pg.* 618, *pg.* 152
APPLIED MATERIALS, INC., 3050 Bowers Ave, **Santa Clara,** CA 95054-3201, *pg.* 618, *pg.* 264
APPLIED MICRO CIRCUITS CORPORATION, 215 Moffett Park Dr, **Sunnyvale,** CA 94089, *pg.* 618, *pg.* 283
ASANTE TECHNOLOGIES, INC., 2223 Oakland Rd, **San Jose,** CA 95131-1402, *pg.* 619, *pg.* 238
ATMEL CORPORATION, 1600 Technology Dr, **San Jose,** CA 95110, *pg.* 621, *pg.* 238
AVAYA INC., 4655 Great American Pkwy, **Santa Clara,** CA 95054, *pg.* 621, *pg.* 264
AWR CORPORATION, 1960 E Grand Ave Ste 430, **El Segundo,** CA 90245, *pg.* 623, *pg.* 78
AXXCELERA BROADBAND WIRELESS INC., 82 Coromar Dr, **Santa Barbara,** CA 93117, *pg.* 623, *pg.* 263
BAND PRO FILM & DIGITAL INC., 3403 W Pacific Ave, **Burbank,** CA 91505, *pg.* 623, *pg.* 51
BEATS ELECTRONICS LLC, 1601 Cloverfield Blvd, **Santa Monica,** CA 90404, *pg.* 624, *pg.* 272
BENMAR MARINE ELECTRONICS, INC., PO Box 4007, **Idyllwild,** CA 92549, *pg.* 624, *pg.* 105
BEXEL CORPORATION, 2701 N Ontario St, **Burbank,** CA 91504, *pg.* 624, *pg.* 51
BOINGO WIRELESS, INC., 10960 Wilshire Blvd Ste 800, **Los Angeles,** CA 90024, *pg.* 625, *pg.* 127
BOURNS, INC., 1200 Columbia Ave, **Riverside,** CA 92507-2114, *pg.* 627, *pg.* 193
CEVA, INC., 1943 Landings Dr, **Mountain View,** CA 94043, *pg.* 628, *pg.* 153
CLARION CORPORATION OF AMERICA, 6200 Gateway Dr, **Cypress,** CA 90630, *pg.* 629, *pg.* 75
CPI INTERNATIONAL, INC., 811 Hansen Way, **Palo Alto,** CA 94303, *pg.* 631, *pg.* 175
CTS ELECTRONICS MANUFACTURING SOLUTIONS, 200 Science Dr, **Moorpark,** CA 93021-2003, *pg.* 632, *pg.* 151
CUBIC CORPORATION, 9333 Balboa Ave, **San Diego,** CA 92123-1515, *pg.* 632, *pg.* 201
THE CW TELEVISION NETWORK, 3300 W Olive, **Burbank,** CA 91505, *pg.* 632, *pg.* 52
CXR LARUS CORPORATION, 894 Faulstich Ct, **San Jose,** CA 95112, *pg.* 632, *pg.* 243
DEI HOLDINGS, INC., 1 Viper Way, **Vista,** CA 92081-7853, *pg.* 633, *pg.* 302
DIGITAL VIDEO SYSTEMS, INC., 357 Castro St Ste 5, **Mountain View,** CA 94041-1258, *pg.* 634, *pg.* 153
DTS, INC., 5220 Las Virgenes Rd, **Calabasas,** CA 91302, *pg.* 634, *pg.* 55
DUCOMMUN TECHNOLOGIES, INC., 23301 Wilmington Ave, **Carson,** CA 90745-6209, *pg.* 634, *pg.* 63
DYNATEX INTERNATIONAL, 5577 Skylane Blvd, **Santa Rosa,** CA 95403-1048, *pg.* 636, *pg.* 277
ELECTROCUBE INCORPORATED, 3366 Pomona Blvd, **Pomona,** CA 91768, *pg.* 635, *pg.* 185
ELO TOUCH SOLUTIONS, 1033 McCarthy Blvd, **Milpitas,** CA 95035-7920, *pg.* 635, *pg.* 145
EMCORE CORPORATION, 2015 W Chestnut St, **Alhambra,** CA 91803, *pg.* 636, *pg.* 39
EMG, INC., 3165 Coffey Ln, **Santa Rosa,** CA 95403, *pg.* 636, *pg.* 277
EMPOWER RF SYSTEMS, INC., 316 W Florence Ave, **Inglewood,** CA 90301, *pg.* 637, *pg.* 105
EVERETT CHARLES TECHNOLOGIES, 700 E Harrison Ave, **Pomona,** CA 91767, *pg.* 638, *pg.* 185
FAIRCHILD SEMICONDUCTOR CORPORATION, 3030 Orchard Pkwy, **San Jose,** CA 95134, *pg.* 638, *pg.* 245
FILEMAKER, INC., 5201 Patrick Henry Dr, **Santa Clara,** CA 95054, *pg.* 639, *pg.* 265
FINISAR CORPORATION, 1389 Moffett Park Dr, **Sunnyvale,** CA 94089-1134, *pg.* 639, *pg.* 285
FITBIT INC., 405 Howard St, **San Francisco,** CA 94105, *pg.* 639, *pg.* 218
FRY'S ELECTRONICS, INC., 600 E Brokaw Rd, **San Jose,** CA 95112-1006, *pg.* 640, *pg.* 245
FUNMOBILITY, INC., 4234 Hacienda Dr Ste 200, **Pleasanton,** CA 94588-2721, *pg.* 640, *pg.* 183
GIGA-TRONICS INCORPORATED, 4650 Norris Canyon Rd, **San Ramon,** CA 94583-1320, *pg.* 640, *pg.* 260
GRASS VALLEY, INC., 400 Providence Mine Rd, **Nevada City,** CA 95959-2953, *pg.* 641, *pg.* 164
HYPERSOUND, 13771 Danielson St Ste L, **Poway,** CA 92064, *pg.* 643, *pg.* 186
INDUSTRIAL ELECTRONIC ENGINEERS, INC., 7723 Kester Ave, **Van Nuys,** CA 91405, *pg.* 644, *pg.* 300
INFINEON TECHNOLOGIES NORTH AMERICA CORP., 640 N McCarthy Blvd, **Milpitas,** CA 95035, *pg.* 644, *pg.* 145
INFINERA CORPORATION, 140 Caspian Ct, **Sunnyvale,** CA 94089, *pg.* 644, *pg.* 286
INFOSONICS CORPORATION, 4350 Executive Dr Ste 100, **San Diego,** CA 92121-4204, *pg.* 644, *pg.* 203
INTEGRATED SILICON SOLUTION, INC., 1623 Buckeye Dr, **Milpitas,** CA 95035, *pg.* 645, *pg.* 145
INTEL CORPORATION, 2200 Mission College Blvd, **Santa Clara,** CA 95054-1537, *pg.* 645, *pg.* 266
INTERNATIONAL RECTIFIER CORPORATION, 101 N Sepulveda Blvd, **El Segundo,** CA 90245, *pg.* 647, *pg.* 80
INTERSIL CORPORATION, 1001 Murphy Ranch Rd, **Milpitas,** CA 95035, *pg.* 647, *pg.* 146
IPMOBILENET, LLC, 1221 E Dyer Rd Ste 250, **Santa Ana,** CA 92705, *pg.* 648, *pg.* 261
IRIDEX CORPORATION, 1212 Terra Bella Ave, **Mountain View,** CA 94043-1824, *pg.* 648, *pg.* 160
KENWOOD USA CORPORATION, 2201 E Dominguez St, **Long Beach,** CA 90801, *pg.* 649, *pg.* 123
L-3 INTERSTATE ELECTRONICS CORPORATION, 602 E Vermont Ave, **Anaheim,** CA 92805, *pg.* 650, *pg.* 43
LINEAR TECHNOLOGY CORP., 1630 McCarthy Blvd, **Milpitas,** CA 95035-7417, *pg.* 652, *pg.* 147
LRAD CORPORATION, 15378 Ave of Science Ste 100, **San Diego,** CA 92128-3407, *pg.* 652, *pg.* 204
MARTEK POWER ABBOTT, INC., 1111 Knox St, **Torrance,** CA 90502, *pg.* 652, *pg.* 294
MAXIM INTEGRATED PRODUCTS, INC., 160 Rio Robles, **San Jose,** CA 95134, *pg.* 653, *pg.* 247
MAXWELL TECHNOLOGIES, INC., 9244 Balboa Ave, **San Diego,** CA 92123-1505, *pg.* 653, *pg.* 204
MEGGITT SAFETY SYSTEMS, INC., 1915 Voyager Ave, **Simi Valley,** CA 93063-3386, *pg.* 653, *pg.* 279
MICREL, INC., 2180 Fortune Dr, **San Jose,** CA 95131, *pg.* 654, *pg.* 247
MITSUBISHI DIGITAL ELECTRONICS AMERICA, INC., 9351 Jeronimo Rd, **Irvine,** CA 92618-1904, *pg.* 655, *pg.* 113
MONSTER INC., 455 Valley Dr, **Brisbane,** CA 94005, *pg.* 656, *pg.* 50
MOSYS INC., 3301 Olcott S, **Santa Clara,** CA 95054, *pg.* 657, *pg.* 268
MTONE WIRELESS CORPORATION, 3080 Olcott St Ste 100-A, **Santa Clara,** CA 95054, *pg.* 658, *pg.* 268
MULTI-FINELINE ELECTRONIX, INC., 8659 Research Dr, Ste 100, **Irvine,** CA 92618, *pg.* 658, *pg.* 114
NAVCOM DEFENSE ELECTRONICS, INC., 9129 Stellar Ct, **Corona,** CA 92883, *pg.* 658, *pg.* 70
NEONODE, INC., 2350 Mission College Blvd Ste 190, **Santa Clara,** CA 95054, *pg.* 659, *pg.* 268
NEW AGE ELECTRONICS, INC., 21950 Arnold Ctr Rd, **Carson,** CA 90810, *pg.* 659, *pg.* 63
NHT AUDIO, LLC, 140 W Industrial Way, **Benicia,** CA 94510, *pg.* 659, *pg.* 45
NORTEK SECURITY & CONTROL LLC, 1950 Camino Vida Roble Ste 150, **Carlsbad,** CA 92008-6517, *pg.* 659, *pg.* 59
NTN BUZZTIME, INC., 2231 Rutherford Rd Ste 200, **Carlsbad,** CA 92008-8820, *pg.* 659, *pg.* 60
NXP SEMICONDUCTORS, 411 E Plumeria Dr, **San Jose,** CA 95134, *pg.* 660, *pg.* 248
OPLINK COMMUNICATIONS, INC., 46335 Landing Pkwy, **Fremont,** CA 94538, *pg.* 660, *pg.* 91
PALOMAR TECHNOLOGIES INC., 2728 Loker Ave W, **Carlsbad,** CA 92010, *pg.* 661, *pg.* 60
PIONEER ELECTRONICS (USA) INC., 1925 E Dominguez, **Long Beach,** CA 90810, *pg.* 663, *pg.* 124
PLANTRONICS, INC., 345 Encinal St, **Santa Cruz,** CA 95060-2132, *pg.* 663, *pg.* 270
PMC-SIERRA, INC., 1380 Bordeaux Dr, **Sunnyvale,** CA 94089, *pg.* 664, *pg.* 287
POLYCOM, INC., 6001 America Center Dr, **San Jose,** CA 95002, *pg.* 664, *pg.* 249
PROVISION HOLDING, INC., 9253 Eton Ave, **Chatsworth,** CA 91311, *pg.* 665, *pg.* 65
PULSE ELECTRONICS CORPORATION, 12220 World Trade Dr, **San Diego,** CA 92128-3765, *pg.* 666, *pg.* 206
Q-TECH CORPORATION, 10150 W Jefferson Blvd, **Culver City,** CA 90232-3502, *pg.* 666, *pg.* 72
QUALITAU, INC., 830 Maude Ave, **Mountain View,** CA 94043, *pg.* 666, *pg.* 161
RANTEC MICROWAVE SYSTEMS, INC., 31186 La Baya Dr, **Westlake Village,** CA 91362, *pg.* 666, *pg.* 307
RAYTHEON APPLIED SIGNAL TECHNOLOGY, INC., 460 W California Ave, **Sunnyvale,** CA 94086-5151, *pg.* 667, *pg.* 288
RED PEACOCK INTERNATIONAL, INC., 19859 Nordhoff St, **Northridge,** CA 91324, *pg.* 667, *pg.* 168
RENESAS ELECTRONICS AMERICA INC., 2880 Scott Blvd, **Santa Clara,** CA 95050-2554, *pg.* 667, *pg.* 269
RETZLAFF INCORPORATED, 50 Mitchell Blvd, **San Rafael,** CA 94903-2035, *pg.* 667, *pg.* 258
SAE ENGINEERING, INC., 365 Reed St, **Santa Clara,** CA 95050, *pg.* 669, *pg.* 269
SAMSUNG SEMICONDUCTOR, INC., 3655 N 1st St, **San Jose,** CA 95134-1707, *pg.* 670, *pg.* 250
SANMINA-SCI CORPORATION, 2700 N 1st St, **San Jose,** CA 95134, *pg.* 671, *pg.* 250
SEMTECH CORPORATION, 200 Flynn Rd, **Camarillo,** CA 93012-8790, *pg.* 671, *pg.* 57
SOLAR POWER, INC., 2240 Douglas Blvd Ste 200, **Roseville,** CA 95661-3875, *pg.* 675, *pg.* 195
SONICS, INC., 890 N McCarthy Blvd Ste 200, **Milpitas,** CA 95035, *pg.* 675, *pg.* 148
SONOS, INC., 223 E De La Guerra St, **Santa Barbara,** CA 93101, *pg.* 675, *pg.* 263
SONY ELECTRONICS, INC., 16450 W Bernardo Dr, **San Diego,** CA 92177, *pg.* 676, *pg.* 209
TAITRON COMPONENTS INCORPORATED, 28040 Harrison Pkwy, **Valencia,** CA 91355-4162, *pg.* 677, *pg.* 299
TEAC AMERICA, INC., 7733 Telegraph Rd, **Montebello,** CA 90640-6537, *pg.* 678, *pg.* 151
TELEDYNE MICROELECTRONIC TECHNOLOGIES, 12964 Panama St, **Los Angeles,** CA 90066, *pg.* 678, *pg.* 140
TELENAV, INC., 1130 Kifer Rd, **Sunnyvale,** CA 94086, *pg.* 678, *pg.* 288
THE TENNIS CHANNEL, INC., 2850 Ocean Park Blvd, **Santa Monica,** CA 90405, *pg.* 679, *pg.* 276

First page reference indicates Business Class Edition
Second page reference indicates Geographic Edition

TRANSICO INCORPORATED, 1240 Pioneer St Ste A, **Brea,** CA 92821, *pg.* 682, *pg.* 49
UNIVERSAL ELECTRONICS, INC., 201 Sandpointe Ave, Ste 800, **Santa Ana,** CA 92707, *pg.* 683, *pg.* 262
VANSAN CORPORATION, 16735 E Johnson Dr, **City of Industry,** CA 91745, *pg.* 685, *pg.* 68
VELATEL GLOBAL COMMUNICATIONS, INC., 12526 High Bluff Dr Ste 155, **San Diego,** CA 92130, *pg.* 685, *pg.* 210
VELODYNE ACOUSTICS, INC., 345 Digital Dr, **Morgan Hill,** CA 95037, *pg.* 685, *pg.* 152
VITAL CONNECT, 900 E Hamilton Ave Ste 500, **Campbell,** CA 95008, *pg.* 686, *pg.* 58
VITESSE SEMICONDUCTOR CORPORATION, 741 Calle Plano, **Camarillo,** CA 93012-8543, *pg.* 686, *pg.* 57
VIZIO, INC., 39 Tesla, **Irvine,** CA 92618, *pg.* 686, *pg.* 118
WESTINGHOUSE SOLAR, 1475 S Bascom Ave Ste 101, **Campbell,** CA 95008, *pg.* 688, *pg.* 58
YAMAHA ELECTRONICS CORPORATION USA, 6660 Orangethorpe Ave, **Buena Park,** CA 90620, *pg.* 689, *pg.* 51
ZACK ELECTRONICS, INC., 1075 Hamilton Rd, **Duarte,** CA 91010, *pg.* 690, *pg.* 77

Colorado

ADVANCED ENERGY INDUSTRIES, INC., 1625 Sharp Point Dr, **Fort Collins,** CO 80525-4423, *pg.* 613, *pg.* 328
ARROW ELECTRONICS, INC., 7459 S. Lima St, **Englewood,** CO 80112, *pg.* 619, *pg.* 325
LIBERTY MEDIA CORPORATION, 12300 Liberty Blvd, **Englewood,** CO 80112, *pg.* 652, *pg.* 326
UQM TECHNOLOGIES, INC., 4120 Speciality Pl, **Longmont,** CO 80504, *pg.* 684, *pg.* 334
ZYNEX, INC., 9990 Park Meadows Dr, **Lone Tree,** CO 80124, *pg.* 690, *pg.* 333

Connecticut

AMPHENOL CORPORATION, 358 Hall Ave, **Wallingford,** CT 06492, *pg.* 616, *pg.* 381
DEVAR, INC., 706 Bostwick Ave, **Bridgeport,** CT 06605-2396, *pg.* 633, *pg.* 339
DURACELL, 14 Research Dr Berkshire Corporate Pk, **Bethel,** CT 06801, *pg.* 635, *pg.* 337
HARMAN INTERNATIONAL INDUSTRIES, INCORPORATED, 400 Atlantic St 15th Fl, **Stamford,** CT 06901, *pg.* 641, *pg.* 374
KRELL INDUSTRIES, INC., 45 Connair Rd, **Orange,** CT 06477-3650, *pg.* 650, *pg.* 367
MORSE WATCHMANS INC., 2 Morse Rd, **Oxford,** CT 06478-1040, *pg.* 656, *pg.* 368
NOTIFIER CO., 12 Clintonville Rd, **Northford,** CT 06472, *pg.* 659, *pg.* 360
RADIO FREQUENCY SYSTEMS, INC., 200 Pond View Dr, **Meriden,** CT 06450-7195, *pg.* 666, *pg.* 354
TIMES FIBER COMMUNICATIONS, INC., 358 Hall Ave, **Wallingford,** CT 06492, *pg.* 681, *pg.* 382
TRANS-LUX CORPORATION, 26 Pearl St, **Norwalk,** CT 06850, *pg.* 681, *pg.* 365
VISHAY AMERICAS, 1 Greenwich Place, **Shelton,** CT 06484, *pg.* 686, *pg.* 371
WARD LEONARD ELECTRIC COMPANY, INC., 401 Watertown Rd, **Thomaston,** CT 06787, *pg.* 687, *pg.* 380
WINCHESTER ELECTRONICS CORP., 62 Barnes Industrial Rd N, **Wallingford,** CT 06492, *pg.* 688, *pg.* 382
WIREMOLD/LEGRAND, 60 Woodlawn St, **West Hartford,** CT 06110-2326, *pg.* 689, *pg.* 383

Florida

ACR ELECTRONICS, INC., 5757 Ravenswood Rd, **Fort Lauderdale,** FL 33312-6603, *pg.* 612, *pg.* 422
THE ADT CORPORATION, 1501 Yamato Rd, **Boca Raton,** FL 33431, *pg.* 612, *pg.* 409
API TECHNOLOGIES CORP., 4705 S Apopka Vineland Rd Ste 210, **Orlando,** FL 32819, *pg.* 618, *pg.* 452
AUDIO VISUAL INNOVATIONS, INC., 6301 Benjamin Rd Ste 101, **Tampa,** FL 33634-5181, *pg.* 621, *pg.* 471
BRANDSMART USA, 3200 SW 42nd St, **Hollywood,** FL 33312-6813, *pg.* 627, *pg.* 430
BRIGHTSTAR CORPORATION, 9725 NW 117th Ave #300, **Miami,** FL 33178, *pg.* 627, *pg.* 440
CODA OCTOPUS GROUP, INC., 4020 Kidron Rd Ste 4, **Lakeland,** FL 33811, *pg.* 629, *pg.* 437
CRANE AEROSPACE & ELECTRONICS, KELTEC OPERATION, 84 Hill Ave NW, **Fort Walton Beach,** FL 32548-3858, *pg.* 631, *pg.* 428
DIGITAL LIGHTWAVE, INC., 1780 102nd Ave N Ste 500, **Saint Petersburg,** FL 33716-3603, *pg.* 634, *pg.* 462
FOX ELECTRONICS, 5570 Enterprise Pkwy, **Fort Myers,** FL 33905, *pg.* 639, *pg.* 428
HARRIS CORPORATION, 1025 W NASA Blvd, **Melbourne,** FL 32919-0001, *pg.* 642, *pg.* 439
THE LGL GROUP, INC., 2525 Shader Rd, **Orlando,** FL 32804, *pg.* 652, *pg.* 454
POSITIVEID CORPORATION, 1690 S Congress Ave, Ste 201, **Delray Beach,** FL 33445, *pg.* 665, *pg.* 422
SBA COMMUNICATIONS CORPORATION, 5900 Broken Sound Pkwy NW, **Boca Raton,** FL 33487, *pg.* 671, *pg.* 413
SENSOR SYSTEMS, LLC, 2800 Anvil St N, **Saint Petersburg,** FL 33710-2943, *pg.* 672, *pg.* 464
THE SINGING MACHINE COMPANY, INC., 6301 NW 5th Way Ste 2900, **Fort Lauderdale,** FL 33309-6191, *pg.* 674, *pg.* 426
TRACFONE WIRELESS, INC., 9700 NW 112 Ave, **Miami,** FL 33178-1504, *pg.* 681, *pg.* 447
VERIZON TERREMARK, 2 S Biscayne Blvd Ste 2800, **Miami,** FL 33131, *pg.* 685, *pg.* 447

Georgia

AT&T MOBILITY LLC, 1055 Lenox Park Blvd NE Room A325, **Atlanta,** GA 30319, *pg.* 619, *pg.* 488
MURATA ELECTRONICS NORTH AMERICA, INC., 2200 Lake Park Dr, **Smyrna,** GA 30080-7604, *pg.* 658, *pg.* 540
NUMEREX CORP., 3330 Cumberland Blvd SE, Ste 700, **Atlanta,** GA 30339, *pg.* 660, *pg.* 517
POLYVISION CORPORATION, 10700 Abbotts Bridge Rd Ste 100, **Duluth,** GA 30097, *pg.* 665, *pg.* 531
SIEMENS PROCESS INDUSTRIES AND DRIVES, 3333 Old Milton Pkwy, **Alpharetta,** GA 30005-4437, *pg.* 673, *pg.* 485
SUPERIOR ESSEX, INC., 6120 Powers Ferry Rd Ste 150, **Atlanta,** GA 30339, *pg.* 676, *pg.* 521
VIDEO DISPLAY CORPORATION, 1868 Tucker Industrial Rd, **Tucker,** GA 30084, *pg.* 685, *pg.* 542
WEGENER CORPORATION, 11350 Technology Circle, **Johns Creek,** GA 30097-1502, *pg.* 687, *pg.* 533
WHITE ELECTRICAL CONSTRUCTION CO., 1730 Chattahoochee Ave NW, **Atlanta,** GA 30318-2112, *pg.* 688, *pg.* 524

Illinois

ABT ELECTRONICS, INC., 1200 Milwaukee Ave, **Glenview,** IL 60025, *pg.* 612, *pg.* 614
ACTIVE ELECTRICAL SUPPLY COMPANY, 4240 W Lawrence Ave, **Chicago,** IL 60630-2730, *pg.* 612, *pg.* 563
BASLER ELECTRIC COMPANY, Rte 143, **Highland,** IL 62249, *pg.* 623, *pg.* 616
BRK BRANDS, INC., 3901 Liberty St Rd, **Aurora,** IL 60504-8122, *pg.* 627, *pg.* 554
BROADCAST ELECTRONICS, INC., 4100 N 24th St, **Quincy,** IL 62305-3606, *pg.* 627, *pg.* 653
COBRA ELECTRONICS CORPORATION, 6500 W Cortland St, **Chicago,** IL 60707-4000, *pg.* 629, *pg.* 572
COMMSCOPE, 3 Westbrook Corporate Ctr Ste 900, **Westchester,** IL 60154, *pg.* 630, *pg.* 668
CONSOLIDATED COMMUNICATIONS HOLDINGS, INC., 121 S 17th St, **Mattoon,** IL 61938-3987, *pg.* 630, *pg.* 631
DEXTER MAGNETIC TECHNOLOGIES, INC., 1050 Morse Ave, **Elk Grove Village,** IL 60007-5110, *pg.* 634, *pg.* 610
DUKANE CORPORATION, 2900 Dukane Dr, **Saint Charles,** IL 60174, *pg.* 634, *pg.* 658
EPSON ELECTRONICS AMERICA, 1827 Walden Office Sq, **Schaumburg,** IL 60173, *pg.* 638, *pg.* 658
FEDERAL SIGNAL CORPORATION, 1415 W 22nd St Ste 1100, **Oak Brook,** IL 60523-2074, *pg.* 638, *pg.* 645
GUARDIAN ELECTRIC MANUFACTURING COMPANY, 1425 Lk Ave, **Woodstock,** IL 60098-7419, *pg.* 641, *pg.* 672
HAPP CONTROLS INC., 1743 S Linneman Rd, **Mount Prospect,** IL 60056-5100, *pg.* 641, *pg.* 634
INTERNATIONAL COMPONENTS CORPORATION, 4 Westbrook Corporate Ctr Ste 900, **Westchester,** IL 60154, *pg.* 647, *pg.* 669
KESTER, INC., 800 W Thorndale, **Itasca,** IL 60143, *pg.* 649, *pg.* 620
METHODE ELECTRONICS, INC., 7401 W Wilson Ave, **Chicago,** IL 60706-4548, *pg.* 654, *pg.* 581
MOLEX INCORPORATED, 2222 Wellington Ct, **Lisle,** IL 60532-1682, *pg.* 655, *pg.* 628
MOTOROLA MOBILITY LLC, 600 N US Highway 45, **Libertyville,** IL 60048, *pg.* 657, *pg.* 627
MOTOROLA SOLUTIONS, INC., 1303 E Algonquin Rd, **Schaumburg,** IL 60196-4041, *pg.* 657, *pg.* 659
OHMITE MANUFACTURING COMPANY, 85 W Algonquin Rd Ste 230, **Arlington Heights,** IL 60005-4442, *pg.* 660, *pg.* 553
PANDUIT CORP., 17301 Ridgeland Ave, **Tinley Park,** IL 60477-3093, *pg.* 661, *pg.* 663
QUAM-NICHOLS COMPANY, 234 E Marquette Rd, **Chicago,** IL 60637-4091, *pg.* 666, *pg.* 588
RAULAND-BORG CORPORATION, 1802 W Central Rd, **Mount Prospect,** IL 60052, *pg.* 666, *pg.* 634
RICHARDSON ELECTRONICS, LTD., 40W267 Keslinger Road, **Lafox,** IL 60147, *pg.* 667, *pg.* 622
SHURE INCORPORATED, 5800 Touhy Ave, **Niles,** IL 60714, *pg.* 672, *pg.* 638
SIEMENS HEALTHCARE DIAGNOSTICS, 1717 Deerfield Rd, **Deerfield,** IL 60015-0778, *pg.* 673, *pg.* 604
SIGMATRON INTERNATIONAL, INC., 2201 Landmeier Rd, **Elk Grove Village,** IL 60007-2620, *pg.* 674, *pg.* 611
SYSTEM SENSOR, 3825 Ohio Ave, **Saint Charles,** IL 60174, *pg.* 676, *pg.* 658
TELLABS, INC., 1 Tellabs Ctr 1415 W Diehl Rd, **Naperville,** IL 60563, *pg.* 678, *pg.* 637
ZEBRA TECHNOLOGIES CORPORATION, 475 Half Day Rd Ste 500, **Lincolnshire,** IL 60069, *pg.* 690, *pg.* 628

Indiana

BELL INDUSTRIES, INC., 4400 W 96th St, **Indianapolis, IN** 46268, *pg.* 624, *pg.* 683
CTS CORPORATION, 905 West Blvd N, **Elkhart,** IN 46514-1875, *pg.* 631, *pg.* 677
DA-LITE SCREEN COMPANY, 3100 N Detroit St, **Warsaw,** IN 46581, *pg.* 632, *pg.* 698
DELPHI ELECTRONICS & SAFETY, 2151 E Lincoln Rd, **Kokomo,** IN 46902, *pg.* 633, *pg.* 692
ESSEX GROUP, INC., 1601 Wall St, **Fort Wayne,** IN 46802, *pg.* 638, *pg.* 680
JUNO LIGHTING GROUP, 12001 Exit 5 Pkwy, **Fishers,** IN 46038-7940, *pg.* 648, *pg.* 679
KLIPSCH GROUP, INC., 3502 Woodview Trace Ste 200, **Indianapolis,** IN 46268, *pg.* 649, *pg.* 688
POSITRON CORP., 9715 Kincaid Blvd Ste 1000, **Fishers,** IN 46038, *pg.* 665, *pg.* 680

Iowa

WINEGARD COMPANY, 3000 Kirkwood St, **Burlington,** IA 52601-2000, *pg.* 688, *pg.* 702

Kansas

ELECSYS CORPORATION, 846 N Market-Way Ct, **Olathe,** KS 66061, *pg.* 635, *pg.* 717
PROTECTION ONE, INC., 1035 N 3rd St Ste 101, **Lawrence,** KS 66044, *pg.* 665, *pg.* 715

Louisiana

VALENTINO HOME ENTERTAINMENT, 7150 Jefferson Hwy., Ste 760, **Baton Rouge,** LA 70806, *pg.* 684, *pg.* 742

Maryland

CIENA CORPORATION, 7035 Ridge Rd, **Hanover,** MD 21076, *pg.* 628, *pg.* 771
FUSION UV SYSTEMS, INC., 910 Clopper Rd, **Gaithersburg,** MD 20878-1361, *pg.* 640, *pg.* 770
HUGHES NETWORK SYSTEMS LLC, 11717 Exploration Ln, **Germantown,** MD 20876, *pg.* 643, *pg.* 770
POLK AUDIO, INC., 5601 Metro Dr, **Baltimore,** MD 21215, *pg.* 664, *pg.* 758
TESSCO TECHNOLOGIES, INC., 11126 McCormick Rd, **Hunt Valley,** MD 21031-1494, *pg.* 679, *pg.* 773
UNIVERSAL SECURITY INSTRUMENTS, INC., 11407 Cronhill Dr Ste A, **Owings Mills,** MD 21117, *pg.* 683, *pg.* 775

Massachusetts

ANALOG DEVICES, INC., 1 Technology Way PO Box 9106, **Norwood,** MA 02062-9106, *pg.* 617, *pg.* 839
ATLANTIC TELE-NETWORK, INC., 600 Cummings Ctr, **Beverly,** MA 01915, *pg.* 620, *pg.* 787
AVID TECHNOLOGY, INC., 75 Network Dr, **Burlington,** MA 01803, *pg.* 622, *pg.* 804
BOSE CORPORATION, PO Box 9168, **Framingham,** MA 01701-9168, *pg.* 626, *pg.* 820
CTS VALPEY CORPORATION, 75 South St, **Hopkinton,** MA 01748-2204, *pg.* 632, *pg.* 825
DAVID CLARK COMPANY INCORPORATED, 360 Franklin St, **Worcester,** MA 01615-0054, *pg.* 633, *pg.* 862
THE ENTWISTLE CO., 6 Bigelow St, **Hudson,** MA 01749-2697, *pg.* 637, *pg.* 826
FLOWTRON OUTDOOR PRODUCTS, 15 Highland Ave, **Malden,** MA 02148, *pg.* 639, *pg.* 830
HITTITE MICROWAVE CORPORATION, 2 Elizabeth Dr, **Chelmsford,** MA 01824, *pg.* 642, *pg.* 813
INSULET CORPORATION, 9 Oak Park Dr, **Bedford,** MA 01730, *pg.* 644, *pg.* 785
MICRON CORPORATION, 89 Access Rd Ste 5, **Norwood,** MA 02062-5234, *pg.* 654, *pg.* 840
MINI-SYSTEMS, INC., 20 David Rd, **North Attleboro,** MA 02760, *pg.* 654, *pg.* 837
MONOTYPE IMAGING HOLDINGS, INC., 500 Unicorn Park Dr, **Woburn,** MA 01801, *pg.* 656, *pg.* 861
PARKER CHOMERICS, 77 Dragon Ct, **Woburn,** MA 01801-1039, *pg.* 662, *pg.* 862
PHILIPS ELECTRONICS NORTH AMERICA, 3000 Minuteman Rd, **Andover,** MA 01810, *pg.* 662, *pg.* 782
SKYWORKS SOLUTIONS, INC., 20 Sylvan Rd, **Woburn,** MA 01801-1845, *pg.* 674, *pg.* 862
TERADYNE INC., 600 Riverpark Dr, **North Reading,** MA 01864, *pg.* 679, *pg.* 838
TYCO SIMPLEXGRINNELL LP, 50 Technology Dr, **Westminster,** MA 01441-0001, *pg.* 682, *pg.* 859
XURA, INC., 200 Quannapowitt Pkwy, **Wakefield,** MA 01880-1315, *pg.* 689, *pg.* 849

Michigan

GUARDIAN ALARM COMPANY, 20800 Southfield Rd, **Southfield,** MI 48075-4238, *pg.* 641, *pg.* 907
L-3 AVIONICS SYSTEMS, INC., 5353 52nd St SE, **Grand Rapids,** MI 49512, *pg.* 650, *pg.* 888
POWERMAT USA, LLC, 3000 N Pontiac Trl, **Commerce Township,** MI 48039, *pg.* 665, *pg.* 875
PROGRESSIVE DYNAMICS, INC., 507 Industrial Rd, **Marshall,** MI 49068-1750, *pg.* 665, *pg.* 898
ROFIN-SINAR TECHNOLOGIES, INC., 40984 Concept Dr, **Plymouth,** MI 48170, *pg.* 668, *pg.* 904
ROWE INTERNATIONAL CORP, 4147 Eastern Ave SW Ste 200, **Grand Rapids,** MI 49507, *pg.* 669, *pg.* 889

Minnesota

ATEK, 210 NE 10th Ave, **Brainerd,** MN 56401, *pg.* 620, *pg.* 919
AUDIO RESEARCH CORPORATION, 3900 Annapolis Ln N, **Plymouth,** MN 55447-5447, *pg.* 621, *pg.* 953
BADGER MAGNETICS INC., 501 Apollo Dr, **Lino Lakes,** MN 55014, *pg.* 623, *pg.* 927
BOSCH COMMUNICATIONS INC., 12000 Portland Ave, **Burnsville,** MN 55337-1522, *pg.* 626, *pg.* 919
CINEQUIPT INC., 2601 49th Ave N, **Minneapolis,** MN 55430, *pg.* 629, *pg.* 932
COMMUNICATIONS SYSTEMS, INC., 10900 Red Circle Dr, **Minnetonka,** MN 55343, *pg.* 630, *pg.* 948
ECESSA CORPORATION, 2800 Campus Dr Ste 140, **Plymouth,** MN 55441-3674, *pg.* 635, *pg.* 953
ELECTROSONIC SYSTEMS, INC., 10320 Bren Rd E, **Minnetonka,** MN 55343, *pg.* 635, *pg.* 949
ENVENTIS, 221 E Hickory St, **Mankato,** MN 56001-3610, *pg.* 637, *pg.* 927
INTEGRA TELECOM, INC., 4690 Colorado St SE, **Minneapolis,** MN 55372, *pg.* 644, *pg.* 938
MCT WORLDWIDE LLC, 121 S 8th St Ste 960, **Minneapolis,** MN 55402, *pg.* 653, *pg.* 939
MILESTONE AV TECHNOLOGIES, INC., 8401 Eagle Creek Pkwy, **Savage,** MN 55378, *pg.* 654, *pg.* 964
NORTECH SYSTEMS INCORPORATED, 1120 Wayzata Blvd E Ste 201, **Wayzata,** MN 55391, *pg.* 659, *pg.* 966
RUDOLPH TECHNOLOGIES, INC., 4900 W 78th St, **Bloomington,** MN 55435-5410, *pg.* 669, *pg.* 918
WINLAND ELECTRONICS, INC., 1950 Excel Dr, **Mankato,** MN 56001-5903, *pg.* 688, *pg.* 928
WIRELESS RONIN TECHNOLOGIES INC., Baker Tech N Plz 5929 Baker Rd Ste 475, **Minnetonka,** MN 55345, *pg.* 689, *pg.* 951

Mississippi

C SPIRE WIRELESS, 1018 Highland Colony Pkwy Ste 300, **Ridgeland,** MS 39157-3301, *pg.* 628, *pg.* 971
PEAVEY ELECTRONICS CORPORATION, 5022 Hartley Peavey Dr, **Meridian,** MS 39305-5422, *pg.* 662, *pg.* 970

Missouri

BELDEN, INC., 7733 Forsyth Blvd Ste 800, **Saint Louis,** MO 63105, *pg.* 624, *pg.* 993
DIT-MCO INTERNATIONAL CORPORATION, 5612 Brighton Ter, **Kansas City,** MO 64130-4530, *pg.* 634, *pg.* 982
ENERGIZER HOLDINGS, INC., 533 Maryville University Dr, **Saint Louis,** MO 63141-5801, *pg.* 637, *pg.* 996

Montana

APPLIED MATERIALS, INC, 655 W Reserve Dr, **Kalispell,** MT 59901-2127, *pg.* 618, *pg.* 1009

Nebraska

AMERICAN SHIZUKI CORPORATION, 301 W O St, **Ogallala,** NE 69153, *pg.* 616, *pg.* 1013
BALLANTYNE STRONG, INC., 13710 First Natl Bank Pkwy Ste 400, **Omaha,** NE 68154, *pg.* 623, *pg.* 1013

New Hampshire

AAVID THERMALLOY, LLC, 1 Aavid Circle, **Laconia,** NH 03246, *pg.* 612, *pg.* 1035
BAE SYSTEMS-INFORMATION WARFARE, 144 Daniel Webster Hwy N, **Merrimack,** NH 03054, *pg.* 623, *pg.* 1036
GN NETCOM INC., 77 Northeastern Blvd, **Nashua,** NH 03062-3128, *pg.* 640, *pg.* 1037
ICAD, INC., 98 Spit Brook Rd Ste 100, **Nashua,** NH 03062, *pg.* 643, *pg.* 1037
KEVLIN CORPORATION, 11 Continental Dr, **Exeter,** NH 03833, *pg.* 649, *pg.* 1034

New Jersey

ALCATEL-LUCENT, 600-700 Mountain Ave, **New Providence,** NJ 07974, *pg.* 615, *pg.* 1094
ANADIGICS, INC., 141 Mount Bethel Rd, **Warren,** NJ 07059-5148, *pg.* 617, *pg.* 1128
BEL FUSE INC., 206 Van Vorst St, **Jersey City,** NJ 07302-4421, *pg.* 624, *pg.* 1075
BLONDER TONGUE LABORATORIES, INC., 1 Jake Brown Rd, **Old Bridge,** NJ 08857, *pg.* 625, *pg.* 1100
BOGEN COMMUNICATIONS INTERNATIONAL INC., 50 Spring St, **Ramsey,** NJ 07446, *pg.* 625, *pg.* 1113
COOPER INTERCONNECT, 23 Front St, **Salem,** NJ 08079, *pg.* 630, *pg.* 1118
COOPER WHEELOCK, 273 Branchport Ave, **Long Branch,** NJ 07740-6830, *pg.* 630, *pg.* 1080
CRESTRON ELECTRONICS INC., 15 Volvo Dr, **Rockleigh,** NJ 07647-2507, *pg.* 631, *pg.* 1116
EMERSON RADIO CORP., 85 Oxford Dr, **Moonachie,** NJ 07074, *pg.* 636, *pg.* 1087
FARADAY, 8 Fernwood Rd, **Florham Park,** NJ 07932, *pg.* 638, *pg.* 1066
FUJI ELECTRIC CORPORATION OF AMERICA, Park 80 W Plz II, **Saddle Brook,** NJ 07663, *pg.* 640, *pg.* 1118
I.D. SYSTEMS, INC., 123 Tice Blvd, **Woodcliff Lake,** NJ 07677, *pg.* 643, *pg.* 1134
IDT CORPORATION, 520 Broad St, **Newark,** NJ 07102, *pg.* 643, *pg.* 1096
IKEGAMI ELECTRONICS (U.S.A.), INC., 37 Brook Ave, **Maywood,** NJ 07607, *pg.* 644, *pg.* 1083
IPC SYSTEMS, INC., Harborside Fin Ctr 1500 Plz 10 3 2nd St 15th Fl, **Jersey City,** NJ 07311, *pg.* 648, *pg.* 1075
JOHANSON MANUFACTURING CORPORATION, 301 Rockaway Vly Rd, **Boonton,** NJ 07005, *pg.* 648, *pg.* 1045
JVC AMERICAS CORP., 1700 Valley Rd, **Wayne,** NJ 07470, *pg.* 648, *pg.* 1129
LG ELECTRONICS U.S.A., INC., 1000 Sylvan Ave, **Englewood Cliffs,** NJ 07632, *pg.* 651, *pg.* 1060
MARINE ELECTRIC SYSTEMS, INC., 80 Wesley St, **South Hackensack,** NJ 07606, *pg.* 652, *pg.* 1123
MAXELL CORPORATION OF AMERICA, 3 Garret Mountain Plz 3rd Fl Ste 300, **Little Falls,** NJ 07424, *pg.* 652, *pg.* 1079
MDU COMMUNICATIONS INTERNATIONAL, INC., 60-D Commerce Way, **Totowa,** NJ 07512, *pg.* 653, *pg.* 1126
METAL TEXTILES CORPORATION, 970 New Durham Rd, **Edison,** NJ 08818, *pg.* 654, *pg.* 1057
PANASONIC CORPORATION OF NORTH AMERICA, 1 Panasonic Way, **Secaucus,** NJ 07094-2917, *pg.* 661, *pg.* 1120
PANASONIC ELECTRIC WORKS CORPORATION OF AMERICA, 629 Central Ave, **New Providence,** NJ 07974, *pg.* 661, *pg.* 1095
SAMSUNG ELECTRONICS AMERICA, INC., 85 Challenger Rd, **Ridgefield Park,** NJ 07660, *pg.* 669, *pg.* 1115
SDI TECHNOLOGIES, INC., 1299 Main St, **Rahway,** NJ 07065-5024, *pg.* 671, *pg.* 1113
SHARP ELECTRONICS CORPORATION, 1 Sharp Plz, **Mahwah,** NJ 07430-2135, *pg.* 672, *pg.* 1082
SL INDUSTRIES, INC., 520 Fellowship Rd Ste A114, **Mount Laurel,** NJ 08054-3400, *pg.* 674, *pg.* 1090
TELEGENIX INC., 1930 Olney Ave, **Cherry Hill,** NJ 08003-2016, *pg.* 678, *pg.* 1051
TOSHIBA AMERICA CONSUMER PRODUCTS, LLC, 82 Totowa Rd, **Wayne,** NJ 07470-3114, *pg.* 681, *pg.* 1130
UNILUX, INC., 59 N 5th St, **Saddle Brook,** NJ 07663-6113, *pg.* 682, *pg.* 1118
UNIVERSAL DISPLAY CORPORATION, Princeton Crossroads Corp Ctr 375 Phillips Blvd, **Ewing,** NJ 08618, *pg.* 683, *pg.* 1064
VIRGIN MOBILE USA, LP, 10 Independence Blvd, **Warren,** NJ 07059, *pg.* 685, *pg.* 1129
VONAGE HOLDINGS CORP., 23 Main St, **Holmdel,** NJ 07733, *pg.* 686, *pg.* 1074
WIRELESS TELECOM GROUP, INC., 25 Eastmans Rd, **Parsippany,** NJ 07054-3702, *pg.* 689, *pg.* 1106

New York

AEROFLEX INCORPORATED, 35 S Service Rd, **Plainview,** NY 11803, *pg.* 614, *pg.* 1321
ALLIED MOTION TECHNOLOGIES INC., 455 Commerce Dr Ste 4, **Amherst,** NY 14228, *pg.* 616, *pg.* 1137
AMERICAN TECHNICAL CERAMICS CORP., 1 Norden Ln, **Huntington Station,** NY 11746, *pg.* 616, *pg.* 1168
ANAREN, INC., 6635 Kirkville Rd, **East Syracuse,** NY 13057, *pg.* 617, *pg.* 1157
ANDREA ELECTRONICS CORPORATION, 620 Johnson Ave Ste 1B, **Bohemia,** NY 11716, *pg.* 617, *pg.* 1143
AT&T MOBILITY LLC, Appletree Business Park 2875 Union Rd Ste 35U, **Cheektowaga,** NY 14227, *pg.* 620, *pg.* 1152
AUDIO COMMAND SYSTEMS, INC., 694 Main St, **Westbury,** NY 11590, *pg.* 621, *pg.* 1350
BOSCH SECURITY SYSTEMS, INC., 130 Perinton Pkwy, **Fairport,** NY 14450-9107, *pg.* 626, *pg.* 1158
CANARY CONNECT, INC., 132 E 43rd St, Ste 552, **New York,** NY 10017, *pg.* 628, *pg.* 1209
CVD EQUIPMENT CORPORATION, 355 S Technology Dr, **Central Islip,** NY 11722, *pg.* 632, *pg.* 1152
DGT HOLDINGS, 590 Madison Ave, **New York,** NY 10002, *pg.* 634, *pg.* 1223
FILM EMPORIUM INC., 1890 Palmer Ave, Ste 403, **Larchmont,** NY 10538, *pg.* 639, *pg.* 1173
FREQUENCY ELECTRONICS, INC., 55 Charles Lindbergh Blvd, **Mitchel Field,** NY 11553-3682, *pg.* 639, *pg.* 1182
GLOBECOMM SYSTEMS INC., 45 Oser Ave, **Hauppauge,** NY 11788-3816, *pg.* 640, *pg.* 1164
GRIFFON CORPORATION, 712 5th Ave 18th Fl, **New York,** NY 10019, *pg.* 641, *pg.* 1236
HARMAN CONSUMER, INC., 250 Crossways Pk Dr, **Woodbury,** NY 11797, *pg.* 641, *pg.* 1355
HARRIS CORP. RF COMMUNICATIONS DIVISION, 1680 University Ave, **Rochester,** NY 14610-1839, *pg.* 642, *pg.* 1336
HITACHI AMERICA, LTD., 50 Prospect Ave, **Tarrytown,** NY 10591, *pg.* 642, *pg.* 1344

IEC ELECTRONICS CORP., 105 Norton St, **Newark, NY** 14513-1218, *pg.* 643, *pg.* 1317
JACO ELECTRONICS, INC., 145 Oser Ave, **Hauppauge, NY** 11788, *pg.* 648, *pg.* 1165
KRATOS-GENERAL MICROWAVE, 227A Michael Dr, **Syosset, NY** 11791, *pg.* 650, *pg.* 1344
L-3 COMMUNICATIONS HOLDINGS INC., 600 3rd Ave, **New York, NY** 10016, *pg.* 650, *pg.* 1250
L-3 COMMUNICATIONS NARDA MICROWAVE-EAST, 435 Moreland Rd, **Hauppauge, NY** 11788-3926, *pg.* 650, *pg.* 1165
MEDIACOM COMMUNICATIONS CORPORATION, 100 Crystal Run Rd, **Middletown, NY** 10941, *pg.* 653, *pg.* 1182
MICROWAVE FILTER COMPANY, INC., 6743 Kinne St, **East Syracuse, NY** 13057-1215, *pg.* 654, *pg.* 1157
MTI INSTRUMENTS INC., 325 Washington Ave Ext, **Albany, NY** 12205-5505, *pg.* 658, *pg.* 1137
NAPCO SECURITY SYSTEMS, INC., 333 Bayview Ave, **Amityville, NY** 11701, *pg.* 658, *pg.* 1138
POLAR ELECTRO INC., 1111 Marcus Ave Ste M15, **Lake Success, NY** 11042-1034, *pg.* 664, *pg.* 1173
PROFESSIONAL SOUND SERVICES, INC., 311 W 43rd St Ste 200, **New York, NY** 10036, *pg.* 665, *pg.* 1283
SAM ASH MUSIC CORPORATION, 278 Duffy Ave, **Hicksville, NY** 11801-3605, *pg.* 669, *pg.* 1167
SENTRY TECHNOLOGY CORPORATION, 1881 Lakeland Ave, **Ronkonkoma, NY** 11779, *pg.* 672, *pg.* 1339
SHOKAI FAR EAST LTD., 9 Elena Ct, **Cortlandt Manor, NY** 10567-7012, *pg.* 672, *pg.* 1155
SONY CORPORATION OF AMERICA, 550 Madison Ave, **New York, NY** 10022, *pg.* 675, *pg.* 1293
TII NETWORK TECHNOLOGIES, INC., 141 Rodeo Dr, **Edgewood, NY** 11717-8378, *pg.* 680, *pg.* 1157
TOSHIBA AMERICA, INC., 1251 Ave of the Americas Ste 4100, **New York, NY** 10020-1104, *pg.* 681, *pg.* 1302
TRANSCAT, INC., 35 Vantage Point Dr, **Rochester, NY** 14624-1151, *pg.* 682, *pg.* 1337
TREMOR VIDEO, 122 W 26th St 8th Fl, **New York, NY** 10001, *pg.* 682, *pg.* 1305
UNIVERSAL INSTRUMENTS CORPORATION, 33 Broome Corporate Pkwy, **Conklin, NY** 13748, *pg.* 683, *pg.* 1154
UNIVISION COMMUNICATIONS INC., 605 3rd Ave 12th Fl, **New York, NY** 10158, *pg.* 683, *pg.* 1307
VICON INDUSTRIES, INC., 89 Arkay Dr, **Hauppauge, NY** 11788, *pg.* 685, *pg.* 1166
VOXX INTERNATIONAL, 180 Marcus Blvd, **Hauppauge, NY** 11788, *pg.* 686, *pg.* 1166
VRINGO, INC., 780 3rd Ave, 15th Floor, **New York, NY** 10017, *pg.* 687, *pg.* 1312
VUZIX CORPORATION, 2166 Brighton Henrietta Town Line Rd, Ste B, **Rochester, NY** 14623, *pg.* 687, *pg.* 1337

North Carolina

CREE INC., 4600 Silicon Dr, **Durham, NC** 27703-8475, *pg.* 631, *pg.* 1371
EMRISE CORPORATION, 2530 Meridian Pkwy, **Durham, NC** 27713, *pg.* 637, *pg.* 1371
LAW ENFORCEMENT ASSOCIATES CORPORATION, 2609 Discovery Dr Ste 125, **Raleigh, NC** 27616, *pg.* 651, *pg.* 1387
RF MICRO DEVICES, INC., 7628 Thorndike Rd, **Greensboro, NC** 27409-9421, *pg.* 667, *pg.* 1376
TRION, INC., 101 McNeill Rd, **Sanford, NC** 27330-9451, *pg.* 682, *pg.* 1390
VALENCELL, INC., 4601 Six Forks Rd Ste 103, **Raleigh, NC** 27609, *pg.* 684, *pg.* 1389

Ohio

AGILYSYS, INC., 425 Walnut St Ste 1800, **Cincinnati, OH** 45202, *pg.* 614, *pg.* 1409
AMETEK FLOORCARE SPECIALTY MOTORS DIVISION, 627 Lake St, **Kent, OH** 44240, *pg.* 616, *pg.* 1456
BUD INDUSTRIES, INC., 4605 E 355th St, **Willoughby, OH** 44094-4629, *pg.* 627, *pg.* 1482
CORRPRO COMPANIES, INC., 1055 W smith Rd, **Medina, OH** 44256-1328, *pg.* 631, *pg.* 1464
GATESAIR, INC., 5300 Kings Island Dr Ste 101, **Mason, OH** 45040, *pg.* 640, *pg.* 1460
KIRKWOOD HOLDING, INC., 1239 Rockside Rd, **Parma, OH** 44134, *pg.* 649, *pg.* 1469
PROJECTS UNLIMITED, INC., 6300 Sand Lk Rd, **Dayton, OH** 45414-2649, *pg.* 665, *pg.* 1446

Oklahoma

ADDVANTAGE TECHNOLOGIES GROUP, INC., 1221 E Houston, **Broken Arrow, OK** 74012, *pg.* 612, *pg.* 1484

Oregon

INFOCUS CORPORATION, 13190 SW 68th Parkway Ste 200, **Portland, OR** 97223-8368, *pg.* 644, *pg.* 1503
LATTICE SEMICONDUCTOR CORPORATION, 5555 NE Moore Ct, **Hillsboro, OR** 97124, *pg.* 651, *pg.* 1498
TRIAD SPEAKERS, INC., 15835 NE Cameron Blvd, **Portland, OR** 97230, *pg.* 682, *pg.* 1507
WHITE'S ELECTRONICS, 1011 Pleasant Vly Rd, **Sweet Home, OR** 97386-1034, *pg.* 688, *pg.* 1509

Pennsylvania

ACOPIAN TECHNICAL COMPANY, 131 Loomis St, **Easton, PA** 18045, *pg.* 612, *pg.* 1528
ALLIEDBARTON SECURITY SERVICES, 161 Washington St Ste 600, **Conshohocken, PA** 19428, *pg.* 616, *pg.* 1523
AMUNEAL MANUFACTURING CORPORATION, 4737 Darrah St, **Philadelphia, PA** 19124, *pg.* 617, *pg.* 1558
ANSALDO STS, 1000 Technology Dr, **Pittsburgh, PA** 15219-3120, *pg.* 618, *pg.* 1573
C&D TECHNOLOGIES, INC., 1400 Union Meeting Rd, **Blue Bell, PA** 19422-0858, *pg.* 627, *pg.* 1517
CHECKPOINT SYSTEMS, INC., 1 Commerce Sq 2005 Market St Ste 2410, **Philadelphia, PA** 19103, *pg.* 628, *pg.* 1559
CONTROL CHIEF HOLDINGS, INC., 200 Williams St, **Bradford, PA** 16701-1411, *pg.* 630, *pg.* 1518
DYNAVOX INC., 2100 Wharton St Ste 400, **Pittsburgh, PA** 15203-1942, *pg.* 635, *pg.* 1574
KULICKE & SOFFA INDUSTRIES, INC., 1005 Virginia Dr, **Fort Washington, PA** 19034, *pg.* 650, *pg.* 1533
PHOTONIS USA PENNSYLVANIA, 1000 New Holland Ave, **Lancaster, PA** 17601-5606, *pg.* 663, *pg.* 1547
TE CONNECTIVITY LTD., 1050 Westlakes Dr, **Berwyn, PA** 19312, *pg.* 677, *pg.* 1515
TOPFLIGHT CORPORATION, 277 Commerce Dr, **Glen Rock, PA** 17327-8625, *pg.* 681, *pg.* 1534
WESCO INTERNATIONAL INC., 225 W Station Sq Dr Ste 700, **Pittsburgh, PA** 15219-1136, *pg.* 687, *pg.* 1582
WESTINGHOUSE LIGHTING CORPORATION, 12401 McNulty Rd, **Philadelphia, PA** 19154-1004, *pg.* 687, *pg.* 1571
WIRELESS XCESSORIES GROUP, INC., 1840 County Line Rd Ste 301, **Huntingdon Valley, PA** 19006, *pg.* 689, *pg.* 1541

Rhode Island

ASTRO-MED, INC., 600 E Greenwich Ave, **West Warwick, RI** 02893-7526, *pg.* 619, *pg.* 1609
KVH INDUSTRIES INC, 50 Enterprise Ctr, **Middletown, RI** 02842, *pg.* 650, *pg.* 1602
YARDNEY TECHNICAL PRODUCTS, INC., 2000 S County Trl, **East Greenwich, RI** 02818, *pg.* 690, *pg.* 1601

South Carolina

AVX CORPORATION, 1 AVX Blvd, **Fountain Inn, SC** 29644, *pg.* 623, *pg.* 1616
CERAMTEC NORTH AMERICA ELECTRONIC APPLICATIONS, INC., 1 Technology Pl, **Laurens, SC** 29360, *pg.* 628, *pg.* 1620
CORNELL DUBILIER ELECTRONICS, 140 Technology Pl, **Liberty, SC** 29657-3300, *pg.* 630, *pg.* 1620
HUBBELL POWER SYSTEMS, INC., 200 Center Point Cir Ste 200, **Columbia, SC** 29210, *pg.* 643, *pg.* 1614
KEMET CORPORATION, 2835 KEMET Way, **Simpsonville, SC** 29681, *pg.* 649, *pg.* 1621
SCANSOURCE, INC., 6 Logue Ct, **Greenville, SC** 29615, *pg.* 671, *pg.* 1618

South Dakota

DAKTRONICS, INC., 201 Daktronics Dr, **Brookings, SD** 57006, *pg.* 633, *pg.* 1624

Tennessee

INVISIBLE FENCE, INC., 10427 Petsafe Ave, **Knoxville, TN** 37932, *pg.* 648, *pg.* 1637
POWER & TELEPHONE SUPPLY COMPANY, 2673 Yale Ave, **Memphis, TN** 38112-3335, *pg.* 665, *pg.* 1646
THOMAS & BETTS CORPORATION, 8155 T&B Blvd, **Memphis, TN** 38125-8888, *pg.* 680, *pg.* 1646

Texas

ALCATEL-LUCENT USA, INC., 3400 W Plano Pkwy, **Plano, TX** 75075, *pg.* 615, *pg.* 1728
AMPHENOL FIBER SYSTEMS INTERNATIONAL, INC., 1300 Central Expwy N Ste 100, **Allen, TX** 75013, *pg.* 617, *pg.* 1658
ANTENNA PRODUCTS CORPORATION, 101 SE 25th Ave, **Mineral Wells, TX** 76067, *pg.* 618, *pg.* 1727
ATLAS SOUND, 1601 Jack McKay Blvd, **Ennis, TX** 75119-6507, *pg.* 621, *pg.* 1692
BENCHMARK ELECTRONICS, INC., 3000 Technology Dr, **Angleton, TX** 77515-2524, *pg.* 624, *pg.* 1659
BLACKBERRY, 122 W John Carpenter Pkwy Ste 430, **Irving, TX** 75039, *pg.* 625, *pg.* 1717
CIRRUS LOGIC, INC., 800 W 6th St, **Austin, TX** 78701, *pg.* 629, *pg.* 1661
CONN'S, INC., 3295 College St, **Beaumont, TX** 77701, *pg.* 630, *pg.* 1668
CONTINENTAL ELECTRONICS CORPORATION, 4212 S Buckner Blvd, **Dallas, TX** 75227, *pg.* 630, *pg.* 1678
DETEX CORPORATION, 302 Detex Dr, **New Braunfels, TX** 78130-3045, *pg.* 633, *pg.* 1728
DIODES INCORPORATED, 4949 Hedgcoxe Rd Ste 200, **Plano, TX** 75024-3935, *pg.* 634, *pg.* 1729
ENCORE WIRE CORPORATION, 1329 Millwood Rd, **McKinney, TX** 75069-7158, *pg.* 637, *pg.* 1726
ERICSSON, INC., 6300 Legacy Dr, **Plano, TX** 75024-3607, *pg.* 638, *pg.* 1730
GENBAND, INC., 3605 E Plano Pkwy Ste 100, **Plano, TX** 75074, *pg.* 640, *pg.* 1731
HOUSTON WIRE & CABLE COMPANY, 10201 N Loop E, **Houston, TX** 77029-1415, *pg.* 643, *pg.* 1708
INTERNATIONAL BUSINESS EXCHANGE CORPORATION, Ste 330 1 Chisholm Trl, **Round Rock, TX** 78681-5094, *pg.* 647, *pg.* 1739
MICROPAC INDUSTRIES INC., 905 E Walnut St, **Garland, TX** 75040, *pg.* 654, *pg.* 1698
MONITRONICS INTERNATIONAL, INC., 2350 Valley View Ln Ste 100, **Dallas, TX** 75234-5835, *pg.* 656, *pg.* 1684
NEC CORPORATION OF AMERICA, INC., 6555 N State Hwy 161, **Irving, TX** 75039-2402, *pg.* 658, *pg.* 1723
SABRE INDUSTRIES, INC., 8653 E Highway 67, **Alvarado, TX** 76009, *pg.* 669, *pg.* 1658
SAMSUNG TELECOMMUNICATIONS AMERICA, LLC, 1301 Lookout Dr, **Richardson, TX** 75082, *pg.* 670, *pg.* 1736
SILICON LABORATORIES INC., 400 W Cesar Chavez, **Austin, TX** 78701, *pg.* 674, *pg.* 1666
STMICROELECTRONICS, INC., 750 Kanyon Dr, **Coppell, TX** 75019, *pg.* 676, *pg.* 1671
TEXAS INSTRUMENTS INCORPORATED, 12500 TI Blvd, **Dallas, TX** 75243-4136, *pg.* 679, *pg.* 1688
UNIVERSAL POWER GROUP, INC., 488 S Royal Ln, **Coppell, TX** 75019, *pg.* 683, *pg.* 1671
VALENCE TECHNOLOGY, INC., 12303 Technology Blvd Ste 950, **Austin, TX** 78727-6128, *pg.* 684, *pg.* 1667

Utah

CLEARONE COMMUNICATIONS, INC., 5225 Wiley Post Way Ste 500, **Salt Lake City, UT** 84116, *pg.* 629, *pg.* 1756
EVANS & SUTHERLAND COMPUTER CORPORATION, 770 Komas Dr, **Salt Lake City, UT** 84108, *pg.* 638, *pg.* 1757
SKULLCANDY, INC., 1441 W Ute Blvd Ste 250, **Park City, UT** 84098, *pg.* 674, *pg.* 1754
ZAGG INCORPORATED, 3855 S 500 W Ste J, **Salt Lake City, UT** 84115, *pg.* 690, *pg.* 1762

Virginia

ALION SCIENCE AND TECHNOLOGY CORPORATION, 1750 Tysons Blvd Ste 1300, **McLean, VA** 22102, *pg.* 615, *pg.* 1788
KASTLE SYSTEMS LLC, 1501 Wilson Blvd, **Arlington, VA**

22209, *pg.* 648, *pg.* 1773
LCC INTERNATIONAL, INC., 7900 W Park Dr Ste A315, **McLean,** VA 22102-4235, *pg.* 651, *pg.* 1792
NII HOLDINGS, INC., 1875 Explorer St Ste 1000, **Reston,** VA 20190, *pg.* 659, *pg.* 1799
NTELOS HOLDINGS CORP., 1154 Shenandoah Village Drive, **Waynesboro,** VA 22980-4547, *pg.* 659, *pg.* 1811
PRIMUS TELECOMMUNICATIONS GROUP, INCORPORATED, 7901 Jones Branch Dr Ste 900, **McLean,** VA 22102-3338, *pg.* 665, *pg.* 1794
SHENANDOAH TELECOMMUNICATIONS CO., 500 Shentel Way, **Edinburg,** VA 22824, *pg.* 672, *pg.* 1779
XO HOLDINGS, INC., 13865 Sunrise Valley Dr, **Herndon,** VA 20171, *pg.* 689, *pg.* 1786

Washington

AT&T MOBILITY LLC, 7277 164th Ave NE, **Redmond,** WA 98052, *pg.* 620, *pg.* 1824
BOXLIGHT CORPORATION, NE 151 Hwy 300 Ste A, **Belfair,** WA 98528, *pg.* 627, *pg.* 1813
FURUNO USA, INC., 4400 NW Pacific Rim Blvd, **Camas,** WA 98607-9408, *pg.* 640, *pg.* 1819
INTERPOINT CORPORATION, 10301 Willows Rd Ne, **Redmond,** WA 98052, *pg.* 647, *pg.* 1824
LOUD TECHNOLOGIES INC., 16220 Wood-Red Rd NE, **Woodinville,** WA 98072, *pg.* 652, *pg.* 1847
MAGNOLIA AUDIO VIDEO, 6305 S 231st St, **Kent,** WA 98032-1872, *pg.* 652, *pg.* 1821
MICROVISION, INC., 6222 185th Ave NE, **Redmond,** WA 98052, *pg.* 654, *pg.* 1828
T-MOBILE US, INC., 12920 SE 38th St, **Bellevue,** WA 98006-1350, *pg.* 676, *pg.* 1816
UNIFIED SIGNAL, INC., 5400 Carillon Point Building 5000, 4th FL, **Kirkland,** WA 98033, *pg.* 682, *pg.* 1822

Wisconsin

HELLERMANNTYTON, 7930 N Faulkner Rd, **Milwaukee,** WI 53224-3423, *pg.* 642, *pg.* 1875
KOSS CORPORATION, 4129 N Port Washington Rd, **Milwaukee,** WI 53212, *pg.* 649, *pg.* 1877
ROCHE NIMBLEGEN, INC., 500 S Rosa Rd, **Madison,** WI 53719, *pg.* 667, *pg.* 1867
ROCKWELL AUTOMATION, INC., 1201 S 2nd St, **Milwaukee,** WI 53204-2410, *pg.* 668, *pg.* 1880
SEURA, INC., 1230 Ontario Rd, **Green Bay,** WI 54311, *pg.* 672, *pg.* 1860
TELKONET, INC., 10200 Innovation Dr Ste 300, **Milwaukee,** WI 53226, *pg.* 678, *pg.* 1881
WAUKESHA ELECTRIC SYSTEMS, 400 S Prairie Ave, **Waukesha,** WI 53186-5969, *pg.* 687, *pg.* 1898

Fabrics, Yarns & Sewing Notions

California

MOMENTUM TEXTILES INC., 17811 Fitch, **Irvine,** CA 92614-6001, *pg.* 697, *pg.* 114

Colorado

JHB INTERNATIONAL, INC., 1955 S Quince St, **Denver,** CO 80231, *pg.* 696, *pg.* 320

Florida

UNIROYAL ENGINEERED PRODUCTS, 1800 2nd St Ste 970, **Sarasota,** FL 34236, *pg.* 699, *pg.* 467

Georgia

INTERFACE, INC., 2859 Paces Ferry Rd SE Ste 2000, **Atlanta,** GA 30339-6216, *pg.* 695, *pg.* 512

NAME MAKER INC., PO Box 43821, **Atlanta,** GA 30336-0821, *pg.* 697, *pg.* 515

YKK CORPORATION OF AMERICA, 1 Parkway Ctr 1850 Pkwy Pl SE Ste 300, **Marietta,** GA 30067-8258, *pg.* 699, *pg.* 536

Indiana

BLOCKSOM & COMPANY, 450 St John Rd Ste 710 PO Box 2007, **Michigan City,** IN 46360-7351, *pg.* 691, *pg.* 694

Iowa

HERITAGE LACE INC., 309 S St, **Pella,** IA 50219, *pg.* 694, *pg.* 711

Kentucky

RUSSELL BRANDS LLC, 1 Fruit of the Loom Dr, **Bowling Green,** KY 42103, *pg.* 698, *pg.* 726

Maryland

LION BROTHERS COMPANY, INC., 10246 Reisterstown Rd, **Owings Mills,** MD 21117, *pg.* 696, *pg.* 774

Massachusetts

DRAPER KNITTING CO., INC., 28 Draper Ln, **Canton,** MA 02021-1555, *pg.* 692, *pg.* 810

HARODITE INDUSTRIES, INC., 66 S St, **Taunton,** MA 02780, *pg.* 693, *pg.* 847

JANLYNN CORPORATION, 2070 W Dover Rd, **Chicopee,** MA 01022, *pg.* 696, *pg.* 815

POLARTEC LLC, 46 Stafford St, **Lawrence,** MA 01841, *pg.* 697, *pg.* 827

THE ROBERT ALLEN GROUP, INC., 225 Foxboro Blvd, **Foxboro,** MA 02035, *pg.* 698, *pg.* 819

VICTOR INNOVATIVE TEXTILES, 941 Grinnell St 81 Commerce Dr, **Fall River,** MA 02720-5215, *pg.* 699, *pg.* 819

Michigan

MARY MAXIM, INC., 2001 Holland Ave, **Port Huron,** MI 48060, *pg.* 696, *pg.* 905

Minnesota

G&K SERVICES INC., 5995 Opus Pkwy Ste 500, **Minnetonka,** MN 55343, *pg.* 693, *pg.* 949

Mississippi

HANCOCK FABRICS, INC., 1 Fashion Way, **Baldwyn,** MS 38824-8547, *pg.* 693, *pg.* 968

Nebraska

HORIZON DESIGNS, INC., 5308 Parklane Dr Ste 1, **Kearney,** NE 68847, *pg.* 695, *pg.* 1011

New Hampshire

ALBANY INTERNATIONAL CORP., 216 Airport Dr, **Rochester,** NH 03867, *pg.* 691, *pg.* 1038

VELCRO USA INC., 406 Brown Ave, **Manchester,** NH 03103-7202, *pg.* 699, *pg.* 1036

New Jersey

A.C. MOORE ARTS & CRAFTS, INC., 130 AC Moore Dr, **Berlin,** NJ 08009-9500, *pg.* 691, *pg.* 1044

ALPHA ASSOCIATES, INC., 145 Lehigh Ave, **Lakewood,** NJ 08701, *pg.* 691, *pg.* 1078

ASSOCIATED FABRICS CORPORATION, 15-01 Pollitt Dr Unit 7, **Fair Lawn,** NJ 07410, *pg.* 691, *pg.* 1064

THE DMC CORPORATION, Port Kearny Bldg 10F 77 S Hackensack Ave, **Kearny,** NJ 07032, *pg.* 692, *pg.* 1076

LION BRAND YARN COMPANY, 135 Kero Rd, **Carlstadt,** NJ 07072, *pg.* 696, *pg.* 1050

SEFAR AMERICA, INC., 120 Mt Holly By-Pass, **Lumberton,** NJ 08048, *pg.* 698, *pg.* 1080

TRIMTEX CO. INC., 450 Murray Hill Pkwy Ste F, **East Rutherford,** NJ 07073, *pg.* 699, *pg.* 1055

WESTCHESTER LACE & TEXTILES INC., 3901 Liberty Ave, **North Bergen,** NJ 07047-2538, *pg.* 699, *pg.* 1098

New York

COTTON INCORPORATED CONSUMER MARKETING HEADQUARTERS, 488 Madison Ave, **New York,** NY 10022, *pg.* 692, *pg.* 1218

DESIGNTEX GROUP INC., 200 Varick St 8th Fl, **New York,** NY 10014-7433, *pg.* 692, *pg.* 1223

FAB INDUSTRIES CORP., 98 Cutter Mill Rd Ste 412, **Great Neck,** NY 11021, *pg.* 692, *pg.* 1162

HIRSCH INTERNATIONAL CORP., 50 Engineers Rd, **Hauppauge,** NY 11788, *pg.* 694, *pg.* 1164

NATIONAL SPINNING COMPANY, INC., 1212 Ave of the Americas Ste 1901, **New York,** NY 10036, *pg.* 697, *pg.* 1265

North Carolina

CONRAD INDUSTRIES, INC., PO Box 695, **Weaverville,** NC 28787-0695, *pg.* 691, *pg.* 1392

COPLAND FABRICS, INC., 1714 Carolina Mill Rd, **Burlington,** NC 27217-7837, *pg.* 692, *pg.* 1359

FREUDENBERG NONWOVENS LIMITED PARTNERSHIP, 3500 Industrial Dr Eno Industrial Park, **Durham,** NC 27704, *pg.* 693, *pg.* 1371

GLEN RAVEN, INC., 1831 N Park Ave, **Glen Raven,** NC 27217, *pg.* 693, *pg.* 1373

GUILFORD PERFORMANCE TEXTILES, 1001 Military Cutoff Rd Ste 300, **Wilmington,** NC 28405, *pg.* 693, *pg.* 1393

INTERNATIONAL TEXTILE GROUP, INC., 804 Green Valley Rd Ste 300, **Greensboro,** NC 27408, *pg.* 696, *pg.* 1374

MAKE IT COATS, 3430 Toringdon Way Ste 301, **Charlotte,** NC 28277, *pg.* 696, *pg.* 1367

PARKDALE MILLS INC., 531 Cottonblossom Cir, **Gastonia,** NC 28054, *pg.* 697, *pg.* 1373

POLYMER GROUP, INC., 9335 Harris Corners Pkwy Ste 300, **Charlotte,** NC 28269, *pg.* 698, *pg.* 1368

Ohio

JO-ANN STORES LLC, 5555 Darrow Rd, **Hudson,** OH 44236, *pg.* 696, *pg.* 1455

Oregon

PENDLETON WOOLEN MILLS, INC., 220 NW Broadway, **Portland,** OR 97209-3509, *pg.* 697, *pg.* 1505

Pennsylvania

CALICO CORNERS, 203 Gale Ln, **Kennett Square,** PA 19348-1735, *pg.* 691, *pg.* 1543

HERCULITE PRODUCTS, INC., PO Box 435 105 E Sinking Spring Ln, **Emigsville,** PA 17318-0435, *pg.* 694, *pg.* 1529

WOOLRICH, INC., Two Mill St, **Woolrich,** PA 17779, *pg.* 699, *pg.* 1595

Rhode Island

COOLEY GROUP, INC., 50 Esten Ave, **Pawtucket,** RI 02860-4840, *pg.* 691, *pg.* 1603

RHODE ISLAND TEXTILE COMPANY, INC., 211 Columbus Ave, **Pawtucket,** RI 02861-3404, *pg.* 698, *pg.* 1605

South Carolina

BELTON INDUSTRIES, INC., 1205 Hamby Rd, **Belton,** SC 29627, *pg.* 691, *pg.* 1612

GALEY & LORD LLC, 670 North Main St, **Society Hill,** SC 29593-0157, *pg.* 693, *pg.* 1621

GREENWOOD MILLS, INC., 300 Morgan Ave, **Greenwood,** SC 29646-2641, *pg.* 693, *pg.* 1619

MILLIKEN & COMPANY, 920 Milliken Rd, **Spartanburg,** SC 29304, *pg.* 696, *pg.* 1622

MOUNT VERNON MILLS, INC., 503 S Main St, **Mauldin,** SC 29662, *pg.* 697, *pg.* 1620

PRYM CONSUMER USA, 950 Brisack Rd, **Spartanburg,** SC 29303, *pg.* 698, *pg.* 1622

SPRINGS GLOBAL, INC., 205 N White St, **Fort Mill,** SC 29716-0070, *pg.* 698, *pg.* 1616

Tennessee

THE DIXIE GROUP, INC., 104 Nowlin Ln Ste 101, **Chattanooga,** TN 37421, *pg.* 692, *pg.* 1629

E-Z BOWZ, LLC, 903 Parkway Ste 129, **Gatlinburg,** TN 37738, *pg.* 692, *pg.* 1635

SINGER SEWING COMPANY, 1224 Heil Quaker Blvd, **La Vergne,** TN 37086-3515, *pg.* 698, *pg.* 1639

Texas

NATIONAL BANNER COMPANY, INC., 11938 Harry Hines Blvd, **Dallas,** TX 75234-5919, *pg.* 697, *pg.* 1684

PLAINS COTTON COOPERATIVE ASSOCIATION, 3301 E 50th St, **Lubbock,** TX 79404, *pg.* 697, *pg.* 1726

Wisconsin

FEDERAL FOAM TECHNOLOGIES INC., 600 Wisconsin Dr, **New Richmond,** WI 54017-2608, *pg.* 692, *pg.* 1884

HERRSCHNERS, INC., 2800 Hoover Rd, **Stevens Point,** WI 54481-7103, *pg.* 694, *pg.* 1895

RELIABLE OF MILWAUKEE, 6737 W Washington, Ste 3200, **Milwaukee,** WI 53214-5705, *pg.* 698, *pg.* 1879

First page reference indicates Business Class Edition
Second page reference indicates Geographic Edition

Farm Equipment & Supplies

Alabama

BUSH HOG, INC., 2501 Griffin Ave, **Selma,** AL 36703-1918, *pg.* 702, *pg.* 8

Arizona

SALT RIVER PROJECT, 1521 N Project Dr, **Tempe,** AZ 85281, *pg.* 707, *pg.* 26

California

KUBOTA TRACTOR CORPORATION, 3401 Del Amo Blvd, **Torrance,** CA 90503, *pg.* 705, *pg.* 294
LIMONEIRA COMPANY, 1141 Cummings Rd, **Santa Paula,** CA 93060, *pg.* 705, *pg.* 276
RAIN BIRD CORPORATION, 970 W Sierra Madre Ave, **Azusa,** CA 91702, *pg.* 707, *pg.* 44
VALENT U.S.A. CORP., 1333 N California Blvd Ste 600, **Walnut Creek,** CA 94596-8025, *pg.* 708, *pg.* 305
WEATHERTEC CORPORATION, 5645 E Clinton Ave, **Fresno,** CA 93727-1308, *pg.* 708, *pg.* 93

Georgia

AGCO CORPORATION, 4205 River Green Pkwy, **Duluth,** GA 30096, *pg.* 700, *pg.* 530

Illinois

CNH AMERICA LLC, 6900 Veterans Blvd, **Burr Ridge,** IL 60527, *pg.* 702, *pg.* 560
DEERE & COMPANY, 1 John Deere Pl, **Moline,** IL 61265-8010, *pg.* 703, *pg.* 632
GEA FARM TECHNOLOGIES, 1880 Country Farm Dr, **Naperville,** IL 60563-1089, *pg.* 704, *pg.* 636
SEEDBURO EQUIPMENT CO., 2293 S Mt Prospect Rd, **Chicago,** IL 60018-2914, *pg.* 707, *pg.* 590
YETTER MANUFACTURING CO., INC., 109 S McDonough St, **Colchester,** IL 62326, *pg.* 708, *pg.* 598

Indiana

A.T. FERRELL COMPANY, INC., 1440 S Adams St, **Bluffton,** IN 46714-9793, *pg.* 701, *pg.* 674
WHITE RIVER COOPERATIVE INC., 610 Church St, **Loogootee,** IN 47553, *pg.* 708, *pg.* 693

Iowa

ART'S-WAY MANUFACTURING CO., INC., 5556 Hwy 9, **Armstrong,** IA 50514, *pg.* 701, *pg.* 701
BLOOM MANUFACTURING, INC., 1443 220th St, **Independence,** IA 50644-9124, *pg.* 701, *pg.* 708
HAWKEYE STEEL PRODUCTS, INC., 609 Hwy 16 W, **Houghton,** IA 52631, *pg.* 704, *pg.* 708
HIGHWAY EQUIPMENT COMPANY, 1330 76th Ave SW, **Cedar Rapids,** IA 52404, *pg.* 704, *pg.* 702
LUNDELL ENTERPRISES, INC., 5134 Hwy 3, **Cherokee,** IA 51012, *pg.* 706, *pg.* 703
OMAHA STANDARD PALFINGER, 3501 S 11th St, **Council Bluffs,** IA 51501-3633, *pg.* 706, *pg.* 704
RITCHIE INDUSTRIES, INC., 120 S Main St, **Conrad,** IA 50621, *pg.* 707, *pg.* 703
SHIVVERS INC., 614 W English St, **Corydon,** IA 50060-0467, *pg.* 707, *pg.* 704
VERMEER MANUFACTURING COMPANY, 1210 Vermeer Rd E, **Pella,** IA 50219-7660, *pg.* 708, *pg.* 711

Kansas

CRUSTBUSTER-SPEED KING, INC., 2300 E Trl St, **Dodge City,** KS 67801-9023, *pg.* 702, *pg.* 714
GREAT PLAINS MANUFACTURING, INCORPORATED, 1525 E North St, **Salina,** KS 67402-5060, *pg.* 704, *pg.* 721
HARPER INDUSTRIES, INC., 151 E Hwy 160, **Harper,** KS 67058-8201, *pg.* 704, *pg.* 715
HUTCHINSON/MAYRATH INDUSTRIES INC., 514 W Crawford St, **Clay Center,** KS 67432-2345, *pg.* 704, *pg.* 714
MY-D HAN-D MFG. INC., 10867 McArtor Rd, **Dodge City,** KS 67801-6763, *pg.* 706, *pg.* 714

Kentucky

OWENSBORO GRAIN COMPANY, INC., 822 E 2nd St, **Owensboro,** KY 42303-3301, *pg.* 706, *pg.* 739

Massachusetts

CONRAD FAFARD, INC., 770 Silver St, **Agawam,** MA 01001-0790, *pg.* 702, *pg.* 781
GRIFFIN GREENHOUSE & NURSERY SUPPLIES, INC., 1619 Main St, **Tewksbury,** MA 01876, *pg.* 704, *pg.* 848

Minnesota

CHS INC., 5500 Cenex Dr, **Inver Grove Heights,** MN 55077, *pg.* 702, *pg.* 926
GANDY COMPANY, 815 Rice Lake St, **Owatonna,** MN 55060-0528, *pg.* 703, *pg.* 952
HINIKER COMPANY, 58766 240st St, **Mankato,** MN 56001, *pg.* 704, *pg.* 927
HYPRO, 375 5th Ave NW, **New Brighton,** MN 55112-3239, *pg.* 705, *pg.* 951
MILLER MANUFACTURING COMPANY, 2910 Waters Rd Ste 150, **Eagan,** MN 55121, *pg.* 706, *pg.* 921

Missouri

DANUSER MACHINE COMPANY, INC., 500 E 3rd St, **Fulton,** MO 65251-1679, *pg.* 703, *pg.* 978
NOVUS INTERNATIONAL, INC., 20 Research Park Dr, **Saint Louis,** MO 63304, *pg.* 706, *pg.* 1001
PAUL MUELLER COMPANY, 1600 W Phelps St, **Springfield,** MO 65802, *pg.* 706, *pg.* 1007

Nebraska

BEHLEN MFG. CO., 4025 E 23rd St, **Columbus,** NE 68601-8501, *pg.* 701, *pg.* 1010
BLUE OX, Industrial Park 1 Mill Rd, **Pender,** NE 68047, *pg.* 701, *pg.* 1019
BURDEN SALES COMPANY, 1015 W O St, **Lincoln,** NE 68528, *pg.* 702, *pg.* 1011
FARMERS NATIONAL COMPANY, 11516 Nicholas St Ste 100, **Omaha,** NE 68154-8016, *pg.* 703, *pg.* 1015
KELLY RYAN EQUIPMENT COMPANY, 900 Kelly Ryan Dr, **Blair,** NE 68008, *pg.* 705, *pg.* 1010
REINKE MANUFACTURING COMPANY, INC., 1040 Rd 5300, PO Box 566, **Deshler,** NE 68340, *pg.* 707, *pg.* 1010

New Jersey

ARETT SALES CORPORATION, 9285 Commerce Hwy, **Pennsauken,** NJ 08110, *pg.* 700, *pg.* 1107

New York

GREEN EARTH TECHNOLOGIES, INC., 10 Bank St Ste 680, **White Plains,** NY 10532, *pg.* 704, *pg.* 1352

North Carolina

CRESCENT COMMUNITIES, LLC, 227 W Trade St Ste 1000, **Charlotte,** NC 28202, *pg.* 702, *pg.* 1365
JOHN DEERE CONSUMER & COMMERCIAL EQUIPMENT, INC., 2000 John Deere Run, **Cary,** NC 27513, *pg.* 705, *pg.* 1360

Oregon

R.B. PAMPLIN CORPORATION, 805 SW Broadway Ste 2400, **Portland,** OR 97205-3341, *pg.* 707, *pg.* 1506

Pennsylvania

MILLER CHEMICAL & FERTILIZER CORPORATION, 120 Radio Rd, **Hanover,** PA 17331-1139, *pg.* 706, *pg.* 1535

South Dakota

SIOUX STEEL COMPANY, 196 1/2 E 6th St, **Sioux Falls,** SD 57104-5929, *pg.* 707, *pg.* 1625

Tennessee

TRACTOR SUPPLY COMPANY, 5401 Virginia Way, **Brentwood,** TN 37027, *pg.* 708, *pg.* 1627

Texas

AG-MEIER INDUSTRIES LLC, 920 E 6th Ave, **Belton,** TX 76513-2804, *pg.* 700, *pg.* 1668
THE PERRY COMPANY, 500 S Vly Mills Dr, **Waco,** TX 76711, *pg.* 706, *pg.* 1749
PYCO INDUSTRIES, INC., 2901 Ave A, **Lubbock,** TX 79404-2231, *pg.* 706, *pg.* 1726
RENTZEL PUMP MANUFACTURING, LP, 1301 N Globe Ave, **Lubbock,** TX 79408, *pg.* 707, *pg.* 1726

Utah

INTERMOUNTAIN FARMERS ASSOCIATION, 1147 W 2100 South, **Salt Lake City,** UT 84119-1533, *pg.* 705, *pg.* 1759

Virginia

ALFA LAVAL INC., 5400 International Trade Dr, **Richmond,** VA 23231, *pg.* 700, *pg.* 1800

Wisconsin

AMEREQUIP CORPORATION, 1015 Calumet Ave, **Kiel,** WI 53042, *pg.* 700, *pg.* 1862
ARIENS COMPANY INC., 655 W Ryan St, **Brillion,** WI 54110-1072, *pg.* 700, *pg.* 1855
BLAIN SUPPLY, INC., 3507 E Racine St PO Box 391, **Janesville,** WI 53546, *pg.* 701, *pg.* 1861
BOUMATIC LLC, 1919 S Stoughton Rd, **Madison,** WI 53716, *pg.* 701, *pg.* 1865

First page reference indicates Business Class Edition
Second page reference indicates Geographic Edition

Financial Services

Alabama

BANK OF TUSCALOOSA, 22100 Jack Warner Pkwy, **Tuscaloosa,** AL 35401, *pg.* 722, *pg.* 8
BBVA COMPASS BANK, 15 S 20th St, **Birmingham,** AL 35233-2000, *pg.* 723, *pg.* 2
CB&S BANK, 200 S Jackson Ave, **Russellville,** AL 35653, *pg.* 732, *pg.* 8
CULLMAN BANCORP, INC., 316 2nd Ave SW, **Cullman,** AL 35055, *pg.* 743, *pg.* 5
REGIONS FINANCIAL CORPORATION, 1900 5th Ave N, **Birmingham,** AL 35203, *pg.* 798, *pg.* 4
THE SOUTHERN BANC COMPANY, INC., 221 S 6th St, **Gadsden,** AL 35901, *pg.* 804, *pg.* 5
TRUSTMARK CORPORATION, 107 Saint Francis St, **Mobile,** AL 36602, *pg.* 812, *pg.* 7
UNITED SECURITY BANCSHARES, INC., 131 W Front St, **Thomasville,** AL 36784, *pg.* 814, *pg.* 8

Alaska

NORTHRIM BANCORP, INC., 3111 C St, **Anchorage,** AK 99503, *pg.* 788, *pg.* 10

Arizona

LIFELOCK INC., 60 E Rio Salado Pkwy Ste 400, **Tempe,** AZ 85281, *pg.* 776, *pg.* 26
QUOTEMEDIA, INC., 17100 Shea Blvd Ste 230, **Fountain Hills,** AZ 85268, *pg.* 797, *pg.* 13
SWISS AMERICA TRADING CORPORATION, 15018 N Tatum Blvd, **Phoenix,** AZ 85032, *pg.* 808, *pg.* 20
VIAD CORP., 1850 N Central Ave Ste 1900, **Phoenix,** AZ 85004-4565, *pg.* 816, *pg.* 20
WESTERN ALLIANCE BANCORPORATION, One E Washington St Ste 1400, **Phoenix,** AZ 85004, *pg.* 821, *pg.* 20

Arkansas

BANK OF THE OZARKS, INC., 17901 Chenal Pkwy PO Box 8811, **Little Rock,** AR 72231-8811, *pg.* 721, *pg.* 33
FIRST SECURITY BANCORP INC., 314 N Spring St, **Searcy,** AR 72143, *pg.* 757, *pg.* 35
HOME BANCSHARES, INC., 719 Harkrider St Ste 100, **Conway,** AR 72032, *pg.* 766, *pg.* 31

California

AMERICAN RIVER BANKSHARES, 3100 Zinfandel Dr Ste 450, **Rancho Cordova,** CA 95670, *pg.* 714, *pg.* 186
BANCO POPULAR NORTH AMERICA - CALIFORNIA REGIONAL OFFICE, 888 S Disneyland Dr Ste 500, **Anaheim,** CA 92802-1846, *pg.* 717, *pg.* 42
BANK OF MARIN BANCORP, 504 Redwood Blvd Pell Plaza, **Novato,** CA 94947, *pg.* 720, *pg.* 168
BANK OF THE SIERRA, INC., 86 N Main St, **Porterville,** CA 93257, *pg.* 721, *pg.* 185
BANK OF THE WEST, 180 Montgomery St, **San Francisco,** CA 94104, *pg.* 721, *pg.* 213
BBCN BANCORP, INC., 3731 Wilshire Blvd Ste 1000, **Los Angeles,** CA 90010, *pg.* 723, *pg.* 126
BOFI HOLDING, INC., 12777 High Bluff Dr Ste 100, **San Diego,** CA 92130-2224, *pg.* 726, *pg.* 200
BOSTON PRIVATE, 160 Bovet Rd Ste 100, **San Mateo,** CA 94402, *pg.* 726, *pg.* 254
BROADWAY FEDERAL BANK, F.S.B., 5055 Wilshire Blvd, Ste 500, **Los Angeles,** CA 90036, *pg.* 727, *pg.* 127
CALIFORNIA BANK & TRUST, 11622 El Camino Real 2nd Fl, **San Diego,** CA 92130-2049, *pg.* 728, *pg.* 201
CALIFORNIA FIRST NATIONAL BANCORP, 18201 Von Karman Ave Ste 800, **Irvine,** CA 92612, *pg.* 728, *pg.* 109
CAPITALSOURCE INC., 633 West 5th Street 33rd Floor, **Los Angeles,** CA 90071, *pg.* 731, *pg.* 127
CATHAY GENERAL BANCORP, INC., 777 N Broadway, **Los Angeles,** CA 90012, *pg.* 732, *pg.* 127
CENTRAL VALLEY COMMUNITY BANCORP, 7100 N Financial Dr, **Fresno,** CA 93720, *pg.* 733, *pg.* 93
CHARLES SCHWAB & COMPANY, INC., 211 Main Street, **San Francisco,** CA 94104-4122, *pg.* 734, *pg.* 215
CHASE CARD SERVICES, INC., 360 Bay St, **San Francisco,** CA 94133, *pg.* 734, *pg.* 215
CITY NATIONAL CORPORATION, 555 S Flower St, **Los Angeles,** CA 90071, *pg.* 738, *pg.* 128
COMMUNITY WEST BANCSHARES, 445 Pine Ave, **Goleta,** CA 93117-3709, *pg.* 741, *pg.* 99
CONSUMER PORTFOLIO SERVICES, INC., 19500 Jamboree Rd, **Irvine,** CA 92618, *pg.* 741, *pg.* 109
CRESTLINE FUNDING CORP., 18851 Bardeen Ave, **Irvine,** CA 92612-1520, *pg.* 742, *pg.* 109
DIGITAL INSIGHT, 1300 Seaport Blvd Ste 300, **Redwood City,** CA 94063, *pg.* 744, *pg.* 189
ENCORE CAPITAL GROUP, INC., 8875 Aero Dr Ste 200, **San Diego,** CA 92123, *pg.* 747, *pg.* 202
EXCHANGE BANK, 545 4th St, **Santa Rosa,** CA 95401-6323, *pg.* 750, *pg.* 277
FINANCIAL ENGINES, INC., 1050 Enterprise Way 3rd Fl, **Sunnyvale,** CA 94089, *pg.* 753, *pg.* 285
FRANKLIN RESOURCES, INC., 1 Franklin Pkwy Bldg 970 1st Fl, **San Mateo,** CA 94403, *pg.* 760, *pg.* 254
GENERAL FINANCE CORPORATION, 39 E Union St, **Pasadena,** CA 91103, *pg.* 761, *pg.* 180
GREEN DOT CORPORATION, 3465 E Foothill Blvd, **Pasadena,** CA 91107, *pg.* 763, *pg.* 180
GREENLIGHT FINANCIAL SERVICES, 18200 Von Karman Ave Ste 300, **Irvine,** CA 92612, *pg.* 764, *pg.* 111
HERITAGE COMMERCE CORP., 150 Almaden Blvd, **San Jose,** CA 95113-2000, *pg.* 765, *pg.* 246
HOLMGREN & ASSOCIATES, 1900 Mountain Blvd, **Oakland,** CA 94611, *pg.* 766, *pg.* 171
INTUIT INC., 2700 Coast Ave, **Mountain View,** CA 94043, *pg.* 769, *pg.* 158
IPAYMENT, INC., 30721 Russell Ranch Rd, # 200, **Westlake Village,** CA 91362, *pg.* 771, *pg.* 306
KKR FINANCIAL HOLDINGS LLC, 555 California St 50th Fl, **San Francisco,** CA 94104-1701, *pg.* 774, *pg.* 220
LIBERTY HOME EQUITY SOLUTIONS, INC., 10951 White Rock Rd, Ste 200, **Rancho Cordova,** CA 95670, *pg.* 776, *pg.* 186
LOANDEPOT LLC, Towne Center Dr, **Foothill Ranch,** CA 92610, *pg.* 776, *pg.* 86
MECHANICS BANK, 3170 Hilltop Mall Rd, **Richmond,** CA 94806, *pg.* 781, *pg.* 193
MERRIMAN HOLDINGS INC., 600 California St 9th Fl, **San Francisco,** CA 94108, *pg.* 782, *pg.* 223
ONEUNITED BANK, 3683 Crenshaw Blvd, **Los Angeles,** CA 90016-4849, *pg.* 790, *pg.* 137
PACIFIC INVESTMENT MANAGEMENT COMPANY LLC, 650 Newport Ctr Dr, **Newport Beach,** CA 92660, *pg.* 791, *pg.* 165
PACIFIC PREMIER BANK, 17901 Von Karman Ave, Ste 1200, **Irvine,** CA 92614, *pg.* 791, *pg.* 114
PLUMAS BANCORP, 35 S Lindan Ave, **Quincy,** CA 95971, *pg.* 794, *pg.* 186
PROSPECT MORTGAGE, LLC, 15301 Ventura Blvd, Ste D300, **Sherman Oaks,** CA 91403, *pg.* 796, *pg.* 278
PROVIDENT FINANCIAL HOLDINGS, INC., 3756 Central Ave, **Riverside,** CA 92506, *pg.* 796, *pg.* 194
RABIN WORLDWIDE, INC., 731 Sansome St Fl 2, **San Francisco,** CA 94111-1723, *pg.* 797, *pg.* 225
RBC CAPITAL MARKETS, 2 Embarcadero Ctr Ste 1200, **San Francisco,** CA 94111, *pg.* 798, *pg.* 225
REALTY INCOME CORPORATION, 600 La Terraza Blvd, **Escondido,** CA 92025-3873, *pg.* 798, *pg.* 85
SIERRA BANCORP, 86 N Main St, **Porterville,** CA 93257-1930, *pg.* 803, *pg.* 185
SOUTHWEST SECURITIES, INC., 8350 Wilshire Blvd, **Beverly Hills,** CA 90211, *pg.* 804, *pg.* 47
STEARNS LENDING, LLC., 4 Hutton Centre Dr Ste 500, **Santa Ana,** CA 92707, *pg.* 805, *pg.* 262
SUNWEST BANK, 2050 Main St Ste 300, **Irvine,** CA 92614, *pg.* 807, *pg.* 116
SVB FINANCIAL GROUP, 3003 Tasman Dr, **Santa Clara,** CA 95054-1191, *pg.* 808, *pg.* 270
THOMAS WEISEL PARTNERS LLC, 1 Montgomery St, **San Francisco,** CA 94104, *pg.* 810, *pg.* 228
TRICO BANCSHARES, 63 Constitution Dr, **Chico,** CA 95973, *pg.* 811, *pg.* 65
UNION BANK, N.A., 400 California St, **San Francisco,** CA 94104, *pg.* 813, *pg.* 230
UNIONBANCAL CORPORATION, 400 California St, **San Francisco,** CA 94104, *pg.* 813, *pg.* 230
UNITED SECURITY BANCSHARES, 2126 Inyo St, **Fresno,** CA 93721, *pg.* 814, *pg.* 93
VISA INC., PO Box 8999, **San Francisco,** CA 94128-8999, *pg.* 816, *pg.* 230
VISA U.S.A., INC., PO Box 8999, **San Francisco,** CA 94128-8999, *pg.* 817, *pg.* 231
WELLS FARGO & COMPANY, 420 Montgomery St, **San Francisco,** CA 94104, *pg.* 819, *pg.* 232
WESCO FINANCIAL CORPORATION, 301 E Colorado Blvd Ste 300, **Pasadena,** CA 91101-1901, *pg.* 821, *pg.* 181
WESTAMERICA BANCORPORATION, 1108 Fifth Ave, **San Rafael,** CA 94901, *pg.* 821, *pg.* 258
WESTERN FEDERAL CREDIT UNION, PO Box 10018, **Manhattan Beach,** CA 90267-7565, *pg.* 821, *pg.* 143
WILSHIRE BANCORP INC., 3200 Wilshire Blvd, **Los Angeles,** CA 90010, *pg.* 823, *pg.* 141
ZECCO TRADING, PO Box 60670, **Pasadena,** CA 91116, *pg.* 824, *pg.* 181

Colorado

COLORADO FEDERAL SAVINGS BANK, 8400 E Prentice Ave Ste 545, **Greenwood Village,** CO 80111, *pg.* 739, *pg.* 330
FIRSTBANK HOLDING COMPANY OF COLORADO, INC., 12345 W Colfax Ave, **Lakewood,** CO 80215, *pg.* 758, *pg.* 333
JANUS CAPITAL GROUP, INC., 151 Detroit St, **Denver,** CO 80206, *pg.* 772, *pg.* 320
UDR, INC., 1745 Shea Center Dr Ste 200, **Highlands Ranch,** CO 80129, *pg.* 812, *pg.* 332
UNITED DOMINION REALTY L.P., 1745 Shea Center Dr Ste 200, **Highlands Ranch,** CO 80129, *pg.* 814, *pg.* 332
THE WESTERN UNION COMPANY, 12500 E Belford Ave, **Englewood,** CO 80112, *pg.* 822, *pg.* 327

Connecticut

CLAYTON HOLDINGS, INC., 100 Beard Sawmill Rd Ste 200, **Shelton,** CT 06484, *pg.* 738, *pg.* 370
COMPASS GROUP DIVERSIFIED HOLDINGS LLC, 61 Wilton Rd 2nd Fl, **Westport,** CT 06880, *pg.* 741, *pg.* 383
DISCOVER STUDENT LOANS, 750 Washington Blvd, **Stamford,** CT 06901, *pg.* 744, *pg.* 373
FIRST NIAGARA BANK, 195 Church St, **New Haven,** CT 06510-2009, *pg.* 757, *pg.* 358
GE CAPITAL, 901 Main Ave Ste 800, **Norwalk,** CT 06851, *pg.* 761, *pg.* 362
IHS HEROLD, INC., 200 Connecticut Ave Ste 3A, **Norwalk,** CT 06854-1907, *pg.* 768, *pg.* 362
LIBERTY BANK INC., 315 Main St, **Middletown,** CT 06457, *pg.* 776, *pg.* 356
NAUGATUCK VALLEY FINANCIAL CORPORATION, 333 Church St, **Naugatuck,** CT 06770, *pg.* 786, *pg.* 358
NEW ENGLAND BANCSHARES, INC., 855 Enfield St, **Enfield,** CT 06082, *pg.* 786, *pg.* 346
PEOPLE'S UNITED BANK, 850 Main St, **Bridgeport,** CT 06604-4917, *pg.* 793, *pg.* 340
PEOPLE'S UNITED FINANCIAL, INC., 850 Main St 11th Fl, **Bridgeport,** CT 06604, *pg.* 793, *pg.* 340
SALISBURY BANCORP, INC., 5 Bissell St, **Lakeville,** CT 06039-1868, *pg.* 801, *pg.* 353
SALISBURY BANK & TRUST COMPANY, 5 Bissell St, **Lakeville,** CT 06039-1868, *pg.* 801, *pg.* 353
SI FINANCIAL GROUP, INC., 803 Main St, **Willimantic,** CT 06226, *pg.* 803, *pg.* 385

Delaware

AMERICAN INCORPORATORS LTD., 1220 N Market St Ste 808, **Wilmington,** DE 19801, *pg.* 714, *pg.* 389
SLM CORPORATION, 300 Continental Drive, **Newark,** DE 19713, *pg.* 804, *pg.* 388
WILMINGTON SAVINGS FUND SOCIETY, FEDERAL SAVINGS BANK, 500 Delaware Ave, **Wilmington,** DE 19801, *pg.* 822, *pg.* 392
WILMINGTON TRUST CORPORATION, 1100 N Market St, **Wilmington,** DE 19890-0001, *pg.* 822, *pg.* 392
WSFS FINANCIAL CORPORATION, 500 Delaware Ave, **Wilmington,** DE 19801, *pg.* 823, *pg.* 392

District of Columbia

ARES CAPITAL- WASHINGTON, DC OFFICE, 1919 Pennsylvania Ave NW, **Washington,** DC 20006-3404, *pg.*

716, *pg.* 395
COSTAR GROUP, INC., 1331 L St NW, **Washington,** DC 20005, *pg.* 742, *pg.* 397
FEDERAL AGRICULTURAL MORTGAGE CORPORATION, 1999 K St NW # 4th Fl, **Washington,** DC 20006-1118, *pg.* 751, *pg.* 399
FEDERAL DEPOSIT INSURANCE CORPORATION, 550 17th St Northwest, **Washington,** DC 20429, *pg.* 751, *pg.* 399
FEDERAL NATIONAL MORTGAGE ASSOCIATION, 3900 Wisconsin Ave NW, **Washington,** DC 20016, *pg.* 751, *pg.* 399
IBW FINANCIAL CORP., 4812 Georgia Ave NW, **Washington,** DC 20011, *pg.* 768, *pg.* 401
NATIONAL FOUNDATION FOR CREDIT COUNSELING, 2000 M St NW Ste 505, **Washington,** DC 20036-3307, *pg.* 786, *pg.* 402
PREMIER BANK, 1130 Connecticut Ave, **Washington,** DC 20036, *pg.* 795, *pg.* 404
UNITED STATES MINT, 801 9th St NW, **Washington,** DC 20220, *pg.* 814, *pg.* 406

Florida

ATLANTIC COAST FINANCIAL CORPORATION, 10151 Deerwood Park Blvd, Bldg 200 Ste 100, **Jacksonville,** FL 32256, *pg.* 717, *pg.* 432
AZOY TAX, 4901 NW 17th Way Ste 301, **Fort Lauderdale,** FL 33309, *pg.* 717, *pg.* 423
BB&T, 1750 E Sunrise Blvd, **Fort Lauderdale,** FL 33304-3013, *pg.* 723, *pg.* 423
BBX CAPITAL, 2100 W Cypress Creek Rd, **Fort Lauderdale,** FL 33309, *pg.* 723, *pg.* 423
BFC FINANCIAL CORPORATION, 2100 West Cypress Creek Rd, **Fort Lauderdale,** FL 33309, *pg.* 724, *pg.* 423
CAPITAL CITY BANK GROUP, INC., 217 N Monroe St, **Tallahassee,** FL 32301, *pg.* 730, *pg.* 469
COMMERCEBANK HOLDING CORPORATION, 220 Alhambra Cir, **Coral Gables,** FL 33134, *pg.* 740, *pg.* 418
CONSOLIDATED CREDIT COUNSELING SERVICES, INC., 5701 W Sunrise Blvd, **Fort Lauderdale,** FL 33313, *pg.* 741, *pg.* 424
EMERGENT CAPITAL, INC., 5355 Town Center Rd, Ste 701, **Boca Raton,** FL 33486, *pg.* 747, *pg.* 411
EQUIINSURANCE, LLC, 6839 Main St, **Miami Lakes,** FL 33014, *pg.* 748, *pg.* 448
EVERBANK FINANCIAL CORP., 501 Riverside Rd, **Jacksonville,** FL 32202, *pg.* 749, *pg.* 432
FIRST NATIONWIDE LENDING, INC., 1990 Main St Ste 750, **Sarasota,** FL 34236, *pg.* 756, *pg.* 466
FLORIDA COMMUNITY BANKS, INC., 1400 N 15th St, **Immokalee,** FL 34142, *pg.* 758, *pg.* 431
FLORIDA HOUSING FINANCE CORPORATION, 227 N Bronough St Ste 5000, **Tallahassee,** FL 32301-1329, *pg.* 758, *pg.* 469
FTI CONSULTING, INC., 777 Flagler Dr Ste 1500, **West Palm Beach,** FL 33401, *pg.* 760, *pg.* 478
HOMEBANC, 101 E Kennedy Blvd Ste 4100, **Tampa,** FL 33602, *pg.* 766, *pg.* 473
IDEAL LENDING SOLUTIONS, 5589 Okeechobee Blvd Ste 101, **West Palm Beach,** FL 33417, *pg.* 768, *pg.* 479
INCHARGE INSTITUTE OF AMERICA, INC., 5750 Major Blvd Ste 300, **Orlando,** FL 32819, *pg.* 768, *pg.* 454
JACKSONVILLE BANCORP, INC., 100 N Laura St 10th Fl, **Jacksonville,** FL 32202-3613, *pg.* 771, *pg.* 433
MELITTA USA INC., 13925 58th St N, **Clearwater,** FL 33760-3721, *pg.* 781, *pg.* 416
NEW VALLEY CORPORATION, 100 SE 2nd St 32nd Fl, **Miami,** FL 33131-2158, *pg.* 786, *pg.* 444
NICHOLAS FINANCIAL, INC., 2454 N McMullen-Booth Rd Bldg C, **Clearwater,** FL 33759, *pg.* 787, *pg.* 416
RAYMOND JAMES FINANCIAL, INC., The Raymond James Fin Ctr 880 Carillon Pkwy, **Saint Petersburg,** FL 33716-2749, *pg.* 798, *pg.* 464
TOTALBANK CORP., 2720 Coral Way, **Miami,** FL 33145, *pg.* 811, *pg.* 447
TRADESTATION GROUP, INC., 8050 SW 10th St Ste 4000, **Plantation,** FL 33324, *pg.* 811, *pg.* 459
WEISS RESEARCH, 15430 Endeavour Dr, **Jupiter,** FL 33478, *pg.* 819, *pg.* 436
WIPRO GALLAGHER SOLUTIONS, 18001 Old Cutler Rd 651, **Miami,** FL 33157, *pg.* 823, *pg.* 447

Georgia

1ST FRANKLIN FINANCIAL CORPORATION, 135 E Tugalo St, **Toccoa,** GA 30577, *pg.* 710, *pg.* 542
AGSOUTH FARM CREDIT, 26 S Main St, **Statesboro,** GA 30458, *pg.* 711, *pg.* 540
AMERIS BANCORP, 310 1st St SE, **Moultrie,** GA 31768, *pg.* 715, *pg.* 536
ATLANTICUS CORPORATION, Five Concourse Pkwy Ste 400, **Atlanta,** GA 30328, *pg.* 717, *pg.* 490
CHARTER FINANCIAL CORPORATION, 1233 O.G. Skinner Dr, **West Point,** GA 31833, *pg.* 734, *pg.* 542
COLONY BANKCORP, INC., 115 S Grant St, **Fitzgerald,** GA 31750, *pg.* 739, *pg.* 532
COLUMBUS BANK AND TRUST COMPANY, 1148 Broadway, **Columbus,** GA 31902-0120, *pg.* 739, *pg.* 528
CONSUMER CREDIT COUNSELING SERVICES, 100 Edgewood Ave NE Ste 1500, **Atlanta,** GA 30303, *pg.* 741, *pg.* 501
EQUIFAX INC., 1550 Peachtree St NW, **Atlanta,** GA 30309, *pg.* 748, *pg.* 504
FIDELITY BANK, 3490 Piedmont Rd, **Atlanta,** GA 30305, *pg.* 752, *pg.* 505
FIDELITY SOUTHERN CORPORATION, 3490 Piedmont Rd Ne Ste 1550, **Atlanta,** GA 30305, *pg.* 752, *pg.* 505
FIRST CITIZENS BANK, 10865 Haynes Bridge Rd, **Alpharetta,** GA 30022, *pg.* 754, *pg.* 483
FIRST DATA CORPORATION, 5565 Glenridge Connector NE Ste 2000, **Atlanta,** GA 30342, *pg.* 754, *pg.* 505
FIRST OPTION MORTGAGE, LLC, 400 Interstate N Pkwy SE, Ste 1600, **Atlanta,** GA 30339, *pg.* 757, *pg.* 505
FISERV, INC., 4411 E Jones Bridge Rd, **Norcross,** GA 30092-1615, *pg.* 758, *pg.* 537
FLEETCOR TECHNOLOGIES, INC., 5445 Triangle Parkway Suit 400, **Norcross,** GA 30092-2575, *pg.* 758, *pg.* 537
GLOBAL PAYMENTS INC., 10 Glenlake Pkwy N Tower, **Atlanta,** GA 30328, *pg.* 762, *pg.* 508
HABIF, AROGETI & WYNNE, LLP, 5 Concourse Pkwy Ste 1000, **Atlanta,** GA 30328, *pg.* 764, *pg.* 509
INTERCONTINENTALEXCHANGE, INC., 2100 RiverEdge Pkwy Ste 500, **Atlanta,** GA 30328, *pg.* 769, *pg.* 512
INVESCO LTD., 1555 Peachtree St NE Ste 1800, **Atlanta,** GA 30309, *pg.* 771, *pg.* 513
MICROBILT CORPORATION, 1640 Airport Rd Ste 115, **Kennesaw,** GA 30144, *pg.* 782, *pg.* 534
THE MONEY TREE INC., 114 S Broad St, **Bainbridge,** GA 39817, *pg.* 783, *pg.* 526
PRIMERICA FINANCIAL SERVICES, INC., 3120 Breckinridge Blvd, **Duluth,** GA 30099, *pg.* 795, *pg.* 531
RENASANT BANK, 251 Highway 515 S, **Jasper,** GA 30143-8656, *pg.* 798, *pg.* 533
SOUTHEASTERN BANK FINANCIAL CORPORATION, 3530 Wheeler Rd, **Augusta,** GA 30909, *pg.* 804, *pg.* 525
SOUTHEASTERN BANKING CORP., 1010 Northway St, **Darien,** GA 31305, *pg.* 804, *pg.* 530
SOUTHWEST GEORGIA FINANCIAL CORPORATION, 201 1st St SE, **Moultrie,** GA 31768, *pg.* 804, *pg.* 536
SUN TRUST BANK, ATLANTA, PO Box 4625, **Atlanta,** GA 30302, *pg.* 806, *pg.* 520
SUNTRUST BANKS, INC., 303 Peachtree St NE, **Atlanta,** GA 30308-3201, *pg.* 807, *pg.* 520
TAXSLAYER LLC, 3003 Allen Dr, **Evans,** GA 30809, *pg.* 808, *pg.* 532
TMX FINANCE LLC, 15 Bull St Ste 200, **Savannah,** GA 31401, *pg.* 810, *pg.* 540
UNITED COMMUNITY BANKS, INC., 125 Hwy 515 E, **Blairsville,** GA 30512, *pg.* 814, *pg.* 526

Hawaii

BANK OF HAWAII CORPORATION, 130 Merchant St, **Honolulu,** HI 96813, *pg.* 720, *pg.* 543
CENTRAL PACIFIC FINANCIAL CORPORATION, 220 S King St, **Honolulu,** HI 96813, *pg.* 733, *pg.* 543

Illinois

AVANT, 640 N La Salle Dr Ste 535, **Chicago,** IL 60654, *pg.* 717, *pg.* 566
BANKFINANCIAL CORPORATION, 15W060 N Frontage Rd, **Burr Ridge,** IL 60527, *pg.* 722, *pg.* 560
BMO HARRIS BANK N.A., 111 W Monroe St, **Chicago,** IL 60603-4096, *pg.* 725, *pg.* 567
BRIEFING.COM, 401 N Michigan Ave Ste 2950, **Chicago,** IL 60611, *pg.* 727, *pg.* 568
CALAMOS ASSET MANAGEMENT INC, 2020 Calamos Ct, **Naperville,** IL 60563-2787, *pg.* 728, *pg.* 635
CBOE HOLDINGS, INC., 400 S LaSalle St, **Chicago,** IL 60605, *pg.* 733, *pg.* 569
CME GROUP INC., 20 S Wacker Dr, **Chicago,** IL 60606-7413, *pg.* 738, *pg.* 571
CME GROUP, INC., 141 W Jackson Blvd, **Chicago,** IL 60606-2994, *pg.* 738, *pg.* 571
DISCOVER FINANCIAL SERVICES, 2500 Lake Cook Rd, **Riverwoods,** IL 60015, *pg.* 744, *pg.* 653
E-LOAN, INC., 9600 W Bryn Mawr Ave, **Rosemont,** IL 60018, *pg.* 745, *pg.* 657
ENVESTNET, INC., 35 E Wacker Dr Ste 2400, **Chicago,** IL 60601, *pg.* 748, *pg.* 573
EQUITY GROUP INVESTMENTS, LLC, 2 N Riverside Plz Ste 1500 6 F, **Chicago,** IL 60606, *pg.* 748, *pg.* 573
FIDELITY LIFE ASSOCIATION, PO Box 5030, **Des Plaines,** IL 60017, *pg.* 752, *pg.* 606
FIRST BUSEY CORPORATION, 100 W University Ave, **Champaign,** IL 61820, *pg.* 754, *pg.* 562
FIRST MIDWEST BANCORP INC., 1 Pierce Pl Ste 1500, **Itasca,** IL 60143, *pg.* 756, *pg.* 620
FIRST ROBINSON FINANCIAL CORPORATION, 501 E Main St, **Robinson,** IL 62454, *pg.* 757, *pg.* 654
GRANT THORNTON INTERNATIONAL LTD., 175 W Jackson Blvd 20th Fl, **Chicago,** IL 60604, *pg.* 763, *pg.* 575
GREAT AMERICAN BANCORP, INC., 1311 S Neil St, **Champaign,** IL 61820, *pg.* 763, *pg.* 562
HSBC FINANCE CORPORATION, 26525 N Riverwoods Blvd, **Mettawa,** IL 60045, *pg.* 767, *pg.* 632
HURON CONSULTING GROUP INC., 550 W Van Buren St, **Chicago,** IL 60607, *pg.* 768, *pg.* 577
JPMORGAN CHASE - MIDWEST REGIONAL OFFICE, 10 S Dearborn, **Chicago,** IL 60603, *pg.* 773, *pg.* 579
MB FINANCIAL, INC., 800 W Madison St, **Chicago,** IL 60607-2630, *pg.* 781, *pg.* 581
MORNINGSTAR, INC., 22 W Washington St, **Chicago,** IL 60602, *pg.* 784, *pg.* 583
NAVIGANT CONSULTING, INC., 30 S Wacker Dr Ste 3550, **Chicago,** IL 60606, *pg.* 786, *pg.* 584
THE NORTHERN TRUST COMPANY, 50 S LaSalle St, **Chicago,** IL 60603, *pg.* 787, *pg.* 585
NORTHERN TRUST CORPORATION, 50 S La Salle St, **Chicago,** IL 60603, *pg.* 787, *pg.* 585
NUVEEN INVESTMENTS, INC., 333 W Wacker Dr, **Chicago,** IL 60606, *pg.* 788, *pg.* 586
OLD SECOND BANCORP, INC., 37 S River St, **Aurora,** IL 60506-4173, *pg.* 789, *pg.* 555
OPTIONSXPRESS HOLDINGS, INC., 311 W Monroe St Ste 1000, **Chicago,** IL 60606-4663, *pg.* 790, *pg.* 586
PARK BANCORP, INC., 5400 S Pulaski Rd, **Chicago,** IL 60632, *pg.* 792, *pg.* 587
PRIVATEBANCORP INC., 120 S LaSalle St, **Chicago,** IL 60603, *pg.* 796, *pg.* 587
QCR HOLDINGS, INC., 3551 7th St Ste 204, **Moline,** IL 61265, *pg.* 797, *pg.* 633
TRANSUNION CORP., 555 W Adams St Fl 9, **Chicago,** IL 60661-3614, *pg.* 811, *pg.* 591
WEST SUBURBAN BANCORP, INC., 711 S Meyers Rd, **Lombard,** IL 60148, *pg.* 821, *pg.* 631
WILLIAM BLAIR & COMPANY LLC, 222 W Adams St, **Chicago,** IL 60606-5312, *pg.* 822, *pg.* 596
WIND POINT PARTNERS, 676 N Michigan Ave Ste 3700, **Chicago,** IL 60611, *pg.* 823, *pg.* 596
THE ZIEGLER COMPANIES, INC., 200 S Wacker Dr Ste 2000, **Chicago,** IL 60606, *pg.* 824, *pg.* 597

Indiana

1ST SOURCE BANK, 100 N Michigan St, **South Bend,** IN 46601-1630, *pg.* 710, *pg.* 697
AMB FINANCIAL CORP., 8230 Hohman Ave, **Munster,** IN 46321-1578, *pg.* 711, *pg.* 696
FIFTH THIRD BANK, INDIANA (SOUTHERN), 20 NW 3rd St, **Evansville,** IN 47708-0001, *pg.* 753, *pg.* 678
FIRST BANCORP OF INDIANA, INC., 5001 Davis Lant Dr, **Evansville,** IN 47715, *pg.* 753, *pg.* 678
FIRST HARRISON BANK, 220 Federal Dr NW, **Corydon,** IN 47112, *pg.* 755, *pg.* 676
FIRST MERCHANTS CORPORATION, 200 E Jackson St, **Muncie,** IN 47305, *pg.* 756, *pg.* 695
FIRST SAVINGS FINANCIAL GROUP INC., 501 E Lewis & Clark Pkwy, **Clarksville,** IN 47129, *pg.* 757, *pg.* 675
GERMAN AMERICAN BANCORP, INC., 711 Main St, **Jasper,** IN 47546, *pg.* 762, *pg.* 691

First page reference indicates Business Class Edition
Second page reference indicates Geographic Edition

HORIZON BANCORP, 515 Franklin Sq, **Michigan City, IN** 46360, *pg.* 767, *pg.* 694
LAKELAND FINANCIAL CORPORATION, 202 E Center St PO Box 1387, **Warsaw,** IN 46581-1387, *pg.* 775, *pg.* 699
LAPORTE BANCORP, INC., 710 Indiana Ave, **La Porte,** IN 46350, *pg.* 775, *pg.* 692
MUTUALFIRST FINANCIAL, INC., 110 E Charles St, **Muncie,** IN 47305-2400, *pg.* 785, *pg.* 696
NATIONAL BANK OF INDIANAPOLIS CORPORATION, 107 N Pennsylvania Ste 700, **Indianapolis,** IN 46204, *pg.* 785, *pg.* 688
OLD NATIONAL BANCORP, 1 Main St, **Evansville,** IN 47708, *pg.* 789, *pg.* 679
RIVER VALLEY BANCORP, 430 Clifty Dr, **Madison,** IN 47250, *pg.* 799, *pg.* 694
UNITED COMMUNITY BANCORP, 92 Walnut St, **Lawrenceburg,** IN 47025, *pg.* 813, *pg.* 693
YOUR COMMUNITY BANKSHARES, INC., 101 W Spring St, **New Albany,** IN 47150, *pg.* 824, *pg.* 696

Iowa

AMERICAN EQUITY INVESTMENT LIFE HOLDING COMPANY, 6000 Westown Pkwy, **West Des Moines,** IA 50266, *pg.* 711, *pg.* 712
GREAT WESTERN BANK, 825 Central Ave, **Fort Dodge,** IA 50501, *pg.* 763, *pg.* 708
HEARTLAND FINANCIAL USA, INC., 1398 Central Ave, **Dubuque,** IA 52004, *pg.* 765, *pg.* 707
IOWA FIRST BANCSHARES CORP., 300 E 2nd St, **Muscatine,** IA 52761, *pg.* 771, *pg.* 710
PRINCIPAL FINANCIAL GROUP, INC., 711 High St, **Des Moines,** IA 50392-0001, *pg.* 796, *pg.* 706
WEBSTER CITY FEDERAL BANCORP, 820 Des Moines St, **Webster City,** IA 50595-2120, *pg.* 819, *pg.* 712
WELLS FARGO FINANCIAL, INC., 800 Walnut St, **Des Moines,** IA 50309, *pg.* 821, *pg.* 707

Kansas

BLUE VALLEY BAN CORP, 11935 Riley St, **Overland Park,** KS 66213, *pg.* 725, *pg.* 718
CAPITOL FEDERAL FINANCIAL, INC., 700 S Kansas Ave, **Topeka,** KS 66603-3894, *pg.* 731, *pg.* 721
EMPRISE BANK, 257 N Broadway, **Wichita,** KS 67202, *pg.* 747, *pg.* 723
HILLCREST BANK, N.A., 11111 W 95th St, **Overland Park,** KS 66214-1846, *pg.* 766, *pg.* 719
IVY FUNDS DISTRIBUTOR INC., 6300 Lamar Ave, **Overland Park,** KS 66202, *pg.* 771, *pg.* 719
LANDMARK BANCORP, INC., 701 Poyntz Ave, **Manhattan,** KS 66502-6052, *pg.* 775, *pg.* 717
QC HOLDINGS, INC., 9401 Indian Creek Pwy Ste 1500, **Overland Park,** KS 66210, *pg.* 797, *pg.* 719
WADDELL & REED FINANCIAL, INC., 6300 Lamar Ave, **Shawnee Mission,** KS 66202, *pg.* 818, *pg.* 721

Kentucky

CITIZENS FIRST CORPORATION, 1065 Ashley Street, **Bowling Green,** KY 42103, *pg.* 737, *pg.* 725
CITY NATIONAL BANK, 344 17th St, **Ashland,** KY 41101, *pg.* 737, *pg.* 725
FARMERS CAPITAL BANK CORPORATION, PO Box 309, **Frankfort,** KY 40602-0309, *pg.* 750, *pg.* 728
FASIG-TIPTON CO. INC., 2400 Newtown Pike, **Lexington,** KY 40511-8469, *pg.* 750, *pg.* 729
HOPFED BANCORP, INC., 4155 Lafayette Rd, **Hopkinsville,** KY 42240, *pg.* 766, *pg.* 729
KENTUCKY BANCSHARES, INC., 339 Main St, **Paris,** KY 40362-0157, *pg.* 773, *pg.* 739
REPUBLIC BANCORP, INC., 601 W Market St, **Louisville,** KY 40202-2745, *pg.* 799, *pg.* 737
REPUBLIC BANK & TRUST COMPANY, 601 W Market St, **Louisville,** KY 40202, *pg.* 799, *pg.* 737

Louisiana

HIBERNIA BANK, 325 Carondelet St, **New Orleans,** LA 70130, *pg.* 766, *pg.* 747
HOME BANCORP, INC., 503 Kaliste Saloom Rd, **Lafayette,** LA 70508, *pg.* 766, *pg.* 744
IBERIABANK CORPORATION, 200 W Congress St, **Lafayette,** LA 70501, *pg.* 768, *pg.* 744
LOUISIANA BANCORP, INC., 1600 Veterans Memorial Blvd, **Metairie,** LA 70005, *pg.* 777, *pg.* 745
MIDSOUTH BANCORP, INC., 102 Versailles Blvd, **Lafayette,** LA 70501, *pg.* 783, *pg.* 745
MIDSOUTH BANK N.A., 102 Versailles Blvd, **Lafayette,** LA 70501, *pg.* 783, *pg.* 745
MINDEN BANCORP, INC., 100 MBL Bank Dr, **Minden,** LA 71055, *pg.* 783, *pg.* 746
WHITNEY HOLDING CORPORATION, 228 Saint Charles Ave, **New Orleans,** LA 70130, *pg.* 822, *pg.* 747

Maine

ANDROSCOGGIN SAVINGS BANK, 30 Lisbon St, **Lewiston,** ME 04240, *pg.* 716, *pg.* 751
BAR HARBOR BANK & TRUST, 82 Main St, **Bar Harbor,** ME 04609, *pg.* 722, *pg.* 749
CAMDEN NATIONAL BANK, INC., 2 Elm St, **Camden,** ME 04843-1903, *pg.* 729, *pg.* 749
NORTHEAST BANCORP, 500 Canal St, **Lewiston,** ME 04240, *pg.* 787, *pg.* 751
PEOPLE'S UNITED BANK, 201 Main St, **Bangor,** ME 04401-0925, *pg.* 793, *pg.* 749

Maryland

AMERIX CORPORATION, 8930 Stanford Blvd, **Columbia,** MD 21045-5805, *pg.* 715, *pg.* 767
CALVIN B. TAYLOR BANKSHARES, INC., 24 N Main St, **Berlin,** MD 21811, *pg.* 728, *pg.* 761
CFG COMMUNITY BANK, 1422 Clarkview Rd, **Baltimore,** MD 21209, *pg.* 734, *pg.* 756
THE COLUMBIA BANK, 7168 Columbia Gateway Dr, **Columbia,** MD 21046, *pg.* 739, *pg.* 767
EAGLE BANCORP, INC., 7815 Woodmont Ave, **Bethesda,** MD 20814, *pg.* 745, *pg.* 762
EAGLEBANK, 7815 Woodmont Ave, **Bethesda,** MD 20814, *pg.* 745, *pg.* 762
EDGAR ONLINE, INC., 11200 Rockville Pike Ste 310, **Rockville,** MD 20852, *pg.* 746, *pg.* 776
FIDUCIAL, INC., 10100 Old Columbia Rd, **Columbia,** MD 21046, *pg.* 752, *pg.* 767
FIRST HOME MORTGAGE CORPORATION, 5355 Nottingham Dr, Ste 130, **Baltimore,** MD 21236, *pg.* 755, *pg.* 757
FIRST MARINER BANCORP, 1501 S Clinton St, **Baltimore,** MD 21224, *pg.* 756, *pg.* 757
FIRST MARINER BANK, 3301 Boston St, **Baltimore,** MD 21224, *pg.* 756, *pg.* 757
GLEN BURNIE BANCORP, 101 Crain Hwy SE, **Glen Burnie,** MD 21227, *pg.* 762, *pg.* 771
LEGG MASON, INC., 100 International Dr, **Baltimore,** MD 21202, *pg.* 775, *pg.* 758
OLD LINE BANCSHARES, INC., 1525 Pointer Ridge Place, **Bowie,** MD 20716, *pg.* 789, *pg.* 766
PATAPSCO BANCORP, 1301 Merritt Blvd, **Baltimore,** MD 21222, *pg.* 792, *pg.* 758
SANDY SPRING BANCORP, INC., 17801 Georgia Ave, **Olney,** MD 20832, *pg.* 801, *pg.* 774
SANDY SPRING BANK, 17801 Georgia Ave, **Olney,** MD 20832, *pg.* 801, *pg.* 774
SEVERN BANCORP, INC., 200 Westgate Cir Ste 200, **Annapolis,** MD 21401, *pg.* 803, *pg.* 754
SHORE BANCSHARES, INC., 18 E Dover St, **Easton,** MD 21601, *pg.* 803, *pg.* 769
T. ROWE PRICE GROUP INC., 100 E Pratt St, **Baltimore,** MD 21202-1009, *pg.* 808, *pg.* 759
TRI-COUNTY FINANCIAL CORPORATION, 3035 Leonardtown Rd, **Waldorf,** MD 20601, *pg.* 811, *pg.* 780

Massachusetts

AMERICAN STUDENT ASSISTANCE, 100 Cambridge St Ste 1600, **Boston,** MA 02114, *pg.* 714, *pg.* 789
BANK OF AMERICA GLOBAL WEALTH & INVESTMENT MANAGEMENT, 100 Federal St, **Boston,** MA 02110-1802, *pg.* 720, *pg.* 789
BAY STATE SAVINGS BANK, 28 Franklin St, **Worcester,** MA 01608, *pg.* 722, *pg.* 862
THE BOSTON COMPANY ASSET MANAGEMENT, LLC, 1 Boston Pl, **Boston,** MA 02108-4407, *pg.* 726, *pg.* 790
BOSTON PRIVATE, 10 Post Office Sq, **Boston,** MA 02109, *pg.* 726, *pg.* 791
BROOKLINE BANCORP, INC., 160 Washington St, **Brookline,** MA 02447, *pg.* 727, *pg.* 804
CAMBRIDGE CREDIT COUNSELING CORP., 67 Hunt St, **Agawam,** MA 01001, *pg.* 728, *pg.* 781
CAMBRIDGE SAVINGS BANK, 1374 Massachusetts Ave, **Cambridge,** MA 02138-3822, *pg.* 728, *pg.* 807
CAPE COD FIVE CENTS SAVINGS BANK, 19 W Rd, **Orleans,** MA 02653, *pg.* 730, *pg.* 840
CHICOPEE BANCORP, INC., 70 Center St, **Chicopee,** MA 01013, *pg.* 735, *pg.* 815
EASTERN BANK CORPORATION, 265 Franklin St, **Boston,** MA 02110, *pg.* 745, *pg.* 793
EASTERN BANK CORPORATION-SOUTH REGION HEADQUARTERS, 151 Campanelli Dr, **Middleboro,** MA 02346, *pg.* 745, *pg.* 833
EATON VANCE CORP., 2 International Pl, **Boston,** MA 02110, *pg.* 746, *pg.* 794
ENTERPRISE BANCORP INC., 222 Merrimack St, **Lowell,** MA 01852, *pg.* 747, *pg.* 829
FMR LLC (FIDELITY INVESTMENTS), 82 Devonshire St, **Boston,** MA 02109-3605, *pg.* 759, *pg.* 794
HINGHAM INSTITUTION FOR SAVINGS, 55 Main St, **Hingham,** MA 02043, *pg.* 766, *pg.* 824
INDEPENDENT BANK CORP., 288 Union St, **Rockland,** MA 02370, *pg.* 768, *pg.* 843
INTERACTIVE DATA CORPORATION, 32 Crosby Dr, **Bedford,** MA 01730-1448, *pg.* 769, *pg.* 785
INTERACTIVE DATA PRICING & REFERENCE DATA, INC., 32 Crosby Dr, **Bedford,** MA 01730-1448, *pg.* 769, *pg.* 785
INVESTORS CAPITAL CORPORATION, 230 Broadway East, **Lynnfield,** MA 01940, *pg.* 771, *pg.* 830
KODIAK VENTURE PARTNERS, L.P., 80 William St, Ste 260, **Wellesley Hills,** MA 02481, *pg.* 774, *pg.* 856
LOOMIS, SAYLES & COMPANY, L.P., 1 Financial Ctr, **Boston,** MA 02111-2621, *pg.* 777, *pg.* 798
LPL FINANCIAL CORPORATION, 75 State St, 24th Fl, **Boston,** MA 02109, *pg.* 777, *pg.* 798
MERIDIAN INTERSTATE BANCORP, INC., 10 Meridian St, **East Boston,** MA 02128, *pg.* 782, *pg.* 817
MFS INVESTMENT MANAGEMENT, 111 Huntington Ave, **Boston,** MA 02199-7632, *pg.* 782, *pg.* 798
MICROFINANCIAL INCORPORATED, 16 New England Executive Pk Ste 200, **Burlington,** MA 01803, *pg.* 782, *pg.* 805
NEWBURYPORT FIVE CENTS SAVINGS BANK, 63 State St, **Newburyport,** MA 01950, *pg.* 787, *pg.* 836
OLD MUTUAL ASSET MANAGEMENT, 200 Clarendon St Fl 53, **Boston,** MA 02116, *pg.* 789, *pg.* 799
PIONEER INVESTMENTS, 60 State St, **Boston,** MA 02109-1800, *pg.* 794, *pg.* 800
PUTNAM INVESTMENTS, LLC, 1 Post Office Sq, **Boston,** MA 02109, *pg.* 797, *pg.* 800
READING COOPERATIVE BANK, 180 Haven St, **Reading,** MA 01867, *pg.* 798, *pg.* 842
SALEM FIVE CENTS SAVINGS BANK, 210 Essex St, **Salem,** MA 01970-3705, *pg.* 800, *pg.* 843
SANTANDER HOLDINGS USA, INC., 75 State St, **Boston,** MA 02109, *pg.* 801, *pg.* 800
STATE STREET CORPORATION, 1 Lincoln St, **Boston,** MA 02111, *pg.* 805, *pg.* 801
STONEHAM BANK, 80 Montvale Ave, **Stoneham,** MA 02180, *pg.* 806, *pg.* 846
TAXWARE, 200 Ballardvale St 4th Fl, **Wilmington,** MA 01887, *pg.* 808, *pg.* 860
UPROMISE, INC., 95 Wells Ave Ste 160, **Newton,** MA 02459, *pg.* 815, *pg.* 837
WATERTOWN SAVINGS BANK INC., 60 Main St, **Watertown,** MA 02472-4413, *pg.* 818, *pg.* 855

Michigan

ALLY FINANCIAL INC., 200 Renaissance Ctr, PO Box 200, **Detroit,** MI 48265, *pg.* 711, *pg.* 878
ASSET ACCEPTANCE CAPITAL CORP., 28405 Van Dyke Ave, **Warren,** MI 48093, *pg.* 716, *pg.* 912
CENTURY BANK & TRUST, 100 W Chicago St, **Coldwater,** MI 49036, *pg.* 733, *pg.* 875
CHEMICAL FINANCIAL CORPORATION, 235 E Main St, **Midland,** MI 48640-0569, *pg.* 734, *pg.* 898
CHOICEONE FINANCIAL SERVICES, INC., 109 E Division St, **Sparta,** MI 49345, *pg.* 735, *pg.* 908
COMMUNITY SHORES BANK CORPORATION, 1030 W Norton Ave, **Muskegon,** MI 49441, *pg.* 741, *pg.* 901
CREDIT ACCEPTANCE CORPORATION, 25505 W 12 Mile

Rd Ste 3000, **Southfield,** MI 48034-8339, *pg.* 742, *pg.* 906
FENTURA FINANCIAL, INC., 175 N Leroy St, **Fenton,** MI 48430, *pg.* 752, *pg.* 886
FLAGSTAR BANCORP, INC., 5151 Corporate Dr, **Troy,** MI 48098-2639, *pg.* 758, *pg.* 910
FNBH BANCORP, INC., 101 E Grand River Ave, **Howell,** MI 48843, *pg.* 759, *pg.* 893
INDEPENDENT BANK CORPORATION, 230 W Main St, **Ionia,** MI 48846-1665, *pg.* 768, *pg.* 893
ISABELLA BANK CORPORATION, 401 N Main St, **Mount Pleasant,** MI 48858, *pg.* 771, *pg.* 901
MACATAWA BANK CORPORATION, 10753 Macatawa Dr, **Holland,** MI 49424, *pg.* 778, *pg.* 892
MACKINAC FINANCIAL CORPORATION, 130 S Cedar St, **Manistique,** MI 49854, *pg.* 778, *pg.* 898
MERCANTILE BANK CORPORATION, 310 Leonard St NW, **Grand Rapids,** MI 49504-4224, *pg.* 782, *pg.* 888
QUICKEN LOANS, INC., 1050 Woodward Ave, **Detroit,** MI 48226, *pg.* 797, *pg.* 884
TD AUTO FINANCE, PO Box 9223, **Farmington Hills,** MI 48333-9223, *pg.* 809, *pg.* 886
UNIVERSITY BANCORP, INC., 2015 Washtenaw Ave, **Ann Arbor,** MI 48104-3656, *pg.* 814, *pg.* 867
USA FINANCIAL, 6020 E Fulton St, **Ada,** MI 49301, *pg.* 815, *pg.* 864

Minnesota

AMERIPRISE FINANCIAL, INC., 1099 Ameriprise Financial Ctr, **Minneapolis,** MN 55474, *pg.* 715, *pg.* 930
HMN FINANCIAL, INC., 1016 Civic Center Dr NW, **Rochester,** MN 55903, *pg.* 766, *pg.* 955
MCGLADREY, LLP, 801 Nicollet Ave Ste 1100, **Minneapolis,** MN 55402, *pg.* 781, *pg.* 938
PIPER JAFFRAY COMPANIES, 800 Nicollet Mall, Ste 1000, **Minneapolis,** MN 55402, *pg.* 794, *pg.* 941
SHL, 650 3rd Ave S Ste 1300, **Minneapolis,** MN 55402, *pg.* 803, *pg.* 942
TCF FINANCIAL CORPORATION, 200 Lake St E, **Wayzata,** MN 55391-1693, *pg.* 808, *pg.* 966
U.S. BANCORP, 800 Nicollet Mall, **Minneapolis,** MN 55402, *pg.* 815, *pg.* 945

Mississippi

BANCORPSOUTH, INC., 1 Mississippi Plz 201 S Spring St, **Tupelo,** MS 38804, *pg.* 717, *pg.* 971
BRITTON & KOONTZ FIRST NATIONAL BANK, 500 Main St, **Natchez,** MS 39120-3364, *pg.* 727, *pg.* 970
CADENCE FINANCIAL CORPORATION, 301 E Main St, **Starkville,** MS 39760, *pg.* 728, *pg.* 971
CITIZENS HOLDING COMPANY, 521 Main St, **Philadelphia,** MS 39350, *pg.* 737, *pg.* 971
THE FIRST BANCSHARES, INC., 6480 Hwy 98 W, **Hattiesburg,** MS 39404, *pg.* 753, *pg.* 969
HANCOCK BANK, 1 Hancock Plz, **Gulfport,** MS 39502, *pg.* 765, *pg.* 968
HANCOCK HOLDING COMPANY, 1 Hancock Plz, **Gulfport,** MS 39501-1947, *pg.* 765, *pg.* 968
PEOPLES FINANCIAL CORPORATION, 152 Lameuse Ave, **Biloxi,** MS 39530, *pg.* 793, *pg.* 968
RENASANT CORPORATION, 209 Troy St, **Tupelo,** MS 38804-4827, *pg.* 799, *pg.* 972
TRUSTMARK CORPORATION, 248 E Capitol St, **Jackson,** MS 39201, *pg.* 812, *pg.* 969
TRUSTMARK NATIONAL BANK, 248 E Capitol St, **Jackson,** MS 39201-2503, *pg.* 812, *pg.* 969

Missouri

AMERICAN CENTURY INVESTMENTS, 4500 Main St, **Kansas City,** MO 64111-1816, *pg.* 711, *pg.* 980
AMERICAN EQUITY MORTGAGE INC., 11933 Westline Industrial Dr, **Saint Louis,** MO 63146, *pg.* 712, *pg.* 991
CENTRUE FINANCIAL CORPORATION, 7700 Bonhomme Ave, **Saint Louis,** MO 63105, *pg.* 733, *pg.* 994
CITIZENS BANK & TRUST, 515 Washington St, **Chillicothe,** MO 64601, *pg.* 737, *pg.* 976
COMMERCE BANCSHARES, INC., 1000 Walnut, **Kansas City,** MO 64106, *pg.* 740, *pg.* 982
EDWARD D. JONES & CO., LP, 12555 Manchester Rd, **Saint Louis,** MO 63131, *pg.* 746, *pg.* 995
FCSTONE GROUP, INC., 1251 NW Briarcliff Pkwy Ste 800, **Kansas City,** MO 64116, *pg.* 751, *pg.* 982
FIRST BANKS, INC., 135 N Meramec Ave, **Clayton,** MO 63105-3751, *pg.* 754, *pg.* 976
GREAT SOUTHERN BANCORP, INC., 1451 E Battlefield, **Springfield,** MO 65804, *pg.* 763, *pg.* 1006
GUARANTY BANK, 1341 W Battlefield Rd, **Springfield,** MO 65807, *pg.* 764, *pg.* 1006
H&R BLOCK, INC., 1 H&R Block Way, **Kansas City,** MO 64105, *pg.* 764, *pg.* 983
HAWTHORN BANCSHARES, INC., 300 SW Longview Blvd, **Lees Summit,** MO 64081, *pg.* 765, *pg.* 987
LIBERTY BANCORP, INC., 16 W Franklin St, **Liberty,** MO 64068, *pg.* 775, *pg.* 987
MASTERCARD WORLDWIDE INC., 2200 Mastercard Blvd, **O Fallon,** MO 63366-7263, *pg.* 780, *pg.* 988
NASB FINANCIAL, INC., 12498 S Hwy 71, **Grandview,** MO 64030, *pg.* 785, *pg.* 978
PULASKI FINANCIAL CORP., 12300 Olive Blvd, **Saint Louis,** MO 63141, *pg.* 797, *pg.* 1002
SCOTTRADE, INC., 12800 Corp Hill Dr, **Saint Louis,** MO 63131-1834, *pg.* 802, *pg.* 1003
SOUTHERN MISSOURI BANCORP, INC., 531 Vine St, **Poplar Bluff,** MO 63901, *pg.* 804, *pg.* 989
UMB FINANCIAL CORPORATION, 1010 Grand Blvd, **Kansas City,** MO 64106-2008, *pg.* 812, *pg.* 987
WELLS FARGO ADVISORS, LLC, 1 N Jefferson Ave, **Saint Louis,** MO 63103-2205, *pg.* 819, *pg.* 1005

Montana

FIRST INTERSTATE BANCSYSTEM, INC., 401 N 31st St, **Billings,** MT 59116-0001, *pg.* 755, *pg.* 1008
GLACIER BANCORP, INC., 49 Commons Loop, **Kalispell,** MT 59901-2679, *pg.* 762, *pg.* 1009
GLACIER BANK, 202 Main St, **Kalispell,** MT 59901-4454, *pg.* 762, *pg.* 1009

Nebraska

NELNET, INC., 121 S 13th St Ste 201, **Lincoln,** NE 68508, *pg.* 786, *pg.* 1012
PLATTE VALLEY FINANCIAL SERVICE COMPANIES INC., 1212 Cir Dr, **Scottsbluff,** NE 69363-0137, *pg.* 794, *pg.* 1019
TD AMERITRADE HOLDING CORPORATION, 200 S 108th Ave, **Omaha,** NE 68154, *pg.* 808, *pg.* 1018

Nevada

EVERI HOLDINGS INC., 7250 S Tenaya Way, # 100, **Las Vegas,** NV 89113, *pg.* 749, *pg.* 1023

New Hampshire

BOTTOMLINE TECHNOLOGIES (DE), INC., 325 Corporate Dr, **Portsmouth,** NH 03801, *pg.* 727, *pg.* 1038
INFOGROUP, 10 Vose Farm Rd, **Peterborough,** NH 03458, *pg.* 769, *pg.* 1038
NEW HAMPSHIRE THRIFT BANCSHARES, INC., 9 Main St The Carriage House, **Newport,** NH 03773, *pg.* 786, *pg.* 1038
NORTHWAY FINANCIAL, INC., 9 Main St, **Berlin,** NH 03570, *pg.* 788, *pg.* 1033

New Jersey

AMBOY BANCORPORATION, 3590 US Hwy 9 S, **Old Bridge,** NJ 08857, *pg.* 711, *pg.* 1100
BCB BANCORP, INC., 104 110 Avenue C, **Bayonne,** NJ 07002, *pg.* 723, *pg.* 1042
BEDERSON & COMPANY LLP, 100 Passaic Ave, **Fairfield,** NJ 07004, *pg.* 724, *pg.* 1064
BRUNSWICK BANCORP, 439 Livingston Ave, **New Brunswick,** NJ 08901, *pg.* 727, *pg.* 1091
CAPE BANCORP, INC., 225 N Main St, **Cape May Court House,** NJ 08210, *pg.* 730, *pg.* 1049
CLIFTON SAVINGS BANCORP, INC., 1433 Van Houton Ave, **Clifton,** NJ 07015, *pg.* 738, *pg.* 1052
COHNREZNICK LLP, 4 Becker Farm Rd, **Roseland,** NJ 07068, *pg.* 739, *pg.* 1118
COMMUNITY PARTNERS BANCORP, 1250 Hwy 35 S, **Middletown,** NJ 07748, *pg.* 741, *pg.* 1084
FEDERAL FARM CREDIT BANKS FUNDING CORPORATION, 10 Exchange Pl Ste 1401, **Jersey City,** NJ 07302, *pg.* 751, *pg.* 1075
GAIN CAPITAL HOLDINGS, INC., Bedminster One 135 Route 202/206, **Bedminster,** NJ 07921, *pg.* 760, *pg.* 1043
HEARTLAND PAYMENT SYSTEMS, INC., 90 Nassau St 2nd Fl, **Princeton,** NJ 08542-4520, *pg.* 765, *pg.* 1111
INVESTORS BANCORP, INC., 101 JFK Pkwy, **Short Hills,** NJ 07078, *pg.* 771, *pg.* 1121
JACKSON HEWITT TAX SERVICE INC., 3 Sylvan Way, **Parsippany,** NJ 07054, *pg.* 771, *pg.* 1103
KEARNY FINANCIAL CORP., 120 Passaic Ave, **Fairfield,** NJ 07004-3510, *pg.* 773, *pg.* 1065
KPMG LLP, 3 Chestnut Ridge Rd, **Montvale,** NJ 07645-0435, *pg.* 774, *pg.* 1086
OCEAN SHORE HOLDING CO., 1001 Asbury Ave, **Ocean City,** NJ 08226, *pg.* 789, *pg.* 1100
OCEANFIRST BANK, 975 Hooper Ave, **Toms River,** NJ 08753, *pg.* 789, *pg.* 1125
OCEANFIRST FINANCIAL CORP., 975 Hooper Ave, **Toms River,** NJ 08753, *pg.* 789, *pg.* 1125
ORITANI FINANCIAL CORP., 370 Pascack Rd, **Washington,** NJ 07676, *pg.* 790, *pg.* 1129
PEAPACK-GLADSTONE BANK, 190 Main St, **Gladstone,** NJ 07934, *pg.* 792, *pg.* 1071
PEAPACK-GLADSTONE FINANCIAL CORPORATION, 500 Hills Dr Ste 300, **Bedminster,** NJ 07921, *pg.* 792, *pg.* 1044
PHH CORPORATION, 3000 Leadenhall Rd, **Mount Laurel,** NJ 08054, *pg.* 793, *pg.* 1090
PRINCETON FINANCIAL SYSTEMS, INC., 600 College Rd E, **Princeton,** NJ 08540, *pg.* 795, *pg.* 1112
PROVIDENT FINANCIAL SERVICES, INC., 239 Washington St, **Jersey City,** NJ 07302, *pg.* 796, *pg.* 1075
PRUDENTIAL FINANCIAL, INC., 751 Broad St, **Newark,** NJ 07102-3777, *pg.* 797, *pg.* 1097
STEWARDSHIP FINANCIAL CORPORATION, 630 Godwin Ave, **Midland Park,** NJ 07432, *pg.* 805, *pg.* 1084
SUN BANCORP, INC., 226 W Landis Ave, **Vineland,** NJ 08360, *pg.* 806, *pg.* 1127
SUSSEX BANCORP, 200 Munsonhurst Rd Rt 517, **Franklin,** NJ 07416-0353, *pg.* 807, *pg.* 1068
TD BANK US HOLDING COMPANY, 1701 Rte 70 E, **Cherry Hill,** NJ 08034, *pg.* 809, *pg.* 1051
UNITY BANCORP, INC., 64 Old Highway 22, **Clinton,** NJ 08809-1380, *pg.* 814, *pg.* 1052
UNITY BANK, 64 Old Hwy 22, **Clinton,** NJ 08809, *pg.* 814, *pg.* 1052
VALLEY NATIONAL BANCORP, 1455 Valley Rd, **Wayne,** NJ 07470, *pg.* 815, *pg.* 1130
WISS & COMPANY LLP, 354 Eisenhower Pkwy, **Livingston,** NJ 07039, *pg.* 823, *pg.* 1080

New York

ALMA BANK, 28-31 31st St., **Astoria,** NY 11102, *pg.* 711, *pg.* 1140
AMERICAN EXPRESS COMPANY, World Financial Ctr 200 Vesey St, **New York,** NY 10285-4805, *pg.* 712, *pg.* 1190
AMERICAN SECURITIES LLC, 299 Park Ave 34th Fl, **New York,** NY 10171-4011, *pg.* 714, *pg.* 1193
APPLE BANK FOR SAVINGS, 122 E 42nd St 9th Fl, **New York,** NY 10168, *pg.* 716, *pg.* 1196
ARROW FINANCIAL CORPORATION, 250 Glen St, **Glens Falls,** NY 12801-3505, *pg.* 716, *pg.* 1161
ASTORIA FEDERAL SAVINGS & LOAN, 1 Astoria Federal Plz, **Lake Success,** NY 11042, *pg.* 716, *pg.* 1171
ASTORIA FINANCIAL CORPORATION, 1 Astoria Federal Plz, **Lake Success,** NY 11042-1085, *pg.* 717, *pg.* 1172
AXEL JOHNSON INC., 155 Spring St 6th Fl, **New York,** NY 10012, *pg.* 717, *pg.* 1199
BANK LEUMI USA, 579 5th Ave, **New York,** NY 10017-1917, *pg.* 718, *pg.* 1200
THE BANK OF NEW YORK MELLON CORPORATION, 225 Liberty St, **New York,** NY 10286, *pg.* 720, *pg.* 1200
BDO SEIDMAN, LLP, 100 Pk Ave, **New York,** NY 10017, *pg.* 724, *pg.* 1202
THE BERKSHIRE BANK, 160 Broadway, **New York,** NY 10038, *pg.* 724, *pg.* 1202
BLACKROCK, INC., 55 E 52nd St, **New York,** NY 10055, *pg.* 724, *pg.* 1203
BLOOMBERG L.P., 731 Lexington Ave, **New York,** NY 10022, *pg.* 725, *pg.* 1204
BRIDGE BANCORP, INC., 2200 Montauk Hwy, **Bridgehampton,** NY 11932, *pg.* 727, *pg.* 1144

First page reference indicates Business Class Edition
Second page reference indicates Geographic Edition

BRIDGEHAMPTON NATIONAL BANK, 2200 Montauk Hwy, **Bridgehampton,** NY 11932, *pg.* 727, *pg.* 1144
BROADRIDGE FINANCIAL SOLUTIONS INC., 1981 Marcus Ave, **Lake Success,** NY 11042, *pg.* 727, *pg.* 1172
CAPITAL Z, 230 Park Ave S, **New York,** NY 10003-1528, *pg.* 731, *pg.* 1209
CARVER FEDERAL SAVINGS BANK, 75 W 125th St, **New York,** NY 10027-4512, *pg.* 732, *pg.* 1209
CHEMUNG FINANCIAL CORPORATION, 1 Chemung Canal Plz, **Elmira,** NY 14901, *pg.* 734, *pg.* 1157
CIT GROUP INC., 11 W 42nd St, **New York,** NY 10036, *pg.* 735, *pg.* 1212
CITIGROUP INC., 399 Park Ave, **New York,** NY 10022, *pg.* 735, *pg.* 1212
COMMUNITY BANK, N.A., 5790 Widewaters Pkwy, **De Witt,** NY 13214-1883, *pg.* 741, *pg.* 1155
COMMUNITY BANK SYSTEM, INC., 5790 Widewaters Pkwy, **De Witt,** NY 13214-1883, *pg.* 741, *pg.* 1155
COWEN GROUP, INC., 599 Lexington Ave, **New York,** NY 10022, *pg.* 742, *pg.* 1219
CREDIT SUISSE SECURITIES (USA) LLC, 11 Madison Ave, **New York,** NY 10010, *pg.* 742, *pg.* 1220
DEALERTRACK HOLDINGS, INC., 1111 Marcus Ave Ste M04, **Lake Success,** NY 11042, *pg.* 743, *pg.* 1172
DELOITTE & TOUCHE USA LLP, 30 Rockefeller Plz, **New York,** NY 10112, *pg.* 743, *pg.* 1222
DIME COMMUNITY BANCSHARES, INC., 209 Havemeyer St, **Brooklyn,** NY 11211, *pg.* 744, *pg.* 1146
DOMINICK & DOMINICK, LLC, 150 E 52nd St 3rd Fl, **New York,** NY 10022, *pg.* 744, *pg.* 1225
THE DREYFUS CORPORATION, 225 Liberty St, **New York,** NY 10286, *pg.* 745, *pg.* 1226
DUFF & PHELPS CORPORATION, 55 E 52nd St 31 Fl, **New York,** NY 10055, *pg.* 745, *pg.* 1226
EARLYBIRDCAPITAL INC., 275 Madison Ave, **New York,** NY 10016, *pg.* 745, *pg.* 1226
EDUCATIONAL COIN COMPANY, 291 Uppr N Rd, **Highland,** NY 12528-0892, *pg.* 746, *pg.* 1167
THE ELMIRA SAVINGS BANK, FSB, 333 E Water St, **Elmira,** NY 14902-9967, *pg.* 746, *pg.* 1157
EMIGRANT SAVINGS BANK, 5 E 42nd St, **New York,** NY 10017-6904, *pg.* 747, *pg.* 1227
EMPIRE STATE DEVELOPMENT CORPORATION, 633 3rd Ave, **New York,** NY 10017-6706, *pg.* 747, *pg.* 1227
ERNST & YOUNG GLOBAL LIMITED, 5 Times Sq, **New York,** NY 10036-6530, *pg.* 748, *pg.* 1228
E*TRADE FINANCIAL CORPORATION, 1271 Ave of the Americas 14th Fl, **New York,** NY 10020, *pg.* 749, *pg.* 1230
EVANS BANCORP, INC., 14-16 N Main St, **Angola,** NY 14006, *pg.* 749, *pg.* 1138
FINANCIAL INSTITUTIONS, INC., 220 Liberty St, **Warsaw,** NY 14569-1465, *pg.* 753, *pg.* 1349
FINOTEC GROUP, INC., 228 E 45th St Ste 1801, **New York,** NY 10017, *pg.* 753, *pg.* 1231
FIRST NIAGARA BANK, 6950 S Transit Rd, **Lockport,** NY 14094, *pg.* 756, *pg.* 1174
FIRST NIAGARA FINANCIAL GROUP, INC., 726 Exchange St Ste 618, **Buffalo,** NY 14210, *pg.* 757, *pg.* 1148
FLUSHING FINANCIAL CORPORATION, 1979 Marcus Ave Ste E 140, **Lake Success,** NY 11042, *pg.* 759, *pg.* 1172
FLUSHING SAVINGS BANK INC., 1979 Marcus Ave Ste E 140, **Lake Success,** NY 11042, *pg.* 759, *pg.* 1172
FORSTMANN LITTLE & CO., 1 Bryant Park 44th Fl, **New York,** NY 10036, *pg.* 759, *pg.* 1232
GAMCO INVESTORS, INC., 1 Corp Ctr, **Rye,** NY 10580-1422, *pg.* 761, *pg.* 1339
GFI GROUP INC., 55 Water St, **New York,** NY 10041, *pg.* 762, *pg.* 1234
GILMAN CIOCIA, INC., 11 Raymond Ave, **Poughkeepsie,** NY 12603-2342, *pg.* 762, *pg.* 1324
THE GOLDMAN SACHS GROUP, INC., 200 West St, **New York,** NY 10282, *pg.* 762, *pg.* 1236
GOUVERNEUR BANCORP, INC., 42 Church St, **Gouverneur,** NY 13642, *pg.* 763, *pg.* 1162
GOUVERNEUR SAVINGS & LOAN ASSOCIATION, 42 Church St, **Gouverneur,** NY 13642-1416, *pg.* 763, *pg.* 1162
GREATER HUDSON BANK, N.A., 643 Rte 211 E, **Middletown,** NY 10941, *pg.* 763, *pg.* 1182
GREENE COUNTY BANCORP, INC., 302 Main St, **Catskill,** NY 12414, *pg.* 764, *pg.* 1152
HSBC BANK USA, 452 5th Ave, **New York,** NY 10018-2706, *pg.* 767, *pg.* 1241
INFINITY AUGMENTED REALITY, INC., 45 Broadway 6th Fl, **New York,** NY 10006, *pg.* 768, *pg.* 1243
JEFFERIES GROUP, INC., 520 Madison Ave 12th Fl, **New York,** NY 10022, *pg.* 772, *pg.* 1246
JEFFERSONVILLE BANCORP, 4866 State Rte 52, **Jeffersonville,** NY 12748, *pg.* 772, *pg.* 1170
J.P. MORGAN ASSET MANAGEMENT HOLDINGS INC., 270 Park Ave, **New York,** NY 10017, *pg.* 772, *pg.* 1246
JPMORGAN CHASE & CO., 270 Park Ave, **New York,** NY 10017, *pg.* 772, *pg.* 1246
KEYBANK, 65 Dutch Hill Rd, **Orangeburg,** NY 10962, *pg.* 773, *pg.* 1319
KKR & CO. L.P., 9 W 57th St Ste 4200, **New York,** NY 10019, *pg.* 774, *pg.* 1249
LAKE SHORE BANCORP, INC., 125 E 4th St, **Dunkirk,** NY 14048-2226, *pg.* 775, *pg.* 1156
LAZARD FRERES & CO., LLC, 30 Rockefeller Plz, **New York,** NY 10020-0002, *pg.* 775, *pg.* 1250
LEUCADIA NATIONAL CORPORATION, 315 Park Ave S, **New York,** NY 10010, *pg.* 775, *pg.* 1251
LIQUIDNET HOLDINGS, INC., 498 7th Ave 12th Fl, **New York,** NY 10018, *pg.* 776, *pg.* 1251
LONG POINT CAPITAL LLC, 747 Third Ave 22nd Fl, **New York,** NY 10017, *pg.* 776, *pg.* 1252
THE LYONS NATIONAL BANK, 35 Williams St, **Lyons,** NY 14489, *pg.* 777, *pg.* 1177
M&T BANK CORPORATION, 1 M&T Plaza, **Buffalo,** NY 14203, *pg.* 777, *pg.* 1149
MACANDREWS & FORBES HOLDINGS INC., 35 E 62nd St, **New York,** NY 10021, *pg.* 777, *pg.* 1254
MARKETAXESS HOLDINGS INC., 299 Park Ave, **New York,** NY 10171, *pg.* 778, *pg.* 1256
MASTERCARD INCORPORATED, 2000 Purchase St, **Purchase,** NY 10577-2405, *pg.* 779, *pg.* 1325
MASTERCARD INTERNATIONAL, INC., 2000 Purchase St, **Purchase,** NY 10577, *pg.* 780, *pg.* 1326
MEDALLION FINANCIAL CORP., 437 Madison Ave 38th Fl, **New York,** NY 10022, *pg.* 781, *pg.* 1258
MORGAN STANLEY, 1585 Broadway, **New York,** NY 10036, *pg.* 783, *pg.* 1261
MORGAN STANLEY SMITH BARNEY LLC, 388 Greenwich St, **New York,** NY 10013-2375, *pg.* 784, *pg.* 1262
MSCI INC., 1 Chase Manhattan Plz 44th Fl, **New York,** NY 10005, *pg.* 785, *pg.* 1262
THE NASDAQ OMX GROUP, INC., 1 Liberty Plz, **New York,** NY 10006, *pg.* 785, *pg.* 1263
NEW YORK COMMERCIAL BANK, 1 Suffolk Sq 1601 Veterans Memorial Hwy, **Islandia,** NY 11749, *pg.* 787, *pg.* 1169
NOMURA SECURITIES INTERNATIONAL, INC., 2 World Financial Ctr Bldg B, **New York,** NY 10281-1008, *pg.* 787, *pg.* 1273
NYSE EURONEXT, 11 Wall St, **New York,** NY 10005-1905, *pg.* 789, *pg.* 1274
OLIVER WYMAN, INC., 1166 Ave of the Americas, **New York,** NY 10036-2708, *pg.* 790, *pg.* 1274
ONEIDA FINANCIAL CORP., 182 Main St, **Oneida,** NY 13421-1676, *pg.* 790, *pg.* 1318
ONEIDA SAVINGS BANK, 182 Main St, **Oneida,** NY 13421, *pg.* 790, *pg.* 1319
OPPENHEIMERFUNDS, INC., 2 World Financial Ctr 225 Liberty St 11th Fl, **New York,** NY 10281-1008, *pg.* 790, *pg.* 1274
OTC MARKETS GROUP INC., 304 Hudson St 2nd Fl, **New York,** NY 10013, *pg.* 791, *pg.* 1275
PATHFINDER BANCORP, INC., 214 W 1st St, **Oswego,** NY 13126, *pg.* 792, *pg.* 1320
PAYCHEX, INC., 911 Panorama Trail S, **Rochester,** NY 14625-0397, *pg.* 792, *pg.* 1336
PRICEWATERHOUSECOOPERS LLP, 300 Madison Ave, **New York,** NY 10017-6204, *pg.* 795, *pg.* 1283
RABO CAPITAL SERVICES, INC., 245 Park Ave, **New York,** NY 10167, *pg.* 797, *pg.* 1284
ROTHSCHILD INC., 1251 Ave of the Americas 51st Fl, **New York,** NY 10020-1104, *pg.* 799, *pg.* 1287
ROTHSCHILD NORTH AMERICA INC., 1251 Ave Of The Americas, **New York,** NY 10020-1104, *pg.* 800, *pg.* 1287
SAXBST, 26 Computer Dr W, **Albany,** NY 12205, *pg.* 801, *pg.* 1137
SEAWAY VALLEY CAPITAL CORPORATION, 10 18 Park Str 2nd Fl, **Gouverneur,** NY 13642, *pg.* 802, *pg.* 1162
SIEBERT FINANCIAL CORP., 885 3rd Ave Fl 17, **New York,** NY 10022-4834, *pg.* 803, *pg.* 1291
SIEMENS CORPORATION, 527 Madison Ave 8th Flr, **New York,** NY 10022, *pg.* 803, *pg.* 1291
STANDARD & POOR'S RATINGS SERVICES, 55 Water St, **New York,** NY 10041, *pg.* 805, *pg.* 1296
STERLING BANCORP, 400 Rella Blvd, **Montebello,** NY 10901, *pg.* 805, *pg.* 1183
THOMSON REUTERS MARKETS, 3 Times Sq, **New York,** NY 10006, *pg.* 810, *pg.* 1299
TRUSTCO BANK CORP NY, 5 Sarnowski Dr, **Glenville,** NY 12302, *pg.* 811, *pg.* 1162
UBS FINANCIAL SERVICES INC., 1285 Ave of the Americas, **New York,** NY 10019, *pg.* 812, *pg.* 1306
WISDOMTREE INVESTMENTS, INC., 380 Madison Ave 21st Fl, **New York,** NY 10017, *pg.* 823, *pg.* 1314
W.P. CAREY & CO., LLC, 50 Rockefeller Plz 2nd Fl, **New York,** NY 10020-1605, *pg.* 823, *pg.* 1315

North Carolina

ASHEVILLE SAVINGS BANK SSB, 11 Church St, **Asheville,** NC 28801, *pg.* 716, *pg.* 1358
BANK OF AMERICA CORPORATION, Bank of America Corporate Ctr 100 N Tryon St, **Charlotte,** NC 28255-0001, *pg.* 718, *pg.* 1362
BB&T CORPORATION, 200 W 2nd St, **Winston Salem,** NC 27101-4019, *pg.* 723, *pg.* 1393
BNC BANCORP, 1226 Eastchester Dr, **High Point,** NC 27265, *pg.* 726, *pg.* 1379
CAPITAL BANK, 4605 Country Club Rd, **Winston Salem,** NC 27104, *pg.* 730, *pg.* 1393
CAPITAL BANK CORPORATION, 333 Fayetteville St Ste 700, **Raleigh,** NC 27601, *pg.* 730, *pg.* 1386
CAROLINA BANK HOLDINGS, INC., 101 N Spring St, **Greensboro,** NC 27410, *pg.* 732, *pg.* 1374
COMMUNITYONE BANCORP, 150 S Fayetteville St, **Asheboro,** NC 27203, *pg.* 741, *pg.* 1358
FIRST CITIZENS BANCSHARES, INC., 4300 Six Forks Rd, **Raleigh,** NC 27609, *pg.* 754, *pg.* 1387
FIRST SOUTH BANCORP, INC., 1311 Carolina Ave, **Washington,** NC 27883, *pg.* 757, *pg.* 1392
LENDINGTREE, LLC, 11115 Rushmore Dr, **Charlotte,** NC 28277, *pg.* 775, *pg.* 1367
NEWBRIDGE BANCORP, 1501 Highwoods Blvd Ste 400, **Greensboro,** NC 27410, *pg.* 787, *pg.* 1375
OAK RIDGE FINANCIAL SERVICES, INC., 2211 Oak Ridge Rd, **Oak Ridge,** NC 27310, *pg.* 789, *pg.* 1386
PARK STERLING BANK, 519 S New Hope Rd, **Gastonia,** NC 28054-4040, *pg.* 792, *pg.* 1373
PEOPLES BANCORP OF NORTH CAROLINA, INC., 518 W C St, **Newton,** NC 28658, *pg.* 793, *pg.* 1386
PIEDMONT FEDERAL SAVINGS BANK, 16 W 3rd St, **Winston Salem,** NC 27101, *pg.* 794, *pg.* 1395
SELECT BANK & TRUST, 700 W Cumberland St, **Dunn,** NC 28335, *pg.* 803, *pg.* 1370
WORDEN BROTHERS, INC., Five Oaks Ofc Pk 4905 Pine Cone Dr, **Durham,** NC 27707, *pg.* 823, *pg.* 1372
YADKIN VALLEY FINANCIAL CORPORATION, 209 N Bridge St, **Elkin,** NC 28621-3404, *pg.* 824, *pg.* 1372

North Dakota

CAPITAL FINANCIAL HOLDINGS, INC., 1 Main St N, **Minot,** ND 58703-3189, *pg.* 730, *pg.* 1398
FIRST WESTERN BANK & TRUST, 900 S Broadway, **Minot,** ND 58701, *pg.* 757, *pg.* 1398
GATE CITY BANK, 500 2nd Ave N, **Fargo,** ND 58102, *pg.* 761, *pg.* 1397

Ohio

AMERICAN FINANCIAL GROUP, INC., 301 E 4th St, **Cincinnati,** OH 45202-3715, *pg.* 714, *pg.* 1410
BARTLETT & CO., 600 Vine St Ste 2100, **Cincinnati,** OH 45202-3896, *pg.* 722, *pg.* 1410
CBIZ, INC., 6050 Oaktree Blvd Ste 500, **Cleveland,** OH 44131-6951, *pg.* 733, *pg.* 1429
CENTRAL FEDERAL CORPORATION, 2923 Smith Rd, **Fairlawn,** OH 44333, *pg.* 733, *pg.* 1453
CHEVIOT FINANCIAL CORP., 3723 Glenmore Ave, **Cheviot,** OH 45211-4744, *pg.* 735, *pg.* 1409
CIVISTA BANCSHARES, INC., 100 E Water St, **Sandusky,** OH 44870, *pg.* 738, *pg.* 1472
COMMERCIAL BANCSHARES, INC., 118 S Sandusky Ave, **Upper Sandusky,** OH 43351, *pg.* 740, *pg.* 1477
CORTLAND SAVINGS & BANKING CO., 194 W Main St, **Cortland,** OH 44410-1445, *pg.* 742, *pg.* 1445
CROGHAN BANCSHARES, INC., 323 Croghan St, **Fremont,**

OH 43420, *pg.* 742, *pg.* 1454
DCB FINANCIAL CORP., 110 Riverbend Ave, **Lewis Center,** OH 43035, *pg.* 743, *pg.* 1457
FARMERS & MERCHANTS BANCORP, 307 N Defiance St, **Archbold,** OH 43502, *pg.* 750, *pg.* 1403
FARMERS NATIONAL BANC CORP., 20 S Broad St, **Canfield,** OH 44406, *pg.* 750, *pg.* 1407
FIFTH THIRD BANCORP, Fifth Third Ctr 38 Fountain Sq Plz, **Cincinnati,** OH 45263, *pg.* 752, *pg.* 1413
FIRSTMERIT CORPORATION, 3 Cascade Plz 7th Fl, **Akron,** OH 44308-1103, *pg.* 758, *pg.* 1400
HILL BARTH & KING LLC, 7680 Market St, **Youngstown,** OH 44512, *pg.* 766, *pg.* 1483
HUNTINGTON BANCSHARES INCORPORATED, 41 S High St, **Columbus,** OH 43287, *pg.* 767, *pg.* 1440
THE HUNTINGTON NATIONAL BANK, 41 S High St, **Columbus,** OH 43287, *pg.* 767, *pg.* 1440
KEYCORP, 127 Public Sq, **Cleveland,** OH 44114-1221, *pg.* 774, *pg.* 1432
KIRTLAND CAPITAL PARTNERS, 3201 Enterprise Pkwy Ste 200, **Beachwood,** OH 44122, *pg.* 774, *pg.* 1405
MIDDLEFIELD BANC CORP., 15985 E High St PO Box 35, **Middlefield,** OH 44062, *pg.* 783, *pg.* 1465
PARK NATIONAL CORPORATION, 50 N 3rd St, **Newark,** OH 43058, *pg.* 792, *pg.* 1468
PEOPLES BANCORP INC., 138 Putnam St, **Marietta,** OH 45750-0738, *pg.* 793, *pg.* 1458
THE RESERVE GROUP, 3560 W Market St Ste 300, **Akron,** OH 44333, *pg.* 799, *pg.* 1402
SB FINANCIAL GROUP, 401 Clinton St, PO Box 467, **Defiance,** OH 43512-2662, *pg.* 801, *pg.* 1447
SUNBELT BUSINESS ADVISORS NETWORK, LLC, 7100 E Pleasant Valley Rd Ste 300, **Independence,** OH 44131, *pg.* 806, *pg.* 1456
THIRD FEDERAL SAVINGS & LOAN ASSOCIATION, 7007 Broadway Ave, **Cleveland,** OH 44105, *pg.* 810, *pg.* 1436
THE UNION BANK CO., 100 S High St, **Columbus Grove,** OH 45830, *pg.* 813, *pg.* 1445
UNITED BANCORP, INC., 201 S 4th St, **Martins Ferry,** OH 43935, *pg.* 813, *pg.* 1459
UNITED COMMUNITY FINANCIAL CORP., 275 Federal Plz W, **Youngstown,** OH 44503, *pg.* 814, *pg.* 1483
WAYNE SAVINGS BANCSHARES, INC., 151 N Market St, **Wooster,** OH 44691, *pg.* 819, *pg.* 1482

Oklahoma

BANCFIRST CORPORATION, 101 N Broadway Ave Ste 101, **Oklahoma City,** OK 73102, *pg.* 717, *pg.* 1484
BOK FINANCIAL CORPORATION, Bank of Oklahoma Tower PO Box 2300, **Tulsa,** OK 74192-0001, *pg.* 726, *pg.* 1489
LEGAL SHIELD, 1 Pre-Paid Way, **Ada,** OK 74820-5605, *pg.* 775, *pg.* 1484
URBAN FINANCIAL OF AMERICA, LLC., 8909 S Yale Ave, **Tulsa,** OK 74137, *pg.* 815, *pg.* 1491

Oregon

BANK OF THE CASCADES, 1100 NW Wall St, **Bend,** OR 97701-1935, *pg.* 721, *pg.* 1496
CASCADE BANCORP, 1100 NW Wall St, **Bend,** OR 97701, *pg.* 732, *pg.* 1496
MORLEY FINANCIAL SERVICES, 1300 SW 5th Ave Ste 3300, **Portland,** OR 97201-3193, *pg.* 784, *pg.* 1504
PACIFIC CONTINENTAL CORPORATION, 111 W 7th Ave, **Eugene,** OR 97401-2622, *pg.* 791, *pg.* 1497
PAULSON CAPITAL CORP., 811 SW Naito Pkwy Ste 200, **Portland,** OR 97204, *pg.* 792, *pg.* 1505
RIVERVIEW COMMUNITY BANK, 10401 NE Halsey, **Portland,** OR 97220, *pg.* 799, *pg.* 1506
UMPQUA HOLDINGS CORPORATION, 1 SW Colombia St Ste 1200, **Portland,** OR 97258, *pg.* 813, *pg.* 1507

Pennsylvania

ACNB CORPORATION, 16 Lincoln Sq, **Gettysburg,** PA 17325, *pg.* 710, *pg.* 1534
ADAMS COUNTY NATIONAL BANK INC., 16 Lincoln Sq, **Gettysburg,** PA 17325, *pg.* 710, *pg.* 1534
AMERICAN BANK INCORPORATED, 4029 W Tilghman St, **Allentown,** PA 18104-1619, *pg.* 711, *pg.* 1513
BENEFICIAL BANK, 510 Walnut St, **Philadelphia,** PA 19106, *pg.* 724, *pg.* 1559
BENEFICIAL MUTUAL BANCORP, INC., 510 Walnut St 19th Fl, **Philadelphia,** PA 19106, *pg.* 724, *pg.* 1559
BRYN MAWR BANK CORPORATION, 801 Lancaster Ave, **Bryn Mawr,** PA 19010, *pg.* 728, *pg.* 1519
CCFNB BANCORP, INC., 232 East St, **Bloomsburg,** PA 17815, *pg.* 733, *pg.* 1517
CNB FINANCIAL CORPORATION, 1 S 2nd St, **Clearfield,** PA 16830, *pg.* 739, *pg.* 1522
CODORUS VALLEY BANCORP, INC., 105 Leader Heights Rd PO Box 2887, **York,** PA 17405-2887, *pg.* 739, *pg.* 1596
COMMERCIAL BANK & TRUST OF PENNSYLVANIA, 900 Ligonier St, **Latrobe,** PA 15650, *pg.* 740, *pg.* 1547
COMMERCIAL NATIONAL FINANCIAL CORPORATION, 900 Ligonier St, **Latrobe,** PA 15650, *pg.* 740, *pg.* 1547
DFC GLOBAL CORPORATION, 1436 Lancaster Ave, **Berwyn,** PA 19312-1288, *pg.* 743, *pg.* 1515
DOLLAR FINANCIAL GROUP INC., 1436 Lancaster Ave Ste 300, **Berwyn,** PA 19312, *pg.* 744, *pg.* 1515
EGS FINANCIAL CARE, INC., 507 Prudential Rd, **Horsham,** PA 19044, *pg.* 746, *pg.* 1540
EMCLAIRE FINANCIAL CORP., 612 Main St, **Emlenton,** PA 16373, *pg.* 747, *pg.* 1529
ENB FINANCIAL CORP., 31 E Main St, **Ephrata,** PA 17522, *pg.* 747, *pg.* 1530
ESB FINANCIAL CORPORATION, 600 Lawrence Ave, **Ellwood City,** PA 16117, *pg.* 749, *pg.* 1529
ESSA BANCORP, INC., 200 Palmer St, **Stroudsburg,** PA 18360, *pg.* 749, *pg.* 1587
FEDERATED INVESTORS, INC., Federated Investors Tower 1001 Liberty Ave, **Pittsburgh,** PA 15222-3779, *pg.* 752, *pg.* 1575
FIDELITY D & D BANCORP INC., Blakely & Drinker STS, **Dunmore,** PA 18512, *pg.* 752, *pg.* 1527
FIRST COMMONWEALTH FINANCIAL CORPORATION, 22 N 6th St, **Indiana,** PA 15701, *pg.* 754, *pg.* 1541
FIRST KEYSTONE COMMUNITY BANK, 111 W Front St, **Berwick,** PA 18603, *pg.* 756, *pg.* 1515
FIRST NATIONAL BANK, 4220 William Penn Hwy, **Monroeville,** PA 15146, *pg.* 756, *pg.* 1553
FIRST NATIONAL COMMUNITY BANCORP, INC., 102 E Drinker St, **Dunmore,** PA 18512, *pg.* 756, *pg.* 1527
FIRSTRUST SAVINGS BANK, 15 E Rdg Pike Ste 400, **Conshohocken,** PA 19428, *pg.* 758, *pg.* 1523
F.N.B. CORPORATION, 12 Federal St One North Shore Ctr, **Pittsburgh,** PA 15212, *pg.* 759, *pg.* 1575
FRANKLIN FINANCIAL SERVICES CORPORATION, 20 S Main St, **Chambersburg,** PA 17201, *pg.* 760, *pg.* 1521
FULTON FINANCIAL CORPORATION, 1 Penn Sq, P. O. Box 4887, **Lancaster,** PA 17604-2853, *pg.* 760, *pg.* 1546
THE GLENMEDE TRUST COMPANY, 1650 Market St Ste 1200, **Philadelphia,** PA 19103, *pg.* 762, *pg.* 1566
HFF, INC., 1 Oxford Ctr 301 Grant St Ste 600, **Pittsburgh,** PA 15219, *pg.* 766, *pg.* 1576
JANNEY MONTGOMERY SCOTT LLC, 1717 Arch St, **Philadelphia,** PA 19103, *pg.* 772, *pg.* 1566
JUNIATA VALLEY FINANCIAL CORP., Bridge & Main Streets PO Box 66, **Mifflintown,** PA 17059-0066, *pg.* 773, *pg.* 1553
LINCOLN NATIONAL CORPORATION, 150 N.Radner Chester Rd, Suite A305 Radnor, **Philadelphia,** PA 19087, *pg.* 776, *pg.* 1567
MALVERN FEDERAL BANCORP, INC., 42 E Lancaster Ave, **Paoli,** PA 19301, *pg.* 778, *pg.* 1558
METRO BANCORP, INC., 3801 Paxton St, **Harrisburg,** PA 17111, *pg.* 782, *pg.* 1537
MID PENN BANCORP, INC., 349 Union St, **Millersburg,** PA 17061, *pg.* 782, *pg.* 1553
NATIONAL PENN BANCSHARES, INC., Philadelphia & Reading Aves, **Boyertown,** PA 19512-0547, *pg.* 786, *pg.* 1517
NORTHWEST BANCSHARES, INC., 100 Liberty St, **Warren,** PA 16365-2353, *pg.* 788, *pg.* 1590
NORWOOD FINANCIAL CORP., 717 Main St, **Honesdale,** PA 18431, *pg.* 788, *pg.* 1539
ORRSTOWN FINANCIAL SERVICES, INC., 77 E Kings St, **Shippensburg,** PA 17257, *pg.* 791, *pg.* 1586
PENN TREATY AMERICAN CORPORATION, 3440 Lehigh St, **Allentown,** PA 18103, *pg.* 793, *pg.* 1514
PEOPLES SECURITY BANK & TRUST, 82 Franklin Ave PO Box A, **Hallstead,** PA 18822, *pg.* 793, *pg.* 1535
THE PNC FINANCIAL SERVICES GROUP, INC., 1 PNC Plaza 249 5th Ave, **Pittsburgh,** PA 15222-2707, *pg.* 795, *pg.* 1579
REPUBLIC FIRST BANCORP, INC., 50 S 16th St Ste 2400, **Philadelphia,** PA 19102, *pg.* 799, *pg.* 1570
RIVERVIEW FINANCIAL CORPORATION, 3rd & Market Streets, **Halifax,** PA 17032, *pg.* 799, *pg.* 1535
ROYAL BANCSHARES OF PENNSYLVANIA, INC., 732 Montgomery Ave, **Narberth,** PA 19072, *pg.* 800, *pg.* 1555
SEI INVESTMENTS COMPANY, 1 Freedom Valley Dr, **Oaks,** PA 19456-1100, *pg.* 802, *pg.* 1558
STANDARD FINANCIAL CORP., 2640 Monroeville Blvd, **Monroeville,** PA 15146, *pg.* 805, *pg.* 1553
SUSQUEHANNA BANK, 26 N Cedar St, **Lititz,** PA 17543-7000, *pg.* 807, *pg.* 1548
UNIVEST CORPORATION OF PENNSYLVANIA, 14 N Main St, **Souderton,** PA 18964, *pg.* 814, *pg.* 1586
USA TECHNOLOGIES, INC., 100 Deerfield Ln Ste 140, **Malvern,** PA 19355, *pg.* 815, *pg.* 1550
THE VANGUARD GROUP, INC., 100 Vanguard Blvd, **Malvern,** PA 19355, *pg.* 816, *pg.* 1550
VIST BANK, 1240 Broadcasting Rd, **Wyomissing,** PA 19610, *pg.* 818, *pg.* 1596
VIST FINANCIAL CORP., 1240 Broadcasting Rd, **Wyomissing,** PA 19610-0219, *pg.* 818, *pg.* 1596
WAYNE BANK, 717 Main St, **Honesdale,** PA 18431, *pg.* 819, *pg.* 1540

Puerto Rico

DORAL FINANCIAL CORPORATION, 1451 Franklin D Roosevelt Ave, **San Juan,** PR 00920-2717, *pg.* 744, *pg.* 1599
ORIENTAL FINANCIAL GROUP INC, Oriental Ctr 10th Fl Professional Office Park, **San Juan,** PR 00926, *pg.* 790, *pg.* 1599

Rhode Island

BANK RHODE ISLAND, 1 Turks Head Pl, **Providence,** RI 02903, *pg.* 722, *pg.* 1605
CITIZENS FINANCIAL GROUP, INC., 1 Citizens Plz, **Providence,** RI 02903, *pg.* 737, *pg.* 1606
EMBRACE HOME LOANS, INC., 25 Enterprise Center, **Newport,** RI 02842, *pg.* 747, *pg.* 1603
WASHINGTON TRUST BANCORP, INC., 23 Broad St, **Westerly,** RI 02891-1879, *pg.* 818, *pg.* 1610

South Carolina

ADVANCE AMERICA CASH ADVANCE CENTERS, INC., 135 N Church St, **Spartanburg,** SC 29306, *pg.* 711, *pg.* 1622
BANK OF SOUTH CAROLINA CORPORATION, 256 Meeting St, **Charleston,** SC 29401, *pg.* 721, *pg.* 1613
COASTAL BANKING COMPANY, INC., 36 Sea Island Pkwy, **Beaufort,** SC 29907, *pg.* 739, *pg.* 1612
FIRST COMMUNITY CORPORATION, 5455 Sunset Blvd, **Lexington,** SC 29072, *pg.* 754, *pg.* 1620
FIRST FINANCIAL HOLDINGS, INC., 520 Gervais St, **Columbia,** SC 29201-3046, *pg.* 755, *pg.* 1614
NATIONAL BANK OF SOUTH CAROLINA, 1221 Main St, **Columbia,** SC 29201-3212, *pg.* 785, *pg.* 1614
PALMETTO BANCSHARES, INC., 306 E North St, **Greenville,** SC 29601, *pg.* 791, *pg.* 1618
SCBT FINANCIAL CORPORATION, 520 Gervais St, **Columbia,** SC 29201-3046, *pg.* 801, *pg.* 1614
SECURITY FEDERAL CORPORATION, 238 Richland Ave W, **Aiken,** SC 29801, *pg.* 802, *pg.* 1612
SOUTHCOAST FINANCIAL CORPORATION, 530 Johnnie Dodds Blvd, **Mount Pleasant,** SC 29464, *pg.* 804, *pg.* 1620
TIDELANDS BANCSHARES, INC., 875 Lowcountry Blvd, **Mount Pleasant,** SC 29464, *pg.* 810, *pg.* 1620
WORLD ACCEPTANCE CORPORATION, 108 Frederick St, **Greenville,** SC 29607-2532, *pg.* 823, *pg.* 1619

South Dakota

FIRST PREMIER BANK, 601 S Minnesota Ave, **Sioux Falls,** SD 57104, *pg.* 757, *pg.* 1625
HF FINANCIAL CORP., 225 S Main Ave, **Sioux Falls,** SD 57104, *pg.* 766, *pg.* 1625

Tennessee

ATHENS BANCSHARES CORPORATION, 106 Washington Ave, **Athens,** TN 37303, *pg.* 717, *pg.* 1627
BANK OF NASHVILLE, 401 Church St, **Nashville,** TN 37219-8986, *pg.* 720, *pg.* 1648

First page reference indicates Business Class Edition
Second page reference indicates Geographic Edition

COMDATA CORPORATION, 5301 Maryland Way, **Brentwood,** TN 37027-5055, *pg.* 739, *pg.* 1627
EMDEON, INC., 3055 Lebanon Pike Ste 1000, **Nashville,** TN 37214, *pg.* 747, *pg.* 1650
FIRST HORIZON NATIONAL CORPORATION, 165 Madison Ave, **Memphis,** TN 38103, *pg.* 755, *pg.* 1644
FIRST SECURITY GROUP, INC., 531 Broad St, **Chattanooga,** TN 37402-2613, *pg.* 757, *pg.* 1629
FROST COMPANY, 6830 Lee Hwy, **Chattanooga,** TN 37421-2444, *pg.* 760, *pg.* 1629
MORGAN KEEGAN, INC., Morgan Keegan Tower 50 Frnt St, **Memphis,** TN 38103, *pg.* 783, *pg.* 1645
PINNACLE FINANCIAL PARTNERS, INC., 150 3rd Ave S Ste 900, **Nashville,** TN 37201, *pg.* 794, *pg.* 1653
SUNTRUST BANK, NASHVILLE REGION, 201 4th Ave N, **Nashville,** TN 37219, *pg.* 807, *pg.* 1654
UNITED TENNESSEE BANKSHARES, INC., 170 W Broadway, **Newport,** TN 37821-2857, *pg.* 814, *pg.* 1655
WILSON BANK HOLDING COMPANY, 623 W Main St, **Lebanon,** TN 37087, *pg.* 823, *pg.* 1640

Texas

ACE CASH EXPRESS, INC., 1231 Greenway Dr Ste 600, **Irving,** TX 75038-9904, *pg.* 710, *pg.* 1717
AMEGY BANK, N.A., 4400 Post Oak Pkwy, **Houston,** TX 77027-3421, *pg.* 711, *pg.* 1700
ASHFORD HOSPITALITY TRUST, INC., 14185 Dallas Pkwy Ste 1100, **Dallas,** TX 75254, *pg.* 716, *pg.* 1674
CALIBER HOME LOANS, INC., 3701 Regent Blvd, **Irving,** TX 75063, *pg.* 728, *pg.* 1717
CARDTRONICS, INC., 3250 Briarpark Dr Ste 400, **Houston,** TX 77042, *pg.* 732, *pg.* 1703
COMERICA INCORPORATED, Comerica Bank Tower 1717 Main St, MC 6404, **Dallas,** TX 75201, *pg.* 740, *pg.* 1677
CULLEN/FROST BANKERS, INC., 100 W Houston St, **San Antonio,** TX 78205-1414, *pg.* 742, *pg.* 1740
EDELMAN FINANCIAL SERVICES LLC, JP Morgan Chase Twr 600 Travis St Ste 5900, **Houston,** TX 77002, *pg.* 746, *pg.* 1705
EXTRACO BANKS, 1700 N Valley Mills Dr, **Waco,** TX 76710, *pg.* 750, *pg.* 1749
EZCORP, INC., 1901 Capital Pkwy, **Austin,** TX 78746-7613, *pg.* 750, *pg.* 1662
FARM BUREAU BANK FSB, 17300 Henderson Pass, **San Antonio,** TX 78232-1568, *pg.* 750, *pg.* 1740
FIRST CASH FINANCIAL SERVICES, INC., 690 E Lamar Blvd Ste 400, **Arlington,** TX 76011-3864, *pg.* 754, *pg.* 1659
FIRST FINANCIAL BANKSHARES, INC., 400 Pine St, **Abilene,** TX 79601-5128, *pg.* 755, *pg.* 1657
FIRST FINANCIAL GROUP OF AMERICA, 515 N Sam Houston Pkwy E, **Houston,** TX 77060-4034, *pg.* 755, *pg.* 1705
FIRST INVESTORS FINANCIAL SERVICES GROUP, INC., 675 Bering Dr Ste 710, **Houston,** TX 77057-2129, *pg.* 756, *pg.* 1706
GUARANTY BANCSHARES, INC., 100 W Arkansas St, **Mount Pleasant,** TX 75455, *pg.* 764, *pg.* 1728
H.D. VEST, INC., 6333 N State Hwy 161 4th Fl, **Irving,** TX 75038-2216, *pg.* 765, *pg.* 1720
INTERNATIONAL BANCSHARES CORPORATION, 1200 San Bernardo Ave, **Laredo,** TX 78042-1359, *pg.* 769, *pg.* 1725
MCCOMBS ENTERPRISES, 755 E Mulberry Ave Ste 600, **San Antonio,** TX 78212, *pg.* 781, *pg.* 1741
MONEYGRAM INTERNATIONAL, INC., 2828 N Harwood St 15th Fl, **Dallas,** TX 75201, *pg.* 783, *pg.* 1684
NETSPEND CORPORATION, 701 Brazos St Ste 1300, **Austin,** TX 78701-2582, *pg.* 786, *pg.* 1665
ORTHOSYNETICS, INC., 15305 Dallas Pkwy Ste 100, **Addison,** TX 75001, *pg.* 791, *pg.* 1657
PLAINS CAPITAL CORPORATION, 2323 Victory Ave Ste 1400, **Dallas,** TX 75219, *pg.* 794, *pg.* 1685
PROSPERITY BANCSHARES, INC., Prosperity Bank Plz 4295 San Felipe, **Houston,** TX 77027, *pg.* 796, *pg.* 1713
RAMPART CAPITAL CORPORATION, 16401 Country Club Dr, **Crosby,** TX 77532, *pg.* 798, *pg.* 1672
SCHLUMBERGER LIMITED, 5599 San Felipe 17th Fl, **Houston,** TX 77056, *pg.* 801, *pg.* 1714
SOUTHSIDE BANCSHARES INC., 1201 S Beckham Ave, **Tyler,** TX 75701, *pg.* 804, *pg.* 1748
T BANCSHARES, INC., 16000 Dallas Pkwy Ste 125, **Dallas,** TX 75248, *pg.* 808, *pg.* 1688
TEXAS CAPITAL BANCSHARES, INC., 2350 Lakeside Blvd Ste 800, **Richardson,** TX 75082, *pg.* 809, *pg.* 1737
U.S. GLOBAL INVESTORS, INC., 7900 Callaghan Rd, **San Antonio,** TX 78229-2327, *pg.* 815, *pg.* 1743

Utah

BANK OF AMERICAN FORK, 33 E Main St, **American Fork,** UT 84003, *pg.* 720, *pg.* 1751
BANK OF UTAH, 2605 Washington Blvd, **Ogden,** UT 84401-3626, *pg.* 722, *pg.* 1752
SECURITY NATIONAL FINANCIAL CORPORATION, 5300 S 360 W Ste 250, **Salt Lake City,** UT 84123-4600, *pg.* 802, *pg.* 1760
WEBBANK, 215 S State St Ste 800, **Salt Lake City,** UT 84111-2339, *pg.* 819, *pg.* 1761
ZIONS BANCORPORATION, 1 S Main St, **Salt Lake City,** UT 84133-1109, *pg.* 824, *pg.* 1762
ZIONS FIRST NATIONAL BANK, N.A., 1 S Main St, **Salt Lake City,** UT 84111, *pg.* 824, *pg.* 1762

Vermont

COMMUNITY BANCORP, 4811 US Rte 5, **Derby,** VT 05829, *pg.* 741, *pg.* 1766
MERCHANTS BANCSHARES, INC., 275 Kennedy Dr, **South Burlington,** VT 05403, *pg.* 782, *pg.* 1768
UNION BANKSHARES, INC., 20 Lower Main St, **Morrisville,** VT 05661, *pg.* 813, *pg.* 1767

Virginia

ACCESS NATIONAL CORPORATION, 1800 Robert Fulton Dr Ste 310, **Reston,** VA 20191, *pg.* 710, *pg.* 1798
ACI WORLDWIDE, 4795 Meadow Wood Ln Ste 300, **Chantilly,** VA 20151, *pg.* 710, *pg.* 1777
AMERICAN NATIONAL BANKSHARES INC., 628 Main St, **Danville,** VA 24541, *pg.* 714, *pg.* 1779
ARLINGTON ASSET INVESTMENT CORP., 1001 19th St N, **Arlington,** VA 22209-1722, *pg.* 716, *pg.* 1772
BANK OF MCKENNEY, 20718 First St, **McKenney,** VA 23872, *pg.* 720, *pg.* 1788
BAY BANKS OF VIRGINIA, INC., 100 S Main St, **Kilmarnock,** VA 22482-1869, *pg.* 722, *pg.* 1787
BOTETOURT BANKSHARES, INC., 19747 Main St, **Buchanan,** VA 24066, *pg.* 726, *pg.* 1777
C&F FINANCIAL CORPORATION, 802 Main St, **West Point,** VA 23181, *pg.* 728, *pg.* 1811
CAPITAL ONE BANK (USA), N.A., 1680 Capital One Dr, **McLean,** VA 22102, *pg.* 730, *pg.* 1789
CAPITAL ONE FINANCIAL CORPORATION, 1680 Capital One Dr, **McLean,** VA 22102, *pg.* 730, *pg.* 1789
CARDINAL BANK N.A., 8270 Greensboro Dr Ste 500, **McLean,** VA 22102, *pg.* 732, *pg.* 1790
CARDINAL FINANCIAL CORP., 8270 Greensboro Dr Ste 500, **McLean,** VA 22102, *pg.* 732, *pg.* 1790
CEB INC., 1919 N Lynn St, **Arlington,** VA 22209, *pg.* 733, *pg.* 1773
CHESAPEAKE FINANCIAL SHARES, INC., PO Box 1419, **Kilmarnock,** VA 22482, *pg.* 735, *pg.* 1787
EAGLE FINANCIAL SERVICES, INC., 2 E Main St PO Box 391, **Berryville,** VA 22611, *pg.* 745, *pg.* 1776
EASTERN VIRGINIA BANKSHARES, INC., 330 Hospital Rd, **Tappahannock,** VA 22560, *pg.* 746, *pg.* 1808
ESSEX BANK, 323 Prince St, **Tappahannock,** VA 22560-0965, *pg.* 749, *pg.* 1808
F&M BANK CORP., 205 S Main St PO Box 1111, **Timberville,** VA 22853, *pg.* 750, *pg.* 1808
THE FAUQUIER BANK, 10 Courthouse Sq, **Warrenton,** VA 20186, *pg.* 751, *pg.* 1810
FAUQUIER BANKSHARES INC, 10 Courthouse Sq, **Warrenton,** VA 20186, *pg.* 751, *pg.* 1810
FEDERAL HOME LOAN MORTGAGE CORPORATION, 8200 Jones Branch Dr, **McLean,** VA 22102-3110, *pg.* 751, *pg.* 1790
FIRST BANK, 112 W King St, **Strasburg,** VA 22657, *pg.* 753, *pg.* 1808
FIRST CAPITAL BANCORP, INC., 4222 Cox Rd Ste 200, **Glen Allen,** VA 23060, *pg.* 754, *pg.* 1782
FIRST COMMUNITY BANCSHARES, INC., One Community Pl, **Bluefield,** VA 24605, *pg.* 754, *pg.* 1776
GENWORTH FINANCIAL, INC., 6620 W Broad St, **Richmond,** VA 23230, *pg.* 761, *pg.* 1802
GRAYSON BANKSHARES, INC., 113 W Main St, **Independence,** VA 24348, *pg.* 763, *pg.* 1786
HAMPTON ROADS BANKSHARES, INC., 999 Waterside Dr Ste 200, **Norfolk,** VA 23510, *pg.* 765, *pg.* 1796
INTERSECTIONS INC., 3901 Stonecroft Blvd, **Chantilly,** VA 20151, *pg.* 769, *pg.* 1777
LIBERTY TAX SERVICE, 1716 Corporate Landing Pkwy, **Virginia Beach,** VA 23454, *pg.* 776, *pg.* 1810
MAXIMUS, INC., 11419 Sunset Hills Rd, **Reston,** VA 20190-5207, *pg.* 780, *pg.* 1799
MCG CAPITAL CORPORATION, 1001 19th St N 10th Fl, **Arlington,** VA 22209, *pg.* 781, *pg.* 1774
MIDDLEBURG FINANCIAL CORPORATION, 111 W Washington St, **Middleburg,** VA 20117, *pg.* 782, *pg.* 1795
MONARCH FINANCIAL HOLDINGS, INC., 1435 Crossways Blvd, **Chesapeake,** VA 23320, *pg.* 783, *pg.* 1778
THE MOTLEY FOOL, INC., 2000 Duke St 4th FL, **Alexandria,** VA 22314, *pg.* 784, *pg.* 1771
NATIONAL BANKSHARES, INC., 101 Hubbard St, **Blacksburg,** VA 24062-9002, *pg.* 785, *pg.* 1776
OLD POINT FINANCIAL CORPORATION, 1 W Mellen St, **Hampton,** VA 23663, *pg.* 789, *pg.* 1783
TOWNEBANK, 5716 High St, **Portsmouth,** VA 23703, *pg.* 811, *pg.* 1798
UNION FIRST MARKET BANKSHARES CORPORATION, 1051 E Cary St Ste 103, **Richmond,** VA 23219-4044, *pg.* 813, *pg.* 1804
VILLAGE BANK & TRUST FINANCIAL CORP., 15521 Midlothian Tpke Ste 200, **Midlothian,** VA 23113, *pg.* 816, *pg.* 1796

Washington

AMERICANWEST BANCORPORATION, 41 W Riverside Ave Ste 400, **Spokane,** WA 99201, *pg.* 715, *pg.* 1843
BAKER BOYER BANCORP, 7 W Main St, **Walla Walla,** WA 99362, *pg.* 717, *pg.* 1846
BANNER CORPORATION, 10 S First Ave, **Walla Walla,** WA 99362, *pg.* 722, *pg.* 1846
CAPITALONE INVESTING, 83 S Kings St Ste 700, **Seattle,** WA 98104, *pg.* 731, *pg.* 1834
COLUMBIA BANKING SYSTEM, INC., 1301 A Street, **Tacoma,** WA 98402, *pg.* 739, *pg.* 1844
ELECTRONIC TRANSFER, INC., 3107 E Mission Ave, **Spokane,** WA 99202, *pg.* 746, *pg.* 1843
FINANCIAL PACIFIC LEASING, LLC, 3455 S 344th Way Ste 300, **Federal Way,** WA 98001, *pg.* 753, *pg.* 1820
HERITAGE FINANCIAL CORPORATION, 201 5th Ave SW, **Olympia,** WA 98501, *pg.* 765, *pg.* 1823
NORTHWEST BANCORPORATION INC., 421 W Riverside Ave, **Spokane,** WA 99201, *pg.* 788, *pg.* 1844
OPUS BANK, 2828 Colby Ave, **Everett,** WA 98201, *pg.* 790, *pg.* 1819
PACIFIC FINANCIAL CORPORATION, 1011 S Boone St, **Aberdeen,** WA 98520, *pg.* 791, *pg.* 1813
RIVERVIEW BANCORP, INC., 900 Washington St Ste 900, **Vancouver,** WA 98660, *pg.* 799, *pg.* 1846
RUSSELL INVESTMENT GROUP, 909 A St, **Tacoma,** WA 98402-5111, *pg.* 800, *pg.* 1845
SKAGIT STATE BANCORP, INC., 301 E Fairhaven Ave, **Burlington,** WA 98233, *pg.* 804, *pg.* 1819
TIMBERLAND BANCORP, INC., 624 Simpson Ave, **Hoquiam,** WA 98550, *pg.* 810, *pg.* 1820
WASHINGTON FEDERAL INC., 425 Pike St, **Seattle,** WA 98101, *pg.* 818, *pg.* 1842

West Virginia

BANK OF CHARLES TOWN, 111 E Washington St, **Charles Town,** WV 25414, *pg.* 720, *pg.* 1849
CITY HOLDING COMPANY, 25 Gatewater Rd, **Charleston,** WV 25313, *pg.* 737, *pg.* 1849
FIRST WEST VIRGINIA BANCORP, INC., 1701 Warwood Ave, **Wheeling,** WV 26003, *pg.* 757, *pg.* 1851
UNITED BANKSHARES, INC., 300 United Center 500 Virginia St E, **Charleston,** WV 25301, *pg.* 813, *pg.* 1849
WESBANCO, INC., 1 Bank Plz, **Wheeling,** WV 26003, *pg.* 821, *pg.* 1851

Wisconsin

ASSOCIATED BANC-CORP, 433 Main St, **Green Bay,** WI 54301, *pg.* 716, *pg.* 1859
BAYLAKE CORP., 217 N 4th Ave, **Sturgeon Bay,** WI 54235, *pg.* 722, *pg.* 1895
BIZFILINGS, 8040 Excelsior Dr Ste 200, **Madison,** WI 53717,

pg. 724, *pg.* 1865

BLACKHAWK BANCORP INC., 400 Broad St, **Beloit,** WI 53511, *pg.* 724, *pg.* 1854

CIB MARINE BANCSHARES, INC., 1930 W Bluemound Rd Ste D, **Waukesha,** WI 53186, *pg.* 735, *pg.* 1897

CITIZENS COMMUNITY BANCORP, INC., 2174 EastRidge Ctr, **Eau Claire,** WI 54701, *pg.* 737, *pg.* 1857

COMMUNITY STATE BANK, 1500 Main St, **Union Grove,** WI 53182, *pg.* 741, *pg.* 1896

CUNA MUTUAL INSURANCE SOCIETY, 5910 Mineral Point Rd, **Madison,** WI 53705, *pg.* 743, *pg.* 1865

FAIRWAY INDEPENDENT MORTGAGE CORPORATION, 4801 S Biltmore Ln, **Madison,** WI 53718, *pg.* 750, *pg.* 1866

INTERNATIONAL MONETARY SYSTEMS, LTD., 16901 W Glendale Dr, **New Berlin,** WI 53151, *pg.* 769, *pg.* 1884

PSB HOLDINGS, INC., 1905 W Stewart Ave, **Wausau,** WI 54402-1686, *pg.* 797, *pg.* 1898

TITANIUM ASSET MANAGEMENT CORP., 777 E Wisconsin Ave, **Milwaukee,** WI 53202-5310, *pg.* 810, *pg.* 1881

WATERSTONE FINANCIAL, INC., 11200 W Plank Ct, **Wauwatosa,** WI 53226, *pg.* 818, *pg.* 1899

WAUSAU FINANCIAL SYSTEMS INC., 875 Indianhead Dr, **Mosinee,** WI 54455-9512, *pg.* 819, *pg.* 1882

Flour & Cereals

California

KASHI COMPANY, 4275 Executive Sq Dr, **La Jolla,** CA 92037-1477, *pg.* 830, *pg.* 119
MEGAMEX FOODS, LLC, 4340 Eucalyptus Ave, **Chino,** CA 91710-9705, *pg.* 833, *pg.* 66

Illinois

ARCHER-DANIELS-MIDLAND COMPANY, 77 W Wacker Dr Ste 4600, **Chicago,** IL 60601, *pg.* 825, *pg.* 565
HODGSON MILL, INC., 1100 Stevens Ave, **Effingham,** IL 62401, *pg.* 830, *pg.* 609
THE QUAKER OATS COMPANY, 555 W Monroe Ste 16-01, **Chicago,** IL 60604-9001, *pg.* 834, *pg.* 588

Iowa

AMERICAN POP CORN COMPANY, 1 Fun Pl, **Sioux City,** IA 51108, *pg.* 825, *pg.* 712

Kansas

ADM MILLING, 8000 W 110th St, **Overland Park,** KS 66210, *pg.* 825, *pg.* 718

Michigan

KELLOGG COMPANY, 1 Kellogg Sq, **Battle Creek,** MI 49016-3599, *pg.* 831, *pg.* 870

Minnesota

GENERAL MILLS, INC., 1 General Mills Blvd, **Minneapolis,** MN 55426-1347, *pg.* 828, *pg.* 933
POST CONSUMER BRANDS, 20802 Kensington Blvd, **Lakeville,** MN 55044, *pg.* 833, *pg.* 927

Missouri

CONAGRA FOODS, 800 Market St, **Saint Louis,** MO 63101-2506, *pg.* 826, *pg.* 994
POST HOLDINGS, INC., 2503 S Hanley Rd, **Saint Louis,** MO 63144, *pg.* 833, *pg.* 1002
THE UHLMANN CO., 1009 Central St, **Kansas City,** MO 64105, *pg.* 834, *pg.* 986

Nebraska

CONAGRA FOODS, INC., 1 ConAgra Dr, **Omaha,** NE 68102-5001, *pg.* 826, *pg.* 1014

New York

THE BIRKETT MILLS, 163 Main St, **Penn Yan,** NY 14527, *pg.* 826, *pg.* 1321

North Dakota

NORTH DAKOTA MILL & ELEVATOR ASSOCIATION, 1823 Mill Rd, **Grand Forks,** ND 58203-1535, *pg.* 833, *pg.* 1398

Vermont

THE KING ARTHUR FLOUR COMPANY, INC., 135 Rte 5 S, **Norwich,** VT 05055, *pg.* 833, *pg.* 1767

Washington

CONTINENTAL MILLS, INC., 18100 Andover Park W, **Tukwila,** WA 98188, *pg.* 827, *pg.* 1845
ROMAN MEAL COMPANY, 2101 S Tacoma Way, **Tacoma,** WA 98409, *pg.* 834, *pg.* 1845

First page reference indicates Business Class Edition
Second page reference indicates Geographic Edition

Food Processing & Manufacturing

Alabama

BON SECOUR FISHERIES INC., 17449 Country Rd 49 S, **Bon Secour,** AL 36511, *pg.* 841, *pg.* 5
PECO FOODS INC., 1020 Lurleen Wallace Blvd N, **Tuscaloosa,** AL 35401, *pg.* 888, *pg.* 8
WHITFIELD FOODS, INC., 1101 N Ct St, **Montgomery,** AL 36104, *pg.* 910, *pg.* 8

Arizona

BAR-S FOODS CO., 5090 N 40th St, Ste 300, **Phoenix,** AZ 85018, *pg.* 839, *pg.* 15
FOOD SERVICES OF AMERICA, INC., 16100 N 71st St Ste 400, **Scottsdale,** AZ 85254, *pg.* 856, *pg.* 21
SHAMROCK FOODS COMPANY, 2228 N Black Canyon Hwy, **Phoenix,** AZ 85009-2707, *pg.* 895, *pg.* 20

Arkansas

RICELAND FOODS, INC., 2120 S Park Ave, **Stuttgart,** AR 72160-6822, *pg.* 892, *pg.* 36
SIMMONS FOODS INC., 601 N Hico, **Siloam Springs,** AR 72761, *pg.* 895, *pg.* 35
TYSON FOODS, INC., 2200 Don Tyson Pkwy, **Springdale,** AR 72762-6999, *pg.* 902, *pg.* 35

California

AIDELLS SAUSAGE COMPANY, 2411 Baumann Ave, **San Lorenzo,** CA 94580, *pg.* 836, *pg.* 253
AMY'S KITCHEN, INC., 2330 Northpoint Pkwy, **Santa Rosa,** CA 95407, *pg.* 837, *pg.* 276
ARMANINO FOODS OF DISTINCTION, INC., 30588 San Antonio St, **Hayward,** CA 94544, *pg.* 837, *pg.* 100
BAKER COMMODITIES, INC., 4020 Bandini Blvd, **Vernon,** CA 90058-4605, *pg.* 839, *pg.* 301
BASIC AMERICAN FOODS, INC., 2121 N Califor Blv Ste 400, **Walnut Creek,** CA 94596, *pg.* 839, *pg.* 303
BELL-CARTER FOODS, INC., 3742 Mt Diablo Blvd, **Lafayette,** CA 94549-3682, *pg.* 839, *pg.* 120
BIMBO BAKERIES USA, 480 S Vail Ave, **Montebello,** CA 90640-4900, *pg.* 840, *pg.* 151
BLUE DIAMOND GROWERS, 1701 C St, **Sacramento,** CA 95811, *pg.* 840, *pg.* 195
BOLTHOUSE FARMS, 7200 E Brundage Ln, **Bakersfield,** CA 93304, *pg.* 841, *pg.* 44
BRIDGFORD FOODS CORPORATION, 1308 N Patt St, **Anaheim,** CA 92801-2551, *pg.* 842, *pg.* 42
BUMBLE BEE FOODS LLC, 9655 Gramett Rdg Dr, **San Diego,** CA 92123-2674, *pg.* 842, *pg.* 201
C&H SUGAR COMPANY, INC., 830 Loring Ave, **Crockett,** CA 94525, *pg.* 843, *pg.* 71
CALAVO GROWERS, INC., 1141-A Cummings Rd, **Santa Paula,** CA 93060-9118, *pg.* 843, *pg.* 276
CALIFIA FARMS LLC, 1095 E Green St, **Pasadena,** CA 91106, *pg.* 843, *pg.* 179
CALIFORNIA MILK ADVISORY BOARD, 3800 Cornucopia Way Ste D, **Modesto,** CA 95358-9494, *pg.* 843, *pg.* 149
CIRCLE FOODS, LLC, 8411 Siempre Viva Rd, **San Diego,** CA 92154, *pg.* 848, *pg.* 201
CLIF BAR INC., 1451 66th St, **Emeryville,** CA 94608, *pg.* 848, *pg.* 83
CLOUGHERTY PACKING COMPANY, 3049 E Vernon Ave, **Los Angeles,** CA 90058-1800, *pg.* 848, *pg.* 128
CLOVER STORNETTA FARMS INC., 5401 Old Redwood Hwy, **Petaluma,** CA 94954-1168, *pg.* 848, *pg.* 182
CROWN PRINCE, INC., 18581 Railroad St, **City of Industry,** CA 91748, *pg.* 850, *pg.* 67
CRYSTAL CREAM & BUTTER COMPANY, 529 Kansas Ave, **Modesto,** CA 95321, *pg.* 850, *pg.* 149
DAKLEN INC., 5900 Wilshire Blvd 26th Fl, **Los Angeles,** CA 90036, *pg.* 851, *pg.* 129
D'ARRIGO BROS. COMPANY, 2177 Harris Rd, **Salinas,** CA 93908, *pg.* 852, *pg.* 197
DEL MONTE FOODS, INC., 3003 Oak Rd, **Walnut Creek,** CA 94597, *pg.* 852, *pg.* 304
DOLE FOOD COMPANY, INC., 1 Dole Dr, **Westlake Village,** CA 91362-7300, *pg.* 853, *pg.* 306
DOLE FRESH VEGETABLES, 639 S Sanborn Rd, **Salinas,** CA 93901, *pg.* 854, *pg.* 198
DRISCOLL STRAWBERRY ASSOCIATES INC., 345 Westridge Dr, **Watsonville,** CA 95076-4169, *pg.* 854, *pg.* 305
FARMER BROTHERS COMPANY, 20333 S Normandie Ave, **Torrance,** CA 90502, *pg.* 855, *pg.* 293
FARMERS RICE COOPERATIVE, 2525 Natomas Pk Dr Ste 300, **Sacramento,** CA 95833-2933, *pg.* 855, *pg.* 196
FOSTER FARMS, 1000 Davis St, **Livingston,** CA 95334-0457, *pg.* 856, *pg.* 122
KIKKOMAN INTERNATIONAL INC., 50 California St Ste 3600, **San Francisco,** CA 94111, *pg.* 868, *pg.* 220
KING'S HAWAIIAN BAKERY WEST, INC., 19161 Harborgate Way, **Torrance,** CA 90501, *pg.* 869, *pg.* 293
MAVERICK BRANDS LLC, 2400 Wyndotte St, Ste B103, **Mountain View,** CA 94043, *pg.* 876, *pg.* 161
MONTEREY GOURMET FOODS, INC., 2315 Moore Ave, **Fullerton,** CA 92833, *pg.* 881, *pg.* 94
MONTEREY MUSHROOMS, INC., 260 Westgate Dr, **Watsonville,** CA 95076-2452, *pg.* 881, *pg.* 305
MUSCO FAMILY OLIVE COMPANY, 17950 Via Nicolo, **Tracy,** CA 95377-9767, *pg.* 882, *pg.* 297
NAKED JUICE COMPANY, INC., 935 W 8th St, **Monrovia,** CA 91016, *pg.* 882, *pg.* 150
NATURAL SELECTION FOODS, LLC, 1721 San Juan Hwy, **San Juan Bautista,** CA 95045, *pg.* 882, *pg.* 252
NATURE MADE NUTRITIONAL PRODUCTS INC., 8510 Balboa Blvd PO Box 9606, **Mission Hills,** CA 91325, *pg.* 883, *pg.* 148
NESTLE USA - BEVERAGE DIVISION, INC., 800 N Brand Blvd Fl 21, **Glendale,** CA 91203-1229, *pg.* 883, *pg.* 96
NESTLE USA, INC., 800 N Brand Blvd, **Glendale,** CA 91203-1245, *pg.* 883, *pg.* 96
NULAID FOODS INC., 200 W 5th St, **Ripon,** CA 95366-2766, *pg.* 887, *pg.* 193
OCEAN MIST FARMS CORP., 10855 Ocean Mist Pkwy, **Castroville,** CA 95012-3229, *pg.* 887, *pg.* 64
PLUM ORGANICS, 1485 Park Ave, **Emeryville,** CA 94608, *pg.* 890, *pg.* 85
POM WONDERFUL, LLC, 11444 W Olympic Blvd, **Los Angeles,** CA 90064, *pg.* 890, *pg.* 139
POPCHIPS, 5510 Lincoln Blvd, **Playa Vista,** CA 90094, *pg.* 890, *pg.* 182
Q&B FOODS, INC., 15547 First St, **Irwindale,** CA 91706-6201, *pg.* 891, *pg.* 119
RUIZ FOOD PRODUCTS, INC., 501 S Alta Ave, **Dinuba,** CA 93618-2100, *pg.* 893, *pg.* 77
SAGE V FOODS, LLC, 12100 Wilshire Blvd Ste 605, **Los Angeles,** CA 90025-7122, *pg.* 893, *pg.* 139
STAR FINE FOODS-BORGES USA, 2680 W Shaw Ln, **Fresno,** CA 93711, *pg.* 897, *pg.* 93
SUN-MAID GROWERS OF CALIFORNIA, 13525 S Bethel Ave, **Kingsburg,** CA 93631-9212, *pg.* 899, *pg.* 119
SUNKIST GROWERS, INC., 2770 Entertainment Dr, **Valencia,** CA 91355, *pg.* 899, *pg.* 299
SUNSWEET GROWERS, INC., 901 N Walton Ave, **Yuba City,** CA 95993-8634, *pg.* 900, *pg.* 309
TRADER VIC'S GOURMET PRODUCTS, INC., 5650 Imhoff Dr Ste I, **Concord,** CA 94520, *pg.* 901, *pg.* 69
VALLEY FIG GROWERS, INC., 2028 S 3rd St, **Fresno,** CA 93702, *pg.* 908, *pg.* 93
VAN'S INTERNATIONAL FOODS, INC., 3285 E Vernon Ave, **Vernon,** CA 90058, *pg.* 908, *pg.* 302
VENICE BAKERY, 134 Main St, **El Segundo,** CA 90245, *pg.* 908, *pg.* 83
VENTURA COASTAL LLC, 2325 Vista Del Mar Dr PO Box 69, **Ventura,** CA 93001-3751, *pg.* 908, *pg.* 301
VENTURA FOODS, LLC, 40 Pointe Dr, **Brea,** CA 92821, *pg.* 908, *pg.* 49
WETZEL'S PRETZELS LLC, 35 Hugus Alley Ste 300, **Pasadena,** CA 91103, *pg.* 910, *pg.* 181
YASHENG GROUP, 805 Veterans Blvd Ste 228, **Redwood City,** CA 94063, *pg.* 910, *pg.* 192
ZACKY FARMS, INC., 2020 S East Ave, **Fresno,** CA 93721, *pg.* 911, *pg.* 93

Colorado

ALLEGRO COFFEE CO., 12799 Claude Ct Bldg B Dock 4, **Thornton,** CO 80241, *pg.* 836, *pg.* 336
CELESTIAL SEASONINGS, INC., 4600 Sleepytime Dr, **Boulder,** CO 80301-3292, *pg.* 846, *pg.* 310
JBS USA HOLDING, INC., 1770 Promontory Cir, **Greeley,** CO 80634, *pg.* 865, *pg.* 330
LEPRINO FOODS COMPANY, 1830 W 38th Ave, **Denver,** CO 80211, *pg.* 874, *pg.* 320
NOOSA YOGHURT, PO Box 403, **Bellvue,** CO 80512, *pg.* 886, *pg.* 310
PILGRIM'S PRIDE CORPORATION, 1770 Promontory Cir, **Greeley,** CO 80634-9038, *pg.* 889, *pg.* 330

Connecticut

A.V. OLSSON TRADING CO. INC., 2001 W Main St Ste 215, **Stamford,** CT 06902-4542, *pg.* 838, *pg.* 372
NEW ZEALAND LAMB COOPERATIVE, INC., 372 Danbury Rd, Ste 207, **Wilton,** CT 06897, *pg.* 886, *pg.* 385
NEWMAN'S OWN, INC., 246 Post Rd E, **Westport,** CT 06880, *pg.* 886, *pg.* 384
NORSELAND, INC., 1290 E Main St, **Stamford,** CT 06902-3555, *pg.* 886, *pg.* 376
PEPPERIDGE FARM, INC., 595 Westport Ave, **Norwalk,** CT 06851-4413, *pg.* 888, *pg.* 363
R.C. BIGELOW, INC., 201 Black Rock Tpke, **Fairfield,** CT 06825, *pg.* 891, *pg.* 348

Delaware

BURRIS LOGISTICS, 501 SE 5th St, **Milford,** DE 19963-2022, *pg.* 843, *pg.* 387

Florida

A. DUDA & SONS INC., 1200 Duda Trl, **Oviedo,** FL 32765-4504, *pg.* 835, *pg.* 457
BOAR'S HEAD PROVISIONS CO., INC., 1819 Main St Ste 800, **Sarasota,** FL 34236-5926, *pg.* 841, *pg.* 465
BPI SPORTS, LLC, 3149 SW 42nd St, **Hollywood,** FL 33312, *pg.* 842, *pg.* 430
DUNDEE CITRUS GROWERS ASSOCIATION, PO Box 1739, **Dundee,** FL 33838, *pg.* 854, *pg.* 422
FLORIDA'S NATURAL GROWERS, 20205 US Hwy 27, **Lake Wales,** FL 33853, *pg.* 855, *pg.* 437
FRESH DEL MONTE PRODUCE INC., 241 Sevilla Ave, **Coral Gables,** FL 33134-3125, *pg.* 856, *pg.* 418
THE FRESH DIET, INC., 1545 NE 123rd St, **Miami,** FL 33161, *pg.* 856, *pg.* 442
PARADISE, INC., 1200 Dr Martin Luther King Jr Blvd, **Plant City,** FL 33563-5155, *pg.* 888, *pg.* 458
POINSETTIA GROVES INC., 1481 US Hwy 1, **Vero Beach,** FL 32960-5733, *pg.* 890, *pg.* 478
UNITED STATES SUGAR CORPORATION, 111 Ponce de Leon Ave, **Clewiston,** FL 33440-3032, *pg.* 907, *pg.* 417

Georgia

CARVEL CORPORATION, 200 Glenridge Point Pkwy Ste 200, **Atlanta,** GA 30342, *pg.* 846, *pg.* 492
COCA-COLA NORTH AMERICA, 1 Coca Cola Plaza, **Atlanta,** GA 30313-2499, *pg.* 848, *pg.* 500
FLOWERS FOODS BAKERIES GROUP, LLC, 112 E Jefferson St, **Thomasville,** GA 31792, *pg.* 855, *pg.* 541
FLOWERS FOODS, INC., 1919 Flowers Cir, **Thomasville,** GA 31757-1137, *pg.* 855, *pg.* 541
LAVOI CORPORATION, 1749 Tullie Cir, **Atlanta,** GA 30329, *pg.* 874, *pg.* 513
UNITED EGG PRODUCERS, 1720 Windward Concourse Ste 230, **Alpharetta,** GA 30005-2289, *pg.* 907, *pg.* 485

Hawaii

HAWAII COFFEE COMPANY, 1555 Kalani St, **Honolulu,** HI 96817, *pg.* 861, *pg.* 543
MAUI LAND & PINEAPPLE COMPANY, INC., 200 Village Rd, **Lahaina,** HI 96761, *pg.* 876, *pg.* 545
VIP FOODSERVICE, 74 Hobron Ave, **Kahului,** HI 96732, *pg.* 908, *pg.* 545

Idaho

CLEAR SPRINGS FOODS, INC., 1500 E 4424 N Clear Lk Rd, **Buhl,** ID 83316, *pg.* 848, *pg.* 548
CONAGRA FOODS LAMB WESTON, INC., 599 S Rivershore Ln, **Eagle,** ID 83616, *pg.* 850, *pg.* 549
IDAHO FRESH-PAK INC., 529 N 3500 E, **Lewisville,** ID 83431-5035, *pg.* 864, *pg.* 549

First page reference indicates Business Class Edition
Second page reference indicates Geographic Edition

J.R. SIMPLOT COMPANY, 999 Main St Ste 1300, **Boise,** ID 83702-9000, *pg.* 867, *pg.* 547

Illinois

ALPHA BAKING COMPANY, 5001 W Polk St, **Chicago,** IL 60644, *pg.* 836, *pg.* 564
AZTECA FOODS, INCORPORATED, 5005 S Nagle Ave, **Chicago,** IL 60638, *pg.* 838, *pg.* 566
BARILLA AMERICA, INC., 1200 Lakeside Dr, **Bannockburn,** IL 60015, *pg.* 839, *pg.* 555
BEL BRANDS USA, 30 S Wacker Dr Suite 3000, **Chicago,** IL 60606-7413, *pg.* 839, *pg.* 566
CARL BUDDIG & COMPANY, 950 W 175th St, **Homewood,** IL 60430-2027, *pg.* 846, *pg.* 619
C.J. VITNER CO., 4202 W 45th St, **Chicago,** IL 60632, *pg.* 848, *pg.* 571
CREST FOODS CO. INC., 905 Main St, **Ashton,** IL 61006, *pg.* 850, *pg.* 554
CUSTOM CULINARY, INC., 2021 Swift Dr, **Oak Brook,** IL 60523, *pg.* 851, *pg.* 644
FONA INTERNATIONAL INC., 1900 Averill Rd, **Geneva,** IL 60134-1601, *pg.* 855, *pg.* 613
FRONTERA FOODS, INC., 449 N Clark St, **Chicago,** IL 60654, *pg.* 857, *pg.* 574
GILSTER-MARY LEE CORPORATION, 1037 State St, **Chester,** IL 62233, *pg.* 858, *pg.* 563
GONNELLA BAKING COMPANY, 2006 W Erie St, **Chicago,** IL 60612-1318, *pg.* 859, *pg.* 575
GRECIAN DELIGHT FOODS INC., 1201 Tonne Rd, **Elk Grove Village,** IL 60007-4925, *pg.* 859, *pg.* 610
GRIFFITH LABORATORIES, INC., 1 Griffith Ctr, **Alsip,** IL 60803-3408, *pg.* 860, *pg.* 552
HILLSHIRE BRANDS, 400 S. Jefferson St, **Chicago,** IL 60607, *pg.* 862, *pg.* 576
INGREDION, 5 Westbrook Corporate Ctr, **Westchester,** IL 60154, *pg.* 864, *pg.* 669
INTELLIGENTSIA COFFEE, INC., 1850 W Fulton St, **Chicago,** IL 60612, *pg.* 865, *pg.* 578
INTERNATIONAL FOODS AND INGREDIENTS INC., 760 Lakeside Dr Unit A, **Gurnee,** IL 60031, *pg.* 865, *pg.* 616
THE JEL SERT COMPANY, Route 59 and Conde St, **West Chicago,** IL 60185-0261, *pg.* 865, *pg.* 668
JOHN MORRELL FOOD GROUP, 4225 Naperville Rd Ste 600, **Lisle,** IL 60563, *pg.* 866, *pg.* 628
KAUFFMAN POULTRY FARMS, INC., 8519 Leland Rd, **Waterman,** IL 60556, *pg.* 867, *pg.* 665
KOSTO FOOD PRODUCTS CO., 1325 N Old Rand Rd, **Wauconda,** IL 60084, *pg.* 869, *pg.* 665
THE KRAFT HEINZ COMPANY, 3 Lakes Dr, **Northfield,** IL 60093-2753, *pg.* 871, *pg.* 641
KRONOS PRODUCTS, INC., 1 Kronos Dr Glendale Hts, **Glendale Heights,** IL 60139, *pg.* 872, *pg.* 614
LA PREFERIDA, INC., 3400 W 35th St, **Chicago,** IL 60632, *pg.* 873, *pg.* 579
LIFEWAY FOODS, INC., 6431 W Oakton St, **Morton Grove,** IL 60053, *pg.* 874, *pg.* 634
LITTLE LADY FOODS, INC., 2323 Pratt Blvd, **Elk Grove Village,** IL 60007-5918, *pg.* 875, *pg.* 611
MERISANT COMPANY, 33 N Dearborn St Ste 200, **Chicago,** IL 60602, *pg.* 876, *pg.* 581
MIZKAN AMERICAS, INC., 1661 Feehanville Dr Ste 300, **Mount Prospect,** IL 60056, *pg.* 877, *pg.* 634
MONDELEZ INTERNATIONAL, INC., 3 Pkwy North, **Deerfield,** IL 60015, *pg.* 878, *pg.* 601
MORTON SALT, INC., 123 N Wacker Dr, **Chicago,** IL 60606, *pg.* 881, *pg.* 583
NEWLY WEDS FOODS, INC., 4140 W Fullerton Ave, **Chicago,** IL 60639-2106, *pg.* 886, *pg.* 585
OBERWEIS DAIRY, INC., 951 Ice Cream Dr, **North Aurora,** IL 60542-8193, *pg.* 887, *pg.* 638
PEER FOODS INC., 1200 W 35th St Ste 5 E, **Chicago,** IL 60609-3214, *pg.* 888, *pg.* 587
PLOCHMAN, INC., 1333 N Boudreau Rd, **Manteno,** IL 60950-9384, *pg.* 890, *pg.* 631
PRAIRIE FARMS DAIRY, INC., 1100 N Broadway St, **Carlinville,** IL 62626-1183, *pg.* 890, *pg.* 561
QUANTUM FOODS, INC., 750 S Schmidt Rd, **Bolingbrook,** IL 60440, *pg.* 891, *pg.* 559
ROSE PACKING COMPANY, 65 S Barrington Rd, **Barrington,** IL 60010-9508, *pg.* 892, *pg.* 556
SAPUTO CHEESE USA INC., 1 Overlook Point Ste 300, **Lincolnshire,** IL 60069, *pg.* 893, *pg.* 627
SCHULZE & BURCH BISCUIT COMPANY, 1133 W 35th St, **Chicago,** IL 60609-1447, *pg.* 894, *pg.* 589
SKINNYPOP POPCORN LLC, 8135 Monticello Ave, **Skokie,** IL 60076, *pg.* 895, *pg.* 661
SUBCO FOODS, INC., 1150 Commerce Dr, **West Chicago,** IL 60185, *pg.* 899, *pg.* 668
TAYLOR COMPANY, 750 N Blackhawk Blvd, **Rockton,** IL 61072-2104, *pg.* 901, *pg.* 655
TOPCO HOLDINGS INC., 7711 Gross Point Rd, **Skokie,** IL 60077, *pg.* 901, *pg.* 661
TREEHOUSE FOODS, INC., 2021 Spring Rd Ste 600, **Oak Brook,** IL 60523-1860, *pg.* 901, *pg.* 649
TROPICANA PRODUCTS, INC., 555 West Monroe St, **Chicago,** IL 60661, *pg.* 902, *pg.* 592
V&V SUPREMO FOODS, INC., 2141 S Throop St, **Chicago,** IL 60608, *pg.* 907, *pg.* 595
VITA FOOD PRODUCTS, INC., 2222 W Lake St, **Chicago,** IL 60612-2210, *pg.* 909, *pg.* 595

Indiana

AUNT MILLIE'S BAKERIES, 350 Pearl St, **Fort Wayne,** IN 46802, *pg.* 838, *pg.* 680
CTB INTERNATIONAL CORP., 611 N Higbee St, **Milford,** IN 46542, *pg.* 850, *pg.* 695
HEARTLAND FOOD PRODUCTS GROUP, 14300 Clay Terrace Blvd, Ste 249, **Carmel,** IN 46032, *pg.* 861, *pg.* 675
HULMAN & COMPANY, 900 Wabash Ave, **Terre Haute,** IN 47807-3208, *pg.* 864, *pg.* 698
MORGAN FOODS, INC., 90 W Morgan St, **Austin,** IN 47102-1741, *pg.* 881, *pg.* 673
N.K. HURST CO., INC., 230 W McCarty St, **Indianapolis,** IN 46225-1234, *pg.* 886, *pg.* 689
RED GOLD, INC., 1500 Tomato Country Way, **Elwood,** IN 46036, *pg.* 891, *pg.* 677
REIDCO, INC., 1351 W US Hwy 50, **Brownstown,** IN 47220, *pg.* 891, *pg.* 675
SENSIENT FLAVORS INC., 5600 W Raymond St, **Indianapolis,** IN 46241-4343, *pg.* 895, *pg.* 690

Iowa

AMANA SOCIETY, INC., 506 39th Ave PO Box 189, **Amana,** IA 52203-8229, *pg.* 836, *pg.* 701
ANDERSON ERICKSON DAIRY COMPANY, 2420 E University Ave, **Des Moines,** IA 50317-6559, *pg.* 837, *pg.* 704
GRAIN PROCESSING CORPORATION, 1600 Oregon St, **Muscatine,** IA 52761-1404, *pg.* 859, *pg.* 709
NATIONAL PORK BOARD, 1776 NW 114th St, **Clive,** IA 50325-7073, *pg.* 882, *pg.* 703
WELLS ENTERPRISES, INC., 1 Blue Bunny Dr SW, **Le Mars,** IA 51031, *pg.* 909, *pg.* 709

Kansas

CARGILL MEAT SOLUTIONS, 151 N Main St 1st Fl, **Wichita,** KS 67201, *pg.* 846, *pg.* 722
GOLDEN HERITAGE FOODS, LLC, 120 Santa Fe St, **Hillsboro,** KS 67063, *pg.* 858, *pg.* 715
MGP INGREDIENTS, INC., 100 Commercial St PO Box 130, **Atchison,** KS 66002-2666, *pg.* 877, *pg.* 714
PINES INTERNATIONAL, INC., 1992 E 1400 Rd, **Lawrence,** KS 66044, *pg.* 889, *pg.* 715

Kentucky

ALGOOD FOOD COMPANY, 7401 Tradeport Dr, **Louisville,** KY 40258, *pg.* 836, *pg.* 731
DIPPIN' DOTS LLC, 5101 Charter Oak Dr, **Paducah,** KY 42001, *pg.* 853, *pg.* 739
SPECIALTY FOODS GROUP-FIELD PACKING DIV., 6 Dublin Ln, **Owensboro,** KY 42301, *pg.* 897, *pg.* 739
WILD FLAVORS, INC., 1261 Pacific Ave, **Erlanger,** KY 41018, *pg.* 910, *pg.* 728

Louisiana

BRUCE FOODS CORPORATION, Hwy 182 W, **Cade,** LA 70519, *pg.* 842, *pg.* 743
COMMUNITY COFFEE COMPANY LLC, 3332 Partridge Ln, **Baton Rouge,** LA 70821, *pg.* 849, *pg.* 741
MCILHENNY COMPANY, Hwy 329, **Avery Island,** LA 70513, *pg.* 876, *pg.* 741
REILY FOODS COMPANY, 640 Magazine St, **New Orleans,** LA 70130-3406, *pg.* 891, *pg.* 747
ZATARAIN'S BRANDS, INC., 82 1st St, **Gretna,** LA 70053, *pg.* 911, *pg.* 744

Maine

BARBER FOODS, INC., 56 Milliken St, **Portland,** ME 04103, *pg.* 839, *pg.* 751
OAKHURST DAIRY, 364 Forest Ave, **Portland,** ME 04101-2035, *pg.* 887, *pg.* 752

Maryland

FUCHS NORTH AMERICA., 9740 Reisterstown Rd, **Owings Mills,** MD 21117, *pg.* 857, *pg.* 774
LEDO PIZZA SYSTEM INC., 2001 Tidewater Colony Dr, Ste 103, **Annapolis,** MD 21401, *pg.* 874, *pg.* 754
MURRY'S, INC., 8300 Pennsylvania Ave, **Upper Marlboro,** MD 20772, *pg.* 882, *pg.* 780
PERDUE FARMS INCORPORATED, 31149 Old Ocean City Rd, **Salisbury,** MD 21804-1806, *pg.* 889, *pg.* 777
POMPEIAN, INC., 4201 Pulaski Hwy, **Baltimore,** MD 21224-1603, *pg.* 890, *pg.* 759
SCHMIDT BAKING CO., INC., 7801 Fitch Ln, **Baltimore,** MD 21236-3916, *pg.* 894, *pg.* 759
SEA WATCH INTERNATIONAL, LTD., 8978 Glebe Pk Dr, **Easton,** MD 21601-7004, *pg.* 895, *pg.* 769

Massachusetts

CAINS FOODS, L.P., 114 E Main St, **Ayer,** MA 01432-1832, *pg.* 843, *pg.* 784
CANADIAN FISH EXPORTERS, INC., 134 Rumford Ave Ste 202, **Auburndale,** MA 02466-1377, *pg.* 845, *pg.* 784
CAPE COD POTATO CHIP COMPANY, 100 Breeds Hill Rd, **Hyannis,** MA 02601-1860, *pg.* 845, *pg.* 826
COSTA FRUIT & PRODUCE INC., 18 Bunker Hill Indus Pk, **Boston,** MA 02129-1621, *pg.* 850, *pg.* 793
F.W. BRYCE, INC., 8 Pond Rd, **Gloucester,** MA 01930-1833, *pg.* 857, *pg.* 823
GARELICK FARMS, LLC, 1199 W Central St, **Franklin,** MA 02038, *pg.* 858, *pg.* 823
THE GORTON GROUP, 128 Rogers St, **Gloucester,** MA 01930-5005, *pg.* 859, *pg.* 823
HIGH LINER FOODS (USA) INCORPORATED, 18 Electronics Ave, **Danvers,** MA 01923, *pg.* 862, *pg.* 816
HP HOOD LLC, 6 Kimball Ln, **Lynnfield,** MA 01940, *pg.* 864, *pg.* 829
KAYEM FOODS, INC., 75 Arlington St, **Chelsea,** MA 02150, *pg.* 867, *pg.* 814
KEN'S FOODS, INC., 1 Dangelo Dr, **Marlborough,** MA 01752, *pg.* 867, *pg.* 832
THE LEAVITT CORPORATION, 100 Santilli Hwy, **Everett,** MA 02149-1938, *pg.* 874, *pg.* 818
OCEAN SPRAY CRANBERRIES, INC., 1 Ocean Spray Dr, **Lakeville,** MA 02347-1339, *pg.* 887, *pg.* 827
WELCH FOODS INC., 3 Concord Farms 575 Virginia Rd, **Concord,** MA 01742-9101, *pg.* 909, *pg.* 815
WELCH'S INTERNATIONAL, 300 Baker Ave, Ste 101, **Concord,** MA 01742, *pg.* 909, *pg.* 816

Michigan

CHERRY CENTRAL COOPERATIVE, INC., 1771 N US 31 S, **Traverse City,** MI 49684-0988, *pg.* 847, *pg.* 909
THE COFFEE BEANERY LTD., 3429 Pierson Pl, **Flushing,** MI 48433-2413, *pg.* 849, *pg.* 886
FRY KRISP COMPANY, 3360 Spring Arbor Rd, **Jackson,** MI 49203-3636, *pg.* 857, *pg.* 893
NEOGEN CORPORATION, 620 Lesher Pl, **Lansing,** MI 48912-1509, *pg.* 883, *pg.* 896
NU-VU FOODSERVICE SYSTEMS, 5600 13th St, **Menominee,** MI 49858, *pg.* 887, *pg.* 898
WIN SCHULER FOODS, 27777 Franklin Rd Ste 1520, **Southfield,** MI 48034-8261, *pg.* 910, *pg.* 908

Minnesota

AMERICAN CRYSTAL SUGAR COMPANY, 101 3rd St N, **Moorhead,** MN 56560-1952, *pg.* 837, *pg.* 951
ASSOCIATED MILK PRODUCERS INC., 315 N Broadway,

New Ulm, MN 56073, pg. 838, pg. 951
BELLISIO FOODS, INC., 1201 Harmon Pl Ste 302, **Minneapolis,** MN 55403, pg. 840, pg. 931
BERNATELLO'S PIZZA INC., 220 Congress St, **Maple Lake,** MN 55358, pg. 840, pg. 928
BETTY CROCKER PRODUCTS, 1 General Mills Blvd, **Minneapolis,** MN 55426, pg. 840, pg. 931
CARGILL, INC., 15407 McGinty Rd W, **Wayzata,** MN 55391-2365, pg. 845, pg. 965
CARGILL SALT, 9350 Excelsior Blvd, **Hopkins,** MN 55343, pg. 846, pg. 926
CATALLIA MEXICAN FOODS LLC, 2965 Lone Oak Cir, **Eagan,** MN 55121, pg. 846, pg. 921
FARIBAULT FOODS, INC., 128 15th St NW, **Faribault,** MN 55021-3037, pg. 855, pg. 925
GOLD'N PLUMP POULTRY, INC., 4150 Second St S Ste 200, **Saint Cloud,** MN 56301-3994, pg. 858, pg. 956
GRUMA CORPORATION, 1565 1st Ave NW, **New Brighton,** MN 55112-1948, pg. 860, pg. 951
HORMEL FOODS CORPORATION, 1 Hormel Pl, **Austin,** MN 55912-3680, pg. 863, pg. 915
HORMEL FOODS CORPORATION - FOODSERVICE DIVISION, 1 Hormel Pl, **Austin,** MN 55912-3673, pg. 864, pg. 916
JENNIE-O TURKEY STORE, LLC, 2505 SW Willmar Ave, **Willmar,** MN 56201, pg. 865, pg. 966
KEMPS LLC, 1270 Energy Ln, **Saint Paul,** MN 55108-5225, pg. 867, pg. 961
LAND O'LAKES, INC., 4001 Lexington Ave N, **Arden Hills,** MN 55126-2934, pg. 873, pg. 915
LUND FOOD HOLDINGS, INC., 4100 W 50th St, **Edina,** MN 55424-1200, pg. 875, pg. 924
MICHAEL FOODS, INC., 301 Carlson Pkwy Ste 400, **Minnetonka,** MN 55305, pg. 877, pg. 949
OLD DUTCH FOODS, INC., 2375 Terminal Rd, **Roseville,** MN 55113-2530, pg. 888, pg. 956
THE SCHWAN FOOD COMPANY, 115 W College Dr, **Marshall,** MN 56258, pg. 894, pg. 928
SUNOPTA INGREDIENTS, INC., 7301 Ohms Ln, Ste 600, **Minneapolis,** MN 55439, pg. 900, pg. 942
WATKINS INCORPORATED, 150 Liberty St, **Winona,** MN 55987-3707, pg. 909, pg. 967
YOPLAIT USA, INC., 1 General Mills Blvd, **Minneapolis,** MN 55426-1347, pg. 910, pg. 947

Mississippi

CAL-MAINE FOODS, INC., 3320 W Woodrow Wilson Ave, **Jackson,** MS 39209-3409, pg. 843, pg. 969
CONSOLIDATED CATFISH COMPANIES, LLC, PO Box 271 South City Limits Rd, **Isola,** MS 38754, pg. 850, pg. 969
SANDERSON FARMS, INC., 127 Flynt Rd, **Laurel,** MS 39443, pg. 893, pg. 970

Missouri

AMERICAN ITALIAN PASTA COMPANY, 1251 NW Briarcliff Pkwy Ste 500, **Kansas City,** MO 64116, pg. 837, pg. 980
DAIRY FARMERS OF AMERICA, INC., PO Box 909700, **Kansas City,** MO 64190-9700, pg. 851, pg. 982
HILAND DAIRY FOODS COMPANY, PO Box 2270, **Springfield,** MO 65801, pg. 862, pg. 1006
LOUIS MAULL COMPANY, 219 N Market, **Saint Louis,** MO 63102, pg. 875, pg. 999
NATIONAL BEEF PACKING COMPANY, LLC, 12200 N Ambassador Dr Ste 500, **Kansas City,** MO 64163-1244, pg. 882, pg. 985
NATIONAL ENZYME COMPANY, 15366 US Hwy 160, **Forsyth,** MO 65653, pg. 882, pg. 978
SAVE-A-LOT, LTD., 100 Corporate Office Dr, **Earth City,** MO 63045-1528, pg. 894, pg. 977
U.S. PREMIUM BEEF, LLC, 12200 N Ambassador Dr, **Kansas City,** MO 64163-1244, pg. 907, pg. 987

Nebraska

AG PROCESSING INC., 12700 W Dodge Rd, **Omaha,** NE 68154-2154, pg. 835, pg. 1013
ROTELLAS ITALIAN BAKERY, INC., 6949 S 108th St, **Omaha,** NE 68128, pg. 892, pg. 1018
WESTIN FOODS, INC., 11808 W Ctr Rd, **Omaha,** NE 68144-4397, pg. 909, pg. 1019

Nevada

U-SWIRL, INC., 1175 American Pacific Ste C, **Henderson,** NV 89074, pg. 903, pg. 1021

New Hampshire

STONYFIELD FARM, INC., 10 Burton Dr, **Londonderry,** NH 03053, pg. 899, pg. 1035

New Jersey

ALLIED OLD ENGLISH, INC., 100 Markley St, **Port Reading,** NJ 07064, pg. 836, pg. 1110
APPLEGATE, 750 Rt 202 S Ste 300, **Bridgewater,** NJ 08807-5530, pg. 837, pg. 1045
ATALANTA CORPORATION, 1 Atalanta Plz, **Elizabeth,** NJ 07206, pg. 838, pg. 1057
B&G FOODS, INC., 4 Gatehall Dr, **Parsippany,** NJ 07054, pg. 838, pg. 1102
CAMERICAN INTERNATIONAL, 45 Eisenhower Dr, **Paramus,** NJ 07652-1452, pg. 844, pg. 1101
CAMPBELL SOUP COMPANY, 1 Campbell Pl, **Camden,** NJ 08103-1799, pg. 844, pg. 1048
COLAVITA USA, INC., 1 Runyons Ln, **Edison,** NJ 08817-2219, pg. 849, pg. 1056
COLONNA BROS., INC., 4102 Bergen Tpke, **North Bergen,** NJ 07047-2510, pg. 849, pg. 1098
EASTERN FISH COMPANY, 300 Frank W Burr Blvd, **Teaneck,** NJ 07666-6704, pg. 854, pg. 1124
GERBER PRODUCTS COMPANY, 12 Vreeland Rd, **Florham Park,** NJ 07932, pg. 858, pg. 1067
GOYA FOODS, INC., 350 Country Rd, **Jersey City,** NJ 07307, pg. 859, pg. 1075
J&J SNACK FOODS CORPORATION, 6000 Central Hwy, **Pennsauken,** NJ 08109-4607, pg. 865, pg. 1107
JOHANNA FOODS INC., Johanna Farms Rd, **Flemington,** NJ 08822, pg. 866, pg. 1066
MANISCHEWITZ COMPANY, 80 Avenue K, **Newark,** NJ 07105, pg. 875, pg. 1097
MITSUI FOODS, INC., 35 Maple St, **Norwood,** NJ 07648, pg. 877, pg. 1099
MONDELEZ NORTH AMERICA, 100 DeForest Ave, **East Hanover,** NJ 07936, pg. 881, pg. 1054
PINNACLE FOODS GROUP LLC, 399 Jefferson Rd, **Parsippany,** NJ 07054, pg. 889, pg. 1104
SLIM-FAST FOODS COMPANY, 800 Sylvan Ave, **Englewood Cliffs,** NJ 07632, pg. 896, pg. 1061
STROHMEYER & ARPE COMPANY, 106 Allen Rd, **Basking Ridge,** NJ 07920, pg. 899, pg. 1042
TABATCHNICK FINE FOODS, INC., 1230 Hamilton St, **Somerset,** NJ 08873-3343, pg. 900, pg. 1122
TETLEY USA INC., 890 Mountain Ave Ste 105, **New Providence,** NJ 07974, pg. 901, pg. 1095
UNILEVER UNITED STATES, INC., 800 Sylvan Ave, **Englewood Cliffs,** NJ 07632-3113, pg. 904, pg. 1061
WHITE ROSE FOODS, 380 Middlesex Ave, **Carteret,** NJ 07008-3446, pg. 910, pg. 1050
WORLD FINER FOODS, INC., 1455 Broad St, 4th Fl, **Bloomfield,** NJ 07003, pg. 910, pg. 1044

New York

4C FOODS CORPORATION, 580 Fountain Ave, **Brooklyn,** NY 11208-6002, pg. 835, pg. 1145
BALCHEM CORPORATION, 52 Sunrise Park Rd, **New Hampton,** NY 10958, pg. 839, pg. 1183
BUNGE LIMITED, 50 Main St, **White Plains,** NY 10606-1901, pg. 842, pg. 1351
CHOBANI LLC, 147 State Hwy 320, **Norwich,** NY 13815, pg. 847, pg. 1318
COFFEE HOLDING CO., INC., 3475 Victory Blvd, **Staten Island,** NY 10314, pg. 849, pg. 1343
CUMBERLAND PACKING CORP., 2 Cumberland St, **Brooklyn,** NY 11205-1040, pg. 851, pg. 1146
DAIRYLEA COOPERATIVE INC., 5001 Brittonfield Pkwy, **East Syracuse,** NY 13057-9201, pg. 851, pg. 1157
THE DANNON COMPANY, INC., Fl 3 100 Hillside Ave, **White Plains,** NY 10603-2862, pg. 851, pg. 1351
ENERGY BRANDS, INC., 260 Madison Ave, **New York,** NY 10016, pg. 854, pg. 1227
FRESHDIRECT, LLC, 23-30 Borden Ave, **Long Island City,** NY 11101, pg. 857, pg. 1174
FRIENDSHIP DAIRIES, INC., 1 Jericho Plz, **Jericho,** NY 11753-1680, pg. 857, pg. 1171
GOLD PURE FOOD PRODUCTS CO., INC., 1 Brooklyn Rd, **Hempstead,** NY 11550-6619, pg. 858, pg. 1166
THE HAIN CELESTIAL GROUP, INC., 1111 Marcus Ave, **Lake Success,** NY 11042, pg. 860, pg. 1172
HAYDENERGY, INC., 200 W 58th St Ste 2C, **New York,** NY 10019-1432, pg. 861, pg. 1238
INTERNATIONAL FIBER CORP., 50 Bridge St, **North Tonawanda,** NY 14120-6842, pg. 865, pg. 1317
KIND LLC, PO Box 705 Midtown Station, **New York,** NY 10018, pg. 868, pg. 1249
KOZY SHACK INC., 83 Ludy St, **Hicksville,** NY 11801, pg. 869, pg. 1167
LACTALIS AMERICAN GROUP, 2376 S Park Ave, **Buffalo,** NY 14220, pg. 873, pg. 1149
LAVAZZA PREMIUM COFFEES CORP., 120 Wall St Fl 27, **New York,** NY 10005, pg. 874, pg. 1250
LES TROIS PETITS COCHONS, INC., 4223 1st Ave, 2nd Fl, **Brooklyn,** NY 11232, pg. 874, pg. 1146
LIDESTRI FOODS, INC., 815 W Whitney Rd, **Fairport,** NY 14450-1030, pg. 874, pg. 1159
MONDELEZ INTERNATIONAL, 555 S Broadway, **Tarrytown,** NY 10591-5598, pg. 877, pg. 1344
REDCO FOODS, INC., One Hansen Island, **Little Falls,** NY 13365, pg. 891, pg. 1174
RICH PRODUCTS CORPORATION, 1 Robert Rich Way, **Buffalo,** NY 14213-1714, pg. 892, pg. 1150
SAU-SEA FOODS, INC., 670 Montauk Hwy, **Water Mill,** NY 11976, pg. 894, pg. 1349
SENECA FOODS CORPORATION, 3736 S Main St, **Marion,** NY 14505-9751, pg. 895, pg. 1177
UPSTATE NIAGARA COOPERATIVE, INC., 25 Anderson Rd, **Buffalo,** NY 14225-4905, pg. 907, pg. 1151
VIRGINIA DARE EXTRACT CO., INC., 882 3rd Ave, **Brooklyn,** NY 11232, pg. 908, pg. 1147
WORLDWIDE FOOD PRODUCTS INC., 14707 94th Ave, **Jamaica,** NY 11435-4513, pg. 910, pg. 1170

North Carolina

BUTTERBALL, LLC, 1628 Garner Chapel Rd, **Mount Olive,** NC 28365, pg. 843, pg. 1385
CHIQUITA BRANDS INTERNATIONAL, INC., 550 S Caldwell St Ste 1010, **Charlotte,** NC 28202, pg. 847, pg. 1365
HOUSE OF RAEFORD FARMS, INC., 520 E Central Ave, **Raeford,** NC 28376-3020, pg. 864, pg. 1386
INSTITUTION FOOD HOUSE, INC., 543 12th St Dr NW, **Hickory,** NC 28603, pg. 864, pg. 1378
PAMLICO PACKING COMPANY INCORPORATED, PO Box 336, **Grantsboro,** NC 28529, pg. 888, pg. 1374
SNYDER'S-LANCE, INC., 13515 Ballantyne Pl, **Charlotte,** NC 28277, pg. 896, pg. 1368
SWISHER HYGIENE INC., 4725 Piedmont Row Dr Ste 400, **Charlotte,** NC 28210, pg. 900, pg. 1369

North Dakota

MINN-DAK FARMERS COOPERATIVE, 7525 Red River Rd, **Wahpeton,** ND 58075-9705, pg. 877, pg. 1399

Ohio

ALFRED NICKLES BAKERY, INC., 26 N Main St, **Navarre,** OH 44662-1158, pg. 836, pg. 1466
AVITAE USA LLC, 8500 Memorial Dr Ste C, **Plain City,** OH 43064, pg. 838, pg. 1471
BOB EVANS FARMS, LLC, 8111 Smith's Mill Rd, **New Albany,** OH 43054-1183, pg. 841, pg. 1467
BROUGHTON FOODS COMPANY, 1701 Greene St, **Marietta,** OH 45750-9816, pg. 842, pg. 1458
ELLENBEE-LEGGETT COMPANY INC., 3765 Port Union Rd, **Fairfield,** OH 45014-2207, pg. 854, pg. 1452
THE FREMONT COMPANY, 802 N Front St, **Fremont,** OH 43420-1917, pg. 856, pg. 1454
FRESH MARK, INC., 1888 Southway St SW PO Box 571, **Massillon,** OH 44646, pg. 856, pg. 1461
THE GREAT LAKES CHEESE CO., INC., 17825 Great Lks Pkwy, **Hiram,** OH 44234-9677, pg. 859, pg. 1455
HICKORY FARMS, INC., 1505 Holland Rd, **Maumee,** OH 43537-1620, pg. 862, pg. 1462
THE J.M. SMUCKER COMPANY, 1 Strawberry Lane, **Orrville,** OH 44667-0280, pg. 865, pg. 1468
JOHN MORRELL & CO., 805 E Kemper Rd, **Cincinnati,** OH

First page reference indicates Business Class Edition
Second page reference indicates Geographic Edition

45246, *pg.* 866, *pg.* 1415
KLOSTERMAN BAKING COMPANY, INC., 4760 Paddock Rd, **Cincinnati,** OH 45229-1004, *pg.* 869, *pg.* 1415
LANCASTER COLONY CORPORATION, 37 W Broad St Ste 500, **Columbus,** OH 43215-4132, *pg.* 873, *pg.* 1441
NORSE DAIRY SYSTEMS LLC, 1740 Joyce Ave, **Columbus,** OH 43219-1026, *pg.* 886, *pg.* 1442
RUDOLPH FOODS COMPANY, 6575 Bellefontaine Rd, **Lima,** OH 45804-4415, *pg.* 892, *pg.* 1458
SUGAR CREEK PACKING CO., 2101 1 2 Kenskill Ave, **Washington Court House,** OH 43160-9311, *pg.* 899, *pg.* 1478
SUNNY DELIGHT BEVERAGES CO., 10300 Alliance Rd, # 500, **Cincinnati,** OH 45242, *pg.* 899, *pg.* 1426
T. MARZETTI COMPANY, 1105 Schrock Rd Ste 300, **Columbus,** OH 43229-1174, *pg.* 900, *pg.* 1444
UNITED DAIRY FARMERS, INC., 3955 Montgomery Rd, **Cincinnati,** OH 45212, *pg.* 906, *pg.* 1426

Oklahoma

GRIFFIN FOOD COMPANY, 111 S Cherokee St, **Muskogee,** OK 74403, *pg.* 860, *pg.* 1484
NONNI'S FOOD COMPANY INC., 601 S Boulder Ave Ste 900, **Tulsa,** OK 74119, *pg.* 886, *pg.* 1490

Oregon

BOB'S RED MILL NATURAL FOODS, INC., 13521 SE Pleasant Ct, **Milwaukie,** OR 97222, *pg.* 841, *pg.* 1500
GRAY & COMPANY, 5520 Sw Macadam Ave, Ste 230, **Portland,** OR 97239, *pg.* 859, *pg.* 1503
OREGON FREEZE DRY, INC., 525 25th Ave SW, **Albany,** OR 97322, *pg.* 888, *pg.* 1492
TILLAMOOK COUNTY CREAMERY ASSOCIATION, 4175 Hwy 101 N, **Tillamook,** OR 97141-7770, *pg.* 901, *pg.* 1509
UNITED STATES BAKERY, 315 NE 10th Ave, **Portland,** OR 97232-2712, *pg.* 907, *pg.* 1507

Pennsylvania

ADVANCED FOOD PRODUCTS LLC, 402 S Custer Ave, **New Holland,** PA 17557, *pg.* 835, *pg.* 1555
ATEECO, INC., 600 E Center St, **Shenandoah,** PA 17976, *pg.* 838, *pg.* 1586
BIMBO BAKERIES USA INC., 255 Business Center Dr, **Horsham,** PA 19044, *pg.* 840, *pg.* 1540
BONGRAIN NORTH AMERICA, 400 S Custer Ave, **New Holland,** PA 17557-9220, *pg.* 841, *pg.* 1556
CEDAR FARMS COMPANY, INC., 2100 Hornig Rd, **Philadelphia,** PA 19116, *pg.* 846, *pg.* 1559
DAVID MICHAEL & CO. INC., 10801 Decatur Rd, **Philadelphia,** PA 19154-3209, *pg.* 852, *pg.* 1563
DIETZ & WATSON INC., 5701 Tacony St, **Philadelphia,** PA 19135-4311, *pg.* 853, *pg.* 1563
DUTCH GOLD HONEY INC., 2220 Dutch Gold Dr, **Lancaster,** PA 17601-1941, *pg.* 854, *pg.* 1546
EGGLAND'S BEST, INC., 1400 S. Trooper Rd., Ste 201, **Jeffersonville,** PA 19403, *pg.* 854, *pg.* 1542
EMPIRE KOSHER POULTRY, INC., Rte 5 PO Box 228, **Mifflintown,** PA 17059-9409, *pg.* 854, *pg.* 1553
FARMERS PRIDE, INC., 154 W Main St, **Fredericksburg,** PA 17026, *pg.* 855, *pg.* 1534
FURMANO FOODS, INC., 770 Cannery Rd, **Northumberland,** PA 17857, *pg.* 857, *pg.* 1557
HANOVER FOODS CORPORATION, P.O. Box 334, **Hanover,** PA 17331-9570, *pg.* 861, *pg.* 1535
HATFIELD QUALITY MEATS, INC., 2700 Clemens Rd, **Hatfield,** PA 19440-2834, *pg.* 861, *pg.* 1537
HEINZ FROZEN FOOD COMPANY, 357 6 Avn, **Pittsburgh,** PA 15222, *pg.* 861, *pg.* 1576
HEINZ NORTH AMERICA, 357 6th Ave, **Pittsburgh,** PA 15222-2500, *pg.* 861, *pg.* 1576
HERR FOODS INC., 273 Baltimore Pke, **Nottingham,** PA 19362-9788, *pg.* 861, *pg.* 1557
JOHN PATON INC, 73 E State St, **Doylestown,** PA 18901, *pg.* 866, *pg.* 1526
KNOUSE FOODS COOPERATIVE INC., 800 Peach Glen Idaville Rd, **Peach Glen,** PA 17375, *pg.* 869, *pg.* 1558
THE KRAFT HEINZ COMPANY, 1 PPG Pl, **Pittsburgh,** PA 15222, *pg.* 870, *pg.* 1577
LA COLOMBE TORREFACTION, INC., 2620 E Tioga St, **Philadelphia,** PA 19134, *pg.* 873, *pg.* 1566
MALLET & COMPANY, INC., 51 Arch St, **Carnegie,** PA 15106, *pg.* 875, *pg.* 1521
NEW WORLD PASTA COMPANY, 85 Shannon Rd, **Harrisburg,** PA 17112-2799, *pg.* 885, *pg.* 1537
STARKIST FOODS INC., 323 North Shore Dr Ste 600, **Pittsburgh,** PA 15212, *pg.* 898, *pg.* 1581
SYLVAN INC., 90 Glade Dr, **Kittanning,** PA 16201, *pg.* 900, *pg.* 1544
TURKEY HILL DAIRY, INC., 2601 River Rd, **Conestoga,** PA 17516, *pg.* 902, *pg.* 1522
UTZ QUALITY FOODS, INC., 900 High St, **Hanover,** PA 17331-1639, *pg.* 907, *pg.* 1536

Rhode Island

GALAXY NUTRITIONAL FOODS, INC., 66 Whitecap Dr Fl 2, **North Kingstown,** RI 02852, *pg.* 857, *pg.* 1603
GREAT NORTHERN PRODUCTS, LTD., 804 Centerville Rd, **Warwick,** RI 02886-4397, *pg.* 859, *pg.* 1609
UNITED NATURAL FOODS, INC., 313 Iron Horse Way, **Providence,** RI 02908, *pg.* 907, *pg.* 1608

Tennessee

ACH FOOD COMPANIES, INC., 7171 Goodlett Farms Pkwy, **Cordova,** TN 38016-4909, *pg.* 835, *pg.* 1631
BUSH BROTHERS & COMPANY, 1016 E Weisgarber Rd, **Knoxville,** TN 37909, *pg.* 843, *pg.* 1636
CHATTANOOGA BAKERY INC., 900 Manufacturers Rd, **Chattanooga,** TN 37405-3763, *pg.* 847, *pg.* 1628
KRAFT FOOD INGREDIENTS, 8000 Horizon Ctr Blvd, **Memphis,** TN 38133, *pg.* 870, *pg.* 1645
ODOM'S TENNESSEE PRIDE SAUSAGE, INC., 1201 Neelys Bend Rd, **Madison,** TN 37115-5446, *pg.* 887, *pg.* 1640
PURITY DAIRIES, LLC, 360 Murfreesboro Rd, **Nashville,** TN 37210-2816, *pg.* 891, *pg.* 1653
WILLIAMS SAUSAGE CO., INC., 5132 Old Troy Hickman Hwy, **Union City,** TN 38261, *pg.* 910, *pg.* 1656

Texas

ADAMS EXTRACT & SPICE LLC, 3217 Johnston Rd, **Gonzales,** TX 78629, *pg.* 835, *pg.* 1698
AMERICAN RICE, INC., 10700 N Fwy Ste 800, **Houston,** TX 77037-1158, *pg.* 837, *pg.* 1700
BEN E. KEITH COMPANY, 1805 Record Crossing Rd, **Dallas,** TX 75235, *pg.* 840, *pg.* 1676
BORDEN DAIRY COMPANY, 8750 North Central Expwy Ste 400, **Dallas,** TX 75231, *pg.* 842, *pg.* 1676
DARLING INGREDIENTS, INC., 251 O'Connor Ridge Blvd Ste 300, **Irving,** TX 75038, *pg.* 852, *pg.* 1718
DEAN FOODS COMPANY, 2711 N Haskell Ave Ste 3400, **Dallas,** TX 75204, *pg.* 852, *pg.* 1679
FRESHBREW COFFEE, LLC, 11600 Big John St, **Houston,** TX 77038-3302, *pg.* 857, *pg.* 1706
GLOBAL SMOOTHIE SUPPLY, INC., 4428 University Blvd, **Dallas,** TX 75205, *pg.* 858, *pg.* 1681
GRUMA CORPORATION, 1159 Cottonwood Ln Ste 200, **Irving,** TX 75038, *pg.* 860, *pg.* 1720
IMPERIAL SUGAR COMPANY, 3 Sugar Creek Center Blvd, **Sugar Land,** TX 77478, *pg.* 864, *pg.* 1746
LEON'S FINE FOODS, INC., 2100 N Redbud Blvd, **McKinney,** TX 75069, *pg.* 874, *pg.* 1727
OAK FARMS DAIRY, 3114 S Haskell Ave, **Dallas,** TX 75223-3100, *pg.* 887, *pg.* 1685
RIVIANA FOODS INC., 2777 Allen Pkwy, **Houston,** TX 77019-2141, *pg.* 892, *pg.* 1713
SABRA DIPPING COMPANY LLC, PO Box 660634, **Dallas,** TX 75266-0634, *pg.* 893, *pg.* 1686
SUREQUEST SYSTEMS, INC., 3330 Keller Springs Ste 205, **Carrollton,** TX 75006, *pg.* 900, *pg.* 1669
TURBOCHEF TECHNOLOGIES, INC., 2801 Trade Ctr, **Carrollton,** TX 75007, *pg.* 902, *pg.* 1670
WINDSOR QUALITY FOOD CO., LTD., 3355 W Alabama St Ste 730, **Houston,** TX 77098-1797, *pg.* 910, *pg.* 1717

Utah

JBS, 410 N 200 W, **Hyrum,** UT 84319-1024, *pg.* 865, *pg.* 1751
RHODES INTERNATIONAL, INC., PO Box 25487, **Salt Lake City,** UT 84123-0487, *pg.* 891, *pg.* 1760

Vermont

KEURIG GREEN MOUNTAIN, INC., 33 Coffee Ln, **Waterbury,** VT 05676-8900, *pg.* 868, *pg.* 1768

Virginia

CARGILL TURKEY PRODUCTS, 1 Kratzer Ave, **Harrisonburg,** VA 22802-4567, *pg.* 846, *pg.* 1784
THE C.F. SAUER COMPANY, 2000 W Broad St, **Richmond,** VA 23220-2006, *pg.* 847, *pg.* 1801
CUISINE SOLUTIONS, INC., 2800 Eisenhower Ave Ste 450, **Alexandria,** VA 22314, *pg.* 850, *pg.* 1770
HIGH LINER FOODS, 190 Enterprise Dr, **Newport News,** VA 23603, *pg.* 862, *pg.* 1796
MASSIMO ZANETTI BEVERAGE USA, 1370 Progress Rd, **Suffolk,** VA 23434, *pg.* 876, *pg.* 1808
NATIONAL FRUIT PRODUCT COMPANY, INC., 551 Fairmont Ave, **Winchester,** VA 22601-3931, *pg.* 882, *pg.* 1811
SAN-J INTERNATIONAL, INC., 2880 Sprouse Dr, **Richmond,** VA 23231-6039, *pg.* 893, *pg.* 1803
SMITHFIELD FOODS, INC., 200 Commerce St, **Smithfield,** VA 23430, *pg.* 896, *pg.* 1806
THE SMITHFIELD PACKING CO., INC., 501 N Church St PO Box 447, **Smithfield,** VA 23430, *pg.* 896, *pg.* 1807

Washington

AMERICAN SEAFOODS, LP, Marketplace Tower 2025 1st Ave Ste 900, **Seattle,** WA 98121, *pg.* 837, *pg.* 1833
DARIGOLD, INC., PO Box 34377, **Seattle,** WA 98124-1377, *pg.* 852, *pg.* 1835
HAELAN PRODUCTS, INC., 18568 142nd Ave NE Bldg F, **Woodinville,** WA 98072-8520, *pg.* 860, *pg.* 1847
ICICLE SEAFOODS, INC., 4019 21st Ave W, **Seattle,** WA 98199-1251, *pg.* 864, *pg.* 1836
KEY TECHNOLOGY, INC., 150 Avery St, **Walla Walla,** WA 99362, *pg.* 868, *pg.* 1847
MILNE FOOD PRODUCTS, INC., 804 Bennett Ave, **Prosser,** WA 99350-1267, *pg.* 877, *pg.* 1824
PETER PAN SEAFOODS, INC., 2200 6th Ave Ste 1000, **Seattle,** WA 98121, *pg.* 889, *pg.* 1838
STARBUCKS CORPORATION, 2401 Utah Ave S, **Seattle,** WA 98134, *pg.* 897, *pg.* 1840
TRANS OCEAN PRODUCTS INC., 350 West Orchard, **Bellingham,** WA 98225, *pg.* 901, *pg.* 1818
TREE TOP, INC., 220 E 2nd Ave, **Selah,** WA 98942-0248, *pg.* 901, *pg.* 1843
TRIDENT SEAFOODS CORPORATION, 5303 Shilshole Ave NW, **Seattle,** WA 98107-4000, *pg.* 902, *pg.* 1842
UNISEA FOODS, INC., 15400 NE 90th St Po 97019, **Redmond,** WA 98052-3524, *pg.* 906, *pg.* 1829

Wisconsin

ALTO-SHAAM INC., W 164 N 9221 Water St, **Menomonee Falls,** WI 53051-1401, *pg.* 836, *pg.* 1869
AMERICAN FOODS GROUP, LLC, 544 Acme St, **Green Bay,** WI 54302, *pg.* 837, *pg.* 1859
CHR. HANSEN, 9015 W Maple St, **Milwaukee,** WI 53214-4213, *pg.* 847, *pg.* 1873
COLONY BRANDS INC., 1112 7th Ave, **Monroe,** WI 53566-1364, *pg.* 849, *pg.* 1881
COOPERATIVE REGIONS OF ORGANIC PRODUCER POOLS, 1 Organic Way, **La Farge,** WI 54639, *pg.* 850, *pg.* 1864
FOREMOST FARMS USA COOPERATIVE, E 10889 A Penny Ln, **Baraboo,** WI 53913, *pg.* 856, *pg.* 1854
FRED USINGER, INC., 1030 N Old World 3rd St, **Milwaukee,** WI 53203-1302, *pg.* 856, *pg.* 1874
GLK FOODS, LLC, 158 E Northland Ave, **Appleton,** WI 54911, *pg.* 858, *pg.* 1852
JOHNSONVILLE SAUSAGE, LLC, N6928 Johnsonville Way, **Sheboygan Falls,** WI 53085, *pg.* 867, *pg.* 1894
JONES DAIRY FARM, 800 Jones Ave, **Fort Atkinson,** WI 53538, *pg.* 867, *pg.* 1858
KRAFT FOODS OSCAR MAYER, 910 Mayer Ave, **Madison,** WI 53704-4256, *pg.* 870, *pg.* 1866
LINK SNACKS, INC., 1 Snack Food Ln, **Minong,** WI 54859, *pg.* 874, *pg.* 1881
THE MASTERSON COMPANY, INC., 4023 W Natl Ave, **Milwaukee,** WI 53215, *pg.* 876, *pg.* 1877
PATRICK CUDAHY INC., 1 Sweet Apple Wood Ln, **Cudahy,**

WI 53110, *pg.* 888, *pg.* 1856

SARGENTO FOODS INC., 1 Persnickety Pl, **Plymouth,** WI 53073-3544, *pg.* 894, *pg.* 1886

SCHREIBER FOODS, INC., 425 Pine St, **Green Bay,** WI 54301-5137, *pg.* 894, *pg.* 1859

SENSIENT TECHNOLOGIES CORPORATION, 777 E Wisconsin Ave, **Milwaukee,** WI 53202-5304, *pg.* 895, *pg.* 1881

SUBCO FOODS OF WISCONSIN, 4350 S Taylor Dr, **Sheboygan,** WI 53081-8479, *pg.* 899, *pg.* 1894

Furniture, Floor Coverings & Decorations

Alabama

NATURAL DECORATIONS, INC., 777 Industrial Park Dr, **Brewton,** AL 36426, *pg.* 936, *pg.* 5

Arizona

ARIZONA WHOLESALE SUPPLY COMPANY, 2020 E Univ Dr, **Phoenix,** AZ 85034-6731, *pg.* 914, *pg.* 15
STONE CREEK FURNITURE INC., 4221 E Raymond St Ste 102, **Phoenix,** AZ 85040, *pg.* 944, *pg.* 20

California

3 DAY BLINDS, INC., 25 Technology Dr Ste B100, **Irvine,** CA 92618, *pg.* 912, *pg.* 105
BABY TREND, INC., 1607 S Campus Ave, **Ontario,** CA 91761, *pg.* 916, *pg.* 173
BOGDANCO CONSULTING, 541 F Cowper St, **Palo Alto,** CA 94301, *pg.* 918, *pg.* 174
BURKE INDUSTRIES, INC., 2250 S 10th St, **San Jose,** CA 95112-4114, *pg.* 919, *pg.* 239
CAESARSTONE, 6840 Hayvenhurst Ave. Suite 100, **Van Nuys,** CA 91406, *pg.* 919, *pg.* 299
CONKLIN BROS, 2250 Almaden Expy, **San Jose,** CA 95125, *pg.* 921, *pg.* 242
COST PLUS WORLD MARKET, 200 4th St, **Oakland,** CA 94607-4312, *pg.* 921, *pg.* 170
CROWN CRAFTS INFANT PRODUCTS, INC., 711 W Walnut St, **Compton,** CA 90220, *pg.* 922, *pg.* 68
DESIGN WITHIN REACH, INC., 2299 Alameda St, **San Francisco,** CA 94103, *pg.* 923, *pg.* 216
THE ENKEBOLL COMPANY, 16506 Avalon Blvd, **Carson,** CA 90746-1096, *pg.* 923, *pg.* 63
HUMAN TOUCH, 3030 Walnut Ave, **Long Beach,** CA 90807, *pg.* 928, *pg.* 123
IAC INDUSTRIES, INC., 895 Beacon St, **Brea,** CA 92821-2926, *pg.* 929, *pg.* 48
J. ROBERT SCOTT INC., 500 N Oak St, **Inglewood,** CA 90302, *pg.* 930, *pg.* 105
JBI, INC., 2650 E El Presidio St, **Long Beach,** CA 90810, *pg.* 930, *pg.* 123
RELAX THE BACK CORPORATION, 6 Centerpointe Dr Ste 350, **La Palma,** CA 90623, *pg.* 940, *pg.* 120
TROPITONE FURNITURE CO., INC., 5 Marconi, **Irvine,** CA 92618, *pg.* 945, *pg.* 118
VIRCO MANUFACTURING CORPORATION, 2027 Harpers Way, **Torrance,** CA 90501-1524, *pg.* 946, *pg.* 297
THE WICKER WORKS, 101 Henry Adams St Ste 136, **San Francisco,** CA 94103, *pg.* 946, *pg.* 233

Colorado

WM OHS INC., 5095 Peoria St, **Denver,** CO 80239, *pg.* 947, *pg.* 324

Connecticut

EDELMAN LEATHER, LLC, 80 Pickett District Rd, **New Milford,** CT 06776, *pg.* 923, *pg.* 359
ETHAN ALLEN INTERIORS INC., Ethan Allen Dr, **Danbury,** CT 06811, *pg.* 924, *pg.* 343
HISTORIC HOUSEFITTERS CO., INC., 287 New Milford Tpky, **Litchfield,** CT 06777, *pg.* 927, *pg.* 354
THE STANDARD MATTRESS COMPANY, 261 Weston St, **Hartford,** CT 06120-1209, *pg.* 943, *pg.* 352

Delaware

FLOOR CONCEPTS INC., 4315 Kirkwood Hwy, **Wilmington,** DE 19808, *pg.* 925, *pg.* 391

Florida

ACOUSTIC INNOVATIONS INC., 1101 Holland Dr Ste 17, **Boca Raton,** FL 33487-2734, *pg.* 912, *pg.* 409
BR-111 IMPORT & EXPORT, INC., 12800 NW 107th Ct, **Medley,** FL 33178, *pg.* 919, *pg.* 439
BUTLER CARPET COMPANY INC., 10815 US Hwy 19 N, **Clearwater,** FL 33764, *pg.* 919, *pg.* 415
CLOSETMAID CORPORATION, 650 SW 27th Ave, **Ocala,** FL 34471-2034, *pg.* 920, *pg.* 452
CONCRETE TECHNOLOGY INCORPORATED, 8770 133rd Ave, **Largo,** FL 33773, *pg.* 921, *pg.* 438
DREAM POLISHERS, INC., 2701 Ivy St, **Englewood,** FL 34224, *pg.* 923, *pg.* 422
EL DORADO FURNITURE CORP., 4200 NW 167th St, **Opa Locka,** FL 33054, *pg.* 923, *pg.* 452
EUROTECH CABINETRY, INC., 1609 Desoto Rd, **Sarasota,** FL 34234, *pg.* 924, *pg.* 466
THE GREAT AMERICAN HANGER COMPANY INC., 8250 NW 27th St Ste 304, **Miami,** FL 33122, *pg.* 926, *pg.* 442
HOLLANDER SLEEP PRODUCTS, 6501 Congress Ave, Ste 300, **Boca Raton,** FL 33487, *pg.* 927, *pg.* 411
INTERIORS BY STEVEN G INC., 2818 Centre Port Cir, **Pompano Beach,** FL 33064, *pg.* 929, *pg.* 459
KANE FURNITURE CORPORATION, 5700 70th Ave, **Pinellas Park,** FL 33781-4238, *pg.* 931, *pg.* 458
MARC-MICHAELS INTERIOR DESIGN, INC., 720 W Morse Blvd, **Winter Park,** FL 32789, *pg.* 934, *pg.* 480
PERLA LICHI LLC, 7381 W Sample Rd, **Coral Springs,** FL 33065, *pg.* 940, *pg.* 418
ROBB & STUCKY, LTD., 14550 Plantation Rd, **Fort Myers,** FL 33912, *pg.* 941, *pg.* 428
ROOMS TO GO.COM, INC., 11540 Hwy 92 E, **Seffner,** FL 33584, *pg.* 941, *pg.* 468
ROSARIO SALAZAR DESIGN INC., 358 San Lorenzo Ave #3215, **Coral Gables,** FL 33146, *pg.* 941, *pg.* 418
VICTORIA LESSER, INC., 1011 Truman Ave, **Key West,** FL 33040, *pg.* 946, *pg.* 436
WINDOWS OF THE WORLD, INC., 1855 Griffin Rd Ste A350, **Dania,** FL 33004, *pg.* 946, *pg.* 419
W.S. BADCOCK CORPORATION, 200 N Phosphate Blvd, **Mulberry,** FL 33860-2328, *pg.* 947, *pg.* 449

Georgia

AARON'S, INC., 309 E Paces Ferry Rd NE, **Atlanta,** GA 30305-2377, *pg.* 912, *pg.* 486
BEAULIEU GROUP, LLC, 1502 Coronet Dr, **Dalton,** GA 30720-2664, *pg.* 917, *pg.* 529
HAVERTY FURNITURE COMPANIES, INC., 780 Johnson Ferry Rd Ste 800, **Atlanta,** GA 30342, *pg.* 926, *pg.* 509
INTERFACE FLOORING SYSTEMS INC., 1503 Orchard Hill Rd, **Lagrange,** GA 30241-1503, *pg.* 929, *pg.* 534
LARSON-JUHL US LLC, 3900 Steve Reynolds Blvd, **Norcross,** GA 30093, *pg.* 933, *pg.* 537
MOHAWK HOME, 3090 Sugar Valley Rd NW, **Sugar Valley,** GA 30746-5166, *pg.* 935, *pg.* 541
MOHAWK INDUSTRIES, INC., 160 S Industrial Blvd, **Calhoun,** GA 30701-3030, *pg.* 935, *pg.* 527
RED BARON ANTIQUES INCORPORATED, 8655 Roswell Rd, **Atlanta,** GA 30350, *pg.* 940, *pg.* 519
SHAW INDUSTRIES GROUP, INC., PO Drawer 2128 616 E Walnut Ave, **Dalton,** GA 30722-2128, *pg.* 942, *pg.* 530
SIMMONS COMPANY, 1 Concourse Pkwy Ste 800, **Atlanta,** GA 30328-6188, *pg.* 943, *pg.* 520

Illinois

BAKER KNAPP & TUBBS INC., 222 Merchandise Mart Plz Ste 1414, **Chicago,** IL 60654, *pg.* 916, *pg.* 566
BELVEDERE USA CORPORATION, 1 Belvedere Blvd, **Belvidere,** IL 61008, *pg.* 917, *pg.* 556
CC INDUSTRIES, INC., 222 N La Salle St Ste 1000, **Chicago,** IL 60601, *pg.* 920, *pg.* 569
CENTURY SUPPLY CO. INC., 747 E Roosevelt Rd, **Lombard,** IL 60148-4742, *pg.* 920, *pg.* 631
CRATE & BARREL, INC., 1250 Techny Rd, **Northbrook,** IL 60062, *pg.* 922, *pg.* 640
DARVIN FURNITURE, 15400 La Grange Rd, **Orland Park,** IL 60462, *pg.* 922, *pg.* 649
EMPIRE TODAY, LLC, 333 NW Ave, **Northlake,** IL 60164, *pg.* 923, *pg.* 643
KING KOIL LICENSING COMPANY INC., 7501 S Quincy St Ste 130, **Willowbrook,** IL 60527, *pg.* 932, *pg.* 671
MILLER MULTIPLEX DISPLAY FIXTURE CO., 1610 Design Way, **Dupo,** IL 62239, *pg.* 935, *pg.* 609
NATIONAL BEDDING CO., 2600 Forbs Ave, **Hoffman Estates,** IL 60192, *pg.* 935, *pg.* 618
OLSON RUG COMPANY, 832 S Central Ave, **Chicago,** IL 60644-5501, *pg.* 939, *pg.* 586
RESTONIC MATTRESS CORPORATION, PO Box 755, **Antioch,** IL 60002, *pg.* 941, *pg.* 553
SERTA, INC., 2600 Forbs Ave, **Hoffman Estates,** IL 60192, *pg.* 942, *pg.* 619
THYBONY WALLCOVERINGS INC., 3445 N Kimball, **Chicago,** IL 60618, *pg.* 945, *pg.* 591

Indiana

BUSINESS FURNISHINGS LLC, 4102 Meghan Beeler Ct, **South Bend,** IN 46628-8408, *pg.* 919, *pg.* 697
DOREL JUVENILE GROUP, INC., 2525 State St, **Columbus,** IN 47201-7443, *pg.* 923, *pg.* 676
JASPER GROUP, 225 Clay St, **Jasper,** IN 47546-2821, *pg.* 930, *pg.* 691
JOFCO INC., 402 E 13th St, **Jasper,** IN 47546-2422, *pg.* 931, *pg.* 691
THE KARGES FURNITURE COMPANY, INC., 1501 W Maryland St, **Evansville,** IN 47719-1831, *pg.* 931, *pg.* 679
KIMBALL INTERNATIONAL, INC., 1600 Royal St, **Jasper,** IN 47549-1001, *pg.* 931, *pg.* 692

Iowa

FLEXSTEEL INDUSTRIES, INC., 385 Bell St, **Dubuque,** IA 52001, *pg.* 925, *pg.* 707
HNI CORPORATION, 408 E 2nd St, **Muscatine,** IA 52761-0071, *pg.* 927, *pg.* 709
THE HON COMPANY, 200 Oak St, **Muscatine,** IA 52761-4313, *pg.* 928, *pg.* 709

Kentucky

BROWN JORDAN INTERNATIONAL COMPANY, 20 Kingbrook Pkwy, **Simpsonville,** KY 40067, *pg.* 919, *pg.* 740
DMI FURNITURE, INC., 1 Oxmoor Pl 101 Bullitt Ln Ste 205, **Louisville,** KY 40222, *pg.* 923, *pg.* 733
OFFICE RESOURCES INC., 816 E Broadway, **Louisville,** KY 40204, *pg.* 939, *pg.* 737
OMEGA NATIONAL PRODUCTS, 1190 E Broadway, **Louisville,** KY 40204, *pg.* 939, *pg.* 737
TEMPUR SEALY INTERNATIONAL, INC., 1000 Tempur Way, **Lexington,** KY 40511, *pg.* 944, *pg.* 731

Louisiana

FIRESIDE ANTIQUES, 14007 Perkins Rd, **Baton Rouge,** LA 70810, *pg.* 925, *pg.* 742

Maine

ANGELA ADAMS, 273 Congress St, **Portland,** ME 04101, *pg.* 913, *pg.* 751
HUSSEY SEATING CO., 38 Dyer St Ext, **North Berwick,** ME 03906-6763, *pg.* 929, *pg.* 751
JEREMIAH CAMPBELL & COMPANY, 1537 Route 1, **Cape Neddick,** ME 03902-7432, *pg.* 931, *pg.* 749

Maryland

CARPET FAIR, INC., 7100 Rutherford Rd, **Baltimore,** MD 21244-2702, *pg.* 920, *pg.* 756
FRANK B. RHODES FURNITURE MAKER, 535 Morgnec Rd, **Chestertown,** MD 21620, *pg.* 925, *pg.* 766
MARLO FURNITURE CO., INC., 3300 Marlo Ln, **Forestville,** MD 20747, *pg.* 934, *pg.* 769

Massachusetts

COUNTRY CURTAINS RETAIL INC., 705 Pleasant St, **Lee,** MA 01238, *pg.* 921, *pg.* 827
JS INTERNATIONAL, INC., 485 Commerce Dr, **Fall River,** MA 02720, *pg.* 931, *pg.* 818
LISTA INTERNATIONAL CORPORATION, 106 Lowland St, **Holliston,** MA 01746, *pg.* 934, *pg.* 825
THE SERAPH, 420 Main St, **Sturbridge,** MA 01566, *pg.* 942, *pg.* 847
WITH HEART & HAND, 258 Dedham St Rte 1A, **Norfolk,** MA 02056, *pg.* 946, *pg.* 837

Michigan

ART VAN FURNITURE, INC., 6500 E 14 Mi Rd, **Warren,** MI 48092-1281, *pg.* 914, *pg.* 912
HERMAN MILLER, INC., 855 E Main Ave, **Zeeland,** MI 49464-1366, *pg.* 926, *pg.* 913
IRWIN SEATING COMPANY INC., 3251 Fruit Rdg Ave NW, **Grand Rapids,** MI 49544, *pg.* 929, *pg.* 887
KINDEL FURNITURE COMPANY, 4047 Eastern Ave SE, **Grand Rapids,** MI 49508, *pg.* 931, *pg.* 887
LA-Z-BOY INCORPORATED, 1 La-Z-Boy Drive, **Monroe,** MI 48162-5138, *pg.* 932, *pg.* 901
TRENDWAY CORPORATION, 13467 Quincy St, **Holland,** MI 49424, *pg.* 945, *pg.* 892

Minnesota

BELLACOR INC., 2425 Enterprise Dr Ste 900, **Mendota Heights,** MN 55120-1172, *pg.* 917, *pg.* 920
BLU DOT DESIGN & MANUFACTURING, INC., 1323 Tyler St NE, **Minneapolis,** MN 55413, *pg.* 918, *pg.* 931
HOM FURNITURE, INC., 10301 Woodcrest Dr NW, **Minneapolis,** MN 55433-6519, *pg.* 927, *pg.* 938
MARVIN WINDOWS & DOORS, 401 States Ave, **Warroad,** MN 56763, *pg.* 934, *pg.* 965
SELECT COMFORT CORPORATION, 9800 59th Ave N, **Minneapolis,** MN 55442, *pg.* 942, *pg.* 942

Missouri

THE COMMERCIAL FURNITURE GROUP, 10650 Gateway Blvd, **Saint Louis,** MO 63304-1102, *pg.* 920, *pg.* 994
HOWE FURNITURE CORPORATION, 10650 Gateway Blvd, **Saint Louis,** MO 63132, *pg.* 928, *pg.* 998
LEGGETT & PLATT, INCORPORATED, 1 Leggett Rd, **Carthage,** MO 64836, *pg.* 933, *pg.* 974

Nebraska

ZONGKERS CUSTOM FURNITURE, INC., 1717 S 3rd St, **Omaha,** NE 68108, *pg.* 947, *pg.* 1019

New Hampshire

CARLISLE WIDE PLANK FLOORS, INC., 1676 Rte 9, **Stoddard,** NH 03464, *pg.* 919, *pg.* 1039

New Jersey

ARTISTIC TILE INC., 520 Secaucus Rd, **Secaucus,** NJ 07094-2502, *pg.* 914, *pg.* 1119
BLINDS TO GO INC., 101 E State Rte 4, **Paramus,** NJ 07652, *pg.* 918, *pg.* 1101
CONGOLEUM CORPORATION, 3500 Quaker Bridge Rd, **Mercerville,** NJ 08619, *pg.* 921, *pg.* 1084
COURISTAN INC., 2 Executive Dr Ste 400, **Fort Lee,** NJ 07024-3308, *pg.* 921, *pg.* 1067
MANNINGTON MILLS, INC., 75 Mannington Mills Rd, **Salem,** NJ 08079, *pg.* 934, *pg.* 1119
MANNINGTON RESILIENT FLOORS, 75 Mannington Mills Rd, **Salem,** NJ 08079, *pg.* 934, *pg.* 1119
SCALAMANDRE, INC., 1130 Chestnut St, **Elizabeth,** NJ 07201, *pg.* 941, *pg.* 1058
SUBURBAN FURNITURE CORP., 10 State Rte 10 W, **Succasunna,** NJ 07876, *pg.* 944, *pg.* 1123
THERAPEDIC ASSOCIATES, INC., 103 College Rd E, **Princeton,** NJ 08540, *pg.* 945, *pg.* 1112
WAYNE TILE CO., 2 Doig Rd, **Wayne,** NJ 07470, *pg.* 946, *pg.* 1130
WHITE LOTUS HOME, 431 Raritan Ave, **Highland Park,** NJ 08904, *pg.* 946, *pg.* 1073

New York

ABC CARPET & HOME INC., 888 Broadway Fl 4, **New York,** NY 10003, *pg.* 912, *pg.* 1185
ADELPHI PAPER HANGINGS LLC, PO Box 135, **Sharon Springs,** NY 13459, *pg.* 912, *pg.* 1342
AFD CONTRACT FURNITURE, INC., 810 7th Ave, **New York,** NY 10019, *pg.* 912, *pg.* 1188
BUSH INDUSTRIES INC., 1 Mason Dr, **Jamestown,** NY 14701-9265, *pg.* 919, *pg.* 1170
CHF INDUSTRIES, INC., 1 Park Ave, **New York,** NY 10016, *pg.* 920, *pg.* 1211
F. SCHUMACHER & CO., 79 Madison Ave, **New York,** NY 10016-7802, *pg.* 925, *pg.* 1230
F.E. HALE MANUFACTURING COMPANY, 120 Benson Pl, **Frankfort,** NY 13340, *pg.* 925, *pg.* 1160
THE GUNLOCKE COMPANY, 1 Gunlocke Dr, **Wayland,** NY 14572-9515, *pg.* 926, *pg.* 1349
HARDEN FURNITURE INC., 8550 Mill Pond Way, **McConnellsville,** NY 13401-1800, *pg.* 926, *pg.* 1177
HUNTER DOUGLAS, INC., 1 Blue Hill Plz 20th Fl, **Pearl River,** NY 10965, *pg.* 928, *pg.* 1320
JENNIFER CONVERTIBLES INC., 417 Crossways Park Dr, **Woodbury,** NY 11797, *pg.* 931, *pg.* 1355
KRAVET FABRICS INC., 225 Central Ave S, **Bethpage,** NY 11714, *pg.* 932, *pg.* 1142
LEE JOFA, INC., 201 Central Ave S, **Bethpage,** NY 11714, *pg.* 933, *pg.* 1142
MURPHY BED CO., INC., 42 Central Ave, **Farmingdale,** NY 11735-6906, *pg.* 935, *pg.* 1159
RALPH PUCCI INTERNATIONAL LTD., 44 W 18th St, **New York,** NY 10011, *pg.* 940, *pg.* 1285
RAYMOUR & FLANIGAN FURNITURE CO., 7248 Morgan Rd, **Liverpool,** NY 13090, *pg.* 940, *pg.* 1174
SLEEPY'S, INC., 1000 S Oyster Bay Rd, **Hicksville,** NY 11801, *pg.* 943, *pg.* 1167
STARK CARPET CORPORATION, D&D Bldg 979 3rd Ave Fl 11, **New York,** NY 10022, *pg.* 944, *pg.* 1296
TELESCOPE CASUAL FURNITURE INC., 82 Church St, **Granville,** NY 12832-1621, *pg.* 944, *pg.* 1162
WILLIAM-WAYNE & COMPANY, 850 Lexington Ave & 64th St, **New York,** NY 10021, *pg.* 946, *pg.* 1314
WINDOWS AND WALLS UNLIMITED, INC., 375 County Road 39, **Southampton,** NY 11968, *pg.* 946, *pg.* 1343

North Carolina

AMERICAN DREW, 4620 Grandover Pkwy, **Greensboro,** NC 27407-8202, *pg.* 912, *pg.* 1374
BERNHARDT DESIGN, 1839 Morganton Blvd SW, **Lenoir,** NC 28645-5338, *pg.* 918, *pg.* 1381
BROYHILL FURNITURE INDUSTRIES, INC., 1 Broyhill Pk, **Lenoir,** NC 28633-0003, *pg.* 919, *pg.* 1381
CENTURY FURNITURE INDUSTRIES, 401 11th St NW, **Hickory,** NC 28601, *pg.* 920, *pg.* 1377
HERITAGE HOME GROUP, 1925 Eastchester Dr, **High Point,** NC 27265, *pg.* 926, *pg.* 1379
HICKORY CHAIR COMPANY, 37 9th St SE, **Hickory,** NC 28602, *pg.* 927, *pg.* 1378
HOME MERIDIAN INTERNATIONAL, INC., 3980 Premier Dr Ste 310, **High Point,** NC 27265, *pg.* 928, *pg.* 1379
KEWAUNEE SCIENTIFIC CORPORATION, 2700 W Front St, **Statesville,** NC 28677-2927, *pg.* 931, *pg.* 1391
KINGSDOWN, INC., 126 W Holt St, **Mebane,** NC 27302, *pg.* 932, *pg.* 1383
LANE VENTURE, INC., 1925 Eastchester Dr, **High Point,** NC 27265, *pg.* 933, *pg.* 1379
LEXINGTON HOME BRANDS, 1300 National Hwy, **Thomasville,** NC 27360, *pg.* 933, *pg.* 1391
MITCHELL GOLD & BOB WILLIAMS, 135 One Comfortable Pl, **Taylorsville,** NC 28681-6106, *pg.* 935, *pg.* 1391
RAUCH INDUSTRIES, INC., 2408 Forbes Rd, **Gastonia,** NC 28053, *pg.* 940, *pg.* 1373
SEALY CORPORATION, 1 Office Pkwy at Sealy Dr, **Trinity,** NC 27370-9449, *pg.* 942, *pg.* 1391
STANLEY FURNITURE CO., INC., 200 N Hamilton St, **High Point,** NC 27260, *pg.* 943, *pg.* 1379
STEARNS & FOSTER BEDDING COMPANY, 1 Office Parkway Rd, **Trinity,** NC 27370-9449, *pg.* 944, *pg.* 1392
THOMASVILLE FURNITURE INDUSTRIES, INC., 401 E Main St, **Thomasville,** NC 27360, *pg.* 945, *pg.* 1391
TOMLINSON/ERWIN-LAMBETH, INC., 201 E Holly Hill Rd, **Thomasville,** NC 27360-5819, *pg.* 945, *pg.* 1391

Ohio

CHILD CRAFT INDUSTRIES, INC., 5216 Portside Dr, **Medina,** OH 44256, *pg.* 920, *pg.* 1463
EVENFLO COMPANY, INC., 1801 Commerce Dr, **Piqua,** OH 45356, *pg.* 924, *pg.* 1470
SAUDER MANUFACTURING COMPANY, 930 W Barre Rd, **Archbold,** OH 43502-9320, *pg.* 941, *pg.* 1403
SAUDER WOODWORKING CO., 502 Middle St, **Archbold,** OH 43502-1559, *pg.* 941, *pg.* 1403
STANLEY STEEMER INTERNATIONAL, INC., 5800 Innovation Dr, **Dublin,** OH 43016, *pg.* 944, *pg.* 1450

Oklahoma

HOBBY LOBBY STORES INC., 7707 SW 44th St, **Oklahoma City,** OK 73179, *pg.* 927, *pg.* 1486

Oregon

ANTHRO CORPORATION, 10450 SW Manhasset Dr, **Tualatin,** OR 97062, *pg.* 913, *pg.* 1509

Pennsylvania

ARMSTRONG WORLD INDUSTRIES, INC., 2500 Columbia Ave, **Lancaster,** PA 17603, *pg.* 914, *pg.* 1545
BALL & BALL HARDWARE REPRODUCTIONS, 463 W Lincoln Hwy, **Exton,** PA 19341, *pg.* 916, *pg.* 1531
CONESTOGA WOOD SPECIALTIES CORP., 245 Reading Rd, **East Earl,** PA 17519-9549, *pg.* 921, *pg.* 1527
IKEA NORTH AMERICA SERVICES LLC, 420 Alan Wood Rd, **Conshohocken,** PA 19428, *pg.* 929, *pg.* 1523
MARTIN'S CHAIR, INC., 124 King Ct, **New Holland,** PA 17557, *pg.* 934, *pg.* 1556
RIO BRANDS, INC., 10981 Decatur Rd, **Philadelphia,** PA 19154-3210, *pg.* 941, *pg.* 1570
SURE FIT INC., 6575 Snowdrift Rd Ste 101, **Allentown,** PA 18106-9353, *pg.* 944, *pg.* 1514
UMF MEDICAL, 1316 Eisenhower Blvd, **Johnstown,** PA 15904-3307, *pg.* 946, *pg.* 1542
WOVEN LEGENDS INC., 4700 Wissahickon Ave, **Philadelphia,** PA 19144, *pg.* 947, *pg.* 1572
YORK WALLCOVERINGS INC., 750 Linden Ave, **York,** PA 17404-3364, *pg.* 947, *pg.* 1598

Tennessee

JAMISON BEDDING, INC., 550 E Park Ave, **Nashville,** TN 37066, *pg.* 930, *pg.* 1651

Texas

AMERICAN LEATHER LP, 4501 Mtn Creek Pkwy, **Dallas,** TX 75236, *pg.* 912, *pg.* 1673
CREATIVE BRANCH, 7246 Wynnwood Ln, **Houston,** TX 77008, *pg.* 922, *pg.* 1704
THE FANTASY GALLERY, 804 W Gray St, **Houston,** TX 77019-4317, *pg.* 925, *pg.* 1705
GALLERY MODEL HOMES, INC., 6006 N Fwy, **Houston,** TX 77076-4029, *pg.* 926, *pg.* 1706
IMPERIAL WOODWORKS, INC., 7201 Mars Dr, **Waco,** TX 76712, *pg.* 929, *pg.* 1749
THE MATTRESS FIRM, INC., 5815 Gulf Fwy, **Houston,** TX 77023-5341, *pg.* 934, *pg.* 1711
MATTRESS HOLDING CORP., 5815 Gulf Freeway, **Houston,** TX 77023, *pg.* 935, *pg.* 1711
NEUTRAL POSTURE, INC., 3904 N Texas Ave, **Bryan,** TX 77803-0555, *pg.* 939, *pg.* 1669
PIER 1 IMPORTS, INC., 100 Pier 1 Pl, **Fort Worth,** TX 76102-2600, *pg.* 940, *pg.* 1695
RENT-A-CENTER, INC., 5501 Headquarters Dr, **Plano,** TX 75024, *pg.* 940, *pg.* 1734
STAR FURNITURE COMPANY, 16666 Barker Springs Rd, **Houston,** TX 77084-5032, *pg.* 944, *pg.* 1715

Utah

LIFETIME PRODUCTS INC., Freeport Ctr Bldg D 11, **Clearfield,** UT 84016, *pg.* 933, *pg.* 1751
MITY ENTERPRISES, INC., 1301 W 400 N, **Orem,** UT 84057-4442, *pg.* 935, *pg.* 1753

Vermont

MCGUIRE FAMILY FURNITURE MAKERS, 239 Main St, **Isle La Motte,** VT 05440, *pg.* 935, *pg.* 1766
VERMONT CLOCK COMPANY, 239 Main St, **Isle La Motte,** VT 05463, *pg.* 946, *pg.* 1766

Virginia

First page reference indicates Business Class Edition
Second page reference indicates Geographic Edition

AMERICAN WOODMARK CORPORATION, 3102 Shawnee Dr, **Winchester,** VA 22601-4208, *pg.* 913, *pg.* 1811

BACOVA GUILD, LTD., 1000 Commerce Ctr Dr, **Covington,** VA 24426, *pg.* 916, *pg.* 1779

BASSETT FURNITURE INDUSTRIES, INCORPORATED, 3525 Fairystone Hwy, **Bassett,** VA 24055, *pg.* 916, *pg.* 1776

CARPENTER CO., 5016 Monument Ave, **Richmond,** VA 23230-3620, *pg.* 920, *pg.* 1801

CORT BUSINESS SERVICES CORPORATION, 15000 Conference Center Dr Ste 440, **Chantilly,** VA 20151-3841, *pg.* 921, *pg.* 1777

THE DUMP FURNITURE STORE, 5324 Virginia Beach Blvd, **Virginia Beach,** VA 23462, *pg.* 923, *pg.* 1810

HOOKER FURNITURE CORPORATION, 440 E Commonwealth Blvd, **Martinsville,** VA 24112-1831, *pg.* 928, *pg.* 1788

KINGSLEY-BATE, LTD., 7200 Gateway Ct, **Manassas,** VA 20109-7308, *pg.* 932, *pg.* 1787

NYDREE FLOORING, 1191 Venture Dr, **Forest,** VA 24551, *pg.* 939, *pg.* 1782

Washington

BINW, 10848 E Marginal Way S, **Seattle,** WA 98168, *pg.* 918, *pg.* 1833

SLEEP COUNTRY USA, INC., 6705 S 209th St, **Kent,** WA 98032, *pg.* 943, *pg.* 1822

Wisconsin

ASHLEY FURNITURE INDUSTRIES, INC., 1 Ashley Way, **Arcadia,** WI 54612-1218, *pg.* 914, *pg.* 1852

NEMSCHOFF, INC., 909 N 8th St, **Sheboygan,** WI 53081-4056, *pg.* 936, *pg.* 1890

SPRINGS WINDOW FASHIONS LLC, 7549 Graber Rd, **Middleton,** WI 53562-1001, *pg.* 943, *pg.* 1872

WATERLOO INDUSTRIES, INC., 139 W Forest Hill Avenue, **Oak Creek,** WI 53154, *pg.* 946, *pg.* 1885

Games, Toys, Etc.

California

505 GAMES (US), INC., 5008 Chesebro Rd, **Agoura Hills,** CA 91301, *pg.* 948, *pg.* 38
ACTIVISION BLIZZARD, INC., 3100 Ocean Park Blvd, **Santa Monica,** CA 90405, *pg.* 948, *pg.* 271
ATLUS USA, INC., 6400 Oak Cyn Ste 100, **Irvine,** CA 92618-5204, *pg.* 949, *pg.* 107
B. DAZZLE, INC., 500 Meyer Ln, **Redondo Beach,** CA 90278, *pg.* 949, *pg.* 188
BANDAI AMERICA INCORPORATED, 5551 Katella Ave, **Cypress,** CA 90630, *pg.* 950, *pg.* 75
BLIZZARD ENTERTAINMENT, PO Box 18979, **Irvine,** CA 92623-8979, *pg.* 950, *pg.* 107
CAPCOM USA, INC., 800 Concar Dr Ste 300, **San Mateo,** CA 94402-2649, *pg.* 950, *pg.* 254
EDUCATIONAL INSIGHTS, INC., 18730 S Wilmington Ave, **Rancho Dominguez,** CA 90220, *pg.* 951, *pg.* 187
ELECTRONIC ARTS INC., 209 Redwood Shores Pkwy, **Redwood City,** CA 94065-1175, *pg.* 951, *pg.* 189
FOLKMANIS, INC., 1219 Pk Ave, **Emeryville,** CA 94608, *pg.* 953, *pg.* 83
GAMEFLY, INC., 5340 Alla Rd Ste 110, **Los Angeles,** CA 90066, *pg.* 953, *pg.* 132
GLU MOBILE INC., 45 Fremont St Ste 2800, **San Francisco,** CA 94105, *pg.* 954, *pg.* 219
THE HAPPY COMPANY, 26203 Production Ave Ste 4, **Hayward,** CA 94545-3800, *pg.* 954, *pg.* 101
IMPERIAL TOY CORPORATION, 16641 Roscoe Pl, **North Hills,** CA 91343, *pg.* 957, *pg.* 166
INFANTINO, LLC, 4920 Carroll Canyon Road, Ste 200, **San Diego,** CA 92121, *pg.* 957, *pg.* 203
JADA TOYS, INC., 938 Hatcher Ave, **City of Industry,** CA 91748, *pg.* 960, *pg.* 67
JAKKS PACIFIC, INC., 22619 Pacific Coast Hwy Ste 250, **Malibu,** CA 90265-5080, *pg.* 960, *pg.* 142
JOSEPH ENTERPRISES, INC., 425 California St Ste 300, **San Francisco,** CA 94104, *pg.* 960, *pg.* 220
KONAMI CORPORATION OF AMERICA INC., 2381 Rosecrans Ave Ste 200, **El Segundo,** CA 90245-4922, *pg.* 960, *pg.* 80
LEAPFROG ENTERPRISES, INC., 6401 Hollis St Ste 100, **Emeryville,** CA 94608, *pg.* 961, *pg.* 84
MATTEL GAMES/PUZZLES, 333 Continental Blvd, **El Segundo,** CA 90245-5012, *pg.* 962, *pg.* 80
MATTEL, INC., 333 Continental Blvd, **El Segundo,** CA 90245-5012, *pg.* 962, *pg.* 81
MGA ENTERTAINMENT, INC., 16300 Roscoe Blvd Ste 150, **Van Nuys,** CA 91406, *pg.* 964, *pg.* 300
MUNCHKIN, INC., 7835 Gloria Ave, **Van Nuys,** CA 91406, *pg.* 964, *pg.* 300
PLAYMATES TOYS INC., 909 N Sepulveda Blvd Ste 800, **El Segundo,** CA 90245, *pg.* 965, *pg.* 82
PRO-LINE, INC., 201 W Lincoln St, **Banning,** CA 92220-4933, *pg.* 966, *pg.* 45
SEGA OF AMERICA INC., 350 Rhode Island St, **San Francisco,** CA 94103, *pg.* 966, *pg.* 227
SONY COMPUTER ENTERTAINMENT AMERICA LLC, 2207 Bridgepointe Pkwy, **San Mateo,** CA 94404, *pg.* 966, *pg.* 256
UNIVERSITY GAMES CORPORATION, 2030 Harrison St, **San Francisco,** CA 94110-1310, *pg.* 969, *pg.* 230
THE UPPER DECK COMPANY, LLC, 5909 Sea Otter Pl, **Carlsbad,** CA 92010, *pg.* 969, *pg.* 62
WHAM-O, INC., 6301 Owensmouth Ave Ste 700, **Woodland Hills,** CA 93167, *pg.* 969, *pg.* 308

Colorado

FRACTILES, INC., 2525 Arapahoe Ave Ste E4 110, **Boulder,** CO 80302, *pg.* 953, *pg.* 311

Connecticut

INNOVATIVE USA, INC., 50 Washington St Ste 201, **Norwalk,** CT 06854, *pg.* 957, *pg.* 363
LEGO SYSTEMS, INC., 555 Taylor Rd, **Enfield,** CT 06082, *pg.* 961, *pg.* 346

Florida

THE BRIDGE DIRECT, INC., 301 Yamato Rd Ste 2112, **Boca Raton,** FL 33431, *pg.* 950, *pg.* 410
THE WORLD OF MINIATURE BEARS, INC., 8011 NW 64th St, **Miami,** FL 33166, *pg.* 970, *pg.* 448

Georgia

FACTORY X DISTRIBUTION, 2840 Lafayette Rd, **Fort Oglethorpe,** GA 30742, *pg.* 953, *pg.* 532
MDI ENTERTAINMENT LLC, 1500 Bluegrass Lakes Pkwy, **Alpharetta,** GA 30004, *pg.* 964, *pg.* 484

Illinois

ELENCO ELECTRONICS, INC., 150 W Carpenter Ave, **Wheeling,** IL 60090, *pg.* 953, *pg.* 670
HOBBICO, INC., 2904 Research Rd, **Champaign,** IL 61822, *pg.* 956, *pg.* 562
RADIO FLYER INC., 6515 W Grand Ave, **Chicago,** IL 60707, *pg.* 966, *pg.* 588
REVELL, 1850 Howard St Unit A, **Elk Grove Village,** IL 60007, *pg.* 966, *pg.* 611
ROLLER DERBY SKATE CORP., PO Box 930, **Litchfield,** IL 62056, *pg.* 966, *pg.* 630
SRAM CORPORATION, 1333 N Kingsbury St No 4, **Chicago,** IL 60622-2641, *pg.* 967, *pg.* 590
THE TESTOR CORPORATION, 440 Blackhawk Ave, **Rockford,** IL 61104, *pg.* 968, *pg.* 655
TOMY, 2015 Spring Rd. Ste 400, **Oak Brook,** IL 60523, *pg.* 968, *pg.* 648
VTECH ELECTRONICS NORTH AMERICA, LLC, 1156 W Shure Dr Ste 200, **Arlington Heights,** IL 60004, *pg.* 969, *pg.* 554

Indiana

PRIMA GAMES, 199 Pearson Pkwy, **Lebanon,** IN 46052, *pg.* 965, *pg.* 693

Kentucky

THE UNITED STATES PLAYING CARD COMPANY, 300 Gap Way, **Erlanger,** KY 41018, *pg.* 969, *pg.* 727

Maryland

A&A GLOBAL INDUSTRIES INC., 17 Stenersen Ln, **Cockeysville,** MD 21030, *pg.* 948, *pg.* 767
LIFOAM INDUSTRIES INC., 235 Schilling Cir Ste 111, **Hunt Valley,** MD 21031, *pg.* 961, *pg.* 772

Massachusetts

GAMEWRIGHT, 70 Ridge St Ste 200, **Newton,** MA 02458, *pg.* 953, *pg.* 836
WINNING MOVES GAMES, INC., 75 Sylvan St Ste C-104, **Danvers,** MA 01923, *pg.* 970, *pg.* 816

Michigan

LIONEL LLC, 26750 23 Mile Rd, **Chesterfield,** MI 48051, *pg.* 961, *pg.* 875
SASSY, INC., 2305 Breton Indus Pk Dr SE, **Kentwood,** MI 49508, *pg.* 966, *pg.* 895

Missouri

BUILD-A-BEAR WORKSHOP, INC., 1954 Innerbelt Business Ctr Dr, **Saint Louis,** MO 63114, *pg.* 950, *pg.* 993
HANDI-CRAFT COMPANY, 4433 Fyler Ave, **Saint Louis,** MO 63116-1803, *pg.* 954, *pg.* 998
U.S. TOY CO., INC., 13201 Arrington Rd, **Grandview,** MO 64030-2886, *pg.* 969, *pg.* 978

Nevada

FORTUNET, INC., 2950 S Highland Dr Ste C, **Las Vegas,** NV 89109, *pg.* 953, *pg.* 1024
GAMING PARTNERS INTERNATIONAL CORPORATION, 1700 S Industrial Rd, **Las Vegas,** NV 89102-2620, *pg.* 954, *pg.* 1024
INTERNATIONAL GAME TECHNOLOGY, 6355 S Buffalo Dr, **Las Vegas,** NV 89113, *pg.* 957, *pg.* 1024

New Jersey

COASTAL AMUSEMENTS INC., 1935 Swarthmore Ave, **Lakewood,** NJ 08701, *pg.* 951, *pg.* 1078
GUND, INC., One Runyons Ln, **Edison,** NJ 08817, *pg.* 954, *pg.* 1056
REEVES INTERNATIONAL, INC., 14 Indus Rd, **Pequannock,** NJ 07440-1920, *pg.* 966, *pg.* 1108
TOYS "R" US, INC., 1 Geoffrey Way, **Wayne,** NJ 07470, *pg.* 968, *pg.* 1130

New York

4LICENSING CORPORATION, 767 3rd Ave 17th Fl, **New York,** NY 10017, *pg.* 948, *pg.* 1185
CROSMAN CORPORATION, 7629 Rtes 5 & 20, **Bloomfield,** NY 14469, *pg.* 951, *pg.* 1143
FISHER-PRICE, INC., 636 Girard Ave, **East Aurora,** NY 14052, *pg.* 953, *pg.* 1156
THE GOLDBERGER COMPANY, LLC, 36 W 25th St Fl 14, **New York,** NY 10010, *pg.* 954, *pg.* 1235
STRAT-O-MATIC GAME CO., INC., 46 Railroad Ave, **Glen Head,** NY 11545, *pg.* 968, *pg.* 1161
TONNER DOLL COMPANY, INC., 301 Wall St, **Kingston,** NY 12401, *pg.* 968, *pg.* 1171

Ohio

DUNCAN TOYS COMPANY, 15981 Valplast St, **Middlefield,** OH 44062-0005, *pg.* 951, *pg.* 1465
MAPLE CITY RUBBER COMPANY, 55 Newton St, **Norwalk,** OH 44857, *pg.* 962, *pg.* 1468
THE OHIO ART COMPANY, INC., One Toy St, **Bryan,** OH 43506-0111, *pg.* 965, *pg.* 1406
ZANER-BLOSER, INC., 1201 Dublin Rd, **Columbus,** OH 43215, *pg.* 970, *pg.* 1445

Pennsylvania

ALEXANDER DOLL COMPANY, INC., 805 Estelle Dr Ste 101, **Lancaster,** PA 17601, *pg.* 949, *pg.* 1545
BACHMANN INDUSTRIES, INC., 1400 E Erie Ave, **Philadelphia,** PA 19124, *pg.* 950, *pg.* 1559
CRAYOLA LLC, 1100 Church Ln, **Easton,** PA 18044, *pg.* 951, *pg.* 1528
GRACO CHILDREN'S PRODUCTS INC., 710 Stockton Dr, **Exton,** PA 19341, *pg.* 954, *pg.* 1531
MARTIN/F. WEBER COMPANY, 2727 Southampton Rd, **Philadelphia,** PA 19154-1293, *pg.* 962, *pg.* 1567

Rhode Island

HASBRO, INC., 1027 Newport Ave, **Pawtucket,** RI 02861-2539, *pg.* 954, *pg.* 1603

Texas

CARTA MUNDI, INC., 5101 Highland Pl Dr, **Dallas,** TX 75236, *pg.* 951, *pg.* 1677
ID SOFTWARE, INC., 3819 Towne Crossing Blvd, **Mesquite,** TX 75150-6123, *pg.* 956, *pg.* 1727
PRESSMAN TOY CORPORATION, 3701 W Plano Pkwy Ste 100, **Plano,** TX 75075, *pg.* 965, *pg.* 1734
SPEED COMMERCE, INC., 1303 E Arapaho Rd Ste 200, **Richardson,** TX 75081, *pg.* 967, *pg.* 1737

Vermont

THE VERMONT TEDDY BEAR COMPANY, 6655 Shelburne Rd, **Shelburne,** VT 05482-6500, *pg.* 969, *pg.* 1767

Virginia

THE BABY JOGGER COMPANY, # 1000 8575 Magellan Pkwy, **Richmond,** VA 23227-1150, *pg.* 949, *pg.* 1800

First page reference indicates Business Class Edition
Second page reference indicates Geographic Edition

Washington

MICROSOFT GAME STUDIOS, 1 Microsoft Way, **Redmond,** WA 98052-6399, *pg.* 964, *pg.* 1828
NINTENDO OF AMERICA, INC., 4600 150th Ave NE, **Redmond,** WA 98052-5111, *pg.* 965, *pg.* 1829
OOZ & OZ INC., 3624 46 Ave SW, **Seattle,** WA 98116, *pg.* 965, *pg.* 1838
WIZARDS OF THE COAST, INC., 1600 Lind Ave SW, **Renton,** WA 98055-4068, *pg.* 970, *pg.* 1830
XBOX, 1 Microsoft Way, **Redmond,** WA 98052-6399, *pg.* 970, *pg.* 1829

Wisconsin

AMERICAN GIRL LLC, 8400 Fairway Pl, **Middleton,** WI 53562-2548, *pg.* 949, *pg.* 1871

Gasoline & Lubricants

Alabama

HUNT REFINING COMPANY INC., 1855 Fairlawn Rd, **Tuscaloosa,** AL 35401, *pg.* 979, *pg.* 8

Alaska

BP EXPLORATION (ALASKA) INC., 900 E Benson Blvd, **Anchorage,** AK 99508-4254, *pg.* 973, *pg.* 10

Arizona

EGPI FIRECREEK, INC., 6564 Smoke Tree Ln, **Scottsdale,** AZ 85253, *pg.* 976, *pg.* 21

Arkansas

MURPHY OIL CORPORATION, 200 Peach St, **El Dorado,** AR 71730, *pg.* 982, *pg.* 31

California

CHEVRON CORPORATION, 6001 Bollinger Canyon Rd, **San Ramon,** CA 94583, *pg.* 974, *pg.* 259
CLEAN ENERGY FUELS CORP., 4675 MacArthur Ct Ste 800, **Newport Beach,** CA 92660, *pg.* 974, *pg.* 165
PACIFIC ETHANOL, INC., 400 Capitol Mall St 2060, **Sacramento,** CA 95814, *pg.* 982, *pg.* 197
ROYALE ENERGY, INC., 7676 Hazard Ctr Dr Ste 1500, **San Diego,** CA 92108-4503, *pg.* 984, *pg.* 208
WYNN OIL COMPANY, 1505 S Dupont Ave, Unit #I, **Ontario,** CA 91761, *pg.* 987, *pg.* 173

Colorado

MAGELLAN PETROLEUM CORPORATION, 1775 Sherman St Ste 1950, **Denver,** CO 80203, *pg.* 981, *pg.* 321
MARKWEST ENERGY PARTNERS, L.P., 1515 Arapahoe St Tower 1 Ste 1600, **Denver,** CO 80202-2137, *pg.* 981, *pg.* 321
TRANSMONTAIGNE, INC., 1670 Broadway Ste 3100, **Denver,** CO 80202, *pg.* 986, *pg.* 323

Georgia

G-P GYPSUM CORPORATION, 133 Peach Tree St Fl 8, **Atlanta,** GA 30303, *pg.* 978, *pg.* 505
RACETRAC PETROLEUM, INC., 3225 Cumberland Blvd Ste 100, **Atlanta,** GA 30339-6408, *pg.* 983, *pg.* 519
RPC, INC., 2801 Buford Hwy Ste 520, **Atlanta,** GA 30329, *pg.* 984, *pg.* 519

Illinois

BP CORPORATION NORTH AMERICA INC., 28301 Ferry Rd, **Warrenville,** IL 60555-3018, *pg.* 973, *pg.* 665
ITW FLUIDS NORTH AMERICA, 3624 W Lk Ave, **Glenview,** IL 60026, *pg.* 980, *pg.* 614
TENNECO, INC., 500 N Field Dr, **Lake Forest,** IL 60045-2595, *pg.* 985, *pg.* 625

Indiana

D-A LUBRICANT COMPANY, 801 Edwards Dr, **Lebanon,** IN 46052, *pg.* 975, *pg.* 693

Iowa

RENEWABLE ENERGY GROUP, INC., 416 S Bell Ave PO Box 888, **Ames,** IA 50010, *pg.* 984, *pg.* 701

Kansas

FERRELLGAS PARTNERS, L.P., 7500 College Blvd Ste 1000, **Overland Park,** KS 66210, *pg.* 977, *pg.* 718

Kentucky

ASHLAND INC., 50 E RiverCenter Blvd, PO Box 391, **Covington,** KY 41012-0391, *pg.* 972, *pg.* 726

Louisiana

COMPLEX CHEMICALS COMPANY, INC., 177 Complex Chemical Rd PO Box 1352, **Tallulah,** LA 71284, *pg.* 974, *pg.* 748
EPL OIL & GAS, INC., 201 St Charles Ave Ste 3400, **New Orleans,** LA 70170-3400, *pg.* 976, *pg.* 746

Maryland

CROWN CENTRAL LLC, 1 N Charles St Ste 2100, **Baltimore,** MD 21201-3740, *pg.* 975, *pg.* 756

Massachusetts

ENERNOC, INC., One Marina Park Dr Ste 400, **Boston,** MA 02110, *pg.* 976, *pg.* 794
EVERSOURCE, 800 Boylston St, **Boston,** MA 02199-8003, *pg.* 977, *pg.* 794
GULF OIL LIMITED PARTNERSHIP, 90 Everett Ave, **Chelsea,** MA 02150-2337, *pg.* 978, *pg.* 814

Michigan

AMERICAN GREASE STICK CO., 2651 Hoyt St, **Muskegon Heights,** MI 49444-2141, *pg.* 971, *pg.* 902
CHEM-TREND LIMITED PARTNERSHIP, 1445 McPherson Park Dr, **Howell,** MI 48843-3947, *pg.* 973, *pg.* 892

Mississippi

ERGON, INC., 2829 Lakeland Dr, **Jackson,** MS 39232, *pg.* 976, *pg.* 969

Missouri

ABENGOA BIOENERGY CORP., 16150 Main Cricle Dr Ste 300, **Chesterfield,** MO 63017, *pg.* 971, *pg.* 974
J.D. STREETT & CO., INC., 144 Weldon Pkwy, **Maryland Heights,** MO 63043-3102, *pg.* 980, *pg.* 988
THE LACLEDE GROUP, INC., 720 Olive St, **Saint Louis,** MO 63101, *pg.* 980, *pg.* 999
MFA OIL COMPANY, 1 Ray Young Dr, **Columbia,** MO 65201, *pg.* 981, *pg.* 976

Nevada

SOUTHWEST GAS CORPORATION, 5241 Spring Mountain Rd, **Las Vegas,** NV 89193, *pg.* 984, *pg.* 1029

New Hampshire

IRVING OIL CORPORATION, 190 Commerce Way, **Portsmouth,** NH 03801, *pg.* 980, *pg.* 1038

New Jersey

BEL-RAY COMPANY, INC., Bowman Ave, **Wall,** NJ 07719, *pg.* 972, *pg.* 1128
CASTROL NORTH AMERICA INC., 1500 Valley Rd, **Wayne,** NJ 07470-2040, *pg.* 973, *pg.* 1129
FISKE BROTHERS REFINING COMPANY, 129 Lockwood St, **Newark,** NJ 07105, *pg.* 978, *pg.* 1096
HALOCARBON PRODUCTS CORPORATION, 887 Kinderkamack Rd, **River Edge,** NJ 07661-2307, *pg.* 978, *pg.* 1116
KRONOS WORLDWIDE, INC., 5 Cedarbrook Dr, **Cranbury,** NJ 08512, *pg.* 980, *pg.* 1053
LUBRIPLATE LUBRICANTS, 129 Lockwood St, **Newark,** NJ 07105, *pg.* 980, *pg.* 1097

New York

CH ENERGY GROUP, INC., 284 South Ave, **Poughkeepsie,** NY 12601, *pg.* 973, *pg.* 1324
HESS CORPORATION, 1185 Ave of the Americas, **New York,** NY 10036, *pg.* 979, *pg.* 1240
INCOMING INC., 244 5th Ave Ste V235, **New York,** NY 10001, *pg.* 979, *pg.* 1243
NATIONAL FUEL GAS COMPANY, 6363 Main St, **Williamsville,** NY 14221, *pg.* 982, *pg.* 1355
TRAMMO, 320 Park Ave 10th Fl, **New York,** NY 10022-6022, *pg.* 986, *pg.* 1304
UNITED STATES OIL & GAS CORPORATION, 9322 3rd Ave Ste 475, **Brooklyn,** NY 11209, *pg.* 986, *pg.* 1147

North Dakota

MDU RESOURCES GROUP, INC., 1200 W Century Ave PO Box 5650, **Bismarck,** ND 58506-5650, *pg.* 981, *pg.* 1397

Ohio

ENGLEFIELD OIL COMPANY, 447 James Pkwy, **Heath,** OH 43056-1030, *pg.* 976, *pg.* 1455
MARATHON PETROLEUM COMPANY LLC, 539 S Main St, **Findlay,** OH 45840, *pg.* 981, *pg.* 1454
MATHESON VALLEY, 6500 Rockside Rd Ste 200, **Independence,** OH 44131, *pg.* 981, *pg.* 1456
SPEEDWAY LLC, 500 Speedway Dr, **Enon,** OH 45323, *pg.* 985, *pg.* 1452

Oklahoma

DEVON ENERGY CORPORATION, 333 W Sheridan Ave, **Oklahoma City,** OK 73102, *pg.* 975, *pg.* 1485
ONEOK, INC., 100 W 5th St, **Tulsa,** OK 74103-4240, *pg.* 982, *pg.* 1490
THE WILLIAMS COMPANIES, INC., 1 Williams Ctr, **Tulsa,** OK 74172, *pg.* 987, *pg.* 1491

Pennsylvania

OMEGA FLEX, INC., 451 Creamery Way, **Exton,** PA 19341, *pg.* 982, *pg.* 1532
STONER INC., 1070 Robert Fulton Hwy, **Quarryville,** PA 17566, *pg.* 985, *pg.* 1583
SUNOCO INC., 1818 Market St Ste 1500, **Philadelphia,** PA 19103, *pg.* 985, *pg.* 1571
UNITED REFINING COMPANY, 15 Bradley St, **Warren,** PA 16365-3224, *pg.* 986, *pg.* 1590

Tennessee

DELEK US HOLDINGS, INC., 7102 Commerce Way, **Brentwood,** TN 37027, *pg.* 975, *pg.* 1627
PILOT CORPORATION, 5508 Lonas Rd, **Knoxville,** TN 37909-3221, *pg.* 983, *pg.* 1637
TRI STAR ENERGY, LLC, 1740 Ed Temple Blvd, **Nashville,** TN 37208-1850, *pg.* 986, *pg.* 1655

Texas

ALON USA ENERGY, INC., 12700 Park Central Dr Ste 1600, **Dallas,** TX 75251, *pg.* 971, *pg.* 1673
ANADARKO PETROLEUM CORPORATION, 1201 Lake Robbins Dr, **The Woodlands,** TX 77380, *pg.* 971, *pg.* 1746
BLUE DOLPHIN ENERGY COMPANY, 801 Travis St Ste 2100, **Houston,** TX 77002-5705, *pg.* 972, *pg.* 1701
BP AMERICA INC., 501 Westlake Park Blvd, **Houston,** TX 77079-2604, *pg.* 972, *pg.* 1702
CGGVERITAS SERVICES (U.S.) INC., 10300 Town Park Dr, **Houston,** TX 77072-5236, *pg.* 973, *pg.* 1703
CITGO PETROLEUM CORPORATION, 1293 Eldridge Pkwy, **Houston,** TX 77077-1670, *pg.* 974, *pg.* 1703
CONOCOPHILLIPS, 600 N Dairy Ashford, **Houston,** TX 77079-1100, *pg.* 975, *pg.* 1703
CROSSTEX ENERGY, L.P., 2501 Cedar Springs, **Dallas,** TX 75201-7684, *pg.* 975, *pg.* 1678
DEVON ENERGY CORPORATION, 1200 Smith St Ste 3300, **Houston,** TX 77002-4400, *pg.* 976, *pg.* 1704
DYNEGY, INC., 1000 Louisiana St Ste 5800, **Houston,** TX 77002, *pg.* 976, *pg.* 1705
ENTERPRISE PRODUCTS PARTNERS L.P., 1100 Louisiana St 10th Fl, **Houston,** TX 77002, *pg.* 976, *pg.* 1705
EXCENTUS CORPORATION, 14241 Dallas Pkwy Ste 1200, **Dallas,** TX 75254, *pg.* 977, *pg.* 1681
EXTERRAN HOLDINGS, INC., 16666 Northchase Dr,

First page reference indicates Business Class Edition
Second page reference indicates Geographic Edition

Houston, TX 77060, *pg.* 977, *pg.* 1705
EXXON MOBIL CORPORATION, 5959 Las Colinas Blvd, **Irving,** TX 75039-2298, *pg.* 977, *pg.* 1718
GEOKINETICS INC., 1500 City West Blvd Ste 800, **Houston,** TX 77042, *pg.* 978, *pg.* 1706
HALLIBURTON COMPANY, 3000 N Sam Houston Pkwy E, **Houston,** TX 77032, *pg.* 978, *pg.* 1707
HKN, INC., 180 State St Ste 200, **Southlake, TX** 76092, *pg.* 979, *pg.* 1745
HMT LLC, 24 Waterway Ave Ste 400, **The Woodlands,** TX 77380, *pg.* 979, *pg.* 1747
HUNTING COMPANY, US OFFICE, 2 Northpoint Dr Ste 400, **Houston,** TX 77060, *pg.* 979, *pg.* 1708
HYDROTEX PARTNERS LTD., 12920 Senlac Dr Ste 190, **Farmers Branch,** TX 75234-9237, *pg.* 979, *pg.* 1692
HYPERDYNAMICS CORPORATION, 12012 Wickchester Ln #475, **Houston,** TX 77079, *pg.* 979, *pg.* 1708
KRONOS INTERNATIONAL, INC., 5430 LBJ Freeway Ste 1700, **Dallas,** TX 75240-2697, *pg.* 980, *pg.* 1683
LYONDELLBASELL INDUSTRIES, 1221 McKinney St, **Houston,** TX 77010, *pg.* 980, *pg.* 1710
M-I SWACO, 5950 N Course Dr, **Houston,** TX 77072, *pg.* 980, *pg.* 1710
MARATHON OIL CORPORATION, 5555 San Felipe Rd, **Houston,** TX 77056-2723, *pg.* 981, *pg.* 1710
NEWPARK RESOURCES, INC., 2700 Research Forest Dr Ste 100, **The Woodlands,** TX 77381, *pg.* 982, *pg.* 1747
OCCIDENTAL OIL & GAS CORPORATION, 5 E Greeway Plz Ste 110, **Houston,** TX 77046, *pg.* 982, *pg.* 1712
PARKER DRILLING COMPANY, 5 Greenway Plz Ste 100, **Houston,** TX 77046, *pg.* 982, *pg.* 1712
PLAINS ALL AMERICAN PIPELINE, L.P., 333 Clay St Ste 1600, **Houston,** TX 77002, *pg.* 983, *pg.* 1712
POWER SERVICE PRODUCTS, INC., 513 Peaster Hwy, **Weatherford,** TX 76086, *pg.* 983, *pg.* 1749
QUICKSILVER RESOURCES INC., 801 Cherry St Ste 3700 Unit 19, **Fort Worth,** TX 76102, *pg.* 983, *pg.* 1696
ROWAN COMPANIES, INC., 2800 Post Oak Blvd Ste 5450, **Houston,** TX 77056-6189, *pg.* 984, *pg.* 1713
SASOL NORTH AMERICA INC., 900 Threadneedle Ste 100, **Houston,** TX 77079-2990, *pg.* 984, *pg.* 1713
SHELL OIL COMPANY, 1 Shell Plz 910 Louisiana, **Houston,** TX 77002, *pg.* 984, *pg.* 1714
STALLION OILFIELD SERVICES, INC., 950 Corbindale Rd Ste 300, **Houston,** TX 77024, *pg.* 985, *pg.* 1715
STEWART & STEVENSON, LLC, 1000 Louisiana Ste 5900, **Houston,** TX 77002, *pg.* 985, *pg.* 1715
SUSSER HOLDINGS CORPORATION, 4525 Ayers St, **Corpus Christi,** TX 78415, *pg.* 985, *pg.* 1671
TETRA TECHNOLOGIES, INC., 24955 I 45 N, **The Woodlands,** TX 77380, *pg.* 986, *pg.* 1747
TEXAS REFINERY CORP., 1 Refinery Pl 840 N Main St, **Fort Worth,** TX 76106, *pg.* 986, *pg.* 1696
VALERO ENERGY CORPORATION, 1 Valero Way, **San Antonio,** TX 78249, *pg.* 986, *pg.* 1743
WEATHERFORD PRODUCTION OPTIMIZATION, 22001 N Park Dr, **Kingwood,** TX 77339, *pg.* 987, *pg.* 1725
ZION OIL & GAS, INC., 6510 Abrams Rd Ste 300, **Dallas,** TX 75231, *pg.* 987, *pg.* 1691

Utah

FJ MANAGEMENT, INC., 185 S State St, Ste 201, **Salt Lake City,** UT 84111, *pg.* 978, *pg.* 1758
HEADWATERS INCORPORATED, 10653 S River Front Pkwy Ste 300, **South Jordan,** UT 84095, *pg.* 978, *pg.* 1763
QUESTAR CORPORATION, 333 S State St, **Salt Lake City,** UT 84111, *pg.* 983, *pg.* 1760
SINCLAIR OIL CORPORATION, 550 E S Temple PO Box 30825, **Salt Lake City,** UT 84102-1005, *pg.* 984, *pg.* 1760

Virginia

NEWMARKET CORPORATION, 330 S 4th St, **Richmond,** VA 23219-4350, *pg.* 982, *pg.* 1803

Washington

BARDAHL MANUFACTURING CORPORATION, 1400 NW 52nd St, **Seattle,** WA 98127-5131, *pg.* 972, *pg.* 1833

Wisconsin

AMSOIL INC., 925 Tower Ave, **Superior,** WI 54880, *pg.* 971, *pg.* 1896

Government & State Agencies

Alabama

ALABAMA BUREAU OF TOURISM & TRAVEL, 401 Adams Ave Ste 126, **Montgomery,** AL 36104-4325, *pg.* 988, *pg.* 7

Alaska

ALASKA DEPARTMENT OF COMMERCE, COMMUNITY & ECONOMIC DEVELOPMENT, PO Box 110800, **Juneau,** AK 99811-0801, *pg.* 988, *pg.* 10

Arizona

ARIZONA LOTTERY, 4740 E University Dr, **Phoenix,** AZ 85034-7400, *pg.* 988, *pg.* 14

ARIZONA OFFICE OF TOURISM, 1110 W Washington Ste 155, **Phoenix,** AZ 85007, *pg.* 988, *pg.* 14

GREATER PHOENIX CHAMBER OF COMMERCE, Chase Tower 201 N Central Ave 27th Fl, **Phoenix,** AZ 85004, *pg.* 994, *pg.* 16

METROPOLITAN TUCSON CONVENTION & VISITORS BUREAU, 100 S Church Ave, **Tucson,** AZ 85701-1631, *pg.* 998, *pg.* 27

Arkansas

ARKANSAS DEPARTMENT OF ECONOMIC DEVELOPMENT, 900 W Capitol Ste 400, **Little Rock,** AR 72201-1049, *pg.* 988, *pg.* 33

ARKANSAS DEPARTMENT OF PARKS & TOURISM, 1 Capitol Mall 4A 900, **Little Rock,** AR 72201-1049, *pg.* 988, *pg.* 33

HOT SPRINGS CONVENTION & VISITORS BUREAU, 134 Convention Blvd, **Hot Springs National Park,** AR 71901-4135, *pg.* 995, *pg.* 33

California

ANAHEIM/ORANGE COUNTY VISITOR & CONVENTION BUREAU, 800 W Katella Ave, **Anaheim,** CA 92802-3415, *pg.* 988, *pg.* 42

CALIFORNIA DEPARTMENT OF CONSERVATION, 801 K St MS 24-01, **Sacramento,** CA 95814, *pg.* 989, *pg.* 195

CALIFORNIA DEPARTMENT OF CONSUMER AFFAIRS, 1625 N Market Blvd, **Sacramento,** CA 95834, *pg.* 990, *pg.* 195

CALIFORNIA LOTTERY, 598 N 10th St, **Sacramento,** CA 95811, *pg.* 990, *pg.* 196

CALIFORNIA TRAVEL & TOURISM COMMISSION, 555 Capitol Mall, Fl 11, **Sacramento,** CA 95814, *pg.* 990, *pg.* 196

LOS ANGELES CONVENTION & VISITORS BUREAU, 333 S Hope St 18th Fl, **Los Angeles,** CA 90071, *pg.* 997, *pg.* 135

MEXICO TOURISM BOARD, 2401 W 6th St, **Los Angeles,** CA 90057, *pg.* 998, *pg.* 136

PALM SPRINGS DESERT RESORTS CONVENTION & VISITORS AUTHORITY, 70-100 Hwy 111, **Rancho Mirage,** CA 92270-2853, *pg.* 1003, *pg.* 187

SAN DIEGO CONVENTION & VISITORS BUREAU, 750 B St Ste 1500, **San Diego,** CA 92101-8131, *pg.* 1004, *pg.* 208

SAN FRANCISCO TRAVEL ASSOCIATION, 1 Front St, Ste 2900, **San Francisco,** CA 94111, *pg.* 1005, *pg.* 227

SAN JOSE CONVENTION/VISITORS BUREAU, 408 Almaden Blvd, **San Jose,** CA 95110, *pg.* 1005, *pg.* 250

TAHITI TOURISME NORTH AMERICA, INC., 300 Continental Blvd Ste 160, **El Segundo,** CA 90245, *pg.* 1007, *pg.* 83

TOURISM AUSTRALIA, 6100 Ctr Dr Ste 1150, **Los Angeles,** CA 90045, *pg.* 1007, *pg.* 140

TOURISM NEW ZEALAND, 501 Santa Monica Blvd Ste 300, **Santa Monica,** CA 90401, *pg.* 1008, *pg.* 276

Colorado

COLORADO TOURISM OFFICE, 1625 Broadway Ste 2700, **Denver,** CO 80202-4725, *pg.* 991, *pg.* 318

DENVER METRO CONVENTION & VISITORS BUREAU, 1555 California St Ste 300, **Denver,** CO 80202-4200, *pg.* 991, *pg.* 318

ESTES PARK CONVENTION & VISITORS BUREAU, 500 Big Thompson Ave, **Estes Park,** CO 80517-9649, *pg.* 992, *pg.* 328

Connecticut

CERC, 805 Brook St Bldg 4, **Rocky Hill,** CT 06067, *pg.* 990, *pg.* 369

Delaware

DELAWARE TOURISM OFFICE, 99 Kings Hwy, **Dover,** DE 19901, *pg.* 991, *pg.* 387

District of Columbia

BROADCASTING BOARD OF GOVERNORS, 330 Independence Ave SW, **Washington,** DC 20237, *pg.* 989, *pg.* 396

D.C. LOTTERY & CHARITABLE GAMES CONTROL BOARD, 2101 Martin Luther King Jr Ave SE, **Washington,** DC 20020-5731, *pg.* 991, *pg.* 398

DESTINATION DC, 901 7th St NW 4th Fl, **Washington,** DC 20001, *pg.* 991, *pg.* 398

NATIONAL AERONAUTICS & SPACE ADMINISTRATION (NASA), 300 E St SW, **Washington,** DC 20024-3210, *pg.* 1000, *pg.* 401

NATIONAL PARK FOUNDATION, 1201 Eye St Ste 550B, **Washington,** DC 20005, *pg.* 1000, *pg.* 402

UNITED STATES ARMY, 1500 Army Pentagon, **Washington,** DC 20310-1500, *pg.* 1008, *pg.* 405

UNITED STATES COAST GUARD, 2100 Second St SW, **Washington,** DC 20593, *pg.* 1008, *pg.* 406

UNITED STATES DEPARTMENT OF ENERGY, 1000 Independence Ave SW, **Washington,** DC 20585-0001, *pg.* 1008, *pg.* 406

UNITED STATES DEPARTMENT OF STATE, 2201 C St NW, **Washington,** DC 20520-0001, *pg.* 1008, *pg.* 406

UNITED STATES DEPARTMENT OF THE INTERIOR, 1849 C St NW, **Washington,** DC 20240-0001, *pg.* 1009, *pg.* 406

UNITED STATES ENVIRONMENTAL PROTECTION AGENCY, Ariel Rios Bldg 1200 Pennsylvania Ave NW, **Washington,** DC 20460-0001, *pg.* 1009, *pg.* 406

UNITED STATES POSTAL SERVICE, 475 L'Enfant Plz SW, **Washington,** DC 20260-0004, *pg.* 1009, *pg.* 406

U.S. DEPARTMENT OF HOUSING & URBAN DEVELOPMENT, 451 7th St SW, **Washington,** DC 20410, *pg.* 1009, *pg.* 407

U.S. DEPARTMENT OF VETERANS AFFAIRS, 810 Vermont Ave NW, **Washington,** DC 20420, *pg.* 1009, *pg.* 407

VOICE OF AMERICA, 330 Independence Ave SW, **Washington,** DC 20237-0001, *pg.* 1010, *pg.* 407

Florida

DAYTONA BEACH RESORT AREA CONVENTION & VISITORS BUREAU, 126 E Orange Ave, **Daytona Beach,** FL 32114-4406, *pg.* 991, *pg.* 420

ENTERPRISE FLORIDA, INC., 800 N Magnolia Ave Ste 1100, **Orlando,** FL 32803, *pg.* 992, *pg.* 453

FLORIDA DEPARTMENT OF AGRICULTURE & CONSUMER SERVICES - DIVISION OF MARKETING & DEVELOPMENT, 407 S Calhoun St, **Tallahassee,** FL 32399, *pg.* 992, *pg.* 469

THE FLORIDA LOTTERY, 250 Marriott Dr, **Tallahassee,** FL 32399-4000, *pg.* 992, *pg.* 469

GREATER MIAMI CONVENTION & VISITORS BUREAU, 701 Brickell Ave Ste 2700, **Miami,** FL 33131-2847, *pg.* 993, *pg.* 442

GREATER NAPLES CHAMBER OF COMMERCE, 2390 Tamiami Trl N Ste 210, **Naples,** FL 34103-4484, *pg.* 994, *pg.* 450

GREATER TAMPA CHAMBER OF COMMERCE, 201 N Franklin St Ste 201, **Tampa,** FL 33602, *pg.* 994, *pg.* 473

JAMAICA TOURIST BOARD, 5201 Blue Lagoon Dr Ste 670, **Miami,** FL 33126-7016, *pg.* 996, *pg.* 443

KISSIMMEE-ST. CLOUD CONVENTION & VISITORS BUREAU, 215 Celebration Pl, Ste 200, **Kissimmee,** FL 34747, *pg.* 997, *pg.* 436

MANATEE CHAMBER OF COMMERCE, 222 10th St W, **Bradenton,** FL 34206, *pg.* 998, *pg.* 414

NEW SMYRNA BEACH AREA VISITORS BUREAU, 2238 State Rd 44, **New Smyrna Beach,** FL 32168, *pg.* 1001, *pg.* 451

ORLANDO/ORANGE COUNTY CONVENTION & VISITORS BUREAU, INC., 6700 Forum Dr Ste 100, **Orlando,** FL 32821-8017, *pg.* 1003, *pg.* 455

PALM BEACH COUNTY CONVENTION & VISITORS BUREAU, 1555 Palm Beach Lakes Blvd Ste 800, **West Palm Beach,** FL 33401, *pg.* 1003, *pg.* 479

PENSACOLA BAY AREA CONVENTION & VISITORS BUREAU, 1401 E Gregory St, **Pensacola,** FL 32502, *pg.* 1004, *pg.* 458

PINELLAS COUNTY ECONOMIC DEVELOPMENT, Ste 1-200 13805 58th St N, **Clearwater,** FL 33760-3716, *pg.* 1004, *pg.* 416

SARASOTA CONVENTION & VISITORS BUREAU, 1777 Main St # 302, **Sarasota,** FL 34236-5845, *pg.* 1005, *pg.* 467

ST. AUGUSTINE, PONTE VEDRA & THE BEACHES VISITORS & CONVENTION BUREAU, 29 Old mission Ave, **Saint Augustine,** FL 32084, *pg.* 1006, *pg.* 461

STATE OF FLORIDA DEPARTMENT OF CITRUS, 1115 E Memorial Blvd, **Lakeland,** FL 33801-2021, *pg.* 1006, *pg.* 437

TAMPA BAY & CO., 401 E Jackson St Ste 2100, **Tampa,** FL 33602, *pg.* 1007, *pg.* 476

VISIT FLORIDA INC., 2540 W Executive Ctr Cir Ste 200, **Tallahassee,** FL 32301, *pg.* 1010, *pg.* 470

YBOR CITY CHAMBER OF COMMERCE, 1800 E 9th Ave, **Tampa,** FL 33605-3818, *pg.* 1011, *pg.* 477

Georgia

ATLANTA CONVENTION & VISITORS BUREAU, 233 Peachtree St NE Ste 1400, **Atlanta,** GA 30303-1553, *pg.* 989, *pg.* 489

AUGUSTA METROPOLITAN CONVENTION & VISITORS BUREAU, INC., 1450 Greene St Ste 110, **Augusta,** GA 30901, *pg.* 989, *pg.* 524

THE CENTER FOR DISEASE CONTROL & PREVENTION, 1600 Clifton Rd NE, **Atlanta,** GA 30333, *pg.* 990, *pg.* 492

GEORGIA DEPARTMENT OF ECONOMIC DEVELOPMENT, Ste 1200 75 5th St NW, **Atlanta,** GA 30308-1020, *pg.* 992, *pg.* 506

GEORGIA LOTTERY CORPORATION, 250 Williams St NW #3000, **Atlanta,** GA 30303, *pg.* 993, *pg.* 506

METRO ATLANTA CHAMBER OF COMMERCE, 235 Andrew Young International Blvd NW, **Atlanta,** GA 30303, *pg.* 998, *pg.* 514

SOUTHEAST TOURISM SOCIETY, 555 Sun Valley Dr Ste E5, **Roswell,** GA 30076-5624, *pg.* 1006, *pg.* 539

Hawaii

HAWAII VISITORS & CONVENTION BUREAU, 2270 Kalakaua Ave Ste 801, **Honolulu,** HI 96815, *pg.* 994, *pg.* 543

Idaho

IDAHO DEPARTMENT OF COMMERCE, 700 W State St 2nd Fl, **Boise,** ID 83720-0093, *pg.* 995, *pg.* 547

IDAHO LOTTERY, 1199 Shoreline Ln Ste 100, **Boise,** ID 83702, *pg.* 995, *pg.* 547

Illinois

CHICAGO CONVENTION & TOURISM BUREAU, 301 E Cermak Rd, **Chicago,** IL 60616-1578, *pg.* 990, *pg.* 569

CITY OF CHICAGO-DEPARTMENT OF PLANNING & DEVELOPMENT, 121 N LaSalle St Rm 1111, **Chicago,** IL 60602-1250, *pg.* 991, *pg.* 570

ILLINOIS BUREAU OF TOURISM, 100 W Randolph St Ste 3-400, **Chicago,** IL 60601-3219, *pg.* 995, *pg.* 578

ILLINOIS STATE LOTTERY, 100 W Randolph 7th Fl, **Chicago,** IL 60601, *pg.* 995, *pg.* 578

Indiana

INDIANAPOLIS CONVENTION & VISITORS ASSOCIATION, 30 S Meridian St Ste 410, **Indianapolis,** IN 46204, *pg.* 995, *pg.* 687

THE STATE LOTTERY COMMISSION OF INDIANA, 1302 N

First page reference indicates Business Class Edition
Second page reference indicates Geographic Edition

Meridian St, **Indianapolis,** IN 46202, *pg.* 1006, *pg.* 690

Iowa

IOWA DEPARTMENT OF ECONOMIC DEVELOPMENT, 200 E Grand Ave, **Des Moines,** IA 50309, *pg.* 995, *pg.* 705
IOWA LOTTERY, 2323 Grand Ave, **Des Moines,** IA 50312, *pg.* 996, *pg.* 705

Kansas

KANSAS DEPARTMENT OF COMMERCE, 1000 SW Jackson St Ste 100, **Topeka,** KS 66612, *pg.* 996, *pg.* 722

Kentucky

KENTUCKY DEPARTMENT OF TOURISM, 500 Mero St 22 Fl, **Frankfort,** KY 40601, *pg.* 996, *pg.* 728
KENTUCKY LOTTERY CORPORATION, 1011 W Main St, **Louisville,** KY 40202, *pg.* 996, *pg.* 735
LOUISVILLE CONVENTION & VISITORS BUREAU, 401 W Main St Ste 2300, **Louisville,** KY 40202, *pg.* 998, *pg.* 736

Louisiana

BATON ROUGE AREA CONVENTION & VISITORS BUREAU, 359 Third St, **Baton Rouge,** LA 70801, *pg.* 989, *pg.* 741
LOUISIANA DEPARTMENT OF ECONOMIC DEVELOPMENT, 1051 N Third St, **Baton Rouge,** LA 70802, *pg.* 997, *pg.* 742
LOUISIANA LOTTERY CORPORATION, 555 Laurel St, **Baton Rouge,** LA 70801, *pg.* 997, *pg.* 742
LOUISIANA OFFICE OF TOURISM, 1051 N 3rd St, **Baton Rouge,** LA 70802, *pg.* 997, *pg.* 742
NEW ORLEANS TOURISM MARKETING CORPORATION, 2020 Saint Charles Ave, **New Orleans,** LA 70130-5319, *pg.* 1001, *pg.* 747
THE UNITED STATES AIR FORCE, 9038 Mansfield Rd, **Shreveport,** LA 71118, *pg.* 1008, *pg.* 748

Maryland

CENTERS FOR MEDICARE & MEDICAID SERVICES, 7500 Security Blvd, **Baltimore,** MD 21244-1849, *pg.* 990, *pg.* 756
MARYLAND OFFICE OF TOURISM DEVELOPMENT, World Trade Ctr 401 Pratt St, **Baltimore,** MD 21202, *pg.* 998, *pg.* 758

Massachusetts

BERKSHIRE VISITORS BUREAU, 66 Allen St, **Pittsfield,** MA 01201, *pg.* 989, *pg.* 841
EASTERN STATES EXPOSITION, 1305 Memorial Ave, **West Springfield,** MA 01089-3525, *pg.* 992, *pg.* 857
GREATER BOSTON CONVENTION & VISITORS BUREAU INC., 2 Copley Pl Ste 105, **Boston,** MA 02116-6501, *pg.* 993, *pg.* 795
THE GREATER BOSTON FOOD BANK, 70 S Bay Ave, **Boston,** MA 02118-2701, *pg.* 993, *pg.* 795
MASSACHUSETTS OFFICE OF TRAVEL & TOURISM, 10 Pk Plz Ste 4510, **Boston,** MA 02116, *pg.* 998, *pg.* 798
MASSACHUSETTS STATE LOTTERY, 60 Columbian St, **Braintree,** MA 02184-7342, *pg.* 998, *pg.* 802
SCOTTISH DEVELOPMENT INTERNATIONAL, 28 State St Ste 2300, **Boston,** MA 02109, *pg.* 1005, *pg.* 801

Michigan

THE MICHIGAN ECONOMIC DEVELOPMENT CORPORATION, TOURISM & MARKETING, 300 N Washington Sq, **Lansing,** MI 48913, *pg.* 999, *pg.* 895
MICHIGAN STATE LOTTERY BUREAU, 101 E Hillsdale, **Lansing,** MI 48933-0001, *pg.* 999, *pg.* 895

Minnesota

EXPLORE MINNESOTA TOURISM, 100 Metro Sq 121 7th Pl E, **Saint Paul,** MN 55101, *pg.* 992, *pg.* 960
MINNESOTA STATE LOTTERY, 2645 Long Lk Rd, **Roseville,** MN 55113-2533, *pg.* 999, *pg.* 956

Mississippi

MISSISSIPPI DEVELOPMENT AUTHORITY, 501 NW St, **Jackson,** MS 39201-1008, *pg.* 999, *pg.* 969

Missouri

KANSAS CITY CONVENTION & VISITORS ASSOCIATION, 1100 Main St Ste 2200, **Kansas City,** MO 64105, *pg.* 996, *pg.* 984
MISSOURI LOTTERY, 1823 Southridge Dr, **Jefferson City,** MO 65109-5645, *pg.* 999, *pg.* 979
ST. LOUIS CONVENTION & VISITORS COMMISSION, 701 Convention Plz Ste 300, **Saint Louis,** MO 63101, *pg.* 1006, *pg.* 1003

Montana

MONTANA LOTTERY, 2525 N Montana Ave, **Helena,** MT 59601-0511, *pg.* 1000, *pg.* 1008

Nebraska

NEBRASKA DEPARTMENT OF ECONOMIC DEVELOPMENT, 301 Centenial Mall S 4th Fl, **Lincoln,** NE 68509-4666, *pg.* 1000, *pg.* 1012
NEBRASKA LOTTERY, 1800 O St Ste 101, **Lincoln,** NE 68508, *pg.* 1000, *pg.* 1012

Nevada

LAS VEGAS CONVENTION & VISITORS AUTHORITY, 3150 Paradise Rd, **Las Vegas,** NV 89109, *pg.* 997, *pg.* 1027
NEVADA COMMISSION ON TOURISM, 401 N Carson St, **Carson City,** NV 89701, *pg.* 1000, *pg.* 1021

New Jersey

NEW JERSEY STATE LOTTERY, Lawrence Park Complex, 1333 Brunswick Ave Cir, **Trenton,** NJ 08648, *pg.* 1000, *pg.* 1126

New Mexico

ALBUQUERQUE CONVENTION & VISITORS BUREAU, 20 First Plz NW Ste 601, **Albuquerque,** NM 87102, *pg.* 988, *pg.* 1135
NEW MEXICO ECONOMIC DEVELOPMENT DEPARTMENT, 1100 St Francis Dr PO Box 20003, **Santa Fe,** NM 87505-4147, *pg.* 1001, *pg.* 1136
NEW MEXICO TOURISM DEPARTMENT, 491 Old Santa Fe Trl, **Santa Fe,** NM 87501-0001, *pg.* 1001, *pg.* 1136

New York

AUSTRALIAN TRADE COMMISSION, 150 E 42nd St 34th Fl, **New York,** NY 10017, *pg.* 989, *pg.* 1198
BERMUDA DEPARTMENT OF TOURISM, 675 3rd Ave 20th Fl, **New York,** NY 10017, *pg.* 989, *pg.* 1202
EMPIRE STATE DEVELOPMENT-DIVISION OF TOURISM, 633 3rd Ave, **New York,** NY 10017-6706, *pg.* 992, *pg.* 1227
ENTERTAINMENT SOFTWARE RATING BOARD, 317 Madison Ave 22nd Fl, **New York,** NY 10017, *pg.* 992, *pg.* 1228
FRENCH GOVERNMENT TOURIST OFFICE, 825 3rd Ave, **New York,** NY 10022-6954, *pg.* 992, *pg.* 1233
GREEK NATIONAL TOURIST ORGANIZATION, 645 5th Ave 9th Fl, **New York,** NY 10022-5910, *pg.* 994, *pg.* 1236
INDIA TOURISM, 1270 Ave of the Americas Ste 303 fl3, **New York,** NY 10020-1801, *pg.* 995, *pg.* 1243
ISRAEL MINISTRY OF TOURISM INFORMATION CENTER, 800 2nd Ave, **New York,** NY 10017-4709, *pg.* 996, *pg.* 1244
ITALIAN GOVERNMENT TOURIST BOARD-NORTH AMERICA, 630 5th Ave Ste 1565, **New York,** NY 10111, *pg.* 996, *pg.* 1244
NEW YORK CITY DEPARTMENT OF CITY WIDE ADMINISTRATIVE SERVICES, The Municipal Bldg 1 Centre St 17th Fl S, **New York,** NY 10007, *pg.* 1001, *pg.* 1268
NEW YORK CITY ECONOMIC DEVELOPMENT CORPORATION, 110 William St, **New York,** NY 10038, *pg.* 1001, *pg.* 1268
NEW YORK STATE DEPARTMENT OF HEALTH, Corning Tower Empire State Plz, **Albany,** NY 12237, *pg.* 1001, *pg.* 1137
NEW YORK STATE LOTTERY, 1 Broadway Ctr, **Schenectady,** NY 12305, *pg.* 1001, *pg.* 1340
NYC & COMPANY, INC., 810 7th Ave, **New York,** NY 10019, *pg.* 1002, *pg.* 1274
SOUTH AFRICAN TOURISM, 500 5th Ave 20th Fl Ste 2040, **New York,** NY 10110-2099, *pg.* 1005, *pg.* 1294
SWITZERLAND TOURISM, 608 5th Ave 49th St, **New York,** NY 10020-2303, *pg.* 1006, *pg.* 1297
TOURISM IRELAND, 345 Park Ave 17th Fl, **New York,** NY 10154, *pg.* 1007, *pg.* 1303

North Carolina

GREATER RALEIGH CONVENTION & VISITORS BUREAU, 421 Fayetteville St Mall Ste 1505, **Raleigh,** NC 27601-2946, *pg.* 994, *pg.* 1387
GREENSBORO CONVENTION & VISITORS BUREAU, 2200 Pinecroft Rd Ste 200, **Greensboro,** NC 27407, *pg.* 994, *pg.* 1374
NORTH CAROLINA DEPARTMENT OF COMMERCE DIVISION OF TOURISM, FILM & SPORTS DEVELOPMENT, 301 N Wilmington St, **Raleigh,** NC 27601, *pg.* 1001, *pg.* 1388

North Dakota

NORTH DAKOTA DEPARTMENT OF COMMERCE TOURISM DIVISION, 1600 E Century Ave Ste 2, **Bismarck, ND** 58503-2057, *pg.* 1002, *pg.* 1397
NORTH DAKOTA STATE SEED DEPARTMENT, 1313 18th St N PO Box 5257, **Fargo,** ND 58105-5257, *pg.* 1002, *pg.* 1397

Ohio

GREATER CINCINNATI CONVENTION & VISITORS BUREAU, Ste 1500 525 Vine St, **Cincinnati,** OH 45202, *pg.* 993, *pg.* 1414
OHIO DEPARTMENT OF DEVELOPMENT, 77 S High St, **Columbus,** OH 43215, *pg.* 1002, *pg.* 1442
OHIO LOTTERY COMMISSION, 615 W Superior Ave, **Cleveland,** OH 44113-1897, *pg.* 1002, *pg.* 1433
POSITIVELY CLEVELAND, 334 Euclid Ave, **Cleveland,** OH 44114, *pg.* 1004, *pg.* 1434

Oklahoma

OKLAHOMA CITY CONVENTION & VISITORS BUREAU, 123 Park Ave, **Oklahoma City,** OK 73102, *pg.* 1002, *pg.* 1487
OKLAHOMA TOURISM & RECREATION DEPARTMENT, 900 N Stiles, **Oklahoma City,** OK 73104, *pg.* 1003, *pg.* 1487
TULSA METRO CHAMBER, 2 W 2nd St Williams Center Tower 2 Ste 150, **Tulsa,** OK 74103, *pg.* 1008, *pg.* 1491

Oregon

OREGON STATE LOTTERY, 500 Airport Rd SE, **Salem,** OR 97301, *pg.* 1003, *pg.* 1508
OREGON TOURISM COMMISSION, 670 Hawthorne SE Ste 240, **Salem,** OR 97301-1282, *pg.* 1003, *pg.* 1508
PORTLAND BUSINESS ALLIANCE, 200 SW Market St Ste 150, **Portland,** OR 97201-5718, *pg.* 1004, *pg.* 1505
TRAVEL PORTLAND, 1000 SW Broadway Ste 2300, **Portland,** OR 97205, *pg.* 1008, *pg.* 1507

Pennsylvania

PENNSYLVANIA STATE LOTTERY, 1200 Fulling Mill Rd Ste 1, **Middletown,** PA 17057, *pg.* 1003, *pg.* 1552
PHILADELPHIA CONVENTION & VISITORS BUREAU, 1601 Market St Ste 200, **Philadelphia,** PA 19103, *pg.* 1004, *pg.* 1568

Puerto Rico

PUERTO RICO TOURISM COMPANY, Princes Bulding

Number 2 Princes Work Way, **San Juan,** PR 00902-3960, *pg.* 1004, *pg.* 1599

Rhode Island

RHODE ISLAND COMMERCE CORPORATION, 315 Iron Horse Way Ste 101, **Providence,** RI 02908, *pg.* 1004, *pg.* 1607

RHODE ISLAND LOTTERY, 1425 Pontiac Ave, **Cranston,** RI 02920-4454, *pg.* 1004, *pg.* 1600

South Carolina

THE SOUTH CAROLINA EDUCATION LOTTERY, 1333 Main St 4th Fl, **Columbia,** SC 29201, *pg.* 1005, *pg.* 1614

SOUTH CAROLINA PARKS RECREATION & TOURISM, 1205 Pendleton St Ste 110, **Columbia,** SC 29201-3731, *pg.* 1005, *pg.* 1614

South Dakota

SOUTH DAKOTA LOTTERY, 207 E Capitol Ave, **Pierre,** SD 57501, *pg.* 1006, *pg.* 1624

SOUTH DAKOTA'S DEPARTMENT OF TOURISM, 711 E Wells Ave, **Pierre,** SD 57501-3369, *pg.* 1006, *pg.* 1624

Tennessee

TENNESSEE DEPARTMENT OF TOURIST DEVELOPMENT, 312 Rosa L Parks Ave, **Nashville,** TN 37243, *pg.* 1007, *pg.* 1654

UNITED STATES NAVY, 5722 Integrity Dr Bldg 784, **Millington,** TN 38054, *pg.* 1009, *pg.* 1647

UNITED STATES NAVY RECRUITING COMMAND, Bldg 784 5722 Integrity Dr Bldg 784, **Millington,** TN 38054-5028, *pg.* 1009, *pg.* 1648

Texas

DALLAS CONVENTION & VISITORS BUREAU, 325 N Saint Paul St Ste 700, **Dallas,** TX 75201, *pg.* 991, *pg.* 1678

GOVERNOR'S OFFICE OF ECONOMIC DEVELOPMENT & TOURISM, 221 E 11th St 4th Fl, **Austin,** TX 78701, *pg.* 993, *pg.* 1662

GREATER AUSTIN CHAMBER OF COMMERCE, 535 E 5th St, **Austin,** TX 78701, *pg.* 993, *pg.* 1663

GREATER HOUSTON CONVENTION & VISITORS BUREAU, 4 Houston Ctr 1331 Lamar St Ste 700, **Houston,** TX 77010-3025, *pg.* 993, *pg.* 1706

IRVING CONVENTION & VISITORS BUREAU, 500 Las Colinas Blvd W, **Irving,** TX 75039-3717, *pg.* 996, *pg.* 1720

SAN ANTONIO CONVENTION & VISITORS BUREAU, 203 S Saint Marys St 2nd Fl, **San Antonio,** TX 78205, *pg.* 1004, *pg.* 1742

SAN ANTONIO ECONOMIC DEVELOPMENT FOUNDATION, 602 E Commerce St, **San Antonio,** TX 78205, *pg.* 1004, *pg.* 1742

TEXAS LOTTERY COMMISSION, 611 E 6th St, **Austin,** TX 78701, *pg.* 1007, *pg.* 1666

UNITED STATES AIR FORCE RECRUITING SERVICE, 550 D St W Ste 1, **Randolph AFB,** TX 78150-4527, *pg.* 1008, *pg.* 1735

Vermont

VERMONT DEPARTMENT OF TOURISM & MARKETING, 1 National Life Dr 6th Fl, **Montpelier,** VT 05620, *pg.* 1010, *pg.* 1767

VERMONT LOTTERY COMMISSION, 1311 US Rt 302 Berlin Ste 100, **Barre,** VT 05641, *pg.* 1010, *pg.* 1764

Virginia

HAMPTON ROADS ECONOMIC DEVELOPMENT ALLIANCE, 500 E Main St Ste 1300, **Norfolk,** VA 23510-2206, *pg.* 994, *pg.* 1797

PENINSULA COUNCIL FOR WORKFORCE DEVELOPMENT, 11820 Fountain Way Ste 301, **Newport News,** VA 23606, *pg.* 1003, *pg.* 1796

VIRGINIA ECONOMIC DEVELOPMENT PARTNERSHIP, 901 E Byrd St, **Richmond,** VA 23219, *pg.* 1010, *pg.* 1804

VIRGINIA STATE LOTTERY DEPARTMENT, 900 E Main St, **Richmond,** VA 23219-3548, *pg.* 1010, *pg.* 1804

VIRGINIA TOURISM AUTHORITY, 901 E Byrd St, **Richmond,** VA 23219-4052, *pg.* 1010, *pg.* 1804

Washington

SEATTLE CONVENTION & VISITORS BUREAU, One Convention Pl 701 Pike St Ste 800, **Seattle,** WA 98101-4042, *pg.* 1005, *pg.* 1839

WASHINGTON STATE DEPARTMENT OF COMMUNITY, TRADE & ECONOMIC DEVELOPMENT, 128 10th Ave SW, **Olympia,** WA 98504-2525, *pg.* 1010, *pg.* 1823

WASHINGTON STATE LOTTERY, 814 4th Ave E, **Olympia,** WA 98504, *pg.* 1011, *pg.* 1823

West Virginia

WEST VIRGINIA DEPARTMENT OF COMMERCE, 1900 Kanawha Blvd E State Capital Complex Bldg 6 Rm 553, **Charleston,** WV 25305, *pg.* 1011, *pg.* 1849

WEST VIRGINIA LOTTERY, 312 MacCorkle Ave SE, **Charleston,** WV 25314-1143, *pg.* 1011, *pg.* 1849

Wisconsin

GREATER MILWAUKEE CONVENTION & VISITORS BUREAU, 648 N Plankinton Ave Ste 425, **Milwaukee,** WI 53203-2501, *pg.* 993, *pg.* 1874

WISCONSIN DELLS VISITOR & CONVENTION BUREAU, 115 La Crosse St, **Wisconsin Dells,** WI 53965, *pg.* 1011, *pg.* 1899

WISCONSIN DEPARTMENT OF AGRICULTURE, TRADE & CONSUMER PROTECTION, 2811 Agriculture Dr, **Madison,** WI 53718-6777, *pg.* 1011, *pg.* 1867

WISCONSIN DEPARTMENT OF HEALTH SERVICES, 1 W Wilson St, **Madison,** WI 53703, *pg.* 1011, *pg.* 1868

WISCONSIN DEPARTMENT OF TOURISM, 201 W Washington Ave, **Madison,** WI 53703, *pg.* 1011, *pg.* 1868

Wyoming

WYOMING BUSINESS COUNCIL, 214 W 15th St, **Cheyenne,** WY 82002, *pg.* 1011, *pg.* 1901

First page reference indicates Business Class Edition
Second page reference indicates Geographic Edition

Groceries & Food Retailers

Arizona

BASHAS' SUPERMARKETS, 22402 S Basha Rd, **Chandler,** AZ 85248-4908, *pg.* 1015, *pg.* 12
INVENTURE FOODS, INC., 5050 N 40th St Ste 300, **Phoenix,** AZ 85018, *pg.* 1023, *pg.* 17
KAHALA FRANCHISING LLC, 9311 E Via De Ventura, **Scottsdale,** AZ 85258, *pg.* 1025, *pg.* 23
P.F. CHANG'S CHINA BISTRO, INC., 7676 E Pinnacle Peak Rd, **Scottsdale,** AZ 85255, *pg.* 1030, *pg.* 24

Arkansas

HARPS FOOD STORES, INC., 918 S Gutensohn Rd, **Springdale,** AR 72762-5165, *pg.* 1022, *pg.* 35

California

THE ALMOND BOARD OF CALIFORNIA, 1150 9th St Ste 1500, **Modesto,** CA 95354, *pg.* 1013, *pg.* 149
ARDEN GROUP, INC., 2020 S Central Ave, **Compton,** CA 90220-5302, *pg.* 1014, *pg.* 68
CALIFORNIA RAISIN MARKETING BOARD, 2445 Capitol St Ste 200, **Fresno,** CA 93721, *pg.* 1017, *pg.* 93
CHEESECAKE FACTORY INCORPORATED, 26901 Malibu Hills Rd, **Calabasas Hills,** CA 91301, *pg.* 1017, *pg.* 56
CYTOSPORT, INC., 4795 Industrial Way, **Benicia,** CA 94510, *pg.* 1018, *pg.* 45
FRESH & EASY NEIGHBORHOOD MARKET INC, 2120 Park Pl # 200, **El Segundo,** CA 90245-4741, *pg.* 1020, *pg.* 80
GELSON'S MARKETS, 16400 Ventura Blvd Ste 240 PO Box 1802 91426, **Encino,** CA 91436-2123, *pg.* 1020, *pg.* 85
H&N FOODS INTERNATIONAL, INC., 5580 S Alameda St, **Los Angeles,** CA 90058-3426, *pg.* 1022, *pg.* 132
JAMBA, INC., 6475 Christie Ave Ste 150, **Emeryville,** CA 94608, *pg.* 1024, *pg.* 84
JORDANO'S, INC., 550 S Patterson Ave, **Santa Barbara,** CA 93111, *pg.* 1024, *pg.* 263
MORINAGA NUTRITIONAL FOODS, INC., 2441 W 205th Ste C102, **Torrance,** CA 90501, *pg.* 1028, *pg.* 295
PEET'S COFFEE & TEA, INC., 1400 Park Ave, **Emeryville,** CA 94608-3520, *pg.* 1029, *pg.* 85
RALEY'S INC., 500 W Capitol Ave, **West Sacramento,** CA 95605-2624, *pg.* 1031, *pg.* 305
RALPHS GROCERY COMPANY, 1100 W Artesia Blvd, **Compton,** CA 90220-5108, *pg.* 1031, *pg.* 69
SAFEWAY INC., 5918 Stoneridge Mall Rd, **Pleasanton,** CA 94588-3229, *pg.* 1032, *pg.* 184
SAVE MART SUPERMARKETS, 1800 Standiford Ave, **Modesto,** CA 95350-0180, *pg.* 1033, *pg.* 150
SMART & FINAL, INC., 600 Citadel Dr, **City of Commerce,** CA 90040, *pg.* 1034, *pg.* 66
STATER BROS. MARKETS, 301 S Tippecanoe Ave, **San Bernardino,** CA 92408, *pg.* 1034, *pg.* 198
STATER BROTHERS HOLDINGS, 301 S Tippecanoe Ave, **San Bernardino,** CA 92408, *pg.* 1034, *pg.* 198
UNIFIED GROCERS, INC., 5200 Sheila St, **City of Commerce,** CA 90040, *pg.* 1036, *pg.* 66
VONS A SAFEWAY COMPANY, 618 Michillinda Ave, **Arcadia,** CA 91007-6300, *pg.* 1036, *pg.* 43

Colorado

BOULDER BRANDS, INC., 1600 Pearl St Ste 300, **Boulder,** CO 80302, *pg.* 1016, *pg.* 310
EINSTEIN NOAH RESTAURANT GROUP, INC., 555 Zang St Ste 300, **Lakewood,** CO 80228-1013, *pg.* 1019, *pg.* 332
QDOBA MEXICAN GRILL INC., 4865 Ward Rd Ste 500, **Wheat Ridge,** CO 80033, *pg.* 1031, *pg.* 336
ROCKY MOUNTAIN CHOCOLATE FACTORY, INC., 265 Turner Dr, **Durango,** CO 81303, *pg.* 1032, *pg.* 324
THE WHITEWAVE FOODS COMPANY, 1225 17th St Ste 1000, **Denver,** CO 80202, *pg.* 1037, *pg.* 324

Connecticut

BOZZUTO'S INC., 275 Schoolhouse Rd, **Cheshire,** CT 06410-1241, *pg.* 1016, *pg.* 342
CENTERPLATE, INC., 2187 Atlantic St, **Stamford,** CT 06902, *pg.* 1017, *pg.* 372
GRADE A MARKET INC., 360 Connecticut Ave, **Norwalk,** CT 06854, *pg.* 1021, *pg.* 362

Florida

B&B CORPORATE HOLDINGS, INC., 927 S US Hwy 301, **Tampa,** FL 33619, *pg.* 1015, *pg.* 471
CHECKERS DRIVE-IN RESTAURANTS, INC., 4300 W Cypress St Ste 600, **Tampa,** FL 33607-4159, *pg.* 1017, *pg.* 472
FARM STORES, Grove Forest Plz, 2937 SW 27th Ave Ste 203, **Coconut Grove,** FL 33133, *pg.* 1019, *pg.* 417
ORANGE PEEL ENTERPRISES, INC., 2183 Ponce De Leon Cir, **Vero Beach,** FL 32960, *pg.* 1028, *pg.* 477
PUBLIX SUPER MARKETS, INC., 3300 Publix Corporate Pkwy, **Lakeland,** FL 33811, *pg.* 1031, *pg.* 437
SEDANO'S MANAGEMENT, INC., 3140 W 76th St, **Hialeah,** FL 33018, *pg.* 1033, *pg.* 430
WINN DIXIE STORES, INC., 5050 Edgewood Ct, **Jacksonville,** FL 32254-3699, *pg.* 1038, *pg.* 435

Georgia

ARBY'S RESTAURANT GROUP, INC., 1155 Perimeter Ctr W 9th Fl, **Atlanta,** GA 30338, *pg.* 1014, *pg.* 488
FROSTY ACRES BRANDS, INC., 1225 Old Alpharetta Rd Ste 235, **Alpharetta,** GA 30005, *pg.* 1020, *pg.* 484
MOE'S SOUTHWEST GRILL, LLC, 2915 Peachtree Rd, **Atlanta,** GA 30305, *pg.* 1027, *pg.* 514
MORRISON MANAGEMENT SPECIALISTS, INC., 5801 Peachtree Dunwoody Rd, **Atlanta,** GA 30342-1503, *pg.* 1028, *pg.* 515
OLD FASHION FOODS, INC., 5521 Collins Blvd, **Austell,** GA 30106-3653, *pg.* 1028, *pg.* 525
WAYFIELD FOODS INC., 5145 Wellcome All Rd, **Atlanta,** GA 30349, *pg.* 1037, *pg.* 523

Idaho

ALBERTSON'S LLC, 250 Parkcenter Blvd, **Boise,** ID 83726-0020, *pg.* 1013, *pg.* 546
WINCO FOODS, INC., 650 N Armstrong Pl, **Boise,** ID 83704-0825, *pg.* 1038, *pg.* 548

Illinois

ALDI FOOD INC., 1200 N Kirk Rd, **Batavia,** IL 60510-1443, *pg.* 1013, *pg.* 556
BUTERA MARKET, 1 Clock Twr Plz, **Elgin,** IL 60120-6918, *pg.* 1016, *pg.* 609
DOMINICK'S FINER FOODS, LLC, 711 Jorie Blvd, **Oak Brook,** IL 60523-4425, *pg.* 1019, *pg.* 644
IGA, INC., 8745 W Higgins Rd Ste 350, **Chicago,** IL 60631-2716, *pg.* 1023, *pg.* 578
JEWEL-OSCO, 150 Pierce Rd, **Itasca,** IL 60143, *pg.* 1024, *pg.* 620
JIMMY JOHNS FRANCHISE, LLC, 2212 Fox Dr, **Champaign,** IL 61820, *pg.* 1024, *pg.* 562
JOHN B. SANFILIPPO & SON, INC., 1703 N Randall Rd, **Elgin,** IL 60123-7820, *pg.* 1024, *pg.* 610
NIEMANN FOODS INC., 1501 N 12th St, **Quincy,** IL 62306, *pg.* 1028, *pg.* 653
PEAPOD, LLC, 9933 Woods Dr Ste 375, **Skokie,** IL 60077-1057, *pg.* 1029, *pg.* 661

Indiana

MARSH SUPERMARKETS, INC., 9800 Crosspoint Blvd, **Indianapolis,** IN 46256, *pg.* 1027, *pg.* 688
SUPERVALU, INC., FOOD MARKETING DIVISION, 4815 Executive Blvd, **Fort Wayne,** IN 46808, *pg.* 1035, *pg.* 681

Iowa

CASEY'S GENERAL STORES, INC., 1 Convenience Blvd, **Ankeny,** IA 50021, *pg.* 1017, *pg.* 701
FAREWAY STORES, INC., PO Box 70, 715 8th St, **Boone,** IA 50036, *pg.* 1019, *pg.* 702
HY-VEE, INC., 5820 Westown Pkwy, **West Des Moines,** IA 50266-8223, *pg.* 1023, *pg.* 713
US FOODS, 3550 2nd St, **Coralville,** IA 52241-3205, *pg.* 1036, *pg.* 703

Kansas

ASSOCIATED WHOLESALE GROCERS, INC., 5000 Kansas Ave, **Kansas City,** KS 66106, *pg.* 1015, *pg.* 715
DEAN & DELUCA, INC., 2402 E 37th St, **Wichita,** KS 67219, *pg.* 1018, *pg.* 723

Kentucky

HOUCHENS INDUSTRIES INC., 700 Church St, **Bowling Green,** KY 42101-5112, *pg.* 1023, *pg.* 726

Maine

HANNAFORD BROTHERS CO., 145 Pleasant Hill Rd, **Scarborough,** ME 04074-9309, *pg.* 1022, *pg.* 752

Maryland

GIANT OF MARYLAND LLC, 8301 Professional Pl, **Landover,** MD 20785, *pg.* 1021, *pg.* 773
MCCORMICK & COMPANY, INCORPORATED, 18 Loveton Circle, **Sparks,** MD 21152-6000, *pg.* 1027, *pg.* 779
PHILLIPS FOODS INC., 1215 Fort Ave, **Baltimore,** MD 21220, *pg.* 1030, *pg.* 758

Massachusetts

AGRI-MARK, INC., 100 Milk St, **Methuen,** MA 01844-4600, *pg.* 1012, *pg.* 833
BIG Y FOODS, INC., 2145 Roosevelt Ave, **Springfield,** MA 01102, *pg.* 1015, *pg.* 845
CUMBERLAND FARMS, INC., 100 Crossing Blvd, **Framingham,** MA 01702, *pg.* 1018, *pg.* 820
DEMOULAS SUPER MARKETS INC., 875 E St, **Tewksbury,** MA 01876, *pg.* 1018, *pg.* 848
LATE JULY SNACKS LLC, 3166 Main St, **Barnstable,** MA 02630, *pg.* 1026, *pg.* 784
THE PASTENE COMPANIES, LTD., 330 Tpke St, **Canton,** MA 02021-2357, *pg.* 1029, *pg.* 811
STACY'S PITA CHIP COMPANY, INC., 663 N St, **Randolph,** MA 02368, *pg.* 1034, *pg.* 842
THE STOP & SHOP SUPERMARKET COMPANY LLC, 1385 Hancock St Quincy Ctr Plz, **Quincy,** MA 02169-5100, *pg.* 1034, *pg.* 842
UPTON TEA IMPORTS, 100 Jeffrey Ave # 1, **Holliston,** MA 01746-2028, *pg.* 1036, *pg.* 825

Michigan

AWREY BAKERIES, INC., 12301 Farmington Rd, **Livonia,** MI 48150-1747, *pg.* 1015, *pg.* 896
DAWN FOOD PRODUCTS, INC., 3333 Sargeant Rd, **Jackson,** MI 49201-3473, *pg.* 1018, *pg.* 893
EDEN FOODS INC., 701 Tecumseh Rd, **Clinton,** MI 49236-9589, *pg.* 1019, *pg.* 875
GORDON FOOD SERVICE INC., 1300 Gezon Pkwy SW, **Wyoming,** MI 49509, *pg.* 1021, *pg.* 913
HUNGRY HOWIE'S PIZZA & SUBS INC., 30300 Stephenson Hwy, **Madison Heights,** MI 48071-1600, *pg.* 1023, *pg.* 897
LIVING ESSENTIALS, LLC, 38955 Hills Tech Dr, **Farmington Hills,** MI 48331, *pg.* 1026, *pg.* 886
SHERWOOD FOOD DISTRIBUTORS, 12499 Evergreen Rd, **Detroit,** MI 48228, *pg.* 1033, *pg.* 884
SPARTANNASH CO, 850 76th St SW, **Grand Rapids,** MI 49518, *pg.* 1034, *pg.* 889

Minnesota

SPARTANNASH CO., 7600 France Ave S, **Edina,** MN 55435, *pg.* 1034, *pg.* 925
SUPERVALU, INC., 11840 Valley View Rd, **Eden Prairie,** MN 55344, *pg.* 1035, *pg.* 924

Missouri

DIERBERGS MARKETS INC., 16690 Swingley Rdg Rd, **Chesterfield,** MO 63017-0758, *pg.* 1018, *pg.* 974
MORAN FOODS, INC., 100 Corporate Ofc Dr, **Earth City,** MO 63045-1528, *pg.* 1028, *pg.* 976

PANERA BREAD COMPANY, 3630 S Geyer Rd Ste 100, **Saint Louis,** MO 63127, *pg.* 1029, *pg.* 1001
SCHNUCK MARKETS, INC., 11420 Lackland Rd, **Saint Louis,** MO 63146-3559, *pg.* 1033, *pg.* 1002

Nebraska

AFFILIATED FOODS MIDWEST INC., 1301 Omaha Ave, **Norfolk,** NE 68701, *pg.* 1012, *pg.* 1013

New Hampshire

C&S WHOLESALE GROCERS, INC., 7 Corporate Dr, **Keene,** NH 03431, *pg.* 1016, *pg.* 1035

New Jersey

THE GREAT ATLANTIC & PACIFIC TEA COMPANY, INC., 2 Paragon Dr, **Montvale,** NJ 07645-1718, *pg.* 1021, *pg.* 1000
KINGS FOOD MARKETS, INC., 700 Lanidex Plz, **Parsippany,** NJ 07054, *pg.* 1025, *pg.* 1103
QUICK CHEK FOOD STORES INC., 3 Old Hwy 28, **Whitehouse Station,** NJ 08889, *pg.* 1031, *pg.* 1132
WAKEFERN FOOD CORPORATION, 600 York St, **Elizabeth,** NJ 07207, *pg.* 1037, *pg.* 1058

New York

BLUE APRON, INC., 5 Crosby St, **New York,** NY 10013, *pg.* 1016, *pg.* 1205
CITARELLA, 2135 Broadway, **New York,** NY 10023, *pg.* 1017, *pg.* 1212
CULINART, INC., 175 Sunnyside Blvd, **Plainview,** NY 11803-6769, *pg.* 1017, *pg.* 1321
D'AGOSTINO SUPERMARKETS INC., 1385 Boston Post Rd, **Larchmont,** NY 10538-3904, *pg.* 1018, *pg.* 1173
GOLUB CORPORATION, 461 Nott St, **Schenectady,** NY 12308, *pg.* 1021, *pg.* 1340
INKO'S WHITE ICED TEA, 435 E 70st, **New York,** NY 10021, *pg.* 1023, *pg.* 1243
KEY FOOD STORES CO-OPERATIVE, INC., 1200 S Ave, **Staten Island,** NY 10314, *pg.* 1025, *pg.* 1343
KING KULLEN GROCERY COMPANY, INC., 185 Central Ave, **Bethpage,** NY 11714, *pg.* 1025, *pg.* 1141
LACKMANN CULINARY SERVICES, 303 Crossways Pk Dr, **Woodbury,** NY 11797, *pg.* 1026, *pg.* 1356
PRICE CHOPPER OPERATING CO., INC., 501 Duanesburg Rd, **Schenectady,** NY 12306, *pg.* 1030, *pg.* 1341
SHOPRITE SUPERMARKETS, INC., 176 N Main St, **Florida,** NY 10921-1021, *pg.* 1033, *pg.* 1160
SYSCO FOOD SERVICES OF ALBANY, LLC, 1 Liebich Ln, **Halfmoon,** NY 12065-1421, *pg.* 1035, *pg.* 1163
TOPS HOLDING CORPORATION, 6363 Main St, **Williamsville,** NY 14221, *pg.* 1036, *pg.* 1355
TOPS MARKETS, LLC, 6363 Main St, **Williamsville,** NY 14221, *pg.* 1036, *pg.* 1355
WEGMANS FOOD MARKETS, INC., 1500 Brooks Ave, **Rochester,** NY 14603-0844, *pg.* 1037, *pg.* 1337
WESTERN BEEF, INC., 47-05 Metropolitan Ave, **Ridgewood,** NY 11385-1046, *pg.* 1037, *pg.* 1333

North Carolina

BISCUITVILLE, INC., 1414 Yanceyville St Ste 300, **Greensboro,** NC 27405-1753, *pg.* 1015, *pg.* 1374
FOOD LION, LLC, 2110 Executive Dr, **Salisbury,** NC 28147-9007, *pg.* 1019, *pg.* 1390
THE FRESH MARKET, INC., 628 Green Valley Rd Ste 500, **Greensboro,** NC 27408-7099, *pg.* 1020, *pg.* 1374
HARRIS TEETER, INC., 701 Crestdale Rd, **Matthews,** NC 28105, *pg.* 1022, *pg.* 1383
INGLES MARKETS, INCORPORATED, 2913 US Hwy 70 W, **Black Mountain,** NC 28711, *pg.* 1023, *pg.* 1358
LOWE'S FOOD STORES, INC., 1381 Old Mill Cir Ste 200, **Winston Salem,** NC 27103, *pg.* 1026, *pg.* 1394
MEAT & SEAFOOD SOLUTIONS, LLC, 3500 Old Battleground Rd, **Greensboro,** NC 27410, *pg.* 1027, *pg.* 1375
THE PANTRY, INC., 305 Gregson Dr PO Box 8019, **Cary,** NC 27511, *pg.* 1029, *pg.* 1360
PRIMO WATER CORPORATION, 104 Cambridge Plaza Dr, **Winston Salem,** NC 27104, *pg.* 1030, *pg.* 1395

Ohio

THE FRED W. ALBRECHT GROCERY CO., 2700 Gilchrist Rd, **Akron,** OH 44305-4433, *pg.* 1020, *pg.* 1400
GIANT EAGLE AMERICAN SEAWAY FOODS, 5300 Richmond Rd, **Bedford,** OH 44146, *pg.* 1020, *pg.* 1405
GOLD STAR CHILI INC., 650 Lunken Park Dr, **Cincinnati,** OH 45226, *pg.* 1021, *pg.* 1414
THE KROGER CO., 1014 Vine St, **Cincinnati,** OH 45202-1141, *pg.* 1025, *pg.* 1416
SKYLINE CHILI, INC., 4180 Thunderbird Ln, **Fairfield,** OH 45014, *pg.* 1033, *pg.* 1452

Oklahoma

HOMELAND STORES, INC., 390 NE 36th St, **Oklahoma City,** OK 73105, *pg.* 1023, *pg.* 1486
LOPEZ FOODS INC., 9500 NW 4th St, **Oklahoma City,** OK 73127, *pg.* 1026, *pg.* 1486
QUIKTRIP CORPORATION, 4705 S 129th East Ave, **Tulsa,** OK 74134-7008, *pg.* 1031, *pg.* 1490

Oregon

C&K MARKET, INC., 615 5th St, **Brookings,** OR 97415-9199, *pg.* 1016, *pg.* 1496
HARRY & DAVID HOLDINGS, INC., 2500 S Pacific Hwy, **Medford,** OR 97501-2675, *pg.* 1022, *pg.* 1499
OREGON CHERRY GROWERS, INC., 1520 Woodrow St NE, **Salem,** OR 97301, *pg.* 1028, *pg.* 1508
RESER'S FINE FOODS INC., 15570 SW Jenkins Rd, **Beaverton,** OR 97006, *pg.* 1032, *pg.* 1496
TAZO TEA COMPANY, 301 SE Second Ave, **Portland,** OR 97207, *pg.* 1036, *pg.* 1507
WESTERN FAMILY HOLDING CO., INC., 6700 SW Sandburg St, **Tigard,** OR 97223-8008, *pg.* 1037, *pg.* 1509
YOCREAM INTERNATIONAL INC., 5858 NE 87th Ave, **Portland,** OR 97220-1312, *pg.* 1039, *pg.* 1508

Pennsylvania

ACME MARKETS, INC., 75 Valley Stream Pkwy, **Malvern,** PA 19355-1406, *pg.* 1012, *pg.* 1549
AHOLD USA, INC., 1149 Harrisburg Pk, **Carlisle,** PA 17013, *pg.* 1013, *pg.* 1520
ARAMARK, 1101 Market St, **Philadelphia,** PA 19107, *pg.* 1013, *pg.* 1558
GIANT EAGLE, INC., 101 Kappa Dr, **Pittsburgh,** PA 15238-2809, *pg.* 1020, *pg.* 1575
GIANT FOOD STORES, LLC, 1149 Harrisburg Pike, **Carlisle,** PA 17013-1665, *pg.* 1021, *pg.* 1520
KUNZLER & COMPANY, INC., 652 Manor St, **Lancaster,** PA 17603, *pg.* 1026, *pg.* 1546
QUAKER VALLEY FOODS INC., 2701 Red Lion Rd, **Philadelphia,** PA 19114-1019, *pg.* 1031, *pg.* 1570
SHEETZ, INC., 5700 6th Ave, **Altoona,** PA 16602, *pg.* 1033, *pg.* 1514
SUPERVALU, INC., HARRISBURG DIVISION, 500 S Muddy Creek Rd, **Denver,** PA 17517, *pg.* 1035, *pg.* 1526
WAWA, INC., 260 W Baltimore Pike, **Media,** PA 19063-5620, *pg.* 1037, *pg.* 1552
WEIS MARKETS, INC., 1000 S 2nd St PO Box 471, **Sunbury,** PA 17801-0471, *pg.* 1037, *pg.* 1588

South Carolina

BI-LO, LLC, 208 BI-LO Blvd, **Greenville,** SC 29607, *pg.* 1015, *pg.* 1617

Tennessee

ALADDIN TEMP-RITE, LLC, 250 E Main St, **Hendersonville,** TN 37075, *pg.* 1013, *pg.* 1635
THE H.T. HACKNEY COMPANY, 502 S Gay St, **Knoxville,** TN 37902-1503, *pg.* 1023, *pg.* 1637
MOODY DUNBAR INC., 2000 Waters Edge Dr, **Johnson City,** TN 37604, *pg.* 1028, *pg.* 1635

Texas

7-ELEVEN, INC., One Arts Plaza 1722 Routh St Ste 1000, **Dallas,** TX 75201, *pg.* 1012, *pg.* 1672
AFFILIATED FOODS, INC., 1401 W Farmers, **Amarillo,** TX 79118, *pg.* 1012, *pg.* 1658
ALON BRANDS, INC., 12700 Park Central Dr Ste 1600, **Dallas,** TX 75251, *pg.* 1013, *pg.* 1673
BIGLARI HOLDINGS INC., 17802 IH 10 West Ste 400, **San Antonio,** TX 78257, *pg.* 1015, *pg.* 1739
BROOKSHIRE GROCERY COMPANY, 1600 W SW Loop 323, **Tyler,** TX 75701-8532, *pg.* 1016, *pg.* 1748
DEL FRISCO'S RESTAURANT GROUP, LLC, 3232 McKinney Ave, **Dallas,** TX 75204, *pg.* 1018, *pg.* 1680
FIESTA MART LLC, 5235 Katy Fwy, **Houston,** TX 77007-2210, *pg.* 1019, *pg.* 1705
GERLAND CORPORATION, 3131 Pawnee St, **Houston,** TX 77054-3302, *pg.* 1020, *pg.* 1706
GSC ENTERPRISES, INC., 130 Hillcrest Dr, **Sulphur Springs,** TX 75482, *pg.* 1021, *pg.* 1746
H-E-B, 646 S Main Ave, **San Antonio,** TX 78204-1210, *pg.* 1022, *pg.* 1740
LOCAL & WESTERN OF TEXAS, INC., 5445 La Sierra, **Dallas,** TX 75231, *pg.* 1026, *pg.* 1683
RICE EPICUREAN MARKET, 2020 Fountain View, San Felipe, **Houston,** TX 77057, *pg.* 1032, *pg.* 1713
SYSCO CORPORATION, 1390 Enclave Pkwy, **Houston,** TX 77077-2099, *pg.* 1035, *pg.* 1716
UNITED SUPERMARKETS, L.L.C., 7830 Orlando Ave, **Lubbock,** TX 79423-1942, *pg.* 1036, *pg.* 1726
WHOLE FOODS MARKET, INC., 550 Bowie St, **Austin,** TX 78703, *pg.* 1038, *pg.* 1667

Utah

ASSOCIATED FOOD STORES, INC., 1850 W 2100 S, **Salt Lake City,** UT 84119, *pg.* 1014, *pg.* 1756
MAVERIK COUNTRY STORES, INC., 880 W Ctr St, **North Salt Lake,** UT 84054-2913, *pg.* 1027, *pg.* 1752
SMITH'S FOOD & DRUG CENTERS, INC., 1550 S Redwood Rd, **Salt Lake City,** UT 84104-5105, *pg.* 1034, *pg.* 1761

Virginia

FARM FRESH INC., 853 Chimney Hill Shopping Ctr, **Virginia Beach,** VA 23452, *pg.* 1019, *pg.* 1810
K-VA-T FOOD STORES, INC., 201 Trigg St PO Box 1158, **Abingdon,** VA 24210, *pg.* 1025, *pg.* 1770
PERFORMANCE FOOD GROUP COMPANY, LLC, 12500 W Creek Pkwy, **Richmond,** VA 23238-1110, *pg.* 1030, *pg.* 1803
SUPERVALU, INC. - EASTERN REGION, 8258 Richfood Rd, **Mechanicsville,** VA 23116-2008, *pg.* 1035, *pg.* 1795

Washington

HAGGEN, INC., 2211 Rimland Dr, **Bellingham,** WA 98226, *pg.* 1022, *pg.* 1817
OCEAN BEAUTY SEAFOODS, INC., 1100 W Ewing St, **Seattle,** WA 98127-1321, *pg.* 1028, *pg.* 1838
ROSAUERS SUPERMARKETS, INC., 1815 W Garland Ave, **Spokane,** WA 99205-2522, *pg.* 1032, *pg.* 1844
UNIFIED GROCERS, INC., 3301 S Norfolk St, **Seattle,** WA 98118-5648, *pg.* 1036, *pg.* 1842
URM STORES, INC., 7511 N Freya St PO Box 3365, **Spokane,** WA 99217-8004, *pg.* 1036, *pg.* 1844

West Virginia

GO-MART INC., 915 Riverside Dr, **Gassaway,** WV 26624, *pg.* 1021, *pg.* 1849

Wisconsin

THE COPPS CORPORATION, 2828 Wayne St, **Stevens Point,** WI 54481-4169, *pg.* 1017, *pg.* 1895
COUSINS SUBMARINES, INC., N83 W13400 Leon Rd, **Menomonee Falls,** WI 53051-3306, *pg.* 1017, *pg.* 1870
KWIK TRIP INC., 1626 Oak St, **La Crosse,** WI 54602, *pg.* 1026, *pg.* 1864
ROUNDY'S SUPERMARKETS INC., 875 E Wisconsin Ave, **Milwaukee,** WI 53202, *pg.* 1032, *pg.* 1880

First page reference indicates Business Class Edition
Second page reference indicates Geographic Edition

Hardware

Alabama

T&S PERFECTION CHAIN PRODUCTS, INC., 301 Goodwin Rd, **Cullman,** AL 35058, *pg.* 1065, *pg.* 5

Alaska

ALASKA INDUSTRIAL HARDWARE INC., 2192 Viking Dr, **Anchorage,** AK 99501-1731, *pg.* 1041, *pg.* 10

Arkansas

MKT FASTENING, LLC, 1 Gunnebo Dr, **Lonoke,** AR 72086, *pg.* 1056, *pg.* 34

California

ADAMS RITE AEROSPACE INC., 4141 N Palm St, **Fullerton,** CA 92835, *pg.* 1041, *pg.* 93

ALLFAST FASTENING SYSTEMS, INC., 15200 Don Julian Rd, **City of Industry,** CA 91745, *pg.* 1041, *pg.* 66

ASCO SINTERING CO., 2750 Garfield Ave, **Los Angeles,** CA 90040, *pg.* 1042, *pg.* 126

BOBRICK WASHROOM EQUIPMENT, INC., 11611 Hart St, **North Hollywood,** CA 91605-5882, *pg.* 1043, *pg.* 166

DARNELL-ROSE, 17915 Railroad St, **City of Industry,** CA 91748, *pg.* 1045, *pg.* 67

HOCHIKI AMERICA CORPORATION, 7051 Village Dr Ste 100, **Buena Park,** CA 90621, *pg.* 1050, *pg.* 50

ORCHARD SUPPLY HARDWARE STORES CORP., 6450 Via Del Oro, **San Jose,** CA 95119-1208, *pg.* 1058, *pg.* 248

PFISTER, INC., 19701 Da Vinci, **Foothill Ranch,** CA 92610-2622, *pg.* 1059, *pg.* 88

RESTORATION HARDWARE HOLDINGS, INC., 15 Koch Rd Ste K, **Corte Madera,** CA 94925, *pg.* 1060, *pg.* 70

ROHL LLC, 3 Parker, **Irvine,** CA 92618, *pg.* 1061, *pg.* 116

SNYDER-DIAMOND, 1399 Olympic Blvd, **Santa Monica,** CA 90404-3730, *pg.* 1062, *pg.* 276

THE TORO COMPANY IRRIGATION PRODUCTS, 5825 Jasmine St, **Riverside,** CA 92504-1144, *pg.* 1065, *pg.* 194

Connecticut

ABBOTT BALL COMPANY, 19 Railroad Pl, **West Hartford,** CT 06110-0100, *pg.* 1040, *pg.* 383

ACME UNITED CORPORATION, 55 Walls Dr, **Fairfield,** CT 06824, *pg.* 1040, *pg.* 346

AMATOM ELECTRONIC HARDWARE, INC., 5 Pasco Hill Rd, **Cromwell,** CT 06416-1093, *pg.* 1041, *pg.* 342

ASSA ABLOY DOOR SECURITY SOLUTIONS, 110 Sargent Dr, **New Haven,** CT 06511-5918, *pg.* 1042, *pg.* 358

EAO SWITCH CORPORATION, 98 Washington St, **Milford,** CT 06460-3670, *pg.* 1046, *pg.* 356

GIBBS WIRE & STEEL COMPANY, INC., Metals Dr PO Box 520, **Southington,** CT 06489, *pg.* 1048, *pg.* 371

HENKEL CORPORATION, 1001 Trout Brook Crossing 1 Hanco Way, **Rocky Hill,** CT 06067-3582, *pg.* 1049, *pg.* 369

MOORE TOOL COMPANY, INC., 800 Union Ave, **Bridgeport,** CT 06607-1137, *pg.* 1057, *pg.* 339

NORWALK POWDERED METALS, INC., 1100 Boston Ave Bldg 3, **Bridgeport,** CT 06610-2654, *pg.* 1058, *pg.* 340

SARGENT MANUFACTURING COMPANY, 100 Sargent Dr, **New Haven,** CT 06511-5918, *pg.* 1061, *pg.* 359

STANLEY BLACK & DECKER, INC., 1000 Stanley Dr, **New Britain,** CT 06053, *pg.* 1063, *pg.* 358

UNIVERSAL THREAD GRINDING COMPANY, 30 Chambers St, **Fairfield,** CT 06825, *pg.* 1066, *pg.* 349

District of Columbia

DANAHER CORPORATION, 2200 Pennsylvania Ave. N.W, Suite 800W, **Washington,** DC 20037-1701, *pg.* 1044, *pg.* 397

Florida

AGI-VR/WESSON INC, 2673 NE 9th Ave, **Cape Coral,** FL 33909, *pg.* 1041, *pg.* 415

ELECTRO-OPTIX, INC., 2181 N Powerline Rd Ste 1, **Pompano Beach,** FL 33069, *pg.* 1046, *pg.* 459

FARREY'S WHOLESALE HARDWARE CO., INC., 1850 NE 146th St, **Miami,** FL 33181, *pg.* 1047, *pg.* 442

INTERLINE BRANDS, INC., 701 San Marco Blvd, **Jacksonville,** FL 32207, *pg.* 1051, *pg.* 433

WATERWISE INC., 3608 Pkwy Blvd, **Leesburg,** FL 34748, *pg.* 1066, *pg.* 438

Georgia

HITACHI KOKI USA, LTD., 3950 Steve Reynolds Blvd, **Norcross,** GA 30093, *pg.* 1050, *pg.* 537

THE HOME DEPOT, INC., 2455 Paces Ferry Rd NW, **Atlanta,** GA 30339-4024, *pg.* 1050, *pg.* 510

SOUTHWIRE COMPANY, 1 Southwire Dr, **Carrollton,** GA 30119, *pg.* 1063, *pg.* 527

TOTO USA, INC., 1155 Southern Rd, **Morrow,** GA 30260-2917, *pg.* 1065, *pg.* 536

Idaho

ROCKY MOUNTAIN HARDWARE INC., 1030 Airport Way, **Hailey,** ID 83333, *pg.* 1061, *pg.* 549

Illinois

ACE HARDWARE CORPORATION, 2200 Kensington Ct, **Oak Brook,** IL 60523-2100, *pg.* 1040, *pg.* 644

A.L. HANSEN MANUFACTURING CO., 701 Pershing Rd, **Waukegan,** IL 60085-4079, *pg.* 1041, *pg.* 665

AMERICAN JEBCO CORPORATION, 11330 W Melrose Ave, **Franklin Park,** IL 60131-1367, *pg.* 1041, *pg.* 612

THE CHICAGO FAUCET COMPANY, 2100 S Clearwater Dr, **Des Plaines,** IL 60018-1918, *pg.* 1044, *pg.* 606

DREMEL, 1800 W Central Rd, **Mount Prospect,** IL 60056, *pg.* 1046, *pg.* 634

DRIV-LOK, INC., 1140 Pk Ave, **Sycamore,** IL 60178-2927, *pg.* 1046, *pg.* 662

ECHO INCORPORATED, 400 Oakwood Rd, **Lake Zurich,** IL 60047-1561, *pg.* 1046, *pg.* 626

ELECTRON BEAM TECHNOLOGIES, INC., 1275 Harvard Dr, **Kankakee,** IL 60901-9471, *pg.* 1046, *pg.* 621

ESSENTRA COMPONENTS, 7400 W Industrial Dr, **Forest Park,** IL 60130, *pg.* 1047, *pg.* 612

GERDAU AMERISTEEL JOLIET STEEL MILL, 1 Industry Ave, **Joliet,** IL 60435-2653, *pg.* 1048, *pg.* 621

GREENLEE TEXTRON INC., 4455 Boeing Dr, **Rockford,** IL 61109-2932, *pg.* 1048, *pg.* 655

GROHE AMERICA, INC., 241 Covington Dr, **Bloomingdale,** IL 60108-3109, *pg.* 1048, *pg.* 557

HENRY PRATT COMPANY, 401 S Highland Ave, **Aurora,** IL 60506-5580, *pg.* 1049, *pg.* 555

IDEAL INDUSTRIES, INC., 1375 Park Ave, **Sycamore,** IL 60178-2420, *pg.* 1051, *pg.* 662

KLEIN TOOLS INC., 450 Bond St, **Lincolnshire,** IL 60069-0350, *pg.* 1052, *pg.* 627

PASLODE, 888 Forest Edge Dr, **Vernon Hills,** IL 60061-3105, *pg.* 1059, *pg.* 664

PAYSON CASTERS, INC., 2323 N Delaney Rd, **Gurnee,** IL 60031, *pg.* 1059, *pg.* 616

ROBERT BOSCH TOOL CORP, 1800 W Central Rd, **Mount Prospect,** IL 60056, *pg.* 1060, *pg.* 634

SK HAND TOOL CORPORATION, 1600 S Prairie Dr, **Sycamore,** IL 60178, *pg.* 1062, *pg.* 663

SLOAN VALVE COMPANY, 10500 Seymour Ave, **Franklin Park,** IL 60131, *pg.* 1062, *pg.* 613

SPRAYING SYSTEMS CO., N Ave at Schmale Rd, **Wheaton,** IL 60188, *pg.* 1063, *pg.* 670

TRUE VALUE COMPANY, 8600 W Bryn Mawr Ave, **Chicago,** IL 60631-3579, *pg.* 1065, *pg.* 592

VAUGHAN & BUSHNELL MANUFACTURING COMPANY, INC., 11414 Maple Ave PO Box 390, **Hebron,** IL 60034, *pg.* 1066, *pg.* 616

Indiana

DO IT BEST CORP., 6502 Nelson Rd, **Fort Wayne,** IN 46803-1920, *pg.* 1045, *pg.* 680

THE FORD METER BOX COMPANY, INC., 775 Manchester Ave, **Wabash,** IN 46992, *pg.* 1047, *pg.* 698

LASALLE BRISTOL CORP., 601 County Rd 17, **Elkhart,** IN 46516, *pg.* 1053, *pg.* 677

Iowa

DECO PRODUCTS CO., 506 Sanford St, **Decorah,** IA 52101, *pg.* 1045, *pg.* 704

Kansas

CASHCO, INC., 607 W 15th St, **Ellsworth,** KS 67439, *pg.* 1044, *pg.* 714

WESTLAKE ACE HARDWARE, INC., 14000 Marshall Dr, **Lenexa,** KS 66215, *pg.* 1067, *pg.* 717

Kentucky

BROCK-MCVEY COMPANY, 1100 Brock McVey Dr, **Lexington,** KY 40509-4116, *pg.* 1043, *pg.* 729

REV-A-SHELF, 2409 Plantside Dr, **Louisville,** KY 40299-2527, *pg.* 1060, *pg.* 738

SARGENT & GREENLEAF, INC., 1 Security Dr, **Nicholasville,** KY 40356-2159, *pg.* 1061, *pg.* 739

Maine

EASTMAN INDUSTRIES, 410 Riverside St, **Portland,** ME 04103, *pg.* 1046, *pg.* 751

EMERY-WATERHOUSE COMPANY, 7 Rand Rd, **Portland,** ME 04104, *pg.* 1047, *pg.* 751

Maryland

DIXON VALVE & COUPLING COMPANY, 800 High St, **Chestertown,** MD 21620, *pg.* 1045, *pg.* 766

Massachusetts

AUBUCHON HARDWARE, 95 Aubuchon Dr, **Westminster,** MA 01473-1470, *pg.* 1043, *pg.* 859

HYER INDUSTRIES INC., 91 Schoosett St, **Pembroke,** MA 02359, *pg.* 1051, *pg.* 841

LENOX, 301 Chestnut St, **East Longmeadow,** MA 01028-5601, *pg.* 1053, *pg.* 817

LOWELL CORPORATION, 65 Hartwell St, **West Boylston,** MA 01583-2407, *pg.* 1053, *pg.* 856

MID-CAPE HOME CENTERS, 465 Rte 134, **South Dennis,** MA 02660, *pg.* 1056, *pg.* 844

STERN-LEACH, 49 Pearl St, **Attleboro,** MA 02703, *pg.* 1064, *pg.* 783

VERTEX DISTRIBUTION, 523 Pleasant St Bldg 10, **Attleboro,** MA 02703, *pg.* 1066, *pg.* 784

Michigan

ACO HARDWARE, INC., 23333 Commerce Dr, **Farmington Hills,** MI 48335-2727, *pg.* 1040, *pg.* 885

AROTECH CORPORATION, 1229 Oak Valley Dr, **Ann Arbor,** MI 48108, *pg.* 1042, *pg.* 865

BRASSCRAFT MANUFACTURING COMPANY, 39600 Orchard Hill Pl, **Novi,** MI 48375, *pg.* 1043, *pg.* 902

DE-STA-CO INDUSTRIES, 1025 Doris Rd, **Auburn Hills,** MI 48326, *pg.* 1045, *pg.* 867

KNAPE & VOGT MANUFACTURING COMPANY, 2700 Oak Industrial Dr NE, **Wyoming,** MI 49505-3408, *pg.* 1052, *pg.* 913

Minnesota

K-TEL INTERNATIONAL, INC., 2491 Xenium Ln N, **Plymouth,** MN 55441, *pg.* 1052, *pg.* 953

LAMPERT YARDS, INC., 1850 Como Ave, **Saint Paul,** MN 55108, *pg.* 1053, *pg.* 962

THE TORO COMPANY, 8111 Lyndale Ave S, **Bloomington,** MN 55420-1196, *pg.* 1065, *pg.* 918

TRUTH HARDWARE CORP., 700 W Bridge St, **Owatonna,** MN 55060, *pg.* 1066, *pg.* 952

TWIN CITY DIE CASTINGS CO., 1070 SE 33rd Ave, **Minneapolis,** MN 55414-2707, *pg.* 1066, *pg.* 945

Missouri

DETECTO SCALE COMPANY, 203 E Daugherty St, **Webb City,** MO 64870-1929, *pg.* 1045, *pg.* 1007
FIKE CORPORATION, 704 SW 10th St, **Blue Springs,** MO 64015, *pg.* 1047, *pg.* 973
MEEK'S BUILDING CENTERS, 1311 E Woodhurst Dr, **Springfield,** MO 65804-4282, *pg.* 1055, *pg.* 1006
MITEK, INC., 14515 N Outer Forty Rd Ste 300, **Chesterfield,** MO 63017, *pg.* 1056, *pg.* 975

Nevada

PANAVISE PRODUCTS, INC., 7540 Colbert Dr, **Reno,** NV 89511-1225, *pg.* 1058, *pg.* 1032

New Hampshire

NEW HAMPSHIRE BALL BEARINGS, INC., 175 Jaffrey Rd, **Peterborough,** NH 03458-1767, *pg.* 1058, *pg.* 1038
SOLIDSCAPE, INC., 316 Daniel Webster Hwy, **Merrimack,** NH 03054, *pg.* 1063, *pg.* 1037

New Jersey

ALLIED SECURITY INNOVATIONS, INC., 1709 Rte 34 S, **Farmingdale,** NJ 07727, *pg.* 1041, *pg.* 1066
ARROW FASTENER COMPANY, INC., 271 Mayhill St, **Saddle Brook,** NJ 07663-5303, *pg.* 1042, *pg.* 1118
HAYWARD POOL PRODUCTS, 620 Division St, **Elizabeth,** NJ 07207, *pg.* 1049, *pg.* 1057
JARCO/U.S. CASTINGS, 4407 Park Ave, **Union City,** NJ 07087, *pg.* 1051, *pg.* 1127
MICRO CORP., 140 Belmont Dr, **Somerset,** NJ 08873-1204, *pg.* 1056, *pg.* 1122
OUTWATER PLASTIC INDUSTRIES, INC., 24 River Rd, **Bogota,** NJ 07603, *pg.* 1058, *pg.* 1044
THERMWELL PRODUCTS CO., INC., 420 Rte 17 S, **Mahwah,** NJ 07430, *pg.* 1065, *pg.* 1082

New York

GENERAL TOOLS & INSTRUMENTS LLC, 80 White St, **New York,** NY 10013-3527, *pg.* 1048, *pg.* 1234
JOHN HASSALL, INC., 609-1 Cantiague Rock Rd, **Westbury,** NY 11590, *pg.* 1052, *pg.* 1350
MSC INDUSTRIAL DIRECT CO., INC., 75 Maxess Rd, **Melville,** NY 11747, *pg.* 1057, *pg.* 1181
OXO, 601 W 26th St 10th Fl St 1050, **New York,** NY 10001, *pg.* 1058, *pg.* 1275
POWERS FASTENERS INC., 2 Powers Ln, **Brewster,** NY 10509, *pg.* 1059, *pg.* 1143
PRECISION VALVE CORPORATION, 700 Nepperhan Ave, **Yonkers,** NY 10703, *pg.* 1060, *pg.* 1357
ROBINSON HOME PRODUCTS INC., 170 Lawrence Bell Dr, Ste 110, **Williamsville,** NY 14221, *pg.* 1060, *pg.* 1355
SIGMUND COHN CORP., 121 S Columbus Ave, **Mount Vernon,** NY 10553, *pg.* 1062, *pg.* 1183
SULZER METCO (WESTBURY) INC., 1101 Prospect Ave, **Westbury,** NY 11590-2724, *pg.* 1064, *pg.* 1350

North Carolina

CHARLOTTE PIPE & FOUNDRY COMPANY, 2109 Randolph Rd, **Charlotte,** NC 28207, *pg.* 1044, *pg.* 1365
CRANE CHEMPHARMA & ENERGY, 1 Quality Way, **Marion,** NC 28752, *pg.* 1044, *pg.* 1382
HAYS FLUID CONTROLS, 114 Eason Rd PO Box 580, **Dallas,** NC 28034, *pg.* 1049, *pg.* 1370
IMPULSE NC LLC, 100 IMPulse Way, **Mount Olive,** NC 28365-8691, *pg.* 1051, *pg.* 1385
KABA ILCO CORP., 400 Jeffreys Rd, **Rocky Mount,** NC 27804, *pg.* 1052, *pg.* 1390
LOWE'S COMPANIES, INC., 1000 Lowe's Blvd, **Mooresville,** NC 28117, *pg.* 1053, *pg.* 1383

Ohio

ATLAS BOLT & SCREW COMPANY, 1628 Troy Rd State Rte 511 N, **Ashland,** OH 44805, *pg.* 1042, *pg.* 1403
DORCY INTERNATIONAL INC., 2700 Port Rd, **Columbus,** OH 43217-1136, *pg.* 1046, *pg.* 1439
EBERHARD MANUFACTURING DIVISION, 21944 Drake Rd, **Strongsville,** OH 44149, *pg.* 1046, *pg.* 1475
ELYRIA FOUNDRY COMPANY, 120 Filbert St, **Elyria,** OH 44035, *pg.* 1046, *pg.* 1451
FEDERAL HOSE MANUFACTURING INC., 25 Florence Ave, **Painesville,** OH 44077-1103, *pg.* 1047, *pg.* 1469
THE FERRY CAP & SET SCREW COMPANY, 13300 Bramley Ave, **Lakewood,** OH 44107, *pg.* 1047, *pg.* 1457
GORILLA GLUE CO., 4550 Red Bank Expy, **Cincinnati,** OH 45227, *pg.* 1048, *pg.* 1414
KRAFTMAID CABINETRY, INC., 15535 S State Ave, **Middlefield,** OH 44062, *pg.* 1053, *pg.* 1465
LONG-LOK FASTENERS CORP., 10630 Chester Rd, **Cincinnati,** OH 45215, *pg.* 1053, *pg.* 1416
MATCO TOOLS CORPORATION, 4403 Allen Rd, **Stow,** OH 44224, *pg.* 1055, *pg.* 1474
METTLER-TOLEDO INC., 1900 Polaris Pkwy, **Columbus,** OH 43240, *pg.* 1056, *pg.* 1441
MOEN INCORPORATED, 25300 Al Moen Dr, **North Olmsted,** OH 44070-8022, *pg.* 1056, *pg.* 1468
MTD PRODUCTS, INC., 5965 Grafton Rd, **Valley City,** OH 44280, *pg.* 1057, *pg.* 1478
SENECA WIRE & MANUFACTURING COMPANY, 319 S Vine St, **Fostoria,** OH 44830-1843, *pg.* 1061, *pg.* 1454
SETCO SALES COMPANY, 5880 Hillside Ave, **Cincinnati,** OH 45233-1524, *pg.* 1061, *pg.* 1426
SUPPLY TECHNOLOGIES LLC, 6065 Parkland Blvd, **Cleveland,** OH 44124, *pg.* 1064, *pg.* 1436
SWAGELOK COMPANY, 29500 Solon Rd, **Solon,** OH 44139-3449, *pg.* 1064, *pg.* 1473
UNIVERSAL INDUSTRIAL PRODUCTS CO., 1 Coreway Dr, **Pioneer,** OH 43554-0628, *pg.* 1066, *pg.* 1470

Oklahoma

GERDAU AMERISTEEL SAND SPRINGS STEEL MILL, 2300 S Hwy 97, **Sand Springs,** OK 74063-7914, *pg.* 1048, *pg.* 1488

Oregon

BLOUNT INTERNATIONAL, INC., 4909 SE International Way, **Portland,** OR 97222-4679, *pg.* 1043, *pg.* 1501
JELD-WEN, INC., 401 Harbor Isles Blvd, **Klamath Falls,** OR 97601, *pg.* 1051, *pg.* 1499
LEATHERMAN TOOL GROUP, INC., 12106 NE Ainsworth Cir, **Portland,** OR 97220-9001, *pg.* 1053, *pg.* 1504

Pennsylvania

AMERICAN MACHINE & TOOL COMPANY, INC., 400 Springs St, **Royersford,** PA 19468-0070, *pg.* 1042, *pg.* 1585
ATT HOLDING CO., 465 Railroad Ave, **Camp Hill,** PA 17001, *pg.* 1043, *pg.* 1519
CHANNELLOCK, INC., 1306 S Main St, **Meadville,** PA 16335-3035, *pg.* 1044, *pg.* 1551
KENNAMETAL INC., 1600 Technology Way, **Latrobe,** PA 15650-4647, *pg.* 1052, *pg.* 1547
MORRIS COUPLING COMPANY, 2240 W 15th St, **Erie,** PA 16505, *pg.* 1057, *pg.* 1530
NEWAGE TESTING INSTRUMENTS, INC., 820 Pennsylvania Blvd, **Feasterville Trevose,** PA 19053, *pg.* 1058, *pg.* 1532
ORBEL CORPORATION, 2 Danforth Dr, **Easton,** PA 18045, *pg.* 1058, *pg.* 1528
PCC SPS FASTENER DIVISION, 301 Highland Ave, **Jenkintown,** PA 19046, *pg.* 1059, *pg.* 1542
PENN ENGINEERING & MANUFACTURING CORP., 5190 Old Easton Rd Bldg 3, **Danboro,** PA 18916, *pg.* 1059, *pg.* 1525
PENNENGINEERING FASTENING TECHNOLOGIES, 5190 Old Easton Rd, **Danboro,** PA 18916, *pg.* 1059, *pg.* 1526
PENNSYLVANIA SCALE COMPANY, 1042 New Holland Ave, **Lancaster,** PA 17601, *pg.* 1059, *pg.* 1546
SCHILLER-PFEIFFER, INC., 1028 St Rd, **Southampton,** PA 18966-4227, *pg.* 1061, *pg.* 1587
SFS INTEC, INC., Spring St & Van Reed Rd, **Wyomissing,** PA 19610, *pg.* 1061, *pg.* 1596
SOUTHCO, INC., 210 N Brinton Lk Rd, **Concordville,** PA 19331, *pg.* 1063, *pg.* 1522
VICTAULIC COMPANY, 4901 Kesslersville Rd, **Easton,** PA 18044-0031, *pg.* 1066, *pg.* 1529

Rhode Island

ACS INDUSTRIES, INC., 1 New England Way, **Lincoln,** RI 02865, *pg.* 1040, *pg.* 1602
GRIPNAIL CORPORATION, 97 Dexter Rd, **East Providence,** RI 02914-2045, *pg.* 1048, *pg.* 1601
GROOV-PIN CORPORATION, 331 Farnum Pike, **Smithfield,** RI 02917, *pg.* 1049, *pg.* 1608
HINDLEY MANUFACTURING COMPANY, INC., 9 Havens St, **Cumberland,** RI 02864, *pg.* 1049, *pg.* 1601
KENNEY MANUFACTURING COMPANY, 1000 Jefferson Blvd, **Warwick,** RI 02886, *pg.* 1052, *pg.* 1609

South Carolina

MACLEAN POWER SYSTEMS, Kingsley Park Five 481 Munn Rd Ste 300, **Fort Mill,** SC 29715, *pg.* 1054, *pg.* 1615
STARRETT, 5965 Core Ave Ste 618, **North Charleston,** SC 29406-4909, *pg.* 1064, *pg.* 1621

Tennessee

SHERMAN & REILLY, INC., 400 W 33rd St, **Chattanooga,** TN 37410-1039, *pg.* 1062, *pg.* 1629

Texas

AMERICAN LOCKER GROUP INCORPORATED, 2701 Regent Blvd Ste 200, **Dallas,** TX 75621, *pg.* 1041, *pg.* 1674
AMERICAN LOCKER SECURITY SYSTEMS, INC., 2701 Regent Blvd Ste 200, **Dallas,** TX 75019, *pg.* 1042, *pg.* 1674
COMPX INTERNATIONAL INC., 5430 LBJ Fwy Ste 1700, **Dallas,** TX 75240, *pg.* 1044, *pg.* 1678
FOXWORTH-GALBRAITH LUMBER COMPANY, 4965 Preston Park Blvd Ste 400, **Plano,** TX 75093-5141, *pg.* 1047, *pg.* 1730
MCCOY'S BUILDING SUPPLY CENTERS, 1350 N Interstate 35, **San Marcos,** TX 78666-7118, *pg.* 1055, *pg.* 1744
MG BUILDING MATERIALS, 2651 SW Military Dr, **San Antonio,** TX 78224-1048, *pg.* 1056, *pg.* 1741
MILLERS FORGE INC., 1411 Capital Ave, **Plano,** TX 75074-8119, *pg.* 1056, *pg.* 1733
MR. ROOTER CORPORATION, 1010 N University Parks Dr, **Waco,** TX 76707-3854, *pg.* 1057, *pg.* 1749
SOUTHERN FOLGER DETENTION EQUIPMENT COMPANY, 4634 S Presa St PO Box 2021, **San Antonio,** TX 78223, *pg.* 1063, *pg.* 1743

Vermont

CHAMPLAIN CABLE CORP., 175 Hercules Dr, **Colchester,** VT 05446-5925, *pg.* 1044, *pg.* 1765

Virginia

MEDECO HIGH SECURITY LOCKS, INC., 3625 Alleghany Dr, **Salem,** VA 24153, *pg.* 1055, *pg.* 1806
MELNOR, INC., 109 Tyson Dr, **Winchester,** VA 22603, *pg.* 1055, *pg.* 1811
STIHL, INC., 536 Viking Dr, **Virginia Beach,** VA 23452, *pg.* 1064, *pg.* 1810

Washington

ROMAC INDUSTRIES, INC., 21919 20th Ave SE Ste 100, **Bothell,** WA 98021-4446, *pg.* 1061, *pg.* 1818

Wisconsin

AIR-LEC INDUSTRIES LLC, 3300 Commercial Ave, **Madison,** WI 53714-1458, *pg.* 1041, *pg.* 1864
C&H DISTRIBUTORS, LLC, 770 S 70th St, **Milwaukee,** WI 53214, *pg.* 1044, *pg.* 1873
E.R. WAGNER CASTERS AND WHEELS DIV., 4611 N 32nd St, **Milwaukee,** WI 53209, *pg.* 1047, *pg.* 1874
FISCHER SPINDLE GROUP, 3715 Blue River Ave, **Racine,** WI 53405, *pg.* 1047, *pg.* 1888
HAMMOND VALVE CORP., 16550 W Stratton Dr, **New Berlin,** WI 53151, *pg.* 1049, *pg.* 1883
LAVELLE INDUSTRIES INC., 665 McHenry St, **Burlington,** WI 53105, *pg.* 1053, *pg.* 1856
MASTER APPLIANCE CORP., 2420 18th St, **Racine,** WI

53403, *pg.* 1055, *pg.* 1888
MASTER LOCK COMPANY LLC, 137 W Forrest Hills Ave, **Oak Creek,** WI 53154, *pg.* 1055, *pg.* 1884
MENARD, INC., 5101 Menard Dr, **Eau Claire,** WI 54703-9604, *pg.* 1055, *pg.* 1857
MILWAUKEE ELECTRIC TOOL CORP., 13135 W Lisbon Rd, **Brookfield,** WI 53005-2550, *pg.* 1056, *pg.* 1855
SNAP-ON INCORPORATED, 2801 80th St, **Kenosha,** WI 53143, *pg.* 1062, *pg.* 1862

Heating & Air Conditioning

Arizona

SEELEY INTERNATIONAL AMERICAS, 1202 N 54th Ave Bldg 2 Ste 117, **Phoenix,** AZ 85043, *pg.* 1076, *pg.* 19

Arkansas

RHEEM MANUFACTURING - AIR CONDITIONING DIV, 5600 Old Greenwood Rd, **Fort Smith,** AR 72908-6586, *pg.* 1075, *pg.* 32

California

ACCO ENGINEERED SYSTEMS, 6265 San Fernando Rd, **Glendale,** CA 91201-2214, *pg.* 1068, *pg.* 05
FAFCO INC., 435 Otterson Dr, **Chico,** CA 95928, *pg.* 1071, *pg.* 65
PREMIER POWER RENEWABLE ENERGY, INC., 4961 Windplay Dr Ste 100, **El Dorado Hills,** CA 95762, *pg.* 1075, *pg.* 78
S.T. JOHNSON CO., 925 Stanford Ave, **Oakland,** CA 94608, *pg.* 1077, *pg.* 173

Colorado

REAL GOODS SOLAR, INC., 833 W South Boulder Rd, **Louisville,** CO 80027-2452, *pg.* 1075, *pg.* 334

Connecticut

CARRIER CORPORATION, 1 Carrier Pl, **Farmington,** CT 06032-4015, *pg.* 1070, *pg.* 349
PREFERRED UTILITIES MANUFACTURING CORPORATION, 31 35 South St, **Danbury,** CT 06810-8147, *pg.* 1075, *pg.* 344

Florida

EDD HELMS GROUP, INC., 17850 NE 5th Ave, **Miami,** FL 33162-1008, *pg.* 1071, *pg.* 442
N&M COOL TODAY, INC., 6143 Clark Center Ave, **Sarasota,** FL 34238, *pg.* 1074, *pg.* 466
WATSCO INC., 2665 S Bayshore Dr Ste 901, **Coconut Grove,** FL 33133, *pg.* 1078, *pg.* 417

Georgia

HILL PHOENIX INC., 2016 Gees Mill Rd, **Conyers,** GA 30013, *pg.* 1072, *pg.* 528
RHEEM MANUFACTURING COMPANY, 1100 Abernathy Rd Ste 1400, **Atlanta,** GA 30328, *pg.* 1075, *pg.* 519
RINNAI AMERICA CORP., 103 Intl Dr, **Peachtree City,** GA 30269-1911, *pg.* 1076, *pg.* 538

Illinois

THE GRIEVE CORPORATION, 500 Hart Rd, **Round Lake,** IL 60073-2835, *pg.* 1072, *pg.* 657
IPSEN INTERNATIONAL, INC., 984 Ipsen Rd, **Cherry Valley,** IL 61016, *pg.* 1073, *pg.* 562
MFRI INC., 7720 N Lehigh Ave, **Niles,** IL 60714, *pg.* 1074, *pg.* 637

Indiana

DOMETIC CORPORATION, 2320 Industrial Pkwy, **Elkhart,** IN 46516, *pg.* 1070, *pg.* 677

Maine

VULCAN ELECTRIC COMPANY, 28 Endfield St, **Porter,** ME 04068-3502, *pg.* 1078, *pg.* 751

Maryland

BALTIMORE AIRCOIL COMPANY, 7600 Dorsey Run Rd, **Jessup,** MD 20794-9323, *pg.* 1069, *pg.* 773

Massachusetts

AMERICAN DG ENERGY INC., 45 1st Ave, **Waltham,** MA 02451, *pg.* 1068, *pg.* 850
EMCOR SERVICES NORTHEAST COMMAIR/BALCO, 80 Hawes Way, **Stoughton,** MA 02072, *pg.* 1071, *pg.* 847
LYTRON INCORPORATED, 55 Dragon Ct, **Woburn,** MA 01801, *pg.* 1074, *pg.* 861
MESTEK, INC., 260 N Elm St, **Westfield,** MA 01085-1614, *pg.* 1074, *pg.* 857
WATTS WATER TECHNOLOGIES, INC., 815 Chestnut St, **North Andover,** MA 01845-6098, *pg.* 1078, *pg.* 837

Michigan

ARMSTRONG INTERNATIONAL, INC., 816 Maple St, **Three Rivers,** MI 49093-2345, *pg.* 1069, *pg.* 900
DETROIT STOKER CO., 1510 E 1st St, **Monroe,** MI 48161-1915, *pg.* 1070, *pg.* 900
FLEXFAB HORIZONS INTERNATIONAL, LLC, 1699 W M43 Hwy, **Hastings,** MI 49058-9629, *pg.* 1072, *pg.* 891
GENERAL FILTERS, INC., 43800 Grand River Ave, **Novi,** MI 48375-1115, *pg.* 1072, *pg.* 903
HEAT CONTROLLER, INC., 1900 Wellworth, **Jackson,** MI 49203-6428, *pg.* 1072, *pg.* 893
KADANT JOHNSON INC., 805 Wood St, **Three Rivers,** MI 49093, *pg.* 1073, *pg.* 909

Minnesota

DESPATCH INDUSTRIES, 8860 207th St W, **Lakeville,** MN 55044, *pg.* 1070, *pg.* 927
THERMO KING CORPORATION, 314 W 90th St, **Bloomington,** MN 55420-3630, *pg.* 1077, *pg.* 918

Missouri

EMERSON WHITE-RODGERS, 8100 W Florissant Ave, **Saint Louis,** MO 63136, *pg.* 1071, *pg.* 996
NOOTER/ERIKSEN, INC., 1509 Ocello Dr, **Fenton,** MO 63026, *pg.* 1075, *pg.* 977
NORTEK GLOBAL HVAC, 8000 Phoenix Pkwy, **O Fallon,** MO 63368, *pg.* 1075, *pg.* 989
WATLOW ELECTRIC MANUFACTURING COMPANY, 12001 Lackland Rd, **Saint Louis,** MO 63146, *pg.* 1078, *pg.* 1004

New Jersey

EVERGREEN ELECTRIC, INC., 59 Frog Hollow Rd, **Califon,** NJ 07830-3212, *pg.* 1071, *pg.* 1048
HEAT-TIMER CORPORATION, 20 New Dutch Ln, **Fairfield,** NJ 07004, *pg.* 1072, *pg.* 1065

New York

AERCO INTERNATIONAL INC., 100 Oritani Dr, **Blauvelt,** NY 10913-1022, *pg.* 1068, *pg.* 1142
AMETEK ROTRON, 55 Hasbrouck Ln, **Woodstock,** NY 12498-1807, *pg.* 1068, *pg.* 1356
EMBASSY INDUSTRIES, INC., 315 Oser Ave, **Hauppauge,** NY 11788, *pg.* 1071, *pg.* 1164
HUDSON TECHNOLOGIES, INC., 1 Blue Hill Plz PO Box 1541, **Pearl River,** NY 10965, *pg.* 1073, *pg.* 1320
P&F INDUSTRIES, INC., 445 Broadhollow Rd Ste 100, **Melville,** NY 11747, *pg.* 1075, *pg.* 1182
ROBERTS-GORDON INC., 1250 William St, **Buffalo,** NY 14206, *pg.* 1076, *pg.* 1151
SLANT/FIN CORPORATION, 100 Forest Dr, **Greenvale,** NY 11548, *pg.* 1076, *pg.* 1163
SLOMIN'S INC., 125 Lauman Ln, **Hicksville,** NY 11801-6522, *pg.* 1076, *pg.* 1167
XYLEM INC., 1 International Dr, **Rye Brook,** NY 10573, *pg.* 1078, *pg.* 1339

North Carolina

BUHLER AEROGLIDE, 100 Aeroglide Dr, **Cary,** NC 27511-6900, *pg.* 1069, *pg.* 1359
FIELD CONTROLS LLC, 2630 Airport Rd, **Kinston,** NC 28504-7319, *pg.* 1071, *pg.* 1380

Ohio

BABCOCK & WILCOX POWER GENERATION GROUP, INC., 20 S Van Buren Ave, **Barberton,** OH 44203-0351, *pg.* 1069, *pg.* 1404
BARD MANUFACTURING COMPANY, 1914 Randolph Dr, **Bryan,** OH 43506-2253, *pg.* 1069, *pg.* 1406
CINCINNATI SUB-ZERO PRODUCTS, INC., 12011 Mosteller Rd, **Cincinnati,** OH 45241-1528, *pg.* 1070, *pg.* 1411
DIAMOND POWER INTERNATIONAL, INC., 2600 E Main St, **Lancaster,** OH 43130-8490, *pg.* 1070, *pg.* 1457
EMERSON NETWORK POWER, 610 Exec Campus Dr, **Westerville,** OH 43082-8871, *pg.* 1071, *pg.* 1479
EMERSON NETWORK POWER LIEBERT, 1050 Dearborn Dr, **Columbus,** OH 43085, *pg.* 1071, *pg.* 1439
MEASUREMENT SPECIALTIES/YSI TEMPERATURE, 1700/1725 Brannum Ln, **Yellow Springs,** OH 45387-1107, *pg.* 1074, *pg.* 1482
SURFACE COMBUSTION, INC., 1700 Indian Wood Cir, **Maumee,** OH 43537-4005, *pg.* 1077, *pg.* 1462
YOUNG REGULATOR COMPANY, 7100 Krick Rd, **Walton Hills,** OH 44146, *pg.* 1078, *pg.* 1478

Oklahoma

AAON, INC., 2425 S Yukon Ave, **Tulsa,** OK 74107-2728, *pg.* 1068, *pg.* 1488
JOHNSON CONTROLS UNITARY PRODUCTS, 5005 York Dr, **Norman,** OK 73069, *pg.* 1073, *pg.* 1484

Pennsylvania

AJAX ELECTRIC CO., 60 Tomlinson Rd, **Huntingdon Valley,** PA 19006, *pg.* 1068, *pg.* 1541
BRADFORD-WHITE CORPORATION, 725 Talamore Dr, **Ambler,** PA 19002-1815, *pg.* 1069, *pg.* 1514
BURNHAM HOLDINGS, INC., 1241 Harrisburg Pike, **Lancaster,** PA 17603, *pg.* 1069, *pg.* 1546
CHROMALOX, INC., 103 Gamma Dr, **Pittsburgh,** PA 15238-2919, *pg.* 1070, *pg.* 1574
GEA REFRIGERATION NORTH AMERICA, INC., 3475 Board Rd, **York,** PA 17406-9414, *pg.* 1072, *pg.* 1597
JOHNSON CONTROLS, INC., 631 S Richland Ave, **York,** PA 17403-3445, *pg.* 1073, *pg.* 1597
NAO, INC., 1284 E Sedgley Ave, **Philadelphia,** PA 19134, *pg.* 1074, *pg.* 1567
PEIRCE-PHELPS, INC., 2000 N 59th St, **Philadelphia,** PA 19131-3031, *pg.* 1075, *pg.* 1568
SECO/WARWICK CORPORATION, 180 Mercer St, **Meadville,** PA 16335-3618, *pg.* 1076, *pg.* 1552
SELAS HEAT TECHNOLOGY COMPANY LLC, 130 Keystone Dr, **Montgomeryville,** PA 18936-8375, *pg.* 1076, *pg.* 1553

Rhode Island

C.I. HAYES, 33 Freeway Dr, **Cranston,** RI 02920, *pg.* 1070, *pg.* 1600
TACO INCORPORATED, 1160 Cranston St, **Cranston,** RI 02920-7335, *pg.* 1077, *pg.* 1601

South Carolina

MARLEY ENGINEERED PRODUCTS, 470 Beauty Spot Rd, **Bennettsville,** SC 29512, *pg.* 1074, *pg.* 1612
SPIRAX SARCO, INC., 1150 Northpoint Blvd, **Blythewood,** SC 29016, *pg.* 1076, *pg.* 1612

Tennessee

LOCHINVAR CORPORATION, 300 Maddox Simpson Pkwy, **Lebanon,** TN 37090, *pg.* 1073, *pg.* 1640

Texas

AMOT CONTROLS CORPORATION, 8824 Fallbrook Dr, **Houston,** TX 77064, *pg.* 1068, *pg.* 1700
ECODYNE HEAT EXCHANGERS, INC., 8203 Market St Rd, **Houston,** TX 77029, *pg.* 1071, *pg.* 1705
FRIEDRICH AIR CONDITIONING CO., 10001 Reunion PL Ste 500, **San Antonio,** TX 78216, *pg.* 1072, *pg.* 1740

First page reference indicates Business Class Edition
Second page reference indicates Geographic Edition

GOODMAN GROUP, INC., 5151 San Felipe Ste 500, **Houston,** TX 77056, *pg.* 1072, *pg.* 1706
LENNOX INTERNATIONAL INC., 2140 Lake Park Blvd, **Richardson,** TX 75080, *pg.* 1073, *pg.* 1736
SELKIRK CORPORATION, 1301 W President Bush Hwy Ste 330, **Richardson,** TX 75080, *pg.* 1076, *pg.* 1736
TD INDUSTRIES, INC., 13850 Diplomat Dr, **Dallas,** TX 75234-8812, *pg.* 1077, *pg.* 1688
THERMON AMERICAS INC., 100 Thermon Dr, **San Marcos,** TX 78666-5947, *pg.* 1077, *pg.* 1744

Virginia

AEROFIN CORP., 4621 Murray Pl, **Lynchburg,** VA 24502-2235, *pg.* 1068, *pg.* 1787

Wisconsin

BROAN-NUTONE LLC, 926 W State St, **Hartford,** WI 53027-0140, *pg.* 1069, *pg.* 1860
MODINE MANUFACTURING COMPANY, 1500 DeKoven Ave, **Racine,** WI 53403-2552, *pg.* 1074, *pg.* 1888
RESEARCH PRODUCTS CORPORATION, 1015 E Washington Ave, **Madison,** WI 53703-2938, *pg.* 1075, *pg.* 1867
VILTER MANUFACTURING LLC, 5555 S Packard Ave, **Cudahy,** WI 53110-2658, *pg.* 1078, *pg.* 1856

Hotels, Resorts & Real Estate

Alabama

HONOURS GOLF COMPANY, LLC, 1960 Stonegate Dr, **Birmingham,** AL 35242, *pg.* 1096, *pg.* 3
JIM WILSON & ASSOCIATES, INC., Ste 100 2660 Eastchase Ln, **Montgomery,** AL 36117-7024, *pg.* 1098, *pg.* 7
REALTYSOUTH, 2501 20th Pl S Ste 400, **Birmingham,** AL 35223-1744, *pg.* 1109, *pg.* 4

Arizona

AV HOMES INC., 8601 N Scottsdale Rd Ste 225, **Scottsdale,** AZ 85283, *pg.* 1080, *pg.* 20
BEST WESTERN INTERNATIONAL, INC., 6201 N 24th Pkwy, **Phoenix,** AZ 85016-2023, *pg.* 1081, *pg.* 15
CANYON RANCH MANAGEMENT, LLC, 8600 E Rockcliff Rd, **Tucson,** AZ 85750, *pg.* 1084, *pg.* 27
GILA RIVER GAMING ENTERPRISES, INC., 5040 W Wild Horse Pass Blvd, **Chandler,** AZ 85246, *pg.* 1093, *pg.* 12
INNSUITES HOSPITALITY TRUST, InnSuites Hotel Ctr 1625 E Northern Ave Ste 105, **Phoenix,** AZ 85020, *pg.* 1097, *pg.* 17
KITCHELL CORPORATION, 1707 E Highland Ste 100, **Phoenix,** AZ 85016, *pg.* 1099, *pg.* 17
LONG REALTY COMPANY, 900 E River Rd, **Tucson,** AZ 85718-5600, *pg.* 1101, *pg.* 27
MCO PROPERTIES INC., 13620 N Sagaro Blvd Ste 200, **Fountain Hills,** AZ 85268, *pg.* 1104, *pg.* 13
MIRAVAL RESORT, 5000 E Via Estancia Miraval, **Catalina,** AZ 85739, *pg.* 1105, *pg.* 12
RED DEVELOPMENT, One E Washington Ste 300, **Phoenix,** AZ 85004, *pg.* 1109, *pg.* 19
TAYLOR MORRISON, 4900 N Scottsdale Rd, Ste 2000, **Scottsdale,** AZ 85251, *pg.* 1116, *pg.* 24

California

ARDEN REALTY, INC., 11601 Wilshire Blvd 4th Fl, **Los Angeles,** CA 90025-1740, *pg.* 1080, *pg.* 126
AUBERGE RESORTS, LLC, 591 Redwood Hwy Ste 3150, **Mill Valley,** CA 94941, *pg.* 1080, *pg.* 145
BARONA RESORT & CASINO, 1932 Wildcat Canyon Rd, **Lakeside,** CA 92040, *pg.* 1080, *pg.* 121
BERKSHIRE HATHAWAY HOME SERVICES, 2365 Northside Dr Ste 420, **San Diego,** CA 92130, *pg.* 1081, *pg.* 200
THE BEVERLY HILLS HOTEL, 9641 Sunset Blvd, **Beverly Hills,** CA 90210-2938, *pg.* 1082, *pg.* 46
CALATLANTIC GROUP, INC., 15360 Barranca Pkwy, **Irvine,** CA 92618, *pg.* 1084, *pg.* 108
CB RICHARD ELLIS GROUP, INC., 11150 Santa Monica Blvd Ste 1600, **Los Angeles,** CA 90025, *pg.* 1085, *pg.* 127
ESSEX PROPERTY TRUST, INC., 925 E Meadow Dr, **Palo Alto,** CA 94303-4233, *pg.* 1091, *pg.* 175
GALAXY HOTEL SYSTEMS LLC, 15621 Red Hill Ave Ste 100, **Tustin,** CA 92780-7322, *pg.* 1092, *pg.* 297
THE IRVINE COMPANY INC., 550 Newport Ctr Dr, **Newport Beach,** CA 92660-7011, *pg.* 1098, *pg.* 165
KENNEDY-WILSON, INC., 9701 Wilshire Blvd Ste 700, **Beverly Hills,** CA 90212, *pg.* 1099, *pg.* 46
KILROY REALTY CORPORATION, 12200 W Olympic Blvd Ste 200, **Los Angeles,** CA 90064, *pg.* 1099, *pg.* 134
KIMPTON HOTEL & RESTAURANT GROUP, 222 Kearny St Ste 200, **San Francisco,** CA 94108, *pg.* 1099, *pg.* 220
KSL RESORTS, 50-905 Avenida Bermudas, **La Quinta,** CA 92253, *pg.* 1099, *pg.* 120
THE MACERICH COMPANY, 401 Wilshire Blvd Ste 700, **Santa Monica,** CA 90401, *pg.* 1101, *pg.* 275
MAMMOTH MOUNTAIN SKI AREA, 1 Minaret Rd, **Mammoth Lakes,** CA 93546, *pg.* 1102, *pg.* 142
MARCUS & MILLICHAP REAL ESTATE INVESTMENT COMPANY, 23975 Park Sorrento, Ste 400, **Calabasas,** CA 91302, *pg.* 1102, *pg.* 56
MCGRATH RENTCORP, 5700 Las Positas Rd, **Livermore,** CA 94551-7800, *pg.* 1104, *pg.* 122
NEWLAND REAL ESTATE GROUP, LLC, 9820 Towne Center Dr Ste 100, **San Diego,** CA 92121, *pg.* 1106, *pg.* 205
OJAI VALLEY INN & SPA, 905 Country Club Rd, **Ojai,** CA 93023, *pg.* 1106, *pg.* 173
OVERTON MOORE PROPERTIES, 19300 S Hamilton Ave Ste 200, **Gardena,** CA 90248-4337, *pg.* 1107, *pg.* 94
PACIFICA HOTEL COMPANY, 17300 Red Hill Ste 250, **Irvine,** CA 92614, *pg.* 1107, *pg.* 114
PORTSMOUTH SQUARE, INC., 10940 Wilshire Blvd Ste 2150, **Los Angeles,** CA 90024, *pg.* 1108, *pg.* 139
PRUDENTIAL REAL ESTATE AFFILIATES, INC., 3333 Michelson Dr Ste 1000, **Irvine,** CA 92612-1690, *pg.* 1108, *pg.* 115
PS BUSINESS PARKS, INC., 701 Western Ave, **Glendale,** CA 91201-2397, *pg.* 1108, *pg.* 98
PUEBLO BONITO HOTELS & RESORTS, 4350 La Jolla Village Dr Ste 460, **San Diego,** CA 92122, *pg.* 1108, *pg.* 206
SAVE THE QUEEN, LLC., 1126 Queens Highway, **Long Beach,** CA 90802, *pg.* 1111, *pg.* 124
SUNSTONE HOTEL INVESTORS, INC., 120 Vantis Ste 350, **Aliso Viejo,** CA 92656, *pg.* 1116, *pg.* 41
TEJON RANCH COMPANY, 4436 Lebec Rd, PO Box 1000, **Lebec,** CA 93243, *pg.* 1116, *pg.* 122
VACABOND FRANCHISE SYSTEM, INC., 3101 S Figueroa, **Los Angeles,** CA 90007, *pg.* 1117, *pg.* 141
ZIPREALTY, INC., 2000 Powell St Ste 300, **Emeryville,** CA 94608, *pg.* 1120, *pg.* 85

Colorado

AIMCO PROPERTIES, L.P., 4582 S Ulster St Pkwy Ste 1100, **Denver,** CO 80237, *pg.* 1079, *pg.* 316
APARTMENT INVESTMENT AND MANAGEMENT COMPANY, 4582 S Ulster St Ste 1100, **Denver,** CO 80237, *pg.* 1079, *pg.* 316
BROADMOOR HOTEL, INC., 1 Lk Ave, **Colorado Springs,** CO 80906-4254, *pg.* 1083, *pg.* 315
CRESTED BUTTE MOUNTAIN RESORT, INC., 17 Emmons Loop, **Crested Butte,** CO 81225, *pg.* 1088, *pg.* 316
EXCLUSIVE RESORTS, LLC, 1515 Arapahoe Carver St Ste 300, **Denver,** CO 80202, *pg.* 1091, *pg.* 319
INTRAWEST ULC, 1621 18th St Ste 300, **Denver,** CO 80202, *pg.* 1098, *pg.* 320
M.D.C. HOLDINGS, INC., 4350 S Monaco St Ste 500, **Denver,** CO 80237, *pg.* 1104, *pg.* 321
PROLOGIS, 4545 Airport Way, **Denver,** CO 80239, *pg.* 1108, *pg.* 322
RE/MAX INTERNATIONAL, INC., 5075 S Syracuse St, **Denver,** CO 80237, *pg.* 1109, *pg.* 322
SNOWMASS VILLAGE RESORT ASSOCIATION, 130 Kearns Rd, **Snowmass Village,** CO 81615, *pg.* 1113, *pg.* 335
STEAMBOAT SKI & RESORT CORPORATION, 2305 Mount Werner Cir, **Steamboat Springs,** CO 80487-9023, *pg.* 1115, *pg.* 336
VAIL RESORTS, INC., 390 Interlocken Crescent, **Broomfield,** CO 80021, *pg.* 1117, *pg.* 313

Connecticut

GE CAPITAL REAL ESTATE, 901 Main Ave, **Norwalk,** CT 06902, *pg.* 1093, *pg.* 362
THE SHERATON CORPORATION, One StarPoint, **Stamford,** CT 06902, *pg.* 1112, *pg.* 378
STARWOOD HOTELS & RESORTS WORLDWIDE, INC., One StarPoint, **Stamford,** CT 06902, *pg.* 1114, *pg.* 378
WESTIN HOTELS & RESORTS, One StarPoint, **Stamford,** CT 06902, *pg.* 1118, *pg.* 379

Florida

BAYOU GOLF CLUB, 7979 Bayou Club Blvd, **Largo,** FL 33777-3040, *pg.* 1081, *pg.* 438
BERKSHIRE HATHAWAY HOME SERVICES, 1580 Sawgrass Corp Pkwy, Ste 400, **Sunrise,** FL 33323, *pg.* 1081, *pg.* 469
BLUEGREEN CORPORATION, 4960 Conference Way N Ste 100, **Boca Raton,** FL 33431-4490, *pg.* 1082, *pg.* 410
CANDY SWICK & COMPANY, 2063 Main St, **Sarasota,** FL 34237, *pg.* 1084, *pg.* 465
CENTRAL FLORIDA INVESTMENTS INC., 5601 Windhover Dr, **Orlando,** FL 32819-7914, *pg.* 1085, *pg.* 452
COASTAL CONSTRUCTION GROUP OF SOUTH FLORIDA INC., Ste 200 5959 Blue Lagoon Dr, **Miami,** FL 33126-2052, *pg.* 1087, *pg.* 441
CONSOLIDATED-TOMOKA LAND CO., 1530 Cornerstone Blvd Ste 100, **Daytona Beach,** FL 32117, *pg.* 1087, *pg.* 419
CUSHMAN & WAKEFIELD OF FLORIDA, INC., 200 S Biscayne Blvd Ste 2800, **Miami,** FL 33131-2662, *pg.* 1089, *pg.* 442
DANIEL DECARO REAL ESTATE AUCTIONS, INC., 29 Ave of the Flowers, **Longboat Key,** FL 34228, *pg.* 1089, *pg.* 438
THE DELTONA CORPORATION, 8014 SW 135th St Rd, **Ocala,** FL 34473-6807, *pg.* 1089, *pg.* 452
ESSLINGER-WOOTEN-MAXWELL REALTORS, INC., 1360 S Dixie Hwy, **Coral Gables,** FL 33146, *pg.* 1091, *pg.* 418
FISHER AUCTION COMPANY, INC., 2112 E Atlantic Blvd, **Pompano Beach,** FL 33062, *pg.* 1092, *pg.* 459
HOBE SOUND GOLF CLUB, INC., 11671 SE Plandome Dr, **Hobe Sound,** FL 33455, *pg.* 1095, *pg.* 430
JACOBSEN MANUFACTURING, INC., 600 Packard Ct, **Safety Harbor,** FL 34695-3001, *pg.* 1098, *pg.* 460
LAGO MAR PROPERTIES, INC., 1700 S Ocean Ln, **Fort Lauderdale,** FL 37316, *pg.* 1100, *pg.* 425
LENNAR CORPORATION, 700 NW 107th Ave Ste 400, **Miami,** FL 33172, *pg.* 1100, *pg.* 443
LENNAR HOMES, INC., 700 Northwest 107th Ave Ste 400, **Miami,** FL 33172-3139, *pg.* 1101, *pg.* 443
LIBERTY GROUP OF COMPANIES, 13577 Feather Sound Dr Ste 520, **Clearwater,** FL 33762, *pg.* 1101, *pg.* 416
MARI VESCI REALTORS, INC., 9000 Gulf Shore Dr, **Naples,** FL 34108, *pg.* 1102, *pg.* 451
MICHAEL SAUNDERS & COMPANY, 100 S Washington Blvd, **Sarasota,** FL 34236, *pg.* 1105, *pg.* 466
MISSION INN RESORTS INC., 10400 County Rd 48, **Howey in the Hills,** FL 34737, *pg.* 1105, *pg.* 431
NAPLES BEACH HOTEL & GOLF CLUB, 851 Gulf Shore Blvd N, **Naples,** FL 34102, *pg.* 1106, *pg.* 451
OCEAN PROPERTIES, LTD., 1001 Atlantic Ave, **Delray Beach,** FL 33444-1146, *pg.* 1106, *pg.* 422
ORANGE COUNTY NATIONAL GOLF CENTER & LODGE, 16301 Phil Ritson Way, **Winter Garden,** FL 34787, *pg.* 1107, *pg.* 480
OXFORD REALTY, INC., 7625 W Sand Lake Rd Ste 202, **Orlando,** FL 32819, *pg.* 1107, *pg.* 455
PHILLIPS DEVELOPMENT & REALTY, LLC, 142 W Platt St, **Tampa,** FL 33606, *pg.* 1108, *pg.* 475
THE RESORT AT LONGBOAT KEY CLUB, 301 Gulf of Mexico Dr, **Longboat Key,** FL 34228, *pg.* 1110, *pg.* 438
SADDLEBROOK RESORTS, INC., 5700 Saddlebrook Way, **Wesley Chapel,** FL 33543-4499, *pg.* 1111, *pg.* 478
SALAMANDER INNISBROOK, LLC, 36750 US 19 N, **Palm Harbor,** FL 34684, *pg.* 1111, *pg.* 457
SANDALS RESORTS INTERNATIONAL, 4950 SW 72nd Ave, **Miami,** FL 33155-5533, *pg.* 1111, *pg.* 446
SANDESTIN GOLF & BEACH RESORT, 9300 Emerald Coast Pkwy W, **Destin,** FL 32550, *pg.* 1111, *pg.* 422
SCOTTSDALE COMPANY, 4200 Gulf Shore Blvd N, **Naples,** FL 34103, *pg.* 1111, *pg.* 451
SEASIDE PROPERTIES GROUP, INC., 2100 N Ocean Blvd Ste 402, **Fort Lauderdale,** FL 33305, *pg.* 1112, *pg.* 426
SKYLINE EQUITIES REALTY, LLC, 800 Brickell Ave Ste 201, **Miami,** FL 33131, *pg.* 1113, *pg.* 446
SOUTHWOOD GOLF CLUB, 3750 Grove Park Dr, **Tallahassee,** FL 32311, *pg.* 1113, *pg.* 470
STILES CORPORATION, 301 E Las Olas Blvd, **Fort Lauderdale,** FL 33301-2295, *pg.* 1115, *pg.* 427
STRATUS INVESTMENTS, LLC, 550 Sw 12th Ave, Ste 550, **Deerfield Beach,** FL 33442, *pg.* 1115, *pg.* 421
SUNSTREAM, INC., 6231 Estero Blvd, **Fort Myers Beach,** FL 33931, *pg.* 1116, *pg.* 428
TRADEWINDS ISLANDS RESORTS ON SAINT PETE BEACH, 5500 Gulf Blvd, **Saint Pete Beach,** FL 33706, *pg.* 1116, *pg.* 461
WALDORF ASTORIA NAPLES, 475 Seagate Dr, **Naples,** FL 34103, *pg.* 1118, *pg.* 451
WCI COMMUNITIES, INC., 24301 Walden Ctr Dr Ste 300, **Bonita Springs,** FL 34134, *pg.* 1118, *pg.* 414
WYNDHAM VACATION OWNERSHIP, 8427 S Park Cir Ste 500, **Orlando,** FL 32819-9054, *pg.* 1119, *pg.* 457

Georgia

BEAZER HOMES USA, INC., 1000 Abernathy Rd NE Ste 260, **Atlanta,** GA 30328-5648, *pg.* 1081, *pg.* 491
COUSINS PROPERTIES INCORPORATED, 191 Peachtree St NE Ste 3600, **Atlanta,** GA 30303, *pg.* 1088, *pg.* 501
HARRY NORMAN REALTORS, 532 E Paces Ferry Rd Ste 300, **Atlanta,** GA 30305, *pg.* 1094, *pg.* 509
INTERCONTINENTAL HOTELS CORPORATION, 3 Ravinia Drive Ste 100, **Atlanta,** GA 30346, *pg.* 1097, *pg.* 511

INTOWN SUITES MANAGEMENT, INC., Ste 2-1200 2727 Paces Ferry Rd SE, **Atlanta,** GA 30339-6143, *pg.* 1098, *pg.* 513
LODGIAN INC., 3445 Peachtree Rd NE Ste 700, **Atlanta,** GA 30326, *pg.* 1101, *pg.* 513
POST APARTMENT HOMES, L.P., 4401 Northside Pkwy NW Ste 800, **Atlanta,** GA 30327, *pg.* 1108, *pg.* 518
POST PROPERTIES, INC., 4401 Northside Pkwy Ste 800, **Atlanta,** GA 30327-3057, *pg.* 1108, *pg.* 518
REYNOLDS PLANTATION, 5741 Lake Oconee Pkwy, **Greensboro,** GA 30642, *pg.* 1110, *pg.* 533
SEA ISLAND ACQUISITION LLC, 100 Cloister Dr, **Sea Island,** GA 31561, *pg.* 1111, *pg.* 540
WELLS REAL ESTATE FUNDS, INC., 6200 the Corners Pkwy Ste 250, **Norcross,** GA 30092, *pg.* 1118, *pg.* 538

Hawaii

ALEXANDER & BALDWIN, INC., 822 Bishop St, PO Box 3440, **Honolulu,** HI 96801, *pg.* 1079, *pg.* 543
D.R. HORTON, INC./SCHULER HOMES LLC, 828 Fort St Mall 4th Fl, **Honolulu,** HI 96813-4321, *pg.* 1090, *pg.* 543
OUTRIGGER ENTERPRISES, INC., 2375 Kuhio Ave, **Honolulu,** HI 96815-2939, *pg.* 1107, *pg.* 544
THE SHIDLER GROUP, 841 Bishop St Ste 1700, **Honolulu,** HI 96813-4789, *pg.* 1112, *pg.* 545

Idaho

THE COEUR D'ALENE RESORT, 115 S 2nd St, **Coeur D'Alene,** ID 83814, *pg.* 1087, *pg.* 549
SUN VALLEY COMPANY, 1 Sun Valley Rd, **Sun Valley,** ID 83353, *pg.* 1115, *pg.* 550

Illinois

BROOKFIELD GLOBAL RELOCATION SERVICES, 150 Harvester Dr, # 201, **Burr Ridge,** IL 60527, *pg.* 1083, *pg.* 560
DRAPER & KRAMER RETIREMENT PROPERTY SERVICES, 33 W Monroe St Fl 19, **Chicago,** IL 60603, *pg.* 1090, *pg.* 572
EQUITY LIFESTYLE PROPERTIES, INC., 2 N Riverside Plz Ste 800, **Chicago,** IL 60606, *pg.* 1090, *pg.* 573
GENERAL GROWTH PROPERTIES, INC., 110 N Wacker Dr, **Chicago,** IL 60606-1511, *pg.* 1093, *pg.* 574
HYATT HOTELS CORPORATION, 71 S Wacker Dr, **Chicago,** IL 60606-3414, *pg.* 1096, *pg.* 577
JMB REALTY CORPORATION, 900 N Michigan Ave Ste 1500, **Chicago,** IL 60611-1542, *pg.* 1099, *pg.* 579
JOHN BUCK COMPANY, 1 N Wacker Dr Ste 2400, **Chicago,** IL 60606, *pg.* 1099, *pg.* 579
KOENIG & STREY, 4709 Golf Rd, Ste 1100, **Skokle,** IL 60076, *pg.* 1099, *pg.* 661
PREFERRED HOTEL GROUP, 311 S Wacker Dr Ste 1900, **Chicago,** IL 60606-6676, *pg.* 1108, *pg.* 587
THE RITZ-CARLTON CHICAGO, 160 E Pearson St at Water Tower Pl, **Chicago,** IL 60611-2308, *pg.* 1110, *pg.* 589

Indiana

SIMON PROPERTY GROUP, INC., 225 W Washington St, **Indianapolis,** IN 46204, *pg.* 1112, *pg.* 690
SOUTH BEND CLINIC LLP, 211 N Eddy St, **South Bend,** IN 46617, *pg.* 1113, *pg.* 697

Iowa

DIAMOND JO, LLC, 301 Bell St, **Dubuque,** IA 52001, *pg.* 1089, *pg.* 707

Kansas

REECE & NICHOLS REALTORS, 11601 Granada St, **Leawood,** KS 66211-1455, *pg.* 1110, *pg.* 716

Kentucky

NTS DEVELOPMENT COMPANY, 10172 Linn Sta Rd Ste 200, **Louisville,** KY 40223, *pg.* 1106, *pg.* 737
SEMONIN REALTORS, 600 N Hurstbourne Pkwy, Ste 200, **Louisville,** KY 40222, *pg.* 1112, *pg.* 738

Maryland

CHAMPION REALTY INC., 5418 Baltimore Annapolis Blvd, **Severna Park,** MD 21146-3934, *pg.* 1085, *pg.* 777
CHOICE HOTELS INTERNATIONAL, INC., 1 Choice Hotels Cir Ste 400, **Rockville,** MD 20850, *pg.* 1086, *pg.* 775
ERICKSON LIVING, 701 Maiden Choice Ln, **Catonsville,** MD 21228-3738, *pg.* 1090, *pg.* 766
HOST HOTELS & RESORTS, INC., 6903 Rockledge Dr Ste 1500, **Bethesda,** MD 20817, *pg.* 1096, *pg.* 762
MARRIOTT INTERNATIONAL, INC., 10400 Fernwood Rd, **Bethesda,** MD 20817, *pg.* 1102, *pg.* 764
THE RITZ-CARLTON HOTEL COMPANY LLC, 4445 Willard Ave Ste 800, **Chevy Chase,** MD 20815, *pg.* 1110, *pg.* 766
SUNBURST HOSPITALITY CORPORATION, 10770 Columbia Pike Ste 200, **Silver Spring,** MD 20901-4448, *pg.* 1115, *pg.* 778

Massachusetts

COLDWELL BANKER RESIDENTIAL BROKERAGE, 52 2nd St 3 Fl, **Waltham,** MA 02451, *pg.* 1087, *pg.* 850
THE FLATLEY COMPANY, Bldg 35 Braintree Hill Office Pk, **Braintree,** MA 02184, *pg.* 1092, *pg.* 802
SONESTA INTERNATIONAL HOTELS CORPORATION, 255 Washington St, Ste 270, **Newton,** MA 02458, *pg.* 1113, *pg.* 836
ST. BARTH PROPERTIES, INC., 693 E Central St Ste 201, **Franklin,** MA 02038, *pg.* 1114, *pg.* 823

Michigan

BOYNE USA RESORTS INC., 1 Boyne Mountain Rd, **Boyne Falls,** MI 49713-9642, *pg.* 1082, *pg.* 874
DETROIT ENTERTAINMENT, LLC, 2901 Grand River Ave, **Detroit,** MI 48201, *pg.* 1089, *pg.* 879
FOUR WINDS CASINO RESORT, 11111 Wilson Rd, **New Buffalo,** MI 49117, *pg.* 1092, *pg.* 902
PARK PLACE HOTEL, 300 E State St, **Traverse City,** MI 49684, *pg.* 1107, *pg.* 909
PULTEGROUP, INC., 100 Bloomfield Hills Pkwy Ste 300, **Bloomfield Hills,** MI 48304, *pg.* 1109, *pg.* 873
SUN COMMUNITIES, INC., The American Center 27777 Franklin Rd Ste 200, **Southfield,** MI 48034, *pg.* 1115, *pg.* 907
WYNNESTONE COMMUNITIES, 30215 Southfield Rd Ste 200, **Southfield,** MI 48076-1361, *pg.* 1120, *pg.* 908

Minnesota

BRUTGER EQUITIES, INC., 100 4th Ave S, **Saint Cloud,** MN 56301, *pg.* 1083, *pg.* 956
CARLSON COMPANIES INC., 701 Carlson Pkwy, **Minnetonka,** MN 55305, *pg.* 1084, *pg.* 947
CARLSON REAL ESTATE COMPANY, 301 Carlson Pkwy Ste 100, **Minnetonka,** MN 55305-5358, *pg.* 1084, *pg.* 947
HOMESERVICES OF AMERICA, INC., Ste 2700 333 S 7th St, **Minneapolis,** MN 55402-2438, *pg.* 1096, *pg.* 938

Mississippi

GOLD STRIKE CASINO RESORT, 1010 Casino Ctr Dr, **Robinsonville,** MS 38664, *pg.* 1093, *pg.* 971
PURCELL CO., INC., 4401 E Aloha Dr, **Diamondhead,** MS 39525-3303, *pg.* 1109, *pg.* 968

Missouri

ADAM'S MARK HOTELS & RESORTS, 11330 Olive Blvd, **Saint Louis,** MO 63141, *pg.* 1079, *pg.* 990
JOHN Q. HAMMONS HOTELS INC., 300 S John Q Hammons Pkwy Ste 900, **Springfield,** MO 65806, *pg.* 1099, *pg.* 1006

Nebraska

CBSHOME REAL ESTATE, 15950 W Dodge Rd Ste 300, **Omaha,** NE 68118, *pg.* 1085, *pg.* 1013
HOME REAL ESTATE INC., 3355 Orwell St Ste 102, **Lincoln,** NE 68516, *pg.* 1096, *pg.* 1012
WOODS BROS REALTY, INC., 3355 Orwell St Ste 102, **Lincoln,** NE 68516, *pg.* 1119, *pg.* 1012

Nevada

ARCHON CORPORATION, 2200 Casino Dr, **Laughlin,** NV 89029, *pg.* 1080, *pg.* 1030
BOYD GAMING CORPORATION, 3883 Howard Hughes Pkwy 9th Fl, **Las Vegas,** NV 89169, *pg.* 1082, *pg.* 1022
CAESARS ENTERTAINMENT CORPORATION, 1 Harrahs Ct, **Las Vegas,** NV 89119, *pg.* 1083, *pg.* 1023
CIRCUS CIRCUS CASINOS, INC., 2880 Las Vegas Blvd S, **Las Vegas,** NV 89109-1138, *pg.* 1086, *pg.* 1023
GOLD COAST HOTEL & CASINO, 4000 W Flamingo Rd, **Las Vegas,** NV 89103-5420, *pg.* 1093, *pg.* 1024
HYATT REGENCY LAKE TAHOE RESORT & CASINO, 111 Country Club Dr, **Incline Village,** NV 89451, *pg.* 1097, *pg.* 1021
LAS VEGAS SANDS CORP., 3355 Las Vegas Blvd S, **Las Vegas,** NV 89109, *pg.* 1100, *pg.* 1027
MESQUITE GAMING, LLC, 950 W Mesquite Blvd, **Mesquite,** NV 89027, *pg.* 1104, *pg.* 1030
MGM GRAND HOTEL, LLC, 3799 Las Vegas Blvd S, **Las Vegas,** NV 89109-4319, *pg.* 1104, *pg.* 1028
MGM RESORTS INTERNATIONAL, 3799 S Las Vegas Blvd, **Las Vegas,** NV 89109-4303, *pg.* 1105, *pg.* 1028
MIRAGE RESORTS INCORPORATED, 3400 Las Vegas Blvd S, **Las Vegas,** NV 89109-8923, *pg.* 1105, *pg.* 1028
NEVADA GOLD & CASINOS, INC., 133 E Warm Springs Rd Ste 102, **Las Vegas,** NV 89119, *pg.* 1106, *pg.* 1028
STRATOSPHERE CORPORATION, 2000 Las Vegas Blvd S, **Las Vegas,** NV 89104-2507, *pg.* 1115, *pg.* 1030
WYNN LAS VEGAS, LLC, 3131 Las Vegas Blvd S, **Las Vegas,** NV 89109, *pg.* 1119, *pg.* 1030
WYNN RESORTS LIMITED, 3131 Las Vegas Blvd S, **Las Vegas,** NV 89109, *pg.* 1119, *pg.* 1030

New Hampshire

GUNSTOCK RECREATION AREA, 719 Cherry Valley Rd, **Gilford,** NH 03249, *pg.* 1094, *pg.* 1034

New Jersey

ADVANCE REALTY GROUP, LLC, 1041 US Hwy 202/206, **Bridgewater,** NJ 08807, *pg.* 1079, *pg.* 1045
BALLY'S PARK PLACE, INC., Park Pl & Boardwalk, **Atlantic City,** NJ 08401, *pg.* 1080, *pg.* 1041
BORGATA HOTEL CASINO & SPA, 1 Borgata Way, **Atlantic City,** NJ 08401, *pg.* 1082, *pg.* 1041
CAESARS NEW JERSEY, INC., 2100 Pacific Ave, **Atlantic City,** NJ 08401-6612, *pg.* 1084, *pg.* 1041
CENTURY 21 REAL ESTATE LLC, 175 Park Ave, **Madison,** NJ 07940, *pg.* 1085, *pg.* 1080
COLDWELL BANKER REAL ESTATE LLC, 1 Campus Dr, **Parsippany,** NJ 07054-3826, *pg.* 1087, *pg.* 1103
DAYS INNS WORLDWIDE, INC., 1 Sylvan Way, **Parsippany,** NJ 07054-3887, *pg.* 1089, *pg.* 1103
GLORIA NILSON GMAC REAL ESTATE, 350 Route 35, **Middletown,** NJ 07748, *pg.* 1093, *pg.* 1084
HOVNANIAN ENTERPRISES, INC., 110 W Front St, **Red Bank,** NJ 07701, *pg.* 1096, *pg.* 1114
MACK-CALI REALTY CORPORATION, 343 Thornall St, **Edison,** NJ 08837-2206, *pg.* 1102, *pg.* 1056
MATRIX DEVELOPMENT GROUP INC., Forsgate Dr CN 4000, **Cranbury,** NJ 08512, *pg.* 1104, *pg.* 1053
REALOGY CORPORATION, 175 Park Ave, **Madison,** NJ 07940, *pg.* 1109, *pg.* 1081
RESORTS ATLANTIC CITY, 1133 Boardwalk, **Atlantic City,** NJ 08401, *pg.* 1110, *pg.* 1041
THE SCHULTZ ORGANIZATION, 900 US Hwy 9 N, **Woodbridge,** NJ 07095, *pg.* 1111, *pg.* 1133
TRAVELODGE HOTELS, INC., 22 Sylvan Way, **Parsippany,** NJ 07054, *pg.* 1117, *pg.* 1106
TRUMP ENTERTAINMENT RESORTS, INC., 1000 Boardwalk at Virginia Ave, **Atlantic City,** NJ 08401, *pg.* 1117, *pg.* 1041
WEICHERT REALTORS, 1625 State Rte 10, **Morris Plains,** NJ 07950-2905, *pg.* 1118, *pg.* 1087
WEICHERT RELOCATION RESOURCES INC., 1625 Rte 10, **Morris Plains,** NJ 07950-2905, *pg.* 1118, *pg.* 1087
WYNDHAM WORLDWIDE CORPORATION, 22 Sylvan Way, **Parsippany,** NJ 07054, *pg.* 1119, *pg.* 1107

New Mexico

TAOS SKI VALLEY, INC., 116 Sutton Pl, **Taos Ski Valley,** NM 87525-0090, *pg.* 1116, *pg.* 1136

New York

AMERICAN EXPRESS TRAVEL RELATED SERVICES COMPANY, INC., 200 Vesey St, **New York,** NY 10285, *pg.* 1079, *pg.* 1192
BROOKFIELD FINANCIAL PROPERTIES, INC., 3 World Financial Ctr 200 Vesey St 11Fl, **New York,** NY 10281, *pg.* 1083, *pg.* 1207
CB RICHARD ELLIS, INC., 200 Park Ave, **New York,** NY 10166-0005, *pg.* 1085, *pg.* 1210
CORCORAN SUNSHINE MARKETING GROUP, 888 7th Ave, **New York,** NY 10106, *pg.* 1088, *pg.* 1218
COUNTRY WIDE REALTY INC., 1234 Castle Hill Ave, **Bronx,** NY 10462-4810, *pg.* 1088, *pg.* 1144
CRESA PARTNERS LLC, 100 Pk Ave 24th Fl, **New York,** NY 10017, *pg.* 1088, *pg.* 1220
CUSHMAN & WAKEFIELD, INC., 1290 Avenue of the Americas, **New York,** NY 10104, *pg.* 1088, *pg.* 1220
DELAWARE NORTH COMPANIES, INC., 40 Fountain Plz, **Buffalo,** NY 14202-2229, *pg.* 1089, *pg.* 1148
DENIHAN HOSPITALITY GROUP, LLC, 551 Fifth Ave, **New York,** NY 10176, *pg.* 1089, *pg.* 1223
EMPIRE RESORTS, INC., c/o Monticello Casino & Raceway Rte 17B, **Monticello,** NY 12701, *pg.* 1090, *pg.* 1183
GARDEN CITY HOTEL INC., 45 7th St, **Garden City,** NY 11530, *pg.* 1093, *pg.* 1161
HELMSLEY ENTERPRISES, INC., 230 Pk Ave, **New York,** NY 10169, *pg.* 1094, *pg.* 1240
HOME PROPERTIES INC., 850 Clinton Sq, **Rochester,** NY 14604-1730, *pg.* 1096, *pg.* 1336
HOULIHAN/LAWRENCE INC., 4 Valley Rd, **Bronxville,** NY 10708, *pg.* 1096, *pg.* 1145
ICAHN ENTERPRISES L.P., 767 5th Ave Ste 4700, **New York,** NY 10153, *pg.* 1097, *pg.* 1243
THE LEADING HOTELS OF THE WORLD, LTD., 485 Lexington Ave, Rm 401, **New York,** NY 10017, *pg.* 1100, *pg.* 1250
LEFRAK ORGANIZATION INC., 40 W 57th St, **New York,** NY 10019, *pg.* 1100, *pg.* 1251
LOEWS HOTELS HOLDING CORPORATION, 667 Madison Ave, **New York,** NY 10065, *pg.* 1101, *pg.* 1252
MORGANS HOTEL GROUP CO., 475 10th Ave, **New York,** NY 10018, *pg.* 1105, *pg.* 1262
NEWMARK GRUBB KNIGHT FRANK, 125 Park Ave, **New York,** NY 10017, *pg.* 1106, *pg.* 1271
ROCKEFELLER GROUP, INC., 1221 Ave of The Americas, **New York,** NY 10020-1001, *pg.* 1110, *pg.* 1286
ROGER SMITH HOTELS CORP., 501 Lexington Ave, **New York,** NY 10017-2008, *pg.* 1111, *pg.* 1286
SOTHEBY'S INTERNATIONAL REALTY, INC., 38 E 61st St, **New York,** NY 10065, *pg.* 1113, *pg.* 1294
SPA FINDER, INC., 257 Park Ave S 10th Fl, **New York,** NY 10010, *pg.* 1113, *pg.* 1295
THE TRUMP ORGANIZATION, LLC, 725 5th Ave, **New York,** NY 10022, *pg.* 1117, *pg.* 1305
TURNING STONE RESORT CASINO LLC, 5218 Patrick Rd, **Verona,** NY 13478, *pg.* 1117, *pg.* 1348
UNITED STATES REALTY & INVESTMENT COMPANY, 450 7th Ave 45th Fl, **New York,** NY 12123, *pg.* 1117, *pg.* 1307
VORNADO REALTY TRUST, 888 7th Ave, **New York,** NY 10019, *pg.* 1118, *pg.* 1312

North Carolina

BEVERLY-HANKS & ASSOCIATES INC., 300 Executive Park, **Asheville,** NC 28801, *pg.* 1082, *pg.* 1358
DIVI HOTELS, INC., 6320 Quadrangle Dr Ste 210, **Chapel Hill,** NC 27517, *pg.* 1090, *pg.* 1361
TANGER FACTORY OUTLET CENTERS, INC., 3200 Northline Ave Ste 360, **Greensboro,** NC 27408, *pg.* 1116, *pg.* 1376
TANGER PROPERTIES LIMITED PARTNERSHIP, 3200 Northline Ave Ste 360, **Greensboro,** NC 27408-7612, *pg.* 1116, *pg.* 1376

North Dakota

INVESTORS REAL ESTATE TRUST, 3015 16th St SW, Ste 100, **Minot,** ND 58701, *pg.* 1098, *pg.* 1398

Ohio

ASSOCIATED ESTATES REALTY CORPORATION, 1 AEC Pkwy, **Richmond Heights,** OH 44143-1467, *pg.* 1080, *pg.* 1471
DDR CORP., 3300 Enterprise Pkwy, **Beachwood,** OH 44122, *pg.* 1089, *pg.* 1405
FOREST CITY ENTERPRISES, INC., 50 Public Sq Terminal Tower Ste 1100, **Cleveland,** OH 44113-2203, *pg.* 1092, *pg.* 1430
MRI SOFTWARE, LLC, 28925 Fountain Pkwy, **Solon,** OH 44139, *pg.* 1106, *pg.* 1473
RED ROOF INNS, INC., The Red Roof Bldg 605 S Front St, **Columbus,** OH 43215, *pg.* 1110, *pg.* 1443
TOWNE PROPERTIES, 1055 St Paul Pl, **Cincinnati,** OH 45202-6042, *pg.* 1116, *pg.* 1426
WASHINGTON PRIME GROUP INC., 180 E Broad St, **Columbus,** OH 43215, *pg.* 1118, *pg.* 1444

Pennsylvania

BINSWANGER CORPORATION, 2 Logan Sq, **Philadelphia,** PA 19103, *pg.* 1082, *pg.* 1559
CUBESMART, 460 E Swedesford Rd Ste 3000, **Wayne,** PA 19087, *pg.* 1088, *pg.* 1591
HERSHA HOSPITALITY TRUST, 44 Hersha Dr, **Harrisburg,** PA 17102, *pg.* 1094, *pg.* 1536
HERSHEY ENTERTAINMENT & RESORTS COMPANY, 27 W Chocolate Ave, **Hershey,** PA 17033-0860, *pg.* 1094, *pg.* 1539
LANCASTER HOST RESORT & CONFERENCE CENTER, 2300 Lincoln Hwy E, **Lancaster,** PA 17602, *pg.* 1100, *pg.* 1546
LIBERTY PROPERTY TRUST, 500 Chesterfield Pkwy, **Malvern,** PA 19355-8707, *pg.* 1101, *pg.* 1550
MOUNT AIRY CASINO RESORT, 312 Woodland Rd, **Mount Pocono,** PA 18344, *pg.* 1106, *pg.* 1554
PEDDLER'S VILLAGE, INC., Rt 202 & 263, **Lahaska,** PA 18931, *pg.* 1107, *pg.* 1545
POCONO MANOR GOLF RESORT & SPA, 1 Manor Dr, **Pocono Manor,** PA 18349, *pg.* 1108, *pg.* 1582
SKI ROUNDTOP OPERATING CORP., 925 Roundtop Rd, **Lewisberry,** PA 17339-9762, *pg.* 1113, *pg.* 1548

South Carolina

THE CLIFFS COMMUNITIES, INC., 3598 Hwy 11, **Travelers Rest,** SC 29690, *pg.* 1086, *pg.* 1623
EXTENDED STAY HOTELS LLC, 100 Dunbar St, **Spartanburg,** SC 29306, *pg.* 1091, *pg.* 1622
KIAWAH RESORT ASSOCIATES LP, 1 Kiawah Is Pkwy, **Kiawah Island,** SC 29455, *pg.* 1099, *pg.* 1620
SEA PINES RESORT, LLC, 32 Greenwood Dr, **Hilton Head Island,** SC 29928-4510, *pg.* 1112, *pg.* 1620

Tennessee

CHATTANOOGA CHOO-CHOO HOLIDAY INN, 1400 Market St, **Chattanooga,** TN 37402-4429, *pg.* 1086, *pg.* 1628
CLAYTON HOMES, INC., 500 Alcoa Trl, **Maryville,** TN 37804-5550, *pg.* 1086, *pg.* 1640
EDR TRUST, 999 S Shady Grove Rd, Ste 600, **Memphis,** TN 38120, *pg.* 1090, *pg.* 1642
ELVIS PRESLEY ENTERPRISES, INC., 3734 Elvis Presley Blvd, **Memphis,** TN 38116, *pg.* 1090, *pg.* 1642
LEDIC MANAGEMENT GROUP, 2650 Thousand Oaks Blvd Ste 3100, **Memphis,** TN 38118, *pg.* 1100, *pg.* 1645
PEABODY HOTEL GROUP, INC., 5118 Park Ave Ste 245, **Memphis,** TN 38117, *pg.* 1107, *pg.* 1645
RYMAN HOSPITALITY PROPERTIES, INC, 1 Gaylord Dr, **Nashville,** TN 37214, *pg.* 1111, *pg.* 1653

Texas

1859 HISTORIC HOTELS LTD., 2302 Post Ofc St Ste 500, **Galveston,** TX 77550-1936, *pg.* 1079, *pg.* 1697
ACCOR, 5055 Keller Spring Rd Ste 200, **Addison,** TX 75001, *pg.* 1079, *pg.* 1657
AMERICAN CAMPUS COMMUNITIES, INC., 12700 Hill Country Blvd Ste T-200, **Austin,** TX 78738, *pg.* 1079, *pg.* 1660
BEHRINGER HOLDINGS, LLC, 15601 Dallas Pkwy Ste 600, **Addison,** TX 75001, *pg.* 1081, *pg.* 1657
BENCHMARK HOSPITALITY INTERNATIONAL INC., 4 Waterway Sq Ste 300, **The Woodlands,** TX 77380, *pg.* 1081, *pg.* 1747
CALDWELL WATSON REAL ESTATE GROUP, 7904 N Sam Houston Pkwy W 4th Fl, **Houston,** TX 77064, *pg.* 1084, *pg.* 1702
CAPITAL SENIOR LIVING CORPORATION, 14160 Dallas Pkwy Ste 300, **Dallas,** TX 75240-4383, *pg.* 1084, *pg.* 1677
CLUBCORP, INC., 3030 Lyndon B Johnson Fwy Ste 600, **Dallas,** TX 75234-7763, *pg.* 1086, *pg.* 1677
CRESCENT REAL ESTATE EQUITIES LP, 777 Main St Ste 2100, **Fort Worth,** TX 76102-5304, *pg.* 1088, *pg.* 1694
D.R. HORTON, INC., 301 Commerce St Ste 500, **Fort Worth,** TX 76102, *pg.* 1090, *pg.* 1694
FELCOR LODGING TRUST INCORPORATED, 545 E John Carpenter Fwy Ste 1300, **Irving,** TX 75062 8124, *pg.* 1092, *pg.* 1719
G6 HOSPITALITY LLC, 4001 International Pkwy, **Carrollton,** TX 75007, *pg.* 1092, *pg.* 1669
GH III MANAGEMENT LLC, 10575 Katy Fwy Ste 100, **Houston,** TX 77024, *pg.* 1093, *pg.* 1706
LA QUINTA CORPORATION, 909 Hidden Ridge Ste 600, **Irving,** TX 75038, *pg.* 1099, *pg.* 1722
LA QUINTA INNS, INC., 909 Hidden Ridge Ste 600, **Irving,** TX 75038, *pg.* 1100, *pg.* 1722
LAKE AUSTIN SPA RESORT, 1705 S Quinlan Park Rd, **Austin,** TX 78732, *pg.* 1100, *pg.* 1663
LANTERN ASSET MANAGEMENT, 100 Crescent Ct Ste 260, **Dallas,** TX 75201, *pg.* 1100, *pg.* 1683
MOTEL 6, 4001 International Pkwy, **Carrollton,** TX 75007, *pg.* 1106, *pg.* 1669
OMNI HOTELS & RESORTS, 4001 Maple Avenue, Ste. 500, **Dallas,** TX 75219, *pg.* 1107, *pg.* 1685
PALM HARBOR HOMES, INC., 15303 Dallas Pkwy Ste 800, **Addison,** TX 75001-4600, *pg.* 1107, *pg.* 1658
ROSEWOOD HOTELS & RESORTS LLC, 500 Crescent Ct Ste 300, **Dallas,** TX 75201, *pg.* 1111, *pg.* 1686
SILVERLEAF RESORTS, INC., 1221 River Bend Dr Ste 120, **Dallas,** TX 75247-4919, *pg.* 1112, *pg.* 1686
SRS REAL ESTATE PARTNERS, 8343 Douglas Ave Ste 200, **Dallas,** TX 75225, *pg.* 1113, *pg.* 1687
STRATUS PROPERTIES, INC., 212 Lavaca St Ste 300, **Austin,** TX 78701, *pg.* 1115, *pg.* 1666
TRAMMELL CROW COMPANY, 2100 Mckinney Ave, Ste 900, **Dallas,** TX 75201, *pg.* 1116, *pg.* 1689

Utah

EXTRA SPACE STORAGE, INC., 2795 E Cottonwood Pkwy Ste 400, **Salt Lake City,** UT 84121, *pg.* 1091, *pg.* 1757

Vermont

JAY PEAK, INC., 830 Jay Peak Rd, **Jay Peak,** VT 05859, *pg.* 1098, *pg.* 1766
STOWE AREA ASSOCIATION, INC., 51 Main St, **Stowe,** VT 05672, *pg.* 1115, *pg.* 1768
STRATTON MOUNTAIN RESORT, RR 1 Box 145, **Stratton Mountain,** VT 05155, *pg.* 1115, *pg.* 1768

Virginia

BRIDGESTREET WORLDWIDE INC., 4501 N Fairfax Dr, **Arlington,** VA 22203, *pg.* 1083, *pg.* 1772
COMSTOCK HOLDING COMPANIES INC., 1886 Metro Center Dr, Ste 400, **Reston,** VA 20190, *pg.* 1087, *pg.* 1798
CRESTLINE HOTELS & RESORTS, INC., 3950 University Dr Ste 301, **Fairfax,** VA 22030, *pg.* 1088, *pg.* 1779
EMBASSY SUITES HOTELS, 7930 Jones Branch Dr, **McLean,** VA 22102, *pg.* 1090, *pg.* 1790
EXIT REALTY CENTRAL, 870 N Military Hwy, **Norfolk,** VA 23502, *pg.* 1091, *pg.* 1796
HILTON WORLDWIDE, INC., 7930 Jones Branch Dr, **McLean,** VA 22102, *pg.* 1094, *pg.* 1791
MCLEAN FAULCONER INC., 503 Faulconer Dr Ste 5, **Charlottesville,** VA 22903, *pg.* 1104, *pg.* 1778
THE OMNI HOMESTEAD RESORT, 1766 Homestead Dr, **Hot Springs,** VA 24445, *pg.* 1106, *pg.* 1786

First page reference indicates Business Class Edition
Second page reference indicates Geographic Edition

Washington

COLLIERS INTERNATIONAL, 601 Union St Ste 4800, **Seattle,** WA 98101, *pg.* 1087, *pg.* 1834
MARKET LEADER, INC., 11332 NE 122nd Way, **Kirkland,** WA 98034-6916, *pg.* 1102, *pg.* 1822
RED LION HOTELS CORP., 201 W North River Dr Ste 100, **Spokane,** WA 99201-2262, *pg.* 1110, *pg.* 1844

West Virginia

THE GREENBRIER, 300 W Main St, **White Sulphur Springs,** WV 24986-2414, *pg.* 1094, *pg.* 1851

Wisconsin

GREAT WOLF RESORTS, INC., 525 Junction Rd Ste 6000 S, **Madison,** WI 53717, *pg.* 1093, *pg.* 1866
THE MARCUS CORPORATION, 100 E Wisconsin Ave Ste 1900, **Milwaukee,** WI 53202-4125, *pg.* 1102, *pg.* 1877

Wyoming

JACKSON HOLE MOUNTAIN RESORT, 3395 Cody Ln, **Teton Village,** WY 83025, *pg.* 1098, *pg.* 1901
SNOW KING RESORT, INC., 400 E Snow King Ave, **Jackson,** WY 83001, *pg.* 1113, *pg.* 1901

Housewares

California

DURAFLAME, INC., PO Box 1230, **Stockton,** CA 95201-1230, *pg.* 1123, *pg.* 280
WILLIAMS-SONOMA, INC., 3250 Van Ness Ave, **San Francisco,** CA 94109-1012, *pg.* 1140, *pg.* 234

Connecticut

CUISINART INC., 1 Cummings Point Rd, **Stamford,** CT 06902-7901, *pg.* 1123, *pg.* 373
VICTORINOX SWISS ARMY INC., 7 Victoria Dr, **Monroe,** CT 06484, *pg.* 1139, *pg.* 357

Florida

DECOLAV, INC., 606 Banyan Trl, **Boca Raton,** FL 33431, *pg.* 1123, *pg.* 411
TUPPERWARE BRANDS CORPORATION, 14901 S Orange Blossom Trl, **Orlando,** FL 32837-6600, *pg.* 1139, *pg.* 456

Georgia

THE EVERCARE COMPANY, 3440 Preston Rdg Rd Ste 650, **Alpharetta,** GA 30005, *pg.* 1124, *pg.* 483
NEWELL RUBBERMAID INC., 3 Glenlake Pkwy, **Atlanta,** GA 30328, *pg.* 1128, *pg.* 515

Illinois

ENESCO, LLC, 225 Windsor Dr, **Itasca,** IL 60143-1200, *pg.* 1124, *pg.* 620
EUROMARKET DESIGNS, INC., 1250 Techny Rd, **Northbrook,** IL 60062-2349, *pg.* 1124, *pg.* 640
HAMMACHER SCHLEMMER & CO., INC., 9307 N Milwaukee Ave, **Niles,** IL 60714, *pg.* 1124, *pg.* 637
HOME PRODUCTS INTERNATIONAL, INC., 4501 W 47th St, **Chicago,** IL 60632-4451, *pg.* 1125, *pg.* 577
JOHN BOOS & CO., 3601 S Banker St, **Effingham,** IL 62401, *pg.* 1126, *pg.* 609
THE PAMPERED CHEF, 1 Pampered Chef Ln, **Addison,** IL 60101-5630, *pg.* 1129, *pg.* 552
REYNOLDS CONSUMER PRODUCTS, 1900 W Field Ct, **Lake Forest,** IL 60045, *pg.* 1138, *pg.* 625
WILTON PRODUCTS, INC., 2240 W 75th St, **Woodridge,** IL 60517-2333, *pg.* 1140, *pg.* 672
WORLD KITCHEN LLC, 9525 W Bryn Mawr Ave Ste 300, **Rosemont,** IL 60018, *pg.* 1141, *pg.* 657

Kentucky

STERLING CUT GLASS COMPANY, INC., 3233 Mineola Pke, **Erlanger,** KY 41018-1027, *pg.* 1138, *pg.* 727

Massachusetts

DEXTER-RUSSELL INC., 44 River St, **Southbridge,** MA 01550, *pg.* 1123, *pg.* 844
HOMEGOODS, INC., 770 Cochituate, **Framingham,** MA 01701, *pg.* 1125, *pg.* 821
HYDE TOOLS, INC., 54 Eastford Rd, **Southbridge,** MA 01550-3604, *pg.* 1125, *pg.* 844
STERILITE CORPORATION, 30 Scales Ln, **Townsend,** MA 01469-1010, *pg.* 1138, *pg.* 848

Minnesota

JARDEN HOME BRANDS, 1800 Cloquet Ave, **Cloquet,** MN 55720-2141, *pg.* 1126, *pg.* 920
NORTHLAND ALUMINUM PRODUCTS INC., 5005 County Rd 25, **Minneapolis,** MN 55416-2274, *pg.* 1129, *pg.* 941

Missouri

FORSHAW OF ST. LOUIS, 825 S Lindbergh Blvd, **Saint Louis,** MO 63131, *pg.* 1124, *pg.* 997
KATY INDUSTRIES, INC., 305 Rock Industrial Park Dr, **Bridgeton,** MO 63044, *pg.* 1126, *pg.* 973
WILLERT HOME PRODUCTS, INC., 4044 Pk Ave, **Saint Louis,** MO 63110-2320, *pg.* 1140, *pg.* 1005
ZEPHYR MANUFACTURING COMPANY INC., 200 Mitchell Rd, **Sedalia,** MO 65301-2114, *pg.* 1141, *pg.* 1006

New Jersey

BED BATH & BEYOND INC., 650 Liberty Ave, **Union,** NJ 07083, *pg.* 1121, *pg.* 1127
LALIQUE NORTH AMERICA, 25 Branca Rd, **East Rutherford,** NJ 07073, *pg.* 1126, *pg.* 1054
RECKITT BENCKISER INC., Morris Corp Ctr IV 399 Interpace Pkwy, **Parsippany,** NJ 07054, *pg.* 1136, *pg.* 1105
TOWNECRAFT, INC., 1 De Boer Dr, **Glen Rock,** NJ 07452-3301, *pg.* 1139, *pg.* 1071
VILLEROY & BOCH TABLEWARE, LTD., 3A S Middlesex Ave, **Monroe Township,** NJ 08831, *pg.* 1139, *pg.* 1085

New York

CORNING INCORPORATED, 1 Riverfront Plz, **Corning,** NY 14831-0001, *pg.* 1122, *pg.* 1154
CROSCILL, INC., 295 5th Ave, **New York,** NY 10016, *pg.* 1122, *pg.* 1220
CUTCO CORPORATION, 1116 E State St, **Olean,** NY 14760-3814, *pg.* 1123, *pg.* 1318
LIFETIME BRANDS, INC., 1000 Stewart Ave, **Garden City,** NY 11530, *pg.* 1127, *pg.* 1161
ONEIDA LTD, 163-181 Kenwood Ave, **Oneida,** NY 13421, *pg.* 1129, *pg.* 1318
RELIABLE AUTOMATIC SPRINKLER CO., INC., 103 Fairview Pk Dr, **Elmsford,** NY 10523, *pg.* 1137, *pg.* 1158
VECTOR MARKETING CORPORATION, 1116 E State St, **Olean,** NY 14760-3814, *pg.* 1139, *pg.* 1318

North Carolina

REPLACEMENTS, LTD., 1089 Knox Rd, **McLeansville,** NC 27301-9228, *pg.* 1138, *pg.* 1383
WMF OF AMERICA, INC., 3512 Faith Church Rd, **Indian Trail,** NC 28079, *pg.* 1140, *pg.* 1380

Ohio

ANCHOR HOCKING COMPANY, 519 N Pierce Ave, **Lancaster,** OH 43130, *pg.* 1121, *pg.* 1457
CALPHALON CORPORATION, 3rd D St, **Perrysburg,** OH 43551, *pg.* 1121, *pg.* 1470
E.L. MUSTEE & SONS, INC., 5431 W 164th St, **Cleveland,** OH 44142, *pg.* 1124, *pg.* 1430
LIBBEY, INC., 300 Madison Ave, **Toledo,** OH 43604, *pg.* 1126, *pg.* 1476
LINCOLN FOODSERVICE PRODUCTS, LLC, 1333 E 179th St, **Cleveland,** OH 44110, *pg.* 1127, *pg.* 1432
THE LONGABERGER COMPANY, 1500 E Main St, **Newark,** OH 43055-8847, *pg.* 1127, *pg.* 1467
THE PROCTER & GAMBLE COMPANY, 1 Procter & Gamble Plaza, **Cincinnati,** OH 45202, *pg.* 1129, *pg.* 1418
RUBBERMAID HOME PRODUCTS, 3320 W Market St, **Fairlawn,** OH 44333-3306, *pg.* 1138, *pg.* 1453
VITA-MIX CORPORATION, 8615 Usher Rd, **Cleveland,** OH 44138-2199, *pg.* 1139, *pg.* 1436
WITT INDUSTRIES, INC., 4600 N Mason-Montgomery Rd, **Mason,** OH 45040, *pg.* 1140, *pg.* 1461

Oklahoma

D'VONTZ, 7208 E 38th St, **Tulsa,** OK 74145, *pg.* 1123, *pg.* 1489

Oregon

COAST CUTLERY COMPANY, 8033 NE Holman St, **Portland,** OR 97218-4019, *pg.* 1121, *pg.* 1501
PORTLAND WILLAMETTE, 6800 NE 59th Pl, **Portland,** OR 97218-2714, *pg.* 1129, *pg.* 1505

Pennsylvania

ALL-CLAD METALCRAFTERS LLC, 424 Morganza Rd, **Canonsburg,** PA 15317-5707, *pg.* 1121, *pg.* 1519
LENOX CORPORATION, 1414 Radcliffe St, **Bristol,** PA 19007-0806, *pg.* 1126, *pg.* 1518
W.R. CASE & SONS CUTLERY COMPANY, PO Box 4000 Owens Way, **Bradford,** PA 16701, *pg.* 1141, *pg.* 1518

Rhode Island

SUMMER INFANT, INC., 1275 Park East Dr, **Woonsocket,** RI 02895, *pg.* 1139, *pg.* 1610

South Carolina

SHEEX, INC., 1237 Gadsden St Ste 200E, **Columbia,** SC 29201, *pg.* 1138, *pg.* 1614

Tennessee

KIRKLAND'S INC., 2501 McGavock Pike Ste 1000, **Nashville,** TN 37214, *pg.* 1126, *pg.* 1652

Texas

IGLOO PRODUCTS CORPORATION, 777 Igloo Rd, **Katy,** TX 77494, *pg.* 1126, *pg.* 1724
MICHAELS STORES, INC., 8000 Bent Branch Dr, **Irving,** TX 75234, *pg.* 1127, *pg.* 1722

Vermont

EDLUND COMPANY, INC., 159 Indus Pkwy, **Burlington,** VT 05401-5437, *pg.* 1123, *pg.* 1765

West Virginia

BRIGHT OF AMERICA, INC., 300 Greenbrier Rd, **Summersville,** WV 26651-1826, *pg.* 1121, *pg.* 1851
THE FENTON ART GLASS COMPANY, 700 Elizabeth St, **Williamstown,** WV 26187-1028, *pg.* 1124, *pg.* 1851
THE HOMER LAUGHLIN CHINA COMPANY, 672 Fiesta Dr, **Newell,** WV 26050-1067, *pg.* 1125, *pg.* 1850

Wisconsin

DIVERSEY, INC., 8310 16th St, **Sturtevant,** WI 53177-0902, *pg.* 1123, *pg.* 1896
FISKARS BRANDS, INC., 2537 Daniels St, **Madison,** WI 53718, *pg.* 1124, *pg.* 1866
NATIONAL PRESTO INDUSTRIES, INC, 3925 N Hastings Way, **Eau Claire,** WI 54703-0485, *pg.* 1128, *pg.* 1857
POLAR WARE COMPANY, 502 Hwy 67, **Kiel,** WI 53042, *pg.* 1129, *pg.* 1862
REGAL WARE, INC., 1675 Reigle Dr, **Kewaskum,** WI 53040-8923, *pg.* 1137, *pg.* 1862
THE VOLLRATH COMPANY LLC, 1236 N 18th St, **Sheboygan,** WI 53081-3201, *pg.* 1139, *pg.* 1894

Industrial Chemicals

Arizona

FREEPORT-MCMORAN COPPER & GOLD, INC., 333 N Central Ave, **Phoenix,** AZ 85004-2189, *pg.* 1163, *pg.* 16

Arkansas

FIBER GLASS SYSTEMS L.P., 2700 W 65th St, **Little Rock,** AR 72209, *pg.* 1162, *pg.* 34

California

AEROJET ROCKETDYNE HOLDINGS, INC., 200 Aerojet Rd, **Rancho Cordova,** CA 95742, *pg.* 1145, *pg.* 186

CODEXIS, INC., 200 Penobscot Dr, **Redwood City,** CA 94063, *pg.* 1154, *pg.* 189

CP KELCO, 8225 Aero Dr, **San Diego,** CA 92123-1718, *pg.* 1154, *pg.* 201

EUREKA CHEMICAL COMPANY, 234 Lawrence Ave, **South San Francisco,** CA 94080-6817, *pg.* 1161, *pg.* 279

E.V. ROBERTS & ASSOCIATES, INC., 18027 Bishop Ave, **Carson,** CA 90746, *pg.* 1161, *pg.* 63

THE FLAMEMASTER CORPORATION, 13576 Desmond St, **Pacoima,** CA 91331, *pg.* 1162, *pg.* 174

HURST CHEMICAL COMPANY, 2360 Eastman Ave, Ste 108, **Oxnard,** CA 93030, *pg.* 1168, *pg.* 174

MITSUBISHI RAYON CARBON FIBER AND COMPOSITES, INC.,, 1822 Reynolds Ave, **Irvine,** CA 92614-5714, *pg.* 1173, *pg.* 113

OCCIDENTAL PETROLEUM CORPORATION, 10889 Wilshire Blvd, **Los Angeles,** CA 90024-4201, *pg.* 1175, *pg.* 137

P. KAY METAL SUPPLY INC., 2448 E 25th St, **Los Angeles,** CA 90058, *pg.* 1176, *pg.* 137

PPG AEROSPACE, 12780 San Fernando Rd, **Sylmar,** CA 91342, *pg.* 1178, *pg.* 290

RENTECH, INC., 10877 Wilshire Blvd Ste 710, **Los Angeles,** CA 90024, *pg.* 1179, *pg.* 139

SPECTRUM CHEMICALS & LABORATORY PRODUCTS, INC., 14422 S San Pedro St, **Gardena,** CA 90248-2027, *pg.* 1181, *pg.* 94

SUPER GLUE CORPORATION, 9420 Santa Anita Ave, **Rancho Cucamonga,** CA 91730-6117, *pg.* 1183, *pg.* 187

U.S. PUMICE COMPANY, 20219 Bahama St, **Chatsworth,** CA 91311-6204, *pg.* 1185, *pg.* 65

WILBUR-ELLIS COMPANY, 345 California St 27th Fl, **San Francisco,** CA 94104-2644, *pg.* 1185, *pg.* 234

Colorado

BIRKO CORPORATION, 9152 Yosemite St, **Henderson,** CO 80640, *pg.* 1149, *pg.* 332

BOULDER SCIENTIFIC COMPANY, 598 3rd St, **Mead,** CO 80542, *pg.* 1150, *pg.* 335

MACDERMID, INC., 1401 Blake St, **Denver,** CO 80202, *pg.* 1172, *pg.* 321

PENFORD CORPORATION, 7094 S Revere Pkwy, **Centennial,** CO 80112-3952, *pg.* 1177, *pg.* 314

Connecticut

BIOSAFE SYSTEMS, LLC, 22 Meadow St, **East Hartford,** CT 06108, *pg.* 1149, *pg.* 345

CHEMTURA CORPORATION, 199 Benson Rd, **Middlebury,** CT 06749, *pg.* 1152, *pg.* 355

ENTHONE INC., 55 Corporate Dr, **Trumbull,** CT 06611, *pg.* 1161, *pg.* 381

HUBBARD-HALL, INC., 563 S Leonard St, **Waterbury,** CT 06708-4316, *pg.* 1167, *pg.* 382

MASTER SILICON CARBIDE INDUSTRIES, INC., 558 Lime Rock Rd, **Lakeville,** CT 06039, *pg.* 1172, *pg.* 353

MILLER-STEPHENSON CHEMICAL COMPANY, INC., George Washington Hwy, **Danbury,** CT 06813, *pg.* 1172, *pg.* 344

PRAXAIR, INC., 39 Old Ridgebury Rd, **Danbury,** CT 06810, *pg.* 1178, *pg.* 344

R.T. VANDERBILT COMPANY, INC., 30 Winfield St, **Norwalk,** CT 06855-1329, *pg.* 1180, *pg.* 364

SUMMIT CORPORATION OF AMERICA, 1430 Waterbury Rd, **Thomaston,** CT 06787-2029, *pg.* 1182, *pg.* 380

Delaware

E.I. DU PONT DE NEMOURS & COMPANY, 1007 Market St, **Wilmington,** DE 19898-0001, *pg.* 1159, *pg.* 390

HERCULES INCORPORATED, 500 Hercules Rd, **Wilmington,** DE 19808, *pg.* 1166, *pg.* 392

Florida

ARIZONA CHEMICAL CO. LLC, 4600 Touchton Rd E Ste 1200, **Jacksonville,** FL 32246, *pg.* 1147, *pg.* 431

BLASTGARD INTERNATIONAL INC., 2451 McMullen Booth Rd Ste 242, **Clearwater,** FL 33759, *pg.* 1150, *pg.* 415

NUCO2 INC., 2800 SE Market Pl, **Stuart,** FL 34997-4965, *pg.* 1175, *pg.* 468

RAYONIER INC., 1301 Riverplace Blvd, **Jacksonville,** FL 32207, *pg.* 1179, *pg.* 434

SOUTHERN AGRICULTURAL INSECTICIDES, INC., 7600 Bayshore Rd, **Palmetto,** FL 34221-8363, *pg.* 1181, *pg.* 458

THE STIMPSON COMPANY, INC., 1515 sw 13th Ct, **Pompano Beach,** FL 33069, *pg.* 1182, *pg.* 460

THEOCHEM LABORATORIES, INC., 7373 Rowlett Pk Dr, **Tampa,** FL 33610, *pg.* 1184, *pg.* 476

Georgia

BURGESS PIGMENT COMPANY, 187 Pierce Ave, **Macon,** GA 31204-2821, *pg.* 1150, *pg.* 535

EVOQUA WATER TECHNOLOGIES, 1828 Metcalf Ave, **Thomasville,** GA 31792-6845, *pg.* 1162, *pg.* 541

ROLLINS, INC., 2170 Piedmont Rd NE, **Atlanta,** GA 30324-4135, *pg.* 1179, *pg.* 519

Hawaii

CYANOTECH CORPORATION, 73-4460 Queen Kaahumanu Hwy Ste 102, **Kailua Kona,** HI 96740, *pg.* 1154, *pg.* 545

Idaho

COEUR D'ALENE MINES CORPORATION, 505 Front Ave, **Coeur D'Alene,** ID 83816, *pg.* 1154, *pg.* 549

Illinois

AKZO NOBEL INC., 525 W Van Buren St 14,15,16 Fl, **Chicago,** IL 60607, *pg.* 1146, *pg.* 563

AMERICAN CHEMET CORPORATION, 740 Waukegan Rd Ste 202, **Deerfield,** IL 60015-4374, *pg.* 1147, *pg.* 599

ANGUS CHEMICAL COMPANY, 1500 E Lk Cook Rd, **Buffalo Grove,** IL 60089-6553, *pg.* 1147, *pg.* 560

CABOT MICROELECTRONICS CORPORATION, 870 N Commons Dr, **Aurora,** IL 60504-7963, *pg.* 1151, *pg.* 554

CARUS CORPORATION, 315 5th St, **Peru,** IL 61354-2859, *pg.* 1152, *pg.* 652

CHICAGO WHITE METAL CASTING, INC., Rte 83 & Fairway Dr, **Bensenville,** IL 60106, *pg.* 1153, *pg.* 556

CORAL CHEMICAL COMPANY, 135 LeBaron St, **Waukegan,** IL 60085, *pg.* 1154, *pg.* 666

DAUBERT INDUSTRIES, INC., 1333 Burr Rdg Pkwy Ste150, **Burr Ridge,** IL 60527-0833, *pg.* 1155, *pg.* 561

DOBER CHEMICAL CORP., 11230 Katherine's Crossing Ste 100, **Woodridge,** IL 60517, *pg.* 1156, *pg.* 671

HARRINGTON & KING PERFORATING COMPANY, INC., 5655 W Fillmore St, **Chicago,** IL 60644-5504, *pg.* 1164, *pg.* 576

KRAFT CHEMICAL COMPANY, 1975 N Hawthorne Ave, **Melrose Park,** IL 60160, *pg.* 1170, *pg.* 632

LA-CO INDUSTRIES MARKAL CO., INC., 1201 Pratt Blvd, **Elk Grove Village,** IL 60007, *pg.* 1170, *pg.* 610

MINERALS TECHNOLOGIES INC., 2870 Forbs Ave, **Hoffman Estates,** IL 60192, *pg.* 1173, *pg.* 617

NALCO CO., 1601 W Diehl Rd, **Naperville,** IL 60563-1198, *pg.* 1174, *pg.* 636

NANOPHASE TECHNOLOGIES CORPORATION, 1319 Marquette Dr, **Romeoville,** IL 60446-4055, *pg.* 1174, *pg.* 656

OLD WORLD INDUSTRIES, INC., 4065 Commercial Ave, **Northbrook,** IL 60062-1828, *pg.* 1175, *pg.* 641

PETROFERM INC., 3938 Porett Dr, **Gurnee,** IL 60031, *pg.* 1177, *pg.* 616

POTASH CORP., 1101 Skokie Blvd Ste 400, **Northbrook,** IL 60062-4123, *pg.* 1177, *pg.* 641

ROCK VALLEY OIL & CHEMICAL COMPANY, 1911 Windsor Rd, **Loves Park,** IL 61111, *pg.* 1179, *pg.* 631

SLIDE PRODUCTS, INC., 430 Wheeling Rd, **Wheeling,** IL 60090-4742, *pg.* 1181, *pg.* 670

STEPAN COMPANY, Edens & Winnetka Rd, **Northfield,** IL 60093, *pg.* 1182, *pg.* 643

SUN CHEMICAL INK, 135 W Lake St, **Northlake,** IL 60164, *pg.* 1182, *pg.* 643

VELSICOL CHEMICAL CORPORATION, 10400 W Higgins Rd Ste 700, **Rosemont,** IL 60018-3713, *pg.* 1185, *pg.* 657

Indiana

DOW AGROSCIENCES LLC, 9330 Zionsville Rd, **Indianapolis,** IN 46268-1053, *pg.* 1156, *pg.* 684

MAYS CHEMICAL COMPANY, 5611 E 71st St, **Indianapolis,** IN 46220-3920, *pg.* 1172, *pg.* 688

ROYAL ADHESIVES & SEALANTS LLC, 2001 Washington St, **South Bend,** IN 46628-2032, *pg.* 1179, *pg.* 697

VERTELLUS SPECIALTIES INC., 201 N Illinois St Ste 1800, **Indianapolis,** IN 46204, *pg.* 1185, *pg.* 690

Iowa

JOHNSON MANUFACTURING COMPANY, 114 Lost Grove Rd, **Princeton,** IA 52768, *pg.* 1169, *pg.* 712

Kansas

BRADKEN, 400 S 4th St, **Atchison,** KS 66002, *pg.* 1150, *pg.* 714

COMPASS MINERALS INTERNATIONAL, INC., 9900 W 109th St Ste 100, **Overland Park,** KS 66210, *pg.* 1154, *pg.* 718

FULL VISION, INC., 3017 Full Vision Dr, **Newton,** KS 67114-9750, *pg.* 1163, *pg.* 717

INVISTA B.V., 4123 E 37th St N, **Wichita,** KS 67220, *pg.* 1168, *pg.* 723

SPURRIER CHEMICAL COMPANIES, INC., 1200 E Central Ave, **Wichita,** KS 67214, *pg.* 1182, *pg.* 724

Kentucky

PHARMCO-AAPER, 1101 Isaac Shelby Dr, **Shelbyville,** KY 40065, *pg.* 1177, *pg.* 740

Louisiana

ALBEMARLE CORPORATION, 451 Florida St, **Baton Rouge,** LA 70801, *pg.* 1146, *pg.* 741

Maryland

CRISTAL, 20 Wight Ave Ste 100, **Hunt Valley,** MD 21030, *pg.* 1154, *pg.* 772

IRT, INC., 7100 Holladay Tyler Rd, **Glenn Dale,** MD 20769, *pg.* 1169, *pg.* 771

THE MISTRAL INC., 7910 Woodmont Ave Ste 820, **Bethesda,** MD 20814, *pg.* 1173, *pg.* 765

Massachusetts

BOSTIK INC., 211 Boston St, **Middleton,** MA 01949-2128, *pg.* 1150, *pg.* 833

CABOT CORPORATION, 2 Seaport Ln Ste 1300, **Boston,** MA 02210-2019, *pg.* 1151, *pg.* 792

CHASE CORPORATION, 26 Summer St, **Bridgewater,** MA 02324, *pg.* 1152, *pg.* 803

DOW ELECTRONIC MATERIALS, 455 Forest St, **Marlborough,** MA 01752, *pg.* 1159, *pg.* 832

HEATBATH CORPORATION, 107 Frnt St, **Indian Orchard,** MA 01151-1124, *pg.* 1165, *pg.* 826

LUSTER-ON PRODUCTS, INC., 54 Waltham Ave, **Springfield,** MA 01109-3335, *pg.* 1171, *pg.* 845

Michigan

ANDERSON DEVELOPMENT COMPANY, 1415 E Michigan St, **Adrian,** MI 49221-3499, *pg.* 1147, *pg.* 864

DETREX CORPORATION, 24901 Northwestern Hwy Ste 410,

Southfield, MI 48075-2209, *pg.* 1156, *pg.* 906
THE DOW CHEMICAL COMPANY, 2030 Dow Ctr, **Midland,** MI 48674-0001, *pg.* 1157, *pg.* 898
DOW CORNING CORPORATION, 2200 W Salzburg Rd, **Midland,** MI 48686, *pg.* 1159, *pg.* 900
FLINT GROUP, INC., 14909 N Beck Rd, **Plymouth,** MI 48170-2411, *pg.* 1163, *pg.* 904
GAGE PRODUCTS COMPANY, 821 Wanda St, **Ferndale,** MI 48220, *pg.* 1164, *pg.* 886
HAVILAND ENTERPRISES INC., 421 Ann St NW, **Grand Rapids,** MI 49504-2019, *pg.* 1165, *pg.* 887
HENKEL CORPORATION, 32100 Stephenson Hwy, **Madison Heights,** MI 48071-5514, *pg.* 1166, *pg.* 897
PVS CHEMICALS, INC., 10900 Harper Ave, **Detroit,** MI 48213-3364, *pg.* 1178, *pg.* 884
RENOSOL CORPORATION, 691 S River Rd, **Bay City,** MI 48708, *pg.* 1179, *pg.* 872
WALL COLMONOY CORPORATION, 101 W Girard, **Madison Heights,** MI 48071, *pg.* 1185, *pg.* 898

Minnesota

3M COMPANY, 3M Center, **Saint Paul,** MN 55144-1000, *pg.* 1142, *pg.* 956
HAWKINS, INC., 3100 E Hennepin Ave, **Minneapolis,** MN 55413-2922, *pg.* 1165, *pg.* 937
H.B. FULLER COMPANY, 1200 Willow Lake Blvd, **Saint Paul,** MN 55110-5146, *pg.* 1165, *pg.* 961
IKONICS CORPORATION, 4832 Grand Ave, **Duluth,** MN 55807-2743, *pg.* 1168, *pg.* 921
INTERPLASTIC CORPORATION, 1225 Willow Lk Blvd, **Saint Paul,** MN 55110-5145, *pg.* 1168, *pg.* 961

Missouri

BAYER CROPSCIENCE, 8400 Hawthorne Rd, **Kansas City,** MO 64120-2301, *pg.* 1149, *pg.* 981
BREWER SCIENCE, INC., 2401 Brewer Dr, **Rolla,** MO 65401-7003, *pg.* 1150, *pg.* 989
CARBOLINE CO., 2150 Schuetz Rd, **Saint Louis,** MO 63146, *pg.* 1152, *pg.* 994
CHEMISPHERE CORPORATION, 2101 Clifton Ave, **Saint Louis,** MO 63139, *pg.* 1152, *pg.* 994
CLAYTON CORPORATION, 866 Horan Dr, **Fenton,** MO 63026-2416, *pg.* 1154, *pg.* 977
MONSANTO COMPANY, 800 N Lindbergh Blvd, **Saint Louis,** MO 63167, *pg.* 1173, *pg.* 999
OLIN CORPORATION, 190 Carondelet Plz Ste 1530, **Clayton,** MO 63105, *pg.* 1176, *pg.* 976
PBI/GORDON CORPORATION, 1217 W 12th St, **Kansas City,** MO 64101-1407, *pg.* 1176, *pg.* 985
PEABODY ENERGY CORPORATION, 701 Market St, **Saint Louis,** MO 63101, *pg.* 1176, *pg.* 1001
SENSIENT COLORS INC., 2515 N Jefferson Ave, **Saint Louis,** MO 63106, *pg.* 1180, *pg.* 1003
SIGMA-ALDRICH CORPORATION, 3050 Spruce St, **Saint Louis,** MO 63103-2530, *pg.* 1181, *pg.* 1003

Nevada

ALTAIR NANOTECHNOLOGIES INC., 204 Edison Way, **Reno,** NV 89502-2306, *pg.* 1147, *pg.* 1031
ITRONICS INC., 6490 S McCarren Blvd Bldg C Ste 23, **Reno,** NV 89509, *pg.* 1169, *pg.* 1031

New Jersey

ALPHA, 109 Corporate Blvd, **South Plainfield,** NJ 07080, *pg.* 1146, *pg.* 1123
ATLAS REFINERY, INC., 142 Lockwood St, **Newark,** NJ 07105-4719, *pg.* 1148, *pg.* 1095
BASF CATALYSTS LLC, 25 Middlesex Essex Tpke, **Iselin,** NJ 08830-0770, *pg.* 1148, *pg.* 1074
BASF CORPORATION, 100 Park Ave, **Florham Park,** NJ 07932, *pg.* 1149, *pg.* 1066
CHURCH & DWIGHT CO., INC., Princeton South Corporate Center, 500 Charles Ewiing Blvd, **Ewing,** NJ 08628, *pg.* 1153, *pg.* 1063
CYTEC INDUSTRIES, INC., 5 Garret Mountain Plz, **West Paterson,** NJ 07424-3317, *pg.* 1155, *pg.* 1131
EVONIK CORPORATION, 299 Jefferson Rd, **Parsippany,** NJ 07054, *pg.* 1162, *pg.* 1103
EVONIK CYRO LLC, 299 Jefferson Rd, **Parsippany,** NJ 07054, *pg.* 1162, *pg.* 1103
GENERAL MAGNAPLATE CORPORATION, 1331 US Rte 1, **Linden,** NJ 07036, *pg.* 1164, *pg.* 1079
INTERCHEM CORPORATION, 120 Rte 17 N, **Paramus,** NJ 07653-1579, *pg.* 1168, *pg.* 1101
JARCHEM INDUSTRIES, INC., 414 Wilson Ave, **Newark,** NJ 07105, *pg.* 1169, *pg.* 1096
J.M. HUBER CORPORATION, 333 Thornall St, **Edison,** NJ 08837-2220, *pg.* 1169, *pg.* 1056
JOHNSON MATTHEY PROCESS TECHNOLOGIES, 2399 Hwy 34 South Ste C-1, **Manasquan,** NJ 08736, *pg.* 1169, *pg.* 1083
LIPO CHEMICALS INC., 207 19th Ave, **Paterson,** NJ 07504, *pg.* 1171, *pg.* 1107
LITTLE FALLS ALLOYS, INC., 171-191 Caldwell Ave, **Paterson,** NJ 07501, *pg.* 1171, *pg.* 1107
LONZA INC., 90 Boroline Rd, **Allendale,** NJ 07401-1613, *pg.* 1171, *pg.* 1041
MASTER BOND INC., 154 Hobart St, **Hackensack,** NJ 07601, *pg.* 1172, *pg.* 1072
PHIBROCHEM, 300 Frank W Burr Blvd, Ste 21, **Teaneck,** NJ 07666, *pg.* 1177, *pg.* 1124
RHODIA INC., 8 Cedar Brook Dr, **Cranbury,** NJ 08512-7500, *pg.* 1179, *pg.* 1053
SGS U.S. TESTING COMPANY INC., 291 Fairfield Ave, **Fairfield,** NJ 07004-3833, *pg.* 1181, *pg.* 1065
SYMRISE, INC., 300 N St, **Teterboro,** NJ 07608-1204, *pg.* 1183, *pg.* 1125
TROY CORPORATION, 8 Vreeland Rd, **Florham Park,** NJ 07932-0955, *pg.* 1184, *pg.* 1067
UNETTE CORPORATION, 1578 Sussex Tpke Bldg 5, **Randolph,** NJ 07869-1833, *pg.* 1184, *pg.* 1114

New York

ACCURATE CHEMICAL & SCIENTIFIC CORPORATION, 300 Shames Dr, **Westbury,** NY 11590-1736, *pg.* 1145, *pg.* 1350
ACETO CORPORATION, 4 Tri Harbor Court, **Port Washington,** NY 11050, *pg.* 1145, *pg.* 1323
BAMBERGER POLYMERS, INC., 2 Jericho Plz, **Jericho,** NY 11753-1658, *pg.* 1148, *pg.* 1171
BARTON MINES COMPANY LLC, 6 SIF Warren St, **Lake George,** NY 12801-3438, *pg.* 1148, *pg.* 1171
GLOBE SPECIALTY METALS INC., One Penn Plz 250 West 34th Street Suite 4125, **New York,** NY 10119, *pg.* 1164, *pg.* 1235
SEQUA CORPORATION, 200 Park Ave, **New York,** NY 10166, *pg.* 1180, *pg.* 1290
SI GROUP, INC., 2750 Ball Gown Rd, **Schenectady,** NY 12309, *pg.* 1181, *pg.* 1341
UNITED-GUARDIAN, INC., 230 Marcus Blvd, **Hauppauge,** NY 11788-3731, *pg.* 1184, *pg.* 1165

North Carolina

CLARIANT CORPORATION, 4000 Monroe Rd, **Charlotte,** NC 28205, *pg.* 1153, *pg.* 1365
FMC LITHIUM DIVISION, Ste 300 2801 Yorkmont Rd, **Charlotte,** NC 28208-7377, *pg.* 1163, *pg.* 1366
MOHAWK FINISHING PRODUCTS, INC., 22 S Ctr St PO Box 535414, **Hickory,** NC 28602, *pg.* 1173, *pg.* 1378
REICHHOLD, INC., Research Triangle Park 2400 Ellis Rd, **Durham,** NC 27703, *pg.* 1179, *pg.* 1372
SYNGENTA PROFESSIONAL PRODUCTS, PO Box 18300, **Greensboro,** NC 27419, *pg.* 1183, *pg.* 1376

Ohio

A. SCHULMAN, INC., 3637 Ridgewood Rd, **Fairlawn,** OH 44333, *pg.* 1144, *pg.* 1452
ASHLAND PERFORMANCE MATERIALS, 5200 Blazer Pkwy, **Dublin,** OH 43017-5309, *pg.* 1147, *pg.* 1448
AUSTIN POWDER COMPANY, 25800 Science Park Dr 3rd Fl Ste 300, **Cleveland,** OH 44122-7311, *pg.* 1148, *pg.* 1428
B.J. ALAN COMPANY, 555 Martin Luther King Jr Blvd, **Youngstown,** OH 44502-1102, *pg.* 1150, *pg.* 1483
COHESANT, INC., 3601 Green Rd, Ste 308, **Beachwood,** OH 44122, *pg.* 1154, *pg.* 1405
DOVER CHEMICAL CORPORATION, 3676 Davis Rd NW, **Dover,** OH 44622-0040, *pg.* 1156, *pg.* 1447
EMERALD PERFORMANCE MATERIALS, LLC, 2020 Front St Ste 100, **Cuyahoga Falls,** OH 44221, *pg.* 1161, *pg.* 1445
EVANS ADHESIVE CORPORATION, LTD., 925 Old Henderson Rd, **Columbus,** OH 43220-3722, *pg.* 1161, *pg.* 1440
FAIRMOUNT SANTROL, 8834 Mayfield Rd, Ste A, **Chesterland,** OH 44026, *pg.* 1162, *pg.* 1409
FERRO CORPORATION, 6060 Parkland Blvd, **Mayfield Heights,** OH 44124-4185, *pg.* 1162, *pg.* 1462
GFS CHEMICALS, INC., 3041 Home Rd, **Powell,** OH 43065, *pg.* 1164, *pg.* 1471
HARWICK STANDARD DISTRIBUTION CORPORATION, 60 S Seiberling St, **Akron,** OH 44305-4217, *pg.* 1164, *pg.* 1402
HEXION, 180 E Broad St, **Columbus,** OH 43215, *pg.* 1166, *pg.* 1440
HILL & GRIFFITH COMPANY, 1085 Summer St, **Cincinnati,** OH 45204-2037, *pg.* 1167, *pg.* 1414
JONES-HAMILTON CO., 30354 Tracy Rd, **Walbridge,** OH 43465-9775, *pg.* 1169, *pg.* 1478
THE LUBRIZOL CORPORATION, 29400 Lakeland Blvd, **Wickliffe,** OH 44092-2298, *pg.* 1171, *pg.* 1481
MALCO PRODUCTS, INC., 361 Fairview Ave, **Barberton,** OH 44203, *pg.* 1172, *pg.* 1404
MCGEAN-ROHCO, INC., 2910 Harvard Ave, **Cleveland,** OH 44105, *pg.* 1172, *pg.* 1432
NACCO INDUSTRIES, INC., 5875 Landerbrook Dr Ste 300, **Cleveland,** OH 44124-4069, *pg.* 1174, *pg.* 1433
OMNOVA SOLUTIONS INC, 175 Ghent Rd, **Fairlawn,** OH 44333-3330, *pg.* 1176, *pg.* 1453
POLYONE CORPORATION, 33587 Walker Rd, **Avon Lake,** OH 44012, *pg.* 1177, *pg.* 1404

Oklahoma

DEEPWATER CHEMICALS, INC., 1210 Airpark Rd, **Woodward,** OK 73801-9568, *pg.* 1155, *pg.* 1491

Oregon

THE WILLAMETTE VALLEY COMPANY, 1075 Arrowsmith St, **Eugene,** OR 97402, *pg.* 1186, *pg.* 1497

Pennsylvania

ACTON TECHNOLOGIES, INC., 100 Thompson St, **Pittston,** PA 18640, *pg.* 1145, *pg.* 1582
AIR PRODUCTS AND CHEMICALS, INC., 7201 Hamilton Blvd, **Allentown,** PA 18195-1526, *pg.* 1145, *pg.* 1513
AIRGAS, INC., 259 N Radnor-Chester Rd Ste 100, **Radnor,** PA 19087-5283, *pg.* 1146, *pg.* 1583
ARKEMA INC., 900 1st Ave, **King of Prussia,** PA 19406-1308, *pg.* 1147, *pg.* 1543
AVANTOR PERFORMANCE MATERIALS, INC., 3477 Corporate Pkwy Ste 200, **Center Valley,** PA 18034-8235, *pg.* 1148, *pg.* 1521
CALGON CARBON CORPORATION, 500 Calgon Carbon Dr, **Pittsburgh,** PA 15205, *pg.* 1151, *pg.* 1574
CONSOL ENERGY INC., 1000 CONSOL Energy Dr, **Canonsburg,** PA 15317-4000, *pg.* 1154, *pg.* 1520
DOW CHEMICAL, 100 Independence Mall W, **Philadelphia,** PA 19106-2399, *pg.* 1156, *pg.* 1563
FMC CORPORATION, 1735 Market St, **Philadelphia,** PA 19103-7501, *pg.* 1163, *pg.* 1564
FXI, Rose Tree Corporate Center II 1400 Providence Rd Ste 2000, **Media,** PA 19063-2076, *pg.* 1163, *pg.* 1552
HENKEL CORPORATION, 2200 Renaissance Blvd, **Gulph Mills,** PA 19406, *pg.* 1165, *pg.* 1535
HOUGHTON INTERNATIONAL INC., Madison & Van Buren Ave, **Valley Forge,** PA 19482, *pg.* 1167, *pg.* 1589
INOLEX CHEMICAL COMPANY, 2101 S Swanson St, **Philadelphia,** PA 19148, *pg.* 1168, *pg.* 1566
INOLEX GROUP INC., Jackson and Swanson Sts, **Philadelphia,** PA 19148, *pg.* 1168, *pg.* 1566
KIDDE FIRE FIGHTING, 180 Sheree Blvd Ste 3900, **Exton,** PA 19341, *pg.* 1170, *pg.* 1531
KOPPERS HOLDINGS INC., 436 7th Ave, **Pittsburgh,** PA 15219-1800, *pg.* 1170, *pg.* 1577
LOCKHART COMPANY, 2873 W Hardies Rd, **Gibsonia,** PA 15044, *pg.* 1171, *pg.* 1534
MACE SECURITY INTERNATIONAL, INC., 240 Gibraltar Rd Ste 220, **Horsham,** PA 19044, *pg.* 1172, *pg.* 1541
NEVILLE CHEMICAL COMPANY, 2800 Neville Rd, **Pittsburgh,** PA 15225-1408, *pg.* 1174, *pg.* 1578
PQ CORPORATION, 1200 W Swedesford Rd, **Berwyn,** PA 19312-1077, *pg.* 1178, *pg.* 1515
QUADRANT ENGINEERING PLASTIC PRODUCTS, 2120

First page reference indicates Business Class Edition
Second page reference indicates Geographic Edition

Fairmont Ave, **Reading,** PA 19605-3041, *pg.* 1178, *pg.* 1585
QUAKER CHEMICAL CORP., 1 Quaker Pk 901 Hector St, **Conshohocken,** PA 19428-0809, *pg.* 1178, *pg.* 1524
READING ANTHRACITE COMPANY, 200 Mahantongo St, **Pottsville,** PA 17901-7200, *pg.* 1179, *pg.* 1583
SAINT-GOBAIN ABRASIVES, INC. - PHILADELPHIA, 200 Commerce Dr, **Montgomeryville,** PA 18936-9640, *pg.* 1180, *pg.* 1553
SUNOCO CHEMICALS, 1735 Market St, **Philadelphia,** PA 19103-1699, *pg.* 1182, *pg.* 1570
WHITFORD WORLDWIDE COMPANY, 47 Park Ave, **Elverson,** PA 19520, *pg.* 1185, *pg.* 1529

Puerto Rico

WATERS CORPORATION, Gautier Benitez Ave 230 Ste 20, **Caguas,** PR 00725, *pg.* 1185, *pg.* 1599

Rhode Island

TECHNIC INCORPORATED, 1 Spectacle St, **Cranston,** RI 02910-1032, *pg.* 1183, *pg.* 1601

South Carolina

JPS INDUSTRIES, INC., 55 Beattie Pl Ste 1510, **Greenville,** SC 29601-2146, *pg.* 1169, *pg.* 1617

Tennessee

BUCKMAN, 1256 N Mclean Blvd, **Memphis,** TN 38108-1241, *pg.* 1150, *pg.* 1641
DELTA FOREMOST CHEMICAL CORPORATION, 3915 Air Pk St, **Memphis,** TN 38118-6007, *pg.* 1155, *pg.* 1642
EASTMAN CHEMICAL COMPANY, 200 S Wilcox Dr, **Kingsport,** TN 37662, *pg.* 1159, *pg.* 1636
GEORGIA-PACIFIC CELLULOSE, 1001 Tillman St, **Memphis,** TN 38108, *pg.* 1164, *pg.* 1644
KILGORE FLARES, 155 Kilgore Rd, **Toone,** TN 38381-7850, *pg.* 1170, *pg.* 1656
TOHO TENAX AMERICA, INC., 121 Cardiff Vly Rd, **Rockwood,** TN 37854, *pg.* 1184, *pg.* 1655

Texas

A BRITE COMPANY, 3217 Wood Dr, **Garland,** TX 75041, *pg.* 1144, *pg.* 1697
BAKER PETROLITE CORPORATION, 12645 W Airport Blvd, **Sugar Land,** TX 77478-6120, *pg.* 1148, *pg.* 1745
CAMERON INTERNATIONAL, 11210 Equity Dr Ste 100, **Houston,** TX 77041, *pg.* 1151, *pg.* 1702
GDF SUEZ ENERGY NORTH AMERICA, INC., 1990 Post Oak Blvd Ste 1900, **Houston,** TX 77056-4499, *pg.* 1164, *pg.* 1706
GSE LINING TECHNOLOGY, INC., 19103 Gundle Rd, **Houston,** TX 77073, *pg.* 1164, *pg.* 1706
HENSLEY INDUSTRIES, INC., 2108 Joe Field Rd, **Dallas,** TX 75229-3255, *pg.* 1166, *pg.* 1682
MERICHEM COMPANY, 5455 Old Spanish Trl, **Houston,** TX 77024, *pg.* 1172, *pg.* 1711
NCH CORPORATION, 2727 Chemsearch Blvd, **Irving,** TX 75062-6454, *pg.* 1174, *pg.* 1723
NL INDUSTRIES, INC., 5430 LBJ Fwy Ste 1700, **Dallas,** TX 75240-2697, *pg.* 1174, *pg.* 1684
NOAH TECHNOLOGIES CORPORATION, 1 Noah Park, **San Antonio,** TX 78249-3419, *pg.* 1175, *pg.* 1742
THE NORTH AMERICAN COAL CORPORATION, 5340 Legacy Dr Bldg I Ste 300, **Plano,** TX 75024-3141, *pg.* 1175, *pg.* 1733
OCCIDENTAL CHEMICAL CORPORATION, 5005 Lyndon B Johnson Fwy, **Dallas,** TX 75244-6100, *pg.* 1175, *pg.* 1685
SACHEM INC., 821 E Woodward St, **Austin,** TX 78704, *pg.* 1180, *pg.* 1665
SAFETY-KLEEN HOLDCO, INC., 5360 Legacy Dr Cluster II Bldg 2 Ste 100, **Plano,** TX 75024, *pg.* 1180, *pg.* 1734
STEMCO INC, 300 Industrial Dr, **Longview,** TX 75602-4720, *pg.* 1182, *pg.* 1726
TECH SPRAY, L.P., 1001 NW 1st, **Amarillo,** TX 79107, *pg.* 1183, *pg.* 1659
TOR MINERALS INTERNATIONAL INC., 722 Burleson St, **Corpus Christi,** TX 78402-1344, *pg.* 1184, *pg.* 1672
TOTAL PETROCHEMICALS USA, INC., 1201 Louisiana St Ste 1800, **Houston,** TX 77002, *pg.* 1184, *pg.* 1716
VALHI, INC., 5430 LBJ Fwy Ste 1700, **Dallas,** TX 75240, *pg.* 1185, *pg.* 1690

Utah

HUNTSMAN CORPORATION, 500 Huntsman Way, **Salt Lake City,** UT 84108, *pg.* 1167, *pg.* 1758
KENNECOTT UTAH COPPER CORPORATION, 4700 W Daybreak Pkwy, **South Jordan,** UT 84095, *pg.* 1170, *pg.* 1763

Virginia

HERMES ABRASIVES LTD., 524 Viking Dr, **Virginia Beach,** VA 23452, *pg.* 1166, *pg.* 1810
KYANITE MINING CORPORATION, 30 Willis Mountain Ln, **Dillwyn,** VA 23936, *pg.* 1170, *pg.* 1779

Washington

UNIVAR INC., 17425 NE Union Hill Rd, **Redmond,** WA 98052, *pg.* 1184, *pg.* 1829

West Virginia

U.S. SILICA COMPANY, 2496 Hancock Rd, **Berkeley Springs,** WV 25411, *pg.* 1185, *pg.* 1849

Wisconsin

ANSUL, INCORPORATED, 1 Stanton St, **Marinette,** WI 54143-2542, *pg.* 1147, *pg.* 1869
BOSTIK INC., 11320 Watertown Plank Rd, **Wauwatosa,** WI 53226-3413, *pg.* 1150, *pg.* 1899
MATERION ADVANCED CHEMICALS, 407 N 13th St, **Milwaukee,** WI 53233, *pg.* 1172, *pg.* 1877
SIGMA-ALDRICH CORPORATION, 6000 N Teutonie Ave, **Milwaukee,** WI 53209, *pg.* 1181, *pg.* 1881
TEKRA CORPORATION, 16700 W Lincoln Ave, **New Berlin,** WI 53151-2728, *pg.* 1184, *pg.* 1884

Insurance

Alabama

INFINITY PROPERTY & CASUALTY CORPORATION, 3700 Colonnade Pkwy, **Birmingham,** AL 35243, *pg.* 1205, *pg.* 3
LIBERTY NATIONAL LIFE INSURANCE CO., 100 Concourse Pkwy Ste 350, **Hoover,** AL 35244, *pg.* 1206, *pg.* 5
THE NATIONAL SECURITY GROUP, INC., 661 E Davis St, **Elba,** AL 36323, *pg.* 1210, *pg.* 5
PROASSURANCE CORPORATION, 100 Brookwood Pl, **Birmingham,** AL 35209-6811, *pg.* 1214, *pg.* 3
PROTECTIVE LIFE CORPORATION, 2801 Hwy 280 S, **Birmingham,** AL 35223-2407, *pg.* 1215, *pg.* 4
PROTECTIVE LIFE INSURANCE COMPANY, 2801 Hwy 280 S, **Birmingham,** AL 35223, *pg.* 1215, *pg.* 4

Arizona

OXFORD LIFE INSURANCE COMPANY, 2721 N Central Ave, **Phoenix,** AZ 85004-1121, *pg.* 1213, *pg.* 18

California

AIG ANNUITIES, 2710 Media Ctr Dr Bldg 6 Ste 120, **Los Angeles,** CA 90065, *pg.* 1188, *pg.* 125
ASSET MARKETING SYSTEMS INSURANCE SERVICES, LLC, 15050 Avenue Of Science, Ste 100, **San Diego,** CA 92128, *pg.* 1193, *pg.* 200
BLUE SHIELD OF CALIFORNIA, 50 Beale St, **San Francisco,** CA 94105-1808, *pg.* 1195, *pg.* 214
CORELOGIC, INC., 40 Pacifica Ste 900, **Irvine,** CA 92618, *pg.* 1198, *pg.* 109
CORVEL CORPORATION, 2010 Main St Ste 600, **Irvine,** CA 92614-7203, *pg.* 1198, *pg.* 109
CSE INSURANCE GROUP, 2121 N California Blvd Ste 555, **Walnut Creek,** CA 94596-3501, *pg.* 1199, *pg.* 304
THE DOCTORS COMPANY, 185 Greenwood Rd, **Napa,** CA 94558, *pg.* 1199, *pg.* 163
FARMERS GROUP, INC., 4680 Wilshire Blvd, **Los Angeles,** CA 90010-3807, *pg.* 1199, *pg.* 130
FIREMAN'S FUND INSURANCE COMPANY, 777 San Marin Dr, **Novato,** CA 94998-0001, *pg.* 1200, *pg.* 168
GEOVERA INSURANCE COMPANY INC., 4820 Business Center Dr Ste 200, **Fairfield,** CA 94533, *pg.* 1201, *pg.* 86
INSWEB CORPORATION, 10850 Gold Center Dr Ste 250, **Rancho Cordova,** CA 95670-6178, *pg.* 1205, *pg.* 186
MERCURY INSURANCE COMPANY, 4484 Wilshire Blvd, **Los Angeles,** CA 90010, *pg.* 1208, *pg.* 136
PACIFIC LIFE INSURANCE COMPANY, 700 Newport Ctr Dr, **Newport Beach,** CA 92660, *pg.* 1213, *pg.* 166
REAL INDUSTRY, INC., 15301 Ventura Blvd Ste 400, **Sherman Oaks,** CA 91403, *pg.* 1215, *pg.* 278
TRANSAMERICA INSURANCE & INVESTMENT GROUP, 1150 S Olive St, **Los Angeles,** CA 90015-2211, *pg.* 1219, *pg.* 141
UNICO AMERICAN CORPORATION, 23251 Mulholland Dr, **Woodland Hills,** CA 91364, *pg.* 1220, *pg.* 308
VETERINARY PET INSURANCE CO., 1800 E Imperial Hwy Ste 100, **Brea,** CA 92821-6069, *pg.* 1222, *pg.* 49

Colorado

CIGI DIRECT INSURANCE SERVICES, INC., 232 F St, **Salida,** CO 81201, *pg.* 1197, *pg.* 335

Connecticut

AETNA INC., 151 Farmington Ave, **Hartford,** CT 06156-0001, *pg.* 1187, *pg.* 351
CIGNA CORPORATION, 900 Cottage Grove Rd, **Bloomfield,** CT 06002, *pg.* 1197, *pg.* 338
THE HARTFORD FINANCIAL SERVICES GROUP, INC., 1 Hartford Plz, **Hartford,** CT 06155, *pg.* 1202, *pg.* 352
HSB GROUP, INC., 1 State St, **Hartford,** CT 06103-5024, *pg.* 1204, *pg.* 352
ODYSSEY RE HOLDINGS CORP., 300 First Stamford Pl, **Stamford,** CT 06902, *pg.* 1212, *pg.* 376
THE PHOENIX COMPANIES, INC., 1 American Row, **Hartford,** CT 06102, *pg.* 1214, *pg.* 352
THE TRAVELERS COMPANIES, INC., One Tower Sq 2MS, **Hartford,** CT 06183, *pg.* 1220, *pg.* 352
VERTAFORE INC., 7 Waterside Crossing, **Windsor,** CT 06095, *pg.* 1222, *pg.* 386
W.R. BERKLEY CORPORATION, 475 Steamboat Rd, **Greenwich,** CT 06830, *pg.* 1223, *pg.* 350

Delaware

21ST CENTURY INSURANCE GROUP, 3 Beaver Valley Rd, **Wilmington,** DE 19803, *pg.* 1187, *pg.* 389

District of Columbia

CAREFIRST BLUECROSS BLUESHIELD, 840 First St NE, **Washington,** DC 20065-0001, *pg.* 1196, *pg.* 397
GEICO CORPORATION, 1 Geico Plz, **Washington,** DC 20076, *pg.* 1200, *pg.* 399
PROASSURANCE CORPORATION, 1115 30th St NW, **Washington,** DC 20007, *pg.* 1214, *pg.* 404

Florida

AAA AUTO CLUB SOUTH, 1515 N Westshore Blvd, **Tampa,** FL 33607, *pg.* 1187, *pg.* 470
AMERICAN AUTOMOBILE ASSOCIATION, 1000 AAA Dr, **Heathrow,** FL 32746-5062, *pg.* 1190, *pg.* 429
AMERICAN FAMILY AGENCIES, 555 S Hercules Ave Ste 402, **Clearwater,** FL 33764-6347, *pg.* 1190, *pg.* 415
BB&T - OSWALD TRIPPE & CO., 13515 Bell Twr Dr, **Fort Myers,** FL 33907-5944, *pg.* 1194, *pg.* 427
BROWN & BROWN, INC., 220 S Ridgewood Ave, **Daytona Beach,** FL 32114, *pg.* 1196, *pg.* 419
PATRIOT NATIONAL INSURANCE GROUP, 401 E Las Olas Blvd Ste 1650, **Fort Lauderdale,** FL 33301, *pg.* 1213, *pg.* 426
STAHL & ASSOCIATES INSURANCE, 110 Carillon Pkwy, **Saint Petersburg,** FL 33716, *pg.* 1217, *pg.* 464
UNITED INSURANCE HOLDINGS CORP., 360 Central Ave Ste 900, **Saint Petersburg,** FL 33701, *pg.* 1220, *pg.* 465
WELCOME FUNDS, INC., 6001 Broken Sound Pkwy Ste 320, **Boca Raton,** FL 33487, *pg.* 1223, *pg.* 413
WELLCARE HEALTH PLANS INC., 8725 Henderson Road Renaissance One, **Tampa,** FL 33634, *pg.* 1223, *pg.* 476

Georgia

AFLAC INCORPORATED, 1932 Wynnton Rd, **Columbus,** GA 31999-0001, *pg.* 1188, *pg.* 527
CRAWFORD & COMPANY, 1001 Summit Blvd, **Atlanta,** GA 30319, *pg.* 1199, *pg.* 502

Illinois

THE ALLSTATE CORPORATION, 2775 Sanders Rd, **Northbrook,** IL 60062, *pg.* 1189, *pg.* 639
AON RISK SERVICES INC., 200 E Randolph St, **Chicago,** IL 60601, *pg.* 1193, *pg.* 564
BANKERS LIFE & CASUALTY COMPANY, 111 E Wacker Dr Ste 2100, **Chicago,** IL 60601-4508, *pg.* 1194, *pg.* 566
BITCO INSURANCE, 320 18th St, **Rock Island,** IL 61201-8938, *pg.* 1195, *pg.* 654
BLUE CROSS & BLUE SHIELD ASSOCIATION, 225 N Michigan Ave, **Chicago,** IL 60601-7601, *pg.* 1195, *pg.* 566
CATHOLIC ORDER OF FORESTERS, 355 Shuman Blvd, **Naperville,** IL 60563, *pg.* 1196, *pg.* 635
CENTEGRA NORTHERN ILLINOIS MEDICAL CENTER, 4201 W Medical Ctr Dr, **McHenry,** IL 60050-8409, *pg.* 1196, *pg.* 632
CNA INSURANCE COMPANIES, CNA Ctr 333 S Wabash Ave, **Chicago,** IL 60604-0001, *pg.* 1198, *pg.* 571
COUNTRY FINANCIAL, 1701 Towanda Ave, **Bloomington,** IL 61701, *pg.* 1198, *pg.* 557
HEALTH CARE SERVICE CORPORATION, 300 E Randolph St, **Chicago,** IL 60601-5099, *pg.* 1203, *pg.* 576
HORACE MANN COMPANIES, 1 Horace Mann Plaza, **Springfield,** IL 62715-0001, *pg.* 1203, *pg.* 662
HORTICA INSURANCE, 1 Horticultural Ln, **Edwardsville,** IL 62025-0428, *pg.* 1204, *pg.* 609
KEMPER CORPORATION, 1 E Wacker Dr, **Chicago,** IL 60601-1802, *pg.* 1205, *pg.* 579
LIFE QUOTES, INC., 8205 S Cass Ave Ste 102, **Darien,** IL 60561, *pg.* 1206, *pg.* 598
MODERN WOODMEN OF AMERICA, 1701 1st Ave, **Rock Island,** IL 61201-8724, *pg.* 1209, *pg.* 654
RLI CORP., 9025 N Lindbergh Dr, **Peoria,** IL 61615, *pg.* 1216, *pg.* 652
SAFEWAY INSURANCE COMPANY, 790 Pasquinelli Dr, **Westmont,** IL 60559, *pg.* 1216, *pg.* 669
STATE FARM MUTUAL AUTOMOBILE INSURANCE CO., 1 State Farm Plz, **Bloomington,** IL 61710-0001, *pg.* 1218, *pg.* 557
UTG, INC., 5250 S 6th St Rd PO Box 5147, **Springfield,** IL 62703-5128, *pg.* 1222, *pg.* 662
ZURICH HOLDING COMPANY OF AMERICA, INC., Zurich Towers 1400 American Ln, **Schaumburg,** IL 60196, *pg.* 1224, *pg.* 660

Indiana

ANTHEM, INC., 120 Monument Cir, **Indianapolis,** IN 46204-4906, *pg.* 1192, *pg.* 683
CNO FINANCIAL GROUP, INC., 11825 N Pennsylvania St, **Carmel,** IN 46032, *pg.* 1198, *pg.* 675
INDIANA FARM BUREAU INSURANCE, 225 SE St, **Indianapolis,** IN 46202-4058, *pg.* 1204, *pg.* 687
THE LINCOLN NATIONAL LIFE INSURANCE CO., 1300 S Clinton St, **Fort Wayne,** IN 46802, *pg.* 1207, *pg.* 680
THE MEDICAL PROTECTIVE COMPANY, 5814 Reed Rd, **Fort Wayne,** IN 46835, *pg.* 1208, *pg.* 680

Iowa

AMERICAN REPUBLIC INSURANCE COMPANY, 601 6th Ave, **Des Moines,** IA 50334-0001, *pg.* 1191, *pg.* 704
FARMERS MUTUAL HAIL INSURANCE COMPANY OF IOWA, 6785 Westown Pkwy, **West Des Moines,** IA 50266-7727, *pg.* 1199, *pg.* 713
GRINNELL MUTUAL REINSURANCE COMPANY INC., 4215 Hwy 146, **Grinnell,** IA 50112, *pg.* 1201, *pg.* 708
GUIDEONE INSURANCE COMPANY, 1111 Ashworth Rd, **West Des Moines,** IA 50265-3544, *pg.* 1202, *pg.* 713
NATIONWIDE MUTUAL INSURANCE COMPANY, 1100 Locus St, **Des Moines,** IA 50391-2000, *pg.* 1211, *pg.* 706
UNITED FIRE GROUP, INC, 118 2nd Ave SE, **Cedar Rapids,** IA 52401-1212, *pg.* 1220, *pg.* 703
WELLMARK, INC, 1331 Grand Ave, **Des Moines,** IA 50306-9232, *pg.* 1223, *pg.* 707

Kentucky

HUMANA, INC., 500 W Main St, **Louisville,** KY 40202, *pg.* 1204, *pg.* 734

Louisiana

AMERISAFE, INC., 2301 Hwy 190 W, **Deridder,** LA 70634, *pg.* 1191, *pg.* 743
PAN-AMERICAN LIFE INSURANCE COMPANY, 601 Poydras St, **New Orleans,** LA 70130-6029, *pg.* 1213, *pg.* 747

Maryland

AEGON USA, INC., 2 E Chase St, **Baltimore,** MD 21202, *pg.* 1187, *pg.* 755
AVEMCO INSURANCE COMPANY, Frederick Municipal Airport 411 Aviation Way, **Frederick,** MD 21701, *pg.* 1194, *pg.* 769
GEICO GENERAL INSURANCE COMPANY, 5260 Western Ave, **Chevy Chase,** MD 20815, *pg.* 1201, *pg.* 766
KAISER FOUNDATION HEALTH PLAN OF THE MID-ATLANTIC STATES, INC., 2101 E Jefferson St, **Rockville,** MD 20852, *pg.* 1205, *pg.* 776

Massachusetts

BOSTON MUTUAL LIFE INSURANCE COMPANY, 120 Royall St, **Canton,** MA 02021-1028, *pg.* 1196, *pg.* 810
THE HANOVER INSURANCE COMPANY, 440 Lincoln St, **Worcester,** MA 01653, *pg.* 1202, *pg.* 862
JOHN HANCOCK FINANCIAL SERVICES, John Hancock Pl, **Boston,** MA 02117, *pg.* 1205, *pg.* 796
LIBERTY MUTUAL INSURANCE GROUP INC., 175 Berkeley St, **Boston,** MA 02116, *pg.* 1205, *pg.* 797
MAPFRE INSURANCE, 211 Main St, **Webster,** MA 01570-

First page reference indicates Business Class Edition
Second page reference indicates Geographic Edition

2249, *pg.* 1207, *pg.* 856
MASSACHUSETTS MUTUAL LIFE INSURANCE COMPANY, 1295 State St, **Springfield,** MA 01111, *pg.* 1207, *pg.* 845
NEIGHBORHOOD HEALTH PLAN INC., 253 Summer St 5th Fl, **Boston,** MA 02110-1114, *pg.* 1211, *pg.* 798
QUINCY MUTUAL FIRE INSURANCE COMPANY, 57 Washington St, **Quincy,** MA 02169, *pg.* 1215, *pg.* 842

Michigan

AMERISURE MUTUAL INSURANCE COMPANY, 26777 Halsted Rd, **Farmington Hills,** MI 48331-3560, *pg.* 1191, *pg.* 885
AUTO-OWNERS INSURANCE GROUP, 6101 Anacapri Blvd, **Lansing,** MI 48917, *pg.* 1194, *pg.* 895
BLUE CROSS & BLUE SHIELD OF MICHIGAN, 600 Lafayette E Blvd, **Detroit,** MI 48226, *pg.* 1195, *pg.* 879
KAUFMAN FINANCIAL GROUP, INC., 30833 NW Hwy Ste 220, **Farmington Hills,** MI 48334, *pg.* 1205, *pg.* 886

Minnesota

ALLIANZ LIFE INSURANCE COMPANY OF NORTH AMERICA, 5701 Golden Hills Dr, **Minneapolis,** MN 55416, *pg.* 1188, *pg.* 929
FEDERATED MUTUAL INSURANCE COMPANY, 121 E Pk Sq, **Owatonna,** MN 55060-3046, *pg.* 1200, *pg.* 952
HEALTHPARTNERS, INC., 8170 33rd Ave S, **Bloomington,** MN 55425, *pg.* 1203, *pg.* 918
MEDICA, INC., 401 Carlson Pkwy, **Minnetonka,** MN 55305, *pg.* 1208, *pg.* 949
THE MINNESOTA LIFE INSURANCE COMPANY, 400 Robert St N, **Saint Paul,** MN 55101, *pg.* 1209, *pg.* 962
THRIVENT FINANCIAL FOR LUTHERANS, 625 4th Ave S, **Minneapolis,** MN 55415-1624, *pg.* 1219, *pg.* 944
TRAVELERS INSURANCE, 385 Washington St, **Saint Paul,** MN 55102-1309, *pg.* 1220, *pg.* 963
UNITEDHEALTH GROUP INCORPORATED, UnitedHealth Group Ctr 9900 Bren Rd E, **Minnetonka,** MN 55343, *pg.* 1221, *pg.* 950
WESTERN NATIONAL MUTUAL INSURANCE CO., 5350 W 78th St, **Minneapolis,** MN 55439, *pg.* 1223, *pg.* 946

Missouri

OLD AMERICAN INSURANCE COMPANY, 3520 Broadway St, **Kansas City,** MO 64111-2502, *pg.* 1213, *pg.* 985

Nebraska

AMERITAS LIFE INSURANCE CORP., 5900 O St, **Lincoln,** NE 68510, *pg.* 1192, *pg.* 1011
ASSURITY LIFE INSURANCE COMPANY, 1526 K St, **Lincoln,** NE 68508, *pg.* 1194, *pg.* 1011
BERKSHIRE HATHAWAY INC., 3555 Farnam St, **Omaha,** NE 68131, *pg.* 1195, *pg.* 1013
FINANCIAL BROKERAGE INC., 2238 S 156 Cir, **Omaha,** NE 68130, *pg.* 1200, *pg.* 1015
LINCOLN FINANCIAL BENEFIT PARTNERS, 8801 Indian Hills Dr, **Omaha,** NE 68114, *pg.* 1206, *pg.* 1016
MILLENNIUM MARKETING GROUP, LLC, 11313 Chicago Cir, **Omaha,** NE 68154-2633, *pg.* 1209, *pg.* 1016
MUTUAL OF OMAHA INSURANCE COMPANY, Mutual of Omaha Plz, **Omaha,** NE 68175, *pg.* 1210, *pg.* 1016
PHYSICIANS MUTUAL INSURANCE CO., 2600 Dodge St, **Omaha,** NE 68131-2671, *pg.* 1214, *pg.* 1017
SENIOR MARKET SALES, INC., 8420 W Dodge Rd 5th Fl, **Omaha,** NE 68114, *pg.* 1217, *pg.* 1018

New Hampshire

VISION FINANCIAL CORPORATION, 17 Church St, **Keene,** NH 03431-0506, *pg.* 1222, *pg.* 1035

New Jersey

THE CHUBB CORPORATION, 15 Mountain View Rd, **Warren,** NJ 07059, *pg.* 1196, *pg.* 1128
GALLAGHER BOLLINGER, 101 JFK Pkwy, **Short Hills,** NJ 07078, *pg.* 1200, *pg.* 1121
HORIZON BLUE CROSS BLUE SHIELD OF NEW JERSEY, 3 Penn Plz E, **Newark,** NJ 07105, *pg.* 1203, *pg.* 1096
NEW JERSEY MANUFACTURERS INSURANCE COMPANY, 301 Sullivan Way, **West Trenton,** NJ 08628, *pg.* 1211, *pg.* 1132
QUALCARE, INC., 30 Knightsbridge Rd, **Piscataway,** NJ 08854, *pg.* 1215, *pg.* 1109
RICHARDS & SUMMERS INC., 76 Broadway, **Denville,** NJ 07834-0068, *pg.* 1216, *pg.* 1053
SELECTIVE INSURANCE GROUP, INC., 40 Wantage Ave, **Branchville,** NJ 07890, *pg.* 1216, *pg.* 1045
VERISK ANALYTICS, INC., 545 Washington Blvd, **Jersey City,** NJ 07310-1686, *pg.* 1222, *pg.* 1076
VREELAND INSURANCE INC., Rockaway 80 Corp Ctr 100 Enterprise Dr Ste 501, **Rockaway,** NJ 07866, *pg.* 1223, *pg.* 1116
ZENITH MARKETING GROUP, INC., 303 W Main St Ste 200, **Freehold,** NJ 07728, *pg.* 1224, *pg.* 1071

New York

AMERICAN INTERNATIONAL GROUP, INC., 175 Water St, **New York,** NY 10038, *pg.* 1190, *pg.* 1193
ASSURANT, INC., 1 Chase Manhattan Plz 41st Fl, **New York,** NY 10005, *pg.* 1193, *pg.* 1198
ATHENE ANNUITY & LIFE ASSURANCE COMPANY OF NEW YORK, 69 Lydecker St, **Nyack,** NY 10960-2103, *pg.* 1194, *pg.* 1318
AXA EQUITABLE LIFE INSURANCE COMPANY, 1290 Ave of the Americas, **New York,** NY 10104-0101, *pg.* 1194, *pg.* 1199
COLUMBIAN MUTUAL LIFE INSURANCE COMPANY, Vestal Pkwy E, **Binghamton,** NY 13902, *pg.* 1198, *pg.* 1142
FRENKEL & CO. INC., 1740 Broadway, **New York,** NY 10019, *pg.* 1200, *pg.* 1233
GERBER LIFE INSURANCE COMPANY, 1311 Mamaroneck Ave, **White Plains,** NY 10605-5223, *pg.* 1201, *pg.* 1352
GREATER NEW YORK MUTUAL INSURANCE COMPANY, 200 Madison Ave, **New York,** NY 10016, *pg.* 1201, *pg.* 1236
THE GUARDIAN LIFE INSURANCE COMPANY OF AMERICA, 7 Hanover Sq, **New York,** NY 10004-4025, *pg.* 1202, *pg.* 1237
KINGSTONE COMPANIES, INC., 1154 Broadway, **Hewlett,** NY 11557, *pg.* 1205, *pg.* 1166
MARSH & MCLENNAN COMPANIES INC., 1166 Ave of the Americas, **New York,** NY 10036-2774, *pg.* 1207, *pg.* 1256
MERCHANTS GROUP, INC., 250 Main St, **Buffalo,** NY 14202, *pg.* 1208, *pg.* 1149
METLIFE, INC., 200 Park Ave, **New York,** NY 10166-0188, *pg.* 1208, *pg.* 1258
MUTUAL OF AMERICA LIFE INSURANCE COMPANY, 320 Park Ave, **New York,** NY 10022, *pg.* 1210, *pg.* 1263
NEW YORK LIFE INSURANCE COMPANY, 51 Madison Ave, **New York,** NY 10010, *pg.* 1211, *pg.* 1268
SBLI USA LIFE INSURANCE COMPANY, INC., 460 W 34th St Ste 800, **New York,** NY 10001-2320, *pg.* 1216, *pg.* 1288
SECURITY MUTUAL LIFE INSURANCE COMPANY OF NEW YORK, 100 Court St, **Binghamton,** NY 13901, *pg.* 1216, *pg.* 1142
SIRIUS AMERICA REINSURANCE COMPANY, 140 Broadway 32nd Fl, **New York,** NY 10005, *pg.* 1217, *pg.* 1292
SWISS REINSURANCE AMERICA CORPORATION, 175 King St, **Armonk,** NY 10504, *pg.* 1218, *pg.* 1140
TEACHERS INSURANCE & ANNUITY ASSOCIATION - COLLEGE RETIREMENT EQUITIES FUND, 730 3rd Ave, **New York,** NY 10017-3206, *pg.* 1219, *pg.* 1297
UNITED STATES AIRCRAFT INSURANCE GROUP, 199 Water St, **New York,** NY 10038-3526, *pg.* 1221, *pg.* 1307
USI HOLDINGS CORPORATION, 555 Pleasantville Rd Ste 160 S, **Briarcliff Manor,** NY 10510, *pg.* 1222, *pg.* 1144
UTICA MUTUAL INSURANCE COMPANY, 180 Genesee St, **New Hartford,** NY 13413-2299, *pg.* 1222, *pg.* 1183
WILLIS HRH, INC., 200 Liberty St 3rd Fl, **New York,** NY 10281, *pg.* 1223, *pg.* 1314

North Carolina

ARROWPOINT CAPITAL CORP., Whitehall Corporate Ctr 3 3600 Arco Corporate Dr, **Charlotte,** NC 28273, *pg.* 1193, *pg.* 1361
FINANCIAL INDEPENDENCE GROUP INC., 19250 W Catawba Ave, **Cornelius,** NC 28031-6222, *pg.* 1200, *pg.* 1370
LINCOLN FINANCIAL GROUP, 100 N Greene St, **Greensboro,** NC 27401, *pg.* 1206, *pg.* 1375
NORTH CAROLINA MUTUAL LIFE INSURANCE COMPANY, 411 W Chapel Hill St, **Durham,** NC 27701-3616, *pg.* 1212, *pg.* 1372

Ohio

AMERITAS INVESTMENT CORP., 1876 Waycross Rd, **Cincinnati,** OH 45240, *pg.* 1192, *pg.* 1410
CENTRAL MUTUAL INSURANCE COMPANY, 800 S Washington St, **Van Wert,** OH 45891-2357, *pg.* 1196, *pg.* 1478
INSURANCE.COM, INC., 29000 Aurora Rd, **Solon,** OH 44139, *pg.* 1205, *pg.* 1473
MOTORISTS MUTUAL INSURANCE CO., 471 E Broad St Ste 200, **Columbus,** OH 43215, *pg.* 1210, *pg.* 1442
NATIONWIDE MUTUAL INSURANCE COMPANY, 1 Nationwide Plz, **Columbus,** OH 43215-2220, *pg.* 1210, *pg.* 1442
OHIO FARMERS INSURANCE COMPANY, 1 Park Cir PO Box 5001, **Westfield Center,** OH 44251-5001, *pg.* 1213, *pg.* 1480
THE PROGRESSIVE CORPORATION, 6300 Wilson Mills Rd, **Mayfield Village,** OH 44143-2109, *pg.* 1214, *pg.* 1463
SAFEAUTO INSURANCE COMPANY, 4 Easton Oval, **Columbus,** OH 43213, *pg.* 1216, *pg.* 1443
STATE AUTOMOBILE MUTUAL INSURANCE COMPANY, 518 E Broad St, **Columbus,** OH 43215, *pg.* 1217, *pg.* 1444
THE WESTERN & SOUTHERN FINANCIAL GROUP, 400 Broadway, **Cincinnati,** OH 45202, *pg.* 1223, *pg.* 1427

Oklahoma

GLOBE LIFE & ACCIDENT INSURANCE COMPANY, Globe Life Ctr 204 N Robinson, **Oklahoma City,** OK 73102, *pg.* 1201, *pg.* 1486

Oregon

M FINANCIAL HOLDINGS INC., 1125 NW Couch St Ste 900, **Portland,** OR 97209, *pg.* 1207, *pg.* 1504
REGENCE BLUECROSS BLUESHIELD OF OREGON, 100 SW Market St, **Portland,** OR 97201, *pg.* 1215, *pg.* 1506
STANDARD INSURANCE COMPANY, 1100 SW 6th Ave, **Portland,** OR 97204, *pg.* 1217, *pg.* 1506

Pennsylvania

HIGHMARK BLUE CROSS BLUE SHIELD, 120 5th Ave, **Pittsburgh,** PA 15222, *pg.* 1203, *pg.* 1576
NATIONWIDE MUTUAL INSURANCE COMPANY, 355 Maple Ave, **Harleysville,** PA 19438-2297, *pg.* 1211, *pg.* 1536
PENNSYLVANIA NATIONAL MUTUAL CASUALTY INSURANCE COMPANY, 2 N 2nd St, **Harrisburg,** PA 17101-1619, *pg.* 1214, *pg.* 1537
RELIANCE STANDARD LIFE INSURANCE COMPANY, 2001 Market St Ste 500, **Philadelphia,** PA 19103, *pg.* 1215, *pg.* 1570

Rhode Island

AMICA MUTUAL INSURANCE CO., 100 Amica Way, **Lincoln,** RI 02865, *pg.* 1192, *pg.* 1602
BLUE CROSS & BLUE SHIELD OF RHODE ISLAND, 500 Exchange St, **Providence,** RI 02903-3206, *pg.* 1195, *pg.* 1606
FACTORY MUTUAL INSURANCE COMPANY, 270 Central Ave, **Johnston,** RI 02919, *pg.* 1199, *pg.* 1601

South Carolina

THE SEIBELS BRUCE GROUP, INC., 1501 Lady St, **Columbia,** SC 29201, *pg.* 1216, *pg.* 1614

South Dakota

AVERA HEALTH, 3900 W Avera Dr, **Sioux Falls,** SD 57108, *pg.* 1194, *pg.* 1625

Tennessee

AMERICAN INTERNATIONAL GROUP, American General

Ctr, **Nashville,** TN 37250-0001, *pg.* 1190, *pg.* 1648
FIRST ACCEPTANCE CORPORATION, 3813 Green Hills Village Dr, **Nashville,** TN 37215, *pg.* 1200, *pg.* 1650
UNUM GROUP, 1 Fountain Sq, **Chattanooga,** TN 37402-1307, *pg.* 1222, *pg.* 1629

Texas

AMERICAN NATIONAL INSURANCE COMPANY, 1 Moody Plz, **Galveston,** TX 77550-7999, *pg.* 1191, *pg.* 1697
CITIZENS INC., 400 E Anderson Ln, **Austin,** TX 78752, *pg.* 1197, *pg.* 1661
HALLMARK FINANCIAL SERVICES, INC., 777 Main St Ste 1000, **Fort Worth,** TX 76102, *pg.* 1202, *pg.* 1695
NATIONAL WESTERN LIFE INSURANCE COMPANY, 850 E Anderson Ln, **Austin,** TX 78752-1602, *pg.* 1210, *pg.* 1664
SOLERA HOLDINGS, INC., 7 Village Circle Ste 100, **Westlake,** TX 76262, *pg.* 1217, *pg.* 1749
STANDARD LIFE & ACCIDENT INSURANCE COMPANY, 2450 S Shore Blvd, **League City,** TX 77573, *pg.* 1217, *pg.* 1725
STONEBRIDGE LIFE INSURANCE COMPANY, 2700 W Plano Pkwy, **Plano,** TX 75075-8200, *pg.* 1218, *pg.* 1735
UNITED SERVICES AUTOMOBILE ASSOCIATION, 9800 Fredericksburg Rd, **San Antonio,** TX 78288, *pg.* 1221, *pg.* 1743

Vermont

NATIONAL LIFE INSURANCE COMPANY, 1 National Life Dr, **Montpelier,** VT 05604, *pg.* 1210, *pg.* 1766

Virginia

ANTHEM HEALTH PLANS OF VIRGINIA, 2015 Staples Mill Rd Ste 1, **Richmond,** VA 23279-3119, *pg.* 1192, *pg.* 1800
GENWORTH LIFE AND ANNUITY INSURANCE COMPANY, 6610 W Broad St, **Richmond,** VA 23230, *pg.* 1201, *pg.* 1802
MARKEL CORPORATION, 4521 Highwoods Pkwy, **Glen Allen,** VA 23060-6148, *pg.* 1207, *pg.* 1783

Washington

PREMERA BLUE CROSS, 7001-220 St SW Bldg 1, **Mountlake Terrace,** WA 98043, *pg.* 1214, *pg.* 1823

Wisconsin

AMERICAN FAMILY MUTUAL INSURANCE COMPANY, 6000 American Pkwy, **Madison,** WI 53783, *pg.* 1190, *pg.* 1864
ANTHEM BLUE CROSS BLUE SHIELD, N17 W24340 Riverwood Dr, **Pewaukee,** WI 53188, *pg.* 1192, *pg.* 1886
ASSURANT HEALTH, 501 W Michigan Ave, **Milwaukee,** WI 53203-2706, *pg.* 1193, *pg.* 1873
THE NORTHWESTERN MUTUAL LIFE INSURANCE COMPANY, 720 E Wisconsin Ave, **Milwaukee,** WI 53202-4797, *pg.* 1212, *pg.* 1879
SENTRY INSURANCE GROUP, 1800 Northpoint Dr, **Stevens Point,** WI 54481, *pg.* 1217, *pg.* 1895

Internet/Online

Alabama

RADIANCE TECHNOLOGIES, INC., 350 Wynn Dr, **Huntsville,** AL 35805, *pg.* 1277, *pg.* 6

Arizona

GO DADDY INC., 14455 N Hayden Rd Ste 226, **Scottsdale,** AZ 85260, *pg.* 1249, *pg.* 21
INCENTIVE LOGIC, INC., 7600 E Redfield Rd, Ste 140, **Scottsdale,** AZ 85260, *pg.* 1258, *pg.* 22
LIMELIGHT NETWORKS, INC., 222 South Mill Ave Ste 800, **Tempe,** AZ 85281, *pg.* 1262, *pg.* 26

California

AIRBNB, INC., 888 Brannan St, **San Francisco,** CA 94103, *pg.* 1226, *pg.* 211
ALEXA INTERNET, INC., Presidio of San Francisco Bldg 37, **San Francisco,** CA 94129, *pg.* 1226, *pg.* 212
ART & LOGIC, INC., 2 N Lake Ave Ste 1050, **Pasadena,** CA 91101, *pg.* 1229, *pg.* 179
ART.COM, 2100 Powell St 13th Fl, **Emeryville,** CA 94608, *pg.* 1229, *pg.* 83
AUTOBYTEL INC., 18872 MacArthur Blvd Ste 200, **Irvine,** CA 92612-1400, *pg.* 1230, *pg.* 107
BABYCENTER, LLC, 163 Freelon St, **San Francisco,** CA 94107-1624, *pg.* 1231, *pg.* 212
BIRDSALL INTERACTIVE, INC., 961 Moraga Rd, Ste C, **Lafayette,** CA 94549, *pg.* 1231, *pg.* 120
BIZRATE.COM, 12200 W Olympic Blvd Ste 300, **Los Angeles,** CA 90064, *pg.* 1231, *pg.* 126
BLOGHER INC., 1301 Shoreway Rd, **Belmont,** CA 94002, *pg.* 1232, *pg.* 45
BOX INC., 4440 El Camino Real, **Los Altos,** CA 94022, *pg.* 1232, *pg.* 124
BRILLIANT DIGITAL, 12711 Ventura Blvd Ste 210, **Studio City,** CA 91604, *pg.* 1233, *pg.* 281
BRS MEDIA INC., 55 New Montgonery Suit 622, **San Francisco,** CA 94105, *pg.* 1233, *pg.* 214
CAFEPRESS.COM, INC., 1850 Gateway Dr Ste 300, **San Mateo,** CA 94404, *pg.* 1234, *pg.* 254
CHEMINDUSTRY.COM, INC., 730 E Cypress Ave, **Monrovia,** CA 91016, *pg.* 1235, *pg.* 150
CITRIX ONLINE LLC, 7414 Hollister Ave, **Goleta,** CA 93117-2583, *pg.* 1235, *pg.* 99
CONSUMERREVIEW, INC., 100 Marine Pkwy Ste 550, **Redwood Shores,** CA 94065, *pg.* 1237, *pg.* 193
COOKING.COM, 4086 Del Rey Ave, **Marina Del Rey,** CA 90292, *pg.* 1237, *pg.* 143
DAYBREAK GAME COMPANY, LLC, 8928 Terman Ct, **San Diego,** CA 92121, *pg.* 1237, *pg.* 202
DEMAND MEDIA, INC., 1299 Ocean Ave Ste 500, **Santa Monica,** CA 90401, *pg.* 1238, *pg.* 273
DISCOUNT SCHOOL SUPPLY, 2 Lowr Ragsdale Dr, **Monterey,** CA 93940-5748, *pg.* 1238, *pg.* 151
DISNEY INTERACTIVE MEDIA GROUP, 1200 Grand Central Ave, **Glendale,** CA 91201, *pg.* 1239, *pg.* 95
DISQUS, 301 Howard St Ste 300, **San Francisco,** CA 94105, *pg.* 1239, *pg.* 216
DOLLARSTORE, INC., 2222 Michelson Dr, **Irvine,** CA 92612, *pg.* 1239, *pg.* 109
E! ONLINE, INC., 5750 Wilshire Blvd, **Los Angeles,** CA 90036-3697, *pg.* 1239, *pg.* 129
EBATES.COM, 333 Bryant St Ste 250, **San Francisco,** CA 94107, *pg.* 1240, *pg.* 217
EBAY INC., Whitman Campus 2065 Hamilton Ave, **San Jose,** CA 95125, *pg.* 1240, *pg.* 243
EDMUNDS, INC., 1620 26th St Ste 400 S Tower, **Santa Monica,** CA 90404, *pg.* 1241, *pg.* 273
EFAX.COM INC., 6922 Hollywood Blvd 5th Fl, **Los Angeles,** CA 90028-6128, *pg.* 1242, *pg.* 129
EGAIN COMMUNICATIONS CORPORATION, 1252 Borregas Ave, **Sunnyvale,** CA 94089-1309, *pg.* 1242, *pg.* 284
EHARMONY.COM, INC., 300 N Lake Ave Ste 1111, **Pasadena,** CA 91101, *pg.* 1242, *pg.* 180
EHEALTH, INC., 440 E Middlefield Rd, **Mountain View,** CA 94043, *pg.* 1242, *pg.* 153
ELLIE MAE, INC., 4155 Hopyard Rd Ste 200, **Pleasanton,** CA 94588, *pg.* 1243, *pg.* 183
EN POINTE TECHNOLOGIES, INC., 18701 S Figueroa St, **Gardena,** CA 90248-4506, *pg.* 1243, *pg.* 94
EOS INTERNATIONAL, INC., 2292 Faraday Ave, **Carlsbad,** CA 92008-7208, *pg.* 1243, *pg.* 59
ESURANCE, INC., 650 Davis St, **San Francisco,** CA 94111, *pg.* 1243, *pg.* 217
EVEO INC., 303 2nd St S Tower 6th Fl, **San Francisco,** CA 94107-3629, *pg.* 1244, *pg.* 217
EXPERIAN CONSUMER DIRECT, 475 Anton Blvd, **Costa Mesa,** CA 92626, *pg.* 1245, *pg.* 71
FACEBOOK, INC., 1601 Willow Rd, **Menlo Park,** CA 94025, *pg.* 1245, *pg.* 143
FANDANGO MEDIA, LLC, 12200 W Olympic Blvd Ste 400, **Los Angeles,** CA 90064, *pg.* 1247, *pg.* 130
FREEREALTIME.COM INC., 22365 El Toro Rd 224, **Lake Forest,** CA 92630, *pg.* 1248, *pg.* 121
GOINDUSTRY-DOVEBID, INC., 1900 O'Farrell St Ste 325, **San Mateo,** CA 94403, *pg.* 1249, *pg.* 255
GOOD TECHNOLOGY, INC., 430 N Mary Ave, Ste 200, **Sunnyvale,** CA 94085, *pg.* 1249, *pg.* 285
GOOGLE INC., 1600 Amphitheatre Pkwy, **Mountain View,** CA 94043, *pg.* 1249, *pg.* 153
GREE INTERNATIONAL, INC., 185 Berry St, **San Francisco,** CA 94107, *pg.* 1255, *pg.* 219
GUNGHO ONLINE ENTERTAINMENT AMERICA, 2101 Rosecrans Ave Ste 3220, **El Segundo,** CA 90245, *pg.* 1255, *pg.* 80
HIRERIGHT, INC., 5151 California Ave, **Irvine,** CA 92617, *pg.* 1256, *pg.* 111
HOMEGAIN.COM, INC., 1250 45th St Ste 200, **Emeryville,** CA 94608-2924, *pg.* 1256, *pg.* 83
HOMES.COM, INC., 5510 Morehouse Dr Ste 100, **San Diego,** CA 92121, *pg.* 1256, *pg.* 203
HOOKED MEDIA GROUP, 995 Market St 8th Fl, **San Francisco,** CA 94103, *pg.* 1256, *pg.* 219
HULU LLC, 2500 Broadway, **Santa Monica,** CA 90404, *pg.* 1257, *pg.* 274
IAC SEARCH & MEDIA, INC., 555 12th St Ste 500, **Oakland,** CA 94607, *pg.* 1257, *pg.* 171
IDEALAB, INC., 130 W Union St, **Pasadena,** CA 91103, *pg.* 1258, *pg.* 180
IF(WE), 848 Battery St, **San Francisco,** CA 94111, *pg.* 1258, *pg.* 219
IGN ENTERTAINMENT, INC., 625 2nd St, 3rd Fl, **San Francisco,** CA 94107, *pg.* 1258, *pg.* 220
INTERNET MEDIA SERVICES, INC., 1434 6th St Ste 9, **Santa Monica,** CA 90401-2527, *pg.* 1259, *pg.* 274
IPASS, INC., 3800 Bridge Pkwy, **Redwood Shores,** CA 94065, *pg.* 1259, *pg.* 193
IPOWERWEB INC., 2800 28th St Ste 205, **Santa Monica,** CA 90405, *pg.* 1259, *pg.* 274
IRONPLANET, INC., 3825 Hopyard Rd, Ste 250, **Pleasanton,** CA 94588, *pg.* 1259, *pg.* 183
ITRADE NETWORK, 4160 Dublin Blvd Ste 300, **Dublin,** CA 94568, *pg.* 1259, *pg.* 77
J2 GLOBAL COMMUNICATIONS, INC., 6922 Hollywood Blvd Ste 500, **Los Angeles,** CA 90028, *pg.* 1260, *pg.* 133
JUNIPER NETWORKS, INC., 1194 N Mathilda Ave, **Sunnyvale,** CA 94089-1206, *pg.* 1260, *pg.* 286
KLOUT, INC., 77 Stillman St, **San Francisco,** CA 94107, *pg.* 1261, *pg.* 220
LEGALZOOM.COM, INC., 101 N Brand Blvd 11th Fl, **Glendale,** CA 91203, *pg.* 1261, *pg.* 96
LEXAR MEDIA, INC., 590 Alder Dr, **Milpitas,** CA 95035, *pg.* 1262, *pg.* 146
LINKEDIN CORPORATION, 2029 Stierlin Ct, **Mountain View,** CA 94043, *pg.* 1262, *pg.* 160
LITHIUM TECHNOLOGIES, 225 Bush St 15th Fl, **San Francisco,** CA 94104, *pg.* 1263, *pg.* 221
LIVE365, INC., 950 Tower Ln Ste 400, **Foster City,** CA 94404, *pg.* 1264, *pg.* 89
LIVERAIL, 1 Hacker Way Bldg 12, **Menlo Park,** CA 94025, *pg.* 1264, *pg.* 145
LIVEWORLD, INC., 4340 Stevens Creek Blvd Ste 101, **San Jose,** CA 95129, *pg.* 1264, *pg.* 246
LOCAL.COM CORPORATION, 7555 Irvine Ctr Dr, **Irvine,** CA 92618, *pg.* 1264, *pg.* 113
LOGITECH INC., 7600 Gateway Blvd, **Newark,** CA 94560, *pg.* 1264, *pg.* 164
LOOKSMART, LTD., 55 2nd St, **San Francisco,** CA 94105, *pg.* 1265, *pg.* 221
LOOPNET, INC., 185 Berry St Ste 4000, **San Francisco,** CA 94107, *pg.* 1265, *pg.* 222
MARKETWATCH, INC., 201 California St 13th Fl, **San Francisco,** CA 94111-5002, *pg.* 1265, *pg.* 222
MBLOX INC., 430 N Mary Ave, Ste 100, **Sunnyvale,** CA 94085, *pg.* 1266, *pg.* 286
MESSAGEBROADCAST INC., 4685 MacArthur Court Ste 250, **Newport Beach,** CA 92660-6476, *pg.* 1266, *pg.* 165
METRIXLAB, 201 Mission St Ste 1320, **San Francisco,** CA 94105, *pg.* 1266, *pg.* 223
MILITARY ADVANTAGE, INC., 799 Market St, Ste 700, **San Francisco,** CA 94103, *pg.* 1267, *pg.* 223
MODE MEDIA, 2000 Sierra Point Parkway Suite 1000 10th Floor, **Brisbane,** CA 94005, *pg.* 1267, *pg.* 50
MONDO MEDIA CORPORATION, 444 De Haro St Ste 201, **San Francisco,** CA 94107, *pg.* 1268, *pg.* 223
MOVE, INC., 10 Almaden Blvd Ste 800, **San Jose,** CA 95113, *pg.* 1268, *pg.* 247
MYLIFE.COM, INC., 1100 Glendon Ave Ste 1800, **Los Angeles,** CA 90024, *pg.* 1268, *pg.* 137
MYPOINTS.COM, INC., 525 Markert St Ste 3400, **San Francisco,** CA 94105, *pg.* 1269, *pg.* 223
NETFLIX, INC., 100 Winchester Circle, **Los Gatos,** CA 95032, *pg.* 1269, *pg.* 141
NETSOL TECHNOLOGIES, INC., 23901 Calabasas Rd Ste 2072, **Calabasas,** CA 91302, *pg.* 1270, *pg.* 56
NETSUITE, INC., 2955 Campus Dr Ste 100, **San Mateo,** CA 94403-2511, *pg.* 1270, *pg.* 255
NEWEGG INC., 16839 E Gale Ave, **City of Industry,** CA 91745, *pg.* 1271, *pg.* 67
NEXON AMERICA INC., 222 Sepulveda Blvd, **El Segundo,** CA 90245, *pg.* 1271, *pg.* 82
NOVICA UNITED, INC., 11835 W Olympic Blvd Ste 750, **Los Angeles,** CA 90064-5001, *pg.* 1271, *pg.* 137
ON24, INC., 201 3rd St 3rd Fl, **San Francisco,** CA 94103-2046, *pg.* 1272, *pg.* 224
OPENX TECHNOLOGIES, INC., 888 E Walnut St 2nd Fl, **Pasadena,** CA 91101, *pg.* 1272, *pg.* 180
PANDORA MEDIA INC., 2101 Webster St Ste 1650, **Oakland,** CA 94612, *pg.* 1273, *pg.* 172
PANJO, 1640 5th St Ste 226, **Santa Monica,** CA 90401, *pg.* 1274, *pg.* 275
PAYPAL INC., 2211 N First St, **San Jose,** CA 95131, *pg.* 1274, *pg.* 248
PERISCOPE, 1355 Market St Ste 900, **San Francisco,** CA 94103, *pg.* 1274, *pg.* 224
PINTEREST, 808 Brannan St, **San Francisco,** CA 94103, *pg.* 1275, *pg.* 225
PROVIDE COMMERCE, INC., 4840 Eastgate Mall, **San Diego,** CA 92121, *pg.* 1276, *pg.* 206
QUINSTREET, INC., 950 Tower Lane 6th Floor, **Foster City,** CA 94404, *pg.* 1276, *pg.* 89
QUORA, INC., 261 Hamilton Ave Ste 212, **Palo Alto,** CA 94301, *pg.* 1277, *pg.* 178
RAKUTEN.COM SHOPPING, 85 Enterprise Ste 100, **Aliso Viejo,** CA 92656, *pg.* 1277, *pg.* 41
REACHLOCAL, INC., 21700 Oxnard St Ste 1600, **Woodland Hills,** CA 91367, *pg.* 1277, *pg.* 308
REPLY! INC., 12667 Alcosta Blvd Ste 200, **San Ramon,** CA 94583, *pg.* 1277, *pg.* 260
RIVERBED TECHNOLOGY, INC., 199 Fremont St, **San Francisco,** CA 94105, *pg.* 1277, *pg.* 225
RUBICON PROJECT, 12181 Bluff Creek Dr, **Playa Vista,** CA 90094, *pg.* 1278, *pg.* 182
SALESFORCE.COM, INC., The Landmark 1 Market St Ste 300, **San Francisco,** CA 94105-1420, *pg.* 1278, *pg.* 226
SALON MEDIA GROUP, INC., 870 Market St, Ste 528, **San Francisco,** CA 94102, *pg.* 1278, *pg.* 226
SHOPPING.COM, LTD., 8000 Marina Blvd 5th Fl, **Brisbane,** CA 94005, *pg.* 1280, *pg.* 50
SHUTTERFLY, INC., 2800 Bridge Pkwy, **Redwood City,** CA 94065-1162, *pg.* 1280, *pg.* 192
SINA CORP., 883 N Shoreline Blvd Ste C 200, **Mountain View,** CA 94043, *pg.* 1280, *pg.* 161
SMAATO INC., 240 Stockton St 10th Fl, **San Francisco,** CA 94108, *pg.* 1281, *pg.* 228
SNAPCHAT, INC., 63 Market St, **Venice,** CA 90291, *pg.* 1281, *pg.* 301
SPINMEDIA, 6464 W Sunset Blvd Ste 650, **Hollywood,** CA 90028, *pg.* 1282, *pg.* 104
STAMPS.COM INC., 1990 E Grand Ave, **El Segundo,** CA 90245, *pg.* 1282, *pg.* 82
STRATEGIC FOCUS, 36083 Soapberry Cmn, **Fremont,** CA 94536, *pg.* 1283, *pg.* 92
STREAMING MEDIA HOSTING, INC., 2280 University Dr Ste 104, **Newport Beach,** CA 92660, *pg.* 1283, *pg.* 166
SUPPORT.COM, INC., 900 Chesapeake Dr, **Redwood City,** CA 94063, *pg.* 1283, *pg.* 192

TECHNICAL COMMUNITIES, INC., 111 Bayhill Dr Ste 400, **San Bruno,** CA 94066, *pg.* 1283, *pg.* 198
TICKETMASTER ENTERTAINMENT LLC, 9348 Civic Center Dr, **Beverly Hills,** CA 90210, *pg.* 1284, *pg.* 48
THE TRADE DESK, INC., 505 Poli St 5th Fl, **Ventura,** CA 93001, *pg.* 1284, *pg.* 301
TRUECAR INC., 225 Santa Monica Blvd 6th Fl, **Santa Monica,** CA 90401, *pg.* 1284, *pg.* 276
TWITTER, INC., 1355 Market St Ste 900, **San Francisco,** CA 94103, *pg.* 1285, *pg.* 228
UBER USA, LLC, 405 Howard St, **San Francisco,** CA 94105, *pg.* 1286, *pg.* 229
UBERMEDIA, INC., 130 W Union St, **Pasadena,** CA 91103, *pg.* 1286, *pg.* 181
UNITED ONLINE, INC., 21301 Burbank Blvd, **Woodland Hills,** CA 91367, *pg.* 1286, *pg.* 308
VENDIO, INC., 2800 Campus Dr, **San Mateo,** CA 94403, *pg.* 1287, *pg.* 256
WAL-MART.COM, 7000 Marina Blvd, **Brisbane,** CA 94005, *pg.* 1287, *pg.* 50
XAP CORPORATION, 100 Corporate Pointe Ste 100, **Culver City,** CA 90230, *pg.* 1289, *pg.* 73
XOOM CORPORATION, 301 Brannan St 5th Fl, **San Francisco,** CA 94107, *pg.* 1289, *pg.* 234
YAHOO! INC., 701 1st Ave, **Sunnyvale,** CA 94089, *pg.* 1289, *pg.* 289
YAHOO! MOBILE, 701 1st Ave, **Sunnyvale,** CA 94089, *pg.* 1291, *pg.* 290
YELP! INC., 706 Mission St, **San Francisco,** CA 94103, *pg.* 1291, *pg.* 235
YOUTUBE, LLC, 901 Cherry Ave, **San Bruno,** CA 94066, *pg.* 1291, *pg.* 198
ZOOSK INC., 989 Market St, **San Francisco,** CA 94103, *pg.* 1292, *pg.* 235
ZYNGA INC., 699 8th St, **San Francisco,** CA 94103, *pg.* 1292, *pg.* 235

Colorado

EAGLE:XM, 5105 E 41st Ave, **Denver,** CO 80216-4420, *pg.* 1239, *pg.* 319
EBAGS, INC., 5500 ST 160, **Greenwood Village,** CO 80111-4801, *pg.* 1240, *pg.* 331
HEALTH GRADES, INC., 999 18th St Ste 600, **Denver,** CO 80202, *pg.* 1256, *pg.* 319
LEVEL 3 COMMUNICATIONS, INC., 1025 Eldorado Blvd, **Broomfield,** CO 80021-8869, *pg.* 1262, *pg.* 312
MAPQUEST, INC., 555 17th St Ste 1600, **Denver,** CO 80202, *pg.* 1265, *pg.* 321
TWO RIVERS WATER COMPANY, 2000 S Colorado Blvd, Ste 3100, **Denver,** CO 80222, *pg.* 1286, *pg.* 323
VERIO INC., 8300 E Maplewood Ave # 400, **Greenwood Village,** CO 80111-4804, *pg.* 1287, *pg.* 332
WAND, INC., 820 16th St Ste 605, **Denver,** CO 80202, *pg.* 1288, *pg.* 324
WEBROOT SOFTWARE, INC., 385 Interlocken Crescent Ste 800, **Broomfield,** CO 80021-8067, *pg.* 1289, *pg.* 313

Connecticut

AFFINION GROUP, INC., 6 High Ridge Park, **Stamford,** CT 06905, *pg.* 1225, *pg.* 372
FACTSET RESEARCH SYSTEMS INC., 601 Merritt 7 3rd Fl, **Norwalk,** CT 06851, *pg.* 1247, *pg.* 361
GARTNER, INC., 56 Top Gallant Rd, P.O. Box 10212, **Stamford,** CT 06902-7747, *pg.* 1248, *pg.* 374
KAYAK, 55 N Water St Ste 1, **Norwalk,** CT 06854, *pg.* 1260, *pg.* 363
OLM, LLC, 4 Trefoil Dr, **Trumbull,** CT 06611-1330, *pg.* 1271, *pg.* 381
THE PRICELINE GROUP INC., 800 Connecticut Ave, **Norwalk,** CT 06854-1631, *pg.* 1276, *pg.* 364

District of Columbia

BLACKBOARD INC., 650 Massachusetts Ave NW, **Washington,** DC 20001, *pg.* 1232, *pg.* 396
GRASSROOTS ENTERPRISE, INC., 1875 Eye St NW Ste 900, **Washington,** DC 20006, *pg.* 1255, *pg.* 400
LIQUIDITY SERVICES, INC., 1920 L St NW 6th Fl, **Washington,** DC 20036, *pg.* 1263, *pg.* 401
LIVINGSOCIAL, INC., 829 7th St Ste 301, **Washington,** DC 20001, *pg.* 1264, *pg.* 401

Florida

B-SCADA, INC., 1255 N Vantage Point Dr Ste A, **Crystal River,** FL 34429, *pg.* 1231, *pg.* 419
BANKRATE, INC., 11760 US Hwy 1 Ste 200, **North Palm Beach,** FL 33408, *pg.* 1231, *pg.* 451
CBS SPORTSLINE.COM, INC., 1401 W Cypress Creek Rd, **Fort Lauderdale,** FL 33309-1825, *pg.* 1234, *pg.* 423
CBT DIRECT, LLC, 25400 US Hwy 19 N 285, **Clearwater,** FL 33763, *pg.* 1234, *pg.* 415
CIQ, INC., 611 Druid Rd Ste 405, **Clearwater,** FL 33756, *pg.* 1235, *pg.* 415
THE HACKETT GROUP, INC., 1001 Brickell Bay Dr Ste 3000, **Miami,** FL 33131, *pg.* 1255, *pg.* 443
HOLLYWOOD MEDIA CORP., 2255 Glades Rd Ste 221 A, **Boca Raton,** FL 33431-7382, *pg.* 1256, *pg.* 412
ICRUISE.COM CORP., 220 Congress Park Dr Ste 140, **Delray Beach,** FL 33445, *pg.* 1258, *pg.* 421
KFORCE INC., 1001 E Palm Ave, **Tampa,** FL 33605-3551, *pg.* 1261, *pg.* 473
NETWOLVES CORPORATION, 4710 Eisenhower Blvd Ste E8, **Tampa,** FL 33634-7527, *pg.* 1271, *pg.* 474
NEWSMAX MEDIA, INC., 560 Vlg Blvd Ste 120, **West Palm Beach,** FL 33409, *pg.* 1271, *pg.* 479
OMNICOMM SYSTEMS, INC., 2101 W Commercial Blvd Ste 4000, **Fort Lauderdale,** FL 33309, *pg.* 1272, *pg.* 426
OWENS ONLINE, INC., 10012 N Dale Mabry Hwy Ste B-101, **Tampa,** FL 33618, *pg.* 1273, *pg.* 475
REGISTER.COM, INC., 12808 Gran Bay Pkwy, **Jacksonville,** FL 32258, *pg.* 1277, *pg.* 434
SPECTORSOFT CORPORATION, 1555 Indian River Blvd Bldg B210, **Vero Beach,** FL 32960, *pg.* 1281, *pg.* 478
TECHHEALTH, INC., 14025 Riveredge Dr Ste 400, **Tampa,** FL 33637-2003, *pg.* 1283, *pg.* 476
WEB RESULTS, INC., 440 E Sample Rd, Ste 205, **Pompano Beach,** FL 33064, *pg.* 1288, *pg.* 460
WEB.COM GROUP, INC., 12808 Gran Bay Pkwy W, **Jacksonville,** FL 32258, *pg.* 1288, *pg.* 435

Georgia

A.D.A.M., INC., 10 10th Street NE Ste 525, **Atlanta,** GA 30309-3848, *pg.* 1225, *pg.* 487
AUTOTRADER, INC., 3003 Summit Blvd, Fl 200, **Atlanta,** GA 30319, *pg.* 1230, *pg.* 490
COFFEECUP SOFTWARE INC., 165 Courtland St Ste A, **Atlanta,** GA 30303, *pg.* 1236, *pg.* 501
COMMERCE SCIENCE CORPORATION, 3400 Peachtree Rd NE Ste 630, **Atlanta,** GA 30326-1189, *pg.* 1236, *pg.* 501
COMPUTER MART, 4052 Lawrenceville Hwy, **Tucker,** GA 30084-4621, *pg.* 1236, *pg.* 542
EARTHLINK HOLDINGS CORP., 1170 Peachtree St Ste 900, **Atlanta,** GA 30309, *pg.* 1240, *pg.* 504
EBIX INC., 5 Concourse Pkwy Ste 3200, **Atlanta,** GA 30328, *pg.* 1241, *pg.* 504
ECOMPANYSTORE, INC., 5945 Cabot Pkwy Bldg 200 Ste 150, **Alpharetta,** GA 30005, *pg.* 1241, *pg.* 483
I2SMS, PO Box 421194, **Atlanta,** GA 30342, *pg.* 1257, *pg.* 511
MARKET VELOCITY, INC., 1305 Mall of georgia Blvd Ste 190, **Buford,** GA 30519, *pg.* 1265, *pg.* 527
NETWORK COMMUNICATIONS INC., 2305 Newpoint Pkwy, **Lawrenceville,** GA 30043, *pg.* 1271, *pg.* 534
PREMIERE GLOBAL SERVICES, INC., 3280 Peachtree Rd NW Ste 1000, **Atlanta,** GA 30305, *pg.* 1275, *pg.* 518
THE ROCKET SCIENCE GROUP, LLC, 512 Means St, **Atlanta,** GA 30318, *pg.* 1278, *pg.* 519
VETJOBS, INC., PO Box 71445, **Marietta,** GA 30007-1445, *pg.* 1287, *pg.* 535
WEB.COM, INC., 303 Peachtree Ctr Ave 5th Flr, **Atlanta,** GA 30303-1238, *pg.* 1288, *pg.* 524

Idaho

BODYBUILDING.COM LLC, 2026 Silverstone Way, **Meridian,** ID 83642, *pg.* 1232, *pg.* 549
CRUCIAL TECHNOLOGY DIV OF MICRON, 3475 Commercial Ct, **Meridian,** ID 83642-6041, *pg.* 1237, *pg.* 550

Illinois

CAREERBUILDER, LLC, 200 N LaSalle St Ste 1100, **Chicago,** IL 60601, *pg.* 1234, *pg.* 568
CARS.COM, 175 W Jackson Blvd Ste 800, **Chicago,** IL 60604, *pg.* 1234, *pg.* 568
CLASSIFIED VENTURES, LLC, 175 W Jackson Blvd Ste 800, **Chicago,** IL 60604, *pg.* 1235, *pg.* 571
EOLAS TECHNOLOGIES, INC., 10 E Ontario St Ste 5106, **Chicago,** IL 60611, *pg.* 1243, *pg.* 573
GROUPON, INC., 600 W Chicago Ave Ste 400, **Chicago,** IL 60654, *pg.* 1255, *pg.* 575
GRUBHUB INC., 111 W Washington St Ste 2100, **Chicago,** IL 60602, *pg.* 1255, *pg.* 576
HOME SCHOOL HOLDINGS, INC., 1153 So. Lee Street, Suite 198, **Des Plaines,** IL 60016, *pg.* 1256, *pg.* 606
HOSTWAY CORPORATION, 1 N State St Ste 1200, **Chicago,** IL 60602, *pg.* 1256, *pg.* 577
LOGIKA CORPORATION, 3717 N Ravenswood Ste 244, **Chicago,** IL 60613, *pg.* 1264, *pg.* 581
Q INTERACTIVE INC., 1 N Dearborn St 12th Fl, **Chicago,** IL 60602, *pg.* 1276, *pg.* 588
SHOPLOCAL, LLC, 225 N Michigan Ave Ste 1600, **Chicago,** IL 60601, *pg.* 1280, *pg.* 590
SKINNYCORP L.L.C., 1260 W Madison St, **Chicago,** IL 60607-1933, *pg.* 1280, *pg.* 590
SPORTVISION, INC., 4619 N Ravenswood, **Chicago,** IL 60640, *pg.* 1282, *pg.* 590
STARTSAMPLING, INC., 130 E Saint Charles Rd Ste C, **Carol Stream,** IL 60188-2059, *pg.* 1283, *pg.* 561
TRUSTWAVE HOLDINGS, INC., 70 W Madison Ste 1050, **Chicago,** IL 60602, *pg.* 1285, *pg.* 593
UBID.COM, 740 Hilltop Dr, **Itasca,** IL 60143, *pg.* 1286, *pg.* 621

Indiana

ANGIE'S LIST INC, 1030 E Washington St, **Indianapolis,** IN 46202, *pg.* 1228, *pg.* 682
EXACTTARGET INC., 20 N Meridian St, **Indianapolis,** IN 46204, *pg.* 1244, *pg.* 685
IUNIVERSE, INC., 1663 Liberty Dr Ste 200, **Bloomington,** IN 47403, *pg.* 1259, *pg.* 674

Iowa

DICE.COM, 12150 Meredith Dr, **Urbandale,** IA 50323, *pg.* 1238, *pg.* 712

Kansas

IMODULES SOFTWARE, INC., 5101 College Blvd, **Leawood,** KS 66211, *pg.* 1258, *pg.* 716
MIQ LOGISTICS, LLC, 11501 Outlook St Ste 500, **Overland Park,** KS 66211, *pg.* 1267, *pg.* 719

Kentucky

A BOOK COMPANY, LLC, 2415 Palumbo Dr, **Lexington,** KY 40509-1116, *pg.* 1225, *pg.* 729

Louisiana

GOLFBALLS.COM, INC., 126 Arnould Blvd, **Lafayette,** LA 70506, *pg.* 1249, *pg.* 744

Maryland

ADVERTISING.COM, LLC, 1020 Hull St Ivory Bldg, **Baltimore,** MD 21230, *pg.* 1225, *pg.* 755
BROADSOFT, INC., 9737 Washingtonian Blvd Ste 350, **Gaithersburg,** MD 20878, *pg.* 1233, *pg.* 770
DOD NEWS, 6700 Taylor Ave, **Fort Meade,** MD 20755, *pg.* 1239, *pg.* 769
INO.COM, Discovery Vlg 4800 Atwell Rd, **Shady Side,** MD 20764, *pg.* 1259, *pg.* 777
INVENDA CORPORATION, 6901 Rockledge Dr, **Bethesda,** MD 20817, *pg.* 1259, *pg.* 762
LCG TECHNOLOGIES CORPORATION, 1818 Pot Spring Rd Ste 116, **Timonium,** MD 21286, *pg.* 1261, *pg.* 779
OPENTEXT GXS, 9711 Washingtonian Blvd, **Gaithersburg,** MD 20878, *pg.* 1272, *pg.* 770
TELCOIQ, INC., 4300 Forbes Blvd, Ste 210, **Lanham,** MD 20706, *pg.* 1284, *pg.* 773
WELOCALIZE, INC., 241 E 4th St Ste 207, **Frederick,** MD 21701-3612, *pg.* 1289, *pg.* 769

First page reference indicates Business Class Edition
Second page reference indicates Geographic Edition

Massachusetts

AKAMAI TECHNOLOGIES, INC., 8 Cambridge Ctr, **Cambridge,** MA 02142, *pg.* 1226, *pg.* 807
AVENTION, 300 Baker Ave, **Concord,** MA 01742-2131, *pg.* 1230, *pg.* 815
BULLHORN, INC., 33-41 Farnsworth St, **Boston,** MA 02210, *pg.* 1233, *pg.* 792
BUYERZONE.COM, LLC, 225 Wyman St, **Waltham,** MA 02451-1209, *pg.* 1233, *pg.* 850
BZZAGENT, INC., 500 Harrison Ave, **Boston,** MA 02118, *pg.* 1233, *pg.* 792
CAMBRIDGE SOUNDWORKS, INC., 100 Brickstone Sq, **Andover,** MA 01810-1428, *pg.* 1234, *pg.* 781
CEOEXPRESS COMPANY, 1 Broadway 14th Fl, **Cambridge,** MA 02142, *pg.* 1235, *pg.* 807
HARMONIX MUSIC SYSTEMS, INC., 675 Massachusetts Ave 6th Fl, **Cambridge,** MA 02139, *pg.* 1256, *pg.* 808
HYDRALIGN, 41 Leona Dr, **Middleboro,** MA 02346-1404, *pg.* 1257, *pg.* 833
IDG ENTERPRISE, 492 Old Connecticut Path, PO Box 9208, **Framingham,** MA 01701, *pg.* 1258, *pg.* 821
LYCOS, INC., 52 Second Ave 4th Fl, **Waltham,** MA 02451, *pg.* 1265, *pg.* 852
MICROWAY, INC., Plymouth Indus Pk 12 Richards Rd, **Plymouth,** MA 02360, *pg.* 1267, *pg.* 841
MIRROR IMAGE INTERNET, INC., Ste 101 2 Highwood Dr, **Tewksbury,** MA 01876-1100, *pg.* 1267, *pg.* 848
MONSTER WORLDWIDE, INC., 135 Boston Post Rd Bldg 15, **Weston,** MA 02493, *pg.* 1268, *pg.* 859
NAMEMEDIA, INC., 230 3rd Ave, **Waltham,** MA 02451, *pg.* 1269, *pg.* 852
NAVISITE, INC., 400 Minute Man Rd, **Andover,** MA 01810, *pg.* 1269, *pg.* 782
NET-TEMPS, INC., 55 Middlesex St Ste 220, **North Chelmsford,** MA 01863, *pg.* 1269, *pg.* 838
NETSCOUT SYSTEMS, INC., 310 Littleton Rd, **Westford,** MA 01886-4105, *pg.* 1270, *pg.* 858
NEXAGE, INC., 101 Arch St Ste 1510, **Boston,** MA 02110, *pg.* 1271, *pg.* 799
OPENAIR, INC., 211 Congress St 8th Fl, **Boston,** MA 02110, *pg.* 1272, *pg.* 800
ORACLE CORPORATION, 100 Crosby Dr, **Bedford,** MA 01730, *pg.* 1272, *pg.* 786
PASSKEY INTERNATIONAL, INC., 221 Crescent St, **Waltham,** MA 02453, *pg.* 1274, *pg.* 853
PLANPRESCRIBER, INC., 8 Clock Tower Pl Ste 400, **Maynard,** MA 01754, *pg.* 1275, *pg.* 832
PLASTICS.COM, INC., Montachusett Pk Bldg 225, **Fitchburg,** MA 01420, *pg.* 1275, *pg.* 819
RUE LA LA, 20 Channel Center St, **Boston,** MA 02210-3402, *pg.* 1278, *pg.* 800
SEACHANGE INTERNATIONAL, INC., 50 Nagog Park, **Acton,** MA 01720-3409, *pg.* 1279, *pg.* 781
SONUS NETWORKS INC., 4 Technology Park Dr, **Westford,** MA 01886-3140, *pg.* 1281, *pg.* 858
UNICOM ENGINEERING, 25 Dan Rd, **Canton,** MA 02021-2817, *pg.* 1286, *pg.* 812
VECNA TECHNOLOGIES, INC., 36 Cambridgepark Dr, **Cambridge,** MA 02140, *pg.* 1287, *pg.* 810
WAYFAIR LLC, 177 Huntington Ave Ste 6000, **Boston,** MA 02115, *pg.* 1288, *pg.* 801
YET2.COM, INC., 10 Kearney Rd, **Needham,** MA 02494, *pg.* 1291, *pg.* 835

Michigan

VALASSIS COMMUNICATIONS, INC., 19975 Victor Pkwy, **Livonia,** MI 48152, *pg.* 1287, *pg.* 897

Minnesota

DIGITAL RIVER, INC., 10380 Bren Rd W, **Minnetonka,** MN 55343-9072, *pg.* 1238, *pg.* 948
FAIR ISAAC CORPORATION, 2655 Long Lake Rd, Bldg C, **Roseville,** MN 55113, *pg.* 1247, *pg.* 955
GOVDELIVERY, INC., 408 Saint Peter St Ste 600, **Saint Paul,** MN 55102, *pg.* 1255, *pg.* 961
US INTERNET CORPORATION, 12450 Wayzata Blvd Ste 224, **Minnetonka,** MN 55305, *pg.* 1287, *pg.* 950

Missouri

PERFICIENT, INC., 520 Maryville Ctr Dr Ste 400, **Saint Louis,** MO 63141, *pg.* 1274, *pg.* 1002

Nebraska

GIFTCERTIFICATES.COM, 11510 Blondo St, **Omaha,** NE 68164-3846, *pg.* 1249, *pg.* 1015
MIDWEST MICROSYSTEMS, LLC, Ste 7 3100 O St, **Lincoln,** NE 68510-1532, *pg.* 1267, *pg.* 1012

Nevada

ZAPPOS.COM, INC., 400 Stewart Ave, **Las Vegas,** NV 89101, *pg.* 1291, *pg.* 1030

New Hampshire

NUANCE DOCUMENT IMAGING SOLUTIONS, 1 Oracle Dr, **Nashua,** NH 03062, *pg.* 1271, *pg.* 1037

New Jersey

AUDIBLE, INC., 1 Washington Park, **Newark,** NJ 07102, *pg.* 1230, *pg.* 1095
BIOSPACE, INC., 2399 Hwy 34 Bldg A5, **Manasquan,** NJ 08736-1528, *pg.* 1231, *pg.* 1082
CHERRYROAD TECHNOLOGIES INC., 301 Gibraltar Dr Ste 2C, **Morris Plains,** NJ 07950, *pg.* 1235, *pg.* 1087
DELTATHREE, INC., 1 Bridge Plz Ste 275, **Fort Lee,** NJ 07024, *pg.* 1238, *pg.* 1068
EARTHCAM, INC., 84 Kennedy St, **Hackensack,** NJ 07601-5229, *pg.* 1239, *pg.* 1072
EASYLINK SERVICES CORPORATION, 33 Knightsbridge Rd, **Piscataway,** NJ 08854, *pg.* 1240, *pg.* 1108
INNODATA ISOGEN, INC., 3 University Plz, **Hackensack,** NJ 07601, *pg.* 1259, *pg.* 1072
JET.COM, INC., 221 River St, **Hoboken,** NJ 07030, *pg.* 1260, *pg.* 1073
LAUNCHFAX.COM INC., 623 River Rd, **Fair Haven,** NJ 07704, *pg.* 1261, *pg.* 1064
NET ACCESS CORPORATION, 1719 Rte 10 E, **Parsippany,** NJ 07054, *pg.* 1269, *pg.* 1101
NET2PHONE, INC., 520 Broad St, **Newark,** NJ 07102, *pg.* 1269, *pg.* 1097
QUIDSI, INC., 10 Exchange Place 25th Fl, **Jersey City,** NJ 07302, *pg.* 1276, *pg.* 1076
QUODD FINANCIAL INFORMATION SERVICES, 30 Montgomery St Ste 600, **Jersey City,** NJ 07302, *pg.* 1276, *pg.* 1076
SENDONLINE.COM, INC., 100 Canal Pointe Blvd Ste 204, **Princeton,** NJ 08540-7063, *pg.* 1280, *pg.* 1112

New York

123GREETINGS.COM, INC., 1674 Broadway Ste 403, **New York,** NY 10019, *pg.* 1225, *pg.* 1184
ABOUT, INC., 249 W 17th St, **New York,** NY 10011, *pg.* 1225, *pg.* 1186
ANSWERS CORPORATION, 237 W 35th St Ste 1101, **New York,** NY 10001, *pg.* 1229, *pg.* 1195
AOL INC., 770 Broadway, **New York,** NY 10003, *pg.* 1229, *pg.* 1195
BANDSINTOWN, 215 Lexington Ave Fl 18, **New York,** NY 10016, *pg.* 1231, *pg.* 1200
BLUE PHOENIX MEDIA, 320 W 37th St, Ste 1201, **New York,** NY 10018, *pg.* 1232, *pg.* 1205
BLUEFLY, INC., 42 W 39th St, **New York,** NY 10018-3809, *pg.* 1232, *pg.* 1205
BUSINESS INSIDER, 257 Park Ave South13th fl, **New York,** NY 10010, *pg.* 1233, *pg.* 1208
BUZZFEED, 54 W 21st St, 11th Fl, **New York,** NY 10010, *pg.* 1233, *pg.* 1208
CONDE NAST DIGITAL, 1 World Trade Ctr, **New York,** NY 10007, *pg.* 1237, *pg.* 1217
DEFYMEDIA, 498 7th Ave, 19th Fl, **New York,** NY 10018, *pg.* 1237, *pg.* 1222
DHI GROUP, INC., 1040 Ave of the Americas 8th Fl, **New York,** NY 10018, *pg.* 1238, *pg.* 1223
DIGG, INC., 416 W 13th St #203, **New York,** NY 10014, *pg.* 1238, *pg.* 1224
DIGITAL FIRST MEDIA, 5 Hanover Sq 25th Fl, **New York,** NY 10005, *pg.* 1238, *pg.* 1224
DOUBLECLICK, INC., 111 8th Ave 10th Fl, **New York,** NY 10011, *pg.* 1239, *pg.* 1225
ELLE.COM, 300 W 57th St 24th Fl, **New York,** NY 10019, *pg.* 1242, *pg.* 1227
EMUSIC.COM, INC., 244 5th Ave Ste 2070, **New York,** NY 10001, *pg.* 1243, *pg.* 1227
ETRONICS, INC., 216 Maspeth Ave, **Brooklyn,** NY 11211, *pg.* 1244, *pg.* 1146
FORBES.COM LLC, E 60 5th Ave, **New York,** NY 10011-5204, *pg.* 1247, *pg.* 1232
FOURSQUARE LABS, INC, 36 Cooper Square, 5th Fl, **New York,** NY 10003, *pg.* 1248, *pg.* 1232
FRAGRANCENET.COM, INC., 900 Grand Blvd, **Deer Park,** NY 11729-5745, *pg.* 1248, *pg.* 1155
FUSION TELECOMMUNICATIONS INTERNATIONAL, INC., 420 Lexington Ave Ste 1718, **New York,** NY 10170, *pg.* 1248, *pg.* 1233
GAWKER MEDIA LLC, 210 Elizabeth St 4th Fl, **New York,** NY 10012, *pg.* 1248, *pg.* 1234
INC.COM LLC, 7 World Trade Ctr, **New York,** NY 10007-2195, *pg.* 1258, *pg.* 1243
THE LADDERS.COM, INC., 137 Varick St 8th Fl, **New York,** NY 10013, *pg.* 1261, *pg.* 1250
LIVEPERSON, INC., 475 10th Ave, Fl 5, **New York,** NY 10018, *pg.* 1264, *pg.* 1252
MARITIME BROADBAND, 680 East 18th St, **Brooklyn,** NY 11230, *pg.* 1265, *pg.* 1146
MASTERBEAT CORPORATION, 222 E 31st St, **New York,** NY 10004, *pg.* 1265, *pg.* 1257
MEDIABISTRO, INC., 475 Park Ave S 4th FL, **New York,** NY 10016, *pg.* 1266, *pg.* 1258
MEETUP INC., 632 Broadway 10th Fl, **New York,** NY 10012, *pg.* 1266, *pg.* 1258
MONEY.NET, INC., 9 Desbrosses St Ste 303, **New York,** NY 10013, *pg.* 1268, *pg.* 1261
OOVOO LLC, 44 E 30th St 12th Fl, **New York,** NY 10016, *pg.* 1272, *pg.* 1274
PIKSEL, 1250 Broadway Ste 1902, **New York,** NY 10001, *pg.* 1275, *pg.* 1282
SHUTTERSTOCK, INC., 1133 Broadway Ste 1427, **New York,** NY 10010, *pg.* 1280, *pg.* 1291
SKYAUCTION.COM, INC., 501 Madison Ave, **New York,** NY 10022-5602, *pg.* 1281, *pg.* 1293
SMARTPROS LTD., 12 Skyline Dr, **Hawthorne,** NY 10532-2133, *pg.* 1281, *pg.* 1166
SNAP INTERACTIVE, INC., 363 7th Ave 13th Fl, **New York,** NY 10001, *pg.* 1281, *pg.* 1293
SPOTIFY, 45 W 18th St 7th Fl, **New York,** NY 10011, *pg.* 1282, *pg.* 1295
SQUARESPACE INC., 459 Broadway 5th Fl, **New York,** NY 10013, *pg.* 1282, *pg.* 1295
THE STREET, INC., 14 Wall St 15th Fl, **New York,** NY 10005-2140, *pg.* 1283, *pg.* 1296
STS JEWELS, 42 West 48th St Ste 1600, **New York,** NY 10036, *pg.* 1283, *pg.* 1297
SYNACOR, INC., 40 La Riviere Dr Ste 300, **Buffalo,** NY 14202, *pg.* 1283, *pg.* 1151
TRACK DATA CORPORATION, 1122 Coney Island Ave, **Brooklyn,** NY 11230, *pg.* 1284, *pg.* 1147
TRADEPAQ CORPORATION, 33 Maiden Ln 9th Fl, **New York,** NY 10038-3202, *pg.* 1284, *pg.* 1304
TUMBLR, INC., 35 E 21st St 6E, **New York,** NY 10010, *pg.* 1285, *pg.* 1305
UNCOMMONGOODS LLC, Brooklyn Army Terminal, 140 58th St Bldg B Ste 5A, **Brooklyn,** NY 11220, *pg.* 1286, *pg.* 1147
UNIVERSUM USA, 254 W 31st St 12th Fl, **New York,** NY 10001, *pg.* 1286, *pg.* 1307
USADATA, INC., 477 Madison Ave, Ste 1220, **New York,** NY 10022, *pg.* 1287, *pg.* 1308
WEBMD HEALTH CORPORATION, 111 8th Ave, **New York,** NY 10011, *pg.* 1288, *pg.* 1313
XO GROUP INC., 195 Broadway, Fl 25, **New York,** NY 10007, *pg.* 1289, *pg.* 1316
ZOGBY ANALYTICS, 901 Broad St, **Utica,** NY 13501, *pg.* 1292, *pg.* 1347

North Carolina

ADVANCED INTERNET TECHNOLOGIES INC., 421 Maiden Ln, **Fayetteville,** NC 28301, *pg.* 1225, *pg.* 1372
CONCLUSIVE ANALYTICS, 13620 Reese Blvd E Ste 300, **Huntersville,** NC 28078-6453, *pg.* 1236, *pg.* 1380
IENTERTAINMENT NETWORK, INC., 124-126 Quade Dr,

Cary, NC 27513-7400, *pg.* 1258, *pg.* 1360
MARKET AMERICA WORLDWIDE, INC., 1302 Pleasant Ridge Rd, **Greensboro,** NC 27409, *pg.* 1265, *pg.* 1375
MERGE ECLINICAL INC., 4000 Aerial Center Pkwy, **Morrisville,** NC 27560, *pg.* 1266, *pg.* 1385
MINDBLAZER, INC., 6120 Harish Technology Blvd, **Charlotte,** NC 28269-2325, *pg.* 1267, *pg.* 1367
NET32, INC., 250 Towne Village Dr, **Cary,** NC 27513, *pg.* 1269, *pg.* 1360
TYBIT UNIFIED SEARCH, 421 Maiden Ln, **Fayetteville,** NC 28301, *pg.* 1286, *pg.* 1372

North Dakota

SRT COMMUNICATIONS INC., 3615 N Broadway, **Minot,** ND 58703, *pg.* 1282, *pg.* 1398

Ohio

BESTTRANSPORT, INC., 400 W Wilson Bridge Rd, **Worthington,** OH 43085, *pg.* 1231, *pg.* 1482
INFOACCESS.NET LLC, 8801 E Pleasant Valley Rd, **Independence,** OH 44131, *pg.* 1258, *pg.* 1456
KNOVATION, 3630 Park 42 Dr Ste 170F, **Cincinnati,** OH 45241, *pg.* 1261, *pg.* 1415

Oregon

FLOWERBUD.COM, 155 B Ave Ste 110, **Lake Oswego,** OR 97034-3233, *pg.* 1247, *pg.* 1499
PLUS VISION CORP. OF AMERICA, 9610 Sw Sunshine Ct, Ste 100, **Beaverton,** OR 97005, *pg.* 1275, *pg.* 1496

Pennsylvania

1&1 INTERNET, INC., 701 Lee Rd Ste 300, **Chesterbrook,** PA 19087, *pg.* 1225, *pg.* 1521
BEYOND.COM, INC., 1060 1st Ave Ste 100, **King of Prussia,** PA 19406, *pg.* 1231, *pg.* 1543
BRAVOSOLUTION US, 400 Chester Field Pkwy, **Malvern,** PA 19355, *pg.* 1233, *pg.* 1549
COMCAST INTERACTIVE MEDIA, LLC, 1701 JSK Blvd, **Philadelphia,** PA 19103, *pg.* 1236, *pg.* 1562
ELEMICA, INC., 550 E Swedesford Rd Ste 310, **Wayne,** PA 19087, *pg.* 1242, *pg.* 1591
ERESEARCH TECHNOLOGY INC., 1818 Market St, **Philadelphia,** PA 19103-4001, *pg.* 1243, *pg.* 1564
ESM SOLUTIONS CORPORATION, 2700 Kelly Rd Ste 100, **Warrington,** PA 18976, *pg.* 1243, *pg.* 1591
MEETME, INC., 100 Union Square Dr, **New Hope,** PA 18938, *pg.* 1266, *pg.* 1556

Rhode Island

POLAR COVE, INC., 150 Chestnut St, **Providence,** RI 02903-4645, *pg.* 1275, *pg.* 1607
TOWERSTREAM CORP., 55 Hammarlund Way, **Middletown,** RI 02842, *pg.* 1284, *pg.* 1602

South Carolina

10BEST, INC., 9 Legrand Blvd, **Greenville,** SC 29607-2909, *pg.* 1225, *pg.* 1617

South Dakota

SONIFI SOLUTIONS, 3900 W Innovation St, **Sioux Falls,** SD 57107-7002, *pg.* 1281, *pg.* 1625

Tennessee

MAGAZINES.COM INC., Ste 150 325 Seaboard Ln, **Franklin,** TN 37067-6431, *pg.* 1265, *pg.* 1633
SCRIPPS NETWORKS INTERACTIVE, INC., 9271 Sherrill Blvd, **Knoxville,** TN 37932, *pg.* 1279, *pg.* 1638

Texas

BLACKHAWK ENGAGEMENT SOLUTIONS, INC., 700 St Hwy 121 Bypass Ste 200, **Lewisville,** TX 75067, *pg.* 1232, *pg.* 1725
CHARLES SCHWAB, 12401 Research Blvd Bld 2 Ste 350, **Austin,** TX 78759, *pg.* 1235, *pg.* 1661
CORNERWORLD CORPORATION, 13101 Preston Rd Ste 100, **Dallas,** TX 75240, *pg.* 1237, *pg.* 1678
CREDITCARDS.COM, INC., 13809 Research Blvd Ste 906, **Austin,** TX 78750, *pg.* 1237, *pg.* 1661
FILECONTROL PARTNERS LTD, 77 Sugar Creek Center Blvd Ste 200, **Sugar Land,** TX 77478, *pg.* 1247, *pg.* 1746
HOTELS.COM, L.P., 5400 Lyndon B Johnson Fwy, Ste 500, **Dallas,** TX 75240, *pg.* 1257, *pg.* 1682
INTRUSION INC., 1101 E Arapaho Rd Ste 200, **Richardson,** TX 75081, *pg.* 1259, *pg.* 1736
LEVEL 3 COMMUNICATIONS, INC., 1122 Capital of Texas Hwy S, **Austin,** TX 78746-6426, *pg.* 1262, *pg.* 1664
MATCH.COM, LLC, Ste 800 8300 Douglas Ave, **Dallas,** TX 75225-5826, *pg.* 1265, *pg.* 1683
MAX SOUND CORPORATION, 10685-B Hazelhurst Dr #6572, **Houston,** TX 77043, *pg.* 1266, *pg.* 1711
PFSWEB, INC., 500 N Central Expy 5th Flr, **Plano,** TX 75074-6772, *pg.* 1275, *pg.* 1733
QUESTIA MEDIA INC., 24 E Greenway Plz Ste 1050, **Houston,** TX 77046, *pg.* 1276, *pg.* 1713
RACKSPACE HOSTING, INC., 5000 Walzem Rd, **San Antonio,** TX 78218, *pg.* 1277, *pg.* 1742
REALPAGE, INC., 4000 International Pkwy Ste 1000, **Carrollton,** TX 75007, *pg.* 1277, *pg.* 1669
SPREDFAST, 200 Cesar Chavez, **Austin,** TX 78701, *pg.* 1282, *pg.* 1666
TRAVELOCITY, INC., 3150 Sabre Dr, **Southlake,** TX 76092, *pg.* 1284, *pg.* 1745
US DATAWORKS, INC., One Sugar Creek Center Blvd 5th Fl, **Sugar Land,** TX 77478, *pg.* 1286, *pg.* 1746

Utah

ANCESTRY.COM LLC, 360 W 4800 North, **Provo,** UT 84604, *pg.* 1228, *pg.* 1754
OVERSTOCK.COM, INC., 6350 S 3000 E, **Salt Lake City,** UT 84121-6937, *pg.* 1273, *pg.* 1760

Vermont

MYWEBGROCER.COM CORP., 20 Winooski Falls Way, Ste 5, **Winooski,** VT 05404, *pg.* 1269, *pg.* 1769

Virginia

ASPIRE LIFESTYLES OF THE AMERICAS, 324 N Fairfax St, **Alexandria,** VA 22314-2625, *pg.* 1230, *pg.* 1770
COMSCORE, INC, 11950 Democracy Dr Ste 600, **Reston,** VA 20190, *pg.* 1236, *pg.* 1798
COMTEX NEWS NETWORK, INC., 625 N Washington St Ste 301, **Alexandria,** VA 22314, *pg.* 1236, *pg.* 1770
CROIX CONNECT, 8130 Boone Blvd Ste 240, **Vienna,** VA 22182, *pg.* 1237, *pg.* 1809
CRUTCHFIELD CORPORATION, 1 Crutchfield Park, **Charlottesville,** VA 22911, *pg.* 1237, *pg.* 1777
GEEKNET, INC., 11216 Waples Mill Rd Ste 100, **Fairfax,** VA 22030, *pg.* 1248, *pg.* 1780
HEALTHCENTRAL, 2300 Wilson Blvd Ste 600, **Arlington,** VA 22201, *pg.* 1256, *pg.* 1773
K12, INC., 2300 Corporate Park Dr, **Herndon,** VA 20171, *pg.* 1260, *pg.* 1785
MICROSTRATEGY, INC., 1850 Towers Crescent Plz, **Vienna,** VA 22182, *pg.* 1266, *pg.* 1809
ORANGE BUSINESS SERVICES, 13775 Mclearen Rd, **Herndon,** VA 20171, *pg.* 1273, *pg.* 1785
PANTHEON SOFTWARE, INC., 2020 N 14th St 7th Fl, **Arlington,** VA 22201-1706, *pg.* 1274, *pg.* 1774
SITESTAR CORPORATION, 7109 Timberlake Rd, **Lynchburg,** VA 24502, *pg.* 1280, *pg.* 1787
STRANGE'S FLORIST & GREENHOUSES, 3313 Mechanicsville Pike, **Richmond,** VA 23223-1726, *pg.* 1283, *pg.* 1804
SURETY, INC., 12020 Sunrise Valley Dr, **Reston,** VA 20191, *pg.* 1283, *pg.* 1799
VACATION.COM, INC., 1650 King St Ste 450, **Alexandria,** VA 22314-2747, *pg.* 1287, *pg.* 1772
YELLOWBRIX, INC., 200 N Glebe Rd Ste 1025, **Arlington,** VA 22203-3759, *pg.* 1291, *pg.* 1775

Washington

ALLRECIPES.COM, 3317 Third Ave S Ste D, **Seattle,** WA 98134, *pg.* 1226, *pg.* 1831
AMAZON.COM, INC., 410 Terry Ave N, **Seattle,** WA 98109-5210, *pg.* 1226, *pg.* 1831
AVVO, INC., 1501 4th Ave Ste 1900, **Seattle,** WA 98101-1636, *pg.* 1231, *pg.* 1833
BLUCORA, 10900 NE 8th St Ste 800, **Bellevue,** WA 98004, *pg.* 1232, *pg.* 1813
CLASSMATES ONLINE, INC., 333 Elliott Ave W, Ste 500, **Seattle,** WA 98119, *pg.* 1235, *pg.* 1834
CONCUR TECHNOLOGIES, INC., 601 108th Ave NE, Ste 1000, **Bellevue,** WA 98004, *pg.* 1236, *pg.* 1813
DIABETICSUPPLIES.COM, INC., 614 E Main St Ste 103, **Vancouver,** WA 98604, *pg.* 1238, *pg.* 1846
DRUGSTORE.COM, INC., 411 108th Ave NE, Ste 1600, **Bellevue,** WA 98004, *pg.* 1239, *pg.* 1814
EXPEDIA, INC., 333 108th Ave NE, **Bellevue,** WA 98004, *pg.* 1244, *pg.* 1814
MEDIO SYSTEMS INC., One Convention Place 701 Pike St 15th Fl, **Seattle,** WA 98101, *pg.* 1266, *pg.* 1837
ONVIA, INC., 509 Olive Way Ste 400, **Seattle,** WA 98101, *pg.* 1272, *pg.* 1838
SECUREEYE SYSTEMS, INC., 19504 24th Ave W Ste 5, **Lynnwood,** WA 98036-4868, *pg.* 1280, *pg.* 1822
WHITEPAGES.COM INC., 1301 5th Ave Ste 1600, **Seattle,** WA 98101, *pg.* 1289, *pg.* 1842
ZILLOW GROUP, INC., 1301 2nd Ave Fl 31, **Seattle,** WA 98101, *pg.* 1292, *pg.* 1843
ZONES, INC., 1102 15th St SW Ste 102, **Auburn,** WA 98001-6509, *pg.* 1292, *pg.* 1813

Wisconsin

THE GUILD INC., 931 E Main St Ste 9, **Madison,** WI 53703, *pg.* 1255, *pg.* 1866
MUSICNOTES, INC., 8020 Excelsior Dr Ste 201, **Madison,** WI 53717, *pg.* 1268, *pg.* 1866
NATIONAL BUSINESS FURNITURE INC, 735 N Water St, **Milwaukee,** WI 53202, *pg.* 1269, *pg.* 1879
SAJAN, INC., 625 Whitetail Blvd, **River Falls,** WI 54022, *pg.* 1278, *pg.* 1890

First page reference indicates Business Class Edition
Second page reference indicates Geographic Edition

Law Firms/Legal Services

New York

CELLINO & BARNES, 350 Main St, 2500 Main Place Tower, **Buffalo,** NY 14202, *pg.* 1293, *pg.* 1147

Lighting

Arizona

NKK SWITCHES, 7850 E Gelding Dr, **Scottsdale,** AZ 85260, *pg.* 1302, *pg.* 23

California

CYMER, INC., 17075 Thornmint Ct, **San Diego,** CA 92127-1712, *pg.* 1296, *pg.* 202
LAMPS PLUS INC., 20250 Plummer St, **Chatsworth,** CA 91311, *pg.* 1300, *pg.* 64
MOLE-RICHARDSON CO., 937 N Sycamore Ave, **Hollywood,** CA 90038-2384, *pg.* 1302, *pg.* 103
REULAND ELECTRIC COMPANY, 17969 E Railroad St, **City of Industry,** CA 91748, *pg.* 1304, *pg.* 68
STANDARD WIRE & CABLE CO., 2050 E Vista Bella Way, **Rancho Dominguez,** CA 90220, *pg.* 1306, *pg.* 187
SUREFIRE, LLC, 18300 Mount Baldy Cir, **Fountain Valley,** CA 92708, *pg.* 1307, *pg.* 90
XENONICS HOLDINGS, INC., 3186 Lionshead Ave, **Carlsbad,** CA 92010-4701, *pg.* 1308, *pg.* 62

Connecticut

GENERAL ELECTRIC COMPANY, 3135 Easton Tpke, **Fairfield,** CT 06828-0001, *pg.* 1297, *pg.* 347
HUBBELL INCORPORATED, 40 Waterview Dr, **Shelton,** CT 06484, *pg.* 1299, *pg.* 370
REVOLUTION LIGHTING TECHNOLOGIES, INC., 177 Broad St 12th Fl, **Stamford,** CT 06901, *pg.* 1304, *pg.* 377
THE RIPLEY COMPANY, 46 Nooks Hill Rd, **Cromwell,** CT 06416, *pg.* 1305, *pg.* 342
ROGERS CORPORATION, One Technology Dr, **Rogers,** CT 06263-0217, *pg.* 1305, *pg.* 369

Florida

CARLISLE INTERCONNECT TECHNOLOGIES, 100 Tensolite Dr, **Saint Augustine,** FL 32092-0590, *pg.* 1294, *pg.* 461
LIGHTING SCIENCE GROUP CORPORATION, 1227 S Patrick Dr Bldg 2A, **Satellite Beach,** FL 32937, *pg.* 1301, *pg.* 467
OTTLITE, 220 W 7th Ave, Ste 100, **Tampa,** FL 33602, *pg.* 1303, *pg.* 475

Georgia

ACUITY BRANDS, INC., 1170 Peachtree St NE Ste 2300, **Atlanta,** GA 30309-7676, *pg.* 1294, *pg.* 487
CIRCA LIGHTING, INC., 513 W Jones St, **Savannah,** GA 31401, *pg.* 1295, *pg.* 539
COOPER WIRING DEVICES, 203 Cooper Cir, **Peachtree City,** GA 30269, *pg.* 1295, *pg.* 538

Illinois

AMERICAN LOUVER COMPANY, 7700 Austin Ave, **Skokie,** IL 60077-2603, *pg.* 1294, *pg.* 660
BIG BEAM EMERGENCY SYSTEMS, INC., 290 E Prairie St, **Crystal Lake,** IL 60039-4415, *pg.* 1294, *pg.* 598
EMERSON INDUSTRIAL AUTOMATION, 9377 W Higgins Rd, **Rosemont,** IL 60018-4938, *pg.* 1296, *pg.* 657
HD ELECTRIC COMPANY, 1475 Lakeside Dr, **Waukegan,** IL 60085-8314, *pg.* 1299, *pg.* 666
JUNO LIGHTING, INC., 1300 S Wolf Rd, **Des Plaines,** IL 60017-5065, *pg.* 1300, *pg.* 606
LA MARCHE MANUFACTURING COMPANY, 106 Bradrock Dr, **Des Plaines,** IL 60018, *pg.* 1300, *pg.* 606
LITTELFUSE, INC., 8755 West Higgins Rd Ste 500, **Chicago,** IL 60631, *pg.* 1301, *pg.* 580
ROYAL HAEGER LAMP COMPANY, 1300 W Piper St, **Macomb,** IL 61455, *pg.* 1305, *pg.* 631
S&C ELECTRIC COMPANY, 6601 N Ridge Blvd, **Chicago,** IL 60626-3904, *pg.* 1305, *pg.* 589
SCHNEIDER ELECTRIC USA, INC., 1415 Roselle Rd, **Palatine,** IL 60067, *pg.* 1306, *pg.* 650

Indiana

BUZTRONICS, INC., 4343 W 62nd St, **Indianapolis,** IN 46268, *pg.* 1294, *pg.* 683
TOPBULB.COM LLC, 5204 Indianapolis Blvd, **East Chicago,** IN 46312-3838, *pg.* 1307, *pg.* 677

Kansas

SOR, INC., 14685 W 105th St, **Lenexa,** KS 66215-2003, *pg.* 1306, *pg.* 716

Massachusetts

AFC CABLE SYSTEMS, INC., 272 Duchaine Blvd, **New Bedford,** MA 02745-1222, *pg.* 1294, *pg.* 835
CYALUME TECHNOLOGIES HOLDINGS, INC., 96 Windsor St, **West Springfield,** MA 01089, *pg.* 1295, *pg.* 856
LIGHTOLIER, 631 Airport Rd, **Fall River,** MA 02720-4722, *pg.* 1301, *pg.* 819
LITECONTROL CORPORATION, 65 Spring St, **Plympton,** MA 02367, *pg.* 1301, *pg.* 841
MERSEN, 374 Merrimac St, **Newburyport,** MA 01950-1930, *pg.* 1302, *pg.* 836
OSRAM SYLVANIA, INC., 100 Endicott St, **Danvers,** MA 01923-3623, *pg.* 1302, *pg.* 816
PHILIPS LIGHTING, 3 Burlingtonwoods Woods, **Burlington,** MA 01803, *pg.* 1303, *pg.* 806
PHILIPS SOLID-STATE LIGHTING SOLUTIONS, 3 Burlington Woods Dr, 4th Fl, **Burlington,** MA 01803, *pg.* 1303, *pg.* 806

Michigan

HUMPHREY PRODUCTS CORPORATION, 5070 E N Ave, **Kalamazoo,** MI 49048, *pg.* 1300, *pg.* 894
MECHANICAL PRODUCTS INC., 1824 River St, **Jackson,** MI 49202, *pg.* 1302, *pg.* 894

Minnesota

WENGER CORPORATION, 555 Pk Dr, **Owatonna,** MN 55060-0448, *pg.* 1307, *pg.* 952

Missouri

DAZOR MANUFACTURING CORP., 2079 Congressional Dr, **Saint Louis,** MO 63146, *pg.* 1296, *pg.* 995
GRAYBAR ELECTRIC COMPANY, INC., 34 N Meramec Ave, **Saint Louis,** MO 63105-3844, *pg.* 1299, *pg.* 997
H.E. WILLIAMS, INC., 831 W Fairview Ave, **Carthage,** MO 64836-3736, *pg.* 1299, *pg.* 974
KILLARK ELECTRIC, 3940 Martin Luther King Dr, **Saint Louis,** MO 63113, *pg.* 1300, *pg.* 998

Nebraska

CONDUCTIX INC., 10102 F St, **Omaha,** NE 68127-1104, *pg.* 1295, *pg.* 1015
GEORGE RISK INDUSTRIES, INC., 802 S Elm St, **Kimball,** NE 69145-1599, *pg.* 1298, *pg.* 1011

New Jersey

CAPITOL LIGHTING, 365 Rte 10, **East Hanover,** NJ 07936, *pg.* 1294, *pg.* 1053
CRESCENT/STONCO SUPPLY DIVISION, 200 Franklin Square Dr, **Somerset,** NJ 08873, *pg.* 1295, *pg.* 1121
MULBERRY METAL PRODUCTS, INC., 2199 Stanley Ter PO Box 443, **Union,** NJ 07083-4300, *pg.* 1302, *pg.* 1127
THE OKONITE COMPANY, 102 Hilltop Rd, **Ramsey,** NJ 07446, *pg.* 1302, *pg.* 1113

New York

EATON'S CROUSE-HINDS, 1201 Wolf St, **Syracuse,** NY 13208, *pg.* 1296, *pg.* 1344
LEVITON MANUFACTURING COMPANY, INC., 201 N Service Rd, **Melville,** NY 11747, *pg.* 1301, *pg.* 1180
NIAGARA TRANSFORMER CORP., 1747 Dale Rd, **Buffalo,** NY 14225, *pg.* 1302, *pg.* 1150
PASS & SEYMOUR/LEGRAND, 50 Boyd Ave, **Syracuse,** NY 13209, *pg.* 1303, *pg.* 1344
SAG HARBOR INDUSTRIES, 1668 Sag Harbor Tpke, **Sag Harbor,** NY 11963, *pg.* 1305, *pg.* 1340
SWIVELIER CO., INC., 600 Bradley Hill Rd, **Blauvelt,** NY 10913-1187, *pg.* 1307, *pg.* 1142

Ohio

DUALITE SALES & SERVICE, INC., 1 Dualite Ln, **Williamsburg,** OH 45176-1121, *pg.* 1296, *pg.* 1482
HINKLEY LIGHTING INC., 33000 Pin Oak Pkwy, **Avon Lake,** OH 44012, *pg.* 1299, *pg.* 1404
RADIX WIRE COMPANY, 26000 Lakeland Blvd, **Cleveland,** OH 44132-2638, *pg.* 1304, *pg.* 1434

Oregon

REJUVENATION INC., 2550 NW Nicolai St, **Portland,** OR 97210, *pg.* 1304, *pg.* 1506

Pennsylvania

AMERICAN PERIOD LIGHTING, INC., 3004 Columbia Ave, **Lancaster,** PA 17603, *pg.* 1294, *pg.* 1545
STREAMLIGHT INC., 30 Eagleville Rd, **Eagleville,** PA 19403, *pg.* 1306, *pg.* 1527

South Carolina

HAHL INC., 126 Glassmaster Rd, **Lexington,** SC 29072-3710, *pg.* 1299, *pg.* 1620
HUBBELL LIGHTING - PROGRESS LIGHTING DIVISION, 701 Millenium Blvd, **Greenville,** SC 29607, *pg.* 1300, *pg.* 1617
PRESCOLITE INC., 101 Corporate Dr, **Spartanburg,** SC 29303, *pg.* 1304, *pg.* 1622
QUOIZEL INC., 6 Corp Pkwy, **Goose Creek,** SC 29445-7144, *pg.* 1304, *pg.* 1616

Tennessee

FUSHI COPPERWELD, 254 Cotton Mill Rd, **Fayetteville,** TN 37334-7249, *pg.* 1296, *pg.* 1632
PHILIPS EMERGENCY LIGHTING, 236 Mount Pleasant Rd PO Box 460, **Collierville,** TN 38017-2752, *pg.* 1303, *pg.* 1631
UNIVERSAL LIGHTING TECHNOLOGIES, 26 Century Blvd Ste 500, **Nashville,** TN 37214-3683, *pg.* 1307, *pg.* 1655

Texas

CRAFTMADE INTERNATIONAL, INC., 650 S Royal Ln Ste 100, **Coppell,** TX 75019-3836, *pg.* 1295, *pg.* 1670
HIGH END SYSTEMS, INC., 2105 Gracy Farms Ln, **Austin,** TX 78758-4031, *pg.* 1299, *pg.* 1663

Utah

YOUNG ELECTRIC SIGN COMPANY, 2401 Foothill Dr, **Salt Lake City,** UT 84109, *pg.* 1308, *pg.* 1762

Vermont

WHITNEY BLAKE CO., INC., 20 Indus Dr, **Bellows Falls,** VT 05101-3122, *pg.* 1308, *pg.* 1764

Wisconsin

CREE INC., 9201 Washington Ave, **Racine,** WI 53406, *pg.* 1295, *pg.* 1888
EATON CORPORATION - INDUSTRIAL CONTROLS, 4201 N 27th St, **Milwaukee,** WI 53216-1807, *pg.* 1296, *pg.* 1874
ELECTRONIC THEATRE CONTROLS, INC., 3031 Pleasant View Rd, **Middleton,** WI 53562-1754, *pg.* 1296, *pg.* 1872
MAGNETEK, INC., N49 W13650 Campbell Drive, **Menomonee Falls,** WI 53051, *pg.* 1301, *pg.* 1870
PHOENIX PRODUCTS COMPANY, 8711 W Port Ave, **Milwaukee,** WI 53224-3429, *pg.* 1304, *pg.* 1879

First page reference indicates Business Class Edition
Second page reference indicates Geographic Edition

Machinery & Supplies

Alabama

ALTEC INDUSTRIES INC., 210 Inverness Ctr Dr, **Birmingham,** AL 35242-4834, *pg.* 1312, *pg.* 1

Arizona

MOBILE MINI, INC., 7420 S Kyrene Rd Ste 101, **Tempe,** AZ 85283, *pg.* 1362, *pg.* 26

UNITED RENTALS, 6929 E Greenway Pkwy Ste 200, **Scottsdale,** AZ 85254, *pg.* 1386, *pg.* 24

Arkansas

ADVANCED ENVIRONMENTAL RECYCLING TECHNOLOGIES, INC., 914 N Jefferson St, **Springdale,** AR 72764, *pg.* 1310, *pg.* 35

BALDOR ELECTRIC COMPANY, 5711 RS Boreham Jr St, **Fort Smith,** AR 72901-8301, *pg.* 1316, *pg.* 32

BRUNNER & LAY, INC., 1510 N Old Missouri Rd, **Springdale,** AR 72764, *pg.* 1320, *pg.* 35

California

ADEPT TECHNOLOGY, INC., 5960 Inglewood Dr, **Pleasanton,** CA 94588, *pg.* 1310, *pg.* 182

AIXTRON INC., 1139 Karlstad Dr, **Sunnyvale,** CA 94089-2117, *pg.* 1310, *pg.* 283

ANIXTER PENTACON, INC., 21123 Nordhoff St, **Chatsworth,** CA 91311, *pg.* 1313, *pg.* 64

BARKSDALE, INC., 3211 Fruitland Ave, **Los Angeles,** CA 90058-3717, *pg.* 1317, *pg.* 126

BRION TECHNOLOGIES INC., 4211Burton Dr, **Santa Clara,** CA 95054-1228, *pg.* 1319, *pg.* 265

BROOKTRONICS ENGINEERING CORPORATION, 28231 Ave Crocker Bldg 60 & 70, **Valencia,** CA 91355-1276, *pg.* 1320, *pg.* 299

CLAYTON INDUSTRIES CO., 17477 Hurley St, **City of Industry,** CA 91744-5106, *pg.* 1323, *pg.* 66

COLLABRX, INC., 44 Montgomery St, Ste 800, **San Francisco,** CA 94104, *pg.* 1324, *pg.* 216

CYPRESS SEMICONDUCTOR CORPORATION, 198 Champion Ct, **San Jose,** CA 95134, *pg.* 1326, *pg.* 243

DOWNS CRANE & HOIST CO, INC., 8827 S Juniper St, **Los Angeles,** CA 90002-1827, *pg.* 1330, *pg.* 129

ENERGY RECOVERY, INC., 1717 Doolittle Dr, **San Leandro,** CA 94577, *pg.* 1334, *pg.* 252

FALLBROOK TECHNOLOGIES INC., 9444 Waples St Ste 410, **San Diego,** CA 92121, *pg.* 1336, *pg.* 203

HF GROUP INC., 203 W Artesia Blvd, **Compton,** CA 90220-5517, *pg.* 1346, *pg.* 68

ISC8, 3001 Red Hill Ave Bldg 3 Ste 108, **Costa Mesa,** CA 92626-4532, *pg.* 1350, *pg.* 71

KLA-TENCOR CORPORATION, 1 Technology Dr, **Milpitas,** CA 95035, *pg.* 1353, *pg.* 146

LAM RESEARCH CORPORATION, 4650 Cushing Pkwy, **Fremont,** CA 94538, *pg.* 1354, *pg.* 91

LAM RESEARCH CORPORATION, 4000 N First St, **San Jose,** CA 95134, *pg.* 1354, *pg.* 246

LIQUIDMETAL TECHNOLOGIES, INC., 30452 Esperanza, **Rancho Santa Margarita,** CA 92688, *pg.* 1356, *pg.* 188

MAKITA U.S.A., INC., 14930 Northam St, **La Mirada,** CA 90638, *pg.* 1358, *pg.* 120

MICRO-OHM CORPORATION, 1088 Hamilton Rd, **Duarte,** CA 91010, *pg.* 1360, *pg.* 77

MOREHOUSE-COWLES, 13930 Magnolia Ave, **Chino,** CA 91710-7029, *pg.* 1363, *pg.* 66

NEOMAGIC CORPORATION, 2372-A Qume Dr, **San Jose,** CA 95131, *pg.* 1364, *pg.* 247

POWER INTEGRATIONS, INC., 5245 Hellyer Ave, **San Jose,** CA 95138-1002, *pg.* 1369, *pg.* 249

QUANTUM FUEL SYSTEMS TECHNOLOGIES WORLDWIDE, INC., 17872 Cartwright Rd, **Irvine,** CA 92614-6217, *pg.* 1371, *pg.* 115

RELIANCE STEEL & ALUMINUM CO., 350 S Grand Ave Ste 5100, **Los Angeles,** CA 90071, *pg.* 1371, *pg.* 139

ROLLEM CORPORATION OF AMERICA, 1650 S Lewis St, **Anaheim,** CA 92805, *pg.* 1372, *pg.* 43

SHUR-LOK COMPANY, 2541 White Rd, **Irvine,** CA 92614-6235, *pg.* 1375, *pg.* 116

SIMPSON MANUFACTURING COMPANY, INC., 5956 Las Positas Blvd, **Pleasanton,** CA 94588, *pg.* 1376, *pg.* 185

SOLAR TURBINES INCORPORATED, 2200 Pacific Hwy, **San Diego,** CA 92101-1745, *pg.* 1377, *pg.* 209

TAIYO YUDEN (U.S.A.), INC., 440 Stevens Ave Ste 300, **Solana Beach,** CA 92075, *pg.* 1380, *pg.* 279

TAMURA CORPORATION OF AMERICA, 43352 Bus Pk Dr, **Temecula,** CA 92590-3665, *pg.* 1380, *pg.* 291

TCI PRECISION METALS, INC., 240 E Rosecrans Ave, **Gardena,** CA 90248, *pg.* 1380, *pg.* 95

TESSERA TECHNOLOGIES INC., 3025 Orchard Pkwy, **San Jose,** CA 95134, *pg.* 1382, *pg.* 251

TOWERJAZZ U.S., 4321 Jamboree Rd, **Newport Beach,** CA 92660-3007, *pg.* 1383, *pg.* 166

TRIMBLE NAVIGATION LIMITED, 935 Stewart Dr, **Sunnyvale,** CA 94085, *pg.* 1384, *pg.* 288

TRIO-TECH INTERNATIONAL, 16139 Wyandotte St, **Van Nuys,** CA 91406, *pg.* 1384, *pg.* 300

ZEPHYR MANUFACTURING CO., INC., 201 Hindry Ave, **Inglewood,** CA 90301-1519, *pg.* 1391, *pg.* 105

Colorado

CONERGY, INC., 2460 W 26th Ave, Ste 280C, **Denver,** CO 80211, *pg.* 1325, *pg.* 318

HARSH INTERNATIONAL, INC., 600 Oak Ave, **Eaton,** CO 80615-3404, *pg.* 1345, *pg.* 324

INTERROLL ENGINEERING WEST INC., 1 Forge Rd, **Canon City,** CO 81212, *pg.* 1350, *pg.* 314

Connecticut

APTAR OF STRATFORD, 125 Access Rd, **Stratford,** CT 06615-7414, *pg.* 1313, *pg.* 380

ARBURG, INC., 125 Rockwell Rd, **Newington,** CT 06111, *pg.* 1314, *pg.* 359

ATMI, INC., 7 Commerce Dr, **Danbury,** CT 06810-4131, *pg.* 1314, *pg.* 342

BARNES GROUP INC., 123 Main St, **Bristol,** CT 06010-6307, *pg.* 1317, *pg.* 340

BOLT TECHNOLOGY CORPORATION, 4 Duke Pl, **Norwalk,** CT 06854, *pg.* 1318, *pg.* 360

BRANSON ULTRASONICS CORPORATION, 41 Eagle Rd, **Danbury,** CT 06810, *pg.* 1319, *pg.* 342

BRANSON ULTRASONICS CORPORATION-PRECISION CLEANING DIV, 41 Eagle Rd, **Danbury,** CT 06813-1961, *pg.* 1319, *pg.* 343

THE CARLYLE JOHNSON MACHINE COMPANY, L.L.C., 291 Boston Tpke PO Box 9546, **Bolton,** CT 06043-7252, *pg.* 1321, *pg.* 339

DAVIS-STANDARD LLC, 1 Extrusion Dr, **Pawcatuck,** CT 06379-2313, *pg.* 1328, *pg.* 368

DEL-TRON PRECISION, INC., 5 Trowbridge Dr, **Bethel,** CT 06801, *pg.* 1328, *pg.* 337

THE EASTERN COMPANY, 112 Bridge St PO Box 460, **Naugatuck,** CT 06770-0460, *pg.* 1331, *pg.* 357

EDAC TECHNOLOGIES CORPORATION, 5 McKee Pl, **Cheshire,** CT 06410, *pg.* 1332, *pg.* 342

FARREL CORPORATION, 25 Main St, **Ansonia,** CT 06401-1605, *pg.* 1336, *pg.* 337

GARDNER DENVER NASH, 9 Trefoil Dr, **Trumbull,** CT 06611-1330, *pg.* 1338, *pg.* 381

GOODWAY TECHNOLOGIES CORPORATION, 420 W Ave, **Stamford,** CT 06902-6329, *pg.* 1341, *pg.* 374

HIGHFIELD MANUFACTURING CO., 380 Mountain Grove St, **Bridgeport,** CT 06605, *pg.* 1346, *pg.* 339

JACOBS VEHICLE SYSTEMS, 22 E Dudley Town Rd, **Bloomfield,** CT 06002, *pg.* 1351, *pg.* 338

LOOS & COMPANY, INC., 1 Cable Rd, **Pomfret,** CT 06258, *pg.* 1356, *pg.* 368

LYDALL, INC., 1 Colonial Rd, **Manchester,** CT 06040, *pg.* 1357, *pg.* 354

NORWALK COMPRESSOR COMPANY, INC., 1650 Stratford Ave, **Stratford,** CT 06615-6419, *pg.* 1366, *pg.* 380

P/A INDUSTRIES, INC., 522 Cottage Grove Rd, **Bloomfield,** CT 06002-3111, *pg.* 1367, *pg.* 339

POLYFLON COMPANY, 1 Willard Rd, **Norwalk,** CT 06851, *pg.* 1369, *pg.* 364

SHEFFIELD LABORATORIES, 170 Broad St, **New London,** CT 06320-5313, *pg.* 1375, *pg.* 359

THE SPENCER TURBINE CO., 600 Day Hill Rd, **Windsor,** CT 06095-1703, *pg.* 1378, *pg.* 386

SPIROL INTERNATIONAL CORPORATION, 30 Rock Ave, **Danielson,** CT 06239-1425, *pg.* 1378, *pg.* 345

SPX PRECISION COMPONENTS - FENN DIVISION, 300 Fenn Rd, **Newington,** CT 06111-2244, *pg.* 1378, *pg.* 360

TEREX CORPORATION, 200 Nyala Farm Rd, **Westport,** CT 06880, *pg.* 1381, *pg.* 384

TRC COMPANIES, INC., 21 Griffin Rd N, **Windsor,** CT 06095, *pg.* 1383, *pg.* 386

TRUMPF INC., 111 Hyde Rd, **Farmington,** CT 06032, *pg.* 1385, *pg.* 349

UNITED RENTALS, INC., 5 Greenwich Office Pk, **Greenwich,** CT 06830, *pg.* 1386, *pg.* 350

Delaware

GRAVER TECHNOLOGIES LLC, 200 Lake Dr, **Glasgow,** DE 19702-3319, *pg.* 1343, *pg.* 387

O.A. NEWTON & SON CO, 16356 Sussex Hwy, **Bridgeville,** DE 19933, *pg.* 1366, *pg.* 387

Florida

ABC PACKAGING MACHINE CORPORATION, 811 Live Oak St, **Tarpon Springs,** FL 34689-4137, *pg.* 1309, *pg.* 477

BALDWIN TECHNOLOGY COMPANY, INC., 200 NW Corp Blvd Ste 101, **Boca Raton,** FL 33431, *pg.* 1316, *pg.* 410

FABCO-AIR, INC., 3716 NE 49th Ave, **Gainesville,** FL 32609-1699, *pg.* 1336, *pg.* 429

GENCOR INDUSTRIES, INC., 5201 N Orange Blossom Trl, **Orlando,** FL 32810-1008, *pg.* 1339, *pg.* 453

INTERNATIONAL BALER CORP., 5400 Rio Grande Ave, **Jacksonville,** FL 32254, *pg.* 1350, *pg.* 433

NEW ENGLAND MACHINERY, INC., 6204 29th St E, **Bradenton,** FL 34203-5304, *pg.* 1364, *pg.* 415

Q.E.P. CO., INC., 1001 Broken Sound Pkwy NW Ste A, **Boca Raton,** FL 33487, *pg.* 1371, *pg.* 413

ROPER TECHNOLOGIES, INC., 6901 Professional Pkwy E Ste 200, **Sarasota,** FL 34240, *pg.* 1372, *pg.* 467

Georgia

COMVERGE, INC., 5390 Triangle Pkwy Ste 300, **Norcross,** GA 30092, *pg.* 1325, *pg.* 536

DEUTZ CORPORATION, 3883 Steve Reynolds Blvd, **Norcross,** GA 30093-3051, *pg.* 1328, *pg.* 536

GE ENERGY, 4200 Wildwood Pkwy, **Atlanta,** GA 30339, *pg.* 1338, *pg.* 506

GIW INDUSTRIES, INC., 5000 Wrightsboro Rd, **Grovetown,** GA 30813-2842, *pg.* 1340, *pg.* 533

GRAVOGRAPH-NEW HERMES, 2200 Northmont Pkwy, **Duluth,** GA 30096-5895, *pg.* 1344, *pg.* 531

HARRIS HOLDINGS INC., 1641 Lewis Way, **Stone Mountain,** GA 30083, *pg.* 1345, *pg.* 541

THE HARRIS PRODUCTS GROUP, 2345 Murphy Blvd, **Gainesville,** GA 30504-6001, *pg.* 1345, *pg.* 533

HARRIS WASTE MANAGEMENT GROUP, INC., 340 Jekyll Rd, **Baxley,** GA 31513, *pg.* 1345, *pg.* 526

LYNCH TECHNOLOGIES, INC., 207 Airport Rd, **Bainbridge,** GA 39817, *pg.* 1357, *pg.* 526

PANGBORN CORPORATION, 4630 Coates Dr, **Fairburn,** GA 30213, *pg.* 1367, *pg.* 532

PROCESS CONTROL CORPORATION, 6875 Mimms Dr, **Atlanta,** GA 30340, *pg.* 1370, *pg.* 518

THERMAL CERAMICS INC., 2102 Old Savannah Rd, **Augusta,** GA 30906-2133, *pg.* 1382, *pg.* 525

WEBER-HYDRAULIK, 100 Galleria Pkwy Ste 1000, **Atlanta,** GA 30339, *pg.* 1388, *pg.* 524

Illinois

A. FINKL & SONS CO., 2011 N Southport Ave, **Chicago,** IL 60614-4015, *pg.* 1309, *pg.* 563

ACCURATE PERFORATING COMPANY, INC., 3636 S Kedzie Ave, **Chicago,** IL 60632-2727, *pg.* 1309, *pg.* 563

ANIXTER INTERNATIONAL INC., 2301 Patriot Blvd, **Glenview,** IL 60026-8020, *pg.* 1313, *pg.* 614

BARNES INTERNATIONAL INC., 814 Chestnut St, **Rockford,** IL 61105, *pg.* 1317, *pg.* 654

BIMBA MANUFACTURING COMPANY, Rte 50 N, **Monee,** IL 60449, *pg.* 1317, *pg.* 633

BODINE ELECTRIC COMPANY, 201 Northfield Rd, **Northfield,** IL 60093-3311, *pg.* 1318, *pg.* 641

BOMAG AMERICAS, INC., 2000 Kentville Rd, **Kewanee,** IL 61443-1714, *pg.* 1318, *pg.* 621

BOURN & KOCH MACHINE TOOL COMPANY, 2500 Kishwaukee St, **Rockford,** IL 61104, *pg.* 1319, *pg.* 654
BROADWIND ENERGY, INC., 3240 S Central Ave, **Cicero,** IL 60804, *pg.* 1319, *pg.* 598
BW CONTAINER SYSTEMS, 1305 Lakeview Dr, **Romeoville,** IL 60446-3950, *pg.* 1321, *pg.* 656
CARTER MOTOR COMPANY, 400 S Railroad St, **Warren,** IL 61087, *pg.* 1321, *pg.* 665
CATERPILLAR, INC., 100 NE Adams St, **Peoria,** IL 61629-0001, *pg.* 1321, *pg.* 650
C.H. HANSON COMPANY, 2000 N Aurora Rd, **Naperville,** IL 60563-8793, *pg.* 1322, *pg.* 636
CHICAGO METAL FABRICATORS, INC., 3724 S Rockwell St, **Chicago,** IL 60632-1051, *pg.* 1323, *pg.* 569
CHICAGO RIVET & MACHINE COMPANY, 901 Frontenac Rd, **Naperville,** IL 60563, *pg.* 1323, *pg.* 636
CHICAGO TUBE & IRON CO., 1 Chicago Tube Dr, **Romeoville,** IL 60446, *pg.* 1323, *pg.* 656
COILCRAFT, INC., 1102 Silver Lake Rd, **Cary,** IL 60013-1658, *pg.* 1324, *pg.* 562
COLEMAN CABLE, INC., 1530 Shields Dr, **Waukegan,** IL 60085-8309, *pg.* 1324, *pg.* 665
THE DOALL COMPANY, 1480 S Wolf Rd, **Wheeling,** IL 66090, *pg.* 1329, *pg.* 670
DORMER PRAMET, 2511 Technology Dr Ste 113/114, **Elgin,** IL 60124, *pg.* 1329, *pg.* 609
DOVER CORPORATION, 3005 Highland Pkwy, **Downers Grove,** IL 60515, *pg.* 1329, *pg.* 608
ECLIPSE INC., 1665 Elmwood Rd, **Rockford,** IL 61103-1211, *pg.* 1332, *pg.* 655
ELECTRO-MOTIVE DIESEL, INC., 9301 W 55th St, **La Grange,** IL 60525-3211, *pg.* 1333, *pg.* 621
ELGIN NATIONAL INDUSTRIES, INC., 2001 Butterfield Rd Ste 1020, **Downers Grove,** IL 60515-1084, *pg.* 1333, *pg.* 608
ESTAD STAMPING & MANUFACTURING COMPANY, 1005 Griggs St, **Danville,** IL 61832, *pg.* 1336, *pg.* 598
FLEXIBLE STEEL LACING COMPANY, 2525 Wisconsin Ave, **Downers Grove,** IL 60515-4241, *pg.* 1337, *pg.* 608
G&W ELECTRIC COMPANY, 3500 W 127th St, **Blue Island,** IL 60406, *pg.* 1338, *pg.* 558
GEORGE T. SCHMIDT, INC., 6151 W Howard St, **Niles,** IL 60714-3401, *pg.* 1340, *pg.* 637
HARIG MANUFACTURING CORPORATION, 5757 W Howard St, **Niles,** IL 60714-4012, *pg.* 1345, *pg.* 637
HOLLYMATIC CORPORATION, 600 E Plainfield Rd, **Countryside,** IL 60525-6914, *pg.* 1346, *pg.* 598
IDEX CORPORATION, 1925 W Field Ct Ste 200, **Lake Forest,** IL 60045-4824, *pg.* 1347, *pg.* 623
ILLINOIS TOOL WORKS INC., 155 Harlem Ave, **Glenview,** IL 60025, *pg.* 1348, *pg.* 614
KOMATSU AMERICA INDUSTRIES, LLC, One Continental Twr 1701 W Golf Rd Ste 300, **Rolling Meadows,** IL 60008, *pg.* 1353, *pg.* 656
KOMORI AMERICA CORPORATION, 5520 Meadowbrook Industrial Ct, **Rolling Meadows,** IL 60008, *pg.* 1353, *pg.* 656
KONE INC., 1 Kone Ct, **Moline,** IL 61265, *pg.* 1353, *pg.* 633
LAWSON PRODUCTS, INC., 8770 W Bryn Mawr Ave Ste 900, **Chicago,** IL 60631, *pg.* 1355, *pg.* 580
LAYSTROM MANUFACTURING CO., 3900 W Palmer St, **Chicago,** IL 60647-2208, *pg.* 1355, *pg.* 580
LIQUID CONTROLS, INC., 105 Albrecht Dr, **Lake Bluff,** IL 60044, *pg.* 1356, *pg.* 622
MACLEAN-FOGG COMPANY INC., 1000 Allanson Rd, **Mundelein,** IL 60060, *pg.* 1358, *pg.* 635
MANITEX INTERNATIONAL, INC., 9725 Industrial Dr, **Bridgeview,** IL 60455-2406, *pg.* 1358, *pg.* 559
MARCH MANUFACTURING INC., 1819 Pickwick Ave, **Glenview,** IL 60025, *pg.* 1359, *pg.* 615
THE MIDDLEBY CORPORATION, 1400 Toastmaster Dr, **Elgin,** IL 60120-9274, *pg.* 1361, *pg.* 610
NAYLOR PIPE COMPANY, 1230 E 92nd St, **Chicago,** IL 60619-7991, *pg.* 1364, *pg.* 584
PEACE INDUSTRIES INC., 1100 Hicks Rd, **Rolling Meadows,** IL 60008-1016, *pg.* 1368, *pg.* 656
PETTIBONE, LLC, 2626 Warrenville Rd, **Downers Grove,** IL 60515-1775, *pg.* 1368, *pg.* 609
THE PROTECTOSEAL COMPANY, 225 W Foster Ave, **Bensenville,** IL 60106-1631, *pg.* 1370, *pg.* 556
QUINCY COMPRESSOR INC., 3501 Wisman Ln, **Quincy,** IL 62301-1257, *pg.* 1371, *pg.* 653
ROCKFORD PRODUCTS CORP., 707 Harrison Ave, **Rockford,** IL 61104-7162, *pg.* 1372, *pg.* 655
RYERSON INC., 227 W Monroe St, **Chicago,** IL 60606, *pg.* 1373, *pg.* 589
SCOTSMAN GROUP LLC, 775 Corporate Woods Pkwy, **Vernon Hills,** IL 60061-3112, *pg.* 1374, *pg.* 665
SENIOR FLEXONICS INC., 300 E Devon Ave, **Bartlett,** IL 60103-4608, *pg.* 1375, *pg.* 556
SERFILCO, LTD., 2900 MacArthur Blvd, **Northbrook,** IL 60062-2005, *pg.* 1375, *pg.* 641
SIEMENS BUILDING TECHNOLOGIES, INC., 1000 Deerfield Pkwy, **Buffalo Grove,** IL 60089-4547, *pg.* 1376, *pg.* 560
SPARTON CORPORATION, 425 N Martingale Ste 2050, **Schaumburg,** IL 60173-2213, *pg.* 1377, *pg.* 660
STANDARD SAFETY EQUIPMENT CO., 1407 Ridgeview Dr, **McHenry,** IL 60050, *pg.* 1379, *pg.* 632
THOMAS ENGINEERING INC., 575 W Central Rd, **Hoffman Estates,** IL 60192-1937, *pg.* 1382, *pg.* 619
TORNADO INDUSTRIES, INC., 7401 W Lawrence Ave, **Chicago,** IL 60706, *pg.* 1383, *pg.* 591
TRIANGLE PACKAGE MACHINERY CO., 6655 W Diversey Ave, **Chicago,** IL 60707-2239, *pg.* 1383, *pg.* 592
TRITON INDUSTRIES, INC., 1020 N Kolmar Ave, **Chicago,** IL 60651-3343, *pg.* 1384, *pg.* 592
TUTHILL CORPORATION, 8500 S Madison St, **Burr Ridge,** IL 60527-6284, *pg.* 1385, *pg.* 561
TUTHILL CORPORATION PUMP GROUP, 12500 S Pulaski Rd, **Alsip,** IL 60803-1911, *pg.* 1385, *pg.* 553
ULINE SHIPPING SUPPLIES, 2200 S Lakeside Dr, **Waukegan,** IL 60085, *pg.* 1385, *pg.* 666
UOP LLC, 25 E Algonquin Rd Bldg A, **Des Plaines,** IL 60016-6101, *pg.* 1386, *pg.* 606
WES-TECH AUTOMATION SOLUTIONS, 720 Dartmouth Ln, **Buffalo Grove,** IL 60089, *pg.* 1388, *pg.* 560
W.H. MAZE COMPANY, 100 Church St, **Peru,** IL 61354, *pg.* 1389, *pg.* 652
WHITING CORPORATION, 26000 Whiting Way, **Monee,** IL 60449-8060, *pg.* 1389, *pg.* 633
W.W. GRAINGER, INC., 100 Grainger Pkwy, **Lake Forest,** IL 60045-5201, *pg.* 1390, *pg.* 625
XEIKON AMERICA, INC., 1375 E Irving Park Rd, **Itasca,** IL 60143, *pg.* 1390, *pg.* 621

Indiana

CUMMINS INC., 500 Jackson St, **Columbus,** IN 47201-6258, *pg.* 1326, *pg.* 676
DIAMOND CHAIN COMPANY, 402 Kentucky Ave, **Indianapolis,** IN 46225, *pg.* 1328, *pg.* 684
DIEHL WOODWORKING MACHINERY, INC., 981 S Wabash St, **Wabash,** IN 46992-4125, *pg.* 1328, *pg.* 698
DWYER INSTRUMENTS INC., 102 Indiana Hwy 212, **Michigan City,** IN 46360-1956, *pg.* 1330, *pg.* 694
EAST CHICAGO MACHINE TOOL CORPORATION, 980 Crown Ct, **Crown Point,** IN 46307-2732, *pg.* 1331, *pg.* 676
FIRE KING SECURITY GROUP, 101 Security Pkwy, **New Albany,** IN 47150-9366, *pg.* 1336, *pg.* 696
FOX CONTRACTORS CORP., 5430 W Ferguson Rd, **Fort Wayne,** IN 46809-9612, *pg.* 1337, *pg.* 680
FRANKLIN ELECTRIC CO., INC., 9255 Coverdale Rd, **Fort Wayne,** IN 46809, *pg.* 1337, *pg.* 680
GEMA USA INC., 4141 W 54th St, **Indianapolis,** IN 46254, *pg.* 1339, *pg.* 686
GRC ENTERPRISES, INC., 3477 Watling St, **East Chicago,** IN 46312-1708, *pg.* 1344, *pg.* 677
ILPEA INDUSTRIES, INC., 745 S Gardner St, **Scottsburg,** IN 47170, *pg.* 1348, *pg.* 697
MAXON CORPORATION, 201 E 18th St, **Muncie,** IN 47302, *pg.* 1359, *pg.* 695
QUEST SAFETY PRODUCTS, INC., 1414 S West St Ste 8, **Indianapolis,** IN 46225, *pg.* 1371, *pg.* 689
SANISERV, 451 E Country Line Rd, **Mooresville,** IN 46158-5089, *pg.* 1373, *pg.* 695
SCREW CONVEYOR INDUSTRIES, 700 Hoffman St, **Hammond,** IN 46327-1827, *pg.* 1374, *pg.* 682
SHUTTLEWORTH, INC., 10 Commercial Rd, **Huntington,** IN 46750-8805, *pg.* 1375, *pg.* 682
SMC CORPORATION OF AMERICA, 10100 SMC Blvd, **Noblesville,** IN 46060, *pg.* 1376, *pg.* 696
SPEEDGRIP CHUCK, INC., 2000 Indus Pkwy, **Elkhart,** IN 46516, *pg.* 1377, *pg.* 677
STEDMAN MACHINE COMPANY, 129 Franklin St, **Aurora,** IN 47001, *pg.* 1379, *pg.* 673
SULLAIR CORPORATION, 3700 E Michigan Blvd, **Michigan City,** IN 46360-6527, *pg.* 1379, *pg.* 695
THERMWOOD CORPORATION, 904 Dale Buffaloville Rd, **Dale,** IN 47523-9057, *pg.* 1382, *pg.* 676
URSCHEL LABORATORIES INCORPORATED, 2503 Calumet Ave, **Valparaiso,** IN 46383-2715, *pg.* 1386, *pg.* 698

Iowa

DANFOSS POWER SOLUTIONS COMPANY, 2800 E 13th St, **Ames,** IA 50010, *pg.* 1328, *pg.* 701
LISLE CORPORATION, 807 E Main St PO Box 89, **Clarinda,** IA 51632, *pg.* 1356, *pg.* 703
R.A. JONES & CO., 807 W Kimberly Rd, **Davenport,** IA 52806-5706, *pg.* 1371, *pg.* 704
TEREX CEDARAPIDS, 909 17th St NE, **Cedar Rapids,** IA 52402, *pg.* 1381, *pg.* 703
VAN GORP CORPORATION, 1410 Washington St, **Pella,** IA 50219-1502, *pg.* 1387, *pg.* 711
VIKING PUMP, INC., 406 State St, **Cedar Falls,** IA 50613-3343, *pg.* 1387, *pg.* 702

Kansas

BUNTING MAGNETICS CO., 500 S Spencer Rd, **Newton,** KS 67114-4109, *pg.* 1320, *pg.* 717
JOHN DEERE COFFEYVILLE WORKS INC, 2624 N US Hwy 169, **Coffeyville,** KS 67337, *pg.* 1351, *pg.* 714
WIRECO WORLDGROUP, 2400 W 75th St, **Prairie Village,** KS 66208, *pg.* 1389, *pg.* 721

Kentucky

CLARK MATERIAL HANDLING COMPANY, 700 Enterprise Dr, **Lexington,** KY 40510, *pg.* 1323, *pg.* 729
E.D. BULLARD COMPANY, 1898 Safety Way, **Cynthiana,** KY 41031-9303, *pg.* 1332, *pg.* 727
GUSHER PUMPS, INC., 22 Ruthman Dr, **Dry Ridge,** KY 41035-9784, *pg.* 1344, *pg.* 727
LITTLEFORD DAY INC., 7451 Empire Dr, **Florence,** KY 41042, *pg.* 1356, *pg.* 728
MODERN WELDING COMPANY, INC., 2880 New Hartford Rd, **Owensboro,** KY 42303-1321, *pg.* 1363, *pg.* 739
MULTI-METALS, 715 E Gray St, **Louisville,** KY 40202, *pg.* 1363, *pg.* 737
SWECO, 8029 Dixie Hwy 25, **Florence,** KY 41042-2903, *pg.* 1380, *pg.* 728
THOMPSON INTERNATIONAL INC., 5840 Airline Rd, **Henderson,** KY 42420-9561, *pg.* 1382, *pg.* 729

Louisiana

ANVIL ATTACHMENTS, LLC, 261 Hwy 19, **Slaughter,** LA 70777-0216, *pg.* 1313, *pg.* 748
GIBSONS ENERGY, 4500 NE Evangeline Thruway, **Carencro,** LA 70520-5253, *pg.* 1340, *pg.* 743
INTRALOX LLC, 201 Laitram Ln, **Harahan,** LA 70123, *pg.* 1350, *pg.* 744
THE LAITRAM LLC, 220 Laitram Ln, **Harahan,** LA 70123, *pg.* 1354, *pg.* 744
PELLERIN MILNOR CORPORATION, 700 Jackson St, **Kenner,** LA 70062-7774, *pg.* 1368, *pg.* 744

Maine

PARKER HANNIFIN WATTS FLUID AIR, 9 Cutts Rd, **Kittery,** ME 03904-5567, *pg.* 1368, *pg.* 750

Maryland

COLFAX CORPORATION, 8170 Maple Lawn Blvd Ste 180, **Fulton,** MD 20759, *pg.* 1324, *pg.* 770
DEWALT INDUSTRIAL TOOL COMPANY, 701 E Joppa Rd, **Baltimore,** MD 21286, *pg.* 1328, *pg.* 757
ELLICOTT DREDGES, LLC, 1425 Wicomomico St, **Baltimore,** MD 21230-2020, *pg.* 1333, *pg.* 757
HOLMATRO, INC., 505 McCormick Dr, **Glen Burnie,** MD 21061-3254, *pg.* 1346, *pg.* 771

Massachusetts

A123 SYSTEMS INC., Arsenal on the Charles 321 Arsenal St, **Watertown,** MA 02472, *pg.* 1309, *pg.* 855
ACCURATE FASTENERS INC., 550 E 1st St, **Boston,** MA

First page reference indicates Business Class Edition
Second page reference indicates Geographic Edition

02127-1403, *pg.* 1309, *pg.* 789
ALTRIA INDUSTRIAL MOTION CORP., 300 Granite St Ste 201, **Braintree,** MA 02184, *pg.* 1312, *pg.* 802
A.W. CHESTERTON COMPANY, 500 Unicorn Pk Dr, **Woburn,** MA 01801, *pg.* 1315, *pg.* 861
BARBOUR STOCKWELL INCORPORATED, 45 6th Rd, **Woburn,** MA 01801, *pg.* 1316, *pg.* 861
BARRY CONTROLS, 82 South St, **Hopkinton,** MA 01748-2205, *pg.* 1317, *pg.* 825
BOLTON-EMERSON AMERICAS, INC., 9 Osgood St, **Lawrence,** MA 01843-1859, *pg.* 1318, *pg.* 827
BROOKS AUTOMATION, INC., 15 Elizabeth Dr, **Chelmsford,** MA 01824, *pg.* 1320, *pg.* 813
BTU INTERNATIONAL, INC., 23 Esquire Rd, **North Billerica,** MA 01862, *pg.* 1320, *pg.* 838
BUTLER AUTOMATIC, INC., 41 Leona Dr, **Middleboro,** MA 02346-1404, *pg.* 1320, *pg.* 833
CONNELL LIMITED PARTNERSHIP, 1 Intl Pl 31 Fl, **Boston,** MA 02110-2635, *pg.* 1325, *pg.* 793
GLOUCESTER ENGINEERING, CO., Blackburn Industrial Park 11 Dory Rd, **Gloucester,** MA 01931-0900, *pg.* 1341, *pg.* 823
IMPLANT SCIENCES CORPORATION, 600 Research Dr, **Wilmington,** MA 01887, *pg.* 1348, *pg.* 860
INSTRON CORPORATION, 825 University Ave, **Norwood,** MA 02062-2643, *pg.* 1349, *pg.* 839
KADANT INC., 1 Technology Park Dr, **Westford,** MA 01886, *pg.* 1352, *pg.* 858
MKS INSTRUMENTS, INC., 2 Tech Dr Ste 201, **Andover,** MA 01810, *pg.* 1362, *pg.* 781
MORGAN ADVANCED MATERIALS, 225 Theodore Rice Blvd, **New Bedford,** MA 02745, *pg.* 1363, *pg.* 835
OMG, INC., 153 Bowles Rd, **Agawam,** MA 01001-2900, *pg.* 1367, *pg.* 781
ORBOTECH INC., 44 Manning Rd, **Billerica,** MA 01821-3931, *pg.* 1367, *pg.* 788
RODNEY HUNT COMPANY, 46 Mill St, **Orange,** MA 01364-1251, *pg.* 1372, *pg.* 840
SCHAEFER MARINE INC., 158 Duchaine Blvd, **New Bedford,** MA 02745, *pg.* 1373, *pg.* 835
SIMONDS INTERNATIONAL CORPORATION, 135 Intervale Rd, **Fitchburg,** MA 01420-6519, *pg.* 1376, *pg.* 819
SPEEDLINE TECHNOLOGIES, INC., 16 Forge Park, **Franklin,** MA 02038, *pg.* 1378, *pg.* 823
SPIRE CORPORATION, 1 Patriots Park, **Bedford,** MA 01730-2343, *pg.* 1378, *pg.* 786
STURTEVANT INC., 348 Circuit St, **Hanover,** MA 02339-2129, *pg.* 1379, *pg.* 824
VACUUM TECHNOLOGY ASSOCIATES, INC., 110 Indus Pk Rd, **Hingham,** MA 02043-4369, *pg.* 1386, *pg.* 824
WESTERBEKE CORPORATION, Myles Standish Indus Pk 150 John Hancock Rd, **Taunton,** MA 02780, *pg.* 1388, *pg.* 847

Michigan

ADMIRAL TOOL & MANUFACTURING COMPANY INC., 38010 Amrhein Rd, **Livonia,** MI 48150, *pg.* 1310, *pg.* 896
A.G. DAVIS/AA GAGE, 6533 Sims Dr, **Sterling Heights,** MI 48313, *pg.* 1310, *pg.* 908
ALTAIR CORPORATION, 1820 East Big Beaver Rd, **Troy,** MI 48083, *pg.* 1312, *pg.* 910
BESSER COMPANY, 801 Johnson St, **Alpena,** MI 49707-1870, *pg.* 1317, *pg.* 865
BTM CORPORATION, 300 Davis Rd, **Marysville,** MI 48040, *pg.* 1320, *pg.* 898
THE CHALLENGE MACHINERY COMPANY, 6125 Norton Ctr Dr, **Norton Shores,** MI 49441, *pg.* 1322, *pg.* 902
CMI-SCHNEIBLE COMPANY, 2220 Veterans Memorial Pkwy, **Saginaw,** MI 48601, *pg.* 1324, *pg.* 906
CWC TEXTRON, 1085 W Sherman Blvd, **Muskegon,** MI 49441, *pg.* 1326, *pg.* 901
DAIFUKU WEBB, 34375 W 12 Mi Rd, **Farmington Hills,** MI 48331, *pg.* 1327, *pg.* 885
EAGLE TECHNOLOGIES GROUP, 9850 Red Arrow Hwy, **Bridgman,** MI 49106, *pg.* 1331, *pg.* 874
ESSENTRA COMPONENTS, 2265 Black Creek Rd, **Muskegon,** MI 49444, *pg.* 1335, *pg.* 901
GEERPRES INC., 1780 Harvey St, **Muskegon,** MI 49442-5378, *pg.* 1339, *pg.* 901
HOLCIM (U.S.) INC., 6211 N Ann Arbor Rd, **Dundee,** MI 48131-0122, *pg.* 1346, *pg.* 885
HOUGEN MANUFACTURING INC., 3001 Hougen Dr, **Swartz Creek,** MI 48473-7935, *pg.* 1347, *pg.* 908
KAYDON CORPORATION, 315 E Eisenhower Pkwy Ste 300, **Ann Arbor,** MI 48108-3330, *pg.* 1352, *pg.* 866
LECO CORPORATION, 3000 Lakeview Ave, **Saint Joseph,** MI 49085-2396, *pg.* 1355, *pg.* 906
MAGLINE, INC., 1205 W Cedar St, **Standish,** MI 48658-9535, *pg.* 1358, *pg.* 908
METZGAR CONVEYOR COMPANY, 901 Metzgar Dr, **Comstock Park,** MI 49321-9758, *pg.* 1360, *pg.* 875
NLB CORP., 29830 Beck Rd, **Wixom,** MI 48393-2824, *pg.* 1365, *pg.* 913
OLIVER PRODUCTS COMPANY INC., 445 6th St NW, **Grand Rapids,** MI 49504-5253, *pg.* 1367, *pg.* 888
PRAB, INC., 5944 E Kilgore Rd, **Kalamazoo,** MI 49048, *pg.* 1369, *pg.* 894
TECUMSEH PRODUCTS COMPANY, 5683 Hines Dr, **Ann Arbor,** MI 48108, *pg.* 1381, *pg.* 866
TOLEDO COMMUTATOR CO., 1101 S Chestnut St, **Owosso,** MI 48867-4096, *pg.* 1383, *pg.* 903
TRIMAS CORPORATION, 39400 Woodward Ave Ste 130, **Bloomfield Hills,** MI 48304, *pg.* 1383, *pg.* 874

Minnesota

AVERY WEIGH-TRONIX, INC., 1000 Armstrong Dr, **Fairmont,** MN 56031, *pg.* 1315, *pg.* 925
BADGER EQUIPMENT COMPANY, 217 Patenaude Dr, **Winona,** MN 55987-1463, *pg.* 1315, *pg.* 966
CANNON EQUIPMENT COMPANY, 324 Washington St W, **Cannon Falls,** MN 55009, *pg.* 1321, *pg.* 920
CHRISTIANSON SYSTEMS, INC., 20421 15th St SE, **Blomkest,** MN 56216, *pg.* 1323, *pg.* 917
CORNELIUS INC, 101 Broadway St W Ste 100, **Osseo,** MN 55369-1542, *pg.* 1326, *pg.* 952
CUMMINS POWER GENERATION, 1400 73rd Ave NE, **Minneapolis,** MN 55432-3702, *pg.* 1326, *pg.* 932
DONALDSON COMPANY, INC., 1400 W 94th St, **Bloomington,** MN 55431-2370, *pg.* 1329, *pg.* 917
EATON HYDRAULICS INC., 14615 Lone Oak Rd, **Eden Prairie,** MN 55344-2079, *pg.* 1332, *pg.* 922
ELECTRO-SENSORS, INC., 6111 Blue Circle Dr, **Minnetonka,** MN 55343, *pg.* 1333, *pg.* 948
EMERSON PROCESS MANAGEMENT ROSEMOUNT INC., 8200 Market Blvd, **Chanhassen,** MN 55317-9685, *pg.* 1334, *pg.* 920
GRACO, INC., 88 11th Ave NE, **Minneapolis,** MN 55413, *pg.* 1342, *pg.* 935
INDUSTRIAL RUBBER PRODUCTS, INC., 3516 E 13th Ave, **Hibbing,** MN 55746, *pg.* 1349, *pg.* 926
LIND ELECTRONICS, INC., 6414 Cambridge St, **Minneapolis,** MN 55426, *pg.* 1355, *pg.* 938
METRO MACHINE & ENGINEERING CORP., 8001 Wallace Rd, **Eden Prairie,** MN 55344-2224, *pg.* 1360, *pg.* 923
MOCON, INC., 7500 Mendelssohn Ave N, **Minneapolis,** MN 55428, *pg.* 1363, *pg.* 940
NORTHERN TOOL + EQUIPMENT, 2800 Southcross Dr W, PO Box 1219, **Burnsville,** MN 55306-6936, *pg.* 1366, *pg.* 919
TCR CORPORATION, 1600 67th Ave N, **Minneapolis,** MN 55430-1742, *pg.* 1380, *pg.* 944
TENNANT COMPANY, 701 N Lilac Dr, **Minneapolis,** MN 55440, *pg.* 1381, *pg.* 944
TIMESAVERS INC., 11123 89th Ave N, **Maple Grove,** MN 55369, *pg.* 1382, *pg.* 928
WATEROUS COMPANY, 125 Hardman Ave S, **South Saint Paul,** MN 55075-1129, *pg.* 1387, *pg.* 965

Mississippi

UNIFIED BRANDS INC., 1055 Mendell Davis Dr, **Jackson,** MS 39272-9788, *pg.* 1385, *pg.* 970

Missouri

ACF INDUSTRIES LLC, 101 Clark St, **Saint Charles,** MO 63301, *pg.* 1310, *pg.* 989
CENTRIFUGAL & MECHANICAL INDUSTRIES, INC., 201 President St, **Saint Louis,** MO 63118-4111, *pg.* 1322, *pg.* 994
COIN ACCEPTORS, INC., 300 Hunter Ave, **Saint Louis,** MO 63124-2081, *pg.* 1324, *pg.* 994
D&S CAR WASH EQUIPMENT CO., 4200 Brandi Ln, **High Ridge,** MO 63049, *pg.* 1327, *pg.* 979
EATON BUSSMANN, INC., 114 Old State Rd, **Ellisville,** MO 63021-5942, *pg.* 1331, *pg.* 977
HUSSMANN INTERNATIONAL, INC., 12999 Saint Charles Rock Rd, **Bridgeton,** MO 63044-2419, *pg.* 1347, *pg.* 973
INTELLIGRATED SYSTEMS LLC, 9301 Olive Blvd, **Saint Louis,** MO 63132-3207, *pg.* 1350, *pg.* 998
LINCOLN INDUSTRIAL CORP., 1 Lincoln Way, **Saint Louis,** MO 63120-1508, *pg.* 1355, *pg.* 999
MAC EQUIPMENT, INC., 7901 NW 107th Ter, **Kansas City,** MO 64153-1910, *pg.* 1357, *pg.* 985
MARK ANDY, INC., 18081 Chesterfield Airport Rd, **Chesterfield,** MO 63005, *pg.* 1359, *pg.* 975
MOORE FANS LLC, 800 S Missouri Ave, **Marceline,** MO 64658-1602, *pg.* 1363, *pg.* 987
O'BRIEN CORPORATION, 1900 Crystal Industrial Ct, **Saint Louis,** MO 63114, *pg.* 1366, *pg.* 1001
SOUTHWEST BINDING & LAMINATING, 109 Millwell Ct, **Maryland Heights,** MO 63043, *pg.* 1377, *pg.* 988
SUNNEN PRODUCTS COMPANY, 7910 Manchester Ave, **Saint Louis,** MO 63143-2712, *pg.* 1379, *pg.* 1004
TUTHILL VACUUM & BLOWER SYSTEMS, 4840 W Kearney St, **Springfield,** MO 65803-8702, *pg.* 1385, *pg.* 1007
WILLIAMS PATENT CRUSHER & PULVERIZER CO., INC., 2701 N Broadway, **Saint Louis,** MO 63102-1509, *pg.* 1389, *pg.* 1005
WIRECO WORLDGROUP, 12200 NW Ambassador Dr, **Kansas City,** MO 64163, *pg.* 1389, *pg.* 987
ZIMMERMAN-MCDONALD MACHINERY, INC., 2272 Weldon Pkwy, **Saint Louis,** MO 63146-3206, *pg.* 1391, *pg.* 1005

Nebraska

BALDWIN FILTERS, 4400 E Hwy 30, **Kearney,** NE 68847, *pg.* 1316, *pg.* 1011
CHIEF INDUSTRIES, INC., 3942 W Old Hwy 30, **Grand Island,** NE 68802, *pg.* 1323, *pg.* 1010
INTERSYSTEMS, 9575 N 109th Ave, **Omaha,** NE 68142-1111, *pg.* 1350, *pg.* 1016
LINDSAY CORPORATION, 2222 N 111th St, **Omaha,** NE 68164, *pg.* 1356, *pg.* 1016
SNYDER INDUSTRIES, INC., 4700 Fremont St, **Lincoln,** NE 68504-1646, *pg.* 1377, *pg.* 1012
SURPLUS CENTER, 1015 W O St, **Lincoln,** NE 68528-1322, *pg.* 1380, *pg.* 1012
VALMONT INDUSTRIES, INC., 1 Valmont Plaza, **Omaha,** NE 68154-5214, *pg.* 1387, *pg.* 1019

New Hampshire

ELECTROCRAFT, INC, 1 Progress Dr, **Dover,** NH 03820-5450, *pg.* 1333, *pg.* 1033
INTELITEK, INC., 444 E Industrial Pk Dr, **Manchester,** NH 03109, *pg.* 1349, *pg.* 1036
KINGSBURY CORPORATION, 80 Laurel St, **Keene,** NH 03431-4207, *pg.* 1353, *pg.* 1035
PRAXAIR-TAFA, 146 Pembroke Rd, **Concord,** NH 03301-5706, *pg.* 1370, *pg.* 1033
RSCC AEROSPACE & DEFENSE, 680 Hayward St, **Manchester,** NH 03103, *pg.* 1373, *pg.* 1036
UNIVEX CORPORATION, 3 Old Rockingham Rd, **Salem,** NH 03079-2133, *pg.* 1386, *pg.* 1039

New Jersey

ACRISON, INC., 20 Empire Blvd, **Moonachie,** NJ 07074-1303, *pg.* 1310, *pg.* 1087
A.J. JERSEY INC., 125 St Nicholas Ave, **South Plainfield,** NJ 07080, *pg.* 1310, *pg.* 1123
ARTUS CORPORATION, 201 S Dean St, **Englewood,** NJ 07631-4107, *pg.* 1314, *pg.* 1059
ASCO POWER TECHNOLOGIES, L.P., 50 Hanover Rd, **Florham Park,** NJ 07932-1503, *pg.* 1314, *pg.* 1066
BOMAR INTERCONNECT PRODUCTS, INC., 1850 US Hwy 46, **Ledgewood,** NJ 07852, *pg.* 1318, *pg.* 1079
BOSCH INSPECTION TECHNOLOGY INC., 90 Boroline, **Allendale,** NJ 07401, *pg.* 1319, *pg.* 1041
BREEZE-EASTERN CORPORATION, 35 Melanie Ln, **Whippany,** NJ 07981, *pg.* 1319, *pg.* 1132
CLINTON INDUSTRIES, INC., 207 Redneck Ave, **Little Ferry,** NJ 07643-1320, *pg.* 1324, *pg.* 1079
CROLL-REYNOLDS COMPANY, INC., 6 Campus Dr, **Parsippany,** NJ 07054, *pg.* 1326, *pg.* 1103
THE DEWEY ELECTRONICS CORPORATION, 27 Muller Rd, **Oakland,** NJ 07436, *pg.* 1328, *pg.* 1099
ELECTROID CO, 45 Fadem Rd, **Springfield,** NJ 07081-3115, *pg.* 1333, *pg.* 1123

FANCORT INDUSTRIES, INC., 31 Fairfield Pl, **West Caldwell,** NJ 07006-6206, *pg.* 1336, *pg.* 1131
HOSOKAWA MICRON POWDER SYSTEMS, 10 Chatham Rd, **Summit,** NJ 07901, *pg.* 1347, *pg.* 1124
INDEL, INC., 10 Indel Ave, **Rancocas,** NJ 08073-0157, *pg.* 1348, *pg.* 1113
INDUCTOTHERM CORP., 10 Indel Ave, **Rancocas,** NJ 08073-0157, *pg.* 1348, *pg.* 1114
LEVER MANUFACTURING CORP., 420 Rte 17 S, **Mahwah,** NJ 07430, *pg.* 1355, *pg.* 1082
LINDE GAS LLC, 575 Mountain Ave, **New Providence,** NJ 07974-2097, *pg.* 1356, *pg.* 1095
MAGNETIC METALS CORP., 1900 Hayes Ave, **Camden,** NJ 08105, *pg.* 1358, *pg.* 1049
METALFAB, INC., Prices Switch Rd PO Box 9, **Vernon,** NJ 07462, *pg.* 1360, *pg.* 1127
MIDDLE ATLANTIC PRODUCTS INC., 300 Fairfield Rd, **Fairfield,** NJ 07004, *pg.* 1360, *pg.* 1065
MISTRAS GROUP, INC., 195 Clarksville Rd, **Princeton Junction,** NJ 08550, *pg.* 1362, *pg.* 1113
NATIONAL METAL FINISHING CORP., 897 S Ave, **Middlesex,** NJ 08846-2534, *pg.* 1363, *pg.* 1084
NRG ENERGY, INC., 211 Carnegie Ctr, **Princeton,** NJ 08540-6213, *pg.* 1366, *pg.* 1112
PERRY PRODUCTS CORPORATION, 25 Mount Laurel Rd, **Hainesport,** NJ 08036, *pg.* 1368, *pg.* 1072
PERRY VIDEX LLC, 25 Mt Laurel Rd, **Hainesport,** NJ 08036, *pg.* 1368, *pg.* 1072
POTDEVIN MACHINE COMPANY, 26 Fairfield Pl, **West Caldwell,** NJ 07006-6207, *pg.* 1369, *pg.* 1131
ROYLE SYSTEMS GROUP, 111 Bauer Dr, **Oakland,** NJ 07436, *pg.* 1373, *pg.* 1100
TDK-LAMBDA HIGH POWER DIVISION, 405 Essex Rd, **Neptune,** NJ 07753-7701, *pg.* 1380, *pg.* 1090
TITAN TOOL, INC., 107 Bauer Dr, **Oakland,** NJ 07436, *pg.* 1383, *pg.* 1100
UNEX MANUFACTURING, INC., 50 Progress Pl, **Jackson,** NJ 08527-3002, *pg.* 1385, *pg.* 1075
VALCOR ENGINEERING CORPORATION, 2 Lawrence Rd, **Springfield,** NJ 07081-3121, *pg.* 1386, *pg.* 1123
VIBRA SCREW INC., 755 Union Blvd, **Totowa,** NJ 07512-2207, *pg.* 1387, *pg.* 1126
WYSSMONT CO., INC., 1470 Bergen Blvd, **Fort Lee,** NJ 07024-2116, *pg.* 1390, *pg.* 1068

New York

ACME METAL CAP CO., INC., 3353 62nd St, **Woodside,** NY 11377-2235, *pg.* 1310, *pg.* 1356
ALSTOM SIGNALING, INC., 1025 John St, **West Henrietta,** NY 14586, *pg.* 1312, *pg.* 1350
AMERICAN CASTING & MANUFACTURING CORPORATION, 51 Comml St, **Plainview,** NY 11803-2401, *pg.* 1312, *pg.* 1321
AMERICAN FELT & FILTER COMPANY, 361 Walsh Ave, **New Windsor,** NY 12553-6727, *pg.* 1312, *pg.* 1184
ARGO INTERNATIONAL CORPORATION, 140 Franklin St, **New York,** NY 10013, *pg.* 1314, *pg.* 1196
ATLAS COPCO COMPTEC LLC, 46 School Rd, **Voorheesville,** NY 12186-9608, *pg.* 1314, *pg.* 1349
AWISCO NY CORPORATION, 55-15 43rd St, **Maspeth,** NY 11378, *pg.* 1315, *pg.* 1177
BELMONT METALS, INC., 330 Belmont Ave, **Brooklyn,** NY 11207, *pg.* 1317, *pg.* 1145
CEMTREX, INC., 19 Engineers Ln, **Farmingdale,** NY 11735, *pg.* 1322, *pg.* 1159
COLUMBUS MCKINNON CORPORATION, 140 John James Audubon Pkwy, **Amherst,** NY 14228-1112, *pg.* 1325, *pg.* 1138
CONAX TECHNOLOGIES LLC, 2300 Walden Ave, **Buffalo,** NY 14225-4740, *pg.* 1325, *pg.* 1148
DFCI SOLUTIONS INC., 425 Union Blvd, **West Islip,** NY 11795-3116, *pg.* 1328, *pg.* 1350
EASTMAN MACHINE COMPANY, 779 Washington St, **Buffalo,** NY 14203-1308, *pg.* 1331, *pg.* 1148
EDWARDS VACUUM, INC., 6416 Inducon Dr W, **Sanborn,** NY 14132, *pg.* 1332, *pg.* 1340
FLEXBAR MACHINE CORP., 250 Gibbs Rd, **Islandia,** NY 11749-2612, *pg.* 1337, *pg.* 1169
GIBRALTAR INDUSTRIES, INC., 3556 Lake Shore Rd, **Buffalo,** NY 14219-1445, *pg.* 1340, *pg.* 1148
GLEASON CORPORATION, 1000 University Ave, **Rochester,** NY 14607-1239, *pg.* 1340, *pg.* 1335
THE GLEASON WORKS, 1000 University Ave, **Rochester,** NY 14607-1239, *pg.* 1341, *pg.* 1336
GOULDS PUMPS, INCORPORATED, 240 Fall St, **Seneca Falls,** NY 13148-1590, *pg.* 1342, *pg.* 1341
GRAPHITE METALLIZING CORPORATION, 1050 Nepperhan Ave, **Yonkers,** NY 10703, *pg.* 1343, *pg.* 1356
HANNAY REELS INC., 553 State Rte 143, **Westerlo,** NY 12193-0159, *pg.* 1344, *pg.* 1351
HARDINGE INC., 1 Hardinge Dr, **Elmira,** NY 14903, *pg.* 1344, *pg.* 1157
IMERYS FUSED MINERALS, 2000 College Ave M, **Niagara Falls,** NY 14305-1734, *pg.* 1348, *pg.* 1317
INTERNATIONAL CONTROLS & MEASUREMENTS CORP., 7313 William Barry Blvd, **North Syracuse,** NY 13212, *pg.* 1350, *pg.* 1317
ITOCHU INTERNATIONAL INC., 335 Madison Ave, **New York,** NY 10017-4611, *pg.* 1351, *pg.* 1245
ITT CORPORATION, 1133 Westchester Ave, **White Plains,** NY 10604, *pg.* 1351, *pg.* 1354
KAWASAKI HEAVY INDUSTRIES (U.S.A.), INC., 60 E 42nd St Ste 2501, **New York,** NY 10165, *pg.* 1352, *pg.* 1248
LAKELAND INDUSTRIES, INC., 701 Koehler Ave Ste 7, **Ronkonkoma,** NY 11779-7403, *pg.* 1354, *pg.* 1338
PRECIPART, 80 Finn Ct, **Farmingdale,** NY 11735-1107, *pg.* 1370, *pg.* 1160
RENOLD, INC., 100 Bourne St, **Westfield,** NY 14787-9706, *pg.* 1371, *pg.* 1351
RING PRECISION COMPONENTS, 2980 Turner Rd, **Jamestown,** NY 14701, *pg.* 1372, *pg.* 1170
S. HOWES, INC., 25 Howard St, **Silver Creek,** NY 14136-1007, *pg.* 1373, *pg.* 1342
SENECA FALLS MACHINES, 314 Fall St, **Seneca Falls,** NY 13148-1543, *pg.* 1374, *pg.* 1341
SERVOTRONICS, INC., 1110 Maple Rd, **Elma,** NY 14059-9573, *pg.* 1375, *pg.* 1157
SPX PROCESS EQUIPMENT, 135 Mt Read Blvd, **Rochester,** NY 14611, *pg.* 1378, *pg.* 1337
ULTRALIFE CORPORATION, 2000 Technology Pkwy, **Newark,** NY 14513-2175, *pg.* 1385, *pg.* 1317
WSF INDUSTRIES, INC., 7 Hackett Dr, **Tonawanda,** NY 14150-3711, *pg.* 1390, *pg.* 1346
YOUNG & FRANKLIN, INC., 942 Old Liverpool Rd, **Liverpool,** NY 13088-5552, *pg.* 1391, *pg.* 1174

North Carolina

ABB INC., 9000 Regency, **Cary,** NC 27511, *pg.* 1309, *pg.* 1359
BLUE RHINO CORPORATION, 5620 University Pkwy, # 300, **Winston Salem,** NC 27105, *pg.* 1318, *pg.* 1393
CONBRACO INDUSTRIES INC., 701 Matthews Mint Hill Rd, **Matthews,** NC 28105-1706, *pg.* 1325, *pg.* 1382
ENGINEERED CONTROLS INTERNATIONAL LLC, 100 Rego Dr, **Elon,** NC 27244-9159, *pg.* 1334, *pg.* 1372
ENPRO INDUSTRIES, INC., 5605 Carnegie Blvd Ste 500, **Charlotte,** NC 28209, *pg.* 1334, *pg.* 1366
FLANDERS CORPORATION, 531 Flanders Filters Rd, **Washington,** NC 27889, *pg.* 1336, *pg.* 1392
FLETCHER INDUSTRIES, INC., 1485 Central Dr, **Southern Pines,** NC 28387-2105, *pg.* 1337, *pg.* 1390
GAINES MOTOR LINES INCORPORATED, 2349 13th Ave SW, **Hickory,** NC 28602, *pg.* 1338, *pg.* 1378
GAS-FIRED PRODUCTS, INC., 305 Doggett St, **Charlotte,** NC 28203-4923, *pg.* 1338, *pg.* 1367
INGERSOLL-RAND COMPANY, 800 E Beaty St, **Davidson,** NC 28036, *pg.* 1349, *pg.* 1370
KURZ TRANSFER PRODUCTS, L.P., 3200 Woodpark Blvd, **Charlotte,** NC 28206, *pg.* 1354, *pg.* 1367
LORD CORPORATION, 111 Lord Dr, **Cary,** NC 27511, *pg.* 1357, *pg.* 1360
OKUMA AMERICA CORPORATION, 11900 Westhall Dr, **Charlotte,** NC 28278-7127, *pg.* 1366, *pg.* 1368
TIPPER TIE, INC., 2000 Lufkin Rd, **Apex,** NC 27502, *pg.* 1382, *pg.* 1358
U.S. BOTTLERS MACHINERY COMPANY, 11911 Steele Creek Rd, **Charlotte,** NC 28273-3773, *pg.* 1386, *pg.* 1369

North Dakota

BUTLER MACHINERY COMPANY, 3401 33rd St SW, **Fargo,** ND 58104, *pg.* 1321, *pg.* 1397
TITAN MACHINERY INC., 644 E Beaton Dr, **Fargo,** ND 58078-2648, *pg.* 1383, *pg.* 1398

Ohio

AK STEEL HOLDING CORPORATION, 9227 Centre Point Dr, **West Chester,** OH 45069, *pg.* 1311, *pg.* 1479
AKRON BRASS COMPANY, 343 Venture Blvd, **Wooster,** OH 44691, *pg.* 1311, *pg.* 1482
ALLIED CONSTRUCTION PRODUCTS, LLC, 3900 Kelley Ave, **Cleveland,** OH 44114-4536, *pg.* 1311, *pg.* 1427
ANDERSON INTERNATIONAL CORP., 4545 Boyce Pkwy, **Stow,** OH 44224-1770, *pg.* 1313, *pg.* 1474
AUTOMATIC EQUIPMENT CORPORATION, 4699 Inter State Dr, **Cincinnati,** OH 45246, *pg.* 1315, *pg.* 1410
BARDONS & OLIVER, INC., 5800 Harper Rd, **Solon,** OH 44139-1833, *pg.* 1316, *pg.* 1472
BAYLOFF STAMPED PRODUCTS, 8091 State Route 5, **Kinsman,** OH 44428-9628, *pg.* 1317, *pg.* 1457
BRENNAN INDUSTRIES INC., 6701 Cochran Rd, **Cleveland,** OH 44139, *pg.* 1319, *pg.* 1429
THE CINCINNATI GILBERT MACHINE TOOL COMPANY, L.L.C., 3366 Beekman St, **Cincinnati,** OH 45223-2424, *pg.* 1323, *pg.* 1411
CONSOLIDATED METAL PRODUCTS, INC., 1028 Depot St, **Cincinnati,** OH 45204-2012, *pg.* 1325, *pg.* 1412
CRES-COR, 5925 Heisley Rd, **Mentor,** OH 44060-1833, *pg.* 1326, *pg.* 1464
DAYTON SUPERIOR CORPORATION, 1125 Byers Rd, **Miamisburg,** OH 45342-5765, *pg.* 1328, *pg.* 1464
DOYLE SYSTEMS, 5186 New Haven Cir, **Barberton,** OH 44203, *pg.* 1330, *pg.* 1404
EATON CORPORATION, Eaton Ctr 1111 Superior Ave, **Cleveland,** OH 44114-2584, *pg.* 1331, *pg.* 1429
EMERSON CLIMATE TECHNOLOGIES, INC., 1675 W Campbell Rd, **Sidney,** OH 45365-2479, *pg.* 1333, *pg.* 1472
ERICO INTERNATIONAL CORPORATION, 3100 Solon Rd, **Solon,** OH 44139-2221, *pg.* 1335, *pg.* 1472
FEINTOOL EQUIPMENT CORP., 6833 Creek Rd, **Cincinnati,** OH 45242, *pg.* 1336, *pg.* 1413
FREEWAY CORPORATION, 9301 Allen Dr, **Cleveland,** OH 44125-4632, *pg.* 1338, *pg.* 1431
GLEASON - M&M PRECISION SYSTEMS CORPORATION, 300 Progress Rd, **West Carrollton,** OH 45449, *pg.* 1341, *pg.* 1479
THE GORMAN-RUPP COMPANY, 600 S Airport Rd, **Mansfield,** OH 44903, *pg.* 1341, *pg.* 1458
HEAT SEAL LLC, 4580 E 71 St, **Cleveland,** OH 44125, *pg.* 1345, *pg.* 1431
HOBART BROTHERS COMPANY, 101 Trade Sq E, **Troy,** OH 45373-2463, *pg.* 1346, *pg.* 1477
HOBART CORPORATION, 701 S Rdg Ave, **Troy,** OH 45374, *pg.* 1346, *pg.* 1477
INTELLIGRATED, INC., 7901 Innovation Way, **Mason,** OH 45040, *pg.* 1349, *pg.* 1460
INTELLIGRATED SYSTEMS INC., 10045 International Blvd, **Cincinnati,** OH 45246-4845, *pg.* 1349, *pg.* 1414
KADANT BLACK CLAWSON INC., 7312 Central Parke Blvd, **Mason,** OH 45040, *pg.* 1352, *pg.* 1460
LINCOLN ELECTRIC HOLDINGS, INC., 22801 Saint Clair Ave, **Cleveland,** OH 44117-2524, *pg.* 1355, *pg.* 1432
LINDE HYDRAULICS CORPORATION, 5089 Western Reserve Rd PO Box 82, **Canfield,** OH 44406, *pg.* 1356, *pg.* 1407
LOUIS BERKMAN CO., 330 N 7th St, **Steubenville,** OH 43952, *pg.* 1357, *pg.* 1473
MAKINO INC., 7680 A Innovation Way, **Mason,** OH 45040, *pg.* 1358, *pg.* 1461
MATERION CORPORATION, 6070 Parkland Blvd, **Mayfield Heights,** OH 44124, *pg.* 1359, *pg.* 1463
MAYFRAN INTERNATIONAL, INC., 6650 Beta Dr, **Cleveland,** OH 44143, *pg.* 1359, *pg.* 1432
MCNEIL & NRM INC., 96 E Crosier St, **Akron,** OH 44311, *pg.* 1360, *pg.* 1402
MILACRON LLC, 4165 Half Acre Rd, **Batavia,** OH 45103, *pg.* 1361, *pg.* 1405
MOOG FLO-TORK, 1701 N Main St, **Orrville,** OH 44667-9172, *pg.* 1363, *pg.* 1469
NATIONAL MACHINERY LLC, 161 Greenfield St, **Tiffin,** OH 44883-2422, *pg.* 1363, *pg.* 1475
THE NOLAN COMPANY, 1016 9th St SW, **Canton,** OH 44707-4108, *pg.* 1365, *pg.* 1408
NORDSON CORPORATION, 28601 Clemens Rd, **Westlake,** OH 44145-1148, *pg.* 1365, *pg.* 1480
NOSHOK INC., 1010 W Bagley Rd, **Berea,** OH 44017, *pg.* 1366, *pg.* 1406
OSBORN INTERNATIONAL, 1100 Resource Dr Ste 1, **Brooklyn Heights,** OH 44131, *pg.* 1367, *pg.* 1406

First page reference indicates Business Class Edition
Second page reference indicates Geographic Edition

PARKER HANNIFIN CORPORATION, 6035 Parkland Blvd, **Cleveland,** OH 44124-4141, *pg.* 1368, *pg.* 1434
PLANET PRODUCTS CORPORATION, 4200 Malsbary Rd, **Cincinnati,** OH 45242-5510, *pg.* 1369, *pg.* 1418
PNEUMATICSCALEANGELUS, 10 Ascot Pkwy, **Cuyahoga Falls,** OH 44223-3325, *pg.* 1369, *pg.* 1445
PREFORMED LINE PRODUCTS COMPANY, 660 Beta Dr, **Cleveland,** OH 44143-2355, *pg.* 1370, *pg.* 1434
PRESSCO TECHNOLOGY INC., 29200 Aurora Rd, **Cleveland,** OH 44139, *pg.* 1370, *pg.* 1434
RIDGE TOOL COMPANY, 400 Clark St, **Elyria,** OH 44035-6108, *pg.* 1372, *pg.* 1452
SENCO PRODUCTS, INC., 4270 Ivy Point Blvd, **Cincinnati,** OH 45242, *pg.* 1374, *pg.* 1425
SHILOH INDUSTRIES, INC., 880 Steel Dr, **Valley City,** OH 44280, *pg.* 1375, *pg.* 1478
SHOPSMITH, INC., 6530 Poe Ave, **Dayton,** OH 45414, *pg.* 1375, *pg.* 1446
SIEMENS, 105 N Sandusky St, **Mount Vernon,** OH 43050-2495, *pg.* 1376, *pg.* 1466
SLY, INC., 8300 Dow Cir, **Strongsville,** OH 44136-1760, *pg.* 1376, *pg.* 1475
TECHNIBUS LLC, 1501 Raff Rd SW, **Canton,** OH 44710, *pg.* 1380, *pg.* 1408
TORRMETAL CORPORATION, 12125 Bennington Ave, **Cleveland,** OH 44135, *pg.* 1383, *pg.* 1436
WASHINGTON PRODUCTS INC., 1875 Harsh Ave SE, **Massillon,** OH 44646, *pg.* 1387, *pg.* 1461
WEBSTER INDUSTRIES INC., 325 Hall St, **Tiffin,** OH 44883-1419, *pg.* 1388, *pg.* 1475
WESTERN STATES MACHINE COMPANY, PO Box 327, **Hamilton,** OH 45012-0327, *pg.* 1388, *pg.* 1455
WISCO PRODUCTS, INC., 109 Commercial St, **Dayton,** OH 45402-2211, *pg.* 1389, *pg.* 1447
THE WM. POWELL COMPANY, 2503 Spring Grove Ave, **Cincinnati,** OH 45214-1729, *pg.* 1389, *pg.* 1427
THE WOLF MACHINE CO., 5570 Creek Rd, **Cincinnati,** OH 45242-4004, *pg.* 1389, *pg.* 1427
THE W.W. WILLIAMS COMPANY, 835 W Goodale Blvd, **Columbus,** OH 43212, *pg.* 1390, *pg.* 1444
XTEK, INC., 11451 Reading Rd, **Cincinnati,** OH 45241-2246, *pg.* 1390, *pg.* 1427

Oklahoma

CHARLES MACHINE WORKS, INC., 1959 W Fir Ave, **Perry,** OK 73077-5803, *pg.* 1322, *pg.* 1488
CORKEN, INC., 3805 NW 36th St, **Oklahoma City,** OK 73112, *pg.* 1325, *pg.* 1485
THE GEORGE E. FAILING COMPANY, 2215 S Van Buren St, **Enid,** OK 73701, *pg.* 1340, *pg.* 1484
HILTI, INC., 5400 S 122nd Et Ave, **Tulsa,** OK 74146-6007, *pg.* 1346, *pg.* 1490
LITTLE GIANT PUMP COMPANY, 3810 N Tulsa St, **Oklahoma City,** OK 73112-2935, *pg.* 1356, *pg.* 1486
REEL-O-MATIC, INC., 6408 S Eastern Ave, **Oklahoma City,** OK 73149-5134, *pg.* 1371, *pg.* 1487
T.D. WILLIAMSON, INC., 6120 S Yale Ave Ste 1700, **Tulsa,** OK 74136-4235, *pg.* 1380, *pg.* 1490

Oregon

ATI WAH CHANG, 1600 Old Salem Rd NE, **Albany,** OR 97321-4548, *pg.* 1314, *pg.* 1492
CASCADE CORPORATION, 2201 NE 201st Ave, **Fairview,** OR 97024-9718, *pg.* 1321, *pg.* 1497
ESCO CORPORATION, 2141 NW 25th Ave, **Portland,** OR 97210, *pg.* 1335, *pg.* 1502
HYSTER-YALE MATERIALS HANDLING, 650 NE Holladay St Ste 1600, **Portland,** OR 97232-2045, *pg.* 1347, *pg.* 1503
PECO, INC., 4707 SE 17th Ave, **Portland,** OR 97202-4714, *pg.* 1368, *pg.* 1505
POWIN CORPORATION, 20550 SW 115th Ave, **Tualatin,** OR 97062-6857, *pg.* 1369, *pg.* 1509
SCHMITT INDUSTRIES, INC., 2765 NW Nicolai St, **Portland,** OR 97210, *pg.* 1374, *pg.* 1506

Pennsylvania

AKRION, INC., 6330 Hedgewood Dr Ste 150, **Allentown,** PA 18106, *pg.* 1311, *pg.* 1513
AMERICAN CRANE & EQUIPMENT CORPORATION, 531 Old Swede Rd, **Douglassville,** PA 19518-1205, *pg.* 1312, *pg.* 1526
AMPCO-PITTSBURGH CORPORATION, 600 Grant St Ste 4600, **Pittsburgh,** PA 15219-2700, *pg.* 1313, *pg.* 1573
AUTOMATION DEVICES, INC., 7050 W Ridge Rd, **Fairview,** PA 16415-2099, *pg.* 1315, *pg.* 1532
BOSCH REXROTH CORPORATION, 2315 City Line Rd, **Bethlehem,** PA 18017, *pg.* 1319, *pg.* 1516
BRIDON AMERICAN CORP., 280 New Commerce Blvd, **Wilkes Barre,** PA 18706-1448, *pg.* 1319, *pg.* 1594
DANAHER MOTION, 110 Westtown Rd, **West Chester,** PA 19382-4978, *pg.* 1327, *pg.* 1593
ELLIOTT COMPANY, 901 N 4th St, **Jeannette,** PA 15644-1473, *pg.* 1333, *pg.* 1542
ELLWOOD CITY FORGE, 800 Commercial Ave PO Box 31, **Ellwood City,** PA 16117-2354, *pg.* 1333, *pg.* 1529
ELLWOOD NATIONAL FORGE COMPANY, LLC, 1 Front St, **Irvine,** PA 16329, *pg.* 1333, *pg.* 1542
ENERSYS INC., 2366 Bernville Rd, **Reading,** PA 19605, *pg.* 1334, *pg.* 1584
ERIEZ MANUFACTURING CO. INC., 2200 Asbury Rd, **Erie,** PA 16506-1402, *pg.* 1335, *pg.* 1530
EVOQUA, 181 Thorn Hill Rd, **Warrendale,** PA 15086, *pg.* 1336, *pg.* 1590
FENNER DRIVES, 311 W Stiegel St, **Manheim,** PA 17545-1747, *pg.* 1336, *pg.* 1551
FLIGHT SYSTEMS, INC., 505 Fishing Creek Rd, **Lewisberry,** PA 17339-9517, *pg.* 1337, *pg.* 1548
THE FROG, SWITCH & MANUFACTURING COMPANY, 600 E High St, **Carlisle,** PA 17013-2651, *pg.* 1338, *pg.* 1520
GARDNER DENVER, INC., 1500 Liberty Ridge Dr Ste 300, **Wayne,** PA 19087, *pg.* 1338, *pg.* 1592
GE WATER & PROCESS TECHNOLOGIES, 4636 Somerton Rd, **Trevose,** PA 19053-6742, *pg.* 1339, *pg.* 1588
GREENE, TWEED & CO., 2075 Detwiler Rd, **Kulpsville,** PA 19443, *pg.* 1344, *pg.* 1544
HARRINGTON HOISTS, INC., 401 W End Ave, **Manheim,** PA 17545-1754, *pg.* 1345, *pg.* 1551
HAUCK MANUFACTURING COMPANY, INC., 100 N Harris St, **Cleona,** PA 17042, *pg.* 1345, *pg.* 1522
JLG INDUSTRIES, INC., 1 JLG Dr, **McConnellsburg,** PA 17233-9533, *pg.* 1351, *pg.* 1551
JOY MINING MACHINERY, 177 Thorn Hill Rd, **Warrendale,** PA 15086, *pg.* 1352, *pg.* 1591
KENNAMETAL EXTRUDE HONE, 235 Industry Blvd, **Irwin,** PA 15642-2794, *pg.* 1352, *pg.* 1542
KEYSTONE POWDERED METAL COMPANY, 251 State St, **Saint Marys,** PA 15857, *pg.* 1353, *pg.* 1585
L.B. FOSTER COMPANY, 415 Holiday Dr, **Pittsburgh,** PA 15220, *pg.* 1355, *pg.* 1578
MANITOWOC CRANE SHADY GROVE, 1565 Buchanan Trail E, **Shady Grove,** PA 17256, *pg.* 1359, *pg.* 1586
MARMON/KEYSTONE CORPORATION, 225 E Cunningham St, **Butler,** PA 16001-6018, *pg.* 1359, *pg.* 1519
MEADVILLE FORGING COMPANY INC., 15309 Baldwin St Ext, **Meadville,** PA 16335, *pg.* 1360, *pg.* 1552
MILTON ROY COMPANY, 201 Ivyland Rd, **Ivyland,** PA 18974-1706, *pg.* 1361, *pg.* 1542
MINE SAFETY APPLIANCES COMPANY, MSA Corp Center 1000 Cranberry Woods Dr, **Cranberry,** PA 16066, *pg.* 1361, *pg.* 1525
NETZSCH PUMPS NORTH AMERICA, LLC, 119 Pickering Way, **Exton,** PA 19431-1393, *pg.* 1364, *pg.* 1532
PARAGON TECHNOLOGIES, INC., 600 Kuebler Rd, **Easton,** PA 18040-9201, *pg.* 1367, *pg.* 1528
PHILADELPHIA GEAR CORPORATION, 901 E 8th Ave Ste 100, **King of Prussia,** PA 19406-1354, *pg.* 1368, *pg.* 1544
PRECISION ROLL GRINDERS, INC., 6356 Chapmans Rd, **Allentown,** PA 18106-9364, *pg.* 1370, *pg.* 1514
PTC ALLIANCE CORP., 6051 Wallace Rd Ext Ste 200, **Wexford,** PA 15090, *pg.* 1370, *pg.* 1594
SEASTAR SOLUTIONS, 640 N Lewis Rd, **Limerick,** PA 19468-1228, *pg.* 1374, *pg.* 1548
SHINGLE BELTING COMPANY, 420 Drew Ct, **King of Prussia,** PA 19406, *pg.* 1375, *pg.* 1544
SHOP-VAC CORPORATION, 2323 Reach Rd, **Williamsport,** PA 17701-5579, *pg.* 1375, *pg.* 1595
SIEMENS PROCESS INDUSTRIES AND DRIVE, 1201 Sumneytown Pike, **Spring House,** PA 19477-1019, *pg.* 1376, *pg.* 1587
SMITHCO, INC., 34 West Ave, **Wayne,** PA 19087, *pg.* 1377, *pg.* 1592
SPX PROCESS EQUIPMENT, 5620 W Rd, **McKean,** PA 16426, *pg.* 1378, *pg.* 1551
SPX THERMAL PRODUCT SOLUTIONS, 2821 Old Rt 15, **New Columbia,** PA 17856, *pg.* 1378, *pg.* 1555
STRAHMAN VALVES, INC., 2801 Baglyos Cir Lehigh Vly Indus Pk VI, **Bethlehem,** PA 18020, *pg.* 1379, *pg.* 1517
TEI STRUTHERS WELLS, 36 Clark St, **Warren,** PA 16365, *pg.* 1381, *pg.* 1590
VOITH HYDRO INC., 760 E Berlin Rd, **York,** PA 17408, *pg.* 1387, *pg.* 1598
VOSSLOH TRACK MATERIAL, INC., 5662 Leesport Ave, **Reading,** PA 19605-9802, *pg.* 1387, *pg.* 1585
WELDON SOLUTIONS, 425 E Berlin Rd, **York,** PA 17408, *pg.* 1388, *pg.* 1598
WESTINGHOUSE AIR BRAKE TECHNOLOGIES CORPORATION, 1001 Air Brake Ave, **Wilmerding,** PA 15148-1036, *pg.* 1388, *pg.* 1595
YARDLEY PRODUCTS CORPORATION, 10 W College Ave, **Yardley,** PA 19067-1517, *pg.* 1391, *pg.* 1596

Rhode Island

MAHR FEDERAL, INC., 1144 Eddy St, **Providence,** RI 02905-4511, *pg.* 1358, *pg.* 1606
VIBCO INC., 75 Stilson Rd, **Wyoming,** RI 02898, *pg.* 1387, *pg.* 1611

South Carolina

BOILER TUBE COMPANY OF AMERICA, 506 Charlotte Hwy, **Lyman,** SC 29365, *pg.* 1318, *pg.* 1620
ESAB WELDING & CUTTING PRODUCTS, 411 S Ebenezer Rd, **Florence,** SC 29501-7916, *pg.* 1335, *pg.* 1615
HARSCO RAIL, 2401 Edmund Hwy Box 20, **West Columbia,** SC 29171-0020, *pg.* 1345, *pg.* 1623
THE INTERTECH GROUP, INC., 4838 Jenkins Ave, **Charleston,** SC 29405-4816, *pg.* 1350, *pg.* 1613
KENNAMETAL IPG, 1662 MacMillan Park Dr, **Fort Mill,** SC 29707, *pg.* 1353, *pg.* 1615
MCLAUGHLIN BORING SYSTEMS, 2006 Perimeter Rd, **Greenville,** SC 29605, *pg.* 1360, *pg.* 1617
THE SCHMIDT GROUP, INC., I 385 At Roper Mtn Rd, **Greenville,** SC 29615, *pg.* 1374, *pg.* 1618
SOUTH CAROLINA MANUFACTURING EXTENSION PARTNERSHIP, 1301 Gervais St Ste 910, **Columbia,** SC 29201-3344, *pg.* 1377, *pg.* 1614
TUFFALOY PRODUCTS, INC., 1400 S Batesville Rd, **Greer,** SC 29650-4809, *pg.* 1385, *pg.* 1619

South Dakota

GROSSENBURG IMPLEMENT, INC., 31341 US Hwy 18, **Winner,** SD 57580-6484, *pg.* 1344, *pg.* 1626
KPI-JCI, 700 W 21st St, **Yankton,** SD 57078, *pg.* 1354, *pg.* 1626
NUTTING, 450 Pheasant Ridge Dr, **Watertown,** SD 57201-5610, *pg.* 1366, *pg.* 1626
SCOTCHMAN INDUSTRIES, INC., 180 E Hwy 14, **Philip,** SD 57567, *pg.* 1374, *pg.* 1624

Tennessee

CORLEY MANUFACTURING CO., 2900 Crescent Cir, **Chattanooga,** TN 37407, *pg.* 1326, *pg.* 1628
EMERSON PROCESS MANAGEMENT, 835 Innovation Dr, **Knoxville,** TN 37932-2563, *pg.* 1334, *pg.* 1636
ITW DYNATEC, 31 Volunteer Dr, **Hendersonville,** TN 37075-3156, *pg.* 1351, *pg.* 1635
NN, INC., 2000 Waters Edge Dr Ste 12, **Johnson City,** TN 37604-8318, *pg.* 1365, *pg.* 1635
PIERCE EQUIPMENT, 1247 Northgate Bus Pkwy, **Madison,** TN 37115, *pg.* 1369, *pg.* 1640
POWER EQUIPMENT COMPANY INC, 3300 Alcoa Hwy, **Knoxville,** TN 37920-5558, *pg.* 1369, *pg.* 1637

Texas

ABATIX CORP., 2400 Skyline Dr, **Dallas,** TX 75149, *pg.* 1309, *pg.* 1672
ACTIVE POWER, INC., 2128 W Braker Ln BK 12, **Austin,** TX 78758, *pg.* 1310, *pg.* 1660
ALAMO GROUP INC., 1627 East Walnut, **Seguin,** TX 78155-5202, *pg.* 1311, *pg.* 1745
ALAMO IRON WORKS, 943 AT&T Ctr Pkwy, **San Antonio,** TX 78219, *pg.* 1311, *pg.* 1739
THE ALLIED POWER GROUP, 10131 Mills Rd, **Houston,** TX 77070, *pg.* 1312, *pg.* 1699

AMERICAN GILSONITE CO., 1717 St James Pl Ste 600, **Houston,** TX 77056, *pg.* 1313, *pg.* 1700
APW WYOTT FOOD SERVICE EQUIPMENT, INC., 1307 N Watters Rd Ste 180, **Allen,** TX 75013, *pg.* 1314, *pg.* 1658
BAKER HUGHES INCORPORATED, 2929 Allen Pkwy Ste 2100, **Houston,** TX 77019, *pg.* 1315, *pg.* 1700
BAKER HUGHES INTEQ, 2001 Rankin Rd, **Houston,** TX 77073-5114, *pg.* 1316, *pg.* 1700
CAMERON DRILLING & PRODUCTION SYSTEMS, 4646 W Sam Houston Pkwy N, **Houston,** TX 77041, *pg.* 1321, *pg.* 1702
CAMERON VALVES & MEASUREMENT, 3250 Briarpark Dr Ste 300, **Houston,** TX 77042-4239, *pg.* 1321, *pg.* 1703
DRIL-QUIP, INC., 6401 N.Eldridge Parkway, **Houston,** TX 77040-5851, *pg.* 1330, *pg.* 1704
ENCON SAFETY PRODUCTS, 6825 W Sam Houston Pkwy N, **Houston,** TX 77041-4026, *pg.* 1334, *pg.* 1705
ENTECH SOLAR, INC., 13301 Park Vista Blvd Ste 100, **Fort Worth,** TX 76177, *pg.* 1335, *pg.* 1694
EQUIPMENT DEPOT LTD., 4100 S Interstate 35, **Waco,** TX 76706, *pg.* 1335, *pg.* 1749
THE FLEXITALLIC GROUP, 6915 Hwy 225, **Deer Park,** TX 77536-2414, *pg.* 1337, *pg.* 1691
HACO-ATLANTIC, INC., 11629 N Houston Rosslyn Rd, **Houston,** TX 77086, *pg.* 1344, *pg.* 1707
ION GEOPHYSICAL CORPORATION, 2105 CityWest Blvd Ste 400, **Houston,** TX 77042-2839, *pg.* 1350, *pg.* 1708
LUFKIN INDUSTRIES, INC., 601 S Raguet St, **Lufkin,** TX 75904-3951, *pg.* 1357, *pg.* 1726
MIETHER BEARING PRODUCTS, INC., 8720 N County Rd W, **Odessa,** TX 79764-1926, *pg.* 1361, *pg.* 1728
NATIONAL OILWELL VARCO, INC., 7909 Parkwood Cir Dr, **Houston,** TX 77036, *pg.* 1364, *pg.* 1712
NCI BUILDING SYSTEMS, INC., 10943 N Sam Houston Pkwy W, **Houston,** TX 77064, *pg.* 1364, *pg.* 1712
PMFG, INC., 14651 N Dallas Pkwy Ste 500, **Dallas,** TX 75254, *pg.* 1369, *pg.* 1685
PURVIS BEARING SERVICE LTD., 10500 N Stemmons Fwy, **Dallas,** TX 75220, *pg.* 1371, *pg.* 1686
RUG DOCTOR, LP, 4701 Old Shepard Pl, **Plano,** TX 75093-5218, *pg.* 1373, *pg.* 1734
SAMMONS ENTERPRISES, INC., 5949 Sherry Ln Ste 1900, **Dallas,** TX 75225-8015, *pg.* 1373, *pg.* 1686
SCHLUMBERGER WELL COMPLETIONS, 7030 Ardmore St, **Houston,** TX 77054-2302, *pg.* 1373, *pg.* 1714
SMITH INTERNATIONAL, INC., 1301 Rankin Rd, **Houston,** TX 77073, *pg.* 1377, *pg.* 1715
TELSCO INDUSTRIES, INC., 3301 W Kingsley Rd, **Garland,** TX 75041-2207, *pg.* 1381, *pg.* 1698
TIDEL ENGINEERING, L.P., Ste 114 2025 W Belt Line Rd, **Carrollton,** TX 75006-6453, *pg.* 1382, *pg.* 1670
TRANTER PHE, INC., 1900 Old Burk Hwy, **Wichita Falls,** TX 76307, *pg.* 1383, *pg.* 1749
URS CORPORATION, Amber Oaks 9400 Amberglen Blvd, **Austin,** TX 78729, *pg.* 1386, *pg.* 1667

Utah

ARNOLD MACHINERY COMPANY, 2975 West 2100 South PO Box 30020, **Salt Lake City,** UT 84119-1207, *pg.* 1314, *pg.* 1755

Vermont

BRYANT GRINDER, 65 Pearl St, **Springfield,** VT 05156, *pg.* 1320, *pg.* 1768
DYNAPOWER CORPORATION, 85 Meadowland Dr, **South Burlington,** VT 05403, *pg.* 1330, *pg.* 1768

Virginia

AMF BAKERY SYSTEMS, 2115 W Laburnum Ave, **Richmond,** VA 23227-4315, *pg.* 1313, *pg.* 1800
GE INTELLIGENT PLATFORMS, 2500 Austin Dr, **Charlottesville,** VA 22911, *pg.* 1339, *pg.* 1777
KSB INC., 4415 Sarellen Rd, **Richmond,** VA 23231-4428, *pg.* 1354, *pg.* 1802
MEASUREMENT SPECIALTIES INC., 1000 Lucas Way, **Hampton,** VA 23666-1573, *pg.* 1360, *pg.* 1783
SWISSLOG LOGISTICS, 161 Enterprise Dr, **Newport News,** VA 23603, *pg.* 1380, *pg.* 1796

Washington

ALGAS-SDI, 151 S Michigan, **Seattle,** WA 98108, *pg.* 1311, *pg.* 1831
BELSHAW ADAMATIC BAKERY GROUP, 814 44th St NW Ste 103, **Auburn,** WA 98001, *pg.* 1317, *pg.* 1813
CONSOLIDATED METCO INC., 5701 SE Columbia Way, **Vancouver,** WA 98661, *pg.* 1325, *pg.* 1846
FLOW INTERNATIONAL CORPORATION, 23500 64th Ave S, **Kent,** WA 98032, *pg.* 1337, *pg.* 1821
NORTH STAR ICE EQUIPMENT CORPORATION, 8151 Occidental Ave S, **Seattle,** WA 98108, *pg.* 1366, *pg.* 1838
OUTERWALL INC., 1800 114th Ave SE, **Bellevue,** WA 98004-6946, *pg.* 1367, *pg.* 1816

West Virginia

HELMICK CORPORATION, 998 Minor Ave, **Fairmont,** WV 26554-3682, *pg.* 1346, *pg.* 1849
SPECIAL METALS CORPORATION, 3200 Riverside Dr, **Huntington,** WV 25705, *pg.* 1377, *pg.* 1850
WOODCRAFT SUPPLY CORP., 1177 Rosemar Rd, **Parkersburg,** WV 26105-8272, *pg.* 1390, *pg.* 1850

Wisconsin

A.O. SMITH CORPORATION, 11270 W Park Pl, **Milwaukee,** WI 53224-9508, *pg.* 1313, *pg.* 1872
DORNER MANUFACTURING CORP., 975 Cottonwood Ave, **Hartland,** WI 53029, *pg.* 1329, *pg.* 1861
DUMORE CORPORATION, 1030 Veterans St, **Mauston,** WI 53948-9314, *pg.* 1330, *pg.* 1869
DYNATECT MANUFACTURING INC., 2300 S Calhoun Rd, **New Berlin,** WI 53151-2708, *pg.* 1330, *pg.* 1883
FLAMBEAU, INC., 801 Lynn Ave, **Baraboo,** WI 53913, *pg.* 1336, *pg.* 1854
GEHL COMPANY, 1 Gehl Way, **West Bend,** WI 53095-3415, *pg.* 1339, *pg.* 1899
GENERAC HOLDINGS INC., S45 W29290 Hwy 59, **Waukesha,** WI 53187, *pg.* 1340, *pg.* 1897
GENERAC POWER SYSTEMS INC., Hillside Rd & Hwy 59, **Waukesha,** WI 53187, *pg.* 1340, *pg.* 1898
GLEASON INDUSTRIAL PRODUCTS INC., 8575 W Forest Home Ave #100, **Milwaukee,** WI 53228-3417, *pg.* 1341, *pg.* 1874
HELWIG CARBON PRODUCTS, INC., 8900 W Tower Ave, **Milwaukee,** WI 53224-2849, *pg.* 1346, *pg.* 1875
JOY GLOBAL, INC., 100 E Wisconsin Ave Ste 2780, **Milwaukee,** WI 53202-4127, *pg.* 1351, *pg.* 1876
KAUFMAN MFG. COMPANY, 547 S 29th St, **Manitowoc,** WI 54220, *pg.* 1352, *pg.* 1868
KEMPSMITH MACHINE COMPANY, 1819 S 71st St, **Milwaukee,** WI 53214, *pg.* 1352, *pg.* 1876
M-B COMPANIES, INC., 1615 Wisconsin Ave, **New Holstein,** WI 53061, *pg.* 1357, *pg.* 1884
MADISON-KIPP CORPORATION, 201 Waubesa St, **Madison,** WI 53704, *pg.* 1358, *pg.* 1866
THE MANITOWOC COMPANY, INC., 2400 S 44th St, **Manitowoc,** WI 54221-0066, *pg.* 1358, *pg.* 1868
MARINE TRAVELIFT, INC., 49 E Yew St, **Sturgeon Bay,** WI 54235, *pg.* 1359, *pg.* 1895
MCDONOUGH MANUFACTURING COMPANY, 2320 Melby St, **Eau Claire,** WI 54702, *pg.* 1360, *pg.* 1857
MILLER ELECTRIC MANUFACTURING CO., 1635 W Spencer St, **Appleton,** WI 54914-4911, *pg.* 1361, *pg.* 1852
MILWAUKEE VALVE COMPANY, INC., 16550 W Stratton Dr, **New Berlin,** WI 53151-7301, *pg.* 1361, *pg.* 1884
MODERN EQUIPMENT COMPANY, 369 W Western Ave, **Port Washington,** WI 53074-0993, *pg.* 1363, *pg.* 1887
NATIONAL RIVET & MANUFACTURING COMPANY, 21 E Jefferson St, **Waupun,** WI 53963-1942, *pg.* 1364, *pg.* 1898
NORDCO, INC., 245 W Forest Hill Ave, **Oak Creek,** WI 53154, *pg.* 1365, *pg.* 1884
PUTZMEISTER AMERICA, 1733 90th St, **Sturtevant,** WI 53177-1805, *pg.* 1371, *pg.* 1896
RBS GLOBAL, INC., 4701 W Greenfield Ave, **Milwaukee,** WI 53214, *pg.* 1371, *pg.* 1879
RITE-HITE HOLDING CORPORATION, 8900 N Arbon Dr, **Milwaukee,** WI 53223-2451, *pg.* 1372, *pg.* 1880
SUPERIOR DIE SET CORP., 900 W Drexel Ave, **Oak Creek,** WI 53154, *pg.* 1379, *pg.* 1885
TELSMITH, INC., 10910 N Industrial Dr, **Mequon,** WI 53092-4331, *pg.* 1381, *pg.* 1871
WAUKESHA FOUNDRY INC., 1300 Lincoln Ave, **Waukesha,** WI 53186, *pg.* 1388, *pg.* 1898
WISCONSIN MACHINE TOOL CORPORATION, 3225 Gateway Rd Ste 100, **Brookfield,** WI 53045-5139, *pg.* 1389, *pg.* 1855

First page reference indicates Business Class Edition
Second page reference indicates Geographic Edition

Miscellaneous

California

CONVERSANT, INC., 30699 Russell Ranch Rd Ste 250, **Westlake Village,** CA 91362-7319, *pg.* 1393, *pg.* 306
GREAT AMERICAN GROUP, INC., 21860 Burbank Blvd Ste 300 S, **Woodland Hills,** CA 91367, *pg.* 1394, *pg.* 308
LA FITNESS INTERNATIONAL, LLC, PO Box 55088, **Irvine,** CA 92619, *pg.* 1394, *pg.* 112
ROSE HILLS COMPANY, 3888 Workman Mill Rd, **Whittier,** CA 90601, *pg.* 1395, *pg.* 307
TAPJOY, INC., 111 Sutter St 12th Fl, **San Francisco,** CA 94104, *pg.* 1396, *pg.* 228

Colorado

AEROGROW INTERNATIONAL, INC., 6075 Longbow Dr Ste 200, **Boulder,** CO 80301, *pg.* 1393, *pg.* 310

Florida

AMERICAN MOLD REMOVAL, INC., 1630 N US Hwy 1, **Jupiter,** FL 33469, *pg.* 1393, *pg.* 436
ASK THE SEAL, LLC, 3001 N Rocky Point Dr E Ste 223, **Tampa,** FL 33607, *pg.* 1393, *pg.* 470
BEACON SOLAR ENERGY INC., 6340 Techster Blvd Ste 1, **Fort Myers,** FL 33966-4798, *pg.* 1393, *pg.* 427
FREEDOM RINGS DOCUMENT PREPARATION SERVICES, 3003 S Tamiami Trl, **Sarasota,** FL 34239, *pg.* 1394, *pg.* 466
MIA'S THERAPEUTIC MASSAGE, 5217 Trouble Creek Rd, **New Port Richey,** FL 34652, *pg.* 1395, *pg.* 451
NEOC, 8211 W Broward Blvd PH3, **Plantation,** FL 33324, *pg.* 1395, *pg.* 459

Georgia

LIBERATOR, INC., 2745 Bankers Industrial Dr, **Atlanta,** GA 30360, *pg.* 1395, *pg.* 513

Illinois

JUSTRITE MANUFACTURING COMPANY, LLC, 2454 E Dempster St, **Des Plaines,** IL 60016, *pg.* 1394, *pg.* 606
SELECTIVE SEARCH LLC, 35 E Wacker Dr Ste 1920, **Chicago,** IL 60601, *pg.* 1395, *pg.* 590
SIMS METAL MANAGEMENT, 325 N LaSalle St Ste 550, **Chicago,** IL 60610, *pg.* 1396, *pg.* 590
UNDERWRITERS LABORATORIES INC., 333 Pfingsten Rd, **Northbrook,** IL 60062-2096, *pg.* 1396, *pg.* 641

Indiana

AURORA CASKET COMPANY, INC., 10944 Marsh Rd, **Aurora,** IN 47001, *pg.* 1393, *pg.* 673
BATESVILLE CASKET COMPANY, INC., 1 Batesville Blvd, **Batesville,** IN 47006, *pg.* 1393, *pg.* 673
HILLENBRAND, INC., 1 Batesville Blvd, **Batesville,** IN 47006, *pg.* 1394, *pg.* 673

Massachusetts

BUILDING EDUCATED LEADERS FOR LIFE, 60 Clayton St, **Dorchester,** MA 02122, *pg.* 1393, *pg.* 817
HOLLISTER STAFFING, INC., 75 State St 9th Fl, **Boston,** MA 02109, *pg.* 1394, *pg.* 796

Missouri

BROWN & CROUPPEN, P.C., 211 N Broadway Ste 1600, **Saint Louis,** MO 63102, *pg.* 1393, *pg.* 993

Nebraska

MAIDS INTERNATIONAL INC., 9394 West Dodge Rd, Ste 140, **Omaha,** NE 68114, *pg.* 1395, *pg.* 1016

New Jersey

1-800-DOCTORS, 186 Wood Ave S Ste 102, **Iselin,** NJ 08830, *pg.* 1392, *pg.* 1074
EDUCATIONAL TESTING SERVICE INC., 660 Rosedale Rd, **Princeton,** NJ 08541-0001, *pg.* 1394, *pg.* 1111
TELEBRANDS, INC., 79 Two Bridges Rd, **Fairfield,** NJ 07004, *pg.* 1396, *pg.* 1066

New York

ACCENTURE, 1345 Ave of the Americas, **New York,** NY 10105, *pg.* 1392, *pg.* 1186
ADSTRUC, INC., 241 Centre St 7th Fl, **New York,** NY 10013, *pg.* 1393, *pg.* 1187
APPLIED DNA SCIENCES, INC., 25 Health Sciences Dr Ste 215, **Stony Brook,** NY 11790, *pg.* 1393, *pg.* 1343
GLOBALOPTIONS GROUP, INC., 75 Rockefeller Plz 27th Fl, **New York,** NY 10019, *pg.* 1394, *pg.* 1235
MERCER INC., 1166 Ave of the Americas, **New York,** NY 10036-2708, *pg.* 1395, *pg.* 1258
SANTINELLI INTERNATIONAL INC., 325 Oser Ave, **Hauppauge,** NY 11788, *pg.* 1395, *pg.* 1165
SEQUENTIAL BRANDS GROUP, INC., 5 Bryant Park 30th Fl, **New York,** NY 10018, *pg.* 1395, *pg.* 1290
VISANT HOLDING CORP., 357 Main St, **Armonk,** NY 10504, *pg.* 1396, *pg.* 1140

North Carolina

STOP HUNGER NOW, 615 Hillsborough St Ste 200, **Raleigh,** NC 27603, *pg.* 1396, *pg.* 1389

Ohio

ENVISION, 3030 W Fork Rd, **Cincinnati,** OH 45211-1944, *pg.* 1394, *pg.* 1412

Oregon

XZERES WIND CORP., 9025 SW Hillman Ct Ste 3126, **Wilsonville,** OR 97070, *pg.* 1396, *pg.* 1512

Pennsylvania

STONEMOR PARTNERS L.P., 311 Veterans Hwy Ste B, **Levittown,** PA 19056, *pg.* 1396, *pg.* 1548

Texas

SERVICE CORPORATION INTERNATIONAL, 1929 Allen Pkwy, **Houston,** TX 77019, *pg.* 1395, *pg.* 1714
UNIVERSITY GENERAL HEALTH SYSTEM INC, 7501 Fannin St, **Houston,** TX 77054, *pg.* 1396, *pg.* 1716

Virginia

CX ACT, INC., 1100 Wilson Blvd Ste 950, **Arlington,** VA 22209, *pg.* 1394, *pg.* 1773
EVOLENT HEALTH LLC, 800 N Glebe Rd Ste 500, **Arlington,** VA 22203, *pg.* 1394, *pg.* 1773

Washington

MARCHEX, INC., 520 Pike St Ste 2000, **Seattle,** WA 98101, *pg.* 1395, *pg.* 1837

Optical, Photo & Scientific Instruments

Arizona

ARIZONA INSTRUMENT LLC, 3375 N Delaware St, **Chandler,** AZ 85225, *pg.* 1400, *pg.* 12
MARCOLIN USA INC., 7543 E Tierra Buena Ln, **Scottsdale,** AZ 85260, *pg.* 1421, *pg.* 23

California

ACACIA RESEARCH CORPORATION, 500 Newport Ctr Dr, **Newport Beach,** CA 92660, *pg.* 1398, *pg.* 165
ALAN GORDON ENTERPRISES, INC., 5625 Melrose Ave, **Los Angeles,** CA 90038-3909, *pg.* 1399, *pg.* 125
ALLIANCE FIBER OPTIC PRODUCTS, INC., 275 Gibraltar Dr, **Sunnyvale,** CA 94089-2918, *pg.* 1399, *pg.* 283
AMERICAN MEDICAL SYSTEMS, INC., 3052 Orchard Dr, **San Jose,** CA 95134-2011, *pg.* 1399, *pg.* 238
AXT, INC., 4281 Technology Dr, **Fremont,** CA 94538-6339, *pg.* 1400, *pg.* 90
BECKMAN COULTER, INC., 250 S Kramer Blvd, **Brea,** CA 92821, *pg.* 1402, *pg.* 48
CDI, 26250 Enterprise Ct Ste 100, **Lake Forest,** CA 92630, *pg.* 1405, *pg.* 121
COHERENT, INC., 5100 Patrick Henry Dr, **Santa Clara,** CA 95054, *pg.* 1406, *pg.* 265
COMBIMATRIX CORPORATION, 310 Goddard Ste 150, **Irvine,** CA 92618, *pg.* 1407, *pg.* 109
CUSTOM SENSORS & TECHNOLOGIES, 14401 Princeton Ave, **Moorpark,** CA 93201, *pg.* 1407, *pg.* 152
CVI MELLES GRIOT, 2051 Palomar Airport Rd 200, **Carlsbad,** CA 92011, *pg.* 1407, *pg.* 59
EPSILON SYSTEMS SOLUTIONS, 9242 Lightwave Ave, **San Diego,** CA 92123, *pg.* 1412, *pg.* 202
FLUIDIGM CORPORATION, 7000 Shoreline Ct Ste 100, **South San Francisco,** CA 94080, *pg.* 1413, *pg.* 279
GOPRO, 3000 Clearview Way, **San Mateo,** CA 94402, *pg.* 1414, *pg.* 255
HID GLOBAL CORPORATION, 15370 Barranca Pkwy, **Irvine,** CA 92618-1905, *pg.* 1416, *pg.* 111
KOFAX IMAGE PRODUCTS, INC., 15211 Laguna Canyon Rd, **Irvine,** CA 92618-3603, *pg.* 1419, *pg.* 112
LANDEC CORPORATION, 3603 Haven Ave, **Menlo Park,** CA 94025, *pg.* 1419, *pg.* 145
LEADER INSTRUMENTS CORPORATION, 11095 Knott Ave Ste B, **Cypress,** CA 90630, *pg.* 1419, *pg.* 75
LUNA IMAGING LTD., 2702 Media Center Dr, **Los Angeles,** CA 90065-1733, *pg.* 1421, *pg.* 136
MEADE INSTRUMENTS CORPORATION, 27 Hubble, **Irvine,** CA 92618, *pg.* 1422, *pg.* 113
NANOMETRICS INCORPORATED, 1550 Buckeye Dr, **Milpitas,** CA 95035-7418, *pg.* 1423, *pg.* 147
NDC TECHNOLOGIES, 5314 N Irwindale Ave, **Irwindale,** CA 91706-2089, *pg.* 1423, *pg.* 118
NEW WAVE RESEARCH INCORPORATED, 48660 Kato Rd, **Fremont,** CA 94538, *pg.* 1423, *pg.* 91
NEWPORT CORPORATION, 1791 Deere Ave, **Irvine,** CA 92606, *pg.* 1424, *pg.* 114
OCLARO, INC., 2560 Junction Ave, **San Jose,** CA 95134, *pg.* 1425, *pg.* 248
OHARA CORPORATION, 23141 Arroyo Vista Ste 200, **Rancho Santa Margarita,** CA 92688-2609, *pg.* 1425, *pg.* 188
OMRON SCIENTIFIC TECHNOLOGIES INCORPORATED, 6550 Dumbarton Cir, **Fremont,** CA 94555-3605, *pg.* 1425, *pg.* 91
OPTOSIGMA CORP., 3210 S Croddy Way, **Santa Ana,** CA 92704, *pg.* 1425, *pg.* 262
OSI OPTOELECTRONICS, 12525 Chadron Ave, **Hawthorne,** CA 90250-4807, *pg.* 1425, *pg.* 100
Q A GROUP LLC., 3400 E 3Rd Ave, **Foster City,** CA 94404, *pg.* 1427, *pg.* 89
REALD INC., 100 N Crescent Dr Ste 120, **Beverly Hills,** CA 90210, *pg.* 1427, *pg.* 47
SIGNATURE EYEWEAR, INC., 498 N Oak St, **Inglewood,** CA 90302-3315, *pg.* 1429, *pg.* 105
SIGNET ARMORLITE, INC., 5803 Newton Dr, Ste A, **Carlsbad,** CA 92008, *pg.* 1429, *pg.* 60
SOURCE PHOTONICS, INC., 8521 Fallbrook Ave Ste 200, **West Hills,** CA 91304, *pg.* 1429, *pg.* 305
SOUTHWESTERN INDUSTRIES, INC., 2615 Homestead Pl Rancho Dominguez, **Compton,** CA 90224-9066, *pg.* 1429, *pg.* 69
SYSTRON DONNER INERTIAL DIVISION, 2700 Systron Dr, **Concord,** CA 94518, *pg.* 1430, *pg.* 69
TRIMEDYNE, INC., 25901 Commercentre Dr, **Lake Forest,** CA 92630-8805, *pg.* 1432, *pg.* 121
ULTRATECH, INC., 3050 Zanker Rd, **San Jose,** CA 95134-2126, *pg.* 1433, *pg.* 251
UVP, INC., 2066 W 11th St, **Upland,** CA 91786-3509, *pg.* 1434, *pg.* 298
VARIAN MEDICAL SYSTEMS, INC., 3100 Hansen Way, **Palo Alto,** CA 94304-1030, *pg.* 1434, *pg.* 178
VIAVI SOLUTIONS INC., 430 N McCarthy Blvd, **Milpitas,** CA 95035, *pg.* 1435, *pg.* 148
YOUNGER OPTICS, 2925 California St, **Torrance,** CA 90503-3914, *pg.* 1437, *pg.* 297
ZENNI OPTICAL, INC., 448 Ignacio Blvd #332, **Novato,** CA 94949, *pg.* 1438, *pg.* 168

Colorado

DIGITALGLOBE, INC., 1601 Dry Creek Dr Ste 260, **Longmont,** CO 80503, *pg.* 1408, *pg.* 333
EPILOG CORPORATION, 16371 Table Mountain Pkwy, **Golden,** CO 80403, *pg.* 1412, *pg.* 330
HACH COMPANY, 5600 Lindbergh Dr, **Loveland,** CO 80538-8842, *pg.* 1415, *pg.* 334
LASER TECHNOLOGY, INC., 6912 S Quentin St, **Centennial,** CO 80112, *pg.* 1419, *pg.* 314
QUALMARK CORPORATION, 10390 E 48th Ave, **Denver,** CO 80238-2620, *pg.* 1427, *pg.* 322
ROCKY MOUNTAIN INSTRUMENT, INC., 106 Laser Dr, **Lafayette,** CO 80026, *pg.* 1428, *pg.* 332

Connecticut

BRANSON ULTRASONICS CORPORATION - PLASTICS JOINING DIVISION, 41 Eagle Rd, **Danbury,** CT 06810-4127, *pg.* 1403, *pg.* 343
COOPER-ATKINS CORPORATION, 33 Reeds Gap Rd, **Middlefield,** CT 06455, *pg.* 1407, *pg.* 355
EMERY WINSLOW SCALE COMPANY, 73 Cogwheel Ln, **Seymour,** CT 06483, *pg.* 1411, *pg.* 369
GERBER SCIENTIFIC, INC., 24 Industrial Park Rd, **Tolland,** CT 06084, *pg.* 1414, *pg.* 380
THE LEE COMPANY, 2 Pettipaug Rd, **Westbrook,** CT 06498, *pg.* 1420, *pg.* 383
MARKTIME, 105 Nutmeg Rd S, **South Windsor,** CT 06074, *pg.* 1421, *pg.* 371
ULTRAOPTIX, INC., 17 Commerce St, **East Haven,** CT 06512-4113, *pg.* 1433, *pg.* 346
WALLACH SURGICAL DEVICES, INC., 95 Corporate Dr, **Trumbull,** CT 06611, *pg.* 1436, *pg.* 381

Florida

ACCUSOFT, 4001 N Riverside Dr, **Tampa,** FL 33603, *pg.* 1398, *pg.* 470
COSTA DEL MAR SUNGLASSES, INC., 2361 Mason Ave Ste 100, **Daytona Beach,** FL 32117, *pg.* 1407, *pg.* 419
DANKER LABORATORIES INC., 6805 33rd St E, **Sarasota,** FL 34243-4144, *pg.* 1408, *pg.* 465
ELSTER AMCO WATER, INC., 1100 SW 38th Ave, **Ocala,** FL 34474, *pg.* 1411, *pg.* 452
ICARE INDUSTRIES, INC., 4399 35th St N, **Saint Petersburg,** FL 33714-3717, *pg.* 1417, *pg.* 463
LIGHTPATH TECHNOLOGIES INC, 2603 Challenger Tech Ct Ste 100, **Orlando,** FL 32826, *pg.* 1420, *pg.* 454
PARKERVISION, INC., 7915 Baymeadows Way Ste 400, **Jacksonville,** FL 32256-7517, *pg.* 1426, *pg.* 434
TRANSITIONS OPTICAL, INC., 9251 Belcher Rd, **Pinellas Park,** FL 33782-4200, *pg.* 1432, *pg.* 458
UNILENS VISION INC., 10431 72nd St N, **Largo,** FL 33777-1511, *pg.* 1433, *pg.* 438

Georgia

ALCON, 11460 Johns Creek Pkwy, **Duluth,** GA 30097-1518, *pg.* 1399, *pg.* 530
COLOR IMAGING INC., 4350 Peachtree Industrial Blvd Ste 100, **Norcross,** GA 30071, *pg.* 1407, *pg.* 536
NATIONAL VISION, INC., 296 Grayson Hwy, **Lawrenceville,** GA 30045, *pg.* 1423, *pg.* 534
NUCLETRON CORPORATION, 400 Perimeter Center Ter NE, Ste 50, **Atlanta,** GA 30346, *pg.* 1424, *pg.* 516
SUNLINK HEALTH SYSTEMS, INC., 900 Circle 75 Pkwy Ste 1120, **Atlanta,** GA 30339, *pg.* 1430, *pg.* 520
THERAGENICS CORPORATION, 5203 Bristol Industrial Way, **Buford,** GA 30518-1799, *pg.* 1431, *pg.* 527
WIKA INSTRUMENT CORPORATION, 1000 Wiegand Blvd, **Lawrenceville,** GA 30043, *pg.* 1437, *pg.* 534

Illinois

ASSOCIATED RESEARCH INC., 13860 W Laurel Dr, **Lake Forest,** IL 60045-4531, *pg.* 1400, *pg.* 622
AVALIGN TECHNOLOGIES, 272 E Deerpath Rd Ste 208, **Lake Forest,** IL 60045, *pg.* 1400, *pg.* 622
BUEHLER, LTD., 41 Waukegan Rd, **Lake Bluff,** IL 60044, *pg.* 1403, *pg.* 622
CALUMET PHOTOGRAPHIC, INC., 819 W Eastman St, **Chicago,** IL 60642, *pg.* 1404, *pg.* 568
COLE-PARMER INSTRUMENT COMPANY, 625 E Bunker Ct, **Vernon Hills,** IL 60061-1844, *pg.* 1406, *pg.* 664
DEDERT CORPORATION, 20000 Governors Dr, **Olympia Fields,** IL 60461-1034, *pg.* 1408, *pg.* 649
DYNAPAR, 1675 N Delany Rd, **Gurnee,** IL 60031-1237, *pg.* 1408, *pg.* 616
FLETCHER CHICAGO INC., 1000 N Northbranch St, **Chicago,** IL 60642, *pg.* 1413, *pg.* 574
H. WILSON COMPANY, 2245 Delany Rd, **Waukegan,** IL 60087, *pg.* 1415, *pg.* 666
ITW MAGNAFLUX, 155 Harlem Ave, **Glenview,** IL 60025, *pg.* 1418, *pg.* 615
LEICA MICROSYSTEMS, INC., 2345 Waukegan Rd, **Bannockburn,** IL 60015-1515, *pg.* 1420, *pg.* 555
PHOTOGENIC PROFESSIONAL LIGHTING, 1268 Humbracht Cir, **Bartlett,** IL 60103-1631, *pg.* 1426, *pg.* 556
SELLSTROM MANUFACTURING CO., 2050 Hammond Dr, **Schaumburg,** IL 60173, *pg.* 1428, *pg.* 659
STOELTING CO., 620 Wheat Ln, **Wood Dale,** IL 60191-1164, *pg.* 1430, *pg.* 671

Indiana

BIOANALYTICAL SYSTEMS, INC., 2701 Kent Ave, **West Lafayette,** IN 47906-1350, *pg.* 1402, *pg.* 700

Kansas

BUSHNELL OUTDOOR PRODUCTS, INC., 9200 Cody St, **Overland Park,** KS 66214-1734, *pg.* 1403, *pg.* 718
GARMIN INTERNATIONAL, INC., 1200 E 151st St, **Olathe,** KS 66062-3426, *pg.* 1414, *pg.* 717

Maryland

BRIMROSE CORPORATION, 19 Loveton Cir, **Baltimore,** MD 21152-9201, *pg.* 1403, *pg.* 756
DISTRICT PHOTO INC., 10501 Rhode Is Ave, **Beltsville,** MD 20705-2317, *pg.* 1408, *pg.* 761
ROHDE & SCHWARZ, INC., 8661A Robert Fulton Dr, **Columbia,** MD 21046-2265, *pg.* 1428, *pg.* 768
SHIMADZU SCIENTIFIC INSTRUMENTS, INC., 7102 Riverwood Dr, **Columbia,** MD 21046, *pg.* 1428, *pg.* 768

Massachusetts

AGILTRON, INC., 15 Presidential Way, **Woburn,** MA 01801-1040, *pg.* 1398, *pg.* 860
AMERICAN SCIENCE AND ENGINEERING, INC., 829 Middlesex Tpke, **Billerica,** MA 01821-3907, *pg.* 1399, *pg.* 787
ANALOGIC CORPORATION, 8 Centennial Dr, **Peabody,** MA 01960-7902, *pg.* 1399, *pg.* 840
AXCELIS TECHNOLOGIES, INC., 108 Cherry Hill Dr, **Beverly,** MA 01915, *pg.* 1400, *pg.* 787
AZONIX CORPORATION, 101 Billerica Ave Bldg 4, **Billerica,** MA 01862, *pg.* 1400, *pg.* 788
BROOKFIELD ENGINEERING LABORATORIES, INC., 11 Commerce Blvd, **Middleboro,** MA 02346, *pg.* 1403, *pg.* 833
CANDELA CORPORATION, 530 Boston Post Rd, **Wayland,** MA 01778-1833, *pg.* 1404, *pg.* 855

First page reference indicates Business Class Edition
Second page reference indicates Geographic Edition

COGNEX CORPORATION, 1 Vision Dr, **Natick,** MA 01760-2059, *pg.* 1406, *pg.* 834
ECRM IMAGING SYSTEMS, INC., 554 Clark Rd, **Tewksbury,** MA 01876-1631, *pg.* 1410, *pg.* 848
EXERGEN CORPORATION, 400 Pleasant St, **Watertown,** MA 02172, *pg.* 1412, *pg.* 855
GSI GROUP INC., 125 Middlesex Tpke, **Bedford,** MA 01730, *pg.* 1415, *pg.* 784
THE HILSINGER CO., 33 W Bacon St, **Plainville,** MA 02762-2418, *pg.* 1416, *pg.* 841
HOLOGIC, INC., 35 Crosby Dr, **Bedford,** MA 01730, *pg.* 1416, *pg.* 784
IROBOT CORP., 8 Crosby Dr, **Bedford,** MA 01730, *pg.* 1418, *pg.* 785
THE L.S. STARRETT COMPANY, 121 Crescent St, **Athol,** MA 01331-1913, *pg.* 1421, *pg.* 783
MATEC INSTRUMENT COMPANIES, INC., 56 Hudson St, **Northborough,** MA 01532-1922, *pg.* 1421, *pg.* 839
MILLIPORE CORPORATION, 290 Concord Rd, **Billerica,** MA 01821, *pg.* 1423, *pg.* 788
PERKINELMER, INC., 940 Winter St, **Waltham,** MA 02451, *pg.* 1426, *pg.* 853
POLAROID CORPORATION, 300 Baker Ave, **Concord,** MA 01742-2131, *pg.* 1426, *pg.* 815
SETRA SYSTEMS, INC., 159 Swanson Rd, **Boxboro,** MA 01719-1316, *pg.* 1428, *pg.* 802
TELEDYNE BENTHOS, INC., 49 Edgerton Dr, **North Falmouth,** MA 02556-2821, *pg.* 1431, *pg.* 838
THERMO FISHER SCIENTIFIC INC., 81 Wyman St, **Waltham,** MA 02454-9046, *pg.* 1431, *pg.* 854
VICOR CORPORATION, 25 Frontage Rd, **Andover,** MA 01810-5424, *pg.* 1435, *pg.* 783
WATERS CORPORATION, 34 Maple St, **Milford,** MA 01757, *pg.* 1436, *pg.* 834

Michigan

ADVANCED PHOTONIX, INC., 2925 Boardwalk, **Ann Arbor,** MI 48104, *pg.* 1398, *pg.* 865
ASPEN SURGICAL PRODUCTS, INC., 6945 Southbelt Dr SE, **Caledonia,** MI 49316, *pg.* 1400, *pg.* 874
HOLO-SOURCE CORPORATION, 12280 Hubbard St, **Livonia,** MI 48150-1737, *pg.* 1416, *pg.* 896
X-RITE, INCORPORATED, 4300 44th St SE, **Grand Rapids,** MI 49512, *pg.* 1437, *pg.* 891

Minnesota

CLEARFIELD, INC., 5480 Nathan Lane Ste 120, **Plymouth,** MN 55442, *pg.* 1406, *pg.* 953
CYBEROPTICS CORPORATION, 5900 Golden Hills Dr, **Golden Valley,** MN 55416-1040, *pg.* 1408, *pg.* 925
LIFETOUCH, INC., 11000 Viking Dr Ste 400 W, **Eden Prairie,** MN 55344-7294, *pg.* 1420, *pg.* 922
MEDTOX SCIENTIFIC, INC., 402 W County Rd D, **Saint Paul,** MN 55112-3522, *pg.* 1422, *pg.* 962
PRECISION CONTROL SYSTEMS, INC./ RESEARCH INC., 7128 Shady Oak Rd, **Eden Prairie,** MN 55344, *pg.* 1427, *pg.* 923
S-T INDUSTRIES, INC., 301 Armstrong Blvd N, **Saint James,** MN 56081-1206, *pg.* 1428, *pg.* 956
TSI INCORPORATED, 500 Cardigan Rd, **Shoreview,** MN 55126-3903, *pg.* 1432, *pg.* 965
VASCULAR SOLUTIONS, INC., 6464 Sycamore Ct, **Minneapolis,** MN 55369, *pg.* 1434, *pg.* 946
VISION-EASE LENS CORPORATION, 7000 Sunwood Dr NW, **Ramsey,** MN 55303, *pg.* 1436, *pg.* 954

Missouri

HEMCO CORPORATION, 111 Powell Rd, **Independence,** MO 64056, *pg.* 1416, *pg.* 979

Montana

ILX LIGHTWAVE CORPORATION, 31950 Frontage Rd, **Bozeman,** MT 59715, *pg.* 1417, *pg.* 1008

Nevada

HAMILTON CO., INC., 4970 Energy Way, **Reno,** NV 89502-4123, *pg.* 1415, *pg.* 1031

New Hampshire

JEWELL INSTRUMENTS, LLC, 850 Perimeter Rd, **Manchester,** NH 03103, *pg.* 1418, *pg.* 1036
PRECITECH, INC., 44 Black Brook Rd, **Keene,** NH 03431, *pg.* 1427, *pg.* 1035
PROPHOTONIX LIMITED, 32 Hampshire Rd, **Salem,** NH 03079, *pg.* 1427, *pg.* 1039

New Jersey

AGFA CORPORATION, 100 Challenger Rd, **Ridgefield Park,** NJ 07660, *pg.* 1398, *pg.* 1114
BAUSCH & LOMB INCORPORATED, 400 Somerset Corporate Blvd, **Bridgewater,** NJ 08807, *pg.* 1401, *pg.* 1045
BIO-REFERENCE LABORATORIES, INC., 481 Edward H Ross Dr, **Elmwood Park,** NJ 07407-3118, *pg.* 1402, *pg.* 1058
CANTEL MEDICAL CORP., 150 Clove Rd, **Little Falls,** NJ 07424, *pg.* 1405, *pg.* 1079
CODA INC., 30 Indus Ave, **Mahwah,** NJ 07430, *pg.* 1406, *pg.* 1081
CONTROL PRODUCTS, INC., 280 Ridgedale Ave, **East Hanover,** NJ 07936, *pg.* 1407, *pg.* 1054
EDMUND INDUSTRIAL OPTICS INC., 101 E Gloucester Pike, **Barrington,** NJ 08007-1380, *pg.* 1411, *pg.* 1041
FUJINON INC., 10 Highpoint Dr, **Wayne,** NJ 07470-7431, *pg.* 1414, *pg.* 1129
HAMAMATSU CORPORATION, 360 Foothill Rd, **Bridgewater,** NJ 08807, *pg.* 1415, *pg.* 1046
HASSELBLAD USA, INC., 10 Madison Rd, **Fairfield,** NJ 07004-2330, *pg.* 1416, *pg.* 1065
KONICA MINOLTA BUSINESS SOLUTIONS USA, INC., 100 Williams Dr, **Ramsey,** NJ 07446, *pg.* 1419, *pg.* 1113
L&R MANUFACTURING COMPANY, 577 Elm St, **Kearny,** NJ 07032, *pg.* 1419, *pg.* 1076
LEICA CAMERA, INC., 1 Pearl Ct Unit A, **Allendale,** NJ 07401-1610, *pg.* 1420, *pg.* 1041
SGS NORTH AMERICA INC., 201 Route 17 N, **Rutherford,** NJ 07070, *pg.* 1428, *pg.* 1118
THORLABS INC., 56 Sparta Ave, **Newton,** NJ 07860, *pg.* 1432, *pg.* 1098
THWING-ALBERT INSTRUMENT COMPANY, 14 W Collings Ave, **West Berlin,** NJ 08091, *pg.* 1432, *pg.* 1131
U.S. VISION, INC., 1 Harmon Dr Glen Oaks Industrial Park, **Glendora,** NJ 08029, *pg.* 1433, *pg.* 1071

New York

ADORAMA CAMERA INC., 42 W 18th St, **New York,** NY 10011, *pg.* 1398, *pg.* 1187
BOVIE MEDICAL CORPORATION, 734 Walt Whitman Rd, **Melville,** NY 11747, *pg.* 1402, *pg.* 1178
CANON U.S.A., INC., 1 Cannon Park, **Melville,** NY 11747, *pg.* 1404, *pg.* 1178
CARL ZEISS, INC., 1 Zeiss Dr, **Thornwood,** NY 10594-1939, *pg.* 1405, *pg.* 1345
COHEN'S FASHION OPTICAL INC., 100 Quentin Roosevelt Blvd Ste 400, **Garden City,** NY 11530-1558, *pg.* 1406, *pg.* 1161
COOPERVISION, INC., 370 Woodcliff Dr Ste 200, **Fairport,** NY 14450, *pg.* 1407, *pg.* 1159
EASTMAN KODAK COMPANY, 343 State St, **Rochester,** NY 14650-0001, *pg.* 1408, *pg.* 1333
ECOLOGY AND ENVIRONMENT, INC., 368 Pleasant View Dr, **Lancaster,** NY 14086, *pg.* 1410, *pg.* 1173
EDROY PRODUCTS CO., INC., 245 N Midland Ave, **Nyack,** NY 10960-1907, *pg.* 1411, *pg.* 1318
EMERGING VISION, INC., 520 8th Ave 23 Fl, **New York,** NY 10018, *pg.* 1411, *pg.* 1227
EPPENDORF NORTH AMERICA, 102 Motor Pkwy, **Hauppauge,** NY 11788, *pg.* 1412, *pg.* 1164
EVAPORATED METAL FILMS CORP., 239 Cherry St, **Ithaca,** NY 14850, *pg.* 1412, *pg.* 1170
FONAR CORPORATION, 110 Marcus Dr, **Melville,** NY 11747-4228, *pg.* 1413, *pg.* 1179
FUJIFILM U.S.A., INC., 200 Summit Lake Dr, **Valhalla,** NY 10595, *pg.* 1414, *pg.* 1348
GLASS FAB INC., 257 Ormond St, **Rochester,** NY 14605, *pg.* 1414, *pg.* 1335
JAND, INC., 295 Lafayette Ste 501, **New York,** NY 10012, *pg.* 1418, *pg.* 1245
MAGNETIC ANALYSIS CORPORATION, 103 Fairview Pk Dr, **Elmsford,** NY 10523, *pg.* 1421, *pg.* 1158
MARCHON EYEWEAR, INC., 35 Hub Dr, **Melville,** NY 11747, *pg.* 1421, *pg.* 1180
MECHANICAL TECHNOLOGY, INCORPORATED, 325 Washington Avenue Ext, **Albany,** NY 12205, *pg.* 1422, *pg.* 1137
MELA SCIENCES, INC., 50 S Buckhout St Ste 1, **Irvington,** NY 10533, *pg.* 1422, *pg.* 1168
NIKON INC., 1300 Walt Whitman Rd, **Melville,** NY 11747-3064, *pg.* 1424, *pg.* 1181
NORTH ATLANTIC INDUSTRIES INC., 110 Wilbur Pl, **Bohemia,** NY 11716, *pg.* 1424, *pg.* 1143
SCHNEIDER OPTICS INC., 285 Oser Ave, **Hauppauge,** NY 11788, *pg.* 1428, *pg.* 1165
SIRONA DENTAL SYSTEMS, INC., 30-30 47th Ave Ste 500, **Long Island City,** NY 11101-3492, *pg.* 1429, *pg.* 1175
SOLSTICE MARKETING CONCEPTS, LLC, 404 5th Ave 2nd Fl, **New York,** NY 10018, *pg.* 1429, *pg.* 1293
STEFAN SYDOR OPTICS, INC., 31 Jet Veiw Dr, **Rochester,** NY 14624, *pg.* 1430, *pg.* 1337
TELEDYNE LECROY, 700 Chestnut Ridge Rd, **Chestnut Ridge,** NY 10977, *pg.* 1431, *pg.* 1153
THE TIFFEN COMPANY LLC, 90 Oser Ave, **Hauppauge,** NY 11788-3886, *pg.* 1432, *pg.* 1165
UNITRON INC., 73 Mall Dr, **Commack,** NY 11725, *pg.* 1433, *pg.* 1153
UNIVERSAL PHOTONICS, INC., 495 W John St, **Hicksville,** NY 11801-1028, *pg.* 1433, *pg.* 1167
VEECO INSTRUMENTS INC., Terminal Dr, **Plainview,** NY 11803, *pg.* 1434, *pg.* 1322
WELCH ALLYN INC., 4341 State Street Rd, **Skaneateles Falls,** NY 13153-0220, *pg.* 1436, *pg.* 1342
WILLOUGHBY'S KONICA MINOLTA IMAGING CENTER, 298 5th Ave, **New York,** NY 10001, *pg.* 1437, *pg.* 1314

North Carolina

BD DIAGNOSTICS - TRIPATH, 780 Plantation Dr, **Burlington,** NC 27215, *pg.* 1402, *pg.* 1358
CEM CORPORATION, 3100 Smith Farm Rd, **Matthews,** NC 28104-5044, *pg.* 1405, *pg.* 1382
CORNING CABLE SYSTEMS LLC, 800 17th St NW, **Hickory,** NC 28601, *pg.* 1407, *pg.* 1378
ELSTER AMERICAN METER COMPANY, 208 S Rogers Ln, **Raleigh,** NC 27610, *pg.* 1411, *pg.* 1387
PORTRAIT INNOVATIONS HOLDING COMPANY, 2016 Ayrsley Town Blvd Ste 200, **Charlotte,** NC 28273, *pg.* 1427, *pg.* 1368

Ohio

BATTELLE MEMORIAL INSTITUTE, 505 King Ave, **Columbus,** OH 43201-2696, *pg.* 1401, *pg.* 1437
CHART INDUSTRIES, INC., 1 Infinity Corporate Centre Dr Ste 300, **Garfield Heights,** OH 44125-5370, *pg.* 1405, *pg.* 1454
ENERGY FOCUS, INC., 32000 Aurora Rd, **Solon,** OH 44139, *pg.* 1411, *pg.* 1472
ESCORT, INC., 5440 W Chester Rd, **West Chester,** OH 45069-2950, *pg.* 1412, *pg.* 1479
GILSON COMPANY, INC., 7975 N Central Dr, **Lewis Center,** OH 43035, *pg.* 1414, *pg.* 1457
KEITHLEY INSTRUMENTS, INC., 28775 Aurora Rd, **Solon,** OH 44139-1837, *pg.* 1418, *pg.* 1473
LCA-VISION INC., 7840 Montgomery Rd, **Cincinnati,** OH 45236, *pg.* 1419, *pg.* 1416
LENSCRAFTERS, INC., 4000 Luxottica Pl, **Mason,** OH 45040, *pg.* 1420, *pg.* 1460
MERIDIAN BIOSCIENCE INC., 3471 River Hills Dr, **Cincinnati,** OH 45244-3023, *pg.* 1422, *pg.* 1417
METTLER-TOLEDO INTERNATIONAL INC., 1900 Polaris Pkwy, **Columbus,** OH 43240, *pg.* 1423, *pg.* 1441
THE WILL-BURT CO., INC., 169 S Main St, **Orrville,** OH 44667-1801, *pg.* 1437, *pg.* 1469
YSI INCORPORATED, 1725 Brannum Ln, **Yellow Springs,** OH 45387-1107, *pg.* 1438, *pg.* 1483

Oklahoma

CANDID COLOR SYSTEMS, INC., 1300 Metropolitan Ave, **Oklahoma City,** OK 73108-2042, *pg.* 1404, *pg.* 1485

Oregon

CASCADE MICROTECH, INC., 9100 SW Gemini Dr, **Beaverton,** OR 97008-7127, *pg.* 1405, *pg.* 1492
FEI COMPANY, 5350 NE Dawson Creek Dr, **Hillsboro,** OR 97124, *pg.* 1413, *pg.* 1498
FLIR SYSTEMS, INC., 27700 SW Pkwy Ave, **Wilsonville,** OR 97070, *pg.* 1413, *pg.* 1510
FRYE ELECTRONICS, INC., 9826 SW Tigard St, **Tigard,** OR 97223, *pg.* 1413, *pg.* 1509
HINDS INSTRUMENTS, INC., 3175 NW Aloclek Dr 7245 NW Evergreen Pkwy, **Hillsboro,** OR 97124-7124, *pg.* 1416, *pg.* 1498
LEUPOLD & STEVENS, INC., 14400 NW Greenbrier Pkwy, **Beaverton,** OR 97006-5790, *pg.* 1420, *pg.* 1492
LIFE TECHNOLOGIES, 29851 Willow Creek Rd, **Eugene,** OR 97402, *pg.* 1420, *pg.* 1497
TEKTRONIX, INC., 14150 SW Karl Braun Dr, **Beaverton,** OR 97077-0001, *pg.* 1431, *pg.* 1496

Pennsylvania

ABB INC. - AUTOMATION TECHNOLOGIES INSTRUMENTATION PRODUCTS, 125 E County Line Rd, **Warminster,** PA 18974-4995, *pg.* 1398, *pg.* 1590
BACHARACH INC., 621 Hunt Vly Cir, **New Kensington,** PA 15068-7074, *pg.* 1400, *pg.* 1556
BROOKS INSTRUMENT, LLC, 407 W Vine St, **Hatfield,** PA 19440-0903, *pg.* 1403, *pg.* 1537
CARDIACASSIST, INC., 240 Alpha Dr, **Pittsburgh,** PA 15238, *pg.* 1405, *pg.* 1574
CERORA, INC., 116 Research Dr Ste 2207, **Bethlehem,** PA 18015, *pg.* 1405, *pg.* 1516
ENVIRONMENTAL TECTONICS CORPORATION, 125 James Way, **Southampton,** PA 18966-3877, *pg.* 1411, *pg.* 1587
ERM GROUP, INC., 350 Eagleview Blvd, **Exton,** PA 19341-2843, *pg.* 1412, *pg.* 1531
ESCALON MEDICAL CORP., 435 Devon Park Dr Bldg 100, **Wayne,** PA 19087, *pg.* 1412, *pg.* 1592
II-VI INCORPORATED, 375 Saxonburg Blvd, **Saxonburg,** PA 16056, *pg.* 1417, *pg.* 1585
KRATOS LANCASTER, 3061 Industry Dr, Ste 200, **Lancaster,** PA 17603, *pg.* 1419, *pg.* 1546
MEGGER INC., Megger Vly Forge Corporate Ctr 2621 Van Buren Ave, **Norristown,** PA 19403, *pg.* 1422, *pg.* 1557
OLYMPUS AMERICA INC., 3500 Corporate Pkwy, **Center Valley,** PA 18034-0610, *pg.* 1425, *pg.* 1521
SCHUTTE & KOERTING INC., 2510 Metropolitan Dr, **Trevose,** PA 19053, *pg.* 1428, *pg.* 1589
TINIUS OLSEN, INC., 1065 Easton Rd, **Horsham,** PA 19044-8009, *pg.* 1432, *pg.* 1541
TURA L.P., 123 Girton Dr, **Muncy,** PA 17756-6375, *pg.* 1433, *pg.* 1555
VISHAY INTERTECHNOLOGY, INC., 63 Lancaster Ave, **Malvern,** PA 19355-2143, *pg.* 1435, *pg.* 1551
WESTON SOLUTIONS HOLDINGS, INC., 1400 Weston Way, **West Chester,** PA 19380, *pg.* 1437, *pg.* 1593

Rhode Island

UVEX SAFETY, 900 Douglas Pike, **Smithfield,** RI 02917-1874, *pg.* 1433, *pg.* 1608

South Carolina

HACKER INSTRUMENTS & INDUSTRIES INC., 1132 Kincaid Bridge Rd, **Winnsboro,** SC 29180, *pg.* 1415, *pg.* 1623

Tennessee

HORNER RAUSCH OPTICAL COMPANY EAST, INC., 968 Main St, **Nashville,** TN 37206-3614, *pg.* 1417, *pg.* 1651
MCR SAFETY, 1255 Schilling Blvd W, **Collierville,** TN 38017, *pg.* 1422, *pg.* 1630
PERCEPTICS, LLC, 9737 Cogdill Rd Ste 200N, **Knoxville,** TN 37932-3350, *pg.* 1426, *pg.* 1637

Texas

ASTROTECH CORPORATION, 401 Congress Ave Ste 1650, **Austin,** TX 78701, *pg.* 1400, *pg.* 1660
ATRION CORPORATION, 1 Allentown Pkwy, **Allen,** TX 75002-4206, *pg.* 1400, *pg.* 1658
ESSILOR OF AMERICA, INC., 13555 N Stemmons Fwy, **Dallas,** TX 75234, *pg.* 1412, *pg.* 1680
GLOBAL GEOPHYSICAL SERVICES, INC., 13927 S Gessner Rd, **Missouri City,** TX 77489, *pg.* 1414, *pg.* 1727
HOWELL INSTRUMENTS INC., 8945 South Freeway, **Fort Worth,** TX 76140-5722, *pg.* 1417, *pg.* 1695
LUMINEX CORPORATION, 12212 Technology Blvd, **Austin,** TX 78727, *pg.* 1421, *pg.* 1664
OSTEOMED CORPORATION, 3885 Arapaho Rd, **Addison,** TX 75001, *pg.* 1425, *pg.* 1658
PRECISION FRAC, 407 Walker St, **Midland,** TX 79701, *pg.* 1427, *pg.* 1727
SWIFT OPTICAL INSTRUMENTS, INC., 6508 Tri-County Pkwy, **Schertz,** TX 78154, *pg.* 1430, *pg.* 1744
SWORDFISH FINANCIAL, INC., 142 Wembley Way, **Rockwall,** TX 75032, *pg.* 1430, *pg.* 1737
TOPPAN PHOTOMASKS, INC., 131 E Old Settlers Blvd, **Round Rock,** TX 78664-2211, *pg.* 1432, *pg.* 1739
VERMILLION, INC., 12117 Bee Caves Rd Bldg II Ste 100, **Austin,** TX 78738, *pg.* 1435, *pg.* 1667
VISIONWORKS OF AMERICA, INC., 175 E Houston St, **San Antonio,** TX 78205, *pg.* 1436, *pg.* 1744

Utah

VARIAN MEDICAL SYSTEMS X-RAY PRODUCTS, 1678 Pioneer Rd, **Salt Lake City,** UT 84104-4205, *pg.* 1434, *pg.* 1761

Virginia

CARL ZEISS OPTICAL, INC., 13017 N Kingston Ave, **Chester,** VA 23836-2743, *pg.* 1405, *pg.* 1778
DYNEX TECHNOLOGIES, INC., 14340 Sullyfield Cir, **Chantilly,** VA 20151-1621, *pg.* 1408, *pg.* 1777
ISOMET CORPORATION, 5263 Port Royal Rd, **Springfield,** VA 22151-2103, *pg.* 1418, *pg.* 1807
MICROAIRE SURGICAL INSTRUMENTS INC., 3590 Grand Forks Blvd, **Charlottesville,** VA 22911, *pg.* 1423, *pg.* 1778
NORTHROP GRUMMAN INFORMATION SYSTEMS, 7575 Colshire Dr, **McLean,** VA 22102, *pg.* 1424, *pg.* 1794
ORBITAL ATK, 45101 Warp Drive, **Dulles,** VA 20166-6850, *pg.* 1425, *pg.* 1779
SPERRY MARINE INC., 1070 Seminole Trl, **Charlottesville,** VA 22901-2891, *pg.* 1430, *pg.* 1778
TASC, INC., 4801 Stonecroft Blvd, **Chantilly,** VA 20151, *pg.* 1431, *pg.* 1777
VERSAR, INC., 6850 Versar Ctr, **Springfield,** VA 22151, *pg.* 1435, *pg.* 1807

Washington

ESTERLINE TECHNOLOGIES CORPORATION, City Ctr Bellevue 500 108th Ave NE Ste 1500, **Bellevue,** WA 98004, *pg.* 1412, *pg.* 1814
FLUKE CORPORATION, 6920 Seaway Blvd, **Everett,** WA 98203-5829, *pg.* 1413, *pg.* 1819
SONOSITE, INC., 21919 30th Dr SE, **Bothell,** WA 98021-3904, *pg.* 1429, *pg.* 1818

West Virginia

PREISER SCIENTIFIC, INC., 94 Oliver St, **Saint Albans,** WV 25177, *pg.* 1427, *pg.* 1851

Wisconsin

3M DETECTION SOLUTIONS, 1060 Corporate Ctr Dr, **Oconomowoc,** WI 53066-4828, *pg.* 1398, *pg.* 1885
BADGER METER, INC., 4545 W Brown Deer Rd, **Milwaukee,** WI 53223, *pg.* 1401, *pg.* 1873
VESTA INC., 5400 W Franklin Dr, **Franklin,** WI 53132, *pg.* 1435, *pg.* 1858

First page reference indicates Business Class Edition
Second page reference indicates Geographic Edition

Paints, Varnishes & Enamels

California

DUNN-EDWARDS CORPORATION, 4885 E 52nd Pl, **Los Angeles,** CA 90058, *pg.* 1442, *pg.* 129
FOAMPRO MANUFACTURING, INC., 1791 Kaiser Ave Ste A, **Irvine,** CA 92614, *pg.* 1442, *pg.* 110
KELLY-MOORE PAINT COMPANY, INC., 987 Comml St, **San Carlos,** CA 94070, *pg.* 1443, *pg.* 198
PPG AEROSPACE DEFT FACILITY, 17451 Von Karman Ave, **Irvine,** CA 92614-6205, *pg.* 1445, *pg.* 115

Connecticut

KING INDUSTRIES, INC., Science Rd, **Norwalk,** CT 06852, *pg.* 1443, *pg.* 363
STANCHEM, INC., 401 Berlin St, **East Berlin,** CT 06023-1127, *pg.* 1449, *pg.* 345

Florida

OCEAN BIO CHEM, INC., 4041 SW 47th Ave, **Fort Lauderdale,** FL 33314-4023, *pg.* 1444, *pg.* 426

Illinois

CHROMA CORPORATION, 3900 W Dayton St, **McHenry,** IL 60050, *pg.* 1441, *pg.* 632
FLUID MANAGEMENT, 1023 Wheeling Rd, **Wheeling,** IL 60090-5776, *pg.* 1442, *pg.* 670
LECHLER, INC., 445 Kautz Rd, **Saint Charles,** IL 60174-5301, *pg.* 1444, *pg.* 658
OERLIKON BALZERS COATING USA, INC., 2511 Technology Dr Ste 114, **Elgin,** IL 60123, *pg.* 1444, *pg.* 610
PAASCHE AIRBRUSH COMPANY, 4311 N Normandy, **Chicago,** IL 60634-1395, *pg.* 1444, *pg.* 587
RUST-OLEUM CORPORATION, 11 Hawthorn Pkwy, **Vernon Hills,** IL 60061-1402, *pg.* 1447, *pg.* 664
SEYMOUR OF SYCAMORE, INC., 917 Crosby Ave, **Sycamore,** IL 60178-1343, *pg.* 1447, *pg.* 663

Indiana

RED SPOT PAINT & VARNISH CO., INC., 1107 E Louisiana St, **Evansville,** IN 47711, *pg.* 1446, *pg.* 679

Iowa

DIAMOND VOGEL PAINT, INC., 1110 Albany Pl SE, **Orange City,** IA 51041-1982, *pg.* 1441, *pg.* 710

Louisiana

JOTUN PAINTS, INC., 9203 Hwy 23, **Belle Chasse,** LA 70037, *pg.* 1443, *pg.* 742

Maryland

DAP PRODUCTS, INC., 2400 Boston St Ste 200, **Baltimore,** MD 21224, *pg.* 1441, *pg.* 756

Massachusetts

CALIFORNIA PRODUCTS CORPORATION, 150 Dascomb Rd, **Andover,** MA 01810-5873, *pg.* 1441, *pg.* 781
THE SAVOGRAN COMPANY, 259 Lenox St, **Norwood,** MA 02062-3417, *pg.* 1447, *pg.* 840

Minnesota

HIRSHFIELD'S INC., 725 2nd Ave N, **Minneapolis,** MN 55405-1601, *pg.* 1442, *pg.* 937
THE VALSPAR CORPORATION, 901 Third Ave S, **Minneapolis,** MN 55402, *pg.* 1449, *pg.* 945
WAGNER SPRAY TECH CORPORATION, 1770 Fernbrook Ln, **Plymouth,** MN 55447-4661, *pg.* 1449, *pg.* 954

Missouri

DAVIS PAINT COMPANY, 1311 Iron St PO Box 7589, **Kansas City,** MO 64116-4010, *pg.* 1441, *pg.* 982
MASTERCHEM INDUSTRIES, LLC, 3135 Old Hwy M, **Imperial,** MO 63052, *pg.* 1444, *pg.* 979

Nevada

AERVOE INDUSTRIES INCORPORATED, 1198 Mark Cir, **Gardnerville,** NV 89410, *pg.* 1439, *pg.* 1021

New Jersey

BENJAMIN MOORE & CO., 101 Paragon Dr, **Montvale,** NJ 07645, *pg.* 1440, *pg.* 1085
THE MURALO COMPANY, 148 E 5th St, **Bayonne,** NJ 07002, *pg.* 1444, *pg.* 1042
PETTIT PAINT COMPANY, 36 Pine St, **Rockaway,** NJ 07866, *pg.* 1444, *pg.* 1116
SHERWIN-WILLIAMS WOOD CARE GROUP, 10 Mountainview Rd, **Upper Saddle River,** NJ 07458-1933, *pg.* 1448, *pg.* 1127

Ohio

AKZO NOBEL COATINGS INC., 1313 Windsor Ave, **Columbus,** OH 43211-2851, *pg.* 1439, *pg.* 1437
AKZO NOBEL DECORATIVE PAINTS, USA, 15885 Sprague Rd, **Strongsville,** OH 44136, *pg.* 1439, *pg.* 1474
AKZONOBEL DECORATIVE PAINTS U.S., 15885 W Sprague Rd, **Strongsville,** OH 44136-1772, *pg.* 1439, *pg.* 1474
THE BRON SHOE COMPANY, 1313 Alum Creek Dr, **Columbus,** OH 43209, *pg.* 1440, *pg.* 1438
DAY-GLO COLOR CORP., 4515 Saint Clair Ave, **Cleveland,** OH 44103-1203, *pg.* 1441, *pg.* 1429
ELMER'S PRODUCTS, INC., 460 Polaris Pkwy Ste 5, **Westerville,** OH 43082, *pg.* 1442, *pg.* 1479
HAR ADHESIVE TECHNOLOGIES, 60 S Park, **Bedford,** OH 44146, *pg.* 1442, *pg.* 1405
ITW - EVERCOAT, 6600 Cornell Rd, **Cincinnati,** OH 45242-2033, *pg.* 1443, *pg.* 1415
PRATT & LAMBERT PAINTS, 101 Prospect Ave, **Cleveland,** OH 44115-1093, *pg.* 1446, *pg.* 1434
RPM INTERNATIONAL INC., 2628 Pearl Rd, **Medina,** OH 44258, *pg.* 1447, *pg.* 1464
THE SHERWIN-WILLIAMS COMPANY, 101 W Prospect Ave, **Cleveland,** OH 44115, *pg.* 1447, *pg.* 1435
SHERWIN-WILLIAMS DIVERSIFIED BRANDS DIVISION, 101 Prospect Ave N W, **Cleveland,** OH 44115, *pg.* 1448, *pg.* 1435
SHERWIN WILLIAMS, 101 Prospect Ave nw, **Cleveland,** OH 44115, *pg.* 1448, *pg.* 1436
UES, INC., 4401 Dayton Xenia Rd, **Dayton,** OH 45432-1894, *pg.* 1449, *pg.* 1447
THE WOOSTER BRUSH COMPANY, 604 Madison Ave, **Wooster,** OH 44691-4764, *pg.* 1450, *pg.* 1482
YENKIN-MAJESTIC PAINT CORPORATION, 1920 Leonard Ave, **Columbus,** OH 43219-2514, *pg.* 1450, *pg.* 1445

Oklahoma

ANCHOR PAINT MANUFACTURING CO. INC., 6707 E 14th St, **Tulsa,** OK 74112-6615, *pg.* 1440, *pg.* 1489

Pennsylvania

CERAMIC COLOR & CHEMICAL MFG. CO., PO Box 297, **New Brighton,** PA 15066, *pg.* 1441, *pg.* 1555
KOP-COAT, INC., 436 7th Ave 1850 Koppers Bldg, **Pittsburgh,** PA 15219, *pg.* 1444, *pg.* 1576
PECORA CORPORATION, 165 Wambold Rd, **Harleysville,** PA 19438-2014, *pg.* 1444, *pg.* 1536
PPG INDUSTRIES, INC., 1 PPG Place, **Pittsburgh,** PA 15272-0001, *pg.* 1445, *pg.* 1579
THE REAL MILK PAINT CO., 11 W Pumping Sta Rd, **Quakertown,** PA 18951, *pg.* 1446, *pg.* 1583
UNITED GILSONITE LABORATORIES, 1396 Jefferson Ave, **Dunmore,** PA 18509-2415, *pg.* 1449, *pg.* 1527

Texas

ENGLISH COLOR & SUPPLY INC., 810 N Grove Rd, **Richardson,** TX 75081, *pg.* 1442, *pg.* 1735
JONES-BLAIR COMPANY, 2728 Empire Central, **Dallas,** TX 75235, *pg.* 1443, *pg.* 1682
LAPOLLA INDUSTRIES, INC., 15402 Vantage Pkwy E Ste 322, **Houston,** TX 77032, *pg.* 1444, *pg.* 1710
WILSONART INTERNATIONAL, INC., 2400 Wilson Pl, **Temple,** TX 76504-5131, *pg.* 1450, *pg.* 1746

Washington

HOMAX PRODUCTS INC., 1835 Barkley Blvd Ste 101, **Bellingham,** WA 98226, *pg.* 1442, *pg.* 1817

Wisconsin

HERESITE PROTECTIVE COATINGS, INC., 822 S 14th St, **Manitowoc,** WI 54220, *pg.* 1442, *pg.* 1868

Paper, Packaging & Containers

California

AVERY DENNISON CORPORATION, 207 Goode, **Glendale,** CA 91203, *pg.* 1452, *pg.* 95
ICON DESIGN & DISPLAY, INC., 1733 Sebastopol Rd, **Santa Rosa,** CA 95407-6816, *pg.* 1460, *pg.* 277
POLY PAK AMERICA, INC., 2939 E Washington Blvd, **Los Angeles,** CA 90023-4277, *pg.* 1467, *pg.* 138
PUBLIC STORAGE, 701 Western Ave, **Glendale,** CA 91201-2349, *pg.* 1467, *pg.* 98

Colorado

BALL CORPORATION, 10 Longs Peak Dr, **Broomfield,** CO 80021-2510, *pg.* 1452, *pg.* 311

Connecticut

ATLAS HOLDINGS LLC, 1 Sound Shore Dr Ste 203, **Greenwich,** CT 06830, *pg.* 1452, *pg.* 349
HASLER, INC., 478 Wheelers Farms Rd, **Milford,** CT 06461, *pg.* 1459, *pg.* 356
INLINE PLASTICS CORP., 42 Canal St, **Shelton,** CT 06484-3223, *pg.* 1460, *pg.* 370

Florida

ARDAGH GROUP, 401 E Jackson St Ste 2800, **Tampa,** FL 33602, *pg.* 1452, *pg.* 470
B.H. BUNN COMPANY, 2730 Drane Field Rd, **Lakeland,** FL 33811-1325, *pg.* 1453, *pg.* 437
POINT BLANK SOLUTIONS, INC., 2102 SW 2nd St, **Pompano Beach,** FL 33069, *pg.* 1467, *pg.* 460

Georgia

ANDRITZ INC., 1115 Northmeadow Pkwy, **Roswell,** GA 30076-3857, *pg.* 1451, *pg.* 539
BWAY HOLDING COMPANY, 8607 Roberts Dr Ste 250, **Atlanta,** GA 30350-2230, *pg.* 1454, *pg.* 491
CARAUSTAR INDUSTRIES, INC., 5000 Austell-Powder Springs Rd Ste 300, **Austell,** GA 30106-3227, *pg.* 1455, *pg.* 525
GEORGIA-PACIFIC LLC, 133 Peachtree St NE, **Atlanta,** GA 30303, *pg.* 1458, *pg.* 507
GRAPHIC PACKAGING HOLDING COMPANY, 1500 Riveredge Pkwy Ste 100, **Atlanta,** GA 30328, *pg.* 1459, *pg.* 509
MEADWESTVACO PACKAGING SYSTEMS, LLC, 949 Herndon St Nw, **Atlanta,** GA 30318, *pg.* 1464, *pg.* 514
NEENAH PAPER, INC., 3460 Preston Ridge Rd Ste 600, **Alpharetta,** GA 30005, *pg.* 1465, *pg.* 484

Idaho

BOISE CASCADE HOLDINGS, L.L.C., 1111 W Jefferson St, **Boise,** ID 83702, *pg.* 1453, *pg.* 546
I/D/E/A/ INC., 1 Idea Way, **Caldwell,** ID 83605-6999, *pg.* 1460, *pg.* 548

Illinois

APTARGROUP, INC., 475 W Terra Cotta Ave Ste E, **Crystal Lake,** IL 60014-9695, *pg.* 1451, *pg.* 598
BROWN PAPER GOODS COMPANY, 3530 Birchwood Dr, **Waukegan,** IL 60085-8334, *pg.* 1454, *pg.* 665
CALUMET CARTON COMPANY, 16920 State St, **South Holland,** IL 60473-2841, *pg.* 1454, *pg.* 661
CRESCENT CARDBOARD COMPANY, L.L.C., 100 W Willow Rd, **Wheeling,** IL 60090-6522, *pg.* 1456, *pg.* 670
FLEX-O-GLASS, INC., 1100 N Cicero Ave, **Chicago,** IL 60651, *pg.* 1457, *pg.* 574
FORT DEARBORN COMPANY, 1530 Morse Ave, **Elk Grove Village,** IL 60007, *pg.* 1457, *pg.* 610
ITW HI-CONE, 1140 W Bryn Mawr Ave, **Itasca,** IL 60143-1509, *pg.* 1461, *pg.* 620
LABELQUEST, INC., 578 N Michigan St, **Elmhurst,** IL 60126, *pg.* 1463, *pg.* 611
NETWORK SERVICES COMPANY, 1100 E Woodfield Rd, Ste 200, **Schaumburg,** IL 60173, *pg.* 1465, *pg.* 659
PACKAGING CORPORATION OF AMERICA, 1955 W Field Ct, **Lake Forest,** IL 60045, *pg.* 1466, *pg.* 624
PACTIV CORPORATION, 1900 W Field Ct, **Lake Forest,** IL 60045-4828, *pg.* 1466, *pg.* 624
REXAM BEVERAGE CAN NORTH AMERICA, 8770 W Bryn Mawr Ave, **Chicago,** IL 60631-3515, *pg.* 1468, *pg.* 588
SCHWARZ PAPER COMPANY, 8338 Austin Ave, **Morton Grove,** IL 60053-3209, *pg.* 1468, *pg.* 634
SOLO CUP COMPANY, 150 S Saunders Rd Ste 150, **Lake Forest,** IL 60045, *pg.* 1469, *pg.* 625
TRANSILWRAP COMPANY, INC., 9201 W Belmont Ave, **Franklin Park,** IL 60131, *pg.* 1470, *pg.* 613
VISKASE COMPANIES, INC., 8205 S Cass Ave Ste 115, **Darien,** IL 60561-5319, *pg.* 1471, *pg.* 599
WARP BROTHERS, 4647 W Augusta Blvd, **Chicago,** IL 60651-3310, *pg.* 1471, *pg.* 595
ZIP-PAK, 1800 Sycamore Rd, **Manteno,** IL 60950, *pg.* 1473, *pg.* 631

Kansas

KOCH INDUSTRIES, INC., 4111 E 37th St N, **Wichita,** KS 67220, *pg.* 1463, *pg.* 724
LAWRENCE PAPER COMPANY, 2801 Lakeview Rd PO Box 887, **Lawrence,** KS 66049, *pg.* 1463, *pg.* 715

Maryland

C.R. DANIELS, INC., 3451 Ellicott Ctr Dr, **Ellicott City,** MD 21043, *pg.* 1456, *pg.* 769
INDEPENDENT CAN COMPANY, 1300 Brass Mill Rd, **Belcamp,** MD 21017-1211, *pg.* 1460, *pg.* 760

Massachusetts

BOISE CASCADE, 32 Manning Rd, **Billerica,** MA 01821, *pg.* 1453, *pg.* 788
CRANE & CO., INC., 30 South St, **Dalton,** MA 01226-1751, *pg.* 1456, *pg.* 816
FLEXCON CORPORATION, 1 Flexcon Indus Pk, **Spencer,** MA 01562-2642, *pg.* 1457, *pg.* 844
HAZEN PAPER COMPANY, 240 S Water St, **Holyoke,** MA 01040, *pg.* 1459, *pg.* 825
PELICAN PRODUCTS, 147 N Main St, **South Deerfield,** MA 01373-1026, *pg.* 1467, *pg.* 843
SAPPI FINE PAPER NORTH AMERICA, 255 State St, # 4, **Boston,** MA 02109, *pg.* 1468, *pg.* 801
SOUTHWORTH COMPANY INC., 265 Main St, **Agawam,** MA 01001-1822, *pg.* 1470, *pg.* 781

Michigan

AMCOR PET PACKAGING INC., 10521 South Hwy M 52, **Manchester,** MI 48158, *pg.* 1451, *pg.* 898
ARVCO CONTAINER CORPORATION, 845 Gibson St, **Kalamazoo,** MI 49001-2573, *pg.* 1452, *pg.* 894
TECUMSEH PACKAGING SOLUTIONS, 707 S Evans St, **Tecumseh,** MI 49286-1919, *pg.* 1470, *pg.* 909

Minnesota

BEDFORD INDUSTRIES, INC., 1659 Rowe Ave, **Worthington,** MN 56187, *pg.* 1453, *pg.* 967
DOUGLAS MACHINE, INC., 3404 Iowa St, **Alexandria,** MN 56308-3345, *pg.* 1456, *pg.* 915

Mississippi

RESOLUTE FOREST PRODUCTS, 1000 Papermill Rd, **Grenada,** MS 38901, *pg.* 1468, *pg.* 968

Missouri

ALPHA PACKAGING, 1555 Page Industrial Blvd, **Saint Louis,** MO 63132, *pg.* 1451, *pg.* 990
TRICORBRAUN, 6 CityPlace Dr 1000, **Saint Louis,** MO 63141, *pg.* 1471, *pg.* 1004

Nebraska

AIRLITE PLASTICS COMPANY, 6110 Abbott Dr, **Omaha,** NE 68110, *pg.* 1451, *pg.* 1013
GIBRALTAR PACKAGING GROUP, INC., 2000 Summit Ave, **Hastings,** NE 68901-6703, *pg.* 1459, *pg.* 1011

New Hampshire

MONADNOCK PAPER MILLS, INC., 117 Antrim Rd, **Bennington,** NH 03442-4205, *pg.* 1464, *pg.* 1033

New Jersey

COMAR INC., 1 Comar Pl, **Buena,** NJ 08310-1523, *pg.* 1455, *pg.* 1047
GLUEFAST COMPANY, INC., 3535 State Rte 66 Bldg 1, **Neptune,** NJ 07753, *pg.* 1459, *pg.* 1090
JAMES ALEXANDER CORPORATION, 845 State Rte 94, **Blairstown,** NJ 07825, *pg.* 1461, *pg.* 1044
NETWORK 1 FINANCIAL GROUP, INC., 2 Bridge Ave Ste 241, **Red Bank,** NJ 07701, *pg.* 1465, *pg.* 1114
NEXUS PLASTICS, INC., 1 Loretto Ave, **Hawthorne,** NJ 07506-1303, *pg.* 1465, *pg.* 1073
SEALED AIR CORPORATION, 200 Riverfront Blvd, **Elmwood Park,** NJ 07407, *pg.* 1468, *pg.* 1058
TEKNI-PLEX, INC., 201 Industrial Pkwy, **Somerville,** NJ 08876, *pg.* 1470, *pg.* 1122
UNITED STATES BOX CORP., 1296 McCarter Hwy, **Newark,** NJ 07104-3714, *pg.* 1471, *pg.* 1098

New York

AMERICAN PACKAGING CORPORATION, 777 Driving Pk Ave, **Rochester,** NY 14613-1591, *pg.* 1451, *pg.* 1333
CASE PAPER COMPANY INC., 500 Mamaroneck Ave 2nd Fl, **Harrison,** NY 10528-1633, *pg.* 1455, *pg.* 1163
CHEM-TAINER INDUSTRIES, INC., 361 Neptune Ave, **West Babylon,** NY 11704-5818, *pg.* 1455, *pg.* 1349
COMPLEMAR PARTNERS, 500 Lee Rd, **Rochester,** NY 14606, *pg.* 1455, *pg.* 1333
FINCH PAPER LLC, 1 Glen St, **Glens Falls,** NY 12801-4439, *pg.* 1457, *pg.* 1161
GARAGETEK INC., 145 Pinelawn Rd, Ste 240N, **Melville,** NY 11747, *pg.* 1457, *pg.* 1179
INNOVATIVE PLASTICS CORPORATION, 400 Rte 303, **Orangeburg,** NY 10962, *pg.* 1460, *pg.* 1319
LINDENMEYR MUNROE, 3 Manhattanville Rd, **Purchase,** NY 10577, *pg.* 1464, *pg.* 1325
MARIETTA HOSPITALITY, 37 Huntington St, **Cortland,** NY 13045, *pg.* 1464, *pg.* 1155
MOHAWK FINE PAPERS, INC., 465 Saratoga St, **Cohoes,** NY 12047-4626, *pg.* 1464, *pg.* 1153
MOMENTIVE PERFORMANCE MATERIALS, INC., 260 Hudson River Rd, **Waterford,** NY 12188, *pg.* 1464, *pg.* 1349
NICE-PAK PRODUCTS, INC., 2 Nice Pak Pk, **Orangeburg,** NY 10962-1317, *pg.* 1465, *pg.* 1319
OUTFRONT MEDIA, 405 Lexington Ave, **New York,** NY 10174, *pg.* 1465, *pg.* 1275
TEXPAK INC., 130 New Hyde Pk Rd, **Franklin Square,** NY 11010, *pg.* 1470, *pg.* 1161
UNCLE BOBS SELF-STORAGE, 6367 Main St, **Buffalo,** NY 14221, *pg.* 1471, *pg.* 1151

North Carolina

ATLANTIC CORPORATION, 806 N 23rd St, **Wilmington,** NC 28405, *pg.* 1452, *pg.* 1392
XPEDX, 3900 Spring Garden St, **Greensboro,** NC 27407-1606, *pg.* 1473, *pg.* 1377

Ohio

AUTOMATED PACKAGING SYSTEMS INC., 10175 Philipp Pkwy, **Streetsboro,** OH 44241-4706, *pg.* 1452, *pg.* 1474
BUCKEYE CORRUGATED INC., 275 Springside Dr Ste 200, **Akron,** OH 44333-4551, *pg.* 1454, *pg.* 1400
GREIF INC., 425 Winter Rd, **Delaware,** OH 43015-8903, *pg.* 1459, *pg.* 1447
KLW PLASTICS, INC., 980 Deneen Ave, **Monroe,** OH 45050, *pg.* 1463, *pg.* 1465
OWENS-ILLINOIS, INC., 1 Michael Owens Way, **Perrysburg,** OH 43551-2999, *pg.* 1466, *pg.* 1470
SPINNAKER COATING, LLC, 518 E Water St, **Troy,** OH

First page reference indicates Business Class Edition
Second page reference indicates Geographic Edition

45373-3445, *pg.* 1470, *pg.* 1477
SUMMIT PLASTIC CO., 1169 Brittain Rd PO Box 117, **Akron,** OH 44305, *pg.* 1470, *pg.* 1403
WAUSAU PAPER BAY WEST, 700 Columbia Ave, **Middletown,** OH 45042-1931, *pg.* 1471, *pg.* 1465
XPEDX, 6285 Tri Ridge Blvd, **Loveland,** OH 45140, *pg.* 1472, *pg.* 1458

Oklahoma

CARLISLE FOODSERVICE PRODUCTS INCORPORATED, 4711 E Hefner Rd, **Oklahoma City,** OK 73131, *pg.* 1455, *pg.* 1485
ORCHIDS PAPER PRODUCTS COMPANY, 4826 Hunt St, **Pryor,** OK 74361, *pg.* 1465, *pg.* 1488

Pennsylvania

BERRY PLASTICS LANCASTER, 1706 Hempstead Rd, **Lancaster,** PA 17601-6706, *pg.* 1453, *pg.* 1546
CROWN HOLDINGS, INC., 1 Crown Way, **Philadelphia,** PA 19154, *pg.* 1456, *pg.* 1562
DUNMORE CORPORATION, 145 Wharton Rd, **Bristol,** PA 19007-1621, *pg.* 1456, *pg.* 1518
MCCOURT LABEL COMPANY, 20 Egbert Ln, **Lewis Run,** PA 16738, *pg.* 1464, *pg.* 1548
QUALITY PERFORATING, INC., 166 Dundaff St, **Carbondale,** PA 18407-1565, *pg.* 1468, *pg.* 1520
WEST PHARMACEUTICAL SERVICES, INC., 530 Herman O West Dr, **Exton,** PA 19341-0645, *pg.* 1472, *pg.* 1532

South Carolina

CRYOVAC, INC., 100 Rogers Bridge Rd Bldg A, **Duncan,** SC 29334, *pg.* 1456, *pg.* 1615
PINNACLE COATING & CONVERTING, INC., 212 Natl Ave, **Spartanburg,** SC 29303-6316, *pg.* 1467, *pg.* 1622
SONOCO PRODUCTS COMPANY, 1 N 2nd St, **Hartsville,** SC 29550-3305, *pg.* 1469, *pg.* 1619

Tennessee

CLARCOR, INC., 840 Crescent Ctr Dr Ste 600, **Franklin,** TN 37067, *pg.* 1455, *pg.* 1632
HOLLISTON LLC, 905 Holliston Mills Rd, **Church Hill,** TN 37642, *pg.* 1460, *pg.* 1630
INTERNATIONAL PAPER-BLEACHED BOARD DIV., 6400 Poplar Ave, **Memphis,** TN 38197-0100, *pg.* 1460, *pg.* 1644
INTERNATIONAL PAPER COMPANY, 6400 Poplar Ave, **Memphis,** TN 38197, *pg.* 1460, *pg.* 1644
LANGSTON COMPANIES, INC., 1760 S 3rd St, **Memphis,** TN 38109, *pg.* 1463, *pg.* 1645

Texas

AMERICAN EXCELSIOR COMPANY, 850 Ave H E, **Arlington,** TX 76011-7720, *pg.* 1451, *pg.* 1659
KIMBERLY-CLARK CORPORATION, 351 Phelps Dr, **Irving,** TX 75038-6540, *pg.* 1461, *pg.* 1720
SURFACE COATINGS LLC, 2007 A Industrial Blvd, **Rockwall,** TX 75087, *pg.* 1470, *pg.* 1737

Vermont

FIBERMARK INC., 161 Wellington Rd, **Brattleboro,** VT 05301, *pg.* 1457, *pg.* 1764

Virginia

LIQUI-BOX CORPORATION, 901 E Byrd St Ste 1105, **Richmond,** VA 23219, *pg.* 1464, *pg.* 1802
MIDWESCO FILTER RESOURCES INC., 385 Battaile Dr, **Winchester,** VA 22604, *pg.* 1464, *pg.* 1811
WESTROCK COMPANY, 501 S 5th St, **Richmond,** VA 23219-0501, *pg.* 1472, *pg.* 1805

Washington

POTLATCH CORPORATION, 601 W First Ave Ste 1600, **Spokane,** WA 99201-0603, *pg.* 1467, *pg.* 1844
SAMSON ROPE TECHNOLOGIES, 2090 Thornton St, **Ferndale,** WA 98248-9314, *pg.* 1468, *pg.* 1820

Wisconsin

APPVION INC., 825 E Wisconsin Ave, **Appleton,** WI 54912, *pg.* 1451, *pg.* 1852
BEMIS COMPANY, INC., 1 Neenah Ctr 4th Fl, **Neenah,** WI 54957, *pg.* 1453, *pg.* 1882
BEMIS HEALTHCARE PACKAGING, 3500 N Main St, **Oshkosh,** WI 54901-1233, *pg.* 1453, *pg.* 1885
BPM INC., 200 W Front St, **Peshtigo,** WI 54157, *pg.* 1454, *pg.* 1886
CAMPBELL WRAPPER CORPORATION, 1415 Fortune Ave, **De Pere,** WI 54115, *pg.* 1454, *pg.* 1856
PACON CORPORATION, 2525 N Casaloma Dr, **Appleton,** WI 54912-7068, *pg.* 1466, *pg.* 1852
QUAD/GRAPHICS, INC., N61 W23044 Harry's Way, **Sussex,** WI 53089-3995, *pg.* 1468, *pg.* 1896
WASAU PAPER CORP., 100 Paper Pl, **Mosinee,** WI 54455, *pg.* 1471, *pg.* 1882
WAUSAU PAPER, 202 Second St, **Brokaw,** WI 54417-0305, *pg.* 1471, *pg.* 1855

Pet Food, Livestock & Poultry Feed

Alabama

JEFFERS, INC., 310 W Saunders Rd PO Box 100, **Dothan,** AL 36301, *pg.* 1477, *pg.* 5

Arizona

PETSMART, INC., 19601 N 27th Ave, **Phoenix,** AZ 85027, *pg.* 1481, *pg.* 18

California

ALL AMERICAN PET COMPANY, INC., 1100 Glendon Ave 17th Fl, **Los Angeles,** CA 90024, *pg.* 1474, *pg.* 125

BIG HEART PET BRANDS, 1 Maritime Plz, **San Francisco,** CA 94111, *pg.* 1474, *pg.* 213

CENTRAL GARDEN & PET COMPANY, 1340 Treat Blvd Ste 600, **Walnut Creek,** CA 94597, *pg.* 1475, *pg.* 303

J.D. HEISKELL & CO., 116 W Cedar St, **Tulare,** CA 93274-5348, *pg.* 1477, *pg.* 297

PETCO ANIMAL SUPPLIES, INC., 9125 Rehco Rd, **San Diego,** CA 92121, *pg.* 1480, *pg.* 206

Connecticut

THE BLUE BUFFALO CO., PO Box 770, **Wilton,** CT 06897, *pg.* 1474, *pg.* 385

CHARLES RIVER LABORATORIES, INC., 106 Rte 32, **North Franklin,** CT 06254-1811, *pg.* 1475, *pg.* 360

Delaware

MERCK ANIMAL HEALTH, 29160 Intervet Ln, **Millsboro,** DE 19966, *pg.* 1479, *pg.* 387

Illinois

ADM ALLIANCE NUTRITION, INC., 1000 N 30th St, **Quincy,** IL 62301-3400, *pg.* 1474, *pg.* 653

FURST-MCNESS COMPANY, 120 E Clark St, **Freeport,** IL 61032, *pg.* 1476, *pg.* 613

OIL-DRI CORPORATION OF AMERICA, 410 N Michigan Ave Ste 400, **Chicago,** IL 60611-4213, *pg.* 1480, *pg.* 586

TROUW NUTRITION USA, 115 Executive Dr, **Highland,** IL 62249-0219, *pg.* 1482, *pg.* 616

Indiana

ELANCO ANIMAL HEALTH, 2500 Innovation Way, **Greenfield,** IN 46140, *pg.* 1475, *pg.* 681

Iowa

KENT NUTRITION GROUP, 2905 N Hwy 61, **Muscatine,** IA 52761, *pg.* 1477, *pg.* 710

Kansas

HILL'S PET NUTRITION, INC., 400 SW 8th Ave, **Topeka,** KS 66603-3925, *pg.* 1476, *pg.* 721

Kentucky

KEENELAND ASSOCIATION INC., 4201 Versailles Rd, **Lexington,** KY 40510, *pg.* 1477, *pg.* 730

NATIONAL BAND & TAG CO., 721 York St, **Newport,** KY 41071-1817, *pg.* 1479, *pg.* 739

Massachusetts

PETEDGE, 100 Cumming Centre Ste 307 B, **Beverly,** MA 01915, *pg.* 1481, *pg.* 787

SMARTPAK EQUINE, LLC, 30 Worcester St, **Natick,** MA 01760, *pg.* 1482, *pg.* 834

Michigan

MERCY HEALTH, 200 Jefferson Ave SE, **Grand Rapids,** MI 49503, *pg.* 1479, *pg.* 888

NATIONAL BULK EQUIPMENT, INC., 12838 Stainless Dr, **Holland,** MI 49424-8218, *pg.* 1479, *pg.* 892

Minnesota

CARGILL ANIMAL NUTRITION, 15407 McGinty Rd W, **Wayzata,** MN 55391-2365, *pg.* 1475, *pg.* 965

HUBBARD FEEDS INC., 424 N Riverfront Dr, **Mankato,** MN 56001, *pg.* 1477, *pg.* 928

UNIVERSAL COOPERATIVES, INC., 1300 Corp Ctr Curve, **Eagan,** MN 55121-1233, *pg.* 1482, *pg.* 922

Missouri

BOEHRINGER INGELHEIM VETMEDICA, INC., 2621 N Belt Hwy, **Saint Joseph,** MO 64506, *pg.* 1474, *pg.* 989

MANNA PRO CORPORATION, 707 Spirit 40 Pk Dr Ste 150, **Chesterfield,** MO 63005-1137, *pg.* 1478, *pg.* 975

MFA INCORPORATED, 201 Ray Young Dr, **Columbia,** MO 65201, *pg.* 1479, *pg.* 976

NESTLE PURINA PETCARE COMPANY, 801 Chouteau Ave, **Saint Louis,** MO 63102, *pg.* 1479, *pg.* 1000

Nebraska

THE SCOULAR COMPANY, 2027 Dodge St, **Omaha,** NE 68102, *pg.* 1481, *pg.* 1018

New Jersey

THE HARTZ MOUNTAIN CORP., 400 Plaza Dr, **Secaucus,** NJ 07094-3605, *pg.* 1476, *pg.* 1120

MERCK ANIMAL HEALTH, 556 Morris Ave, **Summit,** NJ 07901, *pg.* 1478, *pg.* 1124

VITUSA CORP., 110 Charlotte Pl, **Englewood Cliffs,** NJ 07632-2606, *pg.* 1482, *pg.* 1063

New York

CONTINENTAL GRAIN COMPANY, 277 Park Ave, **New York,** NY 10172, *pg.* 1475, *pg.* 1218

H.W. NAYLOR COMPANY, INC., 121 Main St, **Morris,** NY 13808, *pg.* 1477, *pg.* 1183

North Carolina

HAPPY JACK INC., 2122 Hwy 258 S, **Snow Hill,** NC 28580, *pg.* 1476, *pg.* 1390

Pennsylvania

PETFOODDIRECT.COM, 189 Main St, **Harleysville,** PA 18936, *pg.* 1481, *pg.* 1536

Tennessee

IAMS COMPANY, 315 Cool Springs Blvd, **Franklin,** TN 37068, *pg.* 1477, *pg.* 1633

MARS PETCARE, 315 Cool Springs Blvd, **Franklin,** TN 37067, *pg.* 1478, *pg.* 1633

Texas

ANIMAL HEALTH INTERNATIONAL, INC., 7 Village Cir Ste 200, **Westlake,** TX 76262, *pg.* 1474, *pg.* 1749

Virginia

SOUTHERN STATES COOPERATIVE, INC., 6606 W Broad St, **Richmond,** VA 23230-1717, *pg.* 1482, *pg.* 1804

Wisconsin

FROMM FAMILY PET FOODS, INC., 13145 N Green Bay Rd 56 W, **Mequon,** WI 53097, *pg.* 1476, *pg.* 1870

First page reference indicates Business Class Edition
Second page reference indicates Geographic Edition

Pharmaceuticals & Health Care Products

Alabama

BIOHORIZONS, INC., 2300 Riverchase Ctr, **Birmingham,** AL 35244, *pg.* 1506, *pg.* 2
EAST ALABAMA MEDICAL CENTER, 2000 Pepperell Pkwy, **Opelika,** AL 36801-5452, *pg.* 1526, *pg.* 8
HEALTHSOUTH CORPORATION, 3660 Grandview Pkwy, **Birmingham,** AL 35243, *pg.* 1540, *pg.* 3

Arizona

BANNER HEALTH SYSTEM, 1441 N 12th St, **Phoenix,** AZ 85006-2837, *pg.* 1498, *pg.* 15
MATRIXX INITIATIVES, INC., 8515 E Anderson Dr, **Scottsdale,** AZ 85255, *pg.* 1559, *pg.* 23
PIMA MEDICAL INSTITUTE, 40 North Swan Ste 100, **Tucson,** AZ 85711, *pg.* 1585, *pg.* 27
RURAL/METRO CORPORATION, 9221 E Via de Ventura, **Scottsdale,** AZ 85258, *pg.* 1591, *pg.* 24

Arkansas

GOLDEN LIVING, 1000 Fianna Way, **Fort Smith,** AR 72919, *pg.* 1538, *pg.* 32
LIFEPLUS INTERNATIONAL, 15 Industrial Dr, **Batesville,** AR 72501-5512, *pg.* 1556, *pg.* 29
SPARKS HEALTH SYSTEM, 1500 Dodson Ave Ste 195, **Fort Smith,** AR 72901, *pg.* 1595, *pg.* 32
WELLQUEST MEDICAL & WELLNESS CORPORATION, 3400 SE Macy Rd Ste 18, **Bentonville,** AR 72712, *pg.* 1610, *pg.* 31

California

3M UNITEK CORPORATION, 2724 S Peck Rd, **Monrovia,** CA 91016-5097, *pg.* 1483, *pg.* 150
ABAXIS, INC., 3240 Whipple Rd, **Union City,** CA 94587-1217, *pg.* 1483, *pg.* 298
ABBOTT DIABETES CARE, INC., 1360 S Loop Rd, **Alameda,** CA 94502-7000, *pg.* 1483, *pg.* 38
ABBOTT MEDICAL OPTICS, INC., 1700 E Saint Andrew Pl, **Santa Ana,** CA 92705-4933, *pg.* 1485, *pg.* 260
ACCURAY INCORPORATED, 1310 Chesapeake Terr, **Sunnyvale,** CA 94089, *pg.* 1486, *pg.* 282
AFFYMAX, INC., 19200 Stevens Creek Blvd, Ste 240, **Cupertino,** CA 95014, *pg.* 1487, *pg.* 73
AFFYMETRIX, INC., 3420 Central Expy, **Santa Clara,** CA 95051, *pg.* 1487, *pg.* 263
ALERE SAN DIEGO, 9975 Summers Ridge Rd, **San Diego,** CA 92121-1205, *pg.* 1489, *pg.* 199
ALIGN TECHNOLOGY, INC., 2560 Orchard Pkwy, **San Jose,** CA 95131, *pg.* 1489, *pg.* 237
ALLERGAN, INC., 2525 Dupont Dr, **Irvine,** CA 92612, *pg.* 1491, *pg.* 106
AMERICAN SHARED HOSPITAL SERVICES, 4 Embarcadero Ctr Ste 3700, **San Francisco,** CA 94111-3823, *pg.* 1493, *pg.* 212
AMGEN INC., 1 Amgen Center Dr, **Thousand Oaks,** CA 91320-1799, *pg.* 1493, *pg.* 291
AMN HEALTHCARE SERVICES, INC., 12400 High Bluff Dr Ste 100, **San Diego,** CA 92130, *pg.* 1494, *pg.* 200
APRIA HEALTHCARE GROUP INC., 26220 Enterprise Ct, **Lake Forest,** CA 92630-8405, *pg.* 1495, *pg.* 120
ARDEA BIOSCIENCES, INC., 9390 Towne Ctr Dr, **San Diego,** CA 92121, *pg.* 1495, *pg.* 200
ARENA PHARMACEUTICALS, INC., 6166 Nancy Ridge Dr, **San Diego,** CA 92121-3223, *pg.* 1495, *pg.* 200
ASTEX PHARMACEUTICALS, INC, 4140 Dublin Blvd Ste 200, **Dublin,** CA 94568-7757, *pg.* 1497, *pg.* 77
AVANIR PHARMACEUTICALS, 20 Enterprise Ste 200, **Aliso Viejo,** CA 92656-7104, *pg.* 1498, *pg.* 40
BAZI INTERNATIONAL, INC., 18552 MacArthur Blvd Ste 325, **Irvine,** CA 92612, *pg.* 1501, *pg.* 107
BEECH STREET CORPORATION, 25500 Commercentre Dr, **Lake Forest,** CA 92630-8855, *pg.* 1503, *pg.* 121
BIO-RAD LABORATORIES, INC., 1000 Alfred Nobel Dr, **Hercules,** CA 94547-1811, *pg.* 1504, *pg.* 101
BIOLASE TECHNOLOGY, INC., 4 Cromwell, **Irvine,** CA 92618, *pg.* 1506, *pg.* 107
BIOMERICA, INC., 17571 Von Karman Ave, **Irvine,** CA 92614, *pg.* 1506, *pg.* 107
BOSLEY INC., 9100 Wilshire Blvd, East Tower Penthouse, **Beverly Hills,** CA 90212, *pg.* 1508, *pg.* 46
CALIFORNIA PACIFIC MEDICAL CENTER, 2333 Buchanan St, **San Francisco,** CA 94115-1925, *pg.* 1511, *pg.* 214
CAREFUSION CORPORATION, 3750 Torrey View Ct, **San Diego,** CA 92130-2622, *pg.* 1513, *pg.* 201
CATASYS, INC., 11150 Santa Monica Blvd Ste 1500, **Los Angeles,** CA 90025, *pg.* 1514, *pg.* 127
CEPHEID, 904 Caribbean Dr, **Sunnyvale,** CA 94089-1189, *pg.* 1514, *pg.* 284
CITY OF HOPE NATIONAL MEDICAL CENTER, 1500 E Duarte Rd, **Duarte,** CA 91010, *pg.* 1516, *pg.* 77
CLARIENT INC., 31 Columbia, **Aliso Viejo,** CA 92656-1460, *pg.* 1516, *pg.* 40
THE COOPER COMPANIES, INC., 6140 Stoneridge Mall Rd Ste 590, **Pleasanton,** CA 94588, *pg.* 1518, *pg.* 183
COVERED CALIFORNIA, 1601 Exposition Blvd, **Sacramento,** CA 95815, *pg.* 1519, *pg.* 196
CUTERA, INC., 3240 Bayshore Blvd, **Brisbane,** CA 94005, *pg.* 1521, *pg.* 49
CYTRX CORPORATION, 11726 San Vicente Blvd Ste 650, **Los Angeles,** CA 90049, *pg.* 1521, *pg.* 129
DAUGHTERS OF CHARITY HEALTH SYSTEM, 26000 Altamont Rd, **Los Altos,** CA 94022-4317, *pg.* 1522, *pg.* 124
DEN-MAT CORPORATION, 2727 Skwy Dr PO Box 1729, **Santa Maria,** CA 93455-1413, *pg.* 1522, *pg.* 271
DEPOMED, INC., 1360 O'Brien Dr, **Menlo Park,** CA 94025-1436, *pg.* 1523, *pg.* 143
DERMALOGICA, INC., 1535 Beachey Place, **Carson,** CA 90746, *pg.* 1523, *pg.* 63
DESIGNING HEALTH, INC., 28410 Witherspoon Pkwy, **Valencia,** CA 91355-4167, *pg.* 1523, *pg.* 299
DEXCOM INC, 6340 Sequence Dr, **San Diego,** CA 92121, *pg.* 1524, *pg.* 202
DIGIRAD CORPORATION, 13950 Stowe Dr, **Poway,** CA 92046-8803, *pg.* 1524, *pg.* 185
DJO INCORPORATED, 1430 Decision St, **Vista,** CA 92081, *pg.* 1524, *pg.* 302
DR. TATTOFF, INC., 8500 Wilshire Blvd Ste 105, **Beverly Hills,** CA 90211, *pg.* 1525, *pg.* 46
ENDOLOGIX, INC., 11 Studebaker, **Irvine,** CA 92618-2013, *pg.* 1528, *pg.* 109
EPOCRATES, INC., 1100 Park Pl Ste 300, **San Mateo,** CA 94403, *pg.* 1529, *pg.* 254
FUTUREDONTICS, INC., 6060 Ctr Dr 7th Fl, **Los Angeles,** CA 90045-1596, *pg.* 1532, *pg.* 131
GENENTECH, INC., 1 DNA Way, **South San Francisco,** CA 94080-4918, *pg.* 1533, *pg.* 279
GENOPTIX, INC., 2110 Rutherford Rd, **Carlsbad,** CA 92008, *pg.* 1534, *pg.* 59
GILEAD SCIENCES, INC., 333 Lakeside Dr, **Foster City,** CA 94404-1147, *pg.* 1535, *pg.* 88
HALOZYME THERAPEUTICS, INC., 11388 Sorrento Valley Rd, **San Diego,** CA 92121, *pg.* 1539, *pg.* 203
HEALTH NET, INC., 21650 Oxnard St, **Woodland Hills,** CA 91367-6607, *pg.* 1540, *pg.* 308
HEMACARE CORPORATION, 15350 Sherman Way Ste 350, **Van Nuys,** CA 91406, *pg.* 1541, *pg.* 300
HERBALIFE INTERNATIONAL OF AMERICA, INC., 800 W Olympic Blvd, **Los Angeles,** CA 90015, *pg.* 1541, *pg.* 132
IMPAX LABORATORIES, INC., 30831 Huntwood Ave, **Hayward,** CA 94544, *pg.* 1544, *pg.* 101
INTUITIVE SURGICAL, INC., 1266 Kifer Rd, **Sunnyvale,** CA 94086, *pg.* 1546, *pg.* 286
IPC THE HOSPITALIST COMPANY, INC., 4605 Lankershim Blvd Ste 617, **North Hollywood,** CA 91602, *pg.* 1547, *pg.* 167
IRIS INTERNATIONAL, INC., 9158 Eton Ave, **Chatsworth,** CA 91311, *pg.* 1547, *pg.* 64
ISIS PHARMACEUTICALS, INC., 2855 Gazelle Ct, **Carlsbad,** CA 92010-6670, *pg.* 1548, *pg.* 59
JENNY CRAIG OPERATIONS, INC., 5770 Fleet St, **Carlsbad,** CA 92008, *pg.* 1548, *pg.* 59
KAISER PERMANENTE, 1 Kaiser Plz Ste 2600, **Oakland,** CA 94612-3673, *pg.* 1552, *pg.* 171
LA JOLLA PHARMACEUTICAL COMPANY, 4365 Executive Dr Ste 300, **San Diego,** CA 92121, *pg.* 1554, *pg.* 204
LIFESCAN INC, 1000 Gibraltar Dr, **Milpitas,** CA 95035, *pg.* 1556, *pg.* 146
LIGAND PHARMACEUTICALS INC., 11085 N Torrey Pines Rd Ste 300, **La Jolla,** CA 92037, *pg.* 1556, *pg.* 119
MANNKIND CORPORATION, 28903 N Ave Paine, **Valencia,** CA 91355, *pg.* 1558, *pg.* 299
MASIMO CORPORATION, 40 Parker, **Irvine,** CA 92618, *pg.* 1558, *pg.* 113
MCKESSON CORPORATION, 1 Post St, **San Francisco,** CA 94104, *pg.* 1560, *pg.* 222
MEDICOOL, INC., 20460 Gramercy Pl, **Torrance,** CA 90501, *pg.* 1562, *pg.* 294
MEDTRONIC, 4280 Hacienda Dr, **Pleasanton,** CA 94588-2719, *pg.* 1563, *pg.* 183
MEMORIAL HEALTH SERVICES INC., 17360 Brookhurst St, **Fountain Valley,** CA 92708, *pg.* 1565, *pg.* 90
MENTOR CORPORATION, 201 Mentor Dr, **Santa Barbara,** CA 93111, *pg.* 1565, *pg.* 263
MERZ AESTHETICS, 1875 S Grant St Ste 200, **San Mateo,** CA 94402, *pg.* 1567, *pg.* 255
MOLECULAR DEVICES CORPORATION, 1311 Orleans Dr, **Sunnyvale,** CA 94089-1136, *pg.* 1568, *pg.* 287
MOLINA HEALTHCARE, INC., 200 Oceangate Ste 100, **Long Beach,** CA 90802-4317, *pg.* 1569, *pg.* 123
MONOGRAM BIOSCIENCES, INC., 345 Oyster Point Blvd, **South San Francisco,** CA 94080-1913, *pg.* 1569, *pg.* 280
NATROL, INC., 21411 Prairie St, **Chatsworth,** CA 91311-5829, *pg.* 1570, *pg.* 64
NATURAL ALTERNATIVES INTERNATIONAL, INC., 1185 Linda Vista Dr, **San Marcos,** CA 92069-3823, *pg.* 1571, *pg.* 253
NATUS MEDICAL INCORPORATED, 1501 Industrial Rd, **San Carlos,** CA 94070-4111, *pg.* 1572, *pg.* 199
NEKTAR THERAPEUTICS, 455 Mission Bay Blvd S, **San Francisco,** CA 94158, *pg.* 1572, *pg.* 224
NORDIC NATURALS, INC., 111 Jennings Dr, **Watsonville,** CA 95076, *pg.* 1573, *pg.* 305
NUVASIVE, INC., 7475 Lusk Blvd, **San Diego,** CA 92121, *pg.* 1577, *pg.* 205
OBAGI MEDICAL PRODUCTS, INC., 3760 Kilroy Airport Way Ste 500, **Long Beach,** CA 90806, *pg.* 1577, *pg.* 123
O'CONNOR HOSPITAL, 2105 Forest Ave, **San Jose,** CA 95128, *pg.* 1577, *pg.* 248
OCULUS INNOVATIVE SCIENCES, 1129 N McDowell Blvd, **Petaluma,** CA 94954, *pg.* 1577, *pg.* 182
OMNICELL INC., 590 E Middlefield Rd, **Mountain View,** CA 94043, *pg.* 1578, *pg.* 161
ONE LAMBDA, INC., 2001 Kittridge St, **Canoga Park,** CA 91303-2801, *pg.* 1578, *pg.* 58
OXIS INTERNATIONAL, INC., 468 N Camden Dr Ste 200, **Beverly Hills,** CA 90210, *pg.* 1579, *pg.* 47
PATIENT SAFETY TECHNOLOGIES, INC., 2 Venture Plz Ste 350, **Irvine,** CA 92618, *pg.* 1580, *pg.* 114
PHARMAVITE LLC, 8510 Balboa Blvd Ste 300, **Northridge,** CA 91325, *pg.* 1584, *pg.* 167
PRO-DEX, INC., 2361 McGaw Ave, **Irvine,** CA 92614, *pg.* 1586, *pg.* 115
PROMETHEUS LABORATORIES, INC., 9410 Carrol Pk Dr, **San Diego,** CA 92121-4203, *pg.* 1586, *pg.* 206
PURETEK CORPORATION, 1245 Aviation Pl, **San Fernando,** CA 91340, *pg.* 1587, *pg.* 211
QUALITY SYSTEMS, INC., 18111 Von Karman Ave, Ste 700, **Irvine,** CA 92612, *pg.* 1587, *pg.* 115
QUANTROS, INC., 475 Sycamore Dr, **Milpitas,** CA 95035, *pg.* 1587, *pg.* 147
QUIDEL CORPORATION, 10165 McKellar Ct, **San Diego,** CA 92121-4201, *pg.* 1588, *pg.* 207
RESMED INC., 9001 Spectrum Center Blvd, **San Diego,** CA 92123, *pg.* 1589, *pg.* 207
RESPONSE GENETICS, INC., 1640 Marengo St 6th Fl, **Los Angeles,** CA 90033, *pg.* 1590, *pg.* 139
SCRIPPS, 4275 Campus Point Ct, **San Diego,** CA 92121-1513, *pg.* 1593, *pg.* 209
SCRIPPS MERCY HOSPITAL, 4077 5th Ave, **San Diego,** CA 92103, *pg.* 1593, *pg.* 209
SECHRIST INDUSTRIES, INC., 4225 E La Palma Ave, **Anaheim,** CA 92807, *pg.* 1593, *pg.* 43
SEQUENOM, INC., 3595 John Hopkins Ct, **San Diego,** CA 92121-1331, *pg.* 1593, *pg.* 209
SHAKLEE CORPORATION, 4747 Willow Rd, **Pleasanton,** CA 94588-2763, *pg.* 1593, *pg.* 184
SMILE BRANDS GROUP INC., 8105 Irvine Center Dr Ste 1500, **Irvine,** CA 92618-4935, *pg.* 1594, *pg.* 116
SOURCE NATURALS, 23 Janis Way, **Scotts Valley,** CA 95066, *pg.* 1595, *pg.* 278
SPECTRASCIENCE, INC., 11568 Sorrento Valley Rd Ste 11, **San Diego,** CA 92121, *pg.* 1595, *pg.* 210
SPECTRUM LABORATORIES INC., 18617 S Broadwick St, **Compton,** CA 90220, *pg.* 1595, *pg.* 69

First page reference indicates Business Class Edition
Second page reference indicates Geographic Edition

SPECTRUM ORGANIC PRODUCTS, INC., 5341 Old Redwood Hwy Ste 400, **Petaluma,** CA 94954, *pg.* 1596, *pg.* 182
ST. VINCENT MEDICAL CENTER, 2131 W 3rd St, **Los Angeles,** CA 90057-1901, *pg.* 1597, *pg.* 140
STAAR SURGICAL COMPANY, 1911 Walker Ave, **Monrovia,** CA 91016-4846, *pg.* 1597, *pg.* 151
SUTTER HEALTH, 2200 River Plz Dr, **Sacramento,** CA 95833-4134, *pg.* 1600, *pg.* 197
THERMO FISHER SCIENTIFIC INC., 5791 Van Allen Way, **Carlsbad,** CA 92008, *pg.* 1602, *pg.* 61
VCA INC., 12401 W Olympic Blvd, **Los Angeles,** CA 90064-1022, *pg.* 1606, *pg.* 141
VITATECH INTERNATIONAL, INC., 2832 Dow Ave, **Tustin,** CA 92780-7212, *pg.* 1608, *pg.* 298
VIVUS, INC., 1172 Castro St, **Mountain View,** CA 94040-2552, *pg.* 1608, *pg.* 163
WHITEWING LABS, INC., 1815 Flower St, **Glendale,** CA 91201, *pg.* 1610, *pg.* 99
XOMA CORPORATION, 2910 7th St, **Berkeley,** CA 94710-2700, *pg.* 1611, *pg.* 46
ZOGENIX, INC., 12400 High Bluff Dr Ste 650, **San Diego,** CA 92130, *pg.* 1612, *pg.* 211
ZONARE MEDICAL SYSTEMS, INC., 420 N Bernardo Ave, **Mountain View,** CA 94043-5209, *pg.* 1612, *pg.* 163

Colorado

ALLOS THERAPEUTICS, INC., 11080 CirclePoint Rd Ste 430, **Westminster,** CO 80020, *pg.* 1492, *pg.* 336
ATKINS NUTRITIONALS, INC., 1050 17th St Ste 1500, **Denver,** CO 80265, *pg.* 1498, *pg.* 316
BIRNER DENTAL MANAGEMENT SERVICES, INC., 1777 S Harrison St Ste 1400, **Denver,** CO 80210, *pg.* 1506, *pg.* 317
COLORADO SERUM CO., 4950 York St, **Denver,** CO 80216-2246, *pg.* 1516, *pg.* 318
CORAM SPECIALTY INFUSION SERVICES, 1675 Broadway Ste 900, **Denver,** CO 80202, *pg.* 1519, *pg.* 318
CORGENIX MEDICAL CORPORATION, 11575 Main St Ste 400, **Broomfield,** CO 80020, *pg.* 1519, *pg.* 312
EMERGENCY MEDICAL SERVICES CORPORATION, 6200 S Syracuse Way, Ste 200, **Greenwood Village,** CO 80111, *pg.* 1528, *pg.* 331
ENCISION INC., 6797 Winchester Cir, **Boulder,** CO 80301, *pg.* 1528, *pg.* 310
GAIAM, INC., 833 W South Boulder Rd, **Louisville,** CO 80027-2452, *pg.* 1532, *pg.* 334
HESKA CORPORATION, 3760 Rocky Mountain Ave, **Loveland,** CO 80538, *pg.* 1542, *pg.* 335
LIFELOC TECHNOLOGIES, INC., 12441 W 49th Ave Unit 4, **Wheat Ridge,** CO 80033, *pg.* 1556, *pg.* 336
MESA LABORATORIES, INC., 12100 W 6th Ave, **Lakewood,** CO 80228-1252, *pg.* 1567, *pg.* 333
SIMILASAN CORPORATION, 1805 Shea Center Dr, Ste 270, **Highlands Ranch,** CO 80129, *pg.* 1594, *pg.* 332
THE SPECTRANETICS CORPORATION, 9965 Federal Dr, **Colorado Springs,** CO 80921, *pg.* 1595, *pg.* 315
WATER PIK, INC., 1730 E Prospect Rd, **Fort Collins,** CO 80553-0001, *pg.* 1609, *pg.* 329

Connecticut

ALEXION PHARMACEUTICALS, INC., 352 Knotter Dr, **Cheshire,** CT 06410-1138, *pg.* 1489, *pg.* 341
THE ARISTOTLE CORPORATION, 96 Cummings Point Rd, **Stamford,** CT 06902, *pg.* 1496, *pg.* 372
BIOTECH CORPORATION, 107 Oakwood Dr, **Glastonbury,** CT 06033, *pg.* 1506, *pg.* 349
BOEHRINGER INGELHEIM PHARMACEUTICALS, INC., 900 Ridgebury Rd, **Ridgefield,** CT 06877-1058, *pg.* 1507, *pg.* 368
CAS MEDICAL SYSTEMS, INC., 44 E Industrial Rd, **Branford,** CT 06405, *pg.* 1513, *pg.* 339
FUJIFILM MEDICAL SYSTEMS USA, INC., 419 W Ave, **Stamford,** CT 06902-6300, *pg.* 1531, *pg.* 374
GRIFFIN HEALTH SERVICES CORPORATION, 130 Division St, **Derby,** CT 06418-1326, *pg.* 1538, *pg.* 345
IMS HEALTH, INC., 83 Wooster Hts Rd Fl 5, **Danbury,** CT 06810-7552, *pg.* 1544, *pg.* 344
MAGELLAN HEALTH SERVICES, INC., 55 Nod Rd, **Avon,** CT 06001, *pg.* 1557, *pg.* 337
MEMRY CORPORATION, 3 Berkshire Blvd, **Bethel,** CT 06801, *pg.* 1565, *pg.* 337
PURDUE PHARMA LP, 1 Stamford Forum 201 Tresser Blvd, **Stamford,** CT 06901-3431, *pg.* 1587, *pg.* 377

Delaware

ASTRAZENECA PHARMACEUTICALS LP, 1800 Concord Pike, **Wilmington,** DE 19850-5437, *pg.* 1497, *pg.* 389
CHRISTIANA CARE CORPORATION, 501 W 14th St, **Wilmington,** DE 19801, *pg.* 1515, *pg.* 390
INCYTE CORPORATION, Rte 141 & Henry Clay Rd Bldg E336, **Wilmington,** DE 19880, *pg.* 1545, *pg.* 392

Florida

21ST CENTURY ONCOLOGY, INC., 2270 Colonial Blvd, **Fort Myers,** FL 33907, *pg.* 1483, *pg.* 427
ALL CHILDREN'S HOSPITAL INC., 501 6th Ave S, **Saint Petersburg,** FL 33701, *pg.* 1490, *pg.* 461
BAYFRONT HEALTH SYSTEM, INC., 701 6th St S, **Saint Petersburg,** FL 33701-4814, *pg.* 1500, *pg.* 461
BEACH PRODUCTS, INC., 5220 S Manhattan Ave, **Tampa,** FL 33611-3420, *pg.* 1501, *pg.* 471
BLUE CROSS & BLUE SHIELD OF FLORIDA, INC., PO Box 1798, **Jacksonville,** FL 32231-0014, *pg.* 1507, *pg.* 432
CANCER TREATMENT CENTERS OF AMERICA, 5900 Broken Sound Pkwy NW, **Boca Raton,** FL 33487, *pg.* 1511, *pg.* 410
CCS MEDICAL HOLDINGS, INC., 14255 49th St N Ste 301, **Clearwater,** FL 33762, *pg.* 1514, *pg.* 415
COMPREHENSIVE CARE CORPORATION, 3405 W Dr Martin Luther King Jr Blvd Ste 101, **Tampa,** FL 33607-3540, *pg.* 1517, *pg.* 472
CONTINUCARE CORPORATION, 7200 Corp Ctr Dr Ste 600, **Miami,** FL 33126, *pg.* 1518, *pg.* 442
CORDIS CORPORATION, 14201 NW 60th Ave, **Hialeah,** FL 33014, *pg.* 1519, *pg.* 430
CROSS COUNTRY HEALTHCARE, INC., 6551 Park of Commerce Blvd Ste 200, **Boca Raton,** FL 33487-8244, *pg.* 1520, *pg.* 411
CRYO-CELL INTERNATIONAL, INC., 700 Brooker Creek Blvd Ste 1800, **Oldsmar,** FL 34677, *pg.* 1520, *pg.* 452
EUROPEAN WAX CENTER, PO Box 802208, **Aventura,** FL 33280, *pg.* 1529, *pg.* 409
EXACTECH, INC., 2320 NW 66th Ct, **Gainesville,** FL 32653-1630, *pg.* 1529, *pg.* 428
FLORIDA HOSPITAL ORLANDO, 601 E Rollins St, **Orlando,** FL 32803, *pg.* 1531, *pg.* 453
GARDEN OF LIFE, INC., 5500 Village Blvd Ste 202, **West Palm Beach,** FL 33407, *pg.* 1532, *pg.* 478
GENELINK, INC., 317 Wekiva Springs Rd Ste 200, **Longwood,** FL 32779, *pg.* 1533, *pg.* 438
HALIFAX MEDICAL CENTER, 303 N Clyde Morris Blvd, **Daytona Beach,** FL 32114, *pg.* 1538, *pg.* 420
HEALTH WATCH INC., 6400 Park of Commerce Blvd Ste 1, **Boca Raton,** FL 33487, *pg.* 1540, *pg.* 411
HEARUSA, INC., 104550 Riverside Dr, **Palm Beach Gardens,** FL 33410, *pg.* 1541, *pg.* 457
HOVEROUND CORP., 2151 Whitfield Industrial Way, **Sarasota,** FL 34243-4047, *pg.* 1543, *pg.* 466
IMAGING DIAGNOSTIC SYSTEMS, INC., 5307 NW 35th Ter, **Fort Lauderdale,** FL 33309, *pg.* 1544, *pg.* 425
INTELLIGENT HEARING SYSTEMS CORP., 6860 SW 81 St, **Miami,** FL 33143-7708, *pg.* 1546, *pg.* 443
JACKSON MEMORIAL HOSPITAL, 1611 N.W. 12th Ave, **Miami,** FL 33136, *pg.* 1548, *pg.* 443
JOHNSON & JOHNSON VISION CARE, INC., 7500 Centurion Pkwy, **Jacksonville,** FL 32256-0517, *pg.* 1552, *pg.* 434
LAKELAND REGIONAL MEDICAL CENTER, 1324 Lakeland Hills Blvd, **Lakeland,** FL 33805, *pg.* 1554, *pg.* 437
LEE MEMORIAL HEALTH SYSTEM, PO Box 2218, **Fort Myers,** FL 33902, *pg.* 1555, *pg.* 428
LIBERATOR MEDICAL HOLDINGS, INC., 2979 SE Gran Park Way, **Stuart,** FL 34997, *pg.* 1555, *pg.* 468
LIBERTY MEDICAL SUPPLY, INC., 10400 S Federal Hwy, **Port Saint Lucie,** FL 34952, *pg.* 1555, *pg.* 460
MANATEE MEMORIAL HOSPITAL & HEALTH SYSTEM, 206 2nd St E, **Bradenton,** FL 34208, *pg.* 1558, *pg.* 415
METROPOLITAN HEALTH NETWORKS, INC., 777 NW 51st St Ste 510, **Boca Raton,** FL 33431-4475, *pg.* 1567, *pg.* 412
MICHAEL DATTOLI MD, LLC, 2803 Fruitville Rd, **Sarasota,** FL 34237, *pg.* 1568, *pg.* 466
MONTICELLO DRUG CO., 592 Ellis Rd S Ste 120, **Jacksonville,** FL 32254, *pg.* 1569, *pg.* 434
MOUNT SINAI MEDICAL CENTER, 4300 Alton Rd, **Miami Beach,** FL 33140-2910, *pg.* 1569, *pg.* 448
NICKLAUS CHILDREN'S HOSPITAL, 3100 SW 62nd Ave, **Miami,** FL 33155, *pg.* 1573, *pg.* 444
NIPRO DIAGNOSTICS, INC., 2400 NW 55th Ct, **Fort Lauderdale,** FL 33309, *pg.* 1573, *pg.* 426
NOVAPRO, 1408 N Westshore Blvd Ste 300, **Tampa,** FL 33607, *pg.* 1574, *pg.* 474
NOVEN PHARMACEUTICALS, INC., 11960 SW 144th St, **Miami,** FL 33186, *pg.* 1576, *pg.* 445
ONEBLOOD, INC., 10100 Dr Martin Luther King Jr St N, **Saint Petersburg,** FL 33716, *pg.* 1578, *pg.* 463
ORAGENICS, INC., 4902 Eisenhower Blvd, Ste 125, **Tampa,** FL 33634, *pg.* 1578, *pg.* 475
ORLANDO REGIONAL MEDICAL CENTER, 1414 Kuhl Ave, **Orlando,** FL 32806, *pg.* 1579, *pg.* 455
SAINT PETERSBURG GENERAL HOSPITAL, 6500 38th Ave N, **Saint Petersburg,** FL 33710, *pg.* 1591, *pg.* 464
SHRINERS HOSPITALS FOR CHILDREN, 2900 Rocky Point Dr, **Tampa,** FL 33607-1460, *pg.* 1594, *pg.* 475
SKULPT INC., 5220 S University Dr Ste 204, **Davie,** FL 33328, *pg.* 1594, *pg.* 419
SOUTH BROWARD HOSPITAL DISTRICT, 3501 Johnson St, **Hollywood,** FL 33021, *pg.* 1595, *pg.* 431
THE STEPHAN COMPANY, 1850 W McNab Rd, **Fort Lauderdale,** FL 33309-1012, *pg.* 1597, *pg.* 426
STRYKER MAKO, 2555 Davie Rd, **Fort Lauderdale,** FL 33317, *pg.* 1598, *pg.* 427
UNIVERSITY HOSPITAL & MEDICAL CENTER, 7201 N University Dr, **Tamarac,** FL 33321-2913, *pg.* 1604, *pg.* 470
VICTUS, INC., 4918 SW 74th Ct, **Miami,** FL 33155, *pg.* 1606, *pg.* 447
VISITING NURSE ASSOCIATION OF FLORIDA, 2400 SE Monterey Rd, **Stuart,** FL 34996, *pg.* 1607, *pg.* 468
VITACOST.COM, INC., 5400 Broken Sound Blvd NW Ste 500, **Boynton Beach,** FL 33487, *pg.* 1607, *pg.* 414
VITAL PHARMACEUTICALS, INC., 1600 N Park Dr, **Weston,** FL 33326, *pg.* 1607, *pg.* 479
VITAS HEALTHCARE CORPORATION, 201 S Biscayne Blvd, #400, **Miami,** FL 33131, *pg.* 1608, *pg.* 447

Georgia

ADCARE HEALTH SYSTEMS, INC., 1145 Hembree Rd, **Roswell,** GA 30076, *pg.* 1486, *pg.* 539
ALERE HEALTH SYSTEMS, INC., 1850 Parkway Pl, **Marietta,** GA 30067, *pg.* 1488, *pg.* 535
ALIMERA SCIENCES, INC., 6120 Winward Pkway Ste 290, **Alpharetta,** GA 30005, *pg.* 1490, *pg.* 482
APYRON TECHNOLOGIES, INC., 3342 International Pk Dr, **Atlanta,** GA 30316, *pg.* 1495, *pg.* 488
ASSOCIATED HYGIENIC PRODUCTS LLC, 3400 River Green Ct Ste 600, **Duluth,** GA 30096-8334, *pg.* 1496, *pg.* 531
CRYOLIFE, INC., 1655 Roberts Blvd NW, **Kennesaw,** GA 30144-3632, *pg.* 1520, *pg.* 534
DIXIE HEALTH, INC., 2161 New Market Pkwy SE Ste 222, **Marietta,** GA 30067-8768, *pg.* 1524, *pg.* 535
EXAMWORKS GROUP, INC., 3280 Peachtree Rd NE Ste 2625, **Atlanta,** GA 30305, *pg.* 1529, *pg.* 505
GENTIVA HEALTH SERVICES, INC., 3350 Riverwood Pkwy Ste 1400, **Atlanta,** GA 30339-3314, *pg.* 1534, *pg.* 506
GF HEALTH PRODUCTS, INC., 2935 NE Pkwy, **Atlanta,** GA 30360, *pg.* 1535, *pg.* 508
HALYARD HEALTH, INC., 5405 Windward Pkwy, **Alpharetta,** GA 30004, *pg.* 1539, *pg.* 484
IMMUCOR, INC., 3130 Gateway Dr PO Box 5265, **Norcross,** GA 30091-5625, *pg.* 1544, *pg.* 537
MEDASSETS INC., 100 N Point Center E Ste 200, **Alpharetta,** GA 30022, *pg.* 1561, *pg.* 484
NORTHSIDE HOSPITAL, 1000 Johnson Ferry Rd NE, **Atlanta,** GA 30342-1606, *pg.* 1574, *pg.* 516
NUANCE TRANSCRIPTION, 1 Glenlake Pkwy Ste 1325, **Atlanta,** GA 30328, *pg.* 1576, *pg.* 516
PS KIDS LLC, 310 Technology Pkwy Ste A, **Norcross,** GA 30092-2932, *pg.* 1587, *pg.* 538
SAVA SENIOR CARE LLC, 1 Ravinia Dr Ste 1500, **Atlanta,** GA 30346-2115, *pg.* 1592, *pg.* 519
SUMMIT INDUSTRIES, INC., 839 Pickens Industrial Dr, **Marietta,** GA 30062-3100, *pg.* 1599, *pg.* 535

Hawaii

First page reference indicates Business Class Edition
Second page reference indicates Geographic Edition

MERA PHARMACEUTICALS, INC., 73-4460 Queen Ka'ahumanu Hwy Ste 110, **Kailua Kona,** HI 96740-2639, *pg.* 1566, *pg.* 545

Idaho

INTERMOUNTAIN HOSPITAL, 303 N Allumbaugh, **Boise,** ID 83704, *pg.* 1546, *pg.* 547
MWI VETERINARY SUPPLY, INC., 3041 Pasadena Dr, **Boise,** ID 83705-4776, *pg.* 1570, *pg.* 548
ST. ALPHONSUS REGIONAL MEDICAL CENTER, 1055 N Curtis Rd, **Boise,** ID 83706-1352, *pg.* 1596, *pg.* 548

Illinois

ABBOTT LABORATORIES, 100 Abbott Park Rd, **Abbott Park,** IL 60064-6400, *pg.* 1484, *pg.* 551
ABBVIE INC., 1 N Waukegan Rd, **North Chicago,** IL 60064, *pg.* 1486, *pg.* 638
ADDUS HOMECARE CORPORATION, 2401 S Plum Grove Rd, **Palatine,** IL 60067, *pg.* 1487, *pg.* 650
ADVOCATE HEALTH CARE, 3075 Highland Pkwy, **Downers Grove,** IL 60515, *pg.* 1487, *pg.* 607
AJINOMOTO HEARTLAND LLC, 8430 W Bryn Mawr Ave Ste 650, **Chicago,** IL 60631-3421, *pg.* 1488, *pg.* 563
AKORN, INC., 1925 W Field Court Ste 300, **Lake Forest,** IL 60045, *pg.* 1488, *pg.* 622
ALEXIAN BROTHERS HEALTH SYSTEM FOUNDATION, 3040 Salt Creek Ln, **Arlington Heights,** IL 60005, *pg.* 1489, *pg.* 553
ALLSCRIPTS HEALTHCARE SOLUTIONS, INC., 222 Merchandise Mart Plz Ste 2024, **Chicago,** IL 60654, *pg.* 1492, *pg.* 563
ALVA/AMCO PHARMACAL COMPANIES, INC., 7711 N Merrimac Ave, **Niles,** IL 60714-3423, *pg.* 1492, *pg.* 637
AMCOR FLEXIBLES INC., 1919 S Butterfield Rd, **Mundelein,** IL 60060-9735, *pg.* 1492, *pg.* 635
ASTELLAS PHARMA US, INC., 1 Astellas Way, **Northbrook,** IL 60062, *pg.* 1496, *pg.* 640
ATI PHYSICAL THERAPY, 790 Remington Blvd, **Bolingbrook,** IL 60440, *pg.* 1498, *pg.* 558
BAXTER INTERNATIONAL INC., 1 Baxter Pkwy, **Deerfield,** IL 60015-4625, *pg.* 1499, *pg.* 599
BELTONE ELECTRONICS LLC, 2601 Patriot Blvd, **Glenview,** IL 60026, *pg.* 1503, *pg.* 614
BEUTLICH PHARMACEUTICALS LP, 1541 S Shields Dr, **Waukegan,** IL 60085-8304, *pg.* 1503, *pg.* 665
CATAMARAN, 2441 Warrenville Rd Ste 610, **Lisle,** IL 60532-3642, *pg.* 1514, *pg.* 628
THE FEMALE HEALTH COMPANY, 515 N State St Ste 2225, **Chicago,** IL 60610, *pg.* 1530, *pg.* 573
FRESENIUS KABI USA, 3 Corporate Dr, **Lake Zurich,** IL 60047, *pg.* 1531, *pg.* 626
HOSPIRA, INC., 275 N Field Dr, **Lake Forest,** IL 60045, *pg.* 1542, *pg.* 623
LANDAUER, INC., 2 Science Rd, **Glenwood,** IL 60425-1586, *pg.* 1554, *pg.* 615
MARIANJOY REHABILITATION HOSPITAL, 26 W 171 Roosevelt Rd, **Wheaton,** IL 60187, *pg.* 1558, *pg.* 669
MEAD JOHNSON NUTRITION COMPANY, 2701 Patriot Blvd, **Glenview,** IL 60026, *pg.* 1561, *pg.* 615
MEDLINE INDUSTRIES, INC., 1 Medline Pl, **Mundelein,** IL 60060, *pg.* 1562, *pg.* 635
NORTHWESTERN MEMORIAL HEALTHCARE, 251 E Huron St, **Chicago,** IL 60611-2908, *pg.* 1574, *pg.* 585
NOW HEALTH GROUP, INC., 395 Glen Ellyn Rd, **Bloomingdale,** IL 60108-2176, *pg.* 1576, *pg.* 557
OSF HEALTHCARE SYSTEM, 800 NE Glen Oak Ave, **Peoria,** IL 61603-3200, *pg.* 1579, *pg.* 652
PHONAK LLC, 4520 Weaver Pkwy, **Warrenville,** IL 60555-3927, *pg.* 1585, *pg.* 665
PRESENCE HEALTH, 200 Wacker Dr, **Chicago,** IL 60606, *pg.* 1586, *pg.* 587
THE ROHO GROUP, 100 N Florida Ave, **Belleville,** IL 62221-5429, *pg.* 1591, *pg.* 556
SAGENT HOLDING CO., 1901 N Roselle Rd Ste 700, **Schaumburg,** IL 60195, *pg.* 1591, *pg.* 659
SUNSTAR AMERICAS INC., 4635 W Foster Ave, **Chicago,** IL 60630-1709, *pg.* 1599, *pg.* 591
TAKEDA PHARMACEUTICALS USA, INC., 1 Takeda Pkwy, **Deerfield,** IL 60015-4832, *pg.* 1600, *pg.* 605
VEIN CLINICS OF AMERICA INC, 2001 Butterfield #300, **Downers Grove,** IL 60515, *pg.* 1606, *pg.* 609
WALGREEN CO., 108 Wilmot Rd, **Deerfield,** IL 60015-4620, *pg.* 1608, *pg.* 605

Indiana

ANCILLA SYSTEMS INCORPORATED, 1419 S Lk Pk Ave, **Hobart,** IN 46342-5958, *pg.* 1494, *pg.* 682
COOK GROUP, INC., PO Box 1608, **Bloomington,** IN 47402, *pg.* 1518, *pg.* 674
DEPUYSYNTHES, 700 Orthopaedic Dr, **Warsaw,** IN 46581, *pg.* 1523, *pg.* 699
ELI LILLY AND COMPANY, Lilly Corporate Ctr, **Indianapolis,** IN 46285, *pg.* 1527, *pg.* 684
HILL-ROM HOLDINGS, INC., 1069 State Rte 46 E, **Batesville,** IN 47006-8928, *pg.* 1542, *pg.* 673
INDIANA UNIVERSITY HEALTH METHODIST HOSPITAL, 1701 North Senate Blvd, **Indianapolis,** IN 46202, *pg.* 1545, *pg.* 687
ROCHE DIAGNOSTICS CORPORATION, 9115 Hague Rd, **Indianapolis,** IN 46250, *pg.* 1590, *pg.* 689
SYMMETRY MEDICAL INC., 3724 N State Rd 15, **Warsaw,** IN 46582, *pg.* 1600, *pg.* 699
ZIMMER BIOMET HOLDINGS, INC., 345 E Main St, **Warsaw,** IN 46580, *pg.* 1611, *pg.* 699

Iowa

UNITYPOINT HEALTH, 1200 Pleasant St, **Des Moines,** IA 50309-1406, *pg.* 1604, *pg.* 706

Kansas

CONTINENTAL ANALYTICAL SERVICES INC., 525 N 8th St, **Salina,** KS 67401, *pg.* 1518, *pg.* 721
HOOPER HOLMES, INC., 560 N Rogers Rd, **Olathe,** KS 66062, *pg.* 1542, *pg.* 718

Kentucky

ALMOST FAMILY, INC., 9510 Ormsby Station Rd Ste 300, **Louisville,** KY 40223, *pg.* 1492, *pg.* 731
GRANDPA BRANDS COMPANY, 1820 Airport Exch Blvd, **Erlanger,** KY 41018-3192, *pg.* 1538, *pg.* 727
KINDRED HEALTHCARE, INC., 680 S 4th St, **Louisville,** KY 40202-2412, *pg.* 1553, *pg.* 736
POST GLOVER RESISTORS INC., 1369 Cox Ave, **Erlanger,** KY 41018, *pg.* 1585, *pg.* 727
RES-CARE, INC., 9901 Linn Station Rd, **Louisville,** KY 40223-3808, *pg.* 1589, *pg.* 738

Louisiana

AMEDISYS, INC., 5959 S Sherwood Forest Blvd, **Baton Rouge,** LA 70816, *pg.* 1493, *pg.* 741

Maine

IDEXX LABORATORIES, INC., 1 IDEXX Dr, **Westbrook,** ME 04092, *pg.* 1543, *pg.* 753
MAINE COAST REGIONAL HEALTH FACILITIES INC., 50 Union St, **Ellsworth,** ME 04605, *pg.* 1557, *pg.* 749

Maryland

BON SECOURS HEALTH SYSTEM, INC., 1505 Marriottsville Rd, **Marriottsville,** MD 21104-1301, *pg.* 1508, *pg.* 774
CAREFIRST, INC., 1501 S Clinton St, **Baltimore,** MD 21224, *pg.* 1513, *pg.* 756
CONMED HEALTHCARE MANAGEMENT, INC., 7250 Parkway Dr Ste 400, **Hanover,** MD 21076, *pg.* 1518, *pg.* 772
COVENTRY HEALTH CARE, INC., 6720 B Rockledge Dr Ste 700, **Bethesda,** MD 20817, *pg.* 1519, *pg.* 761
GLAXOSMITHKLINE, 14200 Shady Grove Rd, **Rockville,** MD 20850-7464, *pg.* 1537, *pg.* 776
MAXIM HEALTHCARE SERVICES, 7227 Lee Deforest Dr, **Columbia,** MD 21046, *pg.* 1559, *pg.* 767
MEDIFAST, INC., 3600 Crondall Ln, **Owings Mills,** MD 21117, *pg.* 1562, *pg.* 774
MEDIMMUNE LLC, One MedImmune Way, **Gaithersburg,** MD 20878-4021, *pg.* 1562, *pg.* 770
MEDSTAR HEALTH INC., 5565 Sterrett Pl 5th Fl, **Columbia,** MD 21044, *pg.* 1563, *pg.* 767
NUTRICIA NORTH AMERICA, 9900 Belward Campus Dr, Ste 100, **Rockville,** MD 20850, *pg.* 1577, *pg.* 776
QIAGEN GAITHERSBURG INC., 19300 Germantown Rd, **Germantown,** MD 20874, *pg.* 1587, *pg.* 771
SUCAMPO PHARMACEUTICALS, INC., 4520 East West Hwy 3rd Fl, **Bethesda,** MD 20814, *pg.* 1599, *pg.* 765
SYNUTRA INTERNATIONAL, INC., 2275 Research Blvd Ste 500, **Rockville,** MD 20850, *pg.* 1600, *pg.* 776
UNITED THERAPEUTICS CORPORATION, 1040 Spring St, **Silver Spring,** MD 20910, *pg.* 1604, *pg.* 778

Massachusetts

A-T SURGICAL MFG. CO., INC., 115 Clemente St, **Holyoke,** MA 01040-5644, *pg.* 1483, *pg.* 825
ALERE INC., 51 Sawyer Rd Ste 200, **Waltham,** MA 02453, *pg.* 1488, *pg.* 849
ALIMED, INC., 297 High St, **Dedham,** MA 02026-2852, *pg.* 1490, *pg.* 816
AMAG PHARMACEUTICALS, INC., 100 Hayden Ave, **Lexington,** MA 02421, *pg.* 1492, *pg.* 827
ARIAD PHARMACEUTICALS, INC., 26 Landsdowne St, **Cambridge,** MA 02139-4234, *pg.* 1496, *pg.* 807
ARRHYTHMIA RESEARCH TECHNOLOGY, INC., 25 Sawyer Passway, **Fitchburg,** MA 01420, *pg.* 1496, *pg.* 819
ATHENAHEALTH, INC., 311 Arsenal St, **Watertown,** MA 02472, *pg.* 1497, *pg.* 855
AVEO PHARMACEUTICALS, INC., 75 Sidney St, **Cambridge,** MA 02139, *pg.* 1498, *pg.* 807
BAYSTATE HEALTH SYSTEM, INC., 280 Chestnut St, **Springfield,** MA 01199-1001, *pg.* 1501, *pg.* 845
BETHANY HEALTH CARE CENTER, 97 Bethany Rd, **Framingham,** MA 01702, *pg.* 1503, *pg.* 820
BLUE CROSS BLUE SHIELD OF MASSACHUSETTS, 101 Huntington Ave Ste 1300, **Boston,** MA 02199-7611, *pg.* 1507, *pg.* 789
BOSTON CHILDREN'S HOSPITAL, 300 Longwood Ave, **Boston,** MA 02115, *pg.* 1508, *pg.* 790
BOSTON HEART DIAGNOSTICS, 175 Crossing Blvd, **Framingham,** MA 01702, *pg.* 1508, *pg.* 820
BOSTON MEDICAL CENTER, One Boston Medical Center Pl, **Boston,** MA 02118, *pg.* 1508, *pg.* 791
BOSTON SCIENTIFIC CORPORATION, 300 Boston Scientifice Way, **Marlborough,** MA 01752, *pg.* 1508, *pg.* 831
BRIGHAM AND WOMEN'S HOSPITAL, 75 Francis St, **Boston,** MA 02115, *pg.* 1509, *pg.* 792
BRUKER CORPORATION, 40 Manning Rd, **Billerica,** MA 01821, *pg.* 1511, *pg.* 788
CALLOWAY LABS, 12 Gill St Ste 4000, **Woburn,** MA 01801, *pg.* 1511, *pg.* 861
CAREGROUP, INC., 109 Brookline Dr Ste 300, **Boston,** MA 02215, *pg.* 1513, *pg.* 792
COMMUNITY NURSE & HOSPICE CARE, 62 Center St, **Fairhaven,** MA 02719, *pg.* 1517, *pg.* 818
CUBIST PHARMACEUTICALS, INC., 65 Hayden Ave, **Lexington,** MA 02421-7994, *pg.* 1521, *pg.* 828
CYBEX INTERNATIONAL, INC., 10 Trotter Dr, **Medway,** MA 02053-2299, *pg.* 1521, *pg.* 832
CYNOSURE, INC., 5 Carlisle Rd, **Westford,** MA 01886, *pg.* 1521, *pg.* 858
DUSA PHARMACEUTICALS, INC., 25 Upton Dr, **Wilmington,** MA 01887, *pg.* 1525, *pg.* 860
DYAX CORP., 55 Network Drive, **Burlington,** MA 01803, *pg.* 1525, *pg.* 805
DYNISCO INSTRUMENTS LLC, 38 Forge Pkwy, **Franklin,** MA 02038, *pg.* 1526, *pg.* 823
FALLON COMMUNITY HEALTH PLAN, One Chestnut Pl, 10 Chestnut St, **Worcester,** MA 01608, *pg.* 1530, *pg.* 862
FRESENIUS MEDICAL CARE NORTH AMERICA, Reservoir Woods 920 Winter St, **Waltham,** MA 02451-1457, *pg.* 1531, *pg.* 851
GENZYME CORPORATION, 500 Kendall St, **Cambridge,** MA 02142, *pg.* 1534, *pg.* 808
GILLETTE, 800 Boylston St, **Boston,** MA 02199, *pg.* 1536, *pg.* 795
HAEMONETICS CORPORATION, 400 Wood Rd, **Braintree,** MA 02184-9114, *pg.* 1538, *pg.* 802
HARVARD BIOSCIENCE, INC., 84 October Hill Rd, **Holliston,** MA 01746-1371, *pg.* 1539, *pg.* 824
HARVARD PILGRIM HEALTH CARE, INC., 93 Worcester St, **Wellesley,** MA 02481, *pg.* 1539, *pg.* 856
HOUSEWORKS, One Gateway Ctr Ste 902, **Newton,** MA 02458, *pg.* 1543, *pg.* 836

IDERA PHARMACEUTICALS, INC., 167 Sidney St, **Cambridge,** MA 02139, *pg.* 1543, *pg.* 808
IMMUNOGEN, INC., 830 Winter St, **Waltham,** MA 02451, *pg.* 1544, *pg.* 851
INTERLEUKIN GENETICS, INC., 135 Beaver St, **Waltham,** MA 02452, *pg.* 1546, *pg.* 851
JUNIPER PHARMACEUTICALS, 4 Liberty Sq 4th Fl, **Boston,** MA 02109, *pg.* 1552, *pg.* 797
LAHEY CLINIC, 41 Mall Rd, **Burlington,** MA 01805, *pg.* 1554, *pg.* 805
LAKE REGION MEDICAL, 100 Fordham Rd, **Wilmington,** MA 01887, *pg.* 1554, *pg.* 860
LEMAITRE VASCULAR, INC., 63 2nd Ave, **Burlington,** MA 01803, *pg.* 1555, *pg.* 805
LONG TERM SOLUTIONS INC., 235 W Central St, **Natick,** MA 01760, *pg.* 1557, *pg.* 834
MAGELLAN DIAGNOSTICS, 101 Billerica Ave Bldg 4, **North Billerica,** MA 01862, *pg.* 1557, *pg.* 838
MASSACHUSETTS MEDICAL SOCIETY, 860 Winter St, Waltham Woods Corporate Ctr, **Waltham,** MA 02451-1411, *pg.* 1559, *pg.* 852
MEDTRONIC, 15 Hampshire St, **Mansfield,** MA 02048, *pg.* 1563, *pg.* 830
MILLENNIUM: THE TAKEDA ONCOLOGY COMPANY, 40 Landsdowne St, **Cambridge,** MA 02139-4134, *pg.* 1568, *pg.* 809
MULTIPLAN, INC., 1100 Winter St, **Waltham,** MA 02451-1440, *pg.* 1570, *pg.* 852
NATIONAL DENTEX CORPORATION, 2 Vision Dr, **Natick,** MA 01760, *pg.* 1570, *pg.* 834
NEUROMETRIX, INC., 62 4th Ave, **Waltham,** MA 02451, *pg.* 1572, *pg.* 852
NOVARTIS VACCINES & DIAGNOSTICS, INC., 350 Massachusetts Ave, **Cambridge,** MA 02139, *pg.* 1575, *pg.* 809
PAREXEL INTERNATIONAL CORPORATION, 195 West St, **Waltham,** MA 02451-1121, *pg.* 1580, *pg.* 853
PARTNERS HEALTHCARE SYSTEM, INC., 800 Boylston St Ste 1150 Prudential Twr, **Boston,** MA 02199, *pg.* 1580, *pg.* 800
PHILIPS HEALTHCARE, 3000 Minuteman Rd, **Andover,** MA 01810-1032, *pg.* 1585, *pg.* 783
PRESSURE BIOSCIENCES, INC., 14 Norfolk Ave, **South Easton,** MA 02375, *pg.* 1586, *pg.* 844
REPLIGEN CORPORATION, 41 Sayon St Bldg 1 Ste 100, **Waltham,** MA 02453, *pg.* 1589, *pg.* 854
THE SALK COMPANY, 1005 Boylston St, #305, **Boston,** MA 02461, *pg.* 1591, *pg.* 800
SERACARE LIFE SCIENCES, INC., 37 Birch St, **Milford,** MA 01757, *pg.* 1593, *pg.* 833
SMITH & NEPHEW, INC., ENDOSCOPY DIVISION, 150 Minuteman Rd, **Andover,** MA 01810-5885, *pg.* 1594, *pg.* 783
SUNOVION PHARMACEUTICALS INC., 84 Waterford Dr, **Marlborough,** MA 01752, *pg.* 1599, *pg.* 832
TUFTS MEDICAL CENTER, 800 Washington St, **Boston,** MA 02111, *pg.* 1603, *pg.* 801
VERTEX PHARMACEUTICALS INCORPORATED, 50 Northern Ave, **Boston,** MA 02210, *pg.* 1606, *pg.* 801
VIACORD, 245 1st St, **Cambridge,** MA 02142, *pg.* 1606, *pg.* 810
W.F. YOUNG, INC., 302 Benton Dr, **East Longmeadow,** MA 01028-5990, *pg.* 1610, *pg.* 817
ZOLL MEDICAL CORPORATION, 269 Mill Rd, **Chelmsford,** MA 01824-4105, *pg.* 1612, *pg.* 814

Michigan

BATTLE CREEK EQUIPMENT CO., 307 W Jackson St, **Battle Creek,** MI 49017-2306, *pg.* 1499, *pg.* 870
THE DETROIT MEDICAL CENTER, 3990 John R, **Detroit,** MI 48201, *pg.* 1524, *pg.* 880
HENRY FORD HEALTH SYSTEM, 1 Ford Pl, **Detroit,** MI 48202, *pg.* 1541, *pg.* 883
MCKEON PRODUCTS, INC., 25460 Guenther, **Warren,** MI 48091, *pg.* 1559, *pg.* 912
MPI RESEARCH, INC., 54943 N Main St, **Mattawan,** MI 49071-9399, *pg.* 1569, *pg.* 898
OAKWOOD HEALTHCARE, INC., 18101 Oakwood Blvd, **Dearborn,** MI 48124-4089, *pg.* 1577, *pg.* 878
ROCKWELL MEDICAL TECHNOLOGIES, INC., 30142 S Wixom Rd, **Wixom,** MI 48393-3440, *pg.* 1590, *pg.* 913
ST. JOHN HEALTH, 28000 Dequindre Rd, **Warren,** MI 48092-2468, *pg.* 1596, *pg.* 912
STRYKER CORPORATION, 2825 Airview Blvd, **Kalamazoo,** MI 49002, *pg.* 1598, *pg.* 894
VENTURI, INC., 2299 Traversefield Dr, **Traverse City,** MI 49686, *pg.* 1606, *pg.* 910

Minnesota

ALLINA HEALTH SYSTEM, INC., 2925 Chicago Ave, **Minneapolis,** MN 55407, *pg.* 1491, *pg.* 929
AMERICAN MEDICAL SYSTEMS HOLDINGS, INC., 10700 Bren Rd W, **Minnetonka,** MN 55343-9679, *pg.* 1493, *pg.* 947
ARKRAY USA, INC., 5198 W 76th St, **Edina,** MN 55439, *pg.* 1496, *pg.* 924
COGENTIX MEDICAL, INC., 5420 Feltl Rd, **Minnetonka,** MN 55343, *pg.* 1516, *pg.* 948
ELECTROMED, INC., 500 6th Ave NW, **New Prague,** MN 56071, *pg.* 1527, *pg.* 951
ENVOY MEDICAL CORPORATION, 5000 Township Pkwy, **Saint Paul,** MN 55110, *pg.* 1529, *pg.* 960
HEALTH FITNESS CORPORATION, 1700 W 82Nd St, Ste 200, **Minneapolis,** MN 55431, *pg.* 1539, *pg.* 937
HYPERTENSION DIAGNOSTICS, INC., 2915 Waters Rd Ste 108, **Eagan,** MN 55121, *pg.* 1543, *pg.* 921
LIFE TIME FITNESS, INC., 2902 Corporate Pl, **Chanhassen,** MN 55317, *pg.* 1556, *pg.* 920
LIFECORE BIOMEDICAL, LLC, 3515 Lyman Blvd, **Chaska,** MN 55318-3050, *pg.* 1556, *pg.* 920
MAYO CLINIC, 200 First St SW, **Rochester,** MN 55905, *pg.* 1559, *pg.* 955
MEDTRONIC, INC., 710 Medtronic Pkwy NE, **Minneapolis,** MN 55432-5604, *pg.* 1564, *pg.* 939
MIRACLE-EAR, INC., 5000 Cheshire Ln N, **Minneapolis,** MN 55446-3706, *pg.* 1568, *pg.* 940
NESTLE HEALTHCARE NUTRITION, 1600 Utica Ave S Ste 600, **Minneapolis,** MN 55416, *pg.* 1572, *pg.* 941
PATTERSON COMPANIES, INC., 1031 Mendota Hts Rd, **Saint Paul,** MN 55120, *pg.* 1580, *pg.* 962
PATTERSON DENTAL SUPPLY, INC., 1031 Mendota Heights Rd, **Saint Paul,** MN 55120-1419, *pg.* 1580, *pg.* 963
SMITHS MEDICAL MD, INC., 1265 Grey Fox Rd, **Saint Paul,** MN 55112-6929, *pg.* 1594, *pg.* 963
ST. JUDE MEDICAL, INC., 1 St.Jude Medical Dr, **Saint Paul,** MN 55117-9983, *pg.* 1596, *pg.* 963
STARKEY LABORATORIES, INC., 6700 Washington Ave S, **Eden Prairie,** MN 55344, *pg.* 1597, *pg.* 923
STEN CORPORATION, 10275 Wayzata Blvd Ste 310, **Minnetonka,** MN 55305, *pg.* 1597, *pg.* 950
SURMODICS, INC., 9924 W 74th St, **Eden Prairie,** MN 55344-3523, *pg.* 1600, *pg.* 924
TECHNE CORPORATION, 614 McKinley Pl NE, **Minneapolis,** MN 55413-2610, *pg.* 1601, *pg.* 944
UNIVERSAL HOSPITAL SERVICES, INC., 6625 W 78th St, Ste 300, **Minneapolis,** MN 55439, *pg.* 1604, *pg.* 945
UROLOGIX, INC., 14405 21st Ave N, **Minneapolis,** MN 55447-4685, *pg.* 1604, *pg.* 945
VIRTUAL RADIOLOGIC CORPORATION, 11995 Singletree Ln Ste 500, **Eden Prairie,** MN 55344, *pg.* 1607, *pg.* 924
VITAL IMAGES, INC., 5850 Opus Parkway Ste 300, **Minnetonka,** MN 55343-4411, *pg.* 1607, *pg.* 950

Missouri

ALLIED HEALTHCARE PRODUCTS, INC., 1720 Sublette Ave, **Saint Louis,** MO 63110-1927, *pg.* 1491, *pg.* 990
ASCENSION HEALTH ALLIANCE, 101 S Hanley Rd Ste 450, **Saint Louis,** MO 63105, *pg.* 1496, *pg.* 992
BARNES-JEWISH HOSPITAL, 1 Barnes-Jewish Hospital Plaza, **Saint Louis,** MO 63110, *pg.* 1498, *pg.* 992
BJC HEALTHCARE, 4444 Forest Pk Ave Ste 500, **Saint Louis,** MO 63108, *pg.* 1506, *pg.* 993
BLUE CROSS & BLUE SHIELD OF KANSAS CITY, INC., 2301 Main St, **Kansas City,** MO 64108, *pg.* 1507, *pg.* 981
CENTRIC GROUP LLC, 1260 Andes Blvd, **Saint Louis,** MO 63132, *pg.* 1514, *pg.* 994
CERNER CORPORATION, 2800 Rockcreek Pkwy, **Kansas City,** MO 64117, *pg.* 1514, *pg.* 981
EDGEWELL PERSONAL CARE, 1350 Timberlake Manor Pkwy, **Saint Louis,** MO 63017, *pg.* 1526, *pg.* 995
EXPRESS SCRIPTS, INC., 1 Express Way, **Saint Louis,** MO 63121, *pg.* 1530, *pg.* 997
LUMARA HEALTH INC., 1 Corporate Woods Dr, **Bridgeton,** MO 63044, *pg.* 1557, *pg.* 973
MALLINCKRODT PHARMACEUTICALS, 675 McDonnell Blvd, **Hazelwood,** MO 63042-2301, *pg.* 1557, *pg.* 978
MEDICINE SHOPPE INTERNATIONAL, INC., 1 Rider Trail Plz Dr Ste 300, **Earth City,** MO 63045, *pg.* 1561, *pg.* 976
RELIV INTERNATIONAL, INC., 136 Chesterfield Industrial Blvd, **Chesterfield,** MO 63005-1220, *pg.* 1589, *pg.* 975
STEREOTAXIS, INC., 4320 Forest Park Ave Ste 100, **Saint Louis,** MO 63108, *pg.* 1597, *pg.* 1004
YOUNG INNOVATIONS, INC., 13705 Shoreline Ct E, **Earth City,** MO 63045-1202, *pg.* 1611, *pg.* 977

Nebraska

COMPLETE NUTRITION, 17220 Wright St, Ste 200, **Omaha,** NE 68130, *pg.* 1517, *pg.* 1014
FITLIFE BRANDS, 4509 S 143rd St, Ste 1, **Omaha,** NE 68137, *pg.* 1531, *pg.* 1015
HOME INSTEAD, INC., 13323 California St, **Omaha,** NE 68154, *pg.* 1542, *pg.* 1016

Nevada

CORD BLOOD AMERICA, INC., 1857 Helm Dr, **Las Vegas,** NV 89119, *pg.* 1519, *pg.* 1023
PDL BIOPHARMA INC., 932 Southwood Blvd, **Incline Village,** NV 89451, *pg.* 1580, *pg.* 1022

New Hampshire

TENDER CORPORATION, 106 Burndy Rd, **Littleton,** NH 03561, *pg.* 1601, *pg.* 1035

New Jersey

ABBOTT POINT OF CARE, INC., 400 College Road East, **Princeton,** NJ 08540, *pg.* 1486, *pg.* 1110
ALLERGAN, Morris Corporate Center III, 400 Interpace Parkway, **Parsippany,** NJ 07054, *pg.* 1490, *pg.* 1101
ANSELL, 200 Schultz Dr, **Red Bank,** NJ 07701-6745, *pg.* 1495, *pg.* 1114
ATLANTIC HEALTH SYSTEM INC., 475 South St, **Morristown,** NJ 07960, *pg.* 1498, *pg.* 1087
BAYADA NURSES INC., 290 Chester Ave, **Moorestown,** NJ 08057, *pg.* 1499, *pg.* 1087
BAYER HEALTHCARE CONSUMER CARE DIVISION, 36 Columbia Rd, **Morristown,** NJ 07962-1910, *pg.* 1500, *pg.* 1087
BAYER HEALTHCARE PHARMACEUTICAL DIVISION, 67 Whippany Rd, **Whippany,** NJ 07981, *pg.* 1500, *pg.* 1132
BECTON, DICKINSON & COMPANY, 1 Becton Dr, **Franklin Lakes,** NJ 07417-1880, *pg.* 1501, *pg.* 1068
BLICKMAN HEALTH INDUSTRIES, INC., 500 Hwy 46 E, **Clifton,** NJ 07011-3808, *pg.* 1506, *pg.* 1051
BRACCO DIAGNOSTICS, INC., 259 Prospect Plains Rd Bldg H, **Monroe Township,** NJ 08831, *pg.* 1509, *pg.* 1085
BRAINSTORM CELL THERAPEUTICS INC., 3 University Plaza Dr, **Hackensack,** NJ 07601, *pg.* 1509, *pg.* 1072
BRISTOL-MYERS SQUIBB U.S. PHARMACEUTICAL GROUP, 206 & Province Line Rd, **Princeton,** NJ 08540, *pg.* 1511, *pg.* 1110
CENTRASTATE HEALTHCARE SYSTEM INC., 901 W Main St, **Freehold,** NJ 07728, *pg.* 1514, *pg.* 1071
CONVATEC LTD., 200 Headquarters Park Dr, **Skillman,** NJ 08558, *pg.* 1518, *pg.* 1121
C.R. BARD, INC., 730 Central Ave, **New Providence,** NJ 07974, *pg.* 1519, *pg.* 1094
CYCLACEL PHARMACEUTICALS, INC., 200 Connell Dr Ste 1500, **Berkeley Heights,** NJ 07922, *pg.* 1521, *pg.* 1044
DERMA SCIENCES, INC., 214 Carnegie Ctr Ste 300, **Princeton,** NJ 08540-6237, *pg.* 1523, *pg.* 1111
EISAI INC., 100 Tice Blvd, **Woodcliff Lake,** NJ 07677, *pg.* 1526, *pg.* 1133
EMISPHERE TECHNOLOGIES, INC., 4 Becker Farm Rd, Ste 103, **Roseland,** NJ 07068, *pg.* 1528, *pg.* 1118
EXPRESS SCRIPTS, 100 Parsons Pond Dr, **Franklin Lakes,** NJ 07417, *pg.* 1530, *pg.* 1070
G&W LABORATORIES INC., 111 Coolidge St, **South Plainfield,** NJ 07080-3801, *pg.* 1532, *pg.* 1123
HACKENSACK UNIVERSITY MEDICAL CENTER, 30 Prospect Ave, **Hackensack,** NJ 07601, *pg.* 1538, *pg.* 1072
HOFFMANN-LA ROCHE INC., 340 Kingsland St, **Nutley,** NJ 07110-1199, *pg.* 1542, *pg.* 1099
IMMUNOMEDICS, INC., 300 American Rd, **Morris Plains,** NJ

First page reference indicates Business Class Edition
Second page reference indicates Geographic Edition

07950-2460, *pg.* 1544, *pg.* 1087
INTEGRA LIFESCIENCES HOLDINGS CORPORATION, 311 Enterprise Dr, **Plainsboro,** NJ 08536, *pg.* 1545, *pg.* 1109
INTEGRATED BIOPHARMA, INC., 225 Long Ave, **Hillside,** NJ 07205, *pg.* 1546, *pg.* 1073
INVENTIV HEALTH CLINICAL, 504 Carnegie Ctr, **Princeton,** NJ 08540, *pg.* 1547, *pg.* 1111
JANSSEN PHARMACEUTICA PRODUCTS, L.P., 1125 Trenton Harbourton Rd, **Titusville,** NJ 08560, *pg.* 1548, *pg.* 1125
JOHNSON & JOHNSON, 1 Johnson & Johnson Plz, **New Brunswick,** NJ 08933-0001, *pg.* 1549, *pg.* 1091
JOHNSON & JOHNSON BABY PRODUCTS, INC., 1 Johnson & Johnson Plz, **New Brunswick,** NJ 08933, *pg.* 1552, *pg.* 1094
KENNEDY HEALTH SYSTEM, 1099 White Horse Rd, **Voorhees,** NJ 08043, *pg.* 1553, *pg.* 1128
LANELABS USA INC., 3 North St, **Waldwick,** NJ 07463, *pg.* 1554, *pg.* 1128
LIFECELL CORPORATION, 1 Millennium Way, **Branchburg,** NJ 08876, *pg.* 1556, *pg.* 1045
MAQUET, 1300 MacArthur Blvd, **Mahwah,** NJ 07430, *pg.* 1558, *pg.* 1082
MAXIMUM HUMAN PERFORMANCE, INC., 21 Dwight Pl, **Fairfield,** NJ 07004, *pg.* 1559, *pg.* 1065
THE MEDICINES COMPANY, 8 Sylvan Way, **Parsippany,** NJ 07054, *pg.* 1561, *pg.* 1104
MERCK & CO., INC., 2000 Galloping Hill Rd, **Kenilworth,** NJ 07033, *pg.* 1566, *pg.* 1077
MILESTONE SCIENTIFIC, INC., 220 S Orange Ave, **Livingston,** NJ 07039, *pg.* 1568, *pg.* 1079
NOVARTIS PHARMACEUTICALS CORP., 1 Health Plz East, **East Hanover,** NJ 07936-1080, *pg.* 1575, *pg.* 1054
NPS PHARMACEUTICALS, INC., 550 Hills Dr 3rd Fl, **Bedminster,** NJ 07921, *pg.* 1576, *pg.* 1043
PACIFICHEALTH LABORATORIES, INC., 100 Matawan Rd Ste 150, **Matawan,** NJ 07747, *pg.* 1579, *pg.* 1083
PACIRA PHARMACEUTICALS, INC., 5 Silvay Way Ste 125, **Parsippany,** NJ 07054, *pg.* 1579, *pg.* 1104
PDI, INC., Morris Corporate Ctr 1 Bldg A 300 Interpace Pkwy, **Parsippany,** NJ 07054, *pg.* 1580, *pg.* 1104
PENTAX MEDICAL COMPANY, 3 Paragon Dr, Ste 1, **Montvale,** NJ 07645, *pg.* 1580, *pg.* 1086
QUEST DIAGNOSTICS INCORPORATED, 3 Giralda Farms, **Madison,** NJ 07940, *pg.* 1587, *pg.* 1080
RICOLA USA, INC., 6 Campus Dr, 2nd Fl S, **Parsippany,** NJ 07054, *pg.* 1590, *pg.* 1106
SANOFI US, 55 Corporate Dr, **Bridgewater,** NJ 08807, *pg.* 1592, *pg.* 1046
STRYKER ORTHOPAEDICS, 325 Corporate Dr, **Mahwah,** NJ 07430, *pg.* 1599, *pg.* 1082
VALEANT PHARMACEUTICALS INTERNATIONAL, 400 Somerset Corporate Blvd, **Bridgewater,** NJ 08807, *pg.* 1605, *pg.* 1047
VISITING NURSE ASSOCIATION OF CENTRAL JERSEY, 176 Riverside Ave, **Red Bank,** NJ 07701-1014, *pg.* 1607, *pg.* 1114
VISITING NURSE ASSOCIATION OF SOMERSET HILLS INC., 200 Mount Airy Rd, **Basking Ridge,** NJ 07920, *pg.* 1607, *pg.* 1042
VITAL SIGNS, INC., 20 Campus Rd, **Totowa,** NJ 07512-1210, *pg.* 1607, *pg.* 1126
VITAMIN SHOPPE, INC., 2101 91st St, **North Bergen,** NJ 07047-6446, *pg.* 1608, *pg.* 1098
ZOETIS INC., 100 Campus Dr, **Florham Park,** NJ 07932, *pg.* 1611, *pg.* 1067

New Mexico

PRESBYTERIAN HEALTHCARE SERVICES, 2501 Buena Vista SE, **Albuquerque,** NM 87106, *pg.* 1586, *pg.* 1135

New York

ACORDA THERAPEUTICS, INC., 420 Saw Mill River Rd, **Ardsley,** NY 10502, *pg.* 1486, *pg.* 1138
ADH HEALTH PRODUCTS, INC., 215 N Rte 303, **Congers,** NY 10920-1726, *pg.* 1487, *pg.* 1154
AFFINIA HOSPITALITY, 551 5th Ave, **New York,** NY 10176, *pg.* 1487, *pg.* 1188
AIR TECHNIQUES, INC., 1295 Walt Whitman Rd, **Melville,** NY 11747, *pg.* 1487, *pg.* 1178
AKORN, 369 Bayview Ave, **Amityville,** NY 11701-2801, *pg.* 1488, *pg.* 1138
ALLIQUA, INC., 850 Third Ave Ste 1801, **New York,** NY 10022, *pg.* 1492, *pg.* 1189
AMERICAN BIO MEDICA CORPORATION, 122 Smith Rd, **Kinderhook,** NY 12106-2819, *pg.* 1493, *pg.* 1171
ANGIODYNAMICS, INC., 14 Plaza Dr, **Latham,** NY 12110, *pg.* 1495, *pg.* 1173
ATC HEALTHCARE, INC., 1983 Marcus Ave, **New Hyde Park,** NY 11042-1016, *pg.* 1497, *pg.* 1184
BACTOLAC PHARMACEUTICAL, INC., 7 Oser Ave Unit 14, **Hauppauge,** NY 11788, *pg.* 1498, *pg.* 1163
BEE-ALIVE INC., 7 New Lake Rd, **Valley Cottage,** NY 10989, *pg.* 1503, *pg.* 1348
BIOSCRIP, INC., 100 Clearbrook Rd, **Elmsford,** NY 10523, *pg.* 1506, *pg.* 1158
BRISTOL-MYERS SQUIBB COMPANY, 345 Park Ave, **New York,** NY 10154-0004, *pg.* 1509, *pg.* 1206
CALADRIUS BIOSCIENCES, INC., 420 Lexington Ave Ste 450, **New York,** NY 10170, *pg.* 1511, *pg.* 1209
CENTERLIGHT HEALTH SYSTEM, 612 Allerton Ave, **Bronx,** NY 10467-7404, *pg.* 1514, *pg.* 1144
COLGATE ORAL PHARMACEUTICAL, 300 Park Ave, **New York,** NY 10022, *pg.* 1516, *pg.* 1214
COMBE INCORPORATED, 1101 Westchester Ave, **White Plains,** NY 10604-3503, *pg.* 1516, *pg.* 1351
CONCIERGE CHOICE PHYSICIANS, 100 Merrick Rd, Ste 410W, **Rockville Centre,** NY 11570, *pg.* 1517, *pg.* 1338
CONMED CORPORATION, 525 French Rd, **Utica,** NY 13502, *pg.* 1517, *pg.* 1347
CROSSTEX INTERNATIONAL INC., 10 Ranick Rd, **Hauppauge,** NY 11788, *pg.* 1520, *pg.* 1164
DAXOR CORPORATION, 350 5th Ave Ste 7120, **New York,** NY 10118-7120, *pg.* 1522, *pg.* 1221
DUANE READE, INC., 40 Wall St, **New York,** NY 10005, *pg.* 1525, *pg.* 1226
ENZO BIOCHEM INC., 527 Madison Ave, **New York,** NY 10022-4304, *pg.* 1529, *pg.* 1228
THE GURWIN JEWISH GERIATRIC CENTER, 68 Hauppauge Rd, **Commack,** NY 11725, *pg.* 1538, *pg.* 1153
HEALTH MANAGEMENT SYSTEMS, INC., 360 Park Ave S, Fl 17, **New York,** NY 10010, *pg.* 1540, *pg.* 1238
HEALTH PRODUCTS CORPORATION, 1060 Nepperhan Ave, **Yonkers,** NY 10703-1432, *pg.* 1540, *pg.* 1356
HENRY SCHEIN, INC., 135 Duryea Rd, **Melville,** NY 11747, *pg.* 1541, *pg.* 1180
HOSPITAL FOR SPECIAL SURGERY, 535 E 70th St, **New York,** NY 10021, *pg.* 1543, *pg.* 1241
IMAGEWORKS, 250 Clearbrook Rd Ste 240, **Elmsford,** NY 10523-1315, *pg.* 1544, *pg.* 1158
INTEGRAMED AMERICA, INC., 2 Manhattanville Rd, **Purchase,** NY 10577-2113, *pg.* 1546, *pg.* 1325
JEWISH HOME LIFECARE, 120 W 106th St, **New York,** NY 10025, *pg.* 1548, *pg.* 1246
KERYX BIOPHARMACEUTICALS, INC., 750 Lexington Ave 20th Fl, **New York,** NY 10022, *pg.* 1553, *pg.* 1248
KYOWA HAKKO U.S.A., INC., 600 3rd Ave, 19th Fl, **New York,** NY 10016, *pg.* 1554, *pg.* 1249
LENOX HILL HOSPITAL, 100 E 77th St, **New York,** NY 10075, *pg.* 1555, *pg.* 1251
LIGHTHOUSE INTERNATIONAL, 111 E 59th St, **New York,** NY 10022, *pg.* 1557, *pg.* 1251
LUITPOLD PHARMACEUTICALS, INC., 1 Luitpold Dr, **Shirley,** NY 11967, *pg.* 1557, *pg.* 1342
MATERION MICROELECTRONICS & SERVICES, 2978 Main St, **Buffalo,** NY 14214-1004, *pg.* 1559, *pg.* 1149
MEMORIAL SLOAN-KETTERING CANCER CENTER INC., 1275 York Ave, **New York,** NY 10065, *pg.* 1565, *pg.* 1258
THE MENTHOLATUM COMPANY, 707 Sterling Dr, **Orchard Park,** NY 14127-1557, *pg.* 1565, *pg.* 1320
METROPOLITAN JEWISH HEALTH SYSTEM, 6323 7th Ave, **Brooklyn,** NY 11220, *pg.* 1568, *pg.* 1146
MISONIX INC., 1938 New Hwy, **Farmingdale,** NY 11735-1204, *pg.* 1568, *pg.* 1159
MONTEFIORE MEDICAL CENTER, 111 E 210 St, **Bronx,** NY 10467-2662, *pg.* 1569, *pg.* 1144
MULTISORB TECHNOLOGIES, INC., 325 Harlem Rd, **Buffalo,** NY 14224-1825, *pg.* 1570, *pg.* 1150
NATIONAL HOME HEALTH CARE CORP., 700 White Plains Rd Ste 275, **Scarsdale,** NY 10583-5013, *pg.* 1570, *pg.* 1340
NATURAL ORGANICS, INC., 548 Broadhollow Rd, **Melville,** NY 11747, *pg.* 1571, *pg.* 1181
NBTY, INC., 2100 Smithtown Ave, **Ronkonkoma,** NY 11779, *pg.* 1572, *pg.* 1338
NEW YORK BLOOD CENTER, INC., 310 E 67th St, **New York,** NY 10065, *pg.* 1573, *pg.* 1268
NEW YORK-PRESBYTERIAN HEALTHCARE SYSTEM, 650 E 68th St, **New York,** NY 10021-4870, *pg.* 1573, *pg.* 1269
NORTH SHORE-LIJ HEALTH SYSTEM, 125 Community Dr, **Great Neck,** NY 11021, *pg.* 1573, *pg.* 1162
NOVARTIS CORPORATION, 230 Park Ave, Fl 21, **New York,** NY 10169, *pg.* 1574, *pg.* 1273
NUTRITION 21, INC., 3 Manhattanville Rd, Ste 201, **Purchase,** NY 10577, *pg.* 1577, *pg.* 1327
PFIZER INC., 235 E 42nd St, **New York,** NY 10017-5755, *pg.* 1581, *pg.* 1278
PROPPER MANUFACTURING COMPANY, INC., 36-04 Skillman Ave, **Long Island City,** NY 11101-1730, *pg.* 1586, *pg.* 1175
QUALITY KING DISTRIBUTORS INC., 2060 9th Ave, **Ronkonkoma,** NY 11779-6253, *pg.* 1587, *pg.* 1339
REGENERON PHARMACEUTICALS, INC., 777 Old Saw Mill River Rd, **Tarrytown,** NY 10591-6717, *pg.* 1588, *pg.* 1345
SIGA TECHNOLOGIES, INC., 35 E 62nd St, **New York,** NY 10065, *pg.* 1594, *pg.* 1292
ST. FRANCIS HOSPITAL, 100 Port Washington Blvd, **Roslyn,** NY 11576, *pg.* 1596, *pg.* 1339
SUMITOMO ELECTRIC, 600 3rd Ave Ste 39, **New York,** NY 10016, *pg.* 1599, *pg.* 1297
TWINLAB CORPORATION, 632 Broadway, Ste 201, **New York,** NY 10012, *pg.* 1603, *pg.* 1306
VISITING NURSE ASSOCIATION OF STATEN ISLAND, 400 Lake Ave, **Staten Island,** NY 10303, *pg.* 1607, *pg.* 1343
VISITING NURSE SERVICE OF NEW YORK, 107 E 70th St, **New York,** NY 10021-5006, *pg.* 1607, *pg.* 1311
VISITING NURSE SERVICES IN WESTCHESTER, INC., 360 Mamaroneck Ave, **White Plains,** NY 10605, *pg.* 1607, *pg.* 1354
WEIGHT WATCHERS INTERNATIONAL, INC., 675 Avenue of the Americas 6th Fl, **New York,** NY 10010, *pg.* 1609, *pg.* 1313
ZEPTOMETRIX CORPORATION, 872 Main St, **Buffalo,** NY 14202-1403, *pg.* 1611, *pg.* 1151

North Carolina

BARNHARDT MANUFACTURING COMPANY, 1100 Hawthorne Ln, **Charlotte,** NC 28205-2918, *pg.* 1498, *pg.* 1364
CAROLINA BIOLOGICAL SUPPLY COMPANY, 2700 York Rd, **Burlington,** NC 27215, *pg.* 1513, *pg.* 1359
CHIESI USA, INC., 1255 Crescent Green Dr Ste 250, **Cary,** NC 27518, *pg.* 1515, *pg.* 1359
GLAXOSMITHKLINE, 5 Moore Drive PO Box 13398, **Research Triangle Park,** NC 27709-3398, *pg.* 1536, *pg.* 1389
LABORATORY CORPORATION OF AMERICA HOLDINGS, 358 S Main St, **Burlington,** NC 27215, *pg.* 1554, *pg.* 1359
NOVANT HEALTH, INC., 2085 Frontis Plz Blvd, **Winston Salem,** NC 27103-3013, *pg.* 1574, *pg.* 1394
PHARMACEUTICAL PRODUCT DEVELOPMENT, INC., 929 N Front St, **Wilmington,** NC 28401, *pg.* 1584, *pg.* 1393
PRAHEALTH SCIENCES, 4130 Park Lake Ave Ste 400, **Raleigh,** NC 27612, *pg.* 1585, *pg.* 1388
PREMIER HEALTHCARE ALLIANCE, 13034 Ballantyne Corporate Pl, **Charlotte,** NC 28277, *pg.* 1586, *pg.* 1368
SALIX PHARMACEUTICALS, INC., 8510 Colonnade Center Dr, **Raleigh,** NC 27615-3273, *pg.* 1591, *pg.* 1388
SWISHER INTERNATIONAL, INC., 4725 Piedmont Row Dr Ste 400, **Charlotte,** NC 28210, *pg.* 1600, *pg.* 1369
TARGACEPT, INC., 100 N Main St Ste 1510, **Winston Salem,** NC 27101, *pg.* 1601, *pg.* 1395
WATAUGA MEDICAL CENTER, PO Box 2600, **Boone,** NC 28607-2600, *pg.* 1609, *pg.* 1358

North Dakota

SWANSON HEALTH PRODUCTS INC., 4075 40th Ave SW, **Fargo,** ND 58104-3912, *pg.* 1600, *pg.* 1397

Ohio

ABBOTT NUTRITION, 3300 Stelzer Rd, **Columbus,** OH 43219, *pg.* 1485, *pg.* 1437
CARDINAL HEALTH, INC., 7000 Cardinal Pl, **Dublin,** OH 43017, *pg.* 1512, *pg.* 1448
CLEVELAND CLINIC, 9500 Euclid Ave, **Cleveland,** OH 44195, *pg.* 1516, *pg.* 1429
DENTAL ONE, INC., 5875 Landerbrook Dr, **Mayfield**

Heights, OH 44124, *pg.* 1522, *pg.* 1462
DIET CENTER WORLDWIDE, INC., 395 Springside Dr, **Akron**, OH 44333, *pg.* 1524, *pg.* 1400
DISCOUNT DRUG MART INC., 211 Commerce Dr, **Medina**, OH 44256-1331, *pg.* 1524, *pg.* 1464
FORM YOU 3 INTERNATIONAL, INC., 395 Springside Dr, **Akron**, OH 44333, *pg.* 1531, *pg.* 1400
GANEDEN BIOTECH, INC., 5800 Landerbrook Dr, Ste 300, **Mayfield Heights**, OH 44124, *pg.* 1532, *pg.* 1463
HCR MANORCARE, INC., 333 N Summit St, **Toledo**, OH 43604-2617, *pg.* 1539, *pg.* 1476
INVACARE CORPORATION, 1 Invacare Way, **Elyria**, OH 44035-4190, *pg.* 1546, *pg.* 1451
OHIOHEALTH, 180 E Broad St, **Columbus**, OH 43201-3201, *pg.* 1578, *pg.* 1443
OMNICARE, INC, 201 E 4th St, Ste 900, **Cincinnati**, OH 45202, *pg.* 1578, *pg.* 1418
PHYSICIANS WEIGHT LOSS CENTERS, INC., 395 Springside Dr, **Akron**, OH 44333, *pg.* 1585, *pg.* 1402
PROGRESSIVE MEDICAL, INC., 250 Progressive Way, **Westerville**, OH 43082, *pg.* 1586, *pg.* 1480
RADIANT RESEARCH INC., 11500 Northlake Dr Ste 320, **Cincinnati**, OH 45249, *pg.* 1588, *pg.* 1425
RADIOMETER AMERICA INC., 810 Sharon Dr, **Westlake**, OH 44145-1521, *pg.* 1588, *pg.* 1481
RELIANCE MEDICAL PRODUCTS, INC., 3535 Kings Mills Rd, **Mason**, OH 45040-2303, *pg.* 1589, *pg.* 1461
STERIS CORPORATION, 5960 Heisley Rd, **Mentor**, OH 44060-1834, *pg.* 1597, *pg.* 1464

Oregon

A-DEC, INC., 2601 Crestview Dr, **Newberg**, OR 97132-9529, *pg.* 1483, *pg.* 1500
BIOJECT MEDICAL TECHNOLOGIES INC., 7180 Sw Sandburg St, Ste 100, **Tigard**, OR 97223, *pg.* 1506, *pg.* 1509
DRAVON MEDICAL, INC., 11465 SE Hwy 212, **Clackamas**, OR 97015-0069, *pg.* 1525, *pg.* 1497
HEMCON MEDICAL TECHNOLOGIES, INC., 10575 SW Cascade Ave Ste 130, **Portland**, OR 97223-4363, *pg.* 1541, *pg.* 1503
LEGACY HEALTH SYSTEM, 1919 NW Lovejoy, **Portland**, OR 97209, *pg.* 1555, *pg.* 1504
NEW EARTH LIFE SCIENCES, INC., 565 Century Ct, **Klamath Falls**, OR 97601, *pg.* 1573, *pg.* 1499
NUNATURALS, INC., 2220 W 2nd Ave Ste 1, **Eugene**, OR 97402, *pg.* 1576, *pg.* 1497
TOTAL NUTRACEUTICAL SOLUTIONS, INC., 13565 SW Tualatin-Sherwood Rd Ste 800, **Sherwood**, OR 97140, *pg.* 1603, *pg.* 1509
WEBMD HEALTH SERVICES GROUP, 2701 NW Vaughn St Ste 700, **Portland**, OR 97210, *pg.* 1609, *pg.* 1508

Pennsylvania

AESCULAP, INC., 3773 Corporate Pkwy, **Center Valley**, PA 18034-8217, *pg.* 1487, *pg.* 1521
AMERISOURCEBERGEN CORPORATION, 1300 Morris Dr, **Chesterbrook**, PA 19087-5594, *pg.* 1493, *pg.* 1522
ANIMAS CORPORATION, 200 Lawrence Dr, **West Chester**, PA 19380-3428, *pg.* 1495, *pg.* 1593
BAYER CORPORATION, 100 Bayer Rd, **Pittsburgh**, PA 15205-9741, *pg.* 1499, *pg.* 1573
BIOCLINICA, INC., 826 Newtown-Yardley Rd, **Newtown**, PA 18940-1721, *pg.* 1506, *pg.* 1556
BOIRON USA INC., 6 Campus Blvd, **Newtown Square**, PA 19073, *pg.* 1507, *pg.* 1556
CARDIONET, INC., 227 Washington St, **Conshohocken**, PA 19428, *pg.* 1513, *pg.* 1523
CHESTER COUNTY HOSPITAL, 701 E Marshall St, **West Chester**, PA 19380, *pg.* 1515, *pg.* 1593
CHILDREN'S HOSPITAL OF PHILADELPHIA, 34th St & Civic Center Blvd, **Philadelphia**, PA 19104, *pg.* 1515, *pg.* 1560
CROZER-KEYSTONE HEALTH SYSTEM INC., 100 W Sproul Rd 3rd Fl, **Springfield**, PA 19064, *pg.* 1520, *pg.* 1587
CSL BEHRING LLC, 1020 1st Ave, **King of Prussia**, PA 19406, *pg.* 1520, *pg.* 1543
DENTSPLY INTERNATIONAL INC., 221 W Philadelphia St, **York**, PA 17405, *pg.* 1522, *pg.* 1596
DEPUY SYNTHES, 1302 Wrights Ln E, **West Chester**, PA 19380, *pg.* 1523, *pg.* 1593
ENCORIUM GROUP, INC., 435 Devon Park Dr Bldg 500, **Wayne**, PA 19087, *pg.* 1528, *pg.* 1591
ENDO PHARMACEUTICALS HOLDINGS, INC., 1400 Atwater Dr, **Malvern**, PA 19355, *pg.* 1528, *pg.* 1549
FIBROCELL SCIENCE, INC., 405 Eagleview Blvd, **Exton**, PA 19341, *pg.* 1530, *pg.* 1531
FUJIREBIO DIAGNOSTICS INC., 201 Great Valley Pkwy, **Malvern**, PA 19355-1307, *pg.* 1531, *pg.* 1550
GEISINGER HEALTH SYSTEM, 100 N Academy Ave, **Danville**, PA 17822-0001, *pg.* 1533, *pg.* 1526
GENERAL NUTRITION CENTERS, INC., 300 6th Ave, **Pittsburgh**, PA 15222, *pg.* 1534, *pg.* 1575
GENESIS HEALTHCARE CORP., 101 E State St, **Kennett Square**, PA 19348-3109, *pg.* 1534, *pg.* 1543
GLAXOSMITHKLINE, 5 Crescent Dr, **Philadelphia**, PA 19112, *pg.* 1536, *pg.* 1565
GNC HOLDINGS INC., 300 6th Ave, **Pittsburgh**, PA 15222, *pg.* 1537, *pg.* 1576
INTEGRA MILTEX, INC., 589 Davies Dr, **York**, PA 17402-8630, *pg.* 1546, *pg.* 1597
JANSSEN BIOTECH, INC., 800 Ridgeview Rd, **Horsham**, PA 19044, *pg.* 1548, *pg.* 1540
JOHNSON & JOHNSON - MERCK CONSUMER PHARMACEUTICALS CO., 7050 Camp Hill Rd, **Fort Washington**, PA 19034-2292, *pg.* 1552, *pg.* 1533
LANNETT COMPANY, INC., 13200 Townsend Rd, **Philadelphia**, PA 19154, *pg.* 1555, *pg.* 1566
MAXIM HEALTHCARE SERVICES INC., 4815 Jonestown Rd Ste 202, **Harrisburg**, PA 17109-1750, *pg.* 1559, *pg.* 1537
MCNEIL-PPC, INC., 7050 Camp Hill Rd, **Fort Washington**, PA 19034-2210, *pg.* 1560, *pg.* 1533
MEDRAD, INC., 100 Global View Dr, **Warrendale**, PA 15086, *pg.* 1563, *pg.* 1591
MYLAN, INC., 1000 Mylan Blvd., **Canonsburg**, PA 15317, *pg.* 1570, *pg.* 1520
NUTRISYSTEM, INC., 600 Office Center Dr, **Fort Washington**, PA 19034, *pg.* 1577, *pg.* 1533
ORASURE TECHNOLOGIES INC, 220 E First St, **Bethlehem**, PA 18015-1338, *pg.* 1578, *pg.* 1516
PHILIPS RESPIRONICS, 1010 Murry Ridge Ln, **Murrysville**, PA 15668-8525, *pg.* 1585, *pg.* 1555
PROPHASE LABS, INC., 621 N Shady Retreat Rd, **Doylestown**, PA 18901, *pg.* 1586, *pg.* 1526
THE RENFREW CENTERS INC., 475 Spring Ln, **Philadelphia**, PA 19128, *pg.* 1589, *pg.* 1570
RITE AID CORPORATION, 30 Hunter Ln, **Camp Hill**, PA 17011-2400, *pg.* 1590, *pg.* 1519
SANOFI PASTEUR, INC, Discovery Dr, **Swiftwater**, PA 18370-0187, *pg.* 1591, *pg.* 1588
SCANDINAVIAN FORMULAS, INC., 140 E Church St, **Sellersville**, PA 18960, *pg.* 1592, *pg.* 1586
SHIRE, 730 Stockton Dr, **Exton**, PA 19341, *pg.* 1593, *pg.* 1532
SYMONS CAPITAL MANAGEMENT, 650 Washington Rd, Ste 800, **Pittsburgh**, PA 15228, *pg.* 1600, *pg.* 1582
TEMPLE UNIVERSITY HEALTH SYSTEM, 3401 N Broad St, **Philadelphia**, PA 19140, *pg.* 1601, *pg.* 1571
UNILIFE CORPORATION, 250 Cross Farm Ln, **York**, PA 17406, *pg.* 1603, *pg.* 1597
UNIVERSAL HEALTH SERVICES INC., 367 S Gulph Rd PO Box 61558, **King of Prussia**, PA 19406, *pg.* 1604, *pg.* 1544
VWR FUNDING, INC., 100 Matsonford Rd PO Box 6660, **Radnor**, PA 19087, *pg.* 1608, *pg.* 1583
WEXFORD HEALTH SOURCES INC., 45 Holiday Dr Foster Plz Two, **Pittsburgh**, PA 15220, *pg.* 1610, *pg.* 1582

Rhode Island

MEDPORT, LLC, 23 Acorn St, **Providence**, RI 02903, *pg.* 1563, *pg.* 1607

South Carolina

GREENVILLE HOSPITAL SYSTEM INC., 701 Grove Rd, **Greenville**, SC 29605-5611, *pg.* 1538, *pg.* 1617
SPAN-AMERICA MEDICAL SYSTEMS, INC., 70 Commerce Ctr, **Greenville**, SC 29615-5814, *pg.* 1595, *pg.* 1618

South Dakota

CIGNA TEL-DRUG, INC., 4901 N 4th Ave, **Sioux Falls**, SD 57104-0444, *pg.* 1515, *pg.* 1625

Tennessee

BROOKDALE SENIOR LIVING INC., 111 Westwood Pl Ste 400, **Brentwood**, TN 37027, *pg.* 1511, *pg.* 1627
CAREMARK PHARMACY SERVICES, 445 Great Cir Rd, **Nashville**, TN 37228, *pg.* 1513, *pg.* 1649
CHATTEM, INC., 1715 W 38th St, **Chattanooga**, TN 37409-1248, *pg.* 1515, *pg.* 1628
CIGNA-HEALTHSPRING, 9009 Carothers Parkway Ste 501, **Franklin**, TN 37067, *pg.* 1515, *pg.* 1632
COMMUNITY HEALTH SYSTEMS, INC., 4000 Meridian Blvd, **Franklin**, TN 37067, *pg.* 1516, *pg.* 1632
CUMBERLAND PHARMACEUTICALS, INC., 2525 West End Ave Ste 950, **Nashville**, TN 37203, *pg.* 1521, *pg.* 1650
ERLANGER HEALTH SYSTEM, 975 E 3rd St, **Chattanooga**, TN 37403-2103, *pg.* 1529, *pg.* 1629
HCA HOLDINGS, INC., 1 Park Plz, **Nashville**, TN 37203-6527, *pg.* 1539, *pg.* 1651
HEALTHWAYS, INC., 701 Cool Springs Blvd, **Franklin**, TN 37067, *pg.* 1540, *pg.* 1632
KING PHARMACEUTICALS, INC., 501 5th St, **Bristol**, TN 37620, *pg.* 1553, *pg.* 1627
LIFE CARE CENTERS OF AMERICA, 3570 Keith St NW, **Cleveland**, TN 37320, *pg.* 1555, *pg.* 1630
METHODIST UNIVERSITY HOSPITAL, 1265 Union Ave, **Memphis**, TN 38104, *pg.* 1567, *pg.* 1645
SAINT THOMAS MIDTOWN HOSPITAL, 2000 Church St, **Nashville**, TN 37236-0002, *pg.* 1591, *pg.* 1654
ST. JUDE CHILDREN'S RESEARCH HOSPITAL, 332 N Lauderdale St, **Memphis**, TN 38105-2729, *pg.* 1596, *pg.* 1646
TEAM HEALTH HOLDINGS, INC., 265 Brookview Centre Way Ste 400, **Knoxville**, TN 37919, *pg.* 1601, *pg.* 1639

Texas

ASD HEALTHCARE, 3101 Gaylord Pkwy 3rd Fl, **Frisco**, TX 75034, *pg.* 1496, *pg.* 1697
BAYLOR HEALTH CARE SYSTEM, 3500 Gaston Ave, **Dallas**, TX 75246, *pg.* 1500, *pg.* 1676
DJO SURGICAL, 9800 Metric Blvd, **Austin**, TX 78758-5445, *pg.* 1525, *pg.* 1661
DYMATIZE ENTERPRISES, INC., 13737 N Stemmons Fwy, **Farmers Branch**, TX 75234, *pg.* 1525, *pg.* 1692
DYNACQ HEALTHCARE, INC., 4301 Vista Rd, **Pasadena**, TX 77504, *pg.* 1526, *pg.* 1728
FIRST SURGICAL PARTNERS INC., 411 1st St, **Bellaire**, TX 77401, *pg.* 1531, *pg.* 1668
GALDERMA LABORATORIES, L.P., 14501 N Freeway, **Fort Worth**, TX 76177-3304, *pg.* 1532, *pg.* 1695
HANGER INC., 10910 Domain Dr Ste 300, **Austin**, TX 78758, *pg.* 1539, *pg.* 1663
HEALTHTRONICS, INC., 9825 Spectrum Dr Bldg 3, **Austin**, TX 78717, *pg.* 1540, *pg.* 1663
KINETIC CONCEPTS, INC., 12930 Interstate 10 W, **San Antonio**, TX 78249, *pg.* 1553, *pg.* 1741
LEXICON PHARMACEUTICALS, INC., 8800 Technology Forest Pl, **The Woodlands**, TX 77381, *pg.* 1555, *pg.* 1747
LIVANOVA, 100 Cyberonics Blvd, **Houston**, TX 77058, *pg.* 1557, *pg.* 1710
MANNATECH, INCORPORATED, 600 S Royal Ln Ste 200, **Coppell**, TX 75019-3823, *pg.* 1558, *pg.* 1671
MEMORIAL HERMANN HEALTHCARE SYSTEM, 6411 Fannin St, **Houston**, TX 77030, *pg.* 1565, *pg.* 1711
METHODIST HOSPITAL, 8109 Fredricksburg Rd, **San Antonio**, TX 78229, *pg.* 1567, *pg.* 1741
MISSION PHARMACAL COMPANY INC., 10999 IH 10 W Ste 1000, **San Antonio**, TX 78230-1355, *pg.* 1568, *pg.* 1742
OXYSURE SYSTEMS, INC., 10880 John W Elliot Dr Ste 600, **Frisco**, TX 75034, *pg.* 1579, *pg.* 1697
PAIN THERAPEUTICS, INC., 7801 N Capital Of Texas Hwy Ste 260, **Austin**, TX 78731-1192, *pg.* 1579, *pg.* 1665
RBC LIFE SCIENCES, INC., 2301 Crown Ct, **Irving**, TX 75038-4305, *pg.* 1588, *pg.* 1723
RETRACTABLE TECHNOLOGIES INC., 511 Lobo Ln, **Little Elm**, TX 75068, *pg.* 1590, *pg.* 1725
TENET HEALTHCARE CORPORATION, 1445 Ross Ave, Ste 1400, **Dallas**, TX 75202, *pg.* 1601, *pg.* 1688
ULURU INC., 4452 Beltway Dr, **Addison**, TX 75001, *pg.* 1603, *pg.* 1658
UNITED SURGICAL PARTNERS INTERNATIONAL, INC., 15305 Dallas Pkwy Ste 1600, **Addison**, TX 75001, *pg.* 1604, *pg.* 1658
UNIVERSITY HEALTH SYSTEM, 4502 Medical Dr, **San**

First page reference indicates Business Class Edition
Second page reference indicates Geographic Edition

Antonio, TX 78229, *pg.* 1604, *pg.* 1743
US ONCOLOGY, INC., 10101 Woodloch Forrest Dr, **The Woodlands,** TX 77380, *pg.* 1604, *pg.* 1747
U.S. PHYSICAL THERAPY, INC., 1300 W Sam Houston Pkwy S Ste 300, **Houston,** TX 77042, *pg.* 1604, *pg.* 1716
VHA INC., 220 Las Colinas Blvd E, **Irving,** TX 75039-5503, *pg.* 1606, *pg.* 1724
VIRBAC CORPORATION, 3200 Meacham Blvd, **Fort Worth,** TX 76137, *pg.* 1606, *pg.* 1696

Utah

BD MEDICAL, 9450 S State St, **Sandy,** UT 84070-3213, *pg.* 1501, *pg.* 1762
BIO-PATH HOLDINGS, INC., 3293 Harrison Blvd Ste 220, **Ogden,** UT 84403, *pg.* 1504, *pg.* 1752
CHG HEALTHCARE SERVICES, INC., 6440 S Newrock Dr, **Salt Lake City,** UT 84121, *pg.* 1515, *pg.* 1756
DYNATRONICS CORPORATION, 7030 Park Centre Dr, **Salt Lake City,** UT 84121-6618, *pg.* 1526, *pg.* 1757
INTERMOUNTAIN HEALTH CARE INC., 36 S State St, **Salt Lake City,** UT 84111, *pg.* 1546, *pg.* 1759
LIFEVANTAGE CORPORATION, 9815 S Monroe St, Ste 100, **Sandy,** UT 84070, *pg.* 1556, *pg.* 1762
MORINDA HOLDINGS INC., 333 W River Prk Dr, **Provo,** UT 84604, *pg.* 1569, *pg.* 1754
NATURE'S SUNSHINE PRODUCTS, INC., 75 E 1700 S, **Provo,** UT 84606, *pg.* 1571, *pg.* 1754
NUTRACEUTICAL INTERNATIONAL CORPORATION, 1400 Kearns Blvd Fl 2, **Park City,** UT 84060-7228, *pg.* 1576, *pg.* 1753
PERSEON CORPORATION, 2188 W 2200 S, **Salt Lake City,** UT 84119-1326, *pg.* 1581, *pg.* 1760
SCHIFF NUTRITION INTERNATIONAL, INC., 2002 S 5070 W, **Salt Lake City,** UT 84104-4726, *pg.* 1592, *pg.* 1760
TRACK GROUP, 405 S Main St Ste 700, **Salt Lake City,** UT 84111, *pg.* 1603, *pg.* 1761
USANA HEALTH SCIENCES, INC., 3838 W Parkway Blvd, **Salt Lake City,** UT 84120-6336, *pg.* 1605, *pg.* 1761
UTAH MEDICAL PRODUCTS, INC., 7043 S 300 W, **Midvale,** UT 84047-1048, *pg.* 1605, *pg.* 1752
XANGO, LLC, 2889 Ashton Blvd, **Lehi,** UT 84043, *pg.* 1610, *pg.* 1751

Virginia

BOSTWICK LABORATORIES, INC., 4355 Innslake Dr, **Glen Allen,** VA 23060, *pg.* 1509, *pg.* 1782
CARILION HEALTH SYSTEM, 1906 Belleview Ave, **Roanoke,** VA 24014, *pg.* 1513, *pg.* 1806
FLEET LABORATORIES, 4615 Murray Pl, **Lynchburg,** VA 24502-2235, *pg.* 1531, *pg.* 1787
INOVA HEALTH SYSTEM, 8110 Gatehouse Rd, **Falls Church,** VA 22042, *pg.* 1545, *pg.* 1781
LUNA INNOVATIONS INC., 1 Riverside Cir Ste 400, **Roanoke,** VA 24016, *pg.* 1557, *pg.* 1806
OWENS & MINOR, INC., 9120 Lockwood Blvd, **Mechanicsville,** VA 23116, *pg.* 1579, *pg.* 1795
SENTARA HEALTHCARE, 6015 Poplar Hall Dr Ste 300, **Norfolk,** VA 23502, *pg.* 1593, *pg.* 1797
SPHERIX INC., 7927 Jones Branch Dr, Ste 3125, **Tysons Corner,** VA 22102, *pg.* 1596, *pg.* 1808
SUNRISE SENIOR LIVING, INC., 7900 Westpark Drive, **McLean,** VA 22102, *pg.* 1599, *pg.* 1795

Washington

THE BARTELL DRUG COMPANY, 4025 Delridge Way SW, Ste 400, **Seattle,** WA 98106, *pg.* 1499, *pg.* 1833
CELL THERAPEUTICS, INC., 3101 Western Ave, Ste 600, **Seattle,** WA 98121, *pg.* 1514, *pg.* 1834
DENDREON CORPORATION, 1301 2nd Ave Ste 3200, **Seattle,** WA 98101-0004, *pg.* 1522, *pg.* 1835
GUS COMMUNICATIONS, INC., 1006 Lonetree Ct, **Bellingham,** WA 98229, *pg.* 1538, *pg.* 1817
ISORAY, INC., 350 Hills St Ste 106, **Richland,** WA 99354, *pg.* 1548, *pg.* 1830
ONCOGENEX PHARMACEUTICALS, INC., 1522 217th Pl SE Ste 100, **Bothell,** WA 98021, *pg.* 1578, *pg.* 1818
ONCOTHYREON INC., 2601 4th Ave Ste 500, **Seattle,** WA 98121, *pg.* 1578, *pg.* 1838
PROVIDENCE HEALTH SYSTEM, 1801 Lind ave SW, **Renton,** WA 98057, *pg.* 1587, *pg.* 1829
SPACELABS HEALTHCARE, 5150 220th Ave SE, **Issaquah,** WA 98029, *pg.* 1595, *pg.* 1821

West Virginia

MEDEXPRESS URGENT CARE, 1751 Earl Core Rd, **Morgantown,** WV 26505, *pg.* 1561, *pg.* 1850

Wisconsin

ACCURAY, 1240 Deming Way, **Madison,** WI 53717-2911, *pg.* 1486, *pg.* 1864
CARDIAC SCIENCE CORPORATION, N7W22025 Johnson Dr, **Waukesha,** WI 53186, *pg.* 1512, *pg.* 1897
CRITICARE SYSTEMS, INC., N7W22025 Johnson Dr, **Waukesha,** WI 53186-1856, *pg.* 1520, *pg.* 1897
ENZYMATIC THERAPY INC., 825 Challenger Dr, **Green Bay,** WI 54311, *pg.* 1529, *pg.* 1859
EXACT SCIENCES CORPORATION, 441 Charmany Dr, **Madison,** WI 53719, *pg.* 1529, *pg.* 1865
EXTENDICARE HEALTH SERVICES INC., 111 W Michigan St, **Milwaukee,** WI 53203-2903, *pg.* 1530, *pg.* 1874
THE F. DOHMEN CO., W194 N11381 McCormick Dr, **Germantown,** WI 53022-3033, *pg.* 1530, *pg.* 1858
GAMMEX RMI INC., 7600 Discovery Dr, **Middleton,** WI 53562-2610, *pg.* 1532, *pg.* 1872
GE HEALTHCARE TECHNOLOGIES, 3000 N Grandview Blvd, **Waukesha,** WI 53188, *pg.* 1533, *pg.* 1897
MARSHFIELD CLINIC, 1000 N Oak Ave, **Marshfield,** WI 54449, *pg.* 1558, *pg.* 1869
MODERN PRODUCTS, INC., 6425 W Executive Dr, **Mequon,** WI 53092-0248, *pg.* 1568, *pg.* 1871
MUELLER SPORTS MEDICINE, INC., 1 Quench Dr, **Prairie Du Sac,** WI 53578-2100, *pg.* 1570, *pg.* 1887
SCIENTIFIC PROTEIN LABORATORIES, INC., 700 E Main St, **Waunakee,** WI 53597-1440, *pg.* 1593, *pg.* 1898
WISCONSIN PHARMACAL COMPANY, LLC, 1 Pharmacal Way, **Jackson,** WI 53037-9583, *pg.* 1610, *pg.* 1861

Publishers, Printers, Engravers, Etc.

Alabama

BOOKS-A-MILLION, INC., 402 Industrial Ln, **Birmingham,** AL 35211-4465, *pg.* 1623, *pg.* 2
EBSCO INDUSTRIES, INC., 5724 Hwy 280 E, **Birmingham,** AL 35242, *pg.* 1638, *pg.* 2
RANDALL-REILLY PUBLISHING COMPANY LLC, 3200 Rice Mine Rd NE, **Tuscaloosa,** AL 35406-1510, *pg.* 1679, *pg.* 8
TRUCKER PUBLICATIONS INC., 610 Noble St, **Anniston,** AL 36201, *pg.* 1696, *pg.* 1

Alaska

JUNEAU EMPIRE, 3100 Channel Dr, **Juneau,** AK 99801, *pg.* 1656, *pg.* 10
THE PENINSULA CLARION, 150 Trading Bay Dr Ste 1, **Kenai,** AK 99611, *pg.* 1676, *pg.* 11

Arizona

THE ARIZONA REPUBLIC, 200 E Van Buren St, **Phoenix,** AZ 85004, *pg.* 1617, *pg.* 14
EAST VALLEY TRIBUNE, 1620 W Fountainhead Pkwy Ste 219, **Tempe,** AZ 85282-1848, *pg.* 1638, *pg.* 25
INFORMA EXHIBITIONS LLC, 3300 N Central Ave, Ste 300, **Phoenix,** AZ 85012, *pg.* 1653, *pg.* 17
NEWS WEST PUBLISHING COMPANY INC., 2435 S Miracle Mile, **Bullhead City,** AZ 86442-7311, *pg.* 1670, *pg.* 12
THE SUN, 2055 Arizona Ave, **Yuma,** AZ 85364-6549, *pg.* 1690, *pg.* 28
WESTERN NEWSPAPERS, INC., 1748 S Arizona Ave, **Yuma,** AZ 85364-5727, *pg.* 1702, *pg.* 28

Arkansas

LOG CABIN DEMOCRAT, LLC, 1111 Main St Ste 102, **Conway,** AR 72032, *pg.* 1660, *pg.* 31

California

ACADEMIC COMMUNICATION ASSOCIATES, INC., Bldg 102 4001 Avenida de la Plata, **Oceanside,** CA 92052-4279, *pg.* 1613, *pg.* 173
ACADEMIC INNOVATIONS, 281 S Magnolia Ave, **Santa Barbara,** CA 93117, *pg.* 1613, *pg.* 262
AMERICAN REPROGRAPHICS COMPANY, 1981 N Broadway Ste 385, **Walnut Creek,** CA 94596, *pg.* 1616, *pg.* 303
AMERICAN SOCIETY OF CINEMATOGRAPHERS, 1782 N Orange Dr, **Hollywood,** CA 90028-4307, *pg.* 1616, *pg.* 103
ANTELOPE VALLEY NEWSPAPER INC., 37404 Sierra Hwy, **Palmdale,** CA 93550, *pg.* 1617, *pg.* 174
ASIAN WEEK FOUNDATION, 564 Market St Ste 320, **San Francisco,** CA 94104, *pg.* 1617, *pg.* 212
ASTARA, INC., 10700 Jersey Blvd Ste 450, **Rancho Cucamonga,** CA 91730, *pg.* 1618, *pg.* 186
BOBIT BUSINESS MEDIA, 3520 Challenger St, **Torrance,** CA 90503, *pg.* 1622, *pg.* 293
BREHM COMMUNICATIONS INC., 16644 W Bernardo Dr Ste 300, **San Diego,** CA 92127-1901, *pg.* 1623, *pg.* 201
BRIDGE PUBLICATIONS INC., 5600 E Olympic Blvd, **Los Angeles,** CA 90022, *pg.* 1623, *pg.* 127
CALIFORNIA OFFSET PRINTERS, INC., 620 W Elk Ave, **Glendale,** CA 91204, *pg.* 1625, *pg.* 95
CENGAGE LEARNING, 500 Terry Francois Blvd 2nd Fl, **San Francisco,** CA 94158, *pg.* 1626, *pg.* 215
CHRONICLE BOOKS, 680 Second St, **San Francisco,** CA 94107, *pg.* 1627, *pg.* 216
COLLECTORS EDITIONS, 9002 Eton Ave, **Canoga Park,** CA 91304-1616, *pg.* 1628, *pg.* 58
CONDE NAST PUBLICATIONS, INC., 6300 Wilshire Blvd, **Los Angeles,** CA 90048-5204, *pg.* 1630, *pg.* 128
CPP, INC., 1055 Joaquin Rd 2nd Fl, **Mountain View,** CA 94043, *pg.* 1631, *pg.* 153
THE DAILY BREEZE, 21250 Hawthorne Blvd Ste 170, **Torrance,** CA 90503, *pg.* 1632, *pg.* 293
DAILY PRESS, 13891 Pk Ave, **Victorville,** CA 92392, *pg.* 1632, *pg.* 302
DESERT DISPATCH, 130 Coolwater Ln, **Barstow,** CA 92311, *pg.* 1635, *pg.* 45
DESERT PUBLICATIONS INC., 303 N Indian Canyon Dr, **Palm Springs,** CA 92262, *pg.* 1635, *pg.* 174
ENTREPRENEUR MEDIA, INC., 2445 McCabe Way Ste 400, **Irvine,** CA 92614-4293, *pg.* 1639, *pg.* 110
EVAN-MOOR CORPORATION, 18 Lower Reagsdale Dr, **Monterey,** CA 93940-5746, *pg.* 1639, *pg.* 151
FILM SCORE MONTHLY, 6311 Romaine St Ste 7109, **Hollywood,** CA 90038-2617, *pg.* 1641, *pg.* 103
FINDLAW, 800 W California Ave 2nd Fl, **Sunnyvale,** CA 94086-4834, *pg.* 1641, *pg.* 285
FREEDOM COMMUNICATIONS, INC., 17666 Fitch, **Irvine,** CA 92614-6022, *pg.* 1643, *pg.* 110
HI-DESERT PUBLISHING CO. INC., 56445 29 Palms Hwy, **Yucca Valley,** CA 92284-2861, *pg.* 1650, *pg.* 309
THE HOLLYWOOD REPORTER INC., 5055 Wilshire Blvd, **Los Angeles,** CA 90036-4396, *pg.* 1650, *pg.* 133
I-5 PUBLISHING LLC, 2401 Beverly Blvd, **Los Angeles,** CA 90057-1001, *pg.* 1651, *pg.* 133
IMPREMEDIA LLC, 700 S Flowers St Ste 3000, **Los Angeles,** CA 90017, *pg.* 1652, *pg.* 133
INVESTORS BUSINESS DAILY, INC., 12655 Beatrice St, **Los Angeles,** CA 90066, *pg.* 1653, *pg.* 133
KELLEY BLUE BOOK CO., INC., 195 Technology Dr, **Irvine,** CA 92618-2402, *pg.* 1656, *pg.* 112
LINCOLN NEWS MESSENGER, 553 F St, **Lincoln,** CA 95648-1849, *pg.* 1659, *pg.* 122
LINE PUBLICATIONS, INC., 10537 Santa Monica Blvd Ste 250, **Los Angeles,** CA 90025, *pg.* 1659, *pg.* 134
LOS ANGELES DAILY NEWS PUBLISHING COMPANY, PO Box 4200, **Woodland Hills,** CA 91365-4200, *pg.* 1660, *pg.* 308
LOS ANGELES MAGAZINE, 5900 Wilshire Blvd 10th Fl, **Los Angeles,** CA 90036, *pg.* 1660, *pg.* 135
LOS ANGELES TIMES COMMUNICATIONS, LLC, 202 W First St, **Los Angeles,** CA 90012, *pg.* 1660, *pg.* 135
THE LUCKY GROUP, INC., 1223 Wilshire Blvd Box #C, **Santa Monica,** CA 90403, *pg.* 1660, *pg.* 275
MARIN INDEPENDENT JOURNAL, 4000 Civic Center Dr Ste 301, **San Rafael,** CA 94903-4171, *pg.* 1661, *pg.* 258
MARSHALL & SWIFT/BOECKH, LLC, 777 S Figueroa St 12th Fl, **Los Angeles,** CA 90017-5882, *pg.* 1661, *pg.* 136
THE MCCLATCHY COMPANY, 2100 Q St, **Sacramento,** CA 95816, *pg.* 1662, *pg.* 196
MCCLATCHY NEWSPAPERS, INC., 2100 Q St, **Sacramento,** CA 95816-6816, *pg.* 1662, *pg.* 197
METRO NEWSPAPERS ADVERTISING SERVICES, INC., 160 Spear St Ste 1875, **San Francisco,** CA 94105, *pg.* 1665, *pg.* 223
THE ORANGE COUNTY REGISTER, 625 N Grand Ave, **Santa Ana,** CA 92701-4347, *pg.* 1673, *pg.* 262
O'REILLY MEDIA, INC., 1005 Gravenstein Hwy N, **Sebastopol,** CA 95472-3858, *pg.* 1673, *pg.* 278
PACIFIC PALISADES POST INC., 839 Via De La Paz PO Box 725, **Pacific Palisades,** CA 90272-3618, *pg.* 1673, *pg.* 174
PAISANO PUBLICATIONS, LLC, 28210 Dorothy Dr, **Agoura Hills,** CA 91301, *pg.* 1674, *pg.* 38
PAZDUR PUBLISHING CO., 2171 Campus Dr Ste 330, **Irvine,** CA 92612-1422, *pg.* 1674, *pg.* 115
PIP PRINTING, INC., 26722 Plaza Dr Ste 200, **Mission Viejo,** CA 92691, *pg.* 1677, *pg.* 149
THE PLANNING SHOP, 555 Bryant St Ste 180, **Palo Alto,** CA 94301, *pg.* 1677, *pg.* 178
PORTERVILLE RECORDER, 115 E Oak Ave, **Porterville,** CA 93257, *pg.* 1677, *pg.* 185
PUBLISHERS GROUP WEST, 1700 4th St, **Berkeley,** CA 94710, *pg.* 1679, *pg.* 46
THE RECORD, 530 E Market St, **Stockton,** CA 95202-3009, *pg.* 1680, *pg.* 281
THE RECORD SEARCHLIGHT, 1101 Twin View Blvd, **Redding,** CA 96003-1531, *pg.* 1680, *pg.* 188
RESEARCH SOLUTIONS, INC., 5435 Balboa Blvd, Ste 202, **Encino,** CA 91316, *pg.* 1680, *pg.* 85
ROBB REPORT, 29160 Heathercliff Rd Ste 200, **Malibu,** CA 90265, *pg.* 1681, *pg.* 142
SAN DIEGO BUSINESS JOURNAL, 4909 Murphy Canyon Rd Ste 200, **San Diego,** CA 92123, *pg.* 1682, *pg.* 208
THE SAN DIEGO UNION-TRIBUNE, LLC, 350 Camino de la Reina, **San Diego,** CA 92108-3003, *pg.* 1682, *pg.* 208
SAN FRANCISCO CHRONICLE, 901 Mission St, **San Francisco,** CA 94103-2905, *pg.* 1683, *pg.* 226
SAN JOSE MERCURY NEWS, 750 Ridder Park Dr, **San Jose,** CA 95190, *pg.* 1683, *pg.* 250
SANTA CRUZ SENTINEL, 1800 Green Hills Rd Ste 210, **Scotts Valley,** CA 95066, *pg.* 1683, *pg.* 278
SF NEWSPAPER COMPANY, LLC, 225 Bush St 17th Fl, **San Francisco,** CA 94104, *pg.* 1686, *pg.* 227
SIR SPEEDY, INC., 26722 Plz Dr, **Mission Viejo,** CA 92691, *pg.* 1687, *pg.* 149
SNAPFISH, 330 2nd St, S Tower Ste 500, **San Francisco,** CA 94107, *pg.* 1687, *pg.* 228
THE SUN, 290 N D St Ste 102, **San Bernardino,** CA 92401, *pg.* 1690, *pg.* 198
TWELVE SIGNS, INC., 3369 S Robertson Blvd, **Los Angeles,** CA 90034-0069, *pg.* 1697, *pg.* 141
VENTURA COUNTY STAR, PO Box 6006, **Camarillo,** CA 93011, *pg.* 1699, *pg.* 57
ZUMA PRESS, INC., 408 N El Camino Real, **San Clemente,** CA 92672, *pg.* 1704, *pg.* 199

Colorado

COLORADO COMMUNITY NEWSPAPERS, 9137 S. Ridgeline Blvd, Ste 210, **Highlands Ranch,** CO 80129, *pg.* 1628, *pg.* 332
DAVID C. COOK, 4050 Lee Vance View, **Colorado Springs,** CO 80918-7102, *pg.* 1633, *pg.* 315
THE DENVER NEWSPAPER AGENCY, 101 W coosas st, **Denver,** CO 80204, *pg.* 1634, *pg.* 318
THE FORT MORGAN TIMES, 329 Main St, **Fort Morgan,** CO 80701-2108, *pg.* 1642, *pg.* 329
THE GAZETTE, 30 S Prospect St, **Colorado Springs,** CO 80903, *pg.* 1644, *pg.* 315
IHS INC., 15 Inverness Way E, **Englewood,** CO 80112, *pg.* 1652, *pg.* 326
LEANIN' TREE, INC., 6055 Longbow Dr, **Boulder,** CO 80301, *pg.* 1658, *pg.* 311
SNOWMASS VILLAGE SUN, 16 Kearns Rd Unit 211, **Snowmass Village,** CO 81615, *pg.* 1687, *pg.* 335
SPS STUDIOS, INC., 2905 Wilderness Pl, **Boulder,** CO 80301-5402, *pg.* 1688, *pg.* 311
WIESNER PUBLISHING, LLC, 7009 S Potomac St Ste 200, **Englewood,** CO 80112, *pg.* 1702, *pg.* 328

Connecticut

BAYARD INC., 1 Montauk Ave Ste 200, **New London,** CT 06320, *pg.* 1620, *pg.* 359
BELVOIR MEDIA GROUP, LLC, 535 Connecticut Ave, PO Box 5656, **Norwalk,** CT 06856-5656, *pg.* 1620, *pg.* 360
BUSINESS & LEGAL REPORTS INC., 141 Mill Rock Rd E, **Old Saybrook,** CT 06475-4217, *pg.* 1624, *pg.* 367
CENVEO INC., 1 Canterbury Green, **Stamford,** CT 06901, *pg.* 1626, *pg.* 372
THE GLOBE PEQUOT PRESS, INC., 246 Goose Ln, **Guilford,** CT 06437, *pg.* 1645, *pg.* 350
HOUR PUBLISHING COMPANY, 1 Selleck St, **Norwalk,** CT 06855, *pg.* 1651, *pg.* 362
LEWTAN INDUSTRIES CORP., 30 High St, **Hartford,** CT 06103, *pg.* 1658, *pg.* 352
MARKET DATA RETRIEVAL, 6 Armstrong Rd, **Shelton,** CT 06484, *pg.* 1661, *pg.* 370
THE NEWS-TIMES, 333 Main St, **Danbury,** CT 06810-5818, *pg.* 1670, *pg.* 344
THE RECORD-JOURNAL PUBLISHING COMPANY, 11 Crown St, **Meriden,** CT 06450-5713, *pg.* 1680, *pg.* 354
STAT RESOURCE GROUP, INC., 69 Kenosia Ave, **Danbury,** CT 06810, *pg.* 1689, *pg.* 345
STREAMING MEDIA, INC., 88 Danbury Rd Ste 1D, **Wilton,** CT 06897, *pg.* 1689, *pg.* 385
STRUCTURAL GRAPHICS, LLC, 38 Plains Rd, **Essex,** CT 06426, *pg.* 1689, *pg.* 346
SUMNER COMMUNICATIONS INC., 24 Stony Hill Rd, **Bethel,** CT 06801, *pg.* 1690, *pg.* 338
SURVEY SAMPLING INTERNATIONAL LLC, 6 Research Dr, **Shelton,** CT 06484, *pg.* 1690, *pg.* 371
TECHNOLOGY MARKETING CORP., 800 Connecticut Ave 1st Fl E, **Norwalk,** CT 06854, *pg.* 1691, *pg.* 364
VALASSIS, 1 Targeting Centre, **Windsor,** CT 06095, *pg.* 1698, *pg.* 386
YALE UNIVERSITY PRESS, 302 Temple St, **New Haven,** CT 06511-8909, *pg.* 1703, *pg.* 359

District of Columbia

First page reference indicates Business Class Edition
Second page reference indicates Geographic Edition

THE ATLANTIC MONTHLY GROUP, 600 New Hampshire Ave NW Ste 400, **Washington,** DC 20037, *pg.* 1618, *pg.* 396
CQ ROLL CALL, 77 K St NE Fl 8, **Washington,** DC 20002-4681, *pg.* 1631, *pg.* 397
THE KIPLINGER WASHINGTON EDITORS, INC., 1100 13th St Nw Ste 750, **Washington,** DC 20005-4364, *pg.* 1657, *pg.* 401
NATIONAL GEOGRAPHIC SOCIETY, 1145 17th St NW, **Washington,** DC 20036-4701, *pg.* 1667, *pg.* 402
NATIONAL JOURNAL GROUP, 600 New Hampshire Ave NW Fl 4, **Washington,** DC 20037-2403, *pg.* 1667, *pg.* 402
THE NEW REPUBLIC INC., 1620 L Street NW, Ste 300C, **Washington,** DC 20036, *pg.* 1667, *pg.* 403
SMITHSONIAN MAGAZINE, 600 Maryland Ave SW Ste 6001 MRC 513, **Washington,** DC 20024, *pg.* 1687, *pg.* 404
UNITED PRESS INTERNATIONAL, INC., 1133 19th St NW Ste 800, **Washington,** DC 20036, *pg.* 1698, *pg.* 405
THE WASHINGTON POST, 1150 15th St NW, **Washington,** DC 20071, *pg.* 1701, *pg.* 407
THE WASHINGTON TIMES, LLC, 3600 New York Ave NE, **Washington,** DC 20002-1947, *pg.* 1701, *pg.* 408
WHITE HOUSE HISTORICAL ASSOCIATION, 740 Jackson Pl NW, **Washington,** DC 20038, *pg.* 1702, *pg.* 408

Florida

AMERICAN MEDIA, INC., 1000 American Media Way, **Boca Raton,** FL 33464, *pg.* 1615, *pg.* 410
BONNIER CORPORATION, 460 N Orlando Ave Ste 200, **Winter Park,** FL 32789, *pg.* 1622, *pg.* 480
CHARISMA MEDIA, 600 Rinehart Rd, **Lake Mary,** FL 32746-4898, *pg.* 1627, *pg.* 436
CITRUS COUNTY CHRONICLE, 1624 N Meadowcrest Blvd, **Crystal River,** FL 34429-5760, *pg.* 1628, *pg.* 419
CREATIVE LOAFING, INC., 19011 N 13th St Ste W200, **Tampa,** FL 33605, *pg.* 1631, *pg.* 472
DATAMAX CORPORATION, 4501 Pkwy Commerce Blvd, **Orlando,** FL 32808-1013, *pg.* 1633, *pg.* 453
DUPONT PUBLISHING, INC., 3051 Tech Dr, **Saint Petersburg,** FL 33716, *pg.* 1637, *pg.* 462
DUPONT REGISTRY, 3051 Tech Dr, **Saint Petersburg,** FL 33716, *pg.* 1637, *pg.* 462
EDITORIAL TELEVISA INTERNATIONAL, 6355 NW 36th St, **Miami,** FL 33166, *pg.* 1638, *pg.* 442
FLORIDA FAMILY MAGAZINE, 1840 Glengary St, **Sarasota,** FL 34231, *pg.* 1641, *pg.* 466
THE FLORIDA TIMES-UNION, 1 Riverside Ave, **Jacksonville,** FL 32202, *pg.* 1641, *pg.* 433
FREDERICK FELL PUBLISHERS, INC., 1403 Shoreline Way, **Hollywood,** FL 33019, *pg.* 1643, *pg.* 431
FRIENDFINDER NETWORKS INC., 6800 Broken Sound Pkwy Ste 100, **Boca Raton,** FL 33487, *pg.* 1643, *pg.* 411
HOUGHTON MIFFLIN HARCOURT PUBLISHING COMPANY, 9400 S Park Cr Loop, **Orlando,** FL 32819, *pg.* 1651, *pg.* 454
ISLANDS MAGAZINE, 460 N Orlando Ave Ste 200, **Winter Park,** FL 32789, *pg.* 1654, *pg.* 480
JACKSONVILLE BUSINESS JOURNAL, 200 W Forsyth St, Ste 1350, **Jacksonville,** FL 32202, *pg.* 1654, *pg.* 433
THE JUPITER COURIER JOURNAL, 1939 S Federal Hwy, **Stuart,** FL 34994, *pg.* 1656, *pg.* 468
LAKE CITY REPORTER, 180 E Duval St, **Lake City,** FL 32055-4083, *pg.* 1657, *pg.* 436
THE MIAMI HERALD, 1 Herald Plz, **Miami,** FL 33132, *pg.* 1665, *pg.* 444
NAPLES DAILY NEWS, 1100 Immokalee Rd, **Naples,** FL 34110-6237, *pg.* 1666, *pg.* 451
THE NATIONAL ENQUIRER, 1000 American Media Way, **Boca Raton,** FL 33464-1000, *pg.* 1667, *pg.* 412
NEWS CHIEF, 455 6th St SW, **Winter Haven,** FL 33881, *pg.* 1669, *pg.* 480
NEWS-LEADER, 511 Ash St, **Fernandina Beach,** FL 32034-3930, *pg.* 1670, *pg.* 422
NEWS-SUN, INC., 2227 US Hwy 27 S, **Sebring,** FL 33870, *pg.* 1670, *pg.* 467
NORTHWEST FLORIDA DAILY NEWS, 2 Eglin Pkwy NE, **Fort Walton Beach,** FL 32548-4915, *pg.* 1672, *pg.* 428
OPEN SKY MEDIA, 1421 Pine Ridge Rd Ste 100, **Naples,** FL 34109, *pg.* 1673, *pg.* 451
PALATKA DAILY NEWS, 1825 Saint Johns Ave, **Palatka,** FL 32177-4442, *pg.* 1674, *pg.* 457
PALM BEACH MEDIA GROUP INC., PO Box 3344, **Palm Beach,** FL 33480, *pg.* 1674, *pg.* 457
QUANTURO PUBLISHING, INC., 4141 NE 2nd Ave Ste 205, **Miami,** FL 33137, *pg.* 1679, *pg.* 445
SOUTHEASTERN PRINTING COMPANY INC., 3601 SE Dixie Hwy, **Stuart,** FL 34997-5246, *pg.* 1687, *pg.* 468
THE ST. AUGUSTINE RECORD, 1 News Pl, **Saint Augustine,** FL 32086, *pg.* 1688, *pg.* 461
TAMPA BAY BUSINESS JOURNAL, 4350 W Cypress St Ste 800, **Tampa,** FL 33607-4176, *pg.* 1691, *pg.* 476
TAMPA BAY MAGAZINE, 2531 Landmark Dr Ste 101, **Clearwater,** FL 33761, *pg.* 1691, *pg.* 416
TAMPA BAY NEWSPAPERS, INC., 9911 Seminole Blvd, **Seminole,** FL 33772, *pg.* 1691, *pg.* 468
TAMPA BAY PUBLICATIONS, INC., 2531 Landmark Dr, **Clearwater,** FL 33761, *pg.* 1691, *pg.* 416
TAMPA BAY TIMES, 490 1st Ave S, **Saint Petersburg,** FL 33701-4204, *pg.* 1691, *pg.* 464
THE TAMPA TRIBUNE, 200 S Parker St, **Tampa,** FL 33606-2308, *pg.* 1691, *pg.* 476
THE TIMES PUBLISHING CO., 490 1st Ave S, **Saint Petersburg,** FL 33701-4204, *pg.* 1695, *pg.* 464
TREND MAGAZINES, INC., 490 1st Ave S 8th Fl, **Saint Petersburg,** FL 33701-4204, *pg.* 1696, *pg.* 465
VALPAK DIRECT MARKETING SYSTEMS, INC., 8605 Largo Lks Dr, **Largo,** FL 33773, *pg.* 1699, *pg.* 438
THE WALTON SUN, 5597 Hwy 98 W Ste 203, **Santa Rosa Beach,** FL 32459, *pg.* 1701, *pg.* 465

Georgia

ACTIVE PARENTING PUBLISHERS, 1220 Kennestone Cir Ste 130, **Marietta,** GA 30066-6022, *pg.* 1613, *pg.* 535
ATHENS BANNER-HERALD, 1 Press Pl, **Athens,** GA 30601, *pg.* 1618, *pg.* 486
THE ATLANTA JOURNAL-CONSTITUTION, 223 Perimeter Center Pkwy NE, **Atlanta,** GA 30346, *pg.* 1618, *pg.* 490
COMMUNITY NEWSPAPERS INC., 2365-A Prince Ave Ste A, **Athens,** GA 30606-6003, *pg.* 1628, *pg.* 486
FAIRWAY OUTDOOR ADVERTISING, 713 Broad St, **Augusta,** GA 30901, *pg.* 1640, *pg.* 525
FAIRWAY OUTDOOR ADVERTISING OF GEORGIA-ALABAMA, 3420 Jefferson Rd, **Athens,** GA 30607-1476, *pg.* 1640, *pg.* 486
MORRIS COMMUNICATIONS COMPANY LLC, 725 Broad St, **Augusta,** GA 30901-1336, *pg.* 1666, *pg.* 525
MORRIS MULTIMEDIA, INC., 27 Abercorn, **Savannah,** GA 31401, *pg.* 1666, *pg.* 540
MORRIS PUBLISHING GROUP, LLC, 725 Broad St, **Augusta,** GA 30901, *pg.* 1666, *pg.* 525
NORTHWEST GEORGIA NEWS, 305 E 6th Ave, **Rome,** GA 30162, *pg.* 1672, *pg.* 539
RENTPATH, INC., 3585 Engineering Dr Ste 100, **Norcross,** GA 30092, *pg.* 1680, *pg.* 538
ROTADYNE, 9126 Industrial Blvd NE, **Covington,** GA 30014-1473, *pg.* 1681, *pg.* 529
SAVANNAH MORNING NEWS, 1375 Chatham Pkwy, **Savannah,** GA 31405, *pg.* 1683, *pg.* 540

Hawaii

THE HONOLULU STAR-ADVERTISER, 500 Ala Moana Blvd #7-210, **Honolulu,** HI 96813, *pg.* 1650, *pg.* 544

Idaho

THE CAXTON PRINTERS LTD., 312 Main St, **Caldwell,** ID 83605-3235, *pg.* 1626, *pg.* 548
PACIFIC PRESS PUBLISHING ASSOCIATION, 1350 N Kings Rd, **Nampa,** ID 83687, *pg.* 1674, *pg.* 550
THE POST COMPANY, 333 Northgate Mile, **Idaho Falls,** ID 83401, *pg.* 1677, *pg.* 549

Illinois

AMERICAN LIBRARY ASSOCIATION, 50 E Huron St, **Chicago,** IL 60611-2729, *pg.* 1615, *pg.* 564
AMERICAN TECHNICAL PUBLISHERS, INC., 10100 Orland Pkwy Ste 200, **Orland Park,** IL 60467, *pg.* 1616, *pg.* 649
CCH, 4025 W Peterson Ave, **Chicago,** IL 60646, *pg.* 1626, *pg.* 569
CCH INC., 2700 Lk Cook Rd, **Riverwoods,** IL 60015-3867, *pg.* 1626, *pg.* 653
CHICAGO READER, INC., 350 N Orleans St, **Chicago,** IL 60654, *pg.* 1627, *pg.* 570
CHICAGO SUN TIMES, 350 N Orleans Ste 9 10, **Chicago,** IL 60654, *pg.* 1627, *pg.* 570
CHICAGO TRIBUNE COMPANY, 435 N Michigan Ave, **Chicago,** IL 60611-4066, *pg.* 1627, *pg.* 570
CHRISTIANITY TODAY INTERNATIONAL, 465 Gundersen Dr, **Carol Stream,** IL 60188-2415, *pg.* 1627, *pg.* 561
COUNTRY SAMPLER INC., 707 Kautz Rd, **Saint Charles,** IL 60174, *pg.* 1630, *pg.* 658
CRAIN'S CHICAGO BUSINESS, 150 N Michigan Ave, 16th Fl, **Chicago,** IL 60601, *pg.* 1631, *pg.* 572
DAILY REPUBLICAN REGISTER, 115 E 4th St, **Mount Carmel,** IL 62863-2110, *pg.* 1633, *pg.* 634
ENCYCLOPAEDIA BRITANNICA, INC., 331 N La Salle St, **Chicago,** IL 60654, *pg.* 1638, *pg.* 573
FOLLETT CORPORATION, 3 Westbrook Corporate Ctr, **Westchester,** IL 60154, *pg.* 1641, *pg.* 669
GANNETT HEALTHCARE GROUP, 1721 Moon Lake Blvd Ste 540, **Hoffman Estates,** IL 60169-2170, *pg.* 1644, *pg.* 617
THE GOODHEART-WILLCOX CO., INC., 18604 W Creek Dr, **Tinley Park,** IL 60477-6243, *pg.* 1645, *pg.* 663
HOUGHTON MIFFLIN HARCOURT, 909 Davis St, **Evanston,** IL 60201, *pg.* 1650, *pg.* 611
H.S. CROCKER CO., INC., 12100 Smith Dr, **Huntley,** IL 60142-9618, *pg.* 1651, *pg.* 619
HUMAN KINETICS PUBLISHERS INC., 1607 N Market St, **Champaign,** IL 61820, *pg.* 1651, *pg.* 562
INDEPENDENT PUBLISHERS GROUP, 814 N Franklin St, **Chicago,** IL 60610, *pg.* 1652, *pg.* 578
JACKSONVILLE JOURNAL-COURIER, 235 W State St, **Jacksonville,** IL 62650, *pg.* 1654, *pg.* 621
JOHNSON PUBLISHING COMPANY, INC., 820 S Michigan Ave, **Chicago,** IL 60605-2103, *pg.* 1655, *pg.* 579
JOURNAL STAR, INC., 1 News Plz, **Peoria,** IL 61643-0001, *pg.* 1656, *pg.* 651
LAW BULLETIN PUBLISHING COMPANY, 415 N State St, **Chicago,** IL 60610, *pg.* 1658, *pg.* 580
MANUFACTURERS' NEWS, INC., 1633 Central St, **Evanston,** IL 60201, *pg.* 1661, *pg.* 612
MILLER GROUP MEDIA, 426 2nd St, **La Salle,** IL 61301, *pg.* 1665, *pg.* 621
MOODY PUBLISHERS, 820 N La Salle Blvd, **Chicago,** IL 60610-3214, *pg.* 1665, *pg.* 583
MULTI-AD, INC., 1720 W Detweiller Dr, **Peoria,** IL 61615-1612, *pg.* 1666, *pg.* 652
NATIONAL ASSOCIATION OF REALTORS, 430 N Michigan Ave, **Chicago,** IL 60611-4011, *pg.* 1666, *pg.* 584
NEWS MEDIA CORPORATION, 211 Hwy 38 E, **Rochelle,** IL 61068, *pg.* 1670, *pg.* 654
OAG WORLDWIDE LIMITED, 3025 Highland Pkwy Ste 200, **Downers Grove,** IL 60515-5561, *pg.* 1672, *pg.* 609
O'MEARA-BROWN PUBLICATIONS, INC., 630 Davis St Ste 301, **Chicago,** IL 60201, *pg.* 1673, *pg.* 586
ONION, INC., 212 W Superior St Ste 200, **Chicago,** IL 60654, *pg.* 1673, *pg.* 586
PADDOCK PUBLICATIONS, INC., 155 E Algonquin Rd, **Arlington Heights,** IL 60005, *pg.* 1674, *pg.* 554
PUBLICATIONS INTERNATIONAL, LTD., 7373 N Cicero Ave, **Lincolnwood,** IL 60712-1613, *pg.* 1679, *pg.* 628
PUTMAN MEDIA, INC., 555 W Pierce Rd Ste 301, **Itasca,** IL 60143-2666, *pg.* 1679, *pg.* 621
RAND MCNALLY & COMPANY, 8255 N Central Park Ave, **Skokie,** IL 60076, *pg.* 1679, *pg.* 661
R.R. DONNELLEY & SONS COMPANY, 111 S Wacker Dr, **Chicago,** IL 60606-4301, *pg.* 1682, *pg.* 589
SCRANTON GILLETTE COMMUNICATIONS, 3030 W Saltcreel Ln Ste 201, **Arlington Heights,** IL 60005, *pg.* 1685, *pg.* 554
SGK, 1 N Dearborn, **Chicago,** IL 60602, *pg.* 1686, *pg.* 590
SRDS, INC., 5600 N River Rd Ste 900, **Rosemont,** IL 60018, *pg.* 1688, *pg.* 657
STAR COURIER, 105 E Central Blvd, **Kewanee,** IL 61443-2245, *pg.* 1689, *pg.* 621
THE STATE JOURNAL-REGISTER, 1 Copley Plz, **Springfield,** IL 62701-1927, *pg.* 1689, *pg.* 662
SUN-TIMES MEDIA GROUP, INC., 350 N Orleans St 10th Fl, **Chicago,** IL 60654, *pg.* 1690, *pg.* 591
THE TELEGRAPH, 111 E Broadway, **Alton,** IL 62002, *pg.* 1691, *pg.* 553
TRIBUNE MEDIA COMPANY, 435 N Michigan Ave, **Chicago,** IL 60611, *pg.* 1696, *pg.* 592
TYNDALE HOUSE PUBLISHERS, INC., 351 Exec Dr, **Carol Stream,** IL 60188, *pg.* 1697, *pg.* 561
UNIVERSITY OF CHICAGO PRESS, 1427 E 60th St, **Chicago,** IL 60637-2902, *pg.* 1698, *pg.* 594
VANCE PUBLISHING CORPORATION, 400 Knightsbridge

Pkwy, **Lincolnshire,** IL 60069, *pg.* 1699, *pg.* 627
WATT PUBLISHING COMPANY, 303 North Main Street Ste 500, **Rockford,** IL 61101, *pg.* 1701, *pg.* 655
WEBSITE MAGAZINE INCORPORATED, 999 E Touhy Ave, **Des Plaines,** IL 60018, *pg.* 1701, *pg.* 607

Indiana

ANNIE'S, 306 E Parr Rd, **Berne,** IN 46711-1138, *pg.* 1617, *pg.* 673
AUTHOR SOLUTIONS, INC., 1663 Liberty Dr Ste 200, **Bloomington,** IN 47403, *pg.* 1618, *pg.* 674
DYNAMIC RESOURCE GROUP, 306 E Parr Rd, **Berne,** IN 46711, *pg.* 1637, *pg.* 674
THE EVANSVILLE COURIER & PRESS, 300 E Walnut St, **Evansville,** IN 47713, *pg.* 1639, *pg.* 678
INDIANAPOLIS STAR, 130 S Meridian St, **Indianapolis,** IN 46225, *pg.* 1652, *pg.* 687
THE JOURNAL GAZETTE, 600 W Main St, **Fort Wayne,** IN 46802, *pg.* 1655, *pg.* 680
THE NEWS-SENTINEL, 600 W Main St, **Fort Wayne,** IN 46802, *pg.* 1670, *pg.* 681
OUR SUNDAY VISITOR, INC., 200 Noll Plz, **Huntington,** IN 46750-4310, *pg.* 1673, *pg.* 682
THE ROUGH NOTES COMPANY, INC., 11690 Technology Dr, **Carmel,** IN 46032-5600, *pg.* 1681, *pg.* 675
SATURDAY EVENING POST SOCIETY, 1100 Waterway Blvd, **Indianapolis,** IN 46202-2156, *pg.* 1683, *pg.* 690
WARNER PRESS, INC., 1201 E 5th St, **Anderson,** IN 46012-3472, *pg.* 1701, *pg.* 673
WARRICK PUBLISHING CO. INC., 204 W Locust St, **Boonville,** IN 47601-1594, *pg.* 1701, *pg.* 675

Iowa

BETTER HOMES & GARDENS BOOKS, 1716 Locust St, **Des Moines,** IA 50309-3023, *pg.* 1620, *pg.* 704
THE DEMOCRAT CO., 1226 Ave H, **Fort Madison,** IA 52627-4544, *pg.* 1634, *pg.* 708
GAZETTE COMMUNICATIONS, INC., 500 3rd Ave SE, **Cedar Rapids,** IA 52401-1608, *pg.* 1644, *pg.* 702
IOWA FARMER TODAY, 1065 Sierra Court NE Ste B, **Cedar Rapids,** IA 52402-6585, *pg.* 1653, *pg.* 702
LEE ENTERPRISES, INCORPORATED, 201 N Harrison St Ste 600, **Davenport,** IA 52801-1924, *pg.* 1658, *pg.* 704
MEREDITH CORPORATION, 1716 Locust St, **Des Moines,** IA 50309-3023, *pg.* 1663, *pg.* 705

Kansas

ALLEN PRESS INC., 810 E Tenth St, **Lawrence,** KS 66044-3018, *pg.* 1614, *pg.* 715
THE ARKANSAS CITY TRAVELER, 200 E 5th Ave, **Arkansas City,** KS 67005, *pg.* 1617, *pg.* 714
DODGE CITY DAILY GLOBE, 705 2nd Ave, **Dodge City,** KS 67801, *pg.* 1636, *pg.* 714
THE MORNING SUN, 701 N Locust St, **Pittsburg,** KS 66762-0570, *pg.* 1666, *pg.* 720
MOTHER EARTH NEWS, 1503 SW 42nd St, **Topeka,** KS 66609, *pg.* 1666, *pg.* 722
THE NEWTON KANSAN, 121 W 6th St, **Newton,** KS 67114-0268, *pg.* 1671, *pg.* 717
OGDEN PUBLICATIONS, INC., 1503 SW 42nd St, **Topeka,** KS 66609-1265, *pg.* 1672, *pg.* 722
PENTON MEDIA, INC., 9800 Metcalf Ave, **Overland Park,** KS 66212-2216, *pg.* 1676, *pg.* 719
THE TOPEKA CAPITAL-JOURNAL, 616 SE Jefferson St, **Topeka,** KS 66607-1137, *pg.* 1695, *pg.* 722
THE WICHITA EAGLE, 825 E Douglas Ave, **Wichita,** KS 67202, *pg.* 1702, *pg.* 724

Kentucky

CYNTHIANA PUBLISHING CO., 302 Webster Ave, **Cynthiana,** KY 41031-1660, *pg.* 1632, *pg.* 726
FASTLINE PUBLICATIONS INC., 4900 Fox Run Rd, **Buckner,** KY 40010, *pg.* 1641, *pg.* 726
THE NEWS-ENTERPRISE, 408 W Dixie Ave, **Elizabethtown,** KY 42701-2455, *pg.* 1669, *pg.* 727
PRESBYTERIAN PUBLISHING CORPORATION, 100 Witherspoon St, **Louisville,** KY 40202-1396, *pg.* 1678, *pg.* 737
SCHROEDER PUBLISHING COMPANY, 5801 Kentucky Dam Rd, **Paducah,** KY 42003-9323, *pg.* 1685, *pg.* 739

Louisiana

CAPITAL CITY PRESS, 7290 Bluebonnet Blvd, **Baton Rouge,** LA 70810-1611, *pg.* 1625, *pg.* 741
NOLA MEDIA GROUP, 365 Canal St., **New Orleans,** LA 70130, *pg.* 1671, *pg.* 747

Maine

KMWORLD, 22 Bayview St, **Camden,** ME 04843, *pg.* 1657, *pg.* 749
LEWISTON DAILY SUN, 104 Pk St, **Lewiston,** ME 04240, *pg.* 1658, *pg.* 751
STENHOUSE PUBLISHERS, Fl 2 480 Congress St PO Box 11020, **Portland,** ME 04101-3400, *pg.* 1689, *pg.* 752
VILLAGE SOUP, 301 Pk St, **Rockland,** ME 04841, *pg.* 1699, *pg.* 752

Maryland

AIIM INTERNATIONAL, 1100 Wayne Ave Ste 1100, **Silver Spring,** MD 20910-5616, *pg.* 1614, *pg.* 777
AMERICAN HERITAGE PUBLISHING, 416 Hungerford Dr Ste 216, **Rockville,** MD 20850-4127, *pg.* 1615, *pg.* 775
THE BALTIMORE SUN COMPANY, 501 N Calvert St, **Baltimore,** MD 21278, *pg.* 1619, *pg.* 755
CAMBRIDGE INFORMATION GROUP, INC., 7200 Wisconsin Ave Ste 601, **Bethesda,** MD 20814-4837, *pg.* 1625, *pg.* 761
CAPITAL GAZETTE COMMUNICATIONS INC., 2000 Capital Dr, **Annapolis,** MD 21401, *pg.* 1625, *pg.* 754
CARROLL COUNTY TIMES, 201 Railroad Ave, **Westminster,** MD 21157, *pg.* 1626, *pg.* 780
CCPRESS.NET INC., 7110 Golden Ring Rd Ste 114, **Baltimore,** MD 21221-3136, *pg.* 1626, *pg.* 756
DAEDALUS BOOKS, INC., 9645 Gerwig Ln, **Columbia,** MD 21046, *pg.* 1632, *pg.* 767
DIAMOND COMIC DISTRIBUTORS, INC., 10150 York Rd Ste 300, **Hunt Valley,** MD 21030, *pg.* 1635, *pg.* 772
HEALTHY DIRECTIONS, 7811 Montrose Rd Ste 2, **Potomac,** MD 20854-3359, *pg.* 1649, *pg.* 775
THE JOHNS HOPKINS UNIVERSITY PRESS, 2715 N Charles St, **Baltimore,** MD 21218, *pg.* 1655, *pg.* 757
MIDNIGHT MARQUEE PRESS, INC., 9721 Britinay Ln, **Baltimore,** MD 21234-1863, *pg.* 1665, *pg.* 758
PUBLISHERS CIRCULATION FULFILLMENT INC., 502 Washington Ave Ste 500, **Towson,** MD 21204-5017, *pg.* 1679, *pg.* 780
RECORDED BOOKS, LLC, 270 Skipjack Rd, **Prince Frederick,** MD 20678-3410, *pg.* 1680, *pg.* 775
ROSEBUD ENTERTAINMENT LLC, 1000 Lancaster St Ste 400, **Baltimore,** MD 21202, *pg.* 1681, *pg.* 759
SCARECROW PRESS, INC., 4501 Forbes Blvd Ste 200, **Lanham,** MD 20706-4310, *pg.* 1683, *pg.* 773
THE SHERIDAN GROUP, INC., 11311 McCormick Rd Ste 260, **Hunt Valley,** MD 21031-8676, *pg.* 1686, *pg.* 772
U.S. NAVAL INSTITUTE, 291 Wood Rd, **Annapolis,** MD 21402, *pg.* 1698, *pg.* 754
YOUNG MONEY, 10950 Gilroy Rd Ste D, **Hunt Valley,** MD 21031, *pg.* 1703, *pg.* 773

Massachusetts

AMERICAN METEOROLOGICAL SOCIETY, 45 Beacon St, **Boston,** MA 02108-3693, *pg.* 1616, *pg.* 789
AMERICA'S TEST KITCHEN, 17 Station St, **Brookline,** MA 02445, *pg.* 1616, *pg.* 803
AMESBURY NEWS, 72 Cherry Hill Dr, **Beverly,** MA 01915, *pg.* 1616, *pg.* 787
THE ARLINGTON ADVOCATE, 9 Meriam St, **Lexington,** MA 02420, *pg.* 1617, *pg.* 828
B&W PRESS, INC., 401 E Main St, **Georgetown,** MA 01833, *pg.* 1619, *pg.* 823
BEVERLY CITIZEN, 75 Sylvan St Ste C105, **Danvers,** MA 01923-2765, *pg.* 1620, *pg.* 816
BILLERICA MINUTEMAN, 150 Baker Ave Ext Ste 101, **Concord,** MA 01742, *pg.* 1621, *pg.* 815
THE BOSTON GLOBE, 135 William T Morrissey Blvd, **Boston,** MA 02125, *pg.* 1623, *pg.* 790
BOSTON HERALD INC., 1 Herald Sq, **Boston,** MA 02106, *pg.* 1623, *pg.* 791
CANSON INC., 21 Industrial Dr, **South Hadley,** MA 01075, *pg.* 1625, *pg.* 844
CAPE COD TIMES, 319 Main St, **Hyannis,** MA 02601, *pg.* 1625, *pg.* 826
CAPE CODDER, 5 Namskaket Rd, **Orleans,** MA 02653, *pg.* 1625, *pg.* 840
CHELMSFORD INDEPENDENT, 150 Baker Ave Ext Ste 105, **Concord,** MA 01742, *pg.* 1627, *pg.* 815
COMPUTERWORLD, INC., 492 Old Connecticut Path, **Framingham,** MA 01701, *pg.* 1629, *pg.* 820
CONCORD JOURNAL, 150 Baker Ave Ext Ste 101, **Concord,** MA 01742, *pg.* 1629, *pg.* 815
COUNTRY GAZETTE, 159 S Main St, **Milford,** MA 01757, *pg.* 1630, *pg.* 833
THE DAILY ITEM, 38 Exchange St, **Lynn,** MA 01901, *pg.* 1632, *pg.* 829
DOVER-SHERBORN PRESS, 254 2nd Ave, **Needham,** MA 02494, *pg.* 1636, *pg.* 835
EAGLE-TRIBUNE PUBLISHING COMPANY INC., 100 Turnpike St, **North Andover,** MA 01845-5033, *pg.* 1638, *pg.* 837
EBSCO INFORMATION SERVICES WALPOLE, 1600 Providence Hwy Ste 145, **Walpole,** MA 02081, *pg.* 1638, *pg.* 849
FORRESTER RESEARCH, INC., 60 Acorn Park Dr, **Cambridge,** MA 02140-2303, *pg.* 1642, *pg.* 807
HAMILTON-WENHAM CHRONICLE, 75 Sylvan St Ste C105, **Danvers,** MA 01923-2765, *pg.* 1647, *pg.* 816
HARVARD UNIVERSITY PRESS, 79 Garden St, **Cambridge,** MA 02138-1423, *pg.* 1648, *pg.* 808
HAVERHILL GAZETTE, 100 Turnpike St, **North Andover,** MA 01845, *pg.* 1648, *pg.* 837
HORIZON HOUSE PUBLICATIONS INC., 685 Canton St, **Norwood,** MA 02062, *pg.* 1650, *pg.* 839
HOUGHTON MIFFLIN HARCOURT PUBLISHING COMPANY, 222 Berkeley St, **Boston,** MA 02116, *pg.* 1651, *pg.* 796
THE INQUIRER & MIRROR, 1 Old S Rd, **Nantucket,** MA 02554-6029, *pg.* 1653, *pg.* 834
INTERNATIONAL DATA GROUP, 1 Exeter Plz 15th Fl, **Boston,** MA 02116, *pg.* 1653, *pg.* 796
LAURIN PUBLISHING CO., INC., 100 West St, PO Box 4949, **Pittsfield,** MA 01202-4949, *pg.* 1658, *pg.* 841
MASSACHUSETTS LAWYERS WEEKLY, INC., 10 Milk St Ste 1000, **Boston,** MA 02108, *pg.* 1662, *pg.* 798
MERRIAM-WEBSTER, INC., 47 Federal St, **Springfield,** MA 01105-1127, *pg.* 1664, *pg.* 846
METROWEST DAILY NEWS, 33 New York Ave, **Framingham,** MA 01701, *pg.* 1665, *pg.* 821
THE NEW ENGLAND JOURNAL OF MEDICINE, 10 Shattuck St, **Boston,** MA 02115, *pg.* 1667, *pg.* 799
PEARSON EDUCATION, 75 Arlington St Ste 300, **Boston,** MA 02116-3936, *pg.* 1675, *pg.* 800
PEOPLE2PEOPLE GROUP INC., 126 Brookline Ave, **Boston,** MA 02215, *pg.* 1676, *pg.* 800
RR DONNELLEY, 15 Wellman Ave, **North Chelmsford,** MA 01863-1334, *pg.* 1682, *pg.* 838
SHAMBHALA PUBLICATIONS INC., 300 Massachusetts Ave, **Boston,** MA 02115, *pg.* 1686, *pg.* 801
SMARTER TRAVEL MEDIA LLC, 500 Rutherford Ave, **Boston,** MA 02129, *pg.* 1687, *pg.* 801
TPR EDUCATION, LLC, 111Speen St, **Framingham,** MA 01701, *pg.* 1695, *pg.* 822
VISTAPRINT USA, INCORPORATED, 95 Hayden Ave, **Lexington,** MA 02421, *pg.* 1700, *pg.* 829
WORCESTER TELEGRAM & GAZETTE CORP., 20 Franklin St, **Worcester,** MA 01608-1904, *pg.* 1702, *pg.* 863

Michigan

ADVISOR-SOURCE NEWSPAPERS, 51180 Bedford St, **New Baltimore,** MI 48047, *pg.* 1614, *pg.* 902
ALLEGRA NETWORK LLC, 47585 Galleon Dr, **Plymouth,** MI 48170, *pg.* 1614, *pg.* 904
ARMADA TIMES, 51180 Bedford St, **New Baltimore,** MI 48047, *pg.* 1617, *pg.* 902
AUTOMOTIVE NEWS, 1155 Gratiot Ave, **Detroit,** MI 48207-2997, *pg.* 1618, *pg.* 879
BAKER PUBLISHING GROUP, 6030 Fulton St E, **Ada,** MI 49301-9106, *pg.* 1619, *pg.* 864
BNP MEDIA, 2401 W Big Beaver Rd Ste 700, **Troy,** MI 48084, *pg.* 1622, *pg.* 910
BROWN CITY BANNER, 4241 Main St, **Brown City,** MI 48416-0250, *pg.* 1624, *pg.* 874
CRAIN COMMUNICATIONS, INC., 1155 Gratiot Ave, **Detroit,**

First page reference indicates Business Class Edition
Second page reference indicates Geographic Edition

MI 48207-2997, *pg.* 1631, *pg.* 879
THE DAILY OAKLAND PRESS, 48 W Huron St, **Pontiac,** MI 48342, *pg.* 1632, *pg.* 905
DETROIT LEGAL NEWS PUBLISHING LLC, 2001 W Lafayette Blvd, **Detroit,** MI 48216, *pg.* 1635, *pg.* 880
THE DETROIT NEWS, INC., 615 W Lafayette Blvd, **Detroit,** MI 48226-3124, *pg.* 1635, *pg.* 880
ENTERTAINMENT PUBLICATIONS, INC., 1414 E Maple Rd, **Troy,** MI 48083, *pg.* 1639, *pg.* 910
FLASHES PUBLISHERS, 595 Jenner Dr, **Allegan,** MI 49010, *pg.* 1641, *pg.* 864
GALE CENGAGE LEARNING, 27500 Drake Rd, **Farmington Hills,** MI 48331-3535, *pg.* 1643, *pg.* 885
HILLSDALE DAILY NEWS, 263 Industrial Dr, **Hillsdale,** MI 49242, *pg.* 1650, *pg.* 891
HOMETOWN COMMUNICATIONS NETWORK, INC., 41304 Concept Dr, **Plymouth,** MI 48170, *pg.* 1650, *pg.* 904
IHS AUTOMOTIVE DRIVEN BY POLK, 26533 Evergreen Rd, Ste 900, **Southfield,** MI 48076, *pg.* 1652, *pg.* 907
JENKINS GROUP, INC., 1129 Woodmere Dr Ste B, **Traverse City,** MI 49686, *pg.* 1654, *pg.* 909
LAPEER COUNTY PRESS, 1521 Imlay City Rd, **Lapeer,** MI 48446-3175, *pg.* 1657, *pg.* 896
MACOMB COUNTY LEGAL NEWS, 148 S Main St Ste 100, **Mount Clemens,** MI 48043, *pg.* 1660, *pg.* 901
MICHIGAN.COM, 160 W Fort St, **Detroit,** MI 48226, *pg.* 1665, *pg.* 884
MLIVE MEDIA GROUP, 169 Monroe NW, Ste 100, **Grand Rapids,** MI 49503, *pg.* 1665, *pg.* 888
THE NEWS-HERALD, 1 Heritage Pl Ste 100, **Southgate,** MI 48195, *pg.* 1670, *pg.* 908
OPTIMIZERX CORPORATION, 400 Water St, Ste 200, **Rochester,** MI 48307, *pg.* 1673, *pg.* 905
TRAVERSE CITY RECORD-EAGLE, 120 W Front St, **Traverse City,** MI 49684, *pg.* 1696, *pg.* 910
TRUVEN HEALTH ANALYTICS, 777 E Eisenhower Pkwy, **Ann Arbor,** MI 48108, *pg.* 1696, *pg.* 867
VOICE COMMUNICATIONS CORP., 51180 Bedford St, **New Baltimore,** MI 48047-2533, *pg.* 1700, *pg.* 902
THE ZONDERVAN CORPORATION, 5300 Patterson SE, **Grand Rapids,** MI 49530-0001, *pg.* 1703, *pg.* 891

Minnesota

AUGSBURG FORTRESS, Ste 600 100 S 5th St PO Box 1209, **Minneapolis,** MN 55402-1242, *pg.* 1618, *pg.* 931
BRAINERD DAILY DISPATCH, 506 James St, **Brainerd,** MN 56401-0974, *pg.* 1623, *pg.* 919
BROWN & BIGELOW, INC., 345 Plato Blvd E, **Saint Paul,** MN 55107-1211, *pg.* 1624, *pg.* 959
CAPSTONE PRESS, INC., 1710 Roe Crest Dr, **North Mankato,** MN 56003, *pg.* 1625, *pg.* 951
DELUXE CORPORATION, 3680 Victoria St N, **Shoreview,** MN 55126, *pg.* 1634, *pg.* 964
THE DOLAN COMPANY, 222 S 9th St Ste 2300, **Minneapolis,** MN 55402, *pg.* 1636, *pg.* 932
JAPS-OLSON COMPANY, 7500 Excelsior Blvd, **Saint Louis Park,** MN 55426, *pg.* 1654, *pg.* 956
LLEWELLYN WORLDWIDE LIMITED, 2143 Wooddale Dr, **Woodbury,** MN 55125-2989, *pg.* 1660, *pg.* 967
MERRILL CORPORATION, 1 Merrill Cir, **Saint Paul,** MN 55108, *pg.* 1664, *pg.* 962
PEARSON ASSESSMENTS, 5601 Green Vly Dr, **Bloomington,** MN 55437-1187, *pg.* 1674, *pg.* 918
THE STAR TRIBUNE COMPANY, 425 Portland Ave, **Minneapolis,** MN 55488, *pg.* 1689, *pg.* 942
TAYLOR CORPORATION, 1725 Roe Crest Dr, **North Mankato,** MN 56003, *pg.* 1691, *pg.* 952
THAYER PUBLISHING, 150 Kingswood Rd, **Mankato,** MN 56001, *pg.* 1692, *pg.* 928

Mississippi

DAILY TIMES LEADER, 227 Ct St, **West Point,** MS 39773-2926, *pg.* 1633, *pg.* 972
DELTA FARM PRESS, 14920 US Hwy 61, **Clarksdale,** MS 38614, *pg.* 1634, *pg.* 968
JOURNAL INC., 1242 S Green St, **Tupelo,** MS 38804, *pg.* 1655, *pg.* 972

Missouri

ANDREWS MCMEEL UNIVERSAL, 1130 Walnut St, **Kansas City,** MO 64106, *pg.* 1616, *pg.* 980
CONCORD PRINTING, 301 Broadway St, **Cape Girardeau,** MO 63701, *pg.* 1629, *pg.* 974
CONCORDIA PUBLISHING HOUSE, 3558 S Jefferson Ave, **Saint Louis,** MO 63118-3968, *pg.* 1629, *pg.* 995
THE EXAMINER, 410 S Liberty St, **Independence,** MO 64050, *pg.* 1640, *pg.* 979
HALLMARK CARDS, INC., 2501 McGee Trafficway, **Kansas City,** MO 64108-2615, *pg.* 1646, *pg.* 983
HANNIBAL COURIER-POST, 200 N 3rd St, **Hannibal,** MO 63401-3504, *pg.* 1647, *pg.* 978
THE KANSAS CITY STAR COMPANY, 1729 Grand Blvd, **Kansas City,** MO 64108-1413, *pg.* 1656, *pg.* 985
NEWS TRIBUNE CO., 210 Monroe St, **Jefferson City,** MO 65101, *pg.* 1670, *pg.* 980
THE SEDALIA DEMOCRAT, 700 S Massachusetts Ave, **Sedalia,** MO 65301, *pg.* 1685, *pg.* 1005
ST. LOUIS POST-DISPATCH LLC, 900 N Tucker Blvd, **Saint Louis,** MO 63101, *pg.* 1688, *pg.* 1004

Nebraska

THE GRAND ISLAND DAILY INDEPENDENT, 422 W 1st St, **Grand Island,** NE 68801, *pg.* 1646, *pg.* 1010
INFOGROUP INC., 5711 S 86th Cir, **Omaha,** NE 68127-4146, *pg.* 1652, *pg.* 1016
THE YORK NEWS-TIMES, 327 Platte Ave, **York,** NE 68467, *pg.* 1703, *pg.* 1020

Nevada

LAS VEGAS SUN, INC., 2360 Corporate Cir 3rd Fl, **Henderson,** NV 89074, *pg.* 1657, *pg.* 1021
SWIFT NEWSPAPERS, INC., 500 Double Eagle Court, **Reno,** NV 89521, *pg.* 1690, *pg.* 1032

New Hampshire

DERRY PUBLISHING CO. INC., 46 W Broadway, **Derry,** NH 03038-2329, *pg.* 1635, *pg.* 1033
GEORGE J. FOSTER CO. INC., 150 Venture Dr, **Dover,** NH 03820, *pg.* 1644, *pg.* 1033
PRESSTEK LLC, 55 Executive Dr, **Hudson,** NH 03051, *pg.* 1678, *pg.* 1034
YANKEE PUBLISHING INC., 1121 Main St, **Dublin,** NH 03444, *pg.* 1703, *pg.* 1033

New Jersey

ADVANTAGE BUSINESS MEDIA, 100 Enterprise Dr Ste 600, **Rockaway,** NJ 07866-0912, *pg.* 1613, *pg.* 1116
A.M. BEST COMPANY, Ambest Rd, **Oldwick,** NJ 08858, *pg.* 1614, *pg.* 1101
AMERICAN BANKNOTE CORPORATION, 2200 Fletcher Ave, **Fort Lee,** NJ 07024, *pg.* 1615, *pg.* 1067
ANDERSON & VREELAND, INC., 8 Evans St, **Fairfield,** NJ 07004-2210, *pg.* 1616, *pg.* 1064
ASBURY PARK PRESS INC., 3601 Hwy 66, **Neptune,** NJ 07754, *pg.* 1617, *pg.* 1090
BAUER PUBLISHING USA, 270 Sylvan Ave, **Englewood Cliffs,** NJ 07632, *pg.* 1620, *pg.* 1059
BELL-MARK CORPORATION, 331 Changebridge Rd, **Pine Brook,** NJ 07058, *pg.* 1620, *pg.* 1108
BLANC INDUSTRIES SIGNAGE & DISPLAY GROUP, 88 King St, **Dover,** NJ 07801, *pg.* 1621, *pg.* 1053
BOOKAZINE COMPANY, INC., 75 Hook Rd, **Bayonne,** NJ 07002-5006, *pg.* 1622, *pg.* 1042
DAILY RECORD, 6th Century Dr, **Parsippany,** NJ 07054, *pg.* 1633, *pg.* 1103
THE DUN & BRADSTREET CORP., 103 JFK Pkwy, **Short Hills,** NJ 07078-2708, *pg.* 1637, *pg.* 1120
THE GALLUP ORGANIZATION-PRINCETON, 502 Carnegie Ctr Ste 300, **Princeton,** NJ 08540, *pg.* 1643, *pg.* 1111
GREATER MEDIA NEWSPAPERS, INC., 3499 US Hwy 9 Ste 1B, **Freehold,** NJ 07728-3281, *pg.* 1646, *pg.* 1071
IN TOUCH WEEKLY, 270 Sylvan Ave Ste 4, **Englewood Cliffs,** NJ 07632, *pg.* 1652, *pg.* 1060
INFORMATION TODAY INC., 143 Old Marlton Pike, **Medford,** NJ 08055-8750, *pg.* 1653, *pg.* 1084
ITC PRINTING & PROMOTIONS, 24 Beechwood Rd, **Summit,** NJ 07901, *pg.* 1654, *pg.* 1124
JERSEY JOURNAL NEWSPAPER, One Harmon Plz Ste 1010, **Secaucus,** NJ 07094, *pg.* 1654, *pg.* 1120
JOC GROUP INC., 2 Penn Plz E 12th Fl, **Newark,** NJ 07015, *pg.* 1654, *pg.* 1096
JOHN WILEY & SONS, INC., 111 River St, **Hoboken,** NJ 07030-5774, *pg.* 1655, *pg.* 1073
JOURNAL OF COMMERCE, INC., 2 Penn Plaza E, **Newark,** NJ 07105, *pg.* 1655, *pg.* 1097
LEXISNEXIS CORPORATE AFFILIATIONS, 121 Chanlon Rd, **New Providence,** NJ 07974, *pg.* 1658, *pg.* 1095
MARQUIS WHO'S WHO, LLC, 300 Connell Dr Ste 2000, **Berkeley Heights,** NJ 07922, *pg.* 1661, *pg.* 1044
MARTINDALE-HUBBELL, INC., 121 Chanlon Rd, **New Providence,** NJ 07974-1541, *pg.* 1662, *pg.* 1095
NEW JERSEY HILLS MEDIA GROUP, 17 19 Morristown Rd, **Bernardsville,** NJ 07924, *pg.* 1667, *pg.* 1044
NEW JERSEY MONTHLY, 55 Park Pl, **Morristown,** NJ 07963, *pg.* 1667, *pg.* 1089
NJBIZ, 220 Davidson Ave Ste 302, **Somerset,** NJ 08873, *pg.* 1671, *pg.* 1122
NORTH JERSEY MEDIA GROUP INC., 150 River St, **Hackensack,** NJ 07601-7110, *pg.* 1672, *pg.* 1072
PHANMEDIA L.L.C., 77 Franklin Ave, **Ocean Grove,** NJ 07756, *pg.* 1677, *pg.* 1100
PRINCETON UNIVERSITY PRESS, 41 William St, **Princeton,** NJ 08540-5237, *pg.* 1678, *pg.* 1112
PRUDENT PUBLISHING COMPANY, INC., 65 Challenger Rd Fl 1, **Ridgefield Park,** NJ 07660, *pg.* 1678, *pg.* 1115
R.R. BOWKER LLC, 630 Central Ave, **New Providence,** NJ 07974-1541, *pg.* 1682, *pg.* 1095
SYS-CON MEDIA, INC., 577 Chestnut Ridge Rd, **Woodcliff Lake,** NJ 07677, *pg.* 1690, *pg.* 1134
TRANSACTION PUBLISHERS, INC., 10 Corportate PL S Ste 102, **Piscataway,** NJ 08854, *pg.* 1695, *pg.* 1109
UNZ & COMPANY, INC., 333 Cedar Ave Bldg B Ste #2, **Middlesex,** NJ 08846, *pg.* 1698, *pg.* 1084

New Mexico

CLOVIS NEWS JOURNAL, 521 Pile St, **Clovis,** NM 88101, *pg.* 1628, *pg.* 1135

New York

AARP PUBLICATIONS, 780 3rd Ave, **New York,** NY 10017, *pg.* 1613, *pg.* 1185
ABRAMS, 115 West 18th St 6th Fl, **New York,** NY 10011, *pg.* 1613, *pg.* 1186
ADVANCE PUBLICATIONS, INC., 950 W Fingerboard Rd, **Staten Island,** NY 10305-1453, *pg.* 1613, *pg.* 1343
ADVERTISING AGE, 685 3rd Ave, **New York,** NY 10017-4024, *pg.* 1613, *pg.* 1187
ALFRED A. KNOPF, INC., 1745 Broadway, **New York,** NY 10019, *pg.* 1614, *pg.* 1189
AMERICAN BABY MAGAZINE, 375 Lexington Ave, **New York,** NY 10017-5529, *pg.* 1614, *pg.* 1190
AMERICAN LAWYER MEDIA, INC., 120 Broadway 5th Fl, **New York,** NY 10271, *pg.* 1615, *pg.* 1193
ARCHITECTURAL DIGEST, 1 World Trade Ctr, **New York,** NY 10007, *pg.* 1617, *pg.* 1196
ASIMOV'S SCIENCE FICTION MAGAZINE, 475 Park Ave S 11th Fl, **New York,** NY 10016, *pg.* 1618, *pg.* 1197
AUDUBON MAGAZINE, 225 Varick St 7 Fl, **New York,** NY 10014-9536, *pg.* 1618, *pg.* 1198
BANNER DIRECT, 222 W 83rd St Ste 7G, **New York,** NY 10024, *pg.* 1619, *pg.* 1200
BARNES & NOBLE, INC., 122 5th Ave 2nd Fl, **New York,** NY 10011-5605, *pg.* 1619, *pg.* 1201
BARRON'S, 1155 Avenue of the Americas 8th Fl, **New York,** NY 10036-2711, *pg.* 1620, *pg.* 1201
BARRON'S EDUCATIONAL SERIES, INC., 250 Wireless Blvd, **Hauppauge,** NY 11788, *pg.* 1620, *pg.* 1164
BIO, 235 E 45th St Ste 1104, **New York,** NY 10017-3303, *pg.* 1621, *pg.* 1202
BIZBASH MEDIA INC., 8 W 38th St, Ste 200, **New York,** NY 10018, *pg.* 1621, *pg.* 1203
BLOOMBERG BUSINESSWEEK, 731 Lexington Ave, **New York,** NY 10022-1331, *pg.* 1621, *pg.* 1204
BONNIER ACTIVE MEDIA, INC., 2 Park Ave, **New York,** NY 10016, *pg.* 1622, *pg.* 1205
BOYS' LIFE MAGAZINE, 1040 Ave of the Americas, Ste 16A, **New York,** NY 10018, *pg.* 1623, *pg.* 1206
BRANT PUBLICATIONS, INC., 110 Greene St 2nd Fl, **New York,** NY 10012, *pg.* 1623, *pg.* 1206
CABLE NEWS NETWORK LP, 1271 Ave Of The Americas, **New York,** NY 10020, *pg.* 1624, *pg.* 1208
CARL FISCHER, LLC, 48 Wall St, 28th Fl, **New York,** NY

10005, *pg.* 1625, *pg.* 1209
CASTLE CONNOLLY MEDICAL LTD., 42 W 24th St 2nd Fl, **New York,** NY 10010, *pg.* 1626, *pg.* 1210
CHRISTIAN HERALD ASSOCIATION, 132 Madison Ave, **New York,** NY 10016-7004, *pg.* 1627, *pg.* 1212
CITY GUIDE MAGAZINE, Empire State Bldg 350 5th Ave Ste 2420, **New York,** NY 10118, *pg.* 1628, *pg.* 1214
COLUMBIA UNIVERSITY PRESS, 61 W 62nd St, **New York,** NY 10023, *pg.* 1628, *pg.* 1216
COMMENTARY, 561 7th Ave Fl 16, **New York,** NY 10018-1816, *pg.* 1628, *pg.* 1216
COMPLEX MEDIA, INC., 40 W 23rd St, **New York,** NY 10010, *pg.* 1628, *pg.* 1217
CONDE NAST PUBLICATIONS, INC., 1 World Trade Ctr, **New York,** NY 10007, *pg.* 1629, *pg.* 1217
CONDE NAST TRAVELER, 4 Times Sq, **New York,** NY 10036-6518, *pg.* 1630, *pg.* 1218
CONSUMERS UNION OF THE UNITED STATES, INC., 101 Truman Ave, **Yonkers,** NY 10703-1044, *pg.* 1630, *pg.* 1356
CORNELL UNIVERSITY PRESS, 512 E State St, **Ithaca,** NY 14850-4412, *pg.* 1630, *pg.* 1169
COSMOPOLITAN, 300 W 57th St, **New York,** NY 10019-3212, *pg.* 1630, *pg.* 1218
CRAIN'S NEW YORK BUSINESS, 685 3rd Ave, **New York,** NY 10017-4036, *pg.* 1631, *pg.* 1220
CREDITRISKMONITOR.COM, INC., 704 Executive Blvd Ste A, **Valley Cottage,** NY 10989, *pg.* 1631, *pg.* 1348
CRM MEDIA, LLC, 237 W 35th St 14th Fl, **New York,** NY 10001-2509, *pg.* 1631, *pg.* 1220
DAILY NEWS, L.P., 4 New York Plaza, **New York,** NY 10004, *pg.* 1632, *pg.* 1221
DAILY RACING FORM, LLC, 315 Hudson St Fl 9, **New York,** NY 10013, *pg.* 1632, *pg.* 1221
THE DAILY STAR, 102 Chestnut St, **Oneonta,** NY 13820, *pg.* 1633, *pg.* 1319
DANCE MAGAZINE, 333 7th Ave 11th Fl, **New York,** NY 10001, *pg.* 1633, *pg.* 1221
DC COMICS, INC., 1700 Brdwy, **New York,** NY 10019-5905, *pg.* 1633, *pg.* 1221
DETAILS MAGAZINE, 1 World Trad Ctr, **New York,** NY 10007, *pg.* 1635, *pg.* 1223
DK PUBLISHING, 375 Hudson St, **New York,** NY 10014, *pg.* 1636, *pg.* 1224
DOVER PUBLICATIONS, INC., 31 E 2nd St, **Mineola,** NY 11501, *pg.* 1636, *pg.* 1182
DOW JONES & COMPANY, INC., 1211 Avenue of the Americas, **New York,** NY 10036, *pg.* 1637, *pg.* 1225
ENTERTAINMENT WEEKLY INC., 135 W 50th St 3 Fl, **New York,** NY 10020, *pg.* 1639, *pg.* 1228
ESSENCE MAGAZINE, 135 W 50th St 4th Fl, **New York,** NY 10020, *pg.* 1639, *pg.* 1229
FAIRCHILD FASHION GROUP, 1 World Trade Ctr, **New York,** NY 10007, *pg.* 1640, *pg.* 1230
THE FAMILY CIRCLE, INC., 375 Lexington Ave, **New York,** NY 10017, *pg.* 1640, *pg.* 1230
FARRAR, STRAUS & GIROUX, INC., 18 W 18th ST, **New York,** NY 10011, *pg.* 1640, *pg.* 1231
FITNESS RX, 690 Rt 25A, **Setauket,** NY 11733, *pg.* 1641, *pg.* 1342
FORBES, INC., 60 5th Ave, **New York,** NY 10011-8802, *pg.* 1641, *pg.* 1232
FORTUNE, 1271 Avenue Of The Americas, **New York,** NY 10020, *pg.* 1642, *pg.* 1232
GATEHOUSE MEDIA, INC., 350 Willowbrook Office Pk, **Fairport,** NY 14450, *pg.* 1644, *pg.* 1159
GEORGE BRAZILLER PUBLISHERS, INC., 277 Broadway Ste 708, **New York,** NY 10017, *pg.* 1644, *pg.* 1234
GLAMOUR, 4 Times Sq 16th Fl, **New York,** NY 10036, *pg.* 1645, *pg.* 1235
GOOD HOUSEKEEPING, 300 W 57th St, **New York,** NY 10019, *pg.* 1645, *pg.* 1236
GREY HOUSE PUBLISHING CORP., PO Box 56, **Amenia,** NY 12501, *pg.* 1646, *pg.* 1137
GROVE/ATLANTIC, INC., 154 W 14th St, 12th Fl, **New York,** NY 10011, *pg.* 1646, *pg.* 1236
HAIGHTS CROSS COMMUNICATIONS, INC., 136 Madison Ave 8th Fl, **New York,** NY 10016, *pg.* 1646, *pg.* 1237
HARLEQUIN MAGAZINES INC, 233 Brdwy Rm 1001 10th Fl, **New York,** NY 10279-0001, *pg.* 1647, *pg.* 1237
HARPERCOLLINS PUBLISHERS INC., 10 E 53rd St, **New York,** NY 10022-5244, *pg.* 1647, *pg.* 1237
HARPER'S MAGAZINE FOUNDATION, 666 Broadway 11th Fl, **New York,** NY 10012-2317, *pg.* 1648, *pg.* 1238
HARRIS CONNECT LLC, 1511 Rte 22 Ste C-25, **Brewster,** NY 10509, *pg.* 1648, *pg.* 1143
HARVARD BUSINESS REVIEW, Ste 1501 75 Rockefeller Plz, **New York,** NY 10019-6908, *pg.* 1648, *pg.* 1238
HBG BOOKS, INC., 237 Park Ave, **New York,** NY 10017, *pg.* 1648, *pg.* 1238
HEALTH MAGAZINE, 1271 Ave Of The Americas 20th Fl, **New York,** NY 10020-1300, *pg.* 1648, *pg.* 1238
THE HEARST CORPORATION, 300 W 57th St, **New York,** NY 10019, *pg.* 1649, *pg.* 1239
HEARST MAGAZINES, 300 W 57th St, **New York,** NY 10019, *pg.* 1649, *pg.* 1239
HOUSE BEAUTIFUL, 300 W 57th St 24th Fl, **New York,** NY 10019, *pg.* 1651, *pg.* 1241
HYPERION BOOKS, 77 W 66th St, **New York,** NY 10023, *pg.* 1651, *pg.* 1242
IN STYLE MAGAZINE, 1271 Ave of the Americas Ste 18-38B2, **New York,** NY 10020, *pg.* 1652, *pg.* 1243
INSTITUTIONAL INVESTOR, INC., 225 Park Ave S 8th Fl, **New York,** NY 10003-1605, *pg.* 1653, *pg.* 1244
JOBSON HEALTHCARE INFORMATION LLC, 100 Ave of the Americas 9th Fl, **New York,** NY 10013-1689, *pg.* 1654, *pg.* 1246
JOHNSON NEWSPAPER CORPORATION, 260 Washington St, **Watertown,** NY 13601-3301, *pg.* 1655, *pg.* 1349
KENSINGTON PUBLISHING CORP., 119 W Forty St 21st Fl, **New York,** NY 10018, *pg.* 1656, *pg.* 1248
THE KNOPF DOUBLEDAY GROUP, 1745 Broadway, **New York,** NY 10019, *pg.* 1657, *pg.* 1249
LADIES' HOME JOURNAL, 125 Park Ave, **New York,** NY 10017, *pg.* 1657, *pg.* 1250
LATINA MEDIA VENTURES, LLC, 625 Madison Ave 3rd Fl, **New York,** NY 10022, *pg.* 1657, *pg.* 1250
LAURA DAMIANO DESIGNS, 500 Pondside Dr, **White Plains,** NY 10607, *pg.* 1658, *pg.* 1354
LEBHAR-FRIEDMAN INC., 150 W 30th St, 19th Fl, **New York,** NY 10001, *pg.* 1658, *pg.* 1250
LITERARY CLASSICS OF THE UNITED STATES, INC., 14 E 60th St, **New York,** NY 10022-1006, *pg.* 1659, *pg.* 1251
LITTLE, BROWN & COMPANY, 237 Park Ave, **New York,** NY 10017, *pg.* 1660, *pg.* 1251
MACFADDEN COMMUNICATIONS GROUP, LLC, 333 7th Ave, **New York,** NY 10001, *pg.* 1660, *pg.* 1254
MANSUETO VENTURES LLC, 7 World Trade Ctr, **New York,** NY 10007-2195, *pg.* 1661, *pg.* 1256
MARTHA STEWART LIVING OMNIMEDIA, INC., 601 W 26th St, **New York,** NY 10001, *pg.* 1661, *pg.* 1256
MARVEL ENTERTAINMENT, LLC, 135 W 50th St 7th Fl, **New York,** NY 10020, *pg.* 1662, *pg.* 1257
MCBOOKS PRESS INC., I D Booth Bldg 520 N Meadow St, **Ithaca,** NY 14850, *pg.* 1662, *pg.* 1170
THE MCGRAW-HILL COMPANIES INC., 1221 Ave of the Americas, **New York,** NY 10020-1001, *pg.* 1663, *pg.* 1257
MEN'S JOURNAL, 1290 Ave of The Americas 2nd Fl, **New York,** NY 10104, *pg.* 1663, *pg.* 1258
METRO NEWSPAPER ADVERTISING SERVICES, INC., 8th W 38th St 4th Fl, **New York,** NY 10018, *pg.* 1664, *pg.* 1259
METRO-PUCK COMICS NETWORK, 8 W 38th St, **New York,** NY 10018, *pg.* 1665, *pg.* 1259
MOD-PAC CORP., 1801 Elmwood Ave, **Buffalo,** NY 14207-2496, *pg.* 1665, *pg.* 1150
MUSIC SALES CORPORATION, 257 Pk Ave S Fl 20, **New York,** NY 10010-7304, *pg.* 1666, *pg.* 1263
NATIONAL REVIEW, INC., 215 Lexington Ave, **New York,** NY 10016-6023, *pg.* 1667, *pg.* 1265
NEW YORK MAGAZINE, 75 Varick St, **New York,** NY 10013, *pg.* 1667, *pg.* 1269
THE NEW YORK OBSERVER, LLC, 321 W 44th St 6th Fl, **New York,** NY 10036, *pg.* 1668, *pg.* 1269
THE NEW YORK POST, 1211 Ave of the Americas, **New York,** NY 10036-8701, *pg.* 1668, *pg.* 1269
THE NEW YORK TIMES, 620 8th Ave, **New York,** NY 10018, *pg.* 1668, *pg.* 1270
THE NEW YORK TIMES COMPANY, 620 8th Ave, **New York,** NY 10018, *pg.* 1668, *pg.* 1270
THE NEW YORKER MAGAZINE, INC., 4 Times Sq, **New York,** NY 10036-6518, *pg.* 1669, *pg.* 1271
NEWS AMERICA INCORPORATED, 1211 Ave of the Americas, **New York,** NY 10036-8701, *pg.* 1669, *pg.* 1271
NEWS CORPORATION, 1211 Ave of the Americas, **New York,** NY 10036, *pg.* 1669, *pg.* 1271
NEWSDAY MEDIA GROUP, 235 Pinelawn Rd, **Melville,** NY 11747, *pg.* 1670, *pg.* 1181
NEWSWEEK DAILY BEAST CO., 395 Hudson St, **New York,** NY 10014, *pg.* 1670, *pg.* 1271
NIELSEN BUSINESS MEDIA, 770 Broadway, **New York,** NY 10003-9595, *pg.* 1671, *pg.* 1272
THE NIELSEN COMPANY B.V., 770 Broadway, **New York,** NY 10003, *pg.* 1671, *pg.* 1272
THE NPD GROUP, INC., 900 W Shore Rd, **Port Washington,** NY 11050-4624, *pg.* 1672, *pg.* 1323
OXFORD UNIVERSITY PRESS, INC., 198 Madison Ave, **New York,** NY 10016-4308, *pg.* 1673, *pg.* 1275
PARADE MAGAZINE, 711 3rd Ave, **New York,** NY 10017, *pg.* 1674, *pg.* 1275
PARADE PUBLICATIONS INC., 711 3rd Ave, **New York,** NY 10017-4014, *pg.* 1674, *pg.* 1276
PC MAGAZINE, 28 E 28th St, **New York,** NY 10016, *pg.* 1674, *pg.* 1276
PENGUIN RANDOM HOUSE, 1745 Broadway, **New York,** NY 10019, *pg.* 1675, *pg.* 1276
PENGUIN RANDOM HOUSE, 375 Hudson St, **New York,** NY 10014-3658, *pg.* 1675, *pg.* 1276
PENGUIN RANDOM HOUSE CHILDREN'S BOOKS, 1745 Broadway, **New York,** NY 10019, *pg.* 1676, *pg.* 1277
PENTON MEDIA, INC., 1166 Ave of the Americas 10th Fl, **New York,** NY 10036, *pg.* 1676, *pg.* 1277
PEOPLE MAGAZINE, Time Life Bldg Rockefeller Ctr, **New York,** NY 10020, *pg.* 1676, *pg.* 1278
THE PERSEUS BOOKS GROUP, 250 W 57th St, Fl 15, **New York,** NY 10107, *pg.* 1676, *pg.* 1278
PLAYBILL INCORPORATED, 525 7th Ave Ste 1801, **New York,** NY 10018-4918, *pg.* 1677, *pg.* 1282
POPULAR MECHANICS, 300 W 57th St, **New York,** NY 10019, *pg.* 1677, *pg.* 1282
PR NEWSWIRE ASSOCIATION LLC, 350 Hudson Ste 300, **New York,** NY 10014, *pg.* 1678, *pg.* 1283
PRESS-REPUBLICAN, 170 Margaret St, **Plattsburgh,** NY 12901, *pg.* 1678, *pg.* 1322
QUESTAR ASSESSMENT, INC., 4 Hardscrabble Hts, **Brewster,** NY 10509-0382, *pg.* 1679, *pg.* 1143
THE READER'S DIGEST ASSOCIATION, INC., Reader's Digest Rd, **Pleasantville,** NY 10570, *pg.* 1679, *pg.* 1322
REDBOOK, 224 W 57th St, **New York,** NY 10019-3212, *pg.* 1680, *pg.* 1285
ROLLING STONE MAGAZINE, 1290 Ave Of The Americas 2nd Fl, **New York,** NY 10104, *pg.* 1681, *pg.* 1287
SCHOLASTIC CORPORATION, 557 Broadway, **New York,** NY 10012-3902, *pg.* 1683, *pg.* 1288
SCHOLASTIC INC., 557 Broadway, **New York,** NY 10012-3919, *pg.* 1683, *pg.* 1288
SCIENTIFIC AMERICAN, INC., 415 Madison Ave, **New York,** NY 10017-1111, *pg.* 1685, *pg.* 1290
SELF MAGAZINE, 4 Times Sq 5th Fl, **New York,** NY 10036-6518, *pg.* 1686, *pg.* 1290
SEVENTEEN MAGAZINE, 300 W 57th St 17Fl, **New York,** NY 10019, *pg.* 1686, *pg.* 1290
SHAREDBOOK INC., 14 Wall St, **New York,** NY 10005, *pg.* 1686, *pg.* 1291
SIMMONS-BOARDMAN PUBLISHING CORP., 345 Hudson St 12 Fl, **New York,** NY 10014-4502, *pg.* 1686, *pg.* 1292
SIMON & SCHUSTER CHILDREN'S PUBLISHING, 1230 Ave of the Americas, **New York,** NY 10020, *pg.* 1686, *pg.* 1292
SIMON & SCHUSTER, INC., 1230 Avenue of the Americas, **New York,** NY 10020, *pg.* 1687, *pg.* 1292
SPAR GROUP, INC., 333 Westchester Ave, Ste 204, **West Harrison,** NY 10604, *pg.* 1687, *pg.* 1349
THE SPORTING NEWS, 475 Park Ave S 27th Fl, **New York,** NY 10016, *pg.* 1688, *pg.* 1295
SPORTS ILLUSTRATED, 1271 Ave Of The Americas, **New York,** NY 10020-1393, *pg.* 1688, *pg.* 1295
SPRINGER SCIENCE+BUSINESS MEDIA, LLC, 233 Spring St, **New York,** NY 10013, *pg.* 1688, *pg.* 1295
ST. MARTINS PRESS, INC., 175 5th Ave, **New York,** NY 10010-7703, *pg.* 1688, *pg.* 1295
STARLOG GROUP, INC., 475 Park Ave S, **New York,** NY 10016-6901, *pg.* 1689, *pg.* 1296
STERLING PUBLISHING CO., INC., 387 Park Ave S, **New York,** NY 10016-8810, *pg.* 1689, *pg.* 1296
SUPERMARKET NEWS, 1166 Ave of the Americas 10th Fl, **New York,** NY 10036, *pg.* 1690, *pg.* 1297
SYRACUSE UNIVERSITY PRESS, 621 Skytop Rd Ste 110, **Syracuse,** NY 13244-5290, *pg.* 1690, *pg.* 1344
TEN: THE ENTHUSIAST NETWORK, 261 Madison Ave 6th Fl, **New York,** NY 10016, *pg.* 1691, *pg.* 1298
TENNIS MAGAZINE, 48 W 21st St 6th Fl, **New York,** NY 10010, *pg.* 1692, *pg.* 1298
THEHUFFINGTONPOST.COM, INC., 770 Broadway 4th Fl, **New York,** NY 10013, *pg.* 1692, *pg.* 1298

THOMAS PUBLISHING COMPANY LLC, 5 Penn Plz, **New York,** NY 10001-1810, *pg.* 1692, *pg.* 1299
THOMAS REGISTER OF AMERICAN MANUFACTURERS, 5 Penn Plz, **New York,** NY 10001-1810, *pg.* 1692, *pg.* 1299
THOMSON REUTERS - CORPORATE HEADQUARTERS, 3 Times Sq, **New York,** NY 10036, *pg.* 1693, *pg.* 1299
THOMSON REUTERS TAX & ACCOUNTING, 195 Broadway, **New York,** NY 10007, *pg.* 1693, *pg.* 1299
TIME INC., Time Life Bldg Rockefeller Ctr 1271 Ave of The Americas, **New York,** NY 10020-1393, *pg.* 1693, *pg.* 1300
TIME OUT NEW YORK, 475 Tenth Ave 12th Fl, **New York,** NY 10018, *pg.* 1694, *pg.* 1301
TIMES HERALD-RECORD, 40 Mulberry St, **Middletown,** NY 10940, *pg.* 1694, *pg.* 1182
TOWN & COUNTRY, 300 W 57th St, **New York,** NY 10019-3794, *pg.* 1695, *pg.* 1303
TV GUIDE MAGAZINE GROUP, INC., 11 W 42nd St, **New York,** NY 10036, *pg.* 1697, *pg.* 1305
UBM ADVANSTAR, 641 Lexington Ave Fl 8, **New York,** NY 10022, *pg.* 1697, *pg.* 1306
UNITED BUSINESS MEDIA LLC, 600 Community Dr, **Manhasset,** NY 11030-3847, *pg.* 1697, *pg.* 1177
U.S. NEWS & WORLD REPORT, L.P., 4 New York Plz Fl 6, **New York,** NY 10004-2473, *pg.* 1698, *pg.* 1308
US WEEKLY LLC, 1290 Ave Of The Americas 2nd Fl, **New York,** NY 10104, *pg.* 1698, *pg.* 1308
VALUE LINE, INC., 220 E 42nd St, **New York,** NY 10017-5806, *pg.* 1699, *pg.* 1308
VANITY FAIR, 4 Times Sq Fl 22, **New York,** NY 10036, *pg.* 1699, *pg.* 1308
VILLAGE VOICE MEDIA HOLDINGS, LLC, 80 Maiden Ln Ste 2105, **New York,** NY 10038, *pg.* 1699, *pg.* 1311
VOGUE MAGAZINE, 4 Times Sq Fl 12, **New York,** NY 10036-6518, *pg.* 1700, *pg.* 1311
THE WALL STREET JOURNAL, 1211 Ave Americas, **New York,** NY 10036, *pg.* 1700, *pg.* 1312
WENNER MEDIA LLC, 1290 Ave of the Americas 2nd Fl, **New York,** NY 10104, *pg.* 1701, *pg.* 1314
WILLIAM H. SADLIER, INC., 9 Pine St, **New York,** NY 10005-1002, *pg.* 1702, *pg.* 1314
WILLIAM S. HEIN & CO., INC., 1285 Main St, **Buffalo,** NY 14209-1911, *pg.* 1702, *pg.* 1151
WORKING MOTHER MEDIA, INC., 60 E 42nd St 27th Fl, **New York,** NY 10165, *pg.* 1702, *pg.* 1315
WORKMAN PUBLISHING COMPANY, 225 Barick St, **New York,** NY 10014, *pg.* 1702, *pg.* 1315
WORTH, 1271 Ave of the Americas 17th Fl, **New York,** NY 10020, *pg.* 1702, *pg.* 1315
W.W. NORTON & COMPANY, INC., 500 5th Ave, **New York,** NY 10110-0002, *pg.* 1702, *pg.* 1316
YELLOW BOOK USA, INC., 398 RXR Plz, **Uniondale,** NY 11556, *pg.* 1703, *pg.* 1347
ZAGAT, 76 9th Ave, 4th Fl, **New York,** NY 10011, *pg.* 1703, *pg.* 1316
ZIFF DAVIS, LLC, 28 E 28th St 11th Fl, **New York,** NY 10016-7930, *pg.* 1703, *pg.* 1316

North Carolina

THE ALDERMAN COMPANY, 325 Model Farm Rd, **High Point,** NC 27263-1825, *pg.* 1614, *pg.* 1379
BAKER & TAYLOR, INC., 2550 W Tyvola Rd Ste 300, **Charlotte,** NC 28217, *pg.* 1619, *pg.* 1362
THE CHARLOTTE OBSERVER PUBLISHING CO., 600 S Tryon St, **Charlotte,** NC 28202-1880, *pg.* 1627, *pg.* 1364
DEX ONE CORPORATION, 1001 Winstead Dr, **Cary,** NC 27513, *pg.* 1635, *pg.* 1360
FAIRWAY OUTDOOR ADVERTISING OF THE PIEDMONT TRIAD, 1920 W Lee St, **Greensboro,** NC 27403, *pg.* 1640, *pg.* 1374
FAIRWAY OUTDOOR ADVERTISING OF THE TRIANGLE EAST, 508 Capital Blvd, **Raleigh,** NC 27605, *pg.* 1640, *pg.* 1387
FAYETTEVILLE PUBLISHING CO., 458 Whitfield St, **Fayetteville,** NC 28306, *pg.* 1641, *pg.* 1372
THE GASTON GAZETTE, 1893 Remount Rd, **Gastonia,** NC 28054, *pg.* 1644, *pg.* 1373
HAVELOCK NEWS, 230 Stonebridge Sq, **Havelock,** NC 28532, *pg.* 1648, *pg.* 1377
THE JACKSONVILLE DAILY NEWS CO., 724 Bell Fork Rd, **Jacksonville,** NC 28540-6311, *pg.* 1654, *pg.* 1380
KINSTON FREE PRESS, 2103 N Queen St, **Kinston,** NC 28501-1622, *pg.* 1656, *pg.* 1380
MCFARLAND & COMPANY, INC., 960 Hwy 88 W, **Jefferson,** NC 28640, *pg.* 1662, *pg.* 1380
NEWS & RECORD, 200 E Market St, **Greensboro,** NC 27420-0848, *pg.* 1669, *pg.* 1375
SUN JOURNAL, 3200 Wellon Blvd, **New Bern,** NC 28562-5234, *pg.* 1690, *pg.* 1386
THE TIMES-NEWS, 707 S Main St, **Burlington,** NC 27215, *pg.* 1694, *pg.* 1359
XERIUM TECHNOLOGIES, INC., 8537 Six Forks Rd, **Raleigh,** NC 27615, *pg.* 1703, *pg.* 1389

North Dakota

FORUM COMMUNICATIONS COMPANY, 101 5th St N, **Fargo,** ND 58102-4826, *pg.* 1642, *pg.* 1397

Ohio

AMERICAN GREETINGS CORPORATION, 1 American Rd, **Cleveland,** OH 44144-2398, *pg.* 1615, *pg.* 1428
AMOS PRESS, INC., 911 Vandemark Rd, **Sidney,** OH 45365, *pg.* 1616, *pg.* 1472
BABCOX MEDIA, 3550 Embassy Pkwy, **Akron,** OH 44333, *pg.* 1619, *pg.* 1400
THE BLADE CO., 541 N Superior St, **Toledo,** OH 43660-1000, *pg.* 1621, *pg.* 1476
BLOCK COMMUNICATIONS, INC., 405 Madison Ave, Ste 2100, **Toledo,** OH 43604, *pg.* 1621, *pg.* 1476
THE CANTON REPOSITORY, 500 Market Ave S, **Canton,** OH 44702, *pg.* 1625, *pg.* 1407
CINCINNATI BUSINESS COURIER, 101 W 7th St, **Cincinnati,** OH 45202-2411, *pg.* 1627, *pg.* 1411
THE CINCINNATI ENQUIRER, INC., 312 Elm St, **Cincinnati,** OH 45202-2739, *pg.* 1628, *pg.* 1411
THE DISPATCH PRINTING COMPANY, 34 S 3rd St, **Columbus,** OH 43215-4201, *pg.* 1636, *pg.* 1439
THE E.W. SCRIPPS COMPANY, 312 Walnut St, **Cincinnati,** OH 45202-4024, *pg.* 1639, *pg.* 1412
GARDNER PUBLICATIONS, INC., 6915 Vly Ave, **Cincinnati,** OH 45244-3029, *pg.* 1644, *pg.* 1413
GREAT LAKES PUBLISHING COMPANY, 1422 Euclid Ave Ste 730, **Cleveland,** OH 44115, *pg.* 1646, *pg.* 1431
HAINES & COMPANY, INC., 8050 Freedom Ave NW, **North Canton,** OH 44720-6912, *pg.* 1646, *pg.* 1468
HIGHLIGHTS FOR CHILDREN, INC., 1800 Watermark Dr, **Columbus,** OH 43215-1060, *pg.* 1650, *pg.* 1440
KAESER & BLAIR INCORPORATED, 4236 Grissom Dr, **Batavia,** OH 45103, *pg.* 1656, *pg.* 1405
LEXISNEXIS GROUP, 9443 Springboro Pike, **Dayton,** OH 45342, *pg.* 1658, *pg.* 1446
LEXISNEXIS LITIGATION SOLUTIONS, 9443 Springboro Pike, **Dayton,** OH 45342, *pg.* 1659, *pg.* 1446
THE LIMA NEWS, 3515 Elida Rd, **Lima,** OH 45807, *pg.* 1659, *pg.* 1457
THE NEWARK ADVOCATE, 22 N 1st St, **Newark,** OH 43055-5608, *pg.* 1669, *pg.* 1467
PLAIN DEALER PUBLISHING CO., 1801 Superior Ave Plain Dealer Plz, **Cleveland,** OH 44114, *pg.* 1677, *pg.* 1434
SANDUSKY NEWSPAPERS INC., 314 W Market St, **Sandusky,** OH 44870, *pg.* 1683, *pg.* 1472
STANDARD PUBLISHING GROUP LLC, 8805 Governor's Dr Ste 400, **Cincinnati,** OH 45249, *pg.* 1689, *pg.* 1426

Oklahoma

THE DAILY ARDMOREITE, 117 W Broadway, **Ardmore,** OK 73401, *pg.* 1632, *pg.* 1484
EDUCATIONAL DEVELOPMENT CORPORATION, 10302 E 55th Pl, **Tulsa,** OK 74146-6515, *pg.* 1638, *pg.* 1490
PENNWELL PUBLISHING COMPANY INC., 1421 S Sheridan Rd, **Tulsa,** OK 74112-6619, *pg.* 1676, *pg.* 1490
SHAWNEE NEWS-STAR, 215 N Bell, **Shawnee,** OK 74801, *pg.* 1686, *pg.* 1488

Oregon

ASHLAND DAILY TIDINGS, 111 N. Fir St., **Medford,** OR 97501, *pg.* 1617, *pg.* 1499
DARK HORSE COMICS, INC., 10956 SE Main St, **Milwaukie,** OR 97222-7644, *pg.* 1633, *pg.* 1500
EAST OREGONIAN PUBLISHING CO., 211 SE Byers Ave, **Pendleton,** OR 97801, *pg.* 1638, *pg.* 1500
HOT OFF THE PRESS, INC., 1250 NW 3rd Ave, **Canby,** OR 97013, *pg.* 1650, *pg.* 1497
INSPIRATION SOFTWARE, INC., 6443 Sw Beaverton Hillsdale Hwy, Ste 370, **Portland,** OR 97221, *pg.* 1653, *pg.* 1503
OREGONIAN PUBLISHING CO., 1320 SW Broadway, **Portland,** OR 97201-3411, *pg.* 1673, *pg.* 1504
PAMPLIN MEDIA GROUP, 6605 SE Lake Rd, **Portland,** OR 97222, *pg.* 1674, *pg.* 1504
POWELL'S BOOKS INC., 7 NW 9th Ave, **Portland,** OR 97209, *pg.* 1677, *pg.* 1505
WESTERN COMMUNICATIONS INC., 1777 SW Chandler Ave, **Bend,** OR 97702, *pg.* 1701, *pg.* 1496

Pennsylvania

BOYDS MILLS PRESS, INC., 815 Church St, **Honesdale,** PA 18431, *pg.* 1623, *pg.* 1539
CALKINS MEDIA INC., 8400 Rt 13, **Levittown,** PA 19057, *pg.* 1625, *pg.* 1548
CLIPPER MAGAZINE INC., 3708 Hempland Rd, **Mountville,** PA 17554, *pg.* 1628, *pg.* 1555
CSS INDUSTRIES, INC., 1845 Walnut St Ste 800, **Philadelphia,** PA 19103-4755, *pg.* 1631, *pg.* 1562
THE DAILY ITEM, 200 Market St, **Sunbury,** PA 17801, *pg.* 1632, *pg.* 1588
DERRICK PUBLISHING CO., 1510 W 1st St, **Oil City,** PA 16301, *pg.* 1635, *pg.* 1558
ELSEVIER HEALTH SCIENCES, 1600 John F Kennedy Blvd Ste 1800, **Philadelphia,** PA 19103-2899, *pg.* 1638, *pg.* 1564
F.A. DAVIS PUBLISHING COMPANY, 1915 Arch St, **Philadelphia,** PA 19103, *pg.* 1640, *pg.* 1564
FARM JOURNAL MEDIA, 110 One Penn Sq W 30 S 15 St Ste 900, **Philadelphia,** PA 19102, *pg.* 1640, *pg.* 1564
JAMESON PUBLISHING INC., Knowledge Park 5340 Fryling Rd Ste 300, **Erie,** PA 16510, *pg.* 1654, *pg.* 1530
LANCASTER NEWSPAPERS INC., 8 W Can Ste, **Lancaster,** PA 17608-1328, *pg.* 1657, *pg.* 1546
LIPPINCOTT WILLIAMS & WILKINS, 323 Norristown Rd Ste 200, **Ambler,** PA 19002, *pg.* 1659, *pg.* 1514
LIPPINCOTT WILLIAMS & WILKINS, INC., 530 Walnut St, **Philadelphia,** PA 19106-3619, *pg.* 1659, *pg.* 1567
LRP PUBLICATIONS, 747 Dresher Rd, Ste 500, **Horsham,** PA 19044, *pg.* 1660, *pg.* 1540
MATTHEWS INTERNATIONAL CORPORATION, 2 N Shore Ctr, **Pittsburgh,** PA 15212-5851, *pg.* 1662, *pg.* 1578
MERION MATTERS, 2900 Horizon Dr, **King of Prussia,** PA 19406-0956, *pg.* 1664, *pg.* 1544
THE MORNING CALL, INC., 101 N 6th St, **Allentown,** PA 18105, *pg.* 1665, *pg.* 1513
NORTH AMERICAN PUBLISHING COMPANY, 1500 Spring Gdn St Ste 1200, **Philadelphia,** PA 19130, *pg.* 1671, *pg.* 1567
OBSERVER PUBLISHING COMPANY, 122 S Main St, **Washington,** PA 15301, *pg.* 1672, *pg.* 1591
PHILADELPHIA DAILY NEWS, 400 N Broad St, **Philadelphia,** PA 19101-4099, *pg.* 1677, *pg.* 1569
THE PHILADELPHIA INQUIRER, 400 N Broad St, **Philadelphia,** PA 19130, *pg.* 1677, *pg.* 1569
RODALE, INC., 400 S 10th St, **Emmaus,** PA 18098-0099, *pg.* 1681, *pg.* 1530
RUNNING PRESS, 2300 Chestnut St, **Philadelphia,** PA 19103, *pg.* 1682, *pg.* 1570
STAGESTEP INC., Ste 4 4701 Bath St, **Philadelphia,** PA 19137-2235, *pg.* 1688, *pg.* 1570
THEODORE PRESSER CO., 588 N Gulph Rd, **King of Prussia,** PA 19406, *pg.* 1692, *pg.* 1544
TIMES PUBLISHING CO. INC., 205 W 12th St, **Erie,** PA 16534, *pg.* 1695, *pg.* 1530

Rhode Island

THE PROVIDENCE JOURNAL, 75 Fountain St, **Providence,** RI 02902, *pg.* 1678, *pg.* 1607
YACHTING MAGAZINE, 55 Hammerlund Way, **Middletown,** RI 02842, *pg.* 1703, *pg.* 1602

South Carolina

FAIRWAY OUTDOOR ADVERTISING OF THE GSA, 814 Duncan Reidville Rd, **Duncan,** SC 29334-1900, *pg.* 1640, *pg.* 1615
GARLINGHOUSE COMPANY, 2121 Boundary St Ste 208 Burnside Bldg, **Beaufort,** SC 29902, *pg.* 1644, *pg.* 1612
MERGENT, INC., 580 Kingsley Park Dr, **Fort Mill,** SC 29715-

6403, *pg.* 1664, *pg.* 1616
OCONEE PUBLISHING INC., 210 W N 1st St, **Seneca,** SC 29678, *pg.* 1672, *pg.* 1621

South Dakota

YANKTON DAILY PRESS & DAKOTAN, 319 Walnut St, **Yankton,** SD 57078-0056, *pg.* 1703, *pg.* 1626

Tennessee

ATHLON SPORTS, INC., 2451 Atrium Way Bldg 2 Ste 320, **Nashville,** TN 37214-5102, *pg.* 1618, *pg.* 1648
C.R. GIBSON, LLC, 402 BNA Dr Bldg 100 Ste 600, **Nashville,** TN 37217, *pg.* 1631, *pg.* 1650
HEALTHSTREAM, INC., 209 10th Ave S Ste 450, **Nashville,** TN 37203, *pg.* 1649, *pg.* 1651
KNOXVILLE NEWS-SENTINEL COMPANY, 2332 News Sentinel Dr, **Knoxville,** TN 37921-5761, *pg.* 1657, *pg.* 1637
THE OAK RIDGER, LLC, 785 Oak Ridge Tpke, **Oak Ridge,** TN 37830-7076, *pg.* 1672, *pg.* 1655
THOMAS NELSON INC., 501 Nelson Pl, **Nashville,** TN 37214, *pg.* 1692, *pg.* 1654
THOMAS NELSON PUBLISHERS, PO Box 141000, **Nashville,** TN 37214-1000, *pg.* 1692, *pg.* 1654
UNIGUEST, 1035 Acorn Dr, **Nashville,** TN 37210, *pg.* 1697, *pg.* 1655
THE UPPER ROOM, 1908 Grand Ave, **Nashville,** TN 37212-2129, *pg.* 1698, *pg.* 1655

Texas

ABILENE REPORTER NEWS, 101 Cypress St, **Abilene,** TX 79601-5816, *pg.* 1613, *pg.* 1657
A.H. BELO CORPORATION, 400 S Record St, **Dallas,** TX 75202-4806, *pg.* 1614, *pg.* 1673
AMARILLO GLOBE-NEWS, PO Box 2091, **Amarillo,** TX 79166, *pg.* 1614, *pg.* 1658
ANTARCTIC PRESS, 7272 Wurzbach Rd Ste 204, **San Antonio,** TX 78240, *pg.* 1617, *pg.* 1739
THE BROWNSVILLE HERALD, 1135 E Van Buren St, **Brownsville,** TX 78520, *pg.* 1624, *pg.* 1668
COMPASSLEARNING, INC., 203 Colorado St, **Austin,** TX 78701, *pg.* 1628, *pg.* 1661
CORPUS CHRISTI CALLER-TIMES, 820 N Lower Broadway St, **Corpus Christi,** TX 78401, *pg.* 1630, *pg.* 1671
THE DALLAS MORNING NEWS CO., 508 Young St, **Dallas,** TX 75202-4808, *pg.* 1633, *pg.* 1679
DENTON PUBLISHING COMPANY, 314 E Hickory St, **Denton,** TX 76201-4272, *pg.* 1634, *pg.* 1691
DEX MEDIA INC, 2200 W Airfield Dr, PO Box 619810, **Dallas,** TX 75261, *pg.* 1635, *pg.* 1680
DRG TEXAS LP, 111 Corporate Dr, **Big Sandy,** TX 75755, *pg.* 1637, *pg.* 1668
FORT WORTH STAR-TELEGRAM, 808 Throckmorton St, **Fort Worth,** TX 76102, *pg.* 1642, *pg.* 1694
FRANK MAYBORN ENTERPRISES, 10 S 3rd St, **Temple,** TX 76501, *pg.* 1642, *pg.* 1746
GULF PUBLISHING COMPANY, 2 Green Way Plz Ste 1020, **Houston,** TX 77046, *pg.* 1646, *pg.* 1707
HARLAND CLARKE HOLDINGS CORP., 10931 Laureate Dr, **San Antonio,** TX 78249, *pg.* 1647, *pg.* 1741
HOUSTON CHRONICLE, 801 Texas Ave, **Houston,** TX 77002-2904, *pg.* 1651, *pg.* 1707
THE LUBBOCK AVALANCHE-JOURNAL, 710 Ave J, **Lubbock,** TX 79401, *pg.* 1660, *pg.* 1726
THE MONITOR, 1400 E Nolana, **McAllen,** TX 78501, *pg.* 1665, *pg.* 1726
ODESSA AMERICAN, 222 E Fourth St, **Odessa,** TX 79760, *pg.* 1672, *pg.* 1728
PEARSON ASSESSMENT & INFORMATION, 19500 Bulverde Rd, **San Antonio,** TX 78259, *pg.* 1674, *pg.* 1742
PUBLICATIONS & COMMUNICATIONS, INC., 13552 Hwy 183 N Ste A, **Austin,** TX 78750, *pg.* 1678, *pg.* 1665
SAN ANGELO STANDARD, INC., 34 W Harris Ave, **San Angelo,** TX 76903-5838, *pg.* 1682, *pg.* 1739
SAN ANTONIO EXPRESS NEWS, Ave E At 3rd St, **San Antonio,** TX 78205, *pg.* 1682, *pg.* 1742
TEXAS MONTHLY, 816 Congress Ave, Ste 1700, **Austin,** TX 78701, *pg.* 1692, *pg.* 1666
TIMES RECORD NEWS, 1301 Lamar St, **Wichita Falls,** TX 76301-7032, *pg.* 1695, *pg.* 1749
TRAVELHOST, INC., 10701 N Stemmons Fwy, **Dallas,** TX 75220-2419, *pg.* 1696, *pg.* 1689
VALLEY MORNING STAR, 1310 S Commerce, **Harlingen,** TX 78550, *pg.* 1699, *pg.* 1699
VICTORIA ADVOCATE PUBLISHING COMPANY, 311 E Constitution St, **Victoria,** TX 77901, *pg.* 1699, *pg.* 1748

Utah

FRANKLIN COVEY CO., 2200 W Parkway Blvd, **Salt Lake City,** UT 84119-2099, *pg.* 1642, *pg.* 1758
OGDEN PUBLISHING CORPORATION, 332 S Standard Way, **Ogden,** UT 84404-1306, *pg.* 1672, *pg.* 1753

Vermont

THE BENNINGTON BANNER, 425 Main St, **Bennington,** VT 05201, *pg.* 1620, *pg.* 1764
INNER TRADITIONS INTERNATIONAL, 1 Park St, **Rochester,** VT 05767, *pg.* 1653, *pg.* 1767

Virginia

BLOOMBERG BNA, 1801 S Bell St, **Arlington,** VA 22202, *pg.* 1621, *pg.* 1772
DIRECT HOLDINGS AMERICAS INC., 8280 Willow Oaks Corporate Dr Ste 800, **Fairfax,** VA 22031-4511, *pg.* 1636, *pg.* 1780
DOMINION ENTERPRISES, 150 Granby St, **Norfolk,** VA 23510, *pg.* 1636, *pg.* 1796
THE FREE LANCE-STAR PUBLISHING CO., 616 Amelia St, **Fredericksburg,** VA 22401, *pg.* 1643, *pg.* 1782
THE FREELANCE-STAR RADIO GROUPS, 616 Amelia St, **Fredericksburg,** VA 22401-3887, *pg.* 1643, *pg.* 1782
GANNETT CO., INC., 7950 Jones Branch Dr, **McLean,** VA 22107-0910, *pg.* 1643, *pg.* 1790
GRAHAM HOLDINGS COMPANY, 1300 N 17th St, 17th Fl, **Arlington,** VA 22209, *pg.* 1645, *pg.* 1773
INSIDE BUSINESS INC., 150 W Brambleton Ave, **Norfolk,** VA 23510, *pg.* 1653, *pg.* 1797
PERSONAL SELLING POWER INC., 1140 Intl Pkwy, **Fredericksburg,** VA 22406-1126, *pg.* 1677, *pg.* 1782
PILOT MEDIA, 150 W Varmvaltom Ave, **Norfolk,** VA 23510, *pg.* 1677, *pg.* 1797
PUBLIC UTILITIES REPORTS, INC., 8229 Boone Blvd Ste 400, **Vienna,** VA 22182-2623, *pg.* 1678, *pg.* 1809
THE ROANOKE TIMES, 201 W Campbell Ave, **Roanoke,** VA 24011, *pg.* 1680, *pg.* 1806
STYLE WEEKLY INC., 24 E 3rd St, **Richmond,** VA 23224, *pg.* 1690, *pg.* 1804
TRANSPORT TOPICS PUBLISHING GROUP, 2200 Mill Rd, **Alexandria,** VA 22314-4654, *pg.* 1696, *pg.* 1772

Washington

BARKER CREEK PUBLISHING INC., 5889 State Hwy 303, **Bremerton,** WA 98383, *pg.* 1619, *pg.* 1818
THE DAILY HERALD CO., 1213 California St, **Everett,** WA 98201, *pg.* 1632, *pg.* 1819
GETTY IMAGES, INC., 605 5th Ave S, Ste 400, **Seattle,** WA 98104, *pg.* 1645, *pg.* 1836
KITSAP SUN, 545 5th St, **Bremerton,** WA 98337-1413, *pg.* 1657, *pg.* 1819
THE NEWS TRIBUNE, 1950 S State St, **Tacoma,** WA 98405, *pg.* 1670, *pg.* 1845
SEATTLE POST-INTELLIGENCER, 2901 3rd Ave Ste 120, **Seattle,** WA 98121, *pg.* 1685, *pg.* 1839
SEATTLE TIMES COMPANY, 1000 Denny Way, **Seattle,** WA 98109, *pg.* 1685, *pg.* 1840
SOUND PUBLISHING, INC., 19351 8th Ave NE Ste 106, **Poulsbo,** WA 98370, *pg.* 1687, *pg.* 1823
THE SPOKESMAN-REVIEW, 999 W Riverside Ave, **Spokane,** WA 99201-1006, *pg.* 1687, *pg.* 1844

West Virginia

CHAMPION INDUSTRIES, INC., 2450 1st Ave, **Huntington,** WV 25728, *pg.* 1626, *pg.* 1849
OGDEN NEWSPAPERS, INC., 1500 Main St, **Wheeling,** WV 26003, *pg.* 1672, *pg.* 1851

Wisconsin

ANCIENT AMERICAN, PO Box 370, **Colfax,** WI 54730, *pg.* 1616, *pg.* 1856
BLISS COMMUNICATIONS INC., 1 S Parker Dr, **Janesville,** WI 53545-3928, *pg.* 1621, *pg.* 1861
EAU CLAIRE PRESS COMPANY, 701 S Farwell St, **Eau Claire,** WI 54701, *pg.* 1638, *pg.* 1857
J.J. KELLER & ASSOCIATES, INC., 3003 W Breezewood Ln, **Neenah,** WI 59456, *pg.* 1654, *pg.* 1883
JOURNAL MEDIA GROUP, INC., 333 W State St, PO Box 661, **Milwaukee,** WI 53201-0661, *pg.* 1655, *pg.* 1876
JOURNAL SENTINEL, INC., 333 W State St, **Milwaukee,** WI 53203-1305, *pg.* 1655, *pg.* 1876
KALMBACH PUBLISHING CO., 21027 Crossroads Cir, **Waukesha,** WI 53186, *pg.* 1656, *pg.* 1898
KRAUSE PUBLICATIONS, INC., 700 E State St, **Iola,** WI 54990-0001, *pg.* 1657, *pg.* 1861
MADISON NEWSPAPERS, INC., 1901 Fish Hatchery Rd, **Madison,** WI 53713-1248, *pg.* 1661, *pg.* 1866
SERIGRAPH, INC., 3801 E Decorah Rd, **West Bend,** WI 53095-9597, *pg.* 1686, *pg.* 1899
TRADE PRESS MEDIA GROUP, 2100 W Florist Ave, **Milwaukee,** WI 53209, *pg.* 1695, *pg.* 1881
TUFCO TECHNOLOGIES, INC., PO Box 23500, **Green Bay,** WI 54305-3500, *pg.* 1697, *pg.* 1860

First page reference indicates Business Class Edition
Second page reference indicates Geographic Edition

Recreational Vehicles

California

CATALINA YACHTS, INC., 21200 Victory Blvd, **Woodland Hills,** CA 91367-2522, *pg.* 1706, *pg.* 307
THE COAST DISTRIBUTION SYSTEM, INC., 350 Woodview Ave, **Morgan Hill,** CA 95037, *pg.* 1706, *pg.* 152
ELECTRA BICYCLE COMPANY, 3275 Corporate Vw, **Vista,** CA 92081, *pg.* 1706, *pg.* 303
FELT RACING LLC, 12 Chrysler, **Irvine,** CA 92618, *pg.* 1707, *pg.* 110
GIANT BICYCLE INC., 3587 Old Conejo Rd, **Newbury Park,** CA 91320, *pg.* 1707, *pg.* 164
HOBIE CAT COMPANY, 4925 Oceanside Blvd, **Oceanside,** CA 92056-3044, *pg.* 1708, *pg.* 173
KAWASAKI MOTORS CORP., U.S.A., 9950 Jeronimo Rd, **Irvine,** CA 92618-2014, *pg.* 1708, *pg.* 111
MARIN BIKES, 265 Bel Marin Keys Blvd, **Novato,** CA 94949, *pg.* 1708, *pg.* 168
REXHALL INDUSTRIES, INC., 45640 23rd St W, **Lancaster,** CA 93536, *pg.* 1710, *pg.* 121
SANTA CRUZ BICYCLES, 2841 Mission St, **Santa Cruz,** CA 95060, *pg.* 1710, *pg.* 271
SPECIALIZED BICYCLE COMPONENTS, INC., 15130 Concord Cir, **Morgan Hill,** CA 95037, *pg.* 1711, *pg.* 152
UTILITY TRAILER MANUFACTURING COMPANY, 17295 E Railroad St, **City of Industry,** CA 91748, *pg.* 1712, *pg.* 68
WEST MARINE, INC., 500 Westridge Dr, **Watsonville,** CA 95076-4171, *pg.* 1712, *pg.* 305
YAMAHA MOTOR CORPORATION USA, 6555 Katella Ave, **Cypress,** CA 90630, *pg.* 1713, *pg.* 76

Colorado

MOOTS CYCLES, 2545 Copper Ridge Dr, **Steamboat Springs,** CO 80487, *pg.* 1709, *pg.* 335

Florida

ACCURATE MOTORCARS, 915 NE 3rd Ave Ste 5, **Fort Lauderdale,** FL 33304, *pg.* 1705, *pg.* 422
BOSTON WHALER, INC., 100 Whaler Way, **Edgewater,** FL 32141, *pg.* 1705, *pg.* 422
CHRIS-CRAFT CORPORATION, 8161 15th St E, **Sarasota,** FL 34243, *pg.* 1706, *pg.* 465
CORRECT CRAFT, INC., 14700 Aerospace Pkwy, **Orlando,** FL 32832, *pg.* 1706, *pg.* 452
GILMAN YACHTS OF FORT LAUDERDALE, INC., 1510 SE 17th St Ste 300, **Fort Lauderdale,** FL 33316-1737, *pg.* 1707, *pg.* 425
HUCKINS YACHT CORPORATION, 3482 Lake Shore Blvd, **Jacksonville,** FL 32210-5391, *pg.* 1708, *pg.* 433
MARINEMAX, INC., 18167 US Hwy 19 N Ste 300, **Clearwater,** FL 33764-6572, *pg.* 1709, *pg.* 416
MARLOW-HUNTER LLC, 14700 441 NW U.S. Hwy, **Alachua,** FL 32615, *pg.* 1709, *pg.* 409

Georgia

BLUE BIRD CORPORATION, 402 Blue Bird Blvd, **Fort Valley,** GA 31030, *pg.* 1705, *pg.* 532
E-Z-GO TEXTRON, 1451 Marvin Griffin Rd, **Augusta,** GA 30906-3852, *pg.* 1706, *pg.* 525
GREAT DANE TRAILERS, 602 E Lathrop Ave, **Savannah,** GA 31415-1062, *pg.* 1707, *pg.* 539
HUDDLE HOUSE, INC., 5901 Peachtree-Dunwoody Ste B450, **Atlanta,** GA 30328, *pg.* 1708, *pg.* 511

Indiana

DUTCHMEN MANUFACTURING, INC., 2164 Carangana Ct, **Goshen,** IN 46526, *pg.* 1706, *pg.* 681
JAYCO INC., 903 S Main St, **Middlebury,** IN 46540-9706, *pg.* 1708, *pg.* 695
SKYLINE CORPORATION, 2520 By-Pass Rd, **Elkhart,** IN 46515, *pg.* 1711, *pg.* 677

Iowa

FEATHERLITE, INC., Hwy 63 & Hwy 9 PO Box 320, **Cresco,** IA 52136, *pg.* 1707, *pg.* 704
WINNEBAGO INDUSTRIES, INC., 605 W Crystal Lake Rd, **Forest City,** IA 50436, *pg.* 1712, *pg.* 707

Maine

SABRE CORPORATION, 12 Hawthorne Rd, **Raymond,** ME 04071, *pg.* 1710, *pg.* 752

Michigan

ATTWOOD CORPORATION, 1016 N Monroe St, **Lowell,** MI 49331, *pg.* 1705, *pg.* 897
HARBORMASTER MARINE, INC., 37654 Amrhein Rd, **Livonia,** MI 48150-1821, *pg.* 1707, *pg.* 896
MICHIGAN WHEEL CORPORATION, 1501 Buchanan Ave SW, **Grand Rapids,** MI 49507-1697, *pg.* 1709, *pg.* 888
S2 YACHTS, INC., 725 E 40th St, **Holland,** MI 49423, *pg.* 1710, *pg.* 892

Minnesota

ALUMACRAFT BOAT COMPANY, 315 W St Julien St, **Saint Peter,** MN 56082, *pg.* 1705, *pg.* 964
ARCTIC CAT INC., 505 Hwy 169 N Ste 1000, **Plymouth,** MN 55441, *pg.* 1705, *pg.* 953
POLARIS INDUSTRIES INC., 2100 Hwy 55, **Medina,** MN 55340-9770, *pg.* 1709, *pg.* 928
QUALITY BICYCLE PRODUCTS, 6400 W 105th St, **Bloomington,** MN 55438, *pg.* 1710, *pg.* 918

Mississippi

TRINITY YACHTS, LLC, 13085 Seaway Rd, **Gulfport,** MS 39503-4607, *pg.* 1712, *pg.* 968

New Jersey

G. JOANNOU CYCLE CO. INC., 151 Ludlow Ave, **Northvale,** NJ 07647-2305, *pg.* 1707, *pg.* 1098
VIKING YACHT COMPANY, Rte 9, **New Gretna,** NJ 08224, *pg.* 1712, *pg.* 1094

New York

SEA EAGLE DIVISION OF HARRISON HOGE INDUSTRIES, INC., 19 N Columbia St Ste 1, **Port Jefferson Station,** NY 11777-2165, *pg.* 1710, *pg.* 1322
TAYLOR MADE GROUP, 66 Kingsboro Ave, **Gloversville,** NY 12078, *pg.* 1711, *pg.* 1162

North Carolina

GRADY-WHITE BOATS, INC., PO Box 1527, **Greenville,** NC 27835-1527, *pg.* 1707, *pg.* 1377
HATTERAS YACHTS, 110 N Glenburnie Rd, **New Bern,** NC 28560, *pg.* 1708, *pg.* 1386
JACOBSEN TEXTRON, 11108 Quality Drive, **Charlotte,** NC 28273, *pg.* 1708, *pg.* 1367

Ohio

THOR INDUSTRIES, INC., 419 W Pike St, **Jackson Center,** OH 45334, *pg.* 1711, *pg.* 1456

Oregon

GUARANTY RV CENTERS, 20 Hwy 99 S, **Junction City,** OR 97448-9714, *pg.* 1707, *pg.* 1499

Pennsylvania

CANNONDALE BICYCLE CORPORATION, 172 Friendship Rd, **Bedford,** PA 15522-6600, *pg.* 1705, *pg.* 1515

Rhode Island

BRISTOL MARINE, 99 Poppasquash Rd, **Bristol,** RI 02809, *pg.* 1705, *pg.* 1600

South Carolina

CONFLUENCE WATERSPORTS CO. INC., 575 Mauldin Rd # 200, **Greenville,** SC 29607-4208, *pg.* 1706, *pg.* 1617

South Dakota

LEHMAN TRIKES INC., 125 Industrial Dr, **Spearfish,** SD 57783, *pg.* 1708, *pg.* 1626

Tennessee

MASTERCRAFT BOAT COMPANY LLC, 100 Cherokee Cove Dr, **Vonore,** TN 37885-2129, *pg.* 1709, *pg.* 1656
SEA RAY BOATS, INC., 2600 Sea Ray Blvd Bldg 1, **Knoxville,** TN 37914, *pg.* 1710, *pg.* 1638
SKIER'S CHOICE INC., 1717 Henry G Lane St, **Maryville,** TN 37801, *pg.* 1711, *pg.* 1640

Virginia

VOLVO PENTA OF THE AMERICAS, INC., 1300 Volvo Penta Dr, **Chesapeake,** VA 23320, *pg.* 1712, *pg.* 1778

Washington

DIAMONDBACK BICYCLES, 6004 S 190th St Ste 101, **Kent,** WA 98032, *pg.* 1706, *pg.* 1821

Wisconsin

MERCURY MARINE, 6250 W Pioneer Rd, **Fond Du Lac,** WI 54935-1939, *pg.* 1709, *pg.* 1857
PACIFIC CYCLE INC., 4902 Hammersley Rd, **Madison,** WI 53711-2614, *pg.* 1709, *pg.* 1867
PALMER JOHNSON INCORPORATED, 128 Kentucky St, **Sturgeon Bay,** WI 54235-0109, *pg.* 1709, *pg.* 1895

Restaurants

Arizona

KONA GRILL INC., 7150 E Camelback Rd Ste 220, **Scottsdale,** AZ 85251, *pg.* 1734, *pg.* 23
PETER PIPER, INC., 950 W Behrend Dr Ste 102, **Phoenix,** AZ 85027, *pg.* 1744, *pg.* 18
STAR BUFFET, INC., 1312 N Scottsdale Rd, **Scottsdale,** AZ 85257-3410, *pg.* 1751, *pg.* 24
TILTED KILT FRANCHISE OPERATING LLC, 664 W Warner Rd, **Tempe,** AZ 85284, *pg.* 1754, *pg.* 27
VENUE OF SCOTTSDALE, 7117 E 3rd Ave, **Scottsdale,** AZ 85251-3821, *pg.* 1754, *pg.* 25

California

BJ'S RESTAURANTS, INC., 7755 Center Ave Ste 300, **Huntington Beach,** CA 92647, *pg.* 1716, *pg.* 104
BLAZE PIZZA LLC, 35 N Lake Ave Ste 710, **Pasadena,** CA 91101, *pg.* 1716, *pg.* 179
CALIFORNIA PIZZA KITCHEN INC., 6053 W Century Blvd 11th Fl, **Los Angeles,** CA 90045-6438, *pg.* 1720, *pg.* 127
CARL KARCHER ENTERPRISES, INC., 6303 Carpinteria Ave Ste A, **Carpinteria,** CA 93013-2901, *pg.* 1720, *pg.* 63
CKE RESTAURANTS INC., 6307 Carpinteria Ave Ste A, **Carpinteria,** CA 93013, *pg.* 1723, *pg.* 63
DEL TACO RESTAURANTS, INC., 25521 Commercentre Dr Ste 200, **Lake Forest,** CA 92630, *pg.* 1725, *pg.* 121
DINEEQUITY, INC., 450 N Brand Blvd, **Glendale,** CA 91203-2306, *pg.* 1725, *pg.* 95
EL POLLO LOCO, INC., 3535 Harbor Blvd Ste 100, **Costa Mesa,** CA 92626, *pg.* 1728, *pg.* 70
FRESH ENTERPRISES, LLC, 320 Commerce Ste 100, **Irvine,** CA 92602-1363, *pg.* 1729, *pg.* 110
GALARDI GROUP, INC., 7700 Irvine Center Dr, Ste 550, **Irvine,** CA 92618, *pg.* 1729, *pg.* 110
GARDEN FRESH RESTAURANT CORP., 15822 Bernardo Ctr Dr Ste A, **San Diego,** CA 92127-2320, *pg.* 1729, *pg.* 203
GRILL CONCEPTS, INC., 6300 Canoga Ave Ste 600, **Woodland Hills,** CA 91367, *pg.* 1730, *pg.* 308
GUCKENHEIMER ENTERPRISES, INC., 3 Lagoon Dr Ste 325, **Redwood City,** CA 94065-5167, *pg.* 1730, *pg.* 190
THE HABIT RESTAURANTS, INC., 17320 Red Hill Ave Ste 140, **Irvine,** CA 92614, *pg.* 1730, *pg.* 111
IL FORNAIO (AMERICA) CORPORATION, 770 Tamalpais Dr Ste 400, **Corte Madera,** CA 94925, *pg.* 1731, *pg.* 70
IN-N-OUT BURGERS, INC., 4199 Campus Dr 9th Fl, **Irvine,** CA 92612, *pg.* 1732, *pg.* 111
INTERNATIONAL HOUSE OF PANCAKES, INC., 450 N Brand Blvd, **Glendale,** CA 91203, *pg.* 1732, *pg.* 96
JACK IN THE BOX INC., 9330 Balboa Ave, **San Diego,** CA 92123-1516, *pg.* 1732, *pg.* 204
JACMAR COMPANIES, INC., 360 N Baldwin Park Blvd, **City of Industry,** CA 91746, *pg.* 1733, *pg.* 67
JERRY'S FAMOUS DELI, INC., 12711 Ventura Blvd Ste 400, **Studio City,** CA 91604, *pg.* 1733, *pg.* 281
THE JOHNNY ROCKETS GROUP, INC., 20 Enterprise, Ste 300, **Aliso Viejo,** CA 92656, *pg.* 1733, *pg.* 41
LAMP POST FRANCHISE CORPORATION, 3002 Dow Ave, Ste 414, **Tustin,** CA 92780, *pg.* 1735, *pg.* 297
LAWRY'S RESTAURANTS, INC., 234 E Colorado Blvd Ste 500, **Pasadena,** CA 91101, *pg.* 1735, *pg.* 180
MIMI'S CAFE, LLC, 17852 E 17th St South Bldg Ste 108, **Tustin,** CA 92780, *pg.* 1741, *pg.* 297
PANDA RESTAURANT GROUP, INC., 1683 Walnut Grove Ave, **Rosemead,** CA 91770, *pg.* 1743, *pg.* 194
PINKBERRY INC., 3130 Wilshire Blvd, Ste 400, **Santa Monica,** CA 90403, *pg.* 1744, *pg.* 275
REAL MEX RESTAURANTS, INC., 5660 Katella Ave Ste 100, **Cypress,** CA 90630, *pg.* 1746, *pg.* 75
ROUND TABLE PIZZA, 1320 Willow Pass Rd Ste 600, **Concord,** CA 94520, *pg.* 1748, *pg.* 69
RUBIO'S RESTAURANTS, INC., 1902 Wright Pl Ste 300, **Carlsbad,** CA 92008-6583, *pg.* 1748, *pg.* 60
SHAKEY'S USA, INC., 2200 W Valley Blvd, **Alhambra,** CA 91803, *pg.* 1749, *pg.* 40
STRAW HAT COOPERATIVE CORPORATION, 18 Crow Cyn Ct Ste 270, **San Ramon,** CA 94583-1669, *pg.* 1751, *pg.* 260
TACO BELL CORP., 1 Glen Bell Way, **Irvine,** CA 92618, *pg.* 1752, *pg.* 117
YARD HOUSE USA, INC., 7700 Irvine Ctr Dr Ste 300, **Irvine,** CA 92618, *pg.* 1756, *pg.* 118
YOSHINOYA AMERICA INC., 991 W Knox St, **Torrance,** CA 90502, *pg.* 1756, *pg.* 297

Colorado

BAKERS SQUARE, 400 W 48th Ave, **Denver,** CO 80216-1806, *pg.* 1715, *pg.* 316
BOSTON MARKET CORPORATION, 14103 Denver W Pkwy, **Golden,** CO 80401-3116, *pg.* 1717, *pg.* 329
CHIPOTLE MEXICAN GRILL, INC., 1401 Wynkoop St Ste 500, **Denver,** CO 80202, *pg.* 1722, *pg.* 317
GOOD TIMES RESTAURANTS, INC., 601 Corporate Cir, **Golden,** CO 80401-5622, *pg.* 1730, *pg.* 330
NOODLES & COMPANY, 520 Zang St D, **Broomfield,** CO 80021, *pg.* 1742, *pg.* 313
THE QUIZNO'S MASTER LLC, 7595 Technology Way, Ste 200, **Denver,** CO 80237, *pg.* 1746, *pg.* 322
RED ROBIN GOURMET BURGERS, INC., 6312 S Fiddlers Green Cir #200N, **Greenwood Village,** CO 80111, *pg.* 1747, *pg.* 331
ROCK BOTTOM RESTAURANTS, INC., 248 Centennial Pkwy, **Louisville,** CO 80027-1675, *pg.* 1748, *pg.* 334
SMASHBURGER MASTER LLC, 1515 Arapahoe St, Tower 1, 10th Fl, **Denver,** CO 80202, *pg.* 1750, *pg.* 323
SPICY PICKLE FRANCHISING, INC., 90 Madison St Ste 700, **Denver,** CO 80206, *pg.* 1751, *pg.* 323

Connecticut

DOCTOR'S ASSOCIATES INC., 325 Bic Dr, **Milford,** CT 06461-3072, *pg.* 1726, *pg.* 356
SANDELLA'S FLATBREAD CAFE, 9 Brookside Place, **West Redding,** CT 06896, *pg.* 1749, *pg.* 383
SUBWAY RESTAURANTS, 325 Bic Dr, **Milford,** CT 06461, *pg.* 1751, *pg.* 356

Florida

AMERICAN RESTAURANT CONCEPTS, INC., 14476 Duval Pl W Ste 103, **Jacksonville,** FL 32218, *pg.* 1715, *pg.* 431
BENIHANA INC., 21500 Biscayne Blvd Ste 900, **Aventura,** FL 33180, *pg.* 1716, *pg.* 409
BLOOMIN' BRANDS, INC., 2202 N West Shore Blvd Ste 500, **Tampa,** FL 33607, *pg.* 1716, *pg.* 471
BONEFISH GRILL, 2202 N West Shore Blvd 5th Fl, **Tampa,** FL 33607, *pg.* 1717, *pg.* 471
BURGER 21 INC., 8810 Twin Lakes Blvd, **Tampa,** FL 33614, *pg.* 1719, *pg.* 472
BURGER KING CORPORATION, 5505 Blue Lagoon Dr, **Miami,** FL 33126, *pg.* 1719, *pg.* 440
CARRABBA'S ITALIAN GRILL, LLC, 2202 NW Shore Blvd, **Tampa,** FL 33607, *pg.* 1720, *pg.* 472
COLUMBIA RESTAURANT GROUP, 2025 E 7th Ave, **Tampa,** FL 33605, *pg.* 1723, *pg.* 472
DARDEN RESTAURANTS, INC., 1000 Darden Ctr Dr, **Orlando,** FL 32837, *pg.* 1724, *pg.* 453
DORAKU CORP., 1104 Lincoln Rd, **Miami Beach,** FL 33139-2425, *pg.* 1727, *pg.* 448
FIREHOUSE SUBS, 3400-8 Kori Rd, **Jacksonville,** FL 32257, *pg.* 1728, *pg.* 433
FSC FRANCHISE CO., LLC, 5660 W Cypress St Ste A, **Tampa,** FL 33607, *pg.* 1729, *pg.* 473
HARD ROCK CAFE INTERNATIONAL, INC., 6100 Old Park Ln, **Orlando,** FL 32835, *pg.* 1730, *pg.* 454
KER, INC., 7491 Ulmerton Rd, **Largo,** FL 33771, *pg.* 1733, *pg.* 438
LOUIS PAPPAS RESTAURANT GROUP, LLC, 731 Wesley Ave, **Tarpon Springs,** FL 34689, *pg.* 1736, *pg.* 477
THE MELTING POT RESTAURANTS INC., 8810 Twin Lakes Blvd, **Tampa,** FL 33614, *pg.* 1741, *pg.* 474
OLIVE GARDEN ITALIAN RESTAURANT, 1000 Darden Ctr Dr, **Orlando,** FL 32837, *pg.* 1742, *pg.* 454
POLLO TROPICAL INC., 7300 N Kendall Dr Fl 8, **Miami,** FL 33156-7840, *pg.* 1745, *pg.* 445
RED LOBSTER, 1000 Darden Ctr Dr, **Orlando,** FL 32837, *pg.* 1747, *pg.* 455
RIB CITY GRILL, INC., 2122 Second St, **Fort Myers,** FL 33901, *pg.* 1748, *pg.* 428
RUTH'S HOSPITALITY GROUP, INC., 1030 W. Canton Avenue, St 100, **Winter Park,** FL 32789, *pg.* 1748, *pg.* 480
SMOKEY BONES BARBEQUE & GRILL, 8427 South Park Cir Ste 250, **Orlando,** FL 32819, *pg.* 1750, *pg.* 456
SONNY'S FRANCHISE COMPANY INC., 201 N New York Ave, Ste 300, **Winter Park,** FL 32789, *pg.* 1751, *pg.* 480
SONNY'S REAL PIT BAR-B-QUE, 1720 US Hwy 1 S, **Saint Augustine,** FL 32084-6016, *pg.* 1751, *pg.* 461

Georgia

THE ATLANTA BREAD COMPANY, 1200 Wilson Way Ste 100, **Smyrna,** GA 30082, *pg.* 1715, *pg.* 540
CHICK-FIL-A, INC., 5200 Buffington Rd, **Atlanta,** GA 30349-2945, *pg.* 1721, *pg.* 492
CHURCH'S CHICKEN, INC., 980 Hammond Dr NE Ste 1100, **Atlanta,** GA 30328-8187, *pg.* 1722, *pg.* 493
CINNABON, INC., 200 Glenridge Point Pkwy Ste 200, **Atlanta,** GA 30342, *pg.* 1723, *pg.* 493
HOOTERS OF AMERICA LLC, 1815 The Exchange SE, **Atlanta,** GA 30339-2027, *pg.* 1731, *pg.* 511
MCALISTER'S DELI, 4501 N Point Pkwy Ste 100, **Alpharetta,** GA 30022, *pg.* 1737, *pg.* 484
POPEYE'S CHICKEN & BISCUITS, 400 Perimeter Center Terr NE Ste 1000, **Atlanta,** GA 30346, *pg.* 1745, *pg.* 517
POPEYES LOUISIANA KITCHEN, INC., 400 Perimeter Ctr Ter NE Ste 1000, **Atlanta,** GA 30346-1234, *pg.* 1745, *pg.* 517
SMITH & SONS FOODS, INC., 2124 Riverside Dr, **Macon,** GA 31204-1747, *pg.* 1750, *pg.* 535
WAFFLE HOUSE, INCORPORATED, 5986 Financial Dr, **Norcross,** GA 30071-2949, *pg.* 1754, *pg.* 538
ZAXBY'S FRANCHISING, INC., 1040 Founders Blvd, **Athens,** GA 30606, *pg.* 1756, *pg.* 486

Hawaii

ZIPPY'S, INC., 1765 S King St 2nd Fl, **Honolulu,** HI 96826-2134, *pg.* 1757, *pg.* 545

Idaho

PITA PIT USA, INC., 105 N 4th St Ste 208, **Coeur D'Alene,** ID 83814, *pg.* 1744, *pg.* 549

Illinois

BAB, INC., 500 Lake Cook Rd Ste 475, **Deerfield,** IL 60015, *pg.* 1715, *pg.* 599
COCO PAZZO OF ILLINOIS LLC, 300 W Hubbard St, **Chicago,** IL 60610, *pg.* 1723, *pg.* 572
COSI, INC., 1751 Lake Cook Rd, **Deerfield,** IL 60015, *pg.* 1723, *pg.* 600
GIORDANO'S ENTERPRISES, INC., 308 W Randolph St, **Chicago,** IL 60606-1710, *pg.* 1729, *pg.* 575
LETTUCE ENTERTAIN YOU ENTERPRISES, INC., 5419 N Sheridan Rd, **Chicago,** IL 60640-1964, *pg.* 1735, *pg.* 580
LEVY RESTAURANTS, INC., 980 N Michigan Ave, **Chicago,** IL 60611-4518, *pg.* 1736, *pg.* 580
MCDONALD'S CORPORATION, 2111 McDonald's Dr, **Oak Brook,** IL 60523, *pg.* 1737, *pg.* 645
MCGONIGAL'S PUB, 105 S Cook St, **Barrington,** IL 60010-4311, *pg.* 1741, *pg.* 555
MORTON'S RESTAURANT GROUP, INC., 325 N LaSalle St Ste 500, **Chicago,** IL 60610, *pg.* 1741, *pg.* 583
PEPE'S INC., 1325 W 15th St, **Chicago,** IL 60608-2107, *pg.* 1744, *pg.* 587
POTBELLY SANDWICH WORKS LLC, 222 Merchandise Mart Plz Ste 2300, **Chicago,** IL 60654, *pg.* 1746, *pg.* 587

Indiana

NOBLE ROMAN'S, INC., 1 Virginia Ave Ste 300, **Indianapolis,** IN 46204-3669, *pg.* 1741, *pg.* 689
QUALITY DINING, INC., 4220 Edison Lks Pkwy, **Mishawaka,** IN 46545-1420, *pg.* 1746, *pg.* 695

Kansas

FOX & HOUND RESTAURANT GROUP, 1551 N Waterfront Pkwy Ste 310, **Wichita,** KS 67206-6611, *pg.* 1729, *pg.* 723
FREDDY'S FROZEN CUSTARD & STEAKBURGERS, 260 N Rock Rd Ste 200, **Wichita,** KS 67206, *pg.* 1729, *pg.* 723
HOULIHAN'S RESTAURANTS, INC., 8700 State Line Rd Ste 100, **Leawood,** KS 66206, *pg.* 1731, *pg.* 716
MCCOLLA ENTERPRISES LTD., 2945 SW Wanamaker Dr,

Topeka, KS 66614, *pg.* 1737, *pg.* 722
NPC INTERNATIONAL, INC., 7300 W 129th St, **Overland Park,** KS 66213, *pg.* 1742, *pg.* 719

Kentucky

A&W ALL-AMERICAN FOOD RESTAURANTS, INC., 1900 Colonel Sanders Ln, **Louisville,** KY 40213, *pg.* 1714, *pg.* 731
BARLEYCORN'S, 1073 Industrial Rd, **Cold Spring,** KY 41076-9097, *pg.* 1716, *pg.* 726
FAZOLI'S MANAGEMENT INC., 2470 Palumbo Dr, **Lexington,** KY 40509, *pg.* 1728, *pg.* 729
KFC CORPORATION, 1441 Gardiner Ln, **Louisville,** KY 40213, *pg.* 1733, *pg.* 735
LONG JOHN SILVER'S, LLC, 9505 Williamsburg Plz Ste 300, **Louisville,** KY 40222, *pg.* 1736, *pg.* 736
PAPA JOHN'S INTERNATIONAL, INC., 2002 Papa Johns Blvd, **Louisville,** KY 40299-2367, *pg.* 1743, *pg.* 737
TEXAS ROADHOUSE, INC., 6040 Dutchmans Ln Ste 200, **Louisville,** KY 40205, *pg.* 1753, *pg.* 738
YUM! BRANDS, INC., 1441 Gardiner Ln, **Louisville,** KY 40213-1914, *pg.* 1756, *pg.* 738

Louisiana

PICCADILLY RESTAURANTS, LLC, 3232 Sherwood Forest Blvd, **Baton Rouge,** LA 70816-2218, *pg.* 1744, *pg.* 742
RAISING CANE'S USA, 400 Convention St, Ste 550, **Baton Rouge,** LA 70802, *pg.* 1746, *pg.* 742
SMOOTHIE KING FRANCHISES, INC., 121 Park Pl, **Covington,** LA 70433, *pg.* 1750, *pg.* 743

Maryland

DAVCO RESTAURANTS INC., 1657 Crofton Blvd, **Crofton,** MD 21114-1305, *pg.* 1724, *pg.* 768
MAMMA ILARDO'S CORP., 110 W Rd Ste 201, **Towson,** MD 21204, *pg.* 1737, *pg.* 779
SILVER DINER, INC., 12276 Rockville Pike, **Rockville,** MD 20852-1664, *pg.* 1750, *pg.* 776

Massachusetts

ABP CORPORATION, 1 Au Bon Pain Way, **Boston,** MA 02210, *pg.* 1714, *pg.* 789
BERTUCCI'S CORP., 155 Otis St, **Northborough,** MA 01532, *pg.* 1716, *pg.* 838
BOSTON RESTAURANT ASSOCIATES, INC., 50 Salem St, **Lynnfield,** MA 01940, *pg.* 1717, *pg.* 829
DUNKIN' BRANDS GROUP, INC., 130 Royall St, **Canton,** MA 02021, *pg.* 1727, *pg.* 810
HONEY DEW ASSOCIATES, INC., 2 Taunton St, **Plainville,** MA 02762, *pg.* 1731, *pg.* 841
LEGAL SEA FOODS INC., 1 Sea Food Wy, **Boston,** MA 02210, *pg.* 1735, *pg.* 797
PAPA GINOS-DEANGELO HOLDING CORPORATION, INC., 600 Providence Hwy, **Dedham,** MA 02026-6804, *pg.* 1743, *pg.* 817
TAVISTOCK RESTAURANT GROUP, 35 Braintree Hill Office Park Ste 107, **Braintree,** MA 02184, *pg.* 1753, *pg.* 803
UFOOD RESTAURANT GROUP, INC., 255 Washington St Ste 150, **Newton,** MA 02458-1649, *pg.* 1754, *pg.* 837
UNO RESTAURANT HOLDINGS CORPORATION, 100 Charles Park Rd, **West Roxbury,** MA 02132, *pg.* 1754, *pg.* 856

Michigan

BIG BOY RESTAURANTS INTERNATIONAL, LLC, 1 Big Boy Dr, **Warren,** MI 48091-1733, *pg.* 1716, *pg.* 912
BIGGBY COFFEE, 2501 Coolidge Rd Ste 302, **East Lansing,** MI 48823, *pg.* 1716, *pg.* 885
DOMINO'S PIZZA, INC., 30 Frank Lloyd Wright Dr, **Ann Arbor,** MI 48106, *pg.* 1726, *pg.* 865
HAPPY'S PIZZA LLC, 30201 Orchard Lake Road, Ste 200, **Farmington Hills,** MI 48334, *pg.* 1730, *pg.* 886
LITTLE CAESARS ENTERPRISES, INC., 2211 Woodward Ave, **Detroit,** MI 48201, *pg.* 1736, *pg.* 883
MERITAGE HOSPITALITY GROUP, INC., 3310 Eagle Prk Dr Ste 205, **Grand Rapids,** MI 49525, *pg.* 1741, *pg.* 888

Minnesota

AMERICAN DAIRY QUEEN CORPORATION, 7505 Metro Blvd, **Minneapolis,** MN 55439-0286, *pg.* 1714, *pg.* 930
BRIDGEMAN'S RESTAURANTS INC., 6201 Brooklyn Blvd, **Brooklyn Center,** MN 55429-4035, *pg.* 1718, *pg.* 919
BUCA, INC., 1300 Nicollet Mall Ste 5003, **Minneapolis,** MN 55403-2606, *pg.* 1718, *pg.* 931
BUFFALO WILD WINGS, INC., 5500 Wayzata Blvd Ste 1600, **Minneapolis,** MN 55416, *pg.* 1718, *pg.* 931
DAIRY QUEEN CORPORATE STORE, 7505 Metro Blvd, **Minneapolis,** MN 55439-0286, *pg.* 1724, *pg.* 932
FAMOUS DAVE'S OF AMERICA, INC., 12701 Whitewater Dr Ste 200, **Hopkins,** MN 55343-4165, *pg.* 1728, *pg.* 926
GRANITE CITY FOOD & BREWERY LTD, 701 Xenia Ave S, Ste 120, **Minneapolis,** MN 55416, *pg.* 1730, *pg.* 937
INTERNATIONAL DAIRY QUEEN, INC., 7505 Metro Blvd, **Minneapolis,** MN 55439-0286, *pg.* 1732, *pg.* 938
NORTHCOTT HOSPITALITY INTERNATIONAL, LLC, 250 Lakek Dr E, **Chanhassen,** MN 55317-9364, *pg.* 1742, *pg.* 920
OVATION BRANDS, 1020 Discovery Rd Ste 100, **Eagan,** MN 55121, *pg.* 1743, *pg.* 921
PARASOLE RESTAURANT HOLDINGS, INC., 5032 France Ave S, **Edina,** MN 55410, *pg.* 1744, *pg.* 925

Missouri

APPLEBEE'S INTERNATIONAL, INC., 8140 Ward Pkwy, **Kansas City,** MO 64114, *pg.* 1715, *pg.* 980
HARDEES FOOD SYSTEMS, INC., 100 N Broadway Ste 1200, **Saint Louis,** MO 63102, *pg.* 1731, *pg.* 998
THE PASTA HOUSE CO., 1143 Macklind Ave, **Saint Louis,** MO 63110-1440, *pg.* 1744, *pg.* 1001
RAMMKERR, INC., 221 W 74th Ter, **Kansas City,** MO 64114-5730, *pg.* 1746, *pg.* 986

Nebraska

GODFATHER'S PIZZA, INC., 2808 N 108th St, **Omaha,** NE 68164, *pg.* 1729, *pg.* 1015

Nevada

CAPRIOTTI'S SANDWICH SHOP INC, 6056 S Durango, Ste 100, **Las Vegas,** NV 89113, *pg.* 1720, *pg.* 1023
PORT OF SUBS INC., 5365 Mae Anne Ave Ste A-29, **Reno,** NV 89523, *pg.* 1746, *pg.* 1032

New Jersey

CHEF'S INTERNATIONAL, INC., 62 Broadway, **Point Pleasant Beach,** NJ 08742-2606, *pg.* 1721, *pg.* 1110
JERSEY MIKE'S SUBS, 2251 Landmark Place, **Manasquan,** NJ 08736, *pg.* 1733, *pg.* 1083

New York

ARK RESTAURANTS CORP., 85 5th Ave, **New York,** NY 10003-3019, *pg.* 1715, *pg.* 1196
BOMBAY PALACE COMPANY, 30 W 52nd St, **New York,** NY 10019-6103, *pg.* 1717, *pg.* 1205
CARROLS CORPORATION, 968 James St, **Syracuse,** NY 13203-2503, *pg.* 1720, *pg.* 1344
CARROLS RESTAURANT GROUP, INC., 968 James St, **Syracuse,** NY 13203, *pg.* 1721, *pg.* 1344
FAMIGLIA - DEBARTOLO, LLC, 199 Main St 8th Fl, **White Plains,** NY 10601, *pg.* 1728, *pg.* 1352
NATHAN'S FAMOUS INC., 1 Jericho Plz, **Jericho,** NY 11753, *pg.* 1741, *pg.* 1171
PRET A MANGER, 857 Broadway, Ste 701, **New York,** NY 10003, *pg.* 1746, *pg.* 1283
RESTAURANT ASSOCIATES CORPORATION, 330 Fifth Ave 5th Fl, **New York,** NY 10001, *pg.* 1747, *pg.* 1285
SBARRO, INC., 401 Broadhollow Rd, **Melville,** NY 11747-4721, *pg.* 1749, *pg.* 1182
SHAKE SHACK INC., 24 Union Square E, 5th Fl, **New York,** NY 10003, *pg.* 1749, *pg.* 1291
THE SMITH & WOLLENSKY RESTAURANT GROUP, INC., 880 3rd Ave, **New York,** NY 10022-4730, *pg.* 1750, *pg.* 1293
TRUFOODS LLC, 14 Penn Plaza Ste 1305, **New York,** NY 10122, *pg.* 1754, *pg.* 1305

North Carolina

BOJANGLES' RESTAURANTS, INC., 9432 Southern Pine Blvd, **Charlotte,** NC 28273, *pg.* 1717, *pg.* 1364
GOLDEN CORRAL CORPORATION, 5151 Glenwood Ave, **Raleigh,** NC 27612-3267, *pg.* 1730, *pg.* 1387
KRISPY KREME DOUGHNUTS, INC., 370 Knollwood St Ste 500, **Winston Salem,** NC 27103-1880, *pg.* 1734, *pg.* 1394

Ohio

ADVANCEPIERRE FOODS, INC., 9987 Carver Rd Ste 500, **Cincinnati,** OH 45242, *pg.* 1714, *pg.* 1409
BOB EVANS RESTAURANTS, INC., 3776 S High St, **Columbus,** OH 43207, *pg.* 1717, *pg.* 1438
BRAVO BRIO RESTAURANT GROUP, INC., 777 Goodale Blvd Ste 100, **Columbus,** OH 43212, *pg.* 1717, *pg.* 1438
DONATOS PIZZERIA CORPORATION, 935 Taylor Station Rd, **Columbus,** OH 43230-6657, *pg.* 1727, *pg.* 1439
FRISCH'S RESTAURANTS, INC., 2800 Gilbert Ave, **Cincinnati,** OH 45206-1206, *pg.* 1729, *pg.* 1413
GOSH ENTERPRISES, INC., 2500 Farmers Dr Ste 140, **Columbus,** OH 43235-5706, *pg.* 1730, *pg.* 1440
LA ROSA'S, INC., 2334 Boudinot Ave, **Cincinnati,** OH 45238, *pg.* 1735, *pg.* 1416
MARCOS PIZZA INC., 5252 Monroe St, **Toledo,** OH 43623, *pg.* 1737, *pg.* 1476
MORGAN'S FOODS, INC., 4829 Galaxy Pkwy Ste S, **Cleveland,** OH 44128, *pg.* 1741, *pg.* 1432
PENN STATION, INC., 1226 US Highway 50, **Milford,** OH 45150, *pg.* 1744, *pg.* 1465
RESTAURANT DEVELOPERS CORP., 7002 Engle Rd # 100, **Middleburg Heights,** OH 44130-3474, *pg.* 1747, *pg.* 1464
STRANG CORPORATION, 8905 Lake Ave, **Cleveland,** OH 44102, *pg.* 1751, *pg.* 1436
THE WENDY'S COMPANY, 1 Dave Thomas Blvd, **Dublin,** OH 43017, *pg.* 1755, *pg.* 1450
WENDY'S INTERNATIONAL, INC., 1 Dave Thomas Blvd, **Dublin,** OH 43017-1442, *pg.* 1755, *pg.* 1451
WHITE CASTLE MANAGEMENT CO., 555 W Goodale St, **Columbus,** OH 43215, *pg.* 1756, *pg.* 1444

Oklahoma

MAZZIO'S CORPORATION, 4441 S 72nd E Ave, **Tulsa,** OK 74145-4692, *pg.* 1737, *pg.* 1490
ORANGE LEAF FROZEN YOGURT, 14201 Caliber Dr, Ste 200, **Oklahoma City,** OK 73134, *pg.* 1742, *pg.* 1487
SONIC CORP., 300 Johnny Bench Dr Ste 400, **Oklahoma City,** OK 73104, *pg.* 1750, *pg.* 1487

Oregon

ELMER'S RESTAURANTS, INC., 11802 SE Stark St, **Portland,** OR 97216-3762, *pg.* 1728, *pg.* 1502

Pennsylvania

AUNTIE ANNE'S INC., 48 50 W Chestnut St Ste 200, **Lancaster,** PA 17603, *pg.* 1715, *pg.* 1546
EAT'N PARK HOSPITALITY GROUP, 285 E Waterfront Dr, **Homestead,** PA 15230, *pg.* 1728, *pg.* 1539
HOSS'S STEAK & SEA HOUSE, INC., 170 Patchway Rd, **Duncansville,** PA 16635, *pg.* 1731, *pg.* 1526
NUTRITION MANAGEMENT SERVICES COMPANY, 2071 Kimberton Rd, **Kimberton,** PA 19442-0725, *pg.* 1742, *pg.* 1543
SALADWORKS, LLC, Eight Tower Bridge, 161 Washington St Ste 300, **Conshohocken,** PA 19428, *pg.* 1749, *pg.* 1524

South Carolina

DENNY'S CORPORATION, 203 E Main St, **Spartanburg,** SC 29319-9966, *pg.* 1725, *pg.* 1622
DENNY'S, INC., 203 E Main St, **Spartanburg,** SC 29319, *pg.* 1725, *pg.* 1622

Tennessee

AMERICAN BLUE RIBBON HOLDINGS, 3038 Sidco Dr, **Nashville,** TN 37204, *pg.* 1714, *pg.* 1648

First page reference indicates Business Class Edition
Second page reference indicates Geographic Edition

BACK YARD BURGERS, INC., 500 Church St Ste 200, **Nashville,** TN 37219, *pg.* 1715, *pg.* 1648
CAPTAIN D'S, LLC, 624 Grassmere Park Dr, Ste 30, **Nashville,** TN 37211, *pg.* 1720, *pg.* 1649
CBOCS, INC., 305 Hartmann Dr, **Lebanon,** TN 37087, *pg.* 1721, *pg.* 1639
CORKY'S BAR-B-Q, 5255 Poplar Ave, **Memphis,** TN 38119-3513, *pg.* 1723, *pg.* 1642
CRACKER BARREL OLD COUNTRY STORE, INC., 305 Hartmann Dr, **Lebanon,** TN 37087, *pg.* 1723, *pg.* 1639
DYNAMIC MANAGEMENT COMPANY LLC, 313 East Main St, **Hendersonville,** TN 37075, *pg.* 1727, *pg.* 1635
J. ALEXANDER'S CORPORATION, 3401 W End Ave Ste 260, **Nashville,** TN 37203, *pg.* 1732, *pg.* 1651
JRN, INC., 209 W 7th St, **Columbia,** TN 38401-3233, *pg.* 1733, *pg.* 1631
THE KRYSTAL COMPANY, 1 Union Sq, **Chattanooga,** TN 37402, *pg.* 1734, *pg.* 1629
LOGAN'S ROADHOUSE, INC., 3011 Armory Dr Ste 300, **Nashville,** TN 37204, *pg.* 1736, *pg.* 1652
MAX & ERMA'S RESTAURANTS, INC., 3038 Sidco Dr, **Nashville,** TN 37204, *pg.* 1737, *pg.* 1652
O'CHARLEY'S INC., 3038 Sidco Dr, **Nashville,** TN 37204, *pg.* 1742, *pg.* 1653
PERKINS & MARIE CALLENDER'S INC., 6075 Poplar Ave Ste 800, **Memphis,** TN 38119, *pg.* 1744, *pg.* 1645
RUBY TUESDAY, INC., 150 W Church Ave, **Maryville,** TN 37801-4936, *pg.* 1748, *pg.* 1640
SHONEY'S NORTH AMERICA, LLC, 1717 Elm Hill Pike Ste B-1, **Nashville,** TN 37210, *pg.* 1749, *pg.* 1654
TASTI D-LITE LLC, 341 Cool Springs Blvd, Ste 420, **Franklin,** TN 37067, *pg.* 1753, *pg.* 1634

Texas

BRINKER INTERNATIONAL, INC., 6820 LBJ Fwy, **Dallas,** TX 75240-6511, *pg.* 1718, *pg.* 1676
BUBBA GUMP SHRIMP COMPANY RESTAURANT & MARKET, 1510 W Loop South, **Houston,** TX 77027, *pg.* 1718, *pg.* 1702
CBC RESTAURANT CORP., 12700 Park Central Dr, Ste 1300, **Dallas,** TX 75251, *pg.* 1721, *pg.* 1677
CEC ENTERTAINMENT, INC., 4441 W Airport Fwy, **Irving,** TX 75062-5834, *pg.* 1721, *pg.* 1717
CHEDDAR'S, INC, 2900 Ranch Trail, **Irving,** TX 75063-2797, *pg.* 1721, *pg.* 1718
CHILI'S, INC., 6820 LBJ Freeway, **Dallas,** TX 75240, *pg.* 1722, *pg.* 1677
CICI ENTERPRISES LP, 1080 W Bethel Rd, **Coppell,** TX 75019, *pg.* 1723, *pg.* 1670
DAVE & BUSTER'S ENTERTAINMENT, INC., 2481 Manana Dr, **Dallas,** TX 75220-1203, *pg.* 1724, *pg.* 1679
DELI MANAGEMENT INC., 2400 Broadway St, **Beaumont,** TX 77702-1904, *pg.* 1725, *pg.* 1668
DICKEY'S BARBECUE RESTAURANTS, INC., 4514 Cole Ave, Ste 1015, **Dallas,** TX 75025, *pg.* 1725, *pg.* 1680
FREEBIRDS WORLD BURRITO, 9050 Capital of Texas Hwy Ste 360, **Austin,** TX 78759, *pg.* 1729, *pg.* 1662
GOLDEN FRANCHISING CORPORATION, 1131 Rockingham Ste 250, **Richardson,** TX 75080, *pg.* 1730, *pg.* 1736
IGNITE RESTAURANT GROUP, INC., 9900 Westpark Dr Ste 300, **Houston,** TX 77063, *pg.* 1731, *pg.* 1708
LANDRY'S, INC., 1510 West Loop S, **Houston,** TX 77027, *pg.* 1735, *pg.* 1709
LONE STAR STEAKHOUSE & SALOON, INC., 5055 W Park Blvd Ste 500, **Plano,** TX 75093, *pg.* 1736, *pg.* 1733
LUBY'S FUDDRUCKERS RESTAURANTS, LLC, 13111 NW Freeway Ste 600, **Houston,** TX 77040, *pg.* 1736, *pg.* 1710
LUBY'S, INC., 13111 Northwest Fwy Ste 600, **Houston,** TX 77040, *pg.* 1736, *pg.* 1710
MCCORMICK & SCHMICK'S SEAFOOD RESTAURANTS, INC., 1510 W Loop S, **Houston,** TX 77027, *pg.* 1737, *pg.* 1711
MEXICAN RESTAURANTS, INC., 12000 Aerospace Ave Ste 400, **Houston,** TX 77034-5576, *pg.* 1741, *pg.* 1711
MR. GATTI'S, LP, 5912 Balcones Dr, **Austin,** TX 78731-5919, *pg.* 1741, *pg.* 1664
PIZZA HUT, INC., 7100 Corporate Dr, **Plano,** TX 75024-4100, *pg.* 1744, *pg.* 1733
PIZZA INN, INC., 3551 Plano Pkwy, **The Colony,** TX 75056, *pg.* 1745, *pg.* 1746
RED MANGO INC., 2811 McKinney Ave Ste 18, **Dallas,** TX 75204, *pg.* 1747, *pg.* 1686
ROMACORP, INC., 1700 Alma Dr Ste 400, **Plano,** TX 75075-6964, *pg.* 1748, *pg.* 1734
SCHLOTZSKY'S, LTD., 11401 Century Oaks Ter Ste 400, **Austin,** TX 78758, *pg.* 1749, *pg.* 1665
SPAGHETTI WAREHOUSE, INC., 5525 N Macarthur Blvd, Ste 200, **Irving,** TX 75038, *pg.* 1751, *pg.* 1724
TACO BUENO RESTAURANTS, L.P., 1605 LBJ Fwy Ste 800, **Farmers Branch,** TX 75234, *pg.* 1753, *pg.* 1692
TACO CABANA, INC., 8918 Tesoro Dr Ste 200, **San Antonio,** TX 78217-6219, *pg.* 1753, *pg.* 1743
T.G.I. FRIDAY'S INC., 4201 Marsh Ln, **Carrollton,** TX 75007, *pg.* 1754, *pg.* 1669
WHATABURGER, INC., 300 Concord Plz Dr, **San Antonio,** TX 78216, *pg.* 1755, *pg.* 1744
WHICH WICH, INC., 1412 Main St, Ste 2000, **Dallas,** TX 75202, *pg.* 1756, *pg.* 1690
WINGSTOP INC., 5501 LBJ Fwy 5th Fl, **Dallas,** TX 75240, *pg.* 1756, *pg.* 1690
ZOES KITCHEN, INC., 5760 State Hwy 121, Ste 250, **Plano,** TX 75024, *pg.* 1757, *pg.* 1735

Vermont

BRUEGGER'S CORPORATION, 159 Bank St, **Burlington,** VT 05402-4420, *pg.* 1718, *pg.* 1764

Virginia

FIVE GUYS ENTERPRISES LLC, 10440 Furnace Rd Ste 205, **Lorton,** VA 22079, *pg.* 1728, *pg.* 1787
WESTERN SIZZLIN CORPORATION, PO Box 12157, **Roanoke,** VA 24023-2157, *pg.* 1755, *pg.* 1806

Washington

BURGERVILLE USA, 109 W 17th St, **Vancouver,** WA 98660, *pg.* 1720, *pg.* 1845
PAPA MURPHY'S INTERNATIONAL, LLC, 8000 NE Pkwy Dr # 350, **Vancouver,** WA 98662, *pg.* 1743, *pg.* 1846
RESTAURANTS UNLIMITED, INC., 411 1st Ave S Ste 200, **Seattle,** WA 98104-3831, *pg.* 1748, *pg.* 1839

Wisconsin

COUNTRY KITCHEN INTERNATIONAL, INC., 1289 Deming Way Ste 212, **Madison,** WI 53717, *pg.* 1723, *pg.* 1865
CULVER FRANCHISING SYSTEM, INC., 1240 Water St, **Prairie Du Sac,** WI 53578, *pg.* 1724, *pg.* 1887
ROCKY ROCOCO CORPORATION, 105 E Wisconsin Ave Ste 101, **Oconomowoc,** WI 53066, *pg.* 1748, *pg.* 1885

Wyoming

TACO JOHN'S INTERNATIONAL, INC., 808 W 20th St, PO Box 1589, **Cheyenne,** WY 82001, *pg.* 1753, *pg.* 1901

Retail

Arkansas

DILLARD'S, INC., 1600 Cantrell Rd, **Little Rock,** AR 72201-1110, *pg.* 1766, *pg.* 34
SAM'S CLUB, 2101 SE Simple Savings Dr, **Bentonville,** AR 72716-0745, *pg.* 1783, *pg.* 29
WAL-MART STORES, INC., 702 SW 8th St, **Bentonville,** AR 72716, *pg.* 1790, *pg.* 29

California

99 CENTS ONLY STORES LLC, 4000 Union Pacific Ave, **City of Commerce,** CA 90023, *pg.* 1759, *pg.* 66
AIRCRAFT SPRUCE & SPECIALTY CO., 225 Airport Cir, **Corona,** CA 92880, *pg.* 1759, *pg.* 69
ALIBRIS, INC., 1250 45th St Ste 100, **Emeryville,** CA 94608, *pg.* 1759, *pg.* 83
ANNA'S LINEN COMPANY INC., 3550 Hyland Ave, **Costa Mesa,** CA 92626-1438, *pg.* 1760, *pg.* 70
ANNIE'S INC., 1610 Fifth St, **Berkeley,** CA 94710, *pg.* 1760, *pg.* 45
BANANA REPUBLIC, 2 Folsom St, **San Francisco,** CA 94105, *pg.* 1760, *pg.* 212
CERAMIC DEVELOPMENT CORP., 1776 Wright Ave, **Richmond,** CA 94804, *pg.* 1764, *pg.* 193
CONCORD MUSIC GROUP, INC., 100 North Crescent Dr, **Beverly Hills,** CA 90210, *pg.* 1765, *pg.* 46
DOMO RECORDS, INC., 11340 W Olympic Blvd Ste 270, **Los Angeles,** CA 90064, *pg.* 1767, *pg.* 129
ERNIE BALL INC., 53973 Polk St, **Coachella,** CA 92236, *pg.* 1768, *pg.* 68
EXCELLIGENCE LEARNING CORP., 2 Lower Ragsdale Dr Ste 200, **Monterey,** CA 93940, *pg.* 1768, *pg.* 151
FLAX ARTIST'S MATERIALS, 1699 Market St, **Brisbane,** CA 94103, *pg.* 1769, *pg.* 49
THE GAP, INC., 2 Folsom St, **San Francisco,** CA 94105, *pg.* 1770, *pg.* 218
GUITAR CENTER, INC., 5795 Lindero Canyon Rd, **Westlake Village,** CA 91362, *pg.* 1771, *pg.* 306
GUMP'S CORP., 135 Post St, **San Francisco,** CA 94108-4701, *pg.* 1772, *pg.* 219
HARBOR FREIGHT TOOLS, 26541 Agoura Rd, **Calabasas,** CA 91302, *pg.* 1772, *pg.* 55
INTRADA INC., 2220 Mountain Blvd Ste 220, **Oakland,** CA 94611, *pg.* 1773, *pg.* 171
PACIFIC SUNWEAR OF CALIFORNIA, INC., 3450 E Miraloma Ave, **Anaheim,** CA 92806-2101, *pg.* 1781, *pg.* 43
ROSS STORES, INC., 5130 Hacienda Dr, **Dublin,** CA 94568, *pg.* 1783, *pg.* 78
SMITH & HAWKEN, LTD., 4 Hamilton Landing ste 100, **Novato,** CA 94949, *pg.* 1786, *pg.* 168
STARCREST PRODUCTS OF CALIFORNIA, 3660 Brennan Ave, **Perris,** CA 92571, *pg.* 1786, *pg.* 181
TRADER JOE'S CO., 800 Shamrock Ave, **Monrovia,** CA 91016, *pg.* 1789, *pg.* 151
VARESE SARABANDE RECORDS, INC., 11846 Ventura Blvd Ste 130, **Studio City,** CA 91604-2620, *pg.* 1789, *pg.* 281
WARNER BROS. RECORDS, INC., 3300 Warner Blvd, **Burbank,** CA 91505, *pg.* 1791, *pg.* 55

Colorado

CURRENT USA, INC., 1005 E Woodman Rd, **Colorado Springs,** CO 80920, *pg.* 1765, *pg.* 315
LILLIAN VERNON CORPORATION, 1005 E Woodmen Rd, **Colorado Springs,** CO 80920, *pg.* 1776, *pg.* 315
PRO GROUP, INC., 8480 E Orchard Rd Ste 3000, **Greenwood Village,** CO 80111-5017, *pg.* 1782, *pg.* 331

Connecticut

BOB'S DISCOUNT FURNITURE INC., 428 Tolland Tpke, **Manchester,** CT 06040-1765, *pg.* 1763, *pg.* 354
EDIBLE ARRANGEMENTS INTERNATIONAL, INC., 95 Barnes Rd, **Wallingford,** CT 06492, *pg.* 1768, *pg.* 382
MBI INC., 47 Richards Ave, **Norwalk,** CT 06857, *pg.* 1778, *pg.* 363
OLYMPIA SALES, INC., 215 Moody Rd, **Enfield,** CT 06082, *pg.* 1780, *pg.* 346
ROSCO LABORATORIES, INC., 52 Harbor View Ave, **Stamford,** CT 06902-5914, *pg.* 1782, *pg.* 378

District of Columbia

GEORGETOWN TOBACCO & PIPE STORES INC., 3144 M St NW, **Washington,** DC 20007, *pg.* 1771, *pg.* 400

Florida

BEALL'S, INC., 1806 38th Ave E, **Bradenton,** FL 34208-4708, *pg.* 1760, *pg.* 414
THE ELYSIAN FIELDS, INC., 1273 S Tamiami Trl, **Sarasota,** FL 34239, *pg.* 1768, *pg.* 466
INTERNATIONAL PLAZA & BAY STREET, 2223 NW Shore Blvd, **Tampa,** FL 33607, *pg.* 1773, *pg.* 473
JOHNSON SMITH COMPANY, 4514 19th St Ct E, **Bradenton,** FL 34203, *pg.* 1774, *pg.* 414
LEVENGER COMPANY, 420 S Congress Ave, **Delray Beach,** FL 33445, *pg.* 1776, *pg.* 421
MACY'S FLORIDA, 22 E Flagler St, **Miami,** FL 33131-1004, *pg.* 1777, *pg.* 444
PETMED EXPRESS, INC., 1441 SW 29th Ave, **Pompano Beach,** FL 33069, *pg.* 1781, *pg.* 460
PRESCRIPTIONS PLUS, INC., 3381 Fairlane Farms Rd, **West Palm Beach,** FL 33414, *pg.* 1782, *pg.* 479
SHORELINE IMAGE WORKS LLC, 331 Sailfish Dr, **Tarpon Springs,** FL 34688, *pg.* 1785, *pg.* 477
STEIN MART, INC., 1200 Riverplace Blvd, **Jacksonville,** FL 32207, *pg.* 1786, *pg.* 435

Georgia

AMC, INC., 240 Peachtree St NW Ste 2200, **Atlanta,** GA 30303-1327, *pg.* 1759, *pg.* 487
GLOBAL FRANCHISE MANAGEMENT LLC, 1346 Oakbrook Dr Ste 170, **Norcross,** GA 30093, *pg.* 1771, *pg.* 537
J.L. TODD AUCTION CO., 28 Bale St SW, **Rome,** GA 30165-2842, *pg.* 1774, *pg.* 539

Illinois

THE BRADFORD GROUP, 9333 N Milwaukee Ave, **Niles,** IL 60714-1381, *pg.* 1763, *pg.* 637
CLAIRE'S STORES, INC., 2400 W Central Rd, **Hoffman Estates,** IL 60192, *pg.* 1764, *pg.* 617
COSMETIQUE, INC., 200 Corporate Woods Pkwy, **Vernon Hills,** IL 60061-3171, *pg.* 1765, *pg.* 664
DICK BLICK COMPANY, 1849 Green Bay Rd Ste 310, **Highland Park,** IL 60035, *pg.* 1766, *pg.* 617
EBY-BROWN CO., 280 W Shuman Blvd Ste 280, **Naperville,** IL 60563-2578, *pg.* 1767, *pg.* 636
FOLLETT HIGHER EDUCATION GROUP, 3 westbrook Corp Ctr Ste 200, **Westchester,** IL 60154, *pg.* 1769, *pg.* 669
FTD.COM INC., 3113 Woodcreek Dr, **Downers Grove,** IL 60515, *pg.* 1770, *pg.* 608
THE GLIK COMPANY, 3248 Nameoki Rd, **Granite City,** IL 62040-5014, *pg.* 1771, *pg.* 615
KMART CORPORATION, 3333 Beverly Rd, **Hoffman Estates,** IL 60179, *pg.* 1775, *pg.* 617
SEARS HOLDINGS CORPORATION, 3333 Beverly Rd, **Hoffman Estates,** IL 60179, *pg.* 1784, *pg.* 618
SEARS, ROEBUCK & CO., 3333 Beverly Rd, **Hoffman Estates,** IL 60179, *pg.* 1785, *pg.* 619
SVM, LP, 200 E Howard Ave ste 220, **Des Plaines,** IL 60018, *pg.* 1786, *pg.* 606

Indiana

AMERICAN ART CLAY CO., INC., 6060 Guion Rd, **Indianapolis,** IN 46254-1222, *pg.* 1759, *pg.* 682
DIRECTBUY, INC., 8450 Broadway, **Merrillville,** IN 46410-6221, *pg.* 1766, *pg.* 694
THE FINISH LINE, INC., 3308 N Mitthoeffer Rd, **Indianapolis,** IN 46235, *pg.* 1769, *pg.* 686

Iowa

KUM & GO, 6400 Westown Pkwy, **West Des Moines,** IA 50266-7709, *pg.* 1775, *pg.* 713

Kansas

SHEPLERS, INC., 6501 W Kellogg Dr, **Wichita,** KS 67209-2211, *pg.* 1785, *pg.* 724
VICTORIAN TRADING COMPANY, 15600 W 99th St, **Lenexa,** KS 66219, *pg.* 1789, *pg.* 717

Maine

L.L. BEAN, INC., 15 Casco St, **Freeport,** ME 04033, *pg.* 1777, *pg.* 750
PINE STATE TRADING COMPANY, 8 Ellis Ave, **Augusta,** ME 04330-7199, *pg.* 1781, *pg.* 749

Maryland

GOODWILL INDUSTRIES INTERNATIONAL, INC., 15810 Indianola Dr, **Rockville,** MD 20855, *pg.* 1771, *pg.* 776
GUYETTE & DEETER, 24718 Beverly Rd, **Saint Michaels,** MD 21663, *pg.* 1772, *pg.* 776
ULLA POPKEN LTD., 12201 Long Green Pk, **Glen Arm,** MD 21057, *pg.* 1789, *pg.* 771

Massachusetts

BJ'S WHOLESALE CLUB, INC., 25 Research Dr, **Westborough,** MA 01581, *pg.* 1762, *pg.* 857
THE J. JILL GROUP, INC., 4 Batterymarch Park, **Quincy,** MA 02169, *pg.* 1774, *pg.* 842
MARSHALLS OF MA, INC., 770 Cochituate Rd, **Framingham,** MA 01701, *pg.* 1778, *pg.* 821
SPECIALTY CATALOG CORPORATION, 400 Manley St, **West Bridgewater,** MA 02379, *pg.* 1786, *pg.* 856
T.J. MAXX, 770 Cochituate Rd, **Framingham,** MA 01701, *pg.* 1788, *pg.* 822
THE TJX COMPANIES, INC., 770 Cochituate Rd, **Framingham,** MA 01701, *pg.* 1788, *pg.* 822
THE YANKEE CANDLE COMPANY, INC., 16 Yankee Candle Way, **South Deerfield,** MA 01373, *pg.* 1792, *pg.* 843

Michigan

MEIJER, INC., 2929 Walker Rd NW, **Grand Rapids,** MI 49544-9424, *pg.* 1779, *pg.* 888
PET SUPPLIES PLUS, 17197 N Laurel Park Dr, **Livonia,** MI 48152, *pg.* 1781, *pg.* 897
THE SHARPER IMAGE, 27725 Stansbury Blvd, Ste 175, **Farmington Hills,** MI 48334, *pg.* 1785, *pg.* 886

Minnesota

BEST BUY CO., INC., 7601 Penn Ave S, **Richfield,** MN 55423, *pg.* 1761, *pg.* 954
BLUESTEM BRANDS, INC., 6509 Flying Cloud Dr, **Eden Prairie,** MN 55344, *pg.* 1763, *pg.* 922
CARIBOU COFFEE COMPANY, INC., 3900 Lakebreeze Ave N, **Minneapolis,** MN 55429, *pg.* 1764, *pg.* 932
EVINE LIVE INC., 6740 Shady Oak Rd, **Eden Prairie,** MN 55344-3433, *pg.* 1768, *pg.* 922
TARGET CORPORATION, 1000 Nicollet Mall, **Minneapolis,** MN 55403-2467, *pg.* 1786, *pg.* 942
WINMARK CORPORATION, 605 Highway 169 N Ste 400, **Minneapolis,** MN 55441, *pg.* 1792, *pg.* 946

Missouri

CRUISIN' USA/BOWLINGSHIRT.COM., 6262 Olive Blvd, **Saint Louis,** MO 63130, *pg.* 1765, *pg.* 995
FRANCHISE CONCEPTS, INC., 221 First Executive Ave, **Saint Peters,** MO 63376, *pg.* 1769, *pg.* 1005

Nebraska

THE BUCKLE, INC., 2407 W 24th St, **Kearney,** NE 68845-4915, *pg.* 1764, *pg.* 1011
GORDMANS STORES INC., 12100 W Ctr Rd, **Omaha,** NE 68144-3969, *pg.* 1771, *pg.* 1016
OMAHA STEAKS INTERNATIONAL, INC., 10909 John Galt Blvd, **Omaha,** NE 68137, *pg.* 1780, *pg.* 1017

New Hampshire

BROOKSTONE, INC., 1 Innovation Way, **Merrimack,** NH 03054-4873, *pg.* 1764, *pg.* 1036
GARNET HILL, 231 Main St, **Franconia,** NH 03580, *pg.* 1771, *pg.* 1034
LITTLETON COIN CO., INC., 1309 Mt Eustis Rd, **Littleton,** NH 03561, *pg.* 1776, *pg.* 1035

New Jersey

BURLINGTON COAT FACTORY, 1830 Rte 130 N, **Burlington,** NJ 08016, *pg.* 1764, *pg.* 1047
EDEN COMPANY, 80 Triangle Blvd, **Carlstadt,** NJ 07072-2701, *pg.* 1768, *pg.* 1050
HABAND COMPANY, INC., 110 Bauer Dr, **Oakland,** NJ 07436-3105, *pg.* 1772, *pg.* 1099
HANOVER DIRECT, INC., 1200 Harbor Blvd, **Weehawken,** NJ 07086, *pg.* 1772, *pg.* 1130
PARTY CITY CORPORATION, 25 Green Pond Rd Ste 1, **Rockaway,** NJ 07866, *pg.* 1781, *pg.* 1116
SPENCER GIFTS LLC, 6826 Black Horse Pike, **Egg Harbor Township,** NJ 08234, *pg.* 1786, *pg.* 1057
UMSI INCORPORATED, 125 Lincoln Blvd, **Middlesex,** NJ 08846-1060, *pg.* 1789, *pg.* 1084

New Mexico

FOREIGN TRADERS, INC., 202 Galisteo St, **Santa Fe,** NM 87501, *pg.* 1769, *pg.* 1135

New York

1-800-FLOWERS.COM, INC., 1 Old Country Rd Ste 500, **Carle Place,** NY 11514-1847, *pg.* 1758, *pg.* 1151
1-800-MATTRESS.COM, 1000 S Oyster Bay Rd, **Hicksville,** NY 11801, *pg.* 1759, *pg.* 1166
AMSCAN HOLDINGS, INC., 80 Grasslands Rd, **Elmsford,** NY 10523, *pg.* 1760, *pg.* 1158
BERGDORF GOODMAN, INC., 754 Fifth Ave, **New York,** NY 10019-2503, *pg.* 1761, *pg.* 1202
BIRCHBOX, 28 East 28th St, **New York,** NY 10016, *pg.* 1762, *pg.* 1203
BLOOMINGDALE'S, INC., 1000 3rd Ave, **New York,** NY 10022-1231, *pg.* 1763, *pg.* 1204
CORE MEDIA GROUP, 650 Madison Ave, **New York,** NY 10022, *pg.* 1765, *pg.* 1218
THE DRESS BARN, INC., 30 Dunnigan Dr, **Suffern,** NY 10901-4101, *pg.* 1767, *pg.* 1343
DRG RECORDS INCORPORATED, 740 Broadway Fl 7, **New York,** NY 10003, *pg.* 1767, *pg.* 1226
E. MISHAN & SONS, INC., 230 5th Ave Ste 800, **New York,** NY 10001-7704, *pg.* 1767, *pg.* 1226
ETSY, INC., 55 Washington St, **New York,** NY 11201, *pg.* 1768, *pg.* 1230
FULLBEAUTY BRANDS, 463 7th Ave, **New York,** NY 10018-7604, *pg.* 1770, *pg.* 1233
HEARST BUSINESS MEDIA, 50 Charles Lindbergh Blvd Ste 100, **Uniondale,** NY 11553, *pg.* 1773, *pg.* 1346
J. CREW GROUP, INC., 770 Broadway, **New York,** NY 10003, *pg.* 1773, *pg.* 1245
LORD & TAYLOR LLC, 424 5th Ave, **New York,** NY 10018-2703, *pg.* 1777, *pg.* 1252
MACY'S EAST, 151 W 34th St 17th Fl, **New York,** NY 10001, *pg.* 1777, *pg.* 1254
NEW YORK & COMPANY, INC., 450 W 33rd St 5th Fl, **New York,** NY 10001-2606, *pg.* 1779, *pg.* 1268
PAUL STUART, INC., Madison Ave and 45th St, **New York,** NY 10017, *pg.* 1781, *pg.* 1276
POPPIN, 44 W 18th St Ste 701, **New York,** NY 10011, *pg.* 1782, *pg.* 1282
PUBLISHERS CLEARING HOUSE, 382 Channel Dr, **Port Washington,** NY 11050-2219, *pg.* 1782, *pg.* 1324
RESTAURANT DEPOT, LLC, 13311 132nd St, **College Point,** NY 11356-2440, *pg.* 1782, *pg.* 1153
SAKS FIFTH AVENUE, INC., 12 E 49th St, **New York,** NY 10017, *pg.* 1783, *pg.* 1287
SAKS INCORPORATED, 12 E 49th St, **New York,** NY 10017, *pg.* 1783, *pg.* 1288

North Carolina

BELK, INC., 2801 W Tyvola Rd, **Charlotte,** NC 28217-4500, *pg.* 1760, *pg.* 1364
FAMILY DOLLAR STORES, INC., 10401 Monroe Rd, **Matthews,** NC 28105, *pg.* 1768, *pg.* 1382
OVERTON'S INC., 111 Red Bank Rd, **Greenville,** NC 27858, *pg.* 1781, *pg.* 1377
PERFORMANCE DIRECT, INC., 144 Old Lystra Rd PO Box 2741, **Chapel Hill,** NC 27515-2741, *pg.* 1781, *pg.* 1361

Ohio

AMERIMARK DIRECT, LLC, 6864 Engle Rd, **Cleveland,** OH 44130, *pg.* 1759, *pg.* 1428
BIG LOTS, INC., 300 Phillipi Rd, **Columbus,** OH 43228, *pg.* 1762, *pg.* 1438
L BRANDS, INC., 3 Limited Pkwy, **Columbus,** OH 43230-1467, *pg.* 1776, *pg.* 1441
LANE BRYANT, 3344 Morse Crossing, **Columbus,** OH 43219, *pg.* 1776, *pg.* 1441
MACY'S, INC., 7 W 7th St, **Cincinnati,** OH 45202-2424, *pg.* 1778, *pg.* 1417
THINGS REMEMBERED, INC., 5500 Avion Park Dr, **Highland Heights,** OH 44143, *pg.* 1788, *pg.* 1455
VICTORIA'S SECRET STORES, LLC, 4 Limited Pkwy E, **Reynoldsburg,** OH 43068-5302, *pg.* 1789, *pg.* 1471

Oklahoma

DRYSDALES INC., 3220 S Memorial Dr, **Tulsa,** OK 74145, *pg.* 1767, *pg.* 1489
SHARPE DRY GOODS CO., INC., 200 N Broadway St, **Checotah,** OK 74426-2432, *pg.* 1785, *pg.* 1484

Oregon

ALLEGRO CORPORATION, 20048 NE San Rafel St, **Portland,** OR 97230, *pg.* 1759, *pg.* 1501
CD BABY, INC., 13909 NE Airport Way, **Portland,** OR 97230-3441, *pg.* 1764, *pg.* 1501
FRED MEYER STORES, INC., 3800 SE 22nd Ave, **Portland,** OR 97202-2918, *pg.* 1769, *pg.* 1502
HANNA ANDERSSON CORPORATION, 1010 NW Flanders St, **Portland,** OR 97209-3119, *pg.* 1772, *pg.* 1503
NORM THOMPSON OUTFITTERS INC., 3188 NW Aloclek Dr, **Hillsboro,** OR 97124-7134, *pg.* 1780, *pg.* 1498

Pennsylvania

BLAIR CORPORATION, 220 Hickory St, **Warren,** PA 16366-0001, *pg.* 1762, *pg.* 1590
BON TON STORES, INC., 2801 E Market St, **York,** PA 17402, *pg.* 1763, *pg.* 1596
BOSCOV'S DEPARTMENT STORE, LLC, 4500 Perkiomen Ave, **Reading,** PA 19606-3202, *pg.* 1763, *pg.* 1583
DAY-TIMERS, INC., 1 Willow Ln, **East Texas,** PA 18046, *pg.* 1766, *pg.* 1528
FLYNN & O'HARA UNIFORMS INC., 10905 Dutton Rd, **Philadelphia,** PA 19154, *pg.* 1769, *pg.* 1564
THE FRANKLIN MINT, LLC, 486 Thomas Jones Way Ste 240, **Franklin Center,** PA 19341-2561, *pg.* 1769, *pg.* 1533
HARRIET CARTER GIFTS, INC., 425 Stump Rd, **Montgomeryville,** PA 18936-9631, *pg.* 1773, *pg.* 1553
MOVIES UNLIMITED INC., 3015 Darnell Rd, **Philadelphia,** PA 19154-3201, *pg.* 1779, *pg.* 1567
OLLIE'S BARGAIN OUTLET INC., 6295 Allentown Blvd Ste A, **Harrisburg,** PA 17112-2606, *pg.* 1780, *pg.* 1537
ORCHARD BRANDS CORPORATION, 100 Murray Dr, **Warren,** PA 16368, *pg.* 1780, *pg.* 1590
URBAN OUTFITTERS, INC., 5000 S Broad St, **Philadelphia,** PA 19112, *pg.* 1789, *pg.* 1571
WM. F. COMLY & SON, INC., 1825 E Boston St, **Philadelphia,** PA 19125-1201, *pg.* 1792, *pg.* 1572

Rhode Island

CVS HEALTH CORPORATION, 1 CVS Dr, **Woonsocket,** RI 02895-6146, *pg.* 1765, *pg.* 1610
ROSS-SIMONS INC., 9 Ross Simons Dr, **Cranston,** RI 02920-4475, *pg.* 1783, *pg.* 1600

South Carolina

SUNBELT RENTALS, 2341 Deerfield Dr, **Fort Mill,** SC 29715, *pg.* 1786, *pg.* 1616

Tennessee

DOLLAR GENERAL CORPORATION, 100 Mission Ridge Dr, **Goodlettsville,** TN 37072-2171, *pg.* 1767, *pg.* 1635
FRED'S INC., 4300 New Getwell Rd, **Memphis,** TN 38118-6801, *pg.* 1769, *pg.* 1644
NAXOS OF AMERICA INC., 416 Mary Lindsay Polk Dr Ste 509, **Franklin,** TN 37067, *pg.* 1779, *pg.* 1633
SMOKY MOUNTAIN KNIFE WORKS INC., 2320 Winfield Dunn Pkwy, **Sevierville,** TN 37876-0557, *pg.* 1786, *pg.* 1655

Texas

AT HOME STORES LLC, 1600 E Plano Pkwy, **Plano,** TX 75074, *pg.* 1760, *pg.* 1729
COLORTYME, INC., 5700 Tennyson Pkwy Ste 180, **Plano,** TX 75024-3585, *pg.* 1765, *pg.* 1729
HASTINGS ENTERTAINMENT, INC., 3601 Plains Blvd, **Amarillo,** TX 79102-1019, *pg.* 1773, *pg.* 1659
J.C. PENNEY COMPANY, INC., 6501 Legacy Dr, **Plano,** TX 75024-3612, *pg.* 1774, *pg.* 1732
JOURNEY EDUCATION MARKETING, INC., 13755 Hutton Dr Ste 500, **Dallas,** TX 75234, *pg.* 1775, *pg.* 1683
POLLO CAMPERO, 5420 Lyndon B Johnson Fwy, Lincoln Centre Tower II Ste 950, **Dallas,** TX 75420, *pg.* 1782, *pg.* 1685
RETAILMENOT INC., 301 Congress Ave Ste 700, **Austin,** TX 78701, *pg.* 1782, *pg.* 1665
TUESDAY MORNING CORPORATION, 6250 LBJ Fwy, **Dallas,** TX 75240, *pg.* 1789, *pg.* 1690
UNIVERSAL COIN & BULLION LTD., 7410 Phelan Blvd, **Beaumont,** TX 77706, *pg.* 1789, *pg.* 1668
WALLPAPERS-TO-GO, INC., 7342 San Pedro Ave, **San Antonio,** TX 78216, *pg.* 1791, *pg.* 1744

Utah

1-800 CONTACTS, INC., 51 W Center St, **Orem,** UT 84057, *pg.* 1758, *pg.* 1753
1-800-VENDING, INC., 1284 W Flint Meadow Dr, **Kaysville,** UT 84037, *pg.* 1759, *pg.* 1751
SUNDANCE CATALOG CO., LTD., 3865 W 2400 S, **Salt Lake City,** UT 84120-7212, *pg.* 1786, *pg.* 1761

Vermont

THE ORVIS COMPANY, INC., 178 Conservation Way, **Arlington,** VT 05250, *pg.* 1781, *pg.* 1764
VERMONT COUNTRY STORE, INC., 5650 Main St PO Box 1108, **Manchester Center,** VT 05255-1108, *pg.* 1789, *pg.* 1766

Virginia

DOLLAR TREE, INC., 500 Volvo Pkwy, **Chesapeake,** VA 23320-1604, *pg.* 1767, *pg.* 1778
TECHNOBRANDS, INC., 1998 Ruffin Mill Rd, **Colonial Heights,** VA 23834-5913, *pg.* 1788, *pg.* 1778

Washington

COSTCO WHOLESALE CORPORATION, 999 Lake Dr, **Issaquah,** WA 98027-8990, *pg.* 1765, *pg.* 1820
DANIEL SMITH INC., 4150 1st Ave S, **Seattle,** WA 98134, *pg.* 1766, *pg.* 1835
NORDSTROM, INC., 1617 6th Ave Ste 700, **Seattle,** WA 98101-1707, *pg.* 1779, *pg.* 1837
ZULILY, 2200 1st Ave S, **Seattle,** WA 98134, *pg.* 1792, *pg.* 1843

Wisconsin

CELEBRATE EXPRESS, INC., 5915 S Moorland Rd, **New Berlin,** WI 53151, *pg.* 1764, *pg.* 1883
KOHL'S CORPORATION, N56W17000 Ridgewood Dr, **Menomonee Falls,** WI 53051, *pg.* 1775, *pg.* 1870
LANDS' END, INC., Lands' End Ln, **Dodgeville,** WI 53595, *pg.* 1776, *pg.* 1857
NASCO INTERNATIONAL, INC., 901 Janesville Ave, **Fort Atkinson,** WI 53538-2402, *pg.* 1779, *pg.* 1858
ONE STEP AHEAD, 1112 7th Ave, **Monroe,** WI 53566-1364,

First page reference indicates Business Class Edition
Second page reference indicates Geographic Edition

pg. 1780, *pg.* 1881
SHOPKO, 700 Pilgrim Way, **Green Bay,** WI 54307-5263, *pg.* 1785, *pg.* 1860
SILVER STAR BRANDS, 250 City Center, **Oshkosh,** WI 54906, *pg.* 1785, *pg.* 1886

Seeds, Plants & Fertilizers

Alabama

BELLINGRATH GARDENS & HOME, 12401 Bellingrath Gardens Rd, **Theodore,** AL 36582-8460, *pg.* 1794, *pg.* 8

California

AMERICAN VANGUARD CORPORATION, 4695 Macarthur Ct Ste 1200, **Newport Beach,** CA 92660-8859, *pg.* 1793, *pg.* 165
ARMSTRONG GARDEN CENTERS, INC., 2200 E Rte 66 Ste 200, **Glendora,** CA 91740, *pg.* 1793, *pg.* 99
HARRIS MORAN SEED CO., 555 Codoni Ave, **Modesto,** CA 95357-0507, *pg.* 1796, *pg.* 150
MONROVIA GROWERS, 817 E Monrovia Pl, **Azusa,** CA 91702-2638, *pg.* 1797, *pg* 44
TELEFLORA LLC, 11444 W Olympic Blvd, **Los Angeles,** CA 90064-1549, *pg.* 1801, *pg.* 140

Colorado

DENVER WHOLESALE FLORISTS COMPANY, 4800 Dahlia St, **Denver,** CO 80216-3121, *pg.* 1794, *pg.* 319

Connecticut

THE CHAS. C. HART SEED CO., 304 Main St, **Wethersfield,** CT 06109-1826, *pg.* 1794, *pg.* 384
THE F.A. BARTLETT TREE EXPERT COMPANY, 1290 E Main St, **Stamford,** CT 06902-3555, *pg.* 1795, *pg.* 373
WILT-PRUF PRODUCTS, INC., PO Box 469, **Essex,** CT 06426-0469, *pg.* 1801, *pg.* 346

Florida

SPEEDLING INCORPORATED, 4300 Old US Hwy 41 S, **Sun City,** FL 33586-7220, *pg.* 1800, *pg.* 468
SUN BULB COMPANY, INC., 1615 SW Hwy 17, **Arcadia,** FL 34266-7101, *pg.* 1800, *pg.* 409
YARA N AMERICA, INC., 100 N Tampa St Ste 3200, **Tampa,** FL 33602, *pg.* 1802, *pg.* 477

Georgia

ORKIN, INC., 2170 Piedmont Rd NE, **Atlanta,** GA 30324-4135, *pg.* 1798, *pg.* 517

Idaho

J.R. SIMPLOT COMPANY, AGRI BUSINESS, 999 Main St Ste 1300, **Boise,** ID 83702, *pg.* 1796, *pg.* 547
SIMPLOT PARTNERS INC., 999 Main St, **Boise,** ID 83702, *pg.* 1800, *pg.* 548

Illinois

BALL HORTICULTURAL COMPANY, 622 Town Rd, **West Chicago,** IL 60185-2614, *pg.* 1793, *pg.* 668
FTD GROUP, INC., 3113 Woodcreek Dr, **Downers Grove,** IL 60515, *pg.* 1795, *pg.* 608
MOEWS SEED CO., INC., Rte 89 S, **Granville,** IL 61326, *pg.* 1797, *pg.* 616
NUFARM AMERICAS INC, 11901 S Austin Ave, **Alsip,** IL 60803, *pg.* 1798, *pg.* 552
PANAMERICAN SEED CO., 622 Town Rd, **West Chicago,** IL 60185-2614, *pg.* 1798, *pg.* 668
POTASHCORP, 1101 Skokie Blvd Ste 400, **Northbrook,** IL 60062, *pg.* 1799, *pg.* 641
SMITHEREEN PEST MANAGEMENT SERVICES, 7400 N Melvina Ave, **Niles,** IL 60714-3908, *pg.* 1800, *pg.* 638
SPRING-GREEN LAWN CARE CORPORATION, 11909 S Spaulding School Dr, **Plainfield,** IL 60585, *pg.* 1800, *pg.* 652
SYNGENTA SEEDS, INC., 4343 Commerce Ct, **Lisle,** IL 60532, *pg.* 1801, *pg.* 630

Indiana

GARDENS ALIVE!, INC., 5100 Schenley Pl, **Lawrenceburg,** IN 47025-2181, *pg.* 1796, *pg.* 693

Iowa

DUPONT PIONEER, 7100 NW 62nd Ave, **Johnston,** IA 50131, *pg.* 1795, *pg.* 708
EARL MAY SEED & NURSERY L.C., 208 N Elm St, **Shenandoah,** IA 51603-1000, *pg.* 1795, *pg.* 712

Kansas

EXCEL INDUSTRIES, INC., 200 S Ridge Rd, **Hesston,** KS 67062, *pg.* 1795, *pg.* 715
KALO, INC., 13200 Metcalf Ave Ste 250, **Overland Park,** KS 66213, *pg.* 1796, *pg.* 719

Kentucky

FERRY-MORSE SEED COMPANY, 600 Stethen Beale Dr, **Fulton,** KY 42041, *pg.* 1795, *pg.* 728

Louisiana

TERRAL SEED, INC., 111 Ellington Dr, **Rayville,** LA 71269, *pg.* 1801, *pg.* 748

Maryland

LILYPONS WATER GARDENS INC., 6800 Lilypons Rd, **Buckeystown,** MD 21710, *pg.* 1797, *pg.* 766
PLANTABBS PRODUCTS COMPANY, 8839 H Kelso Dr, **Baltimore,** MD 21221, *pg.* 1799, *pg.* 758
SYNAGRO TECHNOLOGIES, INC., 435 Williams Ct, # 100, **Baltimore,** MD 21220, *pg.* 1800, *pg.* 759

Massachusetts

PLANTATION PRODUCTS INC, 202 S Washington St, **Norton,** MA 02766, *pg.* 1799, *pg.* 839
WALTHAM SERVICES, INC., 817 Moody St, **Waltham,** MA 02453, *pg.* 1801, *pg.* 855

Minnesota

MCLAUGHLIN GORMLEY KING COMPANY, 8810 10th Ave N, **Minneapolis,** MN 55427, *pg.* 1797, *pg.* 939
SYNGENTA SEEDS, INC., 11055 Wayzata Blvd, **Minnetonka,** MN 55305, *pg.* 1801, *pg.* 950

Mississippi

MONSANTO, 1 Cotton Row, **Scott,** MS 38772-0157, *pg.* 1798, *pg.* 971

Missouri

BASF, 3568 Tree Ct Industrial Blvd, **Saint Louis,** MO 63122-6620, *pg.* 1793, *pg.* 992
FORREST KEELING NURSERY, INC., 88 Forest Keeling Ln, **Elsberry,** MO 63343, *pg.* 1795, *pg.* 977
GILBERT H. WILD & SON, LLC, 3044 State Hwy 37, **Sarcoxie,** MO 64862, *pg.* 1796, *pg.* 1005

New Jersey

LAWN DOCTOR INC., 142 State Rte 34, **Holmdel,** NJ 07733, *pg.* 1796, *pg.* 1074

New York

BONIDE PRODUCTS, INC., 6301 Sutliff Rd, **Oriskany,** NY 13424-4326, *pg.* 1794, *pg.* 1320
CROSMAN SEED CORPORATION, 511 W Comml St, **East Rochester,** NY 14445, *pg.* 1794, *pg.* 1156
THE PAGE SEED CO., 1A Green St, **Greene,** NY 13778-1108, *pg.* 1798, *pg.* 1163

North Dakota

MONSANTO, 304 Ctr St, **West Fargo,** ND 58078-3134, *pg.* 1798, *pg.* 1399

Ohio

THE ANDERSONS INCORPORATED, 480 W Dussel Dr, **Maumee,** OH 43537-1639, *pg.* 1793, *pg.* 1461
ARIS HORTICULTURE, INC., 115 3rd St SE, **Barberton,** OH 44203-4208, *pg.* 1793, *pg.* 1404
THE CIVIC GARDEN CENTER OF GREATER CINCINNATI, 2715 Reading Rd, **Cincinnati,** OH 45206, *pg.* 1794, *pg.* 1412
THE DAVEY TREE EXPERT COMPANY, 1500 N Mantua St, **Kent,** OH 44240, *pg.* 1794, *pg.* 1456
THE SCOTTS MIRACLE-GRO COMPANY, 14111 Scottslawn Rd, **Marysville,** OH 43041, *pg.* 1799, *pg.* 1459
THE SIEBENTHALER CO., 3001 Catalpa Dr, **Dayton,** OH 45405-1745, *pg.* 1800, *pg.* 1446

Pennsylvania

THE CONARD-PYLE COMPANY, 25 Lewis Rd, **West Grove,** PA 19390-9701, *pg.* 1794, *pg.* 1594
LEBANON SEABOARD CORPORATION, 1600 E Cumberland St, **Lebanon,** PA 17042-8323, *pg.* 1797, *pg.* 1547
W. ATLEE BURPEE & CO., 300 Pk Ave, **Warminster,** PA 18974-4808, *pg.* 1801, *pg.* 1590
THE WOODSTREAM CORPORATION, 69 N Locust St, **Lititz,** PA 17543-1714, *pg.* 1801, *pg.* 1549

Tennessee

TRUGREEN-CHEMLAWN, 860 Ridge Lake Blvd, **Memphis,** TN 38120-9421, *pg.* 1801, *pg.* 1647

Texas

CALLOWAY'S NURSERY, INC., 4200 Airport Fwy Ste 200, **Fort Worth,** TX 76117-6200, *pg.* 1794, *pg.* 1694
CORNELIUS NURSERIES, 4200 Airport Frwy Ste 200, **Fort Worth,** TX 76117, *pg.* 1794, *pg.* 1694

Utah

MORGRO, INC., 145 W Central Ave, **Salt Lake City,** UT 84107-1418, *pg.* 1798, *pg.* 1759

Virginia

LANCASTER LEAF TOBACCO CO., 205 W Main St, **Kenbridge,** VA 23944, *pg.* 1796, *pg.* 1786
WAYNESBORO NURSERIES, INC., 2597 Lyndhurst Rd, **Waynesboro,** VA 22980, *pg.* 1801, *pg.* 1811

First page reference indicates Business Class Edition
Second page reference indicates Geographic Edition

Shoes

California

BIRKENSTOCK DISTRIBUTION USA INC., 8171 Redwood Blvd, **Novato,** CA 94945-1403, *pg.* 1805, *pg.* 168
COBIAN CORP., 1739 Melrose Dr #101, **San Marcos,** CA 92078-2100, *pg.* 1806, *pg.* 253
DECKERS OUTDOOR CORPORATION, 250 Coromar Dr, **Goleta,** CA 93117, *pg.* 1807, *pg.* 100
HI-TEC SPORTS USA, INC., 4801 Stoddard Rd, **Modesto,** CA 95356-9318, *pg.* 1809, *pg.* 150
L.A. GEAR, INC., 844 Moraga Dr, **Los Angeles,** CA 90049, *pg.* 1811, *pg.* 134
PHOENIX FOOTWEAR GROUP, INC., 5937 Darwin Ct Ste 109, **Carlsbad,** CA 92008, *pg.* 1815, *pg.* 60
PRINCIPLE PLASTICS, INC., 1136 W 135th St, **Gardena,** CA 90247-1919, *pg.* 1816, *pg.* 94
SKECHERS U.S.A., INC., 228 Manhattan Beach Blvd, **Manhattan Beach,** CA 90266-5347, *pg.* 1819, *pg.* 143
TOMS SHOE'S INC, 3025 Olympic Blvd Ste C, **Santa Monica,** CA 90404, *pg.* 1821, *pg.* 276
VANS, INC., 6550 Katella Ave, **Cypress,** CA 90630, *pg.* 1821, *pg.* 76
THE WALKING COMPANY, INC., 2475 Townsgate Ste 200, **Westlake Village,** CA 91361, *pg.* 1822, *pg.* 307

Colorado

CROCS, INC., 7477 E Dry Creek Pkwy, **Niwot,** CO 80503-8021, *pg.* 1806, *pg.* 335

Florida

CHAMPS SPORTS, 311 Manatee Ave W, **Bradenton,** FL 34205, *pg.* 1806, *pg.* 414

Indiana

SHOE CARNIVAL, INC., 7500 E Columbia St, **Evansville,** IN 47715-9127, *pg.* 1819, *pg.* 679

Maine

EASTLAND SHOE CORPORATION, 4 Meetinghouse Rd, **Freeport,** ME 04032, *pg.* 1808, *pg.* 750

Maryland

FILA USA, 930 Ridgebrook Rd # 200, **Sparks,** MD 21152-9390, *pg.* 1808, *pg.* 779
RICHLEE SHOE COMPANY, 7311 Grove Rd Ste K, **Frederick,** MD 21704-3300, *pg.* 1818, *pg.* 769

Massachusetts

THE ALDEN SHOE COMPANY, 1 Taunton St, **Middleboro,** MA 02346-1426, *pg.* 1804, *pg.* 833
CLARKS COMPANIES, 156 Oak St, **Newton,** MA 02464-1440, *pg.* 1806, *pg.* 836
ETONIC WORLDWIDE LLC, 2400 Computer Dr, **Westborough,** MA 01581, *pg.* 1808, *pg.* 857
HITCHCOCK SHOES, INC., 225 Beal St, **Hingham,** MA 02043-1543, *pg.* 1810, *pg.* 824
KEDS LLC, 191 Spring St, **Lexington,** MA 02420, *pg.* 1810, *pg.* 828
MERCURY INTERNATIONAL TRADING CORP., 20 Alice Agnew Dr, **North Attleboro,** MA 02763, *pg.* 1811, *pg* 837
NEW BALANCE ATHLETIC SHOE, INC., 20 Guest St Ste 20, **Boston,** MA 02135-2040, *pg.* 1811, *pg.* 798
PUMA NORTH AMERICA, INC., 10 Lyberty Way, **Westford,** MA 01886, *pg.* 1816, *pg.* 858
REEBOK INTERNATIONAL LTD., 1895 JW Foster Blvd, **Canton,** MA 02021-1099, *pg.* 1817, *pg.* 811
THE ROCKPORT GROUP, 1895 J W Foster Blvd, **Canton,** MA 02021, *pg.* 1818, *pg.* 812
SAUCONY, INC., 191 Spring St, **Lexington,** MA 02421-8045, *pg.* 1818, *pg.* 828
THE STRIDE RITE CORPORATION, 191 Spring St, **Lexington,** MA 02421-8045, *pg.* 1820, *pg.* 828
TEXON MATERIALS INC., 1190 Huntington Rd, **Russell,** MA 01071, *pg.* 1820, *pg.* 843

Michigan

WOLVERINE WORLD WIDE, INC., 9341 Courtland Dr NE, **Rockford,** MI 49351-0001, *pg.* 1822, *pg.* 905

Minnesota

RED WING SHOE COMPANY, INC., 314 Main St, **Red Wing,** MN 55066-2300, *pg.* 1817, *pg.* 954

Missouri

CALERES, INC., 8300 Maryland Ave, **Saint Louis,** MO 63105-3645, *pg.* 1805, *pg.* 993
FAMOUS FOOTWEAR, 8300 Maryland Ave, **Saint Louis,** MO 63105, *pg.* 1808, *pg.* 997

New Hampshire

COLE-HAAN LLC, 150 Ocean Rd, **Greenland,** NH 03840, *pg.* 1806, *pg.* 1034
THE TIMBERLAND COMPANY, 200 Domain Dr, **Stratham,** NH 03885-2575, *pg.* 1821, *pg.* 1039

New Jersey

AEROGROUP INTERNATIONAL, INC., 201 Meadow Rd, **Edison,** NJ 08817-6002, *pg.* 1803, *pg.* 1055
CAPEZIO BALLET MAKERS INC., 1 Campus Rd, **Totowa,** NJ 07512, *pg.* 1805, *pg.* 1125
STANBEE COMPANY, INC., 70 Broad St, **Carlstadt,** NJ 07072-2006, *pg.* 1819, *pg.* 1050

New York

BALLY NORTH AMERICA, INC., 689 5th Ave 4th Fl, **New York,** NY 10022, *pg.* 1804, *pg.* 1200
DEER STAGS INC., 1414 Ave of the Americas, **New York,** NY 10019-2514, *pg.* 1807, *pg.* 1222
FOOT LOCKER, INC., 112 W 34th St, **New York,** NY 10120-0101, *pg.* 1808, *pg.* 1231
G.H. BASS & CO., 200 Madison Ave, **New York,** NY 10016, *pg.* 1809, *pg.* 1234
HUNTER BOOT USA, 140 W 57th St Ste 7B, **New York,** NY 10019, *pg.* 1810, *pg.* 1242
JACK SCHWARTZ SHOES, INC., 155 Ave Of The Americas 9th Fl, **New York,** NY 10013, *pg.* 1810, *pg.* 1245
JIMLAR CORPORATION, 350 5th Ave, Lbby 8, **New York,** NY 10118, *pg.* 1810, *pg.* 1246
KENNETH COLE PRODUCTIONS, INC., 603 W 50th St, **New York,** NY 10019, *pg.* 1810, *pg.* 1248
MAURICE J. MARKELL SHOE CO., INC., PO Box 246, **Yonkers,** NY 10702-0246, *pg.* 1811, *pg.* 1356
NINE WEST HOLDINGS, INC., 1411 Broadway, **New York,** NY 10018, *pg.* 1815, *pg.* 1272
P.W. MINOR & SON, INC., 3 Treadeasy Ave, **Batavia,** NY 14020-3009, *pg.* 1816, *pg.* 1140
SCHWARTZ & BENJAMIN, INC., 20 W 57th St 4th Fl, **New York,** NY 10019, *pg.* 1818, *pg.* 1290
STEVEN MADDEN, LTD., 52-16 Barnett Ave, **Long Island City,** NY 11104, *pg.* 1819, *pg.* 1176

North Carolina

WELLCO ENTERPRISES, INC., 150 Westwood Cir, **Waynesville,** NC 28786-1987, *pg.* 1822, *pg.* 1392

Ohio

DSW, INC., 810 DSW Dr, **Columbus,** OH 43219-1802, *pg.* 1807, *pg.* 1439
R.G. BARRY CORPORATION, 13405 Yarmouth Rd NW, **Pickerington,** OH 43147-8493, *pg.* 1818, *pg.* 1470
ROCKY BRANDS, INC., 39 E Canal St, **Nelsonville,** OH 45764, *pg.* 1818, *pg.* 1466

Oregon

ADIDAS AMERICA INC., 5055 N Greeley Ave, **Portland,** OR 97217, *pg.* 1803, *pg.* 1500
DR. MARTENS AIRWAIR USA LLC, 10 NW 10th Ave, **Portland,** OR 97209, *pg.* 1807, *pg.* 1502
LACROSSE FOOTWEAR, INC., 17634 NE Airport Way, **Portland,** OR 97230, *pg.* 1811, *pg.* 1503
NIKE, INC., 1 Bowerman Dr, **Beaverton,** OR 97005-6453, *pg.* 1812, *pg.* 1492

Pennsylvania

DANSKO INC., 33 Federal Rd, **West Grove,** PA 19390, *pg.* 1807, *pg.* 1594

Tennessee

GENESCO INC., Genesco Park 1415 Murfreesboro Rd, **Nashville,** TN 37217-2895, *pg.* 1809, *pg.* 1650
JOHNSTON & MURPHY CO., 1415 Murfreesboro Pike, **Nashville,** TN 37201, *pg.* 1810, *pg.* 1651

Texas

EL CHARRO LLC, 2509 Wyoming St, **El Paso,** TX 79903, *pg.* 1808, *pg.* 1691
HEELYS, INC., 3200 Belmeade Dr Ste 100, **Carrollton,** TX 75006, *pg.* 1809, *pg.* 1669
JUSTIN BRANDS, INC., 610 W Daggett Ave, **Fort Worth,** TX 76104-1103, *pg.* 1810, *pg.* 1695

Washington

BROOKS SPORTS INC., 19910 N Creek Pkwy Ste 200, **Bothell,** WA 98011-8223, *pg.* 1805, *pg.* 1818

Wisconsin

ALLEN-EDMONDS SHOE CORP., 201 E Seven Hills Rd, **Port Washington,** WI 53074-2504, *pg.* 1804, *pg.* 1887
MASON COMPANIES, INC., 1251 1st Ave, **Chippewa Falls,** WI 54729-1408, *pg.* 1811, *pg.* 1856
WEINBRENNER SHOE COMPANY, INC., 108 S Polk St, **Merrill,** WI 54452-2348, *pg.* 1822, *pg.* 1871
WEYCO GROUP, INC., 333 W Estabrook Blvd, **Glendale,** WI 53212-1067, *pg.* 1822, *pg.* 1858

Wyoming

SIERRA TRADING POST INC., 5025 Campstool Rd, **Cheyenne,** WY 82007, *pg.* 1819, *pg.* 1901

Sporting Goods

Alabama

BEAR & SON CUTLERY, INC., 1111 Bear Blvd SW, **Jacksonville,** AL 36265, *pg.* 1827, *pg.* 7
HIBBETT SPORTS, INC., 451 Industrial Ln, **Birmingham,** AL 35211-4464, *pg.* 1836, *pg.* 3

Arizona

KARSTEN MANUFACTURING CORPORATION, 2201 W Desert Cove Ave, **Phoenix,** AZ 85029, *pg.* 1838, *pg.* 17
LESLIE'S POOLMART, INC., 3925 E Broadway Rd, **Phoenix,** AZ 85040, *pg.* 1838, *pg.* 17
PING INC., 2201 W Desert Cove Ave, **Phoenix,** AZ 85029-4912, *pg.* 1842, *pg.* 19
SUPERCOACH, LLC, 1535 W Parkside Ln, **Scottsdale,** AZ 85027-1361, *pg.* 1847, *pg.* 24

Arkansas

DAISY MANUFACTURING COMPANY, 400 W Stribling Dr, **Rogers,** AR 72756-2411, *pg.* 1831, *pg.* 35

California

ALDILA, INC., 14145 Danielson St Ste B, **Poway,** CA 92064, *pg.* 1825, *pg.* 185
ASICS AMERICA CORPORATION, 80 Technology Dr, **Irvine,** CA 92618, *pg.* 1826, *pg.* 106
BALANCED BODY, INC., 8220 Ferguson Ave, **Sacramento,** CA 95828, *pg.* 1826, *pg.* 195
BIANCHI U.S.A., INC., 21325A Cabot Blvd, **Hayward,** CA 94545-1650, *pg.* 1827, *pg.* 100
BIG 5 SPORTING GOODS CORPORATION, 2525 E El Segundo Blvd, **El Segundo,** CA 90245, *pg.* 1827, *pg.* 78
CALLAWAY GOLF COMPANY, 2180 Rutherford Rd, **Carlsbad,** CA 92008-7328, *pg.* 1829, *pg.* 58
CONTINENTAL MARKETING, 15381 E Proctor Ave, **City of Industry,** CA 91745, *pg.* 1831, *pg.* 66
DAIWA CORPORATION, 11137 Warland Dr, **Cypress,** CA 90630-5034, *pg.* 1832, *pg.* 75
EASTON SPORTS, INC., 7855 Haskell Ave Ste 200, **Van Nuys,** CA 91406-1907, *pg.* 1833, *pg.* 299
EASYTURF, 2750 La Mirada Dr, **Vista,** CA 92081, *pg.* 1833, *pg.* 302
JANDD MOUNTAINEERING, INC., 2365 Marconi Ct Ste F, **San Diego,** CA 92154-7265, *pg.* 1837, *pg.* 204
JANSPORT, 2601 Harbor Bay Parkway, **Alameda,** CA 94502, *pg.* 1837, *pg.* 38
K-SWISS, 31248 Oak Crest Dr, **Westlake Village,** CA 91361, *pg.* 1837, *pg.* 306
MOUNTAIN HARDWEAR, INC., 1414 Harbour Way S Ford Point Ste 1005, **Richmond,** CA 94804, *pg.* 1839, *pg.* 193
THE NORTH FACE, INC., 14450 Doolittle Dr, **San Leandro,** CA 94577, *pg.* 1840, *pg.* 252
OAKLEY, INC., 1 Icon, **Foothill Ranch,** CA 92610-3000, *pg.* 1840, *pg.* 86
O'NEILL INC., 1071 41st Ave, **Santa Cruz,** CA 95062-4400, *pg.* 1842, *pg.* 270
PARAMOUNT FITNESS CORP., 6450 E Bandini Blvd, **Los Angeles,** CA 90040-3118, *pg.* 1842, *pg.* 138
PELICAN PRODUCTS, INC., 23215 Early Ave, **Torrance,** CA 90505, *pg.* 1842, *pg.* 295
ROGER CLEVELAND GOLF COMPANY, INC., 5601 Skylab Rd, **Huntington Beach,** CA 92647, *pg.* 1844, *pg.* 105
SHIMANO AMERICAN CORPORATION, 1 Holland Dr, **Irvine,** CA 92618-2506, *pg.* 1845, *pg.* 116
SPORT CHALET, INC., 1 Sports Chalet Dr, **La Canada,** CA 91011-3338, *pg.* 1846, *pg.* 119
TAYLORMADE-ADIDAS GOLF, 5545 Fermi Ct, **Carlsbad,** CA 92008-7324, *pg.* 1847, *pg.* 60
VOLCOM, INC., 1740 Monrovia Ave, **Costa Mesa,** CA 92627, *pg.* 1847, *pg.* 71
WEATHERBY, INC., 1605 Commerce Way, **Paso Robles,** CA 93446, *pg.* 1848, *pg.* 181

Colorado

EXXEL OUTDOORS LLC, 6235 Lookout Rd Ste B, **Boulder,** CO 80301, *pg.* 1833, *pg.* 311
SPORT OBERMEYER LTD., 115 ABC, **Aspen,** CO 81611, *pg.* 1846, *pg.* 310
THE SPORTS AUTHORITY, INC., 1050 W Hampden Ave, **Englewood,** CO 80110, *pg.* 1846, *pg.* 326
WRIGHT & MCGILL CO., 4245 E 46th Ave, **Denver,** CO 80216, *pg.* 1848, *pg.* 324

Connecticut

LYMAN PRODUCTS CORPORATION, 475 Smith St, **Middletown,** CT 06457, *pg.* 1839, *pg.* 356
O.F. MOSSBERG & SONS, INC., 7 Grasso Ave, **North Haven,** CT 06473-3237, *pg.* 1842, *pg.* 360
STURM, RUGER & COMPANY, INC., 1 Lacey Pl, **Southport,** CT 06890, *pg.* 1846, *pg.* 371
THE WIFFLE BALL INC., 275 Bridgeport Ave, **Shelton,** CT 06484, *pg.* 1848, *pg.* 371

Florida

FEEL GOLF CO., INC., 510 Central Park Dr, **Sanford,** FL 32771, *pg.* 1834, *pg.* 465
RON JON SURF SHOP OF FLORIDA INC., 3850 S Banana River Blvd, **Cocoa Beach,** FL 32931-3481, *pg.* 1844, *pg.* 417
TARPON TOTAL FITNESS, 1888 Alt 19 S, **Tarpon Springs,** FL 34689, *pg.* 1847, *pg.* 477

Georgia

BRIDGESTONE GOLF, INC., 14230 Lochridge Blvd Ste G, **Covington,** GA 30014-4953, *pg.* 1828, *pg.* 528
CLUB CAR, INC., 4125 Washington Rd, **Evans,** GA 30809-3067, *pg.* 1830, *pg.* 532
L.A. T SPORTSWEAR, LLC, 1200 Airport Dr, **Ball Ground,** GA 30107-4545, *pg.* 1838, *pg.* 526
MEGGITT TRAINING SYSTEMS, 296 Brogdon Rd, **Suwanee,** GA 30024, *pg.* 1839, *pg.* 541
MIZUNO USA, INC., 4925 Avalon Ridge Pkwy, **Norcross,** GA 30071-1571, *pg.* 1839, *pg.* 538

Idaho

BUCK KNIVES, INC., 660 S Lochsa St, **Post Falls,** ID 83854-5200, *pg.* 1828, *pg.* 550

Illinois

BRUNSWICK BOWLING & BILLIARDS CORP., 1 N Field Ct, **Lake Forest,** IL 60045-4811, *pg.* 1828, *pg.* 622
BRUNSWICK CORPORATION, 1 N Field Ct, **Lake Forest,** IL 60045-4811, *pg.* 1828, *pg.* 623
GILL ATHLETICS, INC., 2808 Gemini Ct, **Champaign,** IL 61822, *pg.* 1835, *pg.* 562
HILLERICH & BRADSBY CO., INC., 8750 W Bryn Mawr Ave, **Chicago,** IL 60631, *pg.* 1836, *pg.* 576
WILSON SPORTING GOODS CO., 8750 W Bryn Mawr Ave, **Chicago,** IL 60631, *pg.* 1848, *pg.* 596

Indiana

ANCHOR INDUSTRIES, INC., 7701 Hwy 41 N, **Evansville,** IN 47725-1702, *pg.* 1825, *pg.* 678
ESCALADE INC., 817 Maxwell Ave, **Evansville,** IN 47711, *pg.* 1833, *pg.* 678

Kansas

THE COLEMAN COMPANY, INC., 3600 N Hydraulic St, **Wichita,** KS 67219-3812, *pg.* 1830, *pg.* 723

Kentucky

CAMPING WORLD, INC., 650 3 Springs Rd, **Bowling Green,** KY 42104-7520, *pg.* 1830, *pg.* 725

Louisiana

POOL CORPORATION, 109 Northpark Blvd, **Covington,** LA 70433-5005, *pg.* 1843, *pg.* 743

Maryland

180S, LLC, 700 S Caroline St, **Baltimore,** MD 21231, *pg.* 1824, *pg.* 754
BENELLI USA CORPORATION, 17603 Indian Head Hwy Ste 200, **Accokeek,** MD 20607, *pg.* 1827, *pg.* 754

Massachusetts

ACUSHNET COMPANY, 333 Bridge St, **Fairhaven,** MA 02719-4905, *pg.* 1824, *pg.* 818
AMPAC ENTERPRISES, INC., PO Box 1356, **Shirley,** MA 01464-1356, *pg.* 1825, *pg.* 843
CALLAWAY GOLF BALL OPERATIONS, INC., 425 Meadow St, **Chicopee,** MA 01013-2201, *pg.* 1829, *pg.* 814
CITY SPORTS, 64 Industrial Way, **Wilmington,** MA 01887-3434, *pg.* 1830, *pg.* 860
CONVERSE INC., 160 North Washington St, **Boston,** MA 02114, *pg.* 1831, *pg.* 793
CREATIVE PLAYTHINGS LTD., 33 Loring Dr, **Framingham,** MA 01702, *pg.* 1831, *pg.* 820
DOVER SADDLERY, INC., 525 Great Rd PO Box 1100, **Littleton,** MA 01460, *pg.* 1833, *pg.* 829
EXERCYCLE CORPORATION, 31 Hayward St, **Franklin,** MA 02038, *pg.* 1833, *pg.* 823
FRANKLIN SPORTS, INC., 17 Campanelli Parkway, **Stoughton,** MA 02072-0508, *pg.* 1834, *pg.* 847
SMITH & WESSON HOLDING CORPORATION, 2100 Roosevelt Ave, **Springfield,** MA 01104, *pg.* 1845, *pg.* 846
SPALDING, 150 Brookdale Dr, **Springfield,** MA 01104, *pg.* 1845, *pg.* 846

Michigan

ALVIMAR GENESIS, 640 Three Mile Rd NW, **Grand Rapids,** MI 49544, *pg.* 1825, *pg.* 886
CAMERON BALLOONS U.S., 7399 Newman Blvd, **Dexter,** MI 48130, *pg.* 1829, *pg.* 884
EPPINGER MANUFACTURING CO., 6340 Schaefer Rd, **Dearborn,** MI 48126-2285, *pg.* 1833, *pg.* 876
SCHOOL-TECH, INC., 745 State Cir, **Ann Arbor,** MI 48106-1647, *pg.* 1844, *pg.* 866

Minnesota

FEDERAL PREMIUM AMMUNITION, 900 Bob Ehlen Dr, **Anoka,** MN 55303-1778, *pg.* 1834, *pg.* 915
GANDER MOUNTAIN COMPANY, 180 E 5th St Ste 1300, **Saint Paul,** MN 55101-1664, *pg.* 1834, *pg.* 960
RAPALA VMC CORPORATION, 10395 Yellow Cir Dr, **Minnetonka,** MN 55343-9101, *pg.* 1843, *pg.* 949
THE SPORTSMAN'S GUIDE, INC., 411 Farwell Ave, **South Saint Paul,** MN 55075, *pg.* 1846, *pg.* 965

Missouri

BASS PRO SHOPS, INC., 2500 E Kearney St, **Springfield,** MO 65898-0001, *pg.* 1826, *pg.* 1006
MIRACLE RECREATION EQUIPMENT COMPANY, 878 E Hwy 60, **Monett,** MO 65708, *pg.* 1839, *pg.* 988
RAWLINGS SPORTING GOODS CO., INC., 510 Maryville University Dr Ste 110, **Saint Louis,** MO 63141, *pg.* 1843, *pg.* 1002

Montana

SIMMS FISHING PRODUCTS CORP., 101 Evergreen Dr, **Bozeman,** MT 59715-2400, *pg.* 1845, *pg.* 1008

Nebraska

HORNADY MANUFACTURING COMPANY, 3625 Old Potash Hwy, **Grand Island,** NE 68803, *pg.* 1836, *pg.* 1010

New Hampshire

PFIP, LLC, 26 Fox Run Rd, **Newington,** NH 03801, *pg.* 1842, *pg.* 1037

New Jersey

First page reference indicates Business Class Edition
Second page reference indicates Geographic Edition

HENRY BONA POOLS & SPAS, 878 Rte 46, **Kenvil,** NJ 07847-2632, *pg.* 1836, *pg.* 1078
IMPERIAL INTERNATIONAL, 303 Paterson Plank Rd E, **Carlstadt,** NJ 07072, *pg.* 1837, *pg.* 1050

New York

ANC SPORTS ENTERPRISES, LLC, 2 Manhattanville Rd Ste 402, **Purchase,** NY 10577, *pg.* 1825, *pg.* 1325
BLATT BOWLING & BILLIARD CORP., 809 Broadway, **New York,** NY 10003, *pg.* 1827, *pg.* 1203
BOWLMOR AMF, 222 W 44th St, **New York,** NY 10036, *pg.* 1828, *pg.* 1206
CORTLAND LINE COMPANY, 3736 Kellogg Rd, **Cortland,** NY 13045-8818, *pg.* 1831, *pg.* 1155
EVERLAST WORLDWIDE INC., 183 Madison Ave Ste 1701, **New York,** NY 10016, *pg.* 1833, *pg.* 1230
HENRY MODELL & COMPANY, INC., 498 7th Ave 20th Fl, **New York,** NY 10018-6738, *pg.* 1836, *pg.* 1240
LOOP-LOC LTD., 390 Motor Pkwy, **Hauppauge,** NY 11788, *pg.* 1838, *pg.* 1165
NEW ERA CAP COMPANY INC., 8061 Erie Rd, **Derby,** NY 14047, *pg.* 1840, *pg.* 1155
SEA EAGLE BOATS, 19 N Columbia St, **Port Jefferson Station,** NY 11777-2165, *pg.* 1845, *pg.* 1322
SOULCYCLE HOLDINGS LLC, 609 Greenwich St, **New York,** NY 10014, *pg.* 1845, *pg.* 1294

North Carolina

DIAMOND BRAND CANVAS PRODUCTS CO., INC., 145 Cane Creek Industrial Pk Rd Ste 1, **Fletcher,** NC 28732, *pg.* 1832, *pg.* 1372
ECHO FARMS GOLF & COUNTRY CLUB, INC., 4114 Echo Farms Blvd, **Wilmington,** NC 28412, *pg.* 1833, *pg.* 1392
FREEDOM GROUP, INC., 870 Remington Dr, **Madison,** NC 27025-1776, *pg.* 1834, *pg.* 1382
REMINGTON ARMS COMPANY, LLC, 870 Remington Dr, **Madison,** NC 27025-0700, *pg.* 1844, *pg.* 1382

Ohio

ANTHONY & SYLVAN POOLS CORPORATION, 6690 Beta Dr Ste 300, **Cleveland,** OH 44143-2359, *pg.* 1826, *pg.* 1428
HUFFY CORPORATION, 6551 Centerville Business Pkwy, **Centerville,** OH 45459, *pg.* 1836, *pg.* 1409
OHIO AWNING & MANUFACTURING CO., 5777 Grant Ave, **Cleveland,** OH 44105, *pg.* 1842, *pg.* 1433

Oklahoma

ZEBCO, 6101 E Apache St, **Tulsa,** OK 74115-3370, *pg.* 1848, *pg.* 1491

Oregon

COLUMBIA SPORTSWEAR COMPANY, 14375 NW Science Park Dr, **Portland,** OR 97229-5418, *pg.* 1830, *pg.* 1501
GERBER LEGENDARY BLADES, 14200 SW 72nd Ave, **Portland,** OR 97224, *pg.* 1834, *pg.* 1503
SOLOFLEX, INC., 22590 NW Badertscher Rd, **Hillsboro,** OR 97124, *pg.* 1845, *pg.* 1498

Pennsylvania

AMERICAN SPORTS LICENSING, INC., 345 Court St, **Coraopolis,** PA 15108, *pg.* 1825, *pg.* 1524
BRODER BROS., CO., 6 Neshaminy Interplex Dr 6th Fl, **Trevose,** PA 19053, *pg.* 1828, *pg.* 1588
DICK'S SPORTING GOODS, INC., 345 Court St, **Coraopolis,** PA 15108, *pg.* 1832, *pg.* 1524
ENDLESS POOLS, INC., 1601 Dutton Mill Rd, **Aston,** PA 19014, *pg.* 1833, *pg.* 1515
GOLF GALAXY, INC., 345 Crt St, **Coraopolis,** PA 15108, *pg.* 1835, *pg.* 1525
INNOVATIVE DESIGNS, INC., 223 N Main St Ste 1, **Pittsburgh,** PA 15215, *pg.* 1837, *pg.* 1576

Rhode Island

ASHAWAY LINE & TWINE MFG. CO., 24 Laurel St, **Ashaway,** RI 02804-1515, *pg.* 1826, *pg.* 1600

South Carolina

PURE FISHING, INC., 7 Science Ct, **Columbia,** SC 29203, *pg.* 1843, *pg.* 1614

Tennessee

OLHAUSEN BILLIARD MFG, INC., 1124 Vaughn Pkwy, **Portland,** TN 37148, *pg.* 1842, *pg.* 1655
TRUE TEMPER SPORTS, INC., 8275 Tournament Dr Ste 200, **Memphis,** TN 38125-8871, *pg.* 1847, *pg.* 1647
VARSITY BRANDS, INC., 6745 Lenox Ctr Ct Ste 300, **Memphis,** TN 38115, *pg.* 1847, *pg.* 1647

Texas

ACADEMY SPORTS & OUTDOORS, LTD., 565 S Mason Rd #419, **Katy,** TX 77450, *pg.* 1824, *pg.* 1724
ALLIANCE SPORTS GROUP, L.P., 3025 N Great Southwest Pkwy, **Grand Prairie,** TX 75050-1407, *pg.* 1825, *pg.* 1698
BURNHAM BROTHERS, INC., PO Box 427, **Menard,** TX 76859, *pg.* 1829, *pg.* 1727
GOLFSMITH INTERNATIONAL HOLDINGS, INC., 11000 N Hwy 35, **Austin,** TX 78753-3195, *pg.* 1835, *pg.* 1662
SPORT SUPPLY GROUP, INC., 1901 Diplomat Dr, **Dallas,** TX 75234-8914, *pg.* 1846, *pg.* 1687

Utah

BLACK DIAMOND, INC., 2084 E 3900 S, **Salt Lake City,** UT 84124, *pg.* 1827, *pg.* 1756
BROWNING, One Browning Pl, **Morgan,** UT 84050, *pg.* 1828, *pg.* 1752
HUGGER MUGGER YOGA PRODUCTS LLC, 1190 South Pioneer Rd, **Salt Lake City,** UT 84104, *pg.* 1836, *pg.* 1758
ICON HEALTH & FITNESS, INC., 1500 S 1000 W, **Logan,** UT 84321-8206, *pg.* 1837, *pg.* 1752
REVOLUTION MFG., 1185 N 1200 W, **Orem,** UT 84057-2841, *pg.* 1844, *pg.* 1753
SALOMON NORTH AMERICA, INC., 2030 Lincoln Ave, **Ogden,** UT 84401, *pg.* 1844, *pg.* 1753
SPORT COURT INTERNATIONAL INC., 939 South 700 West, **Salt Lake City,** UT 84104, *pg.* 1846, *pg.* 1761

Vermont

BURTON SNOWBOARD COMPANY, 80 Industrial Pkwy, **Burlington,** VT 05401-5434, *pg.* 1829, *pg.* 1765
KOMBI, LTD., 6 Thompson Dr, **Essex Junction,** VT 05452-3405, *pg.* 1838, *pg.* 1766

Virginia

DATREK GOLF, 2701 Emerywood Pkwy Ste 101, **Richmond,** VA 23294, *pg.* 1832, *pg.* 1801
FITNESS RESOURCE, INC., 22714 Glenn Dr Ste 130, **Sterling,** VA 20164, *pg.* 1834, *pg.* 1807
QUBICAAMF, 8100 AMF Dr, **Mechanicsville,** VA 23111, *pg.* 1843, *pg.* 1795

Washington

CEDARBROOK SAUNA & STEAM, PO Box 535, **Cashmere,** WA 98815, *pg.* 1830, *pg.* 1819
MCNETT CORPORATION, 1411 Meador Ave, **Bellingham,** WA 98229, *pg.* 1839, *pg.* 1817
NAUTILUS, INC., 17750 SE 6th Way, **Vancouver,** WA 98683-5535, *pg.* 1840, *pg.* 1846
PRECOR, INC., 20031 142nd Ave NE, **Woodinville,** WA 98072-4002, *pg.* 1843, *pg.* 1847
RECREATIONAL EQUIPMENT, INC., 6750 S 228th St, **Kent,** WA 98032, *pg.* 1843, *pg.* 1821

Wisconsin

CARRON NET COMPANY, INC., 1623 17th St, **Two Rivers,** WI 54241-2916, *pg.* 1830, *pg.* 1896
GLD PRODUCTS, INC., S84 W 19093 Enterprise Dr, **Muskego,** WI 53150, *pg.* 1835, *pg.* 1882
GOLF GIFTS & GALLERY, N 1675 Powers Lk Rd, **Powers Lake,** WI 53159, *pg.* 1835, *pg.* 1887
JOHNSON OUTDOORS INC., 555 Main St, **Racine,** WI 53403, *pg.* 1837, *pg.* 1888
TREK BICYCLE CORPORATION, 801 W Madison St, **Waterloo,** WI 53594-1379, *pg.* 1847, *pg.* 1896
THE WORTH COMPANY, 214 Sherman Ave, **Stevens Point,** WI 54481-5847, *pg.* 1848, *pg.* 1895

Sweets

Alabama

GOLDEN ENTERPRISES INC., 1 Golden Flake Dr, **Birmingham,** AL 35201, *pg.* 1854, *pg.* 2
GOLDEN FLAKE SNACK FOODS, INC., 1 Golden Flake Dr, **Birmingham,** AL 35205, *pg.* 1854, *pg.* 3

California

ANNABELLE CANDY COMPANY, INC., 27211 Industrial Blvd, **Hayward,** CA 94545-3347, *pg.* 1850, *pg.* 100
DIAMOND FOODS, INC., 600 Montgomery St 13th Fl, **San Francisco,** CA 94111, *pg.* 1851, *pg.* 216
DREYER'S GRAND ICE CREAM HOLDINGS, INC., 5929 College Ave, **Oakland,** CA 94618, *pg.* 1852, *pg.* 171
GHIRARDELLI CHOCOLATE COMPANY, 1111 139th Ave, **San Leandro,** CA 94578-2631, *pg.* 1854, *pg.* 252
GUITTARD CHOCOLATE COMPANY, 10 Guittard Rd, **Burlingame,** CA 94010-2203, *pg.* 1855, *pg.* 55
JELLY BELLY CANDY COMPANY, 1 Jelly Belly Ln, **Fairfield,** CA 94533, *pg.* 1857, *pg.* 86

Connecticut

PEZ CANDY, INC., 35 Prindle Hill Rd, **Orange,** CT 06477-3616, *pg.* 1861, *pg.* 367

Georgia

BENSON'S, INC., 134 Elder St, **Bogart,** GA 30622-1500, *pg.* 1850, *pg.* 526
GOLDEN PEANUT COMPANY, L.L.C., 100 N Point Ctr E Ste 400, **Alpharetta,** GA 30022-8262, *pg.* 1854, *pg.* 484

Illinois

BALDWIN RICHARDSON FOODS COMPANY, 20201 S LaGrange Rd Ste 200, **Frankfort,** IL 60423, *pg.* 1850, *pg.* 612
BEER NUTS, INC., 103 N Robinson St, **Bloomington,** IL 61701-5424, *pg.* 1850, *pg.* 557
BLOMMER CHOCOLATE COMPANY, 600 W Kinzie St, **Chicago,** IL 60654, *pg.* 1851, *pg.* 566
ELI'S CHEESECAKE COMPANY, 6701 W Forest Preserve Dr, **Chicago,** IL 60634, *pg.* 1852, *pg.* 572
FERRARA CANDY CO., 7301 W Harrison St, **Forest Park,** IL 60130-2016, *pg.* 1852, *pg.* 612
THE NUTRASWEET COMPANY, 222 Merchandise Mart Plz Ste 936, **Chicago,** IL 60654-1001, *pg.* 1860, *pg.* 585
THE POPCORN FACTORY, 13970 W Laurel Dr, **Lake Forest,** IL 60045-4533, *pg.* 1861, *pg.* 625
PURECIRCLE USA INC., 915 Harger Rd Ste 250, **Oak Brook,** IL 60523, *pg.* 1861, *pg.* 648
SOKOL & COMPANY, 5315 Dansher Rd, **Countryside,** IL 60525-3101, *pg.* 1862, *pg.* 598
STORCK USA, L.P., 325 N LaSalle Ste 400, **Chicago,** IL 60654, *pg.* 1862, *pg.* 591
TOOTSIE ROLL INDUSTRIES, INC., 7401 S Cicero Ave, **Chicago,** IL 60629-5818, *pg.* 1863, *pg.* 591
WM. WRIGLEY JR. COMPANY, 410 N Michigan Ave Wrigley Bldg, **Chicago,** IL 60611, *pg.* 1863, *pg.* 596
WORLD'S FINEST CHOCOLATE, INC., 4801 S Lawndale Ave, **Chicago,** IL 60632-3065, *pg.* 1864, *pg.* 597

Indiana

AMERICAN LICORICE CO. INC., 1900 Whirlpool Dr S, **La Porte,** IN 94587, *pg.* 1850, *pg.* 692

Kentucky

PERFETTI VAN MELLE USA, INC., 3645 Turfway Rd, **Erlanger,** KY 41018, *pg.* 1860, *pg.* 727

Louisiana

ZAPP'S POTATO CHIPS, INC., 307 E Airline Hwy, **Gramercy,** LA 70052, *pg.* 1864, *pg.* 743

Massachusetts

F.B. WASHBURN CANDY CORP., 137 Perkins Ave, **Brockton,** MA 02302-3850, *pg.* 1852, *pg.* 803
FRIENDLY ICE CREAM, LLC, 1855 Boston Rd, **Wilbraham,** MA 01095-1002, *pg.* 1853, *pg.* 859
NEW ENGLAND CONFECTIONERY COMPANY INC., 135 American Legion Hwy, **Revere,** MA 02151, *pg.* 1860, *pg.* 842

Minnesota

BARREL O'FUN SNACK FOODS CO., 800 4th St NW, **Perham,** MN 56573-1226, *pg.* 1850, *pg.* 952

Missouri

HAMMONS PRODUCTS COMPANY, 105 Hammons Dr, **Stockton,** MO 65785, *pg.* 1855, *pg.* 1007
HOSTESS BRANDS LLC, PO Box 419593, **Kansas City,** MO 64141, *pg.* 1856, *pg.* 984
RUSSELL STOVER CANDIES, INC., 4900 Oak St, **Kansas City,** MO 64112-2702, *pg.* 1861, *pg.* 986
WHITMAN'S CANDIES, INC., 4900 Oak St, **Kansas City,** MO 64112-2702, *pg.* 1863, *pg.* 987

New Hampshire

LINDT & SPRUNGLI (USA) INC., 1 Fine Chocolate Pl, **Stratham,** NH 03885, *pg.* 1857, *pg.* 1039

New Jersey

CIAO BELLA GELATO COMPANY, 25A Vreeland Rd Ste 104, **Florham Park,** NJ 07932, *pg.* 1851, *pg.* 1066
FERRERO U.S.A., INC., 600 Cottontail Ln, **Somerset,** NJ 08873, *pg.* 1852, *pg.* 1121
MAFCO WORLDWIDE CORPORATION, 3rd St & Jefferson Ave, **Camden,** NJ 08104, *pg.* 1858, *pg.* 1049
MARS NORTH AMERICA, 800 High St, **Hackettstown,** NJ 07840-1552, *pg.* 1859, *pg.* 1072
PROMOTION IN MOTION, INC., 25 Commerce Dr, P.O. Box 8, **Closter,** NJ 07401, *pg.* 1861, *pg.* 1052
SMARTIES CANDY COMPANY, 1091 Lousons Rd, **Union,** NJ 07083, *pg.* 1861, *pg.* 1127

New York

FIELDBROOK FOODS INC., 1 Ice Cream Dr, **Dunkirk,** NY 14048-6318, *pg.* 1852, *pg.* 1156
GODIVA CHOCOLATIER, INC., 333 W 34th St 6th Fl, **New York,** NY 10001, *pg.* 1854, *pg.* 1235
JOYVA CORPORATION, 53 Varick Ave, **Brooklyn,** NY 11237, *pg.* 1857, *pg.* 1146
PERRY'S ICE CREAM CO., INC., 1 Ice Cream Plz, **Akron,** NY 14001-1036, *pg.* 1861, *pg.* 1137

North Carolina

BESTSWEET INC., 288 Mazeppa Rd, **Mooresville,** NC 28115, *pg.* 1851, *pg.* 1383

Ohio

GRAETER'S, INC., 1175 Regina Graeter Way, **Cincinnati,** OH 45216, *pg.* 1854, *pg.* 1414
KANAN ENTERPRISES, INC., 31900 Solon Rd, **Solon,** OH 44139, *pg.* 1857, *pg.* 1473
MIKE-SELL'S POTATO CHIP COMPANY, 333 Leo St, **Dayton,** OH 45404-1007, *pg.* 1860, *pg.* 1446
SPANGLER CANDY COMPANY, 400 N Portland St, **Bryan,** OH 43506-1200, *pg.* 1862, *pg.* 1407

Pennsylvania

BOYER CANDY COMPANY INC., 821 17th St, **Altoona,** PA 16601-2074, *pg.* 1851, *pg.* 1514
THE HERSHEY CO., 100 Crystal A Dr, **Hershey,** PA 17033-9529, *pg.* 1855, *pg.* 1538
JUST BORN, INC., 1300 Stefko Blvd, **Bethlehem,** PA 18017-6620, *pg.* 1857, *pg.* 1516
R.M. PALMER COMPANY, 77 S Second Ave, **Reading,** PA 19611, *pg.* 1861, *pg.* 1585
SNYDER'S OF HANOVER, INC., 1250 York St, **Hanover,** PA 17331, *pg.* 1862, *pg.* 1536
SORBEE INTERNATIONAL, LLC, 9990 Global Rd, **Philadelphia,** PA 19115, *pg.* 1862, *pg.* 1570
TASTY BAKING COMPANY, Navy Yard Corporate Ctr 3 Crescent Dr Ste 200, **Philadelphia,** PA 19112, *pg.* 1862, *pg.* 1571

South Carolina

YOUNG PECAN, INC., 1831 W Evans St, Ste 200, **Florence,** SC 29501, *pg.* 1864, *pg.* 1615

Tennessee

MCKEE FOODS CORPORATION, 10260 McKee Rd, **Collegedale,** TN 37315, *pg.* 1860, *pg.* 1630
STANDARD FUNCTIONAL FOODS GROUP(SFFG), 715 Massman Dr, **Nashville,** TN 37210-3723, *pg.* 1862, *pg.* 1654

Texas

BLUE BELL CREAMERIES, L.P., 1101 S Blue Bell Rd, **Brenham,** TX 77833, *pg.* 1851, *pg.* 1668
COLLIN STREET BAKERY, 401 W 7th Ave, **Corsicana,** TX 75110-6362, *pg.* 1851, *pg.* 1672
FRITO-LAY NORTH AMERICA, INC., 7701 Legacy Dr, **Plano,** TX 75024-4002, *pg.* 1853, *pg.* 1730
MRS. BAIRD'S BAKERIES, INC., 7301 S Fwy, **Fort Worth,** TX 76134-4004, *pg.* 1860, *pg.* 1695

Utah

COOKIE TREE BAKERIES, 4122 South 500 West, **Salt Lake City,** UT 84123, *pg.* 1851, *pg.* 1756
MILLER'S HONEY COMPANY, 3000 South W Temple, **Salt Lake City,** UT 84165, *pg.* 1860, *pg.* 1759
SWEET CANDY COMPANY, 3780 W Directors Row 1100 S, **Salt Lake City,** UT 84104-5502, *pg.* 1862, *pg.* 1761

Vermont

BEN & JERRY'S HOMEMADE, INC., 30 Community Dr, **South Burlington,** VT 05403-6828, *pg.* 1850, *pg.* 1767

Virginia

BIRDSONG CORPORATION, 612 Madison Ave, **Suffolk,** VA 23434-4028, *pg.* 1851, *pg.* 1808
MARS, INCORPORATED, 6885 Elm St, **McLean,** VA 22101, *pg.* 1858, *pg.* 1792

Washington

BROWN & HALEY, 3500 20th St E Ste C, **Fife,** WA 98424-1700, *pg.* 1851, *pg.* 1820
LIBERTY ORCHARDS CO., INC., 117 Mission St, **Cashmere,** WA 98815, *pg.* 1857, *pg.* 1819

Telecom

Alabama

MOMENTUM TELECOM, INC., 880 Montclair Rd Ste 400, **Birmingham,** AL 35213, *pg.* 1872, *pg.* 3

Alaska

GENERAL COMMUNICATION, INC., 2550 Denali St Ste 1000, **Anchorage,** AK 99503-2751, *pg.* 1871, *pg.* 10

Arizona

MITEL NETWORKS, INC., 1146 N Alma School Rd, **Mesa,** AZ 85201, *pg.* 1872, *pg.* 13

Arkansas

ALLTEL WIRELESS COMMUNICATIONS CORPORATION, 1001 Technology Dr, **Little Rock,** AR 72223, *pg.* 1865, *pg.* 33

California

8X8, INC., 810 W Maude Ave, **Sunnyvale,** CA 94085, *pg.* 1865, *pg.* 282

AT&T, 2600 Camino Ramon, **San Ramon,** CA 94583-4328, *pg.* 1865, *pg.* 258

AT&T WEST, 525 Market St, **San Francisco,** CA 94105, *pg.* 1869, *pg.* 212

BOOST MOBILE, 8845 Irvine Center Dr Ste 200, **Irvine,** CA 92618, *pg.* 1869, *pg.* 107

CHANNELL COMMERCIAL CORP., 26040 Ynez Rd, **Temecula,** CA 92591-6033, *pg.* 1870, *pg.* 291

QUALCOMM INCORPORATED, 5775 Morehouse Dr, **San Diego,** CA 92121-1714, *pg.* 1873, *pg.* 207

Colorado

CENTURYLINK, INC, 1801 California St, **Denver,** CO 80202, *pg.* 1870, *pg.* 317

GOGO BUSINESS AIR, 11001 W 120th Ave Ste 310, **Broomfield,** CO 80021-3493, *pg.* 1871, *pg.* 312

ZAYO GROUP, LLC, 400 Centennial Pkwy, Ste 200, **Louisville,** CO 80027, *pg.* 1877, *pg.* 334

Connecticut

AT&T INC., 310 Orange St, **New Haven,** CT 06510, *pg.* 1868, *pg.* 358

FRONTIER COMMUNICATIONS CORPORATION, 401 Merritt 7, **Norwalk,** CT 06851, *pg.* 1871, *pg.* 362

Georgia

AT&T SOUTHEAST, 472 Ivy Park Ln NE, **Atlanta,** GA 30342-4554, *pg.* 1868, *pg.* 489

INTERACTIVE COMMUNICATIONS INC, 250 Williams St Ste M-100, **Atlanta,** GA 30303, *pg.* 1872, *pg.* 511

Hawaii

HAWAIIAN TELCOM COMMUNICATIONS, INC., 1177 Bishop St, **Honolulu,** HI 96813, *pg.* 1872, *pg.* 544

Illinois

T-SYSTEMS NORTH AMERICA INC., 701 Warrenville Rd Ste 100, **Lisle,** IL 60532, *pg.* 1875, *pg.* 630

TELEPHONE & DATA SYSTEMS, INC., 30 N LaSalle St Ste 4000, **Chicago,** IL 60602-2590, *pg.* 1875, *pg.* 591

UNITED STATES CELLULAR CORPORATION, 8410 W Bryn Mawr Ave Ste 700, **Chicago,** IL 60631-3463, *pg.* 1875, *pg.* 594

Kansas

SPRINT CORPORATION, 6200 Sprint Pkwy, **Overland Park,** KS 66251, *pg.* 1874, *pg.* 719

Louisiana

CENTURYLINK, INC., 100 CenturyLink Dr, **Monroe,** LA 71203, *pg.* 1870, *pg.* 746

Maryland

STARTEC GLOBAL COMMUNICATIONS CORPORATION, 7361 Calhoun Pl Ste 650, **Derwood,** MD 20855-2775, *pg.* 1874, *pg.* 768

New Jersey

AT&T COMMUNICATIONS CORP., 1 AT&T Way, **Bedminster,** NJ 07921, *pg.* 1866, *pg.* 1043

CELLCO PARTNERSHIP, 1 Verizon Way, **Basking Ridge,** NJ 07920, *pg.* 1869, *pg.* 1042

LATTICE INC., 7150 N Park Dr Ste 500, **Pennsauken,** NJ 08109, *pg.* 1872, *pg.* 1108

New York

VERIZON COMMUNICATIONS INC., 1095 Ave of the Americas, **New York,** NY 10036, *pg.* 1875, *pg.* 1309

WARWICK VALLEY TELEPHONE CO., 47 Main St, **Warwick,** NY 10990, *pg.* 1877, *pg.* 1349

North Carolina

FAIRPOINT COMMUNICATIONS, INC., 521 E Morehead St Ste 250, **Charlotte,** NC 28202, *pg.* 1871, *pg.* 1366

Ohio

THE BERRY COMPANY LLC, 3170 Kettering Blvd, **Dayton,** OH 45439-1924, *pg.* 1869, *pg.* 1445

CINCINNATI BELL INC., 221 E 4th St, **Cincinnati,** OH 45202-4137, *pg.* 1871, *pg.* 1410

Pennsylvania

ADVANCED TELECOM SERVICES, 996 Old Eagle School Rd Ste 1105, **Wayne,** PA 19087, *pg.* 1865, *pg.* 1591

CONSOLIDATED COMMUNICATIONS, INC., 4008 Gibsonia Rd, **Gibsonia,** PA 15044-9311, *pg.* 1871, *pg.* 1534

INTERDIGITAL, INC., 781 3rd Ave, **King of Prussia,** PA 19406, *pg.* 1872, *pg.* 1543

Texas

AT&T INC., 208 S Akard St, **Dallas,** TX 75202, *pg.* 1867, *pg.* 1674

GRANDE COMMUNICATIONS NETWORKS LLC, 401 Carlson Cir, **San Marcos,** TX 78666, *pg.* 1871, *pg.* 1744

METROPCS, INC., PO Box 601119, **Dallas,** TX 75360, *pg.* 1872, *pg.* 1683

Virginia

NEUSTAR, INC., 46000 Center Oak Plz, **Sterling,** VA 20166, *pg.* 1872, *pg.* 1807

SPOK, 6850 Versar Ctr Ste 420, **Springfield,** VA 22151-4148, *pg.* 1873, *pg.* 1807

Tires, Tubes, Rubber Molded Products & Plastics

Arizona

THE ZIPPERTUBING COMPANY, 7150 W Erie St, **Chandler,** AZ 85226, *pg.* 1892, *pg.* 12

California

ELKAY PLASTICS COMPANY, INC., 6000 Sheila St, **Commerce,** CA 90040, *pg.* 1882, *pg.* 68
FORMFACTOR, INC., 7005 S Front St, **Livermore,** CA 94551, *pg.* 1882, *pg.* 122
NUSIL TECHNOLOGY LLC, 1050 Cindy Ln, **Carpinteria,** CA 93013, *pg.* 1887, *pg.* 63
PROFESSIONAL PLASTICS, INC., 1810 E Valencia Dr, **Fullerton,** CA 92831-4847, *pg.* 1888, *pg.* 94
RYAN HERCO PRODUCTS CORPORATION, 3010 N San Fernando Blvd, **Burbank,** CA 91503, *pg.* 1889, *pg.* 52
TOYO TIRE (U.S.A.) CORPORATION, 5665 Plaza Dr, Fl 3, **Cypress,** CA 90630, *pg.* 1890, *pg.* 76
YOKOHAMA TIRE CORPORATION, 601 S Acacia Ave, **Fullerton,** CA 92831-5106, *pg.* 1892, *pg.* 94

Connecticut

HEXCEL CORPORATION, 2 Stamford Plz 281 Tresser Blvd, **Stamford,** CT 06901-3238, *pg.* 1884, *pg.* 375
PTA CORPORATION, 148 Christian St, **Oxford,** CT 06478, *pg.* 1888, *pg.* 368

Delaware

DELSTAR TECHNOLOGIES, INC., 601 Industrial Dr, **Middletown,** DE 19709, *pg.* 1881, *pg.* 387

Florida

JARDEN CORPORATION, 1800 N Military Trl, **Boca Raton,** FL 33431, *pg.* 1885, *pg.* 412
NATIONAL MOLDING, LLC, 14427 Northwest 60th Ave, **Hialeah,** FL 33014, *pg.* 1887, *pg.* 430
TBC CORPORATION, 4300 TBC Way, **Palm Beach Gardens,** FL 33410, *pg.* 1889, *pg.* 457
TERVIS TUMBLER COMPANY, 201 Triple Diamond Blvd N, **Venice,** FL 34285, *pg.* 1890, *pg.* 477

Georgia

KAUFFMAN TIRE INC., 2832 Anivelle Block Rd, **Ellenwood,** GA 30294-6009, *pg.* 1885, *pg.* 532
PIRELLI TIRE NORTH AMERICA, 100 Pirelli Dr, **Rome,** GA 30161, *pg.* 1887, *pg.* 539
TEXTILE RUBBER & CHEMICAL COMPANY, 1300 Tiarco Dr, **Dalton,** GA 30721-1907, *pg.* 1890, *pg.* 530
VYSTAR CORPORATION, 3235 Satellite Blvd Bldg 400 Ste 290, **Duluth,** GA 30096, *pg.* 1891, *pg.* 532

Illinois

ALESSCO INC., 2525 N Elston Ave, **Chicago,** IL 60647, *pg.* 1878, *pg.* 563
CAPSONIC GROUP LLC, 460 2nd St, **Elgin,** IL 60123-7008, *pg.* 1880, *pg.* 609
CTI INDUSTRIES CORPORATION, 22160 N Pepper Rd, **Barrington,** IL 60010, *pg.* 1881, *pg.* 555
HONEYWELL SALISBURY ELECTRICAL SAFETY, 101 E Crossroads Pkwy Ste A, **Bolingbrook,** IL 60440, *pg.* 1884, *pg.* 558
MAPA PROFESSIONAL, 3901 Liberty St, **Aurora,** IL 60504, *pg.* 1885, *pg.* 555
MHI INJECTION MOLDING MACHINERY, INC., 1051 W Ardmore, **Itasca,** IL 60143, *pg.* 1886, *pg.* 620
PLANO MOLDING COMPANY, 431 E S St, **Plano,** IL 60545-1676, *pg.* 1887, *pg.* 652
SAFE-HIT CORPORATION, 70 W Madison St, Ste 2350, **Chicago,** IL 60602, *pg.* 1889, *pg.* 589
WINZELER GEAR, 7355 W Wilson Ave, **Harwood Heights,** IL 60706-4707, *pg.* 1892, *pg.* 616

Indiana

BERRY PLASTICS, 3245 Kansas Rd, **Evansville,** IN 47725-9757, *pg.* 1879, *pg.* 678
CRESLINE PLASTIC PIPE CO., INC., 600 Cross Pointe Blvd, **Evansville,** IN 47715, *pg.* 1881, *pg.* 678
FIRESTONE INDUSTRIAL PRODUCTS DIVISION, 250 W 96th St, **Indianapolis,** IN 46260, *pg.* 1882, *pg.* 686
KITCHEN-QUIP, INC., 405 E Marion St, **Waterloo,** IN 46793, *pg.* 1885, *pg.* 699
THE TIRE RACK INC., 7101 Vorden Pkwy, **South Bend,** IN 46628, *pg.* 1890, *pg.* 697

Iowa

CUSTOM PAK, INC., 86 16th Ave N, **Clinton,** IA 52732, *pg.* 1881, *pg.* 703

Kansas

CONTINENTAL AMERICAN CORP., 5000 E 29th St N, **Wichita,** KS 67220-2111, *pg.* 1880, *pg.* 723

Kentucky

INDUSTRIAL SERVICES OF AMERICA, INC., 7100 Grade Ln, **Louisville,** KY 40213-3424, *pg.* 1884, *pg.* 734

Maryland

MARYLAND PLASTICS, INC., 251 E Central Ave, **Federalsburg,** MD 21632, *pg.* 1885, *pg.* 769

Massachusetts

ABNOTE NORTH AMERICA, 225 Rivermoor St, **Boston,** MA 02132-4905, *pg.* 1878, *pg.* 789
AMERICAN BILTRITE INC., 57 River St Ste 302, **Wellesley Hills,** MA 02481-2097, *pg.* 1878, *pg.* 856
THE BILTRITE CORPORATION, 51 Sawyer Rd, **Waltham,** MA 02454, *pg.* 1879, *pg.* 850
ENTEGRIS, INC., 129 Concord Road, **Billerica,** MA 01821, *pg.* 1882, *pg.* 788
FABREEKA INTERNATIONAL, INC., 1023 Tpke St, **Stoughton,** MA 02072-1156, *pg.* 1882, *pg.* 847
GLOBE COMPOSITE SOLUTIONS, LTD., 254 Beech St, **Rockland,** MA 02370-2749, *pg.* 1883, *pg.* 842
PILGRIM PLASTIC PRODUCTS COMPANY, 1200 W Chestnut St, **Brockton,** MA 02301-5574, *pg.* 1887, *pg.* 803
UFP TECHNOLOGIES, INC., 172 E Main St, **Georgetown,** MA 01833-2107, *pg.* 1891, *pg.* 823

Michigan

AVON RUBBER & PLASTICS INC., 805 W 13th St, **Cadillac,** MI 49601-9281, *pg.* 1879, *pg.* 874
COOPER-STANDARD AUTOMOTIVE INC., 39550 Orchard Hill Pl Dr, **Novi,** MI 48375, *pg.* 1880, *pg.* 903
FREUDENBERG-NOK, 47690 E Anchor Ct, **Plymouth,** MI 48170-2400, *pg.* 1882, *pg.* 904
JANESVILLE ACOUSTICS, 29200 Northwestern Hwy, Ste 400, **Southfield,** MI 48034, *pg.* 1885, *pg.* 907
MOTAN, INC., 320 N Acorn St, **Plainwell,** MI 49080, *pg.* 1886, *pg.* 903
VAIL RUBBER WORKS, INC., 521 Langley Ave, **Saint Joseph,** MI 49085-1725, *pg.* 1891, *pg.* 906

Minnesota

MAAX INC.-MINNEAPOLIS, 9224 73rd Ave N, **Minneapolis,** MN 55428, *pg.* 1885, *pg.* 938
PEERLESS CHAIN COMPANY, 1416 E Sanborn St, **Winona,** MN 55987, *pg.* 1887, *pg.* 967
QUADION CORPORATION, 1100 Xenium Ln N, **Minneapolis,** MN 55441-4405, *pg.* 1888, *pg.* 941
REESE ENTERPRISES, INC., 16350 Asher Ave PO Box 459, **Rosemount,** MN 55068, *pg.* 1888, *pg.* 955
VALLEY CASTING, INC., 9462 Deerwood Ln N, **Maple Grove,** MN 55369, *pg.* 1891, *pg.* 928

Nevada

AMERITYRE CORPORATION, 1501 Industrial Rd, **Boulder City,** NV 89005, *pg.* 1879, *pg.* 1021

New Hampshire

ANVIL INTERNATIONAL, INC., 110 Corporate Dr Ste 10, **Portsmouth,** NH 03801, *pg.* 1879, *pg.* 1038

New Jersey

AEP INDUSTRIES INC., 95 Chestnut Ridge Rd, **Montvale,** NJ 07645, *pg.* 1878, *pg.* 1085
BEL-ART PRODUCTS, INC., 661 St Rte 23, **Wayne,** NJ 07470, *pg.* 1879, *pg.* 1129
PERMALITH PLASTICS LLC, 6901 N Crescent Blvd, **Pennsauken,** NJ 08110, *pg.* 1887, *pg.* 1108
REMA TIP TOP/NORTH AMERICA, INC., 119 Rockland Ave, **Northvale,** NJ 07647, *pg.* 1889, *pg.* 1099
STULL TECHNOLOGIES INC., 17 Veronica Ave, **Somerset,** NJ 08873-3448, *pg.* 1889, *pg.* 1122
TYCO INTERNATIONAL (US) INC., 9 Roszel Rd, **Princeton,** NJ 08540, *pg.* 1891, *pg.* 1113

New York

THE MERCER RUBBER COMPANY, 350 Rabro Dr, **Hauppauge,** NY 11788-4257, *pg.* 1886, *pg.* 1165
PARKER HANNIFIN - WEBSTER PLASTICS INC, 83 Estates Dr W, **Fairport,** NY 14450, *pg.* 1887, *pg.* 1159
SEALING DEVICES INC., 4400 Walden Ave, **Lancaster,** NY 14086-9716, *pg.* 1889, *pg.* 1173

North Carolina

HSM SOLUTIONS, 235 2nd Ave NW, **Hickory,** NC 28601-4950, *pg.* 1884, *pg.* 1378
OLIVER RUBBER COMPANY, 408 Telephone Ave, **Asheboro,** NC 27205, *pg.* 1887, *pg.* 1358

Ohio

ADVANCED DRAINAGE SYSTEMS, INC., 4640 Truman Rd, **Hilliard,** OH 43026-2438, *pg.* 1878, *pg.* 1455
COOPER TIRE & RUBBER COMPANY, 701 Lima Ave, **Findlay,** OH 45840-2315, *pg.* 1881, *pg.* 1453
CORE MOLDING TECHNOLOGIES, INC., 800 Manor Park Dr, **Columbus,** OH 43228, *pg.* 1881, *pg.* 1439
CRANE PLASTICS HOLDING COMPANY, 330 W Spring St, **Columbus,** OH 43215, *pg.* 1881, *pg.* 1439
DIMCO-GRAY COMPANY, 900 Dimco Way, **Centerville,** OH 45458-2710, *pg.* 1881, *pg.* 1409
THE GOODYEAR TIRE & RUBBER COMPANY, 200 Innovation Way, **Akron,** OH 44316-0001, *pg.* 1883, *pg.* 1401
THE HERCULES TIRE & RUBBER COMPANY, 16380 E US Rte 224 Ste 200, **Findlay,** OH 45840, *pg.* 1884, *pg.* 1454
MOLDED FIBER GLASS COMPANIES, 2925 MFG Pl PO Box 675, **Ashtabula,** OH 44005-0675, *pg.* 1886, *pg.* 1403
MULTI-PLASTICS, INC., 7770 N Central Dr, **Lewis Center,** OH 43035-9404, *pg.* 1886, *pg.* 1457
MYERS INDUSTRIES, INC., 1293 S Main St, **Akron,** OH 44301-1302, *pg.* 1887, *pg.* 1402
PLASKOLITE, INC., 1770 Joyce Ave, **Columbus,** OH 43219-1026, *pg.* 1888, *pg.* 1443
PLASTIC SUPPLIERS, INC., 2887 Johnstown Rd, **Columbus,** OH 43219-1719, *pg.* 1888, *pg.* 1443
R.C.A. RUBBER COMPANY, 1833 E Market St, **Akron,** OH 44305-4214, *pg.* 1888, *pg.* 1402
ROCHLING GLASTIC COMPOSITES, 4321 Glenridge Rd, **Cleveland,** OH 44121-2805, *pg.* 1889, *pg.* 1435
THE STEP2 COMPANY LLC, 10010 Aurora-Hudson Rd, **Streetsboro,** OH 44241, *pg.* 1889, *pg.* 1474
VERNAY LABORATORIES, INC., 120 E S College St, **Yellow Springs,** OH 45387, *pg.* 1891, *pg.* 1482

Oklahoma

CONTINENTAL INDUSTRIES INC., 1140 N 129th E Ave, **Tulsa,** OK 74116, *pg.* 1880, *pg.* 1489

First page reference indicates Business Class Edition
Second page reference indicates Geographic Edition

Pennsylvania

ALLIED RUBBER & RIGGING SUPPLY, 101 Hindman Ln, **Butler,** PA 16001, *pg.* 1878, *pg.* 1519
CPG INTERNATIONAL, INC., 888 N Keyser Ave, **Scranton,** PA 18504, *pg.* 1881, *pg.* 1586
HYGRADE METAL MOULDING MANUFACTURING CORP., 1990 Highland Ave, **Bethlehem,** PA 18020-9083, *pg.* 1884, *pg.* 1516
WESTLAKE PLASTICS COMPANY, 490 Lenni Rd, **Lenni,** PA 19052, *pg.* 1892, *pg.* 1548
WHIRLEY INDUSTRIES, INC., 618 4th Ave, **Warren,** PA 16365-0988, *pg.* 1892, *pg.* 1590

Rhode Island

TEKNOR APEX COMPANY, 505 Central Ave, **Pawtucket,** RI 02861-1945, *pg.* 1889, *pg.* 1605

South Carolina

CARLISLE TIRE & WHEEL COMPANY, 23 Windham Blvd, **Aiken,** SC 29805-9320, *pg.* 1880, *pg.* 1612
CONTINENTAL TIRE NORTH AMERICA, INC., 1830 MacMillan Park Dr, **Fort Mill,** SC 29707, *pg.* 1880, *pg.* 1615
MICHELIN AMERICAS SMALL TIRES (MAST), 1 Parkway S, **Greenville,** SC 29615-5022, *pg.* 1886, *pg.* 1618
MICHELIN NORTH AMERICA INC., 1 Pkwy S, **Greenville,** SC 29615, *pg.* 1886, *pg.* 1618

South Dakota

RAVEN INDUSTRIES, INC., 205 E 6th St, **Sioux Falls,** SD 57104-5931, *pg.* 1888, *pg.* 1625

Tennessee

BRIDGESTONE AMERICAS, INC., 535 Marriott Dr, PO Box 140990, **Nashville,** TN 37214-0990, *pg.* 1879, *pg.* 1648
BRYCE CORPORATION, 4505 Old Lamar Ave, **Memphis,** TN 38118, *pg.* 1879, *pg.* 1641
COKER TIRE COMPANY, 1317 Chestnut St, **Chattanooga,** TN 37402-4418, *pg.* 1880, *pg.* 1628

Texas

ALLFLEX USA, INC., 2805 E 14th St DFW Airport, **Irving,** TX 75261, *pg.* 1878, *pg.* 1717
VALERON STRENGTH FILMS, 9505 Bamboo Rd, **Houston,** TX 77041-7705, *pg.* 1891, *pg.* 1716

Utah

ZERO MANUFACTURING, INC., 500 West 200 North, **North Salt Lake,** UT 84054, *pg.* 1892, *pg.* 1752

Virginia

DYNARIC, INC., 5740 Bayside Rd, **Virginia Beach,** VA 23455, *pg.* 1882, *pg.* 1810
KLOCKNER PENTAPLAST OF AMERICA, INC., 3585 Klockner Rd, **Gordonsville,** VA 22942-0500, *pg.* 1885, *pg.* 1783
TREDEGAR CORPORATION, 1100 Boulders Pkwy, **Richmond,** VA 23225-4035, *pg.* 1890, *pg.* 1804

Washington

SPENCER FLUID POWER, 19308 68th Ave S, **Kent,** WA 98032, *pg.* 1889, *pg.* 1822

West Virginia

MARSH BELLOFRAM CORPORATION, State Rte 2 PO Box 305, **Newell,** WV 26050, *pg.* 1885, *pg.* 1850

Wisconsin

TRIENDA, LLC, N7660 Industrial Rd, **Portage,** WI 53901-9451, *pg.* 1890, *pg.* 1887

Tobacco Products & Supplies

Connecticut

SWISHER INTERNATIONAL, INC., 20 Thorndal Cir, **Darien,** CT 06820-5421, *pg.* 1895, *pg.* 345

Florida

ALTADIS USA, INC., 5900 N Andrews Ave Ste 1100, **Fort Lauderdale,** FL 33309-2300, *pg.* 1893, *pg.* 423

ROCK CREEK PHARMACEUTICALS, INC., 2040 Whitfield Ave Ste 300, **Sarasota,** FL 34243, *pg.* 1895, *pg.* 466

VECTOR GROUP LTD., 100 SE 2nd St 32nd Fl, **Miami,** FL 33131, *pg.* 1895, *pg.* 447

Georgia

SWM, 100 North Point Ctr E Ste 600, **Alpharetta,** GA 30022-8263, *pg.* 1895, *pg.* 485

Illinois

REPUBLIC TOBACCO LP, 2301 Ravine Way, **Glenview,** IL 60025, *pg.* 1894, *pg.* 615

Indiana

REPUBLIC AIRWAYS HOLDINGS INC., 8909 Perdu Rd Ste 300, **Indianapolis,** IN 46268, *pg.* 1894, *pg.* 689

New York

PHILIP MORRIS INTERNATIONAL INC., 120 Park Ave, **New York,** NY 10017-5579, *pg.* 1894, *pg.* 1282

North Carolina

ALLIANCE ONE INTERNATIONAL, INC., 8001 Aerial Center Pkwy PO Box 2009, **Morrisville,** NC 27560-2009, *pg.* 1893, *pg.* 1384

REYNOLDS AMERICAN INC., 401 N Main St, **Winston Salem,** NC 27102-2866, *pg.* 1894, *pg.* 1395

R.J. REYNOLDS TOBACCO CO., 401 N Main St, **Winston Salem,** NC 27102-2866, *pg.* 1895, *pg.* 1395

Pennsylvania

AVANTI CIGAR CORPORATION, 200 Keystone Industrial Park, **Dunmore,** PA 18512, *pg.* 1894, *pg.* 1527

ZIPPO MANUFACTURING COMPANY, INC., 33 Barbour St, **Bradford,** PA 16701-1973, *pg.* 1895, *pg.* 1518

Tennessee

AMERICAN SNUFF COMPANY, 5106 Tradeport Dr, **Memphis,** TN 38141, *pg.* 1893, *pg.* 1641

Texas

FINCK CIGAR CO., 414 Vera Cruz, **San Antonio,** TX 78207-5642, *pg.* 1894, *pg.* 1740

Virginia

ALTRIA GROUP, INC., 6601 W Broad St, **Richmond,** VA 23230, *pg.* 1893, *pg.* 1800

PHILIP MORRIS USA INC., 6601 W Broad St, **Richmond,** VA 23230, *pg.* 1894, *pg.* 1803

U.S. SMOKELESS TOBACCO COMPANY, 6601 W Broad St, **Richmond,** VA 23230, *pg.* 1895, *pg.* 1804

Travel & Transportation

Alabama

INTERNATIONAL SHIPHOLDING CORPORATION, 11 N Water St Ste 18290, **Mobile,** AL 36602, *pg.* 1912, *pg.* 7
SILVER SHIPS, INC., 9243 Bellingrath Rd, **Theodore,** AL 36582-2710, *pg.* 1923, *pg.* 8

Arizona

MESA AIR GROUP, INC., 410 N 44th St Ste 700, **Phoenix,** AZ 85008-7608, *pg.* 1915, *pg.* 18
SWIFT TRANSPORTATION, 2200 S 75th Ave, **Phoenix,** AZ 85043, *pg.* 1924, *pg.* 20
U-HAUL INTERNATIONAL, INC., 2727 N Central Ave, **Phoenix,** AZ 85004-1155, *pg.* 1926, *pg.* 20

Arkansas

ABF FREIGHT SYSTEM, INC., 3801 Old Greenwood Rd, **Fort Smith,** AR 72903-5937, *pg.* 1896, *pg.* 31
ARKANSAS BEST CORPORATION, 3801 Old Greenwood Rd, **Fort Smith,** AR 72903-5937, *pg.* 1899, *pg.* 32
J.B. HUNT TRANSPORT SERVICES, INC., 615 JB Hunt Corporate Dr, **Lowell,** AR 72745-0130, *pg.* 1913, *pg.* 34
MAVERICK TRANSPORTATION, INC., 13301 Valentine Rd, **North Little Rock,** AR 72117, *pg.* 1915, *pg.* 35
P.A.M. TRANSPORTATION SERVICES, INC., 297 Henri Detonti Blvd, **Tontitown,** AR 72770, *pg.* 1919, *pg.* 36
USA TRUCK, INC., 3200 Industrial Park Rd, **Van Buren,** AR 72956-6110, *pg.* 1929, *pg.* 36

California

AIR NEW ZEALAND LTD. (U.S.A.), 1960 E Grand Ave, **El Segundo,** CA 90245-5000, *pg.* 1897, *pg.* 78
AMERICAN FREIGHTWAYS, 10845 Rancho Bernardo Rd Ste 100, **San Diego,** CA 92127, *pg.* 1899, *pg.* 200
ASIANA AIRLINES, 3530 Wilshire Blvd Ste 1700, **Los Angeles,** CA 90010-2341, *pg.* 1899, *pg.* 126
CLASSIC VACATIONS, LLC, 5893 Rue Ferrari, **San Jose,** CA 95138, *pg.* 1903, *pg.* 242
CROWLEY MARITIME CORPORATION, 155 Grand Ave, **Oakland,** CA 94612-3758, *pg.* 1904, *pg.* 170
CRYSTAL CRUISES LLC, 11755 Wilshire Blvd Ste 900, **Los Angeles,** CA 90025, *pg.* 1904, *pg.* 128
CUBIC TRANSPORTATION SYSTEMS, INC., 5650 Kearny Mesa Rd, **San Diego,** CA 92111-5587, *pg.* 1905, *pg.* 202
CUNARD LINE LTD., 24303 Town Ctr Dr Ste 200, **Valencia,** CA 91355, *pg.* 1905, *pg.* 299
EXECUTIVE CAR LEASING CO., 7807 Santa Monica Blvd, **Los Angeles,** CA 90046-5302, *pg.* 1907, *pg.* 130
HOTWIRE, INC., 333 Market St Ste 100, **San Francisco,** CA 94105-2146, *pg.* 1912, *pg.* 219
LOS ANGELES COUNTY METROPOLITAN TRANSPORTATION AUTHORITY, 1 Gateway Plz, **Los Angeles,** CA 90012, *pg.* 1914, *pg.* 135
MATSON NAVIGATION COMPANY, INC., 555 12th St 7th Fl, **Oakland,** CA 94607, *pg.* 1915, *pg.* 172
MENLO WORLDWIDE, LLC, 2855 Campus Dr Ste 300, **San Mateo,** CA 94403-2512, *pg.* 1915, *pg.* 255
PLAN ASIA, INC, 360 N Sepulveda Blvd Ste 3008, **El Segundo,** CA 90245, *pg.* 1919, *pg.* 82
PLEASANT HOLIDAYS LLC, 2404 Townsgate Rd, **Westlake Village,** CA 91361-2505, *pg.* 1919, *pg.* 307
PORT OF OAKLAND, 530 Water St, **Oakland,** CA 94607-3746, *pg.* 1920, *pg.* 172
PRINCESS CRUISE LINES LTD., 24305 Town Center Dr, **Santa Clarita,** CA 91355, *pg.* 1920, *pg.* 270
QANTAS AIRWAYS - USA, 6080 Ctr Dr Ste 400, **Los Angeles,** CA 90045, *pg.* 1920, *pg.* 139
SAN LUIS OBISPO COUNTY VISITORS & CONFERENCE BUREAU, 811 El Capitan Way, **San Luis Obispo,** CA 93401, *pg.* 1922, *pg.* 253
SINGAPORE AIRLINES, 222 N Sepulveda Blvd Ste 1600, **El Segundo,** CA 90245, *pg.* 1923, *pg.* 82
THAI AIRWAYS INTERNATIONAL LTD., 222 N Sepulveda Blvd Ste 1950, **El Segundo,** CA 90245, *pg.* 1925, *pg.* 83
VIRGIN AMERICA INC., 555 Airport Blvd, **Burlingame,** CA 94010, *pg.* 1930, *pg.* 55
YMT VACATIONS, 100 N Sepulveda Blvd Ste 1700, **El Segundo,** CA 90245, *pg.* 1931, *pg.* 83

Colorado

FRONTIER AIRLINES, INC., 7001 Tower Rd, **Denver,** CO 80249-7312, *pg.* 1909, *pg.* 319
GROUP VOYAGERS, INC., 5301 S Federal Cir, **Littleton,** CO 80123-2980, *pg.* 1910, *pg.* 333
INSPIRATO LLC, 1637 Wazee St, **Denver,** CO 80202, *pg.* 1912, *pg.* 320
JOHNSON STORAGE & MOVING COMPANY, 221 Broadway, **Denver,** CO 80203-3918, *pg.* 1913, *pg.* 320

Connecticut

CITATIONAIR, Greenwich American Ctr 5 American Ln, **Greenwich,** CT 06831, *pg.* 1903, *pg.* 350
THE MOTORLEASE CORPORATION, 1506 New Britain Ave, **Farmington,** CT 06032-3126, *pg.* 1916, *pg.* 349
XPO LOGISTICS, INC., 5 Greenwich Office Park, **Greenwich,** CT 06831, *pg.* 1931, *pg.* 350

District of Columbia

ACADEMIC TRAVEL ABROAD, INC., 1920 N St NW Ste 200, **Washington,** DC 20036, *pg.* 1896, *pg.* 393
BRAND USA, 1725 Eye St NW Eighth Fl, **Washington,** DC 20006, *pg.* 1901, *pg.* 396
CAREY INTERNATIONAL, INC., 4530 Wisconsin Ave NW, **Washington,** DC 20016, *pg.* 1902, *pg.* 397
NATIONAL RAILROAD PASSENGER CORPORATION, 60 Massachusetts Ave NE, **Washington,** DC 20002-4285, *pg.* 1916, *pg.* 403
WASHINGTON METROPOLITAN AREA TRANSIT AUTHORITY, 600 5th St NW, **Washington,** DC 20001-2610, *pg.* 1930, *pg.* 407

Florida

AEROLINEAS ARGENTINAS, 1000 NW 57 Ct Ste 120, **Miami,** FL 33126, *pg.* 1896, *pg.* 439
BAHAMAS TOURISM CENTER, 1200 S Pine Is Rd Ste 750, **Plantation,** FL 33324, *pg.* 1900, *pg.* 459
CARNIVAL CORPORATION, 3655 NW 87th Ave, **Miami,** FL 33178-2428, *pg.* 1902, *pg.* 441
CARNIVAL CRUISE LINES, Carnival Pl 3655 NW 87th Ave, **Miami,** FL 33178-2428, *pg.* 1902, *pg.* 441
CENTRAL FLORIDA REGIONAL TRANSPORT AUTHORITY, 455 N Garland Ave, **Orlando,** FL 32801, *pg.* 1903, *pg.* 452
CLUB MED SALES, INC., 65005 Blue Lagoon Dr Ste 225, **Miami,** FL 33126, *pg.* 1903, *pg.* 441
COSTA CRUISE LINES N.V., St 200 S Park Rd, **Hollywood,** FL 33021-8592, *pg.* 1904, *pg.* 431
CSX CORPORATION, 500 Water St 15th Fl, **Jacksonville,** FL 32202, *pg.* 1904, *pg.* 432
CSX TRANSPORTATION, INC., 500 Water St, **Jacksonville,** FL 32202-4423, *pg.* 1904, *pg.* 432
DHL HOLDINGS (USA), INC., 1200 S Pine Island Rd Ste 600, **Plantation,** FL 33324, *pg.* 1906, *pg.* 459
FLORIDA EAST COAST INDUSTRIES, INC., 7411 Fullerton St Ste 300, **Jacksonville,** FL 32256, *pg.* 1909, *pg.* 433
THE HERTZ CORPORATION, 999 Vanderbilt Beach Rd, **Naples,** FL 34108, *pg.* 1911, *pg.* 450
INTERVAL LEISURE GROUP, INC., 6262 Sunset Dr, **Miami,** FL 33143-4843, *pg.* 1912, *pg.* 443
LANDSTAR SYSTEM, INC., 13410 Sutton Park Dr S, **Jacksonville,** FL 32224, *pg.* 1914, *pg.* 434
MIAMI INTERNATIONAL AIRPORT, PO Box 592075, **Miami,** FL 33159, *pg.* 1916, *pg.* 444
NCL CORPORATION LTD., 7665 Corporate Center Dr, **Miami,** FL 33126, *pg.* 1916, *pg.* 444
NORWEGIAN CRUISE LINE, 7665 Corporate Center Dr, **Miami,** FL 33126-1201, *pg.* 1917, *pg.* 444
ODYSSEY MARINE EXPLORATION, INC., 5215 W Laurel St Ste 210, **Tampa,** FL 33607, *pg.* 1918, *pg.* 475
PINELLAS SUNCOAST TRANSIT AUTHORITY, 3201 Scherer Dr N, **Saint Petersburg,** FL 33716-1004, *pg.* 1919, *pg.* 463
PODS ENTERPRISES, INC., 5585 Rio Vista Dr, **Clearwater,** FL 33760, *pg.* 1919, *pg.* 416
PORT OF MIAMI TERMINAL OPERATING COMPANY, LC, 1007 N America Way Ste 400, **Miami,** FL 33132, *pg.* 1920, *pg.* 445
ROYAL CARIBBEAN CRUISES LTD, 1050 Caribbean Way, **Miami,** FL 33132-2096, *pg.* 1921, *pg.* 446 .
RYDER SYSTEM, INC., 11690 NW 105 St, **Miami,** FL 33178, *pg.* 1922, *pg.* 446
SEACOR HOLDINGS INC., 2200 Eller Dr, **Fort Lauderdale,** FL 33316, *pg.* 1923, *pg.* 426
SOVEREIGN CRUISES LLC, 118 Woodland Ct, **Safety Harbor,** FL 34695, *pg.* 1924, *pg.* 461
THE SUDDATH COMPANIES INC., 815 S Main St, **Jacksonville,** FL 32207-9050, *pg.* 1924, *pg.* 435
TAMPA PORT AUTHORITY INC., 1101 Channelside Dr, **Tampa,** FL 33602, *pg.* 1925, *pg.* 476

Georgia

BULLDOG MOVERS, INC., 4194 Northeast Expy, Ste E, **Atlanta,** GA 30340, *pg.* 1901, *pg.* 491
CONCUR TECHNOLOGIES, 2970 Clairmont Rd Ste 300, **Atlanta,** GA 30329, *pg.* 1903, *pg.* 501
DELTA AIR LINES, INC., 1030 Delta Blvd, **Atlanta,** GA 30354-1989, *pg.* 1905, *pg.* 503
RAILSERVE INC., 1691 Phoenix Blvd Ste 250, **Atlanta,** GA 30349-5565, *pg.* 1921, *pg.* 519
SAIA, INC., 11465 Johns Creek Pkwy Ste 400, **Johns Creek,** GA 30097, *pg.* 1922, *pg.* 533
TRAVELPORT LIMITED, 300 Galleria Pkwy, **Atlanta,** GA 30339, *pg.* 1925, *pg.* 521
UNITED PARCEL SERVICE, INC., 55 Glenlake Pkwy NE, **Atlanta,** GA 30328, *pg.* 1928, *pg.* 522
UPS SUPPLY CHAIN SOLUTIONS, INC., 12380 Morris Rd, **Alpharetta,** GA 30005, *pg.* 1929, *pg.* 485

Hawaii

HAWAIIAN AIRLINES, INC., 3375 Koapaka St Ste G-350, **Honolulu,** HI 96819, *pg.* 1910, *pg.* 543
HAWAIIAN HOLDINGS, INC., 3375 Koapaka St Ste G-350, **Honolulu,** HI 96819, *pg.* 1910, *pg.* 544
MOKULELE FLIGHT SERVICE, INC., 73-350 U'u St, **Kailua,** HI 96740, *pg.* 1916, *pg.* 545
PACIFIC MARINE & SUPPLY CO. LTD. INC., 841 Bishop St Ste 1110, **Honolulu,** HI 96813-3908, *pg.* 1918, *pg.* 544

Illinois

ABERCROMBIE & KENT USA, LLC, 1411 Opus Pl Exec Towers W II Ste 300, **Downers Grove,** IL 60515-1182, *pg.* 1896, *pg.* 607
AUTO DRIVEAWAY CO., 11 E Adams Ste 1402, **Chicago,** IL 60603, *pg.* 1900, *pg.* 566
CARAVAN TOURS, INC., 401 N Michigan Ave, **Chicago,** IL 60611-4255, *pg.* 1902, *pg.* 568
EMKAY, INC., 805 W Thorndale Ave, **Itasca,** IL 60143-1338, *pg.* 1906, *pg.* 619
ESSENDANT INC., 1 N Pkwy Blvd Ste 100, **Deerfield,** IL 60015, *pg.* 1907, *pg.* 600
NATIONAL TRUCK LEASING SYSTEM, 1 S 450 Summit Ave Ste 300, **Oakbrook Terrace,** IL 60181, *pg.* 1916, *pg.* 649
NATIONAL VAN LINES, INC., 2800 W Roosevelt Rd, **Broadview,** IL 60155-3756, *pg.* 1916, *pg.* 559
ORBITZ WORLDWIDE, INC., 500 W Madison St Ste 1000, **Chicago,** IL 60661, *pg.* 1918, *pg.* 586
OSHKOSH SPECIALTY VEHICLES, 2150 E Dolton Rd, **Calumet City,** IL 60409, *pg.* 1918, *pg.* 561
PACE, 550 W Algonquin Rd, **Arlington Heights,** IL 60005-4412, *pg.* 1918, *pg.* 553
REGIONAL TRANSPORTATION AUTHORITY, 175 W Jackson St Ste 1550, **Chicago,** IL 60602-4501, *pg.* 1921, *pg.* 588
SIRVA, INC., 700 Oakmont Ln, **Westmont,** IL 60559, *pg.* 1923, *pg.* 669
UNITED AIRLINES, INC., 233 S Wacker Dr, **Chicago,** IL 60606, *pg.* 1927, *pg.* 593
UNITED CONTINENTAL HOLDINGS, INC., 233 S Wacker Dr, **Chicago,** IL 60606, *pg.* 1927, *pg.* 593
WHEELS INC., 666 Garland Pl, **Des Plaines,** IL 60016-4725, *pg.* 1931, *pg.* 607

Indiana

ALLIED VAN LINES, 5001 US Hwy 30W, **Fort Wayne,** IN

46818, *pg.* 1898, *pg.* 680

AMERICAN RED BALL TRANSIT CO. INC., 1335 Sadlier Cir E, **Indianapolis,** IN 46239-1051, *pg.* 1899, *pg.* 682

ATLAS VAN LINES, INC., 1212 Saint George Rd, **Evansville,** IN 47711-2364, *pg.* 1900, *pg.* 678

CELADON GROUP, INC., 9503 E 33rd St, **Indianapolis,** IN 46235-4207, *pg.* 1903, *pg.* 683

GRAMMER INDUSTRIES INC., 18375 E 345 S, **Grammer,** IN 47236, *pg.* 1909, *pg.* 681

NORTH AMERICAN VAN LINES, 5001 US Hwy 30W, **Fort Wayne,** IN 46818, *pg.* 1917, *pg.* 681

RCI, LLC, 9998 North Michigan Rd, **Carmel,** IN 46032, *pg.* 1921, *pg.* 675

US 1 INDUSTRIES, INC., 336 W US Hwy 30 Ste 201, **Valparaiso,** IN 46385-5345, *pg.* 1929, *pg.* 698

WHEATON VAN LINES, INC., 8010 Castleton Rd, **Indianapolis,** IN 46250-2005, *pg.* 1930, *pg.* 691

Iowa

HEARTLAND EXPRESS, INC., 901 N Kansas Ave, **North Liberty,** IA 52317, *pg.* 1910, *pg.* 710

Kansas

YRC WORLDWIDE INC., 10990 Roe Ave, **Overland Park,** KS 66211-1213, *pg.* 1931, *pg.* 720

Maine

AUTO EUROPE, LLC, 39 Commercial St, **Portland,** ME 04101, *pg.* 1900, *pg.* 751

Maryland

RENT-A-WRECK OF AMERICA, INC., 13900 Laurel Lakes Ave, Ste 100, **Laurel,** MD 20707, *pg.* 1921, *pg.* 773

Massachusetts

EXPLORICA, INC., 145 Tremont St 6th Fl, **Boston,** MA 02111-1208, *pg.* 1907, *pg.* 794

ICELANDAIR NORTH AMERICA, 1900 Crown Colony Dr, 1st Fl, **Quincy,** MA 02169, *pg.* 1912, *pg.* 841

PETER PAN BUS LINES, INC., 1776 Main St, **Springfield,** MA 01102-1776, *pg.* 1919, *pg.* 846

SENTIENT JET, LLC, 97 Libbey Pkwy, **Weymouth,** MA 02189, *pg.* 1923, *pg.* 859

TNT VACATIONS, 2 Charlesgate W, **Boston,** MA 02215, *pg.* 1925, *pg.* 801

TRIPADVISOR, INC., 141 Needham Street, **Needham,** MA 02464, *pg.* 1926, *pg.* 835

WORLD TRAVEL HOLDINGS, 100 Fordham Rd Bldg C, **Wilmington,** MA 01887, *pg.* 1931, *pg.* 860

ZIPCAR, INC., 25 First St 4th Fl, **Cambridge,** MA 02141, *pg.* 1931, *pg.* 810

Michigan

STEVENS GROUP, INC., 527 Morley Dr, **Saginaw,** MI 48601, *pg.* 1924, *pg.* 906

TWO MEN AND A TRUCK INTERNATIONAL, INC., 3400 Belle Chase Way, **Lansing,** MI 48911, *pg.* 1926, *pg.* 896

WEST MICHIGAN TOURIST ASSOCIATION, 741 Kenmoor Ave Ste E, **Grand Rapids,** MI 49546, *pg.* 1930, *pg.* 891

Minnesota

CARLSON WAGONLIT TRAVEL, 701 Carlson Pkwy, **Minnetonka,** MN 55305, *pg.* 1902, *pg.* 948

DART TRANSIT COMPANY, 800 Lone Oak Rd, **Eagan,** MN 55121-2212, *pg.* 1905, *pg.* 921

SAINT PAUL PORT AUTHORITY, 380 St Peter St, Ste 850, **Saint Paul,** MN 55102, *pg.* 1922, *pg.* 963

Mississippi

KLLM TRANSPORT SERVICES, INC., 134 Riverview Dr, **Richland,** MS 39218, *pg.* 1914, *pg.* 971

Missouri

ENTERPRISE HOLDINGS, INC., 600 Corporate Park Dr, **Saint Louis,** MO 63105-4204, *pg.* 1906, *pg.* 996

THE KANSAS CITY SOUTHERN RAILWAY COMPANY, 427 W 12th St, **Kansas City,** MO 64105, *pg.* 1913, *pg.* 985

MARITZ INC., 1375 N Hwy Dr, **Fenton,** MO 63099, *pg.* 1914, *pg.* 977

TRI-STATE MOTOR TRANSIT CO., 8141 E 7th St, **Joplin,** MO 64801, *pg.* 1926, *pg.* 980

UNIGROUP, INC., 1 Premier Dr, **Fenton,** MO 63026, *pg.* 1927, *pg.* 977

UNITED VAN LINES, LLC, 1 United Dr, **Fenton,** MO 63026-2535, *pg.* 1929, *pg.* 978

WAGNER INDUSTRIES, INC., 1201 E 12th Ave, **Kansas City,** MO 64116, *pg.* 1930, *pg.* 987

Nebraska

UNION PACIFIC CORPORATION, 1400 Douglas St, **Omaha,** NE 68179, *pg.* 1927, *pg.* 1018

UNION PACIFIC RAILROAD COMPANY, 1400 Douglas St, **Omaha,** NE 68179-0001, *pg.* 1927, *pg.* 1019

WERNER ENTERPRISES, INC., 14507 Frontier Rd, **Omaha,** NE 68138-3808, *pg.* 1930, *pg.* 1019

Nevada

AMERCO, 5555 Kietzke Ln Ste 100, **Reno,** NV 89511, *pg.* 1898, *pg.* 1031

New Hampshire

ALEXANDER+ROBERTS, 53 Summer St, **Keene,** NH 03431-3318, *pg.* 1898, *pg.* 1034

SEGWAY INC., 14 Technology Dr, **Bedford,** NH 03110, *pg.* 1923, *pg.* 1033

New Jersey

AIR CHARTERS, INC., 333 Industrial Ave Ste 3, **Teterboro,** NJ 07608, *pg.* 1897, *pg.* 1124

ALLSTATES WORLDCARGO, INC., 1 Telican Dr, **Bayville,** NJ 08721, *pg.* 1898, *pg.* 1042

AUTOMOTIVE RESOURCES INTERNATIONAL (ARI), 4001 Leadenhall Rd, **Mount Laurel,** NJ 08054-1539, *pg.* 1900, *pg.* 1090

AVIS BUDGET GROUP, INC., 6 Sylvan Way, **Parsippany,** NJ 07054, *pg.* 1900, *pg.* 1102

BUDGET RENT A CAR SYSTEM, INC., 6 Sylvan Way, **Parsippany,** NJ 07054, *pg.* 1901, *pg.* 1102

DELAWARE RIVER PORT AUTHORITY OF PENNSYLVANIA & NEW JERSEY, 1 Port Ctr 2 Riverside Dr, **Camden,** NJ 08101-1003, *pg.* 1905, *pg.* 1049

EDISON PROPERTIES, LLC, 100 Washington St, **Newark,** NJ 07102, *pg.* 1906, *pg.* 1096

FLEXI-VAN LEASING, INC., 251 Monroe Ave, **Kenilworth,** NJ 07033-1106, *pg.* 1909, *pg.* 1077

KUWAIT AIRWAYS CORP., Parker Plz 400 Kelby St, **Fort Lee,** NJ 07024, *pg.* 1914, *pg.* 1068

LIBERTY TRAVEL, INC., 69 Spring St, **Ramsey,** NJ 07446, *pg.* 1914, *pg.* 1113

MAERSK INC., 2 Giralda Farms Madison Ave, **Madison,** NJ 07940, *pg.* 1914, *pg.* 1080

NFI INDUSTRIES INC., 71 W Park Ave, **Vineland,** NJ 08360-3508, *pg.* 1917, *pg.* 1127

NJ TRANSIT CORPORATION, 1 Penn Plz E, **Newark,** NJ 07105-2245, *pg.* 1917, *pg.* 1097

ROYAL COACHMAN WORLDWIDE, 88 Ford Rd Unit 26, **Denville,** NJ 07834, *pg.* 1922, *pg.* 1053

TAP PORTUGAL, 263 Lafayette St 3rd Flr, **Newark,** NJ 07105, *pg.* 1925, *pg.* 1098

New York

AER LINGUS, 300 Jericho Quandrangle Ste 130, **Jericho,** NY 11753, *pg.* 1896, *pg.* 1171

AIR FRANCE, USA, 125 W 55th St 2nd Fl, **New York,** NY 10019, *pg.* 1897, *pg.* 1188

AIR INDIA, 570 Lexington Ave 15th Fl, **New York,** NY 10022, *pg.* 1897, *pg.* 1188

ALBA WHEELS UP INTERNATIONAL, INC., 150 30 132nd Ave, **Jamaica,** NY 11434, *pg.* 1898, *pg.* 1170

ASSOCIATED GLOBAL SYSTEMS, INC., 3333 New Hyde Pk Rd, **New Hyde Park,** NY 11042-1205, *pg.* 1899, *pg.* 1184

BARBADOS TOURISM AUTHORITY, 820 2nd Ave 5th Fl, **New York,** NY 10017-4709, *pg.* 1900, *pg.* 1200

BLUE STAR JETS, INC., 805 3rd Ave Fl 16, **New York,** NY 10022, *pg.* 1901, *pg.* 1205

BRITISH AIRWAYS, 2 Park Ave Ste 1100, **New York,** NY 10016, *pg.* 1901, *pg.* 1207

BUFFALO NIAGARA CONVENTION & VISITORS BUREAU, INC., 617 Main St Ste 200, **Buffalo,** NY 14203-1400, *pg.* 1901, *pg.* 1147

COOK MOVING SYSTEMS, INC., 1845 Dale Rd, **Buffalo,** NY 14225-4909, *pg.* 1904, *pg.* 1148

EL AL ISRAEL AIRLINES, LTD., 15 E 26th St 6th Fl, **New York,** NY 10010, *pg.* 1906, *pg.* 1226

FINNAIR OYJ-NEW YORK, 228 E 45th St Fl 8, **New York,** NY 10017-3303, *pg.* 1909, *pg.* 1231

FUGAZY INTERNATIONAL CORPORATION, 1270 Ave Of The Americas, **New York,** NY 10020, *pg.* 1909, *pg.* 1233

HONG KONG TOURISM BOARD - NEW YORK, 370 Lexington Ave Ste 1812, **New York,** NY 10017-6579, *pg.* 1911, *pg.* 1241

ISRAM WHOLESALE TOURS & TRAVEL LTD., 233 Pk Ave S, **New York,** NY 10003, *pg.* 1913, *pg.* 1244

JAPAN AIRLINES COMPANY, LTD., 461 5th Ave, **New York,** NY 10017, *pg.* 1913, *pg.* 1245

JETBLUE AIRWAYS CORPORATION, 27-01 Queens Plz N, Ste 1, **Long Island City,** NY 11101, *pg.* 1913, *pg.* 1174

KLM ROYAL DUTCH AIRLINES, 565 Taxter Rd 3rd Fl, **Elmsford,** NY 10523, *pg.* 1914, *pg.* 1158

LONG ISLAND RAIL ROAD, Jamaica Sta, **Jamaica,** NY 11435, *pg.* 1914, *pg.* 1170

MARQUIS JET PARTNERS INC., 230 Park Ave Ste 840, **New York,** NY 10169, *pg.* 1915, *pg.* 1256

METROPOLITAN TRANSPORTATION AUTHORITY, 347 Madison Ave, **New York,** NY 10017-3706, *pg.* 1915, *pg.* 1260

NIAGARA FRONTIER TRANSPORTATION AUTHORITY, 181 Ellicott St, **Buffalo,** NY 14203, *pg.* 1917, *pg.* 1150

PORT AUTHORITY OF NEW YORK & NEW JERSEY, 4 World Trade Ctr, 150 Greenwich St, **New York,** NY 10007, *pg.* 1919, *pg.* 1283

RAIL EUROPE INC., 44 S Broadway Fl 11, **White Plains,** NY 10601-4411, *pg.* 1920, *pg.* 1354

TRAVEL-BY-NET, INC., 195 N Bedford Rd, **Mount Kisco,** NY 10549-1140, *pg.* 1925, *pg.* 1183

TRAVELZOO INC, 590 Madison Ave 37th Fl, **New York,** NY 10022, *pg.* 1926, *pg.* 1304

North Carolina

OLD DOMINION FREIGHT LINE, INC., 500 Old Dominion Way, **Thomasville,** NC 27360, *pg.* 1918, *pg.* 1391

OUTER BANKS VISITORS BUREAU, One Visitors Center Cir, **Manteo,** NC 27954, *pg.* 1918, *pg.* 1382

Ohio

THE ANDREWS MOVING & STORAGE COMPANY INC., 10235 Philipp Pkwy, **Streetsboro,** OH 44241, *pg.* 1899, *pg.* 1474

GREATER CLEVELAND REGIONAL TRANSIT AUTHORITY, 1240 W 6th St, **Cleveland,** OH 44113-1302, *pg.* 1909, *pg.* 1431

THE KENAN ADVANTAGE GROUP, INC., 4366 MT Pleasent St, **Canton,** OH 44720, *pg.* 1914, *pg.* 1408

NETJETS INC., 4111 Bridgeway Ave, **Columbus,** OH 43219, *pg.* 1917, *pg.* 1442

PLANES MOVING & STORAGE, INC., 9823 Cincinnati Dayton Rd, **West Chester,** OH 45069-3825, *pg.* 1919, *pg.* 1479

TRAVEL LEADERS, 9895 Montgomery Rd, **Cincinnati,** OH 45242-6424, *pg.* 1925, *pg.* 1426

TRAVELCENTERS OF AMERICA, LLC, 24601 Center Ridge Rd Ste 200, **Westlake,** OH 44145, *pg.* 1925, *pg.* 1481

ULTIMATE JETCHARTERS, INC., 6060 W Airport Dr, **Canton,** OH 44720, *pg.* 1927, *pg.* 1409

Oklahoma

ALAMO RENT-A-CAR, LLC, 6929 N Lakewood Ave Ste 100, **Tulsa,** OK 74117, *pg.* 1897, *pg.* 1489

GROENDYKE TRANSPORT, INC., 2510 Rock Island Blvd, **Enid,** OK 73701, *pg.* 1910, *pg.* 1484

NATIONAL CAR RENTAL, 6929 N Lakewood Ave Ste 100, **Tulsa,** OK 74117-1808, *pg.* 1916, *pg.* 1490

First page reference indicates Business Class Edition
Second page reference indicates Geographic Edition

Oregon

MAY TRUCKING COMPANY INC., 4185 Brooklake Rd, **Salem,** OR 97303, *pg.* 1915, *pg.* 1508
PORT OF PORTLAND, 7200 NE Airport Way, **Portland,** OR 97218-4049, *pg.* 1920, *pg.* 1505

Pennsylvania

APPLE VACATIONS INC., 7 Campus Blvd, **Newtown Square,** PA 19073, *pg.* 1899, *pg.* 1556
BDP INTERNATIONAL INC., 510 Walnut St Fl 2A, **Philadelphia,** PA 19106-3621, *pg.* 1900, *pg.* 1559
CHEAPCARIBBEAN.COM, 2003 S Easton Rd Ste 100, **Doylestown,** PA 18901, *pg.* 1903, *pg.* 1526
CONSOLIDATED RAIL CORPORATION, 1717 Arch St, **Philadelphia,** PA 19103, *pg.* 1903, *pg.* 1562
SOUTHEASTERN PENNSYLVANIA TRANSPORTATION AUTHORITY, 1234 Market St, **Philadelphia,** PA 19107-3721, *pg.* 1923, *pg.* 1570

Rhode Island

PAUL ARPIN VAN LINES, INC., 99 James P Murphy Hwy, **West Warwick,** RI 02893, *pg.* 1919, *pg.* 1610

Tennessee

FEDEX CORPORATION, 3875 Airways, Module H3 Department 4634, **Memphis,** TN 38116, *pg.* 1907, *pg.* 1642
FEDEX EXPRESS CORPORATION, 3875 Airways, Module H3 Department 4634, **Memphis,** TN 38116, *pg.* 1908, *pg.* 1644
MILAN EXPRESS CO., INC., 1091 Kefauver Dr, **Milan,** TN 38358-3412, *pg.* 1916, *pg.* 1647
U.S. XPRESS ENTERPRISES, INC., 4080 Jenkins Rd, **Chattanooga,** TN 37421-1174, *pg.* 1929, *pg.* 1630

Texas

AMERICAN AIRLINES INC., 4333 Amon Carter Blvd, **Fort Worth,** TX 76155-2604, *pg.* 1898, *pg.* 1693
ANDREW HARPER, INC., 1601 Rio Grande St Ste 410, **Austin,** TX 78701-1149, *pg.* 1899, *pg.* 1660
BRINK'S U.S., 555 Dividend Dr, **Coppell,** TX 75019, *pg.* 1901, *pg.* 1670
BURLINGTON NORTHERN SANTA FE, LLC, 2650 Lou Menk Dr, **Fort Worth,** TX 76131-2830, *pg.* 1901, *pg.* 1694
DYNAMEX, INC., 5429 LBJ Fwy Ste 1000, **Dallas,** TX 75240, *pg.* 1906, *pg.* 1680
FORETRAVEL INC., 1221 NW Stallings Dr, **Nacogdoches,** TX 75964, *pg.* 1909, *pg.* 1728
FRONTIER LOGISTICS, LP, 101 E Barbours Cut Blvd, **Morgan's Point,** TX 77571, *pg.* 1909, *pg.* 1728
GREYHOUND LINES, INC., 350 N St Paul, **Dallas,** TX 75201, *pg.* 1910, *pg.* 1681
HOMEAWAY, INC., 1011 W Fifth St Ste 300, **Austin,** TX 78703, *pg.* 1911, *pg.* 1663
PORT OF GALVESTON, 123 25th St 8th Fl, **Galveston,** TX 77550-1494, *pg.* 1919, *pg.* 1697
PORT OF HOUSTON AUTHORITY, 111 E Loop N, **Houston,** TX 77029-4326, *pg.* 1920, *pg.* 1713
SABRE HOLDINGS CORPORATION, 3150 Sabre Dr, **Southlake,** TX 76092-2103, *pg.* 1922, *pg.* 1745
SOUTHWEST AIRLINES CO., 2702 Love Field Dr, **Dallas,** TX 75235-1908, *pg.* 1923, *pg.* 1687
VIRTUOSO LTD., 505 Main St Ste 500, **Fort Worth,** TX 76102-3941, *pg.* 1930, *pg.* 1696

Utah

A&K RAILROAD MATERIALS INC., 1505 S Redwood Rd, **Salt Lake City,** UT 84104, *pg.* 1896, *pg.* 1755
CR ENGLAND, INC., 4701 W 2100 S, **Salt Lake City,** UT 84120-1223, *pg.* 1904, *pg.* 1756
SKYWEST INC., 444 S River Rd, **Saint George,** UT 84790, *pg.* 1923, *pg.* 1755

Virginia

AIRBUS NORTH AMERICA HOLDINGS, INC., 198 Van Buren St, **Herndon,** VA 20170, *pg.* 1897, *pg.* 1784
INTERSTATE WORLDWIDE RELOCATION, INC., 5801 Rolling Rd, **Springfield,** VA 22152-1064, *pg.* 1912, *pg.* 1807
NORFOLK SOUTHERN CORPORATION, 3 Commercial Pl, **Norfolk,** VA 23510-2191, *pg.* 1917, *pg.* 1797
RELIANT ASSET MANAGEMENT LLC, 2900 S Quincy St Ste 300 A, **Arlington,** VA 22206, *pg.* 1921, *pg.* 1774
UPS GROUND FREIGHT, INC., 1000 Semmes Ave, **Richmond,** VA 23224, *pg.* 1929, *pg.* 1804
VIRGINIA PORT AUTHORITY, 600 World Trade Ctr, **Norfolk,** VA 23510, *pg.* 1930, *pg.* 1797
ZIM-AMERICAN ISRAELI SHIPPING CO., 5801 Lk Wright Dr, **Norfolk,** VA 23502-1862, *pg.* 1931, *pg.* 1798

Washington

ALASKA AIR GROUP, INC., 19300 International Blvd, **Seattle,** WA 98188-5304, *pg.* 1897, *pg.* 1830
ALASKA AIRLINES, INC., 19300 Pacific Hwy S, **Seattle,** WA 98188-5304, *pg.* 1897, *pg.* 1830
AMBASSADORS GROUP, INC., 2001 S Flint Rd, **Spokane,** WA 99224, *pg.* 1898, *pg.* 1843
DOWN UNDER ANSWERS, LLC, 400 108th Ave NE, Ste 200, **Bellevue,** WA 98004, *pg.* 1906, *pg.* 1814
HOLLAND AMERICA LINE INC., 300 Elliott Ave W, **Seattle,** WA 98119-4198, *pg.* 1911, *pg.* 1836
HORIZON AIR INDUSTRIES, 19521 International Blvd, **Seattle,** WA 98188-5402, *pg.* 1912, *pg.* 1836
PRINCESS TOURS, 800 5th Ave Ste 2600, **Seattle,** WA 98104, *pg.* 1920, *pg.* 1838
WINDSTAR CRUISES, 2101 4th Ave Ste 210, **Seattle,** WA 98121, *pg.* 1931, *pg.* 1843

Wisconsin

FEDEX SMARTPOST, INC., 16555 W Rogers Dr, **New Berlin,** WI 53151, *pg.* 1909, *pg.* 1883
MARK TRAVEL CORPORATION, 8969 N Port Washington Rd, **Milwaukee,** WI 53217-1634, *pg.* 1915, *pg.* 1877
SCHNEIDER, 3101 Packerland Dr, **Green Bay,** WI 54313-6187, *pg.* 1922, *pg.* 1859
TRAVEL GUARD GROUP, INC., 3300 Business Pk Dr, **Stevens Point,** WI 54481, *pg.* 1925, *pg.* 1895

Wyoming

GREAT LAKES AVIATION, LTD., 1022 Airport Pkwy, **Cheyenne,** WY 82001-1551, *pg.* 1909, *pg.* 1901

Utilities

Alabama

ALABAMA GAS CORPORATION, 20th St S, **Birmingham,** AL 35295, *pg.* 1933, *pg.* 1
ALABAMA POWER COMPANY, 600 N 18th St, **Birmingham,** AL 35291-0001, *pg.* 1933, *pg.* 1
ENERGEN CORPORATION, 605 Richard Arrington Jr Blvd N, **Birmingham,** AL 35203-2707, *pg.* 1941, *pg.* 2

Arizona

ARIZONA PUBLIC SERVICE COMPANY, 400 N 5th St, **Phoenix,** AZ 85004-3902, *pg.* 1935, *pg.* 14
TUCSON ELECTRIC POWER COMPANY, 88 E Broadway Blvd, **Tucson,** AZ 85701, *pg.* 1953, *pg.* 27
UNS ENERGY CORPORATION, 88 E Broadway Blvd, **Tucson,** AZ 85702, *pg.* 1954, *pg.* 27

California

EDISON INTERNATIONAL, 2244 Walnut Grove Ave Ste 369, **Rosemead,** CA 91770-3714, *pg.* 1941, *pg.* 194
PG&E CORPORATION, 77 Beale St, P.O. Box 770000, **San Francisco,** CA 94177, *pg.* 1949, *pg.* 224
SEMPRA ENERGY, 101 Ash St, **San Diego,** CA 92101-3017, *pg.* 1951, *pg.* 209
SOUTHERN CALIFORNIA EDISON COMPANY, 2244 Walnut Grove Ave, **Rosemead,** CA 91770-3714, *pg.* 1952, *pg.* 194
SOUTHERN CALIFORNIA GAS COMPANY, 555 W 5th St, **Los Angeles,** CA 90013-1010, *pg.* 1952, *pg.* 140
SUNPOWER CORPORATION, 77 Rio Robles, **San Jose,** CA 95134-1859, *pg.* 1952, *pg.* 250
VERENGO, INC., 20285 South Western Ave, Ste 200, **Torrance,** CA 90501, *pg.* 1954, *pg.* 297

Colorado

WESTMORELAND COAL COMPANY, 9540 S Maroon Cir Ste 200, **Englewood,** CO 80112, *pg.* 1955, *pg.* 328

Connecticut

AQUARION WATER COMPANY, 200 Monroe Tpke, **Monroe,** CT 06468, *pg.* 1935, *pg.* 357
CONNECTICUT WATER SERVICE, INC., 93 W Main St, **Clinton,** CT 06413, *pg.* 1938, *pg.* 342
CONSTELLATION, 595 Summer St Ste 300, **Stamford,** CT 06901, *pg.* 1938, *pg.* 373
EVERSOURCE, 107 Selden St, **Berlin,** CT 06037, *pg.* 1942, *pg.* 337
UIL HOLDINGS CORPORATION, 157 Church St, **New Haven,** CT 06506, *pg.* 1953, *pg.* 359

Delaware

CHESAPEAKE UTILITIES CORPORATION, 909 Silver Lake Blvd, **Dover,** DE 19904-2409, *pg.* 1937, *pg.* 387

District of Columbia

EDISON ELECTRIC INSTITUTE, 701 Pennsylvania Ave NW, **Washington,** DC 20004-2696, *pg.* 1941, *pg.* 398
PEPCO HOLDINGS, INC., 701 9th St NW, **Washington,** DC 20068, *pg.* 1949, *pg.* 404
POTOMAC ELECTRIC POWER COMPANY, 701 9th St NW, **Washington,** DC 20068-0001, *pg.* 1950, *pg.* 404
WASHINGTON GAS LIGHT CO., 101 Constitution Ave NW, **Washington,** DC 20080, *pg.* 1954, *pg.* 407

Florida

DUKE ENERGY PROGRESS, 299 First Ave N, **Saint Petersburg,** FL 33701-3324, *pg.* 1940, *pg.* 462
FLORIDA POWER & LIGHT COMPANY, 700 Universe Blvd, **Juno Beach,** FL 33408-2657, *pg.* 1943, *pg.* 435
FLORIDA PUBLIC UTILITIES, 780 Amelia Island Pkwy, **Fernandina Beach,** FL 32034, *pg.* 1943, *pg.* 422
GAINESVILLE REGIONAL UTILITIES INC., 301 SE 4th Ave, **Gainesville,** FL 32601-6857, *pg.* 1943, *pg.* 429
GULF POWER COMPANY, 1 Energy Pl, **Pensacola,** FL 32520-0001, *pg.* 1944, *pg.* 458
TAMPA ELECTRIC COMPANY, 702 N Franklin St, **Tampa,** FL 33602-4429, *pg.* 1952, *pg.* 476

Georgia

AGL RESOURCES INC., 10 Peachtree Pl NE, **Atlanta,** GA 30309, *pg.* 1933, *pg.* 487
GEORGIA POWER COMPANY, 241 Ralph McGill Blvd NE, **Atlanta,** GA 30308-3374, *pg.* 1943, *pg.* 508
MUNICIPAL ELECTRIC AUTHORITY OF GEORGIA, 1470 Riveredge Pkwy NW, **Atlanta,** GA 30328-4686, *pg.* 1946, *pg.* 515
SOUTHERN COMPANY, 30 Ivan Allen Jr Blvd NW, **Atlanta,** GA 30308, *pg.* 1952, *pg.* 520

Hawaii

THE GAS COMPANY LLC, 515 Kamakee St, **Honolulu,** HI 96814, *pg.* 1943, *pg.* 543
HAWAIIAN ELECTRIC COMPANY, INC., 900 Richards St, **Honolulu,** HI 96813-2919, *pg.* 1944, *pg.* 544

Idaho

IDACORP, INC., 1221 W Idaho St, **Boise,** ID 83702-5627, *pg.* 1944, *pg.* 546
INTERMOUNTAIN GAS COMPANY, 555 S Cole Rd, **Boise,** ID 83709-0940, *pg.* 1945, *pg.* 547

Illinois

AMEREN ILLINOIS COMPANY, 300 Liberty St, **Peoria,** IL 61602, *pg.* 1934, *pg.* 650
EXELON CORPORATION, 10 S Dearborn St 48th Fl, **Chicago,** IL 60680, *pg.* 1942, *pg.* 573
NICOR GAS AN AGL RESOURCES COMPANY, 1844 W Ferry Rd, **Naperville,** IL 60563-9600, *pg.* 1947, *pg.* 636
NORTHERN ILLINOIS GAS COMPANY, 1844 W Ferry Rd, **Naperville,** IL 60563-9600, *pg.* 1947, *pg.* 637

Indiana

CITIZENS ENERGY GROUP, 2020 N Meridian St, **Indianapolis,** IN 46202, *pg.* 1937, *pg.* 683
DUKE ENERGY INDIANA, INC., 1000 E Main St, **Plainfield,** IN 46168, *pg.* 1940, *pg.* 696
HOOSIER ENERGY RURAL ELECTRIC COOPERATIVE INC., 7398 N State Rd 37, **Bloomington,** IN 47404-9424, *pg.* 1944, *pg.* 674
INDIANAPOLIS POWER & LIGHT COMPANY, 1 Monument Cir, **Indianapolis,** IN 46206, *pg.* 1945, *pg.* 687
NORTHERN INDIANA PUBLIC SERVICE COMPANY, 801 E 86th Ave, **Merrillville,** IN 46410-6271, *pg.* 1947, *pg.* 694

Iowa

MIDAMERICAN ENERGY HOLDINGS COMPANY, 666 Grand Ave Ste 500, **Des Moines,** IA 50309-2580, *pg.* 1946, *pg.* 706

Kentucky

KENTUCKY UTILITIES COMPANY, 1 Quality St, **Lexington,** KY 40507-1428, *pg.* 1945, *pg.* 730
LG&E AND KU ENERGY LLC, 220 W Main St, **Louisville,** KY 40232, *pg.* 1946, *pg.* 736

Louisiana

CLECO CORPORATION, 2030 Donahue Ferry Rd, **Pineville,** LA 71360, *pg.* 1937, *pg.* 748
ENTERGY CORPORATION, 639 Loyola Ave, **New Orleans,** LA 70113, *pg.* 1941, *pg.* 746
ENTERGY NEW ORLEANS, INC., 1600 Perdido St, **New Orleans,** LA 70112, *pg.* 1942, *pg.* 746

Maine

CENTRAL MAINE POWER COMPANY, 83 Edison Dr, **Augusta,** ME 04336, *pg.* 1937, *pg.* 749

Maryland

BALTIMORE GAS AND ELECTRIC COMPANY, PO Box 1475, **Baltimore,** MD 21203-1475, *pg.* 1936, *pg.* 755
CONSTELLATION ENERGY RESOURCES, LLC, 100 Constellation Way, **Baltimore,** MD 21202, *pg.* 1938, *pg.* 756

Massachusetts

BEACON POWER, LLC, 65 Middlesex Rd, **Tyngsboro,** MA 01879, *pg.* 1936, *pg.* 848
EVERSOURCE, One Federal Street Building 111-4, **Springfield,** MA 01105, *pg.* 1942, *pg.* 845
NATIONAL GRID USA, 40 Sylvin Rd, **Waltham,** MA 02451, *pg.* 1946, *pg.* 852

Michigan

CMS ENERGY CORPORATION, One Energy Plaza, **Jackson,** MI 49201, *pg.* 1937, *pg.* 893
CONSUMERS ENERGY COMPANY, 1 Energy Plz, **Jackson,** MI 49201, *pg.* 1938, *pg.* 893
DTE ENERGY COMPANY, 1 Energy Plz, **Detroit,** MI 48226-1279, *pg.* 1940, *pg.* 880
ITC HOLDINGS CORP., 27175 Energy Way, **Novi,** MI 48377, *pg.* 1945, *pg.* 903

Minnesota

ALLETE, INC., 30 W Superior St, **Duluth,** MN 55802, *pg.* 1933, *pg.* 921
DAKOTA ELECTRIC ASSOCIATION, 4300 220th St W, **Farmington,** MN 55024, *pg.* 1939, *pg.* 925
XCEL ENERGY INC., 414 Nicollet Mall, **Minneapolis,** MN 55401, *pg.* 1955, *pg.* 946

Missouri

AMEREN CORPORATION, 1901 Chouteau Ave, **Saint Louis,** MO 63103, *pg.* 1934, *pg.* 990
THE EMPIRE DISTRICT ELECTRIC COMPANY, 602 Joplin St, **Joplin,** MO 64801, *pg.* 1941, *pg.* 980
GREAT PLAINS ENERGY INCORPORATED, 1200 Main St, **Kansas City,** MO 64105, *pg.* 1944, *pg.* 983
KANSAS CITY POWER & LIGHT COMPANY, 1200 Main St, **Kansas City,** MO 64105, *pg.* 1945, *pg.* 985
LACLEDE GAS COMPANY, 720 Olive St, **Saint Louis,** MO 63101, *pg.* 1945, *pg.* 999

Montana

NORTHWESTERN ENERGY, 40 E Broadway St, **Butte,** MT 59701, *pg.* 1947, *pg.* 1008

Nebraska

NEBRASKA PUBLIC POWER DISTRICT, 1414 15th St, **Columbus,** NE 68601-5226, *pg.* 1947, *pg.* 1010
OMAHA PUBLIC POWER DISTRICT, OPPD Energy Plz 444 S 16th St Mall, **Omaha,** NE 68102-2247, *pg.* 1948, *pg.* 1017

Nevada

NV ENERGY, 6100 Neil Rd, **Reno,** NV 89511-1132, *pg.* 1948, *pg.* 1032
NV ENERGY, INC., 6226 W Sahara Ave, **Las Vegas,** NV 89146, *pg.* 1948, *pg.* 1028

New Hampshire

EVERSOURCE, 780 N Commercial St, **Manchester,** NH 03101-1134, *pg.* 1942, *pg.* 1035

New Jersey

First page reference indicates Business Class Edition
Second page reference indicates Geographic Edition

AMERICAN WATER WORKS COMPANY, INC., 1025 Laurel Oak Rd, **Voorhees, NJ** 08043-3506, *pg.* 1934, *pg.* 1128
MIDDLESEX WATER COMPANY, 1500 Ronson Rd, **Iselin,** NJ 08830-3049, *pg.* 1946, *pg.* 1075
OCEAN POWER TECHNOLOGIES, INC., 1590 Reed Rd, **Pennington, NJ** 08534, *pg.* 1948, *pg.* 1107
PUBLIC SERVICE ENTERPRISE GROUP INCORPORATED, 80 Park Plaza, **Newark, NJ** 07101-1171, *pg.* 1950, *pg.* 1097
SOUTH JERSEY GAS COMPANY, 1 S Jersey Plz, **Folsom,** NJ 08037, *pg.* 1951, *pg.* 1067
UNITED WATER RESOURCES INC., 200 Old Hook Rd, **Harrington Park, NJ** 07640-1716, *pg.* 1954, *pg.* 1073

New Mexico

PNM RESOURCES, INC., Alvarado Sq, **Albuquerque,** NM 87158-0001, *pg.* 1949, *pg.* 1135

New York

CENTRAL HUDSON GAS & ELECTRIC CORPORATION, 284 South Ave, **Poughkeepsie,** NY 12601, *pg.* 1937, *pg.* 1324
CONSOLIDATED EDISON, INC., 4 Irving Pl, **New York,** NY 10003-3502, *pg.* 1938, *pg.* 1218
LAPP INSULATOR COMPANY, LLC, 130 Gilbert St, **Le Roy,** NY 14482, *pg.* 1946, *pg.* 1173
LONG ISLAND POWER AUTHORITY, 333 Earle Ovington Blvd Ste 403, **Uniondale,** NY 11553, *pg.* 1946, *pg.* 1346
NATIONAL FUEL GAS DISTRIBUTION CORP., 6363 Main St, **Williamsville,** NY 14221, *pg.* 1946, *pg.* 1355
NEW YORK POWER AUTHORITY, INC., 30 S Pearl St, **Albany,** NY 12207-3425, *pg.* 1947, *pg.* 1137
ORANGE & ROCKLAND UTILITIES, INC., 1 Blue Hill Plz, **Pearl River,** NY 10965, *pg.* 1949, *pg.* 1321
RGS ENERGY, 36 Midland Ave, **Port Chester,** NY 10573, *pg.* 1951, *pg.* 1322

North Carolina

DUKE ENERGY CORPORATION, 526 S Church St, **Charlotte,** NC 28202-1904, *pg.* 1940, *pg.* 1366
DUKE ENERGY PROGRESS, 410 S Wilmington St, **Raleigh,** NC 27601, *pg.* 1940, *pg.* 1387
PIEDMONT NATURAL GAS COMPANY, INC., 4720 Piedmont Row Dr, **Charlotte,** NC 28210, *pg.* 1949, *pg.* 1368

North Dakota

BASIN ELECTRIC POWER COOPERATIVE, 1717 E Interstate Ave, **Bismarck,** ND 58503, *pg.* 1936, *pg.* 1397
CASS COUNTY ELECTRIC COOPERATIVE, INC., 4100 32nd Ave SW, **Fargo,** ND 58104-8608, *pg.* 1937, *pg.* 1397
VERENDRYE ELECTRIC COOPERATIVE, 615 Hwy 52 W, **Velva,** ND 58790, *pg.* 1954, *pg.* 1398

Ohio

AEP OHIO, 850 Tech Ctr Dr, **Gahanna,** OH 43230, *pg.* 1933, *pg.* 1454
AMERICAN ELECTRIC POWER COMPANY, INC., 1 Riverside Plz, **Columbus,** OH 43215-2373, *pg.* 1934, *pg.* 1437
AMERICAN ELECTRIC POWER SERVICE CORPORATION, 1 Riverside Plz, **Columbus,** OH 43215-2355, *pg.* 1934, *pg.* 1437
COLUMBIA GAS OF OHIO, INC., 200 Civic Ctr Dr, **Columbus,** OH 43215, *pg.* 1938, *pg.* 1438
DPL INC., 1065 Woodman Dr, **Dayton,** OH 45432, *pg.* 1939, *pg.* 1445
FIRSTENERGY CORP., 76 S Main St, **Akron,** OH 44308-1812, *pg.* 1942, *pg.* 1400
JERSEY CENTRAL POWER & LIGHT COMPANY, c/o FirstEnergy Corp 76 S Main St, **Akron,** OH 44308, *pg.* 1945, *pg.* 1402
OHIO GAS COMPANY, 200 W High St, **Bryan,** OH 43506-0528, *pg.* 1948, *pg.* 1407
PUBLIC SERVICE COMPANY OF OKLAHOMA, 1 Riverside Plz, **Columbus,** OH 43215, *pg.* 1950, *pg.* 1443

Oklahoma

CHESAPEAKE ENERGY CORPORATION, 6100 N Western Ave, **Oklahoma City,** OK 73118-1044, *pg.* 1937, *pg.* 1485
OGE ENERGY CORP., 321 N Harvey Ave, **Oklahoma City,** OK 73102-3405, *pg.* 1948, *pg.* 1486

Oregon

NORTHWEST NATURAL GAS COMPANY, 220 NW 2nd Ave, **Portland,** OR 97209, *pg.* 1947, *pg.* 1504
PACIFICORP, 825 NE Multnomah St, **Portland,** OR 97232, *pg.* 1949, *pg.* 1504
PORTLAND GENERAL ELECTRIC COMPANY, 121 SW Salmon St, **Portland,** OR 97204-2901, *pg.* 1950, *pg.* 1505

Pennsylvania

AQUA AMERICA, INC., 762 W Lancaster Ave, **Bryn Mawr,** PA 19010-3402, *pg.* 1935, *pg.* 1518
DUQUESNE LIGHT COMPANY, 411 7th Ave, **Pittsburgh,** PA 15219-1919, *pg.* 1940, *pg.* 1574
PECO ENERGY COMPANY, 2301 Market St, **Philadelphia,** PA 19101, *pg.* 1949, *pg.* 1568
PPL CORPORATION, 2 N 9th St, **Allentown,** PA 18101-1179, *pg.* 1950, *pg.* 1514
UGI CORPORATION, 460 N Gulph Rd, **King of Prussia,** PA 19406, *pg.* 1953, *pg.* 1544

South Carolina

SANTEE COOPER, 1 Riverwood Dr, **Moncks Corner,** SC 29461, *pg.* 1951, *pg.* 1620
SCANA CORPORATION, 100 SCANA Pkwy, **Cayce,** SC 29033, *pg.* 1951, *pg.* 1612

South Dakota

NORTHWESTERN CORPORATION, 3010 W 69th St, **Sioux Falls,** SD 57108, *pg.* 1947, *pg.* 1625

Tennessee

MEMPHIS LIGHT, GAS & WATER, 220 S Main St, **Memphis,** TN 38103-3917, *pg.* 1946, *pg.* 1645

Texas

APACHE CORPORATION, One Post Oak Central 2000 Post Oak Blvd Ste 100, **Houston,** TX 77056-4400, *pg.* 1934, *pg.* 1700
ATMOS ENERGY CORPORATION, 3 Lincoln Centre Ste 1800 5430 LBJ Fwy, **Dallas,** TX 75240-2615, *pg.* 1935, *pg.* 1675
CALPINE CORPORATION, 717 Texas Ave Ste 1000, **Houston,** TX 77002, *pg.* 1936, *pg.* 1702
CPS ENERGY, 145 Navarro St, **San Antonio,** TX 78205, *pg.* 1939, *pg.* 1739
DIRECT ENERGY, 12 Greenway Plz, Ste 250, **Houston,** TX 77046, *pg.* 1939, *pg.* 1704
ENERGY FUTURE HOLDINGS CORP., 1601 Bryan St, **Dallas,** TX 75201-3411, *pg.* 1941, *pg.* 1680
ENERGY TRANSFER EQUITY, L.P., 3738 Oak Lawn Ave, **Dallas,** TX 75219, *pg.* 1941, *pg.* 1680
ENVIROGEN TECHNOLOGIES, INC., Two Kingwood Pl 700 Rockmead Dr Ste 105, **Kingwood,** TX 77339, *pg.* 1942, *pg.* 1724
GREEN MOUNTAIN ENERGY COMPANY, 300 W 6th St, **Austin,** TX 78701, *pg.* 1944, *pg.* 1663
KINDER MORGAN, Kinder Morgan Bldg 1001 Louisiana St, **Houston,** TX 77002, *pg.* 1945, *pg.* 1709
NRG ENERGY, INC., 1000 Main St, **Houston,** TX 77002, *pg.* 1948, *pg.* 1712
SOUTHERN UNION COMPANY, 5051 Westheimer Rd Ste 1428, **Houston,** TX 77056-5720, *pg.* 1952, *pg.* 1715
TXU ENERGY RETAIL COMPANY LLC, 1601 Bryan St, **Dallas,** TX 75201, *pg.* 1953, *pg.* 1690
WASTE CONNECTIONS, INC., 3 Waterway Sq PL Ste 110, **The Woodlands,** TX 77380, *pg.* 1954, *pg.* 1747
WASTE MANAGEMENT, INC., 1001 Fannin St Ste 4000, **Houston,** TX 77002-6711, *pg.* 1954, *pg.* 1716

Utah

ENERGYSOLUTIONS INC., 423 W 300 S Ste 200, **Salt Lake City,** UT 84101, *pg.* 1941, *pg.* 1757

Vermont

GREEN MOUNTAIN POWER CORPORATION, 163 Acorn Ln, **Colchester,** VT 05446-6612, *pg.* 1944, *pg.* 1765

Virginia

DOMINION EAST OHIO ENERGY, 120 Tredegar St, **Richmond,** VA 23219, *pg.* 1939, *pg.* 1801
DOMINION RESOURCES, INC., 120 Tredegar St, **Richmond,** VA 23219-4306, *pg.* 1939, *pg.* 1802
DOMINION VIRGINIA POWER, 120 Tredegar St, **Richmond,** VA 23219, *pg.* 1939, *pg.* 1802
RGC RESOURCES, INC., 519 Kimball Ave NE, **Roanoke,** VA 24016-2103, *pg.* 1951, *pg.* 1806
TOUCHSTONE ENERGY COOPERATIVES, 4301 Wilson Blvd, **Arlington,** VA 22203, *pg.* 1953, *pg.* 1775

Washington

AVISTA CORPORATION, 1411 E Mission Ave, **Spokane,** WA 99202-2600, *pg.* 1935, *pg.* 1843
PUGET ENERGY, INC., 10885 NE 4th St Ste 1200, **Bellevue,** WA 98004-5515, *pg.* 1950, *pg.* 1816
SEATTLE CITY LIGHT, 700 Fifth Ave Ste 3200, **Seattle,** WA 98104-5031, *pg.* 1951, *pg.* 1839

Wisconsin

ALLIANT ENERGY CORPORATION, 4902 N Biltmore Ln, **Madison,** WI 53718, *pg.* 1933, *pg.* 1864
DAIRYLAND POWER COOPERATIVE, 3200 E Ave S, PO Box 817, **La Crosse,** WI 54602-0817, *pg.* 1939, *pg.* 1864
WEC ENERGY GROUP, INC., 231 W Michigan St, **Milwaukee,** WI 53201, *pg.* 1954, *pg.* 1881

Wines & Liquors

California

CAMERON HUGHES WINE, 444 De Haro St Ste 101, **San Francisco,** CA 94107-2349, *pg.* 1960, *pg.* 214
CAMPARI AMERICA, 1255 Battery St Ste 500, **San Francisco,** CA 94111, *pg.* 1960, *pg.* 214
DELICATO FAMILY VINEYARDS, 455 Devlin Rd Ste 201, **Napa,** CA 94558, *pg.* 1961, *pg.* 163
DOMAINE CHANDON, INC., One California Dr, **Yountville,** CA 94599, *pg.* 1962, *pg.* 308
THE DONUM ESTATE, INC, PO Box 154, **Sonoma,** CA 95476-0154, *pg.* 1962, *pg.* 279
E&J GALLO WINERY, 600 Yosemite Blvd, **Modesto,** CA 95354-2760, *pg.* 1962, *pg.* 149
F. KORBEL BROS. INC., 13250 River Rd, **Guerneville,** CA 95446-9593, *pg.* 1963, *pg.* 100
FETZER VINEYARDS, 12901 Old River Rd, **Hopland,** CA 95449, *pg.* 1963, *pg.* 104
FREIXENET U.S.A., 23555 Hwy 121, **Sonoma,** CA 95476-9285, *pg.* 1963, *pg.* 279
GEYSER PEAK WINERY, 2306 Magnolia Dr, **Healdsburg,** CA 92407, *pg.* 1964, *pg.* 101
GIUMARRA VINEYARDS CORPORATION, PO Box 1969, **Bakersfield,** CA 93303-1969, *pg.* 1964, *pg.* 45
GLOBAL WINE COMPANY, 10 Liberty Ship Way Ste 300, **Sausalito,** CA 94965, *pg.* 1964, *pg.* 278
INTERNATIONAL WINE ACCESSORIES, INC., 531 Mercantile Dr, **Cotati,** CA 94931, *pg.* 1964, *pg.* 71
KENDALL-JACKSON WINE ESTATES, LTD., 421 Aviation Blvd, **Santa Rosa,** CA 95403, *pg.* 1965, *pg.* 277
NOLET SPIRITS USA INC., 30 Journey, **Aliso Viejo,** CA 92656, *pg.* 1967, *pg.* 41
PARTIDA TEQUILA, LLC, 150 California St Ste 500, **San Francisco,** CA 94111, *pg.* 1967, *pg.* 224
PHOENIX VINTNERS, LLC, 755 Baywood Dr 2nd Fl, **Petaluma,** CA 94954, *pg.* 1968, *pg.* 182
ROBERT MONDAVI WINERY, 7801 Saint Helena Hwy, **Oakville,** CA 94562, *pg.* 1969, *pg.* 173
SAPPORO U.S.A., INC., 1821250 Hawthorne Blvd, **Torrance,** CA 90503, *pg.* 1969, *pg.* 295
SCHEID VINEYARDS INC., 305 Hilltown Rd, **Salinas,** CA 93908-8902, *pg.* 1970, *pg.* 198
STONE BRIDGE CELLARS INC., 200 Taplin Rd, **Saint Helena,** CA 94574-9601, *pg.* 1971, *pg.* 197
TREASURY WINE ESTATES, 610 Airpark Rd, **Napa,** CA 94558-7516, *pg.* 1971, *pg.* 164
TRINCHERO FAMILY ESTATES, 100 Main St, **Saint Helena,** CA 94574-2166, *pg.* 1971, *pg.* 197
VEEV ACAI SPIRITS, 5979 W 3rd St Ste 204, **Los Angeles,** CA 90036, *pg.* 1972, *pg.* 141
WEIBEL, INC., 1 Winemaster Way, **Lodi,** CA 95240-0860, *pg.* 1972, *pg.* 122
WENTE VINEYARDS, 5565 Tesla Rd, **Livermore,** CA 94550-9149, *pg.* 1972, *pg.* 122
THE WINE GROUP, INC., 240 Stockton St Ste 800, **San Francisco,** CA 94108-5325, *pg.* 1972, *pg.* 234
WINE.COM, INC., 114 Sansome St Ste 300, **San Francisco,** CA 94104, *pg.* 1972, *pg.* 234

Connecticut

DIAGEO NORTH AMERICA, INC., 801 Main Ave, **Norwalk,** CT 06851, *pg.* 1961, *pg.* 361
NEW ENGLAND BREWING COMPANY, 7 Seldon St, **Woodbridge,** CT 06525, *pg.* 1967, *pg.* 386

Florida

B-21 FINE WINE & SPIRITS INC., 43380 Hwy 19 N, **Tarpon Springs,** FL 34689-0849, *pg.* 1956, *pg.* 477
BACARDI GLOBAL BRANDS INC., 866 Ponce De Leon Blvd Fl 2, **Coral Gables,** FL 33134-3039, *pg.* 1956, *pg.* 417
BACARDI USA, INC., 2701 Le Jeu Rd, **Coral Gables,** FL 33134-5014, *pg.* 1956, *pg.* 417
FLANIGAN'S ENTERPRISES, INC., 5059 NE 18th Ave, **Fort Lauderdale,** FL 33334-5724, *pg.* 1963, *pg.* 425
SHAW ROSS INTERNATIONAL IMPORTERS, 2400 SW 145th Ave Ste 201, **Miramar,** FL 33027, *pg.* 1970, *pg.* 449

Georgia

UNITED DISTRIBUTORS, INC., 5500 United Dr, **Smyrna,** GA 30082-4755, *pg.* 1971, *pg.* 540

Illinois

BEAM SUNTORY INC., 510 Lake Cook Rd Ste 200, **Deerfield,** IL 60015, *pg.* 1957, *pg.* 599
JIM BEAM BRANDS CO., 510 Lake Cook Rd, **Deerfield,** IL 60015, *pg.* 1965, *pg.* 601
MAGNET ENTERPRISES, INC., 2211 N Elston Ave, **Chicago,** IL 60614, *pg.* 1966, *pg.* 581
MIKE'S HARD LEMONADE CO., 328 S Jefferson, **Chicago,** IL 60661, *pg.* 1966, *pg.* 582
THE TERLATO WINE GROUP, 2401 Waukegan Rd, **Bannockburn,** IL 60044, *pg.* 1971, *pg.* 555

Indiana

NATIONAL WINE & SPIRITS, INC., 700 W Morris St, **Indianapolis,** IN 46206, *pg.* 1967, *pg.* 689

Kentucky

BROWN-FORMAN BEVERAGES, 850 Dixie Hwy, **Louisville,** KY 40210-1038, *pg.* 1958, *pg.* 731
BROWN-FORMAN CORPORATION, 850 Dixie Hwy, **Louisville,** KY 40210-1038, *pg.* 1958, *pg.* 732
HEAVEN HILL DISTILLERIES, INC., 1064 Loretto Rd, **Bardstown,** KY 40004-2229, *pg.* 1964, *pg.* 725
MAKER'S MARK DISTILLERY, INC., 3350 Burks Springs Rd, **Loretto,** KY 40037, *pg.* 1966, *pg.* 731

Louisiana

SAZERAC COMPANY, INC., 3850 N Causeway Blvd, Ste 1695, **Metairie,** LA 70002, *pg.* 1969, *pg.* 745

Maryland

MONTEBELLO BRANDS INC., 1919 Willow Spring Rd, **Baltimore,** MD 21222-2939, *pg.* 1967, *pg.* 758
TOTAL WINE & MORE, 11325 Seven Locks Rd Ste 214, **Potomac,** MD 20854, *pg.* 1971, *pg.* 775

Massachusetts

CARE.COM, 77 Fourth Ave 5th Fl, **Waltham,** MA 02451, *pg.* 1960, *pg.* 850
M.S. WALKER, INC., 20 3rd Ave, **Somerville,** MA 02143-4450, *pg.* 1967, *pg.* 843

Michigan

GRAND TRAVERSE DISTILLERY, 781 Industrial Cir Ste 5, **Traverse City,** MI 49686, *pg.* 1964, *pg.* 909

Minnesota

JOHNSON BROTHERS LIQUOR COMPANY, 1999 Shepard Rd, **Saint Paul,** MN 55116, *pg.* 1965, *pg.* 961

Missouri

MCCORMICK DISTILLING CO., INC., 1 McCormick Ln, **Weston,** MO 64098-9558, *pg.* 1966, *pg.* 1007

Nevada

THE PATRON SPIRITS COMPANY, 6670 S Vly View, **Las Vegas,** NV 89118-4516, *pg.* 1967, *pg.* 1029

New Jersey

GARY'S WINE & MARKETPLACE, 121 Main St, **Madison,** NJ 07940-2115, *pg.* 1964, *pg.* 1080
LAIRD & COMPANY, INC., 1 Laird Rd, **Scobeyville,** NJ 07724-9724, *pg.* 1966, *pg.* 1119
OPICI WINE GROUP INC., 25 De Boer Dr, **Glen Rock,** NJ 07452-3301, *pg.* 1967, *pg.* 1071
PROXIMO SPIRITS, INC., 333 Washington St, **Jersey City,** NJ 07302, *pg.* 1969, *pg.* 1076
WILLIAM GRANT & SONS, INC., 130 Fieldcrest Ave, **Edison,** NJ 08837, *pg.* 1972, *pg.* 1057

New York

THE ABSOLUT SPIRITS COMPANY INC., 100 Manhattanville Rd, **Purchase,** NY 10577, *pg.* 1956, *pg.* 1325
ADAMBA IMPORTS INTERNATIONAL, 585 Meserole St, **Brooklyn,** NY 11237, *pg.* 1956, *pg.* 1145
BANFI VINTNERS, 1111 Cedar Swamp Rd, **Glen Head,** NY 11545-2109, *pg.* 1957, *pg.* 1161
CONSTELLATION BRANDS, INC., 207 High Point Dr Bldg 100, **Victor,** NY 14564, *pg.* 1960, *pg.* 1348
DREYFUS ASHBY INC., 630 3rd Ave 15th Fl, **New York,** NY 10017, *pg.* 1962, *pg.* 1226
FREDERICK WILDMAN & SONS LTD., 307 E 53rd St, **New York,** NY 10022-4985, *pg.* 1963, *pg.* 1233
KOBRAND CORPORATION, 1 Manhattanville Rd Fl 4, **Purchase,** NY 10577-2126, *pg.* 1965, *pg.* 1325
MARNIER-LAPOSTOLLE INC., 717 5th Ave, **New York,** NY 10022, *pg.* 1966, *pg.* 1256
MOET HENNESSY, 85 10th Ave Fl 2, **New York,** NY 10011, *pg.* 1966, *pg.* 1260
PERNOD RICARD USA, INC., 100 Manhattanville Rd, **Purchase,** NY 10577, *pg.* 1968, *pg.* 1332
REMY COINTREAU USA INC., 1290 Avenue of the Americas 10th Fl, **New York,** NY 10104, *pg.* 1969, *pg.* 1285
SIDNEY FRANK IMPORTING CO., INC., 20 Cedar St, **New Rochelle,** NY 10801, *pg.* 1970, *pg.* 1184
STOLI GROUP USA LLC, 135 E 57th St, **New York,** NY 10022, *pg.* 1970, *pg.* 1296
TEQUILA AVION, 584 Broadway, Suite 903, **New York,** NY 10012, *pg.* 1971, *pg.* 1298

North Carolina

BILTMORE ESTATE WINE COMPANY, 1 Lodge St, **Asheville,** NC 28803, *pg.* 1958, *pg.* 1358

Oregon

HOOD RIVER DISTILLERS INC., 660 Riverside Dr, **Hood River,** OR 97031-1177, *pg.* 1964, *pg.* 1498
KING ESTATE OREGON WINES, 80854 Territorial Hwy, **Eugene,** OR 97405, *pg.* 1965, *pg.* 1497
REX HILL VINEYARDS, 30835 N Hwy 99 W, **Newberg,** OR 97132, *pg.* 1969, *pg.* 1500
WILLAMETTE VALLEY VINEYARDS, INC., 8800 Enchanted Way SE, **Turner,** OR 97392-9580, *pg.* 1972, *pg.* 1510

Tennessee

JACK DANIEL'S DISTILLERY, Hwy 55, **Lynchburg,** TN 37352, *pg.* 1964, *pg.* 1640

Texas

DEEP EDDY VODKA, 2250 E Hwy 290, **Dripping Springs,** TX 78620, *pg.* 1961, *pg.* 1691
FIFTH GENERATION, INC., 12101 Moore Rd, **Austin,** TX 78719, *pg.* 1963, *pg.* 1662
SPEC'S FAMILY PARTNERS LTD., 2410 Smith St, **Houston,** TX 77006, *pg.* 1970, *pg.* 1715

Washington

STE. MICHELLE WINE ESTATES LTD., 14111 NE 145th St, **Woodinville,** WA 98072, *pg.* 1970, *pg.* 1847

First page reference indicates Business Class Edition
Second page reference indicates Geographic Edition

BRANDS AND PRODUCTS INDEX

0

0-IN - Software System - MENTOR GRAPHICS CORPORATION; *pg.* 432, *pg.* 1510

1

1-2-3 FAMILY TREE - Software - ANCESTRY.COM LLC; *pg.* 1228, *pg.* 1754
1/2 LUNEMOON - Bakery Product - SAPUTO, INC.; *pg.* 893, *pg.* 1956
1-800-4MY-HOME - Technical Services - SEARS HOLDINGS CORPORATION; *pg.* 1784, *pg.* 618
1-800-BASKETS.COM - Online Store - 1-800-FLOWERS.COM, INC.; *pg.* 1758, *pg.* 1151
1-800-CANDIES.COM - Online Store - 1-800-FLOWERS.COM, INC.; *pg.* 1758, *pg.* 1151
1-800-DENTIST - Dental Marketing Service - FUTUREDONTICS, INC.; *pg.* 1532, *pg.* 131
1-800/DIAL BEN - Fund Information Phone Number - FRANKLIN RESOURCES, INC.; *pg.* 760, *pg.* 254
1-800-FASTFILE - Customer Response Number - IRON MOUNTAIN INCORPORATED; *pg.* 421, *pg.* 796
1-800-FLEURISTE - Florist Network - 1-800-FLOWERS.COM, INC.; *pg.* 1758, *pg.* 1151
1-800-FLORES - Floral Network - 1-800-FLOWERS.COM, INC.; *pg.* 1758, *pg.* 1151
1-800-FLOWERS - Flower Delivery Service - 1-800-FLOWERS.COM, INC.; *pg.* 1758, *pg.* 1151
1-800-FLOWERS.BIZ - Website - 1-800-FLOWERS.COM, INC.; *pg.* 1758, *pg.* 1151
1-800-GET-REAL - Advertising And Publishing - AT&T SOUTHEAST; *pg.* 1868, *pg.* 489
1-800-GIFTHOUSE - Gift Network - 1-800-FLOWERS.COM, INC.; *pg.* 1758, *pg.* 1151
1-800-GO-UHAUL - Moving Equipment - U-HAUL INTERNATIONAL, INC.; *pg.* 1926, *pg.* 20
1-800-GOODIES.COM - Website - 1-800-FLOWERS.COM, INC.; *pg.* 1758, *pg.* 1151
1-800-GREETINGS.COM - Website - 1-800-FLOWERS.COM, INC.; *pg.* 1758, *pg.* 1151
1-800-GROWERS.COM - Website - 1-800-FLOWERS.COM, INC.; *pg.* 1758, *pg.* 1151
1-800-LAS-FLORES.COM - Retail Store Services - 1-800-FLOWERS.COM, INC.; *pg.* 1758, *pg.* 1151
1-800-MC1-STCK - Information Services - MCDONALD'S CORPORATION; *pg.* 1737, *pg.* 645
1-800-MY-YAHOO - Internet Services - YAHOO! INC.; *pg.* 1289, *pg.* 289
1-800-PICK-UPS - Software - UNITED PARCEL SERVICE, INC.; *pg.* 1928, *pg.* 522
1-800-PROGRESSIVE - Insurance - THE PROGRESSIVE CORPORATION; *pg.* 1214, *pg.* 1463
1-800-SCHOLASTIC - Educational Materials - SCHOLASTIC INC.; *pg.* 1683, *pg.* 1288
1-800-THE-ROSE - Florist Network - 1-800-FLOWERS.COM, INC.; *pg.* 1758, *pg.* 1151
1-800-WIGGLE-1 - Educational Materials - SCHOLASTIC INC.; *pg.* 1683, *pg.* 1288
1-877-GO-DIGITAL - Customer Service Center - AT&T SOUTHEAST; *pg.* 1868, *pg.* 489
1-877-ON YOUR SIDE - Insurance Service - NATIONWIDE MUTUAL INSURANCE COMPANY; *pg.* 1210, *pg.* 1442
1-888-FLEURISTE - Florist Network - 1-800-FLOWERS.COM, INC.; *pg.* 1758, *pg.* 1151
1-888-FLOWERS - Florist Network - 1-800-FLOWERS.COM, INC.; *pg.* 1758, *pg.* 1151
1-888-FRANKLIN - Fund Information Phone Number - FRANKLIN RESOURCES, INC.; *pg.* 760, *pg.* 254
1-888-KB-HOMES - Homebuilding Services - KB HOME; *pg.* 90, *pg.* 134
1-CLIC - Prescription Vial System - OWENS-ILLINOIS, INC.; *pg.* 1466, *pg.* 1470
1-D ANALYST - Software - BIO-RAD LABORATORIES, INC.; *pg.* 1504, *pg.* 101
1-DAY ACUVUE - Contact Lens - JOHNSON & JOHNSON VISION CARE, INC.; *pg.* 1552, *pg.* 434
1 DAY PASS OUT - Video Game - INTERNATIONAL GAME TECHNOLOGY; *pg.* 957, *pg.* 1024
1 MILLION JACKPOT SLOT - Services - DOVER DOWNS GAMING & ENTERTAINMENT, INC.; *pg.* 545, *pg.* 387
1 SR - Steel Product - AK STEEL HOLDING CORPORATION; *pg.* 1311, *pg.* 1479
1-STITCH - Fasteners - HABAND COMPANY, INC.; *pg.* 1772, *pg.* 1099
1-STROKE ENVIRON - Disinfectant Cleaner - STERIS CORPORATION; *pg.* 1597, *pg.* 1464
1-TOUCH - Helmet Suspension Design - MINE SAFETY APPLIANCES COMPANY; *pg.* 1361, *pg.* 1525
1 WIRE - Communications Product - MAXIM INTEGRATED PRODUCTS, INC.; *pg.* 653, *pg.* 247
1+1 - Upholstery Fabrics - DESIGNTEX GROUP INC.; *pg.* 692, *pg.* 1223
10 10 056 - Phone Savings Plan - CENTURYLINK, INC; *pg.* 1870, *pg.* 317
10//2 - Footwear - NIKE, INC.; *pg.* 1812, *pg.* 1492
10/22 - Autoloading Carbine - STURM, RUGER & COMPANY, INC.; *pg.* 1846, *pg.* 371
10 CANE - Rum - MOET HENNESSY; *pg.* 1966, *pg.* 1260
10 CARAT WINS - Game - WMS INDUSTRIES INC.; *pg.* 593, *pg.* 666
10 DAYS OF CHOCOLATE - Weight Loss System - RBC LIFE SCIENCES, INC.; *pg.* 1588, *pg.* 1723
10 G ENTERPRISE EDITION - Software - ORACLE CORPORATION; *pg.* 450, *pg.* 191
10 G JAVA EDITION - Software - ORACLE CORPORATION; *pg.* 450, *pg.* 191
10-MAR - Steel Product - RUSSEL METALS INC.; *pg.* 1180, *pg.* 1928
10 SQUIRTIN SEA BUDDIES - Baby Care Product - MUNCHKIN, INC.; *pg.* 964, *pg.* 300
10 TEN TIMES PAY - Video Game - INTERNATIONAL GAME TECHNOLOGY; *pg.* 957, *pg.* 1024
10 UNIVERSITY - Apparels - UNDER ARMOUR, INC.; *pg.* 49, *pg.* 759
100 CALORIE BARS - Calorie Bars - THE HERSHEY CO.; *pg.* 1855, *pg.* 1538
100 DEGREES - Video Game - INTERNATIONAL GAME TECHNOLOGY; *pg.* 957, *pg.* 1024
100 GRAND - Chocolate Bar - NESTLE USA, INC.; *pg.* 883, *pg.* 96
100 HUNDRED OR NOTHING - Slots - INTERNATIONAL GAME TECHNOLOGY; *pg.* 957, *pg.* 1024
100 LADIES - Video Game - INTERNATIONAL GAME TECHNOLOGY; *pg.* 957, *pg.* 1024
100 MILLION DOLLAR BLOCKBUSTER - Lottery Card - MISSOURI LOTTERY; *pg.* 999, *pg.* 979
100 PANDAS - Video Game - INTERNATIONAL GAME TECHNOLOGY; *pg.* 957, *pg.* 1024
100% CHICKEN. NATURALLY. - Slogan - SANDERSON FARMS, INC.; *pg.* 893, *pg.* 970
100 WOLVES - Video Game - INTERNATIONAL GAME TECHNOLOGY; *pg.* 957, *pg.* 1024
10,000 STEPS - Health Program - HEALTHPARTNERS, INC.; *pg.* 1203, *pg.* 918
100,000 BONUS BINGO - Lottery Game - OHIO LOTTERY COMMISSION; *pg.* 1002, *pg.* 1433
$100,000 PAYDAY - Game - MISSOURI LOTTERY; *pg.* 999, *pg.* 979
$100,000 RICHES - Lottery Game - MISSOURI LOTTERY; *pg.* 999, *pg.* 979
$100,000 TREASURE HUNT - Lottery Game - MINNESOTA STATE LOTTERY; *pg.* 999, *pg.* 956
$100,000 VEGAS MONEY - Lottery Game - MISSOURI LOTTERY; *pg.* 999, *pg.* 979
1,000,000 DEGREES - Video Game - BALLY TECHNOLOGIES, INC.; *pg.* 531, *pg.* 1022
100X ONE HUNDRED TIMES PAY - Video Game - INTERNATIONAL GAME TECHNOLOGY; *pg.* 957, *pg.* 1024
101 GT - Conveyor-Based System - AMERICAN SCIENCE AND ENGINEERING, INC.; *pg.* 1399, *pg.* 787
101 Z - Stationary Conveyor-Based System - AMERICAN SCIENCE AND ENGINEERING, INC.; *pg.* 1399, *pg.* 787
101 ZZ - Stationary Conveyor-Based System - AMERICAN SCIENCE AND ENGINEERING, INC.; *pg.* 1399, *pg.* 787
101GT - Image Simulator Software - AMERICAN SCIENCE AND ENGINEERING, INC.; *pg.* 1399, *pg.* 787
101VAN - Image Simulator Software - AMERICAN SCIENCE AND ENGINEERING, INC.; *pg.* 1399, *pg.* 787
101Z - Image Simulator Software - AMERICAN SCIENCE AND ENGINEERING, INC.; *pg.* 1399, *pg.* 787
10221 - Electronic Component - EMCORE CORPORATION; *pg.* 636, *pg.* 39
10347A - Electronic Component - EMCORE CORPORATION; *pg.* 636, *pg.* 39
10357A - Electronic Component - EMCORE CORPORATION; *pg.* 636, *pg.* 39
10381 - Electronic Component - EMCORE CORPORATION; *pg.* 636, *pg.* 39
10382 - Electronic Component - EMCORE CORPORATION; *pg.* 636, *pg.* 39
10383 - Electronic Component - EMCORE CORPORATION; *pg.* 636, *pg.* 39
10384 - Electronic Component - EMCORE CORPORATION; *pg.* 636, *pg.* 39
104+ - Performance Additives - GOLD EAGLE COMPANY; *pg.* 206, *pg.* 575
1040 EXPRESS ANSWERS - Reference Material - CCH INC.; *pg.* 1626, *pg.* 653
1040 PREPARATION & PLANNING GUIDE - Reference Material - CCH INC.; *pg.* 1626, *pg.* 653
1041 EXPRESS ANSWEERS - Reference Material - CCH INC.; *pg.* 1626, *pg.* 653
1041 PREPARATION & PLANNING GUIDE - Reference Material - CCH INC.; *pg.* 1626, *pg.* 653
10447A - Electronic Component - EMCORE CORPORATION; *pg.* 636, *pg.* 39
10457A - Electronic Component - EMCORE CORPORATION; *pg.* 636, *pg.* 39
10481 - Electronic Component - EMCORE CORPORATION; *pg.* 636, *pg.* 39
10482 - Electronic Component - EMCORE CORPORATION; *pg.* 636, *pg.* 39
10483 - Electronic Component - EMCORE CORPORATION; *pg.* 636, *pg.* 39
10484 - Electronic Component - EMCORE CORPORATION; *pg.* 636, *pg.* 39
105 - Desk Stapler - ARROW FASTENER COMPANY, INC.; *pg.* 1042, *pg.* 1118
10501 - Electronic Component - EMCORE CORPORATION; *pg.* 636, *pg.* 39
1065 & 1120S EXPRESS ANWSERS - Reference Material - CCH INC.; *pg.* 1626, *pg.* 653
1065 EXPRESS ANSWERS - Reference Material - CCH INC.; *pg.* 1626, *pg.* 653
107C - Desk Stapler - ARROW FASTENER COMPANY, INC.; *pg.* 1042, *pg.* 1118
10901G - Electronic Component - EMCORE CORPORATION; *pg.* 636, *pg.* 39
10990 - Electronic Component - EMCORE CORPORATION; *pg.* 636, *pg.* 39
10G 17-PIN - Electronic Components - EMCORE CORPORATION; *pg.* 636, *pg.* 39
10G ROSA - Electronic Components - EMCORE CORPORATION; *pg.* 636, *pg.* 39
10GB CX4 - Transceiver - EMCORE CORPORATION; *pg.* 636, *pg.* 39
10GB LX4 - Transceiver - EMCORE CORPORATION; *pg.* 636, *pg.* 39
10K - Piston Seals - A.W. CHESTERTON COMPANY; *pg.* 1315, *pg.* 861
10TO10 - Biopharmaceutical Product - LEXICON PHARMACEUTICALS, INC.; *pg.* 1555, *pg.* 1747
10X PAY STRIKE - Video Game - INTERNATIONAL GAME TECHNOLOGY; *pg.* 957, *pg.* 1024
11 - Beer - SLEEMAN UNIBROUE QUEBEC; *pg.* 265, *pg.* 1950
11 CR-CB - Steel Product - AK STEEL HOLDING

CORPORATION; *pg.* 1311, *pg.* 1479
110 SE - Plasma Etch System - COLLABRX, INC.; *pg.* 1324, *pg.* 216
1100/1200 SERIES - Tables - HOWE FURNITURE CORPORATION; *pg.* 928, *pg.* 998
12 BAND - Laser Speed Detectors - COBRA ELECTRONICS CORPORATION; *pg.* 629, *pg.* 572
12 COUNTRY - Sausage & Biscuits - WILLIAMS SAUSAGE CO., INC.; *pg.* 910, *pg.* 1656
12 DAYS OF GIVING - Gift Registry Services - YAHOO! INC.; *pg.* 1289, *pg.* 289
12 MESES - Spanish-Language Parenting Magazine - MEREDITH CORPORATION; *pg.* 1663, *pg.* 705
12-PETTE - Multi-Channel Pipetter - CORNING INCORPORATED; *pg.* 1122, *pg.* 1154
12 SR - Steel Product - AK STEEL HOLDING CORPORATION; *pg.* 1311, *pg.* 1479
12 TIMES PAY - Slot Machine Game - INTERNATIONAL GAME TECHNOLOGY; *pg.* 957, *pg.* 1024
1200 SERIES - Service Fittings - WIREMOLD/LEGRAND; *pg.* 689, *pg.* 383
1200EPX - Medical Apparatus - ARRHYTHMIA RESEARCH TECHNOLOGY, INC.; *pg.* 1496, *pg.* 819
123 CLEANING SERVICES - Residential & Office Cleaning Temporary Staffing - 123 STAFFING, INC.; *pg.* 339, *pg.* 1123
123 EAST - Temporary Staffing - 123 STAFFING, INC.; *pg.* 339, *pg.* 1123
123 HOME HEALTHCARE - Home Healthcare Temporary Staffing - 123 STAFFING, INC.; *pg.* 339, *pg.* 1123
123 MOVERS.COM - Real Estate Website - DOMINION ENTERPRISES; *pg.* 1636, *pg.* 1796
123 PAYCHECKS - Payroll Services for Temporary Staff - 123 STAFFING, INC.; *pg.* 339, *pg.* 1123
123 STAFFING - Temporary Staffing - 123 STAFFING, INC.; *pg.* 339, *pg.* 1123
1.2.3 SUCCESS - Weight Loss Program - WEIGHT WATCHERS INTERNATIONAL, INC.; *pg.* 1609, *pg.* 1313
123 WEST - Temporary Staffing - 123 STAFFING, INC.; *pg.* 339, *pg.* 1123
123CONTRACTORQUOTES.COM - Real Estate Website - DOMINION ENTERPRISES; *pg.* 1636, *pg.* 1796
1313 DEADEND DRIVE - Game - HASBRO, INC.; *pg.* 954, *pg.* 1603
13TH STREET - International Channel - NBC UNIVERSAL, INC.; *pg.* 300, *pg.* 1266
14 KARAT CASH - Lotto Game - SOUTH DAKOTA LOTTERY; *pg.* 1006, *pg.* 1624
14 KARAT PLATINUM - Jewelry - KARAT PLATINUM LLC; *pg.* 7, *pg.* 1168
1400 - Tape - A.W. CHESTERTON COMPANY; *pg.* 1315, *pg.* 861
14KT.PT - Jewelry - KARAT PLATINUM LLC; *pg.* 7, *pg.* 1168
15-15LC - Stainless Steels - CARPENTER TECHNOLOGY CORPORATION; *pg.* 73, *pg.* 1584
15-5 PH - Steel Product - AK STEEL HOLDING CORPORATION; *pg.* 1311, *pg.* 1479
15-BAND - Laser Detectors - COBRA ELECTRONICS CORPORATION; *pg.* 629, *pg.* 572
15 BEAN SOUP - Dried Beans for Soup - N.K. HURST CO., INC.; *pg.* 886, *pg.* 689
150 RPX - Fluid Handling System - GRACO, INC.; *pg.* 1342, *pg.* 935
1500 CHEM/BIO - Filtration System - IRT, INC.; *pg.* 1169, *pg.* 771
1500 HEPA - Filtration System - IRT, INC.; *pg.* 1169, *pg.* 771
1500 SERIES - Wiring System - WIREMOLD/LEGRAND; *pg.* 689, *pg.* 383
150,000,000 PRIZE PAYOUT BONANZA - Lottery Game - NEW YORK STATE LOTTERY; *pg.* 1001, *pg.* 1340
155 - Standard Cartridge Single Seal - A.W. CHESTERTON COMPANY; *pg.* 1315, *pg.* 861
1554 - Beer - NEW BELGIUM BREWING COMPANY, INC.; *pg.* 258, *pg.* 328
155MBITS S APD-TIA T0-46 - Electronic Components - EMCORE CORPORATION; *pg.* 636, *pg.* 39
156 - Slurry Cartridge Singe Seal - A.W. CHESTERTON COMPANY; *pg.* 1315, *pg.* 861
1600 L-R WALL - Curtain Wall System - KAWNEER COMPANY, INC.; *pg.* 90, *pg.* 537
1600 POWERWALL - Curtain Wall System - KAWNEER COMPANY, INC.; *pg.* 90, *pg.* 537
1600 SUNSHADE - Pre-Engineered Sunshade - KAWNEER COMPANY, INC.; *pg.* 90, *pg.* 537
1600 WALL POWERSHADE - Pre-Engineered Sunshade System - KAWNEER COMPANY, INC.; *pg.* 90, *pg.* 537
1600 WALL SYSTEM - Curtain Wall Systems - KAWNEER COMPANY, INC.; *pg.* 90, *pg.* 537
1612A DFB - Electronic Component - EMCORE CORPORATION; *pg.* 636, *pg.* 39
1612B DFB - Electronic Component - EMCORE CORPORATION; *pg.* 636, *pg.* 39
1614W DFB - Electronic Component - EMCORE CORPORATION; *pg.* 636, *pg.* 39
1622 DFB - Electronic Component - EMCORE CORPORATION; *pg.* 636, *pg.* 39
17-14 CU MO - Steel Product - AK STEEL HOLDING CORPORATION; *pg.* 1311, *pg.* 1479
17-22-A - Steel - THE TIMKEN COMPANY; *pg.* 218, *pg.* 1408
17-22-AS - Steel - THE TIMKEN COMPANY; *pg.* 218, *pg.* 1408
17-4 PH - Steel Product - AK STEEL HOLDING CORPORATION; *pg.* 1311, *pg.* 1479
17-7 PH - Steel Product - AK STEEL HOLDING CORPORATION; *pg.* 1311, *pg.* 1479
1724 - Non-Hardening Yarn - A.W. CHESTERTON COMPANY; *pg.* 1315, *pg.* 861
175TH ANNIVERSARY STOCKMAN KNIFE - Knife - WOOLRICH, INC.; *pg.* 699, *pg.* 1595
18-9 LW - Steel Product - AK STEEL HOLDING CORPORATION; *pg.* 1311, *pg.* 1479
18 CR-CB - Steel Product - AK STEEL HOLDING CORPORATION; *pg.* 1311, *pg.* 1479
18 HOUR - Bra - PLAYTEX APPAREL, INC.; *pg.* 31, *pg.* 1395
18 REELER - Video Game - INTERNATIONAL GAME TECHNOLOGY; *pg.* 957, *pg.* 1024
18 SR - Steel Product - AK STEEL HOLDING CORPORATION; *pg.* 1311, *pg.* 1479
180 SEAL - Heavy Duty Cartridge Seal - A.W. CHESTERTON COMPANY; *pg.* 1315, *pg.* 861
1800 TEQUILA - Spirits - PROXIMO SPIRITS, INC.; *pg.* 1969, *pg.* 1076
1800FLOWERS.BIZ - Online Store - 1-800-FLOWERS.COM, INC.; *pg.* 1758, *pg.* 1151
180PLUS - Transducer - SONOSITE, INC.; *pg.* 1429, *pg.* 1818
1837 - Beer - SLEEMAN UNIBROUE QUEBEC; *pg.* 265, *pg.* 1950
1837 - Jewelry Collection - TIFFANY & CO.; *pg.* 13, *pg.* 1299
1837 COLLECTION - Silver Jewelry - TIFFANY & CO.; *pg.* 13, *pg.* 1299
1881 - Silverware - ONEIDA LTD; *pg.* 1129, *pg.* 1318
1889 - Jacket - CARHARTT, INC.; *pg.* 39, *pg.* 875
19-9DL - Steel Product - AK STEEL HOLDING CORPORATION; *pg.* 1311, *pg.* 1479
19 PLATFORM - Computer Support Worktools - STEELCASE INC.; *pg.* 475, *pg.* 889
190ES - Electric Airless Sprayer - GRACO, INC.; *pg.* 1342, *pg.* 935
1920'S - Women's Clothing & Accessories - WOODEN SHIPS OF HOBOKEN; *pg.* 35, *pg.* 1315
1CLICK ANSWERS - Search Engine for Windows Software - ANSWERS CORPORATION; *pg.* 1229, *pg.* 1195
1MR VORTEX - Pre-Training Powder - BPI SPORTS, LLC; *pg.* 842, *pg.* 430
1T-FLASH - Flash Memory Technology - MOSYS INC.; *pg.* 657, *pg.* 268
1T-SRAM - Memory Technology - MOSYS INC.; *pg.* 657, *pg.* 268

2

2-26 - Multi-Purpose Precision Lubricant - CRC INDUSTRIES, INC.; *pg.* 329, *pg.* 1590
2 BELOW - Seasonal Beer - NEW BELGIUM BREWING COMPANY, INC.; *pg.* 258, *pg.* 328
2-D ANALYST - Software - BIO-RAD LABORATORIES, INC.; *pg.* 1504, *pg.* 101
2-D DOCTOR - Software - BIO-RAD LABORATORIES, INC.; *pg.* 1504, *pg.* 101
2 IN 1 - Flea & Tick Products - THE HARTZ MOUNTAIN CORP.; *pg.* 1476, *pg.* 1120
2-IN-1 - Wick-Equipped Drip Bottle Deodorant - SURCO PRODUCTS, INC.; *pg.* 336, *pg.* 1581
2-IN-1 TUMMY TIME GYM - Toy & Game - HASBRO, INC.; *pg.* 954, *pg.* 1603
2-PHASE EXTRACTION - Manual - XEROX CORPORATION; *pg.* 494, *pg.* 365
2 PLEX - Laminated Exterior Engravable Plastic - GRAVOGRAPH-NEW HERMES; *pg.* 1344, *pg.* 531
2 PLUS 4 - Extended Warranty & Protection Services - VOLVO PENTA OF THE AMERICAS, INC.; *pg.* 1712, *pg.* 1778
2 SR - Steel Product - AK STEEL HOLDING CORPORATION; *pg.* 1311, *pg.* 1479
20-20 - Adhesive - SPINNAKER COATING, LLC; *pg.* 1470, *pg.* 1477
20 QUESTIONS - Game - UNIVERSITY GAMES CORPORATION; *pg.* 969, *pg.* 230
200 SE - Plasma Etch System - COLLABRX, INC.; *pg.* 1324, *pg.* 216
200 SERIES - Banquet Tables - HOWE FURNITURE CORPORATION; *pg.* 928, *pg.* 998
2000 FLUSHES - Toilet Bowl Cleaner - WD-40 COMPANY; *pg.* 337, *pg.* 210
2000 SERIES - Highly Durable Pliers - KLEIN TOOLS INC.; *pg.* 1052, *pg.* 627
$200,000 A YEAR FOR LIFE - Lottery Card - MISSOURI LOTTERY; *pg.* 999, *pg.* 979
$200,000 MEGA SLOTS - Lottery Game - MINNESOTA STATE LOTTERY; *pg.* 999, *pg.* 956
2000A - Flatbed Trailer - UTILITY TRAILER MANUFACTURING COMPANY; *pg.* 1712, *pg.* 68
2001 - Carpet Extraction Chemical - NILODOR, INC.; *pg.* 332, *pg.* 1406
2020TC IMAGER - Digital Gamma Camera - DIGIRAD CORPORATION; *pg.* 1524, *pg.* 185
20300 SERIES - Compact Office Shredders - DAHLE USA; *pg.* 382, *pg.* 1038
20400 SERIES - Intermediate Office Shredders - DAHLE USA; *pg.* 382, *pg.* 1038
20500 SERIES - Economy Office Shredders - DAHLE USA; *pg.* 382, *pg.* 1038
20600 SERIES - General Office Shredders - DAHLE USA; *pg.* 382, *pg.* 1038
206B-3 - Turbine Helicopter - BELL HELICOPTER TEXTRON, INC.; *pg.* 224, *pg.* 1693
206L-4 - Seven Passenger Helicopter - BELL HELICOPTER TEXTRON, INC.; *pg.* 224, *pg.* 1693
20800 SERIES - Computer Forms Shredders - DAHLE USA; *pg.* 382, *pg.* 1038
20CB-3 - Stainless Steel Products - CARPENTER TECHNOLOGY CORPORATION; *pg.* 73, *pg.* 1584
20K - Microprocessor Core - IMAGINATION TECHNOLOGIES; *pg.* 412, *pg.* 285
20KC - Microprocessor Core - IMAGINATION TECHNOLOGIES; *pg.* 412, *pg.* 285
20MO-6 - Stainless Steel Products - CARPENTER TECHNOLOGY CORPORATION; *pg.* 73, *pg.* 1584
20TH CENTURY FOX - Films & Television Shows - 20TH CENTURY FOX FILM CORP.; *pg.* 267, *pg.* 124
20X - Jeanswear - V.F. CORPORATION; *pg.* 34, *pg.* 1376
21 GAMBLER - Video Game - INTERNATIONAL GAME TECHNOLOGY; *pg.* 957, *pg.* 1024
210 - Helicopter - BELL HELICOPTER TEXTRON, INC.; *pg.* 224, *pg.* 1693
21ST SENTRY - Security System - NORTEK, INC.; *pg.* 100, *pg.* 1607
22 CHARGER - Autoloading Pistols - STURM, RUGER & COMPANY, INC.; *pg.* 1846, *pg.* 371
22-OCT - Autoloading Rifles - STURM, RUGER & COMPANY, INC.; *pg.* 1846, *pg.* 371
2200 SERIES - Conveyors - DORNER MANUFACTURING CORP.; *pg.* 1329, *pg.* 1861
221 - Jumbo Split Seal - A.W. CHESTERTON COMPANY; *pg.* 1315, *pg.* 861
225 - Standard Cartridge Dual Seal - A.W. CHESTERTON COMPANY; *pg.* 1315, *pg.* 861
2300 SERIES - Nonmetallic Raceway - WIREMOLD/LEGRAND; *pg.* 689, *pg.* 383
2300 VERSYS - Etch Systems - LAM RESEARCH CORPORATION; *pg.* 1354, *pg.* 91
2300D SERIES - Nonmetallic Raceway - WIREMOLD/LEGRAND; *pg.* 689, *pg.* 383
230ES - Fluid Handling System - GRACO, INC.; *pg.* 1342, *pg.* 935
2.4-D - Weedkilling Compound - NUFARM AMERICAS INC; *pg.* 1798, *pg.* 552
24 HOUR ODOR ABSORBER - Odor Neutralizer - SURCO PRODUCTS, INC.; *pg.* 336, *pg.* 1581
24 HOURS OF DAYTONA - Motorsports Event - INTERNATIONAL SPEEDWAY CORPORATION; *pg.* 553,

pg. 420
24 SEVEN - Nutritional Supplement - RBC LIFE SCIENCES, INC.; *pg.* 1588, *pg.* 1723
24C - Effervescent Vitamin Drink Mix - JONES SODA CO.; *pg.* 253, *pg.* 1836
24K - Microprocessor Core - IMAGINATION TECHNOLOGIES; *pg.* 412, *pg.* 285
24K - Lottery Game - MISSOURI LOTTERY; *pg.* 999, *pg.* 979
24KC - Microprocessor Core - IMAGINATION TECHNOLOGIES; *pg.* 412, *pg.* 285
24KE - Microprocessor Core - IMAGINATION TECHNOLOGIES; *pg.* 412, *pg.* 285
24KEC - Microprocessor Core - IMAGINATION TECHNOLOGIES; *pg.* 412, *pg.* 285
24KEF - Microprocessor Core - IMAGINATION TECHNOLOGIES; *pg.* 412, *pg.* 285
24KF - Microprocessor Core - IMAGINATION TECHNOLOGIES; *pg.* 412, *pg.* 285
2500 PG WALL - Wall Entrances - KAWNEER COMPANY, INC.; *pg.* 90, *pg.* 537
$25,000 BANKROLL - Lottery Card - MISSOURI LOTTERY; *pg.* 999, *pg.* 979
$25,000 CASH VAULT - Lottery Game - MISSOURI LOTTERY; *pg.* 999, *pg.* 979
25,000 HOLD 'EM POKER - Lottery Game - OHIO LOTTERY COMMISSION; *pg.* 1002, *pg.* 1433
$250,000 MEGA CASH - Lottery Card - MISSOURI LOTTERY; *pg.* 999, *pg.* 979
255 - Standard Cartridge Dual Seal - A.W. CHESTERTON COMPANY; *pg.* 1315, *pg.* 861
25KF - Microprocessor Core - IMAGINATION TECHNOLOGIES; *pg.* 412, *pg.* 285
2600 SERIES - Wiring System - WIREMOLD/LEGRAND; *pg.* 689, *pg.* 383
26000 VODKA - Beer - UNITED STATES BEVERAGE LLC; *pg.* 266, *pg.* 379
270ES - Fluid Handling System - GRACO, INC.; *pg.* 1342, *pg.* 935
280 - Heavy Duty Cartridge Dual Seal - A.W. CHESTERTON COMPANY; *pg.* 1315, *pg.* 861
2800 TRUSSWALL - Curtain Wall System - KAWNEER COMPANY, INC.; *pg.* 90, *pg.* 537
2801 PRO - Transmitters - EMCORE CORPORATION; *pg.* 636, *pg.* 39
2802 PRO - Transmitters - EMCORE CORPORATION; *pg.* 636, *pg.* 39
2804 CATV - Transmitters - EMCORE CORPORATION; *pg.* 636, *pg.* 39
2805 CATV - Transmitters - EMCORE CORPORATION; *pg.* 636, *pg.* 39
2806 CATV - Transmitter - EMCORE CORPORATION; *pg.* 636, *pg.* 39
2807 CATV - Receiver - EMCORE CORPORATION; *pg.* 636, *pg.* 39
2808 CATV - Receiver - EMCORE CORPORATION; *pg.* 636, *pg.* 39
2809 CATV - Receiver - EMCORE CORPORATION; *pg.* 636, *pg.* 39
2860E - Receiver - EMCORE CORPORATION; *pg.* 636, *pg.* 39
2860F - Receiver - EMCORE CORPORATION; *pg.* 636, *pg.* 39
290 EASY - Fluid Handling System - GRACO, INC.; *pg.* 1342, *pg.* 935
2990 PRO - Electronic Component - EMCORE CORPORATION; *pg.* 636, *pg.* 39
2991R - Electronic Component - EMCORE CORPORATION; *pg.* 636, *pg.* 39
2991T - Electronic Component - EMCORE CORPORATION; *pg.* 636, *pg.* 39
2B BEBE - Apparel - BEBE STORES, INC.; *pg.* 19, *pg.* 49
2BE - Apparel - BEBE STORES, INC.; *pg.* 19, *pg.* 49
2BY2 - Lottery Game - ARIZONA LOTTERY; *pg.* 988, *pg.* 14
2GO - Food Product - 4C FOODS CORPORATION; *pg.* 835, *pg.* 1145
2GR - Medical Equipment - INVACARE CORPORATION; *pg.* 1546, *pg.* 1451
2GT - Medical Equipment - INVACARE CORPORATION; *pg.* 1546, *pg.* 1451
2GTR - Medical Equipment - INVACARE CORPORATION; *pg.* 1546, *pg.* 1451
2K SPORTS - Game - TAKE-TWO INTERACTIVE SOFTWARE, INC.; *pg.* 481, *pg.* 1297
2KNOW - Educational Materials - RENAISSANCE LEARNING, INC.; *pg.* 607, *pg.* 1899
2MB MIND STATION - Educational Toys - LEAPFROG ENTERPRISES, INC.; *pg.* 961, *pg.* 84
2ND CHANCE ROYAL - Video Game - INTERNATIONAL GAME TECHNOLOGY; *pg.* 957, *pg.* 1024
2ND DRAW ROYAL - Video Game - INTERNATIONAL GAME TECHNOLOGY; *pg.* 957, *pg.* 1024
2ND-SKINZ - Gloves - FRANKLIN SPORTS, INC.; *pg.* 1834, *pg.* 847
2SQUARED - Software - SUREQUEST SYSTEMS, INC.; *pg.* 900, *pg.* 1669
2TAB - Side & Top Tab Folders - TAB PRODUCTS CO. LLC; *pg.* 481, *pg.* 1869
2UV - Multiple Wavelengths in One Unit - UVP, INC.; *pg.* 1434, *pg.* 298
2X JACKPOT JEWELS - Video Game - INTERNATIONAL GAME TECHNOLOGY; *pg.* 957, *pg.* 1024
2X PAY RED WHITE & BLUE - Video Game - INTERNATIONAL GAME TECHNOLOGY; *pg.* 957, *pg.* 1024
2X SHERIFF'S STARS - Game - WMS INDUSTRIES INC.; *pg.* 593, *pg.* 666
2X WILD & CRAZY - Game - WMS INDUSTRIES INC.; *pg.* 593, *pg.* 666
2X2 - Cheeseburger Sandwiches - IN-N-OUT BURGERS, INC.; *pg.* 1732, *pg.* 111
2X3X RED WHITE & BLUE - Video Game - INTERNATIONAL GAME TECHNOLOGY; *pg.* 957, *pg.* 1024
2X3X4X HOT WIRE - Video Game - INTERNATIONAL GAME TECHNOLOGY; *pg.* 957, *pg.* 1024
2X3X4X JADE - Video Game - INTERNATIONAL GAME TECHNOLOGY; *pg.* 957, *pg.* 1024
2X3X4X WHITE PEARL - Video Game - INTERNATIONAL GAME TECHNOLOGY; *pg.* 957, *pg.* 1024
2X3X4X5X DRAGON - Video Game - INTERNATIONAL GAME TECHNOLOGY; *pg.* 957, *pg.* 1024
2X3X4X5X LUCKY 7S - Video Game - INTERNATIONAL GAME TECHNOLOGY; *pg.* 957, *pg.* 1024
2X3X4X5X LUCKY PAYS - Video Game - INTERNATIONAL GAME TECHNOLOGY; *pg.* 957, *pg.* 1024
2X3X4X5X RED HOT 7S - Video Game - INTERNATIONAL GAME TECHNOLOGY; *pg.* 957, *pg.* 1024
2X3X4X5X SUPER LUCKY TIMES PAY - Video Game - INTERNATIONAL GAME TECHNOLOGY; *pg.* 957, *pg.* 1024

3

3-36 - Multi-Purpose Lubricant & Corrosion Inhibitor - CRC INDUSTRIES, INC.; *pg.* 329, *pg.* 1590
3/4 LENGTH SKINNY PANT - Clothing - K-SWISS; *pg.* 1837, *pg.* 306
3/4 RUN CAPRI - Clothing - K-SWISS; *pg.* 1837, *pg.* 306
3 ALARM FIRE - Game - WMS INDUSTRIES INC.; *pg.* 593, *pg.* 666
3 DAY SELECT - Software - UNITED PARCEL SERVICE, INC.; *pg.* 1928, *pg.* 522
3-DEC - Software - AUTODESK INC.; *pg.* 356, *pg.* 257
3-DNS - Controller - F5 NETWORKS, INC.; *pg.* 396, *pg.* 1835
3-IN-ONE - Oil - WD-40 COMPANY; *pg.* 337, *pg.* 210
3-MINUTE DRILL - Trademark - NATIONAL COLLEGIATE ATHLETIC ASSOCIATION; *pg.* 567, *pg.* 688
3 MINUTOS MIXED CEREAL - Cereal - THE QUAKER OATS COMPANY; *pg.* 834, *pg.* 588
3 MUSKETEERS - Candy Bar - MARS, INCORPORATED; *pg.* 1858, *pg.* 1792
3 ON 3 - Youth Hockey League - CANLAN ICE SPORTS CORPORATION; *pg.* 536, *pg.* 1907
3 OZ HANDY - Household Product - WD-40 COMPANY; *pg.* 337, *pg.* 210
3+1 - Guitar - ERNIE BALL INC.; *pg.* 1768, *pg.* 68
30 ROCK - Television Show - NBC UNIVERSAL, INC.; *pg.* 300, *pg.* 1266
300 PIN - Transceiver - FINISAR CORPORATION; *pg.* 639, *pg.* 285
3000 - Electronic Component - EMCORE CORPORATION; *pg.* 636, *pg.* 39
3000 SERIES - Eductors - AKRON BRASS COMPANY; *pg.* 1311, *pg.* 1482
$300,000 CASH SPECTACULAR - Lottery Game - MISSOURI LOTTERY; *pg.* 999, *pg.* 979
$300,000 CASINO NIGHTS - Lottery Game - MISSOURI LOTTERY; *pg.* 999, *pg.* 979
$300,000 CASINO THRILLS - Lottery Game - MISSOURI LOTTERY; *pg.* 999, *pg.* 979
$300,000 CLUB CASINO - Lottery Game - MISSOURI LOTTERY; *pg.* 999, *pg.* 979
$300,000 FORTUNE - Lottery Game - MISSOURI LOTTERY; *pg.* 999, *pg.* 979
$300,000 MEGA MONEY - Lottery Game - MISSOURI LOTTERY; *pg.* 999, *pg.* 979
$300,000 PAYOUT - Lottery Game - MISSOURI LOTTERY; *pg.* 999, *pg.* 979
3000C - Electronic Component - EMCORE CORPORATION; *pg.* 636, *pg.* 39
3000R - Reefers - UTILITY TRAILER MANUFACTURING COMPANY; *pg.* 1712, *pg.* 68
3000UB - Electronic Component - EMCORE CORPORATION; *pg.* 636, *pg.* 39
3000UC - Electronic Component - EMCORE CORPORATION; *pg.* 636, *pg.* 39
3005 - Electronic Component - EMCORE CORPORATION; *pg.* 636, *pg.* 39
3010 - Electronic Component - EMCORE CORPORATION; *pg.* 636, *pg.* 39
3015 - Electronic Component - EMCORE CORPORATION; *pg.* 636, *pg.* 39
3020 - Electronic Component - EMCORE CORPORATION; *pg.* 636, *pg.* 39
302HQ-FM - Stainless Steel Products - CARPENTER TECHNOLOGY CORPORATION; *pg.* 73, *pg.* 1584
3030 - Electronic Component - EMCORE CORPORATION; *pg.* 636, *pg.* 39
3035 - Electronic Component - EMCORE CORPORATION; *pg.* 636, *pg.* 39
303MA - Steel Product - AK STEEL HOLDING CORPORATION; *pg.* 1311, *pg.* 1479
304-SCQ - Stainless Steel Products - CARPENTER TECHNOLOGY CORPORATION; *pg.* 73, *pg.* 1584
3058 - Electronic Component - EMCORE CORPORATION; *pg.* 636, *pg.* 39
3060 SHOWERTUB - Shower Enclosure - E.L. MUSTEE & SONS, INC.; *pg.* 1124, *pg.* 1430
309 A.B.Q. - Stainless Steel Products - CARPENTER TECHNOLOGY CORPORATION; *pg.* 73, *pg.* 1584
3091 ODU - Electronic Component - EMCORE CORPORATION; *pg.* 636, *pg.* 39
3091 PS-24 ODU - Electronic Component - EMCORE CORPORATION; *pg.* 636, *pg.* 39
3091A - Electronic Component - EMCORE CORPORATION; *pg.* 636, *pg.* 39
311 DQ - Steel Product - AK STEEL HOLDING CORPORATION; *pg.* 1311, *pg.* 1479
3112A - Electronic Component - EMCORE CORPORATION; *pg.* 636, *pg.* 39
3120 - Semiconductor Chip - ECHELON CORPORATION; *pg.* 389, *pg.* 245
3120A - Electronic Component - EMCORE CORPORATION; *pg.* 636, *pg.* 39
3150 - Semiconductor Chip - ECHELON CORPORATION; *pg.* 389, *pg.* 245
316L-SCQ - Stainless Steel Products - CARPENTER TECHNOLOGY CORPORATION; *pg.* 73, *pg.* 1584
319 EXECUTIVE - Office Furniture - STEELCASE INC.; *pg.* 475, *pg.* 889
3200 SE - Plasma Etch System - COLLABRX, INC.; *pg.* 1324, *pg.* 216
321 PENGUINS - Video - BIG IDEA, INC.; *pg.* 271, *pg.* 1632
3270 SUPEROPTIMIZER/CICS - Network Optimization - BMC SOFTWARE, INC.; *pg.* 362, *pg.* 1701
330GS - Fluid Handling System - GRACO, INC.; *pg.* 1342, *pg.* 935
333HT - Fly Lines - CORTLAND LINE COMPANY; *pg.* 1831, *pg.* 1155
340 GOLD - Epoxy Primer - PETTIT PAINT COMPANY; *pg.* 1444, *pg.* 1116
34K - Microprocessor Core - IMAGINATION TECHNOLOGIES; *pg.* 412, *pg.* 285
34KC - Microprocessor Core - IMAGINATION TECHNOLOGIES; *pg.* 412, *pg.* 285
34KF - Microprocessor Core - IMAGINATION TECHNOLOGIES; *pg.* 412, *pg.* 285
35 MILLION SPECTACULAR - Lottery Game - OHIO LOTTERY COMMISSION; *pg.* 1002, *pg.* 1433
35 SOUTH - Wine - SHAW ROSS INTERNATIONAL IMPORTERS; *pg.* 1970, *pg.* 449
350 HEAVY WALL - Doorway Entrances - KAWNEER COMPANY, INC.; *pg.* 90, *pg.* 537
350 TUFFLINE - Heavy Duty Entrances - KAWNEER COMPANY, INC.; *pg.* 90, *pg.* 537

350 XL SERIES - Electric Slicers - EDLUND COMPANY, INC.; *pg.* 1123, *pg.* 1765
3500-II - Assembly Cell - PALOMAR TECHNOLOGIES INC.; *pg.* 661, *pg.* 60
3500S - Medical Equipment - INVACARE CORPORATION; *pg.* 1546, *pg.* 1451
35XA - Electronic Component - EMCORE CORPORATION; *pg.* 636, *pg.* 39
360 DEGREES CUSTOM LABELS - Labels - ENNIS, INC.; *pg.* 393, *pg.* 1727
360 VODKA - Vodka - MCCORMICK DISTILLING CO., INC.; *pg.* 1966, *pg.* 1007
3641 DFB - Electronic Component - EMCORE CORPORATION; *pg.* 636, *pg.* 39
365 - Placing Insurance With Underwriters - AMERICAN AUTOMOBILE ASSOCIATION; *pg.* 1190, *pg.* 429
365 EVERYDAY VALUE - Food Product - WHOLE FOODS MARKET, INC.; *pg.* 1038, *pg.* 1667
3688A - Electronic Component - EMCORE CORPORATION; *pg.* 636, *pg.* 39
3688D - Electronic Component - EMCORE CORPORATION; *pg.* 636, *pg.* 39
3688M - Electronic Component - EMCORE CORPORATION; *pg.* 636, *pg.* 39
3688U - Electronic Component - EMCORE CORPORATION; *pg.* 636, *pg.* 39
38 - Varnish - PRATT & LAMBERT PAINTS; *pg.* 1446, *pg.* 1434
380 - Machinery Coolant - A.W. CHESTERTON COMPANY; *pg.* 1315, *pg.* 861
380 MACHINERY COOLANT - Synthetic Metal Working Fluid - A.W. CHESTERTON COMPANY; *pg.* 1315, *pg.* 861
390 - Fluid Handling System - GRACO, INC.; *pg.* 1342, *pg.* 935
392 - Brewer - BUNN-O-MATIC CORPORATION; *pg.* 53, *pg.* 661
3988 - Electronic Component - EMCORE CORPORATION; *pg.* 636, *pg.* 39
3B2 - Book Projects - CENVEO INC.; *pg.* 1626, *pg.* 372
3C-XP - Flashlight - STREAMLIGHT INC.; *pg.* 1306, *pg.* 1527
(3)CENTER - Colocation Package - LEVEL 3 COMMUNICATIONS, INC.; *pg.* 1262, *pg.* 312
3CHEM - Liquid Delivery System - ATMI, INC.; *pg.* 1314, *pg.* 342
(3)CONNECT - Telecommunications Gateway - LEVEL 3 COMMUNICATIONS, INC.; *pg.* 1262, *pg.* 312
(3)CROSSROADS - Telecommunications Gateway - LEVEL 3 COMMUNICATIONS, INC.; *pg.* 1262, *pg.* 312
3D AUDIO THAT WORKS - Audio System - QSOUND LABS, INC.; *pg.* 666, *pg.* 1904
3D DESIGN - Software System - MENTOR GRAPHICS CORPORATION; *pg.* 432, *pg.* 1510
3D DINOSAURS - Educational Materials - SCHOLASTIC INC.; *pg.* 1683, *pg.* 1288
3D GRID HURRICANE 6 - Men's & Women's Training Shoe - SAUCONY, INC.; *pg.* 1818, *pg.* 828
3D GRID TRIUMPH - Men's & Women's Training Shoe - SAUCONY, INC.; *pg.* 1818, *pg.* 828
3D IMANUAL - Interactive 3D Assembly Guides - ALION SCIENCE AND TECHNOLOGY CORPORATION; *pg.* 615, *pg.* 1788
3D LIGHTYEAR - Software - 3D SYSTEMS CORPORATION; *pg.* 339, *pg.* 1621
3D-LUX - Decorating Technology - SERIGRAPH, INC.; *pg.* 1686, *pg.* 1899
3D MANAGE - Software - 3D SYSTEMS CORPORATION; *pg.* 339, *pg.* 1621
3D NETWORK VISUALIZER - Software Product Module - RIVERBED PERFORMANCE MANAGEMENT; *pg.* 462, *pg.* 765
3D PRINT - Software - 3D SYSTEMS CORPORATION; *pg.* 339, *pg.* 1621
3D VIEWIT - Software - BIO-RAD LABORATORIES, INC.; *pg.* 1504, *pg.* 101
3DANN - Three-D Artificial Neutral Network Technology - ISC8; *pg.* 1350, *pg.* 71
3DC - Graphics Card - ADVANCED MICRO DEVICES, INC.; *pg.* 613, *pg.* 282
3DKNEE - Orthopedic Implant Product - DJO SURGICAL; *pg.* 1525, *pg.* 1661
3DMATRIX - Orthopedic Product - DJO SURGICAL; *pg.* 1525, *pg.* 1661
3DMAX - Medical Device - C.R. BARD, INC.; *pg.* 1519, *pg.* 1094
3DMETRIX - Video Game - INTERNATIONAL GAME TECHNOLOGY; *pg.* 957, *pg.* 1024
3DNOW! - Graphics Card - ADVANCED MICRO DEVICES, INC.; *pg.* 613, *pg.* 282
3D'S - Snack - FRITO-LAY NORTH AMERICA, INC.; *pg.* 1853, *pg.* 1730
3DS MAX - Animation Software - AUTODESK INC.; *pg.* 356, *pg.* 257
(3)FLEX - Telecommunications Gateway - LEVEL 3 COMMUNICATIONS, INC.; *pg.* 1262, *pg.* 312
3G ARROW RWD - Power Wheelchair - INVACARE CORPORATION; *pg.* 1546, *pg.* 1451
3G CHARGER - Fruit Drink - JAMBA, INC.; *pg.* 1024, *pg.* 84
3G TORQUE SP RWD - Power Wheelchair - INVACARE CORPORATION; *pg.* 1546, *pg.* 1451
3GPP MULTIMEDIA TELEPHONY - Mobile Solutions - SONUS NETWORKS INC.; *pg.* 1281, *pg.* 858
(3)HUB - Telecommunications Gateway - LEVEL 3 COMMUNICATIONS, INC.; *pg.* 1262, *pg.* 312
(3)LINK - Telecommunications Gateway - LEVEL 3 COMMUNICATIONS, INC.; *pg.* 1262, *pg.* 312
3M - Abrasives, Adhesives & Chemical Additives - 3M COMPANY; *pg.* 1142, *pg.* 956
3M-MATIC - Automatic & Semi-Automatic Business Equipment - 3M COMPANY; *pg.* 1142, *pg.* 956
(3)PACKET - Telecommunications Gateway - LEVEL 3 COMMUNICATIONS, INC.; *pg.* 1262, *pg.* 312
3RV - Game - WMS INDUSTRIES INC.; *pg.* 593, *pg.* 666
3RV DESIGN - Game - WMS INDUSTRIES INC.; *pg.* 593, *pg.* 666
3SIGMA - Laser Measurement Instrument - COHERENT, INC.; *pg.* 1406, *pg.* 265
3SIXTY5 - Vitamin & Mineral Supplement - XANGO, LLC; *pg.* 1610, *pg.* 1751
3UV - Multiple Wavelengths in One Unit - UVP, INC.; *pg.* 1434, *pg.* 298
(3)VOICE - Telecommunications Gateway - LEVEL 3 COMMUNICATIONS, INC.; *pg.* 1262, *pg.* 312
(3)VOIP - Telecommunications Gateway - LEVEL 3 COMMUNICATIONS, INC.; *pg.* 1262, *pg.* 312
3X 2X BURNING BARS - Video Game - INTERNATIONAL GAME TECHNOLOGY; *pg.* 957, *pg.* 1024
3X 777 2X - Video Game - INTERNATIONAL GAME TECHNOLOGY; *pg.* 957, *pg.* 1024
3X HOT HOT 777 - Game - WMS INDUSTRIES INC.; *pg.* 593, *pg.* 666
3X PAY RED WHITE & BLUE - Video Game - INTERNATIONAL GAME TECHNOLOGY; *pg.* 957, *pg.* 1024
3X TRIPLE JACKPOT 9X - Video Game - INTERNATIONAL GAME TECHNOLOGY; *pg.* 957, *pg.* 1024
3X2X SUPER 7 SEVENS - Video Game - INTERNATIONAL GAME TECHNOLOGY; *pg.* 957, *pg.* 1024
3X2X SUPER 7S - Video Game - INTERNATIONAL GAME TECHNOLOGY; *pg.* 957, *pg.* 1024
3X3 - Cheeseburger Sandwiches - IN-N-OUT BURGERS, INC.; *pg.* 1732, *pg.* 111
3XDRY - Microcheck Shirt - SIMMS FISHING PRODUCTS CORP.; *pg.* 1845, *pg.* 1008

4

4-5 BONUS POKER - Video Game - INTERNATIONAL GAME TECHNOLOGY; *pg.* 957, *pg.* 1024
THE 4 DISCIPLINES OF EXECUTION - Core Offerings - FRANKLIN COVEY CO.; *pg.* 1642, *pg.* 1758
4 FOUR TIMES PAY - Video Game - INTERNATIONAL GAME TECHNOLOGY; *pg.* 957, *pg.* 1024
4 GIVE - Shoe - AEROGROUP INTERNATIONAL, INC.; *pg.* 1803, *pg.* 1055
4-IN-1 - Carseat/Stroller - GRACO CHILDREN'S PRODUCTS INC.; *pg.* 954, *pg.* 1531
4 MILLION DOLLAR CASH BONANZA - Lottery Card - MISSOURI LOTTERY; *pg.* 999, *pg.* 979
4 O'CLOCK - Office Furniture - STEELCASE INC.; *pg.* 475, *pg.* 889
THE 4 ROLES OF LEADERSHIP - Workshop - FRANKLIN COVEY CO.; *pg.* 1642, *pg.* 1758
4 SIGHT - Imaging Product - JACK HENRY & ASSOCIATES, INC.; *pg.* 422, *pg.* 988
4 TEL - Line Tester - TERADYNE INC.; *pg.* 679, *pg.* 838
4 TO GROW - Plant Starter Kit - THE PAGE SEED CO.; *pg.* 1798, *pg.* 1163
4-WAY - Floor Deck - HOMASOTE COMPANY; *pg.* 87, *pg.* 1126
4-WINDOW PULL - Advertising & Promotional Brochure Design - STRUCTURAL GRAPHICS, LLC; *pg.* 1689, *pg.* 346
4+2 - Guitar - ERNIE BALL INC.; *pg.* 1768, *pg.* 68
40 FATHOMS - Frozen Seafood - HIGH LINER FOODS INCORPORATED; *pg.* 862, *pg.* 1917
400 CHEM/BIO - Filtration System - IRT, INC.; *pg.* 1169, *pg.* 771
400 CIRCLE TOP - Windows - ANDERSEN CORPORATION; *pg.* 67, *pg.* 916
400 FLEXIFRAME - Windows - ANDERSEN CORPORATION; *pg.* 67, *pg.* 916
400 FRENCHWOOD - Patio Doors - ANDERSEN CORPORATION; *pg.* 67, *pg.* 916
400 HEPA - Filtration System - IRT, INC.; *pg.* 1169, *pg.* 771
400 SERIES - Nonmetallic Raceway - WIREMOLD/LEGRAND; *pg.* 689, *pg.* 383
400 SPRINGLINE - Windows - ANDERSEN CORPORATION; *pg.* 67, *pg.* 916
400 WOODWRIGHT - Windows - ANDERSEN CORPORATION; *pg.* 67, *pg.* 916
4000 D-X - Trailer - UTILITY TRAILER MANUFACTURING COMPANY; *pg.* 1712, *pg.* 68
4000 SERIES - Self-propelled Lawn Mower - EXCEL INDUSTRIES, INC.; *pg.* 1795, *pg.* 715
4000 SERIES - Electronic Locks - KABA ILCO CORP.; *pg.* 1052, *pg.* 1390
4000DSI - Surveyor - TRIMBLE NAVIGATION LIMITED; *pg.* 1384, *pg.* 288
4000IM MSK - Receiver - TRIMBLE NAVIGATION LIMITED; *pg.* 1384, *pg.* 288
4000MSK DGPS - Modulator - TRIMBLE NAVIGATION LIMITED; *pg.* 1384, *pg.* 288
4000RSI - Receiver - TRIMBLE NAVIGATION LIMITED; *pg.* 1384, *pg.* 288
4000SSI - Software - TRIMBLE NAVIGATION LIMITED; *pg.* 1384, *pg.* 288
406 PLB - Personal Locator Beacon - ACR ELECTRONICS, INC.; *pg.* 612, *pg.* 422
407 - Helicopter - BELL HELICOPTER TEXTRON, INC.; *pg.* 224, *pg.* 1693
410 COLLECTION - Bedding - CROSCILL, INC.; *pg.* 1122, *pg.* 1220
4100 SERIES - Conveyors - DORNER MANUFACTURING CORP.; *pg.* 1329, *pg.* 1861
4112A - Electronic Component - EMCORE CORPORATION; *pg.* 636, *pg.* 39
4120A - Electronic Component - EMCORE CORPORATION; *pg.* 636, *pg.* 39
412EP - 15 Place Four Bladed Twin Engine Helicopter - BELL HELICOPTER TEXTRON, INC.; *pg.* 224, *pg.* 1693
415 - Bicycle Accessories - SPECIALIZED BICYCLE COMPONENTS, INC.; *pg.* 1711, *pg.* 152
4200 SE - Plasma Etch System - COLLABRX, INC.; *pg.* 1324, *pg.* 216
420M - Stainless Steel - A. FINKL & SONS CO.; *pg.* 1309, *pg.* 563
427 - Seven Place Twin Engine Helicopter - BELL HELICOPTER TEXTRON, INC.; *pg.* 224, *pg.* 1693
430 - Eleven Place Twin Engine Four Bladed Helicopter - BELL HELICOPTER TEXTRON, INC.; *pg.* 224, *pg.* 1693
431-X MERCURY VAPOR ANALYZER - Analyzer - ARIZONA INSTRUMENT LLC; *pg.* 1400, *pg.* 12
4340 GURLEY AUTOMATIC DENSOMETER - Surface Measurement Instrument - THWING-ALBERT INSTRUMENT COMPANY; *pg.* 1432, *pg.* 1131
44 MAGNUM - Power Tool - MILWAUKEE ELECTRIC TOOL CORP.; *pg.* 1056, *pg.* 1855
440 SOUNDBARRIER - Sidewall Sheathing - HOMASOTE COMPANY; *pg.* 87, *pg.* 1126
440-XH - Alloys - CARPENTER TECHNOLOGY CORPORATION; *pg.* 73, *pg.* 1584
442 - Mixer Split Seal - A.W. CHESTERTON COMPANY; *pg.* 1315, *pg.* 861
444 - Fly Lines - CORTLAND LINE COMPANY; *pg.* 1831, *pg.* 1155
444 LAZERLINE - Fly Lines - CORTLAND LINE COMPANY; *pg.* 1831, *pg.* 1155
444 SL - Fly Lines - CORTLAND LINE COMPANY; *pg.* 1831, *pg.* 1155
4540NS - Sunflower Hybrids - MONSANTO; *pg.* 1798, *pg.* 1399
4575NS/CL - Sunflower Hybrids - MONSANTO; *pg.* 1798, *pg.* 1399
4595 - Printer - XEROX CORPORATION; *pg.* 494, *pg.* 365

First page reference indicates Business Class Edition
Second page reference indicates Geographic Edition

45NRTH - Bicycle Tires - QUALITY BICYCLE PRODUCTS; *pg.* 1710, *pg.* 918
4600 LS - Navigation Aid - TRIMBLE NAVIGATION LIMITED; *pg.* 1384, *pg.* 288
4635 - Printer - XEROX CORPORATION; *pg.* 494, *pg.* 365
470 PARADE - Waiting Seating - STEELCASE INC.; *pg.* 475, *pg.* 889
4700 - Printer - XEROX CORPORATION; *pg.* 494, *pg.* 365
4704NS - Sunflower Hybrids - MONSANTO; *pg.* 1798, *pg.* 1399
470CX - Printer - XEROX CORPORATION; *pg.* 494, *pg.* 365
470NS - Sunflower Hybrids - MONSANTO; *pg.* 1798, *pg.* 1399
472 MAX STACKER - Waiting Seating - STEELCASE INC.; *pg.* 475, *pg.* 889
4850 - Printer - XEROX CORPORATION; *pg.* 494, *pg.* 365
4890 - Printer - XEROX CORPORATION; *pg.* 494, *pg.* 365
495 - Printer - XEROX CORPORATION; *pg.* 494, *pg.* 365
495ST - Airless Paint Sprayer - GRACO, INC.; *pg.* 1342, *pg.* 935
49ERS - Sport Company - SAN FRANCISCO FORTY NINERS, LTD.; *pg.* 581, *pg.* 270
4B'S - Restaurant - STAR BUFFET, INC.; *pg.* 1751, *pg.* 24
4C + - Anti Fog, Anti Scratch, Anti UV Scratch Resistant Coating - UVEX SAFETY; *pg.* 1433, *pg.* 1608
4D - Treatment Optimization - ACCURAY INCORPORATED; *pg.* 1486, *pg.* 282
4D-MSPECT - Software - DIGIRAD CORPORATION; *pg.* 1524, *pg.* 185
4FFATC FLUSH - Wiring Products - WIREMOLD/LEGRAND; *pg.* 689, *pg.* 383
4K - Microprocessor Core - IMAGINATION TECHNOLOGIES; *pg.* 412, *pg.* 285
4KC - Microprocessor Core - IMAGINATION TECHNOLOGIES; *pg.* 412, *pg.* 285
4KE - Microprocessor Core - IMAGINATION TECHNOLOGIES; *pg.* 412, *pg.* 285
4KEC - Microprocessor Core - IMAGINATION TECHNOLOGIES; *pg.* 412, *pg.* 285
4KEM - Microprocessor Core - IMAGINATION TECHNOLOGIES; *pg.* 412, *pg.* 285
4KEP - Microprocessor Core - IMAGINATION TECHNOLOGIES; *pg.* 412, *pg.* 285
4KM - Microprocessor Core - IMAGINATION TECHNOLOGIES; *pg.* 412, *pg.* 285
4KP - Microprocessor Core - IMAGINATION TECHNOLOGIES; *pg.* 412, *pg.* 285
4KS - Microprocessor Core - IMAGINATION TECHNOLOGIES; *pg.* 412, *pg.* 285
4KSC - Microprocessor Core - IMAGINATION TECHNOLOGIES; *pg.* 412, *pg.* 285
4KSD - Microprocessor Core - IMAGINATION TECHNOLOGIES; *pg.* 412, *pg.* 285
4RUNNER - Sports Utility Vehicle - TOYOTA MOTOR NORTH AMERICA, INC.; *pg.* 192, *pg.* 1303
4S - Container Closure System - GREIF INC.; *pg.* 1459, *pg.* 1447
4TITUDE - Orthopedic Product - DJO INCORPORATED; *pg.* 1524, *pg.* 302
4X4 - Cheeseburger Sandwiches - IN-N-OUT BURGERS, INC.; *pg.* 1732, *pg.* 111
4X4 DDS - Networking Products - ADTRAN, INC.; *pg.* 344, *pg.* 6

5

5 - Sugar-Free Gum - WM. WRIGLEY JR. COMPANY; *pg.* 1863, *pg.* 596
5 ALIVE - Card Game - MATTEL GAMES/PUZZLES; *pg.* 962, *pg.* 80
5 EYEWITNESS NEWS - News Broadcast - KSTP-TV, LLC; *pg.* 295, *pg.* 962
5 FIVE TIMES PAY - Video Game - INTERNATIONAL GAME TECHNOLOGY; *pg.* 957, *pg.* 1024
5-HOUR ENERGY - Liquid Energy Shot - LIVING ESSENTIALS, LLC; *pg.* 1026, *pg.* 886
5 LEVEL DEUCES WILD PLUS - Game - WMS INDUSTRIES INC.; *pg.* 593, *pg.* 666
5 LEVEL TENS OR BETTER - Game - WMS INDUSTRIES INC.; *pg.* 593, *pg.* 666
5-MINUTE CHALLENGE - Puzzle - B. DAZZLE, INC.; *pg.* 949, *pg.* 188
5 SECOND - Nail Glue - AMERICAN INTERNATIONAL INDUSTRIES COMPANY; *pg.* 498, *pg.* 126
5 SECOUND NAIL - Nail Care - AMERICAN INTERNATIONAL INDUSTRIES COMPANY; *pg.* 498, *pg.* 126
5-STAR - Lottery Game - LOUISIANA LOTTERY CORPORATION; *pg.* 997, *pg.* 742
5 STAR SERVICE PLAN DESIGN - Service Plan Design - INVACARE CORPORATION; *pg.* 1546, *pg.* 1451
5 WIZARDS - Video Game - INTERNATIONAL GAME TECHNOLOGY; *pg.* 957, *pg.* 1024
50 STATE QUARTERS - Commemorative Coins - UNITED STATES MINT; *pg.* 814, *pg.* 406
$500 A WEEK FOR LIFE - Lottery Game - NEW YORK STATE LOTTERY; *pg.* 1001, *pg.* 1340
500 II SERIES - Table System - HOWE FURNITURE CORPORATION; *pg.* 928, *pg.* 998
$500,000 CASH BLOWOUT - Lottery Game - MINNESOTA STATE LOTTERY; *pg.* 999, *pg.* 956
$500,000 CASH EXPLOSION - Lottery Game - MINNESOTA STATE LOTTERY; *pg.* 999, *pg.* 956
$500,000 CASH SPECTACULAR - Lottery Card - MISSOURI LOTTERY; *pg.* 999, *pg.* 979
$500,000 HIGH ROLLER - Lottery Game - MINNESOTA STATE LOTTERY; *pg.* 999, *pg.* 956
500,000 PAYDAY - Lottery Game - OHIO LOTTERY COMMISSION; *pg.* 1002, *pg.* 1433
5009 - Copier - XEROX CORPORATION; *pg.* 494, *pg.* 365
501 ORIGINAL - Jean - LEVI STRAUSS & CO.; *pg.* 43, *pg.* 220
5011 - Copier - XEROX CORPORATION; *pg.* 494, *pg.* 365
5012 - Copier - XEROX CORPORATION; *pg.* 494, *pg.* 365
5014 - Copier - XEROX CORPORATION; *pg.* 494, *pg.* 365
5016 RF - Transceiver - EMCORE CORPORATION; *pg.* 636, *pg.* 39
5017 - Electronic Component - EMCORE CORPORATION; *pg.* 636, *pg.* 39
5018 - Copier - XEROX CORPORATION; *pg.* 494, *pg.* 365
5021 - Photocopiers - XEROX CORPORATION; *pg.* 494, *pg.* 365
5028 - Copier - XEROX CORPORATION; *pg.* 494, *pg.* 365
503 - Jean - LEVI STRAUSS & CO.; *pg.* 43, *pg.* 220
5034 - Photocopiers - XEROX CORPORATION; *pg.* 494, *pg.* 365
504 - Jean - LEVI STRAUSS & CO.; *pg.* 43, *pg.* 220
505 - Jean - LEVI STRAUSS & CO.; *pg.* 43, *pg.* 220
5052 - Copier - XEROX CORPORATION; *pg.* 494, *pg.* 365
5053 - Copier - XEROX CORPORATION; *pg.* 494, *pg.* 365
506 DXN - Healthcare System - CRITICARE SYSTEMS, INC.; *pg.* 1520, *pg.* 1897
5065 - Copier - XEROX CORPORATION; *pg.* 494, *pg.* 365
5080 - Printer - XEROX CORPORATION; *pg.* 494, *pg.* 365
5090 - Copier - XEROX CORPORATION; *pg.* 494, *pg.* 365
5100 - Copier - XEROX CORPORATION; *pg.* 494, *pg.* 365
5114 - Photocopiers - XEROX CORPORATION; *pg.* 494, *pg.* 365
512 - Jean - LEVI STRAUSS & CO.; *pg.* 43, *pg.* 220
512 VENTROW - Thermal Insert Ventilator - KAWNEER COMPANY, INC.; *pg.* 90, *pg.* 537
515 - Jean - LEVI STRAUSS & CO.; *pg.* 43, *pg.* 220
516 ISOPORT - Window Framing - KAWNEER COMPANY, INC.; *pg.* 90, *pg.* 537
518 - Jean - LEVI STRAUSS & CO.; *pg.* 43, *pg.* 220
5201 - Copier - XEROX CORPORATION; *pg.* 494, *pg.* 365
5203 - Copier - XEROX CORPORATION; *pg.* 494, *pg.* 365
5205 - Copier - XEROX CORPORATION; *pg.* 494, *pg.* 365
5210 - Copier - XEROX CORPORATION; *pg.* 494, *pg.* 365
5220 - Copier - XEROX CORPORATION; *pg.* 494, *pg.* 365
524 - Jean - LEVI STRAUSS & CO.; *pg.* 43, *pg.* 220
5240 - Copier - XEROX CORPORATION; *pg.* 494, *pg.* 365
525 - Jean - LEVI STRAUSS & CO.; *pg.* 43, *pg.* 220
525 SERIES - Service Fittings - WIREMOLD/LEGRAND; *pg.* 689, *pg.* 383
5260 - Copier - XEROX CORPORATION; *pg.* 494, *pg.* 365
527 - Jean - LEVI STRAUSS & CO.; *pg.* 43, *pg.* 220
5280 - Copier - XEROX CORPORATION; *pg.* 494, *pg.* 365
5305 - Copier - XEROX CORPORATION; *pg.* 494, *pg.* 365
5306 - Copier - XEROX CORPORATION; *pg.* 494, *pg.* 365
5309 - Copier - XEROX CORPORATION; *pg.* 494, *pg.* 365
531 - Jean - LEVI STRAUSS & CO.; *pg.* 43, *pg.* 220
5310 - Copier - XEROX CORPORATION; *pg.* 494, *pg.* 365
5313 - Copier - XEROX CORPORATION; *pg.* 494, *pg.* 365
5318 - Copier - XEROX CORPORATION; *pg.* 494, *pg.* 365
5320 - Copier - XEROX CORPORATION; *pg.* 494, *pg.* 365
5322 - Copier - XEROX CORPORATION; *pg.* 494, *pg.* 365
5328 - Copier - XEROX CORPORATION; *pg.* 494, *pg.* 365
5335 - Copier - XEROX CORPORATION; *pg.* 494, *pg.* 365
5337 - Copier - XEROX CORPORATION; *pg.* 494, *pg.* 365
5340 - Copier - XEROX CORPORATION; *pg.* 494, *pg.* 365
5343C - Copier - XEROX CORPORATION; *pg.* 494, *pg.* 365
5350 - Copier - XEROX CORPORATION; *pg.* 494, *pg.* 365
5352C - Copier - XEROX CORPORATION; *pg.* 494, *pg.* 365
5365 - Copier - XEROX CORPORATION; *pg.* 494, *pg.* 365
5380 - Copier - XEROX CORPORATION; *pg.* 494, *pg.* 365
5388 - Copier - XEROX CORPORATION; *pg.* 494, *pg.* 365
5390 - Copier - XEROX CORPORATION; *pg.* 494, *pg.* 365
5400 SERIES - Nonmetallic Raceway - WIREMOLD/LEGRAND; *pg.* 689, *pg.* 383
545 - Jean - LEVI STRAUSS & CO.; *pg.* 43, *pg.* 220
54G - Computer Hardware - BROADCOM CORPORATION; *pg.* 364, *pg.* 108
THE 55 - Knife - BUCK KNIVES, INC.; *pg.* 1828, *pg.* 550
550 - Jean - LEVI STRAUSS & CO.; *pg.* 43, *pg.* 220
5500 ISOWEB - Thermal Windows - KAWNEER COMPANY, INC.; *pg.* 90, *pg.* 537
555 - Copier - XEROX CORPORATION; *pg.* 494, *pg.* 365
561 - Silicone Transformer Liquid - DOW CORNING CORPORATION; *pg.* 1159, *pg.* 900
5614 - Copier - XEROX CORPORATION; *pg.* 494, *pg.* 365
5624 - Copier - XEROX CORPORATION; *pg.* 494, *pg.* 365
5626 - Copier - XEROX CORPORATION; *pg.* 494, *pg.* 365
5680 - Copier - XEROX CORPORATION; *pg.* 494, *pg.* 365
569 - Jean - LEVI STRAUSS & CO.; *pg.* 43, *pg.* 220
'57 CLASSIC - Electrical Pickups for Guitars - GIBSON GUITAR CORP.; *pg.* 550, *pg.* 1650
575 - Printer - XEROX CORPORATION; *pg.* 494, *pg.* 365
5818 - Copier - XEROX CORPORATION; *pg.* 494, *pg.* 365
5820 - Copier - XEROX CORPORATION; *pg.* 494, *pg.* 365
5837 - Copier - XEROX CORPORATION; *pg.* 494, *pg.* 365
5845C - Copier - XEROX CORPORATION; *pg.* 494, *pg.* 365
5855C - Copier - XEROX CORPORATION; *pg.* 494, *pg.* 365
5885 - Copier - XEROX CORPORATION; *pg.* 494, *pg.* 365
5890 - Copier - XEROX CORPORATION; *pg.* 494, *pg.* 365
5895 - Copier - XEROX CORPORATION; *pg.* 494, *pg.* 365
59FIFTY - Cap - NEW ERA CAP COMPANY INC.; *pg.* 1840, *pg.* 1155
5ESS - Telecommunications Switching Units & Computer Programming - ALCATEL-LUCENT; *pg.* 615, *pg.* 1094
5EXC - Telecommunications Equipment - ALCATEL-LUCENT; *pg.* 615, *pg.* 1094
5F RF MARINR - Electrophysiology Catheter - MEDTRONIC, INC.; *pg.* 1564, *pg.* 939
5K - Abrasion Resistant Wiper - A.W. CHESTERTON COMPANY; *pg.* 1315, *pg.* 861
5K - Microprocessor Core - IMAGINATION TECHNOLOGIES; *pg.* 412, *pg.* 285
5KC - Microprocessor Core - IMAGINATION TECHNOLOGIES; *pg.* 412, *pg.* 285
5KF - Microprocessor Core - IMAGINATION TECHNOLOGIES; *pg.* 412, *pg.* 285
5STAR - Candy Bar - MONDELEZ INTERNATIONAL, INC.; *pg.* 878, *pg.* 601
5STARMAX - Movie Channel - HOME BOX OFFICE, INC.; *pg.* 290, *pg.* 1240
5TH AVENUE - Furniture - BASSETT FURNITURE INDUSTRIES, INCORPORATED; *pg.* 916, *pg.* 1776
5TH AVENUE - Coffee Product - COFFEE HOLDING CO., INC.; *pg.* 849, *pg.* 1343
5TH AVENUE - Fan - CRAFTMADE INTERNATIONAL, INC.; *pg.* 1295, *pg.* 1670
5TH AVENUE - Perfume - ELIZABETH ARDEN, INC.; *pg.* 507, *pg.* 448
5TH AVENUE - Chocolate And Candy - THE HERSHEY CO.; *pg.* 1855, *pg.* 1538
5TH AVENUE AFTER FIVE - Fragrance - ELIZABETH ARDEN, INC.; *pg.* 507, *pg.* 448
5X LUCKY - Lottery Card - MISSOURI LOTTERY; *pg.* 999, *pg.* 979
5X RAILROAD - Game - WMS INDUSTRIES INC.; *pg.* 593, *pg.* 666
5X5 - Cheeseburger - IN-N-OUT BURGERS, INC.; *pg.* 1732, *pg.* 111

6

6 BAND - Laser Detectors - COBRA ELECTRONICS CORPORATION; *pg.* 629, *pg.* 572
THE 6 MOST IMPORTANT DECISIONS YOU'LL EVER MAKE - Publication - FRANKLIN COVEY CO.; *pg.* 1642, *pg.* 1758
6-PAK - Electronic Components - MOLEX INCORPORATED;

pg. 655, *pg.* 628
6 SR - Steel Product - AK STEEL HOLDING CORPORATION; *pg.* 1311, *pg.* 1479
60 MINUTE CANADA SAVINGS - Communication Product - CENTURYLINK, INC; *pg.* 1870, *pg.* 317
600 SE - Instant Camera for Color & Black & White Prints - POLAROID CORPORATION; *pg.* 1426, *pg.* 815
6060 - Healthcare Product - BAXTER INTERNATIONAL INC.; *pg.* 1499, *pg.* 599
61 - Paints, Varnishes, Enamels - PRATT & LAMBERT PAINTS; *pg.* 1446, *pg.* 1434
631-X HYDROGEN SULFIDE ANALYZER - Analyzer - ARIZONA INSTRUMENT LLC; *pg.* 1400, *pg.* 12
636 - Jet Transports - THE BOEING COMPANY; *pg.* 225, *pg.* 567
6400 HILLSIDER - Self-propelled Lawn Mower - EXCEL INDUSTRIES, INC.; *pg.* 1795, *pg.* 715
65 TEAMS...ONE DREAM - Trademark - NATIONAL COLLEGIATE ATHLETIC ASSOCIATION; *pg.* 567, *pg.* 688
6500 - Die Bonder - PALOMAR TECHNOLOGIES INC.; *pg.* 661, *pg.* 60
666 - Cold Preparations - MONTICELLO DRUG CO.; *pg.* 1569, *pg.* 434
66Z - Image Simulator Software - AMERICAN SCIENCE AND ENGINEERING, INC.; *pg.* 1399, *pg.* 787
6925 CWDM - Electronic Component - EMCORE CORPORATION; *pg.* 636, *pg.* 39
6D - Skull Tracking - ACCURAY INCORPORATED; *pg.* 1486, *pg.* 282
6INONERIDER - Infant Carrier - INFANTINO, LLC; *pg.* 957, *pg.* 203
6K - Hydraulic Equipment - A.W. CHESTERTON COMPANY; *pg.* 1315, *pg.* 861
6S-HC - Color Wheel - REVOLUTION LIGHTING TECHNOLOGIES, INC.; *pg.* 1304, *pg.* 377

7

7-11-21 - Game - MISSOURI LOTTERY; *pg.* 999, *pg.* 979
7 CROWN - Blended Whisky - DIAGEO CANADA, INC.; *pg.* 1961, *pg.* 1937
7-ELEVEN - Convenience Food Stores - 7-ELEVEN, INC.; *pg.* 1012, *pg.* 1672
7-FLEX - Wire Rope - WIRECO WORLDGROUP; *pg.* 1389, *pg.* 987
7-FOOTER - Socks - WIGWAM MILLS, INC.; *pg.* 15, *pg.* 1894
7 FOR ALL MANKIND - Denim Pants & Sportswear - V.F. CORPORATION; *pg.* 34, *pg.* 1376
THE 7 HABITS FOR MANAGERS - Workshop - FRANKLIN COVEY CO.; *pg.* 1642, *pg.* 1758
THE 7 HABITS OF HIGHLY EFFECTIVE FAMILIES - Publication - FRANKLIN COVEY CO.; *pg.* 1642, *pg.* 1758
THE 7 HABITS OF HIGHLY EFFECTIVE PEOPLE - Address Alphabetized Page - FRANKLIN COVEY CO.; *pg.* 1642, *pg.* 1758
THE 7 HABITS OF HIGHLY EFFECTIVE TEENS - Publication - FRANKLIN COVEY CO.; *pg.* 1642, *pg.* 1758
7-JOURS - Convenience Store Banner - ALIMENTATION COUCHE-TARD INC.; *pg.* 1013, *pg.* 1951
7-LAYER BURRITO - Burritos - TACO BELL CORP.; *pg.* 1752, *pg.* 117
7 SAFARI - Game - GAMEWRIGHT; *pg.* 953, *pg.* 836
7-SELECT - Private-Label Foods - 7-ELEVEN, INC.; *pg.* 1012, *pg.* 1672
7 STORM - Video Game - INTERNATIONAL GAME TECHNOLOGY; *pg.* 957, *pg.* 1024
70 SERIES - Thermostats - EMERSON WHITE-RODGERS; *pg.* 1071, *pg.* 996
7.0 SYSTEM - Athletic Shoes - K-SWISS; *pg.* 1837, *pg.* 306
700 - Ventilator - MEDTRONIC; *pg.* 1563, *pg.* 183
7009 - Fax - XEROX CORPORATION; *pg.* 494, *pg.* 365
7033 - Fax - XEROX CORPORATION; *pg.* 494, *pg.* 365
7041 - Fax - XEROX CORPORATION; *pg.* 494, *pg.* 365
707 - Airplane - THE BOEING COMPANY; *pg.* 225, *pg.* 567
7085 - Copier - XEROX CORPORATION; *pg.* 494, *pg.* 365
70K SERIES - Bronchoscopes - PENTAX MEDICAL COMPANY; *pg.* 1580, *pg.* 1086
711 - Lubricant - SHERWIN-WILLIAMS DIVERSIFIED BRANDS DIVISION; *pg.* 1448, *pg.* 1435
722 SOLUTION - Copier - XEROX CORPORATION; *pg.* 494, *pg.* 365
723 - Oil - A.W. CHESTERTON COMPANY; *pg.* 1315, *pg.* 861
727 - Airplane - THE BOEING COMPANY; *pg.* 225, *pg.* 567
727 QTL - Lubricant - SHERWIN-WILLIAMS DIVERSIFIED BRANDS DIVISION; *pg.* 1448, *pg.* 1435
7346 - Copier - XEROX CORPORATION; *pg.* 494, *pg.* 365
7356 - Copier - XEROX CORPORATION; *pg.* 494, *pg.* 365
737 - Airplane - THE BOEING COMPANY; *pg.* 225, *pg.* 567
7399 - Copier - XEROX CORPORATION; *pg.* 494, *pg.* 365
747 - Airplane - THE BOEING COMPANY; *pg.* 225, *pg.* 567
747 - Socks - WIGWAM MILLS, INC.; *pg.* 15, *pg.* 1894
74K - Microprocessor Core - IMAGINATION TECHNOLOGIES; *pg.* 412, *pg.* 285
74KC - Microprocessor Core - IMAGINATION TECHNOLOGIES; *pg.* 412, *pg.* 285
74KF - Microprocessor Core - IMAGINATION TECHNOLOGIES; *pg.* 412, *pg.* 285
7500 WALL - Curtain Wall System - KAWNEER COMPANY, INC.; *pg.* 90, *pg.* 537
757 - Airplane - THE BOEING COMPANY; *pg.* 225, *pg.* 567
76 - Petroleum Product - CONOCOPHILLIPS; *pg.* 975, *pg.* 1703
76 COLLECTION - Vinyl Siding - NORTEK, INC.; *pg.* 100, *pg.* 1607
760 SERIES - Laser Diode Mount - NEWPORT CORPORATION; *pg.* 1424, *pg.* 114
765 - Copier - XEROX CORPORATION; *pg.* 494, *pg.* 365
767 - Airplane - THE BOEING COMPANY; *pg.* 225, *pg.* 567
76ERS - Basketball Team Slogan - PHILADELPHIA 76ERS, L.P.; *pg.* 575, *pg.* 1568
77/22 - Rimfire Rifles - STURM, RUGER & COMPANY, INC.; *pg.* 1846, *pg.* 371
77/44 - Rimfire Rifles - STURM, RUGER & COMPANY, INC.; *pg.* 1846, *pg.* 371
77/50 - Rimfire Rifles - STURM, RUGER & COMPANY, INC.; *pg.* 1846, *pg.* 371
772 - Nickel Anti-Seize Compound - A.W. CHESTERTON COMPANY; *pg.* 1315, *pg.* 861
777 - Airplane - THE BOEING COMPANY; *pg.* 225, *pg.* 567
777 SUNSHINE - Video Game - INTERNATIONAL GAME TECHNOLOGY; *pg.* 957, *pg.* 1024
7777 CLASSIC SEVENS - Video Game - INTERNATIONAL GAME TECHNOLOGY; *pg.* 957, *pg.* 1024
77KIDS - Online Only Kids Clothing & Accessories Store - AMERICAN EAGLE OUTFITTERS, INC.; *pg.* 37, *pg.* 1572
7810 - Video Receiver Module - EMCORE CORPORATION; *pg.* 636, *pg.* 39
785 - Parting Lubricant - A.W. CHESTERTON COMPANY; *pg.* 1315, *pg.* 861
785 - Copier - XEROX CORPORATION; *pg.* 494, *pg.* 365
7TH DIMENSION - Hair Care Product - ZOTOS INTERNATIONAL, INC.; *pg.* 524, *pg.* 345
7TH HEAVEN - Fabric - NEUTRAL POSTURE, INC.; *pg.* 939, *pg.* 1669
7UP - Carbonated Soft Drink - DR PEPPER SNAPPLE GROUP, INC.; *pg.* 250, *pg.* 1729
7X PAY - Video Game - INTERNATIONAL GAME TECHNOLOGY; *pg.* 957, *pg.* 1024
7X SEVEN TIMES PAY - Video Game - INTERNATIONAL GAME TECHNOLOGY; *pg.* 957, *pg.* 1024

8

8 IMMORTALS - Video Game - INTERNATIONAL GAME TECHNOLOGY; *pg.* 957, *pg.* 1024
8 IN 1 - Pet Product - PETSMART, INC.; *pg.* 1481, *pg.* 18
8 OVER 8 - Lottery Game - NEW YORK STATE LOTTERY; *pg.* 1001, *pg.* 1340
8-PETTE - Multi-Channel Pipetter - CORNING INCORPORATED; *pg.* 1122, *pg.* 1154
80 SERIES - Thermostats - EMERSON WHITE-RODGERS; *pg.* 1071, *pg.* 996
800 - Tape - A.W. CHESTERTON COMPANY; *pg.* 1315, *pg.* 861
800-588-2300 - Toll Free Number - EMPIRE TODAY, LLC; *pg.* 923, *pg.* 643
800-BASKETS - Gift Baskets Network - 1-800-FLOWERS.COM, INC.; *pg.* 1758, *pg.* 1151
800-CANDIES - Candy Sales Network - 1-800-FLOWERS.COM, INC.; *pg.* 1758, *pg.* 1151
800 CONNECT - Communication Product - CENTURYLINK, INC; *pg.* 1870, *pg.* 317
800-FLORIST - Florist Network - 1-800-FLOWERS.COM, INC.; *pg.* 1758, *pg.* 1151
800-FLOWERS - Floral Network - 1-800-FLOWERS.COM, INC.; *pg.* 1758, *pg.* 1151
800-GOODIES - Candy Sales Network - 1-800-FLOWERS.COM, INC.; *pg.* 1758, *pg.* 1151
800-GROWERS - Florist Network - 1-800-FLOWERS.COM, INC.; *pg.* 1758, *pg.* 1151
800-LAS-FLORES - Florist Network - 1-800-FLOWERS.COM, INC.; *pg.* 1758, *pg.* 1151
800 PAGELINE - Communication Product - CENTURYLINK, INC; *pg.* 1870, *pg.* 317
800 SERIES - Nonmetallic Raceway - WIREMOLD/LEGRAND; *pg.* 689, *pg.* 383
800 SERIES KTP/YAG - Surgical Laser System Designed for the Hospital Market - AMERICAN MEDICAL SYSTEMS, INC.; *pg.* 1399, *pg.* 238
8000 SERIES - Serial Dot Matrix Printers - RICOH PRINTING SYSTEMS AMERICA, INC.; *pg.* 462, *pg.* 279
800SAMEDAY.COM - Delivery Services & Distribution Solutions - ASSOCIATED GLOBAL SYSTEMS, INC.; *pg.* 1899, *pg.* 1184
810 BASIC - Dental X-Ray Processor - IMAGEWORKS; *pg.* 1544, *pg.* 1158
810 PLUS - Film Processor - IMAGEWORKS; *pg.* 1544, *pg.* 1158
8142 - Copier - XEROX CORPORATION; *pg.* 494, *pg.* 365
8160 - Copier - XEROX CORPORATION; *pg.* 494, *pg.* 365
8254E - Copier - XEROX CORPORATION; *pg.* 494, *pg.* 365
8264E - Copier - XEROX CORPORATION; *pg.* 494, *pg.* 365
8265 - Copier - XEROX CORPORATION; *pg.* 494, *pg.* 365
8290 - Copier - XEROX CORPORATION; *pg.* 494, *pg.* 365
8365 - Copier - XEROX CORPORATION; *pg.* 494, *pg.* 365
8390 - Copier - XEROX CORPORATION; *pg.* 494, *pg.* 365
841-PE - Optical Power & Energy Meter - NEWPORT CORPORATION; *pg.* 1424, *pg.* 114
860 - Moldable Polymer Gasketing - A.W. CHESTERTON COMPANY; *pg.* 1315, *pg.* 861
8603A - Electronic Component - EMCORE CORPORATION; *pg.* 636, *pg.* 39
8604A - Electronic Component - EMCORE CORPORATION; *pg.* 636, *pg.* 39
862 SERIES - Floor Boxes - WIREMOLD/LEGRAND; *pg.* 689, *pg.* 383
863 SERIES - Floor Boxes - WIREMOLD/LEGRAND; *pg.* 689, *pg.* 383
8710A - Electronic Component - EMCORE CORPORATION; *pg.* 636, *pg.* 39
8720A - Electronic Component - EMCORE CORPORATION; *pg.* 636, *pg.* 39
880 CROWN & CHASSIS GREASE - Extreme Pressure Grease - TEXAS REFINERY CORP.; *pg.* 986, *pg.* 1696
880 TRADITION - Fire Helmet - MINE SAFETY APPLIANCES COMPANY; *pg.* 1361, *pg.* 1525
880MP MODULINK - Floor Boxes - WIREMOLD/LEGRAND; *pg.* 689, *pg.* 383
881 RACHET PRO - Floor Boxes - WIREMOLD/LEGRAND; *pg.* 689, *pg.* 383
8810 - Electronic Component - EMCORE CORPORATION; *pg.* 636, *pg.* 39
8820 - Electronic Component - EMCORE CORPORATION; *pg.* 636, *pg.* 39
8825 DDS - Copier - XEROX CORPORATION; *pg.* 494, *pg.* 365
882C SERIES - Floor Boxes - WIREMOLD/LEGRAND; *pg.* 689, *pg.* 383
883 XL - Motorcycle - HARLEY-DAVIDSON, INC.; *pg.* 178, *pg.* 1874
8830 - Copier - XEROX CORPORATION; *pg.* 494, *pg.* 365
884C SERIES - Floor Boxes - WIREMOLD/LEGRAND; *pg.* 689, *pg.* 383
8850A - Electronic Component - EMCORE CORPORATION; *pg.* 636, *pg.* 39
8860A - Electronic Component - EMCORE CORPORATION; *pg.* 636, *pg.* 39
888-KB-HOMES - Homebuilding Services - KB HOME; *pg.* 90, *pg.* 134
891 - Rotary Inside Single Seal - A.W. CHESTERTON COMPANY; *pg.* 1315, *pg.* 861
8910 - Electronic Component - EMCORE CORPORATION; *pg.* 636, *pg.* 39
8920 - Electronic Component - EMCORE CORPORATION; *pg.* 636, *pg.* 39
8K - Hydraulic Set - A.W. CHESTERTON COMPANY; *pg.* 1315, *pg.* 861
8S-SB - Color Wheel - REVOLUTION LIGHTING TECHNOLOGIES, INC.; *pg.* 1304, *pg.* 377
THE 8TH HABIT: FROM EFFECTIVENESS TO GREATNESS

First page reference indicates Business Class Edition
Second page reference indicates Geographic Edition

- Publication - FRANKLIN COVEY CO.; pg. 1642, pg. 1758

9

9-1-1 NET - Web-Based 9-1-1 Data Management Service - INTRADO INC.; pg. 420, pg. 334
9-1-1 PINPOINT - Service - AT&T SOUTHEAST; pg. 1868, pg. 489
9 KOI - Video Game - INTERNATIONAL GAME TECHNOLOGY; pg. 957, pg. 1024
9-LIVES - Canned Cat Food - HEINZ NORTH AMERICA; pg. 861, pg. 1576
9 LIVES - Video Game - INTERNATIONAL GAME TECHNOLOGY; pg. 957, pg. 1024
9-LIVES MATURE - Soft/Moist Cat Food - HEINZ NORTH AMERICA; pg. 861, pg. 1576
9 SUNS - Game - WMS INDUSTRIES INC.; pg. 593, pg. 666
90-75 - Water Conserving Metering Faucet - BRADLEY CORPORATION; pg. 71, pg. 1870
90 SERIES - Thermostats - EMERSON WHITE-RODGERS; pg. 1071, pg. 996
9000 SERIES - Serial Dot Matrix Printers - RICOH PRINTING SYSTEMS AMERICA, INC.; pg. 462, pg. 279
900UDX - Urine Pathology System - IRIS INTERNATIONAL, INC.; pg. 1547, pg. 64
904 - Pump - GARDNER DENVER NASH; pg. 1338, pg. 381
911 SERIES - Fire Apparatus Seating - SEATS INCORPORATED; pg. 217, pg. 1890
911EP - Warning Light Systems Using LED Technology - BAE SYSTEMS PRODUCTS GROUP; pg. 359, pg. 432
928 - Young Men's Suited Separates - OXFORD INDUSTRIES, INC.; pg. 30, pg. 517
92C LPS - Copier - XEROX CORPORATION; pg. 494, pg. 365
92C NPS - Copier - XEROX CORPORATION; pg. 494, pg. 365
939UDX - Urine Pathology System - IRIS INTERNATIONAL, INC.; pg. 1547, pg. 64
9400DSIE - Silicon Etch System - LAM RESEARCH CORPORATION; pg. 1354, pg. 91
950 INDUSTRIAL - Semi-Commercial Sewing Machines - BERNINA OF AMERICA INC.; pg. 51, pg. 554
960 - Fluid Handling System - GRACO, INC.; pg. 1342, pg. 935
99 BOTTLES OF BEER - Video Game - BALLY TECHNOLOGIES, INC.; pg. 531, pg. 1022
99 CALORIE CARLING - Beer - MOLSON COORS BREWING COMPANY; pg. 256, pg. 321
9936F - Electronic Component - EMCORE CORPORATION; pg. 636, pg. 39
9937D - Electronic Component - EMCORE CORPORATION; pg. 636, pg. 39
999 - Tools - VAUGHAN & BUSHNELL MANUFACTURING COMPANY, INC.; pg. 1066, pg. 616
9LIVES - Cat Food - BIG HEART PET BRANDS; pg. 1474, pg. 213
9ROUND - Kickboxing Club Franchise - LIFT BRANDS; pg. 557, pg. 920
9S IN A LINE - Lottery Game - OHIO LOTTERY COMMISSION; pg. 1002, pg. 1433

A

A - Brokerage - COUSINS PROPERTIES INCORPORATED; pg. 1088, pg. 501
A-100 - Paint - THE SHERWIN-WILLIAMS COMPANY; pg. 1447, pg. 1435
A-101 - Fire Suppression System Data Sheet - ANSUL, INCORPORATED; pg. 1147, pg. 1869
A-11 - Gypsum Cement - USG CORPORATION; pg. 118, pg. 594
A&A AUTO PARTS - Automotive Parts Stores - KEYSTONE AUTOMOTIVE OPERATIONS, INC.; pg. 210, pg. 1531
A&D OINTMENT - Skincare - MERCK & CO., INC.; pg. 1566, pg. 1077
A&E - Television Channel - A&E TELEVISION NETWORKS, LLC; pg. 267, pg. 1185
A&P - Food Stores - THE GREAT ATLANTIC & PACIFIC TEA COMPANY, INC.; pg. 1021, pg. 1086
A & V - Ink Jet Proofer - ANDERSON & VREELAND, INC.; pg. 1616, pg. 1064
A&W - Fast Food - A&W FOOD SERVICES OF CANADA INC.; pg. 1714, pg. 1908
A&W - Carbonated Soft Drink - DR PEPPER SNAPPLE GROUP, INC.; pg. 250, pg. 1729
A & W - Fast Foods & Beverages - YUM! BRANDS, INC.; pg. 1756, pg. 738
A&W ROOT BEER - Fast Food - A&W FOOD SERVICES OF CANADA INC.; pg. 1714, pg. 1908
A-B-C - Asbestos Binding Compound - CALIFORNIA PRODUCTS CORPORATION; pg. 1441, pg. 781
A-B IN OCTAGON - Software - ROCKWELL AUTOMATION, INC.; pg. 668, pg. 1880
A BANK INVESTED IN PEOPLE - Slogan - HUNTINGTON BANCSHARES INCORPORATED; pg. 767, pg. 1440
A BANK INVESTED IN PEOPLE - Tag Line - THE HUNTINGTON NATIONAL BANK; pg. 767, pg. 1440
A BEAUTIFUL IDEA - Tag Line - THE BONNE BELL COMPANY; pg. 502, pg. 1480
A BETTER DECISION - Health Care Insurance - HEALTH NET, INC.; pg. 1540, pg. 308
A BETTER GAME BY DESIGN - Slogan - CALLAWAY GOLF COMPANY; pg. 1829, pg. 58
A BETTER PLACE FOR YOU. - Slogan - THE CO-OPERATORS GROUP LIMITED; pg. 1198, pg. 1920
A BETTER VIEW OF LIFE - Slogan - EASTMAN KODAK COMPANY; pg. 1408, pg. 1333
A BETTER WAY... - Tagline - COLD SPRING GRANITE COMPANY; pg. 76, pg. 920
A BETTER WAY TO TREAT A DOOR - Tagline - ODL INCORPORATED; pg. 101, pg. 914
A BLUEPRINT FOR DELIVERING BETTER HEALTH CARE - Service - VHA INC.; pg. 1606, pg. 1724
A-BOMB - Nutritional Supplement - MAXIMUM HUMAN PERFORMANCE, INC.; pg. 1559, pg. 1065
A BUSINESS OF CARING - Tagline - CIGNA CORPORATION; pg. 1197, pg. 338
A BUYERS GALLERY OF FINE AUTOMOBILES - Magazine - DUPONT PUBLISHING, INC.; pg. 1637, pg. 462
A BUYER'S GALLERY OF FINE AUTOMOBILES - Magazine - DUPONT REGISTRY; pg. 1637, pg. 462
A BUYERS GALLERY OF FINE BOATS - Magazine - DUPONT PUBLISHING, INC.; pg. 1637, pg. 462
A BUYER'S GALLERY OF FINE BOATS - Magazine - DUPONT REGISTRY; pg. 1637, pg. 462
A BUYERS GALLERY OF FINE HOMES - Magazine - DUPONT PUBLISHING, INC.; pg. 1637, pg. 462
A BUYER'S GALLERY OF FINE HOMES - Magazine - DUPONT REGISTRY; pg. 1637, pg. 462
A/C PRO - Automotive Air Conditioner - ARMORED AUTOGROUP INC.; pg. 199, pg. 342
A-C PUMP - Wastewater & Fire Pumps - GOULDS PUMPS, INCORPORATED; pg. 1342, pg. 1341
A-C PUMP - Fluid Technology - ITT CORPORATION; pg. 1351, pg. 1354
A/C QUIET - Air Conditioner Parts Lubricant - MOC PRODUCTS COMPANY, INC.; pg. 332, pg. 174
A CAPITAL FOURTH - Annual 4th of July Celebration - JOHN F. KENNEDY CENTER FOR THE PERFORMING ARTS; pg. 555, pg. 401
A-CLASS - Bar Code System - DATAMAX CORPORATION; pg. 1633, pg. 453
A CLEANER CLEAN - Slogan - METHOD PRODUCTS INC.; pg. 332, pg. 223
A CODE - Blind Rivet - ALLFAST FASTENING SYSTEMS, INC.; pg. 1041, pg. 66
A COMPANY WITH A SMART VISION - Tag Line - LSI INDUSTRIES INC.; pg. 58, pg. 1416
A CREATIVE CLEANTECH COMPANY - Slogan - ITRONICS INC.; pg. 1169, pg. 1031
A CREATIVE ENVIRONMENTAL TECHNOLOGY COMPANY - Slogan - ITRONICS INC.; pg. 1169, pg. 1031
A-DRUM - Plastic Drum - GREIF INC.; pg. 1459, pg. 1447
A FAMILY OF COMMUNITY BANKS - Tagline - CFG COMMUNITY BANK; pg. 734, pg. 756
A FEW SECONDS - Slogan - PFIZER INC.; pg. 1581, pg. 1270
A-FOCUS - Steerable Diagnostic Catheters - BOSTON SCIENTIFIC CORPORATION; pg. 1508, pg. 831
A FRESH APPROACH TO CHICKEN - Slogan - ZAXBY'S FRANCHISING, INC.; pg. 1756, pg. 486
A GALAXY OF SMART FOOD CHOICES - Slogan - GALAXY NUTRITIONAL FOODS, INC.; pg. 857, pg. 1603
A GIRL'S BEST FRIEND - Toy Dogs & Accessories - AMERICAN GIRL LLC; pg. 949, pg. 1871
A GOOD PLACE TO PUT YOUR INFORMATION - Memory Product - CAMBEX CORPORATION; pg. 368, pg. 844
A GREAT CANDY ISN'T MADE . . . IT'S JUST BORN - Slogan - JUST BORN, INC.; pg. 1857, pg. 1516
A GREAT DAY IN THE O.R. - Slogan - EXACTECH, INC.; pg. 1529, pg. 428
A GREAT DENTIST CAN CHANGE YOUR LIFE - Slogan - FUTUREDONTICS, INC.; pg. 1532, pg. 131
A GREAT PLACE TO BE - Tagline - UNITED PARCEL SERVICE, INC.; pg. 1928, pg. 522
A GREAT SOUNDING WEB ADDRESS ENDS IN DOTFM! - Slogan - BRS MEDIA INC.; pg. 1233, pg. 214
A GREATER MEASURE OF CONFIDENCE - Tagline - KEITHLEY INSTRUMENTS, INC.; pg. 1418, pg. 1473
A-HD ELITE - Test Booster - BPI SPORTS, LLC; pg. 842, pg. 430
A HEALTHY WAY OF LIFE COMPANY - Tag Line - LIFE TIME FITNESS, INC.; pg. 1556, pg. 920
A HEALTHY WAY TO START YOUR DAY - Tag Line - CHIQUITA BRANDS INTERNATIONAL, INC.; pg. 847, pg. 1365
A HISTORY OF MAKING OUR MARK - Slogan - MATTHEWS INTERNATIONAL CORPORATION; pg. 1662, pg. 1578
A JIGSAW JONES MYSTERY - Educational Materials - SCHOLASTIC INC.; pg. 1683, pg. 1288
A KID'S SCIENCE MUSEUM IN A BOOK - Educational Materials - SCHOLASTIC INC.; pg. 1683, pg. 1288
A LA CARTE - Office Furniture - STEELCASE INC.; pg. 475, pg. 889
A LEGEND IN WORK - Slogan - WILLIAMSON-DICKIE MANUFACTURING COMPANY; pg. 50, pg. 1696
A. LINCOLN - Signature Design of All Lincoln Life Products - LINCOLN NATIONAL CORPORATION; pg. 776, pg. 1567
A LITTLE BIT OF SATELLITE GOES A LONG WAY - Tagline - GLOBECOMM SYSTEMS INC.; pg. 640, pg. 1164
A LITTLE SEXY - Designer Fragrance - PARFUMS DE COEUR LTD.; pg. 519, pg. 376
A. MELLOT - Sancerre - DREYFUS ASHBY INC.; pg. 1962, pg. 1226
A MIND IS A TERRIBLE THING TO WASTE - Tag Line - UNITED NEGRO COLLEGE FUND, INC.; pg. 159, pg. 405
A MOTHER'S LOVE - Pillow & Throw - HERITAGE LACE INC.; pg. 694, pg. 711
A MOTHER'S TOUCH NAO - Flower Arrangement - 1-800-FLOWERS.COM, INC.; pg. 1758, pg. 1151
A NAME YOU CAN TRUST FOR LIFE - Slogan - SBLI USA LIFE INSURANCE COMPANY, INC.; pg. 1216, pg. 1288
A NEW KIND A BUZZ - Beverage - MONSTER BEVERAGE CORPORATION; pg. 257, pg. 69
A NEW STANDARD OF RESPONSIBILITY - Tagline - ROCK CREEK PHARMACEUTICALS, INC.; pg. 1895, pg. 466
A NEW STATEMENT OF STYLE - Tagline - THE CATO CORPORATION; pg. 21, pg. 1364
A/P LITE - Joint Compound - USG CORPORATION; pg. 118, pg. 594
A PARTNER FOR LIFE - Tag Line - VARIAN MEDICAL SYSTEMS, INC.; pg. 1434, pg. 178
A PASSION FOR EXCELLENCE - Tagline - THE GREAT LAKES CHEESE CO., INC.; pg. 859, pg. 1455
A PASSION FOR LIFE, THE PURSUIT OF EXCELLENCE - Tagline - SPARTAN MOTORS, INC.; pg. 217, pg. 874
A PEA IN THE POD - Maternity Apparel - DESTINATION MATERNITY CORPORATION; pg. 23, pg. 1563
A PERFECT CHISEL - Bathroom Design - DECOLAV, INC.; pg. 1123, pg. 411
A REAL MEXICAN FOOD COMPANY - Slogan - RUIZ FOOD PRODUCTS, INC.; pg. 893, pg. 77
A ROOKIE READER - Educational Materials - SCHOLASTIC INC.; pg. 1683, pg. 1288
A-ROSE AT DAWN - Nail Care Product - OPI PRODUCTS INC.; pg. 518, pg. 167
A-SERIES - Cage Mill/Pulverizer - STEDMAN MACHINE COMPANY; pg. 1379, pg. 673
A SHORTS STORY - Slacks & Shorts - HABAND COMPANY, INC.; pg. 1772, pg. 1099
A SIMPLE WAY OF DOING BUSINESS BETTER Tag Line TESSCO TECHNOLOGIES, INC.; pg. 679, pg. 773
A SMART GIRL'S GUIDE - Dolls - AMERICAN GIRL LLC; pg. 949, pg. 1871
A SMARTER PLANET - Slogan - INTERNATIONAL BUSINESS MACHINES CORPORATION; pg. 418, pg. 1138
A SMARTER VISION - Slogan - GENTEX CORPORATION; pg. 206, pg. 913
A SMARTER WAY TO BANK SINCE 1905 - Slogan - MECHANICS BANK; pg. 781, pg. 193
A SMARTER WAY TO INVEST FOR COLLEGE - Slogan -

FRANKLIN RESOURCES, INC.; *pg.* 760, *pg.* 254
A SMARTER WAY TO PRINT - Tagline - PRESSTEK LLC; *pg.* 1678, *pg.* 1034
A SMARTER WAY TO WORK - Tag Line - STEELCASE INC.; *pg.* 475, *pg.* 889
A SOLID CONNECTION - Tagline - MKT FASTENING, LLC; *pg.* 1056, *pg.* 34
A SOLUTION FOR EVERY LIFESTYLE - Tagline - PNY TECHNOLOGIES, INC.; *pg.* 455, *pg.* 1105
A SOUND WEB ADDRESS. - Slogan - BRS MEDIA INC.; *pg.* 1233, *pg.* 214
A SPECIAL BIRTHDAY WISH - Flower Arrangement - 1-800-FLOWERS.COM, INC.; *pg.* 1758, *pg.* 1151
A STEAKHOUSE TO END ALL ARGUMENTS - Slogan - THE SMITH & WOLLENSKY RESTAURANT GROUP, INC.; *pg.* 1750, *pg.* 1293
A-T - Health Products - A-T SURGICAL MFG. CO., INC.; *pg.* 1483, *pg.* 825
A-T - Medical Equipment - INVACARE CORPORATION; *pg.* 1546, *pg.* 1451
A/T 2000 - X-Ray Film Processor - AIR TECHNIQUES, INC.; *pg.* 1487, *pg.* 1178
A/T SCANX - Intraoral Digital Imaging System - AIR TECHNIQUES, INC.; *pg.* 1487, *pg.* 1178
A/T SLC - Digital Video Imaging System - AIR TECHNIQUES, INC.; *pg.* 1487, *pg.* 1178
A TASTE OF CALIFORNIA - Wine Catalog - MAGNET ENTERPRISES, INC.; *pg.* 1966, *pg.* 581
A-TEAM - Healthcare Facilities - ATC HEALTHCARE, INC.; *pg.* 1497, *pg.* 1184
A TIMELESS PLEASURE - Tag Line - GHIRARDELLI CHOCOLATE COMPANY; *pg.* 1854, *pg.* 252
A TO ZOO - Subject Access to Children's Picture Books - R.R. BOWKER LLC; *pg.* 1682, *pg.* 1095
A TOUCH OF ELEGANCE - Dozen Roses - 1-800-FLOWERS.COM, INC.; *pg.* 1758, *pg.* 1151
A TRADIITON OF GROWTH - Slogan - WILLIAM BLAIR & COMPANY LLC; *pg.* 822, *pg.* 596
A TRADITION OF GOOD EATING - Slogan - REILY FOODS COMPANY; *pg.* 891, *pg.* 747
A TRUE BOOK - Educational Materials - SCHOLASTIC INC.; *pg.* 1683, *pg.* 1288
A TRUSTED SOURCE OF NEWS AND INFORMATION - Tag Line - VOICE OF AMERICA; *pg.* 1010, *pg.* 407
A TURN FOR THE BETTER - Tagline - LOWELL CORPORATION; *pg.* 1053, *pg.* 856
A-TYPE - Hot Air Balloon - CAMERON BALLOONS U.S.; *pg.* 1829, *pg.* 884
A UNIQUE CANADIAN OPPORTUNITY - Tagline - TIGRENT INC.; *pg.* 608, *pg.* 415
A VERY HEALTHY WAY TO SHOP - Tagline - DRUGSTORE.COM, INC.; *pg.* 1239, *pg.* 1814
A VISIBLE DIFFERENCE - Slogan - H.E. WILLIAMS, INC.; *pg.* 1299, *pg.* 974
A VISION FOR OUR ENERGY FUTURE - Tagline - NV ENERGY, INC.; *pg.* 1948, *pg.* 1028
A WHOLE LOT OF MEXICAN - Mexican Restaurants - TACO JOHN'S INTERNATIONAL, INC.; *pg.* 1753, *pg.* 1901
A WIRE - Eyewear - OAKLEY, INC.; *pg.* 1840, *pg.* 86
A WORLD BEYOND THE MAIN STREAM - Slogan - SEA RAY BOATS, INC.; *pg.* 1710, *pg.* 1638
A WORLD OF ADVANTAGES FOR OUR CUSTOMERS - Tag Line - FUCHS NORTH AMERICA.; *pg.* 857, *pg.* 774
A WORLD OF CAPABILITIES - Tag Line - KENNEY MANUFACTURING COMPANY; *pg.* 1052, *pg.* 1609
A WORLD OF EXPERTS - Tagline - LIVEPERSON, INC.; *pg.* 1264, *pg.* 1252
A WORLD OF HEALTH & COMFORT - Tagline - KAZ, INC.; *pg.* 58, *pg.* 844
A WORLD OF LEARNING - Service Mark - MENTOR GRAPHICS CORPORATION; *pg.* 432, *pg.* 1510
A WORLD OF SOLUTIONS - Tagline - CONMED CORPORATION; *pg.* 1517, *pg.* 1347
A WORLD OF SOLUTIONS - Tagline - INFOGROUP INC.; *pg.* 1652, *pg.* 1016
A-XGMAC - Software System - MENTOR GRAPHICS CORPORATION; *pg.* 432, *pg.* 1510
A-ZOOM - Rifle Snap Caps - LYMAN PRODUCTS CORPORATION; *pg.* 1839, *pg.* 356
A.1. - Steak Sauce - THE KRAFT HEINZ COMPANY; *pg.* 870, *pg.* 1577
A1 - Bicycle Accessories - SPECIALIZED BICYCLE COMPONENTS, INC.; *pg.* 1711, *pg.* 152
A100 - Wireless Product - HEMISPHERE GPS INC.; *pg.* 642, *pg.* 1903
A125 SHARPLET-2 - Pencil - PENTEL OF AMERICA, LTD.; *pg.* 453, *pg.* 295
A2 - Shoe - AEROGROUP INTERNATIONAL, INC.; *pg.* 1803, *pg.* 1055
A2 - Microarray System Absorbance Detectors - BECKMAN COULTER, INC.; *pg.* 1402, *pg.* 48
A2100 - Spacecraft - LOCKHEED MARTIN CORPORATION; *pg.* 229, *pg.* 762
A31 - DC-AC Inverter - LA MARCHE MANUFACTURING COMPANY; *pg.* 1300, *pg.* 606
A4 - Folding Wheelchair - INVACARE CORPORATION; *pg.* 1546, *pg.* 1451
A40R - Railroad Battery Charger - LA MARCHE MANUFACTURING COMPANY; *pg.* 1300, *pg.* 606
A45M - Mine Battery Charger - LA MARCHE MANUFACTURING COMPANY; *pg.* 1300, *pg.* 606
A5 - Sports Apparel - THE NORTH FACE, INC.; *pg.* 1840, *pg.* 252
A55 - Horizontal Machining Center - MAKINO INC.; *pg.* 1358, *pg.* 1461
A85MD - Mine Battery Charger - LA MARCHE MANUFACTURING COMPANY; *pg.* 1300, *pg.* 606
AA - Window - ALCOA INC.; *pg.* 65, *pg.* 1188
AA - Rice - AMERICAN RICE, INC.; *pg.* 837, *pg.* 1700
AA - Engineered Sound Products; Electronic Speakers, Microphones - PEAVEY ELECTRONICS CORPORATION; *pg.* 662, *pg.* 970
AA PLUS - Valves - GRACO, INC.; *pg.* 1342, *pg.* 935
AA SERIES - Fluid Handling System - GRACO, INC.; *pg.* 1342, *pg.* 935
AAA - American Automobile Association - AMERICAN AUTOMOBILE ASSOCIATION; *pg.* 1190, *pg.* 429
AAA - Epitaxial System - COHERENT, INC.; *pg.* 1406, *pg.* 265
AAA AUTOEASE - Automobile Pricing & Buying Services - AMERICAN AUTOMOBILE ASSOCIATION; *pg.* 1190, *pg.* 429
AAA AUTOMAKER - Automobile Selection Services - AMERICAN AUTOMOBILE ASSOCIATION; *pg.* 1190, *pg.* 429
AAA AUTOMANAGER - Vehicle Maintenance & Repair Management Services - AMERICAN AUTOMOBILE ASSOCIATION; *pg.* 1190, *pg.* 429
AAA CAMPBOOK - Regional Camping Guidebooks - AMERICAN AUTOMOBILE ASSOCIATION; *pg.* 1190, *pg.* 429
AAA CITIBOOK - City Guidebooks - AMERICAN AUTOMOBILE ASSOCIATION; *pg.* 1190, *pg.* 429
AAA NORTH AMERICAN ROAD ATLAS - Road Atlas - AMERICAN AUTOMOBILE ASSOCIATION; *pg.* 1190, *pg.* 429
AAA TOURBOOK - U.S. & Canada Guidebooks - AMERICAN AUTOMOBILE ASSOCIATION; *pg.* 1190, *pg.* 429
AAA TRAVELBOOK - Europe, Caribbean & Mexico Guidebooks - AMERICAN AUTOMOBILE ASSOCIATION; *pg.* 1190, *pg.* 429
AAA TRIPTIK - Travel Routings & Trip Plans - AMERICAN AUTOMOBILE ASSOCIATION; *pg.* 1190, *pg.* 429
AABR - Medical Device - NATUS MEDICAL INCORPORATED; *pg.* 1572, *pg.* 199
AADVANTAGE - Frequent Flyer Program - AMERICAN AIRLINES INC.; *pg.* 1898, *pg.* 1693
AADVANTAGE - Cash Card - CITIGROUP INC.; *pg.* 735, *pg.* 1212
AAI - Gymnastics Equipment - RUSSELL BRANDS LLC; *pg.* 698, *pg.* 726
AALTO - Furniture - HERMAN MILLER, INC.; *pg.* 926, *pg.* 913
AAM-RAS - Confectionery - THE HERSHEY CO.; *pg.* 1855, *pg.* 1538
AAMCO TRANSMISSIONS - Transmissions - AAMCO TRANSMISSIONS, INC.; *pg.* 197, *pg.* 1540
AAMUX - Storage Hardware - AVAGO TECHNOLOGIES; *pg.* 358, *pg.* 238
AANALYST - Atomic Absorption Spectrometer - PERKINELMER, INC.; *pg.* 1426, *pg.* 853
AAONAIRE - Heating Equipment - AAON, INC.; *pg.* 1068, *pg.* 1488
AAONECAT - Software - AAON, INC.; *pg.* 1068, *pg.* 1488
AAONECAT32 - Software - AAON, INC.; *pg.* 1068, *pg.* 1488
AAPAK - Packing Drums - SONOCO PRODUCTS COMPANY; *pg.* 1469, *pg.* 1619
AAPER - Alcohol - PHARMCO-AAPER; *pg.* 1177, *pg.* 740
AAPRI - Facial Scrub, Replenishing Cream & Lotion - THE GILLETTE COMPANY; *pg.* 509, *pg.* 795
AARON - Electrosurgery Generators & Accessories - BOVIE MEDICAL CORPORATION; *pg.* 1402, *pg.* 1178
AARON 1250 - Electrosurgery Generator - BOVIE MEDICAL CORPORATION; *pg.* 1402, *pg.* 1178
AARON 2250 - Electrosurgery Generator - BOVIE MEDICAL CORPORATION; *pg.* 1402, *pg.* 1178
AARON 3250 - Electrosurgery Generator - BOVIE MEDICAL CORPORATION; *pg.* 1402, *pg.* 1178
AARON 900 - Electrosurgery Generator - BOVIE MEDICAL CORPORATION; *pg.* 1402, *pg.* 1178
AARON 950 - Electrosurgery Generator - BOVIE MEDICAL CORPORATION; *pg.* 1402, *pg.* 1178
AARP - The American Association of Retired Persons - AARP; *pg.* 124, *pg.* 393
AARP BULLETIN - Magazine - AARP; *pg.* 124, *pg.* 393
AARP SEGUNDA JUVENTUD - Magazine - AARP; *pg.* 124, *pg.* 393
AARP THE MAGAZINE - Magazine - AARP; *pg.* 124, *pg.* 393
AASAY - Confectionery - THE HERSHEY CO.; *pg.* 1855, *pg.* 1538
AATON-A MINIMA - Film - EASTMAN KODAK COMPANY; *pg.* 1408, *pg.* 1333
AB-100 - Broadband Wireless Equipment - AXXCELERA BROADBAND WIRELESS INC.; *pg.* 623, *pg.* 263
AB-ACCESS - Fixed Broadband Wireless Access Equipment - AXXCELERA BROADBAND WIRELESS INC.; *pg.* 623, *pg.* 263
AB CODE RIVET - Blind Rivet - ALLFAST FASTENING SYSTEMS, INC.; *pg.* 1041, *pg.* 66
A.B. DICK - Pre-Press, Press & Post-Press Equipment & Supplies - PRESSTEK, INC.; *pg.* 456, *pg.* 606
AB-E1/T1 - Broadband Wireless Equipment - AXXCELERA BROADBAND WIRELESS INC.; *pg.* 623, *pg.* 263
AB-EXTENDER - Broadband Wireless System - AXXCELERA BROADBAND WIRELESS INC.; *pg.* 623, *pg.* 263
AB-FULL ACCESS - Broadband Wireless Equipment - AXXCELERA BROADBAND WIRELESS INC.; *pg.* 623, *pg.* 263
AB-MUX - Broadband Wireless Equipment - AXXCELERA BROADBAND WIRELESS INC.; *pg.* 623, *pg.* 263
AB139 - Twin Engine Helicopter - BELL HELICOPTER TEXTRON, INC.; *pg.* 224, *pg.* 1693
ABA TRUST LETTER - Legislative & Regulatory Banking News - THE AMERICAN BANKERS ASSOCIATION; *pg.* 126, *pg.* 394
ABACUS - Surface Material - STEELCASE INC.; *pg.* 475, *pg.* 889
ABACUS - Medical System - VARIAN MEDICAL SYSTEMS, INC.; *pg.* 1434, *pg.* 178
ABACUS PCR - Reprographic Product - AMERICAN REPROGRAPHICS COMPANY; *pg.* 1616, *pg.* 303
ABAK - Furniture - HERMAN MILLER, INC.; *pg.* 926, *pg.* 913
ABALON BEECH - Wood & Building Material - WEYERHAEUSER COMPANY; *pg.* 121, *pg.* 1820
ABALYN - Resin - EASTMAN CHEMICAL COMPANY; *pg.* 1159, *pg.* 1636
ABBA-ZABA - Chewy Taffy - ANNABELLE CANDY COMPANY, INC.; *pg.* 1850, *pg.* 100
ABBA-ZABA CHERRY APPLE - Candy Bar - ANNABELLE CANDY COMPANY, INC.; *pg.* 1850, *pg.* 100
ABBEY - Beer - NEW BELGIUM BREWING COMPANY, INC.; *pg.* 258, *pg.* 328
ABBEY CARPETS - Floor Carpets - CONKLIN BROS; *pg.* 921, *pg.* 242
ABBEY HILL - Home Goods - KMART CORPORATION; *pg.* 1775, *pg.* 617
ABBEY TRIPLE - Beverage - SPRECHER BREWING COMPANY; *pg.* 265, *pg.* 1858
ABBIE - Women's Clothing & Accessories - WOODEN SHIPS OF HOBOKEN; *pg.* 35, *pg.* 1315
ABBO-VAC - Medical Device - HOSPIRA, INC.; *pg.* 1542, *pg.* 623
ABBOCATH - Medical Device - HOSPIRA, INC.; *pg.* 1542, *pg.* 623
ABBOJECT - Syringes - HOSPIRA, INC.; *pg.* 1542, *pg.* 623
ABBOKINASE - Clot-Dissolving Drug - ABBOTT LABORATORIES; *pg.* 1484, *pg.* 551
ABBOTIC - Pharmaceutical Products - ABBOTT LABORATORIES; *pg.* 1484, *pg.* 551
ABBOTT PRISM - Blood Screening Product - ABBOTT LABORATORIES; *pg.* 1484, *pg.* 551
ABBOTTBALL - Ball Bearing - ABBOTT BALL COMPANY; *pg.* 1040, *pg.* 383
ABC - Case Erector - ABC PACKAGING MACHINE CORPORATION; *pg.* 1309, *pg.* 477

First page reference indicates Business Class Edition
Second page reference indicates Geographic Edition

ABC - Medical Product - CONMED CORPORATION; *pg.* 1517, *pg.* 1347
ABC - Food Product - THE KRAFT HEINZ COMPANY; *pg.* 870, *pg.* 1577
ABC - Coating & Finish - NOV AMERON; *pg.* 100, *pg.* 187
ABC - Educational Resources - SCHOOL SPECIALTY, INC.; *pg.* 467, *pg.* 1860
ABC CERVICAL PLATING SYSTEM - Cervical Plating System - AESCULAP, INC.; *pg.* 1487, *pg.* 1521
ABC INVESTMENT PLAN - Investing Service - U.S. GLOBAL INVESTORS, INC.; *pg.* 815, *pg.* 1743
ABC SONG GAME - Toy & Game - HASBRO, INC.; *pg.* 954, *pg.* 1603
ABCGONLINE - Telephone Service - IDT CORPORATION; *pg.* 643, *pg.* 1096
ABCHAIR - Chair - NEUTRAL POSTURE, INC.; *pg.* 939, *pg.* 1669
ABCORP - Medical Product - UTAH MEDICAL PRODUCTS, INC.; *pg.* 1605, *pg.* 1752
ABE - Offline Telemetry Analysis & Display Tool - INTEGRAL SYSTEMS, INC.; *pg.* 416, *pg.* 767
ABE - Accelerated Benefit Election Rider - LINCOLN NATIONAL CORPORATION; *pg.* 776, *pg.* 1567
ABE & LOUIE'S - Restaurants - TAVISTOCK RESTAURANT GROUP; *pg.* 1753, *pg.* 803
ABECO - Cable Preparation Tool - THE RIPLEY COMPANY; *pg.* 1305, *pg.* 342
ABEND-AID - Software - COMPUWARE CORPORATION; *pg.* 379, *pg.* 879
ABERCROMBIE - Clothing - ABERCROMBIE & FITCH CO.; *pg.* 37, *pg.* 1466
ABERCROMBIE & FITCH - Clothing - ABERCROMBIE & FITCH CO.; *pg.* 37, *pg.* 1466
ABERDEEN - Area Lighting - JUNO LIGHTING, INC.; *pg.* 1300, *pg.* 606
ABERDEEN - Kitchen Faucet - MOEN INCORPORATED; *pg.* 1056, *pg.* 1468
ABERDEEN - Fabric - NEMSCHOFF, INC.; *pg.* 936, *pg.* 1890
ABEX - Friction Products - FEDERAL-MOGUL HOLDINGS CORPORATION; *pg.* 205, *pg.* 907
ABEX - Fabric - NEMSCHOFF, INC.; *pg.* 936, *pg.* 1890
ABF - Freight Transportation - ABF FREIGHT SYSTEM, INC.; *pg.* 1896, *pg.* 31
ABFREE - Online Account Checking - ANDROSCOGGIN SAVINGS BANK; *pg.* 716, *pg.* 751
ABIGAIL - Furniture - HOOKER FURNITURE CORPORATION; *pg.* 928, *pg.* 1788
ABIGAIL ADAMS - Lighting Product - QUOIZEL INC.; *pg.* 1304, *pg.* 1616
THE ABILENE REPORTER-NEWS - Newspaper - THE E.W. SCRIPPS COMPANY; *pg.* 1639, *pg.* 1412
ABILIFY - Antidepressant Medication - BRISTOL-MYERS SQUIBB COMPANY; *pg.* 1509, *pg.* 1206
ABILITATIONS - Educational Resources - SCHOOL SPECIALTY, INC.; *pg.* 467, *pg.* 1860
ABILITEC - Data Products - ACXIOM CORPORATION; *pg.* 342, *pg.* 33
ABILITY EQUIPPED - Recreation Vehicle - WINNEBAGO INDUSTRIES, INC.; *pg.* 1712, *pg.* 707
ABINGTON - Fabric - NEMSCHOFF, INC.; *pg.* 936, *pg.* 1890
ABINGTON - Lighting Product - WESTINGHOUSE LIGHTING CORPORATION; *pg.* 687, *pg.* 1571
ABISKO - Ceramic, Glass, Stone Tiles & Slabs - WALKER & ZANGER, INC.; *pg.* 119, *pg.* 281
ABIST - Software System - MENTOR GRAPHICS CORPORATION; *pg.* 432, *pg.* 1510
ABITA AMBER - Beer - ABITA BREWING COMPANY; *pg.* 237, *pg.* 741
ABITA GOLDEN - Beer - ABITA BREWING COMPANY; *pg.* 237, *pg.* 741
ABITA LIGHT - Beer - ABITA BREWING COMPANY; *pg.* 237, *pg.* 741
ABITO - Fabric - NEMSCHOFF, INC.; *pg.* 936, *pg.* 1890
ABITOL - Alcohol - EASTMAN CHEMICAL COMPANY; *pg.* 1159, *pg.* 1636
ABJ - Fluid Technology - ITT CORPORATION; *pg.* 1351, *pg.* 1354
ABLEWARE - Shampoo - ALIMED, INC.; *pg.* 1490, *pg.* 816
ABMS - Software - HEALTHSTREAM, INC.; *pg.* 1649, *pg.* 1651
ABOLITE - Lighting - LSI INDUSTRIES INC.; *pg.* 58, *pg.* 1416
ABOUT FACE - Furniture - HERMAN MILLER, INC.; *pg.* 926, *pg.* 913
ABOUT FACE - Surface Material - STEELCASE INC.; *pg.* 475, *pg.* 889
ABOUT.COM - Interactive Web Site - ABOUT, INC.; *pg.* 1225, *pg.* 1186
ABOVE & BEYOND - Tagline - LOCKHEED MARTIN CORPORATION; *pg.* 229, *pg.* 762
ABOVE AND BEYOND HONING - Tag Line - SUNNEN PRODUCTS COMPANY; *pg.* 1379, *pg.* 1004
ABOVE THE CROWD - Slogan - RE/MAX INTERNATIONAL, INC.; *pg.* 1109, *pg.* 322
ABOVE THE RIM - Athletic Shoes - REEBOK INTERNATIONAL LTD.; *pg.* 1817, *pg.* 811
ABOVE THE RIM HOOPWEAR - Athletic Apparel - REEBOK INTERNATIONAL LTD.; *pg.* 1817, *pg.* 811
ABOVEALL - Automatic Under Cabinet Can Opener; Can Opener Plus - NATIONAL PRESTO INDUSTRIES, INC; *pg.* 1128, *pg.* 1857
ABRA - Clothing - ABERCROMBIE & FITCH CO.; *pg.* 37, *pg.* 1466
ABRA - Lounge Chairs & Modern Occasional Tables - BERNHARDT DESIGN; *pg.* 918, *pg.* 1381
ABRA-CASH-DABRA - Video Game - INTERNATIONAL GAME TECHNOLOGY; *pg.* 957, *pg.* 1024
ABRA SUITE - HR & Payroll Software - SAGE SOFTWARE, INC.; *pg.* 464, *pg.* 116
ABRACADABRA - Video Game - INTERNATIONAL GAME TECHNOLOGY; *pg.* 957, *pg.* 1024
ABRACADABRA - Fabric - NEMSCHOFF, INC.; *pg.* 936, *pg.* 1890
ABRASI-BLAST - Air Respirator - MINE SAFETY APPLIANCES COMPANY; *pg.* 1361, *pg.* 1525
ABRASIMATIC - Automatic Abrasive Cutter - BUEHLER, LTD.; *pg.* 1403, *pg.* 622
ABRASIMET - Cut Off Machine - BUEHLER, LTD.; *pg.* 1403, *pg.* 622
ABRASION ACE - Carbide Enhanced Wear Parts - HENSLEY INDUSTRIES, INC.; *pg.* 1166, *pg.* 1682
ABRATEL - Medicine - PFIZER INC.; *pg.* 1581, *pg.* 1278
ABREVA - Therapeutic Product - AVANIR PHARMACEUTICALS; *pg.* 1498, *pg.* 40
ABSCESSION - Electrosurgical Devices - ANGIODYNAMICS, INC.; *pg.* 1495, *pg.* 1173
ABSKYN - Thermoplastic Sheet - SCHNELLER, INC.; *pg.* 234, *pg.* 1456
ABSOLUT VODKA - Liquor - PERNOD RICARD USA, INC.; *pg.* 1968, *pg.* 1332
ABSOLUTE - Chemical Products - AIR PRODUCTS AND CHEMICALS, INC.; *pg.* 1145, *pg.* 1513
ABSOLUTE - Medical Equipment - INVACARE CORPORATION; *pg.* 1546, *pg.* 1451
ABSOLUTE PRO - Stent System - ABBOTT LABORATORIES; *pg.* 1484, *pg.* 551
ABSOLUTE PUNK - Alternative Music News & Commentary Site - SPINMEDIA; *pg.* 1282, *pg.* 104
ABSOLUTE-S - Molecular Probe Product - THERMO FISHER SCIENTIFIC INC.; *pg.* 1602, *pg.* 61
ABSOLUTELY FABULOUS - Lipstick - REVLON, INC.; *pg.* 521, *pg.* 1286
ABSOLUTELY, POSITIVELY, PERFECT AND ON-TIME - Slogan - IEC ELECTRONICS CORP.; *pg.* 643, *pg.* 1317
ABSOLUTEPROOF - Data Integrity System - SURETY, INC.; *pg.* 1283, *pg.* 1799
ABSOLVE - Decontaminant & Cleaner - PERKINELMER, INC.; *pg.* 1426, *pg.* 853
ABSOLYTE - Battery - EXIDE TECHNOLOGIES; *pg.* 204, *pg.* 483
ABSORB - Apparel - OAKLEY, INC.; *pg.* 1840, *pg.* 86
ABSORBALEAN - Nutritional Supplements - NATURAL ALTERNATIVES INTERNATIONAL, INC.; *pg.* 1571, *pg.* 253
ABSORBINE JR. - Liniment - W.F. YOUNG, INC.; *pg.* 1610, *pg.* 817
ABSORBINE PRO CMC - Gastric Relief Formula - W.F. YOUNG, INC.; *pg.* 1610, *pg.* 817
ABSORBINE VETPATCH - Muscle Care Product - W.F. YOUNG, INC.; *pg.* 1610, *pg.* 817
ABSORBOND - Elastomer Semiconductor Adhesive - W.L. GORE & ASSOCIATES, INC.; *pg.* 122, *pg.* 388
ABSORBOTRON - Fixture-Unit Sizing Method - JOSAM COMPANY; *pg.* 89, *pg.* 695
ABSPLUS - 3D Production System - STRATASYS, INC.; *pg.* 476, *pg.* 923
ABSTRACT - Pillow - AMERICAN LEATHER LP; *pg.* 912, *pg.* 1673
ABSYLUX - Compression Molded Product - WESTLAKE PLASTICS COMPANY; *pg.* 1892, *pg.* 1548
ABTCO - Vinyl Siding - LOUISIANA-PACIFIC CORPORATION; *pg.* 94, *pg.* 1652
ABTHRAX - Biopharmaceutical Product - GLAXOSMITHKLINE; *pg.* 1537, *pg.* 776
ABU BINT - Rice - AMERICAN RICE, INC.; *pg.* 837, *pg.* 1700
ABU BINT/GOLDEN CHOPSTICK - Rice - AMERICAN RICE, INC.; *pg.* 837, *pg.* 1700
ABUNDANCE - Wall Decor - HERITAGE LACE INC.; *pg.* 694, *pg.* 711
ABUNDANT LOVE - Flower Arrangement - 1-800-FLOWERS.COM, INC.; *pg.* 1758, *pg.* 1151
ABUSED WORLD WIDE - Tag Line - MILE MARKER INTERNATIONAL INC.; *pg.* 213, *pg.* 459
ABZOL - Chemical Product - ALBEMARLE CORPORATION; *pg.* 1146, *pg.* 741
AC-90 - Cable - AFC CABLE SYSTEMS, INC.; *pg.* 1294, *pg.* 835
AC-90 LITE - Cable - AFC CABLE SYSTEMS, INC.; *pg.* 1294, *pg.* 835
AC-DI-SOL - Pharmaceutical Ingredient - FMC CORPORATION; *pg.* 1163, *pg.* 1564
AC FEEL - Men's & Women's Golf Gloves - ETONIC WORLDWIDE LLC; *pg.* 1808, *pg.* 857
AC GRIP - Men's & Women's Golf Gloves - ETONIC WORLDWIDE LLC; *pg.* 1808, *pg.* 857
AC SERIES - Floor Boxes - WIREMOLD/LEGRAND; *pg.* 689, *pg.* 383
AC TEC 100 - Chemical Product - BIRKO CORPORATION; *pg.* 1149, *pg.* 332
AC TOUR - Men's & Women's Golf Gloves - ETONIC WORLDWIDE LLC; *pg.* 1808, *pg.* 857
AC100 PLUS - Injection Adhesive System - POWERS FASTENERS INC.; *pg.* 1059, *pg.* 1143
AC100+ GOLD - Adhesive Anchors & Foam - POWERS FASTENERS INC.; *pg.* 1059, *pg.* 1143
ACADEMIA - Fabric - NEMSCHOFF, INC.; *pg.* 936, *pg.* 1890
ACADEMIC - Carpet - INTERFACE, INC.; *pg.* 695, *pg.* 512
ACADEMIC AMERICAN - Magazine - SCHOLASTIC INC.; *pg.* 1683, *pg.* 1288
ACADEMIC SYSTEMS - Instructional Solutions - EDMENTUM, INC.; *pg.* 390, *pg.* 917
ACADEMY AWARDS - Movie Awards - ACADEMY OF MOTION PICTURE ARTS & SCIENCES; *pg.* 526, *pg.* 46
ACADIA - Paper & Nonwoven Material - FIBERMARK INC.; *pg.* 1457, *pg.* 1764
ACADIA - Mid-Sized Sport Utility Vehicle - GENERAL MOTORS COMPANY; *pg.* 175, *pg.* 881
ACADIA - Footwear - LACROSSE FOOTWEAR, INC.; *pg.* 1811, *pg.* 1503
ACADIA - Surface Material - STEELCASE INC.; *pg.* 475, *pg.* 889
ACADIA CRUISER - Bicycle - L.L. BEAN, INC.; *pg.* 1777, *pg.* 750
ACAI SUPER-ANTIOXIDANT - Fruit Drink - JAMBA, INC.; *pg.* 1024, *pg.* 84
ACAI TOPPER - Fruit Drink - JAMBA, INC.; *pg.* 1024, *pg.* 84
ACANTHUS - Furniture - J. ROBERT SCOTT INC.; *pg.* 930, *pg.* 105
ACAP - Patient Care - ST. JUDE MEDICAL, INC.; *pg.* 1596, *pg.* 963
ACAPPELLA - Utility Routing Switcher - GRASS VALLEY, INC.; *pg.* 641, *pg.* 164
ACAPULCO MEXICAN RESTAURANT - Mexican Restaurants - REAL MEX RESTAURANTS, INC.; *pg.* 1746, *pg.* 75
ACAREXX - Pharmaceutical Product - IDEXX LABORATORIES, INC.; *pg.* 1543, *pg.* 753
ACAROSAN - Floor Care Product - BISSELL HOMECARE, INC.; *pg.* 52, *pg.* 887
ACARTUS - Software - EMC CORPORATION; *pg.* 391, *pg.* 825
ACAT - Software System - ALION SCIENCE AND TECHNOLOGY CORPORATION; *pg.* 615, *pg.* 1788
ACB - Pharmaceutical Product - ALERE INC.; *pg.* 1488, *pg.* 849
ACB - Paper Tubes & Cores - SONOCO PRODUCTS COMPANY; *pg.* 1469, *pg.* 1619
ACC-U-BAR - Rectangular Steel Product - ALCOA INC.; *pg.* 65, *pg.* 1188
ACC-U-SOL - Tamper-Evident Trigger System Sprayers - PRECISION VALVE CORPORATION; *pg.* 1060, *pg.* 1357
ACCEAVA - Pharmaceutical Product - ALERE INC.; *pg.* 1488, *pg.* 849

ACCEE - Footwear - STEVEN MADDEN, LTD.; *pg.* 1819, *pg.* 1176
ACCEL - Microelectronics Cleaning Equipment - SPEEDLINE TECHNOLOGIES, INC.; *pg.* 1378, *pg.* 823
ACCEL GEL - Energy Gel - PACIFICHEALTH LABORATORIES, INC.; *pg.* 1579, *pg.* 1083
ACCEL-T - Cure Accelerator - SMOOTH-ON INC.; *pg.* 111, *pg.* 1528
ACCELA-COTA - Tablet Coating Machine - THOMAS ENGINEERING INC.; *pg.* 1382, *pg.* 619
ACCELDSP - Synthesis Tool - XILINX, INC.; *pg.* 496, *pg.* 252
ACCELENET - Broadband Satellite Network - VIASAT, INC.; *pg.* 489, *pg.* 62
ACCELEPORT - Computer Peripheral Equipment - DIGI INTERNATIONAL INC.; *pg.* 387, *pg.* 948
ACCELERADE - Sports Drink - PACIFICHEALTH LABORATORIES, INC.; *pg.* 1579, *pg.* 1083
ACCELERADE HYDRO - Sport Drink - PACIFICHEALTH LABORATORIES, INC.; *pg.* 1579, *pg.* 1083
ACCELERATE - Voice Over IP Solutions - ALCATEL-LUCENT; *pg.* 615, *pg.* 38
ACCELERATE PERFORMANCE. ACCELERATE PROFITS. - Slogan - SUMTOTAL SYSTEMS, INC.; *pg.* 477, *pg.* 429
ACCELERATED GRAMMAR & SPELLING - Educational Materials - RENAISSANCE LEARNING, INC.; *pg.* 607, *pg.* 1899
ACCELERATED MATH - Educational Materials - RENAISSANCE LEARNING, INC.; *pg.* 607, *pg.* 1899
ACCELERATED READER - Educational Materials - RENAISSANCE LEARNING, INC.; *pg.* 607, *pg.* 1899
ACCELERATED VOCABULARY - Educational Materials - RENAISSANCE LEARNING, INC.; *pg.* 607, *pg.* 1899
ACCELERATED WRITER - Educational Materials - RENAISSANCE LEARNING, INC.; *pg.* 607, *pg.* 1899
ACCELERATING DATA DELIVERY - Slogan - ALACRITECH, INC.; *pg.* 346, *pg.* 237
ACCELERATING POSSIBILITIES - Tagline - PRO-DEX, INC.; *pg.* 1586, *pg.* 115
ACCELERATING YOUR GLOBAL SUCCESS - Tagline - LIONBRIDGE TECHNOLOGIES INC.; *pg.* 428, *pg.* 851
ACCELERATING YOUR PROFIT - Slogan - BROOKS AUTOMATION, INC.; *pg.* 1320, *pg.* 813
ACCELERATING YOUR SUCESS - Slogan - AVNET, INC.; *pg.* 622, *pg.* 15
ACCELERATION ALLEY - Motorsports Event - INTERNATIONAL SPEEDWAY CORPORATION; *pg.* 553, *pg.* 420
ACCELERATOR - Automatic Processing System - ABBOTT LABORATORIES; *pg.* 1484, *pg.* 551
ACCELERATOR - Power Semiconductor Device - INTERNATIONAL RECTIFIER CORPORATION; *pg.* 647, *pg.* 80
ACCELERATOR 3 - Healthcare Product - MANNATECH, INCORPORATED; *pg.* 1558, *pg.* 1671
ACCELEREX - Digital Accelerometer - HONEYWELL AEROSPACE ELECTRONIC SYSTEMS; *pg.* 228, *pg.* 17
ACCELERON - Bag Machines - TRIANGLE PACKAGE MACHINERY CO.; *pg.* 1383, *pg.* 592
ACCELERON - Optical Product - UNIVERSAL PHOTONICS, INC.; *pg.* 1433, *pg.* 1167
ACCELL - Software Product - DAEGIS INC; *pg.* 381, *pg.* 195
ACCELL - Cartridge - WATERS CORPORATION; *pg.* 1436, *pg.* 834
ACCELL/IDS - Software Product - DAEGIS INC; *pg.* 381, *pg.* 195
ACCELL/SQL - Software Product - DAEGIS INC; *pg.* 381, *pg.* 195
ACCELL/WEB - Software Product - DAEGIS INC; *pg.* 381, *pg.* 195
ACCELPORT RAS - Computer Peripheral Equipment - DIGI INTERNATIONAL INC.; *pg.* 387, *pg.* 948
ACCELSCAN - Educational Materials - RENAISSANCE LEARNING, INC.; *pg.* 607, *pg.* 1899
ACCELTEST - Educational Materials - RENAISSANCE LEARNING, INC.; *pg.* 607, *pg.* 1899
AC'CENT - Flavor Enhancer - B&G FOODS, INC.; *pg.* 838, *pg.* 1102
ACCENT - Angioplasty - COOK GROUP, INC.; *pg.* 1518, *pg.* 674
ACCENT - Herbicide - E.I. DU PONT DE NEMOURS & COMPANY; *pg.* 1159, *pg.* 390
ACCENT - Dinnerware - THE HOMER LAUGHLIN CHINA COMPANY; *pg.* 1125, *pg.* 1850
ACCENT - Paper - INTERNATIONAL PAPER COMPANY; *pg.* 1460, *pg.* 1644
ACCENT - Furniture - JASPER GROUP; *pg.* 930, *pg.* 691
ACCENT - Tableware - PACTIV CORPORATION; *pg.* 1466, *pg.* 624
ACCENT - Pace Maker - ST. JUDE MEDICAL, INC.; *pg.* 1596, *pg.* 963
ACCENT OPAQUE - Paper - INTERNATIONAL PAPER COMPANY; *pg.* 1460, *pg.* 1644
ACCENTRIM - Tape - 3M COMPANY; *pg.* 1142, *pg.* 956
ACCENTS - Area Rugs - COURISTAN INC.; *pg.* 921, *pg.* 1067
ACCEPTOR - Plug & Receptacles - KILLARK ELECTRIC; *pg.* 1300, *pg.* 998
ACCESS - Software - AXEDA SYSTEMS INC.; *pg.* 359, *pg.* 819
ACCESS - Testing Instrument System - BECKMAN COULTER, INC.; *pg.* 1402, *pg.* 48
ACCESS - Hearing Aid - BELTONE ELECTRONICS LLC; *pg.* 1503, *pg.* 614
ACCESS - Books - HARPERCOLLINS PUBLISHERS INC.; *pg.* 1647, *pg.* 1237
ACCESS - Energy Management Systems - SIEMENS PROCESS INDUSTRIES AND DRIVES; *pg.* 673, *pg.* 485
ACCESS - Wireless Telecommunication Product - SYNIVERSE HOLDINGS, INC.; *pg.* 479, *pg.* 475
ACCESS - Motor Homes - WINNEBAGO INDUSTRIES, INC.; *pg.* 1712, *pg.* 707
ACCESS 5000 - Nonmetallic Raceway - WIREMOLD/LEGRAND; *pg.* 689, *pg.* 383
ACCESS & LD TANDEM - Wireline Solutions - SONUS NETWORKS INC.; *pg.* 1281, *pg.* 858
ACCESS GATEWAY CONTROL FUNCTION - Wireline Solutions - SONUS NETWORKS INC.; *pg.* 1281, *pg.* 858
ACCESS LOGIX - Software - EMC CORPORATION; *pg.* 391, *pg.* 825
ACCESS MANAGER - Software - DELL SOFTWARE; *pg.* 385, *pg.* 40
ACCESS MANAGER - Computer Software - NOVELL INC.; *pg.* 446, *pg.* 852
ACCESS MASTER - Access Control - NORTEK, INC.; *pg.* 100, *pg.* 1607
ACCESS NP - Central Office Platform for Switching in Storage of Voice Messages - XURA, INC.; *pg.* 689, *pg.* 849
ACCESS PLUS - Medical Device - HOSPIRA, INC.; *pg.* 1542, *pg.* 623
ACCESS PRO - Access Control - NORTEK, INC.; *pg.* 100, *pg.* 1607
ACCESS REGISTRAR - Computer Programs - CISCO SYSTEMS, INC.; *pg.* 372, *pg.* 240
ACCESSAWARE - Computer Software - NOVELL INC.; *pg.* 446, *pg.* 852
ACCESSBASE 2000 - Access Control System Programming & Networking Software - NORTEK SECURITY & CONTROL LLC; *pg.* 659, *pg.* 59
ACCESSIBILITY - Wireless Telecommunication Product - SYNIVERSE HOLDINGS, INC.; *pg.* 479, *pg.* 475
ACCESSIBILITY LIFT - Wheelchair Lift - INCLINATOR COMPANY OF AMERICA; *pg.* 88, *pg.* 1536
ACCESSINGRAM.COM - Website for Customer Base - INGRAM ENTERTAINMENT INC.; *pg.* 292, *pg.* 1639
ACCESSMAX - Software - TELLABS, INC.; *pg.* 678, *pg.* 637
ACCESSMAX - Object Oriented Software for Network Based Enhanced Telecomm. Services - XURA, INC.; *pg.* 689, *pg.* 849
ACCESSNS - Transportation Logistics Information - NORFOLK SOUTHERN CORPORATION; *pg.* 1917, *pg.* 1797
ACCESSORY MERCHANDISING - Magazine - VANCE PUBLISHING CORPORATION; *pg.* 1699, *pg.* 627
ACCESSORY MOTOR CONTROLLER - Remote Control - LIONEL LLC; *pg.* 961, *pg.* 875
ACCESSORY SWITCH CONTROLLER - Remote Control - LIONEL LLC; *pg.* 961, *pg.* 875
ACCESSPLUS - Automatic Meter Reading System - BADGER METER, INC.; *pg.* 1401, *pg.* 1873
ACCESSPOINT - Audio Solution - VIQ SOLUTIONS INC.; *pg.* 490, *pg.* 1905
ACCESSPOINTE - Information Technology Product Portal - EN POINTE TECHNOLOGIES, INC.; *pg.* 1243, *pg.* 94
ACCESSPOINTE PRO - EBusiness Platform - EN POINTE TECHNOLOGIES, INC.; *pg.* 1243, *pg.* 94
ACCLAIM - Intraoral Camera - AIR TECHNIQUES, INC.; *pg.* 1487, *pg.* 1178
ACCLAIM - Software - BIO-RAD LABORATORIES, INC.; *pg.* 1504, *pg.* 101
ACCLAIM - Towing Product - BLUE OX; *pg.* 701, *pg.* 1019
ACCLAIM - Cosmetic Product - CYNOSURE, INC.; *pg.* 1521, *pg.* 858
ACCLAIM - Bathroom Tissue - GEORGIA-PACIFIC LLC; *pg.* 1458, *pg.* 507
ACCLAIM - Medical Product - HOLOGIC, INC.; *pg.* 1416, *pg.* 784
ACCLAIM - Perm, Shampoos, Conditioners & Styling Aids - ZOTOS INTERNATIONAL, INC.; *pg.* 524, *pg.* 345
ACCLIMATE - Multi-Criteria Smoke Detector - SYSTEM SENSOR; *pg.* 676, *pg.* 658
ACCO - Office Products - ACCO BRANDS CORPORATION; *pg.* 340, *pg.* 626
ACCO FEEDS - Feeds - CARGILL, INC.; *pg.* 845, *pg.* 965
ACCO-PHOS - Chemical Product - CYTEC INDUSTRIES, INC.; *pg.* 1155, *pg.* 1131
ACCOCARB - Minerals - MINERALS TECHNOLOGIES INC.; *pg.* 1173, *pg.* 617
ACCOFORM - Minerals - MINERALS TECHNOLOGIES INC.; *pg.* 1173, *pg.* 617
ACCOLADE - Light - CRAFTMADE INTERNATIONAL, INC.; *pg.* 1295, *pg.* 1670
ACCOLADE - Progressive Lenses - ESSILOR OF AMERICA, INC.; *pg.* 1412, *pg.* 1680
ACCOLADE - Office Furniture - HAWORTH, INC.; *pg.* 402, *pg.* 891
ACCOLADE - Furniture - JASPER GROUP; *pg.* 930, *pg.* 691
ACCOLADE - Fabric - NEMSCHOFF, INC.; *pg.* 936, *pg.* 1890
ACCOLADE - Latex Enamel Paints - PRATT & LAMBERT PAINTS; *pg.* 1446, *pg.* 1434
ACCOLADE - Medical Product - STRYKER CORPORATION; *pg.* 1598, *pg.* 894
ACCOLADE - Drug Delivery System - SURMODICS, INC.; *pg.* 1600, *pg.* 924
ACCOMODATION - Carpet - BEAULIEU GROUP, LLC; *pg.* 917, *pg.* 529
ACCOMPLI - Telephones - MOTOROLA SOLUTIONS, INC.; *pg.* 657, *pg.* 659
ACCOMPLISH - Athletic Shoes - K-SWISS; *pg.* 1837, *pg.* 306
ACCOMPLISH CREW - Clothing - K-SWISS; *pg.* 1837, *pg.* 306
ACCOMPLISH JACKET - Clothing - K-SWISS; *pg.* 1837, *pg.* 306
ACCOMPLISH KNT SHORT - Clothing - K-SWISS; *pg.* 1837, *pg.* 306
ACCOMPLISH PANT - Clothing - K-SWISS; *pg.* 1837, *pg.* 306
ACCOMPLISH POLO - Clothing - K-SWISS; *pg.* 1837, *pg.* 306
ACCOMPLISH RACR TANK - Clothing - K-SWISS; *pg.* 1837, *pg.* 306
ACCOMPLISH SHORT - Clothing - K-SWISS; *pg.* 1837, *pg.* 306
ACCOMPLISH SKIRT - Clothing - K-SWISS; *pg.* 1837, *pg.* 306
ACCOMPLISH TANK - Clothing - K-SWISS; *pg.* 1837, *pg.* 306
ACCOPURE - Minerals - MINERALS TECHNOLOGIES INC.; *pg.* 1173, *pg.* 617
ACCORD - Automobile - AMERICAN HONDA MOTOR CO., INC.; *pg.* 163, *pg.* 292
ACCORD - Valve - FLOWSERVE CORPORATION; *pg.* 82, *pg.* 1719
ACCORD - Fabric - NEMSCHOFF, INC.; *pg.* 936, *pg.* 1890
ACCORD - Network Service - POLYCOM, INC.; *pg.* 664, *pg.* 249
ACCORDANT - HealthCare Management - CVS HEALTH CORPORATION; *pg.* 1765, *pg.* 1610
ACCORDION REELS - Video Game - INTERNATIONAL GAME TECHNOLOGY; *pg.* 957, *pg.* 1024
ACCOSOFT - Chemical Product - STEPAN COMPANY; *pg.* 1182, *pg.* 643
ACCOSORB - Minerals - MINERALS TECHNOLOGIES INC.; *pg.* 1173, *pg.* 617
ACCOUNT - Software - ELEKTA; *pg.* 391, *pg.* 284
ACCOUNTANCY AGE - Trade Magazine - THE NIELSEN COMPANY B.V.; *pg.* 1671, *pg.* 1272
ACCOUNTEMPS - Specialized Temporary Financial Staffing - ROBERT HALF INTERNATIONAL INC.; *pg.* 462, *pg.* 145
ACCOUNTING.21 - Software - ASPEN TECHNOLOGY, INC.; *pg.* 354, *pg.* 804
ACCOUNTLINK - Software - KANSAS CITY POWER & LIGHT COMPANY; *pg.* 1945, *pg.* 985
ACCOUSTIMASS - Audio Product - BOSE CORPORATION;

pg. 626, *pg.* 820

ACCRETROPIN - Drug - EMERGENT BIOSOLUTIONS; *pg.* 1528, *pg.* 1914

ACCU-BEEP - Thermometer - BECTON, DICKINSON & COMPANY; *pg.* 1501, *pg.* 1068

ACCU-CARE - Software System - OMNICARE, INC; *pg.* 1578, *pg.* 1418

ACCU-CAT - Proportioning & Dispensing Machines - GRACO, INC.; *pg.* 1342, *pg.* 935

ACCU-CHEK - Health & Wellness Product - EXPRESS SCRIPTS; *pg.* 1530, *pg.* 1070

ACCU-CHOKE - Shotgun Barrels - O.F. MOSSBERG & SONS, INC.; *pg.* 1842, *pg.* 360

ACCU-COUNT - Scale & Counter - AUTOMATED PACKAGING SYSTEMS INC.; *pg.* 1452, *pg.* 1474

ACCU-CUT - Automated Packaging System - SEALED AIR CORPORATION; *pg.* 1468, *pg.* 1058

ACCU-CYCLE - Chargers - HOBBICO, INC.; *pg.* 956, *pg.* 562

ACCU-DERMATOME - Battery Powered Dermatone - AESCULAP, INC.; *pg.* 1487, *pg.* 1521

ACCU-DISC - Medical Device - INTEGRA LIFESCIENCES HOLDINGS CORPORATION; *pg.* 1545, *pg.* 1109

ACCU DRAIN - Drainage System - INTEGRA LIFESCIENCES HOLDINGS CORPORATION; *pg.* 1545, *pg.* 1109

ACCU-DRIVE - Gear Drive - EDELBROCK CORPORATION; *pg.* 204, *pg.* 293

ACCU-LEVEL - Hydraulic Leveling System - ALTEC INDUSTRIES INC.; *pg.* 1312, *pg.* 1

ACCU-LOK - Bolts - ALCOA INC.; *pg.* 65, *pg.* 1188

ACCU-LUBE - Metalworking Lubricants - ITW FLUIDS NORTH AMERICA; *pg.* 980, *pg.* 614

ACCU-PEEP - Threshold Resistor - VITAL SIGNS, INC.; *pg.* 1607, *pg.* 1126

ACCU-PRICE - Guarantee Program - SCHNUCK MARKETS, INC.; *pg.* 1033, *pg.* 1002

ACCU-SCALE - Scale & Counter - AUTOMATED PACKAGING SYSTEMS INC.; *pg.* 1452, *pg.* 1474

ACCU-SORT - Scanning Systems - DATALOGIC; *pg.* 382, *pg.* 1588

ACCU-SWIPE - Testing Equipment - ASTEC INDUSTRIES, INC.; *pg.* 69, *pg.* 1628

ACCU-TAB - Chemical Product - PPG INDUSTRIES, INC.; *pg.* 1445, *pg.* 1579

ACCU-THERM - Diary Farm Equipment - PAUL MUELLER COMPANY; *pg.* 706, *pg.* 1007

ACCU-TRAC - Electronic Cattle Management Systems (ECM) - MIDWEST MICROSYSTEMS, LLC; *pg.* 1267, *pg.* 1012

ACCU-TRAK - Measurement While Drilling - BAKER HUGHES INTEQ; *pg.* 1316, *pg.* 1700

ACCU-TRIM - P.C. Flor Control Adjustment - BOSCH REXROTH CORPORATION; *pg.* 1319, *pg.* 1516

ACCU-VOICE - Guitars - GIBSON GUITAR CORP.; *pg.* 550, *pg.* 1650

ACCU-VU - Electrosurgical Devices - ANGIODYNAMICS, INC.; *pg.* 1495, *pg.* 1173

ACCU-WRAP - CSR Wrap - MEDLINE INDUSTRIES, INC.; *pg.* 1562, *pg.* 635

ACCUAUDIO PLUS - Data Management Services - HDI SOLUTIONS, INC.; *pg.* 403, *pg.* 1

ACCUBAKE - Home Appliance Product - WHIRLPOOL CORPORATION; *pg.* 62, *pg.* 872

ACCUBALANCE - Plus Air Capture Hood - TSI INCORPORATED; *pg.* 1432, *pg.* 965

ACCUBAR - Control & Detection System - NORDSON CORPORATION; *pg.* 1365, *pg.* 1480

ACCUBIND - Starch - CARGILL LIMITED; *pg.* 1475, *pg.* 1914

ACCUBINDPRO2 - Binding System - STANDARD DUPLICATING MACHINES CORPORATION; *pg.* 473, *pg.* 783

ACCUBOND - Cartridge - AGILENT TECHNOLOGIES, INC.; *pg.* 614, *pg.* 264

ACCUBRAZE - Software - SECO/WARWICK CORPORATION; *pg.* 1076, *pg.* 1552

ACCUBUMP - Stud Bumping Technology - KULICKE & SOFFA INDUSTRIES, INC.; *pg.* 650, *pg.* 1533

ACCUCAP - Breath Monitor - MAQUET; *pg.* 1558, *pg.* 1082

ACCUCAPTURE PLUS - Data Management Services - HDI SOLUTIONS, INC.; *pg.* 403, *pg.* 1

ACCUCHANGE - Coin Dispenser - GLORY GLOBAL SOLUTIONS; *pg.* 401, *pg.* 628

ACCUCHART - Quality Control Data Management Software - PRESSURE BIOSCIENCES, INC.; *pg.* 1586, *pg.* 844

ACCUCLEAN - Food Safety Product - NEOGEN CORPORATION; *pg.* 883, *pg.* 896

ACCUCOAT - Spray Product - SPRAYING SYSTEMS CO.; *pg.* 1063, *pg.* 670

ACCUCUP - Measurement Cup - COMAR INC.; *pg.* 1455, *pg.* 1047

ACCUDACS - Automated Telecommunications Units with Multiple Applications in Voice/Data - ALCATEL-LUCENT USA, INC.; *pg.* 615, *pg.* 1728

ACCUDART - Sporting Good Product - ESCALADE INC.; *pg.* 1833, *pg.* 678

ACCUDB PLUS - Data Management Services - HDI SOLUTIONS, INC.; *pg.* 403, *pg.* 1

ACCUDEPTH - Conventional Trolling Reels - DAIWA CORPORATION; *pg.* 1832, *pg.* 75

ACCUDIL - Zero-Dead-Volume Syringes - HAMILTON CO., INC.; *pg.* 1415, *pg.* 1031

ACCUDUR - Solid Imaging Material - 3D SYSTEMS CORPORATION; *pg.* 339, *pg.* 1621

ACCUENTRY PLUS - Data Management Services - HDI SOLUTIONS, INC.; *pg.* 403, *pg.* 1

ACCUFEED - Repair Services - LEXMARK INTERNATIONAL, INC.; *pg.* 427, *pg.* 730

ACCUFILL - Electronic Material - HONEYWELL INTERNATIONAL INC.; *pg.* 407, *pg.* 1088

ACCUFLO - Starch - CARGILL LIMITED; *pg.* 1475, *pg.* 1914

ACCUFLO - Electronic Material - HONEYWELL INTERNATIONAL INC.; *pg.* 407, *pg.* 1088

ACCUFLOOD - Flood Lighting - JUNO LIGHTING, INC.; *pg.* 1300, *pg.* 606

ACCUFLOW - Piston Filler - PNEUMATICSCALEANGELUS; *pg.* 1369, *pg.* 1445

ACCUGEL - Corn Starch - CARGILL LIMITED; *pg.* 1475, *pg.* 1914

ACCUGEN - Solid Imaging Material - 3D SYSTEMS CORPORATION; *pg.* 339, *pg.* 1621

ACCUGLASS - Electronic Material - HONEYWELL INTERNATIONAL INC.; *pg.* 407, *pg.* 1088

ACCUGLASS - Light Fixtures - JUNO LIGHTING, INC.; *pg.* 1300, *pg.* 606

ACCUGLIDE - Taping Head - 3M COMPANY; *pg.* 1142, *pg.* 956

ACCUGLIDE - Package Conveying Machinery - INTELLIGRATED SYSTEMS LLC; *pg.* 1350, *pg.* 998

ACCUGLIDE PLUS - Accumulation Conveyor - INTELLIGRATED SYSTEMS LLC; *pg.* 1350, *pg.* 998

ACCUGLO - Commercial Retail Lighting - JUNO LIGHTING, INC.; *pg.* 1300, *pg.* 606

ACCUGREEN - Spreader - THE SCOTTS MIRACLE-GRO COMPANY; *pg.* 1799, *pg.* 1459

ACCUGROW - Lawn Care Product - GARDENS ALIVE!, INC.; *pg.* 1796, *pg.* 693

ACCUHELP - Web Tool - ACCUWEATHER, INC.; *pg.* 268, *pg.* 1587

ACCUIMAGE PLUS - Data Management Services - HDI SOLUTIONS, INC.; *pg.* 403, *pg.* 1

ACCUJECT - Dental Product - DENTSPLY INTERNATIONAL INC.; *pg.* 1522, *pg.* 1596

ACCULAB - Chart & Marking System - GRAPHIC CONTROLS LLC; *pg.* 401, *pg.* 1148

ACCULINE - Software - AMERISOURCEBERGEN CORPORATION; *pg.* 1493, *pg.* 1522

ACCULINK - Carotid Stent System - ABBOTT LABORATORIES; *pg.* 1484, *pg.* 551

ACCULITE - Data Cable - CARLISLE INTERCONNECT TECHNOLOGIES; *pg.* 1294, *pg.* 461

ACCULOBE - Pump Product - IDEX CORPORATION; *pg.* 1347, *pg.* 623

ACCULUME - Light Fixtures - JUNO LIGHTING, INC.; *pg.* 1300, *pg.* 606

ACCUMALL - Online Store - ACCUWEATHER, INC.; *pg.* 268, *pg.* 1587

ACCUMARK - Pattern Development & Marketing Software - GERBER SCIENTIFIC, INC.; *pg.* 1414, *pg.* 380

ACCUMARK - Rifle - WEATHERBY, INC.; *pg.* 1848, *pg.* 181

ACCUMATCH - Electronic Color Matching Equipment - PPG INDUSTRIES, INC.; *pg.* 1445, *pg.* 1579

ACCUMAX - Graphic Arts Film - EASTMAN KODAK COMPANY; *pg.* 1408, *pg.* 1333

ACCUMAX - Healthcare Product - GF HEALTH PRODUCTS, INC.; *pg.* 1535, *pg.* 508

ACCUMEASURE - Gaging System - MECHANICAL TECHNOLOGY, INCORPORATED; *pg.* 1422, *pg.* 1137

ACCUMEASURE 1500 - Measuring System - MTI INSTRUMENTS INC.; *pg.* 658, *pg.* 1137

ACCUMEASURE 5000 - Measuring System - MTI INSTRUMENTS INC.; *pg.* 658, *pg.* 1137

ACCUMEASURE 9000 - Measuring System - MTI INSTRUMENTS INC.; *pg.* 658, *pg.* 1137

ACCUMIC - Audio Conferencing System - CLEARONE COMMUNICATIONS, INC.; *pg.* 629, *pg.* 1756

ACCUMINE PLUS - Data Management Services - HDI SOLUTIONS, INC.; *pg.* 403, *pg.* 1

ACCUMIX - Aerospace Syntactic & Potting Compounds - HUNTSMAN CORPORATION; *pg.* 1167, *pg.* 1758

ACCUMOULD - Food Starch - CARGILL LIMITED; *pg.* 1475, *pg.* 1914

ACCUNET - Embolic Protection System - ABBOTT LABORATORIES; *pg.* 1484, *pg.* 551

ACCUPAK - Security Lighting - JUNO LIGHTING, INC.; *pg.* 1300, *pg.* 606

ACCUPARK - Parking Garage & Canopy Lighting - JUNO LIGHTING, INC.; *pg.* 1300, *pg.* 606

ACCUPARTGEN - Software System - MENTOR GRAPHICS CORPORATION; *pg.* 432, *pg.* 1510

ACCUPARTNER - Software System - MENTOR GRAPHICS CORPORATION; *pg.* 432, *pg.* 1510

ACCUPARTS - Software System - MENTOR GRAPHICS CORPORATION; *pg.* 432, *pg.* 1510

ACCUPHASE - Telemetry System - MTS SYSTEMS CORPORATION; *pg.* 442, *pg.* 923

ACCUPIC - Light-Directed Picking Technology - PARAGON TECHNOLOGIES, INC.; *pg.* 1367, *pg.* 1528

ACCUPLUS - Data Management Services - HDI SOLUTIONS, INC.; *pg.* 403, *pg.* 1

ACCUPOINT - Food Safety Product - NEOGEN CORPORATION; *pg.* 883, *pg.* 896

ACCUPOP - Meteorological Workstation - ACCUWEATHER, INC.; *pg.* 268, *pg.* 1587

ACCUPRIL - Medicine - PFIZER INC.; *pg.* 1581, *pg.* 1278

ACCUPRIME - Molecular Biology Product - THERMO FISHER SCIENTIFIC INC.; *pg.* 1602, *pg.* 61

ACCUPRO - Bath & Plumbing Product - JACUZZI BRANDS CORPORATION; *pg.* 554, *pg.* 65

ACCUPULSE - Wireless Communication System - AT&T SOUTHEAST; *pg.* 1868, *pg.* 489

ACCUPUMP - Healthcare - WESTROCK COMPANY; *pg.* 1472, *pg.* 1805

ACCURA - Solid Imaging Material - 3D SYSTEMS CORPORATION; *pg.* 339, *pg.* 1621

ACCURA - CRRT Instrument - BAXTER INTERNATIONAL INC.; *pg.* 1499, *pg.* 599

ACCURA - Electron Microscope - FEI COMPANY; *pg.* 1413, *pg.* 1498

ACCURA - Modems - ZOOM TECHNOLOGIES, INC.; *pg.* 497, *pg.* 1317

ACCURACY - Carpet - BEAULIEU GROUP, LLC; *pg.* 917, *pg.* 529

ACCURACY POLO - Apparels - UNDER ARMOUR, INC.; *pg.* 49, *pg.* 759

ACCURETIC - Medicine - PFIZER INC.; *pg.* 1581, *pg.* 1278

ACCURLOY - Electric Furnace Process Steel - RUSSEL METALS INC.; *pg.* 1180, *pg.* 1928

ACCUROL - Roller Conveyor - PARAGON TECHNOLOGIES, INC.; *pg.* 1367, *pg.* 1528

ACCUROUTE - Document Capture & Routing Solution Products - OMTOOL, LTD.; *pg.* 449, *pg.* 782

ACCURUN - External Run Controls for Infectious Disease Testing - PRESSURE BIOSCIENCES, INC.; *pg.* 1586, *pg.* 844

ACCURX - Bleached Usp Grade Starch - CARGILL LIMITED; *pg.* 1475, *pg.* 1914

ACCUSCAN - Test Reader - NEOGEN CORPORATION; *pg.* 883, *pg.* 896

ACCUSCAPE - Garden Tools - STANLEY BLACK & DECKER, INC.; *pg.* 1063, *pg.* 358

ACCUSCORE - Software - SCAN-OPTICS, LLC; *pg.* 467, *pg.* 354

ACCUSCORE XL - Bowling Product - BOWLMOR AMF; *pg.* 1828, *pg.* 1206

ACCUSCREEN - Medical Device - NATUS MEDICAL INCORPORATED; *pg.* 1572, *pg.* 199

ACCUSEED - Software - ELEKTA; *pg.* 391, *pg.* 987

ACCUSEP - Filters for Industrial Purification, Separation and Clarification - PALL CORPORATION; *pg.* 232, *pg.* 1323

ACCUSET - Thin Boiling Starches - CARGILL LIMITED; *pg.* 1475, *pg.* 1914

ACCUSHAKE - Dispensing Containers - SONOCO PRODUCTS COMPANY; *pg.* 1469, *pg.* 1619

ACCUSIM - Software System - MENTOR GRAPHICS CORPORATION; *pg.* 432, *pg.* 1510

ACCUSIMMER - Home Appliance Product - WHIRLPOOL CORPORATION; *pg.* 62, *pg.* 872
ACCUSLITTER - Electric Mail Openers - THE STAPLEX COMPANY, INC.; *pg.* 474, *pg.* 1146
ACCUSOL - Dialysis System - BAXTER INTERNATIONAL INC.; *pg.* 1499, *pg.* 599
ACCUSQUARE - Parking Garage & Canopy Lighting - JUNO LIGHTING, INC.; *pg.* 1300, *pg.* 606
ACCUSTAR - Sensor System - MEASUREMENT SPECIALTIES INC.; *pg.* 1360, *pg.* 1783
ACCUSTART - Electronic Ballasts - UNIVERSAL LIGHTING TECHNOLOGIES; *pg.* 1307, *pg.* 1655
ACCUSTAT - Surgical Tool - AMERICAN MEDICAL SYSTEMS, INC.; *pg.* 1399, *pg.* 238
ACCUSTICK - Medical Device - BOSTON SCIENTIFIC CORPORATION; *pg.* 1508, *pg.* 831
ACCUTAC - Medical Equipment - CONMED CORPORATION; *pg.* 1517, *pg.* 1347
ACCUTACK - Ink Testing Instrument - THWING-ALBERT INSTRUMENT COMPANY; *pg.* 1432, *pg.* 1131
ACCUTANE - Pharmaceutical Product - HOFFMANN-LA ROCHE INC.; *pg.* 1542, *pg.* 1099
ACCUTAPE - Driving Tool - MEASUREMENT SPECIALTIES INC.; *pg.* 1360, *pg.* 1783
ACCUTERRA - Handheld Product - INTERMAP TECHNOLOGIES CORPORATION; *pg.* 417, *pg.* 1903
ACCUTEST - Software - SCAN-OPTICS, LLC; *pg.* 467, *pg.* 354
ACCUTICK - Software - WORDEN BROTHERS, INC.; *pg.* 823, *pg.* 1372
ACCUTINTER - Dispensing Equipment - IDEX CORPORATION; *pg.* 1347, *pg.* 623
ACCUTIRE - Tire Gauge - MEASUREMENT SPECIALTIES INC.; *pg.* 1360, *pg.* 1783
ACCUTITLES PLUS - Data Management Services - HDI SOLUTIONS, INC.; *pg.* 403, *pg.* 1
ACCUTNI - Testing Instrument System - BECKMAN COULTER, INC.; *pg.* 1402, *pg.* 48
ACCUTORR - Non-Invasive Blood Pressure Monitor With Or Without Recorder - MAQUET; *pg.* 1558, *pg.* 1082
ACCUTORR PLUS - Non-Invasive Blood Pressure Monitor - MAQUET; *pg.* 1558, *pg.* 1082
ACCUTOUCH - Hardware & Software - IMMERSION CORPORATION; *pg.* 413, *pg.* 246
ACCUTRAC - Mail Management System - PITNEY BOWES INC.; *pg.* 454, *pg.* 376
ACCUTRAC SA - Mail Management System - PITNEY BOWES INC.; *pg.* 454, *pg.* 376
ACCUTRACK - Mousepad - ALLSOP, INC.; *pg.* 347, *pg.* 1817
ACCUTRAK - Control & Monitoring Equipment - GE WATER & PROCESS TECHNOLOGIES; *pg.* 1339, *pg.* 1588
ACCUTRIMMER - Case Trimmer - LYMAN PRODUCTS CORPORATION; *pg.* 1839, *pg.* 356
ACCUTRON - Quartz Watches - BULOVA CORPORATION; *pg.* 2, *pg.* 1356
ACCUTUFF - Food Safety Instrument - COOPER-ATKINS CORPORATION; *pg.* 1407, *pg.* 355
ACCUVERIFY - Data Management Services - HDI SOLUTIONS, INC.; *pg.* 403, *pg.* 1
ACCUVIEW ANTIALIASING - Multi-Display Technology System - NVIDIA CORPORATION; *pg.* 447, *pg.* 268
ACCUVISION - Scanner - DATALOGIC; *pg.* 382, *pg.* 1588
ACCUVOTE-OS - Optical Scan System - DIEBOLD, INCORPORATED; *pg.* 387, *pg.* 1407
ACCUWAVE - Wall Clock - HOWARD MILLER COMPANY; *pg.* 7, *pg.* 914
ACCUWAVE - Home Appliance Product - WHIRLPOOL CORPORATION; *pg.* 62, *pg.* 872
ACCUWAVE DS - Wall Clocks - HOWARD MILLER COMPANY; *pg.* 7, *pg.* 914
ACCUWEATHER.COM - Weather Information - ACCUWEATHER, INC.; *pg.* 268, *pg.* 1587
ACCUWIK - Membrane - PALL CORPORATION; *pg.* 232, *pg.* 1323
ACCUWIPE - Eyeglass Wiping Cloth - GEORGIA-PACIFIC LLC; *pg.* 1458, *pg.* 507
ACCXES - Xerox Engineering System - XEROX CORPORATION; *pg.* 494, *pg.* 365
ACCXES & DESIGN - Xerox Engineering System - XEROX CORPORATION; *pg.* 494, *pg.* 365
ACD - Software - ACD SYSTEMS INTERNATIONAL INC.; *pg.* 340, *pg.* 1913
ACD - Soccer Socks - FRANKLIN SPORTS, INC.; *pg.* 1834, *pg.* 847
ACD FOTOANGELO - Image Management System - ACD SYSTEMS INTERNATIONAL INC.; *pg.* 340, *pg.* 1913
ACD FOTOSLATE - Image Management System - ACD SYSTEMS INTERNATIONAL INC.; *pg.* 340, *pg.* 1913
ACD VIDEOMAGIC - Image Management System - ACD SYSTEMS INTERNATIONAL INC.; *pg.* 340, *pg.* 1913
ACDELCO - Auto Parts - GENERAL MOTORS COMPANY; *pg.* 175, *pg.* 881
ACDINTOUCH - Software - ACD SYSTEMS INTERNATIONAL INC.; *pg.* 340, *pg.* 1913
ACDSEE - Software - ACD SYSTEMS INTERNATIONAL INC.; *pg.* 340, *pg.* 1913
ACDZIP - Software - ACD SYSTEMS INTERNATIONAL INC.; *pg.* 340, *pg.* 1913
ACE - Elastic Compression Bandages - 3M COMPANY; *pg.* 1142, *pg.* 956
ACE - Financial Services - ACE CASH EXPRESS, INC.; *pg.* 710, *pg.* 1717
ACE - Hardware - ACE HARDWARE CORPORATION; *pg.* 1040, *pg.* 644
ACE - Bandage - BECTON, DICKINSON & COMPANY; *pg.* 1501, *pg.* 1068
ACE - Medical Device - BOSTON SCIENTIFIC CORPORATION; *pg.* 1508, *pg.* 831
ACE - Electrical Device - BOURNS, INC.; *pg.* 627, *pg.* 193
ACE - Web Application Firewall - CISCO SYSTEMS, INC.; *pg.* 372, *pg.* 240
ACE - Anti-Corrosion Exterior Chain - DIAMOND CHAIN COMPANY; *pg.* 1328, *pg.* 684
ACE - Footwear - EASTLAND SHOE CORPORATION; *pg.* 1808, *pg.* 750
ACE - Combs - GOODY PRODUCTS, INC.; *pg.* 510, *pg.* 509
ACE - Shock Absorbers - KAYDON CORPORATION; *pg.* 1352, *pg.* 866
ACE - Energy Drinks - MONSTER BEVERAGE CORPORATION; *pg.* 257, *pg.* 69
ACE - Bleach - THE PROCTER & GAMBLE COMPANY; *pg.* 1129, *pg.* 1418
ACE ANALYST - Analytics For Networked Applications - RIVERBED PERFORMANCE MANAGEMENT; *pg.* 462, *pg.* 765
ACE & DEUCE BONUS POKER - Video Game - INTERNATIONAL GAME TECHNOLOGY; *pg.* 957, *pg.* 1024
ACE ASPHALT - Parking Lot Paving Services - ACE ASPHALT OF ARIZONA, INC.; *pg.* 64, *pg.* 13
ACE BEST BUYS - Hardware Retail Store Services - ACE HARDWARE CORPORATION; *pg.* 1040, *pg.* 644
ACE GSS 4400 - Switch - CISCO SYSTEMS, INC.; *pg.* 372, *pg.* 240
ACE HARDWARE - Hardware Retail Store Services - ACE HARDWARE CORPORATION; *pg.* 1040, *pg.* 644
ACE HARDWARE AND GARDEN CENTER - Lawn & Garden Services - ACE HARDWARE CORPORATION; *pg.* 1040, *pg.* 644
ACE HARDWARE COMMITTED TO A QUALITY ENVIRONMENT - Promotional Program - ACE HARDWARE CORPORATION; *pg.* 1040, *pg.* 644
ACE III GPS - Navigation Aid - TRIMBLE NAVIGATION LIMITED; *pg.* 1384, *pg.* 288
ACE IN THE HOLE - Lottery Game - MISSOURI LOTTERY; *pg.* 999, *pg.* 979
ACE INVADERS - Video Game - INTERNATIONAL GAME TECHNOLOGY; *pg.* 957, *pg.* 1024
ACE IS THE PLACE - Slogan - ACE HARDWARE CORPORATION; *pg.* 1040, *pg.* 644
ACE IS THE PLACE WITH THE HELPFUL HARDWARE FOLKS - Slogan - ACE HARDWARE CORPORATION; *pg.* 1040, *pg.* 644
ACE KIDZ - Bandage - BECTON, DICKINSON & COMPANY; *pg.* 1501, *pg.* 1068
ACE LIVE - Real-Time Network Analytics - RIVERBED PERFORMANCE MANAGEMENT; *pg.* 462, *pg.* 765
ACE MODULE - Switch - CISCO SYSTEMS, INC.; *pg.* 372, *pg.* 240
ACE PACKAGING - Packaging Product - INTERNATIONAL PAPER COMPANY; *pg.* 1460, *pg.* 1644
ACE PRO - Hardware - ACE HARDWARE CORPORATION; *pg.* 1040, *pg.* 644
ACE SPECIALTY FOODS - Candy & Confectionery Gifts - HICKORY FARMS, INC.; *pg.* 862, *pg.* 1462
ACE-THE HELPFUL PLACE - Slogan - ACE HARDWARE CORPORATION; *pg.* 1040, *pg.* 644
ACE-TUF - Wheel - HAMILTON CASTER & MFG. CO.; *pg.* 206, *pg.* 1454
ACE UTC - Navigation Aid - TRIMBLE NAVIGATION LIMITED; *pg.* 1384, *pg.* 288
ACE XML - Software - CISCO SYSTEMS, INC.; *pg.* 372, *pg.* 240
ACEC CENTRIFUGAL - Pump - FLOWSERVE CORPORATION; *pg.* 82, *pg.* 1719
ACELA EXPRESS - Spectrum Train Set - BACHMANN INDUSTRIES, INC.; *pg.* 950, *pg.* 1559
ACELEPRYN - Insecticide - E.I. DU PONT DE NEMOURS & COMPANY; *pg.* 1159, *pg.* 390
ACEMANAGER - Air Link Control Product - SIERRA WIRELESS INCORPORATED; *pg.* 673, *pg.* 1909
ACENET - Computer Database - ACE HARDWARE CORPORATION; *pg.* 1040, *pg.* 644
ACENET - Air Link Control Product - SIERRA WIRELESS INCORPORATED; *pg.* 673, *pg.* 1909
ACENTI - Electronic Component - LEVITON MANUFACTURING COMPANY, INC.; *pg.* 1301, *pg.* 1180
ACEPHEN - Pharmaceutical Product - G&W LABORATORIES INC.; *pg.* 1532, *pg.* 1123
ACES - Network Installation & Maintenance Services - ADTRAN, INC.; *pg.* 344, *pg.* 6
ACES DEUCES BONUS POKER - Video Game - INTERNATIONAL GAME TECHNOLOGY; *pg.* 957, *pg.* 1024
ACE'S WILD - Lottery Game - IOWA LOTTERY; *pg.* 996, *pg.* 705
ACETA-GESIC - Pharmaceutical Product - ALLERGAN; *pg.* 1490, *pg.* 1101
ACETAZOLAMIDE - Pharmaceutical Product - LANNETT COMPANY, INC.; *pg.* 1555, *pg.* 1566
ACEVIEW - On-Screen Dashboard - SIERRA WIRELESS INCORPORATED; *pg.* 673, *pg.* 1909
ACEWARE - Air Link Control Product - SIERRA WIRELESS INCORPORATED; *pg.* 673, *pg.* 1909
ACEX - FPGA Device - ALTERA CORPORATION; *pg.* 348, *pg.* 237
ACEX 1K - Gate Array - ALTERA CORPORATION; *pg.* 348, *pg.* 237
ACF - Optics - MEADE INSTRUMENTS CORPORATION; *pg.* 1422, *pg.* 113
ACFB - Motor Brakes & Brake Motors - ELECTROID CO; *pg.* 1333, *pg.* 1123
ACGT - Seal & Thermoplastic Component - GREENE, TWEED & CO.; *pg.* 1344, *pg.* 1544
ACGTL - Seal & Thermoplastic Component - GREENE, TWEED & CO.; *pg.* 1344, *pg.* 1544
ACH - Banking Software - JACK HENRY & ASSOCIATES, INC.; *pg.* 422, *pg.* 988
ACHIEVA - Fabric - NEMSCHOFF, INC.; *pg.* 936, *pg.* 1890
ACHILLON - Medical Device - INTEGRA LIFESCIENCES HOLDINGS CORPORATION; *pg.* 1545, *pg.* 1109
ACHOPHOS - Aqueous Cleaner - HUBBARD-HALL, INC.; *pg.* 1167, *pg.* 382
ACHROLYTE - Chemical Coating - ENTHONE INC.; *pg.* 1161, *pg.* 381
ACI - Motor Product - STANDARD MOTOR PRODUCTS, INC.; *pg.* 218, *pg.* 1176
ACI MATERIALS JOURNAL - Journal on Concrete Materials - AMERICAN CONCRETE INSTITUTE; *pg.* 127, *pg.* 885
ACI STRUCTURAL JOURNAL - Journal on Concrete Structures - AMERICAN CONCRETE INSTITUTE; *pg.* 127, *pg.* 885
ACID BRITE - Aqueous Cleaner - HUBBARD-HALL, INC.; *pg.* 1167, *pg.* 382
ACID BRITE NO 2 - Chemical Product - BIRKO CORPORATION; *pg.* 1149, *pg.* 332
ACID DEFENSE - Health Supplement - GARDEN OF LIFE, INC.; *pg.* 1532, *pg.* 478
ACID KLEEN - Acid Cleaner - BIRKO CORPORATION; *pg.* 1149, *pg.* 332
ACID-V - Animal Nutrition Product - VITUSA CORP.; *pg.* 1482, *pg.* 1063
ACIDALL - Cleaning And Conditioning Product - HEATBATH CORPORATION; *pg.* 1165, *pg.* 826
ACIDMASTER - Total Encapsulating Garment - STANDARD SAFETY EQUIPMENT CO.; *pg.* 1379, *pg.* 632
ACIDOMIX - Health & Nutrition Product - NOVUS INTERNATIONAL, INC.; *pg.* 706, *pg.* 1001
ACIDOPHILUS PEARLS - Intestinal Supplement - ENZYMATIC THERAPY INC.; *pg.* 1529, *pg.* 1859
ACIMA - Industrial Product - DOW CHEMICAL; *pg.* 1156, *pg.* 1563
ACIPHEX - Pharmaceutical - EISAI INC.; *pg.* 1526, *pg.* 1133
ACIPHEX - Pharmaceutical - JANSSEN PHARMACEUTICA

PRODUCTS, L.P.; pg. 1548, pg. 1125
ACKLANDS-GRAINGER - Sourcing Service - W.W. GRAINGER, INC.; pg. 1390, pg. 625
ACL - Coagulation Analyzer - BECKMAN COULTER, INC.; pg. 1402, pg. 48
ACL - Chlorinated Isocyanurates - OCCIDENTAL CHEMICAL CORPORATION; pg. 1175, pg. 1685
ACLAR - Fluoropolymer Film - HONEYWELL INTERNATIONAL INC.; pg. 407, pg. 1088
ACLON - Wettable, Bondable PTFE Whisker for Polymers - ACTON TECHNOLOGIES, INC.; pg. 1145, pg. 1582
ACLON - Resin - HONEYWELL INTERNATIONAL INC.; pg. 407, pg. 1088
ACM - Cashier Machine - EVERI HOLDINGS INC.; pg. 749, pg. 1023
ACME - Grocery Store - THE FRED W. ALBRECHT GROCERY CO.; pg. 1020, pg. 1400
ACME - Air Distribution Product - STANDEX INTERNATIONAL CORPORATION; pg. 60, pg. 1039
ACME UNITED - Scissors & Shears - ACME UNITED CORPORATION; pg. 1040, pg. 346
ACNE CLARIFYING COMPLEX - Skin Treatment - SHAKLEE CORPORATION; pg. 1593, pg. 184
ACNIELSEN - Sales Tracker - THE NIELSEN COMPANY B.V.; pg. 1671, pg. 1272
ACOLYSIS - Medical Device - VASCULAR SOLUTIONS, INC.; pg. 1434, pg. 946
ACOPIA - Software - F5 NETWORKS, INC.; pg. 396, pg. 1835
ACOPIA NETWORKS - Software - F5 NETWORKS, INC.; pg. 396, pg. 1835
ACORGA - Extraction Reagents - CYTEC INDUSTRIES, INC.; pg. 1155, pg. 1131
ACORN - Software - ENVIRONMENTAL SYSTEMS RESEARCH INSTITUTE INC.; pg. 393, pg. 188
ACORN II - Medication Nebulizer - VITAL SIGNS, INC.; pg. 1607, pg. 1126
ACOT (APPLE CLASSROOMS OF TOMORROW) - Education Service - APPLE INC.; pg. 350, pg. 73
ACOUSTASONIC - Guitar - FENDER MUSICAL INSTRUMENTS CORPORATION; pg. 547, pg. 21
ACOUSTASONIC STRAT - Electric Guitar - FENDER MUSICAL INSTRUMENTS CORPORATION; pg. 547, pg. 21
ACOUSTI-SEAL - Partitions - MODERNFOLD, INC.; pg. 98, pg. 681
ACOUSTIC - Window & Door - HARVEY INDUSTRIES, INC.; pg. 86, pg. 851
ACOUSTIC NOISE CANCELLING - Headphones - BOSE CORPORATION; pg. 626, pg. 820
ACOUSTIC PORTRAIT - Digital Organ Sound System - ALLEN ORGAN COMPANY; pg. 527, pg. 1549
ACOUSTIC PROPERTIES EXPLORER - Drilling System - BAKER HUGHES INTEQ; pg. 1316, pg. 1700
ACOUSTIC RESEARCH - Mobile & Consumer Electronics - VOXX INTERNATIONAL; pg. 686, pg. 1166
ACOUSTIC STAGE PACK - Musical Instrument - PEAVEY ELECTRONICS CORPORATION; pg. 662, pg. 970
ACOUSTIC WAVE - Audio Product - BOSE CORPORATION; pg. 626, pg. 820
ACOUSTICAIR - Blower - TUTHILL CORPORATION; pg. 1385, pg. 561
ACOUSTIKOTE - Interior Acoustic Paint - DUNN-EDWARDS CORPORATION; pg. 1442, pg. 129
ACOUSTIMASS - Speaker Systems - BOSE CORPORATION; pg. 626, pg. 820
ACP - Cell Washing Technology - HAEMONETICS CORPORATION; pg. 1538, pg. 802
ACP - Accelerated Claim Processing - HEALTH MANAGEMENT SYSTEMS, INC.; pg. 1540, pg. 1238
ACP - Anti-Piracy Software - ROVI CORPORATION; pg. 463, pg. 269
ACPI ARCHITECT - Software - PHOENIX TECHNOLOGIES LTD.; pg. 454, pg. 147
ACQ - Pressure Treated Forest Product - J.H. BAXTER & COMPANY; pg. 89, pg. 255
ACQUA - Priceline - TIMEX CORPORATION; pg. 14, pg. 355
ACQUA DI GIO - Designer Fragrance - PARFUMS DE COEUR LTD.; pg. 519, pg. 376
ACQUA PANNA - Water - NESTLE WATERS NORTH AMERICA INC.; pg. 257, pg. 375
ACQUEST - Software - MOLECULAR DEVICES CORPORATION; pg. 1568, pg. 287
ACQUILINE - Software - CACI INTERNATIONAL INC.; pg. 367, pg. 1773
ACQUIRE - Game - HASBRO, INC.; pg. 954, pg. 1603
ACQUITY UPLC - Liquid Chromatography Instrument - WATERS CORPORATION; pg. 1436, pg. 834
ACR - Hoist - TECHNIC INCORPORATED; pg. 1183, pg. 1601
ACR/DETAIL - Software - INFOGIX INC.; pg. 414, pg. 636
ACR ESSENTIALS - Software - INFOGIX INC.; pg. 414, pg. 636
ACR/FILE - Software - INFOGIX INC.; pg. 414, pg. 636
ACR/INMATCH - Software - INFOGIX INC.; pg. 414, pg. 636
ACR/INSTREAM - Software - INFOGIX INC.; pg. 414, pg. 636
ACR/PC WORKBENCH - Software - INFOGIX INC.; pg. 414, pg. 636
ACR/SUMMARY - Software - INFOGIX INC.; pg. 414, pg. 636
ACR/WEBVIEW - Software - INFOGIX INC.; pg. 414, pg. 636
ACRA-VECTOR - Logic Decoder - SHURE INCORPORATED; pg. 672, pg. 638
ACRALANE - Automotive Adhesives & Sealants - PPG INDUSTRIES, INC.; pg. 1445, pg. 1579
ACRAMITE - Miticide - CHEMTURA CORPORATION; pg. 1152, pg. 355
ACRASIL - Wirewound Resistor - OHMITE MANUFACTURING COMPANY; pg. 660, pg. 553
ACRAWAX C - Plastic Additives - LONZA INC.; pg. 1171, pg. 1041
ACREAGE - Wood & Building Material - WEYERHAEUSER COMPANY; pg. 121, pg. 1820
ACRES - Surface Material - STEELCASE INC.; pg. 475, pg. 889
ACRES ADVANTAGE - Game - INTERNATIONAL GAME TECHNOLOGY; pg. 957, pg. 1024
ACRES BONUSING - Game - INTERNATIONAL GAME TECHNOLOGY; pg. 957, pg. 1024
ACRES CASHLESS - Game - INTERNATIONAL GAME TECHNOLOGY; pg. 957, pg. 1024
ACRI-ADD - Acrylic Fortifier - USG CORPORATION; pg. 118, pg. 594
ACRI-DATA - Software - ACRISON, INC.; pg. 1310, pg. 1087
ACRI-FLAT - Wood Stain & Flat Paint - DUNN-EDWARDS CORPORATION; pg. 1442, pg. 129
ACRI-LOC - Masonry Primer & Sealer - DUNN-EDWARDS CORPORATION; pg. 1442, pg. 129
ACRI-PRO - Coating Product - PPG INDUSTRIES, INC.; pg. 1445, pg. 1579
ACRI-SHIELD - Coating Product - PPG INDUSTRIES, INC.; pg. 1445, pg. 1579
ACRO - Vent & Air Filter - PALL CORPORATION; pg. 232, pg. 1323
ACRO-FLEX - Non-Woven Book Binding Material - HOLLISTON LLC; pg. 1460, pg. 1630
ACRO-SET - Bearing - THE TIMKEN COMPANY; pg. 218, pg. 1408
ACROBAT - Software - ADOBE SYSTEMS INCORPORATED; pg. 342, pg. 235
ACROBAT - Desk Stand - LAPWORKS, INC.; pg. 426, pg. 187
ACROBAT 9 PRO EXTENDED - Software - ADOBE SYSTEMS INCORPORATED; pg. 342, pg. 235
ACROBAT CAPTURE - Conversion System - ADOBE SYSTEMS INCORPORATED; pg. 342, pg. 235
ACROBAT CONNECT - Software - ADOBE SYSTEMS INCORPORATED; pg. 342, pg. 235
ACROBAT CONNECT PRO - Software - ADOBE SYSTEMS INCORPORATED; pg. 342, pg. 235
ACROBAT DISTILLER - File Conversion Server - ADOBE SYSTEMS INCORPORATED; pg. 342, pg. 235
ACROBAT E-BOOK READER - E-Book Display System - ADOBE SYSTEMS INCORPORATED; pg. 342, pg. 235
ACROBAT MESSENGER - Software - ADOBE SYSTEMS INCORPORATED; pg. 342, pg. 235
ACROCAP - Positive Pressure Device - PALL CORPORATION; pg. 232, pg. 1323
ACRODISC - Syringe Filter - PALL CORPORATION; pg. 232, pg. 1323
ACROLOC - Controlled Drilling & Milling Machine - HURCO COMPANIES, INC.; pg. 409, pg. 686
ACROPAK - Capsule - PALL CORPORATION; pg. 232, pg. 1323
ACROPREP - Filter Plate - PALL CORPORATION; pg. 232, pg. 1323
ACROS - Home Appliance Product - WHIRLPOOL CORPORATION; pg. 62, pg. 872
ACROSS - Electrophysiology Products - ST. JUDE MEDICAL, INC.; pg. 1596, pg. 963
ACROSS THE STREET. ACROSS THE COUNTRY. - Slogan - INTERIM HEALTHCARE INC.; pg. 417, pg. 469
ACROVENT - Vent & Air Filter - PALL CORPORATION; pg. 232, pg. 1323
ACROWELL - Filter Plate - PALL CORPORATION; pg. 232, pg. 1323
ACRUF - Gear Cutting Tools - GLEASON CORPORATION; pg. 1340, pg. 1335
ACRY-BOND - Low-Sheen Paint - DUNN-EDWARDS CORPORATION; pg. 1442, pg. 129
ACRY GLO - Paint - THE SHERWIN-WILLIAMS COMPANY; pg. 1447, pg. 1435
ACRY-LUSTRE - Paint - KELLY-MOORE PAINT COMPANY, INC.; pg. 1443, pg. 198
ACRY-PLEX - Paint - KELLY-MOORE PAINT COMPANY, INC.; pg. 1443, pg. 198
ACRY-PRIME - Primer-Sealer - KELLY-MOORE PAINT COMPANY, INC.; pg. 1443, pg. 198
ACRY-SHEILD - Paint Product - KELLY-MOORE PAINT COMPANY, INC.; pg. 1443, pg. 198
ACRY-TRED - Paint - KELLY-MOORE PAINT COMPANY, INC.; pg. 1443, pg. 198
ACRYFLOW - Chemical Product - LYONDELLBASELL INDUSTRIES; pg. 980, pg. 1710
ACRYGEN - Chemical Product - OMNOVA SOLUTIONS INC; pg. 1176, pg. 1453
ACRYJET - Pigment Dispersion - DOW CHEMICAL; pg. 1156, pg. 1563
ACRYLI-CLEAN - Professional-Quality Automotive Wax & Grease Remover - PPG INDUSTRIES, INC.; pg. 1445, pg. 1579
ACRYLIC - Lens - STAAR SURGICAL COMPANY; pg. 1597, pg. 151
ACRYLIC FUSION - Backboard - LIFETIME PRODUCTS INC.; pg. 933, pg. 1751
ACRYLITE - Polymers - EVONIK CYRO LLC; pg. 1162, pg. 1103
ACRYLITHANE C - Acrylic Coating - JONES-BLAIR COMPANY; pg. 1443, pg. 1682
ACRYLOTEX - Acrylic Coating - CALIFORNIA PRODUCTS CORPORATION; pg. 1441, pg. 781
ACRYLOX - Oxidized Polyacrylonitrile Fiber - TOHO TENAX AMERICA, INC.; pg. 1184, pg. 1655
ACRYNAR - Coating Product - PPG INDUSTRIES, INC.; pg. 1445, pg. 1579
ACRYPTER - Plastics Product - AEP INDUSTRIES INC.; pg. 1878, pg. 1085
ACRYSOL - Additive - DOW CHEMICAL; pg. 1156, pg. 1563
ACRYSOL - Rheology Modifiers - THE DOW CHEMICAL COMPANY; pg. 1157, pg. 898
ACRYTHANE - Paint Product - AKZO NOBEL; pg. 1439, pg. 1952
ACS - Banking Software - JACK HENRY & ASSOCIATES, INC.; pg. 422, pg. 988
ACSIUM - Chemical Product - E.I. DU PONT DE NEMOURS & COMPANY; pg. 1159, pg. 390
ACSM'S HEALTH AND FITNESS JOURNAL - Medical Journal - LIPPINCOTT WILLIAMS & WILKINS, INC.; pg. 1659, pg. 1567
ACT - Chemical Products - AIR PRODUCTS AND CHEMICALS, INC.; pg. 1145, pg. 1513
ACT - Snowmobile Drive Technology - ARCTIC CAT INC.; pg. 1705, pg. 953
AC*T - Hematology Analyzer - BECKMAN COULTER, INC.; pg. 1402, pg. 48
ACT - Dental Hygiene Product - CHATTEM, INC.; pg. 1515, pg. 1628
ACT - Braking System - GREENE, TWEED & CO.; pg. 1344, pg. 1544
ACT 1900/2300 - Network Channel Banks - ADTRAN, INC.; pg. 344, pg. 6
ACT ASSESSMENT - College Entrance & Placement Exam - ACT INC.; pg. 597, pg. 708
ACT CENTERS - Network of Technology-Enabled Training & Career Planning Sites - ACT INC.; pg. 597, pg. 708
AC*T DIFF - Hematology Analyzer - BECKMAN COULTER, INC.; pg. 1402, pg. 48
AC*T DIFF 2 - Hematology Analyzer - BECKMAN COULTER, INC.; pg. 1402, pg. 48
ACT I - Flatware - ONEIDA LTD; pg. 1129, pg. 1318
ACT II - Food Product - CONAGRA FOODS, INC.; pg. 826, pg. 1014
ACT II - Diagnostic Devices - MEDTRONIC, INC.; pg. 1564, pg. 939

ACT-O-MATIC - Plumbing Product - SLOAN VALVE COMPANY; pg. 1062, pg. 613

ACT RESTORING - Mouth Wash - CHATTEM, INC.; pg. 1515, pg. 1628

ACT1241 - Software - ADTRAN, INC.; pg. 344, pg. 6

ACTA - Chart & Marking System - GRAPHIC CONTROLS LLC; pg. 401, pg. 1148

ACTAFOAM - Polymer Product - CHEMTURA CORPORATION; pg. 1152, pg. 355

ACTAFOAM R-3 - Activator - CHEMTURA CORPORATION; pg. 1152, pg. 355

ACTAIR - Software Development - AEROFLEX INCORPORATED; pg. 614, pg. 1321

ACTANE - Chemical Coating - ENTHONE INC.; pg. 1161, pg. 381

ACTAR-DFIB - Emergence Care Product - VITAL SIGNS, INC.; pg. 1607, pg. 1126

ACTAZENE - Bag - PACTIV CORPORATION; pg. 1466, pg. 624

ACTEV - Biomolecule Product - THERMO FISHER SCIENTIFIC INC.; pg. 1602, pg. 61

ACTHIB - Haemophilus b Conjugate Vaccine - SANOFI PASTEUR, INC; pg. 1591, pg. 1588

ACTI-ZYME - Digestant - DELTA FOREMOST CHEMICAL CORPORATION; pg. 1155, pg. 1642

ACTI-ZYME - Nutritional Supplement - NATURAL ORGANICS, INC.; pg. 1571, pg. 1181

ACTICEL - Cosmetic Ingredient - ACTIVE ORGANICS, INC.; pg. 498, pg. 1725

ACTICON - Healthcare System - AMERICAN MEDICAL SYSTEMS HOLDINGS, INC.; pg. 1493, pg. 947

ACTIFED - Medicine - MCNEIL-PPC, INC.; pg. 1560, pg. 1533

ACTIFIRM - Performance Ingredient - ACTIVE ORGANICS, INC.; pg. 498, pg. 1725

ACTIGEN - Performance Ingredient - ACTIVE ORGANICS, INC.; pg. 498, pg. 1725

ACTIGLIDE - Cosmetic Ingredient - ACTIVE ORGANICS, INC.; pg. 498, pg. 1725

ACTIGLOW - Cosmetic Ingredient - ACTIVE ORGANICS, INC.; pg. 498, pg. 1725

ACTILAC - Cosmetic Ingredient - ACTIVE ORGANICS, INC.; pg. 498, pg. 1725

ACTILON - Therapeutic Product - IDERA PHARMACEUTICALS, INC.; pg. 1543, pg. 808

ACTIMEL - Cultured Dairy Drink - THE DANNON COMPANY, INC.; pg. 851, pg. 1351

ACTIMET - Catalyst - BASF CATALYSTS LLC; pg. 1148, pg. 1074

ACTIMETER - Automatic Replenishing Apparatus - EASTMAN KODAK COMPANY; pg. 1408, pg. 1333

ACTIMOIST - Cosmetic Ingredient - ACTIVE ORGANICS, INC.; pg. 498, pg. 1725

ACTION - Statistical Process Control Software Package - GE WATER & PROCESS TECHNOLOGIES; pg. 1339, pg. 1588

ACTION - Magazine - SCHOLASTIC INC.; pg. 1683, pg. 1288

ACTION 99 - Nonionic Organosilicone - UNIVERSAL COOPERATIVES, INC.; pg. 1482, pg. 922

ACTION! AN ADVENTURE IN MOVIE MAKING - Museum Exhibition Services - MUSEUM OF SCIENCE AND INDUSTRY; pg. 565, pg. 583

ACTION FOR HUMAN RIGHTS. HOPE FOR HUMANITY. - Tagline - AMNESTY INTERNATIONAL USA; pg. 131, pg. 1194

ACTION GRIP - Basketball Equipment - LIFETIME PRODUCTS INC.; pg. 933, pg. 1751

ACTION LABS - Nutritional Product - NUTRACEUTICAL INTERNATIONAL CORPORATION; pg. 1576, pg. 1753

THE ACTION LEVEL - Education Program - AMERICAN CONFERENCE OF GOVERNMENTAL INDUSTRIAL HYGIENISTS; pg. 127, pg. 1409

ACTION MAN - Toy & Game - HASBRO, INC.; pg. 954, pg. 1603

ACTION OFFICE - Desks & Tables - HERMAN MILLER, INC.; pg. 926, pg. 913

ACTION RECORDER - Toy Train - LIONEL LLC; pg. 961, pg. 875

ACTION REQUEST SYSTEM - Software - BMC SOFTWARE, INC.; pg. 362, pg. 1701

ACTION TECH - Clock - BROWN & BIGELOW, INC.; pg. 1624, pg. 959

THE ACTION TRACK - Motorsports Facility - INTERNATIONAL SPEEDWAY CORPORATION; pg. 553, pg. 420

ACTIONABLE INFRASTRUCTURE - Software - SYMANTEC CORPORATION; pg. 478, pg. 161

ACTIONAIR - Valve - MAXON CORPORATION; pg. 1359, pg. 695

ACTIONAL - Software - PROGRESS SOFTWARE CORPORATION; pg. 457, pg. 786

ACTIONALERTS PLUS - Online News - THE STREET, INC.; pg. 1283, pg. 1296

ACTIONMANAGER - Software - PARK CITY GROUP, INC.; pg. 452, pg. 1760

ACTIONMAX - Movie Channel - HOME BOX OFFICE, INC.; pg. 290, pg. 1240

ACTIONPACKER - Storage Container Line - RUBBERMAID HOME PRODUCTS; pg. 1138, pg. 1453

ACTIONS SPEAK LOUDER - Tagline - EQ WORKS; pg. 1243, pg. 1938

ACTIPET - Nutritional Product - NUTRACEUTICAL INTERNATIONAL CORPORATION; pg. 1576, pg. 1753

ACTIPHY - Ethernet Network Equipment - VITESSE SEMICONDUCTOR CORPORATION; pg. 686, pg. 57

ACTIPHYTE - Botanical Extract - ACTIVE ORGANICS, INC.; pg. 498, pg. 1725

ACTIPLEX - Cosmetic Ingredient - ACTIVE ORGANICS, INC.; pg. 498, pg. 1725

ACTIPLEX - Electronic Device - CTS CORPORATION; pg. 631, pg. 677

ACTIPRESS - Steam Iron - ROWENTA (USA), INC.; pg. 60, pg. 1084

ACTIPURE - Separation Product - LYDALL, INC.; pg. 1357, pg. 354

ACTIS - Pharmaceutical Product - VIVUS, INC.; pg. 1608, pg. 163

ACTISEA - Performance Ingredient - ACTIVE ORGANICS, INC.; pg. 498, pg. 1725

ACTISLIM - Performance Ingredient - ACTIVE ORGANICS, INC.; pg. 498, pg. 1725

ACTISORB - Healthcare Product - JOHNSON & JOHNSON; pg. 1549, pg. 1091

ACTISTAR - Starch - CARGILL, INC.; pg. 845, pg. 965

ACTIV-8 - Chemical Product - R.T. VANDERBILT COMPANY, INC.; pg. 1180, pg. 364

ACTIV A.C. - Therapy System - KINETIC CONCEPTS, INC.; pg. 1553, pg. 1741

ACTIVA - DVD Player - CSR; pg. 280, pg. 284

ACTIVA - Tremor Control Therapy - MEDTRONIC, INC.; pg. 1564, pg. 939

ACTIVA - Medical Device - RESMED INC.; pg. 1589, pg. 207

ACTIVA 220 - Sewing Machines - BERNINA OF AMERICA INC.; pg. 51, pg. 554

ACTIVA 230 PE - Sewing Machines - BERNINA OF AMERICA INC.; pg. 51, pg. 554

ACTIVA 240 - Sewing Machines - BERNINA OF AMERICA INC.; pg. 51, pg. 554

ACTIVASE - Tissue-Plasminogen Activator to Dissolve Blood Clots - GENENTECH, INC.; pg. 1533, pg. 279

ACTIVATE - Health & Nutrition Product - NOVUS INTERNATIONAL, INC.; pg. 706, pg. 1001

ACTIVATION - Facility Access Control Equipment - TYCO SIMPLEXGRINNELL LP; pg. 682, pg. 859

ACTIVATIONNOW - Software Platform - SYNCHRONOSS TECHNOLOGIES, INC.; pg. 479, pg. 1047

THE ACTIVATOR - Automotive Equipment - THEXTON MANUFACTURING COMPANY, INC.; pg. 218, pg. 925

ACTIVE - Chemicals - HUNTSMAN CORPORATION; pg. 1167, pg. 1758

ACTIVE ADMINISTRATOR - Software - DELL SOFTWARE; pg. 385, pg. 40

ACTIVE BALANCING - Spinal Cord Stimulation - ST. JUDE MEDICAL, INC.; pg. 1596, pg. 963

ACTIVE CHEMISTRY - Educational Materials - HERFF JONES, INC.; pg. 7, pg. 686

ACTIVE CHRISTIAN PARENTING - Educational Program - ACTIVE PARENTING PUBLISHERS; pg. 1613, pg. 535

ACTIVE DOG - Dog Food - KENT NUTRITION GROUP; pg. 1477, pg. 710

ACTIVE EXTENSIONS - Software - SYMANTEC CORPORATION; pg. 478, pg. 161

ACTIVE INPUT - Electronic Sign System - DAKTRONICS, INC.; pg. 633, pg. 1624

ACTIVE JOE - Pants - HABAND COMPANY, INC.; pg. 1772, pg. 1099

ACTIVE LABEL - Card Product - ABNOTE NORTH AMERICA; pg. 1878, pg. 789

ACTIVE LEARNING CENTER - Baby Toy - EVENFLO COMPANY, INC.; pg. 924, pg. 1470

ACTIVE LIFE - Ostomy Supplies - ALIMED, INC.; pg. 1490, pg. 816

ACTIVE MATCHING NETWORK - Network - ADVANCED ENERGY INDUSTRIES, INC.; pg. 613, pg. 328

ACTIVE-MATRIX - Light Emitting Device - UNIVERSAL DISPLAY CORPORATION; pg. 683, pg. 1064

ACTIVE PARENTING NOW - Parenting Education Programs - ACTIVE PARENTING PUBLISHERS; pg. 1613, pg. 535

ACTIVE PARENTING OF TEENS - Educational Program - ACTIVE PARENTING PUBLISHERS; pg. 1613, pg. 535

ACTIVE PARENTING TODAY - Educational Program - ACTIVE PARENTING PUBLISHERS; pg. 1613, pg. 535

ACTIVE POWER SAVE - Hard Drive - WESTERN DIGITAL CORPORATION; pg. 492, pg. 118

ACTIVE RECTIFIER - Regulator - MAXIM INTEGRATED PRODUCTS, INC.; pg. 653, pg. 247

ACTIVE RESPONSE FORMULA - Medicine Product - SIMILASAN CORPORATION; pg. 1594, pg. 332

ACTIVE TEACHING - Educational Program - ACTIVE PARENTING PUBLISHERS; pg. 1613, pg. 535

ACTIVEADMIN - Software - SYMANTEC CORPORATION; pg. 478, pg. 161

ACTIVEARMOR - Secure Networking Engine - NVIDIA CORPORATION; pg. 447, pg. 268

ACTIVECELL - Medical Device - RESMED INC.; pg. 1589, pg. 207

ACTIVECONNECT - Software - SEMTECH CORPORATION GENNUM PRODUCTS; pg. 671, pg. 1919

ACTIVEFIBER - Satellite Communication Product - KVH INDUSTRIES INC; pg. 650, pg. 1602

ACTIVEGROUPS - Software - DELL SOFTWARE; pg. 385, pg. 40

ACTIVELIFE - Ostomy Care Product - CONVATEC LTD.; pg. 1518, pg. 1121

ACTIVEPAY - Card Services - THE PNC FINANCIAL SERVICES GROUP, INC.; pg. 795, pg. 1579

ACTIVEROLES DIRECT - Software - DELL SOFTWARE; pg. 385, pg. 40

ACTIVEROLES SERVER - Software - DELL SOFTWARE; pg. 385, pg. 40

ACTIVESERVICE - Computer Server Architecture - STRATUS TECHNOLOGIES, INC.; pg. 477, pg. 832

ACTIVESTAFFER - Human Resources Software - API HEALTHCARE CORP.; pg. 350, pg. 1860

ACTIVETECH - Tray - PACTIV CORPORATION; pg. 1466, pg. 624

ACTIVEX/32 - SDK - ALLIED SECURITY INNOVATIONS, INC.; pg. 1041, pg. 1066

ACTIVIN - Nutritional Product - NATROL, INC.; pg. 1570, pg. 64

ACTIVISION - Action & Simulation Games - ACTIVISION BLIZZARD, INC.; pg. 948, pg. 271

ACTO 140 - Chemical Product - BIRKO CORPORATION; pg. 1149, pg. 332

ACTON RECORDER CONTROLLER - Remote Control - LIONEL LLC; pg. 961, pg. 875

ACTRABASE - Emulsifier Packages - GEORGIA-PACIFIC LLC; pg. 1458, pg. 507

ACTRACOR - Metalworking Chemicals - GEORGIA-PACIFIC LLC; pg. 1458, pg. 507

ACTRAFOS - Phosphate Esters - GEORGIA-PACIFIC LLC; pg. 1458, pg. 507

ACTRALUBE - Lubricant Additives - GEORGIA-PACIFIC LLC; pg. 1458, pg. 507

ACTRAMER - Oxidized Oils - GEORGIA-PACIFIC LLC; pg. 1458, pg. 507

ACTRAMIDE - Fatty Acid Alkanomide - GEORGIA-PACIFIC LLC; pg. 1458, pg. 507

ACTRASOL - Sulfated Oils - GEORGIA-PACIFIC LLC; pg. 1458, pg. 507

ACTRAVIS - Computer Software - LOCKHEED MARTIN CORPORATION; pg. 229, pg. 762

ACTRONAL - Activator - DOW CHEMICAL; pg. 1156, pg. 1563

ACTUATE ANALYTICS - Software - ACTUATE CORPORATION; pg. 342, pg. 253

ACTUATED GATE VALVES - Gate Valves - DRIL-QUIP, INC.; pg. 1330, pg. 1704

ACTUREL - Medical Product - E.I. DU PONT DE NEMOURS & COMPANY; pg. 1159, pg. 390

ACTYSSE - Pigment - BASF CATALYSTS LLC; pg. 1148, pg. 1074

ACU-RATE - Geochemical Service - W.L. GORE & ASSOCIATES, INC.; pg. 122, pg. 388

ACUAJEL - Personal Care Product - UNITED-GUARDIAN, INC.; *pg.* 1184, *pg.* 1165

ACUBLOCK - Digital Lens Layout Blocking System - GERBER SCIENTIFIC, INC.; *pg.* 1414, *pg.* 380

ACUBRIGHT - Bleaching & Stabilizing Chemicals for Industrial Use - DOW CHEMICAL; *pg.* 1156, *pg.* 1563

ACUCUT - Processing System - HOSOKAWA MICRON POWDER SYSTEMS; *pg.* 1347, *pg.* 1124

ACUDOSE-RX - Storage, Dispensing & Tracking System - MCKESSON CORPORATION; *pg.* 1560, *pg.* 222

ACUDRIVER - Orthopedic Implant Device - EXACTECH, INC.; *pg.* 1529, *pg.* 428

ACUDYNE - Hair Fixatives - THE DOW CHEMICAL COMPANY; *pg.* 1157, *pg.* 898

ACUEDUCTO - Soft Drink - THE COCA-COLA COMPANY; *pg.* 240, *pg.* 493

ACUFEED - Control Equipment - GE WATER & PROCESS TECHNOLOGIES; *pg.* 1339, *pg.* 1588

ACUFORM - Delivery Technology - DEPOMED, INC.; *pg.* 1523, *pg.* 143

ACUGARD 2 - Activating Device - NABCO ENTRANCES, INC.; *pg.* 99, *pg.* 1882

ACUITY - Medical Device - BOSTON SCIENTIFIC CORPORATION; *pg.* 1508, *pg.* 831

ACUITY - Finer & Polisher - GERBER SCIENTIFIC, INC.; *pg.* 1414, *pg.* 380

ACUITY - Software - MOLECULAR DEVICES CORPORATION; *pg.* 1568, *pg.* 287

ACUITY - Laser Measuring Sensor - SCHMITT INDUSTRIES, INC.; *pg.* 1374, *pg.* 1506

ACUITY - Simulation & Verification System - VARIAN MEDICAL SYSTEMS, INC.; *pg.* 1434, *pg.* 178

ACUITY - Central Station - WELCH ALLYN INC.; *pg.* 1436, *pg.* 1342

ACUITY BT - Medical System - VARIAN MEDICAL SYSTEMS, INC.; *pg.* 1434, *pg.* 178

ACUITY PLUS - Herbal Formula - SHAKLEE CORPORATION; *pg.* 1593, *pg.* 184

ACUITY RESEARCH - Laser Sensor - SCHMITT INDUSTRIES, INC.; *pg.* 1374, *pg.* 1506

ACUITYXPRESS - Software - MOLECULAR DEVICES CORPORATION; *pg.* 1568, *pg.* 287

ACULAR - Eye Care Product - ALLERGAN, INC.; *pg.* 1491, *pg.* 106

ACULAR LS - Eye Care Product - ALLERGAN, INC.; *pg.* 1491, *pg.* 106

ACULYN - Rheology Modifiers - THE DOW CHEMICAL COMPANY; *pg.* 1157, *pg.* 898

ACUMATCH - Orthopedic Implant Device - EXACTECH, INC.; *pg.* 1529, *pg.* 428

ACUMAX PLUS - Warehouse Management System - MCKESSON CORPORATION; *pg.* 1560, *pg.* 222

ACUMEDIA - Medical Tests - IDEXX LABORATORIES, INC.; *pg.* 1543, *pg.* 753

ACUMEDIA - Pharmaceuticals Product - NEOGEN CORPORATION; *pg.* 883, *pg.* 896

ACUMER - Dispersant - DOW CHEMICAL; *pg.* 1156, *pg.* 1563

ACUMER - Scale Inhibitors & Dispersants - THE DOW CHEMICAL COMPANY; *pg.* 1157, *pg.* 898

ACUMOTION - Activation Device - NABCO ENTRANCES, INC.; *pg.* 99, *pg.* 1882

ACUPLANE - Slurries - THE DOW CHEMICAL COMPANY; *pg.* 1157, *pg.* 898

ACURA - Automobile - AMERICAN HONDA MOTOR CO., INC.; *pg.* 163, *pg.* 292

ACURA 1.7 EL - Automobile - HONDA CANADA INC.; *pg.* 179, *pg.* 1938

ACURA MDX - Automobile - HONDA CANADA INC.; *pg.* 179, *pg.* 1938

ACUSEAL - Cardiothoracic Product - W.L. GORE & ASSOCIATES, INC.; *pg.* 122, *pg.* 388

ACUSENSOR - Activation Device - NABCO ENTRANCES, INC.; *pg.* 99, *pg.* 1882

ACUSHAPE - Inspection System - KLA-TENCOR CORPORATION; *pg.* 1353, *pg.* 146

ACUSHNET - Golf Equipment - ACUSHNET COMPANY; *pg.* 1824, *pg.* 818

ACUSNARE - Medical Device - COOK GROUP, INC.; *pg.* 1518, *pg.* 674

ACUTE-KARE - Skin Care Product - STERIS CORPORATION; *pg.* 1597, *pg.* 1464

ACUTIME - Navigation Aid - TRIMBLE NAVIGATION LIMITED; *pg.* 1384, *pg.* 288

ACUTIP 500 - Laser Products - CUTERA, INC.; *pg.* 1521, *pg.* 49

ACUTORQUE - Automation Product - CONBRACO INDUSTRIES INC.; *pg.* 1325, *pg.* 1382

ACUTRAK - Furnace - INDUCTOTHERM CORP.; *pg.* 1348, *pg.* 1114

ACUTRAN - Wafer Handling Platforms - BROOKS AUTOMATION, INC.; *pg.* 1320, *pg.* 813

ACUTRAY - Atmospheric Tool - BROOKS AUTOMATION, INC.; *pg.* 1320, *pg.* 813

ACUVUE - Contact Lens - JOHNSON & JOHNSON VISION CARE, INC.; *pg.* 1552, *pg.* 434

ACUVUE 2 COLOURS - Contact Lens - JOHNSON & JOHNSON VISION CARE, INC.; *pg.* 1552, *pg.* 434

ACXIOM - Innovative Marketing Solutions - ACXIOM CORPORATION; *pg.* 342, *pg.* 33

ACYCLOPRIME - Detection System - PERKINELMER, INC.; *pg.* 1426, *pg.* 853

ACZONE - Acne Treatment - ALLERGAN, INC.; *pg.* 1491, *pg.* 106

AD ADVANTAGE - Software - CINCOM SYSTEMS, INC.; *pg.* 372, *pg.* 1411

AD-BUILDER - Art Illustration System - MULTI-AD, INC.; *pg.* 1666, *pg.* 652

AD-FX - Natural Health Product - AFEXA LIFE SCIENCES INC.; *pg.* 1487, *pg.* 1905

AD-TYPE - Photo Paper - EASTMAN KODAK COMPANY; *pg.* 1408, *pg.* 1333

AD WORLD - Publication - MADISON NEWSPAPERS, INC.; *pg.* 1661, *pg.* 1866

ADACOR - Pressed & Monolithic Refractory - RESCO PRODUCTS, INC.; *pg.* 107, *pg.* 1581

ADAGIO - Lounge Chairs - BERNHARDT DESIGN; *pg.* 918, *pg.* 1381

ADAGIO - Software - CRESTRON ELECTRONICS INC.; *pg.* 631, *pg.* 1116

ADAGIO - Bathtub - MAAX INC.-MINNEAPOLIS; *pg.* 1885, *pg.* 938

ADAGIO - Flooring Product - ROSCO LABORATORIES, INC.; *pg.* 1782, *pg.* 378

ADAGIO TOUR - Flooring Product - ROSCO LABORATORIES, INC.; *pg.* 1782, *pg.* 378

ADALAT - Pharmaceutical Product - BAYER HEALTHCARE PHARMACEUTICAL DIVISION; *pg.* 1500, *pg.* 1132

ADALINE - Footwear - STEVEN MADDEN, LTD.; *pg.* 1819, *pg.* 1176

ADAM - Furniture - ETHAN ALLEN INTERIORS INC.; *pg.* 924, *pg.* 343

ADAM - Furniture - J. ROBERT SCOTT INC.; *pg.* 930, *pg.* 105

ADAMANT - Pressed & Monolithic Refractory - RESCO PRODUCTS, INC.; *pg.* 107, *pg.* 1581

ADAMAS - Musical Instrument - KAMAN CORPORATION; *pg.* 229, *pg.* 338

ADAMO - Computers - DELL INC.; *pg.* 383, *pg.* 1737

ADAMS - Cap - BROWN & BIGELOW, INC.; *pg.* 1624, *pg.* 959

ADAMS - Peanut Butter - THE J.M. SMUCKER COMPANY; *pg.* 865, *pg.* 1468

ADAMS - Motion Simulation Software - MSC SOFTWARE CORPORATION; *pg.* 441, *pg.* 262

ADAMS BEST - Vanilla Extract - ADAMS EXTRACT & SPICE LLC; *pg.* 835, *pg.* 1698

ADAMS CLEANAIRE - Electronic Air Cleaner - ADAMS MFG. CO.; *pg.* 51, *pg.* 1427

ADAMS EXTRACT - Seasonings, Food Coloring & Spices - ADAMS EXTRACT & SPICE LLC; *pg.* 835, *pg.* 1698

THE ADAM'S FAMILY - Game - INTERNATIONAL GAME TECHNOLOGY; *pg.* 957, *pg.* 1024

ADAM'S MARK - Hotels - ADAM'S MARK HOTELS & RESORTS; *pg.* 1079, *pg.* 990

ADAMS MCCLURE - POP Displays - ENNIS, INC.; *pg.* 393, *pg.* 1727

ADAMS MOUNTAIN - Clothing - ABERCROMBIE & FITCH CO.; *pg.* 37, *pg.* 1466

ADAMS RESERVE - Spices - ADAMS EXTRACT & SPICE LLC; *pg.* 835, *pg.* 1698

ADANO - Lighting Product - QUOIZEL INC.; *pg.* 1304, *pg.* 1616

ADAPDEV - Development Workstation - MERCURY COMPUTER SYSTEMS, INC.; *pg.* 434, *pg.* 813

ADAPHOS - Pressed & Monolithic Refractory - RESCO PRODUCTS, INC.; *pg.* 107, *pg.* 1581

ADAPLET - Software - DASSAULT SYSTEMS ENOVIA; *pg.* 382, *pg.* 851

ADAPT-A-LITE - Lighting - SWIVELIER CO., INC.; *pg.* 1307, *pg.* 1142

ADAPT SV - Ventilator - RESMED INC.; *pg.* 1589, *pg.* 207

ADAPTA - Orthopedic Device - DJO SURGICAL; *pg.* 1525, *pg.* 1661

ADAPTABLE WORKSPACE - Office Product - HAWORTH, INC.; *pg.* 402, *pg.* 891

ADAPTAMAX - Health Care Product - NATURE'S SUNSHINE PRODUCTS, INC.; *pg.* 1571, *pg.* 1754

ADAPTATIONS - Carpet - INTERFACE, INC.; *pg.* 695, *pg.* 512

ADAPTEST - Software - KEITHLEY INSTRUMENTS, INC.; *pg.* 1418, *pg.* 1473

ADAPTIC - Healthcare Product - JOHNSON & JOHNSON; *pg.* 1549, *pg.* 1091

ADAPTIV - Software Product - SUNGARD DATA SYSTEMS INC.; *pg.* 477, *pg.* 1592

ADAPTIVE - Software - SUNGARD DATA SYSTEMS INC.; *pg.* 477, *pg.* 1592

ADAPTIVE GAMING - Game - WMS INDUSTRIES INC.; *pg.* 593, *pg.* 666

ADAPTIVE RECALL - Language Learning Solutions - ROSETTA STONE INC.; *pg.* 462, *pg.* 1774

ADAPTIVE SERVER ENTERPRISE - Software - SAP; *pg.* 465, *pg.* 78

ADAPTOR - Cushion - THE ROHO GROUP; *pg.* 1591, *pg.* 556

ADAPTSIM - Software System - MENTOR GRAPHICS CORPORATION; *pg.* 432, *pg.* 1510

ADASET - Refractory Product - RESCO PRODUCTS, INC.; *pg.* 107, *pg.* 1581

ADATO - Silicone Oil - BAUSCH & LOMB INCORPORATED; *pg.* 1401, *pg.* 1045

ADAWNA - Medicine - PFIZER INC.; *pg.* 1581, *pg.* 1278

ADC ALERE - Pharmaceutical Product - ALERE INC.; *pg.* 1488, *pg.* 849

ADC ANALYZER - Software - ANALOG DEVICES, INC.; *pg.* 617, *pg.* 839

ADCO - Detergent - ADCO, INC.; *pg.* 325, *pg.* 482

ADCO BOOSTER - Detergent - ADCO, INC.; *pg.* 325, *pg.* 482

ADCO-LITE CHARGE - Dry Cleaning & Laundry Product - ADCO, INC.; *pg.* 325, *pg.* 482

ADCO SILK-RESTORER - Dry Cleaning & Laundry Product - ADCO, INC.; *pg.* 325, *pg.* 482

ADCO TIGER - Dry Cleaning & Laundry Product - ADCO, INC.; *pg.* 325, *pg.* 482

ADCOTE - Adhesive & Sealant - DOW CHEMICAL; *pg.* 1156, *pg.* 1563

ADCOTE - Laminating Adhesives - THE DOW CHEMICAL COMPANY; *pg.* 1157, *pg.* 898

ADD-A-GIRL - Dolls - AMERICAN GIRL LLC; *pg.* 949, *pg.* 1871

ADD-A-PAD - Furniture - TROPITONE FURNITURE CO., INC.; *pg.* 945, *pg.* 118

ADD-A-PIPES - Lighting Fixtures - SWIVELIER CO., INC.; *pg.* 1307, *pg.* 1142

ADD ON - Software System - OMNICARE, INC; *pg.* 1578, *pg.* 1418

ADD/STAT - Side-Firing Laser Delivery Device - AMERICAN MEDICAL SYSTEMS, INC.; *pg.* 1399, *pg.* 238

ADD-VANTAGE - Pharmaceutical Product - HOSPIRA, INC.; *pg.* 1542, *pg.* 623

ADDABOY - Food Product - WHATABURGER, INC.; *pg.* 1755, *pg.* 1744

ADDERALL XR - Pharmaceutical Product - IMPAX LABORATORIES, INC.; *pg.* 1544, *pg.* 101

ADDICTINGGAMES.COM - Gaming Website - DEFYMEDIA; *pg.* 1237, *pg.* 1222

ADDING VALUE AT EVERY STOP! - Slogan - REPUBLIC SERVICES, INC.; *pg.* 107, *pg.* 19

ADDING VALUE THROUGH INNOVATION - Tag Line - NULAID FOODS INC.; *pg.* 887, *pg.* 193

ADDISON - Leather Products - COACH, INC.; *pg.* 3, *pg.* 1214

ADDISON - Furniture - JASPER GROUP; *pg.* 930, *pg.* 691

ADDISON - Kitchen Product - KOHLER CO.; *pg.* 91, *pg.* 1862

ADDISONN - Footwear - STEVEN MADDEN, LTD.; *pg.* 1819, *pg.* 1176

ADDITIONS - Nutrition Supplement - NESTLE USA, INC.; *pg.* 883, *pg.* 96

ADDITIVE 601 - Water Softener & Foam Suppressor - ECOLAB INC.; *pg.* 329, *pg.* 960

ADDITOL - Additives - CYTEC INDUSTRIES, INC.; *pg.* 1155, *pg.* 1131

ADDITROL - Mineral Binders - MINERALS TECHNOLOGIES INC.; *pg.* 1173, *pg.* 617
ADDREESSOBJECT - Software - MELISSA DATA CORP.; *pg.* 432, *pg.* 188
ADDRESS SAVER - Envelopes - TENSION ENVELOPE CORPORATION; *pg.* 483, *pg.* 986
ADDRESSBUILDER - Software - SCAN-OPTICS, LLC; *pg.* 467, *pg.* 354
ADDRESSDOCTOR - Software - MELISSA DATA CORP.; *pg.* 432, *pg.* 188
ADDRESSGUARD - Internet Services - YAHOO! INC.; *pg.* 1289, *pg.* 289
ADDRESSRIGHT - Addressing System - PITNEY BOWES INC.; *pg.* 454, *pg.* 376
ADDRESSVALIDATOR - Software - MELISSA DATA CORP.; *pg.* 432, *pg.* 188
ADDVANTAGE - Software - SUNGARD DATA SYSTEMS INC.; *pg.* 477, *pg.* 1592
ADDY - Dolls - AMERICAN GIRL LLC; *pg.* 949, *pg.* 1871
ADDY WALKER - Dolls - AMERICAN GIRL LLC; *pg.* 949, *pg.* 1871
ADDY'S BIRTHDAY TEA - Dolls - AMERICAN GIRL LLC; *pg.* 949, *pg.* 1871
ADE - Encoder Register - BADGER METER, INC.; *pg.* 1401, *pg.* 1873
ADELAIDE - Fabric - SCALAMANDRE, INC.; *pg.* 941, *pg.* 1058
ADELAIDES - Dark Chocolate - RUSSELL STOVER CANDIES, INC.; *pg.* 1861, *pg.* 986
ADELPHI - Lounge Chairs - BERNHARDT DESIGN; *pg.* 918, *pg.* 1381
ADELPHI - Furniture - J. ROBERT SCOTT INC.; *pg.* 930, *pg.* 105
ADEMCO - Touchscreen Keypad - HONEYWELL INTERNATIONAL INC.; *pg.* 407, *pg.* 1088
ADEN - Furniture - AMISCO INDUSTRIES LTD.; *pg.* 913, *pg.* 1958
ADENCOCARD - Pharmaceutical Drug - FRESENIUS KABI USA; *pg.* 1531, *pg.* 626
ADENOCLONE - Diagnostic Test Product - MERIDIAN BIOSCIENCE INC.; *pg.* 1422, *pg.* 1417
ADENOVIRUS - Biomolecule Product - THERMO FISHER SCIENTIFIC INC.; *pg.* 1602, *pg.* 61
ADEPT - Insect Growth Regulator - CHEMTURA CORPORATION; *pg.* 1152, *pg.* 355
ADEPT - Software System - MENTOR GRAPHICS CORPORATION; *pg.* 432, *pg.* 1510
ADEPT ACE - Software - ADEPT TECHNOLOGY, INC.; *pg.* 1310, *pg.* 182
ADEPT ANYFEEDER - Feeder - ADEPT TECHNOLOGY, INC.; *pg.* 1310, *pg.* 182
ADEPT APPROFLEX - Feeder - ADEPT TECHNOLOGY, INC.; *pg.* 1310, *pg.* 182
ADEPT COBRA - Robot - ADEPT TECHNOLOGY, INC.; *pg.* 1310, *pg.* 182
ADEPT COBRA SMART600 - SCARA Robot - ADEPT TECHNOLOGY, INC.; *pg.* 1310, *pg.* 182
ADEPT MOTIONBLOX - Amplifier - ADEPT TECHNOLOGY, INC.; *pg.* 1310, *pg.* 182
ADEPT PYTHON - Linear Modules - ADEPT TECHNOLOGY, INC.; *pg.* 1310, *pg.* 182
ADEPT QUATTRO - Delta Robot - ADEPT TECHNOLOGY, INC.; *pg.* 1310, *pg.* 182
ADEPT SIGHT - Software - ADEPT TECHNOLOGY, INC.; *pg.* 1310, *pg.* 182
ADEPT SMARTCONTROLLER - Robot Controller - ADEPT TECHNOLOGY, INC.; *pg.* 1310, *pg.* 182
ADEPT SMARTMOTION - Robot Controller - ADEPT TECHNOLOGY, INC.; *pg.* 1310, *pg.* 182
ADEPT SMARTSERVO - Digital Network for Robot & Motion Control Products - ADEPT TECHNOLOGY, INC.; *pg.* 1310, *pg.* 182
ADEPT V+ - Automation Software Programming Language - ADEPT TECHNOLOGY, INC.; *pg.* 1310, *pg.* 182
ADEPT VIPER - Robot - ADEPT TECHNOLOGY, INC.; *pg.* 1310, *pg.* 182
ADEPT VISION - Vision Controller - ADEPT TECHNOLOGY, INC.; *pg.* 1310, *pg.* 182
ADEPT-XL - SCARA Robot - ADEPT TECHNOLOGY, INC.; *pg.* 1310, *pg.* 182
ADEPTONE-XL - Direct Drive Robot Designed for Medium-sized Payloads - ADEPT TECHNOLOGY, INC.; *pg.* 1310, *pg.* 182
ADEPTSIX - Compact, High-Performance Robot System Equipped with Six-Axis Articulation - ADEPT TECHNOLOGY, INC.; *pg.* 1310, *pg.* 182
ADEPTVICRON 300S - Robot Designed for Substrate Handling & Semiconductor Manufacturing - ADEPT TECHNOLOGY, INC.; *pg.* 1310, *pg.* 182
ADEQUAN - Veterinary Joint Disease Medicine - LUITPOLD PHARMACEUTICALS, INC.; *pg.* 1557, *pg.* 1342
ADES - Soft Drink - THE COCA-COLA COMPANY; *pg.* 240, *pg.* 493
ADESCO - Safe & Security Product - FIRE KING SECURITY GROUP; *pg.* 1336, *pg.* 696
ADEX - Additives - THE LUBRIZOL CORPORATION; *pg.* 1171, *pg.* 1481
AD*GRAPH - Advertising Research & Tracking Service - IPSOS-ASI, INC.; *pg.* 421, *pg.* 363
ADHAESIUM - Machinery Mounting Material - FLEXBAR MACHINE CORP.; *pg.* 1337, *pg.* 1169
ADHESIUM - Wallpaper Adhesives - THE MURALO COMPANY; *pg.* 1444, *pg.* 1042
ADHESIVE MOCK-UP PAPER - Paper Products - BOISE CASCADE HOLDINGS, L.L.C.; *pg.* 1453, *pg.* 546
ADHESIVE REMOVER - Automotive Reconditioning Product - MOC PRODUCTS COMPANY, INC.; *pg.* 332, *pg.* 174
ADI - Software - AUTODESK INC.; *pg.* 356, *pg.* 257
ADI-PURE - Adipic Acid for Nylon Fabrics - INVISTA B.V.; *pg.* 1168, *pg.* 723
ADI-ZYME - Enzyme - STERIS CORPORATION; *pg.* 1597, *pg.* 1464
ADIANA - Contraception System - HOLOGIC, INC.; *pg.* 1416, *pg.* 784
ADIPRENE - Polymer Product - CHEMTURA CORPORATION; *pg.* 1152, *pg.* 355
ADIPRENE BL16 - Liquid Urethane Elastomer - CHEMTURA CORPORATION; *pg.* 1152, *pg.* 355
ADIPRENE EXTREME - Cast Elastomers - CHEMTURA CORPORATION; *pg.* 1152, *pg.* 355
ADIPRENE L 200 - Prepolymer - CHEMTURA CORPORATION; *pg.* 1152, *pg.* 355
ADIPRENE L100 - Polyether/TDI Urethane Prepolymer - CHEMTURA CORPORATION; *pg.* 1152, *pg.* 355
ADIPRENE L167 - Prepolymer - CHEMTURA CORPORATION; *pg.* 1152, *pg.* 355
ADIRONDACK - Table - BLATT BOWLING & BILLIARD CORP.; *pg.* 1827, *pg.* 1203
ADIRONDACK - Paper & Nonwoven Material - FIBERMARK INC.; *pg.* 1457, *pg.* 1764
ADIRONDACK - Apparel - LACROSSE FOOTWEAR, INC.; *pg.* 1811, *pg.* 1503
ADIRONDACK - Athletic Equipment & Sporting Goods - RAWLINGS SPORTING GOODS CO., INC.; *pg.* 1843, *pg.* 1002
ADISIMADC - Virtual Evolution Board - ANALOG DEVICES, INC.; *pg.* 617, *pg.* 839
ADISIMPOWER - Regulators - ANALOG DEVICES, INC.; *pg.* 617, *pg.* 839
ADISON - Furniture - ETHAN ALLEN INTERIORS INC.; *pg.* 924, *pg.* 343
ADIT - Software System - MENTOR GRAPHICS CORPORATION; *pg.* 432, *pg.* 1510
ADJACENT KEY SUPPRESSION - Integrated Circuit - ATMEL CORPORATION; *pg.* 621, *pg.* 238
ADJUST-A-SHORE - Adjustable Shoring System - SAFWAY SERVICES, LLC; *pg.* 109, *pg.* 1898
ADJUST-A-STAT - Anti-Static Device - WALTER G. LEGGE COMPANY, INC.; *pg.* 337, *pg.* 1321
ADJUST-A-STROKE - Sanitary Priming Piston Pump - GRACO, INC.; *pg.* 1342, *pg.* 935
ADJUSTA-LOCK - Security Lock-Combination - SARGENT & GREENLEAF, INC.; *pg.* 1061, *pg.* 739
ADJUSTA-MAGIC - Adjustable Electric Beds - LEGGETT & PLATT, INCORPORATED; *pg.* 933, *pg.* 974
ADJUSTABENCH - Adjustable Workstation Bench - KEWAUNEE SCIENTIFIC CORPORATION; *pg.* 931, *pg.* 1391
ADJUSTABLE TOP - Clothing - K-SWISS; *pg.* 1837, *pg.* 306
ADJUSTMENT SUB - Surface Equipment - DRIL-QUIP, INC.; *pg.* 1330, *pg.* 1704
ADLER - Furniture - LA-Z-BOY INCORPORATED; *pg.* 932, *pg.* 901
ADLER POPPIES COLOR KHAKI - Bath Accessory - CROSCILL, INC.; *pg.* 1122, *pg.* 1220
ADM CLINTOSE - Fermentation Enhancer - ARCHER-DANIELS-MIDLAND COMPANY; *pg.* 825, *pg.* 565
ADMA - Chemical Product - ALBEMARLE CORPORATION; *pg.* 1146, *pg.* 741
ADMAX - Gateway - NEXAGE, INC.; *pg.* 1271, *pg.* 799
ADMC - Software - DELL SOFTWARE; *pg.* 385, *pg.* 40
ADME PARTNERS - Pharmaceutical Licensing Program - SIMULATIONS PLUS, INC.; *pg.* 470, *pg.* 121
ADMET MODELER - Pharmaceutical Software - SIMULATIONS PLUS, INC.; *pg.* 470, *pg.* 121
ADMET PREDICTOR - Pharmaceutical Software - SIMULATIONS PLUS, INC.; *pg.* 470, *pg.* 121
ADMETOX - Workstation - BECKMAN COULTER, INC.; *pg.* 1402, *pg.* 48
ADMINISTAR - Software - SUNGARD DATA SYSTEMS INC.; *pg.* 477, *pg.* 1592
ADMINISTRATION - Software - AXEDA SYSTEMS INC.; *pg.* 359, *pg.* 819
ADMINISTRATOR - Software - MICROSTRATEGY, INC.; *pg.* 1266, *pg.* 1809
ADMINSTUDIO - Software - FLEXERA SOFTWARE INC.; *pg.* 398, *pg.* 658
ADMIRAL - Polymer Suspensions - HERCULES INCORPORATED; *pg.* 1166, *pg.* 392
ADMIRAL - Maintenance Service - THE MILLARD GROUP; *pg.* 440, *pg.* 628
ADMIRAL - Shares - THE VANGUARD GROUP, INC.; *pg.* 816, *pg.* 1550
ADMIRAL - Home Appliance - WHIRLPOOL CORPORATION; *pg.* 62, *pg.* 872
ADMIRE - Furniture Polish - BLUE CROSS LABORATORIES; *pg.* 326, *pg.* 277
ADMISSION - Online Ticket Service - IAC/INTERACTIVECORP; *pg.* 292, *pg.* 1242
ADMISSIONS XPRESS - Software - XEROX CORPORATION; *pg.* 494, *pg.* 365
ADMOB - Mobile Advertising Services - GOOGLE INC.; *pg.* 1249, *pg.* 153
ADMORE - Presentation Products - ENNIS, INC.; *pg.* 393, *pg.* 1727
ADMS - Simulator - ENVIRONMENTAL TECTONICS CORPORATION; *pg.* 1411, *pg.* 1587
ADOBE - Fabric - NEMSCHOFF, INC.; *pg.* 936, *pg.* 1890
ADOBE AFTER EFFECTS - Motion Graphics & Visual Effect System - ADOBE SYSTEMS INCORPORATED; *pg.* 342, *pg.* 235
ADOBE ATMOSHERE - 3D Interactive Stage Set for Web - ADOBE SYSTEMS INCORPORATED; *pg.* 342, *pg.* 235
ADOBE CREATIVE SUITE - Software - ADOBE SYSTEMS INCORPORATED; *pg.* 342, *pg.* 235
ADOBE ENCORE - Software - ADOBE SYSTEMS INCORPORATED; *pg.* 342, *pg.* 235
ADOBE FRAMEMAKER - Desktop Publishing System - ADOBE SYSTEMS INCORPORATED; *pg.* 342, *pg.* 235
ADOBE MEDIA PLAYER - Software - ADOBE SYSTEMS INCORPORATED; *pg.* 342, *pg.* 235
ADOBE ONLOCATION - Software - ADOBE SYSTEMS INCORPORATED; *pg.* 342, *pg.* 235
ADOBE PREMIERE - Real-Time Video Editing System - ADOBE SYSTEMS INCORPORATED; *pg.* 342, *pg.* 235
ADOBE VILLAGE - Carpet - BEAULIEU GROUP, LLC; *pg.* 917, *pg.* 529
ADOLPHUS - Rice - AMERICAN RICE, INC.; *pg.* 837, *pg.* 1700
ADONIS - Table - BLATT BOWLING & BILLIARD CORP.; *pg.* 1827, *pg.* 1203
ADORABL - Footwear - STEVEN MADDEN, LTD.; *pg.* 1819, *pg.* 1176
ADORN - Healthcare Product - MEDICOOL, INC.; *pg.* 1562, *pg.* 294
ADOX - Sodium Chlorite Products - E.I. DU PONT DE NEMOURS & COMPANY; *pg.* 1159, *pg.* 390
ADPER - Easy Bond Adhesive - 3M COMPANY; *pg.* 1142, *pg.* 956
ADPLUS - Advertising Solution - SEACHANGE INTERNATIONAL, INC.; *pg.* 1279, *pg.* 781
ADR - Automatic Defect Removal System - KEY TECHNOLOGY, INC.; *pg.* 868, *pg.* 1847
ADR COMBO - Medical Tests - IDEXX LABORATORIES, INC.; *pg.* 1543, *pg.* 753
ADRAS - Aircraft Data Recovery Computer System - HONEYWELL AEROSPACE ELECTRONIC SYSTEMS; *pg.* 228, *pg.* 17
ADRCHEK - Medical Tests - IDEXX LABORATORIES, INC.; *pg.* 1543, *pg.* 753
ADREACH - Wireless Communication System - AT&T SOUTHEAST; *pg.* 1868, *pg.* 489
ADREACH IMPRESSIONS - Wireless Communication System - AT&T SOUTHEAST; *pg.* 1868, *pg.* 489
ADRENALINE GTS - Trainer Shoe - BROOKS SPORTS INC.;

pg. 1805, *pg.* 1818
ADRENALINE SPX - Knife - BUCK KNIVES, INC.; *pg.* 1828, *pg.* 550
ADRIAMYCIN - Pharmaceutical Drug - FRESENIUS KABI USA; *pg.* 1531, *pg.* 626
ADRIAN DELAFIELD - Embroidered Pant Set - HABAND COMPANY, INC.; *pg.* 1772, *pg.* 1099
ADRIANA - Clothing - ABERCROMBIE & FITCH CO.; *pg.* 37, *pg.* 1466
ADRIANNA - Furniture - J. ROBERT SCOTT INC.; *pg.* 930, *pg.* 105
ADRIEN ARPEL - Skin Care - COLOR ME BEAUTIFUL, INC.; *pg.* 505, *pg.* 1787
ADRISTES - Medicine - PFIZER INC.; *pg.* 1581, *pg.* 1278
ADRUCIL - Pharmaceutical Drug - FRESENIUS KABI USA; *pg.* 1531, *pg.* 626
ADS - Track - COILCRAFT, INC.; *pg.* 1324, *pg.* 562
ADS 3000 - Pipe - ADVANCED DRAINAGE SYSTEMS, INC.; *pg.* 1878, *pg.* 1455
ADS 6000 - Triple-Wall Drainage Pipe - ADVANCED DRAINAGE SYSTEMS, INC.; *pg.* 1878, *pg.* 1455
ADSENSE - Internet Application - GOOGLE INC.; *pg.* 1249, *pg.* 153
ADSIM - Software - ASPEN TECHNOLOGY, INC.; *pg.* 354, *pg.* 804
ADSL - Copper Connectivity - CHANNELL COMMERCIAL CORP.; *pg.* 1870, *pg.* 291
ADSMART - Internet Ad Delivery - ADVERTISING CHECKING BUREAU INCORPORATED; *pg.* 345, *pg.* 1187
ADSPRAY - Cleaning Product - HILLYARD, INC.; *pg.* 331, *pg.* 990
ADSPRING - Software - R.R. DONNELLEY & SONS COMPANY; *pg.* 1682, *pg.* 589
ADT - Electronic Protection Systems - THE ADT CORPORATION; *pg.* 612, *pg.* 409
ADT ALWAYS THERE - Tag Line - THE ADT CORPORATION; *pg.* 612, *pg.* 409
ADTELLIGENCE - Metered Advertising Measurement Program - AT&T SOUTHEAST; *pg.* 1868, *pg.* 489
ADTRAN - Networking Products - ADTRAN, INC.; *pg.* 344, *pg.* 6
ADTRAN HAS THE FORMULA FOR BUSINESS SUCCESS - Slogan - ADTRAN, INC.; *pg.* 344, *pg.* 6
ADTRAN SOLUTIONS = BUSINESS SUCCESS - Slogan - ADTRAN, INC.; *pg.* 344, *pg.* 6
ADULATION - Sandals - AEROGROUP INTERNATIONAL, INC.; *pg.* 1803, *pg.* 1055
ADULT GOLD - Food for Adult Dogs - FROMM FAMILY PET FOODS, INC.; *pg.* 1476, *pg.* 1870
ADULT LEARNING SATELLITE SERVICE - Satellite Distribution of Educational Programming Directly to Colleges - PUBLIC BROADCASTING SERVICE; *pg.* 305, *pg.* 1774
ADULT LEARNING SERVICE - Distribution of Telecourses for College Credit - PUBLIC BROADCASTING SERVICE; *pg.* 305, *pg.* 1774
ADULT PLUS - Veterinary Food - IAMS COMPANY; *pg.* 1477, *pg.* 1633
ADULT PRIME - Dog Food - KENT NUTRITION GROUP; *pg.* 1477, *pg.* 710
ADULT SUPER SPECS - Safety Goggle - SCHOOL-TECH, INC.; *pg.* 1844, *pg.* 866
ADULT SWIM - Game & TV Show - THE CARTOON NETWORK; *pg.* 273, *pg.* 492
ADURA - Polyurethane Product - AIR PRODUCTS AND CHEMICALS, INC.; *pg.* 1145, *pg.* 1513
ADURA - Flooring - MANNINGTON MILLS, INC.; *pg.* 934, *pg.* 1119
ADVACAL - Health System Product - LANELABS USA INC.; *pg.* 1554, *pg.* 1128
ADVACARE - Textile Care Product - ECOLAB INC.; *pg.* 329, *pg.* 960
ADVACOR - Absorption Refrigerant - FMC CORPORATION; *pg.* 1163, *pg.* 1564
ADVAGUARD - Inhibitor - FMC CORPORATION; *pg.* 1163, *pg.* 1564
ADVAJOINT - Health System Product - LANELABS USA INC.; *pg.* 1554, *pg.* 1128
ADVALUBE - Lubricant - DOW CHEMICAL; *pg.* 1156, *pg.* 1563
ADVAN TIP - Precision Pipette Tip - HAMILTON CO., INC.; *pg.* 1415, *pg.* 1031
ADVANCAP - Seal & Thermoplastic Component - GREENE, TWEED & CO.; *pg.* 1344, *pg.* 1544
ADVANCE - Nutritional Supplement - ABBOTT LABORATORIES; *pg.* 1484, *pg.* 551
ADVANCE - Medical Device - AMERICAN MEDICAL SYSTEMS HOLDINGS, INC.; *pg.* 1493, *pg.* 947
ADVANCE - Pest-Control Equipment - BASF; *pg.* 1793, *pg.* 992
ADVANCE - Fiberglass Boat Product - GRADY-WHITE BOATS, INC.; *pg.* 1707, *pg.* 1377
ADVANCE - Software System - MENTOR GRAPHICS CORPORATION; *pg.* 432, *pg.* 1510
ADVANCE - Nerve Conduction Studies - NEUROMETRIX, INC.; *pg.* 1572, *pg.* 852
ADVANCE - Low TSNA Cigarettes - ROCK CREEK PHARMACEUTICALS, INC.; *pg.* 1895, *pg.* 466
ADVANCE - Software - SUNGARD DATA SYSTEMS INC.; *pg.* 477, *pg.* 1592
ADVANCE - Concrete Mixer - TEREX CORPORATION; *pg.* 1381, *pg.* 384
ADVANCE ADVENGER - Floor Care - NILFISK-ADVANCE, INC.; *pg.* 332, *pg.* 953
ADVANCE FOR ADMINISTRATORS OF THE LABORATORY - Publication - MERION MATTERS; *pg.* 1664, *pg.* 1544
ADVANCE FOR AUDIOLOGISTS - Publication - MERION MATTERS; *pg.* 1664, *pg.* 1544
ADVANCE FOR CAREERS - Publication - MERION MATTERS; *pg.* 1664, *pg.* 1544
ADVANCE FOR DIRECTORS IN REHABILITATION - Publication - MERION MATTERS; *pg.* 1664, *pg.* 1544
ADVANCE FOR HEALTH INFORMATION EXECUTIVES - Publication - MERION MATTERS; *pg.* 1664, *pg.* 1544
ADVANCE FOR HEALTH INFORMATION PROFESSIONALS - Publication - MERION MATTERS; *pg.* 1664, *pg.* 1544
ADVANCE FOR IMAGING AND ONCOLOGY ADMINISTRATORS - Publication - MERION MATTERS; *pg.* 1664, *pg.* 1544
ADVANCE FOR LPNS - Publication - MERION MATTERS; *pg.* 1664, *pg.* 1544
ADVANCE FOR MANAGERS OF RESPIRATORY CARE - Publication - MERION MATTERS; *pg.* 1664, *pg.* 1544
ADVANCE FOR MEDICAL LABORATORY PROFESSIONALS - Publication - MERION MATTERS; *pg.* 1664, *pg.* 1544
ADVANCE FOR NURSE PRACTITIONERS - Publication - MERION MATTERS; *pg.* 1664, *pg.* 1544
ADVANCE FOR NURSES - Publication - MERION MATTERS; *pg.* 1664, *pg.* 1544
ADVANCE FOR OCCUPATIONAL THERAPY PRACTITIONERS - Publication - MERION MATTERS; *pg.* 1664, *pg.* 1544
ADVANCE FOR PHYSICAL THERAPISTS AND PT ASSISTANTS - Publication - MERION MATTERS; *pg.* 1664, *pg.* 1544
ADVANCE FOR PHYSICIAN ASSISTANTS - Publication - MERION MATTERS; *pg.* 1664, *pg.* 1544
ADVANCE FOR PROVIDERS OF POST-ACUTE CARE - Publication - MERION MATTERS; *pg.* 1664, *pg.* 1544
ADVANCE FOR RESPIRATORY CARE PRACTITIONERS - Publication - MERION MATTERS; *pg.* 1664, *pg.* 1544
ADVANCE FOR SLEEP.COM - Publication - MERION MATTERS; *pg.* 1664, *pg.* 1544
ADVANCE FOR SPEECH LANGUAGE PATHOLOGISTS AND AUDIO - Publication - MERION MATTERS; *pg.* 1664, *pg.* 1544
ADVANCE GUARD INSECT PROTECTED WOOD - Pressure Treated Wood - OSMOSE, INC.; *pg.* 102, *pg.* 533
ADVANCE JED - Software System - MENTOR GRAPHICS CORPORATION; *pg.* 432, *pg.* 1510
ADVANCE JOB FAIRS & CE EVENTS - Publication - MERION MATTERS; *pg.* 1664, *pg.* 1544
ADVANCE KLEEN - Detergent - ADCO, INC.; *pg.* 325, *pg.* 482
ADVANCE MS - Software System - MENTOR GRAPHICS CORPORATION; *pg.* 432, *pg.* 1510
ADVANCE PRODUCTS - Audio Visual Carts & Monitor Mounts - DA-LITE SCREEN COMPANY; *pg.* 632, *pg.* 698
ADVANCE QUICK LINK - Screen - DA-LITE SCREEN COMPANY; *pg.* 632, *pg.* 698
ADVANCE RELENTLESSLY - Tag Line - LEAR CORPORATION; *pg.* 229, *pg.* 907
ADVANCE RFIC - Software System - MENTOR GRAPHICS CORPORATION; *pg.* 432, *pg.* 1510
ADVANCE VCB - Software System - MENTOR GRAPHICS CORPORATION; *pg.* 432, *pg.* 1510
ADVANCED - Medical Device - MANNATECH, INCORPORATED; *pg.* 1558, *pg.* 1671
ADVANCED - Loss Weight Food - NUTRISYSTEM, INC.; *pg.* 1577, *pg.* 1533
ADVANCED ACPI - Software - PHOENIX TECHNOLOGIES LTD.; *pg.* 454, *pg.* 147
ADVANCED CARE BRAND - Pet Products - THE HARTZ MOUNTAIN CORP.; *pg.* 1476, *pg.* 1120
ADVANCED CLIENT AUTHENTICATION - Software - F5 NETWORKS, INC.; *pg.* 396, *pg.* 1835
ADVANCED COATINGS FOR A WORLD OF PLASTICS - Slogan - RED SPOT PAINT & VARNISH CO., INC.; *pg.* 1446, *pg.* 679
ADVANCED COMA- FREE - Optics - MEADE INSTRUMENTS CORPORATION; *pg.* 1422, *pg.* 113
ADVANCED CONSUMER LENDING SYSTEM (ACLS) - Software - CGI TECHNOLOGIES & SOLUTIONS INC.; *pg.* 371, *pg.* 1779
ADVANCED DUNGEONS & DRAGONS - Game - WIZARDS OF THE COAST, INC.; *pg.* 970, *pg.* 1830
ADVANCED ESSENTIAL ENERGY - Body Care - SHISEIDO COSMETICS AMERICA OF SAC; *pg.* 522, *pg.* 1291
ADVANCED ESTIMATICS - Educational Program - VALE NATIONAL TRAINING CENTER INC.; *pg.* 610, *pg.* 1660
ADVANCED EXTREMITY SOLUTIONS - Slogan - INTEGRA LIFESCIENCES HOLDINGS CORPORATION; *pg.* 1545, *pg.* 1109
ADVANCED FOCUS SYSTEM - Laser Technology - COAST CUTLERY COMPANY; *pg.* 1121, *pg.* 1501
ADVANCED GENERATION SEALY POSTUREPEDIC - Mattresses - SEALY CORPORATION; *pg.* 942, *pg.* 1391
ADVANCED HYBRID - Filter Technology - W.L. GORE & ASSOCIATES, INC.; *pg.* 122, *pg.* 388
ADVANCED MATERIALS & PROCESSES - Business-to-Business Technical Magazine - ASM INTERNATIONAL; *pg.* 132, *pg.* 1461
ADVANCED MC - Hardware Product - INTERPHASE CORPORATION; *pg.* 420, *pg.* 1732
ADVANCED MEMORY FORMULA - Nutritional Product - NUTRITION 21, INC.; *pg.* 1577, *pg.* 1327
ADVANCED MICRO DEVICES - Integrated Circuit - ADVANCED MICRO DEVICES, INC.; *pg.* 613, *pg.* 282
ADVANCED PERFORMANCE LEATHER - Golf Equipment - ACUSHNET COMPANY; *pg.* 1824, *pg.* 818
ADVANCED PHOTO SYSTEM - Film - EASTMAN KODAK COMPANY; *pg.* 1408, *pg.* 1333
ADVANCED PICK - Software - TIGERLOGIC CORPORATION; *pg.* 484, *pg.* 117
ADVANCED POLYMER ALLOYS - Polymer Blends - FERRO CORPORATION; *pg.* 1162, *pg.* 1462
ADVANCED POLYMER CONJUGATE TECHNOLOGY - Technology - NEKTAR THERAPEUTICS; *pg.* 1572, *pg.* 224
ADVANCED PROFORMANCE PROFILE STAINLESS - Hockey Ice Skate Blade Steel Perforated Runner - REEBOK-CCM HOCKEY, INC.; *pg.* 1844, *pg.* 1960
THE ADVANCED PROPERTY INVESTMENT SYSTEM - Prerecorded Audio Discs - NIGHTINGALE-CONANT CORPORATION; *pg.* 152, *pg.* 670
ADVANCED ROUTING - Software - F5 NETWORKS, INC.; *pg.* 396, *pg.* 1835
ADVANCED SCIENCE FOR REAL LIVING - Slogan - ZIMMER BIOMET HOLDINGS, INC.; *pg.* 1611, *pg.* 699
ADVANCED SCREENLOK - Water Heater - BRADFORD-WHITE CORPORATION; *pg.* 1069, *pg.* 1514
ADVANCED STORE - Grocery Checkout System - NCR CORPORATION; *pg.* 443, *pg.* 531
ADVANCED SYSTEMS DESIGN & SERVICES - Tagline - ELECTRO STANDARDS LABORATORIES INC.; *pg.* 390, *pg.* 1600
ADVANCED TASER M18 - Non-Lethal Energy Weapons - TASER INTERNATIONAL, INC.; *pg.* 677, *pg.* 24
ADVANCED TASER M26 - Non-Lethal Energy Weapons - TASER INTERNATIONAL, INC.; *pg.* 677, *pg.* 24
ADVANCED TCA - Hardware Product - INTERPHASE CORPORATION; *pg.* 420, *pg.* 1732
ADVANCED TECHNIQUES - Beauty Product - AVON PRODUCTS, INC.; *pg.* 500, *pg.* 1198
ADVANCED TECHNOLOGY. EXACTING STANDARDS. - Tagline - IMPLANT SCIENCES CORPORATION; *pg.* 1348, *pg.* 860
ADVANCED TECHNOLOGY FOR ESSENTIAL PRACTICE - Slogan - RENAISSANCE LEARNING, INC.; *pg.* 607, *pg.* 1899
ADVANCED UV PROTECTION DR RECOMMENDED - Tagline - FGX INTERNATIONAL, INC.; *pg.* 5, *pg.* 1608
ADVANCED VIDEO PLATFORM - Video Streaming

Technology - INTERNATIONAL GAME TECHNOLOGY; *pg.* 957, *pg.* 1024
ADVANCED WHITENING WRAPS - Whitening - RANIR LLC; *pg.* 520, *pg.* 888
ADVANCEDVOICE - Software - TELLABS, INC.; *pg.* 678, *pg.* 637
ADVANCEMAN - Remote Isolation Devices - TII NETWORK TECHNOLOGIES, INC.; *pg.* 680, *pg.* 1157
ADVANCERTK - Performance Enhancer - NOVATEL INC.; *pg.* 1424, *pg.* 1904
ADVANCING CONCRETE KNOWLEDGE - Tagline - AMERICAN CONCRETE INSTITUTE; *pg.* 127, *pg.* 885
ADVANCING LOCAL SEARCH & PERFORMANCE ADVERTISING - Slogan - MARCHEX, INC.; *pg.* 1395, *pg.* 1837
ADVANCING RESUSCITATION. TODAY. - Slogan - ZOLL MEDICAL CORPORATION; *pg.* 1612, *pg.* 814
ADVANCING SCIENCE. SERVING SOCIETY - Tagline - AMERICAN ASSOCIATION FOR THE ADVANCEMENT OF SCIENCE; *pg.* 126, *pg.* 394
ADVANCING SECURITY & WELL BEING - Tagline - FEDERAL SIGNAL CORPORATION; *pg.* 638, *pg.* 645
ADVANCING THE DELIVERY OF HEALTH CARE - Slogan - C.R. BARD, INC.; *pg.* 1519, *pg.* 1094
ADVANCING THE PROFESSION - Slogan - INSTITUTE OF MANAGEMENT ACCOUNTANTS, INC.; *pg.* 144, *pg.* 1086
ADVANCING THE WORLD'S TECHNOLOGIES - Tagline - MATERION CORPORATION; *pg.* 1359, *pg.* 1463
ADVANCING TOPICAL DELIVERY - Tagline - ULURU INC.; *pg.* 1603, *pg.* 1658
ADVANCING WELLNESS - Medical Device - HOSPIRA, INC.; *pg.* 1542, *pg.* 623
ADVANEDGE - Pipe - ADVANCED DRAINAGE SYSTEMS, INC.; *pg.* 1878, *pg.* 1455
ADVANEX - Chemical Cleaner Product - TECH SPRAY, L.P.; *pg.* 1183, *pg.* 1659
ADVANTACAL - Graphic Film - FLEXCON CORPORATION; *pg.* 1457, *pg.* 844
ADVANTAGE - Portable Suction Unit - ALLIED HEALTHCARE PRODUCTS, INC.; *pg.* 1491, *pg.* 990
ADVANTAGE - Medical Device - BOSTON SCIENTIFIC CORPORATION; *pg.* 1508, *pg.* 831
ADVANTAGE - Billiard Table - BOWLMOR AMF; *pg.* 1828, *pg.* 1206
ADVANTAGE - Cap - BROWN & BIGELOW, INC.; *pg.* 1624, *pg.* 959
ADVANTAGE - Smooth-Pour, No-Splash Bleach - THE CLOROX COMPANY; *pg.* 327, *pg.* 169
ADVANTAGE - Vinyl Tile - CONGOLEUM CORPORATION; *pg.* 921, *pg.* 1084
ADVANTAGE - Transportation Service - DART TRANSIT COMPANY; *pg.* 1905, *pg.* 921
ADVANTAGE - Electrical Product - EATON CORPORATION; *pg.* 1331, *pg.* 1429
ADVANTAGE - Toothbrush - GILLETTE; *pg.* 1536, *pg.* 795
ADVANTAGE - Fluid Handling System - GRACO, INC.; *pg.* 1342, *pg.* 935
ADVANTAGE - Furniture - GREAT LAKES CASE & CABINET CO., INC.; *pg.* 401, *pg.* 1529
ADVANTAGE - Additive - HERCULES INCORPORATED; *pg.* 1166, *pg.* 392
ADVANTAGE - Steel Laboratory Cabinets - KEWAUNEE SCIENTIFIC CORPORATION; *pg.* 931, *pg.* 1391
ADVANTAGE - Rubber Floor Mats - MACNEIL AUTOMOTIVE PRODUCTS, LTD.; *pg.* 211, *pg.* 559
ADVANTAGE - Respirator - MINE SAFETY APPLIANCES COMPANY; *pg.* 1361, *pg.* 1525
ADVANTAGE - Electronic Components - MOLEX INCORPORATED; *pg.* 655, *pg.* 628
ADVANTAGE - Grips - MTS SYSTEMS CORPORATION; *pg.* 442, *pg.* 923
ADVANTAGE - Commercial Knitting Yarn - NATIONAL SPINNING COMPANY, INC.; *pg.* 697, *pg.* 1265
THE ADVANTAGE - Servo Roll Feed - P/A INDUSTRIES, INC.; *pg.* 1367, *pg.* 339
ADVANTAGE - Pet Medication - PETMED EXPRESS, INC.; *pg.* 1781, *pg.* 460
ADVANTAGE - Economy Goggles - SELLSTROM MANUFACTURING CO.; *pg.* 1428, *pg.* 659
ADVANTAGE - Bag Machines - TRIANGLE PACKAGE MACHINERY CO.; *pg.* 1383, *pg.* 592
ADVANTAGE - Brush - THE WOOSTER BRUSH COMPANY; *pg.* 1450, *pg.* 1482
ADVANTAGE 1000 - Facepiece - MINE SAFETY APPLIANCES COMPANY; *pg.* 1361, *pg.* 1525
ADVANTAGE 900 - Coating Product - PPG INDUSTRIES, INC.; *pg.* 1445, *pg.* 1579
ADVANTAGE BONUSING - Video Game - INTERNATIONAL GAME TECHNOLOGY; *pg.* 957, *pg.* 1024
ADVANTAGE DATABASE SERVER - Data Management System - SAP; *pg.* 465, *pg.* 78
ADVANTAGE DELUXE ELECTROL - Screen - DA-LITE SCREEN COMPANY; *pg.* 632, *pg.* 698
ADVANTAGE DIGEST - Transportation Service - DART TRANSIT COMPANY; *pg.* 1905, *pg.* 921
ADVANTAGE DRIVE - Fluid Handling System - GRACO, INC.; *pg.* 1342, *pg.* 935
ADVANTAGE ELECTROL - Electric Screen - DA-LITE SCREEN COMPANY; *pg.* 632, *pg.* 698
ADVANTAGE FIT - Medical Device - BOSTON SCIENTIFIC CORPORATION; *pg.* 1508, *pg.* 831
THE ADVANTAGE IS UNDENIABLE - Slogan - UNDER ARMOUR, INC.; *pg.* 49, *pg.* 759
THE ADVANTAGE LINE - Cable - AMPHENOL CORPORATION; *pg.* 616, *pg.* 381
ADVANTAGE MANUAL - Ceiling Recessed Manually Operated Screen - DA-LITE SCREEN COMPANY; *pg.* 632, *pg.* 698
ADVANTAGE MATCH PLAY - Video Game - INTERNATIONAL GAME TECHNOLOGY; *pg.* 957, *pg.* 1024
ADVANTAGE PLUS - Towel - CROSSTEX INTERNATIONAL INC.; *pg.* 1520, *pg.* 1164
ADVANTAGE SCAN - Video Game - INTERNATIONAL GAME TECHNOLOGY; *pg.* 957, *pg.* 1024
ADVANTAGE SERVICES - Distribution Services - BARRISTER GLOBAL SERVICES NETWORK, INC.; *pg.* 360, *pg.* 744
ADVANTAGE TIMBER - Cap - BROWN & BIGELOW, INC.; *pg.* 1624, *pg.* 959
ADVANTAGE90 - Pharmacy Services - WALGREEN CO.; *pg.* 1608, *pg.* 605
ADVANTAGEBED - Mattress System - TEMPUR SEALY INTERNATIONAL, INC.; *pg.* 944, *pg.* 731
ADVANTAGELOFT - Coated Polyester Fibers - KING KOIL LICENSING COMPANY INC.; *pg.* 932, *pg.* 671
ADVANTASOY - Soy - CARGILL LIMITED; *pg.* 1475, *pg.* 1914
ADVANTEDGE - Drug Delivery System - ABBOTT LABORATORIES; *pg.* 1484, *pg.* 551
ADVANTEDGE - Software - EMC CORPORATION; *pg.* 391, *pg.* 825
ADVANTEDGE - Cookware - POLAR WARE COMPANY; *pg.* 1129, *pg.* 1862
ADVANTEK - Engine Parts - DANA HOLDING CORPORATION; *pg.* 203, *pg.* 1461
ADVANTER - Rim Exit Device - DETEX CORPORATION; *pg.* 633, *pg.* 1728
ADVANTEX - Architectural Hardware - DETEX CORPORATION; *pg.* 633, *pg.* 1728
ADVANTIS - Electric Instrument - UNIVERSAL INSTRUMENTS CORPORATION; *pg.* 683, *pg.* 1154
ADVANTIUM - Oven - GENERAL ELECTRIC COMPANY; *pg.* 1297, *pg.* 347
ADVANTIV - Electronic Device - ANALOG DEVICES, INC.; *pg.* 617, *pg.* 839
ADVANTIX - Disposable Camera - EASTMAN KODAK COMPANY; *pg.* 1408, *pg.* 1333
ADVANTRA - Medicare Risk Product - COVENTRY HEALTH CARE, INC.; *pg.* 1519, *pg.* 761
ADVANTRA - Industrial Adhesive for Packaging Applications - H.B. FULLER COMPANY; *pg.* 1165, *pg.* 961
ADVANTRA Z - Nutritional Product - RELIV INTERNATIONAL, INC.; *pg.* 1589, *pg.* 975
ADVANTUS - Insurance Product - THE MINNESOTA LIFE INSURANCE COMPANY; *pg.* 1209, *pg.* 962
ADVANZ - Band Saw Blades - THE L.S. STARRETT COMPANY; *pg.* 1421, *pg.* 783
ADVASTAB - Heat Stabilizer - DOW CHEMICAL; *pg.* 1156, *pg.* 1563
ADVATE - Biopharmaceutical Product - BAXTER INTERNATIONAL INC.; *pg.* 1499, *pg.* 599
ADVENT - Fire Helmet - E.D. BULLARD COMPANY; *pg.* 1332, *pg.* 727
ADVENT - Door - SIMPSON DOOR COMPANY; *pg.* 110, *pg.* 1823
ADVENT - Mobile & Consumer Electronics - VOXX INTERNATIONAL; *pg.* 686, *pg.* 1166
ADVENT BROWSER REPORTING - Reporting Distribution Service - ADVENT SOFTWARE, INC.; *pg.* 345, *pg.* 211
ADVENT CORPORATE ACTIONS - Integrated Corporate Action Solution - ADVENT SOFTWARE, INC.; *pg.* 345, *pg.* 211
ADVENT CUSTODIAL DATA - Web-Based Custodial Data - ADVENT SOFTWARE, INC.; *pg.* 345, *pg.* 211
ADVENT INX - Business Solutions - ADVENT SOFTWARE, INC.; *pg.* 345, *pg.* 211
ADVENT MARKET DATA MANAGER - Business Management Solutions - ADVENT SOFTWARE, INC.; *pg.* 345, *pg.* 211
ADVENT OFFICE - Investment Management System - ADVENT SOFTWARE, INC.; *pg.* 345, *pg.* 211
ADVENT PACKAGER - Business Management Solutions - ADVENT SOFTWARE, INC.; *pg.* 345, *pg.* 211
ADVENT PARTNER - Tax Layering & Partnership Accounting Solution - ADVENT SOFTWARE, INC.; *pg.* 345, *pg.* 211
ADVENT PORTFOLIO EXCHANGE - Business Management Solution - ADVENT SOFTWARE, INC.; *pg.* 345, *pg.* 211
ADVENT REPORT CENTER - Business Management Solutions - ADVENT SOFTWARE, INC.; *pg.* 345, *pg.* 211
ADVENT REVENUE CENTER - Software - ADVENT SOFTWARE, INC.; *pg.* 345, *pg.* 211
ADVENT TRUSTEDNETWORK - Business Management Solutions - ADVENT SOFTWARE, INC.; *pg.* 345, *pg.* 211
ADVENT WAREHOUSE - Data Warehouse Solution - ADVENT SOFTWARE, INC.; *pg.* 345, *pg.* 211
ADVENTURE - Shoe - AEROGROUP INTERNATIONAL, INC.; *pg.* 1803, *pg.* 1055
ADVENTURE - Outdoor Lights - DORCY INTERNATIONAL INC.; *pg.* 1046, *pg.* 1439
ADVENTURE - Fiberglass Boat Product - GRADY-WHITE BOATS, INC.; *pg.* 1707, *pg.* 1377
ADVENTURE - Medical Equipment - INVACARE CORPORATION; *pg.* 1546, *pg.* 1451
ADVENTURE AWARDS - Video Game - INTERNATIONAL GAME TECHNOLOGY; *pg.* 957, *pg.* 1024
ADVENTURE CLUB CARD - Membership Card - MAVERIK COUNTRY STORES, INC.; *pg.* 1027, *pg.* 1752
ADVENTURE OCEAN - Cruise Ship - ROYAL CARIBBEAN CRUISES LTD; *pg.* 1921, *pg.* 446
ADVENTURE OF THE SEAS - Cruise Ship - ROYAL CARIBBEAN CRUISES LTD; *pg.* 1921, *pg.* 446
ADVENTURE PLANNER - Software - TRIMBLE NAVIGATION LIMITED; *pg.* 1384, *pg.* 288
ADVENTURE POWER - Batteries - UNIVERSAL POWER GROUP, INC.; *pg.* 683, *pg.* 1671
ADVENTURE SLOTS - Games - PENN NATIONAL GAMING, INC.; *pg.* 574, *pg.* 1595
ADVENTURELAND - Amusement Park - THE WALT DISNEY COMPANY; *pg.* 317, *pg.* 52
ADVENTURELESS CAPITAL - Definitive Investment Theory - LITTLEFIELD CORPORATION; *pg.* 558, *pg.* 1664
ADVENTURER - Towing Product - BLUE OX; *pg.* 701, *pg.* 1019
ADVENTURER - Motor Homes - WINNEBAGO INDUSTRIES, INC.; *pg.* 1712, *pg.* 707
ADVENTURERS' - Dolls - 1-800-FLOWERS.COM, INC.; *pg.* 1758, *pg.* 1151
ADVENTURE'S FIRST STOP - Tagline - MAVERIK COUNTRY STORES, INC.; *pg.* 1027, *pg.* 1752
THE ADVENTURES OF THE BAILEY SCHOOL KIDS - Educational Materials - SCHOLASTIC INC.; *pg.* 1683, *pg.* 1288
ADVERA - Zeolite - PQ CORPORATION; *pg.* 1178, *pg.* 1515
ADVERTISING AGE - Newspaper - CRAIN COMMUNICATIONS, INC.; *pg.* 1631, *pg.* 879
ADVICE LIGHT - Online Investment Notification Product - FINANCIAL ENGINES, INC.; *pg.* 753, *pg.* 285
ADVICESERVER - Investing Products & Services - FINANCIAL ENGINES, INC.; *pg.* 753, *pg.* 285
ADVICOR - Tablets - ABBOTT LABORATORIES; *pg.* 1484, *pg.* 551
ADVIL - Cold & Sinus Relief - PFIZER INC.; *pg.* 1581, *pg.* 1278
ADVION - Insecticide - E.I. DU PONT DE NEMOURS & COMPANY; *pg.* 1159, *pg.* 390
ADVISION - Network Management - ADTRAN, INC.; *pg.* 344, *pg.* 6
ADVISOR - Software - ASPEN TECHNOLOGY, INC.; *pg.* 354, *pg.* 804
ADVISOR - ATM Status Monitoring System - DIEBOLD, INCORPORATED; *pg.* 387, *pg.* 1407
ADVISOR - Bicycle Accessories - SPECIALIZED BICYCLE COMPONENTS, INC.; *pg.* 1711, *pg.* 152
ADVISOR BUSINESS BUILDERS - Slogan - FRANKLIN

RESOURCES, INC.; *pg.* 760, *pg.* 254
ADVISOR INSIGHT - Reference Tool - STANDARD & POOR'S RATINGS SERVICES; *pg.* 805, *pg.* 1296
ADVISOR INSIGHT STREET - Wall Street at a Glance - STANDARD & POOR'S RATINGS SERVICES; *pg.* 805, *pg.* 1296
ADVISORWARE - Software - SS&C TECHNOLOGIES HOLDINGS, INC.; *pg.* 473, *pg.* 386
ADVISORWARE ENTERPRISE - Software - SS&C TECHNOLOGIES HOLDINGS, INC.; *pg.* 473, *pg.* 386
THE ADVOCATE - Newspaper - CAPITAL CITY PRESS; *pg.* 1625, *pg.* 741
ADVOCATE - Paper - INTERNATIONAL PAPER COMPANY; *pg.* 1460, *pg.* 1644
ADVX - Integrated Circuit - ATMEL CORPORATION; *pg.* 621, *pg.* 238
ADWATCH - Wireless Communication System - AT&T SOUTHEAST; *pg.* 1868, *pg.* 489
ADWORDS - Internet Application - GOOGLE INC.; *pg.* 1249, *pg.* 153
ADWORDS EXPRESS - Advertising App - GOOGLE INC.; *pg.* 1249, *pg.* 153
AE - Pistons - FEDERAL-MOGUL HOLDINGS CORPORATION; *pg.* 205, *pg.* 907
AE-500 - Telephone Entry System - NORTEK SECURITY & CONTROL LLC; *pg.* 659, *pg.* 59
AEC - Automation Electronics Corporation - ELECTRONIC TELE-COMMUNICATIONS, INC.; *pg.* 390, *pg.* 1897
AEC PREMIER STRAW - Erosion Control Product - AMERICAN EXCELSIOR COMPANY; *pg.* 1451, *pg.* 1659
AE.COM - Website - AMERICAN EAGLE OUTFITTERS, INC.; *pg.* 37, *pg.* 1572
AED 10 - Defibrillator - WELCH ALLYN INC.; *pg.* 1436, *pg.* 1342
AED 20 - Defibrillator - WELCH ALLYN INC.; *pg.* 1436, *pg.* 1342
AED PLUS - Defibrillator - ZOLL MEDICAL CORPORATION; *pg.* 1612, *pg.* 814
AED PRO - Defibrillator - ZOLL MEDICAL CORPORATION; *pg.* 1612, *pg.* 814
AEDATS III/IV - Test Cell Instrumentation System - HOWELL INSTRUMENTS INC.; *pg.* 1417, *pg.* 1695
AEGIS - Sport Product - FRANKLIN SPORTS, INC.; *pg.* 1834, *pg.* 847
AEGIS - Nylon Resin - HONEYWELL INTERNATIONAL INC.; *pg.* 407, *pg.* 1088
AEGIS - Weapon System - LOCKHEED MARTIN CORPORATION; *pg.* 229, *pg.* 762
AEGIS QUBE - Beam Routing System - NEWPORT CORPORATION; *pg.* 1424, *pg.* 114
AEGIS THERAPIES - Therapy Services - GOLDEN LIVING; *pg.* 1538, *pg.* 32
AEM - Surgical Instruments - ENCISION INC.; *pg.* 1528, *pg.* 310
AEMR - Copper Connectivity - CHANNELL COMMERCIAL CORP.; *pg.* 1870, *pg.* 291
AEOLIAN - Musical Instrument - GIBSON GUITAR CORP.; *pg.* 550, *pg.* 1650
AEON - Synthetic Oils - GARDNER DENVER, INC.; *pg.* 1338, *pg.* 1592
AEP - Agricultural Products - AG PROCESSING INC.; *pg.* 835, *pg.* 1013
AEPLEX - Plastics Product - AEP INDUSTRIES INC.; *pg.* 1878, *pg.* 1085
AEPRO - Plastics Product - AEP INDUSTRIES INC.; *pg.* 1878, *pg.* 1085
AEQUASCREEN - Assays & Reagents - PERKINELMER, INC.; *pg.* 1426, *pg.* 853
AEQUOZEN - Assays & Reagents - PERKINELMER, INC.; *pg.* 1426, *pg.* 853
AER-O-BUOY - Life Ring - TAYLOR MADE GROUP; *pg.* 1711, *pg.* 1162
AER-O-WATER - Fire Protection Equipment - KIDDE FIRE FIGHTING; *pg.* 1170, *pg.* 1531
AERA - Digital Mass Flow Product - ADVANCED ENERGY INDUSTRIES, INC.; *pg.* 613, *pg.* 328
AERA2 - Mask Inspection System - APPLIED MATERIALS, INC.; *pg.* 618, *pg.* 264
AERBUS - Motor Homes - REXHALL INDUSTRIES, INC.; *pg.* 1710, *pg.* 121
AERECON - Film - EASTMAN KODAK COMPANY; *pg.* 1408, *pg.* 1333
AERFILM - Film Laminate - SCHNELLER, INC.; *pg.* 234, *pg.* 1456
AERFORM - Thermoplastic Sheet - SCHNELLER, INC.; *pg.* 234, *pg.* 1456
AERIAL - Footwear - CAPEZIO BALLET MAKERS INC.; *pg.* 1805, *pg.* 1125
AERIAL - Medical Device - RESMED INC.; *pg.* 1589, *pg.* 207
AERIALACE - Wireless Product - HEMISPHERE GPS INC.; *pg.* 642, *pg.* 1903
AERIE - Clothing - AMERICAN EAGLE OUTFITTERS, INC.; *pg.* 37, *pg.* 1572
AERLAM - Film Laminate - SCHNELLER, INC.; *pg.* 234, *pg.* 1456
AERLINGUS.COM - Web Site - AER LINGUS; *pg.* 1896, *pg.* 1171
AERMAT - Utility Floor Laminate - SCHNELLER, INC.; *pg.* 234, *pg.* 1456
AERMET - Alloy - CARPENTER TECHNOLOGY CORPORATION; *pg.* 73, *pg.* 1584
AERO - Chemical Product - CYTEC INDUSTRIES, INC.; *pg.* 1155, *pg.* 1131
AERO - Photo Film - EASTMAN KODAK COMPANY; *pg.* 1408, *pg.* 1333
AERO - Grease that Provides Low Torque & Outstanding Oxidation Resistance - LUBRIPLATE LUBRICANTS; *pg.* 980, *pg.* 1097
AERO - Integrated Circuit Product - SILICON LABORATORIES INC.; *pg.* 674, *pg.* 1666
AERO-90 - Aerospace Test System - MTS SYSTEMS CORPORATION; *pg.* 442, *pg.* 923
AERO ATHLETICS - Clothing - AEROPOSTALE, INC.; *pg.* 17, *pg.* 1188
AERO-CLICK - Exhalation Outlet - RESMED INC.; *pg.* 1589, *pg.* 207
AERO-DUSTER - Chemical - MILLER-STEPHENSON CHEMICAL COMPANY, INC.; *pg.* 1172, *pg.* 344
AERO-FIX - Mask - RESMED INC.; *pg.* 1589, *pg.* 207
AERO-MOTIVE - Electronic Components - MOLEX INCORPORATED; *pg.* 655, *pg.* 628
AERO-NEG - Photographic Process - EASTMAN KODAK COMPANY; *pg.* 1408, *pg.* 1333
AERO PLUS - Carpet Extractor - NSS ENTERPRISES, INC.; *pg.* 59, *pg.* 1476
AERO SPREAD - Sludge, Compost & Lime Spreaders - HIGHWAY EQUIPMENT COMPANY; *pg.* 704, *pg.* 702
AERO STRIKE - Training Balls - FRANKLIN SPORTS, INC.; *pg.* 1834, *pg.* 847
AERO TRADER - Magazine - DOMINION ENTERPRISES; *pg.* 1636, *pg.* 1796
AEROBAR - Ionizer - MKS INSTRUMENTS, INC.; *pg.* 1362, *pg.* 781
AEROBAR - Electronic Components - MOLEX INCORPORATED; *pg.* 655, *pg.* 628
AEROCAB - Sleeper Cab - KENWORTH TRUCK CO.; *pg.* 181, *pg.* 1822
AEROCARB - Carbon Fiber Product - ASHLAND INC.; *pg.* 972, *pg.* 726
AEROCELL - Healthcare Product - GF HEALTH PRODUCTS, INC.; *pg.* 1535, *pg.* 508
AEROCHROME - Film - EASTMAN KODAK COMPANY; *pg.* 1408, *pg.* 1333
AEROCIDE - Healthcare Product - GF HEALTH PRODUCTS, INC.; *pg.* 1535, *pg.* 508
AEROCOLOR - Film - EASTMAN KODAK COMPANY; *pg.* 1408, *pg.* 1333
AEROCRAFT - Systems Integration & Aeronautics - LOCKHEED MARTIN CORPORATION; *pg.* 229, *pg.* 762
AERODECK - Engineered Powder Coating System - NORDSON CORPORATION; *pg.* 1365, *pg.* 1480
AERODRI - Chemical Product - CYTEC INDUSTRIES, INC.; *pg.* 1155, *pg.* 1131
AERODUCT - Hose - HBD INDUSTRIES, INC.; *pg.* 207, *pg.* 1449
AERODUSTER - Chemical Product - MILLER-STEPHENSON CHEMICAL COMPANY, INC.; *pg.* 1172, *pg.* 344
AERODYNAMIC - Spectrometer - TSI INCORPORATED; *pg.* 1432, *pg.* 965
AERODYNAMIC MOTOMIRROR - Mirror System - COMMERCIAL VEHICLE GROUP, INC.; *pg.* 203, *pg.* 1467
AERODYNE - Sleeper Cab - KENWORTH TRUCK CO.; *pg.* 181, *pg.* 1822
AEROFIN - Heat Exchangers - AEROFIN CORP.; *pg.* 1068, *pg.* 1787
AEROFLEX - Electronic Components - AEROFLEX INCORPORATED; *pg.* 614, *pg.* 1321
AEROFLEX - Fiber Glass Duct Liner - OWENS CORNING; *pg.* 102, *pg.* 1476
AEROFLEX PLUS - Edge Coated Glass Fiber Duct Liner - OWENS CORNING; *pg.* 102, *pg.* 1476
AEROFLOAT - Chemical Product - CYTEC INDUSTRIES, INC.; *pg.* 1155, *pg.* 1131
AEROFLOC - Chemical Product - CYTEC INDUSTRIES, INC.; *pg.* 1155, *pg.* 1131
AEROFLOWER - Live Plants - AEROGROW INTERNATIONAL, INC.; *pg.* 1393, *pg.* 310
AEROFONE - Integrated Circuit Product - SILICON LABORATORIES INC.; *pg.* 674, *pg.* 1666
AEROFROTH - Chemical Product - CYTEC INDUSTRIES, INC.; *pg.* 1155, *pg.* 1131
AEROGARDEN - Indoor Garden - AEROGROW INTERNATIONAL, INC.; *pg.* 1393, *pg.* 310
AEROGLAZE - Coating - LORD CORPORATION; *pg.* 1357, *pg.* 1360
AEROGLIDE - Industrial Dryers & Dehydrators - BUHLER AEROGLIDE; *pg.* 1069, *pg.* 1359
AEROGRAPHIC - Film - EASTMAN KODAK COMPANY; *pg.* 1408, *pg.* 1333
AEROGROW - Live Plants - AEROGROW INTERNATIONAL, INC.; *pg.* 1393, *pg.* 310
AEROHOT - Steamtables - DUKE MANUFACTURING COMPANY, INC.; *pg.* 54, *pg.* 995
AEROLITH - Filter Cartridge - PALL CORPORATION; *pg.* 232, *pg.* 1323
AEROLIZER - Medical Apparatus - MERCK & CO., INC.; *pg.* 1566, *pg.* 1077
AEROLOGY - Shoes - AEROGROUP INTERNATIONAL, INC.; *pg.* 1803, *pg.* 1055
AEROMASTER - Vehicles - SPARTAN MOTORS, INC.; *pg.* 217, *pg.* 874
AEROMAT - Glass Fiber Duct Liner - OWENS CORNING; *pg.* 102, *pg.* 1476
AEROMET - Pot Room - WEINBRENNER SHOE COMPANY, INC.; *pg.* 1822, *pg.* 1871
AEROMINE - Chemical Product - CYTEC INDUSTRIES, INC.; *pg.* 1155, *pg.* 1131
AERON - Chairs - HERMAN MILLER, INC.; *pg.* 926, *pg.* 913
AERONEB - Nebulizer - NEKTAR THERAPEUTICS; *pg.* 1572, *pg.* 224
AERONEX - Purifiers - ENTEGRIS, INC.; *pg.* 1882, *pg.* 788
AEROPHINE - Chemical Product - CYTEC INDUSTRIES, INC.; *pg.* 1155, *pg.* 1131
AEROPLANE - Food Product - MCCORMICK & COMPANY, INCORPORATED; *pg.* 1027, *pg.* 779
AEROPOSTALE - Teen Clothing - AEROPOSTALE, INC.; *pg.* 17, *pg.* 1188
AEROPRO - Data Acquisition Software for Use in Aerospace Testing - MTS SYSTEMS CORPORATION; *pg.* 442, *pg.* 923
AEROQUIP - Hydraulic Component - EATON CORPORATION; *pg.* 1331, *pg.* 1429
AEROSERV - Serving Systems - DUKE MANUFACTURING COMPANY, INC.; *pg.* 54, *pg.* 995
AEROSET - Clinical System - ABBOTT LABORATORIES; *pg.* 1484, *pg.* 551
AEROSHADE - Louvered Side Window Covers - LUND INTERNATIONAL, INC.; *pg.* 211, *pg.* 526
AEROSHIELD - Heavy Truck Bug Deflector - LUND INTERNATIONAL, INC.; *pg.* 211, *pg.* 526
AEROSHIELD CUSTOM - Heavy Truck Bug Deflector - LUND INTERNATIONAL, INC.; *pg.* 211, *pg.* 526
AEROSHIELD-PLUS - Heavy Truck Bug Deflector - LUND INTERNATIONAL, INC.; *pg.* 211, *pg.* 526
AEROSHIELD WAVE - Heavy Truck Bug Deflector - LUND INTERNATIONAL, INC.; *pg.* 211, *pg.* 526
AEROSIZER - Measurement Device - TSI INCORPORATED; *pg.* 1432, *pg.* 965
AEROSOL - Chemical Product - CYTEC INDUSTRIES, INC.; *pg.* 1155, *pg.* 1131
AEROSOLV - Absorbent - SAFETY-KLEEN HOLDCO, INC.; *pg.* 1180, *pg.* 1734
AEROSPACEWARRIOR - Systems Integration & Aeronautics - LOCKHEED MARTIN CORPORATION; *pg.* 229, *pg.* 762
AEROSPRAY - Chemical Product - CYTEC INDUSTRIES, INC.; *pg.* 1155, *pg.* 1131
AEROSYSTEM - Lighting - LSI INDUSTRIES INC.; *pg.* 58, *pg.* 1416
AEROTEX - Chemical Product - CYTEC INDUSTRIES, INC.; *pg.* 1155, *pg.* 1131
AEROTIL - Chemical Product - CYTEC INDUSTRIES, INC.; *pg.* 1155, *pg.* 1131
AEROTRAK - Particle Counter - TSI INCORPORATED; *pg.* 1432, *pg.* 965

AEROTRAN - Software - ASPEN TECHNOLOGY, INC.; *pg.* 354, *pg.* 804
AEROWASH - Engineered Powder Coating System - NORDSON CORPORATION; *pg.* 1365, *pg.* 1480
AEROWAVE - Welding & Cutting Equipment - MILLER ELECTRIC MANUFACTURING CO.; *pg.* 1361, *pg.* 1852
AEROWHIP - Polymer - HERCULES INCORPORATED; *pg.* 1166, *pg.* 392
AERTRIM - Reinforced Laminate - SCHNELLER, INC.; *pg.* 234, *pg.* 1456
AERUS - Foam Product - FXI; *pg.* 1163, *pg.* 1552
AERVOE SHIPPING ESSENTIALS - Shipping Products - AERVOE INDUSTRIES INCORPORATED; *pg.* 1439, *pg.* 1021
AERVOE TOOLMATES - Lubricant - AERVOE INDUSTRIES INCORPORATED; *pg.* 1439, *pg.* 1021
AESA - Defense System - RAYTHEON COMPANY; *pg.* 233, *pg.* 854
AESCULA - Pacing Leads - ST. JUDE MEDICAL, INC.; *pg.* 1596, *pg.* 963
AESOP - Robotic Endoscope Positioner - INTUITIVE SURGICAL, INC.; *pg.* 1546, *pg.* 286
AETHOXYSKLEROL - Sclerosing Agent - MERZ AESTHETICS; *pg.* 1567, *pg.* 255
AETI - Power Delivery Product - AMERICAN ELECTRIC TECHNOLOGIES, INC.; *pg.* 349, *pg.* 1700
AETNA EZCONNECT - Patient Information Tool - AETNA INC.; *pg.* 1187, *pg.* 351
AETNA EZENROLL - Insurance Enrollment Tool - AETNA INC.; *pg.* 1187, *pg.* 351
AETNA EZLINK - Healthcare Information Tool - AETNA INC.; *pg.* 1187, *pg.* 351
AETNA NAGIVATOR - Consumer Decision-Making Tool - AETNA INC.; *pg.* 1187, *pg.* 351
AETNA RX HOME DELIVERY - Prescription Mail Service - AETNA INC.; *pg.* 1187, *pg.* 351
AEWIN - Emission Testing System - MISTRAS GROUP, INC.; *pg.* 1362, *pg.* 1113
AEWINPOST - Emission Testing System - MISTRAS GROUP, INC.; *pg.* 1362, *pg.* 1113
AF-50 - Plastics Product - AEP INDUSTRIES INC.; *pg.* 1878, *pg.* 1085
AF LIGHTING - Lighting - INTERLINE BRANDS, INC.; *pg.* 1051, *pg.* 433
AF SERIES - Floor Boxes - WIREMOLD/LEGRAND; *pg.* 689, *pg.* 383
AF SUPPRESSION - ICD Products - ST. JUDE MEDICAL, INC.; *pg.* 1596, *pg.* 963
AFARIA - Mobile Device Management & Security - SAP; *pg.* 465, *pg.* 78
AFEDITAB - Pharmaceutical Product - ALLERGAN; *pg.* 1490, *pg.* 1101
AFFCO - Felt Color - AMERICAN FELT & FILTER COMPANY; *pg.* 1312, *pg.* 1184
AFFECTION - Flatware - ONEIDA LTD; *pg.* 1129, *pg.* 1318
AFFECTIONATELY YOURS - Carpet - BEAULIEU GROUP, LLC; *pg.* 917, *pg.* 529
AFFI-GEL - Software - BIO-RAD LABORATORIES, INC.; *pg.* 1504, *pg.* 101
AFFI-PREP - Software - BIO-RAD LABORATORIES, INC.; *pg.* 1504, *pg.* 101
AFFILIATEDIRECT - Software - QSOUND LABS, INC.; *pg.* 666, *pg.* 1904
AFFINA - Platform Management Architecture - DATACARD CORPORATION; *pg.* 382, *pg.* 948
AFFINIA HOTELS - Hotels - DENIHAN HOSPITALITY GROUP, LLC; *pg.* 1089, *pg.* 1223
AFFINITY - Chemical Product - THE DOW CHEMICAL COMPANY; *pg.* 1157, *pg.* 898
AFFINITY - Herbicide - E.I. DU PONT DE NEMOURS & COMPANY; *pg.* 1159, *pg.* 390
AFFINITY - Medical Product - HOLOGIC, INC.; *pg.* 1416, *pg.* 784
AFFINITY - Healthcare Product - JOHNSON & JOHNSON; *pg.* 1549, *pg.* 1091
AFFINITY - Vinyl Windows - LINDAL CEDAR HOMES, INC.; *pg.* 94, *pg.* 1837
AFFINITY - Thermal Control Unit - LYDALL, INC.; *pg.* 1357, *pg.* 354
AFFINITY - Flooring - MANNINGTON MILLS, INC.; *pg.* 934, *pg.* 1119
AFFINITY - Personalized Application - SEACHANGE INTERNATIONAL, INC.; *pg.* 1279, *pg.* 781
AFFINITY - Pacemakers - ST. JUDE MEDICAL, INC.; *pg.* 1596, *pg.* 963
AFFINITY PLATINUM - Medical Product - HOLOGIC, INC.; *pg.* 1416, *pg.* 784
AFFINITY QS - Aesthetic Spa Treatment System - CYNOSURE, INC.; *pg.* 1521, *pg.* 858
AFFIRM - Anti-Aging Workstation - CYNOSURE, INC.; *pg.* 1521, *pg.* 858
AFFIRM - Plastic Clad Metals - THE DOW CHEMICAL COMPANY; *pg.* 1157, *pg.* 898
AFFLAB - Cleaning Chemicals - PERFORMANCE FOOD GROUP COMPANY, LLC; *pg.* 1030, *pg.* 1803
AFFORDABLE GOLD - Gold Mortgages - FEDERAL HOME LOAN MORTGAGE CORPORATION; *pg.* 751, *pg.* 1790
AFFORDABLE MERIT RATE - Mortgage - FEDERAL HOME LOAN MORTGAGE CORPORATION; *pg.* 751, *pg.* 1790
AFFORDABLE PORTABLE - Cold Food Station - THE VOLLRATH COMPANY LLC; *pg.* 1139, *pg.* 1894
AFFORDABLE SECONDS - Financial Services - FEDERAL HOME LOAN MORTGAGE CORPORATION; *pg.* 751, *pg.* 1790
AFFRESH - Home Appliance Product - WHIRLPOOL CORPORATION; *pg.* 62, *pg.* 872
AFFYMETRIX EXPRESSION CONSOLE - Software - AFFYMETRIX, INC.; *pg.* 1487, *pg.* 263
AFGEN - Software - SYNOPSYS, INC.; *pg.* 480, *pg.* 162
AFINITY - Collamer IOL - STAAR SURGICAL COMPANY; *pg.* 1597, *pg.* 151
AFIS - Airborne Flight Information System - HONEYWELL AEROSPACE ELECTRONIC SYSTEMS; *pg.* 228, *pg.* 17
AFOCUS - Medical Device - BOSTON SCIENTIFIC CORPORATION; *pg.* 1508, *pg.* 831
AFOP - Fiber Optic Product - ALLIANCE FIBER OPTIC PRODUCTS, INC.; *pg.* 1399, *pg.* 283
AFP-CIDE - Humanized Y-90 Labeled Antibody for Alpha Fetoprotein - IMMUNOMEDICS, INC.; *pg.* 1544, *pg.* 1087
AFP-SCAN - In-Vivo Liver & Germ Cell Imaging Agent - IMMUNOMEDICS, INC.; *pg.* 1544, *pg.* 1087
AFP4 - Biochemical Screening Test - GENZYME CORPORATION; *pg.* 1534, *pg.* 808
AFRC - Acid Free Restroom Cleaner - HILLYARD, INC.; *pg.* 331, *pg.* 990
AFRC - Ski & Sportswear - RAVEN INDUSTRIES, INC.; *pg.* 1888, *pg.* 1625
AFREZZA - Insulin Inhalation Powder - MANNKIND CORPORATION; *pg.* 1558, *pg.* 299
AFRICA - Lamp - ASHLEY FURNITURE INDUSTRIES, INC.; *pg.* 914, *pg.* 1852
AFRICAN CHIEF - Video Game - INTERNATIONAL GAME TECHNOLOGY; *pg.* 957, *pg.* 1024
AFRICAN GOLD - Ethnic Hair Care Products - J. STRICKLAND & COMPANY; *pg.* 512, *pg.* 970
AFRICASPAN - Portfolio Management - ION GEOPHYSICAL CORPORATION; *pg.* 1350, *pg.* 1708
AFRIN - Medicine - MERCK & CO., INC.; *pg.* 1566, *pg.* 1077
AFTER BITE - Insect Bite Treatment - TENDER CORPORATION; *pg.* 1601, *pg.* 1035
AFTER CUTS & SCRAPES - Insect Repellent Product - TENDER CORPORATION; *pg.* 1601, *pg.* 1035
AFTER RUN - Oil - HOBBICO, INC.; *pg.* 956, *pg.* 562
AFTER SHOCK - Schnapps - JIM BEAM BRANDS CO.; *pg.* 1965, *pg.* 601
AFTER STING - Gel - TENDER CORPORATION; *pg.* 1601, *pg.* 1035
AFTER SUN - Hair & Skin Product - AUBREY ORGANICS INC.; *pg.* 499, *pg.* 470
AFTER THE FALL - Fruit Juices - THE J.M. SMUCKER COMPANY; *pg.* 865, *pg.* 1468
THE AFTERMATH - Video Game - ELECTRONIC ARTS INC.; *pg.* 951, *pg.* 189
AFTON - Footwear - K-SWISS; *pg.* 1837, *pg.* 306
AFURIA - Pharmaceutical Product - AKORN, INC.; *pg.* 1488, *pg.* 622
AG - Software - BIO-RAD LABORATORIES, INC.; *pg.* 1504, *pg.* 101
AG-12-28 - Resins - NEVILLE CHEMICAL COMPANY; *pg.* 1174, *pg.* 1578
AG-20 - Agriculture - NOVATEL INC.; *pg.* 1424, *pg.* 1904
AG BOARD - Insulation - THE DOW CHEMICAL COMPANY; *pg.* 1157, *pg.* 898
AG-CHEM - Field Sprayer - AGCO CORPORATION; *pg.* 700, *pg.* 530
AG FICTION - Contemporary Novels for Girls Ten & Up - AMERICAN GIRL LLC; *pg.* 949, *pg.* 1871
A.G. GEAR - Dolls - AMERICAN GIRL LLC; *pg.* 949, *pg.* 1871
AG-MASTER - Metal Building System - BUTLER MANUFACTURING COMPANY; *pg.* 72, *pg.* 981
A.G. MINIS - Dolls - AMERICAN GIRL LLC; *pg.* 949, *pg.* 1871
AG STAR - Livestock Equipment - BEHLEN MFG. CO.; *pg.* 701, *pg.* 1010
AG-TEK - Animal Safety Product - NEOGEN CORPORATION; *pg.* 883, *pg.* 896
AGAPETOS - Fabric - NEMSCHOFF, INC.; *pg.* 936, *pg.* 1890
AGATE PORTABLE - Lighting Product - QUOIZEL INC.; *pg.* 1304, *pg.* 1616
AGAVE PLUS - Granola - NATURE'S PATH FOODS INC.; *pg.* 833, *pg.* 1908
AGAVERO LIQUEUR - Spirits - PROXIMO SPIRITS, INC.; *pg.* 1969, *pg.* 1076
AGC TOTAL KNEE SYSTEM - Knee Product - ZIMMER BIOMET HOLDINGS, INC.; *pg.* 1611, *pg.* 699
AGCAREERS.COM - Consulting And Marketing Service - FARMS.COM LTD.; *pg.* 1247, *pg.* 1922
AGCL LIGHT SPEED - Horse Clipper - ANDIS COMPANY; *pg.* 498, *pg.* 1895
AGE DEFENSE - Nutritional Supplement - PHARMAVITE LLC; *pg.* 1584, *pg.* 167
AGED SUMATRA - Coffee - PEET'S COFFEE & TEA, INC.; *pg.* 1029, *pg.* 85
AGELESS BEAUTY - Carpet - BEAULIEU GROUP, LLC; *pg.* 917, *pg.* 529
AGELESS RESULTS - Beauty Product - AVON PRODUCTS, INC.; *pg.* 500, *pg.* 1198
AGENCY - Boot Bindings - VANS, INC.; *pg.* 1821, *pg.* 76
AGENCY CLAIMVIEW - Computer Software - THE CHUBB CORPORATION; *pg.* 1196, *pg.* 1128
AGENCY E-LOSS - Computer Software - THE CHUBB CORPORATION; *pg.* 1196, *pg.* 1128
THE AGENCY MANAGER - Software - APPLIED SYSTEMS INC.; *pg.* 352, *pg.* 663
AGENDA - Apparel - OAKLEY, INC.; *pg.* 1840, *pg.* 86
AGENERASE - Pharmaceutical Product - VERTEX PHARMACEUTICALS INCORPORATED; *pg.* 1606, *pg.* 801
AGENT - Software - AXEDA SYSTEMS INC.; *pg.* 359, *pg.* 819
AGENT BUCK - Game - INTERNATIONAL GAME TECHNOLOGY; *pg.* 420, *pg.* 1606
AGENT PROJECT CREATION - Software - AXEDA SYSTEMS INC.; *pg.* 359, *pg.* 819
AGENT USA - Educational Materials - SCHOLASTIC INC.; *pg.* 1683, *pg.* 1288
AGENTADVANTAGE - Personal Agent Website Service - HOMES.COM, INC.; *pg.* 1256, *pg.* 203
AGENTEVALUATOR - Real Estate Agent Marketing Solution - HOMEGAIN.COM, INC.; *pg.* 1256, *pg.* 83
AGENTINSIDER - Information For Agents - INSWEB CORPORATION; *pg.* 1205, *pg.* 186
AGENTSONLINE - Computer Services - WESTERN NATIONAL MUTUAL INSURANCE CO.; *pg.* 1223, *pg.* 946
AGENTVIEW - Real Estate Agent Profile Solution - HOMEGAIN.COM, INC.; *pg.* 1256, *pg.* 83
AGERITE - Antioxidants - R.T. VANDERBILT COMPANY, INC.; *pg.* 1180, *pg.* 364
AGESA - Video Card - ADVANCED MICRO DEVICES, INC.; *pg.* 613, *pg.* 282
AGGPS - Navigation Aid - TRIMBLE NAVIGATION LIMITED; *pg.* 1384, *pg.* 288
AGGRAVATION - Game - HASBRO, INC.; *pg.* 954, *pg.* 1603
AGGRECOR - Minerals - MINERALS TECHNOLOGIES INC.; *pg.* 1173, *pg.* 617
AGGRESSOR - Saw Blades - KENNAMETAL IPG; *pg.* 1353, *pg.* 1615
AGILE MFG. - Poultry System - CTB INTERNATIONAL CORP.; *pg.* 850, *pg.* 695
AGILENT - Track - COILCRAFT, INC.; *pg.* 1324, *pg.* 562
AGILI-T - Lighting - STEELCASE INC.; *pg.* 475, *pg.* 889
AGILIA - Concrete - LAFARGE NORTH AMERICA INC.; *pg.* 93, *pg.* 579
AGILIS - Line of ATM Terminal Software - DIEBOLD, INCORPORATED; *pg.* 387, *pg.* 1407
THE AGILIS - Software - DIEBOLD, INCORPORATED; *pg.* 387, *pg.* 1407
AGILIS - Piezo Motor Driven Optical Mounts - NEWPORT CORPORATION; *pg.* 1424, *pg.* 114
AGILIS - Electrophysiology Products - ST. JUDE MEDICAL, INC.; *pg.* 1596, *pg.* 963
AGILIS 3X - Software - DIEBOLD, INCORPORATED; *pg.* 387, *pg.* 1407

First page reference indicates Business Class Edition
Second page reference indicates Geographic Edition

AGILIS 91X - Software - DIEBOLD, INCORPORATED; *pg.* 387, *pg.* 1407
AGILIS EMPOWER - Software - DIEBOLD, INCORPORATED; *pg.* 387, *pg.* 1407
AGILIS NDX - Software - DIEBOLD, INCORPORATED; *pg.* 387, *pg.* 1407
AGILIS POWER - Software - DIEBOLD, INCORPORATED; *pg.* 387, *pg.* 1407
AGILITY - Polyurethane Dispersions - THE DOW CHEMICAL COMPANY; *pg.* 1157, *pg.* 898
AGILITY - Herbicide - E.I. DU PONT DE NEMOURS & COMPANY; *pg.* 1159, *pg.* 390
AGILITY - Disposable Razors - THE GILLETTE COMPANY; *pg.* 509, *pg.* 795
AGILITY RXT - Sneaker - REEBOK INTERNATIONAL LTD.; *pg.* 1817, *pg.* 811
AGILTRAC - Peripheral Dilatation Catheter - ABBOTT LABORATORIES; *pg.* 1484, *pg.* 551
AGIO - Writing Instrument - SHEAFFER PEN CORPORATION; *pg.* 469, *pg.* 371
AGLON - Antimicrobial Coated Stainless Steel - L&R MANUFACTURING COMPANY; *pg.* 1419, *pg.* 1076
AGMATE - Insulation - THE DOW CHEMICAL COMPANY; *pg.* 1157, *pg.* 898
AGN4 - Grinder - WELDON SOLUTIONS; *pg.* 1388, *pg.* 1598
AGNES DREARY - Doll - TONNER DOLL COMPANY, INC.; *pg.* 968, *pg.* 1171
AGNONA - Carpet - INTERFACE, INC.; *pg.* 695, *pg.* 512
AGO RAPID - Chemicals - HUNTSMAN CORPORATION; *pg.* 1167, *pg.* 1758
AGODA - Online Hotel Reservations - THE PRICELINE GROUP INC.; *pg.* 1276, *pg.* 364
AGOMET - Adhesives - HUNTSMAN CORPORATION; *pg.* 1167, *pg.* 1758
AGOMET TWIN - Chemicals - HUNTSMAN CORPORATION; *pg.* 1167, *pg.* 1758
AGORA - Fabric - NEMSCHOFF, INC.; *pg.* 936, *pg.* 1890
AGOREX - Chemicals - HUNTSMAN CORPORATION; *pg.* 1167, *pg.* 1758
AGPOWER - Financial Services - FEDERAL AGRICULTURAL MORTGAGE CORPORATION; *pg.* 751, *pg.* 399
AGPRO GRAIN - Grain Elevator - VITERRA INC.; *pg.* 834, *pg.* 1962
AGR - Professional Clipper for Animals - ANDIS COMPANY; *pg.* 498, *pg.* 1895
AGRADO - Health & Nutrition Product - NOVUS INTERNATIONAL, INC.; *pg.* 706, *pg.* 1001
AGRI-BUILDER - Metal Building System - BUTLER MANUFACTURING COMPANY; *pg.* 72, *pg.* 981
AGRI-COMP - Dairy Herd Management Computer Systems - BOUMATIC LLC; *pg.* 701, *pg.* 1865
AGRI POWER - Diesel Additive - POWER SERVICE PRODUCTS, INC.; *pg.* 983, *pg.* 1749
AGRI-SCREEN - Food Safety Product - NEOGEN CORPORATION; *pg.* 883, *pg.* 896
AGRI-SCREEN TICKET - Pesticide Residue Test - NEOGEN CORPORATION; *pg.* 883, *pg.* 896
AGRI-VIEW - Publication - MADISON NEWSPAPERS, INC.; *pg.* 1661, *pg.* 1866
AGRI-WEATHER - Weather Information - ACCUWEATHER, INC.; *pg.* 268, *pg.* 1587
AGRIPRO - Branded Seeds - MONSANTO COMPANY; *pg.* 1173, *pg.* 999
AGRO GEL S - Minerals - MINERALS TECHNOLOGIES INC.; *pg.* 1173, *pg.* 617
AGRO LIG - Minerals - MINERALS TECHNOLOGIES INC.; *pg.* 1173, *pg.* 617
AGROBLEN - Lawn & Garden Product - THE SCOTTS MIRACLE-GRO COMPANY; *pg.* 1799, *pg.* 1459
AGROCERES - Seeds - MONSANTO COMPANY; *pg.* 1173, *pg.* 999
AGROCOTE - Lawn & Garden Product - THE SCOTTS MIRACLE-GRO COMPANY; *pg.* 1799, *pg.* 1459
AGROLABS SPIRULINA - Healthful Nutritional Product - INTEGRATED BIOPHARMA, INC.; *pg.* 1546, *pg.* 1073
AGROMEN - Seeds - DOW AGROSCIENCES LLC; *pg.* 1156, *pg.* 684
AGROPUR SIGNATURE - Cheese - AGROPUR COOPERATIVE; *pg.* 836, *pg.* 1950
AGRYLIN - Pharmaceutical Product - IMPAX LABORATORIES, INC.; *pg.* 1544, *pg.* 101
AGS - Sport Product - FRANKLIN SPORTS, INC.; *pg.* 1834, *pg.* 847
THE AGS INBOUND PROCUREMENT PROGRAM - Multi-Benefit Inbound Shipping Program - ASSOCIATED GLOBAL SYSTEMS, INC.; *pg.* 1899, *pg.* 1184
AGSIL - Fertilizer - PQ CORPORATION; *pg.* 1178, *pg.* 1515
AGSILVER - Hand Sanitizer - ALIMED, INC.; *pg.* 1490, *pg.* 816
AGSORB - Agricultural Chemical Product - OIL-DRI CORPORATION OF AMERICA; *pg.* 1480, *pg.* 586
AGT - Braking System - GREENE, TWEED & CO.; *pg.* 1344, *pg.* 1544
AGTL - Braking System - GREENE, TWEED & CO.; *pg.* 1344, *pg.* 1544
AGTV - TV Children Programs Distribution & Production - AMERICAN GIRL LLC; *pg.* 949, *pg.* 1871
AGUARDIENTE CRISTAL - Liqueurs - SHAW ROSS INTERNATIONAL IMPORTERS; *pg.* 1970, *pg.* 449
AGVANTAGE - Agricultural Mortgage-backed Security - FEDERAL AGRICULTURAL MORTGAGE CORPORATION; *pg.* 751, *pg.* 399
AH - Burner - ECLIPSE INC.; *pg.* 1332, *pg.* 655
AH-1Z - Military Helicopter - BELL HELICOPTER TEXTRON, INC.; *pg.* 224, *pg.* 1693
AH CARAMEL! - Bakery Product - VACHON BAKERY INC.; *pg.* 907, *pg.* 1959
AH MCCAIN, YOU'VE DONE IT AGAIN! - Slogan - MCCAIN FOODS LIMITED; *pg.* 876, *pg.* 1915
AH-SO - Chinese Condiments - ALLIED OLD ENGLISH, INC.; *pg.* 836, *pg.* 1110
AHAM TOR - Manufacturer of Heat Sinks - WAKEFIELD-VETTE; *pg.* 119, *pg.* 1038
AHC - Machinery - HARDINGE INC.; *pg.* 1344, *pg.* 1157
AHCARAMEL! - Bakery Product - SAPUTO, INC.; *pg.* 893, *pg.* 1956
AHFS FRAMEWORK - Software - FIRST DATABANK, INC.; *pg.* 397, *pg.* 217
AHFSFIRSTFAX - Drug Reference Materials - AMERICAN SOCIETY OF HEALTH-SYSTEM PHARMACISTS; *pg.* 131, *pg.* 761
AHH, THE POWER OF CHEESE - Tagline - AMERICAN DAIRY ASSOCIATION; *pg.* 127, *pg.* 656
AHI - Eyewear - MAUI JIM, INC.; *pg.* 9, *pg.* 651
AHORA - Educational Materials - SCHOLASTIC INC.; *pg.* 1683, *pg.* 1288
A.I. SERIES - Software - ROCKWELL AUTOMATION, INC.; *pg.* 668, *pg.* 1880
AI THE ART INSTITUTES INTERNATIONAL - Art Schools - EDUCATION MANAGEMENT CORPORATION; *pg.* 601, *pg.* 1575
AIC - High-Speed Document Imaging Solutions for Physicians - ALLSCRIPTS HEALTHCARE SOLUTIONS, INC.; *pg.* 1492, *pg.* 563
AIC - Automotive Information Center - AUTOBYTEL INC.; *pg.* 1230, *pg.* 107
AIDA - Passenger Cruises & Tours - CARNIVAL CORPORATION; *pg.* 1902, *pg.* 441
AIDAN - Sunglasses - COACH, INC.; *pg.* 3, *pg.* 1214
AIDA'S NILE - Tile - ARTISTIC TILE INC.; *pg.* 914, *pg.* 1119
AIDELLS - Chicken Sausages - TYSON FOODS, INC.; *pg.* 902, *pg.* 35
AIGLIFE - Life Insurance - AMERICAN INTERNATIONAL GROUP, INC.; *pg.* 1190, *pg.* 1193
AIM - National Media Watchdog - ACCURACY IN MEDIA, INC.; *pg.* 125, *pg.* 761
AIM - Toothpaste - CHURCH & DWIGHT CO., INC.; *pg.* 1153, *pg.* 1063
AIM - Plastic Resins - THE DOW CHEMICAL COMPANY; *pg.* 1157, *pg.* 898
AIM - Investment Products - INVESCO LTD.; *pg.* 771, *pg.* 513
AIM - Bicycle Accessories - SPECIALIZED BICYCLE COMPONENTS, INC.; *pg.* 1711, *pg.* 152
AIM - Mutual Funds Statistics - STANDARD & POOR'S RATINGS SERVICES; *pg.* 805, *pg.* 1296
AIM - Drift Reduction - UNIVERSAL COOPERATIVES, INC.; *pg.* 1482, *pg.* 922
AIM RITE - Trouble Light - COLEMAN CABLE, INC.; *pg.* 1324, *pg.* 665
AIMPOINT - Systems Integration & Aeronautics - LOCKHEED MARTIN CORPORATION; *pg.* 229, *pg.* 762
AIMS - Game - FORTUNET, INC.; *pg.* 953, *pg.* 1024
AIMS - Real Estate Agent Lead Generation Solution - HOMEGAIN.COM, INC.; *pg.* 1256, *pg.* 83
AIQ SYSTEMS - Artificial Intelligence Based Stock Market Analysis Charting & Software - TRACK DATA CORPORATION; *pg.* 1284, *pg.* 1147
AIR - Protective Packaging System - PACTIV CORPORATION; *pg.* 1466, *pg.* 624
AIR-1000 - Inclinometer Angle Readout - JEWELL INSTRUMENTS, LLC; *pg.* 1418, *pg.* 1036
AIR BANSHEE - Bicycle Accessories - SPECIALIZED BICYCLE COMPONENTS, INC.; *pg.* 1711, *pg.* 152
AIR BLITZ - Hockey Table - SCHOOL-TECH, INC.; *pg.* 1844, *pg.* 866
AIR BOSS - Industrial Oil Mist & Air Pollution Cleaner - TRION, INC.; *pg.* 682, *pg.* 1390
AIR BRUTE - Cutting Room Equipment - EASTMAN MACHINE COMPANY; *pg.* 1331, *pg.* 1148
AIR CANADA CENTRE - Sports & Entertainment Complex - MAPLE LEAF SPORTS & ENTERTAINMENT LTD.; *pg.* 560, *pg.* 1940
AIR CARGO WORLD - Air Cargo Publication - JOC GROUP INC.; *pg.* 1654, *pg.* 1096
AIR CEL - Fishing Lines - 3M COMPANY; *pg.* 1142, *pg.* 956
AIR CELL - Microcellular Urethane Spring - AIR LIFT COMPANY; *pg.* 198, *pg.* 895
AIR CHANNEL - Floor System - ROBBINS, INC.; *pg.* 108, *pg.* 1425
AIR-CHANNEL STAR - Sport Surface - ROBBINS, INC.; *pg.* 108, *pg.* 1425
AIR CHIEF - Couplings - DIXON VALVE & COUPLING COMPANY; *pg.* 1045, *pg.* 766
AIR CLASSIC BW - Footwear - NIKE, INC.; *pg.* 1812, *pg.* 1492
AIR COBRA - Bicycle Accessories - SPECIALIZED BICYCLE COMPONENTS, INC.; *pg.* 1711, *pg.* 152
AIR COIL - Sleeper Mattress - FLEXSTEEL INDUSTRIES, INC.; *pg.* 925, *pg.* 707
AIR CORE SPRING - Designer Kit - COILCRAFT, INC.; *pg.* 1324, *pg.* 562
AIR CUT - Bicycle Accessories - SPECIALIZED BICYCLE COMPONENTS, INC.; *pg.* 1711, *pg.* 152
AIR DEFENSE - Dietary Supplement - NOW HEALTH GROUP, INC.; *pg.* 1576, *pg.* 557
AIR DIAMOND TURF - Athletic Shoe - NIKE, INC.; *pg.* 1812, *pg.* 1492
AIR-EASE - Heating & Cooling Product - LENNOX INTERNATIONAL INC.; *pg.* 1073, *pg.* 1736
AIR EXPRESS - Systems Integration & Aeronautics - LOCKHEED MARTIN CORPORATION; *pg.* 229, *pg.* 762
AIR FLEX - Fluid Handling System - GRACO, INC.; *pg.* 1342, *pg.* 935
AIR FLITETRAC - Wireless Product - HEMISPHERE GPS INC.; *pg.* 642, *pg.* 1903
AIR FLYING FLAGMAN - Wireless Product - HEMISPHERE GPS INC.; *pg.* 642, *pg.* 1903
AIR FORCE - Bicycle Pumps - SPECIALIZED BICYCLE COMPONENTS, INC.; *pg.* 1711, *pg.* 152
AIR FORCE I - Bicycle Pumps - SPECIALIZED BICYCLE COMPONENTS, INC.; *pg.* 1711, *pg.* 152
AIR FORCE II - Bicycle Pumps - SPECIALIZED BICYCLE COMPONENTS, INC.; *pg.* 1711, *pg.* 152
AIR FORCE III - Bicycle Pumps - SPECIALIZED BICYCLE COMPONENTS, INC.; *pg.* 1711, *pg.* 152
AIR-FRAME - Ceiling Systems - DAW TECHNOLOGIES, INC.; *pg.* 78, *pg.* 1756
AIR-GARD - Housewrap Air Barrier - BUILDING PRODUCTS OF CANADA CORP.; *pg.* 72, *pg.* 1951
AIR GUARD - Fluid Handling System - GRACO, INC.; *pg.* 1342, *pg.* 935
AIR HANDLER - Air Filtration Equipment - W.W. GRAINGER, INC.; *pg.* 1390, *pg.* 625
AIR HEAD - Bicycle Accessories - SPECIALIZED BICYCLE COMPONENTS, INC.; *pg.* 1711, *pg.* 152
AIR HOCKEY - Bowling Equipment - BRUNSWICK BOWLING & BILLIARDS CORP.; *pg.* 1828, *pg.* 622
AIR HOCKEY - Toy - WHAM-O, INC.; *pg.* 969, *pg.* 308
AIR HOGS - Toy - SPIN MASTER LTD.; *pg.* 967, *pg.* 1943
AIR-INDIA - Airline - AIR INDIA; *pg.* 1897, *pg.* 1188
AIR INTELLIFLOW - Wireless Product - HEMISPHERE GPS INC.; *pg.* 642, *pg.* 1903
AIR INTELLIGATE - Wireless Product - HEMISPHERE GPS INC.; *pg.* 642, *pg.* 1903
AIR JET QUENCH - Thermal Processing Equipment - SURFACE COMBUSTION, INC.; *pg.* 1077, *pg.* 1462
AIR JORDAN - Footwear - NIKE, INC.; *pg.* 1812, *pg.* 1492
AIR JORDAN XX3 - Footwear - NIKE, INC.; *pg.* 1812, *pg.* 1492
AIR KING - Couplings - DIXON VALVE & COUPLING COMPANY; *pg.* 1045, *pg.* 766
AIR KING - Fluid Handling System - GRACO, INC.; *pg.* 1342, *pg.* 935
AIR-KRAFT - Protective Packaging Material - PACTIV

CORPORATION; *pg.* 1466, *pg.* 624
AIR LEAF - Suspension - PETERBILT MOTORS CO.; *pg.* 188, *pg.* 1691
AIR-LEC - Automatic Door Operating Equipment & Accessories - AIR-LEC INDUSTRIES LLC; *pg.* 1041, *pg.* 1864
AIR LEGEND - Footwear - NIKE, INC.; *pg.* 1812, *pg.* 1492
AIR LIFT 1000 - Air Spring Kit - AIR LIFT COMPANY; *pg.* 198, *pg.* 895
AIR LITESTAR II - Wireless Product - HEMISPHERE GPS INC.; *pg.* 642, *pg.* 1903
AIR LOCK - Bicycle Tire - SPECIALIZED BICYCLE COMPONENTS, INC.; *pg.* 1711, *pg.* 152
AIR M3 - Wireless Product - HEMISPHERE GPS INC.; *pg.* 642, *pg.* 1903
AIR MAPSTAR - Wireless Product - HEMISPHERE GPS INC.; *pg.* 642, *pg.* 1903
AIR MASTER - Compressor & Pump - CUSTOM ACCESSORIES INC.; *pg.* 203, *pg.* 653
AIR-MATE - Air Respirator - 3M COMPANY; *pg.* 1142, *pg.* 956
AIR MAX - Footwear - NIKE, INC.; *pg.* 1812, *pg.* 1492
AIR MAX 360 - Footwear - NIKE, INC.; *pg.* 1812, *pg.* 1492
AIR MAX 90 - Footwear - NIKE, INC.; *pg.* 1812, *pg.* 1492
AIR MAX 97 - Footwear - NIKE, INC.; *pg.* 1812, *pg.* 1492
AIR MAX MVP - Footwear - NIKE, INC.; *pg.* 1812, *pg.* 1492
AIR MAX TURBULENCE - Footwear - NIKE, INC.; *pg.* 1812, *pg.* 1492
AIR MOGAN MID - Footwear - NIKE, INC.; *pg.* 1812, *pg.* 1492
AIR NAUTIQUE - Wakeboard Boat - CORRECT CRAFT, INC.; *pg.* 1706, *pg.* 452
AIR ONE RADIO - Christian Music Station - EDUCATIONAL MEDIA FOUNDATION; *pg.* 284, *pg.* 194
AIR-OPAQUE - Paint - BADGER AIR BRUSH COMPANY; *pg.* 359, *pg.* 612
AIR-PAQ - Packaging Product - PACTIV CORPORATION; *pg.* 1466, *pg.* 624
AIR PEGASUS - Footwear - NIKE, INC.; *pg.* 1812, *pg.* 1492
AIR PLAS - Chemical Product - WESTROCK COMPANY; *pg.* 1472, *pg.* 1805
AIR POWER - Hose - HBD INDUSTRIES, INC.; *pg.* 207, *pg.* 1449
AIR PRODUCTS - Polymers - AIR PRODUCTS AND CHEMICALS, INC.; *pg.* 1145, *pg.* 1513
AIR R100 - Wireless Product - HEMISPHERE GPS INC.; *pg.* 642, *pg.* 1903
AIR-RANGEMENT - Balloons - 1-800-FLOWERS.COM, INC.; *pg.* 1758, *pg.* 1151
AIR RANGER - Hunting Knives - GERBER LEGENDARY BLADES; *pg.* 1834, *pg.* 1503
AIR RELIEF - Compressor - GARDNER DENVER, INC.; *pg.* 1338, *pg.* 1592
AIR RIFT - Footwear - NIKE, INC.; *pg.* 1812, *pg.* 1492
AIR-SAVERS - Fan Freshener Refills - SURCO PRODUCTS, INC.; *pg.* 336, *pg.* 1581
AIR-SCENT - Fan Air Freshener Systems - SURCO PRODUCTS, INC.; *pg.* 336, *pg.* 1581
AIR SCOOP - Cleaning Product - HILLYARD, INC.; *pg.* 331, *pg.* 990
AIR SCOOPS - Air Separator - TACO INCORPORATED; *pg.* 1077, *pg.* 1601
AIR-SHOT - Fluid Handling System - GRACO, INC.; *pg.* 1342, *pg.* 935
AIR SPEED - Bicycle Accessories - SPECIALIZED BICYCLE COMPONENTS, INC.; *pg.* 1711, *pg.* 152
AIR STAB - Footwear - NIKE, INC.; *pg.* 1812, *pg.* 1492
AIR-STAR - Vacuum Pump - BOUMATIC LLC; *pg.* 701, *pg.* 1865
AIR STEP - Shoes - CALERES, INC.; *pg.* 1805, *pg.* 993
AIR STRUCTURE TRIAX - Footwear - NIKE, INC.; *pg.* 1812, *pg.* 1492
AIR SWEEP - Deaerator - PETERBILT MOTORS CO.; *pg.* 188, *pg.* 1691
AIR TASER - Non-Lethal Energy Weapons - TASER INTERNATIONAL, INC.; *pg.* 677, *pg.* 24
AIR TECH - Sponge PVC Football - FRANKLIN SPORTS, INC.; *pg.* 1834, *pg.* 847
AIR TECHNIQUE - X-Ray - AIR TECHNIQUES, INC.; *pg.* 1487, *pg.* 1178
AIR-TEX - Paint - BADGER AIR BRUSH COMPANY; *pg.* 359, *pg.* 612
AIR TIEMPO RIVAL - Footwear - NIKE, INC.; *pg.* 1812, *pg.* 1492
AIR TRAC - Suspension - PETERBILT MOTORS CO.; *pg.* 188, *pg.* 1691
AIR UNLIMITED - Footwear - NIKE, INC.; *pg.* 1812, *pg.* 1492
AIR VOS - Footwear - NIKE, INC.; *pg.* 1812, *pg.* 1492
AIR WAVE - Bicycle Helmets - SPECIALIZED BICYCLE COMPONENTS, INC.; *pg.* 1711, *pg.* 152
AIR WAVE BLOB - Bicycle Accessories - SPECIALIZED BICYCLE COMPONENTS, INC.; *pg.* 1711, *pg.* 152
AIR WAVE MEGA - Bicycle Accessories - SPECIALIZED BICYCLE COMPONENTS, INC.; *pg.* 1711, *pg.* 152
AIR WICK - Color Changing Candle - RECKITT BENCKISER INC.; *pg.* 1136, *pg.* 1105
AIR ZOOM - Footwear - NIKE, INC.; *pg.* 1812, *pg.* 1492
AIR ZOOM FLIGHT FIVE - Footwear - NIKE, INC.; *pg.* 1812, *pg.* 1492
AIR ZOOM MOIRE - Footwear - NIKE, INC.; *pg.* 1812, *pg.* 1492
AIR ZOOM SUPER BAD - Footwear - NIKE, INC.; *pg.* 1812, *pg.* 1492
AIR ZOOM SUPER SPEED - Footwear - NIKE, INC.; *pg.* 1812, *pg.* 1492
AIRBEAM - Software - MOTOROLA ENTERPRISE MOBILITY; *pg.* 441, *pg.* 1167
AIRBOND - Chemical Product - AIR PRODUCTS AND CHEMICALS, INC.; *pg.* 1145, *pg.* 1513
AIRBORNE - Immune System Support Supplement - RECKITT BENCKISER INC.; *pg.* 1136, *pg.* 1105
AIRBORNE - Immune Support Products - SCHIFF NUTRITION INTERNATIONAL, INC.; *pg.* 1592, *pg.* 1760
AIRCAP - High-Performance Air Cellular Cushioning - SEALED AIR CORPORATION; *pg.* 1468, *pg.* 1058
AIRCARD EXPRESSCARDS - Wireless Card - SIERRA WIRELESS INCORPORATED; *pg.* 673, *pg.* 1909
AIRCHARGER - Performance Intake Kit - K&N ENGINEERING INC.; *pg.* 210, *pg.* 194
AIRCLEAN - Technical Furniture - IAC INDUSTRIES, INC.; *pg.* 929, *pg.* 48
AIRCON - Electrically Heated Laminated Panels - PPG INDUSTRIES, INC.; *pg.* 1445, *pg.* 1579
AIRCOPLANAR - Wafer Probing System - CASCADE MICROTECH, INC.; *pg.* 1405, *pg.* 1492
AIRCRAFT - Hand Dryer - BOBRICK WASHROOM EQUIPMENT, INC.; *pg.* 1043, *pg.* 166
AIRCUSHION - Wind & Rain Deflectors - MACNEIL AUTOMOTIVE PRODUCTS, LTD.; *pg.* 211, *pg.* 559
AIRDEFENSE - Pest Elimination System - ECOLAB INC.; *pg.* 329, *pg.* 960
AIRDENT II - Dental Air Abrasion Machine - AIR TECHNIQUES, INC.; *pg.* 1487, *pg.* 1178
AIRDEX - Stretchable Spandex Backs - WELLS LAMONT CORPORATION; *pg.* 15, *pg.* 638
AIRE - Apparel - HANESBRANDS INC.; *pg.* 26, *pg.* 1394
AIRE-FLO - Heating & Cooling Product - LENNOX INTERNATIONAL INC.; *pg.* 1073, *pg.* 1736
AIRE SERVE HEATING & AIR CONDITIONING - HVAC Businesses - THE DWYER GROUP, INC.; *pg.* 79, *pg.* 1748
AIREASE - Heating & Cooling Systems - LENNOX INTERNATIONAL INC.; *pg.* 1073, *pg.* 1736
AIREDALE - Furniture - ASHLEY FURNITURE INDUSTRIES, INC.; *pg.* 914, *pg.* 1852
AIREPLEX - Fabric - BROOKS SPORTS INC.; *pg.* 1805, *pg.* 1818
AIRES - Patient Handling Equipment - STRYKER CORPORATION; *pg.* 1598, *pg.* 894
AIRES - Airline Passenger Service System - TRAVELPORT LIMITED; *pg.* 1925, *pg.* 521
AIRESEARCH - Products for Aircraft, Missile & Commercial Applications - HONEYWELL AEROSPACE; *pg.* 228, *pg.* 16
AIREWEAVE - Furniture - HERMAN MILLER, INC.; *pg.* 926, *pg.* 913
AIREX - Gel - ALIMED, INC.; *pg.* 1490, *pg.* 816
AIREX - Mat - HUGGER MUGGER YOGA PRODUCTS LLC; *pg.* 1836, *pg.* 1758
AIREZE - Odor Eliminator - THEOCHEM LABORATORIES, INC.; *pg.* 1184, *pg.* 476
AIRFAREWATCHDOG.COM - Airfare Deals Aggregator - SMARTER TRAVEL MEDIA LLC; *pg.* 1687, *pg.* 801
AIRFLEX - Emulsions - AIR PRODUCTS AND CHEMICALS, INC.; *pg.* 1145, *pg.* 1513
AIRFLEX - Clutch & Brake System - EATON CORPORATION; *pg.* 1331, *pg.* 1429
AIRFLEX - Hose - HBD INDUSTRIES, INC.; *pg.* 207, *pg.* 1449
AIRFLEXTRA - Cleaning Product - HILLYARD, INC.; *pg.* 331, *pg.* 990
AIRFLO - Wheelchair Cushions - INVACARE CORPORATION; *pg.* 1546, *pg.* 1451
AIRFLO - Burner - MAXON CORPORATION; *pg.* 1359, *pg.* 695
AIRFLOW SYSTEM - Material Construction - TEMPUR SEALY INTERNATIONAL, INC.; *pg.* 944, *pg.* 731
AIRFORCE - Integrated Circuits & Software - BROADCOM CORPORATION; *pg.* 364, *pg.* 108
AIRFORCE ONE - Wireless Technology - BROADCOM CORPORATION; *pg.* 364, *pg.* 108
AIRFORCE XPRESS - Wireless Technology - BROADCOM CORPORATION; *pg.* 364, *pg.* 108
AIRFUGE - Testing Instrument System - BECKMAN COULTER, INC.; *pg.* 1402, *pg.* 48
AIRGARD - Fume Scrubber - MKS INSTRUMENTS, INC.; *pg.* 1362, *pg.* 781
AIRGARD - Air Flow Monitor - TSI INCORPORATED; *pg.* 1432, *pg.* 965
AIRGARD LAB HOOD MONITOR - Hood Monitor - TSI INCORPORATED; *pg.* 1432, *pg.* 965
AIRGLIDE - Gun Case - PLANO MOLDING COMPANY; *pg.* 1887, *pg.* 652
AIRGLIDE - Drive Axle - TUTHILL CORPORATION; *pg.* 1385, *pg.* 561
AIRGRIT - Marking Unit - MATTHEWS INTERNATIONAL CORPORATION; *pg.* 1662, *pg.* 1578
AIRGUARD - Hand Dryer - BOBRICK WASHROOM EQUIPMENT, INC.; *pg.* 1043, *pg.* 166
AIRHAWK - Air Mask - MINE SAFETY APPLIANCES COMPANY; *pg.* 1361, *pg.* 1525
AIRHAWK - End Cutter - THE WOLF MACHINE CO.; *pg.* 1389, *pg.* 1427
AIRHEAD - Bicycle Accessories - SPECIALIZED BICYCLE COMPONENTS, INC.; *pg.* 1711, *pg.* 152
AIRIA - Furniture - HERMAN MILLER, INC.; *pg.* 926, *pg.* 913
AIRJECTOR - Heat & Smoke Units - SWARTWOUT DIVISION; *pg.* 114, *pg.* 978
AIRLESS - Fluid Handling System - GRACO, INC.; *pg.* 1342, *pg.* 935
AIRLESS SPRAY CENTER - Fluid Handling System - GRACO, INC.; *pg.* 1342, *pg.* 935
AIRLIFT - Daypack - JANSPORT; *pg.* 1837, *pg.* 38
AIRLINK - Antenna - BALL CORPORATION; *pg.* 1452, *pg.* 311
AIRLINK - Mobile Wireless Data - SIERRA WIRELESS INCORPORATED; *pg.* 673, *pg.* 1909
AIRLINK HELIX - Routing Device - SIERRA WIRELESS INCORPORATED; *pg.* 673, *pg.* 1909
AIRLINK PINPOINT X - Mobile Communications Platform - SIERRA WIRELESS INCORPORATED; *pg.* 673, *pg.* 1909
AIRLINK PINPOINT XT - Tracking Device - SIERRA WIRELESS INCORPORATED; *pg.* 673, *pg.* 1909
AIRLINK RAVEN X - Modem - SIERRA WIRELESS INCORPORATED; *pg.* 673, *pg.* 1909
AIRLITE - Seat Cushion - THE ROHO GROUP; *pg.* 1591, *pg.* 556
AIRLOCK - Field Repair Manual - ION GEOPHYSICAL CORPORATION; *pg.* 1350, *pg.* 1708
AIRLOCK - Eyewear - MARCHON EYEWEAR, INC.; *pg.* 1421, *pg.* 1180
AIRLOCK - Protective Clothing - W.L. GORE & ASSOCIATES, INC.; *pg.* 122, *pg.* 388
AIRLUX - Home Air Pollutants Purifier - AERUS LLC; *pg.* 51, *pg.* 1673
AIRMAC - Wireless Hardware/Software Solution - APPLE INC.; *pg.* 350, *pg.* 73
AIRMAX VS - Connector - AMPHENOL CORPORATION; *pg.* 616, *pg.* 381
AIRMAXXIS - Mattress - KINETIC CONCEPTS, INC.; *pg.* 1553, *pg.* 1741
AIRMIST - Tables - THE CINCINNATI GILBERT MACHINE TOOL COMPANY, L.L.C.; *pg.* 1323, *pg.* 1411
AIRMOUNT - Air Spring - FIRESTONE INDUSTRIAL PRODUCTS DIVISION; *pg.* 1882, *pg.* 686
AIROCOOL - Burner - NAO, INC.; *pg.* 1074, *pg.* 1567
AIRONET - Software - CISCO SYSTEMS, INC.; *pg.* 372, *pg.* 240
AIROUT - Chemicals - HUNTSMAN CORPORATION; *pg.* 1167, *pg.* 1758
AIROVENT - Burner - NAO, INC.; *pg.* 1074, *pg.* 1567
AIROX - Transmitter - MINE SAFETY APPLIANCES COMPANY; *pg.* 1361, *pg.* 1525
AIRPAL - Patient Air Lift - KINETIC CONCEPTS, INC.; *pg.* 1553, *pg.* 1741

AIRPLAY - Streaming Service - APPLE INC.; *pg.* 350, *pg.* 73
AIRPORT - Wireless Hardware/Software Solution - APPLE INC.; *pg.* 350, *pg.* 73
AIRPORT ACCESS - Internet Services - IPASS, INC.; *pg.* 1259, *pg.* 193
AIRPORT EXPRESS - Wireless Hardware - APPLE INC.; *pg.* 350, *pg.* 73
AIRPORT EXTREME - Wireless Hardware - APPLE INC.; *pg.* 350, *pg.* 73
AIRPORTMONITOR - Software - PASSUR AEROSPACE, INC.; *pg.* 233, *pg.* 376
AIRPORTS - Footwear - VANS, INC.; *pg.* 1821, *pg.* 76
AIRPOT - Air Actuator - DEL-TRON PRECISION, INC.; *pg.* 1328, *pg.* 337
AIRPOUCH - Void Fill System - AUTOMATED PACKAGING SYSTEMS INC.; *pg.* 1452, *pg.* 1474
AIRPRO - Hand Dryer - BOBRICK WASHROOM EQUIPMENT, INC.; *pg.* 1043, *pg.* 166
AIRRIDE - Air Spring - FIRESTONE INDUSTRIAL PRODUCTS DIVISION; *pg.* 1882, *pg.* 686
AIRSHIELD - Patented Air Seal Design Used in Spindles - SETCO SALES COMPANY; *pg.* 1061, *pg.* 1426
AIRSHOW - Cabin Electronic System - ROCKWELL COLLINS, INC.; *pg.* 234, *pg.* 702
AIRSOFT - Medical Equipment - CONMED CORPORATION; *pg.* 1517, *pg.* 1347
AIRSPACE - Packaging System - POLYAIR INTER PACK INC.; *pg.* 1467, *pg.* 1941
AIRSPANACCESS - Wireless Network Product - AIRSPAN NETWORKS INC.; *pg.* 346, *pg.* 410
AIRSPEED TECHNOLOGY - Menu Driven Control System - TURBOCHEF TECHNOLOGIES, INC.; *pg.* 902, *pg.* 1670
AIRSPERSE - Adhesive - H.B. FULLER COMPANY; *pg.* 1165, *pg.* 961
AIRSTAR - Air Compressor - AIR TECHNIQUES, INC.; *pg.* 1487, *pg.* 1178
AIRSTAR - Data Sheet - AMERICAN FELT & FILTER COMPANY; *pg.* 1312, *pg.* 1184
AIRSTAR - Wireless Product - HEMISPHERE GPS INC.; *pg.* 642, *pg.* 1903
AIRSTREAM - Recreation Vehicle - THOR INDUSTRIES, INC.; *pg.* 1711, *pg.* 1456
AIRSTREAM MOTOR HOMES & TRAVEL TRAILERS - Trailer - AIRSTREAM, INC.; *pg.* 163, *pg.* 1456
AIRSTROKE - Air Spring - FIRESTONE INDUSTRIAL PRODUCTS DIVISION; *pg.* 1882, *pg.* 686
AIRTHOTIC Footwear - LACROSSE FOOTWEAR, INC.; *pg.* 1811, *pg.* 1503
AIRTOUCH - Office Furniture - STEELCASE INC.; *pg.* 475, *pg.* 889
AIRTRACK - Golf Equipment - ACUSHNET COMPANY; *pg.* 1824, *pg.* 818
AIRTROL - Plaster - USG CORPORATION; *pg.* 118, *pg.* 594
AIRTUNES - Application Program - APPLE INC.; *pg.* 350, *pg.* 73
AIRVANTAGE - All-Weather Fabric - W.L. GORE & ASSOCIATES, INC.; *pg.* 122, *pg.* 388
AIRWALK - Bag - DATREK GOLF; *pg.* 1832, *pg.* 1801
AIRWAVE - Software - IDEALAB, INC.; *pg.* 1258, *pg.* 180
AIRWAVE - Apparel - OAKLEY, INC.; *pg.* 1840, *pg.* 86
AIRWAVES - Gum - WM. WRIGLEY JR. COMPANY; *pg.* 1863, *pg.* 596
AIRWEAR - Balloon - CONTINENTAL AMERICAN CORP.; *pg.* 1880, *pg.* 723
AIRWEIGHS - Landing System - CRANE CO.; *pg.* 227, *pg.* 373
AIRWEIGHT - Golf Equipment - ACUSHNET COMPANY; *pg.* 1824, *pg.* 818
AIS CAMERA - Video Vehicle Detection System - IMAGE SENSING SYSTEMS, INC.; *pg.* 412, *pg.* 961
AIT - Inspection System - KLA-TENCOR CORPORATION; *pg.* 1353, *pg.* 146
AIT UV - Inspection System - KLA-TENCOR CORPORATION; *pg.* 1353, *pg.* 146
AIT XUV - Inspection System - KLA-TENCOR CORPORATION; *pg.* 1353, *pg.* 146
AJ - Musical Instrument - GIBSON GUITAR CORP.; *pg.* 550, *pg.* 1650
AJAX - Professional Dry Cleaning Machines - ALLIANCE LAUNDRY HOLDINGS LLC; *pg.* 51, *pg.* 1890
AJAX - Fabric Care Product - COLGATE-PALMOLIVE COMPANY; *pg.* 504, *pg.* 1215
AJAX FLEXIBLE COUPLINGS - Gear Type Couplings and Spindle Couplings - RENOLD, INC.; *pg.* 1371, *pg.* 1351
AJAX PRESS - Forging Product - SUPERIOR DIE SET CORP.; *pg.* 1379, *pg.* 1885
AJAX SHAKER - Shaker Gearbox for Vibratory Drives - RENOLD, INC.; *pg.* 1371, *pg.* 1351
AJS - Building Products - BOISE CASCADE HOLDINGS, L.L.C.; *pg.* 1453, *pg.* 546
AK-CON - Pharmaceutical Product - AKORN, INC.; *pg.* 1488, *pg.* 622
AK-DILATE - Pharmaceutical Product - AKORN, INC.; *pg.* 1488, *pg.* 622
AK-FLUOR - Ophthalmic Pharmaceutical Product - AKORN, INC.; *pg.* 1488, *pg.* 622
AK FORMTUBE - Steel Product - AK STEEL HOLDING CORPORATION; *pg.* 1311, *pg.* 1479
AK-PENTOLATE - Pharmaceutical Product - AKORN, INC.; *pg.* 1488, *pg.* 622
AK-POLYBOC - Pharmaceutical Product - AKORN, INC.; *pg.* 1488, *pg.* 622
AK SPECIALTY VEHICLES - Mobile MRI Trailers - OSHKOSH SPECIALTY VEHICLES; *pg.* 1918, *pg.* 561
AK-SPECTRA - Steel Product - AK STEEL HOLDING CORPORATION; *pg.* 1311, *pg.* 1479
AK-TOB - Pharmaceutical Product - AKORN, INC.; *pg.* 1488, *pg.* 622
AKAMAI - Eyewear - MAUI JIM, INC.; *pg.* 9, *pg.* 651
AKBAR - Garage Door - WAYNE-DALTON CORP.; *pg.* 120, *pg.* 1465
AKERS - Furniture - AMISCO INDUSTRIES LTD.; *pg.* 913, *pg.* 1958
AKERSTROMS - Wireless Control - CONTROL CHIEF HOLDINGS, INC.; *pg.* 630, *pg.* 1518
AKG - Microphones & Headphones - HARMAN INTERNATIONAL INDUSTRIES, INCORPORATED; *pg.* 641, *pg.* 374
AKIRA - Tables - STEELCASE INC.; *pg.* 475, *pg.* 889
AKONI - Eyewear - MAUI JIM, INC.; *pg.* 9, *pg.* 651
AKONUA GUITAR - Knife - BUCK KNIVES, INC.; *pg.* 1828, *pg.* 550
AKOS - Staffing Services - CROSS COUNTRY HEALTHCARE, INC.; *pg.* 1520, *pg.* 411
AKREOS - Acrylic Intraocular Lenses - BAUSCH & LOMB INCORPORATED; *pg.* 1401, *pg.* 1045
AKRO-MILS - Plastic Product - MYERS INDUSTRIES, INC.; *pg.* 1887, *pg.* 1402
AKROBINS - Plastic Bins - MYERS INDUSTRIES, INC.; *pg.* 1887, *pg.* 1402
AKROCLEN - Janitorial Cart - MEDLINE INDUSTRIES, INC.; *pg.* 1562, *pg.* 635
AKROS - Tile - ARTISTIC TILE INC.; *pg.* 914, *pg.* 1119
AKROS - Healthcare Product - GF HEALTH PRODUCTS, INC.; *pg.* 1535, *pg.* 508
AKROSAIR - Medical Product - GF HEALTH PRODUCTS, INC.; *pg.* 1535, *pg.* 508
AKS - Integrated Circuit - ATMEL CORPORATION; *pg.* 621, *pg.* 238
AKSV - Mobile MRI Trailers - OSHKOSH SPECIALTY VEHICLES; *pg.* 1918, *pg.* 561
AKTEN - Ophthalmic Pharmaceutical Product - AKORN, INC.; *pg.* 1488, *pg.* 622
AKTUELL - Educational Materials - SCHOLASTIC INC.; *pg.* 1683, *pg.* 1288
AKTULU - Carpet - WOVEN LEGENDS INC.; *pg.* 947, *pg.* 1572
AKWA TEARS - Pharmaceutical Product - AKORN, INC.; *pg.* 1488, *pg.* 622
AL-COTE - Dental Product - DENTSPLY INTERNATIONAL INC.; *pg.* 1522, *pg.* 1596
AL-MAX - Pressed & Monolithic Refractory - RESCO PRODUCTS, INC.; *pg.* 107, *pg.* 1581
AL PLUS - Spray Guns - GRACO, INC.; *pg.* 1342, *pg.* 935
AL-SHIELD - Monolithic Refractory Product - PLIBRICO CO. LLC; *pg.* 104, *pg.* 587
ALA TECHSOURCE - Publication - AMERICAN LIBRARY ASSOCIATION; *pg.* 1615, *pg.* 564
ALABANZA - Web Hosting Services - NAVISITE, INC.; *pg.* 1269, *pg.* 782
ALABASTER - Lighting Product - QUOIZEL INC.; *pg.* 1304, *pg.* 1616
ALABASTRO - Ceramic, Glass, Stone Tiles & Slabs - WALKER & ZANGER, INC.; *pg.* 119, *pg.* 281
ALACRA BOOK - Business Information Retrieval Service - ALACRA, INC.; *pg.* 346, *pg.* 1188
ALACRA COMPLIANCE - Business Information Service - ALACRA, INC.; *pg.* 346, *pg.* 1188
ALACRA CONCORDANCE - Business Information Service - ALACRA, INC.; *pg.* 346, *pg.* 1188
ALACRA CONNECTIONS - Business Information Service - ALACRA, INC.; *pg.* 346, *pg.* 1188
ALACRA CORPORATE CONNECTIONS - Business Information Service - ALACRA, INC.; *pg.* 346, *pg.* 1188
ALACRA CURRENT AWARENESS - Business Information Service - ALACRA, INC.; *pg.* 346, *pg.* 1188
ALACRA PCAN - Business Information Service - ALACRA, INC.; *pg.* 346, *pg.* 1188
ALACRA PORTALS - Business Information Service - ALACRA, INC.; *pg.* 346, *pg.* 1188
ALACRA PREMIUM - Business Information Service - ALACRA, INC.; *pg.* 346, *pg.* 1188
ALACRA PULSE - Business Information Service - ALACRA, INC.; *pg.* 346, *pg.* 1188
ALADDIN - Carpet - MOHAWK INDUSTRIES, INC.; *pg.* 935, *pg.* 527
ALADDIN PAPERBACKS - Children's Paperback Publisher - SIMON & SCHUSTER, INC.; *pg.* 1687, *pg.* 1292
ALADDIO - Furniture - ASHLEY FURNITURE INDUSTRIES, INC.; *pg.* 914, *pg.* 1852
ALADIN - Dive Computers - JOHNSON OUTDOORS INC.; *pg.* 1837, *pg.* 1888
ALAGA HOT SAUCE - Hot Sauce Blended With Cane & Corn Syrups - WHITFIELD FOODS, INC.; *pg.* 910, *pg.* 8
ALAGA LIGHT CORN SYRUP - Low Sodium All-Natural Corn Syrups - WHITFIELD FOODS, INC.; *pg.* 910, *pg.* 8
ALAGA ORIGINAL SYRUP - Blended Corn & Cane Syrups - WHITFIELD FOODS, INC.; *pg.* 910, *pg.* 8
ALAGA SPICED APPLE CIDER - Apple Cider Blended With Cane Syrup - WHITFIELD FOODS, INC.; *pg.* 910, *pg.* 8
ALAM - Systems Integration & Aeronautics - LOCKHEED MARTIN CORPORATION; *pg.* 229, *pg.* 762
ALAMAC - Fatty Amine Acetates - HENKEL CORPORATION; *pg.* 1165, *pg.* 1535
ALAMARBLUE - Molecular Probe Product - THERMO FISHER SCIENTIFIC INC.; *pg.* 1602, *pg.* 61
ALAMCO SMC - Front-End Loader - ALAMO GROUP INC.; *pg.* 1311, *pg.* 1745
ALAMGIR - Rug - COURISTAN INC.; *pg.* 921, *pg.* 1067
ALAMINE - Fatty Amines - HENKEL CORPORATION; *pg.* 1165, *pg.* 1535
ALAMO - Car Rental - ALAMO RENT-A-CAR, LLC; *pg.* 1897, *pg.* 1489
ALAMO - Fabric - NEMSCHOFF, INC.; *pg.* 936, *pg.* 1890
ALAMO INDUSTRIAL - Track Mounted Mowers - ALAMO GROUP INC.; *pg.* 1311, *pg.* 1745
ALAMO INDUSTRIAL MAVERICK - Boom Movers - ALAMO GROUP INC.; *pg.* 1311, *pg.* 1745
ALAN SCOTT - Character - DC COMICS, INC.; *pg.* 1633, *pg.* 1221
ALANA - Clothing - ABERCROMBIE & FITCH CO.; *pg.* 37, *pg.* 1466
ALANA - Eyewear - MAUI JIM, INC.; *pg.* 9, *pg.* 651
ALANAP - Water-Soluble Herbicide - CHEMTURA CORPORATION; *pg.* 1152, *pg.* 355
ALANTRO - Cable Modems & Wireless Computer Products - TEXAS INSTRUMENTS INCORPORATED; *pg.* 679, *pg.* 1688
ALARIS - Health Care Automation Technology - CARDINAL HEALTH, INC.; *pg.* 1512, *pg.* 1448
ALARM - Hose - HBD INDUSTRIES, INC.; *pg.* 207, *pg.* 1449
ALARM - Software - MICROSTRATEGY, INC.; *pg.* 1266, *pg.* 1809
ALARMPOINT - Software - BMC SOFTWARE, INC.; *pg.* 362, *pg.* 1701
ALASKA - Airlines - ALASKA AIRLINES, INC.; *pg.* 1897, *pg.* 1830
ALASKAN GUIDE - Rainwear - CABELA'S INCORPORATED; *pg.* 535, *pg.* 1019
ALASKAN OUTFITTER - Fire Starters & Lighters - CABELA'S INCORPORATED; *pg.* 535, *pg.* 1019
ALAVERT - Allergy Relief - PFIZER INC.; *pg.* 1581, *pg.* 1278
ALAYA - Fabric - NEMSCHOFF, INC.; *pg.* 936, *pg.* 1890
ALAZAR WINERY - Beverage - PHOENIX VINTNERS, LLC; *pg.* 1968, *pg.* 182
ALBA BOTANICA - Personal Care Products - THE HAIN CELESTIAL GROUP, INC.; *pg.* 860, *pg.* 1172
ALBA DAIRY - Dairy Beverage Products - THE HAIN CELESTIAL GROUP, INC.; *pg.* 860, *pg.* 1172
ALBANY - Automotive Brake Pads & Shoes - AUTOZONE, INC.; *pg.* 200, *pg.* 1641
ALBANY - Furniture - FLEXSTEEL INDUSTRIES, INC.; *pg.* 925, *pg.* 707
ALBANY TIMES UNION - Newspaper - THE HEARST CORPORATION; *pg.* 1649, *pg.* 1239

ALBERGER - Salt - CARGILL, INC.; *pg.* 845, *pg.* 965
ALBERGER - Salt - CARGILL LIMITED; *pg.* 1475, *pg.* 1914
ALBEROX - High Alumina Ceramic Components - MORGAN ADVANCED MATERIALS; *pg.* 1363, *pg.* 835
ALBERS - Food Product - NESTLE USA, INC.; *pg.* 883, *pg.* 96
ALBERT - Sunglasses - COACH, INC.; *pg.* 3, *pg.* 1214
ALBERT - Furniture - ETHAN ALLEN INTERIORS INC.; *pg.* 924, *pg.* 343
ALBERTA - Beer - BIG ROCK BREWERY INCOME TRUST; *pg.* 239, *pg.* 1902
ALBERTSONS - Store - SUPERVALU, INC.; *pg.* 1035, *pg.* 924
ALBI CLAD - Intumescent Coating - STANCHEM, INC.; *pg.* 1449, *pg.* 345
ALBI DRICLAD - Fireproofing System - STANCHEM, INC.; *pg.* 1449, *pg.* 345
ALBION - Jewelry - YURMAN DESIGN, INC.; *pg.* 15, *pg.* 1316
ALBLEND - Chemical Product - ALBEMARLE CORPORATION; *pg.* 1146, *pg.* 741
ALBOGRAFT - Medical Device - LEMAITRE VASCULAR, INC.; *pg.* 1555, *pg.* 805
ALBRAZE - Heat Transfer Products - MODINE MANUFACTURING COMPANY; *pg.* 1074, *pg.* 1888
ALBROM - Chemical Product - ALBEMARLE CORPORATION; *pg.* 1146, *pg.* 741
ALBUFERON - Biopharmaceutical Product - GLAXOSMITHKLINE; *pg.* 1537, *pg.* 776
ALBUMAX - Biomolecule Product - THERMO FISHER SCIENTIFIC INC.; *pg.* 1602, *pg.* 61
ALBUMINAR - Albumin (Human) U.S.P. 5% - CSL BEHRING LLC; *pg.* 1520, *pg.* 1543
ALBUQUERQUE - Footwear - EASTLAND SHOE CORPORATION; *pg.* 1808, *pg.* 750
THE ALBUQUERQUE TRIBUNE - Newspaper - THE E.W. SCRIPPS COMPANY; *pg.* 1639, *pg.* 1412
ALCARE - Antiseptic Handrub - STERIS CORPORATION; *pg.* 1597, *pg.* 1464
ALCARE PLUS - Skin Care Product - STERIS CORPORATION; *pg.* 1597, *pg.* 1464
ALCATRAZ - Bike - MARIN BIKES; *pg.* 1708, *pg.* 168
ALCHEMIST - Bike - MARIN BIKES; *pg.* 1708, *pg.* 168
ALCHEMY - Fabric - NEMSCHOFF, INC.; *pg.* 936, *pg.* 1890
ALCHEMY - Software - WIND RIVER SYSTEMS, INC.; *pg.* 493, *pg.* 38
ALCHROME - Alloy - CARPENTER TECHNOLOGY CORPORATION; *pg.* 73, *pg.* 1584
ALCHROME - Metal Finishing Product - HEATBATH CORPORATION; *pg.* 1165, *pg.* 826
ALCO - Air Distribution Product - STANDEX INTERNATIONAL CORPORATION; *pg.* 60, *pg.* 1039
ALCOA - Aluminum Products - ALCOA INC.; *pg.* 65, *pg.* 1188
ALCOA-DIRECT - Web Service - ALCOA INC.; *pg.* 65, *pg.* 1188
ALCOHOLISM - Medical Journal Devoted to the Study & Treatment of Alcoholism - LIPPINCOTT WILLIAMS & WILKINS, INC.; *pg.* 1659, *pg.* 1567
ALCOJET - Cleaning Detergent - ALCONOX, INC.; *pg.* 325, *pg.* 1351
ALCONOX - Cleaning Detergent - ALCONOX, INC.; *pg.* 325, *pg.* 1351
ALCORD - Shoe Dressings - HENKEL CORPORATION; *pg.* 1165, *pg.* 1535
ALCOTABS - Cleaning Detergent - ALCONOX, INC.; *pg.* 325, *pg.* 1351
ALCOTT - Kitchen Product - KOHLER CO.; *pg.* 91, *pg.* 1862
ALCOTT RIDGE - Wine - E&J GALLO WINERY; *pg.* 1962, *pg.* 149
ALCOVE - Office Furniture - STEELCASE INC.; *pg.* 475, *pg.* 889
ALCRYN - Synthetic Rubber - FERRO CORPORATION; *pg.* 1162, *pg.* 1462
ALCRYN - Heater - WATLOW ELECTRIC MANUFACTURING COMPANY; *pg.* 1078, *pg.* 1004
ALDACTAZIDE - Medicine - PFIZER INC.; *pg.* 1581, *pg.* 1278
ALDACTONE - Medicine - PFIZER INC.; *pg.* 1581, *pg.* 1278
ALDEK - Aluminum Scaffolding - WERNER HOLDING CO.; *pg.* 121, *pg.* 1534
ALDEN - Furniture - JASPER GROUP; *pg.* 930, *pg.* 691
ALDEN NEW ENGLAND - Shoes - THE ALDEN SHOE COMPANY; *pg.* 1804, *pg.* 833
ALDEN PEDIC - Shoes - THE ALDEN SHOE COMPANY; *pg.* 1804, *pg.* 833
ALDEOX - Pre-Treatment Cleaner - A BRITE COMPANY; *pg.* 1144, *pg.* 1697
ALDER - Guest Chairs - BERNHARDT DESIGN; *pg.* 918, *pg.* 1381
ALDI - Grocery Stores - ALDI FOOD INC.; *pg.* 1013, *pg.* 556
ALDILA - Golf Club Shafts - ALDILA, INC.; *pg.* 1825, *pg.* 185
ALDINE - Fabric - NEMSCHOFF, INC.; *pg.* 936, *pg.* 1890
ALDO - Footwear - ALDO GROUP; *pg.* 1804, *pg.* 1959
ALDO - Emulsifier - LONZA INC.; *pg.* 1171, *pg.* 1041
ALDON AFFINITI - Software - ROCKET ALDON; *pg.* 462, *pg.* 85
ALDON CMS - Software - ROCKET ALDON; *pg.* 462, *pg.* 85
ALDRICH - Pump - FLOWSERVE CORPORATION; *pg.* 82, *pg.* 1719
ALDRICH - Organics & Inorganics for Chemical Synthesis - SIGMA-ALDRICH CORPORATION; *pg.* 1181, *pg.* 1003
ALDRICH - Wallcovering - YORK WALLCOVERINGS INC.; *pg.* 947, *pg.* 1598
ALDURAZYME - Lysosomal Storage Disorder - GENZYME CORPORATION; *pg.* 1534, *pg.* 808
ALDUTI RUPTER - Switch - S&C ELECTRIC COMPANY; *pg.* 1305, *pg.* 589
ALEGRIA - Show And Ticket - CIRQUE DU SOLEIL INC.; *pg.* 540, *pg.* 1954
ALENCON LACE - Kitchen Product - KOHLER CO.; *pg.* 91, *pg.* 1862
ALEQUEL - Crohn's Disease Treatment - ENZO BIOCHEM INC.; *pg.* 1529, *pg.* 1228
ALERA - Lighting Product - HUBBELL INCORPORATED; *pg.* 1299, *pg.* 370
ALERE - Pharmaceutical Product - ALERE INC.; *pg.* 1488, *pg.* 849
ALERION - Office Furniture - STEELCASE INC.; *pg.* 475, *pg.* 889
ALERIS - Inspection System - KLA-TENCOR CORPORATION; *pg.* 1353, *pg.* 146
ALERON - Lighting - STEELCASE INC.; *pg.* 475, *pg.* 889
ALERT - Statistical Process Control Software Package - GE WATER & PROCESS TECHNOLOGIES; *pg.* 1339, *pg.* 1588
ALERT - Leak Detectors - LA-CO INDUSTRIES MARKAL CO., INC.; *pg.* 1170, *pg.* 610
ALERT - Systems Integration & Aeronautics - LOCKHEED MARTIN CORPORATION; *pg.* 229, *pg.* 762
ALERT - Food Safety Product - NEOGEN CORPORATION; *pg.* 883, *pg.* 896
ALERT-O.A.D - Sterilization Product - PROPPER MANUFACTURING COMPANY, INC.; *pg.* 1586, *pg.* 1175
ALERT.COM - Software - MICROSTRATEGY, INC.; *pg.* 1266, *pg.* 1809
ALERTIT - Video Card - ADVANCED MICRO DEVICES, INC.; *pg.* 613, *pg.* 282
ALERTLINK - Security System - NORTEK, INC.; *pg.* 100, *pg.* 1607
ALERTS - Wireless Communication Product - TELECOMMUNICATION SYSTEMS INC.; *pg.* 483, *pg.* 754
ALESSANDRIA - Fabric - NEMSCHOFF, INC.; *pg.* 936, *pg.* 1890
ALESSE - Oral Contraceptive - PFIZER INC.; *pg.* 1581, *pg.* 1278
ALESTA - Powder Coatings - E.I. DU PONT DE NEMOURS & COMPANY; *pg.* 1159, *pg.* 390
ALETHOS PLUS - Fabric - NEMSCHOFF, INC.; *pg.* 936, *pg.* 1890
ALEVE - Arthritis Medication - BAYER HEALTHCARE CONSUMER CARE DIVISION; *pg.* 1500, *pg.* 1087
ALEX - Acrylic Latex Caulk - DAP PRODUCTS, INC.; *pg.* 1441, *pg.* 756
ALEX - Apparel - OAKLEY, INC.; *pg.* 1840, *pg.* 86
ALEX PLUS - Acrylic Latex Caulk Plus Silicone - DAP PRODUCTS, INC.; *pg.* 1441, *pg.* 756
ALEXA - Toolbar - ALEXA INTERNET, INC.; *pg.* 1226, *pg.* 212
ALEXA - Medical Test System - HOLOGIC, INC.; *pg.* 1416, *pg.* 784
ALEXA - Dinnerware - THE HOMER LAUGHLIN CHINA COMPANY; *pg.* 1125, *pg.* 1850
ALEXA FLUOR - Molecular Probe Product - THERMO FISHER SCIENTIFIC INC.; *pg.* 1602, *pg.* 61
ALEXANDER - Guest Chairs - BERNHARDT DESIGN; *pg.* 918, *pg.* 1381
ALEXANDER KEITH'S - Beer - LABATT BREWING COMPANY LIMITED; *pg.* 253, *pg.* 1939
ALEXANDRA - Women's Clothing & Accessories - WOODEN SHIPS OF HOBOKEN; *pg.* 35, *pg.* 1315
ALEXANDRIA - Window Treatment - CROSCILL, INC.; *pg.* 1122, *pg.* 1220
ALEXANDRIA - Furniture - FLEXSTEEL INDUSTRIES, INC.; *pg.* 925, *pg.* 707
ALEXIS - Lamp - ASHLEY FURNITURE INDUSTRIES, INC.; *pg.* 914, *pg.* 1852
ALEXIS - Cart Bag - DATREK GOLF; *pg.* 1832, *pg.* 1801
ALEXIS - Puff-Sleeved Blouse - RALPH LAUREN CORPORATION; *pg.* 46, *pg.* 1284
ALEXTRIVANTAGE - Aesthetic Skin Lesion & Tattoo Removal Laser - CANDELA CORPORATION; *pg.* 1404, *pg.* 855
ALFA - Orthopedic Implant Product - DJO SURGICAL; *pg.* 1525, *pg.* 1661
ALFA - Laboratory Sample Cutter - THWING-ALBERT INSTRUMENT COMPANY; *pg.* 1432, *pg.* 1131
ALFA-CHEWS - Alfalfa Pet Treat - THE HARTZ MOUNTAIN CORP.; *pg.* 1476, *pg.* 1120
ALFA-I - Material & Alloy - ALLEGHENY TECHNOLOGIES INCORPORATED; *pg.* 66, *pg.* 1572
ALFALFA BLOSSOM - Honey - MILLER'S HONEY COMPANY; *pg.* 1860, *pg.* 1759
ALFANI - Apparel for Men & Women - MACY'S, INC.; *pg.* 1778, *pg.* 1417
ALFENTA - Pharmaceutical Product - AKORN, INC.; *pg.* 1488, *pg.* 622
ALFLEX - Conduit - SOUTHWIRE COMPANY; *pg.* 1063, *pg.* 527
ALFLO - Ladder Product - WERNER HOLDING CO.; *pg.* 121, *pg.* 1534
ALFONIC - Biodegradeable Nonionics - SASOL NORTH AMERICA INC.; *pg.* 984, *pg.* 1713
ALFRED PENNYWORTH - Character - DC COMICS, INC.; *pg.* 1633, *pg.* 1221
ALFRESCO - Furniture - TELESCOPE CASUAL FURNITURE INC.; *pg.* 944, *pg.* 1162
ALFUSE - Heat Transfer Products - MODINE MANUFACTURING COMPANY; *pg.* 1074, *pg.* 1888
ALGA-GRO - Biological Supplies - CAROLINA BIOLOGICAL SUPPLY COMPANY; *pg.* 1513, *pg.* 1359
ALGAAS HBT - Transistor Wafer - KOPIN CORPORATION; *pg.* 425, *pg.* 847
ALGAE BLOCK - Copper Roofing System - 3M COMPANY; *pg.* 1142, *pg.* 956
ALGAE MAX - Nutritional Supplement - NATURAL ORGANICS, INC.; *pg.* 1571, *pg.* 1181
ALGAS-SDI - LPG Gas & Air Standby Systems - ALGAS-SDI; *pg.* 1311, *pg.* 1831
ALGAS-SDI - Burner System - ECLIPSE INC.; *pg.* 1332, *pg.* 655
ALGEBRA - Sandals - AEROGROUP INTERNATIONAL, INC.; *pg.* 1803, *pg.* 1055
ALGEBRA SHOP - Educational Materials - SCHOLASTIC INC.; *pg.* 1683, *pg.* 1288
ALGENE - Cationic Surfactant - HUNTSMAN CORPORATION; *pg.* 1167, *pg.* 1758
ALGICELL - Wound Dressing - DERMA SCIENCES, INC.; *pg.* 1523, *pg.* 1111
ALGISITE - Medical & Aesthetic Product - DYNATRONICS CORPORATION; *pg.* 1526, *pg.* 1757
ALGO - Hearing Screener - NATUS MEDICAL INCORPORATED; *pg.* 1572, *pg.* 199
ALGO 3I - Newborn Hearing Screener - NATUS MEDICAL INCORPORATED; *pg.* 1572, *pg.* 199
ALGO 5 - Newborn Hearing Screener - NATUS MEDICAL INCORPORATED; *pg.* 1572, *pg.* 199
ALGO FLEXICOUPLER - Valu-Pak Earphones Designed for Accurate Newborn Hearing Screenings - NATUS MEDICAL INCORPORATED; *pg.* 1572, *pg.* 199
ALGO PORTABLE - Medical Device - NATUS MEDICAL INCORPORATED; *pg.* 1572, *pg.* 199
ALGOLI - Beauty Product - GRANDPA BRANDS COMPANY; *pg.* 1538, *pg.* 727
ALGONQUIN - Lounge Chairs - BERNHARDT DESIGN; *pg.* 918, *pg.* 1381
ALGONQUIN - Fly Rod - DAIWA CORPORATION; *pg.* 1832, *pg.* 75
ALGONQUIN - Footwear - P.W. MINOR & SON, INC.; *pg.* 1816, *pg.* 1140
ALGOOD OLD FASHIONED - Peanut Butter - ALGOOD FOOD COMPANY; *pg.* 836, *pg.* 731
ALGOOD RED LABEL - Peanut Butter - ALGOOD FOOD COMPANY; *pg.* 836, *pg.* 731
ALGORITHMIC C - Software System - MENTOR GRAPHICS

First page reference indicates Business Class Edition
Second page reference indicates Geographic Edition

CORPORATION; *pg.* 432, *pg.* 1510

ALHAMBRA - Fabric - NEMSCHOFF, INC.; *pg.* 936, *pg.* 1890

ALI - Soft Drink - THE COCA-COLA COMPANY; *pg.* 240, *pg.* 493

ALIANZA - Wireless Communication System - AT&T SOUTHEAST; *pg.* 1868, *pg.* 489

ALIAS - Software - AUTODESK INC.; *pg.* 356, *pg.* 257

ALIAS - Electric Car - ZAP; *pg.* 222, *pg.* 277

ALIASSTUDIO - Software - AUTODESK INC.; *pg.* 356, *pg.* 257

ALICCE - Footwear - STEVEN MADDEN, LTD.; *pg.* 1819, *pg.* 1176

ALICE - Clothing - ABERCROMBIE & FITCH CO.; *pg.* 37, *pg.* 1466

ALICE - Fabric - NEMSCHOFF, INC.; *pg.* 936, *pg.* 1890

ALICIA - Bedding - CROSCILL, INC.; *pg.* 1122, *pg.* 1220

ALICLIMBER - Mast Climbing Work Platforms - ALIMAK HEK INC; *pg.* 66, *pg.* 1749

ALIEDGE - Economical Edge Rest - ALIMED, INC.; *pg.* 1490, *pg.* 816

ALIEN ATTACK - Game - INTERNATIONAL GAME TECHNOLOGY; *pg.* 420, *pg.* 1606

ALIEN HOTSHOTS - Game - GAMEWRIGHT; *pg.* 953, *pg.* 836

ALIEN RACERS - Doll - MGA ENTERTAINMENT, INC.; *pg.* 964, *pg.* 300

ALIENGUISE - Computer Product - ALIENWARE CORPORATION; *pg.* 346, *pg.* 439

ALIENICE - Video Cooling System - ALIENWARE CORPORATION; *pg.* 346, *pg.* 439

ALIENWARE BOT - Computer Product - ALIENWARE CORPORATION; *pg.* 346, *pg.* 439

ALIGHT - Office Furniture - STEELCASE INC.; *pg.* 475, *pg.* 889

ALIGN - Workbenches - LISTA INTERNATIONAL CORPORATION; *pg.* 934, *pg.* 825

ALIGN - Fabric - NEMSCHOFF, INC.; *pg.* 936, *pg.* 1890

ALIGN - Probiotic Supplement - THE PROCTER & GAMBLE COMPANY; *pg.* 1129, *pg.* 1418

ALIGNFLOW - Molecular Probe Product - THERMO FISHER SCIENTIFIC INC.; *pg.* 1602, *pg.* 61

ALIGNGUIDE - Alignment System Software - HUNTER ENGINEERING COMPANY; *pg.* 208, *pg.* 973

ALIMAK SE - Hoist - ALIMAK HEK INC; *pg.* 66, *pg.* 1749

ALIMED BED STUFFER - Bed Positioning & Safety Product - ALIMED, INC.; *pg.* 1490, *pg.* 816

ALIMENTUM - Infant Formula - ABBOTT LABORATORIES; *pg.* 1484, *pg.* 551

ALIMENTUM ADVANCE - Infant Nutritional Formulas - ABBOTT LABORATORIES; *pg.* 1484, *pg.* 551

ALIMET - Health & Nutrition Product - NOVUS INTERNATIONAL, INC.; *pg.* 706, *pg.* 1001

ALIMTA - Pharmaceutical Product - ELI LILLY AND COMPANY; *pg.* 1527, *pg.* 684

ALINA - Office Furniture - STEELCASE INC.; *pg.* 475, *pg.* 889

ALINCO - Industrial Oils - ARCHER-DANIELS-MIDLAND COMPANY; *pg.* 825, *pg.* 565

ALIPHATIC NAPHTHAS - Organic Solvent - ROCK VALLEY OIL & CHEMICAL COMPANY; *pg.* 1179, *pg.* 631

ALIQUAT - Ammonium Chlorides - HENKEL CORPORATION; *pg.* 1165, *pg.* 1535

ALISAH - Footwear - STEVEN MADDEN, LTD.; *pg.* 1819, *pg.* 1176

ALISLIDE - Half Shifter - ALIMED, INC.; *pg.* 1490, *pg.* 816

ALISO - Office Furniture - STEELCASE INC.; *pg.* 475, *pg.* 889

ALISTA - Treatment for Female Sexual Arousal Disorder - VIVUS, INC.; *pg.* 1608, *pg.* 163

ALITRA Q - Nutritional Products - ABBOTT LABORATORIES; *pg.* 1484, *pg.* 551

ALIVE - Beverages - THE COCA-COLA COMPANY; *pg.* 240, *pg.* 493

ALIVE - Soil Activator - GARDENS ALIVE!, INC.; *pg.* 1796, *pg.* 693

ALIVE NOW - Small Group Study - THE UPPER ROOM; *pg.* 1698, *pg.* 1655

ALIZE VS - Cognac - KOBRAND CORPORATION; *pg.* 1965, *pg.* 1325

ALIZE VSOP - Cognac - KOBRAND CORPORATION; *pg.* 1965, *pg.* 1325

ALJ - Health Care Product - NATURE'S SUNSHINE PRODUCTS, INC.; *pg.* 1571, *pg.* 1754

ALJA-SAFE - Ceramic Product - SMOOTH-ON INC.; *pg.* 111, *pg.* 1528

ALJO - Towable Recreational Vehicle - SKYLINE CORPORATION; *pg.* 1711, *pg.* 677

ALKA-MINTS - Chewable Antacid Tablets - BAYER HEALTHCARE CONSUMER CARE DIVISION; *pg.* 1500, *pg.* 1087

ALKA-SELTZER - Effervescent Pain Reliever & Antacid - BAYER HEALTHCARE CONSUMER CARE DIVISION; *pg.* 1500, *pg.* 1087

ALKADET - Alkyl Polysaccharide - HUNTSMAN CORPORATION; *pg.* 1167, *pg.* 1758

ALKANATE - Anionic Surfactants - HUNTSMAN CORPORATION; *pg.* 1167, *pg.* 1758

ALKANOX - Antioxidants - CHEMTURA CORPORATION; *pg.* 1152, *pg.* 355

ALKAT-XL - Aklylation Catalyst - GE WATER & PROCESS TECHNOLOGIES; *pg.* 1339, *pg.* 1588

ALKATROL - Pressed & Monolithic Refractory - RESCO PRODUCTS, INC.; *pg.* 107, *pg.* 1581

ALKAWET - Surfactant for Household & Industrial Products - LONZA INC.; *pg.* 1171, *pg.* 1041

ALKCO - Lighting - PHILIPS LIGHTING; *pg.* 1303, *pg.* 806

ALKLEEN - Pre-Treatment Cleaner - A BRITE COMPANY; *pg.* 1144, *pg.* 1697

ALKOR - Corrosion Resistant Mortar - ATLAS MINERALS & CHEMICALS, INC.; *pg.* 69, *pg.* 1552

ALKYD ZONE - Marking Paint - JONES-BLAIR COMPANY; *pg.* 1443, *pg.* 1682

ALKYDEX - Stain - KELLY-MOORE PAINT COMPANY, INC.; *pg.* 1443, *pg.* 198

ALKYFALL - Dry-Fall Coatings - DUNN-EDWARDS CORPORATION; *pg.* 1442, *pg.* 129

ALKYLPHENOLS - Insulating Varnishes - SI GROUP, INC.; *pg.* 1181, *pg.* 1341

ALKYLSEAL - Sealer - DUNN-EDWARDS CORPORATION; *pg.* 1442, *pg.* 129

ALL - Laundry Detergent - THE SUN PRODUCTS CORPORATION; *pg.* 336, *pg.* 385

ALL-AMERICAN - Tires - THE GOODYEAR TIRE & RUBBER COMPANY; *pg.* 1883, *pg.* 1401

ALL AMERICAN - Footwear - P.W. MINOR & SON, INC.; *pg.* 1816, *pg.* 1140

ALL-AMERICAN - Sound Systems - RAULAND-BORG CORPORATION; *pg.* 666, *pg.* 634

ALL-AMERICAN - Fabric - UNIROYAL ENGINEERED PRODUCTS; *pg.* 699, *pg.* 467

ALL ANIMALS - Magazine - THE HUMANE SOCIETY OF THE UNITED STATES; *pg.* 143, *pg.* 400

ALL-AROUND BORDERS - Educational Product - BARKER CREEK PUBLISHING INC.; *pg.* 1619, *pg.* 1818

ALL CAFE ESCAPES - Coffee - KEURIG GREEN MOUNTAIN, INC.; *pg.* 868, *pg.* 1768

ALL CASH ADVANCE - Video Game - INTERNATIONAL GAME TECHNOLOGY; *pg.* 957, *pg.* 1024

ALL-CAST - Scraper Blade And Router - ESCO CORPORATION; *pg.* 1335, *pg.* 1502

ALL-CITY - Urban Bicycles - QUALITY BICYCLE PRODUCTS; *pg.* 1710, *pg.* 918

ALL-CLEAR - Eye Drop & Ointment - BAUSCH & LOMB INCORPORATED; *pg.* 1401, *pg.* 1045

ALL CLIMATE - Men's Underwear - STANFIELD'S LIMITED; *pg.* 48, *pg.* 1917

ALL DAY EVERY DAY. OUR GAME. - Trademark (Women's Basketball) - NATIONAL COLLEGIATE ATHLETIC ASSOCIATION; *pg.* 567, *pg.* 688

ALL-FI - Drum - GREIF INC.; *pg.* 1459, *pg.* 1447

ALL-FLASH - Roof Flashing - OATEY SUPPLY CHAIN SERVICES; *pg.* 30, *pg.* 1433

ALL-FLEX - Healthcare Product - JOHNSON & JOHNSON; *pg.* 1549, *pg.* 1091

ALL FOR YOU - Slogan - BELK, INC.; *pg.* 1760, *pg.* 1364

ALL FRUIT SMOOTHIES - Slogan - JAMBA, INC.; *pg.* 1024, *pg.* 84

ALL GAME GUIDE - Video Game Database - ROVI CORPORATION; *pg.* 463, *pg.* 269

ALL HANDS - Magazine - UNITED STATES NAVY; *pg.* 1009, *pg.* 1647

ALL-IN-ONE - Clipper Kit - ANDIS COMPANY; *pg.* 498, *pg.* 1895

ALL-IN-ONE - Batteries - UNIVERSAL POWER GROUP, INC.; *pg.* 683, *pg.* 1671

ALL IN THE CARDS - Game - WMS INDUSTRIES INC.; *pg.* 593, *pg.* 666

ALL-IN-WONDER - Graphics Card - ADVANCED MICRO DEVICES, INC.; *pg.* 613, *pg.* 282

ALL-IN-WONDER - 3D Graphical Technology - ADVANCED MICRO DEVICES, INC.-MARKHAM; *pg.* 345, *pg.* 1922

ALL IS WELL - Slogan - DESIGNING HEALTH, INC.; *pg.* 1523, *pg.* 299

ALL MUSIC GUIDE - Music Database - ROVI CORPORATION; *pg.* 463, *pg.* 269

ALL OR NUT'N KENO - Video Game - INTERNATIONAL GAME TECHNOLOGY; *pg.* 957, *pg.* 1024

ALL-POLYMER - Mechanical & Electrical System - JOHNSON CONTROLS, INC.; *pg.* 209, *pg.* 1876

ALL-PRO - Toothbrush - RANIR LLC; *pg.* 520, *pg.* 888

ALL PRO DAD - Training Aid - FAMILY FIRST; *pg.* 140, *pg.* 472

ALL PURPOSE - Paint & Coating - AERVOE INDUSTRIES INCORPORATED; *pg.* 1439, *pg.* 1021

ALL SEASON - Paint & Coating - DIAMOND VOGEL PAINT, INC.; *pg.* 1441, *pg.* 710

ALL-SEASON BRUSH-NO-MORE - Homeowner Product - PBI/GORDON CORPORATION; *pg.* 1176, *pg.* 985

ALL SEASON SELECT - Lubricant - INGERSOLL-RAND COMPANY; *pg.* 1349, *pg.* 1370

ALL-SEASON WASHER SOLVENT - Battery & Windshield Treatment - MOC PRODUCTS COMPANY, INC.; *pg.* 332, *pg.* 174

ALL SEASONS - Household Insect Control - BONIDE PRODUCTS, INC.; *pg.* 1794, *pg.* 1320

ALL-SIZE - Corrugated Product - BUCKEYE CORRUGATED INC.; *pg.* 1454, *pg.* 1400

ALL SMILES BOUQUET - Flower Arrangement - 1-800-FLOWERS.COM, INC.; *pg.* 1758, *pg.* 1151

ALL SPORT - Scoreboard & Sports Product - DAKTRONICS, INC.; *pg.* 633, *pg.* 1624

ALL SPORT BODY QUENCHER - Non-Carbonated Sports Beverage - THE MONARCH BEVERAGE COMPANY, INC.; *pg.* 257, *pg.* 514

ALL SPORT PLUS - Beverage - THE MONARCH BEVERAGE COMPANY, INC.; *pg.* 257, *pg.* 514

ALL STAR - Sport Surface - ROBBINS, INC.; *pg.* 108, *pg.* 1425

ALL STAR 2000 - Foot Apparel - CONVERSE INC.; *pg.* 1831, *pg.* 793

ALL STAR COLLECTION - Foot Apparel - CONVERSE INC.; *pg.* 1831, *pg.* 793

ALL-STAR POKER - Video Game - INTERNATIONAL GAME TECHNOLOGY; *pg.* 957, *pg.* 1024

ALL STARS - Food Product - ANNIE'S INC.; *pg.* 1760, *pg.* 45

ALL STEER - Steering - OSHKOSH CORPORATION; *pg.* 187, *pg.* 1885

ALL SURFACE - Primer - THE SHERWIN-WILLIAMS COMPANY; *pg.* 1447, *pg.* 1435

ALL-TACH - Attachment System - GEHL COMPANY; *pg.* 1339, *pg.* 1899

ALL THAT GLITTERS - Game - WMS INDUSTRIES INC.; *pg.* 593, *pg.* 666

ALL THAT JAZZ - Music Publisher - CARL FISCHER, LLC; *pg.* 1625, *pg.* 1209

ALL THAT JAZZ - Women's Active Wear - CHEROKEE GLOBAL BRANDS; *pg.* 21, *pg.* 278

ALL THAT RAZZ-BERRY - Nail Care Product - OPI PRODUCTS INC.; *pg.* 518, *pg.* 167

ALL THE MONEY - Lottery Game - NEW YORK STATE LOTTERY; *pg.* 1001, *pg.* 1340

ALL THE RIGHT CONNECTIONS - Slogan - ASANTE TECHNOLOGIES, INC.; *pg.* 619, *pg.* 238

ALL THE RIGHT STUFF FOR YOUR LABORATORY - Tagline - PREISER SCIENTIFIC, INC.; *pg.* 1427, *pg.* 1851

ALL THE WAY - Clothing - SPANX INC.; *pg.* 32, *pg.* 520

ALL THINGS FINANCIAL - Slogan - FIRST HORIZON NATIONAL CORPORATION; *pg.* 755, *pg.* 1644

ALL TIME FAVORITES - Music Publisher - CARL FISCHER, LLC; *pg.* 1625, *pg.* 1209

ALL TOGETHER - Slogan - CERNER CORPORATION; *pg.* 1514, *pg.* 981

ALL TRAIL - Trademark & ATV Tires - CARLISLE TIRE & WHEEL COMPANY; *pg.* 1880, *pg.* 1612

ALL-TUFF - Plastic Refractory - PLIBRICO CO. LLC; *pg.* 104, *pg.* 587

ALL-U-NEED - Fuel - BARDAHL MANUFACTURING CORPORATION; *pg.* 972, *pg.* 1833

ALL-WEATHER - Alkyd House Paints & Primer; Wood Stains - AKZONOBEL DECORATIVE PAINTS U.S.; *pg.* 1439, *pg.* 1474

ALL-WEATHER - Rifle - STURM, RUGER & COMPANY, INC.; *pg.* 1846, *pg.* 371

ALL WHEEL ABS - Brake System - GENERAL ENGINES COMPANY INC.; *pg.* 174, *pg.* 437
ALL WOMAN - Cigarette - PHILIP MORRIS USA INC.; *pg.* 1894, *pg.* 1803
ALL YOU CAN MEET - Pricing Structure - CITRIX SYSTEMS, INC.; *pg.* 375, *pg.* 424
ALL YOU CAN READ - Educational Materials - SCHOLASTIC INC.; *pg.* 1683, *pg.* 1288
ALL YOU CAN SEE AND SAY - Video Communication System - GLOWPOINT, INC.; *pg.* 401, *pg.* 1094
ALL YOU NEED FOR THE LIFE OF YOUR PET - Tagline - PETSMART, INC.; *pg.* 1481, *pg.* 18
ALL YOUR PROTECTION UNDER ONE ROOF - Slogan - AMERICAN FAMILY MUTUAL INSURANCE COMPANY; *pg.* 1190, *pg.* 1864
ALLA CASA - Kiosk - DONATOS PIZZERIA CORPORATION; *pg.* 1727, *pg.* 1439
ALLAGASH - Shirts - L.L. BEAN, INC.; *pg.* 1777, *pg.* 750
ALLAN QUATERMAIN - Game - WMS INDUSTRIES INC.; *pg.* 593, *pg.* 666
ALLANTE - Carpet - BEAULIEU GROUP, LLC; *pg.* 917, *pg.* 529
ALLAROUND - Portable Wet/Dry Vacuum - SHOP-VAC CORPORATION; *pg.* 1375, *pg.* 1595
ALLBEE - B-Complex Vitamins - ALERE INC.; *pg.* 1488, *pg.* 849
ALLCASE - Thermal Processing Equipment - SURFACE COMBUSTION, INC.; *pg.* 1077, *pg.* 1462
ALLCORR - Material & Alloy - ALLEGHENY TECHNOLOGIES INCORPORATED; *pg.* 66, *pg.* 1572
ALLEGORY - Fabric - NEMSCHOFF, INC.; *pg.* 936, *pg.* 1890
ALLEGRA - Testing Instrument System - BECKMAN COULTER, INC.; *pg.* 1402, *pg.* 48
ALLEGRA - Sunglasses - COACH, INC.; *pg.* 3, *pg.* 1214
ALLEGRA - Fexofenadine HC1 - SANOFI US; *pg.* 1592, *pg.* 1046
ALLEGRA - Pharmaceutical Product - SUNOVION PHARMACEUTICALS INC.; *pg.* 1599, *pg.* 832
ALLEGRA ALLERGY - Allergy Relief Medication - CHATTEM, INC.; *pg.* 1515, *pg.* 1628
ALLEGRA-D - Pharmaceutical Product - IMPAX LABORATORIES, INC.; *pg.* 1544, *pg.* 101
ALLEGRA NETWORK - Quick Printing Services - ALLEGRA NETWORK LLC; *pg.* 1614, *pg.* 904
ALLEGRA PRINT & IMAGING - Quick Printing Services - ALLEGRA NETWORK LLC; *pg.* 1614, *pg.* 904
ALLEGRO - Cheeses - AGROPUR COOPERATIVE; *pg.* 836, *pg.* 1950
ALLEGRO - Sport Reformer - BALANCED BODY, INC.; *pg.* 1826, *pg.* 195
ALLEGRO - Software - CADENCE DESIGN SYSTEMS, INC.; *pg.* 367, *pg.* 239
ALLEGRO - Cordless LED - DEN-MAT CORPORATION; *pg.* 1522, *pg.* 271
ALLEGRO - Folding Wheelchair - INVACARE CORPORATION; *pg.* 1546, *pg.* 1451
ALLEGRO - Seating Product - IRWIN SEATING COMPANY INC.; *pg.* 929, *pg.* 887
ALLEGRO - Furniture - NEMSCHOFF, INC.; *pg.* 936, *pg.* 1890
ALLEN - Clinical Furniture - ALIMED, INC.; *pg.* 1490, *pg.* 816
ALLEN - Instrument Table - BLICKMAN HEALTH INDUSTRIES, INC.; *pg.* 1506, *pg.* 1051
ALLEN - Hand Tools - DANAHER CORPORATION; *pg.* 1044, *pg.* 397
ALLEN - Food Products - RICH PRODUCTS CORPORATION; *pg.* 892, *pg.* 1150
ALLEN-BRADLEY - Industrial Automation Products - ROCKWELL AUTOMATION, INC.; *pg.* 668, *pg.* 1880
ALLEN-BRADLEY 1771 REMOTE I/O - Software - ROCKWELL AUTOMATION, INC.; *pg.* 668, *pg.* 1880
ALLEN-EDMONDS - Men's Shoes - ALLEN-EDMONDS SHOE CORP.; *pg.* 1804, *pg.* 1887
ALLEN ELITE - Organs - ALLEN ORGAN COMPANY; *pg.* 527, *pg.* 1549
ALLEN ENSEMBLE - Sound Module - ALLEN ORGAN COMPANY; *pg.* 527, *pg.* 1549
ALLENRX - Pharmaceutical Product - CHIESI USA, INC.; *pg.* 1515, *pg.* 1359
ALLEN'S SAL-AMMONIAC - Soldering Blocks - JOHNSON MANUFACTURING COMPANY; *pg.* 1169, *pg.* 712
ALLER-7 - Nutritional Supplement - NATURAL ORGANICS, INC.; *pg.* 1571, *pg.* 1181
ALLER-CHLOR - Pharmaceutical Product - ALLERGAN; *pg.* 1490, *pg.* 1101
ALLER-MELTS - Allergy Relief Medication - WALGREEN CO.; *pg.* 1608, *pg.* 605
ALLER-RESPONSE - Vitamin & Herbal Supplement - SOURCE NATURALS; *pg.* 1595, *pg.* 278
ALLER-RX - Anti-Allergen Spray - STEAMATIC INC.; *pg.* 60, *pg.* 1696
ALLERCEPT - Allergy Treatment System - HESKA CORPORATION; *pg.* 1542, *pg.* 335
ALLERCETIN - Vitamin & Herbal Supplement - SOURCE NATURALS; *pg.* 1595, *pg.* 278
ALLERCOAT - Software - BIO-RAD LABORATORIES, INC.; *pg.* 1504, *pg.* 101
ALLERDERM - Veterinary Product - VIRBAC CORPORATION; *pg.* 1606, *pg.* 1696
ALLERFRIM - Pharmaceutical Product - ALLERGAN; *pg.* 1490, *pg.* 1101
ALLERQUANT - Allergy Product - BIOMERICA, INC.; *pg.* 1506, *pg.* 107
ALLERX - Pharmaceutical Product - CHIESI USA, INC.; *pg.* 1515, *pg.* 1359
ALLESANDRO - Furniture - ASHLEY FURNITURE INDUSTRIES, INC.; *pg.* 914, *pg.* 1852
ALLESON - Sportswear - ALLESON OF ROCHESTER, INC.; *pg.* 37, *pg.* 1333
ALLESON ATHLETIC - Athletic Wear - ALLESON OF ROCHESTER, INC.; *pg.* 37, *pg.* 1333
ALLEVYN - Medical & Aesthetic Product - DYNATRONICS CORPORATION; *pg.* 1526, *pg.* 1757
ALLEY CAT - Pet Food - BIG HEART PET BRANDS; *pg.* 1474, *pg.* 213
ALLEY CAT KENO - Video Game - INTERNATIONAL GAME TECHNOLOGY; *pg.* 957, *pg.* 1024
ALLEZ - Bicycle - SPECIALIZED BICYCLE COMPONENTS, INC.; *pg.* 1711, *pg.* 152
ALLFUSION - Life Cycle Management Software - CA TECHNOLOGIES; *pg.* 366, *pg.* 1168
ALLGONE - Air Cleaning System - CALGON CARBON CORPORATION; *pg.* 1151, *pg.* 1574
ALLIANCE - Table System - HOWE FURNITURE CORPORATION; *pg.* 928, *pg.* 998
ALLIANCE - Wafer Processing Line - LAM RESEARCH CORPORATION; *pg.* 1354, *pg.* 91
ALLIANCE BIZ TALK - Business Technology - ASTEA INTERNATIONAL INC.; *pg.* 355, *pg.* 1540
ALLIANCE BUSINESS INTELLIGENCE - Business Application Services - ASTEA INTERNATIONAL INC.; *pg.* 355, *pg.* 1540
ALLIANCE CHECK IMAGE SOLUTIONS - Check Imaging Solutions - JACK HENRY & ASSOCIATES, INC.; *pg.* 422, *pg.* 988
ALLIANCE CONTACT CENTER - Business Management Services - ASTEA INTERNATIONAL INC.; *pg.* 355, *pg.* 1540
ALLIANCE CUSTOMER PORTAL - Business Application Services - ASTEA INTERNATIONAL INC.; *pg.* 355, *pg.* 1540
ALLIANCE DEPOT REPAIR - Business Management Services - ASTEA INTERNATIONAL INC.; *pg.* 355, *pg.* 1540
ALLIANCE DSE - Business Management Services - ASTEA INTERNATIONAL INC.; *pg.* 355, *pg.* 1540
ALLIANCE ENEWSLETTER - Online Publication - PORTLAND BUSINESS ALLIANCE; *pg.* 1004, *pg.* 1505
ALLIANCE FIELD SERVICE - Business Management Services - ASTEA INTERNATIONAL INC.; *pg.* 355, *pg.* 1540
ALLIANCE GENERATION - Platform - ONMOBILE LIVE, INC.; *pg.* 449, *pg.* 829
ALLIANCE GLOBAL DATABASE - Business Technology - ASTEA INTERNATIONAL INC.; *pg.* 355, *pg.* 1540
ALLIANCE II - Inflation Device - BOSTON SCIENTIFIC CORPORATION; *pg.* 1508, *pg.* 831
ALLIANCE LINK - Business Technology - ASTEA INTERNATIONAL INC.; *pg.* 355, *pg.* 1540
ALLIANCE LOGISTICS - Business Management Services - ASTEA INTERNATIONAL INC.; *pg.* 355, *pg.* 1540
ALLIANCE MARKETING - Business Management Services - ASTEA INTERNATIONAL INC.; *pg.* 355, *pg.* 1540
ALLIANCE MOBILE - Business Application Services - ASTEA INTERNATIONAL INC.; *pg.* 355, *pg.* 1540
ALLIANCE NUTRITION - Food Products - ADM ALLIANCE NUTRITION, INC.; *pg.* 1474, *pg.* 653
ALLIANCE PROFESSIONAL SERVICES - Business Management Services - ASTEA INTERNATIONAL INC.; *pg.* 355, *pg.* 1540
ALLIANCE REPORTING - Business Application Services - ASTEA INTERNATIONAL INC.; *pg.* 355, *pg.* 1540
ALLIANCE RT - Material Test Systems - MTS SYSTEMS CORPORATION; *pg.* 442, *pg.* 923
ALLIANCE SALES - Business Management Services - ASTEA INTERNATIONAL INC.; *pg.* 355, *pg.* 1540
ALLIANCE STUDIO - Business Technology - ASTEA INTERNATIONAL INC.; *pg.* 355, *pg.* 1540
ALLIANT ENERGY - Electricity & Natural Gas - ALLIANT ENERGY CORPORATION; *pg.* 1933, *pg.* 1864
ALLIBERT BUCKHORN - Reusable Plastic Material Handling Products - MYERS INDUSTRIES, INC.; *pg.* 1887, *pg.* 1402
ALLIED - Relocation Services - SIRVA, INC.; *pg.* 1923, *pg.* 669
ALLIED GROUP - Insurance & Related Services - NATIONWIDE MUTUAL INSURANCE COMPANY; *pg.* 1211, *pg.* 706
ALLIED PICKFORDS - Relocation Services - SIRVA, INC.; *pg.* 1923, *pg.* 669
ALLIED SPECIAL PRODUCTS - Relocation Services - SIRVA, INC.; *pg.* 1923, *pg.* 669
ALLIGATOR - Multiple Rivet Installation Tool - FLEXIBLE STEEL LACING COMPANY; *pg.* 1337, *pg.* 608
ALLIGATOR CAPITAL OF THE WORLD - Slogan - GODWIN'S GATORLAND, INC.; *pg.* 550, *pg.* 453
ALLISION TRANSMISSION - Truck, Bus & Military Transmissions - GENERAL MOTORS COMPANY; *pg.* 175, *pg.* 881
ALLISON EMBROIDERY - Window Treatment - CROSCILL, INC.; *pg.* 1122, *pg.* 1220
ALLISON TRANSMISSION - Auto Transmissions - ALLISON TRANSMISSION, INC.; *pg.* 198, *pg.* 682
ALLIUM - Window Treatment - HERITAGE LACE INC.; *pg.* 694, *pg.* 711
ALLJOIST - Wood Product - BOISE CASCADE HOLDINGS, L.L.C.; *pg.* 1453, *pg.* 546
ALLKARE - Protective Barrier Wipes - ALIMED, INC.; *pg.* 1490, *pg.* 816
ALLMAX - Rivet - ALLFAST FASTENING SYSTEMS, INC.; *pg.* 1041, *pg.* 66
ALLMAX RIVET - Blind Rivet - ALLFAST FASTENING SYSTEMS, INC.; *pg.* 1041, *pg.* 66
ALLMET - Roofing Material - METALS USA, INC.; *pg.* 97, *pg.* 425
ALLOCATION - Software - JDA SOFTWARE GROUP, INC.; *pg.* 423, *pg.* 22
ALLOCATIONMASTER - Software - SUNGARD DATA SYSTEMS INC.; *pg.* 477, *pg.* 1592
ALLOCRAFT - Spinal System - STRYKER CORPORATION; *pg.* 1598, *pg.* 894
ALLOMATIC - Motor Vehicle Parts & Accessories - ALLOMATIC PRODUCTS COMPANY; *pg.* 198, *pg.* 1160
ALLONGD - Furniture - J. ROBERT SCOTT INC.; *pg.* 930, *pg.* 105
ALLONS-Y - Educational Materials - SCHOLASTIC INC.; *pg.* 1683, *pg.* 1288
ALLOVER - Voice & Data Network - AT&T MOBILITY LLC; *pg.* 619, *pg.* 488
ALLOY - Paper & Nonwoven Material - FIBERMARK INC.; *pg.* 1457, *pg.* 1764
ALLOY - Ceiling Fan - WESTINGHOUSE LIGHTING CORPORATION; *pg.* 687, *pg.* 1571
ALLOY DIGEST - Trade Publication - ASM INTERNATIONAL; *pg.* 132, *pg.* 1461
ALLOYA - Furniture - JOFCO INC.; *pg.* 931, *pg.* 691
ALLPAC - Valves - FLOWSERVE CORPORATION; *pg.* 82, *pg.* 1719
ALLPRINT - Laser Printers - VIDEOJET TECHNOLOGIES INC.; *pg.* 489, *pg.* 671
ALLRECIPES.COM - Culinary Website - THE READER'S DIGEST ASSOCIATION, INC.; *pg.* 1679, *pg.* 1322
ALLSCAPE - Lighting - PHILIPS LIGHTING; *pg.* 1303, *pg.* 806
ALLSCRIPTS DIRECT - Prescription Software - ALLSCRIPTS HEALTHCARE SOLUTIONS, INC.; *pg.* 1492, *pg.* 563
ALLSEASONGEAR - Sport Apparel - UNDER ARMOUR, INC.; *pg.* 49, *pg.* 759
ALLSOLUTIONS - Dental Product - DENTSPLY INTERNATIONAL INC.; *pg.* 1522, *pg.* 1596
ALLSTATE FINANCIAL - Individual Life Insurance & Annuity Products - THE ALLSTATE CORPORATION; *pg.* 1189, *pg.* 639
ALLSTATE INDEMNITY & CASUALTY INSURANCE COMPANY - Property-Liability Insurance - THE ALLSTATE

First page reference indicates Business Class Edition
Second page reference indicates Geographic Edition

CORPORATION; *pg.* 1189, *pg.* 639
ALLSTATE INSURANCE COMPANY - Multi-Line Property-Liability Insurance Company - THE ALLSTATE CORPORATION; *pg.* 1189, *pg.* 639
ALLSTATE MOTOR CLUB - Emergency Road Service - THE ALLSTATE CORPORATION; *pg.* 1189, *pg.* 639
ALLSTEEL - Office Furniture - HNI CORPORATION; *pg.* 927, *pg.* 709
ALLTEC - Laser Marking System - DANAHER CORPORATION; *pg.* 1044, *pg.* 397
ALLTEC - Laser Printers - VIDEOJET TECHNOLOGIES INC.; *pg.* 489, *pg.* 671
ALLURA - Mixing Valve - SYMMONS INDUSTRIES, INC.; *pg.* 114, *pg.* 803
ALLURABED - Mattress System - TEMPUR SEALY INTERNATIONAL, INC.; *pg.* 944, *pg.* 731
ALLURE - Furniture - ASHLEY FURNITURE INDUSTRIES, INC.; *pg.* 914, *pg.* 1852
ALLURE - Range Hoods - BROAN-NUTONE LLC; *pg.* 1069, *pg.* 1860
ALLURE - Beauty Magazine - CONDE NAST PUBLICATIONS, INC.; *pg.* 1629, *pg.* 1217
ALLURE - Rug - COURISTAN INC.; *pg.* 921, *pg.* 1067
ALLURE - Faucet - ELKAY MANUFACTURING COMPANY; *pg.* 80, *pg.* 645
ALLURE - Door Glass - ODL INCORPORATED; *pg.* 101, *pg.* 914
ALLURE - Fabric - UNIROYAL ENGINEERED PRODUCTS; *pg.* 699, *pg.* 467
ALLUSION - Bath & Plumbing Product - JACUZZI BRANDS CORPORATION; *pg.* 554, *pg.* 65
ALLUVER - Chemical Reagent - HACH COMPANY; *pg.* 1415, *pg.* 334
ALLWOOD - Wood Flooring Product - ARMSTRONG WORLD INDUSTRIES, INC.; *pg.* 914, *pg.* 1545
ALLY - Herbicide - E.I. DU PONT DE NEMOURS & COMPANY; *pg.* 1159, *pg.* 390
ALLY - Office Furniture - STEELCASE INC.; *pg.* 475, *pg.* 889
ALLYMER - Polymerizable Synthetic Resin - PPG INDUSTRIES, INC.; *pg.* 1445, *pg.* 1579
ALMA - Lamp - ASHLEY FURNITURE INDUSTRIES, INC.; *pg.* 914, *pg.* 1852
ALMACONE - Pharmaceutical Product - ALLERGAN; *pg.* 1490, *pg.* 1101
ALMADEN - Wine - CONSTELLATION BRANDS, INC.; *pg.* 1960, *pg.* 1348
ALMAY - Cosmetics - REVLON, INC.; *pg.* 521, *pg.* 1286
ALMETA XS - Laser & Laser System - COHERENT, INC.; *pg.* 1406, *pg.* 265
ALMIRA - Lamp - ASHLEY FURNITURE INDUSTRIES, INC.; *pg.* 914, *pg.* 1852
ALMOND ACCENTS - Almonds - BLUE DIAMOND GROWERS; *pg.* 840, *pg.* 195
ALMOND FACTS - Almonds - BLUE DIAMOND GROWERS; *pg.* 840, *pg.* 195
THE ALMOND PEOPLE - Almonds - BLUE DIAMOND GROWERS; *pg.* 840, *pg.* 195
ALMOND PLAZA - Candy, Nut & Confectionery Gifts - HICKORY FARMS, INC.; *pg.* 862, *pg.* 1462
ALMOND ROCA - Buttercrunch Toffee - BROWN & HALEY; *pg.* 1851, *pg.* 1820
ALMOST BARE - Hosiery - KAYSER-ROTH CORPORATION; *pg.* 28, *pg.* 1374
ALMOST FOREVER - Envelope - POLY PAK AMERICA, INC.; *pg.* 1467, *pg.* 138
ALMOST PERFECT - Fabric - NEMSCHOFF, INC.; *pg.* 936, *pg.* 1890
ALOCRIL - Eye Care Product - ALLERGAN, INC.; *pg.* 1491, *pg.* 106
ALODINE - Metalworking Chemical - HENKEL CORPORATION; *pg.* 1166, *pg.* 897
ALOE BAN - Pet Supplies - HAPPY JACK INC.; *pg.* 1476, *pg.* 1390
ALOE CREME - Personal Care Product - RBC LIFE SCIENCES, INC.; *pg.* 1588, *pg.* 1723
ALOE ESSENCE - Hair & Skin Product - AUBREY ORGANICS INC.; *pg.* 499, *pg.* 470
ALOE GELEE - Personal Care Product - RBC LIFE SCIENCES, INC.; *pg.* 1588, *pg.* 1723
ALOE SOFT TEAT DIP - Wash Spray - BOUMATIC LLC; *pg.* 701, *pg.* 1865
ALOE-STAT - Conductive Skin Lotion - WALTER G. LEGGE COMPANY, INC.; *pg.* 337, *pg.* 1321
ALOE VESTA - Skin Care Product - CONVATEC LTD.; *pg.* 1518, *pg.* 1121
ALOECARE - Hand Care Product - CROSSTEX INTERNATIONAL INC.; *pg.* 1520, *pg.* 1164
ALOEMANNAN - Nutritional Product - RBC LIFE SCIENCES, INC.; *pg.* 1588, *pg.* 1723
ALOEPURE - Skin Care Product - ALOETTE COSMETICS, INC.; *pg.* 498, *pg.* 487
ALOESEPT - Cleaning Preparation - WALTER G. LEGGE COMPANY, INC.; *pg.* 337, *pg.* 1321
ALOESPA - Skin Care Product - ALOETTE COSMETICS, INC.; *pg.* 498, *pg.* 487
ALOETOUCH - Medical Gloves - MEDLINE INDUSTRIES, INC.; *pg.* 1562, *pg.* 635
ALOFT - Hotels - STARWOOD HOTELS & RESORTS WORLDWIDE, INC.; *pg.* 1114, *pg.* 378
ALOHA - Eyewear - MAUI JIM, INC.; *pg.* 9, *pg.* 651
ALOHA BREEZE - Embroidered Tees - HABAND COMPANY, INC.; *pg.* 1772, *pg.* 1099
ALOHA PINEAPPLE - Fruit Drink - JAMBA, INC.; *pg.* 1024, *pg.* 84
ALOMATIK - Sodium Tablets - THE PROCTER & GAMBLE COMPANY; *pg.* 1129, *pg.* 1418
ALONG THE BLUES HIGHWAY - Publisher - VARESE SARABANDE RECORDS, INC.; *pg.* 1789, *pg.* 281
ALORA - Pharmaceutical Product - ALLERGAN; *pg.* 1490, *pg.* 1101
ALOS - Reader & Printer - ANACOMP, INC.; *pg.* 350, *pg.* 1777
ALOUETTE - Whipped Cream Cheese Based Products - BONGRAIN NORTH AMERICA; *pg.* 841, *pg.* 1556
ALOUETTE - Light Louvers - HUNTER DOUGLAS, INC.; *pg.* 928, *pg.* 1320
ALOX - Polishing Agent for Hard & Soft Contact Lenses - FERRO CORPORATION; *pg.* 1162, *pg.* 1462
ALOX - Optical Product - UNIVERSAL PHOTONICS, INC.; *pg.* 1433, *pg.* 1167
ALOXI - Pharmaceutical - EISAI INC.; *pg.* 1526, *pg.* 1133
ALP/4500 - Print & Apply System - DIAGRAPH; *pg.* 387, *pg.* 989
ALP PLUS - Orthopedic Product - DJO INCORPORATED; *pg.* 1524, *pg.* 302
ALPAC - Semi-Conductor Devices - SEMTECH CORPORATION; *pg.* 671, *pg.* 57
ALPEN GOLD - Chocolate - MONDELEZ INTERNATIONAL, INC.; *pg.* 878, *pg.* 601
ALPENA - Dinnerware - THE HOMER LAUGHLIN CHINA COMPANY; *pg.* 1125, *pg.* 1850
ALPHA - Furniture - AMISCO INDUSTRIES LTD.; *pg.* 913, *pg.* 1958
ALPHA - Thermal Paper - APPVION INC.; *pg.* 1451, *pg.* 1852
ALPHA - Video Game - BALLY TECHNOLOGIES, INC.; *pg.* 531, *pg.* 1022
ALPHA - Wire & Cable Products - BELDEN, INC.; *pg.* 624, *pg.* 993
ALPHA - Shampoo Bowl - BELVEDERE USA CORPORATION; *pg.* 917, *pg.* 556
ALPHA - Software - BIO-RAD LABORATORIES, INC.; *pg.* 1504, *pg.* 101
ALPHA - Filtration Product - FLANDERS CORPORATION; *pg.* 1336, *pg.* 1392
ALPHA - Fluid Handling System - GRACO, INC.; *pg.* 1342, *pg.* 935
ALPHA - Surgical System - INTUITIVE SURGICAL, INC.; *pg.* 1546, *pg.* 286
ALPHA - Boots - LACROSSE FOOTWEAR, INC.; *pg.* 1811, *pg.* 1503
ALPHA - Workstation - MICROWAY, INC.; *pg.* 1267, *pg.* 841
ALPHA - Fabric - NEMSCHOFF, INC.; *pg.* 936, *pg.* 1890
ALPHA - Fog Product - ROSCO LABORATORIES, INC.; *pg.* 1782, *pg.* 378
ALPHA-7 - Clostridia Vaccine - BOEHRINGER INGELHEIM VETMEDICA, INC.; *pg.* 1474, *pg.* 989
ALPHA AIRCON - Cone Mask - ALPHA PRO TECH, LTD.; *pg.* 1492, *pg.* 1922
ALPHA-ALAFLEX - Coated & Laminated Fabrics - ALPHA ASSOCIATES, INC.; *pg.* 691, *pg.* 1078
ALPHA AROMA THERAPY - Personal Care Product - GARDEN OF LIFE, INC.; *pg.* 1532, *pg.* 478
ALPHA BAK - Filtration System - WATERS CORPORATION; *pg.* 1436, *pg.* 834
ALPHA BITS - Cereal - POST HOLDINGS, INC.; *pg.* 833, *pg.* 1002
ALPHA-CEL - Powdered Cellulose - INTERNATIONAL FIBER CORP.; *pg.* 865, *pg.* 1317
ALPHA CROSSLOCK - Knife - BUCK KNIVES, INC.; *pg.* 1828, *pg.* 550
ALPHA DORADO - Knife - BUCK KNIVES, INC.; *pg.* 1828, *pg.* 550
ALPHA FACTOR - Competition Leotards - PERFORM GROUP, LLC; *pg.* 31, *pg.* 1597
ALPHA FACTOR AERIALS - Gymnastic Apparel - PERFORM GROUP, LLC; *pg.* 31, *pg.* 1597
ALPHA FOAMER - Chemical Product - STEPAN COMPANY; *pg.* 1182, *pg.* 643
ALPHA GOLD - Supplement & Food Product - NEW EARTH LIFE SCIENCES, INC.; *pg.* 1573, *pg.* 1499
ALPHA-HU-AL - Indoor-Outdoor Jacketing - ALPHA ASSOCIATES, INC.; *pg.* 691, *pg.* 1078
ALPHA HUNTER - Knife - BUCK KNIVES, INC.; *pg.* 1828, *pg.* 550
ALPHA-MARITEX - Marine & Power Plant Insulation Fabrics & Lagging Materials - ALPHA ASSOCIATES, INC.; *pg.* 691, *pg.* 1078
ALPHA-MOTIVE - Under-the-Hood Insulating & Noise Attenuating Applications - ALPHA ASSOCIATES, INC.; *pg.* 691, *pg.* 1078
ALPHA NIR - Thermal Imaging System - FLIR SYSTEMS, INC.; *pg.* 1413, *pg.* 1510
ALPHA OMEGA - Car Seat - DOREL JUVENILE GROUP, INC.; *pg.* 923, *pg.* 676
ALPHA PLUS - Spray Guns - GRACO, INC.; *pg.* 1342, *pg.* 935
ALPHA-PROBE - Software - BIO-RAD LABORATORIES, INC.; *pg.* 1504, *pg.* 101
ALPHA-SIL - High Temperature Silica Fabric - ALPHA ASSOCIATES, INC.; *pg.* 691, *pg.* 1078
ALPHA-SONIC - Lead-Free Acoustical Products - ALPHA ASSOCIATES, INC.; *pg.* 691, *pg.* 1078
ALPHA-STEP - Chemical Product - STEPAN COMPANY; *pg.* 1182, *pg.* 643
ALPHA-STEP IQ - Surface Profiler - KLA-TENCOR CORPORATION; *pg.* 1353, *pg.* 146
ALPHA SUN - Supplement & Food Product - NEW EARTH LIFE SCIENCES, INC.; *pg.* 1573, *pg.* 1499
ALPHA SWAMPFOX - Apparel - LACROSSE FOOTWEAR, INC.; *pg.* 1811, *pg.* 1503
ALPHA SYSTEM - Modular Steel & Wood Furniture - KEWAUNEE SCIENTIFIC CORPORATION; *pg.* 931, *pg.* 1391
ALPHA-WELD - Insulation Product - ALPHA ASSOCIATES, INC.; *pg.* 691, *pg.* 1078
ALPHA-Z - Color Code Labels - SMEAD MANUFACTURING COMPANY; *pg.* 470, *pg.* 926
ALPHAAIR - Masks - ALPHA PRO TECH, LTD.; *pg.* 1492, *pg.* 1922
ALPHAAVE 35 - Start-Up Software Support for Businesses - XEROX CORPORATION; *pg.* 494, *pg.* 365
ALPHABET FUN BLOCKS - Educational Materials - SCHOLASTIC INC.; *pg.* 1683, *pg.* 1288
ALPHABET PAL - Educational Toys - LEAPFROG ENTERPRISES, INC.; *pg.* 961, *pg.* 84
ALPHABURLY - Footwear - LACROSSE FOOTWEAR, INC.; *pg.* 1811, *pg.* 1503
ALPHACENE - Plastics Product - AEP INDUSTRIES INC.; *pg.* 1878, *pg.* 1085
ALPHAGAN - Eye Care Product - ALLERGAN, INC.; *pg.* 1491, *pg.* 106
ALPHAGLAS - Tape - ALPHA ASSOCIATES, INC.; *pg.* 691, *pg.* 1078
ALPHAGUARD - Protective Apparel - ALPHA PRO TECH, LTD.; *pg.* 1492, *pg.* 1922
ALPHALAIN - Dinnerware - THE HOMER LAUGHLIN CHINA COMPANY; *pg.* 1125, *pg.* 1850
ALPHALISA - Assays & Reagents - PERKINELMER, INC.; *pg.* 1426, *pg.* 853
ALPHAMAX - Labeling - FLEXCON CORPORATION; *pg.* 1457, *pg.* 844
ALPHAPET EXPLORER - Educational Product - LEAPFROG ENTERPRISES, INC.; *pg.* 961, *pg.* 84
ALPHAPLATE - Light Gray Microplate - PERKINELMER, INC.; *pg.* 1426, *pg.* 853
ALPHAQUIZ - Educational Materials - RENAISSANCE LEARNING, INC.; *pg.* 607, *pg.* 1899
ALPHASAN - Chemical - MILLIKEN & COMPANY; *pg.* 696, *pg.* 1622
ALPHASCREEN - Assay & Reagents - PERKINELMER, INC.; *pg.* 1426, *pg.* 853
ALPHASORB-C - Nutritional Product - NOW HEALTH GROUP, INC.; *pg.* 1576, *pg.* 557
ALPHASTAT - Nutritional Supplement - NATURAL

ORGANICS, INC.; *pg.* 1571, *pg.* 1181
ALPHASTOR - Software System - EMC CORPORATION; *pg.* 391, *pg.* 825
ALPHATRAK - Blood Glucose Monitoring System - ABBOTT LABORATORIES; *pg.* 1484, *pg.* 551
ALPHAWORD - Educational Materials - RENAISSANCE LEARNING, INC.; *pg.* 607, *pg.* 1899
ALPINE - Mobile Audio Systems - ALPINE ELECTRONICS OF AMERICA, INC.; *pg.* 616, *pg.* 292
ALPINE - Furniture - ASHLEY FURNITURE INDUSTRIES, INC.; *pg.* 914, *pg.* 1852
ALPINE - Food Product - CONTINENTAL MILLS, INC.; *pg.* 827, *pg.* 1845
ALPINE - Play System - CREATIVE PLAYTHINGS LTD.; *pg.* 1831, *pg.* 820
THE ALPINE - Naturaline Swing Set - CREATIVE PLAYTHINGS LTD.; *pg.* 1831, *pg.* 820
ALPINE - Bedding - CROSCILL, INC.; *pg.* 1122, *pg.* 1220
ALPINE - Switch - EXTREME NETWORKS INC; *pg.* 287, *pg.* 245
ALPINE - Eye Protection Product - MINE SAFETY APPLIANCES COMPANY; *pg.* 1361, *pg.* 1525
ALPINE - Fabric - NEMSCHOFF, INC.; *pg.* 936, *pg.* 1890
ALPINE - Cigarettes - PHILIP MORRIS USA INC.; *pg.* 1894, *pg.* 1803
ALPINE - Gum - WM. WRIGLEY JR. COMPANY; *pg.* 1863, *pg.* 596
ALPINE 3800 - Switch - EXTREME NETWORKS INC; *pg.* 287, *pg.* 245
ALPINE ADVENTURE - Game - WMS INDUSTRIES INC.; *pg.* 593, *pg.* 666
ALPINE LACE - Deli Cheese - LAND O'LAKES, INC.; *pg.* 873, *pg.* 915
ALPINE PINE - Household Product - BLUE CROSS LABORATORIES; *pg.* 326, *pg.* 277
ALPINE SPICE - Fragrances - S.C. JOHNSON & SON, INC.; *pg.* 334, *pg.* 1889
ALPINE TRAIL - Bike - MARIN BIKES; *pg.* 1708, *pg.* 168
ALPO - Pet Food - NESTLE PURINA PETCARE COMPANY; *pg.* 1479, *pg.* 1000
ALPO CHEW-EEZ - Dog Treats - NESTLE USA, INC.; *pg.* 883, *pg.* 96
ALPO DOG TREATS - Dog Food - NESTLE USA, INC.; *pg.* 883, *pg.* 96
ALPO MASTER'S CHOICE - Dog Food - NESTLE USA, INC.; *pg.* 883, *pg.* 96
ALREADY IN TOUCH WITH THE FUTURE - Tagline - AT&T SOUTHEAST; *pg.* 1868, *pg.* 489
ALREX - Pharmaceutical Product - BAUSCH & LOMB INCORPORATED; *pg.* 1401, *pg.* 1045
ALSIBRONZ - Mica Additive - BASF CATALYSTS LLC; *pg.* 1148, *pg.* 1074
ALSIDE - Building Product - ASSOCIATED MATERIALS LLC; *pg.* 69, *pg.* 1445
ALSONS - Plumbing Product - MASCO CORPORATION; *pg.* 96, *pg.* 909
ALSTO'S - Online Gift Store - IAC/INTERACTIVECORP; *pg.* 292, *pg.* 1242
ALSTYLE APPAREL - Apparel - ENNIS, INC.; *pg.* 393, *pg.* 1727
ALTA - Mass Flow Control - MKS INSTRUMENTS, INC.; *pg.* 1362, *pg.* 781
ALTA - Catheter - SPIRE CORPORATION; *pg.* 1378, *pg.* 786
ALTA DENA - Milk Product - DEAN FOODS COMPANY; *pg.* 852, *pg.* 1679
ALTACE - Pharmaceutical Product - KING PHARMACEUTICALS, INC.; *pg.* 1553, *pg.* 1627
ALTACOR - Insect Control Product - E.I. DU PONT DE NEMOURS & COMPANY; *pg.* 1159, *pg.* 390
ALTACOVER - Insurance - PROASSURANCE CORPORATION; *pg.* 1214, *pg.* 3
ALTADYNE - Healthcare Product - GF HEALTH PRODUCTS, INC.; *pg.* 1535, *pg.* 508
ALTAIR - Software - FLIR SYSTEMS, INC.; *pg.* 1413, *pg.* 1510
ALTAIR - Aircraft Digital Photographs - LOCKHEED MARTIN CORPORATION; *pg.* 229, *pg.* 762
ALTAIR - Multigas Detector - MINE SAFETY APPLIANCES COMPANY; *pg.* 1361, *pg.* 1525
ALTAIR - Furniture - NEMSCHOFF, INC.; *pg.* 936, *pg.* 1890
ALTAIR - Software - SS&C TECHNOLOGIES HOLDINGS, INC.; *pg.* 473, *pg.* 386
ALTAMA - Footwear - PHOENIX FOOTWEAR GROUP, INC.; *pg.* 1815, *pg.* 60
ALTASEC - Information Encryptor - VIASAT, INC.; *pg.* 489, *pg.* 62
ALTAX - Accelerators - R.T. VANDERBILT COMPANY, INC.; *pg.* 1180, *pg.* 364
ALTEC DIRECT - Retail Store Services - ALTEC INDUSTRIES INC.; *pg.* 1312, *pg.* 1
ALTEC SENTRY - Video Cassette Tapes - ALTEC INDUSTRIES INC.; *pg.* 1312, *pg.* 1
ALTEMP - Material & Alloy - ALLEGHENY TECHNOLOGIES INCORPORATED; *pg.* 66, *pg.* 1572
ALTER - Software - BMC SOFTWARE, INC.; *pg.* 362, *pg.* 1701
ALTER-LITE - Replacement Window & Door - TRUE HOME VALUE, INC.; *pg.* 117, *pg.* 738
ALTERA CYCLONE - Circuit Board - XILINX, INC.; *pg.* 496, *pg.* 252
ALTERA STRATIX - Circuit Board - XILINX, INC.; *pg.* 496, *pg.* 252
ALTERNA - Bath Product - KOHLER CO.; *pg.* 91, *pg.* 1862
ALTERNAPLUS - Window & Door - JELD-WEN, INC.; *pg.* 1051, *pg.* 1499
ALTERNATE - Carpet - BEAULIEU GROUP, LLC; *pg.* 917, *pg.* 529
ALTERNATIVE - Fabric - NEMSCHOFF, INC.; *pg.* 936, *pg.* 1890
ALTERNATIVE INVESTMENT LAW REPORT - Publisher - BLOOMBERG BNA; *pg.* 1621, *pg.* 1772
ALTERNATIVE POWER - Online Publication - TECHNOLOGY MARKETING CORP.; *pg.* 1691, *pg.* 364
ALTERNATIVE ROCKS - Diamond Product - STULLER, INC.; *pg.* 13, *pg.* 745
ALTERRA - Coffee - MARS, INCORPORATED; *pg.* 1858, *pg.* 1792
ALTERREX - Replacement Bridge System - BASLER ELECTRIC COMPANY; *pg.* 623, *pg.* 616
ALTI-PHY - Computer Products - BROADCOM CORPORATION; *pg.* 364, *pg.* 108
ALTIMA - Integrated Circuits & Software - BROADCOM CORPORATION; *pg.* 364, *pg.* 108
ALTIMA - Bag - DATREK GOLF; *pg.* 1832, *pg.* 1801
ALTIMA - Automobile - NISSAN NORTH AMERICA, INC.; *pg.* 186, *pg.* 1633
ALTIMETER - Barometers - SWIFT OPTICAL INSTRUMENTS, INC.; *pg.* 1430, *pg.* 1744
ALTIMIRA - Wine - GEYSER PEAK WINERY; *pg.* 1964, *pg.* 101
ALTIRIS - Software - SYMANTEC CORPORATION; *pg.* 478, *pg.* 161
ALTITUDE - Switch - EXTREME NETWORKS INC; *pg.* 287, *pg.* 245
ALTITUDE - Software System - KRONOS INCORPORATED; *pg.* 425, *pg.* 813
ALTITUDE - Fabric - NEMSCHOFF, INC.; *pg.* 936, *pg.* 1890
ALTITUDE 350-2 - Wireless Components - EXTREME NETWORKS INC; *pg.* 287, *pg.* 245
ALTITUDE 450 - Wireless Components - EXTREME NETWORKS INC; *pg.* 287, *pg.* 245
ALTITUDE 451 - Wireless Components - EXTREME NETWORKS INC; *pg.* 287, *pg.* 245
ALTIVEC - Software - MERCURY COMPUTER SYSTEMS, INC.; *pg.* 434, *pg.* 813
ALTOIDS - Mints - WM. WRIGLEY JR. COMPANY; *pg.* 1863, *pg.* 596
ALTON - Heating & Ventilation Equipment - MESTEK, INC.; *pg.* 1074, *pg.* 857
ALTON BELLE - Games - PENN NATIONAL GAMING, INC.; *pg.* 574, *pg.* 1595
ALTOS - Dielectric Cable - CORNING INCORPORATED; *pg.* 1122, *pg.* 1154
ALTRA - Testing Instrument System - BECKMAN COULTER, INC.; *pg.* 1402, *pg.* 48
ALTRAZEAL - Transforming Powder Dressing - ULURU INC.; *pg.* 1603, *pg.* 1658
ALTRO - Fabric - NEMSCHOFF, INC.; *pg.* 936, *pg.* 1890
ALTRUA - Medical Device - BOSTON SCIENTIFIC CORPORATION; *pg.* 1508, *pg.* 831
ALTURA - Furniture - ASHLEY FURNITURE INDUSTRIES, INC.; *pg.* 914, *pg.* 1852
ALTURA - Ion & Electron Beam - FEI COMPANY; *pg.* 1413, *pg.* 1498
ALTURA - Lottery Terminal - INTERNATIONAL GAME TECHNOLOGY; *pg.* 420, *pg.* 1606
ALTUS - Tungsten Deposition System - LAM RESEARCH CORPORATION; *pg.* 1354, *pg.* 246
ALU - Steel Product - A. FINKL & SONS CO.; *pg.* 1309, *pg.* 563
ALU-C - Aluminum Mold - A. FINKL & SONS CO.; *pg.* 1309, *pg.* 563
ALU-KLEEN - Cleaning And Etching Material - HEATBATH CORPORATION; *pg.* 1165, *pg.* 826
ALU-PLATE - Sidewall Panels - ALCOA INC.; *pg.* 65, *pg.* 1188
ALU-X - Aluminum Mold - A. FINKL & SONS CO.; *pg.* 1309, *pg.* 563
ALUM-A-LEAD - Metallic Filler - PPG INDUSTRIES, INC.; *pg.* 1445, *pg.* 1579
ALUM-ETCH - Cleaning And Etching Material - HEATBATH CORPORATION; *pg.* 1165, *pg.* 826
ALUMA ETCH - Pre-Treatment Cleaner - A BRITE COMPANY; *pg.* 1144, *pg.* 1697
ALUMA-PERF - Metal Rain Gutters - ALCOA INC.; *pg.* 65, *pg.* 1188
ALUMA-PLANK - Ladder Product - WERNER HOLDING CO.; *pg.* 121, *pg.* 1534
ALUMACOAT - Antifouling Paint-Aluminum Boats - PETTIT PAINT COMPANY; *pg.* 1444, *pg.* 1116
ALUMAFLEX - Cover - DYNATECT MANUFACTURING INC.; *pg.* 1330, *pg.* 1883
ALUMALOCK - Folding Knife - WERNER HOLDING CO.; *pg.* 121, *pg.* 1534
ALUMASEAL - Radiator Stop Leak - GOLD EAGLE COMPANY; *pg.* 206, *pg.* 575
ALUMEL - Tester - HOWELL INSTRUMENTS INC.; *pg.* 1417, *pg.* 1695
ALUMEX - Pressed & Monolithic Refractory - RESCO PRODUCTS, INC.; *pg.* 107, *pg.* 1581
ALUMI-BLAST - Aerosol - SEYMOUR OF SYCAMORE, INC.; *pg.* 1447, *pg.* 663
ALUMI-BRITE - Automotive Cleaner - DELTA FOREMOST CHEMICAL CORPORATION; *pg.* 1155, *pg.* 1642
ALUMI-MATCH - Touch-Up Paint - SEYMOUR OF SYCAMORE, INC.; *pg.* 1447, *pg.* 663
ALUMI-THERM - Steel Product - AK STEEL HOLDING CORPORATION; *pg.* 1311, *pg.* 1479
ALUMICUBE - Lighting Diffusers - AMERICAN LOUVER COMPANY; *pg.* 1294, *pg.* 660
ALUMIDE - Coating Product - PPG INDUSTRIES, INC.; *pg.* 1445, *pg.* 1579
ALUMIGATOR - Irrigation Equipment Center Pivot - REINKE MANUFACTURING COMPANY, INC.; *pg.* 707, *pg.* 1010
ALUMINALL - Aluminum Paint - HENKEL CORPORATION; *pg.* 1165, *pg.* 1535
ALUMINATOR - Chrome Cover - HARLEY-DAVIDSON, INC.; *pg.* 178, *pg.* 1874
ALUMINUM SHIELD SYSTEM II - Metal Roofing System - TEXAS REFINERY CORP.; *pg.* 986, *pg.* 1696
ALUMINWELD - Electrode - LINCOLN ELECTRIC HOLDINGS, INC.; *pg.* 1355, *pg.* 1432
ALUMITEX - Papers - DAUBERT INDUSTRIES, INC.; *pg.* 1155, *pg.* 561
ALUMITRAK - Aluminum Track Power & Free Conveyors - DAIFUKU WEBB; *pg.* 1327, *pg.* 885
ALUMIX - Coating Product - PPG INDUSTRIES, INC.; *pg.* 1445, *pg.* 1579
ALUMON - Aluminum Preparation - ENTHONE INC.; *pg.* 1161, *pg.* 381
ALUPOWER - Aluminum-Air Batteries - YARDNEY TECHNICAL PRODUCTS, INC.; *pg.* 690, *pg.* 1601
ALUPREM - Mineral Product - TOR MINERALS INTERNATIONAL INC.; *pg.* 1184, *pg.* 1672
ALUPREP - Cleaner - DOW CHEMICAL; *pg.* 1156, *pg.* 1563
ALURA - Power Boats - MARLOW-HUNTER LLC; *pg.* 1709, *pg.* 409
ALUSHIELD - Animal Safety Product - NEOGEN CORPORATION; *pg.* 883, *pg.* 896
ALUVIA - Tablet - ABBOTT LABORATORIES; *pg.* 1484, *pg.* 551
ALVALLE - Gazpacho Fruit Juice & Vegetable Juice Drinks - TROPICANA PRODUCTS, INC.; *pg.* 902, *pg.* 592
ALVAREZ - Acoustic Instruments - LOUD TECHNOLOGIES INC.; *pg.* 652, *pg.* 1847
ALVINA VALENTA - Wedding Gowns - JLM COUTURE, INC.; *pg.* 27, *pg.* 1246
ALWAYS - Feminine Protection - THE PROCTER & GAMBLE COMPANY; *pg.* 1129, *pg.* 1418
ALWAYS A LADY - Slogan - PHILIP MORRIS USA INC.; *pg.* 1894, *pg.* 1803
ALWAYS ABLE - Consulting Service - CIBER, INC.; *pg.* 372, *pg.* 330
ALWAYS FRIENDS - Educational Materials - SCHOLASTIC INC.; *pg.* 1683, *pg.* 1288

First page reference indicates Business Class Edition
Second page reference indicates Geographic Edition

ALWAYS LOOKING OUT FOR YOU. - Slogan - SECUREEYE SYSTEMS, INC.; *pg.* 1280, *pg.* 1822
ALWAYS ON, ALWAYS CONNECTED - Slogan - BLACKBERRY LIMITED; *pg.* 625, *pg.* 1947
ALWAYS RIPE, ALWAYS READY - Tagline - PACIFIC NORTHWEST CANNED PEAR SERVICE, INC.; *pg.* 153, *pg.* 1847
ALWAYS SAVE - Extra Standard Grocery & Grocery Related Products - ASSOCIATED WHOLESALE GROCERS, INC.; *pg.* 1015, *pg.* 715
ALWAYS TENDER - Food Product - HORMEL FOODS CORPORATION; *pg.* 863, *pg.* 915
ALYSSA - Beer - COASTAL EXTREME BREWING COMPANY; *pg.* 240, *pg.* 1602
ALYX - Blood Collection & Transfusion - BAXTER INTERNATIONAL INC.; *pg.* 1499, *pg.* 599
ALZHEMED - Alzheimer's Disease Treatment - BELLUS HEALTH INC.; *pg.* 1503, *pg.* 1951
AM&P TESTING BUYERS' GUIDE - Trade Magazine - ASM INTERNATIONAL; *pg.* 132, *pg.* 1461
AM/PM - 24 Hour Odor Absorber - SURCO PRODUCTS, INC.; *pg.* 336, *pg.* 1581
AM186 - Microcontroller - ADVANCED MICRO DEVICES, INC.; *pg.* 613, *pg.* 282
AM188 - Microcontroller - ADVANCED MICRO DEVICES, INC.; *pg.* 613, *pg.* 282
AM486 - Microcontroller - ADVANCED MICRO DEVICES, INC.; *pg.* 613, *pg.* 282
AMA EVOICE - Medical Journal - AMERICAN MEDICAL ASSOCIATION; *pg.* 130, *pg.* 564
AMA VOICE - Publication - AMERICAN MEDICAL ASSOCIATION; *pg.* 130, *pg.* 564
AMADEO CHIANTI - Italian Wine - LAIRD & COMPANY, INC.; *pg.* 1966, *pg.* 1119
AMAGE - Dry Cleaning & Laundry Product - ADCO, INC.; *pg.* 325, *pg.* 482
AMALFI - Lighting Product - QUOIZEL INC.; *pg.* 1304, *pg.* 1616
AMANA - Meat - HY-VEE, INC.; *pg.* 1023, *pg.* 713
AMANA - Home Appliances - WHIRLPOOL CORPORATION; *pg.* 62, *pg.* 872
AMANDA - Leather Product - COACH, INC.; *pg.* 3, *pg.* 1214
AMANDA - Footwear - PHOENIX FOOTWEAR GROUP, INC.; *pg.* 1815, *pg.* 60
AMANDA - Polo Dress - RALPH LAUREN CORPORATION; *pg.* 46, *pg.* 1284
AMARETTO - Bath Product - KOHLER CO.; *pg.* 91, *pg.* 1862
AMARETTO DI PADRINO - Liqueur - SAZERAC COMPANY, INC.; *pg.* 1969, *pg.* 745
AMARETTO NOG - Oil & Spray - AROMATIQUE INC.; *pg.* 499, *pg.* 32
AMARILLO BONE - Knife - BEAR & SON CUTLERY, INC.; *pg.* 1827, *pg.* 7
AMARINTH - Table - BLATT BOWLING & BILLIARD CORP.; *pg.* 1827, *pg.* 1203
AMARIS - Waiting Seating - STEELCASE INC.; *pg.* 475, *pg.* 889
AMARTA - Software - SUNGARD DATA SYSTEMS INC.; *pg.* 477, *pg.* 1592
AMASS - Software - QUANTUM CORPORATION; *pg.* 458, *pg.* 250
AMATEUR CITY ELITE - Event - CHICAGO WHITE SOX LTD.; *pg.* 539, *pg.* 570
AMATOM - Electronic Hardware - AMATOM ELECTRONIC HARDWARE, INC.; *pg.* 1041, *pg.* 342
AMAX - Match Bullets - HORNADY MANUFACTURING COMPANY; *pg.* 1836, *pg.* 1010
AMAZE - Detergent - ADCO, INC.; *pg.* 325, *pg.* 482
THE AMAZEMENT PARK - Amusement & Water Park - CEDAR FAIR, L.P.; *pg.* 537, *pg.* 1471
AMAZIN - Pet Shampoo - BLUE CROSS LABORATORIES; *pg.* 326, *pg.* 277
AMAZING - Carpet - INTERFACE, INC.; *pg.* 695, *pg.* 512
AMAZING 8'S - Lottery Card - MISSOURI LOTTERY; *pg.* 999, *pg.* 979
THE AMAZING DAYS OF ABBY HAYES - Educational Materials - SCHOLASTIC INC.; *pg.* 1683, *pg.* 1288
THE AMAZING EXTEND-O-TOTE - Bags - HABAND COMPANY, INC.; *pg.* 1772, *pg.* 1099
AMAZING GAME BOARD BOOK - Toy And Game - INNOVATIVE USA, INC.; *pg.* 957, *pg.* 363
AMAZING SEVENS - Game - WMS INDUSTRIES INC.; *pg.* 593, *pg.* 666
AMAZING SOLUTIONS - Slogan - COORSTEK, INC.; *pg.* 77, *pg.* 330
AMAZING STORIES - Magazine - WIZARDS OF THE COAST, INC.; *pg.* 970, *pg.* 1830
AMAZING STRETCH LACE - Blouses - HABAND COMPANY, INC.; *pg.* 1772, *pg.* 1099
AMAZON - Breakfast Cereals - NATURE'S PATH FOODS INC.; *pg.* 833, *pg.* 1908
AMAZON - Fabric - NEMSCHOFF, INC.; *pg.* 936, *pg.* 1890
AMAZON - Mountain Gear - W.L. GORE & ASSOCIATES, INC.; *pg.* 122, *pg.* 388
AMAZON HANDMADE - Online Store with Artistic and Craft Products - AMAZON.COM, INC.; *pg.* 1226, *pg.* 1831
AMAZON PRIME - Delivery Service - AMAZON.COM, INC.; *pg.* 1226, *pg.* 1831
AMAZON STORM - Ice Cream - WELLS ENTERPRISES, INC.; *pg.* 909, *pg.* 709
AMAZON.COM - Online Store - AMAZON.COM, INC.; *pg.* 1226, *pg.* 1831
AMBANJA - Chocolate Product - GUITTARD CHOCOLATE COMPANY; *pg.* 1855, *pg.* 55
AMBAR MARINE - Welded Aluminum Boat - SILVER SHIPS, INC.; *pg.* 1923, *pg.* 8
AMBASA - Beverages - THE COCA-COLA COMPANY; *pg.* 240, *pg.* 493
AMBASSADOR - Locker - AMERICAN LOCKER GROUP INCORPORATED; *pg.* 1041, *pg.* 1674
AMBASSADOR - Computer Telephony Integration - AVAGO TECHNOLOGIES; *pg.* 358, *pg.* 238
AMBASSADOR - Lounge Chairs - BERNHARDT DESIGN; *pg.* 918, *pg.* 1381
AMBASSADOR - Table - BLATT BOWLING & BILLIARD CORP.; *pg.* 1827, *pg.* 1203
AMBASSADOR - Towing Product - BLUE OX; *pg.* 701, *pg.* 1019
AMBASSADOR - Seating Product - IRWIN SEATING COMPANY INC.; *pg.* 929, *pg.* 887
AMBER - Flat Panel Display - EPSILON SYSTEMS SOLUTIONS; *pg.* 1412, *pg.* 202
AMBER - Fabric - NEMSCHOFF, INC.; *pg.* 936, *pg.* 1890
AMBER SUNSET - Candle - THE YANKEE CANDLE COMPANY, INC.; *pg.* 1792, *pg.* 843
AMBERCHROM - Resin - DOW CHEMICAL; *pg.* 1156, *pg.* 1563
AMBEREDGE - Resin - DOW CHEMICAL; *pg.* 1156, *pg.* 1563
AMBERGUM - Polymer - HERCULES INCORPORATED; *pg.* 1166, *pg.* 392
AMBERJET - Resin - DOW CHEMICAL; *pg.* 1156, *pg.* 1563
AMBERLEY ESTATE - Wine - CONSTELLATION BRANDS CANADA; *pg.* 1960, *pg.* 1925
AMBERLITE - Resin - DOW CHEMICAL; *pg.* 1156, *pg.* 1563
AMBERLITE - Ion Exchange Resins - THE DOW CHEMICAL COMPANY; *pg.* 1157, *pg.* 898
AMBERLITE - Chemical Product - SPECTRUM CHEMICALS & LABORATORY PRODUCTS, INC.; *pg.* 1181, *pg.* 94
AMBERLYST - Resin - DOW CHEMICAL; *pg.* 1156, *pg.* 1563
AMBERSYNTH - Resin - DOW CHEMICAL; *pg.* 1156, *pg.* 1563
AMBERWARE - Microwave Cookware - VENTURI, INC.; *pg.* 1606, *pg.* 910
AMBERZYME - Resin - DOW CHEMICAL; *pg.* 1156, *pg.* 1563
AMBI - Furniture - HERMAN MILLER, INC.; *pg.* 926, *pg.* 913
AMBIANCE - Electronics - CAMBRIDGE SOUNDWORKS, INC.; *pg.* 1234, *pg.* 781
AMBIEN CIV - Zolpidem Tartrate - SANOFI US; *pg.* 1592, *pg.* 1046
AMBIENT - Mattress Pad - CARPENTER CO.; *pg.* 920, *pg.* 1801
AMBION - Gene Array - AFFYMETRIX, INC.; *pg.* 1487, *pg.* 263
AMBISOME - Biopharmaceutical Product - GILEAD SCIENCES, INC.; *pg.* 1535, *pg.* 88
AMBIT - Security Systems - MAXXESS SYSTEMS, INC.; *pg.* 431, *pg.* 43
AMBITROL - Coolant - THE DOW CHEMICAL COMPANY; *pg.* 1157, *pg.* 898
AMBOND - Resins - GEORGIA-PACIFIC LLC; *pg.* 1458, *pg.* 507
AMBRA - Tile - ARTISTIC TILE INC.; *pg.* 914, *pg.* 1119
AMBRIA - Home Fragrance Product - BLYTH, INC.; *pg.* 502, *pg.* 349
AMBRIA - Fine Dining Restaurant - LETTUCE ENTERTAIN YOU ENTERPRISES, INC.; *pg.* 1735, *pg.* 580
AMBRODERM - Skin Care Product - MANNATECH, INCORPORATED; *pg.* 1558, *pg.* 1671
AMBROSIA - Wines - 1-800-FLOWERS.COM, INC.; *pg.* 1758, *pg.* 1151
AMBROSTART - Nutritional Product - MANNATECH, INCORPORATED; *pg.* 1558, *pg.* 1671
AMBROTOSE - Medical Device - MANNATECH, INCORPORATED; *pg.* 1558, *pg.* 1671
AMBROTOSE AO - Medical Device - MANNATECH, INCORPORATED; *pg.* 1558, *pg.* 1671
AMBROTOSE COMPLEX - Healthcare Product - MANNATECH, INCORPORATED; *pg.* 1558, *pg.* 1671
AMBUSH - Boat Propeller - MICHIGAN WHEEL CORPORATION; *pg.* 1709, *pg.* 888
AMBUSH - Apparel - OAKLEY, INC.; *pg.* 1840, *pg.* 86
AMBX - PC Gaming Peripherals - PHILIPS ELECTRONICS NORTH AMERICA; *pg.* 662, *pg.* 782
AMC - Television Network - AMC NETWORKS INC.; *pg.* 269, *pg.* 1189
AMC THEATRES - Motion Picture Theaters - AMC ENTERTAINMENT INC.; *pg.* 527, *pg.* 716
AMC TRADE SHOWS, LTD. - Trade Show Operating Company - AMC, INC.; *pg.* 1759, *pg.* 487
AMCAL - Home Product - WESTROCK COMPANY; *pg.* 1472, *pg.* 1805
AMCO CLEAR - Chemical Product - GFS CHEMICALS, INC.; *pg.* 1164, *pg.* 1471
AMD - Integrated Circuits - ADVANCED MICRO DEVICES, INC.; *pg.* 613, *pg.* 282
AMD-750 - Chipset - ADVANCED MICRO DEVICES, INC.; *pg.* 613, *pg.* 282
AMD-751 - Chipset - ADVANCED MICRO DEVICES, INC.; *pg.* 613, *pg.* 282
AMD-756 - Chipset - ADVANCED MICRO DEVICES, INC.; *pg.* 613, *pg.* 282
AMD-760 - Chipset - ADVANCED MICRO DEVICES, INC.; *pg.* 613, *pg.* 282
AMD-761 - Chipset - ADVANCED MICRO DEVICES, INC.; *pg.* 613, *pg.* 282
AMD-762 - Chipset - ADVANCED MICRO DEVICES, INC.; *pg.* 613, *pg.* 282
AMD-766 - Chipset - ADVANCED MICRO DEVICES, INC.; *pg.* 613, *pg.* 282
AMD-768 - Chipset - ADVANCED MICRO DEVICES, INC.; *pg.* 613, *pg.* 282
AMD-8000 - Chipset - ADVANCED MICRO DEVICES, INC.; *pg.* 613, *pg.* 282
AMD-8100 - Chipset - ADVANCED MICRO DEVICES, INC.; *pg.* 613, *pg.* 282
AMD-8111 - Chipset - ADVANCED MICRO DEVICES, INC.; *pg.* 613, *pg.* 282
AMD-8113 - Chipset - ADVANCED MICRO DEVICES, INC.; *pg.* 613, *pg.* 282
AMD-8114 - Chipset - ADVANCED MICRO DEVICES, INC.; *pg.* 613, *pg.* 282
AMD-8115 - Chipset - ADVANCED MICRO DEVICES, INC.; *pg.* 613, *pg.* 282
AMD-8131 - Chipset - ADVANCED MICRO DEVICES, INC.; *pg.* 613, *pg.* 282
AMD-8132 - Connectivity Product - ADVANCED MICRO DEVICES, INC.; *pg.* 613, *pg.* 282
AMD-8151 - Chipset - ADVANCED MICRO DEVICES, INC.; *pg.* 613, *pg.* 282
AMD-8152 - Chipset - ADVANCED MICRO DEVICES, INC.; *pg.* 613, *pg.* 282
AMD-8161 - Chipset - ADVANCED MICRO DEVICES, INC.; *pg.* 613, *pg.* 282
AMD ATHLON - Microprocessor - ADVANCED MICRO DEVICES, INC.; *pg.* 613, *pg.* 282
AMD COOLCORE - Chipset - ADVANCED MICRO DEVICES, INC.; *pg.* 613, *pg.* 282
AMD DIGITAL MEDIA XPRESS - Video Software - ADVANCED MICRO DEVICES, INC.; *pg.* 613, *pg.* 282
AMD DURON - Microprocessor - ADVANCED MICRO DEVICES, INC.; *pg.* 613, *pg.* 282
AMD EFFICEON - Microprocessor - ADVANCED MICRO DEVICES, INC.; *pg.* 613, *pg.* 282
AMD GEODE - Connectivity Product - ADVANCED MICRO DEVICES, INC.; *pg.* 613, *pg.* 282
AMD IMAGEON - Mobile Processor - ADVANCED MICRO DEVICES, INC.; *pg.* 613, *pg.* 282
AMD-K6 - Microprocessor - ADVANCED MICRO DEVICES, INC.; *pg.* 613, *pg.* 282
AMD-K7 - Microprocessor - ADVANCED MICRO DEVICES, INC.; *pg.* 613, *pg.* 282
AMD-K8 - Microprocessor - ADVANCED MICRO DEVICES, INC.; *pg.* 613, *pg.* 282

AMD LIVE! - Video Software - ADVANCED MICRO DEVICES, INC.; *pg.* 613, *pg.* 282
AMD OPTERON - Microprocessor - ADVANCED MICRO DEVICES, INC.; *pg.* 613, *pg.* 282
AMD OVERDRIVE - Graphics Card - ADVANCED MICRO DEVICES, INC.; *pg.* 613, *pg.* 282
AMD PHENOM - Microprocessor - ADVANCED MICRO DEVICES, INC.; *pg.* 613, *pg.* 282
AMD POWERNOW! - Software - ADVANCED MICRO DEVICES, INC.; *pg.* 613, *pg.* 282
AMD SEMPRON - Microprocessor - ADVANCED MICRO DEVICES, INC.; *pg.* 613, *pg.* 282
AMD TURION - Microprocessor - ADVANCED MICRO DEVICES, INC.; *pg.* 613, *pg.* 282
AMD VIRTUALIZATION - Chipset - ADVANCED MICRO DEVICES, INC.; *pg.* 613, *pg.* 282
AMD XILLEON - Microprocessor - ADVANCED MICRO DEVICES, INC.; *pg.* 613, *pg.* 282
AMD XPRESS - Microprocessor - ADVANCED MICRO DEVICES, INC.; *pg.* 613, *pg.* 282
AMD XPRESSNOW! - Microprocessor - ADVANCED MICRO DEVICES, INC.; *pg.* 613, *pg.* 282
AMD8 POKE-THRU - Wiring Products - WIREMOLD/LEGRAND; *pg.* 689, *pg.* 383
AMDD - Inspection System - KLA-TENCOR CORPORATION; *pg.* 1353, *pg.* 146
AMDEBUG - Chipset - ADVANCED MICRO DEVICES, INC.; *pg.* 613, *pg.* 282
AMDIRECT - Chipset - ADVANCED MICRO DEVICES, INC.; *pg.* 613, *pg.* 282
AME - Marine Resins - ASHLAND INC.; *pg.* 972, *pg.* 726
AMECO - Construction Product - FLUOR CORPORATION; *pg.* 82, *pg.* 1719
AMELIA - Decorative Accessory - ETHAN ALLEN INTERIORS INC.; *pg.* 924, *pg.* 343
AMELIE - Hat - WOODEN SHIPS OF HOBOKEN; *pg.* 35, *pg.* 1315
AMENITY - Fabric - MOMENTUM TEXTILES INC.; *pg.* 697, *pg.* 114
AMERCOAT - Coating & Finish - NOV AMERON; *pg.* 100, *pg.* 187
AMERCOR - Controlling Corrosion - ASHLAND INC.; *pg.* 972, *pg.* 726
AMEREQUIP - Utility Vehicle Attachments - AMEREQUIP CORPORATION; *pg.* 700, *pg.* 1862
AMERFLOC - Water Treatment - ASHLAND INC.; *pg.* 972, *pg.* 726
AMERFLON - Packing Valves - ASHLAND INC.; *pg.* 972, *pg.* 726
AMERI-KART - Plastic Product - MYERS INDUSTRIES, INC.; *pg.* 1887, *pg.* 1402
AMERICA - Restaurant - ARK RESTAURANTS CORP.; *pg.* 1715, *pg.* 1196
AMERICA AT SCHOOL - Teaching Materials - AMERICAN GIRL LLC; *pg.* 949, *pg.* 1871
AMERICA@WORK - Magazine - AMERICAN FEDERATION OF LABOR - CONGRESS OF INDUSTRIAL ORGANIZATIONS; *pg.* 128, *pg.* 394
AMERICA. CHAPTER I. - Editorial Advertisement - COLONIAL WILLIAMSBURG FOUNDATION; *pg.* 541, *pg.* 1811
AMERICA COOKS - Kitchen Products - ROBINSON HOME PRODUCTS INC.; *pg.* 1060, *pg.* 1355
AMERICA UNDERCOVER - Cable Television Show - HOME BOX OFFICE, INC.; *pg.* 290, *pg.* 1240
AMERICAL - Ophthalmic Polish for Hard Resin Lenses - FERRO CORPORATION; *pg.* 1162, *pg.* 1462
AMERICAL PLUS - Ophthalmic Polish - FERRO CORPORATION; *pg.* 1162, *pg.* 1462
AMERICAN - Lockers - AMERICAN LOCKER GROUP INCORPORATED; *pg.* 1041, *pg.* 1674
AMERICAN - Metal Vault Doors - DIEBOLD, INCORPORATED; *pg.* 387, *pg.* 1407
AMERICAN - Meters - ELSTER AMERICAN METER COMPANY; *pg.* 1411, *pg.* 1387
AMERICAN 7'S - Game - WMS INDUSTRIES INC.; *pg.* 593, *pg.* 666
AMERICAN 7'S PLUS - Game - WMS INDUSTRIES INC.; *pg.* 593, *pg.* 666
AMERICAN ADVENTURES - Magazine - SCHOLASTIC INC.; *pg.* 1683, *pg.* 1288
AMERICAN AIRLINES - Airline - AMERICAN AIRLINES INC.; *pg.* 1898, *pg.* 1693
AMERICAN APPRAISAL CANADA - Appraisal Services - AMERICAN APPRAISAL ASSOCIATES, INC.; *pg.* 349, *pg.* 1872
AMERICAN ARTIST - Trade Publication - THE NIELSEN COMPANY B.V.; *pg.* 1671, *pg.* 1272
AMERICAN AUGERS - Paving Equipment - ASTEC INDUSTRIES, INC.; *pg.* 69, *pg.* 1628
AMERICAN BABY - Magazine - MEREDITH CORPORATION; *pg.* 1663, *pg.* 705
AMERICAN BANDSTAND - Music & Dance Television Program - DICK CLARK PRODUCTIONS, INC.; *pg.* 281, *pg.* 273
AMERICAN BANDSTAND - Game - INTERNATIONAL GAME TECHNOLOGY; *pg.* 957, *pg.* 1024
AMERICAN BASKET - Shopping Basket - AMERICAN LOUVER COMPANY; *pg.* 1294, *pg.* 660
AMERICAN BEAUTY - Beauty Products - THE ESTEE LAUDER COMPANIES INC.; *pg.* 508, *pg.* 1229
AMERICAN BEAUTY - Food Product - NEW WORLD PASTA COMPANY; *pg.* 885, *pg.* 1537
AMERICAN BLACK - Granite - ROCK OF AGES CORPORATION; *pg.* 108, *pg.* 1766
AMERICAN BODY ARMOR - Ballistic Protective Vests - BAE SYSTEMS PRODUCTS GROUP; *pg.* 359, *pg.* 432
AMERICAN BOOK TRADE DIRECTORY - Directory to Retail & Antiquarian Book Dealers, Wholesalers & Distributors - R.R. BOWKER LLC; *pg.* 1682, *pg.* 1095
AMERICAN BUSINESS AWARDS - Award - STEVIE AWARDS, INC.; *pg.* 157, *pg.* 1780
AMERICAN BUSINESS DIRECTORIES - National Directories - INFOGROUP INC.; *pg.* 1652, *pg.* 1016
AMERICAN CANCER SOCIETY - Cancer Awareness Programs - AMERICAN CANCER SOCIETY, INC.; *pg.* 126, *pg.* 487
AMERICAN CELEBRATIONS - Swoop Tray Basket - THE LONGABERGER COMPANY; *pg.* 1127, *pg.* 1467
AMERICAN CINEMATOGRAPHER - Magazine - AMERICAN SOCIETY OF CINEMATOGRAPHERS; *pg.* 1616, *pg.* 103
AMERICAN CLASSIC - Motor Oil - BARDAHL MANUFACTURING CORPORATION; *pg.* 972, *pg.* 1833
AMERICAN CLASSICS - Salads - RESER'S FINE FOODS INC.; *pg.* 1032, *pg.* 1496
AMERICAN CLASSICS - Gift Basket - RUSSELL STOVER CANDIES, INC.; *pg.* 1861, *pg.* 986
AMERICAN CLIPPER - Motorhome - REXHALL INDUSTRIES, INC.; *pg.* 1710, *pg.* 121
AMERICAN COIN-OP - Trade Magazine - CRAIN COMMUNICATIONS, INC.; *pg.* 1631, *pg.* 879
AMERICAN COLA - Beverage - THE MONARCH BEVERAGE COMPANY, INC.; *pg.* 257, *pg.* 514
THE AMERICAN COLLECTION - Misses' & Women's Apparel - KELLWOOD COMPANY; *pg.* 28, *pg.* 975
AMERICAN CONTRACTOR - Extension Cords - COLEMAN CABLE, INC.; *pg.* 1324, *pg.* 665
AMERICAN COUNTRY - Book Series - DIRECT HOLDINGS AMERICAS INC.; *pg.* 1636, *pg.* 1780
AMERICAN DAIRY ASSOCIATION - Dairy Product - DAIRY MANAGEMENT, INC.; *pg.* 138, *pg.* 656
AMERICAN DIAMOND - Apparel - ENNIS, INC.; *pg.* 393, *pg.* 1727
AMERICAN DREW - Wood Bedroom & Dining Room Furniture - AMERICAN DREW; *pg.* 912, *pg.* 1374
THE AMERICAN DRUMMERS ACHIEVEMENT AWARDS - Musical Instrument - AVEDIS ZILDJIAN COMPANY; *pg.* 531, *pg.* 839
AMERICAN DRYCLEANER - Trade Magazine - CRAIN COMMUNICATIONS, INC.; *pg.* 1631, *pg.* 879
AMERICAN EAGLE - Casual Clothing - AMERICAN EAGLE OUTFITTERS, INC.; *pg.* 37, *pg.* 1572
AMERICAN EAGLE - Footwear - JIMLAR CORPORATION; *pg.* 1810, *pg.* 1246
AMERICAN EDUCATION PUBLISHING - Educational Resources - SCHOOL SPECIALTY, INC.; *pg.* 467, *pg.* 1860
AMERICAN ELECT - Office Furniture - STEELCASE INC.; *pg.* 475, *pg.* 889
AMERICAN ELECTRIC LIGHTING - Lighting Fixture Product - ACUITY BRANDS, INC.; *pg.* 1294, *pg.* 487
AMERICAN ELECTRONICS - Precision Power Electromechanical Equipment - DUCOMMUN TECHNOLOGIES, INC.; *pg.* 634, *pg.* 63
AMERICAN ENCORES - Magazine - NASHVILLE SYMPHONY ASSOCIATION; *pg.* 565, *pg.* 1653
THE AMERICAN ENTERPRISE - Bi-Monthly Policy Magazine - AMERICAN ENTERPRISE INSTITUTE FOR PUBLIC POLICY RESEARCH; *pg.* 128, *pg.* 394
AMERICAN EXPRESS - Gift Cheques - GATE CITY BANK; *pg.* 761, *pg.* 1397
AMERICAN FARMLAND - Tank - TRACTOR SUPPLY COMPANY; *pg.* 708, *pg.* 1627
AMERICAN FLYER - Toy Train - LIONEL LLC; *pg.* 961, *pg.* 875
AMERICAN FORESTS - Magazine - AMERICAN FORESTS; *pg.* 128, *pg.* 394
AMERICAN GARDEN - Table Knives - TIFFANY & CO.; *pg.* 13, *pg.* 1299
AMERICAN GIRL - Dolls - AMERICAN GIRL LLC; *pg.* 949, *pg.* 1871
AMERICAN GIRL - Dolls and Books for Adolescent Girls - MATTEL, INC.; *pg.* 962, *pg.* 81
AMERICAN GIRL ATHLETE - Dolls - AMERICAN GIRL LLC; *pg.* 949, *pg.* 1871
AMERICAN GIRL CAFE - Dolls - AMERICAN GIRL LLC; *pg.* 949, *pg.* 1871
AMERICAN GIRL CLUB - Club Membership Association - AMERICAN GIRL LLC; *pg.* 949, *pg.* 1871
AMERICAN GIRL FASHION SHOW - Games - AMERICAN GIRL LLC; *pg.* 949, *pg.* 1871
AMERICAN GIRL GEAR - Girls Clothes & Accessories - AMERICAN GIRL LLC; *pg.* 949, *pg.* 1871
AMERICAN GIRL ICE CREAM FUN DAY - Dolls - AMERICAN GIRL LLC; *pg.* 949, *pg.* 1871
AMERICAN GIRL LIBRARY - Activity Books for Girls 7-12 - AMERICAN GIRL LLC; *pg.* 949, *pg.* 1871
AMERICAN GIRL MAGAZINE - Publication - AMERICAN GIRL LLC; *pg.* 949, *pg.* 1871
AMERICAN GIRL OF TODAY - Dolls, Books & Doll Accessories - AMERICAN GIRL LLC; *pg.* 949, *pg.* 1871
AMERICAN GIRL THEATER - Dolls - AMERICAN GIRL LLC; *pg.* 949, *pg.* 1871
AMERICAN GIRL TODAY - Dolls & Doll Accessories - AMERICAN GIRL LLC; *pg.* 949, *pg.* 1871
AMERICAN GIRL TODAY - Toy - MATTEL, INC.; *pg.* 962, *pg.* 81
AMERICAN GIRLS - Dolls - AMERICAN GIRL LLC; *pg.* 949, *pg.* 1871
THE AMERICAN GIRLS ART STUDIO - Doll And Toy - AMERICAN GIRL LLC; *pg.* 949, *pg.* 1871
THE AMERICAN GIRLS CHRISTMAS - Games - AMERICAN GIRL LLC; *pg.* 949, *pg.* 1871
THE AMERICAN GIRLS CLUB - Doll And Toy - AMERICAN GIRL LLC; *pg.* 949, *pg.* 1871
THE AMERICAN GIRLS COLLECTION - Doll And Toy - AMERICAN GIRL LLC; *pg.* 949, *pg.* 1871
AMERICAN GIRLS COLLECTION - Toy - MATTEL, INC.; *pg.* 962, *pg.* 81
THE AMERICAN GIRLS GAME - Doll And Toy - AMERICAN GIRL LLC; *pg.* 949, *pg.* 1871
AMERICAN GIRLS HISTORIAN - Dolls - AMERICAN GIRL LLC; *pg.* 949, *pg.* 1871
THE AMERICAN GIRLS NEWS - Games - AMERICAN GIRL LLC; *pg.* 949, *pg.* 1871
AMERICAN GIRLS PASTIMES - Dolls - AMERICAN GIRL LLC; *pg.* 949, *pg.* 1871
THE AMERICAN GIRLS POSTCARD COLLECTION - Doll And Toy - AMERICAN GIRL LLC; *pg.* 949, *pg.* 1871
THE AMERICAN GIRLS PUZZLE - Doll And Toy - AMERICAN GIRL LLC; *pg.* 949, *pg.* 1871
THE AMERICAN GIRLS REVUE - Doll And Toy - AMERICAN GIRL LLC; *pg.* 949, *pg.* 1871
THE AMERICAN GIRLS SAVINGS GAME - Doll And Toy - AMERICAN GIRL LLC; *pg.* 949, *pg.* 1871
AMERICAN GIRLS SHORT STORIES - Games - AMERICAN GIRL LLC; *pg.* 949, *pg.* 1871
THE AMERICAN GIRLS TEA - Games - AMERICAN GIRL LLC; *pg.* 949, *pg.* 1871
AMERICAN GIRLS TRADING CARDS - Play Cards - AMERICAN GIRL LLC; *pg.* 949, *pg.* 1871
AMERICAN GREETINGS SAYS IT BEST - Tagline - AMERICAN GREETINGS CORPORATION; *pg.* 1615, *pg.* 1428
AMERICAN GROWN BOTTLE - Water Bottles - PRIMO WATER CORPORATION; *pg.* 1030, *pg.* 1395
AMERICAN HARMONY - Flatware - ONEIDA LTD; *pg.* 1129, *pg.* 1318
AMERICAN HEALTH - Nutritional Supplements - NBTY, INC.; *pg.* 1572, *pg.* 1338
AMERICAN HEALTH CONSULTANTS - Healthcare Newletters - TRUVEN HEALTH ANALYTICS; *pg.* 1696, *pg.* 867
AMERICAN HERITAGE - Candy - MARS, INCORPORATED; *pg.* 1858, *pg.* 1792

First page reference indicates Business Class Edition
Second page reference indicates Geographic Edition

AMERICAN HERITAGE - Cheese - SCHREIBER FOODS, INC.; *pg.* 894, *pg.* 1859
AMERICAN HERITAGE LIFE - Workplace Insurance - THE ALLSTATE CORPORATION; *pg.* 1189, *pg.* 639
AMERICAN HEWN - Furniture - BASSETT FURNITURE INDUSTRIES, INCORPORATED; *pg.* 916, *pg.* 1776
AMERICAN HOME - Plate & Utensils - THE LONGABERGER COMPANY; *pg.* 1127, *pg.* 1467
AMERICAN HOME COLLECTION - Furniture - LA-Z-BOY INCORPORATED; *pg.* 932, *pg.* 901
AMERICAN HOME SHIELD - Home Warranty Contracts - THE SERVICEMASTER COMPANY, LLC; *pg.* 335, *pg.* 1646
AMERICAN INTERNATIONAL TOY FAIR - Show - TOY INDUSTRY ASSOCIATION, INC.; *pg.* 158, *pg.* 1303
AMERICAN JOURNAL OF NURSING - Nursing Journal - LIPPINCOTT WILLIAMS & WILKINS, INC.; *pg.* 1659, *pg.* 1567
AMERICAN JOURNAL OF THERAPEUTICS - Medical Journal - LIPPINCOTT WILLIAMS & WILKINS, INC.; *pg.* 1659, *pg.* 1567
AMERICAN KENNEL CLUB - Dog Owner Association - AMERICAN KENNEL CLUB, INC.; *pg.* 129, *pg.* 1193
AMERICAN LAUNDRY NEWS - Trade Magazine - CRAIN COMMUNICATIONS, INC.; *pg.* 1631, *pg.* 879
THE AMERICAN LAWYER - Legal Publication - AMERICAN LAWYER MEDIA, INC.; *pg.* 1615, *pg.* 1193
AMERICAN LEGACY - Financial Product - LINCOLN NATIONAL CORPORATION; *pg.* 776, *pg.* 1567
AMERICAN LEGACY FOUNDATION - Anti-Smoking Foundation - TRUTH INITIATIVE; *pg.* 158, *pg.* 405
AMERICAN LEVEL - Electronic Levels - M-D BUILDING PRODUCTS, INC.; *pg.* 95, *pg.* 1486
AMERICAN LIBRARIES - Publication - AMERICAN LIBRARY ASSOCIATION; *pg.* 1615, *pg.* 564
AMERICAN LIBRARY DIRECTORY - Reference Guide of Information on Libraries & Library-Related Organizations - R.R. BOWKER LLC; *pg.* 1682, *pg.* 1095
AMERICAN LIFESTYLE - Bed Linen - SPRINGS GLOBAL, INC.; *pg.* 698, *pg.* 1616
AMERICAN LIFTS - Lift Tables - COLUMBUS MCKINNON CORPORATION; *pg.* 1325, *pg.* 1138
AMERICAN LIVING - Clothing, Accessories & Home Furnishings - RALPH LAUREN CORPORATION; *pg.* 46, *pg.* 1284
AMERICAN LOCK - Hardware - FORTUNE BRANDS HOME & SECURITY, INC.; *pg.* 55, *pg.* 600
AMERICAN MARKING SYSTEMS - Marking Devices - AMERICAN MARKING SYSTEMS, INC.; *pg.* 349, *pg.* 1051
AMERICAN MEDICAL NEWS - Medical Newspaper - AMERICAN MEDICAL ASSOCIATION; *pg.* 130, *pg.* 564
AMERICAN MEN & WOMEN OF SCIENCE - Reference Book - R.R. BOWKER LLC; *pg.* 1682, *pg.* 1095
AMERICAN METAL PRODUCTS - Air Distribution Products - MASCO CORPORATION; *pg.* 96, *pg.* 909
AMERICAN METAL WARE - Coffee & Tea Systems - GRINDMASTER CORPORATION; *pg.* 56, *pg.* 734
AMERICAN MIRROR - Mirror - AMERICAN LOUVER COMPANY; *pg.* 1294, *pg.* 660
AMERICAN MODERN - Furniture - STANLEY FURNITURE CO., INC.; *pg.* 943, *pg.* 1379
AMERICAN MOSS - Excelsior Fiber - AMERICAN EXCELSIOR COMPANY; *pg.* 1451, *pg.* 1659
AMERICAN MUSIC AWARDS - Music Awards - DICK CLARK PRODUCTIONS, INC.; *pg.* 281, *pg.* 273
AMERICAN OBSERVER - Magazine - SCHOLASTIC INC.; *pg.* 1683, *pg.* 1288
AMERICAN OLEAN - Ceramic Tile - DAL-TILE CORPORATION; *pg.* 78, *pg.* 1678
AMERICAN OLEAN - Flooring - MOHAWK INDUSTRIES, INC.; *pg.* 935, *pg.* 527
AMERICAN ORIGINAL - Women's Fragrance - COTY, INC.; *pg.* 506, *pg.* 1219
THE AMERICAN ORIGINAL - Slogan - SUN VALLEY COMPANY; *pg.* 1115, *pg.* 550
AMERICAN PATCHWORK & QUILTING - Magazine - MEREDITH CORPORATION; *pg.* 1663, *pg.* 705
AMERICAN PERIOD - Lighting Fixtures - AMERICAN PERIOD LIGHTING, INC.; *pg.* 1294, *pg.* 1545
THE AMERICAN QUARTER HORSE JOURNAL - Horse Breeding Magazine - AMERICAN QUARTER HORSE ASSOCIATION; *pg.* 130, *pg.* 1658
THE AMERICAN QUARTER HORSE RACING JOURNAL - Horse Breeding Magazine - AMERICAN QUARTER HORSE ASSOCIATION; *pg.* 130, *pg.* 1658
AMERICAN QUILTERS SOCIETY - Publisher - SCHROEDER PUBLISHING COMPANY; *pg.* 1685, *pg.* 739
AMERICAN REELS - Game - WMS INDUSTRIES INC.; *pg.* 593, *pg.* 666
AMERICAN REPROGRAPHICS COMPANY - Reprographic Services - AMERICAN REPROGRAPHICS COMPANY; *pg.* 1616, *pg.* 303
AMERICAN RESIDENTIAL SERVICES/RESCUE ROOTER - Heating, Air Conditioning & Plumbing Service - THE SERVICEMASTER COMPANY, LLC; *pg.* 335, *pg.* 1646
AMERICAN RIVERS - Door - RAYNOR GARAGE DOORS; *pg.* 106, *pg.* 607
AMERICAN ROSE - Dinnerware - THE HOMER LAUGHLIN CHINA COMPANY; *pg.* 1125, *pg.* 1850
AMERICAN RUG CRAFTSMEN - Carpet Line - MOHAWK INDUSTRIES, INC.; *pg.* 935, *pg.* 527
AMERICAN SALON - Trade Publication - UBM ADVANSTAR; *pg.* 1697, *pg.* 1306
AMERICAN SEAWAY FOODS - Wholesale Foods - GIANT EAGLE AMERICAN SEAWAY FOODS; *pg.* 1020, *pg.* 1405
AMERICAN SERIES - Metal Building System - BUTLER MANUFACTURING COMPANY; *pg.* 72, *pg.* 981
AMERICAN SHIELD OF HONOR - Pin - STULLER, INC.; *pg.* 13, *pg.* 745
AMERICAN SHOWER & BATH - Tub & Shower Units - MASCO CORPORATION; *pg.* 96, *pg.* 909
AMERICAN SIGMA - Water Quality Instrument - DANAHER CORPORATION; *pg.* 1044, *pg.* 397
AMERICAN SLICE - Cheese - THE GREAT LAKES CHEESE CO., INC.; *pg.* 859, *pg.* 1455
AMERICAN SNOWMOBILER - Magazine - KALMBACH PUBLISHING CO.; *pg.* 1656, *pg.* 1898
AMERICAN SONGBOOK - Performing Arts Program - LINCOLN CENTER FOR THE PERFORMING ARTS, INC.; *pg.* 557, *pg.* 1251
AMERICAN SPEEDY PRINTING - Quick Printing Services - ALLEGRA NETWORK LLC; *pg.* 1614, *pg.* 904
AMERICAN SPIRIT - Gaming Product - GLD PRODUCTS, INC.; *pg.* 1835, *pg.* 1882
AMERICAN SPIRIT - Game - WMS INDUSTRIES INC.; *pg.* 593, *pg.* 666
AMERICAN STOCKMAN - Mineral Salt - COMPASS MINERALS INTERNATIONAL, INC.; *pg.* 1154, *pg.* 718
AMERICAN SWEETHEART - Canvas - HABAND COMPANY, INC.; *pg.* 1772, *pg.* 1099
AMERICAN THEATRE - Magazine - THEATRE COMMUNICATIONS GROUP, INC.; *pg.* 587, *pg.* 1298
AMERICAN TOOL - Machine Tool Product - BOURN & KOCH MACHINE TOOL COMPANY; *pg.* 1319, *pg.* 654
AMERICAN TOURISTER - Luggage - SAMSONITE CORPORATION; *pg.* 11, *pg.* 830
AMERICAN TRADITION - Fan - CRAFTMADE INTERNATIONAL, INC.; *pg.* 1295, *pg.* 1670
AMERICAN VIEW - Furniture - STANLEY FURNITURE CO., INC.; *pg.* 943, *pg.* 1379
AMERICANA - Chimes - CRAFTMADE INTERNATIONAL, INC.; *pg.* 1295, *pg.* 1670
AMERICANA - Musical Instrument - GIBSON GUITAR CORP.; *pg.* 550, *pg.* 1650
AMERICANA - Furniture - JASPER GROUP; *pg.* 930, *pg.* 691
AMERICANA ANNUAL - Magazine - SCHOLASTIC INC.; *pg.* 1683, *pg.* 1288
AMERICAN'S BEST - Microwave Pop Corn - AMERICAN POP CORN COMPANY; *pg.* 825, *pg.* 712
AMERICANSINGLES - Online Dating Service - SPARK NETWORKS, INC.; *pg.* 472, *pg.* 140
AMERICA'S BATTERY EXPERTS - Slogan - BATTERIES PLUS BULBS LLC; *pg.* 360, *pg.* 1860
AMERICA'S BUSINESS FLORIST - Retail Store Services - 1-800-FLOWERS.COM, INC.; *pg.* 1758, *pg.* 1151
AMERICA'S CAR & TRUCK STORE - Tag Line - LITHIA MOTORS INC; *pg.* 183, *pg.* 1499
AMERICA'S CHOCOLATIER - Tagline - ROCKY MOUNTAIN CHOCOLATE FACTORY, INC.; *pg.* 1032, *pg.* 324
AMERICA'S CHOICE - Food Products - THE GREAT ATLANTIC & PACIFIC TEA COMPANY, INC.; *pg.* 1021, *pg.* 1086
AMERICA'S CLASSROOM NEWSPAPER - Educational Materials - SCHOLASTIC INC.; *pg.* 1683, *pg.* 1288
AMERICA'S CREDIT UNIONS - Collective Membership Mark - CREDIT UNION NATIONAL ASSOCIATION; *pg.* 138, *pg.* 1865
AMERICA'S DRIVE-IN - Slogan - SONIC CORP.; *pg.* 1750, *pg.* 1487
AMERICA'S ENERGY PARTNER - Electricity Generators - AMERICAN ELECTRIC POWER COMPANY, INC.; *pg.* 1934, *pg.* 1437
AMERICA'S FAVORITE DRIVE-IN - Slogan - SONIC CORP.; *pg.* 1750, *pg.* 1487
AMERICA'S FAVORITE FAMILY RESTAURANT - Slogan - EAT'N PARK HOSPITALITY GROUP; *pg.* 1728, *pg.* 1539
AMERICA'S FAVOURITE HOLIDAY CANDY - Tag Line - R.M. PALMER COMPANY; *pg.* 1861, *pg.* 1585
AMERICA'S FISHING LURES - Tagline - EPPINGER MANUFACTURING CO.; *pg.* 1833, *pg.* 876
AMERICA'S HORRIBLE HISTORIES - Educational Materials - SCHOLASTIC INC.; *pg.* 1683, *pg.* 1288
AMERICA'S HORSE - Members-only Magazine - AMERICAN QUARTER HORSE ASSOCIATION; *pg.* 130, *pg.* 1658
AMERICA'S LUXURY HOME BUILDER - Slogan - TOLL BROTHERS, INC.; *pg.* 115, *pg.* 1541
AMERICAS MOST TRUSTED NAME IN WOMEN'S HEALTH - Tagline - PLANNED PARENTHOOD FEDERATION OF AMERICA, INC.; *pg.* 154, *pg.* 1282
AMERICA'S NEIGHBORHOOD AUTO CARE EXPERTS - Slogan - PRECISION AUTO CARE, INC.; *pg.* 215, *pg.* 1787
AMERICA'S OLDEST SPEED SHOP - Slogan - SPEEDWAY MOTORS INC.; *pg.* 218, *pg.* 1012
AMERICA'S ON SWITCH - Tagline - CONSOL ENERGY INC.; *pg.* 1154, *pg.* 1520
AMERICA'S OPTICS AUTHORITY - Slogan - LEUPOLD & STEVENS, INC.; *pg.* 1420, *pg.* 1492
AMERICA'S PET STORE ON THE WEB! - Tagline - PETFOODDIRECT.COM; *pg.* 1481, *pg.* 1536
AMERICA'S PLACE TO WORK AMERICA'S PLACE TO EAT - Slogan - WAFFLE HOUSE, INCORPORATED; *pg.* 1754, *pg.* 538
AMERICA'S PREMIER CERTIFIED ORGANIC DISTRIBUTOR - Slogan - UNITED NATURAL FOODS, INC.; *pg.* 907, *pg.* 1608
AMERICA'S PREMIUM CHOCOLATE - Tagline - GHIRARDELLI CHOCOLATE COMPANY; *pg.* 1854, *pg.* 252
AMERICA'S PREMIUM WOOD FINISHES - Slogan - PRATT & LAMBERT PAINTS; *pg.* 1446, *pg.* 1434
AMERICA'S PRETZEL BAKERY SINCE 1909 - Slogan - SNYDER'S OF HANOVER, INC.; *pg.* 1862, *pg.* 1536
AMERICA'S PRINT SHOP - Tagline - PRINTINGFORLESS.COM, INC.; *pg.* 456, *pg.* 1009
AMERICA'S SILENT HERO - Systems Integration & Aeronautics - LOCKHEED MARTIN CORPORATION; *pg.* 229, *pg.* 762
AMERICA'S STORYTELLER - Photo Products & Services - EASTMAN KODAK COMPANY; *pg.* 1408, *pg.* 1333
AMERICA'S TROUBLESHOOTER - Sewer & Drain Cleaning Business - THE DWYER GROUP, INC.; *pg.* 79, *pg.* 1748
AMERICASMART - Trade Show Operating Company - AMC, INC.; *pg.* 1759, *pg.* 487
AMERICASMART ALPHA - Menswear Show - AMC, INC.; *pg.* 1759, *pg.* 487
AMERICASMART FIRSTLOOK - Bridal, Prom & Special Occasion Clothing - AMC, INC.; *pg.* 1759, *pg.* 487
AMERICASMART PREMIER - Trade Show - AMC, INC.; *pg.* 1759, *pg.* 487
AMERICAST - Wireless Communication System - AT&T SOUTHEAST; *pg.* 1868, *pg.* 489
AMERICAST ADVANTAGE - Wireless Communication System - AT&T SOUTHEAST; *pg.* 1868, *pg.* 489
AMERICAST PREMIERCAST - Wireless Communication System - AT&T SOUTHEAST; *pg.* 1868, *pg.* 489
AMERICAST VIEWCAST - Wireless Communication System - AT&T SOUTHEAST; *pg.* 1868, *pg.* 489
AMERICHOICE - Government-Sponsored Healthcare Services - UNITEDHEALTH GROUP INCORPORATED; *pg.* 1221, *pg.* 950
AMERICINN - Motels - NORTHCOTT HOSPITALITY INTERNATIONAL, LLC; *pg.* 1742, *pg.* 920
AMERICO - Floor Pads - AMERICO MANUFACTURING CO., INC.; *pg.* 325, *pg.* 482
AMERICRAFTERS - Craft Tables - RIO BRANDS, INC.; *pg.* 941, *pg.* 1570
AMERICROWN - Catering Service - INTERNATIONAL SPEEDWAY CORPORATION; *pg.* 553, *pg.* 420
AMERIFILL - Tires - AMERITYRE CORPORATION; *pg.* 1879, *pg.* 1021
AMERIGEL - Wound Wash - ALIMED, INC.; *pg.* 1490, *pg.*

816
AMERIHOST INN - Hotels - WYNDHAM WORLDWIDE CORPORATION; *pg.* 1119, *pg.* 1107
AMERIPHONE - Communication Headset Product - PLANTRONICS, INC.; *pg.* 663, *pg.* 270
AMERISPEC - Home Inspection - THE SERVICEMASTER COMPANY, LLC; *pg.* 335, *pg.* 1646
AMERISURE - Insurance - AMERISURE MUTUAL INSURANCE COMPANY; *pg.* 1191, *pg.* 885
AMERITAS - Insurance & Financial Products - AMERITAS LIFE INSURANCE CORP.; *pg.* 1192, *pg.* 1011
AMERITONE - Paint - AKZONOBEL DECORATIVE PAINTS U.S.; *pg.* 1439, *pg.* 1474
AMERITRADE - Financial Services - TD AMERITRADE HOLDING CORPORATION; *pg.* 808, *pg.* 1018
AMERITRADE ADVANCED ANALYZER - Stock Trading Tool - TD AMERITRADE HOLDING CORPORATION; *pg.* 808, *pg.* 1018
AMERITRADE ADVISOR SERVICES - Financial Services - TD AMERITRADE HOLDING CORPORATION; *pg.* 808, *pg.* 1018
AMERITRADE APEX - Brokerage Svc for Frequent Traders - TD AMERITRADE HOLDING CORPORATION; *pg.* 808, *pg.* 1018
AMERITRADE CLEARING SERVICES - Stock Trading Tool - TD AMERITRADE HOLDING CORPORATION; *pg.* 808, *pg.* 1018
AMERITRADE CORPORATE SERVICES - Online Institutional Brokerage Services - TD AMERITRADE HOLDING CORPORATION; *pg.* 808, *pg.* 1018
AMERITRADE IZONE - Electronic Brokerage Svc - TD AMERITRADE HOLDING CORPORATION; *pg.* 808, *pg.* 1018
AMERITRADE PLUS - Financial Services - TD AMERITRADE HOLDING CORPORATION; *pg.* 808, *pg.* 1018
AMERITRADE PRO - Stock Trading Tool - TD AMERITRADE HOLDING CORPORATION; *pg.* 808, *pg.* 1018
AMERITRADE STREAMER - Stock Trading Tool - TD AMERITRADE HOLDING CORPORATION; *pg.* 808, *pg.* 1018
AMERITYRE - Tires - AMERITYRE CORPORATION; *pg.* 1879, *pg.* 1021
AMERIVEST - Online Advisory Svc - TD AMERITRADE HOLDING CORPORATION; *pg.* 808, *pg.* 1018
AMERIWHITE - Dinnerware - THE HOMER LAUGHLIN CHINA COMPANY; *pg.* 1125, *pg.* 1850
AMERIX - Credit Counseling - AMERIX CORPORATION; *pg.* 715, *pg.* 767
AMERLOCK - Coating & Finish - NOV AMERON; *pg.* 100, *pg.* 187
AMEROCK - Tools - NEWELL RUBBERMAID INC.; *pg.* 1128, *pg.* 515
AMEROID - Chemicals - ASHLAND INC.; *pg.* 972, *pg.* 726
AMERPACK - Packing Valves - ASHLAND INC.; *pg.* 972, *pg.* 726
AMERSCENT - Neutralizing Agents - ASHLAND INC.; *pg.* 972, *pg.* 726
AMERSE - Instrument Disinfectant - STERIS CORPORATION; *pg.* 1597, *pg.* 1464
AMERSHIELD - Graffiti-Resistant Coating - NOV AMERON; *pg.* 100, *pg.* 187
AMERSTAT - Controlling Chemicals - ASHLAND INC.; *pg.* 972, *pg.* 726
AMESEAL - Oral Lesion Relief Spray - 3M COMPANY; *pg.* 1142, *pg.* 956
AMETHYST - Solid Imaging Material - 3D SYSTEMS CORPORATION; *pg.* 339, *pg.* 1621
AMETHYST - Dinnerware - THE HOMER LAUGHLIN CHINA COMPANY; *pg.* 1125, *pg.* 1850
AMETHYST - Video Game - INTERNATIONAL GAME TECHNOLOGY; *pg.* 957, *pg.* 1024
AMEYAL - Beverages - THE COCA-COLA COMPANY; *pg.* 240, *pg.* 493
AMF - Bowling Products - BOWLMOR AMF; *pg.* 1828, *pg.* 1206
AMFLITE II - Bowling Product - BOWLMOR AMF; *pg.* 1828, *pg.* 1206
AMG - Data Solutions - ROVI CORPORATION; *pg.* 463, *pg.* 269
AMG ALL-GAME GUIDE - Data Solutions - ROVI CORPORATION; *pg.* 463, *pg.* 269
AMG ALL-MEDIA GUIDE - Data Solutions - ROVI CORPORATION; *pg.* 463, *pg.* 269
AMG ALL-MOVIE GUIDE - Data Solutions - ROVI CORPORATION; *pg.* 463, *pg.* 269
AMHERST - Lighting Product - QUOIZEL INC.; *pg.* 1304, *pg.* 1616
AMI - Apnea Monitor - CAS MEDICAL SYSTEMS, INC.; *pg.* 1513, *pg.* 339
AMI DODUCO - Electrical Contact Products Segment - PULSE ELECTRONICS CORPORATION; *pg.* 666, *pg.* 206
AMIA - Office Furniture - STEELCASE INC.; *pg.* 475, *pg.* 889
AMICAL - Antifungel Agent - THE DOW CHEMICAL COMPANY; *pg.* 1157, *pg.* 898
AMICELLI - Food Product - MARS, INCORPORATED; *pg.* 1858, *pg.* 1792
AMICO-KLEMP - Riveted Carbon Steel - ALABAMA METAL INDUSTRIES CORPORATION; *pg.* 65, *pg.* 1
AMICURE - Epoxy Curatives - AIR PRODUCTS AND CHEMICALS, INC.; *pg.* 1145, *pg.* 1513
AMICUS - Blood Collection & Transfusion - BAXTER INTERNATIONAL INC.; *pg.* 1499, *pg.* 599
AMIDA - Light Equipment - TEREX CORPORATION; *pg.* 1381, *pg.* 384
AMIGA - Bath & Plumbing Product - JACUZZI BRANDS CORPORATION; *pg.* 554, *pg.* 65
AMIGO - Bananas - CHIQUITA BRANDS INTERNATIONAL, INC.; *pg.* 847, *pg.* 1365
AMILOX - Lubricants - THE DOW CHEMICAL COMPANY; *pg.* 1157, *pg.* 898
AMINA - Furniture - AMISCO INDUSTRIES LTD.; *pg.* 913, *pg.* 1958
AMINE - Farm & Ranch Product - PBI/GORDON CORPORATION; *pg.* 1176, *pg.* 985
AMINE CS-1135 - Buffering Agent and Corrosion Inhibitor - THE DOW CHEMICAL COMPANY; *pg.* 1157, *pg.* 898
AMINE CS-1246 - Corrosion Inhibitor - THE DOW CHEMICAL COMPANY; *pg.* 1157, *pg.* 898
AMINE MANAGEMENT - Program - THE DOW CHEMICAL COMPANY; *pg.* 1157, *pg.* 898
AMINEX - Software - BIO-RAD LABORATORIES, INC.; *pg.* 1504, *pg.* 101
AMINOGEN - Enzyme Supplement - HERBALIFE INTERNATIONAL OF AMERICA, INC.; *pg.* 1541, *pg.* 132
AMINOPLUS - Grain - AG PROCESSING INC.; *pg.* 835, *pg.* 1013
AMINOX - Polymer Product - CHEMTURA CORPORATION; *pg.* 1152, *pg.* 355
AMIRA - Software - MERCURY COMPUTER SYSTEMS, INC.; *pg.* 434, *pg.* 813
AMIRANTE - Surface Material - STEELCASE INC.; *pg.* 475, *pg.* 889
AMISCO - Furniture - AMISCO INDUSTRIES LTD.; *pg.* 913, *pg.* 1958
AMISH KITCHEN - Egg Noodles - LANCASTER COLONY CORPORATION; *pg.* 873, *pg.* 1441
AMISH KITCHEN - Noodles - T. MARZETTI COMPANY; *pg.* 900, *pg.* 1444
AMISTAD - Books - HARPERCOLLINS PUBLISHERS INC.; *pg.* 1647, *pg.* 1237
AMITIZA - Pharmaceutical - SUCAMPO PHARMACEUTICALS, INC.; *pg.* 1599, *pg.* 765
AMKARD - Packaging System - AMKOR TECHNOLOGY, INC.; *pg.* 67, *pg.* 25
AML HIP - Orthopedic Product - DEPUYSYNTHES; *pg.* 1523, *pg.* 699
AMMBER - Footwear - STEVEN MADDEN, LTD.; *pg.* 1819, *pg.* 1176
AMMCO - Brake Lathes - HENNESSY INDUSTRIES, INC.; *pg.* 207, *pg.* 1639
AMMO - Bag - OAKLEY, INC.; *pg.* 1840, *pg.* 86
AMMOGAS - Heat Treating Equipment - SECO/WARWICK CORPORATION; *pg.* 1076, *pg.* 1552
AMMONASORB - Vapor Phase Activated Carbons - CALGON CARBON CORPORATION; *pg.* 1151, *pg.* 1574
AMMONYX - Chemical Product - STEPAN COMPANY; *pg.* 1182, *pg.* 643
AMN HEALTHCARE - Healthcare Staffing - AMN HEALTHCARE SERVICES, INC.; *pg.* 1494, *pg.* 200
AMNIOMAX - Cell Culture Product - THERMO FISHER SCIENTIFIC INC.; *pg.* 1602, *pg.* 61
AMO - Accredited Management Organization - INSTITUTE OF REAL ESTATE MANAGEMENT; *pg.* 144, *pg.* 578
AMOR 93.1 FM - Radio Station - SPANISH BROADCASTING SYSTEM INC.; *pg.* 310, *pg.* 446
AMORE - Canned Cat Food - HEINZ NORTH AMERICA; *pg.* 861, *pg.* 1576
AMOREPACIFIC - Beauty & Skin Care Products - AMOREPACIFIC US, INC.; *pg.* 498, *pg.* 1195
AMORINO - Beverages - THE COCA-COLA COMPANY; *pg.* 240, *pg.* 493
AMORPHOUS SILICON - X-Ray Detector - PERKINELMER, INC.; *pg.* 1426, *pg.* 853
AMOXI-DROP - Medicine - PFIZER INC.; *pg.* 1581, *pg.* 1278
AMOXI-TABS - Medicine - PFIZER INC.; *pg.* 1581, *pg.* 1278
AMOXIVET - Pharmaceutical Product - VALEANT PHARMACEUTICALS INTERNATIONAL; *pg.* 1605, *pg.* 1047
AMP - Adapters - BMC SOFTWARE, INC.; *pg.* 362, *pg.* 1701
AMP - Energy Drink - PEPSICO, INC.; *pg.* 259, *pg.* 1327
AMP - Electrical & Electronic Components - TE CONNECTIVITY LTD.; *pg.* 677, *pg.* 1515
AMP-90 - Dispersant - THE DOW CHEMICAL COMPANY; *pg.* 1157, *pg.* 898
AMP-95 - Dispersant - THE DOW CHEMICAL COMPANY; *pg.* 1157, *pg.* 898
AMP CAN - Battery Powered Amplifier - FENDER MUSICAL INSTRUMENTS CORPORATION; *pg.* 547, *pg.* 21
AMP/OAM - Footwear - COBIAN CORP.; *pg.* 1806, *pg.* 253
AMP-REGULAR - Neutralizing Amine - THE DOW CHEMICAL COMPANY; *pg.* 1157, *pg.* 898
AMP-TRAP - Feeder Circuits - MERSEN; *pg.* 1302, *pg.* 836
AMP-TRAP 2000 - Time Delay Low Voltage Fuse - MERSEN; *pg.* 1302, *pg.* 836
AMP-TRAP E RATED - Power Fuse - MERSEN; *pg.* 1302, *pg.* 836
AMP-TRAP FORM 101 - Semiconductor - MERSEN; *pg.* 1302, *pg.* 836
AMP-TRAP FORM 480 - Feeder Circuits with Time Delay - MERSEN; *pg.* 1302, *pg.* 836
AMP-TRAP II - Feeder Circuits with Time Delay - MERSEN; *pg.* 1302, *pg.* 836
AMP-TRAP R RATED - Medium Voltage Motor Fuse - MERSEN; *pg.* 1302, *pg.* 836
AMP-ULTRA - Neutralizing Amine - THE DOW CHEMICAL COMPANY; *pg.* 1157, *pg.* 898
AMPAK - Skin Packaging Equipment - HEAT SEAL LLC; *pg.* 1345, *pg.* 1431
A.M.P.A.S. - Academy of Motion Picture Arts & Sciences - ACADEMY OF MOTION PICTURE ARTS & SCIENCES; *pg.* 526, *pg.* 46
AMPEG - Electric Bass & Guitar Amplification Products - LOUD TECHNOLOGIES INC.; *pg.* 652, *pg.* 1847
AMPEREX - Electronics - RICHARDSON ELECTRONICS, LTD.; *pg.* 667, *pg.* 622
AMPGARD - Electrical Product - EATON CORPORATION; *pg.* 1331, *pg.* 1429
AMPHOCIN - Medicine - PFIZER INC.; *pg.* 1581, *pg.* 1278
AMPHORA - Fan - CRAFTMADE INTERNATIONAL, INC.; *pg.* 1295, *pg.* 1670
AMPHORA - Lamp - J. ROBERT SCOTT INC.; *pg.* 930, *pg.* 105
AMPHOSOL - Chemical Product - STEPAN COMPANY; *pg.* 1182, *pg.* 643
AMPHOTERGE - Amphoteric Surfactant - LONZA INC.; *pg.* 1171, *pg.* 1041
AMPHOTO - Books on Photography - NIELSEN BUSINESS MEDIA; *pg.* 1671, *pg.* 1272
AMPHYL - Disinfectant Deodorant Spray - RECKITT BENCKISER INC.; *pg.* 1136, *pg.* 1105
AMPLATZ SUPER STIFF - Medical Guidewires - BOSTON SCIENTIFIC CORPORATION; *pg.* 1508, *pg.* 831
AMPLE - Software System - MENTOR GRAPHICS CORPORATION; *pg.* 432, *pg.* 1510
AMPLEX - Molecular Probe Product - THERMO FISHER SCIENTIFIC INC.; *pg.* 1602, *pg.* 61
AMPLICHEK - Software - BIO-RAD LABORATORIES, INC.; *pg.* 1504, *pg.* 101
AMPLICLEAR - Software - BIO-RAD LABORATORIES, INC.; *pg.* 1504, *pg.* 101
AMPLICOMM - Microelectronics - AEROFLEX INCORPORATED; *pg.* 614, *pg.* 1321
AMPLIFIED - Carpet - INTERFACE, INC.; *pg.* 695, *pg.* 512
AMPLIFIRE - Heat Extractor - PORTLAND WILLAMETTE; *pg.* 1129, *pg.* 1505
AMPLIFIT - Hearing Test - MIRACLE-EAR, INC.; *pg.* 1568, *pg.* 940
AMPLIFLOW - Valves - FLOWSERVE CORPORATION; *pg.* 82, *pg.* 1719
AMPLIFY - Virtual Receptionist - BULLSEYE TELECOM INC.; *pg.* 366, *pg.* 906
AMPLIFY - Polymer - THE DOW CHEMICAL COMPANY; *pg.* 1157, *pg.* 898
AMPLIFY - Strategic Advertiser Program - TWITTER, INC.; *pg.* 1285, *pg.* 228

AMPLIGHT - Software - BIO-RAD LABORATORIES, INC.; *pg.* 1504, *pg.* 101
AMPLIPROBE - Software - BIO-RAD LABORATORIES, INC.; *pg.* 1504, *pg.* 101
AMPLISIZE - Software - BIO-RAD LABORATORIES, INC.; *pg.* 1504, *pg.* 101
AMPLITEK - Software - BIO-RAD LABORATORIES, INC.; *pg.* 1504, *pg.* 101
AMPLITROL - Software - BIO-RAD LABORATORIES, INC.; *pg.* 1504, *pg.* 101
AMPLIVAX - Therapeutic Product - IDERA PHARMACEUTICALS, INC.; *pg.* 1543, *pg.* 808
AMPLIXA - Pharmaceutical Preparations - TARGACEPT, INC.; *pg.* 1601, *pg.* 1395
AMPLOCK - Fluid Handling System - GRACO, INC.; *pg.* 1342, *pg.* 935
AMPS - Industrial Chemicals - THE LUBRIZOL CORPORATION; *pg.* 1171, *pg.* 1481
AMPS - Software - SYNOPSYS, INC.; *pg.* 480, *pg.* 162
AMPUSCAN - High-Speed Inspection System - ATS AUTOMATION TOOLING SYSTEMS INC.; *pg.* 355, *pg.* 1919
AMPWORKS B - Bass Effects Processor - KORG USA, INC.; *pg.* 556, *pg.* 1180
AMPWORKS G - Guitar Effects Processor - KORG USA, INC.; *pg.* 556, *pg.* 1180
AMR - Recording, Studio, Broadcast Products - PEAVEY ELECTRONICS CORPORATION; *pg.* 662, *pg.* 970
AMRAMM - Defense System - RAYTHEON COMPANY; *pg.* 233, *pg.* 854
AMRES - Synthetic Resins Used in Manufacturing Paper - GEORGIA-PACIFIC LLC; *pg.* 1458, *pg.* 507
AMRITZAR - Rug - ETHAN ALLEN INTERIORS INC.; *pg.* 924, *pg.* 343
AMRIX - Pharmaceutical Product - IMPAX LABORATORIES, INC.; *pg.* 1544, *pg.* 101
AMS - Automatic Microphone System - SHURE INCORPORATED; *pg.* 672, *pg.* 638
AMS 650/600M - Non-Inflatable Penile Implant - AMERICAN MEDICAL SYSTEMS HOLDINGS, INC.; *pg.* 1493, *pg.* 947
AMS 700 - Inflatable Penile Implant - AMERICAN MEDICAL SYSTEMS HOLDINGS, INC.; *pg.* 1493, *pg.* 947
AMS 800 - Urinary Control System - AMERICAN MEDICAL SYSTEMS HOLDINGS, INC.; *pg.* 1493, *pg.* 947
AMS AMBICOR - Medical Device - AMERICAN MEDICAL SYSTEMS HOLDINGS, INC.; *pg.* 1493, *pg.* 947
AMS COMPLETE - Liquid Ammonium - UNIVERSAL COOPERATIVES, INC.; *pg.* 1482, *pg.* 922
AMS DURA II - Medical Device - AMERICAN MEDICAL SYSTEMS HOLDINGS, INC.; *pg.* 1493, *pg.* 947
AMS-OILER - Charger - AMSOIL INC.; *pg.* 971, *pg.* 1896
AMSCO - Sterilizer - STERIS CORPORATION; *pg.* 1597, *pg.* 1464
AMSCO CENTURY - Sterilizer - STERIS CORPORATION; *pg.* 1597, *pg.* 1464
AMSCRUB - Multipurpose Cleaner - STERIS CORPORATION; *pg.* 1597, *pg.* 1464
AMSOIL - Lubricants & Lubricating Equipment - AMSOIL INC.; *pg.* 971, *pg.* 1896
AMSTEL - Beer - HEINEKEN USA INC.; *pg.* 252, *pg.* 1352
AMSTERDAM - Bike - ELECTRA BICYCLE COMPANY; *pg.* 1706, *pg.* 303
AMSTERDAM - Seating Product - IRWIN SEATING COMPANY INC.; *pg.* 929, *pg.* 887
AMT - Pumps - AMERICAN MACHINE & TOOL COMPANY, INC.; *pg.* 1042, *pg.* 1585
AMTAK - Fastener - GRIPNAIL CORPORATION; *pg.* 1048, *pg.* 1601
AMTECH - Wireless Product - TRANSCORE HOLDINGS INC.; *pg.* 485, *pg.* 1541
AMTICO - Flooring - AMERICAN BILTRITE INC.; *pg.* 1878, *pg.* 856
AMTRAK - National Passenger Rail System - NATIONAL RAILROAD PASSENGER CORPORATION; *pg.* 1916, *pg.* 403
AMUMETAL - Shielding Alloys - AMUNEAL MANUFACTURING CORPORATION; *pg.* 617, *pg.* 1558
AMUNEAL - Magnetic Shields - AMUNEAL MANUFACTURING CORPORATION; *pg.* 617, *pg.* 1558
AMUNICKEL - Shielding Alloys - AMUNEAL MANUFACTURING CORPORATION; *pg.* 617, *pg.* 1558
AMUSEMENT BUSINESS - Trade Publication - THE NIELSEN COMPANY B.V.; *pg.* 1671, *pg.* 1272
AMV - Fluid Handling System - GRACO, INC.; *pg.* 1342, *pg.* 935
AMVET - Animal Safety Product - NEOGEN CORPORATION; *pg.* 883, *pg.* 896
AMY - Footwear - PHOENIX FOOTWEAR GROUP, INC.; *pg.* 1815, *pg.* 60
AMYL ACETATE - Dry Cleaning & Laundry Product - ADCO, INC.; *pg.* 325, *pg.* 482
AMYLOTEX - Polymer - HERCULES INCORPORATED; *pg.* 1166, *pg.* 392
AMZIRC - Zirconium Copper Wire - LITTLE FALLS ALLOYS, INC.; *pg.* 1171, *pg.* 1107
AN AMERICAN GIRLS EVENT - Dolls - AMERICAN GIRL LLC; *pg.* 949, *pg.* 1871
AN AMERICAN GIRLS EXPERIENCE - Games - AMERICAN GIRL LLC; *pg.* 949, *pg.* 1871
AN AMERICAN GIRLS LIVING HISTORY PROGRAM - Games - AMERICAN GIRL LLC; *pg.* 949, *pg.* 1871
AN AMERICAN GIRLS MUSEUM PROGRAM - Museum-Related Activities - AMERICAN GIRL LLC; *pg.* 949, *pg.* 1871
AN/APG-67 - Systems Integration & Aeronautics - LOCKHEED MARTIN CORPORATION; *pg.* 229, *pg.* 762
AN/APS-145 - Systems Integration & Aeronautics - LOCKHEED MARTIN CORPORATION; *pg.* 229, *pg.* 762
AN AUTHENTIC AMERICAN CLASSIC - Tagline - SILVER DINER, INC.; *pg.* 1750, *pg.* 776
AN ENABLING THIN FILM EQUIPMENT COMPANY - Slogan - AIXTRON INC.; *pg.* 1310, *pg.* 283
AN EXPERIENCE AT EVERY TABLE - Slogan - BENIHANA INC.; *pg.* 1716, *pg.* 409
AN INTRODUCTION TO APERTURE - Training Course - APPLE INC.; *pg.* 350, *pg.* 73
AN INTRODUCTION TO FINAL CUT PRO - Training Course - APPLE INC.; *pg.* 350, *pg.* 73
AN INTRODUCTION TO LOGIC EXPRESS & LOGIC PRO - Training Course - APPLE INC.; *pg.* 350, *pg.* 73
AN/PAS-13 THERMAL WEAPON SIGHT - Defense System - RAYTHEON COMPANY; *pg.* 233, *pg.* 854
AN UNFAIR ADVANTAGE - Pharmaceutical Product - ALERE INC.; *pg.* 1488, *pg.* 849
A.N.A. - Retail - J.C. PENNEY COMPANY, INC.; *pg.* 1774, *pg.* 1732
ANA GUEVARA MAG - Eyewear - OAKLEY, INC.; *pg.* 1840, *pg.* 86
ANACONDA - Wire & Cable Product - GENERAL CABLE CORPORATION; *pg.* 83, *pg.* 729
ANADROX - Nutritional Supplement - MAXIMUM HUMAN PERFORMANCE, INC.; *pg.* 1559, *pg.* 1065
ANAFRANIL - Pharmaceutical Product - MALLINCKRODT PHARMACEUTICALS; *pg.* 1557, *pg.* 978
ANAHEIM - Footwear - VANS, INC.; *pg.* 1821, *pg.* 76
ANAIS - Fabric - NEMSCHOFF, INC.; *pg.* 936, *pg.* 1890
ANALOG - Apparel - BURTON SNOWBOARD COMPANY; *pg.* 1829, *pg.* 1765
ANALOG ANALYST - Software System - MENTOR GRAPHICS CORPORATION; *pg.* 432, *pg.* 1510
ANALOG MASTER - Semiconductor Product - RENESAS ELECTRONICS AMERICA INC.; *pg.* 667, *pg.* 269
ANALOG OFFICE - Computer Software - AWR CORPORATION; *pg.* 623, *pg.* 78
ANALOG STATION - Software System - MENTOR GRAPHICS CORPORATION; *pg.* 432, *pg.* 1510
ANALOG TRUNK SAFETY PLUS - Communication Product - CENTURYLINK, INC; *pg.* 1870, *pg.* 317
ANALOGUE PLANNER - Software System - IMS HEALTH, INC.; *pg.* 1544, *pg.* 344
ANALYSIS 5 - Software - CTI GROUP HOLDINGS INC.; *pg.* 381, *pg.* 684
ANALYSLIDE - Petri Dish - PALL CORPORATION; *pg.* 232, *pg.* 1323
ANALYST - Software - MOLECULAR DEVICES CORPORATION; *pg.* 1568, *pg.* 287
ANALYST ACEL - ICD Product - ST. JUDE MEDICAL, INC.; *pg.* 1596, *pg.* 963
ANALYSTPERSPECTIVES - Software - SKILLSOFT PLC; *pg.* 470, *pg.* 1037
ANALYSTS HANDBOOK - Evaluation Tool - STANDARD & POOR'S RATINGS SERVICES; *pg.* 805, *pg.* 1296
ANALYSTVIEW - Software - OPENTEXT; *pg.* 450, *pg.* 1665
ANALYTIC BUSINESS COMPONENTS - Software - INFORMATICA CORPORATION; *pg.* 414, *pg.* 190
ANALYTICS - Video Analysis Reporting - APPLIED GLOBAL TECHNOLOGIES; *pg.* 352, *pg.* 460
ANALYTICS - Software Application - BMC SOFTWARE, INC.; *pg.* 362, *pg.* 1701
ANALYTYX - Systems Integration & Aeronautics - LOCKHEED MARTIN CORPORATION; *pg.* 229, *pg.* 762
ANALYZEIT - Software - BIO-RAD LABORATORIES, INC.; *pg.* 1504, *pg.* 101
ANALYZER - Software - KULICKE & SOFFA INDUSTRIES, INC.; *pg.* 650, *pg.* 1533
ANALYZIR - Software - FLIR SYSTEMS, INC.; *pg.* 1413, *pg.* 1510
ANAPAMU - Wine - E&J GALLO WINERY; *pg.* 1962, *pg.* 149
ANAPROX - Pharmaceutical Product - HOFFMANN-LA ROCHE INC.; *pg.* 1542, *pg.* 1099
ANARCHY - Sunglasses - FGX INTERNATIONAL, INC.; *pg.* 5, *pg.* 1608
ANASOFT - Software - WATLOW ELECTRIC MANUFACTURING COMPANY; *pg.* 1078, *pg.* 1004
ANASTASIA - Carpet - BEAULIEU GROUP, LLC; *pg.* 917, *pg.* 529
ANASTASIA - Silverware - ONEIDA LTD; *pg.* 1129, *pg.* 1318
ANASTOCLIP - Implantable Vessel Closure System - LEMAITRE VASCULAR, INC.; *pg.* 1555, *pg.* 805
ANATEL - Organic Carbon Analysis - DANAHER CORPORATION; *pg.* 1044, *pg.* 397
ANAWIN - Software - WATLOW ELECTRIC MANUFACTURING COMPANY; *pg.* 1078, *pg.* 1004
ANBESOL - Antiseptic & Anesthetic - PFIZER INC.; *pg.* 1581, *pg.* 1278
ANC-300 - Active Noise Cancellation - ANDREA ELECTRONICS CORPORATION; *pg.* 617, *pg.* 1143
ANC-700 - Active Noise Cancellation - ANDREA ELECTRONICS CORPORATION; *pg.* 617, *pg.* 1143
ANC-750 - Stereo Headset - ANDREA ELECTRONICS CORPORATION; *pg.* 617, *pg.* 1143
ANCAMIDE - Chemical Products - AIR PRODUCTS AND CHEMICALS, INC.; *pg.* 1145, *pg.* 1513
ANCAMINE - Epoxy Curing Agent - AIR PRODUCTS AND CHEMICALS, INC.; *pg.* 1145, *pg.* 1513
ANCAMINE - Chemical - MILLER-STEPHENSON CHEMICAL COMPANY, INC.; *pg.* 1172, *pg.* 344
ANCAREZ - Chemical Products - AIR PRODUCTS AND CHEMICALS, INC.; *pg.* 1145, *pg.* 1513
ANCEF - Pharmaceutical Drug - FRESENIUS KABI USA; *pg.* 1531, *pg.* 626
ANCESTRY MAGAZINE - Magazine - ANCESTRY.COM LLC; *pg.* 1228, *pg.* 1754
ANCESTRY.COM - Website - ANCESTRY.COM LLC; *pg.* 1228, *pg.* 1754
ANCHO GRILL - Tex-Mex Food Service Option - TYSON FOODS, INC.; *pg.* 902, *pg.* 35
ANCHOR - Exchange Device - ABBOTT LABORATORIES; *pg.* 1484, *pg.* 551
ANCHOR - Corrosion Inhibitor - AIR PRODUCTS AND CHEMICALS, INC.; *pg.* 1145, *pg.* 1513
ANCHOR - Bandshells & Pool Covers - ANCHOR INDUSTRIES, INC.; *pg.* 1825, *pg.* 678
ANCHOR - Paint - ANCHOR PAINT MANUFACTURING CO. INC.; *pg.* 1440, *pg.* 1489
ANCHOR - Embroidery Threads - MAKE IT COATS; *pg.* 696, *pg.* 1367
ANCHOR BIBLE - Publishing Imprint - THE KNOPF DOUBLEDAY GROUP; *pg.* 1657, *pg.* 1249
ANCHOR CARRY-ALLS - Canvas Bags & Back Packs - ANCHOR INDUSTRIES, INC.; *pg.* 1825, *pg.* 678
ANCHOR-DOWN - Specialty Nails - W.H. MAZE COMPANY; *pg.* 1389, *pg.* 652
ANCHOR FENCE PRODUCTS - Fencing - MASTER HALCO; *pg.* 96, *pg.* 474
ANCHOR FLOOR SWEEPS - Floor Sweeps - CARLISLE FOODSERVICE PRODUCTS INCORPORATED; *pg.* 1455, *pg.* 1485
ANCHOR-LOK - Thermoplastic Sheet Lining for Concrete - ATLAS MINERALS & CHEMICALS, INC.; *pg.* 69, *pg.* 1552
ANCHOR OPTICAL - Surplus Lenses - EDMUND INDUSTRIAL OPTICS INC.; *pg.* 1411, *pg.* 1041
ANCHOR-STOCK - Hydraulic-set Anchor Run - SMITH INTERNATIONAL, INC.; *pg.* 1377, *pg.* 1715
ANCHOR-TITE - Patch - SUPER GLUE CORPORATION; *pg.* 1183, *pg.* 187
ANCHORDARLING - Valve - FLOWSERVE CORPORATION; *pg.* 82, *pg.* 1719
ANCHORED FOR WEAR - Tagline - ANCHOR PAINT MANUFACTURING CO. INC.; *pg.* 1440, *pg.* 1489
ANCHORMATE - Reel - THE WORTH COMPANY; *pg.* 1848, *pg.* 1895
ANCHORMATE II - Matched Set - THE WORTH COMPANY; *pg.* 1848, *pg.* 1895
ANCHORMATE ST - Metal Product - THE WORTH

COMPANY; *pg.* 1848, *pg.* 1895
ANCHORSPAN - Clearspan Fabric Structures - ANCHOR INDUSTRIES, INC.; *pg.* 1825, *pg.* 678
ANCIENT AMERICAN - Bi-monthly Magazine Publication - ANCIENT AMERICAN; *pg.* 1616, *pg.* 1856
ANCIENT ARCADIA - Video Game - INTERNATIONAL GAME TECHNOLOGY; *pg.* 957, *pg.* 1024
ANCIENT CHINESE SECRET - Video Game - INTERNATIONAL GAME TECHNOLOGY; *pg.* 957, *pg.* 1024
ANCIENT GOLD - Video Game - INTERNATIONAL GAME TECHNOLOGY; *pg.* 957, *pg.* 1024
ANCIENT SPIRAL - Carpet - INTERFACE, INC.; *pg.* 695, *pg.* 512
ANCIENTS - Fabric - NEMSCHOFF, INC.; *pg.* 936, *pg.* 1890
ANCO - Windshield Wiper Products - FEDERAL-MOGUL HOLDINGS CORPORATION; *pg.* 205, *pg.* 907
ANCOBON - Pharmaceutical Product - VALEANT PHARMACEUTICALS INTERNATIONAL; *pg.* 1605, *pg.* 1047
ANCONA - Shoes - ALLEN-EDMONDS SHOE CORP.; *pg.* 1804, *pg.* 1887
ANCORA - Paperboard Product - POTLATCH CORPORATION; *pg.* 1467, *pg.* 1844
ANCOTIL - Pharmaceutical Product - VALEANT PHARMACEUTICALS INTERNATIONAL; *pg.* 1605, *pg.* 1047
AND AWAY GO TROUBLES DOWN THE DRAIN - Slogan - ROTO-ROOTER, INC.; *pg.* 108, *pg.* 1425
AND THEN THERE WERE FOUR - Trademark - NATIONAL COLLEGIATE ATHLETIC ASSOCIATION; *pg.* 567, *pg.* 688
AND1 - Basketball Products - SEQUENTIAL BRANDS GROUP, INC.; *pg.* 1395, *pg.* 1290
ANDAFRAC - Pressed & Monolithic Refractory - RESCO PRODUCTS, INC.; *pg.* 107, *pg.* 1581
ANDALUSIA - Fabric - NEMSCHOFF, INC.; *pg.* 936, *pg.* 1890
ANDERSEN - Wood Window Units, Patio Doors & Roof Windows - ANDERSEN CORPORATION; *pg.* 67, *pg.* 916
ANDERSON - Food Processing Equipment - ANDERSON INTERNATIONAL CORP.; *pg.* 1313, *pg.* 1474
ANDERSON - Sanitary Process Instrumentation - DANAHER CORPORATION; *pg.* 1044, *pg.* 397
ANDERSON & VREELAND - Printing Equipment & Materials - ANDERSON & VREELAND, INC.; *pg.* 1616, *pg.* 1064
ANDERSON HARDWOOD FLOORS - Wood Floor - ANDERSON HARDWOOD FLOORS; *pg.* 67, *pg.* 1613
ANDERSON INDEPENDENT-MAIL - Newspaper - THE E.W. SCRIPPS COMPANY; *pg.* 1639, *pg.* 1412
ANDERSON-MIDWEST - Sight Flow Indicator - DWYER INSTRUMENTS INC.; *pg.* 1330, *pg.* 694
ANDERSON'S - Tomato Soup - ADVANCED FOOD PRODUCTS LLC; *pg.* 835, *pg.* 1555
ANDES - Ice Cream Product - PERRY'S ICE CREAM CO., INC.; *pg.* 1861, *pg.* 1137
ANDES - Mints - TOOTSIE ROLL INDUSTRIES, INC.; *pg.* 1863, *pg.* 591
ANDI - Fabric - NEMSCHOFF, INC.; *pg.* 936, *pg.* 1890
ANDINA - Beverages - THE COCA-COLA COMPANY; *pg.* 240, *pg.* 493
ANDINA FORTIFIED - Beverages - THE COCA-COLA COMPANY; *pg.* 240, *pg.* 493
ANDINA FRESH - Beverages - THE COCA-COLA COMPANY; *pg.* 240, *pg.* 493
ANDINA FRUT - Beverages - THE COCA-COLA COMPANY; *pg.* 240, *pg.* 493
ANDINA LIGHT - Beverages - THE COCA-COLA COMPANY; *pg.* 240, *pg.* 493
ANDINA NECTAR - Beverages - THE COCA-COLA COMPANY; *pg.* 240, *pg.* 493
ANDINA NECTAR LIGHT - Beverages - THE COCA-COLA COMPANY; *pg.* 240, *pg.* 493
ANDORA - Bathroom Accessories - SYMMONS INDUSTRIES, INC.; *pg.* 114, *pg.* 803
ANDORRA - Bathtub - MAAX INC.-MINNEAPOLIS; *pg.* 1885, *pg.* 938
ANDRE - Sparkling Wine - E&J GALLO WINERY; *pg.* 1962, *pg.* 149
ANDREA - Bodycare & Skincare - AMERICAN INTERNATIONAL INDUSTRIES COMPANY; *pg.* 498, *pg.* 126
ANDREA - Footwear - PHOENIX FOOTWEAR GROUP, INC.; *pg.* 1815, *pg.* 60
ANDRENALINE - Splitters & Combiners - ANAREN, INC.; *pg.* 617, *pg.* 1157
ANDRES - Wine - ANDREW PELLER LIMITED; *pg.* 1956, *pg.* 1920
ANDREW - Furniture - AMISCO INDUSTRIES LTD.; *pg.* 913, *pg.* 1958
ANDREW - Wireless Products - COMMSCOPE, INC.; *pg.* 278, *pg.* 1378
ANDREW - Messenger Bag - JANDD MOUNTAINEERING, INC.; *pg.* 1837, *pg.* 204
ANDREW - Corrugated Cable Connector - RF INDUSTRIES, LTD.; *pg.* 461, *pg.* 208
ANDROID - Program - GOOGLE INC.; *pg.* 1249, *pg.* 153
ANDROID - Pharmaceutical Product - IMPAX LABORATORIES, INC.; *pg.* 1544, *pg.* 101
ANDROID - Pharmaceutical Product - VALEANT PHARMACEUTICALS INTERNATIONAL; *pg.* 1605, *pg.* 1047
ANDROID KITKAT - Operating System for Smartphones & Tablets - GOOGLE INC.; *pg.* 1249, *pg.* 153
ANDROMEDA - Video Game - INTERNATIONAL GAME TECHNOLOGY; *pg.* 957, *pg.* 1024
ANDROMEDA - Furniture - J. ROBERT SCOTT INC.; *pg.* 930, *pg.* 105
ANDROS - Rug - COURISTAN INC.; *pg.* 921, *pg.* 1067
ANDRX - Generic Pharmaceuticals - ALLERGAN; *pg.* 1490, *pg.* 1101
ANDY - Furniture - AMISCO INDUSTRIES LTD.; *pg.* 913, *pg.* 1958
ANDY ARMADILLO - Restaurant & Bar Services - TEXAS ROADHOUSE, INC.; *pg.* 1753, *pg.* 738
ANDY CAPP'S - Food Product - CONAGRA FOODS, INC.; *pg.* 826, *pg.* 1014
ANECDOTE - Fabric - NEMSCHOFF, INC.; *pg.* 936, *pg.* 1890
ANESTAR - Anesthesia Delivery System - MAQUET; *pg.* 1558, *pg.* 1082
ANESTHESIA-RX - Software - MCKESSON CORPORATION; *pg.* 1560, *pg.* 222
ANEURX - Endovascular Stent Graft Sys. - MEDTRONIC, INC.; *pg.* 1564, *pg.* 939
ANEUVYSION - Diagnostic Kits - ABBOTT LABORATORIES; *pg.* 1484, *pg.* 551
ANEW - Beauty Product - AVON PRODUCTS, INC.; *pg.* 500, *pg.* 1198
ANGEL - Sunglasses - FGX INTERNATIONAL, INC.; *pg.* 5, *pg.* 1608
ANGEL - Bookmark - HERITAGE LACE INC.; *pg.* 694, *pg.* 711
ANGEL - Software - MICROSTRATEGY, INC.; *pg.* 1266, *pg.* 1809
ANGEL - Container Grown Plant - MONROVIA GROWERS; *pg.* 1797, *pg.* 44
ANGEL BOWZ - Bows - E-Z BOWZ, LLC; *pg.* 692, *pg.* 1635
ANGEL KITS - Cleaning Supply Kit - ANGELICA CORPORATION; *pg.* 38, *pg.* 483
ANGEL MATS - Floor Mats - ANGELICA CORPORATION; *pg.* 38, *pg.* 483
ANGEL SLIDERS - Bed Patient Positioning Blanket - ANGELICA CORPORATION; *pg.* 38, *pg.* 483
ANGEL SOFT - Disposable Paper Tissues, Bathroom Tissue, Towels & Napkins - GEORGIA-PACIFIC LLC; *pg.* 1458, *pg.* 507
ANGEL TREADS - Slippers - R.G. BARRY CORPORATION; *pg.* 1818, *pg.* 1470
ANGELA - Women's Clothing & Accessories - WOODEN SHIPS OF HOBOKEN; *pg.* 35, *pg.* 1315
ANGELA MIA - Food Product - CONAGRA FOODS, INC.; *pg.* 826, *pg.* 1014
ANGELICA - Hair & Skin Product - AUBREY ORGANICS INC.; *pg.* 499, *pg.* 470
ANGELINA - Clothing - ABERCROMBIE & FITCH CO.; *pg.* 37, *pg.* 1466
ANGELIQUE - Ceiling Fan - WESTINGHOUSE LIGHTING CORPORATION; *pg.* 687, *pg.* 1571
ANGELO - Decorative Electrical Products - WESTINGHOUSE LIGHTING CORPORATION; *pg.* 687, *pg.* 1571
ANGELO FAN BRACE - Support Boxes & Braces for Ceiling Fans & Fixtures - WESTINGHOUSE LIGHTING CORPORATION; *pg.* 687, *pg.* 1571
ANGELO SUITE - Decorative Lighting Fixtures for the Home Center Market - WESTINGHOUSE LIGHTING CORPORATION; *pg.* 687, *pg.* 1571
ANGELS - Lace - HERITAGE LACE INC.; *pg.* 694, *pg.* 711
ANGELS BASEBALL FOUNDATION - Foundation - ANGELS BASEBALL, L.P.; *pg.* 529, *pg.* 42
ANGEL'S BLUSH - Container Grown Plant - MONROVIA GROWERS; *pg.* 1797, *pg.* 44
ANGELS BY VICTORIA'S SECRET - Apparel - VICTORIA'S SECRET STORES, LLC; *pg.* 1789, *pg.* 1471
ANGELS SCHOLARS - Scholars Program - ANGELS BASEBALL, L.P.; *pg.* 529, *pg.* 42
ANGELSTAT - Scrub - ALIMED, INC.; *pg.* 1490, *pg.* 816
ANGIO-SEAL - Vascular Closure Device - ST. JUDE MEDICAL, INC.; *pg.* 1596, *pg.* 963
ANGIOFLOW - Electrosurgical Devices - ANGIODYNAMICS, INC.; *pg.* 1495, *pg.* 1173
ANGIOFLUSH III - Electrosurgical Devices - ANGIODYNAMICS, INC.; *pg.* 1495, *pg.* 1173
ANGIOMAX - Pharmaceutical Products - THE MEDICINES COMPANY; *pg.* 1561, *pg.* 1104
ANGIOPTIC - Electrosurgical Devices - ANGIODYNAMICS, INC.; *pg.* 1495, *pg.* 1173
ANGIOSTATIN - Molecular Probe Product - THERMO FISHER SCIENTIFIC INC.; *pg.* 1602, *pg.* 61
ANGIOX - Pharmaceutical Products - THE MEDICINES COMPANY; *pg.* 1561, *pg.* 1104
ANGLAMOL - Additive Concentrates for Preparing Lubricating Compositions - THE LUBRIZOL CORPORATION; *pg.* 1171, *pg.* 1481
ANGLE DRIVER - Cross-Connect Fuse - TII NETWORK TECHNOLOGIES, INC.; *pg.* 680, *pg.* 1157
ANGLE EDGE+ - Toothbrush - RANIR LLC; *pg.* 520, *pg.* 888
ANGLE SHEER - Balloon - CONTINENTAL AMERICAN CORP.; *pg.* 1880, *pg.* 723
ANGLED MICROSTATS - Surgical Instrument - AMERICAN MEDICAL SYSTEMS, INC.; *pg.* 1399, *pg.* 238
ANGLESTAR - Sensor System - MEASUREMENT SPECIALTIES INC.; *pg.* 1360, *pg.* 1783
ANGOVE'S - Beverage - TRINCHERO FAMILY ESTATES; *pg.* 1971, *pg.* 197
ANGUILLA - Footwear - EASTLAND SHOE CORPORATION; *pg.* 1808, *pg.* 750
ANGUS BEEF - Meat - CARGILL LIMITED; *pg.* 1475, *pg.* 1914
ANGUS PRIDE - Meat - CARGILL LIMITED; *pg.* 1475, *pg.* 1914
ANGUS PRIDE - Beef Product Line - FOOD LION, LLC; *pg.* 1019, *pg.* 1390
ANHEUSER-BUSCH - Beer - ANHEUSER-BUSCH COMPANIES, LLC; *pg.* 237, *pg.* 991
ANIMAL - Hamburger & Cheeseburger Sandwiches - IN-N-OUT BURGERS, INC.; *pg.* 1732, *pg.* 111
ANIMAL HOUSE - Game - INTERNATIONAL GAME TECHNOLOGY; *pg.* 957, *pg.* 1024
ANIMAL MATRIX - Animal & Plantcare Product - NEW EARTH LIFE SCIENCES, INC.; *pg.* 1573, *pg.* 1499
ANIMAL PARADE - Games - AMERICAN GIRL LLC; *pg.* 949, *pg.* 1871
ANIMAL PARADE - Nutritional Supplement - NATURAL ORGANICS, INC.; *pg.* 1571, *pg.* 1181
ANIMAL PLANET - Television Station - DISCOVERY COMMUNICATIONS, INC.; *pg.* 282, *pg.* 777
ANIMAL SHELTERING - Magazine - THE HUMANE SOCIETY OF THE UNITED STATES; *pg.* 143, *pg.* 400
ANIMAS - Diabetes Treatment Products - ANIMAS CORPORATION; *pg.* 1495, *pg.* 1593
ANIMATE - Pet Product - PETSMART, INC.; *pg.* 1481, *pg.* 18
ANIMATTE - Video Keying - AVID TECHNOLOGY, INC.; *pg.* 622, *pg.* 804
ANIMORPHS - Educational Materials - SCHOLASTIC INC.; *pg.* 1683, *pg.* 1288
ANIXTER INTERNATIONAL - Supply Chain Services - ANIXTER INTERNATIONAL INC.; *pg.* 1313, *pg.* 614
ANKARA - Bath Product - KOHLER CO.; *pg.* 91, *pg.* 1862
ANKLE TOUGH - Medical & Aesthetic Product - DYNATRONICS CORPORATION; *pg.* 1526, *pg.* 1757
ANKOR - Chemical Coating - ENTHONE INC.; *pg.* 1161, *pg.* 381
ANKYLOS - Dental Product - DENTSPLY INTERNATIONAL INC.; *pg.* 1522, *pg.* 1596
ANLC 1 - Chemical Product - BIRKO CORPORATION; *pg.* 1149, *pg.* 332
ANM - Software - CISCO SYSTEMS, INC.; *pg.* 372, *pg.* 240
ANN - Furniture - AMISCO INDUSTRIES LTD.; *pg.* 913, *pg.* 1958
ANN - Fragrance & Personal Care Products - ANN INC.; *pg.* 18, *pg.* 1195
THE ANN ARBOR NEWS - Newspaper - MLIVE MEDIA GROUP; *pg.* 1665, *pg.* 888
ANN SACKS - Furniture - KOHLER CO.; *pg.* 91, *pg.* 1862

First page reference indicates Business Class Edition
Second page reference indicates Geographic Edition

ANN TAYLOR LOFT - Women's Clothing, Shoes, Accessories, Fragrance & Personal Care - ANN INC.; *pg.* 18, *pg.* 1195
ANNA - Clothing - ABERCROMBIE & FITCH CO.; *pg.* 37, *pg.* 1466
ANNA - Mattress - ETHAN ALLEN INTERIORS INC.; *pg.* 924, *pg.* 343
ANNA SERVICE BUREAU - ISIN Numbers Reference Source - STANDARD & POOR'S RATINGS SERVICES; *pg.* 805, *pg.* 1296
ANNABEL - Women's Clothing & Accessories - WOODEN SHIPS OF HOBOKEN; *pg.* 35, *pg.* 1315
ANNABELLE - Furniture - AMISCO INDUSTRIES LTD.; *pg.* 913, *pg.* 1958
ANNABELLE - Lamp - ASHLEY FURNITURE INDUSTRIES, INC.; *pg.* 914, *pg.* 1852
ANNE BOLYN CREWEL - Fabric - SCALAMANDRE, INC.; *pg.* 941, *pg.* 1058
ANNELISE - Women's Clothing & Accessories - WOODEN SHIPS OF HOBOKEN; *pg.* 35, *pg.* 1315
ANNESLEY - Furniture - JOFCO INC.; *pg.* 931, *pg.* 691
ANNETTE - Lamp - ASHLEY FURNITURE INDUSTRIES, INC.; *pg.* 914, *pg.* 1852
ANNETTE - Bedding - CROSCILL, INC.; *pg.* 1122, *pg.* 1220
ANNETTE HIMSTEDT - Collector Dolls - MATTEL, INC.; *pg.* 962, *pg.* 81
ANNIE - Footwear - PHOENIX FOOTWEAR GROUP, INC.; *pg.* 1815, *pg.* 60
ANNIHILATOR - Insecticide Premise Spray - BOEHRINGER INGELHEIM VETMEDICA, INC.; *pg.* 1474, *pg.* 989
ANNIKA - Furniture - ASHLEY FURNITURE INDUSTRIES, INC.; *pg.* 914, *pg.* 1852
ANNIVERSARY BLEND - Coffee - PEET'S COFFEE & TEA, INC.; *pg.* 1029, *pg.* 85
ANNIVERSARY BOUQUET - Floral Bouquet - FTD GROUP, INC.; *pg.* 1795, *pg.* 608
ANNIVERSARY CASH - Lottery Game - KENTUCKY LOTTERY CORPORATION; *pg.* 996, *pg.* 735
ANNIVERSARY SPLENDOR - Flower Arrangement - 1-800-FLOWERS.COM, INC.; *pg.* 1758, *pg.* 1151
ANN'S CHOICE - Retirement Community - ERICKSON LIVING; *pg.* 1090, *pg.* 766
ANNUAL REGISTER OF GRANT SUPPORT - Guide to Grant-Giving Organizations - R.R. BOWKER LLC; *pg.* 1682, *pg.* 1095
ANNULAR - Air Gun - BOLT TECHNOLOGY CORPORATION; *pg.* 1318, *pg.* 360
ANO-KLEEN - Chemical for Metal Finishing - HAVILAND ENTERPRISES INC.; *pg.* 1165, *pg.* 887
ANON - Opticwear - BURTON SNOWBOARD COMPANY; *pg.* 1829, *pg.* 1765
ANORAD - Air Bearing System - ROCKWELL AUTOMATION, INC.; *pg.* 668, *pg.* 1880
ANORAK - Apparel - OAKLEY, INC.; *pg.* 1840, *pg.* 86
ANOX - Antioxidants - CHEMTURA CORPORATION; *pg.* 1152, *pg.* 355
ANQUAMINE - Chemical Products - AIR PRODUCTS AND CHEMICALS, INC.; *pg.* 1145, *pg.* 1513
ANQUAWHITE - Chemical Product - AIR PRODUCTS AND CHEMICALS, INC.; *pg.* 1145, *pg.* 1513
ANSAC - Cognac - HEAVEN HILL DISTILLERIES, INC.; *pg.* 1964, *pg.* 725
ANSAID - Medicine - PFIZER INC.; *pg.* 1581, *pg.* 1278
ANSER - Golf Club - KARSTEN MANUFACTURING CORPORATION; *pg.* 1838, *pg.* 17
ANSILEX - Pigment - BASF CATALYSTS LLC; *pg.* 1148, *pg.* 1074
ANSO - Nylon - HONEYWELL INTERNATIONAL INC.; *pg.* 407, *pg.* 1088
ANSUL - Fire Protection & Suppression Products - ANSUL, INCORPORATED; *pg.* 1147, *pg.* 1869
ANSWER - Pregnancy Test - CHURCH & DWIGHT CO., INC.; *pg.* 1153, *pg.* 1063
ANSWER - Toiletries - THE GILLETTE COMPANY; *pg.* 509, *pg.* 795
ANSWER - Office Furniture - STEELCASE INC.; *pg.* 475, *pg.* 889
ANSWER HIP SYSTEM - Hip Product - ZIMMER BIOMET HOLDINGS, INC.; *pg.* 1611, *pg.* 699
ANSWERS FOR THE INFORMATION AGE - Slogan - INTERNATIONAL DATA GROUP; *pg.* 1653, *pg.* 796
ANSWERS.COM - Free Search Engine Website - ANSWERS CORPORATION; *pg.* 1229, *pg.* 1195
ANSWERTIPS - Software - ANSWERS CORPORATION; *pg.* 1229, *pg.* 1195
ANSYR - Pharmaceutical Product - HOSPIRA, INC.; *pg.* 1542, *pg.* 623
ANT RID - Insecticides - THE CLOROX COMPANY; *pg.* 327, *pg.* 169
ANTARCTICA - Cinema Theater Services - MUSEUM OF SCIENCE AND INDUSTRY; *pg.* 565, *pg.* 583
ANTARES - Software - SS&C TECHNOLOGIES HOLDINGS, INC.; *pg.* 473, *pg.* 386
ANTARIS - Semiconductor Integrated Circuits - ATMEL CORPORATION; *pg.* 621, *pg.* 238
ANTE UP - Lottery Game - IOWA LOTTERY; *pg.* 996, *pg.* 705
ANTE UP - Lottery Game - KENTUCKY LOTTERY CORPORATION; *pg.* 996, *pg.* 735
ANTENNA SPECIALISTS - Antenna Product - PCTEL, INC.; *pg.* 452, *pg.* 557
ANTEQUERA - Ceramic, Glass, Stone Tiles & Slabs - WALKER & ZANGER, INC.; *pg.* 119, *pg.* 281
ANTHEA - Lamp - ASHLEY FURNITURE INDUSTRIES, INC.; *pg.* 914, *pg.* 1852
ANTHELCIDE - Medicine - PFIZER INC.; *pg.* 1581, *pg.* 1278
ANTHEM - Air Brush - BADGER AIR BRUSH COMPANY; *pg.* 359, *pg.* 612
ANTHEM - Furniture - JASPER GROUP; *pg.* 930, *pg.* 691
ANTHEM - Herbicide - MONSANTO COMPANY; *pg.* 1173, *pg.* 999
ANTHEM - Chemistry-Free CTP - PRESSTEK LLC; *pg.* 1678, *pg.* 1034
ANTHEM - Class "A" Motor Homes - REXHALL INDUSTRIES, INC.; *pg.* 1710, *pg.* 121
ANTHEM - CRT System - ST. JUDE MEDICAL, INC.; *pg.* 1596, *pg.* 963
ANTHIUM DIOXCIDE - Disinfectant - E.I. DU PONT DE NEMOURS & COMPANY; *pg.* 1159, *pg.* 390
ANTHOLOGY - Game - ACTIVISION BLIZZARD, INC.; *pg.* 948, *pg.* 271
ANTHOLOGY - Branded Video Program - FACEBOOK, INC.; *pg.* 1245, *pg.* 143
ANTHONY LOG HOMES - Log Homes - ANTHONY FOREST PRODUCTS CO., INC.; *pg.* 67, *pg.* 31
ANTHONY POWER PLANK - Scaffold Board - ANTHONY FOREST PRODUCTS CO., INC.; *pg.* 67, *pg.* 31
ANTHONY'S - Pasta - AMERICAN ITALIAN PASTA COMPANY; *pg.* 837, *pg.* 980
ANTHROBENCH - Furniture - ANTHRO CORPORATION; *pg.* 913, *pg.* 1509
ANTHROCART - Furniture - ANTHRO CORPORATION; *pg.* 913, *pg.* 1509
ANTHROPOLOGIE - Apparel - URBAN OUTFITTERS, INC.; *pg.* 1789, *pg.* 1571
ANTI-AGING PHYSICIAN - Health System Product - LANELABS USA INC.; *pg.* 1554, *pg.* 1128
ANTI-CREEP - Linear Motion Component - DEL-TRON PRECISION, INC.; *pg.* 1328, *pg.* 337
ANTI-FOAM - Foam Preventer - KALO, INC.; *pg.* 1796, *pg.* 719
ANTI-FREEZE - Software - SYMANTEC CORPORATION; *pg.* 478, *pg.* 161
ANTI-GLOOM - Nutritional Supplement - WHITEWING LABS, INC.; *pg.* 1610, *pg.* 99
ANTI-HIS - Biomolecule Product - THERMO FISHER SCIENTIFIC INC.; *pg.* 1602, *pg.* 61
ANTI-HISG - Biomolecule Product - THERMO FISHER SCIENTIFIC INC.; *pg.* 1602, *pg.* 61
ANTI-ITCH - Hair & Skin Product - AUBREY ORGANICS INC.; *pg.* 499, *pg.* 470
ANTI-LEXA - Biomolecule Product - THERMO FISHER SCIENTIFIC INC.; *pg.* 1602, *pg.* 61
ANTI-OX - Beverage - MONSTER BEVERAGE CORPORATION; *pg.* 257, *pg.* 69
ANTI OXIDANT POWER - Boost - JAMBA, INC.; *pg.* 1024, *pg.* 84
ANTI-REFLECTIVE COATING - Coating - BREWER SCIENCE, INC.; *pg.* 1150, *pg.* 989
ANTI-SIPHON DEVICES - Medical Device - INTEGRA LIFESCIENCES HOLDINGS CORPORATION; *pg.* 1545, *pg.* 1109
ANTI-SLIP - Coating Agent - DELTA FOREMOST CHEMICAL CORPORATION; *pg.* 1155, *pg.* 1642
ANTI STICK - Steel Product - AK STEEL HOLDING CORPORATION; *pg.* 1311, *pg.* 1479
ANTI-THIO - Biomolecule Product - THERMO FISHER SCIENTIFIC INC.; *pg.* 1602, *pg.* 61
ANTI-WASH - Fabric Product - BELTON INDUSTRIES, INC.; *pg.* 691, *pg.* 1612
ANTI-XPRESS - Molecular Biology Product - THERMO FISHER SCIENTIFIC INC.; *pg.* 1602, *pg.* 61
ANTIALIASING - Software - NVIDIA CORPORATION; *pg.* 447, *pg.* 268
ANTIBES - Women's Clothing & Accessories - WOODEN SHIPS OF HOBOKEN; *pg.* 35, *pg.* 1315
ANTIBLAZE - Chemical Product - ALBEMARLE CORPORATION; *pg.* 1146, *pg.* 741
ANTIBODY BEACON - Molecular Probe Product - THERMO FISHER SCIENTIFIC INC.; *pg.* 1602, *pg.* 61
ANTICO POSTO - Italian Restaurant - LETTUCE ENTERTAIN YOU ENTERPRISES, INC.; *pg.* 1735, *pg.* 580
ANTIGO - Furniture - AMERICAN LEATHER LP; *pg.* 912, *pg.* 1673
ANTIGO - Furniture - ASHLEY FURNITURE INDUSTRIES, INC.; *pg.* 914, *pg.* 1852
ANTIGUA - Broadloom - COURISTAN INC.; *pg.* 921, *pg.* 1067
ANTIGUITY - Fabric - NEMSCHOFF, INC.; *pg.* 936, *pg.* 1890
ANTINORI - Wine - REMY COINTREAU USA INC.; *pg.* 1969, *pg.* 1285
ANTIOCH - Peripheral Controller - CYPRESS SEMICONDUCTOR CORPORATION; *pg.* 1326, *pg.* 243
ANTIOXIDANT ESSENTIALS - Supplement & Food Product - NEW EARTH LIFE SCIENCES, INC.; *pg.* 1573, *pg.* 1499
ANTIOXIDANT EXTRA - Wellness Tea - CELESTIAL SEASONINGS, INC.; *pg.* 846, *pg.* 310
THE ANTIOXIDANT SUPERPOWER - Tag Line - POM WONDERFUL, LLC; *pg.* 890, *pg.* 139
ANTIPHLOGISTINE - Muscle Care Product - W.F. YOUNG, INC.; *pg.* 1610, *pg.* 817
ANTIQUE - Furniture - ASHLEY FURNITURE INDUSTRIES, INC.; *pg.* 914, *pg.* 1852
ANTIQUE - Kitchen Product - KOHLER CO.; *pg.* 91, *pg.* 1862
ANTIQUE APPRAISAL - Video Slots INTERNATIONAL GAME TECHNOLOGY; *pg.* 957, *pg.* 1024
ANTIQUE ROSE SHEER - Window Treatment - CROSCILL, INC.; *pg.* 1122, *pg.* 1220
ANTIQUENCH - Performance Ingredient - ACTIVE ORGANICS, INC.; *pg.* 498, *pg.* 1725
ANTIQUES ROADSHOW INSIDER - Newsletter - BELVOIR MEDIA GROUP, LLC; *pg.* 1620, *pg.* 360
ANTIROBE - Pharmaceutical Product - PFIZER INC.; *pg.* 1581, *pg.* 1278
ANTIUM - Ceramic, Glass, Stone Tiles & Slabs - WALKER & ZANGER, INC.; *pg.* 119, *pg.* 281
ANTIVERT - Medicine - PFIZER INC.; *pg.* 1581, *pg.* 1278
ANTLER KING - Deer & Elk Feeds - KENT NUTRITION GROUP; *pg.* 1477, *pg.* 710
ANTOINETTE - Doll - TONNER DOLL COMPANY, INC.; *pg.* 968, *pg.* 1171
ANTON - Furniture - ETHAN ALLEN INTERIORS INC.; *pg.* 924, *pg.* 343
ANTONELLI - Italian Wine - LAIRD & COMPANY, INC.; *pg.* 1966, *pg.* 1119
ANTONINA VELLA DESIGNS - Wallpaper - YORK WALLCOVERINGS INC.; *pg.* 947, *pg.* 1598
ANTONIO - Fabric - NEMSCHOFF, INC.; *pg.* 936, *pg.* 1890
ANTRON - Commercial Carpet Fibers - INVISTA B.V.; *pg.* 1168, *pg.* 723
ANTS IN THE PANTS - Toy & Game - HASBRO, INC.; *pg.* 954, *pg.* 1603
ANUCORT-HC - Pharmaceutical Product - G&W LABORATORIES INC.; *pg.* 1532, *pg.* 1123
ANUSOL-HC - Pharmaceutical Product - SALIX PHARMACEUTICALS, INC.; *pg.* 1591, *pg.* 1388
ANVIL - Bulk Material Handling - ANVIL ATTACHMENTS, LLC; *pg.* 1313, *pg.* 748
ANVIL - Cap - BROWN & BIGELOW, INC.; *pg.* 1624, *pg.* 959
ANVIL - Display Product - RICHARDSON ELECTRONICS, LTD.; *pg.* 667, *pg.* 622
ANVILANE - Bowling Equipment - BRUNSWICK BOWLING & BILLIARDS CORP.; *pg.* 1828, *pg.* 622
ANXIRON - Pharmaceutical Product - VALEANT PHARMACEUTICALS INTERNATIONAL; *pg.* 1605, *pg.* 1047
ANY-ANGLE - Stereotaxic Equipment - STOELTING CO.; *pg.* 1430, *pg.* 671
ANY JET. ANY TIME. ANY PLACE. - Slogan - BLUE STAR JETS, INC.; *pg.* 1901, *pg.* 1205
ANY LIGHT BULB ANYTIME - Slogan - TOPBULB.COM LLC; *pg.* 1307, *pg.* 677
ANY-MAZE - Software - STOELTING CO.; *pg.* 1430, *pg.* 671
ANY TIME'S A GOOD TIME FOR IHOP - Tagline - DINEEQUITY, INC.; *pg.* 1725, *pg.* 95

ANYCAP - Regulator - ANALOG DEVICES, INC.; *pg.* 617, *pg.* 839

ANYCARD ATM - Automated Teller Machines - TIDEL ENGINEERING, L.P.; *pg.* 1382, *pg.* 1670

ANYCLOCK - Precision Frequency Synthesizer - MICREL, INC.; *pg.* 654, *pg.* 247

ANYGATE - Integrated Circuits - MICREL, INC.; *pg.* 654, *pg.* 247

ANYGEL - Software - BIO-RAD LABORATORIES, INC.; *pg.* 1504, *pg.* 101

ANYPLACE LIGHT - Flashlight - ENERGIZER HOLDINGS, INC.; *pg.* 637, *pg.* 996

ANYRATE - Receiver & Transmitter - MICREL, INC.; *pg.* 654, *pg.* 247

ANYSTREAM - Shower Heads - SPEAKMAN COMPANY; *pg.* 112, *pg.* 388

ANYTHING BUT SIX - Video Game - INTERNATIONAL GAME TECHNOLOGY; *pg.* 957, *pg.* 1024

ANYTHING ELSE IS A COMPROMISE - Slogan - INVACARE CORPORATION; *pg.* 1546, *pg.* 1451

ANYTHING ELSE IS A SUBSTITUTE - Knitwear - WIGWAM MILLS, INC.; *pg.* 15, *pg.* 1894

ANYTHING LESS COSTS MORE - Slogan - BOBRICK WASHROOM EQUIPMENT, INC.; *pg.* 1043, *pg.* 166

ANYTHING YOU CAN IMAGINE, UVP CAN IMAGE! - Slogan - UVP, INC.; *pg.* 1434, *pg.* 298

ANYTHING'S WILD POKER - Video Game - INTERNATIONAL GAME TECHNOLOGY; *pg.* 957, *pg.* 1024

ANYTIME! - Tag Line - BARLEYCORN'S; *pg.* 1716, *pg.* 726

ANYTIME - Firelog - DURAFLAME, INC.; *pg.* 1123, *pg.* 280

ANYTIME! - Gourmet Cinnamon Rolls & Cinnamon Rolls - RHODES INTERNATIONAL, INC.; *pg.* 891, *pg.* 1760

ANYTIME. ANYWHERE - Tagline - HARRIS CORPORATION; *pg.* 642, *pg.* 439

ANYWHERE CHAIR - Pneumatic Seating - THE HON COMPANY; *pg.* 928, *pg.* 709

ANYWHERE RN - Automated Medication Management - OMNICELL INC.; *pg.* 1578, *pg.* 161

ANYWHERE VOICEMAIL - Communication Product - CENTURYLINK, INC; *pg.* 1870, *pg.* 317

ANYWHERESCOPE - Microscope - UNITRON INC.; *pg.* 1433, *pg.* 1153

ANYWHEREUSB - Computer Peripheral Equipment - DIGI INTERNATIONAL INC.; *pg.* 387, *pg.* 948

ANZEA - Fabric - NEMSCHOFF, INC.; *pg.* 936, *pg.* 1890

AO - Furniture - HERMAN MILLER, INC.; *pg.* 926, *pg.* 913

AOA - Tissue Treatment - MEDTRONIC, INC.; *pg.* 1564, *pg.* 939

AOAE - Medical Device - NATUS MEDICAL INCORPORATED; *pg.* 1572, *pg.* 199

AOL - Entertainment Product - TIME WARNER INC.; *pg.* 312, *pg.* 1302

AOL TIME WARNER FOUNDATION - Entertainment Product - TIME WARNER INC.; *pg.* 312, *pg.* 1302

AON MODULE - Router - CISCO SYSTEMS, INC.; *pg.* 372, *pg.* 240

AOSTA - Rubber - K-SWISS; *pg.* 1837, *pg.* 306

AOYOU.COM - Tourism Website - ORBITZ WORLDWIDE, INC.; *pg.* 1918, *pg.* 586

AP - Advanced Placement Program - EDUCATIONAL TESTING SERVICE INC.; *pg.* 1394, *pg.* 1111

AP - Foam Sheathing - JOHNS MANVILLE CORPORATION; *pg.* 89, *pg.* 320

AP - Bearing - THE TIMKEN COMPANY; *pg.* 218, *pg.* 1408

AP-2 - Bearing - THE TIMKEN COMPANY; *pg.* 218, *pg.* 1408

AP-24 - Oral Health Care - NU SKIN ENTERPRISES, INC.; *pg.* 518, *pg.* 1755

AP ARCHIVE - Online Application - THE ASSOCIATED PRESS, INC.; *pg.* 270, *pg.* 1197

AP EXCHANGE - Online Application - THE ASSOCIATED PRESS, INC.; *pg.* 270, *pg.* 1197

AP IMAGES - Online Application - THE ASSOCIATED PRESS, INC.; *pg.* 270, *pg.* 1197

AP MOBILE - Mobile Application - THE ASSOCIATED PRESS, INC.; *pg.* 270, *pg.* 1197

AP STYLEBOOK - Online Application - THE ASSOCIATED PRESS, INC.; *pg.* 270, *pg.* 1197

AP-WARE - Software - CLEARONE COMMUNICATIONS, INC.; *pg.* 629, *pg.* 1756

AP2 - Fluid Handling System - GRACO, INC.; *pg.* 1342, *pg.* 935

APA - Performance Rated Panels - APA-THE ENGINEERED WOOD ASSOCIATION; *pg.* 132, *pg.* 1844

APA - Amateur Putters Association - THE PROFESSIONAL PUTTERS ASSOCIATION; *pg.* 154, *pg.* 1735

APA PRI-400 - I-Joists - APA-THE ENGINEERED WOOD ASSOCIATION; *pg.* 132, *pg.* 1844

APACHE - Clinical Decision Support System - CERNER CORPORATION; *pg.* 1514, *pg.* 981

APACHI - Fuels & Fuel Gases - AIR PRODUCTS AND CHEMICALS, INC.; *pg.* 1145, *pg.* 1513

APACS - Distributed Control Systems - SIEMENS PROCESS INDUSTRIES AND DRIVE; *pg.* 1376, *pg.* 1587

APAK - Fiber Packing Drums or Fiber with Metallic Ends - SONOCO PRODUCTS COMPANY; *pg.* 1469, *pg.* 1619

APARTMENT FINDER - Apartment Guide - NETWORK COMMUNICATIONS INC.; *pg.* 1271, *pg.* 534

APARTMENT GUIDE - Magazine - RENTPATH, INC.; *pg.* 1680, *pg.* 538

APARTMENT SHOWCASE - Classifieds Publication - MADISON NEWSPAPERS, INC.; *pg.* 1661, *pg.* 1866

APARTMENTS.COM - Residential Advertising Website - CLASSIFIED VENTURES, LLC; *pg.* 1235, *pg.* 571

APC - Adhesive System - 3M UNITEK CORPORATION; *pg.* 1483, *pg.* 150

APC - Lubricant - AERVOE INDUSTRIES INCORPORATED; *pg.* 1439, *pg.* 1021

APC - Polymer Compounds - FERRO CORPORATION; *pg.* 1162, *pg.* 1462

APC FOR INTUNE - Software - BMC SOFTWARE, INC.; *pg.* 362, *pg.* 1701

APC TODAY - Healthcare Publication - LEBHAR-FRIEDMAN INC.; *pg.* 1658, *pg.* 1250

APCOS - Melting Product - AIR PRODUCTS AND CHEMICALS, INC.; *pg.* 1145, *pg.* 1513

APE - Modulator - VIAVI SOLUTIONS INC.; *pg.* 1435, *pg.* 148

APECS - Actuator - WOODWARD, INC.; *pg.* 122, *pg.* 329

APEEL - Catheter Delivery Systems - ST. JUDE MEDICAL, INC.; *pg.* 1596, *pg.* 963

APERITIF - Kitchen Product - KOHLER CO.; *pg.* 91, *pg.* 1862

APERTURE - Application Program - APPLE INC.; *pg.* 350, *pg.* 73

APERTURE - Fabric - MOMENTUM TEXTILES INC.; *pg.* 697, *pg.* 114

APEX - Power Supply System - ADVANCED ENERGY INDUSTRIES, INC.; *pg.* 613, *pg.* 328

APEX - FPGA Device - ALTERA CORPORATION; *pg.* 348, *pg.* 237

APEX - Grinder & Polisher - BUEHLER, LTD.; *pg.* 1403, *pg.* 622

APEX - Sleever - DOUGLAS MACHINE, INC.; *pg.* 1456, *pg.* 915

APEX - Radar Gauge - EMERSON PROCESS MANAGEMENT ROSEMOUNT INC.; *pg.* 1334, *pg.* 920

APEX - Valves - FLOWSERVE CORPORATION; *pg.* 82, *pg.* 1719

APEX - Fluid Handling System - GRACO, INC.; *pg.* 1342, *pg.* 935

APEX - Audio Routing Switcher - GRASS VALLEY, INC.; *pg.* 641, *pg.* 164

APEX - Software - HOLOGIC, INC.; *pg.* 1416, *pg.* 784

APEX - Flight Deck - HONEYWELL INTERNATIONAL INC.; *pg.* 407, *pg.* 1088

APEX - Thinner - JONES-BLAIR COMPANY; *pg.* 1443, *pg.* 1682

APEX - Fertilizers - J.R. SIMPLOT COMPANY; *pg.* 867, *pg.* 547

APEX - Fabric - POLYMER GROUP, INC.; *pg.* 698, *pg.* 1368

APEX - Programming Language - SALESFORCE.COM, INC.; *pg.* 1278, *pg.* 226

APEX - USB Modem - SIERRA WIRELESS INCORPORATED; *pg.* 673, *pg.* 1909

APEX - Surgical & Medical Product - STRYKER CORPORATION; *pg.* 1598, *pg.* 894

APEX - Plastic & Rubber - TEKNOR APEX COMPANY; *pg.* 1889, *pg.* 1605

APEX - Veneer Finish Plaster - USG CORPORATION; *pg.* 118, *pg.* 594

APEX 20K - High-Density Field-Programmable Gate Array - ALTERA CORPORATION; *pg.* 348, *pg.* 237

APEX 20KC - High-density Field-programmable Gate Array - ALTERA CORPORATION; *pg.* 348, *pg.* 237

APEX 20KE - High-density Field-programmable Gate Array - ALTERA CORPORATION; *pg.* 348, *pg.* 237

APEX II - High-Density Field-Programmable Gate Array - ALTERA CORPORATION; *pg.* 348, *pg.* 237

APEX SENTRY - Radar Gauge - EMERSON PROCESS MANAGEMENT ROSEMOUNT INC.; *pg.* 1334, *pg.* 920

APEX STEP - Rubber Stair Tread - R.C.A. RUBBER COMPANY; *pg.* 1888, *pg.* 1402

APHRODITE - Apparel - BEBE STORES, INC.; *pg.* 19, *pg.* 49

APHRODITE - Fabric - NEMSCHOFF, INC.; *pg.* 936, *pg.* 1890

APHRODITE'S PINK NIGHTIE - Nail Care Product - OPI PRODUCTS INC.; *pg.* 518, *pg.* 167

API - Opto-Electronic Solutions - ADVANCED PHOTONIX, INC.; *pg.* 1398, *pg.* 865

API INTEGRATION WORKSHOP - Software - SONUS NETWORKS INC.; *pg.* 1281, *pg.* 858

API LABORWORKX - Healthcare Industry Software - API HEALTHCARE CORP.; *pg.* 350, *pg.* 1860

APIEZON - High-Vacuum Oils, Greases & Waxes - MEGGER INC.; *pg.* 1422, *pg.* 1557

APLAC - Simulation Engine - AWR CORPORATION; *pg.* 623, *pg.* 78

APLE - Software - ASPEN TECHNOLOGY, INC.; *pg.* 354, *pg.* 804

APLETS - Candies - LIBERTY ORCHARDS CO., INC.; *pg.* 1857, *pg.* 1819

APLICAP - Ionomer Cement Restorative - 3M COMPANY; *pg.* 1142, *pg.* 956

APLITE - Silica - U.S. SILICA COMPANY; *pg.* 1185, *pg.* 1849

APNEAL - Screening - RESMED INC.; *pg.* 1589, *pg.* 207

APNEALINK - Sleep Screening Tool - RESMED INC.; *pg.* 1589, *pg.* 207

APO-BRDU - Molecular Probe Product - THERMO FISHER SCIENTIFIC INC.; *pg.* 1602, *pg.* 61

APO-SYMMAR - Lenses - SCHNEIDER OPTICS INC.; *pg.* 1428, *pg.* 1165

APOGE - Shower - MAAX INC.-MINNEAPOLIS; *pg.* 1885, *pg.* 938

APOGEE - Pens - A. T. CROSS COMPANY; *pg.* 339, *pg.* 1602

APOGEE - Medical Device - AMERICAN MEDICAL SYSTEMS HOLDINGS, INC.; *pg.* 1493, *pg.* 947

APOGEE ELITE - Hair Removal System - CYNOSURE, INC.; *pg.* 1521, *pg.* 858

APOGEE EXECUTIVE - Pen - A. T. CROSS COMPANY; *pg.* 339, *pg.* 1602

APOHEAT - Power Steamer Carpet Deep Cleaner - BISSELL HOMECARE, INC.; *pg.* 52, *pg.* 887

APOKYN - Pharmaceutical Product - MYLAN, INC.; *pg.* 1570, *pg.* 1520

APOLLINARIS - Beverages - THE COCA-COLA COMPANY; *pg.* 240, *pg.* 493

APOLLO - Audio Visual Products - ACCO BRANDS CORPORATION; *pg.* 340, *pg.* 626

APOLLO - Monitors - AKRON BRASS COMPANY; *pg.* 1311, *pg.* 1482

APOLLO - Furniture - ASHLEY FURNITURE INDUSTRIES, INC.; *pg.* 914, *pg.* 1852

APOLLO - Software - ASPEN TECHNOLOGY, INC.; *pg.* 354, *pg.* 804

APOLLO - Braking System - BLUE OX; *pg.* 701, *pg.* 1019

APOLLO - Biofilter - CALGON CARBON CORPORATION; *pg.* 1151, *pg.* 1574

APOLLO - Software - COMVERGE, INC.; *pg.* 1325, *pg.* 536

APOLLO - Valve - CONBRACO INDUSTRIES INC.; *pg.* 1325, *pg.* 1382

APOLLO - Medical Equipment - CONMED CORPORATION; *pg.* 1517, *pg.* 1347

APOLLO - Rug - COURISTAN INC.; *pg.* 921, *pg.* 1067

APOLLO - Reels - DAIWA CORPORATION; *pg.* 1832, *pg.* 75

APOLLO - Medical Equipment - INVACARE CORPORATION; *pg.* 1546, *pg.* 1451

APOLLO - Software - IRI GROUP; *pg.* 421, *pg.* 579

APOLLO - Storage Trailer - M-B COMPANIES, INC.; *pg.* 1357, *pg.* 1884

APOLLO - Silverware - ONEIDA LTD; *pg.* 1129, *pg.* 1318

APOLLO - Ingredient System - PENFORD CORPORATION; *pg.* 1177, *pg.* 314

APOLLO - Software - SYNOPSYS, INC.; *pg.* 480, *pg.* 162

APOLLO - Ceiling Fan - WESTINGHOUSE LIGHTING CORPORATION; *pg.* 687, *pg.* 1571

APOLLO 11 - Gaming Product - GLD PRODUCTS, INC.; *pg.* 1835, *pg.* 1882

APOLLO 3 AC - Medical Equipment - CONMED CORPORATION; *pg.* 1517, *pg.* 1347

APOLLO ELITE - Ceiling Fan - WESTINGHOUSE LIGHTING CORPORATION; *pg.* 687, *pg.* 1571

APOLLO II - Thermoplastic Hand Applicator - M-B COMPANIES, INC.; *pg.* 1357, *pg.* 1884

First page reference indicates Business Class Edition
Second page reference indicates Geographic Edition

APOLLO PLATFORM - Software - COMVERGE, INC.; *pg.* 1325, *pg.* 536
APOLLO SMARTGRID - Software Technology - COMVERGE, INC.; *pg.* 1325, *pg.* 536
APOLLO3 - Medical Equipment - CONMED CORPORATION; *pg.* 1517, *pg.* 1347
APOSTROPHE - Apparel - SEARS HOLDINGS CORPORATION; *pg.* 1784, *pg.* 618
APOTARGET - Molecular Probe Product - THERMO FISHER SCIENTIFIC INC.; *pg.* 1602, *pg.* 61
APOTHECARY - Skincare Product - WATKINS INCORPORATED; *pg.* 909, *pg.* 967
APP-1 - Micropipette Puller for Research - STOELTING CO.; *pg.* 1430, *pg.* 671
APP STORE - Online Store - APPLE INC.; *pg.* 350, *pg.* 73
APPARENET - Software - APPNETA; *pg.* 352, *pg.* 1909
APPARMOR - Computer Software - NOVELL INC.; *pg.* 446, *pg.* 852
APPCACHE - Software - CITRIX SYSTEMS, INC.; *pg.* 375, *pg.* 424
APPCATCHER - Software - WEBSENSE, INC.; *pg.* 491, *pg.* 210
APPCOMPRESS - Software - CITRIX SYSTEMS, INC.; *pg.* 375, *pg.* 424
APPCRITICAL - Support System - APPNETA; *pg.* 352, *pg.* 1909
APPDEV STUDIO - Software - SAS INSTITUTE INC.; *pg.* 466, *pg.* 1361
APPEAL-DEMOCRAT - California Newspaper - FREEDOM COMMUNICATIONS, INC.; *pg.* 1643, *pg.* 110
APPEEL - Lidding Sealant Resins - E.I. DU PONT DE NEMOURS & COMPANY; *pg.* 1159, *pg.* 390
APPETIZERS - Mexican Food - RUIZ FOOD PRODUCTS, INC.; *pg.* 893, *pg.* 77
APPEX 4.5M - APP Modified Bitumen Sheet - JOHNS MANVILLE CORPORATION; *pg.* 89, *pg.* 320
APPEXCHANGE - On-Demand Application - SALESFORCE.COM, INC.; *pg.* 1278, *pg.* 226
APPIAN WAY - Pizza - HENKEL CONSUMER GOODS; *pg.* 511, *pg.* 22
APPLAUSE - Honeycomb Shades - HUNTER DOUGLAS, INC.; *pg.* 928, *pg.* 1320
APPLAUSE - Musical Instrument - KAMAN CORPORATION; *pg.* 229, *pg.* 338
APPLAUSE - Process-Free CTP - PRESSTEK LLC; *pg.* 1678, *pg.* 1034
APPLE - Accessories - THE MEN'S WEARHOUSE, INC.; *pg.* 44, *pg.* 1711
APPLE - Educational Materials - SCHOLASTIC INC.; *pg.* 1683, *pg.* 1288
APPLE BASKET - Scarf - HERITAGE LACE INC.; *pg.* 694, *pg.* 711
APPLE BLOSSOM - Fruit Arrangements - EDIBLE ARRANGEMENTS INTERNATIONAL, INC.; *pg.* 1768, *pg.* 382
APPLE BOXES - Grip Equipment - ALAN GORDON ENTERPRISES, INC.; *pg.* 1399, *pg.* 125
APPLE CINEMA DISPLAY - Computer Monitor - APPLE INC.; *pg.* 350, *pg.* 73
APPLE CINNAMON - Herb Teas - R.C. BIGELOW, INC.; *pg.* 891, *pg.* 348
APPLE CINNAMON CHEERIOS - Cereal - GENERAL MILLS, INC.; *pg.* 828, *pg.* 933
APPLE CINNAMON TOASTY O'S - Cereal - POST CONSUMER BRANDS; *pg.* 833, *pg.* 927
APPLE CONSULTANTS NETWORK - Consultant Services - APPLE INC.; *pg.* 350, *pg.* 73
APPLE CRISP - Donut Mixes - DAWN FOOD PRODUCTS, INC.; *pg.* 1018, *pg.* 893
THE APPLE EXPERTS - Tag Line - KNOUSE FOODS COOPERATIVE INC.; *pg.* 869, *pg.* 1558
APPLE FANTASY - Fragrance - PARFUMS DE COEUR LTD.; *pg.* 519, *pg.* 376
APPLE GRANDE - Dessert - TACO JOHN'S INTERNATIONAL, INC.; *pg.* 1753, *pg.* 1901
APPLE ISERVICES - Internet Services - APPLE INC.; *pg.* 350, *pg.* 73
APPLE JACK - Chewing Tobacco - SWISHER INTERNATIONAL, INC.; *pg.* 1895, *pg.* 345
APPLE JACKS - Food Product - KELLOGG COMPANY; *pg.* 831, *pg.* 870
APPLE JUICE - Beverage - MONSTER BEVERAGE CORPORATION; *pg.* 257, *pg.* 69
APPLE LED CINEMA DISPLAY - Display - APPLE INC.; *pg.* 350, *pg.* 73
APPLE MEDIA SERIES - Training Materials - APPLE INC.; *pg.* 350, *pg.* 73
APPLE PAPERBACKS - Educational Materials - SCHOLASTIC INC.; *pg.* 1683, *pg.* 1288
APPLE PIE MINIS - Desserts - KFC CORPORATION; *pg.* 1733, *pg.* 735
APPLE RAISIN CRISP - Flakes of Rice & Rye Cereal with Apples & Raisins - KELLOGG COMPANY; *pg.* 831, *pg.* 870
APPLE REMOTE DESKTOP - Remote Desktop Software - APPLE INC.; *pg.* 350, *pg.* 73
APPLE STORE - Retail Store Services - APPLE INC.; *pg.* 350, *pg.* 73
APPLE TIME - Apple Products - KNOUSE FOODS COOPERATIVE INC.; *pg.* 869, *pg.* 1558
APPLE TV - Digital Media Player - APPLE INC.; *pg.* 350, *pg.* 73
APPLE ZINGS - Cereal - POST CONSUMER BRANDS; *pg.* 833, *pg.* 927
APPLEBEE'S NEIGHBORHOOD GRILL & BAR - Restaurants - APPLEBEE'S INTERNATIONAL, INC.; *pg.* 1715, *pg.* 980
APPLECARE - Service & Support Programs - APPLE INC.; *pg.* 350, *pg.* 73
APPLESCRIPT - Application Program - APPLE INC.; *pg.* 350, *pg.* 73
APPLESEED - Fabric - NEMSCHOFF, INC.; *pg.* 936, *pg.* 1890
APPLETON - Electrical Products - EMERSON INDUSTRIAL AUTOMATION; *pg.* 1296, *pg.* 657
APPLETON & LANGE - Medical-Science Books - THE MCGRAW-HILL COMPANIES INC.; *pg.* 1663, *pg.* 1257
APPLEWAY - Car Dealerships - AUTONATION, INC.; *pg.* 165, *pg.* 423
APPLEWISE - Food Product - SUN-RYPE PRODUCTS LTD.; *pg.* 899, *pg.* 1908
APPLIANCE $MART - Appliance Retail Store - APPLIANCE RECYCLING CENTERS OF AMERICA, INC.; *pg.* 51, *pg.* 930
APPLIANCE RECYCLING CENTERS OF AMERICA - Recycling Programs - APPLIANCE RECYCLING CENTERS OF AMERICA, INC.; *pg.* 51, *pg.* 930
APPLIANCESMART - Factory Outlet - APPLIANCE RECYCLING CENTERS OF AMERICA, INC.; *pg.* 51, *pg.* 930
APPLIANCEWATCH - Software - NETAPP, INC.; *pg.* 444, *pg.* 287
APPLICAT - Catalyst - BASF CATALYSTS LLC; *pg.* 1148, *pg.* 1074
APPLICATION ACCELERATOR - Software - F5 NETWORKS, INC.; *pg.* 396, *pg.* 1835
APPLICATION ASSURANCE SUITE - Software - DELL SOFTWARE; *pg.* 385, *pg.* 40
APPLICATION BUILDER - Software - CRESTRON ELECTRONICS INC.; *pg.* 631, *pg.* 1116
APPLICATION EXCHANGE FRAMEWORK - Software - DASSAULT SYSTEMS ENOVIA; *pg.* 382, *pg.* 851
APPLICATION LOCKDOWN - Software - WEBSENSE, INC.; *pg.* 491, *pg.* 210
APPLICATION PERFORMANCE MANAGEMENT SUITE - Software - DELL SOFTWARE; *pg.* 385, *pg.* 40
APPLICATION PROBLEM RESOLUTION SYSTEM - Software Application - BMC SOFTWARE, INC.; *pg.* 362, *pg.* 1701
APPLICATION RESTART CONTROL - Software Application - BMC SOFTWARE, INC.; *pg.* 362, *pg.* 1701
APPLICATION SAVER - Software - SYMANTEC CORPORATION; *pg.* 478, *pg.* 161
APPLICATIONS - Office Furniture - JOFCO INC.; *pg.* 931, *pg.* 691
APPLICATIONS ATLAS - Service Program - GE WATER & PROCESS TECHNOLOGIES; *pg.* 1339, *pg.* 1588
APPLICATIONXTENDER - Software - EMC CORPORATION; *pg.* 391, *pg.* 825
APPLICOM - Electronic Components - MOLEX INCORPORATED; *pg.* 655, *pg.* 628
APPLIED AIR - Heating & Ventilating Equipment - MESTEK, INC.; *pg.* 1074, *pg.* 857
APPLIED CONVEYOR ENGINEERING - Electric Instrument - UNIVERSAL INSTRUMENTS CORPORATION; *pg.* 683, *pg.* 1154
APPLIED ENTERPRISE - Technical Services - COMPUTER SCIENCES CORPORATION; *pg.* 378, *pg.* 1780
APPLIED MEMS - Desert Imaging Solutions - ION GEOPHYSICAL CORPORATION; *pg.* 1350, *pg.* 1708
APPLIED SIGNAL TECHNOLOGY - Signal Processing Product - RAYTHEON APPLIED SIGNAL TECHNOLOGY, INC.; *pg.* 667, *pg.* 288
APPLIED THERMAL INNOVATON - Slogan - MODINE MANUFACTURING COMPANY; *pg.* 1074, *pg.* 1888
APPLOCK - Software - WATCHGUARD TECHNOLOGIES, INC.; *pg.* 491, *pg.* 1842
APPLYING GENOMICS TO ERADICATE CANCER - Slogan - EXACT SCIENCES CORPORATION; *pg.* 1529, *pg.* 1865
APPLYING TECHNOLOGY, DELIVERING RESULTS. - Slogan - MSX INTERNATIONAL, INC.; *pg.* 98, *pg.* 912
APPNOTES - Software System - MENTOR GRAPHICS CORPORATION; *pg.* 432, *pg.* 1510
APPNOTES - Magazines - NOVELL INC.; *pg.* 446, *pg.* 852
APPRAISE - Testing Instrument System - BECKMAN COULTER, INC.; *pg.* 1402, *pg.* 48
APPRENTICE - Floor - ROSCO LABORATORIES, INC.; *pg.* 1782, *pg.* 378
APPROACH - Footwear - K-SWISS; *pg.* 1837, *pg.* 306
APPROACH 5C - Multimedia Processor - CSR; *pg.* 280, *pg.* 284
APPROACH 7 - Processor - CSR; *pg.* 280, *pg.* 284
APPROACH MESH - Footwear - K-SWISS; *pg.* 1837, *pg.* 306
APPROPRIATE ROAST - Coffee - KEURIG GREEN MOUNTAIN, INC.; *pg.* 868, *pg.* 1768
APPROVE - Bar Soap - SWISHER HYGIENE INC.; *pg.* 336, *pg.* 1507
APPSERVER - Software - PROGRESS SOFTWARE CORPORATION; *pg.* 457, *pg.* 786
APPSIGHT - Software Development Application - BMC SOFTWARE, INC.; *pg.* 362, *pg.* 1701
APPSIGHT APPLICATION PROBLEM RESOLUTION SYSTEM - Software Application - BMC SOFTWARE, INC.; *pg.* 362, *pg.* 1701
APPSTV - TV - POWER INTEGRATIONS, INC.; *pg.* 1369, *pg.* 249
APPTUNE - Software - BMC SOFTWARE, INC.; *pg.* 362, *pg.* 1701
APRES SKI - Footwear - RALPH LAUREN CORPORATION; *pg.* 46, *pg.* 1284
APRESOLINE - Pharmaceutical Drug - FRESENIUS KABI USA; *pg.* 1531, *pg.* 626
APRICOT DRIFT - Garden Roses - THE CONARD-PYLE COMPANY; *pg.* 1794, *pg.* 1594
APRICOT HONEY - Fragrance - PARFUMS DE COEUR LTD.; *pg.* 519, *pg.* 376
APRILAIRE - Air Cleaner - RESEARCH PRODUCTS CORPORATION; *pg.* 1075, *pg.* 1867
APRILIA - Scooter - PIAGGIO USA, INC.; *pg.* 188, *pg.* 1282
APRISO - Pharmaceutical Product - SALIX PHARMACEUTICALS, INC.; *pg.* 1591, *pg.* 1388
APRIVERA - Healthcare Product - DERMA SCIENCES, INC.; *pg.* 1523, *pg.* 1111
APRON'S - Book - PUBLIX SUPER MARKETS, INC.; *pg.* 1031, *pg.* 437
APROPOS - Fabric - NEMSCHOFF, INC.; *pg.* 936, *pg.* 1890
APS - Energy Services - ARIZONA PUBLIC SERVICE COMPANY; *pg.* 1935, *pg.* 14
APS - Banking Software - JACK HENRY & ASSOCIATES, INC.; *pg.* 422, *pg.* 988
APS - Inserters - PITNEY BOWES INC.; *pg.* 454, *pg.* 376
APS-100 - Auxiliary Power Supply - ANDREA ELECTRONICS CORPORATION; *pg.* 617, *pg.* 1143
APSIRO - Pharmaceutical Product - SALIX PHARMACEUTICALS, INC.; *pg.* 1591, *pg.* 1388
APSYS - Software - SUNGARD DATA SYSTEMS INC.; *pg.* 477, *pg.* 1592
APT FROM YAHOO! - Internet Services - YAHOO! INC.; *pg.* 1289, *pg.* 289
APT.5 - Cosmetic Line - DUANE READE, INC.; *pg.* 1525, *pg.* 1226
APTAC - Adiabatic Calorimeter - TIAX LLC; *pg.* 115, *pg.* 829
APTERA - Connector - AMPHENOL CORPORATION; *pg.* 616, *pg.* 381
APTERA - Medical Product - W.L. GORE & ASSOCIATES, INC.; *pg.* 122, *pg.* 388
APTERA STACKER - Connector - AMPHENOL CORPORATION; *pg.* 616, *pg.* 381
APTIX - Software System - MENTOR GRAPHICS CORPORATION; *pg.* 432, *pg.* 1510
APTRA - Self-Service Software Products - NCR CORPORATION; *pg.* 443, *pg.* 531
APTURA - Self-Retracting Lanyard - MINE SAFETY APPLIANCES COMPANY; *pg.* 1361, *pg.* 1525

APX - Computer Hardware - ALCATEL-LUCENT; *pg.* 615, *pg.* 1094
APX - Burner - MAXON CORPORATION; *pg.* 1359, *pg.* 695
APX 8000 - Access Switch - ALCATEL-LUCENT; *pg.* 615, *pg.* 38
AQC-21 - Air Quality Detector - BOSCH SECURITY SYSTEMS, INC.; *pg.* 626, *pg.* 1158
AQCB - Communication Product - CENTURYLINK, INC; *pg.* 1870, *pg.* 317
AQUA - Dish Detergents - BLUE CROSS LABORATORIES; *pg.* 326, *pg.* 277
AQUA - Beverages - THE COCA-COLA COMPANY; *pg.* 240, *pg.* 493
AQUA - Fabric - NEMSCHOFF, INC.; *pg.* 936, *pg.* 1890
AQUA BASE - Cosmetic Product - MERLE NORMAN COSMETICS, INC.; *pg.* 517, *pg.* 136
AQUA BASE PLUS - Felxographic Inks - VAN SON HOLLAND INK CORPORATION OF AMERICA; *pg.* 487, *pg.* 1169
AQUA-BIND - Chemical Product - APYRON TECHNOLOGIES, INC.; *pg.* 1495, *pg.* 488
AQUA BLOCK - Soft Flanged Earplugs - MCKEON PRODUCTS, INC.; *pg.* 1559, *pg.* 912
AQUA BOWL - Toilet Bowl Cleaner - THETFORD CORPORATION; *pg.* 337, *pg.* 867
AQUA-CAL - Uncalcined Gypsum - USG CORPORATION; *pg.* 118, *pg.* 594
AQUA CAST - Ultimate Cement - USG CORPORATION; *pg.* 118, *pg.* 594
AQUA CHEM - Swimming Pool Cleaners - AKZONOBEL DECORATIVE PAINTS U.S.; *pg.* 1439, *pg.* 1474
AQUA CLEAR - Pool Chemicals - OCCIDENTAL CHEMICAL CORPORATION; *pg.* 1175, *pg.* 1685
AQUA COVER - Solar Blanket - POLYAIR INTER PACK INC.; *pg.* 1467, *pg.* 1941
AQUA DOODLE - Toy - SPIN MASTER LTD.; *pg.* 967, *pg.* 1943
AQUA-DUCTOR - Vacuum Pump - CROLL-REYNOLDS COMPANY, INC.; *pg.* 1326, *pg.* 1103
AQUA EC - Coating - E.I. DU PONT DE NEMOURS & COMPANY; *pg.* 1159, *pg.* 390
AQUA EDGE - Plastic & Rubber - TEKNOR APEX COMPANY; *pg.* 1889, *pg.* 1605
AQUA-GEL - Wire Pulling Lubricant - IDEAL INDUSTRIES, INC.; *pg.* 1051, *pg.* 662
AQUA-GEL - Disposable Underpad - THE SALK COMPANY; *pg.* 1591, *pg.* 800
AQUA GLASS - Plumbing Product - MASCO CORPORATION; *pg.* 96, *pg.* 909
AQUA-GUN - Spray Gun - MELNOR, INC.; *pg.* 1055, *pg.* 1811
AQUA-IMAGE - Lithographic Plates, Chemicals, Equipment - EASTMAN KODAK COMPANY; *pg.* 1408, *pg.* 1333
AQUA-KEM - Liquid Holding Tank Deodorant - THETFORD CORPORATION; *pg.* 337, *pg.* 867
AQUA-KEM TOSS-TABS - Tablet Holding Tank Deodorant - THETFORD CORPORATION; *pg.* 337, *pg.* 867
AQUA KINGLITE - Flashlight - PELICAN PRODUCTS, INC.; *pg.* 1842, *pg.* 295
AQUA-KOTE - Paperboard Packaging System - GRAPHIC PACKAGING HOLDING COMPANY; *pg.* 1459, *pg.* 509
AQUA-LAM - Adhesive & Sealant - DOW CHEMICAL; *pg.* 1156, *pg.* 1563
AQUA-LAM - Laminating Adhesives - THE DOW CHEMICAL COMPANY; *pg.* 1157, *pg.* 898
AQUA LINER - Vinyl Liners - POLYAIR INTER PACK INC.; *pg.* 1467, *pg.* 1941
AQUA LOGIC - Pool & Spa - HAYWARD POOL PRODUCTS; *pg.* 1049, *pg.* 1057
AQUA-LUBE - Skincare Product - MERLE NORMAN COSMETICS, INC.; *pg.* 517, *pg.* 136
AQUA MAG - Chemical Product - CARUS CORPORATION; *pg.* 1152, *pg.* 652
AQUA MAG DP - Phosphate - CARUS CORPORATION; *pg.* 1152, *pg.* 652
AQUA-MAGIC - Permanent Toilet - THETFORD CORPORATION; *pg.* 337, *pg.* 867
AQUA MATE - Dinnerware - THE HOMER LAUGHLIN CHINA COMPANY; *pg.* 1125, *pg.* 1850
AQUA-MATE - Marine Head - THETFORD CORPORATION; *pg.* 337, *pg.* 867
AQUA-MELT - Adhesive - H.B. FULLER COMPANY; *pg.* 1165, *pg.* 961
AQUA MER - Dry Film - MACDERMID, INC.; *pg.* 1172, *pg.* 321
AQUA POD - Automatic Pool Cleaner - HAYWARD POOL PRODUCTS; *pg.* 1049, *pg.* 1057
AQUA POX - Paint & Coating - DIAMOND VOGEL PAINT, INC.; *pg.* 1441, *pg.* 710
AQUA PRIME - Penetrating Oil Additive - DUNN-EDWARDS CORPORATION; *pg.* 1442, *pg.* 129
AQUA PRUF - Conveyor - DORNER MANUFACTURING CORP.; *pg.* 1329, *pg.* 1861
AQUA-QUENCH - Heat Treating Product - HOUGHTON INTERNATIONAL INC.; *pg.* 1167, *pg.* 1589
AQUA RITE - Generator - HAYWARD POOL PRODUCTS; *pg.* 1049, *pg.* 1057
AQUA SAVER - Flushing Platform - GERBER PLUMBING FIXTURES CORPORATION; *pg.* 84, *pg.* 672
AQUA SENTRY - Water Conservation - MELNOR, INC.; *pg.* 1055, *pg.* 1811
AQUA-SHED - Rinse Aids for Metals - GE WATER & PROCESS TECHNOLOGIES; *pg.* 1339, *pg.* 1588
AQUA SOFT - 2-Ply Toilet Tissue - THETFORD CORPORATION; *pg.* 337, *pg.* 867
AQUA SUNSHINE FRESH - Dry Cleaning & Laundry Product - ADCO, INC.; *pg.* 325, *pg.* 482
AQUA TEMP HOLDING CABINETS - Heated Food Warmer Cabinets - CRES-COR; *pg.* 1326, *pg.* 1464
AQUA TIGER - Centrifugal Pump - HYPRO; *pg.* 705, *pg.* 951
AQUA TORCH - Welding Machine - L&R MANUFACTURING COMPANY; *pg.* 1419, *pg.* 1076
AQUA-TOUGH - Interior Panels - USG CORPORATION; *pg.* 118, *pg.* 594
AQUA-TRED - Paint Product - KELLY-MOORE PAINT COMPANY, INC.; *pg.* 1443, *pg.* 198
AQUA TROL - Generator - HAYWARD POOL PRODUCTS; *pg.* 1049, *pg.* 1057
AQUA-VACTOR - Water Jet - CROLL-REYNOLDS COMPANY, INC.; *pg.* 1326, *pg.* 1103
AQUA VELVA - Health & Beauty Product - COMBE INCORPORATED; *pg.* 1516, *pg.* 1351
AQUA-VU - Video Viewing System - SWORDFISH FINANCIAL, INC.; *pg.* 1430, *pg.* 1737
AQUA ZYME - Enzymatic Waste Digester - THETFORD CORPORATION; *pg.* 337, *pg.* 867
AQUABAR - Floor Protection System - FORTIFIBER CORPORATION; *pg.* 83, *pg.* 1021
AQUABASE - Autobody Refinish Paint - AKZONOBEL DECORATIVE PAINTS U.S.; *pg.* 1439, *pg.* 1474
AQUABLEND - Mining Product - QUIKRETE COMPANIES; *pg.* 106, *pg.* 519
AQUABONA - Beverages - THE COCA-COLA COMPANY; *pg.* 240, *pg.* 493
AQUABROWSER - Visual Faceted Search Solutions - R.R. BOWKER LLC; *pg.* 1682, *pg.* 1095
AQUACADE - Textiles - BERNHARDT DESIGN; *pg.* 918, *pg.* 1381
AQUACEL - Wound Care Product - CONVATEC LTD.; *pg.* 1518, *pg.* 1121
AQUACOAT - Adhesive & Sealant - DOW CHEMICAL; *pg.* 1156, *pg.* 1563
AQUACOAT - Pharmaceutical Ingredient - FMC CORPORATION; *pg.* 1163, *pg.* 1564
AQUACRON - Coating Product - PPG INDUSTRIES, INC.; *pg.* 1445, *pg.* 1579
AQUACTIVEDE AQUARIUS - Beverages - THE COCA-COLA COMPANY; *pg.* 240, *pg.* 493
AQUACURE - Graphic Art UV System - NORDSON CORPORATION; *pg.* 1365, *pg.* 1480
AQUACURE - Turf Product - PBI/GORDON CORPORATION; *pg.* 1176, *pg.* 985
AQUADRAIN - Hose - TEKNOR APEX COMPANY; *pg.* 1889, *pg.* 1605
AQUADRAN - Transformer Testing - GE ENERGY; *pg.* 1338, *pg.* 506
AQUADRIVE - Controller - ENTECH SOLAR, INC.; *pg.* 1335, *pg.* 1694
AQUAEASE - Aqueous Cleaner - HUBBARD-HALL, INC.; *pg.* 1167, *pg.* 382
AQUAFALL - Latex Dry-Fall Coatings - DUNN-EDWARDS CORPORATION; *pg.* 1442, *pg.* 129
AQUAFIEL - Carbonated Soft Drink - DR PEPPER SNAPPLE GROUP, INC.; *pg.* 250, *pg.* 1729
AQUAFILM - Water Soluble Laundry Bag - MONOSOL, LLC; *pg.* 59, *pg.* 694
AQUAFINA - Bottled Water - PEPSICO, INC.; *pg.* 259, *pg.* 1327
AQUAFINA SPARKLING - Carbonated Beverage - PEPSICO, INC.; *pg.* 259, *pg.* 1327
AQUAFLEX - Medical & Aesthetic Product - DYNATRONICS CORPORATION; *pg.* 1526, *pg.* 1757
AQUAFLO - Polymer - HERCULES INCORPORATED; *pg.* 1166, *pg.* 392
AQUAFLOR - Medicine - MERCK & CO., INC.; *pg.* 1566, *pg.* 1077
AQUAFLOW - Polymer - HERCULES INCORPORATED; *pg.* 1166, *pg.* 392
AQUAFLOW - Drainage Device - STAAR SURGICAL COMPANY; *pg.* 1597, *pg.* 151
AQUAFORCE - Floor Cleaning Product - NSS ENTERPRISES, INC.; *pg.* 59, *pg.* 1476
AQUAGEL - Pressure Management Pads - STERIS CORPORATION; *pg.* 1597, *pg.* 1464
AQUAGLO - Paint And Stain Product - BENJAMIN MOORE & CO.; *pg.* 1440, *pg.* 1085
AQUAGUARD - Hot Melt Equipment - NORDSON CORPORATION; *pg.* 1365, *pg.* 1480
AQUAKLEEN - Pre-Treatment Cleaner - A BRITE COMPANY; *pg.* 1144, *pg.* 1697
AQUAKNOX - Restaurants - TAVISTOCK RESTAURANT GROUP; *pg.* 1753, *pg.* 803
AQUALIBRIUM - Bath & Plumbing Product - JACUZZI BRANDS CORPORATION; *pg.* 554, *pg.* 65
AQUALIGHT - Mining Product - QUIKRETE COMPANIES; *pg.* 106, *pg.* 519
AQUALINE - Solder Paste - ALPHA; *pg.* 1146, *pg.* 1123
AQUALINE - Chemical Product - GFS CHEMICALS, INC.; *pg.* 1164, *pg.* 1471
AQUALINER - Electrosurgical Devices - ANGIODYNAMICS, INC.; *pg.* 1495, *pg.* 1173
AQUALITE - Wheel - HAMILTON CASTER & MFG. CO.; *pg.* 206, *pg.* 1454
AQUALITE - Molecular Probe Product - THERMO FISHER SCIENTIFIC INC.; *pg.* 1602, *pg.* 61
AQUALON - Polymer - HERCULES INCORPORATED; *pg.* 1166, *pg.* 392
AQUALOY - Plastic Compound & Resin - A. SCHULMAN, INC.; *pg.* 1144, *pg.* 1452
AQUALURE - Can Coatings - AKZONOBEL DECORATIVE PAINTS U.S.; *pg.* 1439, *pg.* 1474
AQUALUX - Paint Product - AKZO NOBEL; *pg.* 1439, *pg.* 1952
AQUAMAGIC IV - Perm Fresh Water Toilet - THETFORD CORPORATION; *pg.* 337, *pg.* 867
AQUAMAN - Character - DC COMICS, INC.; *pg.* 1633, *pg.* 1221
AQUAMARINE - Video Game - INTERNATIONAL GAME TECHNOLOGY; *pg.* 957, *pg.* 1024
AQUAMASTER - Herbicide - MONSANTO COMPANY; *pg.* 1173, *pg.* 999
AQUAMATIC - Residential & Commercial Valves for Softeners & Media Filters - GE WATER & PROCESS TECHNOLOGIES; *pg.* 1339, *pg.* 1588
AQUAMATIC SELECTRIC - Self Propelled Carpet Extractor - HILLYARD, INC.; *pg.* 331, *pg.* 990
AQUAMAX - Solar Electric System - ENTECH SOLAR, INC.; *pg.* 1335, *pg.* 1694
AQUAMAX - Liquid Handling System - MOLECULAR DEVICES CORPORATION; *pg.* 1568, *pg.* 287
AQUAMAX - Floor Care - NILFISK-ADVANCE, INC.; *pg.* 332, *pg.* 953
AQUAMET - Steel Product - AK STEEL HOLDING CORPORATION; *pg.* 1311, *pg.* 1479
AQUAMETER - Water Meter - ENTECH SOLAR, INC.; *pg.* 1335, *pg.* 1694
AQUAMINE - Piping System - VICTAULIC COMPANY; *pg.* 1066, *pg.* 1529
AQUAMIRA - Water Filter System - MCNETT CORPORATION; *pg.* 1839, *pg.* 1817
AQUAMIX - Additive - POLYONE CORPORATION; *pg.* 1177, *pg.* 1404
AQUANA - Soft Drink - THE COCA-COLA COMPANY; *pg.* 240, *pg.* 493
AQUANET - Apparel - VANS, INC.; *pg.* 1821, *pg.* 76
AQUANOX - Cleaning Chemical Product - KYZEN CORPORATION; *pg.* 331, *pg.* 1652
AQUAOIL - Sensor - GE ENERGY; *pg.* 1338, *pg.* 506
AQUAPAC - Polymer - HERCULES INCORPORATED; *pg.* 1166, *pg.* 392
AQUAPART - Metal Casting Product - HILL & GRIFFITH COMPANY; *pg.* 1167, *pg.* 1414
AQUAPEARL - Paint And Stain Product - BENJAMIN MOORE & CO.; *pg.* 1440, *pg.* 1085
AQUAPEL - Sizing Agent - HERCULES INCORPORATED;

pg. 1166, *pg.* 392
AQUAPEL - Pesticide - MCLAUGHLIN GORMLEY KING COMPANY; *pg.* 1797, *pg.* 939
AQUAPEL - Glass Treatment - PPG INDUSTRIES, INC.; *pg.* 1445, *pg.* 1579
AQUAPEL - Glass Treatment - ZIEBART INTERNATIONAL CORPORATION; *pg.* 222, *pg.* 912
AQUAPERM - Lens - DANKER LABORATORIES INC.; *pg.* 1408, *pg.* 465
AQUAPHOR - Chemical Product - SPECTRUM CHEMICALS & LABORATORY PRODUCTS, INC.; *pg.* 1181, *pg.* 94
AQUAPON - Coating Product - PPG INDUSTRIES, INC.; *pg.* 1445, *pg.* 1579
AQUAPURE - Software - BIO-RAD LABORATORIES, INC.; *pg.* 1504, *pg.* 101
AQUAPURE - Waste Water Treatment - HUBBARD-HALL, INC.; *pg.* 1167, *pg.* 382
AQUAQUARTZ - Pool Filter Sand - FAIRMOUNT SANTROL; *pg.* 1162, *pg.* 1409
AQUAREALEASE - Coating - FERRO CORPORATION; *pg.* 1162, *pg.* 1462
AQUARIAN - Petcare Product - MARS, INCORPORATED; *pg.* 1858, *pg.* 1792
AQUARIAN - Pet Product - PETSMART, INC.; *pg.* 1481, *pg.* 18
AQUARIDE - Floor Care - NILFISK-ADVANCE, INC.; *pg.* 332, *pg.* 953
AQUARION - Safety & Protective Equipment - ENCON SAFETY PRODUCTS; *pg.* 1334, *pg.* 1705
AQUARIUM FISH MAGAZINE - Magazine - I-5 PUBLISHING LLC; *pg.* 1651, *pg.* 133
AQUARIUS - Soft Drink - THE COCA-COLA COMPANY; *pg.* 240, *pg.* 493
AQUARIUS - Dispensing Equipment - IDEX CORPORATION; *pg.* 1347, *pg.* 623
AQUARIUS - Fabric - NEMSCHOFF, INC.; *pg.* 936, *pg.* 1890
AQUARIUS - Flatware - ONEIDA LTD; *pg.* 1129, *pg.* 1318
AQUARIUS 421 - Fluid Handling System - GRACO, INC.; *pg.* 1342, *pg.* 935
AQUARIUS ACTIVE DIET - Beverages - THE COCA-COLA COMPANY; *pg.* 240, *pg.* 493
AQUARIUS FREESTYLE - Beverages - THE COCA-COLA COMPANY; *pg.* 240, *pg.* 493
AQUASAFE - Water Surveillance Monitors - PALL CORPORATION; *pg.* 232, *pg.* 1323
AQUASEAL - Adhesive Tape & Patch - MCNETT CORPORATION; *pg.* 1839, *pg.* 1817
AQUASEAL - Fishing Gear Product - SIMMS FISHING PRODUCTS CORP.; *pg.* 1845, *pg.* 1008
AQUASEP - Coalescer System - PALL CORPORATION; *pg.* 232, *pg.* 1323
AQUASET - Acrylic Thermosetting Resins - THE DOW CHEMICAL COMPANY; *pg.* 1157, *pg.* 898
AQUASIL - Dental Product - DENTSPLY INTERNATIONAL INC.; *pg.* 1522, *pg.* 1596
AQUASIL - Coating - SILBERLINE MANUFACTURING CO., INC.; *pg.* 110, *pg.* 1588
AQUASIL ULTRA SMART WETTING - Dental Product - DENTSPLY INTERNATIONAL INC.; *pg.* 1522, *pg.* 1596
AQUASITE - Wound Dressing - DERMA SCIENCES, INC.; *pg.* 1523, *pg.* 1111
AQUASOL - Plastic Compound & Resin - A. SCHULMAN, INC.; *pg.* 1144, *pg.* 1452
AQUASONIC - Transmission Gel - ALIMED, INC.; *pg.* 1490, *pg.* 816
AQUASONIC - Medical & Aesthetic Product - DYNATRONICS CORPORATION; *pg.* 1526, *pg.* 1757
AQUASORB - Polymer - HERCULES INCORPORATED; *pg.* 1166, *pg.* 392
AQUASOUND - Bath & Plumbing Product - JACUZZI BRANDS CORPORATION; *pg.* 554, *pg.* 65
AQUASPEXX - Bearing - THE TIMKEN COMPANY; *pg.* 218, *pg.* 1408
AQUASPOT - Floor Care - NILFISK-ADVANCE, INC.; *pg.* 332, *pg.* 953
AQUASTAB - Chemical Additive - EASTMAN CHEMICAL COMPANY; *pg.* 1159, *pg.* 1636
AQUASTAR - Chemical Product - GFS CHEMICALS, INC.; *pg.* 1164, *pg.* 1471
AQUASTAR - Chemical Product - SPECTRUM CHEMICALS & LABORATORY PRODUCTS, INC.; *pg.* 1181, *pg.* 94
AQUASTAX - Puzzle Game - BLUCORA; *pg.* 1232, *pg.* 1813
AQUASTEALTH - Footwear - SIMMS FISHING PRODUCTS CORP.; *pg.* 1845, *pg.* 1008
AQUASTORM - Printed Circuit Board Cleaning Systems - SPEEDLINE TECHNOLOGIES, INC.; *pg.* 1378, *pg.* 823
AQUASURE - Adhesive & Sealant - MCNETT CORPORATION; *pg.* 1839, *pg.* 1817
AQUATAC - Tackifier Resin Dispersions - ARIZONA CHEMICAL CO. LLC; *pg.* 1147, *pg.* 431
AQUATAPOXY - Coating - COHESANT, INC.; *pg.* 1154, *pg.* 1405
AQUATECH - Sewer Cleaning Equipment - HI-VAC CORPORATION; *pg.* 56, *pg.* 1458
AQUATEX - Patterned Glass - AGC GLASS NORTH AMERICA, INC.; *pg.* 65, *pg.* 482
AQUATEX - Pleasure Boating Fabrics - HERCULITE PRODUCTS, INC.; *pg.* 694, *pg.* 1529
AQUATEX II - Industrial Fabric - HERCULITE PRODUCTS, INC.; *pg.* 694, *pg.* 1529
AQUATHERM - Medical Product - GF HEALTH PRODUCTS, INC.; *pg.* 1535, *pg.* 508
AQUATITE - Corrugating & Bag - GRAIN PROCESSING CORPORATION; *pg.* 859, *pg.* 709
AQUATITE RESIN ADDITION SYSTEM - Corrugating & Bag - GRAIN PROCESSING CORPORATION; *pg.* 859, *pg.* 709
AQUATRACE - Sensor - MOCON, INC.; *pg.* 1363, *pg.* 940
AQUATRAIN - Transportation Service - CANADIAN NATIONAL RAILWAY COMPANY; *pg.* 1902, *pg.* 1953
AQUATRAK - Shoe & Boot Cover - ALPHA PRO TECH, LTD.; *pg.* 1492, *pg.* 1922
AQUATRAN - Water Vapor Permeation Test System - MOCON, INC.; *pg.* 1363, *pg.* 940
AQUATRAP - Refrigeration - BROOKS AUTOMATION, INC.; *pg.* 1320, *pg.* 813
AQUATRED - Wet Traction Tire - THE GOODYEAR TIRE & RUBBER COMPANY; *pg.* 1883, *pg.* 1401
AQUAVAIRE - Gas-Fired Waterbath LPG Vaporizer - ALGAS-SDI; *pg.* 1311, *pg.* 1831
AQUAVELVET - Paint And Stain Product - BENJAMIN MOORE & CO.; *pg.* 1440, *pg.* 1085
AQUAVET - Ink - SILBERLINE MANUFACTURING CO., INC.; *pg.* 110, *pg.* 1588
AQUAVEX - Ink - SILBERLINE MANUFACTURING CO., INC.; *pg.* 110, *pg.* 1588
AQUAXCEL - Fish & Shrimp Feeds - CARGILL, INC.; *pg.* 845, *pg.* 965
AQUAZONE - Plastics - FXI; *pg.* 1163, *pg.* 1552
AQUAZONE - Software - SMITH MICRO SOFTWARE, INC.; *pg.* 471, *pg.* 41
AQUCAR - Microbiocide - THE DOW CHEMICAL COMPANY; *pg.* 1157, *pg.* 898
AQUEON - Pet Product - PETSMART, INC.; *pg.* 1481, *pg.* 18
AQUEOUS - Farm & Ranch Product - PBI/GORDON CORPORATION; *pg.* 1176, *pg.* 985
AQUIDRY - Film Product - TREDEGAR CORPORATION; *pg.* 1890, *pg.* 1804
AQUIFER - Kitchen Product - KOHLER CO.; *pg.* 91, *pg.* 1862
AQUIS - Fishing Gear Product - SIMMS FISHING PRODUCTS CORP.; *pg.* 1845, *pg.* 1008
AQUOX - Chemical Product - CARUS CORPORATION; *pg.* 1152, *pg.* 652
AQUQGENE 90 - Non-Ionic Surfactant - UNIVERSAL COOPERATIVES, INC.; *pg.* 1482, *pg.* 922
AQUS - Greywater System - SLOAN VALVE COMPANY; *pg.* 1062, *pg.* 613
AR - Anti-Reflective Coatings - THE DOW CHEMICAL COMPANY; *pg.* 1157, *pg.* 898
AR - Thermoplastic Composite Material - GREENE, TWEED & CO.; *pg.* 1344, *pg.* 1544
AR (ACOUSTIC RESEARCH) - Loud Speakers - NHT AUDIO, LLC; *pg.* 659, *pg.* 45
AR AIRCOIL - Evaporator - BALTIMORE AIRCOIL COMPANY; *pg.* 1069, *pg.* 773
AR BOOKFINDER - Educational Materials - RENAISSANCE LEARNING, INC.; *pg.* 607, *pg.* 1899
AR BOOKGUIDE - Educational Materials - RENAISSANCE LEARNING, INC.; *pg.* 607, *pg.* 1899
AR-EL - Resin Laminated Tubes & Cores - SONOCO PRODUCTS COMPANY; *pg.* 1469, *pg.* 1619
AR-MET - Control Measurement - BROOKS INSTRUMENT, LLC; *pg.* 1403, *pg.* 1537
AR SERIES - Impact Hammer - ALLIED CONSTRUCTION PRODUCTS, LLC; *pg.* 1311, *pg.* 1427
AR SYSTEM - Software Platform - BMC SOFTWARE, INC.; *pg.* 362, *pg.* 1701
ARA - Chemicals - HUNTSMAN CORPORATION; *pg.* 1167, *pg.* 1758
ARA-LARIX - Nutritional Supplement - NATURAL ORGANICS, INC.; *pg.* 1571, *pg.* 1181
ARABELLA - Bedding - CROSCILL, INC.; *pg.* 1122, *pg.* 1220
ARABELLA STUART - Beauty Product - COSMETIQUE, INC.; *pg.* 1765, *pg.* 664
ARABESQUE - Furniture - JOFCO INC.; *pg.* 931, *pg.* 691
ARABESQUE - Flooring Product - ROSCO LABORATORIES, INC.; *pg.* 1782, *pg.* 378
ARABIA 2000 - Arab World News Service - UNITED PRESS INTERNATIONAL, INC.; *pg.* 1698, *pg.* 405
ARABIAN MOCHA JAVA - Coffee - PEET'S COFFEE & TEA, INC.; *pg.* 1029, *pg.* 85
ARABIAN MOCHA SANANI - Coffee - PEET'S COFFEE & TEA, INC.; *pg.* 1029, *pg.* 85
ARABIAN RICHES - Video Game - INTERNATIONAL GAME TECHNOLOGY; *pg.* 957, *pg.* 1024
ARACAST - Chemicals - HUNTSMAN CORPORATION; *pg.* 1167, *pg.* 1758
ARACON - Metal Clad Fibers - E.I. DU PONT DE NEMOURS & COMPANY; *pg.* 1159, *pg.* 390
ARADUR - Amine Hardener - HUNTSMAN CORPORATION; *pg.* 1167, *pg.* 1758
ARAFAST - Adhesives - HUNTSMAN CORPORATION; *pg.* 1167, *pg.* 1758
ARAFLOOR - Synthetic Resin Binder System - HUNTSMAN CORPORATION; *pg.* 1167, *pg.* 1758
ARAG - Monitor - VIEWSONIC CORPORATION; *pg.* 489, *pg.* 303
ARAGON - Bicycle - G. JOANNOU CYCLE CO. INC.; *pg.* 1707, *pg.* 1098
ARALDIT - Adhesives - HUNTSMAN CORPORATION; *pg.* 1167, *pg.* 1758
ARALDIT RAPID - Adhesives - HUNTSMAN CORPORATION; *pg.* 1167, *pg.* 1758
ARALDITE - Structural Adhesives - HUNTSMAN CORPORATION; *pg.* 1167, *pg.* 1758
ARALDITE BUILDER - Adhesives - HUNTSMAN CORPORATION; *pg.* 1167, *pg.* 1758
ARALDITE BUILDER BARRIER KOAT - Adhesives - HUNTSMAN CORPORATION; *pg.* 1167, *pg.* 1758
ARALDITE BUILDER INTEGRA - Adhesives - HUNTSMAN CORPORATION; *pg.* 1167, *pg.* 1758
ARALDITE BUILDER KLAD-X - Adhesives - HUNTSMAN CORPORATION; *pg.* 1167, *pg.* 1758
ARALDITE BUILDER RENOVA - Adhesives - HUNTSMAN CORPORATION; *pg.* 1167, *pg.* 1758
ARALDITE FUSION - Adhesives - HUNTSMAN CORPORATION; *pg.* 1167, *pg.* 1758
ARALEN - Pharmaceutical Product - IMPAX LABORATORIES, INC.; *pg.* 1544, *pg.* 101
ARALL - Industrial Laminate - ALCOA INC.; *pg.* 65, *pg.* 1188
ARAMIS - Men's Products - THE ESTEE LAUDER COMPANIES INC.; *pg.* 508, *pg.* 1229
ARANESP - Human Therapeutic Product - AMGEN INC.; *pg.* 1493, *pg.* 291
ARANOX - Polymer Product - CHEMTURA CORPORATION; *pg.* 1152, *pg.* 355
ARASEAL - Epoxy Putty - HUNTSMAN CORPORATION; *pg.* 1167, *pg.* 1758
ARATHAN - Adhesives - HUNTSMAN CORPORATION; *pg.* 1167, *pg.* 1758
ARATHANE - Polurethane Encapsulating Materials - HUNTSMAN CORPORATION; *pg.* 1167, *pg.* 1758
ARATHERM - Thermal Conductive Epoxy Materials - HUNTSMAN CORPORATION; *pg.* 1167, *pg.* 1758
ARATRONIC - Resins - HUNTSMAN CORPORATION; *pg.* 1167, *pg.* 1758
ARAVITE - Chemicals - HUNTSMAN CORPORATION; *pg.* 1167, *pg.* 1758
ARAVON - Women Footwear - NEW BALANCE ATHLETIC SHOE, INC.; *pg.* 1811, *pg.* 798
ARAVON - Footwear - THE ROCKPORT GROUP; *pg.* 1818, *pg.* 812
ARBITRENDS - Data Services - NIELSEN AUDIO; *pg.* 446, *pg.* 768
ARBITRON DATA EXPRESS - Registration Form - NIELSEN AUDIO; *pg.* 446, *pg.* 768
ARBITRON EBOOK - Data Services - NIELSEN AUDIO; *pg.* 446, *pg.* 768
ARBITRON ON DEMAND - Tool - NIELSEN AUDIO; *pg.* 446, *pg.* 768
ARBITRON PORTABLE PEOPLE METER - Measurement System - NIELSEN AUDIO; *pg.* 446, *pg.* 768
ARBITRON PPM - Software - NIELSEN AUDIO; *pg.* 446, *pg.* 768
ARBO - Forest Product - TEMBEC INC.; *pg.* 114, *pg.* 1957

ARBOR - Fabric - NEMSCHOFF, INC.; *pg.* 936, *pg.* 1890
ARBOR - Office Furniture - STEELCASE INC.; *pg.* 475, *pg.* 889
ARBOR GREEN - Tree & Lawn Care Services - THE DAVEY TREE EXPERT COMPANY; *pg.* 1794, *pg.* 1456
ARBOR GREEN PRO - Tree Fertilization - THE DAVEY TREE EXPERT COMPANY; *pg.* 1794, *pg.* 1456
ARBOR MIST - Bedding - CROSCILL, INC.; *pg.* 1122, *pg.* 1220
ARBOR ROSE - Flatware - ONEIDA LTD; *pg.* 1129, *pg.* 1318
ARBORA TANK - Apparels - UNDER ARMOUR, INC.; *pg.* 49, *pg.* 759
ARBORTEXT - Document Publishing - PARAMETRIC TECHNOLOGY CORPORATION; *pg.* 452, *pg.* 835
ARBURG - Injection Molding Machines - ARBURG, INC.; *pg.* 1314, *pg.* 359
ARBY'S - Fast Food Restaurants - THE WENDY'S COMPANY; *pg.* 1755, *pg.* 1450
ARBY'S MARKET FRESH - Food Product - THE WENDY'S COMPANY; *pg.* 1755, *pg.* 1450
ARC - Anti-Reflective Coatings - BREWER SCIENCE, INC.; *pg.* 1150, *pg.* 989
ARC - Athletic Shoe - JACK SCHWARTZ SHOES, INC.; *pg.* 1810, *pg.* 1245
ARC - Apparel - OAKLEY, INC.; *pg.* 1840, *pg.* 86
ARC - Exterior Automotive Coating - RED SPOT PAINT & VARNISH CO., INC.; *pg.* 1446, *pg.* 679
ARC - Adiabatic Calorimeter - TIAX LLC; *pg.* 115, *pg.* 829
ARC LIGHT - Curing & Bleaching System - AIR TECHNIQUES, INC.; *pg.* 1487, *pg.* 1178
ARC T U872 D CAR FOR F250 - Soy Protein - ARCHER-DANIELS-MIDLAND COMPANY; *pg.* 825, *pg.* 565
ARC T871 LT CARML F125 - Soy Protein - ARCHER-DANIELS-MIDLAND COMPANY; *pg.* 825, *pg.* 565
ARC TRAINER - Cross Training Equipment - CYBEX INTERNATIONAL, INC.; *pg.* 1521, *pg.* 832
ARC4 - Software System - MENTOR GRAPHICS CORPORATION; *pg.* 432, *pg.* 1510
ARCA - Hearing Aid - BELTONE ELECTRONICS LLC; *pg.* 1503, *pg.* 614
ARCA BELLA - Table - BLATT BOWLING & BILLIARD CORP.; *pg.* 1827, *pg.* 1203
ARCADE AMERICA - Family Apparel - A&E STORES, INC.; *pg.* 17, *pg.* 1124
ARCADE BALL - Multi-Game Table - SCHOOL-TECH, INC.; *pg.* 1844, *pg.* 866
ARCADIA - Dinnerware - THE HOMER LAUGHLIN CHINA COMPANY; *pg.* 1125, *pg.* 1850
ARCALYST - Pharmaceutical & Medicinal Product - REGENERON PHARMACEUTICALS, INC.; *pg.* 1588, *pg.* 1345
ARCATA - Furniture - JASPER GROUP; *pg.* 930, *pg.* 691
ARCATLAS - Software - ENVIRONMENTAL SYSTEMS RESEARCH INSTITUTE INC.; *pg.* 393, *pg.* 188
ARCCAD - Software - ENVIRONMENTAL SYSTEMS RESEARCH INSTITUTE INC.; *pg.* 393, *pg.* 188
ARCCATALOG - Software - ENVIRONMENTAL SYSTEMS RESEARCH INSTITUTE INC.; *pg.* 393, *pg.* 188
ARCCOGO - Software - ENVIRONMENTAL SYSTEMS RESEARCH INSTITUTE INC.; *pg.* 393, *pg.* 188
ARCDATA - Software - ENVIRONMENTAL SYSTEMS RESEARCH INSTITUTE INC.; *pg.* 393, *pg.* 188
ARCDOC - Software - ENVIRONMENTAL SYSTEMS RESEARCH INSTITUTE INC.; *pg.* 393, *pg.* 188
ARCEDIT - Software - ENVIRONMENTAL SYSTEMS RESEARCH INSTITUTE INC.; *pg.* 393, *pg.* 188
ARCEDITOR - Software - ENVIRONMENTAL SYSTEMS RESEARCH INSTITUTE INC.; *pg.* 393, *pg.* 188
ARCEL - Expandable Polystyrene - NOVA CHEMICALS CORPORATION; *pg.* 1175, *pg.* 1904
ARCEUROPE - Software - ENVIRONMENTAL SYSTEMS RESEARCH INSTITUTE INC.; *pg.* 393, *pg.* 188
ARCEXPLORER - Software - ENVIRONMENTAL SYSTEMS RESEARCH INSTITUTE INC.; *pg.* 393, *pg.* 188
ARCEXPRESS - Software - ENVIRONMENTAL SYSTEMS RESEARCH INSTITUTE INC.; *pg.* 393, *pg.* 188
ARCFLASH - Faceshield - SELLSTROM MANUFACTURING CO.; *pg.* 1428, *pg.* 659
ARCGIS - Software - ENVIRONMENTAL SYSTEMS RESEARCH INSTITUTE INC.; *pg.* 393, *pg.* 188
ARCGLOBE - Software - ENVIRONMENTAL SYSTEMS RESEARCH INSTITUTE INC.; *pg.* 393, *pg.* 188
ARCGRID - Software - ENVIRONMENTAL SYSTEMS RESEARCH INSTITUTE INC.; *pg.* 393, *pg.* 188
ARCH - Wood Preservation Chemical - KOPPERS HOLDINGS INC.; *pg.* 1170, *pg.* 1577
ARCH BOOKS - Book - CONCORDIA PUBLISHING HOUSE; *pg.* 1629, *pg.* 995
ARCHAEOLOGY OF THE AMERICAS BEFORE COLUMBUS - Tagline - ANCIENT AMERICAN; *pg.* 1616, *pg.* 1856
ARCHER - Metrology Product - KLA-TENCOR CORPORATION; *pg.* 1353, *pg.* 146
ARCHER 10 - Automated Optical Overlay Metrology - KLA-TENCOR CORPORATION; *pg.* 1353, *pg.* 146
ARCHER 10XT - Automated Optical Overlay Metrology - KLA-TENCOR CORPORATION; *pg.* 1353, *pg.* 146
ARCHER AIM - Advanced Optical Overlay Metrology - KLA-TENCOR CORPORATION; *pg.* 1353, *pg.* 146
ARCHER FARMS - Grocery Products - TARGET CORPORATION; *pg.* 1786, *pg.* 942
ARCHER III - Aircraft - PIPER AIRCRAFT, INC.; *pg.* 233, *pg.* 477
ARCHER RC - Non-Hazardous Latex Paints - ARCHER-DANIELS-MIDLAND COMPANY; *pg.* 825, *pg.* 565
ARCHER SOYBEAN OIL - Food Ingredient - ARCHER-DANIELS-MIDLAND COMPANY; *pg.* 825, *pg.* 565
ARCHER VERIFICATION - Software System - MENTOR GRAPHICS CORPORATION; *pg.* 432, *pg.* 1510
ARCHIPELAGO - Office Furniture - STEELCASE INC.; *pg.* 475, *pg.* 889
ARCHITECH - Mounting Hardware Designed to Complement Surroundings - VICON INDUSTRIES, INC.; *pg.* 685, *pg.* 1166
ARCHITECT - Clinical System - ABBOTT LABORATORIES; *pg.* 1484, *pg.* 551
ARCHITECT - Bathroom Fan - HUNTER FAN COMPANY; *pg.* 57, *pg.* 1631
ARCHITECT - Software - MICROSTRATEGY, INC.; *pg.* 1266, *pg.* 1809
ARCHITECT SERIES - EnduraClad Wood Doors & Windows - PELLA CORPORATION; *pg.* 104, *pg.* 711
ARCHITECTURAL DIGEST - Magazine - CONDE NAST PUBLICATIONS, INC.; *pg.* 1629, *pg.* 1217
ARCHITECTURAL ELEMENTS - Furniture - HAWORTH, INC.; *pg.* 402, *pg.* 891
ARCHITECTURAL LIGHTING - Trade Publication - THE NIELSEN COMPANY B.V.; *pg.* 1671, *pg.* 1272
ARCHITECTURAL SERIES - Affordable Made-to-Order Cabinets - WM OHS INC.; *pg.* 947, *pg.* 324
ARCHITECTURE - Carpet - INTERFACE, INC.; *pg.* 695, *pg.* 512
ARCHITECTURE - Magazine - NIELSEN BUSINESS MEDIA; *pg.* 1671, *pg.* 1272
ARCHITECTURE - Trade Publication - THE NIELSEN COMPANY B.V.; *pg.* 1671, *pg.* 1272
ARCHITENT - Tent Fabrics - HERCULITE PRODUCTS, INC.; *pg.* 694, *pg.* 1529
ARCHITENT WIDESIDE - Industrial Fabric - HERCULITE PRODUCTS, INC.; *pg.* 694, *pg.* 1529
ARCHITEX - Stainless Steel Product - PETERSEN ALUMINUM CORPORATION; *pg.* 104, *pg.* 611
ARCHIV - Banking Software - JACK HENRY & ASSOCIATES, INC.; *pg.* 422, *pg.* 988
ARCHIVE MANAGEMENT SUITE - Software - DELL SOFTWARE; *pg.* 385, *pg.* 40
ARCHIVE MANAGER - Software - DELL SOFTWARE; *pg.* 385, *pg.* 40
ARCHIVE MANAGER - End-to-End Satellite Data Management Solution - INTEGRAL SYSTEMS, INC.; *pg.* 416, *pg.* 767
ARCHIVEXTENDER - Software System - EMC CORPORATION; *pg.* 391, *pg.* 825
ARCHWAY - Cookies - SNYDER'S-LANCE, INC.; *pg.* 896, *pg.* 1368
ARCIMS - Software - ENVIRONMENTAL SYSTEMS RESEARCH INSTITUTE INC.; *pg.* 393, *pg.* 188
ARCINFO - Software - ENVIRONMENTAL SYSTEMS RESEARCH INSTITUTE INC.; *pg.* 393, *pg.* 188
ARCLOCATION - Software - ENVIRONMENTAL SYSTEMS RESEARCH INSTITUTE INC.; *pg.* 393, *pg.* 188
ARCLOGISTICS - Software - ENVIRONMENTAL SYSTEMS RESEARCH INSTITUTE INC.; *pg.* 393, *pg.* 188
ARCNETWORK - Software - ENVIRONMENTAL SYSTEMS RESEARCH INSTITUTE INC.; *pg.* 393, *pg.* 188
ARCNEWS - Software - ENVIRONMENTAL SYSTEMS RESEARCH INSTITUTE INC.; *pg.* 393, *pg.* 188
ARCO IRIS - Laundry Additives - THE CLOROX COMPANY; *pg.* 327, *pg.* 169
ARCOBJECTS - Software - ENVIRONMENTAL SYSTEMS RESEARCH INSTITUTE INC.; *pg.* 393, *pg.* 188
ARCOFLEX - Paper & Nonwoven Material - FIBERMARK INC.; *pg.* 1457, *pg.* 1764
ARCON - Soy Protein Concentrates - ARCHER-DANIELS-MIDLAND COMPANY; *pg.* 825, *pg.* 565
ARCON - Paper & Nonwoven Material - FIBERMARK INC.; *pg.* 1457, *pg.* 1764
ARCON F - Soy Protein - ARCHER-DANIELS-MIDLAND COMPANY; *pg.* 825, *pg.* 565
ARCON S - Soy Protein - ARCHER-DANIELS-MIDLAND COMPANY; *pg.* 825, *pg.* 565
ARCON SM - Soy Protein - ARCHER-DANIELS-MIDLAND COMPANY; *pg.* 825, *pg.* 565
ARCON T - Soy Protein - ARCHER-DANIELS-MIDLAND COMPANY; *pg.* 825, *pg.* 565
ARCON T F125 - Soy Protein - ARCHER-DANIELS-MIDLAND COMPANY; *pg.* 825, *pg.* 565
ARCON T F125 CARAMEL - Soy Protein - ARCHER-DANIELS-MIDLAND COMPANY; *pg.* 825, *pg.* 565
ARCON T F250 - Soy Protein - ARCHER-DANIELS-MIDLAND COMPANY; *pg.* 825, *pg.* 565
ARCON T F250 CARAMEL - Soy Protein - ARCHER-DANIELS-MIDLAND COMPANY; *pg.* 825, *pg.* 565
ARCON T MINCED - Soy Protein - ARCHER-DANIELS-MIDLAND COMPANY; *pg.* 825, *pg.* 565
ARCON T MINCED 180 - Soy Protein - ARCHER-DANIELS-MIDLAND COMPANY; *pg.* 825, *pg.* 565
ARCON T MINCED 180 CARAMEL - Soy Protein - ARCHER-DANIELS-MIDLAND COMPANY; *pg.* 825, *pg.* 565
ARCON T MINCED 300 - Soy Protein - ARCHER-DANIELS-MIDLAND COMPANY; *pg.* 825, *pg.* 565
ARCON T MINCED 300 CARAMEL - Soy Protein - ARCHER-DANIELS-MIDLAND COMPANY; *pg.* 825, *pg.* 565
ARCON T STRIP - Soy Protein - ARCHER-DANIELS-MIDLAND COMPANY; *pg.* 825, *pg.* 565
ARCON T STRIP 5 CARAMEL - Soy Protein - ARCHER-DANIELS-MIDLAND COMPANY; *pg.* 825, *pg.* 565
ARCON VF - Soy Protein - ARCHER-DANIELS-MIDLAND COMPANY; *pg.* 825, *pg.* 565
ARCONATE - Chemical Product - LYONDELLBASELL INDUSTRIES; *pg.* 980, *pg.* 1710
ARCOPEN - Software - ENVIRONMENTAL SYSTEMS RESEARCH INSTITUTE INC.; *pg.* 393, *pg.* 188
ARCOPLUS - Chemical Product - LYONDELLBASELL INDUSTRIES; *pg.* 980, *pg.* 1710
ARCOPURE - Chemical Product - LYONDELLBASELL INDUSTRIES; *pg.* 980, *pg.* 1710
ARCOS - Lighting System - LITECONTROL CORPORATION; *pg.* 1301, *pg.* 841
ARCOSOLV - Chemical Product - LYONDELLBASELL INDUSTRIES; *pg.* 980, *pg.* 1710
ARCOXIA - Medicine - MERCK & CO., INC.; *pg.* 1566, *pg.* 1077
ARCPAD - Software - ENVIRONMENTAL SYSTEMS RESEARCH INSTITUTE INC.; *pg.* 393, *pg.* 188
ARCPLOT - Software - ENVIRONMENTAL SYSTEMS RESEARCH INSTITUTE INC.; *pg.* 393, *pg.* 188
ARCPRESS - Software - ENVIRONMENTAL SYSTEMS RESEARCH INSTITUTE INC.; *pg.* 393, *pg.* 188
ARCPRO V.2 - Software Program - HD ELECTRIC COMPANY; *pg.* 1299, *pg.* 666
ARCQUEST - Software - ENVIRONMENTAL SYSTEMS RESEARCH INSTITUTE INC.; *pg.* 393, *pg.* 188
ARCREADER - Software - ENVIRONMENTAL SYSTEMS RESEARCH INSTITUTE INC.; *pg.* 393, *pg.* 188
ARCSAFE - Body Harness - MINE SAFETY APPLIANCES COMPANY; *pg.* 1361, *pg.* 1525
ARCSCAN - Software - ENVIRONMENTAL SYSTEMS RESEARCH INSTITUTE INC.; *pg.* 393, *pg.* 188
ARCSCENE - Software - ENVIRONMENTAL SYSTEMS RESEARCH INSTITUTE INC.; *pg.* 393, *pg.* 188
ARCSCHOOL - Software - ENVIRONMENTAL SYSTEMS RESEARCH INSTITUTE INC.; *pg.* 393, *pg.* 188
ARCSDE - Software - ENVIRONMENTAL SYSTEMS RESEARCH INSTITUTE INC.; *pg.* 393, *pg.* 188
ARCSDL - Software - ENVIRONMENTAL SYSTEMS RESEARCH INSTITUTE INC.; *pg.* 393, *pg.* 188
ARCSKETCH - Software - ENVIRONMENTAL SYSTEMS RESEARCH INSTITUTE INC.; *pg.* 393, *pg.* 188
ARCSTORM - Software - ENVIRONMENTAL SYSTEMS RESEARCH INSTITUTE INC.; *pg.* 393, *pg.* 188
ARCSURVEY - Software - ENVIRONMENTAL SYSTEMS RESEARCH INSTITUTE INC.; *pg.* 393, *pg.* 188
ARCTIC - Tile - ARTISTIC TILE INC.; *pg.* 914, *pg.* 1119
ARCTIC - Eye Protection Product - MINE SAFETY

APPLIANCES COMPANY; *pg.* 1361, *pg.* 1525

ARCTIC BLAST - Semi-Frozen Carbonated Beverage - J&J SNACK FOODS CORPORATION; *pg.* 865, *pg.* 1107

ARCTIC BREEZE - Cooler - SEELEY INTERNATIONAL AMERICAS; *pg.* 1076, *pg.* 19

ARCTIC CAT - Snowmobile - ARCTIC CAT INC.; *pg.* 1705, *pg.* 953

ARCTIC CIRCLE - Video Game - INTERNATIONAL GAME TECHNOLOGY; *pg.* 957, *pg.* 1024

ARCTIC EXPRESS - Diesel Fuel - POWER SERVICE PRODUCTS, INC.; *pg.* 983, *pg.* 1749

ARCTIC EXPRESS - Frozen Dessert Dispenser - THE SCHWAN FOOD COMPANY; *pg.* 894, *pg.* 928

ARCTIC FOX - Video Game - INTERNATIONAL GAME TECHNOLOGY; *pg.* 957, *pg.* 1024

ARCTIC FROST - Skin Creams - WALGREEN CO.; *pg.* 1608, *pg.* 605

ARCTIC ICE - Health & Beauty Product - BLUE CROSS LABORATORIES; *pg.* 326, *pg.* 277

ARCTIC ICE - Seafood - TRIDENT SEAFOODS CORPORATION; *pg.* 902, *pg.* 1842

ARCTICFLOW - Orthopedic Product - DJO INCORPORATED; *pg.* 1524, *pg.* 302

ARCTICWEAR - Snowmobile - ARCTIC CAT INC.; *pg.* 1705, *pg.* 953

ARCTICWELD - Solvent & Roof Flashing - GENOVA PRODUCTS, INC.; *pg.* 83, *pg.* 875

ARCTIKOAT - Packaging Product - CASCADES, INC.; *pg.* 73, *pg.* 1950

ARCTOOLBOX - Software - ENVIRONMENTAL SYSTEMS RESEARCH INSTITUTE INC.; *pg.* 393, *pg.* 188

ARCTOOLS - Software - ENVIRONMENTAL SYSTEMS RESEARCH INSTITUTE INC.; *pg.* 393, *pg.* 188

ARCTUBE - Fluid Systems Product - COOPER-STANDARD AUTOMOTIVE INC.; *pg.* 1880, *pg.* 903

ARCUS - Tires - AMERITYRE CORPORATION; *pg.* 1879, *pg.* 1021

ARCUSA - Software - ENVIRONMENTAL SYSTEMS RESEARCH INSTITUTE INC.; *pg.* 393, *pg.* 188

ARCUSER - Software - ENVIRONMENTAL SYSTEMS RESEARCH INSTITUTE INC.; *pg.* 393, *pg.* 188

ARCVAUL 24 - Data Backup & Recovery - OVERLAND STORAGE, INC.; *pg.* 451, *pg.* 205

ARCVAULT - Tape-Based Storage Appliance - OVERLAND STORAGE, INC.; *pg.* 451, *pg.* 205

ARCVAULT 12 - Data Backup & Recovery - OVERLAND STORAGE, INC.; *pg.* 451, *pg.* 205

ARCVIEW - Software - ENVIRONMENTAL SYSTEMS RESEARCH INSTITUTE INC.; *pg.* 393, *pg.* 188

ARCVOYAGER - Software - ENVIRONMENTAL SYSTEMS RESEARCH INSTITUTE INC.; *pg.* 393, *pg.* 188

ARCWATCH - Software - ENVIRONMENTAL SYSTEMS RESEARCH INSTITUTE INC.; *pg.* 393, *pg.* 188

ARCWEB - Software - ENVIRONMENTAL SYSTEMS RESEARCH INSTITUTE INC.; *pg.* 393, *pg.* 188

ARCWORLD - Software - ENVIRONMENTAL SYSTEMS RESEARCH INSTITUTE INC.; *pg.* 393, *pg.* 188

ARCXML - Software - ENVIRONMENTAL SYSTEMS RESEARCH INSTITUTE INC.; *pg.* 393, *pg.* 188

ARDBEG - Single Islay Malt Scotch Whisky - BROWN-FORMAN CORPORATION; *pg.* 1958, *pg.* 732

ARDBERG - Scotch - MOET HENNESSY; *pg.* 1966, *pg.* 1260

ARDEA - Furniture - HERMAN MILLER, INC.; *pg.* 926, *pg.* 913

ARDEE - Lighting - PHILIPS LIGHTING; *pg.* 1303, *pg.* 806

ARDEL - Resin - WESTLAKE PLASTICS COMPANY; *pg.* 1892, *pg.* 1548

ARDELL - Bodycare & Skincare - AMERICAN INTERNATIONAL INDUSTRIES COMPANY; *pg.* 498, *pg.* 126

ARDEN B. - Clothing Stores - THE WET SEAL, LLC; *pg.* 35, *pg.* 88

ARDEN COURTS - Assisted Living Alzheimer's Units - HCR MANORCARE, INC.; *pg.* 1539, *pg.* 1476

ARDENBEAUTY - Fragrance - ELIZABETH ARDEN, INC.; *pg.* 507, *pg.* 448

ARDENCE - Software - INTERVALZERO INC.; *pg.* 420, *pg.* 851

ARDEX - Soy Proteins - ARCHER-DANIELS-MIDLAND COMPANY; *pg.* 825, *pg.* 565

ARDEX AF - Soy Protein - ARCHER-DANIELS-MIDLAND COMPANY; *pg.* 825, *pg.* 565

ARDEX- F - Soy Protein - ARCHER-DANIELS-MIDLAND COMPANY; *pg.* 825, *pg.* 565

ARDMORE FARMS - Fruit Juice Drinks - COUNTRY PURE FOODS, INC.; *pg.* 247, *pg.* 1400

ARE YOU A PLAYER - Tagline - ALDILA, INC.; *pg.* 1825, *pg.* 185

ARE YOU SMARTER THAN A 5TH GRADER? - Toy & Game - HASBRO, INC.; *pg.* 954, *pg.* 1603

AREA - Computer System - ALIENWARE CORPORATION; *pg.* 346, *pg.* 439

AREA-51 - Computer Gaming Desktop System - ALIENWARE CORPORATION; *pg.* 346, *pg.* 439

AREA-51 SENTIA - Notebook Personal Computer - ALIENWARE CORPORATION; *pg.* 346, *pg.* 439

AREA-51M - Mobile Computer Gaming System - ALIENWARE CORPORATION; *pg.* 346, *pg.* 439

AREA ARRAY - Probe Card - KULICKE & SOFFA INDUSTRIES, INC.; *pg.* 650, *pg.* 1533

AREA PLUS - Calling Plan - AT&T SOUTHEAST; *pg.* 1868, *pg.* 489

AREACODEINFO - Area Code Boundary Tool - PITNEY BOWES SOFTWARE INC.; *pg.* 455, *pg.* 1346

AREDIA - Pharmaceutical Drug - FRESENIUS KABI USA; *pg.* 1531, *pg.* 626

ARELA - Laundry Additives, Cleaners, Waxes, Candles - THE CLOROX COMPANY; *pg.* 327, *pg.* 169

ARENA - Game - ACTIVISION BLIZZARD, INC.; *pg.* 948, *pg.* 271

ARENA - Hemodialysis Instrument - BAXTER INTERNATIONAL INC.; *pg.* 1499, *pg.* 599

ARENA - Software - ROCKWELL AUTOMATION, INC.; *pg.* 668, *pg.* 1880

ARENA PHARMACEUTICALS - Pharmaceuticals - ARENA PHARMACEUTICALS, INC.; *pg.* 1495, *pg.* 200

AREN'T YOU GLAD YOU USE DIAL? - Slogan - HENKEL CONSUMER GOODS; *pg.* 511, *pg.* 22

ARES - Automated Real-Time Execution Suite - INTEGRAL SYSTEMS, INC.; *pg.* 416, *pg.* 767

ARES - Software System - MENTOR GRAPHICS CORPORATION; *pg.* 432, *pg.* 1510

ARES - Molecular Probe Product - THERMO FISHER SCIENTIFIC INC.; *pg.* 1602, *pg.* 61

ARETJA - Lamp - ASHLEY FURNITURE INDUSTRIES, INC.; *pg.* 914, *pg.* 1852

AREX F-DISP - Soy Protein - ARCHER-DANIELS-MIDLAND COMPANY; *pg.* 825, *pg.* 565

AREZZO - Faucet - ELKAY MANUFACTURING COMPANY; *pg.* 80, *pg.* 645

ARGENTA - Bike - MARIN BIKES; *pg.* 1708, *pg.* 168

ARGENTEENY PINKINI - Nail Care Product - OPI PRODUCTS INC.; *pg.* 518, *pg.* 167

ARGILE BLANCHE - Beauty Product - GRANDPA BRANDS COMPANY; *pg.* 1538, *pg.* 727

ARGIMIEL - Beauty Product - GRANDPA BRANDS COMPANY; *pg.* 1538, *pg.* 727

ARGINAID - Pharmaceutical Product - NESTLE HEALTHCARE NUTRITION; *pg.* 1572, *pg.* 941

ARGLAES - Medical Product - MEDLINE INDUSTRIES, INC.; *pg.* 1562, *pg.* 635

ARGMATCH - Fingerprint Identification & Matching Software - LOCKHEED MARTIN CORPORATION; *pg.* 229, *pg.* 762

ARGO - Flashlight - STREAMLIGHT INC.; *pg.* 1306, *pg.* 1527

ARGO HP - Flashlight - STREAMLIGHT INC.; *pg.* 1306, *pg.* 1527

ARGO-TECH - Aerospace Product - EATON CORPORATION; *pg.* 1331, *pg.* 1429

ARGONAUT - Water Current Meter - YSI INCORPORATED; *pg.* 1438, *pg.* 1483

ARGOSHIELD - Shielding Gases - LINDE GAS LLC; *pg.* 1356, *pg.* 1095

ARGOSY UNIVERSITY - Universities - EDUCATION MANAGEMENT CORPORATION; *pg.* 601, *pg.* 1575

ARGUS - Valve - FLOWSERVE CORPORATION; *pg.* 82, *pg.* 1719

ARGUS - Bear Puppet - GUND, INC.; *pg.* 954, *pg.* 1056

ARGUS - Plasma Display Modules - INDUSTRIAL ELECTRONIC ENGINEERS, INC.; *pg.* 644, *pg.* 300

ARGUS - Medical System - VARIAN MEDICAL SYSTEMS, INC.; *pg.* 1434, *pg.* 178

ARGYLE - Medical Device - MALLINCKRODT PHARMACEUTICALS; *pg.* 1557, *pg.* 978

ARGYLE - Nasopharyngeal Airway - MEDTRONIC; *pg.* 1563, *pg.* 183

ARGYLE - Women's Clothing & Accessories - WOODEN SHIPS OF HOBOKEN; *pg.* 35, *pg.* 1315

ARI MAILSMART - Software - ARI NETWORK SERVICES, INC.; *pg.* 353, *pg.* 1873

ARIA - Case - ANTEC INCORPORATED; *pg.* 350, *pg.* 90

ARIA - Guest Chairs - BERNHARDT DESIGN; *pg.* 918, *pg.* 1381

ARIA - Servingware for Buffets - CARLISLE FOODSERVICE PRODUCTS INCORPORATED; *pg.* 1455, *pg.* 1485

ARIA - Pest Control Product - FMC CORPORATION; *pg.* 1163, *pg.* 1564

ARIA - Resort & Casino - MGM RESORTS INTERNATIONAL; *pg.* 1105, *pg.* 1028

ARIA - Fabric - NEMSCHOFF, INC.; *pg.* 936, *pg.* 1890

ARIA - Flatware - ONEIDA LTD; *pg.* 1129, *pg.* 1318

ARIA - China Toilet - THETFORD CORPORATION; *pg.* 337, *pg.* 867

ARIA - Cosmetics - WESTROCK COMPANY; *pg.* 1472, *pg.* 1805

ARIAKE - Footwear - K-SWISS; *pg.* 1837, *pg.* 306

ARIAKE LITE MESH - Footwear - K-SWISS; *pg.* 1837, *pg.* 306

ARIBA ANALYSIS - Software - ARIBA, INC.; *pg.* 353, *pg.* 283

ARIBA BUYER - Software - ARIBA, INC.; *pg.* 353, *pg.* 283

ARIBA CATEGORY MANAGEMENT - Software - ARIBA, INC.; *pg.* 353, *pg.* 283

ARIBA CATEGORY PROCUREMENT - Software - ARIBA, INC.; *pg.* 353, *pg.* 283

ARIBA CONTENT PROCUREMENT - Software - ARIBA, INC.; *pg.* 353, *pg.* 283

ARIBA CONTRACT COMPLIANCE - Software - ARIBA, INC.; *pg.* 353, *pg.* 283

ARIBA CONTRACT MANAGEMENT - Software - ARIBA, INC.; *pg.* 353, *pg.* 283

ARIBA CONTRACT WORKBENCH - Software - ARIBA, INC.; *pg.* 353, *pg.* 283

ARIBA CONTRACTS - Software - ARIBA, INC.; *pg.* 353, *pg.* 283

ARIBA DATA ENRICHMENT - Software - ARIBA, INC.; *pg.* 353, *pg.* 283

ARIBA EFORMS - Software - ARIBA, INC.; *pg.* 353, *pg.* 283

ARIBA ELECTRONIC INVOICE PRESENTMENT & PAYMENT - Software - ARIBA, INC.; *pg.* 353, *pg.* 283

ARIBA INVOICE - Software - ARIBA, INC.; *pg.* 353, *pg.* 283

ARIBA LIVE - Software - ARIBA, INC.; *pg.* 353, *pg.* 283

ARIBA PAYMENT - Software - ARIBA, INC.; *pg.* 353, *pg.* 283

ARIBA PROCURE-TO-PAY - Software - ARIBA, INC.; *pg.* 353, *pg.* 283

ARIBA PUNCHOUT - Software - ARIBA, INC.; *pg.* 353, *pg.* 283

ARIBA QUICKSOURCE - Software - ARIBA, INC.; *pg.* 353, *pg.* 283

ARIBA READY - Software - ARIBA, INC.; *pg.* 353, *pg.* 283

ARIBA SETTLEMENT - Software - ARIBA, INC.; *pg.* 353, *pg.* 283

ARIBA SOLUTIONS DELIVERY - Software - ARIBA, INC.; *pg.* 353, *pg.* 283

ARIBA SOURCING - Software - ARIBA, INC.; *pg.* 353, *pg.* 283

ARIBA SPEND MANAGEMENT - Software - ARIBA, INC.; *pg.* 353, *pg.* 283

ARIBA SPEND MANAGEMENT. FIND IT. GET IT. KEEP IT. - Slogan - ARIBA, INC.; *pg.* 353, *pg.* 283

ARIBA SPEND MANAGEMENT KNOWLEDGE BASE - Software - ARIBA, INC.; *pg.* 353, *pg.* 283

ARIBA SPEND VISIBILITY - Software - ARIBA, INC.; *pg.* 353, *pg.* 283

ARIBA SUPPLIER CONNECTIVITY - Software - ARIBA, INC.; *pg.* 353, *pg.* 283

ARIBA SUPPLIER NETWORK - Software - ARIBA, INC.; *pg.* 353, *pg.* 283

ARIBA SUPPLIER PERFORMANCE MANAGEMENT - Software - ARIBA, INC.; *pg.* 353, *pg.* 283

ARIBA SUPPLY LINES - Software - ARIBA, INC.; *pg.* 353, *pg.* 283

ARIBA SUPPLY MANAGER - Software - ARIBA, INC.; *pg.* 353, *pg.* 283

ARIBA. THIS IS SPEND MANAGEMENT - Slogan - ARIBA, INC.; *pg.* 353, *pg.* 283

ARIBA TRAVEL & EXPENSE - Software - ARIBA, INC.; *pg.* 353, *pg.* 283

ARIBA WORKFORCE - Software - ARIBA, INC.; *pg.* 353, *pg.* 283

ARIBA.COM - Software - ARIBA, INC.; *pg.* 353, *pg.* 283

ARIBA.COM NETWORK - Software - ARIBA, INC.; *pg.* 353, *pg.* 283

ARIBALIVE - Software - ARIBA, INC.; *pg.* 353, *pg.* 283

ARICA - Bath Product - KOHLER CO.; *pg.* 91, *pg.* 1862
ARICEPT - Intestinal Treatment - EISAI INC.; *pg.* 1526, *pg.* 1133
ARICEPT - Alzheimer's Medication - PFIZER INC.; *pg.* 1581, *pg.* 1278
ARICID - Metal Finishing Product - HEATBATH CORPORATION; *pg.* 1165, *pg.* 826
ARID-CORE - Cable - COMMSCOPE, INC.; *pg.* 278, *pg.* 1378
ARIDEX - Screws - USG CORPORATION; *pg.* 118, *pg.* 594
ARIEL - Laundry Detergent - THE PROCTER & GAMBLE COMPANY; *pg.* 1129, *pg.* 1418
ARIES - Area Lighting - JUNO LIGHTING, INC.; *pg.* 1300, *pg.* 606
ARIMAX - Chemicals - ASHLAND INC.; *pg.* 972, *pg.* 726
ARION - Furniture - HOOKER FURNITURE CORPORATION; *pg.* 928, *pg.* 1788
ARIOSO - Air Filtration - LYDALL, INC.; *pg.* 1357, *pg.* 354
ARIS - Voice Processing Platform - ELECTRONIC TELE-COMMUNICATIONS, INC.; *pg.* 390, *pg.* 1897
ARISE - Food Product - MGP INGREDIENTS, INC.; *pg.* 877, *pg.* 714
ARISTA - Hair Preparations - THE GILLETTE COMPANY; *pg.* 509, *pg.* 795
ARISTA RECORDS - Artist - SONY MUSIC ENTERTAINMENT; *pg.* 309, *pg.* 1294
ARISTALOY - Dental Amalgam - BASF CATALYSTS LLC; *pg.* 1148, *pg.* 1074
ARISTOCRAT - Table - BLATT BOWLING & BILLIARD CORP.; *pg.* 1827, *pg.* 1203
ARISTOCRAT - Gaming Product - GLD PRODUCTS, INC.; *pg.* 1835, *pg.* 1882
ARISTOCRAT - Fishing Rods & Reels - WRIGHT & MCGILL CO.; *pg.* 1848, *pg.* 324
ARISTOKRAFT - Hardware - FORTUNE BRANDS HOME & SECURITY, INC.; *pg.* 55, *pg.* 600
ARISTOKRAFT - Cabinetry - MASTERBRAND CABINETS, INC.; *pg.* 96, *pg.* 692
ARISTOSHEEN - Interior Alkyd Low Semi-Gloss Enamel - DUNN-EDWARDS CORPORATION; *pg.* 1442, *pg.* 129
ARISTOSHELL - Interior Alkyd Eggshell Enamel - DUNN-EDWARDS CORPORATION; *pg.* 1442, *pg.* 129
ARISTOWAX - Chemical Product - SPECTRUM CHEMICALS & LABORATORY PRODUCTS, INC.; *pg.* 1181, *pg.* 94
ARITHMETIC BIST - Software System - MENTOR GRAPHICS CORPORATION; *pg.* 432, *pg.* 1510
ARIVA - Dissolvable Hard & Smokeless Tobacco Product - ROCK CREEK PHARMACEUTICALS, INC.; *pg.* 1895, *pg.* 466
ARIZONA - Fabric - NEMSCHOFF, INC.; *pg.* 936, *pg.* 1890
ARIZONA DIAMONDBACKS - Baseball Team - ARIZONA DIAMONDBACKS; *pg.* 529, *pg.* 14
ARIZONA RATTLERS - Game - PHOENIX SUNS; *pg.* 576, *pg.* 19
ARIZONA'S ORIGINAL WESTERN STORE - Tagline - SABAS BUNCH LIMITED PARTNERSHIP; *pg.* 47, *pg.* 12
ARKANSAS CANCER RESEARCH CENTER - Cancer Research & Treatment - UNIVERSITY OF ARKANSAS FOR MEDICAL SCIENCES; *pg.* 608, *pg.* 34
ARKITEKT - Sunglasses - FOSSIL GROUP, INC.; *pg.* 5, *pg.* 1735
ARKONLINE - Software - SEMTECH CORPORATION GENNUM PRODUCTS; *pg.* 671, *pg.* 1919
ARLAC P - Potassium Lactate - ARCHER-DANIELS-MIDLAND COMPANY; *pg.* 825, *pg.* 565
ARLAC S - Sodium Lactate - ARCHER-DANIELS-MIDLAND COMPANY; *pg.* 825, *pg.* 565
ARLI$$ - Cable Television Show - HOME BOX OFFICE, INC.; *pg.* 290, *pg.* 1240
ARLINGTON - Furniture - ASHLEY FURNITURE INDUSTRIES, INC.; *pg.* 914, *pg.* 1852
ARLINGTON - Furniture - JASPER GROUP; *pg.* 930, *pg.* 691
ARLINGTON PARK - Race Course - CHURCHILL DOWNS, INC.; *pg.* 540, *pg.* 733
ARLIZ - Footwear - STEVEN MADDEN, LTD.; *pg.* 1819, *pg.* 1176
ARLON - Seal & Thermoplastic Component - GREENE, TWEED & CO.; *pg.* 1344, *pg.* 1544
ARM - Accredited Residential Mgr. - INSTITUTE OF REAL ESTATE MANAGEMENT; *pg.* 144, *pg.* 578
ARM & HAMMER - Health & Beauty & Household Products - CHURCH & DWIGHT CANADA CORP.; *pg.* 503, *pg.* 1925
ARM & HAMMER - Cleaning, Baking, Laundry Detergent & Deodorizing Products - CHURCH & DWIGHT CO., INC.; *pg.* 1153, *pg.* 1063
ARM AND HAMMER - Filtration Product - FLANDERS CORPORATION; *pg.* 1336, *pg.* 1392
ARM & HAMMER DENTAL CARE - Toothpaste, Gel & Tooth Powder - CHURCH & DWIGHT CO., INC.; *pg.* 1153, *pg.* 1063
ARM & HAMMER ESSENTIALS - Cleaning Products - CHURCH & DWIGHT CO., INC.; *pg.* 1153, *pg.* 1063
ARM & HAMMER ORALCARE - Toothpaste - CHURCH & DWIGHT CO., INC.; *pg.* 1153, *pg.* 1063
ARM & HAMMER SUPER SCOOP - Cat Litter - CHURCH & DWIGHT CO., INC.; *pg.* 1153, *pg.* 1063
ARM & HAMMER VACUUM FREE - Foam Carpet Cleaner - CHURCH & DWIGHT CO., INC.; *pg.* 1153, *pg.* 1063
ARM MAKERS FOR RESPONSIBLE CITIZENS - Slogan - STURM, RUGER & COMPANY, INC.; *pg.* 1846, *pg.* 371
ARMACOR - Alloy Coating - LIQUIDMETAL TECHNOLOGIES, INC.; *pg.* 1356, *pg.* 188
ARMACOR - Fabric - W.L. GORE & ASSOCIATES, INC.; *pg.* 122, *pg.* 388
ARMADA - Game - WMS INDUSTRIES INC.; *pg.* 593, *pg.* 666
ARMADALE - Vodka - WILLIAM GRANT & SONS, INC., *pg.* 1972, *pg.* 1057
ARMADILLO - Aerator - AG-MEIER INDUSTRIES LLC; *pg.* 700, *pg.* 1668
ARMAGRIP - Protective & Decorative Coatings - PPG INDUSTRIES, INC.; *pg.* 1445, *pg.* 1579
ARMAKLEEN - Aqueous Cleaner for Printed Wiring Assemblies - CHURCH & DWIGHT CO., INC.; *pg.* 1153, *pg.* 1063
ARMAKLEEN - Liquid Cleaner And Rust - SAFETY-KLEEN HOLDCO, INC.; *pg.* 1180, *pg.* 1734
ARMALOC - Plastics Product - AEP INDUSTRIES INC.; *pg.* 1878, *pg.* 1085
ARMAND DUPREE - Kitchenware - TUPPERWARE BRANDS CORPORATION; *pg.* 1139, *pg.* 456
ARMANI CASA - Apparel & Fragrance - GIORGIO ARMANI CORPORATION; *pg.* 25, *pg.* 1234
ARMANI COLLEZIONI - Apparel & Fragrance - GIORGIO ARMANI CORPORATION; *pg.* 25, *pg.* 1234
ARMANI EXCHANGE - Apparel & Fragrance - GIORGIO ARMANI CORPORATION; *pg.* 25, *pg.* 1234
ARMANI JEANS - Apparel & Fragrance - GIORGIO ARMANI CORPORATION; *pg.* 25, *pg.* 1234
ARMANI JUNIOR - Apparel & Fragrance - GIORGIO ARMANI CORPORATION; *pg.* 25, *pg.* 1234
ARMASAFE PLUS - Battery - ENERSYS INC.; *pg.* 1334, *pg.* 1584
ARMASEAL - Plastics Product - AEP INDUSTRIES INC.; *pg.* 1878, *pg.* 1085
ARMASTUFF - Plastics Product - AEP INDUSTRIES INC.; *pg.* 1878, *pg.* 1085
ARMATHENE - Plastics Product - AEP INDUSTRIES INC.; *pg.* 1878, *pg.* 1085
ARMATUFF - Plastics Product - AEP INDUSTRIES INC.; *pg.* 1878, *pg.* 1085
ARMATUFF TWIN - Plastics Product - AEP INDUSTRIES INC.; *pg.* 1878, *pg.* 1085
ARMCO - Steel Product - AK STEEL HOLDING CORPORATION; *pg.* 1311, *pg.* 1479
ARMEX BLAST MEDIA - Paint Stripper - CHURCH & DWIGHT CO., INC.; *pg.* 1153, *pg.* 1063
ARMITRON - Watches - ARMITRON WATCH DIVISION; *pg.* 1, *pg.* 1174
ARMO-COT - Amniotomy Finger Cots - UTAH MEDICAL PRODUCTS, INC.; *pg.* 1605, *pg.* 1752
ARMO-DUR - Impact Resistant Material - SHURE INCORPORATED; *pg.* 672, *pg.* 638
ARMOR - Crayon Dispenser - C.H. HANSON COMPANY; *pg.* 1322, *pg.* 636
ARMOR - Orthopedic Product - DJO INCORPORATED; *pg.* 1524, *pg.* 302
ARMOR - Blade - LENOX; *pg.* 1053, *pg.* 817
ARMOR - Apparel - OAKLEY, INC.; *pg.* 1840, *pg.* 86
ARMOR - Software - ROCKWELL AUTOMATION, INC.; *pg.* 668, *pg.* 1880
ARMOR ALL - Automotive Aftermarket Appearance Products - ARMORED AUTOGROUP INC.; *pg.* 199, *pg.* 342
ARMOR ALL - Protectants, Cleaners, Tire Products, Waxes & Washes - THE CLOROX COMPANY; *pg.* 327, *pg.* 169
ARMOR ALL - Paint - W.M. BARR & COMPANY, INC.; *pg.* 338, *pg.* 1647
ARMOR ALL FIERCE SHINE TIRE FOAM - All-Purpose Cleaner - THE CLOROX COMPANY; *pg.* 327, *pg.* 169
ARMOR ALL PROFESSIONAL - Vehicle Care Products - ZEP INC.; *pg.* 338, *pg.* 524
ARMOR-LITE - Packaging - PACTIV CORPORATION; *pg.* 1466, *pg.* 624
ARMOR-NIT - Protector & Pillowcover - MEDLINE INDUSTRIES, INC.; *pg.* 1562, *pg.* 635
ARMOR PIERCING BLACK - Knife - BEAR & SON CUTLERY, INC.; *pg.* 1827, *pg.* 7
ARMOR SHELL - Vinyl Extruded Membrane - COOLEY GROUP, INC.; *pg.* 691, *pg.* 1603
ARMOR-TAN - Sport Gloves - FRANKLIN SPORTS, INC.; *pg.* 1834, *pg.* 847
ARMOR TEK 3 - Tires - COOPER TIRE & RUBBER COMPANY; *pg.* 1881, *pg.* 1453
ARMOR-TOUGH - Tents - KELLWOOD COMPANY; *pg.* 28, *pg.* 975
ARMORBLOCK - Auxiliary Power Connection - ROCKWELL AUTOMATION, INC.; *pg.* 668, *pg.* 1880
ARMORCOIL - Spring Covers & Safety Curtains - DYNATECT MANUFACTURING INC.; *pg.* 1330, *pg.* 1883
ARMORED - Seam Construction for Protective Garments - STANDARD SAFETY EQUIPMENT CO.; *pg.* 1379, *pg.* 632
ARMOREZ - Chemical Product - WESTROCK COMPANY; *pg.* 1472, *pg.* 1805
ARMORFLEX - Recreational Vehicle - CLUB CAR, INC.; *pg.* 1830, *pg.* 532
ARMORGARD - Lens Treatment Product - EMERGING VISION, INC.; *pg.* 1411, *pg.* 1227
ARMORKRAFT - Safety Storage Cabinet - EAGLE MANUFACTURING COMPANY; *pg.* 79, *pg.* 1851
ARMORLINE - Bullet Resistant Doors & Door Frames - KAWNEER COMPANY, INC.; *pg.* 90, *pg.* 537
ARMORLITE - Cable - AMPHENOL CORPORATION; *pg.* 616, *pg.* 381
ARMORLITE - Plastic Ophthalmic Lenses - SIGNET ARMORLITE, INC.; *pg.* 1429, *pg.* 60
ARMORLITE - Cable - SOUTHWIRE COMPANY; *pg.* 1063, *pg.* 527
ARMORPOINT - Software - ROCKWELL AUTOMATION, INC.; *pg.* 668, *pg.* 1880
ARMORWALL - Heavy Wall Tubular Heater - VULCAN ELECTRIC COMPANY; *pg.* 1078, *pg.* 751
ARMORWARE - Construction Material - CRANE PLASTICS HOLDING COMPANY; *pg.* 1881, *pg.* 1439
ARMOUR - Canned Meats - HENKEL CONSUMER GOODS; *pg.* 511, *pg.* 22
ARMOUR - Meat Products - JOHN MORRELL FOOD GROUP; *pg.* 866, *pg.* 628
ARMOUR - Canned Meal - PINNACLE FOODS GROUP LLC; *pg.* 889, *pg.* 1104
ARMOUR - Food Products - SMITHFIELD FOODS, INC.; *pg.* 896, *pg.* 1806
ARMOUR - Apparels - UNDER ARMOUR, INC.; *pg.* 49, *pg.* 759
ARMOUR STORM - Accessories - UNDER ARMOUR, INC.; *pg.* 49, *pg.* 759
ARMS - Automated Rental Management System - ENTERPRISE HOLDINGS, INC.; *pg.* 1906, *pg.* 996
ARMSTRONG - Heating & Cooling Product - LENNOX INTERNATIONAL INC.; *pg.* 1073, *pg.* 1736
ARMSTRONG - Cheese - SAPUTO, INC.; *pg.* 893, *pg.* 1956
ARMSTRONG - Floor Cleaner - S.C. JOHNSON & SON, INC.; *pg.* 334, *pg.* 1889
ARMSTRONG AIR - Heating & Cooling Systems - LENNOX INTERNATIONAL INC.; *pg.* 1073, *pg.* 1736
ARMSTRONG SERVICE - Energy Solution - ARMSTRONG INTERNATIONAL, INC.; *pg.* 1069, *pg.* 909
ARMSTRONG TOOLS - Hand Tool - DANAHER CORPORATION; *pg.* 1044, *pg.* 397
ARMY - Shoe - AEROGROUP INTERNATIONAL, INC.; *pg.* 1803, *pg.* 1055
ARMY OF TWO - Video Game - ELECTRONIC ARTS INC.; *pg.* 951, *pg.* 189
ARMY TACTICAL MISSILE SYSTEM - Vehicle-Mounted Guided Missiles - LOCKHEED MARTIN CORPORATION; *pg.* 229, *pg.* 762
ARNDT - Endobronchial Blocker Set - COOK GROUP, INC.; *pg.* 1518, *pg.* 674
ARNESON - Surface Drives - TWIN DISC, INCORPORATED; *pg.* 220, *pg.* 1889
ARNO - Dinnerware - THE HOMER LAUGHLIN CHINA COMPANY; *pg.* 1125, *pg.* 1850
ARNOTT'S - Biscuits - CAMPBELL SOUP COMPANY; *pg.* 844, *pg.* 1048
AROCURE - Pressure Sensitive Adhesives - ASHLAND INC.;

First page reference indicates Business Class Edition
Second page reference indicates Geographic Edition

pg. 972, *pg.* 726
AROCY - Cyanate Ester Resins - HUNTSMAN CORPORATION; *pg.* 1167, *pg.* 1758
AROFENE - Paper Resins - ASHLAND INC.; *pg.* 972, *pg.* 726
AROGUARD - Synthetic Resins - ASHLAND INC.; *pg.* 972, *pg.* 726
AROM-COT - Medical Product - UTAH MEDICAL PRODUCTS, INC.; *pg.* 1605, *pg.* 1752
AROMA - Yoga Mat - HUGGER MUGGER YOGA PRODUCTS LLC; *pg.* 1836, *pg.* 1758
AROMA CLEAN - Cleaner - SUNSHINE MAKERS, INC.; *pg.* 336, *pg.* 105
AROMA EXPRESS - Kitchen Appliance - HAMILTON BEACH BRANDS, INC.; *pg.* 56, *pg.* 1783
AROMA SIGN - Fragrance - NU SKIN ENTERPRISES, INC.; *pg.* 518, *pg.* 1755
AROMA SPA - Health & Beauty Product - BLUE CROSS LABORATORIES; *pg.* 326, *pg.* 277
AROMA STREET - Food Products - SPARTANNASH CO; *pg.* 1034, *pg.* 889
AROMAE - Hair Shampoo - MARIETTA HOSPITALITY; *pg.* 1464, *pg.* 1155
AROMAFREE - Body Care - AROMALAND INC.; *pg.* 499, *pg.* 1135
AROMALACQUER - Olfactory Sampling System - ARCADE MARKETING, INC.; *pg.* 352, *pg.* 1196
AROMASENSE - Candles - HENKEL CONSUMER GOODS; *pg.* 511, *pg.* 22
AROMASIN - Breast Cancer Medication - PFIZER INC.; *pg.* 1581, *pg.* 1278
AROMATIC - Organic Solvent - ROCK VALLEY OIL & CHEMICAL COMPANY; *pg.* 1179, *pg.* 631
AROMATIQUE - Fragrance - AROMATIQUE INC.; *pg.* 499, *pg.* 32
AROMATRAN - Electronic Instruments - MOCON, INC.; *pg.* 1363, *pg.* 940
AROMELT - Adhesives - ASHLAND INC.; *pg.* 972, *pg.* 726
AROMETRICS - Automobile Air Fresheners - ASHLAND INC.; *pg.* 972, *pg.* 726
AROPOL - Resins - ASHLAND INC.; *pg.* 972, *pg.* 726
AROSET - Industrial Polymers - ASHLAND INC.; *pg.* 972, *pg.* 726
AROSURF - Chemical Product - WESTROCK COMPANY; *pg.* 1472, *pg.* 1805
AROTECH - Defense & Security Product - AROTECH CORPORATION; *pg.* 1042, *pg.* 865
AROTRAN - Low-Profile Resin Transfer Molding System - ASHLAND INC.; *pg.* 972, *pg.* 726
AROUND - Fabric - NEMSCHOFF, INC.; *pg.* 936, *pg.* 1890
AROUND THE BEND - Dog Toy - THE HARTZ MOUNTAIN CORP.; *pg.* 1476, *pg.* 1120
AROUND THE CORNER - AROUND THE WORLD - Banking Service - SALEM FIVE CENTS SAVINGS BANK; *pg.* 800, *pg.* 843
AROUND THE HORN - Sports Discussion Program - ESPN, INC.; *pg.* 285, *pg.* 340
ARQUEST - Computer Software - LOCKHEED MARTIN CORPORATION; *pg.* 229, *pg.* 762
ARRA - Table Grape Label - GIUMARRA VINEYARDS CORPORATION; *pg.* 1964, *pg.* 45
ARRAY - Testing Instrument System - BECKMAN COULTER, INC.; *pg.* 1402, *pg.* 48
ARRAY - Hair Preparations - THE GILLETTE COMPANY; *pg.* 509, *pg.* 795
ARRAY - Cleaning System - GORDON FOOD SERVICE INC.; *pg.* 1021, *pg.* 913
ARRAY LED G4 - Lighting Systems - REVOLUTION LIGHTING TECHNOLOGIES, INC.; *pg.* 1304, *pg.* 377
ARRAY LED MR16 - Lighting Systems - REVOLUTION LIGHTING TECHNOLOGIES, INC.; *pg.* 1304, *pg.* 377
ARRAY LED PAR16 - Lighting Systems - REVOLUTION LIGHTING TECHNOLOGIES, INC.; *pg.* 1304, *pg.* 377
ARRAY LED PAR30 - Lighting Systems - REVOLUTION LIGHTING TECHNOLOGIES, INC.; *pg.* 1304, *pg.* 377
ARRAY OF ARRAYS - Array - ILLUMINA, INC.; *pg.* 412, *pg.* 203
ARRAY VCSELS - Electronic Component - EMCORE CORPORATION; *pg.* 636, *pg.* 39
ARRAYASSIST LITE - Software - AFFYMETRIX, INC.; *pg.* 1487, *pg.* 263
ARRAYTUBE - Pharmaceutical Product - ALERE INC.; *pg.* 1488, *pg.* 849
ARRESTOX - Aqueous-Coated Book Cloth - HOLLISTON LLC; *pg.* 1460, *pg.* 1630
ARRETIN - Pharmaceutical Product - VALEANT PHARMACEUTICALS INTERNATIONAL; *pg.* 1605, *pg.* 1047
ARRIA - Transceiver - ALTERA CORPORATION; *pg.* 348, *pg.* 237
ARRIA GX - Transceiver - ALTERA CORPORATION; *pg.* 348, *pg.* 237
ARRID - Deodorant - CHURCH & DWIGHT CO., INC.; *pg.* 1153, *pg.* 1063
ARRIO - Furniture - HERMAN MILLER, INC.; *pg.* 926, *pg.* 913
ARRIVA - Radial Tire - THE GOODYEAR TIRE & RUBBER COMPANY; *pg.* 1883, *pg.* 1401
ARRIVA - Eye Protection - MCR SAFETY; *pg.* 1422, *pg.* 1630
ARRIVA - Tables - STEELCASE INC.; *pg.* 475, *pg.* 889
ARRIVAL - Software - PITNEY BOWES INC.; *pg.* 454, *pg.* 376
ARRIVALS SUITES - Airline Service - UNITED CONTINENTAL HOLDINGS, INC.; *pg.* 1927, *pg.* 593
ARRIVEDERCI - Fabric - NEMSCHOFF, INC.; *pg.* 936, *pg.* 1890
ARRIVL - Paper Product - BOISE CASCADE HOLDINGS, L.L.C.; *pg.* 1453, *pg.* 546
ARRIX - Semiconductor Chips - SAJAN, INC.; *pg.* 1278, *pg.* 1890
ARRONDI - Seating - STEELCASE INC.; *pg.* 475, *pg.* 889
ARROW - Houseware Product - ARROW FASTENER COMPANY, INC.; *pg.* 1042, *pg.* 1118
ARROW - Wheelchair - INVACARE CORPORATION; *pg.* 1546, *pg.* 1451
ARROW - Heating & Ventilation Equipment - MESTEK, INC.; *pg.* 1074, *pg.* 857
ARROW - Fabric - NEMSCHOFF, INC.; *pg.* 936, *pg.* 1890
ARROW - Aircraft - PIPER AIRCRAFT, INC.; *pg.* 233, *pg.* 477
ARROW - Apparel - PVH CORP.; *pg.* 46, *pg.* 1283
ARROW - Footwear - P.W. MINOR & SON, INC.; *pg.* 1816, *pg.* 1140
ARROW - Educational Materials - SCHOLASTIC INC.; *pg.* 1683, *pg.* 1288
ARROW - Engine Company - TRIMAS CORPORATION; *pg.* 1383, *pg.* 874
ARROW ACES - Prototype Development Service - ARROW ELECTRONICS, INC.; *pg.* 619, *pg.* 325
ARROW ALERT - Real Time Notifications - ARROW ELECTRONICS, INC.; *pg.* 619, *pg.* 325
ARROW ASIC - Prototype Development Team - ARROW ELECTRONICS, INC.; *pg.* 619, *pg.* 325
ARROW COLLABORATOR - Web-Based Inventory Service - ARROW ELECTRONICS, INC.; *pg.* 619, *pg.* 325
ARROW FASTENER - Staple Guns - MASCO CORPORATION; *pg.* 96, *pg.* 909
ARROW FWD - Power Wheelchair - INVACARE CORPORATION; *pg.* 1546, *pg.* 1451
ARROW-LOCK - Protective Lining Product - NOV AMERON; *pg.* 100, *pg.* 187
ARROW RISK MANAGER - Part Selection System - ARROW ELECTRONICS, INC.; *pg.* 619, *pg.* 325
ARROWEDGE - Technical Presentations - ARROW ELECTRONICS, INC.; *pg.* 619, *pg.* 325
ARROWHEAD - Video Game - INTERNATIONAL GAME TECHNOLOGY; *pg.* 957, *pg.* 1024
ARROWHEAD - Electronic Targeting Apparatus - LOCKHEED MARTIN CORPORATION; *pg.* 229, *pg.* 762
ARROWHEAD MILLS - Food Product - THE HAIN CELESTIAL GROUP, INC.; *pg.* 860, *pg.* 1172
ARROYO GRANDE - Furniture - FLEXSTEEL INDUSTRIES, INC.; *pg.* 925, *pg.* 707
ARS LINK - Software - BMC SOFTWARE, INC.; *pg.* 362, *pg.* 1701
ARS TECHNICA - IT Magazine - CONDE NAST PUBLICATIONS, INC.; *pg.* 1629, *pg.* 1217
ARSENAL - Cleaning Product - HILLYARD, INC.; *pg.* 331, *pg.* 990
ART - Asphalt Residual Treating Process - BASF CATALYSTS LLC; *pg.* 1148, *pg.* 1074
THE ART & SCIENCE OF FIBER OPTICS - Tagline - ALLIANCE FIBER OPTIC PRODUCTS, INC.; *pg.* 1399, *pg.* 283
ART DECO - Fan - WESTINGHOUSE LIGHTING CORPORATION; *pg.* 687, *pg.* 1571
ART GLASS - Optical Design Accessory - HIGH END SYSTEMS, INC.; *pg.* 1299, *pg.* 1663
ART-GUARD - Glass Product - GUARDIAN INDUSTRIES CORP.; *pg.* 85, *pg.* 869
ART IN AMERICA - Magazine - BRANT PUBLICATIONS, INC.; *pg.* 1623, *pg.* 1206
THE ART INSTITUE ONLINE - Internet Educational Services - EDUCATION MANAGEMENT CORPORATION; *pg.* 601, *pg.* 1575
THE ART INSTITUTE OF ATLANTA - Art School - EDUCATION MANAGEMENT CORPORATION; *pg.* 601, *pg.* 1575
THE ART INSTITUTE OF CALIFORNIA - Art School - EDUCATION MANAGEMENT CORPORATION; *pg.* 601, *pg.* 1575
THE ART INSTITUTE OF CHARLOTTE - Art School - EDUCATION MANAGEMENT CORPORATION; *pg.* 601, *pg.* 1575
THE ART INSTITUTE OF COLORADO - Art School - EDUCATION MANAGEMENT CORPORATION; *pg.* 601, *pg.* 1575
THE ART INSTITUTE OF DALLAS - Art School - EDUCATION MANAGEMENT CORPORATION; *pg.* 601, *pg.* 1575
THE ART INSTITUTE OF FORT LAUDERDALE - Art School - EDUCATION MANAGEMENT CORPORATION; *pg.* 601, *pg.* 1575
THE ART INSTITUTE OF HOUSTON - Art School - EDUCATION MANAGEMENT CORPORATION; *pg.* 601, *pg.* 1575
THE ART INSTITUTE OF LAS VEGAS - Art School - EDUCATION MANAGEMENT CORPORATION; *pg.* 601, *pg.* 1575
THE ART INSTITUTE OF NEW YORK CITY - Art School - EDUCATION MANAGEMENT CORPORATION; *pg.* 601, *pg.* 1575
THE ART INSTITUTE OF PHILADELPHIA - Art School - EDUCATION MANAGEMENT CORPORATION; *pg.* 601, *pg.* 1575
THE ART INSTITUTE OF PHOENIX - Art School - EDUCATION MANAGEMENT CORPORATION; *pg.* 601, *pg.* 1575
THE ART INSTITUTE OF PITTSBURGH - Art School - EDUCATION MANAGEMENT CORPORATION; *pg.* 601, *pg.* 1575
THE ART INSTITUTE OF PORTLAND - Art School - EDUCATION MANAGEMENT CORPORATION; *pg.* 601, *pg.* 1575
THE ART INSTITUTE OF SEATTLE - Art School - EDUCATION MANAGEMENT CORPORATION; *pg.* 601, *pg.* 1575
THE ART INSTITUTE OF TAMPA - Art School - EDUCATION MANAGEMENT CORPORATION; *pg.* 601, *pg.* 1575
THE ART INSTITUTE OF WASHINGTON - Art School - EDUCATION MANAGEMENT CORPORATION; *pg.* 601, *pg.* 1575
THE ART INSTITUTES INTERNATIONAL MINNESOTA - Art School - EDUCATION MANAGEMENT CORPORATION; *pg.* 601, *pg.* 1575
ART KRAFT - Heavyweight Paper - PACON CORPORATION; *pg.* 1466, *pg.* 1852
ART MASKOID - Art Product - DANIEL SMITH INC.; *pg.* 1766, *pg.* 1835
ART METRO - Ceiling Fan - WESTINGHOUSE LIGHTING CORPORATION; *pg.* 687, *pg.* 1571
ART OF CARE - Recliners & Chairs - HILL-ROM HOLDINGS, INC.; *pg.* 1542, *pg.* 673
THE ART OF FIT - Design Tool - GLAMORISE FOUNDATIONS, INC.; *pg.* 25, *pg.* 1235
THE ART OF JOSEPHINE WALL - Deluxe Cards - LEANIN' TREE, INC.; *pg.* 1658, *pg.* 311
ART OF NEGOTIATING - Educational Negotiation Program - NEGOTIATION INSTITUTE, INC.; *pg.* 151, *pg.* 1268
THE ART OF PUTTING - Tag Line - ACUSHNET COMPANY; *pg.* 1824, *pg.* 818
ARTBIN - Art Product - DANIEL SMITH INC.; *pg.* 1766, *pg.* 1835
ARTBIN - Storage Container - FLAMBEAU, INC.; *pg.* 1336, *pg.* 1854
ARTCAT - Fluidizeable Contact Material - BASF CATALYSTS LLC; *pg.* 1148, *pg.* 1074
ARTCOLOUR - Printing Ink and Cartridges - VAN SON HOLLAND INK CORPORATION OF AMERICA; *pg.* 487, *pg.* 1169
ARTCRAFT - Line of Craft Organizing Products - RUBBERMAID HOME PRODUCTS; *pg.* 1138, *pg.* 1453
ARTEC - Office Furniture - KIMBALL INTERNATIONAL, INC.; *pg.* 931, *pg.* 692

ARTECON - Storage System - DOT HILL SYSTEMS CORP.; *pg.* 388, *pg.* 333
ARTEFFECTS - Wood Flooring Product - ARMSTRONG WORLD INDUSTRIES, INC.; *pg.* 914, *pg.* 1545
ARTEFFEX - Hair Care Products - LUSTER PRODUCTS INC.; *pg.* 515, *pg.* 581
ARTEK - Door - MASONITE INTERNATIONAL CORPORATION; *pg.* 1054, *pg.* 1920
ARTEMIS - Airborne Radar System - LOCKHEED MARTIN CORPORATION; *pg.* 229, *pg.* 762
ARTESIA - Community Name - WCI COMMUNITIES, INC.; *pg.* 1118, *pg.* 414
ARTESIAN - Fabric - NEMSCHOFF, INC.; *pg.* 936, *pg.* 1890
ARTESIAN - Fabric - NEUTRAL POSTURE, INC.; *pg.* 939, *pg.* 1669
ARTGRID - Software System - MENTOR GRAPHICS CORPORATION; *pg.* 432, *pg.* 1510
ARTHAFFECT - Nutritional Product - RELIV INTERNATIONAL, INC.; *pg.* 1589, *pg.* 975
ARTHRED - Hydrolysed Collagen - CARGILL, INC.; *pg.* 845, *pg.* 965
ARTHRED - Nutritional Product - RELIV INTERNATIONAL, INC.; *pg.* 1589, *pg.* 975
ARTHRI-MEND - Nutritional Product - NUTRACEUTICAL INTERNATIONAL CORPORATION; *pg.* 1576, *pg.* 1753
ARTHRIFIX - Nutritional Product - NUTRACEUTICAL INTERNATIONAL CORPORATION; *pg.* 1576, *pg.* 1753
ARTHRITEN - Pharmaceutical Product - ALVA/AMCO PHARMACAL COMPANIES, INC.; *pg.* 1492, *pg.* 637
ARTHRITIS ADVISOR - Newsletter - BELVOIR MEDIA GROUP, LLC; *pg.* 1620, *pg.* 360
ARTHRITIS HOT - Health & Beauty Product - CHATTEM, INC.; *pg.* 1515, *pg.* 1628
ARTHRIVIVE - Nutritional Supplement - WHITEWING LABS, INC.; *pg.* 1610, *pg.* 99
ARTHRIVIVE BLUE - Pharmaceutical Product - WHITEWING LABS, INC.; *pg.* 1610, *pg.* 99
ARTHRO-FLO - Arthroscopy Irrigation System - C.R. BARD, INC.; *pg.* 1519, *pg.* 1094
ARTHRO-KNIFE - Medical Equipment - CONMED CORPORATION; *pg.* 1517, *pg.* 1347
ARTHROTEC - Medicine - PFIZER INC.; *pg.* 1581, *pg.* 1278
ARTHUR - Food Product - ANNIE'S INC.; *pg.* 1760, *pg.* 45
ARTHUR - Software - JDA SOFTWARE GROUP, INC.; *pg.* 423, *pg.* 22
ARTHUR LOOPS - Food Product - ANNIE'S INC.; *pg.* 1760, *pg.* 45
ARTHUR TREACHER'S - Chips - NATHAN'S FAMOUS INC.; *pg.* 1741, *pg.* 1171
ARTHUR TREACHER'S - Fish & Chips - TRUFOODS LLC; *pg.* 1754, *pg.* 1305
ARTIC - Italian Liqueur - LAIRD & COMPANY, INC.; *pg.* 1966, *pg.* 1119
ARTIC - Embedded Computer System - RADISYS CORPORATION; *pg.* 458, *pg.* 1498
ARTICHOKE NANOCLUSTERS - Nutritional Product - RBC LIFE SCIENCES, INC.; *pg.* 1588, *pg.* 1723
ARTICLE - Fabric - NEMSCHOFF, INC.; *pg.* 936, *pg.* 1890
ARTICULATOR - Medical Equipment - CONMED CORPORATION; *pg.* 1517, *pg.* 1347
ARTICULATOR 35 - Medical Product - CONMED CORPORATION; *pg.* 1517, *pg.* 1347
ARTIFACT - Fabric - NEMSCHOFF, INC.; *pg.* 936, *pg.* 1890
ARTIFLEX - Medical & Aesthetic Product - DYNATRONICS CORPORATION; *pg.* 1526, *pg.* 1757
ARTISAN - Table - BLATT BOWLING & BILLIARD CORP.; *pg.* 1827, *pg.* 1203
ARTISAN - Medical Device - OLIVER PRODUCTS COMPANY INC.; *pg.* 1367, *pg.* 888
ARTISAN - Electric Beating - WHIRLPOOL CORPORATION; *pg.* 62, *pg.* 872
ARTISAN BLENDS - Shredded Cheese - SARGENTO FOODS INC.; *pg.* 894, *pg.* 1886
ARTISAN COLLECTION - Decorative Molding & Hardware - REV-A-SHELF; *pg.* 1060, *pg.* 738
ARTISAN PAVE - Diamond Setting Technique - HARRY KOTLAR & CO., INC.; *pg.* 6, *pg.* 132
ARTIST - Sketch Pads - PACON CORPORATION; *pg.* 1466, *pg.* 1852
ARTIST CHOICE - Glass Product - GUARDIAN INDUSTRIES CORP.; *pg.* 85, *pg.* 869
ARTISTA - Porcelain Dolls - CHARISMA BRANDS, LLC; *pg.* 2, *pg.* 120
ARTISTA - Custom Card Printer - DATACARD CORPORATION; *pg.* 382, *pg.* 948
ARTISTA 165E HERITAGE EDITION - Sewing Machines - BERNINA OF AMERICA INC.; *pg.* 51, *pg.* 554
ARTISTA 185 QEE - Sewing Machines - BERNINA OF AMERICA INC.; *pg.* 51, *pg.* 554
ARTISTA 200 - Sewing System - BERNINA OF AMERICA INC.; *pg.* 51, *pg.* 554
ARTISTA 200 E - Sewing Machines - BERNINA OF AMERICA INC.; *pg.* 51, *pg.* 554
ARTISTRI - Ink & Printing Systems - E.I. DU PONT DE NEMOURS & COMPANY; *pg.* 1159, *pg.* 390
ARTISTRY - Cosmetics - AMWAY CORPORATION; *pg.* 326, *pg.* 864
ARTISTRY - Fan - CRAFTMADE INTERNATIONAL, INC.; *pg.* 1295, *pg.* 1670
ARTIX - Software - PROGRESS SOFTWARE CORPORATION; *pg.* 457, *pg.* 786
ARTOPAQUE - Paper - BPM INC.; *pg.* 1454, *pg.* 1886
ARTPRO - Artwork System - ANDERSON & VREELAND, INC.; *pg.* 1616, *pg.* 1064
ARTRA - Skin Bleach - J. STRICKLAND & COMPANY; *pg.* 512, *pg.* 970
ARTROUTER - Software System - MENTOR GRAPHICS CORPORATION; *pg.* 432, *pg.* 1510
THE ARTS AND CRAFTS STORE - Slogan - MICHAELS STORES, INC.; *pg.* 1127, *pg.* 1722
ARTS FOR THE SPIRIT - Entertainment Services - OAKWOOD HEALTHCARE, INC.; *pg.* 1577, *pg.* 878
ART'S WAY A TRADITION OF QUALITY SINCE 1956 - Tagline - ART'S-WAY MANUFACTURING CO., INC.; *pg.* 701, *pg.* 701
ARTSEARCH - Magazine - THEATRE COMMUNICATIONS GROUP, INC.; *pg.* 587, *pg.* 1298
ARTSEDGE - Educational Program - JOHN F. KENNEDY CENTER FOR THE PERFORMING ARTS; *pg.* 555, *pg.* 401
ARTSHAPE - Software System - MENTOR GRAPHICS CORPORATION; *pg.* 432, *pg.* 1510
ARTURO FUENTE PREMIUM - Cigars - FINCK CIGAR CO.; *pg.* 1894, *pg.* 1740
ARTURO'S - Meat - GRECIAN DELIGHT FOODS INC.; *pg.* 859, *pg.* 610
ARTUS - Shims - ARTUS CORPORATION; *pg.* 1314, *pg.* 1059
ARTUS - Aerospace & Defense Product - DANAHER CORPORATION; *pg.* 1044, *pg.* 397
ARTWORKS - Business Support Software - INTEGRAMED AMERICA, INC.; *pg.* 1546, *pg.* 1325
ARUBA - Rug - COURISTAN INC.; *pg.* 921, *pg.* 1067
ARUBA - Electronic Catalog & Ordering System - HENRY SCHEIN, INC.; *pg.* 1541, *pg.* 1180
ARUBA - Fabric - NEMSCHOFF, INC.; *pg.* 936, *pg.* 1890
ARUBA - Furniture - TELESCOPE CASUAL FURNITURE INC.; *pg.* 944, *pg.* 1162
ARV2 - Footwear - COBIAN CORP.; *pg.* 1806, *pg.* 253
ARVAULT 48 - Data Backup & Recovery - OVERLAND STORAGE, INC.; *pg.* 451, *pg.* 205
ARWA - Beverages - THE COCA-COLA COMPANY; *pg.* 240, *pg.* 493
ARYLZENE - Resins - GEORGIA-PACIFIC LLC; *pg.* 1458, *pg.* 507
A'S AMIGOS - Baseball Program - OAKLAND ATHLETICS LIMITED PARTNERSHIP; *pg.* 571, *pg.* 172
AS&E-EDS - Automatic Explosives Detection Systems - AMERICAN SCIENCE AND ENGINEERING, INC.; *pg.* 1399, *pg.* 787
AS GOOD AS GOLD - Video Game - INTERNATIONAL GAME TECHNOLOGY; *pg.* 957, *pg.* 1024
AS3010 - Wireless Network Product - AIRSPAN NETWORKS INC.; *pg.* 346, *pg.* 410
AS3030 - Wireless Network Product - AIRSPAN NETWORKS INC.; *pg.* 346, *pg.* 410
AS3030 PTP - Wireless Network Product - AIRSPAN NETWORKS INC.; *pg.* 346, *pg.* 410
AS3600I - Scanner - OPEX CORPORATION; *pg.* 450, *pg.* 1087
AS4000 - Wireless Network Product - AIRSPAN NETWORKS INC.; *pg.* 346, *pg.* 410
AS4020 - Wireless Network Product - AIRSPAN NETWORKS INC.; *pg.* 346, *pg.* 410
AS4030 - Wireless Network Product - AIRSPAN NETWORKS INC.; *pg.* 346, *pg.* 410
AS700 PELLETS - Medicated Feeds for Weight Management - KENT NUTRITION GROUP; *pg.* 1477, *pg.* 710
ASA AROMA - Pump Product - IDEX CORPORATION; *pg.* 1347, *pg.* 623
ASA TIRE SYSTEMS - Automotive Aftermarket Accounting & Management Software - ASA INTERNATIONAL LTD.; *pg.* 353, *pg.* 1036
ASAHI - Coronary Guide Wires - ABBOTT LABORATORIES; *pg.* 1484, *pg.* 551
ASAHI CONFIANZA - Coronary Guide Wires - ABBOTT LABORATORIES; *pg.* 1484, *pg.* 551
ASAHI GRAND SLAM - Coronary Guide Wires - ABBOTT LABORATORIES; *pg.* 1484, *pg.* 551
ASAHI MIRACLE BROS - Coronary Guide Wires - ABBOTT LABORATORIES; *pg.* 1484, *pg.* 551
ASAHI PROWATER - Coronary Guide Wires - ABBOTT LABORATORIES; *pg.* 1484, *pg.* 551
ASAHI TORNUS - Catheter - ABBOTT LABORATORIES; *pg.* 1484, *pg.* 551
ASAMANEX - Medicine - MERCK & CO., INC.; *pg.* 1566, *pg.* 1077
ASANA - Insecticide - E.I. DU PONT DE NEMOURS & COMPANY; *pg.* 1159, *pg.* 390
ASANA - Waiting Seating - STEELCASE INC.; *pg.* 475, *pg.* 889
ASANTE - Vitamin Water - NATIONAL BEVERAGE CORP.; *pg.* 257, *pg.* 425
THE ASBURY PARK PRESS - Daily/Sunday Newspaper & Direct Mail - ASBURY PARK PRESS INC.; *pg.* 1617, *pg.* 1090
ASC - Capacitors - AMERICAN SHIZUKI CORPORATION; *pg.* 616, *pg.* 1013
ASCARITE - Chemical Product - SPECTRUM CHEMICALS & LABORATORY PRODUCTS, INC.; *pg.* 1181, *pg.* 94
ASCEND - Chemical Products - AIR PRODUCTS AND CHEMICALS, INC.; *pg.* 1145, *pg.* 1513
ASCEND - Pharmaceutical Product - ALERE INC.; *pg.* 1488, *pg.* 849
ASCEND COLLECTION - Historic & Boutique Hotels - CHOICE HOTELS INTERNATIONAL, INC.; *pg.* 1086, *pg.* 775
ASCEND MULTIMMUNOASSAY - Pharmaceutical Product - ALERE INC.; *pg.* 1488, *pg.* 849
ASCENDER ELECTROL - Screen - DA-LITE SCREEN COMPANY; *pg.* 632, *pg.* 698
ASCENDOR - Footwear - K-SWISS; *pg.* 1837, *pg.* 306
ASCENSION - Outdoor Products - BLACK DIAMOND, INC.; *pg.* 1827, *pg.* 1756
ASCENT - Furniture - HAWORTH, INC.; *pg.* 402, *pg.* 891
ASCENT - Fabric - NEMSCHOFF, INC.; *pg.* 936, *pg.* 1890
ASCENT REVISION KNEE SYSTEM - Knee Product - ZIMMER BIOMET HOLDINGS, INC.; *pg.* 1611, *pg.* 699
ASCENTIALS - Sports Apparel - THE NORTH FACE, INC.; *pg.* 1840, *pg.* 252
ASCERI - Bathroom Faucet - MOEN INCORPORATED; *pg.* 1056, *pg.* 1468
ASCERTAIN - Software Solution - CARTESIAN; *pg.* 369, *pg.* 718
ASCO - Controls Rebuilding Services - FLIGHT SYSTEMS, INC.; *pg.* 1337, *pg.* 1548
ASCOM - Wireless Phone System - RAULAND-BORG CORPORATION; *pg.* 666, *pg.* 634
ASCOT - Cookie - A.V. OLSSON TRADING CO. INC.; *pg.* 838, *pg.* 372
ASCOT - Fabric - NEMSCHOFF, INC.; *pg.* 936, *pg.* 1890
ASCOT - Office Furniture - STEELCASE INC.; *pg.* 475, *pg.* 889
ASE - Avionics Support Equipment - BAE SYSTEMS-INFORMATION WARFARE; *pg.* 623, *pg.* 1036
ASENTINEL - Software - CA TECHNOLOGIES; *pg.* 366, *pg.* 1168
ASEPTIK - Valves - FLOWSERVE CORPORATION; *pg.* 82, *pg.* 1719
ASEPTROL - Release Agent - BASF CATALYSTS LLC; *pg.* 1148, *pg.* 1074
ASET-FSX - Metrology Product - KLA-TENCOR CORPORATION; *pg.* 1353, *pg.* 146
ASG - Custom Automated Equipment - TE CONNECTIVITY LTD.; *pg.* 677, *pg.* 1515
ASG-ADDERS - Software - ALLEN SYSTEMS GROUP, INC.; *pg.* 346, *pg.* 449
ASG-ADMIN - Software - ALLEN SYSTEMS GROUP, INC.; *pg.* 346, *pg.* 449
ASG-AUTOCHANGE - Software - ALLEN SYSTEMS GROUP, INC.; *pg.* 346, *pg.* 449
ASG-BATCH BRIDGE - Software - ALLEN SYSTEMS GROUP, INC.; *pg.* 346, *pg.* 449
ASG-BECUBIC - Software - ALLEN SYSTEMS GROUP, INC.; *pg.* 346, *pg.* 449

First page reference indicates Business Class Edition
Second page reference indicates Geographic Edition

ASG-BIP - Software - ALLEN SYSTEMS GROUP, INC.; pg. 346, pg. 449
ASG-BRIDGE - Software - ALLEN SYSTEMS GROUP, INC.; pg. 346, pg. 449
ASG-CATS - Software - ALLEN SYSTEMS GROUP, INC.; pg. 346, pg. 449
ASG-CORTEX-MS - Software - ALLEN SYSTEMS GROUP, INC.; pg. 346, pg. 449
ASG-CORTEX-OMS - Software - ALLEN SYSTEMS GROUP, INC.; pg. 346, pg. 449
ASG-CORTEX-PDB - Software - ALLEN SYSTEMS GROUP, INC.; pg. 346, pg. 449
ASG-CORTEX-PLAN - Software - ALLEN SYSTEMS GROUP, INC.; pg. 346, pg. 449
ASG-CORTEX-PREP - Software - ALLEN SYSTEMS GROUP, INC.; pg. 346, pg. 449
ASG-CORTEX-RE - Software - ALLEN SYSTEMS GROUP, INC.; pg. 346, pg. 449
ASG-CYPRESS - Software - ALLEN SYSTEMS GROUP, INC.; pg. 346, pg. 449
ASG-DBOL - Software - ALLEN SYSTEMS GROUP, INC.; pg. 346, pg. 449
ASG-DOC-AID - Software - ALLEN SYSTEMS GROUP, INC.; pg. 346, pg. 449
ASG-ECORA - Software - ALLEN SYSTEMS GROUP, INC.; pg. 346, pg. 449
ASG-ENCORE - Software - ALLEN SYSTEMS GROUP, INC.; pg. 346, pg. 449
ASG-ENTACT - Software - ALLEN SYSTEMS GROUP, INC.; pg. 346, pg. 449
ASG-ENTACT ID - Software - ALLEN SYSTEMS GROUP, INC.; pg. 346, pg. 449
ASG-ESTIMATE - Software - ALLEN SYSTEMS GROUP, INC.; pg. 346, pg. 449
ASG-FAST ACCESS - Software - ALLEN SYSTEMS GROUP, INC.; pg. 346, pg. 449
ASG-FOCAL POINT - Software - ALLEN SYSTEMS GROUP, INC.; pg. 346, pg. 449
ASG-IMPACT WEB - Software - ALLEN SYSTEMS GROUP, INC.; pg. 346, pg. 449
ASG-INSIGHT - Software - ALLEN SYSTEMS GROUP, INC.; pg. 346, pg. 449
ASG-INTELLITEST - Software - ALLEN SYSTEMS GROUP, INC.; pg. 346, pg. 449
ASG-JCLPREP - Software - ALLEN SYSTEMS GROUP, INC.; pg. 346, pg. 449
ASG-JOURNAL MANAGER - Software - ALLEN SYSTEMS GROUP, INC.; pg. 346, pg. 449
ASG-KEYPLUS - Software - ALLEN SYSTEMS GROUP, INC.; pg. 346, pg. 449
ASG-LIFE CYCLE MANAGER - Software - ALLEN SYSTEMS GROUP, INC.; pg. 346, pg. 449
ASG-MANAGER PRODUCT - Software - ALLEN SYSTEMS GROUP, INC.; pg. 346, pg. 449
ASG-MANAGERVIEW - Software - ALLEN SYSTEMS GROUP, INC.; pg. 346, pg. 449
ASG-MOBILECONTROL ADMINISTRATOR - Software - ALLEN SYSTEMS GROUP, INC.; pg. 346, pg. 449
ASG-MQENTERPRISE - Software - ALLEN SYSTEMS GROUP, INC.; pg. 346, pg. 449
ASG-NAVIGRAPH - Software - ALLEN SYSTEMS GROUP, INC.; pg. 346, pg. 449
ASG-NAVIPLEX - Software - ALLEN SYSTEMS GROUP, INC.; pg. 346, pg. 449
ASG-ODE - Software - ALLEN SYSTEMS GROUP, INC.; pg. 346, pg. 449
ASG-OPSCENTRAL - Software - ALLEN SYSTEMS GROUP, INC.; pg. 346, pg. 449
ASG-OUTBOUND ENTERPRISE - Software - ALLEN SYSTEMS GROUP, INC.; pg. 346, pg. 449
ASG-PATHPOINT - Software - ALLEN SYSTEMS GROUP, INC.; pg. 346, pg. 449
ASG-PREALERT - Software - ALLEN SYSTEMS GROUP, INC.; pg. 346, pg. 449
ASG-RADIANTONE - Software - ALLEN SYSTEMS GROUP, INC.; pg. 346, pg. 449
ASG-RECAP - Software - ALLEN SYSTEMS GROUP, INC.; pg. 346, pg. 449
ASG-REPLICATION SUITE - Software - ALLEN SYSTEMS GROUP, INC.; pg. 346, pg. 449
ASG-REPORT.WEB - Software - ALLEN SYSTEMS GROUP, INC.; pg. 346, pg. 449
ASG-ROCHADE - Software - ALLEN SYSTEMS GROUP, INC.; pg. 346, pg. 449
ASG-SAFARI - Software - ALLEN SYSTEMS GROUP, INC.; pg. 346, pg. 449
ASG-SAFARI.OLAP - Software - ALLEN SYSTEMS GROUP, INC.; pg. 346, pg. 449
ASG-SENTRY - Software - ALLEN SYSTEMS GROUP, INC.; pg. 346, pg. 449
ASG-SMARTDOT - Software - ALLEN SYSTEMS GROUP, INC.; pg. 346, pg. 449
ASG-SMARTEDIT - Software - ALLEN SYSTEMS GROUP, INC.; pg. 346, pg. 449
ASG-SMARTFILE - Software - ALLEN SYSTEMS GROUP, INC.; pg. 346, pg. 449
ASG-SMARTSCOPE - Software - ALLEN SYSTEMS GROUP, INC.; pg. 346, pg. 449
ASG-SMARTTEST - Software - ALLEN SYSTEMS GROUP, INC.; pg. 346, pg. 449
ASG-SMARTTUNE - Software - ALLEN SYSTEMS GROUP, INC.; pg. 346, pg. 449
ASG-SPACEFINDER - Software - ALLEN SYSTEMS GROUP, INC.; pg. 346, pg. 449
ASG-SYNC - Software - ALLEN SYSTEMS GROUP, INC.; pg. 346, pg. 449
ASG-TAPEFINDER - Software - ALLEN SYSTEMS GROUP, INC.; pg. 346, pg. 449
ASG-TEVISTA - Software - ALLEN SYSTEMS GROUP, INC.; pg. 346, pg. 449
ASG-TMON - Software - ALLEN SYSTEMS GROUP, INC.; pg. 346, pg. 449
ASG-TOTAL RECALL - Software - ALLEN SYSTEMS GROUP, INC.; pg. 346, pg. 449
ASG-TRACER - Software - ALLEN SYSTEMS GROUP, INC.; pg. 346, pg. 449
ASG-TRACKBIED - Software - ALLEN SYSTEMS GROUP, INC.; pg. 346, pg. 449
ASG-VALIDDATE - Software - ALLEN SYSTEMS GROUP, INC.; pg. 346, pg. 449
ASG-VIRTUAL DB - Software - ALLEN SYSTEMS GROUP, INC.; pg. 346, pg. 449
ASG-VISUAL PROCESS - Software - ALLEN SYSTEMS GROUP, INC.; pg. 346, pg. 449
ASG-WEB ENABLER - Software - ALLEN SYSTEMS GROUP, INC.; pg. 346, pg. 449
ASG-WEBDOCUMENTZ - Software - ALLEN SYSTEMS GROUP, INC.; pg. 346, pg. 449
ASG-WORKLOAD ANALYZER - Software - ALLEN SYSTEMS GROUP, INC.; pg. 346, pg. 449
ASG-WORKLOAD OPTIMIZATION SUITE - Software - ALLEN SYSTEMS GROUP, INC.; pg. 346, pg. 449
ASG-WORKLOAD PLANNER - Software - ALLEN SYSTEMS GROUP, INC.; pg. 346, pg. 449
ASG-WORKLOAD SCHEDULER - Software - ALLEN SYSTEMS GROUP, INC.; pg. 346, pg. 449
ASG-ZACK - Software - ALLEN SYSTEMS GROUP, INC.; pg. 346, pg. 449
ASG-ZARA - Software - ALLEN SYSTEMS GROUP, INC.; pg. 346, pg. 449
ASG-ZEBB - Software - ALLEN SYSTEMS GROUP, INC.; pg. 346, pg. 449
ASG-ZEKE - Software - ALLEN SYSTEMS GROUP, INC.; pg. 346, pg. 449
ASG-ZEKE AGENTS - Software - ALLEN SYSTEMS GROUP, INC.; pg. 346, pg. 449
ASG-ZENA - Software - ALLEN SYSTEMS GROUP, INC.; pg. 346, pg. 449
ASG-ZEUS - Software - ALLEN SYSTEMS GROUP, INC.; pg. 346, pg. 449
ASGROW - Seeds - MONSANTO COMPANY; pg. 1173, pg. 999
ASH - Footwear - PHOENIX FOOTWEAR GROUP, INC.; pg. 1815, pg. 60
ASHANTI - Surface Material - STEELCASE INC.; pg. 475, pg. 889
ASHAWAY - Squash Racket - ASHAWAY LINE & TWINE MFG. CO.; pg. 1826, pg. 1600
ASHAWAY MONOGUT - String - ASHAWAY LINE & TWINE MFG. CO.; pg. 1826, pg. 1600
ASHBEE - Table - BLATT BOWLING & BILLIARD CORP.; pg. 1827, pg. 1203
ASHBURY - Bathroom Fan - HUNTER FAN COMPANY; pg. 57, pg. 1631
ASHBY PONDS - Retirement Community - ERICKSON LIVING; pg. 1090, pg. 766
ASHEARDON.COM - Radio & Multimedia Service - BRS MEDIA INC.; pg. 1233, pg. 214
ASHEVILLE - Furniture - ASHLEY FURNITURE INDUSTRIES, INC.; pg. 914, pg. 1852
ASHFAIR - Furniture - ASHLEY FURNITURE INDUSTRIES, INC.; pg. 914, pg. 1852
ASHFORD.COM - Watch - DIAMOND.COM; pg. 1238, pg. 1954
ASHL (ADULT SAFE HOCKEY LEAGUE) - Recreational Ice Sport League - CANLAN ICE SPORTS CORPORATION; pg. 536, pg. 1907
ASHLAND - Chemicals - ASHLAND PERFORMANCE MATERIALS; pg. 1147, pg. 1448
ASHLAND - Footwear - EASTLAND SHOE CORPORATION; pg. 1808, pg. 750
ASHLAND - Kitchen Product - KOHLER CO.; pg. 91, pg. 1862
ASHLAND STAKES - Horse Race - KEENELAND ASSOCIATION INC.; pg. 1477, pg. 730
ASHLEE - Footwear - PHOENIX FOOTWEAR GROUP, INC.; pg. 1815, pg. 60
ASHLEY - Bath Accessory - CROSCILL, INC.; pg. 1122, pg. 1220
ASHLEY - Fabric - NEMSCHOFF, INC.; pg. 936, pg. 1890
ASHN - Recreational Hockey League - CANLAN ICE SPORTS CORPORATION; pg. 536, pg. 1907
ASHTON - Shoes - ALLEN-EDMONDS SHOE CORP.; pg. 1804, pg. 1887
ASHTON - Furniture - ASHLEY FURNITURE INDUSTRIES, INC.; pg. 914, pg. 1852
ASHTON - Bedcovering - ETHAN ALLEN INTERIORS INC.; pg. 924, pg. 343
ASHTON - Furniture - JOFCO INC.; pg. 931, pg. 691
ASHTON CLASSIC - Cigars - FINCK CIGAR CO.; pg. 1894, pg. 1740
ASHTON DRAKE - Collectors Plates - THE BRADFORD GROUP; pg. 1763, pg. 637
ASHVILLE - Furniture - HAWORTH, INC.; pg. 402, pg. 891
ASIA MARKETSCOPE - Market Analysis - STANDARD & POOR'S RATINGS SERVICES; pg. 805, pg. 1296
ASIAN GOLD - Bath Collection - CROSCILL, INC.; pg. 1122, pg. 1220
ASIAN RHYTHMS - Food Product - PHILLIPS FOODS INC.; pg. 1030, pg. 758
ASIAN SENSATIONS - Asian Food Products - THE SCHWAN FOOD COMPANY; pg. 894, pg. 928
ASIAN TAPESTRY - Wallcovering - YORK WALLCOVERINGS INC.; pg. 947, pg. 1598
THE ASIAN WALL STREET JOURNAL - Daily Business & Financial Publication Circulated in Asia - DOW JONES & COMPANY, INC.; pg. 1637, pg. 1225
ASIANWEEK - Publisher - ASIAN WEEK FOUNDATION; pg. 1617, pg. 212
ASIC-FRIENDLY - Network Product - VITESSE SEMICONDUCTOR CORPORATION; pg. 686, pg. 57
ASICPLAN - Software System - MENTOR GRAPHICS CORPORATION; pg. 432, pg. 1510
ASICS - Sporting Goods - ASICS AMERICA CORPORATION; pg. 1826, pg. 106
ASICS TIGER - Sporting Goods - ASICS AMERICA CORPORATION; pg. 1826, pg. 106
ASICVECTOR INTERFACES - Software System - MENTOR GRAPHICS CORPORATION; pg. 432, pg. 1510
ASIDE - Furniture - HERMAN MILLER, INC.; pg. 926, pg. 913
ASK - Digital Projector - INFOCUS CORPORATION; pg. 644, pg. 1503
ASK - Apparel - OAKLEY, INC.; pg. 1840, pg. 86
ASK-A-NURSE - Healthcare Information Service - MCKESSON CORPORATION; pg. 1560, pg. 222
ASK ACE - Hardware Retail Services - ACE HARDWARE CORPORATION; pg. 1040, pg. 644
ASK AMD - Technical Services - ADVANCED MICRO DEVICES, INC.; pg. 613, pg. 282
ASK DIANE - Medical Program - MENTOR CORPORATION; pg. 1565, pg. 263
ASK IT ALREADY - Online Trivia Game - NTN BUZZTIME, INC.; pg. 659, pg. 60
ASK JEEVES FOR KIDS - Children's Search Engine - IAC SEARCH & MEDIA, INC.; pg. 1257, pg. 171
ASK JEEVES UK - Search Engine - IAC SEARCH & MEDIA, INC.; pg. 1257, pg. 171
ASK KIDS - Online Services - IAC/INTERACTIVECORP; pg. 292, pg. 1242
ASK ME 3 - Printed Materials - PFIZER INC.; pg. 1581, pg. 1278
ASK SERVICE LISTING - Online Services - IAC/INTERACTIVECORP; pg. 292, pg. 1242
ASK THE EXPERTS - Online Webinar - QUALMARK

CORPORATION; *pg.* 1427, *pg.* 322
ASK US HOW - Slogan - LORD CORPORATION; *pg.* 1357, *pg.* 1360
ASK.COM - Search Engine - IAC/INTERACTIVECORP; *pg.* 292, *pg.* 1242
ASKERASER - Internet Privacy Tool - IAC SEARCH & MEDIA, INC.; *pg.* 1257, *pg.* 171
ASKEW - Fabric - NEMSCHOFF, INC.; *pg.* 936, *pg.* 1890
ASK.FM - Social Media Q&A Site - IAC SEARCH & MEDIA, INC.; *pg.* 1257, *pg.* 171
ASKPROXIMA - Mobile Projector - INFOCUS CORPORATION; *pg.* 644, *pg.* 1503
ASM - Software - F5 NETWORKS, INC.; *pg.* 396, *pg.* 1835
ASM - Fluid Handling System - GRACO, INC.; *pg.* 1342, *pg.* 935
ASM COMPANY INC. - Fluid Handling System - GRACO, INC.; *pg.* 1342, *pg.* 935
ASM NEWS - Member Newspaper - ASM INTERNATIONAL; *pg.* 132, *pg.* 1461
ASMA - Deep Water Imaging - ION GEOPHYSICAL CORPORATION; *pg.* 1350, *pg.* 1708
AS.MAX - Wireless Network Product - AIRSPAN NETWORKS INC.; *pg.* 346, *pg.* 410
ASMBL - Software - XILINX, INC.; *pg.* 496, *pg.* 252
ASMR - Radar System - RAYTHEON COMPANY; *pg.* 233, *pg.* 854
AS.NET - Wireless Network Product - AIRSPAN NETWORKS INC.; *pg.* 346, *pg.* 410
ASNIS III - Surgical & Medical Product - STRYKER CORPORATION; *pg.* 1598, *pg.* 894
ASOKA GARDEN - Bath Product - KOHLER CO.; *pg.* 91, *pg.* 1862
ASOS - Software Services - THE DOW CHEMICAL COMPANY; *pg.* 1157, *pg.* 898
ASP - Hydrous Kaolin Aluminum Silicate Pigments - BASF CATALYSTS LLC; *pg.* 1148, *pg.* 1074
ASPECT - Server - ADVANCED MICRO DEVICES, INC.; *pg.* 613, *pg.* 282
ASPECT - Software - ASPECT SOFTWARE, INC.; *pg.* 354, *pg.* 813
ASPECT - Motor Homes - WINNEBAGO INDUSTRIES, INC.; *pg.* 1712, *pg.* 707
ASPECTS - Carpet - BEAULIEU GROUP, LLC; *pg.* 917, *pg.* 529
ASPEKT - Waiting Seating - STEELCASE INC.; *pg.* 475, *pg.* 889
ASPEN - Furniture - BASSETT FURNITURE INDUSTRIES, INCORPORATED; *pg.* 916, *pg.* 1776
ASPEN - Paper Product - BOISE CASCADE HOLDINGS, L.L.C.; *pg.* 1453, *pg.* 546
ASPEN - Men's Fragrance - COTY, INC.; *pg.* 506, *pg.* 1219
ASPEN - Heat Exchangers - LYTRON INCORPORATED; *pg.* 1074, *pg.* 861
ASPEN - Eye Protection - MCR SAFETY; *pg.* 1422, *pg.* 1630
ASPEN - Software - SUMTOTAL SYSTEMS, INC.; *pg.* 477, *pg.* 429
ASPEN 1QMODEL POWERTOOLS - Logistics Software - ASPEN TECHNOLOGY, INC.; *pg.* 354, *pg.* 804
ASPEN ADSORPTION - Logistics Software - ASPEN TECHNOLOGY, INC.; *pg.* 354, *pg.* 804
ASPEN ADVISOR - Logistics Software - ASPEN TECHNOLOGY, INC.; *pg.* 354, *pg.* 804
ASPEN AEROTRAN - Logistics Software - ASPEN TECHNOLOGY, INC.; *pg.* 354, *pg.* 804
ASPEN AIR COOLED EXCHANGER - Software - ASPEN TECHNOLOGY, INC.; *pg.* 354, *pg.* 804
ASPEN APOLLO - Logistics Software - ASPEN TECHNOLOGY, INC.; *pg.* 354, *pg.* 804
ASPEN ASSETBUILDER - Logistics Software - ASPEN TECHNOLOGY, INC.; *pg.* 354, *pg.* 804
ASPEN ATOMS - Software - ASPEN TECHNOLOGY, INC.; *pg.* 354, *pg.* 804
ASPEN AUDIT COMPLIANCE MANAGER - Software - ASPEN TECHNOLOGY, INC.; *pg.* 354, *pg.* 804
ASPEN BASIC ENGINEERING - Software - ASPEN TECHNOLOGY, INC.; *pg.* 354, *pg.* 804
ASPEN BATCH DISTILLATION - Logistics Software - ASPEN TECHNOLOGY, INC.; *pg.* 354, *pg.* 804
ASPEN BATCH PROCESS DEVELOPER - Software - ASPEN TECHNOLOGY, INC.; *pg.* 354, *pg.* 804
ASPEN BATCH.21 - Software - ASPEN TECHNOLOGY, INC.; *pg.* 354, *pg.* 804
ASPEN BLEND - Logistics Software - ASPEN TECHNOLOGY, INC.; *pg.* 354, *pg.* 804
ASPEN BUSINESS PROCESS - Logistics Software - ASPEN TECHNOLOGY, INC.; *pg.* 354, *pg.* 804
ASPEN CALC - Logistics Software - ASPEN TECHNOLOGY, INC.; *pg.* 354, *pg.* 804
ASPEN CAPABLE-TO-PROMISE - Logistics Software - ASPEN TECHNOLOGY, INC.; *pg.* 354, *pg.* 804
ASPEN CAPITAL COST ESTIMATOR - Logistics Software - ASPEN TECHNOLOGY, INC.; *pg.* 354, *pg.* 804
ASPEN CATREF - Logistics Software - ASPEN TECHNOLOGY, INC.; *pg.* 354, *pg.* 804
ASPEN CHROMATOGRAPHY - Software - ASPEN TECHNOLOGY, INC.; *pg.* 354, *pg.* 804
ASPEN CIM-IO - Software - ASPEN TECHNOLOGY, INC.; *pg.* 354, *pg.* 804
ASPEN COLLABORATIVE DEMAND MANAGEMENT - Logistics Software - ASPEN TECHNOLOGY, INC.; *pg.* 354, *pg.* 804
ASPEN COLLABORATIVE FORECASTING - Logistics Software - ASPEN TECHNOLOGY, INC.; *pg.* 354, *pg.* 804
ASPEN COMPLIANCE.21 - Software - ASPEN TECHNOLOGY, INC.; *pg.* 354, *pg.* 804
ASPEN CUSTOM MODELER - Logistics Software - ASPEN TECHNOLOGY, INC.; *pg.* 354, *pg.* 804
ASPEN DECISION ANALYZER - Logistics Software - ASPEN TECHNOLOGY, INC.; *pg.* 354, *pg.* 804
ASPEN DISTIL - Software - ASPEN TECHNOLOGY, INC.; *pg.* 354, *pg.* 804
ASPEN DISTILLATION SYNTHESIS - Software - ASPEN TECHNOLOGY, INC.; *pg.* 354, *pg.* 804
ASPEN DYNAMICS - Logistics Software - ASPEN TECHNOLOGY, INC.; *pg.* 354, *pg.* 804
ASPEN EBRS - Logistics Software - ASPEN TECHNOLOGY, INC.; *pg.* 354, *pg.* 804
ASPEN ECONOMIC EVALUATION - Software - ASPEN TECHNOLOGY, INC.; *pg.* 354, *pg.* 804
ASPEN ENERGY ANALYZER - Software - ASPEN TECHNOLOGY, INC.; *pg.* 354, *pg.* 804
ASPEN ENTERPRISECONNECT - Logistics Software - ASPEN TECHNOLOGY, INC.; *pg.* 354, *pg.* 804
ASPEN EVENT.21 - Logistics Software - ASPEN TECHNOLOGY, INC.; *pg.* 354, *pg.* 804
ASPEN FCC - Logistics Software - ASPEN TECHNOLOGY, INC.; *pg.* 354, *pg.* 804
ASPEN FIRED HEATER - Simulator - ASPEN TECHNOLOGY, INC.; *pg.* 354, *pg.* 804
ASPEN FLARE SYSTEM ANALYZER - Software - ASPEN TECHNOLOGY, INC.; *pg.* 354, *pg.* 804
ASPEN FRAMEWORK - Logistics Software - ASPEN TECHNOLOGY, INC.; *pg.* 354, *pg.* 804
ASPEN GENEALOGY - Software - ASPEN TECHNOLOGY, INC.; *pg.* 354, *pg.* 804
ASPEN GOLD - Food Product - SHAMROCK FOODS COMPANY; *pg.* 895, *pg.* 20
ASPEN HETRAN - Software - ASPEN TECHNOLOGY, INC.; *pg.* 354, *pg.* 804
ASPEN HTFS RESEARCH NETWORK - Logistics Software - ASPEN TECHNOLOGY, INC.; *pg.* 354, *pg.* 804
ASPEN HTFS+ - Logistics Software - ASPEN TECHNOLOGY, INC.; *pg.* 354, *pg.* 804
ASPEN HYDROTREATER - Logistics Software - ASPEN TECHNOLOGY, INC.; *pg.* 354, *pg.* 804
ASPEN HYSYS AMINES - Software - ASPEN TECHNOLOGY, INC.; *pg.* 354, *pg.* 804
ASPEN HYSYS CRUDE - Software - ASPEN TECHNOLOGY, INC.; *pg.* 354, *pg.* 804
ASPEN HYSYS DYNAMICS - Software - ASPEN TECHNOLOGY, INC.; *pg.* 354, *pg.* 804
ASPEN HYSYS PIPELINE HYDRAULICS - Software - ASPEN TECHNOLOGY, INC.; *pg.* 354, *pg.* 804
ASPEN HYSYS PIPELINE HYDRAULICS-OLGAS 2-PHASE - Software - ASPEN TECHNOLOGY, INC.; *pg.* 354, *pg.* 804
ASPEN HYSYS UPSTREAM - Software - ASPEN TECHNOLOGY, INC.; *pg.* 354, *pg.* 804
ASPEN ICARUS - Logistics Software - ASPEN TECHNOLOGY, INC.; *pg.* 354, *pg.* 804
ASPEN ICARUS PROCESS EVALUATOR - Logistics Software - ASPEN TECHNOLOGY, INC.; *pg.* 354, *pg.* 804
ASPEN ICARUS PROJECT MANAGER - Logistics Software - ASPEN TECHNOLOGY, INC.; *pg.* 354, *pg.* 804
ASPEN IMAGING INTERNATIONAL - Printer Supplies - PUBCO CORPORATION; *pg.* 457, *pg.* 1434
ASPEN IN-PLANT COST ESTIMATOR - Software - ASPEN TECHNOLOGY, INC.; *pg.* 354, *pg.* 804
ASPEN INFOPLUS.21 - Software - ASPEN TECHNOLOGY, INC.; *pg.* 354, *pg.* 804
ASPEN INTEGRATION INFRASTRUCTURE - Software - ASPEN TECHNOLOGY, INC.; *pg.* 354, *pg.* 804
ASPEN INVENTORY PLANNER - Logistics Software - ASPEN TECHNOLOGY, INC.; *pg.* 354, *pg.* 804
ASPEN IQ - Logistics Software - ASPEN TECHNOLOGY, INC.; *pg.* 354, *pg.* 804
ASPEN MBO - Logistics Software - ASPEN TECHNOLOGY, INC.; *pg.* 354, *pg.* 804
ASPEN MEMORY - Memory Product - MICRON TECHNOLOGY, INC.; *pg.* 435, *pg.* 547
ASPEN MIMI - Logistics Software - ASPEN TECHNOLOGY, INC.; *pg.* 354, *pg.* 804
ASPEN MODEL RUNNER - Software - ASPEN TECHNOLOGY, INC.; *pg.* 354, *pg.* 804
ASPEN MULTIVARIATE - Logistics Software - ASPEN TECHNOLOGY, INC.; *pg.* 354, *pg.* 804
ASPEN MUSE - Software - ASPEN TECHNOLOGY, INC.; *pg.* 354, *pg.* 804
ASPEN ONLINE DEPLOYMENT - Online Service - ASPEN TECHNOLOGY, INC.; *pg.* 354, *pg.* 804
ASPEN OPERATIONS DOMAIN MODEL - Software - ASPEN TECHNOLOGY, INC.; *pg.* 354, *pg.* 804
ASPEN OPSKPI - Software - ASPEN TECHNOLOGY, INC.; *pg.* 354, *pg.* 804
ASPEN ORION - Logistics Software - ASPEN TECHNOLOGY, INC.; *pg.* 354, *pg.* 804
ASPEN ORION XT - Software - ASPEN TECHNOLOGY, INC.; *pg.* 354, *pg.* 804
ASPEN OTISS - Logistics Software - ASPEN TECHNOLOGY, INC.; *pg.* 354, *pg.* 804
ASPEN PERFORMANCE SCORECARD - Logistics Software - ASPEN TECHNOLOGY, INC.; *pg.* 354, *pg.* 804
ASPEN PETROVANTAGE - Logistics Software - ASPEN TECHNOLOGY, INC.; *pg.* 354, *pg.* 804
ASPEN PIMS - Logistics Software - ASPEN TECHNOLOGY, INC.; *pg.* 354, *pg.* 804
ASPEN PINCH - Logistics Software - ASPEN TECHNOLOGY, INC.; *pg.* 354, *pg.* 804
ASPEN PLANT SCHEDULER - Software - ASPEN TECHNOLOGY, INC.; *pg.* 354, *pg.* 804
ASPEN PLATE EXCHANGER - Software - ASPEN TECHNOLOGY, INC.; *pg.* 354, *pg.* 804
ASPEN PLATE FIN EXCHANGER - Software - ASPEN TECHNOLOGY, INC.; *pg.* 354, *pg.* 804
ASPEN PLUS - Logistics Software - ASPEN TECHNOLOGY, INC.; *pg.* 354, *pg.* 804
ASPEN PLUS DYNAMICS - Industry Standard Simulator - ASPEN TECHNOLOGY, INC.; *pg.* 354, *pg.* 804
ASPEN PLUS ONLINE - Software - ASPEN TECHNOLOGY, INC.; *pg.* 354, *pg.* 804
ASPEN POLYMERS - Software - ASPEN TECHNOLOGY, INC.; *pg.* 354, *pg.* 804
ASPEN PROCESS ECONOMIC ANALYZER - Software - ASPEN TECHNOLOGY, INC.; *pg.* 354, *pg.* 804
ASPEN PROCESS EXPLORER - Logistics Software - ASPEN TECHNOLOGY, INC.; *pg.* 354, *pg.* 804
ASPEN PROCESS MANUAL - Software - ASPEN TECHNOLOGY, INC.; *pg.* 354, *pg.* 804
ASPEN PROCESS RECIPE - Logistics Software - ASPEN TECHNOLOGY, INC.; *pg.* 354, *pg.* 804
ASPEN PROCESS TOOLS - Software - ASPEN TECHNOLOGY, INC.; *pg.* 354, *pg.* 804
ASPEN PROPERTIES - Logistics Software - ASPEN TECHNOLOGY, INC.; *pg.* 354, *pg.* 804
ASPEN Q SERVER - Performance Management Tool - ASPEN TECHNOLOGY, INC.; *pg.* 354, *pg.* 804
ASPEN RATE-BASED DISTILLATION - Distillation Model - ASPEN TECHNOLOGY, INC.; *pg.* 354, *pg.* 804
ASPEN REFSYS - Software - ASPEN TECHNOLOGY, INC.; *pg.* 354, *pg.* 804
ASPEN RETAIL - Management Solution - ASPEN TECHNOLOGY, INC.; *pg.* 354, *pg.* 804
ASPEN RICHARDSON - Logistics Software - ASPEN TECHNOLOGY, INC.; *pg.* 354, *pg.* 804
ASPEN ROLE-BASED VISUALIZATION - Operations Management - ASPEN TECHNOLOGY, INC.; *pg.* 354, *pg.* 804
ASPEN SHELL & TUBE MECHANICAL - Logistics Software - ASPEN TECHNOLOGY, INC.; *pg.* 354, *pg.* 804
ASPEN SHELL TUBE EXCHANGER - Software - ASPEN TECHNOLOGY, INC.; *pg.* 354, *pg.* 804
ASPEN SIMULATION WORKBOOK - Integrated Software Module - ASPEN TECHNOLOGY, INC.; *pg.* 354, *pg.* 804
ASPEN SMARTSEP ADVANCED - Software - ASPEN TECHNOLOGY, INC.; *pg.* 354, *pg.* 804
ASPEN SMARTSIM - Logistics Software - ASPEN

First page reference indicates Business Class Edition
Second page reference indicates Geographic Edition

TECHNOLOGY, INC.; *pg.* 354, *pg.* 804
ASPEN SMARTSTEP - Logistics Software - ASPEN TECHNOLOGY, INC.; *pg.* 354, *pg.* 804
ASPEN STRATEGIC ANALYZER - Logistics Software - ASPEN TECHNOLOGY, INC.; *pg.* 354, *pg.* 804
ASPEN SUPPLY PLANNER - Logistics Software - ASPEN TECHNOLOGY, INC.; *pg.* 354, *pg.* 804
ASPEN TRANSITION MANAGER - Logistics Software - ASPEN TECHNOLOGY, INC.; *pg.* 354, *pg.* 804
ASPEN UTILITIES OPERATIONS - Software - ASPEN TECHNOLOGY, INC.; *pg.* 354, *pg.* 804
ASPEN UTILITIES PLANNER - Logistics Software - ASPEN TECHNOLOGY, INC.; *pg.* 354, *pg.* 804
ASPEN VIRTUAL CLASSROOM SERVER - Software - SUMTOTAL SYSTEMS, INC.; *pg.* 477, *pg.* 429
ASPEN WATCH - Logistics Software - ASPEN TECHNOLOGY, INC.; *pg.* 354, *pg.* 804
ASPEN WATER - Logistics Software - ASPEN TECHNOLOGY, INC.; *pg.* 354, *pg.* 804
ASPEN WEB.21 - Logistics Software - ASPEN TECHNOLOGY, INC.; *pg.* 354, *pg.* 804
ASPEN WEBMODELS - Software - ASPEN TECHNOLOGY, INC.; *pg.* 354, *pg.* 804
ASPEN WINRACE DATABASE - Database - ASPEN TECHNOLOGY, INC.; *pg.* 354, *pg.* 804
ASPEN ZYGAD - Logistics Software - ASPEN TECHNOLOGY, INC.; *pg.* 354, *pg.* 804
ASPENONE - Software - ASPEN TECHNOLOGY, INC.; *pg.* 354, *pg.* 804
ASPENTECH - Software - ASPEN TECHNOLOGY, INC.; *pg.* 354, *pg.* 804
ASPERCREME - Health & Beauty Product - CHATTEM, INC.; *pg.* 1515, *pg.* 1628
ASPHALTUM - Asphalt Varnish - JONES-BLAIR COMPANY; *pg.* 1443, *pg.* 1682
ASPHERO-B - Lens - DANKER LABORATORIES INC.; *pg.* 1408, *pg.* 465
ASPHERO-F - Lens - DANKER LABORATORIES INC.; *pg.* 1408, *pg.* 465
ASPHERO-FB - Lens - DANKER LABORATORIES INC.; *pg.* 1408, *pg.* 465
ASPI COR - Aspirin - HEALTH PRODUCTS CORPORATION; *pg.* 1540, *pg.* 1356
ASPIRA - Line of Office Furniture - RUBBERMAID HOME PRODUCTS; *pg.* 1138, *pg.* 1453
ASPIRATOR - Arterial Blood Gas Sampler - VITAL SIGNS, INC.; *pg.* 1607, *pg.* 1126
ASPIRE - Medical Device - LEMAITRE VASCULAR, INC.; *pg.* 1555, *pg.* 805
ASPIRE - Software System - MENTOR GRAPHICS CORPORATION; *pg.* 432, *pg.* 1510
ASPIRE - Suitcase - SAMSONITE CORPORATION; *pg.* 11, *pg.* 830
ASPIRE - Cleaning Products - ZEP INC.; *pg.* 338, *pg.* 524
ASPIRE CLASSIC - Bank Card - ATLANTICUS CORPORATION; *pg.* 717, *pg.* 490
ASPIRE DIAMOND - Bank Card - ATLANTICUS CORPORATION; *pg.* 717, *pg.* 490
ASPIRE PLATINUM - Bank Card - ATLANTICUS CORPORATION; *pg.* 717, *pg.* 490
ASPIRE VISA - Bank Card - ATLANTICUS CORPORATION; *pg.* 717, *pg.* 490
ASPM - Power Modules - MICROSEMI CORPORATION; *pg.* 435, *pg.* 41
ASPR-LITE - Dairy Product - TROUW NUTRITION USA; *pg.* 1482, *pg.* 616
ASPUN - Resin - THE DOW CHEMICAL COMPANY; *pg.* 1157, *pg.* 898
ASQUARE - Folding Tool - C.H. HANSON COMPANY; *pg.* 1322, *pg.* 636
ASR - Automatic Scrap Recovery - PROCESS CONTROL CORPORATION; *pg.* 1370, *pg.* 518
ASRX - Thermal Processing Equipment - SURFACE COMBUSTION, INC.; *pg.* 1077, *pg.* 1462
ASSASSIN'S CREED - Video Game - UBISOFT INC.; *pg.* 589, *pg.* 229
ASSAULT - Nozzles - AKRON BRASS COMPANY; *pg.* 1311, *pg.* 1482
ASSAULT - Cleaning Product - HILLYARD, INC.; *pg.* 331, *pg.* 990
ASSENT CONSULTING - Staffing Services - CROSS COUNTRY HEALTHCARE, INC.; *pg.* 1520, *pg.* 411
ASSERT - Magnetic Coronary Guidewire - STEREOTAXIS, INC.; *pg.* 1597, *pg.* 1004
ASSESS2000 - Software System - MENTOR GRAPHICS CORPORATION; *pg.* 432, *pg.* 1510
ASSESS2LEARN - Online Testing Program - HOUGHTON MIFFLIN HARCOURT PUBLISHING COMPANY; *pg.* 1651, *pg.* 796
ASSESSMENT CONNECTION - Software - SCANTRON CORPORATION; *pg.* 467, *pg.* 922
ASSESSMENTMASTER - Educational Materials - RENAISSANCE LEARNING, INC.; *pg.* 607, *pg.* 1899
ASSESSOR - Software - INTELLICORP, INC.; *pg.* 417, *pg.* 268
ASSET - Provider of Course Placement Assistance - ACT INC.; *pg.* 597, *pg.* 708
ASSET FOCUS - Technical Support Service - MAXIMUS, INC.; *pg.* 780, *pg.* 1799
ASSET-LINK - Wireless Product - HEMISPHERE GPS INC.; *pg.* 642, *pg.* 1903
ASSET PRESERVER - Universal Life Policy - NEW YORK LIFE INSURANCE COMPANY; *pg.* 1211, *pg.* 1268
ASSET SURVEYOR - Software - TRIMBLE NAVIGATION LIMITED; *pg.* 1384, *pg.* 288
ASSETBUILDER - Software - ASPEN TECHNOLOGY, INC.; *pg.* 354, *pg.* 804
ASSETMANAGER - Software - AMX CORPORATION; *pg.* 349, *pg.* 1735
ASSETMAXX - Software Product - MAXIMUS, INC.; *pg.* 780, *pg.* 1799
ASSETPAD - Navigation Aid - TRIMBLE NAVIGATION LIMITED; *pg.* 1384, *pg.* 288
ASSETPRO - Surveillance Equipment - THE ADT CORPORATION; *pg.* 612, *pg.* 409
ASSIGNIT - Software - BIO-RAD LABORATORIES, INC.; *pg.* 1504, *pg.* 101
ASSIGNMENT AMERICA - Staffing Services - CROSS COUNTRY HEALTHCARE, INC.; *pg.* 1520, *pg.* 411
ASSISA - Office Furniture - STEELCASE INC.; *pg.* 475, *pg.* 889
THE ASSISTED LIVING PLUS - Home Health Care - PENN TREATY AMERICAN CORPORATION; *pg.* 793, *pg.* 1514
ASSISTED PAYROLL - Software - INTUIT INC.; *pg.* 769, *pg.* 158
ASSISTINA - Maintenance System - A-DEC, INC.; *pg.* 1483, *pg.* 1500
ASSOCIATED OVERNIGHT - Overnight Delivery Service - ASSOCIATED GLOBAL SYSTEMS, INC.; *pg.* 1899, *pg.* 1184
ASSOCIATED PUBLISHING CO. - Directory Publishing - THE HEARST CORPORATION; *pg.* 1649, *pg.* 1239
ASSOCIATED SAME DAY - Same-day Door-to-door Delivery Service - ASSOCIATED GLOBAL SYSTEMS, INC.; *pg.* 1899, *pg.* 1184
ASSOCIATED WHOLESALE GROCERS - Co-Operative Grocery Distributor - ASSOCIATED WHOLESALE GROCERS, INC.; *pg.* 1015, *pg.* 715
ASST - Manual - XEROX CORPORATION; *pg.* 494, *pg.* 365
ASSURA - Design Rule Checker - CADENCE DESIGN SYSTEMS, INC.; *pg.* 367, *pg.* 239
ASSURA - Car Seat - GRACO CHILDREN'S PRODUCTS INC.; *pg.* 954, *pg.* 1531
ASSURANCE - Tires - THE GOODYEAR TIRE & RUBBER COMPANY; *pg.* 1883, *pg.* 1401
ASSURANCE - Cleaning Product - HILLYARD, INC.; *pg.* 331, *pg.* 990
ASSURANCE COMFORTRED - Tires - THE GOODYEAR TIRE & RUBBER COMPANY; *pg.* 1883, *pg.* 1401
ASSURANCE TRIPLETRED - Tires - THE GOODYEAR TIRE & RUBBER COMPANY; *pg.* 1883, *pg.* 1401
ASSURE - Software - DIEBOLD, INCORPORATED; *pg.* 387, *pg.* 1407
ASSURE - Herbicide - E.I. DU PONT DE NEMOURS & COMPANY; *pg.* 1159, *pg.* 390
ASSURE - Kitchen Product - KOHLER CO.; *pg.* 91, *pg.* 1862
ASSURED - Pillow - SELECT COMFORT CORPORATION; *pg.* 942, *pg.* 942
ASSURED COMMUNICATIONS - Slogan - HARRIS CORPORATION; *pg.* 642, *pg.* 439
ASSUREDETHERNET - Software - TELLABS, INC.; *pg.* 678, *pg.* 637
ASSUREDSNAP - Storage System - DOT HILL SYSTEMS CORP.; *pg.* 388, *pg.* 333
AST - Scrap Recycling System - PROCESS CONTROL CORPORATION; *pg.* 1370, *pg.* 518
AST-100 - Viscometer - BROOKFIELD ENGINEERING LABORATORIES, INC.; *pg.* 1403, *pg.* 833
ASTAFACTOR - Nutritional Supplement - MERA PHARMACEUTICALS, INC.; *pg.* 1566, *pg.* 545
ASTAR - Model Helicopter - AIRBUS HELICOPTERS, INC.; *pg.* 223, *pg.* 1698
ASTEC - Asphalt Mixing Equipment - ASTEC INDUSTRIES, INC.; *pg.* 69, *pg.* 1628
ASTEX - Microwave Plasma Source - MKS INSTRUMENTS, INC.; *pg.* 1362, *pg.* 781
ASTHMA WALK - Educational Campaign - AMERICAN LUNG ASSOCIATION; *pg.* 129, *pg.* 395
ASTON - Ventilation Systems - NORTEK, INC.; *pg.* 100, *pg.* 1607
AS.TONE - Wireless Network Product - AIRSPAN NETWORKS INC.; *pg.* 346, *pg.* 410
ASTONISHING LENGTHS - Beauty Product - AVON PRODUCTS, INC.; *pg.* 500, *pg.* 1198
ASTOR - Decorative Accessory - ETHAN ALLEN INTERIORS INC.; *pg.* 924, *pg.* 343
ASTOR - Defense System - RAYTHEON COMPANY; *pg.* 233, *pg.* 854
ASTOR - Office Furniture - STEELCASE INC.; *pg.* 475, *pg.* 889
ASTOR PLACE - Table - BLATT BOWLING & BILLIARD CORP.; *pg.* 1827, *pg.* 1203
ASTORIA - Table - BLATT BOWLING & BILLIARD CORP.; *pg.* 1827, *pg.* 1203
ASTORIA - Lighting Product - QUOIZEL INC.; *pg.* 1304, *pg.* 1616
ASTORIA - Manual - XEROX CORPORATION; *pg.* 494, *pg.* 365
ASTR - Filtration Product - FLANDERS CORPORATION; *pg.* 1336, *pg.* 1392
ASTRA - Disposable Rubber Gloves - THE CLOROX COMPANY; *pg.* 327, *pg.* 169
ASTRAL - Power Supply System - ADVANCED ENERGY INDUSTRIES, INC.; *pg.* 613, *pg.* 328
ASTRAL - Jewelry - LAGOS INC.; *pg.* 8, *pg.* 1566
ASTRAL - Fabric - NEUTRAL POSTURE, INC.; *pg.* 939, *pg.* 1669
ASTRAMORPH - Pharmaceutical Drug - FRESENIUS KABI USA; *pg.* 1531, *pg.* 626
ASTRIA - Digital Video Processing - MOTOROLA SOLUTIONS, INC.; *pg.* 657, *pg.* 659
ASTRID - Flatware - ONEIDA LTD; *pg.* 1129, *pg.* 1318
ASTRINGYN - Astringents for Medical Uses - THE COOPER COMPANIES, INC.; *pg.* 1518, *pg.* 183
ASTRO - Pest Control Product - FMC CORPORATION; *pg.* 1163, *pg.* 1564
ASTRO - Gaming Product - GLD PRODUCTS, INC.; *pg.* 1835, *pg.* 1882
ASTRO - Popcorn Machine - GOLD MEDAL PRODUCTS CO.; *pg.* 55, *pg.* 1414
ASTRO - Binoculars - MEADE INSTRUMENTS CORPORATION; *pg.* 1422, *pg.* 113
ASTRO - Communications Product - MOTOROLA SOLUTIONS, INC.; *pg.* 657, *pg.* 659
ASTRO - Food Product - PARMALAT CANADA INC.; *pg.* 888, *pg.* 1941
ASTRO - Software - SYNOPSYS, INC.; *pg.* 480, *pg.* 162
ASTRO CELL - Protective Packaging Material - PACTIV CORPORATION; *pg.* 1466, *pg.* 624
ASTRO CLIMAPLUS - Ceiling System - CGC INC.; *pg.* 75, *pg.* 1925
ASTRO-FOAM - Cushion - PACTIV CORPORATION; *pg.* 1466, *pg.* 624
ASTRO-GRAPH - Digital Chart Recorders - ASTRO-MED, INC.; *pg.* 619, *pg.* 1609
ASTRO GUM 21 - Anionic Corn Starch - PENFORD CORPORATION; *pg.* 1177, *pg.* 314
ASTRO GUMS - Carboxymethylated Corn Starches - PENFORD CORPORATION; *pg.* 1177, *pg.* 314
ASTRO ORBITER - Amusement Ride - THE WALT DISNEY COMPANY; *pg.* 317, *pg.* 52
ASTRO PLASTICS - Extruded Plastic - REESE ENTERPRISES, INC.; *pg.* 1888, *pg.* 955
ASTRO PUNCH - Cold-Forming Header Tools - PRECISION CASTPARTS CORP.; *pg.* 105, *pg.* 1506
ASTRO-RAIL - Software - SYNOPSYS, INC.; *pg.* 480, *pg.* 162
ASTRO X - Cationic Potato Starch - PENFORD CORPORATION; *pg.* 1177, *pg.* 314
ASTRO-XTALK - Software - SYNOPSYS, INC.; *pg.* 480, *pg.* 162
ASTROBARRIER - Packaging - PACTIV CORPORATION; *pg.* 1466, *pg.* 624
ASTROBRIGHTS - Paper Product - WASAU PAPER CORP.; *pg.* 1471, *pg.* 1882

ASTROCOM NX1 - Network Tool - ECESSA CORPORATION; *pg.* 635, *pg.* 953
ASTROCOM SP-100 - Communication Service Components - ECESSA CORPORATION; *pg.* 635, *pg.* 953
ASTROCOM SP1000 - Communication Service Components - ECESSA CORPORATION; *pg.* 635, *pg.* 953
ASTROCOM T-1000 - Communication Service Components - ECESSA CORPORATION; *pg.* 635, *pg.* 953
ASTROCOTE 75 - Potato Starch - PENFORD CORPORATION; *pg.* 1177, *pg.* 314
ASTRODAQ - Data Acquisition System - ASTRO-MED, INC.; *pg.* 619, *pg.* 1609
ASTROFLEX - Automobile Electronics - DEI HOLDINGS, INC.; *pg.* 633, *pg.* 302
ASTROLINK - Satellite-Based Communications Services - LOCKHEED MARTIN CORPORATION; *pg.* 229, *pg.* 762
ASTROLITE - Lighting Product - HAYWARD POOL PRODUCTS; *pg.* 1049, *pg.* 1057
ASTROLITE - Graphic Art Paper - MONADNOCK PAPER MILLS, INC.; *pg.* 1464, *pg.* 1033
ASTROLITE PC - Paper - MONADNOCK PAPER MILLS, INC.; *pg.* 1464, *pg.* 1033
ASTRON - Reactive Gas Generators - MKS INSTRUMENTS, INC.; *pg.* 1362, *pg.* 781
ASTRONOMY - Magazine - KALMBACH PUBLISHING CO.; *pg.* 1656, *pg.* 1898
ASTRONOMY.COM - Web Site - KALMBACH PUBLISHING CO.; *pg.* 1656, *pg.* 1898
ASTROPAQUE - Paper Product - WASAU PAPER CORP.; *pg.* 1471, *pg.* 1882
ASTROPARCHE - Paper Product - WASAU PAPER CORP.; *pg.* 1471, *pg.* 1882
ASTROSPEC - Industrial Safety Eyewear - UVEX SAFETY; *pg.* 1433, *pg.* 1608
ASTROTECH SPACE OPERATIONS - Satellite Launch Processing Service - ASTROTECH CORPORATION; *pg.* 1400, *pg.* 1660
ASUR - Chemical Product - ALBEMARLE CORPORATION; *pg.* 1146, *pg.* 741
ASURECALL - Software - NETWOLVES CORPORATION; *pg.* 1271, *pg.* 474
ASURENET - Software - NETWOLVES CORPORATION; *pg.* 1271, *pg.* 474
ASUREROUTE - Software - NETWOLVES CORPORATION; *pg.* 1271, *pg.* 474
ASX FEATURE SERVER - Server - SONUS NETWORKS INC.; *pg.* 1281, *pg.* 858
ASYMMETRIA - Lamp - DAZOR MANUFACTURING CORP.; *pg.* 1296, *pg.* 995
ASYMTEK - Dispensing System - NORDSON CORPORATION; *pg.* 1365, *pg.* 1480
AT-100 - Leakage Tester - HD ELECTRIC COMPANY; *pg.* 1299, *pg.* 666
AT-200 - Electronic Components - MOLEX INCORPORATED; *pg.* 655, *pg.* 628
AT-2000 - Helicopter Transportable Drilling Rigs - PARKER DRILLING COMPANY; *pg.* 982, *pg.* 1712
AT-A-GLANCE - Office Product - WESTROCK COMPANY; *pg.* 1472, *pg.* 1805
AT&T 1-800-YELLOWPAGES - Directory Assistance - AT&T INC.; *pg.* 1867, *pg.* 1674
AT&T CONNECTECH - High Speed Internet - AT&T INC.; *pg.* 1867, *pg.* 1674
AT&T FAST ACCESS - High Speed Internet - AT&T INC.; *pg.* 1867, *pg.* 1674
AT&T U-VERSE - Internet Protocol Based Television Services - AT&T INC.; *pg.* 1867, *pg.* 1674
AT&T UNIVERSAL SAVINGS & REWARDS CARD - Cash Card - CITIGROUP INC.; *pg.* 735, *pg.* 1212
AT&T UNIVERSAL SAVINGS PLATINUM CARD - Cash Card - CITIGROUP INC.; *pg.* 735, *pg.* 1212
AT EASE - Lounge Set - HABAND COMPANY, INC.; *pg.* 1772, *pg.* 1099
AT FEEL - Glove - ETONIC WORLDWIDE LLC; *pg.* 1808, *pg.* 857
A.T. FERRELL - Hammermill - A.T. FERRELL COMPANY, INC.; *pg.* 701, *pg.* 674
AT HOME IN ARKANSAS - Magazine - NETWORK COMMUNICATIONS INC.; *pg.* 1271, *pg.* 534
AT LAST - Shoe - AEROGROUP INTERNATIONAL, INC.; *pg.* 1803, *pg.* 1055
AT LAST - Herbal Products - AT LAST NATURALS, INC.; *pg.* 499, *pg.* 1347
AT-MRAM - Semiconductor Device - NVE CORPORATION; *pg.* 447, *pg.* 923
AT PLAY - Dog Toy - THE HARTZ MOUNTAIN CORP.; *pg.* 1476, *pg.* 1120
@RADIO.AM - Radio & Multimedia Service - BRS MEDIA INC.; *pg.* 1233, *pg.* 214
@RADIO.FM - Radio & Multimedia Service - BRS MEDIA INC.; *pg.* 1233, *pg.* 214
AT THE CORE OF THE USER EXPERIENCE - Slogan - IMAGINATION TECHNOLOGIES; *pg.* 412, *pg.* 285
AT THE CORNER OF HAPPY AND HEALTHY - Tagline - WALGREEN CO.; *pg.* 1608, *pg.* 605
AT THE FOREFRONT OF NEW CANCER THERAPIES - Tagline - ALLOS THERAPEUTICS, INC.; *pg.* 1492, *pg.* 336
AT THE HEART OF HEALTH - Slogan - EXPRESS SCRIPTS; *pg.* 1530, *pg.* 1070
AT THE HEART OF SAVING LIVES - Tagline - CARDIAC SCIENCE CORPORATION; *pg.* 1512, *pg.* 1897
AT THE HEART OF WHAT DRIVES YOUR WORLD - Slogan - REGAL BELOIT CORPORATION; *pg.* 106, *pg.* 1854
@UTO REVENUE - Advertising Publication - DOMINION ENTERPRISES; *pg.* 1636, *pg.* 1796
@VENTURE - Web Portal - THE HARTFORD FINANCIAL SERVICES GROUP, INC.; *pg.* 1202, *pg.* 352
@XI - Workstation - @XI COMPUTER CORPORATION; *pg.* 355, *pg.* 199
AT500 - Preventative Pacing System - MEDTRONIC, INC.; *pg.* 1564, *pg.* 939
ATA 990 - Skate - ROLLER DERBY SKATE CORP.; *pg.* 966, *pg.* 630
ATA PC CARD - Storage System - HGST; *pg.* 406, *pg.* 260
ATAC - Clothing - LAKELAND INDUSTRIES, INC.; *pg.* 1354, *pg.* 1338
ATACMS - Guided Missiles - LOCKHEED MARTIN CORPORATION; *pg.* 229, *pg.* 762
ATACT - Software System - ALION SCIENCE AND TECHNOLOGY CORPORATION; *pg.* 615, *pg.* 1788
ATALANTA - Packaged Foods - ATALANTA CORPORATION; *pg.* 838, *pg.* 1057
ATARAX - Medicine - PFIZER INC.; *pg.* 1581, *pg.* 1278
ATASOL - Pharmaceutical Product - CHURCH & DWIGHT CANADA CORP.; *pg.* 503, *pg.* 1925
ATC - Professional Training Providers - AUTODESK INC.; *pg.* 356, *pg.* 257
ATC - Outdoor Products - BLACK DIAMOND, INC.; *pg.* 1827, *pg.* 1756
ATC - Applied Technology Center - MILWAUKEE SCHOOL OF ENGINEERING; *pg.* 605, *pg.* 1878
ATD ACTUATOR - Automatic Door Opener - DYNATECT MANUFACTURING INC.; *pg.* 1330, *pg.* 1883
ATDAQ - Data Acquisition System - CYBERRESEARCH INC.; *pg.* 381, *pg.* 339
ATDONLINE - Online Ordering Service - AMERICAN TIRE DISTRIBUTORS HOLDINGS, INC.; *pg.* 199, *pg.* 1379
ATDSERVICEBAY - Warranty & Other Benefit Services - AMERICAN TIRE DISTRIBUTORS HOLDINGS, INC.; *pg.* 199, *pg.* 1379
ATEC - Breast Biopsy - HOLOGIC, INC.; *pg.* 1416, *pg.* 784
ATELIER - Fabric - NEMSCHOFF, INC.; *pg.* 936, *pg.* 1890
ATFS - Fighting System - ENVIRONMENTAL TECTONICS CORPORATION; *pg.* 1411, *pg.* 1587
ATFS-400 - Fighting System - ENVIRONMENTAL TECTONICS CORPORATION; *pg.* 1411, *pg.* 1587
ATGAM - Medicine - PFIZER INC.; *pg.* 1581, *pg.* 1278
ATHALIE - Lamp - ASHLEY FURNITURE INDUSTRIES, INC.; *pg.* 914, *pg.* 1852
ATHENA - Vanity Lights - CRAFTMADE INTERNATIONAL, INC.; *pg.* 1295, *pg.* 1670
ATHENA - Software - LAM RESEARCH CORPORATION; *pg.* 1354, *pg.* 246
ATHENA - Space Launch Vehicles - LOCKHEED MARTIN CORPORATION; *pg.* 229, *pg.* 762
ATHENA - Shot Gun - WEATHERBY, INC.; *pg.* 1848, *pg.* 181
ATHENA CHANDELIER - Lamp - J. ROBERT SCOTT INC.; *pg.* 930, *pg.* 105
ATHENA KNOWLEDGE BASE - Software Modules - LAM RESEARCH CORPORATION; *pg.* 1354, *pg.* 246
ATHENA REMOTE - Software Modules - LAM RESEARCH CORPORATION; *pg.* 1354, *pg.* 246
ATHENA V - O/U Shotgun - WEATHERBY, INC.; *pg.* 1848, *pg.* 181
ATHENA WALL SCONCES - Lamp - J. ROBERT SCOTT INC.; *pg.* 930, *pg.* 105
ATHENACLINICALS - Medical Records Management - ATHENAHEALTH, INC.; *pg.* 1497, *pg.* 855
ATHENACOLLECTOR - Medical Records Management - ATHENAHEALTH, INC.; *pg.* 1497, *pg.* 855
ATHENACOMMUNICATOR - Communication Device - ATHENAHEALTH, INC.; *pg.* 1497, *pg.* 855
ATHENAEUM - Fabric - NEMSCHOFF, INC.; *pg.* 936, *pg.* 1890
ATHENANET - Webbased Software - ATHENAHEALTH, INC.; *pg.* 1497, *pg.* 855
ATHENEUM BOOKS FOR YOUNG READERS - Children's Books - SIMON & SCHUSTER, INC.; *pg.* 1687, *pg.* 1292
ATHENIAN - Footwear - CAPEZIO BALLET MAKERS INC.; *pg.* 1805, *pg.* 1125
ATHENOS - Greek Flatbread - THE KRAFT HEINZ COMPANY; *pg.* 870, *pg.* 1577
ATHENS - Sandals - AEROGROUP INTERNATIONAL, INC.; *pg.* 1803, *pg.* 1055
ATHENS - Furniture - JASPER GROUP; *pg.* 930, *pg.* 691
ATHENS - Fabric - NEMSCHOFF, INC.; *pg.* 936, *pg.* 1890
ATHERTON - Guest Chairs - BERNHARDT DESIGN; *pg.* 918, *pg.* 1381
ATHLETA - Retail Clothing Store - THE GAP, INC.; *pg.* 1770, *pg.* 218
ATHLETIC - Footwear - NIKE, INC.; *pg.* 1812, *pg.* 1492
ATHLETIC BABY - Toy - THE OHIO ART COMPANY, INC.; *pg.* 965, *pg.* 1406
THE ATHLETIC CONNECTION - Sporting Goods - SPORT SUPPLY GROUP, INC.; *pg.* 1846, *pg.* 1687
ATHLETIC WORKS - Clothes & Equipment - WAL-MART STORES, INC.; *pg.* 1790, *pg.* 29
ATHLITE - Watches - REEBOK INTERNATIONAL LTD.; *pg.* 1817, *pg.* 811
ATHLON - Cluster - MICROWAY, INC.; *pg.* 1267, *pg.* 841
ATHOS - Software - SCHLUMBERGER LIMITED; *pg.* 801, *pg.* 1714
ATI - Chipset - ADVANCED MICRO DEVICES, INC.; *pg.* 613, *pg.* 282
ATI - Tools & Equipment for Aerospace & Industrial Applications - SNAP-ON INCORPORATED; *pg.* 1062, *pg.* 1862
ATI - Manufacturer of Heat Sinks - WAKEFIELD-VETTE; *pg.* 119, *pg.* 1038
ATI & DESIGN - Graphics Software - ADVANCED MICRO DEVICES, INC.; *pg.* 613, *pg.* 282
ATI AVIVO - Video Converter - ADVANCED MICRO DEVICES, INC.; *pg.* 613, *pg.* 282
ATI CATALYST - Software Driver - ADVANCED MICRO DEVICES, INC.; *pg.* 613, *pg.* 282
ATI FIREMV - Graphics Card - ADVANCED MICRO DEVICES, INC.; *pg.* 613, *pg.* 282
ATI FIREPRO - Graphics Card - ADVANCED MICRO DEVICES, INC.; *pg.* 613, *pg.* 282
ATI HYPERMEMORY - Chipset - ADVANCED MICRO DEVICES, INC.; *pg.* 613, *pg.* 282
ATI MOBILITY RADEON - Graphics Card - ADVANCED MICRO DEVICES, INC.; *pg.* 613, *pg.* 282
ATI MULTIMEDIA CENTER - Multimedia Processor - ADVANCED MICRO DEVICES, INC.; *pg.* 613, *pg.* 282
ATI RADEON - Graphics Card - ADVANCED MICRO DEVICES, INC.; *pg.* 613, *pg.* 282
ATI TV WONDER - Graphics Card - ADVANCED MICRO DEVICES, INC.; *pg.* 613, *pg.* 282
ATIVAN - Pharmaceutical Product - VALEANT PHARMACEUTICALS INTERNATIONAL, INC.; *pg.* 1605, *pg.* 1957
ATJ - Space Solar Cell - EMCORE CORPORATION; *pg.* 636, *pg.* 39
ATJM - Space Solar Cell - EMCORE CORPORATION; *pg.* 636, *pg.* 39
ATL-140 - Zipper - ZIP-PAK; *pg.* 1473, *pg.* 631
ATLANTA APPAREL MART - Men's, Women's & Children's Fashions - AMC, INC.; *pg.* 1759, *pg.* 487
ATLANTA DECORATIVE ARTS CENTER - Residential & Contract Design - AMC, INC.; *pg.* 1759, *pg.* 487
ATLANTA FASHION PREVIEW - Apparel & Fashion Publication - AMC, INC.; *pg.* 1759, *pg.* 487
ATLANTA HOME IMPROVEMENT - Magazine - NETWORK COMMUNICATIONS INC.; *pg.* 1271, *pg.* 534
ATLANTA HOMES & LIFESTYLES - Magazine - NETWORK COMMUNICATIONS INC.; *pg.* 1271, *pg.* 534
ATLANTA MARKET DIRECTORY - Industry-Secific Directories - AMC, INC.; *pg.* 1759, *pg.* 487
ATLANTA MARKET PREVIEW - Gifts Periodical & Home Furnishings Periodical - AMC, INC.; *pg.* 1759, *pg.* 487
ATLANTA MERCHANDISE MART - Residential, Commercial & Contract Furnishings - AMC, INC.; *pg.* 1759, *pg.* 487

First page reference indicates Business Class Edition
Second page reference indicates Geographic Edition

ATLANTA MOTOR SPEEDWAY - Entertainment Venue - SPEEDWAY MOTORSPORTS, INC.; *pg.* 584, *pg.* 1370
ATLANTIC - Record Label - WARNER MUSIC GROUP CORP.; *pg.* 590, *pg.* 1313
ATLANTIC AMBER - Beer - NEW ENGLAND BREWING COMPANY; *pg.* 1967, *pg.* 386
ATLANTIC COAST IN-HOUSE - In-House Publication - MASSACHUSETTS LAWYERS WEEKLY, INC.; *pg.* 1662, *pg.* 798
ATLANTIC FISH - Restaurants - TAVISTOCK RESTAURANT GROUP; *pg.* 1753, *pg.* 803
ATLANTIC FLUIDICS - Pump - TUTHILL CORPORATION; *pg.* 1385, *pg.* 561
THE ATLANTIC MONTHLY MAGAZINE - Magazine - THE ATLANTIC MONTHLY GROUP; *pg.* 1618, *pg.* 396
ATLANTIC OCEAN - Frozen Seafood Product - F.W. BRYCE, INC.; *pg.* 857, *pg.* 823
ATLANTIC OLEFIN - Plastic & Rubber - TEKNOR APEX COMPANY; *pg.* 1889, *pg.* 1605
ATLANTIC TRUST - Investment Management Products & Services - INVESCO LTD.; *pg.* 771, *pg.* 513
ATLANTICA - Glass Product - PPG INDUSTRIES, INC.; *pg.* 1445, *pg.* 1579
ATLANTICVILLE - Newspaper - GREATER MEDIA NEWSPAPERS, INC.; *pg.* 1646, *pg.* 1071
ATLANTIS - SR Pro Coronary Imaging Catheter - BOSTON SCIENTIFIC CORPORATION; *pg.* 1508, *pg.* 831
ATLANTIS - Dinnerware - THE HOMER LAUGHLIN CHINA COMPANY; *pg.* 1125, *pg.* 1850
ATLANTIS - Casino Resort - MONARCH CASINO & RESORT, INC.; *pg.* 564, *pg.* 1031
ATLANTIS - Protective Eyewear - SELLSTROM MANUFACTURING CO.; *pg.* 1428, *pg.* 659
ATLANTIS - Analytical Column - WATERS CORPORATION; *pg.* 1436, *pg.* 834
ATLAS - Network Integrated Access - ADTRAN, INC.; *pg.* 344, *pg.* 6
ATLAS - Fatliquor & Chemical Auxiliary - ATLAS REFINERY, INC.; *pg.* 1148, *pg.* 1095
ATLAS - Fitness & Body Building - CHARLES ATLAS, LTD.; *pg.* 538, *pg.* 1211
ATLAS - Orthopedic Product - DJO INCORPORATED; *pg.* 1524, *pg.* 302
ATLAS - Hose - HBD INDUSTRIES, INC.; *pg.* 207, *pg.* 1449
ATLAS - Chemicals - HUNTSMAN CORPORATION; *pg.* 1167, *pg.* 1758
ATLAS - Development Board - IMAGINATION TECHNOLOGIES; *pg.* 412, *pg.* 285
ATLAS - Display Mounting Bezel - INDUSTRIAL ELECTRONIC ENGINEERS, INC.; *pg.* 644, *pg.* 300
ATLAS - Medical Device - INTEGRA LIFESCIENCES HOLDINGS CORPORATION; *pg.* 1545, *pg.* 1109
ATLAS - Medical Equipment - INVACARE CORPORATION; *pg.* 1546, *pg.* 1451
ATLAS - Bonding Tool - KULICKE & SOFFA INDUSTRIES, INC.; *pg.* 650, *pg.* 1533
ATLAS - Furniture - LA-Z-BOY INCORPORATED; *pg.* 932, *pg.* 901
ATLAS - Basketball Standards - LIFETIME PRODUCTS INC.; *pg.* 933, *pg.* 1751
ATLAS - Space Launch Vehicles - LOCKHEED MARTIN CORPORATION; *pg.* 229, *pg.* 762
ATLAS - Fabric - NEMSCHOFF, INC.; *pg.* 936, *pg.* 1890
ATLAS - Fastener Product - PENN ENGINEERING & MANUFACTURING CORP.; *pg.* 1059, *pg.* 1525
ATLAS - Footwear - P.W. MINOR & SON, INC.; *pg.* 1816, *pg.* 1140
ATLAS - Polyurethane Foam - SPAN-AMERICA MEDICAL SYSTEMS, INC.; *pg.* 1595, *pg.* 1618
ATLAS - ICD Products - ST. JUDE MEDICAL, INC.; *pg.* 1596, *pg.* 963
ATLAS - Restaurants - TAVISTOCK RESTAURANT GROUP; *pg.* 1753, *pg.* 803
ATLAS - Crane & Excavator - TEREX CORPORATION; *pg.* 1381, *pg.* 384
ATLAS - Gravity Feed Oiler - TRICO MFG. CORP.; *pg.* 219, *pg.* 1886
ATLAS - Wireless Control Product - UNIVERSAL ELECTRONICS, INC.; *pg.* 683, *pg.* 262
ATLAS - Telecommunication Product - VERISIGN, INC.; *pg.* 488, *pg.* 1799
ATLAS - Monitor - WELCH ALLYN INC.; *pg.* 1436, *pg.* 1342
ATLAS 2 - Display Mounting Bezel - INDUSTRIAL ELECTRONIC ENGINEERS, INC.; *pg.* 644, *pg.* 300
ATLAS A - Space Launch Vehicles - LOCKHEED MARTIN CORPORATION; *pg.* 229, *pg.* 762
ATLAS ACCOUNT - Financial Purchase Program - MONEX DEPOSIT COMPANY; *pg.* 10, *pg.* 165
ATLAS-AGO-INFRA - Chemicals - HUNTSMAN CORPORATION; *pg.* 1167, *pg.* 1758
ATLAS-AGO-RAPID - Chemicals - HUNTSMAN CORPORATION; *pg.* 1167, *pg.* 1758
ATLAS BASKETBALL EQUIPMENT - Basketball Backboards - LIFETIME PRODUCTS INC.; *pg.* 933, *pg.* 1751
ATLAS BORE PLANNER - Construction Equipment - VERMEER MANUFACTURING COMPANY; *pg.* 708, *pg.* 711
ATLAS G - Chemical Product - SPECTRUM CHEMICALS & LABORATORY PRODUCTS, INC.; *pg.* 1181, *pg.* 94
ATLAS GIS - Software - ENVIRONMENTAL SYSTEMS RESEARCH INSTITUTE INC.; *pg.* 393, *pg.* 188
ATLAS GLASSMASTER - Building Product - BLUELINX HOLDINGS, INC.; *pg.* 70, *pg.* 491
ATLAS II - ICD Product - ST. JUDE MEDICAL, INC.; *pg.* 1596, *pg.* 963
ATLAS-II - Control Platform - WOODWARD, INC.; *pg.* 122, *pg.* 329
ATLAS III - Systems Integration & Aeronautics - LOCKHEED MARTIN CORPORATION; *pg.* 229, *pg.* 762
ATLAS LEATHER OIL - Fatliquor & Chemical Auxiliary - ATLAS REFINERY, INC.; *pg.* 1148, *pg.* 1095
ATLAS OCAP - Remote Control Device - UNIVERSAL ELECTRONICS, INC.; *pg.* 683, *pg.* 262
ATLAS PINNACLE - Building Product - BLUELINX HOLDINGS, INC.; *pg.* 70, *pg.* 491
ATLAS/SOUNDOLIER - Communication Products - ATLAS SOUND; *pg.* 621, *pg.* 1692
ATLAS STRATFORD - Building Product - BLUELINX HOLDINGS, INC.; *pg.* 70, *pg.* 491
ATLAS TRANSMISSION - Automotive Repair Service - MORAN INDUSTRIES, INC.; *pg.* 213, *pg.* 632
ATLAS V - Rockets - LOCKHEED MARTIN CORPORATION; *pg.* 229, *pg.* 762
ATLAS VAC - Tray Sealer - PLANET PRODUCTS CORPORATION; *pg.* 1369, *pg.* 1418
ATLAS VAN LINES - Moving Services - ATLAS VAN LINES, INC.; *pg.* 1900, *pg.* 678
ATLAS WHITE - White Titanium - SENSIENT COLORS INC.; *pg.* 1180, *pg.* 1003
ATLASENE - Fatliquor & Chemical Auxiliary - ATLAS REFINERY, INC.; *pg.* 1148, *pg.* 1095
ATLASOL - Fatliquor & Chemical Auxiliary - ATLAS REFINERY, INC.; *pg.* 1148, *pg.* 1095
ATLASPC - Software Product - WOODWARD, INC.; *pg.* 122, *pg.* 329
ATLASSC - Control System - WOODWARD, INC.; *pg.* 122, *pg.* 329
ATLASTAN - Fatliquor & Chemical Auxiliary - ATLAS REFINERY, INC.; *pg.* 1148, *pg.* 1095
ATLASWARE - Software - ENVIRONMENTAL SYSTEMS RESEARCH INSTITUTE INC.; *pg.* 393, *pg.* 188
ATLER - Fire Counter Shutter - WAYNE-DALTON CORP.; *pg.* 120, *pg.* 1465
ATLV - Vacuum Type Trash Collectors - TENNANT COMPANY; *pg.* 1381, *pg.* 944
ATLYS - Billing Service - CONVERGYS CORPORATION; *pg.* 379, *pg.* 1412
ATM - Reflective Marking Tape - MYERS INDUSTRIES, INC.; *pg.* 1887, *pg.* 1402
ATM MOWERS - All Terrain Mowers - HARPER INDUSTRIES, INC.; *pg.* 704, *pg.* 715
ATMI - Semiconductor Process Technology - ATMI, INC.; *pg.* 1314, *pg.* 342
ATMOPLAS - Engine Parts - DANA HOLDING CORPORATION; *pg.* 203, *pg.* 1461
ATMOS - Software - EMC CORPORATION; *pg.* 391, *pg.* 825
ATMOSAIR - Mattress - KINETIC CONCEPTS, INC.; *pg.* 1553, *pg.* 1741
ATMOSPHERE - Fabric - NEMSCHOFF, INC.; *pg.* 936, *pg.* 1890
ATMOSPHERE GAS - Thermal Processing Equipment - SURFACE COMBUSTION, INC.; *pg.* 1077, *pg.* 1462
ATMOSPHERIC - Tires - AMERITYRE CORPORATION; *pg.* 1879, *pg.* 1021
ATMOTROL - Thermal Processing Equipment - SURFACE COMBUSTION, INC.; *pg.* 1077, *pg.* 1462
ATO - Standard Blade Type Fuse - LITTELFUSE, INC.; *pg.* 1301, *pg.* 580
ATOGA - Cable - ARRIS GROUP, INC.; *pg.* 353, *pg.* 541
ATOMAC - Valve - FLOWSERVE CORPORATION; *pg.* 82, *pg.* 1719
ATOMIC BEE - Gaming Product - GLD PRODUCTS, INC.; *pg.* 1835, *pg.* 1882
ATOMIC FIREBALL LOLLIPOPS - Suckers - SPANGLER CANDY COMPANY; *pg.* 1862, *pg.* 1407
ATOMIC FIREBALLS - Candy - FERRARA CANDY CO.; *pg.* 1852, *pg.* 612
ATOMIC OIL - Motorsports Entertainment - SPEEDWAY MOTORSPORTS, INC.; *pg.* 584, *pg.* 1370
ATOS - Educational Materials - RENAISSANCE LEARNING, INC.; *pg.* 607, *pg.* 1899
ATP - Adhesive - SPINNAKER COATING, LLC; *pg.* 1470, *pg.* 1477
ATP-201 - Electronic Components - MOLEX INCORPORATED; *pg.* 655, *pg.* 628
ATP/CASEMATE - Endothermic Gas Generator Microprocessor Controller - SURFACE COMBUSTION, INC.; *pg.* 1077, *pg.* 1462
ATPLITE - Luminescence Assay System - PERKINELMER, INC.; *pg.* 1426, *pg.* 853
ATR - Footwear - REEBOK INTERNATIONAL LTD.; *pg.* 1817, *pg.* 811
ATRA - Pivoting Head Razors & Blades - THE GILLETTE COMPANY; *pg.* 509, *pg.* 795
ATRA PLUS - Pivoting Head Razor & Blades - THE GILLETTE COMPANY; *pg.* 509, *pg.* 795
ATRAX - Carbide - KENNAMETAL IPG; *pg.* 1353, *pg.* 1615
ATRIA - Electrocardiography Product - CARDIAC SCIENCE CORPORATION; *pg.* 1512, *pg.* 1897
ATRIA BOOKS - Adult Publishing Imprint - SIMON & SCHUSTER, INC.; *pg.* 1687, *pg.* 1292
ATRIMMEC - Turf Product - PBI/GORDON CORPORATION; *pg.* 1176, *pg.* 985
ATRIPLA - HIV Medication - BRISTOL-MYERS SQUIBB COMPANY; *pg.* 1509, *pg.* 1206
ATRIUM - Software - BMC SOFTWARE, INC.; *pg.* 362, *pg.* 1701
ATRO - Pneumatic Tools - STANLEY BLACK & DECKER, INC.; *pg.* 1063, *pg.* 358
ATROPINE CARE - Pharmaceutical Product - AKORN, INC.; *pg.* 1488, *pg.* 622
ATS - Adhesive Melter - NORDSON CORPORATION; *pg.* 1365, *pg.* 1480
ATS - Skate - ROLLER DERBY SKATE CORP.; *pg.* 966, *pg.* 630
ATS-600 - Absorbency Test System - THWING-ALBERT INSTRUMENT COMPANY; *pg.* 1432, *pg.* 1131
ATTACHE - Bag - AEP INDUSTRIES INC.; *pg.* 1878, *pg.* 1085
ATTACHE - Fabric - MOMENTUM TEXTILES INC.; *pg.* 697, *pg.* 114
ATTACHE PLUS - Software - WIND RIVER SYSTEMS, INC.; *pg.* 493, *pg.* 38
ATTACHMATE - Software - ATTACHMATE CORPORATION; *pg.* 356, *pg.* 1833
ATTACHMATE FTPLUS - High-Speed FTP File Transfer Solution for the Unisys 2200 & ClearPath IX - ATTACHMATE CORPORATION; *pg.* 356, *pg.* 1833
ATTACK - Laundry & Cleaning Products - KAO BRANDS CO. INC.; *pg.* 513, *pg.* 1415
ATTACK - Bicycle Component - SRAM CORPORATION; *pg.* 967, *pg.* 590
ATTACK LIFE - Golf Equipment - REEBOK INTERNATIONAL LTD.; *pg.* 1817, *pg.* 811
ATTACK TRAIL - Bike - MARIN BIKES; *pg.* 1708, *pg.* 168
THE ATTACKER - Staple Gun - ARROW FASTENER COMPANY, INC.; *pg.* 1042, *pg.* 1118
ATTACLAY - Earth Used In Insecticide Formulations - BASF CATALYSTS LLC; *pg.* 1148, *pg.* 1074
ATTACOTE - Attapulgite Clay for use as Anti-Caking Agent - BASF CATALYSTS LLC; *pg.* 1148, *pg.* 1074
ATTAFLOW - Additive - BASF CATALYSTS LLC; *pg.* 1148, *pg.* 1074
ATTAGEL - Additive - BASF CATALYSTS LLC; *pg.* 1148, *pg.* 1074
ATTANE - Copolymer - THE DOW CHEMICAL COMPANY; *pg.* 1157, *pg.* 898
ATTAPULGITE - Fullers Earth Having Oil & Water Absorption Properties - BASF CATALYSTS LLC; *pg.* 1148, *pg.* 1074
ATTASORB - Additive - BASF CATALYSTS LLC; *pg.* 1148, *pg.* 1074
ATTENDANT CONSOLE - Software System - MITEL NETWORKS, INC.; *pg.* 1872, *pg.* 13
ATTENTIVE CHILD - Vitamin & Herbal Supplement - SOURCE NATURALS; *pg.* 1595, *pg.* 278

ATTIC BLANKET - Glass Fiber Insulation - OWENS CORNING; pg. 102, pg. 1476
ATTIC PROTECTOR - Fiber Glass Insulation - JOHNS MANVILLE CORPORATION; pg. 89, pg. 320
ATTO-TAG - Molecular Probe Product - THERMO FISHER SCIENTIFIC INC.; pg. 1602, pg. 61
ATTOFLUOR - Molecular Probe Product - THERMO FISHER SCIENTIFIC INC.; pg. 1602, pg. 61
ATTOGUARD - Wafer Probing System - CASCADE MICROTECH, INC.; pg. 1405, pg. 1492
ATTORNEY NETWORK SERVICES - Network Service - EGS FINANCIAL CARE, INC.; pg. 746, pg. 1540
ATTRIBUTE - Carpet - BEAULIEU GROUP, LLC; pg. 917, pg. 529
ATTUNE - Flexible Ring - ST. JUDE MEDICAL, INC.; pg. 1596, pg. 963
ATV - Integrated Circuit - ATMEL CORPORATION; pg. 621, pg. 238
ATV HUMMER - Sport Product - FRANKLIN SPORTS, INC.; pg. 1834, pg. 847
ATVTRADERONLINE.COM - Advertising Website - DOMINION ENTERPRISES; pg. 1636, pg. 1796
ATWATER CAREY - Safety Product - WISCONSIN PHARMACAL COMPANY, LLC; pg. 1610, pg. 1861
ATX - Pens - A. T. CROSS COMPANY; pg. 339, pg. 1602
ATX - Electrical Products - EMERSON INDUSTRIAL AUTOMATION; pg. 1296, pg. 657
ATZ - Self-propelled Lawn Mower - EXCEL INDUSTRIES, INC.; pg. 1795, pg. 715
AU EAGLES - Athletic Teams - AMERICAN UNIVERSITY; pg. 597, pg. 395
AU LAIT TABLE - Tables - STEELCASE INC.; pg. 475, pg. 889
AU1000 - Technical Documentation - ADVANCED MICRO DEVICES, INC.; pg. 613, pg. 282
AU1100 - Technical Documentation - ADVANCED MICRO DEVICES, INC.; pg. 613, pg. 282
AU1500 - Technical Documentation - ADVANCED MICRO DEVICES, INC.; pg. 613, pg. 282
AUBREY - Sunglasses - COACH, INC.; pg. 3, pg. 1214
AUBURN MAPLE - Furniture - BUSH INDUSTRIES INC.; pg. 919, pg. 1170
AUBURN RIDGE - Furniture - ASHLEY FURNITURE INDUSTRIES, INC.; pg. 914, pg. 1852
AUBUSSON - Pillow - ETHAN ALLEN INTERIORS INC.; pg. 924, pg. 343
AUCKLAND - Furniture - ASHLEY FURNITURE INDUSTRIES, INC.; pg. 914, pg. 1852
AUCTION JET - Diagnostic Urinalysis System - IRIS INTERNATIONAL, INC.; pg. 1547, pg. 64
AUCTION MAX - Diagnostic Urinalysis System - IRIS INTERNATIONAL, INC.; pg. 1547, pg. 64
AUCTION VIDEO - Video Processing - ONSTREAM MEDIA CORPORATION; pg. 449, pg. 459
AUDEX - Apparel - BURTON SNOWBOARD COMPANY; pg. 1829, pg. 1765
AUDI - Automobile Brand - AUDI OF AMERICA, INC.; pg. 164, pg. 1784
AUDIBLEENTERPRISE - Audio Publication Business Partnership Plan - AUDIBLE, INC.; pg. 1230, pg. 1095
AUDIBLELISTENER - Audio Publication Membership Plan - AUDIBLE, INC.; pg. 1230, pg. 1095
AUDIBLEREADY - Audio Publication Partnership Plan - AUDIBLE, INC.; pg. 1230, pg. 1095
AUDIBLEWIRELESS - Audio Publication Wireless Delivery - AUDIBLE, INC.; pg. 1230, pg. 1095
AUDICHRON - Voice Processing Platform - ELECTRONIC TELE-COMMUNICATIONS, INC.; pg. 390, pg. 1897
AUDICHRON 410 - Time, Weather & Temperature Announcers - ELECTRONIC TELE-COMMUNICATIONS, INC.; pg. 390, pg. 1897
AUDIE - Footwear - VANS, INC.; pg. 1821, pg. 76
AUDIO ADVENTURES - Publisher - HAIGHTS CROSS COMMUNICATIONS, INC.; pg. 1646, pg. 1237
AUDIO-ANIMATRONICS - Audio Story - THE WALT DISNEY COMPANY; pg. 317, pg. 52
AUDIO COMPANION - Language Learning Solutions - ROSETTA STONE INC.; pg. 462, pg. 1774
AUDIO MASTER - Powermixer - SHURE INCORPORATED; pg. 672, pg. 638
AUDIO PERFECT - Audio Conferencing System - CLEARONE COMMUNICATIONS, INC.; pg. 629, pg. 1756
AUDIO TRACKMASTER - Fluid Handling System - GRACO, INC.; pg. 1342, pg. 935
AUDIO VAULT - Digital Audio Storage System - BROADCAST ELECTRONICS, INC.; pg. 627, pg. 653
AUDIOACCESS - Audio Equipment - HARMAN INTERNATIONAL INDUSTRIES, INCORPORATED; pg. 641, pg. 374
AUDIOCOM - Communication System - BOSCH COMMUNICATIONS INC.; pg. 626, pg. 919
AUDIOCOMMANDER - Software - ANDREA ELECTRONICS CORPORATION; pg. 617, pg. 1143
AUDIOMETRICS - Electronic Product - GATESAIR, INC.; pg. 640, pg. 1460
AUDIOPIX - Software - QSOUND LABS, INC.; pg. 666, pg. 1904
AUDITGUARD - Cleaner - ROCHESTER MIDLAND CORPORATION; pg. 334, pg. 1337
AUDITION - Software - ADOBE SYSTEMS INCORPORATED; pg. 342, pg. 235
AUDITOR - Software - TELEDYNE LECROY; pg. 1431, pg. 1153
AUDITOR PROFESSIONAL - Software - ECORA SOFTWARE CORPORATION; pg. 389, pg. 1662
AUDITORIUM - Telecom Product - PREMIERE GLOBAL SERVICES, INC.; pg. 1275, pg. 518
AUDITSCAN - Software - WATCHGUARD TECHNOLOGIES, INC.; pg. 491, pg. 1842
AUDIX - Telecommunication Product - AVAYA INC.; pg. 621, pg. 264
AUDREY - Footwear - PHOENIX FOOTWEAR GROUP, INC.; pg. 1815, pg. 60
AUDREY WS - Footwear - PHOENIX FOOTWEAR GROUP, INC.; pg. 1815, pg. 60
AUDUBON - Publication - AUDUBON MAGAZINE; pg. 1618, pg. 1198
AUDUBON - Magazine - NATIONAL AUDUBON SOCIETY; pg. 148, pg. 1263
AUDUBON ADVISORY - Newsletter - NATIONAL AUDUBON SOCIETY; pg. 148, pg. 1263
AUGERVAC - Grain Conveyors - CHRISTIANSON SYSTEMS, INC.; pg. 1323, pg. 917
AUGMENTIN - Pharmaceutical Product - CUBIST PHARMACEUTICALS, INC.; pg. 1521, pg. 828
AUGUR LAKE - T-Shirts - ABERCROMBIE & FITCH CO.; pg. 37, pg. 1466
AUGUSTA - Clock - BROWN & BIGELOW, INC.; pg. 1624, pg. 959
AUGUSTA - Lighting - LSI INDUSTRIES INC.; pg. 58, pg. 1416
AUGUSTINE - Furniture - ETHAN ALLEN INTERIORS INC.; pg. 924, pg. 343
AULTRA-THIN - Pastes for Electronic Circuits - FERRO CORPORATION; pg. 1162, pg. 1462
AUNT HATTIE'S - Split Top Breads - UNITED STATES BAKERY; pg. 907, pg. 1507
AUNT JEMIMA - Frozen Breakfast - PINNACLE FOODS GROUP LLC; pg. 889, pg. 1104
AUNT JEMIMA - Mixes & Syrups - THE QUAKER OATS COMPANY; pg. 834, pg. 588
AUNT LYDIA - Crochet Threads - MAKE IT COATS; pg. 696, pg. 1367
AUNT M'S - Convenience Stores - THE PANTRY, INC.; pg. 1029, pg. 1360
AUNT NELLIES - Pickled Beets, Red Cabbage & Onions - SENECA FOODS CORPORATION; pg. 895, pg. 1177
AUNT SWEETIES - Bakery Goods - TASTY BAKING COMPANY; pg. 1862, pg. 1571
AUOTSPEC - Mass Spectrometer - WATERS CORPORATION; pg. 1436, pg. 834
AUP - Systems Integration & Aeronautics - LOCKHEED MARTIN CORPORATION; pg. 229, pg. 762
AURA - Laser System - AMERICAN MEDICAL SYSTEMS, INC.; pg. 1399, pg. 238
AURA - Database - COBRA ELECTRONICS CORPORATION; pg. 629, pg. 572
AURA - Automotive Air Conditioning Products - DELPHI AUTOMOTIVE LLP; pg. 204, pg. 910
AURA - Stroller - EVENFLO COMPANY, INC.; pg. 924, pg. 1470
AURA - System Providing Support to Maturing Generation of Active Patients - EXACTECH, INC.; pg. 1529, pg. 428
AURA - Gaming Machine - INTERNATIONAL GAME TECHNOLOGY; pg. 420, pg. 1606
AURA - Bath & Plumbing Product - JACUZZI BRANDS CORPORATION; pg. 554, pg. 65
AURA - Electronic Security Devices - MASTER LOCK COMPANY LLC; pg. 1055, pg. 1884
AURA - Medical Device - MISONIX INC.; pg. 1568, pg. 1159
AURA - Apparel - V.F. CORPORATION; pg. 34, pg. 1376
AURA CACIA - Aromatherapy Products - FRONTIER NATURAL PRODUCTS CO-OP; pg. 509, pg. 710
AURA-I - Portable Single Wavelength Laser - AMERICAN MEDICAL SYSTEMS, INC.; pg. 1399, pg. 238
AURA-I - Medical Laser System - IRIDEX CORPORATION; pg. 648, pg. 160
AURA OF AROMA - Scent Extraction Technology - INTERNATIONAL FLAVORS & FRAGRANCES INC.; pg. 512, pg. 1244
AURACOR - Encapsulated Corrosion Inhibitor - BAKER PETROLITE CORPORATION; pg. 1148, pg. 1745
AURALAST - Treated Wood - JELD-WEN, INC.; pg. 1051, pg. 1499
AURALL - Brightener - DOW CHEMICAL; pg. 1156, pg. 1563
AURASPERSE - Pigment & Dispersion - BASF CATALYSTS LLC; pg. 1148, pg. 1074
AURATONE - Acoustical Ceiling Tile - CGC INC.; pg. 75, pg. 1925
AUREOMYCIN - Prevent Cattle Disease - MANNA PRO CORPORATION; pg. 1478, pg. 975
AUREUS - Semiconductors - TEXAS INSTRUMENTS INCORPORATED; pg. 679, pg. 1688
AURIFLUSH - Medicine - MERCK & CO., INC.; pg. 1566, pg. 1077
AUROLECTROLESS - Immersion Process - THE DOW CHEMICAL COMPANY; pg. 1157, pg. 898
AURORA - Computer System - ALIENWARE CORPORATION; pg. 346, pg. 439
AURORA - Highway Crossing Signals - ALSTOM SIGNALING, INC.; pg. 1312, pg. 1350
AURORA - Special Effect Film - BASF CATALYSTS LLC; pg. 1148, pg. 1074
AURORA - Hemodialysis Instrument - BAXTER INTERNATIONAL INC.; pg. 1499, pg. 599
AURORA - Bicycle - G. JOANNOU CYCLE CO. INC.; pg. 1707, pg. 1098
AURORA - Medical Equipment - INVACARE CORPORATION; pg. 1546, pg. 1451
AURORA - Window & Door - JELD-WEN, INC.; pg. 1051, pg. 1499
AURORA - Flooring - MANNINGTON MILLS, INC.; pg. 934, pg. 1119
AURORA - Eye Protection Product - MINE SAFETY APPLIANCES COMPANY; pg. 1361, pg. 1525
AURORA - Toothbrush - RANIR LLC; pg. 520, pg. 888
AURORA - Rotor Crusher - STEDMAN MACHINE COMPANY; pg. 1379, pg. 673
AURORA - Software - SYNOPSYS, INC.; pg. 480, pg. 162
AURORA - Closed Circuit Television Equipment - VICON INDUSTRIES, INC.; pg. 685, pg. 1166
AURORA-3 - Near-field Scanning Optical Microscope - VEECO INSTRUMENTS INC.; pg. 1434, pg. 1322
AURORA 430 E - Sewing Machines - BERNINA OF AMERICA INC.; pg. 51, pg. 554
AURORA 440 QE - Quilting Machines - BERNINA OF AMERICA INC.; pg. 51, pg. 554
AURORA 440 QEE - Quilting Machines - BERNINA OF AMERICA INC.; pg. 51, pg. 554
AURORA BOREALIS - Video Game - INTERNATIONAL GAME TECHNOLOGY; pg. 957, pg. 1024
AURORACORD - Digital Video Multiplexer & Recorder - VICON INDUSTRIES, INC.; pg. 685, pg. 1166
AUROUS - Catheter - COOK GROUP, INC.; pg. 1518, pg. 674
AURUM - Software - BIO-RAD LABORATORIES, INC.; pg. 1504, pg. 101
AURUM - Preamplifier - KLIPSCH GROUP, INC.; pg. 649, pg. 688
AUS-QUENCH - Quenching Salt - HEATBATH CORPORATION; pg. 1165, pg. 826
AUSCO - Brakes for Off-Highway Vehicles - AUSCO PRODUCTS, INC.; pg. 199, pg. 872
AUSRIA - Diagnostic Product - ABBOTT LABORATORIES; pg. 1484, pg. 551
AUSSIE - Hair Care Products - THE PROCTER & GAMBLE COMPANY; pg. 1129, pg. 1418
AUSSIE SERIES - Golf Equipment - ACUSHNET COMPANY; pg. 1824, pg. 818
AUSTENITIC - Industrial Fabric - HERCULITE PRODUCTS, INC.; pg. 694, pg. 1529
AUSTERE - Flatware - ONEIDA LTD; pg. 1129, pg. 1318
AUSTIL-FOCAL - Lens - DANKER LABORATORIES INC.; pg. 1408, pg. 465
AUSTIN - Boots - COACH, INC.; pg. 3, pg. 1214

AUSTIN - Window Treatment - CROSCILL, INC.; *pg.* 1122, *pg.* 1220
AUSTIN - Food Product - KELLOGG COMPANY; *pg.* 831, *pg.* 870
THE AUSTIN COMPANY - Consultants, Designers, Engineer & Constructors - THE AUSTIN COMPANY; *pg.* 69, *pg.* 1428
THE AUSTIN METHOD - Proprietary Concept of Single-Source Approach to Design, Engrng. & Constr. - THE AUSTIN COMPANY; *pg.* 69, *pg.* 1428
AUSTIN POWERS - Game - INTERNATIONAL GAME TECHNOLOGY; *pg.* 957, *pg.* 1024
AUSTOFT - Agricultural Equipment - CNH AMERICA LLC; *pg.* 702, *pg.* 560
AUSTORIA - Lighting Product - WESTINGHOUSE LIGHTING CORPORATION; *pg.* 687, *pg.* 1571
AUSTRALIA GONE WILD - Video Game - INTERNATIONAL GAME TECHNOLOGY; *pg.* 957, *pg.* 1024
AUSTRALIAN CYPRESS - Hardware Flooring - LUMBER LIQUIDATORS HOLDINGS, INC.; *pg.* 94, *pg.* 1808
AUSZYME - Diagnostic Product - ABBOTT LABORATORIES; *pg.* 1484, *pg.* 551
AUTAN - Cleaning Product - S.C. JOHNSON & SON, INC.; *pg.* 334, *pg.* 1889
AUTEL - Bath Product - KOHLER CO.; *pg.* 91, *pg.* 1862
AUTEX - Financial Publications - THOMSON REUTERS CORPORATION; *pg.* 1693, *pg.* 1944
AUTEX BLOCKDATA - Software - THOMSON REUTERS CORPORATION; *pg.* 1693, *pg.* 1944
AUTHENTEC - Fabric - NEMSCHOFF, INC.; *pg.* 936, *pg.* 1890
AUTHENTECH COLLECTION - Fabric - INTERNATIONAL TEXTILE GROUP, INC.; *pg.* 696, *pg.* 1374
AUTHENTIC - Bakery Product - SAPUTO, INC.; *pg.* 893, *pg.* 1956
AUTHENTIC - Footwear - VANS, INC.; *pg.* 1821, *pg.* 76
AUTHENTIC HAND-CARVED - Woodcarvings - WHITE RIVER HARDWOODS-WOODWORKS, INC.; *pg.* 121, *pg.* 31
AUTHENTIC LUXURY FOR KITCHEN AND BATH - Slogan - ROHL LLC; *pg.* 1061, *pg.* 116
AUTHENTIC PITA - Handmade Pita Bread - KRONOS PRODUCTS, INC.; *pg.* 872, *pg.* 614
AUTHENTIC PROBLEMS - Software - EMC CORPORATION; *pg.* 391, *pg.* 825
AUTHENTIC TACTICAL FIGHTING SYSTEM - Fighting System - ENVIRONMENTAL TECTONICS CORPORATION; *pg.* 1411, *pg.* 1587
AUTHENTICA - Software - EMC CORPORATION; *pg.* 391, *pg.* 825
AUTHENTICATION SERVICES - Software - DELL SOFTWARE; *pg.* 385, *pg.* 40
AUTHENTICO - Frozen Food - BELLISIO FOODS, INC.; *pg.* 840, *pg.* 931
AUTHEXPRESS - Software System - MENTOR GRAPHICS CORPORATION; *pg.* 432, *pg.* 1510
AUTHOR ONCE - Technology - EGAIN COMMUNICATIONS CORPORATION; *pg.* 1242, *pg.* 284
AUTHOR SERVICE - Software - SAS INSTITUTE INC.; *pg.* 466, *pg.* 1361
AUTHORHOUSE - Self-Publishing Services - AUTHOR SOLUTIONS, INC.; *pg.* 1618, *pg.* 674
AUTHORING CENTER - Software System - HEALTHSTREAM, INC.; *pg.* 1649, *pg.* 1651
AUTHORITY - Pet Supplies - PETSMART, INC.; *pg.* 1481, *pg.* 18
AUTHORITY ASSIST - Herbicides - FMC CORPORATION; *pg.* 1163, *pg.* 1564
AUTHORITY FIRST DF - Herbicides - FMC CORPORATION; *pg.* 1163, *pg.* 1564
AUTHORITY MTZ - Herbicides - FMC CORPORATION; *pg.* 1163, *pg.* 1564
AUTHORWARE - Software - ADOBE SYSTEMS INCORPORATED; *pg.* 342, *pg.* 235
AUTION JET AJ-4270 - Urine Chemistry Analyzer - IRIS INTERNATIONAL, INC.; *pg.* 1547, *pg.* 64
AUTION MAX AX-4280 - Automated Urine Chemistry Analyzer - IRIS INTERNATIONAL, INC.; *pg.* 1547, *pg.* 64
AUTO ADVANTAGE - Life Insurance - METLIFE, INC.; *pg.* 1208, *pg.* 1258
AUTO ARMOR - Rust Protection - DAUBERT INDUSTRIES, INC.; *pg.* 1155, *pg.* 561
AUTO-BAND - Wireless LAN Chipset - TEXAS INSTRUMENTS INCORPORATED; *pg.* 679, *pg.* 1688
AUTO-BULB - Clamp - ALCOA INC.; *pg.* 65, *pg.* 1188
AUTO-CORRELATION - Medical Device - STAAR SURGICAL COMPANY; *pg.* 1597, *pg.* 151
AUTO-DRIVE - Surgical Screws - OSTEOMED CORPORATION; *pg.* 1425, *pg.* 1658
AUTO FILM ID - Medical Product - HOLOGIC, INC.; *pg.* 1416, *pg.* 784
AUTO-FIT - Baby Carrier Straps - EVENFLO COMPANY, INC.; *pg.* 924, *pg.* 1470
AUTO-FLO - Tumbler - LYMAN PRODUCTS CORPORATION; *pg.* 1839, *pg.* 356
AUTO-FLO - Dispensing Valves - NORDSON CORPORATION; *pg.* 1365, *pg.* 1480
AUTO GRADE - Wheel Hardware - DORMAN PRODUCTS, INC.; *pg.* 204, *pg.* 1522
AUTO-GROUND - Auto Grounding - PASS & SEYMOUR/LEGRAND; *pg.* 1303, *pg.* 1344
AUTO-GUIDE - Agricultural Information System - AGCO CORPORATION; *pg.* 700, *pg.* 530
AUTO-JACK - Modular Device for Telephone Network Interface - TII NETWORK TECHNOLOGIES, INC.; *pg.* 680, *pg.* 1157
AUTO-LAYOUT - Fluid Handling System - GRACO, INC.; *pg.* 1342, *pg.* 935
AUTO-LOCK - Tape - IDEAL INDUSTRIES, INC.; *pg.* 1051, *pg.* 662
AUTO-LOCK - Fiber Partitions - SONOCO PRODUCTS COMPANY; *pg.* 1469, *pg.* 1619
AUTO-LYTE - Oral-Specimen Collection Devices - ORASURE TECHNOLOGIES INC; *pg.* 1578, *pg.* 1516
AUTO-MATE - Plastic Grocery Bags - SONOCO PRODUCTS COMPANY; *pg.* 1469, *pg.* 1619
AUTO-MAX - Forage Harvest System - GEHL COMPANY; *pg.* 1339, *pg.* 1899
AUTO-OWNERS - Insurance - AUTO-OWNERS INSURANCE GROUP; *pg.* 1194, *pg.* 895
AUTO PANEL - Touch Up - SHERWIN-WILLIAMS DIVERSIFIED BRANDS DIVISION; *pg.* 1448, *pg.* 1435
AUTO-PARTICLE RECOGNITION - Urinalysis Proprietary Technology - IRIS INTERNATIONAL, INC.; *pg.* 1547, *pg.* 64
AUTO PLUS - Fluid Handling System - GRACO, INC.; *pg.* 1342, *pg.* 935
AUTO PLUS - Retail Store Service - UNI-SELECT INC.; *pg.* 220, *pg.* 1950
AUTO REEL - Machinery/Accessories - REEL-O-MATIC, INC.; *pg.* 1371, *pg.* 1487
AUTO RENTAL NEWS - Magazine - BOBIT BUSINESS MEDIA; *pg.* 1622, *pg.* 293
AUTO RESTORER - Magazine - I-5 PUBLISHING LLC; *pg.* 1651, *pg.* 133
AUTO-SOFT - Vacuum Valve - MKS INSTRUMENTS, INC.; *pg.* 1362, *pg.* 781
AUTO SPRAY - Touch-Up Spray Paint - SHERWIN-WILLIAMS DIVERSIFIED BRANDS DIVISION; *pg.* 1448, *pg.* 1435
AUTO STOP - Healthcare Product - GF HEALTH PRODUCTS, INC.; *pg.* 1535, *pg.* 508
AUTO-STRIP - Power Door - RITE-HITE HOLDING CORPORATION; *pg.* 1372, *pg.* 1880
AUTO TRAC - Convertible Car Seat with Easy to Use Retractor - DOREL JUVENILE GROUP, INC.; *pg.* 923, *pg.* 676
AUTO TRADER ON-LINE - Magazine - DOMINION ENTERPRISES; *pg.* 1636, *pg.* 1796
AUTO-TRADING WITH XECUTE - Application Service Provider - OPTIONSXPRESS HOLDINGS, INC.; *pg.* 790, *pg.* 586
AUTO-TRANS - Unit Load Automatic Guided Vehicles - DAIFUKU WEBB; *pg.* 1327, *pg.* 885
AUTO TRIM & RESTYLING - Magazine - BOBIT BUSINESS MEDIA; *pg.* 1622, *pg.* 293
AUTO TUNE - Fluid Handling System - GRACO, INC.; *pg.* 1342, *pg.* 935
AUTO TUNE - LCD Display - VIEWSONIC CORPORATION; *pg.* 489, *pg.* 303
AUTO VENTSHADE - Vehicle Product - LUND INTERNATIONAL, INC.; *pg.* 211, *pg.* 526
AUTOACTIVE - Software System - MENTOR GRAPHICS CORPORATION; *pg.* 432, *pg.* 1510
AUTOAHORROS.COM - Online Car-Buying Site - AUTOBYTEL INC.; *pg.* 1230, *pg.* 107
AUTOALERTS - Accounting Services - THE PNC FINANCIAL SERVICES GROUP, INC.; *pg.* 795, *pg.* 1579
AUTOALIGN - Telescope - MEADE INSTRUMENTS CORPORATION; *pg.* 1422, *pg.* 113
AUTOALIGN - Epoxy Bond Device - NEWPORT CORPORATION; *pg.* 1424, *pg.* 114
AUTOARMOR - Car Protection - DAUBERT INDUSTRIES, INC.; *pg.* 1155, *pg.* 561
AUTOBAG AB 145 - Bagger - AUTOMATED PACKAGING SYSTEMS INC.; *pg.* 1452, *pg.* 1474
AUTOBAG AB 180 - Packaging System - AUTOMATED PACKAGING SYSTEMS INC.; *pg.* 1452, *pg.* 1474
AUTOBAG AB 180 ONESTEP - Bagger - AUTOMATED PACKAGING SYSTEMS INC.; *pg.* 1452, *pg.* 1474
AUTOBAG AB 255 - Bagger - AUTOMATED PACKAGING SYSTEMS INC.; *pg.* 1452, *pg.* 1474
AUTOBAG AB 255 ONESTEP - Bagger - AUTOMATED PACKAGING SYSTEMS INC.; *pg.* 1452, *pg.* 1474
AUTOBAG CTS4000 - Bagger - AUTOMATED PACKAGING SYSTEMS INC.; *pg.* 1452, *pg.* 1474
AUTOBAG PACESETTER - Bagger - AUTOMATED PACKAGING SYSTEMS INC.; *pg.* 1452, *pg.* 1474
AUTOBAG PACESETTER PS 125 - Bagger - AUTOMATED PACKAGING SYSTEMS INC.; *pg.* 1452, *pg.* 1474
AUTOBEND - Gauging Systems for Metal Fabricating Machine Tools - HURCO COMPANIES, INC.; *pg.* 409, *pg.* 686
AUTOBYTEL.COM - Online Car-Buying Site - AUTOBYTEL INC.; *pg.* 1230, *pg.* 107
AUTOCAD - 3D Software - AUTODESK INC.; *pg.* 356, *pg.* 257
AUTOCAD - Software - EAGLE POINT SOFTWARE CORPORATION; *pg.* 389, *pg.* 707
AUTOCAD - Bonder Connectivity Product - KULICKE & SOFFA INDUSTRIES, INC.; *pg.* 650, *pg.* 1533
AUTOCAD LEARNING ASSISTANCE - Software - AUTODESK INC.; *pg.* 356, *pg.* 257
AUTOCAD REVIT SERIES - Building Information Modeling - AUTODESK INC.; *pg.* 356, *pg.* 257
AUTOCAD SIMULATOR - Software - AUTODESK INC.; *pg.* 356, *pg.* 257
AUTOCAD SQL EXTENSION - Software - AUTODESK INC.; *pg.* 356, *pg.* 257
AUTOCAD SQL INTERFACE - Software - AUTODESK INC.; *pg.* 356, *pg.* 257
AUTOCALL - Fire Detection & Alarm Products - TYCO SIMPLEXGRINNELL LP; *pg.* 682, *pg.* 859
AUTOCAPTURE - Pacing System - ST. JUDE MEDICAL, INC.; *pg.* 1596, *pg.* 963
AUTOCAR - Class 8 Truck & Tractors - VOLVO TRUCKS NORTH AMERICA, INC.; *pg.* 195, *pg.* 1377
AUTOCARB - Thermal Processing Equipment - SURFACE COMBUSTION, INC.; *pg.* 1077, *pg.* 1462
AUTOCELLS - Software System - MENTOR GRAPHICS CORPORATION; *pg.* 432, *pg.* 1510
AUTOCHECK - Automated Quality Control for ABL700 Automated Blood Gas Analyzer - RADIOMETER AMERICA INC.; *pg.* 1588, *pg.* 1481
AUTOCHEMI - Imaging System - UVP, INC.; *pg.* 1434, *pg.* 298
AUTOCLASS - Photo Printer Accessories - EASTMAN KODAK COMPANY; *pg.* 1408, *pg.* 1333
AUTOCLAVE - Healthcare Product - MEDICOOL, INC.; *pg.* 1562, *pg.* 294
AUTOCLEAN - Cleaning System - ATMI, INC.; *pg.* 1314, *pg.* 342
AUTOCLEAN - Oil & Water Separator - DONALDSON COMPANY, INC.; *pg.* 1329, *pg.* 917
AUTOCLEAN - Fluid Handling System - GRACO, INC.; *pg.* 1342, *pg.* 935
AUTOCLIPS - Stereotaxic Equipment - STOELTING CO.; *pg.* 1430, *pg.* 671
AUTOCOMP - Digital Compass Product - KVH INDUSTRIES INC; *pg.* 650, *pg.* 1602
AUTOCOMP - Battery Charge Control Integrated Circuits - TEXAS INSTRUMENTS INCORPORATED; *pg.* 679, *pg.* 1688
AUTOCREASER - Creaser - STANDARD DUPLICATING MACHINES CORPORATION; *pg.* 473, *pg.* 783
AUTOCROSS - Pens - A. T. CROSS COMPANY; *pg.* 339, *pg.* 1602
AUTOCROWD - Underground Construction Equipment - CHARLES MACHINE WORKS, INC.; *pg.* 1322, *pg.* 1488
AUTODESK - Software - RAND WORLDWIDE, INC.; *pg.* 459, *pg.* 821
AUTODESK DESIGN REVIEW - Design Software - AUTODESK INC.; *pg.* 356, *pg.* 257
AUTODESK DWF - Viewing & Printing Designs - AUTODESK INC.; *pg.* 356, *pg.* 257
AUTODESK ENVISION - Software - AUTODESK INC.; *pg.*

356, *pg.* 257
AUTODESK INTENT - Project Management - AUTODESK INC.; *pg.* 356, *pg.* 257
AUTODESK INVENTOR - 2D & 3D Drafting - AUTODESK INC.; *pg.* 356, *pg.* 257
AUTODESK INVENTOR - Software - RAND WORLDWIDE, INC.; *pg.* 459, *pg.* 821
AUTODESK LAND DESKTOP - Integrated Surveyor Tool - AUTODESK INC.; *pg.* 356, *pg.* 257
AUTODESK MAP 3D - 3D Mapping Tool - AUTODESK INC.; *pg.* 356, *pg.* 257
AUTODESK MAPGUIDE - Geospatial Software - AUTODESK INC.; *pg.* 356, *pg.* 257
AUTODESK MOLDFLOW ADVISER - Software - AUTODESK INC.; *pg.* 356, *pg.* 257
AUTODESK MOLDFLOW COMMUNICATOR - Software - AUTODESK INC.; *pg.* 356, *pg.* 257
AUTODESK MOLDFLOW INSIGHT - Software - AUTODESK INC.; *pg.* 356, *pg.* 257
AUTODESK ONSITE ENTERPRISE - Group Mobile Access - AUTODESK INC.; *pg.* 356, *pg.* 257
AUTODESK ONSITE VIEW - Remote Design Access - AUTODESK INC.; *pg.* 356, *pg.* 257
AUTODESK PRE-PLAN - Stand-Alone Emergency Response Tool - AUTODESK INC.; *pg.* 356, *pg.* 257
AUTODESK PRODUCTSTREAM - Design Change Management - AUTODESK INC.; *pg.* 356, *pg.* 257
AUTODESK RASTER DESIGN - Vector & Raster Editing - AUTODESK INC.; *pg.* 356, *pg.* 257
AUTODESK REALDWG - DWG Support - AUTODESK INC.; *pg.* 356, *pg.* 257
AUTODESK REVIT BUILDING - Architectural Design & Documentation - AUTODESK INC.; *pg.* 356, *pg.* 257
AUTODESK REVIT STRUCTURE - Engineering & Documentation Software - AUTODESK INC.; *pg.* 356, *pg.* 257
AUTODESK STREAMLINE - Email-Based Group Communication - AUTODESK INC.; *pg.* 356, *pg.* 257
AUTODESK VAULT - Data Management - AUTODESK INC.; *pg.* 356, *pg.* 257
AUTODESK VIZ - 3D & Animation - AUTODESK INC.; *pg.* 356, *pg.* 257
AUTODISSOLVE - Software System - MENTOR GRAPHICS CORPORATION; *pg.* 432, *pg.* 1510
AUTODOME INDOOR SYSTEMS - Surveillance Camera - BOSCH SECURITY SYSTEMS, INC.; *pg.* 626, *pg.* 1158
AUTOETCH - Silicon Etch System - LAM RESEARCH CORPORATION; *pg.* 1354, *pg.* 91
AUTOFAIR - Motorsports Entertainment - SPEEDWAY MOTORSPORTS, INC.; *pg.* 584, *pg.* 1370
AUTOFEED II - Construction Equipment - VERMEER MANUFACTURING COMPANY; *pg.* 708, *pg.* 711
AUTOFILE - File - I/D/E/A/ INC.; *pg.* 1460, *pg.* 548
AUTOFILTER - Software System - MENTOR GRAPHICS CORPORATION; *pg.* 432, *pg.* 1510
AUTOFIT - Gap & Flush - PERCEPTRON, INC.; *pg.* 215, *pg.* 904
AUTOFLARE - Gas Piping Systems - OMEGA FLEX, INC.; *pg.* 982, *pg.* 1532
AUTOFLOW - Software System - MENTOR GRAPHICS CORPORATION; *pg.* 432, *pg.* 1510
AUTOFLUSH - Toilet Flushing System - HILLYARD, INC.; *pg.* 331, *pg.* 990
AUTOFUSE - Automotive Fuse - LITTELFUSE, INC.; *pg.* 1301, *pg.* 580
AUTOGATE - Software - VITAL IMAGES, INC.; *pg.* 1607, *pg.* 950
AUTOGAUGE - Gauging System - PERCEPTRON, INC.; *pg.* 215, *pg.* 904
AUTOGEN - Sealer - MTS MEDICATION TECHNOLOGIES, INC.; *pg.* 442, *pg.* 463
AUTOGENICS - Bio-Feedback Instruments - STOELTING CO.; *pg.* 1430, *pg.* 671
AUTOGRAFT EXPRESS - Medical Apparatus - MAQUET; *pg.* 1558, *pg.* 1082
AUTOGRAPH - Magazine For New Car Buyers - AMERICAN AUTOMOBILE ASSOCIATION; *pg.* 1190, *pg.* 429
AUTOGRAPH - Non-Stick Coating - E.I. DU PONT DE NEMOURS & COMPANY; *pg.* 1159, *pg.* 390
AUTOGRAPH COLLECTION - Hotels - MARRIOTT INTERNATIONAL, INC.; *pg.* 1102, *pg.* 764
AUTOGRAPHICS - Systems Integration & Aeronautics - LOCKHEED MARTIN CORPORATION; *pg.* 229, *pg.* 762
AUTOGRAV - Gravity Meter - SCINTREX LTD.; *pg.* 1374, *pg.* 1920
AUTOGUIDE - Robot Guidance System - PERCEPTRON, INC.; *pg.* 215, *pg.* 904
AUTOHYGIENE - Restroom Cleaning System - HILLYARD, INC.; *pg.* 331, *pg.* 990
AUTOIMMUNE ATLAS - Clinical Diagnostic Product - BIO-RAD LABORATORIES, INC.; *pg.* 1504, *pg.* 101
AUTOJET - Spray Controller - SPRAYING SYSTEMS CO.; *pg.* 1063, *pg.* 670
AUTOLABEL - Universal Printer Interface - AUTOMATED PACKAGING SYSTEMS INC.; *pg.* 1452, *pg.* 1474
AUTOLABEL PI 412C - Imprinter - AUTOMATED PACKAGING SYSTEMS INC.; *pg.* 1452, *pg.* 1474
AUTOLABEL PI 412CW - Imprinter - AUTOMATED PACKAGING SYSTEMS INC.; *pg.* 1452, *pg.* 1474
AUTOLIB - Software System - MENTOR GRAPHICS CORPORATION; *pg.* 432, *pg.* 1510
AUTOLINE - Process Control System - ROYLE SYSTEMS GROUP; *pg.* 1373, *pg.* 1100
AUTOLINEAR - Software System - MENTOR GRAPHICS CORPORATION; *pg.* 432, *pg.* 1510
AUTOLINK - HF Frequency Management System - HARRIS CORP. RF COMMUNICATIONS DIVISION; *pg.* 642, *pg.* 1336
AUTOLINK - Software System - MENTOR GRAPHICS CORPORATION; *pg.* 432, *pg.* 1510
AUTOLISP - Software - AUTODESK INC.; *pg.* 356, *pg.* 257
AUTOLITE - Spark Plugs - HONEYWELL INTERNATIONAL INC.; *pg.* 407, *pg.* 1088
AUTOLITE - Aviation Spark Plugs - UNISON INDUSTRIES, LLC; *pg.* 235, *pg.* 435
AUTOLOAD - Machinery - HARDINGE INC.; *pg.* 1344, *pg.* 1157
AUTOLOCK - Expandable Police Batons - BAE SYSTEMS PRODUCTS GROUP; *pg.* 359, *pg.* 432
AUTOLOCK - Software - TRIMBLE NAVIGATION LIMITED; *pg.* 1384, *pg.* 288
AUTOLOGIC - Software System - MENTOR GRAPHICS CORPORATION; *pg.* 432, *pg.* 1510
AUTOLOGIC BLOCKS - Software System - MENTOR GRAPHICS CORPORATION; *pg.* 432, *pg.* 1510
AUTOLOGIC FPGA - Software System - MENTOR GRAPHICS CORPORATION; *pg.* 432, *pg.* 1510
AUTOLOGIC VHDL - Software System - MENTOR GRAPHICS CORPORATION; *pg.* 432, *pg.* 1510
AUTOLYNX - Banking Services - MERCHANTS BANCSHARES, INC.; *pg.* 782, *pg.* 1768
AUTOMAC - Service - MCDONALD'S CORPORATION; *pg.* 1737, *pg.* 645
AUTOMAGIC - Can Opener - HABAND COMPANY, INC.; *pg.* 1772, *pg.* 1099
AUTOMASK - Stripping Film - TRANSILWRAP COMPANY, INC.; *pg.* 1470, *pg.* 613
AUTOMASK MX - Stripping Film - TRANSILWRAP COMPANY, INC.; *pg.* 1470, *pg.* 613
AUTOMATE - Sample Processing System - BECKMAN COULTER, INC.; *pg.* 1402, *pg.* 48
AUTOMATE - Mobile Audio & Video Products - DEI HOLDINGS, INC.; *pg.* 633, *pg.* 302
AUTOMATE - Liquid Dyestuff - DOW CHEMICAL; *pg.* 1156, *pg.* 1563
AUTOMATED CREDIT APPLICATION PROCESSING SYSTEM - Software - CGI TECHNOLOGIES & SOLUTIONS INC.; *pg.* 371, *pg.* 1779
AUTOMATED DOCUMENT FACTORIES - Scale Print - PITNEY BOWES INC.; *pg.* 454, *pg.* 376
AUTOMATED POSTAL CENTERS - Postal Services - UNITED STATES POSTAL SERVICE; *pg.* 1009, *pg.* 406
AUTOMATED RESOURCE MANAGER - Software - EMC CORPORATION; *pg.* 391, *pg.* 825
AUTOMATED SOLUTIONS FOR PROCESSORS WORLDWIDE - Tagline - KEY TECHNOLOGY, INC.; *pg.* 868, *pg.* 1847
AUTOMATED WORK DISTRIBUTOR - Software - DST SYSTEMS, INC.; *pg.* 388, *pg.* 982
AUTOMATIC DECISION SUPPORT - Software - MCKESSON CORPORATION; *pg.* 1560, *pg.* 222
AUTOMATIC DEFINITIVE - Cosmetic Product - MERLE NORMAN COSMETICS, INC.; *pg.* 517, *pg.* 136
AUTOMATIC ELECTRONIC MAIL OPENERS - Mailer - PITNEY BOWES INC.; *pg.* 454, *pg.* 376
AUTOMATIC EYELINER - Eye Liner - MERLE NORMAN COSMETICS, INC.; *pg.* 517, *pg.* 136
AUTOMATIC RAIN MOTOR - Water Conservation - MELNOR, INC.; *pg.* 1055, *pg.* 1811
AUTOMATIC SHADOW BASE - Eye Makeup - MERLE NORMAN COSMETICS, INC.; *pg.* 517, *pg.* 136
AUTOMATION FAIR - Software - ROCKWELL AUTOMATION, INC.; *pg.* 668, *pg.* 1880
AUTOMATION XPRESS - Software - GIGA-TRONICS INCORPORATED; *pg.* 640, *pg.* 260
AUTOMATRIX - Dental Product - DENTSPLY INTERNATIONAL INC.; *pg.* 1522, *pg.* 1596
AUTOMATT - Engineering Services - THE DOW CHEMICAL COMPANY; *pg.* 1157, *pg.* 898
AUTOMAX - Valve - FLOWSERVE CORPORATION; *pg.* 82, *pg.* 1719
AUTOMAX - Software - ROCKWELL AUTOMATION, INC.; *pg.* 668, *pg.* 1880
AUTOMED FDS - Repackaging System - AMERISOURCEBERGEN CORPORATION; *pg.* 1493, *pg.* 1522
AUTOMET - Automatic Sample Holing Grinding & Polishing Device - BUEHLER, LTD.; *pg.* 1403, *pg.* 622
AUTOMIX - Compounding System - BAXTER INTERNATIONAL INC.; *pg.* 1499, *pg.* 599
AUTOMOBILE - Magazine - RENTPATH, INC.; *pg.* 1680, *pg.* 538
AUTOMOBILE DEALERS PROTECTOR PLAN - Insurance Package Program - BROWN & BROWN, INC.; *pg.* 1196, *pg.* 419
AUTOMOBILE REDBOOK - Magazine - RENTPATH, INC.; *pg.* 1680, *pg.* 538
AUTOMOBILWOCHE - Automotive Newspaper - CRAIN COMMUNICATIONS, INC.; *pg.* 1631, *pg.* 879
AUTOMOBL - Semiconductor Solution - CYPRESS SEMICONDUCTOR CORPORATION; *pg.* 1326, *pg.* 243
AUTOMOTIVE ESTIMATICS - Workbook - VALE NATIONAL TRAINING CENTER INC.; *pg.* 610, *pg.* 1660
AUTOMOTIVE FLEET - Magazine - BOBIT BUSINESS MEDIA; *pg.* 1622, *pg.* 293
AUTOMOTIVE INTELLIGENCE - Analysis of Industry Trends - IHS AUTOMOTIVE DRIVEN BY POLK; *pg.* 1652, *pg.* 907
AUTOMOTIVE MANUFACTURING & PRODUCTION - Business to Business Magazine - GARDNER PUBLICATIONS, INC.; *pg.* 1644, *pg.* 1413
AUTOMOTIVE NEWS - Newspaper - CRAIN COMMUNICATIONS, INC.; *pg.* 1631, *pg.* 879
AUTOMOTIVE STRENGTH PRESTONE - Stain Remover - HONEYWELL CONSUMER PRODUCTS GROUP; *pg.* 208, *pg.* 344
AUTOMOTIVELIB - Software System - MENTOR GRAPHICS CORPORATION; *pg.* 432, *pg.* 1510
AUTONET - Auto Industry Service - CONSOLIDATED RAIL CORPORATION; *pg.* 1903, *pg.* 1562
AUTOOPERATOR ACCESS NV - Software Application - BMC SOFTWARE, INC.; *pg.* 362, *pg.* 1701
AUTOOPTIMIZER - Software - CITRIX SYSTEMS, INC.; *pg.* 375, *pg.* 424
AUTOPAC 1000 - Concrete Product Machine - BESSER COMPANY; *pg.* 1317, *pg.* 865
AUTOPAR - Software System - MENTOR GRAPHICS CORPORATION; *pg.* 432, *pg.* 1510
AUTOPART INTERNATIONAL - Land Vehicle Part - ADVANCE AUTO PARTS, INC.; *pg.* 197, *pg.* 1805
AUTOPAY - Utility Service - CPS ENERGY; *pg.* 1939, *pg.* 1739
AUTOPHERESIS-C - Blood Collection & Transfusion - BAXTER INTERNATIONAL INC.; *pg.* 1499, *pg.* 599
AUTOPHORETIC - Metalworking Chemical - HENKEL CORPORATION; *pg.* 1166, *pg.* 897
AUTOPILOT - Banking Service - THE BANK OF NOVA SCOTIA; *pg.* 721, *pg.* 1935
AUTOPILOT - Software For Airlines - BMC SOFTWARE, INC.; *pg.* 362, *pg.* 1701
AUTOPILOT - Software - EMULEX CORPORATION; *pg.* 392, *pg.* 70
AUTOPILOT - Navigation Aid - TRIMBLE NAVIGATION LIMITED; *pg.* 1384, *pg.* 288
AUTOPILOT COMP - Bicycle Accessories - SPECIALIZED BICYCLE COMPONENTS, INC.; *pg.* 1711, *pg.* 152
AUTOPIPE - Software - BENTLEY SYSTEMS, INC.; *pg.* 361, *pg.* 1531
AUTOPLANT - Software - BENTLEY SYSTEMS, INC.; *pg.* 361, *pg.* 1531
AUTOPM - Software - LAM RESEARCH CORPORATION; *pg.* 1354, *pg.* 91
AUTOPOSITIVE - Photographic Film, Paper & Plates, Photographic Developer - EASTMAN KODAK COMPANY; *pg.* 1408, *pg.* 1333
AUTOPREP - Software - BIO-RAD LABORATORIES, INC.;

First page reference indicates Business Class Edition
Second page reference indicates Geographic Edition

pg. 1504, pg. 101

AUTOPULSE - Fire Detection & Control System - ANSUL, INCORPORATED; pg. 1147, pg. 1869

AUTOPULSE - Circulation Product - ZOLL MEDICAL CORPORATION; pg. 1612, pg. 814

AUTOSAVER - Thermostat - HUNTER FAN COMPANY; pg. 57, pg. 1631

AUTOSCAN - Flexible Ring Gauge - PERCEPTRON, INC.; pg. 215, pg. 904

AUTOSCAN - Software - RESMED INC.; pg. 1589, pg. 207

AUTOSCAN - Diagnostic Product - SIEMENS HEALTHCARE DIAGNOSTICS; pg. 673, pg. 604

AUTOSCOPE - Video Vehicle Detection System - IMAGE SENSING SYSTEMS, INC.; pg. 412, pg. 961

AUTOSCOPE ATLAS - Junction Detection System - IMAGE SENSING SYSTEMS, INC.; pg. 412, pg. 961

AUTOSCOPE RACKVISION - Video Vehicle Detection System - IMAGE SENSING SYSTEMS, INC.; pg. 412, pg. 961

AUTOSCOPE SOLO - Video Vehicle Detection System - IMAGE SENSING SYSTEMS, INC.; pg. 412, pg. 961

AUTOSCOPE SOLO PRO - Video Vehicle/Pedestrian Detection - IMAGE SENSING SYSTEMS, INC.; pg. 412, pg. 961

AUTOSEAL - Adhesive & Coating - LORD CORPORATION; pg. 1357, pg. 1360

AUTOSEED - Navigation Aid - TRIMBLE NAVIGATION LIMITED; pg. 1384, pg. 288

AUTOSET - Medical Device - RESMED INC.; pg. 1589, pg. 207

AUTOSET ADVANTAGE - Medical Device - RESMED INC.; pg. 1589, pg. 207

AUTOSET CS - Medical Device - RESMED INC.; pg. 1589, pg. 207

AUTOSET CS 2 - Medical Device - RESMED INC.; pg. 1589, pg. 207

AUTOSET RESPOND - Autotitration Device - RESMED INC.; pg. 1589, pg. 207

AUTOSET SPIRIT - Autotitration Device - RESMED INC.; pg. 1589, pg. 207

AUTOSET T - Medical Device - RESMED INC.; pg. 1589, pg. 207

AUTOSET VANTAGE - Medical Device - RESMED INC.; pg. 1589, pg. 207

AUTOSFIG - Diagnostic Instrument - PROPPER MANUFACTURING COMPANY, INC.; pg. 1586, pg. 1175

AUTOSHAPES - Software - AUTODESK INC.; pg. 356, pg. 257

AUTOSHARE - Software - ACD SYSTEMS INTERNATIONAL INC.; pg. 340, pg. 1913

AUTOSHIFT - Valves - FLOWSERVE CORPORATION; pg. 82, pg. 1719

AUTOSHOW - Car Wash Products - ARMALY BRANDS; pg. 326, pg. 912

AUTOSHUTDOWN - Integrated Circuits - MAXIM INTEGRATED PRODUCTS, INC.; pg. 653, pg. 247

AUTOSHUTDOWN PLUS - Transceiver - MAXIM INTEGRATED PRODUCTS, INC.; pg. 653, pg. 247

AUTOSITE.COM - Online Linkage Site - AUTOBYTEL INC.; pg. 1230, pg. 107

AUTOSKETCH - Drawing Software - AUTODESK INC.; pg. 356, pg. 257

AUTOSLIPPER - Coverglass Cartridge - HACKER INSTRUMENTS & INDUSTRIES INC.; pg. 1415, pg. 1623

AUTOSMART - Amplifier - SKYWORKS SOLUTIONS, INC.; pg. 674, pg. 862

AUTOSNAP - Markers - AUTODESK INC.; pg. 356, pg. 257

AUTOSOLVE - Complaint Arbitration Services - AMERICAN AUTOMOBILE ASSOCIATION; pg. 1190, pg. 429

AUTOSONIX - Medical Device - MISONIX INC.; pg. 1568, pg. 1159

AUTOSORT - Nondestructive Testing - MAGNETIC ANALYSIS CORPORATION; pg. 1421, pg. 1158

AUTOSPEC - Fastener Product - PENN ENGINEERING & MANUFACTURING CORP.; pg. 1059, pg. 1525

AUTOSPEC-ULTIMA - Mass Spectrometer - WATERS CORPORATION; pg. 1436, pg. 834

AUTOSPECT - Painted Surface - PERCEPTRON, INC.; pg. 215, pg. 904

AUTOSPECT QMS - Products that Control Vehicle Painting Process - PERCEPTRON, INC.; pg. 215, pg. 904

AUTOSTAR - Telescope Controller - MEADE INSTRUMENTS CORPORATION; pg. 1422, pg. 113

AUTOSTAR SUITE - Software - MEADE INSTRUMENTS CORPORATION; pg. 1422, pg. 113

AUTOSTART - Automobile Electronics - DEI HOLDINGS, INC.; pg. 633, pg. 302

AUTOSTART - Software - EMC CORPORATION; pg. 391, pg. 825

AUTOSTEP - Otoscopes - WELCH ALLYN INC.; pg. 1436, pg. 1342

AUTOSTIC - High Temperature Cements - FLEXBAR MACHINE CORP.; pg. 1337, pg. 1169

AUTOSTOP - Tow Car Brake System - BLUE OX; pg. 701, pg. 1019

AUTOSTRADA - Office Furniture - KNOLL, INC.; pg. 425, pg. 1527

AUTOSWAP - Software - EMC CORPORATION; pg. 391, pg. 825

AUTOSWEEP - Construction Equipment - VERMEER MANUFACTURING COMPANY; pg. 708, pg. 711

AUTOTAK - Monitor - HOWELL INSTRUMENTS INC.; pg. 1417, pg. 1695

AUTOTASKING - Supercomputing System - CRAY INC.; pg. 380, pg. 1834

AUTOTEMP - Monitor - HOWELL INSTRUMENTS INC.; pg. 1417, pg. 1695

AUTOTEST - Magazine For New Car Buyers - AMERICAN AUTOMOBILE ASSOCIATION; pg. 1190, pg. 429

AUTOTHANE - Microcellular Elastomers - THE DOW CHEMICAL COMPANY; pg. 1157, pg. 898

AUTOTHERM - Software System - MENTOR GRAPHICS CORPORATION; pg. 432, pg. 1510

AUTOTHERM DUO - Software System - MENTOR GRAPHICS CORPORATION; pg. 432, pg. 1510

AUTOTHERM MCM - Software System - MENTOR GRAPHICS CORPORATION; pg. 432, pg. 1510

AUTOTOME RX - Cannulating Sphincterotome Distal Catheter - BOSTON SCIENTIFIC CORPORATION; pg. 1508, pg. 831

AUTOTOUCH - Information Handling/Retrieval Equipment - EASTMAN KODAK COMPANY; pg. 1408, pg. 1333

AUTOTRAC - Steering Kits - DEERE & COMPANY; pg. 703, pg. 632

AUTOTRACK - Software - AUTODESK INC.; pg. 356, pg. 257

AUTOTRACKER - Computer Software - GEMA USA INC.; pg. 1339, pg. 686

AUTOTRADER.COM - Vehicle Dealer Website - DOMINION ENTERPRISES; pg. 1636, pg. 1796

AUTOTRAK - Drilling System - BAKER HUGHES INTEQ; pg. 1316, pg. 1700

AUTOTROL - Residential & Commercial Valves for Softeners & Media Filters - GE WATER & PROCESS TECHNOLOGIES; pg. 1339, pg. 1588

AUTOVANTAGE - Vehicle Maintenance & Repair Program - AFFINION GROUP, INC.; pg. 1225, pg. 372

AUTOVENT - Transport Ventilator - ALLIED HEALTHCARE PRODUCTS, INC.; pg. 1491, pg. 990

AUTOVENT - Filter - PALL CORPORATION; pg. 232, pg. 1323

AUTOVIEW - Software System - MENTOR GRAPHICS CORPORATION; pg. 432, pg. 1510

AUTOVIEW - Medical Device - RESMED INC.; pg. 1589, pg. 207

AUTOVISION - Mechanical & Electrical System - JOHNSON CONTROLS, INC.; pg. 209, pg. 1876

AUTOVPAP - Medical Device - RESMED INC.; pg. 1589, pg. 207

AUTOVUE - Collision Warning System - ITERIS, INC.; pg. 293, pg. 261

AUTOVUE - Software - ORACLE CORPORATION; pg. 450, pg. 191

AUTOWAY - Car Dealerships - AUTONATION, INC.; pg. 165, pg. 423

AUTOWEB.COM - Automotive E-Commerce Site - AUTOBYTEL INC.; pg. 1230, pg. 107

AUTOWEEK - Automotive Magazine - CRAIN COMMUNICATIONS, INC.; pg. 1631, pg. 879

AUTOWEST - Car Dealerships - AUTONATION, INC.; pg. 165, pg. 423

AUTOWIRE STATION - Software System - MENTOR GRAPHICS CORPORATION; pg. 432, pg. 1510

AUTOWRAP - Protection Film - AMERICAN BILTRITE INC.; pg. 1878, pg. 856

AUTOZONE - Automotive Products Including Batteries, Fan Belts, Engines & Hoses - AUTOZONE, INC.; pg. 200, pg. 1641

AUTUMN - Fabric - NEMSCHOFF, INC.; pg. 936, pg. 1890

AUTUMN CELEBRATION CENTERPIECE - Flower Arrangement - 1-800-FLOWERS.COM, INC.; pg. 1758, pg. 1151

AUTUMN HARVEST BLEND - Coffee - KEURIG GREEN MOUNTAIN, INC.; pg. 868, pg. 1768

AUTUMN INSPIRATION - Autumn Bouquet - 1-800-FLOWERS.COM, INC.; pg. 1758, pg. 1151

AUTUMN LEAF - Rug - COURISTAN INC.; pg. 921, pg. 1067

AUTUMN SMOKE - Brick & Tile Product - CHEROKEE BRICK & TILE COMPANY; pg. 75, pg. 535

AUTUMN SPLENDOR BOUQUET - Floral Bouquet - FTD GROUP, INC.; pg. 1795, pg. 608

AUTUMN SUNRISE - Video Game - INTERNATIONAL GAME TECHNOLOGY; pg. 957, pg. 1024

AUXACOLOR - Software - BIO-RAD LABORATORIES, INC.; pg. 1504, pg. 101

AUXAL - Fabric - NEMSCHOFF, INC.; pg. 936, pg. 1890

AUXPANDER - Auxiliary Expander - SHURE INCORPORATED; pg. 672, pg. 638

AV - Distributorship Services - AVNET, INC.; pg. 622, pg. 15

AV-OK - Total Vacation Security Plan - APPLE VACATIONS INC.; pg. 1899, pg. 1556

AV PLUS - Pacing Leads - ST. JUDE MEDICAL, INC.; pg. 1596, pg. 963

AV3 POKE-THRU - Wiring Products - WIREMOLD/LEGRAND; pg. 689, pg. 383

AVA - Clothing - ABERCROMBIE & FITCH CO.; pg. 37, pg. 1466

AVA - Lighting - ETHAN ALLEN INTERIORS INC.; pg. 924, pg. 343

AVA PUHI MONI - Ethnobotanical Product - NU SKIN ENTERPRISES, INC.; pg. 518, pg. 1755

AVAC - Acetylene Vacuum Carburizing Technology - IPSEN INTERNATIONAL, INC.; pg. 1073, pg. 562

AVAGARD - Antiseptic - 3M COMPANY; pg. 1142, pg. 956

AVAGE - Skin Care Product - ALLERGAN, INC.; pg. 1491, pg. 106

AVAIL - Agricultural Product - J.R. SIMPLOT COMPANY; pg. 867, pg. 547

AVAILABILITY MANAGER - Software - DELL SOFTWARE; pg. 385, pg. 40

AVALANCHE - Pick-Up Truck - GENERAL MOTORS COMPANY; pg. 175, pg. 881

AVALANCHE - Ales - JIM BEAM BRANDS CO.; pg. 1965, pg. 601

AVALANCHE - Thermal Storage Product - PAUL MUELLER COMPANY; pg. 706, pg. 1007

AVALANCHE - Protective Eyewear - SELLSTROM MANUFACTURING CO.; pg. 1428, pg. 659

AVALANCHE MOUNTAIN - T-Shirts - ABERCROMBIE & FITCH CO.; pg. 37, pg. 1466

AVALANCHE PASS SOLID OXFORD - Shirts - ABERCROMBIE & FITCH CO.; pg. 37, pg. 1466

AVALIGN TECHNOLOGIES - Company Name - AVALIGN TECHNOLOGIES; pg. 1400, pg. 622

AVALON - Corporate Furniture - BERNHARDT DESIGN; pg. 918, pg. 1381

AVALON - Table - BLATT BOWLING & BILLIARD CORP.; pg. 1827, pg. 1203

AVALON - Seal & Thermoplastic Component - GREENE, TWEED & CO.; pg. 1344, pg. 1544

AVALON - Budget Escorted Tours - GROUP VOYAGERS, INC.; pg. 1910, pg. 333

AVALON - Furniture - JASPER GROUP; pg. 930, pg. 691

AVALON - Car - TOYOTA MOTOR NORTH AMERICA, INC.; pg. 192, pg. 1303

AVALON HILL - Toy & Game - HASBRO, INC.; pg. 954, pg. 1603

AVALON HYBRID - Hybrid Car - TOYOTA MOTOR NORTH AMERICA, INC.; pg. 192, pg. 1303

AVALON ORGANICS - Organic Products - THE HAIN CELESTIAL GROUP, INC.; pg. 860, pg. 1172

AVALONIDM - Software System - EMC CORPORATION; pg. 391, pg. 825

AVALUNG - Outdoor Products - BLACK DIAMOND, INC.; pg. 1827, pg. 1756

AVAMAR - Software - EMC CORPORATION; pg. 391, pg. 825

AVANSE - Acrylics - THE DOW CHEMICAL COMPANY; pg. 1157, pg. 898

AVANT - Door Glass - ODL INCORPORATED; pg. 101, pg. 914

AVANT - Wallcovering - OMNOVA SOLUTIONS INC; pg. 1176, pg. 1453

AVANT GARDE - Fabric - NEMSCHOFF, INC.; pg. 936, pg. 1890

First page reference indicates Business Class Edition
Second page reference indicates Geographic Edition

AVANT GAUZE - Medical Product - MEDLINE INDUSTRIES, INC.; *pg.* 1562, *pg.* 635
AVANTA AC - Ceramics Solutions - SACHEM INC.; *pg.* 1180, *pg.* 1665
AVANTAGE - Loader - GEHL COMPANY; *pg.* 1339, *pg.* 1899
AVANTE - Software - EPICOR SOFTWARE CORPORATION; *pg.* 393, *pg.* 110
AVANTE - Musical Instrument - GIBSON GUITAR CORP.; *pg.* 550, *pg.* 1650
AVANTGARD - Software - SUNGARD DATA SYSTEMS INC.; *pg.* 477, *pg.* 1592
AVANTGLIDE - Chair - GROUPE DUTAILIER INC.; *pg.* 926, *pg.* 1960
AVANTGO - Windows Mobile Smartphone Beta - SAP; *pg.* 465, *pg.* 78
AVANTI - Cigars - AVANTI CIGAR CORPORATION; *pg.* 1894, *pg.* 1527
AVANTI - Testing Instrument System - BECKMAN COULTER, INC.; *pg.* 1402, *pg.* 48
AVANTI - Table - BLATT BOWLING & BILLIARD CORP.; *pg.* 1827, *pg.* 1203
AVANTI - Competition Air Rifles - DAISY MANUFACTURING COMPANY; *pg.* 1831, *pg.* 35
AVANTI - Furniture - ETHAN ALLEN INTERIORS INC.; *pg.* 924, *pg.* 343
AVANTIGE - Stretch Fabrics for Furniture Upholstery - INVISTA B.V.; *pg.* 1168, *pg.* 723
AVANWAVES - Software - SYNOPSYS, INC.; *pg.* 480, *pg.* 162
AVANZA - Supermarkets - SPARTANNASH CO.; *pg.* 1034, *pg.* 925
AVARI - Office Furniture - HAWORTH, INC.; *pg.* 402, *pg.* 891
AVASTIN - Anti-VEGF Antibody for Metastatic Colorectal Cancer - GENENTECH, INC.; *pg.* 1533, *pg.* 279
AVASTIN - Therapeutic Product - IDERA PHARMACEUTICALS, INC.; *pg.* 1543, *pg.* 808
AVATAR - Home Builders - AV HOMES INC.; *pg.* 1080, *pg.* 20
AVATAR - Kitchen Product - KOHLER CO.; *pg.* 91, *pg.* 1862
AVAUNT - Insecticide - E.I. DU PONT DE NEMOURS & COMPANY; *pg.* 1159, *pg.* 390
AVBLEND - Engine Lubricant - SPEEDWAY MOTORSPORTS, INC.; *pg.* 584, *pg.* 1370
AVCARB - Carbon Fiber Product - BALLARD POWER SYSTEMS, INC.; *pg.* 70, *pg.* 1907
AVDEL - Fastening Systems - TEXTRON INC.; *pg.* 235, *pg.* 1607
AVEDA - Cosmetics - AVEDA CORPORATION; *pg.* 499, *pg.* 917
AVEDA - Professional Hair Products - THE ESTEE LAUDER COMPANIES INC.; *pg.* 508, *pg.* 1229
AVEDA LOVE - Perfume - AVEDA CORPORATION; *pg.* 499, *pg.* 917
AVEDIS ZILDJIAN - Cymbals & Drumsticks - AVEDIS ZILDJIAN COMPANY; *pg.* 531, *pg.* 839
AVEENO - Healthcare Product - JOHNSON & JOHNSON; *pg.* 1549, *pg.* 1091
AVELOX - Pharmaceutical Product - BAYER HEALTHCARE PHARMACEUTICAL DIVISION; *pg.* 1500, *pg.* 1132
AVENEL - Jacket - I. SPIEWAK & SONS, INC.; *pg.* 42, *pg.* 1242
AVENGER - Hood/Fender Shield - LUND INTERNATIONAL, INC.; *pg.* 211, *pg.* 526
AVENGER - Hockey Table - SCHOOL-TECH, INC.; *pg.* 1844, *pg.* 866
AVENGER - Floating Scraper - YETTER MANUFACTURING CO., INC.; *pg.* 708, *pg.* 598
AVENIR - Boat Seats - ATTWOOD CORPORATION; *pg.* 1705, *pg.* 897
AVENIR - Office Furniture - STEELCASE INC.; *pg.* 475, *pg.* 889
AVENSIS - Footwear - STEVEN MADDEN, LTD.; *pg.* 1819, *pg.* 1176
AVENTA II - Towing Product - BLUE OX; *pg.* 701, *pg.* 1019
AVENTINE - Bathroom Fan - HUNTER FAN COMPANY; *pg.* 57, *pg.* 1631
AVENTINO - Leather Seats - LEAR CORPORATION; *pg.* 229, *pg.* 907
AVENTURA - Clothing - SPORTIF USA INC.; *pg.* 33, *pg.* 1032
AVENUE - Office Chairs - BERNHARDT DESIGN; *pg.* 918, *pg.* 1381
THE AVENUE - Specialty Realty Center - COUSINS PROPERTIES INCORPORATED; *pg.* 1088, *pg.* 501
AVENUE - Software - ENVIRONMENTAL SYSTEMS RESEARCH INSTITUTE INC.; *pg.* 393, *pg.* 188
AVENUE - Fabric - NEMSCHOFF, INC.; *pg.* 936, *pg.* 1890
AVENUE OF AMERICAS - Watch - GEVRIL USA; *pg.* 6, *pg.* 1348
THE AVENUE OF THE PENINSULA - Brokerage - COUSINS PROPERTIES INCORPORATED; *pg.* 1088, *pg.* 501
THE AVENUE PEACHTREE CITY - Brokerage - COUSINS PROPERTIES INCORPORATED; *pg.* 1088, *pg.* 501
THE AVENUE WEST COBB - Brokerage - COUSINS PROPERTIES INCORPORATED; *pg.* 1088, *pg.* 501
AVEO - Sedan - GENERAL MOTORS COMPANY; *pg.* 175, *pg.* 881
AVERSANA - Community Name - WCI COMMUNITIES, INC.; *pg.* 1118, *pg.* 414
AVERY - Self-Adhesive Labeling Products - AVERY DENNISON CORPORATION; *pg.* 1452, *pg.* 95
AVERY - Furniture - ETHAN ALLEN INTERIORS INC.; *pg.* 924, *pg.* 343
AVERY DENNISON - Adhesive & Office Products - AVERY DENNISON CORPORATION; *pg.* 1452, *pg.* 95
AVERY GRAPHICS - Shell Signs - AVERY DENNISON CORPORATION; *pg.* 1452, *pg.* 95
AVIA - Laser & Laser System - COHERENT, INC.; *pg.* 1406, *pg.* 265
AVIA - Battery Charger - LA MARCHE MANUFACTURING COMPANY; *pg.* 1300, *pg.* 606
AVIA - Running & Acitvewear Products - SEQUENTIAL BRANDS GROUP, INC.; *pg.* 1395, *pg.* 1290
AVIAN - Bird Feed - DESIGNING HEALTH, INC.; *pg.* 1523, *pg.* 299
AVIANCE NIGHT MUSK - Fragrance - PARFUMS DE COEUR LTD.; *pg.* 519, *pg.* 376
AVIATION WEEK - Publication - THE MCGRAW-HILL COMPANIES INC.; *pg.* 1663, *pg.* 1257
AVIATOR - Valves - FLOWSERVE CORPORATION; *pg.* 82, *pg.* 1719
AVIATOR - Car & Van - FORD MOTOR COMPANY OF CANADA, LIMITED; *pg.* 174, *pg.* 1930
AVIATOR - Playing Cards - THE UNITED STATES PLAYING CARD COMPANY; *pg.* 969, *pg.* 727
AVIATOR - Ceiling Fan - WESTINGHOUSE LIGHTING CORPORATION; *pg.* 687, *pg.* 1571
AVIAX - Animal Health Product - PHIBROCHEM; *pg.* 1177, *pg.* 1124
AVICEL - Food Ingredient - FMC CORPORATION; *pg.* 1163, *pg.* 1564
AVICINE - Pharmaceutical Product - ASTEX PHARMACEUTICALS, INC; *pg.* 1497, *pg.* 77
AVID - Editing & Audio Systems - AVID TECHNOLOGY, INC.; *pg.* 622, *pg.* 804
AVID 3D - Video Editing Product - AVID TECHNOLOGY, INC.; *pg.* 622, *pg.* 804
AVID ACTIVE CONTENTMANAGER FOR BROADCAST - Asset Management & Distribution Solution - AVID TECHNOLOGY, INC.; *pg.* 622, *pg.* 804
AVID ACTIVE CONTENTMANAGER SDK - Asset Management & Distribution Solution - AVID TECHNOLOGY, INC.; *pg.* 622, *pg.* 804
AVID ADRENALINE - Editing System - AVID TECHNOLOGY, INC.; *pg.* 622, *pg.* 804
AVID AIRSPACE - High-Performance Digital Video Servers & Applications - AVID TECHNOLOGY, INC.; *pg.* 622, *pg.* 804
AVID AIRSPEED - Workflow Integration System - AVID TECHNOLOGY, INC.; *pg.* 622, *pg.* 804
AVID CAPTURE MANAGER - Video Servers - AVID TECHNOLOGY, INC.; *pg.* 622, *pg.* 804
AVID DNA FAMILY - Media Processing Hardware - AVID TECHNOLOGY, INC.; *pg.* 622, *pg.* 804
AVID DNXCHANGE - Media Devices - AVID TECHNOLOGY, INC.; *pg.* 622, *pg.* 804
AVID DS - Editing System - AVID TECHNOLOGY, INC.; *pg.* 622, *pg.* 804
AVID DS ASSIST STATION - Media Software - AVID TECHNOLOGY, INC.; *pg.* 622, *pg.* 804
AVID DS NITRIS - Finishing & Mastering System - AVID TECHNOLOGY, INC.; *pg.* 622, *pg.* 804
AVID DS NITRIS EDITOR - Editing System - AVID TECHNOLOGY, INC.; *pg.* 622, *pg.* 804
AVID DVD BY SONIC - DVD Authoring System - AVID TECHNOLOGY, INC.; *pg.* 622, *pg.* 804
AVID FX - Special Effects System - AVID TECHNOLOGY, INC.; *pg.* 622, *pg.* 804
AVID INEWS - News Collection & Management System - AVID TECHNOLOGY, INC.; *pg.* 622, *pg.* 804
AVID INEWS CONTROLAIR - News Collection & Management System - AVID TECHNOLOGY, INC.; *pg.* 622, *pg.* 804
AVID INEWS FAMILY - News Collection & Management System - AVID TECHNOLOGY, INC.; *pg.* 622, *pg.* 804
AVID INEWS MULTIBYTE - Asian-Language Newsroom Automation System - AVID TECHNOLOGY, INC.; *pg.* 622, *pg.* 804
AVID INTERPLAY - Workgroup Services - AVID TECHNOLOGY, INC.; *pg.* 622, *pg.* 804
AVID LEADERPLUS - Election Data Organizer & Publisher - AVID TECHNOLOGY, INC.; *pg.* 622, *pg.* 804
AVID MEDIA BROWSE - Browsing & Editing System - AVID TECHNOLOGY, INC.; *pg.* 622, *pg.* 804
AVID MEDIA COMPOSER - Digital Nonlinear Editing System - AVID TECHNOLOGY, INC.; *pg.* 622, *pg.* 804
AVID MEDIA COMPOSER ADRENALINE - Digital Nonlinear Editing System - AVID TECHNOLOGY, INC.; *pg.* 622, *pg.* 804
AVID MEDIA STATION XL - Digitizing & Output System - AVID TECHNOLOGY, INC.; *pg.* 622, *pg.* 804
AVID MEDIADOCK ULTRA320 - Media Hardware - AVID TECHNOLOGY, INC.; *pg.* 622, *pg.* 804
AVID MEDIARRAY ZX - Shared Storage Solution - AVID TECHNOLOGY, INC.; *pg.* 622, *pg.* 804
AVID MOJO - Media Hardware - AVID TECHNOLOGY, INC.; *pg.* 622, *pg.* 804
AVID NEARCHIVE - Nearline Storage - AVID TECHNOLOGY, INC.; *pg.* 622, *pg.* 804
AVID NEWSCUTTER - News Editing System - AVID TECHNOLOGY, INC.; *pg.* 622, *pg.* 804
AVID NEWSCUTTER ADRENALINE FX - Nonlinear News Editing System - AVID TECHNOLOGY, INC.; *pg.* 622, *pg.* 804
AVID NEWSCUTTER EFFECTS - News Editing System - AVID TECHNOLOGY, INC.; *pg.* 622, *pg.* 804
AVID NEWSCUTTER FAMILY - News Editing System - AVID TECHNOLOGY, INC.; *pg.* 622, *pg.* 804
AVID PRO TOOLS LE - Digital Audio Production System - AVID TECHNOLOGY, INC.; *pg.* 622, *pg.* 804
AVID UNITY FOR NEWS - News Production Environment - AVID TECHNOLOGY, INC.; *pg.* 622, *pg.* 804
AVID UNITY LANSHARE EX - Ethernet-Based Shared Storage Network - AVID TECHNOLOGY, INC.; *pg.* 622, *pg.* 804
AVID UNITY LANSHARE FOR NEWS - Collaborative News Workgroup System - AVID TECHNOLOGY, INC.; *pg.* 622, *pg.* 804
AVID UNITY MEDIAMANAGER - Media Processing System - AVID TECHNOLOGY, INC.; *pg.* 622, *pg.* 804
AVID UNITY MEDIAMANAGER SELECT - Editing Tool - AVID TECHNOLOGY, INC.; *pg.* 622, *pg.* 804
AVID UNITY MEDIANETWORK - High-Bandwidth Shared Storage Network - AVID TECHNOLOGY, INC.; *pg.* 622, *pg.* 804
AVID UNITY PROENCODE - Media to Web Translation System - AVID TECHNOLOGY, INC.; *pg.* 622, *pg.* 804
AVID UNITY TRANSFERMANAGER - Media Transfer System - AVID TECHNOLOGY, INC.; *pg.* 622, *pg.* 804
AVID XDECK - Direct Ingest Solution - AVID TECHNOLOGY, INC.; *pg.* 622, *pg.* 804
AVID XPRESS - Editing & Audio Systems - AVID TECHNOLOGY, INC.; *pg.* 622, *pg.* 804
AVID XPRESS DV - DV-Only Editing System - AVID TECHNOLOGY, INC.; *pg.* 622, *pg.* 804
AVID XPRESS PRO - Professional Editing Software - AVID TECHNOLOGY, INC.; *pg.* 622, *pg.* 804
AVID XPRESS STUDIO - Editing System - AVID TECHNOLOGY, INC.; *pg.* 622, *pg.* 804
AVIGNON - Ceramic Tile - WALKER & ZANGER, INC.; *pg.* 119, *pg.* 281
AVIIA - Audio & Video Solution - SEMTECH CORPORATION GENNUM PRODUCTS; *pg.* 671, *pg.* 1919
AVIKRIMP - Electronic Components - MOLEX INCORPORATED; *pg.* 655, *pg.* 628
AVILA - Dinnerware - THE HOMER LAUGHLIN CHINA COMPANY; *pg.* 1125, *pg.* 1850
AVIMARK - Software - HENRY SCHEIN, INC.; *pg.* 1541, *pg.* 1180
AVIMID - Chemical Product - CYTEC INDUSTRIES, INC.; *pg.* 1155, *pg.* 1131
AVINO - Footwear - STEVEN MADDEN, LTD.; *pg.* 1819, *pg.* 1176
AVINZA - Capsules - KING PHARMACEUTICALS, INC.; *pg.*

First page reference indicates Business Class Edition
Second page reference indicates Geographic Edition

1553, *pg.* 1627
AVINZA - Pharmaceutical Product - LIGAND PHARMACEUTICALS INC.; *pg.* 1556, *pg.* 119
AVIROL - Fatty Alcohol Sulfates - HENKEL CORPORATION; *pg.* 1165, *pg.* 1535
AVIS - Car Rental Services - AVIS BUDGET GROUP, INC.; *pg.* 1900, *pg.* 1102
AVISTA COMMUNICATIONS - Telecommunications - AVISTA CORPORATION; *pg.* 1935, *pg.* 1843
AVISTA ENERGY - Energy Trading & Marketing - AVISTA CORPORATION; *pg.* 1935, *pg.* 1843
AVISTA VENTURES - Strategic Investments - AVISTA CORPORATION; *pg.* 1935, *pg.* 1843
AVITAL - Mobile Electronics Equipment - DEI HOLDINGS, INC.; *pg.* 633, *pg.* 302
AVITEX - Fiber Softener - E.I. DU PONT DE NEMOURS & COMPANY; *pg.* 1159, *pg.* 390
AVIVA - Intravenous Solutions - BAXTER INTERNATIONAL INC.; *pg.* 1499, *pg.* 599
AVIVA - Lighting System - LITECONTROL CORPORATION; *pg.* 1301, *pg.* 841
AVIVA - Furniture - NEMSCHOFF, INC.; *pg.* 936, *pg.* 1890
AVIVA - Wallcovering - YORK WALLCOVERINGS INC.; *pg.* 947, *pg.* 1598
AVIVE - Furniture - HERMAN MILLER, INC.; *pg.* 926, *pg.* 913
AVL MANAGER - Navigation Aid - TRIMBLE NAVIGATION LIMITED; *pg.* 1384, *pg.* 288
AVNETDIRECT - Electronic Retailing Services - AVNET, INC.; *pg.* 622, *pg.* 15
AVOCADO BLOSSOM - Honey - MILLER'S HONEY COMPANY; *pg.* 1860, *pg.* 1759
AVOCET - production Software - SCHLUMBERGER LIMITED; *pg.* 801, *pg.* 1714
AVOJUICE - Nail Care Product - OPI PRODUCTS INC.; *pg.* 518, *pg.* 167
AVON - Beauty Product - AVON PRODUCTS, INC.; *pg.* 500, *pg.* 1198
AVON - Books - HARPERCOLLINS PUBLISHERS INC.; *pg.* 1647, *pg.* 1237
AVON - Fabric - NEMSCHOFF, INC.; *pg.* 936, *pg.* 1890
AVON - Tables - STEELCASE INC.; *pg.* 475, *pg.* 889
AVON BASICS - Skincare - AVON PRODUCTS, INC.; *pg.* 500, *pg.* 1198
AVON COLOR - Cosmetics - AVON PRODUCTS, INC.; *pg.* 500, *pg.* 1198
AVON SOLUTIONS - Skincare - AVON PRODUCTS, INC.; *pg.* 500, *pg.* 1198
AVON TYRES - Automobile & Motorcycle Tires - COOPER TIRE & RUBBER COMPANY; *pg.* 1881, *pg.* 1453
AVONEX - Pharmaceutical Products - ABBOTT LABORATORIES; *pg.* 1484, *pg.* 551
AVOPLEX NAIL - Oil - OPI PRODUCTS INC.; *pg.* 518, *pg.* 167
AVOPTION - Video Interface - AVID TECHNOLOGY, INC.; *pg.* 622, *pg.* 804
AVORA - Flame Resistant Fabrics - INVISTA B.V.; *pg.* 1168, *pg.* 723
AVOSET - Food Products - RICH PRODUCTS CORPORATION; *pg.* 892, *pg.* 1150
AVP - Video Game - INTERNATIONAL GAME TECHNOLOGY; *pg.* 957, *pg.* 1024
AVR - Microcontroller - ATMEL CORPORATION; *pg.* 621, *pg.* 238
AVR DRAGON - Integrated Circuit - ATMEL CORPORATION; *pg.* 621, *pg.* 238
AVR FREAKS - Web Maintaining - ATMEL CORPORATION; *pg.* 621, *pg.* 238
AVR STUDIO - Computer Studio - ATMEL CORPORATION; *pg.* 621, *pg.* 238
AVRAMP - Vehicle Management System - I.D. SYSTEMS, INC.; *pg.* 643, *pg.* 1134
AVROY SHALIN - Beauty Product - TUPPERWARE BRANDS CORPORATION; *pg.* 1139, *pg.* 456
AVS - Spinal System - STRYKER CORPORATION; *pg.* 1598, *pg.* 894
AVS 3100 - Router - CISCO SYSTEMS, INC.; *pg.* 372, *pg.* 240
AVTEC - Foodservice - UNIFIED BRANDS INC.; *pg.* 1385, *pg.* 970
AVWEB - Aviation Magazine - BELVOIR MEDIA GROUP, LLC; *pg.* 1620, *pg.* 360
AWAIT - Office Furniture - STEELCASE INC.; *pg.* 475, *pg.* 889
AWAKE - Tea - STARBUCKS CORPORATION; *pg.* 897, *pg.* 1840
AWAKENING - Fabric - NEMSCHOFF, INC.; *pg.* 936, *pg.* 1890
AWAPUHI - Hair Care System - JOHN PAUL MITCHELL SYSTEMS; *pg.* 512, *pg.* 133
AWAPUHI MOISTURE MIST - Hair Care Product - JOHN PAUL MITCHELL SYSTEMS; *pg.* 512, *pg.* 133
AWARD - Food Product - CONAGRA FOODS, INC.; *pg.* 826, *pg.* 1014
AWARD - Cooler - SEELEY INTERNATIONAL AMERICAS; *pg.* 1076, *pg.* 19
AWARD - Writing Instrument - SHEAFFER PEN CORPORATION; *pg.* 469, *pg.* 371
AWARDBIOS - Software - PHOENIX TECHNOLOGIES LTD.; *pg.* 454, *pg.* 147
AWARE - Medical Test Product - BIOMERICA, INC.; *pg.* 1506, *pg.* 107
AWARENESS - Safety & Protective Equipment - ENCON SAFETY PRODUCTS; *pg.* 1334, *pg.* 1705
AWARENET - Telecommunications Hardware & Software - LOCKHEED MARTIN CORPORATION; *pg.* 229, *pg.* 762
AWARETEST - Software - AGILENT TECHNOLOGIES, INC.; *pg.* 614, *pg.* 264
AWAY FROM HOME - Food Product - CAMPBELL SOUP COMPANY; *pg.* 844, *pg.* 1048
THE AWAY NETWORK - Travel Portal Websites - ORBITZ WORLDWIDE, INC.; *pg.* 1918, *pg.* 586
AWAY WE GO - Book - SCIENTIFIC LEARNING CORPORATION; *pg.* 607, *pg.* 172
AWD - Software - DST SYSTEMS, INC.; *pg.* 388, *pg.* 982
AWD BUSINESS INTELLIGENCE - Software - DST SYSTEMS, INC.; *pg.* 388, *pg.* 982
AWD/CONTACT - Software - DST SYSTEMS, INC.; *pg.* 388, *pg.* 982
AWD/EMAIL - Software - DST SYSTEMS, INC.; *pg.* 388, *pg.* 982
AWD/ICR - Software - DST SYSTEMS, INC.; *pg.* 388, *pg.* 982
AWD/KNOWLEDGE ENABLER - Software - DST SYSTEMS, INC.; *pg.* 388, *pg.* 982
AWD/NETSERVER - Software - DST SYSTEMS, INC.; *pg.* 388, *pg.* 982
AWD/RIP - Software - DST SYSTEMS, INC.; *pg.* 388, *pg.* 982
AWD/SCAN - Software - DST SYSTEMS, INC.; *pg.* 388, *pg.* 982
AWD/ST - Software - DST SYSTEMS, INC.; *pg.* 388, *pg.* 982
AWD/THIN CLIENT - Software - DST SYSTEMS, INC.; *pg.* 388, *pg.* 982
AWD/VOICE - Software - DST SYSTEMS, INC.; *pg.* 388, *pg.* 982
AWE-SLIM - Nutritional Supplement - NOW HEALTH GROUP, INC.; *pg.* 1576, *pg.* 557
AWESIM - Chipset - ADVANCED MICRO DEVICES, INC.; *pg.* 613, *pg.* 282
AWESOME - Foaming Tub & Tile Cleaner - SWISHER HYGIENE INC.; *pg.* 336, *pg.* 1507
AWESOME 8'S - Game - WMS INDUSTRIES INC.; *pg.* 593, *pg.* 666
AWGM1 - Fiber Optic Component - OPLINK COMMUNICATIONS, INC.; *pg.* 660, *pg.* 91
AWGM5 - Fiber Optic Component - OPLINK COMMUNICATIONS, INC.; *pg.* 660, *pg.* 91
AWREY - Pastries - AWREY BAKERIES, INC.; *pg.* 1015, *pg.* 896
AWS - Snowmobile - ARCTIC CAT INC.; *pg.* 1705, *pg.* 953
THE AX - Power Tool - MILWAUKEE ELECTRIC TOOL CORP.; *pg.* 1056, *pg.* 1855
AX - Ammonia Dissociators - SURFACE COMBUSTION, INC.; *pg.* 1077, *pg.* 1462
AX3 - Medical Equipment - INVACARE CORPORATION; *pg.* 1546, *pg.* 1451
AXAREL - Cleaning Product - PETROFERM INC.; *pg.* 1177, *pg.* 616
AXAREL - Chemical Cleaner Product - TECH SPRAY, L.P.; *pg.* 1183, *pg.* 1659
AXCELIS - Semiconductor Processing Equipment - AXCELIS TECHNOLOGIES, INC.; *pg.* 1400, *pg.* 787
AXCESS - Software - MILLER ELECTRIC MANUFACTURING CO.; *pg.* 1361, *pg.* 1852
AXE - Deodorant - UNILEVER UNITED STATES, INC.; *pg.* 904, *pg.* 1061
AXEDA ACCESS - Software - AXEDA SYSTEMS INC.; *pg.* 359, *pg.* 819
AXEDA ADMINISTRATION - Software - AXEDA SYSTEMS INC.; *pg.* 359, *pg.* 819
AXEDA AGENT CUSTOMIZATION - Software - AXEDA SYSTEMS INC.; *pg.* 359, *pg.* 819
AXEDA APPLICATION ADMINISTRATION - Software - AXEDA SYSTEMS INC.; *pg.* 359, *pg.* 819
AXEDA DASHBOARD - Software - AXEDA SYSTEMS INC.; *pg.* 359, *pg.* 819
AXEDA DEVICE - Software - AXEDA SYSTEMS INC.; *pg.* 359, *pg.* 819
AXEDA DEVICE RELATIONSHIP MANAGEMENT SYSTEM - Software - AXEDA SYSTEMS INC.; *pg.* 359, *pg.* 819
AXEDA DRM - Enterprise Software System - AXEDA SYSTEMS INC.; *pg.* 359, *pg.* 819
AXEDA ENTERPRISE - Software - AXEDA SYSTEMS INC.; *pg.* 359, *pg.* 819
AXEDA ENTERPRISE SDK - Software - AXEDA SYSTEMS INC.; *pg.* 359, *pg.* 819
AXEDA POLICY MANGER - Software - AXEDA SYSTEMS INC.; *pg.* 359, *pg.* 819
AXEDA QUERY STUDIO - Software - AXEDA SYSTEMS INC.; *pg.* 359, *pg.* 819
AXEDA REPORT - Software - AXEDA SYSTEMS INC.; *pg.* 359, *pg.* 819
AXEDA SERVICE - Software - AXEDA SYSTEMS INC.; *pg.* 359, *pg.* 819
AXEDA SERVICELINK - Software - AXEDA SYSTEMS INC.; *pg.* 359, *pg.* 819
AXEDA SERVICELINK BASICS - Software - AXEDA SYSTEMS INC.; *pg.* 359, *pg.* 819
AXEDA SOFTWARE MANAGEMENT - Software - AXEDA SYSTEMS INC.; *pg.* 359, *pg.* 819
AXEDA USAGE - Software - AXEDA SYSTEMS INC.; *pg.* 359, *pg.* 819
AXEL - Xenon Lightsource - AESCULAP, INC.; *pg.* 1487, *pg.* 1521
AXEL - Software System - MENTOR GRAPHICS CORPORATION; *pg.* 432, *pg.* 1510
AXEL SYMBOL GENIE - Software System - MENTOR GRAPHICS CORPORATION; *pg.* 432, *pg.* 1510
AXELL - Organic & Inorganic Chemicals & Biochemicals - ACCURATE CHEMICAL & SCIENTIFIC CORPORATION; *pg.* 1145, *pg.* 1350
AXESS - Software - WEATHERFORD PRODUCTION OPTIMIZATION; *pg.* 987, *pg.* 1725
AXIAL FLOW VALVE - Regulators - ELSTER AMERICAN METER COMPANY; *pg.* 1411, *pg.* 1387
AXID - Electronic Components - MOLEX INCORPORATED; *pg.* 655, *pg.* 628
AXIDYNE - Shoes - MASON COMPANIES, INC.; *pg.* 1811, *pg.* 1856
AXIEM - Electromagnetic Software - AWR CORPORATION; *pg.* 623, *pg.* 78
AXILOK - Vehicle System - MACLEAN-FOGG COMPANY INC.; *pg.* 1358, *pg.* 635
AXIOHM - Resistor Product - OHMITE MANUFACTURING COMPANY; *pg.* 660, *pg.* 553
AXIOM - Wood Flooring Product - ARMSTRONG WORLD INDUSTRIES, INC.; *pg.* 914, *pg.* 1545
AXIOM - Furniture - ASHLEY FURNITURE INDUSTRIES, INC.; *pg.* 914, *pg.* 1852
AXIOM - Coffee Brewer - BUNN-O-MATIC CORPORATION; *pg.* 53, *pg.* 661
AXIOM - Tray Packer - DOUGLAS MACHINE, INC.; *pg.* 1456, *pg.* 915
AXIOM - Fabric - NEMSCHOFF, INC.; *pg.* 936, *pg.* 1890
AXIOM - Advertising Solution - SEACHANGE INTERNATIONAL, INC.; *pg.* 1279, *pg.* 781
AXIOM 360 - Hand Trucks - MAGLINE, INC.; *pg.* 1358, *pg.* 908
AXION - Polymer Product - CHEMTURA CORPORATION; *pg.* 1152, *pg.* 355
AXION - Household Care Product - COLGATE-PALMOLIVE COMPANY; *pg.* 504, *pg.* 1215
AXIOS - Suspension Product - TENNECO, INC.; *pg.* 985, *pg.* 625
AXIS - Furniture - ASHLEY FURNITURE INDUSTRIES, INC.; *pg.* 914, *pg.* 1852
AXIS - Textiles - BERNHARDT DESIGN; *pg.* 918, *pg.* 1381
AXIS - Guitar - ERNIE BALL INC.; *pg.* 1768, *pg.* 68
AXIS - Flatware - ONEIDA LTD; *pg.* 1129, *pg.* 1318
AXIS - Apparel - PERRY ELLIS INTERNATIONAL, INC.; *pg.* 45, *pg.* 445
AXIS & ALLIES - Toy & Game - HASBRO, INC.; *pg.* 954, *pg.* 1603
AXIS NEWS - Online Service - CHYRONHEGO; *pg.* 371, *pg.* 1179

AXIS STORAGE MANAGER - Storage System - DOT HILL SYSTEMS CORP.; *pg.* 388, *pg.* 333
AXIST - Apparel - PERRY ELLIS INTERNATIONAL, INC.; *pg.* 45, *pg.* 445
AXIUS - Rupture Disc Product - FIKE CORPORATION; *pg.* 1047, *pg.* 973
AXIUS - Automotive Accessories - SHELL LUBRICANTS; *pg.* 217, *pg.* 1714
AXIUS SC - Rupture Disc Product - FIKE CORPORATION; *pg.* 1047, *pg.* 973
AXLE-SAVER - Rail Seals - THE TIMKEN COMPANY; *pg.* 218, *pg.* 1408
AXM - Atmospheric Mount Robots - BROOKS AUTOMATION, INC.; *pg.* 1320, *pg.* 813
AXOKINE - Second Generation Ciliary Neurotrophic Factor Causes Weight Loss in Animal - REGENERON PHARMACEUTICALS, INC.; *pg.* 1588, *pg.* 1345
AXON - Medical Device - DEPUY SYNTHES; *pg.* 1523, *pg.* 1593
AXON - Electronic Control Device - TASER INTERNATIONAL, INC.; *pg.* 677, *pg.* 24
AXOR - Faucets - MASCO CORPORATION; *pg.* 96, *pg.* 909
AXSYM - Clinical System - ABBOTT LABORATORIES; *pg.* 1484, *pg.* 551
AXXESS - Communication System - MITEL NETWORKS, INC.; *pg.* 1872, *pg.* 13
AXXESS NS - Proprietary Encryption Software - MAXXESS SYSTEMS, INC.; *pg.* 431, *pg.* 43
AXXSYS ORION - Earth Management Systems - GLOBECOMM SYSTEMS INC.; *pg.* 640, *pg.* 1164
AXYS - Software - ADVENT SOFTWARE, INC.; *pg.* 345, *pg.* 211
AY CARAMBA - Game - WMS INDUSTRIES INC.; *pg.* 593, *pg.* 666
AYATAKA - Beverages - THE COCA-COLA COMPANY; *pg.* 240, *pg.* 493
AYBAL-KIN - Beverages - THE COCA-COLA COMPANY; *pg.* 240, *pg.* 493
AYC GRENADIERS - Domestic Cigars - ALTADIS USA, INC.; *pg.* 1893, *pg.* 423
AYLESBURY - Carpet - BEAULIEU GROUP, LLC; *pg.* 917, *pg.* 529
AYR - Womenswear - BONOBOS; *pg.* 39, *pg.* 1205
AYTEX P - Starch - ARCHER-DANIELS-MIDLAND COMPANY; *pg.* 825, *pg.* 565
AYUDIN - Total Toilet Bowl Cleaner - THE CLOROX COMPANY; *pg.* 327, *pg.* 169
AYURVEDIC - Healthcare Product - SWANSON HEALTH PRODUCTS INC.; *pg.* 1600, *pg.* 1397
AZACTAM - Health Care Product - BRISTOL-MYERS SQUIBB COMPANY; *pg.* 1509, *pg.* 1206
AZASAN - Pharmaceutical Product - SALIX PHARMACEUTICALS, INC.; *pg.* 1591, *pg.* 1388
AZATROL - Turf Product - PBI/GORDON CORPORATION; *pg.* 1176, *pg.* 985
AZAVOR - Medicine - PFIZER INC.; *pg.* 1581, *pg.* 1278
AZDEL - Plastic Film & Sheeting - PPG INDUSTRIES, INC.; *pg.* 1445, *pg.* 1579
AZEK - Building Products - CPG INTERNATIONAL, INC.; *pg.* 1881, *pg.* 1586
AZELEX - Skin Care Product - ALLERGAN, INC.; *pg.* 1491, *pg.* 106
AZEOVAIRE - Steam & Hot Water LPG Vaporizer - ALGAS-SDI; *pg.* 1311, *pg.* 1831
AZIMUTH - Satellite Communication Product - KVH INDUSTRIES INC; *pg.* 650, *pg.* 1602
AZLOY - Fiber Reinforced Plastic Sheeting - PPG INDUSTRIES, INC.; *pg.* 1445, *pg.* 1579
AZMACORT - Inhalation Aerosol - ABBOTT LABORATORIES; *pg.* 1484, *pg.* 551
AZMET - Fiber Reinforced Plastic Sheeting - PPG INDUSTRIES, INC.; *pg.* 1445, *pg.* 1579
AZO - Photographic Paper - EASTMAN KODAK COMPANY; *pg.* 1408, *pg.* 1333
AZTEC - Vanity Lights - CRAFTMADE INTERNATIONAL, INC.; *pg.* 1295, *pg.* 1670
AZTEC - Fabric - NEMSCHOFF, INC.; *pg.* 936, *pg.* 1890
AZTEC ADVENTURE - Game - WMS INDUSTRIES INC.; *pg.* 593, *pg.* 666
AZTEC CHERRY - Flooring - LUMBER LIQUIDATORS HOLDINGS, INC.; *pg.* 94, *pg.* 1808
AZTEC GOLD - Lottery Game - KENTUCKY LOTTERY CORPORATION; *pg.* 996, *pg.* 735
AZTEC PYRAMID - Video Game - INTERNATIONAL GAME TECHNOLOGY; *pg.* 957, *pg.* 1024
AZTEC TEMPLE - Video Game - INTERNATIONAL GAME TECHNOLOGY; *pg.* 957, *pg.* 1024
AZTEK - Airbrush & Accessories - THE TESTOR CORPORATION; *pg.* 968, *pg.* 655
AZUB - Polymer Product - CHEMTURA CORPORATION; *pg.* 1152, *pg.* 355
AZUL TEQUILA - Spirits - PROXIMO SPIRITS, INC.; *pg.* 1969, *pg.* 1076
AZULFIDINE - Medicine - PFIZER INC.; *pg.* 1581, *pg.* 1278
AZULFIDINE EN-TABS - Pharmaceutical Product - PFIZER INC.; *pg.* 1581, *pg.* 1278
AZURE - Laser & Laser System - COHERENT, INC.; *pg.* 1406, *pg.* 265
AZURIA - Glass Product - PPG INDUSTRIES, INC.; *pg.* 1445, *pg.* 1579
AZURICO - Color - FERRO CORPORATION; *pg.* 1162, *pg.* 1462
AZURLITE - Flat Glass - PPG INDUSTRIES, INC.; *pg.* 1445, *pg.* 1579
AZYRAL - Laminating System - HUNTSMAN CORPORATION; *pg.* 1167, *pg.* 1758

B

B-11 - Gypsum Cement - USG CORPORATION; *pg.* 118, *pg.* 594
B-122 - Emulsions - SPINNAKER COATING, LLC; *pg.* 1470, *pg.* 1477
B-17 - Bike - MARIN BIKES; *pg.* 1708, *pg.* 168
B-24 - Systems Integration & Aeronautics - LOCKHEED MARTIN CORPORATION; *pg.* 229, *pg.* 762
B-5 DESIGN - Hair & Skin Product - AUBREY ORGANICS INC.; *pg.* 499, *pg.* 470
B&G - Food Products - B&G FOODS, INC.; *pg.* 838, *pg.* 1102
B&G - French Wines - DIAGEO CANADA, INC.; *pg.* 1961, *pg.* 1937
B&H - Underground Connector & Joint Box Products - TE CONNECTIVITY LTD.; *pg.* 677, *pg.* 1515
B&M - Baked Beans - B&G FOODS, INC.; *pg.* 838, *pg.* 1102
B&T FACTORY DIRECT - Clothing - DESTINATION XL GROUP, INC.; *pg.* 40, *pg.* 810
B&T STEEL - Metal Products - RUSSEL METALS INC.; *pg.* 1180, *pg.* 1928
B-CAP - Wire Connector - IDEAL INDUSTRIES, INC.; *pg.* 1051, *pg.* 662
B CDMA - Telecommunications Services - INTERDIGITAL, INC.; *pg.* 1872, *pg.* 1543
B. DALTON - Book Stores - BARNES & NOBLE, INC.; *pg.* 1619, *pg.* 1201
B-F - Metalworking Fluid Additive - TROY CORPORATION; *pg.* 1184, *pg.* 1067
B-FAMILY - Food Products - MODERN PRODUCTS, INC.; *pg.* 1568, *pg.* 1871
B-LINE - Paper Products - BOISE CASCADE HOLDINGS, L.L.C.; *pg.* 1453, *pg.* 546
B MAGAZINE - Magazine - BLOOMINGDALE'S, INC.; *pg.* 1763, *pg.* 1204
B-NINE - Polymer Product - CHEMTURA CORPORATION; *pg.* 1152, *pg.* 355
B-NINE WSG - Plant Growth Regulator - CHEMTURA CORPORATION; *pg.* 1152, *pg.* 355
B P SERIES - Line Printer - RICOH PRINTING SYSTEMS AMERICA, INC.; *pg.* 462, *pg.* 279
B-PAK - Motor - AMETEK FLOORCARE SPECIALTY MOTORS DIVISION; *pg.* 616, *pg.* 1456
B SERIES - Line Printer - RICOH PRINTING SYSTEMS AMERICA, INC.; *pg.* 462, *pg.* 279
B SHARP - Traction Liquid - MUELLER SPORTS MEDICINE, INC.; *pg.* 1570, *pg.* 1887
B-SQUARE - Security Product - BAE SYSTEMS PRODUCTS GROUP; *pg.* 359, *pg.* 432
B-TOO - Drilling & Tapping Machine - ROMAC INDUSTRIES, INC.; *pg.* 1061, *pg.* 1818
B-TRADE - Trading Services - BLOOMBERG L.P.; *pg.* 725, *pg.* 1204
B-W - Sodium Silicate - PQ CORPORATION; *pg.* 1178, *pg.* 1515
B-WELL - Beverage - MONSTER BEVERAGE CORPORATION; *pg.* 257, *pg.* 69
B1000 - Steel Rule - ARROW FASTENER COMPANY, INC.; *pg.* 1042, *pg.* 1118
B120 - Chrome Tape Measure - ARROW FASTENER COMPANY, INC.; *pg.* 1042, *pg.* 1118
B160 - Chrome Tape Measure - ARROW FASTENER COMPANY, INC.; *pg.* 1042, *pg.* 1118
B1OS BEADEX - Paper Faced Metal Outside Corner Nail-On Bead - USG CORPORATION; *pg.* 118, *pg.* 594
B1WNB BEADEX - Paper Faced Metal Outside Corner Tape-On Bead - USG CORPORATION; *pg.* 118, *pg.* 594
B1XW BEADEX - Paper Faced Metal Outside Corner Tape-On Bead - USG CORPORATION; *pg.* 118, *pg.* 594
B1XWEL BEADEX - Paper Faced Metal Outside Corner Tape-On Bead - USG CORPORATION; *pg.* 118, *pg.* 594
B1XWELNB BEADEX - Paper Faced Metal Outside Corner Tape-On Bead - USG CORPORATION; *pg.* 118, *pg.* 594
B1XWNB BEADEX - Paper Faced Metal Outside Corner Tape-On Bead - USG CORPORATION; *pg.* 118, *pg.* 594
B2 - Engine Oil - BARDAHL MANUFACTURING CORPORATION; *pg.* 972, *pg.* 1833
B2 BEADEX - Paper Faced Metal Inside Corner Tape-On Trim - USG CORPORATION; *pg.* 118, *pg.* 594
B250 - Chrome Tape Measure - ARROW FASTENER COMPANY, INC.; *pg.* 1042, *pg.* 1118
B25G - Tape Measure - ARROW FASTENER COMPANY, INC.; *pg.* 1042, *pg.* 1118
B25T - Tape Measure - ARROW FASTENER COMPANY, INC.; *pg.* 1042, *pg.* 1118
B25Y - Tape Measure - ARROW FASTENER COMPANY, INC.; *pg.* 1042, *pg.* 1118
B2B FOUNDATION - Software - ASPEN TECHNOLOGY, INC.; *pg.* 354, *pg.* 804
B300 - Tape Measure - ARROW FASTENER COMPANY, INC.; *pg.* 1042, *pg.* 1118
B30Y - Tape Measure - ARROW FASTENER COMPANY, INC.; *pg.* 1042, *pg.* 1118
B3BASICS - Electric Blenders & Can Openers - THERMOS L.L.C.; *pg.* 61, *pg.* 660
B3D - Trademark - BRILLIANT DIGITAL; *pg.* 1233, *pg.* 281
B4 - Pre-Training Fat Burner - BPI SPORTS, LLC; *pg.* 842, *pg.* 430
B4 - Dental Pre-Impression Surface Optimizer - DENTSPLY INTERNATIONAL INC.; *pg.* 1522, *pg.* 1596
B5 - Protective Eyewear - SELLSTROM MANUFACTURING CO.; *pg.* 1428, *pg.* 659
B500 - Tape Measure - ARROW FASTENER COMPANY, INC.; *pg.* 1042, *pg.* 1118
B7200 - Battery Pack - ARROW FASTENER COMPANY, INC.; *pg.* 1042, *pg.* 1118
B806 - Conveyor Scales - AVERY WEIGH-TRONIX, INC.; *pg.* 1315, *pg.* 925
BA-59P - Flame Retardants - CHEMTURA CORPORATION; *pg.* 1152, *pg.* 355
BA609 - Tilt Rotor Aircraft - BELL HELICOPTER TEXTRON, INC.; *pg.* 224, *pg.* 1693
BAA BAA BLACK SHEEP - Game - HASBRO, INC.; *pg.* 954, *pg.* 1603
BAA BAA BUCKS - Lottery Game - WEST VIRGINIA LOTTERY; *pg.* 1011, *pg.* 1849
BABBLE - Furniture - HERMAN MILLER, INC.; *pg.* 926, *pg.* 913
BABBLE.COM - Parental Blogging Platform - DISNEY INTERACTIVE MEDIA GROUP; *pg.* 1239, *pg.* 95
BABBLE.COM - Online Social Network - THE WALT DISNEY COMPANY; *pg.* 317, *pg.* 52
BABE - Designer Fragrance - PARFUMS DE COEUR LTD.; *pg.* 519, *pg.* 376
BABIES "R" US - Retail Baby Good Stores - TOYS "R" US, INC.; *pg.* 968, *pg.* 1130
BABOOM - Drug Delivery System - GENEREX BIOTECHNOLOGY CORPORATION; *pg.* 1534, *pg.* 1938
BABY ALIVE - Toy & Game - HASBRO, INC.; *pg.* 954, *pg.* 1603
BABY BLUE II - Resuscitator - VITAL SIGNS, INC.; *pg.* 1607, *pg.* 1126
BABY BODY CARE - Body Care Product - THE HAIN CELESTIAL GROUP, INC.; *pg.* 860, *pg.* 1172
BABY BOTTLE POP - Candy & Gum - THE TOPPS COMPANY, INC.; *pg.* 588, *pg.* 1302
BABY BRIGHT EYES - Doll - PLAYMATES TOYS INC.; *pg.* 965, *pg.* 82
BABY BULL - Corner Trim - USG CORPORATION; *pg.* 118, *pg.* 594
BABY BULLET - Baby Food Making System - CAPITAL BRANDS, LLC; *pg.* 53, *pg.* 127
BABY BURGER - Fast Food - A&W FOOD SERVICES OF CANADA INC.; *pg.* 1714, *pg.* 1908
BABY COUNTING PAL - Educational Toys - LEAPFROG ENTERPRISES, INC.; *pg.* 961, *pg.* 84
BABY CROKI - Toys - LEAPFROG ENTERPRISES, INC.; *pg.*

First page reference indicates Business Class Edition
Second page reference indicates Geographic Edition

961, *pg.* 84
BABY DAYS - Baby Lotion - BLUE CROSS LABORATORIES; *pg.* 326, *pg.* 277
BABY DON'T CRY - Hair Care Product - JOHN PAUL MITCHELL SYSTEMS; *pg.* 512, *pg.* 133
BABY GUESS - Apparel - GUESS?, INC.; *pg.* 25, *pg.* 132
BABY HEALTHTEX - Baby Apparel - LT APPAREL GROUP; *pg.* 29, *pg.* 1254
BABY LOAF - Cheese Products - TILLAMOOK COUNTY CREAMERY ASSOCIATION; *pg.* 901, *pg.* 1509
BABY-LOC - Removable Fencing - LOOP-LOC LTD.; *pg.* 1838, *pg.* 1165
BABY MAGIC - Baby Care Product - NATERRA INTERNATIONAL INC.; *pg.* 59, *pg.* 1684
BABY PAN!PAN - Deep Dish Pizza - LITTLE CAESARS ENTERPRISES, INC.; *pg.* 1736, *pg.* 883
BABY PIERCER - Ear Piercing System - INVERNESS CORPORATION; *pg.* 512, *pg.* 783
BABY PLEX - Nutritional Supplement - NATURAL ORGANICS, INC.; *pg.* 1571, *pg.* 1181
BABY Q - Gas Grill - WEBER-STEPHEN PRODUCTS LLC; *pg.* 62, *pg.* 650
BABY RUTH - Candy - NESTLE USA, INC.; *pg.* 883, *pg.* 96
THE BABY-SITTERS CLUB - Books - SCHOLASTIC INC.; *pg.* 1683, *pg.* 1288
BABY-SITTERS LITTLE SISTER - Educational Materials - SCHOLASTIC INC.; *pg.* 1683, *pg.* 1288
BABY TREND - Infant Products - BABY TREND, INC.; *pg.* 916, *pg.* 173
BABYCENTER - Baby Information Website - BABYCENTER, LLC; *pg.* 1231, *pg.* 212
BABYDJ - Baby Music Station - EVENFLO COMPANY, INC.; *pg.* 924, *pg.* 1470
BABYGO - Portable Playpen - EVENFLO COMPANY, INC.; *pg.* 924, *pg.* 1470
BABYGUND - Stuffed Animals - GUND, INC.; *pg.* 954, *pg.* 1056
BABYLINE - Pharmaceutical Product - ALERE INC.; *pg.* 1488, *pg.* 849
BABYLINK - Pharmaceutical Product - ALERE INC.; *pg.* 1488, *pg.* 849
BABYLISS - Personal Care Products - CONAIR CORPORATION; *pg.* 505, *pg.* 1055
BABYPLACE - Children's Clothing Stores - THE CHILDREN'S PLACE, INC.; *pg.* 22, *pg.* 1119
BABY'S FIRST BOUQUET - Fruit Arrangements - EDIBLE ARRANGEMENTS INTERNATIONAL, INC.; *pg.* 1768, *pg.* 382
BABYSAFE - Infant Resuscitator - VITAL SIGNS, INC.; *pg.* 1607, *pg.* 1126
BABYSLING - Baby Carrier - CROWN CRAFTS INFANT PRODUCTS, INC.; *pg.* 922, *pg.* 68
BABYTALK - Magazine - BONNIER CORPORATION; *pg.* 1622, *pg.* 480
B.A.C. - Company Name - BALTIMORE AIRCOIL COMPANY; *pg.* 1069, *pg.* 773
BAC-N-BLUE - Molecular Biology Product - THERMO FISHER SCIENTIFIC INC.; *pg.* 1602, *pg.* 61
BAC-OUT - Stain & Odor Eliminator - BI-O-KLEEN INDUSTRIES, INC.; *pg.* 326, *pg.* 1845
BAC-TO-BAC - Molecular Biology Product - THERMO FISHER SCIENTIFIC INC.; *pg.* 1602, *pg.* 61
BACALARICO - Salt Fish - CANADIAN FISH EXPORTERS, INC.; *pg.* 845, *pg.* 784
BACANO - Footwear - STEVEN MADDEN, LTD.; *pg.* 1819, *pg.* 1176
BACCARAT ROYALE - Video Game - INTERNATIONAL GAME TECHNOLOGY; *pg.* 957, *pg.* 1024
BACCHUS - Wine - WILLAMETTE VALLEY VINEYARDS, INC.; *pg.* 1972, *pg.* 1510
BACDANOL - Fragrance Ingredient - INTERNATIONAL FLAVORS & FRAGRANCES INC.; *pg.* 512, *pg.* 1244
BACHELOR - Brew - DESCHUTES BREWERY INC.; *pg.* 248, *pg.* 1496
BACI - Food Product - NESTLE USA, INC.; *pg.* 883, *pg.* 96
BACITRACIN - Ointment - G&W LABORATORIES INC.; *pg.* 1532, *pg.* 1123
BACITRACIN - Medicine - PFIZER INC.; *pg.* 1581, *pg.* 1278
BACK-2-BACK SUPPORT - Guaranteed Services - COMPONENTSOURCE HOLDING CORPORATION; *pg.* 378, *pg.* 533
BACK 2 LIFE - Back Pain Solution - CAPITAL BRANDS, LLC; *pg.* 53, *pg.* 127
BACK AGAIN - Fabric - NEMSCHOFF, INC.; *pg.* 936, *pg.* 1890
BACK BAY BOOKS - Publication - LITTLE, BROWN & COMPANY; *pg.* 1660, *pg.* 1251
BACK IT UP - Video Game - INTERNATIONAL GAME TECHNOLOGY; *pg.* 957, *pg.* 1024
BACK PACKER - Knife - COAST CUTLERY COMPANY; *pg.* 1121, *pg.* 1501
BACK PAXE - Lightweight Hatchet - GERBER LEGENDARY BLADES; *pg.* 1834, *pg.* 1503
BACK SENSE - Mattress - THERAPEDIC ASSOCIATES, INC.; *pg.* 945, *pg.* 1112
BACK STAGE - Fabric - NEMSCHOFF, INC.; *pg.* 936, *pg.* 1890
BACK STAGE - Magazine; Books on Theatre & Film; Directories - NIELSEN BUSINESS MEDIA; *pg.* 1671, *pg.* 1272
BACK STAGE WEST - Magazine for Advertising Commercial Business - NIELSEN BUSINESS MEDIA; *pg.* 1671, *pg.* 1272
BACK STREET BREWERY - Microbreweries - LAMP POST FRANCHISE CORPORATION; *pg.* 1735, *pg.* 297
BACK TO NATURE - Dinners - THE KRAFT HEINZ COMPANY; *pg.* 870, *pg.* 1577
BACK-UP - Wireless Communication System - AT&T SOUTHEAST; *pg.* 1868, *pg.* 489
BACK-UPS - Power Protection Product - SCHNEIDER ELECTRIC; *pg.* 467, *pg.* 1609
BACK-UPS OFFICE - Uninterruptible Power Supply - SCHNEIDER ELECTRIC; *pg.* 467, *pg.* 1609
BACK-UPS PRO - Uninterruptible Power Supplies - SCHNEIDER ELECTRIC; *pg.* 467, *pg.* 1609
BACKAID - Pharmaceutical Product - ALVA/AMCO PHARMACAL COMPANIES, INC.; *pg.* 1492, *pg.* 637
BACKBLADE - Universal Rear Spoiler - LUND INTERNATIONAL, INC.; *pg.* 211, *pg.* 526
BACKBONE NETVAULT - Software - OVERLAND STORAGE, INC.; *pg.* 451, *pg.* 205
BACKBURNER - Conform Software - AUTODESK INC.; *pg.* 356, *pg.* 257
BACKCARE - Mattress - SIMMONS COMPANY; *pg.* 943, *pg.* 520
BACKCARE KIDS - Mattress - SIMMONS COMPANY; *pg.* 943, *pg.* 520
BACKCOUNTRY II - Glove - KOMBI, LTD.; *pg.* 1838, *pg.* 1766
BACKCYCLER - Vehicle Seat - COMMERCIAL VEHICLE GROUP, INC.; *pg.* 203, *pg.* 1467
BACKDRAFT - Tailgate Spoiler - LUND INTERNATIONAL, INC.; *pg.* 211, *pg.* 526
BACKFLIP - Electronic Components - MOLEX INCORPORATED; *pg.* 655, *pg.* 628
BACKHAUL - Broadband Wireless Product - AIRSPAN NETWORKS INC.; *pg.* 346, *pg.* 410
BACKLESS - Apparel - OAKLEY, INC.; *pg.* 1840, *pg.* 86
BACKLITE - Ink - BASF CATALYSTS LLC; *pg.* 1148, *pg.* 1074
BACKNOBBER - Massage Product - RELAX THE BACK CORPORATION; *pg.* 940, *pg.* 120
BACKPACK - Leather Bag - COACH, INC.; *pg.* 3, *pg.* 1214
BACKPACKER - Self-Retracting Lanyard - MINE SAFETY APPLIANCES COMPANY; *pg.* 1361, *pg.* 1525
BACKPACKER - Safety Product - WISCONSIN PHARMACAL COMPANY, LLC; *pg.* 1610, *pg.* 1861
BACKPLANE - Software - WIND RIVER SYSTEMS, INC.; *pg.* 493, *pg.* 38
BACKSAVER - Pillow - RELAX THE BACK CORPORATION; *pg.* 940, *pg.* 120
BACKSAVER - Belt - SIMMS FISHING PRODUCTS CORP.; *pg.* 1845, *pg.* 1008
BACKTRACK - Medical Product - HOLOGIC, INC.; *pg.* 1416, *pg.* 784
BACKTRACKER - Software - BIO-RAD LABORATORIES, INC.; *pg.* 1504, *pg.* 101
BACKUP & RECOVERY SOLUTION - Software Application - BMC SOFTWARE, INC.; *pg.* 362, *pg.* 1701
BACKUP EXEC - Quick Start Software - QUANTUM CORPORATION; *pg.* 458, *pg.* 250
BACKUP EXEC - Software - SYMANTEC CORPORATION; *pg.* 478, *pg.* 161
BACKUP NOW - Software - NTI CORPORATION; *pg.* 446, *pg.* 114
BACKUPCARE - Outsourced Solution - IRON MOUNTAIN INCORPORATED; *pg.* 421, *pg.* 796
BACKWOODS - Domestic Cigars - ALTADIS USA, INC.; *pg.* 1893, *pg.* 423
THE BACKYARDIGANS - Toy & Game - HASBRO, INC.; *pg.* 954, *pg.* 1603
THE BACKYARDIGANS - Games - LEAPFROG ENTERPRISES, INC.; *pg.* 961, *pg.* 84
BACL2EAN - Barium Chloride Detoxification System - AJAX ELECTRIC CO.; *pg.* 1068, *pg.* 1541
BACLIGHT - Molecular Probe Product - THERMO FISHER SCIENTIFIC INC.; *pg.* 1602, *pg.* 61
BACO - Global Finishes - THE SHERWIN-WILLIAMS COMPANY; *pg.* 1447, *pg.* 1435
BACON LETTUCE TOSS - Lettuce - DOLE FRESH VEGETABLES; *pg.* 854, *pg.* 198
BACON N' EGGER - Fast Food - A&W FOOD SERVICES OF CANADA INC.; *pg.* 1714, *pg.* 1908
BACON SNAPS - Snack Food Product - RUDOLPH FOODS COMPANY; *pg.* 892, *pg.* 1458
BACOS BITS - Imitation Bacon Bits - GENERAL MILLS, INC.; *pg.* 828, *pg.* 933
BACOUNT - Wet Deck Surface - BALTIMORE AIRCOIL COMPANY; *pg.* 1069, *pg.* 773
BACOVA - Floor Mats & Rugs - BACOVA GUILD, LTD.; *pg.* 916, *pg.* 1779
BACROSS - Wet Deck Surface - BALTIMORE AIRCOIL COMPANY; *pg.* 1069, *pg.* 773
BACTODERM - Medicine - PFIZER INC.; *pg.* 1581, *pg.* 1278
BACTOSHIELD - Skin Care Product - STERIS CORPORATION; *pg.* 1597, *pg.* 1464
BACTURCULT - Pharmaceutical Product - ALERE INC.; *pg.* 1488, *pg.* 849
BACTURTEST - Pharmaceutical Product - ALERE INC.; *pg.* 1488, *pg.* 849
BACULODIRECT - Molecular Biology Product - THERMO FISHER SCIENTIFIC INC.; *pg.* 1602, *pg.* 61
B.A.C.ULOGIC - Computer Control System; Control Panel - BALTIMORE AIRCOIL COMPANY; *pg.* 1069, *pg.* 773
BAD BOY - Record Label - WARNER MUSIC GROUP CORP.; *pg.* 590, *pg.* 1313
BAD BOY RECORDS - Music Records - BAD BOY WORLDWIDE ENTERTAINMENT GROUP; *pg.* 270, *pg.* 1199
BAD MONKEY - Game - MULTIMEDIA GAMES INC.; *pg.* 442, *pg.* 1664
BADA - Wheel Weights & Accessories - HENNESSY INDUSTRIES, INC.; *pg.* 207, *pg.* 1639
BADGEMASTER - Dissolvable Embroidery Films - MONOSOL, LLC; *pg.* 59, *pg.* 694
BADGER - Hydraulic Excavators & RT Cranes - BADGER EQUIPMENT COMPANY; *pg.* 1315, *pg.* 966
BADGER - Meter Reading Systems - BADGER METER, INC.; *pg.* 1401, *pg.* 1873
BADGER - Shirt - BROWN & BIGELOW, INC.; *pg.* 1624, *pg.* 959
BADGER - Footwear - EASTLAND SHOE CORPORATION; *pg.* 1808, *pg.* 750
BADGER - Home Garbage Disposal Unit - IN-SINK-ERATOR; *pg.* 57, *pg.* 1888
BADGER - Power Supply System - VICOR CORPORATION; *pg.* 1435, *pg.* 783
BADGER PAPER MILLS - Paper Products - BPM INC.; *pg.* 1454, *pg.* 1886
BADGERTOUCH - Automated Meter Reading System - BADGER METER, INC.; *pg.* 1401, *pg.* 1873
BADGES - Apparel - VANS, INC.; *pg.* 1821, *pg.* 76
BADGLEY MISCHKA - Apparel - ICONIX BRAND GROUP, INC.; *pg.* 26, *pg.* 1243
BADLANDER - Goggle - HARLEY-DAVIDSON, INC.; *pg.* 178, *pg.* 1874
BADLANDS - Car Part Accessory - PRO-LINE, INC.; *pg.* 966, *pg.* 45
BADMINTON - Shoe - AEROGROUP INTERNATIONAL, INC.; *pg.* 1803, *pg.* 1055
BAERVELDT - Medical Device - ABBOTT MEDICAL OPTICS, INC.; *pg.* 1485, *pg.* 260
BAG-IN-A-BOTTLE - Packaging System - ATMI, INC.; *pg.* 1314, *pg.* 342
BAG-IN-A-CAN - Container - ATMI, INC.; *pg.* 1314, *pg.* 342
BAG-IN-A-DRUM - High Purity Packaging System - ATMI, INC.; *pg.* 1314, *pg.* 342
BAG IT - Insulated Lunch Bag - IGLOO PRODUCTS CORPORATION; *pg.* 1126, *pg.* 1724
BAG-O-MATIC - Curing Press - MCNEIL & NRM INC.; *pg.* 1360, *pg.* 1402
BAG-ON-A-ROLL - Protective Bags - PACTIV CORPORATION; *pg.* 1466, *pg.* 624
BAG-TAG - Twist Tie Closure - BEDFORD INDUSTRIES, INC.; *pg.* 1453, *pg.* 967

BAGEL BITES - Bite Sized Bagels - THE KRAFT HEINZ COMPANY; *pg.* 870, *pg.* 1577
BAGGIES - Bag - PACTIV CORPORATION; *pg.* 1466, *pg.* 624
BAGSBUY.COM - Online Services - IAC/INTERACTIVECORP; *pg.* 292, *pg.* 1242
BAGTRAK - Travel Insurance - TRAVEL GUARD GROUP, INC.; *pg.* 1925, *pg.* 1895
BAH HUMBUCKS - Lottery Game - MASSACHUSETTS STATE LOTTERY; *pg.* 998, *pg.* 802
BAHA-MOSAIC - Furniture - ASHLEY FURNITURE INDUSTRIES, INC.; *pg.* 914, *pg.* 1852
BAHAMA BALM - Health & Beauty Product - BLUE CROSS LABORATORIES; *pg.* 326, *pg.* 277
BAHAMA BREEZE - Restaurant Chain - DARDEN RESTAURANTS, INC.; *pg.* 1724, *pg.* 453
BAILEY - Clothing - ABERCROMBIE & FITCH CO.; *pg.* 37, *pg.* 1466
BAILEY - Lamp - ASHLEY FURNITURE INDUSTRIES, INC.; *pg.* 914, *pg.* 1852
BAILEY - Footwear - COBIAN CORP.; *pg.* 1806, *pg.* 253
BAILEY - Fabric - NEMSCHOFF, INC.; *pg.* 936, *pg.* 1890
THE BAILEY CITY MONSTERS - Educational Materials - SCHOLASTIC INC.; *pg.* 1683, *pg.* 1288
THE BAILEY SCHOOL KIDS MAGAZINE - Magazine - SCHOLASTIC INC.; *pg.* 1683, *pg.* 1288
BAILEYS - Whisky - DIAGEO NORTH AMERICA, INC.; *pg.* 1961, *pg.* 361
BAILEY'S - Restaurant - FOX & HOUND RESTAURANT GROUP; *pg.* 1729, *pg.* 723
BAILEY'S PUB & GRILLE - Restaurant - FOX & HOUND RESTAURANT GROUP; *pg.* 1729, *pg.* 723
BAILEY'S SMOKEHOUSE & TAVERN - Restaurant - FOX & HOUND RESTAURANT GROUP; *pg.* 1729, *pg.* 723
BAILEY'S SPORTS GRILLE - Restaurant - FOX & HOUND RESTAURANT GROUP; *pg.* 1729, *pg.* 723
BAIN DE SOLEIL - Sunscreen Products - BAYER HEALTHCARE CONSUMER CARE DIVISION; *pg.* 1500, *pg.* 1087
BAIN DE SOLEIL - Pharmaceutical Product - PFIZER INC.; *pg.* 1581, *pg.* 1278
BAIN DE TERRE - Perm Shampoos & Conditioners - ZOTOS INTERNATIONAL, INC.; *pg.* 524, *pg.* 345
BAIRD - Investment Products & Services - THE NORTHWESTERN MUTUAL LIFE INSURANCE COMPANY; *pg.* 1212, *pg.* 1879
BAIROCADE - Coating Product - PPG INDUSTRIES, INC.; *pg.* 1445, *pg.* 1579
BAITMATE - Safety Product - WISCONSIN PHARMACAL COMPANY, LLC; *pg.* 1610, *pg.* 1861
BAJA - Fabric - NEMSCHOFF, INC.; *pg.* 936, *pg.* 1890
BAJA CAFE - Food Product - RESER'S FINE FOODS INC.; *pg.* 1032, *pg.* 1496
BAJA FRESH MEXICAN GRILL - Fast Food Mexican Restaurant - FRESH ENTERPRISES, LLC; *pg.* 1729, *pg.* 110
BAJORU GIRA - Beverages - THE COCA-COLA COMPANY; *pg.* 240, *pg.* 493
BAK-N-BEANS - Dry Beans - FURMANO FOODS, INC.; *pg.* 857, *pg.* 1557
BAK-V-SPAR - Paints - PETTIT PAINT COMPANY; *pg.* 1444, *pg.* 1116
BAKE-AND-SERVE - Cookie - COOKIE TREE BAKERIES; *pg.* 1851, *pg.* 1756
THE BAKE SHOP - Bakery Product - GIANT EAGLE, INC.; *pg.* 1020, *pg.* 1575
BAKEALL - Food Product - BUNGE LIMITED; *pg.* 842, *pg.* 1351
BAKED DORITOS - Tortilla Chips - FRITO-LAY NORTH AMERICA, INC.; *pg.* 1853, *pg.* 1730
BAKED FLAKE - Baked, Low-Fat Potato Chips - GOLDEN FLAKE SNACK FOODS, INC.; *pg.* 1854, *pg.* 3
BAKED RUFFLES - Potato Chips - FRITO-LAY NORTH AMERICA, INC.; *pg.* 1853, *pg.* 1730
BAKED TOSTITOS - Tortilla Chips - FRITO-LAY NORTH AMERICA, INC.; *pg.* 1853, *pg.* 1730
BAKELITE - Phenolic & Epoxy Resins - HEXION; *pg.* 1166, *pg.* 1440
BAKEN-EATS - Fried Pork Skins - PEPSICO, INC.; *pg.* 259, *pg.* 1327
BAKEN-ETS - Pork Skin Snack - FRITO-LAY NORTH AMERICA, INC.; *pg.* 1853, *pg.* 1730
BAKER - Furniture - BAKER KNAPP & TUBBS INC.; *pg.* 916, *pg.* 566
BAKER - Furniture - KOHLER CO.; *pg.* 91, *pg.* 1862
BAKER - Cake & Pastry Fillings - SOKOL & COMPANY; *pg.* 1862, *pg.* 598
BAKER - Steel Reels - SONOCO PRODUCTS COMPANY; *pg.* 1469, *pg.* 1619
BAKER BOYER - Banking Services - BAKER BOYER BANCORP; *pg.* 717, *pg.* 1846
BAKER HUGHES - Process Equipment - BAKER HUGHES INCORPORATED; *pg.* 1315, *pg.* 1700
BAKER MOUNTAIN - Clothing - ABERCROMBIE & FITCH CO.; *pg.* 37, *pg.* 1466
BAKER STREET - Ceiling Fan - HUNTER FAN COMPANY; *pg.* 57, *pg.* 1631
BAKERS - Footwear - BAKERS FOOTWEAR GROUP, INC.; *pg.* 19, *pg.* 992
BAKER'S - Bourbon - JIM BEAM BRANDS CO.; *pg.* 1965, *pg.* 601
BAKER'S - Supermarket - THE KROGER CO.; *pg.* 1025, *pg.* 1416
BAKERS - Food Product - MCCORMICK & COMPANY, INCORPORATED; *pg.* 1027, *pg.* 779
BAKERS BEST - Soft Pretzels - J&J SNACK FOODS CORPORATION; *pg.* 865, *pg.* 1107
BAKERS CHOCOLATE - Food Product - THE KRAFT HEINZ COMPANY; *pg.* 870, *pg.* 1577
BAKER'S DOZEN - Video Game - INTERNATIONAL GAME TECHNOLOGY; *pg.* 957, *pg.* 1024
BAKERS EASE - Cake Mixes & Base - DAWN FOOD PRODUCTS, INC.; *pg.* 1018, *pg.* 893
BAKERS IDEAL - Food Product - BUNGE LIMITED; *pg.* 842, *pg.* 1351
BAKERS SELECT - Icing And Filling - DAWN FOOD PRODUCTS, INC.; *pg.* 1018, *pg.* 893
BAKER'S SPECIAL - Bakery Ingredient - FOREMOST FARMS USA COOPERATIVE; *pg.* 856, *pg.* 1854
BAKERS SQUARE - Restaurants - AMERICAN BLUE RIBBON HOLDINGS; *pg.* 1714, *pg.* 1648
BAKERS SQUARE - Carpet - BEAULIEU GROUP, LLC; *pg.* 917, *pg.* 529
BAKERSFIELD - Kitchen Product - KOHLER CO.; *pg.* 91, *pg.* 1862
BAKERY - Compressor - BADGER AIR BRUSH COMPANY; *pg.* 359, *pg.* 612
BAKESHURE - Nutrition & Food Product - BALCHEM CORPORATION; *pg.* 839, *pg.* 1183
BAKING SODA - Soap - GRANDPA BRANDS COMPANY; *pg.* 1538, *pg.* 727
BAKKIE - Glove - KOMBI, LTD.; *pg.* 1838, *pg.* 1766
BAKOS IRON - White Iron - WEBSTER INDUSTRIES INC.; *pg.* 1388, *pg.* 1475
BAKU - Fabric - NEMSCHOFF, INC.; *pg.* 936, *pg.* 1890
BAKUGAN - Toy - SPIN MASTER LTD.; *pg.* 967, *pg.* 1943
BAL-IN-OIL - Pharmaceutical Product - AKORN, INC.; *pg.* 1488, *pg.* 622
BALAC - Chucks & Arbors - GLEASON CORPORATION; *pg.* 1340, *pg.* 1335
BALACET - Pharmaceutical Product - CHIESI USA, INC.; *pg.* 1515, *pg.* 1359
BALACET 325 - Pharmaceutical Product - CHIESI USA, INC.; *pg.* 1515, *pg.* 1359
BALANCE - Printing Product - ELECTRONICS FOR IMAGING, INC.; *pg.* 390, *pg.* 88
BALANCE - Sports Drink - ENERGY BRANDS, INC.; *pg.* 854, *pg.* 1227
BALANCE - Carpet - INTERFACE, INC.; *pg.* 695, *pg.* 512
BALANCE - Fabric - NEMSCHOFF, INC.; *pg.* 936, *pg.* 1890
BALANCE - Furniture - NEUTRAL POSTURE, INC.; *pg.* 939, *pg.* 1669
BALANCE - Cereal - POST CONSUMER BRANDS; *pg.* 833, *pg.* 927
BALANCE - Writing Instrument - SHEAFFER PEN CORPORATION; *pg.* 469, *pg.* 371
BALANCE - Floor Cleaner - SWISHER HYGIENE INC.; *pg.* 336, *pg.* 1507
BALANCE ACTIV - Pharmaceutical Product - ALERE INC.; *pg.* 1488, *pg.* 849
BALANCE BALL - Fitness DVD - GAIAM, INC.; *pg.* 1532, *pg.* 334
BALANCE BAR - Nutrition Bar - NBTY, INC.; *pg.* 1572, *pg.* 1338
BALANCE BODY - Exercise Systems - BALANCED BODY, INC.; *pg.* 1826, *pg.* 195
BALANCE CHECK - Portable Instrument - LORD CORPORATION; *pg.* 1357, *pg.* 1360
BALANCE HIP SYSTEM - Hip Product - ZIMMER BIOMET HOLDINGS, INC.; *pg.* 1611, *pg.* 699
BALANCE OF POWER - Software - WORDEN BROTHERS, INC.; *pg.* 823, *pg.* 1372
BALANCE PROJECT - Fabric - W.L. GORE & ASSOCIATES, INC.; *pg.* 122, *pg.* 388
BALANCING THE BOOKS - Financial Products - DOW JONES & COMPANY, INC.; *pg.* 1637, *pg.* 1225
BALANOX - Spice - FUCHS NORTH AMERICA.; *pg.* 857, *pg.* 774
BALBLAIR - Scotch - CONSTELLATION BRANDS, INC.; *pg.* 1960, *pg.* 1348
BALBOA SUNSET - Container Grown Plant - MONROVIA GROWERS; *pg.* 1797, *pg.* 44
BALCO - Thermal Processing Equipment - SURFACE COMBUSTION, INC.; *pg.* 1077, *pg.* 1462
BALDERSON - Cheese - PARMALAT CANADA INC.; *pg.* 888, *pg.* 1941
BALDFADER - Hair Cutting Kit - WAHL CLIPPER CORPORATION; *pg.* 524, *pg.* 662
BALDOR - Motors, Drives, Gear Boxes & Starters - JASPER ELECTRIC MOTORS; *pg.* 209, *pg.* 691
BALDOR SMARTMOTOR - Integrated Motor - BALDOR ELECTRIC COMPANY; *pg.* 1316, *pg.* 32
BALDWIN - Filters - BALDWIN FILTERS; *pg.* 1316, *pg.* 1011
BALDWIN - Food Product - BALDWIN RICHARDSON FOODS COMPANY; *pg.* 1850, *pg.* 612
BALDWIN - Musical Instrument - GIBSON GUITAR CORP.; *pg.* 550, *pg.* 1650
BALDWIN - Hardware - STANLEY BLACK & DECKER, INC.; *pg.* 1063, *pg.* 358
BALDY - Hat - CORTLAND LINE COMPANY; *pg.* 1831, *pg.* 1155
BALEWEL - Baling Equipment - EAST CHICAGO MACHINE TOOL CORPORATION; *pg.* 1331, *pg.* 676
BALI - Furniture - BASSETT FURNITURE INDUSTRIES, INCORPORATED; *pg.* 916, *pg.* 1776
BALI - Intimate Apparel - HANESBRANDS INC.; *pg.* 26, *pg.* 1394
BALI - Window - SPRINGS GLOBAL, INC.; *pg.* 698, *pg.* 1616
BALI - Window Blinds & Shades - SPRINGS WINDOW FASHIONS LLC; *pg.* 943, *pg.* 1872
BALI - Outdoor Lighting - SWIVELIER CO., INC.; *pg.* 1307, *pg.* 1142
BALI - Furniture - TROPITONE FURNITURE CO., INC.; *pg.* 945, *pg.* 118
BALI BLACK RASPBERRY - Herbal Tea - CELESTIAL SEASONINGS, INC.; *pg.* 846, *pg.* 310
BALINIT - Industrial Coating - OERLIKON BALZERS COATING USA, INC.; *pg.* 1444, *pg.* 610
BALISTO - Chocolate Covered Grain Bar - MARS, INCORPORATED; *pg.* 1858, *pg.* 1792
BALKAMP - Automotive Products - GENUINE PARTS COMPANY; *pg.* 206, *pg.* 506
BALL - Glass & Metal Containers - BALL CORPORATION; *pg.* 1452, *pg.* 311
BALL - Home Canning Products - JARDEN CORPORATION; *pg.* 1885, *pg.* 412
BALL BUSTER - Gaming Product - GLD PRODUCTS, INC.; *pg.* 1835, *pg.* 1882
BALL FRAME 25 - Picture Frame - BOGDANCO CONSULTING; *pg.* 918, *pg.* 174
BALL HOG - Backboard - LIFETIME PRODUCTS INC.; *pg.* 933, *pg.* 1751
BALL PAINT MARKER - Liquid Paint Marker - LA-CO INDUSTRIES MARKAL CO., INC.; *pg.* 1170, *pg.* 610
BALL PARK - Frankfurters - TYSON FOODS, INC.; *pg.* 902, *pg.* 35
BALL WALL - Bowling Equipment - BRUNSWICK BOWLING & BILLIARDS CORP.; *pg.* 1828, *pg.* 622
BALLAD - Furniture - JASPER GROUP; *pg.* 930, *pg.* 691
BALLANTINE - Beer - PABST BREWING COMPANY; *pg.* 258, *pg.* 137
BALLANTRAE WINE MERCHANTS - Wine - COSTCO WHOLESALE CORPORATION; *pg.* 1765, *pg.* 1820
BALLANTYNE - Movie Theater Equipment - BALLANTYNE STRONG, INC.; *pg.* 623, *pg.* 1013
BALLARD DESIGN - Online Gift Store - IAC/INTERACTIVECORP; *pg.* 292, *pg.* 1242
BALLASET - Thermally Stable Diamond Bits - BAKER HUGHES INTEQ; *pg.* 1316, *pg.* 1700
BALLASTAR - Dimming Ballasts - UNIVERSAL LIGHTING TECHNOLOGIES; *pg.* 1307, *pg.* 1655
BALLATORE - Spumante - E&J GALLO WINERY; *pg.* 1962, *pg.* 149
BALLDRIVER - Allen Wrench - NEWPORT CORPORATION; *pg.* 1424, *pg.* 114

First page reference indicates Business Class Edition
Second page reference indicates Geographic Edition

BALLERINA - Cookie - A.V. OLSSON TRADING CO. INC.; *pg.* 838, *pg.* 372
BALLERINA - Ceiling Fan - WESTINGHOUSE LIGHTING CORPORATION; *pg.* 687, *pg.* 1571
BALLET - Office Paper - INTERNATIONAL PAPER COMPANY; *pg.* 1460, *pg.* 1644
BALLET - Office Furniture - STEELCASE INC.; *pg.* 475, *pg.* 889
BALLET - Women's Clothing & Accessories - WOODEN SHIPS OF HOBOKEN; *pg.* 35, *pg.* 1315
BALLETON - Furniture - J. ROBERT SCOTT INC.; *pg.* 930, *pg.* 105
BALLETONE - Fitness Product - BALLY TOTAL FITNESS HOLDINGS CORPORATION; *pg.* 532, *pg.* 1200
BALLINA - Bathroom Accessories - SYMMONS INDUSTRIES, INC.; *pg.* 114, *pg.* 803
BALLISTIC - Stainless Steel Propeller - MICHIGAN WHEEL CORPORATION; *pg.* 1709, *pg.* 888
BALLISTIC - Apparel - OAKLEY, INC.; *pg.* 1840, *pg.* 86
BALLISTIC POINT - Pin - POWERS FASTENERS INC.; *pg.* 1059, *pg.* 1143
BALLISTIX - Computer Memory - CRUCIAL TECHNOLOGY DIV OF MICRON; *pg.* 1237, *pg.* 550
BALLISTIX - Hardware - MICRON TECHNOLOGY, INC.; *pg.* 435, *pg.* 547
BALLISTIX TRACER - Hardware - MICRON TECHNOLOGY, INC.; *pg.* 435, *pg.* 547
BALLOON BARS - Video Game - INTERNATIONAL GAME TECHNOLOGY; *pg.* 957, *pg.* 1024
BALLOON BOUTIQUE - Balloons - 1-800-FLOWERS.COM, INC.; *pg.* 1758, *pg.* 1151
BALLOON JAMZ - Foil Balloons - CTI INDUSTRIES CORPORATION; *pg.* 1881, *pg.* 555
BALLOON MAGIC - Balloon Instruction Book - CONTINENTAL AMERICAN CORP.; *pg.* 1880, *pg.* 723
BALLOON TIME - Low-Pressure Helium Balloon Kit - WORTHINGTON INDUSTRIES, INC.; *pg.* 123, *pg.* 1444
BALLOON TWINKLERS - Balloon Light - CONTINENTAL AMERICAN CORP.; *pg.* 1880, *pg.* 723
BALLOTINI - Solid Glass Beads for Impact Blasting - POTTERS INDUSTRIES, INC.; *pg.* 105, *pg.* 1515
BALLOTINI - Impact Beads - PQ CORPORATION; *pg.* 1178, *pg.* 1515
BALLROOM - Fabric - NEMSCHOFF, INC.; *pg.* 936, *pg.* 1890
BALLY COOL SIGN - Software - BALLY TECHNOLOGIES, INC.; *pg.* 531, *pg.* 1022
BALLY LIVE REWARDS - Bonus Solutions - BALLY TECHNOLOGIES, INC.; *pg.* 531, *pg.* 1022
BALLY ONE SYSTEM - Software - BALLY TECHNOLOGIES, INC.; *pg.* 531, *pg.* 1022
BALLY SMS - Slot Machine - BALLY TECHNOLOGIES, INC.; *pg.* 531, *pg.* 1022
BALLY SPORTS CLUBS - Health Club Services - BALLY TOTAL FITNESS HOLDINGS CORPORATION; *pg.* 532, *pg.* 1200
BALLY TOTAL FITNESS - Fitness Equipment - BALLY TOTAL FITNESS HOLDINGS CORPORATION; *pg.* 532, *pg.* 1200
BALLYMORE - Carpet - BEAULIEU GROUP, LLC; *pg.* 917, *pg.* 529
BALLY'S - Casino - CAESARS ENTERTAINMENT CORPORATION; *pg.* 1083, *pg.* 1023
BALM BARR - Lotion & Cream - THE STEPHAN COMPANY; *pg.* 1597, *pg.* 426
BALM PROOFER - Protector - THE TIMBERLAND COMPANY; *pg.* 1821, *pg.* 1039
BALMEX - Diaper Rash Ointment - CHATTEM, INC.; *pg.* 1515, *pg.* 1628
BALMORAL - Rug - COURISTAN INC.; *pg.* 921, *pg.* 1067
BALMORAL - Paper & Nonwoven Material - FIBERMARK INC.; *pg.* 1457, *pg.* 1764
BALMORAL - Door Panel - MASONITE INTERNATIONAL CORPORATION; *pg.* 1054, *pg.* 1920
BALMORAL COLORS - Rug - COURISTAN INC.; *pg.* 921, *pg.* 1067
BALOMETER JR. - Balometer - TSI INCORPORATED; *pg.* 1432, *pg.* 965
BALSA - Dome - PRECISION VALVE CORPORATION; *pg.* 1060, *pg.* 1357
BALSALAZIDE - Enteritis Treatment - SALIX PHARMACEUTICALS, INC.; *pg.* 1591, *pg.* 1388
BALSAM - Health & Beauty Product - BLUE CROSS LABORATORIES; *pg.* 326, *pg.* 277
BALSAM AND CEDAR HOUSEWARMER - Candle - THE YANKEE CANDLE COMPANY, INC.; *pg.* 1792, *pg.* 843
BALSAM COLOR - Hair Coloring - P&G-CLAIROL, INC.; *pg.* 519, *pg.* 1418
BALSAM LAKE - T-Shirts - ABERCROMBIE & FITCH CO.; *pg.* 37, *pg.* 1466
BALTA - Furniture - ETHAN ALLEN INTERIORS INC.; *pg.* 924, *pg.* 343
BALTIBOND - Corrosion Protection System - BALTIMORE AIRCOIL COMPANY; *pg.* 1069, *pg.* 773
BALTIDRIVE - Power Train - BALTIMORE AIRCOIL COMPANY; *pg.* 1069, *pg.* 773
BALTIMORE ESTATE - Decorative Flower - NATURAL DECORATIONS, INC.; *pg.* 936, *pg.* 5
BALTIMORE MAGAZINE - Magazine - ROSEBUD ENTERTAINMENT LLC; *pg.* 1681, *pg.* 759
BALTIMORE SPICE - Spices & Seasonings - FUCHS NORTH AMERICA.; *pg.* 857, *pg.* 774
BALUSTRADE - Lighting - ETHAN ALLEN INTERIORS INC.; *pg.* 924, *pg.* 343
BALUSTRADE - Fabric - NEMSCHOFF, INC.; *pg.* 936, *pg.* 1890
BALVENIE - Scotch - WILLIAM GRANT & SONS, INC.; *pg.* 1972, *pg.* 1057
BAM - Video Game - INTERNATIONAL GAME TECHNOLOGY; *pg.* 957, *pg.* 1024
BAM - Musical Instrument - PEAVEY ELECTRONICS CORPORATION; *pg.* 662, *pg.* 970
BAMA - Mayonnaise - THE C.F. SAUER COMPANY; *pg.* 847, *pg.* 1801
BAMA - Fruit Spreads & Fruit Juice Cocktails - WELCH FOODS INC.; *pg.* 909, *pg.* 815
BAMBI - Footwear - BEBE STORES, INC.; *pg.* 19, *pg.* 49
BAMBOLA - Footwear - STEVEN MADDEN, LTD.; *pg.* 1819, *pg.* 1176
BAMBOO - Bath Accessory - CROSCILL, INC.; *pg.* 1122, *pg.* 1220
BAMBOO - Black Panda Puppet - GUND, INC.; *pg.* 954, *pg.* 1056
BAMBOO - Eyewear - MAUI JIM, INC.; *pg.* 9, *pg.* 651
BAMBOO - Faucets - MOEN INCORPORATED; *pg.* 1056, *pg.* 1468
BAMBOO - Fabric - NEMSCHOFF, INC.; *pg.* 936, *pg.* 1890
BAMBOO GROVE - Carpet - INTERFACE, INC.; *pg.* 695, *pg.* 512
BAMBOOZLED - Game - WMS INDUSTRIES INC.; *pg.* 593, *pg.* 666
BAMM - Book Publishing - BOOKS-A-MILLION, INC.; *pg.* 1623, *pg.* 2
BAN - Deodorant & Antiperspirant - KAO BRANDS CO. INC.; *pg.* 513, *pg.* 1415
BAN-A-STAIN - Health & Beauty Product - COMBE INCORPORATED; *pg.* 1516, *pg.* 1351
BANAMEX - Financial Services - CITIGROUP INC.; *pg.* 735, *pg.* 1212
BANAMINE - Medicine - MERCK & CO., INC.; *pg.* 1566, *pg.* 1077
BANANA BAGS - Storage Bags - FLEX-O-GLASS, INC.; *pg.* 1457, *pg.* 574
BANANA BERRY - Fruit Drink - JAMBA, INC.; *pg.* 1024, *pg.* 84
BANANA BOAT - Sun Care - EDGEWELL PERSONAL CARE; *pg.* 1526, *pg.* 995
BANANA FLIPS - Cakes - ALFRED NICKLES BAKERY, INC.; *pg.* 836, *pg.* 1466
BANANA PEEL - Wire & Cable Products - BELDEN, INC.; *pg.* 624, *pg.* 993
BANANA REPUBLIC - Apparel And Accessory - BANANA REPUBLIC; *pg.* 1760, *pg.* 212
BANANA REPUBLIC - Retail Clothing Store - THE GAP, INC.; *pg.* 1770, *pg.* 218
BANANA SHUFFLE - CD-Rom - DOLE FRESH VEGETABLES; *pg.* 854, *pg.* 198
BANANA SPLIT - Pre-Treatment Cleaner - A BRITE COMPANY; *pg.* 1144, *pg.* 1697
BANANA SPLIT - Container Grown Plant - MONROVIA GROWERS; *pg.* 1797, *pg.* 44
BANANA SPLIT PEG BAG - Candy - NEW ENGLAND CONFECTIONERY COMPANY INC.; *pg.* 1860, *pg.* 842
BANANA WAX - Automotive Reconditioning Product - MOC PRODUCTS COMPANY, INC.; *pg.* 332, *pg.* 174
BANAWBERRY - Side Dish - BIGLARI HOLDINGS INC.; *pg.* 1015, *pg.* 1739
BANBURY - Internal Batch Mixer - FARREL CORPORATION; *pg.* 1336, *pg.* 337
BANC MALL - Software - SS&C TECHNOLOGIES HOLDINGS, INC.; *pg.* 473, *pg.* 386
BANC TRUST - Banking Service - TRUSTMARK CORPORATION; *pg.* 812, *pg.* 7
BANCROFT - Bath Product - KOHLER CO.; *pg.* 91, *pg.* 1862
BANCTEC - Document Processing Products - BANCTEC, INC.; *pg.* 360, *pg.* 1717
BANCWARE - Software - SUNGARD DATA SYSTEMS INC.; *pg.* 477, *pg.* 1592
BAND-ADE - Sawing Fluid - LENOX; *pg.* 1053, *pg.* 817
BAND-AID - Butterfly Closures - ALIMED, INC.; *pg.* 1490, *pg.* 816
BAND-AID - Bandage Products - JOHNSON & JOHNSON; *pg.* 1549, *pg.* 1091
BAND-IT - Clamps, Banding Devices - IDEX CORPORATION; *pg.* 1347, *pg.* 623
BAND-IT JR. - Clamping Systems - IDEX CORPORATION; *pg.* 1347, *pg.* 623
BAND-LOK - Clamping Systems - IDEX CORPORATION; *pg.* 1347, *pg.* 623
BAND OF VIKINGS - Game - WMS INDUSTRIES INC.; *pg.* 593, *pg.* 666
BANDAG - Commercial Tires - BRIDGESTONE AMERICAS, INC.; *pg.* 201, *pg.* 1649
BANDAGEGARD - Healthcare Product - GF HEALTH PRODUCTS, INC.; *pg.* 1535, *pg.* 508
BANDEROLE - Fabric - NEMSCHOFF, INC.; *pg.* 936, *pg.* 1890
BANDIDO - Industrial Safety Eyewear - UVEX SAFETY; *pg.* 1433, *pg.* 1608
BANDIT - Computer Services - NOVELL INC.; *pg.* 446, *pg.* 852
BANDIT - Musical Instrument - PEAVEY ELECTRONICS CORPORATION; *pg.* 662, *pg.* 970
BANDIT - Beverage - TRINCHERO FAMILY ESTATES; *pg.* 1971, *pg.* 197
BANDIT - Industrial Safety Eyewear - UVEX SAFETY; *pg.* 1433, *pg.* 1608
BANDITO - Medical Equipment - CONMED CORPORATION; *pg.* 1517, *pg.* 1347
BANDITO SALSA - Salsa Sauce - NEWMAN'S OWN, INC.; *pg.* 886, *pg.* 384
BANDOLERO - Motorsports Entertainment - SPEEDWAY MOTORSPORTS, INC.; *pg.* 584, *pg.* 1370
BANDOLINO - Women's Shoes - NINE WEST HOLDINGS, INC.; *pg.* 1815, *pg.* 1272
BANDS OF LOVE - Bangles - DE HAGO, INC.; *pg.* 4, *pg.* 1222
BANDSTAND - Fabric - NEMSCHOFF, INC.; *pg.* 936, *pg.* 1890
BANDWIDTH - Fabric - MOMENTUM TEXTILES INC.; *pg.* 697, *pg.* 114
BANDWIDTH OPTIMIZER - Software - WEBSENSE, INC.; *pg.* 491, *pg.* 210
BANDWIDTH PG - Software - WEBSENSE, INC.; *pg.* 491, *pg.* 210
BANDWIDTH SAVER - Telecommunication Services - VONAGE HOLDINGS CORP.; *pg.* 686, *pg.* 1074
BANERAS - Furniture - ASHLEY FURNITURE INDUSTRIES, INC.; *pg.* 914, *pg.* 1852
BANFIELD PET HOSPITAL - Pet Health Care - MARS, INCORPORATED; *pg.* 1858, *pg.* 1792
BANFIELD PET HOSPITAL - Pet Care - MARS PETCARE; *pg.* 1478, *pg.* 1633
BANG-IT - Mechanical Anchor & Fastener - POWERS FASTENERS INC.; *pg.* 1059, *pg.* 1143
BANGLES - Fabric - NEMSCHOFF, INC.; *pg.* 936, *pg.* 1890
BANGUARD - Banner Fabric - GLEN RAVEN, INC.; *pg.* 693, *pg.* 1373
BANJO - Clock - ETHAN ALLEN INTERIORS INC.; *pg.* 924, *pg.* 343
BANJOS - Musical Instrument - GIBSON GUITAR CORP.; *pg.* 550, *pg.* 1650
BANK A BIT - Video Game - INTERNATIONAL GAME TECHNOLOGY; *pg.* 957, *pg.* 1024
BANK BUSINESS RECOVERY SERVICE - Banking Software - JACK HENRY & ASSOCIATES, INC.; *pg.* 422, *pg.* 988
BANK EXPRESS - Online Banking - SANDY SPRING BANCORP, INC.; *pg.* 801, *pg.* 774
BANK LEUMI - Full Service Commercial Bank - BANK LEUMI USA; *pg.* 718, *pg.* 1200
BANK LOAN AND RECOVERY RATINGS - Credit Ratings Plus - STANDARD & POOR'S RATINGS SERVICES; *pg.* 805, *pg.* 1296
BANK-LOK - Locker - AMERICAN LOCKER SECURITY SYSTEMS, INC.; *pg.* 1042, *pg.* 1674

BANK MART - Banking Centers - FIFTH THIRD BANCORP; *pg.* 752, *pg.* 1413
BANK OF AMERICA MERRILL LYNCH - Investment Services - BANK OF AMERICA CORPORATION; *pg.* 718, *pg.* 1362
BANK OF INTERNET USA - Online Savings Bank Services - BOFI HOLDING, INC.; *pg.* 726, *pg.* 200
THE BANK THAT SERVICE BUILT - Slogan - UNITED COMMUNITY BANKS, INC.; *pg.* 814, *pg.* 526
BANK WITH TOTAL CONFIDENCE - Tagline - TOTALBANK CORP.; *pg.* 811, *pg.* 447
THE BANK YOU CAN TALK TO - Slogan - BRIDGE BANCORP, INC.; *pg.* 727, *pg.* 1144
BANKCONNECT - Banking Services - OLD NATIONAL BANCORP; *pg.* 789, *pg.* 679
BANKDIRECT - Banking Services - TEXAS CAPITAL BANCSHARES, INC.; *pg.* 809, *pg.* 1737
BANKERS CLUB - Whiskey - LAIRD & COMPANY, INC.; *pg.* 1966, *pg.* 1119
BANKERS HEALTH ADVANTAGE PROGRAM - Health Care Discount & Information Program for Seniors - BANKERS LIFE & CASUALTY COMPANY; *pg.* 1194, *pg.* 566
BANKGUARD PLUS - Capacitor Control - S&C ELECTRIC COMPANY; *pg.* 1305, *pg.* 589
BANKIA - Beverages - THE COCA-COLA COMPANY; *pg.* 240, *pg.* 493
BANKING DAILY - Publisher - BLOOMBERG BNA; *pg.* 1621, *pg.* 1772
BANKING. INSURANCE. INVESTMENTS. - Tagline - SHORE BANCSHARES, INC.; *pg.* 803, *pg.* 769
BANKING REPORT - Publisher - BLOOMBERG BNA; *pg.* 1621, *pg.* 1772
BANKING WITH YOU IN MIND - Banking Service - SALEM FIVE CENTS SAVINGS BANK; *pg.* 800, *pg.* 843
BANKJET - Ink Jet Printers - TRANSACT TECHNOLOGIES INCORPORATED; *pg.* 484, *pg.* 351
BANKLINK - Software System - FISERV, INC.; *pg.* 397, *pg.* 1855
BANKNOW - Online Banking - TEXAS CAPITAL BANCSHARES, INC.; *pg.* 809, *pg.* 1737
BANKROLL DOUBLER - Lottery Game - KENTUCKY LOTTERY CORPORATION; *pg.* 996, *pg.* 735
BANKRUPTCY LAW DAILY - Publisher - BLOOMBERG BNA; *pg.* 1621, *pg.* 1772
BANKRUPTCY LAW REPORTER - Publisher - BLOOMBERG BNA; *pg.* 1621, *pg.* 1772
BANKSTON - Car Dealerships - AUTONATION, INC.; *pg.* 165, *pg.* 423
BANMINTH - Animal Health Product - PHIBROCHEM; *pg.* 1177, *pg.* 1124
BANNER - Riflescope - BUSHNELL OUTDOOR PRODUCTS, INC.; *pg.* 1403, *pg.* 718
BANNER - Balloon - CONTINENTAL AMERICAN CORP.; *pg.* 1880, *pg.* 723
BANNERLINE - Graphic Arts Materials - HOLLISTON LLC; *pg.* 1460, *pg.* 1630
BANNERS DEN - Denim Banner - BROWN & BIGELOW, INC.; *pg.* 1624, *pg.* 959
BANNING - Forging Product - SUPERIOR DIE SET CORP.; *pg.* 1379, *pg.* 1885
BANNOK - Sitting Bench - BERNHARDT DESIGN; *pg.* 918, *pg.* 1381
BANQUET - Food Product - CONAGRA FOODS, INC.; *pg.* 826, *pg.* 1014
BANQUET - Fabric - NEMSCHOFF, INC.; *pg.* 936, *pg.* 1890
BANQUET - Folding Furniture - TELESCOPE CASUAL FURNITURE INC.; *pg.* 944, *pg.* 1162
BANSHEE - Computer Software - NOVELL INC.; *pg.* 446, *pg.* 852
BANSHEE - All Terrain Vehicle - YAMAHA MOTOR CORPORATION USA; *pg.* 1713, *pg.* 76
BANSHEE MOUSE - Pet Toy - THE HARTZ MOUNTAIN CORP.; *pg.* 1476, *pg.* 1120
BANTAM - Knife - BUCK KNIVES, INC.; *pg.* 1828, *pg.* 550
BANTAM - Knife - COAST CUTLERY COMPANY; *pg.* 1121, *pg.* 1501
BANTAM BOOKS FOR YOUNG READERS - Publishing Imprint - PENGUIN RANDOM HOUSE CHILDREN'S BOOKS; *pg.* 1676, *pg.* 1277
BANTAM PLUG - Wall Anchor - POWERS FASTENERS INC.; *pg.* 1059, *pg.* 1143
BANTEX - Fabrics - HERCULITE PRODUCTS, INC.; *pg.* 694, *pg.* 1529
BANTEX UNIVERSAL - Banner Media - HERCULITE PRODUCTS, INC.; *pg.* 694, *pg.* 1529
BANYAN - Fabric - NEMSCHOFF, INC.; *pg.* 936, *pg.* 1890
BANYANS - Eyewear - MAUI JIM, INC.; *pg.* 9, *pg.* 651
BANZEL - Pharmaceutical - EISAI INC.; *pg.* 1526, *pg.* 1133
BAPOR PRO RX - Moisture Analyzer - ARIZONA INSTRUMENT LLC; *pg.* 1400, *pg.* 12
BAPS - Medical & Aesthetic Product - DYNATRONICS CORPORATION; *pg.* 1526, *pg.* 1757
THE BAR - Heighted Bars - ALLIANCE SPORTS GROUP, L.P.; *pg.* 1825, *pg.* 1698
BAR-B-CHEF - Charcoal Grill - BARBEQUES GALORE, INC.; *pg.* 51, *pg.* 173
BAR-H STEAKHOUSE - Restaurant - STAR BUFFET, INC.; *pg.* 1751, *pg.* 24
BAR NONE - Candy Bar - THE HERSHEY CO.; *pg.* 1855, *pg.* 1538
BAR OX - Alkyd Primer & Enamel - AKZONOBEL DECORATIVE PAINTS U.S.; *pg.* 1439, *pg.* 1474
BAR RUST - Ship Coating - AKZONOBEL DECORATIVE PAINTS U.S.; *pg.* 1439, *pg.* 1474
BAR-SCHEEZE - Cheese - WIN SCHULER FOODS; *pg.* 910, *pg.* 908
BAR-SCHIPS - Crackers - WIN SCHULER FOODS; *pg.* 910, *pg.* 908
BARA - Lamp - ASHLEY FURNITURE INDUSTRIES, INC.; *pg.* 914, *pg.* 1852
BARA-LAB - Hyperbaric Chamber - ENVIRONMENTAL TECTONICS CORPORATION; *pg.* 1411, *pg.* 1587
BARA-MED - Medical Hyperbaric Chamber - ENVIRONMENTAL TECTONICS CORPORATION; *pg.* 1411, *pg.* 1587
BARA-PRESS - Software - ENVIRONMENTAL TECTONICS CORPORATION; *pg.* 1411, *pg.* 1587
BARABOO NEWS REPUBLIC - Newspaper - MADISON NEWSPAPERS, INC.; *pg.* 1661, *pg.* 1866
BARACLUDE - HBV Medication - BRISTOL-MYERS SQUIBB COMPANY; *pg.* 1509, *pg.* 1206
BARAKA - Bakery Product - SAPUTO, INC.; *pg.* 893, *pg.* 1956
BARALYME - Absorbent - ALLIED HEALTHCARE PRODUCTS, INC.; *pg.* 1491, *pg.* 990
BARANOF - Vodka - JIM BEAM BRANDS CO.; *pg.* 1965, *pg.* 601
BARATRON - Transducer - MKS INSTRUMENTS, INC.; *pg.* 1362, *pg.* 781
BARB-LOK - Press Fit Fastener - DRIV-LOK, INC.; *pg.* 1046, *pg.* 662
BARB-SERT - Threaded Insert - GROOV-PIN CORPORATION; *pg.* 1049, *pg.* 1608
BARBADOS - Rug - COURISTAN INC.; *pg.* 921, *pg.* 1067
BARBARA GORDON - Character - DC COMICS, INC.; *pg.* 1633, *pg.* 1221
BARBECUE KING - Ovens & Baking Equipment - STANDEX INTERNATIONAL CORPORATION; *pg.* 60, *pg.* 1039
BARBECUE RANCH - Hamburger - INTERNATIONAL DAIRY QUEEN, INC.; *pg.* 1732, *pg.* 938
BARBELL - Metal Locks - MASTER LOCK COMPANY LLC; *pg.* 1055, *pg.* 1884
THE BARBEQUE BIBLE - Book - BARBEQUES GALORE, INC.; *pg.* 51, *pg.* 173
BARBER COLMAN - Machine Tool Product - BOURN & KOCH MACHINE TOOL COMPANY; *pg.* 1319, *pg.* 654
BARBER'S - Milk Products - DEAN FOODS COMPANY; *pg.* 852, *pg.* 1679
BARBE'S - Dairy Product - DEAN FOODS COMPANY; *pg.* 852, *pg.* 1679
BARBIE - Real Vacuum - BISSELL HOMECARE, INC.; *pg.* 52, *pg.* 887
BARBIE - Toy - MATTEL, INC.; *pg.* 962, *pg.* 81
BARBIE BLOOM BOX - CD Player - EMERSON RADIO CORP.; *pg.* 636, *pg.* 1087
BARBIE BLOOM TUBE - Television - EMERSON RADIO CORP.; *pg.* 636, *pg.* 1087
BARBIE BLOSSOM PLAYER - DVD - EMERSON RADIO CORP.; *pg.* 636, *pg.* 1087
BARBIE TRUE BLOSSOM - CD Player - EMERSON RADIO CORP.; *pg.* 636, *pg.* 1087
BARBIERI - Tile - ARTISTIC TILE INC.; *pg.* 914, *pg.* 1119
BARBOUR - Beaufort Jacket - THE ORVIS COMPANY, INC.; *pg.* 1781, *pg.* 1764
BARBYY - Footwear - STEVEN MADDEN, LTD.; *pg.* 1819, *pg.* 1176
BARCELONA - Furniture - AMISCO INDUSTRIES LTD.; *pg.* 913, *pg.* 1958
BARCELONA - Door & Wood Product - CONESTOGA WOOD SPECIALTIES CORP.; *pg.* 921, *pg.* 1527
BARCELONA - Rug - COURISTAN INC.; *pg.* 921, *pg.* 1067
BARCELONA - Fan - CRAFTMADE INTERNATIONAL, INC.; *pg.* 1295, *pg.* 1670
BARCELONA - Footwear - PHOENIX FOOTWEAR GROUP, INC.; *pg.* 1815, *pg.* 60
BARCLAY JEWELERS - Jewelry Store - THE KROGER CO.; *pg.* 1025, *pg.* 1416
BARCO - Professional Apparel - BARCO UNIFORMS, INC.; *pg.* 19, *pg.* 94
BARCO'S BEST - Apparel - BARCO UNIFORMS, INC.; *pg.* 19, *pg.* 94
BARDAC - Biocide for Germicidal Application - LONZA INC.; *pg.* 1171, *pg.* 1041
BARDAC-22 - Topical Biocide - LONZA INC.; *pg.* 1171, *pg.* 1041
BARDON - Hooks & Fittings for Wire Rope - ESCO CORPORATION; *pg.* 1335, *pg.* 1502
BARE BY SOLO - Cups - SOLO CUP COMPANY; *pg.* 1469, *pg.* 625
BARE ELEGANCE - Body Shampoo - THE GILLETTE COMPANY; *pg.* 509, *pg.* 795
BARE ENDOSTATS - Disposable Instrument - AMERICAN MEDICAL SYSTEMS, INC.; *pg.* 1399, *pg.* 238
BARE METAL RESTORE - Software - SYMANTEC CORPORATION; *pg.* 478, *pg.* 161
BAREBOAT - Wine - REMY COINTREAU USA INC.; *pg.* 1969, *pg.* 1285
BAREFOOT - Lawncare Products & Services - TRUGREEN-CHEMLAWN; *pg.* 1801, *pg.* 1647
BARELY THERE - Intimate Apparel - HANESBRANDS INC.; *pg.* 26, *pg.* 1394
BARENJAGER LIQUEUR - Beverage - SIDNEY FRANK IMPORTING CO., INC.; *pg.* 1970, *pg.* 1184
BARENTHAL - Fabric - NEMSCHOFF, INC.; *pg.* 936, *pg.* 1890
BARGAIN CALL - Communication Product - CENTURYLINK, INC; *pg.* 1870, *pg.* 317
BARGAIN CAVE - Shop - CABELA'S INCORPORATED; *pg.* 535, *pg.* 1019
BARGAIN HOUND - Pet Supplies - PETSMART, INC.; *pg.* 1481, *pg.* 18
BARGAIN TRADER - Magazine - DOMINION ENTERPRISES; *pg.* 1636, *pg.* 1796
BARI - Footwear - PHOENIX FOOTWEAR GROUP, INC.; *pg.* 1815, *pg.* 60
BARI - Cheese - SAPUTO, INC.; *pg.* 893, *pg.* 1956
BARIAIR - Therapy System - KINETIC CONCEPTS, INC.; *pg.* 1553, *pg.* 1741
BARIATRIC - Metal Furniture - UMF MEDICAL; *pg.* 946, *pg.* 1542
BARIATRIC SOLUTIONS DESIGN - Service Plan Design - INVACARE CORPORATION; *pg.* 1546, *pg.* 1451
BARIATRIC SUPPORT - Therapy System - KINETIC CONCEPTS, INC.; *pg.* 1553, *pg.* 1741
BARIKARE - Mattress - KINETIC CONCEPTS, INC.; *pg.* 1553, *pg.* 1741
BARILLA - Pastas & Sauces - BARILLA AMERICA, INC.; *pg.* 839, *pg.* 555
BARILLA PLUS - Fortified Pasta Products - BARILLA AMERICA, INC.; *pg.* 839, *pg.* 555
BARIMAXX - Bed System - KINETIC CONCEPTS, INC.; *pg.* 1553, *pg.* 1741
BARIOLAGE - Surface Material - STEELCASE INC.; *pg.* 475, *pg.* 889
BARISELECT - Support Surface Product - THE ROHO GROUP; *pg.* 1591, *pg.* 556
BARISTA - Coffee Bartender - STARBUCKS CORPORATION; *pg.* 897, *pg.* 1840
BARISTA PRIMA COFFEEHOUSE - Coffee - KEURIG GREEN MOUNTAIN, INC.; *pg.* 868, *pg.* 1768
BARIVER - Chemical Reagent - HACH COMPANY; *pg.* 1415, *pg.* 334
BARK AVENUE - Video Game - INTERNATIONAL GAME TECHNOLOGY; *pg.* 957, *pg.* 1024
BARKLEY - Bear - GUND, INC.; *pg.* 954, *pg.* 1056
BARKLEY - Furniture - J. ROBERT SCOTT INC.; *pg.* 930, *pg.* 105
BARKO HYDRAULIC - Log Loaders - PETTIBONE, LLC; *pg.* 1368, *pg.* 609
BARKOFF - Dog Training - TELEBRANDS, INC.; *pg.* 1396, *pg.* 1066
BARKWORTH GOURMET - Pet Cookies - PETEDGE; *pg.* 1481, *pg.* 787
BARLETTA ANTIQUE - Furniture - ASHLEY FURNITURE INDUSTRIES, INC.; *pg.* 914, *pg.* 1852
BARLEY - Lighting - ETHAN ALLEN INTERIORS INC.; *pg.*

First page reference indicates Business Class Edition
Second page reference indicates Geographic Edition

924, *pg.* 343
BARLEYS CASINO AND BREWERY - Casino & Brewery - STATION CASINOS, INC.; *pg.* 585, *pg.* 1030
BARLIV - Barley Betafiber - CARGILL, INC.; *pg.* 845, *pg.* 965
BARLOCK - Security Card Processors, Readers & Keypads - MAXXESS SYSTEMS, INC.; *pg.* 431, *pg.* 43
BARLOK - Commutator - KIRKWOOD HOLDING, INC.; *pg.* 649, *pg.* 1469
BARLOX - Amine Oxide for Detergents, Shampoos, Textile Processing - LONZA INC.; *pg.* 1171, *pg.* 1041
BARN - Container - PACTIV CORPORATION; *pg.* 1466, *pg.* 624
BARNES & NOBLE - Book Stores - BARNES & NOBLE, INC.; *pg.* 1619, *pg.* 1201
BARNESITE - Precision Polish for Glass - FERRO CORPORATION; *pg.* 1162, *pg.* 1462
BARNETT - Maintenance, Repair & Operations Products - INTERLINE BRANDS, INC.; *pg.* 1051, *pg.* 433
BARNETT - Furniture - LA-Z-BOY INCORPORATED; *pg.* 932, *pg.* 901
BARNETT - Apparel - OAKLEY, INC.; *pg.* 1840, *pg.* 86
BARNEYS NEW YORK - Retail Clothing Stores - BARNEYS NEW YORK, INC.; *pg.* 38, *pg.* 1201
BARNEY'S NEW YORK CO-OP - Men's & Women's Designer Clothing - BARNEYS NEW YORK, INC.; *pg.* 38, *pg.* 1201
BARNEY'S NEW YORK OUTLET - Outlet Clothing Stores - BARNEYS NEW YORK, INC.; *pg.* 38, *pg.* 1201
BARNHARDT - Batting & Absorbent Cotton - BARNHARDT MANUFACTURING COMPANY; *pg.* 1498, *pg.* 1364
BARNI - Soft Biscuit - MONDELEZ INTERNATIONAL, INC.; *pg.* 878, *pg.* 601
BARNUM'S KALEIDOSCAPE - One Ring Circus - FELD ENTERTAINMENT, INC.; *pg.* 547, *pg.* 458
BARNYARD - Book - TRACTOR SUPPLY COMPANY; *pg.* 708, *pg.* 1627
BARO-PAK - Thermostat Wire Packaging - COLEMAN CABLE, INC.; *pg.* 1324, *pg.* 665
BARO-SPLIT - Coaxial Cables - COLEMAN CABLE, INC.; *pg.* 1324, *pg.* 665
BAROGATION - Sprinkler Cable - COLEMAN CABLE, INC.; *pg.* 1324, *pg.* 665
BARON - Air-Conditioner Whips - COLEMAN CABLE, INC.; *pg.* 1324, *pg.* 665
BARON VON SCHEUTERS - Schnapps - JIM BEAM BRANDS CO.; *pg.* 1965, *pg.* 601
BARONS - Beer - UNITED STATES BEVERAGE LLC; *pg.* 266, *pg.* 379
BAROPLEN - Cable - COLEMAN CABLE, INC.; *pg.* 1324, *pg.* 665
BAROQUE - Apparel - BEBE STORES, INC.; *pg.* 19, *pg.* 49
BAROQUE - Lighting Product - WESTINGHOUSE LIGHTING CORPORATION; *pg.* 687, *pg.* 1571
BAROSTAT - Cable - COLEMAN CABLE, INC.; *pg.* 1324, *pg.* 665
BARQ'S - Root Beer - THE COCA-COLA COMPANY; *pg.* 240, *pg.* 493
BARQUAT/HYAMINE 3500 Biocide - LONZA INC.; *pg.* 1171, *pg.* 1041
BARQUAT/UNIQUAT - Oil Field Chemicals - LONZA INC.; *pg.* 1171, *pg.* 1041
BARRACUDA - Knife Sharpener - HABAND COMPANY, INC.; *pg.* 1772, *pg.* 1099
BARRAGE - Apparel - OAKLEY, INC.; *pg.* 1840, *pg.* 86
BARRE GRAY - Granite - ROCK OF AGES CORPORATION; *pg.* 108, *pg.* 1766
BARREL OF FUN - Shoe - AEROGROUP INTERNATIONAL, INC.; *pg.* 1803, *pg.* 1055
BARREL OF MONKEYS - Toy & Game - HASBRO, INC.; *pg.* 954, *pg.* 1603
BARREL O'FUN - Potato Chips & Snacks in Assorted Flavors & Sizes - BARREL O'FUN SNACK FOODS CO.; *pg.* 1850, *pg.* 952
BARREL SEAL - Seal - GREENE, TWEED & CO.; *pg.* 1344, *pg.* 1544
BARRETTA - Lamp - ASHLEY FURNITURE INDUSTRIES, INC.; *pg.* 914, *pg.* 1852
BARRETT'S BACKERS - Ticket Program - BUCCANEERS LIMITED PARTNERSHIP; *pg.* 534, *pg.* 471
BARRICADE - Coating - YENKIN-MAJESTIC PAINT CORPORATION; *pg.* 1450, *pg.* 1445
BARRIER - Turf Product - PBI/GORDON CORPORATION; *pg.* 1176, *pg.* 985
BARRIER - Personal Care Product - STRAIGHT ARROW PRODUCTS, INC.; *pg.* 523, *pg.* 1517
BARRIER BAG - Oxygen Barrier Vacuum Shrink Bag - SEALED AIR CORPORATION; *pg.* 1468, *pg.* 1058
BARRIER BUBBLE - Cushioning Material - SEALED AIR CORPORATION; *pg.* 1468, *pg.* 1058
BARRIER GLIDER - Cold Storage Door System - RITE-HITE HOLDING CORPORATION; *pg.* 1372, *pg.* 1880
BARRIERTECH - Shoe Cover - ALPHA PRO TECH, LTD.; *pg.* 1492, *pg.* 1922
BARRINGTON - Bath Product - KOHLER CO.; *pg.* 91, *pg.* 1862
BARRINGTON - Door - MASONITE INTERNATIONAL CORPORATION; *pg.* 1054, *pg.* 1920
BARRINGTON - Lighting Product - QUOIZEL INC.; *pg.* 1304, *pg.* 1616
BARRINGTON - Ethernet Product - VITESSE SEMICONDUCTOR CORPORATION; *pg.* 686, *pg.* 57
BARRISTER - Furniture - ETHAN ALLEN INTERIORS INC.; *pg.* 924, *pg.* 343
BARRISTERS SCOTCH - Scotch - LAIRD & COMPANY, INC.; *pg.* 1966, *pg.* 1119
BARRON'S - Business & Financial Publication - BARRON'S; *pg.* 1620, *pg.* 1201
BARRON'S - Weekly Business & Financial Publication - DOW JONES & COMPANY, INC.; *pg.* 1637, *pg.* 1225
BARRY - Isolators & Bearings - BARRY CONTROLS; *pg.* 1317, *pg.* 825
BARRY ALLEN - Character - DC COMICS, INC.; *pg.* 1633, *pg.* 1221
BARRYMORE - Office Furniture - STEELCASE INC.; *pg.* 475, *pg.* 889
BARRYMOUNT - Machinery & Vibration Mounts - BARRY CONTROLS; *pg.* 1317, *pg.* 825
BARRYS TRICOPHEROUS - Hair Tonic - LANMAN & KEMP-BARCLAY CO., INC.; *pg.* 514, *pg.* 1132
BARRYS TRICOPHEROUS TRADITIONAL - Hair Tonic - LANMAN & KEMP-BARCLAY CO., INC.; *pg.* 514, *pg.* 1132
BARSTOW AVE - Furniture - ASHLEY FURNITURE INDUSTRIES, INC.; *pg.* 914, *pg.* 1852
BART SIMPSON - Game - HASBRO, INC.; *pg.* 954, *pg.* 1603
BARTACT - Apparel - OAKLEY, INC.; *pg.* 1840, *pg.* 86
BARTELL - Vibratory Plate Compactor - TEREX CORPORATION; *pg.* 1381, *pg.* 384
BARTELS - Pure Beer - THE LION BREWERY, INC.; *pg.* 254, *pg.* 1594
BARTEX - Mineral Product - TOR MINERALS INTERNATIONAL INC.; *pg.* 1184, *pg.* 1672
BARTLES & JAYMES - Wine Coolers - E&J GALLO WINERY; *pg.* 1962, *pg.* 149
BARTLETT - Pear - PACIFIC NORTHWEST CANNED PEAR SERVICE, INC.; *pg.* 153, *pg.* 1847
BARTLETT BOOST - Fertilizer for Trees & Shrubs - THE F.A. BARTLETT TREE EXPERT COMPANY; *pg.* 1795, *pg.* 373
BARTLETT POND - Clothing - ABERCROMBIE & FITCH CO.; *pg.* 37, *pg.* 1466
BARTON - Footwear - RALPH LAUREN CORPORATION; *pg.* 46, *pg.* 1284
BARWORKS - Beverage Ware - WHIRLEY INDUSTRIES, INC.; *pg.* 1892, *pg.* 1590
BASE A - Donut Mixes - DAWN FOOD PRODUCTS, INC.; *pg.* 1018, *pg.* 893
BASE/LINE - Heating System - SLANT/FIN CORPORATION; *pg.* 1076, *pg.* 1163
BASE24 - Financial Services - ACI WORLDWIDE INC.; *pg.* 341, *pg.* 1010
BASE24-ATM - Financial Services - ACI WORLDWIDE INC.; *pg.* 341, *pg.* 1010
BASE24-CARD - Card Services - ACI WORLDWIDE INC.; *pg.* 341, *pg.* 1010
BASE24-CHECK AUTH - Financial Services - ACI WORLDWIDE INC.; *pg.* 341, *pg.* 1010
BASE24-ES - Integrated Payment Engine - ACI WORLDWIDE INC.; *pg.* 341, *pg.* 1010
BASE24-FREQUENT SHOPPER - Financial Services - ACI WORLDWIDE INC.; *pg.* 341, *pg.* 1010
BASE24-INFOBASE - Financial Services - ACI WORLDWIDE INC.; *pg.* 341, *pg.* 1010
BASE24-POS - Marketing Services - ACI WORLDWIDE INC.; *pg.* 341, *pg.* 1010
BASE24-REFUNDS - Financial Services - ACI WORLDWIDE INC.; *pg.* 341, *pg.* 1010
BASE24-TELLER - Financial Services - ACI WORLDWIDE INC.; *pg.* 341, *pg.* 1010
BASEBALL - Ceiling Fan - WESTINGHOUSE LIGHTING CORPORATION; *pg.* 687, *pg.* 1571
BASEBALL ACADEMY - Summer Camp - THE PHILLIES, L.P.; *pg.* 575, *pg.* 1569
BASELINE - Inclinometer - ALIMED, INC.; *pg.* 1490, *pg.* 816
BASELINE - Medical & Aesthetic Product - DYNATRONICS CORPORATION; *pg.* 1526, *pg.* 1757
BASELINE - Furniture - HERMAN MILLER, INC.; *pg.* 926, *pg.* 913
BASELINE - Portable Basketball Standards - LIFETIME PRODUCTS INC.; *pg.* 933, *pg.* 1751
BASELINE - Software Tool And Application - THOMSON REUTERS MARKETS; *pg.* 810, *pg.* 1299
BASELINE - Gradient Separation - WATERS CORPORATION; *pg.* 1436, *pg.* 834
BASEMAP LEGGING - Apparels - UNDER ARMOUR, INC.; *pg.* 49, *pg.* 759
BASEMENT BLANKET - Glass Fiber Insulation - OWENS CORNING; *pg.* 102, *pg.* 1476
BASHA - Footwear - VANS, INC.; *pg.* 1821, *pg.* 76
BASIC - Cigarettes - PHILIP MORRIS USA INC.; *pg.* 1894, *pg.* 1803
BASIC - Lawn Fertilizer - THE SCOTTS MIRACLE-GRO COMPANY; *pg.* 1799, *pg.* 1459
BASIC 2 - Product Line for Small System Users - VICON INDUSTRIES, INC.; *pg.* 685, *pg.* 1166
BASIC 4 - Cereal - GENERAL MILLS, INC.; *pg.* 828, *pg.* 933
BASIC BLINDZ - Window Blinds - LOWE'S COMPANIES, INC.; *pg.* 1053, *pg.* 1383
BASIC EARLY ASSESSMENT OF READING - Reading Assessment Tool - HOUGHTON MIFFLIN HARCOURT PUBLISHING COMPANY; *pg.* 1651, *pg.* 796
BASIC FLEECE 200 - Glove - 180S, LLC; *pg.* 1824, *pg.* 754
BASIC PAYROLL - Software - INTUIT INC.; *pg.* 769, *pg.* 158
BASIC RED - Paper Towels to Disposable Tableware Products - SAFEWAY INC.; *pg.* 1032, *pg.* 184
BASIC VALUE CHECKING - Personal Checking Account - APPLE BANK FOR SAVINGS; *pg.* 716, *pg.* 1196
BASICALLY U - Cosmetics - ULTA SALON, COSMETICS & FRAGRANCE, INC.; *pg.* 524, *pg.* 559
BASICLISTENER - Audio Publication Membership Plan - AUDIBLE, INC.; *pg.* 1230, *pg.* 1095
BASICS - Bag - PACTIV CORPORATION; *pg.* 1466, *pg.* 624
BASICS PLUS - Food Product - LIFEWAY FOODS, INC.; *pg.* 874, *pg.* 634
BASIKBENCH - Workstations - KEWAUNEE SCIENTIFIC CORPORATION; *pg.* 931, *pg.* 1391
BASIL - Furniture - ASHLEY FURNITURE INDUSTRIES, INC.; *pg.* 914, *pg.* 1852
BASIL - Fabric - NEMSCHOFF, INC.; *pg.* 936, *pg.* 1890
BASIL - Bedding Dispenser - STERIS CORPORATION; *pg.* 1597, *pg.* 1464
BASIL HAYDEN'S - Bourbon - JIM BEAM BRANDS CO.; *pg.* 1965, *pg.* 601
BASILE - Plethysmometer - STOELTING CO.; *pg.* 1430, *pg.* 671
BASIS - Telecommunication Switches, Controller, And Cross-Connect Devices - ALCATEL-LUCENT USA, INC.; *pg.* 615, *pg.* 1728
BASIS - Herbicide - E.I. DU PONT DE NEMOURS & COMPANY; *pg.* 1159, *pg.* 390
BASIS - Fitness & Sleep Tracking Products - INTEL CORPORATION; *pg.* 645, *pg.* 266
BASIS PEAK - Fitness Watch - INTEL CORPORATION; *pg.* 645, *pg.* 266
BASKET OF SPRING - Flower Arrangement - 1-800-FLOWERS.COM, INC.; *pg.* 1758, *pg.* 1151
BASKET OF TREATS BOUQUET - Floral Bouquet - FTD GROUP, INC.; *pg.* 1795, *pg.* 608
BASKET WEAVE - Pillow & Throw - HERITAGE LACE INC.; *pg.* 694, *pg.* 711
BASKET WEAVE - Furniture - J. ROBERT SCOTT INC.; *pg.* 930, *pg.* 105
BASKETWRAP - Paperboard Packaging Product - WESTROCK COMPANY; *pg.* 1472, *pg.* 1805
BASKIN-ROBBINS - Ice Cream - DUNKIN' BRANDS GROUP, INC.; *pg.* 1727, *pg.* 810
BASKIN-ROBBINS CANDY - Frozen Dessert And Beverage - BESTSWEET INC.; *pg.* 1851, *pg.* 1383
BASLER - Generator Controls Rebuilding Services - FLIGHT SYSTEMS, INC.; *pg.* 1337, *pg.* 1548
BASO - Mechanical & Electrical System - JOHNSON CONTROLS, INC.; *pg.* 209, *pg.* 1876
BASOFIL - Fiber - DRAPER KNITTING CO., INC.; *pg.* 692, *pg.* 810
BASS - Shoes - G.H. BASS & CO.; *pg.* 1809, *pg.* 1234
BASS - Musical Instrument - GIBSON GUITAR CORP.; *pg.* 550, *pg.* 1650

BASS - Apparel - PVH CORP.; *pg.* 46, *pg.* 1283
B.A.S.S. FISHING TECHNIQUES - Magazine - B.A.S.S., L.L.C.; *pg.* 270, *pg.* 1
BASS OPTIMIZATION SYSTEM - Audio & Video Product - HARMAN INTERNATIONAL INDUSTRIES, INCORPORATED; *pg.* 641, *pg.* 374
BASS STAGE PACK - Musical Instrument - PEAVEY ELECTRONICS CORPORATION; *pg.* 662, *pg.* 970
B.A.S.S. TIMES - Newspaper - B.A.S.S., L.L.C.; *pg.* 270, *pg.* 1
BASSCASE - Electronics - CAMBRIDGE SOUNDWORKS, INC.; *pg.* 1234, *pg.* 781
BASSCUBE - Electronics - CAMBRIDGE SOUNDWORKS, INC.; *pg.* 1234, *pg.* 781
BASSETT - Tools - KENNAMETAL INC.; *pg.* 1052, *pg.* 1547
BASSETT - Metalworking Tools - KENNAMETAL IPG; *pg.* 1353, *pg.* 1615
BASSETT - Mattresses - SEALY CORPORATION; *pg.* 942, *pg.* 1391
BASSETT FURNITURE DIRECT - Furniture - BASSETT FURNITURE INDUSTRIES, INCORPORATED; *pg.* 916, *pg.* 1776
BASSMAN - Amplifier - FENDER MUSICAL INSTRUMENTS CORPORATION; *pg.* 547, *pg.* 21
BASSMASTER - Magazine - B.A.S.S., L.L.C.; *pg.* 270, *pg.* 1
BASSMASTER CLASSIC REPORT - Magazine - B.A.S.S., L.L.C.; *pg.* 270, *pg.* 1
BASSMASTER ELITE 50 SERIES - Tournament Fishing Trail - B.A.S.S., L.L.C.; *pg.* 270, *pg.* 1
BASSMASTER TOP BASS DESTINATIONS - Magazine - B.A.S.S., L.L.C.; *pg.* 270, *pg.* 1
THE BASSMASTER TOUR - Magazine - B.A.S.S., L.L.C.; *pg.* 270, *pg.* 1
BASSMASTER TOURNAMENT TRAIL - Trail Providers for BASS Tournaments - B.A.S.S., L.L.C.; *pg.* 270, *pg.* 1
THE BASSMASTERS - TV Show - B.A.S.S., L.L.C.; *pg.* 270, *pg.* 1
BASTA SOLE - Furniture - TROPITONE FURNITURE CO., INC.; *pg.* 945, *pg.* 118
BASWEBALL 101 CLINIC - Clinic & Luncheon For Women - THE PHILLIES, L.P.; *pg.* 575, *pg.* 1569
BATAVIA - Footwear - VANS, INC.; *pg.* 1821, *pg.* 76
BATCH CONNECT - Software - ASPEN TECHNOLOGY, INC.; *pg.* 354, *pg.* 804
BATCH DISCOVERY - Software Application - BMC SOFTWARE, INC.; *pg.* 362, *pg.* 1701
BATCH DISPENSE SYSTEM - Meter & Control - GRACO, INC.; *pg.* 1342, *pg.* 935
BATCH IMPACT MANAGER - Software - BMC SOFTWARE, INC.; *pg.* 362, *pg.* 1701
BATCHCAD - Software - ASPEN TECHNOLOGY, INC.; *pg.* 354, *pg.* 804
BATCHELORS - Instant Dry Soups, Noodles, Dry Side Dishes, Canned Vegetables & Dry Sauces - CAMPBELL SOUP COMPANY; *pg.* 844, *pg.* 1048
BATCHMASTER - Batch Oven Furnaces - SURFACE COMBUSTION, INC.; *pg.* 1077, *pg.* 1462
BATCHPAC - Modular Induction Batch Melting Systems - INDUCTOTHERM CORP.; *pg.* 1348, *pg.* 1114
BATCHSEP - Software - ASPEN TECHNOLOGY, INC.; *pg.* 354, *pg.* 804
BATERIA III WOODCOCK-MUNOZ - Testing Assessment Tool - HOUGHTON MIFFLIN HARCOURT PUBLISHING COMPANY; *pg.* 1651, *pg.* 796
BATES - Needlecraft Accessories - MAKE IT COATS; *pg.* 696, *pg.* 1367
BATES - Footwear - WOLVERINE WORLD WIDE, INC.; *pg.* 1822, *pg.* 905
BATGIRL - Character - DC COMICS, INC.; *pg.* 1633, *pg.* 1221
BATH DOLLS - Toy - THE OHIO ART COMPANY, INC.; *pg.* 965, *pg.* 1406
BATH DUNKERS - Baby Care Product - MUNCHKIN, INC.; *pg.* 964, *pg.* 300
BATH MANAGER - Bath Management System - TECK RESOURCES LIMITED; *pg.* 1183, *pg.* 1912
BATH SALTS - Personal Care Product - RBC LIFE SCIENCES, INC.; *pg.* 1588, *pg.* 1723
BATH UNLIMITED - Decorative Architectural Product - MASCO CORPORATION; *pg.* 96, *pg.* 909
BATHE AWAY - Healthcare Product - DERMA SCIENCES, INC.; *pg.* 1523, *pg.* 1111
BATHERAPY - Toiletries - THE HAIN CELESTIAL GROUP, INC.; *pg.* 860, *pg.* 1172
BATHMASTER - Thermal Processing Equipment - SURFACE COMBUSTION, INC.; *pg.* 1077, *pg.* 1462
BATHMINDER - Control Your Plating Bath - HEATBATH CORPORATION; *pg.* 1165, *pg.* 826
BATIK - Pillow - ETHAN ALLEN INTERIORS INC.; *pg.* 924, *pg.* 343
BATIK - Hat - WOODEN SHIPS OF HOBOKEN; *pg.* 35, *pg.* 1315
BATLIGHT - Flashlight - THE FULLER BRUSH COMPANY; *pg.* 330, *pg.* 715
BATLLO - Fabric - NEMSCHOFF, INC.; *pg.* 936, *pg.* 1890
BATLOCK - Component Part - COMMERCIAL VEHICLE GROUP, INC.; *pg.* 203, *pg.* 1467
BATMAN - Character - DC COMICS, INC.; *pg.* 1633, *pg.* 1221
BATMOD - Power Converter - VICOR CORPORATION; *pg.* 1435, *pg.* 783
BATTABOUT - Pet Toy - THE HARTZ MOUNTAIN CORP.; *pg.* 1476, *pg.* 1120
BATTER GOLD - Frozen Food - TYSON FOODS, INC.; *pg.* 902, *pg.* 35
BATTERSWEET - Frozen Poultry - TYSON FOODS, INC.; *pg.* 902, *pg.* 35
BATTERY-VOLTAGE - Hard Disk Drive - ATMEL CORPORATION; *pg.* 621, *pg.* 238
BATTIG - Valve - FLOWSERVE CORPORATION; *pg.* 82, *pg.* 1719
BATTLE BALL - Toy & Game - HASBRO, INC.; *pg.* 954, *pg.* 1603
BATTLE CRY - Game - HASBRO, INC.; *pg.* 954, *pg.* 1603
BATTLE READY COTS - Product Description - MERCURY COMPUTER SYSTEMS, INC.; *pg.* 434, *pg.* 813
BATTLEBOTS - Toy & Game - HASBRO, INC.; *pg.* 954, *pg.* 1603
BATTLEGROUND - Toy - SPIN MASTER LTD.; *pg.* 967, *pg.* 1943
BATTLESHIP - Game - HASBRO, INC.; *pg.* 954, *pg.* 1603
BATTLESTAR GALACTICA - Toy & Game - HASBRO, INC.; *pg.* 954, *pg.* 1603
BATTPAC - Compression & Cutting Tool - THOMAS & BETTS CORPORATION; *pg.* 680, *pg.* 1646
BATTRAX - Protection Thyristor - LITTELFUSE, INC.; *pg.* 1301, *pg.* 580
BATTSLIDE - Batten Receptacle - SCHAEFER MARINE INC.; *pg.* 1373, *pg.* 835
BATYA - Lamp - ASHLEY FURNITURE INDUSTRIES, INC.; *pg.* 914, *pg.* 1852
BAUBLE - Fabric - NEMSCHOFF, INC.; *pg.* 936, *pg.* 1890
BAUER & BLACK - Supporters, Briefs & Suspensions - BECTON, DICKINSON & COMPANY; *pg.* 1501, *pg.* 1068
BAUHAUS - Fabric - NEMSCHOFF, INC.; *pg.* 936, *pg.* 1890
BAUHAUS USA - Furniture - LA-Z-BOY INCORPORATED; *pg.* 932, *pg.* 901
BAUKNECHT - Home Appliance Product - WHIRLPOOL CORPORATION; *pg.* 62, *pg.* 872
BAUM - Paper Cutters & Drills - BAUMFOLDER CORPORATION; *pg.* 360, *pg.* 1472
BAUME & MERCIER - Watches - BAUME & MERCIER, INC.; *pg.* 1, *pg.* 1201
BAUMFOLDER GRAPHIC ARTS EQUIPMENT - Paper Folding Machines - BAUMFOLDER CORPORATION; *pg.* 360, *pg.* 1472
BAUTZ - Motor Drive - DANAHER CORPORATION; *pg.* 1044, *pg.* 397
BAVARIA - Furniture - ASHLEY FURNITURE INDUSTRIES, INC.; *pg.* 914, *pg.* 1852
BAVARIAN - Soft Pretzels - J&J SNACK FOODS CORPORATION; *pg.* 865, *pg.* 1107
BAVARIAN VILLAGE - Ski & Snowboard Retailer - BOYNE USA RESORTS INC.; *pg.* 1082, *pg.* 874
BAX - Pathogen Detection System - E.I. DU PONT DE NEMOURS & COMPANY; *pg.* 1159, *pg.* 390
BAXJECT - Biopharmaceutical Product - BAXTER INTERNATIONAL INC.; *pg.* 1499, *pg.* 599
BAXTER - Clothing - ABERCROMBIE & FITCH CO.; *pg.* 37, *pg.* 1466
BAXTER - Furniture - ASHLEY FURNITURE INDUSTRIES, INC.; *pg.* 914, *pg.* 1852
BAXTER - Fabric - NEMSCHOFF, INC.; *pg.* 936, *pg.* 1890
BAXTER - Dairy Products - SAPUTO, INC.; *pg.* 893, *pg.* 1956
THE BAY - Merchandise Store - HUDSON'S BAY COMPANY; *pg.* 1773, *pg.* 1938
BAY BEAUTY - Canned Salmon - OCEAN BEAUTY SEAFOODS, INC.; *pg.* 1028, *pg.* 1838
BAY CITY - Italian-Style Food - ARMANINO FOODS OF DISTINCTION, INC.; *pg.* 837, *pg.* 100
BAY CITY - Deli & Specialty Bread Items - UNITED STATES BAKERY; *pg.* 907, *pg.* 1507
THE BAY CITY TIMES - Newspaper - MLIVE MEDIA GROUP; *pg.* 1665, *pg.* 888
BAY STATE ONLINE - Online Banking Services - BAY STATE SAVINGS BANK; *pg.* 722, *pg.* 862
BAY WEST - Paper Products - WAUSAU PAPER BAY WEST; *pg.* 1471, *pg.* 1465
BAY WINDS - Seafood - PERFORMANCE FOOD GROUP COMPANY, LLC; *pg.* 1030, *pg.* 1803
BAYBLADE GALEON ATTACKER - Toy & Game - HASBRO, INC.; *pg.* 954, *pg.* 1603
BAYFOL - Plastic Film - TEKRA CORPORATION; *pg.* 1184, *pg.* 1884
BAYFRONT - Eyewear - MAUI JIM, INC.; *pg.* 9, *pg.* 651
BAYGONE - Electric Mosquito Killer - S.C. JOHNSON & SON, INC.; *pg.* 334, *pg.* 1889
BAYLINER - Boats - BRUNSWICK CORPORATION; *pg.* 1828, *pg.* 623
BAYMONT INN & SUITES - Hotels - WYNDHAM WORLDWIDE CORPORATION; *pg.* 1119, *pg.* 1107
BAYMONT INNS AND SUITES - Economy Hotels - THE MARCUS CORPORATION; *pg.* 1102, *pg.* 1877
BAYONET MICROSTATS - Surgical Instrument - AMERICAN MEDICAL SYSTEMS, INC.; *pg.* 1399, *pg.* 238
BAYOU - All-Terrain Vehicle - KAWASAKI MOTORS CORP., U.S.A.; *pg.* 1708, *pg.* 111
BAYPOINT - Carpet - BEAULIEU GROUP, LLC; *pg.* 917, *pg.* 529
BAYPORT - Furniture - ASHLEY FURNITURE INDUSTRIES, INC.; *pg.* 914, *pg.* 1852
BAYPORT - Bed Linen - SPRINGS GLOBAL, INC.; *pg.* 698, *pg.* 1616
BAYSHORE - Footwear - K-SWISS; *pg.* 1837, *pg.* 306
BAYSHORE MESH - Footwear - K-SWISS; *pg.* 1837, *pg.* 306
BAYSTATE HEALTH SYSTEM - Health Care System - BAYSTATE HEALTH SYSTEM, INC.; *pg.* 1501, *pg.* 845
BAYTOWNE - Carpet - BEAULIEU GROUP, LLC; *pg.* 917, *pg.* 529
BAYVIEW - Kitchen Product - KOHLER CO.; *pg.* 91, *pg.* 1862
BAYVIEW TRAIL - Bike - MARIN BIKES; *pg.* 1708, *pg.* 168
BAZAAR - Magazine - COSMOPOLITAN; *pg.* 1630, *pg.* 1218
BAZI - Dietary Supplement Drink - BAZI INTERNATIONAL, INC.; *pg.* 1501, *pg.* 107
BAZOOKA - Candy & Gum - THE TOPPS COMPANY, INC.; *pg.* 588, *pg.* 1302
BB GUN-ITE - Blend of Cement, Sand & Alkali Resistant Glass Fibers - QUIKRETE COMPANIES; *pg.* 106, *pg.* 519
BBEDIT - Software - BARE BONES SOFTWARE, INC.; *pg.* 360, *pg.* 838
BBG - Baffle-Type Industrial Burner - HAUCK MANUFACTURING COMPANY, INC.; *pg.* 1345, *pg.* 1522
BBOND - Mining Product - QUIKRETE COMPANIES; *pg.* 106, *pg.* 519
BBOND MS - Mine Sealant - QUIKRETE COMPANIES; *pg.* 106, *pg.* 519
BBONE - Software - BLACKBOARD INC.; *pg.* 1232, *pg.* 396
BC-20 - Adhesive - SPINNAKER COATING, LLC; *pg.* 1470, *pg.* 1477
BC-52 - Flame Retardants - CHEMTURA CORPORATION; *pg.* 1152, *pg.* 355
BC-58 - Flame Retardants - CHEMTURA CORPORATION; *pg.* 1152, *pg.* 355
BC CALC - Software - BOISE CASCADE HOLDINGS, L.L.C.; *pg.* 1453, *pg.* 546
BC FRAMER - Software - BOISE CASCADE HOLDINGS, L.L.C.; *pg.* 1453, *pg.* 546
BC HIKE - Glove Liner - KOMBI, LTD.; *pg.* 1838, *pg.* 1766
B.C. LIFE - Cleaner & Conditioner - MCNETT CORPORATION; *pg.* 1839, *pg.* 1817
BC PERSONAL - Standby UPS Systems - TRIPPE MANUFACTURING COMPANY; *pg.* 220, *pg.* 592
BC PRO - Standby UPS Systems - TRIPPE MANUFACTURING COMPANY; *pg.* 220, *pg.* 592
BC RIM BOARD - Rimboard - BOISE CASCADE HOLDINGS, L.L.C.; *pg.* 1453, *pg.* 546
BC TRACKER - Building Products - BOISE CASCADE HOLDINGS, L.L.C.; *pg.* 1453, *pg.* 546
BCA - Bottom Cracking Additive - JOHNSON MATTHEY PROCESS TECHNOLOGIES; *pg.* 1169, *pg.* 1083
BCBGMAXAZRIA RUNWAY - Clothing & Accessories for Women - BCBG MAX AZRIA GROUP LLC; *pg.* 19, *pg.* 301

First page reference indicates Business Class Edition
Second page reference indicates Geographic Edition

BCC TAP - Type of Taper Pipe Tap - REGAL BELOIT CORPORATION; *pg.* 106, *pg.* 1854
BCE MOBILE - Wireless Communication Product - BCE INC.; *pg.* 1936, *pg.* 1960
BCE NEXXIA - Wireless Communication Product - BCE INC.; *pg.* 1936, *pg.* 1960
BCI - Building Products - BOISE CASCADE HOLDINGS, L.L.C.; *pg.* 1453, *pg.* 546
BCI JOIST - Precision-Engineered I-Joists - BOISE CASCADE HOLDINGS, L.L.C.; *pg.* 1453, *pg.* 546
BCO - Security Programs - LANDSTAR SYSTEM, INC.; *pg.* 1914, *pg.* 434
BCPAPER - Paper Products - BOISE CASCADE HOLDINGS, L.L.C.; *pg.* 1453, *pg.* 546
BCS - Software - TRIMBLE NAVIGATION LIMITED; *pg.* 1384, *pg.* 288
BD - Medical Products - BECTON, DICKINSON & COMPANY; *pg.* 1501, *pg.* 1068
BD A-CATH - Medical Surgical System - BECTON, DICKINSON & COMPANY; *pg.* 1501, *pg.* 1068
BD A-LINE - Preanalytical Products - BECTON, DICKINSON & COMPANY; *pg.* 1501, *pg.* 1068
BD ACCU-GLASS - Diagnostic Products - BECTON, DICKINSON & COMPANY; *pg.* 1501, *pg.* 1068
BD ACCUCELL - Discovery Labware - BECTON, DICKINSON & COMPANY; *pg.* 1501, *pg.* 1068
BD ACCUSPRAY - Nasal Spray System - BECTON, DICKINSON & COMPANY; *pg.* 1501, *pg.* 1068
BD ACIDCASE - Diagnostic Products - BECTON, DICKINSON & COMPANY; *pg.* 1501, *pg.* 1068
BD ACTIV 8 - Medical Surgical System - BECTON, DICKINSON & COMPANY; *pg.* 1501, *pg.* 1068
BD ACTIVATION ASSIST - Medical Surgical System - BECTON, DICKINSON & COMPANY; *pg.* 1501, *pg.* 1068
BD ACTONE - Bioscience Products - BECTON, DICKINSON & COMPANY; *pg.* 1501, *pg.* 1068
BD ADAMS - Diagnostic Products - BECTON, DICKINSON & COMPANY; *pg.* 1501, *pg.* 1068
BD ADENO-X - Bioscience Products - BECTON, DICKINSON & COMPANY; *pg.* 1501, *pg.* 1068
BD ADSYTE - Catheter - BECTON, DICKINSON & COMPANY; *pg.* 1501, *pg.* 1068
BD ADVANTAGE - Bioscience Products - BECTON, DICKINSON & COMPANY; *pg.* 1501, *pg.* 1068
BD AFFIRM - Diagnostic Products - BECTON, DICKINSON & COMPANY; *pg.* 1501, *pg.* 1068
BD AMPHOPACK - Bioscience Products - BECTON, DICKINSON & COMPANY; *pg.* 1501, *pg.* 1068
BD AMPLATZ - Needle - BECTON, DICKINSON & COMPANY; *pg.* 1501, *pg.* 1068
BD ANGIO-SET - Intravenous Catheter Placement Set - BECTON, DICKINSON & COMPANY; *pg.* 1501, *pg.* 1068
BD ANGIOCATH - Intravenous Catheter Placement Unit - BECTON, DICKINSON & COMPANY; *pg.* 1501, *pg.* 1068
BD ANGIOCATH AUTOGUARD - Catheter - BECTON, DICKINSON & COMPANY; *pg.* 1501, *pg.* 1068
BD ANGIOCATH-N AUTOGUARD - Catheter - BECTON, DICKINSON & COMPANY; *pg.* 1501, *pg.* 1068
BD ANGIOCATH PLUS/PRO - Catheter - BECTON, DICKINSON & COMPANY; *pg.* 1501, *pg.* 1068
BD APEM - Medical Surgical System - BECTON, DICKINSON & COMPANY; *pg.* 1501, *pg.* 1068
BD AQUEO PREMIUM - Ophthalmic System - BECTON, DICKINSON & COMPANY; *pg.* 1501, *pg.* 1068
BD ARTHRO-LOK - Surgical Blade - BECTON, DICKINSON & COMPANY; *pg.* 1501, *pg.* 1068
BD ARTHRO-TRAC - Retractable Cannula Handle - BECTON, DICKINSON & COMPANY; *pg.* 1501, *pg.* 1068
BD ASEPTA-CELL - Medical Surgical System - BECTON, DICKINSON & COMPANY; *pg.* 1501, *pg.* 1068
BD ASEPTO - Medical Surgical System - BECTON, DICKINSON & COMPANY; *pg.* 1501, *pg.* 1068
BD ATOMIC EDGE - Silicon Disposable Blades - BECTON, DICKINSON & COMPANY; *pg.* 1501, *pg.* 1068
BD ATTO - Bioscience Products - BECTON, DICKINSON & COMPANY; *pg.* 1501, *pg.* 1068
BD ATTOFLUOR - Bioscience Products - BECTON, DICKINSON & COMPANY; *pg.* 1501, *pg.* 1068
BD ATTOVISION - Software - BECTON, DICKINSON & COMPANY; *pg.* 1501, *pg.* 1068
BD ATTRACTORS - Immunocytometry Products - BECTON, DICKINSON & COMPANY; *pg.* 1501, *pg.* 1068
BD AUTOCRIT - Diagnostic Products - BECTON, DICKINSON & COMPANY; *pg.* 1501, *pg.* 1068
BD AUTOGUARD - Catheter - BECTON, DICKINSON & COMPANY; *pg.* 1501, *pg.* 1068
BD AUTOGUARD-N PRO - Catheter - BECTON, DICKINSON & COMPANY; *pg.* 1501, *pg.* 1068
BD AUTOGUARD PRO - Catheter - BECTON, DICKINSON & COMPANY; *pg.* 1501, *pg.* 1068
BD AUTOMAGIC - Medical Surgical System - BECTON, DICKINSON & COMPANY; *pg.* 1501, *pg.* 1068
BD AUTONUTRIENT - Diagnostic Products - BECTON, DICKINSON & COMPANY; *pg.* 1501, *pg.* 1068
BD AUTOSCEPTOR - Diagnostic Products - BECTON, DICKINSON & COMPANY; *pg.* 1501, *pg.* 1068
BD AUTOSHIELD - Pen Needle - BECTON, DICKINSON & COMPANY; *pg.* 1501, *pg.* 1068
BD AYRE CERVI-SCRAPER - Diagnostic Products - BECTON, DICKINSON & COMPANY; *pg.* 1501, *pg.* 1068
BD BACT-PLATE - Diagnostic Products - BECTON, DICKINSON & COMPANY; *pg.* 1501, *pg.* 1068
BD BACTEC - Medical Instruments - BECTON, DICKINSON & COMPANY; *pg.* 1501, *pg.* 1068
BD BACTEC MGIT - Reagent - BECTON, DICKINSON & COMPANY; *pg.* 1501, *pg.* 1068
BD BACTO - Diagnostic Products - BECTON, DICKINSON & COMPANY; *pg.* 1501, *pg.* 1068
BD BACTROL - Diagnostic Products - BECTON, DICKINSON & COMPANY; *pg.* 1501, *pg.* 1068
BD BACULOGOLD - Bioscience Products - BECTON, DICKINSON & COMPANY; *pg.* 1501, *pg.* 1068
BD BARD-PARKER - Surgical Blade - BECTON, DICKINSON & COMPANY; *pg.* 1501, *pg.* 1068
BD BAUER & BLACK PRECISION - Diabetes Care Product - BECTON, DICKINSON & COMPANY; *pg.* 1501, *pg.* 1068
BD BBL - Diagnostic Reagents & Culture Media - BECTON, DICKINSON & COMPANY; *pg.* 1501, *pg.* 1068
BD BBL CRYSTAL - Identification System - BECTON, DICKINSON & COMPANY; *pg.* 1501, *pg.* 1068
BD BBLCRYSTAL - Diagnostic Products - BECTON, DICKINSON & COMPANY; *pg.* 1501, *pg.* 1068
BD BEAVER - Ophthalmology Product - BECTON, DICKINSON & COMPANY; *pg.* 1501, *pg.* 1068
BD BEAVER-TAIL - Ophthalmology Product - BECTON, DICKINSON & COMPANY; *pg.* 1501, *pg.* 1068
BD BEAVERGUARD - Ophthalmology Product - BECTON, DICKINSON & COMPANY; *pg.* 1501, *pg.* 1068
BD BEAWARE - Diagnostic Products - BECTON, DICKINSON & COMPANY; *pg.* 1501, *pg.* 1068
BD BIO-BAG - Diagnostic Products - BECTON, DICKINSON & COMPANY; *pg.* 1501, *pg.* 1068
BD BIOCOAT - Laboratory Product - BECTON, DICKINSON & COMPANY; *pg.* 1501, *pg.* 1068
BD BIOSATE - Diagnostic Products - BECTON, DICKINSON & COMPANY; *pg.* 1501, *pg.* 1068
BD BITEK - Diagnostic Products - BECTON, DICKINSON & COMPANY; *pg.* 1501, *pg.* 1068
BD BONNANO - Catheter Tray - BECTON, DICKINSON & COMPANY; *pg.* 1501, *pg.* 1068
BD BUSHER - Injector - BECTON, DICKINSON & COMPANY; *pg.* 1501, *pg.* 1068
BD CALIBRITE - Immunocytometry Products - BECTON, DICKINSON & COMPANY; *pg.* 1501, *pg.* 1068
BD CALPHOS - Bioscience Products - BECTON, DICKINSON & COMPANY; *pg.* 1501, *pg.* 1068
BD CAMPYPAK - Diagnostic Products - BECTON, DICKINSON & COMPANY; *pg.* 1501, *pg.* 1068
BD CAMPYPAK PLUS - Disposable Gas Generator Envelope - BECTON, DICKINSON & COMPANY; *pg.* 1501, *pg.* 1068
BD CAMPYPOUCH - Microbiology Product - BECTON, DICKINSON & COMPANY; *pg.* 1501, *pg.* 1068
BD CAMPYSLIDE - Diagnostic Products - BECTON, DICKINSON & COMPANY; *pg.* 1501, *pg.* 1068
BD CAREFLOW - Catheter - BECTON, DICKINSON & COMPANY; *pg.* 1501, *pg.* 1068
BD CARV II - Confocal Imager - BECTON, DICKINSON & COMPANY; *pg.* 1501, *pg.* 1068
BD CDT - Diagnostic Products - BECTON, DICKINSON & COMPANY; *pg.* 1501, *pg.* 1068
BD CEFINASE - Diagnostic Products - BECTON, DICKINSON & COMPANY; *pg.* 1501, *pg.* 1068
BD CELL - Diagnostic Products - BECTON, DICKINSON & COMPANY; *pg.* 1501, *pg.* 1068
BD CELL TAK - Cell & Tissue Adhesive - BECTON, DICKINSON & COMPANY; *pg.* 1501, *pg.* 1068
BD CELLFIT - Immunocytometry Products - BECTON, DICKINSON & COMPANY; *pg.* 1501, *pg.* 1068
BD CELLFIX - Immunocytometry Products - BECTON, DICKINSON & COMPANY; *pg.* 1501, *pg.* 1068
BD CELLMATICS - Diagnostic Products - BECTON, DICKINSON & COMPANY; *pg.* 1501, *pg.* 1068
BD CELLQUEST PRO - Immunocytometry Products - BECTON, DICKINSON & COMPANY; *pg.* 1501, *pg.* 1068
BD CELLWASH - Immunocytometry Products - BECTON, DICKINSON & COMPANY; *pg.* 1501, *pg.* 1068
BD CHAMPION - Medical Surgical System - BECTON, DICKINSON & COMPANY; *pg.* 1501, *pg.* 1068
BD CHEK - Diagnostic Products - BECTON, DICKINSON & COMPANY; *pg.* 1501, *pg.* 1068
BD CHG - Antimicrobial Skin Cleanser - BECTON, DICKINSON & COMPANY; *pg.* 1501, *pg.* 1068
BD CLAY ADAMS - Diagnostic Products - BECTON, DICKINSON & COMPANY; *pg.* 1501, *pg.* 1068
BD CLINIJECT - Medical Surgical System - BECTON, DICKINSON & COMPANY; *pg.* 1501, *pg.* 1068
BD CLONECYT - Immunocytometry Products - BECTON, DICKINSON & COMPANY; *pg.* 1501, *pg.* 1068
BD CLONFECTIN - Bioscience Products - BECTON, DICKINSON & COMPANY; *pg.* 1501, *pg.* 1068
BD CLONTECH PCR-SELECT - Bioscience Products - BECTON, DICKINSON & COMPANY; *pg.* 1501, *pg.* 1068
BD CMVSCAN - Diagnostic Products - BECTON, DICKINSON & COMPANY; *pg.* 1501, *pg.* 1068
BD COLORPAC - Diagnostic Products - BECTON, DICKINSON & COMPANY; *pg.* 1501, *pg.* 1068
BD COMPRE-KNIT - Home Care Product - BECTON, DICKINSON & COMPANY; *pg.* 1501, *pg.* 1068
BD CONNECTA - Critical Care Product - BECTON, DICKINSON & COMPANY; *pg.* 1501, *pg.* 1068
BD CORNWALL - Injection Product - BECTON, DICKINSON & COMPANY; *pg.* 1501, *pg.* 1068
BD CPT - Preanalytical System - BECTON, DICKINSON & COMPANY; *pg.* 1501, *pg.* 1068
BD CREATOR - Bioscience Products - BECTON, DICKINSON & COMPANY; *pg.* 1501, *pg.* 1068
BD CRITICATH - Pressure Monitoring Catheter - BECTON, DICKINSON & COMPANY; *pg.* 1501, *pg.* 1068
BD CRITIFLO - Critical Care Product - BECTON, DICKINSON & COMPANY; *pg.* 1501, *pg.* 1068
BD CRITIKIT - Critical Care Product - BECTON, DICKINSON & COMPANY; *pg.* 1501, *pg.* 1068
BD CRYSTAL - Diagnostic Products - BECTON, DICKINSON & COMPANY; *pg.* 1501, *pg.* 1068
BD CRYSTALSPEC - Diagnostic Products - BECTON, DICKINSON & COMPANY; *pg.* 1501, *pg.* 1068
BD CSI - Medical Surgical System - BECTON, DICKINSON & COMPANY; *pg.* 1501, *pg.* 1068
BD CTA MEDIUM - Diagnostic Products - BECTON, DICKINSON & COMPANY; *pg.* 1501, *pg.* 1068
BD CULTURESWAB - Diagnostic Products - BECTON, DICKINSON & COMPANY; *pg.* 1501, *pg.* 1068
BD CULTURETTE - Diagnostic Products - BECTON, DICKINSON & COMPANY; *pg.* 1501, *pg.* 1068
BD CUSTOMEYES - Ophthalmic Kit - BECTON, DICKINSON & COMPANY; *pg.* 1501, *pg.* 1068
BD CYCLETEST - Immunocytometry Products - BECTON, DICKINSON & COMPANY; *pg.* 1501, *pg.* 1068
BD CYTOFIX - Cytokine Staining Starter Kit - BECTON, DICKINSON & COMPANY; *pg.* 1501, *pg.* 1068
BD CYTOFIX/CYTOPERM - Bioscience Products - BECTON, DICKINSON & COMPANY; *pg.* 1501, *pg.* 1068
BD CYTOPERM - BrdU Flow Kit - BECTON, DICKINSON & COMPANY; *pg.* 1501, *pg.* 1068
BD CYTOPRINT - Bioscience Products - BECTON, DICKINSON & COMPANY; *pg.* 1501, *pg.* 1068
BD CYTORICH - Fixative System - BECTON, DICKINSON & COMPANY; *pg.* 1501, *pg.* 1068
BD DECISIV - Process Model - BECTON, DICKINSON & COMPANY; *pg.* 1501, *pg.* 1068
BD DELTACATH - Medical Surgical System - BECTON, DICKINSON & COMPANY; *pg.* 1501, *pg.* 1068
BD DESCARTEX - Disposable Collector - BECTON, DICKINSON & COMPANY; *pg.* 1501, *pg.* 1068
BD DESTRUCLIP - Medical Surgical System - BECTON, DICKINSON & COMPANY; *pg.* 1501, *pg.* 1068
BD DIFCO - Diagnostic Products - BECTON, DICKINSON & COMPANY; *pg.* 1501, *pg.* 1068
BD DIRECTIGEN - Diagnostic Products - BECTON, DICKINSON & COMPANY; *pg.* 1501, *pg.* 1068
BD DIRECTOR - Diagnostic Products - BECTON, DICKINSON & COMPANY; *pg.* 1501, *pg.* 1068
BD DISCARDIT - Syringe - BECTON, DICKINSON & COMPANY; *pg.* 1501, *pg.* 1068

BD DISCARDPLUS - Medical Surgical System - BECTON, DICKINSON & COMPANY; *pg.* 1501, *pg.* 1068

BD DISCOVERY - Labware - BECTON, DICKINSON & COMPANY; *pg.* 1501, *pg.* 1068

BD DISPENSTIRS - Diagnostic Products - BECTON, DICKINSON & COMPANY; *pg.* 1501, *pg.* 1068

BD DISPENSTUBE - Diagnostic Products - BECTON, DICKINSON & COMPANY; *pg.* 1501, *pg.* 1068

BD DRIHEP - Preanalytical System - BECTON, DICKINSON & COMPANY; *pg.* 1501, *pg.* 1068

BD DRIHEP-PLUS - Preanalytical System - BECTON, DICKINSON & COMPANY; *pg.* 1501, *pg.* 1068

BD DRYSLIDE - Diagnostic Products - BECTON, DICKINSON & COMPANY; *pg.* 1501, *pg.* 1068

BD DTX - Medical Surgical System - BECTON, DICKINSON & COMPANY; *pg.* 1501, *pg.* 1068

BD DTXPLUS - Blood Sampling System - BECTON, DICKINSON & COMPANY; *pg.* 1501, *pg.* 1068

BD DUOVIAL - Medical Surgical System - BECTON, DICKINSON & COMPANY; *pg.* 1501, *pg.* 1068

BD DURASAFE - Injection Product - BECTON, DICKINSON & COMPANY; *pg.* 1501, *pg.* 1068

BD DYNAC - Diagnostic Products - BECTON, DICKINSON & COMPANY; *pg.* 1501, *pg.* 1068

BD E-Z CARE - Surgical Product - BECTON, DICKINSON & COMPANY; *pg.* 1501, *pg.* 1068

BD E-Z SCRUB - Disposable Scrub - BECTON, DICKINSON & COMPANY; *pg.* 1501, *pg.* 1068

BD E-Z SET - Blood Collection & Infusion Set - BECTON, DICKINSON & COMPANY; *pg.* 1501, *pg.* 1068

BD EASY - Medical Surgical System - BECTON, DICKINSON & COMPANY; *pg.* 1501, *pg.* 1068

BD EASY SAFE - Medical Surgical System - BECTON, DICKINSON & COMPANY; *pg.* 1501, *pg.* 1068

BD EASYVENT - Blood Sampling System - BECTON, DICKINSON & COMPANY; *pg.* 1501, *pg.* 1068

BD ECLIPSE - Syringe & Needle - BECTON, DICKINSON & COMPANY; *pg.* 1501, *pg.* 1068

BD ECOPACK - Bioscience Products - BECTON, DICKINSON & COMPANY; *pg.* 1501, *pg.* 1068

BD EDGEAHEAD - Ophthalmology Product - BECTON, DICKINSON & COMPANY; *pg.* 1501, *pg.* 1068

BD ELECTRACODE - Diagnostic Products - BECTON, DICKINSON & COMPANY; *pg.* 1501, *pg.* 1068

BD EMPIRE - Medical Surgical System - BECTON, DICKINSON & COMPANY; *pg.* 1501, *pg.* 1068

BD ENSURE-IT - Infusion Therapy Product - BECTON, DICKINSON & COMPANY; *pg.* 1501, *pg.* 1068

BD ENTEROCOCCOSEL - Diagnostic Products - BECTON, DICKINSON & COMPANY; *pg.* 1501, *pg.* 1068

BD ENTEROTUBE - Diagnostic Products - BECTON, DICKINSON & COMPANY; *pg.* 1501, *pg.* 1068

BD EPICENTER - Diagnostic Products - BECTON, DICKINSON & COMPANY; *pg.* 1501, *pg.* 1068

BD EPILOR - Syringe & Needle - BECTON, DICKINSON & COMPANY; *pg.* 1501, *pg.* 1068

BD EPLEX - Diagnostic System - BECTON, DICKINSON & COMPANY; *pg.* 1501, *pg.* 1068

BD EUGONAGAR - Diagnostic Products - BECTON, DICKINSON & COMPANY; *pg.* 1501, *pg.* 1068

BD EUGONBROTH - Diagnostic Products - BECTON, DICKINSON & COMPANY; *pg.* 1501, *pg.* 1068

BD EXACTA - Medical Surgical System - BECTON, DICKINSON & COMPANY; *pg.* 1501, *pg.* 1068

BD EXPRESS - Laboratory Product - BECTON, DICKINSON & COMPANY; *pg.* 1501, *pg.* 1068

BD EXTRALIGHT - Diagnostic Products - BECTON, DICKINSON & COMPANY; *pg.* 1501, *pg.* 1068

BD FACS - Immunocytometry Products - BECTON, DICKINSON & COMPANY; *pg.* 1501, *pg.* 1068

BD FACSANALYSIS - Cell Analysis Product - BECTON, DICKINSON & COMPANY; *pg.* 1501, *pg.* 1068

BD FACSARIA - Immunocytometry Products - BECTON, DICKINSON & COMPANY; *pg.* 1501, *pg.* 1068

BD FACSARRAY - Immunocytometry Products - BECTON, DICKINSON & COMPANY; *pg.* 1501, *pg.* 1068

BD FACSCALIBUR - Flow Cytometer - BECTON, DICKINSON & COMPANY; *pg.* 1501, *pg.* 1068

BD FACSCAN - Flow Cytometry - BECTON, DICKINSON & COMPANY; *pg.* 1501, *pg.* 1068

BD FACSCANTO - Immunocytometry Products - BECTON, DICKINSON & COMPANY; *pg.* 1501, *pg.* 1068

BD FACSCOMP - Immunocytometry Products - BECTON, DICKINSON & COMPANY; *pg.* 1501, *pg.* 1068

BD FACSCOUNT - Clinical System Providing Absolute Counts for Monitoring HIV Patients - BECTON, DICKINSON & COMPANY; *pg.* 1501, *pg.* 1068

BD FACSDIVA - Immunocytometry Products - BECTON, DICKINSON & COMPANY; *pg.* 1501, *pg.* 1068

BD FACSERVICE - Immunocytometry Products - BECTON, DICKINSON & COMPANY; *pg.* 1501, *pg.* 1068

BD FACSFLOW - Immunocytometry Products - BECTON, DICKINSON & COMPANY; *pg.* 1501, *pg.* 1068

BD FACSORT - Benchtop Cell Sorter - BECTON, DICKINSON & COMPANY; *pg.* 1501, *pg.* 1068

BD FACSTAR - Cell Sorter - BECTON, DICKINSON & COMPANY; *pg.* 1501, *pg.* 1068

BD FACSTATION - Immunocytometry Products - BECTON, DICKINSON & COMPANY; *pg.* 1501, *pg.* 1068

BD FACSVANTAGE - Immunocytometry Products - BECTON, DICKINSON & COMPANY; *pg.* 1501, *pg.* 1068

BD FALCON - Microbiology Product - BECTON, DICKINSON & COMPANY; *pg.* 1501, *pg.* 1068

BD FASTIMMUNE - Immunocytometry Products - BECTON, DICKINSON & COMPANY; *pg.* 1501, *pg.* 1068

BD FC BLOCK - Bioscience Products - BECTON, DICKINSON & COMPANY; *pg.* 1501, *pg.* 1068

BD FIBROMETER - Diagnostic Products - BECTON, DICKINSON & COMPANY; *pg.* 1501, *pg.* 1068

BD FIBROSYSTEM - Diagnostic Products - BECTON, DICKINSON & COMPANY; *pg.* 1501, *pg.* 1068

BD FIBROTIP - Diagnostic Products - BECTON, DICKINSON & COMPANY; *pg.* 1501, *pg.* 1068

BD FIBROTUBE - Diagnostic Products - BECTON, DICKINSON & COMPANY; *pg.* 1501, *pg.* 1068

BD FILL - Medical Surgical System - BECTON, DICKINSON & COMPANY; *pg.* 1501, *pg.* 1068

BD FINGER DAB - Diagnostic Products - BECTON, DICKINSON & COMPANY; *pg.* 1501, *pg.* 1068

BD FIRELIGHT - Diagnostic Products - BECTON, DICKINSON & COMPANY; *pg.* 1501, *pg.* 1068

BD FIRST MIDCATH - Infusion Therapy Product - BECTON, DICKINSON & COMPANY; *pg.* 1501, *pg.* 1068

BD FIRST PICC - Infusion Therapy Product - BECTON, DICKINSON & COMPANY; *pg.* 1501, *pg.* 1068

BD FLOPRO - Medical Surgical System - BECTON, DICKINSON & COMPANY; *pg.* 1501, *pg.* 1068

BD FLOSWITCH - Critical Care Product - BECTON, DICKINSON & COMPANY; *pg.* 1501, *pg.* 1068

BD FLUOROSENSOR - Bioscience Products - BECTON, DICKINSON & COMPANY; *pg.* 1501, *pg.* 1068

BD FLUROBLOK - Laboratory Product - BECTON, DICKINSON & COMPANY; *pg.* 1501, *pg.* 1068

BD FOCALPOINT - Slide Profiler - BECTON, DICKINSON & COMPANY; *pg.* 1501, *pg.* 1068

BD FOS - Diagnostic Products - BECTON, DICKINSON & COMPANY; *pg.* 1501, *pg.* 1068

BD FUSION-BLUE - Bioscience Products - BECTON, DICKINSON & COMPANY; *pg.* 1501, *pg.* 1068

BD G-FLEX - Diabetes Care - BECTON, DICKINSON & COMPANY; *pg.* 1501, *pg.* 1068

BD GABARITH - Medical Surgical System - BECTON, DICKINSON & COMPANY; *pg.* 1501, *pg.* 1068

BD GASPAK - Laboratory Products - BECTON, DICKINSON & COMPANY; *pg.* 1501, *pg.* 1068

BD GC-LECT - Diagnostic Products - BECTON, DICKINSON & COMPANY; *pg.* 1501, *pg.* 1068

BD GELYSATE - Diagnostic Products - BECTON, DICKINSON & COMPANY; *pg.* 1501, *pg.* 1068

BD GENEOHM - Lysis Kit - BECTON, DICKINSON & COMPANY; *pg.* 1501, *pg.* 1068

BD GENIE - Blood Collection Product - BECTON, DICKINSON & COMPANY; *pg.* 1501, *pg.* 1068

BD GENTEST - Solubility Scanner - BECTON, DICKINSON & COMPANY; *pg.* 1501, *pg.* 1068

BD GETTING STARTED - Fast Food Guide - BECTON, DICKINSON & COMPANY; *pg.* 1501, *pg.* 1068

BD GLASPAK - Syringe & Needle - BECTON, DICKINSON & COMPANY; *pg.* 1501, *pg.* 1068

BD GLIDE - Diabetes Care - BECTON, DICKINSON & COMPANY; *pg.* 1501, *pg.* 1068

BD GOLGIPLUG - Bioscience Products - BECTON, DICKINSON & COMPANY; *pg.* 1501, *pg.* 1068

BD GOLGISTOP - Bioscience Products - BECTON, DICKINSON & COMPANY; *pg.* 1501, *pg.* 1068

BD HARDPAK - Carton - BECTON, DICKINSON & COMPANY; *pg.* 1501, *pg.* 1068

BD HEMOGARD - Microbiology Product - BECTON, DICKINSON & COMPANY; *pg.* 1501, *pg.* 1068

BD H.E.R.O. - Diagnostic System - BECTON, DICKINSON & COMPANY; *pg.* 1501, *pg.* 1068

BD HORIZON - Reagent - BECTON, DICKINSON & COMPANY; *pg.* 1501, *pg.* 1068

BD HUBER - Medical Surgical System - BECTON, DICKINSON & COMPANY; *pg.* 1501, *pg.* 1068

BD HYCHECK - Diagnostic Products - BECTON, DICKINSON & COMPANY; *pg.* 1501, *pg.* 1068

BD HYDROCATH - Catheter Kit - BECTON, DICKINSON & COMPANY; *pg.* 1501, *pg.* 1068

BD HYDROCATH ASSURE - Catheter Kit - BECTON, DICKINSON & COMPANY; *pg.* 1501, *pg.* 1068

BD HYPAK - Syringe - BECTON, DICKINSON & COMPANY; *pg.* 1501, *pg.* 1068

BD HYPAK PHYSIOLIS - Syringe - BECTON, DICKINSON & COMPANY; *pg.* 1501, *pg.* 1068

BD HYPAK SCF - Syringe - BECTON, DICKINSON & COMPANY; *pg.* 1501, *pg.* 1068

BD HYPOINT - Needle - BECTON, DICKINSON & COMPANY; *pg.* 1501, *pg.* 1068

BD I PLATE - Diagnostic Products - BECTON, DICKINSON & COMPANY; *pg.* 1501, *pg.* 1068

BD I.C.E./HEAT - Cloth Wrap - BECTON, DICKINSON & COMPANY; *pg.* 1501, *pg.* 1068

BD IMAGN - Immunocytometry Products - BECTON, DICKINSON & COMPANY; *pg.* 1501, *pg.* 1068

BD INFLUX - Cell Sorter - BECTON, DICKINSON & COMPANY; *pg.* 1501, *pg.* 1068

BD INSTAFLASH - Needle - BECTON, DICKINSON & COMPANY; *pg.* 1501, *pg.* 1068

BD INSYTE - Infusion Therapy Product - BECTON, DICKINSON & COMPANY; *pg.* 1501, *pg.* 1068

BD INSYTE-A - Catheter - BECTON, DICKINSON & COMPANY; *pg.* 1501, *pg.* 1068

BD INSYTE AUTOGUARD - Catheter - BECTON, DICKINSON & COMPANY; *pg.* 1501, *pg.* 1068

BD INSYTE AUTOGUARD-P - Catheter - BECTON, DICKINSON & COMPANY; *pg.* 1501, *pg.* 1068

BD INSYTE AUTOGUARD-W - Catheter - BECTON, DICKINSON & COMPANY; *pg.* 1501, *pg.* 1068

BD INSYTE-N - Catheter - BECTON, DICKINSON & COMPANY; *pg.* 1501, *pg.* 1068

BD INSYTE-N AUTOGUARD - Catheter - BECTON, DICKINSON & COMPANY; *pg.* 1501, *pg.* 1068

BD INSYTE-W - Catheter - BECTON, DICKINSON & COMPANY; *pg.* 1501, *pg.* 1068

BD INTEGRA - Syringe - BECTON, DICKINSON & COMPANY; *pg.* 1501, *pg.* 1068

BD INTERACTIV - Diabetes Care Product - BECTON, DICKINSON & COMPANY; *pg.* 1501, *pg.* 1068

BD INTIMA - Infusion Therapy Product - BECTON, DICKINSON & COMPANY; *pg.* 1501, *pg.* 1068

BD INTIMA II - Catheter - BECTON, DICKINSON & COMPANY; *pg.* 1501, *pg.* 1068

BD INTRACATH - Critical Care Product - BECTON, DICKINSON & COMPANY; *pg.* 1501, *pg.* 1068

BD INTRAMEDIC - Diagnostic Products - BECTON, DICKINSON & COMPANY; *pg.* 1501, *pg.* 1068

BD INTROSYTE - Infusion Therapy Product - BECTON, DICKINSON & COMPANY; *pg.* 1501, *pg.* 1068

BD INTROSYTE-N - Shielded Introducer - BECTON, DICKINSON & COMPANY; *pg.* 1501, *pg.* 1068

BD INTROSYTE-N AUTOGUARD - Shielded Introducer - BECTON, DICKINSON & COMPANY; *pg.* 1501, *pg.* 1068

BD IPLAB - Software - BECTON, DICKINSON & COMPANY; *pg.* 1501, *pg.* 1068

BD ISOVITALEX - Diagnostic Products - BECTON, DICKINSON & COMPANY; *pg.* 1501, *pg.* 1068

BD IV START PAK - Site Prep Kit - BECTON, DICKINSON & COMPANY; *pg.* 1501, *pg.* 1068

BD JAWZONE - Mouthguard - BECTON, DICKINSON & COMPANY; *pg.* 1501, *pg.* 1068

BD JUSTRITE - Medical Surgical System - BECTON, DICKINSON & COMPANY; *pg.* 1501, *pg.* 1068

BD L-CATH - Infusion Therapy Product - BECTON, DICKINSON & COMPANY; *pg.* 1501, *pg.* 1068

BD LABO - Diagnostic Products - BECTON, DICKINSON & COMPANY; *pg.* 1501, *pg.* 1068

BD LACTINEX - Diagnostic Products - BECTON, DICKINSON & COMPANY; *pg.* 1501, *pg.* 1068

BD LEUCOCOUNT - Immunocytometry Products - BECTON, DICKINSON & COMPANY; *pg.* 1501, *pg.* 1068

BD LEUCOGATE - Immunocytometry Products - BECTON, DICKINSON & COMPANY; *pg.* 1501, *pg.* 1068

BD LINK2 - Diagnostic Products - BECTON, DICKINSON & COMPANY; *pg.* 1501, *pg.* 1068

BD LIQUI/DRY - Pharmaceutical System - BECTON, DICKINSON & COMPANY; *pg.* 1501, *pg.* 1068
BD LIQUIHEP - Medical Surgical System - BECTON, DICKINSON & COMPANY; *pg.* 1501, *pg.* 1068
BD LITREPAK - Diagnostic Products - BECTON, DICKINSON & COMPANY; *pg.* 1501, *pg.* 1068
BD LIVING COLORS - Bioscience Products - BECTON, DICKINSON & COMPANY; *pg.* 1501, *pg.* 1068
BD LO-DOSE - Diabetes Care Product - BECTON, DICKINSON & COMPANY; *pg.* 1501, *pg.* 1068
BD LOGIC - Diabetes Care Product - BECTON, DICKINSON & COMPANY; *pg.* 1501, *pg.* 1068
BD LOK-COLLET - Ophthalmology Product - BECTON, DICKINSON & COMPANY; *pg.* 1501, *pg.* 1068
BD LUER-LOK - Microbiology Product - BECTON, DICKINSON & COMPANY; *pg.* 1501, *pg.* 1068
BD LYOPLATE - Cell Analysis Product - BECTON, DICKINSON & COMPANY; *pg.* 1501, *pg.* 1068
BD MACRO-VUE Diagnostic Products - BECTON, DICKINSON & COMPANY; *pg.* 1501, *pg.* 1068
BD MACROSORT - Immunocytometry Products - BECTON, DICKINSON & COMPANY; *pg.* 1501, *pg.* 1068
BD MAGNETIX - Home Care Product - BECTON, DICKINSON & COMPANY; *pg.* 1501, *pg.* 1068
BD MAGNI-GUIDE - Diabetes Care Product - BECTON, DICKINSON & COMPANY; *pg.* 1501, *pg.* 1068
BD MAKE IT SAFE - Slogan - BECTON, DICKINSON & COMPANY; *pg.* 1501, *pg.* 1068
BD MAPAD - Medical Surgical System - BECTON, DICKINSON & COMPANY; *pg.* 1501, *pg.* 1068
BD MARINER - Medical Surgical System - BECTON, DICKINSON & COMPANY; *pg.* 1501, *pg.* 1068
BD MARSTERS INCUBATOR - Diagnostic Products - BECTON, DICKINSON & COMPANY; *pg.* 1501, *pg.* 1068
BD MATRIGEL - Laboratory Product - BECTON, DICKINSON & COMPANY; *pg.* 1501, *pg.* 1068
BD MED-SAFE - Medical Surgical System - BECTON, DICKINSON & COMPANY; *pg.* 1501, *pg.* 1068
BD MEDSAVER - Syringe - BECTON, DICKINSON & COMPANY; *pg.* 1501, *pg.* 1068
BD MGIT - Diagnostic Products - BECTON, DICKINSON & COMPANY; *pg.* 1501, *pg.* 1068
BD MICRO-BLADE - Ophthalmology Product - BECTON, DICKINSON & COMPANY; *pg.* 1501, *pg.* 1068
BD MICRO-FINE - Diabetes Care Product - BECTON, DICKINSON & COMPANY; *pg.* 1501, *pg.* 1068
BD MICRO-SHARP - Ophthalmology Product - BECTON, DICKINSON & COMPANY; *pg.* 1501, *pg.* 1068
BD MICRO-UNITOME - Ophthalmology Product - BECTON, DICKINSON & COMPANY; *pg.* 1501, *pg.* 1068
BD MICROGARD - Closure - BECTON, DICKINSON & COMPANY; *pg.* 1501, *pg.* 1068
BD MICROLANCE - Needle - BECTON, DICKINSON & COMPANY; *pg.* 1501, *pg.* 1068
BD MICROMGIT - Diagnostic Product - BECTON, DICKINSON & COMPANY; *pg.* 1501, *pg.* 1068
BD MICROPROBE - Diagnostic Products - BECTON, DICKINSON & COMPANY; *pg.* 1501, *pg.* 1068
BD MICROTAINER - Blood Collection Product - BECTON, DICKINSON & COMPANY; *pg.* 1501, *pg.* 1068
BD MINICATH - Needle - BECTON, DICKINSON & COMPANY; *pg.* 1501, *pg.* 1068
BD MONOLIGHT - Bioscience Products - BECTON, DICKINSON & COMPANY; *pg.* 1501, *pg.* 1068
BD MONORINSE - Diagnostic Products - BECTON, DICKINSON & COMPANY; *pg.* 1501, *pg.* 1068
BD MONOSLIDE - Diagnostic Products - BECTON, DICKINSON & COMPANY; *pg.* 1501, *pg.* 1068
BD MONOVIAL - Pharmaceutical System - BECTON, DICKINSON & COMPANY; *pg.* 1501, *pg.* 1068
BD MP READACRIT - Diagnostic Products - BECTON, DICKINSON & COMPANY; *pg.* 1501, *pg.* 1068
BD MULTI-DOSER - Pharmaceutical System - BECTON, DICKINSON & COMPANY; *pg.* 1501, *pg.* 1068
BD MULTIFIT - Injection Product - BECTON, DICKINSON & COMPANY; *pg.* 1501, *pg.* 1068
BD MULTIFLO - Medical Surgical System - BECTON, DICKINSON & COMPANY; *pg.* 1501, *pg.* 1068
BD MULTISET - Immunocytometry Products - BECTON, DICKINSON & COMPANY; *pg.* 1501, *pg.* 1068
BD MULTITEST - Immunocytometry Products - BECTON, DICKINSON & COMPANY; *pg.* 1501, *pg.* 1068
BD MULTIVISC - Vicoadaptive Solution - BECTON, DICKINSON & COMPANY; *pg.* 1501, *pg.* 1068
BD MYCOBACTOSEL - Diagnostic Products - BECTON, DICKINSON & COMPANY; *pg.* 1501, *pg.* 1068
BD MYCOFLASK - Diagnostic Products - BECTON, DICKINSON & COMPANY; *pg.* 1501, *pg.* 1068
BD MYCOPHIL - Diagnostic Products - BECTON, DICKINSON & COMPANY; *pg.* 1501, *pg.* 1068
BD MYCOPREP - Diagnostic Products - BECTON, DICKINSON & COMPANY; *pg.* 1501, *pg.* 1068
BD MYCOSEL - Diagnostic Products - BECTON, DICKINSON & COMPANY; *pg.* 1501, *pg.* 1068
BD MYOSATE - Diagnostic Products - BECTON, DICKINSON & COMPANY; *pg.* 1501, *pg.* 1068
BD NA/LE - Bioscience Products - BECTON, DICKINSON & COMPANY; *pg.* 1501, *pg.* 1068
BD NANOPLEX - Diagnostic System - BECTON, DICKINSON & COMPANY; *pg.* 1501, *pg.* 1068
BD NATRIX - Discovery Labware - BECTON, DICKINSON & COMPANY; *pg.* 1501, *pg.* 1068
BD NEOFLON - Cannula - BECTON, DICKINSON & COMPANY; *pg.* 1501, *pg.* 1068
BD NEURO-SHARP - Ophthalmology Product - BECTON, DICKINSON & COMPANY; *pg.* 1501, *pg.* 1068
BD NEXIVA - Catheter System - BECTON, DICKINSON & COMPANY; *pg.* 1501, *pg.* 1068
BD NOKOR - Injection Product - BECTON, DICKINSON & COMPANY; *pg.* 1501, *pg.* 1068
BD NU-SERUM - Discovery Labware - BECTON, DICKINSON & COMPANY; *pg.* 1501, *pg.* 1068
BD OCUSEAL - Liquid Ocular Bandage - BECTON, DICKINSON & COMPANY; *pg.* 1501, *pg.* 1068
BD OMNICOMP - Immunocytometry Products - BECTON, DICKINSON & COMPANY; *pg.* 1501, *pg.* 1068
BD ONCOMARK - Immunocytometry Products - BECTON, DICKINSON & COMPANY; *pg.* 1501, *pg.* 1068
BD ONECATH - Medical Surgical System - BECTON, DICKINSON & COMPANY; *pg.* 1501, *pg.* 1068
BD OPTEIA - Bioscience Products - BECTON, DICKINSON & COMPANY; *pg.* 1501, *pg.* 1068
BD OPTI-FINE - Diabetes Care Product - BECTON, DICKINSON & COMPANY; *pg.* 1501, *pg.* 1068
BD OPTILUX - Laboratory Product - BECTON, DICKINSON & COMPANY; *pg.* 1501, *pg.* 1068
BD OPTIMUM - Ophthalmology Product - BECTON, DICKINSON & COMPANY; *pg.* 1501, *pg.* 1068
BD OPTIMUS - Lancing Device - BECTON, DICKINSON & COMPANY; *pg.* 1501, *pg.* 1068
BD ORALPAK - Pharmaceutical System - BECTON, DICKINSON & COMPANY; *pg.* 1501, *pg.* 1068
BD OXI/FERM - Diagnostic Products - BECTON, DICKINSON & COMPANY; *pg.* 1501, *pg.* 1068
BD P10EZ - Medical Surgical System - BECTON, DICKINSON & COMPANY; *pg.* 1501, *pg.* 1068
BD P23XL - Medical Surgical System - BECTON, DICKINSON & COMPANY; *pg.* 1501, *pg.* 1068
BD PAINT-A-GATE - Immunocytometry Products - BECTON, DICKINSON & COMPANY; *pg.* 1501, *pg.* 1068
BD PANTA - Diagnostic Products - BECTON, DICKINSON & COMPANY; *pg.* 1501, *pg.* 1068
BD PARASIGHT - Diagnostic Products - BECTON, DICKINSON & COMPANY; *pg.* 1501, *pg.* 1068
BD PASCO - Diagnostic Products - BECTON, DICKINSON & COMPANY; *pg.* 1501, *pg.* 1068
BD PATHWAY - Bioscience Products - BECTON, DICKINSON & COMPANY; *pg.* 1501, *pg.* 1068
BD PEDS PLUS - Diagnostic Products - BECTON, DICKINSON & COMPANY; *pg.* 1501, *pg.* 1068
BD PEG - Self-Adhering Elastic - BECTON, DICKINSON & COMPANY; *pg.* 1501, *pg.* 1068
BD PENJECTOR - Medical Surgical System - BECTON, DICKINSON & COMPANY; *pg.* 1501, *pg.* 1068
BD PERISAFE - Injection Product - BECTON, DICKINSON & COMPANY; *pg.* 1501, *pg.* 1068
BD PERM/WASH - Bioscience Products - BECTON, DICKINSON & COMPANY; *pg.* 1501, *pg.* 1068
BD PERSIST - Infusion Therapy Product - BECTON, DICKINSON & COMPANY; *pg.* 1501, *pg.* 1068
BD PERTRACH - Medical Surgical System - BECTON, DICKINSON & COMPANY; *pg.* 1501, *pg.* 1068
BD PHARM LYSE - Bioscience Products - BECTON, DICKINSON & COMPANY; *pg.* 1501, *pg.* 1068
BD PHARMINGEN - Bioscience Products - BECTON, DICKINSON & COMPANY; *pg.* 1501, *pg.* 1068
BD PHOENIX - Diagnostic Products - BECTON, DICKINSON & COMPANY; *pg.* 1501, *pg.* 1068
BD PHOENIX PREFERRED - Diagnostic Products - BECTON, DICKINSON & COMPANY; *pg.* 1501, *pg.* 1068
BD PHYSIOJECT - AutoInjector - BECTON, DICKINSON & COMPANY; *pg.* 1501, *pg.* 1068
BD PHYTONE - Diagnostic Products - BECTON, DICKINSON & COMPANY; *pg.* 1501, *pg.* 1068
BD PLASTICAT - Medical Surgical System - BECTON, DICKINSON & COMPANY; *pg.* 1501, *pg.* 1068
BD PLASTIPAK - Syringe - BECTON, DICKINSON & COMPANY; *pg.* 1501, *pg.* 1068
BD PLASTIPAK PROTECT - Syringe - BECTON, DICKINSON & COMPANY; *pg.* 1501, *pg.* 1068
BD PLASTISET - Medical Surgical System - BECTON, DICKINSON & COMPANY; *pg.* 1501, *pg.* 1068
BD PNEUMOSLIDE - Diagnostic Products - BECTON, DICKINSON & COMPANY; *pg.* 1501, *pg.* 1068
BD POCKET - Ophthalmology Product - BECTON, DICKINSON & COMPANY; *pg.* 1501, *pg.* 1068
BD POLAR-PREENE - Wrap - BECTON, DICKINSON & COMPANY; *pg.* 1501, *pg.* 1068
BD POLYPEPTONE - Diagnostic Products - BECTON, DICKINSON & COMPANY; *pg.* 1501, *pg.* 1068
BD PORT-A-CUL - Diagnostic Products - BECTON, DICKINSON & COMPANY; *pg.* 1501, *pg.* 1068
BD POSIFLOW - IV Access System - BECTON, DICKINSON & COMPANY; *pg.* 1501, *pg.* 1068
BD POSIFLUSH - Infusion Therapy Product - BECTON, DICKINSON & COMPANY; *pg.* 1501, *pg.* 1068
BD POWERBLOT - Bioscience Products - BECTON, DICKINSON & COMPANY; *pg.* 1501, *pg.* 1068
BD PPT - Tube - BECTON, DICKINSON & COMPANY; *pg.* 1501, *pg.* 1068
BD PRECISION - Diabetes Care Product - BECTON, DICKINSON & COMPANY; *pg.* 1501, *pg.* 1068
BD PRECISIONCUT - Needle - BECTON, DICKINSON & COMPANY; *pg.* 1501, *pg.* 1068
BD PRECISIONGLIDE - Needles - BECTON, DICKINSON & COMPANY; *pg.* 1501, *pg.* 1068
BD PREPSTAIN - Slide Processor - BECTON, DICKINSON & COMPANY; *pg.* 1501, *pg.* 1068
BD PRESET - Syringe - BECTON, DICKINSON & COMPANY; *pg.* 1501, *pg.* 1068
BD PREVENTIS - Automatic Needle Shielding System - BECTON, DICKINSON & COMPANY; *pg.* 1501, *pg.* 1068
BD PRIMAFILL - Medical Surgical System - BECTON, DICKINSON & COMPANY; *pg.* 1501, *pg.* 1068
BD PRIMARIA - Laboratory Product - BECTON, DICKINSON & COMPANY; *pg.* 1501, *pg.* 1068
BD PROBETEC - Diagnostic Products - BECTON, DICKINSON & COMPANY; *pg.* 1501, *pg.* 1068
BD PROCOUNT - Immunocytometry Products - BECTON, DICKINSON & COMPANY; *pg.* 1501, *pg.* 1068
BD PROEX - C Reagent - BECTON, DICKINSON & COMPANY; *pg.* 1501, *pg.* 1068
BD PRONTO - Blood Collection Product - BECTON, DICKINSON & COMPANY; *pg.* 1501, *pg.* 1068
BD PSEUDOSEL - Diagnostic Products - BECTON, DICKINSON & COMPANY; *pg.* 1501, *pg.* 1068
BD PST - Tube - BECTON, DICKINSON & COMPANY; *pg.* 1501, *pg.* 1068
BD PURECOAT - Discovery Labware - BECTON, DICKINSON & COMPANY; *pg.* 1501, *pg.* 1068
BD PUREFILL - Pharmaceutical System - BECTON, DICKINSON & COMPANY; *pg.* 1501, *pg.* 1068
BD Q-SYTE - Needleless System - BECTON, DICKINSON & COMPANY; *pg.* 1501, *pg.* 1068
BD QBC - Malaria Test Kit - BECTON, DICKINSON & COMPANY; *pg.* 1501, *pg.* 1068
BD QBC STAR - Diagnostic Products - BECTON, DICKINSON & COMPANY; *pg.* 1501, *pg.* 1068
BD QTEST - Diagnostic Products - BECTON, DICKINSON & COMPANY; *pg.* 1501, *pg.* 1068
BD QUALISWAB - Diagnostic Products - BECTON, DICKINSON & COMPANY; *pg.* 1501, *pg.* 1068
BD QUANTIBRITE - Immunocytometry Products - BECTON, DICKINSON & COMPANY; *pg.* 1501, *pg.* 1068
BD QUIKHEEL - Blood Collection Product - BECTON, DICKINSON & COMPANY; *pg.* 1501, *pg.* 1068
BD READACRIT - Diagnostic Products - BECTON, DICKINSON & COMPANY; *pg.* 1501, *pg.* 1068
BD READYFILL - Pharmaceutical System - BECTON, DICKINSON & COMPANY; *pg.* 1501, *pg.* 1068
BD READYPAK - Ophthalmic System - BECTON, DICKINSON & COMPANY; *pg.* 1501, *pg.* 1068
BD RECTIC-COUNT - Immunocytometry Products - BECTON, DICKINSON & COMPANY; *pg.* 1501, *pg.* 1068
BD RETRO-X - Bioscience Products - BECTON, DICKINSON

& COMPANY; *pg.* 1501, *pg.* 1068
BD RETROPACK - Bioscience Products - BECTON, DICKINSON & COMPANY; *pg.* 1501, *pg.* 1068
BD RFSCAN - Diagnostic Products - BECTON, DICKINSON & COMPANY; *pg.* 1501, *pg.* 1068
BD RIB-BACK - Carbon Steel Blade - BECTON, DICKINSON & COMPANY; *pg.* 1501, *pg.* 1068
BD RIBOQUANT - Bioscience Products - BECTON, DICKINSON & COMPANY; *pg.* 1501, *pg.* 1068
BD RIGHTBORE - Medical Surgical System - BECTON, DICKINSON & COMPANY; *pg.* 1501, *pg.* 1068
BD RODAC - Diagnostic Products - BECTON, DICKINSON & COMPANY; *pg.* 1501, *pg.* 1068
BD R.O.S.E - Critical Care Product - BECTON, DICKINSON & COMPANY; *pg.* 1501, *pg.* 1068
BD RUBASCAN - Diagnostic Products - BECTON, DICKINSON & COMPANY; *pg.* 1501, *pg.* 1068
BD RX - Medication Management System - BECTON, DICKINSON & COMPANY; *pg.* 1501, *pg.* 1068
BD SAF-T-CATH - Medical Surgical System - BECTON, DICKINSON & COMPANY; *pg.* 1501, *pg.* 1068
BD SAF-T E-Z SET - Blood Collection & Infusion Set - BECTON, DICKINSON & COMPANY; *pg.* 1501, *pg.* 1068
BD SAF-T-INTIMA - Catheter - BECTON, DICKINSON & COMPANY; *pg.* 1501, *pg.* 1068
BD SAF-T PRN - Medical Surgical System - BECTON, DICKINSON & COMPANY; *pg.* 1501, *pg.* 1068
BD SAFE-CLIP - Diabetes Care Product - BECTON, DICKINSON & COMPANY; *pg.* 1501, *pg.* 1068
BD SAFEDRAW - Critical Care Product - BECTON, DICKINSON & COMPANY; *pg.* 1501, *pg.* 1068
BD SAFEDWELL - Medical Surgical System - BECTON, DICKINSON & COMPANY; *pg.* 1501, *pg.* 1068
BD SAFEGUARD - Diagnostic Products - BECTON, DICKINSON & COMPANY; *pg.* 1501, *pg.* 1068
BD SAFELON - Medical Surgical System - BECTON, DICKINSON & COMPANY; *pg.* 1501, *pg.* 1068
BD SAFESTART - Medical Surgical System - BECTON, DICKINSON & COMPANY; *pg.* 1501, *pg.* 1068
BD SAFETY CRADLE - Medical Surgical System - BECTON, DICKINSON & COMPANY; *pg.* 1501, *pg.* 1068
BD SAFETY FLOW - Blood Collection Product - BECTON, DICKINSON & COMPANY; *pg.* 1501, *pg.* 1068
BD SAFETY-GARD - Needles - BECTON, DICKINSON & COMPANY; *pg.* 1501, *pg.* 1068
BD SAFETY-HEAD - Diagnostic Products - BECTON, DICKINSON & COMPANY; *pg.* 1501, *pg.* 1068
BD SAFETY-LOK - Blood Collection Product - BECTON, DICKINSON & COMPANY; *pg.* 1501, *pg.* 1068
BD SAFETY-MED - Chemotherapy Dispensing Pin - BECTON, DICKINSON & COMPANY; *pg.* 1501, *pg.* 1068
BD SAFETYGLIDE - Needles - BECTON, DICKINSON & COMPANY; *pg.* 1501, *pg.* 1068
BD SAFETYLOCK - Disposable Scalpel - BECTON, DICKINSON & COMPANY; *pg.* 1501, *pg.* 1068
BD SAFTI - Medical Surgical System - BECTON, DICKINSON & COMPANY; *pg.* 1501, *pg.* 1068
BD SANA-LOK - Medical Surgical System - BECTON, DICKINSON & COMPANY; *pg.* 1501, *pg.* 1068
BD SCEPTOR - Diagnostic Products - BECTON, DICKINSON & COMPANY; *pg.* 1501, *pg.* 1068
BD SCF - Prefilled Syringe - BECTON, DICKINSON & COMPANY; *pg.* 1501, *pg.* 1068
BD SCLEROTOME - Ophthalmology Product - BECTON, DICKINSON & COMPANY; *pg.* 1501, *pg.* 1068
BD SEAL-EASE - Tube Sealer - BECTON, DICKINSON & COMPANY; *pg.* 1501, *pg.* 1068
BD SECALON - Catheter - BECTON, DICKINSON & COMPANY; *pg.* 1501, *pg.* 1068
BD SECALON-T - Catheter - BECTON, DICKINSON & COMPANY; *pg.* 1501, *pg.* 1068
BD SEDI-15 - Bench-top Instrument - BECTON, DICKINSON & COMPANY; *pg.* 1501, *pg.* 1068
BD SEDI-CAL - Diagnostic Products - BECTON, DICKINSON & COMPANY; *pg.* 1501, *pg.* 1068
BD SEDI-STAIN - Microbiology Product - BECTON, DICKINSON & COMPANY; *pg.* 1501, *pg.* 1068
BD SEDISCAN - Preanalytical System - BECTON, DICKINSON & COMPANY; *pg.* 1501, *pg.* 1068
BD SEDISYSTEM - Preanalytical System - BECTON, DICKINSON & COMPANY; *pg.* 1501, *pg.* 1068
BD SEDITAINER - Blood Collection Tube - BECTON, DICKINSON & COMPANY; *pg.* 1501, *pg.* 1068
BD SEDITUBE - Preanalytical System - BECTON, DICKINSON & COMPANY; *pg.* 1501, *pg.* 1068
BD SELECT APS - Diagnostic Products - BECTON, DICKINSON & COMPANY; *pg.* 1501, *pg.* 1068
BD SENSABILITY - Breast Self-Examination Aid - BECTON, DICKINSON & COMPANY; *pg.* 1501, *pg.* 1068
BD SENSI-DISC - Diagnostic Products - BECTON, DICKINSON & COMPANY; *pg.* 1501, *pg.* 1068
BD SENTINEL - Microbiology Product - BECTON, DICKINSON & COMPANY; *pg.* 1501, *pg.* 1068
BD SEPTI-CHEK - Diagnostic Products - BECTON, DICKINSON & COMPANY; *pg.* 1501, *pg.* 1068
BD SERO-FUGE - Diagnostic Products - BECTON, DICKINSON & COMPANY; *pg.* 1501, *pg.* 1068
BD SERO-LINER - Diagnostic Products - BECTON, DICKINSON & COMPANY; *pg.* 1501, *pg.* 1068
BD SIMULSET - Immunocytometry Products - BECTON, DICKINSON & COMPANY; *pg.* 1501, *pg.* 1068
BD SIMULTEST - Immunocytometry Products - BECTON, DICKINSON & COMPANY; *pg.* 1501, *pg.* 1068
BD SLIDEWIZARD - Diagnostics Product - BECTON, DICKINSON & COMPANY; *pg.* 1501, *pg.* 1068
BD SOLOMED - Syringe - BECTON, DICKINSON & COMPANY; *pg.* 1501, *pg.* 1068
BD SOLOSHOT - Injection Product - BECTON, DICKINSON & COMPANY; *pg.* 1501, *pg.* 1068
BD SOLUVIA - Microinjection System - BECTON, DICKINSON & COMPANY; *pg.* 1501, *pg.* 1068
BD SPECTRAJECT - Critical Care Product - BECTON, DICKINSON & COMPANY; *pg.* 1501, *pg.* 1068
BD SPOTTEST - Diagnostic Products - BECTON, DICKINSON & COMPANY; *pg.* 1501, *pg.* 1068
BD SPRAY-CYTE - Diagnostic Products - BECTON, DICKINSON & COMPANY; *pg.* 1501, *pg.* 1068
BD SSA - Diagnostic Products - BECTON, DICKINSON & COMPANY; *pg.* 1501, *pg.* 1068
BD SST - Tube - BECTON, DICKINSON & COMPANY; *pg.* 1501, *pg.* 1068
BD STACKER - Diagnostic Products - BECTON, DICKINSON & COMPANY; *pg.* 1501, *pg.* 1068
BD STAPHYLOSLIDE - Diagnostic Products - BECTON, DICKINSON & COMPANY; *pg.* 1501, *pg.* 1068
BD STERIFILL - Plastic Syringe - BECTON, DICKINSON & COMPANY; *pg.* 1501, *pg.* 1068
BD STERIFILL SCF - Plastic Syringe - BECTON, DICKINSON & COMPANY; *pg.* 1501, *pg.* 1068
BD STIMEX - Injection Product - BECTON, DICKINSON & COMPANY; *pg.* 1501, *pg.* 1068
BD STREPTOCARD - Diagnostic Products - BECTON, DICKINSON & COMPANY; *pg.* 1501, *pg.* 1068
BD STREPTOSEL - Diagnostic Products - BECTON, DICKINSON & COMPANY; *pg.* 1501, *pg.* 1068
BD SUPER-WARD - Medical Surgical System - BECTON, DICKINSON & COMPANY; *pg.* 1501, *pg.* 1068
BD SUPERMIX - Discovery Labware - BECTON, DICKINSON & COMPANY; *pg.* 1501, *pg.* 1068
BD SUPERSOMES - Discovery Labware - BECTON, DICKINSON & COMPANY; *pg.* 1501, *pg.* 1068
BD SURE-MED - Dispensing Pin - BECTON, DICKINSON & COMPANY; *pg.* 1501, *pg.* 1068
BD SUREPATH - Pap Test - BECTON, DICKINSON & COMPANY; *pg.* 1501, *pg.* 1068
BD SUREPREP - Diagnostic Products - BECTON, DICKINSON & COMPANY; *pg.* 1501, *pg.* 1068
BD SURESAVE - Medical Surgical System - BECTON, DICKINSON & COMPANY; *pg.* 1501, *pg.* 1068
BD SURESTART - Medical Surgical System - BECTON, DICKINSON & COMPANY; *pg.* 1501, *pg.* 1068
BD SWUBE - Diagnostic Products - BECTON, DICKINSON & COMPANY; *pg.* 1501, *pg.* 1068
BD SYPHILIGEN - Diagnostic Products - BECTON, DICKINSON & COMPANY; *pg.* 1501, *pg.* 1068
BD SYSTEO - Pharmaceutical System - BECTON, DICKINSON & COMPANY; *pg.* 1501, *pg.* 1068
BD T-PLUS - Medical Surgical System - BECTON, DICKINSON & COMPANY; *pg.* 1501, *pg.* 1068
BD TAMPER-TUF - Medication Container - BECTON, DICKINSON & COMPANY; *pg.* 1501, *pg.* 1068
BD TAXO - Diagnostic Products - BECTON, DICKINSON & COMPANY; *pg.* 1501, *pg.* 1068
BD TEMPAWAY - Diabetes Care Product - BECTON, DICKINSON & COMPANY; *pg.* 1501, *pg.* 1068
BD THIOGEL - Diagnostic Products - BECTON, DICKINSON & COMPANY; *pg.* 1501, *pg.* 1068
BD THIOTONE - Diagnostic Products - BECTON, DICKINSON & COMPANY; *pg.* 1501, *pg.* 1068
BD TITANIUM - Bioscience Products - BECTON, DICKINSON & COMPANY; *pg.* 1501, *pg.* 1068
BD TOUCHGUARD - Blood Sampling System - BECTON, DICKINSON & COMPANY; *pg.* 1501, *pg.* 1068
BD TRANSDUCTION LABORATORIES - Bioscience Products - BECTON, DICKINSON & COMPANY; *pg.* 1501, *pg.* 1068
BD TRANSFERETTES - Diagnostic Products - BECTON, DICKINSON & COMPANY; *pg.* 1501, *pg.* 1068
BD TRIAC - Diagnostic Products - BECTON, DICKINSON & COMPANY; *pg.* 1501, *pg.* 1068
BD TRICHOSEL - Diagnostic Products - BECTON, DICKINSON & COMPANY; *pg.* 1501, *pg.* 1068
BD TRITEST - Immunocytometry Products - BECTON, DICKINSON & COMPANY; *pg.* 1501, *pg.* 1068
BD TRUCOUNT - Immunocytometry Products - BECTON, DICKINSON & COMPANY; *pg.* 1501, *pg.* 1068
BD TRYPTICASE - Diagnostic Products - BECTON, DICKINSON & COMPANY; *pg.* 1501, *pg.* 1068
BD TUFFLINK - Medical Surgical System - BECTON, DICKINSON & COMPANY; *pg.* 1501, *pg.* 1068
BD TUFROL - Laboratory Product - BECTON, DICKINSON & COMPANY; *pg.* 1501, *pg.* 1068
BD TURBOSORT - Immunocytometry Products - BECTON, DICKINSON & COMPANY; *pg.* 1501, *pg.* 1068
BD TWINPAK - Dual Cannula Device - BECTON, DICKINSON & COMPANY; *pg.* 1501, *pg.* 1068
BD ULTRA-FINE - Diabetes Care Product - BECTON, DICKINSON & COMPANY; *pg.* 1501, *pg.* 1068
BD ULTRADEX - Surgical Product - BECTON, DICKINSON & COMPANY; *pg.* 1501, *pg.* 1068
BD ULTRAPOOL - Reagent - BECTON, DICKINSON & COMPANY; *pg.* 1501, *pg.* 1068
BD UNI-LANCE - Medical Surgical System - BECTON, DICKINSON & COMPANY; *pg.* 1501, *pg.* 1068
BD UNI-PAK - Medical Surgical System - BECTON, DICKINSON & COMPANY; *pg.* 1501, *pg.* 1068
BD UNIJECT - Prefill Injection Device - BECTON, DICKINSON & COMPANY; *pg.* 1501, *pg.* 1068
BD UNITOME - Ophthalmology Product - BECTON, DICKINSON & COMPANY; *pg.* 1501, *pg.* 1068
BD UNOPETTE - Diagnostic Products - BECTON, DICKINSON & COMPANY; *pg.* 1501, *pg.* 1068
BD VACUTAINER - Microbiology Product - BECTON, DICKINSON & COMPANY; *pg.* 1501, *pg.* 1068
BD VALU-SET - Medical Surgical System - BECTON, DICKINSON & COMPANY; *pg.* 1501, *pg.* 1068
BD VASCULON - Medical Surgical System - BECTON, DICKINSON & COMPANY; *pg.* 1501, *pg.* 1068
BD VAXINET - Medical Surgical System - BECTON, DICKINSON & COMPANY; *pg.* 1501, *pg.* 1068
BD VECA-C - Sterile Fixation Dressing - BECTON, DICKINSON & COMPANY; *pg.* 1501, *pg.* 1068
BD VECAFIX - Medical Surgical System - BECTON, DICKINSON & COMPANY; *pg.* 1501, *pg.* 1068
BD VENAGUIDE - Medical Surgical System - BECTON, DICKINSON & COMPANY; *pg.* 1501, *pg.* 1068
BD VENFLON - Catheter - BECTON, DICKINSON & COMPANY; *pg.* 1501, *pg.* 1068
BD VIA-PROBE - Bioscience Products - BECTON, DICKINSON & COMPANY; *pg.* 1501, *pg.* 1068
BD VIACATH - Medical Surgical System - BECTON, DICKINSON & COMPANY; *pg.* 1501, *pg.* 1068
BD VIALON - Infusion Therapy Product - BECTON, DICKINSON & COMPANY; *pg.* 1501, *pg.* 1068
BD VIGGO - Medical Surgical System - BECTON, DICKINSON & COMPANY; *pg.* 1501, *pg.* 1068
BD VIPER - Diagnostic Products - BECTON, DICKINSON & COMPANY; *pg.* 1501, *pg.* 1068
BD VISC - Viscoelastic - BECTON, DICKINSON & COMPANY; *pg.* 1501, *pg.* 1068
BD VISCOFLOW - Ophthalmology Product - BECTON, DICKINSON & COMPANY; *pg.* 1501, *pg.* 1068
BD VISIDRAIN - Ophthalmology Product - BECTON, DICKINSON & COMPANY; *pg.* 1501, *pg.* 1068
BD VISIDRAPE - Ophthalmology Product - BECTON, DICKINSON & COMPANY; *pg.* 1501, *pg.* 1068
BD VISIFLEX - Ophthalmology Product - BECTON, DICKINSON & COMPANY; *pg.* 1501, *pg.* 1068
BD VISIMARK - Ophthalmology Product - BECTON, DICKINSON & COMPANY; *pg.* 1501, *pg.* 1068
BD VISISORB - Ophthalmology Product - BECTON, DICKINSON & COMPANY; *pg.* 1501, *pg.* 1068
BD VISISPEAR - Ophthalmology Product - BECTON, DICKINSON & COMPANY; *pg.* 1501, *pg.* 1068
BD VISISWAB - Ophthalmology Product - BECTON,

First page reference indicates Business Class Edition
Second page reference indicates Geographic Edition

DICKINSON & COMPANY; pg. 1501, pg. 1068
BD VISITEC - Ophthalmology Product - BECTON, DICKINSON & COMPANY; pg. 1501, pg. 1068
BD VISITREC - Ophthalmology Product - BECTON, DICKINSON & COMPANY; pg. 1501, pg. 1068
BD VISIWIPE - Ophthalmology Product - BECTON, DICKINSON & COMPANY; pg. 1501, pg. 1068
BD VITAFLON - Medical Surgical System - BECTON, DICKINSON & COMPANY; pg. 1501, pg. 1068
BD VITAFLOW - Medical Surgical System - BECTON, DICKINSON & COMPANY; pg. 1501, pg. 1068
BD VITALFLON - Medical Surgical System - BECTON, DICKINSON & COMPANY; pg. 1501, pg. 1068
BD VZVSCAN - Diagnostic Products - BECTON, DICKINSON & COMPANY; pg. 1501, pg. 1068
BD WALLMATE - Surgical Product - BECTON, DICKINSON & COMPANY; pg. 1501, pg. 1068
BD XCALIBER - Critical Care Product - BECTON, DICKINSON & COMPANY; pg. 1501, pg. 1068
BD XSTAR - Ophthalmology Product - BECTON, DICKINSON & COMPANY; pg. 1501, pg. 1068
BD YALE - Injection Product - BECTON, DICKINSON & COMPANY; pg. 1501, pg. 1068
BD YANKEE - Diagnostic Products - BECTON, DICKINSON & COMPANY; pg. 1501, pg. 1068
BD+ - Anti-Piracy Software - ROVI CORPORATION; pg. 463, pg. 269
BD112 - Receiver - TRIMBLE NAVIGATION LIMITED; pg. 1384, pg. 288
BD122 - Receiver - TRIMBLE NAVIGATION LIMITED; pg. 1384, pg. 288
BD750 - Receiver - TRIMBLE NAVIGATION LIMITED; pg. 1384, pg. 288
BDF - Oxygen Barrier Shrink Film - SEALED AIR CORPORATION; pg. 1468, pg. 1058
BDM - Semiconductor Material - KOPIN CORPORATION; pg. 425, pg. 847
BDM-230K - Module Products - KOPIN CORPORATION; pg. 425, pg. 847
BDM-922K - Module Products - KOPIN CORPORATION; pg. 425, pg. 847
BDMODEM - Diagnostic Products - BECTON, DICKINSON & COMPANY; pg. 1501, pg. 1068
BDP XPEDION - Freight Tracking Services - BDP INTERNATIONAL INC.; pg. 1900, pg. 1559
BE-51 - Flame Retardants - CHEMTURA CORPORATION; pg. 1152, pg. 355
BE CERTAIN - Tagline - MTS SYSTEMS CORPORATION; pg. 442, pg. 923
BE DIRECT - Computer Product - DELL INC.; pg. 383, pg. 1737
BE EXTREME - Slogan - EXTREME NETWORKS INC; pg. 287, pg. 245
BE-FAST - Mold Base & Component - SUPERIOR DIE SET CORP.; pg. 1379, pg. 1885
BE MAGAZINE - Magazine - BENTLEY SYSTEMS, INC.; pg. 361, pg. 1531
BE MORE PRODUCTIVE - Tagline - SOUTHWEST AIRLINES CO.; pg. 1923, pg. 1687
BE SAFE, BE SURE, WEAR LAKELAND - Tag Line - LAKELAND INDUSTRIES, INC.; pg. 1354, pg. 1338
BE SAFE REPLACE - Safety Campaign - BRK BRANDS, INC.; pg. 627, pg. 554
BE THE DREAM - Slogan - SBLI USA LIFE INSURANCE COMPANY, INC.; pg. 1216, pg. 1288
BE TRANSFORMED - Tagline - CYNOSURE, INC.; pg. 1521, pg. 858
BE2 - Video Game - INTERNATIONAL GAME TECHNOLOGY; pg. 957, pg. 1024
BEACH - Lace Curtain - HERITAGE LACE INC.; pg. 694, pg. 711
BEACH BEACON - Newspaper - TAMPA BAY NEWSPAPERS, INC.; pg. 1691, pg. 468
BEACH BLANKET SLINGO - Lottery Game - IDAHO LOTTERY; pg. 995, pg. 547
BEACH GLASS - Bath Accessory - CROSCILL, INC.; pg. 1122, pg. 1220
BEACH HAVEN - Bath Accessory - CROSCILL, INC.; pg. 1122, pg. 1220
BEACH MEMORIES - Bath Accessory - CROSCILL, INC.; pg. 1122, pg. 1220
BEACH MILL - T-Shirts - ABERCROMBIE & FITCH CO.; pg. 37, pg. 1466
BEACH PRISMS - Wall System - SMITH-MIDLAND CORPORATION; pg. 111, pg. 1795
BEACHCOMBER - Eyewear - MAUI JIM, INC.; pg. 9, pg. 651
BEACHES - Resort - SANDALS RESORTS INTERNATIONAL; pg. 1111, pg. 446
BEACHHUNTER - Metal Detector - WHITE'S ELECTRONICS; pg. 688, pg. 1509
BEACHHUNTER ID - Metal Detector - WHITE'S ELECTRONICS; pg. 688, pg. 1509
BEACON - Catheter - COOK GROUP, INC.; pg. 1518, pg. 674
BEACON - Customer Assessment Product - CX ACT, INC.; pg. 1394, pg. 1773
BEACON - Inspection Lighting System - UNILUX, INC.; pg. 682, pg. 1118
BEACON - Gasoline Retail Outlets - VALERO ENERGY CORPORATION; pg. 986, pg. 1743
BEACON/MORRIS - Heating & Ventilation Equipment - MESTEK, INC.; pg. 1074, pg. 857
BEAD & BUTTON - Magazine - KALMBACH PUBLISHING CO.; pg. 1656, pg. 1898
BEAD CHAIN - Industrial Chain - BEAD INDUSTRIES INC.; pg. 200, pg. 356
BEAD MAX - Car Care Product - STONER INC.; pg. 985, pg. 1583
BEADARRAY - Array - ILLUMINA, INC.; pg. 412, pg. 203
BEADED - Hat - WOODEN SHIPS OF HOBOKEN; pg. 35, pg. 1315
BEADED SOFFIT - Vinyl Soffit - NORTEK, INC.; pg. 100, pg. 1607
BEADEX - Drywall Joint Tape - USG CORPORATION; pg. 118, pg. 594
BEADEX B4 - Bead Trim - USG CORPORATION; pg. 118, pg. 594
BEADEX B8 - Bead Trim - USG CORPORATION; pg. 118, pg. 594
BEADEX B9 - Outside L Trim - USG CORPORATION; pg. 118, pg. 594
BEADIMALS - Educational Materials - SCHOLASTIC INC.; pg. 1683, pg. 1288
BEADLINGS - Educational Materials - SCHOLASTIC INC.; pg. 1683, pg. 1288
BEADLOCK - Bicycle Accessories - SPECIALIZED BICYCLE COMPONENTS, INC.; pg. 1711, pg. 152
BEADRETRIEVER - Molecular Probe Product - THERMO FISHER SCIENTIFIC INC.; pg. 1602, pg. 61
BEADS - Bath Accessory - CROSCILL, INC.; pg. 1122, pg. 1220
BEADS TERRY - Bath Accessory - CROSCILL, INC.; pg. 1122, pg. 1220
BEADSEAL - Plastics Product - AEP INDUSTRIES INC.; pg. 1878, pg. 1085
BEADSTATION - Software - ILLUMINA, INC.; pg. 412, pg. 203
BEADSTUDIO - Data Analysis Software - ILLUMINA, INC.; pg. 412, pg. 203
BEADSTYLE - Magazine - KALMBACH PUBLISHING CO.; pg. 1656, pg. 1898
BEADXPRESS - Reader System - ILLUMINA, INC.; pg. 412, pg. 203
BEAGLE - Desktop Search - NOVELL INC.; pg. 446, pg. 852
BEAK APPETIT - Pet Product - PETSMART, INC.; pg. 1481, pg. 18
BEAKIN - Complex Lecithins for Food Manufacturers - ARCHER-DANIELS-MIDLAND COMPANY; pg. 825, pg. 565
BEALL'S - Department Stores - BEALL'S, INC.; pg. 1760, pg. 414
BEALLS - Department Stores - STAGE STORES, INC.; pg. 33, pg. 1715
BEALS - Dress Shoes - JOHNSTON & MURPHY CO.; pg. 1810, pg. 1651
BEAM - Fabric - NEMSCHOFF, INC.; pg. 936, pg. 1890
BEAM - Defense Communication System - ROCKWELL COLLINS, INC.; pg. 234, pg. 702
THE BEAM - Halogen Spotlight - UNITY MANUFACTURING COMPANY; pg. 221, pg. 594
BEAM & COLA - Prepared Alcoholic Beverage - JIM BEAM BRANDS CO.; pg. 1965, pg. 601
BEAMDIRECTOR - Industrial Laser Systems - GSI GROUP INC.; pg. 1415, pg. 784
BEAMER - Medical Equipment - CONMED CORPORATION; pg. 1517, pg. 1347
BEAMER MATE - Medical Equipment - CONMED CORPORATION; pg. 1517, pg. 1347
BEAMER PLUS - Medical Equipment - CONMED CORPORATION; pg. 1517, pg. 1347
BEAMERO - Tequila - JIM BEAM BRANDS CO.; pg. 1965, pg. 601
BEAMGLIDE - Rescue Equipment - MINE SAFETY APPLIANCES COMPANY; pg. 1361, pg. 1525
BEAMGRIP - Rescue Equipment - MINE SAFETY APPLIANCES COMPANY; pg. 1361, pg. 1525
BEAMMASTER - Analyzer - COHERENT, INC.; pg. 1406, pg. 265
BEAM'S EIGHT STAR - Whiskey - JIM BEAM BRANDS CO.; pg. 1965, pg. 601
BEAMSAFE - Safety Light Curtain - OMRON SCIENTIFIC TECHNOLOGIES INCORPORATED; pg. 1425, pg. 91
BEAMVIEW - Analyzer - COHERENT, INC.; pg. 1406, pg. 265
BEAN BAG BALL - Bean Bag Set - SCHOOL-TECH, INC.; pg. 1844, pg. 866
BEAN POD - Storage Pouch - JELLY BELLY CANDY COMPANY; pg. 1857, pg. 86
BEAN STREET COFFEE - Convenience Stores - THE PANTRY, INC.; pg. 1029, pg. 1360
BEANBOOZLED - Jelly Beans - JELLY BELLY CANDY COMPANY; pg. 1857, pg. 86
BEANERY BLEND - Coffee - THE COFFEE BEANERY LTD.; pg. 849, pg. 886
BEAN'S - Sporting Specialties - L.L. BEAN, INC.; pg. 1777, pg. 750
BEANSTALK - Fabric - NEMSCHOFF, INC.; pg. 936, pg. 1890
BEAR - Multi-tools & Knives - BEAR & SON CUTLERY, INC.; pg. 1827, pg. 7
BEAR - Sporting Good Product - ESCALADE INC.; pg. 1833, pg. 678
BEAR BUILDER - Bear Projects - BUILD-A-BEAR WORKSHOP, INC.; pg. 950, pg. 993
BEAR CLAW - Tools - VAUGHAN & BUSHNELL MANUFACTURING COMPANY, INC.; pg. 1066, pg. 616
BEAR CREEK - Fruit & Vegetable Product - GIUMARRA VINEYARDS CORPORATION; pg. 1964, pg. 45
BEAR CREEK COUNTRY KITCHENS - Soup Mixes - B&G FOODS, INC.; pg. 838, pg. 1102
BEAR CUBS - Candy - ROCKY MOUNTAIN CHOCOLATE FACTORY, INC.; pg. 1032, pg. 324
BEAR ESSENTIALS BOUQUET - Floral Bouquet - FTD GROUP, INC.; pg. 1795, pg. 608
BEAR-GRAM - Teddy Bear Delivery Service - THE VERMONT TEDDY BEAR COMPANY; pg. 969, pg. 1767
BEAR I - Respirator - VITAL SIGNS, INC.; pg. 1607, pg. 1126
BEAR II - Respirator - VITAL SIGNS, INC.; pg. 1607, pg. 1126
BEAR IN THE BIG BLUE HOUSE - Toy - MATTEL, INC.; pg. 962, pg. 81
BEAR IN THE BIG BLUE HOUSE - Game - THE WALT DISNEY COMPANY; pg. 317, pg. 52
BEAR MOUNTAIN - T-Shirts - ABERCROMBIE & FITCH CO.; pg. 37, pg. 1466
BEAR MOUNTAIN - Video Game - INTERNATIONAL GAME TECHNOLOGY; pg. 957, pg. 1024
BEAR-N-BRONZ - Hard Bronze Cylindrical Bearing - BOSTON GEAR; pg. 201, pg. 802
BEAR NAKED - Granola - KELLOGG COMPANY; pg. 831, pg. 870
BEAR NECESSITIES - Candy - SWEET CANDY COMPANY; pg. 1862, pg. 1761
BEAR PEPPER SPRAY - Personal Defense Sprays - MACE SECURITY INTERNATIONAL, INC.; pg. 1172, pg. 1541
BEAR VALLEY - Bike - MARIN BIKES; pg. 1708, pg. 168
BEAR-WITH-ME - Baby Care Product - MUNCHKIN, INC.; pg. 964, pg. 300
BEARCAT - Snowmobile - ARCTIC CAT INC.; pg. 1705, pg. 953
BEARCAT - Single-Action Revolvers - STURM, RUGER & COMPANY, INC.; pg. 1846, pg. 371
BEARITOS - Food Product - THE HAIN CELESTIAL GROUP, INC.; pg. 860, pg. 1172
BEARS - Chocolates - ROCKY MOUNTAIN CHOCOLATE FACTORY, INC.; pg. 1032, pg. 324
BEARSAW - Hand Saw - VAUGHAN & BUSHNELL MANUFACTURING COMPANY, INC.; pg. 1066, pg. 616
BEASLEY - Pet Product - PETSMART, INC.; pg. 1481, pg. 18
BEAST - Motion Control Running Shoe - BROOKS SPORTS INC.; pg. 1805, pg. 1818
BEAST BOY - Character - DC COMICS, INC.; pg. 1633, pg. 1221

BEAT - Soft Drink - THE COCA-COLA COMPANY; *pg.* 240, *pg.* 493
BEAT THE EXPERTS - Game - UNIVERSITY GAMES CORPORATION; *pg.* 969, *pg.* 230
BEAT THE HEAT - Lottery Game - NEW JERSEY STATE LOTTERY; *pg.* 1000, *pg.* 1126
BEATS THE NAIL - All Purpose Construction Adhesive - DAP PRODUCTS, INC.; *pg.* 1441, *pg.* 756
BEAU - Terminal Block - MOLEX INCORPORATED; *pg.* 655, *pg.* 628
BEAU NOUVEAU - Furniture - STANLEY FURNITURE CO., INC.; *pg.* 943, *pg.* 1379
BEAU RIVAGE - Resort & Casino - MGM RESORTS INTERNATIONAL; *pg.* 1105, *pg.* 1028
BEAU RIVAGE RESORTS - Gaming Casinos & Resorts - MIRAGE RESORTS INCORPORATED; *pg.* 1105, *pg.* 1028
BEAUFORD - Lighting - ETHAN ALLEN INTERIORS INC.; *pg.* 924, *pg.* 343
BEAUFORT - Rug - COURISTAN INC.; *pg.* 921, *pg.* 1067
BEAUJOLAIS - Carpet - BEAULIEU GROUP, LLC; *pg.* 917, *pg.* 529
BEAULIEU - Window - SPRINGS GLOBAL, INC.; *pg.* 698, *pg.* 1616
BEAULIEU VINEYARD WINES - Wine - DIAGEO NORTH AMERICA, INC.; *pg.* 1961, *pg.* 361
BEAUMONT - Brick & Tile Product - CHEROKEE BRICK & TILE COMPANY; *pg.* 75, *pg.* 535
BEAUMONT - Fan - CRAFTMADE INTERNATIONAL, INC.; *pg.* 1295, *pg.* 1670
BEAUPLUG - Electronic Components - MOLEX INCORPORATED; *pg.* 655, *pg.* 628
BEAUTE MASTER - Clipper - ANDIS COMPANY; *pg.* 498, *pg.* 1895
BEAUTIA - Beverages - THE COCA-COLA COMPANY; *pg.* 240, *pg.* 493
BEAUTICONTROL - Skin Care Products & Cosmetics - BEAUTICONTROL COSMETICS, INC.; *pg.* 501, *pg.* 1669
BEAUTIFUL INVESTMENTS TO PLAY WITH - Slogan - BLATT BOWLING & BILLIARD CORP.; *pg.* 1827, *pg.* 1203
BEAUTIFULLY DESIGNED. MASTERFULLY ENGINEERED. - Tagline - INCLINATOR COMPANY OF AMERICA; *pg.* 88, *pg.* 1536
BEAUTISEAL - Beauty Product Sampling System - ARCADE MARKETING, INC.; *pg.* 352, *pg.* 1196
BEAUTITOUCH - Beauty Product Sampling System - ARCADE MARKETING, INC.; *pg.* 352, *pg.* 1196
BEAUTLICH - Gel - BEUTLICH PHARMACEUTICALS LP; *pg.* 1503, *pg.* 665
BEAUTY BIZ - Newspaper - FAIRCHILD FASHION GROUP; *pg.* 1640, *pg.* 1230
THE BEAUTY GOES ON - Tagline - THE VALSPAR CORPORATION; *pg.* 1449, *pg.* 945
BEAUTY INC - Beauty Magazine - CONDE NAST PUBLICATIONS, INC.; *pg.* 1629, *pg.* 1217
BEAUTY-LINE - Window - ANDERSEN CORPORATION; *pg.* 67, *pg.* 916
BEAUTY MASTER - Clipper - ANDIS COMPANY; *pg.* 498, *pg.* 1895
THE BEAUTY OF IT ALL - Slogan - STULLER, INC.; *pg.* 13, *pg.* 745
BEAUTY REPORT INTERNATIONAL - Newspaper - FAIRCHILD FASHION GROUP; *pg.* 1640, *pg.* 1230
BEAUTY SPAS - Jewelry Cleaner - CONNOISSEURS PRODUCTS CORPORATION; *pg.* 329, *pg.* 861
BEAUTY SUPPLY OUTLET - Beauty Supply Store - REGIS CORPORATION; *pg.* 521, *pg.* 941
BEAUTY TREATMENTS FOR JEWELRY - Slogan - CONNOISSEURS PRODUCTS CORPORATION; *pg.* 329, *pg.* 861
BEAUTY WITHOUT THE BANDWIDTH - Slogan - AVID TECHNOLOGY, INC.; *pg.* 622, *pg.* 804
BEAUTYBAR.COM - Personal Goods - QUIDSI, INC.; *pg.* 1276, *pg.* 1076
BEAUTYGARD - Fabric - UNIROYAL ENGINEERED PRODUCTS; *pg.* 699, *pg.* 467
BEAUTYREST - Mattress - SIMMONS COMPANY; *pg.* 943, *pg.* 520
BEAUTYREST BEGINNINGS - Mattress - SIMMONS COMPANY; *pg.* 943, *pg.* 520
BEAUTYREST BLACK - Mattress - SIMMONS COMPANY; *pg.* 943, *pg.* 520
BEAUTYREST FEELINGS - Flotation Bed - SIMMONS COMPANY; *pg.* 943, *pg.* 520
BEAUTYREST STUDIO - Mattress - SIMMONS COMPANY; *pg.* 943, *pg.* 520
BEAUTYSLEEP - Mattress - SIMMONS COMPANY; *pg.* 943, *pg.* 520
BEAVER CREEK - Mountain - VAIL RESORTS, INC.; *pg.* 1117, *pg.* 313
BEAVER FALLS - Meat Products - HATFIELD QUALITY MEATS, INC.; *pg.* 861, *pg.* 1537
BEAVER FEVER - Game - INTERNATIONAL GAME TECHNOLOGY; *pg.* 420, *pg.* 1606
BEAVER RIVER - T-Shirts - ABERCROMBIE & FITCH CO.; *pg.* 37, *pg.* 1466
BEBAX - Pediatric Orthotics - ALIMED, INC.; *pg.* 1490, *pg.* 816
BEBE - Apparel And Accessory - BEBE STORES, INC.; *pg.* 19, *pg.* 49
BEBE - Furniture - HOOKER FURNITURE CORPORATION; *pg.* 928, *pg.* 1788
BEBE O - Apparel - BEBE STORES, INC.; *pg.* 19, *pg.* 49
BEBE SPORT - Apparel And Accessory - BEBE STORES, INC.; *pg.* 19, *pg.* 49
BEBE.COM - Apparel - BEBE STORES, INC.; *pg.* 19, *pg.* 49
BEBOP - Fabric - NEMSCHOFF, INC.; *pg.* 936, *pg.* 1890
BEC TO BASICS - Shoe - AEROGROUP INTERNATIONAL, INC.; *pg.* 1803, *pg.* 1055
BECAUSE IT'S IMPORTANT - Slogan - SOUTHWORTH COMPANY INC.; *pg.* 1470, *pg.* 781
BECAUSE LIFE IS TOO SHORT TO DRINK CHEAP BEER - Tag line - WARSTEINER IMPORTERS AGENCY, INC.; *pg.* 266, *pg.* 1479
BECAUSE TESTING MATTERS - Tag Line - TERADYNE INC.; *pg.* 679, *pg.* 838
BECAUSE WEALTH KNOWS NO BORDERS - Tagline - TIGRENT INC.; *pg.* 608, *pg.* 415
BECAUSE YOU CARE - Tag Line - AURORA CASKET COMPANY, INC.; *pg.* 1393, *pg.* 673
BECAUSE YOU'RE SPECIAL BOUQUET - Floral Bouquet - FTD GROUP, INC.; *pg.* 1795, *pg.* 608
BECHE - Forging Product - SUPERIOR DIE SET CORP.; *pg.* 1379, *pg.* 1885
BECKER - Audio & Video Product - HARMAN INTERNATIONAL INDUSTRIES, INCORPORATED; *pg.* 641, *pg.* 374
BECKER - External Drainage & Monitoring Sys. - MEDTRONIC, INC.; *pg.* 1564, *pg.* 939
BECKER CPA REVIEW - Education Services - DEVRY EDUCATION GROUP INC.; *pg.* 600, *pg.* 607
BECKER'S - Convenience Store & Gas Station - ALIMENTATION COUCHE-TARD INC.; *pg.* 1013, *pg.* 1951
BECKETT - Paper - INTERNATIONAL PAPER COMPANY; *pg.* 1460, *pg.* 1644
BECKETT - Women's Clothing & Accessories - WOODEN SHIPS OF HOBOKEN; *pg.* 35, *pg.* 1315
BECKETT CONCEPT - Printing Paper - MOHAWK FINE PAPERS, INC.; *pg.* 1464, *pg.* 1153
BECKETT EXPRESSION - Printing Paper - MOHAWK FINE PAPERS, INC.; *pg.* 1464, *pg.* 1153
BECKMAN COULTER - Diagnostic Product - ALERE SAN DIEGO; *pg.* 1489, *pg.* 199
BECKON - Fabric - NEMSCHOFF, INC.; *pg.* 936, *pg.* 1890
BECKOPOX - Solventborne - CYTEC INDUSTRIES, INC.; *pg.* 1155, *pg.* 1131
BECK'S SAPPHIRE - Beer - ANHEUSER-BUSCH COMPANIES, LLC; *pg.* 237, *pg.* 991
BECKWORTH - Dress Shoes - JOHNSTON & MURPHY CO.; *pg.* 1810, *pg.* 1651
BECKY THATCHER - Girlswear - ELDER MANUFACTURING COMPANY, INC.; *pg.* 40, *pg.* 996
BECOME A PART OF THE STRENGTH WITHIN - Tag Line - HEXCEL CORPORATION; *pg.* 1884, *pg.* 375
BECOMING - Beauty Collection - AVON PRODUCTS, INC.; *pg.* 500, *pg.* 1198
BECON N EGGS - Shoe - AEROGROUP INTERNATIONAL, INC.; *pg.* 1803, *pg.* 1055
BED GLOVE - Mattress Pads - HOLLANDER SLEEP PRODUCTS; *pg.* 927, *pg.* 411
BED-O' COBS - Pet Litter - THE ANDERSONS INCORPORATED; *pg.* 1793, *pg.* 1461
BEDAZZLED - 2 - Lottery Game - KENTUCKY LOTTERY CORPORATION; *pg.* 996, *pg.* 735
BEDDAR WITH CHEDDAR - Sausage - JOHNSONVILLE SAUSAGE, LLC; *pg.* 867, *pg.* 1894
BEDDING & DREAM MAKER - Mattresses - BASSETT FURNITURE INDUSTRIES, INCORPORATED; *pg.* 916, *pg.* 1776
BEDFORD - Dinnerware - THE HOMER LAUGHLIN CHINA COMPANY; *pg.* 1125, *pg.* 1850
BEDFORD - Furniture - NEMSCHOFF, INC.; *pg.* 936, *pg.* 1890
BEDFORD VILLAGE - Wall Panel - BLUELINX HOLDINGS, INC.; *pg.* 70, *pg.* 491
BEDLITE - Lighting System - LITECONTROL CORPORATION; *pg.* 1301, *pg.* 841
BEDOYECTA - Pharmaceutical Product - VALEANT PHARMACEUTICALS INTERNATIONAL; *pg.* 1605, *pg.* 1047
BEDSECURE - Furniture - HSM SOLUTIONS; *pg.* 1884, *pg.* 1378
BEDSIDE BASSINET - Bassinet - GRACO CHILDREN'S PRODUCTS INC.; *pg.* 954, *pg.* 1531
BEDTIME - Mattresses - SEALY CORPORATION; *pg.* 942, *pg.* 1391
BEE - Playing Cards - THE UNITED STATES PLAYING CARD COMPANY; *pg.* 969, *pg.* 727
BEE-ALIVE BUFFERED VITAMIN C - Herbal And Vitamin Supplement - BEE-ALIVE INC.; *pg.* 1503, *pg.* 1348
BEE-ALIVE DEFENSE FORMULA - Herbal And Vitamin Supplement - BEE-ALIVE INC.; *pg.* 1503, *pg.* 1348
BEE-ALIVE FEEL GOOD FORMULA - Jelly Product - BEE-ALIVE INC.; *pg.* 1503, *pg.* 1348
BEE-ALIVE PICK-ME-UP - Jelly Product - BEE-ALIVE INC.; *pg.* 1503, *pg.* 1348
BEE-ALIVE PURE & NATURAL - Jelly Product - BEE-ALIVE INC.; *pg.* 1503, *pg.* 1348
BEE-ALIVE SWEET ENERGY - Jelly Product - BEE-ALIVE INC.; *pg.* 1503, *pg.* 1348
BEE-ALLURE - Honey Bee Attractant - GARDENS ALIVE!, INC.; *pg.* 1796, *pg.* 693
BEE BUCKS - Game - WMS INDUSTRIES INC.; *pg.* 593, *pg.* 666
BEE-HAPPY PLUS - Herbal And Vitamin Supplement - BEE-ALIVE INC.; *pg.* 1503, *pg.* 1348
BEE HIVE - Syringe Pump Controller - BIOANALYTICAL SYSTEMS, INC.; *pg.* 1402, *pg.* 700
BEE HIVE - Gaming Product - GLD PRODUCTS, INC.; *pg.* 1835, *pg.* 1882
BEE-LICIOUS - Potato Chip Flavor - ZAPP'S POTATO CHIPS, INC.; *pg.* 1864, *pg.* 743
BEE LINE - All Models - BEE LINE COMPANY; *pg.* 200, *pg.* 701
BEE LUCKY - Lottery Game - KENTUCKY LOTTERY CORPORATION; *pg.* 996, *pg.* 735
BEE LUCKY - Lottery Game - LOUISIANA LOTTERY CORPORATION; *pg.* 997, *pg.* 742
BEE-MOISTURIZED - Skin Care Product - BEE-ALIVE INC.; *pg.* 1503, *pg.* 1348
BEE-SCENT - Insect Pest Control Product - GARDENS ALIVE!, INC.; *pg.* 1796, *pg.* 693
BEECH - Furniture - BUSH INDUSTRIES INC.; *pg.* 919, *pg.* 1170
BEECHCRAFT - Defense System - RAYTHEON COMPANY; *pg.* 233, *pg.* 854
BEECHMONT AUTOMILE - Automobile - BEECHMONT AUTOMOTIVE GROUP; *pg.* 166, *pg.* 1410
BEECHWOOD FARMS - Prepared Food Products - UNITED DAIRY FARMERS, INC.; *pg.* 906, *pg.* 1426
BEEF 15 BEAN SOUP - Soup - N.K. HURST CO., INC.; *pg.* 886, *pg.* 689
BEEF BRATS - Bratwurst - JOHNSONVILLE SAUSAGE, LLC; *pg.* 867, *pg.* 1894
BEEF. IT'S STILL WHAT'S FOR DINNER - Tagline - CATTLEMEN'S BEEF PROMOTION & RESEARCH BOARD; *pg.* 136, *pg.* 314
BEEF. IT'S WHAT'S FOR DINNER! - Tagline - CATTLEMEN'S BEEF PROMOTION & RESEARCH BOARD; *pg.* 136, *pg.* 314
BEEF MATE - Flavoring - DAVID MICHAEL & CO. INC.; *pg.* 852, *pg.* 1563
BEEF SMOKIES - Cocktail Wieners - JOHNSONVILLE SAUSAGE, LLC; *pg.* 867, *pg.* 1894
BEEFEATER - Gin - PERNOD RICARD USA, INC.; *pg.* 1968, *pg.* 1332
BEEF'O'BRADY'S - Family Sports Pubs - FSC FRANCHISE CO., LLC; *pg.* 1729, *pg.* 473
BEEFSTICK - Freshwater Fishing Rod - DAIWA CORPORATION; *pg.* 1832, *pg.* 75
BEEFY FIVE LAYER BURRITO - Burritos - TACO BELL CORP.; *pg.* 1752, *pg.* 117
BEEFY-T - Apparel - HANESBRANDS INC.; *pg.* 26, *pg.* 1394

First page reference indicates Business Class Edition
Second page reference indicates Geographic Edition

BEEHIVE - Vehicle Safety System - GROTE INDUSTRIES, INC.; *pg.* 206, *pg.* 693
BEEHIVE CUT FRINGE - Fabric - SCALAMANDRE, INC.; *pg.* 941, *pg.* 1058
BEEKMAN - Leather Product - COACH, INC.; *pg.* 3, *pg.* 1214
BEELINE - Fabric - NEMSCHOFF, INC.; *pg.* 936, *pg.* 1890
BEELINE - Real Time Azimuth Determination & Kinematic Positioning System - NOVATEL INC.; *pg.* 1424, *pg.* 1904
BEELINER - Collision Correction-Automotive - BEE LINE COMPANY; *pg.* 200, *pg.* 701
BEELITH - Pharmaceuticals - BEACH PRODUCTS, INC.; *pg.* 1501, *pg.* 471
BEEP2TALK - Telephone Service - IDT CORPORATION; *pg.* 643, *pg.* 1096
BEEPLEX - Nutritional Product - NUTRACEUTICAL INTERNATIONAL CORPORATION; *pg.* 1576, *pg.* 1753
BEER BRATS - Bratwurst - JOHNSONVILLE SAUSAGE, LLC; *pg.* 867, *pg.* 1894
BEER MUG OF BLOOMS - Flower Arrangement - 1-800-FLOWERS.COM, INC.; *pg.* 1758, *pg.* 1151
BEER 'N BRATWURST - Sausage - JOHNSONVILLE SAUSAGE, LLC; *pg.* 867, *pg.* 1894
BEER 'N CHEDDAR - Food Product - JOHNSONVILLE SAUSAGE, LLC; *pg.* 867, *pg.* 1894
BEERNADINE - Lamp - ASHLEY FURNITURE INDUSTRIES, INC.; *pg.* 914, *pg.* 1852
BEEVIVE - Nutritional Product - NUTRACEUTICAL INTERNATIONAL CORPORATION; *pg.* 1576, *pg.* 1753
BEFORE - Cleaning Product - VON SCHRADER COMPANY; *pg.* 62, *pg.* 1890
BEFORE I MADE HISTORY - Educational Materials - SCHOLASTIC INC.; *pg.* 1683, *pg.* 1288
BEGGIN' STRIPS - Dog Treats - NESTLE PURINA PETCARE COMPANY; *pg.* 1479, *pg.* 1000
BEGIN TODAY. - Tag Line - MUTUAL OF OMAHA INSURANCE COMPANY; *pg.* 1210, *pg.* 1016
BEGINNER BOOKS - Publishing Imprint - PENGUIN RANDOM HOUSE CHILDREN'S BOOKS; *pg.* 1676, *pg.* 1277
BEGINNINGS - Furniture - SAUDER WOODWORKING CO.; *pg.* 941, *pg.* 1403
BEGREEN - Carbon Offset - GREEN MOUNTAIN ENERGY COMPANY; *pg.* 1944, *pg.* 1663
BEGUES - Restaurant - SONESTA INTERNATIONAL HOTELS CORPORATION; *pg.* 1113, *pg.* 836
BEGUILE - Fabric - NEMSCHOFF, INC.; *pg.* 936, *pg.* 1890
BEHAVE - Hair Preparations - THE GILLETTE COMPANY; *pg.* 509, *pg.* 795
BEHAVIOR EXTRACTING SYNTHESIS TECHNOLOGY - Software - SYNOPSYS, INC.; *pg.* 480, *pg.* 162
BEHAVIOR SCAN - Test Marketing - IRI GROUP; *pg.* 421, *pg.* 579
BEHLEN - Water Tanks - BEHLEN MFG. CO.; *pg.* 701, *pg.* 1010
BEHLEN COUNTRY - Animal Drinkers - BEHLEN MFG. CO.; *pg.* 701, *pg.* 1010
BEHR - Paints & Stains - MASCO CORPORATION; *pg.* 96, *pg.* 909
BEHR PREMIUM PLUS - Decorative Architectural Product - MASCO CORPORATION; *pg.* 96, *pg.* 909
BEHR PROCESS - Paints & Stains - MASCO CORPORATION; *pg.* 96, *pg.* 909
BEI - Sensor And Motion Controller - CUSTOM SENSORS & TECHNOLOGIES; *pg.* 1407, *pg.* 152
BEI ENCODER - Encoders - CUSTOM SENSORS & TECHNOLOGIES; *pg.* 1407, *pg.* 152
BEIGE SHANGRILA - Bedcovering - ETHAN ALLEN INTERIORS INC.; *pg.* 924, *pg.* 343
BEIJING - Furniture - J. ROBERT SCOTT INC.; *pg.* 930, *pg.* 105
BEING MAGAZINE - Magazine - JOCKEY INTERNATIONAL, INC.; *pg.* 27, *pg.* 1861
BEING TOGETHER - Designer Fragrance - PARFUMS DE COEUR LTD.; *pg.* 519, *pg.* 376
BEL AIR - Carpet - BEAULIEU GROUP, LLC; *pg.* 917, *pg.* 529
BEL ARBOR - California Wines - BROWN-FORMAN CORPORATION; *pg.* 1958, *pg.* 732
BEL-RAY - Lubricant - BEL-RAY COMPANY, INC.; *pg.* 972, *pg.* 1128
BEL ROCK - Carpet - BEAULIEU GROUP, LLC; *pg.* 917, *pg.* 529
BELAGIO - Footwear - STEVEN MADDEN, LTD.; *pg.* 1819, *pg.* 1176
BELCARE - Patient Care - BELTONE ELECTRONICS LLC; *pg.* 1503, *pg.* 614
BELCO - Clean Air Technologies - E.I. DU PONT DE NEMOURS & COMPANY; *pg.* 1159, *pg.* 390
BELCOMBO - Connector Modules - BEL FUSE INC.; *pg.* 624, *pg.* 1075
BELCOR - Intimate Apparel - V.F. CORPORATION; *pg.* 34, *pg.* 1376
BELCOURT - Flatware - ONEIDA LTD; *pg.* 1129, *pg.* 1318
BELDEN - Wire & Cable Products - BELDEN, INC.; *pg.* 624, *pg.* 993
BELDENCABLE - Cables - BELDEN, INC.; *pg.* 624, *pg.* 993
BELDFOIL - Aluminum Mylar Shield - BELDEN, INC.; *pg.* 624, *pg.* 993
BELENOS - Fabric - NEMSCHOFF, INC.; *pg.* 936, *pg.* 1890
BELFIORE - Furniture - ETHAN ALLEN INTERIORS INC.; *pg.* 924, *pg.* 343
BELFUSE - Electrical Components - BEL FUSE INC.; *pg.* 624, *pg.* 1075
BELGIAN CREMES - Chocolates - BROWN & HALEY; *pg.* 1851, *pg.* 1820
BELIEVE IN THE POWER OF PLAY - Tag Line - TONNER DOLL COMPANY, INC.; *pg.* 968, *pg.* 1171
BELINI - Footwear - STEVEN MADDEN, LTD.; *pg.* 1819, *pg.* 1176
BELIZE - Carpet - BEAULIEU GROUP, LLC; *pg.* 917, *pg.* 529
BELIZE - Furniture - BUSH INDUSTRIES INC.; *pg.* 919, *pg.* 1170
BELIZE - Bedcovering - ETHAN ALLEN INTERIORS INC.; *pg.* 924, *pg.* 343
BELIZE IT OR NOT - Nail Care Product - OPI PRODUCTS INC.; *pg.* 518, *pg.* 167
BELL - Telecommunications Services - AT&T SOUTHEAST; *pg.* 1868, *pg.* 489
BELL - Aroma Chemical - BELL FLAVORS & FRAGRANCES, INC.; *pg.* 501, *pg.* 640
BELL - Electrical Product - HUBBELL INCORPORATED; *pg.* 1299, *pg.* 370
BELL - Supermarket - THE KROGER CO.; *pg.* 1025, *pg.* 1416
BELL & GOSSETT - Fluid Technology - ITT CORPORATION; *pg.* 1351, *pg.* 1354
BELL & GOSSETT - Pumps - XYLEM INC.; *pg.* 1078, *pg.* 1339
BELL CARTER - Olives - BELL-CARTER FOODS, INC.; *pg.* 839, *pg.* 120
BELL EXPRESSVU - Television Services - BCE INC.; *pg.* 1936, *pg.* 1960
BELL-MARK - Printers - BELL-MARK CORPORATION; *pg.* 1620, *pg.* 1108
BELL MOBILITY - Wireless Telephone Service - BCE INC.; *pg.* 1936, *pg.* 1960
BELL OUTDOOR - Electrical Product - HUBBELL INCORPORATED; *pg.* 1299, *pg.* 370
BELL SYMPATICO - Internet Services - BCE INC.; *pg.* 1936, *pg.* 1960
BELLA - Footwear - BEBE STORES, INC.; *pg.* 19, *pg.* 49
BELLA - Shirt - BROWN & BIGELOW, INC.; *pg.* 1624, *pg.* 959
BELLA - Bedding - CROSCILL, INC.; *pg.* 1122, *pg.* 1220
BELLA - Decorative Accessory - ETHAN ALLEN INTERIORS INC.; *pg.* 924, *pg.* 343
BELLA - Footwear - PHOENIX FOOTWEAR GROUP, INC.; *pg.* 1815, *pg.* 60
BELLA DANCERELLA - Toy - SPIN MASTER LTD.; *pg.* 967, *pg.* 1943
BELLA LUCCA - Furniture - TELESCOPE CASUAL FURNITURE INC.; *pg.* 944, *pg.* 1162
BELLA SERA - Wine - E&J GALLO WINERY; *pg.* 1962, *pg.* 149
BELLA VISTA - Furniture - ASHLEY FURNITURE INDUSTRIES, INC.; *pg.* 914, *pg.* 1852
BELLA VISTA - Prepackaged Food - FURMANO FOODS, INC.; *pg.* 857, *pg.* 1557
BELLACERE - Rug - COURISTAN INC.; *pg.* 921, *pg.* 1067
BELLAFINA - Mattress System - TEMPUR SEALY INTERNATIONAL, INC.; *pg.* 944, *pg.* 731
BELLAGIO - Guest Chairs - BERNHARDT DESIGN; *pg.* 918, *pg.* 1381
BELLAGIO - Furniture - HOOKER FURNITURE CORPORATION; *pg.* 928, *pg.* 1788
BELLAGIO - Door Panel - MASONITE INTERNATIONAL CORPORATION; *pg.* 1054, *pg.* 1920
BELLAGIO - Resort & Casino - MGM RESORTS INTERNATIONAL; *pg.* 1105, *pg.* 1028
BELLAGIO RESORTS - Entertainment Product - MIRAGE RESORTS INCORPORATED; *pg.* 1105, *pg.* 1028
BELLALAGO - Home Builders - AV HOMES INC.; *pg.* 1080, *pg.* 20
THE BELLAPILLOW - Pillow - TEMPUR SEALY INTERNATIONAL, INC.; *pg.* 944, *pg.* 731
BELLAROSE - Surface Material - STEELCASE INC.; *pg.* 475, *pg.* 889
BELLASERA - Hotel - SUNSTREAM, INC.; *pg.* 1116, *pg.* 428
BELLASONNA - Mattress System - TEMPUR SEALY INTERNATIONAL, INC.; *pg.* 944, *pg.* 731
BELLAVISTA - Bedding - CROSCILL, INC.; *pg.* 1122, *pg.* 1220
BELLAVISTA - Bath & Plumbing Product - JACUZZI BRANDS CORPORATION; *pg.* 554, *pg.* 65
BELLAWOOD - Flooring - LUMBER LIQUIDATORS HOLDINGS, INC.; *pg.* 94, *pg.* 1808
BELLE - Footwear - COBIAN CORP.; *pg.* 1806, *pg.* 253
BELLE - Furniture - JASPER GROUP; *pg.* 930, *pg.* 691
BELLE - Lighting Product - QUOIZEL INC.; *pg.* 1304, *pg.* 1616
BELLE - Hat - WOODEN SHIPS OF HOBOKEN; *pg.* 35, *pg.* 1315
BELLE KLIPSCH - Loudspeaker - KLIPSCH GROUP, INC.; *pg.* 649, *pg.* 688
BELLE MEADE - Ceiling Fans - HUNTER FAN COMPANY; *pg.* 57, *pg.* 1631
BELLE OF SIOUX CITY - Games - PENN NATIONAL GAMING, INC.; *pg.* 574, *pg.* 1595
BELLEAIR BEE - Newspaper - TAMPA BAY NEWSPAPERS, INC.; *pg.* 1691, *pg.* 468
BELLES & BEAUS - Games - PENN NATIONAL GAMING, INC.; *pg.* 574, *pg.* 1595
BELLES & BEAUS THE 50 & BETTER SENIOR CLUB - Games - PENN NATIONAL GAMING, INC.; *pg.* 574, *pg.* 1595
BELLEVILLE - Furniture - ASHLEY FURNITURE INDUSTRIES, INC.; *pg.* 914, *pg.* 1852
BELLEVILLE - Door - MASONITE INTERNATIONAL CORPORATION; *pg.* 1054, *pg.* 1920
BELLEVUE - Beauty Salon Furniture - BELVEDERE USA CORPORATION; *pg.* 917, *pg.* 556
BELLEVUE - Footwear - EASTLAND SHOE CORPORATION; *pg.* 1808, *pg.* 750
BELLINGHAM - Fabric - NEMSCHOFF, INC.; *pg.* 936, *pg.* 1890
BELLINGHAM - Fabric - UNIROYAL ENGINEERED PRODUCTS; *pg.* 699, *pg.* 467
BELLINI - Flatware - ONEIDA LTD; *pg.* 1129, *pg.* 1318
BELLIS & MORCOM - Compressors - GARDNER DENVER, INC.; *pg.* 1338, *pg.* 1592
BELLOWS - Whiskey & Scotch - JIM BEAM BRANDS CO.; *pg.* 1965, *pg.* 601
BELLOWSFLEX - Hose - HBD INDUSTRIES, INC.; *pg.* 207, *pg.* 1449
BELLSOUTH 411 NATIONWIDE - Directory Assistance - AT&T SOUTHEAST; *pg.* 1868, *pg.* 489
BELLSOUTH ANSWERS - Phone Service - AT&T SOUTHEAST; *pg.* 1868, *pg.* 489
BELLSOUTH BEYOND PROTECTION PLAN - Wireless Communication System - AT&T SOUTHEAST; *pg.* 1868, *pg.* 489
BELLSOUTH BUSINESS ADVANTAGE - Business Phone Service - AT&T SOUTHEAST; *pg.* 1868, *pg.* 489
BELLSOUTH BUSINESS CHOICE - Business Calling Plan - AT&T SOUTHEAST; *pg.* 1868, *pg.* 489
BELLSOUTH BUSINESS PLUS - Calling Plan - AT&T SOUTHEAST; *pg.* 1868, *pg.* 489
BELLSOUTH CLASSIC - Wireless Communication System - AT&T SOUTHEAST; *pg.* 1868, *pg.* 489
BELLSOUTH CONNECTED COMMUNITY - Wireless Communication System - AT&T SOUTHEAST; *pg.* 1868, *pg.* 489
BELLSOUTH ENHANCED SOLUTIONS - Wireless Communication System - AT&T SOUTHEAST; *pg.* 1868, *pg.* 489
BELLSOUTH. ESCUCHAMOS. RESPONDEMOS. - Slogan (Spanish) - AT&T SOUTHEAST; *pg.* 1868, *pg.* 489
BELLSOUTH ESSENTIALS - Wireless Communication System - AT&T SOUTHEAST; *pg.* 1868, *pg.* 489
BELLSOUTH GEAR - Wireless Communication System - AT&T SOUTHEAST; *pg.* 1868, *pg.* 489
BELLSOUTH INSITE - Wireless Communication System - AT&T SOUTHEAST; *pg.* 1868, *pg.* 489

BELLSOUTH INTELLIGENT WIRELESS NETWORK - Wireless Communication System - AT&T SOUTHEAST; *pg.* 1868, *pg.* 489
BELLSOUTH INTERACTIVE PAGING - Paging Service - AT&T SOUTHEAST; *pg.* 1868, *pg.* 489
BELLSOUTH. LISTENING. ANSWERING. - Slogan - AT&T SOUTHEAST; *pg.* 1868, *pg.* 489
BELLSOUTH MAKES YOU FEEL AT HOME WHEN YOU'RE NOT - Tagline - AT&T SOUTHEAST; *pg.* 1868, *pg.* 489
BELLSOUTH MOBILITY - Cellular Telephone - AT&T SOUTHEAST; *pg.* 1868, *pg.* 489
BELLSOUTH POWERTOOL - Software - AT&T SOUTHEAST; *pg.* 1868, *pg.* 489
BELLSOUTH PREMIUM SYSTEMS - Wireless Communication System - AT&T SOUTHEAST; *pg.* 1868, *pg.* 489
BELLSOUTH PREPAID TO GO - Cellular Service - AT&T SOUTHEAST; *pg.* 1868, *pg.* 489
BELLSOUTH PROFESSIONAL SERVICES - Wireless Communication System - AT&T SOUTHEAST; *pg.* 1868, *pg.* 489
BELLSOUTH PSP REWARD - Wireless Communication System - AT&T SOUTHEAST; *pg.* 1868, *pg.* 489
BELLSOUTH SELECT - Wireless Communication System - AT&T SOUTHEAST; *pg.* 1868, *pg.* 489
BELLSOUTH SELECT BUSINESS - Wireless Communication System - AT&T SOUTHEAST; *pg.* 1868, *pg.* 489
BELLSOUTH SOLUTIONS - Wireless Communication System - AT&T SOUTHEAST; *pg.* 1868, *pg.* 489
BELLSOUTH TELECOMMUNICATIONS - Communication - AT&T SOUTHEAST; *pg.* 1868, *pg.* 489
BELLSOUTH.NET - Internet - AT&T SOUTHEAST; *pg.* 1868, *pg.* 489
BELLWETHER - Customer Experience Product - CX ACT, INC.; *pg.* 1394, *pg.* 1773
BELLY OFF! DIET - Book - RODALE, INC.; *pg.* 1681, *pg.* 1530
BELMAG - Connector Modules - BEL FUSE INC.; *pg.* 624, *pg.* 1075
BELMOR - Vehicle Product - LUND INTERNATIONAL, INC.; *pg.* 211, *pg.* 526
BELSHAW - Bakery Equipment - BELSHAW ADAMATIC BAKERY GROUP; *pg.* 1317, *pg.* 1813
BELSON - Personal Care Electrical Product - HELEN OF TROY L.P.; *pg.* 511, *pg.* 1692
BELSON PRO - Personal Care Electrical Product - HELEN OF TROY L.P.; *pg.* 511, *pg.* 1692
BELSTACK - Connector Modules - BEL FUSE INC.; *pg.* 624, *pg.* 1075
BELSTICK - Connector Modules - BEL FUSE INC.; *pg.* 624, *pg.* 1075
BELT-EASE - Belt Dressing - AMERICAN GREASE STICK CO.; *pg.* 971, *pg.* 902
BELT-FLO - Fluid Sealing Product - A.W. CHESTERTON COMPANY; *pg.* 1315, *pg.* 861
BELT-MAGIC - Lubricant - AMERICAN GREASE STICK CO.; *pg.* 971, *pg.* 902
BELT-TY - Cable Tie - PANDUIT CORP.; *pg.* 661, *pg.* 663
BELT VEYOR - Grain Drills - CRUSTBUSTER-SPEED KING, INC.; *pg.* 702, *pg.* 714
BELTERRA - Casinos - PINNACLE ENTERTAINMENT, INC.; *pg.* 576, *pg.* 1029
BELTMATE - Thermal Processing Equipment - SURFACE COMBUSTION, INC.; *pg.* 1077, *pg.* 1462
BELTRAC - Belt Trackers - HYDRALIGN; *pg.* 1257, *pg.* 833
BELTRAC - Public Guidance System - LAVI INDUSTRIES INC.; *pg.* 93, *pg.* 299
BELVEDERE - Table - BLATT BOWLING & BILLIARD CORP.; *pg.* 1827, *pg.* 1203
BELVEDERE - Bike - MARIN BIKES; *pg.* 1708, *pg.* 168
BELVEDERE - Vodka - MOET HENNESSY; *pg.* 1966, *pg.* 1260
BELVITA - Breakfast Biscuits - MONDELEZ INTERNATIONAL, INC.; *pg.* 878, *pg.* 601
BEM-600 - Shale Shaker - M-I SWACO; *pg.* 980, *pg.* 1710
BEMISTAPE - Paper Product - BEMIS COMPANY, INC.; *pg.* 1453, *pg.* 1882
BEN - Furniture - AMISCO INDUSTRIES LTD.; *pg.* 913, *pg.* 1958
BEN & JERRY'S - Ice Cream - BEN & JERRY'S HOMEMADE, INC.; *pg.* 1850, *pg.* 1767
BEN & JERRY'S - Ice Cream - UNILEVER UNITED STATES, INC.; *pg.* 904, *pg.* 1061
BEN & JERRY'S LIGHT - Ice Cream - BEN & JERRY'S HOMEMADE, INC.; *pg.* 1850, *pg.* 1767
BEN & JERRY'S LOW FAT FROZEN YOGURT - Low Fat Frozen Yogurt - BEN & JERRY'S HOMEMADE, INC.; *pg.* 1850, *pg.* 1767
BEN & JERRY'S PEACE POPS - Ice Cream Novelty - BEN & JERRY'S HOMEMADE, INC.; *pg.* 1850, *pg.* 1767
BEN FRANKLIN - Domestic Cigars - ALTADIS USA, INC.; *pg.* 1893, *pg.* 423
BEN FRANKLIN - Agricultural Gypsum - USG CORPORATION; *pg.* 118, *pg.* 594
BEN HOGAN - Golf Balls, Irons, Wedges, Putters, Accessories - PERRY ELLIS INTERNATIONAL, INC.; *pg.* 45, *pg.* 445
BEN HOGAN - Apparel - SPORT HALEY, INC.; *pg.* 33, *pg.* 333
BEN PAO - Chinese Restaurant - LETTUCE ENTERTAIN YOU ENTERPRISES, INC.; *pg.* 1735, *pg.* 580
BEN SHERMAN - Clothing Line - OXFORD INDUSTRIES, INC.; *pg.* 30, *pg.* 517
BEN SILVER COLLECTION - Classically Styled Men's Clothing - THE BEN SILVER CORPORATION; *pg.* 38, *pg.* 1613
BENADRYL - Allergy Medicine - JOHNSON & JOHNSON; *pg.* 1549, *pg.* 1091
BENADRYL - Allergy Medicine - MCNEIL-PPC, INC.; *pg.* 1560, *pg.* 1533
BENALLURE - Insect Pest Control Product - GARDENS ALIVE!, INC.; *pg.* 1796, *pg.* 693
BENAROYA HALL - Music Hall - SEATTLE SYMPHONY ORCHESTRA; *pg.* 582, *pg.* 1840
BENCH - Fabric - NEMSCHOFF, INC.; *pg.* 936, *pg.* 1890
BENCHMARK - Boilers - AERCO INTERNATIONAL INC.; *pg.* 1068, *pg.* 1142
BENCHMARK - Software - BIO-RAD LABORATORIES, INC.; *pg.* 1504, *pg.* 101
BENCHMARK - Aqueous Cleaning Consoles - BRANSON ULTRASONICS CORPORATION-PRECISION CLEANING DIV; *pg.* 1319, *pg.* 343
BENCHMARK - Foam Marker - KALO, INC.; *pg.* 1796, *pg.* 719
BENCHMARK - Software - MAQUET; *pg.* 1558, *pg.* 1082
BENCHMARK - Residential Door Systems - THERMA-TRU CORP.; *pg.* 115, *pg.* 1462
BENCHMARK - Molecular Biology Product - THERMO FISHER SCIENTIFIC INC.; *pg.* 1602, *pg.* 61
BENCHMARK FACTORY - Software - DELL SOFTWARE; *pg.* 385, *pg.* 40
BENCHMARK HT - Foam Concentrate - KALO, INC.; *pg.* 1796, *pg.* 719
BENCHMARQ - Electronic Components & Integrated Circuits - TEXAS INSTRUMENTS INCORPORATED; *pg.* 679, *pg.* 1688
BENCHMASTER - Test Equipment - SPX THERMAL PRODUCT SOLUTIONS; *pg.* 1378, *pg.* 1555
BENCHTOP - Isolation Platform - NEWPORT CORPORATION; *pg.* 1424, *pg.* 114
BENCHTOP UV INCUBATOR - Ultraviolet Product - UVP, INC.; *pg.* 1434, *pg.* 298
BENCIL - Shoe - AEROGROUP INTERNATIONAL, INC.; *pg.* 1803, *pg.* 1055
BEND OVER - Slacks - HABAND COMPANY, INC.; *pg.* 1772, *pg.* 1099
BENDEEZ - Stress Relief Stick - BROWN & BIGELOW, INC.; *pg.* 1624, *pg.* 959
BENDINI - Crane - TEREX CORPORATION; *pg.* 1381, *pg.* 384
BENDIX - Refrigerants - HONEYWELL INTERNATIONAL INC.; *pg.* 407, *pg.* 1088
BENDIX/KING - Commercial & General Aviation Avionics Products; Radio Products - HONEYWELL AEROSPACE; *pg.* 228, *pg.* 16
BENECALORIE - Pharmaceutical Product - NESTLE HEALTHCARE NUTRITION; *pg.* 1572, *pg.* 941
BENECARDIA - Dietary Supplement - NATROL, INC.; *pg.* 1570, *pg.* 64
BENECEL - Polymer - HERCULES INCORPORATED; *pg.* 1166, *pg.* 392
BENECOL - Healthcare Product - JOHNSON & JOHNSON; *pg.* 1549, *pg.* 1091
BENEDETTO - Guitar - FENDER MUSICAL INSTRUMENTS CORPORATION; *pg.* 547, *pg.* 21
BENEDORM - Pharmaceutical Product - VALEANT PHARMACEUTICALS INTERNATIONAL; *pg.* 1605, *pg.* 1047
BENEFIBER - Pharmaceutical Product - NESTLE HEALTHCARE NUTRITION; *pg.* 1572, *pg.* 941
BENEFIT - Shoe - AEROGROUP INTERNATIONAL, INC.; *pg.* 1803, *pg.* 1055
BENEFIT - Cookie Product - J&J SNACK FOODS CORPORATION; *pg.* 865, *pg.* 1107
BENEFIT - Fabric - NEMSCHOFF, INC.; *pg.* 936, *pg.* 1890
BENEFIT COSMETICS - Cosmetics - BENEFIT COSMETICS LLC; *pg.* 501, *pg.* 213
BENEFITS OF CHEWING - Research Program - WM. WRIGLEY JR. COMPANY; *pg.* 1863, *pg.* 596
BENEFITS SELLING - Business-to-Business Magazine - WIESNER PUBLISHING, LLC; *pg.* 1702, *pg.* 328
BENEFIX - Blood Cell Growth Promotion Pharmaceutical - PFIZER INC.; *pg.* 1581, *pg.* 1278
BENEFOCUS - Medicine - PFIZER INC.; *pg.* 1581, *pg.* 1278
BENEFUL - Pet Care Product - NESTLE PURINA PETCARE COMPANY; *pg.* 1479, *pg.* 1000
BENEFUL - Petcare - TRACTOR SUPPLY COMPANY; *pg.* 708, *pg.* 1627
BENELLI - Firearm - BENELLI USA CORPORATION; *pg.* 1827, *pg.* 754
BENEPROTEIN - Pharmaceutical Product - NESTLE HEALTHCARE NUTRITION; *pg.* 1572, *pg.* 941
BENFORD - Compact Equipment - TEREX CORPORATION; *pg.* 1381, *pg.* 384
BENGAL FEVER - Video Game - INTERNATIONAL GAME TECHNOLOGY; *pg.* 957, *pg.* 1024
BENGAL ROAD - Bedding - CROSCILL, INC.; *pg.* 1122, *pg.* 1220
BENGAY - Pain Relief Cream - JOHNSON & JOHNSON; *pg.* 1549, *pg.* 1091
BENITAA - Footwear - STEVEN MADDEN, LTD.; *pg.* 1819, *pg.* 1176
THE BENJAMIN - Hotels - DENIHAN HOSPITALITY GROUP, LLC; *pg.* 1089, *pg.* 1223
BENJAMIN MOORE - Paint, Stains & Enamels - BENJAMIN MOORE & CO.; *pg.* 1440, *pg.* 1085
BENJAMIN MOORE CLASSIC COLOR COLLECTION - Paint Colors Collection - BENJAMIN MOORE & CO.; *pg.* 1440, *pg.* 1085
BENJAMIN MOORE CLASSIC COLORS - Paint And Stain Product - BENJAMIN MOORE & CO.; *pg.* 1440, *pg.* 1085
BENJAMIN MOORE FRESH START - Paint And Stain Product - BENJAMIN MOORE & CO.; *pg.* 1440, *pg.* 1085
BENJAMIN MOORE PAINTS - Paint And Stain Product - BENJAMIN MOORE & CO.; *pg.* 1440, *pg.* 1085
BENJAMIN SHERIDAN - Airguns & Pellet Gun Rifles - CROSMAN CORPORATION; *pg.* 951, *pg.* 1143
BENNET - Furniture - AMERICAN LEATHER LP; *pg.* 912, *pg.* 1673
BENNETT - Furniture - AMISCO INDUSTRIES LTD.; *pg.* 913, *pg.* 1958
BENNETT - Furniture - ETHAN ALLEN INTERIORS INC.; *pg.* 924, *pg.* 343
BENNETT'S - Sauces & Syrups - TREEHOUSE FOODS, INC.; *pg.* 901, *pg.* 649
BENNI - Clothing - ABERCROMBIE & FITCH CO.; *pg.* 37, *pg.* 1466
BENNINGTON TOO - Fabric - NEMSCHOFF, INC.; *pg.* 936, *pg.* 1890
BENNY BIG GAME - Video Slots - INTERNATIONAL GAME TECHNOLOGY; *pg.* 957, *pg.* 1024
BENOMYL - Fungicide - BONIDE PRODUCTS, INC.; *pg.* 1794, *pg.* 1320
BEN'S - Bread - MAPLE LEAF FOODS INC.; *pg.* 875, *pg.* 1927
BEN'S - Tick and Insect Repellent - TENDER CORPORATION; *pg.* 1601, *pg.* 1035
BENSINGER - Table - BLATT BOWLING & BILLIARD CORP.; *pg.* 1827, *pg.* 1203
BENSON & HEDGES - Cigarettes - PHILIP MORRIS USA INC.; *pg.* 1894, *pg.* 1803
BENSON & HEDGES 100'S - Cigarettes - PHILIP MORRIS USA INC.; *pg.* 1894, *pg.* 1803
BENSON & HEDGES BLUES - Cigarettes - PHILIP MORRIS USA INC.; *pg.* 1894, *pg.* 1803
BENSON & HEDGES SIGNATURE COLLECTION - Mail Order Services - PHILIP MORRIS USA INC.; *pg.* 1894, *pg.* 1803
BENSON'S OLD HOME - Fruit Cake - BENSON'S, INC.; *pg.* 1850, *pg.* 526
BENSUMEC - Turf Product - PBI/GORDON CORPORATION; *pg.* 1176, *pg.* 985
BENT - Apparel - OAKLEY, INC.; *pg.* 1840, *pg.* 86
BENT METAL - Snowboard Bindings - QUIKSILVER, INC.; *pg.* 31, *pg.* 104

BENTASIL - Pharmaceutical Product - CHURCH & DWIGHT CANADA CORP.; *pg.* 503, *pg.* 1925
BENTHOS - Oceanographic And Offshore Equipment - TELEDYNE BENTHOS, INC.; *pg.* 1431, *pg.* 838
BENTLEY - Furniture - ETHAN ALLEN INTERIORS INC.; *pg.* 924, *pg.* 343
BENTLEY ARENIUM - Software - BENTLEY SYSTEMS, INC.; *pg.* 361, *pg.* 1531
BENTLEY AXSYS - Software - BENTLEY SYSTEMS, INC.; *pg.* 361, *pg.* 1531
BENTLEY-HARRIS - Systems Protection - FEDERAL-MOGUL HOLDINGS CORPORATION; *pg.* 205, *pg.* 907
BENTLEY PRINCE STREET - Carpet - INTERFACE, INC.; *pg.* 695, *pg.* 512
BENTLEY SELECT - Technology & Service Subscription Program - BENTLEY SYSTEMS, INC.; *pg.* 361, *pg.* 1531
BENTO - Software - FILEMAKER, INC.; *pg.* 639, *pg.* 265
BENTOMAT - Geosynthetic Clay Liners - MINERALS TECHNOLOGIES INC.; *pg.* 1173, *pg.* 617
BENTON - Shoes - ALLEN-EDMONDS SHOE CORP.; *pg.* 1804, *pg.* 1887
BENTYL - Pharmaceutical Product - LANNETT COMPANY, INC.; *pg.* 1555, *pg.* 1566
BENWOOD - Wood Finishes, Varnishes, Stains - BENJAMIN MOORE & CO.; *pg.* 1440, *pg.* 1085
BENWOOD FINISHES - Paint And Stain Product - BENJAMIN MOORE & CO.; *pg.* 1440, *pg.* 1085
BENYLIN - Medicine - MCNEIL-PPC, INC.; *pg.* 1560, *pg.* 1533
BENZA - Footwear - STEVEN MADDEN, LTD.; *pg.* 1819, *pg.* 1176
BENZAC AC - Pharmaceutical Products - GALDERMA LABORATORIES, L.P.; *pg.* 1532, *pg.* 1695
BENZAC AC WASH - Pharmaceutical Products - GALDERMA LABORATORIES, L.P.; *pg.* 1532, *pg.* 1695
BENZAC W - Pharmaceutical Products - GALDERMA LABORATORIES, L.P.; *pg.* 1532, *pg.* 1695
BENZAC W WASH - Pharmaceutical Products - GALDERMA LABORATORIES, L.P.; *pg.* 1532, *pg.* 1695
BENZODENT - Health & Beauty Product - CHATTEM, INC.; *pg.* 1515, *pg.* 1628
BEP - Diagnostic Product - SIEMENS HEALTHCARE DIAGNOSTICS; *pg.* 673, *pg.* 604
BEPREVE - Ophthalmology Product - BAUSCH & LOMB INCORPORATED; *pg.* 1401, *pg.* 1045
BEPUZZLED - Game - UNIVERSITY GAMES CORPORATION; *pg.* 969, *pg.* 230
BERAL - Friction Products - FEDERAL-MOGUL HOLDINGS CORPORATION; *pg.* 205, *pg.* 907
BERENTZEN APPEL - Liquor - WILLIAM GRANT & SONS, INC.; *pg.* 1972, *pg.* 1057
BERGADUR - Polyester Compounds - POLYONE CORPORATION; *pg.* 1177, *pg.* 1404
BERGAMID - Polyamide Compounds - POLYONE CORPORATION; *pg.* 1177, *pg.* 1404
BERGAMO - Shoes - ALLEN-EDMONDS SHOE CORP.; *pg.* 1804, *pg.* 1887
BERGAN - Pet Product - PETSMART, INC.; *pg.* 1481, *pg.* 18
BERGDORF GOODMAN - Retail Stores - NEIMAN MARCUS, INC.; *pg.* 30, *pg.* 1684
BERGIO - Jewelry - BERGIO INTERNATIONAL, INC.; *pg.* 1, *pg.* 1065
BERGLAND - Shoes - ALLEN-EDMONDS SHOE CORP.; *pg.* 1804, *pg.* 1887
BERGMANN - Acoustic Pianos - YOUNG CHANG NORTH AMERICA; *pg.* 595, *pg.* 77
BERGSMA GALLERY - Deluxe Cards - LEANIN' TREE, INC.; *pg.* 1658, *pg.* 311
BERICO DRYERS - Grain Conditioning Equipment - BEHLEN MFG. CO.; *pg.* 701, *pg.* 1010
BERIGARD - Basket - PACTIV CORPORATION; *pg.* 1466, *pg.* 624
BERKELEY FARMS - Milk Products - DEAN FOODS COMPANY; *pg.* 852, *pg.* 1679
BERKELEY TRAINING CENTER - Workforce Training Service - THE JUDGE GROUP, INC.; *pg.* 424, *pg.* 1594
BERKLEY - Door & Wood Product - CONESTOGA WOOD SPECIALTIES CORP.; *pg.* 921, *pg.* 1527
BERKO - Heaters - MARLEY ENGINEERED PRODUCTS; *pg.* 1074, *pg.* 1612
BERKSHIRE - Furniture - HAWORTH, INC.; *pg.* 402, *pg.* 891
BERKSHIRE INTIMATES - Lingerie; Panties - MAYER/BERKSHIRE CORPORATION; *pg.* 29, *pg.* 1129
BERKSHIRE PLACE - Hotel - OMNI HOTELS & RESORTS; *pg.* 1107, *pg.* 1685
BERLIN - Textiles - BERNHARDT DESIGN; *pg.* 918, *pg.* 1381
BERLIN - Furniture - HAWORTH, INC.; *pg.* 402, *pg.* 891
BERLIN CITIZEN - Weekly Newspaper - THE RECORD-JOURNAL PUBLISHING COMPANY; *pg.* 1680, *pg.* 354
BERLITZ TOTAL IMMERSION - Intensive Language Training - BERLITZ INTERNATIONAL, INC.; *pg.* 598, *pg.* 1110
BERLO - Footwear - K-SWISS; *pg.* 1837, *pg.* 306
BERLO L - Footwear - K-SWISS; *pg.* 1837, *pg.* 306
BERMUDA - Food Product - A. DUDA & SONS INC.; *pg.* 835, *pg.* 457
BERMUDA - Furniture - ETHAN ALLEN INTERIORS INC.; *pg.* 924, *pg.* 343
BERMUDA - Commercial Lighting - SWIVELIER CO., INC.; *pg.* 1307, *pg.* 1142
BERMUDA LITE - Short Pant - CORTLAND LINE COMPANY; *pg.* 1831, *pg.* 1155
BERMUDA LITE MESH - Short Pant - CORTLAND LINE COMPANY; *pg.* 1831, *pg.* 1155
BERNADINE - Lamp - ASHLEY FURNITURE INDUSTRIES, INC.; *pg.* 914, *pg.* 1852
BERNARDI - Food Product - WINDSOR QUALITY FOOD CO., LTD.; *pg.* 910, *pg.* 1717
BERNATELLOS - Food Product - BERNATELLO'S PIZZA INC.; *pg.* 840, *pg.* 928
BERNETTE 55 - Sewing Machines - BERNINA OF AMERICA INC.; *pg.* 51, *pg.* 554
BERNETTE 80E - Sewing Machines - BERNINA OF AMERICA INC.; *pg.* 51, *pg.* 554
BERNETTE 90E - Sewing Machines - BERNINA OF AMERICA INC.; *pg.* 51, *pg.* 554
BERNHARDT - JUBILEE - Fabric - NEMSCHOFF, INC.; *pg.* 936, *pg.* 1890
BERNIEOS - Food Product - ANNIE'S INC.; *pg.* 1760, *pg.* 45
BERNINA 1008 - Mechanical Machines - BERNINA OF AMERICA INC.; *pg.* 51, *pg.* 554
BERNSTEIN'S - Salad Dressing - PINNACLE FOODS GROUP LLC; *pg.* 889, *pg.* 1104
BERNZOMATIC - Propane Torches - NEWELL RUBBERMAID INC.; *pg.* 1128, *pg.* 515
BERRI-MAGIC - Container Grown Plant - MONROVIA GROWERS; *pg.* 1797, *pg.* 44
BERRIE - Footwear - STEVEN MADDEN, LTD.; *pg.* 1819, *pg.* 1176
BERRIES - Decorative Fragrance - AROMATIQUE INC.; *pg.* 499, *pg.* 32
BERRIES JUBILEE - Container Grown Plant - MONROVIA GROWERS; *pg.* 1797, *pg.* 44
BERRINGER - Furniture - ASHLEY FURNITURE INDUSTRIES, INC.; *pg.* 914, *pg.* 1852
BERRY BERRY KIX - Cereal - GENERAL MILLS, INC.; *pg.* 828, *pg.* 933
BERRY BEST - Fruit Arrangements - EDIBLE ARRANGEMENTS INTERNATIONAL, INC.; *pg.* 1768, *pg.* 382
BERRY BURST CHEERIOS - Cereal - GENERAL MILLS, INC.; *pg.* 828, *pg.* 933
BERRY CHOCLATE BOUQUET - Fruit Arrangements - EDIBLE ARRANGEMENTS INTERNATIONAL, INC.; *pg.* 1768, *pg.* 382
BERRY COLOSSAL CRUNCH - Bag Cereal - POST CONSUMER BRANDS; *pg.* 833, *pg.* 927
BERRY DELIGHTS - Confections - LIBERTY ORCHARDS CO., INC.; *pg.* 1857, *pg.* 1819
BERRY FULFILLING - Low Calorie Fruit Drink - JAMBA, INC.; *pg.* 1024, *pg.* 84
BERRY LIME SUBLIME - Smoothie - JAMBA, INC.; *pg.* 1024, *pg.* 84
BERRY OPTIMIZER - Advertising Services - AT&T SOUTHEAST; *pg.* 1868, *pg.* 489
BERRY TOPPER - Fruit Smoothie With Granola - JAMBA, INC.; *pg.* 1024, *pg.* 84
BERRYDOPHILUS - Dietary Supplement - NOW HEALTH GROUP, INC.; *pg.* 1576, *pg.* 557
BERRYPRO - Cellular Phone - AT&T SOUTHEAST; *pg.* 1868, *pg.* 489
BERRYQUEST - Cellular Phone - AT&T SOUTHEAST; *pg.* 1868, *pg.* 489
BERTAN HIGH VOLTAGE - High Voltage Power Supplies - DGT HOLDINGS; *pg.* 634, *pg.* 1223
BERTOLINIS AUTHENTIC TRATTORIAS - Italian Restaurants - MORTON'S RESTAURANT GROUP, INC.; *pg.* 1741, *pg.* 583
BERTOLLI - Pasta - MIZKAN AMERICAS, INC.; *pg.* 877, *pg.* 634
BERTOLLI'S - Frozen Meals - CONAGRA FOODS, INC.; *pg.* 826, *pg.* 1014
BERWICK - Furniture - ETHAN ALLEN INTERIORS INC.; *pg.* 924, *pg.* 343
BES - Product & Technology Development Center - GE WATER & PROCESS TECHNOLOGIES; *pg.* 1339, *pg.* 1588
BES 300 - Bin Evacuation System - GRACO, INC.; *pg.* 1342, *pg.* 935
BESCO - Genuine Besser Replacement Parts - BESSER COMPANY; *pg.* 1317, *pg.* 865
BESCOPAC - Block Machine - BESSER COMPANY; *pg.* 1317, *pg.* 865
BESIDE - Fabric - NEMSCHOFF, INC.; *pg.* 936, *pg.* 1890
BESPOKE STRIPE - Fabric - NEMSCHOFF, INC.; *pg.* 936, *pg.* 1890
BESSER - Concrete Product Equipment - BESSER COMPANY; *pg.* 1317, *pg.* 865
BESSIE - Lamp - ASHLEY FURNITURE INDUSTRIES, INC.; *pg.* 914, *pg.* 1852
BESSIE - Buckwheat Food Product - THE BIRKETT MILLS; *pg.* 826, *pg.* 1321
BEST - Clock - BROWN & BIGELOW, INC.; *pg.* 1624, *pg.* 959
BEST - Security Systems - STANLEY BLACK & DECKER, INC.; *pg.* 1063, *pg.* 358
BEST - Software - SYNOPSYS, INC.; *pg.* 480, *pg.* 162
BEST AMERICAN SERIES - Fiction - HOUGHTON MIFFLIN HARCOURT PUBLISHING COMPANY; *pg.* 1651, *pg.* 796
BEST AMERICAN SHORT STORIES - Fiction - HOUGHTON MIFFLIN HARCOURT PUBLISHING COMPANY; *pg.* 1651, *pg.* 796
BEST BCAA - Branched Chain Aminos - BPI SPORTS, LLC; *pg.* 842, *pg.* 430
BEST BOOKS FOR CHILDREN - Selection Guide to Children's Recreational & Curriculum-Based Reading - R.R. BOWKER LLC; *pg.* 1682, *pg.* 1095
BEST BOSS BOUQUET - Floral Bouquet - FTD GROUP, INC.; *pg.* 1795, *pg.* 608
BEST BRAND - Fertilizers - J.R. SIMPLOT COMPANY, AGRI BUSINESS; *pg.* 1796, *pg.* 547
THE BEST BUSINESS BANK IN TEXAS - Slogan - TEXAS CAPITAL BANCSHARES, INC.; *pg.* 809, *pg.* 1737
BEST BUSINESS WORLDWIDE - Hotel - BEST WESTERN INTERNATIONAL, INC.; *pg.* 1081, *pg.* 15
BEST BUY MOBILE - Mobile - BEST BUY CO., INC.; *pg.* 1761, *pg.* 954
BEST BY BROAN - Range Hoods - BROAN-NUTONE LLC; *pg.* 1069, *pg.* 1860
BEST BY FRUIT OF THE LOOM - Apparel for Imprinting - FRUIT OF THE LOOM, INC.; *pg.* 41, *pg.* 725
BEST CELLARS - Food Stores - THE GREAT ATLANTIC & PACIFIC TEA COMPANY, INC.; *pg.* 1021, *pg.* 1086
BEST CHINA - Chinaware - THE HOMER LAUGHLIN CHINA COMPANY; *pg.* 1125, *pg.* 1850
THE BEST CONNECTION IN THE BUSINESS - Tagline - GENERAL DATACOMM INDUSTRIES, INC.; *pg.* 400, *pg.* 357
BEST CREATINE - Strength Enhancer - BPI SPORTS, LLC; *pg.* 842, *pg.* 430
BEST CUTS - Hair Salon - REGIS CORPORATION; *pg.* 521, *pg.* 941
THE BEST EXPERIENCE COMPANY - Tagline - SPRINGS WINDOW FASHIONS LLC; *pg.* 943, *pg.* 1872
THE BEST GAME IN TOWN - Slogan - PENN NATIONAL GAMING, INC.; *pg.* 574, *pg.* 1595
BEST GARLIC SUPPLEMENTS - Healthcare Product - SWANSON HEALTH PRODUCTS INC.; *pg.* 1600, *pg.* 1397
BEST IN BUSINESS INTELLIGENCE - Slogan - MICROSTRATEGY, INC.; *pg.* 1266, *pg.* 1809
BEST IN GLASS - Cleaner - METHOD PRODUCTS INC.; *pg.* 332, *pg.* 223
BEST IN THE GAME - Basketball Backboards - LIFETIME PRODUCTS INC.; *pg.* 933, *pg.* 1751
THE BEST IN WORLD CINEMA - Tagline - KINO INTERNATIONAL CORP.; *pg.* 294, *pg.* 1249
THE BEST JUST KEEP GETTING BETTER - Slogan - RE/MAX INTERNATIONAL, INC.; *pg.* 1109, *pg.* 322
BEST LIFE - Weight Management Products - BOULDER BRANDS, INC.; *pg.* 1016, *pg.* 310
THE BEST ME I CAN BE - Educational Materials - SCHOLASTIC INC.; *pg.* 1683, *pg.* 1288
THE BEST MOVE FOR YOUR LIFE - Assisted Living Services - SUNRISE SENIOR LIVING, INC.; *pg.* 1599, *pg.* 1795

BEST OF 7'S - Instant Lottery Game - NEW YORK STATE LOTTERY; *pg.* 1001, *pg.* 1340
THE BEST OF EVERYTHING - Slogan - DOMINION HOMES, INC.; *pg.* 79, *pg.* 1449
BEST PIE IN AMERICA - Slogan - AMERICAN BLUE RIBBON HOLDINGS; *pg.* 1714, *pg.* 1648
THE BEST PIE IN AMERICA - Tagline - BAKERS SQUARE; *pg.* 1715, *pg.* 316
THE BEST POSTURE IS THE NEXT POSTURE - Slogan - HAWORTH, INC.; *pg.* 402, *pg.* 891
BEST PROTEIN - Muscle Mass Enhancement - BPI SPORTS, LLC; *pg.* 842, *pg.* 430
BEST RATINGS - Insurance Information - A.M. BEST COMPANY; *pg.* 1614, *pg.* 1101
BEST REQUESTS - Hotel & Motel - BEST WESTERN INTERNATIONAL, INC.; *pg.* 1081, *pg.* 15
THE BEST SECURITY IN AN UNSECURED WORLD - Slogan - WEBROOT SOFTWARE, INC.; *pg.* 1289, *pg.* 313
THE BEST THINGS IN LIFE - Game - WMS INDUSTRIES INC.; *pg.* 593, *pg.* 666
THE BEST WAY TO PAY FOR EVERYTHING THAT MATTERS - Slogan - MASTERCARD INCORPORATED; *pg.* 779, *pg.* 1325
THE BEST WAY TO TEST - Slogan - ALERE INC.; *pg.* 1488, *pg.* 849
THE BEST WEATHER ON THE WEB - Slogan - ACCUWEATHER, INC.; *pg.* 268, *pg.* 1587
BEST WEIGHT-CONTROL FORMULAS - Healthcare Product - SWANSON HEALTH PRODUCTS INC.; *pg.* 1600, *pg.* 1397
BEST WESTERN BEST RATES - Hotel & Motel - BEST WESTERN INTERNATIONAL, INC.; *pg.* 1081, *pg.* 15
BEST WESTERN PREMIER - Hotel - BEST WESTERN INTERNATIONAL, INC.; *pg.* 1081, *pg.* 15
BEST WESTERN TRAVEL CARD - Issuing Stored Value Cards - BEST WESTERN INTERNATIONAL, INC.; *pg.* 1081, *pg.* 15
BEST WISHES - Greeting Cards - LEANIN' TREE, INC.; *pg.* 1658, *pg.* 311
BESTCARRIERS.COM - Transportation System - BESTTRANSPORT, INC.; *pg.* 1231, *pg.* 1482
BESTCHEQUE - Check Issuing Services - BEST WESTERN INTERNATIONAL, INC.; *pg.* 1081, *pg.* 15
BESTDAY - Insurance Information - A.M. BEST COMPANY; *pg.* 1614, *pg.* 1101
BESTER - Saturated Polyester - DOW CHEMICAL; *pg.* 1156, *pg.* 1563
BESTESP - Software - A.M. BEST COMPANY; *pg.* 1614, *pg.* 1101
BESTFORM - Intimate Apparel - V.F. CORPORATION; *pg.* 34, *pg.* 1376
BESTHEALTH - Confectionery Product - BESTSWEET INC.; *pg.* 1851, *pg.* 1383
BESTILE - Roof Cement - JOHNS MANVILLE CORPORATION; *pg.* 89, *pg.* 320
BESTLAC - Animal Nutrition Product - VITUSA CORP.; *pg.* 1482, *pg.* 1063
BESTLIFE - Food Products - NONNI'S FOOD COMPANY INC.; *pg.* 886, *pg.* 1490
BESTLINK - Information Service - A.M. BEST COMPANY; *pg.* 1614, *pg.* 1101
BESTMARK - Service - A.M. BEST COMPANY; *pg.* 1614, *pg.* 1101
BESTOBELL - Steam Trap - RICHARDS INDUSTRIES VALVE GROUP; *pg.* 107, *pg.* 1425
BESTOBELL STEAM TRAPS - Steam Traps & Related Products - RICHARDS INDUSTRIES VALVE GROUP; *pg.* 107, *pg.* 1425
BEST'S REVIEW - Monthly Magazine - A.M. BEST COMPANY; *pg.* 1614, *pg.* 1101
BESTSHIPPERS.COM - Transportation System - BESTTRANSPORT, INC.; *pg.* 1231, *pg.* 1482
BESTSHORING DELIVERS BESTSOLUTION - Slogan - NETSOL TECHNOLOGIES, INC.; *pg.* 1270, *pg.* 56
BESTT LIEBCO - Paints & Coatings - THE SHERWIN-WILLIAMS COMPANY; *pg.* 1447, *pg.* 1435
BESTTRANSPORT.COM - Transportation System - BESTTRANSPORT, INC.; *pg.* 1231, *pg.* 1482
BESTWATER - Water Purification System - SHAKLEE CORPORATION; *pg.* 1593, *pg.* 184
BESTWAY - Furniture & Home Appliance - BESTWAY, INC.; *pg.* 52, *pg.* 1676
BESTWEEK - Insurance Information - A.M. BEST COMPANY; *pg.* 1614, *pg.* 1101
BESTWESTERN.COM - Website - BEST WESTERN INTERNATIONAL, INC.; *pg.* 1081, *pg.* 15
BESTWIRE - News Service - A.M. BEST COMPANY; *pg.* 1614, *pg.* 1101
BET - Black Entertainment Television - BET HOLDINGS LLC; *pg.* 271, *pg.* 396
BET - Metal Fabricated Enclosures - CHANNELL COMMERCIAL CORP.; *pg.* 1870, *pg.* 291
BET J - Adult Programming - BET HOLDINGS LLC; *pg.* 271, *pg.* 396
BET ON THE ROUGE - Games - PENN NATIONAL GAMING, INC.; *pg.* 574, *pg.* 1595
BET THE FARM - Game - WMS INDUSTRIES INC.; *pg.* 593, *pg.* 666
BETA - Fabric - NEMSCHOFF, INC.; *pg.* 936, *pg.* 1890
BETA - Financial Publications - THOMSON REUTERS CORPORATION; *pg.* 1693, *pg.* 1944
BETA 57 - Microphones - SHURE INCORPORATED; *pg.* 672, *pg.* 638
BETA 58 - Microphones - SHURE INCORPORATED; *pg.* 672, *pg.* 638
BETA 98 - Clip-On Microphone - SHURE INCORPORATED; *pg.* 672, *pg.* 638
BETA C - Wire - CARPENTER TECHNOLOGY CORPORATION; *pg.* 73, *pg.* 1584
BETA II - Helicopter - ROBINSON HELICOPTER COMPANY; *pg.* 234, *pg.* 295
BETA-PRO - Antioxidant Nutritional Supplement - NATURAL ORGANICS, INC.; *pg.* 1571, *pg.* 1181
BETA SERIES - Vocal Microphone - SHURE INCORPORATED; *pg.* 672, *pg.* 638
BETA STAR - Antibiotic Test Kit - CHR. HANSEN; *pg.* 847, *pg.* 1873
BETA YAM 900 - Health & Beauty Product - DIXIE HEALTH, INC.; *pg.* 1524, *pg.* 535
BETACLEAN - Industrial Cleaners - THE DOW CHEMICAL COMPANY; *pg.* 1157, *pg.* 898
BETADAMP - Vibration Damping Systems - THE DOW CHEMICAL COMPANY; *pg.* 1157, *pg.* 898
BETAFOAM - Polyols and Isocyanates - THE DOW CHEMICAL COMPANY; *pg.* 1157, *pg.* 898
BETAGUARD - Sealant - THE DOW CHEMICAL COMPANY; *pg.* 1157, *pg.* 898
BETAGUN - Applicator - THE DOW CHEMICAL COMPANY; *pg.* 1157, *pg.* 898
BETAPACE - Pharmaceutical Product - IMPAX LABORATORIES, INC.; *pg.* 1544, *pg.* 101
BETAPRIME - Primer - THE DOW CHEMICAL COMPANY; *pg.* 1157, *pg.* 898
BETASET - Phenolic Foundry Resins - HEXION; *pg.* 1166, *pg.* 1440
BETASTAR - Food Safety Product - NEOGEN CORPORATION; *pg.* 883, *pg.* 896
BETCHA CAN'T EAT JUST ONE! - Tag Line - FRITO-LAY NORTH AMERICA, INC.; *pg.* 1853, *pg.* 1730
BETH - Shoe - AEROGROUP INTERNATIONAL, INC.; *pg.* 1803, *pg.* 1055
BETH - Footwear - PHOENIX FOOTWEAR GROUP, INC.; *pg.* 1815, *pg.* 60
BETHA GENE - Clinical Diagnostic Product - BIO-RAD LABORATORIES, INC.; *pg.* 1504, *pg.* 101
BETHANY - Ceiling Fan - WESTINGHOUSE LIGHTING CORPORATION; *pg.* 687, *pg.* 1571
BETHEL WHITE - Granite - ROCK OF AGES CORPORATION; *pg.* 108, *pg.* 1766
BETHENNY - Food Products - CHEROKEE GLOBAL BRANDS; *pg.* 21, *pg.* 278
BETHESDA - Furniture - J. ROBERT SCOTT INC.; *pg.* 930, *pg.* 105
BETHLEHEM - Scarf - HERITAGE LACE INC.; *pg.* 694, *pg.* 711
BETHLEHEM - Toy Train - LIONEL LLC; *pg.* 961, *pg.* 875
BETSY - Fabric - NEMSCHOFF, INC.; *pg.* 936, *pg.* 1890
BETSY - Footwear - PHOENIX FOOTWEAR GROUP, INC.; *pg.* 1815, *pg.* 60
BETTA PREMIUM FOOD - Fish Food - THE HARTZ MOUNTAIN CORP.; *pg.* 1476, *pg.* 1120
BETTER ALTERNATIVE - Towel Dispenser - GEORGIA-PACIFIC LLC; *pg.* 1458, *pg.* 507
BETTER-BE-READY BLAZIN - Sauces - BUFFALO WILD WINGS, INC.; *pg.* 1718, *pg.* 931
BETTER BENEFITS AT WORK - Tag Line - UNUM GROUP; *pg.* 1222, *pg.* 1629
BETTER BREAD BETTER SUBS - Slogan - COUSINS SUBMARINES, INC.; *pg.* 1017, *pg.* 1870
BETTER BUILDING BEGINS HERE - Tagline - LOUISIANA-PACIFIC CORPORATION; *pg.* 94, *pg.* 1652
BETTER BY EVERY MEASURE - Tag Line - TRANSCAT, INC.; *pg.* 682, *pg.* 1337
BETTER CHOICE - Software - IDEXX LABORATORIES, INC.; *pg.* 1543, *pg.* 753
BETTER CONNECTIONS - Wireless Communication System - AT&T SOUTHEAST; *pg.* 1868, *pg.* 489
BETTER DATA. BETTER LEARNING - Tag Line - RENAISSANCE LEARNING, INC.; *pg.* 607, *pg.* 1899
BETTER GRO - Fertilizer - SUN BULB COMPANY, INC.; *pg.* 1800, *pg.* 409
BETTER HOMES - Magazine - MEREDITH CORPORATION; *pg.* 1663, *pg.* 705
BETTER HOMES AND GARDENS - Magazine - MEREDITH CORPORATION; *pg.* 1663, *pg.* 705
BETTER INGREDIENTS.BETTER PIZZA - Tagline - PAPA JOHN'S INTERNATIONAL, INC.; *pg.* 1743, *pg.* 737
BETTER MEATS. BETTER MEALS. BETTER MENU - Tagline - ROSE PACKING COMPANY; *pg.* 892, *pg.* 556
BETTER PANT - Undergarment - MEDLINE INDUSTRIES, INC.; *pg.* 1562, *pg.* 635
BETTER PET NUTRITION - Tagline - PET VALU CANADA, INC.; *pg.* 1480, *pg.* 1924
THE BETTER PIZZA PEOPLE - Slogan - NOBLE ROMAN'S, INC.; *pg.* 1741, *pg.* 689
BETTER RESULTS MEAN BETTER MEDICINE - Slogan - ALERE INC.; *pg.* 1488, *pg.* 849
THE BETTER ROOF - Building Product - CENTRIA, INC.; *pg.* 74, *pg.* 1554
BETTER SLEEP THROUGH SCIENCE - Slogan - SIMMONS COMPANY; *pg.* 943, *pg.* 520
BETTER TASTE. BETTER NUTRITION. BETTER EGGS - Tagline - EGGLAND'S BEST, INC.; *pg.* 854, *pg.* 1542
BETTER THAN BARE - Hosiery & Related Apparel - MAYER/BERKSHIRE CORPORATION; *pg.* 29, *pg.* 1129
BETTER THAN THE BEST YOU'VE EVER TASTED - Slogan - AUNTIE ANNE'S INC.; *pg.* 1715, *pg.* 1546
BETTER THERMAL SOLUTIONS...FASTER - Tag Line - WATLOW ELECTRIC MANUFACTURING COMPANY; *pg.* 1078, *pg.* 1004
BETTER VALUE THROUGH BETTER DESIGN - Apparel - GILDAN ACTIVEWEAR INC.; *pg.* 1835, *pg.* 1955
BETTER WAYS TO GET BETTER - Slogan - MATRIXX INITIATIVES, INC.; *pg.* 1559, *pg.* 23
BETTER-WEIGH - Belt Feeder - METALFAB, INC.; *pg.* 1360, *pg.* 1127
BETTER WORLD HOT COCOA - Coffee Service - KEURIG GREEN MOUNTAIN, INC.; *pg.* 868, *pg.* 1768
BETTER YET - Carpet - BEAULIEU GROUP, LLC; *pg.* 917, *pg.* 529
BETTERBOOK - Binding System - NORDSON CORPORATION; *pg.* 1365, *pg.* 1480
BETTERCREME - Icing & Filling - RICH PRODUCTS CORPORATION; *pg.* 892, *pg.* 1150
BETTER'N EGGS - Egg Substitute - MICHAEL FOODS, INC.; *pg.* 877, *pg.* 949
BETTERSTATE - Software - WIND RIVER SYSTEMS, INC.; *pg.* 493, *pg.* 38
BETTI THE YETTI - Video Game - INTERNATIONAL GAME TECHNOLOGY; *pg.* 957, *pg.* 1024
BETTOR BONUS CHANCE - Video Game - INTERNATIONAL GAME TECHNOLOGY; *pg.* 957, *pg.* 1024
BETTOR CHANCE - Video Game - INTERNATIONAL GAME TECHNOLOGY; *pg.* 957, *pg.* 1024
BETTOR CHANCE BONUS - Video Game - INTERNATIONAL GAME TECHNOLOGY; *pg.* 957, *pg.* 1024
BETTOR CHANCE FEATURE - Video Game - INTERNATIONAL GAME TECHNOLOGY; *pg.* 957, *pg.* 1024
BETTOR CHANCE PAY - Video Game - INTERNATIONAL GAME TECHNOLOGY; *pg.* 957, *pg.* 1024
BETTOR CHANCE SYMBOL - Video Game - INTERNATIONAL GAME TECHNOLOGY; *pg.* 957, *pg.* 1024
BETTOR CHANCE WAY - Video Game - INTERNATIONAL GAME TECHNOLOGY; *pg.* 957, *pg.* 1024
BETTOR CHANCE WIN - Video Game - INTERNATIONAL GAME TECHNOLOGY; *pg.* 957, *pg.* 1024
BETTOR PAY CHANCE - Video Game - INTERNATIONAL GAME TECHNOLOGY; *pg.* 957, *pg.* 1024
BETTOR SYMBOL CHANCE - Video Game - INTERNATIONAL GAME TECHNOLOGY; *pg.* 957, *pg.* 1024
BETTOR WAY CHANCE - Video Game - INTERNATIONAL GAME TECHNOLOGY; *pg.* 957, *pg.* 1024

BETTOR WIN CHANCE - Video Game - INTERNATIONAL GAME TECHNOLOGY; *pg.* 957, *pg.* 1024
BETT'S - Vehicle Safety System - GROTE INDUSTRIES, INC.; *pg.* 206, *pg.* 693
BETTY - Toy - THE OHIO ART COMPANY, INC.; *pg.* 965, *pg.* 1406
BETTY BOOP - Lottery Game - D.C. LOTTERY & CHARITABLE GAMES CONTROL BOARD; *pg.* 991, *pg.* 398
BETTY BOOP - Lottery Game - MICHIGAN STATE LOTTERY BUREAU; *pg.* 999, *pg.* 895
BETTY BOOP'S ROARING 20'S - Game - MULTIMEDIA GAMES INC.; *pg.* 442, *pg.* 1664
BETTY CROCKER - Food Product - GENERAL MILLS, INC.; *pg.* 828, *pg.* 933
BETTY CROCKER KITCHENS - Homemade Kitchen - BETTY CROCKER PRODUCTS; *pg.* 840, *pg.* 931
BETTY LOU - Furniture - HOOKER FURNITURE CORPORATION; *pg.* 928, *pg.* 1788
BETTY SPAGHETTY - Fashion & Play Doll - THE OHIO ART COMPANY, INC.; *pg.* 965, *pg.* 1406
BETTYS ATTIC - Mail Order Catalog - JOHNSON SMITH COMPANY; *pg.* 1774, *pg.* 414
BETULA - Fabric - MOMENTUM TEXTILES INC.; *pg.* 697, *pg.* 114
BETWEEN COATS - Abrasive - 3M COMPANY; *pg.* 1142, *pg.* 956
BETWEEN THE ACTS - Little Cigars - ALTADIS USA, INC.; *pg.* 1893, *pg.* 423
BETWEEN THE LINES - Slogan - DEXCOM INC; *pg.* 1524, *pg.* 202
BETWIXT - Fabric - NEMSCHOFF, INC.; *pg.* 936, *pg.* 1890
BETZDEARBORN KLEEN - Cleaners for Metals - GE WATER & PROCESS TECHNOLOGIES; *pg.* 1339, *pg.* 1588
BEV-L-EDGE - Laboratory Product - PROPPER MANUFACTURING COMPANY, INC.; *pg.* 1586, *pg.* 1175
BEVAN - Footwear - STEVEN MADDEN, LTD.; *pg.* 1819, *pg.* 1176
BEVELED ELEGANCE - Door Glass - ODL INCORPORATED; *pg.* 101, *pg.* 914
BEVELLINE - Doors - THERMA-TRU CORP.; *pg.* 115, *pg.* 1462
BEVERAGE WRENCH - Can Opener - BROWN & BIGELOW, INC.; *pg.* 1624, *pg.* 959
BEVERLY - Beverages - THE COCA-COLA COMPANY; *pg.* 240, *pg.* 493
THE BEVERLY HILLBILLIES - Game - INTERNATIONAL GAME TECHNOLOGY; *pg.* 957, *pg.* 1024
BEVERLY HILLS - Fabric - NEMSCHOFF, INC.; *pg.* 936, *pg.* 1890
BEWARE - Paper Product - BOISE CASCADE HOLDINGS, L.L.C.; *pg.* 1453, *pg.* 546
BEXLEY - Furniture - FLEXSTEEL INDUSTRIES, INC.; *pg.* 925, *pg.* 707
BEXLEY - Furniture - JOFCO INC.; *pg.* 931, *pg.* 691
BEXPRINT - Software - USA TECHNOLOGIES, INC.; *pg.* 815, *pg.* 1550
BEYBLADE - Game - HASBRO, INC.; *pg.* 954, *pg.* 1603
BEYOND AVAILABILITY - Slogan - VERIZON TERREMARK; *pg.* 685, *pg.* 447
BEYOND BI - Slogan - SAS INSTITUTE INC.; *pg.* 466, *pg.* 1361
BEYOND CHOCOLATE - Ice Cream Sundaes - FRIENDLY ICE CREAM, LLC; *pg.* 1853, *pg.* 859
BEYOND COLOR - Beauty Product - AVON PRODUCTS, INC.; *pg.* 500, *pg.* 1198
BEYOND COMPARISON - Slogan - 3M; *pg.* 339, *pg.* 179
BEYOND CONTACTS - Software - DATAVIZ, INC.; *pg.* 383, *pg.* 356
BEYOND GOURMET - Coffee - A.V. OLSSON TRADING CO. INC.; *pg.* 838, *pg.* 372
BEYOND OMEGA-3 - Health Supplement - GARDEN OF LIFE, INC.; *pg.* 1532, *pg.* 478
BEYOND THE LIMITS OF THE HUMAN HAND - Slogan - INTUITIVE SURGICAL, INC.; *pg.* 1546, *pg.* 286
BEYOND-THE-RAILS - Comparator - MAXIM INTEGRATED PRODUCTS, INC.; *pg.* 653, *pg.* 247
BEYOND WOOD - Hardwood Blinds-New Surfacing Technique, Warp-Free - HUNTER DOUGLAS, INC.; *pg.* 928, *pg.* 1320
B.F. PERKINS - Engraving - STANDEX INTERNATIONAL CORPORATION; *pg.* 60, *pg.* 1039
BFF - Glove - KOMBI, LTD.; *pg.* 1838, *pg.* 1766
BFGOODRICH - Tires - MICHELIN NORTH AMERICA INC.; *pg.* 1886, *pg.* 1618
B.G. - Twist Tobaccos - AMERICAN SNUFF COMPANY; *pg.* 1893, *pg.* 1641
BG 44K POWER ENHANCER - Engine Cleaner - BG PRODUCTS, INC.; *pg.* 200, *pg.* 722
BG BAR - Supplement & Food Product - NEW EARTH LIFE SCIENCES, INC.; *pg.* 1573, *pg.* 1499
BG BIG DAWG - Power Flush & Fluid Exchange System - BG PRODUCTS, INC.; *pg.* 200, *pg.* 722
BG CF5 - Gasoline Supplement - BG PRODUCTS, INC.; *pg.* 200, *pg.* 722
BG FRIGI-CHARGE - Auto Air Conditioning System Product - BG PRODUCTS, INC.; *pg.* 200, *pg.* 722
BG FRIGI-CLEAN - Auto Air Conditioning Evaporator Cleaner - BG PRODUCTS, INC.; *pg.* 200, *pg.* 722
BG FRIGI-FLUSH - Auto Air Conditioning System Cleaning Fluid - BG PRODUCTS, INC.; *pg.* 200, *pg.* 722
BG FRIGI-FRESH - Auto Air Conditioning System Deodorizer - BG PRODUCTS, INC.; *pg.* 200, *pg.* 722
BG INJECT-A-FLUSH - Fuel System Cleaning Apparatus - BG PRODUCTS, INC.; *pg.* 200, *pg.* 722
BG ISC INDUCTION SYSTEM CLEANER - Auto Fuel Injectors Cleaner - BG PRODUCTS, INC.; *pg.* 200, *pg.* 722
BG MGC - Gear Oil Supplement - BG PRODUCTS, INC.; *pg.* 200, *pg.* 722
BG MOA - Engine Oil Additive - BG PRODUCTS, INC.; *pg.* 200, *pg.* 722
BG SERIES - Microphones - SHURE INCORPORATED; *pg.* 672, *pg.* 638
BG SHEAR POWER - Engine Oil Additive - BG PRODUCTS, INC.; *pg.* 200, *pg.* 722
BG SYNCRO SHIFT - Gear Lubricant - BG PRODUCTS, INC.; *pg.* 200, *pg.* 722
BG UNIVERSAL FRIGI-QUIET - Compressor Lubricant - BG PRODUCTS, INC.; *pg.* 200, *pg.* 722
BG UNIVERSAL SUPER COOL - Coolant Additive - BG PRODUCTS, INC.; *pg.* 200, *pg.* 722
BGA PROTEIN - Hair & Skin Product - AUBREY ORGANICS INC.; *pg.* 499, *pg.* 470
BGE - Public Utility Service - CONSTELLATION ENERGY RESOURCES, LLC; *pg.* 1938, *pg.* 756
BGR - Professional Clipper for Barbering - ANDIS COMPANY; *pg.* 498, *pg.* 1895
BHA - Editor Software - SCHLUMBERGER LIMITED; *pg.* 801, *pg.* 1714
BHA TEX - Fabric Filter - GE ENERGY; *pg.* 1338, *pg.* 506
BHOTSTUDHB - Footwear - STEVEN MADDEN, LTD.; *pg.* 1819, *pg.* 1176
BI-FLO - Fluid Handling System - GRACO, INC.; *pg.* 1342, *pg.* 935
BI-FLOW - Golf Equipment - ACUSHNET COMPANY; *pg.* 1824, *pg.* 818
BI-FUEL - Power Generator System - GENERAC POWER SYSTEMS INC.; *pg.* 1340, *pg.* 1898
BI-LITE - Pigment - BASF CATALYSTS LLC; *pg.* 1148, *pg.* 1074
BI-METAL UNIQUE - Band Saw Blades - THE L.S. STARRETT COMPANY; *pg.* 1421, *pg.* 783
BI-METRIC HIP SYSTEM - Hip Stem - ZIMMER BIOMET HOLDINGS, INC.; *pg.* 1611, *pg.* 699
BI-O-KLEEN - Cleaning Product - BI-O-KLEEN INDUSTRIES, INC.; *pg.* 326, *pg.* 1845
BI-O.K. - Sterilization Product - PROPPER MANUFACTURING COMPANY, INC.; *pg.* 1586, *pg.* 1175
BI-SERT - Inserts - YARDLEY PRODUCTS CORPORATION; *pg.* 1391, *pg.* 1596
BI-STABLE BRAKE - Pulse Brake - ELECTROID CO; *pg.* 1333, *pg.* 1123
BI TEC 77H - Chemical Product - BIRKO CORPORATION; *pg.* 1149, *pg.* 332
BIAC - Crystal Polymer Film - W.L. GORE & ASSOCIATES, INC.; *pg.* 122, *pg.* 388
BIANCA - Furniture - AMISCO INDUSTRIES LTD.; *pg.* 913, *pg.* 1958
BIANCA - Bath & Plumbing Product - JACUZZI BRANDS CORPORATION; *pg.* 554, *pg.* 65
BIANCHI - Security Product - BAE SYSTEMS PRODUCTS GROUP; *pg.* 359, *pg.* 432
BIANNA - Footwear - STEVEN MADDEN, LTD.; *pg.* 1819, *pg.* 1176
B.I.A.S - Built In Ankle Support - WEINBRENNER SHOE COMPANY, INC.; *pg.* 1822, *pg.* 1871
BIAS HOLLAND - Hat - WOODEN SHIPS OF HOBOKEN; *pg.* 35, *pg.* 1315
BIASILL - Sand - E.I. DU PONT DE NEMOURS & COMPANY; *pg.* 1159, *pg.* 390
BIAXIAL - Drill & Pick Resistant High Security Locks - MEDECO HIGH SECURITY LOCKS, INC.; *pg.* 1055, *pg.* 1806
BIAXIN - Tablet - ABBOTT LABORATORIES; *pg.* 1484, *pg.* 551
BIAXIN - Pharmaceutical Product - CUBIST PHARMACEUTICALS, INC.; *pg.* 1521, *pg.* 828
BIAXIN XL - Anti-Infective - ABBOTT LABORATORIES; *pg.* 1484, *pg.* 551
THE BIBLE STUDY HOUR - Radio Broadcast - ALLIANCE OF CONFESSING EVANGELICALS, INC.; *pg.* 126, *pg.* 1545
BIBLER - Outdoor Products - BLACK DIAMOND, INC.; *pg.* 1827, *pg.* 1756
BIBO - Beverages - THE COCA-COLA COMPANY; *pg.* 240, *pg.* 493
BIC - Pen - KEY INDUSTRIES, INC.; *pg.* 43, *pg.* 714
BICAP - Medical Equipment - CONMED CORPORATION; *pg.* 1517, *pg.* 1347
BICAP SUPERCONDUCTOR - Medical Equipment - CONMED CORPORATION; *pg.* 1517, *pg.* 1347
BICC - Tray Cables - GENERAL CABLE CORPORATION; *pg.* 83, *pg.* 729
BICE - Misses' Sportswear - KELLWOOD COMPANY; *pg.* 28, *pg.* 975
BICILLIN - Pharmaceutical Product - KING PHARMACEUTICALS, INC.; *pg.* 1553, *pg.* 1627
BICKEL'S - Snack Food Product - HANOVER FOODS CORPORATION; *pg.* 861, *pg.* 1535
BICK'S - Pickle - THE J.M. SMUCKER COMPANY; *pg.* 865, *pg.* 1468
BICK'S - Pickles & Condiments - SMUCKER FOODS OF CANADA CO.; *pg.* 896, *pg.* 1924
BICLAR - Pharmaceutical Products - ABBOTT LABORATORIES; *pg.* 1484, *pg.* 551
BICNU - Health Care Product - BRISTOL-MYERS SQUIBB COMPANY; *pg.* 1509, *pg.* 1206
BICOFIL - Meltblown Systems - NORDSON CORPORATION; *pg.* 1365, *pg.* 1480
BICOR - Medical Product - ST. JUDE MEDICAL, INC.; *pg.* 1596, *pg.* 963
BICYCLE - Playing Cards - THE UNITED STATES PLAYING CARD COMPANY; *pg.* 969, *pg.* 727
BICYCLING - Magazine - RODALE, INC.; *pg.* 1681, *pg.* 1530
BICYCLING.COM - Website - RODALE, INC.; *pg.* 1681, *pg.* 1530
BID-WELL - Concrete Paving - TEREX CORPORATION; *pg.* 1381, *pg.* 384
BIDDING FRENZY - Video Game - INTERNATIONAL GAME TECHNOLOGY; *pg.* 957, *pg.* 1024
BIDDING WILD - Video Game - INTERNATIONAL GAME TECHNOLOGY; *pg.* 957, *pg.* 1024
BIDI - Concrete Pipe Machinery - BESSER COMPANY; *pg.* 1317, *pg.* 865
BIDIRECTIONALL - Pig - T.D. WILLIAMSON, INC.; *pg.* 1380, *pg.* 1490
BIDS - Dispensing Closure - OWENS-ILLINOIS, INC.; *pg.* 1466, *pg.* 1470
BIEDERMEIER FLOOR - Lamp - J. ROBERT SCOTT INC.; *pg.* 930, *pg.* 105
BIENVILLE BAY BUFFET - Games - PENN NATIONAL GAMING, INC.; *pg.* 574, *pg.* 1595
BIER MARKT - Restaurants - PRIME RESTAURANTS INC.; *pg.* 1746, *pg.* 1947
BIFA-15 - Tube - EDEN FOODS INC.; *pg.* 1019, *pg.* 875
BIFIDOPHILUS FLORA FORCE - Health Care Product - NATURE'S SUNSHINE PRODUCTS, INC.; *pg.* 1571, *pg.* 1754
BIFIDUS - Supplement & Food Product - NEW EARTH LIFE SCIENCES, INC.; *pg.* 1573, *pg.* 1499
BIG 4 - 4-Digit Drawing - PENNSYLVANIA STATE LOTTERY; *pg.* 1003, *pg.* 1552
BIG 40 - Welding Generator - MILLER ELECTRIC MANUFACTURING CO.; *pg.* 1361, *pg.* 1852
BIG 5 SPORTING GOODS - Stores - BIG 5 SPORTING GOODS CORPORATION; *pg.* 1827, *pg.* 78
BIG 7 - Video Game - INTERNATIONAL GAME TECHNOLOGY; *pg.* 957, *pg.* 1024
BIG & TALL - Furniture - NEUTRAL POSTURE, INC.; *pg.* 939, *pg.* 1669
BIG&TALL - Apparel - RALPH LAUREN CORPORATION; *pg.* 46, *pg.* 1284
THE BIG APPLE - Marketing Program - NYC & COMPANY, INC.; *pg.* 1002, *pg.* 1274
BIG APPLE BAGELS - Restaurant - BAB, INC.; *pg.* 1715,

pg. 599
BIG APPLE RED - Nail Care Product - OPI PRODUCTS INC.; *pg.* 518, *pg.* 167
BIG AZ - Food Product - ADVANCEPIERRE FOODS, INC.; *pg.* 1714, *pg.* 1409
BIG BALLS OF CASH - Video Game - INTERNATIONAL GAME TECHNOLOGY; *pg.* 957, *pg.* 1024
BIG BAMBINO - Eighteen Inch Pizzas - STRAW HAT COOPERATIVE CORPORATION; *pg.* 1751, *pg.* 260
BIG BAND PIGGY BANKIN - Game - WMS INDUSTRIES INC.; *pg.* 593, *pg.* 666
BIG BANG - Automotive Reconditioning Product - MOC PRODUCTS COMPANY, INC.; *pg.* 332, *pg.* 174
BIG BANG - Game - WMS INDUSTRIES INC.; *pg.* 593, *pg.* 666
BIG BANG BUCKS - Lottery Game - D.C. LOTTERY & CHARITABLE GAMES CONTROL BOARD; *pg.* 991, *pg.* 398
BIG BANG BUCKS - Lottery Game - OHIO LOTTERY COMMISSION; *pg.* 1002, *pg.* 1433
BIG BEEFS - Hamburger Sandwich - FRIENDLY ICE CREAM, LLC; *pg.* 1853, *pg.* 859
BIG BEN - Puzzles - HASBRO, INC.; *pg.* 954, *pg.* 1603
BIG BENN - Fabric - NEMSCHOFF, INC.; *pg.* 936, *pg.* 1890
BIG BERTHA - Golf Product - CALLAWAY GOLF COMPANY; *pg.* 1829, *pg.* 58
BIG BERTHA - Dump Truck Vibrators - VIBCO INC.; *pg.* 1387, *pg.* 1611
BIG BERTHA TITANIUM DRIVER - Titanium Golf Driver - CALLAWAY GOLF COMPANY; *pg.* 1829, *pg.* 58
BIG BIG DOGS - Big-Sized Apparel - THE WALKING COMPANY HOLDINGS, INC.; *pg.* 50, *pg.* 263
BIG BIN - Grain Storage Tanks - BEHLEN MFG. CO.; *pg.* 701, *pg.* 1010
BIG BIRTHDAY BASH - Birthday Gifts - 1-800-FLOWERS.COM, INC.; *pg.* 1758, *pg.* 1151
BIG BITE - Hot Dog - 7-ELEVEN, INC.; *pg.* 1012, *pg.* 1672
BIG BLAST CAN - Household Product - WD-40 COMPANY; *pg.* 337, *pg.* 210
BIG BLAZIN' BUCKS - Lottery Game - KENTUCKY LOTTERY CORPORATION; *pg.* 996, *pg.* 735
BIG BLUE - Welding & Cutting Equip. - MILLER ELECTRIC MANUFACTURING CO.; *pg.* 1361, *pg.* 1852
BIG BLUE - Fire Proofing Pump - PUTZMEISTER AMERICA; *pg.* 1371, *pg.* 1896
BIG BLUE PE - Conduit - ELECTRON BEAM TECHNOLOGIES, INC.; *pg.* 1046, *pg.* 621
BIG BODY - Perm Rods - THE GILLETTE COMPANY; *pg.* 509, *pg.* 795
BIG BONES - Video Game - INTERNATIONAL GAME TECHNOLOGY; *pg.* 957, *pg.* 1024
BIG BOPPER - Ice Cream Sandwich - WELLS ENTERPRISES, INC.; *pg.* 909, *pg.* 709
BIG BOWL - Chinese & Thai Restaurant - LETTUCE ENTERTAIN YOU ENTERPRISES, INC.; *pg.* 1735, *pg.* 580
BIG BOWL CHINESE EXPRESS - Thai Restaurant - LETTUCE ENTERTAIN YOU ENTERPRISES, INC.; *pg.* 1735, *pg.* 580
BIG BOY - Sauce & Pies - FRISCH'S RESTAURANTS, INC.; *pg.* 1729, *pg.* 1413
BIG BREAKFAST - Breakfast Entree - MCDONALD'S CORPORATION; *pg.* 1737, *pg.* 645
BIG BREW - Coffee - 7-ELEVEN, INC.; *pg.* 1012, *pg.* 1672
BIG BROTHER - Software - DELL SOFTWARE; *pg.* 385, *pg.* 40
BIG BROWN TRUCK - Shipping Services - UNITED PARCEL SERVICE, INC.; *pg.* 1928, *pg.* 522
BIG BUFORD - Food Product - CHECKERS DRIVE-IN RESTAURANTS, INC.; *pg.* 1017, *pg.* 472
BIG BUTT - Handmade Cigar - ALTADIS USA, INC.; *pg.* 1893, *pg.* 423
BIG CASH BINGO - Game - MULTIMEDIA GAMES INC.; *pg.* 442, *pg.* 1664
BIG CATCH BONUS HUNTER - Game - INTERNATIONAL GAME TECHNOLOGY; *pg.* 420, *pg.* 1606
THE BIG CHEEZ - Cheddar Cheese Pop Corn - AMERICAN POP CORN COMPANY; *pg.* 825, *pg.* 712
BIG CHIEF - Footwear - LACROSSE FOOTWEAR, INC.; *pg.* 1811, *pg.* 1503
BIG CHILL - Convenience Stores - THE PANTRY, INC.; *pg.* 1029, *pg.* 1360
BIG CRUSH - Beverages - THE COCA-COLA COMPANY; *pg.* 240, *pg.* 493
BIG CUSHION - Mousepads - LEWTAN INDUSTRIES CORP.; *pg.* 1658, *pg.* 352
BIG DADDY - Bakery Product - SAPUTO, INC.; *pg.* 893, *pg.* 1956
BIG DADDY'S - Liquor Stores & Lounges - FLANIGAN'S ENTERPRISES, INC.; *pg.* 1963, *pg.* 425
THE BIG DANCE - Trademark (Div. I Basketball) - NATIONAL COLLEGIATE ATHLETIC ASSOCIATION; *pg.* 567, *pg.* 688
THE BIG DIG - Outdoor Shovel - REEVES INTERNATIONAL, INC.; *pg.* 966, *pg.* 1108
BIG DOG SPORTSWEAR - Athletic Apparel - THE WALKING COMPANY HOLDINGS, INC.; *pg.* 50, *pg.* 263
BIG DON - Oven-baked Subs - DONATOS PIZZERIA CORPORATION; *pg.* 1727, *pg.* 1439
BIG DOUBLE STRAWBERRY - Ice Cream Sandwich - WELLS ENTERPRISES, INC.; *pg.* 909, *pg.* 709
THE BIG DRIVE - Automotive Product - THE DAILY OAKLAND PRESS; *pg.* 1632, *pg.* 905
BIG EASY - Grill - W.C. BRADLEY CO.; *pg.* 62, *pg.* 528
BIG EATS BAKERY - Baked Goods - 7-ELEVEN, INC.; *pg.* 1012, *pg.* 1672
BIG EATS DELI - Sandwiches - 7-ELEVEN, INC.; *pg.* 1012, *pg.* 1672
BIG EATS DELUXE - Sandwiches - 7-ELEVEN, INC.; *pg.* 1012, *pg.* 1672
BIG ED - Flashlight - PELICAN PRODUCTS, INC.; *pg.* 1842, *pg.* 295
BIG ENOUGH FOR THE JOB, SMALL ENOUGH TO CARE - Tagline - GSC ENTERPRISES, INC.; *pg.* 1021, *pg.* 1746
BIG EVENT - Game - WMS INDUSTRIES INC.; *pg.* 593, *pg.* 666
BIG EYE - Electronic Control - GOLD MEDAL PRODUCTS CO.; *pg.* 55, *pg.* 1414
BIG FLYER - Trikes - RADIO FLYER INC.; *pg.* 966, *pg.* 588
BIG FOOT - Flooring Compounds - HENKEL CORPORATION; *pg.* 1049, *pg.* 369
BIG G CEREALS - Food Product - GENERAL MILLS, INC.; *pg.* 828, *pg.* 933
BIG GAME - Multi-State Lotto Game - NEW JERSEY STATE LOTTERY; *pg.* 1000, *pg.* 1126
BIG GREEN - Canister Deep Cleaner - BISSELL HOMECARE, INC.; *pg.* 52, *pg.* 887
BIG GULP - Fountain Soft Drink - 7-ELEVEN, INC.; *pg.* 1012, *pg.* 1672
BIG HAULER - Fluid Handling System - GRACO, INC.; *pg.* 1342, *pg.* 935
BIG HEAT - Heater - BROAN-NUTONE LLC; *pg.* 1069, *pg.* 1860
BIG HIT - Bicycle - SPECIALIZED BICYCLE COMPONENTS, INC.; *pg.* 1711, *pg.* 152
BIG HOOK - Dressing Stick - ALIMED, INC.; *pg.* 1490, *pg.* 816
BIG HUG BOUQUET - Floral Bouquet - FTD GROUP, INC.; *pg.* 1795, *pg.* 608
BIG HUNK - Chewy Nougat - ANNABELLE CANDY COMPANY, INC.; *pg.* 1850, *pg.* 100
BIG I - Virtual University - INDEPENDENT INSURANCE AGENTS & BROKERS OF AMERICA, INC.; *pg.* 144, *pg.* 1770
BIG I, LITTLE T - Manual - XEROX CORPORATION; *pg.* 494, *pg.* 365
THE BIG IDEA - Gift Shops - MUSEUM OF SCIENCE AND INDUSTRY; *pg.* 565, *pg.* 583
BIG IDEA CHAIR - Internet Services - YAHOO! INC.; *pg.* 1289, *pg.* 289
BIG-IP - Software - F5 NETWORKS, INC.; *pg.* 396, *pg.* 1835
BIG ISLAND - Eyewear - MAUI JIM, INC.; *pg.* 9, *pg.* 651
BIG JAMBOX - Wireless Speakers - ALIPHCOM, INC.; *pg.* 616, *pg.* 212
BIG JAMMER - Security & Law Enforcement Products - MACE SECURITY INTERNATIONAL, INC.; *pg.* 1172, *pg.* 1541
BIG JOHN - Submersible Sump Pumps - LITTLE GIANT PUMP COMPANY; *pg.* 1356, *pg.* 1486
THE BIG KAHUNA - Lottery Game - MICHIGAN STATE LOTTERY BUREAU; *pg.* 999, *pg.* 895
BIG KID - Baby Care Product - MUNCHKIN, INC.; *pg.* 964, *pg.* 300
BIG KID TRAINER - Toilet Trainer - GRACO CHILDREN'S PRODUCTS INC.; *pg.* 954, *pg.* 1531
BIG KMART - Discount Stores - KMART CORPORATION; *pg.* 1775, *pg.* 617
BIG LEAGUE CHEW - Gum - WM. WRIGLEY JR. COMPANY; *pg.* 1863, *pg.* 596
THE BIG LIST - Real Estate Product - THE DAILY OAKLAND PRESS; *pg.* 1632, *pg.* 905
BIG MAC - Entertainment - ENVIRONMENTAL TECTONICS CORPORATION; *pg.* 1411, *pg.* 1587
BIG MAC - Sandwich - MCDONALD'S CORPORATION; *pg.* 1737, *pg.* 645
BIG MAC - Enclosures - TII NETWORK TECHNOLOGIES, INC.; *pg.* 680, *pg.* 1157
BIG MAMA SAUSAGE - Food Product - CONAGRA FOODS, INC.; *pg.* 826, *pg.* 1014
BIG MAN ELANCE - Knit Boxer - JOCKEY INTERNATIONAL, INC.; *pg.* 27, *pg.* 1861
BIG MAN MIDWAY - Brief - JOCKEY INTERNATIONAL, INC.; *pg.* 27, *pg.* 1861
BIG MAX - Turbo Muffler - AP EXHAUST PRODUCTS, INC.; *pg.* 199, *pg.* 1373
BIG MAX - Valves - FLOWSERVE CORPORATION; *pg.* 82, *pg.* 1719
BIG MISSISSIPPI MUD - Ice Cream Sandwich - WELLS ENTERPRISES, INC.; *pg.* 909, *pg.* 709
BIG MONEY - Lottery Game - KENTUCKY LOTTERY CORPORATION; *pg.* 996, *pg.* 735
BIG MONEY - Game - MISSOURI LOTTERY; *pg.* 999, *pg.* 979
BIG MONEY BOARD - Game - WMS INDUSTRIES INC.; *pg.* 593, *pg.* 666
BIG MONEY CHEESE CAPER - Game - WMS INDUSTRIES INC.; *pg.* 593, *pg.* 666
BIG MONEY DOUBLER - Lottery Game - KENTUCKY LOTTERY CORPORATION; *pg.* 996, *pg.* 735
BIG MONEY SHOT - Game - WMS INDUSTRIES INC.; *pg.* 593, *pg.* 666
BIG MOUTH - Kitchen Appliance - HAMILTON BEACH BRANDS, INC.; *pg.* 56, *pg.* 1783
BIG MOUTH - Bicycle Accessories - SPECIALIZED BICYCLE COMPONENTS, INC.; *pg.* 1711, *pg.* 152
BIG-MOUTH SERVERS - Plastic Beverage Server - THE VOLLRATH COMPANY LLC; *pg.* 1139, *pg.* 1894
BIG N' TASTY - Fast Food - MCDONALD'S CORPORATION; *pg.* 1737, *pg.* 645
BIG NEAPOLITAN - Ice Cream Sandwich - WELLS ENTERPRISES, INC.; *pg.* 909, *pg.* 709
BIG O - Tire Stores - TBC CORPORATION; *pg.* 1889, *pg.* 457
BIG O - Round Knife - THE WOLF MACHINE CO.; *pg.* 1389, *pg.* 1427
THE BIG ONE - Employment Product - THE DAILY OAKLAND PRESS; *pg.* 1632, *pg.* 905
BIG OR SMALL WE SHIP IT ALL - Tagline - UNITED PARCEL SERVICE, INC.; *pg.* 1928, *pg.* 522
BIG ORANGE - Chain - COLUMBUS MCKINNON CORPORATION; *pg.* 1325, *pg.* 1138
BIG PAK - Injection Molded Product - TRIENDA, LLC; *pg.* 1890, *pg.* 1887
BIG PICK POKER - Video Game - INTERNATIONAL GAME TECHNOLOGY; *pg.* 957, *pg.* 1024
THE BIG PICTURE - Slogan - INFOCUS CORPORATION; *pg.* 644, *pg.* 1503
BIG PIG - Video Game - INTERNATIONAL GAME TECHNOLOGY; *pg.* 957, *pg.* 1024
BIG PLANET - Software - NU SKIN ENTERPRISES, INC.; *pg.* 518, *pg.* 1755
BIG PUNCTURE - Seal - RADIATOR SPECIALTY COMPANY; *pg.* 215, *pg.* 1380
BIG RED - Hand Soap - BIRKO CORPORATION; *pg.* 1149, *pg.* 332
BIG RED - Play System - CREATIVE PLAYTHINGS LTD.; *pg.* 1831, *pg.* 820
BIG RED - Conveyor Belting - HBD INDUSTRIES, INC.; *pg.* 207, *pg.* 1449
BIG RED - Concentrated Cleaner - TEXAS REFINERY CORP.; *pg.* 986, *pg.* 1696
BIG RED - Gum - WM. WRIGLEY JR. COMPANY; *pg.* 1863, *pg.* 596
BIG RED CLASSIC ATW - Wagon - RADIO FLYER INC.; *pg.* 966, *pg.* 588
BIG RIG - Fluid Handling System - GRACO, INC.; *pg.* 1342, *pg.* 935
BIG SCIENCE COMICS - Educational Materials - SCHOLASTIC INC.; *pg.* 1683, *pg.* 1288
BIG SCOOP - Hard Ice Cream Cone - INTERNATIONAL DAIRY QUEEN, INC.; *pg.* 1732, *pg.* 938
BIG SHOT - Soft Drink - NATIONAL BEVERAGE CORP.; *pg.* 257, *pg.* 425
BIG SKY - Bedding - CROSCILL, INC.; *pg.* 1122, *pg.* 1220
BIG SLICE - Ice Cream Slices - WELLS ENTERPRISES, INC.; *pg.* 909, *pg.* 709

First page reference indicates Business Class Edition
Second page reference indicates Geographic Edition

BIG SPARK - Spark Plug - OLD WORLD INDUSTRIES, INC.; *pg.* 1175, *pg.* 641
BIG SPIN - Skate - ROLLER DERBY SKATE CORP.; *pg.* 966, *pg.* 630
BIG SPLIT POKER - Video Poker - INTERNATIONAL GAME TECHNOLOGY; *pg.* 957, *pg.* 1024
BIG STEP - Step Stool Series with Roomy Molded Steps - DOREL JUVENILE GROUP, INC.; *pg.* 923, *pg.* 676
BIG SUR - Golf Equipment - ACUSHNET COMPANY; *pg.* 1824, *pg.* 818
BIG TAI - Beverages - THE COCA-COLA COMPANY; *pg.* 240, *pg.* 493
BIG TEE - Apparel - OAKLEY, INC.; *pg.* 1840, *pg.* 86
BIG TEX - Food - WESTERN SIZZLIN CORPORATION; *pg.* 1755, *pg.* 1806
BIG TEXAS SUN CLUB - Promoting Research - GREEN MOUNTAIN ENERGY COMPANY; *pg.* 1944, *pg.* 1663
BIG THINKING IN LITTLE SIZES - Children's Shoes & Clothing - REEBOK INTERNATIONAL LTD.; *pg.* 1817, *pg.* 811
BIG TIC - Watch - FOSSIL GROUP, INC.; *pg.* 5, *pg.* 1735
BIG TIME PAYROLL - Video Game - INTERNATIONAL GAME TECHNOLOGY; *pg.* 957, *pg.* 1024
BIG TIMES DRAW POKER - Video Game - INTERNATIONAL GAME TECHNOLOGY; *pg.* 957, *pg.* 1024
BIG TIMES PAY - Slots - INTERNATIONAL GAME TECHNOLOGY; *pg.* 957, *pg.* 1024
BIG TIMES RED WHITE & BLUE - Video Game - INTERNATIONAL GAME TECHNOLOGY; *pg.* 957, *pg.* 1024
BIG TIMES WILD CHERRY - Video Game - INTERNATIONAL GAME TECHNOLOGY; *pg.* 957, *pg.* 1024
BIG TIPPERS - Game - WMS INDUSTRIES INC.; *pg.* 593, *pg.* 666
BIG TRUCK TRADER - Magazine - DOMINION ENTERPRISES; *pg.* 1636, *pg.* 1796
BIG TWIN - Pumps - HYPRO; *pg.* 705, *pg.* 951
BIG TWIST - Twist Tobacco - AMERICAN SNUFF COMPANY; *pg.* 1893, *pg.* 1641
BIG VAC - Turf Maintenance Machinery - SMITHCO, INC.; *pg.* 1377, *pg.* 1592
BIG VALLEY - Cattle Handling System - BEHLEN MFG. CO.; *pg.* 701, *pg.* 1010
BIG VANILLA - Ice Cream Sandwich - WELLS ENTERPRISES, INC.; *pg.* 909, *pg.* 709
BIG WALLY - Wall Cleaning Brush - THE FULLER BRUSH COMPANY; *pg.* 330, *pg.* 715
BIG WHITE - Bread - KLOSTERMAN BAKING COMPANY, INC.; *pg.* 869, *pg.* 1415
BIG WOOLLY - Socks - WOOLRICH, INC.; *pg.* 699, *pg.* 1595
BIG X WILD - Game - WMS INDUSTRIES INC.; *pg.* 593, *pg.* 666
BIG YANK - Medical Equipment - CONMED CORPORATION; *pg.* 1517, *pg.* 1347
BIG ZAX SNAK - Food Product - ZAXBY'S FRANCHISING, INC.; *pg.* 1756, *pg.* 486
BIGBERTHA DIABLO - Golf Ball - CALLAWAY GOLF COMPANY; *pg.* 1829, *pg.* 58
BIGBORE - Subsea Wellhead System - DRIL-QUIP, INC.; *pg.* 1330, *pg.* 1704
BIGELOIL - Muscle Care Product - W.F. YOUNG, INC.; *pg.* 1610, *pg.* 817
BIGELOW - Carpets & Rugs - MOHAWK INDUSTRIES, INC.; *pg.* 935, *pg.* 527
BIGFOLD - Paper Towel - GEORGIA-PACIFIC LLC; *pg.* 1458, *pg.* 507
BIGFOLD JR - Paper Towel - GEORGIA-PACIFIC LLC; *pg.* 1458, *pg.* 507
BIGFOLD Z - Paper Towel - GEORGIA-PACIFIC LLC; *pg.* 1458, *pg.* 507
BIGFOOT RAPIDS - Water Ride - KNOTT'S BERRY FARM; *pg.* 556, *pg.* 50
BIGGER BETTER BURGERS - Entrees - EAT'N PARK HOSPITALITY GROUP; *pg.* 1728, *pg.* 1539
BIGGER THAN BIGGER - Tagline - APPLE INC.; *pg.* 350, *pg.* 73
BIGGEST BIG BERTHA - Golf Product - CALLAWAY GOLF COMPANY; *pg.* 1829, *pg.* 58
THE BIGGEST CHILDREN'S BOOK IN THE WORLD - Educational Materials - SCHOLASTIC INC.; *pg.* 1683, *pg.* 1288
BIGGEST LOSER 30-DAY JUMP START - Book - RODALE, INC.; *pg.* 1681, *pg.* 1530
BIGGIE - Apparel - VANS, INC.; *pg.* 1821, *pg.* 76
BIGHAM - Furniture - ASHLEY FURNITURE INDUSTRIES, INC.; *pg.* 914, *pg.* 1852
BIGJOB - Rubber - HBD INDUSTRIES, INC.; *pg.* 207, *pg.* 1449
BIGMOUTH - Apparel - VANS, INC.; *pg.* 1821, *pg.* 76
BIGTIME - Processed Poultry - TYSON FOODS, INC.; *pg.* 902, *pg.* 35
BIJOU - Bath Collection - CROSCILL, INC.; *pg.* 1122, *pg.* 1220
BIJU - Pigment - BASF CATALYSTS LLC; *pg.* 1148, *pg.* 1074
BIK OT - Activator - CHEMTURA CORPORATION; *pg.* 1152, *pg.* 355
BIKE - Athletic Wear - RUSSELL BRANDS LLC; *pg.* 698, *pg.* 726
BIKE BUG - Bicycle Accessories - SPECIALIZED BICYCLE COMPONENTS, INC.; *pg.* 1711, *pg.* 152
BIKE SPIRITS - Motorcycle Cleaning & Maintenance Products - ZEP INC.; *pg.* 338, *pg.* 524
BIKER - Magazine - PAISANO PUBLICATIONS, LLC; *pg.* 1674, *pg.* 38
BIKER SKULL - Apparel - VANS, INC.; *pg.* 1821, *pg.* 76
BIKINI - Eyewear - MAUI JIM, INC.; *pg.* 9, *pg.* 651
BIKINI ZONE - Hair Removal Product - CCA INDUSTRIES, INC.; *pg.* 503, *pg.* 1114
BIKINO - Video Game - INTERNATIONAL GAME TECHNOLOGY; *pg.* 957, *pg.* 1024
BILD-R-TAPE - Insulating System - OWENS CORNING; *pg.* 102, *pg.* 1476
BILETIX - Online Ticket Service - IAC/INTERACTIVECORP; *pg.* 292, *pg.* 1242
BILIBAND - Jaundice Management Product - NATUS MEDICAL INCORPORATED; *pg.* 1572, *pg.* 199
BILIBOTTOMS - Neonatal Product - CAS MEDICAL SYSTEMS, INC.; *pg.* 1513, *pg.* 339
BILINX TECHNOLOGY - Camera Control System - BOSCH SECURITY SYSTEMS, INC.; *pg.* 626, *pg.* 1158
BILL - Electrical Product - EATON CORPORATION; *pg.* 1331, *pg.* 1429
BILL BURNS SIGNATURE - Misses' Suits, Sportswear & Dresses - KELLWOOD COMPANY; *pg.* 28, *pg.* 975
BILL ME LATER - Electronic Payment System - CYBERSOURCE CORPORATION; *pg.* 381, *pg.* 216
BILL-TAINERS - Billfolds - BUXTON ACQUISITION CO., LLC; *pg.* 2, *pg.* 845
BILL TITE - Bill Board Adhesives - EVANS ADHESIVE CORPORATION, LTD.; *pg.* 1161, *pg.* 1440
BILLBOARD - Magazine; Books on Music & Entertainment - NIELSEN BUSINESS MEDIA; *pg.* 1671, *pg.* 1272
BILLBOARD BULLETIN - Newsletter - NIELSEN BUSINESS MEDIA; *pg.* 1671, *pg.* 1272
BILLBOARD INFORMATION NETWORK - Marketing Information Services - NIELSEN BUSINESS MEDIA; *pg.* 1671, *pg.* 1272
BILLBOARD RADIO MONITOR - Trade Publication - THE NIELSEN COMPANY B.V.; *pg.* 1671, *pg.* 1272
BILLING & OSS WORLD - Publication - INFORMA EXHIBITIONS LLC; *pg.* 1653, *pg.* 17
BILLING MEDIATION - Cable Solutions - SONUS NETWORKS INC.; *pg.* 1281, *pg.* 858
BILLINGWATCH - Credit Card Charges - AMERICAN EXPRESS COMPANY; *pg.* 712, *pg.* 1190
BILLION-AIR - Compressor - BADGER AIR BRUSH COMPANY; *pg.* 359, *pg.* 612
BILLMATE - Communication Product - CENTURYLINK, INC; *pg.* 1870, *pg.* 317
BILLO - Ceiling Panel - USG CORPORATION; *pg.* 118, *pg.* 594
BILLPRO - Bill Acceptor - COIN ACCEPTORS, INC.; *pg.* 1324, *pg.* 994
BILL'S - Casino - CAESARS ENTERTAINMENT CORPORATION; *pg.* 1083, *pg.* 1023
BILLWISE - Billing Service - XCEL ENERGY INC.; *pg.* 1955, *pg.* 946
BILLXCHANGE - Software - XEROX CORPORATION; *pg.* 494, *pg.* 365
BILLY BEE - Honey Products - MCCORMICK & COMPANY, INCORPORATED; *pg.* 1027, *pg.* 779
BILLY MARTIN - Guitar - PAUL REED SMITH GUITARS; *pg.* 574, *pg.* 779
BILTMORE - Furniture - ASHLEY FURNITURE INDUSTRIES, INC.; *pg.* 914, *pg.* 1852
BILTMORE ESTATE - Hardwood Floor - ANDERSON HARDWOOD FLOORS; *pg.* 67, *pg.* 1613
BILTRITE - Shoe Repair Products - AMERICAN BILTRITE INC.; *pg.* 1878, *pg.* 856
BIMBO - Beverages - THE COCA-COLA COMPANY; *pg.* 240, *pg.* 493
BIMBO BREAK - Beverages - THE COCA-COLA COMPANY; *pg.* 240, *pg.* 493
BIMINI - Fiberglass Boat Product - GRADY-WHITE BOATS, INC.; *pg.* 1707, *pg.* 1377
BIMS - Sourcing Solution - ESM SOLUTIONS CORPORATION; *pg.* 1243, *pg.* 1591
BIN EVACUATION SYSTEM - Fluid Handling System - GRACO, INC.; *pg.* 1342, *pg.* 935
BINACTIVATOR - Oil-Lubricated Gyrator - VIBRA SCREW INC.; *pg.* 1387, *pg.* 1126
BINARY - Fabric - NEMSCHOFF, INC.; *pg.* 936, *pg.* 1890
BINAXNOW - Rapid Membrane Test Products - ALERE INC.; *pg.* 1488, *pg.* 849
BIND-FAST - Office Machinery - STANDARD DUPLICATING MACHINES CORPORATION; *pg.* 473, *pg.* 783
BINDER TEX 45 - Binder - CARAUSTAR INDUSTRIES, INC.; *pg.* 1455, *pg.* 525
BINDRIGHT - Food Product - NEWLY WEDS FOODS, INC.; *pg.* 886, *pg.* 585
BINDVIEW - Compliance Software - SYMANTEC CORPORATION; *pg.* 478, *pg.* 161
BINEXIS - Medicine - PFIZER INC.; *pg.* 1581, *pg.* 1278
BING - Search Engine - MICROSOFT CORPORATION; *pg.* 435, *pg.* 1824
BINGO - Game - FORTUNET, INC.; *pg.* 953, *pg.* 1024
BINGO - Instant Lottery Game - NEW YORK STATE LOTTERY; *pg.* 1001, *pg.* 1340
BINGO - Lottery Game - OHIO LOTTERY COMMISSION; *pg.* 1002, *pg.* 1433
BINGO BUGS - Video Game - INTERNATIONAL GAME TECHNOLOGY; *pg.* 957, *pg.* 1024
BINGO II - Lottery Game - KENTUCKY LOTTERY CORPORATION; *pg.* 996, *pg.* 735
BINGO NIGHT - Lottery Game - D.C. LOTTERY & CHARITABLE GAMES CONTROL BOARD; *pg.* 991, *pg.* 398
BINGOOO - Soft Drink - THE COCA-COLA COMPANY; *pg.* 240, *pg.* 493
BINGOSTAR - Electronic Bingo System - FORTUNET, INC.; *pg.* 953, *pg.* 1024
BINGOVISION - T.V.-Based Lottery Game - INTERNATIONAL GAME TECHNOLOGY; *pg.* 420, *pg.* 1606
BINYON'S - Eye Care Centers - VISIONWORKS OF AMERICA, INC.; *pg.* 1436, *pg.* 1744
BIO - Television Channel and Magazine - A&E TELEVISION NETWORKS, LLC; *pg.* 267, *pg.* 1185
BIO 90 - Nonionic Spreader Activator - KALO, INC.; *pg.* 1796, *pg.* 719
BIO-ACTION - Surgical Instrument - OSTEOMED CORPORATION; *pg.* 1425, *pg.* 1658
BIO-ADE - Ammonia & Odor Control - TROUW NUTRITION USA; *pg.* 1482, *pg.* 616
BIO-ANCHOR - Medical Equipment - CONMED CORPORATION; *pg.* 1517, *pg.* 1347
BIO-BEADS - Software - BIO-RAD LABORATORIES, INC.; *pg.* 1504, *pg.* 101
BIO BEEDS - Detergents - KAO BRANDS CO. INC.; *pg.* 513, *pg.* 1415
BIO-BEL H1R - Valve Cleaner - BEL-RAY COMPANY, INC.; *pg.* 972, *pg.* 1128
BIO-CAP - Pulp Capping - DEN-MAT CORPORATION; *pg.* 1522, *pg.* 271
BIO-CHALLENGE TEST-PAK - Sterilization Product - PROPPER MANUFACTURING COMPANY, INC.; *pg.* 1586, *pg.* 1175
BIO-CHANNEL - Sport Surface - ROBBINS, INC.; *pg.* 108, *pg.* 1425
BIO CHANNEL LP - Floor System - ROBBINS, INC.; *pg.* 108, *pg.* 1425
BIO-CONSOLE - Control Console with Heart Design - MEDTRONIC, INC.; *pg.* 1564, *pg.* 939
BIO CUSHION - Suspended Maple Sports Flooring - ROBBINS, INC.; *pg.* 108, *pg.* 1425
BIO-DIMENSION - Software - BIO-RAD LABORATORIES, INC.; *pg.* 1504, *pg.* 101
BIO-DOME - Seed Pods - AEROGROW INTERNATIONAL, INC.; *pg.* 1393, *pg.* 310
BIO-DOT - Software - BIO-RAD LABORATORIES, INC.; *pg.* 1504, *pg.* 101
BIO FEEDBACK - Ankle Support System - K-SWISS; *pg.* 1837, *pg.* 306
BIO-FILM - Spreader Sticker - KALO, INC.; *pg.* 1796, *pg.* 719
BIO-FREEZE - Medical & Aesthetic Product - DYNATRONICS

CORPORATION; *pg.* 1526, *pg.* 1757
BIO-FUSE - Hair Replacement - HAIR CLUB FOR MEN, LTD., INC.; *pg.* 511, *pg.* 411
BIO-GEL - Software - BIO-RAD LABORATORIES, INC.; *pg.* 1504, *pg.* 101
BIO GENTLE - Fabric Softener - LONZA INC.; *pg.* 1171, *pg.* 1041
BIO-ICE - Software - BIO-RAD LABORATORIES, INC.; *pg.* 1504, *pg.* 101
BIO-IN-A-BOX - Bioremediation Services - WASTE MANAGEMENT, INC.; *pg.* 1954, *pg.* 1716
BIO-KLEAN - Degreaser - TEXAS REFINERY CORP.; *pg.* 986, *pg.* 1696
BIO-KLEEN - Flux Residue Remover - KESTER, INC.; *pg.* 649, *pg.* 620
BIO KLEEN - Diesel Fuel - POWER SERVICE PRODUCTS, INC.; *pg.* 983, *pg.* 1749
BIO LAB - Lab Science Material - CAROLINA BIOLOGICAL SUPPLY COMPANY; *pg.* 1513, *pg.* 1359
BIO-LYTE - Software - BIO-RAD LABORATORIES, INC.; *pg.* 1504, *pg.* 101
BIO-MARK - Software - BIO-RAD LABORATORIES, INC.; *pg.* 1504, *pg.* 101
BIO-MATRIX - Hair Replacement - HAIR CLUB FOR MEN, LTD., INC.; *pg.* 511, *pg.* 411
BIO-MEDICUS - Cardiopulmonary Equipment - MEDTRONIC, INC.; *pg.* 1564, *pg.* 939
BIO-MODULAR - Implant System - ZIMMER BIOMET HOLDINGS, INC.; *pg.* 1611, *pg.* 699
BIO NC - Pharmaceutical Product - BIOSPACE, INC.; *pg.* 1231, *pg.* 1082
BIO-PLEX - Software - BIO-RAD LABORATORIES, INC.; *pg.* 1504, *pg.* 101
BIO-PLEX MANAGER - Software - BIO-RAD LABORATORIES, INC.; *pg.* 1504, *pg.* 101
BIO-PLEX PRECISION PRO - Software - BIO-RAD LABORATORIES, INC.; *pg.* 1504, *pg.* 101
BIO-PLEX PRO - Software - BIO-RAD LABORATORIES, INC.; *pg.* 1504, *pg.* 101
BIO-PLEX UNIVERSITY - Software - BIO-RAD LABORATORIES, INC.; *pg.* 1504, *pg.* 101
BIO-PREP - Software - BIO-RAD LABORATORIES, INC.; *pg.* 1504, *pg.* 101
BIO-PROBE - Blood Flow Monitoring System - MEDTRONIC, INC.; *pg.* 1564, *pg.* 939
BIO PROTECTIVE CLOTHING - Medical Apparel - I. SPIEWAK & SONS, INC.; *pg.* 42, *pg.* 1242
BIO-PSA - Medical Grade Adhesive - DOW CORNING CORPORATION; *pg.* 1159, *pg.* 900
BIO-QUENCH - Heat Treating Product - HOUGHTON INTERNATIONAL INC.; *pg.* 1167, *pg.* 1589
BIO-RAD & THE BIO-RAD LOGO - Software - BIO-RAD LABORATORIES, INC.; *pg.* 1504, *pg.* 101
BIO-RAD EASYPACK - Software - BIO-RAD LABORATORIES, INC.; *pg.* 1504, *pg.* 101
BIO-RAD GELTEC - Software - BIO-RAD LABORATORIES, INC.; *pg.* 1504, *pg.* 101
BIO-RAD INPLACE - Software - BIO-RAD LABORATORIES, INC.; *pg.* 1504, *pg.* 101
BIO-RAD MAINFRAME - Software - BIO-RAD LABORATORIES, INC.; *pg.* 1504, *pg.* 101
BIO-RAD OCS - Software - BIO-RAD LABORATORIES, INC.; *pg.* 1504, *pg.* 101
BIO-RAD PLUS - Software - BIO-RAD LABORATORIES, INC.; *pg.* 1504, *pg.* 101
BIO-RAD UBZ - Software - BIO-RAD LABORATORIES, INC.; *pg.* 1504, *pg.* 101
BIO-RELEASE - Silicone-Based Pharmaceutically Inactive Compositions - DOW CORNING CORPORATION; *pg.* 1159, *pg.* 900
BIO-REX - Software - BIO-RAD LABORATORIES, INC.; *pg.* 1504, *pg.* 101
BIO-SAFE - Software - BIO-RAD LABORATORIES, INC.; *pg.* 1504, *pg.* 101
BIO-SCALE - Software - BIO-RAD LABORATORIES, INC.; *pg.* 1504, *pg.* 101
BIO-SIL - Software - BIO-RAD LABORATORIES, INC.; *pg.* 1504, *pg.* 101
BIO-SILECT - Software - BIO-RAD LABORATORIES, INC.; *pg.* 1504, *pg.* 101
BIO-SOFT - Chemical Product - STEPAN COMPANY; *pg.* 1182, *pg.* 643
BIO-SPIN - Software - BIO-RAD LABORATORIES, INC.; *pg.* 1504, *pg.* 101
BIO ST. JOHN'S - Nutritional Supplement - NU SKIN ENTERPRISES, INC.; *pg.* 518, *pg.* 1755
BIO-TERGE - Chemical Product - STEPAN COMPANY; *pg.* 1182, *pg.* 643
BIO TRACK - Poured-in-Place Urethane - ROBBINS, INC.; *pg.* 108, *pg.* 1425
BIO-TROL - Biocides - GE WATER & PROCESS TECHNOLOGIES; *pg.* 1339, *pg.* 1588
BIOACT - Cleaning Product - PETROFERM INC.; *pg.* 1177, *pg.* 616
BIOAQUEOUS - Pharmaceutical Product - THE DOW CHEMICAL COMPANY; *pg.* 1157, *pg.* 898
BIOARC - Medical Device - AMERICAN MEDICAL SYSTEMS HOLDINGS, INC.; *pg.* 1493, *pg.* 947
BIOASTIN - Dietary Supplement - CYANOTECH CORPORATION; *pg.* 1154, *pg.* 545
BIOAUS - Pharmaceutical Product - BIOSPACE, INC.; *pg.* 1231, *pg.* 1082
BIOBAC - Fabric - INTERFACE, INC.; *pg.* 695, *pg.* 512
BIOBALANCE - Polymer - THE DOW CHEMICAL COMPANY; *pg.* 1157, *pg.* 898
BIOBASE - Personal Care Product - TRI-K INDUSTRIES, INC.; *pg.* 523, *pg.* 1099
BIOBEADS - Nutritional Product - NATROL, INC.; *pg.* 1570, *pg.* 64
BIOBLEND - Dental Product - DENTSPLY INTERNATIONAL INC.; *pg.* 1522, *pg.* 1596
BIOBLOCK - Pharmaceutical - INTEGRA LIFESCIENCES HOLDINGS CORPORATION; *pg.* 1545, *pg.* 1109
BIOBLOX - Chemical Product - STEPAN COMPANY; *pg.* 1182, *pg.* 643
BIOBOND II - Dental Product - DENTSPLY INTERNATIONAL INC.; *pg.* 1522, *pg.* 1596
BIOBOOST - Vegetable Gardening - GARDENS ALIVE!, INC.; *pg.* 1796, *pg.* 693
BIOCAP - Software - BIO-RAD LABORATORIES, INC.; *pg.* 1504, *pg.* 101
BIOCARE - Polymer - THE DOW CHEMICAL COMPANY; *pg.* 1157, *pg.* 898
BIOCHARTER - Biomolecule Product - THERMO FISHER SCIENTIFIC INC.; *pg.* 1602, *pg.* 61
BIOCHEMI - Imaging System - UVP, INC.; *pg.* 1434, *pg.* 298
BIOCLUSIVE - Healthcare Product - JOHNSON & JOHNSON; *pg.* 1549, *pg.* 1091
BIOCORE - Digestive Supplement - NATIONAL ENZYME COMPANY; *pg.* 882, *pg.* 978
BIOCORRIDOR - Pharmaceutical Product - BIOSPACE, INC.; *pg.* 1231, *pg.* 1082
BIOCURVE - Hammer - ALIMED, INC.; *pg.* 1490, *pg.* 816
BIODEGRADABLE STAKES - Garden Product - E.I. DU PONT DE NEMOURS & COMPANY; *pg.* 1159, *pg.* 390
BIODOC-IT - Gel Documentation Equipment - UVP, INC.; *pg.* 1434, *pg.* 298
BIODUR - Alloy - CARPENTER TECHNOLOGY CORPORATION; *pg.* 73, *pg.* 1584
BIODYNE - Nylon Membrane - PALL CORPORATION; *pg.* 232, *pg.* 1323
BIOEASE - Molecular Biology Product - THERMO FISHER SCIENTIFIC INC.; *pg.* 1602, *pg.* 61
BIOEXTEND - High Performance Additive - EASTMAN CHEMICAL COMPANY; *pg.* 1159, *pg.* 1636
BIOFOCUS - Software - BIO-RAD LABORATORIES, INC.; *pg.* 1504, *pg.* 101
BIOFORCE - Dental Product - DENTSPLY INTERNATIONAL INC.; *pg.* 1522, *pg.* 1596
BIOFORM - Dental Product - DENTSPLY INTERNATIONAL INC.; *pg.* 1522, *pg.* 1596
BIOFRAC - Software - BIO-RAD LABORATORIES, INC.; *pg.* 1504, *pg.* 101
BIOFX - Secondary Antibody - SURMODICS, INC.; *pg.* 1600, *pg.* 924
BIOGARDEN - Pharmaceutical Product - BIOSPACE, INC.; *pg.* 1231, *pg.* 1082
BIOGINKGO - Nutritional Supplement - NU SKIN ENTERPRISES, INC.; *pg.* 518, *pg.* 1755
BIOGLUE - Bioadhesive Product - CRYOLIFE, INC.; *pg.* 1520, *pg.* 534
BIOGLUE - Surgical Adhesive - MERZ AESTHETICS; *pg.* 1567, *pg.* 255
BIOGRADE - Fluorochemical Product - HALOCARBON PRODUCTS CORPORATION; *pg.* 978, *pg.* 1116
BIOGROOVE - Implant Product - ZIMMER BIOMET HOLDINGS, INC.; *pg.* 1611, *pg.* 699
BIOGUARD - Spa Products - HENRY BONA POOLS & SPAS; *pg.* 1836, *pg.* 1078
BIOH - Non-Petroleum Based Polyol - CARGILL, INC.; *pg.* 845, *pg.* 965
BIOJECTOR - Injection System - BIOJECT MEDICAL TECHNOLOGIES INC.; *pg.* 1506, *pg.* 1509
BIOKIT - Biological Products - CAROLINA BIOLOGICAL SUPPLY COMPANY; *pg.* 1513, *pg.* 1359
BIOKNOWLEDGE LIBRARY - Biology Database - INCYTE CORPORATION; *pg.* 1545, *pg.* 392
BIOLASTIC - Material for Pulomonary Repairs & Patching - CRYOLIFE, INC.; *pg.* 1520, *pg.* 534
BIOLOGIC - Software - BIO-RAD LABORATORIES, INC.; *pg.* 1504, *pg.* 101
BIOLOGIC - Food Safety System - NATIONAL BEEF PACKING COMPANY, LLC; *pg.* 882, *pg.* 985
BIOLOGIC DUOFLOW - Software - BIO-RAD LABORATORIES, INC.; *pg.* 1504, *pg.* 101
BIOLOGIC DUOFLOW MAXIMIZER - Software - BIO-RAD LABORATORIES, INC.; *pg.* 1504, *pg.* 101
BIOLOGIC DUOFLOW PATHFINDER - Software - BIO-RAD LABORATORIES, INC.; *pg.* 1504, *pg.* 101
BIOLOGIC DUOFLOW QUADTEC - Software - BIO-RAD LABORATORIES, INC.; *pg.* 1504, *pg.* 101
BIOLOGIC LP DATA VIEW - Software - BIO-RAD LABORATORIES, INC.; *pg.* 1504, *pg.* 101
BIOLOGIC MAXIMIZER - Software - BIO-RAD LABORATORIES, INC.; *pg.* 1504, *pg.* 101
BIOLOGIC QUADTEC - Software - BIO-RAD LABORATORIES, INC.; *pg.* 1504, *pg.* 101
BIOLOGICARE - Bone & Tissue Management - MEDIWARE INFORMATION SYSTEMS, INC.; *pg.* 431, *pg.* 716
BIOMARKER DISCOVERY CENTER - Diagnostic Test - VERMILLION, INC.; *pg.* 1435, *pg.* 1667
BIOMARKER PATTERNS - Software - BIO-RAD LABORATORIES, INC.; *pg.* 1504, *pg.* 101
BIOMARKER PATTERNS - Software - VERMILLION, INC.; *pg.* 1435, *pg.* 1667
BIOMAX - Film - EASTMAN KODAK COMPANY; *pg.* 1408, *pg.* 1333
BIOMAX - Compost - PREMIER TECH HORTICULTURE LTD.; *pg.* 1799, *pg.* 1958
BIOMEGA - Nutritional Supplement - USANA HEALTH SCIENCES, INC.; *pg.* 1605, *pg.* 1761
BIOMEK - Testing Instrument System - BECKMAN COULTER, INC.; *pg.* 1402, *pg.* 48
BIOMEND - Medical Device - INTEGRA LIFESCIENCES HOLDINGS CORPORATION; *pg.* 1545, *pg.* 1109
BIOMET - Implant Product - ZIMMER BIOMET HOLDINGS, INC.; *pg.* 1611, *pg.* 699
BIOMETRIC ENGINE - Software - IMAGEWARE SYSTEMS, INC.; *pg.* 412, *pg.* 203
BIOMETRITECH - Online Publication - TECHNOLOGY MARKETING CORP.; *pg.* 1691, *pg.* 364
BIOMOORE - Implant Product - ZIMMER BIOMET HOLDINGS, INC.; *pg.* 1611, *pg.* 699
BIOMOORE HIP SYSTEM - Hip Product - ZIMMER BIOMET HOLDINGS, INC.; *pg.* 1611, *pg.* 699
BIOMORPH - Carpet - INTERFACE, INC.; *pg.* 695, *pg.* 512
BIONAIRE - Home Air Filtration System - JARDEN CONSUMER SOLUTIONS; *pg.* 57, *pg.* 412
BIONDI SANTI - Wine - REMY COINTREAU USA INC.; *pg.* 1969, *pg.* 1285
BIONEEM - Spray - THE WOODSTREAM CORPORATION; *pg.* 1801, *pg.* 1549
BIONET - Pharmaceutical Product - CHURCH & DWIGHT CANADA CORP.; *pg.* 503, *pg.* 1925
BIONIC - Batting Glove - HILLERICH & BRADSBY CO., INC.; *pg.* 1836, *pg.* 576
BIONIC - Wetting Agent and Emulsifier - HUNTSMAN CORPORATION; *pg.* 1167, *pg.* 1758
BIONICAM - Video Microscope - JAKKS PACIFIC, INC.; *pg.* 960, *pg.* 142
BIONICK - Biomolecule Product - THERMO FISHER SCIENTIFIC INC.; *pg.* 1602, *pg.* 61
BIONOX - Animal Nutrition Product - VITUSA CORP.; *pg.* 1482, *pg.* 1063
BIOODYSSEY - Software - BIO-RAD LABORATORIES, INC.; *pg.* 1504, *pg.* 101
BIOPARTICLES - Molecular Probe Product - THERMO FISHER SCIENTIFIC INC.; *pg.* 1602, *pg.* 61
BIOPATCH - Medical Device - INTEGRA LIFESCIENCES HOLDINGS CORPORATION; *pg.* 1545, *pg.* 1109
BIOPATCH - Healthcare Product - JOHNSON & JOHNSON; *pg.* 1549, *pg.* 1091
BIOPENN - Pharmaceutical Product - BIOSPACE, INC.; *pg.* 1231, *pg.* 1082
BIOPERFORM.COM - Trade Website - ADVANTAGE

First page reference indicates Business Class Edition
Second page reference indicates Geographic Edition

BUSINESS MEDIA; *pg.* 1613, *pg.* 1116
BIOPERINE - Nutritional Supplement - NATURAL ORGANICS, INC.; *pg.* 1571, *pg.* 1181
BIOPERINE 10 - Nutrition Supplement to Aid in Digestion - NATURAL ORGANICS, INC.; *pg.* 1571, *pg.* 1181
BIOPHARMALYNX - Software - WATERS CORPORATION; *pg.* 1436, *pg.* 834
BIOPHOTO - Biological Supplies - CAROLINA BIOLOGICAL SUPPLY COMPANY; *pg.* 1513, *pg.* 1359
BIOPHOTONICS INTERNATIONAL - International Photonics Industry Magazine - LAURIN PUBLISHING CO., INC.; *pg.* 1658, *pg.* 841
BIOPLASTIQUE - Medical Devices - COGENTIX MEDICAL, INC.; *pg.* 1516, *pg.* 948
BIOPLEX - Software - BIO-RAD LABORATORIES, INC.; *pg.* 1504, *pg.* 101
BIOPLEX - Pharmaceutical Preparation - MAQUET; *pg.* 1558, *pg.* 1082
BIOPLUS - Biopsy Kits - MEDTRONIC, INC.; *pg.* 1564, *pg.* 939
BIOPLUS 2B - Feed And Nutrition Product - CHR. HANSEN; *pg.* 847, *pg.* 1873
BIOPRIME - Biomolecule Product - THERMO FISHER SCIENTIFIC INC.; *pg.* 1602, *pg.* 61
BIOPTY - Urological Instrument - C.R. BARD, INC.; *pg.* 1519, *pg.* 1094
BIOPROTECT - Dietary Supplement - GARDEN OF LIFE, INC.; *pg.* 1532, *pg.* 478
BIOPURE - Dental Product - DENTSPLY INTERNATIONAL INC.; *pg.* 1522, *pg.* 1596
BIORAM - Sampling Valve - STRAHMAN VALVES, INC.; *pg.* 1379, *pg.* 1517
BIORAPTR FRD - Workstation - BECKMAN COULTER, INC.; *pg.* 1402, *pg.* 48
BIORE - Facial Care - KAO BRANDS CO. INC.; *pg.* 513, *pg.* 1415
BIORELIANCE - Biologic Safety Test - THERMO FISHER SCIENTIFIC INC.; *pg.* 1602, *pg.* 61
BIOREVIEW - Biological Supplies - CAROLINA BIOLOGICAL SUPPLY COMPANY; *pg.* 1513, *pg.* 1359
BIOS AGENT - PC Setup Software - PHOENIX TECHNOLOGIES LTD.; *pg.* 454, *pg.* 147
BIOS ENHANCEMENTS & MODULES - Software - PHOENIX TECHNOLOGIES LTD.; *pg.* 454, *pg.* 147
BIOSAGENTPLUS - Software - PHOENIX TECHNOLOGIES LTD.; *pg.* 454, *pg.* 147
BIOSAN - Cleaner SWISHER HYGIENE INC.; *pg.* 336, *pg.* 1507
BIOSAP - Absobents - ARCHER-DANIELS-MIDLAND COMPANY; *pg.* 825, *pg.* 565
BIOSCIENCE TECHNOLOGY - Trade Magazine - ADVANTAGE BUSINESS MEDIA; *pg.* 1613, *pg.* 1116
BIOSCOPE SPM - Scanning Probe Microscope - VEECO INSTRUMENTS INC.; *pg.* 1434, *pg.* 1322
BIOSCREW - Medical Equipment - CONMED CORPORATION; *pg.* 1517, *pg.* 1347
BIOSENSOR - Chemical Agent Detector - MINE SAFETY APPLIANCES COMPANY; *pg.* 1361, *pg.* 1525
BIOSENTRY - Disinfectant - NEOGEN CORPORATION; *pg.* 883, *pg.* 896
BIOSENTRY ACID-A-FOAM - Disinfectant - NEOGEN CORPORATION; *pg.* 883, *pg.* 896
BIOSENTRY BIOCRES - Disinfectants - NEOGEN CORPORATION; *pg.* 883, *pg.* 896
BIOSENTRY BIOPHENE - Disinfectant - NEOGEN CORPORATION; *pg.* 883, *pg.* 896
BIOSENTRY BIOQUAT - Disinfectant - NEOGEN CORPORATION; *pg.* 883, *pg.* 896
BIOSENTRY CHLOR-A-FOAM - Disinfectant - NEOGEN CORPORATION; *pg.* 883, *pg.* 896
BIOSEPRA - Chromatography Product - VERMILLION, INC.; *pg.* 1435, *pg.* 1667
BIOSERT - Vaginally or Rectally Administered Bioadhesive Delivery System - LUMARA HEALTH INC.; *pg.* 1557, *pg.* 973
BIOSHAPE - Nutritional Product - RBC LIFE SCIENCES, INC.; *pg.* 1588, *pg.* 1723
BIOSHIELD - Chemical Preparation - GEERPRES INC.; *pg.* 1339, *pg.* 901
BIOSITE - Pharmaceutical Product - ALERE INC.; *pg.* 1488, *pg.* 849
BIOSITE - Bioremediation Services - WASTE MANAGEMENT, INC.; *pg.* 1954, *pg.* 1716
BIOSITE DISCOVERY AN UNFAIR ADVANTAGE - Pharmaceutical Product - ALERE INC.; *pg.* 1488, *pg.* 849
BIOSOLV - Chemical Product - SPECTRUM CHEMICALS & LABORATORY PRODUCTS, INC.; *pg.* 1181, *pg.* 94
BIOSPECTRUM - 2D Imaging System - UVP, INC.; *pg.* 1434, *pg.* 298
BIOSPERSE - Chemicals For Agriculture - ASHLAND INC.; *pg.* 972, *pg.* 726
BIOSTAR - Rapid Membrane Test Products - ALERE INC.; *pg.* 1488, *pg.* 849
BIOSTEON - Wedge Interference Screw - STRYKER CORPORATION; *pg.* 1598, *pg.* 894
BIOSTINGER - Medical Equipment - CONMED CORPORATION; *pg.* 1517, *pg.* 1347
BIOSUITE - Protein & Peptide - WATERS CORPORATION; *pg.* 1436, *pg.* 834
BIOSUPPORT - Software - BIO-RAD LABORATORIES, INC.; *pg.* 1504, *pg.* 101
BIOSURF - Iodophor for Topical Biocide - LONZA INC.; *pg.* 1171, *pg.* 1041
BIOSWIPE - Software - 3M; *pg.* 339, *pg.* 179
BIOSYN - Reagent - HONEYWELL INTERNATIONAL INC.; *pg.* 407, *pg.* 1088
BIOTECH BAY - Pharmaceutical Product - BIOSPACE, INC.; *pg.* 1231, *pg.* 1082
BIOTECH BEACH - Pharmaceutical Product - BIOSPACE, INC.; *pg.* 1231, *pg.* 1082
BIOTECH WATCH - Publisher - BLOOMBERG BNA; *pg.* 1621, *pg.* 1772
BIOTECHNOLOGIES FOR MEDICINE - Slogan - CRYOLIFE, INC.; *pg.* 1520, *pg.* 534
BIOTECHNOLOGY EXPLORER - Software - BIO-RAD LABORATORIES, INC.; *pg.* 1504, *pg.* 101
BIOTIN - Biomolecule Product - THERMO FISHER SCIENTIFIC INC.; *pg.* 1602, *pg.* 61
BIOTIN-BLOT - Software - BIO-RAD LABORATORIES, INC.; *pg.* 1504, *pg.* 101
BIOTINTAG - Biotinylation Kit - SIGMA-ALDRICH CORPORATION; *pg.* 1181, *pg.* 1003
BIOTOMIC - Bicycle Accessories - SPECIALIZED BICYCLE COMPONENTS, INC.; *pg.* 1711, *pg.* 152
BIOTRACE - Nylon Membrane - PALL CORPORATION; *pg.* 232, *pg.* 1323
BIOTRACK - Software - BIOCLINICA, INC.; *pg.* 1506, *pg.* 1556
BIOTRUST - Finger Print Identification - 3M; *pg.* 339, *pg.* 179
BIOTWIST - Medical Equipment - CONMED CORPORATION; *pg.* 1517, *pg.* 1347
BIOUNIQUE - Identification Verification Systems - LOCKHEED MARTIN CORPORATION; *pg.* 229, *pg.* 762
BIOVAC - Smoke Evacuator - WALLACH SURGICAL DEVICES, INC.; *pg.* 1436, *pg.* 381
BIOVEST - Dental Product - DENTSPLY INTERNATIONAL INC.; *pg.* 1522, *pg.* 1596
BIOWAX - Dental Product - DENTSPLY INTERNATIONAL INC.; *pg.* 1522, *pg.* 1596
BIOZIP - Suture Anchor - STRYKER CORPORATION; *pg.* 1598, *pg.* 894
BIPHOR - White Pigment - BUNGE LIMITED; *pg.* 842, *pg.* 1351
BIRD GRUB - High Energy Food - GARDENS ALIVE!, INC.; *pg.* 1796, *pg.* 693
BIRD NETTING - Shrubbery & Garden Protection - E.I. DU PONT DE NEMOURS & COMPANY; *pg.* 1159, *pg.* 390
BIRD TALK - Magazine - I-5 PUBLISHING LLC; *pg.* 1651, *pg.* 133
BIRDERS WORLD - Magazine - KALMBACH PUBLISHING CO.; *pg.* 1656, *pg.* 1898
BIRDHOUSE - Lace Curtain - HERITAGE LACE INC.; *pg.* 694, *pg.* 711
BIRDIE - Golf Shoes - JOHNSTON & MURPHY CO.; *pg.* 1810, *pg.* 1651
BIRDIE - Fast Food - MCDONALD'S CORPORATION; *pg.* 1737, *pg.* 645
BIRDOLA - Pet Product - PETSMART, INC.; *pg.* 1481, *pg.* 18
BIRDOLA PLUS - Pet Product - PETSMART, INC.; *pg.* 1481, *pg.* 18
BIRDS EYE FOODS - Frozen Vegetables - PINNACLE FOODS GROUP LLC; *pg.* 889, *pg.* 1104
BIRDS OF A FEATHER - Video Game - INTERNATIONAL GAME TECHNOLOGY; *pg.* 957, *pg.* 1024
BIRDS USA - Magazine - I-5 PUBLISHING LLC; *pg.* 1651, *pg.* 133
BIRDSNACK - Bird Seed - INTERMOUNTAIN FARMERS ASSOCIATION; *pg.* 705, *pg.* 1759
BIRKETT'S - Buckwheat Food Product - THE BIRKETT MILLS; *pg.* 826, *pg.* 1321
BIRKO - Antifoam - BIRKO CORPORATION; *pg.* 1149, *pg.* 332
BIRKO ANTIFOAM 10 - Chemical Product - BIRKO CORPORATION; *pg.* 1149, *pg.* 332
BIRKO ANTIFOAM 100 - Chemical Product - BIRKO CORPORATION; *pg.* 1149, *pg.* 332
BIRKO D FOAM - Chemical Product - BIRKO CORPORATION; *pg.* 1149, *pg.* 332
BIRKODYNE - Sanitizer - BIRKO CORPORATION; *pg.* 1149, *pg.* 332
BIRKOSIDE - Hide Processing Agent - BIRKO CORPORATION; *pg.* 1149, *pg.* 332
BIRKS - Jewelry - BIRKS & MAYORS INC.; *pg.* 1, *pg.* 1953
BIRMINGHAM - Furniture - BUSH INDUSTRIES INC.; *pg.* 919, *pg.* 1170
BIRMINGHAM - Flatware - ONEIDA LTD; *pg.* 1129, *pg.* 1318
BIRMINGHAM POST-HERALD - Newspaper - THE E.W. SCRIPPS COMPANY; *pg.* 1639, *pg.* 1412
BIROX - Film - E.I. DU PONT DE NEMOURS & COMPANY; *pg.* 1159, *pg.* 390
BIRT - Software - ACTUATE CORPORATION; *pg.* 342, *pg.* 253
BIRTHDAY BLOWOUT - Lottery Game - NEW YORK STATE LOTTERY; *pg.* 1001, *pg.* 1340
BIRTHDAY CASH - Game - WMS INDUSTRIES INC.; *pg.* 593, *pg.* 666
BIRTHDAY EXPRESS - Apparel - CELEBRATE EXPRESS, INC.; *pg.* 1764, *pg.* 1883
BIRTHDAY EXPRESS.COM - Apparel - CELEBRATE EXPRESS, INC.; *pg.* 1764, *pg.* 1883
BIRTHDAY FLOWER CAKE - Flower Arrangement - 1-800-FLOWERS.COM, INC.; *pg.* 1758, *pg.* 1151
BIRTHDAY PARTY BOUQUET - Floral Bouquet - FTD GROUP, INC.; *pg.* 1795, *pg.* 608
BIRTHSTONES - Lottery Game - KENTUCKY LOTTERY CORPORATION; *pg.* 996, *pg.* 735
BIS - Brain Activity Monitor - MEDTRONIC; *pg.* 1563, *pg.* 830
BIS - Biscuit Wafer - MONDELEZ INTERNATIONAL, INC.; *pg.* 878, *pg.* 601
BISAC-EVAC - Pharmaceutical Product - G&W LABORATORIES INC.; *pg.* 1532, *pg.* 1123
BISCAYNE - Paper & Nonwoven Material - FIBERMARK INC.; *pg.* 1457, *pg.* 1764
BISCO SILICONES - Silicone Foams - ROGERS CORPORATION; *pg.* 1305, *pg.* 369
BISLEY - Single Action Revolver - STURM, RUGER & COMPANY, INC.; *pg.* 1846, *pg.* 371
BISLEY VAQUERO - Single-Action Revolver - STURM, RUGER & COMPANY, INC.; *pg.* 1846, *pg.* 371
BISO - Italian Wine - LAIRD & COMPANY, INC.; *pg.* 1966, *pg.* 1119
BISOCARD - Pharmaceutical Product - VALEANT PHARMACEUTICALS INTERNATIONAL; *pg.* 1605, *pg.* 1047
BISON - Furniture - JASPER GROUP; *pg.* 930, *pg.* 691
BISON - Dairy Food Products - UPSTATE NIAGARA COOPERATIVE, INC.; *pg.* 907, *pg.* 1151
BISPEED - Floor Machine - TORNADO INDUSTRIES, INC.; *pg.* 1383, *pg.* 591
BISPHENOL AF - Flurochemical - HALOCARBON PRODUCTS CORPORATION; *pg.* 978, *pg.* 1116
BISQUICK - Food Product - GENERAL MILLS, INC.; *pg.* 828, *pg.* 933
BISSELL TO GO - Floor Care Product - BISSELL HOMECARE, INC.; *pg.* 52, *pg.* 887
BISSETT - Mutual Funds - FRANKLIN RESOURCES, INC.; *pg.* 760, *pg.* 254
BIST COMPILER - Software System - MENTOR GRAPHICS CORPORATION; *pg.* 432, *pg.* 1510
BIST-IN-PLACE - Software System - MENTOR GRAPHICS CORPORATION; *pg.* 432, *pg.* 1510
BIST-READY - Software System - MENTOR GRAPHICS CORPORATION; *pg.* 432, *pg.* 1510
BISTARCHITECT - Software System - MENTOR GRAPHICS CORPORATION; *pg.* 432, *pg.* 1510
BISTATIX - Radio Frequency Identification - MOTOROLA SOLUTIONS, INC.; *pg.* 657, *pg.* 659
BISTO - Food Product - CAMPBELL COMPANY OF CANADA LTD; *pg.* 844, *pg.* 1935
BISTRA - Beverages - THE COCA-COLA COMPANY; *pg.* 240, *pg.* 493
BISTRO - Tumblers - CARLISLE FOODSERVICE PRODUCTS INCORPORATED; *pg.* 1455, *pg.* 1485
BISTRO - Furniture - ETHAN ALLEN INTERIORS INC.; *pg.* 924, *pg.* 343

BISTRO - Lighting Product - QUOIZEL INC.; *pg.* 1304, *pg.* 1616
BISTRO 100 - Restaurant - LEVY RESTAURANTS, INC.; *pg.* 1736, *pg.* 580
BISTRO 110 - Restaurant - LEVY RESTAURANTS, INC.; *pg.* 1736, *pg.* 580
BISTRO TOUJOURS - Restaurant - LEVY RESTAURANTS, INC.; *pg.* 1736, *pg.* 580
BISTRONE - Beverages - THE COCA-COLA COMPANY; *pg.* 240, *pg.* 493
BISYMMETRIK - Vacuum Process Tool - BROOKS AUTOMATION, INC.; *pg.* 1320, *pg.* 813
BIT - Software Consulting - CIBER, INC.; *pg.* 372, *pg.* 330
BIT & BRIDLE - Apparel - TRACTOR SUPPLY COMPANY; *pg.* 708, *pg.* 1627
BIT-O-HONEY - Candy - NESTLE USA, INC.; *pg.* 883, *pg.* 96
BITE - Footwear - CROCS, INC.; *pg.* 1806, *pg.* 335
BITREX - Cleaner - THE SAVOGRAN COMPANY; *pg.* 1447, *pg.* 840
BITS CRASHERS - Yogurt-Covered Fruity Dots - KELLOGG COMPANY; *pg.* 831, *pg.* 870
BITS N PIECES - Milk Shakes - BIGLARI HOLDINGS INC.; *pg.* 1015, *pg.* 1739
BITTERR - Footwear - STEVEN MADDEN, LTD.; *pg.* 1819, *pg.* 1176
BITTERSWEET - Furniture - ASHLEY FURNITURE INDUSTRIES, INC.; *pg.* 914, *pg.* 1852
BITTERSWEET PARTNERSHIP - Beer - MOLSON COORS BREWING COMPANY; *pg.* 256, *pg.* 321
BITTY BABY - Toys - AMERICAN GIRL LLC; *pg.* 949, *pg.* 1871
BITTY BABY COLLECTION - Toys - AMERICAN GIRL LLC; *pg.* 949, *pg.* 1871
BITTY BABY DESIGN - Toys - AMERICAN GIRL LLC; *pg.* 949, *pg.* 1871
BITTY BEAR - Toys - AMERICAN GIRL LLC; *pg.* 949, *pg.* 1871
BITTY BEAR'S BUNCH - Toys - AMERICAN GIRL LLC; *pg.* 949, *pg.* 1871
BITTY BUNNY - Toys - AMERICAN GIRL LLC; *pg.* 949, *pg.* 1871
BITTY DUCKY - Toys - AMERICAN GIRL LLC; *pg.* 949, *pg.* 1871
BITTY FROGGY - Toys - AMERICAN GIRL LLC; *pg.* 949, *pg.* 1871
BITTY KITTY - Toys - AMERICAN GIRL LLC; *pg.* 949, *pg.* 1871
BITTY LAMBIE - Toys - AMERICAN GIRL LLC; *pg.* 949, *pg.* 1871
BITTY PIGGY - Toys - AMERICAN GIRL LLC; *pg.* 949, *pg.* 1871
BITTY PUPPY - Toys - AMERICAN GIRL LLC; *pg.* 949, *pg.* 1871
BITTY TWINS - Toys - AMERICAN GIRL LLC; *pg.* 949, *pg.* 1871
BITUMASTIC - Bituminous Coatings - PETTIT PAINT COMPANY; *pg.* 1444, *pg.* 1116
BITZ & PIZZAS - Video Game - INTERNATIONAL GAME TECHNOLOGY; *pg.* 957, *pg.* 1024
BIVCAP - Patient Care - ST. JUDE MEDICAL, INC.; *pg.* 1596, *pg.* 963
BIVER - Chemical Reagent - HACH COMPANY; *pg.* 1415, *pg.* 334
BIVERT - Agricultural Chemicals - WILBUR-ELLIS COMPANY; *pg.* 1185, *pg.* 234
BIX - Office Furniture - STEELCASE INC.; *pg.* 475, *pg.* 889
BIX SIDE TABLE - Tables - STEELCASE INC.; *pg.* 475, *pg.* 889
BIXCUT - Surgical & Medical Product - STRYKER CORPORATION; *pg.* 1598, *pg.* 894
BIZ - Athletic Shoe - JACK SCHWARTZ SHOES, INC.; *pg.* 1810, *pg.* 1245
BIZGRAPH - Software - CHYRONHEGO; *pg.* 371, *pg.* 1179
BIZZY BALLS - Cat Toy - THE HARTZ MOUNTAIN CORP.; *pg.* 1476, *pg.* 1120
BJ - Sodium Silicate - PQ CORPORATION; *pg.* 1178, *pg.* 1515
B.J. HOLLADAY - Distilled Spirits - MCCORMICK DISTILLING CO., INC.; *pg.* 1966, *pg.* 1007
BJARE - Beverages - THE COCA-COLA COMPANY; *pg.* 240, *pg.* 493
BJ'S AUTO BUYING PROGRAM - Membership Plan - BJ'S WHOLESALE CLUB, INC.; *pg.* 1762, *pg.* 857
BJ'S BERRY BURST CIDER - Beer - BJ'S RESTAURANTS, INC.; *pg.* 1716, *pg.* 104
BJ'S CHICAGO PIZZERIA - Restaurants - BJ'S RESTAURANTS, INC.; *pg.* 1716, *pg.* 104
BJ'S FAMOUS PIZOOKIE - Cookie - BJ'S RESTAURANTS, INC.; *pg.* 1716, *pg.* 104
BJ'S GAS - Membership Plan - BJ'S WHOLESALE CLUB, INC.; *pg.* 1762, *pg.* 857
BJ'S HOME IMPROVEMENT - Membership Plan - BJ'S WHOLESALE CLUB, INC.; *pg.* 1762, *pg.* 857
BJ'S JEREMIAH RED - Beer - BJ'S RESTAURANTS, INC.; *pg.* 1716, *pg.* 104
BJ'S OPTICAL DEPARTMENT - Membership Plan - BJ'S WHOLESALE CLUB, INC.; *pg.* 1762, *pg.* 857
BJ'S PIZZA & GRILL - Restaurant - BJ'S RESTAURANTS, INC.; *pg.* 1716, *pg.* 104
BJ'S P.M. PORTER - Beer - BJ'S RESTAURANTS, INC.; *pg.* 1716, *pg.* 104
BJ'S PROPANE - Membership Plan - BJ'S WHOLESALE CLUB, INC.; *pg.* 1762, *pg.* 857
BJ'S RESTAURANT & BREWERY - Restaurant - BJ'S RESTAURANTS, INC.; *pg.* 1716, *pg.* 104
BJ'S RESTAURANT & BREWHOUSE - Restaurant - BJ'S RESTAURANTS, INC.; *pg.* 1716, *pg.* 104
BJ'S REWARDS - Membership Plan - BJ'S WHOLESALE CLUB, INC.; *pg.* 1762, *pg.* 857
BJ'S REWARDS MEMBERSHIP - Membership Plan - BJ'S WHOLESALE CLUB, INC.; *pg.* 1762, *pg.* 857
BJ'S TIRE CENTER - Membership Plan - BJ'S WHOLESALE CLUB, INC.; *pg.* 1762, *pg.* 857
BJ'S.COM - E-Commerce Website - BJ'S WHOLESALE CLUB, INC.; *pg.* 1762, *pg.* 857
BK BIG FISH - Fish Sandwich - BURGER KING CORPORATION; *pg.* 1719, *pg.* 440
BK BREAKFAST SHOTS - Burger - BURGER KING CORPORATION; *pg.* 1719, *pg.* 440
BK BURGER SHOTS - Burger - BURGER KING CORPORATION; *pg.* 1719, *pg.* 440
BK FLAME BROILED FLAVORED POTATO - Snack Food - INVENTURE FOODS, INC.; *pg.* 1023, *pg.* 17
BK FUSION - Ice Cream - BURGER KING CORPORATION; *pg.* 1719, *pg.* 440
BK JOE - Coffee - BURGER KING CORPORATION; *pg.* 1719, *pg.* 440
BK STACKER - Burger - BURGER KING CORPORATION; *pg.* 1719, *pg.* 440
BK VEGGIE - Burger - BURGER KING CORPORATION; *pg.* 1719, *pg.* 440
BK WRAPPER - Cheesy Bacon - BURGER KING CORPORATION; *pg.* 1719, *pg.* 440
BKE - Apparel - THE BUCKLE, INC.; *pg.* 1764, *pg.* 1011
BKI - Food Service Equipment - BKI; *pg.* 52, *pg.* 1621
BKI - Food Service Equipment - STANDEX INTERNATIONAL CORPORATION; *pg.* 60, *pg.* 1039
BLA BRAND - Food Product - CAMPBELL SOUP COMPANY; *pg.* 844, *pg.* 1048
BLACK - Video Game - ELECTRONIC ARTS INC.; *pg.* 951, *pg.* 189
BLACK - Pillow & Throw - HERITAGE LACE INC.; *pg.* 694, *pg.* 711
BLACK ADAM - Character - DC COMICS, INC.; *pg.* 1633, *pg.* 1221
BLACK AMBER - Ale - BIG ROCK BREWERY INCOME TRUST; *pg.* 239, *pg.* 1902
BLACK & BEAUTIFUL - Conditioners, Hair Spray - E.T. BROWNE DRUG COMPANY, INC.; *pg.* 509, *pg.* 1060
BLACK & DECKER - Tools - STANLEY BLACK & DECKER, INC.; *pg.* 1063, *pg.* 358
BLACK & SILVER - Putty Knives, Scrapers - HYDE TOOLS, INC.; *pg.* 1125, *pg.* 844
BLACK & TAN - Lager Beer - ANHEUSER-BUSCH COMPANIES, LLC; *pg.* 237, *pg.* 991
BLACK & WHITE - Fabric - MOMENTUM TEXTILES INC.; *pg.* 697, *pg.* 114
BLACK & WHITE - Game - MULTIMEDIA GAMES INC.; *pg.* 442, *pg.* 1664
BLACK ANGUS RESERVE - Beef Products - AMERICAN FOODS GROUP, LLC; *pg.* 837, *pg.* 1859
BLACK APRON EXCLUSIVES - Coffee - STARBUCKS CORPORATION; *pg.* 897, *pg.* 1840
BLACK BAVARIAN - Beverage - SPRECHER BREWING COMPANY; *pg.* 265, *pg.* 1858
BLACK BOX - Computer Equipment - BLACK BOX CORPORATION; *pg.* 361, *pg.* 1547
BLACK BOX - Software Application - BMC SOFTWARE, INC.; *pg.* 362, *pg.* 1701
BLACK BROS - Coater & Spreader - BLACK BROTHERS COMPANY; *pg.* 70, *pg.* 632
BLACK BROWN 1826 - Menswear - LORD & TAYLOR LLC; *pg.* 1777, *pg.* 1252
BLACK BUTTE - Brew - DESCHUTES BREWERY INC.; *pg.* 248, *pg.* 1496
BLACK BUTTERFLY - Knife - BEAR & SON CUTLERY, INC.; *pg.* 1827, *pg.* 7
BLACK CANYON - Beef Products - NATIONAL BEEF PACKING COMPANY, LLC; *pg.* 882, *pg.* 985
BLACK CATHODE - Display - XEROX CORPORATION; *pg.* 494, *pg.* 365
BLACK CHERRY - Video Game - INTERNATIONAL GAME TECHNOLOGY; *pg.* 957, *pg.* 1024
BLACK CHERRY DOUBLER - Lottery Game - IDAHO LOTTERY; *pg.* 995, *pg.* 547
BLACK CHERRY VANILLA COKE - Soft Drink - THE COCA-COLA COMPANY; *pg.* 240, *pg.* 493
BLACK CHOCOLATE STOUT - Seasonal Beer - THE BROOKLYN BREWERY; *pg.* 239, *pg.* 1145
BLACK COAT - Stainless Steel Product - AK STEEL HOLDING CORPORATION; *pg.* 1311, *pg.* 1479
BLACK DERLIN - Knife - BEAR & SON CUTLERY, INC.; *pg.* 1827, *pg.* 7
BLACK DIAMOND - Outdoor Equipment - BLACK DIAMOND, INC.; *pg.* 1827, *pg.* 1756
BLACK DIAMOND - Lens - LIGHTPATH TECHNOLOGIES INC; *pg.* 1420, *pg.* 454
BLACK DIAMOND - Cheese - PARMALAT CANADA INC.; *pg.* 888, *pg.* 1941
BLACK DOG ALE - Beer - UNITED STATES BEVERAGE LLC; *pg.* 266, *pg.* 379
BLACK EAGLE - Rods - WRIGHT & MCGILL CO.; *pg.* 1848, *pg.* 324
BLACK EYED PEA - Home-Style Restaurants - DYNAMIC MANAGEMENT COMPANY LLC; *pg.* 1727, *pg.* 1635
BLACK FLAG - Ant, Roach & Other Flying Insect Aerosols - THE CLOROX COMPANY; *pg.* 327, *pg.* 169
BLACK FOREST GUMMIES - Candy - FERRARA CANDY CO.; *pg.* 1852, *pg.* 612
BLACK GOLD - Saltwater Spinning Reels - DAIWA CORPORATION; *pg.* 1832, *pg.* 75
BLACK GOLD - Art Product - DANIEL SMITH INC.; *pg.* 1766, *pg.* 1835
BLACK GOLD - Golf Shaft - TRUE TEMPER SPORTS, INC.; *pg.* 1847, *pg.* 1647
BLACK HAWK STOUT - Beer - MENDOCINO BREWING COMPANY; *pg.* 254, *pg.* 298
BLACK HILLS - Minerals - MINERALS TECHNOLOGIES INC.; *pg.* 1173, *pg.* 617
BLACK ICE - Gaming Product - GLD PRODUCTS, INC.; *pg.* 1835, *pg.* 1882
BLACK JACK - Video Game - INTERNATIONAL GAME TECHNOLOGY; *pg.* 957, *pg.* 1024
BLACK KNIGHT - Game - WMS INDUSTRIES INC.; *pg.* 593, *pg.* 666
BLACK LABEL - Fragrance - RALPH LAUREN CORPORATION; *pg.* 46, *pg.* 1284
BLACK MAGIC - Gaming Product - GLD PRODUCTS, INC.; *pg.* 1835, *pg.* 1882
BLACK MAGIC - Blackening Products - HUBBARD-HALL, INC.; *pg.* 1167, *pg.* 382
BLACK MAGIC - Video Game - INTERNATIONAL GAME TECHNOLOGY; *pg.* 957, *pg.* 1024
BLACK MAGIC - Car Wax - SHELL LUBRICANTS; *pg.* 217, *pg.* 1714
BLACK MAGIC - Vehicle Care - ZEP INC.; *pg.* 338, *pg.* 524
BLACK MAGNUM - Coal Slag Abrasive - FAIRMOUNT SANTROL; *pg.* 1162, *pg.* 1409
BLACK MARIA - Tobacco Product - AMERICAN SNUFF COMPANY; *pg.* 1893, *pg.* 1641
BLACK MARIAH - Gaming Product - GLD PRODUCTS, INC.; *pg.* 1835, *pg.* 1882
BLACK MAX - Airless Paint Spray Guns - GRACO, INC.; *pg.* 1342, *pg.* 935
BLACK MAX - Hose - HBD INDUSTRIES, INC.; *pg.* 207, *pg.* 1449
BLACK MAXI-SHARP - File Product - SIMONDS INTERNATIONAL CORPORATION; *pg.* 1376, *pg.* 819
BLACK OLIVE - Pigment - BASF CATALYSTS LLC; *pg.* 1148, *pg.* 1074
BLACK ONYX - Nail Care Product - OPI PRODUCTS INC.; *pg.* 518, *pg.* 167
BLACK PEARL - Chemical Coating - ENTHONE INC.; *pg.* 1161, *pg.* 381
BLACK PEARLS - Carbon Black - CABOT CORPORATION;

First page reference indicates Business Class Edition
Second page reference indicates Geographic Edition

pg. 1151, *pg.* 792

BLACK PLATE - Chemical Product - HURST CHEMICAL COMPANY; *pg.* 1168, *pg.* 174

BLACK POWDER GOLD - Bullet Lube - LYMAN PRODUCTS CORPORATION; *pg.* 1839, *pg.* 356

BLACK RACER - Hose - HBD INDUSTRIES, INC.; *pg.* 207, *pg.* 1449

BLACK RADIANCE - Cosmetics - MARKWINS INTERNATIONAL CORP.; *pg.* 516, *pg.* 67

BLACK RHINO - Video Slots - INTERNATIONAL GAME TECHNOLOGY; *pg.* 957, *pg.* 1024

BLACK RIVET - Apparel - G-III APPAREL GROUP, LTD.; *pg.* 41, *pg.* 1233

BLACK ROCK - Roller Cover - VAIL RUBBER WORKS, INC.; *pg.* 1891, *pg.* 906

BLACK SAPPHIRE - Substrate - SPINNAKER COATING, LLC; *pg.* 1470, *pg.* 1477

BLACK SHEEP - Video Game - INTERNATIONAL GAME TECHNOLOGY; *pg.* 957, *pg.* 1024

BLACK SPOODLE - Utensil - THE VOLLRATH COMPANY LLC; *pg.* 1139, *pg.* 1894

BLACK STEEL - Fluid Handling System - GRACO, INC.; *pg.* 1342, *pg.* 935

BLACK SUEDE - Beauty Product - AVON PRODUCTS, INC.; *pg.* 500, *pg.* 1198

BLACK SWAN - Wine - E&J GALLO WINERY; *pg.* 1962, *pg.* 149

BLACK TIE - Slots - INTERNATIONAL GAME TECHNOLOGY; *pg.* 957, *pg.* 1024

BLACK TIE - Fragrance - OLEG CASSINI, INC.; *pg.* 30, *pg.* 1274

BLACK TOWER - Wine - SAZERAC COMPANY, INC.; *pg.* 1969, *pg.* 745

BLACK TRIGGERFOAM - Foam - POWERS FASTENERS INC.; *pg.* 1059, *pg.* 1143

BLACK VALUFLEX - General Service Hose - HBD INDUSTRIES, INC.; *pg.* 207, *pg.* 1449

BLACK WATCH - Tape Cartridges for Enterprise Storage - IMATION CORP.; *pg.* 413, *pg.* 952

BLACK WIDOW - Bait Casting Reels - DAIWA CORPORATION; *pg.* 1832, *pg.* 75

BLACK WIDOW - Gaming Product - GLD PRODUCTS, INC.; *pg.* 1835, *pg.* 1882

BLACK WIDOW - Slots - INTERNATIONAL GAME TECHNOLOGY; *pg.* 957, *pg.* 1024

BLACKBAUD DIRECT MARKETING - Direct Marketing Services - BLACKBAUD, INC.; *pg.* 361, *pg.* 1613

BLACKBAUD ENTERPRISE CRM - Constituent Relationship Management Software - BLACKBAUD, INC.; *pg.* 361, *pg.* 1613

BLACKBAUD STUDENT INFORMATION SYSTEM - Education Administration - BLACKBAUD, INC.; *pg.* 361, *pg.* 1613

BLACKBEARD'S DOUBLE DOUBLOONS - Video Game - INTERNATIONAL GAME TECHNOLOGY; *pg.* 957, *pg.* 1024

BLACKBEARD'S GOLD - Video Game - INTERNATIONAL GAME TECHNOLOGY; *pg.* 957, *pg.* 1024

BLACKBERRY 10 - Smartphone - BLACKBERRY; *pg.* 625, *pg.* 1717

BLACKBERRY 10 - Smartphone - BLACKBERRY LIMITED; *pg.* 625, *pg.* 1947

BLACKBERRY BLISS - Fruit Drink - JAMBA, INC.; *pg.* 1024, *pg.* 84

BLACKBERRY BOLD - Smartphone - BLACKBERRY LIMITED; *pg.* 625, *pg.* 1947

BLACKBERRY BUILT-IN - Software - BLACKBERRY LIMITED; *pg.* 625, *pg.* 1947

BLACKBERRY CONNECTION - Smartphone - BLACKBERRY LIMITED; *pg.* 625, *pg.* 1947

BLACKBERRY CURVE - Smartphone - BLACKBERRY LIMITED; *pg.* 625, *pg.* 1947

BLACKBERRY ENTERPRISE EDITION - Wireless Email Solution - BLACKBERRY LIMITED; *pg.* 625, *pg.* 1947

BLACKBERRY EXCHANGE EDITION - Wireless Handheld - BLACKBERRY LIMITED; *pg.* 625, *pg.* 1947

BLACKBERRY INTERNET EDITION - Wireless Internet Service - BLACKBERRY LIMITED; *pg.* 625, *pg.* 1947

BLACKBERRY NOTES EDITION - Wireless Handheld - BLACKBERRY LIMITED; *pg.* 625, *pg.* 1947

BLACKBERRY PEARL - Smartphone - BLACKBERRY LIMITED; *pg.* 625, *pg.* 1947

BLACKBERRY PLAYBOOK - Tablet - BLACKBERRY; *pg.* 625, *pg.* 1717

BLACKBERRY PLAYBOOK - Tablet - BLACKBERRY LIMITED; *pg.* 625, *pg.* 1947

BLACKBERRY STORM - Smartphone - BLACKBERRY LIMITED; *pg.* 625, *pg.* 1947

BLACKBERRY SUREPRESS - Touch Screen Technology - BLACKBERRY LIMITED; *pg.* 625, *pg.* 1947

BLACKBERRY TOUR - Smartphone - BLACKBERRY LIMITED; *pg.* 625, *pg.* 1947

BLACKBERRY UNITE! - Software - BLACKBERRY LIMITED; *pg.* 625, *pg.* 1947

BLACKBIRCH PRESS - Publisher - GALE CENGAGE LEARNING; *pg.* 1643, *pg.* 885

BLACKBIRD - Systems Integration & Aeronautics - LOCKHEED MARTIN CORPORATION; *pg.* 229, *pg.* 762

BLACKBOARD ACADEMIC SUITE - Software - BLACKBOARD INC.; *pg.* 1232, *pg.* 396

BLACKBOARD COMMERCE SUITE - Software - BLACKBOARD INC.; *pg.* 1232, *pg.* 396

BLACKBOARD COMMUNITY SYSTEM - Software - BLACKBOARD INC.; *pg.* 1232, *pg.* 396

BLACKBOARD CONNECT - Software - BLACKBOARD INC.; *pg.* 1232, *pg.* 396

BLACKBOARD CONTENT SYSTEM - Software - BLACKBOARD INC.; *pg.* 1232, *pg.* 396

BLACKBOARD LEARN - Software - BLACKBOARD INC.; *pg.* 1232, *pg.* 396

BLACKBOARD LEARNING SYSTEM - Software - BLACKBOARD INC.; *pg.* 1232, *pg.* 396

BLACKBOARD TRANSACT - Software - BLACKBOARD INC.; *pg.* 1232, *pg.* 396

BLACKBOARD TRANSACTION SYSTEM - Software - BLACKBOARD INC.; *pg.* 1232, *pg.* 396

BLACKBURN - Compression Connector - THOMAS & BETTS CORPORATION; *pg.* 680, *pg.* 1646

BLACKDIAMOND - Switch - EXTREME NETWORKS INC; *pg.* 287, *pg.* 245

BLACKDIAMOND 10808 - Switch - EXTREME NETWORKS INC; *pg.* 287, *pg.* 245

BLACKDIAMOND 12800R - Switch - EXTREME NETWORKS INC; *pg.* 287, *pg.* 245

BLACKDIAMOND 20809 - Switch - EXTREME NETWORKS INC; *pg.* 287, *pg.* 245

BLACKDIAMOND 8800 - Switch - EXTREME NETWORKS INC; *pg.* 287, *pg.* 245

BLACKDIAMOND12804C - Switch - EXTREME NETWORKS INC; *pg.* 287, *pg.* 245

BLACKFIN - Embedded Processor - ANALOG DEVICES, INC.; *pg.* 617, *pg.* 839

BLACKFIRE - Beverages - THE COCA-COLA COMPANY; *pg.* 240, *pg.* 493

BLACKFOOT POND - T-Shirts - ABERCROMBIE & FITCH CO.; *pg.* 37, *pg.* 1466

BLACKGLAMA - Mink - AMERICAN LEGEND COOPERATIVE; *pg.* 18, *pg.* 1833

BLACKHAWK - Air Respirator - MINE SAFETY APPLIANCES COMPANY; *pg.* 1361, *pg.* 1525

BLACKHAWK - Collision Repair Equipment - SNAP-ON INCORPORATED; *pg.* 1062, *pg.* 1862

BLACKHAWK - Mechanic Tools - STANLEY BLACK & DECKER, INC.; *pg.* 1063, *pg.* 358

BLACKHAWK - Revolver - STURM, RUGER & COMPANY, INC.; *pg.* 1846, *pg.* 371

BLACKHAWK GRILLE - Restaurants - TAVISTOCK RESTAURANT GROUP; *pg.* 1753, *pg.* 803

BLACKHEART - Amplifier Products - LOUD TECHNOLOGIES INC.; *pg.* 652, *pg.* 1847

BLACKHOOK PORTER - Beverage - CRAFT BREWERS ALLIANCE, INC; *pg.* 247, *pg.* 1502

BLACKMAC - Airplane Propellers - MCCAULEY PROPELLER SYSTEMS; *pg.* 231, *pg.* 724

BLACKOUT - Kitchen Bags - PACTIV CORPORATION; *pg.* 1466, *pg.* 624

BLACKOUT PAYS - Video Game - INTERNATIONAL GAME TECHNOLOGY; *pg.* 957, *pg.* 1024

BLACK'S GUIDE - Real Estate Guide - NETWORK COMMUNICATIONS INC.; *pg.* 1271, *pg.* 534

BLACKSINGLES.COM - Internet Dating Service for African American Singles - SPARK NETWORKS, INC.; *pg.* 472, *pg.* 140

BLACKSPIDER - Software - WEBSENSE, INC.; *pg.* 491, *pg.* 210

BLACKSTONE - Cigar And Tobacco - SWISHER INTERNATIONAL, INC.; *pg.* 1895, *pg.* 345

BLACKTOP - Athletic Shoes - REEBOK INTERNATIONAL LTD.; *pg.* 1817, *pg.* 811

BLADDERCHEK - Pharmaceutical Product - ALERE INC.; *pg.* 1488, *pg.* 849

THE BLADE - Daily Newspaper - THE BLADE CO.; *pg.* 1621, *pg.* 1476

THE BLADE - Newspaper - BLOCK COMMUNICATIONS, INC.; *pg.* 1621, *pg.* 1476

THE BLADE - Lighting Product - H.E. WILLIAMS, INC.; *pg.* 1299, *pg.* 974

BLADE - Watch - OAKLEY, INC.; *pg.* 1840, *pg.* 86

BLADE - Turf Product - PBI/GORDON CORPORATION; *pg.* 1176, *pg.* 985

BLADEFRAME - Software - EGENERA, INC.; *pg.* 390, *pg.* 802

BLADEPRO - Dicing Blade - KULICKE & SOFFA INDUSTRIES, INC.; *pg.* 650, *pg.* 1533

BLADERUNNER - Chip - BROADCOM CORPORATION; *pg.* 364, *pg.* 108

BLADERUNNER 175 - Wafer Test Product - FORMFACTOR, INC.; *pg.* 1882, *pg.* 122

BLADESAVER - Loader Bucket Lip System - HENSLEY INDUSTRIES, INC.; *pg.* 1166, *pg.* 1682

BLAGDON - Pump Product - IDEX CORPORATION; *pg.* 1347, *pg.* 623

THE BLAIR WITCH PROJECT - Motion Pictures - LIONS GATE ENTERTAINMENT CORP.; *pg.* 296, *pg.* 274

BLAK-RAY - Long Wave Lamps - UVP, INC.; *pg.* 1434, *pg.* 298

BLAKE & MANLEY - Men's Sweaters - KELLWOOD COMPANY; *pg.* 28, *pg.* 975

BLAKELEY - Sport Knife - MCNETT CORPORATION; *pg.* 1839, *pg.* 1817

BLAKELY - Ceiling Fan - WESTINGHOUSE LIGHTING CORPORATION; *pg.* 687, *pg.* 1571

BLANCA - Fabric - NEMSCHOFF, INC.; *pg.* 936, *pg.* 1890

BLANCHARD - Machine Tool Product - BOURN & KOCH MACHINE TOOL COMPANY; *pg.* 1319, *pg.* 654

BLANCHE DE CHAMBLY - Beer - SLEEMAN UNIBROUE QUEBEC; *pg.* 265, *pg.* 1950

BLANCO - Furniture - AMERICAN LEATHER LP; *pg.* 912, *pg.* 1673

BLANCO - Tripe Processing Product - BIRKO CORPORATION; *pg.* 1149, *pg.* 332

BLANCS-BRUT - Wine - BILTMORE ESTATE WINE COMPANY; *pg.* 1958, *pg.* 1358

BLANK CHECK - Auto Financing - CAPITAL ONE FINANCIAL CORPORATION; *pg.* 730, *pg.* 1789

BLANKET BUDDIES - Blanket - 1-800-FLOWERS.COM, INC.; *pg.* 1758, *pg.* 1151

BLANKET WRAP - Fabric - NEMSCHOFF, INC.; *pg.* 936, *pg.* 1890

BLANKETROL - Medical Product - CINCINNATI SUB-ZERO PRODUCTS, INC.; *pg.* 1070, *pg.* 1411

BLANKETROL II - Hyper-Hypothermia System - CINCINNATI SUB-ZERO PRODUCTS, INC.; *pg.* 1070, *pg.* 1411

BLANKIT - Coating Product - PPG INDUSTRIES, INC.; *pg.* 1445, *pg.* 1579

BLANOSE - Polymer - HERCULES INCORPORATED; *pg.* 1166, *pg.* 392

BLANQUITA - Bleaches - THE CLOROX COMPANY; *pg.* 327, *pg.* 169

BLAST - Motorcycles - HARLEY-DAVIDSON, INC.; *pg.* 178, *pg.* 1874

BLAST - Cutting Tool - LEATHERMAN TOOL GROUP, INC.; *pg.* 1053, *pg.* 1504

BLAST - Software System - MENTOR GRAPHICS CORPORATION; *pg.* 432, *pg.* 1510

THE BLAST - Theme Park Ride - WET 'N WILD, INC.; *pg.* 592, *pg.* 457

BLAST-FLEX - Hose - HBD INDUSTRIES, INC.; *pg.* 207, *pg.* 1449

BLAST FROM THE PAST - Game - WMS INDUSTRIES INC.; *pg.* 593, *pg.* 666

BLAST GATE - Valve - ECLIPSE INC.; *pg.* 1332, *pg.* 655

BLAST O BUTTER - Microwave Pop Corn - AMERICAN POP CORN COMPANY; *pg.* 825, *pg.* 712

BLAST O BUTTER LIGHT - Microwave Pop Corn - AMERICAN POP CORN COMPANY; *pg.* 825, *pg.* 712

BLAST OFF - Video Game - INTERNATIONAL GAME TECHNOLOGY; *pg.* 957, *pg.* 1024

BLAST TOO - Footwear - PHOENIX FOOTWEAR GROUP, INC.; *pg.* 1815, *pg.* 60

BLASTED - Apparel - OAKLEY, INC.; *pg.* 1840, *pg.* 86

BLASTER - Video Game Controller - MAD CATZ INTERACTIVE INC.; *pg.* 429, *pg.* 204

BLASTER - Software - ZILOG INC.; *pg.* 497, *pg.* 252

BLASTS - Candy & Gum - THE TOPPS COMPANY, INC.; *pg.*

588, *pg.* 1302
BLASTWRAP - Explosives Mitigation Technology - BLASTGARD INTERNATIONAL INC.; *pg.* 1150, *pg.* 415
BLATZ - Beer - PABST BREWING COMPANY; *pg.* 258, *pg.* 137
BLAUNE - Hair Color - KAO BRANDS CO. INC.; *pg.* 513, *pg.* 1415
BLAW-KNOX - Paver - INGERSOLL-RAND COMPANY; *pg.* 1349, *pg.* 1370
BLAZE - Eye Protection - MCR SAFETY; *pg.* 1422, *pg.* 1630
BLAZE - Software System - MENTOR GRAPHICS CORPORATION; *pg.* 432, *pg.* 1510
BLAZE PIZZA - Pizza Franchise - BLAZE PIZZA LLC; *pg.* 1716, *pg.* 179
BLAZEMASTER - Sprinkler System - THE LUBRIZOL CORPORATION; *pg.* 1171, *pg.* 1481
BLAZER - Medical Device - BOSTON SCIENTIFIC CORPORATION; *pg.* 1508, *pg.* 831
BLAZER - Circular Cloth Cutters - THE WOLF MACHINE CO.; *pg.* 1389, *pg.* 1427
BLAZER DX-20 - Medical Device - BOSTON SCIENTIFIC CORPORATION; *pg.* 1508, *pg.* 831
BLAZER II - XP Catheter - BOSTON SCIENTIFIC CORPORATION; *pg.* 1508, *pg.* 831
BLAZER II XP - Medical Device - BOSTON SCIENTIFIC CORPORATION; *pg.* 1508, *pg.* 831
BLAZER INTERNATIONAL - Trailer Light Kit - TRACTOR SUPPLY COMPANY; *pg.* 708, *pg.* 1627
BLAZER MID - Footwear - NIKE, INC.; *pg.* 1812, *pg.* 1492
BLAZIN' BUCKS - Lottery Game - KENTUCKY LOTTERY CORPORATION; *pg.* 996, *pg.* 735
BLAZIN GLAZE - Professional Wax - TURTLE WAX, INC.; *pg.* 220, *pg.* 671
BLAZIN' HOT BUCKS - Lottery Game - KENTUCKY LOTTERY CORPORATION; *pg.* 996, *pg.* 735
BLAZIN' RED HOT BUCKS - Lottery Game - KENTUCKY LOTTERY CORPORATION; *pg.* 996, *pg.* 735
BLAZING 7S - Slot Machine & Video Game - BALLY TECHNOLOGIES, INC.; *pg.* 531, *pg.* 1022
BLAZING 7S DOUBLE - Slot Machine - BALLY TECHNOLOGIES, INC.; *pg.* 531, *pg.* 1022
BLAZING BUCKS - Lottery Game - OHIO LOTTERY COMMISSION; *pg.* 1002, *pg.* 1433
BLC - Backplane Connector System - MOLEX INCORPORATED; *pg.* 655, *pg.* 628
BLE - Polymer Product - CHEMTURA CORPORATION; *pg.* 1152, *pg.* 355
BLEACH PEN - Gel - THE CLOROX COMPANY; *pg.* 327, *pg.* 169
BLEACHAID - Adsorbent - BASF CATALYSTS LLC; *pg.* 1148, *pg.* 1074
BLEECKER - Leather Product - COACH, INC.; *pg.* 3, *pg.* 1214
BLEND 101 - Coffee - PEET'S COFFEE & TEA, INC.; *pg.* 1029, *pg.* 85
BLEND A DENT - Personal & Household Product - THE PROCTER & GAMBLE COMPANY; *pg.* 1129, *pg.* 1418
BLEND-A-MED - Toothpaste & Toothbrushes - THE PROCTER & GAMBLE COMPANY; *pg.* 1129, *pg.* 1418
BLEND N GLOW - Bronzing Powder - THE BONNE BELL COMPANY; *pg.* 502, *pg.* 1480
BLEND # 27 - Cigarettes - PHILIP MORRIS USA INC.; *pg.* 1894, *pg.* 1803
BLEND STICK - Touch Up Stick - DAP PRODUCTS, INC.; *pg.* 1441, *pg.* 756
BLEND2 - Medical Equipment - INVACARE CORPORATION; *pg.* 1546, *pg.* 1451
BLENDAIRE - LPG/Air Mixers - ALGAS-SDI; *pg.* 1311, *pg.* 1831
BLENDAL STICKS - Staining Tool - MOHAWK FINISHING PRODUCTS, INC.; *pg.* 1173, *pg.* 1378
BLENDED KEVLAR - Gloves - LAKELAND INDUSTRIES, INC.; *pg.* 1354, *pg.* 1338
BLENDERM - Surgical Tape, Waterproof - 3M COMPANY; *pg.* 1142, *pg.* 956
BLENDEX - Polymer Product - CHEMTURA CORPORATION; *pg.* 1152, *pg.* 355
BLENDORAMA - Dispensing Equipment - IDEX CORPORATION; *pg.* 1347, *pg.* 623
BLENDZ ALL - Thinner - AKZONOBEL DECORATIVE PAINTS U.S.; *pg.* 1439, *pg.* 1474
BLESSING OF CHRISTMAS - Pillow & Throw - HERITAGE LACE INC.; *pg.* 694, *pg.* 711
BLICK - Security Systems - STANLEY BLACK & DECKER, INC.; *pg.* 1063, *pg.* 358
BLICKMAN BUILT - Stainless Steel Product - BLICKMAN HEALTH INDUSTRIES, INC.; *pg.* 1506, *pg.* 1051
BLIND SIGHT - Boots - AEROGROUP INTERNATIONAL, INC.; *pg.* 1803, *pg.* 1055
BLING ME THE MONEY - Lottery Game - KENTUCKY LOTTERY CORPORATION; *pg.* 996, *pg.* 735
BLINGKIT - Videogame Accessories - MAD CATZ INTERACTIVE INC.; *pg.* 429, *pg.* 204
BLINGTONES - Mobile Phone Ring Tones - BANDSINTOWN; *pg.* 1231, *pg.* 1200
BLINK - Medical Device - ABBOTT MEDICAL OPTICS, INC.; *pg.* 1485, *pg.* 260
BLINK - Car Cleaning Wipes, Bags & Stain Removers - HONEYWELL CONSUMER PRODUCTS GROUP; *pg.* 208, *pg.* 344
BLINK BLINK - Dog Toy - THE HARTZ MOUNTAIN CORP.; *pg.* 1476, *pg.* 1120
BLINX - Headphone - ANDREA ELECTRONICS CORPORATION; *pg.* 617, *pg.* 1143
BLISS - Beauty Products - BLISSWORLD LLC; *pg.* 501, *pg.* 1204
BLISS - Chocolate Candy - THE HERSHEY CO.; *pg.* 1855, *pg.* 1538
BLISSTREE.COM - Website - DEFYMEDIA; *pg.* 1237, *pg.* 1222
BLISTEX CLEAR ADVANCE - Lip Care Product - BLISTEX, INC.; *pg.* 502, *pg.* 644
BLISTEX COMPLETE MOISTURE - Lip Care Product - BLISTEX, INC.; *pg.* 502, *pg.* 644
BLISTEX FRUIT SMOOTHIES - Lip Care Product - BLISTEX, INC.; *pg.* 502, *pg.* 644
BLISTEX HERBAL ANSWER - Lip Care Product - BLISTEX, INC.; *pg.* 502, *pg.* 644
BLISTEX LIP BALM - Lip Balm - BLISTEX, INC.; *pg.* 502, *pg.* 644
BLISTEX LIP MEDEX - Lip Care Product - BLISTEX, INC.; *pg.* 502, *pg.* 644
BLISTEX LIP OINTMENT - Lip Dryness - BLISTEX, INC.; *pg.* 502, *pg.* 644
BLISTEX LIP REVITALIZER - Lip Care Product - BLISTEX, INC.; *pg.* 502, *pg.* 644
BLISTEX LIP TONE - Lip Care Product - BLISTEX, INC.; *pg.* 502, *pg.* 644
BLISTEX PRO CARE - Lip Care Product - BLISTEX, INC.; *pg.* 502, *pg.* 644
BLISTEX PRO RELIEF - Lip Care Product - BLISTEX, INC.; *pg.* 502, *pg.* 644
BLISTEX SILK & SHINE - Lip Care Product - BLISTEX, INC.; *pg.* 502, *pg.* 644
BLISTEX ULTRA PROTECTION - Element - BLISTEX, INC.; *pg.* 502, *pg.* 644
BLITZ - Office Chairs - BERNHARDT DESIGN; *pg.* 918, *pg.* 1381
BLITZ - Medical Equipment - CONMED CORPORATION; *pg.* 1517, *pg.* 1347
BLITZ - Gaming Product - GLD PRODUCTS, INC.; *pg.* 1835, *pg.* 1882
BLIZ-WHIZ - Sno-Kone Machine - GOLD MEDAL PRODUCTS CO.; *pg.* 55, *pg.* 1414
BLIZZAK - Passenger Tires - BRIDGESTONE AMERICAS, INC.; *pg.* 201, *pg.* 1649
BLIZZARD - Ice Cream Treat - AMERICAN DAIRY QUEEN CORPORATION; *pg.* 1714, *pg.* 930
BLIZZARD - Polymer Product - CHEMTURA CORPORATION; *pg.* 1152, *pg.* 355
BLIZZARD BEACH - Cartoon - THE WALT DISNEY COMPANY; *pg.* 317, *pg.* 52
BLIZZARD FLAVOR TREAT - Soft Serve Ice Milk Combined with Toppings - INTERNATIONAL DAIRY QUEEN, INC.; *pg.* 1732, *pg.* 938
BLIZZARD PORTER - Beverage - COASTAL EXTREME BREWING COMPANY; *pg.* 240, *pg.* 1602
BLO-PRUF - Industrial Material - DOW CHEMICAL; *pg.* 1156, *pg.* 1563
BLOAT GUARD - Animal Health Product - PHIBROCHEM; *pg.* 1177, *pg.* 1124
BLOBOOST - Vegetable Gardening - GARDENS ALIVE!, INC.; *pg.* 1796, *pg.* 693
BLOC-IT - Heat Absorbing Paste - LA-CO INDUSTRIES MARKAL CO., INC.; *pg.* 1170, *pg.* 610
BLOC-RUST - Red Oxide Primer - DUNN-EDWARDS CORPORATION; *pg.* 1442, *pg.* 129
BLOCBOND - Mining Product - QUIKRETE COMPANIES; *pg.* 106, *pg.* 519
BLOCFIL - Concrete Block Filler - DUNN-EDWARDS CORPORATION; *pg.* 1442, *pg.* 129
BLOCH & GUGGENHEIMER - Pickles, Peppers & Relish - B&G FOODS, INC.; *pg.* 838, *pg.* 1102
BLOCK COLLECTION - Alcoholic Beverage - JIM BEAM BRANDS CO.; *pg.* 1965, *pg.* 601
BLOCK GRAPHICS - Business Forms - ENNIS, INC.; *pg.* 393, *pg.* 1727
BLOCK I/O - Software - ROCKWELL AUTOMATION, INC.; *pg.* 668, *pg.* 1880
BLOCK-IT - Fabric - KIMBERLY-CLARK CORPORATION; *pg.* 1461, *pg.* 1720
BLOCK-IT - Biomolecule Product - THERMO FISHER SCIENTIFIC INC.; *pg.* 1602, *pg.* 61
BLOCK LOCK - Protection Tool - INTERSIL CORPORATION; *pg.* 647, *pg.* 146
BLOCK N LEARN - Toy - THE OHIO ART COMPANY, INC.; *pg.* 965, *pg.* 1406
BLOCK PARTY - Carpet - BEAULIEU GROUP, LLC; *pg.* 917, *pg.* 529
BLOCK POWER - Toy Train - LIONEL LLC; *pg.* 961, *pg.* 875
BLOCK POWER CONTROLLER - Remote Control - LIONEL LLC; *pg.* 961, *pg.* 875
BLOCK PREMIUM - Tax Preparation Service - H&R BLOCK, INC.; *pg.* 764, *pg.* 983
BLOCKADE - Caulk And Sealant - DAP PRODUCTS, INC.; *pg.* 1441, *pg.* 756
BLOCKADE - Cleaning Product - VON SCHRADER COMPANY; *pg.* 62, *pg.* 1890
BLOCKAID - Paint - AKZONOBEL DECORATIVE PAINTS U.S.; *pg.* 1439, *pg.* 1474
BLOCKAID - Pharmaceutical Product - ALERE INC.; *pg.* 1488, *pg.* 849
BLOCKAID - Molecular Probe Product - THERMO FISHER SCIENTIFIC INC.; *pg.* 1602, *pg.* 61
BLOCKBUSTER CASH - Lottery Game - KENTUCKY LOTTERY CORPORATION; *pg.* 996, *pg.* 735
BLOCKS - Software - WORDEN BROTHERS, INC.; *pg.* 823, *pg.* 1372
BLOCKTALK - Software - SS&C TECHNOLOGIES HOLDINGS, INC.; *pg.* 473, *pg.* 386
BLOCKTALKPLUS - Software - SS&C TECHNOLOGIES HOLDINGS, INC.; *pg.* 473, *pg.* 386
BLOCKWAY SHOW - Toy - THE OHIO ART COMPANY, INC.; *pg.* 965, *pg.* 1406
BLODGETT - Cooking & Warming Equipment - THE MIDDLEBY CORPORATION; *pg.* 1361, *pg.* 610
BLODGETT COMBI - Cooking Equipment - THE MIDDLEBY CORPORATION; *pg.* 1361, *pg.* 610
BLODGETT RANGE - Ovens - THE MIDDLEBY CORPORATION; *pg.* 1361, *pg.* 610
BLOG FOR HOPE - Internet Services - YAHOO! INC.; *pg.* 1289, *pg.* 289
BLOGGER - Internet Application - GOOGLE INC.; *pg.* 1249, *pg.* 153
BLOGLINES - Online Services - IAC/INTERACTIVECORP; *pg.* 292, *pg.* 1242
BLOK-TITE - Plaster - USG CORPORATION; *pg.* 118, *pg.* 594
BLOKEE - Sneaker - STEVEN MADDEN, LTD.; *pg.* 1819, *pg.* 1176
BLOLITE - Blown Fiber System - GENERAL CABLE CORPORATION; *pg.* 83, *pg.* 729
BLONDIE - Hair Care Product - ZOTOS INTERNATIONAL, INC.; *pg.* 524, *pg.* 345
THE BLOOD MANAGEMENT COMPANY - Tagline - HAEMONETICS CORPORATION; *pg.* 1538, *pg.* 802
BLOODHOUND - Tobacco Product - AMERICAN SNUFF COMPANY; *pg.* 1893, *pg.* 1641
BLOODHOUND - Character - DC COMICS, INC.; *pg.* 1633, *pg.* 1221
BLOODHOUND - Software - SYMANTEC CORPORATION; *pg.* 478, *pg.* 161
BLOODHOUND THICK - Plug Tobacco - AMERICAN SNUFF COMPANY; *pg.* 1893, *pg.* 1641
BLOODLINES - Game - ACTIVISION BLIZZARD, INC.; *pg.* 948, *pg.* 271
BLOODSAFE - Intelligent Remote Release System - MEDIWARE INFORMATION SYSTEMS, INC.; *pg.* 431, *pg.* 716
BLOOM - Fan - CRAFTMADE INTERNATIONAL, INC.; *pg.* 1295, *pg.* 1670
BLOOM OF THE MONTH - Flower Continuity Program - 1-800-FLOWERS.COM, INC.; *pg.* 1758, *pg.* 1151
BLOOMBERG BONDTRADER - Software - BLOOMBERG L.P.; *pg.* 725, *pg.* 1204

First page reference indicates Business Class Edition
Second page reference indicates Geographic Edition

BLOOMBERG CLIENTBOOK - Software - BLOOMBERG L.P.; *pg.* 725, *pg.* 1204
BLOOMBERG EXCHANGETRADER - Software - BLOOMBERG L.P.; *pg.* 725, *pg.* 1204
BLOOMBERG FINANCIAL MARKETS - Securities Markets Analysis - BLOOMBERG L.P.; *pg.* 725, *pg.* 1204
BLOOMBERG LEGAL - Software - BLOOMBERG L.P.; *pg.* 725, *pg.* 1204
BLOOMBERG MARKETS - Software - BLOOMBERG L.P.; *pg.* 725, *pg.* 1204
BLOOMBERG NEWS - Software - BLOOMBERG L.P.; *pg.* 725, *pg.* 1204
BLOOMBERG PERSONAL BOOKSHELF - Trade & Professional Books Publication Services - BLOOMBERG L.P.; *pg.* 725, *pg.* 1204
BLOOMBERG POWERMATCH - Software - BLOOMBERG L.P.; *pg.* 725, *pg.* 1204
BLOOMBERG PRESS - Software - BLOOMBERG L.P.; *pg.* 725, *pg.* 1204
BLOOMBERG PROFESSIONAL - Software - BLOOMBERG L.P.; *pg.* 725, *pg.* 1204
BLOOMBERG PROFESSIONAL LIBRARY - Trade & Professional Books Publication Services - BLOOMBERG L.P.; *pg.* 725, *pg.* 1204
BLOOMBERG RADIO - Software - BLOOMBERG L.P.; *pg.* 725, *pg.* 1204
BLOOMBERG TELEVISION - Software - BLOOMBERG L.P.; *pg.* 725, *pg.* 1204
BLOOMBERG TRADEBOOK - Software - BLOOMBERG L.P.; *pg.* 725, *pg.* 1204
BLOOMBERG UNIVERSITY - Software - BLOOMBERG L.P.; *pg.* 725, *pg.* 1204
BLOOMBERG VOICE - Business Information Services - BLOOMBERG L.P.; *pg.* 725, *pg.* 1204
BLOOMBERG.COM - Software - BLOOMBERG L.P.; *pg.* 725, *pg.* 1204
BLOOMFIELD - Kitchen Equipment - THE MIDDLEBY CORPORATION; *pg.* 1361, *pg.* 610
BLOOMING COOKIES - Flower - FTD GROUP, INC.; *pg.* 1795, *pg.* 608
BLOOMING DAISIES - Fruit Arrangements - EDIBLE ARRANGEMENTS INTERNATIONAL, INC.; *pg.* 1768, *pg.* 382
BLOOMING LOVE - Flower Arrangement - 1-800-FLOWERS.COM, INC.; *pg.* 1758, *pg.* 1151
BLOOMING MASTERPIECE BOUQUET - Arrangement of Roses - FTD GROUP, INC.; *pg.* 1795, *pg.* 608
BLOOMING WILD - Figurines - ENESCO, LLC; *pg.* 1124, *pg.* 620
BLOOMINGDALE'S CREDIT CARD - Credit Card - CITIGROUP INC.; *pg.* 735, *pg.* 1212
BLOOMLINK - Flower Delivery Services - 1-800-FLOWERS.COM, INC.; *pg.* 1758, *pg.* 1151
BLOOMNET - Florist Network - 1-800-FLOWERS.COM, INC.; *pg.* 1758, *pg.* 1151
BLOOMS - Scissors - ACME UNITED CORPORATION; *pg.* 1040, *pg.* 346
BLOOPERS - Television Clip Program - DICK CLARK PRODUCTIONS, INC.; *pg.* 281, *pg.* 273
BLOPRESS - Pharmaceutical Products - ABBOTT LABORATORIES; *pg.* 1484, *pg.* 551
BLOSSOM - Wall Decor - HERITAGE LACE INC.; *pg.* 694, *pg.* 711
BLOSSOM HILL - Wine - DIAGEO NORTH AMERICA, INC.; *pg.* 1961, *pg.* 361
BLOSSOM HILL - Honey - DUTCH GOLD HONEY INC.; *pg.* 854, *pg.* 1546
BLOW POPS - Candy - TOOTSIE ROLL INDUSTRIES, INC.; *pg.* 1863, *pg.* 591
BLOW THE WHISTLE ON ASTHMA - Slogan - AMERICAN LUNG ASSOCIATION; *pg.* 129, *pg.* 395
BLOWER VAC - Wet/Dry Vacuum with Blower Attachment - SHOP-VAC CORPORATION; *pg.* 1375, *pg.* 1595
BLOWERGARD - Filtration System - CHRISTIANSON SYSTEMS, INC.; *pg.* 1323, *pg.* 917
BLOWERXPERT - Blower - TUTHILL CORPORATION; *pg.* 1385, *pg.* 561
BLOWIN' BUBBLES - Cat Toy - THE HARTZ MOUNTAIN CORP.; *pg.* 1476, *pg.* 1120
BLOXFIL - Block Filler - AKZONOBEL DECORATIVE PAINTS U.S.; *pg.* 1439, *pg.* 1474
BLOYAL - Footwear - STEVEN MADDEN, LTD.; *pg.* 1819, *pg.* 1176
BLP25 - Lipsome Vaccine - ONCOTHYREON INC.; *pg.* 1578, *pg.* 1838
BLT SALAD - Salad - KFC CORPORATION; *pg.* 1733, *pg.* 735
BLU - Bag - BROWN & BIGELOW, INC.; *pg.* 1624, *pg.* 959
BLU-109 - Aerial Bombs - LOCKHEED MARTIN CORPORATION; *pg.* 229, *pg.* 762
BLU-COAT - Fastener Product - PENN ENGINEERING & MANUFACTURING CORP.; *pg.* 1059, *pg.* 1525
BLU-MOL - Saw Blades - KENNAMETAL IPG; *pg.* 1353, *pg.* 1615
BLU-U - Biopharmaceutical Product - DUSA PHARMACEUTICALS, INC.; *pg.* 1525, *pg.* 860
BLUCHER-JOSAM - Stainless Steel Drainage & Piping System - JOSAM COMPANY; *pg.* 89, *pg.* 695
BLUE - Plastic Foam - THE DOW CHEMICAL COMPANY; *pg.* 1157, *pg.* 898
BLUE & RYE - Turfgrass Seed Mixture - CROSMAN SEED CORPORATION; *pg.* 1794, *pg.* 1156
BLUE BEETLE - Character - DC COMICS, INC.; *pg.* 1633, *pg.* 1221
BLUE BELL - Quilt & Comforter - CROSCILL, INC.; *pg.* 1122, *pg.* 1220
BLUE BIRD - Buses - BLUE BIRD CORPORATION; *pg.* 1705, *pg.* 532
BLUE BIRD VISION - School Bus - BLUE BIRD CORPORATION; *pg.* 1705, *pg.* 532
BLUE BLAZES - Video Game - INTERNATIONAL GAME TECHNOLOGY; *pg.* 957, *pg.* 1024
BLUE BONNET - Food Product - CONAGRA FOODS, INC.; *pg.* 826, *pg.* 1014
BLUE BOX - Data Collection System - MKS INSTRUMENTS, INC.; *pg.* 1362, *pg.* 781
BLUE BOY - Canned Vegetables - SENECA FOODS CORPORATION; *pg.* 895, *pg.* 1177
BLUE BULLET - Medical Equipment - CONMED CORPORATION; *pg.* 1517, *pg.* 1347
BLUE BUNNY - Dairy Product - WELLS ENTERPRISES, INC.; *pg.* 909, *pg.* 709
BLUE CANOE BODYWEAR - Sportswear & Underwear - BLUE CANOE BODYWEAR; *pg.* 20, *pg.* 94
BLUE CASH - Credit Card - AMERICAN EXPRESS COMPANY; *pg.* 712, *pg.* 1190
BLUE CHECK - Pillow & Throw - HERITAGE LACE INC.; *pg.* 694, *pg.* 711
BLUE CHIP - Stop, Tail & Turn Lamp - GROTE INDUSTRIES, INC.; *pg.* 206, *pg.* 693
BLUE CHIP HOTEL & CASINO - Hotel & Casino - BOYD GAMING CORPORATION; *pg.* 1082, *pg.* 1022
BLUE COAT - Roller Cover - VAIL RUBBER WORKS, INC.; *pg.* 1891, *pg.* 906
BLUE COAT II - Premium Roll Covers - VAIL RUBBER WORKS, INC.; *pg.* 1891, *pg.* 906
BLUE COAT III - Premium Roll Covers - VAIL RUBBER WORKS, INC.; *pg.* 1891, *pg.* 906
BLUE COAT X - Super Premium Roll Covers - VAIL RUBBER WORKS, INC.; *pg.* 1891, *pg.* 906
BLUE COLOR - Fluid Handling System - GRACO, INC.; *pg.* 1342, *pg.* 935
BLUE COLOR FILTER - Filter Cartridges - DONALDSON COMPANY, INC.; *pg.* 1329, *pg.* 917
BLUE CORAL - Car Wax - SHELL LUBRICANTS; *pg.* 217, *pg.* 1714
BLUE CORAL SEAFOOD & SPIRITS - Restaurant - BLOOMIN' BRANDS, INC.; *pg.* 1716, *pg.* 471
BLUE CORRAL - Vehicle Care - ZEP INC.; *pg.* 338, *pg.* 524
BLUE CREEPER - Container Grown Plant - MONROVIA GROWERS; *pg.* 1797, *pg.* 44
BLUE CYPRESS - Hair & Skin Product - AUBREY ORGANICS INC.; *pg.* 499, *pg.* 470
BLUE DEVIL - Fluid Handling System - GRACO, INC.; *pg.* 1342, *pg.* 935
BLUE DIAMOND CLASSICS - Pedal Car Catalog - SPEEDWAY MOTORS INC.; *pg.* 218, *pg.* 1012
BLUE DIAMONDS - Game - WMS INDUSTRIES INC.; *pg.* 593, *pg.* 666
BLUE DISTINCTION - Health Care Service - BLUE CROSS & BLUE SHIELD ASSOCIATION; *pg.* 1195, *pg.* 566
BLUE DISTINCTION CENTERS FOR BARIATRIC SURGERY - Health Care Service - BLUE CROSS & BLUE SHIELD ASSOCIATION; *pg.* 1195, *pg.* 566
BLUE DISTINCTION CENTERS FOR CARDIAC CARE - Health Care Service - BLUE CROSS & BLUE SHIELD ASSOCIATION; *pg.* 1195, *pg.* 566
BLUE DISTINCTION CENTERS FOR SPINE SURGERY - Health Care Service - BLUE CROSS & BLUE SHIELD ASSOCIATION; *pg.* 1195, *pg.* 566
BLUE DISTINCTION CENTERS FOR TRANSPLANTS - Health Care Service - BLUE CROSS & BLUE SHIELD ASSOCIATION; *pg.* 1195, *pg.* 566
BLUE DOLPHIN - Video Game - INTERNATIONAL GAME TECHNOLOGY; *pg.* 957, *pg.* 1024
BLUE DOT - Receptors - MAXIM INTEGRATED PRODUCTS, INC.; *pg.* 653, *pg.* 247
BLUE FLAME DRYER - Crop Dryer - SHIVVERS INC.; *pg.* 707, *pg.* 704
BLUE FLAME GEO - Lubricant - D-A LUBRICANT COMPANY; *pg.* 975, *pg.* 693
BLUE FLAME MARKETING + ADVERTISING - Internal Licensing & Marketing Services - BAD BOY WORLDWIDE ENTERTAINMENT GROUP; *pg.* 270, *pg.* 1199
BLUE FOR BUSINESS - Credit Card - AMERICAN EXPRESS COMPANY; *pg.* 712, *pg.* 1190
BLUE FOR STUDENTS - Personal Card - AMERICAN EXPRESS COMPANY; *pg.* 712, *pg.* 1190
BLUE FORCE TRACKING - Broadband Satellite Network - VIASAT, INC.; *pg.* 489, *pg.* 62
BLUE FROM AMERICAN EXPRESS - Personal Card - AMERICAN EXPRESS COMPANY; *pg.* 712, *pg.* 1190
BLUE GENE - Boots - AEROGROUP INTERNATIONAL, INC.; *pg.* 1803, *pg.* 1055
BLUE GLOSS - Automotive Reconditioning Product - MOC PRODUCTS COMPANY, INC.; *pg.* 332, *pg.* 174
BLUE GRASS - Perfume - ELIZABETH ARDEN, INC.; *pg.* 507, *pg.* 448
BLUE GREEN ALGAE - Hair & Skin Product - AUBREY ORGANICS INC.; *pg.* 499, *pg.* 470
BLUE HERON PALE ALE - Ale - MENDOCINO BREWING COMPANY; *pg.* 254, *pg.* 298
BLUE HIGHWAY - Cable - COMMSCOPE, INC.; *pg.* 278, *pg.* 1378
BLUE ICE - Ice Substitute - NEWELL RUBBERMAID INC.; *pg.* 1128, *pg.* 515
BLUE JAY - Cutting Room Equipment - EASTMAN MACHINE COMPANY; *pg.* 1331, *pg.* 1148
BLUE JEAN TEDDY - Bed Linen - SPRINGS GLOBAL, INC.; *pg.* 698, *pg.* 1616
BLUE LABEL - Fixatif - MARTIN/F. WEBER COMPANY; *pg.* 962, *pg.* 1567
BLUE LABEL - Clothes - RALPH LAUREN CORPORATION; *pg.* 46, *pg.* 1284
BLUE LABEL AIR - Software - UNITED PARCEL SERVICE, INC.; *pg.* 1928, *pg.* 522
BLUE LAGOON - Game - WMS INDUSTRIES INC.; *pg.* 593, *pg.* 666
BLUE LETTER - Apparel - VANS, INC.; *pg.* 1821, *pg.* 76
BLUE LIGHTNING - Head Lamp - BAE SYSTEMS PRODUCTS GROUP; *pg.* 359, *pg.* 432
BLUE MAGIC - Pressing Oil & Hair Conditioners - J. STRICKLAND & COMPANY; *pg.* 512, *pg.* 970
BLUE MAX - Garage Door Opener - THE GENIE COMPANY; *pg.* 55, *pg.* 1403
BLUE MAX - Airless Hose - GRACO, INC.; *pg.* 1342, *pg.* 935
BLUE MAX - Electrode - LINCOLN ELECTRIC HOLDINGS, INC.; *pg.* 1355, *pg.* 1432
BLUE MAX - Right Angle Speed Reducer Product Line - REGAL BELOIT CORPORATION; *pg.* 106, *pg.* 1854
BLUE MAX - Striking Tool - VAUGHAN & BUSHNELL MANUFACTURING COMPANY, INC.; *pg.* 1066, *pg.* 616
BLUE MAX 20 - Balloon Catheters - BOSTON SCIENTIFIC CORPORATION; *pg.* 1508, *pg.* 831
BLUE MIST - Drinking Water - CAROLINA BEVERAGE CORPORATION; *pg.* 239, *pg.* 1390
BLUE MOON - Beer - MILLERCOORS; *pg.* 254, *pg.* 1877
BLUE MOON - Beverages - MOLSON COORS BREWING COMPANY; *pg.* 256, *pg.* 321
BLUE MOON - Game - WMS INDUSTRIES INC.; *pg.* 593, *pg.* 666
BLUE MOON BELGIAN WHITE ALE - Beer - MOLSON COORS BREWING COMPANY; *pg.* 256, *pg.* 321
BLUE MOON BUCKS - Lottery Game - KENTUCKY LOTTERY CORPORATION; *pg.* 996, *pg.* 735
BLUE OX - Towing Products - BLUE OX; *pg.* 701, *pg.* 1019
BLUE PADDLE - Beer - NEW BELGIUM BREWING COMPANY, INC.; *pg.* 258, *pg.* 328
BLUE PE - Conduit - ELECTRON BEAM TECHNOLOGIES, INC.; *pg.* 1046, *pg.* 621
BLUE POINT - Hand Tools - SNAP-ON INCORPORATED; *pg.* 1062, *pg.* 1862
BLUE Q. RED CHEK. GREAT STUFF. - Tag Line - QUALITY CHEKD DAIRIES, INC.; *pg.* 154, *pg.* 630
BLUE RASPBERRY ICEE - Drink - AUNTIE ANNE'S INC.;

pg. 1715, pg. 1546

BLUE-RELEASE - Medical Equipment - INVACARE CORPORATION; pg. 1546, pg. 1451

BLUE RIBBON - Rice - AMERICAN RICE, INC.; pg. 837, pg. 1700

BLUE RIBBON - Furniture - FLEXSTEEL INDUSTRIES, INC.; pg. 925, pg. 707

BLUE RIBBON - Building Product - GEORGIA-PACIFIC LLC; pg. 1458, pg. 507

BLUE RIBBON - Meat - HY-VEE, INC.; pg. 1023, pg. 713

BLUE RIBBON - Bread - SCHMIDT BAKING CO., INC.; pg. 894, pg. 759

BLUE RIBBON - Educational Materials - SCHOLASTIC INC.; pg. 1683, pg. 1288

BLUE RIBBON - Fig - VALLEY FIG GROWERS, INC.; pg. 908, pg. 93

BLUE RIBBON GOLDEN - Rice - AMERICAN RICE, INC.; pg. 837, pg. 1700

BLUE RIBBON SAMPLER - Cigars - FINCK CIGAR CO.; pg. 1894, pg. 1740

BLUE RIDGE - Wall System - SMITH-MIDLAND CORPORATION; pg. 111, pg. 1795

BLUE RIDGE SMOKIES - Sauce - ROMACORP, INC.; pg. 1748, pg. 1734

BLUE RUSH - Fragrances - AVON PRODUCTS, INC.; pg. 500, pg. 1198

BLUE SHOWER - Chemical Cleaner Product - TECH SPRAY, L.P.; pg. 1183, pg. 1659

BLUE SKIES - Container Grown Plant - MONROVIA GROWERS; pg. 1797, pg. 44

BLUE SKY - Beverage - MONSTER BEVERAGE CORPORATION; pg. 257, pg. 69

THE BLUE SKY PRESS - Educational Materials - SCHOLASTIC INC.; pg. 1683, pg. 1288

BLUE SPOT BINGO - Rewards Game - BALLY TECHNOLOGIES, INC.; pg. 531, pg. 1022

BLUE STAR - Fuel Capacity - MILLER ELECTRIC MANUFACTURING CO.; pg. 1361, pg. 1852

BLUE STAR LEATHER - Leather - MELE COMPANIES, INC.; pg. 9, pg. 1347

BLUE STARBURST - Sapphire Ring - HABAND COMPANY, INC.; pg. 1772, pg. 1099

BLUE STONE GRILL - Food Product - ADVANCEPIERRE FOODS, INC.; pg. 1714, pg. 1409

BLUE STREAK - Cutting Room Equipment - EASTMAN MACHINE COMPANY; pg. 1331, pg. 1148

BLUE STREAK - Auto Products - STANDARD MOTOR PRODUCTS, INC.; pg. 218, pg. 1176

BLUE STUFF - Chemical Cleaner Product - TECH SPRAY, L.P.; pg. 1183, pg. 1659

BLUE-TEN - Chemical Product - SPECTRUM CHEMICALS & LABORATORY PRODUCTS, INC.; pg. 1181, pg. 94

BLUE TEQ - Watch - FOSSIL GROUP, INC.; pg. 5, pg. 1735

BLUE THUNDER - Software - WIND RIVER SYSTEMS, INC.; pg. 493, pg. 38

BLUE TIP - Saw Blade - SIMONDS INTERNATIONAL CORPORATION; pg. 1376, pg. 819

BLUE TOO - Solid Automatic Bowl Cleaner - BLUE CROSS LABORATORIES; pg. 326, pg. 277

BLUE WONDER - Security Product - BAE SYSTEMS PRODUCTS GROUP; pg. 359, pg. 432

BLUE XS - Glue - SUPER GLUE CORPORATION; pg. 1183, pg. 187

BLUE365 - Health Service - BLUE CROSS & BLUE SHIELD OF RHODE ISLAND; pg. 1195, pg. 1606

BLUEBELL - Cleaners - THE CLOROX COMPANY; pg. 327, pg. 169

BLUEBERRY GINGER COTTAGE CHEESE - Food Product - GAY LEA FOODS CO-OPERATIVE LIMITED; pg. 858, pg. 1926

BLUEBERRY MUFFIN - Schnapps - JIM BEAM BRANDS CO.; pg. 1965, pg. 601

BLUEBIRD - Food Product - FLOWERS FOODS, INC.; pg. 855, pg. 541

BLUEBIRD - Software - WMS INDUSTRIES INC.; pg. 593, pg. 666

BLUEBIRD 2 DESIGN - Game - WMS INDUSTRIES INC.; pg. 593, pg. 666

BLUEBOARD - Insulation - THE DOW CHEMICAL COMPANY; pg. 1157, pg. 898

BLUEBOARD DIGEST - Newsletter - THE DOW CHEMICAL COMPANY; pg. 1157, pg. 898

BLUECARD - Healthcare Program - HORIZON BLUE CROSS BLUE SHIELD OF NEW JERSEY; pg. 1203, pg. 1096

BLUECARD PROGRAM - Health Care Service - BLUE CROSS & BLUE SHIELD ASSOCIATION; pg. 1195, pg. 566

BLUECARD WORLDWIDE - Ambulatory Services - BLUE CROSS & BLUE SHIELD ASSOCIATION; pg. 1195, pg. 566

BLUECAT - Software - LYNX SOFTWARE TECHNOLOGIES; pg. 429, pg. 247

BLUECHECK - Fingerprint Sensor - 3M; pg. 339, pg. 179

BLUECHIP - Health Plan - BLUE CROSS & BLUE SHIELD OF RHODE ISLAND; pg. 1195, pg. 1606

BLUECONNECT - Mechanical & Electrical System - JOHNSON CONTROLS, INC.; pg. 209, pg. 1876

BLUECOR - Insulation - THE DOW CHEMICAL COMPANY; pg. 1157, pg. 898

BLUEDOMINO - Software - COFFEECUP SOFTWARE INC.; pg. 1236, pg. 501

BLUEFIN - Newspaper Publishing System - ECRM IMAGING SYSTEMS, INC.; pg. 1410, pg. 848

BLUEGRASS CLUB - Motorsports Entertainment - SPEEDWAY MOTORSPORTS, INC.; pg. 584, pg. 1370

BLUEJUICE - Biomolecule Product - THERMO FISHER SCIENTIFIC INC.; pg. 1602, pg. 61

BLUELINK - Semiconductors - TEXAS INSTRUMENTS INCORPORATED; pg. 679, pg. 1688

BLUELOOT - Credit Card Service - AMERICAN EXPRESS COMPANY; pg. 712, pg. 1190

BLUEMAX - ECG Electrodes - CARDIAC SCIENCE CORPORATION; pg. 1512, pg. 1897

BLUEMIX - Cloud Platform - INTERNATIONAL BUSINESS MACHINES CORPORATION; pg. 418, pg. 1138

BLUEPRINT - Software - VIDEOJET TECHNOLOGIES INC.; pg. 489, pg. 671

BLUEPRINTS - Information Services - THE DOW CHEMICAL COMPANY; pg. 1157, pg. 898

BLUE'S CLUES - Toy - MATTEL, INC.; pg. 962, pg. 81

BLUES HAWK - Guitars - GIBSON GUITAR CORP.; pg. 550, pg. 1650

BLUETOOTH - Wireless Headset - PLANTRONICS, INC.; pg. 663, pg. 270

BLUEWATER - Shirt - SIMMS FISHING PRODUCTS CORP.; pg. 1845, pg. 1008

BLUEWAVE - Antenna Products - PCTEL, INC.; pg. 452, pg. 557

BLUEWAVE - Antenna - RF INDUSTRIES, LTD.; pg. 461, pg. 208

BLUFF MOUNTAIN - Clothing - ABERCROMBIE & FITCH CO.; pg. 37, pg. 1466

BLUFF'S RUN - Casino - CAESARS ENTERTAINMENT CORPORATION; pg. 1083, pg. 1023

BLUMEN - Fabric - NEMSCHOFF, INC.; pg. 936, pg. 1890

BLUMENTHAL - Cloth Wall Coverings & Vinyl Coverings - STEELCASE INC.; pg. 475, pg. 889

BLUNDERBUSS OLD ALE - Seasonal Beer - THE BROOKLYN BREWERY; pg. 239, pg. 1145

THE BLUSH - Online Beauty Resource - XO GROUP INC.; pg. 1289, pg. 1316

BLUSH MINUS MINERAL OIL - Blush - AVEDA CORPORATION; pg. 499, pg. 917

BLUSH ROUGE - Blush - MERLE NORMAN COSMETICS, INC.; pg. 517, pg. 136

BLUSHING KNOCK OUT - Garden Roses - THE CONARD-PYLE COMPANY; pg. 1794, pg. 1594

BLUSHINGHAM PALACE - Nail Care Product - OPI PRODUCTS INC.; pg. 518, pg. 167

BLUTO - Fabric - NEMSCHOFF, INC.; pg. 936, pg. 1890

BLUTONIUM - Computer Products - BROADCOM CORPORATION; pg. 364, pg. 108

BLUWAVE - Signal Processing - STARKEY LABORATORIES, INC.; pg. 1597, pg. 923

BLYTHE - Fabric - SCALAMANDRE, INC.; pg. 941, pg. 1058

BM-75 - Truck Scales - AVERY WEIGH-TRONIX, INC.; pg. 1315, pg. 925

BMA - Building Supply Stores - GUARDIAN BUILDING PRODUCTS DISTRIBUTION; pg. 85, pg. 1619

BMA PLUS - Loyalty Program - GUARDIAN BUILDING PRODUCTS DISTRIBUTION; pg. 85, pg. 1619

BMC - Software - BMC SOFTWARE, INC.; pg. 362, pg. 1701

BMD - Animal Product - KENT NUTRITION GROUP; pg. 1477, pg. 710

BMG CLASSICS - Artist - SONY MUSIC ENTERTAINMENT; pg. 309, pg. 1294

BMG HERITAGE - Artist - SONY MUSIC ENTERTAINMENT; pg. 309, pg. 1294

BMG INTERNATIONAL - Artist - SONY MUSIC ENTERTAINMENT; pg. 309, pg. 1294

BMGR - Power Drive Systems - ELECTROID CO; pg. 1333, pg. 1123

BMST - Thermoplastic Enclosures - CHANNELL COMMERCIAL CORP.; pg. 1870, pg. 291

BMT - Thermoplastic Enclosure - CHANNELL COMMERCIAL CORP.; pg. 1870, pg. 291

BMXONLINE.COM - Web Site - BONNIER ACTIVE MEDIA, INC.; pg. 1622, pg. 1205

BN - Piston Pin - BURGESS-NORTON MANUFACTURING COMPANY; pg. 202, pg. 613

BNACOMPANYDASH - Publisher - BLOOMBERG BNA; pg. 1621, pg. 1772

BNACONVERGENCE - Publisher - BLOOMBERG BNA; pg. 1621, pg. 1772

BNACUSTOMCLIP - Publisher - BLOOMBERG BNA; pg. 1621, pg. 1772

BNAINFODASH - Publisher - BLOOMBERG BNA; pg. 1621, pg. 1772

BNB MASTER MONEY - Debit Card - BRIDGE BANCORP, INC.; pg. 727, pg. 1144

BNET - Classic & Current Business Data Website - CBS INTERACTIVE, INC.; pg. 369, pg. 215

BNPCARE - Pharmaceutical Product - ALERE INC.; pg. 1488, pg. 849

BO - Glove - 180S, LLC; pg. 1824, pg. 754

BO-PRO - Molecular Probe Product - THERMO FISHER SCIENTIFIC INC.; pg. 1602, pg. 61

BOARD ARCHITECT - Software System - MENTOR GRAPHICS CORPORATION; pg. 432, pg. 1510

BOARD DESIGNER - Software System - MENTOR GRAPHICS CORPORATION; pg. 432, pg. 1510

BOARD LAYOUT - Software System - MENTOR GRAPHICS CORPORATION; pg. 432, pg. 1510

BOARD PROCESS LIBRARY - Software System - MENTOR GRAPHICS CORPORATION; pg. 432, pg. 1510

BOARD STATION - Software System - MENTOR GRAPHICS CORPORATION; pg. 432, pg. 1510

BOARDROOM - Screen - DA-LITE SCREEN COMPANY; pg. 632, pg. 698

BOARDROOM ELECTROL - Electric Screen - DA-LITE SCREEN COMPANY; pg. 632, pg. 698

BOARDSIM - Software System - MENTOR GRAPHICS CORPORATION; pg. 432, pg. 1510

BOARDWALK - Carpet - INTERFACE, INC.; pg. 695, pg. 512

BOARDWALK - Fabric - NEMSCHOFF, INC.; pg. 936, pg. 1890

BOARDWATCH - Electronic Component - TERADYNE INC.; pg. 679, pg. 838

BOARS HEAD - Food Product - BOAR'S HEAD PROVISIONS CO., INC.; pg. 841, pg. 465

BOAT AND CAMPER - Hose - TEKNOR APEX COMPANY; pg. 1889, pg. 1605

BOAT BASIC - Boat Cleaner - MCNETT CORPORATION; pg. 1839, pg. 1817

BOAT GUARD - Mooring Whip - TAYLOR MADE GROUP; pg. 1711, pg. 1162

BOAT TRADER - Magazine - DOMINION ENTERPRISES; pg. 1636, pg. 1796

BOATBUILDER - Magazine - BELVOIR MEDIA GROUP, LLC; pg. 1620, pg. 360

BOATING LIFE - Magazine - BONNIER CORPORATION; pg. 1622, pg. 480

BOATNECK - Women's Clothing & Accessories - WOODEN SHIPS OF HOBOKEN; pg. 35, pg. 1315

BOATS.COM - Advertising Website - DOMINION ENTERPRISES; pg. 1636, pg. 1796

BOATWORKS - Magazine - RENTPATH, INC.; pg. 1680, pg. 538

BOB - Navigation Aid - TRIMBLE NAVIGATION LIMITED; pg. 1384, pg. 288

BOB-CAT - Golf, Turf & Specialty Products - TEXTRON INC.; pg. 235, pg. 1607

BOB EVANS CARRY HOME KITCHEN - Carryout Food - BOB EVANS FARMS, LLC; pg. 841, pg. 1467

BOB EVANS FARMS - Food Products - BOB EVANS FARMS, LLC; pg. 841, pg. 1467

BOB EVANS RESTAURANTS - Family Restaurants - BOB EVANS RESTAURANTS, INC.; pg. 1717, pg. 1438

BOB GUEST - Office Furniture - STEELCASE INC.; pg. 475, pg. 889

BOB LOUNGE - Office Furniture - STEELCASE INC.; pg. 475, pg. 889

BOB TABLES - Tables - STEELCASE INC.; pg. 475, pg. 889

BOBBEE BEAR.IT - Stuffed Animal - 1-800-FLOWERS.COM,

INC.; *pg.* 1758, *pg.* 1151

BOBBI - Home Permanent - THE GILLETTE COMPANY; *pg.* 509, *pg.* 795

BOBBI BROWN - Beauty Products - THE ESTEE LAUDER COMPANIES INC.; *pg.* 508, *pg.* 1229

BOBBLE BEE - Toy - MUNCHKIN, INC.; *pg.* 964, *pg.* 300

BOBBLE TIME - Video Game - INTERNATIONAL GAME TECHNOLOGY; *pg.* 957, *pg.* 1024

BOBBY - Pillow - THE BOPPY COMPANY, LLC; *pg.* 20, *pg.* 329

BOBBYHOOD - Baby Product - THE BOPPY COMPANY, LLC; *pg.* 20, *pg.* 329

BOBCAT - Gaming Product - GLD PRODUCTS, INC.; *pg.* 1835, *pg.* 1882

BOBCAT - Welding & Cutting Equip. - MILLER ELECTRIC MANUFACTURING CO.; *pg.* 1361, *pg.* 1852

BOBCAT - Paper Product - WEYERHAEUSER COMPANY; *pg.* 121, *pg.* 1820

BOBCAT TRAIL - Bike - MARIN BIKES; *pg.* 1708, *pg.* 168

BOBO - Molecular Probe Product - THERMO FISHER SCIENTIFIC INC.; *pg.* 1602, *pg.* 61

BOBOLI - Bakery Product - GEORGE WESTON LIMITED; *pg.* 858, *pg.* 1938

BOBRICK - Soap Dispenser - BOBRICK WASHROOM EQUIPMENT, INC.; *pg.* 1043, *pg.* 166

BOB'S TEXAS STYLE - Snack Food Product - INVENTURE FOODS, INC.; *pg.* 1023, *pg.* 17

BOB'S TEXAS STYLE BAR B QUE CHIPS - Snack Food - INVENTURE FOODS, INC.; *pg.* 1023, *pg.* 17

BOB'S TEXAS STYLE JALAPENO CHIPS - Snack Food - INVENTURE FOODS, INC.; *pg.* 1023, *pg.* 17

BOB'S TEXAS STYLE ORIGINAL POTATO CHIPS - Snack Food Product - INVENTURE FOODS, INC.; *pg.* 1023, *pg.* 17

BOB'S TEXAS STYLE SALT & CRACKED PEPPER - Snack Food Product - INVENTURE FOODS, INC.; *pg.* 1023, *pg.* 17

BOB'S TEXAS STYLE SALT & VINEGAR CHIPS - Snack Food - INVENTURE FOODS, INC.; *pg.* 1023, *pg.* 17

BOB'S TEXAS STYLE SWEET MAUI ONION POTATO CHIPS - Snack Food Product - INVENTURE FOODS, INC.; *pg.* 1023, *pg.* 17

BOB'S TEXAS STYLE THREE CHEESE JALAPENO - Snack Food - INVENTURE FOODS, INC.; *pg.* 1023, *pg.* 17

BOC - Industrial Gases - LINDE GAS LLC; *pg.* 1356, *pg.* 1095

BOCABITS - Wheat Snack - FRITO-LAY NORTH AMERICA, INC.; *pg.* 1853, *pg.* 1730

BOCABITS - Wheat Snacks - PEPSICO, INC.; *pg.* 259, *pg.* 1327

BOCCIE - Surface Material - STEELCASE INC.; *pg.* 475, *pg.* 889

BOCILLIN - Molecular Probe Product - THERMO FISHER SCIENTIFIC INC.; *pg.* 1602, *pg.* 61

BOCO - Beverages - THE COCA-COLA COMPANY; *pg.* 240, *pg.* 493

BOD - Mens Fragrance - PARFUMS DE COEUR LTD.; *pg.* 519, *pg.* 376

BOD-A-BING! - Body-Shaping Clothing - SPANX INC.; *pg.* 32, *pg.* 520

BODIPY - Molecular Probe Product - THERMO FISHER SCIENTIFIC INC.; *pg.* 1602, *pg.* 61

BODRUM - Fabric - NEMSCHOFF, INC.; *pg.* 936, *pg.* 1890

BODY - Bikini - JOCKEY INTERNATIONAL, INC.; *pg.* 27, *pg.* 1861

BODY + SOUL - Television Program - MARTHA STEWART LIVING OMNIMEDIA, INC.; *pg.* 1661, *pg.* 1256

BODY BUNKER - Hard Armor - BAE SYSTEMS PRODUCTS GROUP; *pg.* 359, *pg.* 432

BODY CLEAR - Skin Care Product - NEUTROGENA CORPORATION; *pg.* 517, *pg.* 137

BODY DOUBLE - Silicone Rubber - SMOOTH-ON INC.; *pg.* 111, *pg.* 1528

BODY DRENCH - Bodycare & Skincare - AMERICAN INTERNATIONAL INDUSTRIES COMPANY; *pg.* 498, *pg.* 126

BODY FANTASIES - Fragrance - PARFUMS DE COEUR LTD.; *pg.* 519, *pg.* 376

BODY FLOWERS - Body Spray - THE GILLETTE COMPANY; *pg.* 509, *pg.* 795

BODY GEM - Fitness Product - BALLY TOTAL FITNESS HOLDINGS CORPORATION; *pg.* 532, *pg.* 1200

BODY GEOMETRY - Bicycle - SPECIALIZED BICYCLE COMPONENTS, INC.; *pg.* 1711, *pg.* 152

BODY GLOVE - Sunglasses - FGX INTERNATIONAL, INC.; *pg.* 5, *pg.* 1608

BODY GLOVE OPTICAL - Sunglasses - FGX INTERNATIONAL, INC.; *pg.* 5, *pg.* 1608

BODY GRIP - Tool - MILWAUKEE ELECTRIC TOOL CORP.; *pg.* 1056, *pg.* 1855

BODY MAGIC - Compounds & Glazes - ITW - EVERCOAT; *pg.* 1443, *pg.* 1415

BODY PERFECT - Mattress & Box Spring Sets - KINGSDOWN, INC.; *pg.* 932, *pg.* 1383

BODY PUMP - Video & Barbell Workout System - ALLIANCE SPORTS GROUP, L.P.; *pg.* 1825, *pg.* 1698

BODY RESCUE - Healthcare Product - SWANSON HEALTH PRODUCTS INC.; *pg.* 1600, *pg.* 1397

BODY ROX - Nutritional Supplement - USANA HEALTH SCIENCES, INC.; *pg.* 1605, *pg.* 1761

BODY SCHUTZ - Applicator - 3M COMPANY; *pg.* 1142, *pg.* 956

BODY SHINE - Automotive Reconditioning Product - MOC PRODUCTS COMPANY, INC.; *pg.* 332, *pg.* 174

BODY SOOTHER - Massager - CONAIR CORPORATION; *pg.* 505, *pg.* 1055

BODY SYSTEM - Bed - KINGSDOWN, INC.; *pg.* 932, *pg.* 1383

BODY-TITE! - Body Hardware - DORMAN PRODUCTS, INC.; *pg.* 204, *pg.* 1522

BODY WRAPPERS - Apparel - ATTITUDES IN DRESSING INC.; *pg.* 19, *pg.* 1057

BODYARRAY - Medical System - VARIAN MEDICAL SYSTEMS, INC.; *pg.* 1434, *pg.* 178

BODYCOLOGY - Bath and Body Collection - ADVANCED BEAUTY SYSTEMS INC.; *pg.* 498, *pg.* 1672

BODY.COM - Advertising Website - LIVE CURRENT MEDIA INC.; *pg.* 1263, *pg.* 1911

BODYGROOM - Shaver - PHILIPS ELECTRONICS NORTH AMERICA; *pg.* 662, *pg.* 782

BODYICE - Medical & Aesthetic Product - DYNATRONICS CORPORATION; *pg.* 1526, *pg.* 1757

BODYLOGIC - Breast Implant Product - MENTOR CORPORATION; *pg.* 1565, *pg.* 263

BODYMATE - Weight Loss Product - PROPHASE LABS, INC.; *pg.* 1586, *pg.* 1526

BODYMEDIA - Wearable Technology - ALIPHCOM, INC.; *pg.* 616, *pg.* 212

THE BODYPILLOW - Pillow - TEMPUR SEALY INTERNATIONAL, INC.; *pg.* 944, *pg.* 731

BODYSEARCH - Personnel Inspection System - AMERICAN SCIENCE AND ENGINEERING, INC.; *pg.* 1399, *pg.* 787

BODYSMART - Personal Care Product - LIFEPLUS INTERNATIONAL; *pg.* 1556, *pg.* 29

BODYSPA - Bath Product - KOHLER CO.; *pg.* 91, *pg.* 1862

BOEING - Airplane - THE BOEING COMPANY; *pg.* 225, *pg.* 567

BOEING - Software - RAND A TECHNOLOGY CORPORATION; *pg.* 459, *pg.* 774

BOEING BUSINESS JET - Airplane - THE BOEING COMPANY; *pg.* 225, *pg.* 567

BOESNER - Fastening Systems - TEXTRON INC.; *pg.* 235, *pg.* 1607

BOG - Lace Flag - HERITAGE LACE INC.; *pg.* 694, *pg.* 711

BOG HORN - Shoe - AEROGROUP INTERNATIONAL, INC.; *pg.* 1803, *pg.* 1055

BOG WILD - Shoe - AEROGROUP INTERNATIONAL, INC.; *pg.* 1803, *pg.* 1055

BOGADERA - Beverages - THE COCA-COLA COMPANY; *pg.* 240, *pg.* 493

BOGGLE - Game - HASBRO, INC.; *pg.* 954, *pg.* 1603

BOGGLE JR. - Toy & Game - HASBRO, INC.; *pg.* 954, *pg.* 1603

BOGOTA BLACKBERRY - Nail Care Product - OPI PRODUCTS INC.; *pg.* 518, *pg.* 167

BOHEMIAN - Beer - MOLSON COORS BREWING COMPANY; *pg.* 256, *pg.* 321

BOHEMIAN KITCHEN - Food Product - SOKOL & COMPANY; *pg.* 1862, *pg.* 598

BOHN - Refrigeration Product - LENNOX INTERNATIONAL INC.; *pg.* 1073, *pg.* 1736

BOILER COMPOUND - Dry Cleaning & Laundry Product - ADCO, INC.; *pg.* 325, *pg.* 482

BOINGO - Wireless Software - BOINGO WIRELESS, INC.; *pg.* 625, *pg.* 127

BOINGO WIRELESS - Wireless Software - BOINGO WIRELESS, INC.; *pg.* 625, *pg.* 127

BOIRON - Healthcare Product - SWANSON HEALTH PRODUCTS INC.; *pg.* 1600, *pg.* 1397

BOISE ALLBEAM - Building Products - BOISE CASCADE HOLDINGS, L.L.C.; *pg.* 1453, *pg.* 546

BOISE CLASSIC - Building Products - BOISE CASCADE HOLDINGS, L.L.C.; *pg.* 1453, *pg.* 546

BOISE GLULAM - Wood Product - BOISE CASCADE HOLDINGS, L.L.C.; *pg.* 1453, *pg.* 546

BOISE GOLD - Building Products - BOISE CASCADE HOLDINGS, L.L.C.; *pg.* 1453, *pg.* 546

BOISE. IT COULDN'T BE EASIER - Slogan - BOISE CASCADE HOLDINGS, L.L.C.; *pg.* 1453, *pg.* 546

BOISE SELECT - Wood Product - BOISE CASCADE HOLDINGS, L.L.C.; *pg.* 1453, *pg.* 546

BOJANGLES' FAMOUS CHICKEN N' BISCUITS - Slogan - BOJANGLES' RESTAURANTS, INC.; *pg.* 1717, *pg.* 1364

BOKAY - Flower Boxes & Brackets, Plant Tubs, Seed Flats, Window Trays, Floor Trays - MOLDED FIBER GLASS COMPANIES; *pg.* 1886, *pg.* 1403

BOKS - Curved Strike Shield - REEBOK INTERNATIONAL LTD.; *pg.* 1817, *pg.* 811

BOL - Bath Product - KOHLER CO.; *pg.* 91, *pg.* 1862

BOLD - Medical Device - INTEGRA LIFESCIENCES HOLDINGS CORPORATION; *pg.* 1545, *pg.* 1109

BOLD - Laundry Products - THE PROCTER & GAMBLE COMPANY; *pg.* 1129, *pg.* 1418

BOLD ADMINISTRATOR - Software System - MENTOR GRAPHICS CORPORATION; *pg.* 432, *pg.* 1510

BOLD BROWSER - Software System - MENTOR GRAPHICS CORPORATION; *pg.* 432, *pg.* 1510

BOLD COMPOSER - Software System - MENTOR GRAPHICS CORPORATION; *pg.* 432, *pg.* 1510

BOLENS - Garden Equipment - MTD PRODUCTS, INC.; *pg.* 1057, *pg.* 1478

BOLERO - Fabric - NEMSCHOFF, INC.; *pg.* 936, *pg.* 1890

BOLERO - Intimate Apparel - V.F. CORPORATION; *pg.* 34, *pg.* 1376

BOLEROPAQ - Software - TRADEPAQ CORPORATION; *pg.* 1284, *pg.* 1304

BOLINAS RIDGE - Bike - MARIN BIKES; *pg.* 1708, *pg.* 168

BOLL BUGGY - Cotton Harvesting Machinery - CRUSTBUSTER-SPEED KING, INC.; *pg.* 702, *pg.* 714

BOLLA - Italian Wines - BROWN-FORMAN CORPORATION; *pg.* 1958, *pg.* 732

BOLLE - Sport Optic Product - BUSHNELL OUTDOOR PRODUCTS, INC.; *pg.* 1403, *pg.* 718

BOLLGARD - Cotton Seed Product - MONSANTO; *pg.* 1798, *pg.* 971

BOLLGARD - Insect Resistant Seeds - MONSANTO COMPANY; *pg.* 1173, *pg.* 999

BOLLGARD II - Insecticides - MONSANTO COMPANY; *pg.* 1173, *pg.* 999

BOLLINGER - Champagne - DREYFUS ASHBY INC.; *pg.* 1962, *pg.* 1226

BOLT ACTION 695 - Gun - O.F. MOSSBERG & SONS, INC.; *pg.* 1842, *pg.* 360

BOLTA - Wallcovering - OMNOVA SOLUTIONS INC; *pg.* 1176, *pg.* 1453

BOLTAFLEX - Upholstery - OMNOVA SOLUTIONS INC; *pg.* 1176, *pg.* 1453

BOLTASOFT - Upholstery - OMNOVA SOLUTIONS INC; *pg.* 1176, *pg.* 1453

BOLTHOUSE FARMS - Food & Beverage Products - BOLTHOUSE FARMS; *pg.* 841, *pg.* 44

BOLTMAKER - Machinery - NATIONAL MACHINERY LLC; *pg.* 1363, *pg.* 1475

BOLTOBAR - Jordan Filling - BOLTON-EMERSON AMERICAS, INC.; *pg.* 1318, *pg.* 827

BOLTON - Carpet - BEAULIEU GROUP, LLC; *pg.* 917, *pg.* 529

BOLU - Footwear - STEVEN MADDEN, LTD.; *pg.* 1819, *pg.* 1176

BOLUFLEX - Medical Device - GAMMEX RMI INC.; *pg.* 1532, *pg.* 1872

BOM BIT MAESIL - Beverages - THE COCA-COLA COMPANY; *pg.* 240, *pg.* 493

BOM EXPLORER 6.0 - Software System - MENTOR GRAPHICS CORPORATION; *pg.* 432, *pg.* 1510

BOMAG - Polymer Product - CHEMTURA CORPORATION; *pg.* 1152, *pg.* 355

BOMAG-A - Butyloctylmagnesium in Heptane - CHEMTURA CORPORATION; *pg.* 1152, *pg.* 355

BOMB POP - Novelty Ice Cream - WELLS ENTERPRISES, INC.; *pg.* 909, *pg.* 709

BOMBAY - Video Game - INTERNATIONAL GAME TECHNOLOGY; *pg.* 957, *pg.* 1024

BOMBER - Jacket - SANTA FE LEATHER CORPORATION; *pg.* 12, *pg.* 1059

BOMBS AWAY - Video Game - INTERNATIONAL GAME TECHNOLOGY; *pg.* 957, *pg.* 1024
BOMFORD - Mowers - ALAMO GROUP INC.; *pg.* 1311, *pg.* 1745
BON AMI - Ironing & Cleaning Product - FAULTLESS STARCH/BON AMI COMPANY; *pg.* 330, *pg.* 982
BON AMI - Glass Cleaner - S.C. JOHNSON & SON, INC.; *pg.* 334, *pg.* 1889
BON APPETIT - Magazine - CONDE NAST PUBLICATIONS, INC.; *pg.* 1629, *pg.* 1217
BON BRIL - Cleaning Utensils - THE CLOROX COMPANY; *pg.* 327, *pg.* 169
BON OEUF - Fabric - SCALAMANDRE, INC.; *pg.* 941, *pg.* 1058
BON PETITES - Ice Cream - WELLS ENTERPRISES, INC.; *pg.* 909, *pg.* 709
BON TON - Snack Food Product - HANOVER FOODS CORPORATION; *pg.* 861, *pg.* 1535
BON VIE - Restaurants - BRAVO BRIO RESTAURANT GROUP, INC.; *pg.* 1717, *pg.* 1438
BON VOYAGE - Video Game - INTERNATIONAL GAME TECHNOLOGY; *pg.* 957, *pg.* 1024
BONAFIDE - Food Product - POPEYES LOUISIANA KITCHEN, INC.; *pg.* 1745, *pg.* 517
BONAIRE - Bath & Plumbing Product - JACUZZI BRANDS CORPORATION; *pg.* 554, *pg.* 65
BONANZA - Small Pet Food - THE HARTZ MOUNTAIN CORP.; *pg.* 1476, *pg.* 1120
BONANZA'S - Building Product - LESTER BUILDING SYSTEMS, LLC; *pg.* 93, *pg.* 927
BONAQUA - Beverages - THE COCA-COLA COMPANY; *pg.* 240, *pg.* 493
BONARIL - Sand Additive - THE DOW CHEMICAL COMPANY; *pg.* 1157, *pg.* 898
BOND 1STEP SURETY - Issuance System - THE HARTFORD FINANCIAL SERVICES GROUP, INC.; *pg.* 1202, *pg.* 352
BOND GUIDE - Data Guide on Convertible Bonds - STANDARD & POOR'S RATINGS SERVICES; *pg.* 805, *pg.* 1296
BOND LOK - Concrete Coating System - QUIKRETE COMPANIES; *pg.* 106, *pg.* 519
BOND STREET BROWN - Brew - DESCHUTES BREWERY INC.; *pg.* 248, *pg.* 1496
BONDAPAK - Analytical Column - WATERS CORPORATION; *pg.* 1436, *pg.* 834
BONDBRITE - Metalworking Chemical - HENKEL CORPORATION; *pg.* 1166, *pg.* 897
BONDER - Basecoats - ORLY INTERNATIONAL, INC.; *pg.* 518, *pg.* 137
BONDEX - Silicone Sealant - DAP PRODUCTS, INC.; *pg.* 1441, *pg.* 756
BONDINI - Glue - SUPER GLUE CORPORATION; *pg.* 1183, *pg.* 187
BONDMASTER - Software - SUNGARD DATA SYSTEMS INC.; *pg.* 477, *pg.* 1592
BONDSTRAND - Fiberglass Pipe Product - NOV AMERON; *pg.* 100, *pg.* 187
BONDTEX - Chart & Marking System - GRAPHIC CONTROLS LLC; *pg.* 401, *pg.* 1148
BONDTICKER - Online Trading Services - MARKETAXESS HOLDINGS INC.; *pg.* 778, *pg.* 1256
BONDURA - Cartridge - DONALDSON COMPANY, INC.; *pg.* 1329, *pg.* 917
BONDWELL - Polymer - HERCULES INCORPORATED; *pg.* 1166, *pg.* 392
BONE PROTECTOR - Vitamin & Dietary Supplement - NATROL, INC.; *pg.* 1570, *pg.* 64
BONE SHAKIN' RICHES - Lottery Game - MICHIGAN STATE LOTTERY BUREAU; *pg.* 999, *pg.* 895
BONE STRENGTH - Nutritional Product - NOW HEALTH GROUP, INC.; *pg.* 1576, *pg.* 557
BONE X TANK - Apparel - VANS, INC.; *pg.* 1821, *pg.* 76
BONEFISH GRILL - Restaurant - BLOOMIN' BRANDS, INC.; *pg.* 1716, *pg.* 471
BONEMAX - Pharmaceutical Product - ALERE INC.; *pg.* 1488, *pg.* 849
BONESOURCE - Micro Implant System - STRYKER CORPORATION; *pg.* 1598, *pg.* 894
BONFIRE - Lighting Product - GERBER LEGENDARY BLADES; *pg.* 1834, *pg.* 1503
BONGO - Stain Remover - A.L. WILSON CHEMICAL CO.; *pg.* 325, *pg.* 1076
BONGO - Furniture - ASHLEY FURNITURE INDUSTRIES, INC.; *pg.* 914, *pg.* 1852
BONGO - Junior Apparel - ICONIX BRAND GROUP, INC.; *pg.* 26, *pg.* 1243
BONHAM - Furniture - HOOKER FURNITURE CORPORATION; *pg.* 928, *pg.* 1788
BONICI - Pizzeria Style Products - TYSON FOODS, INC.; *pg.* 902, *pg.* 35
BONICI ITALIAN - Eatery Branded Solution - TYSON FOODS, INC.; *pg.* 902, *pg.* 35
BONIFACE - Towing & Recovery Equipment - MILLER INDUSTRIES, INC.; *pg.* 185, *pg.* 1655
BONITA DAILY NEWS - Newspaper - THE E.W. SCRIPPS COMPANY; *pg.* 1639, *pg.* 1412
BONIVA - Pharmaceutical Product - HOFFMANN-LA ROCHE INC.; *pg.* 1542, *pg.* 1099
BONJOUR - Educational Materials - SCHOLASTIC INC.; *pg.* 1683, *pg.* 1288
BONKIN' BUCKS - Game - WMS INDUSTRIES INC.; *pg.* 593, *pg.* 666
BONNAVILLA - Houses - CHIEF INDUSTRIES, INC.; *pg.* 1323, *pg.* 1010
BONNIE - Fabric - NEMSCHOFF, INC.; *pg.* 936, *pg.* 1890
BONNIE - Bicycle - TREK BICYCLE CORPORATION; *pg.* 1847, *pg.* 1896
BONNNY - Footwear - STEVEN MADDEN, LTD.; *pg.* 1819, *pg.* 1176
BONOBOS - Menswear - BONOBOS; *pg.* 39, *pg.* 1205
BONTERRA VINEYARDS - California Wines - BROWN-FORMAN CORPORATION; *pg.* 1958, *pg.* 732
BONTONE - Household Insect Control - BONIDE PRODUCTS, INC.; *pg.* 1794, *pg.* 1320
BONTRAGER - Wheels & Components - TREK BICYCLE CORPORATION; *pg.* 1847, *pg.* 1896
BONTRIL - Pharmaceutical Product - VALEANT PHARMACEUTICALS INTERNATIONAL; *pg.* 1605, *pg.* 1047
BONUS - Filing System - FELLOWES, INC.; *pg.* 397, *pg.* 620
BONUS - Lawn Fertilizer - THE SCOTTS MIRACLE-GRO COMPANY; *pg.* 1799, *pg.* 1459
BONUS BELLS - Video Game - INTERNATIONAL GAME TECHNOLOGY; *pg.* 957, *pg.* 1024
BONUS BOOSTER - Game - WMS INDUSTRIES INC.; *pg.* 593, *pg.* 666
BONUS CASHWORD - Scratch Lottery Game - IDAHO LOTTERY; *pg.* 995, *pg.* 547
BONUS CASHWORD - Lottery Game - OHIO LOTTERY COMMISSION; *pg.* 1002, *pg.* 1433
BONUS ENGINE - Video Game - INTERNATIONAL GAME TECHNOLOGY; *pg.* 957, *pg.* 1024
BONUS FRENZY - Video Game - BALLY TECHNOLOGIES, INC.; *pg.* 531, *pg.* 1022
BONUS HAND TRIPLE PLAY DRAW POKER - Video Game - INTERNATIONAL GAME TECHNOLOGY; *pg.* 957, *pg.* 1024
BONUS JACKS POKER - Game - WMS INDUSTRIES INC.; *pg.* 593, *pg.* 666
BONUS KING - Video Game - INTERNATIONAL GAME TECHNOLOGY; *pg.* 957, *pg.* 1024
BONUS POKER - Video Game - INTERNATIONAL GAME TECHNOLOGY; *pg.* 957, *pg.* 1024
BONUS POKER DELUXE - Video Game - INTERNATIONAL GAME TECHNOLOGY; *pg.* 957, *pg.* 1024
BONUS S - Southern Weed & Feed - THE SCOTTS MIRACLE-GRO COMPANY; *pg.* 1799, *pg.* 1459
BONUS SPIN DIAMOND FIVES - Slots - INTERNATIONAL GAME TECHNOLOGY; *pg.* 957, *pg.* 1024
BONUS SPIN FIVE TIMES PAY - Slots - INTERNATIONAL GAME TECHNOLOGY; *pg.* 957, *pg.* 1024
BONUS SPIN RED WHITE & BLUE - Slots - INTERNATIONAL GAME TECHNOLOGY; *pg.* 957, *pg.* 1024
BONUS TIMES PAY - Slots - INTERNATIONAL GAME TECHNOLOGY; *pg.* 957, *pg.* 1024
BONUX - Personal & Household Product - THE PROCTER & GAMBLE COMPANY; *pg.* 1129, *pg.* 1418
BONZAI - Flash Drive - HGST; *pg.* 406, *pg.* 260
BONZAI - Video Game - INTERNATIONAL GAME TECHNOLOGY; *pg.* 957, *pg.* 1024
BOO BERRY - Cereal - GENERAL MILLS, INC.; *pg.* 828, *pg.* 933
BOO BUCKS - Lottery Game - ILLINOIS STATE LOTTERY; *pg.* 995, *pg.* 578
BOO-QUET - Floral Bouquet - FTD GROUP, INC.; *pg.* 1795, *pg.* 608
BOODLES BRITISH GIN - Gin - DIAGEO CANADA, INC.; *pg.* 1961, *pg.* 1937
BOODLES GIN - Spirits - PROXIMO SPIRITS, INC.; *pg.* 1969, *pg.* 1076
BOOGIE - Video Game - ELECTRONIC ARTS INC.; *pg.* 951, *pg.* 189
BOOGIE - Adjustable Keyboard Pad - HAWORTH, INC.; *pg.* 402, *pg.* 891
BOOGIE WOOGIE - Fabric - NEMSCHOFF, INC.; *pg.* 936, *pg.* 1890
BOOGLE - Footwear - STEVEN MADDEN, LTD.; *pg.* 1819, *pg.* 1176
BOOHBAH - Toy & Game - HASBRO, INC.; *pg.* 954, *pg.* 1603
BOOK ANALYSIS SYSTEM - Electronic Reports Identifying Gaps or Duplicates in Collections - R.R. BOWKER LLC; *pg.* 1682, *pg.* 1095
BOOK-CUBE - Advertising & Promotional Brochure Design - STRUCTURAL GRAPHICS, LLC; *pg.* 1689, *pg.* 346
BOOK-END - Video Game - INTERNATIONAL GAME TECHNOLOGY; *pg.* 957, *pg.* 1024
BOOK FACTORY - Educational Materials - SCHOLASTIC INC.; *pg.* 1683, *pg.* 1288
BOOK IN TIME - Manual - XEROX CORPORATION; *pg.* 494, *pg.* 365
BOOK LINKS - Publication - AMERICAN LIBRARY ASSOCIATION; *pg.* 1615, *pg.* 564
BOOKAZINE - Magazine - BOOKAZINE COMPANY, INC.; *pg.* 1622, *pg.* 1042
BOOKER'S - Bourbon - JIM BEAM BRANDS CO.; *pg.* 1965, *pg.* 601
BOOKINGBUDDY.COM - Travel Search Tool - SMARTER TRAVEL MEDIA LLC; *pg.* 1687, *pg.* 801
BOOKING.COM - Online Accomodations Service - THE PRICELINE GROUP INC.; *pg.* 1276, *pg.* 364
BOOKLAND - Book - BOOKS-A-MILLION, INC.; *pg.* 1623, *pg.* 2
BOOKLIST - Publication - AMERICAN LIBRARY ASSOCIATION; *pg.* 1615, *pg.* 564
BOOKLIST ONLINE - Online Publication - AMERICAN LIBRARY ASSOCIATION; *pg.* 1615, *pg.* 564
BOOKMARK35 - Library Copier - XEROX CORPORATION; *pg.* 494, *pg.* 365
BOOKS-A-MILLION - Book Retailer - BOOKS-A-MILLION, INC.; *pg.* 1623, *pg.* 2
BOOKS & CO - Book - BOOKS-A-MILLION, INC.; *pg.* 1623, *pg.* 2
BOOKS & CULTURE - Magazine - CHRISTIANITY TODAY INTERNATIONAL; *pg.* 1627, *pg.* 561
BOOKS ARE FUN - Magazine - THE READER'S DIGEST ASSOCIATION, INC.; *pg.* 1679, *pg.* 1322
BOOKS IN A CUP - Educational Materials - SCHOLASTIC INC.; *pg.* 1683, *pg.* 1288
BOOKS IN PRINT - Information Source on Books Published & Distributed in the United States - R.R. BOWKER LLC; *pg.* 1682, *pg.* 1095
BOOKS IN PRINT INTELLIMARKET - Publication - R.R. BOWKER LLC; *pg.* 1682, *pg.* 1095
BOOKS ON BREAK - Educational Materials - SCHOLASTIC INC.; *pg.* 1683, *pg.* 1288
BOOKS24X7 - Software - SKILLSOFT PLC; *pg.* 470, *pg.* 1037
BOOKSTAR - Book Stores - BARNES & NOBLE, INC.; *pg.* 1619, *pg.* 1201
BOOKSTOP - Book Stores - BARNES & NOBLE, INC.; *pg.* 1619, *pg.* 1201
BOOKTRACK - Software - R.R. DONNELLEY & SONS COMPANY; *pg.* 1682, *pg.* 589
BOOKWIRE - Online Information Source - R.R. BOWKER LLC; *pg.* 1682, *pg.* 1095
BOOM - Game - MULTIMEDIA GAMES INC.; *pg.* 442, *pg.* 1664
BOOM BLOX - Video Game - ELECTRONIC ARTS INC.; *pg.* 951, *pg.* 189
BOOM BOOM ROCKET - Video Game - ELECTRONIC ARTS INC.; *pg.* 951, *pg.* 189
BOOM-O - Toy - MATTEL, INC.; *pg.* 962, *pg.* 81
BOOMER - Gum - WM. WRIGLEY JR. COMPANY; *pg.* 1863, *pg.* 596
BOOMERANG - Furniture - HERMAN MILLER, INC.; *pg.* 926, *pg.* 913
BOOMERANG - Roller Coaster - KNOTT'S BERRY FARM; *pg.* 556, *pg.* 50
BOOMERANG - Medical Device - RESMED INC.; *pg.* 1589, *pg.* 207
BOOMERANG WRIST - Orthopedic Product - DJO INCORPORATED; *pg.* 1524, *pg.* 302

First page reference indicates Business Class Edition
Second page reference indicates Geographic Edition

BOOMTOWN - Casinos - PINNACLE ENTERTAINMENT, INC.; *pg.* 576, *pg.* 1029
BOONE - Office Product - ACCO BRANDS CORPORATION; *pg.* 340, *pg.* 626
BOONE - Fabric - NEMSCHOFF, INC.; *pg.* 936, *pg.* 1890
BOONE'S FARM - Wine - E&J GALLO WINERY; *pg.* 1962, *pg.* 149
BOONVILLE STANDARD - Newspaper - WARRICK PUBLISHING CO. INC.; *pg.* 1701, *pg.* 675
BOORUM & PEASE - Bound Books - ESSELTE BUSINESS CORP; *pg.* 395, *pg.* 1179
BOOS BLOCKS - Butcher Blocks & Cutting Boards - JOHN BOOS & CO.; *pg.* 1126, *pg.* 609
BOOST - Wireless Systems - BOOST MOBILE; *pg.* 1869, *pg.* 107
BOOST - Complete Nutritional Energy Drink - MEAD JOHNSON NUTRITION COMPANY; *pg.* 1561, *pg.* 615
BOOST - Medical Product - MEDLINE INDUSTRIES, INC.; *pg.* 1562, *pg.* 635
BOOSTCAP - Ultracapacitor - MAXWELL TECHNOLOGIES, INC.; *pg.* 653, *pg.* 204
BOOSTER - Dry Cleaning & Laundry Product - ADCO, INC.; *pg.* 325, *pg.* 482
BOOSTER - Floor Care Product - BISSELL HOMECARE, INC.; *pg.* 52, *pg.* 887
BOOSTER - Resin - E.I. DU PONT DE NEMOURS & COMPANY; *pg.* 1159, *pg.* 390
BOOSTER - Cleaning Chemical Product - KYZEN CORPORATION; *pg.* 331, *pg.* 1652
BOOSTER GOLD - Character - DC COMICS, INC.; *pg.* 1633, *pg.* 1221
BOOSTER-IN-A-BAG - Air-Conditioner Whips - COLEMAN CABLE, INC.; *pg.* 1324, *pg.* 665
BOOSTER PAC - Battery Charging Product - CLORE AUTOMOTIVE LLC; *pg.* 202, *pg.* 716
BOOSTPAK - Pump - ECLIPSE INC.; *pg.* 1332, *pg.* 655
BOOSTXP - Software - SMITH MICRO SOFTWARE, INC.; *pg.* 471, *pg.* 41
THE BOOT - Underslab Vapor Retarder - FORTIFIBER CORPORATION; *pg.* 83, *pg.* 1021
BOOT CUT 517 - Jean - LEVI STRAUSS & CO.; *pg.* 43, *pg.* 220
BOOT-IN - Ski Boot Tree - ALLSOP, INC.; *pg.* 347, *pg.* 1817
BOOT SAUCE - Conditioner - THE TIMBERLAND COMPANY; *pg.* 1821, *pg.* 1039
BOOTGUARD - Software - SYMANTEC CORPORATION; *pg.* 478, *pg.* 161
BOOTHE - Tables - STEELCASE INC.; *pg.* 475, *pg.* 889
BOOTSTAT - Static Control Device - WALTER G. LEGGE COMPANY, INC.; *pg.* 337, *pg.* 1321
BOP IT - Game - HASBRO, INC.; *pg.* 954, *pg.* 1603
BOR-CAP - Euipment Maintenance Products - BAE SYSTEMS PRODUCTS GROUP; *pg.* 359, *pg.* 432
BORA - Remote Control Device - UNIVERSAL ELECTRONICS, INC.; *pg.* 683, *pg.* 262
BORATEEM - Color Safe Bleach - HENKEL CONSUMER GOODS; *pg.* 511, *pg.* 22
BORDEAUX - Bar Stool - BLATT BOWLING & BILLIARD CORP.; *pg.* 1827, *pg.* 1203
BORDEAUX - Cookies - PEPPERIDGE FARM, INC.; *pg.* 888, *pg.* 363
BORDEN - Dairy Product - DAIRY FARMERS OF AMERICA, INC.; *pg.* 851, *pg.* 982
BORDEN - Phenolic & Amino Resins - HEXION; *pg.* 1166, *pg.* 1440
BORDER BATTLES - Lottery Game - MINNESOTA STATE LOTTERY; *pg.* 999, *pg.* 956
BORDER BREAKFASTS - Breakfast Entrees - BOB EVANS FARMS, LLC; *pg.* 841, *pg.* 1467
BORDER FINE ARTS - Collectibles - ENESCO, LLC; *pg.* 1124, *pg.* 620
BORDER SCRAMBLE - Flour Tortillas Filled with Meat & Vegetables - BOB EVANS FARMS, LLC; *pg.* 841, *pg.* 1467
BORDERMANAGER - Computer Operations - NOVELL INC.; *pg.* 446, *pg.* 852
BORDERMANAGER FASTCACHE - Computer Software - NOVELL INC.; *pg.* 446, *pg.* 852
BORDETTE - Decorative Border - PACON CORPORATION; *pg.* 1466, *pg.* 1852
BORDEX - Plastics Product - AEP INDUSTRIES INC.; *pg.* 1878, *pg.* 1085
BOREALIS - Medical Device Platform Designed to Measure & Record Brainwave Activity - CERORA, INC.; *pg.* 1405, *pg.* 1516
BOREAS - Textiles - BERNHARDT DESIGN; *pg.* 918, *pg.* 1381
BOREAS - Fabric - NEMSCHOFF, INC.; *pg.* 936, *pg.* 1890
BOREAS MOUNTAIN - Clothing - ABERCROMBIE & FITCH CO.; *pg.* 37, *pg.* 1466
BORGHESE - Furniture - J. ROBERT SCOTT INC.; *pg.* 930, *pg.* 105
BORGIA - Ceramic, Glass, Stone Tiles & Slabs - WALKER & ZANGER, INC.; *pg.* 119, *pg.* 281
BORGOGNO - Imported Brand - BANFI VINTNERS; *pg.* 1957, *pg.* 1161
BORICS - Hair Service Center - REGIS CORPORATION; *pg.* 521, *pg.* 941
BORIDE - Tooling System - KENNAMETAL INC.; *pg.* 1052, *pg.* 1547
BORN BLONDE - Hair Coloring - P&G-CLAIROL, INC.; *pg.* 519, *pg.* 1418
BORN IN A GREAT STEAK HOUSE - Slogan - KEN'S FOODS, INC.; *pg.* 867, *pg.* 832
BORN TO FRY - T-Shirt - ZAPP'S POTATO CHIPS, INC.; *pg.* 1864, *pg.* 743
BORNAFIX - Fragrance Ingredient - INTERNATIONAL FLAVORS & FRAGRANCES INC.; *pg.* 512, *pg.* 1244
BORNEO - Luggage - JANSPORT; *pg.* 1837, *pg.* 38
BOROL - Mechanical Pulp - DOW CHEMICAL; *pg.* 1156, *pg.* 1563
BOROL - Bleaching Solution - THE DOW CHEMICAL COMPANY; *pg.* 1157, *pg.* 898
BORON STEEL - Steel Product - AK STEEL HOLDING CORPORATION; *pg.* 1311, *pg.* 1479
BOROVER - Chemical Reagent - HACH COMPANY; *pg.* 1415, *pg.* 334
BORROW SMART.BUY SMART - Motor Vehicle Dealership Services - ENTERPRISE HOLDINGS, INC.; *pg.* 1906, *pg.* 996
BORTEX - Software - SCHLUMBERGER LIMITED; *pg.* 801, *pg.* 1714
BORU - Vodka - CASTLE BRANDS INC.; *pg.* 239, *pg.* 1209
BORVIEW - Software - SCHLUMBERGER LIMITED; *pg.* 801, *pg.* 1714
BORZOI - Publishing Imprint - ALFRED A. KNOPF, INC.; *pg.* 1614, *pg.* 1189
BOS - Home & Garden Product - WESTROCK COMPANY; *pg.* 1472, *pg.* 1805
BOSCH - Appliances - BSH HOME APPLIANCES CORPORATION; *pg.* 53, *pg.* 108
BOSCH PNEUMATICS & HYDRAULICS - Pumps - BOSCH REXROTH CORPORATION; *pg.* 1319, *pg.* 1516
BOSCIA - Skin Care Product - FANCL INTERNATIONAL, INC.; *pg.* 509, *pg.* 110
BOSCO - Fabric - NEMSCHOFF, INC.; *pg.* 936, *pg.* 1890
BOSCO'S PIZZA COMPANY - Pizza Products & Bread Sticks - TYSON FOODS, INC.; *pg.* 902, *pg.* 35
BOSFET - Power Semiconductor Device - INTERNATIONAL RECTIFIER CORPORATION; *pg.* 647, *pg.* 80
B.O.S.S. - Tactical Eyewear - BAE SYSTEMS PRODUCTS GROUP; *pg.* 359, *pg.* 432
THE BOSS - Flashlight - BROWN & BIGELOW, INC.; *pg.* 1624, *pg.* 959
BOSS - Rubber Flashlights - DORCY INTERNATIONAL INC.; *pg.* 1046, *pg.* 1439
BOSS - Electronic Components - MOLEX INCORPORATED; *pg.* 655, *pg.* 628
THE BOSS - Guard Tour System - MORSE WATCHMANS INC.; *pg.* 656, *pg.* 368
B.O.S.S. - Brinell Optical Scanning System - NEWAGE TESTING INSTRUMENTS, INC.; *pg.* 1058, *pg.* 1532
BOSS CRUISER 7 - Bicycles - G. JOANNOU CYCLE CO. INC.; *pg.* 1707, *pg.* 1098
BOSS CRUISER COASTER - Bicycles - G. JOANNOU CYCLE CO. INC.; *pg.* 1707, *pg.* 1098
BOSS GUARD TOUR SYSTEM - Guard Tour System - MORSE WATCHMANS INC.; *pg.* 656, *pg.* 368
BOSS SKIN - Personal & Household Product - THE PROCTER & GAMBLE COMPANY; *pg.* 1129, *pg.* 1418
BOSSA NOVA - Fabric - NEMSCHOFF, INC.; *pg.* 936, *pg.* 1890
BOST-BRONZ - Hard Bronze Lubricated Cylindrical Bearing - BOSTON GEAR; *pg.* 201, *pg.* 802
BOST PASTORINO - Facom Tools - STANLEY BLACK & DECKER, INC.; *pg.* 1063, *pg.* 358
BOSTITCH - Pneumatic Tools - STANLEY BLACK & DECKER, INC.; *pg.* 1063, *pg.* 358
BOSTON - Contact Lens - BAUSCH & LOMB INCORPORATED; *pg.* 1401, *pg.* 1045
BOSTON - Hydraulic Component - EATON CORPORATION; *pg.* 1331, *pg.* 1429
BOSTON - Furniture - JASPER GROUP; *pg.* 930, *pg.* 691
BOSTON - Pianos - STEINWAY & SONS; *pg.* 586, *pg.* 1176
BOSTON ADVANCE - Contact Lens Care - BAUSCH & LOMB INCORPORATED; *pg.* 1401, *pg.* 1045
BOSTON BAKED BEANS - Candy - FERRARA CANDY CO.; *pg.* 1852, *pg.* 612
BOSTON CELTICS - Professional Basketball Team - BOSTON CELTICS LIMITED PARTNERSHIP; *pg.* 533, *pg.* 790
THE BOSTON GLOBE - Newspaper - THE NEW YORK TIMES COMPANY; *pg.* 1668, *pg.* 1270
THE BOSTON HERALD - Publisher - NEWS AMERICA INCORPORATED; *pg.* 1669, *pg.* 1271
BOSTON MARKET - Trade Name - BOSTON MARKET CORPORATION; *pg.* 1717, *pg.* 329
BOSTON POPS - Orchestra - BOSTON SYMPHONY ORCHESTRA INC.; *pg.* 534, *pg.* 791
BOSTON PROPER - Apparel - BOSTON PROPER, INC.; *pg.* 20, *pg.* 410
BOSTON PROPER - Women's Apparel & Accessories - CHICO'S FAS, INC.; *pg.* 21, *pg.* 427
BOSTON SIMPLUS - Contact Lens Care - BAUSCH & LOMB INCORPORATED; *pg.* 1401, *pg.* 1045
BOSTON SPORTS CLUBS - Fitness Center - TOWN SPORTS INTERNATIONAL HOLDINGS, INC.; *pg.* 589, *pg.* 1303
BOSTON TEA PARTY - Video Game - INTERNATIONAL GAME TECHNOLOGY; *pg.* 957, *pg.* 1024
BOSTON WHALER - Boats - BRUNSWICK CORPORATION; *pg.* 1828, *pg.* 623
BOSTONIAN - Shoes - CLARKS COMPANIES; *pg.* 1806, *pg.* 836
BOSTONIAN - Furniture - J. ROBERT SCOTT INC.; *pg.* 930, *pg.* 105
BOSTONIAN - Shoes - THE MEN'S WEARHOUSE, INC.; *pg.* 44, *pg.* 1711
BOSTONIAN BLUE - Footwear - CLARKS COMPANIES; *pg.* 1806, *pg.* 836
BOSTON'S - Food Product - THE HAIN CELESTIAL GROUP, INC.; *pg.* 860, *pg.* 1172
BOSTON'S BRICKOVEN PIZZA - Tag Line - BOSTON RESTAURANT ASSOCIATES, INC.; *pg.* 1717, *pg.* 829
BOSU - Fitness Product - BALLY TOTAL FITNESS HOLDINGS CORPORATION; *pg.* 532, *pg.* 1200
BOSUN - Toy Sailboat - REEVES INTERNATIONAL, INC.; *pg.* 966, *pg.* 1108
BOTANICAL - Wall Decor - ETHAN ALLEN INTERIORS INC.; *pg.* 924, *pg.* 343
BOTANICAL FIELDS - Plate - THE LONGABERGER COMPANY; *pg.* 1127, *pg.* 1467
BOTANICAL STUDY - Bath Product - KOHLER CO.; *pg.* 91, *pg.* 1862
BOTANICAL WEAVE LARGE BOARDWALK - Basket - THE LONGABERGER COMPANY; *pg.* 1127, *pg.* 1467
BOTANICLEANSE - Nutritional Supplement - NATURAL ORGANICS, INC.; *pg.* 1571, *pg.* 1181
BOTANIQUE - Fabric - MOMENTUM TEXTILES INC.; *pg.* 697, *pg.* 114
BOTANY - Fabric - NEMSCHOFF, INC.; *pg.* 936, *pg.* 1890
BOTANY 500 - Shoes - HABAND COMPANY, INC.; *pg.* 1772, *pg.* 1099
BOTOX - Cosmetic - ALLERGAN, INC.; *pg.* 1491, *pg.* 106
BOTOX COSMETIC - Cosmetic Care Product - ALLERGAN, INC.; *pg.* 1491, *pg.* 106
BOTTICELLI - Bath Product - KOHLER CO.; *pg.* 91, *pg.* 1862
BOTTLECAP - Eyewear - OAKLEY, INC.; *pg.* 1840, *pg.* 86
BOTTLECAPS - Candy - NESTLE USA, INC.; *pg.* 883, *pg.* 96
BOTTOM LINE - Game - WMS INDUSTRIES INC.; *pg.* 593, *pg.* 666
BOTTOM-OF-THE-BOTTLE - Pumps - IDEX CORPORATION; *pg.* 1347, *pg.* 623
BOTTOMHOOF - Animal Safety Product - NEOGEN CORPORATION; *pg.* 883, *pg.* 896
BOTTOMLESS STEAK FRIES - Food Product - RED ROBIN GOURMET BURGERS, INC.; *pg.* 1747, *pg.* 331
BOTTOMLINE - Lighting - STEELCASE INC.; *pg.* 475, *pg.* 889
BOTTOMLINE BUSINESS EXCHANGE - Software - BOTTOMLINE TECHNOLOGIES (DE), INC.; *pg.* 727, *pg.* 1038
BOTTOMLINE PRINT MANAGER - Software - BOTTOMLINE

TECHNOLOGIES (DE), INC.; pg. 727, pg. 1038
BOTTOMS UP - Booster Seat with Reversible Heights - DOREL JUVENILE GROUP, INC.; pg. 923, pg. 676
BOTTOMS UP - Video Game - INTERNATIONAL GAME TECHNOLOGY; pg. 957, pg. 1024
BOTVAX - Equine Botulism Vaccine - NEOGEN CORPORATION; pg. 883, pg. 896
BOU-MATIC PULSATOR - Electric Twin Pulsator - BOUMATIC LLC; pg. 701, pg. 1865
BOU-MATIC ROBOTICS - Milking System - BOUMATIC LLC; pg. 701, pg. 1865
BOU-MATIC SHELL - SDhell Barrel - BOUMATIC LLC; pg. 701, pg. 1865
BOUCLE - Bath Product - KOHLER CO.; pg. 91, pg. 1862
BOUCLE GRID - Carpet - INTERFACE, INC.; pg. 695, pg. 512
BOUCLE STRIPE - Fabric - NEMSCHOFF, INC.; pg. 936, pg. 1890
BOUILLOTTE - Lighting - ETHAN ALLEN INTERIORS INC.; pg. 924, pg. 343
THE BOULDER Naturaline Swing Set - CREATIVE PLAYTHINGS LTD.; pg. 1831, pg. 820
BOULDER CANYON - Snack Food Product - INVENTURE FOODS, INC.; pg. 1023, pg. 17
BOULDER CANYON CANYON CUT SALT & PEPPER - Snack Food - INVENTURE FOODS, INC.; pg. 1023, pg. 17
BOULDER CANYON CANYON CUT SOUR CREAM & CHIVE - Snack Food - INVENTURE FOODS, INC.; pg. 1023, pg. 17
BOULDER CANYON CANYON CUT TOTALLY NATURAL - Snack Food - INVENTURE FOODS, INC.; pg. 1023, pg. 17
BOULDER CANYON RICE & ADZUKI BEAN - Snack Food - INVENTURE FOODS, INC.; pg. 1023, pg. 17
BOULDER CANYON RICE & ADZUKI CHIPOTLE - Snack Food - INVENTURE FOODS, INC.; pg. 1023, pg. 17
BOULDER CANYON TOMATO & BASIL - Snack Food - INVENTURE FOODS, INC.; pg. 1023, pg. 17
BOULDER CREEK - Casual Dining Steak Restaurant - SBARRO, INC.; pg. 1749, pg. 1182
BOULDER STATION HOTEL AND CASINO - Hotel & Casino - STATION CASINOS, INC.; pg. 585, pg. 1030
BOULEVARD - Furniture - ASHLEY FURNITURE INDUSTRIES, INC.; pg. 914, pg. 1852
BOULEVARD - Textiles - BERNHARDT DESIGN; pg. 918, pg. 1381
BOULEVARD - Fabric - NEMSCHOFF, INC.; pg. 936, pg. 1890
BOUNCE - Fabric - NEMSCHOFF, INC.; pg. 936, pg. 1890
BOUNCE - Laundry Product - THE PROCTER & GAMBLE COMPANY; pg. 1129, pg. 1418
BOUNCE - Footwear - WOLVERINE WORLD WIDE, INC.; pg. 1822, pg. 905
BOUNCE BACK - Electrolyte Energy Supplement for Dehydrated Calves - MANNA PRO CORPORATION; pg. 1478, pg. 975
BOUNCE ROUND - Toy - SPIN MASTER LTD.; pg. 967, pg. 1943
BOUNCEBACK - Healthcare Product - MANNATECH, INCORPORATED; pg. 1558, pg. 1671
BOUNCER III - Pitchers - RUBBERMAID HOME PRODUCTS; pg. 1138, pg. 1453
BOUNCING BUCKS - Game - WMS INDUSTRIES INC.; pg. 593, pg. 666
BOUND TO IMPRESS - Manual - XEROX CORPORATION; pg. 494, pg. 365
BOUNDARY - Furniture - ASHLEY FURNITURE INDUSTRIES, INC.; pg. 914, pg. 1852
BOUNDARY WATERS - Dry Bags - CABELA'S INCORPORATED; pg. 535, pg. 1019
BOUNDARYSCAN - Software System - MENTOR GRAPHICS CORPORATION; pg. 432, pg. 1510
BOUNTIFUL HARVEST - Food Product - SHAMROCK FOODS COMPANY; pg. 895, pg. 20
BOUNTY - Candy - MARS, INCORPORATED; pg. 1858, pg. 1792
BOUNTY - Fabric - NEMSCHOFF, INC.; pg. 936, pg. 1890
BOUNTY - Paper Product - THE PROCTER & GAMBLE COMPANY; pg. 1129, pg. 1418
BOUQUET - Fabric - NEMSCHOFF, INC.; pg. 936, pg. 1890
BOURBON STREET - Fabric - NEMSCHOFF, INC.; pg. 936, pg. 1890
BOURBON STREET - Fabric - UNIROYAL ENGINEERED PRODUCTS; pg. 699, pg. 467
BOURSIN - Cheese - BEL BRANDS USA; pg. 839, pg. 566
BOUTIQUE - Fabric - NEMSCHOFF, INC.; pg. 936, pg. 1890
BOV-A-MURA - Homeowner Product - PBI/GORDON CORPORATION; pg. 1176, pg. 985
BOVI-KOTE - Moisturizing Barrier Dip - BOUMATIC LLC; pg. 701, pg. 1865
BOVI-SHIELD FP - Medicine - PFIZER INC.; pg. 1581, pg. 1278
BOVI-SHIELD GOLD - Pharmaceutical Product - PFIZER INC.; pg. 1581, pg. 1278
BOVIE FCFS - Electrosurgery Product - BOVIE MEDICAL CORPORATION; pg. 1402, pg. 1178
BOVIEDED - Electrosurgery Product - BOVIE MEDICAL CORPORATION; pg. 1402, pg. 1178
BOVIEFDFS - Electrosurgery Product - BOVIE MEDICAL CORPORATION; pg. 1402, pg. 1178
BOVIENEM - Electrosurgery Product - BOVIE MEDICAL CORPORATION; pg. 1402, pg. 1178
BOVILIS - Vaccine Lines - MERCK & CO., INC.; pg. 1566, pg. 1077
BOVINE VETERINARIAN - Magazine - VANCE PUBLISHING CORPORATION; pg. 1699, pg. 627
BOVISHIELD - Pharmaceutical Product - PFIZER INC.; pg. 1581, pg. 1278
BOVRIL - Soup, Sauce and Seasoning - UNILEVER CANADA INC.; pg. 903, pg. 1946
BOW BANGLES - Jewelry - CLAIRE'S STORES, INC.; pg. 1764, pg. 617
BOW-MAX - Storage Product - PLANO MOLDING COMPANY; pg. 1887, pg. 652
BOW-TIE - Car Part Accessory - PRO-LINE, INC.; pg. 966, pg. 45
BOW TYE - Footwear - OAKLEY, INC.; pg. 1840, pg. 86
BOWDEN CABLE CONTROLS - Remote Damper Controls - YOUNG REGULATOR COMPANY; pg. 1078, pg. 1478
BOWENS - Lighting - CALUMET PHOTOGRAPHIC, INC.; pg. 1404, pg. 568
BOWERS - Box & Cover - THOMAS & BETTS CORPORATION; pg. 680, pg. 1646
BOWFLEX - Health & Fitness Product - NAUTILUS, INC.; pg. 1840, pg. 1846
BOWHUNTER XTREME - Apparel - CABELA'S INCORPORATED; pg. 535, pg. 1019
THE BOWIE BLADE-NEWS - Newspaper - CAPITAL GAZETTE COMMUNICATIONS INC.; pg. 1625, pg. 754
BOWJAK - Hook - VAUGHAN & BUSHNELL MANUFACTURING COMPANY, INC.; pg. 1066, pg. 616
BOWKER ISBN - Official ISBN Agency for the United States - R.R. BOWKER LLC; pg. 1682, pg. 1095
BOWKERLINK - Publisher Access System for New Release Titles - R.R. BOWKER LLC; pg. 1682, pg. 1095
BOWL APPETIT - Food Product - GENERAL MILLS, INC.; pg. 828, pg. 933
BOWL BEAUTIFUL - Cleaning Product - ORECK CORPORATION; pg. 59, pg. 1653
BOWL FOR THE CURE - Event - UNITED STATES BOWLING CONGRESS; pg. 159, pg. 1660
BOWL FRESH - Toilet Deodorizer - WILLERT HOME PRODUCTS, INC.; pg. 1140, pg. 1005
BOWL WITH US - Slogan - UNITED STATES BOWLING CONGRESS; pg. 159, pg. 1660
BOWS & BLOOMS - Dresses & Sets - HABAND COMPANY, INC.; pg. 1772, pg. 1099
BOWWOW BREAKFAST - Dog Food - ALL AMERICAN PET COMPANY, INC.; pg. 1474, pg. 125
BOWWOW BREAKFAST CEREAL - Dog Food - ALL AMERICAN PET COMPANY, INC.; pg. 1474, pg. 125
BOWZER'S ROCK N' ROLL PARTY - Video Game - INTERNATIONAL GAME TECHNOLOGY; pg. 957, pg. 1024
BOX-A-BUBBLE - Durabubble Product - POLYAIR INTER PACK INC.; pg. 1467, pg. 1941
BOX GARDEN - Carpet - INTERFACE, INC.; pg. 695, pg. 512
BOX HILL - Storage System - DOT HILL SYSTEMS CORP.; pg. 388, pg. 333
BOX OF BUNCO - Game - WINNING MOVES GAMES, INC.; pg. 970, pg. 816
BOX OFFICE - Furniture - ASHLEY FURNITURE INDUSTRIES, INC.; pg. 914, pg. 1852
BOX OFFICE ESSENTIALS - Software - RENTRAK CORPORATION; pg. 306, pg. 1506
BOX SPRING 2.0 - Frames - OAKLEY, INC.; pg. 1840, pg. 86
BOX SPRING 4.0 - Frames - OAKLEY, INC.; pg. 1840, pg. 86
BOX TOP - Footwear - OAKLEY, INC.; pg. 1840, pg. 86
BOXCAR BONUS - Video Game - BALLY TECHNOLOGIES, INC.; pg. 531, pg. 1022
BOXER - Furniture - J. ROBERT SCOTT INC.; pg. 930, pg. 105
BOXERJAM - Online Games - MEDIA GENERAL, INC.; pg. 297, pg. 1803
BOXING AFTER DARK - Cable Television Show - HOME BOX OFFICE, INC.; pg. 290, pg. 1240
BOXVELOPE - Envelopes - TENSION ENVELOPE CORPORATION; pg. 483, pg. 986
BOXWEAVE - Carpet - BEAULIEU GROUP, LLC; pg. 917, pg. 529
BOXXER - Bicycle Component - SRAM CORPORATION; pg. 967, pg. 590
BOY SCOUTS OF AMERICA - Non-Profit Youth Organization - BOY SCOUTS OF AMERICA; pg. 134, pg. 1717
BOYNE - Resorts - BOYNE USA RESORTS INC.; pg. 1082, pg. 874
BOYS' LIFE - Magazine - BOYS' LIFE MAGAZINE; pg. 1623, pg. 1200
BP CEILING CLASSICS - Wood Fibre Ceiling Tiles & Panels, Fibreglass & Mineralite Ceilings - BUILDING PRODUCTS OF CANADA CORP.; pg. 72, pg. 1951
BP CLONASE - Molecular Biology Product - THERMO FISHER SCIENTIFIC INC.; pg. 1602, pg. 61
BP HEALTHCARD - Card - NU SKIN ENTERPRISES, INC.; pg. 518, pg. 1755
BP INTERNET SECURITY - Software - NU SKIN ENTERPRISES, INC.; pg. 518, pg. 1755
BP RANGER - Floor Cleaning Product - NSS ENTERPRISES, INC.; pg. 59, pg. 1476
BP SECURITY ANALYZER - Computer System - NU SKIN ENTERPRISES, INC.; pg. 518, pg. 1755
BP TELECOM - Telecommunication Tool - NU SKIN ENTERPRISES, INC.; pg. 518, pg. 1755
BPH - Thermoplastic Enclosures - CHANNELL COMMERCIAL CORP.; pg. 1870, pg. 291
BPI ENTERTAINMENT NEWS WIRE - Marketing Information Services - NIELSEN BUSINESS MEDIA; pg. 1671, pg. 1272
BPL - Activated Vapor Phase Carbons - CALGON CARBON CORPORATION; pg. 1151, pg. 1574
BPM - Beverages - THE COCA-COLA COMPANY; pg. 240, pg. 493
BPODIRECT - Financial Services - FEDERAL HOME LOAN MORTGAGE CORPORATION; pg. 751, pg. 1790
BPR - Metal Reinforcing Compounds - PPG INDUSTRIES, INC.; pg. 1445, pg. 1579
BQTINY - Power Products - TEXAS INSTRUMENTS INCORPORATED; pg. 679, pg. 1688
BR - Engineered Materials - CYTEC INDUSTRIES, INC.; pg. 1155, pg. 1131
BR1/10 - Network Accessing Product - ADTRAN, INC.; pg. 344, pg. 6
BR75 - Heavy Duty Digger w/Optional Down Pressure Kit - AG-MEIER INDUSTRIES LLC; pg. 700, pg. 1668
BRA-LLELUJAH - Clothing - SPANX INC.; pg. 32, pg. 520
BRABOURNE - Carpet - INTERFACE, INC.; pg. 695, pg. 512
THE BRACELET - Bracelet - UNTIL THERE'S A CURE FOUNDATION; pg. 160, pg. 192
BRACH'S - Candy - FERRARA CANDY CO.; pg. 1852, pg. 612
BRACHYVISION - Software - VARIAN MEDICAL SYSTEMS, INC.; pg. 1434, pg. 178
BRACKEN - Surface Material - STEELCASE INC.; pg. 475, pg. 889
BRAD - Electronic Components - MOLEX INCORPORATED; pg. 655, pg. 628
BRAD HARRISON & DESIGN - Electronic Components - MOLEX INCORPORATED; pg. 655, pg. 628
BRADBURY - Furniture - ASHLEY FURNITURE INDUSTRIES, INC.; pg. 914, pg. 1852
BRADBURY - Furniture - JASPER GROUP; pg. 930, pg. 691
BRADBURY - Office Furniture - STEELCASE INC.; pg. 475, pg. 889
BRADCOMMUNICATIONS - Electronic Components - MOLEX INCORPORATED; pg. 655, pg. 628
BRADCONNECTIVITY - Electronic Components - MOLEX INCORPORATED; pg. 655, pg. 628
BRADCONTROL - Electronic Components - MOLEX INCORPORATED; pg. 655, pg. 628
BRADEN - Winches - PACCAR INC.; pg. 187, pg. 1816
BRADFORD - Table - BLATT BOWLING & BILLIARD CORP.;

pg. 1827, *pg.* 1203
BRADFORD - Furniture - JASPER GROUP; *pg.* 930, *pg.* 691
BRADFORD EXCHANGE - Collectors Plates - THE BRADFORD GROUP; *pg.* 1763, *pg.* 637
BRADINGTON - Furniture - ASHLEY FURNITURE INDUSTRIES, INC.; *pg.* 914, *pg.* 1852
BRADLEY - Shoes - ALLEN-EDMONDS SHOE CORP.; *pg.* 1804, *pg.* 1887
BRADLEY - Furniture - AMISCO INDUSTRIES LTD.; *pg.* 913, *pg.* 1958
BRADLEY POND - T-Shirts - ABERCROMBIE & FITCH CO.; *pg.* 37, *pg.* 1466
BRADPACK - Modular Wash Center - BRADLEY CORPORATION; *pg.* 71, *pg.* 1870
BRADPOWER - Electronic Components - MOLEX INCORPORATED; *pg.* 655, *pg.* 628
BRADPOWER & DESIGN - Electronic Components - MOLEX INCORPORATED; *pg.* 655, *pg.* 628
BRADSTONE - Washfountain - BRADLEY CORPORATION; *pg.* 71, *pg.* 1870
BRADY - Furniture - LA-Z-BOY INCORPORATED; *pg.* 932, *pg.* 901
BRADYGAMES - PC & Video Game Strategy Grids - PRIMA GAMES; *pg.* 965, *pg.* 693
BRADYPRINTER - Label Printer - BRADY CORPORATION; *pg.* 363, *pg.* 1873
BRADY'S IRISH CREAM - Liqueur - CASTLE BRANDS INC.; *pg.* 239, *pg.* 1209
BRAG - Buell Riders Adventure Group - HARLEY-DAVIDSON, INC.; *pg.* 178, *pg.* 1874
BRAID - Carpet - BEAULIEU GROUP, LLC; *pg.* 917, *pg.* 529
BRAID - Fabric - NEMSCHOFF, INC.; *pg.* 936, *pg.* 1890
BRAIDED - Belt - COACH, INC.; *pg.* 3, *pg.* 1214
BRAIDS PRETZELS - Snack Food - INVENTURE FOODS, INC.; *pg.* 1023, *pg.* 17
BRAIN - Laptop Business Backpack - JANSPORT; *pg.* 1837, *pg.* 38
BRAIN ELEVATE - Nutritional Product - NOW HEALTH GROUP, INC.; *pg.* 1576, *pg.* 557
BRAIN FOOD - Museum Restaurant Services - MUSEUM OF SCIENCE AND INDUSTRY; *pg.* 565, *pg.* 583
BRAIN JAM - Educational Materials - SCHOLASTIC INC.; *pg.* 1683, *pg.* 1288
BRAIN PEP - Nutritional Product - NUTRACEUTICAL INTERNATIONAL CORPORATION; *pg.* 1576, *pg.* 1753
BRAIN PLAY - Educational Materials - SCHOLASTIC INC.; *pg.* 1683, *pg.* 1288
BRAIN QUEST - Game - UNIVERSITY GAMES CORPORATION; *pg.* 969, *pg.* 230
BRAIN WARP - Game - HASBRO, INC.; *pg.* 954, *pg.* 1603
BRAINAPPS - Brain Fitness Exercise - SCIENTIFIC LEARNING CORPORATION; *pg.* 607, *pg.* 172
BRAINCONNECTION - Software - SCIENTIFIC LEARNING CORPORATION; *pg.* 607, *pg.* 172
BRAINERD - Decorative Architectural Product - MASCO CORPORATION; *pg.* 96, *pg.* 909
BRAINIAC - Character - DC COMICS, INC.; *pg.* 1633, *pg.* 1221
BRAINLINK - Lab Science Material - CAROLINA BIOLOGICAL SUPPLY COMPANY; *pg.* 1513, *pg.* 1359
BRAINSHARE - Computer Software - NOVELL INC.; *pg.* 446, *pg.* 852
BRAINSPEED ATTENTION - Vitamin & Dietary Supplement - NATROL, INC.; *pg.* 1570, *pg.* 64
BRAINSPEED MEMORY - Nutritional Product - NATROL, INC.; *pg.* 1570, *pg.* 64
BRAINSPEED PERFORM - Vitamin & Dietary Supplement - NATROL, INC.; *pg.* 1570, *pg.* 64
BRAINSTAIN - Molecular Probe Product - THERMO FISHER SCIENTIFIC INC.; *pg.* 1602, *pg.* 61
BRAINWARE - Engineered Product And System - SULZER METCO (WESTBURY) INC.; *pg.* 1064, *pg.* 1350
BRAINWARE DISTILLER - Data Capture Platform - PERCEPTIVE SOFTWARE; *pg.* 453, *pg.* 1775
BRAINZ - Medical Device - NATUS MEDICAL INCORPORATED; *pg.* 1572, *pg.* 199
BRAKECRAWLER - Bicycle Component - SRAM CORPORATION; *pg.* 967, *pg.* 590
BRAKESAFE PULL - Tow Car Brake System - BLUE OX; *pg.* 701, *pg.* 1019
BRAKESAFE PUSH - Braking System - BLUE OX; *pg.* 701, *pg.* 1019
BRAMMALL - Security Entry Barrier Seals - THE VIKING GROUP; *pg.* 119, *pg.* 891
BRAMPTON - Shoe - ALDO GROUP; *pg.* 1804, *pg.* 1959
BRAN BUDS - High-Fiber Morsels of Wheat Bran & Psyllium Cereal - KELLOGG COMPANY; *pg.* 831, *pg.* 870
BRAN FLAKES - Cereal - POST HOLDINGS, INC.; *pg.* 833, *pg.* 1002
BRANCH FLORAL - Wallcovering - YORK WALLCOVERINGS INC.; *pg.* 947, *pg.* 1598
BRANCH REPEATER - Software - CITRIX SYSTEMS, INC.; *pg.* 375, *pg.* 424
BRANCOTT ESTATE - Wine - PERNOD RICARD USA, INC.; *pg.* 1968, *pg.* 1332
BRAND BAG - Newspaper - VALASSIS COMMUNICATIONS, INC.; *pg.* 1287, *pg.* 897
BRAND BAG+ - Newspaper - VALASSIS COMMUNICATIONS, INC.; *pg.* 1287, *pg.* 897
BRAND CUBED - Marketing Tool - THE NIELSEN COMPANY B.V.; *pg.* 1671, *pg.* 1272
BRAND G - Apparel - GUESS?, INC.; *pg.* 25, *pg.* 132
BRAND NAMES YOU KNOW AND TRUST - Tagline - LOWE'S COMPANIES, INC.; *pg.* 1053, *pg.* 1383
BRAND REX - Cable - GENERAL CABLE CORPORATION; *pg.* 83, *pg.* 729
BRAND X - Amplifier - FENDER MUSICAL INSTRUMENTS CORPORATION; *pg.* 547, *pg.* 21
BRAND X - Carbonated Soft Drink - LEADING BRANDS, INC.; *pg.* 1026, *pg.* 1911
BRAND X ORIGINALS - Beverage - LEADING BRANDS, INC.; *pg.* 1026, *pg.* 1911
BRANDAU - Lounge Chairs - BERNHARDT DESIGN; *pg.* 918, *pg.* 1381
BRANDDYY - Footwear - STEVEN MADDEN, LTD.; *pg.* 1819, *pg.* 1176
BRANDE - Footwear - STEVEN MADDEN, LTD.; *pg.* 1819, *pg.* 1176
BRANDGUARD - Sanitizer - ROCHESTER MIDLAND CORPORATION; *pg.* 334, *pg.* 1337
BRANDIE - Footwear - PHOENIX FOOTWEAR GROUP, INC.; *pg.* 1815, *pg.* 60
BRANDOL - Filter Cartridge - PALL CORPORATION; *pg.* 232, *pg.* 1323
BRANDONITE - High Performance Composite Polymers - GLOBE COMPOSITE SOLUTIONS, LTD.; *pg.* 1883, *pg.* 842
THE BRANDS OF EVERYDAY LIFE - Slogan - JARDEN CORPORATION; *pg.* 1885, *pg.* 412
BRANDS THAT MATTER - Tag Line - NEWELL RUBBERMAID INC.; *pg.* 1128, *pg.* 515
BRANDS YOU TRUST. PEOPLE YOU KNOW. - Tagline - SOUTHERN STATES COOPERATIVE, INC.; *pg.* 1482, *pg.* 1804
BRANDT - Money Handling System - GLORY GLOBAL SOLUTIONS; *pg.* 401, *pg.* 628
BRANDWATCHER - Software - WEBSENSE, INC.; *pg.* 491, *pg.* 210
BRANDXCELLENCE - Process for Improving Overall Performance of Independent Distribution - MARITZ INC.; *pg.* 1914, *pg.* 977
BRANDYWINE - Semisweet Chocolate - CARGILL LIMITED; *pg.* 1475, *pg.* 1914
BRAQUETTE - Adjustable Frame - MARTIN/F. WEBER COMPANY; *pg.* 962, *pg.* 1567
BRASIL SLINGO - Game - INTERNATIONAL GAME TECHNOLOGY; *pg.* 957, *pg.* 1024
BRASILIA BLUEBERRY - Beverage - BAI BRANDS; *pg.* 238, *pg.* 1073
BRASS - Software - SUNGARD DATA SYSTEMS INC.; *pg.* 477, *pg.* 1592
BRASS BELL BAKERY - Bakery Good - GOLDEN CORRAL CORPORATION; *pg.* 1730, *pg.* 1387
BRASS BOOT - Footwear - WEYCO GROUP, INC.; *pg.* 1822, *pg.* 1858
BRASS DELUXE - Gaming Product - GLD PRODUCTS, INC.; *pg.* 1835, *pg.* 1882
BRASS LINGUINI - Sensor System - MEASUREMENT SPECIALTIES INC.; *pg.* 1360, *pg.* 1783
BRASS-TITE! - Brass Unions & Fittings - DORMAN PRODUCTS, INC.; *pg.* 204, *pg.* 1522
BRASSCRAFT - Plumbing Product - MASCO CORPORATION; *pg.* 96, *pg.* 909
BRASSERIE JO - French Restaurant - LETTUCE ENTERTAIN YOU ENTERPRISES, INC.; *pg.* 1735, *pg.* 580
BRASSO - Metal Polish - RECKITT BENCKISER INC.; *pg.* 1136, *pg.* 1105
BRASSTECH - Plumbing Product - MASCO CORPORATION; *pg.* 96, *pg.* 909
BRASTEM - Home Appliance Product - WHIRLPOOL CORPORATION; *pg.* 62, *pg.* 872
BRASTEMP - Kitchen Appliance - WHIRLPOOL CORPORATION; *pg.* 62, *pg.* 872
BRATWURSHIP - Food Product - KAYEM FOODS, INC.; *pg.* 867, *pg.* 814
BRATZ PASSION - Game - HASBRO, INC.; *pg.* 954, *pg.* 1603
BRAUD - Agricultural Equipment - CNH AMERICA LLC; *pg.* 702, *pg.* 560
BRAUN - Appliance - THE GILLETTE COMPANY; *pg.* 509, *pg.* 795
BRAUN - Premium Small Electric Appliances - HELEN OF TROY L.P.; *pg.* 511, *pg.* 1692
BRAUN - Personal & Household Product - THE PROCTER & GAMBLE COMPANY; *pg.* 1129, *pg.* 1418
BRAUN AROMASTER - Coffee Makers - BRAUN NORTH AMERICA; *pg.* 52, *pg.* 792
BRAUN AROMATIC - Coffee Grinders - BRAUN NORTH AMERICA; *pg.* 52, *pg.* 792
BRAUN CITROMATIC - Press Juicers - BRAUN NORTH AMERICA; *pg.* 52, *pg.* 792
BRAUN DENTAL CENTER - Electric Dental Prods. - BRAUN NORTH AMERICA; *pg.* 52, *pg.* 792
BRAUN ELECTRIC RAZOR - Electric Razor - BRAUN NORTH AMERICA; *pg.* 52, *pg.* 792
BRAUN HAND BLENDER - Hand Blender - THE GILLETTE COMPANY; *pg.* 509, *pg.* 795
BRAUN INDEPENDENT 2000 - Cordless Hair Curler - BRAUN NORTH AMERICA; *pg.* 52, *pg.* 792
BRAUN MULTIPRACTIC - Hand Blender - BRAUN NORTH AMERICA; *pg.* 52, *pg.* 792
BRAUN MULTIPRESS - Spin Juicers - BRAUN NORTH AMERICA; *pg.* 52, *pg.* 792
BRAUN QUARTZ - Battery Clocks - BRAUN NORTH AMERICA; *pg.* 52, *pg.* 792
BRAUN QUICKSTYLE - Electric Curlers - BRAUN NORTH AMERICA; *pg.* 52, *pg.* 792
BRAUN QUICKSTYLE COMBI - Electric Curlers - BRAUN NORTH AMERICA; *pg.* 52, *pg.* 792
BRAUN REFLEX CONTROL - Battery Clocks - BRAUN NORTH AMERICA; *pg.* 52, *pg.* 792
BRAUN SILENTIME - Battery Clocks - BRAUN NORTH AMERICA; *pg.* 52, *pg.* 792
BRAUN SLIMSTYLE - Electric Curlers - BRAUN NORTH AMERICA; *pg.* 52, *pg.* 792
BRAUN SYNCRO - Oral Care Product - THE GILLETTE COMPANY; *pg.* 509, *pg.* 795
BRAUN THERMOSCAN - Thermometry - WELCH ALLYN INC.; *pg.* 1436, *pg.* 1342
BRAUN VOICE CONTROL - Battery Clocks - BRAUN NORTH AMERICA; *pg.* 52, *pg.* 792
BRAUNLOK - Caps - TRICORBRAUN; *pg.* 1471, *pg.* 1004
BRAVA - Publishing Imprint - KENSINGTON PUBLISHING CORP.; *pg.* 1656, *pg.* 1248
BRAVA TERRA - Beverage - PHOENIX VINTNERS, LLC; *pg.* 1968, *pg.* 182
BRAVADA - Furniture - ASHLEY FURNITURE INDUSTRIES, INC.; *pg.* 914, *pg.* 1852
BRAVADA - Rug - COURISTAN INC.; *pg.* 921, *pg.* 1067
BRAVADO - Eyewear - SIGNATURE EYEWEAR, INC.; *pg.* 1429, *pg.* 105
BRAVAL - Pipe - ADVANCED DRAINAGE SYSTEMS, INC.; *pg.* 1878, *pg.* 1455
BRAVE EAGLE - Fishing Equipment - WRIGHT & MCGILL CO.; *pg.* 1848, *pg.* 324
BRAVE HEARTS - Publication - OGDEN PUBLICATIONS, INC.; *pg.* 1672, *pg.* 722
BRAVO! - Restaurants - BRAVO BRIO RESTAURANT GROUP, INC.; *pg.* 1717, *pg.* 1438
BRAVO - Knife - BUCK KNIVES, INC.; *pg.* 1828, *pg.* 550
BRAVO - Servingware for Buffets - CARLISLE FOODSERVICE PRODUCTS INCORPORATED; *pg.* 1455, *pg.* 1485
BRAVO - Fabric - NEMSCHOFF, INC.; *pg.* 936, *pg.* 1890
BRAVO - Drug Delivery System - SURMODICS, INC.; *pg.* 1600, *pg.* 924
BRAVO - Stand - WENGER CORPORATION; *pg.* 1307, *pg.* 952
BRAVO! CUCINA ITALIANA - Restaurants - BRAVO BRIO RESTAURANT GROUP, INC.; *pg.* 1717, *pg.* 1438
BRAVO! ITALIAN KITCHEN - Restaurants - BRAVO BRIO RESTAURANT GROUP, INC.; *pg.* 1717, *pg.* 1438
BRAVO RESCUE - Knife - BUCK KNIVES, INC.; *pg.* 1828, *pg.* 550

BRAVOPRO - Disc Publisher - MICROBOARDS TECHNOLOGY, LLC; *pg.* 434, *pg.* 920
BRAVOS - Laundry Machines - WHIRLPOOL CORPORATION; *pg.* 62, *pg.* 872
BRAVURA - Perm Freshwater Flush Toilet - THETFORD CORPORATION; *pg.* 337, *pg.* 867
BRAVVOO - Footwear - STEVEN MADDEN, LTD.; *pg.* 1819, *pg.* 1176
BRAWNY - Cleaning Product - THE EVERCARE COMPANY; *pg.* 1124, *pg.* 483
BRAWNY - Paper Towel - GEORGIA-PACIFIC LLC; *pg.* 1458, *pg.* 507
BRAWNY - Footwear - LACROSSE FOOTWEAR, INC.; *pg.* 1811, *pg.* 1503
BRAWNY LAD - Sandwiches - FRISCH'S RESTAURANTS, INC.; *pg.* 1729, *pg.* 1413
BRAXTON - Furniture - AMERICAN LEATHER LP; *pg.* 912, *pg.* 1673
BRAXTON - Restaurant - HOULIHAN'S RESTAURANTS, INC.; *pg.* 1731, *pg.* 716
BRAXTON - Lighting Product - QUOIZEL INC.; *pg.* 1304, *pg.* 1616
BRAYTON - Office Furniture - STEELCASE INC.; *pg.* 475, *pg.* 889
BRAZBOND - Engineered Product And System - SULZER METCO (WESTBURY) INC.; *pg.* 1064, *pg.* 1350
BRAZEN XL - Men's Shoe - JACK SCHWARTZ SHOES, INC.; *pg.* 1810, *pg.* 1245
BRAZIL IPANEMA BOURBON - Coffee - STARBUCKS CORPORATION; *pg.* 897, *pg.* 1840
BRAZIL.COM - Travel Website - LIVE CURRENT MEDIA INC.; *pg.* 1263, *pg.* 1911
BRAZILIAN BEAUTY - Game - WMS INDUSTRIES INC.; *pg.* 593, *pg.* 666
BRAZILIAN MAPLE - Carpet - BEAULIEU GROUP, LLC; *pg.* 917, *pg.* 529
BRAZILIAN MESQUITE - Hardware Flooring - LUMBER LIQUIDATORS HOLDINGS, INC.; *pg.* 94, *pg.* 1808
BRAZZI - Beverages - THE COCA-COLA COMPANY; *pg.* 240, *pg.* 493
BRD - Recycling & De-inking Chemicals - BUCKMAN; *pg.* 1150, *pg.* 1641
BREA - Fabric - NEMSCHOFF, INC.; *pg.* 936, *pg.* 1890
BREAD AND BUTTER COMBO - Cigars - FINCK CIGAR CO.; *pg.* 1894, *pg.* 1740
BREAD READY - Food Product - HORMEL FOODS CORPORATION; *pg.* 863, *pg.* 915
BREAD SMART - Kitchenware - TUPPERWARE BRANDS CORPORATION; *pg.* 1139, *pg.* 456
BREADED NUGGETS - Poultry Product - PILGRIM'S PRIDE CORPORATION; *pg.* 889, *pg.* 330
BREADED TENDER - Poultry Product - PILGRIM'S PRIDE CORPORATION; *pg.* 889, *pg.* 330
BREADSHOP - Food Product - THE HAIN CELESTIAL GROUP, INC.; *pg.* 860, *pg.* 1172
BREAK-DOWN - Defoaming Agent - KALO, INC.; *pg.* 1796, *pg.* 719
BREAK-FREE - Equipment Maintenance Products - BAE SYSTEMS PRODUCTS GROUP; *pg.* 359, *pg.* 432
BREAK FREE CLP - Security Product - BAE SYSTEMS PRODUCTS GROUP; *pg.* 359, *pg.* 432
BREAK THE BANK - Lottery Game - KENTUCKY LOTTERY CORPORATION; *pg.* 996, *pg.* 735
BREAK THE BANK - Lottery Game - MASSACHUSETTS STATE LOTTERY; *pg.* 998, *pg.* 802
BREAK THE BANK - Lottery Game - OHIO LOTTERY COMMISSION; *pg.* 1002, *pg.* 1433
BREAK TIME - Convenience Stores - MFA OIL COMPANY; *pg.* 981, *pg.* 976
BREAK.COM - Website - DEFYMEDIA; *pg.* 1237, *pg.* 1222
BREAKER - Semiconductor Dicing Equipment - DYNATEX INTERNATIONAL; *pg.* 635, *pg.* 277
BREAKFAST JACK - Breakfast Sandwich - JACK IN THE BOX INC.; *pg.* 1732, *pg.* 204
BREAKFAST SMILE - Breakfast Special - EAT'N PARK HOSPITALITY GROUP; *pg.* 1728, *pg.* 1539
BREAKFAST'N FRUIT BUFFET - Morning Food Service - EAT'N PARK HOSPITALITY GROUP; *pg.* 1728, *pg.* 1539
BREAKFREE - Herbicide - E.I. DU PONT DE NEMOURS & COMPANY; *pg.* 1159, *pg.* 390
BREAKING THE RULES - Tagline - WISCONSIN MACHINE TOOL CORPORATION; *pg.* 1389, *pg.* 1855
BREAKOPENS - Lottery Game - OREGON STATE LOTTERY; *pg.* 1003, *pg.* 1508
BREAKSTONES - Cottage Cheeses & Sour Creams - THE KRAFT HEINZ COMPANY; *pg.* 870, *pg.* 1577
BREAKTHROUGH - Resistant Glass - ODL INCORPORATED; *pg.* 101, *pg.* 914
BREAKTHROUGH SCIENCE. BREAKTHROUGH MEDICINE - Slogan - MILLENNIUM: THE TAKEDA ONCOLOGY COMPANY; *pg.* 1568, *pg.* 809
BREAKTHROUGH SIMPLICITY - Tagline - SKYWORKS SOLUTIONS, INC.; *pg.* 674, *pg.* 862
BREAKTHROUGHS EVERY DAY - Tagline - MEMORIAL HERMANN HEALTHCARE SYSTEM; *pg.* 1565, *pg.* 1711
BREAKWATER - Eyewear - MAUI JIM, INC.; *pg.* 9, *pg.* 651
BREAS - Humidifier - VITAL SIGNS, INC.; *pg.* 1607, *pg.* 1126
BREASE - Wallcovering - OMNOVA SOLUTIONS INC; *pg.* 1176, *pg.* 1453
BREAST SELF EXAM SHOWER CARD - Plastic Card to Instruct Proper Technique for Self Exam for Breast Cancer - PILGRIM PLASTIC PRODUCTS COMPANY; *pg.* 1887, *pg.* 803
BREASTIQUE - Health & Beauty Product - DIXIE HEALTH, INC.; *pg.* 1524, *pg.* 535
BREATH-O-PINE - Cleanser, Deodorant & Disinfectant - BRONDOW, INC.; *pg.* 327, *pg.* 1346
BREATH-O-PRENE - Adjustable Compression - 3M COMPANY; *pg.* 1142, *pg.* 956
BREATH RELIEF - Pharmaceutical Product - PURETEK CORPORATION; *pg.* 1587, *pg.* 211
BREATH STRIPS - Dental Products for Dogs - THE HARTZ MOUNTAIN CORP.; *pg.* 1476, *pg.* 1120
BREATH TEK - Therapy System - PROMETHEUS LABORATORIES, INC.; *pg.* 1586, *pg.* 206
BREATHE - Health System Product - LANELABS USA INC.; *pg.* 1554, *pg.* 1128
BREATHE-EASY - Suction Valve - VITAL SIGNS, INC.; *pg.* 1607, *pg.* 1126
BREATHE IN THE FREEDOM - Slogan - INVACARE CORPORATION; *pg.* 1546, *pg.* 1451
BREATHE SAFE - Interior Paint - THE MURALO COMPANY; *pg.* 1444, *pg.* 1042
BREATHE WITH EASE - Asthma Program - MOLINA HEALTHCARE, INC.; *pg.* 1569, *pg.* 123
BREATHER BAG - Vented Poly Bags - BEMIS HEALTHCARE PACKAGING; *pg.* 1453, *pg.* 1885
BREATHESAFE - Respirator - CALGON CARBON CORPORATION; *pg.* 1151, *pg.* 1574
BREATHEWAY - Food Product - LANDEC CORPORATION; *pg.* 1419, *pg.* 145
BREATHSAVERS - Mints - THE HERSHEY CO.; *pg.* 1855, *pg.* 1538
BRECKENRIDGE - Furniture - AMERICAN LEATHER LP; *pg.* 912, *pg.* 1673
BRECKENRIDGE - Ski Resort - VAIL RESORTS, INC.; *pg.* 1117, *pg.* 313
BREE - Fabric - NEMSCHOFF, INC.; *pg.* 936, *pg.* 1890
BREEDER AIDE - Animal Treatment - KENT NUTRITION GROUP; *pg.* 1477, *pg.* 710
BREENA - Fabric - NEMSCHOFF, INC.; *pg.* 936, *pg.* 1890
BREEZAIR - EVAP Coolers - SEELEY INTERNATIONAL AMERICAS; *pg.* 1076, *pg.* 19
BREEZE - Software - ADOBE SYSTEMS INCORPORATED; *pg.* 342, *pg.* 235
BREEZE - Almond Milk - BLUE DIAMOND GROWERS; *pg.* 840, *pg.* 195
BREEZE - Safety & Protective Equipment - ENCON SAFETY PRODUCTS; *pg.* 1334, *pg.* 1705
BREEZE - Fabric - NEMSCHOFF, INC.; *pg.* 936, *pg.* 1890
BREEZE - Liquid Chromatography Instrument - WATERS CORPORATION; *pg.* 1436, *pg.* 834
BREEZE EASTERN - Clamps & Adapters - BREEZE-EASTERN CORPORATION; *pg.* 1319, *pg.* 1132
BREEZE-EASTERN CORPORATION - Rescue Hoist System - BREEZE-EASTERN CORPORATION; *pg.* 1319, *pg.* 1132
BREEZE WEAVE - Outerwear - UNIFIRST CORPORATION; *pg.* 50, *pg.* 860
BREEZY BLOOMS - Twin Set - HABAND COMPANY, INC.; *pg.* 1772, *pg.* 1099
BRELLIN - Lounge Chairs - BERNHARDT DESIGN; *pg.* 918, *pg.* 1381
BREMERTON SUN - Newspaper - THE E.W. SCRIPPS COMPANY; *pg.* 1639, *pg.* 1412
BREMNER - Crackers - CONAGRA FOODS; *pg.* 826, *pg.* 994
BRENNAN - Furniture - ASHLEY FURNITURE INDUSTRIES, INC.; *pg.* 914, *pg.* 1852
BRENT - Furniture - AMISCO INDUSTRIES LTD.; *pg.* 913, *pg.* 1958
BRENT - Beer - COASTAL EXTREME BREWING COMPANY; *pg.* 240, *pg.* 1602
BRENTWOOD - Shoes - ALLEN-EDMONDS SHOE CORP.; *pg.* 1804, *pg.* 1887
BRENTWOOD - Vinyl Siding - PLY GEM SIDING GROUP; *pg.* 105, *pg.* 986
BRER RABBIT - Molasses - B&G FOODS, INC.; *pg.* 838, *pg.* 1102
BRETER - Software - ROCKWELL AUTOMATION, INC.; *pg.* 668, *pg.* 1880
BRETHINE - Pharmaceutical Product - IMPAX LABORATORIES, INC.; *pg.* 1544, *pg.* 101
BRETON - Office Furniture - STEELCASE INC.; *pg.* 475, *pg.* 889
BRETTELLES - Textiles - BERNHARDT DESIGN; *pg.* 918, *pg.* 1381
BREVIA - Bath Product - KOHLER CO.; *pg.* 91, *pg.* 1862
BREVIBLOC - Pharmaceutical Product - BAXTER INTERNATIONAL INC.; *pg.* 1499, *pg.* 599
BREVICON - Pharmaceutical Product - ALLERGAN; *pg.* 1490, *pg.* 1101
BREW - Wireless Communication Product - CRICKET WIRELESS LLC; *pg.* 381, *pg.* 483
BREW - Software Development Kit - QUALCOMM INCORPORATED; *pg.* 1873, *pg.* 207
BREW HA HA - Video Game - INTERNATIONAL GAME TECHNOLOGY; *pg.* 957, *pg.* 1024
BREW-THRU - Beverage - BUNN-O-MATIC CORPORATION; *pg.* 53, *pg.* 661
BREWCO - Frame Straightening Equipment - SNAP-ON INCORPORATED; *pg.* 1062, *pg.* 1862
BREWLINE - Hose - THE GOODYEAR TIRE & RUBBER COMPANY; *pg.* 1883, *pg.* 1401
BREWLOGIC - Brewer - BUNN-O-MATIC CORPORATION; *pg.* 53, *pg.* 661
BREWSTATION - Kitchen Appliance - HAMILTON BEACH BRANDS, INC.; *pg.* 56, *pg.* 1783
BREWSTER'S - Coffee - BAB, INC.; *pg.* 1715, *pg.* 599
BREWWISE - Beverage - BUNN-O-MATIC CORPORATION; *pg.* 53, *pg.* 661
BREWWIZARD - Beverage Dispensing Product - BUNN-O-MATIC CORPORATION; *pg.* 53, *pg.* 661
BREYER - Toys - TRACTOR SUPPLY COMPANY; *pg.* 708, *pg.* 1627
BREYERS - Ice Cream and Frozen Novelties - UNILEVER CANADA INC.; *pg.* 903, *pg.* 1946
BREYERS - Ice Cream - UNILEVER UNITED STATES, INC.; *pg.* 904, *pg.* 1061
BRIAR STRE - Food Product - ELLENBEE-LEGGETT COMPANY INC.; *pg.* 854, *pg.* 1452
BRIARWOOD - Table - BLATT BOWLING & BILLIARD CORP.; *pg.* 1827, *pg.* 1203
BRIARWOOD - Musical Instrument - PEAVEY ELECTRONICS CORPORATION; *pg.* 662, *pg.* 970
BRIC - Interface Controller - PMC-SIERRA, INC.; *pg.* 664, *pg.* 287
BRICK HOUSE TAVERN + TAP - Restaurants - IGNITE RESTAURANT GROUP, INC.; *pg.* 1731, *pg.* 1708
BRICK QUADRANT - Pillow & Throw - HERITAGE LACE INC.; *pg.* 694, *pg.* 711
BRICK TOWNSHIP BULLETIN - Newspaper - GREATER MEDIA NEWSPAPERS, INC.; *pg.* 1646, *pg.* 1071
BRICKFIRE BAKERY - Food Product - SHAMROCK FOODS COMPANY; *pg.* 895, *pg.* 20
BRICKMAN'S - Premium Sandwich - GORDON FOOD SERVICE INC.; *pg.* 1021, *pg.* 913
BRICO - Powder Metal Products - FEDERAL-MOGUL HOLDINGS CORPORATION; *pg.* 205, *pg.* 907
BRICSCAD - Software - EAGLE POINT SOFTWARE CORPORATION; *pg.* 389, *pg.* 707
BRIDAL BOUQUET - Container Grown Plant - MONROVIA GROWERS; *pg.* 1797, *pg.* 44
BRIDAL VEIL - Container Grown Plant - MONROVIA GROWERS; *pg.* 1797, *pg.* 44
BRIDES - Magazine - CONDE NAST PUBLICATIONS, INC.; *pg.* 1629, *pg.* 1217
BRIDES.COM - Bridal Website - CONDE NAST PUBLICATIONS, INC.; *pg.* 1629, *pg.* 1217
BRIDGE - Software - ADOBE SYSTEMS INCORPORATED; *pg.* 342, *pg.* 235
BRIDGE - Stents - MEDTRONIC, INC.; *pg.* 1564, *pg.* 939
BRIDGE BREAKER - Bin & Hopper Discharger - HYER INDUSTRIES INC.; *pg.* 1051, *pg.* 841

BRIDGE E-PAY - Online Banking - BRIDGE BANCORP, INC.; *pg.* 727, *pg.* 1144

BRIDGE PROGRAM - Pharmaceutical Product - PFIZER INC.; *pg.* 1581, *pg.* 1278

BRIDGEMONT - Truck Scales - AVERY WEIGH-TRONIX, INC.; *pg.* 1315, *pg.* 925

BRIDGEPOINT - Software System - MENTOR GRAPHICS CORPORATION; *pg.* 432, *pg.* 1510

BRIDGEPORT - Furniture - ASHLEY FURNITURE INDUSTRIES, INC.; *pg.* 914, *pg.* 1852

BRIDGEPORT - Milling Machine - HARDINGE INC.; *pg.* 1344, *pg.* 1157

BRIDGES - Greeting Cards - LEANIN' TREE, INC.; *pg.* 1658, *pg.* 311

BRIDGES - Educational Materials - SCHOLASTIC INC.; *pg.* 1683, *pg.* 1288

BRIDGESTONE - Tires - BRIDGESTONE AMERICAS, INC.; *pg.* 1879, *pg.* 1648

BRIDGESTONE J33 - Golf Equipment - BRIDGESTONE GOLF, INC.; *pg.* 1828, *pg.* 528

BRIDGESTONE OR NOTHING - Tagline - BRIDGESTONE AMERICAS, INC.; *pg.* 1879, *pg.* 1648

BRIDGESTONE TOUR B330 - Golf Balls - BRIDGESTONE GOLF, INC.; *pg.* 1828, *pg.* 528

BRIDGESTONE TRUCK TIRES - Commercial Tires - BRIDGESTONE AMERICAS, INC.; *pg.* 201, *pg.* 1649

BRIDGET - Footwear - PHOENIX FOOTWEAR GROUP, INC.; *pg.* 1815, *pg.* 60

BRIDGING THE BAY - Games - PENN NATIONAL GAMING, INC.; *pg.* 574, *pg.* 1595

BRIDGIT - Watch - COACH, INC.; *pg.* 3, *pg.* 1214

BRIDION - Pharmaceutical Preparation - MERCK & CO., INC.; *pg.* 1566, *pg.* 1077

BRIDLEWOOD - Wine - E&J GALLO WINERY; *pg.* 1962, *pg.* 149

BRIEFCASE - Beverage Bottle - THERMOS L.L.C.; *pg.* 61, *pg.* 660

BRIEFING ADVISOR - Online Newsletter - BRIEFING.COM; *pg.* 727, *pg.* 568

BRIEFING IN PLAY - Market Coverage & Analysis - BRIEFING.COM; *pg.* 727, *pg.* 568

BRIEFING INSTITUTIONAL - Market Coverage & Analysis - BRIEFING.COM; *pg.* 727, *pg.* 568

BRIEFING PROFESSIONAL - Market Coverage & Analysis - BRIEFING.COM; *pg.* 727, *pg.* 568

BRIEFING TRADER - Market Coverage & Analysis - BRIEFING.COM; *pg.* 727, *pg.* 568

BRIETTA - Lamp - ASHLEY FURNITURE INDUSTRIES, INC.; *pg.* 914, *pg.* 1852

BRIGADE 2EC - Insecticides & Miticides - FMC CORPORATION; *pg.* 1163, *pg.* 1564

BRIGADE WSB - Insecticides & Miticides - FMC CORPORATION; *pg.* 1163, *pg.* 1564

BRIGADIER - Insecticides & Miticides - FMC CORPORATION; *pg.* 1163, *pg.* 1564

BRIGGHT - Footwear - STEVEN MADDEN, LTD.; *pg.* 1819, *pg.* 1176

BRIGGS NEW YORK - Women's Apparel - KELLWOOD COMPANY; *pg.* 28, *pg.* 975

BRIGHAM'S - Ice Cream - HP HOOD LLC; *pg.* 864, *pg.* 829

BRIGHT - Cheese - AGROPUR COOPERATIVE; *pg.* 836, *pg.* 1950

BRIGHT & EARLY - Beverages - THE COCA-COLA COMPANY; *pg.* 240, *pg.* 493

BRIGHT BEAUTY - Spray Paints - SHERWIN-WILLIAMS DIVERSIFIED BRANDS DIVISION; *pg.* 1448, *pg.* 1435

BRIGHT DIAMONDS - Game - WMS INDUSTRIES INC.; *pg.* 593, *pg.* 666

BRIGHT-EDGE - Cutting Fluid - THE DOALL COMPANY; *pg.* 1329, *pg.* 670

BRIGHT EYED AND BLUEBERRY - Yogurt & Fruit Blend Drink - JAMBA, INC.; *pg.* 1024, *pg.* 84

BRIGHT EYES - Residential Lighting Playmate - SWIVELIER CO., INC.; *pg.* 1307, *pg.* 1142

BRIGHT GREEN - Environmentally Safe Household Cleaners & Detergents - SAFEWAY INC.; *pg.* 1032, *pg.* 184

BRIGHT HORIZONS FAMILY SOLUTIONS - Logo - BRIGHT HORIZONS FAMILY SOLUTIONS INC.; *pg.* 598, *pg.* 855

BRIGHT LIFE - Paints - SHERWIN WILLIAMS; *pg.* 1448, *pg.* 1436

BRIGHT LIGHTS - Paints - SHERWIN WILLIAMS; *pg.* 1448, *pg.* 1436

BRIGHT MAGIC - Shampoo - PETEDGE; *pg.* 1481, *pg.* 787

BRIGHT 'N TIGHT - Container Grown Plant - MONROVIA GROWERS; *pg.* 1797, *pg.* 44

BRIGHT NOW! - Dental Services - SMILE BRANDS GROUP INC.; *pg.* 1594, *pg.* 116

BRIGHT SPOT - Halogen Exam Light - MEDLINE INDUSTRIES, INC.; *pg.* 1562, *pg.* 635

BRIGHT TEA CO. - Teas - MARS, INCORPORATED; *pg.* 1858, *pg.* 1792

BRIGHTAMP - Optical Amplifier - VIAVI SOLUTIONS INC.; *pg.* 1435, *pg.* 148

BRIGHTBELLS - Vinyl Dumbbells - ALLIANCE SPORTS GROUP, L.P.; *pg.* 1825, *pg.* 1698

BRIGHTBOY - Rubber Bonded Abrasives - CRATEX MANUFACTURING CO., INC.; *pg.* 77, *pg.* 85

BRIGHTER CHILD - Educational Resources - SCHOOL SPECIALTY, INC.; *pg.* 467, *pg.* 1860

BRIGHTFIRE - Burner - ECLIPSE INC.; *pg.* 1332, *pg.* 655

BRIGHTJACK - Monitoring Solution - VIAVI SOLUTIONS INC.; *pg.* 1435, *pg.* 148

BRIGHTLIFE - Sheet Vinyl Flooring - CONGOLEUM CORPORATION; *pg.* 921, *pg.* 1084

BRIGHTMAIL - Software - SYMANTEC CORPORATION; *pg.* 478, *pg.* 161

BRIGHTON - Cart Bag - DATREK GOLF; *pg.* 1832, *pg.* 1801

BRIGHTON - Dinnerware - THE HOMER LAUGHLIN CHINA COMPANY; *pg.* 1125, *pg.* 1850

BRIGHTPATH - FTTH Solution - COMMSCOPE, INC.; *pg.* 278, *pg.* 1378

BRIGHTPOINT ONLINE - Wireless Product - INGRAM MICRO MOBILITY; *pg.* 415, *pg.* 697

BRIGHTRAY - Alloy Product - SPECIAL METALS CORPORATION; *pg.* 1377, *pg.* 1850

BRIGHTSCORE - Report Analysis - INCHARGE INSTITUTE OF AMERICA, INC.; *pg.* 768, *pg.* 454

BRIGHTSTOR - Storage Management Software - CA TECHNOLOGIES; *pg.* 366, *pg.* 1168

BRIGHTSUN - Antimony Trioxide - ALBEMARLE CORPORATION; *pg.* 1146, *pg.* 741

BRIGHTSWITCH - Switch - VIAVI SOLUTIONS INC.; *pg.* 1435, *pg.* 148

BRIGHTWIRE - Cable - COMMSCOPE, INC.; *pg.* 278, *pg.* 1378

BRIJ - Chemical Product - SPECTRUM CHEMICALS & LABORATORY PRODUCTS, INC.; *pg.* 1181, *pg.* 94

BRILES - Rivet - ALLFAST FASTENING SYSTEMS, INC.; *pg.* 1041, *pg.* 66

BRILEY - Furniture - ASHLEY FURNITURE INDUSTRIES, INC.; *pg.* 914, *pg.* 1852

BRILLIANCE - Wire & Cable Products - BELDEN, INC.; *pg.* 624, *pg.* 993

BRILLIANCE - Finish - DELTA FAUCET COMPANY; *pg.* 78, *pg.* 684

BRILLIANCE - Custom Pleated Shades - HUNTER DOUGLAS, INC.; *pg.* 928, *pg.* 1320

BRILLIANCE - Shortenings & Oils - PERFORMANCE FOOD GROUP COMPANY, LLC; *pg.* 1030, *pg.* 1803

BRILLIANCE OF THE SEAS - Cruise Ship - ROYAL CARIBBEAN CRUISES LTD; *pg.* 1921, *pg.* 446

BRILLIANT COATINGS - Magazine - BENJAMIN MOORE & CO.; *pg.* 1440, *pg.* 1085

BRILLIANT MEMORY SOLUTIONS - Hardware - MICRON TECHNOLOGY, INC.; *pg.* 435, *pg.* 547

BRILLIANT NOVELTY - Table - BLATT BOWLING & BILLIARD CORP.; *pg.* 1827, *pg.* 1203

BRILLIANT PAPER - Inkjet Paper & Ink - CALUMET PHOTOGRAPHIC, INC.; *pg.* 1404, *pg.* 568

BRILLIANTCOLOR - Color Technology - INFOCUS CORPORATION; *pg.* 644, *pg.* 1503

BRILLIANTCOLOR - Projectors - PLANAR SYSTEMS, INC.; *pg.* 455, *pg.* 1495

BRILLIANTCOLOR - Image Technology - TEXAS INSTRUMENTS INCORPORATED; *pg.* 679, *pg.* 1688

BRILLO - Steel Wool - ARMALY BRANDS; *pg.* 326, *pg.* 912

BRIMAX - Cleaners - THE CLOROX COMPANY; *pg.* 327, *pg.* 169

BRINDA - Lamp - ASHLEY FURNITURE INDUSTRIES, INC.; *pg.* 914, *pg.* 1852

BRINE - Athletic Equipment - NEW BALANCE ATHLETIC SHOE, INC.; *pg.* 1811, *pg.* 798

BRINE - Soccerball - SCHOOL-TECH, INC.; *pg.* 1844, *pg.* 866

BRINER'S CHOICE - Calcium Chloride - THE DOW CHEMICAL COMPANY; *pg.* 1157, *pg.* 898

BRING YOUR MOM TO WORK DAY - Educational Services - 1-800-FLOWERS.COM, INC.; *pg.* 1758, *pg.* 1151

BRINGING AMERICA HOME. BRINGING AMERICA FUN. - Slogan - SKYLINE CORPORATION; *pg.* 1711, *pg.* 677

BRINGING EARTH'S RESOURCES TO LIFE - Tag Line - J.R. SIMPLOT COMPANY; *pg.* 867, *pg.* 547

BRINGING HOPE TO LIFE - Slogan - ONCOGENEX PHARMACEUTICALS, INC.; *pg.* 1578, *pg.* 1818

BRINGING INNOVATION TOGETHER - Slogan - SURMODICS, INC.; *pg.* 1600, *pg.* 924

BRINGING OUR STAINLESS REPUTATION TO PLASTICS - Slogan - SWAGELOK COMPANY; *pg.* 1064, *pg.* 1473

BRINGING SOLUTIONS TO VASCULAR MEDICINE - Tagline - VASCULAR SOLUTIONS, INC.; *pg.* 1434, *pg.* 946

BRINGING THE BEST TO EVERYONE WE TOUCH. - Slogan - THE ESTEE LAUDER COMPANIES INC.; *pg.* 508, *pg.* 1229

BRINGING THE MEETING TO YOU - Teleconferencing Services - CISCO SYSTEMS, INC.; *pg.* 372, *pg.* 240

BRINGING THE OCEAN TO LIFE - Tag Line - MERA PHARMACEUTICALS, INC.; *pg.* 1566, *pg.* 545

BRINGING YOUR CATHOLIC FAITH TO LIFE - Slogan - OUR SUNDAY VISITOR, INC.; *pg.* 1673, *pg.* 682

BRINKER - Fabric - SCALAMANDRE, INC.; *pg.* 941, *pg.* 1058

BRINKMAN SMOKER - Charcoal Water Smoker - BARBEQUES GALORE, INC.; *pg.* 51, *pg.* 173

BRINK'S - Security Services - THE BRINK'S COMPANY; *pg.* 364, *pg.* 1800

BRINK'S HOME SECURITY - Home Security Services - THE BRINK'S COMPANY; *pg.* 364, *pg.* 1800

BRIO - Restaurants - BRAVO BRIO RESTAURANT GROUP, INC.; *pg.* 1717, *pg.* 1438

BRIO - Fabric - NEMSCHOFF, INC.; *pg.* 936, *pg.* 1890

BRIO - Ceiling Panel - USG CORPORATION; *pg.* 118, *pg.* 594

BRIO TUSCAN GRILLE - Restaurants - BRAVO BRIO RESTAURANT GROUP, INC.; *pg.* 1717, *pg.* 1438

BRIQUETTER - Briquetting System - PRAB, INC.; *pg.* 1369, *pg.* 894

BRISA - Textiles - BERNHARDT DESIGN; *pg.* 918, *pg.* 1381

BRISCO - Footwear - VANS, INC.; *pg.* 1821, *pg.* 76

BRISCOE - Apparels - UNDER ARMOUR, INC.; *pg.* 49, *pg.* 759

BRISE - Cleaning Product - S.C. JOHNSON & SON, INC.; *pg.* 334, *pg.* 1889

BRISE AUTO - Car Air Freshener - S.C. JOHNSON & SON, INC.; *pg.* 334, *pg.* 1889

BRISE CIRCUL AIR - Air Freshener - S.C. JOHNSON & SON, INC.; *pg.* 334, *pg.* 1889

BRISE HOME FRAGRANCE - Car Air Freshener - S.C. JOHNSON & SON, INC.; *pg.* 334, *pg.* 1889

BRISE ON & ON - Cleaner - S.C. JOHNSON & SON, INC.; *pg.* 334, *pg.* 1889

BRISE TOUCH & FRESH - Cleaner - S.C. JOHNSON & SON, INC.; *pg.* 334, *pg.* 1889

BRISTAN - Faucet - MASCO CORPORATION; *pg.* 96, *pg.* 909

BRISTO - Shredded Cheese - SARGENTO FOODS INC.; *pg.* 894, *pg.* 1886

BRISTOL - Lamp - J. ROBERT SCOTT INC.; *pg.* 930, *pg.* 105

BRISTOL - Furniture - JOFCO INC.; *pg.* 931, *pg.* 691

BRISTOL - Door Glass - ODL INCORPORATED; *pg.* 101, *pg.* 914

BRISTOL - Cigarettes - PHILIP MORRIS USA INC.; *pg.* 1894, *pg.* 1803

BRISTOL BAR & GRILL - Restaurant - HOULIHAN'S RESTAURANTS, INC.; *pg.* 1731, *pg.* 716

BRISTOL MANOR - Lighting Product - QUOIZEL INC.; *pg.* 1304, *pg.* 1616

BRISTOL MOTOR SPEEDWAY - Entertainment Venue - SPEEDWAY MOTORSPORTS, INC.; *pg.* 584, *pg.* 1370

BRISTOL RIDGE - Plastic & Rubber - TEKNOR APEX COMPANY; *pg.* 1889, *pg.* 1605

BRISTOL YACHTS - Yacht Yard - BRISTOL MARINE; *pg.* 1705, *pg.* 1600

BRISTOLINE - Healthcare Product - GF HEALTH PRODUCTS, INC.; *pg.* 1535, *pg.* 508

BRISTOW - Control Cable - TUTHILL CORPORATION; *pg.* 1385, *pg.* 561

BRITA - Water Filter Systems, Pitcher & Faucet - THE CLOROX COMPANY; *pg.* 327, *pg.* 169

BRITANNIA ALCOHOLIC BEVERAGES - Whiskey - MONTEBELLO BRANDS INC.; *pg.* 1967, *pg.* 758

BRITANNICA - Books & Educational Services - ENCYCLOPAEDIA BRITANNICA, INC.; *pg.* 1638, *pg.* 573

BRITE - Floor Polish - S.C. JOHNSON & SON, INC.; *pg.* 334,

pg. 1889
BRITE - Paint - W.M. BARR & COMPANY, INC.; pg. 338, pg. 1647
BRITE-BAK - Cleaner - HILLYARD, INC.; pg. 331, pg. 990
BRITE BULB - Bulb Fixer - AMERICAN GREASE STICK CO.; pg. 971, pg. 902
BRITE GALVANIZE - Paint & Coating - AERVOE INDUSTRIES INCORPORATED; pg. 1439, pg. 1021
BRITE LEGS - Hosiery & Related Apparel - MAYER/BERKSHIRE CORPORATION; pg. 29, pg. 1129
BRITE STAR - Rangefinder - FLIR SYSTEMS, INC.; pg. 1413, pg. 1510
BRITE-STAY - Cable - LOOS & COMPANY, INC.; pg. 1356, pg. 368
BRITE TOUCH - Spray Paint - SHERWIN-WILLIAMS DIVERSIFIED BRANDS DIVISION; pg. 1448, pg. 1435
BRITE UMBRELLA GROUP - Insurance Agency - GREATER NEW YORK MUTUAL INSURANCE COMPANY; pg. 1201, pg. 1236
BRITE WHITE - Airbrush Paper - BADGER AIR BRUSH COMPANY; pg. 359, pg. 612
BRITEBOND - Powder Coatings for Application to Metal & Nonmetallic Substrates - DOW CHEMICAL; pg. 1156, pg. 1563
BRITECORE TT - Fiber Optic Lighting System - ENERGY FOCUS, INC.; pg. 1411, pg. 1472
BRITEGUARD - Coating - A BRITE COMPANY; pg. 1144, pg. 1697
BRITEGUARD PITCHBLACK - Plating Process - A BRITE COMPANY; pg. 1144, pg. 1697
BRITEHUE - Paper - INTERNATIONAL PAPER COMPANY; pg. 1460, pg. 1644
BRITEHUE - Printing Paper - MOHAWK FINE PAPERS, INC.; pg. 1464, pg. 1153
BRITELIGHT - Specialty Illumination Products - BALLANTYNE STRONG, INC.; pg. 623, pg. 1013
BRITELITE - Assays & Reagents - PERKINELMER, INC.; pg. 1426, pg. 853
BRITEN-ZIT - Cleaning Product - HILLYARD, INC.; pg. 331, pg. 990
BRITEPAK - Fiber Optic Lighting System - ENERGY FOCUS, INC.; pg. 1411, pg. 1472
BRITEPLUS - Galvanising Alloy - TECK RESOURCES LIMITED; pg. 1183, pg. 1912
BRITESIL - Sodium Polysilicates - PQ CORPORATION; pg. 1178, pg. 1515
BRITESORB - Adsorbent Gel - PQ CORPORATION; pg. 1178, pg. 1515
BRITESPOT - Fabric - NEMSCHOFF, INC.; pg. 936, pg. 1890
BRITETOUCH - Software - CRESTRON ELECTRONICS INC.; pg. 631, pg. 1116
BRITISH CLASSICS - Furniture - ETHAN ALLEN INTERIORS INC.; pg. 924, pg. 343
BRITISH COLONIAL - Bedding - CROSCILL, INC.; pg. 1122, pg. 1220
BRITISH COLONIAL - Furniture - HOOKER FURNITURE CORPORATION; pg. 928, pg. 1788
BRITISH OPEN - Furniture Collection - CENTURY FURNITURE INDUSTRIES; pg. 920, pg. 1377
BRITISH ROYAL NAVY IMPERIAL RUM - Rum - CASTLE BRANDS INC.; pg. 239, pg. 1209
BRITISH SATEEN - Fabric - NEMSCHOFF, INC.; pg. 936, pg. 1890
BRITNEY - Glove - KOMBI, LTD.; pg. 1838, pg. 1766
BRITOOL - Facom Tools - STANLEY BLACK & DECKER, INC.; pg. 1063, pg. 358
BRITTANIA - Jeanswear - V.F. CORPORATION; pg. 34, pg. 1376
BRITTANY - Furniture - AMISCO INDUSTRIES LTD.; pg. 913, pg. 1958
BRITTANY - Furniture - ASHLEY FURNITURE INDUSTRIES, INC.; pg. 914, pg. 1852
BRIVA - Kitchen Appliance - WHIRLPOOL CORPORATION; pg. 62, pg. 872
BRIZO - Faucet - DELTA FAUCET COMPANY; pg. 78, pg. 684
BRIZO - Faucet Product - MASCO CORPORATION; pg. 96, pg. 909
BRK - Safety Products - BRK BRANDS, INC.; pg. 627, pg. 554
BRK - Transseptal Needles - ST. JUDE MEDICAL, INC.; pg. 1596, pg. 963
BROAD AXE STOUT - Beer - GRANITE CITY FOOD & BREWERY LTD; pg. 1730, pg. 937
BROADBAND ESSENTIALS - Software - RENTRAK CORPORATION; pg. 306, pg. 1506
BROADBAND MARITIME - Broadband Communication System - MARITIME BROADBAND; pg. 1265, pg. 1146
BROADBAND PROTECTION PLUS - Online Security Program - WINDSTREAM CORPORATION; pg. 321, pg. 34
BROADBAND-TODAY.COM - Trade Website - ADVANTAGE BUSINESS MEDIA; pg. 1613, pg. 1116
BROADBAND TUBING - Heat Shrink - CHANNELL COMMERCIAL CORP.; pg. 1870, pg. 291
BROADCAST - Food Product - CONAGRA FOODS, INC.; pg. 826, pg. 1014
BROADCAST - Furniture - JOFCO INC.; pg. 931, pg. 691
BROADCAST NETWORK GATEWAY - Digital Video Product - HARMONIC, INC.; pg. 402, pg. 246
BROADCAST RICHARDSON - Broadcast Products - RICHARDSON ELECTRONICS, LTD.; pg. 667, pg. 622
BROADCORE - Computer Products - BROADCOM CORPORATION; pg. 364, pg. 108
BROADMOOR - Office Furniture - STEELCASE INC.; pg. 475, pg. 889
BROADRANGE - Wireless Technology - BROADCOM CORPORATION; pg. 364, pg. 108
BROADSTREET - Shoes - ALLEN-EDMONDS SHOE CORP.; pg. 1804, pg. 1887
BROADVISION COMMAND CENTER - Software - BROADVISION, INC.; pg. 365, pg. 189
BROADVISION ONE-TO-ONE COMMERCE - Software - BROADVISION, INC.; pg. 365, pg. 189
BROADVISION ONE-TO-ONE ENTERPRISE - Software - BROADVISION, INC.; pg. 365, pg. 189
BROADVISION ONE-TO-ONE PORTAL - Software - BROADVISION, INC.; pg. 365, pg. 189
BROADVOICE - Computer Products - BROADCOM CORPORATION; pg. 364, pg. 108
BROADWATER - Footwear - PHOENIX FOOTWEAR GROUP, INC.; pg. 1815, pg. 60
BROADWAY - Shoe - ALIMED, INC.; pg. 1490, pg. 816
BROADWAY - Furniture - BASSETT FURNITURE INDUSTRIES, INCORPORATED; pg. 916, pg. 1776
BROADWAY - Table - BLATT BOWLING & BILLIARD CORP.; pg. 1827, pg. 1203
BROADWAY - Publishing Imprint - THE KNOPF DOUBLEDAY GROUP; pg. 1657, pg. 1249
BROADWAY - Furniture - LA-Z-BOY INCORPORATED; pg. 932, pg. 901
BROADWAY - Fabric - NEMSCHOFF, INC.; pg. 936, pg. 1890
BROADWAY - Ceramic, Glass, Stone Tiles & Slabs - WALKER & ZANGER, INC.; pg. 119, pg. 281
THE BROADWAY SERIES - Musical Theater Production - CALIFORNIA MUSICAL THEATRE CORPORATION; pg. 536, pg. 196
BROAN - Range Hoods, Ventilating Fans, Bathroom Heaters & Cabinets - BROAN-NUTONE LLC; pg. 1069, pg. 1860
BROCADE - Carpet - BEAULIEU GROUP, LLC; pg. 917, pg. 529
BROCADE - Fiber Channel Switch - BROCADE COMMUNICATIONS SYSTEMS, INC.; pg. 365, pg. 239
BROCADE ENCRYPTION - Software - NETAPP, INC.; pg. 444, pg. 287
BROCCOLOGY - Nutritional Product - NOW HEALTH GROUP, INC.; pg. 1576, pg. 557
BROCK SHUR-STEP - Bin Stairs - CTB INTERNATIONAL CORP.; pg. 850, pg. 695
BROCKTON - Furniture - JASPER GROUP; pg. 930, pg. 691
BROD DUGAN - Protective & Decorative Paint coatings - THE SHERWIN-WILLIAMS COMPANY; pg. 1447, pg. 1435
BRODA - Geriatric Seating - MITY ENTERPRISES, INC.; pg. 935, pg. 1753
BRODBECK - Seeds - DOW AGROSCIENCES LLC; pg. 1156, pg. 684
BRODERICK & BASCOM - Wire Rope - WIRECO WORLDGROUP; pg. 1389, pg. 987
BRODHEAD GARRET - Educational Resources - SCHOOL SPECIALTY, INC.; pg. 467, pg. 1860
BRODIE - Furniture - AMISCO INDUSTRIES LTD.; pg. 913, pg. 1958
BRODY - Glass Vases - LANCASTER COLONY CORPORATION; pg. 873, pg. 1441
BROGAN - Furniture - JASPER GROUP; pg. 930, pg. 691
BROKEN ARROW - Fabric - NEMSCHOFF, INC.; pg. 936, pg. 1890
BROKEN HALO IPA - Beer - CRAFT BREWERS ALLIANCE, INC.; pg. 247, pg. 1502
BROKEN LINE - Rug - ETHAN ALLEN INTERIORS INC.; pg. 924, pg. 343
BROKERADVANTAGE - Broker Office Website Service - HOMES.COM, INC.; pg. 1256, pg. 203
BROKERAUDIT - Software - SUNGARD DATA SYSTEMS INC.; pg. 477, pg. 1592
BROKERLINK - Health Plan & Publication - MEDICA, INC.; pg. 1208, pg. 949
BROKERS GIN - Distilled Spirits - HOOD RIVER DISTILLERS INC.; pg. 1964, pg. 1498
BROMALINE - Pharmaceutical Product - ALLERGAN; pg. 1490, pg. 1101
BROMDAY - Ophthalmology Product - BAUSCH & LOMB INCORPORATED; pg. 1401, pg. 1045
BRON-SHOE CO. - Baby Shoe - THE BRON SHOE COMPANY; pg. 1440, pg. 1438
BRONCHO - Medical Equipment - CONMED CORPORATION; pg. 1517, pg. 1347
BRONCHO-CATH - Endobronchial Tube - MALLINCKRODT PHARMACEUTICALS; pg. 1557, pg. 978
BRONCO - Rotary Cutter - AG-MEIER INDUSTRIES LLC; pg. 700, pg. 1668
BRONCO - Floor Cleaning Product - NSS ENTERPRISES, INC.; pg. 59, pg. 1476
BRONCO-CATH - Endobronchial Tube - MEDTRONIC; pg. 1563, pg. 183
BRONKAID - Medicine - BAYER HEALTHCARE CONSUMER CARE DIVISION; pg. 1500, pg. 1087
BRONTO SKYLIFT - Vehicle-Mounted Aerial Access Platforms - FEDERAL SIGNAL CORPORATION; pg. 638, pg. 645
BRONZE MEDAL - Semisweet Chocolate - CARGILL LIMITED; pg. 1475, pg. 1914
BRONZE-RITE - Mold Base & Component - SUPERIOR DIE SET CORP.; pg. 1379, pg. 1885
BRONZELITE - Lighting Fixture & Control - PHILIPS LIGHTING; pg. 1303, pg. 806
BROOK - Footwear - COBIAN CORP.; pg. 1806, pg. 253
BROOK - Waiting Seating - STEELCASE INC.; pg. 475, pg. 889
BROOKDALE SENIOR LIVING - Senior Living Communities - BROOKDALE SENIOR LIVING INC.; pg. 1511, pg. 1627
BROOKFIELD - Carpet - BEAULIEU GROUP, LLC; pg. 917, pg. 529
BROOKFIELD - Kitchen Product - KOHLER CO.; pg. 91, pg. 1862
BROOKLINE - Bath Product - KOHLER CO.; pg. 91, pg. 1862
BROOKLYN - Footwear - EASTLAND SHOE CORPORATION; pg. 1808, pg. 750
BROOKLYN BROWN ALE - Seasonal Beer - THE BROOKLYN BREWERY; pg. 239, pg. 1145
BROOKLYN CUVEE DE CARDOZ - Seasonal Beer - THE BROOKLYN BREWERY; pg. 239, pg. 1145
BROOKLYN LAGER - Seasonal Beer - THE BROOKLYN BREWERY; pg. 239, pg. 1145
BROOKLYN PENNANT ALE 55 - Seasonal Beer - THE BROOKLYN BREWERY; pg. 239, pg. 1145
BROOKLYN PILSNER - Seasonal Beer - THE BROOKLYN BREWERY; pg. 239, pg. 1145
BROOKLYN VEGAN - Indie Music Blog - SPINMEDIA; pg. 1282, pg. 104
BROOKLYNER WEISSE - Seasonal Beer - THE BROOKLYN BREWERY; pg. 239, pg. 1145
BROOKS - Running Shoes, Apparel & Accessories - BROOKS SPORTS INC.; pg. 1805, pg. 1818
BROOKS - Chili, Chili Beans & Powdered Chili Mix - PINNACLE FOODS GROUP LLC; pg. 889, pg. 1104
BROOKS - Pharmacies - RITE AID CORPORATION; pg. 1590, pg. 1519
BROOKS BROTHERS - Beauty Product - BROOKS BROTHERS GROUP, INC.; pg. 39, pg. 1208
BROOKS EQUILIBRIUM - Apparel Technology - BROOKS SPORTS INC.; pg. 1805, pg. 1818
BROOKS SHELTER - Apparel Technology - BROOKS SPORTS INC.; pg. 1805, pg. 1818
BROOKSBY VILLAGE - Retirement Community - ERICKSON LIVING; pg. 1090, pg. 766
BROOKSHIRE.S. THANK YOU FOR YOUR LOYALTY. - Slogan - BROOKSHIRE GROCERY COMPANY; pg. 1016, pg. 1748
BROOKSIDE - Chocolate - THE HERSHEY CO.; pg. 1855, pg. 1538
BROOKSMITE - Control Measurement - BROOKS

First page reference indicates Business Class Edition
Second page reference indicates Geographic Edition

INSTRUMENT, LLC; *pg.* 1403, *pg.* 1537
BROOKSTONE - Table - BLATT BOWLING & BILLIARD CORP.; *pg.* 1827, *pg.* 1203
THE BROOKTRON PROCESS - Brush Plating Process - BROOKTRONICS ENGINEERING CORPORATION; *pg.* 1320, *pg.* 299
BROOKTROUT LAKE - T-Shirts - ABERCROMBIE & FITCH CO.; *pg.* 37, *pg.* 1466
BROOKWOOD CABINETRY - Semi-custom Cabinetry - NORCRAFT HOLDINGS, LP; *pg.* 100, *pg.* 921
BROOKYLN LOCAL 1 - Seasonal Beer - THE BROOKLYN BREWERY; *pg.* 239, *pg.* 1145
BROOKYLN LOCAL 2 - Seasonal Beer - THE BROOKLYN BREWERY; *pg.* 239, *pg.* 1145
BROOKYLNER SCHNEIDER HOPFEN WEISSE - Seasonal Beer - THE BROOKLYN BREWERY; *pg.* 239, *pg.* 1145
BROTHER BENEDICT'S BOCK - Beer - GRANITE CITY FOOD & BREWERY LTD; *pg.* 1730, *pg.* 937
BROUGHTON - Dairy Products - BROUGHTON FOODS COMPANY; *pg.* 842, *pg.* 1458
BROUGHTON - Dairy Product - DEAN FOODS COMPANY; *pg.* 852, *pg.* 1679
BROUWER - Golf, Turf & Specialty Products - TEXTRON INC.; *pg.* 235, *pg.* 1607
BROVANA - Pharmaceutical Product - SUNOVION PHARMACEUTICALS INC.; *pg.* 1599, *pg.* 832
BROW SEALER - Brow Sealer - MERLE NORMAN COSMETICS, INC.; *pg.* 517, *pg.* 136
BROWER - Poultry & Livestock Equipment - HAWKEYE STEEL PRODUCTS, INC.; *pg.* 704, *pg.* 708
BROWMOUSSE - Styling Gel - TWEEZERMAN INTERNATIONAL; *pg.* 524, *pg.* 1324
BROWN & BIG - Miniature - BROWN & BIGELOW, INC.; *pg.* 1624, *pg.* 959
BROWN & BIGELOW - Calendar - BROWN & BIGELOW, INC.; *pg.* 1624, *pg.* 959
BROWN & BIGGER - Miniature - BROWN & BIGELOW, INC.; *pg.* 1624, *pg.* 959
BROWN & SHARPE - Machine Tool Product - BOURN & KOCH MACHINE TOOL COMPANY; *pg.* 1319, *pg.* 654
BROWN DEVIL - Vitreous Enamel Power Resistor - OHMITE MANUFACTURING COMPANY; *pg.* 660, *pg.* 553
BROWN-FOREMAN - Beverages - BROWN-FORMAN CORPORATION; *pg.* 1958, *pg.* 732
BROWN JORDAN - Furniture Company - BROWN JORDAN INTERNATIONAL COMPANY; *pg.* 919, *pg.* 740
BROWN MACKIE COLLEGE - Colleges - EDUCATION MANAGEMENT CORPORATION; *pg.* 601, *pg.* 1575
BROWN 'N SERVE - Food Product - CONAGRA FOODS, INC.; *pg.* 826, *pg.* 1014
BROWN SHOE - Footwear - CALERES, INC.; *pg.* 1805, *pg.* 993
BROWNIE EXTREME - Premium Ice Cream - WELLS ENTERPRISES, INC.; *pg.* 909, *pg.* 709
BROWNING - Fishing Reels - ZEBCO; *pg.* 1848, *pg.* 1491
BROWN'S DAIRY - Dairy Product - DEAN FOODS COMPANY; *pg.* 852, *pg.* 1679
BROWNSTONE - Fan - CRAFTMADE INTERNATIONAL, INC.; *pg.* 1295, *pg.* 1670
BROWNSTONE STUDIO - Apparel & Shoes - ASCENA RETAIL GROUP, INC.; *pg.* 18, *pg.* 1081
BROWNSVILLE - Guitar Amplifiers, Guitars - SAM ASH MUSIC CORPORATION; *pg.* 669, *pg.* 1167
THE BROWNSVILLE HERALD - Texas Newspaper - FREEDOM COMMUNICATIONS, INC.; *pg.* 1643, *pg.* 110
BROWSEIT - Software - BIO-RAD LABORATORIES, INC.; *pg.* 1504, *pg.* 101
BROYHILL - Furniture - HERITAGE HOME GROUP; *pg.* 926, *pg.* 1379
BRU-R-EZ - Cleaner - BIRKO CORPORATION; *pg.* 1149, *pg.* 332
BRUCE - Furniture - AMISCO INDUSTRIES LTD.; *pg.* 913, *pg.* 1958
BRUCE - Wood Flooring & Cabinetry Products - ARMSTRONG WORLD INDUSTRIES, INC.; *pg.* 914, *pg.* 1545
BRUCE WAYNE - Character - DC COMICS, INC.; *pg.* 1633, *pg.* 1221
BRUCE'S - Southern Vegetables - BRUCE FOODS CORPORATION; *pg.* 842, *pg.* 743
BRUCE'S YAMS - Food Product - BRUCE FOODS CORPORATION; *pg.* 842, *pg.* 743
BRUFEN - Pharmaceutical Products - ABBOTT LABORATORIES; *pg.* 1484, *pg.* 551
BRUINS STREET BRIGADE - Street Hockey Programs - BOSTON PROFESSIONAL HOCKEY ASSOCIATION, INC.; *pg.* 534, *pg.* 791
BRULERIE MONT ROYAL - Coffee - VAN HOUTTE, INC.; *pg.* 908, *pg.* 1957
BRULERIE ST. DENIS - Coffee - VAN HOUTTE, INC.; *pg.* 908, *pg.* 1957
BRUNELLA - Footwear - STEVEN MADDEN, LTD.; *pg.* 1819, *pg.* 1176
BRUNER - Water Treatment Products - CULLIGAN INTERNATIONAL COMPANY; *pg.* 54, *pg.* 656
BRUNNER & LAY - Demolition & Drill Tools - BRUNNER & LAY, INC.; *pg.* 1320, *pg.* 35
BRUNO - Fabric - NEMSCHOFF, INC.; *pg.* 936, *pg.* 1890
BRUNSWICK - Bowling & Billiards Equipment - BRUNSWICK CORPORATION; *pg.* 1828, *pg.* 623
BRUNSWICK - Seafood Products - BUMBLE BEE FOODS LLC; *pg.* 842, *pg.* 201
BRUNSWICK - Surface Material - STEELCASE INC.; *pg.* 475, *pg.* 889
BRUNSWICK HOME & BILLIARD - Billiard Equipment - BRUNSWICK BOWLING & BILLIARDS CORP.; *pg.* 1828, *pg.* 622
BRUNSWICK PAVILION - Bowling Equipment - BRUNSWICK BOWLING & BILLIARDS CORP.; *pg.* 1828, *pg.* 622
BRUNSWICK ZONE - Bowling Equipment - BRUNSWICK BOWLING & BILLIARDS CORP.; *pg.* 1828, *pg.* 622
BRUSH BLUSH BRONZER - Blusher - MAYBELLINE LLC; *pg.* 516, *pg.* 1257
BRUSH 'N CLEAN - Dental Products for Dogs - THE HARTZ MOUNTAIN CORP.; *pg.* 1476, *pg.* 1120
BRUSH-ON - Liquid Rubber - SMOOTH-ON INC.; *pg.* 111, *pg.* 1528
BRUSH-ON-BLUSH - Blusher - COVER GIRL COSMETICS; *pg.* 506, *pg.* 772
BRUSH PLUS - Shaving System - THE GILLETTE COMPANY; *pg.* 509, *pg.* 795
BRUSH STUFF - Brush & Roller Cover Conditioner - AKZO NOBEL DECORATIVE PAINTS, USA; *pg.* 1439, *pg.* 1474
BRUSH-TUFF - Apparel - LACROSSE FOOTWEAR, INC.; *pg.* 1811, *pg.* 1503
BRUSH UP - Denture Cleanser - THE GILLETTE COMPANY; *pg.* 509, *pg.* 795
BRUSHCAL - Polyester Film - FLEXCON CORPORATION; *pg.* 1457, *pg.* 844
BRUSHETTA - Tile - ARTISTIC TILE INC.; *pg.* 914, *pg.* 1119
BRUSHKILLER - Agricultural Product - PBI/GORDON CORPORATION; *pg.* 1176, *pg.* 985
BRUSHMASTER - Turf Product - PBI/GORDON CORPORATION; *pg.* 1176, *pg.* 985
BRUSHSTROKE - Fabric - NEMSCHOFF, INC.; *pg.* 936, *pg.* 1890
BRUSKI GIFT SET - Barware - GORDON INDUSTRIES LTD.; *pg.* 6, *pg.* 1184
BRUSSELS - Cookies - PEPPERIDGE FARM, INC.; *pg.* 888, *pg.* 363
BRUT - Personal Care Electrical Product - HELEN OF TROY L.P.; *pg.* 511, *pg.* 1692
BRUT FORCE - Utility Vehicle - KAWASAKI MOTORS CORP., U.S.A.; *pg.* 1708, *pg.* 111
BRUT REVOLUTION - Personal Care Electrical Product - HELEN OF TROY L.P.; *pg.* 511, *pg.* 1692
THE BRUTE - Steel Rule - ARROW FASTENER COMPANY, INC.; *pg.* 1042, *pg.* 1118
BRUTE - Cutting Room Equipment - EASTMAN MACHINE COMPANY; *pg.* 1331, *pg.* 1148
BRUTE - Mop Bucket - HILLYARD, INC.; *pg.* 331, *pg.* 990
BRUTE - Commercial Storage & Cleaning Products - NEWELL RUBBERMAID INC.; *pg.* 1128, *pg.* 515
BRUTE - Electronic Deadbolt - SARGENT & GREENLEAF, INC.; *pg.* 1061, *pg.* 739
BRUTE - Vacuum - SHOP-VAC CORPORATION; *pg.* 1375, *pg.* 1595
BRUTE FORCE - Exercise Machines - SPORT SUPPLY GROUP, INC.; *pg.* 1846, *pg.* 1687
BRUTE FORCE - Pressure Washers - TORNADO INDUSTRIES, INC.; *pg.* 1383, *pg.* 591
BRUZZANO - Shoes - ALLEN-EDMONDS SHOE CORP.; *pg.* 1804, *pg.* 1887
BRYAN - Artificial Disc for Back Treatment - MEDTRONIC, INC.; *pg.* 1564, *pg.* 939
BRYAN STEAM - Commercial & Industrial Boilers - BURNHAM HOLDINGS, INC.; *pg.* 1069, *pg.* 1546
BRYANT - Furniture - ASHLEY FURNITURE INDUSTRIES, INC.; *pg.* 914, *pg.* 1852
BRYANT - Wiring System - HUBBELL INCORPORATED; *pg.* 1299, *pg.* 370
BRYANT PARK GRILL - Restaurant - ARK RESTAURANTS CORP.; *pg.* 1715, *pg.* 1196
BRYANT'S BUCAROOS - Ticket Program - BUCCANEERS LIMITED PARTNERSHIP; *pg.* 534, *pg.* 471
BRYLANE - Sewing Machine - FULLBEAUTY BRANDS; *pg.* 1770, *pg.* 1233
BRYLCREEM - Hair Cream - COMBE INCORPORATED; *pg.* 1516, *pg.* 1351
BRYON - Reading Glass - A. T. CROSS COMPANY; *pg.* 339, *pg.* 1602
BSAFARIHB - Footwear - STEVEN MADDEN, LTD.; *pg.* 1819, *pg.* 1176
BSC - Backplane Connector System - MOLEX INCORPORATED; *pg.* 655, *pg.* 628
BSC II - Backplane Connector System - MOLEX INCORPORATED; *pg.* 655, *pg.* 628
BSD - Software - WIND RIVER SYSTEMS, INC.; *pg.* 493, *pg.* 38
BSDARCHITECT - Software System - MENTOR GRAPHICS CORPORATION; *pg.* 432, *pg.* 1510
BSDCASSETTE - Molecular Biology Product - THERMO FISHER SCIENTIFIC INC.; *pg.* 1602, *pg.* 61
BSDI - Software - WIND RIVER SYSTEMS, INC.; *pg.* 493, *pg.* 38
BSIMPRO - Software - KEITHLEY INSTRUMENTS, INC.; *pg.* 1418, *pg.* 1473
BSK - Fastening Systems - TEXTRON INC.; *pg.* 235, *pg.* 1607
BSN - Mail Order Catalog - SPORT SUPPLY GROUP, INC.; *pg.* 1846, *pg.* 1687
BSPBUILDER - Software System - MENTOR GRAPHICS CORPORATION; *pg.* 432, *pg.* 1510
BSS - Audio Processors - HARMAN INTERNATIONAL INDUSTRIES, INCORPORATED; *pg.* 641, *pg.* 374
BST - Software - BIO-RAD LABORATORIES, INC.; *pg.* 1504, *pg.* 101
BSY-2 - Systems Integration & Aeronautics - LOCKHEED MARTIN CORPORATION; *pg.* 229, *pg.* 762
BT-CATH - Balloon Tamponade Catheters - UTAH MEDICAL PRODUCTS, INC.; *pg.* 1605, *pg.* 1752
BTEX BUSTER - Flare - CAMERON INTERNATIONAL; *pg.* 1151, *pg.* 1702
BTJ - Space Solar Cell - EMCORE CORPORATION; *pg.* 636, *pg.* 39
BTJM - Space Solar Cell - EMCORE CORPORATION; *pg.* 636, *pg.* 39
BTMS - Power Monitor - OPLINK COMMUNICATIONS, INC.; *pg.* 660, *pg.* 91
BTOB - Business-to-Business Marketing Magazine - CRAIN COMMUNICATIONS, INC.; *pg.* 1631, *pg.* 879
BTRD - Trading Services - BLOOMBERG L.P.; *pg.* 725, *pg.* 1204
BTV - Trading Services - BLOOMBERG L.P.; *pg.* 725, *pg.* 1204
BTV - Carry-Out Restaurant Services - IN-N-OUT BURGERS, INC.; *pg.* 1732, *pg.* 111
BU - Beverages - THE COCA-COLA COMPANY; *pg.* 240, *pg.* 493
BUB - Bath Additives - KAO BRANDS CO. INC.; *pg.* 513, *pg.* 1415
BUBBALOO - Bubble Gum - MONDELEZ INTERNATIONAL, INC.; *pg.* 878, *pg.* 601
BUBBLE BALLOON - Balloon - CONTINENTAL AMERICAN CORP.; *pg.* 1880, *pg.* 723
BUBBLE BLOX - Chewing Gum - TOOTSIE ROLL INDUSTRIES, INC.; *pg.* 1863, *pg.* 591
BUBBLE CUSHION - Medical Device - RESMED INC.; *pg.* 1589, *pg.* 207
BUBBLE GUM - Automotive Reconditioning Product - MOC PRODUCTS COMPANY, INC.; *pg.* 332, *pg.* 174
BUBBLE GUM BOOSTER - Candy & Gum - THE TOPPS COMPANY, INC.; *pg.* 588, *pg.* 1302
BUBBLE JUG - Bubble Gum - WM. WRIGLEY JR. COMPANY; *pg.* 1863, *pg.* 596
BUBBLE MANIA - Toy - SPIN MASTER LTD.; *pg.* 967, *pg.* 1943
BUBBLE MASK - Medical Device - RESMED INC.; *pg.* 1589, *pg.* 207
BUBBLE MASK - Adhesive Air Cellular Cushioning Materials - SEALED AIR CORPORATION; *pg.* 1468, *pg.* 1058
BUBBLE-OUT - Bag - PACTIV CORPORATION; *pg.* 1466, *pg.* 624
BUBBLE PAK - Air Cellular Cushioning Materials - SEALED AIR CORPORATION; *pg.* 1468, *pg.* 1058

BUBBLE TAPE - Gum - WM. WRIGLEY JR. COMPANY; *pg.* 1863, *pg.* 596
BUBBLE UP - Cat Toy - THE HARTZ MOUNTAIN CORP.; *pg.* 1476, *pg.* 1120
BUBBLE UP - Video Game - INTERNATIONAL GAME TECHNOLOGY; *pg.* 957, *pg.* 1024
BUBBLE-UP - Soft Drink - THE MONARCH BEVERAGE COMPANY, INC.; *pg.* 257, *pg.* 514
BUBBLE WRAP - Packaging Product - SEALED AIR CORPORATION; *pg.* 1468, *pg.* 1058
BUBBLE YUM - Gum - THE HERSHEY CO.; *pg.* 1855, *pg.* 1538
BUBBLEARIUM - Educational Materials - SCHOLASTIC INC.; *pg.* 1683, *pg.* 1288
BUBBLEBAGS - Plastic Bags - SEALED AIR CORPORATION; *pg.* 1468, *pg.* 1058
BUBBLES - Hair Care Salon - THE RATNER COMPANIES; *pg.* 520, *pg.* 1809
BUBBLES THE WHALE - Children's Hamper - RUBBERMAID HOME PRODUCTS; *pg.* 1138, *pg.* 1453
BUBBLETACK - Furniture - HERMAN MILLER, INC.; *pg.* 926, *pg.* 913
BUBBLIN CRUDE - Video Game - INTERNATIONAL GAME TECHNOLOGY; *pg.* 957, *pg.* 1024
BUBBLY - Beverages - THE COCA-COLA COMPANY; *pg.* 240, *pg.* 493
BUCA DI BEPPO - Restaurant - BUCA, INC.; *pg.* 1718, *pg.* 931
BUCA LARGE - Restaurant - BUCA, INC.; *pg.* 1718, *pg.* 931
BUCA SMALL - Restaurant - BUCA, INC.; *pg.* 1718, *pg.* 931
BUCHANAN - Screw-On-Connector - IDEAL INDUSTRIES, INC.; *pg.* 1051, *pg.* 662
BUCHANAN TERMEND - Terminal - IDEAL INDUSTRIES, INC.; *pg.* 1051, *pg.* 662
BUCHANAN'S - Whisky - DIAGEO NORTH AMERICA, INC.; *pg.* 1961, *pg.* 361
BUCK - Furniture - AMERICAN LEATHER LP; *pg.* 912, *pg.* 1673
BUCK - Knife - BUCK KNIVES, INC.; *pg.* 1828, *pg.* 550
BUCK - Utility Vehicle - DEERE & COMPANY; *pg.* 703, *pg.* 632
BUCK CADET - Knife - BUCK KNIVES, INC.; *pg.* 1828, *pg.* 550
BUCK KNIVES - Knife - BUCK KNIVES, INC.; *pg.* 1828, *pg.* 550
BUCK/MAYO KAALA - Knife - BUCK KNIVES, INC.; *pg.* 1828, *pg.* 550
BUCK 'N WIN - Game - WMS INDUSTRIES INC.; *pg.* 593, *pg.* 666
BUCK/SIMONICH RAVEN LEGACY - Knife - BUCK KNIVES, INC.; *pg.* 1828, *pg.* 550
BUCK ZIPPER - Knife - BUCK KNIVES, INC.; *pg.* 1828, *pg.* 550
BUCKET BOSS - Truck Equipment - AMERICAN VAN EQUIPMENT INC.; *pg.* 199, *pg.* 1078
BUCKET BUDDIES - Toy - INFANTINO, LLC; *pg.* 957, *pg.* 203
BUCKET-FREE - Automobile Cleaner - ASHLAND INC.; *pg.* 972, *pg.* 726
BUCKET OF BIRTHDAY WISHES - Flower Arrangement - 1-800-FLOWERS.COM, INC.; *pg.* 1758, *pg.* 1151
BUCKETPRO - Excavating System - TRIMBLE NAVIGATION LIMITED; *pg.* 1384, *pg.* 288
BUCKEYE - Container - BUCKEYE CORRUGATED INC.; *pg.* 1454, *pg.* 1400
BUCKEYE 5 - Lottery Game - OHIO LOTTERY COMMISSION; *pg.* 1002, *pg.* 1433
BUCKHORN - Plastic Product - MYERS INDUSTRIES, INC.; *pg.* 1887, *pg.* 1402
BUCKHORN RUBBER - Plastic Product - MYERS INDUSTRIES, INC.; *pg.* 1887, *pg.* 1402
BUCKINGHAM - Furniture - JOFCO INC.; *pg.* 931, *pg.* 691
BUCKINGHAM - Door Panel - MASONITE INTERNATIONAL CORPORATION; *pg.* 1054, *pg.* 1920
BUCKLE - Apparel - THE BUCKLE, INC.; *pg.* 1764, *pg.* 1011
BUCKLITE - Cutlery - BUCK KNIVES, INC.; *pg.* 1828, *pg.* 550
BUCKLITE MAX - Knife - BUCK KNIVES, INC.; *pg.* 1828, *pg.* 550
BUCKS - Cigarettes - PHILIP MORRIS USA INC.; *pg.* 1894, *pg.* 1803
BUCKS AHOY - Casino Game - INTERNATIONAL GAME TECHNOLOGY; *pg.* 957, *pg.* 1024
BUCKSHOT - Apparel - OAKLEY, INC.; *pg.* 1840, *pg.* 86
BUCKSPORT - Footwear - EASTLAND SHOE CORPORATION; *pg.* 1808, *pg.* 750
BUCKWHEAT BLOSSOM - Honey - MILLER'S HONEY COMPANY; *pg.* 1860, *pg.* 1759
BUCKY LASEK - Footwear - VANS, INC.; *pg.* 1821, *pg.* 76
BUCYRUS BLADE - Excavator Product - ESCO CORPORATION; *pg.* 1335, *pg.* 1502
BUD - Electronic Enclosures - BUD INDUSTRIES, INC.; *pg.* 627, *pg.* 1482
BUD DRY - Beer - ANHEUSER-BUSCH COMPANIES, LLC; *pg.* 237, *pg.* 991
BUD EXTRA - Beer - ANHEUSER-BUSCH COMPANIES, LLC; *pg.* 237, *pg.* 991
BUD ICE - Beer - ANHEUSER-BUSCH COMPANIES, LLC; *pg.* 237, *pg.* 991
BUD ICE LIGHT - Beer - ANHEUSER-BUSCH COMPANIES, LLC; *pg.* 237, *pg.* 991
BUD LIGHT - Beer - ANHEUSER-BUSCH COMPANIES, LLC; *pg.* 237, *pg.* 991
BUD LIGHT GOLDEN WHEAT - Beer - ANHEUSER-BUSCH COMPANIES, LLC; *pg.* 237, *pg.* 991
BUD LIGHT PLATINUM - Beer - ANHEUSER-BUSCH COMPANIES, LLC; *pg.* 237, *pg.* 991
BUD SPECIAL - Footwear - P.W. MINOR & SON, INC.; *pg.* 1816, *pg.* 1140
BUDDE - Medical Device - INTEGRA LIFESCIENCES HOLDINGS CORPORATION; *pg.* 1545, *pg.* 1109
BUDDIE BOY - Sandwiches - FRISCH'S RESTAURANTS, INC.; *pg.* 1729, *pg.* 1413
BUDDY - Knife - COAST CUTLERY COMPANY; *pg.* 1121, *pg.* 1501
BUDDY - Fabric - SCALAMANDRE, INC.; *pg.* 941, *pg.* 1058
BUDDY BEARS - Gummi Bear - PROMOTION IN MOTION, INC.; *pg.* 1861, *pg.* 1052
BUDDY BEARS GUMMY BEARS - Gummy Candies - PROMOTION IN MOTION, INC.; *pg.* 1861, *pg.* 1052
BUDDY GUY POLKA DOT STRATOCASTER - Electric Guitar - FENDER MUSICAL INSTRUMENTS CORPORATION; *pg.* 547, *pg.* 21
BUDDY GUY STRATOCASTER - Electric Guitar - FENDER MUSICAL INSTRUMENTS CORPORATION; *pg.* 547, *pg.* 21
BUDDY L - Toy - IMPERIAL TOY CORPORATION; *pg.* 957, *pg.* 166
BUDDY LEE - Advertising Icon - V.F. CORPORATION; *pg.* 34, *pg.* 1376
THE BUDDY SYSTEM - Software System - ALION SCIENCE AND TECHNOLOGY CORPORATION; *pg.* 615, *pg.* 1788
BUDDYFREDDY'S COUNTRY BUFFET - Eateries - STAR BUFFET, INC.; *pg.* 1751, *pg.* 24
BUDENE - Polbutadiene Rubber - THE GOODYEAR TIRE & RUBBER COMPANY; *pg.* 1883, *pg.* 1401
BUDGET MANAGER - Information Management System - PITNEY BOWES INC.; *pg.* 454, *pg.* 376
BUDGET RENT A CAR - Car Rental Services - AVIS BUDGET GROUP, INC.; *pg.* 1900, *pg.* 1102
BUDGET TRAVEL - Magazine - GRAHAM HOLDINGS COMPANY; *pg.* 1645, *pg.* 1773
BUDGET TRUCK RENTAL - Truck Rental Services - AVIS BUDGET GROUP, INC.; *pg.* 1900, *pg.* 1102
BUDGETEL - Hotel Chain - LA QUINTA CORPORATION; *pg.* 1099, *pg.* 1722
BUDGETSMART - Financial Service - XCEL ENERGY INC.; *pg.* 1955, *pg.* 946
BUDGIT - Hoist - COLUMBUS MCKINNON CORPORATION; *pg.* 1325, *pg.* 1138
BUDOKON - DVD - GAIAM, INC.; *pg.* 1532, *pg.* 334
BUDWEISER - Beer - ANHEUSER-BUSCH COMPANIES, LLC; *pg.* 237, *pg.* 991
BUDWEISER BLACK CROWN - Beer - ANHEUSER-BUSCH COMPANIES, LLC; *pg.* 237, *pg.* 991
BUDWEISER SELECT - Beer - ANHEUSER-BUSCH COMPANIES, LLC; *pg.* 237, *pg.* 991
BUEHLER - Abrasive Cutter - BUEHLER, LTD.; *pg.* 1403, *pg.* 622
BUEHLERVANGUARD - Automatic Grinder & Polisher - BUEHLER, LTD.; *pg.* 1403, *pg.* 622
BUELL - Motorcycle - HARLEY-DAVIDSON, INC.; *pg.* 178, *pg.* 1874
BUENA - Apparel - VANS, INC.; *pg.* 1821, *pg.* 76
BUENA VENTRURA - Salt Fish - CANADIAN FISH EXPORTERS, INC.; *pg.* 845, *pg.* 784
BUENA VIDA - Tortillas - AZTECA FOODS, INCORPORATED; *pg.* 838, *pg.* 566
BUENDIA - Coffee - COLOMBIAN COFFEE FEDERATION, INC.; *pg.* 137, *pg.* 1216
BUF-PUF - Facial Cleansing Sponge - 3M COMPANY; *pg.* 1142, *pg.* 956
BUFALO - Mexican Foods - HORMEL FOODS CORPORATION; *pg.* 863, *pg.* 915
BUFF - Head Wear - HUGGER MUGGER YOGA PRODUCTS LLC; *pg.* 1836, *pg.* 1758
BUFFALO - China - ONEIDA LTD; *pg.* 1129, *pg.* 1318
BUFFALO FINGERZ - Food Product - ZAXBY'S FRANCHISING, INC.; *pg.* 1756, *pg.* 486
BUFFALO HARP - Wire - BUFFALO WIRE WORKS CO., INC.; *pg.* 72, *pg.* 1147
BUFFALO SABRES - Hockey Team - HOCKEY WESTERN NEW YORK, LLC; *pg.* 552, *pg.* 1149
BUFFALO WILD WINGS GRILL & BAR - Restaurants - BUFFALO WILD WINGS, INC.; *pg.* 1718, *pg.* 931
BUFFALO WINGS - Poultry Product - PILGRIM'S PRIDE CORPORATION; *pg.* 889, *pg.* 330
BUFFALO WIRE WORKS - Wire Cloth & Vibrator Screen Replacements - BUFFALO WIRE WORKS CO., INC.; *pg.* 72, *pg.* 1147
BUFFET MANIA - Video Slots - INTERNATIONAL GAME TECHNOLOGY; *pg.* 957, *pg.* 1024
BUFFETT - Fabric - NEMSCHOFF, INC.; *pg.* 936, *pg.* 1890
BUFLOC - Flocculating Agents - BUCKMAN; *pg.* 1150, *pg.* 1641
BUG-B-GON - Lawn & Garden Products - THE SCOTTS MIRACLE-GRO COMPANY; *pg.* 1799, *pg.* 1459
BUG-B-GONE - Automotive Reconditioning Product - MOC PRODUCTS COMPANY, INC.; *pg.* 332, *pg.* 174
BUG BEATER - Household Insect Control - BONIDE PRODUCTS, INC.; *pg.* 1794, *pg.* 1320
BUG BLOCK - Insecticide - W.F. YOUNG, INC.; *pg.* 1610, *pg.* 817
BUG BLOCK EASY SWIPE - Insecticide - W.F. YOUNG, INC.; *pg.* 1610, *pg.* 817
THE BUG BUNCH - Educational Materials - SCHOLASTIC INC.; *pg.* 1683, *pg.* 1288
BUG BUSTER - Automotive Cleaner - DELTA FOREMOST CHEMICAL CORPORATION; *pg.* 1155, *pg.* 1642
BUG FACTOR LOLLIPOP - Toy & Game - HASBRO, INC.; *pg.* 954, *pg.* 1603
BUG-NO-MORE - Homeowner Product - PBI/GORDON CORPORATION; *pg.* 1176, *pg.* 985
BUG OFF - Car Wash Equipment - D&S CAR WASH EQUIPMENT CO.; *pg.* 1327, *pg.* 979
BUG OFF! - Insecticide - DELTA FOREMOST CHEMICAL CORPORATION; *pg.* 1155, *pg.* 1642
BUGABOO - Footwear - COLUMBIA SPORTSWEAR COMPANY; *pg.* 1830, *pg.* 1501
BUGABOOT - Footwear - COLUMBIA SPORTSWEAR COMPANY; *pg.* 1830, *pg.* 1501
BUGFLECTOR - Bug Deflector - LUND INTERNATIONAL, INC.; *pg.* 211, *pg.* 526
BUGFLECTOR II - Bug Deflector - LUND INTERNATIONAL, INC.; *pg.* 211, *pg.* 526
BUGGIES - Toy - MUNCHKIN, INC.; *pg.* 964, *pg.* 300
BUGLES - Food Product - GENERAL MILLS, INC.; *pg.* 828, *pg.* 933
BUGSCREEN - Grille Cover - LUND INTERNATIONAL, INC.; *pg.* 211, *pg.* 526
BUGSHIELD - Screen Door - RITE-HITE HOLDING CORPORATION; *pg.* 1372, *pg.* 1880
BUGSTATION - Defect Tracking Server - BUGOPOLIS, INC.; *pg.* 366, *pg.* 278
BUGVILLE - Toy - SPIN MASTER LTD.; *pg.* 967, *pg.* 1943
BUGZONE - Software - BUGOPOLIS, INC.; *pg.* 366, *pg.* 278
BUHLER MONTEC - Wastewater Monitoring Equipment - DANAHER CORPORATION; *pg.* 1044, *pg.* 397
BUICK - Automobile - GENERAL MOTORS COMPANY; *pg.* 175, *pg.* 881
BUILD-A-BEAR WORKSHOP TEDDY BEARS - Teddy Bear - FTD GROUP, INC.; *pg.* 1795, *pg.* 608
BUILD-A-BOX - Chocolate - RUSSELL STOVER CANDIES, INC.; *pg.* 1861, *pg.* 986
BUILD-A-DINO - Make-Your-Own Bear in Various Store Locations - BUILD-A-BEAR WORKSHOP, INC.; *pg.* 950, *pg.* 993
BUILD-A-SOUND - Bear Projects - BUILD-A-BEAR WORKSHOP, INC.; *pg.* 950, *pg.* 993
BUILD AROUND YOU - Slogan - MARVIN WINDOWS & DOORS; *pg.* 934, *pg.* 965
BUILD BELIEVE ACHIEVE - Tagline - BELL INDUSTRIES, INC.; *pg.* 624, *pg.* 683
BUILD FOR CHANGE - Slogan - PEGASYSTEMS INC.; *pg.* 453, *pg.* 809

BUILD. POWER. SERVICE. PROTECT - Tagline - EMCOR GROUP, INC.; *pg.* 80, *pg.* 361
BUILD-RITE - Wood Product - BOISE CASCADE HOLDINGS, L.L.C.; *pg.* 1453, *pg.* 546
BUILD WITH US. - Slogan - LOUISIANA-PACIFIC CORPORATION; *pg.* 94, *pg.* 1652
BUILDABEARVILLE.COM - Virtual World of Fun Bear Projects - BUILD-A-BEAR WORKSHOP, INC.; *pg.* 950, *pg.* 993
BUILDER'S - Food Product - CLIF BAR INC.; *pg.* 848, *pg.* 83
BUILDERS - Chandeliers - CRAFTMADE INTERNATIONAL, INC.; *pg.* 1295, *pg.* 1670
BUILDERS CHOICE - Acrylic Whirlpools - AQUATIC; *pg.* 68, *pg.* 42
BUILDERS SPEC - Coating Product - PPG INDUSTRIES, INC.; *pg.* 1445, *pg.* 1579
BUILDER'S TUBE - Wound Fiber Tubes - SONOCO PRODUCTS COMPANY; *pg.* 1469, *pg.* 1619
BUILDING AMERICA - Slogan - UNION PACIFIC CORPORATION; *pg.* 1927, *pg.* 1018
BUILDING AND CONSTRUCTION SAFETY CODE - Fire Safety Book - NATIONAL FIRE PROTECTION ASSOCIATION; *pg.* 149, *pg.* 842
BUILDING CONNECTIONS - Tagline - IMODULES SOFTWARE, INC.; *pg.* 1258, *pg.* 716
BUILDING FOREMOST COMPANIES - Financial Investment Services - BFC FINANCIAL CORPORATION; *pg.* 724, *pg.* 423
BUILDING INTEGRITY INTO EVERY CUSTOMER EXPERIENCE - Tagline - INTEGRITY SOLUTIONS; *pg.* 145, *pg.* 22
BUILDING LANGUAGE FOR LITERACY - Educational Materials - SCHOLASTIC INC.; *pg.* 1683, *pg.* 1288
BUILDING OUR NAVY'S FUTURE, ONE SAILOR AT A TIME! - Tag Line - UNITED STATES NAVY RECRUITING COMMAND; *pg.* 1009, *pg.* 1648
BUILDING PEACE OF MIND - Slogan - BOISE CASCADE HOLDINGS, L.L.C.; *pg.* 1453, *pg.* 546
BUILDING PROFIT - Magazine - BUTLER MANUFACTURING COMPANY; *pg.* 72, *pg.* 981
BUILDING PROTECTION - Slogan - BOISE CASCADE HOLDINGS, L.L.C.; *pg.* 1453, *pg.* 546
BUILDING QUALITY BRANDS - Tagline - REGAL LAGER, INC.; *pg.* 32, *pg.* 534
BUILDING SOMETHING MORE. - Slogan - GRAYCOR INC.; *pg.* 84, *pg.* 619
BUILDING TECHNOLOGY FOR TOMORROW - Tagline - ACTON TECHNOLOGIES, INC.; *pg.* 1145, *pg.* 1582
BUILDING TRUST EVERY DAY - Tagline - ROCKWELL COLLINS, INC.; *pg.* 234, *pg.* 702
BUILDING VALUE INTO BUILDING PRODUCTS - Slogan - ODL INCORPORATED; *pg.* 101, *pg.* 914
BUILDINGCALK-3G - Concrete System - L.M. SCOFIELD COMPANY; *pg.* 94, *pg.* 134
BUILDINGCALK-3S - Concrete System - L.M. SCOFIELD COMPANY; *pg.* 94, *pg.* 134
BUILDSTATION - Software - 3D SYSTEMS CORPORATION; *pg.* 339, *pg.* 1621
BUILT FOR THE REAL WORLD - Tag Line - IGLOO PRODUCTS CORPORATION; *pg.* 1126, *pg.* 1724
BUILT ON PRODUCT. POWERED BY PEOPLE. - Slogan - MARKET AMERICA WORLDWIDE, INC.; *pg.* 1265, *pg.* 1375
BUILT TO FIT. BUILT TO LAST. - Tagline - RED WING SHOE COMPANY, INC.; *pg.* 1817, *pg.* 954
BUILT TO ORDER - Homebuilding Services - KB HOME; *pg.* 90, *pg.* 134
BUILT-TO-ORDER - Hoagies & Sandwiches - WAWA, INC.; *pg.* 1037, *pg.* 1552
BUITONI - Pasta & Sauces - NESTLE USA, INC.; *pg.* 883, *pg.* 96
BUITONI REFRIGERATED PASTAS & SAUCES - Food - NESTLE USA, INC.; *pg.* 883, *pg.* 96
BULB RIVET - Blind Rivet - ALLFAST FASTENING SYSTEMS, INC.; *pg.* 1041, *pg.* 66
BULBS ALIVE! - Flower Gardening - GARDENS ALIVE!, INC.; *pg.* 1796, *pg.* 693
BULFINCH PRESS - Publication - LITTLE, BROWN & COMPANY; *pg.* 1660, *pg.* 1251
BULGARI - Hotel & Resort - MARRIOTT INTERNATIONAL, INC.; *pg.* 1102, *pg.* 764
BULK - Fabric - NEMSCHOFF, INC.; *pg.* 936, *pg.* 1890
BULK METAL - Foil Resistors - VISHAY INTERTECHNOLOGY, INC.; *pg.* 1435, *pg.* 1551
BULK MUSCLE - Anabolic Mass Gainer - BPI SPORTS, LLC; *pg.* 842, *pg.* 430
BULKFILL - Manifold - ATMI, INC.; *pg.* 1314, *pg.* 342
BULKTOBAC - Tobacco Curing System - GAS-FIRED PRODUCTS, INC.; *pg.* 1338, *pg.* 1367
BULL BLASTER - Gaming Product - GLD PRODUCTS, INC.; *pg.* 1835, *pg.* 1882
BULL DOG - Tape - AMERICAN BILTRITE INC.; *pg.* 1878, *pg.* 856
BULL DOG - Vacuum for Automobiles, Vans, Trucks & RVs - SHOP-VAC CORPORATION; *pg.* 1375, *pg.* 1595
BULL DRIVER - Large-handled Screwdrivers - KLEIN TOOLS INC.; *pg.* 1052, *pg.* 627
BULL OF THE WOODS - Tobacco Product - AMERICAN SNUFF COMPANY; *pg.* 1893, *pg.* 1641
BULL RUN - Textiles - BERNHARDT DESIGN; *pg.* 918, *pg.* 1381
BULLARD - Machine Tool Product - BOURN & KOCH MACHINE TOOL COMPANY; *pg.* 1319, *pg.* 654
BULLDOG - Pumps - GRACO, INC.; *pg.* 1342, *pg.* 935
BULLDOG - Ergonomic Seating - KNOLL, INC.; *pg.* 425, *pg.* 1527
BULLDOG - Hardware - NEWELL RUBBERMAID INC.; *pg.* 1128, *pg.* 515
BULLDOZE - Apparel - OAKLEY, INC.; *pg.* 1840, *pg.* 86
BULLEIT BOURBON - Whisky - DIAGEO NORTH AMERICA, INC.; *pg.* 1961, *pg.* 361
BULLET - Guitar Amplifier - FENDER MUSICAL INSTRUMENTS CORPORATION; *pg.* 547, *pg.* 21
BULLET - Watch - OAKLEY, INC.; *pg.* 1840, *pg.* 86
BULLET - Navigation Aid - TRIMBLE NAVIGATION LIMITED; *pg.* 1384, *pg.* 288
BULLET - Micrologic Semiconductor Device - ZILOG INC.; *pg.* 497, *pg.* 252
BULLET SHADE - Commercial Lighting - SWIVELIER CO., INC.; *pg.* 1307, *pg.* 1142
BULLFROG - Sunblock & Sunscreen - CHATTEM, INC.; *pg.* 1515, *pg.* 1628
BULLFROGGIN - Game - INTERNATIONAL GAME TECHNOLOGY; *pg.* 420, *pg.* 1606
BULLPEN CASINO - Games - PENN NATIONAL GAMING, INC.; *pg.* 574, *pg.* 1595
BULLS EYE - Golf Clubs - ACUSHNET COMPANY; *pg.* 1824, *pg.* 818
BULLS-EYE - Insect Pest Control Product - GARDENS ALIVE!, INC.; *pg.* 1796, *pg.* 693
BULLS EYE - Sundry - KELLY-MOORE PAINT COMPANY, INC.; *pg.* 1443, *pg.* 198
BULLS EYE BALL - Toy & Game - HASBRO, INC.; *pg.* 954, *pg.* 1603
BULLS-EYE BASEBALL - Toy & Game - HASBRO, INC.; *pg.* 954, *pg.* 1603
BULLS EYE KENO - Video Game - INTERNATIONAL GAME TECHNOLOGY; *pg.* 957, *pg.* 1024
BULLSEYE - Fish Products - THE HARTZ MOUNTAIN CORP.; *pg.* 1476, *pg.* 1120
BULLSEYE - Airline Service - UNITED CONTINENTAL HOLDINGS, INC.; *pg.* 1927, *pg.* 593
BULLSEYE DESIGN - Trademark - TARGET CORPORATION; *pg.* 1786, *pg.* 942
BULLSEYE DOG - Trademark - TARGET CORPORATION; *pg.* 1786, *pg.* 942
BULLSEYE PINPOINTER - Metal Detector - WHITE'S ELECTRONICS; *pg.* 688, *pg.* 1509
BULLY - Apparel - OAKLEY, INC.; *pg.* 1840, *pg.* 86
BULOVA - Watches and Clocks - BULOVA CORPORATION; *pg.* 2, *pg.* 1356
BULWARK - Apparel - V.F. CORPORATION; *pg.* 34, *pg.* 1376
BUMBLE AND BUMBLE - Hair Care Products - THE ESTEE LAUDER COMPANIES INC.; *pg.* 508, *pg.* 1229
BUMBLE BEE - Seafood Products - BUMBLE BEE FOODS LLC; *pg.* 842, *pg.* 201
BUMBLE BEE - Musical Instrument - GIBSON GUITAR CORP.; *pg.* 550, *pg.* 1650
BUMEX - Pharmaceutical Product - HOFFMANN-LA ROCHE INC.; *pg.* 1542, *pg.* 1099
BUMINATE - Biopharmaceutical Product - BAXTER INTERNATIONAL INC.; *pg.* 1499, *pg.* 599
BUMMBLE - Footwear - STEVEN MADDEN, LTD.; *pg.* 1819, *pg.* 1176
BUMP - Footwear - COBIAN CORP.; *pg.* 1806, *pg.* 253
THE BUMP - Online Resource for Expectant Mothers - XO GROUP INC.; *pg.* 1289, *pg.* 1316
BUMP PUMP - Rotary Pumps - TUTHILL CORPORATION PUMP GROUP; *pg.* 1385, *pg.* 553
BUMPABELL - Dog Toy - THE HARTZ MOUNTAIN CORP.; *pg.* 1476, *pg.* 1120
BUMPON - Molded Protective Shapes - 3M COMPANY; *pg.* 1142, *pg.* 956
BUMPS - Glove - KOMBI, LTD.; *pg.* 1838, *pg.* 1766
BUMPTZ SCIENCE CARNIVAL - Educational Materials - SCHOLASTIC INC.; *pg.* 1683, *pg.* 1288
BUN RUN - Food Product - SCHLOTZSKY'S, LTD.; *pg.* 1749, *pg.* 1665
BUNA - Rubber - THE DOW CHEMICAL COMPANY; *pg.* 1157, *pg.* 898
BUNCO NIGHT - Video Game - INTERNATIONAL GAME TECHNOLOGY; *pg.* 957, *pg.* 1024
BUNDLE OF JOY - Flower Arrangement - 1-800-FLOWERS.COM, INC.; *pg.* 1758, *pg.* 1151
BUNDLE OF JOY - Fruit Arrangements - EDIBLE ARRANGEMENTS INTERNATIONAL, INC.; *pg.* 1768, *pg.* 382
BUNDLE OF JOY - Dolls - THE GOLDBERGER COMPANY, LLC; *pg.* 954, *pg.* 1235
BUNDT - Baking Mold - NORTHLAND ALUMINUM PRODUCTS INC.; *pg.* 1129, *pg.* 941
BUNGALOW SERIES - Door - SIMPSON DOOR COMPANY; *pg.* 110, *pg.* 1823
BUNGLE - Apparel - VANS, INC.; *pg.* 1821, *pg.* 76
BUNICCI - Food Product - BUNGE LIMITED; *pg.* 842, *pg.* 1351
BUNKER RAKE IMPLEMENTS - Turf Maintenance Machinery - SMITHCO, INC.; *pg.* 1377, *pg.* 1592
BUNN ESPRESS - Electric Beverage Machines - BUNN-O-MATIC CORPORATION; *pg.* 53, *pg.* 661
BUNN GOURMET ICE - Coffee & Beverage Equipment - BUNN-O-MATIC CORPORATION; *pg.* 53, *pg.* 661
BUNN-O-MATIC - Coffee & Beverage Equipment - BUNN-O-MATIC CORPORATION; *pg.* 53, *pg.* 661
BUNN POUR-O-MATIC - Coffee Brewer - BUNN-O-MATIC CORPORATION; *pg.* 53, *pg.* 661
BUNNLINK - Coffee & Beverage Equipment - BUNN-O-MATIC CORPORATION; *pg.* 53, *pg.* 661
BUNNSERVE - Beverage Equipment - BUNN-O-MATIC CORPORATION; *pg.* 53, *pg.* 661
BUNNY BREAD - Food Product - FLOWERS FOODS, INC.; *pg.* 855, *pg.* 541
BUNNY CRISP - Candy - R.M. PALMER COMPANY; *pg.* 1861, *pg.* 1585
BUNNY TRACKS - Ice Cream - WELLS ENTERPRISES, INC.; *pg.* 909, *pg.* 709
BUNTING BABY - Dolls - THE GOLDBERGER COMPANY, LLC; *pg.* 954, *pg.* 1235
BUNTON - Golf, Turf & Specialty Products - TEXTRON INC.; *pg.* 235, *pg.* 1607
BUPAP - Analgesic - VALEANT PHARMACEUTICALS INTERNATIONAL, INC.; *pg.* 1605, *pg.* 1957
BUPRENEX - Pain Reliever - RECKITT BENCKISER INC.; *pg.* 1136, *pg.* 1105
BUR - Adhesive - JOHNS MANVILLE CORPORATION; *pg.* 89, *pg.* 320
BURAN - Air Dryer - DONALDSON COMPANY, INC.; *pg.* 1329, *pg.* 917
BURBANK LEADER - Newspaper - LOS ANGELES TIMES COMMUNICATIONS, LLC; *pg.* 1660, *pg.* 135
BURBER/CORD - Broadloom - COURISTAN INC.; *pg.* 921, *pg.* 1067
BURBER/KNIT - Broadloom - COURISTAN INC.; *pg.* 921, *pg.* 1067
BURDICK - Medical Device - CARDIAC SCIENCE CORPORATION; *pg.* 1512, *pg.* 1897
BURDICK - Furniture - HERMAN MILLER, INC.; *pg.* 926, *pg.* 913
BURDICK AND JACKSON - Reagent - HONEYWELL INTERNATIONAL INC.; *pg.* 407, *pg.* 1088
BUREAULINK - Software - CGI TECHNOLOGIES & SOLUTIONS INC.; *pg.* 371, *pg.* 1779
BUREAUXLINK - Server Based Applications - FAIR ISAAC CORPORATION; *pg.* 1247, *pg.* 955
BURGER KING - Fast Food Restaurants - RESTAURANT BRANDS INTERNATIONAL INC.; *pg.* 1747, *pg.* 1930
BURGER TELEVISION - Carry-Out Restaurant Services - IN-N-OUT BURGERS, INC.; *pg.* 1732, *pg.* 111
BURGESS BSC-SD - Hydrous Kaolin Clay - BURGESS PIGMENT COMPANY; *pg.* 1150, *pg.* 535
BURGESS HC-77 - Air Floated Clay - BURGESS PIGMENT COMPANY; *pg.* 1150, *pg.* 535
BURGESS ICECAP K - Calcined Kaolin - BURGESS PIGMENT COMPANY; *pg.* 1150, *pg.* 535

BURGESS ICECAP KSF - Calcined Kaolin - BURGESS PIGMENT COMPANY; *pg.* 1150, *pg.* 535
BURGESS NO. 10 - Hydrous Kaolin Clay - BURGESS PIGMENT COMPANY; *pg.* 1150, *pg.* 535
BURGESS NO. 17 - Hydrous Kaolin Clay - BURGESS PIGMENT COMPANY; *pg.* 1150, *pg.* 535
BURGESS NO. 20 - Hydrous Kaolin Clay - BURGESS PIGMENT COMPANY; *pg.* 1150, *pg.* 535
BURGESS NO. 28 - Hydrous Kaolin Clay - BURGESS PIGMENT COMPANY; *pg.* 1150, *pg.* 535
BURGESS NO. 40 - Hydrous Kaolin Clay - BURGESS PIGMENT COMPANY; *pg.* 1150, *pg.* 535
BURGESS NO. 50 - Calcined Kaolin - BURGESS PIGMENT COMPANY; *pg.* 1150, *pg.* 535
BURGESS NO. 60 - Hydrous Kaolin Clay - BURGESS PIGMENT COMPANY; *pg.* 1150, *pg.* 535
BURGESS NO. 80 - Air Floated Clay - BURGESS PIGMENT COMPANY; *pg.* 1150, *pg.* 535
BURGESS NO. 86 - Air Floated Clay - BURGESS PIGMENT COMPANY; *pg.* 1150, *pg.* 535
BURGESS NO. 97 - Hydrous Kaolin Clay - BURGESS PIGMENT COMPANY; *pg.* 1150, *pg.* 535
BURGESS NO. 98 - Hydrous Kaolin Clay - BURGESS PIGMENT COMPANY; *pg.* 1150, *pg.* 535
BURGESS OPTIPOZZ - High Reactivity Metakaolin - BURGESS PIGMENT COMPANY; *pg.* 1150, *pg.* 535
BURGESS POLYCLAY - Hydrous Kaolin Clay - BURGESS PIGMENT COMPANY; *pg.* 1150, *pg.* 535
BURGESS THERMOGLACE H - Hydrous Kaolin Clay - BURGESS PIGMENT COMPANY; *pg.* 1150, *pg.* 535
BURIED CAPACITANCE - Laminators - SANMINA-SCI CORPORATION; *pg.* 671, *pg.* 250
BURKAY GENESIS - Gas Boilers - A.O. SMITH CORPORATION; *pg.* 1313, *pg.* 1872
BURKEBASE - Rubber Wall Base - BURKE INDUSTRIES, INC.; *pg.* 919, *pg.* 239
BURKELINE ROOFING SYSTEMS - Single-Ply Membrane Roofing Systems - BURKE INDUSTRIES, INC.; *pg.* 919, *pg.* 239
BURKEMERCER - Vinyl Wall Base & Stair Treads - BURKE INDUSTRIES, INC.; *pg.* 919, *pg.* 239
BURKSHIRE - Fabric - NEMSCHOFF, INC.; *pg.* 936, *pg.* 1890
BURKSHIRE - Fabric - UNIROYAL ENGINEERED PRODUCTS; *pg.* 699, *pg.* 467
BURLE - Electron Multiplier - PHOTONIS USA PENNSYLVANIA; *pg.* 663, *pg.* 1547
BURLED YORK - Table - BLATT BOWLING & BILLIARD CORP.; *pg.* 1827, *pg.* 1203
BURLINGTON - Furniture - ASHLEY FURNITURE INDUSTRIES, INC.; *pg.* 914, *pg.* 1852
BURLINGTON - Fabric - INTERNATIONAL TEXTILE GROUP, INC.; *pg.* 696, *pg.* 1374
BURLINGTON HOUSE - Bed Linen - SPRINGS GLOBAL, INC.; *pg.* 698, *pg.* 1616
BURLY - Footwear - LACROSSE FOOTWEAR, INC.; *pg.* 1811, *pg.* 1503
BURN - Software - AUTODESK INC.; *pg.* 356, *pg.* 257
BURN - Soft Drink - THE COCA-COLA COMPANY; *pg.* 240, *pg.* 493
BURN SHORT - Sport Apparel - UNDER ARMOUR, INC.; *pg.* 49, *pg.* 759
BURNER - Apparel - OAKLEY, INC.; *pg.* 1840, *pg.* 86
BURNETTS - Gin - DIAGEO CANADA, INC.; *pg.* 1961, *pg.* 1937
BURNHAM - Residential & Commercial Boilers & Radiators - BURNHAM HOLDINGS, INC.; *pg.* 1069, *pg.* 1546
BURNING REELS - Game - WMS INDUSTRIES INC.; *pg.* 593, *pg.* 666
BURNISHED METALS - Fabric - NEMSCHOFF, INC.; *pg.* 936, *pg.* 1890
BURNOUT - Video Game - ELECTRONIC ARTS INC.; *pg.* 951, *pg.* 189
BURNS - Misses' Sportswear Collection - KELLWOOD COMPANY; *pg.* 28, *pg.* 975
BURNS - Hot Dogs - MAPLE LEAF FOODS INC.; *pg.* 875, *pg.* 1927
BURR-BROWN - Amplifiers & Converters - TEXAS INSTRUMENTS INCORPORATED; *pg.* 679, *pg.* 1688
BURR SANITIZER - Healthcare Product - MEDICOOL, INC.; *pg.* 1562, *pg.* 294
BURRO - R.R. Locomotive Cranes - BADGER EQUIPMENT COMPANY; *pg.* 1315, *pg.* 966
BURROWS - Furniture - AMERICAN LEATHER LP; *pg.* 912, *pg.* 1673
BURROWS - Moisture Tester - SEEDBURO EQUIPMENT CO.; *pg.* 707, *pg.* 590
BURSINE - Poultry Vaccine - PFIZER INC.; *pg.* 1581, *pg.* 1278
BURST - Fabric - NEMSCHOFF, INC.; *pg.* 936, *pg.* 1890
BURSTBUCKER - Electrical Pickups for String Musical Instruments - GIBSON GUITAR CORP.; *pg.* 550, *pg.* 1650
BURSTPROOF - Hose - HBD INDUSTRIES, INC.; *pg.* 207, *pg.* 1449
BURTEK - Security Products - RICHARDSON ELECTRONICS, LTD.; *pg.* 667, *pg.* 622
BURTON - Snowboards & Gear - BURTON SNOWBOARD COMPANY; *pg.* 1829, *pg.* 1765
BURTON - Office Furniture - STEELCASE INC.; *pg.* 475, *pg.* 889
BURTON & DOYLE - Steak Restaurant - SBARRO, INC.; *pg.* 1749, *pg.* 1182
BURT'S BEES - Personal Care - THE CLOROX COMPANY; *pg.* 327, *pg.* 169
BUS DOCTOR - Analyzer - FINISAR CORPORATION; *pg.* 639, *pg.* 285
BUS STOP - Sandals - AEROGROUP INTERNATIONAL, INC.; *pg.* 1803, *pg.* 1055
BUSAN - Microbicides - BUCKMAN; *pg.* 1150, *pg.* 1641
BUSART - Graphic Film - FLEXCON CORPORATION; *pg.* 1457, *pg.* 844
BUSBRIDGE - Core Interface - IMAGINATION TECHNOLOGIES; *pg.* 412, *pg.* 285
BUSCANDO A NEMO - Educational Kit - LEAPFROG ENTERPRISES, INC.; *pg.* 961, *pg.* 84
BUSCH - Beer - ANHEUSER-BUSCH COMPANIES, LLC; *pg.* 237, *pg.* 991
BUSCH ICE - Beer - ANHEUSER-BUSCH COMPANIES, LLC; *pg.* 237, *pg.* 991
BUSCH LIGHT - Light Beer - ANHEUSER-BUSCH COMPANIES, LLC; *pg.* 237, *pg.* 991
BUSCH NA - Non-Alcoholic Brew - ANHEUSER-BUSCH COMPANIES, LLC; *pg.* 237, *pg.* 991
BUSENGINE - Analyzer - TELEDYNE LECROY; *pg.* 1431, *pg.* 1153
BUSES-ALL-READY-TO-BUY - Program - THOMAS BUILT BUSES, INC.; *pg.* 191, *pg.* 1379
BUSH BUSINESS FURNITURE - Commercial Office Furniture - BUSH INDUSTRIES INC.; *pg.* 919, *pg.* 1170
BUSHMILLS - Whisky - DIAGEO NORTH AMERICA, INC.; *pg.* 1961, *pg.* 361
BUSHNELL - Computer Software - BROWN & BIGELOW, INC.; *pg.* 1624, *pg.* 959
BUSINESS ANALYST ONLINE - Software - ENVIRONMENTAL SYSTEMS RESEARCH INSTITUTE INC.; *pg.* 393, *pg.* 188
BUSINESS AND HEALTH - Healthcare Publication - TRUVEN HEALTH ANALYTICS; *pg.* 1696, *pg.* 867
THE BUSINESS BEHIND BUSINESS - Slogan - AUTOMATIC DATA PROCESSING, INC.; *pg.* 357, *pg.* 1117
BUSINESS BOOSTER PACK - Digital Printing Sales & Marketing Services - RICOH AMERICA; *pg.* 461, *pg.* 1550
BUSINESS BROWSER - Business Tool - AVENTION; *pg.* 1230, *pg.* 815
BUSINESS BUILDERS - Display Baskets - PETEDGE; *pg.* 1481, *pg.* 787
BUSINESS CASHLINE - Credit Line - CALIFORNIA BANK & TRUST; *pg.* 728, *pg.* 201
THE BUSINESS CHANNEL - Distribution of Education & Training Programs for Campus & Workplace Use - PUBLIC BROADCASTING SERVICE; *pg.* 305, *pg.* 1774
BUSINESS CLASS CONTROLLER - Briefcase - SANTA FE LEATHER CORPORATION; *pg.* 12, *pg.* 1059
BUSINESS DRIVER - Magazine - BOBIT BUSINESS MEDIA; *pg.* 1622, *pg.* 293
BUSINESS EMPOWERMENT - Software - PROGRESS SOFTWARE CORPORATION; *pg.* 457, *pg.* 786
THE BUSINESS EQUITY PROTECTOR - Insurance Policy - STANDARD INSURANCE COMPANY; *pg.* 1217, *pg.* 1506
BUSINESS EXPRESS - Software - USA TECHNOLOGIES, INC.; *pg.* 815, *pg.* 1550
BUSINESS FLEET - Magazine - BOBIT BUSINESS MEDIA; *pg.* 1622, *pg.* 293
BUSINESS FORMS & SYSTEMS - Magazine - NORTH AMERICAN PUBLISHING COMPANY; *pg.* 1671, *pg.* 1567
BUSINESS FORMS LABELS & SYSTEMS - Publisher - NORTH AMERICAN PUBLISHING COMPANY; *pg.* 1671, *pg.* 1567
BUSINESS GUARDIAN - Disaster Recovery Services - AT&T SOUTHEAST; *pg.* 1868, *pg.* 489
BUSINESS INFORMATION REPORT - Business Summary - THE DUN & BRADSTREET CORP.; *pg.* 1637, *pg.* 1120
BUSINESS INSIGHT - Software - DELL SOFTWARE; *pg.* 385, *pg.* 40
BUSINESS INSURANCE - Newspaper - CRAIN COMMUNICATIONS, INC.; *pg.* 1631, *pg.* 879
BUSINESS INTELLIGENCE ESSENTIALS - Software - RENTRAK CORPORATION; *pg.* 306, *pg.* 1506
BUSINESS MAKING PROGRESS - Software - PROGRESS SOFTWARE CORPORATION; *pg.* 457, *pg.* 786
BUSINESS MANAGEMENT PERSONNEL - Staffing Firm - GENERAL EMPLOYMENT ENTERPRISES, INC.; *pg.* 400, *pg.* 636
BUSINESS MANAGER - Information Management System - PITNEY BOWES INC.; *pg.* 454, *pg.* 376
BUSINESS MASTERCARD - Credit Card - PACIFIC CONTINENTAL CORPORATION; *pg.* 791, *pg.* 1497
BUSINESS MOBILITY FRAMEWORK - Software - SPRINT CORPORATION; *pg.* 1874, *pg.* 719
BUSINESS MOBILITY NOW! - Slogan - SOCKET MOBILE, INC.; *pg.* 471, *pg.* 164
BUSINESS ONE - Wireless Communication System - AT&T SOUTHEAST; *pg.* 1868, *pg.* 489
BUSINESS ONE - Bag - SAMSONITE CORPORATION; *pg.* 11, *pg.* 830
BUSINESS PACKAGE - Level Monitoring System - BMC SOFTWARE, INC.; *pg.* 362, *pg.* 1701
BUSINESS PLATFORM - Personal Computer - NVIDIA CORPORATION; *pg.* 447, *pg.* 268
BUSINESS PLUS - Hotel - BEST WESTERN INTERNATIONAL, INC.; *pg.* 1081, *pg.* 15
THE BUSINESS PROTECTOR - Insurance Policy - STANDARD INSURANCE COMPANY; *pg.* 1217, *pg.* 1506
BUSINESS TRAVEL NEWS - Trade Publication - THE NIELSEN COMPANY B.V.; *pg.* 1671, *pg.* 1272
BUSINESSCARE - Hardware & Software Solution - DELL INC.; *pg.* 383, *pg.* 1737
BUSINESSDIRECT - Software System - AT&T COMMUNICATIONS CORP.; *pg.* 1866, *pg.* 1043
BUSINESSEASE - Hardware & Software Services - DELL INC.; *pg.* 383, *pg.* 1737
BUSINESSELITE - Air Transportation - DELTA AIR LINES, INC.; *pg.* 1905, *pg.* 503
BUSINESSFACTOR - Computer Software - TIBCO SOFTWARE INC.; *pg.* 484, *pg.* 178
BUSINESSHARE - Computer Software - NOVELL INC.; *pg.* 446, *pg.* 852
BUSINESSMAP - Software - ENVIRONMENTAL SYSTEMS RESEARCH INSTITUTE INC.; *pg.* 393, *pg.* 188
BUSINESSONE - Airline Service - UNITED CONTINENTAL HOLDINGS, INC.; *pg.* 1927, *pg.* 593
BUSINESSPRO - Software - SKILLSOFT PLC; *pg.* 470, *pg.* 1037
BUSINESSWARE - Software - VITRIA TECHNOLOGY, INC.; *pg.* 490, *pg.* 289
BUSINESSWEEK - Publication - THE MCGRAW-HILL COMPANIES INC.; *pg.* 1663, *pg.* 1257
BUSINESSWISE - Online Banking - FIRST NIAGARA FINANCIAL GROUP, INC.; *pg.* 757, *pg.* 1148
BUSINESSWORKS - Computer Software - TIBCO SOFTWARE INC.; *pg.* 484, *pg.* 178
BUSMARK - Graphic Film - FLEXCON CORPORATION; *pg.* 1457, *pg.* 844
BUSPAR - Anti-Anxiety Agent for Mngmt. of Anxiety Disorders - BRISTOL-MYERS SQUIBB U.S. PHARMACEUTICAL GROUP; *pg.* 1511, *pg.* 1110
BUSPERSE - Dispersants - BUCKMAN; *pg.* 1150, *pg.* 1641
BUST-SCULPT - Beauty Product - AVON PRODUCTS, INC.; *pg.* 500, *pg.* 1198
BUSTEDTEES - Online Services - IAC/INTERACTIVECORP; *pg.* 292, *pg.* 1242
BUSTER BAR - Frozen Novelties - INTERNATIONAL DAIRY QUEEN, INC.; *pg.* 1732, *pg.* 938
BUSTER BROWN - Shoes - CALERES, INC.; *pg.* 1805, *pg.* 993
BUSTER THE TORTOISE - Children's Step Stool - RUBBERMAID HOME PRODUCTS; *pg.* 1138, *pg.* 1453
BUSY BALL POPPER - Toy & Game - HASBRO, INC.; *pg.* 954, *pg.* 1603
BUSY BASICS - Toy & Game - HASBRO, INC.; *pg.* 954, *pg.* 1603
BUSY BEE - Processed Honey - GOLDEN HERITAGE FOODS, LLC; *pg.* 858, *pg.* 715
BUSY CONNECT - Calling Feature - AT&T SOUTHEAST; *pg.* 1868, *pg.* 489

First page reference indicates Business Class Edition
Second page reference indicates Geographic Edition

BUT-R-CREME - Icing & Base - DAWN FOOD PRODUCTS, INC.; *pg.* 1018, *pg.* 893
BUT WAIT THERE'S MORE - Video Game - INTERNATIONAL GAME TECHNOLOGY; *pg.* 957, *pg.* 1024
BUT WAIT! WIN MORE - Video Game - INTERNATIONAL GAME TECHNOLOGY; *pg.* 957, *pg.* 1024
BUTACITE - Pliable Sheeting Used in Safety Glass - E.I. DU PONT DE NEMOURS & COMPANY; *pg.* 1159, *pg.* 390
BUTALBITAL - Pharmaceutical Product - LANNETT COMPANY, INC.; *pg.* 1555, *pg.* 1566
BUTAZATE - Polymer Product - CHEMTURA CORPORATION; *pg.* 1152, *pg.* 355
BUTCHER BO - Food Product - ELLENBEE-LEGGETT COMPANY INC.; *pg.* 854, *pg.* 1452
BUTCHER WAGON - Sausages - HATFIELD QUALITY MEATS, INC.; *pg.* 861, *pg.* 1537
BUTCHER'S BLOCK - Meat Product - SYSCO CORPORATION; *pg.* 1035, *pg.* 1716
BUTLER - Floor Care Product - BISSELL HOMECARE, INC.; *pg.* 52, *pg.* 887
BUTLER - Pre-Engineered Metal Buildings - BUTLER MANUFACTURING COMPANY; *pg.* 72, *pg.* 981
BUTLER - Automatic Dumbwaiters & Wheelchair Lifts - THE FLINCHBAUGH CO., INC.; *pg.* 82, *pg.* 1551
BUTLER - Preventive Dentistry Aids - SUNSTAR AMERICAS INC.; *pg.* 1599, *pg.* 591
BUTLER ADVANTAGE - Computer Software System - BUTLER MANUFACTURING COMPANY; *pg.* 72, *pg.* 981
BUTLER BUILDER - Metal Building System - BUTLER MANUFACTURING COMPANY; *pg.* 72, *pg.* 981
BUTLER CLASSIC - Metal Building System - BUTLER MANUFACTURING COMPANY; *pg.* 72, *pg.* 981
BUTLER-COTE - Metal Building System - BUTLER MANUFACTURING COMPANY; *pg.* 72, *pg.* 981
BUTLER ELECTRONIC SPECIFICATIONS - Metal Building System - BUTLER MANUFACTURING COMPANY; *pg.* 72, *pg.* 981
BUTLER GUM ANGLE - Toothbrush - SUNSTAR AMERICAS INC.; *pg.* 1599, *pg.* 591
BUTLER LITE PANL - Metal Building System - BUTLER MANUFACTURING COMPANY; *pg.* 72, *pg.* 981
BUTLER REFERENCE LIBRARY - Metal Building System - BUTLER MANUFACTURING COMPANY; *pg.* 72, *pg.* 981
BUTLER SMILE CENTER - Dental Floss, Floss Threaders, Toothbrushes - SUNSTAR AMERICAS INC.; *pg.* 1599, *pg.* 591
BUTLER SMILE FACTORY - Dental Care Products - SUNSTAR AMERICAS INC.; *pg.* 1599, *pg.* 591
BUTLER WHEELCHAIR LIFT - Wheelchair - THE FLINCHBAUGH CO., INC.; *pg.* 82, *pg.* 1551
BUTLERIB II - Metal Roof & Wall Systems - BUTLER MANUFACTURING COMPANY; *pg.* 72, *pg.* 981
BUTLERWEAVE - Floss - SUNSTAR AMERICAS INC.; *pg.* 1599, *pg.* 591
BUTOX - Antiparasitic Drug - MERCK & CO., INC.; *pg.* 1566, *pg.* 1077
BUTRALIN - Polymer Product - CHEMTURA CORPORATION; *pg.* 1152, *pg.* 355
BUTTER - Fabric - NEMSCHOFF, INC.; *pg.* 936, *pg.* 1890
BUTTER BOOM - Microwave Popcorn - NEWMAN'S OWN, INC.; *pg.* 886, *pg.* 384
BUTTER BUDS - Butter-flavored Granules - CUMBERLAND PACKING CORP.; *pg.* 851, *pg.* 1146
BUTTER-LICIOUS - Pop Corn - AMERICAN POP CORN COMPANY; *pg.* 825, *pg.* 712
BUTTER LICIOUS LIGHT - Microwave Pop Corn - AMERICAN POP CORN COMPANY; *pg.* 825, *pg.* 712
BUTTER PRETZEL BRAIDS - Snack Food - INVENTURE FOODS, INC.; *pg.* 1023, *pg.* 17
BUTTERBALL - Turkey Products - BUTTERBALL, LLC; *pg.* 843, *pg.* 1385
BUTTERBALL BUTTERFLY - Valves - MILWAUKEE VALVE COMPANY, INC.; *pg.* 1361, *pg.* 1884
BUTTERCREAM - Candle - THE YANKEE CANDLE COMPANY, INC.; *pg.* 1792, *pg.* 843
BUTTERCUP - Dry Snuff - SWISHER INTERNATIONAL, INC.; *pg.* 1895, *pg.* 345
BUTTERCUTT - Lubricant - AERVOE INDUSTRIES INCORPORATED; *pg.* 1439, *pg.* 1021
BUTTERFINGER - Candy - NESTLE USA, INC.; *pg.* 883, *pg.* 96
BUTTERFINGER BB'S - Candy - NESTLE USA, INC.; *pg.* 883, *pg.* 96
BUTTERFINGER PEANUT BUTTER CUPS - Candy Bar - NESTLE USA, INC.; *pg.* 883, *pg.* 96
BUTTERFLIES - Lace - HERITAGE LACE INC.; *pg.* 694, *pg.* 711
BUTTERFLY - Valves - FLOWSERVE CORPORATION; *pg.* 82, *pg.* 1719
BUTTERFLY - Fabric - SCALAMANDRE, INC.; *pg.* 941, *pg.* 1058
BUTTERFLY BALLET - Earring - STULLER, INC.; *pg.* 13, *pg.* 745
BUTTERFUL - Butter Product - FROSTY ACRES BRANDS, INC.; *pg.* 1020, *pg.* 484
BUTTERKRUST - Food Product - FLOWERS FOODS, INC.; *pg.* 855, *pg.* 541
BUTTERSKULLS - Apparel - VANS, INC.; *pg.* 1821, *pg.* 76
BUTTON DOWN - Apparel - OAKLEY, INC.; *pg.* 1840, *pg.* 86
BUTTONS 'N BOWS - Container Grown Plant - MONROVIA GROWERS; *pg.* 1797, *pg.* 44
BUTYL EIGHT - Accelerators - R.T. VANDERBILT COMPANY, INC.; *pg.* 1180, *pg.* 364
BUTYL NAMATE - Accelerators - R.T. VANDERBILT COMPANY, INC.; *pg.* 1180, *pg.* 364
BUTYLFLEX - Caulk And Sealant - DAP PRODUCTS, INC.; *pg.* 1441, *pg.* 756
BUXTON - Case - BROWN & BIGELOW, INC.; *pg.* 1624, *pg.* 959
BUY IT FOR LOOKS. BUY IT FOR LIFE - Tag Line - MOEN INCORPORATED; *pg.* 1056, *pg.* 1468
BUY ON DEMAND - Software System - MENTOR GRAPHICS CORPORATION; *pg.* 432, *pg.* 1510
BUYERBASE - Ad Targeting Platform - ZIFF DAVIS, LLC; *pg.* 1703, *pg.* 1316
BUYERLINK - Real Estate Buyer Marketing Solution - HOMEGAIN.COM, INC.; *pg.* 1256, *pg.* 83
BUYERS ADVANTAGE - Purchase Protection Services - AFFINION GROUP, INC.; *pg.* 1225, *pg.* 372
BUYRATE - Hand Tool - IDEAL INDUSTRIES, INC.; *pg.* 1051, *pg.* 662
BUZLINE - Light Product - BUZTRONICS, INC.; *pg.* 1294, *pg.* 683
BUZZ - Wireless Communication System - AT&T SOUTHEAST; *pg.* 1868, *pg.* 489
BUZZ - Beverages - THE COCA-COLA COMPANY; *pg.* 240, *pg.* 493
BUZZ CLUB - Club - BIG LOTS, INC.; *pg.* 1762, *pg.* 1438
BUZZ HMV - HMV Scooter - INVACARE CORPORATION; *pg.* 1546, *pg.* 1451
BUZZ OFF - Pour-on Insecticide - BOEHRINGER INGELHEIM VETMEDICA, INC.; *pg.* 1474, *pg.* 989
BUZZ OFF - Clothing - EX OFFICIO, LLC; *pg.* 40, *pg.* 1835
BUZZ OFF - Insect Repellent Apparel - THE ORVIS COMPANY, INC.; *pg.* 1781, *pg.* 1764
BUZZ STIX - Ice Fishing Equipment - SWORDFISH FINANCIAL, INC.; *pg.* 1430, *pg.* 1737
BUZZAIRD - Cutting Room Equipment - EASTMAN MACHINE COMPANY; *pg.* 1331, *pg.* 1148
BUZZBAR - Mower - ALAMO GROUP INC.; *pg.* 1311, *pg.* 1745
BUZZNET - Pop Culture Social Media Site - SPINMEDIA; *pg.* 1282, *pg.* 104
BUZZSAW - Software - AUTODESK INC.; *pg.* 356, *pg.* 257
BUZZTIME TRIVIA - Trivia Book Series - NTN BUZZTIME, INC.; *pg.* 659, *pg.* 60
BV-ADMIN - Software - SYMANTEC CORPORATION; *pg.* 478, *pg.* 161
BV-CONTROL - Software - SYMANTEC CORPORATION; *pg.* 478, *pg.* 161
BVA 100 - Blood Volume Analyzer - DAXOR CORPORATION; *pg.* 1522, *pg.* 1221
BVD - Underwear - FRUIT OF THE LOOM, INC.; *pg.* 41, *pg.* 725
BW SEALS - Seal - FLOWSERVE CORPORATION; *pg.* 82, *pg.* 1719
BWA - Wireless Network Product - AIRSPAN NETWORKS INC.; *pg.* 346, *pg.* 410
BWANDERHB - Footwear - STEVEN MADDEN, LTD.; *pg.* 1819, *pg.* 1176
BWD - Motor Product - STANDARD MOTOR PRODUCTS, INC.; *pg.* 218, *pg.* 1176
BWOVSTUDT - Footwear - STEVEN MADDEN, LTD.; *pg.* 1819, *pg.* 1176
BX-3 - Double Manual Organ - KORG USA, INC.; *pg.* 556, *pg.* 1180
BXP - Software - INTERVALZERO INC.; *pg.* 420, *pg.* 851
BY ALL ACCOUNTS, BETTER. - Tagline - WESBANCO, INC.; *pg.* 821, *pg.* 1851
BY ENGINEERS. FOR ENGINEERS. - Slogan - CYPRESS SEMICONDUCTOR CORPORATION; *pg.* 1326, *pg.* 243
BY GEORGE - Video Game - INTERNATIONAL GAME TECHNOLOGY; *pg.* 957, *pg.* 1024
BYE BYE BLEMISH - Anti Acne Regime - AMERICAN INTERNATIONAL INDUSTRIES COMPANY; *pg.* 498, *pg.* 126
BYETTA - Pharmaceutical Product - ELI LILLY AND COMPANY; *pg.* 1527, *pg.* 684
BYNEL - Adhesive Resins - E.I. DU PONT DE NEMOURS & COMPANY; *pg.* 1159, *pg.* 390
BYRON - Shoes - ALLEN-EDMONDS SHOE CORP.; *pg.* 1804, *pg.* 1887
BYRON BAY - Carpet - BEAULIEU GROUP, LLC; *pg.* 917, *pg.* 529
BYRON JACKSON - Pump - FLOWSERVE CORPORATION; *pg.* 82, *pg.* 1719
BYRON'S - Barbecue Products - RICH PRODUCTS CORPORATION; *pg.* 892, *pg.* 1150
BZZ OUT - Game - GAMEWRIGHT; *pg.* 953, *pg.* 836

C

C-130 - Systems Integration & Aeronautics - LOCKHEED MARTIN CORPORATION; *pg.* 229, *pg.* 762
C-141 - Systems Integration & Aeronautics - LOCKHEED MARTIN CORPORATION; *pg.* 229, *pg.* 762
C-1508 - Liquid Plastic - SMOOTH-ON INC.; *pg.* 111, *pg.* 1528
C-1509 - Liquid Plastic - SMOOTH-ON INC.; *pg.* 111, *pg.* 1528
C-1515 - Liquid Plastic - SMOOTH-ON INC.; *pg.* 111, *pg.* 1528
C-1520 - Liquid Plastic - SMOOTH-ON INC.; *pg.* 111, *pg.* 1528
C-20 - Detergent - SWISHER HYGIENE INC.; *pg.* 336, *pg.* 1507
C-3 - Cell Stand - BIOANALYTICAL SYSTEMS, INC.; *pg.* 1402, *pg.* 700
C-5 - Systems Integration & Aeronautics - LOCKHEED MARTIN CORPORATION; *pg.* 229, *pg.* 762
C-6500 - Digital Piano - KORG USA, INC.; *pg.* 556, *pg.* 1180
C-7B - Automatic Aerosol Dispensers - SURCO PRODUCTS, INC.; *pg.* 336, *pg.* 1581
C&C CALIFORNIA - Apparel - PERRY ELLIS INTERNATIONAL, INC.; *pg.* 45, *pg.* 445
C&D - Power System - C&D TECHNOLOGIES, INC.; *pg.* 627, *pg.* 1517
C&H - Sugar - C&H SUGAR COMPANY, INC.; *pg.* 843, *pg.* 71
C & S - Pet Product - PETSMART, INC.; *pg.* 1481, *pg.* 18
C&W - Frozen Foods - PINNACLE FOODS GROUP LLC; *pg.* 889, *pg.* 1104
C-ASCORBS - Nutritional Supplement - NATURAL ORGANICS, INC.; *pg.* 1571, *pg.* 1181
C-ASPIN - Automated Shipping System - ASSOCIATED GLOBAL SYSTEMS, INC.; *pg.* 1899, *pg.* 1184
C-BALANCE - Switch - POWER INTEGRATIONS, INC.; *pg.* 1369, *pg.* 249
C-BELT - Sorting Technology - KEY TECHNOLOGY, INC.; *pg.* 868, *pg.* 1847
C BLADES - Ceramic - DYNATEX INTERNATIONAL; *pg.* 635, *pg.* 277
C-BYTE - Compression Connector - AMPHENOL CORPORATION; *pg.* 616, *pg.* 381
C-CLIP - Software - EMC CORPORATION; *pg.* 391, *pg.* 825
C-CO2 - Colorimetric CO2 Indicator - VITAL SIGNS, INC.; *pg.* 1607, *pg.* 1126
C/D-SOLV - Chemical Cleaner Product - TECH SPRAY, L.P.; *pg.* 1183, *pg.* 1659
C-F - Under Hook Lifters - BADGER EQUIPMENT COMPANY; *pg.* 1315, *pg.* 966
C-GRID - Stackable Linear Product - MOLEX INCORPORATED; *pg.* 655, *pg.* 628
C-GRID III - Electronic Components - MOLEX INCORPORATED; *pg.* 655, *pg.* 628
C-L-X - Metallic Sheathed Cables - THE OKONITE COMPANY; *pg.* 1302, *pg.* 1113
C-LETZ - Conization Electrode for Management of Deep Endocervical Disease - UTAH MEDICAL PRODUCTS, INC.; *pg.* 1605, *pg.* 1752
C-LIGHT - Signaling Emergency Light - ACR ELECTRONICS, INC.; *pg.* 612, *pg.* 422
C-LINE - Material Handling Equipment - C&D

TECHNOLOGIES, INC.; pg. 627, pg. 1517
C-LINK - Software - INTELLICHECK MOBILISA, INC.; pg. 416, pg. 1823
C-LOC - Construction Material - CRANE PLASTICS HOLDING COMPANY; pg. 1881, pg. 1439
C-MAX - Software - BIO-RAD LABORATORIES, INC.; pg. 1504, pg. 101
C-MIX - Video Mixer - CHYRONHEGO; pg. 371, pg. 1179
C-MORE - Electronic Control Systems - AERCO INTERNATIONAL INC.; pg. 1068, pg. 1142
C# TOOLKIT - Software - RECURSION SOFTWARE, INC.; pg. 460, pg. 1697
C/P LIFT - Software - BIO-RAD LABORATORIES, INC.; pg. 1504, pg. 101
C. PLATH - Marine Navigation - SPERRY MARINE INC.; pg. 1430, pg. 1778
C-PORT - Semiconductor Product - FREESCALE SEMICONDUCTOR, INC.; pg. 398, pg. 1662
C RADIANT - Overhead Warming Oven - APW WYOTT FOOD SERVICE EQUIPMENT, INC.; pg. 1314, pg. 1658
C STROBE - Signaling Emergency Strobe - ACR ELECTRONICS, INC.; pg. 612, pg. 422
C-THROUGH - Show Control - ELECTROSONIC SYSTEMS, INC.; pg. 635, pg. 949
C-THRU - Glass Cleaner - SWISHER HYGIENE INC.; pg. 336, pg. 1507
C-VI-COMPLEX TABLETS - 500 Mg. Vitamin C Tablets - SCHIFF NUTRITION INTERNATIONAL, INC.; pg. 1592, pg. 1760
C-WING - Heat Spreaders - PARKER CHOMERICS; pg. 662, pg. 862
C-WORTHY - Computer Software - NOVELL INC.; pg. 446, pg. 852
C++ TOOLKIT - Software - RECURSION SOFTWARE, INC.; pg. 460, pg. 1697
C+E REPAIR P.M. - Skin Treatment - SHAKLEE CORPORATION; pg. 1593, pg. 184
C100 - Digital Compass Product - KVH INDUSTRIES INC; pg. 650, pg. 1602
C1000 - Software - BIO-RAD LABORATORIES, INC.; pg. 1504, pg. 101
C1000 MANAGER - Software - BIO-RAD LABORATORIES, INC.; pg. 1504, pg. 101
C12 - High-Performance Coating & Corrosion Inhibitor Products - INVISTA B.V.; pg. 1168, pg. 723
C20 - Printer - XEROX CORPORATION; pg. 494, pg. 365
C2000 - Integrated Circuits - TEXAS INSTRUMENTS INCORPORATED; pg. 679, pg. 1688
C20X - Integrated Circuits - TEXAS INSTRUMENTS INCORPORATED; pg. 679, pg. 1688
C24X - Integrated Circuits - TEXAS INSTRUMENTS INCORPORATED; pg. 679, pg. 1688
C28X - Integrated Circuits - TEXAS INSTRUMENTS INCORPORATED; pg. 679, pg. 1688
C3 - Telecommunications System - ARRIS GROUP, INC.; pg. 353, pg. 541
C3 - Membrane Product - COOLEY GROUP, INC.; pg. 691, pg. 1603
C3 - Single-Wafer Clean - LAM RESEARCH CORPORATION; pg. 1354, pg. 91
C3 - High Speed Oven - TURBOCHEF TECHNOLOGIES, INC.; pg. 902, pg. 1670
C32 COLOR - Printer - XEROX CORPORATION; pg. 494, pg. 365
C35 - Printer - XEROX CORPORATION; pg. 494, pg. 365
C4 - Telecommunications System - ARRIS GROUP, INC.; pg. 353, pg. 541
C4 - Flashlight - STREAMLIGHT INC.; pg. 1306, pg. 1527
C40 COLOR - Printer - XEROX CORPORATION; pg. 494, pg. 365
C420 PAPR SYSTEM - Air Respirator - IRT, INC.; pg. 1169, pg. 771
C45 - Printer - XEROX CORPORATION; pg. 494, pg. 365
C5-A - Anti-Seize Lubricant - HENKEL CORPORATION; pg. 1049, pg. 369
C500 - Trucks - KENWORTH TRUCK CO.; pg. 181, pg. 1822
C5000 - Integrated Circuits - TEXAS INSTRUMENTS INCORPORATED; pg. 679, pg. 1688
C54X - Integrated Circuits - TEXAS INSTRUMENTS INCORPORATED; pg. 679, pg. 1688
C55 - Printer - XEROX CORPORATION; pg. 494, pg. 365
C55X - Integrated Circuits - TEXAS INSTRUMENTS INCORPORATED; pg. 679, pg. 1688
C5X - Integrated Circuits - TEXAS INSTRUMENTS INCORPORATED; pg. 679, pg. 1688
C6000 - Integrated Circuits - TEXAS INSTRUMENTS INCORPORATED; pg. 679, pg. 1688
C62X - Integrated Circuits - TEXAS INSTRUMENTS INCORPORATED; pg. 679, pg. 1688
C64X - Integrated Circuits - TEXAS INSTRUMENTS INCORPORATED; pg. 679, pg. 1688
C65 - Printer - XEROX CORPORATION; pg. 494, pg. 365
C67X - Integrated Circuits - TEXAS INSTRUMENTS INCORPORATED; pg. 679, pg. 1688
C75 - Printer - XEROX CORPORATION; pg. 494, pg. 365
C8 - Semiconductor Solution - CYPRESS SEMICONDUCTOR CORPORATION; pg. 1326, pg. 243
C8051F01X - Precision Mixed-Signal Microcontroller - SILICON LABORATORIES INC.; pg. 674, pg. 1666
C8051F02X - Precision Mixed-Signal Microcontroller - SILICON LABORATORIES INC.; pg. 674, pg. 1666
C8051F04X - Precision Mixed-Signal Microcontroller - SILICON LABORATORIES INC.; pg. 674, pg. 1666
C8051F06X - Precision Mixed-Signal Microcontroller - SILICON LABORATORIES INC.; pg. 674, pg. 1666
C8051F0XX - Precision Mixed-Signal Microcontroller - SILICON LABORATORIES INC.; pg. 674, pg. 1666
C8051F12X/3X - Precision Mixed-Signal Microcontroller - SILICON LABORATORIES INC.; pg. 674, pg. 1666
C8051F2XX - Small Form Factor MCU - SILICON LABORATORIES INC.; pg. 674, pg. 1666
C8051F30X - Small Form Factor MCU - SILICON LABORATORIES INC.; pg. 674, pg. 1666
C8051F31X - Small Form Factor MCU - SILICON LABORATORIES INC.; pg. 674, pg. 1666
C8051F336 - Small Form Factor MCU - SILICON LABORATORIES INC.; pg. 674, pg. 1666
C8051F33X - Small Form Factor MCU - SILICON LABORATORIES INC.; pg. 674, pg. 1666
C8051F35X - Precision Mixed-Signal Microcontroller - SILICON LABORATORIES INC.; pg. 674, pg. 1666
C8051F36X - Small Form Factor MCU - SILICON LABORATORIES INC.; pg. 674, pg. 1666
C8051F41X - Small Form Factor MCU - SILICON LABORATORIES INC.; pg. 674, pg. 1666
C8051F70X/71X - Precision Mixed-Signal Microcontroller - SILICON LABORATORIES INC.; pg. 674, pg. 1666
C8051F9XX - Low-Voltage & Low-Power MCUs - SILICON LABORATORIES INC.; pg. 674, pg. 1666
C8051T606 - Small Form Factor MCU - SILICON LABORATORIES INC.; pg. 674, pg. 1666
C8051T60X - OTP-EPROM - SILICON LABORATORIES INC.; pg. 674, pg. 1666
C8051T61X - OTP-EPROM - SILICON LABORATORIES INC.; pg. 674, pg. 1666
C8051T63X - OTP-EPROM - SILICON LABORATORIES INC.; pg. 674, pg. 1666
C9 - Semiconductor Solution - CYPRESS SEMICONDUCTOR CORPORATION; pg. 1326, pg. 243
C9 - Apparel - HANESBRANDS INC.; pg. 26, pg. 1394
C9 BY CHAMPION - Sunglasses - FGX INTERNATIONAL, INC.; pg. 5, pg. 1608
C9 POKE-THRU - Wiring Products - WIREMOLD/LEGRAND; pg. 689, pg. 383
C90 - Printer - XEROX CORPORATION; pg. 494, pg. 365
CA - Hemodialysis Dialyzer - BAXTER INTERNATIONAL INC.; pg. 1499, pg. 599
CA 1 TAPE MANAGEMENT - Software - CA TECHNOLOGIES; pg. 366, pg. 1168
CA 11 WORKLOAD AUTOMATION RESTART & TRACKING - Software - CA TECHNOLOGIES; pg. 366, pg. 1168
CA 2E - Software - CA TECHNOLOGIES; pg. 366, pg. 1168
CA-5 - Filler - USG CORPORATION; pg. 118, pg. 594
CA 7WORKLOAD AUTOMATION - Software - CA TECHNOLOGIES; pg. 366, pg. 1168
CA-9 - Medical Therapy - DENDREON CORPORATION; pg. 1522, pg. 1835
CA-910 - Call Center Amplifier - ANDREA ELECTRONICS CORPORATION; pg. 617, pg. 1143
CA ACCESS CONTROL - Software - CA TECHNOLOGIES; pg. 366, pg. 1168
CA ACCUCHEK - Software - CA TECHNOLOGIES; pg. 366, pg. 1168
CA ACF2 - Software - CA TECHNOLOGIES; pg. 366, pg. 1168
CA ADS - Software - CA TECHNOLOGIES; pg. 366, pg. 1168
CA AION BUSINESS RULES EXPERT - Software - CA TECHNOLOGIES; pg. 366, pg. 1168
CA ALLOCATE DASD SPACE & PLACEMENT - Software - CA TECHNOLOGIES; pg. 366, pg. 1168
CA ANTI-SPYWARE FOR THE ENTERPRISE - Software - CA TECHNOLOGIES; pg. 366, pg. 1168
CA ANTI-VIRUS FOR THE ENTERPRISE - Software - CA TECHNOLOGIES; pg. 366, pg. 1168
CA APAS INSIGHT MONITOR FOR ADABAS - Software - CA TECHNOLOGIES; pg. 366, pg. 1168
CA ARCSERVE - Software - CA TECHNOLOGIES; pg. 366, pg. 1168
CA ASM2 BACKUP & RESTORE - Software - CA TECHNOLOGIES; pg. 366, pg. 1168
CA ASSET CONVERTER FOR MICROSOFT SMS - Software - CA TECHNOLOGIES; pg. 366, pg. 1168
CA ASSET INTELLIGENCE - Software - CA TECHNOLOGIES; pg. 366, pg. 1168
CA ASSET PORTFOLIO MANAGEMENT - Software - CA TECHNOLOGIES; pg. 366, pg. 1168
CA ASTEX PERFORMANCE - Software - CA TECHNOLOGIES; pg. 366, pg. 1168
CA AUDIT - Software - CA TECHNOLOGIES; pg. 366, pg. 1168
CA AUDITOR FOR Z/OS - Software - CA TECHNOLOGIES; pg. 366, pg. 1168
CA AUTOMATION POINT - Software - CA TECHNOLOGIES; pg. 366, pg. 1168
CA AUTOSYS WORKLOAD AUTOMATION - Software - CA TECHNOLOGIES; pg. 366, pg. 1168
CA BALANCING REPORT CONTROL - Software - CA TECHNOLOGIES; pg. 366, pg. 1168
CA BIND ANALYZER FOR DB2 FOR Z/OS - Software - CA TECHNOLOGIES; pg. 366, pg. 1168
CA BUNDL - Software - CA TECHNOLOGIES; pg. 366, pg. 1168
CA-CALC - Emissions Analyzer - TSI INCORPORATED; pg. 1432, pg. 965
CA CHANGE MANAGER ENTERPRISE WORKBENCH - Software - CA TECHNOLOGIES; pg. 366, pg. 1168
CA CICSORT - Software - CA TECHNOLOGIES; pg. 366, pg. 1168
CA CLARITY - Software - CA TECHNOLOGIES; pg. 366, pg. 1168
CA CLEANUP - Software - CA TECHNOLOGIES; pg. 366, pg. 1168
CA COHESION APPLICATION CONFIGURATION MANAGER - Software - CA TECHNOLOGIES; pg. 366, pg. 1168
CA COMPLIANCE MANAGER FOR Z/OS - Software - CA TECHNOLOGIES; pg. 366, pg. 1168
CA COMPRESS DATA COMPRESSION - Software - CA TECHNOLOGIES; pg. 366, pg. 1168
CA CONFLICTS MANAGER - Software - CA TECHNOLOGIES; pg. 366, pg. 1168
CA CONSOLE MANAGEMENT FOR OPENVMS - Software - CA TECHNOLOGIES; pg. 366, pg. 1168
CA CREWS CATALOG RECOVERY - Software - CA TECHNOLOGIES; pg. 366, pg. 1168
CA CULPRIT - Software - CA TECHNOLOGIES; pg. 366, pg. 1168
CA DADS PLUS FOR CICS - Software - CA TECHNOLOGIES; pg. 366, pg. 1168
CA DATA COMPRESSOR FOR DB2 FOR Z/OS - Software - CA TECHNOLOGIES; pg. 366, pg. 1168
CA DATABASE ANALYZER FOR DB2 FOR Z/OS - Software - CA TECHNOLOGIES; pg. 366, pg. 1168
CA DATABASE ANALYZER FOR IMS FOR Z/OS - Software - CA TECHNOLOGIES; pg. 366, pg. 1168
CA DATABASE COMMAND CENTER - Software - CA TECHNOLOGIES; pg. 366, pg. 1168
CA DATABASE COPIER FOR IMS FOR Z/OS - Software - CA TECHNOLOGIES; pg. 366, pg. 1168
CA DATABASE ORGANIZER FOR IMS FOR Z/OS - Software - CA TECHNOLOGIES; pg. 366, pg. 1168
CA DATACOM - Software - CA TECHNOLOGIES; pg. 366, pg. 1168
CA DATAMACS - Software - CA TECHNOLOGIES; pg. 366, pg. 1168
CA DATE SIMULATOR - Software - CA TECHNOLOGIES; pg. 366, pg. 1168
CA DC MONITOR EXTENSIONS FOR IMS FOR Z/OS - Software - CA TECHNOLOGIES; pg. 366, pg. 1168
CA DELIVER - Software - CA TECHNOLOGIES; pg. 366, pg. 1168
CA DESKTOP MANAGEMENT SUITE FOR WINDOWS - Software - CA TECHNOLOGIES; pg. 366, pg. 1168
CA DESKTOP MIGRATION MANAGER - Software - CA

TECHNOLOGIES; *pg.* 366, *pg.* 1168
CA DETECTOR FOR DB2 FOR Z/OS - Software - CA TECHNOLOGIES; *pg.* 366, *pg.* 1168
CA DIRECTORY - Software - CA TECHNOLOGIES; *pg.* 366, *pg.* 1168
CA DISK BACKUP & RESTORE - Software - CA TECHNOLOGIES; *pg.* 366, *pg.* 1168
CA DISPATCH - Software - CA TECHNOLOGIES; *pg.* 366, *pg.* 1168
CA DLP - Software - CA TECHNOLOGIES; *pg.* 366, *pg.* 1168
CA DUO - Software - CA TECHNOLOGIES; *pg.* 366, *pg.* 1168
CA DYNAM/D DISK MANAGEMENT FOR VSE - Software - CA TECHNOLOGIES; *pg.* 366, *pg.* 1168
CA DYNAM FASTVTOC - Software - CA TECHNOLOGIES; *pg.* 366, *pg.* 1168
CA DYNAM/FI FILE INDEPENDENCE - Software - CA TECHNOLOGIES; *pg.* 366, *pg.* 1168
CA DYNAM/T TAPE MANAGEMENT FOR VSE - Software - CA TECHNOLOGIES; *pg.* 366, *pg.* 1168
CA DYNAM/T TAPE MANAGEMENT FOR Z/VM - Software - CA TECHNOLOGIES; *pg.* 366, *pg.* 1168
CA EARL - Software - CA TECHNOLOGIES; *pg.* 366, *pg.* 1168
CA EASYTRIEVE - Software - CA TECHNOLOGIES; *pg.* 366, *pg.* 1168
CA EHEALTH FOR VOICE - Software - CA TECHNOLOGIES; *pg.* 366, *pg.* 1168
CA EHEALTH PERFORMANCE MANAGER - Software - CA TECHNOLOGIES; *pg.* 366, *pg.* 1168
CA EMBEDDED ENTITLEMENTS MANAGER - Software - CA TECHNOLOGIES; *pg.* 366, *pg.* 1168
CA ENDEVOR SOFTWARE CHANGE MANAGER - Software - CA TECHNOLOGIES; *pg.* 366, *pg.* 1168
CA ENTERPRISE LOG MANAGER - Software - CA TECHNOLOGIES; *pg.* 366, *pg.* 1168
CA EPIC FOR Z/VSE - Software - CA TECHNOLOGIES; *pg.* 366, *pg.* 1168
CA ERWIN - Data Modeler - CA TECHNOLOGIES; *pg.* 366, *pg.* 1168
CA ERWIN SAPHIR OPTION - Software - CA TECHNOLOGIES; *pg.* 366, *pg.* 1168
CA ESP WORKLOAD AUTOMATION - Software - CA TECHNOLOGIES; *pg.* 366, *pg.* 1168
CA ETRUST ANTIVIRUS - Software - OVERLAND STORAGE, INC.; *pg.* 451, *pg.* 205
CA EXPLORE PERFORMANCE MANAGEMENT - Software - CA TECHNOLOGIES; *pg.* 366, *pg.* 1168
CA EXPLORE PERFORMANCE MANAGEMENT FOR Z/VM - Software - CA TECHNOLOGIES; *pg.* 366, *pg.* 1168
CA EXPRESSPRINT - Software - CA TECHNOLOGIES; *pg.* 366, *pg.* 1168
CA EXTEND/DASD VSAM COMPRESSION - Software - CA TECHNOLOGIES; *pg.* 366, *pg.* 1168
CA FAQS AUTOMATED SYSTEMS OPERATION - Software - CA TECHNOLOGIES; *pg.* 366, *pg.* 1168
CA FAQS PRODUCTION CONTROL SYSTEM - Software - CA TECHNOLOGIES; *pg.* 366, *pg.* 1168
CA FAST CHECK - Software - CA TECHNOLOGIES; *pg.* 366, *pg.* 1168
CA FAST INDEX - Software - CA TECHNOLOGIES; *pg.* 366, *pg.* 1168
CA FAST LOAD - Software - CA TECHNOLOGIES; *pg.* 366, *pg.* 1168
CA FAST RECOVER - Software - CA TECHNOLOGIES; *pg.* 366, *pg.* 1168
CA FAST UNLOAD - Software - CA TECHNOLOGIES; *pg.* 366, *pg.* 1168
CA FAVER VSAM DATA PROTECTION - Software - CA TECHNOLOGIES; *pg.* 366, *pg.* 1168
CA FEDERATION MANAGER - Software - CA TECHNOLOGIES; *pg.* 366, *pg.* 1168
CA FILE MASTER PLUS - Software - CA TECHNOLOGIES; *pg.* 366, *pg.* 1168
CA FILE SYSTEM MANAGER - Software - CA TECHNOLOGIES; *pg.* 366, *pg.* 1168
CA FILEAGE - Software - CA TECHNOLOGIES; *pg.* 366, *pg.* 1168
CA FILESAVE RCS AUTOMATED RECOVERY - Software - CA TECHNOLOGIES; *pg.* 366, *pg.* 1168
CA GATEWAY SECURITY - Software - CA TECHNOLOGIES; *pg.* 366, *pg.* 1168
CA GEL - Metal & Trim - LORD CORPORATION; *pg.* 1357, *pg.* 1360
CA GEN - Software - CA TECHNOLOGIES; *pg.* 366, *pg.* 1168
CA GENER/OL - Software - CA TECHNOLOGIES; *pg.* 366, *pg.* 1168
CA GOVERNANCE, RISK & COMPLIANCE MANAGER - Software - CA TECHNOLOGIES; *pg.* 366, *pg.* 1168
CA GRC MANAGER ON DEMAND - Software - CA TECHNOLOGIES; *pg.* 366, *pg.* 1168
CA HIGH PERFORMANCE RECOVERY FOR IMS FOR Z/OS - Software - CA TECHNOLOGIES; *pg.* 366, *pg.* 1168
CA HOST-BASED INTRUSION PREVENTION SYSTEM - Software - CA TECHNOLOGIES; *pg.* 366, *pg.* 1168
CA HYPER-BUF VSAM BUFFER OPTIMIZER - Software - CA TECHNOLOGIES; *pg.* 366, *pg.* 1168
CA IDEAL - Software - CA TECHNOLOGIES; *pg.* 366, *pg.* 1168
CA IDENTITY MANAGER - Software - CA TECHNOLOGIES; *pg.* 366, *pg.* 1168
CA IDMS - Software - CA TECHNOLOGIES; *pg.* 366, *pg.* 1168
CA INDEX EXPERT FOR DB2 FOR Z/OS - Software - CA TECHNOLOGIES; *pg.* 366, *pg.* 1168
CA INFOREFINER - Software - CA TECHNOLOGIES; *pg.* 366, *pg.* 1168
CA INFOSESSION - Software - CA TECHNOLOGIES; *pg.* 366, *pg.* 1168
CA INFOTRANSPORT - Software - CA TECHNOLOGIES; *pg.* 366, *pg.* 1168
CA INSIGHT PERFORMANCE MONITOR FOR DB2 FOR Z/OS - Software - CA TECHNOLOGIES; *pg.* 366, *pg.* 1168
CA INSTANT RECOVERY ON DEMAND - Software - CA TECHNOLOGIES; *pg.* 366, *pg.* 1168
CA INTERTEST BATCH - Software - CA TECHNOLOGIES; *pg.* 366, *pg.* 1168
CA INTERTEST FOR CICS - Software - CA TECHNOLOGIES; *pg.* 366, *pg.* 1168
CA IT ASSET MANAGER - Software - CA TECHNOLOGIES; *pg.* 366, *pg.* 1168
CA IT CLIENT MANAGER - Software - CA TECHNOLOGIES; *pg.* 366, *pg.* 1168
CA IT INVENTORY MANAGER - Software - CA TECHNOLOGIES; *pg.* 366, *pg.* 1168
CA IT PROCESS AUTOMATION MANAGER - Software - CA TECHNOLOGIES; *pg.* 366, *pg.* 1168
CA JARS RESOURCE ACCOUNTING - Software - CA TECHNOLOGIES; *pg.* 366, *pg.* 1168
CA JCLCHECK WORKLOAD AUTOMATION - Software - CA TECHNOLOGIES; *pg.* 366, *pg.* 1168
CA JMR - Software - CA TECHNOLOGIES; *pg.* 366, *pg.* 1168
CA JOB MANAGEMENT FOR OPENVMS - Software - CA TECHNOLOGIES; *pg.* 366, *pg.* 1168
CA JOBTRAC JOB MANAGEMENT - Software - CA TECHNOLOGIES; *pg.* 366, *pg.* 1168
CA LIBRARIAN - Software - CA TECHNOLOGIES; *pg.* 366, *pg.* 1168
CA LOG ANALYZER - Software - CA TECHNOLOGIES; *pg.* 366, *pg.* 1168
CA LOGCOMPRESS - Software - CA TECHNOLOGIES; *pg.* 366, *pg.* 1168
CA MERGE/MODIFY - Software - CA TECHNOLOGIES; *pg.* 366, *pg.* 1168
CA MESSAGE MANAGER - Software - CA TECHNOLOGIES; *pg.* 366, *pg.* 1168
CA MICS RESOURCE MANAGEMENT - Software - CA TECHNOLOGIES; *pg.* 366, *pg.* 1168
CA MIGRATE COBOL - Software - CA TECHNOLOGIES; *pg.* 366, *pg.* 1168
CA MIM RESOURCE SHARING - Software - CA TECHNOLOGIES; *pg.* 366, *pg.* 1168
CA MOBILE DEVICE MANAGEMENT - Software - CA TECHNOLOGIES; *pg.* 366, *pg.* 1168
CA NETCOMPRESS DATA STREAM COMPRESSION - Software - CA TECHNOLOGIES; *pg.* 366, *pg.* 1168
CA NETMAN - Software - CA TECHNOLOGIES; *pg.* 366, *pg.* 1168
CA NETMASTER FILE TRANSFER MANAGEMENT - Software - CA TECHNOLOGIES; *pg.* 366, *pg.* 1168
CA NETMASTER NETWORK MANAGEMENT - Software - CA TECHNOLOGIES; *pg.* 366, *pg.* 1168
CA NETSPY NETWORK PERFORMANCE - Software - CA TECHNOLOGIES; *pg.* 366, *pg.* 1168
CA NETVIZ - Software - CA TECHNOLOGIES; *pg.* 366, *pg.* 1168
CA NSM - Software - CA TECHNOLOGIES; *pg.* 366, *pg.* 1168
CA OPERA - Software - CA TECHNOLOGIES; *pg.* 366, *pg.* 1168
CA OPTIMIZER/II - Software - CA TECHNOLOGIES; *pg.* 366, *pg.* 1168
CA OUTPUT MANAGEMENT WEB VIEWER - Software - CA TECHNOLOGIES; *pg.* 366, *pg.* 1168
CA PANAPT - Software - CA TECHNOLOGIES; *pg.* 366, *pg.* 1168
CA PANAUDIT PLUS - Software - CA TECHNOLOGIES; *pg.* 366, *pg.* 1168
CA PANEXEC - Software - CA TECHNOLOGIES; *pg.* 366, *pg.* 1168
CA PANVALET - Software - CA TECHNOLOGIES; *pg.* 366, *pg.* 1168
CA PARTITION EXPERT - Software - CA TECHNOLOGIES; *pg.* 366, *pg.* 1168
CA PATCH MANAGER - Software - CA TECHNOLOGIES; *pg.* 366, *pg.* 1168
CA PDSMAN PDS LIBRARY MANAGEMENT - Software - CA TECHNOLOGIES; *pg.* 366, *pg.* 1168
CA PLAN ANALYZER - Software - CA TECHNOLOGIES; *pg.* 366, *pg.* 1168
CA PLEX - Software - CA TECHNOLOGIES; *pg.* 366, *pg.* 1168
CA PMA CHARGEBACK - Software - CA TECHNOLOGIES; *pg.* 366, *pg.* 1168
CA PMO RUNTIME PERFORMANCE OPTIMIZER - Software - CA TECHNOLOGIES; *pg.* 366, *pg.* 1168
CA QUICKFETCH RUNTIME PERFORMANCE OPTIMIZER - Software - CA TECHNOLOGIES; *pg.* 366, *pg.* 1168
CA RAMIS - Software - CA TECHNOLOGIES; *pg.* 366, *pg.* 1168
CA RAPID REORG - Software - CA TECHNOLOGIES; *pg.* 366, *pg.* 1168
CA RAPS - Software - CA TECHNOLOGIES; *pg.* 366, *pg.* 1168
CA RC/COMPARE - Software - CA TECHNOLOGIES; *pg.* 366, *pg.* 1168
CA RC/EXTRACT - Software - CA TECHNOLOGIES; *pg.* 366, *pg.* 1168
CA RC/MIGRATOR - Software - CA TECHNOLOGIES; *pg.* 366, *pg.* 1168
CA RC/QUERY - Software - CA TECHNOLOGIES; *pg.* 366, *pg.* 1168
CA RC/SECURE - Software - CA TECHNOLOGIES; *pg.* 366, *pg.* 1168
CA RC/UPDATE - Software - CA TECHNOLOGIES; *pg.* 366, *pg.* 1168
CA RECORDS MANAGER - Software - CA TECHNOLOGIES; *pg.* 366, *pg.* 1168
CA RECOVERY ANALYZER - Software - CA TECHNOLOGIES; *pg.* 366, *pg.* 1168
CA REMOTE CONSOLE - Software - CA TECHNOLOGIES; *pg.* 366, *pg.* 1168
CA REMOTE CONTROL - Software - CA TECHNOLOGIES; *pg.* 366, *pg.* 1168
CA REPORT FACILITY - Software - CA TECHNOLOGIES; *pg.* 366, *pg.* 1168
CA RUGATE - Wine - LAIRD & COMPANY, INC.; *pg.* 1966, *pg.* 1119
CA SAN DESIGNER - Software - CA TECHNOLOGIES; *pg.* 366, *pg.* 1168
CA SAN MANAGER - Software - CA TECHNOLOGIES; *pg.* 366, *pg.* 1168
CA SCHEDULER JOB MANAGEMENT - Software - CA TECHNOLOGIES; *pg.* 366, *pg.* 1168
CA SCHEDULER JOB MANAGEMENT FOR Z/VSE - Software - CA TECHNOLOGIES; *pg.* 366, *pg.* 1168
CA SECURITY COMMAND CENTER - Software - CA TECHNOLOGIES; *pg.* 366, *pg.* 1168
CA SERVICE ACCOUNTING - Software - CA TECHNOLOGIES; *pg.* 366, *pg.* 1168
CA SITEMINDER - Software - CA TECHNOLOGIES; *pg.* 366, *pg.* 1168
CA SMF DIRECTOR - Software - CA TECHNOLOGIES; *pg.* 366, *pg.* 1168
CA SMR - Software - CA TECHNOLOGIES; *pg.* 366, *pg.* 1168
CA SOA SECURITY MANAGER - Software - CA TECHNOLOGIES; *pg.* 366, *pg.* 1168
CA SOFTWARE CHANGE MANAGER - Software - CA TECHNOLOGIES; *pg.* 366, *pg.* 1168
CA SOFTWARE COMPLIANCE MANAGER - Software - CA TECHNOLOGIES; *pg.* 366, *pg.* 1168

CA SOLVE:ACCESS SESSION MANAGEMENT - Software - CA TECHNOLOGIES; *pg.* 366, *pg.* 1168
CA UNICENTER TNG - Software Product - CLARY CORPORATION; *pg.* 226, *pg.* 150
CA VA? - Educational Materials - SCHOLASTIC INC.; *pg.* 1683, *pg.* 1288
CAB-1 - Toy Train - LIONEL LLC; *pg.* 961, *pg.* 875
CAB 3 - Cable Marking System - PASS & SEYMOUR/LEGRAND; *pg.* 1303, *pg.* 1344
CAB AIR SUSPENSION - COE Cab Suspension - PETERBILT MOTORS CO.; *pg.* 188, *pg.* 1691
CAB-O-JET - Inkjet Colorant - CABOT CORPORATION; *pg.* 1151, *pg.* 792
CAB-O-SIL - Chemical Product - CABOT CORPORATION; *pg.* 1151, *pg.* 792
CAB-O-SIL - Chemical Product - MILLER-STEPHENSON CHEMICAL COMPANY, INC.; *pg.* 1172, *pg.* 344
CAB-O-SIL - Bonding Compound - SMOOTH-ON INC.; *pg.* 111, *pg.* 1528
CAB-O-SPERSE - Chemical Product - CABOT CORPORATION; *pg.* 1151, *pg.* 792
CABA WIN - Software - GE ENERGY; *pg.* 1338, *pg.* 506
CABALLERO - Lighting Product - QUOIZEL INC.; *pg.* 1304, *pg.* 1616
CABANA - Rug - COURISTAN INC.; *pg.* 921, *pg.* 1067
CABANA - Snack Food Product - HANOVER FOODS CORPORATION; *pg.* 861, *pg.* 1535
CABANA - Carpet - INTERFACE, INC.; *pg.* 695, *pg.* 512
CABANA - Eyewear - MAUI JIM, INC.; *pg.* 9, *pg.* 651
CABANA - Fabric - NEMSCHOFF, INC.; *pg.* 936, *pg.* 1890
CABARET - Table - BLATT BOWLING & BILLIARD CORP.; *pg.* 1827, *pg.* 1203
CABARET - Footwear - CAPEZIO BALLET MAKERS INC.; *pg.* 1805, *pg.* 1125
CABARET - Furniture - JASPER GROUP; *pg.* 930, *pg.* 691
CABELA'S CLUB - Loyalty Program - CABELA'S INCORPORATED; *pg.* 535, *pg.* 1019
CABELEC - Chemical Product - CABOT CORPORATION; *pg.* 1151, *pg.* 792
CABERNET FRANC - Wine - BILTMORE ESTATE WINE COMPANY; *pg.* 1958, *pg.* 1358
CABIN CRAFTS - Carpets - SHAW INDUSTRIES GROUP, INC.; *pg.* 942, *pg.* 530
CABIN IN THE WOODS - Lace Curtain - HERITAGE LACE INC.; *pg.* 694, *pg.* 711
CABINET MAID - Cabinet Organizers - CLOSETMAID CORPORATION; *pg.* 920, *pg.* 452
CABINETMATE - Surge Protector - WIREMOLD/LEGRAND; *pg.* 689, *pg.* 383
CABLE ANALYZER - Software System - MENTOR GRAPHICS CORPORATION; *pg.* 432, *pg.* 1510
CABLE BALLET - Women's Clothing & Accessories - WOODEN SHIPS OF HOBOKEN; *pg.* 35, *pg.* 1315
CABLE BUTTON - Women's Clothing & Accessories - WOODEN SHIPS OF HOBOKEN; *pg.* 35, *pg.* 1315
CABLE CAGE - Jewelry - YURMAN DESIGN, INC.; *pg.* 15, *pg.* 1316
CABLE CAR - Bakery Products - ALPHA BAKING COMPANY; *pg.* 836, *pg.* 564
CABLE CAR CASH - Video Game - INTERNATIONAL GAME TECHNOLOGY; *pg.* 957, *pg.* 1024
CABLE GUARD - Cable - COMMSCOPE, INC.; *pg.* 278, *pg.* 1378
CABLE GUIDE - Magazine - TV GUIDE MAGAZINE GROUP, INC.; *pg.* 1697, *pg.* 1305
CABLE KEEPER - Worktools - STEELCASE INC.; *pg.* 475, *pg.* 889
CABLE KIDS - Cup - YURMAN DESIGN, INC.; *pg.* 15, *pg.* 1316
CABLE KNIT - Ear Warmer - 180S, LLC; *pg.* 1824, *pg.* 754
CABLE MANAGER - Worktools - STEELCASE INC.; *pg.* 475, *pg.* 889
CABLE RINGS - Computer Support Worktools - STEELCASE INC.; *pg.* 475, *pg.* 889
CABLE SPOOL - Computer Support Worktools - STEELCASE INC.; *pg.* 475, *pg.* 889
CABLE STATION - Software System - MENTOR GRAPHICS CORPORATION; *pg.* 432, *pg.* 1510
CABLE V-NECK - Women's Clothing & Accessories - WOODEN SHIPS OF HOBOKEN; *pg.* 35, *pg.* 1315
CABLE YOKE - Women's Clothing & Accessories - WOODEN SHIPS OF HOBOKEN; *pg.* 35, *pg.* 1315
CABLEACCESS - Wall Mount Cabinet - PANDUIT CORP.; *pg.* 661, *pg.* 663
CABLECRAFT - Control Products - TUTHILL CORPORATION; *pg.* 1385, *pg.* 561
CABLEGUARD - Bridge Product - THE D.S. BROWN COMPANY; *pg.* 79, *pg.* 1468
CABLEJET - System for Installing Fiber Optic Cable - SHERMAN & REILLY, INC.; *pg.* 1062, *pg.* 1629
CABLELABS - Cable - ARRIS GROUP, INC.; *pg.* 353, *pg.* 541
CABLEMATE - Cord Control - WIREMOLD/LEGRAND; *pg.* 689, *pg.* 383
CABLEMATIC - Cable - THE RIPLEY COMPANY; *pg.* 1305, *pg.* 342
CABLEMEDEA - Software - BROADCOM CORPORATION; *pg.* 364, *pg.* 108
CABLEOPTICS - AM & FM Fibre Optic Equipment - MOTOROLA CANADA LIMITED; *pg.* 657, *pg.* 1924
CABLEPRO - Automotive Inline Fuse - LITTELFUSE, INC.; *pg.* 1301, *pg.* 580
CABLESMART - Nonmetallic Raceway - WIREMOLD/LEGRAND; *pg.* 689, *pg.* 383
CABLESPAN - Cable System - TELLABS, INC.; *pg.* 678, *pg.* 637
CABLEWARE - Hardware - LOOS & COMPANY, INC.; *pg.* 1356, *pg.* 368
CABLEXCHANGE - Software - BROADCOM CORPORATION; *pg.* 364, *pg.* 108
CABLOFIL - Wiring System - WIREMOLD/LEGRAND; *pg.* 689, *pg.* 383
CABMATIC - Train Control System - ALSTOM SIGNALING, INC.; *pg.* 1312, *pg.* 1350
CABO - Carpet - BEAULIEU GROUP, LLC; *pg.* 917, *pg.* 529
CABO DE HORNOS - Wine - SHAW ROSS INTERNATIONAL IMPORTERS; *pg.* 1970, *pg.* 449
CABO STRIPE - Rug - COURISTAN INC.; *pg.* 921, *pg.* 1067
CABOOSE PLUS - Fabric - NEMSCHOFF, INC.; *pg.* 936, *pg.* 1890
CABOSIL - Powder Feeder - HYER INDUSTRIES INC.; *pg.* 1051, *pg.* 841
CABOT - Dairy Products - AGRI-MARK, INC.; *pg.* 1012, *pg.* 833
CABOT - Chemical Product - CABOT CORPORATION; *pg.* 1151, *pg.* 792
CABOT MICROELECTRONICS - Polishing Compounds - CABOT MICROELECTRONICS CORPORATION; *pg.* 1151, *pg.* 554
CABRIO - Steam Dryer - WHIRLPOOL CORPORATION; *pg.* 62, *pg.* 872
CABRIOLE - Flooring Product - ROSCO LABORATORIES, INC.; *pg.* 1782, *pg.* 378
CAC PRODUCTS - Well Control Systems - WEATHERFORD PRODUCTION OPTIMIZATION; *pg.* 987, *pg.* 1725
CACAO RESERVE BY HERSHEY'S - Roasted Cacao Beans - THE HERSHEY CO.; *pg.* 1855, *pg.* 1538
CACHAREL - Apparel - HANESBRANDS INC.; *pg.* 26, *pg.* 1394
CACHE-FORWARD - Software - PROGRESS SOFTWARE CORPORATION; *pg.* 457, *pg.* 786
CACHE LOGIC - Integrated Circuit Chips - ATMEL CORPORATION; *pg.* 621, *pg.* 238
CACHE VALLEY - Dairy Product - DAIRY FARMERS OF AMERICA, INC.; *pg.* 851, *pg.* 982
CACHEMIRE - Consumer Products - AKZO NOBEL; *pg.* 1439, *pg.* 1952
CACHET - Bath Product - KOHLER CO.; *pg.* 91, *pg.* 1862
CACHET - Fragrance - PARFUMS DE COEUR LTD.; *pg.* 519, *pg.* 376
CACHET - Office Furniture - STEELCASE INC.; *pg.* 475, *pg.* 889
CACHET STACK - Multi-purpose Seating - STEELCASE INC.; *pg.* 475, *pg.* 889
CACI - Systems, Software & Simulation Consulting Services - CACI INTERNATIONAL INC.; *pg.* 367, *pg.* 1773
CACIHEALTH - HIPAA Compliance Methodology - CACI INTERNATIONAL INC.; *pg.* 367, *pg.* 1773
CACIQUE - Apparel - ASCENA RETAIL GROUP, INC.; *pg.* 18, *pg.* 1081
CACIQUE - Lingerie - LANE BRYANT; *pg.* 1776, *pg.* 1441
CACTAS - Software - DESPATCH INDUSTRIES; *pg.* 1070, *pg.* 927
CACTUS - Apparel - OAKLEY, INC.; *pg.* 1840, *pg.* 86
CACTUS BLOSSOM - Appetizers - TEXAS ROADHOUSE, INC.; *pg.* 1753, *pg.* 738
CACTUS CONTROL - Bicycle Accessories - SPECIALIZED BICYCLE COMPONENTS, INC.; *pg.* 1711, *pg.* 152
CACTUS FLOWER - Video Game - INTERNATIONAL GAME TECHNOLOGY; *pg.* 957, *pg.* 1024
CACTUS MASTER - Bicycle Accessories - SPECIALIZED BICYCLE COMPONENTS, INC.; *pg.* 1711, *pg.* 152
CAD BLOCKS - CAD Drawings on CD ROM & Print - THOMAS REGISTER OF AMERICAN MANUFACTURERS; *pg.* 1692, *pg.* 1299
CAD-CONNECT - Software - PANDUIT CORP.; *pg.* 661, *pg.* 663
CADABRA - Software - SYNOPSYS, INC.; *pg.* 480, *pg.* 162
CADANT - Cable - ARRIS GROUP, INC.; *pg.* 353, *pg.* 541
CADBURY - Chocolates - MONDELEZ INTERNATIONAL, INC.; *pg.* 878, *pg.* 601
CADBURY CREME EGG - Chocolate - MONDELEZ INTERNATIONAL, INC.; *pg.* 878, *pg.* 601
CADBURY DAIRY MILK - Milk Chocolate - MONDELEZ INTERNATIONAL, INC.; *pg.* 878, *pg.* 601
CADBURY ECLAIRS - Chocolates - MONDELEZ INTERNATIONAL, INC.; *pg.* 878, *pg.* 601
CADD - Drug Delivery System - SMITHS MEDICAL MD, INC.; *pg.* 1594, *pg.* 963
CADD-LEGACY - Drug Delivery Systems - SMITHS MEDICAL MD, INC.; *pg.* 1594, *pg.* 963
CADD-MICRO - Drug Delivery Systems - SMITHS MEDICAL MD, INC.; *pg.* 1594, *pg.* 963
CADD-PCA - Drug Delivery Systems - SMITHS MEDICAL MD, INC.; *pg.* 1594, *pg.* 963
CADD-PLUS - Drug Delivery Systems - SMITHS MEDICAL MD, INC.; *pg.* 1594, *pg.* 963
CADD-PRIZM - Drug Delivery Systems - SMITHS MEDICAL MD, INC.; *pg.* 1594, *pg.* 963
CADD TPN - Drug Delivery Systems - SMITHS MEDICAL MD, INC.; *pg.* 1594, *pg.* 963
CADDIE - Electrical Grill - W.C. BRADLEY CO.; *pg.* 62, *pg.* 528
CADDIS - Pet Product - PETSMART, INC.; *pg.* 1481, *pg.* 18
CADDS 5I - Shipbuilding Solution - PARAMETRIC TECHNOLOGY CORPORATION; *pg.* 452, *pg.* 835
CADDY - Fastener - ERICO INTERNATIONAL CORPORATION; *pg.* 1335, *pg.* 1472
CADENCE - Clothing - ABERCROMBIE & FITCH CO.; *pg.* 37, *pg.* 1466
CADENCE - Film Resin - EASTMAN CHEMICAL COMPANY; *pg.* 1159, *pg.* 1636
CADENCE - Spreader - KALO, INC.; *pg.* 1796, *pg.* 719
CADENCE - Fabric - NEMSCHOFF, INC.; *pg.* 936, *pg.* 1890
CADENCE - Door Glass - ODL INCORPORATED; *pg.* 101, *pg.* 914
CADENZA - Fabric - NEMSCHOFF, INC.; *pg.* 936, *pg.* 1890
CADET - Knife - BUCK KNIVES, INC.; *pg.* 1828, *pg.* 550
CADET - Herbicides - FMC CORPORATION; *pg.* 1163, *pg.* 1564
CADET - Furniture - JASPER GROUP; *pg.* 930, *pg.* 691
CADET - Inspection Lighting System - UNILUX, INC.; *pg.* 682, *pg.* 1118
CADETTE - Beauty Product - COSMETIQUE, INC.; *pg.* 1765, *pg.* 664
CADEXTAN - Software - SUNGARD DATA SYSTEMS INC.; *pg.* 477, *pg.* 1592
CADFX - Medical Product - HOLOGIC, INC.; *pg.* 1416, *pg.* 784
CADILLAC - Automobile - GENERAL MOTORS COMPANY; *pg.* 175, *pg.* 881
CADILLAC SLS - Automobile - GENERAL MOTORS COMPANY; *pg.* 175, *pg.* 881
CADILLAC'S KIDS - Ticket Program - BUCCANEERS LIMITED PARTNERSHIP; *pg.* 534, *pg.* 471
CADIZ - Furniture - TELESCOPE CASUAL FURNITURE INC.; *pg.* 944, *pg.* 1162
CADOGAN GUIDES - Publishers of Travel Books - THE GLOBE PEQUOT PRESS, INC.; *pg.* 1645, *pg.* 350
CADPLAN PLUS - Treatment Planning Software - VARIAN MEDICAL SYSTEMS, INC.; *pg.* 1434, *pg.* 178
CADRE - VOC Emission System - CALGON CARBON CORPORATION; *pg.* 1151, *pg.* 1574
CADRE - Ceiling Panel - USG CORPORATION; *pg.* 118, *pg.* 594
CADUET - High Blood Pressure & Cholesterol Medication - PFIZER INC.; *pg.* 1581, *pg.* 1278
CADVUE - Software Solutions - ICAD, INC.; *pg.* 643, *pg.* 1037
CADWELD - Welded Electrical Connection - ERICO INTERNATIONAL CORPORATION; *pg.* 1335, *pg.* 1472
CADY - Hoist - COLUMBUS MCKINNON CORPORATION; *pg.* 1325, *pg.* 1138
CAE-ASTT - Simulation-Based System - CAE INC.; *pg.* 226, *pg.* 1959

CAE AVS - Aviation System - CAE INC.; *pg.* 226, *pg.* 1959
CAE C2-SIM - Geographic Information System - CAE INC.; *pg.* 226, *pg.* 1959
CAE DEPLOY - Decision Support Tool - CAE INC.; *pg.* 226, *pg.* 1959
CAE ENVISION - Simulation-Based Analysis - CAE INC.; *pg.* 226, *pg.* 1959
CAE GESI - Constructive Simulation System - CAE INC.; *pg.* 226, *pg.* 1959
CAE INFRONT 3D - Computer-Based Training System - CAE INC.; *pg.* 226, *pg.* 1959
CAE MAD - Magnetic Anomaly Detection System - CAE INC.; *pg.* 226, *pg.* 1959
CAE TRUE - Electric Motion System - CAE INC.; *pg.* 226, *pg.* 1959
CAECO DESIGNER - Software System - MENTOR GRAPHICS CORPORATION; *pg.* 432, *pg.* 1510
CAEDMON - Books - HARPERCOLLINS PUBLISHERS INC.; *pg.* 1647, *pg.* 1237
CAEFORM - Software System - MENTOR GRAPHICS CORPORATION; *pg.* 432, *pg.* 1510
CAELYX - Doxorubicin - MERCK & CO., INC.; *pg.* 1566, *pg.* 1077
CAESAR SALAD - Salad - KFC CORPORATION; *pg.* 1733, *pg.* 735
CAESAR WINGS - Chicken Wings - LITTLE CAESARS ENTERPRISES, INC.; *pg.* 1736, *pg.* 883
CAESARS - Casino - CAESARS ENTERTAINMENT CORPORATION; *pg.* 1083, *pg.* 1023
CAESAR'S - Tomato Based Beverages - LEADING BRANDS, INC.; *pg.* 1026, *pg.* 1911
CAESARS PALACE - Casino - CAESARS ENTERTAINMENT CORPORATION; *pg.* 1083, *pg.* 1023
CAESARS PALACE - Lottery Game - MASSACHUSETTS STATE LOTTERY; *pg.* 998, *pg.* 802
CAFE - Trays - CARLISLE FOODSERVICE PRODUCTS INCORPORATED; *pg.* 1455, *pg.* 1485
CAFE BA-BA-REEBA! - Spanish Restaurant - LETTUCE ENTERTAIN YOU ENTERPRISES, INC.; *pg.* 1735, *pg.* 580
CAFE BOUQUET - Flower Arrangement - 1-800-FLOWERS.COM, INC.; *pg.* 1758, *pg.* 1151
CAFE CARIBE - Coffee Product - COFFEE HOLDING CO., INC.; *pg.* 849, *pg.* 1343
CAFE CARMEL - Coffee - THE COFFEE BEANERY LTD.; *pg.* 849, *pg.* 886
CAFE CHICAGO - Restaurant - LEVY RESTAURANTS, INC.; *pg.* 1736, *pg.* 580
CAFE DEL REY - Restaurants - TAVISTOCK RESTAURANT GROUP; *pg.* 1753, *pg.* 803
CAFE DUET - Software - AMX CORPORATION; *pg.* 349, *pg.* 1735
CAFE ESTIMA BLEND - Coffee - STARBUCKS CORPORATION; *pg.* 897, *pg.* 1840
CAFE H - Food Product - HORMEL FOODS CORPORATION; *pg.* 863, *pg.* 915
CAFE KARUBA - Coffee - KWIK TRIP INC.; *pg.* 1026, *pg.* 1864
CAFE MULA - Game - WMS INDUSTRIES INC.; *pg.* 593, *pg.* 666
CAFE PTINR - Pharmaceutical Product - ALERE INC.; *pg.* 1488, *pg.* 849
CAFE SPAGGIA - Restaurant - LEVY RESTAURANTS, INC.; *pg.* 1736, *pg.* 580
CAFE SPECIAL - Coffee - COMMUNITY COFFEE COMPANY LLC; *pg.* 849, *pg.* 741
CAFE STEAMERS - Frozen Food - CONAGRA FOODS, INC.; *pg.* 826, *pg.* 1014
CAFE SUPREMO - Coffee Product - COFFEE HOLDING CO., INC.; *pg.* 849, *pg.* 1343
CAFE TOP - Women's Clothing & Accessories - WOODEN SHIPS OF HOBOKEN; *pg.* 35, *pg.* 1315
CAFE VERDE - Coffee - KEURIG GREEN MOUNTAIN, INC.; *pg.* 868, *pg.* 1768
CAFE VERMONT - Coffee - KEURIG GREEN MOUNTAIN, INC.; *pg.* 868, *pg.* 1768
CAFE ZU - Beverages - THE COCA-COLA COMPANY; *pg.* 240, *pg.* 493
CAFFE VERONA - Coffee - STARBUCKS CORPORATION; *pg.* 897, *pg.* 1840
CAFFEINE-FREE BARQ'S - Beverages - THE COCA-COLA COMPANY; *pg.* 240, *pg.* 493
CAFFEINE-FREE COCA-COLA - Beverages - THE COCA-COLA COMPANY; *pg.* 240, *pg.* 493
CAFFEINE-FREE COCA-COLA LIGHT - Beverages - THE COCA-COLA COMPANY; *pg.* 240, *pg.* 493
CAFFEINE-FREE DIET COKE - Beverages - THE COCA-COLA COMPANY; *pg.* 240, *pg.* 493
CAFFEINE FREE DIET PEPSI - Soft Drink - PEPSICO, INC.; *pg.* 259, *pg.* 1327
CAFFEINE FREE MOUNTAIN DEW - Soft Drink - PEPSICO, INC.; *pg.* 259, *pg.* 1327
CAFFEINE FREE PEPSI - Soft Drink - PEPSICO, INC.; *pg.* 259, *pg.* 1327
CAFFEINE FREE SKI - Soft Drink - DOUBLE-COLA CO.-USA; *pg.* 249, *pg.* 1629
CAFFREY'S - Beverages - MOLSON COORS BREWING COMPANY; *pg.* 256, *pg.* 321
CAFIS - Software - 3M; *pg.* 339, *pg.* 179
CAFSPRO - Fire Pumps - IDEX CORPORATION; *pg.* 1347, *pg.* 623
CAGE - Software - GLEASON CORPORATION; *pg.* 1340, *pg.* 1335
CAGE - Apparel - OAKLEY, INC.; *pg.* 1840, *pg.* 86
CAGE-KLENZ - Cage Wash Detergent - STERIS CORPORATION; *pg.* 1597, *pg.* 1464
CAGED - Footwear - STEVEN MADDEN, LTD.; *pg.* 1819, *pg.* 1176
CAGIVA - Motorcycle - HARLEY-DAVIDSON, INC.; *pg.* 178, *pg.* 1874
CAHP - Hemodialysis Dialyzer - BAXTER INTERNATIONAL INC.; *pg.* 1499, *pg.* 599
CAHTS - Heat Treating Control System - BODYCOTE THERMAL PROCESSING; *pg.* 71, *pg.* 632
CAICE - Visual Transportation Software - AUTODESK INC.; *pg.* 356, *pg.* 257
CAINE - Fabric - NEMSCHOFF, INC.; *pg.* 936, *pg.* 1890
CAINS - Mayonnaise - CAINS FOODS, L.P.; *pg.* 843, *pg.* 784
CAINS COUNTRY - Salad Dressing - CAINS FOODS, L.P.; *pg.* 843, *pg.* 784
CAIRE - Cryogenic Product - CHART INDUSTRIES, INC.; *pg.* 1405, *pg.* 1454
CAIRNS - Fire Helmet - MINE SAFETY APPLIANCES COMPANY; *pg.* 1361, *pg.* 1525
CAIROX - Chemical Product - CARUS CORPORATION; *pg.* 1152, *pg.* 652
CAIROX-CR - Potassium Permanganate - CARUS CORPORATION; *pg.* 1152, *pg.* 652
CAITLYN - Bedding - CROSCILL, INC.; *pg.* 1122, *pg.* 1220
CAJON - Cold Plate - LYTRON INCORPORATED; *pg.* 1074, *pg.* 861
CAJON - Plastic Tube - SWAGELOK COMPANY; *pg.* 1064, *pg.* 1473
CAJUN 15 BEAN SOUP - Soup - N.K. HURST CO., INC.; *pg.* 886, *pg.* 689
CAJUN CRAWTATOR - Potato Chip Flavor - ZAPP'S POTATO CHIPS, INC.; *pg.* 1864, *pg.* 743
CAJUN DILL - Potato Chip Flavor - ZAPP'S POTATO CHIPS, INC.; *pg.* 1864, *pg.* 743
CAJUN FIRE - Game - WMS INDUSTRIES INC.; *pg.* 593, *pg.* 666
CAJUN INJECTOR - Food Product - BRUCE FOODS CORPORATION; *pg.* 842, *pg.* 743
CAJUN KING - Seasoning Mixes - BRUCE FOODS CORPORATION; *pg.* 842, *pg.* 743
CAJUN LINE - Fishing Tackle - PURE FISHING, INC.; *pg.* 1843, *pg.* 1614
CAJUN SHRIMP - Nail Care Product - OPI PRODUCTS INC.; *pg.* 518, *pg.* 167
CAJUN STYLE - Poultry Product - PILGRIM'S PRIDE CORPORATION; *pg.* 889, *pg.* 330
CAKE PLATE - Flower Arrangement - 1-800-FLOWERS.COM, INC.; *pg.* 1758, *pg.* 1151
CAKE WALK - Video Game - INTERNATIONAL GAME TECHNOLOGY; *pg.* 957, *pg.* 1024
CAL - Activated Carbon Product - CALGON CARBON CORPORATION; *pg.* 1151, *pg.* 1574
CAL-ALERT - Electrical Test Instruments - ASSOCIATED RESEARCH INC.; *pg.* 1400, *pg.* 622
CAL-C-TOSE - Infant Health Care Product - MEAD JOHNSON NUTRITION COMPANY; *pg.* 1561, *pg.* 615
CAL-CHECK - Sensor - HUNTER ENGINEERING COMPANY; *pg.* 208, *pg.* 973
CAL/GANG - Software - SRA INTERNATIONAL, INC.; *pg.* 473, *pg.* 1780
CAL/MAG - Nutritional Supplement - NATURAL ORGANICS, INC.; *pg.* 1571, *pg.* 1181
CAL-MAINE FOODS - Eggs - CAL-MAINE FOODS, INC.; *pg.* 843, *pg.* 969
CAL-Q-CLUTCH - Business Case - BUXTON ACQUISITION CO., LLC; *pg.* 2, *pg.* 845
CAL-SEAL - Calcined Gypsum Plaster - USG CORPORATION; *pg.* 118, *pg.* 594
CAL-SMART - Detection System - MOCON, INC.; *pg.* 1363, *pg.* 940
CAL STAT - Skin Care Product - STERIS CORPORATION; *pg.* 1597, *pg.* 1464
CALA - Lamp - ASHLEY FURNITURE INDUSTRIES, INC.; *pg.* 914, *pg.* 1852
CALA - Supermarket - THE KROGER CO.; *pg.* 1025, *pg.* 1416
CALABASAS - Fabric - NEMSCHOFF, INC.; *pg.* 936, *pg.* 1890
CALADERA - Carpet - BEAULIEU GROUP, LLC; *pg.* 917, *pg.* 529
CALAGUALA - Hair & Skin Product - AUBREY ORGANICS INC.; *pg.* 499, *pg.* 470
CALAIS - Furniture - ASHLEY FURNITURE INDUSTRIES, INC.; *pg.* 914, *pg.* 1852
CALAIS - Fabric - NEMSCHOFF, INC.; *pg.* 936, *pg.* 1890
CALAL - Hair & Skin Product - AUBREY ORGANICS INC.; *pg.* 499, *pg.* 470
CALAN - Medicine - PFIZER INC.; *pg.* 1581, *pg.* 1278
CALAN SR - Pharmaceutical Product - PFIZER INC.; *pg.* 1581, *pg.* 1278
CALAS - Diagnostic Test Product - MERIDIAN BIOSCIENCE INC.; *pg.* 1422, *pg.* 1417
CALBOX - Software - CHYRONHEGO; *pg.* 371, *pg.* 1179
CALC - Software - ASPEN TECHNOLOGY, INC.; *pg.* 354, *pg.* 804
CALC U LOSS - Cable - COMMSCOPE, INC.; *pg.* 278, *pg.* 1378
CALCANEA - Medical Device - INTEGRA LIFESCIENCES HOLDINGS CORPORATION; *pg.* 1545, *pg.* 1109
CALCI-CHEW - Pharmaceutical Product - ALLERGAN; *pg.* 1490, *pg.* 1101
CALCI-MIX - Pharmaceutical Product - ALLERGAN; *pg.* 1490, *pg.* 1101
CALCIBIND - Supplement - MISSION PHARMACAL COMPANY INC.; *pg.* 1568, *pg.* 1742
CALCIFIBER - Nutritional Product - NUTRACEUTICAL INTERNATIONAL CORPORATION; *pg.* 1576, *pg.* 1753
CALCIGEN - Bone Cement - ZIMMER BIOMET HOLDINGS, INC.; *pg.* 1611, *pg.* 699
CALCIJEX - IV Drug for Bone Loss Disease - ABBOTT LABORATORIES; *pg.* 1484, *pg.* 551
CALCIKIDS - Health Care Product - HEALTH PRODUCTS CORPORATION; *pg.* 1540, *pg.* 1356
CALCILO XD - Pharmaceutical Products - ABBOTT LABORATORIES; *pg.* 1484, *pg.* 551
CALCILYTICS - Pharmaceutical - NPS PHARMACEUTICALS, INC.; *pg.* 1576, *pg.* 1043
CALCINATE - Polymer Product - CHEMTURA CORPORATION; *pg.* 1152, *pg.* 355
CALCIUM - Boost - JAMBA, INC.; *pg.* 1024, *pg.* 84
CALCIUM SHIELD - Strengtheners - ORLY INTERNATIONAL, INC.; *pg.* 518, *pg.* 137
CALCOLOR - Filter - ROSCO LABORATORIES, INC.; *pg.* 1782, *pg.* 378
CALCULATIONS THROUGH OPERATIONS - Healthcare Solutions - MULTISORB TECHNOLOGIES, INC.; *pg.* 1570, *pg.* 1150
CALCULITE - Recessed Lighting - LIGHTOLIER; *pg.* 1301, *pg.* 819
CALCULITE - Lighting - STEELCASE INC.; *pg.* 475, *pg.* 889
CALCULUS - Furniture - JASPER GROUP; *pg.* 930, *pg.* 691
CALCULUS - Fabric - NEMSCHOFF, INC.; *pg.* 936, *pg.* 1890
CALCUTTA - Rug - COURISTAN INC.; *pg.* 921, *pg.* 1067
CALDECOTT - Fabric - NEMSCHOFF, INC.; *pg.* 936, *pg.* 1890
CALDER RACE COURSE - Race Course - CHURCHILL DOWNS, INC.; *pg.* 540, *pg.* 733
CALEB'S KOLA - Craft Cola - PEPSICO, INC.; *pg.* 259, *pg.* 1327
CALEDONIA - Footwear - EASTLAND SHOE CORPORATION; *pg.* 1808, *pg.* 750
CALENDAR - Fabric - NEMSCHOFF, INC.; *pg.* 936, *pg.* 1890
CALENDER SIZE 2283 - Oxidized Corn Starch - PENFORD CORPORATION; *pg.* 1177, *pg.* 314
CALENDULA - Hair & Skin Product - AUBREY ORGANICS INC.; *pg.* 499, *pg.* 470
CALEY - Lamp - ASHLEY FURNITURE INDUSTRIES, INC.; *pg.* 914, *pg.* 1852
CALF COMPASS - Animal Nutritional Supplement -

HUBBARD FEEDS INC.; *pg.* 1477, *pg.* 928
CALF EZE - Animal Safety Product - NEOGEN CORPORATION; *pg.* 883, *pg.* 896
CALF-MANNA - Mixed Calf Food - MANNA PRO CORPORATION; *pg.* 1478, *pg.* 975
CALFGUARD - Veterinary Cattle Vaccine - PFIZER INC.; *pg.* 1581, *pg.* 1278
CALFIX - Surgical Instrument - OSTEOMED CORPORATION; *pg.* 1425, *pg.* 1658
CALFORMA - Dental Implant System - LIFECORE BIOMEDICAL, LLC; *pg.* 1556, *pg.* 920
CALGARY CARPET - Container Grown Plant - MONROVIA GROWERS; *pg.* 1797, *pg.* 44
THE CALGARY SUN - Publisher - THE CALGARY SUN; *pg.* 1625, *pg.* 1903
CALGO CARBON - Activated Carbon & Treatment - CALGON CARBON CORPORATION; *pg.* 1151, *pg.* 1574
CALGON - Water Softener - RECKITT BENCKISER INC.; *pg.* 1136, *pg.* 1105
CALI - Footwear - COBIAN CORP.; *pg.* 1806, *pg.* 253
CALIBAN - Fabric - SCALAMANDRE, INC.; *pg.* 941, *pg.* 1058
CALIBER - De-Icer - ARCHER-DANIELS-MIDLAND COMPANY; *pg.* 825, *pg.* 565
CALIBER - Hot Air Balloon Fabric - CAMERON BALLOONS U.S.; *pg.* 1829, *pg.* 884
CALIBER - Fabric - NEMSCHOFF, INC.; *pg.* 936, *pg.* 1890
CALIBER - Car Part Accessory - PRO-LINE, INC.; *pg.* 966, *pg.* 45
CALIBER 3 - Clostridia Vaccine - BOEHRINGER INGELHEIM VETMEDICA, INC.; *pg.* 1474, *pg.* 989
CALIBER-7 - Clostridia Vaccine - BOEHRINGER INGELHEIM VETMEDICA, INC.; *pg.* 1474, *pg.* 989
CALIBER DC - Dust Control - ARCHER-DANIELS-MIDLAND COMPANY; *pg.* 825, *pg.* 565
CALIBER SAFETY STRIPS - Fastener - POWERS FASTENERS INC.; *pg.* 1059, *pg.* 1143
CALIBRA - Dental Product - DENTSPLY INTERNATIONAL INC.; *pg.* 1522, *pg.* 1596
CALIBRATED - Business Forms - ENNIS, INC.; *pg.* 393, *pg.* 1727
CALIBRE - Resin - THE DOW CHEMICAL COMPANY; *pg.* 1157, *pg.* 898
CALIBRE - Software System - MENTOR GRAPHICS CORPORATION; *pg.* 432, *pg.* 1510
CALIBRE CB - Software System - MENTOR GRAPHICS CORPORATION; *pg.* 432, *pg.* 1510
CALIBRE DESIGNREV - Software System - MENTOR GRAPHICS CORPORATION; *pg.* 432, *pg.* 1510
CALIBRE DRC - Software System - MENTOR GRAPHICS CORPORATION; *pg.* 432, *pg.* 1510
CALIBRE DRC-H - Software System - MENTOR GRAPHICS CORPORATION; *pg.* 432, *pg.* 1510
CALIBRE FRACTUREH - Software System - MENTOR GRAPHICS CORPORATION; *pg.* 432, *pg.* 1510
CALIBRE FRACTUREJ - Software System - MENTOR GRAPHICS CORPORATION; *pg.* 432, *pg.* 1510
CALIBRE FRACTUREK - Software System - MENTOR GRAPHICS CORPORATION; *pg.* 432, *pg.* 1510
CALIBRE FRACTUREM - Software System - MENTOR GRAPHICS CORPORATION; *pg.* 432, *pg.* 1510
CALIBRE FRACTURET - Software System - MENTOR GRAPHICS CORPORATION; *pg.* 432, *pg.* 1510
CALIBRE FRACTUREV - Software System - MENTOR GRAPHICS CORPORATION; *pg.* 432, *pg.* 1510
CALIBRE INTERACTIVE - Software System - MENTOR GRAPHICS CORPORATION; *pg.* 432, *pg.* 1510
CALIBRE LFD - Software System - MENTOR GRAPHICS CORPORATION; *pg.* 432, *pg.* 1510
CALIBRE LITHOVIEW - Software System - MENTOR GRAPHICS CORPORATION; *pg.* 432, *pg.* 1510
CALIBRE LVS-H - Software System - MENTOR GRAPHICS CORPORATION; *pg.* 432, *pg.* 1510
CALIBRE MDP EMBEDDED SVRF - Software System - MENTOR GRAPHICS CORPORATION; *pg.* 432, *pg.* 1510
CALIBRE MDPMERGE - Software System - MENTOR GRAPHICS CORPORATION; *pg.* 432, *pg.* 1510
CALIBRE MDPSTAT - Software System - MENTOR GRAPHICS CORPORATION; *pg.* 432, *pg.* 1510
CALIBRE MDPVERIFY - Software System - MENTOR GRAPHICS CORPORATION; *pg.* 432, *pg.* 1510
CALIBRE MDPVIEW - Software System - MENTOR GRAPHICS CORPORATION; *pg.* 432, *pg.* 1510
CALIBRE MGC - Software System - MENTOR GRAPHICS CORPORATION; *pg.* 432, *pg.* 1510
CALIBRE MTFLEX - Software System - MENTOR GRAPHICS CORPORATION; *pg.* 432, *pg.* 1510
CALIBRE OPCPRO - Software System - MENTOR GRAPHICS CORPORATION; *pg.* 432, *pg.* 1510
CALIBRE OPCSBAR - Software System - MENTOR GRAPHICS CORPORATION; *pg.* 432, *pg.* 1510
CALIBRE OPCVERIFY - Software System - MENTOR GRAPHICS CORPORATION; *pg.* 432, *pg.* 1510
CALIBRE ORC - Software System - MENTOR GRAPHICS CORPORATION; *pg.* 432, *pg.* 1510
CALIBRE PRINTIMAGE - Software System - MENTOR GRAPHICS CORPORATION; *pg.* 432, *pg.* 1510
CALIBRE PSMCHECK - Software System - MENTOR GRAPHICS CORPORATION; *pg.* 432, *pg.* 1510
CALIBRE PSMGATE - Software System - MENTOR GRAPHICS CORPORATION; *pg.* 432, *pg.* 1510
CALIBRE RVE - Software System - MENTOR GRAPHICS CORPORATION; *pg.* 432, *pg.* 1510
CALIBRE TDOPC - Software System - MENTOR GRAPHICS CORPORATION; *pg.* 432, *pg.* 1510
CALIBRE VERIFICATION CENTER - Software System - MENTOR GRAPHICS CORPORATION; *pg.* 432, *pg.* 1510
CALIBRE WORKBENCH - Software System - MENTOR GRAPHICS CORPORATION; *pg.* 432, *pg.* 1510
CALIBRE XRC - Software System - MENTOR GRAPHICS CORPORATION; *pg.* 432, *pg.* 1510
CALICO - Health Focused Organization - ALPHABET INC.; *pg.* 347, *pg.* 153
CALIFLOW - Standard Flow Calibrator - MKS INSTRUMENTS, INC.; *pg.* 1362, *pg.* 781
CALIFONE - Educational Resources - SCHOOL SPECIALTY, INC.; *pg.* 467, *pg.* 1860
CALIFORNIA - Paints - CALIFORNIA PRODUCTS CORPORATION; *pg.* 1441, *pg.* 781
CALIFORNIA - Beverage - MONSTER BEVERAGE CORPORATION; *pg.* 257, *pg.* 69
CALIFORNIA AVOCADOS - Food Product - CALIFORNIA AVOCADO COMMISSION; *pg.* 135, *pg.* 108
CALIFORNIA CAFE - Restaurants - TAVISTOCK RESTAURANT GROUP; *pg.* 1753, *pg.* 803
CALIFORNIA CLUB MYSTERIES - Books - SCHOLASTIC INC.; *pg.* 1683, *pg.* 1288
CALIFORNIA DESIGN COLLEGE - Art School - EDUCATION MANAGEMENT CORPORATION; *pg.* 601, *pg.* 1575
CALIFORNIA DIARIES - Educational Materials - SCHOLASTIC INC.; *pg.* 1683, *pg.* 1288
CALIFORNIA DREAMER - Carpet - BEAULIEU GROUP, LLC; *pg.* 917, *pg.* 529
CALIFORNIA FRAMER - Hammer - VAUGHAN & BUSHNELL MANUFACTURING COMPANY, INC.; *pg.* 1066, *pg.* 616
CALIFORNIA GARDENER - Magazine - ARMSTRONG GARDEN CENTERS, INC.; *pg.* 1793, *pg.* 99
CALIFORNIA GOLDMINER - Sourdough Breads & Rolls - MAPLE LEAF FOODS INC.; *pg.* 875, *pg.* 1927
CALIFORNIA HOTEL & CASINO - Hotel & Casino - BOYD GAMING CORPORATION; *pg.* 1082, *pg.* 1022
CALIFORNIA INFLUENCE - Sportswear for Women & Children - KELLWOOD COMPANY; *pg.* 28, *pg.* 975
CALIFORNIA MARKETPLACE - Shopping & Dining Venue - KNOTT'S BERRY FARM; *pg.* 556, *pg.* 50
CALIFORNIA NATURAL - Food Product - HORMEL FOODS CORPORATION; *pg.* 863, *pg.* 915
CALIFORNIA PASTURES - Milk - COOPERATIVE REGIONS OF ORGANIC PRODUCER POOLS; *pg.* 850, *pg.* 1864
CALIFORNIA PIZZA KITCHEN - Pizza Segment - CALIFORNIA PIZZA KITCHEN INC.; *pg.* 1720, *pg.* 127
CALIFORNIA PIZZA KITCHEN - Frozen Pizza - NESTLE USA, INC.; *pg.* 883, *pg.* 96
CALIFORNIA RASPBERRY - Nail Care Product - OPI PRODUCTS INC.; *pg.* 518, *pg.* 167
CALIFORNIA SEA SALT - Salt - CARGILL LIMITED; *pg.* 1475, *pg.* 1914
THE CALIFORNIA SERIES - Homes - KB HOME; *pg.* 90, *pg.* 134
CALIFORNIA SPEEDWAY - Motorsports Facility - INTERNATIONAL SPEEDWAY CORPORATION; *pg.* 553, *pg.* 420
CALIFORNIA TI-COAT - Epoxy Primer - CALIFORNIA PRODUCTS CORPORATION; *pg.* 1441, *pg.* 781
CALIFORNIA'S GREAT AMERICA - Amusement Park - CEDAR FAIR, L.P.; *pg.* 537, *pg.* 1471
CALIFORNIA'S PREMIER PRIVATE AND BUSINESS BANK - Slogan - CITY NATIONAL CORPORATION; *pg.* 738, *pg.* 128
CALIPER ELAN - Overlay Control System - NANOMETRICS INCORPORATED; *pg.* 1423, *pg.* 147
CALIPER MOSAIC - Overlay Metrology System - NANOMETRICS INCORPORATED; *pg.* 1423, *pg.* 147
CALISSE - Skin Care Product - DYNATRONICS CORPORATION; *pg.* 1526, *pg.* 1757
CALISTO - Software - BROADCOM CORPORATION; *pg.* 364, *pg.* 108
CALK-IN - Bolt & Shield Anchor - POWERS FASTENERS INC.; *pg.* 1059, *pg.* 1143
CALK-SCREW - Specialty Nails - W.H. MAZE COMPANY; *pg.* 1389, *pg.* 652
CALL 1-800-FLOWERS - Floral Network - 1-800-FLOWERS.COM, INC.; *pg.* 1758, *pg.* 1151
CALL LOGIX - Telephone Call Management Services - AT&T SOUTHEAST; *pg.* 1868, *pg.* 489
CALL OF DUTY - Game - ACTIVISION BLIZZARD, INC.; *pg.* 948, *pg.* 271
CALL ON US - Slogan - AT&T SOUTHEAST; *pg.* 1868, *pg.* 489
CALL SCIENCES - Communication Product - J2 GLOBAL COMMUNICATIONS, INC.; *pg.* 1260, *pg.* 133
CALL STAT - Business Communications - SIEMENS CORPORATION; *pg.* 803, *pg.* 1291
CALLA - Casegoods - STEELCASE INC.; *pg.* 475, *pg.* 889
CALLAWAY - Furniture - JASPER GROUP; *pg.* 930, *pg.* 691
CALLAWAY COLLECTION - Golfing Accessories - CALLAWAY GOLF COMPANY; *pg.* 1829, *pg.* 58
CALLAWAY-CONNECT - Golfing Accessories - CALLAWAY GOLF COMPANY; *pg.* 1829, *pg.* 58
CALLAWAY GOLF - Apparel - PERRY ELLIS INTERNATIONAL, INC.; *pg.* 45, *pg.* 445
CALLAWAY GOLF PERFORMANCE CENTER - Center - CALLAWAY GOLF COMPANY; *pg.* 1829, *pg.* 58
CALLAWAY GOLF X SERIES - Glove - CALLAWAY GOLF COMPANY; *pg.* 1829, *pg.* 58
CALLAWAY PUTTERS - Line of Golf Putters - CALLAWAY GOLF COMPANY; *pg.* 1829, *pg.* 58
CALLAWAY YOUR WAY - Slogan - CALLAWAY GOLF COMPANY; *pg.* 1829, *pg.* 58
CALLE - Fabric - NEMSCHOFF, INC.; *pg.* 936, *pg.* 1890
CALLFINDER - Communication Product - MULTI-TECH SYSTEMS INC.; *pg.* 442, *pg.* 951
CALLIDUS TRUEANALYTICS - Software - CALLIDUS SOFTWARE INC.; *pg.* 368, *pg.* 183
CALLIGRAPHER - Software - BIO-RAD LABORATORIES, INC.; *pg.* 1504, *pg.* 101
CALLINGAREAINFO - Telecommunications Software - PITNEY BOWES SOFTWARE INC.; *pg.* 455, *pg.* 1346
CALLINGEST CALLS MADE - Slogan - BURNHAM BROTHERS, INC.; *pg.* 1829, *pg.* 1727
CALLMANAGER - Software - CISCO SYSTEMS, INC.; *pg.* 372, *pg.* 240
CALLMASTER - Telecommunication Product - AVAYA INC.; *pg.* 621, *pg.* 264
CALLOWAY - Furniture - LA-Z-BOY INCORPORATED; *pg.* 932, *pg.* 901
CALLTOUGH - Stainless Steel Products - CARPENTER TECHNOLOGY CORPORATION; *pg.* 73, *pg.* 1584
CALLUSAN CREME MOUSSE - Healthcare Product - MEDICOOL, INC.; *pg.* 1562, *pg.* 294
CALLVANTAGE - Software System - AT&T COMMUNICATIONS CORP.; *pg.* 1866, *pg.* 1043
C.A.L.M - Combating and Living with Youth Migraines - PFIZER INC.; *pg.* 1581, *pg.* 1278
CALM - Tea - STARBUCKS CORPORATION; *pg.* 897, *pg.* 1840
CALM TABLES - Tables - STEELCASE INC.; *pg.* 475, *pg.* 889
CALMADY - Wall Decor - ETHAN ALLEN INTERIORS INC.; *pg.* 924, *pg.* 343
CALMAG PLUS - Nutritional Care Product - LIFEPLUS INTERNATIONAL; *pg.* 1556, *pg.* 29
CALMATRIX - Dental Implant System - LIFECORE BIOMEDICAL, LLC; *pg.* 1556, *pg.* 920
CALMEDIA - Adsorbent - CALGON CARBON CORPORATION; *pg.* 1151, *pg.* 1574
CALMING COMPLEX - Skin Treatment - SHAKLEE CORPORATION; *pg.* 1593, *pg.* 184
CALMING TOUCH - Ethnobotanical Product - NU SKIN ENTERPRISES, INC.; *pg.* 518, *pg.* 1755
CALPACK - Robotic Product - HAMILTON CO., INC.; *pg.* 1415, *pg.* 1031
CALPHALON - Cookware - NEWELL RUBBERMAID INC.; *pg.* 1128, *pg.* 515
CALPHALON COMMERCIAL NON-STICK - Cookware -

First page reference indicates Business Class Edition
Second page reference indicates Geographic Edition

CALPHALON CORPORATION; *pg.* 1121, *pg.* 1470
CALPHALON COMMERCIAL TRI-PLY - Stainless Cookware - CALPHALON CORPORATION; *pg.* 1121, *pg.* 1470
CALPRO - Dairy Product - DAIRY FARMERS OF AMERICA, INC.; *pg.* 851, *pg.* 982
CALRES - Ion Exchange Resin - CALGON CARBON CORPORATION; *pg.* 1151, *pg.* 1574
CALROD - Electrical Resistance Heater - GENERAL ELECTRIC COMPANY; *pg.* 1297, *pg.* 347
CALSAN - Calcium Stearate Dispersion for use in the Paper Industry - PPG INDUSTRIES, INC.; *pg.* 1445, *pg.* 1579
CALSTAND - Calibrator - MKS INSTRUMENTS, INC.; *pg.* 1362, *pg.* 781
CALSTAR - Data Sheet - AMERICAN FELT & FILTER COMPANY; *pg.* 1312, *pg.* 1184
CALSURANCE - Insurance Package Program - BROWN & BROWN, INC.; *pg.* 1196, *pg.* 419
CALTAG - Molecular Biology Product - THERMO FISHER SCIENTIFIC INC.; *pg.* 1602, *pg.* 61
CALTAR LENSES - Large Format (View Camera) Lenses - CALUMET PHOTOGRAPHIC, INC.; *pg.* 1404, *pg.* 568
CALTEX - Oil Fuel - CHEVRON CORPORATION; *pg.* 974, *pg.* 259
CALTRAK - Tracking System - TRANSCAT, INC.; *pg.* 682, *pg.* 1337
CALTRATE - Nutritional Supplement - PFIZER INC.; *pg.* 1581, *pg.* 1278
CALUMET CAMERAS - View Cameras - CALUMET PHOTOGRAPHIC, INC.; *pg.* 1404, *pg.* 568
CALUMET LIGHT STANDS - Studio Lights Stands & Boom Assemblies - CALUMET PHOTOGRAPHIC, INC.; *pg.* 1404, *pg.* 568
CALVER - Chemical Reagent - HACH COMPANY; *pg.* 1415, *pg.* 334
CALVERT - Gin - JIM BEAM BRANDS CO.; *pg.* 1965, *pg.* 601
CALVERT EXTRA - Whiskey - JIM BEAM BRANDS CO.; *pg.* 1965, *pg.* 601
CALVET - Fabric - NEMSCHOFF, INC.; *pg.* 936, *pg.* 1890
CALVIN - Furniture - LA-Z-BOY INCORPORATED; *pg.* 932, *pg.* 901
CALVIN KLEIN - Apparel - G-III APPAREL GROUP, LTD.; *pg.* 41, *pg.* 1233
CALVIN KLEIN - Apparel - PVH CORP.; *pg.* 46, *pg.* 1283
CALVIN KLEIN SPORT - Men's, Women's & Juniors Apparel - CALVIN KLEIN, INC.; *pg.* 20, *pg.* 1209
CALVIN KLEIN UNDERWEAR - Men's Underwear - CALVIN KLEIN, INC.; *pg.* 20, *pg.* 1209
CALYPPSO - Footwear - STEVEN MADDEN, LTD.; *pg.* 1819, *pg.* 1176
CALYPSO - Packaged Foods - ATALANTA CORPORATION; *pg.* 838, *pg.* 1057
CALYPSO - Beverages - THE COCA-COLA COMPANY; *pg.* 240, *pg.* 493
CALYPSO - Dinnerware - THE HOMER LAUGHLIN CHINA COMPANY; *pg.* 1125, *pg.* 1850
CALYPSO - Fabric - NEMSCHOFF, INC.; *pg.* 936, *pg.* 1890
CALYPSO - Bicycle - TREK BICYCLE CORPORATION; *pg.* 1847, *pg.* 1896
CALYPSO - Furniture - TROPITONE FURNITURE CO., INC.; *pg.* 945, *pg.* 118
CALYPSO - Home Appliance Product - WHIRLPOOL CORPORATION; *pg.* 62, *pg.* 872
CALYPSO BREEZE - Blended Fruit Juice Drinks - CHIQUITA BRANDS INTERNATIONAL, INC.; *pg.* 847, *pg.* 1365
CALYPSO MAGIC - Video Game - INTERNATIONAL GAME TECHNOLOGY; *pg.* 957, *pg.* 1024
CALYX - Fabric - NEMSCHOFF, INC.; *pg.* 936, *pg.* 1890
CALYX & COROLLA - Bouquet - THE VERMONT TEDDY BEAR COMPANY; *pg.* 969, *pg.* 1767
CALZONE RING - Starter - MAZZIO'S CORPORATION; *pg.* 1737, *pg.* 1490
CALZONI S.R.L. - Ship Handling System - DANAHER CORPORATION; *pg.* 1044, *pg.* 397
CAM - Apparel - OAKLEY, INC.; *pg.* 1840, *pg.* 86
CAM-LOCK - Trimmer - HORNADY MANUFACTURING COMPANY; *pg.* 1836, *pg.* 1010
CAM-NOIR - Thermal Camera - ISC8; *pg.* 1350, *pg.* 71
CAM-O-FLAGE - Monofilament - CORTLAND LINE COMPANY; *pg.* 1831, *pg.* 1155
CAMA - Software - THOMSON REUTERS TAX & ACCOUNTING; *pg.* 484, *pg.* 905
CAMALOT - Outdoor Products - BLACK DIAMOND, INC.; *pg.* 1827, *pg.* 1756
CAMALOT - Dispensing Systems - SPEEDLINE TECHNOLOGIES, INC.; *pg.* 1378, *pg.* 823
CAMARILLO FIESTA - Container Grown Plant - MONROVIA GROWERS; *pg.* 1797, *pg.* 44
CAMAY - Personal & Beauty Product - THE PROCTER & GAMBLE COMPANY; *pg.* 1129, *pg.* 1418
CAMBER - Bath Product - KOHLER CO.; *pg.* 91, *pg.* 1862
CAMBERLEY HOMES - Wood & Building Material - WEYERHAEUSER COMPANY; *pg.* 121, *pg.* 1820
CAMBIA - Bath & Plumbing Product - JACUZZI BRANDS CORPORATION; *pg.* 554, *pg.* 65
CAMBIO - Teen Website - AOL INC.; *pg.* 1229, *pg.* 1195
CAMBO CAMERAS - View Cameras - CALUMET PHOTOGRAPHIC, INC.; *pg.* 1404, *pg.* 568
CAMBO STUDIO STANDS - Camera Supports for All Format Cameras - CALUMET PHOTOGRAPHIC, INC.; *pg.* 1404, *pg.* 568
CAMBON - Furniture - J. ROBERT SCOTT INC.; *pg.* 930, *pg.* 105
CAMBRIA - Community Name - WCI COMMUNITIES, INC.; *pg.* 1118, *pg.* 414
CAMBRIA - Motor Homes - WINNEBAGO INDUSTRIES, INC.; *pg.* 1712, *pg.* 707
CAMBRIA & TAYLOR - Hair Shampoo - MARIETTA HOSPITALITY; *pg.* 1464, *pg.* 1155
CAMBRIA SUITES - Hotels - CHOICE HOTELS INTERNATIONAL, INC.; *pg.* 1086, *pg.* 775
CAMBRIDGE - Apparel - BARCO UNIFORMS, INC.; *pg.* 19, *pg.* 94
CAMBRIDGE - Furniture - BASSETT FURNITURE INDUSTRIES, INCORPORATED; *pg.* 916, *pg.* 1776
CAMBRIDGE - Lectern - DA-LITE SCREEN COMPANY; *pg.* 632, *pg.* 698
CAMBRIDGE - Footwear - EASTLAND SHOE CORPORATION; *pg.* 1808, *pg.* 750
CAMBRIDGE - Decorative Accessory - ETHAN ALLEN INTERIORS INC.; *pg.* 924, *pg.* 343
CAMBRIDGE - Furniture - FLEXSTEEL INDUSTRIES, INC.; *pg.* 925, *pg.* 707
CAMBRIDGE - Outerwear - HABAND COMPANY, INC.; *pg.* 1772, *pg.* 1099
CAMBRIDGE - Dinnerware - THE HOMER LAUGHLIN CHINA COMPANY; *pg.* 1125, *pg.* 1850
CAMBRIDGE - Furniture - J. ROBERT SCOTT INC.; *pg.* 930, *pg.* 105
CAMBRIDGE - Furniture - JASPER GROUP; *pg.* 930, *pg.* 691
CAMBRIDGE - Office Furniture - JOFCO INC.; *pg.* 931, *pg.* 691
CAMBRIDGE - Cigarettes - PHILIP MORRIS USA INC.; *pg.* 1894, *pg.* 1803
CAMBRIDGE - Writing Pad - WESTROCK COMPANY; *pg.* 1472, *pg.* 1805
CAMBRIDGE BRASS - Brass Service - CAMBRIDGE BRASS; *pg.* 73, *pg.* 1919
CAMBRIDGESOUNDWORKS.COM - Website - CAMBRIDGE SOUNDWORKS, INC.; *pg.* 1234, *pg.* 781
CAMCAD - Software System - MENTOR GRAPHICS CORPORATION; *pg.* 432, *pg.* 1510
CAMCAD GRAPHIC 4.5 - Software System - MENTOR GRAPHICS CORPORATION; *pg.* 432, *pg.* 1510
CAMCAD PCB TRANSLATOR 4.5 - Software System - MENTOR GRAPHICS CORPORATION; *pg.* 432, *pg.* 1510
CAMCAD PROFESSIONAL 4.5 - Software System - MENTOR GRAPHICS CORPORATION; *pg.* 432, *pg.* 1510
CAMCAD VISION 4.5 - Software System - MENTOR GRAPHICS CORPORATION; *pg.* 432, *pg.* 1510
CAMCAR - Fastening Systems - TEXTRON INC.; *pg.* 235, *pg.* 1607
CAMDEN - Table - BLATT BOWLING & BILLIARD CORP.; *pg.* 1827, *pg.* 1203
CAMDEN CREEK - Bakery Products - J&J SNACK FOODS CORPORATION; *pg.* 865, *pg.* 1107
CAMDEN TOO - Fabric - NEMSCHOFF, INC.; *pg.* 936, *pg.* 1890
CAMEL - Pillow & Throw - HERITAGE LACE INC.; *pg.* 694, *pg.* 711
CAMEL - Cigarette - REYNOLDS AMERICAN INC.; *pg.* 1894, *pg.* 1395
CAMELIA - Furniture - AMISCO INDUSTRIES LTD.; *pg.* 913, *pg.* 1958
CAMELOT - Bath Accessory - CROSCILL, INC.; *pg.* 1122, *pg.* 1220
CAMELOT - Wine - KENDALL-JACKSON WINE ESTATES, LTD.; *pg.* 1965, *pg.* 277
CAMELOT - Garage Door - MARTIN DOOR MANUFACTURING, INC.; *pg.* 96, *pg.* 1759
CAMELOT - Fabric - NEMSCHOFF, INC.; *pg.* 936, *pg.* 1890
CAMELOT - Fittings, Quick Connect for Hose & Pipe - SERFILCO, LTD.; *pg.* 1375, *pg.* 641
CAMEO - Table - BLATT BOWLING & BILLIARD CORP.; *pg.* 1827, *pg.* 1203
CAMEO - Linens - CHF INDUSTRIES, INC.; *pg.* 920, *pg.* 1211
CAMEO - Cleaner - CHURCH & DWIGHT CO., INC.; *pg.* 1153, *pg.* 1063
CAMEO - Software - CRESTRON ELECTRONICS INC.; *pg.* 631, *pg.* 1116
CAMEO - Footwear - EASTLAND SHOE CORPORATION; *pg.* 1808, *pg.* 750
CAMEO - Camera Support Accessory - EASTMAN KODAK COMPANY; *pg.* 1408, *pg.* 1333
CAMEO - Furniture - ETHAN ALLEN INTERIORS INC.; *pg.* 924, *pg.* 343
CAMEO - Syringe Filters - GE WATER & PROCESS TECHNOLOGIES; *pg.* 1339, *pg.* 1588
CAMEO - Laboratory Equipment - LECO CORPORATION; *pg.* 1355, *pg.* 906
CAMEO - Fabric - NEMSCHOFF, INC.; *pg.* 936, *pg.* 1890
CAMEO - Furniture - TRENDWAY CORPORATION; *pg.* 945, *pg.* 892
CAMERA 101 - Video Camera - DUKANE CORPORATION; *pg.* 634, *pg.* 658
CAMERA LINK - Machine Vision System - COGNEX CORPORATION; *pg.* 1406, *pg.* 834
CAMERA LINK - Computer Product - RADIANCE TECHNOLOGIES, INC.; *pg.* 1277, *pg.* 6
CAMERAMAN - Video Camera Control System - PARKERVISION, INC.; *pg.* 1426, *pg.* 434
CAMERAWASH - Wash - COMMERCIAL VEHICLE GROUP, INC.; *pg.* 203, *pg.* 1467
CAMERON - Clothing - ABERCROMBIE & FITCH CO.; *pg.* 37, *pg.* 1466
CAMERON - Shoes - ALLEN-EDMONDS SHOE CORP.; *pg.* 1804, *pg.* 1887
CAMERON - Furniture - AMISCO INDUSTRIES LTD.; *pg.* 913, *pg.* 1958
CAMERON - Office Chairs - BERNHARDT DESIGN; *pg.* 918, *pg.* 1381
CAMERON - Hot Air Balloons - CAMERON BALLOONS U.S.; *pg.* 1829, *pg.* 884
CAMERON - Footwear - EASTLAND SHOE CORPORATION; *pg.* 1808, *pg.* 750
CAMERON - Furniture - ETHAN ALLEN INTERIORS INC.; *pg.* 924, *pg.* 343
CAMERON - Pump - FLOWSERVE CORPORATION; *pg.* 82, *pg.* 1719
CAMERON - Hydraulic Chuck - SPEEDGRIP CHUCK, INC.; *pg.* 1377, *pg.* 677
CAMERONDC - Subsea Production System - CAMERON DRILLING & PRODUCTION SYSTEMS; *pg.* 1321, *pg.* 1702
CAMET - Catalyst - BASF CATALYSTS LLC; *pg.* 1148, *pg.* 1074
CAMI - Footwear - STEVEN MADDEN, LTD.; *pg.* 1819, *pg.* 1176
CAMILLA - Lighting - ETHAN ALLEN INTERIORS INC.; *pg.* 924, *pg.* 343
CAMILLE ALBANE - Hair Salon - DESSANGE INTERNATIONAL, INC.; *pg.* 506, *pg.* 787
CAMINO - Textiles - BERNHARDT DESIGN; *pg.* 918, *pg.* 1381
CAMINO - Medical Device - INTEGRA LIFESCIENCES HOLDINGS CORPORATION; *pg.* 1545, *pg.* 1109
CAMIO - Software - CHYRONHEGO; *pg.* 371, *pg.* 1179
CAMLOK - Hoist - COLUMBUS MCKINNON CORPORATION; *pg.* 1325, *pg.* 1138
CAMM - Alignment System Software - HUNTER ENGINEERING COMPANY; *pg.* 208, *pg.* 973
CAMMINI - Digital Camera - CSR; *pg.* 280, *pg.* 284
CAMO - Apparel - OAKLEY, INC.; *pg.* 1840, *pg.* 86
CAMO FORM - Protective Camouflage Wrap - MCNETT CORPORATION; *pg.* 1839, *pg.* 1817
CAMO-LIGHT - Flashlight - STREAMLIGHT INC.; *pg.* 1306, *pg.* 1527
CAMO VAT - Multi-Purpose Cravat - MCNETT CORPORATION; *pg.* 1839, *pg.* 1817
CAMOHIDE - Footwear - LACROSSE FOOTWEAR, INC.; *pg.* 1811, *pg.* 1503
CAMOMILE - Hair & Skin Product - AUBREY ORGANICS INC.; *pg.* 499, *pg.* 470

CAMORA - Footwear - STEVEN MADDEN, LTD.; *pg.* 1819, *pg.* 1176
CAMOUFLAGE - Paint & Coating - AERVOE INDUSTRIES INCORPORATED; *pg.* 1439, *pg.* 1021
CAMP AXE - Lightweight Axe - GERBER LEGENDARY BLADES; *pg.* 1834, *pg.* 1503
CAMP CARNIVAL - Cruise Line - CARNIVAL CRUISE LINES; *pg.* 1902, *pg.* 441
CAMP TRAILS - Backpacks - JOHNSON OUTDOORS INC.; *pg.* 1837, *pg.* 1888
CAMP ZONE - Summer Camp Program - NOBEL LEARNING COMMUNITIES, INC.; *pg.* 605, *pg.* 1593
CAMP4CASH - Video Game - INTERNATIONAL GAME TECHNOLOGY; *pg.* 957, *pg.* 1024
CAMPA CHEM - Powder & Liquid Deodorant; Toilet Tissue - THETFORD CORPORATION; *pg.* 337, *pg.* 867
CAMPAIGN - Herbicide - MONSANTO COMPANY; *pg.* 1173, *pg.* 999
CAMPAIGN ACCELERATOR ADVANCED - Marketing Tool - PREMIERE GLOBAL SERVICES, INC.; *pg.* 1275, *pg.* 518
CAMPAIGN ACCELERATOR PROFESSIONAL - Marketing Service - PREMIERE GLOBAL SERVICES, INC.; *pg.* 1275, *pg.* 518
CAMPANA - Carpet - INTERFACE, INC.; *pg.* 695, *pg.* 512
CAMPATH - Oncology - GENZYME CORPORATION; *pg.* 1534, *pg.* 808
CAMPATH - Pharmaceutical Product - MILLENNIUM: THE TAKEDA ONCOLOGY COMPANY; *pg.* 1568, *pg.* 809
CAMPBELL - Ethernet Product - VITESSE SEMICONDUCTOR CORPORATION; *pg.* 686, *pg.* 57
CAMPBELL-I - Semiconductor Solution - VITESSE SEMICONDUCTOR CORPORATION; *pg.* 686, *pg.* 57
CAMPBELLS - Toy Train - LIONEL LLC; *pg.* 961, *pg.* 875
CAMPBELL'S FOR LIFE - Food Product - CAMPBELL COMPANY OF CANADA LTD; *pg.* 844, *pg.* 1935
CAMPBELL'S GO - Soups - CAMPBELL SOUP COMPANY; *pg.* 844, *pg.* 1048
CAMPHO-PHENIQUE - Medicine - BAYER HEALTHCARE CONSUMER CARE DIVISION; *pg.* 1500, *pg.* 1087
THE CAMPING COMPANY - Tag Line - EXXEL OUTDOORS LLC; *pg.* 1833, *pg.* 311
CAMPTOSAR - Therapeutic Product - IDERA PHARMACEUTICALS, INC.; *pg.* 1543, *pg.* 808
CAMPTOSAR - Colorectal Cancer Medication - PFIZER INC.; *pg.* 1581, *pg.* 1278
CAMPUS LIFE - Magazine - CHRISTIANITY TODAY INTERNATIONAL; *pg.* 1627, *pg.* 561
CAMPUS STORE - Convenience Stores - THE PANTRY, INC.; *pg.* 1029, *pg.* 1360
CAMPUSERP - Software - HTC GLOBAL SERVICES INC.; *pg.* 409, *pg.* 911
CAMPUSLINK - Bus Transportation Service - GREYHOUND LINES, INC.; *pg.* 1910, *pg.* 1681
CAMPZEN - Testing - PERKINELMER, INC.; *pg.* 1426, *pg.* 853
CAMR - Image Data Management Software - BIOCLINICA, INC.; *pg.* 1506, *pg.* 1556
CAMRA - Software - SS&C TECHNOLOGIES HOLDINGS, INC.; *pg.* 473, *pg.* 386
CAMRA D CLASS - Software - SS&C TECHNOLOGIES HOLDINGS, INC.; *pg.* 473, *pg.* 386
CAMRY - Car - TOYOTA MOTOR NORTH AMERICA, INC.; *pg.* 192, *pg.* 1303
CAMRY HYBRID - Hybrid Car - TOYOTA MOTOR NORTH AMERICA, INC.; *pg.* 192, *pg.* 1303
CAMS - Comprehensive Account Management Services - HEALTH MANAGEMENT SYSTEMS, INC.; *pg.* 1540, *pg.* 1238
CAMTAP - Self Drilling Screws - ROBERTSON INC.; *pg.* 1372, *pg.* 1924
CAMTILE - Content Addressable Memory - INTEGRATED SILICON SOLUTION, INC.; *pg.* 645, *pg.* 145
CAN AVR - Technical Support Service - ATMEL CORPORATION; *pg.* 621, *pg.* 238
CAN-CAN - Footwear - CAPEZIO BALLET MAKERS INC.; *pg.* 1805, *pg.* 1125
CAN-DO - Medical & Aesthetic Product - DYNATRONICS CORPORATION; *pg.* 1526, *pg.* 1757
CAN GO - Comfort Set - HABAND COMPANY, INC.; *pg.* 1772, *pg.* 1099
CAN HAND'LER - Paint & Coating - AERVOE INDUSTRIES INCORPORATED; *pg.* 1439, *pg.* 1021
CAN KEY - Can Opener - BROWN & BIGELOW, INC.; *pg.* 1624, *pg.* 959
CAN MASTER - Can opener - LINCOLN FOODSERVICE PRODUCTS, LLC; *pg.* 1127, *pg.* 1432
CAN SLIM - Investment Research Tool - INVESTORS BUSINESS DAILY, INC.; *pg.* 1653, *pg.* 133
CANA - Lamp - ASHLEY FURNITURE INDUSTRIES, INC.; *pg.* 914, *pg.* 1852
CANADA DRY - Carbonated Soft Drink - DR PEPPER SNAPPLE GROUP, INC.; *pg.* 250, *pg.* 1729
CANADA'S WONDERLAND - Amusement Park - CEDAR FAIR, L.P.; *pg.* 537, *pg.* 1471
CANADEK - International Trade Forms - UNZ & COMPANY, INC.; *pg.* 1698, *pg.* 1084
CANADIAN - Beer - MOLSON COORS CANADA INC.; *pg.* 256, *pg.* 1955
CANADIAN ADDRESSER - Software - MELISSA DATA CORP.; *pg.* 432, *pg.* 188
CANADIAN CLUB - Whiskey - JIM BEAM BRANDS CO.; *pg.* 1965, *pg.* 601
CANADIAN GOLD - Whiskey - LAIRD & COMPANY, INC.; *pg.* 1966, *pg.* 1119
CANADIAN ICE - Beer - MOLSON COORS CANADA INC.; *pg.* 256, *pg.* 1955
CANADIAN INTER@CTIVE - Online Service Via the Internet - AIR CANADA; *pg.* 1896, *pg.* 1902
CANADIAN LIGHT - Low Calorie Beer - MOLSON COORS CANADA INC.; *pg.* 256, *pg.* 1955
CANADIAN LIVING - Publication Service - TRANSCONTINENTAL INC.; *pg.* 1695, *pg.* 1957
CANADIAN MIST - Blended Canadian Whiskey - BROWN-FORMAN CORPORATION; *pg.* 1958, *pg.* 732
CANADIAN PLUS - Frequent Flyer Program - AIR CANADA; *pg.* 1896, *pg.* 1902
CANADIAN RESERVE - Cheddar Cheese - AGROPUR COOPERATIVE; *pg.* 836, *pg.* 1950
CANADIAN SAILINGS - Shipping Publication - JOC GROUP INC.; *pg.* 1654, *pg.* 1096
CANADIAN SHUTTLE - Domestic Route Brand - AIR CANADA; *pg.* 1896, *pg.* 1902
CANADIAN SUPER V - Headwear - MINE SAFETY APPLIANCES COMPANY; *pg.* 1361, *pg.* 1525
CANADIAN TIRE COMMERCIAL LINK - Online Sales Service - CANADIAN TIRE CORPORATION LIMITED; *pg.* 202, *pg.* 1936
CANADIAN TIRE FOUNDATION FOR FAMILIES - Recreational Sport - CANADIAN TIRE CORPORATION LIMITED; *pg.* 202, *pg.* 1936
CANADIAN TIRE JUMPSTART - Charitable Program - CANADIAN TIRE CORPORATION LIMITED; *pg.* 202, *pg.* 1936
CANADIAN TIRE MONEY - Rewards Program - CANADIAN TIRE CORPORATION LIMITED; *pg.* 202, *pg.* 1936
CANADIAN WESTERN TRUST - Bank - CANADIAN WESTERN BANK; *pg.* 729, *pg.* 1906
CANADIAN WOODS - Whisky - MCCORMICK DISTILLING CO., INC.; *pg.* 1966, *pg.* 1007
CANADIAN.COM - Travel Website - LIVE CURRENT MEDIA INC.; *pg.* 1263, *pg.* 1911
CANADIZE - Coating - GENERAL MAGNAPLATE CORPORATION; *pg.* 1164, *pg.* 1079
CANALETTO - Restaurants - IL FORNAIO (AMERICA) CORPORATION; *pg.* 1731, *pg.* 70
CANALIGATOR - Motion Controller - PRO-DEX, INC.; *pg.* 1586, *pg.* 115
CANARY - Accessories - THE MEN'S WEARHOUSE, INC.; *pg.* 44, *pg.* 1711
CANASTA CALIENTE - Game - HASBRO, INC.; *pg.* 954, *pg.* 1603
CANCEL STAT - Anti-Static Fabrics - GUILFORD PERFORMANCE TEXTILES; *pg.* 693, *pg.* 1393
CANCELLATION - Software - CLEARONE COMMUNICATIONS, INC.; *pg.* 629, *pg.* 1756
CANCER EPIPANEL - Diagnostic Tool - SEQUENOM, INC.; *pg.* 1593, *pg.* 209
CANCER SCREENING & PREVENTION PROGRAM - Cancer Treatment - CITY OF HOPE NATIONAL MEDICAL CENTER; *pg.* 1516, *pg.* 77
CANCERPAGE.COM - Pharmaceutical Product - ALERE INC.; *pg.* 1488, *pg.* 849
CANCUN - Bath Product - KOHLER CO.; *pg.* 91, *pg.* 1862
CANDELA - Personal Care Electrical Product - HELEN OF TROY L.P.; *pg.* 511, *pg.* 1692
CANDELA - Optical Surface Analyzer - KLA-TENCOR CORPORATION; *pg.* 1353, *pg.* 146
CANDEREL - Sweetener - MERISANT COMPANY; *pg.* 876, *pg.* 581
CANDESCE - Paperboard Product - POTLATCH CORPORATION; *pg.* 1467, *pg.* 1844
CANDID - Furniture - JOFCO INC.; *pg.* 931, *pg.* 691
CANDID - Fabric - NEMSCHOFF, INC.; *pg.* 936, *pg.* 1890
CANDIDA FORTE - Nutritional Supplement - NATURAL ORGANICS, INC.; *pg.* 1571, *pg.* 1181
CANDIDNET - Online Customer Tools - CANDID COLOR SYSTEMS, INC.; *pg.* 1404, *pg.* 1485
CANDIGEN - Medical Test Product - BIOMERICA, INC.; *pg.* 1506, *pg.* 107
CANDIQUANT - Medical Test Product - BIOMERICA, INC.; *pg.* 1506, *pg.* 107
CANDISELECT - Software - BIO-RAD LABORATORIES, INC.; *pg.* 1504, *pg.* 101
CANDLE - Ornament - HERITAGE LACE INC.; *pg.* 694, *pg.* 711
CANDLE-LITE - Candles - LANCASTER COLONY CORPORATION; *pg.* 873, *pg.* 1441
CANDLES ON MY CAKE - Nail Care Product - OPI PRODUCTS INC.; *pg.* 518, *pg.* 167
CANDLESTICK - Lamp - J. ROBERT SCOTT INC.; *pg.* 930, *pg.* 105
CANDLEWOOD SUITES - Extended Stay Hotel - INTERCONTINENTAL HOTELS CORPORATION; *pg.* 1097, *pg.* 511
CANDRIL - Sheet Metal Screws - ROBERTSON INC.; *pg.* 1372, *pg.* 1924
CANDY CANE CASH - Lottery Game - THE SOUTH CAROLINA EDUCATION LOTTERY; *pg.* 1005, *pg.* 1614
CANDY CANE CHRISTMAS BOUQUET - Floral Bouquet - FTD GROUP, INC.; *pg.* 1795, *pg.* 608
CANDY CONE - Ornament - HERITAGE LACE INC.; *pg.* 694, *pg.* 711
CANDY FASHION - Porcelain Dolls - CHARISMA BRANDS, LLC; *pg.* 2, *pg.* 120
CANDY LAND - Game - HASBRO, INC.; *pg.* 954, *pg.* 1603
CANDY STRIPE - Brush - THE WOOSTER BRUSH COMPANY; *pg.* 1450, *pg.* 1482
CANDY WATCHES - Sweet Candy Digital Watches on Stretch Strings Covered with Candy Beads - SMARTIES CANDY COMPANY; *pg.* 1861, *pg.* 1127
CANDYCANE - Molecular Probe Product - THERMO FISHER SCIENTIFIC INC.; *pg.* 1602, *pg.* 61
CANE CLASSICS - Candy Canes - SPANGLER CANDY COMPANY; *pg.* 1862, *pg.* 1407
CANECREEK - Office Furniture - STEELCASE INC.; *pg.* 475, *pg.* 889
CANEXEL - Hardboard Siding - LOUISIANA-PACIFIC CORPORATION; *pg.* 94, *pg.* 1652
CANFIELD - Shoes - ALLEN-EDMONDS SHOE CORP.; *pg.* 1804, *pg.* 1887
CANFIELD - Brazing Alloys & Fluxes - KAYDON CORPORATION; *pg.* 1352, *pg.* 866
CANFOR - Forest Products - CANFOR CORPORATION; *pg.* 1454, *pg.* 1910
CANGENUS - Drug - EMERGENT BIOSOLUTIONS; *pg.* 1528, *pg.* 1914
CANGRELOR - Pharmaceutical Product - THE MEDICINES COMPANY; *pg.* 1561, *pg.* 1104
CANGUARD - Preservatives - THE DOW CHEMICAL COMPANY; *pg.* 1157, *pg.* 898
CANICA - Vertical Shaft Impact Crusher - TEREX CORPORATION; *pg.* 1381, *pg.* 384
CANIGOU - Food Product - MARS, INCORPORATED; *pg.* 1858, *pg.* 1792
CANILLA - Rice - GOYA FOODS, INC.; *pg.* 859, *pg.* 1075
CANINE - Dog Food - DESIGNING HEALTH, INC.; *pg.* 1523, *pg.* 299
CANINE CARRY OUTS - Pet Food - BIG HEART PET BRANDS; *pg.* 1474, *pg.* 213
CANINE CLUB - Dog Food - COSTCO WHOLESALE CORPORATION; *pg.* 1765, *pg.* 1820
CANINE ELEMENTS - Pet Supplies - PETSMART, INC.; *pg.* 1481, *pg.* 18
CANINE GOOD CITIZEN - Certification Program - AMERICAN KENNEL CLUB, INC.; *pg.* 129, *pg.* 1193
CANINE PLUS - Dog Food - MAPLE LEAF FOODS INC.; *pg.* 875, *pg.* 1927
CANLAN CLASSIC TOURNAMENTS - Recreational Hockey League - CANLAN ICE SPORTS CORPORATION; *pg.* 536, *pg.* 1907
CANLAN HOCKEY CAMPS - Recreational Hockey League - CANLAN ICE SPORTS CORPORATION; *pg.* 536, *pg.* 1907
CANLAN ICE SPORTS HOCKEY ACADEMY - Recreational Hockey League - CANLAN ICE SPORTS CORPORATION;

First page reference indicates Business Class Edition
Second page reference indicates Geographic Edition

pg. 536, *pg.* 1907
CANLAN ICE SPORTS SKATING ACADEMY - Recreational Hockey League - CANLAN ICE SPORTS CORPORATION; *pg.* 536, *pg.* 1907
CANLAN SPORTS CAMPS - Recreational Hockey League - CANLAN ICE SPORTS CORPORATION; *pg.* 536, *pg.* 1907
CANLYTE - Lighting Fixture & Control - PHILIPS LIGHTING; *pg.* 1303, *pg.* 806
CANMORE - Fabric - W.L. GORE & ASSOCIATES, INC.; *pg.* 122, *pg.* 388
CANNECK - Nozzle - NORDSON CORPORATION; *pg.* 1365, *pg.* 1480
CANNON - Apparel - ICONIX BRAND GROUP, INC.; *pg.* 26, *pg.* 1243
CANNON - Fishing Equipment - JOHNSON OUTDOORS INC.; *pg.* 1837, *pg.* 1888
CANNON BALL - Tobacco Product - AMERICAN SNUFF COMPANY; *pg.* 1893, *pg.* 1641
CANNONDALE - Shoes - ALLEN-EDMONDS SHOE CORP.; *pg.* 1804, *pg.* 1887
CANOE - Bath Bars & Bath Arms - CRAFTMADE INTERNATIONAL, INC.; *pg.* 1295, *pg.* 1670
CANOES - Eyewear - MAUI JIM, INC.; *pg.* 9, *pg.* 651
CANOIN - Candida Albicans Skin Test Antigen for Cellular Hypersensitivity - SANOFI PASTEUR, INC; *pg.* 1591, *pg.* 1588
CANOLA - Soy Oil - ARCHER-DANIELS-MIDLAND COMPANY; *pg.* 825, *pg.* 565
CANONDA - Furniture - J. ROBERT SCOTT INC.; *pg.* 930, *pg.* 105
CANONITA - Restaurants - TAVISTOCK RESTAURANT GROUP; *pg.* 1753, *pg.* 803
CANOPY - Herbicide - E.I. DU PONT DE NEMOURS & COMPANY; *pg.* 1159, *pg.* 390
CANOPY - Carpet - INTERFACE, INC.; *pg.* 695, *pg.* 512
CANOPY - Communications Product - MOTOROLA SOLUTIONS, INC.; *pg.* 657, *pg.* 659
CANOPY - Fabric - NEMSCHOFF, INC.; *pg.* 936, *pg.* 1890
CANOPY - Lighting - STEELCASE INC.; *pg.* 475, *pg.* 889
CANOPY - Home Decor - WAL-MART STORES, INC.; *pg.* 1790, *pg.* 29
CANSTRUT - Cable Tray Systems - THOMAS & BETTS CORPORATION; *pg.* 680, *pg.* 1646
CAN'T LOSE - Game - WMS INDUSTRIES INC.; *pg.* 593, *pg.* 666
CANTAB - Ingredient System - PENFORD CORPORATION; *pg.* 1177, *pg.* 314
CANTATA - Guest Chairs - BERNHARDT DESIGN; *pg.* 918, *pg.* 1381
CANTATA - Bath Product - KOHLER CO.; *pg.* 91, *pg.* 1862
CANTATA - Flatware - ONEIDA LTD; *pg.* 1129, *pg.* 1318
CANTEEN - Fabric - NEMSCHOFF, INC.; *pg.* 936, *pg.* 1890
CANTERBURY - Rug - COURISTAN INC.; *pg.* 921, *pg.* 1067
CANTERBURY - Bathroom Accessories - SYMMONS INDUSTRIES, INC.; *pg.* 114, *pg.* 803
CANTINA - Kitchen Product - KOHLER CO.; *pg.* 91, *pg.* 1862
CANTINA BURRITOS - Burritos - TACO BELL CORP.; *pg.* 1752, *pg.* 117
CANTO - Entertainment Lighting Product - BALLANTYNE STRONG, INC.; *pg.* 623, *pg.* 1013
CANTO - Office Furniture - STEELCASE INC.; *pg.* 475, *pg.* 889
CANVAS - Software - ACD SYSTEMS INTERNATIONAL INC.; *pg.* 340, *pg.* 1913
CANVAS CHELSEA - Hat - WOODEN SHIPS OF HOBOKEN; *pg.* 35, *pg.* 1315
CANVAS HOLLAND - Hat - WOODEN SHIPS OF HOBOKEN; *pg.* 35, *pg.* 1315
CANVAS ROMEO - Footwear - CAPEZIO BALLET MAKERS INC.; *pg.* 1805, *pg.* 1125
CANVEX - Film - RAVEN INDUSTRIES, INC.; *pg.* 1888, *pg.* 1625
CANVEYOR - Cable - LOOS & COMPANY, INC.; *pg.* 1356, *pg.* 368
CANWORKS - Spray Monitor System - NORDSON CORPORATION; *pg.* 1365, *pg.* 1480
CANYEN - Shoe - AEROGROUP INTERNATIONAL, INC.; *pg.* 1803, *pg.* 1055
CANYON - Bedcovering - ETHAN ALLEN INTERIORS INC.; *pg.* 924, *pg.* 343
CANYON - Pick-Up Truck - GENERAL MOTORS COMPANY; *pg.* 175, *pg.* 881
CANYON - Dinnerware - THE HOMER LAUGHLIN CHINA COMPANY; *pg.* 1125, *pg.* 1850
CANYON CUT - Snack Food Style - INVENTURE FOODS, INC.; *pg.* 1023, *pg.* 17
CANYON RIVER BLUES - Denim Apparel - SEARS HOLDINGS CORPORATION; *pg.* 1784, *pg.* 618
CANYON ROAD - Restaurant - ARK RESTAURANTS CORP.; *pg.* 1715, *pg.* 1196
CANYON ROAD - Table Wines - GEYSER PEAK WINERY; *pg.* 1964, *pg.* 101
CANZONE - Fabric - NEMSCHOFF, INC.; *pg.* 936, *pg.* 1890
CAP - Integrated Circuit - ATMEL CORPORATION; *pg.* 621, *pg.* 238
CAP-1000+ - Viscometer - BROOKFIELD ENGINEERING LABORATORIES, INC.; *pg.* 1403, *pg.* 833
CAP-2000+ - Viscometer - BROOKFIELD ENGINEERING LABORATORIES, INC.; *pg.* 1403, *pg.* 833
CAP CHECK - Electrical Test & Measurement - HD ELECTRIC COMPANY; *pg.* 1299, *pg.* 666
CAP CHECK I - Capacitor Tester - HD ELECTRIC COMPANY; *pg.* 1299, *pg.* 666
CAP CHECK II - Capacitor Tester - HD ELECTRIC COMPANY; *pg.* 1299, *pg.* 666
CAP CHECK III - Capacitor Tester - HD ELECTRIC COMPANY; *pg.* 1299, *pg.* 666
CAP GEMINI AMERICA - Computer Services - CAPGEMINI U.S.; *pg.* 368, *pg.* 1209
CAP RANGER - Resistor Product - OHMITE MANUFACTURING COMPANY; *pg.* 660, *pg.* 553
CAP-SAC - Packaging Product - GRAPHIC PACKAGING HOLDING COMPANY; *pg.* 1459, *pg.* 509
CAPA - Office Furniture - STEELCASE INC.; *pg.* 475, *pg.* 889
CAPABLE-TO-PROMISE - Software - ASPEN TECHNOLOGY, INC.; *pg.* 354, *pg.* 804
CAPACITY MANAGER FOR SQL SERVER - Software - DELL SOFTWARE; *pg.* 385, *pg.* 40
CAPASONIC - Switch - CAPSONIC GROUP LLC; *pg.* 1880, *pg.* 609
CAPCALC - Software - BROOKFIELD ENGINEERING LABORATORIES, INC.; *pg.* 1403, *pg.* 833
CAPCELLIA - Software - BIO-RAD LABORATORIES, INC.; *pg.* 1504, *pg.* 101
CAPD - Peritoneal Dialysis - BAXTER INTERNATIONAL INC.; *pg.* 1499, *pg.* 599
CAPE COD - Potato Chips - CAPE COD POTATO CHIP COMPANY; *pg.* 845, *pg.* 826
CAPE COD - Bath Product - KOHLER CO.; *pg.* 91, *pg.* 1862
CAPE COD - Fabric - NEMSCHOFF, INC.; *pg.* 936, *pg.* 1890
CAPE COD - Potato Chips - SNYDER'S-LANCE, INC.; *pg.* 896, *pg.* 1368
CAPE COD COLLECTION - Shoes - THE ALDEN SHOE COMPANY; *pg.* 1804, *pg.* 833
CAPE COD FIVE - Logo - CAPE COD FIVE CENTS SAVINGS BANK; *pg.* 730, *pg.* 840
CAPE COD SPORTSWEAR - Misses' & Women's Apparel - KELLWOOD COMPANY; *pg.* 28, *pg.* 975
CAPE CODDER - Newspaper - CAPE CODDER; *pg.* 1625, *pg.* 840
CAPE COD'S COMMUNITY BANK - Bank - CAPE COD FIVE CENTS SAVINGS BANK; *pg.* 730, *pg.* 840
CAPE DORY - Kitchen Product - KOHLER CO.; *pg.* 91, *pg.* 1862
CAPE HATTERAS - Bath Product - KOHLER CO.; *pg.* 91, *pg.* 1862
CAPE MARCO - Community Name - WCI COMMUNITIES, INC.; *pg.* 1118, *pg.* 414
CAPE MAY - Furniture - ASHLEY FURNITURE INDUSTRIES, INC.; *pg.* 914, *pg.* 1852
CAPE MAY - Furniture - TELESCOPE CASUAL FURNITURE INC.; *pg.* 944, *pg.* 1162
CAPE MENTELLE - Wine - MOET HENNESSY; *pg.* 1966, *pg.* 1260
CAPE X - Fabric - NEMSCHOFF, INC.; *pg.* 936, *pg.* 1890
CAPELAND - Watches - BAUME & MERCIER, INC.; *pg.* 1, *pg.* 1201
CAPELLA - Wood Flooring Products - ARMSTRONG WORLD INDUSTRIES, INC.; *pg.* 914, *pg.* 1545
CAPELLA - Bath & Plumbing Product - JACUZZI BRANDS CORPORATION; *pg.* 554, *pg.* 65
CAPELLA - Furniture - NEMSCHOFF, INC.; *pg.* 936, *pg.* 1890
CAPELLA ABC - Furniture - NEMSCHOFF, INC.; *pg.* 936, *pg.* 1890
CAPELLI - Furniture - HERMAN MILLER, INC.; *pg.* 926, *pg.* 913
CAPELLO - Flatware - ONEIDA LTD; *pg.* 1129, *pg.* 1318
CAPER - Furniture - HERMAN MILLER, INC.; *pg.* 926, *pg.* 913
CAPEWELL - Saw Blades - KENNAMETAL IPG; *pg.* 1353, *pg.* 1615
CAPEX TOPICAL SHAMPOO - Rx Product - GALDERMA LABORATORIES, L.P.; *pg.* 1532, *pg.* 1695
CAPEZIO - Footwear - CAPEZIO BALLET MAKERS INC.; *pg.* 1805, *pg.* 1125
CAPFIS - Software - 3M; *pg.* 339, *pg.* 179
CAPFIS PRIME - Software - 3M; *pg.* 339, *pg.* 179
CAPIO - Open Access & Standard Suture Capturing Devices - BOSTON SCIENTIFIC CORPORATION; *pg.* 1508, *pg.* 831
CAPISTRANO - Ceiling Fan - WESTINGHOUSE LIGHTING CORPORATION; *pg.* 687, *pg.* 1571
CAPITAL - Investment Vehicle - ALPHABET INC.; *pg.* 347, *pg.* 153
THE CAPITAL - Newspaper - CAPITAL GAZETTE COMMUNICATIONS INC.; *pg.* 1625, *pg.* 754
CAPITAL - Furniture - ETHAN ALLEN INTERIORS INC.; *pg.* 924, *pg.* 343
CAPITAL - Software System - MENTOR GRAPHICS CORPORATION; *pg.* 432, *pg.* 1510
CAPITAL 1900 - Circa 1900 American Pilsner - CAPITAL BREWERY CO., INC.; *pg.* 239, *pg.* 1872
CAPITAL ANALYSIS - Software System - MENTOR GRAPHICS CORPORATION; *pg.* 432, *pg.* 1510
CAPITAL ARCHIVE - Software System - MENTOR GRAPHICS CORPORATION; *pg.* 432, *pg.* 1510
CAPITAL AUTUMNAL FIRE - Strong Marzen Style Bock Beer - CAPITAL BREWERY CO., INC.; *pg.* 239, *pg.* 1872
CAPITAL BAVARIAN LAGER - German Hellas Lager - CAPITAL BREWERY CO., INC.; *pg.* 239, *pg.* 1872
CAPITAL BLONDE DOPPELBOCK - Golden Strong Bock Beer - CAPITAL BREWERY CO., INC.; *pg.* 239, *pg.* 1872
CAPITAL BRIDGES - Software System - MENTOR GRAPHICS CORPORATION; *pg.* 432, *pg.* 1510
CAPITAL BROWN ALE - English Brown Ale - CAPITAL BREWERY CO., INC.; *pg.* 239, *pg.* 1872
CAPITAL CABINET - Cabinetry - MASTERBRAND CABINETS, INC.; *pg.* 96, *pg.* 692
CAPITAL CLUB - Offer Program - DOVER DOWNS GAMING & ENTERTAINMENT, INC.; *pg.* 545, *pg.* 387
CAPITAL DARK - Bavarian Dark Lager - CAPITAL BREWERY CO., INC.; *pg.* 239, *pg.* 1872
CAPITAL DARK DOPPELBOCK - Dark, Strong Bock Beer - CAPITAL BREWERY CO., INC.; *pg.* 239, *pg.* 1872
CAPITAL DIRECTIONS - Banking Services - THE PNC FINANCIAL SERVICES GROUP, INC.; *pg.* 795, *pg.* 1579
CAPITAL DOCUMENTS - Software System - MENTOR GRAPHICS CORPORATION; *pg.* 432, *pg.* 1510
CAPITAL E - Jean - LEVI STRAUSS & CO.; *pg.* 43, *pg.* 220
CAPITAL GOLD - Services - DOVER DOWNS GAMING & ENTERTAINMENT, INC.; *pg.* 545, *pg.* 387
THE CAPITAL GRILLE - Restaurant Chain - DARDEN RESTAURANTS, INC.; *pg.* 1724, *pg.* 453
CAPITAL H - Software System - MENTOR GRAPHICS CORPORATION; *pg.* 432, *pg.* 1510
CAPITAL H THE COMPLETE DESKTOP ENGINEER - Software System - MENTOR GRAPHICS CORPORATION; *pg.* 432, *pg.* 1510
CAPITAL HARNESS - Software System - MENTOR GRAPHICS CORPORATION; *pg.* 432, *pg.* 1510
CAPITAL HARNESSXC - Software System - MENTOR GRAPHICS CORPORATION; *pg.* 432, *pg.* 1510
CAPITAL INSIGHT - Software System - MENTOR GRAPHICS CORPORATION; *pg.* 432, *pg.* 1510
CAPITAL INTEGRATION - Software System - MENTOR GRAPHICS CORPORATION; *pg.* 432, *pg.* 1510
CAPITAL KLOSTER WEIZEN - German Heffe Weizen Style - CAPITAL BREWERY CO., INC.; *pg.* 239, *pg.* 1872
CAPITAL LETTERS - Apparel - VANS, INC.; *pg.* 1821, *pg.* 76
CAPITAL MAIBOCK - German Style Golden Bock Beer - CAPITAL BREWERY CO., INC.; *pg.* 239, *pg.* 1872
CAPITAL MANAGER - Software System - MENTOR GRAPHICS CORPORATION; *pg.* 432, *pg.* 1510
CAPITAL MANUFACTURE - Software System - MENTOR GRAPHICS CORPORATION; *pg.* 432, *pg.* 1510
CAPITAL OKTOBERFEST - Marzen Style Lager Beer - CAPITAL BREWERY CO., INC.; *pg.* 239, *pg.* 1872
CAPITAL ONE - Credit Card - CAPITAL ONE FINANCIAL CORPORATION; *pg.* 730, *pg.* 1789
CAPITAL ONE BUSINESS - Credit Card - CAPITAL ONE FINANCIAL CORPORATION; *pg.* 730, *pg.* 1789

CAPITAL PLATINUM - Services - DOVER DOWNS GAMING & ENTERTAINMENT, INC.; *pg.* 545, *pg.* 387
CAPITAL SOURCE & DESIGN - Providing Financial Solutions - CAPITALSOURCE INC.; *pg.* 731, *pg.* 127
CAPITAL SPECIAL PILSNER - German Style Pilsner - CAPITAL BREWERY CO., INC.; *pg.* 239, *pg.* 1872
CAPITAL SUPPORT - Software System - MENTOR GRAPHICS CORPORATION; *pg.* 432, *pg.* 1510
CAPITAL SYSTEMS - Software System - MENTOR GRAPHICS CORPORATION; *pg.* 432, *pg.* 1510
THE CAPITAL TIMES - Online Newspaper - MADISON NEWSPAPERS, INC.; *pg.* 1661, *pg.* 1866
CAPITAL WEIZEN DOPPELBOCK - Strong Wheat Bock Beer - CAPITAL BREWERY CO., INC.; *pg.* 239, *pg.* 1872
CAPITAL WILD RICE - Wild Rice Lager Beer - CAPITAL BREWERY CO., INC.; *pg.* 239, *pg.* 1872
CAPITAL WINTER SKAL - Rich, Malty Winter Lager - CAPITAL BREWERY CO., INC.; *pg.* 239, *pg.* 1872
CAPITAL WISCONSIN AMBER - Vienna Amber Style - CAPITAL BREWERY CO., INC.; *pg.* 239, *pg.* 1872
CAPITOL FEDERAL - Banking Services - CAPITOL FEDERAL FINANCIAL, INC.; *pg.* 731, *pg.* 721
CAPITOL GEARS - Marine Transmission - REGAL BELOIT CORPORATION; *pg.* 106, *pg.* 1854
CAPKOLD - Cook-Chill System - UNIFIED BRANDS INC.; *pg.* 1385, *pg.* 970
CAPLC - Liquid Chromatography Instrument - WATERS CORPORATION; *pg.* 1436, *pg.* 834
CAP'N CRUNCH - Cereal - PEPSICO, INC.; *pg.* 259, *pg.* 1327
CAP'N CRUNCH - Cereal - THE QUAKER OATS COMPANY; *pg.* 834, *pg.* 588
CAP'N KID - Peanut Butter - ALGOOD FOOD COMPANY; *pg.* 836, *pg.* 731
CAPNO-FLO - Medical Device - MALLINCKRODT PHARMACEUTICALS; *pg.* 1557, *pg.* 978
CAPNOPROBE - Patient Safety Monitoring Products - MEDTRONIC; *pg.* 1563, *pg.* 183
CAPPER'S - Bi-Weekly Magazine - OGDEN PUBLICATIONS, INC.; *pg.* 1672, *pg.* 722
CAPPUCCINO DREAM - Ice Cream Sundaes - FRIENDLY ICE CREAM, LLC; *pg.* 1853, *pg.* 859
CAPPY - Beverages - THE COCA-COLA COMPANY; *pg.* 240, *pg.* 493
CAPPY'S - Brand - TRAVEL-BY-NET, INC.; *pg.* 1925, *pg.* 1183
CAPRAN - Nylon Film - HONEYWELL INTERNATIONAL INC.; *pg.* 407, *pg.* 1088
CAPRAN - Cast Nylon Film - TRANSILWRAP COMPANY, INC.; *pg.* 1470, *pg.* 613
CAPRATON - Glass - LYDALL, INC.; *pg.* 1357, *pg.* 354
CAPRESSO - Furniture - ASHLEY FURNITURE INDUSTRIES, INC.; *pg.* 914, *pg.* 1852
CAPRI - Guest Chairs - BERNHARDT DESIGN; *pg.* 918, *pg.* 1381
CAPRI - Footwear - CAPEZIO BALLET MAKERS INC.; *pg.* 1805, *pg.* 1125
CAPRI - Bicycle - G. JOANNOU CYCLE CO. INC.; *pg.* 1707, *pg.* 1098
CAPRI - Furniture - J. ROBERT SCOTT INC.; *pg.* 930, *pg.* 105
CAPRI - Door Panel - MASONITE INTERNATIONAL CORPORATION; *pg.* 1054, *pg.* 1920
CAPRI - Personal Care - NORTHERN LABS, INC.; *pg.* 517, *pg.* 1869
CAPRI - Lighting Fixture & Control - PHILIPS LIGHTING; *pg.* 1303, *pg.* 806
CAPRI - Outdoor Lighting - SWIVELIER CO., INC.; *pg.* 1307, *pg.* 1142
CAPRI SATIN - Window Treatment - CROSCILL, INC.; *pg.* 1122, *pg.* 1220
CAPRICE - Beverages - THE COCA-COLA COMPANY; *pg.* 240, *pg.* 493
CAPRICE - Freshwater Spinning Reels - DAIWA CORPORATION; *pg.* 1832, *pg.* 75
CAPRICE - Automobile - GENERAL MOTORS COMPANY; *pg.* 175, *pg.* 881
CAPRICORN - Freshwater Spinning Reels - DAIWA CORPORATION; *pg.* 1832, *pg.* 75
CAPRICORN - Digital Weather Station - HINDS INSTRUMENTS, INC.; *pg.* 1416, *pg.* 1498
CAPRICORN - Composite Decking - UNIVERSAL FOREST PRODUCTS, INC.; *pg.* 117, *pg.* 890
CAPRIE - Footwear - STEVEN MADDEN, LTD.; *pg.* 1819, *pg.* 1176
CAPRISUN - Flavored Water Beverage - THE KRAFT HEINZ COMPANY; *pg.* 870, *pg.* 1577
CAPSCARE - Charity - WASHINGTON CAPITALS; *pg.* 591, *pg.* 1775
CAPSENSE - Software - CYPRESS SEMICONDUCTOR CORPORATION; *pg.* 1326, *pg.* 243
CAPSENSE EXPRESS - Software - CYPRESS SEMICONDUCTOR CORPORATION; *pg.* 1326, *pg.* 243
CAPSET - Dental Implant System - LIFECORE BIOMEDICAL, LLC; *pg.* 1556, *pg.* 920
CAPSLEEVE POLO - Clothing - K-SWISS; *pg.* 1837, *pg.* 306
CAPSPACE - Online Video Conferencing Directory - POLYCOM, INC.; *pg.* 664, *pg.* 249
CAPSTONE - Enterprise Access Management System - CERNER CORPORATION; *pg.* 1514, *pg.* 981
CAPSTONE - Repellents & Surfactants - E.I. DU PONT DE NEMOURS & COMPANY; *pg.* 1159, *pg.* 390
CAPSTONE - Decision Accelerator Strategy Design Solutions - FAIR ISAAC CORPORATION; *pg.* 1247, *pg.* 955
CAPSU-PHOTOHELIC - Pressure Switch - DWYER INSTRUMENTS INC.; *pg.* 1330, *pg.* 694
CAPSUHELIC - Differential Pressure Gage - DWYER INSTRUMENTS INC.; *pg.* 1330, *pg.* 694
CAPSULE - Semiconductor Device - APPLIED MATERIALS, INC; *pg.* 618, *pg.* 1009
CAPSULEC - Soft-Gel Lecithin Nutritional Products - ARCHER-DANIELS-MIDLAND COMPANY; *pg.* 825, *pg.* 565
CAPSURE SP NOVUS - Pacing Lead - MEDTRONIC, INC.; *pg.* 1564, *pg.* 939
CAPTAIN - Household Insect Control - BONIDE PRODUCTS, INC.; *pg.* 1794, *pg.* 1320
CAPTAIN APPLEJACK - Brandy - LAIRD & COMPANY, INC.; *pg.* 1966, *pg.* 1119
CAPTAIN B - Gluing Machine - GLUEFAST COMPANY, INC.; *pg.* 1459, *pg.* 1090
CAPTAIN COLD - Character - DC COMICS, INC.; *pg.* 1633, *pg.* 1221
CAPTAIN COMET - Character - DC COMICS, INC.; *pg.* 1633, *pg.* 1221
CAPTAIN JOHN DERST'S - Food Product - FLOWERS FOODS, INC.; *pg.* 855, *pg.* 541
CAPTAIN MARVEL - Character - DC COMICS, INC.; *pg.* 1633, *pg.* 1221
CAPTAIN MIDNIGHT - Educational Materials - SCHOLASTIC INC.; *pg.* 1683, *pg.* 1288
CAPTAIN MORGAN - Rum - DIAGEO NORTH AMERICA, INC.; *pg.* 1961, *pg.* 361
CAPTAIN PAYBACK - Video Game - INTERNATIONAL GAME TECHNOLOGY; *pg.* 957, *pg.* 1024
CAPTAIN'S CATCH - Breaded Fillets - HIGH LINER FOODS INCORPORATED; *pg.* 862, *pg.* 1917
CAPTAIN'S CHOICE - Snack Food - SNYDER'S-LANCE, INC.; *pg.* 896, *pg.* 1368
CAPTAIN'S COVE - Game - WMS INDUSTRIES INC.; *pg.* 593, *pg.* 666
CAPTAIN'S WAFERS - Food Product - SNYDER'S-LANCE, INC.; *pg.* 896, *pg.* 1368
CAPTAVIDIN - Molecular Probe Product - THERMO FISHER SCIENTIFIC INC.; *pg.* 1602, *pg.* 61
CAPTAX - Accelerators - R.T. VANDERBILT COMPANY, INC.; *pg.* 1180, *pg.* 364
CAPTIVA - Software - EMC CORPORATION; *pg.* 391, *pg.* 825
CAPTIVA - Bath Product - KOHLER CO.; *pg.* 91, *pg.* 1862
THE CAPTIVA 2 - Home Floor Plan - JACOBSEN MANUFACTURING, INC.; *pg.* 1098, *pg.* 460
CAPTIVATE - Software - ADOBE SYSTEMS INCORPORATED; *pg.* 342, *pg.* 235
CAPTIVATE - Molecular Probe Product - THERMO FISHER SCIENTIFIC INC.; *pg.* 1602, *pg.* 61
CAPTIVATOR - Medical Device - BOSTON SCIENTIFIC CORPORATION; *pg.* 1508, *pg.* 831
CAPTIVUE - Electronic LED Message - TRANS-LUX CORPORATION; *pg.* 681, *pg.* 365
CAPT'N COOK - Gas Grill - BARBEQUES GALORE, INC.; *pg.* 51, *pg.* 173
CAPTOR - Floor Care - NILFISK-ADVANCE, INC.; *pg.* 332, *pg.* 953
CAPTOUCH - Sensors - ANALOG DEVICES, INC.; *pg.* 617, *pg.* 839
CAPTRA - Software - MOTOROLA ENTERPRISE MOBILITY; *pg.* 441, *pg.* 1167
CAPTURE - Software - EASTMAN KODAK COMPANY; *pg.* 1408, *pg.* 1333
CAPTURE - Insecticide - FMC CORPORATION; *pg.* 1163, *pg.* 1564
CAPTURE - Antibody Screening & Identification Technology - IMMUCOR, INC.; *pg.* 1544, *pg.* 537
CAPTURE - Treatment - PARFUMS CHRISTIAN DIOR, INC; *pg.* 519, *pg.* 1276
CAPTURE LFR - Insecticides & Miticides - FMC CORPORATION; *pg.* 1163, *pg.* 1564
CAPTURE LIQUIDREADY SYSTEM - Insecticides & Miticides - FMC CORPORATION; *pg.* 1163, *pg.* 1564
CAPTURE OUTFIT - Sport Apparel - UNDER ARMOUR, INC.; *pg.* 49, *pg.* 759
CAPTURE STATION - Software System - MENTOR GRAPHICS CORPORATION; *pg.* 432, *pg.* 1510
CAPTURE THE SPIRIT - Slogan - RIO BRANDS, INC.; *pg.* 941, *pg.* 1570
CAPTUREPLUS - Organosilane-Treated Particles - DOW CORNING CORPORATION; *pg.* 1159, *pg.* 900
CAPTUREVIEW - Binoculars - MEADE INSTRUMENTS CORPORATION; *pg.* 1422, *pg.* 113
CAPTURING THE EXCITEMENT OF NOW - Tagline - PEPSICO, INC.; *pg.* 259, *pg.* 1327
CAPULET - Furniture - J. ROBERT SCOTT INC.; *pg.* 930, *pg.* 105
CAPZ - Ceilings & Walls - ARMSTRONG WORLD INDUSTRIES, INC.; *pg.* 914, *pg.* 1545
CAPZASIN-HP - Arthritis Pain Reliever - CHATTEM, INC.; *pg.* 1515, *pg.* 1628
CAPZASIN-P - Arthritis Pain Reliever - CHATTEM, INC.; *pg.* 1515, *pg.* 1628
CAR AND DRIVER - Magazine - THE HEARST CORPORATION; *pg.* 1649, *pg.* 1239
CAR AND TRAVEL - Magazine for Members of Auto Clubs - AMERICAN AUTOMOBILE ASSOCIATION; *pg.* 1190, *pg.* 429
CAR BRITE - Automotive Product - ASHLAND INC.; *pg.* 972, *pg.* 726
CAR2U - Seating System - LEAR CORPORATION; *pg.* 229, *pg.* 907
CARA - Clothing - ABERCROMBIE & FITCH CO.; *pg.* 37, *pg.* 1466
CARA - Footwear - COBIAN CORP.; *pg.* 1806, *pg.* 253
CARA - Mattress - ETHAN ALLEN INTERIORS INC.; *pg.* 924, *pg.* 343
CARA MIA CRIMSON - Nail Care Product - OPI PRODUCTS INC.; *pg.* 518, *pg.* 167
CARADCO - Window & Door - JELD-WEN, INC.; *pg.* 1051, *pg.* 1499
CARAMEL APPLE POPS - Candy - TOOTSIE ROLL INDUSTRIES, INC.; *pg.* 1863, *pg.* 591
CARAMEL CAPPUCCINO - Ice Cream - DIPPIN' DOTS LLC; *pg.* 853, *pg.* 739
CARAMEL CORRETTO - Coffee Beverage - THE SECOND CUP LTD.; *pg.* 1749, *pg.* 1928
CARAMEL DUTCH LATTE - Drink - AUNTIE ANNE'S INC.; *pg.* 1715, *pg.* 1546
CARAMEL MUD SPLASH - Ice Cream - WELLS ENTERPRISES, INC.; *pg.* 909, *pg.* 709
CARAMEL PECANBON - Baked Goods - CINNABON, INC.; *pg.* 1723, *pg.* 493
CARAMEL PECANBON CENTER OF THE ROLL - Baked Goods - CINNABON, INC.; *pg.* 1723, *pg.* 493
CARAMEL PORTER - Premium Beer - THE LION BREWERY, INC.; *pg.* 254, *pg.* 1594
CARAMELLA - Confectionery - THE HERSHEY CO.; *pg.* 1855, *pg.* 1538
CARAMELLO - Candy Bar - THE HERSHEY CO.; *pg.* 1855, *pg.* 1538
CARAMELO - Flavored Coffee - THE SECOND CUP LTD.; *pg.* 1749, *pg.* 1928
CARAMELS WHIRLS - Chocolate Product - WORLD'S FINEST CHOCOLATE, INC.; *pg.* 1864, *pg.* 597
CARANDO - Food Products - SMITHFIELD FOODS, INC.; *pg.* 896, *pg.* 1806
CARAPELLI - Olive Oils - HORMEL FOODS CORPORATION; *pg.* 863, *pg.* 915
CARAT - Fabric - NEMSCHOFF, INC.; *pg.* 936, *pg.* 1890
CARAT - Actuator - PRECISION VALVE CORPORATION; *pg.* 1060, *pg.* 1357
CARAVAN - Textiles - BERNHARDT DESIGN; *pg.* 918, *pg.* 1381
CARAVAN - Travel Brochure - CARAVAN TOURS, INC.; *pg.* 1902, *pg.* 568
CARAVAN - Aircraft - CESSNA AIRCRAFT COMPANY; *pg.* 226, *pg.* 723

CARAVAN - Video Game - INTERNATIONAL GAME TECHNOLOGY; *pg.* 957, *pg.* 1024
CARAVAN - Cast Iron Modular Boiler - SLANT/FIN CORPORATION; *pg.* 1076, *pg.* 1163
CARAVELLE - Lounge Chairs - BERNHARDT DESIGN; *pg.* 918, *pg.* 1381
CARAVELLE - Watches - BULOVA CORPORATION; *pg.* 2, *pg.* 1356
CARB - Bearing - KADANT JOHNSON INC.; *pg.* 1073, *pg.* 909
CARB ALTERNATIVES - Candy - THE HERSHEY CO.; *pg.* 1855, *pg.* 1538
CARB CONSCIOUS - Tortillas - TYSON FOODS, INC.; *pg.* 902, *pg.* 35
CARB DELITE - Ice Cream Product - PERRY'S ICE CREAM CO., INC.; *pg.* 1861, *pg.* 1137
CARB FIT - Food Product - THE HAIN CELESTIAL GROUP, INC.; *pg.* 860, *pg.* 1172
CARB INTERCEPT - Vitamin & Dietary Supplement - NATROL, INC.; *pg.* 1570, *pg.* 64
CARB-MEDIC - Carburetor Cleaner - RADIATOR SPECIALTY COMPANY; *pg.* 215, *pg.* 1380
CARB-N-SERT - Medical Instrument - INTEGRA MILTEX, INC.; *pg.* 1546, *pg.* 1597
CARB-O-PROF - Carbon Profiling System - IPSEN INTERNATIONAL, INC.; *pg.* 1073, *pg.* 562
CARB SMART - Diabetes Treatment Products - ANIMAS CORPORATION; *pg.* 1495, *pg.* 1593
CARB SMART PLUS - Diabetes Treatment Products - ANIMAS CORPORATION; *pg.* 1495, *pg.* 1593
CARB-X - Nutritional Product - NUTRACEUTICAL INTERNATIONAL CORPORATION; *pg.* 1576, *pg.* 1753
CARBENIX - Aircraft Landing System - HONEYWELL INTERNATIONAL INC.; *pg.* 407, *pg.* 1088
CARBIDE PLUS - Imbedded Plate - ESCO CORPORATION; *pg.* 1335, *pg.* 1502
CARBIDIE - Tooling System - KENNAMETAL INC.; *pg.* 1052, *pg.* 1547
CARBITOL - Oxygenated Solvent - THE DOW CHEMICAL COMPANY; *pg.* 1157, *pg.* 898
CARBITOL - Solvents & Acetates - PVS CHEMICALS, INC.; *pg.* 1178, *pg.* 884
CARBO - Filter Cartridge - PALL CORPORATION; *pg.* 232, *pg.* 1323
CARBO CATCHER - Pharmaceutical Product - ALERE INC.; *pg.* 1488, *pg.* 849
CARBO-CHARGER - Beverage System - CHART INDUSTRIES, INC.; *pg.* 1405, *pg.* 1454
CARBO CLAD - Type of Carbide Tap - REGAL BELOIT CORPORATION; *pg.* 106, *pg.* 1854
CARBO-DRAUGHT - Beer Dispense System - CHART INDUSTRIES, INC.; *pg.* 1405, *pg.* 1454
CARBO GRABBERS - Health Care Product - NATURE'S SUNSHINE PRODUCTS, INC.; *pg.* 1571, *pg.* 1754
CARBO-MAX - Beverage System - CHART INDUSTRIES, INC.; *pg.* 1405, *pg.* 1454
CARBO-MITE - Beverage System - CHART INDUSTRIES, INC.; *pg.* 1405, *pg.* 1454
CARBO-MIZER - Beverage System - CHART INDUSTRIES, INC.; *pg.* 1405, *pg.* 1454
CARBO ZINC - Protective Coatings - CARBOLINE CO.; *pg.* 1152, *pg.* 994
CARBOCAP - Mechanical & Electrical System - JOHNSON CONTROLS, INC.; *pg.* 209, *pg.* 1876
CARBOCRYLIC - Waterborne Acrylic - CARBOLINE CO.; *pg.* 1152, *pg.* 994
CARBOFAST - Pharmaceutical Product - ALVA/AMCO PHARMACAL COMPANIES, INC.; *pg.* 1492, *pg.* 637
CARBOFLEX - Carbon Fiber Product - ASHLAND INC.; *pg.* 972, *pg.* 726
CARBOFLEX - Wound Care Product - CONVATEC LTD.; *pg.* 1518, *pg.* 1121
CARBOFORM - Chemical Product - CYTEC INDUSTRIES, INC.; *pg.* 1155, *pg.* 1131
CARBOGUARD - Epoxy Coatings - CARBOLINE CO.; *pg.* 1152, *pg.* 994
CARBOMASTIC - Protective Coatings - CARBOLINE CO.; *pg.* 1152, *pg.* 994
CARBON - Apparel - RUE21, INC.; *pg.* 32, *pg.* 1591
CARBON BLACK - Apparel - RUE21, INC.; *pg.* 32, *pg.* 1591
CARBON COPY - Software - SYMANTEC CORPORATION; *pg.* 478, *pg.* 161
CARBON FIBRE - Sport Product - FRANKLIN SPORTS, INC.; *pg.* 1834, *pg.* 847
CARBONCONX - Connector - XEROX CORPORATION; *pg.* 494, *pg.* 365
CARBONITE - Metal Casting Product - HILL & GRIFFITH COMPANY; *pg.* 1167, *pg.* 1414
CARBONITE - Silicon Carbide - IMERYS FUSED MINERALS; *pg.* 1348, *pg.* 1317
CARBONLESS-RECEIPT - Envelopes - TENSION ENVELOPE CORPORATION; *pg.* 483, *pg.* 986
CARBONO - Tile - ARTISTIC TILE INC.; *pg.* 914, *pg.* 1119
CARBOPOL - Polymers - THE LUBRIZOL CORPORATION; *pg.* 1171, *pg.* 1481
CARBOSPERSE - Polymers - THE LUBRIZOL CORPORATION; *pg.* 1171, *pg.* 1481
CARBOTHANE - Medical Device - SPIRE CORPORATION; *pg.* 1378, *pg.* 786
CARBOWAX - Polyethylene Glycols - THE DOW CHEMICAL COMPANY; *pg.* 1157, *pg.* 898
CARBOXANE - Organic Phosphate Esters - HENKEL CORPORATION; *pg.* 1165, *pg.* 1535
CARBS IN-LINE - Bar Chocolate - BROWN & HALEY; *pg.* 1851, *pg.* 1820
CARBSMART - Gourmet Pasta & Sauce - MONTEREY GOURMET FOODS, INC.; *pg.* 881, *pg.* 94
CARBSORB - Water Treatment Activated Carbons - CALGON CARBON CORPORATION; *pg.* 1151, *pg.* 1574
CARCO - Winches - PACCAR INC.; *pg.* 187, *pg.* 1816
CAR.COM - Online Car-Buying Site - AUTOBYTEL INC.; *pg.* 1230, *pg.* 107
CARD BOILED - Online Services - IAC/INTERACTIVECORP; *pg.* 292, *pg.* 1242
CARD FACTORY - Educational Materials - SCHOLASTIC INC.; *pg.* 1683, *pg.* 1288
CARD GAME - Shoe - AEROGROUP INTERNATIONAL, INC.; *pg.* 1803, *pg.* 1055
CARD MASK - Pre Press Film - PLASTIC SUPPLIERS, INC.; *pg.* 1888, *pg.* 1443
CARD PARTY - Video Game - INTERNATIONAL GAME TECHNOLOGY; *pg.* 957, *pg.* 1024
CARDACCESS - Access Control System - NAPCO SECURITY SYSTEMS, INC.; *pg.* 658, *pg.* 1138
CARDBUS - PCI Expansion System - IGO, INC.; *pg.* 644, *pg.* 22
CARDENAL MENDOZA - Brandy - SHAW ROSS INTERNATIONAL IMPORTERS; *pg.* 1970, *pg.* 449
CARDEX - Men's Wallet - BUXTON ACQUISITION CO., LLC; *pg.* 2, *pg.* 845
CARDIAC HEALTHWAYS - Disease Management - HEALTHWAYS, INC.; *pg.* 1540, *pg.* 1632
CARDIAC STATUS - Diagnostic Product - SPECTRAL DIAGNOSTICS INC.; *pg.* 1430, *pg.* 1943
CARDIALL - Nutritional Product - NUTRACEUTICAL INTERNATIONAL CORPORATION; *pg.* 1576, *pg.* 1753
CARDIN - Furniture - AMISCO INDUSTRIES LTD.; *pg.* 913, *pg.* 1958
CARDINAL - Cutting Room Equipment - EASTMAN MACHINE COMPANY; *pg.* 1331, *pg.* 1148
CARDINAL - Fabric - NEMSCHOFF, INC.; *pg.* 936, *pg.* 1890
CARDINAL ESCROW MANAGER - Software - CARDINAL BANK N.A.; *pg.* 732, *pg.* 1790
CARDINAL ONLINE BANKING - Software - CARDINAL BANK N.A.; *pg.* 732, *pg.* 1790
CARDINAL ONLINE COMMERCIAL BANKING - Software - CARDINAL BANK N.A.; *pg.* 732, *pg.* 1790
CARDINALS' CHOICE - Bird Seed - INTERMOUNTAIN FARMERS ASSOCIATION; *pg.* 705, *pg.* 1759
CARDINAL'S CREST - Wine - BILTMORE ESTATE WINE COMPANY; *pg.* 1958, *pg.* 1358
CARDINI'S - Salad Dressings & Sauces - LANCASTER COLONY CORPORATION; *pg.* 873, *pg.* 1441
CARDINI'S - Salad Dressing & Marinades - T. MARZETTI COMPANY; *pg.* 900, *pg.* 1444
CARDIO BALANCE - Nutritional Product - MANNATECH, INCORPORATED; *pg.* 1558, *pg.* 1671
CARDIO CRP - Blood Test - QUEST DIAGNOSTICS INCORPORATED; *pg.* 1587, *pg.* 1080
CARDIO FULL - Apparels - UNDER ARMOUR, INC.; *pg.* 49, *pg.* 759
CARDIO OMEGA SOLUTIONS - Nutritional Product - NATROL, INC.; *pg.* 1570, *pg.* 64
CARDIO PROFILER - Pharmaceutical Product - ALERE INC.; *pg.* 1488, *pg.* 849
CARDIO TANK - Apparels - UNDER ARMOUR, INC.; *pg.* 49, *pg.* 759
CARDIO TOCONOX - Antioxidant Supplement - HERBALIFE INTERNATIONAL OF AMERICA, INC.; *pg.* 1541, *pg.* 132
CARDIOACTIN - Nutritional Supplement - NATURAL ORGANICS, INC.; *pg.* 1571, *pg.* 1181
CARDIOAID - Plant Sterols - ARCHER-DANIELS-MIDLAND COMPANY; *pg.* 825, *pg.* 565
CARDIOAID-CZ - Plant Sterols - ARCHER-DANIELS-MIDLAND COMPANY; *pg.* 825, *pg.* 565
CARDIOAID-M - Plant Sterols - ARCHER-DANIELS-MIDLAND COMPANY; *pg.* 825, *pg.* 565
CARDIOAID-S - Plant Sterols - ARCHER-DANIELS-MIDLAND COMPANY; *pg.* 825, *pg.* 565
CARDIOBLATE - Surgical Ablation System - MEDTRONIC, INC.; *pg.* 1564, *pg.* 939
CARDIODRIVE - Automated Catheter Advancer - STEREOTAXIS, INC.; *pg.* 1597, *pg.* 1004
CARDIOGRAM - Medical Device - COMPUMED, INC.; *pg.* 378, *pg.* 128
CARDIOLINK - Pharmaceutical Product - PURETEK CORPORATION; *pg.* 1587, *pg.* 211
CARDIOPAT - Blood Salvage System - HAEMONETICS CORPORATION; *pg.* 1538, *pg.* 802
CARDIOPET - Diagnose Heart Disease - IDEXX LABORATORIES, INC.; *pg.* 1543, *pg.* 753
CARDIOPLEGIA PLUS - Blood Filter - PALL CORPORATION; *pg.* 232, *pg.* 1323
CARDIOQUET - Medical Product - PROPPER MANUFACTURING COMPANY, INC.; *pg.* 1586, *pg.* 1175
CARDIORHYTHM - Subsidiary - MEDTRONIC, INC.; *pg.* 1564, *pg.* 939
CARDIOSENS - Electrodes - CARDIAC SCIENCE CORPORATION; *pg.* 1512, *pg.* 1897
CARDIOSENTIALS - Nutritional Product - RELIV INTERNATIONAL, INC.; *pg.* 1589, *pg.* 975
CARDIOSYNC - Cardiac Arrhythmia Tracking System - MAQUET; *pg.* 1558, *pg.* 1082
CARDIOVIVE - Automated External Defibrillator - CARDIAC SCIENCE CORPORATION; *pg.* 1512, *pg.* 1897
CARDIOWRAP - Bioresorbable Protective Sheet - CRYOLIFE, INC.; *pg.* 1520, *pg.* 534
CARDIUS - Digital Gamma Camera - DIGIRAD CORPORATION; *pg.* 1524, *pg.* 185
CARDIZEM LA - Tablets - ABBOTT LABORATORIES; *pg.* 1484, *pg.* 551
CARDMEMBER - Cards - AMERICAN EXPRESS COMPANY; *pg.* 712, *pg.* 1190
CARDSCAN - Business Card Scanner - NEWELL RUBBERMAID INC.; *pg.* 1128, *pg.* 515
CARDURA - Automotive Coatings - HEXION; *pg.* 1166, *pg.* 1440
CARDURA - Chemical - MILLER-STEPHENSON CHEMICAL COMPANY, INC.; *pg.* 1172, *pg.* 344
CARDURA - Medicine - PFIZER INC.; *pg.* 1581, *pg.* 1278
CARDURA XL - Pharmaceutical Product - PFIZER INC.; *pg.* 1581, *pg.* 1278
THE CARE COMPANY - Slogan - AMERICAN REPUBLIC INSURANCE COMPANY; *pg.* 1191, *pg.* 704
CARE FREE - Humidifier - HUNTER FAN COMPANY; *pg.* 57, *pg.* 1631
CARE FREE KITTY - Minerals - MINERALS TECHNOLOGIES INC.; *pg.* 1173, *pg.* 617
CARE LABEL - Paper & Nonwoven Material - FIBERMARK INC.; *pg.* 1457, *pg.* 1764
CARE MAIL - Mailing Supplies - HENKEL CONSUMER ADHESIVES, INC.; *pg.* 403, *pg.* 1480
CARE MANAGEMENT RESOURCE - Missouri PPO Product - COVENTRY HEALTH CARE, INC.; *pg.* 1519, *pg.* 761
CAREADVANCE - Software - TRIZETTO CORPORATION; *pg.* 485, *pg.* 327
CAREAWARE - Device Connectivity Architecture - CERNER CORPORATION; *pg.* 1514, *pg.* 981
CARECAST - Software - GE HEALTHCARE; *pg.* 399, *pg.* 1765
CARECENTRIX - Healthcare Service - GENTIVA HEALTH SERVICES, INC.; *pg.* 1534, *pg.* 506
CARECHAIR - Stretcher - KINETIC CONCEPTS, INC.; *pg.* 1553, *pg.* 1741
CARECHECK - Health Program - HEALTHPARTNERS, INC.; *pg.* 1203, *pg.* 918
CAREDRAPE - Cardiac & Warming Blanket - MEDTRONIC; *pg.* 1563, *pg.* 183
CAREER CHOICES - Interdisciplinary Curriculum - ACADEMIC INNOVATIONS; *pg.* 1613, *pg.* 262
CAREER CHOICES AND CHANGES - Textbook - AMERICAN CONFERENCE OF GOVERNMENTAL INDUSTRIAL HYGIENISTS; *pg.* 127, *pg.* 1409
CAREER FITNESS - Magazine Article - GANNETT HEALTHCARE GROUP; *pg.* 1644, *pg.* 617

CAREERCHOICES.COM - Web-Based Curriculum - ACADEMIC INNOVATIONS; *pg.* 1613, *pg.* 262
CAREERS IN GEAR - Advertising Publication - DOMINION ENTERPRISES; *pg.* 1636, *pg.* 1796
CAREFOR - Disposable Wipes & Towelettes - THE SALK COMPANY; *pg.* 1591, *pg.* 800
CAREFREE - Shoe - AEROGROUP INTERNATIONAL, INC.; *pg.* 1803, *pg.* 1055
CAREFREE - Vinyl Tile - CONGOLEUM CORPORATION; *pg.* 921, *pg.* 1084
CAREFREE - Feminine Care - EDGEWELL PERSONAL CARE; *pg.* 1526, *pg.* 995
CAREFREE - Chewing Gum - THE HERSHEY CO.; *pg.* 1855, *pg.* 1538
CAREFREE - Healthcare Product - JOHNSON & JOHNSON; *pg.* 1549, *pg.* 1091
CAREFREE LIVING - Carpet - BEAULIEU GROUP, LLC; *pg.* 917, *pg.* 529
CAREFRESH - Petcare - TRACTOR SUPPLY COMPANY; *pg.* 708, *pg.* 1627
CAREFUSION - Patent Identification System - CARDINAL HEALTH, INC.; *pg.* 1512, *pg.* 1448
CAREGIVER - Shower - E.L. MUSTEE & SONS, INC.; *pg.* 1124, *pg.* 1430
CAREGUARD - Mattress - INVACARE CORPORATION; *pg.* 1546, *pg.* 1451
CARELINK - Pharmaceutical Product - ALERE INC.; *pg.* 1488, *pg.* 849
CAREMC - Online Managed Care Website - CORVEL CORPORATION; *pg.* 1198, *pg.* 109
CARENET - Nursing Information System - CERNER CORPORATION; *pg.* 1514, *pg.* 981
CAREPATTERNS - Pharmaceutical Product - CAREMARK PHARMACY SERVICES; *pg.* 1513, *pg.* 1649
CAREPLAN - Pharmaceutical Product - ALERE INC.; *pg.* 1488, *pg.* 849
CAREPLANNER - Case Management Software - MEDECISION, INC.; *pg.* 431, *pg.* 1592
CAREPLUS - Health Product - CVS HEALTH CORPORATION; *pg.* 1765, *pg.* 1610
CAREPRICER - Computer Software - MEDASSETS INC.; *pg.* 1561, *pg.* 484
CAREQUILT - Warming Blanket - MEDTRONIC; *pg.* 1563, *pg.* 183
CARERRA - Lighting Product - WESTINGHOUSE LIGHTING CORPORATION; *pg.* 687, *pg.* 1571
CARESCIENCE - Company Name - PREMIER HEALTHCARE ALLIANCE; *pg.* 1586, *pg.* 1368
CARESPAN - Health Program - HEALTHPARTNERS, INC.; *pg.* 1203, *pg.* 918
CARESS - Furniture - ASHLEY FURNITURE INDUSTRIES, INC.; *pg.* 914, *pg.* 1852
CARESS - Broadloom - COURISTAN INC.; *pg.* 921, *pg.* 1067
CARESS - Graphic Art Paper - MONADNOCK PAPER MILLS, INC.; *pg.* 1464, *pg.* 1033
CARESS - Footwear - P.W. MINOR & SON, INC.; *pg.* 1816, *pg.* 1140
CARESS - Soap - UNILEVER UNITED STATES, INC.; *pg.* 904, *pg.* 1061
CARESSA - Beauty Bar - BLUE CROSS LABORATORIES; *pg.* 326, *pg.* 277
CARESSA - Fabric - NEMSCHOFF, INC.; *pg.* 936, *pg.* 1890
CARESTEPP - Computer Software - COMPUTER SCIENCES CORPORATION; *pg.* 378, *pg.* 1780
CAREX - Soaps, Scrubs & Dispensers - GEORGIA-PACIFIC LLC; *pg.* 1458, *pg.* 507
CAREX 3000 - Soaps, Scrubs & Dispensers - GEORGIA-PACIFIC LLC; *pg.* 1458, *pg.* 507
CAREY LIND DESIGNS - Wallpaper - YORK WALLCOVERINGS INC.; *pg.* 947, *pg.* 1598
CAREZZA - Rug - COURISTAN INC.; *pg.* 921, *pg.* 1067
CAREZZA - Passport Jacket - LEVENGER COMPANY; *pg.* 1776, *pg.* 421
CARFAX - Information Retrieval Services - CARFAX INC.; *pg.* 202, *pg.* 1777
CARFAX BUYBACK GUARANTEE - Information Retrieval Services - CARFAX INC.; *pg.* 202, *pg.* 1777
CARFLECTOR - Stone & Bug Deflector - LUND INTERNATIONAL, INC.; *pg.* 211, *pg.* 526
CARGILL - Seeds, Salt, Poultry & Processed Meats - CARGILL, INC.; *pg.* 845, *pg.* 965
CARGO - Beverage Chest - IGLOO PRODUCTS CORPORATION; *pg.* 1126, *pg.* 1724
CARGO - Sport Utility & Van Cargo Mats - KRACO ENTERPRISES, LLC; *pg.* 210, *pg.* 68
CARGO LINER - Cargo Area Protector - LUND INTERNATIONAL, INC.; *pg.* 211, *pg.* 526
CARGO-LOGIC - Cargo Area Protection Liner - LUND INTERNATIONAL, INC.; *pg.* 211, *pg.* 526
CARGO STAR - Dry Freight Truck Bodies - KIDRON, INC.; *pg.* 181, *pg.* 1457
CARGOFLEX - Mechanical & Electrical System - JOHNSON CONTROLS, INC.; *pg.* 209, *pg.* 1876
CARGOMASTER - Fastening System - TEXTRON INC.; *pg.* 235, *pg.* 1607
CARGOSEARCH - Cargo Inspection System - AMERICAN SCIENCE AND ENGINEERING, INC.; *pg.* 1399, *pg.* 787
CARHA - Lamp - ASHLEY FURNITURE INDUSTRIES, INC.; *pg.* 914, *pg.* 1852
CARHARTT - Footwear - RED WING SHOE COMPANY, INC.; *pg.* 1817, *pg.* 954
CARHARTT - Apparels - TRACTOR SUPPLY COMPANY; *pg.* 708, *pg.* 1627
CARHIDE - Liquid & Paste Paints - PPG INDUSTRIES, INC.; *pg.* 1445, *pg.* 1579
CARIBBEAN - Carpet - INTERFACE, INC.; *pg.* 695, *pg.* 512
CARIBBEAN - Bath Product - KOHLER CO.; *pg.* 91, *pg.* 1862
CARIBBEAN BLISS - Video Game - INTERNATIONAL GAME TECHNOLOGY; *pg.* 957, *pg.* 1024
CARIBBEAN BREEZE - Video Game - INTERNATIONAL GAME TECHNOLOGY; *pg.* 957, *pg.* 1024
CARIBBEAN COLADA - Cranberry Pineapple Juice Drink - OCEAN SPRAY CRANBERRIES, INC.; *pg.* 887, *pg.* 827
CARIBBEAN COOL - Personal Care Product - COLGATE-PALMOLIVE COMPANY; *pg.* 504, *pg.* 1215
CARIBBEAN DREAMS - Video Game - INTERNATIONAL GAME TECHNOLOGY; *pg.* 957, *pg.* 1024
CARIBBEAN JOE - Lifestyle Brand - SEQUENTIAL BRANDS GROUP, INC.; *pg.* 1395, *pg.* 1290
CARIBBEAN PASSION - Fruit Drink - JAMBA, INC.; *pg.* 1024, *pg.* 84
CARIBBEAN TRANSPORTATION SERVICES - Shipping Service - FEDEX CORPORATION; *pg.* 1907, *pg.* 1642
CARIBBEAN TRAVEL & LIFE - Magazine - BONNIER CORPORATION; *pg.* 1622, *pg.* 480
CARIBE - Flood Lighting - JUNO LIGHTING, INC.; *pg.* 1300, *pg.* 606
CARIBE - Heater - ROBERTS-GORDON INC.; *pg.* 1076, *pg.* 1151
CARIBE - Publication - THOMAS NELSON INC.; *pg.* 1692, *pg.* 1654
CARIBESPAN - Risk Mitigation - ION GEOPHYSICAL CORPORATION; *pg.* 1350, *pg.* 1708
CARIBIA - Glass Product - PPG INDUSTRIES, INC.; *pg.* 1445, *pg.* 1579
CARIBOU ICED COFFEE - Ready-to-Drink Beverage - CARIBOU COFFEE COMPANY, INC.; *pg.* 1764, *pg.* 932
CARING BEYOND PRESCRIPTION - Tag Line - MEDICINE SHOPPE INTERNATIONAL, INC.; *pg.* 1561, *pg.* 976
CARING CONNECTING DOING THE RIGHT THING - Tagline - SOUTHEASTERN BANK FINANCIAL CORPORATION; *pg.* 804, *pg.* 525
CARING FOR CUSTOMERS LIKE ONLY A FAMILY CAN - Slogan - RICH PRODUCTS CORPORATION; *pg.* 892, *pg.* 1150
CARIOCA - Beverages - THE COCA-COLA COMPANY; *pg.* 240, *pg.* 493
CARIPACK - Conveyor Belting - HBD INDUSTRIES, INC.; *pg.* 207, *pg.* 1449
CARL - Puppet - GUND, INC.; *pg.* 954, *pg.* 1056
CARL FISCHER PERFORMANCE SERIES - Music Publisher - CARL FISCHER, LLC; *pg.* 1625, *pg.* 1209
CARL'S TABLE - Furniture - ANTHRO CORPORATION; *pg.* 913, *pg.* 1509
CARLESTA - Pharmaceutical Product - G&W LABORATORIES INC.; *pg.* 1532, *pg.* 1123
CARLETON - Footwear - EASTLAND SHOE CORPORATION; *pg.* 1808, *pg.* 750
CARLETON - Commercial Retail Lighting - JUNO LIGHTING, INC.; *pg.* 1300, *pg.* 606
CARLETON - Lighting Product - QUOIZEL INC.; *pg.* 1304, *pg.* 1616
CARLETON H. SHEETS - Real Estate Tool Kit - PROFESSIONAL EDUCATION INSTITUTE; *pg.* 457, *pg.* 561
CARLING - Beer - MOLSON COORS BREWING COMPANY; *pg.* 256, *pg.* 321
CARLING BLACK LABEL - Beer - MOLSON COORS BREWING COMPANY; *pg.* 256, *pg.* 321
CARLING BLACK LABEL - Beer - PABST BREWING COMPANY; *pg.* 258, *pg.* 137
CARLING C2 - Lager - MOLSON COORS BREWING COMPANY; *pg.* 256, *pg.* 321
CARLINN - Footwear - STEVEN MADDEN, LTD.; *pg.* 1819, *pg.* 1176
CARLISLE - Furniture - AMERICAN LEATHER LP; *pg.* 912, *pg.* 1673
CARLISLE - Tire And Wheel Company - CARLISLE TIRE & WHEEL COMPANY; *pg.* 1880, *pg.* 1612
CARLISLE - Wood Flooring Products & Accessories - CARLISLE WIDE PLANK FLOORS, INC.; *pg.* 919, *pg.* 1039
CARLISLE - Window Treatment - CROSCILL, INC.; *pg.* 1122, *pg.* 1220
CARLISLE - Paddles - JOHNSON OUTDOORS INC.; *pg.* 1837, *pg.* 1888
THE CARLISLE COMPANY - Wallpaper - YORK WALLCOVERINGS INC.; *pg.* 947, *pg.* 1598
CARLISLE SHOWER - Bath Accessory - CROSCILL, INC.; *pg.* 1122, *pg.* 1220
CARLISLE STRIPE - Window Treatment - CROSCILL, INC.; *pg.* 1122, *pg.* 1220
CARLISLE VERSAPOUR - Polycarbonate Pitchers - CARLISLE FOODSERVICE PRODUCTS INCORPORATED; *pg.* 1455, *pg.* 1485
CARLITE - Steel Product - AK STEEL HOLDING CORPORATION; *pg.* 1311, *pg.* 1479
CARLO ROBELLI - Guitars & Violin Family Instruments - SAM ASH MUSIC CORPORATION; *pg.* 669, *pg.* 1167
CARLO ROSSI - Wine - E&J GALLO WINERY; *pg.* 1962, *pg.* 149
CARLON - Conduit Fittings - THOMAS & BETTS CORPORATION; *pg.* 680, *pg.* 1646
CARLON FLEX-PLUS - Floor Boxes & Covers - THOMAS & BETTS CORPORATION; *pg.* 680, *pg.* 1646
CARLON MULTI-GARD - Floor Boxes & Covers - THOMAS & BETTS CORPORATION; *pg.* 680, *pg.* 1646
CARLON PLENUM-GARD - Floor Boxes & Covers - THOMAS & BETTS CORPORATION; *pg.* 680, *pg.* 1646
CARLON RESI-GARD - Floor Boxes & Covers - THOMAS & BETTS CORPORATION; *pg.* 680, *pg.* 1646
CARLON RISER-GARD - Floor Boxes & Covers - THOMAS & BETTS CORPORATION; *pg.* 680, *pg.* 1646
CARL'S JR. - Quick Service Restaurant - CKE RESTAURANTS INC.; *pg.* 1723, *pg.* 63
CARLSON DESTINATION MARKETING SERVICES - Marketing Service - CARLSON COMPANIES INC.; *pg.* 1084, *pg.* 947
CARLSON LEISURE TRAVEL SERVICES - Travel Services - CARLSON COMPANIES INC.; *pg.* 1084, *pg.* 947
CARLSON MARKETING - Marketing - CARLSON COMPANIES INC.; *pg.* 1084, *pg.* 947
CARLSON WAGONLIT TRAVEL - Travel Planning - CARLSON WAGONLIT TRAVEL; *pg.* 1902, *pg.* 948
CARLTON - Card - AMERICAN GREETINGS CORPORATION; *pg.* 1615, *pg.* 1428
CARLTON - Furniture - JOFCO INC.; *pg.* 931, *pg.* 691
CARLTON - Paper Plate - KIMBERLY-CLARK CORPORATION; *pg.* 1461, *pg.* 1720
CARLTON CARDS - Greeting Cards & Gifts - AMERICAN GREETINGS CORPORATION; *pg.* 1615, *pg.* 1428
CARLTON HAIR - Hair Salons - REGIS CORPORATION; *pg.* 521, *pg.* 941
CARLY - Furniture - AMISCO INDUSTRIES LTD.; *pg.* 913, *pg.* 1958
CARLY - Ladles & Tongs - CARLISLE FOODSERVICE PRODUCTS INCORPORATED; *pg.* 1455, *pg.* 1485
CARLY - Watch - COACH, INC.; *pg.* 3, *pg.* 1214
CARLYLE - Furniture - ASHLEY FURNITURE INDUSTRIES, INC.; *pg.* 914, *pg.* 1852
CARLYLE - Lounge Chairs - BERNHARDT DESIGN; *pg.* 918, *pg.* 1381
CARLYLE - Table - BLATT BOWLING & BILLIARD CORP.; *pg.* 1827, *pg.* 1203
CARMA - Cream-Based Liqueur - JIM BEAM BRANDS CO.; *pg.* 1965, *pg.* 601
CARMEL - Ladies' Wallets - BUXTON ACQUISITION CO., LLC; *pg.* 2, *pg.* 845
CARMEL COVE - Carpet - BEAULIEU GROUP, LLC; *pg.* 917, *pg.* 529
CARMELA'S OF BROOKLYN - Italian Restaurant - SBARRO, INC.; *pg.* 1749, *pg.* 1182
CARMELITA - Footwear - EASTLAND SHOE CORPORATION; *pg.* 1808, *pg.* 750

First page reference indicates Business Class Edition
Second page reference indicates Geographic Edition

CARMELLA - Footwear - EASTLAND SHOE CORPORATION; *pg.* 1808, *pg.* 750
CARMEN - Footwear - BEBE STORES, INC.; *pg.* 19, *pg.* 49
CARMEN - Furniture - LA-Z-BOY INCORPORATED; *pg.* 932, *pg.* 901
CARMET - Tooling System - KENNAMETAL INC.; *pg.* 1052, *pg.* 1547
CARMILAX - Rumen Stimulant-Mild Laxative-Carminative-Antacid - PFIZER INC.; *pg.* 1581, *pg.* 1278
CARMINE - Fabric - NEMSCHOFF, INC.; *pg.* 936, *pg.* 1890
CARNATION - Breakfast Drinks, Milk Products - THE J.M. SMUCKER COMPANY; *pg.* 865, *pg.* 1468
CARNATION ALSOY - Infant Formula - NESTLE USA, INC.; *pg.* 883, *pg.* 96
CARNATION BABY CEREAL - Baby Food - NESTLE USA, INC.; *pg.* 883, *pg.* 96
CARNATION COCO SUPREME - Food Product - NESTLE USA, INC.; *pg.* 883, *pg.* 96
CARNATION COFFEE-MATE - Food & Beverage Product - NESTLE USA, INC.; *pg.* 883, *pg.* 96
CARNATION EVAPORATED MILK - Food Product - NESTLE USA, INC.; *pg.* 883, *pg.* 96
CARNATION FOLLOW-UP FORMULA - Food Product - NESTLE USA, INC.; *pg.* 883, *pg.* 96
CARNATION GOOD START - Food Product - NESTLE USA, INC.; *pg.* 883, *pg.* 96
CARNATION HOT COCOA - Food Product - NESTLE USA, INC.; *pg.* 883, *pg.* 96
CARNATION INSTANT BREAKFAST - Food & Beverage Product - NESTLE USA, INC.; *pg.* 883, *pg.* 96
CARNEBON - Disinfectant - E.I. DU PONT DE NEMOURS & COMPANY; *pg.* 1159, *pg.* 390
CARNEGIE - Fabric - NEMSCHOFF, INC.; *pg.* 936, *pg.* 1890
THE CARNEGIE COACH - Educational Training Service - DALE CARNEGIE TRAINING; *pg.* 600, *pg.* 1221
CARNEO ROSE - Lace Curtain - HERITAGE LACE INC.; *pg.* 694, *pg.* 711
CARNILLE - Furniture - HOOKER FURNITURE CORPORATION; *pg.* 928, *pg.* 1788
CARNIVAL - Cruise Line - CARNIVAL CRUISE LINES; *pg.* 1902, *pg.* 441
THE CARNIVAL - Shoe Stores - SHOE CARNIVAL, INC.; *pg.* 1819, *pg.* 679
CARNIVAL CRUISE LINES - Passenger Cruises & Tours - CARNIVAL CORPORATION; *pg.* 1902, *pg.* 441
CARNIVAL LITES - Shoes - SHOE CARNIVAL, INC.; *pg* 1819, *pg.* 679
CARNIVAL OF CASH - Game - WMS INDUSTRIES INC.; *pg.* 593, *pg.* 666
CARNIVAL OF MYSTERY - Video Game - INTERNATIONAL GAME TECHNOLOGY; *pg.* 957, *pg.* 1024
CARNIVAL OF MYSTERY MASQUERADE - Video Game - INTERNATIONAL GAME TECHNOLOGY; *pg.* 957, *pg.* 1024
CARNIVALE - Cable Television Show - HOME BOX OFFICE, INC.; *pg.* 290, *pg.* 1240
CARNIVALE - Fabric - NEMSCHOFF, INC.; *pg.* 936, *pg.* 1890
CARNIVORES & DESIGN - Restaurant Services - JACK IN THE BOX INC.; *pg.* 1732, *pg.* 204
CARNU - No Buff Wax - S.C. JOHNSON & SON, INC.; *pg.* 334, *pg.* 1889
CAROL - Wire & Cable Product - GENERAL CABLE CORPORATION; *pg.* 83, *pg.* 729
CAROL ROWAN - Home & Garden Product - ENESCO, LLC; *pg.* 1124, *pg.* 620
CAROLE LITTLE - Apparel - CHEROKEE GLOBAL BRANDS; *pg.* 21, *pg.* 278
CAROLENA SHEER - Window Treatment - CROSCILL, INC.; *pg.* 1122, *pg.* 1220
CAROLINA - Shoe - AEROGROUP INTERNATIONAL, INC.; *pg.* 1803, *pg.* 1055
CAROLINA - Absorbent Cotton - BARNHARDT MANUFACTURING COMPANY; *pg.* 1498, *pg.* 1364
CAROLINA - Home Fragrance Product - BLYTH, INC.; *pg.* 502, *pg.* 349
CAROLINA - Paper - INTERNATIONAL PAPER COMPANY; *pg.* 1460, *pg.* 1644
CAROLINA BIOLOGICAL - Lab Science Material - CAROLINA BIOLOGICAL SUPPLY COMPANY; *pg.* 1513, *pg.* 1359
CAROLINA CASH - Lottery Game - THE SOUTH CAROLINA EDUCATION LOTTERY; *pg.* 1005, *pg.* 1614
CAROLINA CLUB - Club - SONIC CORP.; *pg.* 1750, *pg.* 1487
CAROLINA DESK COMPANY - All Products - DMI FURNITURE, INC.; *pg.* 923, *pg.* 733
CAROLINA HONEYS - Sauce - ROMACORP, INC.; *pg.* 1748, *pg.* 1734
CAROLINA HURRICANES - Professional Hockey Team - CAROLINA HURRICANES HOCKEY CLUB; *pg.* 537, *pg.* 1386
CAROLINA MATHEMATICS - Math Supplies - CAROLINA BIOLOGICAL SUPPLY COMPANY; *pg.* 1513, *pg.* 1359
CAROLINA RICE - Rice - RIVIANA FOODS INC.; *pg.* 892, *pg.* 1713
CAROLINA TIPS - Educational Product - CAROLINA BIOLOGICAL SUPPLY COMPANY; *pg.* 1513, *pg.* 1359
CAROLINA TURKEY - Turkey Products - BUTTERBALL, LLC; *pg.* 843, *pg.* 1385
CAROLINA'S PERFECT SOLUTION - Lab Science Material - CAROLINA BIOLOGICAL SUPPLY COMPANY; *pg.* 1513, *pg.* 1359
CAROLINE'S DRESSING - Food Product - CAINS FOODS, L.P.; *pg.* 843, *pg.* 784
CAROLPRENE - Jacketed Electrical Cords, Insulated Electrical Portable Cord - GENERAL CABLE CORPORATION; *pg.* 83, *pg.* 729
CAROL'S DAUGHTER - Hair and Skin Products - L'OREAL USA; *pg.* 514, *pg.* 1252
CAROLS OF CHRISTMAS II - Clocks - HOWARD MILLER COMPANY; *pg.* 7, *pg.* 914
CAROLYN - Clothing - ABERCROMBIE & FITCH CO.; *pg.* 37, *pg.* 1466
CAROLYN - Furniture - AMISCO INDUSTRIES LTD.; *pg.* 913, *pg.* 1958
CAROLYN - Women's Clothing & Accessories - WOODEN SHIPS OF HOBOKEN; *pg.* 35, *pg.* 1315
CAROMED - Post-Surgery Garments - MENTOR CORPORATION; *pg.* 1565, *pg.* 263
CARON - Lamp - ASHLEY FURNITURE INDUSTRIES, INC.; *pg.* 914, *pg.* 1852
CARON - Consumer Knitting Yarn & Craft Kits - NATIONAL SPINNING COMPANY, INC.; *pg.* 697, *pg.* 1265
CARON - Cheese - SAPUTO, INC.; *pg.* 893, *pg.* 1956
CARON - Fabric - SCALAMANDRE, INC.; *pg.* 941, *pg.* 1058
CAROPAK - Biological Supplies - CAROLINA BIOLOGICAL SUPPLY COMPANY; *pg.* 1513, *pg.* 1359
CAROSAFE - Lab Science Material - CAROLINA BIOLOGICAL SUPPLY COMPANY; *pg.* 1513, *pg.* 1359
CAROUSEL - Slide Projectors, Trays & Projector Accessories - EASTMAN KODAK COMPANY; *pg.* 1408, *pg.* 1333
CAROWINDS - Amusement Park - CEDAR FAIR, L.P.; *pg.* 537, *pg.* 1471
CARPAL LOCK - Medical & Aesthetic Product - DYNATRONICS CORPORATION; *pg.* 1526, *pg.* 1757
CARPENTER 20CB-3LR - Alloy - CARPENTER TECHNOLOGY CORPORATION; *pg.* 73, *pg.* 1584
CARPENTER ANT & TERMITE AEROSOL - Ant Control Products - SENORET CHEMICAL COMPANY; *pg.* 335, *pg.* 1548
CARPENTER CCM - Medical Alloys - CARPENTER TECHNOLOGY CORPORATION; *pg.* 73, *pg.* 1584
CARPENTER CUP - Baseball Tournament - THE PHILLIES, L.P.; *pg.* 575, *pg.* 1569
CARPENTER GLASS SEALING 49 - Alloy - CARPENTER TECHNOLOGY CORPORATION; *pg.* 73, *pg.* 1584
CARPENTER HIGH PERMEABILITY - Alloys - CARPENTER TECHNOLOGY CORPORATION; *pg.* 73, *pg.* 1584
CARPENTER HYMU - Alloys - CARPENTER TECHNOLOGY CORPORATION; *pg.* 73, *pg.* 1584
CARPENTER INVAR - Alloys - CARPENTER TECHNOLOGY CORPORATION; *pg.* 73, *pg.* 1584
CARPENTER LOW EXPANSION - Alloys - CARPENTER TECHNOLOGY CORPORATION; *pg.* 73, *pg.* 1584
CARPENTER NO 158 - Steel - CARPENTER TECHNOLOGY CORPORATION; *pg.* 73, *pg.* 1584
CARPENTER TEMPERATURE COMPENSATOR - Alloys - CARPENTER TECHNOLOGY CORPORATION; *pg.* 73, *pg.* 1584
CARPENTER'S PRIDE - Tools - VAUGHAN & BUSHNELL MANUFACTURING COMPANY, INC.; *pg.* 1066, *pg.* 616
CARPET CARE - Household Product - BLUE CROSS LABORATORIES; *pg.* 326, *pg.* 277
CARPET FRESH - Rug & Room Deodorizer - WD-40 COMPANY; *pg.* 337, *pg.* 210
CARPET SCIENCE - Carpet Cleaner - S.C. JOHNSON & SON, INC.; *pg.* 334, *pg.* 1889
CARPET SHAMPOO 877 - Cleaning Preparation - WALTER G. LEGGE COMPANY, INC.; *pg.* 337, *pg.* 1321
CARPETKEEPERS - Carpet Care Machines - TORNADO INDUSTRIES, INC.; *pg.* 1383, *pg.* 591
CARPETRIEVER - Carpet Vacuum - HILLYARD, INC.; *pg.* 331, *pg.* 990
CARPETWIN - Carpet Vacuum - HILLYARD, INC.; *pg.* 331, *pg.* 990
CARPOL - Carpet Cushion - CARPENTER CO.; *pg.* 920, *pg.* 1801
CARPUJECT - Pharmaceutical Product - HOSPIRA, INC.; *pg.* 1542, *pg.* 623
CARRABBA'S - Italian Restaurant - BLOOMIN' BRANDS, INC.; *pg.* 1716, *pg.* 471
CARRARA - Carpet - BEAULIEU GROUP, LLC; *pg.* 917, *pg.* 529
CARRARA - Ornamental Structural Glass - PPG INDUSTRIES, INC.; *pg.* 1445, *pg.* 1579
CARRARA MARBLE - Bath Collection - CROSCILL, INC.; *pg.* 1122, *pg.* 1220
CARRIAGE - Furniture - JASPER GROUP; *pg.* 930, *pg.* 691
CARRIAGE - Watches - TIMEX CORPORATION; *pg.* 14, *pg.* 355
CARRIAGE HOUSE - Food Products - CONAGRA FOODS; *pg.* 826, *pg.* 994
CARRIAGE HOUSE - Garage Door - MARTIN DOOR MANUFACTURING, INC.; *pg.* 96, *pg.* 1759
CARRIAGE HOUSE SERIES - Garage Doors - JELD-WEN, INC.; *pg.* 1051, *pg.* 1499
CARRIDEX - Bulking Agent for Low-Calorie Sweeteners - PENFORD CORPORATION; *pg.* 1177, *pg.* 314
CARRIE - Lamp - ASHLEY FURNITURE INDUSTRIES, INC.; *pg.* 914, *pg.* 1852
CARRIER - Air Conditioning, Heating & Refrigeration - CARRIER CORPORATION; *pg.* 1070, *pg.* 349
CARRIER - Cargo Shorts - LEVI STRAUSS & CO.; *pg.* 43, *pg.* 220
CARRIER - Heating & Air Conditioning - UNITED TECHNOLOGIES CORPORATION; *pg.* 235, *pg.* 353
CARRIER KOTE - Paperboard Packaging Product - WESTROCK COMPANY; *pg.* 1472, *pg.* 1805
CARRIER MOUNTED LUBRICATING SYSTEM - Machinery Lubricating System - ALLIED CONSTRUCTION PRODUCTS, LLC; *pg.* 1311, *pg.* 1427
CARRIER PICKUP - Postal Services - UNITED STATES POSTAL SERVICE; *pg.* 1009, *pg.* 406
CARRIER PRO - Polyurethane - WEINBRENNER SHOE COMPANY, INC.; *pg.* 1822, *pg.* 1871
CARRIERSCAN - Software - SYMANTEC CORPORATION; *pg.* 478, *pg.* 161
CARRINGTON - Furniture - LA-Z-BOY INCORPORATED; *pg.* 932, *pg.* 901
CARRINGTON - Bathroom Accessories - SYMMONS INDUSTRIES, INC.; *pg.* 114, *pg.* 803
CARRINGTON-CHASE - Mattresses - SEALY CORPORATION; *pg.* 942, *pg.* 1391
CARRINGTON STRIPE - Bedding - CROSCILL, INC.; *pg.* 1122, *pg.* 1220
CARROLTOUCH - Infrared Touch Screens - ELO TOUCH SOLUTIONS; *pg.* 635, *pg.* 145
CARRONNET - Sport Net - CARRON NET COMPANY, INC.; *pg.* 1830, *pg.* 1896
CARROT-TEIN - Nutritional Supplement - NATURAL ORGANICS, INC.; *pg.* 1571, *pg.* 1181
CARROWS RESTAURANTS - Eating Place - DENNY'S CORPORATION; *pg.* 1725, *pg.* 1622
CARRY-HOME COVERALL - Polyethylene Sheeting - WARP BROTHERS; *pg.* 1471, *pg.* 595
CARRY IN COMFORT - Dual Support Sling - THE BOPPY COMPANY, LLC; *pg.* 20, *pg.* 329
CARRY MATE - Cleaning Supply Caddy - GEERPRES INC.; *pg.* 1339, *pg.* 901
CARRY-ON TRAILER - Heavy-Duty HitchPacker - TRACTOR SUPPLY COMPANY; *pg.* 708, *pg.* 1627
CARRY-OUT - Container - PACTIV CORPORATION; *pg.* 1466, *pg.* 624
CARRY RIGHT - Infant Car Seat Handle - EVENFLO COMPANY, INC.; *pg.* 924, *pg.* 1470
CARRY-SAFE - Cup - PACTIV CORPORATION; *pg.* 1466, *pg.* 624
CARRYALL - Utility Vehicles - CLUB CAR, INC.; *pg.* 1830, *pg.* 532
CARRYDECK - 8.5 & 20 Ton Industrial Cranes - MARINE TRAVELIFT, INC.; *pg.* 1359, *pg.* 1895
CARS - Software - COMPUWARE CORPORATION; *pg.* 379, *pg.* 879
CARS & PARTS - Publication - AMOS PRESS, INC.; *pg.*

1616, *pg.* 1472

CARS.COM - Automobile Advertising Website - CLASSIFIED VENTURES, LLC; *pg.* 1235, *pg.* 571

CARSMART.COM - Automotive Information Site - AUTOBYTEL INC.; *pg.* 1230, *pg.* 107

CARSON - Furniture - AMERICAN LEATHER LP; *pg.* 912, *pg.* 1673

CARSON - Guest Chairs - BERNHARDT DESIGN; *pg.* 918, *pg.* 1381

CARSOQUAT - Quaternary Compound for Hair Conditioners - LONZA INC.; *pg.* 1171, *pg.* 1041

CARSTAIRS' WHITE SEAL AMERICAN - Blended Whiskey - SAZERAC COMPANY, INC.; *pg.* 1969, *pg.* 745

CART - GPCR Technology - ARENA PHARMACEUTICALS, INC.; *pg.* 1495, *pg.* 200

CART - Operations & Management Enterprise Tracking - CANNON EQUIPMENT COMPANY; *pg.* 1321, *pg.* 920

CART SAFARI - Shopping Cart Cover - INFANTINO, LLC; *pg.* 957, *pg.* 203

CART TUNES - Shopping Cart Cover - INFANTINO, LLC; *pg.* 957, *pg.* 203

CARTALL - Material Handling Products - PECO, INC.; *pg.* 1368, *pg.* 1505

CARTE NOIRE - Coffee - MONDELEZ INTERNATIONAL, INC.; *pg.* 878, *pg.* 601

CARTECSAL - Neutral Salt - HEATBATH CORPORATION; *pg.* 1165, *pg.* 826

CARTEL - Fabric - NEMSCHOFF, INC.; *pg.* 936, *pg.* 1890

CARTEL - Apparel - OAKLEY, INC.; *pg.* 1840, *pg.* 86

CARTEOL - Glaucoma Treatment - BAUSCH & LOMB INCORPORATED; *pg.* 1401, *pg.* 1045

CARTER - Fuel Systems - FEDERAL-MOGUL HOLDINGS CORPORATION; *pg.* 205, *pg.* 907

CARTER HOFFMAN - Kitchen Equipment - THE MIDDLEBY CORPORATION; *pg.* 1361, *pg.* 610

CARTER'S - Laxative - CHURCH & DWIGHT CO., INC.; *pg.* 1153, *pg.* 1063

CARTER'S CLASSIC COLLECTION - Children's Clothes - CARTER'S, INC.; *pg.* 21, *pg.* 491

CARTERS STARTERS - Baby Product - CARTER'S, INC.; *pg.* 21, *pg.* 491

CARTICEL - Orthopaedic - GENZYME CORPORATION; *pg.* 1534, *pg.* 808

CARTILAGE - Orthopedic Product - DJO INCORPORATED; *pg.* 1524, *pg.* 302

CARTIVA - Image Management Platform - DATACARD CORPORATION; *pg.* 382, *pg.* 948

CARTO - Healthcare Product - JOHNSON & JOHNSON; *pg.* 1549, *pg.* 1091

CARTOGRAPHER - Software - BIO-RAD LABORATORIES, INC.; *pg.* 1504, *pg.* 101

CARTON - Adhesive - AERVOE INDUSTRIES INCORPORATED; *pg.* 1439, *pg.* 1021

THE CARTON FLOW AUTHORITY - Tagline - UNEX MANUFACTURING, INC.; *pg.* 1385, *pg.* 1075

CARTON WINDOW FILM - Plastic Film - MULTI-PLASTICS, INC.; *pg.* 1886, *pg.* 1457

CARTRAC - Material Handling System - PARAGON TECHNOLOGIES, INC.; *pg.* 1367, *pg.* 1528

CARTUS - Relocation Management Services - REALOGY CORPORATION; *pg.* 1109, *pg.* 1081

CARTV.COM - Online Car-Buying Site - AUTOBYTEL INC.; *pg.* 1230, *pg.* 107

CARTWHEEL BOOKS - Books - SCHOLASTIC INC.; *pg.* 1683, *pg.* 1288

CARULITE - Chemical Product - CARUS CORPORATION; *pg.* 1152, *pg.* 652

CARUS - Chemical Product - CARUS CORPORATION; *pg.* 1152, *pg.* 652

CARUS ORTHOPHOS - Phosphate - CARUS CORPORATION; *pg.* 1152, *pg.* 652

CARUS UPZ - Phosphate - CARUS CORPORATION; *pg.* 1152, *pg.* 652

CARUSEL - Lithium Manganese Spinel Material - CARUS CORPORATION; *pg.* 1152, *pg.* 652

CARUSMATIC - Feed System - CARUS CORPORATION; *pg.* 1152, *pg.* 652

CARUSO - Personal Care Electrical Product - HELEN OF TROY L.P.; *pg.* 511, *pg.* 1692

CARUSOL - Chemical Product - CARUS CORPORATION; *pg.* 1152, *pg.* 652

CARVE 'N SET - Kitchen Appliance - HAMILTON BEACH BRANDS, INC.; *pg.* 56, *pg.* 1783

CARVEDWOOD2 SERIES - Vinyl Siding - PLY GEM SIDING GROUP; *pg.* 105, *pg.* 986

CARVER - Casual Shoes - JOHNSTON & MURPHY CO.; *pg.* 1810, *pg.* 1651

CARVER'S - Beverages - THE COCA-COLA COMPANY; *pg.* 240, *pg.* 493

CAS-20 - Filler - USG CORPORATION; *pg.* 118, *pg.* 594

CAS 200 - Dual-Color Image Analysis System For Quantitative Biochemical Data - BECTON, DICKINSON & COMPANY; *pg.* 1501, *pg.* 1068

CAS EXPRESS - Software - CAS MEDICAL SYSTEMS, INC.; *pg.* 1513, *pg.* 339

CASA - Faucets - MOEN INCORPORATED; *pg.* 1056, *pg.* 1468

CASA - Fabric - NEMSCHOFF, INC.; *pg.* 936, *pg.* 1890

CASA AT CASTELLA - Community Name - WCI COMMUNITIES, INC.; *pg.* 1118, *pg.* 414

CASA BONITA - Restaurants - STAR BUFFET, INC.; *pg.* 1751, *pg.* 24

THE CASA COLLECTION - Furniture Collection - CENTURY FURNITURE INDUSTRIES; *pg.* 920, *pg.* 1377

CASA DIBERTACCHI - Food Products - RICH PRODUCTS CORPORATION; *pg.* 892, *pg.* 1150

CASA DIVA - Packaged Foods - ATALANTA CORPORATION; *pg.* 838, *pg.* 1057

CASA FIESTA - Mexican Food - BRUCE FOODS CORPORATION; *pg.* 842, *pg.* 743

CASA GALLARDO - Mexican Restaurants - REAL MEX RESTAURANTS, INC.; *pg.* 1746, *pg.* 75

CASA HERRADURA - Tequila - BROWN-FORMAN CORPORATION; *pg.* 1958, *pg.* 732

CASA MOLLINO - Furniture - ASHLEY FURNITURE INDUSTRIES, INC.; *pg.* 914, *pg.* 1852

CASA MONTEREY - Lighting Product - WESTINGHOUSE LIGHTING CORPORATION; *pg.* 687, *pg.* 1571

CASA NOBLE - Tequila - CONSTELLATION BRANDS, INC.; *pg.* 1960, *pg.* 1348

CASA OLE - Restaurant - MEXICAN RESTAURANTS, INC.; *pg.* 1741, *pg.* 1711

CASABLANCA - Furniture - HOOKER FURNITURE CORPORATION; *pg.* 928, *pg.* 1788

CASABLANCA - Container Grown Plant - MONROVIA GROWERS; *pg.* 1797, *pg.* 44

CASABLANCA - Ceramic Tile - WALKER & ZANGER, INC.; *pg.* 119, *pg.* 281

CASABLANCA HOTEL - Resort, Casino, Golf & Spa - MESQUITE GAMING, LLC; *pg.* 1104, *pg.* 1030

CASABLANCA JARDINIER - Flower Arrangement - 1-800-FLOWERS.COM, INC.; *pg.* 1758, *pg.* 1151

CASAL BORDINA WINES ITALY - Wines - LEONARD KREUSCH, INC.; *pg.* 254, *pg.* 1099

CASAMODA - Barware & Serveware Accessories - LIFETIME BRANDS, INC.; *pg.* 1127, *pg.* 1161

CASANOVA - Carpet - BEAULIEU GROUP, LLC; *pg.* 917, *pg.* 529

CASANOVA - Fabric - NEMSCHOFF, INC.; *pg.* 936, *pg.* 1890

CASANOVA - Ceiling Fan - WESTINGHOUSE LIGHTING CORPORATION; *pg.* 687, *pg.* 1571

CASAVA - Software - ILLUMINA, INC.; *pg.* 412, *pg.* 203

CASBAH - Food Product - THE HAIN CELESTIAL GROUP, INC.; *pg.* 860, *pg.* 1172

CASBAH - Fabric - NEMSCHOFF, INC.; *pg.* 936, *pg.* 1890

CASCADA DE DIAMANTES - Video Game - INTERNATIONAL GAME TECHNOLOGY; *pg.* 957, *pg.* 1024

CASCADE - Dental Chair - A-DEC, INC.; *pg.* 1483, *pg.* 1500

CASCADE - Furniture - THE COMMERCIAL FURNITURE GROUP; *pg.* 920, *pg.* 994

CASCADE - Window Treatment - CROSCILL, INC.; *pg.* 1122, *pg.* 1220

CASCADE - Brew - DESCHUTES BREWERY INC.; *pg.* 248, *pg.* 1496

CASCADE - Binocular - LEUPOLD & STEVENS, INC.; *pg.* 1420, *pg.* 1492

CASCADE - House Care Product - THE PROCTER & GAMBLE COMPANY; *pg.* 1129, *pg.* 1418

CASCADE BANCORP - Banking Service - CASCADE BANCORP; *pg.* 732, *pg.* 1496

CASCADE BANK - Banking Service - OPUS BANK; *pg.* 790, *pg.* 1819

CASCADE BLUE - Biomolecule Product - THERMO FISHER SCIENTIFIC INC.; *pg.* 1602, *pg.* 61

CASCADE BLUES - Menswear - KELLWOOD COMPANY; *pg.* 28, *pg.* 975

CASCADE BOOK - Paper Products - BOISE CASCADE HOLDINGS, L.L.C.; *pg.* 1453, *pg.* 546

CASCADE COMPLETE ALL-IN-1 ACTIONPACS - Dishwashing Detergent - THE PROCTER & GAMBLE COMPANY; *pg.* 1129, *pg.* 1418

CASCADE CREST - Building Products - BOISE CASCADE HOLDINGS, L.L.C.; *pg.* 1453, *pg.* 546

CASCADE MOUNTAIN - Game - WMS INDUSTRIES INC.; *pg.* 593, *pg.* 666

CASCADE SELECT - Seafood Products - UNISEA FOODS, INC.; *pg.* 906, *pg.* 1829

CASCADE YELLOW - Biomolecule Product - THERMO FISHER SCIENTIFIC INC.; *pg.* 1602, *pg.* 61

CASCADIA - Soft Drink - NATIONAL BEVERAGE CORP.; *pg.* 257, *pg.* 425

CASCADIA - Fabric - NEMSCHOFF, INC.; *pg.* 936, *pg.* 1890

CASCADIA ONLY 2 CALORIES - Soft Drink - NATIONAL BEVERAGE CORP.; *pg.* 257, *pg.* 425

CASCADIA SPARKLING CLEAR - Soft Drink - NATIONAL BEVERAGE CORP.; *pg.* 257, *pg.* 425

CASCADIAN FARM - Organic Food Products - GENERAL MILLS, INC.; *pg.* 828, *pg.* 933

CASCADIAN FARM PURELY O'S - Cereal - GENERAL MILLS, INC.; *pg.* 828, *pg.* 933

CASCADING HEARTS - Necklace - HABAND COMPANY, INC.; *pg.* 1772, *pg.* 1099

CASCO - Fabric - NEMSCHOFF, INC.; *pg.* 936, *pg.* 1890

CASE - Construction Equipment - CNH AMERICA LLC; *pg.* 702, *pg.* 560

CASE IH - Agricultural Equipment - CNH AMERICA LLC; *pg.* 702, *pg.* 560

CASE360 - Software - OPENTEXT; *pg.* 450, *pg.* 1665

CASEALERT - Predictive Modeling Tool - MEDECISION, INC.; *pg.* 431, *pg.* 1592

CASEC - Powdered Protein Supplement - MEAD JOHNSON NUTRITION COMPANY; *pg.* 1561, *pg.* 615

CASEMASTER - Gaming Product - GLD PRODUCTS, INC.; *pg.* 1835, *pg.* 1882

CASEMASTER - Heat Treating Equipment - SECO/WARWICK CORPORATION; *pg.* 1076, *pg.* 1552

CASEMATE - Thermal Processing Equipment - SURFACE COMBUSTION, INC.; *pg.* 1077, *pg.* 1462

CASEMENT - Room Air Conditioner - FRIEDRICH AIR CONDITIONING CO.; *pg.* 1072, *pg.* 1740

CASEN-FLEET - Laxative Product - FLEET LABORATORIES; *pg.* 1531, *pg.* 1787

CASEWORKS - Office Furniture - JOFCO INC.; *pg.* 931, *pg.* 691

CASEY - Clothing - ABERCROMBIE & FITCH CO.; *pg.* 37, *pg.* 1466

CASEY - Lamp - ASHLEY FURNITURE INDUSTRIES, INC.; *pg.* 914, *pg.* 1852

CASEY'S - Pubs - PRIME RESTAURANTS INC.; *pg.* 1746, *pg.* 1947

CASEY'S CHOICE - Dog Food - PET VALU CANADA, INC.; *pg.* 1480, *pg.* 1924

CASH 3 - Lottery Game - THE FLORIDA LOTTERY; *pg.* 992, *pg.* 469

CASH 3 - Lottery Game - GEORGIA LOTTERY CORPORATION; *pg.* 993, *pg.* 506

CASH 4 - Lottery Game - GEORGIA LOTTERY CORPORATION; *pg.* 993, *pg.* 506

CASH 5 - Cash Game - PENNSYLVANIA STATE LOTTERY; *pg.* 1003, *pg.* 1552

CASH 5 - Lottery Game - THE SOUTH CAROLINA EDUCATION LOTTERY; *pg.* 1005, *pg.* 1614

CASH 5 - Lottery - TEXAS LOTTERY COMMISSION; *pg.* 1007, *pg.* 1666

CASH BALL - Video Game - INTERNATIONAL GAME TECHNOLOGY; *pg.* 957, *pg.* 1024

CASH BLIZZARD - Lottery Game - MASSACHUSETTS STATE LOTTERY; *pg.* 998, *pg.* 802

CASH BLOCKBUSTER - Lottery Game - LOUISIANA LOTTERY CORPORATION; *pg.* 997, *pg.* 742

CASH BLOWOUT - Lottery Game - OHIO LOTTERY COMMISSION; *pg.* 1002, *pg.* 1433

CASH BONUS DOUBLE PLAY - Lottery Game - OHIO LOTTERY COMMISSION; *pg.* 1002, *pg.* 1433

CASH CELEBRATION - Lottery Game - KENTUCKY LOTTERY CORPORATION; *pg.* 996, *pg.* 735

CASH CLIMB - Game - INTERNATIONAL GAME TECHNOLOGY; *pg.* 420, *pg.* 1606

CASH COASTER - Video Game - INTERNATIONAL GAME TECHNOLOGY; *pg.* 957, *pg.* 1024

CASH CONNECT - ATM Services Division - WSFS FINANCIAL CORPORATION; *pg.* 823, *pg.* 392

CASH CONVOY - Video Game - INTERNATIONAL GAME

TECHNOLOGY; *pg.* 957, *pg.* 1024
CASH COVE - Video Game - INTERNATIONAL GAME TECHNOLOGY; *pg.* 957, *pg.* 1024
CASH COW - Lottery Game - IOWA LOTTERY; *pg.* 996, *pg.* 705
CASH CROP - Game - WMS INDUSTRIES INC.; *pg.* 593, *pg.* 666
CASH DASH - Video Game - INTERNATIONAL GAME TECHNOLOGY; *pg.* 957, *pg.* 1024
CASH DELUXE - Insurance Product - SBLI USA LIFE INSURANCE COMPANY, INC.; *pg.* 1216, *pg.* 1288
CASH EXPLOSION - Lottery Card - MISSOURI LOTTERY; *pg.* 999, *pg.* 979
CASH EXPLOSION DOUBLE PLAY - TV Game Show - OHIO LOTTERY COMMISSION; *pg.* 1002, *pg.* 1433
CASH EXPRESS - Lottery Game - MASSACHUSETTS STATE LOTTERY; *pg.* 998, *pg.* 802
CASH EXTRAVAGANZA - Lottery Game - KENTUCKY LOTTERY CORPORATION; *pg.* 996, *pg.* 735
CASH FIESTA - Lottery Game - D.C. LOTTERY & CHARITABLE GAMES CONTROL BOARD; *pg.* 991, *pg.* 398
CASH FIREWORKS - Lottery Game - MINNESOTA STATE LOTTERY; *pg.* 999, *pg.* 956
CASH FLOW GENERATOR - Conducting Seminars - TIGRENT INC.; *pg.* 608, *pg.* 415
CASH FOR LIFE - Lottery Game - OHIO LOTTERY COMMISSION; *pg.* 1002, *pg.* 1433
CASH KING CHECKERS - Game - INTERNATIONAL GAME TECHNOLOGY; *pg.* 957, *pg.* 1024
CASH ON THE SPOT - Lottery Card - MISSOURI LOTTERY; *pg.* 999, *pg.* 979
CASH OUT - Lottery Game - OHIO LOTTERY COMMISSION; *pg.* 1002, *pg.* 1433
CASH QUEST - Video Game - INTERNATIONAL GAME TECHNOLOGY; *pg.* 957, *pg.* 1024
CASH QUEST - Lottery Game - LOUISIANA LOTTERY CORPORATION; *pg.* 997, *pg.* 742
CASH ROULETTE - Lottery Game - MASSACHUSETTS STATE LOTTERY; *pg.* 998, *pg.* 802
CASH SPLASH - Lottery Game - IOWA LOTTERY; *pg.* 996, *pg.* 705
CASH STASH - Lottery Game - LOUISIANA LOTTERY CORPORATION; *pg.* 997, *pg.* 742
CASH WINFALL - Lottery Game - MASSACHUSETTS STATE LOTTERY; *pg.* 998, *pg.* 802
CASH25 - Lottery Game - WEST VIRGINIA LOTTERY; *pg.* 1011, *pg.* 1849
CASHBALL - Video Game - INTERNATIONAL GAME TECHNOLOGY; *pg.* 957, *pg.* 1024
CASHBUILDER - Credit Card - GREAT SOUTHERN BANCORP, INC.; *pg.* 763, *pg.* 1006
CASHCONNECT - Banking Software - JACK HENRY & ASSOCIATES, INC.; *pg.* 422, *pg.* 988
CASHIER - Coin Dispenser - GLORY GLOBAL SOLUTIONS; *pg.* 401, *pg.* 628
CASHMERAN - Fragrance Ingredient - INTERNATIONAL FLAVORS & FRAGRANCES INC.; *pg.* 512, *pg.* 1244
CASHMERE - Milk Chocolate - CARGILL LIMITED; *pg.* 1475, *pg.* 1914
CASHMERE - Fabric - NEMSCHOFF, INC.; *pg.* 936, *pg.* 1890
CASHMERE - Paint - THE SHERWIN-WILLIAMS COMPANY; *pg.* 1447, *pg.* 1435
CASHMERE BOUQUET - Talc - THE STEPHAN COMPANY; *pg.* 1597, *pg.* 426
CASHMIRACLE - Cardigan - HABAND COMPANY, INC.; *pg.* 1772, *pg.* 1099
CASHSQUATCH - Game - INTERNATIONAL GAME TECHNOLOGY; *pg.* 420, *pg.* 1606
CASHSTOP - Banking Service - THE BANK OF NOVA SCOTIA; *pg.* 721, *pg.* 1935
CASHTACTIC - Lottery Game - NEW YORK STATE LOTTERY; *pg.* 1001, *pg.* 1340
CASHWORD - Lottery Game - NEW YORK STATE LOTTERY; *pg.* 1001, *pg.* 1340
CASHWORD - Lottery Game - OHIO LOTTERY COMMISSION; *pg.* 1002, *pg.* 1433
CASINO - Bath Accessory - CROSCILL, INC.; *pg.* 1122, *pg.* 1220
CASINO - Fabric - NEMSCHOFF, INC.; *pg.* 936, *pg.* 1890
CASINO - Bicycle Accessories - SPECIALIZED BICYCLE COMPONENTS, INC.; *pg.* 1711, *pg.* 152
CASINO CASH PLUS - ATM Withdrawals - EVERI HOLDINGS INC.; *pg.* 749, *pg.* 1023
CASINO CHALLENGE - Rewards Game - BALLY TECHNOLOGIES, INC.; *pg.* 531, *pg.* 1022
CASINO MAGIC - Casinos - PINNACLE ENTERTAINMENT, INC.; *pg.* 576, *pg.* 1029
CASINO MARKETING SERVICES - Marketing Services - EVERI HOLDINGS INC.; *pg.* 749, *pg.* 1023
CASINO RICHES - Lottery Game - KENTUCKY LOTTERY CORPORATION; *pg.* 996, *pg.* 735
CASINO ROUGE - Riverboat Gaming Facility - PENN NATIONAL GAMING, INC.; *pg.* 574, *pg.* 1595
CASINO ROYALE - Gaming Product - GLD PRODUCTS, INC.; *pg.* 1835, *pg.* 1882
CASINO ROYALE - Lottery Game - OHIO LOTTERY COMMISSION; *pg.* 1002, *pg.* 1433
CASINO SPIN - Lottery Game - IOWA LOTTERY; *pg.* 996, *pg.* 705
CASK & CREAM - Liqueur - E&J GALLO WINERY; *pg.* 1962, *pg.* 149
CASLON - Apparels - NORDSTROM, INC.; *pg.* 1779, *pg.* 1837
CASON - Integrated Chip Array - AMKOR TECHNOLOGY, INC.; *pg.* 67, *pg.* 25
CASORON - Polymer Product - CHEMTURA CORPORATION; *pg.* 1152, *pg.* 355
CASORON 4G - Herbicide - CHEMTURA CORPORATION; *pg.* 1152, *pg.* 355
CASPIAN - Furniture Collection - CENTURY FURNITURE INDUSTRIES; *pg.* 920, *pg.* 1377
CASS - Systems Integration & Aeronautics - LOCKHEED MARTIN CORPORATION; *pg.* 229, *pg.* 762
CASS - Software - PITNEY BOWES INC.; *pg.* 454, *pg.* 376
CASS CREEK GAME CALLS - Video Viewing System - SWORDFISH FINANCIAL, INC.; *pg.* 1430, *pg.* 1737
CASSANDRA - Clothing - ABERCROMBIE & FITCH CO.; *pg.* 37, *pg.* 1466
CASSANDRA - Bath Accessory - CROSCILL, INC.; *pg.* 1122, *pg.* 1220
CASSARINA - Bedding - CROSCILL, INC.; *pg.* 1122, *pg.* 1220
CASSATT - Furniture - ETHAN ALLEN INTERIORS INC.; *pg.* 924, *pg.* 343
CASSELLA - Furniture - ASHLEY FURNITURE INDUSTRIES, INC.; *pg.* 914, *pg.* 1852
CASSIA - Clothing - ABERCROMBIE & FITCH CO.; *pg.* 37, *pg.* 1466
CASSIE - Footwear - P.W. MINOR & SON, INC.; *pg.* 1816, *pg.* 1140
CASSIFIX - Fragrance Ingredient - INTERNATIONAL FLAVORS & FRAGRANCES INC.; *pg.* 512, *pg.* 1244
CASSINI - Men's Fragrance - OLEG CASSINI, INC.; *pg.* 30, *pg.* 1274
CAST - Current Audio Signal Transmission Technology - KRELL INDUSTRIES, INC.; *pg.* 650, *pg.* 367
CAST COAT - Engine Paint - SHERWIN-WILLIAMS DIVERSIFIED BRANDS DIVISION; *pg.* 1448, *pg.* 1435
CAST FOR CASH - Game - WMS INDUSTRIES INC.; *pg.* 593, *pg.* 666
CAST-IT - Chemicals - HUNTSMAN CORPORATION; *pg.* 1167, *pg.* 1758
CAST-RITE - Carbon Sand - MINERALS TECHNOLOGIES INC.; *pg.* 1173, *pg.* 617
CASTALUM - Aluminum Finishes - PPG INDUSTRIES, INC.; *pg.* 1445, *pg.* 1579
CASTAWAY - Carpet - BEAULIEU GROUP, LLC; *pg.* 917, *pg.* 529
CASTAWAY BAY - Water Park - CEDAR FAIR, L.P.; *pg.* 537, *pg.* 1471
CASTE - Air System Test Equipment - BAE SYSTEMS-INFORMATION WARFARE; *pg.* 623, *pg.* 1036
CASTEEL - Heavy Duty Storage Systems - CLOSETMAID CORPORATION; *pg.* 920, *pg.* 452
CASTELLANA - Cordial - JIM BEAM BRANDS CO.; *pg.* 1965, *pg.* 601
CASTELLARI - Food Product - MARS, INCORPORATED; *pg.* 1858, *pg.* 1792
CASTELLI - Bicycle Clothing & Accessories - BIANCHI U.S.A., INC.; *pg.* 1827, *pg.* 100
CASTELLI - Furniture - HAWORTH, INC.; *pg.* 402, *pg.* 891
CASTELLO BANFI - Super Premium Wines - BANFI VINTNERS; *pg.* 1957, *pg.* 1161
CASTELLO DI VOLPAIA - Chianti - WILLIAM GRANT & SONS, INC.; *pg.* 1972, *pg.* 1057
CASTERJET - Spray Nozzle - SPRAYING SYSTEMS CO.; *pg.* 1063, *pg.* 670
CASTFORM - Solid Imaging Material - 3D SYSTEMS CORPORATION; *pg.* 339, *pg.* 1621
CASTGARD - Healthcare Product - GF HEALTH PRODUCTS, INC.; *pg.* 1535, *pg.* 508
CASTILLO DE MOLINA - Wine - SHAW ROSS INTERNATIONAL IMPORTERS; *pg.* 1970, *pg.* 449
CASTING KIDS - Magazine - B.A.S.S., L.L.C.; *pg.* 270, *pg.* 1
CASTLE - Bakery Products - ALPHA BAKING COMPANY; *pg.* 836, *pg.* 564
CASTLE BAY - Carpet - INTERFACE, INC.; *pg.* 695, *pg.* 512
CASTLE CRASHER - Rewards Game - BALLY TECHNOLOGIES, INC.; *pg.* 531, *pg.* 1022
CASTLE HILL - Furniture - ASHLEY FURNITURE INDUSTRIES, INC.; *pg.* 914, *pg.* 1852
CASTLE METALS - Metals & Alloys - A. M. CASTLE & CO.; *pg.* 64, *pg.* 644
CASTLEBY - Kitchen & Bathroom Faucets - MOEN INCORPORATED; *pg.* 1056, *pg.* 1468
CASTLETON - Furniture - TELESCOPE CASUAL FURNITURE INC.; *pg.* 944, *pg.* 1162
CASTLETOWN - Carpet - BEAULIEU GROUP, LLC; *pg.* 917, *pg.* 529
CASTLOK - Hardware - LOOS & COMPANY, INC.; *pg.* 1356, *pg.* 368
CASTONE - Dental Product - DENTSPLY INTERNATIONAL INC.; *pg.* 1522, *pg.* 1596
CASUAL CANINE - Pet Clothing - PETEDGE; *pg.* 1481, *pg.* 787
CASUAL CLASSICS - Roman Shades - SPRINGS WINDOW FASHIONS LLC; *pg.* 943, *pg.* 1872
CASUAL COLORS - Decorative Architectural Product - MASCO CORPORATION; *pg.* 96, *pg.* 909
CASUAL COMFORT - Slacks & Shorts - HABAND COMPANY, INC.; *pg.* 1772, *pg.* 1099
CASUAL GEAR - Apparel & Accessories - WALGREEN CO.; *pg.* 1608, *pg.* 605
CASUAL GOURMET - Food Products - MONTEREY GOURMET FOODS, INC.; *pg.* 881, *pg.* 94
CASUAL JOE - Sleepwear - HABAND COMPANY, INC.; *pg.* 1772, *pg.* 1099
CASUAL KITTY - Pet Clothing - PETEDGE; *pg.* 1481, *pg.* 787
CASUAL LIVING - Furniture - BROWN JORDAN INTERNATIONAL COMPANY; *pg.* 919, *pg.* 740
CASUAL MALE XL - Big & Tall Shops for Men - DESTINATION XL GROUP, INC.; *pg.* 40, *pg.* 810
CASUAL WALKERS - Shoes - ACUSHNET COMPANY; *pg.* 1824, *pg.* 818
CAT - Snowmobile - ARCTIC CAT INC.; *pg.* 1705, *pg.* 953
CAT - Machinery - CATERPILLAR, INC.; *pg.* 1321, *pg.* 650
CAT - Adapter - ESCO CORPORATION; *pg.* 1335, *pg.* 1502
CAT - Software - IMMERSION CORPORATION; *pg.* 413, *pg.* 246
CAT - Biomolecule Product - THERMO FISHER SCIENTIFIC INC.; *pg.* 1602, *pg.* 61
CAT - Footwear - WOLVERINE WORLD WIDE, INC.; *pg.* 1822, *pg.* 905
CAT-AID - Enhancement Additive - JOHNSON MATTHEY PROCESS TECHNOLOGIES; *pg.* 1169, *pg.* 1083
CAT-AID V - Catalyst Additive - JOHNSON MATTHEY PROCESS TECHNOLOGIES; *pg.* 1169, *pg.* 1083
CAT AND THE FIDDLE - Toy & Game - HASBRO, INC.; *pg.* 954, *pg.* 1603
CAT CHOW - Cat Food - NESTLE PURINA PETCARE COMPANY; *pg.* 1479, *pg.* 1000
CAT COMM - Snowmobile - ARCTIC CAT INC.; *pg.* 1705, *pg.* 953
CAT FANCY - Magazine - I-5 PUBLISHING LLC; *pg.* 1651, *pg.* 133
CAT GYM - Cat Toy - THE HARTZ MOUNTAIN CORP.; *pg.* 1476, *pg.* 1120
CAT TAILS - Bentonite Clay - MINERALS TECHNOLOGIES INC.; *pg.* 1173, *pg.* 617
CAT/TRANSCABLE - Software System - MENTOR GRAPHICS CORPORATION; *pg.* 432, *pg.* 1510
CATA-CHEK - Catalysts - FERRO CORPORATION; *pg.* 1162, *pg.* 1462
CATACOMBS 3D - Video Game - ID SOFTWARE, INC.; *pg.* 956, *pg.* 1727
CATALAN - Fabric - NEMSCHOFF, INC.; *pg.* 936, *pg.* 1890
CATALINA - Furniture - ASHLEY FURNITURE INDUSTRIES, INC.; *pg.* 914, *pg.* 1852
CATALINA - Cruiser - CHRIS-CRAFT CORPORATION; *pg.* 1706, *pg.* 465
CATALINA - Footwear - COBIAN CORP.; *pg.* 1806, *pg.* 253
CATALINA - Furniture - ETHAN ALLEN INTERIORS INC.;

pg. 924, *pg.* 343
CATALINA - Commercial Lighting - SWIVELIER CO., INC.; *pg.* 1307, *pg.* 1142
CATALINA DOUBLE CABIN - Cruiser - CHRIS-CRAFT CORPORATION; *pg.* 1706, *pg.* 465
CATALOG MANAGER - Software Application - BMC SOFTWARE, INC.; *pg.* 362, *pg.* 1701
CATALOG SOLUTION - Software - EMC CORPORATION; *pg.* 391, *pg.* 825
CATALOGNA - Fabric - NEMSCHOFF, INC.; *pg.* 936, *pg.* 1890
CATALYST - Apparel - 180S, LLC; *pg.* 1824, *pg.* 754
CATALYST - Driver Software - ADVANCED MICRO DEVICES, INC.; *pg.* 613, *pg.* 282
CATALYST - Software Suite - ADVANCED MICRO DEVICES, INC.-MARKHAM; *pg.* 345, *pg.* 1922
CATALYST - Business Tool - AVENTION; *pg.* 1230, *pg.* 815
CATALYST - Microsurgical Equipment - BAUSCH & LOMB INCORPORATED; *pg.* 1401, *pg.* 1045
CATALYST - Furniture - HAWORTH, INC.; *pg.* 402, *pg.* 891
CATALYST - Software - HIGH END SYSTEMS, INC.; *pg.* 1299, *pg.* 1663
CATALYST - Remote Control Device - UNIVERSAL ELECTRONICS, INC.; *pg.* 683, *pg.* 262
CATALYST 6500 - Switch - CISCO SYSTEMS, INC.; *pg.* 372, *pg.* 240
CATALYST DX - Chemistry Analyzer - IDEXX LABORATORIES, INC.; *pg.* 1543, *pg.* 753
CATALYST EX - Software - STRATASYS, INC.; *pg.* 476, *pg.* 923
CATALYST MEDIA CENTER - Software - ADVANCED MICRO DEVICES, INC.; *pg.* 613, *pg.* 282
CATALYST TELECOMM - Business Telephones - SCANSOURCE, INC.; *pg.* 671, *pg.* 1618
CATAMOUNT - Cable Tie - THOMAS & BETTS CORPORATION; *pg.* 680, *pg.* 1646
CATAPOSIT - Catalyst - DOW CHEMICAL; *pg.* 1156, *pg.* 1563
CATAPULT - Athletic Shoes - L.A. GEAR, INC.; *pg.* 1811, *pg.* 134
CATAPULT - Software System - MENTOR GRAPHICS CORPORATION; *pg.* 432, *pg.* 1510
CATASAIL - Chemical Product - SACHEM INC.; *pg.* 1180, *pg.* 1665
CATAWBA - Building Product - BLUELINX HOLDINGS, INC.; *pg.* 70, *pg.* 491
CATAWBA - Hardboard Siding - GEORGIA-PACIFIC LLC; *pg.* 1458, *pg.* 507
CATC TRACE - Software - TELEDYNE LECROY; *pg.* 1431, *pg.* 1153
CATCH A WAVE - Video Slots - INTERNATIONAL GAME TECHNOLOGY; *pg.* 957, *pg.* 1024
CATCH-ALL - Floor Protection - LUND INTERNATIONAL, INC.; *pg.* 211, *pg.* 526
CATCH-ALL X-RACING - Performance Floor Protection - LUND INTERNATIONAL, INC.; *pg.* 211, *pg.* 526
CATCH-ALL X-TREME - Heavy-Duty Floor Protection - LUND INTERNATIONAL, INC.; *pg.* 211, *pg.* 526
CATCH ME IF YOU CAN - Dog Toy - THE HARTZ MOUNTAIN CORP.; *pg.* 1476, *pg.* 1120
CATCH PHRASE - Game - HASBRO, INC.; *pg.* 954, *pg.* 1603
CATCH THE GREEN - Video Game - INTERNATIONAL GAME TECHNOLOGY; *pg.* 957, *pg.* 1024
CATCHALL - Floor Care Product - BISSELL HOMECARE, INC.; *pg.* 52, *pg.* 887
CATCHBALL - Toss and Catch Game - SCHOOL-TECH, INC.; *pg.* 1844, *pg.* 866
CATCHET - Office Furniture - STEELCASE INC.; *pg.* 475, *pg.* 889
CATCHMASTER - Disposable Fly Bag - TRACTOR SUPPLY COMPANY; *pg.* 708, *pg.* 1627
CATCHPOINT - Reagent - MOLECULAR DEVICES CORPORATION; *pg.* 1568, *pg.* 287
CATCMM - Software - MSC SOFTWARE CORPORATION; *pg.* 441, *pg.* 262
CATE - Furniture - AMISCO INDUSTRIES LTD.; *pg.* 913, *pg.* 1958
CATEGORYADVISOR - Software - JDA SOFTWARE GROUP, INC.; *pg.* 423, *pg.* 22
CATELINA - Footwear - STEVEN MADDEN, LTD.; *pg.* 1819, *pg.* 1176
CATER-TIME - Bowls, Lids & Utensils - ALCOA INC.; *pg.* 65, *pg.* 1188
CATERACK - Kitchenware - THE VOLLRATH COMPANY LLC; *pg.* 1139, *pg.* 1894
CATERAIDES - Insulated Food & Beverage Carriers - CARLISLE FOODSERVICE PRODUCTS INCORPORATED; *pg.* 1455, *pg.* 1485
CATERBOWL - Bowl - PACTIV CORPORATION; *pg.* 1466, *pg.* 624
CATERMATE - Utensil - PACTIV CORPORATION; *pg.* 1466, *pg.* 624
CATERPAC - French Fries - MCCAIN FOODS LIMITED; *pg.* 876, *pg.* 1915
CATERPILLAR - Toy Train - LIONEL LLC; *pg.* 961, *pg.* 875
CATERPILLAR SPILLERS - Baby Care Product - MUNCHKIN, INC.; *pg.* 964, *pg.* 300
CATERPILLAR YELLOW - Work Tools & Engines - CATERPILLAR, INC.; *pg.* 1321, *pg.* 650
CATERWARE - Cookware - PACTIV CORPORATION; *pg.* 1466, *pg.* 624
CATEZOMES - Personal Care Material - BASF CATALYSTS LLC; *pg.* 1148, *pg.* 1074
CATH-STRIP - Wound Dressing - DERMA SCIENCES, INC.; *pg.* 1523, *pg.* 1111
CATHA COAT - Ship Coating - AKZONOBEL DECORATIVE PAINTS U.S.; *pg.* 1439, *pg.* 1474
CATHALOYS - Metal Tubing - SUPERIOR TUBE COMPANY INC.; *pg.* 113, *pg.* 1522
CATHEDRAL - Fabric - NEMSCHOFF, INC.; *pg.* 936, *pg.* 1890
CATHERINE MALANDRINO COLLECTION - Women's Clothing - AIDAN INDUSTRIES, INC.; *pg.* 17, *pg.* 1188
CATHERINES - Apparel - ASCENA RETAIL GROUP, INC.; *pg.* 18, *pg.* 1081
CATHERINES PLUS SIZES - Apparel - ASCENA RETAIL GROUP, INC.; *pg.* 18, *pg.* 1081
CATHFLO - Vascular Medicine - GENENTECH, INC.; *pg.* 1533, *pg.* 279
CATHFLO ACTIVASE - Tissue Plasminogen Activator - GENENTECH, INC.; *pg.* 1533, *pg.* 279
THE CATHOLIC ANSWER - Online Magazine - OUR SUNDAY VISITOR, INC.; *pg.* 1673, *pg.* 682
CATHOLIC DIGEST - Magazine - BAYARD INC.; *pg.* 1620, *pg.* 359
CATHOLIC DIGEST LARGE PRINT READER - Magazine - BAYARD INC.; *pg.* 1620, *pg.* 359
CATHOLIC FORESTER - Fraternal Benefits - CATHOLIC ORDER OF FORESTERS; *pg.* 1196, *pg.* 635
CATHOLICMINGLE.COM - Online Dating Service for Catholic Singles - SPARK NETWORKS, INC.; *pg.* 472, *pg.* 140
CATHRYN - Vanity Lights - CRAFTMADE INTERNATIONAL, INC.; *pg.* 1295, *pg.* 1670
CATHSIM - Hardware & Software - IMMERSION CORPORATION; *pg.* 413, *pg.* 246
CATIA - Software - MSC SOFTWARE CORPORATION; *pg.* 441, *pg.* 262
CATMASTER - Snowmobile - ARCTIC CAT INC.; *pg.* 1705, *pg.* 953
CATNIP LEAVES 'N HERBS - Cat Toy - THE HARTZ MOUNTAIN CORP.; *pg.* 1476, *pg.* 1120
CATO - Women's Clothing - THE CATO CORPORATION; *pg.* 21, *pg.* 1364
CATO FASHIONS - Women's Clothing - THE CATO CORPORATION; *pg.* 21, *pg.* 1364
CATO PLUS - Women's Specialty Apparel Stores - THE CATO CORPORATION; *pg.* 21, *pg.* 1364
CATREF - Software - ASPEN TECHNOLOGY, INC.; *pg.* 354, *pg.* 804
CATRIX - Pharmaceutical Product - VALEANT PHARMACEUTICALS INTERNATIONAL; *pg.* 1605, *pg.* 1047
CATS - Software - SYNOPSYS, INC.; *pg.* 480, *pg.* 162
CATS CRADLE - Educational Materials - SCHOLASTIC INC.; *pg.* 1683, *pg.* 1288
CATS HAVE STAFF - Pillow and Throw - HERITAGE LACE INC.; *pg.* 694, *pg.* 711
CATS MEOW - Lace Curtain - HERITAGE LACE INC.; *pg.* 694, *pg.* 711
CAT'S MEOW - Game - WMS INDUSTRIES INC.; *pg.* 593, *pg.* 666
CATS 'N' DOGS - Slots - INTERNATIONAL GAME TECHNOLOGY; *pg.* 957, *pg.* 1024
CAT'S PAW - Heels & Soles - AMERICAN BILTRITE INC.; *pg.* 1878, *pg.* 856
CATS PRIDE - Snowmobile - ARCTIC CAT INC.; *pg.* 1705, *pg.* 953
CAT'S PRIDE - Cat Litter - OIL-DRI CORPORATION OF AMERICA; *pg.* 1480, *pg.* 586
CATS USA - Magazine - I-5 PUBLISHING LLC; *pg.* 1651, *pg.* 133
CATSAN - Cat Litter - MARS, INCORPORATED; *pg.* 1858, *pg.* 1792
CATTITUDES - Bear - GUND, INC.; *pg.* 954, *pg.* 1056
CATTLE SAFE-GUARD - De-Wormers - KENT NUTRITION GROUP; *pg.* 1477, *pg.* 710
CATTLEMAN - Men's Westernwear - OXFORD INDUSTRIES, INC.; *pg.* 30, *pg.* 517
CATTLEMASTER - Fountain - RITCHIE INDUSTRIES, INC.; *pg.* 707, *pg.* 703
CATTLEMAXX - Grinder Mixer - ART'S-WAY MANUFACTURING CO., INC.; *pg.* 701, *pg.* 701
CATTLEMEN'S - Barbecue Sauce - RECKITT BENCKISER INC.; *pg.* 1136, *pg.* 1105
CATUABA POWER MAX - Nutritional Product - NUTRACEUTICAL INTERNATIONAL CORPORATION; *pg.* 1576, *pg.* 1753
CATWALK - Fabric - NEMSCHOFF, INC.; *pg.* 936, *pg.* 1890
CATWATCH - Newsletter - BELVOIR MEDIA GROUP, LLC; *pg.* 1620, *pg.* 360
CATWOMAN - Character - DC COMICS, INC.; *pg.* 1633, *pg.* 1221
CAULK - Dental Product - DENTSPLY INTERNATIONAL INC.; *pg.* 1522, *pg.* 1596
CAULK-AWAY PRO - Caulk Tools - HYDE TOOLS, INC.; *pg.* 1125, *pg.* 844
CAULK-BE-GONE - Caulk And Sealant - DAP PRODUCTS, INC.; *pg.* 1441, *pg.* 756
CAULK FYNAL - Dental Product - DENTSPLY INTERNATIONAL INC.; *pg.* 1522, *pg.* 1596
CAULK-RITE PRO - Caulk Tools - HYDE TOOLS, INC.; *pg.* 1125, *pg.* 844
CAUSEWAY - Furniture - HAWORTH, INC.; *pg.* 402, *pg.* 891
CAVA CLADDING - Tile - ARTISTIC TILE INC.; *pg.* 914, *pg.* 1119
CAVALCADE - Fabric - NEMSCHOFF, INC.; *pg.* 936, *pg.* 1890
CAVALIER - Tires - MICHELIN NORTH AMERICA INC.; *pg.* 1886, *pg.* 1618
CAVALIER - Lubricant and Process Oil - ROCK VALLEY OIL & CHEMICAL COMPANY; *pg.* 1179, *pg.* 631
CAVE KING - Video Game - INTERNATIONAL GAME TECHNOLOGY; *pg.* 957, *pg.* 1024
CAVEMAN KENO - Video Game - INTERNATIONAL GAME TECHNOLOGY; *pg.* 957, *pg.* 1024
CAVENDISH - Furniture - HAWORTH, INC.; *pg.* 402, *pg.* 891
CAVERJECT - Medicine - PFIZER INC.; *pg.* 1581, *pg.* 1278
CAVIAR - Jewelry - LAGOS INC.; *pg.* 8, *pg.* 1566
CAVIAR - Fabric - NEMSCHOFF, INC.; *pg.* 936, *pg.* 1890
CAVIAR - Hard Drive - WESTERN DIGITAL CORPORATION; *pg.* 492, *pg.* 118
CAVILON - Creams - 3M COMPANY; *pg.* 1142, *pg.* 956
CAVIRINSE - Dental Caries Prevention - 3M COMPANY; *pg.* 1142, *pg.* 956
CAVIT - Temporary Filling Material - 3M COMPANY; *pg.* 1142, *pg.* 956
CAVITRON - Dental Product - DENTSPLY INTERNATIONAL INC.; *pg.* 1522, *pg.* 1596
CAVITRON 30K SOFTIP - Dental Product - DENTSPLY INTERNATIONAL INC.; *pg.* 1522, *pg.* 1596
CAVITRON BOBCAT PRO - Dental Product - DENTSPLY INTERNATIONAL INC.; *pg.* 1522, *pg.* 1596
CAVITRON JET PLUS - Dental Product - DENTSPLY INTERNATIONAL INC.; *pg.* 1522, *pg.* 1596
CAVITRON STERIMATE - Dental Product - DENTSPLY INTERNATIONAL INC.; *pg.* 1522, *pg.* 1596
CAVITYMATE - Insulation - THE DOW CHEMICAL COMPANY; *pg.* 1157, *pg.* 898
CAVITYSHIELD - Varnish - 3M COMPANY; *pg.* 1142, *pg.* 956
CAVP - Systems Integration & Aeronautics - LOCKHEED MARTIN CORPORATION; *pg.* 229, *pg.* 762
CAXTON - Commercial Printers - THE CAXTON PRINTERS LTD.; *pg.* 1626, *pg.* 548
CAXTON - Bath Product - KOHLER CO.; *pg.* 91, *pg.* 1862
CAYENNE - Fabric - NEMSCHOFF, INC.; *pg.* 936, *pg.* 1890
CAYENNE - Kitchenware - THE VOLLRATH COMPANY LLC; *pg.* 1139, *pg.* 1894
CAYER - Cheese - SAPUTO, INC.; *pg.* 893, *pg.* 1956
CAYLA - Clothing - ABERCROMBIE & FITCH CO.; *pg.* 37, *pg.* 1466
CAYMAN - Carpet - BEAULIEU GROUP, LLC; *pg.* 917, *pg.* 529
CAYMAN - Furniture - FLEXSTEEL INDUSTRIES, INC.; *pg.*

First page reference indicates Business Class Edition
Second page reference indicates Geographic Edition

925, *pg.* 707
CAYTUR - Polymer Product - CHEMTURA CORPORATION; *pg.* 1152, *pg.* 355
CB - Densification Mixers - LITTLEFORD DAY INC.; *pg.* 1356, *pg.* 728
CB-MAP - Monitoring Instrument - GE ENERGY; *pg.* 1338, *pg.* 506
CB1 - Golf Equipment - CALLAWAY GOLF COMPANY; *pg.* 1829, *pg.* 58
CB2 - Apartment, Loft & Home Furnishings - CRATE & BARREL, INC.; *pg.* 922, *pg.* 640
CBA - Balloon Service - CONTINENTAL AMERICAN CORP.; *pg.* 1880, *pg.* 723
CBC-DIFF - Veterinary Hematology System - HESKA CORPORATION; *pg.* 1542, *pg.* 335
CBK - Home Accent - BLYTH, INC.; *pg.* 502, *pg.* 349
C.BOOTH DERMA - Skin Care - RITE AID CORPORATION; *pg.* 1590, *pg.* 1519
CBOT - Futures Exchange - CME GROUP, INC.; *pg.* 738, *pg.* 571
CBR - Lab Science Material - CAROLINA BIOLOGICAL SUPPLY COMPANY; *pg.* 1513, *pg.* 1359
CBREWS - Chemical, Biological & Radiological Early Warning System - LOCKHEED MARTIN CORPORATION; *pg.* 229, *pg.* 762
CBSSPORTSLINE.COM - Web Site - CBS SPORTSLINE.COM, INC.; *pg.* 1234, *pg.* 423
C.B.V. TEMP - Dental Product - DEN-MAT CORPORATION; *pg.* 1522, *pg.* 271
CBW - Continuous Batch Washers - PELLERIN MILNOR CORPORATION; *pg.* 1368, *pg.* 744
CBX 3500 - Edge Switch - ALCATEL-LUCENT; *pg.* 615, *pg.* 1094
CBX 500 - WAN Switch - ALCATEL-LUCENT; *pg.* 615, *pg.* 1094
CC - Educational Materials - SCHOLASTIC INC.; *pg.* 1683, *pg.* 1288
CCAR - Low Temperature Refrigeration - AIR PRODUCTS AND CHEMICALS, INC.; *pg.* 1145, *pg.* 1513
CCDA - Certification - CISCO SYSTEMS, INC.; *pg.* 372, *pg.* 240
CCDE - Certification - CISCO SYSTEMS, INC.; *pg.* 372, *pg.* 240
CCENT - Certification - CISCO SYSTEMS, INC.; *pg.* 372, *pg.* 240
CCH HAND - Software - CCH INC.; *pg.* 1626, *pg.* 653
CCH ONLINE PAY AS YOU GO - Legal Research Systems Software - CCH INC.; *pg.* 1626, *pg.* 653
CCH SWORD - Software - CCH INC.; *pg.* 1626, *pg.* 653
CCH TEAMMATE - Software - CCH INC.; *pg.* 1626, *pg.* 653
CCI - Booster Cables - COLEMAN CABLE, INC.; *pg.* 1324, *pg.* 665
CCIE - Certification - CISCO SYSTEMS, INC.; *pg.* 372, *pg.* 240
CCM - Hockey Equipment - REEBOK-CCM HOCKEY, INC.; *pg.* 1844, *pg.* 1960
CCM MAGAZINE - Radio Broadcasting Product - SALEM MEDIA GROUP, INC.; *pg.* 307, *pg.* 57
CCM PLUS - Alloys - CARPENTER TECHNOLOGY CORPORATION; *pg.* 73, *pg.* 1584
CCMI MARK - Orthopedic Product - DJO INCORPORATED; *pg.* 1524, *pg.* 302
CCNA - Certification - CISCO SYSTEMS, INC.; *pg.* 372, *pg.* 240
CCSFTP - Software - CANDID COLOR SYSTEMS, INC.; *pg.* 1404, *pg.* 1485
CCSI - Certification - CISCO SYSTEMS, INC.; *pg.* 372, *pg.* 240
CCSP - Certification - CISCO SYSTEMS, INC.; *pg.* 372, *pg.* 240
CCT - Pharmaceutical Product - ALERE INC.; *pg.* 1488, *pg.* 849
C(CUBE)150 - Wastewater Disinfection - CALGON CARBON CORPORATION; *pg.* 1151, *pg.* 1574
C(CUBE)500 - Wastewater Disinfection - CALGON CARBON CORPORATION; *pg.* 1151, *pg.* 1574
CD - Couplings - ZERO-MAX, INC.; *pg.* 222, *pg.* 954
CD-2 - High Performance Oil Boost - TURTLE WAX, INC.; *pg.* 220, *pg.* 671
CD/410 - Instrument Equipment - CLAYTON INDUSTRIES CO.; *pg.* 1323, *pg.* 66
CD-75P - Flame Retardants - CHEMTURA CORPORATION; *pg.* 1152, *pg.* 355
CD HORIZON - Thoracolumbar System - MEDTRONIC, INC.; *pg.* 1564, *pg.* 939
CD UNIPACK 201 - Fan - CRAFTMADE INTERNATIONAL, INC.; *pg.* 1295, *pg.* 1670
CD UNIPACK 202 - Fan - CRAFTMADE INTERNATIONAL, INC.; *pg.* 1295, *pg.* 1670
CD UNIPACK 203 - Fan - CRAFTMADE INTERNATIONAL, INC.; *pg.* 1295, *pg.* 1670
CD UNIPACK 204 - Fan - CRAFTMADE INTERNATIONAL, INC.; *pg.* 1295, *pg.* 1670
CDARS - Commercial Banking - PRIVATEBANCORP INC.; *pg.* 796, *pg.* 587
CDC - Cable - GENERAL CABLE CORPORATION; *pg.* 83, *pg.* 729
CDE - Capacitor - CORNELL DUBILIER ELECTRONICS; *pg.* 630, *pg.* 1620
CDE - Computer Software - NOVELL INC.; *pg.* 446, *pg.* 852
CDF CROISIERES DE FRANCE - European Cruises - ROYAL CARIBBEAN CRUISES LTD; *pg.* 1921, *pg.* 446
CDI - Torque Measuring Products & Calibrating Equipment - SNAP-ON INCORPORATED; *pg.* 1062, *pg.* 1862
CDI-X - Customer Data Integration Solution - ACXIOM CORPORATION; *pg.* 342, *pg.* 33
CDICONNECT - Networking Software - OPENCONNECT SYSTEMS, INC.; *pg.* 449, *pg.* 1685
CDM - Software - BIO-RAD LABORATORIES, INC.; *pg.* 1504, *pg.* 101
CDM-75 - Cable Distance Meter - HD ELECTRIC COMPANY; *pg.* 1299, *pg.* 666
CDM MASTER - Computer Software - MEDASSETS INC.; *pg.* 1561, *pg.* 484
CDMA (CONSUMER) - Mobile Solutions - SONUS NETWORKS INC.; *pg.* 1281, *pg.* 858
CDMA (ENTERPRISE) - Mobile Solutions - SONUS NETWORKS INC.; *pg.* 1281, *pg.* 858
CDMA2000 - Telecommunications Mobility Products - ALCATEL-LUCENT; *pg.* 615, *pg.* 1094
CDMA2000 - Graphics Solution - QUALCOMM INCORPORATED; *pg.* 1873, *pg.* 207
CDNA CYCLE - Molecular Biology Product - THERMO FISHER SCIENTIFIC INC.; *pg.* 1602, *pg.* 61
CDO - Treatment System - ATMI, INC.; *pg.* 1314, *pg.* 342
CDO EVALUATOR - Debt Analysis Tool - STANDARD & POOR'S RATINGS SERVICES; *pg.* 805, *pg.* 1296
CDQUICK - Surgical Equipment - MEDASSETS INC.; *pg.* 1561, *pg.* 484
CDR - Dental Radiography System - SIRONA DENTAL SYSTEMS, INC.; *pg.* 1429, *pg.* 1175
CDS ACCELERATOR - Credit Analysis Tool - STANDARD & POOR'S RATINGS SERVICES; *pg.* 805, *pg.* 1296
CDS XPRESS - Credit Analysis Tool - STANDARD & POOR'S RATINGS SERVICES; *pg.* 805, *pg.* 1296
CE - Rivet - THE STIMPSON COMPANY, INC.; *pg.* 1182, *pg.* 460
CE - Bearing - THE TIMKEN COMPANY; *pg.* 218, *pg.* 1408
CE BLUE - Flexible Pipe - CRESLINE PLASTIC PIPE CO., INC.; *pg.* 1881, *pg.* 678
CE MAHOGANY - Guitar - PAUL REED SMITH GUITARS; *pg.* 574, *pg.* 779
CE-RITE - Ophthalmic Polish for Glass - FERRO CORPORATION; *pg.* 1162, *pg.* 1462
C.E. SCHMIDT - Apparel & Footwear - TRACTOR SUPPLY COMPANY; *pg.* 708, *pg.* 1627
CE-VI-SOL - Vitamin C Supplement - MEAD JOHNSON NUTRITION COMPANY; *pg.* 1561, *pg.* 615
CEA - Medical Therapy - DENDREON CORPORATION; *pg.* 1522, *pg.* 1835
CEA-CIDE - CEA Expressing Solid Tumor Therapy - IMMUNOMEDICS, INC.; *pg.* 1544, *pg.* 1087
CEASE - Liquid Deodorant - GEERPRES INC.; *pg.* 1339, *pg.* 901
CEASE-FIRE - Safety Waste Receptacles - JUSTRITE MANUFACTURING COMPANY, LLC; *pg.* 1394, *pg.* 606
CEC - Chemical Product - CABOT CORPORATION; *pg.* 1151, *pg.* 792
CECCHI - Imported Brands - BANFI VINTNERS; *pg.* 1957, *pg.* 1161
CECE - Educational Materials - SCHOLASTIC INC.; *pg.* 1683, *pg.* 1288
CECILE - Dolls - AMERICAN GIRL LLC; *pg.* 949, *pg.* 1871
CECILIA - Furniture - AMISCO INDUSTRIES LTD.; *pg.* 913, *pg.* 1958
CECO - Forging Product - SUPERIOR DIE SET CORP.; *pg.* 1379, *pg.* 1885
CECORR - Microboard - GEORGIA-PACIFIC LLC; *pg.* 1458, *pg.* 507
CED - Trade Magazine - ADVANTAGE BUSINESS MEDIA; *pg.* 1613, *pg.* 1116
CEDAR - Shoes - THE MEN'S WEARHOUSE, INC.; *pg.* 44, *pg.* 1711
CEDAR BREATHER - Roofing Ventilation Product - BENJAMIN OBDYKE, INC.; *pg.* 70, *pg.* 1540
CEDAR CREST - Retirement Community - ERICKSON LIVING; *pg.* 1090, *pg.* 766
CEDAR DISCOVERY - Cedar-Look Shingles & Vinyl Siding - PLY GEM SIDING GROUP; *pg.* 105, *pg.* 986
CEDAR FAIR - Amusement Park - CEDAR FAIR, L.P.; *pg.* 537, *pg.* 1471
CEDAR HEIGHTS - Furniture - ASHLEY FURNITURE INDUSTRIES, INC.; *pg.* 914, *pg.* 1852
CEDAR LUBRICANTS - Micro-Lubricant System - ITW FLUIDS NORTH AMERICA; *pg.* 980, *pg.* 614
CEDAR POINT - Amusement Park - CEDAR FAIR, L.P.; *pg.* 537, *pg.* 1471
CEDAR SPRINGS - Furniture - ASHLEY FURNITURE INDUSTRIES, INC.; *pg.* 914, *pg.* 1852
CEDAR STREET - Carpet - BEAULIEU GROUP, LLC; *pg.* 917, *pg.* 529
CEDARAPIDS - Asphalt Paving - TEREX CORPORATION; *pg.* 1381, *pg.* 384
CEDARONE - Wood & Building Material - WEYERHAEUSER COMPANY; *pg.* 121, *pg.* 1820
CEDEPAL - Chemical Product - STEPAN COMPANY; *pg.* 1182, *pg.* 643
CEDEPHOS - Chemical Product - STEPAN COMPANY; *pg.* 1182, *pg.* 643
CEDRAMBER - Fragrance Ingredient - INTERNATIONAL FLAVORS & FRAGRANCES INC.; *pg.* 512, *pg.* 1244
CEE - Cost Effective Equipment - BREWER SCIENCE, INC.; *pg.* 1150, *pg.* 989
CEE-BEE - Cleaner Product - MCGEAN-ROHCO, INC.; *pg.* 1172, *pg.* 1432
CEE-J - Software System - MENTOR GRAPHICS CORPORATION; *pg.* 432, *pg.* 1510
CEENU - Health Care Product - BRISTOL-MYERS SQUIBB COMPANY; *pg.* 1509, *pg.* 1206
CEFA-DRI - Veterinary Antibiotic - BOEHRINGER INGELHEIM VETMEDICA, INC.; *pg.* 1474, *pg.* 989
CEFA-LAK - Veterinary Antibiotic - BOEHRINGER INGELHEIM VETMEDICA, INC.; *pg.* 1474, *pg.* 989
CEFOBID - Medicine - PFIZER INC.; *pg.* 1581, *pg.* 1278
CEILING DOCCAM - Audio Conferencing System - CLEARONE COMMUNICATIONS, INC.; *pg.* 629, *pg.* 1756
CEJKA SEARCH - Staffing Services - CROSS COUNTRY HEALTHCARE, INC.; *pg.* 1520, *pg.* 411
CELADRIN - Wellness Product - AVON PRODUCTS, INC.; *pg.* 500, *pg.* 1198
CELANO - Footwear - K-SWISS; *pg.* 1837, *pg.* 306
CELARO - Software System - MENTOR GRAPHICS CORPORATION; *pg.* 432, *pg.* 1510
CELCALC - Software - RADIO FREQUENCY SYSTEMS, INC.; *pg.* 666, *pg.* 354
CELCON - Plastic Ball - ABBOTT BALL COMPANY; *pg.* 1040, *pg.* 383
CELCOR - Ceramic Material - CORNING INCORPORATED; *pg.* 1122, *pg.* 1154
CELE-CONNECT - Seal & Thermoplastic Component - GREENE, TWEED & CO.; *pg.* 1344, *pg.* 1544
CELEBRATE FOOD CELEBRATE LIFE - Slogan - RALEY'S INC.; *pg.* 1031, *pg.* 305
CELEBRATING 65 - Educational Program - HARVARD PILGRIM HEALTH CARE, INC.; *pg.* 1539, *pg.* 856
CELEBRATING GIRL OF YESTERDAY AND TODAY - Slogan - AMERICAN GIRL LLC; *pg.* 949, *pg.* 1871
CELEBRATING GIRLS OF TODAY - Slogan - AMERICAN GIRL LLC; *pg.* 949, *pg.* 1871
CELEBRATING GIRLS OF YESTERDAY - Slogan - AMERICAN GIRL LLC; *pg.* 949, *pg.* 1871
CELEBRATING SPECIAL OCCASIONS FOR GENERATIONS - Tag Line - LAWRY'S RESTAURANTS, INC.; *pg.* 1735, *pg.* 180
CELEBRATION - Almonds - BLUE DIAMOND GROWERS; *pg.* 840, *pg.* 195
CELEBRATION CITY - Theme Park - HERSCHEND FAMILY ENTERTAINMENT CORP.; *pg.* 552, *pg.* 973
CELEBRATION GREETINGS - Greeting Cards for the Christian Market - LEANIN' TREE, INC.; *pg.* 1658, *pg.* 311
CELEBRATION OF BLOOMS - Flower Arrangement - 1-800-FLOWERS.COM, INC.; *pg.* 1758, *pg.* 1151
CELEBRATION OF STYLE - Tagline - FGX INTERNATIONAL, INC.; *pg.* 5, *pg.* 1608
CELEBRATION PRIZES - Video Game - INTERNATIONAL

GAME TECHNOLOGY; *pg.* 957, *pg.* 1024
CELEBRATIONS - Candy - MARS, INCORPORATED; *pg.* 1858, *pg.* 1792
CELEBRATIONS.COM - Retail Store Services - 1-800-FLOWERS.COM, INC.; *pg.* 1758, *pg.* 1151
CELEBREX - Arthritis Medication - PFIZER INC.; *pg.* 1581, *pg.* 1278
CELEBRITY - Furniture - ASHLEY FURNITURE INDUSTRIES, INC.; *pg.* 914, *pg.* 1852
CELEBRITY - Canned Meats & Tuna - ATALANTA CORPORATION; *pg.* 838, *pg.* 1057
CELEBRITY - Sink - ELKAY MANUFACTURING COMPANY; *pg.* 80, *pg.* 645
CELEBRITY - Apparel - HANESBRANDS INC.; *pg.* 26, *pg.* 1394
CELEBRITY - Towable Recreational Vehicle - SKYLINE CORPORATION; *pg.* 1711, *pg.* 677
CELEBRITY 1 - Coil Product - AAON, INC.; *pg.* 1068, *pg.* 1488
CELEBRITY CAR - Magazine - DUPONT PUBLISHING, INC.; *pg.* 1637, *pg.* 462
CELEBRITY CARD - Credit & Cash Card - CITGO PETROLEUM CORPORATION; *pg.* 974, *pg.* 1703
CELEBRITY CRUISES - Caribbean Cruises - ROYAL CARIBBEAN CRUISES LTD; *pg.* 1921, *pg.* 446
CELEBRITYBED - Mattress System - TEMPUR SEALY INTERNATIONAL, INC.; *pg.* 944, *pg.* 731
CELEBSLAM - Celebrity Gossip Site - SPINMEDIA; *pg.* 1282, *pg.* 104
CELEBUZZ - Celebrity News Site - SPINMEDIA; *pg.* 1282, *pg.* 104
CELECT - Fuel System - CUMMINS INC.; *pg.* 1326, *pg.* 676
CELERO - Breast Biopsy - HOLOGIC, INC.; *pg.* 1416, *pg.* 784
CELEROMARK - Breast Biopsy - HOLOGIC, INC.; *pg.* 1416, *pg.* 784
CELERRA - Software - EMC CORPORATION; *pg.* 391, *pg.* 825
CELERRA REPLICATOR - Software - EMC CORPORATION; *pg.* 391, *pg.* 825
CELERUS - Fluoroelastomer Composite Gasket - W.L. GORE & ASSOCIATES, INC.; *pg.* 122, *pg.* 388
CELERY CIRCULATION - Dietary Supplement - NOW HEALTH GROUP, INC.; *pg.* 1576, *pg.* 557
CELESTE - Clothing - ABERCROMBIE & FITCH CO.; *pg.* 37, *pg.* 1466
CELESTE - Furniture - HERMAN MILLER, INC.; *pg.* 926, *pg.* 913
CELESTE - Fabric - NEMSCHOFF, INC.; *pg.* 936, *pg.* 1890
CELESTE - Convenience Stores - THE PANTRY, INC.; *pg.* 1029, *pg.* 1360
CELESTE - Frozen Pizza - PINNACLE FOODS GROUP LLC; *pg.* 889, *pg.* 1104
CELESTE CLUB - Active Wear Clothing - BIANCHI U.S.A., INC.; *pg.* 1827, *pg.* 100
CELESTIAL - Tile - ARTISTIC TILE INC.; *pg.* 914, *pg.* 1119
CELESTIAL 3L - Women's Specific Hydration Pack - JANSPORT; *pg.* 1837, *pg.* 38
CELESTIAL SEASONINGS - Tea - THE HAIN CELESTIAL GROUP, INC.; *pg.* 860, *pg.* 1172
CELESTINA - Watch - MOVADO GROUP, INC.; *pg.* 10, *pg.* 1101
CELESTRA - Digital Clock - TYCO SIMPLEXGRINNELL LP; *pg.* 682, *pg.* 859
CELEX - Pharmaceutical Products - ABBOTT LABORATORIES; *pg.* 1484, *pg.* 551
CELEX - Resin - THE DOW CHEMICAL COMPANY; *pg.* 1157, *pg.* 898
CELEXIS - Slurry - DOW CHEMICAL; *pg.* 1156, *pg.* 1563
CELIA - Fabric - NEMSCHOFF, INC.; *pg.* 936, *pg.* 1890
CELINA - Lamp - ASHLEY FURNITURE INDUSTRIES, INC.; *pg.* 914, *pg.* 1852
CELINA - Footwear - EASTLAND SHOE CORPORATION; *pg.* 1808, *pg.* 750
CELINE - Furniture - ASHLEY FURNITURE INDUSTRIES, INC.; *pg.* 914, *pg.* 1852
CELL-AIRE - Packaging Product - SEALED AIR CORPORATION; *pg.* 1468, *pg.* 1058
CELL BUILDER - Software System - MENTOR GRAPHICS CORPORATION; *pg.* 432, *pg.* 1510
CELL-DYN - Medical Instrument - ABBOTT LABORATORIES; *pg.* 1484, *pg.* 551
CELL-FX - Natural Health Product - AFEXA LIFE SCIENCES INC.; *pg.* 1487, *pg.* 1905
CELL LAB QUANTA - Flow Cytometry System - BECKMAN COULTER, INC.; *pg.* 1402, *pg.* 48
CELL REACH - Cable - COMMSCOPE, INC.; *pg.* 278, *pg.* 1378
CELL SAVER - Blood Recovery System - HAEMONETICS CORPORATION; *pg.* 1538, *pg.* 802
CELL STATION - Software System - MENTOR GRAPHICS CORPORATION; *pg.* 432, *pg.* 1510
CELL-U-FOAM - Household Products - ACS INDUSTRIES, INC.; *pg.* 1040, *pg.* 1602
CELL-U-WELD - Vinyl Tabs - SMEAD MANUFACTURING COMPANY; *pg.* 470, *pg.* 926
CELLA - Chairs - HERMAN MILLER, INC.; *pg.* 926, *pg.* 913
CELLA - Wine - SHAW ROSS INTERNATIONAL IMPORTERS; *pg.* 1970, *pg.* 449
CELLAIRTY - Computer Hardware - BROADCOM CORPORATION; *pg.* 364, *pg.* 108
CELLA'S - Candy - TOOTSIE ROLL INDUSTRIES, INC.; *pg.* 1863, *pg.* 591
CELLBIND - Active Surface Coating - CORNING INCORPORATED; *pg.* 1122, *pg.* 1154
CELLBUOY - Utility Systems - OCEAN POWER TECHNOLOGIES, INC.; *pg.* 1948, *pg.* 1107
CELLCEPT - Pharmaceutical Product - HOFFMANN-LA ROCHE INC.; *pg.* 1542, *pg.* 1099
CELLCUBE - Glass & Ceramic Material - CORNING INCORPORATED; *pg.* 1122, *pg.* 1154
CELLE - Furniture - HERMAN MILLER, INC.; *pg.* 926, *pg.* 913
CELLEBRATE - Nutritional Product - RELIV INTERNATIONAL, INC.; *pg.* 1589, *pg.* 975
CELLEMETRY - Wireless Communication System - AT&T SOUTHEAST; *pg.* 1868, *pg.* 489
CELLEMETRY - Communication Product - NUMEREX CORP.; *pg.* 660, *pg.* 517
CELLEX - Orthopedic Device - DJO SURGICAL; *pg.* 1525, *pg.* 1661
CELLEX - Enclosure - THERMON AMERICAS INC.; *pg.* 1077, *pg.* 1744
CELLFECTIN - Molecular Biology Product - THERMO FISHER SCIENTIFIC INC.; *pg.* 1602, *pg.* 61
CELLFLEX - Cable & Antenna System - RADIO FREQUENCY SYSTEMS, INC.; *pg.* 666, *pg.* 354
CELLFLO - Cellulose - MINERALS TECHNOLOGIES INC.; *pg.* 1173, *pg.* 617
CELLFLO - Fluid Purification System - SPECTRUM LABORATORIES INC.; *pg.* 1595, *pg.* 69
CELLFLOOR - Software System - MENTOR GRAPHICS CORPORATION; *pg.* 432, *pg.* 1510
CELLGAS - Filtration System - SPECTRUM LABORATORIES INC.; *pg.* 1595, *pg.* 69
CELLGEN - Software System - MENTOR GRAPHICS CORPORATION; *pg.* 432, *pg.* 1510
CELLGRAPH - Software System - MENTOR GRAPHICS CORPORATION; *pg.* 432, *pg.* 1510
CELLIENT - Medical Product - HOLOGIC, INC.; *pg.* 1416, *pg.* 784
CELLINI - Pigment - BASF CATALYSTS LLC; *pg.* 1148, *pg.* 1074
CELLITE - Software - RADIO FREQUENCY SYSTEMS, INC.; *pg.* 666, *pg.* 354
CELLMASTER - Pump Product - IDEX CORPORATION; *pg.* 1347, *pg.* 623
CELLMASTER - Machine Loader - WES-TECH AUTOMATION SOLUTIONS; *pg.* 1388, *pg.* 560
CELLMAX - Filtration System - SPECTRUM LABORATORIES INC.; *pg.* 1595, *pg.* 69
CELLMITE - Digital Signal Conditioner - ELECTRO STANDARDS LABORATORIES INC.; *pg.* 390, *pg.* 1600
CELLOLYN - Synthetic Resin - EASTMAN CHEMICAL COMPANY; *pg.* 1159, *pg.* 1636
CELLOMICS - Biological Testing System - BECKMAN COULTER, INC.; *pg.* 1402, *pg.* 48
CELLOSIZE - Hydroxyethyl Cellulose - THE DOW CHEMICAL COMPANY; *pg.* 1157, *pg.* 898
CELLOSOLVE - Oxygenated Solvent - THE DOW CHEMICAL COMPANY; *pg.* 1157, *pg.* 898
CELLPIPE - Software System - ALCATEL-LUCENT; *pg.* 615, *pg.* 1094
CELLPLACE - Software System - MENTOR GRAPHICS CORPORATION; *pg.* 432, *pg.* 1510
CELLPOWER - Software System - MENTOR GRAPHICS CORPORATION; *pg.* 432, *pg.* 1510
CELLPROBE - Testing Instrument System - BECKMAN COULTER, INC.; *pg.* 1402, *pg.* 48
CELLQUANT - Biological Testing System - BECKMAN COULTER, INC.; *pg.* 1402, *pg.* 48
CELLROUTE - Software System - MENTOR GRAPHICS CORPORATION; *pg.* 432, *pg.* 1510
CELLSEARCH - Circulating Tumor Cells - QUEST DIAGNOSTICS INCORPORATED; *pg.* 1587, *pg.* 1080
CELLSTACK - Glass & Ceramic Material - CORNING INCORPORATED; *pg.* 1122, *pg.* 1154
CELLTRACE - Molecular Probe Product - THERMO FISHER SCIENTIFIC INC.; *pg.* 1602, *pg.* 61
CELLTRACKER - Molecular Probe Product - THERMO FISHER SCIENTIFIC INC.; *pg.* 1602, *pg.* 61
CELLTREX - Skin Care Product - NU SKIN ENTERPRISES, INC.; *pg.* 518, *pg.* 1755
CELLU-CUSHION - Packaging Product - SEALED AIR CORPORATION; *pg.* 1468, *pg.* 1058
CELLU LINER - Meat & Dairy Case Liners - SEALED AIR CORPORATION; *pg.* 1468, *pg.* 1058
CELLU-MASK - Adhesive Foam Film Laminate - SEALED AIR CORPORATION; *pg.* 1468, *pg.* 1058
CELLU-SCULPT - Beauty Product - AVON PRODUCTS, INC.; *pg.* 500, *pg.* 1198
CELLULAR - Knee Pad - SMITH INTERNATIONAL, INC.; *pg.* 1377, *pg.* 1715
CELLULAR SUSPENSION - Furniture - HERMAN MILLER, INC.; *pg.* 926, *pg.* 913
CELLULARRAM - Semiconductor Device - MICRON TECHNOLOGY, INC.; *pg.* 435, *pg.* 547
CELLULEX - Cartridge - DONALDSON COMPANY, INC.; *pg.* 1329, *pg.* 917
CELLULINK - Wireless Communication System - AT&T SOUTHEAST; *pg.* 1868, *pg.* 489
CELLUMIN - Nutritional Product - NUTRACEUTICAL INTERNATIONAL CORPORATION; *pg.* 1576, *pg.* 1753
CELLUPLANK - Packaging Product - SEALED AIR CORPORATION; *pg.* 1468, *pg.* 1058
CELLUPURE - Filter Cones & Cartridges - HMI INDUSTRIES INC.; *pg.* 56, *pg.* 1475
CELLUTION - Personal Care Product - RBC LIFE SCIENCES, INC.; *pg.* 1588, *pg.* 1723
CELLUVISC - Eye Care Product - ALLERGAN, INC.; *pg.* 1491, *pg.* 106
CELOGEN - Polymer Product - CHEMTURA CORPORATION; *pg.* 1152, *pg.* 355
CELONTIN - Medicine - PFIZER INC.; *pg.* 1581, *pg.* 1278
CELSIUS - Healthy Beverage - CELSIUS HOLDINGS, INC.; *pg.* 239, *pg.* 411
CELSIUS - Healthcare Product - JOHNSON & JOHNSON; *pg.* 1549, *pg.* 1091
CELTIC CROSSING LIQUEUR - Liqueur - CASTLE BRANDS INC.; *pg.* 239, *pg.* 1209
CELTOOLS - Software - RADIO FREQUENCY SYSTEMS, INC.; *pg.* 666, *pg.* 354
CELWAVE - Cable & Antenna System - RADIO FREQUENCY SYSTEMS, INC.; *pg.* 666, *pg.* 354
CELXPRES - Communication System Hardware - AVAGO TECHNOLOGIES; *pg.* 358, *pg.* 238
CEM - Steel Product - AK STEEL HOLDING CORPORATION; *pg.* 1311, *pg.* 1479
CEM APLICAP - Glass Ionomer Luting Cement - 3M COMPANY; *pg.* 1142, *pg.* 956
CEM-SEAL - Sealant - HILLYARD, INC.; *pg.* 331, *pg.* 990
CEMENTHIDE - Paint Coating for Concrete, Brick, Cement & Stucco - PPG INDUSTRIES, INC.; *pg.* 1445, *pg.* 1579
CEMENTONE - Concrete System - L.M. SCOFIELD COMPANY; *pg.* 94, *pg.* 134
CEMEX - Orthopaedic Implant Device - EXACTECH, INC.; *pg.* 1529, *pg.* 428
CEMTRONIC - Chemicals - HUNTSMAN CORPORATION; *pg.* 1167, *pg.* 1758
CENEX - Petroleum Products - CHS INC.; *pg.* 702, *pg.* 926
CENOVA - Software - HOLOGIC, INC.; *pg.* 1416, *pg.* 784
CENSLIDE - Diagnostic Urinalysis System - IRIS INTERNATIONAL, INC.; *pg.* 1547, *pg.* 64
CENTA-FORM - Grinder - BRYANT GRINDER; *pg.* 1320, *pg.* 1768
CENTALIGN - Grinder - BRYANT GRINDER; *pg.* 1320, *pg.* 1768
CENTAP - Anodes - CORRPRO COMPANIES, INC.; *pg.* 631, *pg.* 1464
CENTARI - Acrylic Enamel - E.I. DU PONT DE NEMOURS & COMPANY; *pg.* 1159, *pg.* 390
CENTAUR - Activated Carbon Product - CALGON CARBON CORPORATION; *pg.* 1151, *pg.* 1574
CENTAUR - Fire Pumps - IDEX CORPORATION; *pg.* 1347, *pg.* 623

First page reference indicates Business Class Edition
Second page reference indicates Geographic Edition

CENTAUR - Space Launch Vehicles - LOCKHEED MARTIN CORPORATION; *pg.* 229, *pg.* 762
CENTAUR - Metal Cutting Saw Blade - SIMONDS INTERNATIONAL CORPORATION; *pg.* 1376, *pg.* 819
CENTAUR - Turbine Products - SOLAR TURBINES INCORPORATED; *pg.* 1377, *pg.* 209
CENTAURI - Broadloom - COURISTAN INC.; *pg.* 921, *pg.* 1067
CENTENARIO - Brandy - JIM BEAM BRANDS CO.; *pg.* 1965, *pg.* 601
CENTENNIAL - Carpet - BEAULIEU GROUP, LLC; *pg.* 917, *pg.* 529
CENTENNIAL - Bowling Equipment - BRUNSWICK BOWLING & BILLIARDS CORP.; *pg.* 1828, *pg.* 622
CENTENNIAL - Tire And Rubber Product - THE GOODYEAR TIRE & RUBBER COMPANY; *pg.* 1883, *pg.* 1401
CENTENNIAL - White Gloss Paint - PETTIT PAINT COMPANY; *pg.* 1444, *pg.* 1116
CENTENNIAL - Laundry Machines - WHIRLPOOL CORPORATION; *pg.* 62, *pg.* 872
CENTER CAFE - Restaurant - ARK RESTAURANTS CORP.; *pg.* 1715, *pg.* 1196
CENTER CHANNEL II BY HENRY KLOSS - Speaker - CAMBRIDGE SOUNDWORKS, INC.; *pg.* 1234, *pg.* 781
CENTER CORE - Panel Systems - MITY ENTERPRISES, INC.; *pg.* 935, *pg.* 1753
CENTER FLOW MAGNET - Magnetic Separation - BUNTING MAGNETICS CO.; *pg.* 1320, *pg.* 717
CENTER FOR HEALTHY AGING - Health Plan & Publication - MEDICA, INC.; *pg.* 1208, *pg.* 949
CENTER LOK - Centerlok Demo Kit - THOMAS & BETTS CORPORATION; *pg.* 680, *pg.* 1646
CENTER OF INFLUENCE - Insurance Product - SBLI USA LIFE INSURANCE COMPANY, INC.; *pg.* 1216, *pg.* 1288
CENTER OF THE ROLL - Baked Goods - CINNABON, INC.; *pg.* 1723, *pg.* 493
CENTER SQUARE - Carpet - BEAULIEU GROUP, LLC; *pg.* 917, *pg.* 529
CENTER STAGE - Carpet - BEAULIEU GROUP, LLC; *pg.* 917, *pg.* 529
CENTER STAGE - Modular Playsystem - MIRACLE RECREATION EQUIPMENT COMPANY; *pg.* 1839, *pg.* 988
CENTER STAR WILD - Game - WMS INDUSTRIES INC.; *pg.* 593, *pg.* 666
CENTERA - Software - EMC CORPORATION; *pg.* 391, *pg.* 825
CENTERA - Bicycle Component - SRAM CORPORATION; *pg.* 967, *pg.* 590
CENTERA BY PELLA - Energy-Efficient Vinyl Windows & Patio Doors - PELLA CORPORATION; *pg.* 104, *pg.* 711
CENTERCHARGE - Ticketing System - LINCOLN CENTER FOR THE PERFORMING ARTS, INC.; *pg.* 557, *pg.* 1251
CENTERFIRE - Resistivity System - GE ENERGY; *pg.* 1338, *pg.* 506
CENTERFIRE - Footwear - OAKLEY, INC.; *pg.* 1840, *pg.* 86
CENTERLINE - Software - ROCKWELL AUTOMATION, INC., *pg.* 668, *pg.* 1880
CENTERMASTER - Bowling Equipment - BRUNSWICK BOWLING & BILLIARDS CORP.; *pg.* 1828, *pg.* 622
CENTERONE - Software - ROCKWELL AUTOMATION, INC.; *pg.* 668, *pg.* 1880
CENTERSTAGE - Software - EMC CORPORATION; *pg.* 391, *pg.* 825
CENTERSTAGE BY HENRY KLOSS - Speaker - CAMBRIDGE SOUNDWORKS, INC.; *pg.* 1234, *pg.* 781
CENTERWISE - Software - ELLIE MAE, INC.; *pg.* 1243, *pg.* 183
CENTI-SPLINE - Combination Lock - SARGENT & GREENLEAF, INC.; *pg.* 1061, *pg.* 739
CENTIGRADE - Flatware - ONEIDA LTD; *pg.* 1129, *pg.* 1318
CENTINALE - Furniture - ETHAN ALLEN INTERIORS INC.; *pg.* 924, *pg.* 343
CENTRA - Furniture - BUSH INDUSTRIES INC.; *pg.* 919, *pg.* 1170
CENTRA - Battery - EXIDE TECHNOLOGIES; *pg.* 204, *pg.* 483
CENTRA - Software - SABA SOFTWARE, INC.; *pg.* 464, *pg.* 192
CENTRA-FLO - Catheter - COOK GROUP, INC.; *pg.* 1518, *pg.* 674
CENTRACODE II - Non-vital Interlocking Control - ALSTOM SIGNALING, INC.; *pg.* 1312, *pg.* 1350
CENTRAL - Software - ADOBE SYSTEMS INCORPORATED; *pg.* 342, *pg.* 235
CENTRAL - Software - DELL SOFTWARE; *pg.* 385, *pg.* 40
CENTRAL HUDSON - Your Energy Solutions Company - CENTRAL HUDSON GAS & ELECTRIC CORPORATION; *pg.* 1937, *pg.* 1324
CENTRAL INSURANCE COMPANIES - Mutual Insurance - CENTRAL MUTUAL INSURANCE COMPANY; *pg.* 1196, *pg.* 1478
CENTRAL SHOPPER - Newspaper - NEWS CHIEF; *pg.* 1669, *pg.* 480
CENTRALCREDIT - Transaction Processing System - EVERI HOLDINGS INC.; *pg.* 749, *pg.* 1023
CENTRALIZED ROUTE SERVER - Cable Solutions - SONUS NETWORKS INC.; *pg.* 1281, *pg.* 858
CENTRALIZED ROUTE SERVER (MNP) - Mobile Solutions - SONUS NETWORKS INC.; *pg.* 1281, *pg.* 858
CENTRALUX - Vacuum Cleaner - AERUS LLC; *pg.* 51, *pg.* 1673
CENTRAMATE - Tangential Flow System - PALL CORPORATION; *pg.* 232, *pg.* 1323
CENTRAMATIC 52 - Laundry Liquid Dispenser - ECOLAB INC.; *pg.* 329, *pg.* 960
CENTRASTAR - Software - EMC CORPORATION; *pg.* 391, *pg.* 825
CENTRAVUE - Lens - DANKER LABORATORIES INC.; *pg.* 1408, *pg.* 465
CENTREDIRECT - Printer - XEROX CORPORATION; *pg.* 494, *pg.* 365
CENTREWARE - Software - XEROX CORPORATION; *pg.* 494, *pg.* 365
CENTREX - Community Name - WCI COMMUNITIES, INC.; *pg.* 1118, *pg.* 414
CENTRIC - Boat Seat - ATTWOOD CORPORATION; *pg.* 1705, *pg.* 897
CENTRICITY - Software System - MENTOR GRAPHICS CORPORATION; *pg.* 432, *pg.* 1510
CENTRIFEED - Centrifugal Feeder - AUTOMATION DEVICES, INC.; *pg.* 1315, *pg.* 1532
CENTRIFUSE - Brake Drum - MAXION WHEELS; *pg.* 212, *pg.* 903
CENTRO-MATIC - Automatic Lubrication Equipment for Industry - LINCOLN INDUSTRIAL CORP.; *pg.* 1355, *pg.* 999
CENTRON - Fiberglass Pipe - NOV AMERON; *pg.* 100, *pg.* 187
CENTRULITE - Hub System - MAXION WHEELS; *pg.* 212, *pg.* 903
CENTRUM - Bath Accessory - CROSCILL, INC.; *pg.* 1122, *pg.* 1220
CENTRUM - Dietary Supplement - PFIZER INC.; *pg.* 1581, *pg.* 1278
CENTRUMOUNT - Wheel - MAXION WHEELS; *pg.* 212, *pg.* 903
CENTRUSTEEL - Wheel - MAXION WHEELS; *pg.* 212, *pg.* 903
CENTRX - Logistic Service - BDP INTERNATIONAL INC.; *pg.* 1900, *pg.* 1559
CENTURA - Silicon Etch - APPLIED MATERIALS, INC.; *pg.* 618, *pg.* 264
CENTURA - Building Product - BLUELINX HOLDINGS, INC.; *pg.* 70, *pg.* 491
CENTURA - Actuators - FLOWSERVE CORPORATION; *pg.* 82, *pg.* 1719
CENTURA - Laboratory Products - JUSTRITE MANUFACTURING COMPANY, LLC; *pg.* 1394, *pg.* 606
CENTURIE - Footwear - STEVEN MADDEN, LTD.; *pg.* 1819, *pg.* 1176
CENTURION - Credit Card - AMERICAN EXPRESS COMPANY; *pg.* 712, *pg.* 1190
CENTURION - Fire Control System - ASTRONAUTICS CORPORATION OF AMERICA; *pg.* 224, *pg.* 1873
CENTURION - Security Product - BAE SYSTEMS PRODUCTS GROUP; *pg.* 359, *pg.* 432
CENTURION - Table - BLATT BOWLING & BILLIARD CORP.; *pg.* 1827, *pg.* 1203
CENTURION - Data Storage Product - CAMBEX CORPORATION; *pg.* 368, *pg.* 844
CENTURION - Vanity Lights - CRAFTMADE INTERNATIONAL, INC.; *pg.* 1295, *pg.* 1670
CENTURION - Carrier Chassis - CRANE CARRIER COMPANY; *pg.* 168, *pg.* 1489
CENTURION - Aerospace Product - EATON CORPORATION; *pg.* 1331, *pg.* 1429
CENTURION - Thermal Imaging System - FLIR SYSTEMS, INC.; *pg.* 1413, *pg.* 1510
CENTURION - Seating Product - IRWIN SEATING COMPANY INC.; *pg.* 929, *pg.* 887
CENTURION - Commercial Cookware - LINCOLN FOODSERVICE PRODUCTS, LLC; *pg.* 1127, *pg.* 1432
CENTURION - Defense System - RAYTHEON COMPANY; *pg.* 233, *pg.* 854
CENTURION - Street Sweepers - TENNANT COMPANY; *pg.* 1381, *pg.* 944
CENTURION - Media Publication - TIME INC.; *pg.* 1693, *pg.* 1300
CENTURION - Navigation Aid - TRIMBLE NAVIGATION LIMITED; *pg.* 1384, *pg.* 288
CENTURION - Inspection Lighting System - UNILUX, INC.; *pg.* 682, *pg.* 1118
CENTURION - Metal Product - ZERO MANUFACTURING, INC.; *pg.* 1892, *pg.* 1752
CENTURION 701 - Lighting System - UNILUX, INC.; *pg.* 682, *pg.* 1118
CENTURION BUSINESS RECOVERY CONSULTING GROUP - Multi-Tiered Disaster Recovery Protection - JACK HENRY & ASSOCIATES, INC.; *pg.* 422, *pg.* 988
CENTURY - Gold-Filled Pens & Pencils - A. T. CROSS COMPANY; *pg.* 339, *pg.* 1602
CENTURY - Canopy - ANCHOR INDUSTRIES, INC.; *pg.* 1825, *pg.* 678
CENTURY - Electric Motors - A.O. SMITH CORPORATION; *pg.* 1313, *pg.* 1872
CENTURY - Isostearic Acid Mixture - ARIZONA CHEMICAL CO. LLC; *pg.* 1147, *pg.* 431
CENTURY - Movie Theater Equipment - BALLANTYNE STRONG, INC.; *pg.* 623, *pg.* 1013
CENTURY - Bowling Product - BOWLMOR AMF; *pg.* 1828, *pg.* 1206
CENTURY - Furniture - CENTURY FURNITURE INDUSTRIES; *pg.* 920, *pg.* 1377
CENTURY - Carrier Chassis - CRANE CARRIER COMPANY; *pg.* 168, *pg.* 1489
CENTURY - Paper - DOMTAR CORPORATION; *pg.* 1456, *pg.* 1954
CENTURY - Children's Products & Toys - GRACO CHILDREN'S PRODUCTS INC.; *pg.* 954, *pg.* 1531
CENTURY - Beverage - GREEN SPOT, INC.; *pg.* 251, *pg.* 68
CENTURY - Air Conditioner - HEAT CONTROLLER, INC.; *pg.* 1072, *pg.* 893
CENTURY - Sprayers - HINIKER COMPANY; *pg.* 704, *pg.* 927
CENTURY - Portable Fan - HUNTER FAN COMPANY; *pg.* 57, *pg.* 1631
CENTURY - Information Display - INDUSTRIAL ELECTRONIC ENGINEERS, INC.; *pg.* 644, *pg.* 300
CENTURY - Towing & Recovery Equipment - MILLER INDUSTRIES, INC.; *pg.* 185, *pg.* 1655
CENTURY - B/O Compressor - NORWALK COMPRESSOR COMPANY, INC.; *pg.* 1366, *pg.* 380
CENTURY - Towable Recreational Vehicle - SKYLINE CORPORATION; *pg.* 1711, *pg.* 677
CENTURY - Sterilizer - STERIS CORPORATION; *pg.* 1597, *pg.* 1464
CENTURY - Diesel Engine - WESTERBEKE CORPORATION; *pg.* 1388, *pg.* 847
CENTURY 21 - Residential Real Estate Brokerage - REALOGY CORPORATION; *pg.* 1109, *pg.* 1081
CENTURY 21 CONNECTIONS - Customer Discounts - CENTURY 21 REAL ESTATE LLC; *pg.* 1085, *pg.* 1080
CENTURY 21 FINE HOMES & ESTATES - Real Estate Service - CENTURY 21 REAL ESTATE LLC; *pg.* 1085, *pg.* 1080
CENTURY 21 MATURE MOVES - Real Estate Service - CENTURY 21 REAL ESTATE LLC; *pg.* 1085, *pg.* 1080
CENTURY 21 NEW CONSTRUCTION - Real Estate Service - CENTURY 21 REAL ESTATE LLC; *pg.* 1085, *pg.* 1080
CENTURY 21 RECREATIONAL PROPERTIES - Real Estate Service - CENTURY 21 REAL ESTATE LLC; *pg.* 1085, *pg.* 1080
CENTURY COLORS - Pen - A. T. CROSS COMPANY; *pg.* 339, *pg.* 1602
CENTURY FENCE - Chain Link Fence - CENTURY FENCE COMPANY; *pg.* 74, *pg.* 1886
CENTURY II - Pen - A. T. CROSS COMPANY; *pg.* 339, *pg.* 1602
CENTURY PAC - Seating Product - IRWIN SEATING COMPANY INC.; *pg.* 929, *pg.* 887
CENTURY SIGNET - Pen - A. T. CROSS COMPANY; *pg.* 339, *pg.* 1602
CENTURY SPORT - Pen - A. T. CROSS COMPANY; *pg.* 339, *pg.* 1602

CENTURY XL END MILLS - Rex Twenty-End Mills - REGAL BELOIT CORPORATION; *pg.* 106, *pg.* 1854
CENWAX - Fatty Acid - ARIZONA CHEMICAL CO. LLC; *pg.* 1147, *pg.* 431
C.E.O - Paper Products - BOISE CASCADE HOLDINGS, L.L.C.; *pg.* 1453, *pg.* 546
CEO-TWO - Rectal Suppository - BEUTLICH PHARMACEUTICALS LP; *pg.* 1503, *pg.* 665
CEOC - Software System - MENTOR GRAPHICS CORPORATION; *pg.* 432, *pg.* 1510
CEOEXPRESSSELECT - Subscription Service - CEOEXPRESS COMPANY; *pg.* 1235, *pg.* 807
CEPACOL - Health & Beauty Product - COMBE INCORPORATED; *pg.* 1516, *pg.* 1351
CEPACOL - Sore Throat Relief Lozenge - RECKITT BENCKISER INC.; *pg.* 1136, *pg.* 1105
CEPITA - Soft Drink - THE COCA-COLA COMPANY; *pg.* 240, *pg.* 493
CEPROTIN - Healthcare Product - BAXTER INTERNATIONAL INC.; *pg.* 1499, *pg.* 599
CEQ - Sequencer, Software & Related Consumables - BECKMAN COULTER, INC.; *pg.* 1402, *pg.* 48
CER-COL - Pharmaceutical Product - ALERE INC.; *pg.* 1488, *pg.* 849
CERA BALL - Ball Pen - YASUTOMO & CO.; *pg.* 497, *pg.* 280
CERA-CHECK - Ceramic Instrument - COORSTEK, INC.; *pg.* 77, *pg.* 330
CERA-SLIDE - Ceramic & Plastic Product - COORSTEK, INC.; *pg.* 77, *pg.* 330
CERA-TRIM - Capacitor - JOHANSON MANUFACTURING CORPORATION; *pg.* 648, *pg.* 1045
CERACOL - Waxes - THE CLOROX COMPANY; *pg.* 327, *pg.* 169
CERALASE - Ceramic & Plastic Product - COORSTEK, INC.; *pg.* 77, *pg.* 330
CERAM-A-GRIP - Medical Instrument - INTEGRA MILTEX, INC.; *pg.* 1546, *pg.* 1597
CERAM-BACK-ELBOW - Tubing & Pipe - MORRIS COUPLING COMPANY; *pg.* 1057, *pg.* 1530
CERAM-SPAN - Ceramic Coated Glass in Colors - VIRGINIA GLASS PRODUCTS CORPORATION; *pg.* 119, *pg.* 1788
CERAMAGUARD - Ceilings & Walls - ARMSTRONG WORLD INDUSTRIES, INC.; *pg.* 914, *pg.* 1545
CERAMAX - Technology Drives Ceramic Speakers - MAXIM INTEGRATED PRODUCTS, INC.; *pg.* 653, *pg.* 247
CERAMCO - Dental Product - DENTSPLY INTERNATIONAL INC.; *pg.* 1522, *pg.* 1596
CERAMETALIX - Aircraft Landing System - HONEYWELL INTERNATIONAL INC.; *pg.* 407, *pg.* 1088
CERAMIC CLAYS - Pressed & Monolithic Refractory - RESCO PRODUCTS, INC.; *pg.* 107, *pg.* 1581
CERAMICA ALHAMBRA - Ceramic Tile - WALKER & ZANGER, INC.; *pg.* 119, *pg.* 281
CERAMICAL - Calcined Gypsum - USG CORPORATION; *pg.* 118, *pg.* 594
CERAMICELL - Ceramic & Plastic Product - COORSTEK, INC.; *pg.* 77, *pg.* 330
CERAMIDES - Skin Care Products - ELIZABETH ARDEN, INC.; *pg.* 507, *pg.* 448
CERAMPRESS - Dental Product - DENTSPLY INTERNATIONAL INC.; *pg.* 1522, *pg.* 1596
CERAMTIP - Fluid Handling System - GRACO, INC.; *pg.* 1342, *pg.* 935
CERAMX - Dental Product - DENTSPLY INTERNATIONAL INC.; *pg.* 1522, *pg.* 1596
CERANA - Bath Product - KOHLER CO.; *pg.* 91, *pg.* 1862
CERANO - Agricultural Product - WILBUR-ELLIS COMPANY; *pg.* 1185, *pg.* 234
CERAPURE - Ceramic & Plastic Product - COORSTEK, INC.; *pg.* 77, *pg.* 330
CERASHIELD - Ceramic & Plastic Product - COORSTEK, INC.; *pg.* 77, *pg.* 330
CERASURF - Ceramic & Plastic Product - COORSTEK, INC.; *pg.* 77, *pg.* 330
CERAVE - Pharmaceutical Product - VALEANT PHARMACEUTICALS INTERNATIONAL; *pg.* 1605, *pg.* 1047
CERAZETTE - Desogestrel - MERCK & CO., INC.; *pg.* 1566, *pg.* 1077
CERCOFORM - Ceremic Material - FLOWSERVE CORPORATION; *pg.* 82, *pg.* 1719
CERCON - Dental Product - DENTSPLY INTERNATIONAL INC.; *pg.* 1522, *pg.* 1596
CERDECOAT - Transparent Glaze - FERRO CORPORATION; *pg.* 1162, *pg.* 1462
CERDECOLOR - Decoration Colors - FERRO CORPORATION; *pg.* 1162, *pg.* 1462
CERDECOR - Precious Metal Preparations - FERRO CORPORATION; *pg.* 1162, *pg.* 1462
CEREBRIL - Stroke Prevention Drug - BELLUS HEALTH INC.; *pg.* 1503, *pg.* 1951
CEREBYX - Medicine - PFIZER INC.; *pg.* 1581, *pg.* 1278
CEREC - Conductive Film - 3M COMPANY; *pg.* 1142, *pg.* 956
CEREC - Medical Device - SIEMENS CORPORATION; *pg.* 803, *pg.* 1291
CERECALASE - Food Enzyme Product - NATIONAL ENZYME COMPANY; *pg.* 882, *pg.* 978
CEREDASE - Alglucerase Injection - GENZYME CORPORATION; *pg.* 1534, *pg.* 808
CERENIA - Anti-Emetic for Canines - PFIZER INC.; *pg.* 1581, *pg.* 1278
CERENOL - Polyether Diol - E.I. DU PONT DE NEMOURS & COMPANY; *pg.* 1159, *pg.* 390
CEREPAK - Paperboard Packaging Product - WESTROCK COMPANY; *pg.* 1472, *pg.* 1805
CERES SECRET - Medical & Aesthetic Product - DYNATRONICS CORPORATION; *pg.* 1526, *pg.* 1757
CERESOTA - Unbleached Naturally White Flour - THE UHLMANN CO.; *pg.* 834, *pg.* 986
CEREZYME - Lysosomal Storage Disorder - GENZYME CORPORATION; *pg.* 1534, *pg.* 808
CERFA-KLEEN - Cleaner - HOUGHTON INTERNATIONAL INC.; *pg.* 1167, *pg.* 1589
CERFACE - Decorating Cylinder - BUNTING MAGNETICS CO.; *pg.* 1320, *pg.* 717
CERINATE - Porcelain - DEN-MAT CORPORATION; *pg.* 1522, *pg.* 271
CERMARK - Laser Glass Marking System - FERRO CORPORATION; *pg.* 1162, *pg.* 1462
CERNER BRIDGE - Process Management Solution - CERNER CORPORATION; *pg.* 1514, *pg.* 981
CERNER LIFESCIENCES - Clinical Services - CERNER CORPORATION; *pg.* 1514, *pg.* 981
CERNER MILLENNIUM - Healthcare Information Technology - CERNER CORPORATION; *pg.* 1514, *pg.* 981
CERTAINTY - Selective Herbicide - MONSANTO COMPANY; *pg.* 1173, *pg.* 999
CERTANCE/SEAGATE - Software Back-up Systems - BACKUPWORKS.COM INC.; *pg.* 359, *pg.* 120
CERTE - Software System - MENTOR GRAPHICS CORPORATION; *pg.* 432, *pg.* 1510
CERTI-LITE - Lighting Fixtures - KILLARK ELECTRIC; *pg.* 1300, *pg.* 998
CERTICOM CODESIGN - Software - CERTICOM CORP.; *pg.* 371, *pg.* 1925
CERTICRYPT - Software - CERTICOM CORP.; *pg.* 371, *pg.* 1925
CERTIFICATE OF MAILING - Postal Services - UNITED STATES POSTAL SERVICE; *pg.* 1009, *pg.* 406
CERTIFIED - Protective Apparel - ALPHA PRO TECH, LTD.; *pg.* 1492, *pg.* 1922
CERTIFIED - Software - BIO-RAD LABORATORIES, INC.; *pg.* 1504, *pg.* 101
CERTIFIED LUX - Biomolecule Product - THERMO FISHER SCIENTIFIC INC.; *pg.* 1602, *pg.* 61
CERTIFIED MAIL - Postal Services - UNITED STATES POSTAL SERVICE; *pg.* 1009, *pg.* 406
CERTIFIED MANUFACTURING ENGINEER - Certification Course - SOCIETY OF MANUFACTURING ENGINEERS; *pg.* 157, *pg.* 878
CERTIFIED MANUFACTURING TECHNOLOGIST - Certification Course - SOCIETY OF MANUFACTURING ENGINEERS; *pg.* 157, *pg.* 878
CERTIFIED PERFECT - Jewelry - HELZBERG'S DIAMOND SHOPS, INC.; *pg.* 6, *pg.* 984
CERTIFIED PREMIUM BEEF - Beef Products - NATIONAL BEEF PACKING COMPANY, LLC; *pg.* 882, *pg.* 985
CERTIFIER AIR VELOCITY CALIBRATOR - Calibrator - TSI INCORPORATED; *pg.* 1432, *pg.* 965
CERTIFIER FA - Ventilator Test System - TSI INCORPORATED; *pg.* 1432, *pg.* 965
CERTIFIER FA PLUS - Ventilator Test System - TSI INCORPORATED; *pg.* 1432, *pg.* 965
CERTIFY - Software - SYNOPSYS, INC.; *pg.* 480, *pg.* 162
CERTISOY - Pharmaceutical Product - ALERE INC.; *pg.* 1488, *pg.* 849
CERTMASTER - Software - SUNGARD DATA SYSTEMS INC.; *pg.* 477, *pg.* 1592
CERTUS-3D - Electron Microscope - FEI COMPANY; *pg.* 1413, *pg.* 1498
CERVICAL - Orthopedic Product - DJO INCORPORATED; *pg.* 1524, *pg.* 302
CERVICAL PILLOW BY CORE - Pillow - DYNATRONICS CORPORATION; *pg.* 1526, *pg.* 1757
CERVICORE - Spinal System - STRYKER CORPORATION; *pg.* 1598, *pg.* 894
CERVISTA - Medical Product - HOLOGIC, INC.; *pg.* 1416, *pg.* 784
CESAMET - Pharmaceutical Product - VALEANT PHARMACEUTICALS INTERNATIONAL; *pg.* 1605, *pg.* 1047
CESAR - Power Supply - ADVANCED ENERGY INDUSTRIES, INC.; *pg.* 613, *pg.* 328
CESAR - Petcare Product - MARS, INCORPORATED; *pg.* 1858, *pg.* 1792
CESAR - Pet Food - MARS PETCARE; *pg.* 1478, *pg.* 1633
CESIC - Material System - GE ENERGY; *pg.* 1338, *pg.* 506
CESTEX - Anthelmintic Compound for Veterinary Use - PFIZER INC.; *pg.* 1581, *pg.* 1278
CESTINO - Carpet - INTERFACE, INC.; *pg.* 695, *pg.* 512
CET HOME DENTAL CARE - Veterinary Product - VIRBAC CORPORATION; *pg.* 1606, *pg.* 1696
CETANE BOOST - Diesel Fuel - POWER SERVICE PRODUCTS, INC.; *pg.* 983, *pg.* 1749
CETAPHIL - Pharmaceutical Products - GALDERMA LABORATORIES, L.P.; *pg.* 1532, *pg.* 1695
CETARA WORDSHARE - Certified Document Content Management & Collaboration Tool - MERRILL CORPORATION; *pg.* 1664, *pg.* 962
CETOL - Software - RAND A TECHNOLOGY CORPORATION; *pg.* 459, *pg.* 774
CETONIA - Wall Decor - ETHAN ALLEN INTERIORS INC.; *pg.* 924, *pg.* 343
CETRA - Bath & Plumbing Product - JACUZZI BRANDS CORPORATION; *pg.* 554, *pg.* 65
CETRON - Electronics - RICHARDSON ELECTRONICS, LTD.; *pg.* 667, *pg.* 622
CETS - Contractor Engineering Technical Services - BAE SYSTEMS-INFORMATION WARFARE; *pg.* 623, *pg.* 1036
CETYLPURE - Nutritional Product - NATROL, INC.; *pg.* 1570, *pg.* 64
CEVA - Coating Product - CHASE CORPORATION; *pg.* 1152, *pg.* 803
CEYLON - Fan - CRAFTMADE INTERNATIONAL, INC.; *pg.* 1295, *pg.* 1670
CF - Hot Melt Adhesive Spray Nozzle - NORDSON CORPORATION; *pg.* 1365, *pg.* 1480
CF0I050 - Fiber Optic Component - OPLINK COMMUNICATIONS, INC.; *pg.* 660, *pg.* 91
CFD-TCO - Conductive Display Glass - AGC GLASS NORTH AMERICA, INC.; *pg.* 65, *pg.* 482
CFNY - Media & Entertainment - CORUS ENTERTAINMENT INC.; *pg.* 279, *pg.* 1937
CFO VISION - Financial Management Solution - SAS INSTITUTE INC.; *pg.* 466, *pg.* 1361
CFOI100 - Fiber Optic Component - OPLINK COMMUNICATIONS, INC.; *pg.* 660, *pg.* 91
CFOX - Media & Entertainment - CORUS ENTERTAINMENT INC.; *pg.* 279, *pg.* 1937
CFPLAYER - Audio Solution - VIQ SOLUTIONS INC.; *pg.* 490, *pg.* 1905
CFR-TCO - Conductive Refrigerator Glass - AGC GLASS NORTH AMERICA, INC.; *pg.* 65, *pg.* 482
CFT - Software - BIO-RAD LABORATORIES, INC.; *pg.* 1504, *pg.* 101
CFT - Self-Adjusting Air Therapy - SPAN-AMERICA MEDICAL SYSTEMS, INC.; *pg.* 1595, *pg.* 1618
CFX MANAGER - Software - BIO-RAD LABORATORIES, INC.; *pg.* 1504, *pg.* 101
CFX384 - Software - BIO-RAD LABORATORIES, INC.; *pg.* 1504, *pg.* 101
CFX96 - Software - BIO-RAD LABORATORIES, INC.; *pg.* 1504, *pg.* 101
CG90 - Salt - CARGILL LIMITED; *pg.* 1475, *pg.* 1914
CG90 SURFACE SAVER - Salt - CARGILL LIMITED; *pg.* 1475, *pg.* 1914
CGT - Seal - GREENE, TWEED & CO.; *pg.* 1344, *pg.* 1544
CGW - Glass & Ceramic Material - CORNING INCORPORATED; *pg.* 1122, *pg.* 1154
CH - Automatic Aerosol Dispensers & Refills - SURCO PRODUCTS, INC.; *pg.* 336, *pg.* 1581
CHA-CHING CHERRY - Nail Care Product - OPI PRODUCTS INC.; *pg.* 518, *pg.* 167

First page reference indicates Business Class Edition
Second page reference indicates Geographic Edition

CHABLIS - Bath Product - KOHLER CO.; *pg.* 91, *pg.* 1862
CHACO - Footwear - WOLVERINE WORLD WIDE, INC.; *pg.* 1822, *pg.* 905
CHACOLLET - Purifiers - ENTEGRIS, INC.; *pg.* 1882, *pg.* 788
CHADDOCK - Dress Shoes - JOHNSTON & MURPHY CO.; *pg.* 1810, *pg.* 1651
CHADS FOR VIALS - Labeling System - BIOANALYTICAL SYSTEMS, INC.; *pg.* 1402, *pg.* 700
CHADWICK - Furniture - KNOLL, INC.; *pg.* 425, *pg.* 1527
CHADWICK'S OF BOSTON - Apparel - FULLBEAUTY BRANDS; *pg.* 1770, *pg.* 1233
CHADWOOD - Kitchen Cabinets - KITCHEN KOMPACT, INC.; *pg.* 91, *pg.* 692
CHAI SPIRIT - Nutritional Product - NUTRACEUTICAL INTERNATIONAL CORPORATION; *pg.* 1576, *pg.* 1753
CHAIN - Bicycle Component - SRAM CORPORATION; *pg.* 967, *pg.* 590
CHAIN GLIDE - Door - THE GENIE COMPANY; *pg.* 55, *pg.* 1403
CHAIN STORE AGE - Industry Publication - LEBHAR-FRIEDMAN INC.; *pg.* 1658, *pg.* 1250
CHAINMASTER - Fluid Handling System - GRACO, INC.; *pg.* 1342, *pg.* 935
CHAINSAWS & TOASTERS - Slots - INTERNATIONAL GAME TECHNOLOGY; *pg.* 957, *pg.* 1024
CHAIRMAN OF THE BOARD - Game - WMS INDUSTRIES INC.; *pg.* 593, *pg.* 666
CHAIRMAN SERIES - Furniture - H. WILSON COMPANY; *pg.* 1415, *pg.* 666
CHAIRMAN'S RESERVE - Premium Meats - TYSON FOODS, INC.; *pg.* 902, *pg.* 35
CHAKRA - Perfume - AVEDA CORPORATION; *pg.* 499, *pg.* 917
CHAKRA - Wall Chart - HUGGER MUGGER YOGA PRODUCTS LLC; *pg.* 1836, *pg.* 1758
CHALET - Home Design - LINDAL CEDAR HOMES, INC.; *pg.* 94, *pg.* 1837
CHALICE - Fan - CRAFTMADE INTERNATIONAL, INC.; *pg.* 1295, *pg.* 1670
CHALLENGE - Muffler - AP EXHAUST PRODUCTS, INC.; *pg.* 199, *pg.* 1373
CHALLENGE - Hand Soap - BIRKO CORPORATION; *pg.* 1149, *pg.* 332
CHALLENGE POWER LIFT - Machinery - THE CHALLENGE MACHINERY COMPANY; *pg.* 1322, *pg.* 902
CHALLENGER - Aircraft - BOMBARDIER INC.; *pg.* 1318, *pg.* 1953
CHALLENGER - Paper Driller - THE CHALLENGE MACHINERY COMPANY; *pg.* 1322, *pg.* 902
CHALLENGER - Tires - COOPER TIRE & RUBBER COMPANY; *pg.* 1881, *pg.* 1453
CHALLENGER - Air Rifles - CROSMAN CORPORATION; *pg.* 951, *pg.* 1143
CHALLENGER - Premium Cameras - EASTMAN KODAK COMPANY; *pg.* 1408, *pg.* 1333
CHALLENGER - Lighting - LSI INDUSTRIES INC.; *pg.* 58, *pg.* 1416
CHALLENGER - Truck Storage Box - LUND INTERNATIONAL, INC.; *pg.* 211, *pg.* 526
CHALLENGER - Towing & Recovery Equipment - MILLER INDUSTRIES, INC.; *pg.* 185, *pg.* 1655
CHALLENGER - Press Feeding Equipment - P/A INDUSTRIES, INC.; *pg.* 1367, *pg.* 339
CHALLENGER - Plastic & Rubber - TEKNOR APEX COMPANY; *pg.* 1889, *pg.* 1605
CHALLENGER LITE - Plastic & Rubber - TEKNOR APEX COMPANY; *pg.* 1889, *pg.* 1605
CHALLENGER MARINE - Systems Integration & Aeronautics - LOCKHEED MARTIN CORPORATION; *pg.* 229, *pg.* 762
CHALLENGES DRIVE INNOVATION - Theme - MERCURY COMPUTER SYSTEMS, INC.; *pg.* 434, *pg.* 813
CHALLONER - Tenoner - DIEHL WOODWORKING MACHINERY, INC.; *pg.* 1328, *pg.* 698
CHALMERS - Lighting Product - QUOIZEL INC.; *pg.* 1304, *pg.* 1616
CHALMIT - Electrical Product - HUBBELL INCORPORATED; *pg.* 1299, *pg.* 370
CHAMBERKLEEN - Filter Assembly - PALL CORPORATION; *pg.* 232, *pg.* 1323
CHAMBERLAIN - Fan - CRAFTMADE INTERNATIONAL, INC.; *pg.* 1295, *pg.* 1670
CHAMBERLAIN AND WHISPER DRIVE - Residential Garage Door Openers - THE CHAMBERLAIN GROUP, INC.; *pg.* 75, *pg.* 611
CHAMBERS - Men's & Women's Belts & Accessories - PHOENIX FOOTWEAR GROUP, INC.; *pg.* 1815, *pg.* 60
CHAMBERSBURG ENGINEERING - Forging Product - SUPERIOR DIE SET CORP.; *pg.* 1379, *pg.* 1885
CHAMBIR - Radiant Heater for Extruded Plastic & Rubber - PRECISION CONTROL SYSTEMS, INC./ RESEARCH INC.; *pg.* 1427, *pg.* 923
CHAMBORD - Liqueur - BROWN-FORMAN CORPORATION; *pg.* 1958, *pg.* 732
CHAMBORD - Bedding - CROSCILL, INC.; *pg.* 1122, *pg.* 1220
CHAMBRIL - Offset Printing Paper - INTERNATIONAL PAPER COMPANY; *pg.* 1460, *pg.* 1644
CHAMEA - Fabric - NEMSCHOFF, INC.; *pg.* 936, *pg.* 1890
CHAMEA - Fabric - UNIROYAL ENGINEERED PRODUCTS; *pg.* 699, *pg.* 467
CHAMELEON - Silica Gel - BASF CATALYSTS LLC; *pg.* 1148, *pg.* 1074
CHAMELEON - Cleaner - BIRKO CORPORATION; *pg.* 1149, *pg.* 332
CHAMELEON - Laser & Laser System - COHERENT, INC.; *pg.* 1406, *pg.* 265
CHAMELEON - Color Change Management System - GEMA USA INC.; *pg.* 1339, *pg.* 686
CHAMELEON - Hood Shields - LUND INTERNATIONAL, INC.; *pg.* 211, *pg.* 526
CHAMELEON - Gun System - NORDSON CORPORATION; *pg.* 1365, *pg.* 1480
CHAMELEON - Automated Teller Machines - TIDEL ENGINEERING, L.P.; *pg.* 1382, *pg.* 1670
CHAMELEON 7S - Video Game - INTERNATIONAL GAME TECHNOLOGY; *pg.* 957, *pg.* 1024
CHAMELEON ART - Software System - MENTOR GRAPHICS CORPORATION; *pg.* 432, *pg.* 1510
CHAMEQUINHO - Paper Products - INTERNATIONAL PAPER COMPANY; *pg.* 1460, *pg.* 1644
CHAMOIS - Pillow - ETHAN ALLEN INTERIORS INC.; *pg.* 924, *pg.* 343
CHAMOIS - Fabric - NEMSCHOFF, INC.; *pg.* 936, *pg.* 1890
CHAMOMILE CALM - Nutritional Product - NUTRACEUTICAL INTERNATIONAL CORPORATION; *pg.* 1576, *pg.* 1753
CHAMONIX - Lighting Product - QUOIZEL INC.; *pg.* 1304, *pg.* 1616
CHAMOY - Ice Cream Bar - WELLS ENTERPRISES, INC.; *pg.* 909, *pg.* 709
CHAMP - Bucket - GEERPRES INC.; *pg.* 1339, *pg.* 901
CHAMP - Floor Cleaning Product - NSS ENTERPRISES, INC.; *pg.* 59, *pg.* 1476
CHAMP! - Ice Cream - WELLS ENTERPRISES, INC.; *pg.* 909, *pg.* 709
CHAMP BURGER - Food Product - CHECKERS DRIVE-IN RESTAURANTS, INC.; *pg.* 1017, *pg.* 472
CHAMPAGNE - Burnishing Pad - AMERICO MANUFACTURING CO., INC.; *pg.* 325, *pg.* 482
CHAMPAGNE POPPIES - Bath Accessory - CROSCILL, INC.; *pg.* 1122, *pg.* 1220
CHAMPALE - Beer - PABST BREWING COMPANY; *pg.* 258, *pg.* 137
CHAMPENOISE-BRUT - Wine - BILTMORE ESTATE WINE COMPANY; *pg.* 1958, *pg.* 1358
CHAMPENOISE-SEC - Wine - BILTMORE ESTATE WINE COMPANY; *pg.* 1958, *pg.* 1358
CHAMPFLEURY - Cheese - AGROPUR COOPERATIVE; *pg.* 836, *pg.* 1950
CHAMPION - Car Dealerships - AUTONATION, INC.; *pg.* 165, *pg.* 423
CHAMPION - Memory Controller - BROADCOM CORPORATION; *pg.* 364, *pg.* 108
CHAMPION - Clock - BROWN & BIGELOW, INC.; *pg.* 1624, *pg.* 959
CHAMPION - Paper Cutter - THE CHALLENGE MACHINERY COMPANY; *pg.* 1322, *pg.* 902
CHAMPION - Automotive Accessories - CHAMPION MOTORSPORT; *pg.* 168, *pg.* 459
CHAMPION - Ignition Products - FEDERAL-MOGUL HOLDINGS CORPORATION; *pg.* 205, *pg.* 907
CHAMPION - Guitar Amplifier - FENDER MUSICAL INSTRUMENTS CORPORATION; *pg.* 547, *pg.* 21
CHAMPION - Fluid Handling System - GRACO, INC.; *pg.* 1342, *pg.* 935
CHAMPION - Athletic Apparel - HANESBRANDS INC.; *pg.* 26, *pg.* 1394
CHAMPION - Towing & Recovery Equipment - MILLER INDUSTRIES, INC.; *pg.* 185, *pg.* 1655
CHAMPION - Molecular Biology Product - THERMO FISHER SCIENTIFIC INC.; *pg.* 1602, *pg.* 61
CHAMPION - Plaster - USG CORPORATION; *pg.* 118, *pg.* 594
CHAMPION BARBELL - Pulse Rate Monitor - SPORT SUPPLY GROUP, INC.; *pg.* 1846, *pg.* 1687
CHAMPION BUS - Commercial Bus - THOR INDUSTRIES, INC.; *pg.* 1711, *pg.* 1456
CHAMPION COOK SERIES - Char-broilers, Griddles, Fryers & Ovens - APW WYOTT FOOD SERVICE EQUIPMENT, INC.; *pg.* 1314, *pg.* 1658
CHAMPION POWER EQUIPMENT - Electric Winch - TRACTOR SUPPLY COMPANY; *pg.* 708, *pg.* 1627
CHAMPIONS CHOICE - Salt - CARGILL, INC.; *pg.* 845, *pg.* 965
CHAMPIONS CHOICE - Salt Products - CARGILL LIMITED; *pg.* 1475, *pg.* 1914
CHAMPIONS PLAY HERE - Trademark - NATIONAL COLLEGIATE ATHLETIC ASSOCIATION; *pg.* 567, *pg.* 688
CHAMPIONSHIP CITY - Trademark - NATIONAL COLLEGIATE ATHLETIC ASSOCIATION; *pg.* 567, *pg.* 688
CHAMPLAIN VALLEY - Clothing - ABERCROMBIE & FITCH CO.; *pg.* 37, *pg.* 1466
CHAMPS SPORTS - Athletic Equipment, Footwear & Apparel - FOOT LOCKER, INC.; *pg.* 1808, *pg.* 1231
CHAN-L-WIRE - Wiring System - WIREMOLD/LEGRAND; *pg.* 689, *pg.* 383
CHANCE - Rope - HUBBELL INCORPORATED; *pg.* 1299, *pg.* 370
CHANCE - Fabric - NEMSCHOFF, INC.; *pg.* 936, *pg.* 1890
CHANCEE - Footwear - STEVEN MADDEN, LTD.; *pg.* 1819, *pg.* 1176
CHANCELLOR - Footwear - EASTLAND SHOE CORPORATION; *pg.* 1808, *pg.* 750
CHANCELLOR - Decorative Accessory - ETHAN ALLEN INTERIORS INC.; *pg.* 924, *pg.* 343
CHANCELLOR - Furniture - JASPER GROUP; *pg.* 930, *pg.* 691
CHANCELLOR - Office Furniture - STEELCASE INC.; *pg.* 475, *pg.* 889
CHANCELLOR - Fan - WESTINGHOUSE LIGHTING CORPORATION; *pg.* 687, *pg.* 1571
CHANDLER - Lounge Chairs - BERNHARDT DESIGN; *pg.* 918, *pg.* 1381
CHANDLER - Furniture - ETHAN ALLEN INTERIORS INC.; *pg.* 924, *pg.* 343
CHANDLER - Furniture - JASPER GROUP; *pg.* 930, *pg.* 691
CHANDLER REFRIGERATION - Refrigeration Units - LENNOX INTERNATIONAL INC.; *pg.* 1073, *pg.* 1736
CHANDON - Sparkling Wine - MOET HENNESSY; *pg.* 1966, *pg.* 1260
CHANEL - Table - BLATT BOWLING & BILLIARD CORP.; *pg.* 1827, *pg.* 1203
CHANGE - Electronic Components - MOLEX INCORPORATED; *pg.* 655, *pg.* 628
CHANGE-A-TIP - Electrosurgery Generators & Accessories - BOVIE MEDICAL CORPORATION; *pg.* 1402, *pg.* 1178
CHANGE ACCUMULATION PLUS - Software - BMC SOFTWARE, INC.; *pg.* 362, *pg.* 1701
CHANGE AWARE - Software Product - PEGASYSTEMS INC.; *pg.* 453, *pg.* 809
CHANGE BY DESIGN - Slogan - HAWORTH, INC.; *pg.* 402, *pg.* 891
CHANGE DIRECTOR FOR SQL SERVER - Software - DELL SOFTWARE; *pg.* 385, *pg.* 40
CHANGE GOVERNANCE - Slogan - SERENA SOFTWARE, INC.; *pg.* 468, *pg.* 192
CHANGE MANAGEMENT APPLICATION & AR SYSTEM - Software - BMC SOFTWARE, INC.; *pg.* 362, *pg.* 1701
CHANGE MANAGEMENT DASHBOARD - Software - BMC SOFTWARE, INC.; *pg.* 362, *pg.* 1701
CHANGE MANAGER - Software - BMC SOFTWARE, INC.; *pg.* 362, *pg.* 1701
CHANGE THE WORLD - Tagline - FORBES.COM LLC; *pg.* 1247, *pg.* 1232
CHANGEAUDITOR FOR ACTIVE DIRECTORY - Software - DELL SOFTWARE; *pg.* 385, *pg.* 40
CHANGEAUDITOR FOR EXCHANGE - Software - DELL SOFTWARE; *pg.* 385, *pg.* 40
CHANGEAUDITOR FOR FILE SYSTEMS - Software - DELL SOFTWARE; *pg.* 385, *pg.* 40
CHANGEMAN - Software - SERENA SOFTWARE, INC.; *pg.* 468, *pg.* 192
CHANGEPOINT - Software - COMPUWARE CORPORATION;

pg. 379, *pg.* 879
CHANGING LIVES WITH FITNESS INNOVATION - Slogan - ICON HEALTH & FITNESS, INC.; *pg.* 1837, *pg.* 1752
CHANGING THE STANDARD OF HEALING - Slogan - KINETIC CONCEPTS, INC.; *pg.* 1553, *pg.* 1741
CHANGING THE VALUE EQUATION - Slogan - LAM RESEARCH CORPORATION; *pg.* 1354, *pg.* 91
CHANGING THE WAY GOVERNMENT LOOKS AT INFORMATION - Slogan - MICROSTRATEGY, INC.; *pg.* 1266, *pg.* 1809
CHANGING THE WAY WE WORK,LIVE,PLAY & LEARN - Slogan - CISCO SYSTEMS, INC.; *pg.* 372, *pg.* 240
CHANGING THE WAY YOU THINK ABOUT FIBER MANAGEMENT - Tagline - CLEARFIELD, INC.; *pg.* 1406, *pg.* 953
CHANGING THE WAY YOU VIEW THE BATHROOM - Slogan - DECOLAV, INC.; *pg.* 1123, *pg.* 411
CHANLOCK - Hardware Synchronization - EVANS & SUTHERLAND COMPUTER CORPORATION; *pg.* 638, *pg.* 1757
CHANNEL BOX - Software - CHYRONHEGO; *pg.* 371, *pg.* 1179
CHANNEL CONNECT - Software - WEBSENSE, INC.; *pg.* 491, *pg.* 210
CHANNEL CUSTOM PUBLISHING - Publisher - UNITED BUSINESS MEDIA LLC; *pg.* 1697, *pg.* 1177
CHANNEL DOMAIN PROCESSING - Ultrasound Systems - ZONARE MEDICAL SYSTEMS, INC.; *pg.* 1612, *pg.* 163
CHANNEL FLASH - Manual - XEROX CORPORATION; *pg.* 494, *pg.* 365
CHANNEL MASTER - Medical Equipment - CONMED CORPORATION; *pg.* 1517, *pg.* 1347
CHANNEL ONE NEWS - News Broadcast to High Schools - RENTPATH, INC.; *pg.* 1680, *pg.* 538
CHANNEL PLUS - Integrated Home Network Systems - NORTEK, INC.; *pg.* 100, *pg.* 1607
CHANNELITES - Commercial Lighting - SWIVELIER CO., INC.; *pg.* 1307, *pg.* 1142
CHANNELLOCK BLUE - Grips - CHANNELLOCK, INC.; *pg.* 1044, *pg.* 1551
CHANNELMATE - Insulation - THE DOW CHEMICAL COMPANY; *pg.* 1157, *pg.* 898
CHANNELPLUS - Video Distribution System - NORTEK SECURITY & CONTROL LLC; *pg.* 659, *pg.* 59
CHANNELSTREAM - Valves - FLOWSERVE CORPORATION; *pg.* 82, *pg.* 1719
CHANNELTRON - Electron Multiplier Detector - PHOTONIS USA PENNSYLVANIA; *pg.* 663, *pg.* 1547
CHANNELWEB - Publisher - UNITED BUSINESS MEDIA LLC; *pg.* 1697, *pg.* 1177
CHANTAL - Jewelry - HABAND COMPANY, INC.; *pg.* 1772, *pg.* 1099
CHANTECLERC - Fabric - NEMSCHOFF, INC.; *pg.* 936, *pg.* 1890
CHANTILLY - Home Products - HABAND COMPANY, INC.; *pg.* 1772, *pg.* 1099
CHANTILLY - Cookies - PEPPERIDGE FARM, INC.; *pg.* 888, *pg.* 363
CHANTIX - Smoking Cessation Drug - PFIZER INC.; *pg.* 1581, *pg.* 1278
CHAPARRAL - Fan - CRAFTMADE INTERNATIONAL, INC.; *pg.* 1295, *pg.* 1670
CHAPARRAL - Systems Integration & Aeronautics - LOCKHEED MARTIN CORPORATION; *pg.* 229, *pg.* 762
CHAPARRAL - Lighting Product - QUOIZEL INC.; *pg.* 1304, *pg.* 1616
CHAPEL - Organs - ALLEN ORGAN COMPANY; *pg.* 527, *pg.* 1549
CHAPEL - Wall Decor - HERITAGE LACE INC.; *pg.* 694, *pg.* 711
CHAPEL OF LOVE - Nail Care Product - OPI PRODUCTS INC.; *pg.* 518, *pg.* 167
CHAPERONE - Shoe - AEROGROUP INTERNATIONAL, INC.; *pg.* 1803, *pg.* 1055
CHAPMAN - Furniture - HOOKER FURNITURE CORPORATION; *pg.* 928, *pg.* 1788
CHAPPI - Dog Food - MARS, INCORPORATED; *pg.* 1858, *pg.* 1792
CHAPS - Fabric - NEMSCHOFF, INC.; *pg.* 936, *pg.* 1890
CHAPS - Men's & Women's Wear - RALPH LAUREN CORPORATION; *pg.* 46, *pg.* 1284
CHAPSTICK - Lip Balm - PFIZER INC.; *pg.* 1581, *pg.* 1278
CHAPTER - Fabric - NEMSCHOFF, INC.; *pg.* 936, *pg.* 1890
CHAQWA - Beverages - THE COCA-COLA COMPANY; *pg.* 240, *pg.* 493
CHAR-BROIL - Gas Grill - W.C. BRADLEY CO.; *pg.* 62, *pg.* 528
CHAR-GAS - Thermal Processing Equipment - SURFACE COMBUSTION, INC.; *pg.* 1077, *pg.* 1462
CHAR-LYNN - Hydraulic Component - EATON CORPORATION; *pg.* 1331, *pg.* 1429
CHARACTER STUDIO - Software - AUTODESK INC.; *pg.* 356, *pg.* 257
CHARADE - Furniture - ASHLEY FURNITURE INDUSTRIES, INC.; *pg.* 914, *pg.* 1852
CHARCAT - Catalyst - BASF CATALYSTS LLC; *pg.* 1148, *pg.* 1074
CHARDONNAY SUR LIES - Wine - BILTMORE ESTATE WINE COMPANY; *pg.* 1958, *pg.* 1358
CHARG-CHEK - Automotive Equipment - THEXTON MANUFACTURING COMPANY, INC.; *pg.* 218, *pg.* 925
CHARGE - Cutting Tool - LEATHERMAN TOOL GROUP, INC.; *pg.* 1053, *pg.* 1504
CHARGE N' START - Batteries - UNIVERSAL POWER GROUP, INC.; *pg.* 683, *pg.* 1671
CHARGED WITH INNOVATION - Tagline - ION GEOPHYSICAL CORPORATION; *pg.* 1360, *pg.* 1708
CHARGEMASTER - Corrugating & Bag - GRAIN PROCESSING CORPORATION; *pg.* 859, *pg.* 709
CHARGEPAC - Industrial Water Treatment - ASHLAND INC.; *pg.* 972, *pg.* 726
CHARGER - Physical Vapor Deposition System - APPLIED MATERIALS, INC.; *pg.* 618, *pg.* 264
CHARGER - Compressor for Natural Gas - NORWALK COMPRESSOR COMPANY, INC.; *pg.* 1366, *pg.* 380
CHARGER - Floor Cleaning Product - NSS ENTERPRISES, INC.; *pg.* 59, *pg.* 1476
CHARGESWITCH - Molecular Biology Product - THERMO FISHER SCIENTIFIC INC.; *pg.* 1602, *pg.* 61
CHARIOT - Children's Books, Toys, Games & Videos - DAVID C. COOK; *pg.* 1633, *pg.* 315
CHARIOT - Fabric - NEMSCHOFF, INC.; *pg.* 936, *pg.* 1890
CHARIOT - Airline Service - UNITED CONTINENTAL HOLDINGS, INC.; *pg.* 1927, *pg.* 593
CHARIOT VICTOR - Bible Book - DAVID C. COOK; *pg.* 1633, *pg.* 315
CHARISMA - Furniture - ASHLEY FURNITURE INDUSTRIES, INC.; *pg.* 914, *pg.* 1852
CHARISMA - Book - CHARISMA MEDIA; *pg.* 1627, *pg.* 436
CHARISMA - Apparel - ICONIX BRAND GROUP, INC.; *pg.* 26, *pg.* 1243
CHARISMA - Container Grown Plant - MONROVIA GROWERS; *pg.* 1797, *pg.* 44
CHARISMA - Sturdilite Floodlight - PHOENIX PRODUCTS COMPANY; *pg.* 1304, *pg.* 1879
CHARISMA - Footwear - SAUCONY, INC.; *pg.* 1818, *pg.* 828
CHARISMA - Software - SCHLUMBERGER LIMITED; *pg.* 801, *pg.* 1714
CHARISMA PLUSH - Fabric - NEMSCHOFF, INC.; *pg.* 936, *pg.* 1890
CHARITE - Healthcare Product - JOHNSON & JOHNSON; *pg.* 1549, *pg.* 1091
CHARLEMAGNE - Fabric - NEMSCHOFF, INC.; *pg.* 936, *pg.* 1890
CHARLES - Furniture - AMISCO INDUSTRIES LTD.; *pg.* 913, *pg.* 1958
CHARLES RIVER - Carpet - INTERFACE, INC.; *pg.* 695, *pg.* 512
CHARLES SCRIBNER'S SONS - Reference Books - GALE CENGAGE LEARNING; *pg.* 1643, *pg.* 885
CHARLES THE GREAT - Cigars - FINCK CIGAR CO.; *pg.* 1894, *pg.* 1740
CHARLES TOWN RACES - Racetrack - PENN NATIONAL GAMING, INC.; *pg.* 574, *pg.* 1595
CHARLES WYSOCKI - Toy & Game - HASBRO, INC.; *pg.* 954, *pg.* 1603
CHARLESTON - Window Treatment - CROSCILL, INC.; *pg.* 1122, *pg.* 1220
CHARLESTON - Furniture - JASPER GROUP; *pg.* 930, *pg.* 691
CHARLESTON - Lighting - LSI INDUSTRIES INC.; *pg.* 58, *pg.* 1416
CHARLESTON - Fabric - NEMSCHOFF, INC.; *pg.* 936, *pg.* 1890
CHARLESTON BEADED COLLECTION - Vinyl Siding - PLY GEM SIDING GROUP; *pg.* 105, *pg.* 986
CHARLESTON CHEW - Chocolate & Caramel Candies - TOOTSIE ROLL INDUSTRIES, INC.; *pg.* 1863, *pg.* 591
CHARLESTOWN - Furniture - BUSH INDUSTRIES INC.; *pg.* 919, *pg.* 1170
CHARLESTOWN - Footwear - EASTLAND SHOE CORPORATION; *pg.* 1808, *pg.* 750
CHARLESTOWN - Retirement Community - ERICKSON LIVING; *pg.* 1090, *pg.* 766
CHARLETON - Furniture - ASHLEY FURNITURE INDUSTRIES, INC.; *pg.* 914, *pg.* 1852
CHARLEY 1 HORSE - Hats - HATCO, INC.; *pg.* 6, *pg.* 1698
CHARLEYS CRAB - Restaurant Chain - LANDRY'S, INC.; *pg.* 1735, *pg.* 1709
CHARLEY'S GRILLED SUBS - Restaurants - GOSH ENTERPRISES, INC.; *pg.* 1730, *pg.* 1440
CHARLEYS PHILLY STEAKS - Restaurants - GOSH ENTERPRISES, INC.; *pg.* 1730, *pg.* 1440
CHARLIE - Perfume - REVLON, INC.; *pg.* 521, *pg.* 1286
CHARLIE & THE CHOCOLATE FACTORY - Game - WINNING MOVES GAMES, INC.; *pg.* 970, *pg.* 816
CHARLIE'S LUNCH KIT - Lunch Kit - STARKIST FOODS INC.; *pg.* 898, *pg.* 1581
CHARLOTTE - Furniture - THE COMMERCIAL FURNITURE GROUP; *pg.* 920, *pg.* 994
CHARLOTTE - Bath Accessory - CROSCILL, INC.; *pg.* 1122, *pg.* 1220
CHARLOTTE - Clothing - HUGGER MUGGER YOGA PRODUCTS LLC; *pg.* 1836, *pg.* 1758
CHARLOTTE - Furniture - LA-Z-BOY INCORPORATED; *pg.* 932, *pg.* 901
CHARLOTTE - Fabric - SCALAMANDRE, INC.; *pg.* 941, *pg.* 1058
CHARLOTTE - Software - SUNGARD DATA SYSTEMS INC.; *pg.* 477, *pg.* 1592
CHARLOTTE - Women's Clothing & Accessories - WOODEN SHIPS OF HOBOKEN; *pg.* 35, *pg.* 1315
CHARLOTTE MOTOR SPEEDWAY - Entertainment Venue - SPEEDWAY MOTORSPORTS, INC.; *pg.* 584, *pg.* 1370
THE CHARLOTTE OBSERVER - Newspaper - THE CHARLOTTE OBSERVER PUBLISHING CO.; *pg.* 1627, *pg.* 1364
CHARLOTTE.COM - Website - THE CHARLOTTE OBSERVER PUBLISHING CO.; *pg.* 1627, *pg.* 1364
CHARM - Fabric - NEMSCHOFF, INC.; *pg.* 936, *pg.* 1890
CHARMIN - Toilet Paper Product - THE PROCTER & GAMBLE COMPANY; *pg.* 1129, *pg.* 1418
CHARMIN PLUS - Tissue - THE PROCTER & GAMBLE COMPANY; *pg.* 1129, *pg.* 1418
CHARMIN ULTRA - Tissue - THE PROCTER & GAMBLE COMPANY; *pg.* 1129, *pg.* 1418
CHARMING - Carpet - BEAULIEU GROUP, LLC; *pg.* 917, *pg.* 529
CHARMING CHERRIES - Game - WMS INDUSTRIES INC.; *pg.* 593, *pg.* 666
CHARMO - Thermal Processing Equipment - SURFACE COMBUSTION, INC.; *pg.* 1077, *pg.* 1462
CHARMS - Candy - TOOTSIE ROLL INDUSTRIES, INC.; *pg.* 1863, *pg.* 591
CHARRGER - Footwear - STEVEN MADDEN, LTD.; *pg.* 1819, *pg.* 1176
CHARRITY - Footwear - STEVEN MADDEN, LTD.; *pg.* 1819, *pg.* 1176
CHARRUA - Beverages - THE COCA-COLA COMPANY; *pg.* 240, *pg.* 493
THE CHART HOUSE - Restaurant Chain - LANDRY'S, INC.; *pg.* 1735, *pg.* 1709
CHARTER - Furniture - BROWN JORDAN INTERNATIONAL COMPANY; *pg.* 919, *pg.* 740
THE CHARTER BUNDLE - Communication Product - CHARTER COMMUNICATIONS, INC.; *pg.* 274, *pg.* 372
CHARTER CABLE TV - Communication Product - CHARTER COMMUNICATIONS, INC.; *pg.* 274, *pg.* 372
CHARTER CLUB - Feminine Apparel, Intimate Apparel, Accessories & Home Furnishings - MACY'S, INC.; *pg.* 1778, *pg.* 1417
CHARTER COMMUNICATIONS - Communication Product - CHARTER COMMUNICATIONS, INC.; *pg.* 274, *pg.* 372
CHARTER CONNECT - Communication Product - CHARTER COMMUNICATIONS, INC.; *pg.* 274, *pg.* 372
CHARTER DIGITAL CABLE - Communication Product - CHARTER COMMUNICATIONS, INC.; *pg.* 274, *pg.* 372
CHARTER DIGITAL TV - Communication Product - CHARTER COMMUNICATIONS, INC.; *pg.* 274, *pg.* 372
CHARTER DVR - Communication Product - CHARTER COMMUNICATIONS, INC.; *pg.* 274, *pg.* 372
CHARTER HDTV - Communication Product - CHARTER COMMUNICATIONS, INC.; *pg.* 274, *pg.* 372
CHARTER HIGH-SPEED - Communication Product - CHARTER COMMUNICATIONS, INC.; *pg.* 274, *pg.* 372

First page reference indicates Business Class Edition
Second page reference indicates Geographic Edition

CHARTER MEDICAL - International Hospital Management - MAGELLAN HEALTH SERVICES, INC.; *pg.* 1557, *pg.* 337
CHARTER SECURITY SUITE - Communication Product - CHARTER COMMUNICATIONS, INC.; *pg.* 274, *pg.* 372
CHARTER TELEPHONE - Communication Product - CHARTER COMMUNICATIONS, INC.; *pg.* 274, *pg.* 372
CHARTING THE MARKET - Financial Products - DOW JONES & COMPANY, INC.; *pg.* 1637, *pg.* 1225
CHARTKEEPER - Software - NIGHTINGALE; *pg.* 446, *pg.* 186
CHARTLINK - Software - COMPUTER PROGRAMS & SYSTEMS, INC.; *pg.* 378, *pg.* 7
CHARVEL - Guitar - FENDER MUSICAL INSTRUMENTS CORPORATION; *pg.* 547, *pg.* 21
CHASE - Lounge Chairs - BERNHARDT DESIGN; *pg.* 918, *pg.* 1381
CHASE - Fiberglass Boat Product - GRADY-WHITE BOATS, INC.; *pg.* 1707, *pg.* 1377
CHASE & SONS - Coating & Laminating Product - CHASE CORPORATION; *pg.* 1152, *pg.* 803
CHASE AUTHENTICS - Knitwear - V.F. CORPORATION; *pg.* 34, *pg.* 1376
CHASE BLH2OCK - Water Blocking Compound Sold to the Wire & Cable Industry - CHASE CORPORATION; *pg.* 1152, *pg.* 803
CHASE FACILE - Coating Product - CHASE CORPORATION; *pg.* 1152, *pg.* 803
CHASE LAKE - Clothing - ABERCROMBIE & FITCH CO.; *pg.* 37, *pg.* 1466
CHASE SAPPHIRE - Credit Card - JPMORGAN CHASE & CO.; *pg.* 772, *pg.* 1246
CHASE SAVER - Carriers For Wall-Hung - JOSAM COMPANY; *pg.* 89, *pg.* 695
CHASER - Soft Drink - DOUBLE-COLA CO.-USA; *pg.* 249, *pg.* 1629
CHASER - Fabric - NEMSCHOFF, INC.; *pg.* 936, *pg.* 1890
CHASEX - Software System - MENTOR GRAPHICS CORPORATION; *pg.* 432, *pg.* 1510
CHAT - Fabric - NEMSCHOFF, INC.; *pg.* 936, *pg.* 1890
CHATEAU - Consumer Products - AKZO NOBEL; *pg.* 1439, *pg.* 1952
CHATEAU - Kitchen & Bathroom Faucets - MOEN INCORPORATED; *pg.* 1056, *pg.* 1468
CHATEAU - Fabric - NEMSCHOFF, INC.; *pg.* 936, *pg.* 1890
CHATEAU - Siding & Exterior Products - NORTEK, INC.; *pg.* 100, *pg.* 1607
CHATEAU - Door Glass - ODL INCORPORATED; *pg.* 101, *pg.* 914
CHATEAU - Flatware - ONEIDA LTD; *pg.* 1129, *pg.* 1318
CHATEAU - Lighting Product - WESTINGHOUSE LIGHTING CORPORATION; *pg.* 687, *pg.* 1571
CHATEAU ALTER EGO - Wine - SAZERAC COMPANY, INC.; *pg.* 1969, *pg.* 745
CHATEAU DE BALLEROY - Rug - COURISTAN INC.; *pg.* 921, *pg.* 1067
CHATEAU DE FLEUR - Wine - WEIBEL, INC.; *pg.* 1972, *pg.* 122
CHATEAU FAUTEUIL - Furniture - J. ROBERT SCOTT INC.; *pg.* 930, *pg.* 105
CHATEAU FRONTENAC - Furniture - ASHLEY FURNITURE INDUSTRIES, INC.; *pg.* 914, *pg.* 1852
CHATEAU LEGACY - Siding & Exterior Products - NORTEK, INC.; *pg.* 100, *pg.* 1607
CHATEAU LOUDENNE - Bordeaux Wines - DREYFUS ASHBY INC.; *pg.* 1962, *pg.* 1226
CHATEAU NOBILITY - Siding & Exterior Products - NORTEK, INC.; *pg.* 100, *pg.* 1607
CHATEAU STE. MICHELLE - Wine - STE. MICHELLE WINE ESTATES LTD.; *pg.* 1970, *pg.* 1847
CHATHAM VILLAGE - Croutons - LANCASTER COLONY CORPORATION; *pg.* 873, *pg.* 1441
CHATHAM VILLAGE - Croutons & Stuffing - T. MARZETTI COMPANY; *pg.* 900, *pg.* 1444
CHATITUDE - Game - HASBRO, INC.; *pg.* 954, *pg.* 1603
CHATS - Training Manual - INTELLIGENT HEARING SYSTEMS CORP.; *pg.* 1546, *pg.* 443
CHATTANOOGA - Orthopedic Device - DJO SURGICAL; *pg.* 1525, *pg.* 1661
CHATTANOOGA BAKERY - Bakery Products - CHATTANOOGA BAKERY INC.; *pg.* 847, *pg.* 1628
CHATTANOOGA CHEW - Chewing Tobacco - SWISHER INTERNATIONAL, INC.; *pg.* 1895, *pg.* 345
CHATTERBOX - Fabric - NEMSCHOFF, INC.; *pg.* 936, *pg.* 1890
CHAUDFONTAINE - Beverages - THE COCA-COLA COMPANY; *pg.* 240, *pg.* 493
CHDR - Consulting Service - MAXIMUS, INC.; *pg.* 780, *pg.* 1799
CHECI - Personal Care Products. - AMERICAN INTERNATIONAL INDUSTRIES COMPANY; *pg.* 498, *pg.* 126
CHECK-FLO - Introducer Set - COOK GROUP, INC.; *pg.* 1518, *pg.* 674
CHECK LINK - Service - NATSO, INC.; *pg.* 151, *pg.* 1771
CHECK MARK - Glaze & Enamel Frit & Clay - FERRO CORPORATION; *pg.* 1162, *pg.* 1462
CHECK-MATE - Pumps for Viscous Materials - GRACO, INC.; *pg.* 1342, *pg.* 935
CHECK-MATE - Pump Check Control System - HENRY PRATT COMPANY; *pg.* 1049, *pg.* 555
CHECK-NET - Labels - CHECKPOINT SYSTEMS, INC.; *pg.* 628, *pg.* 1559
CHECK O 2 PLUS - Medical Equipment - INVACARE CORPORATION; *pg.* 1546, *pg.* 1451
CHECK OUT! - Game - GAMEWRIGHT; *pg.* 953, *pg.* 836
CHECK OUTS - Short Pant - CORTLAND LINE COMPANY; *pg.* 1831, *pg.* 1155
CHECK PLUS - Software - BMC SOFTWARE, INC.; *pg.* 362, *pg.* 1701
CHECK-TROL - Isolation Flow Control Flange - XYLEM INC.; *pg.* 1078, *pg.* 1339
CHECK YEARLY SEE CLEARLY - Slogan - MARCHON EYEWEAR, INC.; *pg.* 1421, *pg.* 1180
CHECKCOUNT - Web Host Service - CHECKPOINT SYSTEMS, INC.; *pg.* 628, *pg.* 1559
CHECKDEFENSE - Software System - BOTTOMLINE TECHNOLOGIES (DE), INC.; *pg.* 727, *pg.* 1038
CHECKER - Machine Vision System - COGNEX CORPORATION; *pg.* 1406, *pg.* 834
CHECKER - Wallet - VANS, INC.; *pg.* 1821, *pg.* 76
CHECKER SPLIT - Fabric - NEMSCHOFF, INC.; *pg.* 936, *pg.* 1890
CHECKERBOARD - Educational Materials - SCHOLASTIC INC.; *pg.* 1683, *pg.* 1288
CHECKERS - Fabric - NEMSCHOFF, INC.; *pg.* 936, *pg.* 1890
CHECKERWARE - Software System - MENTOR GRAPHICS CORPORATION; *pg.* 432, *pg.* 1510
CHECKFAST - Laptop Case - SOLO; *pg.* 12, *pg.* 1165
CHECKFIRE - Fire Detection & Control System for Vehicles - ANSUL, INCORPORATED; *pg.* 1147, *pg.* 1869
CHECKIT - Software - SMITH MICRO SOFTWARE, INC.; *pg.* 471, *pg.* 41
CHECKLOCK - Screening Services - TASER INTERNATIONAL, INC.; *pg.* 677, *pg.* 24
CHECKMARK - Software - BIO-RAD LABORATORIES, INC.; *pg.* 1504, *pg.* 101
CHECKMARK CIRCLE DESIGN - Telecommunication Product - VERISIGN, INC.; *pg.* 488, *pg.* 1799
CHECKMARK DESIGN - Healthcare Product - HEALTH GRADES, INC.; *pg.* 1256, *pg.* 319
CHECKMATE - Gage Management System - A.G. DAVIS/AA GAGE; *pg.* 1310, *pg.* 908
CHECKMATE - Medical Product - HOLOGIC, INC.; *pg.* 1416, *pg.* 784
CHECKMATE - Dinnerware - THE HOMER LAUGHLIN CHINA COMPANY; *pg.* 1125, *pg.* 1850
CHECKMATE - Video Game - INTERNATIONAL GAME TECHNOLOGY; *pg.* 957, *pg.* 1024
CHECKMATE - Software System - MENTOR GRAPHICS CORPORATION; *pg.* 432, *pg.* 1510
CHECKMATE - Fabric - NEMSCHOFF, INC.; *pg.* 936, *pg.* 1890
CHECKMATES - Pant Set - HABAND COMPANY, INC.; *pg.* 1772, *pg.* 1099
CHECKMC - Software - MERCURY COMPUTER SYSTEMS, INC.; *pg.* 434, *pg.* 813
CHECKOUT COUPON - Marketing Service - CATALINA MARKETING CORPORATION; *pg.* 369, *pg.* 462
CHECKPOINT - Integrated Solutions - CHECKPOINT SYSTEMS, INC.; *pg.* 628, *pg.* 1559
CHECKPOINT - Machine Vision System - COGNEX CORPORATION; *pg.* 1406, *pg.* 834
CHECKPOINT - Pest Elimination System - ECOLAB INC.; *pg.* 329, *pg.* 960
CHECKPOINT - Software - THOMSON REUTERS TAX & ACCOUNTING; *pg.* 1693, *pg.* 1299
CHECKPOINTE - Shirts - ELBECO INCORPORATED; *pg.* 40, *pg.* 1584
CHECKPRO AUDITOR - Software - CHECKPOINT SYSTEMS, INC.; *pg.* 628, *pg.* 1559
CHECKPRO MANAGER - Data Collection & Management Tool - CHECKPOINT SYSTEMS, INC.; *pg.* 628, *pg.* 1559
CHECKPROTECT - Paper Product - BOISE CASCADE HOLDINGS, L.L.C.; *pg.* 1453, *pg.* 546
CHECKTRONIC - Computerized Security Document Production System - DELPHAX TECHNOLOGIES INC.; *pg.* 386, *pg.* 917
CHECKULATOR - Electronic Register - HABAND COMPANY, INC.; *pg.* 1772, *pg.* 1099
CHECKVISION - Software - COMPUTER SCIENCES CORPORATION; *pg.* 378, *pg.* 1780
CHECKWRITING - Software - TROY GROUP INC.; *pg.* 485, *pg.* 71
CHED 'R' BITES - Food Product - SONIC CORP.; *pg.* 1750, *pg.* 1487
CHED 'R' PEPPERS - Food Product - SONIC CORP.; *pg.* 1750, *pg.* 1487
CHEDDAIRS - Cheddar Cheese Snacks - SNYDER'S OF HANOVER, INC.; *pg.* 1862, *pg.* 1536
CHEDDAR FINGERS - Food Product - PEPPERIDGE FARM, INC.; *pg.* 888, *pg.* 363
CHEER - Laundry Product - THE PROCTER & GAMBLE COMPANY; *pg.* 1129, *pg.* 1418
CHEER LEADER - Shoe - AEROGROUP INTERNATIONAL, INC.; *pg.* 1803, *pg.* 1055
CHEERIOS - Cereal - GENERAL MILLS, INC.; *pg.* 828, *pg.* 933
CHEERLEADERS - Educational Materials - SCHOLASTIC INC.; *pg.* 1683, *pg.* 1288
CHEERS - Soft Drink - THE COCA-COLA COMPANY; *pg.* 240, *pg.* 493
CHEERS - Fabric - NEMSCHOFF, INC.; *pg.* 936, *pg.* 1890
CHEERWINE - Multiflavored Soft Drink - CAROLINA BEVERAGE CORPORATION; *pg.* 239, *pg.* 1390
CHEERY O - Shoe - AEROGROUP INTERNATIONAL, INC.; *pg.* 1803, *pg.* 1055
CHEERY TREE - Shoe - AEROGROUP INTERNATIONAL, INC.; *pg.* 1803, *pg.* 1055
CHEESE BLOCKER - Cheese slicer & cuber - LINCOLN FOODSERVICE PRODUCTS, LLC; *pg.* 1127, *pg.* 1432
CHEESE NIPS - Crackers - MONDELEZ INTERNATIONAL, INC.; *pg.* 878, *pg.* 601
CHEESE ON NIPCHEE - Snacks - SNYDER'S-LANCE, INC.; *pg.* 896, *pg.* 1368
CHEESE-PHOS - Cheese Additive - HAWKINS, INC.; *pg.* 1165, *pg.* 937
CHEESE SMART - Kitchenware - TUPPERWARE BRANDS CORPORATION; *pg.* 1139, *pg.* 456
CHEESE TWISTS - Snacks - SNYDER'S OF HANOVER, INC.; *pg.* 1862, *pg.* 1536
THE CHEESECAKE FACTORY BAKERY - Wholesale Bakery - CHEESECAKE FACTORY INCORPORATED; *pg.* 1017, *pg.* 56
THE CHEESECAKE FACTORY BAKERY CAFE - Restaurant Concepts - CHEESECAKE FACTORY INCORPORATED; *pg.* 1017, *pg.* 56
THE CHEESECAKE FACTORY EXPRESS - Restaurant Concepts - CHEESECAKE FACTORY INCORPORATED; *pg.* 1017, *pg.* 56
CHEESETRODE - Robotic Product - HAMILTON CO., INC.; *pg.* 1415, *pg.* 1031
CHEESY PARCHEESY - Game - WINNING MOVES GAMES, INC.; *pg.* 970, *pg.* 816
CHEESY RAVIOLI - Food Product - ANNIE'S INC.; *pg.* 1760, *pg.* 45
CHEESY TOTS - Golden Brown Tots - BURGER KING CORPORATION; *pg.* 1719, *pg.* 440
CHEETAH - Window Treatment - CROSCILL, INC.; *pg.* 1122, *pg.* 1220
CHEETAH - Fire Protection System - FIKE CORPORATION; *pg.* 1047, *pg.* 973
CHEETAH SYSTEM - Microprocessor-based Analog Addressable Suppression Panel - FIKE CORPORATION; *pg.* 1047, *pg.* 973
CHEETAH XI - Fire Suppression System - FIKE CORPORATION; *pg.* 1047, *pg.* 973
CHEETOS - Cheese Snack - FRITO-LAY NORTH AMERICA, INC.; *pg.* 1853, *pg.* 1730
CHEETOS - Snack Food - PEPSICO, INC.; *pg.* 259, *pg.* 1327
CHEETOS SHOTS - Snack - FRITO-LAY NORTH AMERICA, INC.; *pg.* 1853, *pg.* 1730
CHEEZ-IT - Food Product - KELLOGG COMPANY; *pg.* 831, *pg.* 870
CHEF-AIRE - Range Hoods - NORTEK, INC.; *pg.* 100, *pg.*

1607
CHEF ALLEN'S - Sauce - GOLD PURE FOOD PRODUCTS CO., INC.; *pg.* 858, *pg.* 1166
CHEF BOYARDEE - Food Product - CONAGRA FOODS, INC.; *pg.* 826, *pg.* 1014
CHEF DESIGNS - Apparel - V.F. CORPORATION; *pg.* 34, *pg.* 1376
CHEF-DR - Software - BIO-RAD LABORATORIES, INC.; *pg.* 1504, *pg.* 101
CHEF DRIVEN, INGREDIENT DRIVEN - Tagline - MEAT & SEAFOOD SOLUTIONS, LLC; *pg.* 1027, *pg.* 1375
CHEF MAPPER - Software - BIO-RAD LABORATORIES, INC.; *pg.* 1504, *pg.* 101
CHEF MARK - Food Product - SHAMROCK FOODS COMPANY; *pg.* 895, *pg.* 20
CHEF-MATE - Food Products - NESTLE USA, INC.; *pg.* 883, *pg.* 96
CHEF MICHAEL'S - Dog Food - NESTLE PURINA PETCARE COMPANY; *pg.* 1479, *pg.* 1000
CHEF PLEASER - Bacon - HATFIELD QUALITY MEATS, INC.; *pg.* 861, *pg.* 1537
CHEF SERIES - Kitchenware - TUPPERWARE BRANDS CORPORATION; *pg.* 1139, *pg.* 456
CHEF-WAY - Oil; Shortening; Conditioned Rice - RICELAND FOODS, INC.; *pg.* 892, *pg.* 36
CHEFCO - Cutlery - TOWNECRAFT, INC.; *pg.* 1139, *pg.* 1071
CHEFCOMM PRO - Interface - TURBOCHEF TECHNOLOGIES, INC.; *pg.* 902, *pg.* 1670
CHEFF - Detergent - THE PROCTER & GAMBLE COMPANY; *pg.* 1129, *pg.* 1418
CHEF'S COLLECTION - Food Product - PEPPERIDGE FARM, INC.; *pg.* 888, *pg.* 363
CHEF'S PRIDE - Flavor Base, Salad Oil & Pan Coating - VENTURA FOODS, LLC; *pg.* 908, *pg.* 49
CHEF'S SHORTCUTS - Flavor Systems - WILD FLAVORS, INC.; *pg.* 910, *pg.* 728
CHEF'S WARE - Cookware - TOWNECRAFT, INC.; *pg.* 1139, *pg.* 1071
CHEK - (Complete Hemodialysis Kinetics - FRESENIUS MEDICAL CARE NORTH AMERICA; *pg.* 1531, *pg.* 851
CHEK LO - Sock - VANS, INC.; *pg.* 1821, *pg.* 76
CHEK-LOK - Excess Flow Valves - ENGINEERED CONTROLS INTERNATIONAL LLC; *pg.* 1334, *pg.* 1372
CHEK-MATE - Cadmium Pigments - FERRO CORPORATION; *pg.* 1162, *pg.* 1462
CHEKD FOR QUALITY - Slogan - QUALITY CHEKD DAIRIES, INC.; *pg.* 154, *pg.* 630
CHEKIT - Medical Tests - IDEXX LABORATORIES, INC.; *pg.* 1543, *pg.* 753
CHELAMED - Radiopharmaceutical Services - THE DOW CHEMICAL COMPANY; *pg.* 1157, *pg.* 898
CHELEX - Software - BIO-RAD LABORATORIES, INC.; *pg.* 1504, *pg.* 101
CHELSA - Lamp - ASHLEY FURNITURE INDUSTRIES, INC.; *pg.* 914, *pg.* 1852
CHELSEA - Furniture - ASHLEY FURNITURE INDUSTRIES, INC.; *pg.* 914, *pg.* 1852
CHELSEA - Furniture - ETHAN ALLEN INTERIORS INC.; *pg.* 924, *pg.* 343
CHELSEA - Watch - GEVRIL USA; *pg.* 6, *pg.* 1348
CHELSEA - Furniture - J. ROBERT SCOTT INC.; *pg.* 930, *pg.* 105
CHELSEA - Fabric - NEMSCHOFF, INC.; *pg.* 936, *pg.* 1890
CHELSEA - Fabric - UNIROYAL ENGINEERED PRODUCTS; *pg.* 699, *pg.* 467
CHELSEA HARBOR - Lighting Product - WESTINGHOUSE LIGHTING CORPORATION; *pg.* 687, *pg.* 1571
CHELSEA HOUSE - Publisher - HAIGHTS CROSS COMMUNICATIONS, INC.; *pg.* 1646, *pg.* 1237
CHELSEA TWEED - Hat - WOODEN SHIPS OF HOBOKEN; *pg.* 35, *pg.* 1315
CHEM CALK - Construction Sealants/Caulks - BOSTIK INC.; *pg.* 1150, *pg.* 833
CHEM-F - Seal & Thermoplastic Component - GREENE, TWEED & CO.; *pg.* 1344, *pg.* 1544
CHEM KLEEN - Cleaner - SWISHER HYGIENE INC.; *pg.* 336, *pg.* 1507
CHEM-O-CONE - Enamel - JONES-BLAIR COMPANY; *pg.* 1443, *pg.* 1682
CHEM-O-LITE - Vinyl Finish - JONES-BLAIR COMPANY; *pg.* 1443, *pg.* 1682
CHEM-O-PON - Epoxy Enamel - JONES-BLAIR COMPANY; *pg.* 1443, *pg.* 1682
CHEM-O-THIX - Vinyl Coating - JONES-BLAIR COMPANY; *pg.* 1443, *pg.* 1682
CHEM-O-Z - Zinc Coating - JONES-BLAIR COMPANY; *pg.* 1443, *pg.* 1682
CHEM-O-Z II - Primer - JONES-BLAIR COMPANY; *pg.* 1443, *pg.* 1682
CHEM SEAL - Aircraft, Electrical & Specialty Sealants & Adhesives - THE FLAMEMASTER CORPORATION; *pg.* 1162, *pg.* 174
CHEM-STUD - Adhesive Anchor System - POWERS FASTENERS INC.; *pg.* 1059, *pg.* 1143
CHEM-SURE - Pump Tube - W.L. GORE & ASSOCIATES, INC.; *pg.* 122, *pg.* 388
CHEM-TECH - Pump Product - IDEX CORPORATION; *pg.* 1347, *pg.* 623
CHEM-VAC - Plastic & Industrial Conveyors - CHRISTIANSON SYSTEMS, INC.; *pg.* 1323, *pg.* 917
CHEM-VY-KOTE - Vinyls - AKZONOBEL DECORATIVE PAINTS U.S.; *pg.* 1439, *pg.* 1474
CHEMAWARE - Product Services - THE DOW CHEMICAL COMPANY; *pg.* 1157, *pg.* 898
CHEMBIOPRINT - Health Technology - AFEXA LIFE SCIENCES INC.; *pg.* 1487, *pg.* 1905
CHEMCITE RESEARCH SUITE - Publisher - BLOOMBERG BNA; *pg.* 1621, *pg.* 1772
CHEMCON - Metering Pumps - TUTHILL CORPORATION PUMP GROUP; *pg.* 1385, *pg.* 553
CHEMCOR - Glass & Ceramic Material - CORNING INCORPORATED; *pg.* 1122, *pg.* 1154
CHEMCOR - Corrosion Protection System - JUSTRITE MANUFACTURING COMPANY, LLC; *pg.* 1394, *pg.* 606
CHEMDI - Chemical Indicator - STERIS CORPORATION; *pg.* 1597, *pg.* 1464
CHEMDRAIN - Pipe & Fitting System - CHARLOTTE PIPE & FOUNDRY COMPANY; *pg.* 1044, *pg.* 1365
CHEMESOL - Gloves - LAKELAND INDUSTRIES, INC.; *pg.* 1354, *pg.* 1338
CHEMET CDC - Cuprous Oxide - AMERICAN CHEMET CORPORATION; *pg.* 1147, *pg.* 599
CHEMET DSC - Electrical & Thermal Conductor - AMERICAN CHEMET CORPORATION; *pg.* 1147, *pg.* 599
CHEMETRON - Coupler - ALLIED HEALTHCARE PRODUCTS, INC.; *pg.* 1491, *pg.* 990
CHEMEXPRESS - Monitoring System - STERIS CORPORATION; *pg.* 1597, *pg.* 1464
CHEMFAST - Epoxies - AKZONOBEL DECORATIVE PAINTS U.S.; *pg.* 1439, *pg.* 1474
CHEMFIL - Coatings, Rust Removers, Cleaning Preparations, Stripping Agents - PPG INDUSTRIES, INC.; *pg.* 1445, *pg.* 1579
CHEMFOS - Coating Product - PPG INDUSTRIES, INC.; *pg.* 1445, *pg.* 1579
CHEMGARD - Gas Monitor - MINE SAFETY APPLIANCES COMPANY; *pg.* 1361, *pg.* 1525
CHEMGLAZE - Coating - LORD CORPORATION; *pg.* 1357, *pg.* 1360
CHEMGUARD - Chemical Products - AIR PRODUCTS AND CHEMICALS, INC.; *pg.* 1145, *pg.* 1513
CHEMGUARD - Lubricant - D-A LUBRICANT COMPANY; *pg.* 975, *pg.* 693
CHEMGUARD - Chemical Barrier Sheath - GENERAL CABLE CORPORATION; *pg.* 83, *pg.* 384
CHEMGUARD - Cleaner - ROCHESTER MIDLAND CORPORATION; *pg.* 334, *pg.* 1337
CHEMI-WASHER - Horizontal Belt Washer - KADANT BLACK CLAWSON INC.; *pg.* 1352, *pg.* 1460
CHEMICAL BOND EXPRESS - Chemical Product - SOCIETY OF CHEMICAL MNAUFACTURERS & AFFILIATES, INC.; *pg.* 156, *pg.* 404
CHEMICAL REGULATION REPORTER - Publisher - BLOOMBERG BNA; *pg.* 1621, *pg.* 1772
CHEMIDOC - Software - BIO-RAD LABORATORIES, INC.; *pg.* 1504, *pg.* 101
CHEMIDOC-IT - Imaging System - UVP, INC.; *pg.* 1434, *pg.* 298
CHEMIGUM - Butadiene, Acrylonitrile Latices - THE GOODYEAR TIRE & RUBBER COMPANY; *pg.* 1883, *pg.* 1401
CHEM.INFO - Trade Website - ADVANTAGE BUSINESS MEDIA; *pg.* 1613, *pg.* 1116
CHEMIPALOOZA - Multimedia Educational Programs - THE DOW CHEMICAL COMPANY; *pg.* 1157, *pg.* 898
CHEMISOLID - Paint Product - AKZO NOBEL; *pg.* 1439, *pg.* 1952
CHEMISTRY.COM - Online Dating Service - IAC/INTERACTIVECORP; *pg.* 292, *pg.* 1242
CHEMKLEEN - Coating Product - PPG INDUSTRIES, INC.; *pg.* 1445, *pg.* 1579
CHEMLAWN - Lawn Care Products & Services - TRUGREEN-CHEMLAWN; *pg.* 1801, *pg.* 1647
CHEMLEASE - Release Agents - CHEM-TREND LIMITED PARTNERSHIP; *pg.* 973, *pg.* 892
CHEMLIB - Microplates - BECKMAN COULTER, INC.; *pg.* 1402, *pg.* 48
CHEMLIGHTS - Lights - CYALUME TECHNOLOGIES HOLDINGS, INC.; *pg.* 1295, *pg.* 856
CHEMLOCK - Housing - ENTEGRIS, INC.; *pg.* 1882, *pg.* 788
CHEMLOK - Rubber - LORD CORPORATION; *pg.* 1357, *pg.* 1360
CHEMLON - Plastic & Rubber - TEKNOR APEX COMPANY; *pg.* 1889, *pg.* 1605
CHEMMASTER - Encapsulating Garment - STANDARD SAFETY EQUIPMENT CO.; *pg.* 1379, *pg.* 632
CHEMMAX - Clothing - LAKELAND INDUSTRIES, INC.; *pg.* 1354, *pg.* 1338
CHEMONITE - Pressure Treated Forest Product - J.H. BAXTER & COMPANY; *pg.* 89, *pg.* 255
CHEMOTRODE - Robotic Product - HAMILTON CO., INC.; *pg.* 1415, *pg.* 1031
CHEMPAK - Fabric - W.L. GORE & ASSOCIATES, INC.; *pg.* 122, *pg.* 388
CHEMRAZ - Perfluoroelastomer Material - GREENE, TWEED & CO.; *pg.* 1344, *pg.* 1544
CHEMSEAL - Coating Product - PPG INDUSTRIES, INC.; *pg.* 1445, *pg.* 1579
CHEMSHEEN - Car Washing & Cleaning Composition - PPG INDUSTRIES, INC.; *pg.* 1445, *pg.* 1579
CHEMSTAIN - Concrete System - L.M. SCOFIELD COMPANY; *pg.* 94, *pg.* 134
CHEMSURE - Delivery Service Program - GE WATER & PROCESS TECHNOLOGIES; *pg.* 1339, *pg.* 1588
CHEMTRAQ - Environmental Management System - QUAKER CHEMICAL CORP.; *pg.* 1178, *pg.* 1524
CHEMTRAVELLER - Pump - TUTHILL CORPORATION; *pg.* 1385, *pg.* 561
CHEMTURA - Polymer Product - CHEMTURA CORPORATION; *pg.* 1152, *pg.* 355
CHEMTURE PLUS - Poured-in-Place Urethane - ROBBINS, INC.; *pg.* 108, *pg.* 1425
CHEMTURF - Poured-in-Place Urethane - ROBBINS, INC.; *pg.* 108, *pg.* 1425
CHEMTYTE - Seal & Thermoplastic Component - GREENE, TWEED & CO.; *pg.* 1344, *pg.* 1544
CHEMWINDOW - Software - BIO-RAD LABORATORIES, INC.; *pg.* 1504, *pg.* 101
CHENILLE - Ear Warmer - 180S, LLC; *pg.* 1824, *pg.* 754
CHENILLE STITCH - Fabric - NEMSCHOFF, INC.; *pg.* 936, *pg.* 1890
CHENILLE WARP - Carpet - INTERFACE, INC.; *pg.* 695, *pg.* 512
CHEOS - Software System - MENTOR GRAPHICS CORPORATION; *pg.* 432, *pg.* 1510
CHEQUE - Fabric - NEMSCHOFF, INC.; *pg.* 936, *pg.* 1890
CHEQUERS - Restaurant - HOULIHAN'S RESTAURANTS, INC.; *pg.* 1731, *pg.* 716
CHEQUES FOR TWO - Travelers Checks - AMERICAN EXPRESS COMPANY; *pg.* 712, *pg.* 1190
CHERISH - Fabric - NEMSCHOFF, INC.; *pg.* 936, *pg.* 1890
CHERISHED TEDDIES - Home & Garden Product - ENESCO, LLC; *pg.* 1124, *pg.* 620
CHEROKEE - Apparel & Footwear - CHEROKEE GLOBAL BRANDS; *pg.* 21, *pg.* 278
CHERRIES - Table Textile - HERITAGE LACE INC.; *pg.* 694, *pg.* 711
CHERRY - Fastening Systems - TEXTRON INC.; *pg.* 235, *pg.* 1607
CHERRY BARK BLEND - Nutritional Product - NUTRACEUTICAL INTERNATIONAL CORPORATION; *pg.* 1576, *pg.* 1753
CHERRY BLAST - Game - WMS INDUSTRIES INC.; *pg.* 593, *pg.* 666
CHERRY BLOSSOM - Candy - THE HERSHEY CO.; *pg.* 1855, *pg.* 1538
CHERRY BOMB - Container Grown Plant - MONROVIA GROWERS; *pg.* 1797, *pg.* 44
CHERRY BOMB - Game - WMS INDUSTRIES INC.; *pg.* 593, *pg.* 666
CHERRY CENTRAL - Applesauce - CHERRY CENTRAL COOPERATIVE, INC.; *pg.* 847, *pg.* 909
CHERRY COKE - Soft Drink - THE COCA-COLA COMPANY; *pg.* 240, *pg.* 493

First page reference indicates Business Class Edition
Second page reference indicates Geographic Edition

CHERRY COKE ZERO - Beverages - THE COCA-COLA COMPANY; *pg.* 240, *pg.* 493
CHERRY CORDIAL - Ice Cream - UNITED DAIRY FARMERS, INC.; *pg.* 906, *pg.* 1426
CHERRY GARCIA - Ice Cream - BEN & JERRY'S HOMEMADE, INC.; *pg.* 1850, *pg.* 1767
CHERRY JAM - Pulltab Game - IDAHO LOTTERY; *pg.* 995, *pg.* 547
CHERRY MOON FARMS - Perishable Product - PROVIDE COMMERCE, INC.; *pg.* 1276, *pg.* 206
CHERRY-O - Table Textile - HERITAGE LACE INC.; *pg.* 694, *pg.* 711
CHERRY-O - Air Freshener - SWISHER HYGIENE INC.; *pg.* 336, *pg.* 1507
CHERRY ON TOP - Video Game - INTERNATIONAL GAME TECHNOLOGY; *pg.* 957, *pg.* 1024
CHERRY SKI - Soft Drink - DOUBLE-COLA CO.-USA; *pg.* 249, *pg.* 1629
CHERRY SPLASH - Lip Care Product - BLISTEX, INC.; *pg.* 502, *pg.* 644
CHERRY STICKS - Candy - SWEET CANDY COMPANY; *pg.* 1862, *pg.* 1761
CHERRY TREE - Video Game - INTERNATIONAL GAME TECHNOLOGY; *pg.* 957, *pg.* 1024
CHERRY TRIPLER - Lottery Game - KENTUCKY LOTTERY CORPORATION; *pg.* 996, *pg.* 735
CHERRY TWIST - Lottery Game - NEW YORK STATE LOTTERY; *pg.* 1001, *pg.* 1340
CHERRY VANILLA - Fragrance Product - CCA INDUSTRIES, INC.; *pg.* 503, *pg.* 1114
CHERRYPICKER - Digital Video Product - HARMONIC, INC.; *pg.* 402, *pg.* 246
CHERRYPICKER - Digital Video Processing - MOTOROLA SOLUTIONS, INC.; *pg.* 657, *pg.* 659
CHERYL - Footwear - STEVEN MADDEN, LTD.; *pg.* 1819, *pg.* 1176
CHERYL&CO - Confections - 1-800-FLOWERS.COM, INC.; *pg.* 1758, *pg.* 1151
CHESAPEAK VALLEY FARMS - Hams & Sausages - HATFIELD QUALITY MEATS, INC.; *pg.* 861, *pg.* 1537
THE CHESAPEAKE - Natural Pine Swing Set - CREATIVE PLAYTHINGS LTD.; *pg.* 1831, *pg.* 820
CHESAPEAKE - Cookies - PEPPERIDGE FARM, INC.; *pg.* 888, *pg.* 363
CHESAPEAKE - Furniture - TELESCOPE CASUAL FURNITURE INC.; *pg.* 944, *pg.* 1162
CHESAPEAKE BAGEL BAKERY - Food Store - EINSTEIN NOAH RESTAURANT GROUP, INC.; *pg.* 1019, *pg.* 332
CHESCO - Fluid Sealing Product - A.W. CHESTERTON COMPANY; *pg.* 1315, *pg.* 861
CHESHIRE - Fabric - NEMSCHOFF, INC.; *pg.* 936, *pg.* 1890
CHESHIRE - Graphics Equipment - VIDEOJET TECHNOLOGIES INC.; *pg.* 489, *pg.* 671
CHESHIRE - Computer-Assisted Interviewing System - WESTAT INC.; *pg.* 161, *pg.* 776
CHESHIRE LANE - Furniture - ASHLEY FURNITURE INDUSTRIES, INC.; *pg.* 914, *pg.* 1852
CHESHIRE LINEN - Paper & Nonwoven Material - FIBERMARK INC.; *pg.* 1457, *pg.* 1764
CHESILVALE - Telecommunication Installation, Maintenance & Testing - TEXTRON INC.; *pg.* 235, *pg.* 1607
CHESS CLUB - Carpet - BEAULIEU GROUP, LLC; *pg.* 917, *pg.* 529
CHESS QUEEN - Apparel - VANS, INC.; *pg.* 1821, *pg.* 76
CHESSMEN - Cookies - PEPPERIDGE FARM, INC.; *pg.* 888, *pg.* 363
CHESTER - Shoes - ALLEN-EDMONDS SHOE CORP.; *pg.* 1804, *pg.* 1887
CHESTER - Hoist - COLUMBUS MCKINNON CORPORATION; *pg.* 1325, *pg.* 1138
CHESTER - Dress Shoes - JOHNSTON & MURPHY CO.; *pg.* 1810, *pg.* 1651
CHESTER - Pop Corn - PEPSICO, INC.; *pg.* 259, *pg.* 1327
CHESTER - Lighting - STEELCASE INC.; *pg.* 475, *pg.* 889
CHESTERFIELD - Cigarettes - PHILIP MORRIS USA INC.; *pg.* 1894, *pg.* 1803
CHESTER'S - Popcorn - FRITO-LAY NORTH AMERICA, INC.; *pg.* 1853, *pg.* 1730
CHESTNUT CHANGE - Lottery Game - ILLINOIS STATE LOTTERY; *pg.* 995, *pg.* 578
CHESTNUT HILL - Apparel - BRODER BROS., CO.; *pg.* 1828, *pg.* 1588
CHET ATKINS - Musical Instrument - GIBSON GUITAR CORP.; *pg.* 550, *pg.* 1650
CHEV - Golfing Glove - CALLAWAY GOLF COMPANY; *pg.* 1829, *pg.* 58
CHEVAL DES ANDES - Wine - MOET HENNESSY; *pg.* 1966, *pg.* 1260
CHEVROLET - Automobile - GENERAL MOTORS COMPANY; *pg.* 175, *pg.* 881
CHEVRON - Gasolines, Motor Oils & Industrial Lubricants - CHEVRON CORPORATION; *pg.* 974, *pg.* 259
CHEVRON - Conveyor Belting - HBD INDUSTRIES, INC.; *pg.* 207, *pg.* 1449
CHEVRON - Towing & Recovery Equipment - MILLER INDUSTRIES, INC.; *pg.* 185, *pg.* 1655
CHEVRON - Scientific Detector Product - PHOTONIS USA PENNSYLVANIA; *pg.* 663, *pg.* 1547
CHEVRON CHENILLE - Window Treatment - CROSCILL, INC.; *pg.* 1122, *pg.* 1220
CHEVRONE - Dinnerware - THE HOMER LAUGHLIN CHINA COMPANY; *pg.* 1125, *pg.* 1850
CHEVY HIGH PERFORMANCE - Magazine - RENTPATH, INC.; *pg.* 1680, *pg.* 538
CHEVY'S FRESH MEX - Restaurant Chain - REAL MEX RESTAURANTS, INC.; *pg.* 1746, *pg.* 75
CHEW-ETS - Chocolate & Peanut Candy Bars - JUST BORN, INC.; *pg.* 1857, *pg.* 1516
CHEW 'N CLEAN - Dog Toy - THE HARTZ MOUNTAIN CORP.; *pg.* 1476, *pg.* 1120
CHEWNOT - Anti Chew Training Aid - NILODOR, INC.; *pg.* 332, *pg.* 1406
CHEWY GRANOLA BARS - Granola Bar - KASHI COMPANY; *pg.* 830, *pg.* 119
CHEX - Cereal - GENERAL MILLS, INC.; *pg.* 828, *pg.* 933
CHEX - Footwear - VANS, INC.; *pg.* 1821, *pg.* 76
CHEX-ALL - Sterilization Product - PROPPER MANUFACTURING COMPANY, INC.; *pg.* 1586, *pg.* 1175
CHEX MIX - Snack Mix - GENERAL MILLS, INC.; *pg.* 828, *pg.* 933
CHEX RICE - Food Product - GENERAL MILLS, INC.; *pg.* 828, *pg.* 933
CHEX-WEAR - Paint And Stain Product - BENJAMIN MOORE & CO.; *pg.* 1440, *pg.* 1085
CHEX WHEAT - Food Product - GENERAL MILLS, INC.; *pg.* 828, *pg.* 933
CHEXPRESS - Scanner - NCR CORPORATION; *pg.* 443, *pg.* 531
CHEYENNE - Gaming Product - GLD PRODUCTS, INC.; *pg.* 1835, *pg.* 1882
CHEYENNE - Fabric - NEMSCHOFF, INC.; *pg.* 936, *pg.* 1890
CHEYENNE - Food - WESTERN SIZZLIN CORPORATION; *pg.* 1755, *pg.* 1806
CHEYENNE PEPPER - Nail Care Product - OPI PRODUCTS INC.; *pg.* 518, *pg.* 167
CHEZ NOUS - Educational Materials - SCHOLASTIC INC.; *pg.* 1683, *pg.* 1288
CHI-CHI'S - Mexican Foods - HORMEL FOODS CORPORATION; *pg.* 863, *pg.* 915
CHIA BART SIMPSON - Pottery Planter - JOSEPH ENTERPRISES, INC.; *pg.* 960, *pg.* 220
CHIA BUNNY - Pottery Planter - JOSEPH ENTERPRISES, INC.; *pg.* 960, *pg.* 220
CHIA COW - Pottery Planter - JOSEPH ENTERPRISES, INC.; *pg.* 960, *pg.* 220
CHIA CROCODILE - Pottery Planter - JOSEPH ENTERPRISES, INC.; *pg.* 960, *pg.* 220
CHIA DINOSAUR - Pottery Planter - JOSEPH ENTERPRISES, INC.; *pg.* 960, *pg.* 220
CHIA DONKEY - Pottery Planter - JOSEPH ENTERPRISES, INC.; *pg.* 960, *pg.* 220
CHIA ELEPHANT - Pottery Planter - JOSEPH ENTERPRISES, INC.; *pg.* 960, *pg.* 220
CHIA FROG - Pottery Planter - JOSEPH ENTERPRISES, INC.; *pg.* 960, *pg.* 220
CHIA GARFIELD - Pottery Planter - JOSEPH ENTERPRISES, INC.; *pg.* 960, *pg.* 220
CHIA GUY - Pottery Planter - JOSEPH ENTERPRISES, INC.; *pg.* 960, *pg.* 220
CHIA HEAD - Pottery Planter - JOSEPH ENTERPRISES, INC.; *pg.* 960, *pg.* 220
CHIA HIPPO - Pottery Planter - JOSEPH ENTERPRISES, INC.; *pg.* 960, *pg.* 220
CHIA HOMER SIMPSON - Pottery Planter - JOSEPH ENTERPRISES, INC.; *pg.* 960, *pg.* 220
CHIA KITTEN - Pottery Planter - JOSEPH ENTERPRISES, INC.; *pg.* 960, *pg.* 220
CHIA KUNG FU PANDA - Pottery Planter - JOSEPH ENTERPRISES, INC.; *pg.* 960, *pg.* 220
CHIA MADAGASCAR ALEX - Pottery Planter - JOSEPH ENTERPRISES, INC.; *pg.* 960, *pg.* 220
CHIA MADAGASCAR MARTY - Pottery Planter - JOSEPH ENTERPRISES, INC.; *pg.* 960, *pg.* 220
CHIA PET - Pottery Planters - JOSEPH ENTERPRISES, INC.; *pg.* 960, *pg.* 220
CHIA PIG - Pottery Planter - JOSEPH ENTERPRISES, INC.; *pg.* 960, *pg.* 220
CHIA PROFESSOR - Pottery Planter - JOSEPH ENTERPRISES, INC.; *pg.* 960, *pg.* 220
CHIA PUPPY - Pottery Planter - JOSEPH ENTERPRISES, INC.; *pg.* 960, *pg.* 220
CHIA SCOOBY - DOO - Pottery Planter - JOSEPH ENTERPRISES, INC.; *pg.* 960, *pg.* 220
CHIA SHAGGY - Pottery Planter - JOSEPH ENTERPRISES, INC.; *pg.* 960, *pg.* 220
CHIA SHREK - Pottery Planter - JOSEPH ENTERPRISES, INC.; *pg.* 960, *pg.* 220
CHIA SNOOZING KITTY CAT - Grass Planter - JOSEPH ENTERPRISES, INC.; *pg.* 960, *pg.* 220
CHIA SYLVESTER & TWEETY CAT - Grass Planter - JOSEPH ENTERPRISES, INC.; *pg.* 960, *pg.* 220
CHIA TAZ - Pottery Planter - JOSEPH ENTERPRISES, INC.; *pg.* 960, *pg.* 220
CHIA TWEETY - Pottery Planter - JOSEPH ENTERPRISES, INC.; *pg.* 960, *pg.* 220
CHIARA - Furniture - J. ROBERT SCOTT INC.; *pg.* 930, *pg.* 105
CHIC - Apparel - V.F. CORPORATION; *pg.* 34, *pg.* 1376
CHICA - Container Grown Plant - MONROVIA GROWERS; *pg.* 1797, *pg.* 44
CHICAGO - Watch - A. T. CROSS COMPANY; *pg.* 339, *pg.* 1602
CHICAGO - Quality Chafers - CARLISLE FOODSERVICE PRODUCTS INCORPORATED; *pg.* 1455, *pg.* 1485
CHICAGO - Furniture - FLEXSTEEL INDUSTRIES, INC.; *pg.* 925, *pg.* 707
CHICAGO - Grip - KLEIN TOOLS INC.; *pg.* 1052, *pg.* 627
CHICAGO BULLS - Basketball Team - CHICAGO PROFESSIONAL SPORTS LIMITED PARTNERSHIP; *pg.* 539, *pg.* 570
CHICAGO CHAMPAGNE TOAST - Nail Care Product - OPI PRODUCTS INC.; *pg.* 518, *pg.* 167
CHICAGO CUTLERY - Kitchen Houseware Product - WORLD KITCHEN LLC; *pg.* 1141, *pg.* 657
CHICAGO FLAT SAMMIES - Casual Dining Restaurant - LETTUCE ENTERTAIN YOU ENTERPRISES, INC.; *pg.* 1735, *pg.* 580
CHICAGO GET A MANICURE - Nail Care Product - OPI PRODUCTS INC.; *pg.* 518, *pg.* 167
CHICAGO-LATROBE - Tools - KENNAMETAL INC.; *pg.* 1052, *pg.* 1547
CHICAGO-LATROBE - Drills & Reamers - KENNAMETAL IPG; *pg.* 1353, *pg.* 1615
CHICAGO ORIGINALS - Original Paperbacks - UNIVERSITY OF CHICAGO PRESS; *pg.* 1698, *pg.* 594
CHICAGO PIZZA EXPO - Trade Show - MACFADDEN COMMUNICATIONS GROUP, LLC; *pg.* 1660, *pg.* 1254
THE CHICAGO STYLE SNACKS - Tagline - C.J. VITNER CO.; *pg.* 848, *pg.* 571
CHICAGO TOWN - Frozen Pizza - THE SCHWAN FOOD COMPANY; *pg.* 894, *pg.* 928
CHICAGO TRIBUNE - Newspaper - CHICAGO TRIBUNE COMPANY; *pg.* 1627, *pg.* 570
CHICAGOLAND SPEEDWAY - Motorsports Facility - INTERNATIONAL SPEEDWAY CORPORATION; *pg.* 553, *pg.* 420
CHICAGO'S HOMETOWN AIRLINE - Airline Service - UNITED CONTINENTAL HOLDINGS, INC.; *pg.* 1927, *pg.* 593
CHICAGOSPORTS.COM - Sports News Website - CHICAGO TRIBUNE COMPANY; *pg.* 1627, *pg.* 570
CHICAGOTRIBUNE.COM - News Website - CHICAGO TRIBUNE COMPANY; *pg.* 1627, *pg.* 570
CHICK-FIL-A WAFFLE POTATO FRIES - Prepared Fried Potato - CHICK-FIL-A, INC.; *pg.* 1721, *pg.* 492
CHICK FLICK CHERRY - Nail Care Product - OPI PRODUCTS INC.; *pg.* 518, *pg.* 167
CHICK-GO - Poultry Product - KENT NUTRITION GROUP; *pg.* 1477, *pg.* 710
CHICK-N-STRIPS - Prepared Chicken - CHICK-FIL-A, INC.; *pg.* 1721, *pg.* 492
CHICKADEE - Cutting Room Equipment - EASTMAN MACHINE COMPANY; *pg.* 1331, *pg.* 1148
CHICKADEES' CHOICE - Bird Seed - INTERMOUNTAIN FARMERS ASSOCIATION; *pg.* 705, *pg.* 1759

CHICKEN 15 BEAN SOUP - Soup - N.K. HURST CO., INC.; *pg.* 886, *pg.* 689
CHICKEN BARN - Plastic Containers - PACTIV CORPORATION; *pg.* 1466, *pg.* 624
CHICKEN BITES - Breaded Mini Chicken Breast Patties - TYSON FOODS, INC.; *pg.* 902, *pg.* 35
CHICKEN BURRITO - Burritos - TACO BELL CORP.; *pg.* 1752, *pg.* 117
CHICKEN CAPITAL USA - Slogan - KFC CORPORATION; *pg.* 1733, *pg.* 735
CHICKEN CRITTERS - Chicken Tenders - TEXAS ROADHOUSE, INC.; *pg.* 1753, *pg.* 738
CHICKEN FLORENTINE NORDICA - Food Product - GAY LEA FOODS CO-OPERATIVE LIMITED; *pg.* 858, *pg.* 1926
THE CHICKEN GAME! - Video Slots - INTERNATIONAL GAME TECHNOLOGY; *pg.* 957, *pg.* 1024
CHICKEN GLAZERS - Food Products - TYSON FOODS, INC.; *pg.* 902, *pg.* 35
CHICKEN GRILL - Fast Food - A&W FOOD SERVICES OF CANADA INC.; *pg.* 1714, *pg.* 1908
CHICKEN HELPER - Main Dish Mixes - GENERAL MILLS, INC.; *pg.* 828, *pg.* 933
CHICKEN MCGRILL - Chicken Sandwich - MCDONALD'S CORPORATION; *pg.* 1737, *pg.* 645
CHICKEN MCNUGGETS - Entree - MCDONALD'S CORPORATION; *pg.* 1737, *pg.* 645
CHICKEN SELECTS - Entree - MCDONALD'S CORPORATION; *pg.* 1737, *pg.* 645
CHICKEN SOCKS - Educational Materials - SCHOLASTIC INC.; *pg.* 1683, *pg.* 1288
CHICKEN SOUP BOUQUET - Floral Bouquet - FTD GROUP, INC.; *pg.* 1795, *pg.* 608
CHICKEN TENDERS - Chicken Nuggets - BURGER KING CORPORATION; *pg.* 1719, *pg.* 440
CHICKEN VEGY MEDLEY - Pizza - DONATOS PIZZERIA CORPORATION; *pg.* 1727, *pg.* 1439
CHICKERING - Musical Instrument - GIBSON GUITAR CORP.; *pg.* 550, *pg.* 1650
CHICK'N CRISP - Chicken Sandwich - BURGER KING CORPORATION; *pg.* 1719, *pg.* 440
CHICLETS - Chewing Gum - MONDELEZ INTERNATIONAL, INC.; *pg.* 878, *pg.* 601
CHICO - Bananas & Related Products - CHIQUITA BRANDS INTERNATIONAL, INC.; *pg.* 847, *pg.* 1365
CHICOPEE - Fabric - POLYMER GROUP, INC.; *pg.* 698, *pg.* 1368
CHIEF - Analyzer - TELEDYNE LECROY; *pg.* 1431, *pg.* 1153
CHIEF AGRI INDUSTRIES - Grain Storage System - CHIEF INDUSTRIES, INC.; *pg.* 1323, *pg.* 1010
CHIEF BUILDING - Metal Building System - CHIEF INDUSTRIES, INC.; *pg.* 1323, *pg.* 1010
CHIEF CONSTRUCTION - Building System - CHIEF INDUSTRIES, INC.; *pg.* 1323, *pg.* 1010
CHIEF CUSTOM PRODUCTS - Correctional And Metal Fabrication - CHIEF INDUSTRIES, INC.; *pg.* 1323, *pg.* 1010
CHIEF ETHANOL FUELS - Ethanol Product - CHIEF INDUSTRIES, INC.; *pg.* 1323, *pg.* 1010
CHIEF FABRICATION - Metal Fabrication - CHIEF INDUSTRIES, INC.; *pg.* 1323, *pg.* 1010
CHIEF INTERMODAL - Container Chassis - CHIEF INDUSTRIES, INC.; *pg.* 1323, *pg.* 1010
CHIEF TRANSPORTATION PRODUCTS - Fabricated Steel - CHIEF INDUSTRIES, INC.; *pg.* 1323, *pg.* 1010
CHIEFTAINS - Game - WMS INDUSTRIES INC.; *pg.* 593, *pg.* 666
CHIHUAHUA - Food Product - V&V SUPREMO FOODS, INC.; *pg.* 907, *pg.* 595
CHIK-BITS - Pre-Browned Chicken Patties - TYSON FOODS, INC.; *pg.* 902, *pg.* 35
CHIK PATTIES - Chicken Alternative Products - KELLOGG COMPANY; *pg.* 831, *pg.* 870
CHIKAA - Footwear - STEVEN MADDEN, LTD.; *pg.* 1819, *pg.* 1176
CHILD-CRAFT - Wooden Furniture - CHILD CRAFT INDUSTRIES, INC.; *pg.* 920, *pg.* 1463
CHILD GUIDANCE - Toy & Leisure Product - JAKKS PACIFIC, INC.; *pg.* 960, *pg.* 142
CHILD HEALTH PLUS - Insurance Service - NEW YORK STATE DEPARTMENT OF HEALTH; *pg.* 1001, *pg.* 1137
CHILD OF MINE - Children's Clothing - CARTER'S, INC.; *pg.* 21, *pg.* 491
CHILDALERT - Relief Fund for Emergencies - CHILDFUND INTERNATIONAL; *pg.* 137, *pg.* 1801
CHILDCRAFT - Educational Resources - SCHOOL SPECIALTY, INC.; *pg.* 467, *pg.* 1860
CHILDERS - Canopies & Walkway Covers - CHILDERS CARPORTS AND STRUCTURES, INC.; *pg.* 76, *pg.* 1703
CHILDHOOD'S PUREST TREASURES - Toys - 1-800-FLOWERS.COM, INC.; *pg.* 1758, *pg.* 1151
CHILDLIFE - Sporting Good Product - ESCALADE INC.; *pg.* 1833, *pg.* 678
CHILDREACH - International Development Child Sponsorship - PLAN USA, INC.; *pg.* 154, *pg.* 1609
CHILDREN OF THE INNER LIGHT - Home & Garden Product - ENESCO, LLC; *pg.* 1124, *pg.* 620
CHILDREN OF THE INNER LIGHT - Cards - SPS STUDIOS, INC.; *pg.* 1688, *pg.* 311
CHILDREN'S CIRCLE - Educational Materials - SCHOLASTIC INC.; *pg.* 1683, *pg.* 1288
CHILDREN'S CLASSICS - Publishing Imprint - PENGUIN RANDOM HOUSE; *pg.* 1675, *pg.* 1276
CHILDREN'S MOTRIN - Children's Medication - MCNEIL-PPC, INC.; *pg.* 1560, *pg.* 1533
THE CHILDREN'S OUTLET - Children's Clothing Stores - THE CHILDREN'S PLACE, INC.; *pg.* 22, *pg.* 1119
CHILDREN'S PEPTO - Personal & Household Product - THE PROCTER & GAMBLE COMPANY; *pg.* 1129, *pg.* 1418
THE CHILDREN'S PLACE - Children's Clothing Stores & Children's Clothing - THE CHILDREN'S PLACE, INC.; *pg.* 22, *pg.* 1119
CHILDREN'S PRESS - Educational Materials - SCHOLASTIC INC.; *pg.* 1683, *pg.* 1288
CHILDREN'S TYLENOL - Children's Pain Reliever - MCNEIL-PPC, INC.; *pg.* 1560, *pg.* 1533
CHILDREN'S TYLENOL COLD - Children's Cold Medication - MCNEIL-PPC, INC.; *pg.* 1560, *pg.* 1533
CHILDREN'S VITA-GELS - Nutritional Supplement - NATURAL ORGANICS, INC.; *pg.* 1571, *pg.* 1181
CHILDS FIRST LIBRARY OF LEARNING - Juvenile Book Series - DIRECT HOLDINGS AMERICAS INC.; *pg.* 1636, *pg.* 1780
CHILD'S PLAY - Candy Assortment - TOOTSIE ROLL INDUSTRIES, INC.; *pg.* 1863, *pg.* 591
CHILDTIME - Day Care Centers - LEARNING CARE GROUP INC.; *pg.* 604, *pg.* 903
CHILDWORLD - Magazine - CHILDFUND INTERNATIONAL; *pg.* 137, *pg.* 1801
CHILI 15 BEAN SOUP - Soup - N.K. HURST CO., INC.; *pg.* 886, *pg.* 689
CHILI DOG - Mustard - PLOCHMAN, INC.; *pg.* 890, *pg.* 631
CHILI MAGIC - Food Product - BUSH BROTHERS & COMPANY; *pg.* 843, *pg.* 1636
CHILI PEPPER PARTY - Game - WMS INDUSTRIES INC.; *pg.* 593, *pg.* 666
CHILI'S GRILL & BAR - Grill & Bar - BRINKER INTERNATIONAL, INC.; *pg.* 1718, *pg.* 1676
CHILL - Smooth Ice Beverages - J&J SNACK FOODS CORPORATION; *pg.* 865, *pg.* 1107
CHILL - Footwear - PHOENIX FOOTWEAR GROUP, INC.; *pg.* 1815, *pg.* 60
CHILL CHASERS BY BUSTER - Shoes - CALERES, INC.; *pg.* 1805, *pg.* 993
CHILL-OUT - Software - BIO-RAD LABORATORIES, INC.; *pg.* 1504, *pg.* 101
CHILL SE - Athletic Shoe - JACK SCHWARTZ SHOES, INC.; *pg.* 1810, *pg.* 1245
CHILL-VACTOR - Vacuum Chiller - CROLL-REYNOLDS COMPANY, INC.; *pg.* 1326, *pg.* 1103
THE CHILL ZONE - Convenience Stores - THE PANTRY, INC.; *pg.* 1029, *pg.* 1360
CHILLATTE - Chilled Beverage - THE SECOND CUP LTD.; *pg.* 1749, *pg.* 1928
CHILLBREAKER - Apparel - REFRIGIWEAR, INC.; *pg.* 47, *pg.* 529
CHILLER CHEMISTRY - Refrigerant Service - HUDSON TECHNOLOGIES, INC.; *pg.* 1073, *pg.* 1320
CHILLGARD - Gas Sensor - MINE SAFETY APPLIANCES COMPANY; *pg.* 1361, *pg.* 1525
CHILLI - Catheters - BOSTON SCIENTIFIC CORPORATION; *pg.* 1508, *pg.* 831
CHILLI II - Medical Device - BOSTON SCIENTIFIC CORPORATION; *pg.* 1508, *pg.* 831
CHILLMATE - Optical Product - UNIVERSAL PHOTONICS, INC.; *pg.* 1433, *pg.* 1167
CHILLOW - Pillow - RELAX THE BACK CORPORATION; *pg.* 940, *pg.* 120
CHILLSMART - Analytical Tool - HUDSON TECHNOLOGIES, INC.; *pg.* 1073, *pg.* 1320
CHILLWORKS - Beverage Ware - WHIRLEY INDUSTRIES, INC.; *pg.* 1892, *pg.* 1590
CHILLWRAPPER - Beverage Insulator - SONOCO PRODUCTS COMPANY; *pg.* 1469, *pg.* 1619
CHIME.IN - Social Network - UBERMEDIA, INC.; *pg.* 1286, *pg.* 181
CHINA BLACK - Pipe Tobaccos - ALTADIS USA, INC.; *pg.* 1893, *pg.* 423
CHINA BUTTERFLY - Rice - RICELAND FOODS, INC.; *pg.* 892, *pg.* 36
CHINA CHLORELLA - Nutritional Product - NATROL, INC.; *pg.* 1570, *pg.* 64
CHINA GLAZE - Nail Lacquers - AMERICAN INTERNATIONAL INDUSTRIES COMPANY; *pg.* 498, *pg.* 126
CHINA MOON - Game - WMS INDUSTRIES INC.; *pg.* 593, *pg.* 666
CHINA-PRIDE - Bottled Food Product - ALLIED OLD ENGLISH, INC.; *pg.* 836, *pg.* 1110
CHINACO - Tequila - JIM BEAM BRANDS CO.; *pg.* 1965, *pg.* 601
CHINESE FORTUNE - Tea - R.C. BIGELOW, INC.; *pg.* 891, *pg.* 348
CHINESE ODYSSEY - Video Game - INTERNATIONAL GAME TECHNOLOGY; *pg.* 957, *pg.* 1024
CHINESE SPLENDOUR - Area Rugs - COURISTAN INC.; *pg.* 921, *pg.* 1067
CHINESE TREASURE - Video Game - INTERNATIONAL GAME TECHNOLOGY; *pg.* 957, *pg.* 1024
CHINEX - Paintbrush Filaments - E.I. DU PONT DE NEMOURS & COMPANY; *pg.* 1159, *pg.* 390
CHINICHURRI COTTAGE CHEESE SALAD TOPPER - Food Product - GAY LEA FOODS CO-OPERATIVE LIMITED; *pg.* 858, *pg.* 1926
CHINOISERIE - Bath Accessory - CROSCILL, INC.; *pg.* 1122, *pg.* 1220
CHINOISERIE - Clock - ETHAN ALLEN INTERIORS INC.; *pg.* 924, *pg.* 343
CHINOOK - Textiles - BERNHARDT DESIGN; *pg.* 918, *pg.* 1381
CHINOOK - Ventilation System - UNIFIED BRANDS INC.; *pg.* 1385, *pg.* 970
CHINOTTO - Beverages - THE COCA-COLA COMPANY; *pg.* 240, *pg.* 493
CHIP CLIP - Kitchen Utensils - ROBINSON HOME PRODUCTS INC.; *pg.* 1060, *pg.* 1355
CHIP-MASTER - Vacuum Cleaner - GOODWAY TECHNOLOGIES CORPORATION; *pg.* 1341, *pg.* 374
CHIPARRAY - Packaging System - AMKOR TECHNOLOGY, INC.; *pg.* 67, *pg.* 25
CHIPCLAMP - Flip Chip Device - SEMTECH CORPORATION; *pg.* 671, *pg.* 57
CHIPGRAPH - Software System - MENTOR GRAPHICS CORPORATION; *pg.* 432, *pg.* 1510
CHIPIT - Software - SYNOPSYS, INC.; *pg.* 480, *pg.* 162
CHIPITS - Cocoa, Baking Chocolate, Chocolate Chips - THE HERSHEY CO.; *pg.* 1855, *pg.* 1538
CHIPJET - Electric Instrument - UNIVERSAL INSTRUMENTS CORPORATION; *pg.* 683, *pg.* 1154
CHIPLISTER - Software System - MENTOR GRAPHICS CORPORATION; *pg.* 432, *pg.* 1510
CHIPOTLE - Poultry Product - PILGRIM'S PRIDE CORPORATION; *pg.* 889, *pg.* 330
CHIPPENDALE - Furniture - ETHAN ALLEN INTERIORS INC.; *pg.* 924, *pg.* 343
CHIPPER CLUB - Children's Games & Activities - HERR FOODS INC.; *pg.* 861, *pg.* 1557
CHIPPEWA - Boots - JUSTIN BRANDS, INC.; *pg.* 1810, *pg.* 1695
CHIPS AHOY! - Cookies - MONDELEZ INTERNATIONAL, INC.; *pg.* 878, *pg.* 601
CHIPS DELUXE - Snacks - KELLOGG COMPANY; *pg.* 831, *pg.* 870
CHIPS GALORE! - Ice Cream Sandwich - WELLS ENTERPRISES, INC.; *pg.* 909, *pg.* 709
CHIPSCOPE - Software - XILINX, INC.; *pg.* 496, *pg.* 252
CHIPSKIP - Nail Care Product - OPI PRODUCTS INC.; *pg.* 518, *pg.* 167
CHIPSWITCH - Power Semiconductor Device - INTERNATIONAL RECTIFIER CORPORATION; *pg.* 647, *pg.* 80
CHIPSYNC - Technology - XILINX, INC.; *pg.* 496, *pg.* 252
CHIQUITA - Bananas - CHIQUITA BRANDS INTERNATIONAL, INC.; *pg.* 847, *pg.* 1365
CHIQUITA - Cameras - EASTMAN KODAK COMPANY; *pg.*

First page reference indicates Business Class Edition
Second page reference indicates Geographic Edition

1409, *pg.* 1333

CHIQUITA FRUIT BITES - Fresh Cut Fruit - CHIQUITA BRANDS INTERNATIONAL, INC.; *pg.* 847, *pg.* 1365

CHIQUITA FRUIT SMOOTHIES - Fruit & Vegetable Product - CHIQUITA BRANDS INTERNATIONAL, INC.; *pg.* 847, *pg.* 1365

CHIQUITA JR. - Bananas - CHIQUITA BRANDS INTERNATIONAL, INC.; *pg.* 847, *pg.* 1365

CHIQUITA KIDS - Fruit & Vegetable Product - CHIQUITA BRANDS INTERNATIONAL, INC.; *pg.* 847, *pg.* 1365

CHIQUITA MINI'S - Fruit & Vegetable Product - CHIQUITA BRANDS INTERNATIONAL, INC.; *pg.* 847, *pg.* 1365

CHIQUITA PINEAPPLE BITES - Healthy Snacks - CHIQUITA BRANDS INTERNATIONAL, INC.; *pg.* 847, *pg.* 1365

CHIQUITA SOLUTIONS - Fruit & Vegetable Product - CHIQUITA BRANDS INTERNATIONAL, INC.; *pg.* 847, *pg.* 1365

CHIQUITA TO GO - Food Product - LANDEC CORPORATION; *pg.* 1419, *pg.* 145

CHIQUITA. YOUR PRODUCE SOLUTION - Tag Line - CHIQUITA BRANDS INTERNATIONAL, INC.; *pg.* 847, *pg.* 1365

CHIROTONIC - Mattresses - RESTONIC MATTRESS CORPORATION; *pg.* 941, *pg.* 553

CHISWELL - Carpet - BEAULIEU GROUP, LLC; *pg.* 917, *pg.* 529

CHISYS - Chitosan-based Drug Formulation - WEST PHARMACEUTICAL SERVICES, INC.; *pg.* 1472, *pg.* 1532

CHITO-SEAL - Hemostasis Pad - ABBOTT LABORATORIES; *pg.* 1484, *pg.* 551

CHIVAS REGAL - Scotch Whiskey - PERNOD RICARD USA, INC.; *pg.* 1968, *pg.* 1332

CHIX - Wipe - POLYMER GROUP, INC.; *pg.* 698, *pg.* 1368

CHIX-B-Q - Food Product - ADVANCEPIERRE FOODS, INC.; *pg.* 1714, *pg.* 1409

CHIYOMI - Fabric - SCALAMANDRE, INC.; *pg.* 941, *pg.* 1058

CHLAMYDIAPROBE - Software - BIO-RAD LABORATORIES, INC.; *pg.* 1504, *pg.* 101

CHLOE - Beer - COASTAL EXTREME BREWING COMPANY; *pg.* 240, *pg.* 1602

CHLOE - Furniture - HOOKER FURNITURE CORPORATION; *pg.* 928, *pg.* 1788

CHLOR-TRIMETON - Medicine - MERCK & CO., INC.; *pg.* 1566, *pg.* 1077

CHLORAPREP - Antiseptic Applicator - CARDINAL HEALTH, INC.; *pg.* 1512, *pg.* 1448

CHLORAPREP FREPP - Antiseptic Applicator - CARDINAL HEALTH, INC.; *pg.* 1512, *pg.* 1448

CHLORAPREP SEPP - Antiseptic Applicator - CARDINAL HEALTH, INC.; *pg.* 1512, *pg.* 1448

CHLORAPREP SWABSTICK - Antiseptic Applicator - CARDINAL HEALTH, INC.; *pg.* 1512, *pg.* 1448

CHLORASEPTIC - Healthcare Product - PRESTIGE BRANDS HOLDINGS, INC.; *pg.* 520, *pg.* 1345

CHLORAZENE - Purification Chemical Used to Treat Water in Hospital Hydrotherapy Units - WISCONSIN PHARMACAL COMPANY, LLC; *pg.* 1610, *pg.* 1861

CHLORAZONE - Premium Red Rubber - LAVELLE INDUSTRIES INC.; *pg.* 1053, *pg.* 1856

CHLOREZ - Chemical Product - DOVER CHEMICAL CORPORATION; *pg.* 1156, *pg.* 1447

CHLORIDE SYSTEMS - Lighting Fixture & Control - PHILIPS LIGHTING; *pg.* 1303, *pg.* 806

CHLORIVER - Chemical Reagent - HACH COMPANY; *pg.* 1415, *pg.* 334

CHLOROCHEM - Hose - HBD INDUSTRIES, INC.; *pg.* 207, *pg.* 1449

CHLOROFOAM - Cleaner - BIRKO CORPORATION; *pg.* 1149, *pg.* 332

CHLOROMATIC - Cleaner - BIRKO CORPORATION; *pg.* 1149, *pg.* 332

CHLOROMATIC NO 3 - Chemical Product - BIRKO CORPORATION; *pg.* 1149, *pg.* 332

CHLOROWAX - Chemical Product - DOVER CHEMICAL CORPORATION; *pg.* 1156, *pg.* 1447

CHNC - Machinery - HARDINGE INC.; *pg.* 1344, *pg.* 1157

CHO-BOND - Adhesives - PARKER CHOMERICS; *pg.* 662, *pg.* 862

CHO-CELL - Vents - PARKER CHOMERICS; *pg.* 662, *pg.* 862

CHO-FAB - Laminates - PARKER CHOMERICS; *pg.* 662, *pg.* 862

CHO-FOIL - EMI Shielding Tapes - PARKER CHOMERICS; *pg.* 662, *pg.* 862

CHO-FORM - Automated EMI Gasket Dispensing System - PARKER CHOMERICS; *pg.* 662, *pg.* 862

CHO-JAC - Cable Shielding - PARKER CHOMERICS; *pg.* 662, *pg.* 862

CHO-MASK - Laminates - PARKER CHOMERICS; *pg.* 662, *pg.* 862

CHO-PAT - Medical & Aesthetic Product - DYNATRONICS CORPORATION; *pg.* 1526, *pg.* 1757

CHO-SEAL - Conductive Elastomers - PARKER CHOMERICS; *pg.* 662, *pg.* 862

CHO-SHIELD - Conductive Coatings - PARKER CHOMERICS; *pg.* 662, *pg.* 862

CHO-SHRINK - Cable Shielding - PARKER CHOMERICS; *pg.* 662, *pg.* 862

CHO-SIL - Gaskets - PARKER CHOMERICS; *pg.* 662, *pg.* 862

CHO-SORB - Cable Shielding - PARKER CHOMERICS; *pg.* 662, *pg.* 862

CHO-THERM - Insulator Pads - PARKER CHOMERICS; *pg.* 662, *pg.* 862

CHOBANI - Greek Yogurt - CHOBANI LLC; *pg.* 847, *pg.* 1318

CHOBI - Rug - COURISTAN INC.; *pg.* 921, *pg.* 1067

CHOC-O-LUNCH - Snack Food - SNYDER'S-LANCE, INC.; *pg.* 896, *pg.* 1368

CHOCLATY EC;LAIRS - Confectionery - THE HERSHEY CO.; *pg.* 1855, *pg.* 1538

CHOCO ROCKO - Confectionery - THE HERSHEY CO.; *pg.* 1855, *pg.* 1538

CHOCO TACO - Food Product - TACO JOHN'S INTERNATIONAL, INC.; *pg.* 1753, *pg.* 1901

CHOCO-THIN - Nutritional Supplement - WHITEWING LABS, INC.; *pg.* 1610, *pg.* 99

CHOCOLAT SUISSE CHOCOLATE BARS - Chocolate Bars - PROMOTION IN MOTION, INC.; *pg.* 1861, *pg.* 1052

CHOCOLATE ABUELITA - Hot Chocolate - NESTLE USA, INC.; *pg.* 883, *pg.* 96

CHOCOLATE CHAMPION - Ice Cream - WELLS ENTERPRISES, INC.; *pg.* 909, *pg.* 709

CHOCOLATE DREAMLETS - Candies - LIBERTY ORCHARDS CO., INC.; *pg.* 1857, *pg.* 1819

CHOCOLATE DUTCH MINTS - Chocolate Candies - JELLY BELLY CANDY COMPANY; *pg.* 1857, *pg.* 86

CHOCOLATE FACTORY - Game - WINNING MOVES GAMES, INC.; *pg.* 970, *pg.* 816

CHOCOLATE GARDEN - Pillow - AMERICAN LEATHER LP; *pg.* 912, *pg.* 1673

CHOCOLATE MINT MOOSE TRACKS - Ice Cream - TURKEY HILL DAIRY, INC.; *pg.* 902, *pg.* 1522

CHOCOLATE MOO'D - Smoothie - JAMBA, INC.; *pg.* 1024, *pg.* 84

CHOCOLATE MOOSE - Nail Care Product - OPI PRODUCTS INC.; *pg.* 518, *pg.* 167

CHOCOLATE SHAKE-SPEARE - Nail Care Product - OPI PRODUCTS INC.; *pg.* 518, *pg.* 167

CHOCOLATE SLIM SHAKE - Nutritional Product - RBC LIFE SCIENCES, INC.; *pg.* 1588, *pg.* 1723

CHOCOLATE WORLD - Candy Bar - THE HERSHEY CO.; *pg.* 1855, *pg.* 1538

CHOCOLATES OF THE WORLD - Chocolate - COSTCO WHOLESALE CORPORATION; *pg.* 1765, *pg.* 1820

CHOCOMILK - Infant Health Care Product - MEAD JOHNSON NUTRITION COMPANY; *pg.* 1561, *pg.* 615

CHOCTAW - Paper Product - WEYERHAEUSER COMPANY; *pg.* 121, *pg.* 1820

CHOICE - Diabetes Risk In-Home Test Kit - AKORN; *pg.* 1488, *pg.* 1138

THE CHOICE - Dual Fuel Heat Pump - GEORGIA POWER COMPANY; *pg.* 1943, *pg.* 508

CHOICE - Wireless Communications Service - VERIZON COMMUNICATIONS INC.; *pg.* 1875, *pg.* 1309

CHOICE GENETICS - Agricultural Product - MONSANTO COMPANY; *pg.* 1173, *pg.* 999

THE CHOICE OF A LIFETIME - Slogan - VON SCHRADER COMPANY; *pg.* 62, *pg.* 1890

THE CHOICE OF PROFESSIONAL GUIDES WORLDWIDE - Tagline - SIMMS FISHING PRODUCTS CORP.; *pg.* 1845, *pg.* 1008

CHOICE PLAN - Banking Services - THE PNC FINANCIAL SERVICES GROUP, INC.; *pg.* 795, *pg.* 1579

CHOICE PRIVILEGES - Hotel Service - CHOICE HOTELS INTERNATIONAL, INC.; *pg.* 1086, *pg.* 775

CHOICEPLUS - Financial Product - LINCOLN NATIONAL CORPORATION; *pg.* 776, *pg.* 1567

CHOICEPLY - Wood & Building Material - WEYERHAEUSER COMPANY; *pg.* 121, *pg.* 1820

CHOICES - Educational Materials - SCHOLASTIC INC.; *pg.* 1683, *pg.* 1288

CHOICES - Furniture - TRENDWAY CORPORATION; *pg.* 945, *pg.* 892

CHOICES, CHOICES - Educational Materials - SCHOLASTIC INC.; *pg.* 1683, *pg.* 1288

CHOICES FOR LIFE - Health Plan & Publication - MEDICA, INC.; *pg.* 1208, *pg.* 949

CHOICETRIM - Wood & Building Material - WEYERHAEUSER COMPANY; *pg.* 121, *pg.* 1820

CHOICEWORLD - Online Shopping Directory - QSOUND LABS, INC.; *pg.* 666, *pg.* 1904

CHOLES-RESPONSE - Vitamin & Herbal Supplement - SOURCE NATURALS; *pg.* 1595, *pg.* 278

CHOLEST-LESS - Nutritional Supplement - WHITEWING LABS, INC.; *pg.* 1610, *pg.* 99

CHOLESTAGEL - Tablet - GENZYME CORPORATION; *pg.* 1534, *pg.* 808

CHOLESTECH - Pharmaceutical Product - ALERE INC.; *pg.* 1488, *pg.* 849

CHOLESTECH LDX - Pharmaceutical Product - ALERE INC.; *pg.* 1488, *pg.* 849

CHOLESTER-REG - Health Care Product - NATURE'S SUNSHINE PRODUCTS, INC.; *pg.* 1571, *pg.* 1754

CHOLESTERALL - Health System Product - LANELABS USA INC.; *pg.* 1554, *pg.* 1128

CHOLESTEROL BALANCE - Health Supplement - NATROL, INC.; *pg.* 1570, *pg.* 64

CHOLESTIN - Nutritional Supplement - NU SKIN ENTERPRISES, INC.; *pg.* 518, *pg.* 1755

CHOLESTREX - Vitamin & Herbal Supplement - SOURCE NATURALS; *pg.* 1595, *pg.* 278

CHOLESTROL - Hair Cream - BLUE CROSS LABORATORIES; *pg.* 326, *pg.* 277

CHOMONICX - Geodemographic Segmentation System - ACXIOM CORPORATION; *pg.* 342, *pg.* 33

CHOMP! - Game - GAMEWRIGHT; *pg.* 953, *pg.* 836

CHOMPERS - Processed Chicken - TYSON FOODS, INC.; *pg.* 902, *pg.* 35

CHONDRO-ORAL - Animal Safety Product - NEOGEN CORPORATION; *pg.* 883, *pg.* 896

CHONDROITIN - Nutritional Supplement - NATURAL ORGANICS, INC.; *pg.* 1571, *pg.* 1181

CHOO-CHOO - Toy Train - LIONEL LLC; *pg.* 961, *pg.* 875

CHOOBLES - Variety Pack - PETSMART, INC.; *pg.* 1481, *pg.* 18

CHOOSE AUTHENTICITY - Tagline - PERNOD RICARD USA, INC.; *pg.* 1968, *pg.* 1332

CHOOZERS - Fruit Chews - MARS, INCORPORATED; *pg.* 1858, *pg.* 1792

CHOOZZ - Research Panel - SURVEY SAMPLING INTERNATIONAL LLC; *pg.* 1690, *pg.* 371

CHOP HOUSE - Food Product - ADVANCEPIERRE FOODS, INC.; *pg.* 1714, *pg.* 1409

CHOP HOUSE - Steakhouse & Brewhouse - ROCK BOTTOM RESTAURANTS, INC.; *pg.* 1748, *pg.* 334

CHOP SOOEY - Game - INTERNATIONAL GAME TECHNOLOGY; *pg.* 420, *pg.* 1606

CHORD - Bath Product - KOHLER CO.; *pg.* 91, *pg.* 1862

CHORD - Office Furniture - STEELCASE INC.; *pg.* 475, *pg.* 889

CHORD EXECUTIVE - Office Furniture - STEELCASE INC.; *pg.* 475, *pg.* 889

CHORDIANT FOUNDATION SERVER - Software - PEGASYSTEMS INC.; *pg.* 453, *pg.* 74

CHORE BOY - Sponge & Scrubbing Pad - PRESTIGE BRANDS HOLDINGS, INC.; *pg.* 520, *pg.* 1345

CHORE-MATIC - Broiler Feeding System - CTB INTERNATIONAL CORP.; *pg.* 850, *pg.* 695

CHORE-TIME - Poultry System - CTB INTERNATIONAL CORP.; *pg.* 850, *pg.* 695

CHORIZO SUPREMO - Food Product - V&V SUPREMO FOODS, INC.; *pg.* 907, *pg.* 595

CHORUS - Footwear - CAPEZIO BALLET MAKERS INC.; *pg.* 1805, *pg.* 1125

CHORUS - Fabric - NEMSCHOFF, INC.; *pg.* 936, *pg.* 1890

CHORUS LINE - Women's Active Wear - CHEROKEE GLOBAL BRANDS; *pg.* 21, *pg.* 278

CHOSES - Furniture - J. ROBERT SCOTT INC.; *pg.* 930, *pg.* 105

CHOW - Website for Food & Drink Enthusiasts - CBS INTERACTIVE, INC.; *pg.* 369, *pg.* 215

CHOW WAGON - Restaurant Service - KENTUCKY DERBY FESTIVAL, INC.; *pg.* 556, *pg.* 735

CHOXIE - Chocolate Products - TARGET CORPORATION;

pg. 1786, *pg.* 942
CHRISTA - Footwear - COBIAN CORP.; *pg.* 1806, *pg.* 253
CHRISTIAN ART - Church Worship Bulletins - WARNER PRESS, INC.; *pg.* 1701, *pg.* 673
CHRISTIAN BROTHERS AMBER CREAM - Liqueurs, Brandies & Holiday Nog - HEAVEN HILL DISTILLERIES, INC.; *pg.* 1964, *pg.* 725
CHRISTIAN CHILDREN'S FUND - Children Fund Organization - CHILDFUND INTERNATIONAL; *pg.* 137, *pg.* 1801
CHRISTIAN HISTORY - Magazine - CHRISTIANITY TODAY INTERNATIONAL; *pg.* 1627, *pg.* 561
CHRISTIAN LACROIX ROUGE - Fragrance - AVON PRODUCTS, INC.; *pg.* 500, *pg.* 1198
CHRISTIAN LIFE - Book - CHARISMA MEDIA; *pg.* 1627, *pg.* 436
CHRISTIAN MUSIC PLANET - Christian Music Station - EDUCATIONAL MEDIA FOUNDATION; *pg.* 284, *pg.* 194
CHRISTIAN PARENTING TODAY - Magazine - CHRISTIANITY TODAY INTERNATIONAL; *pg.* 1627, *pg.* 561
CHRISTIAN RETAILING - Magazine - CHARISMA MEDIA; *pg.* 1627, *pg.* 436
CHRISTIANITY TODAY - Magazine - CHRISTIANITY TODAY INTERNATIONAL; *pg.* 1627, *pg.* 561
CHRISTIANITY.COM - Online Christian Bible Study - SALEM MEDIA GROUP, INC.; *pg.* 307, *pg.* 57
CHRISTIANJOBS.COM - Online Community - SALEM MEDIA GROUP, INC.; *pg.* 307, *pg.* 57
CHRISTIANMINGLE - Online Dating Service for Christian Singles - SPARK NETWORKS, INC.; *pg.* 472, *pg.* 140
CHRISTIANSON - Industrial Pneumatic Conveyor Components, Packages & Systems - CHRISTIANSON SYSTEMS, INC.; *pg.* 1323, *pg.* 917
CHRISTIE - Biscuits - MONDELEZ INTERNATIONAL, INC.; *pg.* 878, *pg.* 601
CHRISTINE - Clothing - ABERCROMBIE & FITCH CO.; *pg.* 37, *pg.* 1466
CHRISTMAS CARDS BY MILES KIMBALL OF OSHKOSH - Mail Order - SILVER STAR BRANDS; *pg.* 1785, *pg.* 1886
CHRISTMAS EVA - Candle - THE YANKEE CANDLE COMPANY, INC.; *pg.* 1792, *pg.* 843
CHRISTMAS SEAL CAMPAIGN - Educational Campaign - AMERICAN LUNG ASSOCIATION; *pg.* 129, *pg.* 395
CHRISTMAS SEALS - Stamps & Address Labels - AMERICAN LUNG ASSOCIATION; *pg.* 129, *pg.* 395
CHRISTMAS SLEIGH RIDE - Pillow and Throw - HERITAGE LACE INC.; *pg.* 694, *pg.* 711
CHRISTMAS TREE - Ornament - HERITAGE LACE INC.; *pg.* 694, *pg.* 711
CHRISTMAS WISH - Candle - THE YANKEE CANDLE COMPANY, INC.; *pg.* 1792, *pg.* 843
CHRISTMAS WREATH - Candle - THE YANKEE CANDLE COMPANY, INC.; *pg.* 1792, *pg.* 843
CHRISTOPHER & BANKS - Women's Clothing - CHRISTOPHER & BANKS CORPORATION; *pg.* 22, *pg.* 953
CHRISTY - Clothing - ABERCROMBIE & FITCH CO.; *pg.* 37, *pg.* 1466
CHROM - Chromatography Column - SPECTRUM LABORATORIES INC.; *pg.* 1595, *pg.* 69
CHROMA-BLEND - Colorant & Additive System - CHROMA CORPORATION; *pg.* 1441, *pg.* 632
CHROMA-CLEAN - Colorant & Additive System - CHROMA CORPORATION; *pg.* 1441, *pg.* 632
CHROMA/FILL - Screen Preparation Chemical - IKONICS CORPORATION; *pg.* 1168, *pg.* 921
CHROMA KEY - Paint - ROSCO LABORATORIES, INC.; *pg.* 1782, *pg.* 378
CHROMA LAZER-TEC - Laser Marking Technology - CHROMA CORPORATION; *pg.* 1441, *pg.* 632
CHROMA-LITE - Pigment - BASF CATALYSTS LLC; *pg.* 1148, *pg.* 1074
CHROMA-PEARLS - Colorant & Additive System - CHROMA CORPORATION; *pg.* 1441, *pg.* 632
CHROMA-SHERES - Colorant & Additive System - CHROMA CORPORATION; *pg.* 1441, *pg.* 632
CHROMACLEAN - Chemical Product - SPECTRUM CHEMICALS & LABORATORY PRODUCTS, INC.; *pg.* 1181, *pg.* 94
CHROMACLEAR - Recycled Paper - DOW CHEMICAL; *pg.* 1156, *pg.* 1563
CHROMACORE - Lighting System - PHILIPS SOLID-STATE LIGHTING SOLUTIONS; *pg.* 1303, *pg.* 806
CHROMADOC-IT - Ultraviolet Product - UVP, INC.; *pg.* 1434, *pg.* 298
CHROMAFLAIR - Pigment - VIAVI SOLUTIONS INC.; *pg.* 1435, *pg.* 148
CHROMAFLEX - Protective, Decorative Coatings for Light Industrial Fabricated Metal Prods - PPG INDUSTRIES, INC.; *pg.* 1445, *pg.* 1579
CHROMALINE - Screen Print Product - IKONICS CORPORATION; *pg.* 1168, *pg.* 921
CHROMALOX - Software - CHROMALOX, INC.; *pg.* 1070, *pg.* 1574
CHROMALUSION - Basecoat - E.I. DU PONT DE NEMOURS & COMPANY; *pg.* 1159, *pg.* 390
CHROMAPULSE - Workhorse Inspection System - PRESSCO TECHNOLOGY INC.; *pg.* 1370, *pg.* 1434
CHROMASIC - Lighting System - PHILIPS SOLID-STATE LIGHTING SOLUTIONS; *pg.* 1303, *pg.* 806
CHROMASYSTEM - Automotive Coatings - E.I. DU PONT DE NEMOURS & COMPANY; *pg.* 1159, *pg.* 390
CHROMATIC - Fabric - NEMSCHOFF, INC.; *pg.* 936, *pg.* 1890
CHROMATIDE - Molecular Probe Product - THERMO FISHER SCIENTIFIC INC.; *pg.* 1602, *pg.* 61
CHROMATO-VUE - Viewing Cabinets - UVP, INC.; *pg.* 1434, *pg.* 298
CHROMATOF - Software - LECO CORPORATION; *pg.* 1355, *pg.* 906
CHROMAVER - Chemical Reagent - HACH COMPANY; *pg.* 1415, *pg.* 334
CHROMAVISION ACIS - Imaging System - CLARIENT INC.; *pg.* 1516, *pg.* 40
CHROMAX - Nutritional Product - NUTRITION 21, INC.; *pg.* 1577, *pg.* 1327
CHROMCOAT - Engineered Product And System - SULZER METCO (WESTBURY) INC.; *pg.* 1064, *pg.* 1350
CHROME - Apparel - OAKLEY, INC.; *pg.* 1840, *pg.* 86
CHROME-A-LITE - Lightweight Body Filler - ITW - EVERCOAT; *pg.* 1443, *pg.* 1415
CHROME CORE - Stainless Steel Product - CARPENTER TECHNOLOGY CORPORATION; *pg.* 73, *pg.* 1584
CHROME GALVANIZE - Aerosol - AERVOE INDUSTRIES INCORPORATED; *pg.* 1439, *pg.* 1021
CHROME PLUS - Plating Process - A BRITE COMPANY; *pg.* 1144, *pg.* 1697
CHROMEBOOK - Tablet - GOOGLE INC.; *pg.* 1249, *pg.* 153
CHROMECLASSIC - Kitchen Appliance - HAMILTON BEACH BRANDS, INC.; *pg.* 56, *pg.* 1783
CHROMEL - Tester - HOWELL INSTRUMENTS INC.; *pg.* 1417, *pg.* 1695
CHROMEMATE - Nutritional Product - NATROL, INC.; *pg.* 1570, *pg.* 64
CHROMEPRO - Hair Cutting Kit - WAHL CLIPPER CORPORATION; *pg.* 524, *pg.* 662
CHROMEX - Fluid Handling System - GRACO, INC.; *pg.* 1342, *pg.* 935
CHROMGRAPH - Software - BIOANALYTICAL SYSTEMS, INC.; *pg.* 1402, *pg.* 700
CHROMIX - Concrete System - L.M. SCOFIELD COMPANY; *pg.* 94, *pg.* 134
CHROMLIFT - Metal Stripper - HEATBATH CORPORATION; *pg.* 1165, *pg.* 826
CHROMO4 - Software - BIO-RAD LABORATORIES, INC.; *pg.* 1504, *pg.* 101
CHROMSPUN - Acetate Yarn - EASTMAN CHEMICAL COMPANY; *pg.* 1159, *pg.* 1636
CHROMSTAR II - TV Antenna - WINEGARD COMPANY; *pg.* 688, *pg.* 702
CHROMTRAC - Pumps - IDEX CORPORATION; *pg.* 1347, *pg.* 623
CHRONICLE OF AMERICA - Educational Materials - SCHOLASTIC INC.; *pg.* 1683, *pg.* 1288
CHRONOCOM - Clocks, Communication Systems - RAULAND-BORG CORPORATION; *pg.* 666, *pg.* 634
CHRONOFLEX - Polymer - IMPLANT SCIENCES CORPORATION; *pg.* 1348, *pg.* 860
CHRONOS - Medical Device - DEPUY SYNTHES; *pg.* 1523, *pg.* 1593
CHRYSANTHEMOM - Shoe - AEROGROUP INTERNATIONAL, INC.; *pg.* 1803, *pg.* 1055
CHRYSLER - Automobiles - FCA US LLC; *pg.* 170, *pg.* 868
CHRYSLER 300 - Automobile - FCA US LLC; *pg.* 170, *pg.* 868
CHRYSLER 300 C - Automobile - FCA US LLC; *pg.* 170, *pg.* 868
CHRYSLER 300 M - Automobile - FCA US LLC; *pg.* 170, *pg.* 868
CHRYSLER CIRRUS - Automobile - FCA US LLC; *pg.* 170, *pg.* 868
CHRYSLER CONCORDE - Car - FCA US LLC; *pg.* 170, *pg.* 868
CHRYSLER CROSSFIRE COUPE - Automobile - FCA US LLC; *pg.* 170, *pg.* 868
CHRYSLER CROSSFIRE ROADSTER - Automobile - FCA US LLC; *pg.* 170, *pg.* 868
CHRYSLER FINANCIAL - Automotive Financial Services - FCA US LLC; *pg.* 170, *pg.* 868
CHRYSLER LHS - Automobile - FCA US LLC; *pg.* 170, *pg.* 868
CHRYSLER PACIFICA - Sport Utility - FCA US LLC; *pg.* 170, *pg.* 868
CHRYSLER PT CRUISER - Automobile - FCA US LLC; *pg.* 170, *pg.* 868
CHRYSLER SEBRING - Automobile - FCA US LLC; *pg.* 170, *pg.* 868
CHRYSLER TOWN & COUNTRY - Minivan - FCA US LLC; *pg.* 170, *pg.* 868
CHRYSLER VOYAGER - Minivan - FCA US LLC; *pg.* 170, *pg.* 868
CHRYSTAL - Software - XEROX CORPORATION; *pg.* 494, *pg.* 365
CHT - Software - BIO-RAD LABORATORIES, INC.; *pg.* 1504, *pg.* 101
CHU HAN CHESS GOD - Video Game - INTERNATIONAL GAME TECHNOLOGY; *pg.* 957, *pg.* 1024
CHU HAN CHESS MATCH BONUS - Video Game - INTERNATIONAL GAME TECHNOLOGY; *pg.* 957, *pg.* 1024
CHUBBY CHICKEN - Fast Food Chicken - A&W FOOD SERVICES OF CANADA INC.; *pg.* 1714, *pg.* 1908
CHUBBY DINNER - Fast Food - A&W FOOD SERVICES OF CANADA INC.; *pg.* 1714, *pg.* 1908
CHUBBY 'JUNIOR' - Fast Food - A&W FOOD SERVICES OF CANADA INC.; *pg.* 1714, *pg.* 1908
CHUBMAKER - Filling Machinery - R.A. JONES & CO.; *pg.* 1371, *pg.* 704
CHUCK E CHEESE'S - Restaurants - CEC ENTERTAINMENT, INC.; *pg.* 1721, *pg.* 1717
CHUCK E-CLUB - Entertainment - CEC ENTERTAINMENT, INC.; *pg.* 1721, *pg.* 1717
CHUCK STYLE CAPPER - Capping - U.S. BOTTLERS MACHINERY COMPANY; *pg.* 1386, *pg.* 1369
CHUCK TAYLOR COLLECTION - Foot Apparel - CONVERSE INC.; *pg.* 1831, *pg.* 793
CHUCK WAGON - Processed Meats - BAR-S FOODS CO.; *pg.* 839, *pg.* 15
CHUCKLES - Candy - FERRARA CANDY CO.; *pg.* 1852, *pg.* 612
CHUCURI - Chocolate Product - GUITTARD CHOCOLATE COMPANY; *pg.* 1855, *pg.* 55
CHUKER - Sweetening Ingredient - MERISANT COMPANY; *pg.* 876, *pg.* 581
CHUKKA - Footwear - P.W. MINOR & SON, INC.; *pg.* 1816, *pg.* 1140
CHUKKA - Footwear - VANS, INC.; *pg.* 1821, *pg.* 76
CHUNKY - Food Product - CAMPBELL COMPANY OF CANADA LTD; *pg.* 844, *pg.* 1935
CHUNKY - Soup - CAMPBELL SOUP COMPANY; *pg.* 844, *pg.* 1048
CHUNKY - Candy - NESTLE USA, INC.; *pg.* 883, *pg.* 96
CHUNKY MONKEY - Ice Cream - BEN & JERRY'S HOMEMADE, INC.; *pg.* 1850, *pg.* 1767
CHUNKY STRAWBERRY TOPPER - Fruit Drink - JAMBA, INC.; *pg.* 1024, *pg.* 84
CHUNKY USA - Yarn - LION BRAND YARN COMPANY; *pg.* 696, *pg.* 1050
CHUN'S - Sauces & Marinades - SOKOL & COMPANY; *pg.* 1862, *pg.* 598
CHURCH - Ornament - HERITAGE LACE INC.; *pg.* 694, *pg.* 711
THE CHURCH BOOKSTORE - Magazine - CHARISMA MEDIA; *pg.* 1627, *pg.* 436
CHURCH SOLUTION - Publication - INFORMA EXHIBITIONS LLC; *pg.* 1653, *pg.* 17
CHURCHILL - Door & Wood Product - CONESTOGA WOOD SPECIALTIES CORP.; *pg.* 921, *pg.* 1527
CHURCHILL - Swim Fins - MATTEL, INC.; *pg.* 962, *pg.* 81
CHURCHILL DOWNS - Race Course - CHURCHILL DOWNS, INC.; *pg.* 540, *pg.* 733
CHURCHSTAFFING.COM - Online Church Information - SALEM MEDIA GROUP, INC.; *pg.* 307, *pg.* 57
CHURN SPREAD - Butter Alternative - VENTURA FOODS,

First page reference indicates Business Class Edition
Second page reference indicates Geographic Edition

LLC; *pg.* 908, *pg.* 49
CHURRUMAIS - Fried Corn Strips - FRITO-LAY NORTH AMERICA, INC.; *pg.* 1853, *pg.* 1730
CHURRUMAIS - Fried Corn Strips - PEPSICO, INC.; *pg.* 259, *pg.* 1327
CHUTES & LADDERS - Game - HASBRO, INC.; *pg.* 954, *pg.* 1603
CHUX - Cleaning Cloths - THE CLOROX COMPANY; *pg.* 327, *pg.* 169
CHUX - Sport Product - FRANKLIN SPORTS, INC.; *pg.* 1834, *pg.* 847
CHY-MAX - Coagulant - CHR. HANSEN; *pg.* 847, *pg.* 1873
THE CHYRON CODI - Video System - CHYRONHEGO; *pg.* 371, *pg.* 1179
CI - LED - CREE INC.; *pg.* 631, *pg.* 1371
C.I. HAYES - Electric Heat-Treating Equipment - C.I. HAYES; *pg.* 1070, *pg.* 1600
CIA - Ion Analyzer - WATERS CORPORATION; *pg.* 1436, *pg.* 834
CIA-PAK - Ion Analyzer - WATERS CORPORATION; *pg.* 1436, *pg.* 834
CIAGLIA BLUE RHINO - Tray - COOK GROUP, INC.; *pg.* 1518, *pg.* 674
CIALIS - Pharmaceutical Product - ELI LILLY AND COMPANY; *pg.* 1527, *pg.* 684
CIBC 60 PLUS ADVANTAGE - Banking Service - CANADIAN IMPERIAL BANK OF COMMERCE; *pg.* 729, *pg.* 1935
CIBC ADVANTAGE - Banking Service - CANADIAN IMPERIAL BANK OF COMMERCE; *pg.* 729, *pg.* 1935
CIBC AEROGOLD - Banking Card - CANADIAN IMPERIAL BANK OF COMMERCE; *pg.* 729, *pg.* 1935
CIBC AEROMORTGAGE - Mortgage - CANADIAN IMPERIAL BANK OF COMMERCE; *pg.* 729, *pg.* 1935
CIBC AVENTURA - Banking Service - CANADIAN IMPERIAL BANK OF COMMERCE; *pg.* 729, *pg.* 1935
CIBC BIZLINE - VISA Card - CANADIAN IMPERIAL BANK OF COMMERCE; *pg.* 729, *pg.* 1935
CIBC BUSINESS OPERATING ACCOUNT - Banking Account - CANADIAN IMPERIAL BANK OF COMMERCE; *pg.* 729, *pg.* 1935
CIBC CREDITSMART - Banking Service - CANADIAN IMPERIAL BANK OF COMMERCE; *pg.* 729, *pg.* 1935
CIBC ESCALATING RATE GICS - Banking Service - CANADIAN IMPERIAL BANK OF COMMERCE; *pg.* 729, *pg.* 1935
CIBC EVERYDAY - Checking Account - CANADIAN IMPERIAL BANK OF COMMERCE; *pg.* 729, *pg.* 1935
CIBC EXPRESS SWITCH - Banking Service - CANADIAN IMPERIAL BANK OF COMMERCE; *pg.* 729, *pg.* 1935
CIBC INVESTOR'S EDGE - Banking Service - CANADIAN IMPERIAL BANK OF COMMERCE; *pg.* 729, *pg.* 1935
CIBC PREMIERSERVICE - Banking Service - CANADIAN IMPERIAL BANK OF COMMERCE; *pg.* 729, *pg.* 1935
CIBC PREMIUM GROWTH ACCOUNT - Savings Account - CANADIAN IMPERIAL BANK OF COMMERCE; *pg.* 729, *pg.* 1935
CIBC PRIVATE WEALTH MANAGEMENT - Banking Service - CANADIAN IMPERIAL BANK OF COMMERCE; *pg.* 729, *pg.* 1935
CIBC UNLIMITED - Checking Account - CANADIAN IMPERIAL BANK OF COMMERCE; *pg.* 729, *pg.* 1935
CIBENZA - Health & Nutrition Product - NOVUS INTERNATIONAL, INC.; *pg.* 706, *pg.* 1001
CIBER JOBS - Job Information - CIBER, INC.; *pg.* 372, *pg.* 330
CIBERSPACE - Consulting Service - CIBER, INC.; *pg.* 372, *pg.* 330
CIC - Bonding Tool - KULICKE & SOFFA INDUSTRIES, INC.; *pg.* 650, *pg.* 1533
CICERO - Business Integration Software - CICERO INC.; *pg.* 372, *pg.* 1360
CICHLID PREMIUM FLAKES - Fish Food - THE HARTZ MOUNTAIN CORP.; *pg.* 1476, *pg.* 1120
CICLOPIROX - Pharmaceutical Product - G&W LABORATORIES INC.; *pg.* 1532, *pg.* 1123
CID - Interior Design - CALLAWAY GOLF COMPANY; *pg.* 1829, *pg.* 58
CIDEX - Healthcare Product - JOHNSON & JOHNSON; *pg.* 1549, *pg.* 1091
CIDEX - Activated Dialdehyde Solution - MEDLINE INDUSTRIES, INC.; *pg.* 1562, *pg.* 635
CIE - Electronics Study-Programmed Lessons - CIE DIRECT; *pg.* 599, *pg.* 1429
CIEL - Water - THE COCA-COLA COMPANY; *pg.* 240, *pg.* 493
CIELO 2 - Footwear - COBIAN CORP.; *pg.* 1806, *pg.* 253
CIENEGA - Fabric - NEMSCHOFF, INC.; *pg.* 936, *pg.* 1890
CIF 20/20 - Banking Software - JACK HENRY & ASSOCIATES, INC.; *pg.* 422, *pg.* 988
CIF 36 - Banking Software - JACK HENRY & ASSOCIATES, INC.; *pg.* 422, *pg.* 988
CIF 38 - Banking Software - JACK HENRY & ASSOCIATES, INC.; *pg.* 422, *pg.* 988
CIFALI - Capital Equipment - TEREX CORPORATION; *pg.* 1381, *pg.* 384
CIFS - Software - NETAPP, INC.; *pg.* 444, *pg.* 287
CIGALETT - Tobacco - ROCK CREEK PHARMACEUTICALS, INC.; *pg.* 1895, *pg.* 466
CIGAR - Slots - INTERNATIONAL GAME TECHNOLOGY; *pg.* 957, *pg.* 1024
CIGI DIRECT - Insurance Service - CIGI DIRECT INSURANCE SERVICES, INC.; *pg.* 1197, *pg.* 335
CIGMA 3 - Gear Inspection System - GLEASON - M&M PRECISION SYSTEMS CORPORATION; *pg.* 1341, *pg.* 1479
CIGMA 7 - Gear Inspection System - GLEASON - M&M PRECISION SYSTEMS CORPORATION; *pg.* 1341, *pg.* 1479
CIGNA DENTAL NETWORK ACCESS - Dental Program - CIGNA CORPORATION; *pg.* 1197, *pg.* 338
CIGNAFLEX ADVANTAGE - Dental Plan - CIGNA CORPORATION; *pg.* 1197, *pg.* 338
CIGNAPLUS SAVINGS - Dental Plan - CIGNA CORPORATION; *pg.* 1197, *pg.* 338
CIGRX - Low TSNA Cigarettes - ROCK CREEK PHARMACEUTICALS, INC.; *pg.* 1895, *pg.* 466
CII - Signal Level & Mid-Range Relays - TE CONNECTIVITY LTD.; *pg.* 677, *pg.* 1515
CILANTRO - Kitchen Product - KOHLER CO.; *pg.* 91, *pg.* 1862
CILICON - Computer Products - AVNET, INC.; *pg.* 622, *pg.* 15
CILINDRO - Furniture - J. ROBERT SCOTT INC.; *pg.* 930, *pg.* 105
CIM116-EQUIPMENT PERFORMANCE TRACKING - Computer Software - CIMETRIX INCORPORATED; *pg.* 372, *pg.* 1756
CIM40-PROCESS JOB - Computer Software - CIMETRIX INCORPORATED; *pg.* 372, *pg.* 1756
CIM87-CARRIER MANAGEMENT - Computer Software - CIMETRIX INCORPORATED; *pg.* 372, *pg.* 1756
CIM90-SUBSTRATE TRACKING - Computer Software - CIMETRIX INCORPORATED; *pg.* 372, *pg.* 1756
CIM94-CONTROL JOB - Computer Software - CIMETRIX INCORPORATED; *pg.* 372, *pg.* 1756
CIMARRON - Herbicide - E.I. DU PONT DE NEMOURS & COMPANY; *pg.* 1159, *pg.* 390
CIMARRON - Bath Product - KOHLER CO.; *pg.* 91, *pg.* 1862
CIMFOUNDATION - Computer Software - CIMETRIX INCORPORATED; *pg.* 372, *pg.* 1756
CIMLINK - Electric Instrument - UNIVERSAL INSTRUMENTS CORPORATION; *pg.* 683, *pg.* 1154
CIMMARRON BONDED LEATHER - Paper & Nonwoven Material - FIBERMARK INC.; *pg.* 1457, *pg.* 1764
CIMS - Management Standard - ISSA; *pg.* 145, *pg.* 640
CIMZIA - Therapeutic Product - XOMA CORPORATION; *pg.* 1611, *pg.* 46
CIN-A-YUM - Pretzel - WETZEL'S PRETZELS LLC; *pg.* 910, *pg.* 181
CINCH - Herbicide - E.I. DU PONT DE NEMOURS & COMPANY; *pg.* 1159, *pg.* 390
CINCH - Cornbread Mixes - GILSTER-MARY LEE CORPORATION; *pg.* 858, *pg.* 563
CINCH - Cleaning Product - PRESTIGE BRANDS HOLDINGS, INC.; *pg.* 520, *pg.* 1345
CINCH BAND - Twist Tie Closure - BEDFORD INDUSTRIES, INC.; *pg.* 1453, *pg.* 967
CINCH SAK - Trash Bags - PACTIV CORPORATION; *pg.* 1466, *pg.* 624
CINCH WORM - Shoe - AEROGROUP INTERNATIONAL, INC.; *pg.* 1803, *pg.* 1055
CINCHCERITY - Shoe - AEROGROUP INTERNATIONAL, INC.; *pg.* 1803, *pg.* 1055
CINCHRONIZE - Boots - AEROGROUP INTERNATIONAL, INC.; *pg.* 1803, *pg.* 1055
CINCHSATIONAL - Shoe - AEROGROUP INTERNATIONAL, INC.; *pg.* 1803, *pg.* 1055
CINCINNATI - Shoe - AEROGROUP INTERNATIONAL, INC.; *pg.* 1803, *pg.* 1055
CINCINNATI DELI RYES - Bread - KLOSTERMAN BAKING COMPANY, INC.; *pg.* 869, *pg.* 1415
THE CINCINNATI ENQUIRER - Newspaper - THE CINCINNATI ENQUIRER, INC.; *pg.* 1628, *pg.* 1411
CINCINNATI GILBERT - Boring Machines - THE CINCINNATI GILBERT MACHINE TOOL COMPANY, L.L.C.; *pg.* 1323, *pg.* 1411
CINCINNATI REDS - Baseball Team - REDS BASEBALL PARTNERS, LLC; *pg.* 578, *pg.* 1425
CINCY LIFE - Magazine Depicting Daily Life in Ohio - GREAT LAKES PUBLISHING COMPANY; *pg.* 1646, *pg.* 1431
CINCYBUSINESS - Showcasing Business Sectors - GREAT LAKES PUBLISHING COMPANY; *pg.* 1646, *pg.* 1431
CINDOL - Metal Forming - HOUGHTON INTERNATIONAL INC.; *pg.* 1167, *pg.* 1589
CINDY - Clothing - ABERCROMBIE & FITCH CO.; *pg.* 37, *pg.* 1466
CINDY - Furniture - AMISCO INDUSTRIES LTD.; *pg.* 913, *pg.* 1958
CINE-DIGITAR - Digital Cinema Lenses - SCHNEIDER OPTICS INC.; *pg.* 1428, *pg.* 1165
CINEDICHRO - Filter - ROSCO LABORATORIES, INC.; *pg.* 1782, *pg.* 378
CINEFLURE - X-Ray Film, Chemicals - EASTMAN KODAK COMPANY; *pg.* 1408, *pg.* 1333
CINEFX - Software - NVIDIA CORPORATION; *pg.* 447, *pg.* 268
CINEGEL - Filter - ROSCO LABORATORIES, INC.; *pg.* 1782, *pg.* 378
CINELUX - Filter - ROSCO LABORATORIES, INC.; *pg.* 1782, *pg.* 378
CINEMA - Commercial Lighting - SWIVELIER CO., INC.; *pg.* 1307, *pg.* 1142
CINEMA ART - Exhibition of Acclaimed Films - REGAL ENTERTAINMENT GROUP; *pg.* 579, *pg.* 1638
CINEMA CASH - Lottery Game - MICHIGAN STATE LOTTERY BUREAU; *pg.* 999, *pg.* 895
CINEMA CONTOUR - Projection Screen - DA-LITE SCREEN COMPANY; *pg.* 632, *pg.* 698
CINEMA GOLD - Popcorn Topping - VENTURA FOODS, LLC; *pg.* 908, *pg.* 49
CINEMATE - Audio Product - BOSE CORPORATION; *pg.* 626, *pg.* 820
CINEMAX - Pay Television Service - HOME BOX OFFICE, INC.; *pg.* 290, *pg.* 1240
CINEMAX ON DEMAND - Cable Television Station - HOME BOX OFFICE, INC.; *pg.* 290, *pg.* 1240
CINEOS - Flat TV - PHILIPS ELECTRONICS NORTH AMERICA; *pg.* 662, *pg.* 782
CINEPLEX ODEON THEATRES - Motion Picture Theaters - CINEPLEX ENTERTAINMENT LP; *pg.* 275, *pg.* 1936
CINERGI - Software Development Tool - RECURSION SOFTWARE, INC.; *pg.* 460, *pg.* 1697
CINERRIO H-LINE - Steel Wall Panel - CLESTRA HAUSERMAN, INC.; *pg.* 76, *pg.* 1526
CINERRIO I-LINE - Steel Wall Panel - CLESTRA HAUSERMAN, INC.; *pg.* 76, *pg.* 1526
CINESPHERE - IMAX Movie Theater - ONTARIO PLACE CORPORATION; *pg.* 572, *pg.* 1941
CINESTREAM - Cleaner - AUTODESK INC.; *pg.* 356, *pg.* 257
CINGULAR - Wireless Communications - AT&T MOBILITY LLC; *pg.* 619, *pg.* 488
CINGULAR - Phone Services - AT&T SOUTHEAST; *pg.* 1868, *pg.* 489
CINI-SOPAPILLA BITES - Food Product - TACO JOHN'S INTERNATIONAL, INC.; *pg.* 1753, *pg.* 1901
CINNABAR - Wall Decor - ETHAN ALLEN INTERIORS INC.; *pg.* 924, *pg.* 343
CINNABON - Snack Bar - KELLOGG COMPANY; *pg.* 831, *pg.* 870
CINNABON BITES - Baked Goods - CINNABON, INC.; *pg.* 1723, *pg.* 493
CINNABON CLASSIC ROLL - Baked Goods - CINNABON, INC.; *pg.* 1723, *pg.* 493
CINNABON STIX - Baked Goods - CINNABON, INC.; *pg.* 1723, *pg.* 493
CINNAMINT - Air Freshener - SWISHER HYGIENE INC.; *pg.* 336, *pg.* 1507
CINNAMON CIDER - Oil & Spray - AROMATIQUE INC.; *pg.* 499, *pg.* 32
CINNAMON CINNSATIONS - Cinnamon Rolls - KWIK TRIP INC.; *pg.* 1026, *pg.* 1864
CINNAMON CRUNCH CRISPIX - Cereal - KELLOGG COMPANY; *pg.* 831, *pg.* 870
CINNAMON FINGERS - Food Product - PEPPERIDGE FARM,

INC.; *pg.* 888, *pg.* 363

CINNAMON GRAHAMS - Crackers - GENERAL MILLS, INC.; *pg.* 828, *pg.* 933

CINNAMON MELTS - Sweet Roll - MCDONALD'S CORPORATION; *pg.* 1737, *pg.* 645

CINNAMON N' RAISIN - Breakfast Biscuit - HARDEES FOOD SYSTEMS, INC.; *pg.* 1731, *pg.* 998

CINNAMON ROLL - Snack Cakes - HOSTESS BRANDS LLC; *pg.* 1856, *pg.* 984

CINNAMON STICK - Tea - R.C. BIGELOW, INC.; *pg.* 891, *pg.* 348

CINNAMON TOAST CRUNCH - Cereal - GENERAL MILLS, INC.; *pg.* 828, *pg.* 933

CINNAMON TOASTER - Bag Cereal - POST CONSUMER BRANDS; *pg.* 833, *pg.* 927

CINNAMON ZYLICIOUS - Nutritional Product - NUTRACEUTICAL INTERNATIONAL CORPORATION; *pg.* 1576, *pg.* 1753

CINNAPACKS - Baked Goods - CINNABON, INC.; *pg.* 1723, *pg.* 493

CINRYZE - Prescription Drug - SHIRE; *pg.* 1593, *pg.* 1532

CINRYZESOLUTIONS - Healthcare Program - SHIRE; *pg.* 1593, *pg.* 1532

CINTA AZUL - Rice - AMERICAN RICE, INC.; *pg.* 837, *pg.* 1700

CIO - Technology Magazine - INTERNATIONAL DATA GROUP; *pg.* 1653, *pg.* 796

CIP - Alkaline Cleaner - STERIS CORPORATION; *pg.* 1597, *pg.* 1464

CIP PLUS - Cleaner - DELTA FOREMOST CHEMICAL CORPORATION; *pg.* 1155, *pg.* 1642

CIPHER - Fabric - NEMSCHOFF, INC.; *pg.* 936, *pg.* 1890

CIPHERGENEXPRESS - Software - VERMILLION, INC.; *pg.* 1435, *pg.* 1667

CIPREA - Bath & Plumbing Product - JACUZZI BRANDS CORPORATION; *pg.* 554, *pg.* 65

CIPRO - Medicine - MERCK & CO., INC.; *pg.* 1566, *pg.* 1077

CIPTANE - Synthetic Precipitated Silica - PPG INDUSTRIES, INC.; *pg.* 1445, *pg.* 1579

CIR-Q-LATE - Cleaner - BIRKO CORPORATION; *pg.* 1149, *pg.* 332

CIR SCALD - Tripe & Foot Wash - BIRKO CORPORATION; *pg.* 1149, *pg.* 332

CIRC-ELATION - Nutritional Supplement - WHITEWING LABS, INC.; *pg.* 1610, *pg.* 99

CIRCA - Fabric - NEMSCHOFF, INC.; *pg.* 936, *pg.* 1890

CIRCA - Office Furniture - STEELCASE INC.; *pg.* 475, *pg.* 889

CIRCA 200 - Commercial Lighting - SWIVELIER CO., INC.; *pg.* 1307, *pg.* 1142

CIRCA 250 - Commercial Lighting - SWIVELIER CO., INC.; *pg.* 1307, *pg.* 1142

CIRCA 325 - Commercial Lighting - SWIVELIER CO., INC.; *pg.* 1307, *pg.* 1142

CIRCLE - Tools - KENNAMETAL INC.; *pg.* 1052, *pg.* 1547

CIRCLE-C - Electrosurgical Devices - ANGIODYNAMICS, INC.; *pg.* 1495, *pg.* 1173

CIRCLE K - Convenience Store Banner - ALIMENTATION COUCHE-TARD INC.; *pg.* 1013, *pg.* 1951

CIRCLE O' LOVE - Jewelry - HELZBERG'S DIAMOND SHOPS, INC.; *pg.* 6, *pg.* 984

CIRCLE OF CARE - Healthcare Program - HCR MANORCARE, INC.; *pg.* 1539, *pg.* 1476

CIRCLE OF FRIENDS-AN AMERICAN GIRLS MUSICAL - Doll And Toy - AMERICAN GIRL LLC; *pg.* 949, *pg.* 1871

CIRCLE OF LOVE - Home & Garden Product - ENESCO, LLC; *pg.* 1124, *pg.* 620

CIRCLE OF SISTERS - Educational Services - INNER CITY BROADCASTING CORPORATION; *pg.* 292, *pg.* 1243

CIRCLES - Fabric - NEMSCHOFF, INC.; *pg.* 936, *pg.* 1890

CIRCLESEA - Smoked, Cured & Pickled Fish - OCEAN BEAUTY SEAFOODS, INC.; *pg.* 1028, *pg.* 1838

CIRCPAC - Valves - FLOWSERVE CORPORATION; *pg.* 82, *pg.* 1719

CIRCU-BREEZE - Fan - KAZ, INC.; *pg.* 58, *pg.* 844

CIRCU-LATOR - Grain Dryer - SHIVVERS INC.; *pg.* 707, *pg.* 704

CIRCU-LATOR II - Grain Dryer - SHIVVERS INC.; *pg.* 707, *pg.* 704

CIRCUCOOL PUMP - Medical Device - BOSTON SCIENTIFIC CORPORATION; *pg.* 1508, *pg.* 831

CIRCUIT - Fabric - NEMSCHOFF, INC.; *pg.* 936, *pg.* 1890

CIRCUIT CLOSE CONTACT - Saddle - DOVER SADDLERY, INC.; *pg.* 1833, *pg.* 829

CIRCUIT CLOSE CONTACT JR. - Saddle - DOVER SADDLERY, INC.; *pg.* 1833, *pg.* 829

CIRCUIT ELITE - Saddle - DOVER SADDLERY, INC.; *pg.* 1833, *pg.* 829

CIRCUIT GUARD - Power Distribution Unit - HUBBELL INCORPORATED; *pg.* 1299, *pg.* 370

CIRCUIT-ISOLATOR II - Substation Disconnector - S&C ELECTRIC COMPANY; *pg.* 1305, *pg.* 589

CIRCUIT PATHFINDER - Software System - MENTOR GRAPHICS CORPORATION; *pg.* 432, *pg.* 1510

CIRCUIT PRO - Saddle - DOVER SADDLERY, INC.; *pg.* 1833, *pg.* 829

CIRCUIT SEEKER - Circuit Tracer - GREENLEE TEXTRON INC.; *pg.* 1048, *pg.* 655

CIRCUITBOARD - Fabric - NEMSCHOFF, INC.; *pg.* 936, *pg.* 1890

CIRCUITCITY.COM - Online Computer & Accessory Retailer - SYSTEMAX, INC.; *pg.* 481, *pg.* 1324

CIRCUITSAF - Adhesive - LORD CORPORATION; *pg.* 1357, *pg.* 1360

CIRCUITSWITCHER - Interruption & Transfer Switch - S&C ELECTRIC COMPANY; *pg.* 1305, *pg.* 589

CIRCUITTRIM - Laser System - GSI GROUP INC.; *pg.* 1415, *pg.* 784

CIRCULAR INCINO-PAK - Burner - MAXON CORPORATION; *pg.* 1359, *pg.* 695

CIRCULAR SKYDOMES - Skylight - WASCO PRODUCTS, INC.; *pg.* 120, *pg.* 752

CIRCULIGHT - Lens - LIGHTPATH TECHNOLOGIES INC; *pg.* 1420, *pg.* 454

CIRCUMVENT PCV2 - Vaccine Immunization - MERCK & CO., INC.; *pg.* 1566, *pg.* 1077

CIRCUPOSIT - Electroless Copper System - DOW CHEMICAL; *pg.* 1156, *pg.* 1563

CIRCUS - Furniture - ASHLEY FURNITURE INDUSTRIES, INC.; *pg.* 914, *pg.* 1852

CIRCUS CIRCUS - Resort & Casino - MGM RESORTS INTERNATIONAL; *pg.* 1105, *pg.* 1028

CIRCUS TIME - Bouquet - 1-800-FLOWERS.COM, INC.; *pg.* 1758, *pg.* 1151

CIRE - Gloves - TOTES ISOTONER CORPORATION; *pg.* 14, *pg.* 1426

CIROC - Vodka - DIAGEO NORTH AMERICA, INC.; *pg.* 1961, *pg.* 361

CIROS - Lighting System - LITECONTROL CORPORATION; *pg.* 1301, *pg.* 841

CIRQUE - Modern Occasional Tables - BERNHARDT DESIGN; *pg.* 918, *pg.* 1381

CIRQUE - Fabric - NEMSCHOFF, INC.; *pg.* 936, *pg.* 1890

CIRRASOL - Chemical Product - SPECTRUM CHEMICALS & LABORATORY PRODUCTS, INC.; *pg.* 1181, *pg.* 94

CIRRUS - Ceilings & Walls - ARMSTRONG WORLD INDUSTRIES, INC.; *pg.* 914, *pg.* 1545

CIRRUS - Cash Machine Network - MASTERCARD INCORPORATED; *pg.* 779, *pg.* 1325

CIRRUS - Gas Analyzer - MKS INSTRUMENTS, INC.; *pg.* 1362, *pg.* 781

CIRRUS - Door Glass - ODL INCORPORATED; *pg.* 101, *pg.* 914

CIRTEC CLQR - Cleaner - BIRKO CORPORATION; *pg.* 1149, *pg.* 332

CISA - Locking System - INGERSOLL-RAND COMPANY; *pg.* 1349, *pg.* 1370

CISAL - Classic Bath Product - ROHL LLC; *pg.* 1061, *pg.* 116

CISCO HEALTHPRESENCE - Health Care Service - CISCO SYSTEMS, INC.; *pg.* 372, *pg.* 240

CISCO IOS - Software - CISCO SYSTEMS, INC.; *pg.* 372, *pg.* 240

CISCO LUMIN - Optical Transmission Platform - CISCO SYSTEMS, INC.; *pg.* 372, *pg.* 240

CISCO NEXUS - Virtual Switch - CISCO SYSTEMS, INC.; *pg.* 372, *pg.* 240

CISCO NURSE CONNECT - Industry Solutions - CISCO SYSTEMS, INC.; *pg.* 372, *pg.* 240

CISCO STACKPOWER - Security Appliance - CISCO SYSTEMS, INC.; *pg.* 372, *pg.* 240

CISCO STADIUMVISION - Wireless Applications - CISCO SYSTEMS, INC.; *pg.* 372, *pg.* 240

CISCO STORE - Online Store - CISCO SYSTEMS, INC.; *pg.* 372, *pg.* 240

CISCO TELEPRESENCE - Recording Studio - CISCO SYSTEMS, INC.; *pg.* 372, *pg.* 240

CISCOS EOS - Software - CISCO SYSTEMS, INC.; *pg.* 372, *pg.* 240

CISSY COLLECTION - Collectible Dolls - ALEXANDER DOLL COMPANY, INC.; *pg.* 949, *pg.* 1545

CIT - Metal Fabricated Enclosures - CHANNELL COMMERCIAL CORP.; *pg.* 1870, *pg.* 291

CITADEL - 3-Tab Roofing Shingles - BUILDING PRODUCTS OF CANADA CORP.; *pg.* 72, *pg.* 1951

CITADEL - Medical Product - PATIENT SAFETY TECHNOLOGIES, INC.; *pg.* 1580, *pg.* 114

CITATION - Carpet - BEAULIEU GROUP, LLC; *pg.* 917, *pg.* 529

CITATION - Furniture Collection - CENTURY FURNITURE INDUSTRIES; *pg.* 920, *pg.* 1377

CITATION - Aircraft - CESSNA AIRCRAFT COMPANY; *pg.* 226, *pg.* 723

CITATION - Popcorn Machine - GOLD MEDAL PRODUCTS CO.; *pg.* 55, *pg.* 1414

CITATION - Seating Product - IRWIN SEATING COMPANY INC.; *pg.* 929, *pg.* 887

CITATION - Lighting - LSI INDUSTRIES INC.; *pg.* 58, *pg.* 1416

CITATION - Sturdilite Floodlight - PHOENIX PRODUCTS COMPANY; *pg.* 1304, *pg.* 1879

CITATION - Fastening System - TEXTRON INC.; *pg.* 235, *pg.* 1607

CITATION - Cooking Oil - VENTURA FOODS, LLC; *pg.* 908, *pg.* 49

CITAXIN - Pharmaceutical Product - VALEANT PHARMACEUTICALS INTERNATIONAL; *pg.* 1605, *pg.* 1047

CITGO PLUS CREDIT CARD - Credit Card - CITIGROUP INC.; *pg.* 735, *pg.* 1212

CITI / AADVANTAGE AMERICAN EXPRESS CARD - Credit Card - CITIGROUP INC.; *pg.* 735, *pg.* 1212

CITI ALTERNATIVE INVESTMENTS - Financial Services - CITIGROUP INC.; *pg.* 735, *pg.* 1212

CITI BRONZE / AADVANTAGE MASTERCARD - Credit Card - CITIGROUP INC.; *pg.* 735, *pg.* 1212

CITI BRONZE / AADVANTAGE WORLD MASTERCARD - Credit Card - CITIGROUP INC.; *pg.* 735, *pg.* 1212

CITI CARDS - Credit Cards - CITIGROUP INC.; *pg.* 735, *pg.* 1212

CITI CASHRETURNS MASTERCARD - Cash Card - CITIGROUP INC.; *pg.* 735, *pg.* 1212

CITI CHAIRMAN AMERICAN EXPRESS CARD - Credit Card - CITIGROUP INC.; *pg.* 735, *pg.* 1212

CITI DIAMOND PREFERRED CARD - Credit Card - CITIGROUP INC.; *pg.* 735, *pg.* 1212

CITI DIVIDEND PLATINUM SELECT MASTERCARD - Cash Card - CITIGROUP INC.; *pg.* 735, *pg.* 1212

CITI FORWARD - Credit Card - CITIGROUP INC.; *pg.* 735, *pg.* 1212

CITI FORWARD BY MYSPACE - Cash Card - CITIGROUP INC.; *pg.* 735, *pg.* 1212

CITI GOLD / AADVANTAGE WORLD MASTERCARD - Credit Card - CITIGROUP INC.; *pg.* 735, *pg.* 1212

CITI HILTON HHONORS VISA SIGNATURE CARD - Signature Card - CITIGROUP INC.; *pg.* 735, *pg.* 1212

CITI INSTITUTIONAL CLIENTS GROUP - Financial Services - CITIGROUP INC.; *pg.* 735, *pg.* 1212

CITI INVESTMENT RESEARCH - Financial Services - CITIGROUP INC.; *pg.* 735, *pg.* 1212

CITI MICROFINANCE - Financial Services - CITIGROUP INC.; *pg.* 735, *pg.* 1212

CITI MTVUTM PLATINUM SELECT VISA - Cash Card - CITIGROUP INC.; *pg.* 735, *pg.* 1212

CITI PLATINUM AMERICAN EXPRESS - Cash Card - CITIGROUP INC.; *pg.* 735, *pg.* 1212

CITI PLATINUM SELECT / AADVANTAGE WORLD MASTERCARD - Credit Card - CITIGROUP INC.; *pg.* 735, *pg.* 1212

CITI PLATINUM SELECT MASTERCARD - Credit Card - CITIGROUP INC.; *pg.* 735, *pg.* 1212

CITI PREMIERPASS AMERICAN EXPRESS - Cash Card - CITIGROUP INC.; *pg.* 735, *pg.* 1212

CITI PREMIERPASS CARD - Credit Card - CITIGROUP INC.; *pg.* 735, *pg.* 1212

CITI PREMIERPASS CARD - ELITE LEVEL - Credit Card - CITIGROUP INC.; *pg.* 735, *pg.* 1212

CITI PREMIERPASS / EXPEDIA.COM CARD - Credit Card - CITIGROUP INC.; *pg.* 735, *pg.* 1212

CITI PREMIERPASS / EXPEDIA.COM CARD - ELITE LEVEL - Cash Card - CITIGROUP INC.; *pg.* 735, *pg.* 1212

CITI PRIVATE BANK - Financial Services - CITIGROUP INC.; *pg.* 735, *pg.* 1212

CITI PROFESSIONAL - Cash Card - CITIGROUP INC.; *pg.* 735, *pg.* 1212

CITI PROFESSIONAL CARD WITH THANKYOU NETWORK

Credit Card Service - CITIGROUP INC.; *pg.* 735, *pg.* 1212
CITI SECURED MASTERCARD - Cash Card - CITIGROUP INC.; *pg.* 735, *pg.* 1212
CITI SELECT / AADVANTAGE AMERICAN EXPRESS CARD - Cash Card - CITIGROUP INC.; *pg.* 735, *pg.* 1212
CITIBAG - Plastic Bag Product - AEP INDUSTRIES INC.; *pg.* 1878, *pg.* 1085
CITIBANK - Banking Services - CITIGROUP INC.; *pg.* 735, *pg.* 1212
CITIBUSINESS - Cash Card - CITIGROUP INC.; *pg.* 735, *pg.* 1212
CITIBUSINESS / AADVANTAGE VISA - Cash Card - CITIGROUP INC.; *pg.* 735, *pg.* 1212
CITIBUSINESS CARD WITH THANKYOU - Cash Card - CITIGROUP INC.; *pg.* 735, *pg.* 1212
CITIES - Furniture - NEMSCHOFF, INC.; *pg.* 936, *pg.* 1890
CITIES OF THE WORLD - Educational Materials - SCHOLASTIC INC.; *pg.* 1683, *pg.* 1288
CITIFINANCIAL - Financial Services - CITIGROUP INC.; *pg.* 735, *pg.* 1212
CITIGROUP - Financial Services - CITIGROUP INC.; *pg.* 735, *pg.* 1212
CITIINSURANCE - Insurance Services - CITIGROUP INC.; *pg.* 735, *pg.* 1212
CITIMAP - Tourist Directory Including Road Maps - AMERICAN AUTOMOBILE ASSOCIATION; *pg.* 1190, *pg.* 429
CITIMORTGAGE - Mortgage Services - CITIGROUP INC.; *pg.* 735, *pg.* 1212
CITIRX PROGRAM NEIGHBORHOOD - Software - CITRIX SYSTEMS, INC.; *pg.* 375, *pg.* 424
CITIZEN - Furniture - BUSH INDUSTRIES INC.; *pg.* 919, *pg.* 1170
CITIZEN - Bicycle - G. JOANNOU CYCLE CO. INC.; *pg.* 1707, *pg.* 1098
CITRA - Regular, Caffeine-Free & Diet Soft Drink - THE COCA-COLA COMPANY; *pg.* 240, *pg.* 493
CITRA - Technology - HOLOGIC, INC.; *pg.* 1416, *pg.* 784
CITRACAL - Pharmaceutical Product - MISSION PHARMACAL COMPANY INC.; *pg.* 1568, *pg.* 1742
CITRACAL PRENATAL RX - Vitamin - MISSION PHARMACAL COMPANY INC.; *pg.* 1568, *pg.* 1742
CITRAFECT - Disinfectant - DELTA FOREMOST CHEMICAL CORPORATION; *pg.* 1155, *pg.* 1642
CITRAFLO - Cheese Additive - HAWKINS, INC.; *pg.* 1165, *pg.* 937
CITRAJET - Cleaning Detergent - ALCONOX, INC.; *pg.* 325, *pg.* 1351
CITRALVA - Fragrance Ingredient - INTERNATIONAL FLAVORS & FRAGRANCES INC.; *pg.* 512, *pg.* 1244
CITRANOX - Cleaning Detergent - ALCONOX, INC.; *pg.* 325, *pg.* 1351
CITRANOX - Chemical Product - SPECTRUM CHEMICALS & LABORATORY PRODUCTS, INC.; *pg.* 1181, *pg.* 94
CITRI-KOTE PLUS - Natural Solvent - DELTA FOREMOST CHEMICAL CORPORATION; *pg.* 1155, *pg.* 1642
CITRICAL ULTRADENSE - Vitamin - MISSION PHARMACAL COMPANY INC.; *pg.* 1568, *pg.* 1742
CITRIKLEEN AEROSOL - Cleaner - PENETONE CORPORATION; *pg.* 333, *pg.* 1050
CITRIKLEEN CA - Cleaner - PENETONE CORPORATION; *pg.* 333, *pg.* 1050
CITRIKLEEN HD - Cleaner - PENETONE CORPORATION; *pg.* 333, *pg.* 1050
CITRIKLEEN MIL - Cleaner - PENETONE CORPORATION; *pg.* 333, *pg.* 1050
CITRIKLEEN NST - Cleaner - PENETONE CORPORATION; *pg.* 333, *pg.* 1050
CITRIKLEEN RI - Cleaner - PENETONE CORPORATION; *pg.* 333, *pg.* 1050
CITRIKLEEN XPC - Cleaner - PENETONE CORPORATION; *pg.* 333, *pg.* 1050
CITRILUX - Shampoo - PETEDGE; *pg.* 1481, *pg.* 787
CITRIMAX - Nutritional Product - NATROL, INC.; *pg.* 1570, *pg.* 64
CITRIMAX - Nutritional Supplement - NATURAL ORGANICS, INC.; *pg.* 1571, *pg.* 1181
CITRIMAX - Nutritional Product - RELIV INTERNATIONAL, INC.; *pg.* 1589, *pg.* 975
CITRISOMES - Ethnobotanical Product - NU SKIN ENTERPRISES, INC.; *pg.* 518, *pg.* 1755
CITRISTRIP - Paint - W.M. BARR & COMPANY, INC.; *pg.* 338, *pg.* 1647
CITRIX ACCESS ESSENTIALS - Software - CITRIX SYSTEMS, INC.; *pg.* 375, *pg.* 424
CITRIX ACCESS GATEWAY - Software - CITRIX SYSTEMS, INC.; *pg.* 375, *pg.* 424
CITRIX ACCESS SUITE - Software - CITRIX SYSTEMS, INC.; *pg.* 375, *pg.* 424
CITRIX APPLICATION FIREWALL - Software - CITRIX SYSTEMS, INC.; *pg.* 375, *pg.* 424
CITRIX APPLICATION GATEWAY - Software - CITRIX SYSTEMS, INC.; *pg.* 375, *pg.* 424
CITRIX AUTHORIZED LEARNING CENTER - Software - CITRIX SYSTEMS, INC.; *pg.* 375, *pg.* 424
CITRIX CERTIFIED ADMINISTRATOR - Software - CITRIX SYSTEMS, INC.; *pg.* 375, *pg.* 424
CITRIX CERTIFIED ENTERPRISE ADMINISTRATOR - Software - CITRIX SYSTEMS, INC.; *pg.* 375, *pg.* 424
CITRIX CERTIFIED INSTRUCTOR - Software - CITRIX SYSTEMS, INC.; *pg.* 375, *pg.* 424
CITRIX CERTIFIED INTEGRATION ARCHITECT - Software - CITRIX SYSTEMS, INC.; *pg.* 375, *pg.* 424
CITRIX CERTIFIED SALES PROFESSIONAL - Software - CITRIX SYSTEMS, INC.; *pg.* 375, *pg.* 424
CITRIX CLOUD CENTER - Software - CITRIX SYSTEMS, INC.; *pg.* 375, *pg.* 424
CITRIX COMMUNICATION GATEWAY - Software - CITRIX SYSTEMS, INC.; *pg.* 375, *pg.* 424
CITRIX DELIVERY CENTER - Software - CITRIX SYSTEMS, INC.; *pg.* 375, *pg.* 424
CITRIX DESKTOP RECEIVER - Software - CITRIX SYSTEMS, INC.; *pg.* 375, *pg.* 424
CITRIX DESKTOP SERVER - Software - CITRIX SYSTEMS, INC.; *pg.* 375, *pg.* 424
CITRIX DEVELOPER NETWORK - Software - CITRIX SYSTEMS, INC.; *pg.* 375, *pg.* 424
CITRIX EASYCALL - Software - CITRIX SYSTEMS, INC.; *pg.* 375, *pg.* 424
CITRIX EDUCATION - Software - CITRIX SYSTEMS, INC.; *pg.* 375, *pg.* 424
CITRIX ESSENTIALS - Software - CITRIX SYSTEMS, INC.; *pg.* 375, *pg.* 424
CITRIX EXTRANET - Software - CITRIX SYSTEMS, INC.; *pg.* 375, *pg.* 424
CITRIX GOTOASSIST - Software - CITRIX SYSTEMS, INC.; *pg.* 375, *pg.* 424
CITRIX GOTOMEETING - Software - CITRIX SYSTEMS, INC.; *pg.* 375, *pg.* 424
CITRIX GOTOMYPC CORPORATE - Software - CITRIX SYSTEMS, INC.; *pg.* 375, *pg.* 424
CITRIX ICA - Software - CITRIX SYSTEMS, INC.; *pg.* 375, *pg.* 424
CITRIX MERCHANDISING SERVER - Software - CITRIX SYSTEMS, INC.; *pg.* 375, *pg.* 424
CITRIX PARTNER NETWORK - Software - CITRIX SYSTEMS, INC.; *pg.* 375, *pg.* 424
CITRIX PASSWORD MANAGER - Software - CITRIX SYSTEMS, INC.; *pg.* 375, *pg.* 424
CITRIX PRESENTATION SERVER - Software - CITRIX SYSTEMS, INC.; *pg.* 375, *pg.* 424
CITRIX PROVISIONING SERVER - Software - CITRIX SYSTEMS, INC.; *pg.* 375, *pg.* 424
CITRIX READY - Software - CITRIX SYSTEMS, INC.; *pg.* 375, *pg.* 424
CITRIX RECEIVER - Software - CITRIX SYSTEMS, INC.; *pg.* 375, *pg.* 424
CITRIX REPEATER - Software - CITRIX SYSTEMS, INC.; *pg.* 375, *pg.* 424
CITRIX STREAMING SERVER - Software - CITRIX SYSTEMS, INC.; *pg.* 375, *pg.* 424
CITRIX SUBSCRIPTION ADVANTAGE - Software - CITRIX SYSTEMS, INC.; *pg.* 375, *pg.* 424
CITRIX SYNERGY - Software - CITRIX SYSTEMS, INC.; *pg.* 375, *pg.* 424
CITRIX TECHNICAL SUPPORT - Software - CITRIX SYSTEMS, INC.; *pg.* 375, *pg.* 424
CITRIX WINFRAME - Software - CITRIX SYSTEMS, INC.; *pg.* 375, *pg.* 424
CITRIX WORKFLOW STUDIO - Software - CITRIX SYSTEMS, INC.; *pg.* 375, *pg.* 424
CITRIX XENAPP - Software - CITRIX SYSTEMS, INC.; *pg.* 375, *pg.* 424
CITRO PURE - Fruit Juice - CARGILL LIMITED; *pg.* 1475, *pg.* 1914
CITROLITH - Pharmaceuticals - BEACH PRODUCTS, INC.; *pg.* 1501, *pg.* 471
CITRONEX - Cleaning Preparation - WALTER G. LEGGE COMPANY, INC.; *pg.* 337, *pg.* 1321
CITROSOL 502 - Acidulant - ARCHER-DANIELS-MIDLAND COMPANY; *pg.* 825, *pg.* 565
CITROSOL 503 - Acidulant - ARCHER-DANIELS-MIDLAND COMPANY; *pg.* 825, *pg.* 565
CITRUS - Furniture - THE COMMERCIAL FURNITURE GROUP; *pg.* 920, *pg.* 994
CITRUS AM - Orange Grapefruit Juice Drink - OCEAN SPRAY CRANBERRIES, INC.; *pg.* 887, *pg.* 827
CITRUS & VEGETABLE MAGAZINE - Magazine - VANCE PUBLISHING CORPORATION; *pg.* 1699, *pg.* 627
CITRUS BELLE - Fruit Juice - A. DUDA & SONS INC.; *pg.* 835, *pg.* 457
CITRUS II - Antibacterial Hand Soap - ALIMED, INC.; *pg.* 1490, *pg.* 816
CITRUS LAUNDRY LIQUID - Laundry Liquid - BI-O-KLEEN INDUSTRIES, INC.; *pg.* 326, *pg.* 1845
CITRUS MINT - Personal Care Product - RBC LIFE SCIENCES, INC.; *pg.* 1588, *pg.* 1723
CITRUS PLUM BERRY - Decorative Fragrance - AROMATIQUE INC.; *pg.* 499, *pg.* 32
CITRUS PUBLISHING - Publisher - CITRUS COUNTY CHRONICLE; *pg.* 1628, *pg.* 419
CITRUS-SCRUB - Cleaning Product - HILLYARD, INC.; *pg.* 331, *pg.* 990
CITRUS SQUEEZE - Fruit Drink - JAMBA, INC.; *pg.* 1024, *pg.* 84
CITRUS STIX - Ice Cream and Frozen Novelties - UNILEVER CANADA INC.; *pg.* 903, *pg.* 1946
CITY BLOCK - Carpet - BEAULIEU GROUP, LLC; *pg.* 917, *pg.* 529
CITY CLUB - Bath Product - KOHLER CO.; *pg.* 91, *pg.* 1862
CITY GUIDE - Weekly Tourist Magazine - CITY GUIDE MAGAZINE; *pg.* 1628, *pg.* 1214
CITY JAM - Sneaker - REEBOK INTERNATIONAL LTD.; *pg.* 1817, *pg.* 811
CITY LIGHTS - Skate - ROLLER DERBY SKATE CORP.; *pg.* 966, *pg.* 630
CITY LIGHTS - Fabric - UNIROYAL ENGINEERED PRODUCTS; *pg.* 699, *pg.* 467
CITY LOOKS - Hair Salons - REGIS CORPORATION; *pg.* 521, *pg.* 941
CITY MARKET - Supermarket - THE KROGER CO.; *pg.* 1025, *pg.* 1416
CITY PARK SERIES - Modular Playsystem - MIRACLE RECREATION EQUIPMENT COMPANY; *pg.* 1839, *pg.* 988
CITY SEARCH - Search Engine - IAC/INTERACTIVECORP; *pg.* 292, *pg.* 1242
CITYCENTER RESIDENTIAL DIVISION - Resort & Casino - MGM RESORTS INTERNATIONAL; *pg.* 1105, *pg.* 1028
CITYGREEN - Software Tool - AMERICAN FORESTS; *pg.* 128, *pg.* 394
CITYSCAPE - Furniture - ASHLEY FURNITURE INDUSTRIES, INC.; *pg.* 914, *pg.* 1852
CITYSPHERE - Image - DIGITALGLOBE, INC.; *pg.* 1408, *pg.* 333
CITYVILLE - Online Game - ZYNGA INC.; *pg.* 1292, *pg.* 235
CITYWIDE - Software - PASSKEY INTERNATIONAL, INC.; *pg.* 1274, *pg.* 853
CIVIA - Bicycle - QUALITY BICYCLE PRODUCTS; *pg.* 1710, *pg.* 918
CIVIC - Automobile - AMERICAN HONDA MOTOR CO., INC.; *pg.* 163, *pg.* 292
CIVIC - Fan - CRAFTMADE INTERNATIONAL, INC.; *pg.* 1295, *pg.* 1670
CIVIC UNIPACK - Fan - CRAFTMADE INTERNATIONAL, INC.; *pg.* 1295, *pg.* 1670
CIVIL 3D - Software - AUTODESK INC.; *pg.* 356, *pg.* 257
CIVILSTORM - Software - BENTLEY SYSTEMS, INC.; *pg.* 361, *pg.* 1531
CJ - Electric Clutch - THE CARLYLE JOHNSON MACHINE COMPANY, L.L.C.; *pg.* 1321, *pg.* 339
C.J. BANKS - Women's Clothing - CHRISTOPHER & BANKS CORPORATION; *pg.* 22, *pg.* 953
CJ BLACK - Fragrance - RUE21, INC.; *pg.* 32, *pg.* 1591
CJ RUSH - Security Systems - STANLEY BLACK & DECKER, INC.; *pg.* 1063, *pg.* 358
CJIS - Criminal Justice Information System Solution - MAXIMUS, INC.; *pg.* 780, *pg.* 1799
CK IN2U - Fragrance - CALVIN KLEIN, INC.; *pg.* 20, *pg.* 1209
CKE - Online Medical Database - COMPUTER SCIENCES CORPORATION; *pg.* 378, *pg.* 1780
CL3000 - Color Laser Printer - RICOH AMERICAS CORPORATION; *pg.* 461, *pg.* 1131

CLADMATE - Insulation - THE DOW CHEMICAL COMPANY; *pg.* 1157, *pg.* 898
CLAFLIN - Refiner Machine - BOLTON-EMERSON AMERICAS, INC.; *pg.* 1318, *pg.* 827
CLAIBORNE - Sunglasses & Readers - SAFILO USA INC.; *pg.* 11, *pg.* 1106
CLAIMFACTS - Software - TRIZETTO CORPORATION; *pg.* 485, *pg.* 327
CLAIMPACK - Software - EMC CORPORATION; *pg.* 391, *pg.* 825
CLAIMPLUS - Claim Management - THE HARTFORD FINANCIAL SERVICES GROUP, INC.; *pg.* 1202, *pg.* 352
CLAIMS-MADE PLUS - Insurance - PROASSURANCE CORPORATION; *pg.* 1214, *pg.* 3
CLAIMS MANAGEMENT ACCELERATOR - Computer Program - COMPUTER SCIENCES CORPORATION; *pg.* 378, *pg.* 1780
CLAIMSEDITOR - Software - EMC CORPORATION; *pg.* 391, *pg.* 825
CLAIMSEXCHANGE - Software - TRIZETTO CORPORATION; *pg* 485, *pg.* 327
CLAIMSLINK - Software - TRIZETTO CORPORATION; *pg.* 485, *pg.* 327
CLAIMVIEW - Commercial Insurance - THE CHUBB CORPORATION; *pg.* 1196, *pg.* 1128
CLAIRE - Women's Clothing & Accessories - WOODEN SHIPS OF HOBOKEN; *pg.* 35, *pg.* 1315
CLAIRE ROBINSON'S - Sandwich Thins - BIMBO BAKERIES USA; *pg.* 840, *pg.* 151
CLAIRE'S BOUTIQUES - Women's Fashion Accessories Stores - CLAIRE'S STORES, INC.; *pg.* 1764, *pg.* 617
CLAIRETTE - Kitchen Product - KOHLER CO.; *pg.* 91, *pg.* 1862
CLAIRMONT - Pillow - ETHAN ALLEN INTERIORS INC.; *pg.* 924, *pg.* 343
CLAIROL - Personal & Beauty Product - THE PROCTER & GAMBLE COMPANY; *pg.* 1129, *pg.* 1418
CLAM - Software - IMAGINATION TECHNOLOGIES; *pg.* 412, *pg.* 285
CLAM DIGGER - Fabric - NEMSCHOFF, INC.; *pg.* 936, *pg.* 1890
CLAM-TROL - Mollusk Control Agent - GE WATER & PROCESS TECHNOLOGIES; *pg.* 1339, *pg.* 1588
CLAMATO - Non-Carbonated Soft Drink - DR PEPPER SNAPPLE GROUP, INC.; *pg.* 250, *pg.* 1729
CLAMOR - Carpet - BEAULIEU GROUP, LLC; *pg.* 917, *pg.* 529
CLAMP MASTER - Composite Clamps - DE-STA-CO INDUSTRIES; *pg.* 1045, *pg.* 867
CLAMP-ON - Commercial Lighting - SWIVELIER CO., INC.; *pg.* 1307, *pg.* 1142
CLAMPETT'S CASH - Video Game - INTERNATIONAL GAME TECHNOLOGY; *pg.* 957, *pg.* 1024
CLAMPLESS - Catastrophes - POWER INTEGRATIONS, INC.; *pg.* 1369, *pg.* 249
CLAN MACGREGOR - Scotch - WILLIAM GRANT & SONS, INC.; *pg.* 1972, *pg.* 1057
CLANCY - Reading Glass - A. T. CROSS COMPANY; *pg.* 339, *pg.* 1602
CLAPPDICO - Tools - KENNAMETAL INC.; *pg.* 1052, *pg.* 1547
THE CLAPPER - Sound-Activated On/Off Switch - JOSEPH ENTERPRISES, INC.; *pg.* 960, *pg.* 220
THE CLAPPER PLUS - Sound-Activated On/Off Switch - JOSEPH ENTERPRISES, INC.; *pg.* 960, *pg.* 220
CLARADIGM - Health & Nutrition Product - NOVUS INTERNATIONAL, INC.; *pg.* 706, *pg.* 1001
CLARALERT - Software - EMC CORPORATION; *pg.* 391, *pg.* 825
CLAREMONT - Furniture - AMERICAN LEATHER LP; *pg.* 912, *pg.* 1673
CLAREMONT - Furniture - ASHLEY FURNITURE INDUSTRIES, INC.; *pg.* 914, *pg.* 1852
CLAREMONT - Fabric - NEMSCHOFF, INC.; *pg.* 936, *pg.* 1890
CLAREMORE - Furniture - ASHLEY FURNITURE INDUSTRIES, INC.; *pg.* 914, *pg.* 1852
CLARIDENT - Toothbrush - RANIR LLC; *pg.* 520, *pg.* 888
CLARIDGE - Table - BLATT BOWLING & BILLIARD CORP.; *pg.* 1827, *pg.* 1203
CLARIDGE - Furniture Collection - CENTURY FURNITURE INDUSTRIES; *pg.* 920, *pg.* 1377
CLARIDGE - Fabric - NEMSCHOFF, INC.; *pg.* 936, *pg.* 1890
CLARIE - Clothing - ABERCROMBIE & FITCH CO.; *pg.* 37, *pg.* 1466
CLARIFY - Interface Management Solutions - PCTEL, INC.; *pg.* 452, *pg.* 557
CLARIION - Software - EMC CORPORATION; *pg.* 391, *pg.* 825
CLARINEX - Medicine - MERCK & CO., INC.; *pg.* 1566, *pg.* 1077
CLARINEX - Pharmaceutical Product - SUNOVION PHARMACEUTICALS INC.; *pg.* 1599, *pg.* 832
CLARION - Hotels & Resorts - CHOICE HOTELS INTERNATIONAL, INC.; *pg.* 1086, *pg.* 775
CLARION - Fabric - NEMSCHOFF, INC.; *pg.* 936, *pg.* 1890
CLARIS - Software - APPLE INC.; *pg.* 350, *pg.* 73
CLARIS - Filter Cartridge - PALL CORPORATION; *pg.* 232, *pg.* 1323
CLARISWORKS - Application Program - APPLE INC.; *pg.* 350, *pg.* 73
CLARITEST - Pharmaceutical Product - ALERE INC.; *pg.* 1488, *pg.* 849
CLARITH - Pharmaceutical Products - ABBOTT LABORATORIES; *pg.* 1484, *pg.* 551
CLARITHROMYCIN - Pharmaceutical Products - ABBOTT LABORATORIES; *pg.* 1484, *pg.* 551
CLARITIN - Allergy Medicine - BAYER HEALTHCARE CONSUMER CARE DIVISION; *pg.* 1500, *pg.* 1087
CLARITIN-D - Pharmaceutical Product - IMPAX LABORATORIES, INC.; *pg.* 1544, *pg.* 101
CLARITIN-D 12-HR - Pharmaceutical Product - IMPAX LABORATORIES, INC.; *pg.* 1544, *pg.* 101
CLARITIN REDITAB - Pharmaceutical Product - IMPAX LABORATORIES, INC.; *pg.* 1544, *pg.* 101
CLARITY - Ceramic Bracket - 3M COMPANY; *pg.* 1142, *pg.* 956
CLARITY - Pan-Tilt-Zoom System - CHECKPOINT SYSTEMS, INC.; *pg.* 628, *pg.* 1559
CLARITY - Hot Melt Adhesive for Container Labeling - H.B. FULLER COMPANY; *pg.* 1165, *pg.* 961
CLARITY - Carpet - INTERFACE, INC.; *pg.* 695, *pg.* 512
CLARITY - Kitchen Product - KOHLER CO.; *pg.* 91, *pg.* 1862
CLARITY - Fabric - NEMSCHOFF, INC.; *pg.* 936, *pg.* 1890
CLARITY - Communication Headset Product - PLANTRONICS, INC.; *pg.* 663, *pg.* 270
CLARITY BY POLYCOMM - Acoustic Technology - POLYCOM, INC.; *pg.* 664, *pg.* 249
CLARITY CONCEPT - Joystick Controller - CHECKPOINT SYSTEMS, INC.; *pg.* 628, *pg.* 1559
CLARITYMATTERS - Software System - KRONOS INCORPORATED; *pg.* 425, *pg.* 813
CLARIX - Plastic Compound & Resin - A. SCHULMAN, INC.; *pg.* 1144, *pg.* 1452
CLARK - Guest Chairs - BERNHARDT DESIGN; *pg.* 918, *pg.* 1381
CLARK - Burial Vault - CLARK GRAVE VAULT COMPANY; *pg.* 76, *pg.* 1438
CLARK - Forklift Truck - CLARK MATERIAL HANDLING COMPANY; *pg.* 1323, *pg.* 729
CLARK - Camera Shops - DISTRICT PHOTO INC.; *pg.* 1408, *pg.* 761
CLARK BAR - Candy Bar - NEW ENGLAND CONFECTIONERY COMPANY INC.; *pg.* 1860, *pg.* 842
CLARK JUNIOR TUB - Peanut Butter Candy - NEW ENGLAND CONFECTIONERY COMPANY INC.; *pg.* 1860, *pg.* 842
CLARK KENT - Character - DC COMICS, INC.; *pg.* 1633, *pg.* 1221
CLARK LIFT - Truck - CLARK MATERIAL HANDLING COMPANY; *pg.* 1323, *pg.* 729
CLARKE - Furniture - ETHAN ALLEN INTERIORS INC.; *pg.* 924, *pg.* 343
CLARLET - Ophthalmic Product - CARL ZEISS OPTICAL, INC.; *pg.* 1405, *pg.* 1778
CLARUS - Gas Chromatograph - PERKINELMER, INC.; *pg.* 1426, *pg.* 853
CLASIC 50 - Stand Product - WENGER CORPORATION; *pg.* 1307, *pg.* 952
CLASICA 92.3 FM - Radio Station - SPANISH BROADCASTING SYSTEM INC.; *pg.* 310, *pg.* 446
CLASPCON - Electronic Components - MOLEX INCORPORATED; *pg.* 655, *pg.* 628
CLASS - Student Loan Software Supplement - SLM CORPORATION; *pg.* 804, *pg.* 388
CLASS 1 - Fire Suppression Product - IDEX CORPORATION; *pg.* 1347, *pg.* 623
CLASS 4 OFFLOAD - Wireline Solutions - SONUS NETWORKS INC.; *pg.* 1281, *pg.* 858
CLASS 4 TANDEM - Cable Solutions - SONUS NETWORKS INC.; *pg.* 1281, *pg.* 858
CLASS 5 REPLACEMENT (BUSINESS) - Wireline Solutions - SONUS NETWORKS INC.; *pg.* 1281, *pg.* 858
CLASS 5 REPLACEMENT (RESIDENTIAL) - Wireline Solutions - SONUS NETWORKS INC.; *pg.* 1281, *pg.* 858
CLASS A - Home Stereo Components - KRELL INDUSTRIES, INC.; *pg.* 650, *pg.* 367
CLASS ACT - Furniture - JASPER GROUP; *pg.* 930, *pg.* 691
CLASS ACTION LITIGATION REPORT - Publisher - BLOOMBERG BNA; *pg.* 1621, *pg.* 1772
CLASSACT - Shirt and Trouser - BLAUER MANUFACTURING COMPANY, INC.; *pg.* 20, *pg.* 789
CLASSIAV - Pharmaceutical Preparation - PFIZER INC.; *pg.* 1581, *pg.* 1278
CLASSIC - Fabric - 180S, LLC; *pg.* 1824, *pg.* 754
CLASSIC - Gold-Filled Pens & Pencils - A. T. CROSS COMPANY; *pg.* 339, *pg.* 1602
CLASSIC - Mature Device - ALTERA CORPORATION; *pg.* 348, *pg.* 237
CLASSIC - Aluminum Boat - ALUMACRAFT BOAT COMPANY; *pg.* 1705, *pg.* 964
CLASSIC - Food Warmers - APW WYOTT FOOD SERVICE EQUIPMENT, INC., *pg.* 1314, *pg.* 1658
CLASSIC - Roofing System - BEHLEN MFG. CO.; *pg.* 701, *pg.* 1010
CLASSIC - Engine Type - BRIGGS & STRATTON CORPORATION; *pg.* 201, *pg.* 1899
CLASSIC - Motor - CARTER MOTOR COMPANY; *pg.* 1321, *pg.* 665
CLASSIC - Storage Products - CLOSETMAID CORPORATION; *pg.* 920, *pg.* 452
CLASSIC - Minicomputer Systems - CSPI TECHNOLOGY SOLUTIONS; *pg.* 381, *pg.* 421
CLASSIC - Footwear - EASTLAND SHOE CORPORATION; *pg.* 1808, *pg.* 750
CLASSIC - Head Protection - E.D. BULLARD COMPANY; *pg.* 1332, *pg.* 727
CLASSIC - Herbicide - E.I. DU PONT DE NEMOURS & COMPANY; *pg.* 1159, *pg.* 390
CLASSIC - Chemical Coating - ENTHONE INC.; *pg.* 1161, *pg.* 381
CLASSIC - Battery - EXIDE TECHNOLOGIES; *pg.* 204, *pg.* 483
CLASSIC - Scarf - HERITAGE LACE INC.; *pg.* 694, *pg.* 711
CLASSIC - Steel-Framed Operable Partition - HUFCOR INCORPORATED; *pg.* 87, *pg.* 1861
CLASSIC - Pump Product - IDEX CORPORATION; *pg.* 1347, *pg.* 623
THE CLASSIC - Athletic Shoes - K-SWISS; *pg.* 1837, *pg.* 306
CLASSIC - Rubber Floor Mats - MACNEIL AUTOMOTIVE PRODUCTS, LTD.; *pg.* 211, *pg.* 559
CLASSIC - Apparel - OAKLEY, INC.; *pg.* 1840, *pg.* 86
CLASSIC - Roofing Shingles - OWENS CORNING; *pg.* 102, *pg.* 1476
CLASSIC - Musical Instrument - PEAVEY ELECTRONICS CORPORATION; *pg.* 662, *pg.* 970
CLASSIC - Woman's Apparel - PENDLETON WOOLEN MILLS, INC.; *pg.* 697, *pg.* 1505
CLASSIC - Parallel Bar - SCHOOL-TECH, INC.; *pg.* 1844, *pg.* 866
CLASSIC - Grass Seed - THE SCOTTS MIRACLE-GRO COMPANY; *pg.* 1799, *pg.* 1459
CLASSIC - Brushes - THE SHERWIN-WILLIAMS COMPANY; *pg.* 1447, *pg.* 1435
CLASSIC - Bag - SOLO; *pg.* 12, *pg.* 1165
CLASSIC - Hand Tools - USG CORPORATION; *pg.* 118, *pg.* 594
CLASSIC - Footwear - VANS, INC.; *pg.* 1821, *pg.* 76
CLASSIC - Aluminum Brazier - THE VOLLRATH COMPANY LLC; *pg.* 1139, *pg.* 1894
CLASSIC - Skylighting Product - WASCO PRODUCTS, INC.; *pg.* 120, *pg.* 752
CLASSIC - Hoagie - WAWA, INC.; *pg.* 1037, *pg.* 1552
CLASSIC 300 - Skate - ROLLER DERBY SKATE CORP.; *pg.* 966, *pg.* 630
CLASSIC 7S - Video Game - INTERNATIONAL GAME TECHNOLOGY; *pg.* 957, *pg.* 1024
CLASSIC 99 - Paint - THE SHERWIN-WILLIAMS COMPANY; *pg.* 1447, *pg.* 1435
CLASSIC ALUMINUM - Valve Cover - EDELBROCK CORPORATION; *pg.* 204, *pg.* 293
CLASSIC AMERICAN HOME - Magazine - THE HEARST CORPORATION; *pg.* 1649, *pg.* 1239
CLASSIC BLACK TEA - Tea Product - CELESTIAL

First page reference indicates Business Class Edition
Second page reference indicates Geographic Edition

SEASONINGS, INC.; *pg.* 846, *pg.* 310
CLASSIC BLUE - Indemnity Plan - BLUE CROSS & BLUE SHIELD OF RHODE ISLAND; *pg.* 1195, *pg.* 1606
CLASSIC CALI - Running Shoes - REEBOK INTERNATIONAL LTD.; *pg.* 1817, *pg.* 811
CLASSIC CARRY-OUT - Foil Packaging - PACTIV CORPORATION; *pg.* 1466, *pg.* 624
CLASSIC CASSEROLE - Potato - BASIC AMERICAN FOODS, INC.; *pg.* 839, *pg.* 303
CLASSIC COLUMNS - Paper - NEENAH PAPER, INC.; *pg.* 1465, *pg.* 484
CLASSIC COMEDY - Video Game - INTERNATIONAL GAME TECHNOLOGY; *pg.* 957, *pg.* 1024
CLASSIC COTTON - Paper - NEENAH PAPER, INC.; *pg.* 1465, *pg.* 484
CLASSIC-CRAFT - Fiberglass Exterior Doors - THERMA-TRU CORP.; *pg.* 115, *pg.* 1462
CLASSIC CREST - Printing Paper - NEENAH PAPER, INC.; *pg.* 1465, *pg.* 484
CLASSIC CREST DIGITAL - Paper - NEENAH PAPER, INC.; *pg.* 1465, *pg.* 484
CLASSIC CSM - Battery - EXIDE TECHNOLOGIES; *pg.* 204, *pg.* 483
CLASSIC CUSHION - Mousepads - LEWTAN INDUSTRIES CORP.; *pg.* 1658, *pg.* 352
CLASSIC DECAF BLACK TEA - Tea Product - CELESTIAL SEASONINGS, INC.; *pg.* 846, *pg.* 310
CLASSIC DREAMS - Carpet - BEAULIEU GROUP, LLC; *pg.* 917, *pg.* 529
CLASSIC ELWAY - Furniture - BASSETT FURNITURE INDUSTRIES, INCORPORATED; *pg.* 916, *pg.* 1776
CLASSIC ENGINEERING - Pump Product - IDEX CORPORATION; *pg.* 1347, *pg.* 623
CLASSIC ETCH A SKETCH - Toy - THE OHIO ART COMPANY, INC.; *pg.* 965, *pg.* 1406
CLASSIC FIRST/FLEX - Footwear - CLARKS COMPANIES; *pg.* 1806, *pg.* 836
CLASSIC GLULAM - Wood & Building Material - WEYERHAEUSER COMPANY; *pg.* 121, *pg.* 1820
CLASSIC GOURMET - Flavor Base - VENTURA FOODS, LLC; *pg.* 908, *pg.* 49
CLASSIC HEARTH - Food Product - CONTINENTAL MILLS, INC.; *pg.* 827, *pg.* 1845
CLASSIC III - Manufactured Homes - JACOBSEN MANUFACTURING, INC.; *pg.* 1098, *pg.* 460
CLASSIC IMPRESSIONS - Paper Placemat - GEORGIA-PACIFIC LLC; *pg.* 1458, *pg.* 507
CLASSIC IMPRESSIONS Disposable Dishes - PACTIV CORPORATION; *pg.* 1466, *pg.* 624
CLASSIC KNOT - Jewelry - LAGOS INC.; *pg.* 8, *pg.* 1566
CLASSIC LAID - Paper - NEENAH PAPER, INC.; *pg.* 1465, *pg.* 484
CLASSIC LIGHTS & SOUNDS TRIKE - Trikes - RADIO FLYER INC.; *pg.* 966, *pg.* 588
CLASSIC LINE - Calendars - BROWN & BIGELOW, INC.; *pg.* 1624, *pg.* 959
CLASSIC LINEN - Paper - NEENAH PAPER, INC.; *pg.* 1465, *pg.* 484
CLASSIC LINEN DIGITAL - Paper - NEENAH PAPER, INC.; *pg.* 1465, *pg.* 484
CLASSIC LOTTO 47 - Game - MICHIGAN STATE LOTTERY BUREAU; *pg.* 999, *pg.* 895
THE CLASSIC LUXURY EDITION - Athletic Shoes - K-SWISS; *pg.* 1837, *pg.* 306
CLASSIC MAGNA DOODLE - Toy - THE OHIO ART COMPANY, INC.; *pg.* 965, *pg.* 1406
CLASSIC MANOR - Vinyl Fencing - NORTEK, INC.; *pg.* 100, *pg.* 1607
CLASSIC MIDWAY - Brief - JOCKEY INTERNATIONAL, INC.; *pg.* 27, *pg.* 1861
CLASSIC MODE - Musical Instrument - GIBSON GUITAR CORP.; *pg.* 550, *pg.* 1650
CLASSIC NUTRITIONALS - Dog & Cat Foods - FROMM FAMILY PET FOODS, INC.; *pg.* 1476, *pg.* 1870
CLASSIC ORIGINAL - Footwear - K-SWISS; *pg.* 1837, *pg.* 306
CLASSIC PARCHEES - Game - HASBRO, INC.; *pg.* 954, *pg.* 1603
CLASSIC PLUS - Glove - CROSSTEX INTERNATIONAL INC.; *pg.* 1520, *pg.* 1164
CLASSIC PLUSH - Blanket - SELECT COMFORT CORPORATION; *pg.* 942, *pg.* 942
CLASSIC PREMIER - Fencing - MASTER HALCO; *pg.* 96, *pg.* 474
CLASSIC PRODUCT LINE - Lan-Based PC Software Packages - MAJESCO; *pg.* 429, *pg.* 1089
CLASSIC RECTANGULAR - Computer Support Worktools - STEELCASE INC.; *pg.* 475, *pg.* 889
THE CLASSIC REMASTERED - Footwear - K-SWISS; *pg.* 1837, *pg.* 306
CLASSIC REPP - Fabric - NEMSCHOFF, INC.; *pg.* 936, *pg.* 1890
CLASSIC, RETRO, COOL & FUN - Slogan - WINNING MOVES GAMES, INC.; *pg.* 970, *pg.* 816
CLASSIC RX - Pharmacy System - LOZIER CORPORATION; *pg.* 94, *pg.* 1016
CLASSIC RX SYSTEM - Pharmacy Shelving - LOZIER CORPORATION; *pg.* 94, *pg.* 1016
CLASSIC SCHOOL BOOK FAIRS - Educational Materials - SCHOLASTIC INC.; *pg.* 1683, *pg.* 1288
CLASSIC SELECT - Aluminum Brazier - THE VOLLRATH COMPANY LLC; *pg.* 1139, *pg.* 1894
CLASSIC SERIES - Washroom Equipment, Toilet Partitions - BOBRICK WASHROOM EQUIPMENT, INC.; *pg.* 1043, *pg.* 166
CLASSIC SERIES - Steel Office Furniture - INVINCIBLE OFFICE FURNITURE; *pg.* 420, *pg.* 1868
CLASSIC SERIES - Plastic Stack Chair & Student Desks - VIRCO MANUFACTURING CORPORATION; *pg.* 946, *pg.* 297
CLASSIC SEVENS - Video Game - INTERNATIONAL GAME TECHNOLOGY; *pg.* 957, *pg.* 1024
CLASSIC TASTE WITH AN ATTITUDE - Slogan - NIKAIA, INC.; *pg.* 10, *pg.* 765
CLASSIC TORPEDO - Commercial Lighting - SWIVELIER CO., INC.; *pg.* 1307, *pg.* 1142
CLASSIC TOUCH - Binder and Conference Kit - AMERICAN THERMOPLASTIC COMPANY; *pg.* 349, *pg.* 1573
CLASSIC TOUCH - Incliner Mechanisms for Motion Upholstered Furniture - LEGGETT & PLATT, INCORPORATED; *pg.* 933, *pg.* 974
CLASSIC TOY TRAINS - Magazine - KALMBACH PUBLISHING CO.; *pg.* 1656, *pg.* 1898
CLASSIC TRAINS - Magazine - KALMBACH PUBLISHING CO.; *pg.* 1656, *pg.* 1898
CLASSIC TRIO - Pizza - DONATOS PIZZERIA CORPORATION; *pg.* 1727, *pg.* 1439
CLASSIC TV GAME SHOW - Game - WMS INDUSTRIES INC.; *pg.* 593, *pg.* 666
CLASSIC VACATIONS - Travel Information - EXPEDIA, INC.; *pg.* 1244, *pg.* 1814
CLASSIC-VIEW - Door - LARSON MANUFACTURING COMPANY; *pg.* 93, *pg.* 1624
CLASSIC WATERWORKS - Game - WINNING MOVES GAMES, INC.; *pg.* 970, *pg.* 816
CLASSIC WEAVE - Vinyl Soffit - NORTEK, INC.; *pg.* 100, *pg.* 1607
CLASSICA - Lighting System - LITECONTROL CORPORATION; *pg.* 1301, *pg.* 841
CLASSICAL CHORUS - Toy - MATTEL, INC.; *pg.* 962, *pg.* 81
CLASSICAL PRODUCTIONS - Carpet - BEAULIEU GROUP, LLC; *pg.* 917, *pg.* 529
CLASSICBED - Mattress System - TEMPUR SEALY INTERNATIONAL, INC.; *pg.* 944, *pg.* 731
CLASSICBLUE - Hot Melt Dispensing Gun - NORDSON CORPORATION; *pg.* 1365, *pg.* 1480
CLASSICBOARD - Computer Peripheral Equipment - DIGI INTERNATIONAL INC.; *pg.* 387, *pg.* 948
CLASSICDIRECT - Insurance Analysis Tool - STANDARD & POOR'S RATINGS SERVICES; *pg.* 805, *pg.* 1296
CLASSICO - Bath Accessory - CROSCILL, INC.; *pg.* 1122, *pg.* 1220
CLASSICO - Food Products - THE KRAFT HEINZ COMPANY; *pg.* 870, *pg.* 1577
CLASSICPAK - Packaging Product - INTERNATIONAL PAPER COMPANY; *pg.* 1460, *pg.* 1644
CLASSICPAK7WF - Packaging - INTERNATIONAL PAPER COMPANY; *pg.* 1460, *pg.* 1644
CLASSICPILLOW - Pillow - TEMPUR SEALY INTERNATIONAL, INC.; *pg.* 944, *pg.* 731
CLASSICREST - Sleeper - HSM SOLUTIONS; *pg.* 1884, *pg.* 1378
CLASSICS - Golf Shoes - ACUSHNET COMPANY; *pg.* 1824, *pg.* 818
CLASSICS - Area Rugs - COURISTAN INC.; *pg.* 921, *pg.* 1067
CLASSICS - Toy Scale Model Animal - REEVES INTERNATIONAL, INC.; *pg.* 966, *pg.* 1108
CLASSICS DRY - Shoes - ACUSHNET COMPANY; *pg.* 1824, *pg.* 818
CLASSICS DRY PREMIERE - Shoes - ACUSHNET COMPANY; *pg.* 1824, *pg.* 818
CLASSICS PLUS - Sensitive Film & Adhesive - FLEXCON CORPORATION; *pg.* 1457, *pg.* 844
CLASSICS TOUR - Golf Shoe - ACUSHNET COMPANY; *pg.* 1824, *pg.* 818
CLASSIMA - Watches - BAUME & MERCIER, INC.; *pg.* 1, *pg.* 1201
CLASSIQUE - Mirror - CONAIR CORPORATION; *pg.* 505, *pg.* 1055
CLASSIQUE FARE - Waffle, Pancake & Bake Mixes - MODERN PRODUCTS, INC.; *pg.* 1568, *pg.* 1871
CLASSIQUE SPORT - Casuals - HABAND COMPANY, INC.; *pg.* 1772, *pg.* 1099
CLASSIQUES - Apparels - NORDSTROM, INC.; *pg.* 1779, *pg.* 1837
CLASSMATE - Furniture - JASPER GROUP; *pg.* 930, *pg.* 691
CLASSMATES - Social Networking Application - UNITED ONLINE, INC.; *pg.* 1286, *pg.* 308
CLASSPHARMER - Analysis Software - SIMULATIONS PLUS, INC.; *pg.* 470, *pg.* 121
CLASSROOM KEEPERS - Corrugated Boxes - PACON CORPORATION; *pg.* 1466, *pg.* 1852
CLASSROOM RESPONSE SYSTEM - Educational Materials - RENAISSANCE LEARNING, INC.; *pg.* 607, *pg.* 1899
CLASSROOM SELECT - Educational Resources - SCHOOL SPECIALTY, INC.; *pg.* 467, *pg.* 1860
CLASSROOM WIZARD - Software - SCANTRON CORPORATION; *pg.* 467, *pg.* 922
CLASSSTATION - Distance Learning Solutions - POLYCOM, INC.; *pg.* 664, *pg.* 249
CLASSY - Fabric - NEMSCHOFF, INC.; *pg.* 936, *pg.* 1890
CLASSY TINY TRIKE - Ride-ons - RADIO FLYER INC.; *pg.* 966, *pg.* 588
CLAUDETTE - Furniture - ETHAN ALLEN INTERIORS INC.; *pg.* 924, *pg.* 343
CLAUDETTE - Fabric - SCALAMANDRE, INC.; *pg.* 941, *pg.* 1058
CLAUDIA - Bedding - CROSCILL, INC.; *pg.* 1122, *pg.* 1220
CLAUSS - Cutting Tools - ACME UNITED CORPORATION; *pg.* 1040, *pg.* 346
CLAUSS - Cable - THE RIPLEY COMPANY; *pg.* 1305, *pg.* 342
CLAUSSEN - Pickles - THE KRAFT HEINZ COMPANY; *pg.* 870, *pg.* 1577
CLAVAMOX - Pharmaceutical Product - PFIZER INC.; *pg.* 1581, *pg.* 1278
CLAVE - IV Set - HOSPIRA, INC.; *pg.* 1542, *pg.* 623
CLAVE - Medical Product - VICTUS, INC.; *pg.* 1606, *pg.* 447
CLAVIES - Autoclavable Bags - BEL-ART PRODUCTS, INC.; *pg.* 1879, *pg.* 1129
CLAVOS - Furniture - J. ROBERT SCOTT INC.; *pg.* 930, *pg.* 105
CLAYMAX - Geosynthetic Clay Liners - MINERALS TECHNOLOGIES INC.; *pg.* 1173, *pg.* 617
CLAYS CAR - Trail Utility Vehicle - E-Z-GO TEXTRON; *pg.* 1706, *pg.* 525
CLAYTON - Manufactured Homes - CLAYTON HOMES, INC.; *pg.* 1086, *pg.* 1640
CLAYTON - Steam Generator - CLAYTON INDUSTRIES CO.; *pg.* 1323, *pg.* 66
CLAYTON - Fabric - NEMSCHOFF, INC.; *pg.* 936, *pg.* 1890
CLAYTON'S NEXT GENERATION FOUNDATION - Ticket Program - BUCCANEERS LIMITED PARTNERSHIP; *pg.* 534, *pg.* 471
CLC - Curl Activator & Support Lotion - THE GILLETTE COMPANY; *pg.* 509, *pg.* 795
CLC2000 - Medical Device - HOSPIRA, INC.; *pg.* 1542, *pg.* 623
CLE-LINE - Cutting Tools - KENNAMETAL IPG; *pg.* 1353, *pg.* 1615
CLEAN - Semiconductor Batch-Immersion System - AKRION, INC.; *pg.* 1311, *pg.* 1513
CLEAN + EASY - Bodycare & Skincare - AMERICAN INTERNATIONAL INDUSTRIES COMPANY; *pg.* 498, *pg.* 126
CLEAN ACTION - Cleaning Product - HILLYARD, INC.; *pg.* 331, *pg.* 990
CLEAN AIR CHALLENGE - Fund-Raising Slogan - AMERICAN LUNG ASSOCIATION; *pg.* 129, *pg.* 395
CLEAN AIR CHOICE - No-Voc Paint - AKZONOBEL DECORATIVE PAINTS U.S.; *pg.* 1439, *pg.* 1474
CLEAN AIR WEEK - Educational Campaign - AMERICAN

LUNG ASSOCIATION; *pg.* 129, *pg.* 395
CLEAN & CLEAR - Acne Medication - JOHNSON & JOHNSON; *pg.* 1549, *pg.* 1091
CLEAN AND FRESH - Cleaning Product - BRONDOW, INC.; *pg.* 327, *pg.* 1346
CLEAN ASSIST - Cleaners, Disinfectants & Stripers - HILLYARD, INC.; *pg.* 331, *pg.* 990
CLEAN BLAST - Personal Care Product - COLGATE-PALMOLIVE COMPANY; *pg.* 504, *pg.* 1215
CLEAN COTTON - Candle - THE YANKEE CANDLE COMPANY, INC.; *pg.* 1792, *pg.* 843
CLEAN GETAWAY - Flooring - MANNINGTON MILLS, INC.; *pg.* 934, *pg.* 1119
CLEAN GLIDE - Personal Care Product - COLGATE-PALMOLIVE COMPANY; *pg.* 504, *pg.* 1215
CLEAN GO PET - Pet Care Product - PETEDGE; *pg.* 1481, *pg.* 787
CLEAN LASH - Mascara - COVER GIRL COSMETICS; *pg.* 506, *pg.* 772
CLEAN-MASTER - Steam Cleaner - CLAYTON INDUSTRIES CO.; *pg.* 1323, *pg.* 66
CLEAN 'N LIGHT - Vacuum - BISSELL HOMECARE, INC.; *pg.* 52, *pg.* 887
CLEAN PACK - Collection & Disposal of Laboratory Chemicals - CLEAN HARBORS, INC.; *pg.* 376, *pg.* 839
CLEAN PASSAGE - Conveyor - SHUTTLEWORTH, INC.; *pg.* 1375, *pg.* 682
CLEAN PINE - Cleaning Product - BRONDOW, INC.; *pg.* 327, *pg.* 1346
CLEAN PREP - Nail Product - ORLY INTERNATIONAL, INC.; *pg.* 518, *pg.* 137
CLEAN RELEASE - Cleaning Product - HILLYARD, INC.; *pg.* 331, *pg.* 990
CLEAN RELEASE - Identification/Membership Tags - THE STANDARD REGISTER COMPANY; *pg.* 473, *pg.* 1446
CLEAN ROOM - Paper & Nonwoven Material - FIBERMARK INC.; *pg.* 1457, *pg.* 1764
CLEAN ROOM - Ceiling Panel - USG CORPORATION; *pg.* 118, *pg.* 594
CLEAN SCREEN - Skin Care Product - SCOTT'S LIQUID GOLD-INC.; *pg.* 335, *pg.* 323
CLEAN SCRUB - Cleaning Product - HILLYARD, INC.; *pg.* 331, *pg.* 990
CLEAN SHOWER - Cleaner - CHURCH & DWIGHT CO., INC.; *pg.* 1153, *pg.* 1063
CLEAN-SIGHT - Window - WYSSMONT CO., INC.; *pg.* 1390, *pg.* 1068
CLEAN SLATE - Shoe - AEROGROUP INTERNATIONAL, INC.; *pg.* 1803, *pg.* 1055
CLEAN SLOT - Wire - BUFFALO WIRE WORKS CO., INC.; *pg.* 72, *pg.* 1147
CLEAN SWEEP - Household Product - BLUE CROSS LABORATORIES; *pg.* 326, *pg.* 277
CLEAN TAPE - Repair Tape - MCNETT CORPORATION; *pg.* 1839, *pg.* 1817
CLEAN-TEX - Clean Control Product - MILLIKEN & COMPANY; *pg.* 696, *pg.* 1622
CLEAN THRU - Wire - BUFFALO WIRE WORKS CO., INC.; *pg.* 72, *pg.* 1147
CLEAN TRAC - Rubber Studded Mat - THE BILTRITE CORPORATION; *pg.* 1879, *pg.* 850
CLEAN UP! - Hair Care Product - AUBREY ORGANICS INC.; *pg.* 499, *pg.* 470
CLEAN-UP - Cleaning System - THE CLOROX COMPANY; *pg.* 327, *pg.* 169
CLEAN-UP SOLVENT - Automotive Reconditioning Product - MOC PRODUCTS COMPANY, INC.; *pg.* 332, *pg.* 174
CLEAN WATER FOR THE WORLD. - Tagline - INSITUFORM TECHNOLOGIES INC; *pg.* 88, *pg.* 974
CLEAN WEAVE - Wire - BUFFALO WIRE WORKS CO., INC.; *pg.* 72, *pg.* 1147
CLEANBOX - Software - BIO-RAD LABORATORIES, INC.; *pg.* 1504, *pg.* 101
CLEANCAST - Chemical Products - AIR PRODUCTS AND CHEMICALS, INC.; *pg.* 1145, *pg.* 1513
CLEANCUT - Software - BIO-RAD LABORATORIES, INC.; *pg.* 1504, *pg.* 101
CLEANCUT - Kitchen Appliance - HAMILTON BEACH BRANDS, INC.; *pg.* 56, *pg.* 1783
CLEANER - Software - AUTODESK INC.; *pg.* 356, *pg.* 257
CLEANER - Aqueous Cleaner - HUBBARD-HALL, INC.; *pg.* 1167, *pg.* 382
CLEANER CENTRAL - Software - AUTODESK INC.; *pg.* 356, *pg.* 257
CLEANER PLUS - Chemical Product - MILLER-STEPHENSON CHEMICAL COMPANY, INC.; *pg.* 1172, *pg.* 344
CLEANFIRE - Chemical Product - AIR PRODUCTS AND CHEMICALS, INC.; *pg.* 1145, *pg.* 1513
CLEANFLOW - Valves - FLOWSERVE CORPORATION; *pg.* 82, *pg.* 1719
CLEANGARD - Insulation Product - ALPHA ASSOCIATES, INC.; *pg.* 691, *pg.* 1078
CLEANGLIDE1 - Conveyor System - SHUTTLEWORTH, INC.; *pg.* 1375, *pg.* 682
CLEANGUARD - Fire Extinguishers - ANSUL, INCORPORATED; *pg.* 1147, *pg.* 1869
CLEANHEAD - Head Groomer - CONAIR CORPORATION; *pg.* 505, *pg.* 1055
THE CLEANING RESOURCE - Slogan - HILLYARD, INC.; *pg.* 331, *pg.* 990
CLEANLAB - Modular Room - HEMCO CORPORATION; *pg.* 1416, *pg.* 979
CLEANLINE - Solder Paste - ALPHA; *pg.* 1146, *pg.* 1123
CLEANLINE FILTER - Fluid Handling System - GRACO, INC.; *pg.* 1342, *pg.* 935
CLEANORDER - Software - VITRIA TECHNOLOGY, INC.; *pg.* 490, *pg.* 289
CLEANOUT - Homeowner Product - PBI/GORDON CORPORATION; *pg.* 1176, *pg.* 985
CLEANOX - Additive - BASF CATALYSTS LLC; *pg.* 1148, *pg.* 1074
CLEANPAC - Valves - FLOWSERVE CORPORATION; *pg.* 82, *pg.* 1719
CLEANROOM - Low Particulate Electronic Chemicals - ASHLAND INC.; *pg.* 972, *pg.* 726
CLEANS ALL - Automotive Reconditioning Product - MOC PRODUCTS COMPANY, INC.; *pg.* 332, *pg.* 174
CLEANSCREEN - Clothing - LAKELAND INDUSTRIES, INC.; *pg.* 1354, *pg.* 1338
CLEANSE - Spray Tank Cleaner - UNIVERSAL COOPERATIVES, INC.; *pg.* 1482, *pg.* 922
CLEANSHIELD - Medical Applicator Tape - MASIMO CORPORATION; *pg.* 1558, *pg.* 113
CLEANSHOT - Shutoff Valve - GRACO, INC.; *pg.* 1342, *pg.* 935
CLEANSING GEL AND BRUSH - Jewelry Cleaner - CONNOISSEURS PRODUCTS CORPORATION; *pg.* 329, *pg.* 861
CLEANSOURCE - Battery-Free Power Product - ACTIVE POWER, INC.; *pg.* 1310, *pg.* 1660
CLEANSOURCE2 - Power Storage Products - ACTIVE POWER, INC.; *pg.* 1310, *pg.* 1660
CLEANSPRAY - Nozzle Cleaning System - NORDSON CORPORATION; *pg.* 1365, *pg.* 1480
CLEANSTART - Health Care Product - NATURE'S SUNSHINE PRODUCTS, INC.; *pg.* 1571, *pg.* 1754
CLEANSTREAM - Vacuum - AIR TECHNIQUES, INC.; *pg.* 1487, *pg.* 1178
CLEANSTREAM - Fabric - W.L. GORE & ASSOCIATES, INC.; *pg.* 122, *pg.* 388
CLEANSWEEP - Software - SYMANTEC CORPORATION; *pg.* 478, *pg.* 161
CLEANTEAM - Bath & Body Products - KIMBERLY-CLARK CORPORATION; *pg.* 1461, *pg.* 1720
CLEANVIEW - Floor Care Product - BISSELL HOMECARE, INC.; *pg.* 52, *pg.* 887
CLEANWIZ - Plastic & Rubber Material - AXEL PLASTICS RESEARCH LABORATORIES, INC.; *pg.* 326, *pg.* 1356
CLEAR - Ophthalmic Lenses - SIGNET ARMORLITE, INC.; *pg.* 1429, *pg.* 60
CLEAR - Window Cleaner - SWISHER HYGIENE INC.; *pg.* 336, *pg.* 1507
CLEAR-100 - Plunger Seal - WATERS CORPORATION; *pg.* 1436, *pg.* 834
CLEAR ACRYLIC - Paint & Coating - AERVOE INDUSTRIES INCORPORATED; *pg.* 1439, *pg.* 1021
CLEAR ADVANCE - Long-Lasting Care - BLISTEX, INC.; *pg.* 502, *pg.* 644
CLEAR BATH - Water Bath Algae Inhibitor - SPECTRUM LABORATORIES INC.; *pg.* 1595, *pg.* 69
CLEAR BENEFIT - Hair Preparations - THE GILLETTE COMPANY; *pg.* 509, *pg.* 795
CLEAR-CATH - Medical Device - HOSPIRA, INC.; *pg.* 1542, *pg.* 623
CLEAR CHOICE - Food Product - BUNGE LIMITED; *pg.* 842, *pg.* 1351
THE CLEAR CHOICE - Slogan - RADIO FREQUENCY SYSTEMS, INC.; *pg.* 666, *pg.* 354
CLEAR CLEAN - Toothpaste - KAO BRANDS CO. INC.; *pg.* 513, *pg.* 1415
CLEAR COMMAND - Helmet Communication System - MINE SAFETY APPLIANCES COMPANY; *pg.* 1361, *pg.* 1525
CLEAR CUTS - Boneless, Butterfly & Natural Trout Fillets - CLEAR SPRINGS FOODS, INC.; *pg.* 848, *pg.* 548
CLEAR DIFFERENCE - Hair Setting Gel - THE GILLETTE COMPANY; *pg.* 509, *pg.* 795
CLEAR DIP - Oral Hygiene Aids - SUNSTAR AMERICAS INC.; *pg.* 1599, *pg.* 591
CLEAR ENERGY - Health Supplement - GARDEN OF LIFE, INC.; *pg.* 1532, *pg.* 478
CLEAR EYES - Healthcare Product - PRESTIGE BRANDS HOLDINGS, INC.; *pg.* 520, *pg.* 1345
CLEAR FLEX - Liquid Rubber - SMOOTH-ON INC.; *pg.* 111, *pg.* 1528
CLEAR FOCUS JETVUE - Pressure Sensitive Vinyl - TRANSILWRAP COMPANY, INC.; *pg.* 1470, *pg.* 613
CLEAR-GLO - Acrylic Surface Sealer - CALIFORNIA PRODUCTS CORPORATION; *pg.* 1441, *pg.* 781
CLEAR GO - Urethane Belts - FENNER DRIVES; *pg.* 1336, *pg.* 1551
CLEAR MOBILE - Wireless Communication Product - PURPLE COMMUNICATIONS, INC.; *pg.* 457, *pg.* 194
CLEAR PAK - Films - DAUBERT INDUSTRIES, INC.; *pg.* 1155, *pg.* 561
CLEAR PERFORMANCE - Carpet - BEAULIEU GROUP, LLC; *pg.* 917, *pg.* 529
CLEAR SCALP & HAIR THERAPY - Hair Care Products - UNILEVER UNITED STATES, INC.; *pg.* 904, *pg.* 1061
CLEAR SIGNALTM - Zip Cables - COLEMAN CABLE, INC.; *pg.* 1324, *pg.* 665
CLEAR SOLUTIONS IN A COMPLEX WORLD - Tag Line - LINCOLN NATIONAL CORPORATION; *pg.* 776, *pg.* 1567
CLEAR SPRING - Grain Alcohol - JIM BEAM BRANDS CO.; *pg.* 1965, *pg.* 601
CLEAR SPRINGS KITCHEN - Rainbow Trout Fillet - CLEAR SPRINGS FOODS, INC.; *pg.* 848, *pg.* 548
CLEAR VALLEY - Canola Oil - CARGILL, INC.; *pg.* 845, *pg.* 965
CLEAR VOICE - Hearing Aid Circuits - BELTONE ELECTRONICS LLC; *pg.* 1503, *pg.* 614
CLEAR VUE - Metal Building System - BUTLER MANUFACTURING COMPANY; *pg.* 72, *pg.* 981
CLEAR-VUE - Bathroom Accessories - SYMMONS INDUSTRIES, INC.; *pg.* 114, *pg.* 803
CLEAR WATER - Water Filtration System - ANAHEIM MANUFACTURING COMPANY; *pg.* 51, *pg.* 48
CLEAR WAVE - Water Conditioners - FIELD CONTROLS LLC; *pg.* 1071, *pg.* 1380
CLEARANCE WORLD - Home Decor Furnishings & Accessories - HANOVER DIRECT, INC.; *pg.* 1772, *pg.* 1130
CLEARANCEJOBS.COM - Recruiting & Career Development Website - DHI GROUP, INC.; *pg.* 1238, *pg.* 1223
CLEARASIL - Skin Care Product - RECKITT BENCKISER INC.; *pg.* 1136, *pg.* 1105
CLEARBLUE - Pregnancy & Fertility Test Products - ALERE INC.; *pg.* 1488, *pg.* 849
CLEARBLUE EASY - Personal & Household Product - THE PROCTER & GAMBLE COMPANY; *pg.* 1129, *pg.* 1418
CLEARBREW - Brewing Adjuncts - CARGILL LIMITED; *pg.* 1475, *pg.* 1914
CLEARCOLOUR - Paint - ROSCO LABORATORIES, INC.; *pg.* 1782, *pg.* 378
CLEARCOURSE - Insurance Coverage - GENWORTH FINANCIAL, INC.; *pg.* 761, *pg.* 1802
CLEARCOVER - License Plate Covers - MACNEIL AUTOMOTIVE PRODUCTS, LTD.; *pg.* 211, *pg.* 559
CLEARCUT - Digital Video Product - HARMONIC, INC.; *pg.* 402, *pg.* 246
CLEARDEX - Corn Syrup - CARGILL, INC.; *pg.* 845, *pg.* 965
CLEARDEX - Corn Syrup - CARGILL LIMITED; *pg.* 1475, *pg.* 1914
CLEARFIELD - Seed Corn - MOEWS SEED CO., INC.; *pg.* 1797, *pg.* 616
CLEARFIELD - Cheese - SCHREIBER FOODS, INC.; *pg.* 894, *pg.* 1859
CLEARFRAME - Car Accessories - MACNEIL AUTOMOTIVE PRODUCTS, LTD.; *pg.* 211, *pg.* 559
CLEARFRUIT - Soft Drink - NATIONAL BEVERAGE CORP.; *pg.* 257, *pg.* 425
CLEARFUTURE - 401(k) Portfolio Management Application - MORNINGSTAR, INC.; *pg.* 784, *pg.* 583
CLEARGLIDE - Wire Pulling Lubricant - IDEAL INDUSTRIES, INC.; *pg.* 1051, *pg.* 662

First page reference indicates Business Class Edition
Second page reference indicates Geographic Edition

CLEARGLIDE - Healthcare Product - JOHNSON & JOHNSON; *pg.* 1549, *pg.* 1091
CLEARGUIDE - Endoscopic Vessel Harvesting System - MAQUET; *pg.* 1558, *pg.* 1082
CLEARLANE - Liquid - CARGILL LIMITED; *pg.* 1475, *pg.* 1914
CLEARLINK - Tubing & Access Device - BAXTER INTERNATIONAL INC.; *pg.* 1499, *pg.* 599
CLEARLY BOUND - Polypropylene Product - AMERICAN THERMOPLASTIC COMPANY; *pg.* 349, *pg.* 1573
CLEARLY THE WORLD'S BEST - Slogan - WINEGARD COMPANY; *pg.* 688, *pg.* 702
CLEARLYTE - Chemical Coating - ENTHONE INC.; *pg.* 1161, *pg.* 381
CLEARMOL - Pesticide - MCLAUGHLIN GORMLEY KING COMPANY; *pg.* 1797, *pg.* 939
CLEARMOTIV - LCD Display - VIEWSONIC CORPORATION; *pg.* 489, *pg.* 303
CLEARONE - Resistor Networks - CTS CORPORATION; *pg.* 631, *pg.* 677
CLEARPICTURE - LCD Technology - VIEWSONIC CORPORATION; *pg.* 489, *pg.* 303
CLEARPLAN - Healthcare Product - ALERE INC.; *pg.* 1488, *pg.* 849
CLEARSCALE - Software - AUTODESK INC.; *pg.* 356, *pg.* 257
CLEARSEAL - Plastics Product - AEP INDUSTRIES INC.; *pg.* 1878, *pg.* 1085
CLEARSIGHT - Lens - DANKER LABORATORIES INC.; *pg.* 1408, *pg.* 465
CLEARSIGHT THIN - Lens - DANKER LABORATORIES INC.; *pg.* 1408, *pg.* 465
CLEARSIGNAL - Speaker Cables - COLEMAN CABLE, INC.; *pg.* 1324, *pg.* 665
CLEARSITE - Medical Equipment - CONMED CORPORATION; *pg.* 1517, *pg.* 1347
CLEARSKIN - Beauty Product - AVON PRODUCTS, INC.; *pg.* 500, *pg.* 1198
CLEARSOL GUMS - High-Oxidized Corn Starches - PENFORD CORPORATION; *pg.* 1177, *pg.* 314
CLEARSPIN - Software - BIO-RAD LABORATORIES, INC.; *pg.* 1504, *pg.* 101
CLEARSWEET - Dextrose - CARGILL, INC.; *pg.* 845, *pg.* 965
CLEARSWEET - High Maltose Corn Syrup - CARGILL LIMITED; *pg.* 1475, *pg.* 1914
CLEARTEK - Touch Screen - 3M COMPANY; *pg.* 1142, *pg.* 956
CLEARTEK - Imaging Technology - 3M TOUCH SYSTEMS, INC.; *pg.* 339, *pg.* 833
CLEARTRACE - Medical Equipment - CONMED CORPORATION; *pg.* 1517, *pg.* 1347
CLEARTRAP - Clear Corneal Knives - SURGICAL SPECIALTIES CORPORATION; *pg.* 1600, *pg.* 1912
CLEARVAC - Software - BIO-RAD LABORATORIES, INC.; *pg.* 1504, *pg.* 101
CLEARVIEW - Rapid Membrane Test Products - ALERE INC.; *pg.* 1488, *pg.* 849
CLEARVIEW - Floor Care Product - BISSELL HOMECARE, INC.; *pg.* 52, *pg.* 887
CLEARVIEW - Cassette - CLEARFIELD, INC.; *pg.* 1406, *pg.* 953
CLEARVIEW - Vision System - LEAR CORPORATION; *pg.* 229, *pg.* 907
CLEARVIEW - Eye Protection Product - MINE SAFETY APPLIANCES COMPANY; *pg.* 1361, *pg.* 1525
CLEARVIEW - Container - PACTIV CORPORATION; *pg.* 1466, *pg.* 624
CLEARVIEW - Plastic Houseware Product - STERILITE CORPORATION; *pg.* 1138, *pg.* 848
CLEARVIEW-CS - X-Ray System - FUJIFILM MEDICAL SYSTEMS USA, INC.; *pg.* 1531, *pg.* 374
CLEARVIEW-D - Upright Image Reader - FUJIFILM MEDICAL SYSTEMS USA, INC.; *pg.* 1531, *pg.* 374
CLEARVIEW-ES - Upright Image Reader - FUJIFILM MEDICAL SYSTEMS USA, INC.; *pg.* 1531, *pg.* 374
CLEARVISION - Telephones - MOTOROLA SOLUTIONS, INC.; *pg.* 657, *pg.* 659
CLEARVOX - Communication Headset Product - PLANTRONICS, INC.; *pg.* 663, *pg.* 270
CLEARVUE - Eyewear - MINE SAFETY APPLIANCES COMPANY; *pg.* 1361, *pg.* 1525
CLEARVUE - Professional Auto Glass Cleaner - TURTLE WAX, INC.; *pg.* 220, *pg.* 671
CLEARWATER CITIZEN - Newspaper - TAMPA BAY NEWSPAPERS, INC.; *pg.* 1691, *pg.* 468
CLECINFO - Competitive Local Exchange Carrier Tool - PITNEY BOWES SOFTWARE INC.; *pg.* 455, *pg.* 1346
CLEEN-ABLE - Reusable Blood Pressure Cuff - VITAL SIGNS, INC.; *pg.* 1607, *pg.* 1126
CLEMATIS - Fabric - NEMSCHOFF, INC.; *pg.* 936, *pg.* 1890
CLENCHER - MCC Connectors - KILLARK ELECTRIC; *pg.* 1300, *pg.* 998
CLENZOLOGY - Personal Hygiene Product - GARDEN OF LIFE, INC.; *pg.* 1532, *pg.* 478
CLEO - Clothing - ABERCROMBIE & FITCH CO.; *pg.* 37, *pg.* 1466
CLEOCIN - Medicine - PFIZER INC.; *pg.* 1581, *pg.* 1278
CLEOCIN HCL - Pharmaceutical Product - PFIZER INC.; *pg.* 1581, *pg.* 1278
CLEOCIN PEDIATRIC - Pharmaceutical Product - PFIZER INC.; *pg.* 1581, *pg.* 1278
CLEOCIN PHOSPHATE - Pharmaceutical Product - PFIZER INC.; *pg.* 1581, *pg.* 1278
CLEOCIN T - Pharmaceutical Product - PFIZER INC.; *pg.* 1581, *pg.* 1278
CLEOPATRA - Slots - INTERNATIONAL GAME TECHNOLOGY; *pg.* 957, *pg.* 1024
CLEOPATRA - Fabric - NEMSCHOFF, INC.; *pg.* 936, *pg.* 1890
CLEVELAND - Drills - KENNAMETAL INC.; *pg.* 1052, *pg.* 1547
CLEVELAND BARONS - Sport Good Product - CLEVELAND CAVALIERS/QUICKEN LOANS ARENA; *pg.* 541, *pg.* 1429
CLEVELAND CAVALIERS - Professional Sports Team - CLEVELAND CAVALIERS/QUICKEN LOANS ARENA; *pg.* 541, *pg.* 1429
CLEVELAND HOME DECOR - Home Decorating Magazine - GREAT LAKES PUBLISHING COMPANY; *pg.* 1646, *pg.* 1431
CLEVELAND MAGAZINE - Magazine - GREAT LAKES PUBLISHING COMPANY; *pg.* 1646, *pg.* 1431
CLEVER GEAR & OTHER SMART INNOVATIONS - Mail Order Catalog - JOHNSON SMITH COMPANY; *pg.* 1774, *pg.* 414
CLEVERPATH - Software - CA TECHNOLOGIES; *pg.* 366, *pg.* 1168
CLEVIDIPINE - Pharmaceutical Products - THE MEDICINES COMPANY; *pg.* 1561, *pg.* 1104
CLEVIPREX - Pharmaceutical Products - THE MEDICINES COMPANY; *pg.* 1561, *pg.* 1104
CLEVITE - Engine Parts - DANA HOLDING CORPORATION; *pg.* 203, *pg.* 1461
CLEVITE - Elastomer - TENNECO, INC.; *pg.* 985, *pg.* 625
CLEVITE ELASTOMERS - Noise Vibration Control Systems - TENNECO, INC.; *pg.* 985, *pg.* 625
CLEVVER.COM - Website - DEFYMEDIA; *pg.* 1237, *pg.* 1222
CLGA - Socket Connector - AMPHENOL CORPORATION; *pg.* 616, *pg.* 381
CLIC AQUI - Telephone Service - IDT CORPORATION; *pg.* 643, *pg.* 1096
CLIC IT - Lip Color - THE BONNE BELL COMPANY; *pg.* 502, *pg.* 1480
CLIC-LOC - Child Resistant Closures - OWENS-ILLINOIS, INC.; *pg.* 1466, *pg.* 1470
CLIC STIC - Card - BROWN & BIGELOW, INC.; *pg.* 1624, *pg.* 959
CLICK - Door Accessory - SOUTHCO, INC.; *pg.* 1063, *pg.* 1522
CLICK 2 MAIL - Postal Services - UNITED STATES POSTAL SERVICE; *pg.* 1009, *pg.* 406
CLICK AND STAY - Plastic Screw Caps - MACNEIL AUTOMOTIVE PRODUCTS, LTD.; *pg.* 211, *pg.* 559
CLICK & VIEW - Visual Layout Tool - POLYCOM, INC.; *pg.* 664, *pg.* 249
CLICK-CLACK - Shoes - UNDER ARMOUR, INC.; *pg.* 49, *pg.* 759
CLICK. DONE. - Slogan - CONCUR TECHNOLOGIES, INC.; *pg.* 1236, *pg.* 1813
CLICK INTERACTIVE LEARNING CLUB - Educational Materials - SCHOLASTIC INC.; *pg.* 1683, *pg.* 1288
CLICK-IT - Molecular Probe Product - THERMO FISHER SCIENTIFIC INC.; *pg.* 1602, *pg.* 61
CLICK 'N SAVE - Travel Service - SOUTHWEST AIRLINES CO.; *pg.* 1923, *pg.* 1687
CLICK-N-SHIP - Postal Services - UNITED STATES POSTAL SERVICE; *pg.* 1009, *pg.* 406
CLICK, PAY AND SAIL AWAY - Slogan - AT&T SOUTHEAST; *pg.* 1868, *pg.* 489
CLICK START - Toys - LEAPFROG ENTERPRISES, INC.; *pg.* 961, *pg.* 84
CLICK-TIP - Injection Needle - CONMED CORPORATION; *pg.* 1517, *pg.* 1347
CLICK2COACH - Software - ENVISION; *pg.* 393, *pg.* 1835
CLICK2COACH MULTISITE ADDITION - Software - ENVISION; *pg.* 393, *pg.* 1835
CLICK2LEARN - Software - SUMTOTAL SYSTEMS, INC.; *pg.* 477, *pg.* 429
CLICK2RESERVE - Telephone Service - IDT CORPORATION; *pg.* 643, *pg.* 1096
CLICK2TAKE - Telephone Service - IDT CORPORATION; *pg.* 643, *pg.* 1096
CLICKCAD - Educational Program - ICAD, INC.; *pg.* 643, *pg.* 1037
CLICKER - Remote Control Device - UNIVERSAL ELECTRONICS, INC.; *pg.* 683, *pg.* 262
CLICKON - Software - THE SSI GROUP, INC.; *pg.* 473, *pg.* 7
CLICKON ALLNET - Software - THE SSI GROUP, INC.; *pg.* 473, *pg.* 7
CLICKON PREVENT - Software - THE SSI GROUP, INC.; *pg.* 473, *pg.* 7
CLICKSTOP - Medical Product - PROPPER MANUFACTURING COMPANY, INC.; *pg.* 1586, *pg.* 1175
CLICK'X - Pedicle Screw System - DEPUY SYNTHES; *pg.* 1523, *pg.* 1593
CLIENT APPLICATION MANAGER - Software - WEBSENSE, INC.; *pg.* 491, *pg.* 210
CLIENT CONSOLE - Payment Management Tool - ACI WORLDWIDE; *pg.* 710, *pg.* 1777
CLIENT POLICY MANAGER - Software - WEBSENSE, INC.; *pg.* 491, *pg.* 210
CLIENT32 - Computer Software - NOVELL INC.; *pg.* 446, *pg.* 852
CLIENTELE - Software - EPICOR SOFTWARE CORPORATION; *pg.* 393, *pg.* 110
CLIENTEXPRESS - Facsimile Equipment - MURATEC AMERICA, INC.; *pg.* 443, *pg.* 1733
CLIENTPAK - Software - EMC CORPORATION; *pg.* 391, *pg.* 825
CLIENTWARE - Software - COMPUTER PROGRAMS & SYSTEMS, INC.; *pg.* 378, *pg.* 7
CLIF SHOT - Food Product - CLIF BAR INC.; *pg.* 848, *pg.* 83
CLIF SHOT BLOKS - Food Product - CLIF BAR INC.; *pg.* 848, *pg.* 83
CLIFFHANGER - Super Swing Thrill Ride - CANADA'S WONDERLAND COMPANY; *pg.* 536, *pg.* 1947
CLIFFORD - Automobile Electronics - DEI HOLDINGS, INC.; *pg.* 633, *pg.* 302
CLIFFSNOTES - Literature Guides - JOHN WILEY & SONS, INC.; *pg.* 1655, *pg.* 1073
CLIFTON - Medical Stool - BLICKMAN HEALTH INDUSTRIES, INC.; *pg.* 1506, *pg.* 1051
CLII - Apparel - CHEROKEE GLOBAL BRANDS; *pg.* 21, *pg.* 278
CLIK-MATE - Electronic Components - MOLEX INCORPORATED; *pg.* 655, *pg.* 628
CLIMA-FIT - Apparel - NIKE, INC.; *pg.* 1812, *pg.* 1492
CLIMAGUARD - Glass Product - GUARDIAN INDUSTRIES CORP.; *pg.* 85, *pg.* 869
CLIMAGUARD RLF - Glass Product - GUARDIAN INDUSTRIES CORP.; *pg.* 85, *pg.* 869
CLIMAGUARD SPF - Glass Product - GUARDIAN INDUSTRIES CORP.; *pg.* 85, *pg.* 869
CLIMAPLUS - Ceiling Panel - USG CORPORATION; *pg.* 118, *pg.* 594
CLIMATE CONTROL PERFORMANCE - Shoe And Glove - ACUSHNET COMPANY; *pg.* 1824, *pg.* 818
CLIMATE PRO - Fiber Glass Insulation - JOHNS MANVILLE CORPORATION; *pg.* 89, *pg.* 320
CLIMATE ZONE - Wall Coating - THE VALSPAR CORPORATION; *pg.* 1449, *pg.* 945
CLIMATESEEK.COM - Website - INTELIMAX MEDIA INC.; *pg.* 1259, *pg.* 1911
CLIMB - Pharmaceutical Product - ASTEX PHARMACEUTICALS, INC; *pg.* 1497, *pg.* 77
CLIMBINGPRO - Ladder Product - WERNER HOLDING CO.; *pg.* 121, *pg.* 1534
CLINAC - Medical Linear Accelerators - VARIAN MEDICAL SYSTEMS, INC.; *pg.* 1434, *pg.* 178
CLINBASE - Information Management System - PAREXEL INTERNATIONAL CORPORATION; *pg.* 1580, *pg.* 853
CLINCH-LOK - Vehicle System - MACLEAN-FOGG COMPANY INC.; *pg.* 1358, *pg.* 635

CLINCHECK - Dental Medicine - ALIGN TECHNOLOGY, INC.; *pg.* 1489, *pg.* 237
CLINCHER - Pharmaceutical Products - ABBOTT LABORATORIES; *pg.* 1484, *pg.* 551
CLINCHER - Herbicide - DOW AGROSCIENCES LLC; *pg.* 1156, *pg.* 684
CLINCHER - Wiring Accessory - PANDUIT CORP.; *pg.* 661, *pg.* 663
CLINDAGEL - Topical Drug - GALDERMA LABORATORIES, L.P.; *pg.* 1532, *pg.* 1695
CLINDAMYCIN - Pharmaceutical Product - LANNETT COMPANY, INC.; *pg.* 1555, *pg.* 1566
CLINDAREACH - Biopharmaceutical Product - DUSA PHARMACEUTICALS, INC.; *pg.* 1525, *pg.* 860
CLINFORCE - Staffing Services - CROSS COUNTRY HEALTHCARE, INC.; *pg.* 1520, *pg.* 411
CLING - Plastic Film - AEP INDUSTRIES INC.; *pg.* 1878, *pg.* 1085
CLING-MATE - Printable Plastic Product - TRANSILWRAP COMPANY, INC.; *pg.* 1470, *pg.* 613
CLINGCLASSIC - Plastic Film - AEP INDUSTRIES INC.; *pg.* 1878, *pg.* 1085
CLINGMASTER - Laundry Wrap Film - AEP INDUSTRIES INC.; *pg.* 1878, *pg.* 1085
CLINGZ - Printable Plastic Product - TRANSILWRAP COMPANY, INC.; *pg.* 1470, *pg.* 613
CLINI-RF - Cryostat - HACKER INSTRUMENTS & INDUSTRIES INC.; *pg.* 1415, *pg.* 1623
CLINIC - Fabric - NEMSCHOFF, INC.; *pg.* 936, *pg.* 1890
THE CLINICAL ADVANTAGE - Slogan - KINETIC CONCEPTS, INC.; *pg.* 1553, *pg.* 1741
CLINICAL CAREADVANCE - Software - TRIZETTO CORPORATION; *pg.* 485, *pg.* 327
CLINICAL TRIAL MANAGEMENT SYSTEM (CTMS) - Report - DATATRAK INTERNATIONAL, INC.; *pg.* 383, *pg.* 1462
CLINICALOGIC - Software - TRIZETTO CORPORATION; *pg.* 485, *pg.* 327
CLINICARE - Pharmaceutical Products - ABBOTT LABORATORIES; *pg.* 1484, *pg.* 551
CLINIMIX - Healthcare Product - BAXTER INTERNATIONAL INC.; *pg.* 1499, *pg.* 599
CLINIMIX E - Healthcare Product - BAXTER INTERNATIONAL INC.; *pg.* 1499, *pg.* 599
CLINIQUE - Beauty Products - THE ESTEE LAUDER COMPANIES INC.; *pg.* 508, *pg.* 1229
CLINIQUE MEDICAL - Medical Aesthetics - ALLERGAN, INC.; *pg.* 1491, *pg.* 106
CLINITREND - Software - AMERICAN SOCIETY OF HEALTH-SYSTEM PHARMACISTS; *pg.* 131, *pg.* 761
CLINITRON - Air Fluidized Therapy Bed - HILL-ROM HOLDINGS, INC.; *pg.* 1542, *pg.* 673
CLINOLEIC - Healthcare Product - BAXTER INTERNATIONAL INC.; *pg.* 1499, *pg.* 599
CLINOMYN - Pharmaceutical Product - FLEET LABORATORIES; *pg.* 1531, *pg.* 1787
CLINPRO - Sealant - 3M COMPANY; *pg.* 1142, *pg.* 956
CLINSWOUND - Wound Cleanser - ALIMED, INC.; *pg.* 1490, *pg.* 816
CLINTON - Clinical Furniture - ALIMED, INC.; *pg.* 1490, *pg.* 816
CLINTOSE - Non-Sweet & Bland Sweetener for Food Products - ARCHER-DANIELS-MIDLAND COMPANY; *pg.* 825, *pg.* 565
CLINTOSE CR 18 - Saccharide - ARCHER-DANIELS-MIDLAND COMPANY; *pg.* 825, *pg.* 565
CLINTOSE CR 24 - Saccharide - ARCHER-DANIELS-MIDLAND COMPANY; *pg.* 825, *pg.* 565
CLINTOSE CR10 - Saccharide - ARCHER-DANIELS-MIDLAND COMPANY; *pg.* 825, *pg.* 565
CLINTOSE CR15 - Saccharide - ARCHER-DANIELS-MIDLAND COMPANY; *pg.* 825, *pg.* 565
CLIP - Current Limiting Protector - G&W ELECTRIC COMPANY; *pg.* 1338, *pg.* 558
CLIP CUP - Clip - BROWN & BIGELOW, INC.; *pg.* 1624, *pg.* 959
CLIP-EYELET - Spray Product - SPRAYING SYSTEMS CO.; *pg.* 1063, *pg.* 670
CLIP HANGERS - Hangers - MOORE PUSH PIN CO.; *pg.* 441, *pg.* 1595
CLIP IT - Stretcher Bar Clips - MOORE PUSH PIN CO.; *pg.* 441, *pg.* 1595
CLIP 'N' JECT - Drug Administration System - WEST PHARMACEUTICAL SERVICES, INC.; *pg.* 1472, *pg.* 1532
CLIP 'N STICK - Balloon - CONTINENTAL AMERICAN CORP.; *pg.* 1880, *pg.* 723
CLIPIT - Video Game - INTERNATIONAL GAME TECHNOLOGY; *pg.* 957, *pg.* 1024
CLIPLOK - Electronic Components - MOLEX INCORPORATED; *pg.* 655, *pg.* 628
CLIPMATE - Flashlight - STREAMLIGHT INC.; *pg.* 1306, *pg.* 1527
CLIPO - Toy & Game - HASBRO, INC.; *pg.* 954, *pg.* 1603
CLIPPABLES - Cleaner - BROWN & BIGELOW, INC.; *pg.* 1624, *pg.* 959
CLIPPER - Air Screen Cleaner - A.T. FERRELL COMPANY, INC.; *pg.* 701, *pg.* 674
CLIPPER - Wire Hook - FLEXIBLE STEEL LACING COMPANY; *pg.* 1337, *pg.* 608
CLIPPER - Circular Cloth Cutter - THE WOLF MACHINE CO.; *pg.* 1389, *pg.* 1427
CLIPPER II - Helicopter - ROBINSON HELICOPTER COMPANY; *pg.* 234, *pg.* 295
CLIPPERCOOL - Cooling Spray - PETEDGE; *pg.* 1481, *pg.* 787
CLIPPET - Small Animal Clipper & Trimmer - ANDIS COMPANY; *pg.* 498, *pg.* 1895
CLIQ - Cellular Telephone - MOTOROLA SOLUTIONS, INC.; *pg.* 657, *pg.* 659
CLIQUE - Fabric - NEMSCHOFF, INC.; *pg.* 936, *pg.* 1890
CLIRPATH TURBO - Excimer Laser System - THE SPECTRANETICS CORPORATION; *pg.* 1595, *pg.* 315
CLM-3D - Electron Microscope - FEI COMPANY; *pg.* 1413, *pg.* 1498
CLOCK-KALIPER - Pipeline - T.D. WILLIAMSON, INC.; *pg.* 1380, *pg.* 1490
CLOCKWORK - Furniture - HAWORTH, INC.; *pg.* 402, *pg.* 891
CLOG BUSTER - Drainage Product - OATEY SUPPLY CHAIN SERVICES; *pg.* 30, *pg.* 1433
THE CLOISTER - Resort Hotel - SEA ISLAND ACQUISITION LLC; *pg.* 1111, *pg.* 540
CLOLAR - Oncology - GENZYME CORPORATION; *pg.* 1534, *pg.* 808
CLONASE - Molecular Biology Product - THERMO FISHER SCIENTIFIC INC.; *pg.* 1602, *pg.* 61
CLONDIAG - Pharmaceutical Product - ALERE INC.; *pg.* 1488, *pg.* 849
CLONE - Glove - KOMBI, LTD.; *pg.* 1838, *pg.* 1766
CLONECHECKER - Molecular Biology Product - THERMO FISHER SCIENTIFIC INC.; *pg.* 1602, *pg.* 61
CLONEMINER - Molecular Biology Product - THERMO FISHER SCIENTIFIC INC.; *pg.* 1602, *pg.* 61
CLONERANGER - Molecular Biology Product - THERMO FISHER SCIENTIFIC INC.; *pg.* 1602, *pg.* 61
CLONEWELL - Molecular Biology Product - THERMO FISHER SCIENTIFIC INC.; *pg.* 1602, *pg.* 61
CLONIS - Software - BIO-RAD LABORATORIES, INC.; *pg.* 1504, *pg.* 101
CLONTARF IRISH - Whiskey - CASTLE BRANDS INC.; *pg.* 239, *pg.* 1209
CLOPAMID - Pharmaceutical Product - VALEANT PHARMACEUTICALS INTERNATIONAL; *pg.* 1605, *pg.* 1047
CLOPAY - Garage Doors - CLOPAY BUILDING PRODUCTS COMPANY; *pg.* 76, *pg.* 1459
CLORALEN - Cleaning Product - ALEN AMERICAS INC.; *pg.* 325, *pg.* 1699
CLORINDA - Bleach - THE CLOROX COMPANY; *pg.* 327, *pg.* 169
CLORISOL - Bleach - THE CLOROX COMPANY; *pg.* 327, *pg.* 169
CLOROX - Power Equipment - ECHO INCORPORATED; *pg.* 1046, *pg.* 626
CLOROX 2 - Dry, Liquid, All-Fabric & Color-Safe Bleaches & Bleach-Free Laundry Booster - THE CLOROX COMPANY; *pg.* 327, *pg.* 169
CLOROX ANYWHERE - Anti-Allergen Fabric Spray - THE CLOROX COMPANY; *pg.* 327, *pg.* 169
CLOROX ANYWHERE HARD SURFACE - Daily Sanitizing Spray - THE CLOROX COMPANY; *pg.* 327, *pg.* 169
CLOROX BLEACH PEN - Stain Remover - THE CLOROX COMPANY; *pg.* 327, *pg.* 169
CLOROX CLEAN-UP - Dilutable Household Cleaner, Spray Cleaner & Gel - THE CLOROX COMPANY; *pg.* 327, *pg.* 169
CLOROX COMMERCIAL SOLUTIONS - Hand Sanitizing Spray - THE CLOROX COMPANY; *pg.* 327, *pg.* 169
CLOROX FRESHCARE - Fabric Refresher - THE CLOROX COMPANY; *pg.* 327, *pg.* 169
CLOROX GENTLE - Color-Safe Bleach - THE CLOROX COMPANY; *pg.* 327, *pg.* 169
CLOROX PLUS - Anti-Allergen Bleach - THE CLOROX COMPANY; *pg.* 327, *pg.* 169
CLOROX SCOOBA - Hard Floor Cleaner - THE CLOROX COMPANY; *pg.* 327, *pg.* 169
CLOROX STAIN OUT - Soil & Stain Remover - THE CLOROX COMPANY; *pg.* 327, *pg.* 169
CLOROX ULTIMATE CARE - Premium Bleach - THE CLOROX COMPANY; *pg.* 327, *pg.* 169
CLOROX2 - Bleach - THE CLOROX COMPANY; *pg.* 327, *pg.* 169
CLOS DU BOIS - Wine - CONSTELLATION BRANDS, INC.; *pg.* 1960, *pg.* 1348
CLOS DU BOIS - Wine - JIM BEAM BRANDS CO.; *pg.* 1965, *pg.* 601
CLOSE REACH - Bath Product - KOHLER CO.; *pg.* 91, *pg.* 1862
CLOSE TO METAL - Chipset - ADVANCED MICRO DEVICES, INC.; *pg.* 613, *pg.* 282
CLOSEOUTCENTRAL.COM - Website - SUMNER COMMUNICATIONS INC.; *pg.* 1690, *pg.* 338
CLOSER TO THE HEART - Slogan - MASIMO CORPORATION; *pg.* 1558, *pg.* 113
CLOSETECH SEAMERS - Pharmaceutical Product - PNEUMATICSCALEANGELUS; *pg.* 1369, *pg.* 1445
CLOSETMAID - Vinyl Coated Steel Rod Shelving, Storage Products, Closet Organizers - CLOSETMAID CORPORATION; *pg.* 920, *pg.* 452
CLOSETMAID - Drawer System - LOWE'S COMPANIES, INC.; *pg.* 1053, *pg.* 1383
CLOSIERIE - Furniture - HOOKER FURNITURE CORPORATION; *pg.* 928, *pg.* 1788
CLOSITS - Modular Closet Organization System - SAUDER WOODWORKING CO.; *pg.* 941, *pg.* 1403
CLOTHMASTER - Cloth Replacement Wiper - GEORGIA-PACIFIC LLC; *pg.* 1458, *pg.* 507
CLOTTRAC - Coagulation Tester - MEDTRONIC, INC.; *pg.* 1564, *pg.* 939
CLOUD - Fabric - NEMSCHOFF, INC.; *pg.* 936, *pg.* 1890
CLOUD 9 - Fabric - NEUTRAL POSTURE, INC.; *pg.* 939, *pg.* 1669
CLOUD CHEST - Furniture - J. ROBERT SCOTT INC.; *pg.* 930, *pg.* 105
CLOUD FLEECE - Gowns - HABAND COMPANY, INC.; *pg.* 1772, *pg.* 1099
CLOUD FREE - Cleaning Product - ORECK CORPORATION; *pg.* 59, *pg.* 1653
CLOUDWORX - Software - BENTLEY SYSTEMS, INC.; *pg.* 361, *pg.* 1531
CLOUDY BAY - Wine - MOET HENNESSY; *pg.* 1966, *pg.* 1260
CLOUT - Fabric - NEMSCHOFF, INC.; *pg.* 936, *pg.* 1890
CLOVE LOVE - Sofa - OVERSTOCK.COM, INC.; *pg.* 1273, *pg.* 1760
CLOVER - Grinding & Lapping Compounds - HENKEL CORPORATION; *pg.* 1049, *pg.* 369
CLOVER - Coffee Brewing System - STARBUCKS CORPORATION; *pg.* 897, *pg.* 1840
CLOVER BLOOM - Twist Tobacco - AMERICAN SNUFF COMPANY; *pg.* 1893, *pg.* 1641
CLOVER BLOSSOM - Honey - MILLER'S HONEY COMPANY; *pg.* 1860, *pg.* 1759
CLOVER CASH - Lottery Game - MASSACHUSETTS STATE LOTTERY; *pg.* 998, *pg.* 802
CLOVER LEAF - Food Products - BUMBLE BEE FOODS LLC; *pg.* 842, *pg.* 201
CLOVERFIELD - Toy & Game - HASBRO, INC.; *pg.* 954, *pg.* 1603
CLOVERINE - Skin Care - PRESTIGE BRANDS HOLDINGS, INC.; *pg.* 520, *pg.* 1345
CLOVERS & GOLD - Video Game - INTERNATIONAL GAME TECHNOLOGY; *pg.* 957, *pg.* 1024
CLOVIS - Fabric - NEMSCHOFF, INC.; *pg.* 936, *pg.* 1890
CLOVIS NEWS JOURNAL - New Mexico Newspaper - FREEDOM COMMUNICATIONS, INC.; *pg.* 1643, *pg.* 110
CLOWNHEAD DESIGN - CLOWNHEAD DESIGN (2D) - JACK IN THE BOX INC.; *pg.* 1732, *pg.* 204
CLOZ-IT - Mold Base & Component - SUPERIOR DIE SET CORP.; *pg.* 1379, *pg.* 1885
CLP - Equipment Maintenance Products - BAE SYSTEMS PRODUCTS GROUP; *pg.* 359, *pg.* 432
CLP - Orthopedic Implant Product - DJO SURGICAL; *pg.* 1525, *pg.* 1661
CLP - Skilled Trades Staffing - TRUEBLUE, INC.; *pg.* 485, *pg.* 1845

First page reference indicates Business Class Edition
Second page reference indicates Geographic Edition

CLR - Cleaner Deodorizer - JELMAR COMPANY; *pg.* 331, *pg.* 660
CLR BATHROOM & KITCHEN CLEANER - Bathroom & Kitchen Cleaner - JELMAR COMPANY; *pg.* 331, *pg.* 660
CLR OUTDOOR FURNITURE CLEANER - Outdoor Furniture Cleaner - JELMAR COMPANY; *pg.* 331, *pg.* 660
CLS1 - Livescan Products - 3M; *pg.* 339, *pg.* 179
CLUB - Tires - THE GOODYEAR TIRE & RUBBER COMPANY; *pg.* 1883, *pg.* 1401
CLUB - Snacks - KELLOGG COMPANY; *pg.* 831, *pg.* 870
CLUB - Office Furniture - STEELCASE INC.; *pg.* 475, *pg.* 889
CLUB BARONA - Membership & Gaming Privileges - BARONA RESORT & CASINO; *pg.* 1080, *pg.* 121
CLUB BK - Entertainment Clubs - BURGER KING CORPORATION; *pg.* 1719, *pg.* 440
CLUB CAR - Golf Car - INGERSOLL-RAND COMPANY; *pg.* 1349, *pg.* 1370
THE CLUB COCKTAILS - Cocktails - DIAGEO NORTH AMERICA, INC.; *pg.* 1961, *pg.* 361
CLUB GRANDE - Office Furniture - STEELCASE INC.; *pg.* 475, *pg.* 889
CLUB HOUSE - Seasonings - MCCORMICK & COMPANY, INCORPORATED; *pg.* 1027, *pg.* 779
CLUB INTRAWEST - Resort Club - INTRAWEST ULC; *pg.* 1098, *pg.* 320
CLUB KENO - Lottery Game - MISSOURI LOTTERY; *pg.* 999, *pg.* 979
CLUB LIBBY LU - Specialty Stores - SAKS INCORPORATED; *pg.* 1783, *pg.* 1288
CLUB MOBILE - Office Furniture - STEELCASE INC.; *pg.* 475, *pg.* 889
CLUB MONACO - Clothing - RALPH LAUREN CORPORATION; *pg.* 46, *pg.* 1284
CLUB PENGUIN - Virtual World for Kids - DISNEY INTERACTIVE MEDIA GROUP; *pg.* 1239, *pg.* 95
CLUB PENGUIN - Online Social Network for Children - THE WALT DISNEY COMPANY; *pg.* 317, *pg.* 52
CLUB ROOM - Furniture - BASSETT FURNITURE INDUSTRIES, INCORPORATED; *pg.* 916, *pg.* 1776
CLUB ROYALE - Cruise Ship - ROYAL CARIBBEAN CRUISES LTD; *pg.* 1921, *pg.* 446
CLUB SOCIAL - Crackers - MONDELEZ INTERNATIONAL, INC.; *pg.* 878, *pg.* 601
CLUB SOX - Golf Club Covers - RELIABLE OF MILWAUKEE; *pg.* 698, *pg.* 1879
CLUB TRAINER - Sailboat - MARLOW-HUNTER LLC; *pg.* 1709, *pg.* 409
CLUBHOUSE - Fabric - NEMSCHOFF, INC.; *pg.* 936, *pg.* 1890
CLUBHOUSE LIVING - Printed Periodical - TRAVELHOST, INC.; *pg.* 1696, *pg.* 1689
CLUBLINK - Electronic Telecommunication of Clubs - AMERICAN AUTOMOBILE ASSOCIATION; *pg.* 1190, *pg.* 429
CLUBMAN - Male Grooming Product - AMERICAN INTERNATIONAL INDUSTRIES COMPANY; *pg.* 498, *pg.* 126
CLUBMAN-PINAUD - Toiletries & Grooming Product - AMERICAN INTERNATIONAL INDUSTRIES COMPANY; *pg.* 498, *pg.* 126
CLUBVANTAGE - Club Performance Program - GOLFSMITH INTERNATIONAL HOLDINGS, INC.; *pg.* 1835, *pg.* 1662
CLUE - Game - HASBRO, INC.; *pg.* 954, *pg.* 1603
CLUE FX - Game - HASBRO, INC.; *pg.* 954, *pg.* 1603
CLUE JR. - Toy & Game - HASBRO, INC.; *pg.* 954, *pg.* 1603
CLUMP-N-FLUSH - Pet Litter - THE ANDERSONS INCORPORATED; *pg.* 1793, *pg.* 1461
CLUNY - Fabric - NEMSCHOFF, INC.; *pg.* 936, *pg.* 1890
CLUSTER - Skylighting System - WASCO PRODUCTS, INC.; *pg.* 120, *pg.* 752
CLUSTER BAR - Safety Equipment - CONDUCTIX INC.; *pg.* 1295, *pg.* 1015
CLUSTER-CLIP - Paperboard Packaging Product - WESTROCK COMPANY; *pg.* 1472, *pg.* 1805
CLUSTER GAUGE - Vacuum Gauge System - MKS INSTRUMENTS, INC.; *pg.* 1362, *pg.* 781
CLUSTER-SIDE - Paperboard Packaging Product - WESTROCK COMPANY; *pg.* 1472, *pg.* 1805
CLUSTERBORON - Superior Device Performance - ATMI, INC.; *pg.* 1314, *pg.* 342
CLUSTERCARBON - Diffusion Control - ATMI, INC.; *pg.* 1314, *pg.* 342
CLUSTERPAK - Paperboard Packaging Product - WESTROCK COMPANY; *pg.* 1472, *pg.* 1805
CLUSTERS - Cereals - GENERAL MILLS, INC.; *pg.* 828, *pg.* 933
CLUSTERSLICER - Medical Device - OLIVER PRODUCTS COMPANY INC.; *pg.* 1367, *pg.* 888
CLUTCH-IN! - Clutch pilot accesories - DORMAN PRODUCTS, INC.; *pg.* 204, *pg.* 1522
CLYDE - Bicycle - TREK BICYCLE CORPORATION; *pg.* 1847, *pg.* 1896
CLYSAR - Packaging Film - BEMIS COMPANY, INC.; *pg.* 1453, *pg.* 1882
CM - Electric Hoist - COLUMBUS MCKINNON CORPORATION; *pg.* 1325, *pg.* 1138
CM-15A - Monoxide Detector - BOSCH SECURITY SYSTEMS, INC.; *pg.* 626, *pg.* 1158
CM TESTER - Metalworking Fluid Additive - TROY CORPORATION; *pg.* 1184, *pg.* 1067
CM2IQ - Software - USA TECHNOLOGIES, INC.; *pg.* 815, *pg.* 1550
CMA - Global Certification - INSTITUTE OF MANAGEMENT ACCOUNTANTS, INC.; *pg.* 144, *pg.* 1086
CMA - Management Application - POLYCOM, INC.; *pg.* 664, *pg.* 249
CMA AWARDS - Music Award - COUNTRY MUSIC ASSOCIATION; *pg.* 138, *pg.* 1649
CMA MUSIC FESTIVAL - Music Festival - COUNTRY MUSIC ASSOCIATION; *pg.* 138, *pg.* 1649
CMAX - Software - FIDELITY NATIONAL INFORMATION SERVICES; *pg.* 397, *pg.* 1549
CMAX - Floor Care - NILFISK-ADVANCE, INC.; *pg.* 332, *pg.* 953
CMAX - Medical Apparatus - STERIS CORPORATION; *pg.* 1597, *pg.* 1464
CMF - Salt - CARGILL LIMITED; *pg.* 1475, *pg.* 1914
CMF MONITOR - Software - BMC SOFTWARE, INC.; *pg.* 362, *pg.* 1701
CMI - Centrifuges - CENTRIFUGAL & MECHANICAL INDUSTRIES, INC.; *pg.* 1322, *pg.* 994
CMI - Concrete Paving - TEREX CORPORATION; *pg.* 1381, *pg.* 384
CMI - Medical Service - UTAH MEDICAL PRODUCTS, INC.; *pg.* 1605, *pg.* 1752
CML - Bevel Gear Valve Actuators - REGAL BELOIT CORPORATION; *pg.* 106, *pg.* 1854
CML MACARR - Power Supplies, Battery Chargers & Wide Band Power Amplifiers - MARINE ELECTRIC SYSTEMS, INC.; *pg.* 652, *pg.* 1123
CML-OIL BASE PLUS - Ink - VAN SON HOLLAND INK CORPORATION OF AMERICA; *pg.* 487, *pg.* 1169
CMPLICITY - Copper Integration - ATMI, INC.; *pg.* 1314, *pg.* 342
CMPT - Composite Material Technology - GENERAL MAGNAPLATE CORPORATION; *pg.* 1164, *pg.* 1079
CMR-24 - Roof System - BUTLER MANUFACTURING COMPANY; *pg.* 72, *pg.* 981
CMS - Contractor Maintenance Services - BAE SYSTEMS-INFORMATION WARFARE; *pg.* 623, *pg.* 1036
CMS - Game Management - BALLY TECHNOLOGIES, INC.; *pg.* 531, *pg.* 1022
CMS - Medical Device - NATUS MEDICAL INCORPORATED; *pg.* 1572, *pg.* 199
CMS-JR - Automatic Call Sequencer - ELECTRONIC TELE-COMMUNICATIONS, INC.; *pg.* 390, *pg.* 1897
CMS-SR - Automatic Call Sequencer - ELECTRONIC TELE-COMMUNICATIONS, INC.; *pg.* 390, *pg.* 1897
CMW - Underground Construction Equipment - CHARLES MACHINE WORKS, INC.; *pg.* 1322, *pg.* 1488
CMX - Catalytic Converter - BASF CATALYSTS LLC; *pg.* 1148, *pg.* 1074
CMX - Computer Software - QUALCOMM INCORPORATED; *pg.* 1873, *pg.* 207
CN620 - Network Solutions Product - MOTOROLA SOLUTIONS, INC.; *pg.* 657, *pg.* 659
CNA - Insurance & Insurance Services - CNA INSURANCE COMPANIES; *pg.* 1198, *pg.* 571
CNBC - Consumer News & Business Channel - NBC UNIVERSAL, INC.; *pg.* 300, *pg.* 1266
CNC INTERTAP - Taps for International Tapping System - REGAL BELOIT CORPORATION; *pg.* 106, *pg.* 1854
CNC/XL - Taps for CNC Machining - REGAL BELOIT CORPORATION; *pg.* 106, *pg.* 1854
CNC/XM TAPS - Cobalt Taps for Computer-Numerically Controlled Machinery - REGAL BELOIT CORPORATION; *pg.* 106, *pg.* 1854
CNE - Technical Training - NOVELL INC.; *pg.* 446, *pg.* 852
CNET - Technology & Consumer Electronics Website - CBS INTERACTIVE, INC.; *pg.* 369, *pg.* 215
CNET DOWNLOADS - Digital Content Distribution Website - CBS INTERACTIVE, INC.; *pg.* 369, *pg.* 215
CNET NEWS - News Website - CBS INTERACTIVE, INC.; *pg.* 369, *pg.* 215
CNH CAPITAL - Financial Products & Services - CNH AMERICA LLC; *pg.* 702, *pg.* 560
CNMIPS - Processor - IMAGINATION TECHNOLOGIES; *pg.* 412, *pg.* 285
CNS THIS WEEK - Community Weekly Newspapers - THE DISPATCH PRINTING COMPANY; *pg.* 1636, *pg.* 1439
CO-17 CAMPER - Canoes - ALUMACRAFT BOAT COMPANY; *pg.* 1705, *pg.* 964
CO ACCESS - Central Office Platform for Switching in Storage of Voice Messages - XURA, INC.; *pg.* 689, *pg.* 849
CO-AX - Hose - HBD INDUSTRIES, INC.; *pg.* 207, *pg.* 1449
CO-FLEX - Medical & Aesthetic Product - DYNATRONICS CORPORATION; *pg.* 1526, *pg.* 1757
CO-LO - Enclosure - GREAT LAKES CASE & CABINET CO., INC.; *pg.* 401, *pg.* 1529
CO-LSIM - Software System - MENTOR GRAPHICS CORPORATION; *pg.* 432, *pg.* 1510
CO-OP - Automotive Products, Lubricants & Twine - UNIVERSAL COOPERATIVES, INC.; *pg.* 1482, *pg.* 922
CO-OP INSERT - Promotional Newspaper Insert - VALASSIS COMMUNICATIONS, INC.; *pg.* 1287, *pg.* 897
CO-ORDINATES - Broadloom - COURISTAN INC.; *pg.* 921, *pg.* 1067
CO-STANDBYSERVER - Software - EMC CORPORATION; *pg.* 391, *pg.* 825
CO-VERIFICATION ENVIRONMENT - Software System - MENTOR GRAPHICS CORPORATION; *pg.* 432, *pg.* 1510
COACH - Leatherware - COACH, INC.; *pg.* 3, *pg.* 1214
COACH - Digital Camera Technology - CSR; *pg.* 280, *pg.* 284
COACH - Watches - MOVADO GROUP, INC.; *pg.* 10, *pg.* 1101
COACH - Fabric - NEMSCHOFF, INC.; *pg.* 936, *pg.* 1890
COACH - Office Furniture - STEELCASE INC.; *pg.* 475, *pg.* 889
COACH GRILL - Restaurants - TAVISTOCK RESTAURANT GROUP; *pg.* 1753, *pg.* 803
COACH HERITAGE STRIPE - Leather Products - COACH, INC.; *pg.* 3, *pg.* 1214
COACH VAC - Cleaning Product - HILLYARD, INC.; *pg.* 331, *pg.* 990
COAG DX - Analyzer - IDEXX LABORATORIES, INC.; *pg.* 1543, *pg.* 753
COAIR - Chipset - SIGMA DESIGNS, INC.; *pg.* 469, *pg.* 148
COAL CAT - Coal Tar Epoxy Coatings - PPG INDUSTRIES, INC.; *pg.* 1445, *pg.* 1579
COALOGIC - Software - GE ENERGY; *pg.* 1338, *pg.* 506
COAPTITE - Medical Device - BOSTON SCIENTIFIC CORPORATION; *pg.* 1508, *pg.* 831
COAPTITE - Pharmaceutical Product - MERZ AESTHETICS; *pg.* 1567, *pg.* 255
COASOL - Coalescing Aids - THE DOW CHEMICAL COMPANY; *pg.* 1157, *pg.* 898
COAST - Bar Soap - HENKEL CONSUMER GOODS; *pg.* 511, *pg.* 22
COAST TO COAST HARDWARE - Retail Stores - TRUE VALUE COMPANY; *pg.* 1065, *pg.* 592
COAST TRAIL - Bike - MARIN BIKES; *pg.* 1708, *pg.* 168
COASTAL COTTAGE - Furniture - STANLEY FURNITURE CO., INC.; *pg.* 943, *pg.* 1379
COASTAL INSHORE - Bait Casting Reel - DAIWA CORPORATION; *pg.* 1832, *pg.* 75
COASTAL LIVING - Furniture - STANLEY FURNITURE CO., INC.; *pg.* 943, *pg.* 1379
COASTAL LIVING - Media Publication - TIME INC.; *pg.* 1693, *pg.* 1300
COASTAL WATCH - Automated Marine Scene Understanding - RAYTHEON APPLIED SIGNAL TECHNOLOGY, INC.; *pg.* 667, *pg.* 288
COASTER - Footwear - STEVEN MADDEN, LTD.; *pg.* 1819, *pg.* 1176
COASTER QUEST - Amusement & Water Park - CEDAR FAIR, L.P.; *pg.* 537, *pg.* 1471
COASTLINE - Piping System - VICTAULIC COMPANY; *pg.* 1066, *pg.* 1529
COATED NATURAL KRAFT - Paperboard Packaging Product - WESTROCK COMPANY; *pg.* 1472, *pg.* 1805
THE COATINGS COMPANY - Engineered Product And System - SULZER METCO (WESTBURY) INC.; *pg.* 1064, *pg.* 1350

COATMASTER - Corrugating & Bag - GRAIN PROCESSING CORPORATION; *pg.* 859, *pg.* 709
COATS - Tire Changers & Wheel Balancers - HENNESSY INDUSTRIES, INC.; *pg.* 207, *pg.* 1639
COAXID - Electronic Components - MOLEX INCORPORATED; *pg.* 655, *pg.* 628
COBACTAN - Broad-Spectrum Antibiotic - MERCK & CO., INC.; *pg.* 1566, *pg.* 1077
COBALT - Electronics - DEI HOLDINGS, INC.; *pg.* 633, *pg.* 302
COBALT - Two-Door Coupe - GENERAL MOTORS COMPANY; *pg.* 175, *pg.* 881
COBALT - Stereo Headphones - KOSS CORPORATION; *pg.* 649, *pg.* 1877
COBALT - Fabric - NEMSCHOFF, INC.; *pg.* 936, *pg.* 1890
COBALT - Chewing Gum Flavor - WM. WRIGLEY JR. COMPANY; *pg.* 1863, *pg.* 596
COBAN - Elastic Bandage - 3M COMPANY; *pg.* 1142, *pg.* 956
COBAN - Monensin Sodium - ELANCO ANIMAL HEALTH; *pg.* 1475, *pg.* 881
COBB - Jewelry - W.R. COBB COMPANY; *pg.* 15, *pg.* 1601
COBB HILL - Women's Footwear - NEW BALANCE ATHLETIC SHOE, INC.; *pg.* 1811, *pg.* 798
COBB HILL - Footwear - THE ROCKPORT GROUP; *pg.* 1818, *pg.* 812
COBBLE HILL - Carpet - BEAULIEU GROUP, LLC; *pg.* 917, *pg.* 529
COBBLEHILL - Children's Hardcover Books - PENGUIN RANDOM HOUSE; *pg.* 1675, *pg.* 1276
COBBLESTONE - Furniture - BASSETT FURNITURE INDUSTRIES, INCORPORATED; *pg.* 916, *pg.* 1776
COBBLESTONE MARKET - Food Product - SHAMROCK FOODS COMPANY; *pg.* 895, *pg.* 20
COBBLESTONE MILL - Food Product - FLOWERS FOODS, INC.; *pg.* 855, *pg.* 541
COBI - Footwear - COBIAN CORP.; *pg.* 1806, *pg.* 253
COBI - Office Furniture - STEELCASE INC.; *pg.* 475, *pg.* 889
COBOTICS - Intelligent Assist Device - STANLEY BLACK & DECKER, INC.; *pg.* 1063, *pg.* 358
COBRA - Security System - ANALOGIC CORPORATION; *pg.* 1399, *pg.* 840
COBRA - Medical Device - BOSTON SCIENTIFIC CORPORATION; *pg.* 1508, *pg.* 831
COBRA - Furniture - BUSH INDUSTRIES INC.; *pg.* 919, *pg.* 1170
COBRA - Footwear - CAPEZIO BALLET MAKERS INC.; *pg.* 1805, *pg.* 1125
COBRA - Monofilament Fishing Line - CORTLAND LINE COMPANY; *pg.* 1831, *pg.* 1155
COBRA - Computer Applications - DELTEK, INC.; *pg.* 386, *pg.* 1784
COBRA - Cord Bag - FAULTLESS STARCH/BON AMI COMPANY; *pg.* 330, *pg.* 982
COBRA - Machinery - HARDINGE INC.; *pg.* 1344, *pg.* 1157
COBRA - Chemical Product - MILLER-STEPHENSON CHEMICAL COMPANY, INC.; *pg.* 1172, *pg.* 344
COBRA - Scanner - MOTOROLA ENTERPRISE MOBILITY; *pg.* 441, *pg.* 1167
COBRA - Cassette Basket - PERKINELMER, INC.; *pg.* 1426, *pg.* 853
COBRA - LED Illumination - PROPHOTONIX LIMITED; *pg.* 1427, *pg.* 1039
COBRA - Microtalk Radio - SCHOOL-TECH, INC.; *pg.* 1844, *pg.* 866
COBRA PRODUCTS - Drain Cleaning Hand-Tools - MASCO CORPORATION; *pg.* 96, *pg.* 909
COBRAMARINE - Laser Detectors - COBRA ELECTRONICS CORPORATION; *pg.* 629, *pg.* 572
COBRANET - Audio Networking Technology - CIRRUS LOGIC, INC.; *pg.* 629, *pg.* 1661
COBRATRACK - Mounted Crushers - TEREX CEDARAPIDS; *pg.* 1381, *pg.* 703
COCA-COLA - Beverages - THE COCA-COLA COMPANY; *pg.* 240, *pg.* 493
COCA-COLA BLACK CHERRY VANILLA - Beverages - THE COCA-COLA COMPANY; *pg.* 240, *pg.* 493
COCA-COLA BLAK - Beverages - THE COCA-COLA COMPANY; *pg.* 240, *pg.* 493
COCA-COLA C2 - Beverages - THE COCA-COLA COMPANY; *pg.* 240, *pg.* 493
COCA-COLA CITRA - Beverages - THE COCA-COLA COMPANY; *pg.* 240, *pg.* 493
COCA-COLA CLASSIC - Soft Drink - THE COCA-COLA COMPANY; *pg.* 240, *pg.* 493
COCA-COLA LIFE - Reduced Calorie Soft Drink - THE COCA-COLA COMPANY; *pg.* 240, *pg.* 493
COCA-COLA LIGHT - Beverages - THE COCA-COLA COMPANY; *pg.* 240, *pg.* 493
COCA-COLA LIGHT CITRA - Beverages - THE COCA-COLA COMPANY; *pg.* 240, *pg.* 493
COCA-COLA LIGHT WITH LEMON - Beverages - THE COCA-COLA COMPANY; *pg.* 240, *pg.* 493
COCA-COLA LIGHT WITH LIME - Beverages - THE COCA-COLA COMPANY; *pg.* 240, *pg.* 493
COCA-COLA WITH LEMON - Beverages - THE COCA-COLA COMPANY; *pg.* 240, *pg.* 493
COCA-COLA WITH LIME - Beverages - THE COCA-COLA COMPANY; *pg.* 240, *pg.* 493
COCA-COLA WITH RASPBERRY - Beverages - THE COCA-COLA COMPANY; *pg.* 240, *pg.* 493
COCAL - Flavor Ingredient - INTERNATIONAL FLAVORS & FRAGRANCES INC.; *pg.* 512, *pg.* 1244
COCAT - Catalyst - BASF CATALYSTS LLC; *pg.* 1148, *pg.* 1074
COCCIVAC - Poultry Antibiotic - MERCK & CO., INC.; *pg.* 1566, *pg.* 1077
COCHLEA-SCAN - Medical Device - NATUS MEDICAL INCORPORATED; *pg.* 1572, *pg.* 199
COCINA CASERA - Hispanic Product - FROSTY ACRES BRANDS, INC.; *pg.* 1020, *pg.* 484
COCKBURN'S - Port Wine - JIM BEAM BRANDS CO.; *pg.* 1965, *pg.* 601
COCKTAILS FOR TWO - Cocktails - DIAGEO NORTH AMERICA, INC.; *pg.* 1961, *pg.* 361
COCO - Furniture - ETHAN ALLEN INTERIORS INC.; *pg.* 924, *pg.* 343
COCO - Furniture - HOOKER FURNITURE CORPORATION; *pg.* 928, *pg.* 1788
COCO - Fabric - NEMSCHOFF, INC.; *pg.* 936, *pg.* 1890
COCO BEACH - Rug - COURISTAN INC.; *pg.* 921, *pg.* 1067
COCO LIBRE - Organic Coconut Waters & Protein Beverages - MAVERICK BRANDS LLC; *pg.* 876, *pg.* 161
COCO ROOS - Cereal - POST CONSUMER BRANDS; *pg.* 833, *pg.* 927
COCOA - Software Technology - APPLE INC.; *pg.* 350, *pg.* 73
COCOA - Agriculture Exchange - INTERCONTINENTALEXCHANGE, INC.; *pg.* 769, *pg.* 512
COCOA BEACH - Granola - KASHI COMPANY; *pg.* 830, *pg.* 119
COCOA DYNO-BITES - Cereal - POST CONSUMER BRANDS; *pg.* 833, *pg.* 927
COCOA KRISPES - Cereal - KELLOGG COMPANY; *pg.* 831, *pg.* 870
COCOA PEBBLES - Cereal - POST HOLDINGS, INC.; *pg.* 833, *pg.* 1002
COCOA PUFFS - Cereal - GENERAL MILLS, INC.; *pg.* 828, *pg.* 933
COCOA TOUCH - Software Technology - APPLE INC.; *pg.* 350, *pg.* 73
COCOAVIA - Healthy Snack Foods - MARS, INCORPORATED; *pg.* 1858, *pg.* 1792
COCOCAY - Cruise Ship - ROYAL CARIBBEAN CRUISES LTD; *pg.* 1921, *pg.* 446
COCONUT - Toys - AMERICAN GIRL LLC; *pg.* 949, *pg.* 1871
COCONUT BRONZE - Lotion - E.T. BROWNE DRUG COMPANY, INC.; *pg.* 509, *pg.* 1060
COCONUT OIL FORMULA - Hair Care Product - E.T. BROWNE DRUG COMPANY, INC.; *pg.* 509, *pg.* 1060
COCONUTS MUSIC & MOVIES - Retail Music Stores - TRANS WORLD ENTERTAINMENT CORPORATION; *pg.* 313, *pg.* 1137
COCOON - Chain - STULLER, INC.; *pg.* 13, *pg.* 745
COCOPOP BARS - Portion-Controlled Packaged Popcorn - VENTURA FOODS, LLC; *pg.* 908, *pg.* 49
COCO'S RESTAURANTS - Eating Place - DENNY'S CORPORATION; *pg.* 1725, *pg.* 1622
COCOTEEN - Beverages - THE COCA-COLA COMPANY; *pg.* 240, *pg.* 493
COCOTONIN - Weight-Loss & Wellness Supplement - DIXIE HEALTH, INC.; *pg.* 1524, *pg.* 535
COCREATE - Software - PARAMETRIC TECHNOLOGY CORPORATION; *pg.* 452, *pg.* 835
C.O.D. SECURE - Software - UNITED PARCEL SERVICE, INC.; *pg.* 1928, *pg.* 522
C.O.D. SELECT - Software - UNITED PARCEL SERVICE, INC.; *pg.* 1928, *pg.* 522
CODA - Clinical Diagnostic Product - BIO-RAD LABORATORIES, INC.; *pg.* 1504, *pg.* 101
CODA - Game - WINNING MOVES GAMES, INC.; *pg.* 970, *pg.* 816
CODA COMP - Bicycle - G. JOANNOU CYCLE CO. INC.; *pg.* 1707, *pg.* 1098
CODA ELITE - Bicycle - G. JOANNOU CYCLE CO. INC.; *pg.* 1707, *pg.* 1098
CODA OP/DM - Software - BIO-RAD LABORATORIES, INC.; *pg.* 1504, *pg.* 101
CODA SPORT - Bicycle - G. JOANNOU CYCLE CO. INC.; *pg.* 1707, *pg.* 1098
CODE BLUE - Resuscitator - VITAL SIGNS, INC.; *pg.* 1607, *pg.* 1126
CODE BLUE II - Resuscitator - VITAL SIGNS, INC.; *pg.* 1607, *pg.* 1126
CODE CENTER - Software - VERIFONE SYSTEMS, INC.; *pg.* 487, *pg.* 251
CODE COMPOSER STUDIO - Computer Software Tools - TEXAS INSTRUMENTS INCORPORATED; *pg.* 679, *pg.* 1688
CODE/LAB - Software System - MENTOR GRAPHICS CORPORATION; *pg.* 432, *pg.* 1510
CODE MASTER - Game Book - INNOVATIVE USA, INC.; *pg.* 957, *pg.* 363
CODE ONE - Clothing - LAKELAND INDUSTRIES, INC.; *pg.* 1354, *pg.* 1338
CODE ONE - Systems Integration & Aeronautics - LOCKHEED MARTIN CORPORATION; *pg.* 229, *pg.* 762
CODE-READY - Defibrillator - ZOLL MEDICAL CORPORATION; *pg.* 1612, *pg.* 814
CODE RED - Foam - HSM SOLUTIONS; *pg.* 1884, *pg.* 1378
CODE RED - Apparel - OAKLEY, INC.; *pg.* 1840, *pg.* 86
CODE RED II - Foam - HSM SOLUTIONS; *pg.* 1884, *pg.* 1378
CODE-STAT - Data Management Suite - MEDTRONIC, INC.; *pg.* 1564, *pg.* 939
CODE TAPE - Measuring Product - THE L.S. STARRETT COMPANY; *pg.* 1421, *pg.* 783
CODE TESTER FOR ORACLE - Software - DELL SOFTWARE; *pg.* 385, *pg.* 40
CODEBOOK CORRELATION TECHNOLOGY - Software - EMC CORPORATION; *pg.* 391, *pg.* 825
CODEC - Modem - COMTECH TELECOMMUNICATIONS CORP.; *pg.* 379, *pg.* 1179
CODEFINDER - Medical Computer Program - 3M COMPANY; *pg.* 1142, *pg.* 956
CODEFINDER - Software - COMPUTER PROGRAMS & SYSTEMS, INC.; *pg.* 378, *pg.* 7
CODELINK - Software - EMC CORPORATION; *pg.* 391, *pg.* 825
CODELINK - Activated Slide - SURMODICS, INC.; *pg.* 1600, *pg.* 924
CODEMAESTRO - Software Development Tool - TEXAS INSTRUMENTS INCORPORATED; *pg.* 679, *pg.* 1688
CODENET - Data Management Product - ZOLL MEDICAL CORPORATION; *pg.* 1612, *pg.* 814
CODENET CENTRAL - Data Management Product - ZOLL MEDICAL CORPORATION; *pg.* 1612, *pg.* 814
CODENET WRITER - Data Management Product - ZOLL MEDICAL CORPORATION; *pg.* 1612, *pg.* 814
CODER - Software Product - WOODWARD, INC.; *pg.* 122, *pg.* 329
CODESIGN - Software - CERTICOM CORP.; *pg.* 371, *pg.* 1925
CODESOFT - Label Software - BRADY CORPORATION; *pg.* 363, *pg.* 1873
CODEWARRIOR IDE - Development Tool - LYNX SOFTWARE TECHNOLOGIES; *pg.* 429, *pg.* 247
CODEXIS - Biocatalytic Chemical Processing Technology - CODEXIS, INC.; *pg.* 1154, *pg.* 189
CODICO - Digital Receiver - HARMONIC, INC.; *pg.* 402, *pg.* 246
CODISTRATOR - Software Product - CHYRONHEGO; *pg.* 371, *pg.* 1179
CODMEGA - Nutritional Supplement - GARDEN OF LIFE, INC.; *pg.* 1532, *pg.* 478
CODY - Shoes - ALLEN-EDMONDS SHOE CORP.; *pg.* 1804, *pg.* 1887
COEFFICIENT - Software - DELL SOFTWARE; *pg.* 385, *pg.* 40
COELEX - Pressed & Monolithic Refractory - RESCO PRODUCTS, INC.; *pg.* 107, *pg.* 1581
COENZYME - Nutritional Product - RBC LIFE SCIENCES, INC.; *pg.* 1588, *pg.* 1723
COEUR DE FRANCE - Furniture Collection - CENTURY FURNITURE INDUSTRIES; *pg.* 920, *pg.* 1377

First page reference indicates Business Class Edition
Second page reference indicates Geographic Edition

COEV - Electronic Component Product - TE CONNECTIVITY LTD.; *pg.* 677, *pg.* 1515
COF MATCHING FUNDS PROGRAM - Fraternal Benefits - CATHOLIC ORDER OF FORESTERS; *pg.* 1196, *pg.* 635
COF PHOTO AND POSTER CONTESTS - Fraternal Benefits - CATHOLIC ORDER OF FORESTERS; *pg.* 1196, *pg.* 635
COFFEE AT ITS BEST - Slogan - BUNN-O-MATIC CORPORATION; *pg.* 53, *pg.* 661
COFFEE BEANVAC - Canister - THE COFFEE BEANERY LTD.; *pg.* 849, *pg.* 886
COFFEE BREAK - Ice Cream - WELLS ENTERPRISES, INC.; *pg.* 909, *pg.* 709
COFFEE BUTLER - Insulated Carafe - THERMOS L.L.C.; *pg.* 61, *pg.* 660
COFFEE C - Agriculture Exchange - INTERCONTINENTALEXCHANGE, INC.; *pg.* 769, *pg.* 512
COFFEE CAKES - Snack Cakes - HOSTESS BRANDS LLC; *pg.* 1856, *pg.* 984
COFFEE-MATE - Coffee Creamer - NESTLE USA, INC.; *pg.* 883, *pg.* 96
COFFEE PEOPLE WHO CARE - Tag Line - THE COFFEE BEANERY LTD.; *pg.* 849, *pg.* 886
COFFEE RICH - Non-Dairy Creamer - RICH PRODUCTS CORPORATION; *pg.* 892, *pg.* 1150
COFFEE TOPPER - Coffee Flavorings - DAVID MICHAEL & CO. INC.; *pg.* 852, *pg.* 1563
COFFEEZ - Food Product - SHEETZ, INC.; *pg.* 1033, *pg.* 1514
COFFING - Hoist - COLUMBUS MCKINNON CORPORATION; *pg.* 1325, *pg.* 1138
COGENT SYSTEMS - Software - 3M; *pg.* 339, *pg.* 179
COGNEX - Machine Vision System - COGNEX CORPORATION; *pg.* 1406, *pg.* 834
COGNI-CLEAR - Nutritional Product - NUTRACEUTICAL INTERNATIONAL CORPORATION; *pg.* 1576, *pg.* 1753
COGNIS - Medical Device - BOSTON SCIENTIFIC CORPORATION; *pg.* 1508, *pg.* 831
COGNITA - Furniture - HERMAN MILLER, INC.; *pg.* 926, *pg.* 913
COHEN - Bronchial Blocker Set - COOK GROUP, INC.; *pg.* 1518, *pg.* 674
COHEN'S FASHION OPTICAL - Vision Care Service - COHEN'S FASHION OPTICAL INC.; *pg.* 1406, *pg.* 1161
COHORT - Apparel - OAKLEY, INC.; *pg.* 1840, *pg.* 86
COIFF & CO. - International Salon Brand - REGIS CORPORATION; *pg.* 521, *pg.* 941
COIL COMMANDER - Pull Coil Timer Module - WOODWARD, INC.; *pg.* 122, *pg.* 329
COIL-FLEX - Seating Systems - LEGGETT & PLATT, INCORPORATED; *pg.* 933, *pg.* 974
COIL POLO - Apparels - UNDER ARMOUR, INC.; *pg.* 49, *pg.* 759
COIL-RITE - Air Spring Applications for Personal Vehicles - FIRESTONE INDUSTRIAL PRODUCTS DIVISION; *pg.* 1882, *pg.* 686
COILEX - Extension Cords - COLEMAN CABLE, INC.; *pg.* 1324, *pg.* 665
COILPRO - Coil Cleaning System - GOODWAY TECHNOLOGIES CORPORATION; *pg.* 1341, *pg.* 374
COILWEB - Vibrating Conveyor - WEBSTER INDUSTRIES INC.; *pg.* 1388, *pg.* 1475
COIN CAPER - Lottery Game - IDAHO LOTTERY; *pg.* 995, *pg.* 547
COIN-LOK - Coin-Operated Locker - AMERICAN LOCKER SECURITY SYSTEMS, INC.; *pg.* 1042, *pg.* 1674
COIN WORLD - Publication - AMOS PRESS, INC.; *pg.* 1616, *pg.* 1472
COINCO GLOBAL - Coin Changer - COIN ACCEPTORS, INC.; *pg.* 1324, *pg.* 994
COINCOUNT - Coin Deposit Machine - DIEBOLD, INCORPORATED; *pg.* 387, *pg.* 1407
COINS THAT COUNT - Coin Collection for Non-Profit Agencies - OUTERWALL INC.; *pg.* 1367, *pg.* 1816
COINSAFE - Tamper-Evident Coin Bags - SEALED AIR CORPORATION; *pg.* 1468, *pg.* 1058
COINSTAR 4TH WALL - Product Distributor - OUTERWALL INC.; *pg.* 1367, *pg.* 1816
COIR - Carpet - INTERFACE, INC.; *pg.* 695, *pg.* 512
COIRTEX - Rubberized Fiber - BLOCKSOM & COMPANY; *pg.* 691, *pg.* 694
COKE II - Beverages - THE COCA-COLA COMPANY; *pg.* 240, *pg.* 493
COKE ZERO - Zero Calorie Soft Drink - THE COCA-COLA COMPANY; *pg.* 240, *pg.* 493
COKER - Seed & Wheat - SYNGENTA SEEDS, INC.; *pg.* 1801, *pg.* 950
COKER CLASSIC - Tire - COKER TIRE COMPANY; *pg.* 1880, *pg.* 1628
COL. JOHN PHILLIPS OHOOMPAPA - Amusement & Water Park - CEDAR FAIR, L.P.; *pg.* 537, *pg.* 1471
COL-TY - Cable Ties & Accessories - THOMAS & BETTS CORPORATION; *pg.* 680, *pg.* 1646
COLANDER - Plastic Houseware Product - STERILITE CORPORATION; *pg.* 1138, *pg.* 848
COLAZAL - Pharmaceutical Product - SALIX PHARMACEUTICALS, INC.; *pg.* 1591, *pg.* 1388
COLAZIDE - Balsalazide Disodium - SALIX PHARMACEUTICALS, INC.; *pg.* 1591, *pg.* 1388
COLBY - Furniture - NEMSCHOFF, INC.; *pg.* 936, *pg.* 1890
COLCEMID - Molecular Probe Product - THERMO FISHER SCIENTIFIC INC.; *pg.* 1602, *pg.* 61
COLD-CHEK - Automotive Equipment - THEXTON MANUFACTURING COMPANY, INC.; *pg.* 218, *pg.* 925
COLD CUT TRIO - Turkey Bologna, Turkey Ham & Turkey Salami Sandwich - SUBWAY RESTAURANTS; *pg.* 1751, *pg.* 356
COLD-EEZE - Health Product - PROPHASE LABS, INC.; *pg.* 1586, *pg.* 1526
COLD-FLO - Fibre Drum - GREIF INC.; *pg.* 1459, *pg.* 1447
COLD-FX - Natural Health Product - AFEXA LIFE SCIENCES INC.; *pg.* 1487, *pg.* 1905
COLD-MOUNT - Laminator - CODA INC.; *pg.* 1406, *pg.* 1081
COLD SEAL - Cohesive-Coated Protective Films - SEALED AIR CORPORATION; *pg.* 1468, *pg.* 1058
COLD SPRING - Bullnose Wheel - COLD SPRING GRANITE COMPANY; *pg.* 76, *pg.* 920
COLD STEEL - Gaming Product - GLD PRODUCTS, INC.; *pg.* 1835, *pg.* 1882
COLD STONE CREAMERY - Ice Cream - KAHALA FRANCHISING LLC; *pg.* 1025, *pg.* 23
COLD WATER - Designer Fragrance - PARFUMS DE COEUR LTD.; *pg.* 519, *pg.* 376
COLDBUSTER - Fruit Drink - JAMBA, INC.; *pg.* 1024, *pg.* 84
COLDFIRE - Semiconductor Product - FREESCALE SEMICONDUCTOR, INC.; *pg.* 398, *pg.* 1662
COLDFLOW - Valves - FLOWSERVE CORPORATION; *pg.* 82, *pg.* 1719
COLDFLOW - Fog Product - ROSCO LABORATORIES, INC.; *pg.* 1782, *pg.* 378
COLDFRONT - Winter Grille Insert - LUND INTERNATIONAL, INC.; *pg.* 211, *pg.* 526
COLDFRONT - Nutritional Product - NUTRACEUTICAL INTERNATIONAL CORPORATION; *pg.* 1576, *pg.* 1753
COLDFUSION - Software - ADOBE SYSTEMS INCORPORATED; *pg.* 342, *pg.* 235
COLDGEAR - Sport Apparel - UNDER ARMOUR, INC.; *pg.* 49, *pg.* 759
COLDISC - Flake Ice Maker - NORTH STAR ICE EQUIPMENT CORPORATION; *pg.* 1366, *pg.* 1838
COLDMASTER - Cold Temperature Control Products - CARLISLE FOODSERVICE PRODUCTS INCORPORATED; *pg.* 1455, *pg.* 1485
COLDPRUF - Thermal Underwear - INDERA MILLS COMPANY; *pg.* 26, *pg.* 1396
COLDWARE - Insulated Beverage Containers & Sleeves - THERMOS L.L.C.; *pg.* 61, *pg.* 660
COLDWELL BANKER - Residential Real Estate Brokerage Franchisor - REALOGY CORPORATION; *pg.* 1109, *pg.* 1081
COLDWELL BANKER COMMERCIAL - Commercial Real Estate Brokerage Franchisor - REALOGY CORPORATION; *pg.* 1109, *pg.* 1081
COLE & SON - Wall Coverings - LEE JOFA, INC.; *pg.* 933, *pg.* 1142
COLE-HAAN - Footwear - COLE-HAAN LLC; *pg.* 1806, *pg.* 1034
COLE HAAN - Apparel - G-III APPAREL GROUP, LTD.; *pg.* 41, *pg.* 1233
COLECCION IGUANA - Educational Materials - SCHOLASTIC INC.; *pg.* 1683, *pg.* 1288
COLEMAN - Camping Gear - THE COLEMAN COMPANY, INC.; *pg.* 1830, *pg.* 723
COLEMAN - Controls Rebuilding Service - FLIGHT SYSTEMS, INC.; *pg.* 1337, *pg.* 1548
COLESTID - Pharmaceutical Product - IMPAX LABORATORIES, INC.; *pg.* 1544, *pg.* 101
COLESTID - Medicine - PFIZER INC.; *pg.* 1581, *pg.* 1278
COLETTE - Footwear - CAPEZIO BALLET MAKERS INC.; *pg.* 1805, *pg.* 1125
COLETTE - Furniture - ETHAN ALLEN INTERIORS INC.; *pg.* 924, *pg.* 343
COLETTE - Gaming Product - GLD PRODUCTS, INC.; *pg.* 1835, *pg.* 1882
COLETTE FLOOR - Lamp - J. ROBERT SCOTT INC.; *pg.* 930, *pg.* 105
COLGATE - Toothpaste & Tooth Powder - COLGATE-PALMOLIVE COMPANY; *pg.* 504, *pg.* 1215
COLGATE 360 - Toothbrush - COLGATE-PALMOLIVE COMPANY; *pg.* 504, *pg.* 1215
COLGATE ACTIVE SALT - Toothpaste - COLGATE-PALMOLIVE COMPANY; *pg.* 504, *pg.* 1215
COLGATE ADVANCED WHITENING - Toothpaste - COLGATE-PALMOLIVE COMPANY; *pg.* 504, *pg.* 1215
COLGATE BAKING SODA TOOTHPASTE - Toothpaste - COLGATE-PALMOLIVE COMPANY; *pg.* 504, *pg.* 1215
COLGATE BUBBLE FRUITE - Toothpaste - COLGATE-PALMOLIVE COMPANY; *pg.* 504, *pg.* 1215
COLGATE CIBACA FAMILY PROTECTION - Toothpaste - COLGATE-PALMOLIVE COMPANY; *pg.* 504, *pg.* 1215
COLGATE DENTAL FLOSS - Dental Product - COLGATE-PALMOLIVE COMPANY; *pg.* 504, *pg.* 1215
COLGATE DURAPHAT - Dental Care Product - COLGATE-PALMOLIVE COMPANY; *pg.* 504, *pg.* 1215
COLGATE EXTRA-CLEAN - Toothbrush - COLGATE-PALMOLIVE COMPANY; *pg.* 504, *pg.* 1215
COLGATE FRESH CONFIDENCE - Toothpaste - COLGATE-PALMOLIVE COMPANY; *pg.* 504, *pg.* 1215
COLGATE FRESH ENERGY GEL - Toothpaste - COLGATE-PALMOLIVE COMPANY; *pg.* 504, *pg.* 1215
COLGATE GEL-KAM - Dental Care Product - COLGATE-PALMOLIVE COMPANY; *pg.* 504, *pg.* 1215
COLGATE HERBAL - Toothpaste - COLGATE-PALMOLIVE COMPANY; *pg.* 504, *pg.* 1215
COLGATE KIDS TOOTHPASTE - Toothpaste - COLGATE-PALMOLIVE COMPANY; *pg.* 504, *pg.* 1215
COLGATE MASSAGER - Toothbrush - COLGATE-PALMOLIVE COMPANY; *pg.* 504, *pg.* 1215
COLGATE MAXFRESH - Toothpaste - COLGATE-PALMOLIVE COMPANY; *pg.* 504, *pg.* 1215
COLGATE MOTION - Toothbrush - COLGATE-PALMOLIVE COMPANY; *pg.* 504, *pg.* 1215
COLGATE NAVIGATOR - Toothbrush - COLGATE-PALMOLIVE COMPANY; *pg.* 504, *pg.* 1215
COLGATE OPTIC WHITE - Teeth Whitening Paste - COLGATE-PALMOLIVE COMPANY; *pg.* 504, *pg.* 1215
COLGATE ORABASE - Dental Care Product - COLGATE-PALMOLIVE COMPANY; *pg.* 504, *pg.* 1215
COLGATE PERIOGARD - Dental Care Product - COLGATE-PALMOLIVE COMPANY; *pg.* 504, *pg.* 1215
COLGATE PEROXYL - Dental Care Product - COLGATE-PALMOLIVE COMPANY; *pg.* 504, *pg.* 1215
COLGATE PHOS-FLUR - Dental Care Product - COLGATE-PALMOLIVE COMPANY; *pg.* 504, *pg.* 1215
COLGATE PLATINUM - Toothpaste - COLGATE-PALMOLIVE COMPANY; *pg.* 504, *pg.* 1215
COLGATE PLUS - Toothbrush - COLGATE-PALMOLIVE COMPANY; *pg.* 504, *pg.* 1215
COLGATE PREVIDENT - Dental Care Product - COLGATE-PALMOLIVE COMPANY; *pg.* 504, *pg.* 1215
COLGATE SENSITIVE - Toothpaste - COLGATE-PALMOLIVE COMPANY; *pg.* 504, *pg.* 1215
COLGATE SIMPLY WHITE - Toothpaste - COLGATE-PALMOLIVE COMPANY; *pg.* 504, *pg.* 1215
COLGATE SPARKLING WHITE - Toothpaste - COLGATE-PALMOLIVE COMPANY; *pg.* 504, *pg.* 1215
COLGATE SPONGEBOB - Toothbrush - COLGATE-PALMOLIVE COMPANY; *pg.* 504, *pg.* 1215
COLGATE TARTAR CONTROL - Toothpaste - COLGATE-PALMOLIVE COMPANY; *pg.* 504, *pg.* 1215
COLGATE TOOTHPOWDER - Toothpowder - COLGATE-PALMOLIVE COMPANY; *pg.* 504, *pg.* 1215
COLGATE TOTAL - Toothpaste - COLGATE-PALMOLIVE COMPANY; *pg.* 504, *pg.* 1215
COLGATE TOTAL PROFESSIONAL - Toothbrush - COLGATE-PALMOLIVE COMPANY; *pg.* 504, *pg.* 1215
COLGATE VISIBLE WHITE - Dental Product - COLGATE-PALMOLIVE COMPANY; *pg.* 504, *pg.* 1215
COLGATE WAVE - Toothbrush - COLGATE-PALMOLIVE COMPANY; *pg.* 504, *pg.* 1215
COLGATE WHITENING GEL - Toothpaste - COLGATE-PALMOLIVE COMPANY; *pg.* 504, *pg.* 1215
COLGATE ZIGZAG JUNIOR - Toothpaste - COLGATE-PALMOLIVE COMPANY; *pg.* 504, *pg.* 1215
COLGATE ZIGZAG PLUS - Toothbrush - COLGATE-PALMOLIVE COMPANY; *pg.* 504, *pg.* 1215

COLHOGAR - Kitchen Towel - GEORGIA-PACIFIC LLC; *pg.* 1458, *pg.* 507
COLILERT - Reagent - IDEXX LABORATORIES, INC.; *pg.* 1543, *pg.* 753
COLILERT-18 - Reagent - IDEXX LABORATORIES, INC.; *pg.* 1543, *pg.* 753
COLISTA - Lamp - ASHLEY FURNITURE INDUSTRIES, INC.; *pg.* 914, *pg.* 1852
COLISURE - Reagent - IDEXX LABORATORIES, INC.; *pg.* 1543, *pg.* 753
COLITAG - Food Safety Product - NEOGEN CORPORATION; *pg.* 883, *pg.* 896
COLLABORATION - Office Furniture - STEELCASE INC.; *pg.* 475, *pg.* 889
COLLABORATION CHALLENGES & STRATEGIES - Event - TECHNOLOGY EXECUTIVES CLUB, LTD.; *pg.* 482, *pg.* 627
COLLABORATION SERVICES - Software - DELL SOFTWARE; *pg.* 385, *pg.* 40
COLLABORATION WITHOUT LIMITATION - Web Based Multimedia - CISCO SYSTEMS, INC.; *pg.* 372, *pg.* 240
COLLABORATIVE CLASSIFIER - Software - AUTONOMY, INC.; *pg.* 358, *pg.* 212
COLLABORATIVE FORECASTING - Software - ASPEN TECHNOLOGY, INC.; *pg.* 354, *pg.* 804
COLLACOTE - Medical Device - INTEGRA LIFESCIENCES HOLDINGS CORPORATION; *pg.* 1545, *pg.* 1109
COLLAGE - Wine - KENDALL-JACKSON WINE ESTATES, LTD.; *pg.* 1965, *pg.* 277
COLLAGE - Software - SERENA SOFTWARE, INC.; *pg.* 468, *pg.* 192
COLLAGEN AND ALMOND - Hair & Skin Product - AUBREY ORGANICS INC.; *pg.* 499, *pg.* 470
COLLAMER - Intraocular Lenses - STAAR SURGICAL COMPANY; *pg.* 1597, *pg.* 151
COLLAPLUG - Medical Device - INTEGRA LIFESCIENCES HOLDINGS CORPORATION; *pg.* 1545, *pg.* 1109
COLLATAPE - Medical Device - INTEGRA LIFESCIENCES HOLDINGS CORPORATION; *pg.* 1545, *pg.* 1109
COLLE NERO CHIANTI - Wine - SHAW ROSS INTERNATIONAL IMPORTERS; *pg.* 1970, *pg.* 449
COLLEAGUE - Infusion Pump - BAXTER INTERNATIONAL INC.; *pg.* 1499, *pg.* 599
COLLEAGUE - Knife - BUCK KNIVES, INC.; *pg.* 1828, *pg.* 550
COLLECT ON DELIVERY - Postal Services - UNITED STATES POSTAL SERVICE; *pg.* 1009, *pg.* 406
COLLECTIBLE CHEVY - Die Cast Replicas - REVELL; *pg.* 966, *pg.* 611
COLLECTION - Jewelry - YURMAN DESIGN, INC.; *pg.* 15, *pg.* 1316
COLLECTION 3 - Pacemaker - MEDTRONIC, INC.; *pg.* 1564, *pg.* 939
COLLECTION BEBE - Apparel - BEBE STORES, INC.; *pg.* 19, *pg.* 49
COLLECTIVE LOUNGE - Office Furniture - JOFCO INC.; *pg.* 931, *pg.* 691
COLLECTIVE MOTION - Swivel Furniture - JOFCO INC.; *pg.* 931, *pg.* 691
COLLECTIVE OFFICE - Office Furniture - JOFCO INC.; *pg.* 931, *pg.* 691
COLLECTIVE SPACE - Office Furniture - JOFCO INC.; *pg.* 931, *pg.* 691
COLLECTIVE TABLES - Tables - JOFCO INC.; *pg.* 931, *pg.* 691
COLLECTOR BOOKS - Publisher - SCHROEDER PUBLISHING COMPANY; *pg.* 1685, *pg.* 739
COLLECTOR'S CHOICE - Cigarettes - PHILIP MORRIS USA INC.; *pg.* 1894, *pg.* 1803
COLLECTORS CLASSICS - Furniture - ETHAN ALLEN INTERIORS INC.; *pg.* 924, *pg.* 343
COLLECTORS CLUB - Basket - THE LONGABERGER COMPANY; *pg.* 1127, *pg.* 1467
COLLECTORS CLUB TAMI LONGABERGER HERITAGE SERIES - Basket - THE LONGABERGER COMPANY; *pg.* 1127, *pg.* 1467
COLLEGE ANSWERS - Sweepstakes - SLM CORPORATION; *pg.* 804, *pg.* 388
COLLEGE CUP - Trademark (Div. I Men's & Women's Soccer) - NATIONAL COLLEGIATE ATHLETIC ASSOCIATION; *pg.* 567, *pg.* 688
COLLEGE INN - Food Products - DEL MONTE FOODS, INC.; *pg.* 852, *pg.* 304
COLLEGE WORLD SERIES - Division I Baseball Tournament - NATIONAL COLLEGIATE ATHLETIC ASSOCIATION; *pg.* 567, *pg.* 688
COLLEGEHUMOR.COM - Entertainment Website - IAC/INTERACTIVECORP; *pg.* 292, *pg.* 1242
COLLEGESERV - Magazine - SLM CORPORATION; *pg.* 804, *pg.* 388
COLLEGIAN - Furniture - JASPER GROUP; *pg.* 930, *pg.* 691
COLLEGIATE - Laboratory Product - EPPENDORF NORTH AMERICA; *pg.* 1412, *pg.* 1164
COLLEGIATE ATTACHE - Flash Drive - PNY TECHNOLOGIES, INC.; *pg.* 455, *pg.* 1105
COLLEGIATE SPORT SHELL - Ear Warmer - 180S, LLC; *pg.* 1824, *pg.* 754
COLLEGIS - Software - SUNGARD DATA SYSTEMS INC.; *pg.* 477, *pg.* 1592
COLLEGIUM - Office Furniture - STEELCASE INC.; *pg.* 475, *pg.* 889
COLLIER - Fabric - NEMSCHOFF, INC.; *pg.* 936, *pg.* 1890
COLLIGO - Software - VIEWSONIC CORPORATION; *pg.* 489, *pg.* 303
COLLIN - Furniture - ETHAN ALLEN INTERIORS INC.; *pg.* 924, *pg.* 343
COLLINS - Swing Products - PRYM CONSUMER USA; *pg.* 698, *pg.* 1622
COLLINS AVENUE - Furniture - ASHLEY FURNITURE INDUSTRIES, INC.; *pg.* 914, *pg.* 1852
COLLISION DAMAGE WAIVER - Rental Car Insurance - TRAVEL GUARD GROUP, INC.; *pg.* 1925, *pg.* 1895
COLLOIDAL COOMASSIE - Molecular Biology Product - THERMO FISHER SCIENTIFIC INC.; *pg.* 1602, *pg.* 61
COLMAN - Air Conditioners - NORTEK, INC.; *pg.* 100, *pg.* 1607
COLMONOY - Nickel Alloy - WALL COLMONOY CORPORATION; *pg.* 1185, *pg.* 898
COLO-VADA-PLUS - Nutritional Product - RBC LIFE SCIENCES, INC.; *pg.* 1588, *pg.* 1723
COLOGNE.COM - Advertising Website - LIVE CURRENT MEDIA INC.; *pg.* 1263, *pg.* 1911
COLOMBIA - Coffee - PEET'S COFFEE & TEA, INC.; *pg.* 1029, *pg.* 85
COLOMBIA NARINO SUPREMO - Coffee - STARBUCKS CORPORATION; *pg.* 897, *pg.* 1840
COLOMBO - Yogurt - GENERAL MILLS, INC.; *pg.* 828, *pg.* 933
COLOMBO - Marsala - WILLIAM GRANT & SONS, INC.; *pg.* 1972, *pg.* 1057
COLON PURE - Nutritional Supplement - WHITEWING LABS, INC.; *pg.* 1610, *pg.* 99
COLONEL AG - Gluing Machine - GLUEFAST COMPANY, INC.; *pg.* 1459, *pg.* 1090
COLONEL'S CRISPY STRIPS - Fried Chicken Strips - KFC CORPORATION; *pg.* 1733, *pg.* 735
COLONIAL - Home Fragrance Products - BLYTH, INC.; *pg.* 502, *pg.* 349
COLONIAL - Plain & Iodized Salt - CARGILL LIMITED; *pg.* 1475, *pg.* 1914
COLONIAL - Table Salt - CARGILL SALT; *pg.* 846, *pg.* 926
COLONIAL - Cookies & Biscuits - PARMALAT CANADA INC.; *pg.* 888, *pg.* 1941
COLONIAL - Footwear - STEVEN MADDEN, LTD.; *pg.* 1819, *pg.* 1176
COLONIAL BOSTON - Flatware - ONEIDA LTD; *pg.* 1129, *pg.* 1318
COLONIAL CANDLE OF CAPE COD - Candle - BLYTH, INC.; *pg.* 502, *pg.* 349
COLONIAL KETTLE - Rethermalizer - THE VOLLRATH COMPANY LLC; *pg.* 1139, *pg.* 1894
COLONNADE - Kitchen Faucet - MOEN INCORPORATED; *pg.* 1056, *pg.* 1468
COLONY - Furniture - AMANA SOCIETY, INC.; *pg.* 836, *pg.* 701
COLONY - Furniture - JASPER GROUP; *pg.* 930, *pg.* 691
COLONY - Glassware - LANCASTER COLONY CORPORATION; *pg.* 873, *pg.* 1441
THE COLONY AT PELICAN LANDING - Community Name - WCI COMMUNITIES, INC.; *pg.* 1118, *pg.* 414
COLONY HOMES - Homebuilding Services - KB HOME; *pg.* 90, *pg.* 134
COLONYDOC-IT - Imaging Station - UVP, INC.; *pg.* 1434, *pg.* 298
COLOR ACCESS - Filing Systems - SAFEGUARD BUSINESS SYSTEMS, INC.; *pg.* 464, *pg.* 1686
COLOR ALL - Spray Paint - SHERWIN-WILLIAMS DIVERSIFIED BRANDS DIVISION; *pg.* 1448, *pg.* 1435
THE COLOR AUTHORITY - Paint And Stain Product - BENJAMIN MOORE & CO.; *pg.* 1440, *pg.* 1085
COLOR BLOCK DESIGN - Shoes - SHOE CARNIVAL, INC.; *pg.* 1819, *pg.* 679
COLOR BROWN - Services - UNITED PARCEL SERVICE, INC.; *pg.* 1928, *pg.* 522
COLOR BY DELUXE - Motion Picture Film Processing, Video Mastering - DELUXE LABORATORIES, INC.; *pg.* 281, *pg.* 103
COLOR CHANGE SYSTEM - Fluid Handling System - GRACO, INC.; *pg.* 1342, *pg.* 935
COLOR CHANGING CRYSTALS - Yogurt Additives - THE DANNON COMPANY, INC.; *pg.* 851, *pg.* 1351
COLOR COMMAND - Lighting Product - HIGH END SYSTEMS, INC.; *pg.* 1299, *pg.* 1663
COLOR COVE - Lighting System - PHILIPS SOLID-STATE LIGHTING SOLUTIONS; *pg.* 1303, *pg.* 806
COLOR CUE - Adapter - PEAVEY ELECTRONICS CORPORATION; *pg.* 662, *pg.* 970
COLOR DELIGHTS - Eye Shadow - MAYBELLINE LLC; *pg.* 516, *pg.* 1257
COLOR DOTMATION - Game - WMS INDUSTRIES INC.; *pg.* 593, *pg.* 666
COLOR DYNAMICS - Color System Consultation Services - PPG INDUSTRIES, INC.; *pg.* 1445, *pg.* 1579
COLOR-EZ - Health & Beauty Product - BLUE CROSS LABORATORIES; *pg.* 326, *pg.* 277
COLOR-FLASH - Roof Flashing - OATEY SUPPLY CHAIN SERVICES; *pg.* 30, *pg.* 1433
COLOR-GRAD - Filter - THE TIFFEN COMPANY LLC; *pg.* 1432, *pg.* 1165
THE COLOR INSTITUTE - Cosmetics - MARKWINS INTERNATIONAL CORP.; *pg.* 516, *pg.* 67
COLOR INTRIGUE - Color - ELIZABETH ARDEN, INC.; *pg.* 507, *pg.* 448
COLOR IQC - Software - X-RITE, INCORPORATED; *pg.* 1437, *pg.* 891
COLOR-IT - Dispensing Equipment - IDEX CORPORATION; *pg.* 1347, *pg.* 623
COLOR KEY COMPUTER - Computer Color Matching System - AKZONOBEL DECORATIVE PAINTS U.S.; *pg.* 1439, *pg.* 1474
THE COLOR KEY PROGRAM - Paints - AKZONOBEL DECORATIVE PAINTS U.S.; *pg.* 1439, *pg.* 1474
COLOR-KEYED - Compression Connector - THOMAS & BETTS CORPORATION; *pg.* 680, *pg.* 1646
COLOR LINK - Fencing - MASTER HALCO; *pg.* 96, *pg.* 474
COLOR LOCK - Stainless Steel Product - AK STEEL HOLDING CORPORATION; *pg.* 1311, *pg.* 1479
COLOR MASTER - Filing Systems - SAFEGUARD BUSINESS SYSTEMS, INC.; *pg.* 464, *pg.* 1686
COLOR ME BEAUTIFUL - General Market Color Cosmetics & Skin Care - COLOR ME BEAUTIFUL, INC.; *pg.* 505, *pg.* 1787
COLOR ME NATURAL - Hair & Skin Product - AUBREY ORGANICS INC.; *pg.* 499, *pg.* 470
COLOR MIX - Bridal Wear - ALFRED ANGELO, INC.; *pg.* 17, *pg.* 1532
COLOR NATURALS - Paint - AKZONOBEL DECORATIVE PAINTS U.S.; *pg.* 1439, *pg.* 1474
COLOR-O-METER - Control Assembly - ROYLE SYSTEMS GROUP; *pg.* 1373, *pg.* 1100
COLOR OF THE ZEN-TURY - Nail Care Product - OPI PRODUCTS INC.; *pg.* 518, *pg.* 167
COLOR-ON-DEMAND - Instant Color Selector - NORDSON CORPORATION; *pg.* 1365, *pg.* 1480
COLOR PAK - Confection Processes - SENSIENT COLORS INC.; *pg.* 1180, *pg.* 1003
COLOR PLUS - Fencing - MASTER HALCO; *pg.* 96, *pg.* 474
COLOR PLUS DEFINE - Beauty Product - AVEDA CORPORATION; *pg.* 499, *pg.* 917
COLOR PLUS SHIMMER - Beauty Product - AVEDA CORPORATION; *pg.* 499, *pg.* 917
COLOR PORTABLE - Game - FORTUNET, INC.; *pg.* 953, *pg.* 1024
COLOR POWER - Lighting Product - HIGH END SYSTEMS, INC.; *pg.* 1299, *pg.* 1663
COLOR PREVIEW - Paint And Stain Product - BENJAMIN MOORE & CO.; *pg.* 1440, *pg.* 1085
COLOR PREVIEW STUDIO - Paint And Stain Product - BENJAMIN MOORE & CO.; *pg.* 1440, *pg.* 1085
COLOR PRIME - Primer - THE SHERWIN-WILLIAMS COMPANY; *pg.* 1447, *pg.* 1435
COLOR PRINT - Desk Top Graphics Transfers - THE PENN COMPANIES; *pg.* 10, *pg.* 1568
COLOR PRO - Lighting Product - HIGH END SYSTEMS, INC.; *pg.* 1299, *pg.* 1663

COLOR PROFILER SUITE - Printing Product - ELECTRONICS FOR IMAGING, INC.; *pg.* 390, *pg.* 88
COLOR PROTECT - Hair Care Product - JOHN PAUL MITCHELL SYSTEMS; *pg.* 512, *pg.* 133
COLOR PULSE - Paint And Stain Product - BENJAMIN MOORE & CO.; *pg.* 1440, *pg.* 1085
THE COLOR PURPLE - Art Performance - JOHN F. KENNEDY CENTER FOR THE PERFORMING ARTS; *pg.* 555, *pg.* 401
COLOR SENSATIONAL - Lip Color - MAYBELLINE LLC; *pg.* 516, *pg.* 1257
COLOR SENTRY - Filing Systems - SAFEGUARD BUSINESS SYSTEMS, INC.; *pg.* 464, *pg.* 1686
COLOR SHAMPOO - Hair Care Product - JOHN PAUL MITCHELL SYSTEMS; *pg.* 512, *pg.* 133
COLOR SHIELD - Paint - KELLY-MOORE PAINT COMPANY, INC.; *pg.* 1443, *pg.* 198
COLOR SPECTRUM - Carpet - BEAULIEU GROUP, LLC; *pg.* 917, *pg.* 529
COLOR STYLE - Paints - THE VALSPAR CORPORATION; *pg.* 1449, *pg.* 945
THE COLOR TELLS THE THICKNESS - Tagline - ARTUS CORPORATION; *pg.* 1314, *pg.* 1059
COLOR TREND - Beauty Product - AVON PRODUCTS, INC.; *pg.* 500, *pg.* 1198
COLOR WORKSHOP - Leisure Product - JAKKS PACIFIC, INC.; *pg.* 960, *pg.* 142
THE COLOR WORKSHOP - Cosmetics - MARKWINS INTERNATIONAL CORP.; *pg.* 516, *pg.* 67
COLOR XPRESSIONS - Printer - XEROX CORPORATION; *pg.* 494, *pg.* 365
COLORACCENTS - Paint - THE SHERWIN-WILLIAMS COMPANY; *pg.* 1447, *pg.* 1435
COLORADO - Pick-Up Truck - GENERAL MOTORS COMPANY; *pg.* 175, *pg.* 881
COLORADO AVALANCHE - Hockey Team - COLORADO AVALANCHE, LLC; *pg.* 541, *pg.* 317
COLORADO BIZ - Business-to-Business Magazine - WIESNER PUBLISHING, LLC; *pg.* 1702, *pg.* 328
COLORADO CARNATIONS - Florist Supplies - DENVER WHOLESALE FLORISTS COMPANY; *pg.* 1794, *pg.* 319
COLORADO DAILY - Newspaper - THE E.W. SCRIPPS COMPANY; *pg.* 1639, *pg.* 1412
COLORADO HOMES & LIFESTYLES - Magazine - NETWORK COMMUNICATIONS INC.; *pg.* 1271, *pg.* 534
COLORADO MICRODISSECTION NEEDLE - Micro Implant System - STRYKER CORPORATION; *pg.* 1598, *pg.* 894
COLORADO NEEDLE - Microdissection Needle - STRYKER CORPORATION; *pg.* 1598, *pg.* 894
COLORADO ROCKIES - Baseball Team - COLORADO ROCKIES BASEBALL CLUB, LTD.; *pg.* 542, *pg.* 317
COLORAMA - Display - EASTMAN KODAK COMPANY; *pg.* 1408, *pg.* 1333
COLORATIONS - Paint - DISCOUNT SCHOOL SUPPLY; *pg.* 1238, *pg.* 151
COLORBAR - Label Design System - SMEAD MANUFACTURING COMPANY; *pg.* 470, *pg.* 926
COLORBLAST - Lighting System - PHILIPS SOLID-STATE LIGHTING SOLUTIONS; *pg.* 1303, *pg.* 806
COLORBLAZE - Lighting System - PHILIPS SOLID-STATE LIGHTING SOLUTIONS; *pg.* 1303, *pg.* 806
COLORBLOCK - Hat - WOODEN SHIPS OF HOBOKEN; *pg.* 35, *pg.* 1315
COLORBLOCK LS CREW - Clothing - K-SWISS; *pg.* 1837, *pg.* 306
COLORBLOCKED CREW - Clothing - K-SWISS; *pg.* 1837, *pg.* 306
COLORBRITE - Photographic Print Service - EASTMAN KODAK COMPANY; *pg.* 1408, *pg.* 1333
COLORBURST - One-Time Use Cameras - EASTMAN KODAK COMPANY; *pg.* 1408, *pg.* 1333
COLORBURST - Lighting System - PHILIPS SOLID-STATE LIGHTING SOLUTIONS; *pg.* 1303, *pg.* 806
COLORCAST - Lighting System - PHILIPS SOLID-STATE LIGHTING SOLUTIONS; *pg.* 1303, *pg.* 806
COLORCHECKER - Checkerboard Array - X-RITE, INCORPORATED; *pg.* 1437, *pg.* 891
COLORCOAT - Coating - ROSCO LABORATORIES, INC.; *pg.* 1782, *pg.* 378
COLORCOAT - Thermal Transfer Roll - XEROX CORPORATION; *pg.* 494, *pg.* 365
COLORCOMMAND - Lighting Product - HIGH END SYSTEMS, INC.; *pg.* 1299, *pg.* 1663
COLORCURE - Concrete System - L.M. SCOFIELD COMPANY; *pg.* 94, *pg.* 134
COLORDESIGNER - Color-Matching Computer Software - X-RITE, INCORPORATED; *pg.* 1437, *pg.* 891
COLORDIAL - Lighting System - PHILIPS SOLID-STATE LIGHTING SOLUTIONS; *pg.* 1303, *pg.* 806
COLOREDGE - Color Copiers, Duplicators, & Accessories, Film, Toner, & Developers - EASTMAN KODAK COMPANY; *pg.* 1408, *pg.* 1333
COLORFAST - Software - EAGLE POINT SOFTWARE CORPORATION; *pg.* 389, *pg.* 707
COLORFORMS - Game - UNIVERSITY GAMES CORPORATION; *pg.* 969, *pg.* 230
COLORFORMS. IT.S TIME TO PLAY. - Tag Line - UNIVERSITY GAMES CORPORATION; *pg.* 969, *pg.* 230
COLORFUL IMPRESSIONS - Napkins - GEORGIA-PACIFIC LLC; *pg.* 1458, *pg.* 507
COLORGIN - Coatings - THE SHERWIN-WILLIAMS COMPANY; *pg.* 1447, *pg.* 1435
COLORGO CHEMICAL - Cleanser - A.L. WILSON CHEMICAL CO.; *pg.* 325, *pg.* 1076
COLORGRAFX TONER - Toner - XEROX CORPORATION; *pg.* 494, *pg.* 365
COLORGUARD - Colorants - FERRO CORPORATION; *pg.* 1162, *pg.* 1462
COLORGUARD - Industrial Fabric - HERCULITE PRODUCTS, INC.; *pg.* 694, *pg.* 1529
COLORINE - Paint - ROSCO LABORATORIES, INC.; *pg.* 1782, *pg.* 378
COLORITE - Polymer - TEKNI-PLEX, INC.; *pg.* 1470, *pg.* 1122
COLORITE WATERWORKS - Garden Hose - TEKNI-PLEX, INC.; *pg.* 1470, *pg.* 1122
COLORIZER - Pattern - ROSCO LABORATORIES, INC.; *pg.* 1782, *pg.* 378
COLORIZERS - Gobo Rotator - ROSCO LABORATORIES, INC.; *pg.* 1782, *pg.* 378
COLORLINE - Paint - ROSCO LABORATORIES, INC.; *pg.* 1782, *pg.* 378
COLORLINK PUBLISHING SYSTEM - Manual - XEROX CORPORATION; *pg.* 494, *pg.* 365
COLORLOGIC - Lighting Product - HAYWARD POOL PRODUCTS; *pg.* 1049, *pg.* 1057
COLORLOK - Paper - DOMTAR CORPORATION; *pg.* 1456, *pg.* 1954
COLORLOK - Graphic Supplies - XPEDX; *pg.* 1473, *pg.* 1377
COLORMAIL EXPRESS - Software Utility - X-RITE, INCORPORATED; *pg.* 1437, *pg.* 891
COLORMAN - Press - MANROLAND INC.; *pg.* 430, *pg.* 669
COLORMARK - Sensitive Film & Adhesive - FLEXCON CORPORATION; *pg.* 1457, *pg.* 844
COLORMASTER - Offset Printing Blanket - ROTADYNE; *pg.* 1681, *pg.* 529
COLORMATCH - Liquid Plastic - SMOOTH-ON INC.; *pg.* 111, *pg.* 1528
COLORMAX - Food Product - CHR. HANSEN; *pg.* 847, *pg.* 1873
COLORMAX - Powder Spray System - NORDSON CORPORATION; *pg.* 1365, *pg.* 1480
COLORMERGE - Lighting Product - HIGH END SYSTEMS, INC.; *pg.* 1299, *pg.* 1663
COLORMUNKI - Color Technology - X-RITE, INCORPORATED; *pg.* 1437, *pg.* 891
COLORMUNKI CREATE - Software - X-RITE, INCORPORATED; *pg.* 1437, *pg.* 891
COLORMUNKI DESIGN - Software - X-RITE, INCORPORATED; *pg.* 1437, *pg.* 891
COLORPACK - Fertilizer - SIMPLOT PARTNERS INC.; *pg.* 1800, *pg.* 548
COLORPLAY - Lighting System - PHILIPS SOLID-STATE LIGHTING SOLUTIONS; *pg.* 1303, *pg.* 806
COLORPORT - Connectivity Utility Software - X-RITE, INCORPORATED; *pg.* 1437, *pg.* 891
COLORPRO - Dispensing Equipment - IDEX CORPORATION; *pg.* 1347, *pg.* 623
COLORS - Cameras - EASTMAN KODAK COMPANY; *pg.* 1408, *pg.* 1333
COLORS FOR YOUR LIFE - Tagline - ACE HARDWARE CORPORATION; *pg.* 1040, *pg.* 644
COLORS FROM NATURE - Color - WILD FLAVORS, INC.; *pg.* 910, *pg.* 728
COLORS OF EXCELLENCE - Manual - XEROX CORPORATION; *pg.* 494, *pg.* 365
COLORS OF MILAN - Decorative Coatings - USG CORPORATION; *pg.* 118, *pg.* 594
COLORS OF SIENA - Decorative Coatings - USG CORPORATION; *pg.* 118, *pg.* 594
COLORS OF VENICE - Decorative Coatings - USG CORPORATION; *pg.* 118, *pg.* 594
COLORSAVER - Laser Printers - LEXMARK INTERNATIONAL, INC.; *pg.* 427, *pg.* 730
COLORSCALE - Software - SYMANTEC CORPORATION; *pg.* 478, *pg.* 161
COLORSCAPE - Lighting System - PHILIPS SOLID-STATE LIGHTING SOLUTIONS; *pg.* 1303, *pg.* 806
COLORSCAPES - Paint And Stain Product - BENJAMIN MOORE & CO.; *pg.* 1440, *pg.* 1085
COLORSHIFT - Pigment - VIAVI SOLUTIONS INC.; *pg.* 1435, *pg.* 148
COLORSPEC - ID System - AFC CABLE SYSTEMS, INC.; *pg.* 1294, *pg.* 835
COLORSPLUS - Vinyl Composition Tile - AMERICAN BILTRITE INC.; *pg.* 1878, *pg.* 856
COLORSTAY - Cosmetics - REVLON, INC.; *pg.* 521, *pg.* 1286
COLORSTIX - Ink - XEROX CORPORATION; *pg.* 494, *pg.* 365
COLORSTONE - Concrete System - L.M. SCOFIELD COMPANY; *pg.* 94, *pg.* 134
COLORSYNC - Application Program - APPLE INC.; *pg.* 350, *pg.* 73
COLORTAPE - Label Component System - FLEXCON CORPORATION; *pg.* 1457, *pg.* 844
COLORTEX - Bathroom Tissue & Towel - ORCHIDS PAPER PRODUCTS COMPANY; *pg.* 1465, *pg.* 1488
COLORTOUCH - Software - CRESTRON ELECTRONICS INC.; *pg.* 631, *pg.* 1116
COLORTRAC - Ink - INX INTERNATIONAL INK CO.; *pg.* 421, *pg.* 658
COLORTUNES - Speaker - SDI TECHNOLOGIES, INC.; *pg.* 671, *pg.* 1113
COLORTYME - Rent-To-Own Stores - COLORTYME, INC.; *pg.* 1765, *pg.* 1729
COLORWALL - Electronic Display System - TRANS-LUX CORPORATION; *pg.* 681, *pg.* 365
COLORWASH SHADOW PLUS VITAMINS - Eyeshadow - AVEDA CORPORATION; *pg.* 499, *pg.* 917
COLORWATCH - Photofinishing Quality Monitoring System - EASTMAN KODAK COMPANY; *pg.* 1408, *pg.* 1333
COLORWAVE - LED - CREE INC.; *pg.* 631, *pg.* 1371
COLORWAVES - Clipper - ANDIS COMPANY; *pg.* 498, *pg.* 1895
COLORWAVES - Gobo Rotator - ROSCO LABORATORIES, INC.; *pg.* 1782, *pg.* 378
COLORWAX - Concrete System - L.M. SCOFIELD COMPANY; *pg.* 94, *pg.* 134
COLORWORKS - Hair Care Salon - THE RATNER COMPANIES; *pg.* 520, *pg.* 1809
COLORWORKS - Spray Paints - SHERWIN-WILLIAMS DIVERSIFIED BRANDS DIVISION; *pg.* 1448, *pg.* 1435
COLORZ - Foam Dice - SCHOOL-TECH, INC.; *pg.* 1844, *pg.* 866
COLOSSAL JACKPOTS - Game - WMS INDUSTRIES INC.; *pg.* 593, *pg.* 666
COLOSSEUM - Flatware - ONEIDA LTD; *pg.* 1129, *pg.* 1318
COLOSSUS - Computer Program - COMPUTER SCIENCES CORPORATION; *pg.* 378, *pg.* 1780
COLOSSUS - Navigation Aid - TRIMBLE NAVIGATION LIMITED; *pg.* 1384, *pg.* 288
COLOSTRO-FIX - Animal Nutrition Product - MANNA PRO CORPORATION; *pg.* 1478, *pg.* 975
COLOSTRUM - Nutritional Supplement - NATURAL ORGANICS, INC.; *pg.* 1571, *pg.* 1181
COLOUR MORE - Color-Safe Bleach - THE CLOROX COMPANY; *pg.* 327, *pg.* 169
COLOUR WARPER - Software - AUTODESK INC.; *pg.* 356, *pg.* 257
COLOURFUL BOWLING FRIENDS - Toy - THE OHIO ART COMPANY, INC.; *pg.* 965, *pg.* 1406
COLPAC - Orthopedic Device - DJO SURGICAL; *pg.* 1525, *pg.* 1661
COLPOSTAR - Medical Instrument - WALLACH SURGICAL DEVICES, INC.; *pg.* 1436, *pg.* 381
COLRING - Cable Ties - PASS & SEYMOUR/LEGRAND; *pg.* 1303, *pg.* 1344
COLSIL - Precision Abrasive Product - SAINT-GOBAIN ABRASIVES, INC. - PHILADELPHIA; *pg.* 1180, *pg.* 1553
COLSON - Cable Ties - PASS & SEYMOUR/LEGRAND; *pg.* 1303, *pg.* 1344
COLSPRAY - Metallizing Powder - WALL COLMONOY CORPORATION; *pg.* 1185, *pg.* 898

COLT - Pull Type Finish Mower - AG-MEIER INDUSTRIES LLC; *pg.* 700, *pg.* 1668
COLT - Floor Cleaning Product - NSS ENTERPRISES, INC.; *pg.* 59, *pg.* 1476
COLT 45 - Malt Liquor - PABST BREWING COMPANY; *pg.* 258, *pg.* 137
COLT 45 - Food - WESTERN SIZZLIN CORPORATION; *pg.* 1755, *pg.* 1806
COLT CO2 - Air Pistols - DAISY MANUFACTURING COMPANY; *pg.* 1831, *pg.* 35
COLTS.COM - Website - INDIANAPOLIS COLTS, INC.; *pg.* 553, *pg.* 687
COLUMBIA - Records Group - SONY MUSIC ENTERTAINMENT; *pg.* 309, *pg.* 1294
COLUMBIA - Software - SYNOPSYS, INC.; *pg.* 480, *pg.* 162
COLUMBIA-CE - Software - SYNOPSYS, INC.; *pg.* 480, *pg.* 162
COLUMBIA LIGHTING - Lighting Product - HUBBELL INCORPORATED; *pg.* 1299, *pg.* 370
COLUMBIA UNIVERSITY PRESS - Publisher - COLUMBIA UNIVERSITY PRESS; *pg.* 1628, *pg.* 1216
COLUMBIA VALLEY FARMS - Food Service - FOOD SERVICES OF AMERICA, INC.; *pg.* 856, *pg.* 21
COLUMBIAN - Envelope - WESTROCK COMPANY; *pg.* 1472, *pg.* 1805
COLUMBIANA - Telephone Service - IDT CORPORATION; *pg.* 643, *pg.* 1096
COLUMBO - Yogurt - YOPLAIT USA, INC.; *pg.* 910, *pg.* 947
COLUMBUS - Data Management - PERKINELMER, INC.; *pg.* 1426, *pg.* 853
COLUMBUS BAKERY - Restaurant - ARK RESTAURANTS CORP.; *pg.* 1715, *pg.* 1196
COLUMBUS BLUE JACKETS - Hockey Team - COLUMBUS BLUE JACKETS; *pg.* 542, *pg.* 1439
COLUMBUS CIRCLE - Jewelry - LAGOS INC.; *pg.* 8, *pg.* 1566
THE COLUMBUS DISPATCH - Daily Newspaper - THE DISPATCH PRINTING COMPANY; *pg.* 1636, *pg.* 1439
COLUMN - Decorative Accessory - ETHAN ALLEN INTERIORS INC.; *pg.* 924, *pg.* 343
COLUSA ROSE - Rice - AMERICAN RICE, INC.; *pg.* 837, *pg.* 1700
COLYER - Footwear - K-SWISS; *pg.* 1837, *pg.* 306
COM-FLEX - Spectacle Temples - MCR SAFETY; *pg.* 1422, *pg.* 1630
COMAG - Magazine - THE HEARST CORPORATION; *pg.* 1649, *pg.* 1239
COMAG MARKETING GROUP - Magazine - THE HEARST CORPORATION; *pg.* 1649, *pg.* 1239
COMALLOY - Plastic Compound & Resin - A. SCHULMAN, INC.; *pg.* 1144, *pg.* 1452
COMANCHI - Footwear - STEVEN MADDEN, LTD.; *pg.* 1819, *pg.* 1176
COMAR ORAL DISPENSER - Liquid Medicine Dispenser - COMAR INC.; *pg.* 1455, *pg.* 1047
COMARE - Personal Care Electrical Product - HELEN OF TROY L.P.; *pg.* 511, *pg.* 1692
COMAX - Level Gauge - ECLIPSE INC.; *pg.* 1332, *pg.* 655
COMBAT - Insecticides - THE CLOROX COMPANY; *pg.* 327, *pg.* 169
COMBAT - Insecticides - HENKEL CONSUMER GOODS; *pg.* 511, *pg.* 22
COMBAT SERIES - Toilet Partitions - BOBRICK WASHROOM EQUIPMENT, INC.; *pg.* 1043, *pg.* 166
COMBED - Linens Fabrics - TEMPUR SEALY INTERNATIONAL, INC.; *pg.* 944, *pg.* 731
COMBI - Liquid Handling System - MOLECULAR DEVICES CORPORATION; *pg.* 1568, *pg.* 287
COMBI-SENSE - Mosfet Driver - SEMTECH CORPORATION; *pg.* 671, *pg.* 57
COMBI-SYNC - Rectifier And Regulator - SEMTECH CORPORATION; *pg.* 671, *pg.* 57
COMBI-THERM - Combi Oven - ALTO-SHAAM INC.; *pg.* 836, *pg.* 1869
COMBICOR - Water Heater System - BRADFORD-WHITE CORPORATION; *pg.* 1069, *pg.* 1514
COMBIDERM - Wound Care Product - CONVATEC LTD.; *pg.* 1518, *pg.* 1121
COMBIDEX - Nanoparticle Product - AMAG PHARMACEUTICALS, INC.; *pg.* 1492, *pg.* 827
COMBIFIX - Medical Device - GAMMEX RMI INC.; *pg.* 1532, *pg.* 1872
COMBIGAN - Glaucoma Treatment - ALLERGAN, INC.; *pg.* 1491, *pg.* 106
COMBIGUARD - Water Filtration System - ALTO-SHAAM INC.; *pg.* 836, *pg.* 1869
COMBIPATCH - Estradiol Transdermal System - NOVEN PHARMACEUTICALS, INC.; *pg.* 1576, *pg.* 445
COMBITUBE - Medical Device - MALLINCKRODT PHARMACEUTICALS; *pg.* 1557, *pg.* 978
COMBITUBE - Esophageal & Tracheal Double-Lumen Airway - MEDTRONIC; *pg.* 1563, *pg.* 183
COMBO - Shield Mask - ALPHA PRO TECH, LTD.; *pg.* 1492, *pg.* 1922
COMBO - Burnishing Pad - AMERICO MANUFACTURING CO., INC.; *pg.* 325, *pg.* 482
COMBO - Crusher - ASTEC INDUSTRIES, INC.; *pg.* 69, *pg.* 1628
COMBO - Multi-Angle Scalping Screen - KPI-JCI; *pg.* 1354, *pg.* 1626
COMBO - Musical Instrument - PEAVEY ELECTRONICS CORPORATION; *pg.* 662, *pg.* 970
COMBO CARD - Card Product - ABNOTE NORTH AMERICA; *pg.* 1878, *pg.* 789
COMBO CUT - Haircutting Kit - CONAIR CORPORATION; *pg.* 505, *pg.* 1055
COMBO-LITE - Hospital Lighting - SWIVELIER CO., INC.; *pg.* 1307, *pg.* 1142
COMBO LOCKER - Electronic Data Storage System - MASTER LOCK COMPANY LLC; *pg.* 1055, *pg.* 1884
COMBO-SPREADER - Electronic Material - HONEYWELL INTERNATIONAL INC.; *pg.* 407, *pg.* 1088
COMBO STRIP - Gaskets - PARKER CHOMERICS; *pg.* 662, *pg.* 862
COMBO WARM UP JACKET - Clothing - K-SWISS; *pg.* 1837, *pg.* 306
COMBO WARM UP PANT - Clothing - K-SWISS; *pg.* 1837, *pg.* 306
COMBO WOVEN SHORT - Clothing - K-SWISS; *pg.* 1837, *pg.* 306
COMBOKKULT - Pharmaceutical Product - ALERE INC.; *pg.* 1488, *pg.* 849
COMBOMAT - General Purpose Fiber Glass - PPG INDUSTRIES, INC.; *pg.* 1445, *pg.* 1579
COMBOS - Snack Foods - MARS, INCORPORATED; *pg.* 1858, *pg.* 1792
COMBOTHERM - Chemical Product - THE DOW CHEMICAL COMPANY; *pg.* 1157, *pg.* 898
COMBSCAN - Pharmaceutical Product - ALERE INC.; *pg.* 1488, *pg.* 849
COMBUSTIFUME - Burner - MAXON CORPORATION; *pg.* 1359, *pg.* 695
COMBUSTION - Software - AUTODESK INC.; *pg.* 356, *pg.* 257
COMBUSTION TEC - Burner System - ECLIPSE INC.; *pg.* 1332, *pg.* 655
COMBUSTOR - Flare - NAO, INC.; *pg.* 1074, *pg.* 1567
COMCAST DIGITAL VOICE - Internet Services - COMCAST CORPORATION; *pg.* 276, *pg.* 1560
COMCENTRIX - Integrated Circuits - AVAGO TECHNOLOGIES; *pg.* 358, *pg.* 238
COMCO - Carbon Steel Pipe, Valves, Flanges & Fittings - RUSSEL METALS INC.; *pg.* 1180, *pg.* 1928
COMDIAL DX-120 - Business Communications System - VERTICAL COMMUNICATIONS, INC.; *pg.* 488, *pg.* 270
COMDIAL DX-120FX II - Business Phone System - VERTICAL COMMUNICATIONS, INC.; *pg.* 488, *pg.* 270
COMDIAL MP5000 - Business Phone System - VERTICAL COMMUNICATIONS, INC.; *pg.* 488, *pg.* 270
COME BE OUR GUEST - Iowa State Tourism Campaign - IOWA DEPARTMENT OF ECONOMIC DEVELOPMENT; *pg.* 995, *pg.* 705
COME HOME - Webzine - ANDERSEN CORPORATION; *pg.* 67, *pg.* 916
COME HOME TO THE GOOD STUFF - Slogan - COUNTRY KITCHEN INTERNATIONAL, INC.; *pg.* 1723, *pg.* 1865
COME HUNGRY. LEAVE HAPPY - Slogan - DINEEQUITY, INC.; *pg.* 1725, *pg.* 95
COME PLAY! - Services - DOVER DOWNS GAMING & ENTERTAINMENT, INC.; *pg.* 545, *pg.* 387
COMEDIL - Crane - TEREX CORPORATION; *pg.* 1381, *pg.* 384
COMERICA CENTRAL - Financial Services - COMERICA INCORPORATED; *pg.* 740, *pg.* 1677
COMERICA TM CONNECT - Banking Services - COMERICA INCORPORATED; *pg.* 740, *pg.* 1677
COMERICA TM CONNECT DESKTOP - Banking Services - COMERICA INCORPORATED; *pg.* 740, *pg.* 1677
COMERICA TM CONNECT FILE TRANSFER - Banking Services - COMERICA INCORPORATED; *pg.* 740, *pg.* 1677
COMERICA TM CONNECT WEB - Banking Services - COMERICA INCORPORATED; *pg.* 740, *pg.* 1677
COMERICA WEB BANKING FOR SMALL BUSINESS - Banking Services - COMERICA INCORPORATED; *pg.* 740, *pg.* 1677
COMERICA WEB BILL PAY - Banking Services - COMERICA INCORPORATED; *pg.* 740, *pg.* 1677
COMERICA WEBBANKING - Banking Services - COMERICA INCORPORATED; *pg.* 740, *pg.* 1677
COMERICA'S HOME EQUITY FLEXLINE - Banking Services - COMERICA INCORPORATED; *pg.* 740, *pg.* 1677
COMET - Instant Rice Mixes - AMERICAN RICE, INC.; *pg.* 837, *pg.* 1700
COMET - Software - CANNON EQUIPMENT COMPANY; *pg.* 1321, *pg.* 920
COMET - Bicycle - G. JOANNOU CYCLE CO. INC.; *pg.* 1707, *pg.* 1098
COMET - Medical Equipment - INVACARE CORPORATION; *pg.* 1546, *pg.* 1451
COMET - Fabric - NEMSCHOFF, INC.; *pg.* 936, *pg.* 1890
COMET - Transceiver - PMC-SIERRA, INC.; *pg.* 664, *pg.* 287
COMET - Household Cleaning Product - PRESTIGE BRANDS HOLDINGS, INC.; *pg.* 520, *pg.* 1345
COMET - Detergent - THE PROCTER & GAMBLE COMPANY; *pg.* 1129, *pg.* 1418
COMET - Ceiling Fan - WESTINGHOUSE LIGHTING CORPORATION; *pg.* 687, *pg.* 1571
COMFIES - Bikini - JOCKEY INTERNATIONAL, INC.; *pg.* 27, *pg.* 1861
COMFLEX - Cable & Antenna System - RADIO FREQUENCY SYSTEMS, INC.; *pg.* 666, *pg.* 354
COMFO - Respirator Cartridges - MINE SAFETY APPLIANCES COMPANY; *pg.* 1361, *pg.* 1525
COMFO-CAP - Mining Headwear - MINE SAFETY APPLIANCES COMPANY; *pg.* 1361, *pg.* 1525
COMFO CLASSIC - Gas Mask - MINE SAFETY APPLIANCES COMPANY; *pg.* 1361, *pg.* 1525
COMFO ELITE - Gas Mask - MINE SAFETY APPLIANCES COMPANY; *pg.* 1361, *pg.* 1525
COMFORMAX - Fabric - E.I. DU PONT DE NEMOURS & COMPANY; *pg.* 1159, *pg.* 390
COMFORPEDIC - Mattress - SIMMONS COMPANY; *pg.* 943, *pg.* 520
COMFORT - Veil - ALPHA PRO TECH, LTD.; *pg.* 1492, *pg.* 1922
COMFORT - Orthopedic Product - DJO INCORPORATED; *pg.* 1524, *pg.* 302
COMFORT - Healthcare Fabric - HERCULITE PRODUCTS, INC.; *pg.* 694, *pg.* 1529
COMFORT - Fabric - NEMSCHOFF, INC.; *pg.* 936, *pg.* 1890
COMFORT-AIR - Respirator - MCR SAFETY; *pg.* 1422, *pg.* 1630
COMFORT-AIRE - Air Conditioner - HEAT CONTROLLER, INC.; *pg.* 1072, *pg.* 893
COMFORT ANGLE - Drinking Cup Feature - EVENFLO COMPANY, INC.; *pg.* 924, *pg.* 1470
COMFORT ASSURED - Heat Pump Installations - DOMINION VIRGINIA POWER; *pg.* 1939, *pg.* 1802
COMFORT ASSURED - Lancets - WALGREEN CO.; *pg.* 1608, *pg.* 605
COMFORT BAND - Hearing System - MINE SAFETY APPLIANCES COMPANY; *pg.* 1361, *pg.* 1525
COMFORT BLEND - Clock - BROWN & BIGELOW, INC.; *pg.* 1624, *pg.* 959
COMFORT CARE - Manual Breast Pump - EVENFLO COMPANY, INC.; *pg.* 924, *pg.* 1470
COMFORT CHECK - Handheld Analyzer - BACHARACH INC.; *pg.* 1400, *pg.* 1556
COMFORT COIL - Mattress Pad - CARPENTER CO.; *pg.* 920, *pg.* 1801
COMFORT COLLECTION - Healthcare Apparel - THE SALK COMPANY; *pg.* 1591, *pg.* 800
COMFORT COMES STANDARD - Slogan - INVACARE CORPORATION; *pg.* 1546, *pg.* 1451
COMFORT CURVE - Footwear - WOLVERINE WORLD WIDE, INC.; *pg.* 1822, *pg.* 905
COMFORT-E2 - Low Emissivity Pyrolitic Glass - AGC GLASS NORTH AMERICA, INC.; *pg.* 65, *pg.* 482
COMFORT-EASE - Respirators - MCR SAFETY; *pg.* 1422, *pg.* 1630
COMFORT EQUIPPED - Apparel - HAGGAR CORPORATION; *pg.* 41, *pg.* 1682
COMFORT FIRST - Infant Bath Tub - EVENFLO COMPANY, INC.; *pg.* 924, *pg.* 1470

COMFORT FIT 560 - Jean - LEVI STRAUSS & CO.; *pg.* 43, *pg.* 220
COMFORT GRIP - Flashlight - ENERGIZER HOLDINGS, INC.; *pg.* 637, *pg.* 996
COMFORT-GRIP - Training Cup Handles - EVENFLO COMPANY, INC.; *pg.* 924, *pg.* 1470
COMFORT GRIP - Catheter Handle - ST. JUDE MEDICAL, INC.; *pg.* 1596, *pg.* 963
COMFORT GRIPS - Fluid Handling System - GRACO, INC.; *pg.* 1342, *pg.* 935
COMFORT HEAT - Seat Heater - ROSTRA PRECISION CONTROLS, INC.; *pg.* 216, *pg.* 1381
COMFORT HEIGHT - Bath Product - KOHLER CO.; *pg.* 91, *pg.* 1862
COMFORT INN - Hotels & Resorts - CHOICE HOTELS INTERNATIONAL, INC.; *pg.* 1086, *pg.* 775
COMFORT LITES - Loafers - HABAND COMPANY, INC.; *pg.* 1772, *pg.* 1099
COMFORT MAT - Cushion Mats - MOHAWK HOME; *pg.* 935, *pg.* 541
COMFORT-MATE - Cushion - INVACARE CORPORATION; *pg.* 1546, *pg.* 1451
COMFORT PLUSH - Bicycle Accessories - SPECIALIZED BICYCLE COMPONENTS, INC.; *pg.* 1711, *pg.* 152
COMFORT SEAM - Sock - ACUSHNET COMPANY; *pg.* 1824, *pg.* 818
COMFORT SEAT - Seating System - ROSTRA PRECISION CONTROLS, INC.; *pg.* 216, *pg.* 1381
COMFORT SEATING - Residential Seating - FLEXSTEEL INDUSTRIES, INC.; *pg.* 925, *pg.* 707
COMFORT SELECT - Auto-Cycling Breast Pump - EVENFLO COMPANY, INC.; *pg.* 924, *pg.* 1470
COMFORT SENSATIONS - Mattress - KING KOIL LICENSING COMPANY INC.; *pg.* 932, *pg.* 671
COMFORT-SET - Thermostats for Heating & Air Conditioning - EMERSON WHITE-RODGERS; *pg.* 1071, *pg.* 996
COMFORT-SMOOTH - Baby Wipes - WALGREEN CO.; *pg.* 1608, *pg.* 605
COMFORT SOLUTIONS - Medical Equipment - INVACARE CORPORATION; *pg.* 1546, *pg.* 1451
COMFORT SOLUTIONS - Slogan - KING KOIL LICENSING COMPANY INC.; *pg.* 932, *pg.* 671
COMFORT SUITES - Hotels & Resorts - CHOICE HOTELS INTERNATIONAL, INC.; *pg.* 1086, *pg.* 775
COMFORT TAGS - Pressure-Sensitive Label Materials - AVERY DENNISON CORPORATION; *pg.* 1452, *pg.* 95
COMFORT TI-AC - Low Emissivity Glass - AGC GLASS NORTH AMERICA, INC.; *pg.* 65, *pg.* 482
COMFORT TOUCH - Hair Dryer - CONAIR CORPORATION; *pg.* 505, *pg.* 1055
COMFORT TOUCH - Infant Pads & Pillows - EVENFLO COMPANY, INC.; *pg.* 924, *pg.* 1470
COMFORT TREAD - Footrest (for office) - RUBBERMAID HOME PRODUCTS; *pg.* 1138, *pg.* 1453
COMFORT VENT - Baby Carrier & Pacifier Feature - EVENFLO COMPANY, INC.; *pg.* 924, *pg.* 1470
COMFORT WITH CACHE - Slacks & Shorts - HABAND COMPANY, INC.; *pg.* 1772, *pg.* 1099
COMFORTAB - Closure - ACUSHNET COMPANY; *pg.* 1824, *pg.* 818
COMFORTAIRE - Personal Care Product - TREDEGAR CORPORATION; *pg.* 1890, *pg.* 1804
COMFORTBASE - Building Product - HOMASOTE COMPANY; *pg.* 87, *pg.* 1126
COMFORTCARE - Mattress - RESTONIC MATTRESS CORPORATION; *pg.* 941, *pg.* 553
COMFORTCLEAN - Protective Apparel - TREDEGAR CORPORATION; *pg.* 1890, *pg.* 1804
COMFORTCUFF - Patient Monitoring Device - CRITICARE SYSTEMS, INC.; *pg.* 1520, *pg.* 1897
COMFORTEASE - Scrub - ALIMED, INC.; *pg.* 1490, *pg.* 816
COMFORTEASE - Manual Breast Pump - EVENFLO COMPANY, INC.; *pg.* 924, *pg.* 1470
COMFORTFOLD - Stroller Folding System - EVENFLO COMPANY, INC.; *pg.* 924, *pg.* 1470
COMFORTFORCE - Footwear - RED WING SHOE COMPANY, INC.; *pg.* 1817, *pg.* 954
COMFORTFORM - Orthopedic Product - DJO INCORPORATED; *pg.* 1524, *pg.* 302
COMFORTGLIDE - Stroller Wheels - EVENFLO COMPANY, INC.; *pg.* 924, *pg.* 1470
COMFORTGRIP - Belt - ELBECO INCORPORATED; *pg.* 40, *pg.* 1584
COMFORTGUARD - Generator - CUMMINS INC.; *pg.* 1326, *pg.* 676
COMFORTMATE - Medical Device - MENTOR CORPORATION; *pg.* 1565, *pg.* 263
COMFORTO - Seating - HAWORTH, INC.; *pg.* 402, *pg.* 891
COMFORTPILLOW - Pillow - TEMPUR SEALY INTERNATIONAL, INC.; *pg.* 944, *pg.* 731
COMFORTPLUS - Wholehouse Humidifier - EMERSON WHITE-RODGERS; *pg.* 1071, *pg.* 996
COMFORTQUIT - Diapers - TREDEGAR CORPORATION; *pg.* 1890, *pg.* 1804
COMFORTSEAL - Mask - INVACARE CORPORATION; *pg.* 1546, *pg.* 1451
COMFORTSLIPPERS - Slippers - TEMPUR SEALY INTERNATIONAL, INC.; *pg.* 944, *pg.* 731
COMFORTSOFT - Apparel - HANESBRANDS INC.; *pg.* 26, *pg.* 1394
COMFORTTHERM - Fiber Glass Insulation - JOHNS MANVILLE CORPORATION; *pg.* 89, *pg.* 320
COMFORTTREAD - Foot Rest - ALIMED, INC.; *pg.* 1490, *pg.* 816
COMFORTVEST - Lift Aid - HILL-ROM HOLDINGS, INC.; *pg.* 1542, *pg.* 673
COMFY - Pediatric Orthotics - ALIMED, INC.; *pg.* 1490, *pg.* 816
COMFY COZY - Stuffed Elephant - GUND, INC.; *pg.* 954, *pg.* 1056
COMFY-TRAC - Medical & Aesthetic Product - DYNATRONICS CORPORATION; *pg.* 1526, *pg.* 1757
COMFYPRENE - Pediatric Orthotics - ALIMED, INC.; *pg.* 1490, *pg.* 816
COMIDAS CASERAS - Hispanic Products - SPECIALTY FOODS GROUP-FIELD PACKING DIV.; *pg.* 897, *pg.* 739
COMITE - Polymer Product - CHEMTURA CORPORATION; *pg.* 1152, *pg.* 355
COMITROL - Processor - URSCHEL LABORATORIES INCORPORATED; *pg.* 1386, *pg.* 698
COMLIGHT - Lighting System - REVOLUTION LIGHTING TECHNOLOGIES, INC.; *pg.* 1304, *pg.* 377
COMMAND - Mounting & Adhesive Strips - 3M COMPANY; *pg.* 1142, *pg.* 956
COMMAND - Herbicide - FMC CORPORATION; *pg.* 1163, *pg.* 1564
COMMAND - Home Entertainment Cables - GENERAL CABLE CORPORATION; *pg.* 83, *pg.* 729
COMMAND - Receiver - HOBBICO, INC.; *pg.* 956, *pg.* 562
COMMAND - Helmet - MINE SAFETY APPLIANCES COMPANY; *pg.* 1361, *pg.* 1525
COMMAND 3ME - Herbicides - FMC CORPORATION; *pg.* 1163, *pg.* 1564
COMMAND & CONQUER - Video Game - ELECTRONIC ARTS INC.; *pg.* 951, *pg.* 189
COMMAND & CONQUER 3 TIBERIUM WARS - Video Game - ELECTRONIC ARTS INC.; *pg.* 951, *pg.* 189
COMMAND & CONQUER RED ALERT - Video Game - ELECTRONIC ARTS INC.; *pg.* 951, *pg.* 189
COMMAND & CONQUER RED ALERT COUNTERSTRIKE - Video Game - ELECTRONIC ARTS INC.; *pg.* 951, *pg.* 189
COMMAND & CONQUER RENEGADE - Video Game - ELECTRONIC ARTS INC.; *pg.* 951, *pg.* 189
COMMAND & CONQUER THE COVERT OPERATION - Video Game - ELECTRONIC ARTS INC.; *pg.* 951, *pg.* 189
COMMAND CHIEF - Wireless Remote Control System - CONTROL CHIEF HOLDINGS, INC.; *pg.* 630, *pg.* 1518
COMMAND CONSOLE - Software - AFFYMETRIX, INC.; *pg.* 1487, *pg.* 263
COMMAND LINX - Cable - GENERAL CABLE CORPORATION; *pg.* 83, *pg.* 729
COMMAND SEATING - Automotive Seat Design - FORD MOTOR COMPANY; *pg.* 172, *pg.* 876
COMMAND SERIES - Cables - GENERAL CABLE CORPORATION; *pg.* 83, *pg.* 729
COMMAND VIEW - Software - RAYTHEON COMPANY; *pg.* 233, *pg.* 854
COMMAND ZONE - Electronic System - OSHKOSH CORPORATION; *pg.* 187, *pg.* 1885
COMMAND ZONE - Electronics System - PIERCE MANUFACTURING, INC.; *pg.* 188, *pg.* 1852
COMMANDCENTRAL - Software - SYMANTEC CORPORATION; *pg.* 478, *pg.* 161
COMMANDER - Heated Pressure Washer - GRACO, INC.; *pg.* 1342, *pg.* 935
COMMANDER - Hose - HBD INDUSTRIES, INC.; *pg.* 207, *pg.* 1449
COMMANDER - Head Equipment - MOTOROLA SOLUTIONS, INC.; *pg.* 657, *pg.* 659
COMMANDER - Floor Cleaning Product - NSS ENTERPRISES, INC.; *pg.* 59, *pg.* 1476
COMMANDER - Cigarettes - PHILIP MORRIS USA INC.; *pg.* 1894, *pg.* 1803
COMMANDER - Fountain - RITCHIE INDUSTRIES, INC.; *pg.* 707, *pg.* 703
COMMANDER - Software Product & Module - RIVERBED PERFORMANCE MANAGEMENT; *pg.* 462, *pg.* 765
COMMANDER - Elevator - SAVARIA CONCORD LIFTS INC.; *pg.* 1592, *pg.* 1919
COMMANDER - Lavatory & Sink Fittings - SPEAKMAN COMPANY; *pg.* 112, *pg.* 388
COMMANDER - Light - SUREFIRE, LLC; *pg.* 1307, *pg.* 90
COMMANDER - Construction Equipment - VERMEER MANUFACTURING COMPANY; *pg.* 708, *pg.* 711
COMMANDER KEEN - Video Game - ID SOFTWARE, INC.; *pg.* 956, *pg.* 1727
COMMANDER KEEN GOODBYE GALAXY SET - Video Game - ID SOFTWARE, INC.; *pg.* 956, *pg.* 1727
COMMANDER KEEN INVATION OF THE VORTICONS TRILOGY - Video Game - ID SOFTWARE, INC.; *pg.* 956, *pg.* 1727
COMMANDER KEEN KEEN DREAMS - Video Game - ID SOFTWARE, INC.; *pg.* 956, *pg.* 1727
COMMANDO - Sweater - BLAUER MANUFACTURING COMPANY, INC.; *pg.* 20, *pg.* 789
COMMANDO - Cattle Ear Tag - BOEHRINGER INGELHEIM VETMEDICA, INC.; *pg.* 1474, *pg.* 989
COMMANDO - Nutritional Supplement - NATURAL ORGANICS, INC.; *pg.* 1571, *pg.* 1181
COMMCELL - Software - COMMVAULT SYSTEMS, INC.; *pg.* 377, *pg.* 1125
COMMEND - Athletic Shoes - K-SWISS; *pg.* 1837, *pg.* 306
COMMENT - Communications Manager - GEA REFRIGERATION NORTH AMERICA, INC.; *pg.* 1072, *pg* 1597
COMMENT - Fabric - NEMSCHOFF, INC.; *pg.* 936, *pg.* 1890
COMMENTARY - Magazine - COMMENTARY; *pg.* 1628, *pg.* 1216
COMMERCELYNX - Banking Services - MERCHANTS BANCSHARES, INC.; *pg.* 782, *pg.* 1768
THE COMMERCIAL APPEAL - Newspaper - THE E.W. SCRIPPS COMPANY; *pg.* 1639, *pg.* 1412
COMMERCIAL BUILDING BASICS - Workbook - VALE NATIONAL TRAINING CENTER INC.; *pg.* 610, *pg.* 1660
COMMERCIAL MAXUM - Deadbolt - MEDECO HIGH SECURITY LOCKS, INC.; *pg.* 1055, *pg.* 1806
COMMERCIAL-PAK - Commercial Hot Water Heaters - EMBASSY INDUSTRIES, INC.; *pg.* 1071, *pg.* 1164
COMMERCIAL PROPERTY NEWS - Trade Publication - THE NIELSEN COMPANY B.V.; *pg.* 1671, *pg.* 1272
COMMFLEX - Cable - COMMSCOPE, INC.; *pg.* 278, *pg.* 1378
COMMITMENT AT ALL LEVELS - Tagline - SIMPSON MANUFACTURING COMPANY, INC.; *pg.* 1376, *pg.* 185
COMMITMENT THAT LASTS GENERATIONS - Tag Line - MECHANICS BANK; *pg.* 781, *pg.* 193
COMMITTED TO CUSTOMER SATISFICATION - Tagline - BULLDOG MEDIA GROUP; *pg.* 599, *pg.* 1624
COMMITTED TO DRIVERS. COMMITTED TO YOU. - Tagline - KLLM TRANSPORT SERVICES, INC.; *pg.* 1914, *pg.* 971
COMMITTED TO THE CORE - Slogan - PATAGONIA; *pg.* 31, *pg.* 301
COMMITTED TO THE CRAFT - Plaster - USG CORPORATION; *pg.* 118, *pg.* 594
COMMLIB - Software System - MENTOR GRAPHICS CORPORATION; *pg.* 432, *pg.* 1510
COMMLIB BMC - Software System - MENTOR GRAPHICS CORPORATION; *pg.* 432, *pg.* 1510
COMMLINK - Radio Integrated Circuits - INTERSIL CORPORATION; *pg.* 647, *pg.* 146
COMMNET - Software - COMMVAULT SYSTEMS, INC.; *pg.* 377, *pg.* 1125
COMMODITIES CORNER - Financial Products - DOW JONES & COMPANY, INC.; *pg.* 1637, *pg.* 1225
COMMODITY - Fabric - NEMSCHOFF, INC.; *pg.* 936, *pg.* 1890
COMMODITY MAGIC - Food Product - ADVANCEPIERRE FOODS, INC.; *pg.* 1714, *pg.* 1409
COMMODORE - Fiber Optic Cable - GENERAL CABLE CORPORATION; *pg.* 83, *pg.* 729
COMMON INFORMATION MODEL - Software - EMC CORPORATION; *pg.* 391, *pg.* 825
COMMON THREADS - Carpet - INTERFACE, INC.; *pg.* 695, *pg.* 512
COMMONWEALTH VA PLUS - Variable Annuity Product -

GENWORTH LIFE AND ANNUITY INSURANCE COMPANY; *pg.* 1201, *pg.* 1802
COMMPLETE - Communication Product - MULTI-TECH SYSTEMS INC.; *pg.* 442, *pg.* 951
COMMSCOPE WIRELESS - Cable - COMMSCOPE, INC.; *pg.* 278, *pg.* 1378
COMMSERVE - Software - COMMVAULT SYSTEMS, INC.; *pg.* 377, *pg.* 1125
COMMSOURCE - Peripheral Product - MITEL NETWORKS, INC.; *pg.* 1872, *pg.* 13
COMMUNICATE.COM - Advertising Website - LIVE CURRENT MEDIA INC.; *pg.* 1263, *pg.* 1911
COMMUNICATION WITHOUT BORDERS - Slogan - NET2PHONE, INC.; *pg.* 1269, *pg.* 1097
COMMUNICATIONS DATA SERVICES, INC. - Subscription Services - THE HEARST CORPORATION; *pg.* 1649, *pg.* 1239
COMMUNICATIONS FOR BUSINESS - Tagline - VANCE PUBLISHING CORPORATION; *pg.* 1699, *pg.* 627
COMMUNICATOR - Wireless Remote Control System - CONTROL CHIEF HOLDINGS, INC.; *pg.* 630, *pg.* 1518
COMMUNICATOR - Markers & Ballpoint Pens - DRI MARK PRODUCTS, INC.; *pg.* 388, *pg.* 1323
COMMUNICATORE - Wireless Remote Control System - CONTROL CHIEF HOLDINGS, INC.; *pg.* 630, *pg.* 1518
COMMUNICATORR - Valve - MKS INSTRUMENTS, INC.; *pg.* 1362, *pg.* 781
COMMUNITY - Software - ENVIRONMENTAL SYSTEMS RESEARCH INSTITUTE INC.; *pg.* 393, *pg.* 188
COMMUNITY - Silverware - ONEIDA LTD; *pg.* 1129, *pg.* 1318
COMMUNITY CANTEEN - Restaurant - LETTUCE ENTERTAIN YOU ENTERPRISES, INC.; *pg.* 1735, *pg.* 580
COMMUNITY CODER - Software - ENVIRONMENTAL SYSTEMS RESEARCH INSTITUTE INC.; *pg.* 393, *pg.* 188
COMMUNITY CONSTRUCTION KIT - Educational Materials - SCHOLASTIC INC.; *pg.* 1683, *pg.* 1288
COMMUNITY DAYS - Ticket Program - OAKLAND ATHLETICS LIMITED PARTNERSHIP; *pg.* 571, *pg.* 172
COMMUNITY GAMING - Game - WMS INDUSTRIES INC.; *pg.* 593, *pg.* 666
COMMUNITY GOLD - Financial Services - FEDERAL HOME LOAN MORTGAGE CORPORATION; *pg.* 751, *pg.* 1790
COMMUNITY HERO CHECKING - Banking Services - OLD NATIONAL BANCORP; *pg.* 789, *pg.* 679
COMMUNITY NEWS ADVERTISER - Newspaper - GAZETTE COMMUNICATIONS, INC.; *pg.* 1644, *pg.* 702
COMMUNITY TAPESTRY - Software - ENVIRONMENTAL SYSTEMS RESEARCH INSTITUTE INC.; *pg.* 393, *pg.* 188
COMMUNITYINFO - Software - ENVIRONMENTAL SYSTEMS RESEARCH INSTITUTE INC.; *pg.* 393, *pg.* 188
COMMUTE - Apparel - OAKLEY, INC.; *pg.* 1840, *pg.* 86
COMMUTER - Bicycle - G. JOANNOU CYCLE CO. INC.; *pg.* 1707, *pg.* 1098
COMMWEB - Publisher - UNITED BUSINESS MEDIA LLC; *pg.* 1697, *pg.* 1177
COMP-U-FOLIO - Case - BROWN & BIGELOW, INC.; *pg.* 1624, *pg.* 959
COMPAC - Power Converter - VICOR CORPORATION; *pg.* 1435, *pg.* 783
COMPACDRYER - Hand Dryer - BOBRICK WASHROOM EQUIPMENT, INC.; *pg.* 1043, *pg.* 166
COMPACLINE - Closed Circuit Television Equipment - VICON INDUSTRIES, INC.; *pg.* 685, *pg.* 1166
COMPACT - Pen - A. T. CROSS COMPANY; *pg.* 339, *pg.* 1602
COMPACT - Communication & Test System - AGILENT TECHNOLOGIES, INC.; *pg.* 614, *pg.* 264
COMPACT - Cluster Tool - COLLABRX, INC.; *pg.* 1324, *pg.* 216
COMPACT - Medical Device - DEPUY SYNTHES; *pg.* 1523, *pg.* 1593
COMPACT - Bath Tissue Dispensers - GEORGIA-PACIFIC LLC; *pg.* 1458, *pg.* 507
COMPACT - Beverage Bottle - THERMOS L.L.C.; *pg.* 61, *pg.* 660
COMPACT 3000 - Bath Tissue Dispenser - GEORGIA-PACIFIC LLC; *pg.* 1458, *pg.* 507
COMPACT 360 NLD - Plasma Etch System - COLLABRX, INC.; *pg.* 1324, *pg.* 216
COMPACT 38 - Commercial Lighting - SWIVELIER CO., INC.; *pg.* 1307, *pg.* 1142
COMPACT 600 - Bare Copper - COLEMAN CABLE, INC.; *pg.* 1324, *pg.* 665
COMPACT-AIRE - Air Conditioner - HEAT CONTROLLER, INC.; *pg.* 1072, *pg.* 893
COMPACT COMFORT - Furniture - NEMSCHOFF, INC.; *pg.* 936, *pg.* 1890
COMPACT HAND - Medical Device - DEPUY SYNTHES; *pg.* 1523, *pg.* 1593
COMPACT MF - Medical Device - DEPUY SYNTHES; *pg.* 1523, *pg.* 1593
COMPACT SNO-THROS - Lawn Product - ARIENS COMPANY INC.; *pg.* 700, *pg.* 1855
COMPACTBLOCK I/O - Software - ROCKWELL AUTOMATION, INC.; *pg.* 668, *pg.* 1880
COMPACTFLASH - Flash Card - HGST; *pg.* 406, *pg.* 260
COMPACTFLASH - Memory Card - LEXAR MEDIA, INC.; *pg.* 1262, *pg.* 146
COMPACTFLASH - Memory Card - PNY TECHNOLOGIES, INC.; *pg.* 455, *pg.* 1105
COMPACTLAN - Electronic Components - MOLEX INCORPORATED; *pg.* 655, *pg.* 628
COMPACTLINE - Cable & Antenna System - RADIO FREQUENCY SYSTEMS, INC.; *pg.* 666, *pg.* 354
COMPACTPCI - Board-to-Board Connectors - WINCHESTER ELECTRONICS CORP.; *pg.* 688, *pg.* 382
COMPACTVENDOR - Vending Machine - COIN ACCEPTORS, INC.; *pg.* 1324, *pg.* 994
COMPACVIDEO - Otoscopesa - WELCH ALLYN INC.; *pg.* 1436, *pg.* 1342
COMPAK-LOCK - Electronic Components - MOLEX INCORPORATED; *pg.* 655, *pg.* 628
COMPAKT REDDIES - Dairy Product - ASSOCIATED MILK PRODUCERS INC.; *pg.* 838, *pg.* 951
COMPALOX - Activated Aluminas - ALBEMARLE CORPORATION; *pg.* 1146, *pg.* 741
COMPANERO - Furniture - ASHLEY FURNITURE INDUSTRIES, INC.; *pg.* 914, *pg.* 1852
COMPANION - Enteral Feeding Pump - ABBOTT LABORATORIES; *pg.* 1484, *pg.* 551
COMPANION - Audio Product - BOSE CORPORATION; *pg.* 626, *pg.* 820
COMPANION - Knife - BUCK KNIVES, INC.; *pg.* 1828, *pg.* 550
COMPANION - Healthcare Product - GF HEALTH PRODUCTS, INC.; *pg.* 1535, *pg.* 508
COMPANION - Pad System - THE SALK COMPANY; *pg.* 1591, *pg.* 800
COMPANION LIVING - Retirement Homes - SUNRISE SENIOR LIVING, INC.; *pg.* 1599, *pg.* 1795
COMPANION ROAD - Pet Supplies - PETSMART, INC.; *pg.* 1481, *pg.* 18
COMPANY - Office Furniture - STEELCASE INC.; *pg.* 475, *pg.* 889
THE COMPANY FOR WOMEN - Tagline - AVON PRODUCTS, INC.; *pg.* 500, *pg.* 1198
THE COMPANY IN MOTION - Slogan - PRO-DEX, INC.; *pg.* 1586, *pg.* 115
THE COMPANY STORE - Upscale Direct Marketing of Down Comforters & Home Products - HANOVER DIRECT, INC.; *pg.* 1772, *pg.* 1130
THE COMPANY THAT CONNECTS YOU, NOW PROTECTS YOU - Tagline - AT&T SOUTHEAST; *pg.* 1868, *pg.* 489
THE COMPANY THAT LIVES WHERE YOU DO - Tagline - MFA OIL COMPANY; *pg.* 981, *pg.* 976
THE COMPANY THE WHOLE WORLD WATCHES - Slogan - CHYRONHEGO; *pg.* 371, *pg.* 1179
THE COMPANY YOU KEEP - Slogan - NEW YORK LIFE INSURANCE COMPANY; *pg.* 1211, *pg.* 1268
COMPANYBLUE - Corporate Travel Services - JETBLUE AIRWAYS CORPORATION; *pg.* 1913, *pg.* 1174
COMPAQ - Computer - HEWLETT-PACKARD COMPANY; *pg.* 404, *pg.* 175
COMPAREIT - Software - BIO-RAD LABORATORIES, INC.; *pg.* 1504, *pg.* 101
COMPAREROCKET - Software - DELL SOFTWARE; *pg.* 385, *pg.* 40
COMPAREX - Software - SERENA SOFTWARE, INC.; *pg.* 468, *pg.* 192
COMPAREYOURCARE - Healthcare Product - HEALTH GRADES, INC.; *pg.* 1256, *pg.* 319
COMPARIS - Wood & Building Material - WEYERHAEUSER COMPANY; *pg.* 121, *pg.* 1820
COMPASS - Provider of Course Placement Assistance - ACT INC.; *pg.* 597, *pg.* 708
COMPASS - Laser & Laser System - COHERENT, INC.; *pg.* 1406, *pg.* 265
COMPASS - Shoes - G.H. BASS & CO.; *pg.* 1809, *pg.* 1234
COMPASS - Medical Equipment - INVACARE CORPORATION; *pg.* 1546, *pg.* 1451
COMPASS - Software System - IRON MOUNTAIN INCORPORATED; *pg.* 421, *pg.* 796
COMPASS - Bath Product - KOHLER CO.; *pg.* 91, *pg.* 1862
COMPASS - Fabric - NEMSCHOFF, INC.; *pg.* 936, *pg.* 1890
COMPASS - CTP Imaging System - PRESSTEK LLC; *pg.* 1678, *pg.* 1034
COMPASS - Software - SUNGARD DATA SYSTEMS INC.; *pg.* 477, *pg.* 1592
COMPASS 597 - USB Modem - SIERRA WIRELESS INCORPORATED; *pg.* 673, *pg.* 1909
COMPASS 885 - USB Modem - SIERRA WIRELESS INCORPORATED; *pg.* 673, *pg.* 1909
COMPASS 888 - Wireless Card - SIERRA WIRELESS INCORPORATED; *pg.* 673, *pg.* 1909
THE COMPASS FLOORING SYSTEM - Flooring Product - STAGESTEP INC.; *pg.* 1688, *pg.* 1570
COMPASS PARTNERS - Business Management System - ARI NETWORK SERVICES, INC.; *pg.* 353, *pg.* 1873
COMPASS PROSPECT TRACKING - Software - XEROX CORPORATION; *pg.* 494, *pg.* 365
COMPASSO - Ceiling System - CGC INC.; *pg.* 75, *pg.* 1925
COMPATIBLE - Laser Printer Product - NCR CORPORATION; *pg.* 443, *pg.* 531
COMPATIBLE - Roll Towel Dispenser - WAUSAU PAPER BAY WEST; *pg.* 1471, *pg.* 1465
COMPCORE - Fiberglass Core for Large Storage Reels - HAHL INC.; *pg.* 1299, *pg.* 1620
COMPDRESS - Wound Dressing - DERMA SCIENCES, INC.; *pg.* 1523, *pg.* 1111
COMPEET - Footwear - STEVEN MADDEN, LTD.; *pg.* 1819, *pg.* 1176
COMPEL - Network Control System - WEGENER CORPORATION; *pg.* 687, *pg.* 533
COMPENFLOW - Molecular Probe Product - THERMO FISHER SCIENTIFIC INC.; *pg.* 1602, *pg.* 61
COMPENSATION VISION - Software - SAS INSTITUTE INC.; *pg.* 466, *pg.* 1361
HR.BLR.COM - Website - BUSINESS & LEGAL REPORTS INC.; *pg.* 1624, *pg.* 367
COMPETE - Resin - POLYONE CORPORATION; *pg.* 1177, *pg.* 1404
COMPETE TO WIN - Game - WMS INDUSTRIES INC.; *pg.* 593, *pg.* 666
COMPETENCY COMPASS - Software - HEALTHSTREAM, INC.; *pg.* 1649, *pg.* 1651
COMPETITIVE INTELLIGENCE - Software System - IMS HEALTH, INC.; *pg.* 1544, *pg.* 344
COMPETITOR - Golf Products - FEEL GOLF CO., INC.; *pg.* 1834, *pg.* 465
COMPETITOR - Plastic & Rubber - TEKNOR APEX COMPANY; *pg.* 1889, *pg.* 1605
COMPETITOR - Blower - TUTHILL CORPORATION; *pg.* 1385, *pg.* 561
COMPEX - Compatibility Agent - KALO, INC.; *pg.* 1796, *pg.* 719
COMPEX EXTRA - Liquid Fertilizer - KALO, INC.; *pg.* 1796, *pg.* 719
COMPEXPRO - Excimer Lasers - COHERENT, INC.; *pg.* 1406, *pg.* 265
COMPLAN - Food Products - THE KRAFT HEINZ COMPANY; *pg.* 870, *pg.* 1577
COMPLEATS - Food Product - HORMEL FOODS CORPORATION; *pg.* 863, *pg.* 915
COMPLEMENTS - Healthcare Product - SWANSON HEALTH PRODUCTS INC.; *pg.* 1600, *pg.* 1397
COMPLEMIX - Chemical Product - CYTEC INDUSTRIES, INC.; *pg.* 1155, *pg.* 1131
COMPLEMIX - Animal Nutritional Supplement - HUBBARD FEEDS INC.; *pg.* 1477, *pg.* 928
COMPLETE - Medical Device - ABBOTT MEDICAL OPTICS, INC.; *pg.* 1485, *pg.* 260
COMPLETE-A-CALL - Communication Product - CENTURYLINK, INC; *pg.* 1870, *pg.* 317
COMPLETE AUTOMATION - Software - ROCKWELL AUTOMATION, INC.; *pg.* 668, *pg.* 1880
COMPLETE BALANCE - Nutritional Product - NATROL, INC.; *pg.* 1570, *pg.* 64
COMPLETE BLINK N CLEAN - Contact Lens Care Products - ABBOTT MEDICAL OPTICS, INC.; *pg.* 1485, *pg.* 260
COMPLETE CARE - Wellness Tea - CELESTIAL

First page reference indicates Business Class Edition
Second page reference indicates Geographic Edition

SEASONINGS, INC.; *pg.* 846, *pg.* 310
COMPLETE CHOICE - Wireless Communication System - AT&T SOUTHEAST; *pg.* 1868, *pg.* 489
THE COMPLETE GUIDE TO HERBAL MEDICINES - Medical Journal - LIPPINCOTT WILLIAMS & WILKINS, INC.; *pg.* 1659, *pg.* 1567
COMPLETE IRA - Cash Management Feature - E*TRADE FINANCIAL CORPORATION; *pg.* 749, *pg.* 1230
COMPLETE KITS - Everything Included Plastic Model Kits - REVELL; *pg.* 966, *pg.* 611
COMPLETE MY ALBUM - Online Store Features - APPLE INC.; *pg.* 350, *pg.* 73
COMPLETE SKINCARE - Personal Care Product - THE GILLETTE COMPANY; *pg.* 509, *pg.* 795
THE COMPLETE TREAT COMPANY FOODS - Tag Line - FIELDBROOK FOODS INC.; *pg.* 1852, *pg.* 1156
COMPLETE WHEAT BRAN FLAKES - Cereal - KELLOGG COMPANY; *pg.* 831, *pg.* 870
COMPLETECARE - Support Services - DELL INC.; *pg.* 383, *pg.* 1737
COMPLETEHOME - Home Improvement Program - AFFINION GROUP, INC.; *pg.* 1225, *pg.* 372
COMPLETELY COMFORT - Bra & Shapewear - GLAMORISE FOUNDATIONS, INC.; *pg.* 25, *pg.* 1235
COMPLEX - Skincare Product - MERLE NORMAN COSMETICS, INC.; *pg.* 517, *pg.* 136
COMPLEX MAGAZINE - Young Men's Style & Lifestyle Magazine - COMPLEX MEDIA, INC.; *pg.* 1628, *pg.* 1217
COMPLIANCE - Software - BIO-RAD LABORATORIES, INC.; *pg.* 1504, *pg.* 101
COMPLIANCE SUITE - Software - DELL SOFTWARE; *pg.* 385, *pg.* 40
COMPLIANT SOLUTIONS - Healthcare Service - ATS AUTOMATION TOOLING SYSTEMS INC.; *pg.* 355, *pg.* 1919
COMPLIMENTO - Fabric - NEMSCHOFF, INC.; *pg.* 936, *pg.* 1890
COMPLUS - Wafer Inspection System - APPLIED MATERIALS, INC.; *pg.* 618, *pg.* 264
COMPO - Exterior Alkyd Primer & Undercoater - DUNN-EDWARDS CORPORATION; *pg.* 1442, *pg.* 129
COMPODRE - Connector - MOLEX INCORPORATED; *pg.* 655, *pg.* 628
COMPONENT RPC - Automotive Durability Testing Software - MTS SYSTEMS CORPORATION; *pg.* 442, *pg.* 923
COMPONENTS - Office Furniture - JOFCO INC.; *pg.* 931, *pg.* 691
COMPONENTS FOR A CONNECTED PLANET - Slogan - BEL FUSE INC.; *pg.* 624, *pg.* 1075
COMPONENTS FOR A MODERN WORLD - Tagline - PULSE ELECTRONICS CORPORATION; *pg.* 666, *pg.* 206
COMPONETICS - Stock Components - TRICORBRAUN; *pg.* 1471, *pg.* 1004
COMPOSE - Office Product - HAWORTH, INC.; *pg.* 402, *pg.* 891
COMPOSER - Programmable Hearing Aid - BELTONE ELECTRONICS LLC; *pg.* 1503, *pg.* 614
COMPOSER 2000 - Programmable Hearing Aid - BELTONE ELECTRONICS LLC; *pg.* 1503, *pg.* 614
COMPOSER SABERTOOTH - Software - DAEGIS INC; *pg.* 381, *pg.* 195
COMPOSIPAC - Packaging Product - GRAPHIC PACKAGING HOLDING COMPANY; *pg.* 1459, *pg.* 509
COMPOSITE CATALOG - Catalog - GULF PUBLISHING COMPANY; *pg.* 1646, *pg.* 1707
COMPOSITE TOP - Golf Equipment - ACUSHNET COMPANY; *pg.* 1824, *pg.* 818
COMPOSITE XL PRO - String - ASHAWAY LINE & TWINE MFG. CO.; *pg.* 1826, *pg.* 1600
COMPOSITE XT PRO - String - ASHAWAY LINE & TWINE MFG. CO.; *pg.* 1826, *pg.* 1600
COMPOSITES - Furniture - HAWORTH, INC.; *pg.* 402, *pg.* 891
COMPOSITES MODULAR BUILDING SYSTEM - Corrosive Resistant, Non-Conductive Composite Building Framework System - HAHL INC.; *pg.* 1299, *pg.* 1620
COMPOST ALIVE! - Soil Care Product - GARDENS ALIVE!, INC.; *pg.* 1796, *pg.* 693
COMPOUND W - Wart Removal Product - ORASURE TECHNOLOGIES INC; *pg.* 1578, *pg.* 1516
COMPOUND W FREEZE OFF - Wart Removal Product - ORASURE TECHNOLOGIES INC; *pg.* 1578, *pg.* 1516
COMPOUNDING YOUR SUCCESS - Slogan - A. SCHULMAN, INC.; *pg.* 1144, *pg.* 1452
COMPOUNDINGS - Trade Magazine - THE INDEPENDENT LUBRICANT MANUFACTURERS ASSOCIATION; *pg.* 144, *pg.* 1770
COMPREHEND - Networking Software - OPENCONNECT SYSTEMS, INC.; *pg.* 449, *pg.* 1685
COMPREHENSIVE CONSENSUS CODES - Fire Safety Book - NATIONAL FIRE PROTECTION ASSOCIATION; *pg.* 149, *pg.* 842
COMPREHENSIVE FORMULA - Nutritional Supplement - GUTHY-RENKER LLC; *pg.* 289, *pg.* 273
COMPRESSERATORS - Air Compression - DEERE & COMPANY; *pg.* 703, *pg.* 632
COMPRESSION - Apparel - OAKLEY, INC.; *pg.* 1840, *pg.* 86
COMPRIBAND - Bandage - DERMA SCIENCES, INC.; *pg.* 1523, *pg.* 1111
COMPRILAN - Medical & Aesthetic Product - DYNATRONICS CORPORATION; *pg.* 1526, *pg.* 1757
COMPRIZON - Automated Contracting System - CACI INTERNATIONAL INC.; *pg.* 367, *pg.* 1773
COMPROTENN - Compressor Protection System - SPX THERMAL PRODUCT SOLUTIONS; *pg.* 1378, *pg.* 1555
COMPU-CAPTURE/32 - Law Enforcement Program - ALLIED SECURITY INNOVATIONS, INC.; *pg.* 1041, *pg.* 1066
COMPU-COAT - Coating Equipment Automation - THOMAS ENGINEERING INC.; *pg.* 1382, *pg.* 619
COMPU-COURSE 220 - Autopilot Systems - BENMAR MARINE ELECTRONICS, INC.; *pg.* 624, *pg.* 105
COMPU-LAB - Laboratory Coating Machine - THOMAS ENGINEERING INC.; *pg.* 1382, *pg.* 619
COMPU-LOK - Security Locker - AMERICAN LOCKER GROUP INCORPORATED; *pg.* 1041, *pg.* 1674
COMPU-LOK - Computer-Controlled Lockers - AMERICAN LOCKER SECURITY SYSTEMS, INC.; *pg.* 1042, *pg.* 1674
COMPU-SCENE - Templates - ALLIED SECURITY INNOVATIONS, INC.; *pg.* 1041, *pg.* 1066
COMPU-SCENE - Flight Training Simulators - LOCKHEED MARTIN CORPORATION; *pg.* 229, *pg.* 762
COMPU-SKETCH - Composite Sketching Program - ALLIED SECURITY INNOVATIONS, INC.; *pg.* 1041, *pg.* 1066
COMPUBLEND - Cleaning Chemical - 3M COMPANY; *pg.* 1142, *pg.* 956
COMPUCAL - Labeling - FLEXCON CORPORATION; *pg.* 1457, *pg.* 844
COMPUCALLER - Animal Calls - BURNHAM BROTHERS, INC.; *pg.* 1829, *pg.* 1727
COMPUCESSORY - Office Products - GENUINE PARTS COMPANY; *pg.* 206, *pg.* 506
COMPUCHARGE - Battery - C&D TECHNOLOGIES, INC.; *pg.* 627, *pg.* 1517
COMPUCOLOR - Color & Numerically Coded File Folders & Labels - TAB PRODUCTS CO. LLC; *pg.* 481, *pg.* 1869
COMPUDENT - Anesthetic Injection System - MILESTONE SCIENTIFIC, INC.; *pg.* 1568, *pg.* 1079
COMPUDRY - Computerized Command Center for In-bin Continuous Flow Drying Operations - SHIVVERS INC.; *pg.* 707, *pg.* 704
COMPUFLO - Drug Delivery Injection System - MILESTONE SCIENTIFIC, INC.; *pg.* 1568, *pg.* 1079
COMPUFLOW - Measurement Device - TSI INCORPORATED; *pg.* 1432, *pg.* 965
COMPUHEAT - Heat Loss Program - GAS-FIRED PRODUCTS, INC.; *pg.* 1338, *pg.* 1367
COMPULAB - Pump System - STOELTING CO.; *pg.* 1430, *pg.* 671
COMPUMED - Anesthetic Injection System - MILESTONE SCIENTIFIC, INC.; *pg.* 1568, *pg.* 1079
COMPUND W - Wart Remover - PRESTIGE BRANDS HOLDINGS, INC.; *pg.* 520, *pg.* 1345
COMPUROLLER - Briefcase - SANTA FE LEATHER CORPORATION; *pg.* 12, *pg.* 1059
COMPUSAFE - Logistic Service - BRINK'S U.S.; *pg.* 1901, *pg.* 1670
COMPUSET - Manual - XEROX CORPORATION; *pg.* 494, *pg.* 365
COMPUSTAT DATA - Fundamental & Market Data - STANDARD & POOR'S RATINGS SERVICES; *pg.* 805, *pg.* 1296
COMPUSTAT GLOBAL - Reference Tool - STANDARD & POOR'S RATINGS SERVICES; *pg.* 805, *pg.* 1296
COMPUSTAT NORTH AMERICA - Financial Analysis Tool for US & Canada - STANDARD & POOR'S RATINGS SERVICES; *pg.* 805, *pg.* 1296
COMPUSTAT XPRESSFEED - Reference Tool - STANDARD & POOR'S RATINGS SERVICES; *pg.* 805, *pg.* 1296
COMPUSTAT XPRESSFEED LOADER - Directly Uploaded Financial Analysis Tool - STANDARD & POOR'S RATINGS SERVICES; *pg.* 805, *pg.* 1296
COMPUTABLE - Trade Magazine - THE NIELSEN COMPANY B.V.; *pg.* 1671, *pg.* 1272
COMPUTAR - CCTV Security Product - CBC (AMERICA) CORP.; *pg.* 273, *pg.* 293
COMPUTER HOTLINE - Magazine - DOMINION ENTERPRISES; *pg.* 1636, *pg.* 1796
COMPUTER LEARNING CENTERS - Tagline - NEW HORIZONS WORLDWIDE, INC.; *pg.* 445, *pg.* 43
COMPUTER RESELLER NEWS - Newspaper - UNITED BUSINESS MEDIA LLC; *pg.* 1697, *pg.* 1177
COMPUTER TECHNOLOGY LAW REPORT - Publisher - BLOOMBERG BNA; *pg.* 1621, *pg.* 1772
COMPUTER TELEPHONY EXPO - Publisher - UNITED BUSINESS MEDIA LLC; *pg.* 1697, *pg.* 1177
COMPUTERACTIVE - Trade Magazine - THE NIELSEN COMPANY B.V.; *pg.* 1671, *pg.* 1272
COMPUTERCRAFTS - Craft Kit - JANLYNN CORPORATION; *pg.* 696, *pg.* 815
COMPUTERIZED COLOR RESPONSE - Software - X-RITE, INCORPORATED; *pg.* 1437, *pg.* 891
COMPUTERWORLD - Technology Magazine - INTERNATIONAL DATA GROUP; *pg.* 1653, *pg.* 796
COMPUTING - Trade Magazine - THE NIELSEN COMPANY B.V.; *pg.* 1671, *pg.* 1272
COMPUTRAC - Analyzer - ARIZONA INSTRUMENT LLC; *pg.* 1400, *pg.* 12
COMPUTRACE - Computer Design Programs for Steam & Heat Tracing - THERMON AMERICAS INC.; *pg.* 1077, *pg.* 1744
COMSAT - Systems Integration & Aeronautics - LOCKHEED MARTIN CORPORATION; *pg.* 229, *pg.* 762
COMSAT LABORATORIES - Satellite System - VIASAT, INC.; *pg.* 489, *pg.* 62
COMSAT STAR - Systems Integration & Aeronautics - LOCKHEED MARTIN CORPORATION; *pg.* 229, *pg.* 762
COMSHIELD - Anti-Static Materials - A. SCHULMAN, INC.; *pg.* 1144, *pg.* 1452
COMSPAN - Dental Product - DENTSPLY INTERNATIONAL INC.; *pg.* 1522, *pg.* 1596
COMSTAR - Speakerphone - ZOOM TECHNOLOGIES, INC.; *pg.* 497, *pg.* 1317
COMSTOCK - Pie Fillings - PINNACLE FOODS GROUP LLC; *pg.* 889, *pg.* 1104
COMSTRON - Frequency Synthesizers - AEROFLEX INCORPORATED; *pg.* 614, *pg.* 1321
COMTHERMO - Software - ASPEN TECHNOLOGY, INC.; *pg.* 354, *pg.* 804
COMTRAC - Accounting & Reporting System - COMERICA INCORPORATED; *pg.* 740, *pg.* 1677
COMTUF - Plastic Compound & Resin - A. SCHULMAN, INC.; *pg.* 1144, *pg.* 1452
CON - Copper Connectivity - CHANNELL COMMERCIAL CORP.; *pg.* 1870, *pg.* 291
CON-AX - Thread Locator - A.G. DAVIS/AA GAGE; *pg.* 1310, *pg.* 908
CON-MATE - Screws - ATLAS BOLT & SCREW COMPANY; *pg.* 1042, *pg.* 1403
CON-TACT - Planarization System - BREWER SCIENCE, INC.; *pg.* 1150, *pg.* 989
CON-TACT - Decorative Coverings - RUBBERMAID HOME PRODUCTS; *pg.* 1138, *pg.* 1453
CON-TACT-IT - Bacteria Detection Equipment - BIRKO CORPORATION; *pg.* 1149, *pg.* 332
CONACURE - Chemical Product - CYTEC INDUSTRIES, INC.; *pg.* 1155, *pg.* 1131
CONAGRA - Meat Product - TEXAS BEEF COUNCIL; *pg.* 158, *pg.* 1666
CONAGRA MILLS - Milled Grain Ingredients - CONAGRA FOODS, INC.; *pg.* 826, *pg.* 1014
CONAIR FOR GREAT HAIR...SALON RESULTS AT HOME - Tagline - CONAIR CORPORATION; *pg.* 505, *pg.* 1055
CONAIR PRO STYLE - Hair Dryer - CONAIR CORPORATION; *pg.* 505, *pg.* 1055
CONAP - Chemical Product - CYTEC INDUSTRIES, INC.; *pg.* 1155, *pg.* 1131
CONAPOXY - Chemical Product - CYTEC INDUSTRIES, INC.; *pg.* 1155, *pg.* 1131
CONATHANE - Chemical Product - CYTEC INDUSTRIES, INC.; *pg.* 1155, *pg.* 1131
CONBRACO - Ball Valves - CONBRACO INDUSTRIES INC.; *pg.* 1325, *pg.* 1382
CONCEAL PLUS PROTECT - Concealer - AVEDA CORPORATION; *pg.* 499, *pg.* 917
CONCENSYS - Panel Systems - THE HON COMPANY; *pg.*

928, *pg.* 709
CONCENT - Chemical Centrifugal - WESTERN STATES MACHINE COMPANY; *pg.* 1388, *pg.* 1455
CONCENTRIX - Microsurgical Equipment - BAUSCH & LOMB INCORPORATED; *pg.* 1401, *pg.* 1045
CONCEPT - Fishing Lines, Fly, Floating & Sinking - 3M COMPANY; *pg.* 1142, *pg.* 956
CONCEPT - Hot Air Balloon - CAMERON BALLOONS U.S.; *pg.* 1829, *pg.* 884
CONCEPT - Flooring Product - CONGOLEUM CORPORATION; *pg.* 921, *pg.* 1084
CONCEPT - Medical Equipment - CONMED CORPORATION; *pg.* 1517, *pg.* 1347
CONCEPT 90 - Boats - CHRIS-CRAFT CORPORATION; *pg.* 1706, *pg.* 465
CONCEPT II - Hood Shield - LUND INTERNATIONAL, INC.; *pg.* 211, *pg.* 526
CONCEPT ONE - Deposition System - LAM RESEARCH CORPORATION; *pg.* 1354, *pg.* 246
CONCEPT SERIES - Metal Building Product - CENTRIA, INC.; *pg.* 74, *pg.* 1554
CONCEPT THREE - Chip - LAM RESEARCH CORPORATION; *pg.* 1354, *pg.* 246
CONCEPT TWO - Modular, Integrated Production System - LAM RESEARCH CORPORATION; *pg.* 1354, *pg.* 246
CONCEPT XT - Clipboard - CUSTOM ACCESSORIES INC.; *pg.* 203, *pg.* 653
CONCEPTUAL CREATIONS - Pet Product - PETSMART, INC.; *pg.* 1481, *pg.* 18
CONCERN - Pest Control - THE WOODSTREAM CORPORATION; *pg.* 1801, *pg.* 1549
CONCERN NECESSARY ORGANICS - Lawn & Garden Product - THE WOODSTREAM CORPORATION; *pg.* 1801, *pg.* 1549
CONCERT - Molecular Biology Product - THERMO FISHER SCIENTIFIC INC.; *pg.* 1602, *pg.* 61
CONCERTA - Pharmaceutical Product - IMPAX LABORATORIES, INC.; *pg.* 1544, *pg.* 101
CONCERTAINER - Bulk Container - GREIF INC.; *pg.* 1459, *pg.* 1447
CONCERTINO - Software - BIO-RAD LABORATORIES, INC.; *pg.* 1504, *pg.* 101
CONCERTO - Lounge Chairs - BERNHARDT DESIGN; *pg.* 918, *pg.* 1381
CONCERTO - Software - BIO-RAD LABORATORIES, INC.; *pg.* 1504, *pg.* 101
CONCERTO - Series Routing Switcher - GRASS VALLEY, INC.; *pg.* 641, *pg.* 164
CONCERTO - Furniture - NEMSCHOFF, INC.; *pg.* 936, *pg.* 1890
CONCERTO - Lighting Product - WESTINGHOUSE LIGHTING CORPORATION; *pg.* 687, *pg.* 1571
CONCERTO - Fragrance - WESTROCK COMPANY; *pg.* 1472, *pg.* 1805
CONCERTO - Home Fragrances - WILLERT HOME PRODUCTS, INC.; *pg.* 1140, *pg.* 1005
CONCERTO CONVERSATIONS - Predictive Dialer - ASPECT SOFTWARE, INC.; *pg.* 354, *pg.* 813
CONCERTO ENSEMBLEPRO - Contact Center Management Software - ASPECT SOFTWARE, INC.; *pg.* 354, *pg.* 813
CONCERTO ENTERPRISE SUITE - Software - ASPECT SOFTWARE, INC.; *pg.* 354, *pg.* 813
CONCERTO RIGHTFORCE - Software - ASPECT SOFTWARE, INC.; *pg.* 354, *pg.* 813
CONCERTO SOFTWARE - Software - ASPECT SOFTWARE, INC.; *pg.* 354, *pg.* 813
CONCERTO SPECTRUM - Software - ASPECT SOFTWARE, INC.; *pg.* 354, *pg.* 813
CONCERTO UNIFIED EDITION - Software - ASPECT SOFTWARE, INC.; *pg.* 354, *pg.* 813
CONCERTO UNISON - Outbound & Blended Call Management Solutions - ASPECT SOFTWARE, INC.; *pg.* 354, *pg.* 813
CONCHA Y TORO - Varietal Wines - BANFI VINTNERS; *pg.* 1957, *pg.* 1161
CONCHITA - Furniture - ASHLEY FURNITURE INDUSTRIES, INC.; *pg.* 914, *pg.* 1852
CONCIAIR - Online Reservation System - SIGNATURE FLIGHT SUPPORT CORP.; *pg.* 234, *pg.* 456
CONCIERGE.COM - Travel Site - CONDE NAST DIGITAL; *pg.* 1237, *pg.* 1217
CONCIERGE.COM - Website - CONDE NAST PUBLICATIONS, INC.; *pg.* 1629, *pg.* 1217
CONCISE - Ophthalmic Lenses - SIGNET ARMORLITE, INC.; *pg.* 1429, *pg.* 60
CONCO - Architectural & Industrial Coatings - THE SHERWIN-WILLIAMS COMPANY; *pg.* 1447, *pg.* 1435
CONCORD - Shoes - ALLEN-EDMONDS SHOE CORP.; *pg.* 1804, *pg.* 1887
CONCORD - Software - BIO-RAD LABORATORIES, INC.; *pg.* 1504, *pg.* 101
CONCORD - Corrugated Product - BUCKEYE CORRUGATED INC.; *pg.* 1454, *pg.* 1400
CONCORD - Agricultural Equipment - CNH AMERICA LLC; *pg.* 702, *pg.* 560
THE CONCORD - Ready-to-assemble Swing Set - CREATIVE PLAYTHINGS LTD.; *pg.* 1831, *pg.* 820
CONCORD - Lectern - DA-LITE SCREEN COMPANY; *pg.* 632, *pg.* 698
CONCORD - Heating And Cooling Product - LENNOX INTERNATIONAL INC.; *pg.* 1073, *pg.* 1736
CONCORD - Watch - MOVADO GROUP, INC.; *pg.* 10, *pg.* 1101
CONCORD - Class "A" Motor Homes - REXHALL INDUSTRIES, INC.; *pg.* 1710, *pg.* 121
CONCORD - Elevator - SAVARIA CONCORD LIFTS INC.; *pg.* 1592, *pg.* 1919
CONCORD VINES - Furniture - ASHLEY FURNITURE INDUSTRIES, INC.; *pg.* 914, *pg.* 1852
CONCORDE - Tires - THE GOODYEAR TIRE & RUBBER COMPANY; *pg.* 1883, *pg.* 1401
CONCORDE - Fluid Handling System - GRACO, INC.; *pg.* 1342, *pg.* 935
CONCORDE - Folding Conference Tables - HOWE FURNITURE CORPORATION; *pg.* 928, *pg.* 998
CONCORDER - Computer System - CORRPRO COMPANIES, INC.; *pg.* 631, *pg.* 1464
CONCOTE - Coating - HILL & GRIFFITH COMPANY; *pg.* 1167, *pg.* 1414
CONCOURSE PROSPECT DIALOGS - Manual - XEROX CORPORATION; *pg.* 494, *pg.* 365
CONCRETE - Coating Products - RUSSEL METALS INC.; *pg.* 1180, *pg.* 1928
CONCRETE DEFENSE - Cleaning Product - HILLYARD, INC.; *pg.* 331, *pg.* 990
CONCRETE INTERNATIONAL - Magazine - AMERICAN CONCRETE INSTITUTE; *pg.* 127, *pg.* 885
CONCRETE LOOP - Urban Culture & Lifestyle Site - SPINMEDIA; *pg.* 1282, *pg.* 104
CONCRETE REPAIR BULLETIN - Bimonthly Magazine - AMERICAN CONCRETE INSTITUTE; *pg.* 127, *pg.* 885
CONCRETE SAFETY SYSTEMS - Wall System - SMITH-MIDLAND CORPORATION; *pg.* 111, *pg.* 1795
CONCUR AUDIT - Management Tool - CONCUR TECHNOLOGIES, INC.; *pg.* 1236, *pg.* 1813
CONCUR CLIQBOOK TOOL - Online Travel Booking Tool - CONCUR TECHNOLOGIES, INC.; *pg.* 1236, *pg.* 1813
CONCUR CLIQBOOK TRAVEL - Travel Booking Tool - CONCUR TECHNOLOGIES, INC.; *pg.* 1236, *pg.* 1813
CONCUR CONNECT - Travel Tool - CONCUR TECHNOLOGIES, INC.; *pg.* 1236, *pg.* 1813
CONCUR EXPENSE - Reporting Process - CONCUR TECHNOLOGIES, INC.; *pg.* 1236, *pg.* 1813
CONCUR INTELLIGENCE - Cost Management - CONCUR TECHNOLOGIES, INC.; *pg.* 1236, *pg.* 1813
CONCUR INVOICE - Process Management - CONCUR TECHNOLOGIES, INC.; *pg.* 1236, *pg.* 1813
CONCUR MOBILE - Mobile Management - CONCUR TECHNOLOGIES, INC.; *pg.* 1236, *pg.* 1813
CONCUR PAY - Expense Payment Service - CONCUR TECHNOLOGIES, INC.; *pg.* 1236, *pg.* 1813
CONCUR TRAVEL & EXPENSE - Travel Management - CONCUR TECHNOLOGIES, INC.; *pg.* 1236, *pg.* 1813
CONCURE - Continuous Hose Manufacturing Process - HBD INDUSTRIES, INC.; *pg.* 207, *pg.* 1449
CONCURRENT BOARD PROCESSSM - Software System - MENTOR GRAPHICS CORPORATION; *pg.* 432, *pg.* 1510
CONCURRENT DESIGN ENVIRONMENT - Software System - MENTOR GRAPHICS CORPORATION; *pg.* 432, *pg.* 1510
CONCURVE - Biking Apparel - W.L. GORE & ASSOCIATES, INC.; *pg.* 122, *pg.* 388
CONDE NAST PORTFOLIO - Magazine - CONDE NAST PUBLICATIONS, INC.; *pg.* 1629, *pg.* 1217
CONDE NAST TRAVELER - Magazine - CONDE NAST PUBLICATIONS, INC.; *pg.* 1629, *pg.* 1217
CONDIMIX - Food Product - NESTLE USA, INC.; *pg.* 883, *pg.* 96
CONDIS - High Voltage Capacitor - MAXWELL TECHNOLOGIES, INC.; *pg.* 653, *pg.* 204
CONDITION 3-IN-1 - Personal Care Electrical Product - HELEN OF TROY L.P.; *pg.* 511, *pg.* 1692
CONDITION SPECIFIC FORMULAS - Healthcare Product - SWANSON HEALTH PRODUCTS INC.; *pg.* 1600, *pg.* 1397
THE CONDITIONER - Hair Care Product - JOHN PAUL MITCHELL SYSTEMS; *pg.* 512, *pg.* 133
CONDO CONCIERGE - Magazine - TRAVELHOST, INC.; *pg.* 1696, *pg.* 1689
CONDOR - Lighting - LSI INDUSTRIES INC.; *pg.* 58, *pg.* 1416
CONDOR - Electronic Components - MOLEX INCORPORATED; *pg.* 655, *pg.* 628
CONDOR - Refractory Product - RESCO PRODUCTS, INC.; *pg.* 107, *pg.* 1581
CONDOR - Switch - SL INDUSTRIES, INC.; *pg.* 674, *pg.* 1090
CONDOR - Safety Products - W.W. GRAINGER, INC.; *pg.* 1390, *pg.* 625
CONDOS - Footwear - VANS, INC.; *pg.* 1821, *pg.* 76
CONDUCT-O-FIL - Conductive Particles - POTTERS INDUSTRIES, INC.; *pg.* 105, *pg.* 1515
CONDUCT-TITE! - Electrical Parts & Supplies - DORMAN PRODUCTS, INC.; *pg.* 204, *pg.* 1522
CONDUCTO-O-FIL - Conductive Additive - PQ CORPORATION; *pg.* 1178, *pg.* 1515
CONDUCTOR - Banking Software - JACK HENRY & ASSOCIATES, INC.; *pg.* 422, *pg.* 988
CONDUCTROX - Conductor Paste - FERRO CORPORATION; *pg.* 1162, *pg.* 1462
CONDYLOX - Pharmaceutical Product - ALLERGAN; *pg.* 1490, *pg.* 1101
CONE DENIM - Denim Fabric - INTERNATIONAL TEXTILE GROUP, INC.; *pg.* 696, *pg.* 1374
CONE-O-CORN - Container - GOLD MEDAL PRODUCTS CO.; *pg.* 55, *pg.* 1414
CONE SHADE - Commercial Lighting - SWIVELIER CO., INC.; *pg.* 1307, *pg.* 1142
CONE TOP - Plastic Conveyor Belt - THE LAITRAM LLC; *pg.* 1354, *pg.* 744
THE CONE WITH THE CURL ON TOP - Ice Milk Product in a Cone - INTERNATIONAL DAIRY QUEEN, INC.; *pg.* 1732, *pg.* 938
CONEC - Glass & Ceramic Material - CORNING INCORPORATED; *pg.* 1122, *pg.* 1154
CONEHEAD - Stand Bag - DATREK GOLF; *pg.* 1832, *pg.* 1801
CONEJET - Spray Nozzle - SPRAYING SYSTEMS CO.; *pg.* 1063, *pg.* 670
CONEY BITES - Hot dogs & Cheese in a Crispy Crust with Skyline Chili for Dipping - SKYLINE CHILI, INC.; *pg.* 1033, *pg.* 1452
CONFAIR - Office Furniture - STEELCASE INC.; *pg.* 475, *pg.* 889
CONFECSHURE - Nutrition & Food Product - BALCHEM CORPORATION; *pg.* 839, *pg.* 1183
CONFERENCE - Furniture - BUSH INDUSTRIES INC.; *pg.* 919, *pg.* 1170
CONFERENCE COMPOSER - Configuration Software - POLYCOM, INC.; *pg.* 664, *pg.* 249
CONFERENCE PLACE - Conferencing Service - INTERCALL, INC.; *pg.* 417, *pg.* 578
CONFESS - Designer Fragrance - PARFUMS DE COEUR LTD.; *pg.* 519, *pg.* 376
CONFETTI - Almonds - BLUE DIAMOND GROWERS; *pg.* 840, *pg.* 195
CONFETTI - Rug - COURISTAN INC.; *pg.* 921, *pg.* 1067
CONFETTI - Dinnerware - THE HOMER LAUGHLIN CHINA COMPANY; *pg.* 1125, *pg.* 1850
CONFETTI - Container Grown Plant - MONROVIA GROWERS; *pg.* 1797, *pg.* 44
CONFIDANTE - Speech Privacy Product - STEELCASE INC.; *pg.* 475, *pg.* 889
CONFIDENCE COMES IN A BURGUNDY BOX - Tag Line - HELZBERG'S DIAMOND SHOPS, INC.; *pg.* 6, *pg.* 984
CONFIDENCE IN A CONNECTED WORLD. - Tag Line - SYMANTEC CORPORATION; *pg.* 478, *pg.* 161
CONFIDENCE ONLINE - Software - SYMANTEC CORPORATION; *pg.* 478, *pg.* 161
CONFIDENCE PLUS - Respirator - MINE SAFETY APPLIANCES COMPANY; *pg.* 1361, *pg.* 1525
CONFIENT - Defibrillator - BOSTON SCIENTIFIC CORPORATION; *pg.* 1508, *pg.* 831
CONFIGMAKER - Software - CISCO SYSTEMS, INC.; *pg.* 372, *pg.* 240

CONFIGURATION DISCOVERY - Software - BMC SOFTWARE, INC.; *pg.* 362, *pg.* 1701
CONFIGURATION MANAGER - Software Application Management - BMC SOFTWARE, INC.; *pg.* 362, *pg.* 1701
CONFIGURATION MANAGER EXPRESS - Software Application Management - BMC SOFTWARE, INC.; *pg.* 362, *pg.* 1701
CONFIGURATIONS - Office Furniture - JOFCO INC.; *pg.* 931, *pg.* 691
CONFIGURESOFT - Software - EMC CORPORATION; *pg.* 391, *pg.* 825
CONFINED CHEMICAL CLEANING - Single-Wafer Clean - LAM RESEARCH CORPORATION; *pg.* 1354, *pg.* 91
CONFIRM - Software - BIO-RAD LABORATORIES, INC.; *pg.* 1504, *pg.* 101
CONFIRMA - Software - SYNOPSYS, INC.; *pg.* 480, *pg.* 162
CONFIRMAILER - Confirmation Mailing Box - CALUMET CARTON COMPANY; *pg.* 1454, *pg.* 661
CONFLUENSE - Defense System - RAYTHEON COMPANY; *pg.* 233, *pg.* 854
CONFLUENT - Surgical Product - W.L. GORE & ASSOCIATES, INC.; *pg.* 122, *pg.* 388
CONFORMABLE - Wire & Cable Products - BELDEN, INC.; *pg.* 624, *pg.* 993
CONFUSION - Fabric - NEMSCHOFF, INC.; *pg.* 936, *pg.* 1890
CONGO - Lighting Control Console - ELECTRONIC THEATRE CONTROLS, INC.; *pg.* 1296, *pg.* 1872
CONGO PEAR - Beverage - BAI BRANDS; *pg.* 238, *pg.* 1073
CONGOLEUM - Sheet Vinyl - AMERICAN BILTRITE INC.; *pg.* 1878, *pg.* 856
CONGRESS OF AUTOMOTIVE REPAIR AND SERVICE - Event - AUTOMOTIVE SERVICE ASSOCIATION; *pg.* 134, *pg.* 1670
CONICAL - Tooth Equipment - ESCO CORPORATION; *pg.* 1335, *pg.* 1502
CONIFLEX - Bevel Product - GLEASON CORPORATION; *pg.* 1340, *pg.* 1335
CONJECTO - Thermal Processing Equipment - SURFACE COMBUSTION, INC.; *pg.* 1077, *pg.* 1462
CONKURE - Wet Curing Blanket - RAVEN INDUSTRIES, INC.; *pg.* 1888, *pg.* 1625
CONMED - Medical Equipment - CONMED CORPORATION; *pg.* 1517, *pg.* 1347
CONN SELMER UNIVERSITY - Musical Instrument - CONN-SELMER, INC.; *pg.* 542, *pg.* 677
CONNECT - Online Financial Service - ACI WORLDWIDE; *pg.* 710, *pg.* 1777
CONNECT - Meter Reading Software - BADGER METER, INC.; *pg.* 1401, *pg.* 1873
CONNECT - Computer Peripheral Equipment - DIGI INTERNATIONAL INC.; *pg.* 387, *pg.* 948
CONNECT - Recovery Tool - SANDISK CORPORATION; *pg.* 465, *pg.* 147
CONNECT 4 - Toy & Game - HASBRO, INC.; *pg.* 954, *pg.* 1603
CONNECT-A-BENCH - Floral Display Fixture - CANNON EQUIPMENT COMPANY; *pg.* 1321, *pg.* 920
CONNECT-A-DOT - Balloon - CONTINENTAL AMERICAN CORP.; *pg.* 1880, *pg.* 723
CONNECT-ALL - Nutritional Supplement - NATURAL ORGANICS, INC.; *pg.* 1571, *pg.* 1181
CONNECT EQUIP INSPIRE - Tagline - WARNER PRESS, INC.; *pg.* 1701, *pg.* 673
CONNECT EVERYTHING. ACHIEVE ANYTHING. - Slogan - PROGRESS SOFTWARE CORPORATION; *pg.* 457, *pg.* 786
CONNECT FOUR - Game - HASBRO, INC.; *pg.* 954, *pg.* 1603
CONNECT LINES - Video Game - INTERNATIONAL GAME TECHNOLOGY; *pg.* 957, *pg.* 1024
CONNECT O 2 - Medical Equipment - INVACARE CORPORATION; *pg.* 1546, *pg.* 1451
CONNECT PLUS - Memory Card - SANDISK CORPORATION; *pg.* 465, *pg.* 147
CONNECT-RX - Software - MCKESSON CORPORATION; *pg.* 1560, *pg.* 222
CONNECT TV - Syndicated Television Programming - CWK NETWORK, INC.; *pg.* 281, *pg.* 503
CONNECT WITH INNOVATION - Slogan - NETGEAR, INC.; *pg.* 444, *pg.* 247
CONNECT WITH MOBILE BROADBAND - Tagline - SIERRA WIRELESS INCORPORATED; *pg.* 673, *pg.* 1909
CONNECT YOUR IMAGINATION TO THE NET - Slogan - LANTRONIX, INC.; *pg.* 426, *pg.* 112
CONNECT YOUR WORLD - Software - LAPLINK SOFTWARE, INC.; *pg.* 426, *pg.* 1815
CONNECT2 - Medical Gas - ALLIED HEALTHCARE PRODUCTS, INC.; *pg.* 1491, *pg.* 990
CONNECTCORE - Computer Peripheral Equipment - DIGI INTERNATIONAL INC.; *pg.* 387, *pg.* 948
CONNECTDIRECT - Hardware Services - DELL INC.; *pg.* 383, *pg.* 1737
CONNECTED SITE - Surveyor - TRIMBLE NAVIGATION LIMITED; *pg.* 1384, *pg.* 288
CONNECTICUT WATER - Water Services - CONNECTICUT WATER SERVICE, INC.; *pg.* 1938, *pg.* 342
CONNECTING BUSINESSES & TECHNOLOGY - Tag Line - ZONES, INC.; *pg.* 1292, *pg.* 1813
CONNECTING EVERYTHING - Slogan - BROADCOM CORPORATION; *pg.* 364, *pg.* 108
CONNECTING WITH KIDS - Educational Program - ACTIVE PARENTING PUBLISHERS; *pg.* 1613, *pg.* 535
CONNECTION ASSISTANT - Software System - MITEL NETWORKS, INC.; *pg.* 1872, *pg.* 13
CONNECTIONCENTER - Semiconductor Solution - CYPRESS SEMICONDUCTOR CORPORATION; *pg.* 1326, *pg.* 243
CONNECTIONS - Software - CADENCE DESIGN SYSTEMS, INC.; *pg.* 367, *pg.* 239
CONNECTIONS - Dinnerware - THE HOMER LAUGHLIN CHINA COMPANY; *pg.* 1125, *pg.* 1850
CONNECTIONS THAT MATTER - Wireless Communication Product - TELECOMMUNICATION SYSTEMS INC.; *pg.* 483, *pg.* 754
CONNECTIT - Project Management - HTC GLOBAL SERVICES INC.; *pg.* 409, *pg.* 911
CONNECTIVITY DASHBOARD - Supply Chain Intelligence - ARROW ELECTRONICS, INC.; *pg.* 619, *pg.* 325
CONNECTIVITY DATAPORT - Software System - MENTOR GRAPHICS CORPORATION; *pg.* 432, *pg.* 1510
CONNECTIVITY SECURE SERVER - Software - OPENTEXT CORPORATION; *pg.* 450, *pg.* 1948
CONNECTOLOGY - Technology - ENTEGRIS, INC.; *pg.* 1882, *pg.* 788
CONNECTOR - Software - VIDEOJET TECHNOLOGIES INC.; *pg.* 489, *pg.* 671
CONNECTORWARE - Data Migration - TRANSEND CORPORATION; *pg.* 485, *pg.* 178
CONNECTPAY - Payment Processing Services - FIRST DATA CORPORATION; *pg.* 754, *pg.* 505
CONNECTPORT - Computer Peripheral Equipment - DIGI INTERNATIONAL INC.; *pg.* 387, *pg.* 948
CONNECT'R WARE - Fastener - PENNENGINEERING FASTENING TECHNOLOGIES; *pg.* 1059, *pg.* 1526
CONNECTRIX - Software - EMC CORPORATION; *pg.* 391, *pg.* 825
CONNECTSMART - Utility Service - XCEL ENERGY INC.; *pg.* 1955, *pg.* 946
CONNECTWARE - Computer Peripheral Equipment - DIGI INTERNATIONAL INC.; *pg.* 387, *pg.* 948
CONNEX - Data Management System - WELCH ALLYN INC.; *pg.* 1436, *pg.* 1342
CONNIE - Shoes - CALERES, INC.; *pg.* 1805, *pg.* 993
CONNIE TOO - Shoes - CALERES, INC.; *pg.* 1805, *pg.* 993
CONNOISSEUR - Furniture - ASHLEY FURNITURE INDUSTRIES, INC.; *pg.* 914, *pg.* 1852
CONNOISSEUR - European-Style Spreadable Cheese - BEL BRANDS USA; *pg.* 839, *pg.* 566
CONNOISSEUR - Professional Cutlery - DEXTER-RUSSELL INC.; *pg.* 1123, *pg.* 844
CONNOISSEUR - Fabric - NEMSCHOFF, INC.; *pg.* 936, *pg.* 1890
CONNOISSEUR - Writing Instruments - SHEAFFER PEN CORPORATION; *pg.* 469, *pg.* 371
CONNOR - Leather Product - COACH, INC.; *pg.* 3, *pg.* 1214
CONNOR - Puzzles - PACON CORPORATION; *pg.* 1466, *pg.* 1852
CONOCO - Petroleum Product - CONOCOPHILLIPS; *pg.* 975, *pg.* 1703
CONOLITE - Industrial Laminate Product - PANOLAM INDUSTRIES INTERNATIONAL, INC.; *pg.* 103, *pg.* 370
CONOMATIC - Machine Tool Product - BOURN & KOCH MACHINE TOOL COMPANY; *pg.* 1319, *pg.* 654
CONOR - Upholstery - ETHAN ALLEN INTERIORS INC.; *pg.* 924, *pg.* 343
CONPATCH - Concrete System - L.M. SCOFIELD COMPANY; *pg.* 94, *pg.* 134
CONPOL - Resins - E.I. DU PONT DE NEMOURS & COMPANY; *pg.* 1159, *pg.* 390
CONQUEROR - Table - BLATT BOWLING & BILLIARD CORP.; *pg.* 1827, *pg.* 1203
CONQUEST - Cable - COMMSCOPE, INC.; *pg.* 278, *pg.* 1378
CONQUEST - Piping - CRANE CHEMPHARMA & ENERGY; *pg.* 1044, *pg.* 1382
CONQUEST - Tires - THE GOODYEAR TIRE & RUBBER COMPANY; *pg.* 1883, *pg.* 1401
CONQUEST - Turning Machine - HARDINGE INC.; *pg.* 1344, *pg.* 1157
CONQUEST - French Fries - J.R. SIMPLOT COMPANY; *pg.* 867, *pg.* 547
CONQUEST - All-Purpose Cleaner for Watercraft - MALCO PRODUCTS, INC.; *pg.* 1172, *pg.* 1404
CONQUEST - Kitchen Appliance - WHIRLPOOL CORPORATION; *pg.* 62, *pg.* 872
CONQUEST 80 - Gas Furnaces - HEAT CONTROLLER, INC.; *pg.* 1072, *pg.* 893
CONQUEST 90 - Gas Furnaces - HEAT CONTROLLER, INC.; *pg.* 1072, *pg.* 893
CONQUISTADOR - Carpet - BEAULIEU GROUP, LLC; *pg.* 917, *pg.* 529
CONRAD - Hotels - HILTON WORLDWIDE, INC.; *pg.* 1094, *pg.* 1791
CONRAD-AMERICAN - Grain Bins - HAWKEYE STEEL PRODUCTS, INC.; *pg.* 704, *pg.* 708
CONROY'S 1-800-FLOWERS - Florist Network - 1-800-FLOWERS.COM, INC.; *pg.* 1758, *pg.* 1151
CONROY'S FLOWERS - Florist Network - 1-800-FLOWERS.COM, INC.; *pg.* 1758, *pg.* 1151
CONSCRIPT - Apparel - OAKLEY, INC.; *pg.* 1840, *pg.* 86
CONSEAL - Concrete Coating - DELTA FOREMOST CHEMICAL CORPORATION; *pg.* 1155, *pg.* 1642
CONSENSUS - Communication Product - J2 GLOBAL COMMUNICATIONS, INC.; *pg.* 1260, *pg.* 133
CONSENSUS MATRIX - Manual - XEROX CORPORATION; *pg.* 494, *pg.* 365
CONSERV - Pharmaceutical Product - CUBIST PHARMACEUTICALS, INC.; *pg.* 1521, *pg.* 828
CONSERVATION ENERGY SYSTEMS - Ventilation Systems - NORTEK, INC.; *pg.* 100, *pg.* 1607
CONSERVATIONIST - Water Heaters & Electric Motors - A.O. SMITH CORPORATION; *pg.* 1313, *pg.* 1872
CONSERVE - Insecticide - SOUTHERN AGRICULTURAL INSECTICIDES, INC.; *pg.* 1181, *pg.* 458
CONSET - Light Duty Anchor - MKT FASTENING, LLC; *pg.* 1056, *pg.* 34
CONSEW BIG LITTLE '500+ SERIES - Industrial Cutting Equipment - CONSEW; *pg.* 53, *pg.* 1049
CONSEW/ORGAN - Industrial Sewing Needles - CONSEW; *pg.* 53, *pg.* 1049
CONSIDER - Fabric - NEMSCHOFF, INC.; *pg.* 936, *pg.* 1890
CONSIDER IT DONE - Slogan - SYNTEL, INC.; *pg.* 480, *pg.* 911
CONSISTENTLY GOOD - Tag Line - FARMER BROTHERS COMPANY; *pg.* 855, *pg.* 293
CONSOLEONE - Java-Based Administration Tool - NOVELL INC.; *pg.* 446, *pg.* 852
CONSOLIDATED CAP FEEDERS - Pharmaceutical Product - PNEUMATICSCALEANGELUS; *pg.* 1369, *pg.* 1445
CONSOLIDATED DISABILITY - Insurance Service - STANDARD INSURANCE COMPANY; *pg.* 1217, *pg.* 1506
CONSOLIDATED NUTRITION - Animal Health Product - ADM ALLIANCE NUTRITION, INC.; *pg.* 1474, *pg.* 653
CONSOMATICS - Industrial Automatic Sewing Equipment - CONSEW; *pg.* 53, *pg.* 1049
CONSONANCE - Bath Product - KOHLER CO.; *pg.* 91, *pg.* 1862
CONSORT - Carpet - BEAULIEU GROUP, LLC; *pg.* 917, *pg.* 529
CONSORT - Hair Spray - UNILEVER UNITED STATES, INC.; *pg.* 904, *pg.* 1061
CONSTA-MIX - Natural Gas Air Mixing System - ALGAS-SDI; *pg.* 1311, *pg.* 1831
CONSTA-VOLT - Battery Chargers - LA MARCHE MANUFACTURING COMPANY; *pg.* 1300, *pg.* 606
CONSTANCE - Furniture - HOOKER FURNITURE CORPORATION; *pg.* 928, *pg.* 1788
CONSTANT COMMENT - Tea - R.C. BIGELOW, INC.; *pg.* 891, *pg.* 348
CONSTANTINA - Fan - CRAFTMADE INTERNATIONAL, INC.; *pg.* 1295, *pg.* 1670
CONSTAVAC - Blood Conservation System - STRYKER CORPORATION; *pg.* 1598, *pg.* 894
CONSTEEL - Furnace - TENOVA; *pg.* 114, *pg.* 1525

CONSTELLATION - Medical Device - BOSTON SCIENTIFIC CORPORATION; *pg.* 1508, *pg.* 831
CONSTELLATION - Motor Yachts - CHRIS-CRAFT CORPORATION; *pg.* 1706, *pg.* 465
CONSTELLATION - Systems Integration & Aeronautics - LOCKHEED MARTIN CORPORATION; *pg.* 229, *pg.* 762
CONSTELLATION - Marine/Weather Instrument - SWIFT OPTICAL INSTRUMENTS, INC.; *pg.* 1430, *pg.* 1744
CONSTELLATION - Molecular Probe Product - THERMO FISHER SCIENTIFIC INC.; *pg.* 1602, *pg.* 61
CONSTELLATION POWER - Wholesale Electric Generation and Distribution - BALTIMORE GAS AND ELECTRIC COMPANY; *pg.* 1936, *pg.* 755
CONSTELLATION POWER SOURCE - Energy Marketing - BALTIMORE GAS AND ELECTRIC COMPANY; *pg.* 1936, *pg.* 755
CONSTITUTION - Systems Integration & Aeronautics - LOCKHEED MARTIN CORPORATION; *pg.* 229, *pg.* 762
CONSTITUTION - Marine Clock - SWIFT OPTICAL INSTRUMENTS, INC.; *pg.* 1430, *pg.* 1744
CONSTRAINT EDITOR SYSTEM - Software System - MENTOR GRAPHICS CORPORATION; *pg.* 432, *pg.* 1510
CONSTRUCTEX - Wire Rope Design - BRIDON AMERICAN CORP.; *pg.* 1319, *pg.* 1594
CONSTRUCTION - Magazine - RANDALL-REILLY PUBLISHING COMPANY LLC; *pg.* 1679, *pg.* 8
THE CONSTRUCTION LENDER - Software System - FAIR ISAAC CORPORATION; *pg.* 1247, *pg.* 955
CONSTRUCTIONCAM - Webcam Software - EARTHCAM, INC.; *pg.* 1239, *pg.* 1072
CONSTRUCTIONCAM LITE - Webcam Software - EARTHCAM, INC.; *pg.* 1239, *pg.* 1072
CONSTRUCTWARE - Software - AUTODESK INC.; *pg.* 356, *pg.* 257
CONSUL - Windows & Doors - NORTEK, INC.; *pg.* 100, *pg.* 1607
CONSUL - Home Appliance Product - WHIRLPOOL CORPORATION; *pg.* 62, *pg.* 872
CONSULATE - Furniture Collection - CENTURY FURNITURE INDUSTRIES; *pg.* 920, *pg.* 1377
CONSULTANT DIRECTORY - Pension Fund Consultants - STANDARD & POOR'S RATINGS SERVICES; *pg.* 805, *pg.* 1296
CONSUMER CHOICE - Online Resource - HEALTHPARTNERS, INC.; *pg.* 1203, *pg.* 918
CONSUMER MORTAGE GUIDE - Guide About Mortage - BANKRATE, INC.; *pg.* 1231, *pg.* 451
CONSUMER REPORTS - Magazine - CONSUMERS UNION OF THE UNITED STATES, INC.; *pg.* 1630, *pg.* 1356
CONSUMERSUNION.ORG - Website - CONSUMERS UNION OF THE UNITED STATES, INC.; *pg.* 1630, *pg.* 1356
CONSUMET - Alloy - CARPENTER TECHNOLOGY CORPORATION; *pg.* 73, *pg.* 1584
CONSUMOBL - Semiconductor Solution - CYPRESS SEMICONDUCTOR CORPORATION; *pg.* 1326, *pg.* 243
CONTACT - Cement - DAP PRODUCTS, INC.; *pg.* 1441, *pg.* 756
CONTACT CLEANER - Aerosol Cleaner - TECH SPRAY, L.P.; *pg.* 1183, *pg.* 1659
CONTACT EAST - Industrial Tools - STANLEY BLACK & DECKER, INC.; *pg.* 1063, *pg.* 358
CONTACT RE-NU - Chemical Product - MILLER-STEPHENSON CHEMICAL COMPANY, INC.; *pg.* 1172, *pg.* 344
CONTACTZONE - Software - MELISSA DATA CORP.; *pg.* 432, *pg.* 188
CONTADINA - Food Products - DEL MONTE FOODS, INC.; *pg.* 852, *pg.* 304
CONTAIN - Supplement & Food Product - NEW EARTH LIFE SCIENCES, INC.; *pg.* 1573, *pg.* 1499
CONTAINS SLICKDIESEL - Diesel Fuel - POWER SERVICE PRODUCTS, INC.; *pg.* 983, *pg.* 1749
CONTAK RENEWAL - Medical Device - BOSTON SCIENTIFIC CORPORATION; *pg.* 1508, *pg.* 831
CONTE - Tomato Products - FURMANO FOODS, INC.; *pg.* 857, *pg.* 1557
CONTEGRA - Pediatric Valve - MEDTRONIC, INC.; *pg.* 1564, *pg.* 939
CONTEMPLATE - Fabric - NEMSCHOFF, INC.; *pg.* 936, *pg.* 1890
CONTEMPO - Furniture - ASHLEY FURNITURE INDUSTRIES, INC.; *pg.* 914, *pg.* 1852
CONTEMPO - Furniture - ETHAN ALLEN INTERIORS INC.; *pg.* 924, *pg.* 343
CONTEMPO - Furniture - JASPER GROUP; *pg.* 930, *pg.* 691
CONTEMPO - Greeting Cards - LEANIN' TREE, INC.; *pg.* 1658, *pg.* 311
CONTEMPO CASUALS - Clothing Stores - THE WET SEAL, LLC; *pg.* 35, *pg.* 88
CONTEMPORA - Footwear - CAPEZIO BALLET MAKERS INC.; *pg.* 1805, *pg.* 1125
CONTEMPORARY - Furniture - ASHLEY FURNITURE INDUSTRIES, INC.; *pg.* 914, *pg.* 1852
CONTEMPORARY - Insulated & Traditional Beverage Urns & Soup & Sauce Servers - CARLISLE FOODSERVICE PRODUCTS INCORPORATED; *pg.* 1455, *pg.* 1485
CONTEMPORARY - Chimes - CRAFTMADE INTERNATIONAL, INC.; *pg.* 1295, *pg.* 1670
CONTEMPORARY MAPLE - Laminated 3" Plank-Square Edge - ROBBINS, INC.; *pg.* 108, *pg.* 1425
CONTEMPORARY OB/GYN - Medical Publication - TRUVEN HEALTH ANALYTICS; *pg.* 1696, *pg.* 867
CONTEMPORARY PARQUET - Solid Parquet-Fingerblock - ROBBINS, INC.; *pg.* 108, *pg.* 1425
CONTEMPORARY PEDIATRICS - Medical Publication - TRUVEN HEALTH ANALYTICS; *pg.* 1696, *pg.* 867
CONTEMPORARY PLANK - Laminated 3" Plank Flooring-Eased Edge - ROBBINS, INC.; *pg.* 108, *pg.* 1425
CONTEMPORARY STRIP - Solid 2 1/4" Strip-Beveled Edge - ROBBINS, INC.; *pg.* 108, *pg.* 1425
CONTEMPORARY SURGERY - Healthcare Publication - LEBHAR-FRIEDMAN INC.; *pg.* 1658, *pg.* 1250
CONTEMPORARY UROLOGY - Medical Publication - TRUVEN HEALTH ANALYTICS; *pg.* 1696, *pg.* 867
CONTEMPRA - Ceiling Fan - WESTINGHOUSE LIGHTING CORPORATION; *pg.* 687, *pg.* 1571
CONTEMPRA TRIO - Ceiling Fan - WESTINGHOUSE LIGHTING CORPORATION; *pg.* 687, *pg.* 1571
CONTENDER - Carpet - BEAULIEU GROUP, LLC; *pg.* 917, *pg.* 529
CONTENDER - Hose & Conveyer Belting - THE GOODYEAR TIRE & RUBBER COMPANY; *pg.* 1883, *pg.* 1401
CONTENDER - Cleaning Product - HILLYARD, INC.; *pg.* 331, *pg.* 990
CONTENDER - Truck Storage Box - LUND INTERNATIONAL, INC.; *pg.* 211, *pg.* 526
CONTENDER - Fire Apparatus - PIERCE MANUFACTURING, INC.; *pg.* 188, *pg.* 1852
CONTENT ACCESS POINT - Architecture Network - MIRROR IMAGE INTERNET, INC.; *pg.* 1267, *pg.* 848
CONTENT ADAPTER - Software - EGAIN COMMUNICATIONS CORPORATION; *pg.* 1242, *pg.* 284
CONTENT AUDITOR - Software - WEBSENSE, INC.; *pg.* 491, *pg.* 210
CONTENT DISTRIBUTION - Software Management Process - BMC SOFTWARE, INC.; *pg.* 362, *pg.* 1701
CONTENT ENFORCER - Software - WEBSENSE, INC.; *pg.* 491, *pg.* 210
CONTENT EXPLORER - Software - AUTODESK INC.; *pg.* 356, *pg.* 257
CONTENT SERVER - Software - ADOBE SYSTEMS INCORPORATED; *pg.* 342, *pg.* 235
CONTENT SUPPLY CHAIN - Program - INNODATA ISOGEN, INC.; *pg.* 1259, *pg.* 1072
CONTENTGUARD - Software Product - XEROX CORPORATION; *pg.* 494, *pg.* 365
CONTENTS - Cosmetic Organizers - RUBBERMAID HOME PRODUCTS; *pg.* 1138, *pg.* 1453
CONTESSA - Tile - ARTISTIC TILE INC.; *pg.* 914, *pg.* 1119
CONTESSA - Footwear - P.W. MINOR & SON, INC.; *pg.* 1816, *pg.* 1140
CONTESTOR GT - Blade - LENOX; *pg.* 1053, *pg.* 817
CONTEXT - Office Furniture - STEELCASE INC.; *pg.* 475, *pg.* 889
CONTEXTUAL FORMATION - Language Learning Solutions - ROSETTA STONE INC.; *pg.* 462, *pg.* 1774
CONTINENTAL - Delivery System - A-DEC, INC.; *pg.* 1483, *pg.* 1500
CONTINENTAL - Plumbing Product - SLOAN VALVE COMPANY; *pg.* 1062, *pg.* 613
CONTINENTAL - Chocolate Product - WORLD'S FINEST CHOCOLATE, INC.; *pg.* 1864, *pg.* 597
CONTINENTAL CHAFER - Food Chafer - THE VOLLRATH COMPANY LLC; *pg.* 1139, *pg.* 1894
THE CONTINENTAL DIAMOND COLLECTION - Jewelry - HELZBERG'S DIAMOND SHOPS, INC.; *pg.* 6, *pg.* 984
CONTINENTAL INSTRUMENTS - Access Control Products - NAPCO SECURITY SYSTEMS, INC.; *pg.* 658, *pg.* 1138
CONTINENTAL SKETCHBOOK - Furniture - BASSETT FURNITURE INDUSTRIES, INCORPORATED; *pg.* 916, *pg.* 1776
CONTINUING THE TRADITION OF INDEPENDENCE - Tag Line - HEAVEN HILL DISTILLERIES, INC.; *pg.* 1964, *pg.* 725
CONTINUOUS DATA PROTECTOR - Data Protection Solutions - FALCONSTOR SOFTWARE, INC.; *pg.* 396, *pg.* 1179
THE CONTINUOUS POWER COMPANY - Slogan - CLARY CORPORATION; *pg.* 226, *pg.* 150
CONTINUOUS PROCESSING - Computer Server Architecture - STRATUS TECHNOLOGIES, INC.; *pg.* 477, *pg.* 832
CONTINUOUSTEXTURE - Visual System - EVANS & SUTHERLAND COMPUTER CORPORATION; *pg.* 638, *pg.* 1757
CONTINUOUSWAVE - Programmable AC Power - AMETEK PROGRAMMABLE POWER, INC.; *pg.* 616, *pg.* 200
CONTINUUM - Furniture - ASHLEY FURNITURE INDUSTRIES, INC.; *pg.* 914, *pg.* 1852
CONTINUUM - Resin - THE DOW CHEMICAL COMPANY; *pg.* 1157, *pg.* 898
CONTINUUM - Software System - MENTOR GRAPHICS CORPORATION; *pg.* 432, *pg.* 1510
CONTINUUM - Dog Vaccine - MERCK & CO., INC.; *pg.* 1566, *pg.* 1077
CONTINUUM - Fabric - NEMSCHOFF, INC.; *pg.* 936, *pg.* 1890
CONTINUUM - Furniture - STANLEY FURNITURE CO., INC.; *pg.* 943, *pg.* 1379
CONTINUUM - Computer Servers - STRATUS TECHNOLOGIES, INC.; *pg.* 477, *pg.* 832
CONTINUUM - Software - VIQ SOLUTIONS INC.; *pg.* 490, *pg.* 1905
CONTINUUM AEC - Cooling Water Treatment - GE WATER & PROCESS TECHNOLOGIES; *pg.* 1339, *pg.* 1588
CONTINUUM POWER ANALYST - Software System - MENTOR GRAPHICS CORPORATION; *pg.* 432, *pg.* 1510
CONTOUR - Medical Device - BOSTON SCIENTIFIC CORPORATION; *pg.* 1508, *pg.* 831
CONTOUR - Screen - DA-LITE SCREEN COMPANY; *pg.* 632, *pg.* 698
CONTOUR - Shrink-Wrap System - DOUGLAS MACHINE, INC.; *pg.* 1456, *pg.* 915
CONTOUR - Software - ELLIE MAE, INC.; *pg.* 1243, *pg.* 183
CONTOUR - Medical Product - HOLOGIC, INC.; *pg.* 1416, *pg.* 784
CONTOUR - Steel Laboratory Cabinets - KEWAUNEE SCIENTIFIC CORPORATION; *pg.* 931, *pg.* 1391
CONTOUR - Dispensing Closure - OWENS-ILLINOIS, INC.; *pg.* 1466, *pg.* 1470
CONTOUR - Flash Drive - SANDISK CORPORATION; *pg.* 465, *pg.* 147
CONTOUR - ICD Products - ST. JUDE MEDICAL, INC.; *pg.* 1596, *pg.* 963
CONTOUR - Remote Control Device - UNIVERSAL ELECTRONICS, INC.; *pg.* 683, *pg.* 262
CONTOUR CRIMP - Power & Grounding Connector - PANDUIT CORP.; *pg.* 661, *pg.* 663
CONTOUR ELECTROL - Electric Screen - DA-LITE SCREEN COMPANY; *pg.* 632, *pg.* 698
CONTOUR FIT LOGIC - Sampler Kit - THE HILSINGER CO.; *pg.* 1416, *pg.* 841
CONTOUR FIT SYSTEM - Gloves - FRANKLIN SPORTS, INC.; *pg.* 1834, *pg.* 847
CONTOUR-FLEX - Medical Device - INTEGRA LIFESCIENCES HOLDINGS CORPORATION; *pg.* 1545, *pg.* 1109
CONTOUR-PAK - Carrier - OWENS-ILLINOIS, INC.; *pg.* 1466, *pg.* 1470
CONTOUR PROBE - Laser Sensors - PERCEPTRON, INC.; *pg.* 215, *pg.* 904
CONTOUR PROFILE - Medical Device - MENTOR CORPORATION; *pg.* 1565, *pg.* 263
CONTOUR SELECT - Seat Cushion - THE ROHO GROUP; *pg.* 1591, *pg.* 556
CONTOUR SERIES - Shoes - ACUSHNET COMPANY; *pg.* 1824, *pg.* 818
CONTOUR-TY - Cable Tie - PANDUIT CORP.; *pg.* 661, *pg.* 663
CONTOUR VL VARIABLE LENGTH PERCUFLEX - Medical Device - BOSTON SCIENTIFIC CORPORATION; *pg.* 1508, *pg.* 831
CONTOURA - Medical Equipment - INVACARE CORPORATION; *pg.* 1546, *pg.* 1451
CONTOURED COMFORT - Potty Trainer & Step Stool - EVENFLO COMPANY, INC.; *pg.* 924, *pg.* 1470

First page reference indicates Business Class Edition
Second page reference indicates Geographic Edition

CONTOURS - Furniture - BUSH INDUSTRIES INC.; *pg.* 919, *pg.* 1170
CONTOURS - Window & Door - JELD-WEN, INC.; *pg.* 1051, *pg.* 1499
CONTOURU - Chair Cushion - INVACARE CORPORATION; *pg.* 1546, *pg.* 1451
CONTRACT - Trade Publication - THE NIELSEN COMPANY B.V.; *pg.* 1671, *pg.* 1272
CONTRACT RENEWALS PLUS - Marketing Program Suite - RAINMAKER SYSTEMS INC.; *pg.* 458, *pg.* 58
CONTRACTOR'S CHOICE - Fan - WESTINGHOUSE LIGHTING CORPORATION; *pg.* 687, *pg.* 1571
CONTRACTOR - Flashlight - ENERGIZER HOLDINGS, INC.; *pg.* 637, *pg.* 996
CONTRACTOR - Fluid Handling System - GRACO, INC.; *pg.* 1342, *pg.* 935
CONTRACTOR FTX - Airless Spray Gun - GRACO, INC.; *pg.* 1342, *pg.* 935
CONTRACTOR GRADE - Hand Tools - STANLEY BLACK & DECKER, INC.; *pg.* 1063, *pg.* 358
CONTRACTOR II - Fluid Handling System - GRACO, INC.; *pg.* 1342, *pg.* 935
CONTRACTOR SERIES - Brushes - THE SHERWIN-WILLIAMS COMPANY; *pg.* 1447, *pg.* 1435
CONTRACTOR'S DESIGN - Fan - CRAFTMADE INTERNATIONAL, INC.; *pg.* 1295, *pg.* 1670
CONTRACTOR'S SELECT - Fan - CRAFTMADE INTERNATIONAL, INC.; *pg.* 1295, *pg.* 1670
CONTRACTSLEEPER - Furniture - HSM SOLUTIONS; *pg.* 1884, *pg.* 1378
CONTRACTURE PLATFORM - Medical Equipment - INVACARE CORPORATION; *pg.* 1546, *pg.* 1451
CONTRADA - Furniture - TRENDWAY CORPORATION; *pg.* 945, *pg.* 892
CONTRAST - Biotechnology Product - GENZYME CORPORATION; *pg.* 1534, *pg.* 808
CONTRIBUTE - Software - ADOBE SYSTEMS INCORPORATED; *pg.* 342, *pg.* 235
CONTRO-BULB - Syringe And Tip Protector - MEDLINE INDUSTRIES, INC.; *pg.* 1562, *pg.* 635
CONTRO-PISTON - Irrigation Syringe - MEDLINE INDUSTRIES, INC.; *pg.* 1562, *pg.* 635
CONTROL - Bar Soap - SWISHER HYGIENE INC.; *pg.* 336, *pg.* 1507
CONTROL 2 - Remote Control Device - UNIVERSAL ELECTRONICS, INC.; *pg.* 683, *pg.* 262
CONTROL-3 - Remote Control Device - UNIVERSAL ELECTRONICS, INC.; *pg.* 683, *pg.* 262
CONTROL-A-FLO - Water Conserving Cartridge for Faucets - THE CHICAGO FAUCET COMPANY; *pg.* 1044, *pg.* 606
CONTROL ASSISTANT - Software Product - WOODWARD, INC.; *pg.* 122, *pg.* 329
CONTROL BLADE - Software Product - EGENERA, INC.; *pg.* 390, *pg.* 802
CONTROL CENTER - Software - STRATASYS, INC.; *pg.* 476, *pg.* 923
CONTROL CENTER 5 - Webcam Software - EARTHCAM, INC.; *pg.* 1239, *pg.* 1072
CONTROL COAT - Hot Melt Adhesive Spray Nozzle - NORDSON CORPORATION; *pg.* 1365, *pg.* 1480
CONTROL CONFIDENCE - Electrical Controller - WATLOW ELECTRIC MANUFACTURING COMPANY; *pg.* 1078, *pg.* 1004
CONTROL-D - Software - BMC SOFTWARE, INC.; *pg.* 362, *pg.* 1701
CONTROL-D/AGENT - Monitoring Software - BMC SOFTWARE, INC.; *pg.* 362, *pg.* 1701
CONTROL-D/IMAGE - Software - BMC SOFTWARE, INC.; *pg.* 362, *pg.* 1701
CONTROL-D/PAGE ON DEMAND - Software - BMC SOFTWARE, INC.; *pg.* 362, *pg.* 1701
CONTROL-D/WEBACCESS SERVER - Software - BMC SOFTWARE, INC.; *pg.* 362, *pg.* 1701
CONTROL IS EVERYTHING - Fluid Handling System - GRACO, INC.; *pg.* 1342, *pg.* 935
CONTROL-M/ANALYZER - Software - BMC SOFTWARE, INC.; *pg.* 362, *pg.* 1701
CONTROL-M/ASSIST - Software - BMC SOFTWARE, INC.; *pg.* 362, *pg.* 1701
CONTROL-M BUSINESS PROCESS INTEGRATION SUITE - Software - BMC SOFTWARE, INC.; *pg.* 362, *pg.* 1701
CONTROL-M/CM - Software - BMC SOFTWARE, INC.; *pg.* 362, *pg.* 1701
CONTROL-M/END USER - Software - BMC SOFTWARE, INC.; *pg.* 362, *pg.* 1701
CONTROL-M/ENTERPRISE MANAGER - Software - BMC SOFTWARE, INC.; *pg.* 362, *pg.* 1701
CONTROL-M/FORECAST - Software - BMC SOFTWARE, INC.; *pg.* 362, *pg.* 1701
CONTROL-M/FULL ADMIN USER - Software - BMC SOFTWARE, INC.; *pg.* 362, *pg.* 1701
CONTROL-M INTEGRATION MODULE - Software - BMC SOFTWARE, INC.; *pg.* 362, *pg.* 1701
CONTROL-M/LINKS - Software - BMC SOFTWARE, INC.; *pg.* 362, *pg.* 1701
CONTROL-M OPTION - Software - BMC SOFTWARE, INC.; *pg.* 362, *pg.* 1701
CONTROL-M PLUS MODULE - Software - BMC SOFTWARE, INC.; *pg.* 362, *pg.* 1701
CONTROL-M/RESTART - Software - BMC SOFTWARE, INC.; *pg.* 362, *pg.* 1701
CONTROL-M SMART PLUG-IN - Software - BMC SOFTWARE, INC.; *pg.* 362, *pg.* 1701
CONTROL-M/TAPE - Software - BMC SOFTWARE, INC.; *pg.* 362, *pg.* 1701
CONTROL-M/WEB & PLANNING USER - Software - BMC SOFTWARE, INC.; *pg.* 362, *pg.* 1701
CONTROL MASTER - Electrical Appliance & Housewares - NATIONAL PRESTO INDUSTRIES, INC; *pg.* 1128, *pg.* 1857
CONTROL-O - Software - BMC SOFTWARE, INC.; *pg.* 362, *pg.* 1701
CONTROL PAD PRO - Video Game Controller - MAD CATZ INTERACTIVE INC.; *pg.* 429, *pg.* 204
CONTROL-SA - Software - BMC SOFTWARE, INC.; *pg.* 362, *pg.* 1701
CONTROL-SA/PROVISIONING MODULE - Software - BMC SOFTWARE, INC.; *pg.* 362, *pg.* 1701
THE CONTROL TOWER - Pharmaceutical Product - PFIZER INC.; *pg.* 1581, *pg.* 1278
CONTROL TOWER - Software - ROCKWELL AUTOMATION, INC.; *pg.* 668, *pg.* 1880
CONTROL-V - Software - BMC SOFTWARE, INC.; *pg.* 362, *pg.* 1701
CONTROLBOSS - Cable - AMPHENOL CORPORATION; *pg.* 616, *pg.* 381
CONTROLCENTER - Software System - EMC CORPORATION; *pg.* 391, *pg.* 825
CONTROLCENTRE - Scanner - XEROX CORPORATION; *pg.* 494, *pg.* 365
CONTROLIP - Pharmaceutical Products - ABBOTT LABORATORIES; *pg.* 1484, *pg.* 551
CONTROLIR - Infrared Heaters - PRECISION CONTROL SYSTEMS, INC./ RESEARCH INC.; *pg.* 1427, *pg.* 923
CONTROLLED MAGNETIC - Microphones - SHURE INCORPORATED; *pg.* 672, *pg.* 638
CONTROLLER - Door Locks - KAWNEER COMPANY, INC.; *pg.* 90, *pg.* 537
CONTROLLER - Software - LAPLINK SOFTWARE, INC.; *pg.* 426, *pg.* 1815
CONTROLLOGIX - Software - ROCKWELL AUTOMATION, INC.; *pg.* 668, *pg.* 1880
CONTROLOK - Measuring Product - THE L.S. STARRETT COMPANY; *pg.* 1421, *pg.* 783
CONTROLRX - Sodium Fluoride Dentifrice - 3M COMPANY; *pg.* 1142, *pg.* 956
CONTROLSINSIGHT - Software - INFOGIX INC.; *pg.* 414, *pg.* 636
CONTROLUX - Lighting Fixture - HUBBELL INCORPORATED; *pg.* 1299, *pg.* 370
CONTROLWEB - Ethernet Control System - MKS INSTRUMENTS, INC.; *pg.* 1362, *pg.* 781
CONTROLZ - Paints - THE VALSPAR CORPORATION; *pg.* 1449, *pg.* 945
CONTURA - Stroller - DOREL JUVENILE GROUP, INC.; *pg.* 923, *pg.* 676
CONTURA - Electronic Components - MOLEX INCORPORATED; *pg.* 655, *pg.* 628
CONTURA SERIES - Washroom Equipment - BOBRICK WASHROOM EQUIPMENT, INC.; *pg.* 1043, *pg.* 166
CONVA - Software - DUKANE CORPORATION; *pg.* 634, *pg.* 658
CONVAIR - EVAP Coolers - SEELEY INTERNATIONAL AMERICAS; *pg.* 1076, *pg.* 19
CONVAIR 3 IN 1 - Cooler - SEELEY INTERNATIONAL AMERICAS; *pg.* 1076, *pg.* 19
CONVAQUIP - Bariatric Electric Beds - ALIMED, INC.; *pg.* 1490, *pg.* 816
CONVECT-RITE II - Cook & Chill System - ALADDIN TEMP-RITE, LLC; *pg.* 1013, *pg.* 1635
CONVECTION COMBO - Combination Steamer-Oven - UNIFIED BRANDS INC.; *pg.* 1385, *pg.* 970
CONVENE - Integrated Collaborated Solution - POLYCOM, INC.; *pg.* 664, *pg.* 249
CONVENE - Office Furniture - STEELCASE INC.; *pg.* 475, *pg.* 889
CONVENE TABLE - Tables - STEELCASE INC.; *pg.* 475, *pg.* 889
CONVENIENCE CARD - Banking Card - CANADIAN IMPERIAL BANK OF COMMERCE; *pg.* 729, *pg.* 1935
CONVENIENCE STORE NEWS - Trade Publication - THE NIELSEN COMPANY B.V.; *pg.* 1671, *pg.* 1272
CONVENIENCE WITHOUT COMPROMISE - Food Product - TYSON FOODS, INC.; *pg.* 902, *pg.* 35
CONVENTIONAL CLASSICS - Engine - LIONEL LLC; *pg.* 961, *pg.* 875
CONVERGE - Professional Conferencing - CLEARONE COMMUNICATIONS, INC.; *pg.* 629, *pg.* 1756
CONVERGED MANAGED APPLICATION - Management Application - POLYCOM, INC.; *pg.* 664, *pg.* 249
CONVERGED SENSOR NETWORK - Architecture - MERCURY COMPUTER SYSTEMS, INC.; *pg.* 434, *pg.* 813
CONVERGENCE - Software - EMULEX CORPORATION; *pg.* 392, *pg.* 70
CONVERGENCE - Fabric - NEMSCHOFF, INC.; *pg.* 936, *pg.* 1890
CONVERGENCE GENERATION - Platform - ONMOBILE LIVE, INC.; *pg.* 449, *pg.* 829
CONVERGENCENOW - Software Platform - SYNCHRONOSS TECHNOLOGIES, INC.; *pg.* 479, *pg.* 1047
CONVERGENT HEALTH SOLUTIONS - Healthcare Publication - LEBHAR-FRIEDMAN INC.; *pg.* 1658, *pg.* 1250
CONVERSE - Foot Apparel - CONVERSE INC.; *pg.* 1831, *pg.* 793
CONVERSIONS PLUS - Software - DATAVIZ, INC.; *pg.* 383, *pg.* 356
CONVERT - Apparel - COLUMBIA SPORTSWEAR COMPANY; *pg.* 1830, *pg.* 1501
CONVERT-A-LITE - Commercial Lighting - SWIVELIER CO., INC.; *pg.* 1307, *pg.* 1142
CONVERT-A-TRACK - Commercial Lighting - SWIVELIER CO., INC.; *pg.* 1307, *pg.* 1142
CONVERTAMATIC - Cleaning Product - HILLYARD, INC.; *pg.* 331, *pg.* 990
CONVERTAMATIC - Small Vacuum - NILFISK-ADVANCE, INC.; *pg.* 332, *pg.* 953
CONVERTAMAX - Cleaning Product - HILLYARD, INC.; *pg.* 331, *pg.* 990
CONVERTAMAX - Floor Care - NILFISK-ADVANCE, INC.; *pg.* 332, *pg.* 953
CONVERTAPIPE - Custom Built Pipe - HBD INDUSTRIES, INC.; *pg.* 207, *pg.* 1449
CONVERTER - Additive - BASF CATALYSTS LLC; *pg.* 1148, *pg.* 1074
CONVERTIBLE - Men's Billfold - BUXTON ACQUISITION CO., LLC; *pg.* 2, *pg.* 845
CONVERTIBLE SURVEYS - Publication - VALUE LINE, INC.; *pg.* 1699, *pg.* 1308
CONVERTIBLE ULTRASOUND - Ultrasound Systems - ZONARE MEDICAL SYSTEMS, INC.; *pg.* 1612, *pg.* 163
CONVEX - Furniture - JOFCO INC.; *pg.* 931, *pg.* 691
CONVEX FLEX - Office Furniture - JOFCO INC.; *pg.* 931, *pg.* 691
CONVEY-ALL - Screw Conveyor - METALFAB, INC.; *pg.* 1360, *pg.* 1127
CONVEY-O-QUENCH - Hardening Furnace - AJAX ELECTRIC CO.; *pg.* 1068, *pg.* 1541
CONVIA - Furniture - HERMAN MILLER, INC.; *pg.* 926, *pg.* 913
CONVOI - Furniture - ANTHRO CORPORATION; *pg.* 913, *pg.* 1509
CONVOY - Delivery Sheath Kits - BOSTON SCIENTIFIC CORPORATION; *pg.* 1508, *pg.* 831
CONWAY - Transportation Service - XPO LOGISTICS, INC.; *pg.* 1931, *pg.* 350
COOK - Consumer Paint - DAVIS PAINT COMPANY; *pg.* 1441, *pg.* 982
COOK & LADDER - Entertainment - MCILHENNY COMPANY; *pg.* 876, *pg.* 741
COOK IT! CLUB - Mail/Catalog Order Services - 1-800-FLOWERS.COM, INC.; *pg.* 1758, *pg.* 1151
COOK-N-SHIP - Thermoplastic Bags in Which Processed Meat or Poultry is Cooked & Shipped - SEALED AIR

CORPORATION; *pg.* 1468, *pg.* 1058
COOK NAVIGATOR - Display - TURBOCHEF TECHNOLOGIES, INC.; *pg.* 902, *pg.* 1670
COOK-ON - Gas Grill - BARBEQUES GALORE, INC.; *pg.* 51, *pg.* 173
COOK TOP - Chemical Product - WEIMAN PRODUCTS, LLC; *pg.* 337, *pg.* 616
COOK-WAITE - Dental Anesthetics - EASTMAN KODAK COMPANY; *pg.* 1408, *pg.* 1333
COOK-Z - Medical Device - COOK GROUP, INC.; *pg.* 1518, *pg.* 674
COOKIE - Magazine - CONDE NAST PUBLICATIONS, INC.; *pg.* 1629, *pg.* 1217
COOKIE CRAZE - Friazos - WELLS ENTERPRISES, INC.; *pg.* 909, *pg.* 709
COOKIE CRISP - Cereal - GENERAL MILLS, INC.; *pg.* 828, *pg.* 933
COOKIES 'N' CREME - Chocolate Bar - THE HERSHEY CO.; *pg.* 1855, *pg.* 1538
COOKIN' GOOD - Frozen Poultry - PERDUE FARMS INCORPORATED; *pg.* 889, *pg.* 777
COOKIN' WHAT AMERICA LOVES BEST - Tagline - WESTERN SIZZLIN CORPORATION; *pg.* 1755, *pg.* 1806
COOKING - Software - IDEALAB, INC.; *pg.* 1258, *pg.* 180
COOKING CHANNEL - Television Show - SCRIPPS NETWORKS INTERACTIVE, INC.; *pg.* 1279, *pg.* 1638
COOKING LIGHT - Media Publication - TIME INC.; *pg.* 1693, *pg.* 1300
COOKOUT CASH - Lottery Game - KENTUCKY LOTTERY CORPORATION; *pg.* 996, *pg.* 735
COOK'S - Food Product - CONAGRA FOODS, INC.; *pg.* 826, *pg.* 1014
COOK'S - Food Products - SMITHFIELD FOODS, INC.; *pg.* 896, *pg.* 1806
COOK'S COUNTRY MAGAZINE - Publication - AMERICA'S TEST KITCHEN; *pg.* 1616, *pg.* 803
COOK'S ILLUSTRATED - Publication - AMERICA'S TEST KITCHEN; *pg.* 1616, *pg.* 803
COOKTEK - Cooking Equipment - CHESHER EQUIPMENT LTD.; *pg.* 1323, *pg.* 1925
COOKTEK - Cooking Equipment - THE MIDDLEBY CORPORATION; *pg.* 1361, *pg.* 610
COOKWHEEL - Controller - TURBOCHEF TECHNOLOGIES, INC.; *pg.* 902, *pg.* 1670
COOL 18 - Microfiber Pants - HAGGAR CORPORATION; *pg.* 41, *pg.* 1682
COOL 7'S - Lottery Game - LOUISIANA LOTTERY CORPORATION; *pg.* 997, *pg.* 742
COOL BLUE WAND - Syringe - MILESTONE SCIENTIFIC, INC.; *pg.* 1568, *pg.* 1079
COOL CANADIAN - Spring Water - LEADING BRANDS, INC.; *pg.* 1026, *pg.* 1911
COOL CARE PLUS - Country Fresh Scent - ANDIS COMPANY; *pg.* 498, *pg.* 1895
COOL CARGO - Insulated Lunch Bag - IGLOO PRODUCTS CORPORATION; *pg.* 1126, *pg.* 1724
COOL CASH - Game - MISSOURI LOTTERY; *pg.* 999, *pg.* 979
COOL CASH DOUBLER - Lottery Game - KENTUCKY LOTTERY CORPORATION; *pg.* 996, *pg.* 735
COOL CAT CASH - Game - WMS INDUSTRIES INC.; *pg.* 593, *pg.* 666
COOL COLORS - Extension Cords - COLEMAN CABLE, INC.; *pg.* 1324, *pg.* 665
COOL COLORS - Pigments - FERRO CORPORATION; *pg.* 1162, *pg.* 1462
COOL COMPRESSION - Industrial Refrigeration Compressors - VILTER MANUFACTURING LLC; *pg.* 1078, *pg.* 1856
COOL CONFIDENCE - Beauty Product - AVON PRODUCTS, INC.; *pg.* 500, *pg.* 1198
COOL COVERS - Above-Ground Pool Kit - POOL CORPORATION; *pg.* 1843, *pg.* 743
COOL CREW - Toy & Game - HASBRO, INC.; *pg.* 954, *pg.* 1603
COOL CUTS 4 KIDS - Hair Salons - REGIS CORPORATION; *pg.* 521, *pg.* 941
COOL DRY - Gloves - FRANKLIN SPORTS, INC.; *pg.* 1834, *pg.* 847
COOL EFFECT - Blush, Eye Liner & Shadow - MAYBELLINE LLC; *pg.* 516, *pg.* 1257
COOL FLOW - Baby Care Product - MUNCHKIN, INC.; *pg.* 964, *pg.* 300
COOL-FLOW - Bag - SAMSONITE CORPORATION; *pg.* 11, *pg.* 830
COOL FOREST - Personal Care Product - COLGATE-PALMOLIVE COMPANY; *pg.* 504, *pg.* 1215
COOL-FORM - Lubricant - DAUBERT INDUSTRIES, INC.; *pg.* 1155, *pg.* 561
COOL FROTH - Superautomatic Espresso System - BUNN-O-MATIC CORPORATION; *pg.* 53, *pg.* 661
COOL FUSION - Personal Care Product - COLGATE-PALMOLIVE COMPANY; *pg.* 504, *pg.* 1215
COOL GEL - Spray - LA-CO INDUSTRIES MARKAL CO., INC.; *pg.* 1170, *pg.* 610
COOL-GLO - Commercial Lighting - SWIVELIER CO., INC.; *pg.* 1307, *pg.* 1142
COOL-GUARD - Cooling Product - E.I. DU PONT DE NEMOURS & COMPANY; *pg.* 1159, *pg.* 390
COOL KIDS - Spillproof Cups - EVENFLO COMPANY, INC.; *pg.* 924, *pg.* 1470
COOL LOGIC - Fan Drive - BORGWARNER INC.; *pg.* 167, *pg.* 867
COOL MIST - Humidifier - KAZ, INC.; *pg.* 58, *pg.* 844
COOL MOON - Soft Drink - CAROLINA BEVERAGE CORPORATION; *pg.* 239, *pg.* 1390
COOL OFF - Cooling System - MOC PRODUCTS COMPANY, INC.; *pg.* 332, *pg.* 174
COOL PATH - Catheter - ST. JUDE MEDICAL, INC.; *pg.* 1596, *pg.* 963
COOL POINT - Irrigation Pump - ST. JUDE MEDICAL, INC.; *pg.* 1596, *pg.* 963
COOL POWER - Herbicide Product - NUFARM AMERICAS INC; *pg.* 1798, *pg.* 552
COOL ROLLER - Ice Chest - IGLOO PRODUCTS CORPORATION; *pg.* 1126, *pg.* 1724
COOL SACK - Lunch Kit - IGLOO PRODUCTS CORPORATION; *pg.* 1126, *pg.* 1724
COOL SACK DELUXE - Insulated Lunch Bag - IGLOO PRODUCTS CORPORATION; *pg.* 1126, *pg.* 1724
COOL SOLUTIONS - Refrigeration - BROOKS AUTOMATION, INC.; *pg.* 1320, *pg.* 813
COOL SOLUTIONS - Computer Operations - NOVELL INC.; *pg.* 446, *pg.* 852
COOL-SPEED - Mineral Oil - DAUBERT INDUSTRIES, INC.; *pg.* 1155, *pg.* 561
COOL TECH - Blending System - HAWS CORPORATION; *pg.* 56, *pg.* 1032
COOL TUBES - Ice Cream Bar - WELLS ENTERPRISES, INC.; *pg.* 909, *pg.* 709
COOL WATER - Water Cooler - ANAHEIM MANUFACTURING COMPANY; *pg.* 51, *pg.* 48
COOL WEAVE! - Slacks & Shorts - HABAND COMPANY, INC.; *pg.* 1772, *pg.* 1099
COOL WHIP - Whipped Topping - THE KRAFT HEINZ COMPANY; *pg.* 870, *pg.* 1577
COOL-WICK - Wound Care Boot - ALIMED, INC.; *pg.* 1490, *pg.* 816
COOL WIND - Cooler - SEELEY INTERNATIONAL AMERICAS; *pg.* 1076, *pg.* 19
COOL2GO - Beverage Wrap - E.I. DU PONT DE NEMOURS & COMPANY; *pg.* 1159, *pg.* 390
COOLAM - Industrial Parts - E.I. DU PONT DE NEMOURS & COMPANY; *pg.* 1159, *pg.* 390
COOLANCHOR - Membrane Product - COOLEY GROUP, INC.; *pg.* 691, *pg.* 1603
COOLARC - Ultraviolet Lamphead - NORDSON CORPORATION; *pg.* 1365, *pg.* 1480
COOLBAND - Gelbodies Elbow - ALIMED, INC.; *pg.* 1490, *pg.* 816
COOL.CLICK - Injection System - BIOJECT MEDICAL TECHNOLOGIES INC.; *pg.* 1506, *pg.* 1509
COOLDADDY - Electrical Appliance & Housewares - NATIONAL PRESTO INDUSTRIES, INC; *pg.* 1128, *pg.* 1857
COOLECTIBLZ - Doll - MGA ENTERTAINMENT, INC.; *pg.* 964, *pg.* 300
COOLED THERMO THERAPY - Medical Device - UROLOGIX, INC.; *pg.* 1604, *pg.* 945
COOLED THERMOCATH - Microwave Delivery Catheter - UROLOGIX, INC.; *pg.* 1604, *pg.* 945
COOLERMISER - Software - USA TECHNOLOGIES, INC.; *pg.* 815, *pg.* 1550
COOLERWEAR - Apparel - REFRIGIWEAR, INC.; *pg.* 47, *pg.* 529
COOLEY-BRITE - Sign & Awning Product - COOLEY GROUP, INC.; *pg.* 691, *pg.* 1603
COOLEY-BRITE II - Eradicable Flexible Sign & Awning Membrane - COOLEY GROUP, INC.; *pg.* 691, *pg.* 1603
COOLEY-BRITE LITE - Eradicable Flexible Sign & Awning Membrane - COOLEY GROUP, INC.; *pg.* 691, *pg.* 1603
COOLEY LITE - Resin System - COOLEY GROUP, INC.; *pg.* 691, *pg.* 1603
COOLEY MAGIC - Sign & Awning Product - COOLEY GROUP, INC.; *pg.* 691, *pg.* 1603
COOLFAN - Desk Stand - LAPWORKS, INC.; *pg.* 426, *pg.* 187
COOLFIN - Connector - MOLEX INCORPORATED; *pg.* 655, *pg.* 628
COOLFLEX - Medical Equipment - CONMED CORPORATION; *pg.* 1517, *pg.* 1347
COOLFLEX - Digital Printing Product - COOLEY GROUP, INC.; *pg.* 691, *pg.* 1603
COOLGENIX - Proprietary Cooling Technology - HILL PHOENIX INC.; *pg.* 1072, *pg.* 528
COOLGLIDE - Laser Product - CUTERA, INC.; *pg.* 1521, *pg.* 49
COOLGLIDE EXCEL - Laser Product - CUTERA, INC.; *pg.* 1521, *pg.* 49
COOLGLIDE VANTAGE - Laser Product - CUTERA, INC.; *pg.* 1521, *pg.* 49
COOLGLIDE XEO - Laser Product - CUTERA, INC.; *pg.* 1521, *pg.* 49
COOLGRIP - Building Product - COOLEY GROUP, INC.; *pg.* 691, *pg.* 1603
COOLGUARD - Membrane Product - COOLEY GROUP, INC.; *pg.* 691, *pg.* 1603
COOLGUIDE CV - Light-Based Aesthetic System - CUTERA, INC.; *pg.* 1521, *pg.* 49
COOLIBRIUM - Software - COMVERGE, INC.; *pg.* 1325, *pg.* 536
COOLIFT - Delivery System - MAGLINE, INC.; *pg.* 1358, *pg.* 908
COOLING CALMING COLOR - Beauty Product - AVEDA CORPORATION; *pg.* 499, *pg.* 917
COOLING-SYSTEM MULTI-TREATMENT - Cooling System Treatment - MOC PRODUCTS COMPANY, INC.; *pg.* 332, *pg.* 174
COOLIR - Water Cooler Kit - PRECISION CONTROL SYSTEMS, INC./ RESEARCH INC.; *pg.* 1427, *pg.* 923
COOLITE - Hospital & Industrial Lighting - SWIVELIER CO., INC.; *pg.* 1307, *pg.* 1142
COOLJOYS - Shoes - ACUSHNET COMPANY; *pg.* 1824, *pg.* 818
COOLMAS - Power Device - IXYS CORPORATION; *pg.* 422, *pg.* 146
COOLMASK - Sign & Awning Product - COOLEY GROUP, INC.; *pg.* 691, *pg.* 1603
COOLMAX - Bandana - BROWN & BIGELOW, INC.; *pg.* 1624, *pg.* 959
COOLMAX - Crew Sock - CARHARTT, INC.; *pg.* 39, *pg.* 875
COOLMAX - Sport Product - FRANKLIN SPORTS, INC.; *pg.* 1834, *pg.* 847
COOLMAX - Performance Fabrics - INVISTA B.V.; *pg.* 1168, *pg.* 723
COOLMAX - Liner - JOCKEY INTERNATIONAL, INC.; *pg.* 27, *pg.* 1861
COOLMAX - Fabric - PARKDALE MILLS INC.; *pg.* 697, *pg.* 1373
COOLMAX - Hat - SIMMS FISHING PRODUCTS CORP.; *pg.* 1845, *pg.* 1008
COOLMESH - Coated Polyester - COOLEY GROUP, INC.; *pg.* 691, *pg.* 1603
COOLMESH 5600 - Coated Polyester - COOLEY GROUP, INC.; *pg.* 691, *pg.* 1603
COOLMESH PREMIUM - Coated Polyester - COOLEY GROUP, INC.; *pg.* 691, *pg.* 1603
COOLMESH RENAISSANCE - Coated Polyester - COOLEY GROUP, INC.; *pg.* 691, *pg.* 1603
COOLONE - Masks - ALPHA PRO TECH, LTD.; *pg.* 1492, *pg.* 1922
COOLPAK - Precooler - RESEARCH PRODUCTS CORPORATION; *pg.* 1075, *pg.* 1867
COOLPIX - Digital Camera - NIKON INC.; *pg.* 1424, *pg.* 1181
COOLPOWER - Fabric - W.L. GORE & ASSOCIATES, INC.; *pg.* 122, *pg.* 388
COOLPRO - Membrane Product - COOLEY GROUP, INC.; *pg.* 691, *pg.* 1603
COOLRIDER - Bag - DATREK GOLF; *pg.* 1832, *pg.* 1801
COOLSCAN 4000 - Photo Equipment - NIKON INC.; *pg.* 1424, *pg.* 1181
COOLSCAN 8000 - Photo Equipment - NIKON INC.; *pg.* 1424, *pg.* 1181
COOLSCAN IX - Photo Equipment - NIKON INC.; *pg.* 1424, *pg.* 1181
COOLSHIELD - Membrane Product - COOLEY GROUP, INC.;

pg. 091, *pg.* 1603
COOLSPAN - Thermal Interface Material - ROGERS CORPORATION; *pg.* 1305, *pg.* 369
COOLSPOT - Laser Delivery Device - AMERICAN MEDICAL SYSTEMS, INC.; *pg.* 1399, *pg.* 238
COOLSPOT - Medical Laser System - IRIDEX CORPORATION; *pg.* 648, *pg.* 160
COOLSPOT - Minor Surgery Light - MEDLINE INDUSTRIES, INC.; *pg.* 1562, *pg.* 635
COOLTEK - Cooling Technology - INTERNATIONAL FLAVORS & FRAGRANCES INC.; *pg.* 512, *pg.* 1244
COOLTEMP - Cold Therapy System - CINCINNATI SUB-ZERO PRODUCTS, INC.; *pg.* 1070, *pg.* 1411
COOLTHANE - Membrane Product - COOLEY GROUP, INC.; *pg.* 691, *pg.* 1603
COOLTHANE TANK - Membrane Product - COOLEY GROUP, INC.; *pg.* 691, *pg.* 1603
COOLTRANS - Digital Printing Product - COOLEY GROUP, INC.; *pg.* 691, *pg.* 1603
COOLWAVE - Microwave Ultraviolet Curing System - NORDSON CORPORATION; *pg.* 1365, *pg.* 1480
COOLWAVE - Medical Device - UROLOGIX, INC.; *pg.* 1604, *pg.* 945
COOMASSIE - Chemical Product - SPECTRUM CHEMICALS & LABORATORY PRODUCTS, INC.; *pg.* 1181, *pg.* 94
COOMASSIE - Molecular Probe Product - THERMO FISHER SCIENTIFIC INC.; *pg.* 1602, *pg.* 61
COOMASSIE FLUOR - Molecular Biology Product - THERMO FISHER SCIENTIFIC INC.; *pg.* 1602, *pg.* 61
COOPER - Thermometers - COOPER-ATKINS CORPORATION; *pg.* 1407, *pg.* 355
COOPER - Automobile & Truck Tires, Inner Tubes - COOPER TIRE & RUBBER COMPANY; *pg.* 1881, *pg.* 1453
COOPER - Split Bearings - KAYDON CORPORATION; *pg.* 1352, *pg.* 866
COOPER - Cheese - SCHREIBER FOODS, INC.; *pg.* 894, *pg.* 1859
COOPER ATKINS - Instrument - COOPER-ATKINS CORPORATION; *pg.* 1407, *pg.* 355
COOPER HGP - Rigid, Gas-Permeable Daily-Wear Contact Lens - THE COOPER COMPANIES, INC.; *pg.* 1518, *pg.* 183
COOPER KILN TRAIL - Clothing - ABERCROMBIE & FITCH CO.; *pg.* 37, *pg.* 1466
COOPER LIFELINER CLASSIC - Tires - COOPER TIRE & RUBBER COMPANY; *pg.* 1881, *pg.* 1453
COOPER TIRES ULTIMATE BOWL TOUR - Entertainment Services - COOPER TIRE & RUBBER COMPANY; *pg.* 1881, *pg.* 1453
COOPER VAC - Smoke Evacuator - THE COOPER COMPANIES, INC.; *pg.* 1518, *pg.* 183
COOPERATIVE PARENTING AND DIVORCE - Educational Program - ACTIVE PARENTING PUBLISHERS; *pg.* 1613, *pg.* 535
THE COOPERATORS - Company Name - THE CO-OPERATORS GROUP LIMITED; *pg.* 1198, *pg.* 1920
COOPERCLEAR - Soft, Daily-Wear Contact Lens - THE COOPER COMPANIES, INC.; *pg.* 1518, *pg.* 183
COOPERHEAD - Cutter - HOUGEN MANUFACTURING INC.; *pg.* 1347, *pg.* 908
COOPERSURGICAL SMOKE EVACUATION SYSTEM 6080 - Air Purification Equipment - THE COOPER COMPANIES, INC.; *pg.* 1518, *pg.* 183
COOPERTHIN - Soft, Daily-Wear Contact Lens - THE COOPER COMPANIES, INC.; *pg.* 1518, *pg.* 183
COORDINATOR - Clip - BROWN & BIGELOW, INC.; *pg.* 1624, *pg.* 959
COORS - Beer - MOLSON COORS BREWING COMPANY; *pg.* 256, *pg.* 321
COORS BANQUET - Beer - MOLSON COORS BREWING COMPANY; *pg.* 256, *pg.* 321
COORS LIGHT - Low-Calorie Premium Beer - MOLSON COORS BREWING COMPANY; *pg.* 256, *pg.* 321
COORSTEK - Ceramic & Plastic Product - COORSTEK, INC.; *pg.* 77, *pg.* 330
COOTIE - Toy & Game - HASBRO, INC.; *pg.* 954, *pg.* 1603
COP - Combustion Promoter - JOHNSON MATTHEY PROCESS TECHNOLOGIES; *pg.* 1169, *pg.* 1083
COP-NP - Catalyst Additive - JOHNSON MATTHEY PROCESS TECHNOLOGIES; *pg.* 1169, *pg.* 1083
COPA - Fabric - NEMSCHOFF, INC.; *pg.* 936, *pg.* 1890
COPA DE ORO - Coffee Liqueur - HEAVEN HILL DISTILLERIES, INC.; *pg.* 1964, *pg.* 725
COPAN - Fabric - NEMSCHOFF, INC.; *pg.* 936, *pg.* 1890
COPAXONE - Glatiramer Acetate for Injection - SANOFI US; *pg.* 1592, *pg.* 1046
COPCO - Fashion Kitchenware - WILTON PRODUCTS, INC.; *pg.* 1140, *pg.* 672
COPE - Expansion Process for Claus & Sulfur Recovery Units - AIR PRODUCTS AND CHEMICALS, INC.; *pg.* 1145, *pg.* 1513
COPE ROPE - Minerals - MINERALS TECHNOLOGIES INC.; *pg.* 1173, *pg.* 617
COPEGUS - Pharmaceutical Product - HOFFMANN-LA ROCHE INC.; *pg.* 1542, *pg.* 1099
COPELAND - Compressor - GOODMAN GROUP, INC.; *pg.* 1072, *pg.* 1706
COPELAND LIGHT - Office Light - KNOLL, INC.; *pg.* 425, *pg.* 1527
COPELAND SCROLL - Scroll Compressor - EMERSON CLIMATE TECHNOLOGIES, INC.; *pg.* 1333, *pg.* 1472
COPELAND SCROLL ULTRATECH - Modulated Scroll Compressor Intended for the U.S. Residential Market - EMERSON CLIMATE TECHNOLOGIES, INC.; *pg.* 1333, *pg.* 1472
COPELLA - Food & Beverage - PEPSICO, INC.; *pg.* 259, *pg.* 1327
COPELLA - Juice - TROPICANA PRODUCTS, INC.; *pg.* 902, *pg.* 592
COPENHAGEN - Tobacco Product - U.S. SMOKELESS TOBACCO COMPANY; *pg.* 1895, *pg.* 1804
COPENHAGEN - Lighting Product - WESTINGHOUSE LIGHTING CORPORATION; *pg.* 687, *pg.* 1571
COPERNIC AGENT - Software - COPERNIC INC.; *pg.* 1237, *pg.* 1958
COPERNIC DESKTOP SEARCH - Software - COPERNIC INC.; *pg.* 1237, *pg.* 1958
COPERNIC MEDIA SOLUTIONS - Software - COPERNIC INC.; *pg.* 1237, *pg.* 1958
COPERNIC SUMMARIZER - Software - COPERNIC INC.; *pg.* 1237, *pg.* 1958
COPERNIC TRACKER - Software - COPERNIC INC.; *pg.* 1237, *pg.* 1958
COPICAP - Dispensers - UNETTE CORPORATION; *pg.* 1184, *pg.* 1114
COPICO - Provider of Card & Coin-operated Reprographics Equipment & Services - MAC-GRAY CORPORATION; *pg.* 58, *pg.* 852
COPIER ASSISTANT - Software - XEROX CORPORATION; *pg.* 494, *pg.* 365
COPIERS - Camera - KONICA MINOLTA BUSINESS SOLUTIONS USA, INC.; *pg.* 1419, *pg.* 1113
COPILOT - Control Valve - ABBOTT LABORATORIES; *pg.* 1484, *pg.* 551
COPILOT - Drilling Process Control - BAKER HUGHES INTEQ; *pg.* 1316, *pg.* 1700
COPLAND FABRICS - Textile - COPLAND FABRICS, INC.; *pg.* 692, *pg.* 1359
COPOLYPURE - Tub & Sink - E.L. MUSTEE & SONS, INC.; *pg.* 1124, *pg.* 1430
COPPER - Jeans - LEVI STRAUSS & CO.; *pg.* 43, *pg.* 220
COPPER BRITE - Pots & Pans Cleaner-Instant Cleaner for Soldering - COPPER-BRITE, INC.; *pg.* 329, *pg.* 263
COPPER-FIN - Water Heater - LOCHINVAR CORPORATION; *pg.* 1073, *pg.* 1640
COPPER-FIN II - Water Heater - LOCHINVAR CORPORATION; *pg.* 1073, *pg.* 1640
COPPER-FLEX - Water Heater Connectors - BRASSCRAFT MANUFACTURING COMPANY; *pg.* 1043, *pg.* 902
COPPER GLEAM - Acid Copper Plating Products - THE DOW CHEMICAL COMPANY; *pg.* 1157, *pg.* 898
COPPER LABEL - Audio & Visual Recordings - PHILIP MORRIS USA INC.; *pg.* 1894, *pg.* 1803
COPPER LAKE - Shirts - ABERCROMBIE & FITCH CO.; *pg.* 37, *pg.* 1466
COPPER-PAK - Water Heater - LOCHINVAR CORPORATION; *pg.* 1073, *pg.* 1640
COPPER-TROL - Corrosion Inhibitor - GE WATER & PROCESS TECHNOLOGIES; *pg.* 1339, *pg.* 1588
COPPER XS - Glue - SUPER GLUE CORPORATION; *pg.* 1183, *pg.* 187
COPPERCLAD - Anti-Fouling Coating - FERRO CORPORATION; *pg.* 1162, *pg.* 1462
COPPERFIELD - Cables - COLEMAN CABLE, INC.; *pg.* 1324, *pg.* 665
COPPERHEAD - Airgun Ammunition - CROSMAN CORPORATION; *pg.* 951, *pg.* 1143
COPPERHOOK - Beverage - CRAFT BREWERS ALLIANCE, INC; *pg.* 247, *pg.* 1502
COPPERSTRAP - Power Semiconductor Device - INTERNATIONAL RECTIFIER CORPORATION; *pg.* 647, *pg.* 80
COPPERTEX - Papers - DAUBERT INDUSTRIES, INC.; *pg.* 1155, *pg.* 561
COPPERTONE - Sunscreen Products - BAYER HEALTHCARE CONSUMER CARE DIVISION; *pg.* 1500, *pg.* 1087
COPPERTOP - Battery - DURACELL; *pg.* 635, *pg.* 337
COPPICE - Surface Material - STEELCASE INC.; *pg.* 475, *pg.* 889
COPPS SQUAD FOR KIDS - Fun Newsletter & Healthy Menu Choices for Kids - THE COPPS CORPORATION; *pg.* 1017, *pg.* 1895
COPRA - Oil & Fat Extracting Device - ANDERSON INTERNATIONAL CORP.; *pg.* 1313, *pg.* 1474
COPS & DONUTS - Video Slots - INTERNATIONAL GAME TECHNOLOGY; *pg.* 957, *pg.* 1024
COPY CATS - Video Game - INTERNATIONAL GAME TECHNOLOGY; *pg.* 957, *pg.* 1024
COPY CLAW - Punched Paper Handling Tool - SMEAD MANUFACTURING COMPANY; *pg.* 470, *pg.* 926
COPY KIT - Molecular Biology Product - THERMO FISHER SCIENTIFIC INC.; *pg.* 1602, *pg.* 61
COPY PLUS - Software - BMC SOFTWARE, INC.; *pg.* 362, *pg.* 1701
COPYCAM - Image Capturing System & Software - POLYVISION CORPORATION; *pg.* 665, *pg.* 531
COPYCAM - Office Furniture - STEELCASE INC.; *pg.* 475, *pg.* 889
COPYCENTRE - Software - XEROX CORPORATION; *pg.* 494, *pg.* 365
COPYCODE - Shelf Marking Label - AVERY DENNISON CORPORATION; *pg.* 1452, *pg.* 95
COPYCROSS - Software - EMC CORPORATION; *pg.* 391, *pg.* 825
COPYPOINT - Software - EMC CORPORATION; *pg.* 391, *pg.* 825
COPYRITE - Second Sheets, Bond, Mimeo & Duplicator Paper - BPM INC.; *pg.* 1454, *pg.* 1886
COPYTELE - Communications Product - ITUS CORPORATION; *pg.* 422, *pg.* 1180
COQSKIN - Skin & Haircare Product - NEW EARTH LIFE SCIENCES, INC.; *pg.* 1573, *pg.* 1499
COQUEIRO - Canned Fish - PEPSICO, INC.; *pg.* 259, *pg.* 1327
COQUEIRO - Canned Fish - THE QUAKER OATS COMPANY; *pg.* 834, *pg.* 588
COQUINONE - Nutritional Supplement - USANA HEALTH SCIENCES, INC.; *pg.* 1605, *pg.* 1761
COR - Care Outcome Reports - FRESENIUS MEDICAL CARE NORTH AMERICA; *pg.* 1531, *pg.* 851
COR-AIRE - Air Freshener - SWISHER HYGIENE INC.; *pg.* 336, *pg.* 1507
COR-LOC - Seating System - NEMSCHOFF, INC.; *pg.* 936, *pg.* 1890
COR-PAK - Oxidizers - ABB INC.; *pg.* 1309, *pg.* 1359
COR-TITE - Seaming Adhesive - INTERPLASTIC CORPORATION; *pg.* 1168, *pg.* 961
COR-TROL - Core Chucks - HYDRALIGN; *pg.* 1257, *pg.* 833
COR-WELD - Adhesive - H.B. FULLER COMPANY; *pg.* 1165, *pg.* 961
CORABOND - Adhesives for Motor Vehicle Assembly & Maintenance - PPG INDUSTRIES, INC.; *pg.* 1445, *pg.* 1579
CORADMINISTRATIVE CONNECTIONS - Pharmaceutical Product - ALERE INC.; *pg.* 1488, *pg.* 849
CORAFLON - Coating Product - PPG INDUSTRIES, INC.; *pg.* 1445, *pg.* 1579
CORAGEN - Insect Control Product - E.I. DU PONT DE NEMOURS & COMPANY; *pg.* 1159, *pg.* 390
CORAL - Seafood Products - BUMBLE BEE FOODS LLC; *pg.* 842, *pg.* 201
CORAL - Gaming Product - GLD PRODUCTS, INC.; *pg.* 1835, *pg.* 1882
CORAL - Blood Service - HEMACARE CORPORATION; *pg.* 1541, *pg.* 300
CORAL BAY - Ceiling Fan - HUNTER FAN COMPANY; *pg.* 57, *pg.* 1631
CORAL DRIFT - Garden Roses - THE CONARD-PYLE COMPANY; *pg.* 1794, *pg.* 1594
CORAL ECO-TREAT - Aqueous Compositions - CORAL CHEMICAL COMPANY; *pg.* 1154, *pg.* 666
CORAL REEF - Video Game - INTERNATIONAL GAME TECHNOLOGY; *pg.* 957, *pg.* 1024
CORAL ROSE - Video Game - INTERNATIONAL GAME

TECHNOLOGY; *pg.* 957, *pg.* 1024
CORALAIS - Kitchen Product - KOHLER CO.; *pg.* 91, *pg.* 1862
CORALINE - Footwear - STEVEN MADDEN, LTD.; *pg.* 1819, *pg.* 1176
CORALUBE - Chemical Product - CORAL CHEMICAL COMPANY; *pg.* 1154, *pg.* 666
CORASIL - Silica Packing - WATERS CORPORATION; *pg.* 1436, *pg.* 834
CORAYVAC - Heater - ROBERTS-GORDON INC.; *pg.* 1076, *pg.* 1151
CORBEARATE - Customizable & Personalized Bears for Corporations - BUILD-A-BEAR WORKSHOP, INC.; *pg.* 950, *pg.* 993
CORBETT - Furniture - ETHAN ALLEN INTERIORS INC.; *pg.* 924, *pg.* 343
CORBETT CANYON VINEYARDS - Varietal Wines - THE WINE GROUP, INC.; *pg.* 1972, *pg.* 234
CORBIN - Furniture - JASPER GROUP; *pg.* 930, *pg.* 691
CORCARE - PPO - CORVEL CORPORATION; *pg.* 1198, *pg.* 109
CORCARE RX - Pharmacy Network - CORVEL CORPORATION; *pg.* 1198, *pg.* 109
CORCASE - Case Management Services - CORVEL CORPORATION; *pg.* 1198, *pg.* 109
CORCHO - Heaters - GAS-FIRED PRODUCTS, INC.; *pg.* 1338, *pg.* 1367
CORCHOICES - Pharmaceutical Product - ALERE INC.; *pg.* 1488, *pg.* 849
CORCOM - Electronic Component Product - TE CONNECTIVITY LTD.; *pg.* 677, *pg.* 1515
CORCONNECT - Pharmaceutical Product - ALERE INC.; *pg.* 1488, *pg.* 849
CORD BLOOD BANKING + RESEARCH - Slogan - VIACORD; *pg.* 1606, *pg.* 810
CORD-O-LITE - Temporary Lighting System - COLEMAN CABLE, INC.; *pg.* 1324, *pg.* 665
CORDGUARD - Medical Product - UTAH MEDICAL PRODUCTS, INC.; *pg.* 1605, *pg.* 1752
CORDILLERA - Ceramic, Glass, Stone Tiles & Slabs - WALKER & ZANGER, INC.; *pg.* 119, *pg.* 281
CORDIMENSIONS - Pharmaceutical Product - ALERE INC.; *pg.* 1488, *pg.* 849
CORDLESS - Record Label - WARNER MUSIC GROUP CORP.; *pg.* 590, *pg.* 1313
CORDLESS DRIVER - Surgical Power Tool - STRYKER CORPORATION; *pg.* 1598, *pg.* 894
CORDLESS ZIP VAC - Cleaning Product - ORECK CORPORATION; *pg.* 59, *pg.* 1653
CORDLOCK - Cover & Pad - HOME PRODUCTS INTERNATIONAL, INC.; *pg.* 1125, *pg.* 577
CORDMATE - Cord Control - WIREMOLD/LEGRAND; *pg.* 689, *pg.* 383
CORDMATE II - Cord Control - WIREMOLD/LEGRAND; *pg.* 689, *pg.* 383
CORDOBA - Carpet - BEAULIEU GROUP, LLC; *pg.* 917, *pg.* 529
CORDOBOND - Epoxy Repair System - FERRO CORPORATION; *pg.* 1162, *pg.* 1462
CORDONATOR - Foldable Safety Road Marker - EAGLE MANUFACTURING COMPANY; *pg.* 79, *pg.* 1851
CORDOVA - Footwear - COBIAN CORP.; *pg.* 1806, *pg.* 253
CORDOVA - Fan - CRAFTMADE INTERNATIONAL, INC.; *pg.* 1295, *pg.* 1670
CORDOVAN - Tire - TBC CORPORATION; *pg.* 1889, *pg.* 457
CORDRAN - Pharmaceutical Product - ALLERGAN; *pg.* 1490, *pg.* 1101
CORDUCT - Cord Control - WIREMOLD/LEGRAND; *pg.* 689, *pg.* 383
CORDURA - Case - BROWN & BIGELOW, INC.; *pg.* 1624, *pg.* 959
CORDURA - Workwear - CARHARTT, INC.; *pg.* 39, *pg.* 875
CORDURA - Tough Wear Fabrics - INVISTA B.V.; *pg.* 1168, *pg.* 723
CORDUROY - Medical Product - W.L. GORE & ASSOCIATES, INC.; *pg.* 122, *pg.* 388
CORDYMAX - Nutritional Supplement - NU SKIN ENTERPRISES, INC.; *pg.* 518, *pg.* 1755
CORE - Software - CANDID COLOR SYSTEMS, INC.; *pg.* 1404, *pg.* 1485
CORE - Rescue Reel - HANNAY REELS INC.; *pg.* 1344, *pg.* 1351
CORE - Surgical Power Tool - STRYKER CORPORATION; *pg.* 1598, *pg.* 894
CORE-A-GATOR - Furniture - VIRCO MANUFACTURING CORPORATION; *pg.* 946, *pg.* 297
CORE BUILDER - Software System - MENTOR GRAPHICS CORPORATION; *pg.* 432, *pg.* 1510
CORE DIRECTOR - Banking Software - JACK HENRY & ASSOCIATES, INC.; *pg.* 422, *pg.* 988
CORE FACTORY - Software System - MENTOR GRAPHICS CORPORATION; *pg.* 432, *pg.* 1510
CORE-IN-KETTLE - Heat Exchanger - CHART INDUSTRIES, INC.; *pg.* 1405, *pg.* 1454
CORE KNOWLEDGE - Educational Test - QUESTAR ASSESSMENT, INC.; *pg.* 1679, *pg.* 1143
CORE-LOCK - Electronic Components - MOLEX INCORPORATED; *pg.* 655, *pg.* 628
CORE SECRETS - Fitness Program - GUTHY-RENKER LLC; *pg.* 289, *pg.* 273
CORE TECHNOLOGY - Hydraulic System - HOLMATRO, INC.; *pg.* 1346, *pg.* 771
CORE4LIFE ADVANCED MEMORY FORMULA - Nutritional Product - NUTRITION 21, INC.; *pg.* 1577, *pg.* 1327
COREALLIANCE - Software System - MENTOR GRAPHICS CORPORATION; *pg.* 432, *pg.* 1510
COREARCHITECT - Software - PHOENIX TECHNOLOGIES LTD.; *pg.* 454, *pg.* 147
COREBIST - Software System - MENTOR GRAPHICS CORPORATION; *pg.* 432, *pg.* 1510
COREDIRECTOR - Multiplexing System - CIENA CORPORATION; *pg.* 628, *pg.* 771
COREDIRECTOR CI - Multiplexing System - CIENA CORPORATION; *pg.* 628, *pg.* 771
COREFPGA - Daughter Card - IMAGINATION TECHNOLOGIES; *pg.* 412, *pg.* 285
COREGARD - Low Invasion Coring System - BAKER HUGHES INTEQ; *pg.* 1316, *pg.* 1700
COREL - Office Seating - MITY ENTERPRISES, INC.; *pg.* 935, *pg.* 1753
COREL GALLERY MAGIC - Graphics Software - COREL CORPORATION; *pg.* 380, *pg.* 1931
COREL PAINTER - Software - COREL CORPORATION; *pg.* 380, *pg.* 1931
COREL PARADOX 8 - Business Application - COREL CORPORATION; *pg.* 380, *pg.* 1931
COREL PHOTO-PAINT 8 - Comprehensive Photo-Retouching & Painting Application - COREL CORPORATION; *pg.* 380, *pg.* 1931
COREL PRESENTATIONS - Business Application - COREL CORPORATION; *pg.* 380, *pg.* 1931
COREL PRINT HOUSE MAGIC - Graphics Software - COREL CORPORATION; *pg.* 380, *pg.* 1931
COREL QUATTRO PRO - Business Application - COREL CORPORATION; *pg.* 380, *pg.* 1931
COREL VENTURA 8 - Professional Desktop Publishing Program - COREL CORPORATION; *pg.* 380, *pg.* 1931
COREL WORDPERFECT - Business Application - COREL CORPORATION; *pg.* 380, *pg.* 1931
CORELCENTRAL - Business Application - COREL CORPORATION; *pg.* 380, *pg.* 1931
CORELDRAW - Software - COREL CORPORATION; *pg.* 380, *pg.* 1931
CORELDRAW 8 - Illustration & Image-Editing Software - COREL CORPORATION; *pg.* 380, *pg.* 1931
CORELDRAW GRAPHICS SUITE 12 - Software - COREL CORPORATION; *pg.* 380, *pg.* 1931
CORELLI - Flatware - ONEIDA LTD; *pg.* 1129, *pg.* 1318
CORELV - Daughter Card - IMAGINATION TECHNOLOGIES; *pg.* 412, *pg.* 285
CORELVIDEO - Allows Corporate Customers to Meet Face to Face Company-Wide - COREL CORPORATION; *pg.* 380, *pg.* 1931
COREMASTER - Heavy Duty Core Barrel for Highly Deviated Holes - BAKER HUGHES INTEQ; *pg.* 1316, *pg.* 1700
COREMATE - Core Plugs - SONOCO PRODUCTS COMPANY; *pg.* 1469, *pg.* 1619
CORESTREAM - Multiplexing System - CIENA CORPORATION; *pg.* 628, *pg.* 771
CORETEC - Tube & Pipe Product - DELSTAR TECHNOLOGIES, INC.; *pg.* 1881, *pg.* 387
COREWARE - Storage Semiconductor - AVAGO TECHNOLOGIES; *pg.* 358, *pg.* 238
COREX - Cored Wire - HOBART BROTHERS COMPANY; *pg.* 1346, *pg.* 1477
COREXCELLENCE - Computer Services - COMPUTER SCIENCES CORPORATION; *pg.* 378, *pg.* 1780
COREXTEND - User Defined Instruction - IMAGINATION TECHNOLOGIES; *pg.* 412, *pg.* 285
COREZYN - Vinyl Ester, Modified Vinyl Ester & Isophthalic Corrosion Resistant Resin - INTERPLASTIC CORPORATION; *pg.* 1168, *pg.* 961
CORFU - Rug - COURISTAN INC.; *pg.* 921, *pg.* 1067
CORGARD - Pharmaceutical Product - KING PHARMACEUTICALS, INC.; *pg.* 1553, *pg.* 1627
CORGENIX - Medical Product - CORGENIX MEDICAL CORPORATION; *pg.* 1519, *pg.* 312
CORIAN - Material - E.I. DU PONT DE NEMOURS & COMPANY; *pg.* 1159, *pg.* 390
CORICIDIN - Medicine - MERCK & CO., INC.; *pg.* 1566, *pg.* 1077
CORICIDIN HBP - Medicine - MERCK & CO., INC.; *pg.* 1566, *pg.* 1077
CORINTHIA - Furniture - STANLEY FURNITURE CO., INC.; *pg.* 943, *pg.* 1379
CORINTHIAN - Deli Displayware - CARLISLE FOODSERVICE PRODUCTS INCORPORATED; *pg.* 1455, *pg.* 1485
CORINTHIAN - Toilet Partition - METPAR CORP.; *pg.* 97, *pg.* 1350
CORINTHIAN SUPREME - Fan - WESTINGHOUSE LIGHTING CORPORATION; *pg.* 687, *pg.* 1571
CORKEN - Pump And Compressor - CORKEN, INC.; *pg.* 1325, *pg.* 1485
CORKEN - Pumps & Compressors - IDEX CORPORATION; *pg.* 1347, *pg.* 623
CORKSCRU - Footwear - STEVEN MADDEN, LTD.; *pg.* 1819, *pg.* 1176
CORLAR - Epoxy - E.I. DU PONT DE NEMOURS & COMPANY; *pg.* 1159, *pg.* 390
CORLINE - Pressed & Monolithic Refractory - RESCO PRODUCTS, INC.; *pg.* 107, *pg.* 1581
CORLON - Wood Flooring Product - ARMSTRONG WORLD INDUSTRIES, INC.; *pg.* 914, *pg.* 1545
CORMAG - Refractory Product - RESCO PRODUCTS, INC.; *pg.* 107, *pg.* 1581
CORMATIC - Washroom Tissue, Paper Towels, Soaps & Dispensers - GEORGIA-PACIFIC LLC; *pg.* 1458, *pg.* 507
CORMATIC/ULTIMA - Air Fresheners - GEORGIA-PACIFIC LLC; *pg.* 1458, *pg.* 507
CORMAX - Pharmaceutical Product - ALLERGAN; *pg.* 1490, *pg.* 1101
CORMAX - Electrocoat - E.I. DU PONT DE NEMOURS & COMPANY; *pg.* 1159, *pg.* 390
CORMETECH - Glass & Ceramic Material - CORNING INCORPORATED; *pg.* 1122, *pg.* 1154
CORN BURSTS - Cereal - POST CONSUMER BRANDS; *pg.* 833, *pg.* 927
CORN CRAZE - Lottery Game - IOWA LOTTERY; *pg.* 996, *pg.* 705
CORN DOGS - Dog Food - LEON'S FINE FOODS, INC.; *pg.* 874, *pg.* 1727
CORN KING - Bacon, Ham & Lunchmeats - TYSON FOODS, INC.; *pg.* 902, *pg.* 35
CORN NUTS - Corn Kernels - THE KRAFT HEINZ COMPANY; *pg.* 870, *pg.* 1577
CORN POPS - Ready-Sweetened Puffed Corn Cereal - KELLOGG COMPANY; *pg.* 831, *pg.* 870
CORNADO - Commercial Poppers - GOLD MEDAL PRODUCTS CO.; *pg.* 55, *pg.* 1414
CORNELIUS - Beverage Dispenser - CORNELIUS INC; *pg.* 1326, *pg.* 952
CORNELL PAPERBACKS - Paperback Books - CORNELL UNIVERSITY PRESS; *pg.* 1630, *pg.* 1169
CORNER - Fireplaces - LENNOX HEARTH PRODUCTS; *pg.* 93, *pg.* 1652
CORNER CURL DESIGN - Photo Products & Services - EASTMAN KODAK COMPANY; *pg.* 1408, *pg.* 1333
CORNER EASE - Roller & Tray - HYDE TOOLS, INC.; *pg.* 1125, *pg.* 844
CORNER SHIELD - Flashing System - FORTIFIBER CORPORATION; *pg.* 83, *pg.* 1021
CORNER STORE - Gasoline Retail Outlets - VALERO ENERGY CORPORATION; *pg.* 986, *pg.* 1743
CORNER THE MARKET - Game - WMS INDUSTRIES INC.; *pg.* 593, *pg.* 666
CORNER-VU - Light - RITE-HITE HOLDING CORPORATION; *pg.* 1372, *pg.* 1880
CORNERKEEPER - Packaging - PACTIV CORPORATION; *pg.* 1466, *pg.* 624
CORNERMATE - Cord Control - WIREMOLD/LEGRAND; *pg.* 689, *pg.* 383
CORNERPOST - Wireless Product - HEMISPHERE GPS INC.; *pg.* 642, *pg.* 1903
CORNERSTONE - Floor Sealer/Finish - 3M COMPANY; *pg.*

First page reference indicates Business Class Edition
Second page reference indicates Geographic Edition

1142, *pg.* 956
CORNERSTONE - Cable - ARRIS GROUP, INC.; *pg.* 353, *pg.* 541
CORNERSTONE - Furniture - HERMAN MILLER, INC.; *pg.* 926, *pg.* 913
CORNERSTONE - Software - IDEXX LABORATORIES, INC.; *pg.* 1543, *pg.* 753
CORNERSTONE - Fabric - NEMSCHOFF, INC.; *pg.* 936, *pg.* 1890
CORNERSTONE COLLECTION - Modular Homes - NATIONWIDE HOMES, INC.; *pg.* 99, *pg.* 1788
CORNERSTONES OF FREEDOM - Educational Materials - SCHOLASTIC INC.; *pg.* 1683, *pg.* 1288
CORNFLOWER - Dinnerware - THE HOMER LAUGHLIN CHINA COMPANY; *pg.* 1125, *pg.* 1850
CORNFLOWER - Fabric - NEMSCHOFF, INC.; *pg.* 936, *pg.* 1890
CORNICE - Surface Material - STEELCASE INC.; *pg.* 475, *pg.* 889
CORNING - Glassware - CORNING INCORPORATED; *pg.* 1122, *pg.* 1154
CORNINGWARE - Kitchen Houseware Product - WORLD KITCHEN LLC; *pg.* 1141, *pg.* 657
CORNSWEET - Fructose Syrups - ARCHER-DANIELS-MIDLAND COMPANY; *pg.* 825, *pg.* 565
CORNSWEET 42 - Corn Syrup - ARCHER-DANIELS-MIDLAND COMPANY; *pg.* 825, *pg.* 565
CORNSWEET 42 80% SOLIDS - Corn Syrup - ARCHER-DANIELS-MIDLAND COMPANY; *pg.* 825, *pg.* 565
CORNSWEET 55 - Corn Syrup - ARCHER-DANIELS-MIDLAND COMPANY; *pg.* 825, *pg.* 565
CORNSWEET 90 - Corn Syrup - ARCHER-DANIELS-MIDLAND COMPANY; *pg.* 825, *pg.* 565
CORNSWEET HFCS 90 - Corn Syrup - ARCHER-DANIELS-MIDLAND COMPANY; *pg.* 825, *pg.* 565
CORNUCOPIA - Furniture - J. ROBERT SCOTT INC.; *pg.* 930, *pg.* 105
CORO-FLO - Pump - CORKEN, INC.; *pg.* 1325, *pg.* 1485
CORO-FLO - Pump Product - IDEX CORPORATION; *pg.* 1347, *pg.* 623
CORO-VAC - Purge System - CORKEN, INC.; *pg.* 1325, *pg.* 1485
CORO-VAC - Pump Product - IDEX CORPORATION; *pg.* 1347, *pg.* 623
CORO-VANE - Pump - CORKEN, INC.; *pg.* 1325, *pg.* 1485
CORO-VANE - Pump Product - IDEX CORPORATION; *pg.* 1347, *pg.* 623
COROBUFF - Corrugated Paper - PACON CORPORATION; *pg.* 1466, *pg.* 1852
COROENT - Surgery System - NUVASIVE, INC.; *pg.* 1577, *pg.* 205
COROLLA - Car - TOYOTA MOTOR NORTH AMERICA, INC.; *pg.* 192, *pg.* 1303
CORONA - Beer - CROWN IMPORTS LLC; *pg.* 248, *pg.* 572
CORONA - Ointments & Protectants for Horses - SUMMIT INDUSTRIES, INC.; *pg.* 1599, *pg.* 535
CORONA EXTRA - Beer - CONSTELLATION BRANDS, INC.; *pg.* 1960, *pg.* 1348
CORONADO - Furniture - AMERICAN LEATHER LP; *pg.* 912, *pg.* 1673
CORONADO - Filters & Telescopes - MEADE INSTRUMENTS CORPORATION; *pg.* 1422, *pg.* 113
CORONADO - Jewelry - UNCAS MANUFACTURING COMPANY; *pg.* 15, *pg.* 1608
CORONADO BEACH - Carpet - BEAULIEU GROUP, LLC; *pg.* 917, *pg.* 529
CORONADO GOLD - Game - WMS INDUSTRIES INC.; *pg.* 593, *pg.* 666
CORONADO SST - Paper - NEENAH PAPER, INC.; *pg.* 1465, *pg.* 484
CORONATION - Flatware - ONEIDA LTD; *pg.* 1129, *pg.* 1318
CORONET VSQ - Brandy - HEAVEN HILL DISTILLERIES, INC.; *pg.* 1964, *pg.* 725
CORONUS - Single-Wafer Clean - LAM RESEARCH CORPORATION; *pg.* 1354, *pg.* 91
COROWISE - Dietary Supplement - CARGILL, INC.; *pg.* 845, *pg.* 965
CORPAC - Emission Testing System - MISTRAS GROUP, INC.; *pg.* 1362, *pg.* 1113
CORPATCH - Pressed & Monolithic Refractory - RESCO PRODUCTS, INC.; *pg.* 107, *pg.* 1581
CORPORATE ACCOUNTABILITY REPORT - Publisher - BLOOMBERG BNA; *pg.* 1621, *pg.* 1772
CORPORATE ADVANTAGE - Business Class Program - BULLSEYE TELECOM INC.; *pg.* 366, *pg.* 906
CORPORATE AFFILIATIONS - Business Data Directories - LEXISNEXIS CORPORATE AFFILIATIONS; *pg.* 1658, *pg.* 1095
CORPORATE COUNSEL - Legal Publication - AMERICAN LAWYER MEDIA, INC.; *pg.* 1615, *pg.* 1193
CORPORATE CREDIT RATINGS - Company Creditworthiness - STANDARD & POOR'S RATINGS SERVICES; *pg.* 805, *pg.* 1296
CORPORATE GOVERNANCE EVALUATIONS & SCORES - Evaluation Tool - STANDARD & POOR'S RATINGS SERVICES; *pg.* 805, *pg.* 1296
CORPORATE HOUSING - Advertising Publication - DOMINION ENTERPRISES; *pg.* 1636, *pg.* 1796
CORPORATE LOGO - Publication - INFORMA EXHIBITIONS LLC; *pg.* 1653, *pg.* 17
CORPORATE PROFILES QUANTITATIVE STOCK REPORTS - Company Data - STANDARD & POOR'S RATINGS SERVICES; *pg.* 805, *pg.* 1296
CORPORATE ROLL-UP - Reporting Solution - NIELSEN AUDIO; *pg.* 446, *pg.* 768
CORPORATE TRACKER - CUSIP & Company Changes - STANDARD & POOR'S RATINGS SERVICES; *pg.* 805, *pg.* 1296
CORPORATION RECORDS - Public Company Data - STANDARD & POOR'S RATINGS SERVICES; *pg.* 805, *pg.* 1296
CORPSYSTEM - Software - CCH INC.; *pg.* 1626, *pg.* 653
CORPUS CHRISTI CALLER-TIMES - Newspaper - THE E.W. SCRIPPS COMPANY; *pg.* 1639, *pg.* 1412
CORRACLAD - Fire Alarm Cables - COLEMAN CABLE, INC.; *pg.* 1324, *pg.* 665
CORRAL - Footwear - EASTLAND SHOE CORPORATION; *pg.* 1808, *pg.* 750
CORRAL CARPET - Fabric Product - BELTON INDUSTRIES, INC.; *pg.* 691, *pg.* 1612
CORRECTIONIST - Bodycare & Skincare - AMERICAN INTERNATIONAL INDUSTRIES COMPANY; *pg.* 498, *pg.* 126
CORRECTOL - Laxatives - MERCK & CO., INC.; *pg.* 1566, *pg.* 1077
CORRETEC - Paint Product - AKZO NOBEL; *pg.* 1439, *pg.* 1952
CORREX - Quality Control Tool - CONCUR TECHNOLOGIES; *pg.* 1903, *pg.* 501
CORRGUARD - Amino Alcohol Corrosion Inhibitors - THE DOW CHEMICAL COMPANY; *pg.* 1157, *pg.* 898
CORRIB - Vitreous Enamel Power Resistor - OHMITE MANUFACTURING COMPANY; *pg.* 660, *pg.* 553
CORRIGANS COVE - Carpet - BEAULIEU GROUP, LLC; *pg.* 917, *pg.* 529
CORRO-FOAM - Ribbed Polyethylene Foam - SEALED AIR CORPORATION; *pg.* 1468, *pg.* 1058
CORROBAR - White Alkyd Corrosion Inhibitive Metal Primer - DUNN-EDWARDS CORPORATION; *pg.* 1442, *pg.* 129
CORROSION - Apparel - OAKLEY, INC.; *pg.* 1840, *pg.* 86
CORROSTOP - Consumer Products - AKZO NOBEL; *pg.* 1439, *pg.* 1952
CORROZEX - Padlocks - MASTER LOCK COMPANY LLC; *pg.* 1055, *pg.* 1884
CORRSHIELD - Inhibitor - GE WATER & PROCESS TECHNOLOGIES; *pg.* 1339, *pg.* 1588
CORRUGATED RUNNER - Plastic & Rubber - TEKNOR APEX COMPANY; *pg.* 1889, *pg.* 1605
CORRUGTED - Fabric - NEMSCHOFF, INC.; *pg.* 936, *pg.* 1890
CORSAF - Inhibitor Concentrate - THE DOW CHEMICAL COMPANY; *pg.* 1157, *pg.* 898
CORSAGE - Fabric - NEMSCHOFF, INC.; *pg.* 936, *pg.* 1890
CORSAIR - Racing Boat - CHRIS-CRAFT CORPORATION; *pg.* 1706, *pg.* 465
CORSAIR - Computer Components - CORSAIR COMPONENTS, INC.; *pg.* 380, *pg.* 90
CORSAIR - Oil Well Servicing Rigs - CRANE CARRIER COMPANY; *pg.* 168, *pg.* 1489
CORSICA - Leather Product - COACH, INC.; *pg.* 3, *pg.* 1214
CORSICA - Rug - COURISTAN INC.; *pg.* 921, *pg.* 1067
CORSICA - Ceiling Fan - WESTINGHOUSE LIGHTING CORPORATION; *pg.* 687, *pg.* 1571
CORSINI - Jewelry - UNCAS MANUFACTURING COMPANY; *pg.* 15, *pg.* 1608
CORSOLUTIONS - Pharmaceutical Product - ALERE INC.; *pg.* 1488, *pg.* 849
CORT - Software - NUVIEW WEST; *pg.* 447, *pg.* 1496
CORT HCM - Human Resources Management Software - NUVIEW WEST; *pg.* 447, *pg.* 1496
CORTE MADERA - Bike - MARIN BIKES; *pg.* 1708, *pg.* 168
CORTEF - Medicine - PFIZER INC.; *pg.* 1581, *pg.* 1278
CORTEGA - Wood Flooring Product - ARMSTRONG WORLD INDUSTRIES, INC.; *pg.* 914, *pg.* 1545
CORTEM - Spring - KIRKWOOD HOLDING, INC.; *pg.* 649, *pg.* 1469
CORTEM - Conductive Motor Brush Springs - TOLEDO COMMUTATOR CO.; *pg.* 1383, *pg.* 903
CORTES - Actuator - PRECISION VALVE CORPORATION; *pg.* 1060, *pg.* 1357
CORTEZ - Footwear - NIKE, INC.; *pg.* 1812, *pg.* 1492
CORTINA - Foreign Language Teaching Material - CORTINA LEARNING INTERNATIONAL, INC.; *pg.* 600, *pg.* 385
CORTINA - Bath & Plumbing Product - JACUZZI BRANDS CORPORATION; *pg.* 554, *pg.* 65
CORTINA - Bike - MARIN BIKES; *pg.* 1708, *pg.* 168
CORTISOL FORMULA - Health Care Product - NATURE'S SUNSHINE PRODUCTS, INC.; *pg.* 1571, *pg.* 1754
CORTITROL - Nutritional Supplement - NU SKIN ENTERPRISES, INC.; *pg.* 518, *pg.* 1755
CORTIZONE-10 - Anti-Itch Ointment - CHATTEM, INC.; *pg.* 1515, *pg.* 1628
CORTLAND - Shoes - ALLEN-EDMONDS SHOE CORP.; *pg.* 1804, *pg.* 1887
CORTLAND - Rod - CORTLAND LINE COMPANY; *pg.* 1831, *pg.* 1155
CORTLAND CHAMBRAY - Shirt - CORTLAND LINE COMPANY; *pg.* 1831, *pg.* 1155
CORTROL - Boiler Water Corrosion Inhibitors - GE WATER & PROCESS TECHNOLOGIES; *pg.* 1339, *pg.* 1588
CORTUFF - Packaging Product - SEALED AIR CORPORATION; *pg.* 1468, *pg.* 1058
CORUS - Hearing Device - BELTONE ELECTRONICS LLC; *pg.* 1503, *pg.* 614
CORVEL HEALTHCARD - Healthcare Discount Card - CORVEL CORPORATION; *pg.* 1198, *pg.* 109
CORVERT - Medicine - PFIZER INC.; *pg.* 1581, *pg.* 1278
CORVETTE - Sports Car - GENERAL MOTORS COMPANY; *pg.* 175, *pg.* 881
CORVETTE ENTHUSIAST - Magazine - AMOS PRESS, INC.; *pg.* 1616, *pg.* 1472
CORVETTE SUMMER - Lotto Game - SOUTH DAKOTA LOTTERY; *pg.* 1006, *pg.* 1624
CORVON - Paper & Nonwoven Material - FIBERMARK INC.; *pg.* 1457, *pg.* 1764
CORZAN - Pipe & Fittings - THE LUBRIZOL CORPORATION; *pg.* 1171, *pg.* 1481
CORZIDE - Pharmaceutical Product - KING PHARMACEUTICALS, INC.; *pg.* 1553, *pg.* 1627
COSCO - Folding Furniture, Housewares - DOREL JUVENILE GROUP, INC.; *pg.* 923, *pg.* 676
COSEAL - Adhesive & Sealant - DOW CHEMICAL; *pg.* 1156, *pg.* 1563
COSFECTIN - Software - BIO-RAD LABORATORIES, INC.; *pg.* 1504, *pg.* 101
COSHOCTON STAINLESS - Steel Product - AK STEEL HOLDING CORPORATION; *pg.* 1311, *pg.* 1479
COSMA - Automotive Parts - MAGNA INTERNATIONAL INC.; *pg.* 211, *pg.* 1918
COSMETIC SURGERY TIMES - Trade Publication - UBM ADVANSTAR; *pg.* 1697, *pg.* 1306
COSMIC - Toy & Game - HASBRO, INC.; *pg.* 954, *pg.* 1603
COSMIC - Fabric - NEMSCHOFF, INC.; *pg.* 936, *pg.* 1890
COSMIC BOWLING - Bowling Equipment - BRUNSWICK BOWLING & BILLIARDS CORP.; *pg.* 1828, *pg.* 622
COSMIC CASH - Lottery Game - NEW YORK STATE LOTTERY; *pg.* 1001, *pg.* 1340
COSMIC CATCH - Toy & Game - HASBRO, INC.; *pg.* 954, *pg.* 1603
COSMO - Fabric - NEMSCHOFF, INC.; *pg.* 936, *pg.* 1890
COSMO - Collapsible Storage Unit - NOVA CHEMICALS CORPORATION; *pg.* 1175, *pg.* 1904
COSMODERM - Skin Care Product - ALLERGAN, INC.; *pg.* 1491, *pg.* 106
COSMOGIRL! - Magazine - THE HEARST CORPORATION; *pg.* 1649, *pg.* 1239
COSMOLON - Hook & Loop Fastener - YKK CORPORATION OF AMERICA; *pg.* 699, *pg.* 536
COSMOPLAST - Skin Care Product - ALLERGAN, INC.; *pg.* 1491, *pg.* 106
COSMOPOLITAN - Table - BLATT BOWLING & BILLIARD CORP.; *pg.* 1827, *pg.* 1203
COSMOPOLITAN - Screen - DA-LITE SCREEN COMPANY; *pg.* 632, *pg.* 698
COSMOPOLITAN - Magazine - THE HEARST

CORPORATION; *pg.* 1649, *pg.* 1239

COSMOPOLITAN - Fabric - NEMSCHOFF, INC.; *pg.* 936, *pg.* 1890

COSMOPOLITAN - Shower Heads - SPEAKMAN COMPANY; *pg.* 112, *pg.* 388

COSMOPOLITAN CABARET - Theatre - CALIFORNIA MUSICAL THEATRE CORPORATION; *pg.* 536, *pg.* 196

COSMOPOLITAN ELECTROL - Electric Screen - DA-LITE SCREEN COMPANY; *pg.* 632, *pg.* 698

COSMOPOLITAN TELEVISION - Entertainment & Syndication - THE HEARST CORPORATION; *pg.* 1649, *pg.* 1239

COSMOS - Budget Escorted Tours - GROUP VOYAGERS, INC.; *pg.* 1910, *pg.* 333

COSMOS - Software - SYNOPSYS, INC.; *pg.* 480, *pg.* 162

COSMOS UNIPACK - Fan - CRAFTMADE INTERNATIONAL, INC.; *pg.* 1295, *pg.* 1670

COSMOSLE - Software - SYNOPSYS, INC.; *pg.* 480, *pg.* 162

COSMOSSCOPE - Software - SYNOPSYS, INC.; *pg.* 480, *pg.* 162

COSOM - Hockey Hand Protector - SCHOOL-TECH, INC.; *pg.* 1844, *pg.* 866

COSSU - Cheese - CANADIAN FISH EXPORTERS, INC.; *pg.* 845, *pg.* 784

COST CUTTERS - Hair Salons - REGIS CORPORATION; *pg.* 521, *pg.* 941

COST SAVER CHECKING - Checking Account - CALIFORNIA BANK & TRUST; *pg.* 728, *pg.* 201

COSTA CRUISES - Passenger Cruises & Tours - CARNIVAL CORPORATION; *pg.* 1902, *pg.* 441

COSTA DEL MAR - Sunglasses - A. T. CROSS COMPANY; *pg.* 339, *pg.* 1602

COSTA DEL MAR SUNGLASSES - Sunglasses - COSTA DEL MAR SUNGLASSES, INC.; *pg.* 1407, *pg.* 419

COSTA RICA - Coffee - PEET'S COFFEE & TEA, INC.; *pg.* 1029, *pg.* 85

COSTA RICA CLEMENTINE - Beverage - BAI BRANDS; *pg.* 238, *pg.* 1073

COSTA VERANO - Community Name - WCI COMMUNITIES, INC.; *pg.* 1118, *pg.* 414

COSTAR ADVERTISING - Software - COSTAR GROUP, INC.; *pg.* 742, *pg.* 397

COSTAR COMMERCIAL MLS - Software - COSTAR GROUP, INC.; *pg.* 742, *pg.* 397

COSTAR COMPS EXPRESS - Software - COSTAR GROUP, INC.; *pg.* 742, *pg.* 397

COSTAR COMPS PROFESSIONAL - Software - COSTAR GROUP, INC.; *pg.* 742, *pg.* 397

COSTAR CONNECT - Software - COSTAR GROUP, INC.; *pg.* 742, *pg.* 397

COSTAR EXCHANGE - Software - COSTAR GROUP, INC.; *pg.* 742, *pg.* 397

COSTAR LISTINGS EXPRESS - Software - COSTAR GROUP, INC.; *pg.* 742, *pg.* 397

COSTAR MARKET REPORT - Software - COSTAR GROUP, INC.; *pg.* 742, *pg.* 397

COSTAR PROFESSIONAL DIRECTORY - Software - COSTAR GROUP, INC.; *pg.* 742, *pg.* 397

COSTAR PROPERTY EXPRESS - Software Services - COSTAR GROUP, INC.; *pg.* 742, *pg.* 397

COSTAR PROPERTY PROFESSIONAL - Software - COSTAR GROUP, INC.; *pg.* 742, *pg.* 397

COSTAR SHOWCASE - Software Services - COSTAR GROUP, INC.; *pg.* 742, *pg.* 397

COSTAR TENANT - Software - COSTAR GROUP, INC.; *pg.* 742, *pg.* 397

COSTCO BUSINESS CENTER - Printing Services - COSTCO WHOLESALE CORPORATION; *pg.* 1765, *pg.* 1820

THE COSTCO CONNECTION - Magazine - COSTCO WHOLESALE CORPORATION; *pg.* 1765, *pg.* 1820

COSTCO HOME - Furniture - COSTCO WHOLESALE CORPORATION; *pg.* 1765, *pg.* 1820

COSTCO ONLINE - Online Store - COSTCO WHOLESALE CORPORATION; *pg.* 1765, *pg.* 1820

COSTCO WHOLESALE CASH - Cash Card - COSTCO WHOLESALE CORPORATION; *pg.* 1765, *pg.* 1820

COSTER - Water Vending System - HINIKER COMPANY; *pg.* 704, *pg.* 927

COSTER ENGINEERING - Water Purification & Vending Machines-Municipal, Industrial & Commercial - HINIKER COMPANY; *pg.* 704, *pg.* 927

COSTIMATOR - Software - MTI SYSTEMS INC.; *pg.* 442, *pg.* 857

COSTIMATOR JS - Cost Estimating Software - MTI SYSTEMS INC.; *pg.* 442, *pg.* 857

COSTIMATOR OEM - Cost Estimating Software - MTI SYSTEMS INC.; *pg.* 442, *pg.* 857

COSTPOINT - Computer Applications - DELTEK, INC.; *pg.* 386, *pg.* 1784

COSTTRACK - Software - OWENS & MINOR, INC.; *pg.* 1579, *pg.* 1795

COSTUME - Textiles - BERNHARDT DESIGN; *pg.* 918, *pg.* 1381

COSTUME EXPRESS - Apparel - CELEBRATE EXPRESS, INC.; *pg.* 1764, *pg.* 1883

COSTUME EXPRESS.COM - Apparel - CELEBRATE EXPRESS, INC.; *pg.* 1764, *pg.* 1883

COT-1 DNA - Molecular Biology Product - THERMO FISHER SCIENTIFIC INC.; *pg.* 1602, *pg.* 61

COTCO - LED - CREE INC.; *pg.* 631, *pg.* 1371

COTE-ALL - Paint & Coating - DIAMOND VOGEL PAINT, INC.; *pg.* 1441, *pg.* 710

COTE D OR - Ceramic, Glass, Stone Tiles & Slabs - WALKER & ZANGER, INC.; *pg.* 119, *pg.* 281

COTE D'OR - Chocolate - MONDELEZ INTERNATIONAL, INC.; *pg.* 878, *pg.* 601

COTE D'OR - Chemicals for Electro Plating - TECHNIC INCORPORATED; *pg.* 1183, *pg.* 1601

COTILLION - Textiles - BERNHARDT DESIGN; *pg.* 918, *pg.* 1381

COTLER - Apparel - LT APPAREL GROUP; *pg.* 29, *pg.* 1254

COTLETS - Candies - LIBERTY ORCHARDS CO., INC.; *pg.* 1857, *pg.* 1819

COTOL - Adhesive & Seam Sealer - MCNETT CORPORATION; *pg.* 1839, *pg.* 1817

COTOL 240 - Urethane Cure Accelerator & Pre-Cleaner - MCNETT CORPORATION; *pg.* 1839, *pg.* 1817

COTTAGE - Door & Wood Product - CONESTOGA WOOD SPECIALTIES CORP.; *pg.* 921, *pg.* 1527

COTTAGE GARDEN - Dresses & Sets - HABAND COMPANY, INC.; *pg.* 1772, *pg.* 1099

COTTAGE HEARTH - Bakery Items - UNIFIED GROCERS, INC.; *pg.* 1036, *pg.* 66

COTTAGE RETREAT - Furniture - ASHLEY FURNITURE INDUSTRIES, INC.; *pg.* 914, *pg.* 1852

COTTAGE REVIVAL - Furniture - STANLEY FURNITURE CO., INC.; *pg.* 943, *pg.* 1379

COTTON - Shoes - ALLEN-EDMONDS SHOE CORP.; *pg.* 1804, *pg.* 1887

COTTON BALLET - Women's Clothing & Accessories - WOODEN SHIPS OF HOBOKEN; *pg.* 35, *pg.* 1315

COTTON BOLL - Tobacco Product - AMERICAN SNUFF COMPANY; *pg.* 1893, *pg.* 1641

COTTON CAFE - Women's Clothing & Accessories - WOODEN SHIPS OF HOBOKEN; *pg.* 35, *pg.* 1315

COTTON CANDY - Fragrance - PARFUMS DE COEUR LTD.; *pg.* 519, *pg.* 376

COTTON CANNULATOME - Medical Device - COOK GROUP, INC.; *pg.* 1518, *pg.* 674

COTTON CARESS - Sleepwear - HABAND COMPANY, INC.; *pg.* 1772, *pg.* 1099

COTTON CASHMERE - Apparel - BLUE CANOE BODYWEAR; *pg.* 20, *pg.* 94

COTTON CLOUD - Towel & Washcloth - MEDLINE INDUSTRIES, INC.; *pg.* 1562, *pg.* 635

COTTON COLETTE - Women's Clothing & Accessories - WOODEN SHIPS OF HOBOKEN; *pg.* 35, *pg.* 1315

COTTON DELUXE - Clock - BROWN & BIGELOW, INC.; *pg.* 1624, *pg.* 959

COTTON-EASE - Yarn - LION BRAND YARN COMPANY; *pg.* 696, *pg.* 1050

COTTON FIESTA - Cotton & Cotton Lycra Fabrics - GUILFORD PERFORMANCE TEXTILES; *pg.* 693, *pg.* 1393

COTTON-HUIBREGTSE - Medical Device - COOK GROUP, INC.; *pg.* 1518, *pg.* 674

COTTON-LEUNG - Medical Device - COOK GROUP, INC.; *pg.* 1518, *pg.* 674

COTTON NO. 2 - Agriculture Exchange - INTERCONTINENTALEXCHANGE, INC.; *pg.* 769, *pg.* 512

COTTON SLIP - Women's Clothing & Accessories - WOODEN SHIPS OF HOBOKEN; *pg.* 35, *pg.* 1315

COTTON THEA - Women's Clothing & Accessories - WOODEN SHIPS OF HOBOKEN; *pg.* 35, *pg.* 1315

COTTONBLEND - Entertainment News - IAC/INTERACTIVECORP; *pg.* 292, *pg.* 1242

COTTONELLE - Bathroom Tissue - KIMBERLY-CLARK CORPORATION; *pg.* 1461, *pg.* 1720

COTTONSOF - Shoes - ACUSHNET COMPANY; *pg.* 1824, *pg.* 818

COTTOSINT - Fabric Hand Modifier - HENKEL CORPORATION; *pg.* 1165, *pg.* 1535

COTUBE - Software - BIO-RAD LABORATORIES, INC.; *pg.* 1504, *pg.* 101

COTY PRESTIGE - Fragrances - COTY, INC.; *pg.* 506, *pg.* 1219

COUCH COAT III - Premium Roll Covers - VAIL RUBBER WORKS, INC.; *pg.* 1891, *pg.* 906

COUGAR - Tobacco Product - AMERICAN SNUFF COMPANY; *pg.* 1893, *pg.* 1641

COUGAR - Paper - DOMTAR CORPORATION; *pg.* 1456, *pg.* 1954

COUGAR - Software - SCHLUMBERGER LIMITED; *pg.* 801, *pg.* 1714

COUGAR - Focus Lock Binoculars - SWIFT OPTICAL INSTRUMENTS, INC.; *pg.* 1430, *pg.* 1744

COUGAR - Paper Product - WEYERHAEUSER COMPANY; *pg.* 121, *pg.* 1820

COUGAR TAFFY - Candy - SWEET CANDY COMPANY; *pg.* 1862, *pg.* 1761

COUGARLICIOUS - Video Game - INTERNATIONAL GAME TECHNOLOGY; *pg.* 957, *pg.* 1024

COULOX - Sensor - MOCON, INC.; *pg.* 1363, *pg.* 940

COULTER - Testing Instrument System - BECKMAN COULTER, INC.; *pg.* 1402, *pg.* 48

COULTER CLENZ - Cleaning Agent - BECKMAN COULTER, INC.; *pg.* 1402, *pg.* 48

COULTER CLONE - Monoclonal Antibody - BECKMAN COULTER, INC.; *pg.* 1402, *pg.* 48

COULTER COUNTER - Testing Instrument System - BECKMAN COULTER, INC.; *pg.* 1402, *pg.* 48

COUMADIN - Blod Clot Medication - BRISTOL-MYERS SQUIBB COMPANY; *pg.* 1509, *pg.* 1206

COUNSELOR - Footwear - EASTLAND SHOE CORPORATION; *pg.* 1808, *pg.* 750

COUNT-A-DOSE - Injector - MEDICOOL, INC.; *pg.* 1562, *pg.* 294

COUNT-A-PAK - Seed Counters - SEEDBURO EQUIPMENT CO.; *pg.* 707, *pg.* 590

COUNT CHOCULA - Cereal - GENERAL MILLS, INC.; *pg.* 828, *pg.* 933

COUNT MONEY - Game - WMS INDUSTRIES INC.; *pg.* 593, *pg.* 666

COUNT OF MONTE CRISTO - Video Game - INTERNATIONAL GAME TECHNOLOGY; *pg.* 957, *pg.* 1024

COUNT-OFF - Decontaminant & Cleaner - PERKINELMER, INC.; *pg.* 1426, *pg.* 853

COUNT ON IT. - Tag Line - THE TORO COMPANY; *pg.* 1065, *pg.* 918

COUNTBRIGHT - Molecular Probe Product - THERMO FISHER SCIENTIFIC INC.; *pg.* 1602, *pg.* 61

COUNTDOWN - Playback System - AVID TECHNOLOGY, INC.; *pg.* 622, *pg.* 804

COUNTDOWN - Interactive Trivia Game Using Word Plays - NTN BUZZTIME, INC.; *pg.* 659, *pg.* 60

COUNTDOWN - Health Care Product - PACIFICHEALTH LABORATORIES, INC.; *pg.* 1579, *pg.* 1083

COUNTER-POINT - Commercial Lighting - SWIVELIER CO., INC.; *pg.* 1307, *pg.* 1142

COUNTERPOINT - Computer Software - CHECKPOINT SYSTEMS, INC.; *pg.* 628, *pg.* 1559

COUNTERPRO - Ironing Board - HOME PRODUCTS INTERNATIONAL, INC.; *pg.* 1125, *pg.* 577

COUNTERSCAPE YOUR KITCHEN - Tag Line - HAMILTON BEACH BRANDS, INC.; *pg.* 56, *pg.* 1783

COUNTERSTRIKE - Gas Piping Systems - OMEGA FLEX, INC.; *pg.* 982, *pg.* 1532

COUNTERTOP - Ironing Board - HOME PRODUCTS INTERNATIONAL, INC.; *pg.* 1125, *pg.* 577

COUNTESS - Currency Counter - GLORY GLOBAL SOLUTIONS; *pg.* 401, *pg.* 628

COUNTESS - Theatre Glasses - SWIFT OPTICAL INSTRUMENTS, INC.; *pg.* 1430, *pg.* 1744

COUNTESS MARA - Men's Accessories - COUNTESS MARA, INC.; *pg.* 39, *pg.* 1219

COUNTESS YORK - Bedding Product - HOLLANDER SLEEP PRODUCTS; *pg.* 927, *pg.* 411

COUNTINUOUS SUPPORT - Innerspring - SERTA, INC.; *pg.* 942, *pg.* 619

COUNTOUR - Footwear - P.W. MINOR & SON, INC.; *pg.* 1816, *pg.* 1140

COUNTRY ACCENTS - Rugs - COURISTAN INC.; *pg.* 921, *pg.* 1067

COUNTRY BLEND - Chewing Tobacco - SWISHER INTERNATIONAL, INC.; *pg.* 1895, *pg.* 345

COUNTRY BRIAD - Rug - ETHAN ALLEN INTERIORS INC.; *pg.* 924, *pg.* 343
COUNTRY BUFFET - Restaurants - OVATION BRANDS; *pg.* 1743, *pg.* 921
COUNTRY BUSINESS - Business Publication for Small Retail Stores - COUNTRY SAMPLER INC.; *pg.* 1630, *pg.* 658
COUNTRY-CARVED - Hams - JONES DAIRY FARM; *pg.* 867, *pg.* 1858
COUNTRY CASH - Video Game - INTERNATIONAL GAME TECHNOLOGY; *pg.* 957, *pg.* 1024
COUNTRY CHUNK - Food Product - PEPPERIDGE FARM, INC.; *pg.* 888, *pg.* 363
COUNTRY CLUB - Beverages - THE COCA-COLA COMPANY; *pg.* 240, *pg.* 493
COUNTRY CLUB - Fertilizers & Seeds - LEBANON SEABOARD CORPORATION; *pg.* 1797, *pg.* 1547
COUNTRY CLUB - Malt Liquor - PABST BREWING COMPANY; *pg.* 258, *pg.* 137
COUNTRY CLUB BOURBON - Bourbon Whiskey - LAIRD & COMPANY, INC.; *pg.* 1966, *pg.* 1119
COUNTRY CORN FLAKES - Breakfast Foods - GENERAL MILLS, INC.; *pg.* 828, *pg.* 933
COUNTRY COUSIN - Animal Nutrition Product - MANNA PRO CORPORATION; *pg.* 1478, *pg.* 975
COUNTRY CUPBOARD - Meats - CARL BUDDIG & COMPANY; *pg.* 846, *pg.* 619
COUNTRY DELITE - Dairy Product - DEAN FOODS COMPANY; *pg.* 852, *pg.* 1679
COUNTRY FAIR - Women's Clothing & Accessories - WOODEN SHIPS OF HOBOKEN; *pg.* 35, *pg.* 1315
COUNTRY FRENCH - Door & Wood Product - CONESTOGA WOOD SPECIALTIES CORP.; *pg.* 921, *pg.* 1527
COUNTRY FRENCH - Furniture - ETHAN ALLEN INTERIORS INC.; *pg.* 924, *pg.* 343
COUNTRY FRESH - Dairy Product - DEAN FOODS COMPANY; *pg.* 852, *pg.* 1679
COUNTRY GARDEN - Aerosol - S.C. JOHNSON & SON, INC.; *pg.* 334, *pg.* 1889
COUNTRY HARVEST - Fruit Juices - LEADING BRANDS, INC.; *pg.* 1026, *pg.* 1911
COUNTRY HOME BAKERS - Bakery Product - J&J SNACK FOODS CORPORATION; *pg.* 865, *pg.* 1107
COUNTRY HOSPITALITY - Franchised Family Chain - COUNTRY KITCHEN INTERNATIONAL, INC.; *pg.* 1723, *pg.* 1865
COUNTRY INNS & SUITES BY CARLSON - Hotels & Resorts - CARLSON COMPANIES INC.; *pg.* 1084, *pg.* 947
COUNTRY LIFE - Magazine - MEREDITH CORPORATION; *pg.* 1663, *pg.* 705
COUNTRY LIVING - Magazine - THE HEARST CORPORATION; *pg.* 1649, *pg.* 1239
COUNTRY LIVING GARDENER - Magazine - THE HEARST CORPORATION; *pg.* 1649, *pg.* 1239
COUNTRY LOFT - Acrylic Enamel Spray & Brush On Paints - SHERWIN-WILLIAMS DIVERSIFIED BRANDS DIVISION; *pg.* 1448, *pg.* 1435
COUNTRY MARKET - Restaurant - FJ MANAGEMENT, INC.; *pg.* 978, *pg.* 1758
COUNTRY MARKETPLACE - Magazine - COUNTRY SAMPLER INC.; *pg.* 1630, *pg.* 658
COUNTRY PRIDE - Poultry Products - PILGRIM'S PRIDE CORPORATION; *pg.* 889, *pg.* 330
COUNTRY SAMPLER - Consumer Magazine Featuring Handcrafted Items - COUNTRY SAMPLER INC.; *pg.* 1630, *pg.* 658
COUNTRY SAMPLER DECORATING IDEAS - Magazine Featuring Do-It-Yourself Home Decorating Projects - COUNTRY SAMPLER INC.; *pg.* 1630, *pg.* 658
COUNTRY SELECT - Wireless Communication System - AT&T SOUTHEAST; *pg.* 1868, *pg.* 489
COUNTRY STIR-FRY - Entree - BOB EVANS FARMS, LLC; *pg.* 841, *pg.* 1467
COUNTRY TIME - Lemonade - THE KRAFT HEINZ COMPANY; *pg.* 870, *pg.* 1577
COUNTRY TIME - Apparel - VANS, INC.; *pg.* 1821, *pg.* 76
COUNTRY VET - Agricultural Insect & Odor Control - ZEP INC.; *pg.* 338, *pg.* 524
COUNTRY WEEKLY - Magazine - AMERICAN MEDIA, INC.; *pg.* 1615, *pg.* 410
COUNTRY WOODS - Custom Made Wood Blinds - HUNTER DOUGLAS, INC.; *pg.* 928, *pg.* 1320
COUNTRYHOME - Magazine - MEREDITH CORPORATION; *pg.* 1663, *pg.* 705
COUNTRYLINE - Livestock, Farm & Ranch Equipment - TRACTOR SUPPLY COMPANY; *pg.* 708, *pg.* 1627
COUNTY MARKET - Supermarket Chain - SUPERVALU, INC.; *pg.* 1035, *pg.* 924
COUPE - Office Furniture - STEELCASE INC.; *pg.* 475, *pg.* 889
COUPE GRANDE - Office Furniture - STEELCASE INC.; *pg.* 475, *pg.* 889
COUPE GRANDE MOBILE - Office Furniture - STEELCASE INC.; *pg.* 475, *pg.* 889
COUPE WOOD - Office Furniture - STEELCASE INC.; *pg.* 475, *pg.* 889
COURAGE THE COWARDLY DOG - Animated Series - THE CARTOON NETWORK; *pg.* 273, *pg.* 492
THE COURIER - Briefcase - SANTA FE LEATHER CORPORATION; *pg.* 12, *pg.* 1059
COURIER - Software - WIND RIVER SYSTEMS, INC.; *pg.* 493, *pg.* 38
COURSE SETTER 21 - Autopilot Systems - BENMAR MARINE ELECTRONICS, INC.; *pg.* 624, *pg.* 105
COURSER - Tires - COOPER TIRE & RUBBER COMPANY; *pg.* 1881, *pg.* 1453
COURT CLASSIC - Shoes - COSTCO WHOLESALE CORPORATION; *pg.* 1765, *pg.* 1820
COURT DELUXE - Footwear - K-SWISS; *pg.* 1837, *pg.* 306
COURT DELUXE P - Footwear - K-SWISS; *pg.* 1837, *pg.* 306
COURT GUARD - Cleaning Product - HILLYARD, INC.; *pg.* 331, *pg.* 990
COURT-SIDE GLIDE DESIGN - Service Plan Design - INVACARE CORPORATION; *pg.* 1546, *pg.* 1451
COURT TIME - Basketball Backboards - LIFETIME PRODUCTS INC.; *pg.* 933, *pg.* 1751
COURTABLE - Audio System - VIQ SOLUTIONS INC.; *pg.* 490, *pg.* 1905
COURTESY - Car Dealerships - AUTONATION, INC.; *pg.* 165, *pg.* 423
COURTESYCOMPLETE - Small Business Service - AT&T SOUTHEAST; *pg.* 1868, *pg.* 489
COURTFLOW - Audio System - VIQ SOLUTIONS INC.; *pg.* 490, *pg.* 1905
COURTNEY - Footwear - EASTLAND SHOE CORPORATION; *pg.* 1808, *pg.* 750
COURTSHIP - Carpet - BEAULIEU GROUP, LLC; *pg.* 917, *pg.* 529
COURTSIDE - Portable Basketball System - LIFETIME PRODUCTS INC.; *pg.* 933, *pg.* 1751
COURTSIDER - Lighting - LSI INDUSTRIES INC.; *pg.* 58, *pg.* 1416
COURTVIEW - Software Product - MAXIMUS, INC.; *pg.* 780, *pg.* 1799
COURTYARD - Fabric - NEMSCHOFF, INC.; *pg.* 936, *pg.* 1890
COURTYARD BY MARRIOTT - Hotel Chain - MARRIOTT INTERNATIONAL, INC.; *pg.* 1102, *pg.* 764
COURVOISIER - Cognac - JIM BEAM BRANDS CO.; *pg.* 1965, *pg.* 601
COUSINS SUBS - Uniquely Prepared Submarine Sandwiches - COUSINS SUBMARINES, INC.; *pg.* 1017, *pg.* 1870
COVAC - Container - CHART INDUSTRIES, INC.; *pg.* 1405, *pg.* 1454
COVE - Footwear - EASTLAND SHOE CORPORATION; *pg.* 1808, *pg.* 750
COVELLE - Plastic Film - THE DOW CHEMICAL COMPANY; *pg.* 1157, *pg.* 898
COVENTRYONE - Health Insurance - COVENTRY HEALTH CARE, INC.; *pg.* 1519, *pg.* 761
COVER-ALL - Software - MAJESCO; *pg.* 429, *pg.* 1089
COVER AND CONSERVE - Tagline - FLEXIBLE SOLUTIONS INTERNATIONAL, INC.; *pg.* 1163, *pg.* 1913
COVER COAT - Ready-Mixed Compound - USG CORPORATION; *pg.* 118, *pg.* 594
COVER-CUT - Paper & Nonwoven Material - FIBERMARK INC.; *pg.* 1457, *pg.* 1764
COVER GIRL - Beauty Product - COVER GIRL COSMETICS; *pg.* 506, *pg.* 772
COVER GIRL POWDER - Liquid, Pressed & Tube - COVER GIRL COSMETICS; *pg.* 506, *pg.* 772
COVER KOTE - Interior Latex Flat-Finish - DUNN-EDWARDS CORPORATION; *pg.* 1442, *pg.* 129
COVER MAGAZINE - Magazine - SUMNER COMMUNICATIONS INC.; *pg.* 1690, *pg.* 338
COVER PERFECT - Paint - AKZONOBEL DECORATIVE PAINTS U.S.; *pg.* 1439, *pg.* 1474
COVER-PRO - Tarp System & Component - SHUR-CO, INC.; *pg.* 110, *pg.* 1626
COVER STICK - Concealer - MAYBELLINE LLC; *pg.* 516, *pg.* 1257
COVER TO COVER - Game - HASBRO, INC.; *pg.* 954, *pg.* 1603
COVER UP - Cream - MERLE NORMAN COSMETICS, INC.; *pg.* 517, *pg.* 136
COVER-UP - Tarp System & Component - SHUR-CO, INC.; *pg.* 110, *pg.* 1626
COVERA - Medicine - PFIZER INC.; *pg.* 1581, *pg.* 1278
COVERA-HS - Pharmaceutical Product - PFIZER INC.; *pg.* 1581, *pg.* 1278
COVERAGE - Disinfectant Cleaner - STERIS CORPORATION; *pg.* 1597, *pg.* 1464
COVERAGE PLUS NPD - Disinfectant Cleaner - STERIS CORPORATION; *pg.* 1597, *pg.* 1464
COVERALL - Polyethylene Sheeting - WARP BROTHERS; *pg.* 1471, *pg.* 595
COVERBIND - Document Binder - PITNEY BOWES INC.; *pg.* 454, *pg.* 376
COVERGLOS - Facestock - SPINNAKER COATING, LLC; *pg.* 1470, *pg.* 1477
COVERING YOUR WORLD ONE RISK AT A TIME - Slogan - MARKEL CORPORATION; *pg.* 1207, *pg.* 1783
COVERLET - Medical & Aesthetic Product - DYNATRONICS CORPORATION; *pg.* 1526, *pg.* 1757
COVERMAG.COM - Website - SUMNER COMMUNICATIONS INC.; *pg.* 1690, *pg.* 338
COVERMATTE - Adhesive Coated Paper - SPINNAKER COATING, LLC; *pg.* 1470, *pg.* 1477
COVEROHM - Resistor Paste - FERRO CORPORATION; *pg.* 1162, *pg.* 1462
COVERS - Software - IHS AUTOMOTIVE DRIVEN BY POLK; *pg.* 1652, *pg.* 907
COVERT - Apparel - OAKLEY, INC.; *pg.* 1840, *pg.* 86
COVERWELL - Molecular Probe Product - THERMO FISHER SCIENTIFIC INC.; *pg.* 1602, *pg.* 61
COVEY - Furniture - HERMAN MILLER, INC.; *pg.* 926, *pg.* 913
COVI-OX - Mixed Tocopherols, Antioxidant - HENKEL CORPORATION; *pg.* 1165, *pg.* 1535
COVINGTON - Furniture - AMERICAN LEATHER LP; *pg.* 912, *pg.* 1673
COVINGTON - Brick & Tile Product - CHEROKEE BRICK & TILE COMPANY; *pg.* 75, *pg.* 535
COVINGTON - Furniture - HOOKER FURNITURE CORPORATION; *pg.* 928, *pg.* 1788
COVINGTON - Apparel - SEARS HOLDINGS CORPORATION; *pg.* 1784, *pg.* 618
COVISINT - Software - COMPUWARE CORPORATION; *pg.* 379, *pg.* 879
COVITOL - Vitamin E Products - HENKEL CORPORATION; *pg.* 1165, *pg.* 1535
COW COMM - Individual Animal Management Systems - MIDWEST MICROSYSTEMS, LLC; *pg.* 1267, *pg.* 1012
COW SENSE - Software for Beef Industry - MIDWEST MICROSYSTEMS, LLC; *pg.* 1267, *pg.* 1012
COW TIPPING - Game - WMS INDUSTRIES INC.; *pg.* 593, *pg.* 666
COWARD SHOE - Footwear - ASCENA RETAIL GROUP, INC.; *pg.* 18, *pg.* 1081
COWBOYS - Convenience Stores - THE PANTRY, INC.; *pg.* 1029, *pg.* 1360
COWL RUANA - Women's Clothing & Accessories - WOODEN SHIPS OF HOBOKEN; *pg.* 35, *pg.* 1315
COWLES - Dissolver/Disperser - MOREHOUSE-COWLES; *pg.* 1363, *pg.* 66
COWTRAKKER - Detection Tag - BOUMATIC LLC; *pg.* 701, *pg.* 1865
COWTRAKKER PID - Estrus Detection Tag - BOUMATIC LLC; *pg.* 701, *pg.* 1865
COX-2 CONTROL - Nutritional Product - NUTRACEUTICAL INTERNATIONAL CORPORATION; *pg.* 1576, *pg.* 1753
COX HIGH SPEED INTERNET - Communication Product - COX COMMUNICATIONS, INC.; *pg.* 279, *pg.* 501
COY - Glass & Ceramic Material - CORNING INCORPORATED; *pg.* 1122, *pg.* 1154
COYAH - Shoe - ALDO GROUP; *pg.* 1804, *pg.* 1959
COYOTE - Skate - ROLLER DERBY SKATE CORP.; *pg.* 966, *pg.* 630
COYOTE GRILL - Southwestern Entrees - THE SCHWAN FOOD COMPANY; *pg.* 894, *pg.* 928
COYOTE MOON - Video Game - INTERNATIONAL GAME TECHNOLOGY; *pg.* 957, *pg.* 1024
COYOTES CAUSES - Awareness Program - COYOTES HOCKEY, LLC; *pg.* 542, *pg.* 13
COZEE-CORD - Pants - HABAND COMPANY, INC.; *pg.* 1772, *pg.* 1099

COZY - Footwear - P.W. MINOR & SON, INC.; *pg.* 1816, *pg.* 1140
COZY - Cup - SOLO CUP COMPANY; *pg.* 1469, *pg.* 625
COZY COTTAGE - Lighting Product - QUOIZEL INC.; *pg.* 1304, *pg.* 1616
COZY COTTAGE - Children's Bed - RUBBERMAID HOME PRODUCTS; *pg.* 1138, *pg.* 1453
COZY-LITE - Industrial & Residential Lighting - SWIVELIER CO., INC.; *pg.* 1307, *pg.* 1142
COZYRIDER - Infant Carrier - INFANTINO, LLC; *pg.* 957, *pg.* 203
CP - Educational Materials - SCHOLASTIC INC.; *pg.* 1683, *pg.* 1288
CP-POLY - Fabric - KOPPERS HOLDINGS INC.; *pg.* 1170, *pg.* 1577
CP SERIES II - Internal Batch Mixer - FARREL CORPORATION; *pg.* 1336, *pg.* 337
CP1000S - Intelligent Telecommunications Apparatus - ALCATEL-LUCENT USA, INC.; *pg.* 615, *pg.* 1728
CP2000 - Intelligent Telecommunications Apparatus - ALCATEL-LUCENT USA, INC.; *pg.* 615, *pg.* 1728
CP3000 - Intelligent Telecommunications Apparatus - ALCATEL-LUCENT USA, INC.; *pg.* 615, *pg.* 1728
CP4000 - Intelligent Telecommunications Apparatus - ALCATEL-LUCENT USA, INC.; *pg.* 615, *pg.* 1728
CP820 - Tabletop Payphone - SIEMENS BUILDING TECHNOLOGIES, INC.; *pg.* 1376, *pg.* 560
CPA - Funds - W.P. CAREY & CO., LLC; *pg.* 823, *pg.* 1315
CPA REPORT - Education Program - SMARTPROS LTD.; *pg.* 1281, *pg.* 1166
CPA REPORT ONLINE - Education Program Online Subscription - SMARTPROS LTD.; *pg.* 1281, *pg.* 1166
CPA REPORT VIDEO - Education Program Video Subscription - SMARTPROS LTD.; *pg.* 1281, *pg.* 1166
CPA WEB TRUST - Web Site Seal Certification - AMERICAN INSTITUTE OF CERTIFIED PUBLIC ACCOUNTANTS INC.; *pg.* 129, *pg.* 1192
CPC - Glass & Ceramic Material - CORNING INCORPORATED; *pg.* 1122, *pg.* 1154
CPC - Cores for Winding, Storage & Transport of Web Material - SONOCO PRODUCTS COMPANY; *pg.* 1469, *pg.* 1619
CPC-B - Cores - SONOCO PRODUCTS COMPANY; *pg.* 1469, *pg.* 1619
CPE - Chlorinated Polyethylene Chemical-Resistant Fabric - STANDARD SAFETY EQUIPMENT CO.; *pg.* 1379, *pg.* 632
CPI - Leadership Development Assessments - CPP, INC.; *pg.* 1631, *pg.* 153
CPI - Middleware - MERCURY COMPUTER SYSTEMS, INC.; *pg.* 434, *pg.* 813
CPI 260 - Leadership Development Assessments - CPP, INC.; *pg.* 1631, *pg.* 153
CPK ASAP - Restaurant Services - CALIFORNIA PIZZA KITCHEN INC.; *pg.* 1720, *pg.* 127
CPL - Resolution Enhancement Technology - BRION TECHNOLOGIES INC.; *pg.* 1319, *pg.* 265
CPL - Surveys - CORRPRO COMPANIES, INC.; *pg.* 631, *pg.* 1464
CPM - Certified Property Manager - INSTITUTE OF REAL ESTATE MANAGEMENT; *pg.* 144, *pg.* 578
CPO SCIENCE - Educational Resources - SCHOOL SPECIALTY, INC.; *pg.* 467, *pg.* 1860
CPS - Orthopedic Device - DJO SURGICAL; *pg.* 1525, *pg.* 1661
CPS-3 - Software - SCHLUMBERGER LIMITED; *pg.* 801, *pg.* 1714
CPS AIM - Catheters - ST. JUDE MEDICAL, INC.; *pg.* 1596, *pg.* 963
CPS COURIER - CRT Therapy - ST. JUDE MEDICAL, INC.; *pg.* 1596, *pg.* 963
CPS DIRECT - CRT Therapy - ST. JUDE MEDICAL, INC.; *pg.* 1596, *pg.* 963
CPS DUO - CRT Therapy - ST. JUDE MEDICAL, INC.; *pg.* 1596, *pg.* 963
CPS LUMINARY - CRT Therapy - ST. JUDE MEDICAL, INC.; *pg.* 1596, *pg.* 963
CPS VENTURE - CRT Therapy - ST. JUDE MEDICAL, INC.; *pg.* 1596, *pg.* 963
CPT - Medical Nomenclature - AMERICAN MEDICAL ASSOCIATION; *pg.* 130, *pg.* 564
CPT - Thermoplastic Enclosure - CHANNELL COMMERCIAL CORP.; *pg.* 1870, *pg.* 291
CPU NXT - Software - WMS INDUSTRIES INC.; *pg.* 593, *pg.* 666
CPU TROLLEY - Computer Support Worktools - STEELCASE INC.; *pg.* 475, *pg.* 889
CPV - Capital Equipment - TEREX CORPORATION; *pg.* 1381, *pg.* 384
CQ HOMELAND SECURITY - Political Journalism - CQ ROLL CALL; *pg.* 1631, *pg.* 397
CQ HOUSE ACTION REPORTS - Political Journalism - CQ ROLL CALL; *pg.* 1631, *pg.* 397
CQ MONITOR - Daily Update on Congressional Activity - THE TIMES PUBLISHING CO.; *pg.* 1695, *pg.* 464
CQ PRESS - Political Journalism - CQ ROLL CALL; *pg.* 1631, *pg.* 397
CQ RESEARCHER - Topical Reports-Once a Week - THE TIMES PUBLISHING CO.; *pg.* 1695, *pg.* 464
CQ/T - Optical Product - LEUPOLD & STEVENS, INC.; *pg.* 1420, *pg.* 1492
CQ TODAY - Political Journalism - CQ ROLL CALL; *pg.* 1631, *pg.* 397
CQ WEEKLY - Political Journalism - CQ ROLL CALL; *pg.* 1631, *pg.* 397
CQ WEEKLY - Weekly Report & Analysis on Congress - THE TIMES PUBLISHING CO.; *pg.* 1695, *pg.* 464
CQ.COM - Political Journalism - CQ ROLL CALL; *pg.* 1631, *pg.* 397
CQ.COM - Electronic Media Service on Congress & Politics - THE TIMES PUBLISHING CO.; *pg.* 1695, *pg.* 464
CR-39 - Allyl Diglycol Carbonate - PPG INDUSTRIES, INC.; *pg.* 1445, *pg.* 1579
CR BRAKEMASTER - Air Dryer for Heavy Duty Vehicles - SKF SEALING SOLUTIONS; *pg.* 217, *pg.* 610
C.R. GIBSON - Stationery; Book Publishers - C.R. GIBSON, LLC; *pg.* 1631, *pg.* 1650
CR SEALS - For Automotive, Heavy Duty & Industrial Applications - SKF SEALING SOLUTIONS; *pg.* 217, *pg.* 610
CR U-JOINTS - Universal Joints for Heavy Duty Vehicles - SKF SEALING SOLUTIONS; *pg.* 217, *pg.* 610
CR3 - Steel Fittings - BRENNAN INDUSTRIES INC.; *pg.* 1319, *pg.* 1429
CRA-WAL - Container - BUCKEYE CORRUGATED INC.; *pg.* 1454, *pg.* 1400
THE CRAB HOUSE - Restaurant Chain - LANDRY'S, INC.; *pg.* 1735, *pg.* 1709
CRABMANIA - Video Game - INTERNATIONAL GAME TECHNOLOGY; *pg.* 957, *pg.* 1024
CRACEN - Footwear - K-SWISS; *pg.* 1837, *pg.* 306
CRACK & CREVICE - Pest-Control Equipment - BASF; *pg.* 1793, *pg.* 992
CRACK-BACK - Films Coating - AVERY DENNISON CORPORATION; *pg.* 1452, *pg.* 95
CRACK FILLER - High Solid Filler - CALIFORNIA PRODUCTS CORPORATION; *pg.* 1441, *pg.* 781
CRACKER BARREL CHEESE - Specialty Cheeses - THE KRAFT HEINZ COMPANY; *pg.* 870, *pg.* 1577
CRACKER JACK - Carmel Popcorn & Nuts - FRITO-LAY NORTH AMERICA, INC.; *pg.* 1853, *pg.* 1730
CRACKER JACK - Snack Food - PEPSICO, INC.; *pg.* 259, *pg.* 1327
CRACKIN' UP FOR BREAKFAST - Restaurant Services - TYSON FOODS, INC.; *pg.* 902, *pg.* 35
CRACKLE - Fabric - NEMSCHOFF, INC.; *pg.* 936, *pg.* 1890
CRACKLEFLAME - Firelog - DURAFLAME, INC.; *pg.* 1123, *pg.* 280
CRACKLIN' OAT BRAN - Cereal - KELLOGG COMPANY; *pg.* 831, *pg.* 870
CRACKLIN'OAT BRAN - Cereal - KELLOGG COMPANY; *pg.* 831, *pg.* 870
CRACKSHOT - Repair Product - DAP PRODUCTS, INC.; *pg.* 1441, *pg.* 756
CRADLE - Orthopedic Product - DJO INCORPORATED; *pg.* 1524, *pg.* 302
CRADLE IN COMFORT - Baby Product - THE BOPPY COMPANY, LLC; *pg.* 20, *pg.* 329
CRADLE TO GRAVE - Educational Service - TEMPLE UNIVERSITY HEALTH SYSTEM; *pg.* 1601, *pg.* 1571
CRADLECON - Connector - MOLEX INCORPORATED; *pg.* 655, *pg.* 628
CRAFT KIDS BARRACUTTER - Scissors - ACME UNITED CORPORATION; *pg.* 1040, *pg.* 346
CRAFT KIDS HIPPOSCISSIUS - Scissors - ACME UNITED CORPORATION; *pg.* 1040, *pg.* 346
CRAFT KIDS RHINOSCISSOR - Scissors - ACME UNITED CORPORATION; *pg.* 1040, *pg.* 346
CRAFT KIDS SCISSAGATOR - Scissors - ACME UNITED CORPORATION; *pg.* 1040, *pg.* 346
CRAFT KIDS SCISSAMANDER - Scissors - ACME UNITED CORPORATION; *pg.* 1040, *pg.* 346
CRAFT KIDS SCISSISAURUS - Scissors - ACME UNITED CORPORATION; *pg.* 1040, *pg.* 346
CRAFTEDCLIP - Technology Services - LEAR CORPORATION; *pg.* 229, *pg.* 907
CRAFTKIDS - Scissors - ACME UNITED CORPORATION; *pg.* 1040, *pg.* 346
CRAFTS - Magazine - RENTPATH, INC.; *pg.* 1680, *pg.* 538
CRAFTS' N THINGS - Magazine - AMOS PRESS, INC.; *pg.* 1616, *pg.* 1472
CRAFTSMAN - Door & Wood Product - CONESTOGA WOOD SPECIALTIES CORP.; *pg.* 921, *pg.* 1527
CRAFTSMAN - Footwear - RED WING SHOE COMPANY, INC.; *pg.* 1817, *pg.* 954
CRAFTSMAN - Hand & Power Tool - SEARS HOLDINGS CORPORATION; *pg.* 1784, *pg.* 618
CRAFTSMAN CLUB - Hardware Tool - SEARS HOLDINGS CORPORATION; *pg.* 1784, *pg.* 618
CRAFTSMAN PROFESSIONAL - Hardware Tool - SEARS HOLDINGS CORPORATION; *pg.* 1784, *pg.* 618
CRAFTSMEN COLLECTION - Container Grown Plant - MONROVIA GROWERS; *pg.* 1797, *pg.* 44
CRAFTWORKS - Scissors - ACME UNITED CORPORATION; *pg.* 1040, *pg.* 346
CRAFTY CARL'S CRABMANIA - Video Game - INTERNATIONAL GAME TECHNOLOGY; *pg.* 957, *pg.* 1024
CRAIG PONZIO SIGNATURE COLLECTION - Wood Framing Products - LARSON-JUHL US LLC; *pg.* 933, *pg.* 537
CRAIN'S CHICAGO BUSINESS - Regional Business Newspaper - CRAIN COMMUNICATIONS, INC.; *pg.* 1631, *pg.* 879
CRAIN'S CLEVELAND BUSINESS - Regional Business Newspaper - CRAIN COMMUNICATIONS, INC.; *pg.* 1631, *pg.* 879
CRAIN'S DETROIT BUSINESS - Regional Business Newspaper - CRAIN COMMUNICATIONS, INC.; *pg.* 1631, *pg.* 879
CRAIN'S MANCHESTER BUSINESS - Regional Business Newspaper - CRAIN COMMUNICATIONS, INC.; *pg.* 1631, *pg.* 879
CRAIN'S NEW YORK BUSINESS - Regional Business Newspaper - CRAIN COMMUNICATIONS, INC.; *pg.* 1631, *pg.* 879
CRAISINS - Sweet Fruit Snack - OCEAN SPRAY CRANBERRIES, INC.; *pg.* 887, *pg.* 827
CRAMMER - Toys - LEAPFROG ENTERPRISES, INC.; *pg.* 961, *pg.* 84
CRAN APPLE - Juice Drink - OCEAN SPRAY CRANBERRIES, INC.; *pg.* 887, *pg.* 827
CRAN CHERRY - Juice Drink - OCEAN SPRAY CRANBERRIES, INC.; *pg.* 887, *pg.* 827
CRAN GRAPE - Juice Drink - OCEAN SPRAY CRANBERRIES, INC.; *pg.* 887, *pg.* 827
CRAN MANGO - Juice Drink - OCEAN SPRAY CRANBERRIES, INC.; *pg.* 887, *pg.* 827
CRAN ORANGE - Cranberry Orange Juice Drink - OCEAN SPRAY CRANBERRIES, INC.; *pg.* 887, *pg.* 827
CRAN RASPBERRY - Juice Drink - OCEAN SPRAY CRANBERRIES, INC.; *pg.* 887, *pg.* 827
CRAN STRAWBERRY - Juice Drink - OCEAN SPRAY CRANBERRIES, INC.; *pg.* 887, *pg.* 827
CRAN SUPPORT - Nutritional Product - NATROL, INC.; *pg.* 1570, *pg.* 64
CRAN TANGERINE - Juice Drink - OCEAN SPRAY CRANBERRIES, INC.; *pg.* 887, *pg.* 827
CRANACTIN - Nutritional Product - NUTRACEUTICAL INTERNATIONAL CORPORATION; *pg.* 1576, *pg.* 1753
CRANBERRY-APLETS - Candies - LIBERTY ORCHARDS CO., INC.; *pg.* 1857, *pg.* 1819
CRANBERRY APPLE - Herb Tea - R.C. BIGELOW, INC.; *pg.* 891, *pg.* 348
CRANBERRY CRAZE - Smoothie - JAMBA, INC.; *pg.* 1024, *pg.* 84
CRANBERRY NEWPORT - Decorative Accessory - ETHAN ALLEN INTERIORS INC.; *pg.* 924, *pg.* 343
CRANDAL - Apparel - VANS, INC.; *pg.* 1821, *pg.* 76
CRANE - Furniture - ETHAN ALLEN INTERIORS INC.; *pg.* 924, *pg.* 343
CRANEGLAS - Glass Fiber Paper Products - CRANE & CO., INC.; *pg.* 1456, *pg.* 816
CRANEMART - Crane - COLUMBUS MCKINNON CORPORATION; *pg.* 1325, *pg.* 1138
CRANEMAT - Polyester, Polyphenylene Sulfide & Bicomponent Fiber Paper Products - CRANE & CO., INC.;

First page reference indicates Business Class Edition
Second page reference indicates Geographic Edition

pg. 1456, pg. 816

CRANERGY - Juice Drink - OCEAN SPRAY CRANBERRIES, INC.; pg. 887, pg. 827

CRANE'S BOND - Paper Products - CRANE & CO., INC.; pg. 1456, pg. 816

CRANE'S CHOICE - Paper & Stationery Products - CRANE & CO., INC.; pg. 1456, pg. 816

CRANE'S CREST - Paper & Stationery Products - CRANE & CO., INC.; pg. 1456, pg. 816

CRANE'S PALETTE - Color Paper Products - CRANE & CO., INC.; pg. 1456, pg. 816

CRANFRUIT - Sauces - OCEAN SPRAY CRANBERRIES, INC.; pg. 887, pg. 827

CRANICOT - Cranberry Apricot Juice Drink - OCEAN SPRAY CRANBERRIES, INC.; pg. 887, pg. 827

CRANIOFACIAL REPAIR SYSTEM - Medical Device - DEPUY SYNTHES; pg. 1523, pg. 1593

CRANIOFIX - Cranial Flap Fixation System - AESCULAP, INC.; pg. 1487, pg. 1521

CRANIOFIX 2 - Clamps - STRYKER CORPORATION; pg. 1598, pg. 894

CRANIUM - Toy & Game - HASBRO, INC.; pg. 954, pg. 1603

CRANIUM PALLADIUM - Education Program - THE DOW CHEMICAL COMPANY; pg. 1157, pg. 898

CRANK - Apparel - OAKLEY, INC.; pg. 1840, pg. 86

CRANTASTIC - Cranberry Based Fruit Punch Drink - OCEAN SPRAY CRANBERRIES, INC.; pg. 887, pg. 827

CRASTIN - PBT Thermoplastic Polyester Resin - E.I. DU PONT DE NEMOURS & COMPANY; pg. 1159, pg. 390

CRATE - Instrument Amplification Products - LOUD TECHNOLOGIES INC.; pg. 652, pg. 1847

CRATE & BARREL - Specialty Housewares Stores - EUROMARKET DESIGNS, INC.; pg. 1124, pg. 640

CRATE SECURE - Wooden Crate Tapw - AMERICAN CASTING & MANUFACTURING CORPORATION; pg. 1312, pg. 1321

CRATEC - Glass Fibers Chopped Strands - OWENS CORNING; pg. 102, pg. 1476

CRATEC PLUS - Chopped Strand Mat - OWENS CORNING; pg. 102, pg. 1476

CRATHCO - Frozen Beverage Dispensers - GRINDMASTER CORPORATION; pg. 56, pg. 734

CRAVAT - Textiles - BERNHARDT DESIGN; pg. 918, pg. 1381

CRAVE - Pet Food - MARS, INCORPORATED; pg. 1858, pg. 1792

CRAVE - Cat Treats - MARS PETCARE; pg. 1478, pg. 1633

CRAVE EASE - Nutritional Supplement - NU SKIN ENTERPRISES, INC.; pg. 518, pg. 1755

CRAVE-NX - Drug Delivery System - GENEREX BIOTECHNOLOGY CORPORATION; pg. 1534, pg. 1938

CRAVE THE WAVE - Slogan - OCEAN SPRAY CRANBERRIES, INC.; pg. 887, pg. 827

CRAVEABLE EXPERIENCES. RAVEABLE RESULTS. - Slogan - CENTERPLATE, INC.; pg. 1017, pg. 372

CRAVEX - Nutritional Product - NATROL, INC.; pg. 1570, pg. 64

CRAWDAD - Sandals - AEROGROUP INTERNATIONAL, INC.; pg. 1803, pg. 1055

CRAWFISH CASH - Lottery Game - LOUISIANA LOTTERY CORPORATION; pg. 997, pg. 742

CRAY - Computer Systems - CRAY INC.; pg. 380, pg. 1834

CRAY-1 - Supercomputing System - CRAY INC.; pg. 380, pg. 1834

CRAY-2 - Supercomputing System - CRAY INC.; pg. 380, pg. 1834

CRAY-3 - Supercomputing System - CRAY INC.; pg. 380, pg. 1834

CRAY ANIMATION THEATER - Supercomputing System - CRAY INC.; pg. 380, pg. 1834

CRAY C90 - Supercomputer - CRAY INC.; pg. 380, pg. 1834

CRAY C90D - Supercomputing System - CRAY INC.; pg. 380, pg. 1834

CRAY CF90 - Supercomputing System - CRAY INC.; pg. 380, pg. 1834

CRAY CX1 - Supercomputer - CRAY INC.; pg. 380, pg. 1834

CRAY EL - Supercomputing System - CRAY INC.; pg. 380, pg. 1834

CRAY J90 - Supercomputing System - CRAY INC.; pg. 380, pg. 1834

CRAY J90SE - Supercomputing System - CRAY INC.; pg. 380, pg. 1834

CRAY J916 - Supercomputing System - CRAY INC.; pg. 380, pg. 1834

CRAY J932 - Supercomputing System - CRAY INC.; pg. 380, pg. 1834

CRAY MTA - Supercomputing System - CRAY INC.; pg. 380, pg. 1834

CRAY SV1 - Supercomputer - CRAY INC.; pg. 380, pg. 1834

CRAY SX-6 - Supercomputer - CRAY INC.; pg. 380, pg. 1834

CRAY T3D - Computer System - CRAY INC.; pg. 380, pg. 1834

CRAY T3E - Computer System - CRAY INC.; pg. 380, pg. 1834

CRAY X1 - Supercomputer - CRAY INC.; pg. 380, pg. 1834

CRAY X1E - Computer System - CRAY INC.; pg. 380, pg. 1834

CRAY XD1 - Supercomputer - CRAY INC.; pg. 380, pg. 1834

CRAY XMS - Supercomputing System - CRAY INC.; pg. 380, pg. 1834

CRAY XMT - Supercomputer - CRAY INC.; pg. 380, pg. 1834

CRAY XT - Supercomputing System - CRAY INC.; pg. 380, pg. 1834

CRAY XT4 - Computer System - CRAY INC.; pg. 380, pg. 1834

CRAY XT5 - Computer System - CRAY INC.; pg. 380, pg. 1834

CRAY XT5H - Supercomputing System - CRAY INC.; pg. 380, pg. 1834

CRAY XT5M - Supercomputing System - CRAY INC.; pg. 380, pg. 1834

CRAYDOC - Supercomputing System - CRAY INC.; pg. 380, pg. 1834

CRAYLINK - Supercomputing System - CRAY INC.; pg. 380, pg. 1834

CRAYOLA - Crayons, Chalks, Clay, Markers, Activity Sets, Colored Pencils & Dough - CRAYOLA LLC; pg. 951, pg. 1528

CRAYON - Fabric - NEMSCHOFF, INC.; pg. 936, pg. 1890

CRAYON ARMOR - Lumber Crayon Dispenser - C.H. HANSON COMPANY; pg. 1322, pg. 636

CRAYPACS - Supercomputing System - CRAY INC.; pg. 380, pg. 1834

CRAYPAT - Supercomputing System - CRAY INC.; pg. 380, pg. 1834

CRAYPORT - Supercomputing System - CRAY INC.; pg. 380, pg. 1834

CRAYSOFT - Supercomputing System - CRAY INC.; pg. 380, pg. 1834

CRAYTUTOR - Supercomputing System - CRAY INC.; pg. 380, pg. 1834

CRAZY 8 - Childrens Clothes - THE GYMBOREE CORPORATION; pg. 25, pg. 77

CRAZY 8'S - Game - MISSOURI LOTTERY; pg. 999, pg. 979

CRAZY BREAD - Bread Sticks - LITTLE CAESARS ENTERPRISES, INC.; pg. 1736, pg. 883

CRAZY CASH - Lottery Game - D.C. LOTTERY & CHARITABLE GAMES CONTROL BOARD; pg. 991, pg. 398

CRAZY CRANK - Video Viewing System - SWORDFISH FINANCIAL, INC.; pg. 1430, pg. 1737

CRAZY DIAMONDS - Game - WMS INDUSTRIES INC.; pg. 593, pg. 666

CRAZY DIPS - Candy - SPANGLER CANDY COMPANY; pg. 1862, pg. 1407

CRAZY HORSE - Apparel - KATE SPADE & COMPANY; pg. 27, pg. 1248

CRAZY JOSE'S - Restaurant - MEXICAN RESTAURANTS, INC.; pg. 1741, pg. 1711

CRAZY LEGS - Stilt - SCHOOL-TECH, INC.; pg. 1844, pg. 866

CRAZY MOUNTAIN RANCH - Cigarette - PHILIP MORRIS USA INC.; pg. 1894, pg. 1803

CRAZY SAUCE - Dipping Sauce - LITTLE CAESARS ENTERPRISES, INC.; pg. 1736, pg. 883

CRAZY WILD 10S - Lottery Game - IDAHO LOTTERY; pg. 995, pg. 547

CRAZZY - Footwear - STEVEN MADDEN, LTD.; pg. 1819, pg. 1176

CRB - Eyewear - SEARS HOLDINGS CORPORATION; pg. 1784, pg. 618

CRB-7 - Alloy - CARPENTER TECHNOLOGY CORPORATION; pg. 73, pg. 1584

CRC - Compact Robotic Connectors - MOLEX INCORPORATED; pg. 655, pg. 628

CRD - Cable - COMMSCOPE, INC.; pg. 278, pg. 1378

CRDS - Delivery System - MAGLINE, INC.; pg. 1358, pg. 908

CRE - Medical Device - BOSTON SCIENTIFIC CORPORATION; pg. 1508, pg. 831

CRE8VENTURES - Software System - MENTOR GRAPHICS CORPORATION; pg. 432, pg. 1510

CREAM - Corn Starch - HENKEL CONSUMER GOODS; pg. 511, pg. 22

THE CREAM - Hair Care Product - JOHN PAUL MITCHELL SYSTEMS; pg. 512, pg. 133

CREAM - Beverage - SPRECHER BREWING COMPANY; pg. 265, pg. 1858

CREAM OF RYE - Organic Whole Grain Flaked Rye Cereal - ROMAN MEAL COMPANY; pg. 834, pg. 1845

CREAM OF WHEAT - Hot Cereals - B&G FOODS, INC.; pg. 838, pg. 1102

CREAMETTE - Food Product - NEW WORLD PASTA COMPANY; pg. 885, pg. 1537

CREAMLAND - Milk - DEAN FOODS COMPANY; pg. 852, pg. 1679

CREAMSICLE - Candy Twist - PROMOTION IN MOTION, INC.; pg. 1861, pg. 1052

CREAMSICLE - Ice Cream and Frozen Novelties - UNILEVER CANADA INC.; pg. 903, pg. 1946

CREAMSICLE CANDY TWISTS - Food Product - PROMOTION IN MOTION, INC.; pg. 1861, pg. 1052

CREAMY - Pudding - KOZY SHACK INC.; pg. 869, pg. 1167

CREAMY FLO-MATIC - Cosmetic Product - MERLE NORMAN COSMETICS, INC.; pg. 517, pg. 136

CREAMY HAVARTI - Cheese - A.V. OLSSON TRADING CO. INC.; pg. 838, pg. 372

CREAMY HYDRATING MASQUE - Skin Care Product - NU SKIN ENTERPRISES, INC.; pg. 518, pg. 1755

CREATABLES - Paper-Crafting Products - AMERICAN GREETINGS CORPORATION; pg. 1615, pg. 1428

CREATE - Software - SAS INSTITUTE INC.; pg. 466, pg. 1361

CREATE-A-PRINT - Self Contained Enlargement Center - EASTMAN KODAK COMPANY; pg. 1408, pg. 1333

CREATE SOMETHING GOOD - Slogan - HORMEL FOODS CORPORATION; pg. 863, pg. 915

CREATE SUPPORT FINANCE BUSINESS - Tagline - WINMARK CORPORATION; pg. 1792, pg. 946

CREATE YOUR SPACE - Wood & Plastic Product - TREX COMPANY, INC.; pg. 116, pg. 1812

CREATEARCHIEVE - Software System - BOTTOMLINE TECHNOLOGIES (DE), INC.; pg. 727, pg. 1038

CREATED BY NATURE ADVANCED THROUGH SCIENCE - Slogan - PENFORD CORPORATION; pg. 1177, pg. 314

CREATED BY NATURE. DELIVERED BY DEAN. - Tagline - DEAN FOODS COMPANY; pg. 852, pg. 1679

CREATED BY NATURE. RECREATED BY SCIENCE. - Slogan - VYSTAR CORPORATION; pg. 1891, pg. 532

CREATE!FORM - Software System - BOTTOMLINE TECHNOLOGIES (DE), INC.; pg. 727, pg. 1038

CREATES PRODUCTS FOR PEOPLE AGAINST DIRTY. - Slogan - METHOD PRODUCTS INC.; pg. 332, pg. 223

CREATINE - Nutritional Supplement - MAXIMUM HUMAN PERFORMANCE, INC.; pg. 1559, pg. 1065

CREATING A CLEANER, SAFER WORLD - Slogan - TENNANT COMPANY; pg. 1381, pg. 944

CREATING BASIC ELEMENTS FOR LIFE - Slogan - LYONDELLBASELL INDUSTRIES; pg. 980, pg. 1710

CREATING BETTER SOLUTIONS...NATURALLY - Tagline - MGP INGREDIENTS, INC.; pg. 877, pg. 714

CREATING COMMUNICATIONS SOLUTIONS - Tagline - TALK-A-PHONE CO.; pg. 481, pg. 638

CREATING CUSTOMERS FOR LIFE - Slogan - PAUL ARPIN VAN LINES, INC.; pg. 1919, pg. 1610

CREATING HEALTHIER LIVES - Slogan - SHAKLEE CORPORATION; pg. 1593, pg. 184

CREATING LASTING LIFESTYLES - Slogan - WCI COMMUNITIES, INC.; pg. 1118, pg. 414

CREATING SUPERIOR CARE THROUGH INNOVATION. - Tagline - ELECTROMED, INC.; pg. 1527, pg. 951

CREATING TECHNOLOGY THAT CREATES SOLUTIONS - Slogan - CREE INC.; pg. 631, pg. 1371

CREATING THE NEXT GENERATION OF WEALTH - Tagline - TIGRENT INC.; pg. 608, pg. 415

CREATING TOMMOROW TODAY - Tagline - CYTRX CORPORATION; pg. 1521, pg. 129

CREATING VALUE FROM SORBENT MINERALS - Tagline - OIL-DRI CORPORATION OF AMERICA; pg. 1480, pg. 586

CREATING VALUE THROUGH INNOVATION - Slogan - USA TECHNOLOGIES, INC.; pg. 815, pg. 1550

CREATION HOUSE - Book - CHARISMA MEDIA; pg. 1627, pg. 436

CREATIVE CARRYOUTS - Cups - SOLO CUP COMPANY; pg. 1469, pg. 625

CREATIVE COMPONENTS - Appetizers, Breaded Portions, Stuffed & Marinated Products - CLEAR SPRINGS FOODS, INC.; *pg.* 848, *pg.* 548
CREATIVE EXPRESSIONS - Specialty Products - RESTONIC MATTRESS CORPORATION; *pg.* 941, *pg.* 553
CREATIVE EXPRESSIONS - Paper Party Goods - SOLO CUP COMPANY; *pg.* 1469, *pg.* 625
THE CREATIVE GROUP - Marketing, Web & Creative Professional Staffing - ROBERT HALF INTERNATIONAL INC.; *pg.* 462, *pg.* 145
CREATIVE IDEAS FOR HOME AND GARDEN - Home Improvement Ideas - LOWE'S COMPANIES, INC.; *pg.* 1053, *pg.* 1383
CREATIVE LEARNER - Educational Aids - PACON CORPORATION; *pg.* 1466, *pg.* 1852
CREATIVE PAPERS - Stationery, Gift Wrap, Greeting Cards, Playing Cards - C.R. GIBSON, LLC; *pg.* 1631, *pg.* 1650
CREATIVE SOLUTIONS - Legal Publications - THOMSON REUTERS CORPORATION; *pg.* 1693, *pg.* 1944
CREATIVE SOLUTIONS FOR THE DIGITAL LIFE. - Slogan - ACTIONTEC ELECTRONICS, INC.; *pg.* 342, *pg.* 282
CREATIVE SPACES - Furniture - ASHLEY FURNITURE INDUSTRIES, INC.; *pg.* 914, *pg.* 1852
CREATIVE SPINE TECHNOLOGY - Slogan - NUVASIVE, INC.; *pg.* 1577, *pg.* 205
CREATIVITY - Trade Magazine - CRAIN COMMUNICATIONS, INC.; *pg.* 1631, *pg.* 879
CREDIT CAPACITY INDEX - Predictive Measure - FAIR ISAAC CORPORATION; *pg.* 1247, *pg.* 955
CREDIT RANKINGS - Software - EQUIFAX INC.; *pg.* 748, *pg.* 504
CREDIT REPORT - Software - EQUIFAX INC.; *pg.* 748, *pg.* 504
CREDIT UNION - Magazine - CREDIT UNION NATIONAL ASSOCIATION; *pg.* 138, *pg.* 1865
CREDIT UNION DIRECTORS - Newsletter - CREDIT UNION NATIONAL ASSOCIATION; *pg.* 138, *pg.* 1865
CREDIT UNION FRONT LINE - Newsletter - CREDIT UNION NATIONAL ASSOCIATION; *pg.* 138, *pg.* 1865
CREDIT WATCH - Software - EQUIFAX INC.; *pg.* 748, *pg.* 504
CREDIT WORKS - Financial Services - FEDERAL HOME LOAN MORTGAGE CORPORATION; *pg.* 751, *pg.* 1790
CREDITDESK - Software System - FAIR ISAAC CORPORATION; *pg.* 1247, *pg.* 955
CREDITGARD - Services Provided for Card Holders - AMERICAN AUTOMOBILE ASSOCIATION; *pg.* 1190, *pg.* 429
CREDITMODEL - Credit Scoring Tool - STANDARD & POOR'S RATINGS SERVICES; *pg.* 805, *pg.* 1296
CREDIT.NET - Business Reports - INFOGROUP INC.; *pg.* 1652, *pg.* 1016
CREDITPRO - Credit Tables - STANDARD & POOR'S RATINGS SERVICES; *pg.* 805, *pg.* 1296
CREDITWEEK - Weekly Global Credit Markets Analysis - STANDARD & POOR'S RATINGS SERVICES; *pg.* 805, *pg.* 1296
CREDITWIRE - Real-Time Ratings - STANDARD & POOR'S RATINGS SERVICES; *pg.* 805, *pg.* 1296
CREDITWIRE JAPAN - Credit Ratings Analysis Japanese Version - STANDARD & POOR'S RATINGS SERVICES; *pg.* 805, *pg.* 1296
CREE LED LIGHT - LED - CREE INC.; *pg.* 631, *pg.* 1371
CREE LED LIGHTING SOLUTIONS - LED - CREE INC.; *pg.* 631, *pg.* 1371
CREE LED SOLUTION PROVIDER - LED - CREE INC.; *pg.* 631, *pg.* 1371
CREE LEDS - LED - CREE INC.; *pg.* 631, *pg.* 1371
CREE LIGHTING - LED Lighting - CREE INC.; *pg.* 631, *pg.* 1371
CREEDD - Footwear - STEVEN MADDEN, LTD.; *pg.* 1819, *pg.* 1176
CREEMORE SPRINGS - Lager - MOLSON COORS BREWING COMPANY; *pg.* 256, *pg.* 321
CREEPY CRAWLERS - Toys & Leisure Product - JAKKS PACIFIC, INC.; *pg.* 960, *pg.* 142
CREEPY CRAWLY CASH - Lottery Game - WEST VIRGINIA LOTTERY; *pg.* 1011, *pg.* 1849
CREMA OCCHI INTENSIVA - Skin Cream - BORGHESE, INC.; *pg.* 502, *pg.* 1205
CREMA RANCHERITO - Food Product - V&V SUPREMO FOODS, INC.; *pg.* 907, *pg.* 595
CREMA SUPREMO - Food Product - V&V SUPREMO FOODS, INC.; *pg.* 907, *pg.* 595
CREME BRULEE RISTRETTO - Coffee Beverage - THE SECOND CUP LTD.; *pg.* 1749, *pg.* 1928
CREME DE BRIE - Spreadable Brie Cheese - BONGRAIN NORTH AMERICA; *pg.* 841, *pg.* 1556
CREME EGG - Chocolates - THE HERSHEY CO.; *pg.* 1855, *pg.* 1538
CREME FRAICHE - Cooking Cream - BONGRAIN NORTH AMERICA; *pg.* 841, *pg.* 1556
CREME SAVERS - Candy - WM. WRIGLEY JR. COMPANY; *pg.* 1863, *pg.* 596
CREME STICKS - Donuts - ALFRED NICKLES BAKERY, INC.; *pg.* 836, *pg.* 1466
CREMOGEN - Fragrance - SYMRISE, INC.; *pg.* 1183, *pg.* 1125
CREMOL - Food Product - BUNGE LIMITED; *pg.* 842, *pg.* 1351
CREMORA - Non-Dairy Creamer - TREEHOUSE FOODS, INC.; *pg.* 901, *pg.* 649
CREMORIAL - Gate - MATTHEWS INTERNATIONAL CORPORATION; *pg.* 1662, *pg.* 1578
CREMOSA - Candy - SPANGLER CANDY COMPANY; *pg.* 1002, *pg.* 1407
CREO - Color Servers - EASTMAN KODAK COMPANY; *pg.* 1408, *pg.* 1333
CREOMULSION - Cough Medicines for Adults & Children - SUMMIT INDUSTRIES, INC.; *pg.* 1599, *pg.* 535
CREPEPLUS - Paper Creping Aids - GE WATER & PROCESS TECHNOLOGIES; *pg.* 1339, *pg.* 1588
CREPETROL - Creping Aids - HERCULES INCORPORATED; *pg.* 1166, *pg.* 392
CRES COR - Mobile Cooking Equipment - CHESHER EQUIPMENT LTD.; *pg.* 1323, *pg.* 1925
CRESCAT - Software - CRESTRON ELECTRONICS INC.; *pg.* 631, *pg.* 1116
CRESCENDO - Air Brush - BADGER AIR BRUSH COMPANY; *pg.* 359, *pg.* 612
CRESCENDO - Servingware for Buffets - CARLISLE FOODSERVICE PRODUCTS INCORPORATED; *pg.* 1455, *pg.* 1485
CRESCENDO - Paperboard Packaging Product - WESTROCK COMPANY; *pg.* 1472, *pg.* 1805
CRESCENDO - EMI Shielding - W.L. GORE & ASSOCIATES, INC.; *pg.* 122, *pg.* 388
CRESCENT - Instrument Table - BLICKMAN HEALTH INDUSTRIES, INC.; *pg.* 1506, *pg.* 1051
CRESCENT - Fan - CRAFTMADE INTERNATIONAL, INC.; *pg.* 1295, *pg.* 1670
THE CRESCENT - Naturaline Swing Set - CREATIVE PLAYTHINGS LTD.; *pg.* 1831, *pg.* 820
CRESCENT - Dental Product - DENTSPLY INTERNATIONAL INC.; *pg.* 1522, *pg.* 1596
CRESCENT - Lighting Fixture & Control - PHILIPS LIGHTING; *pg.* 1303, *pg.* 806
CRESCENT - Valves - THE WM. POWELL COMPANY; *pg.* 1389, *pg.* 1427
CRESCENT 1 PIECE - Lens - DANKER LABORATORIES INC.; *pg.* 1408, *pg.* 465
CRESCENT BOOKS - Publishing Imprint - PENGUIN RANDOM HOUSE; *pg.* 1675, *pg.* 1276
CRESCENT FUSED - Lens - DANKER LABORATORIES INC.; *pg.* 1408, *pg.* 465
CRESCENT OEM BOARD - Wireless Product - HEMISPHERE GPS INC.; *pg.* 642, *pg.* 1903
CRESCENT PRODUCTS - Line of Therapeutic Pillows - FEDERAL FOAM TECHNOLOGIES INC.; *pg.* 692, *pg.* 1884
CRESNET - Software - CRESTRON ELECTRONICS INC.; *pg.* 631, *pg.* 1116
CRESNET-TO-LUTRON - Interface - CRESTRON ELECTRONICS INC.; *pg.* 631, *pg.* 1116
CREST - Manufactured Homes - CLAYTON HOMES, INC.; *pg.* 1086, *pg.* 1640
CREST - Oral Care Products - THE PROCTER & GAMBLE COMPANY; *pg.* 1129, *pg.* 1418
CREST AUDIO - Professional Mixers Power Amps & Speakers - PEAVEY ELECTRONICS CORPORATION; *pg.* 662, *pg.* 970
CREST COLLECTION - Mattress - JAMISON BEDDING, INC.; *pg.* 930, *pg.* 1651
CREST GLIDE - Oral Care Product - THE PROCTER & GAMBLE COMPANY; *pg.* 1129, *pg.* 1418
CREST-KUT - Precision Cutting Tool - REGAL BELOIT CORPORATION; *pg.* 106, *pg.* 1854
CREST PRO-HEALTH - Oral Care Products - THE PROCTER & GAMBLE COMPANY; *pg.* 1129, *pg.* 1418
CREST WHITESTRIPS - Oral Care Products - THE PROCTER & GAMBLE COMPANY; *pg.* 1129, *pg.* 1418
CRESTA - Beverages - THE COCA-COLA COMPANY; *pg.* 240, *pg.* 493
CRESTED BUTTE - Ski Resort - CRESTED BUTTE MOUNTAIN RESORT, INC.; *pg.* 1088, *pg.* 316
CRESTON HOME - Software - CRESTRON ELECTRONICS INC.; *pg.* 631, *pg.* 1116
CRESTRON ENGRAVER - Software - CRESTRON ELECTRONICS INC.; *pg.* 631, *pg.* 1116
CRESTRON HOME - Software - CRESTRON ELECTRONICS INC.; *pg.* 631, *pg.* 1116
CRESTRON ROOMVIEW - Software - CRESTRON ELECTRONICS INC.; *pg.* 631, *pg.* 1116
CRESTRON SYSTEMBUILDER - Software - CRESTRON ELECTRONICS INC.; *pg.* 631, *pg.* 1116
CRETACEOUS - Fabric - NEMSCHOFF, INC.; *pg.* 936, *pg.* 1890
CRETE - Fabric - NEMSCHOFF, INC.; *pg.* 936, *pg.* 1890
CREUSLI - Cereal - THE QUAKER OATS COMPANY; *pg.* 834, *pg.* 588
CREW - Office Furniture - STEELCASE INC.; *pg.* 475, *pg.* 889
CREW GUEST - Office Furniture - STEELCASE INC.; *pg.* 475, *pg.* 889
CREWCUTS - Clothing - J. CREW GROUP, INC.; *pg.* 1773, *pg.* 1245
CREWEL - Pillow - ETHAN ALLEN INTERIORS INC.; *pg.* 924, *pg.* 343
CREWTALK - Toy Train - LIONEL LLC; *pg.* 961, *pg.* 875
CRFB SERIES - Floor Boxes - WIREMOLD/LEGRAND; *pg.* 689, *pg.* 383
CRIBBEAN BLISS - Video Game - INTERNATIONAL GAME TECHNOLOGY; *pg.* 957, *pg.* 1024
CRICKET - Leather Product - COACH, INC.; *pg.* 3, *pg.* 1214
CRICKET - Wireless Communication Product - CRICKET WIRELESS LLC; *pg.* 381, *pg.* 483
CRICKET - Industrial Safety Eyewear - UVEX SAFETY; *pg.* 1433, *pg.* 1608
CRICKET BROADBAND - Internet Service - CRICKET WIRELESS LLC; *pg.* 381, *pg.* 483
CRICKET LANE COLLECTION - Misses' & Women's Coordinates - KELLWOOD COMPANY; *pg.* 28, *pg.* 975
CRICKET PAYGO - Internet Service - CRICKET WIRELESS LLC; *pg.* 381, *pg.* 483
CRICKET WIRELESS - Internet Service - CRICKET WIRELESS LLC; *pg.* 381, *pg.* 483
CRICKET.COM - Advertising Website - LIVE CURRENT MEDIA INC.; *pg.* 1263, *pg.* 1911
CRIME FIGHTER - Car Part Accessory - PRO-LINE, INC.; *pg.* 966, *pg.* 45
CRIME SCENE INVESTIGATOR PCR BASICS - Software - BIO-RAD LABORATORIES, INC.; *pg.* 1504, *pg.* 101
THE CRIMPER - Crimping Tool - CHANNELLOCK, INC.; *pg.* 1044, *pg.* 1551
CRIMSON - Pillow and Throw - HERITAGE LACE INC.; *pg.* 694, *pg.* 711
CRIMSON CHECK - Pillow and Throw - HERITAGE LACE INC.; *pg.* 694, *pg.* 711
CRIMSON FIRE - Vehicles - SPARTAN MOTORS, INC.; *pg.* 217, *pg.* 874
CRIMSON JEWEL - Container Grown Plant - MONROVIA GROWERS; *pg.* 1797, *pg.* 44
CRIMSON TOPAZ - Bath Product - KOHLER CO.; *pg.* 91, *pg.* 1862
CRIMSON TRACE - Laser Grip - SMITH & WESSON HOLDING CORPORATION; *pg.* 1845, *pg.* 846
CRIMZON - Micrologic Semiconductor Device - ZILOG INC.; *pg.* 497, *pg.* 252
CRIMZON RC EXPRESS - Software - ZILOG INC.; *pg.* 497, *pg.* 252
CRINFORM - Supercomputing System - CRAY INC.; *pg.* 380, *pg.* 1834
CRINO - Powdered Milk - AGROPUR COOPERATIVE; *pg.* 836, *pg.* 1950
CRINONE - Pharmaceutical Product - JUNIPER PHARMACEUTICALS; *pg.* 1552, *pg.* 797
CRIS - Education Program - MAXIMUS, INC.; *pg.* 780, *pg.* 1799
CRISCO - Shortening - THE J.M. SMUCKER COMPANY; *pg.* 865, *pg.* 1468
CRISISLINK - Service - AT&T SOUTHEAST; *pg.* 1868, *pg.* 489
CRISP 'N CRACKLING RICE - Bag Cereal - POST CONSUMER BRANDS; *pg.* 833, *pg.* 927
CRISP 'N THIN CRUST - Pizza - HUNGRY HOWIE'S PIZZA &

First page reference indicates Business Class Edition
Second page reference indicates Geographic Edition

SUBS INC.; *pg.* 1023, *pg.* 897
CRISP-UMS - Baked Crisps - THE QUAKER OATS COMPANY; *pg.* 834, *pg.* 588
CRISPAC - Polypropylene Wrapping Film - SEALED AIR CORPORATION; *pg.* 1468, *pg.* 1058
CRISPANI - Bakery Product - PANERA BREAD COMPANY; *pg.* 1029, *pg.* 1001
CRISPERS - Restaurant - PUBLIX SUPER MARKETS, INC.; *pg.* 1031, *pg.* 437
CRISPITOS - Food Product - TYSON FOODS, INC.; *pg.* 902, *pg.* 35
CRISPIX - Food Product - KELLOGG COMPANY; *pg.* 831, *pg.* 870
CRISPY CURLS - Seasoned, Curled Fries - HARDEES FOOD SYSTEMS, INC.; *pg.* 1731, *pg.* 998
CRISPY 'N WHITE - Microwave Pop Corn - AMERICAN POP CORN COMPANY; *pg.* 825, *pg.* 712
CRISPY 'N WHITE LIGHT - Microwave Pop Corn - AMERICAN POP CORN COMPANY; *pg.* 825, *pg.* 712
CRISPYWRAP - Perforated Film - SEALED AIR CORPORATION; *pg.* 1468, *pg.* 1058
CRISS+CROSS - Directories - HAINES & COMPANY, INC.; *pg.* 1646, *pg.* 1468
CRISS+CROSS PLUS - Directory - HAINES & COMPANY, INC.; *pg.* 1646, *pg.* 1468
CRISSCROSS - Toothbrush - GILLETTE; *pg.* 1536, *pg.* 795
CRISSCUT - Diamonds - CHRISTOPHER DESIGNS, INC.; *pg.* 3, *pg.* 1212
CRISTAL - Beverages - THE COCA-COLA COMPANY; *pg.* 240, *pg.* 493
CRISTAL - Furniture - ETHAN ALLEN INTERIORS INC.; *pg.* 924, *pg.* 343
CRISTOBAL - Salt Fish - CANADIAN FISH EXPORTERS, INC.; *pg.* 845, *pg.* 784
CRISTOBAL - Dental Product - DENTSPLY INTERNATIONAL INC.; *pg.* 1522, *pg.* 1596
CRIT-KLENZ - Detergent - STERIS CORPORATION; *pg.* 1597, *pg.* 1464
CRITCHLEY - Electronic Component Product - TE CONNECTIVITY LTD.; *pg.* 677, *pg.* 1515
CRITEC - Surge Protection Device - ERICO INTERNATIONAL CORPORATION; *pg.* 1335, *pg.* 1472
CRITERION - Software - BIO-RAD LABORATORIES, INC.; *pg.* 1504, *pg.* 101
CRITERION - Online Writing Evaluation - EDUCATIONAL TESTING SERVICE INC.; *pg.* 1394, *pg.* 1111
CRITERION - Office Furniture - STEELCASE INC.; *pg.* 475, *pg.* 889
CRITERION PLUS - Task Seating - STEELCASE INC.; *pg.* 475, *pg.* 889
CRITERION STAIN FREE - Software - BIO-RAD LABORATORIES, INC.; *pg.* 1504, *pg.* 101
CRITIC - Software - SYNOPSYS, INC.; *pg.* 480, *pg.* 162
CRITICAL CARE - Hardware Services - DELL INC.; *pg.* 383, *pg.* 1737
CRITICAL CARE NUTRITIONALS - Nutritional Supplements for Critical Care Patients - MEAD JOHNSON NUTRITION COMPANY; *pg.* 1561, *pg.* 615
CRITICAL CARE THERAPIES - Therapy System - KINETIC CONCEPTS, INC.; *pg.* 1553, *pg.* 1741
THE CRITICAL COMMUNICATOR - Functional Communication - ALIMED, INC.; *pg.* 1490, *pg.* 816
CRITICAL KETO-NUTRIENTS - Nutritional Supplement - NATURAL ORGANICS, INC.; *pg.* 1571, *pg.* 1181
CRITICS CHOICE - Carpet - BEAULIEU GROUP, LLC; *pg.* 917, *pg.* 529
CRITSPIN - Microhematocrit System - IRIS INTERNATIONAL, INC.; *pg.* 1547, *pg.* 64
CRITTERLAND ADVENTURES - Educational Materials - SCHOLASTIC INC.; *pg.* 1683, *pg.* 1288
CRITTERS - Children's Scissors - ACME UNITED CORPORATION; *pg.* 1040, *pg.* 346
CRITTERS USA - Magazine - I-5 PUBLISHING LLC; *pg.* 1651, *pg.* 133
CRIZAL - Anti Reflective Coating - ICARE INDUSTRIES, INC.; *pg.* 1417, *pg.* 463
CRMS - Software - MCKESSON CORPORATION; *pg.* 1560, *pg.* 222
CROCHET WORLD - Crafts Magazine - ANNIE'S; *pg.* 1617, *pg.* 673
CROCK POT - Cooking Appliances - JARDEN CONSUMER SOLUTIONS; *pg.* 57, *pg.* 412
CROCODILE CASH - Game - WMS INDUSTRIES INC.; *pg.* 593, *pg.* 666
CROCODILE DENTIST - Toy & Game - HASBRO, INC.; *pg.* 954, *pg.* 1603
CROCODILE DENTIST - Game - WINNING MOVES GAMES, INC.; *pg.* 970, *pg.* 816
CROCS - Footwear - CROCS, INC.; *pg.* 1806, *pg.* 335
CROCS RX CUSTOM CLOUD - Healthcare Product - MEDICOOL, INC.; *pg.* 1562, *pg.* 294
CROCS RX SILVER CLOUDS - Healthcare Product - MEDICOOL, INC.; *pg.* 1562, *pg.* 294
CROCSKIN - Glove - LAKELAND INDUSTRIES, INC.; *pg.* 1354, *pg.* 1338
CROCSKINS - Gloves - LAKELAND INDUSTRIES, INC.; *pg.* 1354, *pg.* 1338
CROCSRX - Footwear - CROCS, INC.; *pg.* 1806, *pg.* 335
CROCUS - Fabric - NEMSCHOFF, INC.; *pg.* 936, *pg.* 1890
THE CROFTON NEWS-CRIER - Newspaper - CAPITAL GAZETTE COMMUNICATIONS INC.; *pg.* 1625, *pg.* 754
CROISSAN'WICH - Sandwich - BURGER KING CORPORATION; *pg.* 1719, *pg.* 440
CROM & CRUTHERS - Men's Shaving Oil - ALVA/AMCO PHARMACAL COMPANIES, INC.; *pg.* 1492, *pg.* 637
CROMACHECK - Color Proofing System for Pictures - E.I. DU PONT DE NEMOURS & COMPANY; *pg.* 1159, *pg.* 390
CROMALIN - Color Proofing System - E.I. DU PONT DE NEMOURS & COMPANY; *pg.* 1159, *pg.* 390
CROMANET - Color Management System - E.I. DU PONT DE NEMOURS & COMPANY; *pg.* 1159, *pg.* 390
CROMAPRINT - UV Digital Printing System - E.I. DU PONT DE NEMOURS & COMPANY; *pg.* 1159, *pg.* 390
CROMAPRO - Inkjet Proofing System - E.I. DU PONT DE NEMOURS & COMPANY; *pg.* 1159, *pg.* 390
CROMAX - Basecoat Paint System - E.I. DU PONT DE NEMOURS & COMPANY; *pg.* 1159, *pg.* 390
CROMAX PRO - Paint System - E.I. DU PONT DE NEMOURS & COMPANY; *pg.* 1159, *pg.* 390
CROMOMAN - Press - MANROLAND INC.; *pg.* 430, *pg.* 669
CROMWELL - Table - BLATT BOWLING & BILLIARD CORP.; *pg.* 1827, *pg.* 1203
CROMWELL - Furniture - ETHAN ALLEN INTERIORS INC.; *pg.* 924, *pg.* 343
CROMYLITE - Chemical Coating - ENTHONE INC.; *pg.* 1161, *pg.* 381
CRONAR - Film - E.I. DU PONT DE NEMOURS & COMPANY; *pg.* 1159, *pg.* 390
CRONUS - Magnetic Coronary Guidewire - STEREOTAXIS, INC.; *pg.* 1597, *pg.* 1004
CROOKED CREEK - Shirts - ABERCROMBIE & FITCH CO.; *pg.* 37, *pg.* 1466
CROP COVER WITH DUPONT XAVAN - Crop Protection System - E.I. DU PONT DE NEMOURS & COMPANY; *pg.* 1159, *pg.* 390
CROP PROCESSOR - Forage Harvest System - GEHL COMPANY; *pg.* 1339, *pg.* 1899
CROP SURF - Oil Concentrate - UNIVERSAL COOPERATIVES, INC.; *pg.* 1482, *pg.* 922
CROPLAN GENETICS - Crop Seed - LAND O'LAKES, INC.; *pg.* 873, *pg.* 915
CROPPER CLASSIC - Cropper Guitar - PEAVEY ELECTRONICS CORPORATION; *pg.* 662, *pg.* 970
CROQUET - Textiles - BERNHARDT DESIGN; *pg.* 918, *pg.* 1381
CROQUET - Fabric - NEMSCHOFF, INC.; *pg.* 936, *pg.* 1890
CROQUET - Surface Material - STEELCASE INC.; *pg.* 475, *pg.* 889
CROSCILL - Home Fashions - CROSCILL, INC.; *pg.* 1122, *pg.* 1220
CROSMAN - Air Rifles & Guns - CROSMAN CORPORATION; *pg.* 951, *pg.* 1143
CROSMAN SEED - Flower & Vegetable Packet Seeds - CROSMAN SEED CORPORATION; *pg.* 1794, *pg.* 1156
CROSS - Bookmark - HERITAGE LACE INC.; *pg.* 694, *pg.* 711
CROSS BAR - Furniture - HSM SOLUTIONS; *pg.* 1884, *pg.* 1378
CROSS CHECK - Dresses & Sets - HABAND COMPANY, INC.; *pg.* 1772, *pg.* 1099
CROSS CHECKED - Fast-Paced Trivia Game Devoted to Hockey - NTN BUZZTIME, INC.; *pg.* 659, *pg.* 60
CROSS COUNTRY - Internal Frame Carrier - EVENFLO COMPANY, INC.; *pg.* 924, *pg.* 1470
CROSS COUNTRY 1.0 - Bicycles - G. JOANNOU CYCLE CO. INC.; *pg.* 1707, *pg.* 1098
CROSS COUNTRY 2.0 - Bicycles - G. JOANNOU CYCLE CO. INC.; *pg.* 1707, *pg.* 1098
CROSS-CUT - Nozzle - NORDSON CORPORATION; *pg.* 1365, *pg.* 1480
CROSS FLOW - Recuperator - ECLIPSE INC.; *pg.* 1332, *pg.* 655
CROSS HATCH - Apparel - OAKLEY, INC.; *pg.* 1840, *pg.* 86
CROSS-PILOT - Excimer Laser System - THE SPECTRANETICS CORPORATION; *pg.* 1595, *pg.* 315
CROSS ROADS - Internal Frame Carrier - EVENFLO COMPANY, INC.; *pg.* 924, *pg.* 1470
CROSS STITCHER - Magazine - AMOS PRESS, INC.; *pg.* 1616, *pg.* 1472
CROSS-TERRAIN - Bicycle Design for Use On or Off Road - BIANCHI U.S.A., INC.; *pg.* 1827, *pg.* 100
CROSS TERRAIN - Internal Frame Carrier - EVENFLO COMPANY, INC.; *pg.* 924, *pg.* 1470
CROSS TOWNE - Footwear - PHOENIX FOOTWEAR GROUP, INC.; *pg.* 1815, *pg.* 60
CROSS YOUR HEART - Bra - PLAYTEX APPAREL, INC.; *pg.* 31, *pg.* 1395
CROSSACTION - Toothbrush - GILLETTE; *pg.* 1536, *pg.* 795
CROSSACTION - Dental Hygiene Product - THE GILLETTE COMPANY; *pg.* 509, *pg.* 795
CROSSBOW - Connector System - AMPHENOL CORPORATION; *pg.* 616, *pg.* 381
CROSSCARDS.COM - Online Greeting Cards - SALEM MEDIA GROUP, INC.; *pg.* 307, *pg.* 57
CROSSCHECK - Navigation Aid - TRIMBLE NAVIGATION LIMITED; *pg.* 1384, *pg.* 288
CROSSCODE - Software - WIND RIVER SYSTEMS, INC.; *pg.* 493, *pg.* 38
CROSSCOUNTRY EDUCATION - Training Services - CROSS COUNTRY HEALTHCARE, INC.; *pg.* 1520, *pg.* 411
CROSSCOUNTRY LOCAL - Staffing Services - CROSS COUNTRY HEALTHCARE, INC.; *pg.* 1520, *pg.* 411
CROSSCOUNTRY STAFFING - Staffing Services - CROSS COUNTRY HEALTHCARE, INC.; *pg.* 1520, *pg.* 411
CROSSDAILY.COM - Online Christian Community - SALEM MEDIA GROUP, INC.; *pg.* 307, *pg.* 57
CROSSE & BLACKWELL - Food Products - THE J.M. SMUCKER COMPANY; *pg.* 865, *pg.* 1468
CROSSED - Apparel - OAKLEY, INC.; *pg.* 1840, *pg.* 86
CROSSFIRE - Chipset - ADVANCED MICRO DEVICES, INC.; *pg.* 613, *pg.* 282
CROSSFIRE - Snowmobile - ARCTIC CAT INC.; *pg.* 1705, *pg.* 953
CROSSFIRE - Racket String - ASHAWAY LINE & TWINE MFG. CO.; *pg.* 1826, *pg.* 1600
CROSSFIRE - Freshwater Spinning Reels - DAIWA CORPORATION; *pg.* 1832, *pg.* 75
CROSSFIRE - Medical Equipment - INVACARE CORPORATION; *pg.* 1546, *pg.* 1451
CROSSFIRE - Burner - MAXON CORPORATION; *pg.* 1359, *pg.* 695
CROSSFIRE - Orthopaedic Product - STRYKER CORPORATION; *pg.* 1598, *pg.* 894
CROSSFIRE - Computerized Facility Automation & Alarm System - TYCO SIMPLEXGRINNELL LP; *pg.* 682, *pg.* 859
CROSSFIRE MONOGUT - String - ASHAWAY LINE & TWINE MFG. CO.; *pg.* 1826, *pg.* 1600
CROSSFIRES - Food Product - TYSON FOODS, INC.; *pg.* 902, *pg.* 35
CROSSHAIR - Eyewear - OAKLEY, INC.; *pg.* 1840, *pg.* 86
CROSSINGS - Mobile Furniture - HAWORTH, INC.; *pg.* 402, *pg.* 891
CROSSINGS - Casual Clothing - PERRY ELLIS INTERNATIONAL, INC.; *pg.* 45, *pg.* 445
CROSSLAND ECONOMY STUDIOS - Hotel - EXTENDED STAY HOTELS LLC; *pg.* 1091, *pg.* 1622
CROSSLOCK - New DBL or Single Locking Folding Knife - BUCK KNIVES, INC.; *pg.* 1828, *pg.* 550
CROSSOVER - LED Lighting - LSI INDUSTRIES INC.; *pg.* 58, *pg.* 1416
CROSSPASS - Memory Card - SANDISK CORPORATION; *pg.* 465, *pg.* 147
CROSSPATCH - Fabric - NEMSCHOFF, INC.; *pg.* 936, *pg.* 1890
CROSSPOINT - Medical Product - MEDTRONIC, INC.; *pg.* 1564, *pg.* 939
CROSSROADS - Bicycle Tire - SPECIALIZED BICYCLE COMPONENTS, INC.; *pg.* 1711, *pg.* 152
CROSSTALK - Furniture - ASHLEY FURNITURE INDUSTRIES, INC.; *pg.* 914, *pg.* 1852
CROSSTECH - Outerwear - BLAUER MANUFACTURING COMPANY, INC.; *pg.* 20, *pg.* 789
CROSSTECH - Fabric - W.L. GORE & ASSOCIATES, INC.; *pg.* 122, *pg.* 388
CROSSTIMBERS - Decking Products - GAF MATERIALS

CORP.; pg. 83, pg. 1681
CROSSTOWN - Fabric - NEMSCHOFF, INC.; pg. 936, pg. 1890
CROSSTOWN - Women's Clothing & Accessories - WOODEN SHIPS OF HOBOKEN; pg. 35, pg. 1315
CROSSWALK - Supply Charge Solutions - MEDASSETS INC.; pg. 1561, pg. 484
CROSSWALK.COM - Online Biblically Based Content - SALEM MEDIA GROUP, INC.; pg. 307, pg. 57
CROSSWIND - Software - WIND RIVER SYSTEMS, INC.; pg. 493, pg. 38
CROSSWORD - Game - MISSOURI LOTTERY; pg. 999, pg. 979
CROSSWORDS - Online Game - PROGRAM PARTNERS, INC.; pg. 305, pg. 301
CROSSZYME - Cleaning Solution - CROSSTEX INTERNATIONAL INC.; pg. 1520, pg. 1164
CROWBAR - Goggle - OAKLEY, INC.; pg. 1840, pg. 86
CROWD PLEAZER - Car Part Accessory - PRO-LINE, INC.; pg. 966, pg. 45
CROWN - Paint & Coating - AERVOE INDUSTRIES INCORPORATED; pg. 1439, pg. 1021
CROWN - Petroleum Products - CROWN CENTRAL LLC; pg. 975, pg. 756
CROWN - Loudspeakers & Electronic Equipment - HARMAN INTERNATIONAL INDUSTRIES, INCORPORATED; pg. 641, pg. 374
CROWN - Door - MASONITE INTERNATIONAL CORPORATION; pg. 1054, pg. 1920
CROWN - Fabric - NEMSCHOFF, INC.; pg. 936, pg. 1890
CROWN - Plumbing Product - SLOAN VALVE COMPANY; pg. 1062, pg. 613
CROWN - Right Angle Drives - ZERO-MAX, INC.; pg. 222, pg. 954
CROWN CHILDREN'S BOOKS - Publishing Imprint - PENGUIN RANDOM HOUSE CHILDREN'S BOOKS; pg. 1676, pg. 1277
CROWN COLLECTION - Sauce - GORDON FOOD SERVICE INC.; pg. 1021, pg. 913
CROWN COLLECTION - Mattress & Box Spring - KINGSDOWN, INC.; pg. 932, pg. 1383
CROWN COMFORT - Mattress & Box Spring Sets - KINGSDOWN, INC.; pg. 932, pg. 1383
CROWN CUT - Bevel Product - GLEASON CORPORATION; pg. 1340, pg. 1335
CROWN DEVICE - Paint And Stain Product - BENJAMIN MOORE & CO.; pg. 1440, pg. 1085
CROWN DIAMOND - Consumer Products - AKZO NOBEL; pg. 1439, pg. 1952
CROWN II - Fly Reel - CORTLAND LINE COMPANY; pg. 1831, pg. 1155
CROWN II - Flushometer - SLOAN VALVE COMPANY; pg. 1062, pg. 613
CROWN IMPERIAL - Mattresses & Box Springs - KINGSDOWN, INC.; pg. 932, pg. 1383
THE CROWN JEWEL - Paint - PRATT & LAMBERT PAINTS; pg. 1446, pg. 1434
CROWN NEOLITE - Soles & Heels - THE GOODYEAR TIRE & RUBBER COMPANY; pg. 1883, pg. 1401
CROWN OF EGYPT - Video Game - INTERNATIONAL GAME TECHNOLOGY; pg. 957, pg. 1024
THE CROWN OF EXCELLENCE - Tagline - AMINCO INTERNATIONAL (USA) INC.; pg. 1, pg. 120
CROWN PRINCE - Canned Seafood - CROWN PRINCE, INC.; pg. 850, pg. 67
CROWN PUNCH - Can Openers - EDLUND COMPANY, INC.; pg. 1123, pg. 1765
CROWN ROYAL - Canadian Whisky - DIAGEO CANADA, INC.; pg. 1961, pg. 1937
CROWN ROYAL - Whisky - DIAGEO NORTH AMERICA, INC.; pg. 1961, pg. 361
CROWN ROYAL RESERVE - Whisky - DIAGEO CANADA, INC.; pg. 1961, pg. 1937
CROWN RUSSE - Vodka & Gin - SAZERAC COMPANY, INC.; pg. 1969, pg. 745
CROWN SPOT - Commercial Lighting - SWIVELIER CO., INC.; pg. 1307, pg. 1142
CROWN THIN BOILING - Acid-Modified Corn Starches - PENFORD CORPORATION; pg. 1177, pg. 314
CROWN VICTORIA - Automobile - FORD MOTOR COMPANY; pg. 172, pg. 876
CROWN WINDSOR - Shoes - CLARKS COMPANIES; pg. 1806, pg. 836
CROWNE PLAZA - Hotels & Resorts - INTERCONTINENTAL HOTELS CORPORATION; pg. 1097, pg. 511
CROXLEY - Toy & Game - HASBRO, INC.; pg. 954, pg. 1603
CRS-WRAP - Cryogenic Product - LYDALL, INC.; pg. 1357, pg. 354
CRUCIAL - Brand - CRUCIAL TECHNOLOGY DIV OF MICRON; pg. 1237, pg. 550
CRUCIAL - Memory Product - MICRON TECHNOLOGY, INC.; pg. 435, pg. 547
CRUCIAL - Nutrition Supplement - NESTLE USA, INC.; pg. 883, pg. 96
CRUCIAL TECHNOLOGY - Hardware - MICRON TECHNOLOGY, INC.; pg. 435, pg. 547
CRUESLI - Cereal - PEPSICO, INC.; pg. 259, pg. 1327
CRUISAIR - Suitcase - SAMSONITE CORPORATION; pg. 11, pg. 830
CRUISE - Shirt - CORTLAND LINE COMPANY; pg. 1831, pg. 1155
CRUISE CONTROL - Pump Product - IDEX CORPORATION; pg. 1347, pg. 623
CRUISE CONTROL - Filtering Device - STAAR SURGICAL COMPANY; pg. 1597, pg. 151
CRUISE HOLIDAYS - Cruise Travel - CARLSON COMPANIES INC.; pg. 1084, pg. 947
CRUISE PAL - Accessories - MARLOW-HUNTER LLC; pg. 1709, pg. 409
CRUISE SEMINARS - Trade Seminars - INVESTMENT SEMINARS, INC.; pg. 420, pg. 466
CRUISE, TOUR & TRAVEL - Travel Insurance - TRAVEL GUARD GROUP, INC.; pg. 1925, pg. 1895
CRUISELINER - Bicycle - TREK BICYCLE CORPORATION; pg. 1847, pg. 1896
CRUISEONE - Cruise Franchise - WORLD TRAVEL HOLDINGS; pg. 1931, pg. 860
CRUISER - Medical Equipment - INVACARE CORPORATION; pg. 1546, pg. 1451
CRUISER CLASSIC - Bicycle - TREK BICYCLE CORPORATION; pg. 1847, pg. 1896
CRUISER MOVER - Cup - PACTIV CORPORATION; pg. 1466, pg. 624
CRUISERALLOY - Custom Wheels - AMERICAN TIRE DISTRIBUTORS HOLDINGS, INC.; pg. 199, pg. 1379
CRUISERS - Yacht - KCS INTERNATIONAL, INC.; pg. 556, pg. 1885
CRUISIN' CASH - Lottery Game - NEW YORK STATE LOTTERY; pg. 1001, pg. 1340
CRUISING WORLD - Magazine - BONNIER CORPORATION; pg. 1622, pg. 480
CRUJITOS - Corn Snack - FRITO-LAY NORTH AMERICA, INC.; pg. 1853, pg. 1730
CRUJITOS - Corn Snacks - PEPSICO, INC.; pg. 259, pg. 1327
CRUNCH - Cutting Tool - LEATHERMAN TOOL GROUP, INC.; pg. 1053, pg. 1504
CRUNCH FITNESS - Fitness Equipment - BALLY TOTAL FITNESS HOLDINGS CORPORATION; pg. 532, pg. 1200
CRUNCH 'N MUNCH - Food Product - CONAGRA FOODS, INC.; pg. 826, pg. 1014
CRUNCHEROS - Mexican Food - RUIZ FOOD PRODUCTS, INC.; pg. 893, pg. 77
CRUNCHY TACO - Tacos - TACO BELL CORP.; pg. 1752, pg. 117
CRUNCHY TACO SUPREME - Tacos - TACO BELL CORP.; pg. 1752, pg. 117
CRUNKTASTICAL - Urban Music & Entertainment News Site - SPINMEDIA; pg. 1282, pg. 104
CRUSADER - Seating Product - IRWIN SEATING COMPANY INC.; pg. 929, pg. 887
CRUSADER - Detergent - SWISHER HYGIENE INC.; pg. 336, pg. 1507
CRUSADER - Ceiling Fan - WESTINGHOUSE LIGHTING CORPORATION; pg. 687, pg. 1571
CRUSH - Beverages - THE COCA-COLA COMPANY; pg. 240, pg. 493
CRUSH - Carbonated Soft Drink - DR PEPPER SNAPPLE GROUP, INC.; pg. 250, pg. 1729
CRUSH - Watch - OAKLEY, INC.; pg. 1840, pg. 86
CRUSH 2.0 - Watch - OAKLEY, INC.; pg. 1840, pg. 86
CRUSHABLE.COM - Website - DEFYMEDIA; pg. 1237, pg. 1222
CRUSHED CAN - Office Furniture - STEELCASE INC.; pg. 475, pg. 889
CRUSTANO'S - Cafe - TYSON FOODS, INC.; pg. 902, pg. 35
CRUTCH-MATE - Medical & Aesthetic Product - DYNATRONICS CORPORATION; pg. 1526, pg. 1757
CRUZCONTROL - Automatic Conveyor System - PARAGON TECHNOLOGIES, INC.; pg. 1367, pg. 1528
CRUZER - USB Flash Drive - SANDISK CORPORATION; pg. 465, pg. 147
CRUZER CONTOUR - Flash Drive - SANDISK CORPORATION; pg. 465, pg. 147
CRUZER CROSSFIRE - Memory Card - SANDISK CORPORATION; pg. 465, pg. 147
CRUZER FLEUR - Memory Card - SANDISK CORPORATION; pg. 465, pg. 147
CRUZER FREEDOM - Flash Drive - SANDISK CORPORATION; pg. 465, pg. 147
CRUZER SPECTRUM - Flash Drive - SANDISK CORPORATION; pg. 465, pg. 147
CRUZERLOCK - USB Flash Drive - SANDISK CORPORATION; pg. 465, pg. 147
CRUZERLOGIN - Flash Drive - SANDISK CORPORATION; pg. 465, pg. 147
CRUZERSYNC - Software - SANDISK CORPORATION; pg. 465, pg. 147
CRX - Carbon Black - CABOT CORPORATION; pg. 1151, pg. 792
CRX - Battery Technology - TECK RESOURCES LIMITED; pg. 1183, pg. 1912
CRY BABY - Chewing Gum - TOOTSIE ROLL INDUSTRIES, INC.; pg. 1863, pg. 591
CRYLCOAT - Polyester Resins - CYTEC INDUSTRIES, INC.; pg. 1155, pg. 1131
CRYO-CONDAP - Chemical Products - AIR PRODUCTS AND CHEMICALS, INC.; pg. 1145, pg. 1513
CRYO-CYL - Cryogenic Product - CHART INDUSTRIES, INC.; pg. 1405, pg. 1454
CRYO-GRIND - Recycling Process - AIR PRODUCTS AND CHEMICALS, INC.; pg. 1145, pg. 1513
CRYO-HISTOMAT - Microtome - HACKER INSTRUMENTS & INDUSTRIES INC.; pg. 1415, pg. 1623
CRYO-LITE - Cryogenic Product - LYDALL, INC.; pg. 1357, pg. 354
CRYO-QUICK - Food Freezers - AIR PRODUCTS AND CHEMICALS, INC.; pg. 1145, pg. 1513
CRYO-SURG - Nitrogen Delivery System - THE COOPER COMPANIES, INC.; pg. 1518, pg. 183
CRYO-TORR - Pump System - BROOKS AUTOMATION, INC.; pg. 1320, pg. 813
CRYOARTERY - Tissue Preservation System - CRYOLIFE, INC.; pg. 1520, pg. 534
CRYOCIDE - Disinfectant - E.I. DU PONT DE NEMOURS & COMPANY; pg. 1159, pg. 390
CRYOCYTE - Freezing Container - BAXTER INTERNATIONAL INC.; pg. 1499, pg. 599
CRYOFLEX - Labeling - FLEXCON CORPORATION; pg. 1457, pg. 844
CRYOGENIC - Probe - CASCADE MICROTECH, INC.; pg. 1405, pg. 1492
CRYOGRAFT - Tissue Preservation System - CRYOLIFE, INC.; pg. 1520, pg. 534
CRYOKIDS - Foundation Established to Provide Children Access to Reconstructive Surgery - CRYOLIFE, INC.; pg. 1520, pg. 534
CRYOLIFE-O'BRIEN - Aortic Porcine Valve - CRYOLIFE, INC.; pg. 1520, pg. 534
CRYOLIFE-ROSS - Marked Porcine Stentless Heart Valve, Pulmonary - CRYOLIFE, INC.; pg. 1520, pg. 534
CRYOLITE - Packaging Film - SEALED AIR CORPORATION; pg. 1468, pg. 1058
CRYOPERM 10 - Shielding Alloy - AMUNEAL MANUFACTURING CORPORATION; pg. 617, pg. 1558
CRYOSORB - Sorbent Retainers - MULTISORB TECHNOLOGIES, INC.; pg. 1570, pg. 1150
CRYOTHERM - Cryogenic Product - LYDALL, INC.; pg. 1357, pg. 354
CRYOVAC - Packaging Product - SEALED AIR CORPORATION; pg. 1468, pg. 1058
CRYOVAC BARRIER BAG - Oxygen Barrier Vacuum Shrink Bags - SEALED AIR CORPORATION; pg. 1468, pg. 1058
CRYOVAC BDF - Oxygen Barrier Shrink Films - SEALED AIR CORPORATION; pg. 1468, pg. 1058
CRYOVAC CASE READY - Packaging Systems for Centrally Packaged Fresh Meats - SEALED AIR CORPORATION; pg. 1468, pg. 1058
CRYOVAC MARKET-READY - Packaging Materials & Equipment - SEALED AIR CORPORATION; pg. 1468, pg. 1058
CRYOVAC OSB - Specialty Packaging Materials & Systems - SEALED AIR CORPORATION; pg. 1468, pg. 1058
CRYOVAC PIZZAFRESH - Packaging Materials - SEALED

First page reference indicates Business Class Edition
Second page reference indicates Geographic Edition

AIR CORPORATION; *pg.* 1468, *pg.* 1058
CRYOVAC ROBOLOADER - Packaging System - SEALED AIR CORPORATION; *pg.* 1468, *pg.* 1058
CRYOVAC SLICEPAK - Packaging Materials for Food Products - SEALED AIR CORPORATION; *pg.* 1468, *pg.* 1058
CRYOVALVE - Tissue Preservation System - CRYOLIFE, INC.; *pg.* 1520, *pg.* 534
CRYOVEIN - Tissue Preservation System - CRYOLIFE, INC.; *pg.* 1520, *pg.* 534
CRYPTELE - Telecommunication Product - ITUS CORPORATION; *pg.* 422, *pg.* 1180
CRYPTIC - Apparel - OAKLEY, INC.; *pg.* 1840, *pg.* 86
CRYPTO - Software - CERTICOM CORP.; *pg.* 371, *pg.* 1925
CRYPTO-LA - Pharmaceutical Product - ALERE INC.; *pg.* 1488, *pg.* 849
CRYPTOAUTHENTICATION - Integrated Circuit - ATMEL CORPORATION; *pg.* 621, *pg.* 238
CRYPTOCOMPANION - Embedded Security System - ATMEL CORPORATION; *pg.* 621, *pg.* 238
CRYPTOCONNECT ENCRYPTION TRANSPORT SYSTEM - Legacy System Encrypter Compatible with Unisys & IBM Mainframes - ATTACHMATE CORPORATION; *pg.* 356, *pg.* 1833
CRYPTOCONTROLLER - Integrated Circuit - ATMEL CORPORATION; *pg.* 621, *pg.* 238
CRYPTOLYTE - Silicone Additive - SMOOTH-ON INC.; *pg.* 111, *pg.* 1528
CRYPTOMARK - Downloadable Digital Authentication - NOVELL INC.; *pg.* 446, *pg.* 852
CRYPTOMEMORY - Secure Memory - ATMEL CORPORATION; *pg.* 621, *pg.* 238
CRYPTON TWILL - Fabric - NEMSCHOFF, INC.; *pg.* 936, *pg.* 1890
CRYPTONETX - Computer Products - BROADCOM CORPORATION; *pg.* 364, *pg.* 108
CRYPTORF - Memory Product - ATMEL CORPORATION; *pg.* 621, *pg.* 238
CRYPTOTROL - Software - BIO-RAD LABORATORIES, INC.; *pg.* 1504, *pg.* 101
CRYSTACLEAR - Water White Lacquer 550 VOC - DUNN-EDWARDS CORPORATION; *pg.* 1442, *pg.* 129
CRYSTAL - Power Supply System - ADVANCED ENERGY INDUSTRIES, INC.; *pg.* 613, *pg.* 328
CRYSTAL - Furniture - AMISCO INDUSTRIES LTD.; *pg.* 913, *pg.* 1958
CRYSTAL - Audio Codecs - CIRRUS LOGIC, INC.; *pg.* 629, *pg.* 1661
CRYSTAL - Beverages - THE COCA-COLA COMPANY; *pg.* 240, *pg.* 493
CRYSTAL - Balloon - CONTINENTAL AMERICAN CORP.; *pg.* 1880, *pg.* 723
CRYSTAL - Glass Cleaner - SWISHER HYGIENE INC.; *pg.* 336, *pg.* 1507
CRYSTAL 73 - Lighting Glass - AGC GLASS NORTH AMERICA, INC.; *pg.* 65, *pg.* 482
CRYSTAL AROMA II - Room Freshener - ORECK CORPORATION; *pg.* 59, *pg.* 1653
CRYSTAL BAY - Soft Drink - NATIONAL BEVERAGE CORP.; *pg.* 257, *pg.* 425
CRYSTAL CALCIUM - Nutritional Product - NUTRACEUTICAL INTERNATIONAL CORPORATION; *pg.* 1576, *pg.* 1753
CRYSTAL CHECK - Needle-free Injection System - BIOJECT MEDICAL TECHNOLOGIES INC.; *pg.* 1506, *pg.* 1509
CRYSTAL CLEAN - Personal Care Product - COLGATE-PALMOLIVE COMPANY; *pg.* 504, *pg.* 1215
CRYSTAL CLEAR - Pregnancy Test Products - ALERE INC.; *pg.* 1488, *pg.* 849
CRYSTAL CLEAR - Bath Organizer - HOME PRODUCTS INTERNATIONAL, INC.; *pg.* 1125, *pg.* 577
CRYSTAL CLEAR - Clear Spray Coating - SHERWIN-WILLIAMS DIVERSIFIED BRANDS DIVISION; *pg.* 1448, *pg.* 1435
CRYSTAL CLEAR - Liquid Plastic - SMOOTH-ON INC.; *pg.* 111, *pg.* 1528
CRYSTAL CLEAR TAPE - Clear Adhesive Tape - MOORE PUSH PIN CO.; *pg.* 441, *pg.* 1595
CRYSTAL CLEAR TAPE & DISPENSER - Tape & Dispenser - MOORE PUSH PIN CO.; *pg.* 441, *pg.* 1595
CRYSTAL CRUISES - Luxury Cruise Line - CRYSTAL CRUISES LLC; *pg.* 1904, *pg.* 128
CRYSTAL CUT - Tray - PACTIV CORPORATION; *pg.* 1466, *pg.* 624
CRYSTAL FARMS - Refrigerated Grocery Products - MICHAEL FOODS, INC.; *pg.* 877, *pg.* 949
CRYSTAL FIVES - Slots - INTERNATIONAL GAME TECHNOLOGY; *pg.* 957, *pg.* 1024
CRYSTAL FIVES BONUS WHEEL - Slots - INTERNATIONAL GAME TECHNOLOGY; *pg.* 957, *pg.* 1024
CRYSTAL FOREST - Game - WMS INDUSTRIES INC.; *pg.* 593, *pg.* 666
CRYSTAL FORTUNES - Video Game - INTERNATIONAL GAME TECHNOLOGY; *pg.* 957, *pg.* 1024
CRYSTAL GEYSER - Sparkling Mineral Water - CRYSTAL GEYSER WATER COMPANY; *pg.* 248, *pg.* 57
CRYSTAL GROOVED SERIES - Collection - ODL INCORPORATED; *pg.* 101, *pg.* 914
CRYSTAL HARMONY - Cruise Ship - CRYSTAL CRUISES LLC; *pg.* 1904, *pg.* 128
CRYSTAL KINGDOM - Video Game - INTERNATIONAL GAME TECHNOLOGY; *pg.* 957, *pg.* 1024
CRYSTAL LAN - Ethernet Controller - CIRRUS LOGIC, INC.; *pg.* 629, *pg.* 1661
CRYSTAL LAURA - Fragrance - AVON PRODUCTS, INC.; *pg.* 500, *pg.* 1198
CRYSTAL LIGHT - Beverages - THE KRAFT HEINZ COMPANY; *pg.* 870, *pg.* 1577
CRYSTAL-PANE - Window Material - WARP BROTHERS; *pg.* 1471, *pg.* 595
CRYSTAL PLEAT - Window Shades - SPRINGS GLOBAL, INC.; *pg.* 698, *pg.* 1616
CRYSTAL POLYMER - Professional Wax - TURTLE WAX, INC.; *pg.* 220, *pg.* 671
CRYSTAL ROCK - Bottled Water - CRYSTAL ROCK HOLDINGS, INC.; *pg.* 248, *pg.* 382
CRYSTAL ROD FLOOR - Lamp - J. ROBERT SCOTT INC.; *pg.* 930, *pg.* 105
CRYSTAL ROSE - Video Game - INTERNATIONAL GAME TECHNOLOGY; *pg.* 957, *pg.* 1024
CRYSTAL SERENITY - Cruise Ship - CRYSTAL CRUISES LLC; *pg.* 1904, *pg.* 128
CRYSTAL SEVENS - Slots - INTERNATIONAL GAME TECHNOLOGY; *pg.* 957, *pg.* 1024
CRYSTAL SUGAR - Sugar - AMERICAN CRYSTAL SUGAR COMPANY; *pg.* 837, *pg.* 951
CRYSTAL SYMPHONY - Cruise Ship - CRYSTAL CRUISES LLC; *pg.* 1904, *pg.* 128
CRYSTAL VUE - Square Shaped Plastic Containers for Cakes - INLINE PLASTICS CORP.; *pg.* 1460, *pg.* 370
CRYSTALAS - Optical System - COHERENT, INC.; *pg.* 1406, *pg.* 265
CRYSTALBLAST - Sandblast Equipment - IKONICS CORPORATION; *pg.* 1168, *pg.* 921
CRYSTALGEL - Coating - ROSCO LABORATORIES, INC.; *pg.* 1782, *pg.* 378
CRYSTALINE - Electrosurgical Devices - ANGIODYNAMICS, INC.; *pg.* 1495, *pg.* 1173
CRYSTALITE - Polycarbonate Pitchers - CARLISLE FOODSERVICE PRODUCTS INCORPORATED; *pg.* 1455, *pg.* 1485
CRYSTALON - Tumblers - CARLISLE FOODSERVICE PRODUCTS INCORPORATED; *pg.* 1455, *pg.* 1485
CRYSTALPAK - Wafer Shipping Box - ENTEGRIS, INC.; *pg.* 1882, *pg.* 788
CRYSTALPLEAT - Cellular Shades - SPRINGS WINDOW FASHIONS LLC; *pg.* 943, *pg.* 1872
THE CRYSTALS AT CITYCENTER - Resort & Casino - MGM RESORTS INTERNATIONAL; *pg.* 1105, *pg.* 1028
CRYSTALTINE - Nutritional Supplements - NATURAL ALTERNATIVES INTERNATIONAL, INC.; *pg.* 1571, *pg.* 253
CRYSTALWAVE - Kitchenware - TUPPERWARE BRANDS CORPORATION; *pg.* 1139, *pg.* 456
CRYSTALYX - Animal Nutritional Supplement - HUBBARD FEEDS INC.; *pg.* 1477, *pg.* 928
CRYSTAR - Polyester Resin - E.I. DU PONT DE NEMOURS & COMPANY; *pg.* 1159, *pg.* 390
CRYSTAT - Static Control Product - WESTLAKE PLASTICS COMPANY; *pg.* 1892, *pg.* 1548
CS-10 CASING SUPPORT SYSTEMS - Mudline Equipment - DRIL-QUIP, INC.; *pg.* 1330, *pg.* 1704
CS-3000 - Blood Cell Separators - BAXTER INTERNATIONAL INC.; *pg.* 1499, *pg.* 599
CS-76 - Liquid Nitrogen Delivery & Tissue Monitoring System - THE COOPER COMPANIES, INC.; *pg.* 1518, *pg.* 183
CS/90 - High Quality Chondroitin Sulfate - CARGILL LIMITED; *pg.* 1475, *pg.* 1914
CS-900 - Monaural Noise Canceling Headset - ANDREA ELECTRONICS CORPORATION; *pg.* 617, *pg.* 1143
CS-950 - Binaural Noise Canceling Headset - ANDREA ELECTRONICS CORPORATION; *pg.* 617, *pg.* 1143
CS GOLD 4.0 - Card System - DIEBOLD, INCORPORATED; *pg.* 387, *pg.* 1407
CS PRO - Copiers - KONICA MINOLTA BUSINESS SOLUTIONS USA, INC.; *pg.* 1419, *pg.* 1113
CS UNIPACK - Fan - CRAFTMADE INTERNATIONAL, INC.; *pg.* 1295, *pg.* 1670
CS100 - Intra-Aortic Balloon Pump Monitor - MAQUET; *pg.* 1558, *pg.* 1082
CS7X - Control System - WEATHERFORD PRODUCTION OPTIMIZATION; *pg.* 987, *pg.* 1725
CSA - Imagewear - V.F. CORPORATION; *pg.* 34, *pg.* 1376
CSC - Security Service - COMMAND SECURITY CORPORATION; *pg.* 377, *pg.* 1171
CSC - Computer Products - COMPUTER SCIENCES CORPORATION; *pg.* 378, *pg.* 1780
CSC CONNECT - Electronic Data Transmission Services - COMPUTER SCIENCES CORPORATION; *pg.* 378, *pg.* 1780
CSC CYBERCARE - Educational Services - COMPUTER SCIENCES CORPORATION; *pg.* 378, *pg.* 1780
CSC POWERSOLUTIONS - Computer Software - COMPUTER SCIENCES CORPORATION; *pg.* 378, *pg.* 1780
C:SCAPE - Office Furniture - STEELCASE INC.; *pg.* 475, *pg.* 889
CSCXPRESS - Computer Services - COMPUTER SCIENCES CORPORATION; *pg.* 378, *pg.* 1780
CSE SAFEGUARD - Auto Policy - CSE INSURANCE GROUP; *pg.* 1199, *pg.* 304
CSEP - Ion Exchange Resin - CALGON CARBON CORPORATION; *pg.* 1151, *pg.* 1574
CSL - Chimney Sweeping Log - JOSEPH ENTERPRISES, INC.; *pg.* 960, *pg.* 220
CSN - Software - BIO-RAD LABORATORIES, INC.; *pg.* 1504, *pg.* 101
CSN - Architecture - MERCURY COMPUTER SYSTEMS, INC.; *pg.* 434, *pg.* 813
CSO - Technology Magazine - INTERNATIONAL DATA GROUP; *pg.* 1653, *pg.* 796
CSP 11 - Two Channel Circuit - BELTONE ELECTRONICS LLC; *pg.* 1503, *pg.* 614
CSPNL - Packaging Technology - AMKOR TECHNOLOGY, INC.; *pg.* 67, *pg.* 25
CSPRO - Collaborative Service - ILLUMINA, INC.; *pg.* 412, *pg.* 203
CSS - Command Systems Software - PARAGON TECHNOLOGIES, INC.; *pg.* 1367, *pg.* 1528
CSS/1200 - Instrument Equipment - CLAYTON INDUSTRIES CO.; *pg.* 1323, *pg.* 66
CSSII - Software - SUNGARD DATA SYSTEMS INC.; *pg.* 477, *pg.* 1592
CST - Electronic Measuring Tools - STANLEY BLACK & DECKER, INC.; *pg.* 1063, *pg.* 358
CSTACK - Circuit Assemblies - AMPHENOL CORPORATION; *pg.* 616, *pg.* 381
CSW - Speaker - CAMBRIDGE SOUNDWORKS, INC.; *pg.* 1234, *pg.* 781
CSX - Carbon Black - CABOT CORPORATION; *pg.* 1151, *pg.* 792
CT - Hemodialysis Dialyzer - BAXTER INTERNATIONAL INC.; *pg.* 1499, *pg.* 599
C.T. 3000 - Moisture Analyzer - ARIZONA INSTRUMENT LLC; *pg.* 1400, *pg.* 12
CTC CATTLE MINERAL AFC - Mineral Feed Supplements - KENT NUTRITION GROUP; *pg.* 1477, *pg.* 710
CTC KRUMS - Animal Treatment - KENT NUTRITION GROUP; *pg.* 1477, *pg.* 710
CTG HEALTHCARE SOLUTIONS - IT Services - COMPUTER TASK GROUP, INC.; *pg.* 378, *pg.* 1147
CTG RETAIL SOLUTIONS - IT Services - COMPUTER TASK GROUP, INC.; *pg.* 378, *pg.* 1147
CTI-CRYOGENICS - Compressors - BROOKS AUTOMATION, INC.; *pg.* 1320, *pg.* 813
CTINTEGRATOR - Software System - MENTOR GRAPHICS CORPORATION; *pg.* 432, *pg.* 1510
CTLM - Breast Cancer Imaging Diagnostic System - IMAGING DIAGNOSTIC SYSTEMS, INC.; *pg.* 1544, *pg.* 425
CTM - Stream Processor - ADVANCED MICRO DEVICES, INC.; *pg.* 613, *pg.* 282
CTPVIEW - Software - JUNIPER NETWORKS, INC.; *pg.* 1260, *pg.* 286
CTR - Tree Delimbers, Feller Bunchers - BLOUNT INTERNATIONAL, INC.; *pg.* 1043, *pg.* 1501

CTR600 - Cordless Glue Gun - ARROW FASTENER COMPANY, INC.; *pg.* 1042, *pg.* 1118
CTS - Sedan - GENERAL MOTORS COMPANY; *pg.* 175, *pg.* 881
CTS RELIEF KIT - Medical Equipment - CONMED CORPORATION; *pg.* 1517, *pg.* 1347
CTS-V - Sedan - GENERAL MOTORS COMPANY; *pg.* 175, *pg.* 881
CTU 30 - Golf Equipment - CALLAWAY GOLF COMPANY; *pg.* 1829, *pg.* 58
CTX - Pharmaceutical Product - ALERE INC.; *pg.* 1488, *pg.* 849
CTX - Cooking & Warming Equipment - THE MIDDLEBY CORPORATION; *pg.* 1361, *pg.* 610
CU-BRITE - Coating - HEATBATH CORPORATION; *pg.* 1165, *pg.* 826
CU-STRIP L - Metal Stripper - HEATBATH CORPORATION; *pg.* 1165, *pg.* 826
CUALK IRM - Dental Product - DENTSPLY INTERNATIONAL INC.; *pg.* 1522, *pg.* 1596
CUARTO DE LIBRA - Fast Food - MCDONALD'S CORPORATION; *pg.* 1737, *pg.* 645
CUB - Hand Dryer - BOBRICK WASHROOM EQUIPMENT, INC.; *pg.* 1043, *pg.* 166
CUB CADET - Lawn & Garden Equipment - MTD PRODUCTS, INC.; *pg.* 1057, *pg.* 1478
CUB CADET COMMERCIAL - Lawn & Garden Equipment - MTD PRODUCTS, INC.; *pg.* 1057, *pg.* 1478
CUB CONDO - Bear Projects - BUILD-A-BEAR WORKSHOP, INC.; *pg.* 950, *pg.* 993
CUB FOODS - Bakery Products - ALPHA BAKING COMPANY; *pg.* 836, *pg.* 564
CUB FOODS - Food Product - SUPERVALU, INC.; *pg.* 1035, *pg.* 924
CUB-TOWLS - Towel Dispenser - WAUSAU PAPER BAY WEST; *pg.* 1471, *pg.* 1465
CUBAVERA - Casual Sportswear - PERRY ELLIS INTERNATIONAL, INC.; *pg.* 45, *pg.* 445
CUBE - Laser & Laser System - COHERENT, INC.; *pg.* 1406, *pg.* 265
CUBE - Fabric - NEMSCHOFF, INC.; *pg.* 936, *pg.* 1890
CUBE KING - Cheese slicer & cuber - LINCOLN FOODSERVICE PRODUCTS, LLC; *pg.* 1127, *pg.* 1432
CUBE SAVER - Back Room - LOZIER CORPORATION; *pg.* 94, *pg.* 1016
CUBE SCENTS - Skin Care Product - SCOTT'S LIQUID GOLD-INC.; *pg.* 335, *pg.* 323
CUBED SOLUTIONS - Software - BIO-RAD LABORATORIES, INC.; *pg.* 1504, *pg.* 101
CUBIC - Carpet - INTERFACE, INC.; *pg.* 695, *pg.* 512
CUBICIN - Biopharmaceutical Product - CUBIST PHARMACEUTICALS, INC.; *pg.* 1521, *pg.* 828
CUBISM - Carpet - INTERFACE, INC.; *pg.* 695, *pg.* 512
CUBIT - Packing Cube Organizer - MCNETT CORPORATION; *pg.* 1839, *pg.* 1817
CUBIT - Steam Generators - NORTEK, INC.; *pg.* 100, *pg.* 1607
CUCINA AMERICANA - Furniture - JOHN BOOS & CO.; *pg.* 1126, *pg.* 609
CUCINA BRAVO! ITALIANA - Restaurants - BRAVO BRIO RESTAURANT GROUP, INC.; *pg.* 1717, *pg.* 1438
CUCUMBER MELON - Fragrance - PARFUMS DE COEUR LTD.; *pg.* 519, *pg.* 376
CUDA - Software - NVIDIA CORPORATION; *pg.* 447, *pg.* 268
CUDDLE CLOTH - Fabric - COPLAND FABRICS, INC.; *pg.* 692, *pg.* 1359
CUDDLE-ME - Blanket - CARTER'S, INC.; *pg.* 21, *pg.* 491
CUDDLE TUB - Bath Tub - GRACO CHILDREN'S PRODUCTS INC.; *pg.* 954, *pg.* 1531
CUDDLEBEDS - Bedding Product - HOLLANDER SLEEP PRODUCTS; *pg.* 927, *pg.* 411
CUENTOS FONETICOS DE SCHOLASTIC - Educational Materials - SCHOLASTIC INC.; *pg.* 1683, *pg.* 1288
CUFF-ABLE - Blood Pressure Cuff - VITAL SIGNS, INC.; *pg.* 1607, *pg.* 1126
CUFFMATE - Flashlight - STREAMLIGHT INC.; *pg.* 1306, *pg.* 1527
CUGR - Navigation Aid - TRIMBLE NAVIGATION LIMITED; *pg.* 1384, *pg.* 288
CUISINART - Small Kitchen Appliances - CONAIR CORPORATION; *pg.* 505, *pg.* 1055
CUISINART - Food Processors, Cookware - CUISINART INC.; *pg.* 1123, *pg.* 373
CUISINE IN - Food Product - ELLENBEE-LEGGETT COMPANY INC.; *pg.* 854, *pg.* 1452
CUISINE SOLUTIONS - Food Service - CUISINE SOLUTIONS, INC.; *pg.* 850, *pg.* 1770
CULEX - Automated Blood Sampler - BIOANALYTICAL SYSTEMS, INC.; *pg.* 1402, *pg.* 700
CULINARY - Food Product - GRIFFITH LABORATORIES, INC.; *pg.* 860, *pg.* 552
CULINARY CHOICE - Spices - FUCHS NORTH AMERICA.; *pg.* 857, *pg.* 774
CULINARY CIRCLE - Food Products - SUPERVALU, INC.; *pg.* 1035, *pg.* 924
CULINARY SECRETS - Food Product - SHAMROCK FOODS COMPANY; *pg.* 895, *pg.* 20
CULINOLOGY ONLINE - Publication - INFORMA EXHIBITIONS LLC; *pg.* 1653, *pg.* 17
CULLIGAN - Water Treatment Products - CULLIGAN INTERNATIONAL COMPANY; *pg.* 54, *pg.* 656
CULLIGAN GOLD SERIES - Water Softener - CULLIGAN INTERNATIONAL COMPANY; *pg.* 54, *pg.* 656
CULLIGANAIR - Air Treatment System - CULLIGAN INTERNATIONAL COMPANY; *pg.* 54, *pg.* 656
CULMINAL - Polymer - HERCULES INCORPORATED; *pg.* 1166, *pg.* 392
CULTUR PLATE - Cellular Assays - PERKINELMER, INC.; *pg.* 1426, *pg.* 853
CULTURE - Apparel - OAKLEY, INC.; *pg.* 1840, *pg.* 86
CULTURE SHOCK - Odor Control - SWISHER HYGIENE INC.; *pg.* 336, *pg.* 1507
CULTURED BRICK - Thin Brick Veneer - OWENS CORNING; *pg.* 102, *pg.* 1476
CULTURED STONE - Stone Veneer Product - OWENS CORNING; *pg.* 102, *pg.* 1476
CULTUREGARD - Filtration System - SPECTRUM LABORATORIES INC.; *pg.* 1595, *pg.* 69
CULTURELLE - Food Product - CONAGRA FOODS, INC.; *pg.* 826, *pg.* 1014
CULTURETECH - Yeast Products - ARCHER-DANIELS-MIDLAND COMPANY; *pg.* 825, *pg.* 565
CULTUREWELL - Molecular Probe Product - THERMO FISHER SCIENTIFIC INC.; *pg.* 1602, *pg.* 61
CULVERTMASTER - Software - BENTLEY SYSTEMS, INC.; *pg.* 361, *pg.* 1531
CUMAR - Coumarone-Indene Resin - NEVILLE CHEMICAL COMPANY; *pg.* 1174, *pg.* 1578
CUMBERLAND - Tobacco Product - AMERICAN SNUFF COMPANY; *pg.* 1893, *pg.* 1641
THE CUMBERLAND - Modular Home - NATIONWIDE HOMES, INC.; *pg.* 99, *pg.* 1788
CUMBERLAND OUTFITTERS - Apparel - OXFORD INDUSTRIES, INC.; *pg.* 30, *pg.* 517
CUMBERLAND RIDGE - Pecan Rolls - STANDARD FUNCTIONAL FOODS GROUP(SFFG); *pg.* 1862, *pg.* 1654
CUMMINS ENGINE - Cummins Diesel Engines - CUMMINS INC.; *pg.* 1326, *pg.* 676
CUMULATOR - Reporting Solution - NIELSEN AUDIO; *pg.* 446, *pg.* 768
CUMULUS - Fabric - NEMSCHOFF, INC.; *pg.* 936, *pg.* 1890
CUNARD LINE - Luxury Cruises - CARNIVAL CORPORATION; *pg.* 1902, *pg.* 441
CUNNINGHAM - Rat Transverse Clamp - STOELTING CO.; *pg.* 1430, *pg.* 671
CUPBOARD MOTH TRAP - Insect Pest Control Product - GARDENS ALIVE!, INC.; *pg.* 1796, *pg.* 693
CUPCAKE - Women's Clothing & Accessories - WOODEN SHIPS OF HOBOKEN; *pg.* 35, *pg.* 1315
CUPCAKE IN BLOOM - Flower Arrangement - 1-800-FLOWERS.COM, INC.; *pg.* 1758, *pg.* 1151
CUPCAKES - Snack Cakes - HOSTESS BRANDS LLC; *pg.* 1856, *pg.* 984
CUPID - Chocolate Coating - CARGILL LIMITED; *pg.* 1475, *pg.* 1914
CUPID - Foundations - CUPID FOUNDATIONS, INC.; *pg.* 22, *pg.* 1220
CUPO'CCINO - Coffee Products - SHEETZ, INC.; *pg.* 1033, *pg.* 1514
CUPOSIT - Electroless Copper System - DOW CHEMICAL; *pg.* 1156, *pg.* 1563
CUPRA - Bonding Tool - KULICKE & SOFFA INDUSTRIES, INC.; *pg.* 650, *pg.* 1533
CUPRAKOTE - Metal Finishing Product - HEATBATH CORPORATION; *pg.* 1165, *pg.* 826
CUPRALITE - Chemical Coating - ENTHONE INC.; *pg.* 1161, *pg.* 381
CUPRASELECT - Chemical Products - AIR PRODUCTS AND CHEMICALS, INC.; *pg.* 1145, *pg.* 1513
CUPRINOL - Stain/Preservative - THE SHERWIN-WILLIAMS COMPANY; *pg.* 1447, *pg.* 1435
CUPROBRAZE - Brazing Furnace System - SECO/WARWICK CORPORATION; *pg.* 1076, *pg.* 1552
CUPROCURE - Wood Preservatives - PETTIT PAINT COMPANY; *pg.* 1444, *pg.* 1116
CUPRODIE - Steel Product - A. FINKL & SONS CO.; *pg.* 1309, *pg.* 563
CUPRODIE 2 - Hammer Die Steel - A. FINKL & SONS CO.; *pg.* 1309, *pg.* 563
CUPRODINE - Metalworking Chemical - HENKEL CORPORATION; *pg.* 1166, *pg.* 897
CUPRON - Alloy - CARPENTER TECHNOLOGY CORPORATION; *pg.* 73, *pg.* 1584
THE CUPSICLE - Baby Care Product - MUNCHKIN, INC.; *pg.* 964, *pg.* 300
CURA - Office Furniture - STEELCASE INC.; *pg.* 475, *pg.* 889
CURA-C - Skin Care Product - BORGHESE, INC.; *pg.* 502, *pg.* 1205
CURAFLO - Flow Lining System - COHESANT, INC.; *pg.* 1154, *pg.* 1405
CURAPOXY - Dispensing System - COHESANT, INC.; *pg.* 1154, *pg.* 1405
CURB YOUR ENTHUSIASM - Cable Television Show - HOME BOX OFFICE, INC.; *pg.* 290, *pg.* 1240
CURE 81 - Hams - HORMEL FOODS CORPORATION; *pg.* 863, *pg.* 915
CURE RITE - Dental Product - DENTSPLY INTERNATIONAL INC.; *pg.* 1522, *pg.* 1596
CURED - Skin Care - KAO BRANDS CO. INC.; *pg.* 513, *pg.* 1415
CUREL - Lotion - KAO BRANDS CO. INC.; *pg.* 513, *pg.* 1415
CURENOX - Photoinitiators for UV-Cured Coatings - KING INDUSTRIES, INC.; *pg.* 1443, *pg.* 363
CURESAN - Insolubilizer for Paper Making Applications - PPG INDUSTRIES, INC.; *pg.* 1445, *pg.* 1579
CURESEAL - Concrete System - L.M. SCOFIELD COMPANY; *pg.* 94, *pg.* 134
CUREZOL - Chemical Products - AIR PRODUCTS AND CHEMICALS, INC.; *pg.* 1145, *pg.* 1513
CURIMASTER - Personal Care Electrical Product - HELEN OF TROY L.P.; *pg.* 511, *pg.* 1692
CURIOSITY - Furniture - ASHLEY FURNITURE INDUSTRIES, INC.; *pg.* 914, *pg.* 1852
CURITHANE - Chemical Products - AIR PRODUCTS AND CHEMICALS, INC.; *pg.* 1145, *pg.* 1513
CURL FREE - Curl Relaxer - THE GILLETTE COMPANY; *pg.* 509, *pg.* 795
CURL-OIL MOISTURE BALANCER - Oil Restorative & Curl Revitalizer for Hair - THE GILLETTE COMPANY; *pg.* 509, *pg.* 795
CURLEE - Electrical Products - EMERSON INDUSTRIAL AUTOMATION; *pg.* 1296, *pg.* 657
CURLEX - Excelsior Cooler Pad - AMERICAN EXCELSIOR COMPANY; *pg.* 1451, *pg.* 1659
CURLY FETTUCCINE - Food Product - ANNIE'S INC.; *pg.* 1760, *pg.* 45
CURLY'S - Food Products - SMITHFIELD FOODS, INC.; *pg.* 896, *pg.* 1806
CURRANT - Footwear - P.W. MINOR & SON, INC.; *pg.* 1816, *pg.* 1140
CURRENCY - Publishing Imprint - THE KNOPF DOUBLEDAY GROUP; *pg.* 1657, *pg.* 1249
CURRENCY - Office Furniture - STEELCASE INC.; *pg.* 475, *pg.* 889
CURRENT - Tachycardia Products - ST. JUDE MEDICAL, INC.; *pg.* 1596, *pg.* 963
CURRENT ACCEL - ICD Product - ST. JUDE MEDICAL, INC.; *pg.* 1596, *pg.* 963
CURRENT DRUGS - Science & Healthcare Publications - THOMSON REUTERS CORPORATION; *pg.* 1693, *pg.* 1944
CURRENT PSYCHIATRY - Healthcare Publication - LEBHAR-FRIEDMAN INC.; *pg.* 1658, *pg.* 1250
CURRENT TECHNOLOGY - Filter System Product - DANAHER CORPORATION; *pg.* 1044, *pg.* 397
CURRENT TECHNOLOGY - Cable Ties & Accessories - THOMAS & BETTS CORPORATION; *pg.* 680, *pg.* 1646
CURRENT YIELD - Financial Products - DOW JONES & COMPANY, INC.; *pg.* 1637, *pg.* 1225
CURRENTS - Carpet - BEAULIEU GROUP, LLC; *pg.* 917, *pg.* 529
CURRENTS - Office Furniture - KNOLL, INC.; *pg.* 425, *pg.*

First page reference indicates Business Class Edition
Second page reference indicates Geographic Edition

1527
CURRENTS - Fabric - NEMSCHOFF, INC.; *pg.* 936, *pg.* 1890
CURRICULUM CONNECTIONS SCHOLASTIC - Educational Materials - SCHOLASTIC INC.; *pg.* 1683, *pg.* 1288
CURRICULUM DESIGNER - Software - SCANTRON CORPORATION; *pg.* 467, *pg.* 922
CURRITHANE - Liquid Catalyst - THE DOW CHEMICAL COMPANY; *pg.* 1157, *pg.* 898
CURSORMANIA - Online Services - IAC/INTERACTIVECORP; *pg.* 292, *pg.* 1242
CURTAIN CALL COSTUMES - Dance Apparel - PERFORM GROUP, LLC; *pg.* 31, *pg.* 1597
CURTAIN CALL FOR CLASS - High Quality Basic Dance Apparel - PERFORM GROUP, LLC; *pg.* 31, *pg.* 1597
CURTIS - Computer Products - ESSELTE BUSINESS CORP; *pg.* 395, *pg.* 1179
CURTIS - Creations - UNCAS MANUFACTURING COMPANY; *pg.* 15, *pg.* 1608
CURTIS POND - T-Shirts - ABERCROMBIE & FITCH CO.; *pg.* 37, *pg.* 1466
CURTMAN - Jewelry - UNCAS MANUFACTURING COMPANY; *pg.* 15, *pg.* 1608
CURVACEOUS - Bath slipper - CURVES INTERNATIONAL INC.; *pg.* 542, *pg.* 1748
THE CURVANE - Wheels - PANGBORN CORPORATION; *pg.* 1367, *pg.* 532
CURVATION - Apparel - V.F. CORPORATION; *pg.* 34, *pg.* 1376
CURVATURA - Ceiling Panel - USG CORPORATION; *pg.* 118, *pg.* 594
CURVE - Apparel - KATE SPADE & COMPANY; *pg.* 27, *pg.* 1248
CURVED MICROSTATS - Surgical Instrument - AMERICAN MEDICAL SYSTEMS, INC.; *pg.* 1399, *pg.* 238
CURVED SRS - Metal Building Product - CENTRIA, INC.; *pg.* 74, *pg.* 1554
CURVE'N BODY - Perm Rods - THE GILLETTE COMPANY; *pg.* 509, *pg.* 795
CURVESSMART - Personal Coaching System - CURVES INTERNATIONAL INC.; *pg.* 542, *pg.* 1748
CURVET - Farm Building - BEHLEN MFG. CO.; *pg.* 701, *pg.* 1010
CURVIC - Machines, Cutters, Clutches & Couplings - GLEASON CORPORATION; *pg.* 1340, *pg.* 1335
CURVY - Fabric - NEMSCHOFF, INC.; *pg.* 936, *pg.* 1890
CURZATE - Fungicide - E.I. DU PONT DE NEMOURS & COMPANY; *pg.* 1159, *pg.* 390
CUSA ASPIRATOR - Ultrasonic Surgical Aspirators - INTEGRA LIFESCIENCES HOLDINGS CORPORATION; *pg.* 1545, *pg.* 1109
CUSA DISSECTRON - Ultrasonic Device - INTEGRA LIFESCIENCES HOLDINGS CORPORATION; *pg.* 1545, *pg.* 1109
CUSA EXCEL - Ultrasonic Surgical Aspirators - INTEGRA LIFESCIENCES HOLDINGS CORPORATION; *pg.* 1545, *pg.* 1109
CUSA NXT - Ultrasonic Surgical Aspirators - INTEGRA LIFESCIENCES HOLDINGS CORPORATION; *pg.* 1545, *pg.* 1109
CUSA ULTRASONICS - Ultrasonic Surgical Aspirators - INTEGRA LIFESCIENCES HOLDINGS CORPORATION; *pg.* 1545, *pg.* 1109
CUSEAL - Film Deposition System - KLA-TENCOR CORPORATION; *pg.* 1353, *pg.* 146
CUSH - Skin Care Products - BARE ESCENTUALS, INC.; *pg.* 500, *pg.* 213
CUSH - Footwear - COBIAN CORP.; *pg.* 1806, *pg.* 253
CUSH-N-AIRE - Casters - HAMILTON CASTER & MFG. CO.; *pg.* 206, *pg.* 1454
CUSH-N-FLEX - Rubber Casters - HAMILTON CASTER & MFG. CO.; *pg.* 206, *pg.* 1454
CUSH-N-GRIP - Grips for Fiberglass Hammers - NUPLA CORPORATION; *pg.* 101, *pg.* 281
CUSHE - Footwear - WOLVERINE WORLD WIDE, INC.; *pg.* 1822, *pg.* 905
CUSHION COMB - Honeycomb Product - PACTIV CORPORATION; *pg.* 1466, *pg.* 624
CUSHION DRIVE - Fluid Coupling - REULAND ELECTRIC COMPANY; *pg.* 1304, *pg.* 68
CUSHION FINDER - Retail Store Services - 1-800-FLOWERS.COM, INC.; *pg.* 1758, *pg.* 1151
CUSHION/FLEX - Goggle - MCR SAFETY; *pg.* 1422, *pg.* 1630
CUSHION GRIP - Thermoplastic Denture Adhesive - MERCK & CO., INC.; *pg.* 1566, *pg.* 1077
CUSHION-MOUNT - Tape - 3M COMPANY; *pg.* 1142, *pg.* 956
CUSHION SOFT - Scissors - THE FULLER BRUSH COMPANY; *pg.* 330, *pg.* 715
CUSHIONSHIELD - Aluminum Air Cellular Laminate Materials - SEALED AIR CORPORATION; *pg.* 1468, *pg.* 1058
CUSHIONSTEP - Wood Flooring Product - ARMSTRONG WORLD INDUSTRIES, INC.; *pg.* 914, *pg.* 1545
CUSHMAN - Utility Vehicles - E-Z-GO TEXTRON; *pg.* 1706, *pg.* 525
CUSHMAN - Golf, Turf & Specialty Products - TEXTRON INC.; *pg.* 235, *pg.* 1607
CUSHMAN COMMANDER - Fastening System - TEXTRON INC.; *pg.* 235, *pg.* 1607
CUSHMAN HONEYBELLS - Citrus Fruits - HARRY & DAVID HOLDINGS, INC.; *pg.* 1022, *pg.* 1499
CUSIP ISID PLUS ACCESS - Online CUSIP Access - STANDARD & POOR'S RATINGS SERVICES; *pg.* 805, *pg.* 1296
CUSIP MASTER SERVICE - Reference Tool - STANDARD & POOR'S RATINGS SERVICES; *pg.* 805, *pg.* 1296
CUSIP_DB - CUSIP in Database Format - STANDARD & POOR'S RATINGS SERVICES; *pg.* 805, *pg.* 1296
CUSTARD STYLE - Yogurt - YOPLAIT USA, INC.; *pg.* 910, *pg.* 947
CUSTOM - Binocular - BUSHNELL OUTDOOR PRODUCTS, INC.; *pg.* 1403, *pg.* 718
CUSTOM - Food Products - CUSTOM CULINARY, INC.; *pg.* 851, *pg.* 644
CUSTOM - Guitar - PAUL REED SMITH GUITARS; *pg.* 574, *pg.* 779
CUSTOM 275 - Stainless Steel - CARPENTER TECHNOLOGY CORPORATION; *pg.* 73, *pg.* 1584
CUSTOM 450 - Stainless Steel Products - CARPENTER TECHNOLOGY CORPORATION; *pg.* 73, *pg.* 1584
CUSTOM 455 - Stainless Steel Products - CARPENTER TECHNOLOGY CORPORATION; *pg.* 73, *pg.* 1584
CUSTOM 465 - Stainless Steel Products - CARPENTER TECHNOLOGY CORPORATION; *pg.* 73, *pg.* 1584
CUSTOM 475 - Stainless Steel - CARPENTER TECHNOLOGY CORPORATION; *pg.* 73, *pg.* 1584
CUSTOM AGE 625 PLUS - Resistant Alloy - CARPENTER TECHNOLOGY CORPORATION; *pg.* 73, *pg.* 1584
CUSTOM AIR V - Air Respirator - MINE SAFETY APPLIANCES COMPANY; *pg.* 1361, *pg.* 1525
CUSTOM ARRAY - Microarray - COMBIMATRIX CORPORATION; *pg.* 1407, *pg.* 109
CUSTOM COLOR - Cosmetic Product - NU SKIN ENTERPRISES, INC.; *pg.* 518, *pg.* 1755
CUSTOM COMMUNITY - Online Management Service - IMODULES SOFTWARE, INC.; *pg.* 1258, *pg.* 716
CUSTOM COVERAGE - Data Services - NIELSEN AUDIO; *pg.* 446, *pg.* 768
CUSTOM CREATIONS - Foundation - REVLON, INC.; *pg.* 521, *pg.* 1286
CUSTOM CRYSTAL - Paperweight - BROWN & BIGELOW, INC.; *pg.* 1624, *pg.* 959
CUSTOM CUT - Haircutting Kit - CONAIR CORPORATION; *pg.* 505, *pg.* 1055
CUSTOM DESIGNS - Waterbed Linens - SPRINGS GLOBAL, INC.; *pg.* 698, *pg.* 1616
CUSTOM DIRECT - Retail & Wholesale of Musical Instruments - GIBSON GUITAR CORP.; *pg.* 550, *pg.* 1650
CUSTOM GAUGE - Guitar - ERNIE BALL INC.; *pg.* 1768, *pg.* 68
CUSTOM GOLD LABEL - Food Products - CUSTOM CULINARY, INC.; *pg.* 851, *pg.* 644
CUSTOM GRIND - Kitchen Appliance - HAMILTON BEACH BRANDS, INC.; *pg.* 56, *pg.* 1783
CUSTOM HOISTS - Telescopic & Pistonrod Hydraulic Cylinders - STANDEX INTERNATIONAL CORPORATION; *pg.* 60, *pg.* 1039
CUSTOM IMPERIAL OIL - Food Product - BUNGE LIMITED; *pg.* 842, *pg.* 1351
CUSTOM KOTE - Paperboard Packaging Product - WESTROCK COMPANY; *pg.* 1472, *pg.* 1805
CUSTOM L-5 - Guitars - GIBSON GUITAR CORP.; *pg.* 550, *pg.* 1650
CUSTOM LITE - Golf Shaft - TRUE TEMPER SPORTS, INC.; *pg.* 1847, *pg.* 1647
CUSTOM LUX - Molecular Biology Product - THERMO FISHER SCIENTIFIC INC.; *pg.* 1602, *pg.* 61
CUSTOM MARKETING SOLUTIONS - Marketing Service - UNITED BUSINESS MEDIA LLC; *pg.* 1697, *pg.* 1177
CUSTOM-MEMO - Memo Board - BROWN & BIGELOW, INC.; *pg.* 1624, *pg.* 959
CUSTOM OPTIONS BY MEDICA - Health Plan & Publication - MEDICA, INC.; *pg.* 1208, *pg.* 949
CUSTOM PLUS - Razor - THE GILLETTE COMPANY; *pg.* 509, *pg.* 795
CUSTOM SOFTWARE DEVELOPMENT - Cable Solutions - SONUS NETWORKS INC.; *pg.* 1281, *pg.* 858
CUSTOM WOODWORKER'S ILLUSTRATED BUYING GUIDE - Magazine - VANCE PUBLISHING CORPORATION; *pg.* 1699, *pg.* 627
CUSTOM WOODWORKING BUSINESS - Magazine - VANCE PUBLISHING CORPORATION; *pg.* 1699, *pg.* 627
CUSTOM WRAP - Packaging Product - SEALED AIR CORPORATION; *pg.* 1468, *pg.* 1058
CUSTOMAIR - Seating System - ALIMED, INC.; *pg.* 1490, *pg.* 816
CUSTOMCHOICE - Communication Product - CENTURYLINK, INC; *pg.* 1870, *pg.* 317
THE CUSTOMER - Software - INTEGRITY SOLUTIONS; *pg.* 145, *pg.* 22
CUSTOMER ADVANTAGE TERM - Insurance Product - SBLI USA LIFE INSURANCE COMPANY, INC.; *pg.* 1216, *pg.* 1288
CUSTOMER CARE - Flanged Reels of Wood or Plastic for Wire & Cable - SONOCO PRODUCTS COMPANY; *pg.* 1469, *pg.* 1619
CUSTOMER INSIGHT REPORT - Paper Products - BOISE CASCADE HOLDINGS, L.L.C.; *pg.* 1453, *pg.* 546
CUSTOMER INTELLIGENCE - Computer Information Systems & Services - COMPUTER SCIENCES CORPORATION; *pg.* 378, *pg.* 1780
CUSTOMER INTER@CTION SOLUTIONS - Trade Publication - TECHNOLOGY MARKETING CORP.; *pg.* 1691, *pg.* 364
CUSTOMER INTERACTION CENTER - Software - INTERACTIVE INTELLIGENCE, INC.; *pg.* 417, *pg.* 687
CUSTOMER MANAGER - Database - VENDIO, INC.; *pg.* 1287, *pg.* 256
CUSTOMER RATINGS & COMMENTS - Information Retrieval Services - CARFAX INC.; *pg.* 202, *pg.* 1777
CUSTOMER SATISFACTION GUARANTEE - Mailer - PITNEY BOWES INC.; *pg.* 454, *pg.* 376
CUSTOMER SATISFACTION IS OUR ONLY POLICY - Tagline - ARNOLD MACHINERY COMPANY; *pg.* 1314, *pg.* 1755
CUSTOMER SATISFACTION THROUGH EXCELLENCE - Tag Line - SONOCO PRODUCTS COMPANY; *pg.* 1469, *pg.* 1619
CUSTOMER SERVICE ACCELERATOR - Computer Program - COMPUTER SCIENCES CORPORATION; *pg.* 378, *pg.* 1780
CUSTOMER SERVICE PLATFORM - Manual - XEROX CORPORATION; *pg.* 494, *pg.* 365
CUSTOMER SUCCESS IS OUR MISSION - Slogan - RAYTHEON COMPANY; *pg.* 233, *pg.* 854
CUSTOMERPOINT - Video Communication System - GLOWPOINT, INC.; *pg.* 401, *pg.* 1094
CUSTOMERSAT - Software - METRIXLAB; *pg.* 1266, *pg.* 223
CUSTOMET 286-LNI - Alloy - CARPENTER TECHNOLOGY CORPORATION; *pg.* 73, *pg.* 1584
CUSTOMEXPRESS - Array - AFFYMETRIX, INC.; *pg.* 1487, *pg.* 263
CUSTOMFLOW - Nurser System - EVENFLO COMPANY, INC.; *pg.* 924, *pg.* 1470
CUSTOMIZED BANKING - Banking Services - THE PNC FINANCIAL SERVICES GROUP, INC.; *pg.* 795, *pg.* 1579
CUSTOMIZED TASTE TECHNOLOGY - Tagline - NEWLY WEDS FOODS, INC.; *pg.* 886, *pg.* 585
CUSTOMPOINT - Software - R.R. DONNELLEY & SONS COMPANY; *pg.* 1682, *pg.* 589
CUSTOMS & BORDER PROTECTION - Customs & Border Protection - AMERICAN SCIENCE AND ENGINEERING, INC.; *pg.* 1399, *pg.* 787
CUSTOMSEQ - Array - AFFYMETRIX, INC.; *pg.* 1487, *pg.* 263
CUSTOMSIM - Software - SYNOPSYS, INC.; *pg.* 480, *pg.* 162
CUSTOMVUE - Medical Device - ABBOTT MEDICAL OPTICS, INC.; *pg.* 1485, *pg.* 260
CUSTOM RACING - Jacket - SANTA FE LEATHER CORPORATION; *pg.* 12, *pg.* 1059
CUT CRYSTAL - Door Glass - ODL INCORPORATED; *pg.* 101, *pg.* 914
CUT-EASE - Stick Lubricant - AMERICAN GREASE STICK CO.; *pg.* 971, *pg.* 902

CUT 'N FEED - Coulter Combination - YETTER MANUFACTURING CO., INC.; *pg.* 708, *pg.* 598
CUT-N-FRY - Countertop Fryers - BELSHAW ADAMATIC BAKERY GROUP; *pg.* 1317, *pg.* 1813
CUT-OFF - Beanie - OAKLEY, INC.; *pg.* 1840, *pg.* 86
CUT THE CORD WITH CYPRESS WIRELESS - Slogan - CYPRESS SEMICONDUCTOR CORPORATION; *pg.* 1326, *pg.* 243
CUTBACK - Cleaning Product - HILLYARD, INC.; *pg.* 331, *pg.* 990
CUTCO - Cutlery - CUTCO CORPORATION; *pg.* 1123, *pg.* 1318
CUTCO CUTLERY - Kitchen Cutlery - VECTOR MARKETING CORPORATION; *pg.* 1139, *pg.* 1318
CUTEFTP HOME - Software - GLOBALSCAPE INC.; *pg.* 401, *pg.* 1740
CUTEFTP LITE - Software - GLOBALSCAPE INC.; *pg.* 401, *pg.* 1740
CUTEFTP MACPRO - Software - GLOBALSCAPE INC.; *pg.* 401, *pg.* 1740
CUTEFTP PRO - Software - GLOBALSCAPE INC.; *pg.* 401, *pg.* 1740
CUTEHTML - Software - GLOBALSCAPE INC.; *pg.* 401, *pg.* 1740
CUTEMX - Software - GLOBALSCAPE INC.; *pg.* 401, *pg.* 1740
CUTESITE - Software - GLOBALSCAPE INC.; *pg.* 401, *pg.* 1740
CUTESITE BUILDER - Software - GLOBALSCAPE INC.; *pg.* 401, *pg.* 1740
CUTEST LITTLE BABY - Pillow and Throw - HERITAGE LACE INC.; *pg.* 694, *pg.* 711
CUTEZIP - Software - GLOBALSCAPE INC.; *pg.* 401, *pg.* 1740
CUTI CLIP - Cuticle Clipper - MILLERS FORGE INC.; *pg.* 1056, *pg.* 1733
CUTICLE CARE COMPLEX - Cuticle Care - ORLY INTERNATIONAL, INC.; *pg.* 518, *pg.* 137
CUTIQUE - Cuticle Care - ORLY INTERNATIONAL, INC.; *pg.* 518, *pg.* 137
CUTLER-HAMMER - Electrical Product - EATON CORPORATION; *pg.* 1331, *pg.* 1429
CUTLER-HAMMER - Switches, Relays, Circuit Breakers & Push Buttons - EATON CORPORATION - INDUSTRIAL CONTROLS; *pg.* 1296, *pg.* 1874
CUTLER-HAMMER - Mechanical & Electrical System - JOHNSON CONTROLS, INC.; *pg.* 209, *pg.* 1876
CUTOUT FITNESS TANK - Clothing - K-SWISS; *pg.* 1837, *pg.* 306
CUTTER - Wall Panel - BLUELINX HOLDINGS, INC.; *pg.* 70, *pg.* 491
CUTTER AND BUCK - Case - BROWN & BIGELOW, INC.; *pg.* 1624, *pg.* 959
CUTTER'S BAYHOUSE - Restaurant - RESTAURANTS UNLIMITED, INC.; *pg.* 1748, *pg.* 1839
CUTTING BALLOON ULTRA2 - Medical Device - BOSTON SCIENTIFIC CORPORATION; *pg.* 1508, *pg.* 831
CUTTING THROUGH - Electronic Product - LRAD CORPORATION; *pg.* 652, *pg.* 204
CUTWELL - Dental Product - DENTSPLY INTERNATIONAL INC.; *pg.* 1522, *pg.* 1596
CUTWORKS - Software - GERBER SCIENTIFIC, INC.; *pg.* 1414, *pg.* 380
CV - Online Services - IAC/INTERACTIVECORP; *pg.* 292, *pg.* 1242
CV CRAVAT - Multi-Purpose Cravat - MCNETT CORPORATION; *pg.* 1839, *pg.* 1817
CVD SILICONE CARBIDE - Industrial Material - DOW CHEMICAL; *pg.* 1156, *pg.* 1563
CVIEW PLUS - Software - ITERIS, INC.; *pg.* 293, *pg.* 261
CVINA - Software - IHS AUTOMOTIVE DRIVEN BY POLK; *pg.* 1652, *pg.* 907
CVM 4000 - Vault Management System - GLORY GLOBAL SOLUTIONS; *pg.* 401, *pg.* 628
CVNET - Cardiology Information System - CERNER CORPORATION; *pg.* 1514, *pg.* 981
CVPROFILOR - Cardiovascular Profiling System - HYPERTENSION DIAGNOSTICS, INC.; *pg.* 1543, *pg.* 921
CVPROFILOR DO-2020 - Cardiovascular Profiling System - HYPERTENSION DIAGNOSTICS, INC.; *pg.* 1543, *pg.* 921
CVPROFILOR MD-3000 - Cardiovascular Profiling System - HYPERTENSION DIAGNOSTICS, INC.; *pg.* 1543, *pg.* 921
CVS.COM - Website - CVS HEALTH CORPORATION; *pg.* 1765, *pg.* 1610
CVT - Video Game - INTERNATIONAL GAME TECHNOLOGY; *pg.* 957, *pg.* 1024
CVX-300 - Excimer Laser System - THE SPECTRANETICS CORPORATION; *pg.* 1595, *pg.* 315
CW GOVERNMENT TRAVEL - Soliciting And Managing Travel - CARLSON COMPANIES INC.; *pg.* 1084, *pg.* 947
CW-PULSE - Medical Laser System - IRIDEX CORPORATION; *pg.* 648, *pg.* 160
CW-X - Clothing - HUGGER MUGGER YOGA PRODUCTS LLC; *pg.* 1836, *pg.* 1758
CWC - Iron & Steel Castings - CWC TEXTRON; *pg.* 1326, *pg.* 901
CWD - Windows & Doors - NORTEK, INC.; *pg.* 100, *pg.* 1607
CWDM 4/8 CH - Fiber Optic Component - OPLINK COMMUNICATIONS, INC.; *pg.* 660, *pg.* 91
CWDM OADMG 1X2 - Fiber Optic Component - OPLINK COMMUNICATIONS, INC.; *pg.* 660, *pg.* 91
CWDM OADMG 2X2 - Fiber Optic Component - OPLINK COMMUNICATIONS, INC.; *pg.* 660, *pg.* 91
CWF - Wood Finish - AKZO NOBEL DECORATIVE PAINTS, USA; *pg.* 1439, *pg.* 1474
CWF-UV - Coating & Paint - AKZO NOBEL DECORATIVE PAINTS, USA; *pg.* 1439, *pg.* 1474
CWP - Stock Feeding Equipment for the Metal Forming Industry - MESTEK, INC.; *pg.* 1074, *pg.* 857
CWS - Trademark (Div. I Baseball) - NATIONAL COLLEGIATE ATHLETIC ASSOCIATION; *pg.* 567, *pg.* 688
CX - Hammer Die Steel - A. FINKL & SONS CO.; *pg.* 1309, *pg.* 563
CX - Clinical Analytical Instruments & Reagents - BECKMAN COULTER, INC.; *pg.* 1402, *pg.* 48
CX - Software - EMC CORPORATION; *pg.* 391, *pg.* 825
CX-3 - Combo Organ - KORG USA, INC.; *pg.* 556, *pg.* 1180
CX-7 - Fluid Handling System - GRACO, INC.; *pg.* 1342, *pg.* 935
CX TECHNOLOGY - Technology Services - PEGASYSTEMS INC.; *pg.* 453, *pg.* 74
CXL RANGER - Fan - CRAFTMADE INTERNATIONAL, INC.; *pg.* 1295, *pg.* 1670
CXP NOMEX - Outerwear - UNIFIRST CORPORATION; *pg.* 50, *pg.* 860
CXR - Bike - MARIN BIKES; *pg.* 1708, *pg.* 168
CY-BET - Glass & Ceramic Material - CORNING INCORPORATED; *pg.* 1122, *pg.* 1154
CY-EX - Chemical Product - CYTEC INDUSTRIES, INC.; *pg.* 1155, *pg.* 1131
CY-TEMP - Chemical Product - CYTEC INDUSTRIES, INC.; *pg.* 1155, *pg.* 1131
CYALUME - Lights - CYALUME TECHNOLOGIES HOLDINGS, INC.; *pg.* 1295, *pg.* 856
CYAN - ADP Analyzer - BECKMAN COULTER, INC.; *pg.* 1402, *pg.* 48
CYAN - Laser - NEWPORT CORPORATION; *pg.* 1424, *pg.* 114
CYANAMER - Chemical Product - CYTEC INDUSTRIES, INC.; *pg.* 1155, *pg.* 1131
CYANATROL - Chemical Product - CYTEC INDUSTRIES, INC.; *pg.* 1155, *pg.* 1131
CYANEX - Chemical Product - CYTEC INDUSTRIES, INC.; *pg.* 1155, *pg.* 1131
CYANIVER - Chemical Reagent - HACH COMPANY; *pg.* 1415, *pg.* 334
CYANOX - Chemical Product - CYTEC INDUSTRIES, INC.; *pg.* 1155, *pg.* 1131
CYASORB - Chemical Product - CYTEC INDUSTRIES, INC.; *pg.* 1155, *pg.* 1131
CYASORB THT - Polymer Additives - CYTEC INDUSTRIES, INC.; *pg.* 1155, *pg.* 1131
CYASTAT - Chemical Product - CYTEC INDUSTRIES, INC.; *pg.* 1155, *pg.* 1131
CYBEAR - Virtual World of Stuffed Fun Projects - BUILD-A-BEAR WORKSHOP, INC.; *pg.* 950, *pg.* 993
CYBER BRUSH - Keyboard Brush - BROWN & BIGELOW, INC.; *pg.* 1624, *pg.* 959
CYBER-CHAMP - Guitar Amplifier - FENDER MUSICAL INSTRUMENTS CORPORATION; *pg.* 547, *pg.* 21
CYBER-DELUXE - Guitar Amplifier - FENDER MUSICAL INSTRUMENTS CORPORATION; *pg.* 547, *pg.* 21
CYBER EAGLE - Exercise Equipment - CYBEX INTERNATIONAL, INC.; *pg.* 1521, *pg.* 832
CYBER FOOT CONTROLLER - Guitar Amplifier - FENDER MUSICAL INSTRUMENTS CORPORATION; *pg.* 547, *pg.* 21
CYBER-TWIN SE - Guitar Amplifier - FENDER MUSICAL INSTRUMENTS CORPORATION; *pg.* 547, *pg.* 21
CYBERCAMPUS - Online Education - GOLDEN GATE UNIVERSITY; *pg.* 602, *pg.* 219
CYBERCAT - Fire Alarm System - FIKE CORPORATION; *pg.* 1047, *pg.* 973
CYBERCELL II - Machining Center - KINGSBURY CORPORATION; *pg.* 1353, *pg.* 1035
CYBERCLEAR - Computer Equipment - VIEWSONIC CORPORATION; *pg.* 489, *pg.* 303
CYBERCLIP - Clip - BROWN & BIGELOW, INC.; *pg.* 1624, *pg.* 959
CYBERCLOCKS - Clock & Buffer Product - CYPRESS SEMICONDUCTOR CORPORATION; *pg.* 1326, *pg.* 243
CYBERDISPLAY - Semiconductor Material - KOPIN CORPORATION; *pg.* 425, *pg.* 847
CYBERDISPLAY 1280M - Display - KOPIN CORPORATION; *pg.* 425, *pg.* 847
CYBERDISPLAY 640M - Display - KOPIN CORPORATION; *pg.* 425, *pg.* 847
CYBERDISPLAY 800M - Display - KOPIN CORPORATION; *pg.* 425, *pg.* 847
CYBERDISPLAY SVGA - Display - KOPIN CORPORATION; *pg.* 425, *pg.* 847
CYBERDISPLAY SXGA LVR - Display - KOPIN CORPORATION; *pg.* 425, *pg.* 847
CYBERDISPLAY VGA - Display - KOPIN CORPORATION; *pg.* 425, *pg.* 847
CYBEREVF - Module Products - KOPIN CORPORATION; *pg.* 425, *pg.* 847
CYBEREX - Power Quality Products - THOMAS & BETTS CORPORATION; *pg.* 680, *pg.* 1646
CYBERFORCE - Hardware & Software - IMMERSION CORPORATION; *pg.* 413, *pg.* 246
CYBERFORT - Power Protection Product - SCHNEIDER ELECTRIC; *pg.* 467, *pg.* 1609
CYBERGLOVE - Hardware & Software - IMMERSION CORPORATION; *pg.* 413, *pg.* 246
CYBERGRASP - Hardware & Software - IMMERSION CORPORATION; *pg.* 413, *pg.* 246
CYBERIMPACT - Hardware & Software - IMMERSION CORPORATION; *pg.* 413, *pg.* 246
CYBERKNIFE - Robotic Radiosurgery System - ACCURAY INCORPORATED; *pg.* 1486, *pg.* 282
CYBERLAB - Laboratory Information System - ASPYRA, INC.; *pg.* 355, *pg.* 306
CYBERLIGHT - Luminaire - HIGH END SYSTEMS, INC.; *pg.* 1299, *pg.* 1663
CYBERLIGHT TURBO - Lighting Product - HIGH END SYSTEMS, INC.; *pg.* 1299, *pg.* 1663
CYBERLITE - Semiconductor Material - KOPIN CORPORATION; *pg.* 425, *pg.* 847
CYBERMATE - Mobile Collection Device - ASPYRA, INC.; *pg.* 355, *pg.* 306
CYBERMED - Pharmacy Information System - ASPYRA, INC.; *pg.* 355, *pg.* 306
CYBERPATH - Anatomic Pathology System - ASPYRA, INC.; *pg.* 355, *pg.* 306
CYBERRAD - Radiology Information System - ASPYRA, INC.; *pg.* 355, *pg.* 306
CYBERSCAN - Laser - CYBEROPTICS CORPORATION; *pg.* 1408, *pg.* 925
CYBERSENSOR - Meter Reading System - BADGER METER, INC.; *pg.* 1401, *pg.* 1873
CYBERSOLV - Cleaning Chemical Product - KYZEN CORPORATION; *pg.* 331, *pg.* 1652
CYBERSOURCE CONNECT - Electronic Payment System - CYBERSOURCE CORPORATION; *pg.* 381, *pg.* 216
CYBERSPACE KIDS - Telephone Service - IDT CORPORATION; *pg.* 643, *pg.* 1096
CYBERSPEAK - Sugar Candy - NEW ENGLAND CONFECTIONERY COMPANY INC.; *pg.* 1860, *pg.* 842
CYBERSURFR - Wave Cable Modem - MOTOROLA SOLUTIONS, INC.; *pg.* 657, *pg.* 659
CYBERTECH - Polymer - TEKNI-PLEX, INC.; *pg.* 1470, *pg.* 1122
CYBERTOUCH - Hardware & Software - IMMERSION CORPORATION; *pg.* 413, *pg.* 246
CYBERTRADER - Securities Brokerage & Investment Services - CHARLES SCHWAB & COMPANY, INC.; *pg.* 734, *pg.* 215
CYBERVISION - Computer Equipment - VIEWSONIC CORPORATION; *pg.* 489, *pg.* 303
CYBOND - Chemical Product - CYTEC INDUSTRIES, INC.; *pg.* 1155, *pg.* 1131
CYBORG - Character - DC COMICS, INC.; *pg.* 1633, *pg.* 1221
CYBREAK - Defoamer - CYTEC INDUSTRIES, INC.; *pg.*

First page reference indicates Business Class Edition
Second page reference indicates Geographic Edition

1155, pg. 1131
CYBUL - Footwear - STEVEN MADDEN, LTD.; pg. 1819, pg. 1176
CYC116 - Biopharmaceutical Product - CYCLACEL PHARMACEUTICALS, INC.; pg. 1521, pg. 1044
CYCAT - Chemical Product - CYTEC INDUSTRIES, INC.; pg. 1155, pg. 1131
CYCLACEL - Biopharmaceutical Product - CYCLACEL PHARMACEUTICALS, INC.; pg. 1521, pg. 1044
CYCLACET - Fragrance Ingredient - INTERNATIONAL FLAVORS & FRAGRANCES INC.; pg. 512, pg. 1244
CYCLADES - Fabric - NEMSCHOFF, INC.; pg. 936, pg. 1890
CYCLAPROP - Fragrance Ingredient - INTERNATIONAL FLAVORS & FRAGRANCES INC.; pg. 512, pg. 1244
CYCLE - Canned & Dry Dog Food - HEINZ NORTH AMERICA; pg. 861, pg. 1576
CYCLE-BIN - Feed System - CARUS CORPORATION; pg. 1152, pg. 652
CYCLE TRADER - Magazine - DOMINION ENTERPRISES; pg. 1636, pg. 1796
CYCLECHISER - Healthcare Product - MEDICOOL, INC.; pg. 1562, pg. 294
CYCLEFLO - Electronic Meters & Controls - GRACO, INC.; pg. 1342, pg. 935
CYCLER - Educational Books - WASTE MANAGEMENT, INC.; pg. 1954, pg. 1716
CYCLESAVER - Productivity Enhancing Concentrate - FERRO CORPORATION; pg. 1162, pg. 1462
CYCLESORB - Carbon Adsorption System - CALGON CARBON CORPORATION; pg. 1151, pg. 1574
CYCLETROL - DC Controls - GRAHAM MOTORS AND CONTROLS; pg. 177, pg. 1692
CYCLEWORLD - Motorcycle Magazine - BONNIER CORPORATION; pg. 1622, pg. 480
CYCLEX - Cutting Method - GLEASON CORPORATION; pg. 1340, pg. 1335
CYCLIN-GF - Nutritional Supplement - MAXIMUM HUMAN PERFORMANCE, INC.; pg. 1559, pg. 1065
CYCLINEX-1 - Pharmaceutical Products - ABBOTT LABORATORIES; pg. 1484, pg. 551
CYCLO - Pigment - BASF CATALYSTS LLC; pg. 1148, pg. 1074
CYCLO-INDEX - Motion Control Systems - LEGGETT & PLATT, INCORPORATED; pg. 933, pg. 974
CYCLOBLOWER - Blower - GARDNER DENVER, INC.; pg. 1338, pg. 1592
CYCLOCKS - Semiconductor Solution - CYPRESS SEMICONDUCTOR CORPORATION; pg. 1326, pg. 243
CYCLOCUT - Bevel Product - GLEASON CORPORATION; pg. 1340, pg. 1335
CYCLOGALBANIFF - Fragrance Ingredient - INTERNATIONAL FLAVORS & FRAGRANCES INC.; pg. 512, pg. 1244
CYCLOMAX - Burner - MAXON CORPORATION; pg. 1359, pg. 695
CYCLON - Battery - ENERSYS INC.; pg. 1334, pg. 1584
CYCLONE - FPGA Device - ALTERA CORPORATION; pg. 348, pg. 237
CYCLONE - Compressor - BADGER AIR BRUSH COMPANY; pg. 359, pg. 612
CYCLONE - Separator - CAMERON INTERNATIONAL; pg. 1151, pg. 1702
CYCLONE - Metal Stamper - THE CYCLONE MFG. CO.; pg. 78, pg. 698
CYCLONE - Orthopedic Implant Product - DJO SURGICAL; pg. 1525, pg. 1661
CYCLONE - Electric Guitar - FENDER MUSICAL INSTRUMENTS CORPORATION; pg. 547, pg. 21
CYCLONE - Fluid Handling System - GRACO, INC.; pg. 1342, pg. 935
CYCLONE - Hose - HBD INDUSTRIES, INC.; pg. 207, pg. 1449
CYCLONE - Glove - KOMBI, LTD.; pg. 1838, pg. 1766
CYCLONE - Eyewear - MAUI JIM, INC.; pg. 9, pg. 651
CYCLONE - Adaptive Scanner - MOTOROLA ENTERPRISE MOBILITY; pg. 441, pg. 1167
CYCLONE - Mixer - SANISERV; pg. 1373, pg. 695
CYCLONE HH - Electric Guitar - FENDER MUSICAL INSTRUMENTS CORPORATION; pg. 547, pg. 21
CYCLONE II - High-Density Field-Programmable Gate Array - ALTERA CORPORATION; pg. 348, pg. 237
CYCLONE II - Electric Guitar - FENDER MUSICAL INSTRUMENTS CORPORATION; pg. 547, pg. 21
CYCLONE-MIX - Fluid Handling System - GRACO, INC.; pg. 1342, pg. 935
CYCLONE PLUS - Storage Phosphor System - PERKINELMER, INC.; pg. 1426, pg. 853
CYCLONE XHE - Commercial Water Heater - A.O. SMITH CORPORATION; pg. 1313, pg. 1872
CYCLONIC - Kitchen Appliance - VIKING RANGE CORPORATION; pg. 61, pg. 968
CYCLOPAC - Air Cleaner - DONALDSON COMPANY, INC.; pg. 1329, pg. 917
CYCLOPS - Lighting Product - HD ELECTRIC COMPANY; pg. 1299, pg. 666
CYCLOSET - Pharmaceutical Product - SALIX PHARMACEUTICALS, INC.; pg. 1591, pg. 1388
CYCLOTENE - Electronics Resins - THE DOW CHEMICAL COMPANY; pg. 1157, pg. 898
CYCOM - Chemical Product - CYTEC INDUSTRIES, INC.; pg. 1155, pg. 1131
CYDAS - Software - CYBERRESEARCH INC.; pg. 381, pg. 339
CYDECTIN - Cattle Anthelmintic - BOEHRINGER INGELHEIM VETMEDICA, INC.; pg. 1474, pg. 989
CYDESIGNER - Semiconductor Solution - CYPRESS SEMICONDUCTOR CORPORATION; pg. 1326, pg. 243
CYDRIL - Chemical Product - CYTEC INDUSTRIES, INC.; pg. 1155, pg. 1131
CYDROTHANE - Chemical Product - CYTEC INDUSTRIES, INC.; pg. 1155, pg. 1131
CYFI - Low-Power RF Solution - CYPRESS SEMICONDUCTOR CORPORATION; pg. 1326, pg. 243
CYFLECT - Bunker Accessories - CYALUME TECHNOLOGIES HOLDINGS, INC.; pg. 1295, pg. 856
CYFLOC - Chemical Product - CYTEC INDUSTRIES, INC.; pg. 1155, pg. 1131
CYFORM - Chemical Product - CYTEC INDUSTRIES, INC.; pg. 1155, pg. 1131
CYGNUS - Maneuvering Spacecraft - ORBITAL ATK; pg. 1425, pg. 1779
CYKILL - Animal Safety Product - NEOGEN CORPORATION; pg. 883, pg. 896
CYKLOKAPRON - Medicine - PFIZER INC.; pg. 1581, pg. 1278
CYLINDER BEAM - Commercial & Display Lighting - SWIVELIER CO., INC.; pg. 1307, pg. 1142
CYLINDERMASTER - Glass & Ceramic Material - CORNING INCORPORATED; pg. 1122, pg. 1154
CYLINDRICAL HEATING - Microwave System - THE LAITRAM LLC; pg. 1354, pg. 744
CYLINK - Chemical Product - CYTEC INDUSTRIES, INC.; pg. 1155, pg. 1131
CYLLIND - Pharmaceutical Products - ABBOTT LABORATORIES; pg. 1484, pg. 551
CYMBAL - Blood Collection Technology - HAEMONETICS CORPORATION; pg. 1538, pg. 802
CYMBALTA - Pharmaceutical Product - ELI LILLY AND COMPANY; pg. 1527, pg. 684
CYMBALTA - Pharmaceutical Product - IMPAX LABORATORIES, INC.; pg. 1544, pg. 101
CYMEL - Chemical Product - CYTEC INDUSTRIES, INC.; pg. 1155, pg. 1131
CYMERONLINE - Light Source - CYMER, INC.; pg. 1296, pg. 202
CYMOD - Module - CYBERRESEARCH INC.; pg. 381, pg. 339
CYNAPSE - Network Processing Product - CYPRESS SEMICONDUCTOR CORPORATION; pg. 1326, pg. 243
CYNERGY - Vascular Lesions Treatment System - CYNOSURE, INC.; pg. 1521, pg. 858
CYNERGY - Sanitary Product - ENTEGRIS, INC.; pg. 1882, pg. 788
CYNOFF - Pest Control Product - FMC CORPORATION; pg. 1163, pg. 1564
CYNOSURESPA - Aesthetic Spa Treatment System - CYNOSURE, INC.; pg. 1521, pg. 858
CYNTHIA - Furniture - AMISCO INDUSTRIES LTD.; pg. 913, pg. 1958
CYNTHIA - Lamp - ASHLEY FURNITURE INDUSTRIES, INC.; pg. 914, pg. 1852
THE CYNTHIANA DEMOCRAT - Newspaper - CYNTHIANA PUBLISHING CO.; pg. 1632, pg. 726
CYPAN - Chemical Product - CYTEC INDUSTRIES, INC.; pg. 1155, pg. 1131
CYPHER - Stent - CORDIS CORPORATION; pg. 1519, pg. 430
CYPHER - Healthcare Product - JOHNSON & JOHNSON; pg. 1549, pg. 1091
CYPHER - Access Control System - NAPCO SECURITY SYSTEMS, INC.; pg. 658, pg. 1138
CYPHOS - Chemical Product - CYTEC INDUSTRIES, INC.; pg. 1155, pg. 1131
CYPLY - Chemical Product - CYTEC INDUSTRIES, INC.; pg. 1155, pg. 1131
CYPOXY - Insulator - S&C ELECTRIC COMPANY; pg. 1305, pg. 589
CYPOXYLATED - Devices Employing S&C Cypoxy Resin System - S&C ELECTRIC COMPANY; pg. 1305, pg. 589
CYPRESS - Lighting - LSI INDUSTRIES INC.; pg. 58, pg. 1416
CYPRESS - Sport Knife - MCNETT CORPORATION; pg. 1839, pg. 1817
CYPRESS - Therapy Management Software - OMNICARE, INC; pg. 1578, pg. 1418
CYPRESS.BIZ - Website - CYPRESS SEMICONDUCTOR CORPORATION; pg. 1326, pg. 243
CYPRESS.COM - Website - CYPRESS SEMICONDUCTOR CORPORATION; pg. 1326, pg. 243
CYPROS - Customer-Design Support Network - CYPRESS SEMICONDUCTOR CORPORATION; pg. 1326, pg. 243
CYQUANT - Molecular Probe Product - THERMO FISHER SCIENTIFIC INC.; pg. 1602, pg. 61
CYQUEST - Chemical Product - CYTEC INDUSTRIES, INC.; pg. 1155, pg. 1131
CYRACURE - Cycloaliphatic Epoxide - THE DOW CHEMICAL COMPANY; pg. 1157, pg. 898
CYRANO - Video Game - INTERNATIONAL GAME TECHNOLOGY; pg. 957, pg. 1024
CYRAQ - Monitor - CYBERRESEARCH INC.; pg. 381, pg. 339
CYREL - Printing & Coating of Plates & Platemaking Systems - E.I. DU PONT DE NEMOURS & COMPANY; pg. 1159, pg. 390
CYREX - Acrylic Polycarbonate Alloys - EVONIK CYRO LLC; pg. 1162, pg. 1103
CYREZ - Chemical Product - CYTEC INDUSTRIES, INC.; pg. 1155, pg. 1131
CYRO-TRIM - Cryogenic Deflashing - AIR PRODUCTS AND CHEMICALS, INC.; pg. 1145, pg. 1513
CYROCUP - Medical & Aesthetic Product - DYNATRONICS CORPORATION; pg. 1526, pg. 1757
CYROLITE - Acrylic Based Multipolymer Compound - EVONIK CYRO LLC; pg. 1162, pg. 1103
CYROVU HP2 - Acrylic Sheet for POP Displays - EVONIK CYRO LLC; pg. 1162, pg. 1103
CYSAVE - Pharmaceutical Product - ALERE INC.; pg. 1488, pg. 849
CYSEP - Chemical Product - CYTEC INDUSTRIES, INC.; pg. 1155, pg. 1131
CYSPRAY - Pharmaceutical Product - ALERE INC.; pg. 1488, pg. 849
CYSTALGEL - Styrene Resin - ROSCO LABORATORIES, INC.; pg. 1782, pg. 378
CYSTIC FIBROSIS V 3.0 - Pharmaceutical Products - ABBOTT LABORATORIES; pg. 1484, pg. 551
CYTHANE - Chemical Product - CYTEC INDUSTRIES, INC.; pg. 1155, pg. 1131
CYTO-STAT - Testing Instrument System - BECKMAN COULTER, INC.; pg. 1402, pg. 48
CYTOCARB II - Protein Supplement - CYTOSPORT, INC.; pg. 1018, pg. 45
CYTOFECTENE - Software - BIO-RAD LABORATORIES, INC.; pg. 1504, pg. 101
CYTOFUGE - Diagnostic Urinalysis System - IRIS INTERNATIONAL, INC.; pg. 1547, pg. 64
CYTOGAINER - Protein Supplement - CYTOSPORT, INC.; pg. 1018, pg. 45
CYTOGAM - Medicine - MEDIMMUNE LLC; pg. 1562, pg. 770
CYTOMATE - Cell Processing System - BAXTER INTERNATIONAL INC.; pg. 1499, pg. 599
CYTOMAX - Medical Device - COOK GROUP, INC.; pg. 1518, pg. 674
CYTOMAX - Protein Drink - CYTOSPORT, INC.; pg. 1018, pg. 45
CYTOMAX NATURAL - Protein Supplement - CYTOSPORT, INC.; pg. 1018, pg. 45
CYTOMAX PROTEIN - Protein Supplement - CYTOSPORT, INC.; pg. 1018, pg. 45
CYTOMEL - Pharmaceutical Product - KING PHARMACEUTICALS, INC.; pg. 1553, pg. 1627
CYTOMICS FC 500 - Flow Cytometry System - BECKMAN COULTER, INC.; pg. 1402, pg. 48
CYTOMICS FC 500 MPL - Flow Cytometry System With MXP

Software - BECKMAN COULTER, INC.; *pg.* 1402, *pg.* 48
CYTOP - Chemical Product - CYTEC INDUSTRIES, INC.; *pg.* 1155, *pg.* 1131
CYTORICH - Preservative Liquid - BD DIAGNOSTICS - TRIPATH; *pg.* 1402, *pg.* 1358
CYTOSETS - Molecular Probe Product - THERMO FISHER SCIENTIFIC INC.; *pg.* 1602, *pg.* 61
CYTOTEC - Medicine - PFIZER INC.; *pg.* 1581, *pg.* 1278
CYTOVENE - Pharmaceutical Product - HOFFMANN-LA ROCHE INC.; *pg.* 1542, *pg.* 1099
CYTOX - Chemical Product - CYTEC INDUSTRIES, INC.; *pg.* 1155, *pg.* 1131
CYVLONE - Air Mover - TENNANT COMPANY; *pg.* 1381, *pg.* 944
CZE SERIES - Enclosures - WIREMOLD/LEGRAND; *pg.* 689, *pg.* 383

D

D-10 - Software - BIO-RAD LABORATORIES, INC.; *pg.* 1504, *pg.* 101
D&B MARKET SPECTRUM - Software - THE DUN & BRADSTREET CORP.; *pg.* 1637, *pg.* 1120
D&B SPEND ANALYSIS - Supplier Base Software - THE DUN & BRADSTREET CORP.; *pg.* 1637, *pg.* 1120
D&D MINIATURES - Miniature Figurines - WIZARDS OF THE COAST, INC.; *pg.* 970, *pg.* 1830
D&PL - Seeds - MONSANTO; *pg.* 1798, *pg.* 971
D & S 5000 - High-Pressure, Brushless Automatic Carwash System - D&S CAR WASH EQUIPMENT CO.; *pg.* 1327, *pg.* 979
D-C++ - Software - WIND RIVER SYSTEMS, INC.; *pg.* 493, *pg.* 38
D-CAP - Switching Mode Power Supply - TEXAS INSTRUMENTS INCORPORATED; *pg.* 679, *pg.* 1688
D-CARE - Pharmaceutical Product - PURETEK CORPORATION; *pg.* 1587, *pg.* 211
D-CC - Software - WIND RIVER SYSTEMS, INC.; *pg.* 493, *pg.* 38
D-CON - Rodent Control Solutions - RECKITT BENCKISER INC.; *pg.* 1136, *pg.* 1105
D-CORE - Medical & Aesthetic Product - DYNATRONICS CORPORATION; *pg.* 1526, *pg.* 1757
D-F-B XTRA - Charge Soap - ADCO, INC.; *pg.* 325, *pg.* 482
D-FLAME - Nutritional Product - NOW HEALTH GROUP, INC.; *pg.* 1576, *pg.* 557
D-FLECTOR - Bicycle Accessories - SPECIALIZED BICYCLE COMPONENTS, INC.; *pg.* 1711, *pg.* 152
D GENE - Software - BIO-RAD LABORATORIES, INC.; *pg.* 1504, *pg.* 101
D-GLOSS - Liquid Cleaner - UNITED GILSONITE LABORATORIES; *pg.* 1449, *pg.* 1527
D-I-D - Product Security System - WEST PHARMACEUTICAL SERVICES, INC.; *pg.* 1472, *pg.* 1532
D LOGO - Environmental Control Apparatus - DONALDSON COMPANY, INC.; *pg.* 1329, *pg.* 917
D-LUX - Online Guide - THERMO FISHER SCIENTIFIC INC.; *pg.* 1602, *pg.* 61
D-NET - Diesel Generator - WESTERBEKE CORPORATION; *pg.* 1388, *pg.* 847
D-STAT - Medical Device - VASCULAR SOLUTIONS, INC.; *pg.* 1434, *pg.* 946
D-STRESS - Beverage - MONSTER BEVERAGE CORPORATION; *pg.* 257, *pg.* 69
D-TEC - AC Field Detection System - THE WILL-BURT CO., INC.; *pg.* 1437, *pg.* 1469
D-TEX D-MIX PRO - Lighting Product - HIGH END SYSTEMS, INC.; *pg.* 1299, *pg.* 1663
D-TOPO - Entry Clone - THERMO FISHER SCIENTIFIC INC.; *pg.* 1602, *pg.* 61
D-TR DOOR - Airport Door to Deter Unauthorized Entry - DAIFUKU WEBB; *pg.* 1327, *pg.* 885
D-TRANS - Pesticide - MCLAUGHLIN GORMLEY KING COMPANY; *pg.* 1797, *pg.* 939
D-U-N-S NUMBER - Entity Numbering Methodology - THE DUN & BRADSTREET CORP.; *pg.* 1637, *pg.* 1120
D-W ROD SEAL - Seal - GREENE, TWEED & CO.; *pg.* 1344, *pg.* 1544
D1 - Watch - OAKLEY, INC.; *pg.* 1840, *pg.* 86
D1601 - Transformer - BOSCH SECURITY SYSTEMS, INC.; *pg.* 626, *pg.* 1158
D1640 - Transformer - BOSCH SECURITY SYSTEMS, INC.; *pg.* 626, *pg.* 1158
D1640-32 - Transformer - BOSCH SECURITY SYSTEMS, INC.; *pg.* 626, *pg.* 1158
D16XD - Digital Recorder - KORG USA, INC.; *pg.* 556, *pg.* 1180
D2 - Watch - OAKLEY, INC.; *pg.* 1840, *pg.* 86
D20 - Game System - WIZARDS OF THE COAST, INC.; *pg.* 970, *pg.* 1830
D20 MODERN - Game System - WIZARDS OF THE COAST, INC.; *pg.* 970, *pg.* 1830
D2000 - Clamp Ring Closure - T.D. WILLIAMSON, INC.; *pg.* 1380, *pg.* 1490
D2071A SERIES - Alarm Transmitter - BOSCH SECURITY SYSTEMS, INC.; *pg.* 626, *pg.* 1158
D256A - Heat Detector - BOSCH SECURITY SYSTEMS, INC.; *pg.* 626, *pg.* 1158
D257A - Heat Detector - BOSCH SECURITY SYSTEMS, INC.; *pg.* 626, *pg.* 1158
D263 - Smoke/Heat Detector - BOSCH SECURITY SYSTEMS, INC.; *pg.* 626, *pg.* 1158
D265AW - Smoke Detector Head - BOSCH SECURITY SYSTEMS, INC.; *pg.* 626, *pg.* 1158
D273 - Smoke/Heat Detector - BOSCH SECURITY SYSTEMS, INC.; *pg.* 626, *pg.* 1158
D281A - Detector Head - BOSCH SECURITY SYSTEMS, INC.; *pg.* 626, *pg.* 1158
D282A - Detector Head - BOSCH SECURITY SYSTEMS, INC.; *pg.* 626, *pg.* 1158
D282A-DH - Smoke Detector - BOSCH SECURITY SYSTEMS, INC.; *pg.* 626, *pg.* 1158
D283A - Detector Head - BOSCH SECURITY SYSTEMS, INC.; *pg.* 626, *pg.* 1158
D284 - UV Flame Detector - BOSCH SECURITY SYSTEMS, INC.; *pg.* 626, *pg.* 1158
D285 - Smoke Detector Head - BOSCH SECURITY SYSTEMS, INC.; *pg.* 626, *pg.* 1158
D286 - Smoke Detector Head - BOSCH SECURITY SYSTEMS, INC.; *pg.* 626, *pg.* 1158
D296 - Smoke Detector - BOSCH SECURITY SYSTEMS, INC.; *pg.* 626, *pg.* 1158
D297 - Smoke Detector - BOSCH SECURITY SYSTEMS, INC.; *pg.* 626, *pg.* 1158
D2E VISION - Software - ACTUATE CANADA; *pg.* 1225, *pg.* 1933
D2P - Transmitter/Power Amplifier Technology - PARKERVISION, INC.; *pg.* 1426, *pg.* 434
D3 - Electronic Bill Presentment & Payment - PITNEY BOWES INC.; *pg.* 454, *pg.* 376
D3 - Database Management System - TIGERLOGIC CORPORATION; *pg.* 484, *pg.* 117
D3 PRO - Software - CRESTRON ELECTRONICS INC.; *pg.* 631, *pg.* 1116
D300A - Smoke Detector - BOSCH SECURITY SYSTEMS, INC.; *pg.* 626, *pg.* 1158
D300A-HV - Smoke Detector - BOSCH SECURITY SYSTEMS, INC.; *pg.* 626, *pg.* 1158
D32XD - Digital Recorder - KORG USA, INC.; *pg.* 556, *pg.* 1180
D341P/D341I - Smoke Detector - BOSCH SECURITY SYSTEMS, INC.; *pg.* 626, *pg.* 1158
D342P/D342I - Smoke Detector - BOSCH SECURITY SYSTEMS, INC.; *pg.* 626, *pg.* 1158
D40 - Cameras - NIKON INC.; *pg.* 1424, *pg.* 1181
D5 SOFFIT - Vinyl Soffit - NORTEK, INC.; *pg.* 100, *pg.* 1607
D601 - Heat Detector - BOSCH SECURITY SYSTEMS, INC.; *pg.* 626, *pg.* 1158
D602 - Heat Detector - BOSCH SECURITY SYSTEMS, INC.; *pg.* 626, *pg.* 1158
D61 - Hearing Aid - BELTONE ELECTRONICS LLC; *pg.* 1503, *pg.* 614
D7014 - Converter - BOSCH SECURITY SYSTEMS, INC.; *pg.* 626, *pg.* 1158
D7015 - Converter - BOSCH SECURITY SYSTEMS, INC.; *pg.* 626, *pg.* 1158
D7022 - Control Panel - BOSCH SECURITY SYSTEMS, INC.; *pg.* 626, *pg.* 1158
D7024 - Control Panel - BOSCH SECURITY SYSTEMS, INC.; *pg.* 626, *pg.* 1158
D7025 - Relay Module - BOSCH SECURITY SYSTEMS, INC.; *pg.* 626, *pg.* 1158
D7030X - Remote Module - BOSCH SECURITY SYSTEMS, INC.; *pg.* 626, *pg.* 1158
D7031 - Remote Key Switch - BOSCH SECURITY SYSTEMS, INC.; *pg.* 626, *pg.* 1158
D7032 - Annunciator - BOSCH SECURITY SYSTEMS, INC.; *pg.* 626, *pg.* 1158
D7033 LCD - Keypad Module - BOSCH SECURITY SYSTEMS, INC.; *pg.* 626, *pg.* 1158
D7034 - System Expander Module - BOSCH SECURITY SYSTEMS, INC.; *pg.* 626, *pg.* 1158
D7035 - Relay Board - BOSCH SECURITY SYSTEMS, INC.; *pg.* 626, *pg.* 1158
D7035B - Relay Board - BOSCH SECURITY SYSTEMS, INC.; *pg.* 626, *pg.* 1158
D7036 - Keypad Module - BOSCH SECURITY SYSTEMS, INC.; *pg.* 626, *pg.* 1158
D7038 - Power Supply - BOSCH SECURITY SYSTEMS, INC.; *pg.* 626, *pg.* 1158
D71 - Hearing Aid - BELTONE ELECTRONICS LLC; *pg.* 1503, *pg.* 614
D9068 - Alarm Transmitter - BOSCH SECURITY SYSTEMS, INC.; *pg.* 626, *pg.* 1158
D9133TTL-E - Interface Module - BOSCH SECURITY SYSTEMS, INC.; *pg.* 626, *pg.* 1158
D9142F - Power Supply - BOSCH SECURITY SYSTEMS, INC.; *pg.* 626, *pg.* 1158
D9142LC - Power Supply - BOSCH SECURITY SYSTEMS, INC.; *pg.* 626, *pg.* 1158
D9142M - Power Supply Board - BOSCH SECURITY SYSTEMS, INC.; *pg.* 626, *pg.* 1158
DA-CURVE - Curved Front Projection Screen with Silver Surface - DA-LITE SCREEN COMPANY; *pg.* 632, *pg.* 698
DA-LIFT - Electric Screen - DA-LITE SCREEN COMPANY; *pg.* 632, *pg.* 698
DA-LITE - Projection Screens - DA-LITE SCREEN COMPANY; *pg.* 632, *pg.* 698
DA-LITE/ORAVISUAL - Easels, Lecterns, Communication Cabinets, Credenzas & Scheduling Boards - DA-LITE SCREEN COMPANY; *pg.* 632, *pg.* 698
DA-LITE/WELT - Background Stands - DA-LITE SCREEN COMPANY; *pg.* 632, *pg.* 698
DA-MAT - Screen - DA-LITE SCREEN COMPANY; *pg.* 632, *pg.* 698
DA-SNAP - Projection Screen - DA-LITE SCREEN COMPANY; *pg.* 632, *pg.* 698
DA-TEX - Screen - DA-LITE SCREEN COMPANY; *pg.* 632, *pg.* 698
DA-VIEW - Screen - DA-LITE SCREEN COMPANY; *pg.* 632, *pg.* 698
DA VINCI - Art Product - DANIEL SMITH INC.; *pg.* 1766, *pg.* 1835
DA VINCI - Surgical System - INTUITIVE SURGICAL, INC.; *pg.* 1546, *pg.* 286
DA VINCI - Single-Wafer Clean - LAM RESEARCH CORPORATION; *pg.* 1354, *pg.* 91
DA VINCI DIAMONDS - Video Game - INTERNATIONAL GAME TECHNOLOGY; *pg.* 957, *pg.* 1024
DAAB - Adjustable Downhole Motor - BAKER HUGHES INTEQ; *pg.* 1316, *pg.* 1700
DABCO - Catalysts - AIR PRODUCTS AND CHEMICALS, INC.; *pg.* 1145, *pg.* 1513
DABNEY - Footwear - VANS, INC.; *pg.* 1821, *pg.* 76
D'AC LIGHTING - Lighting - PHILIPS LIGHTING; *pg.* 1303, *pg.* 806
DAC PROFESSIONAL - Hygiene System - SIRONA DENTAL SYSTEMS, INC.; *pg.* 1429, *pg.* 1175
DAC UNIVERSAL - Hygiene System - SIRONA DENTAL SYSTEMS, INC.; *pg.* 1429, *pg.* 1175
DACLIZUMAB - Antibody - PDL BIOPHARMA INC.; *pg.* 1580, *pg.* 1022
DACOGEN - Pharmaceutical - EISAI INC.; *pg.* 1526, *pg.* 1133
DACOMATIC - Photo Film, Processing Chemicals - EASTMAN KODAK COMPANY; *pg.* 1408, *pg.* 1333
DACSS - Mortgage Loan Application Analysis - STANDARD & POOR'S RATINGS SERVICES; *pg.* 805, *pg.* 1296
DADDY RAY'S - Fig & Fruit Bars - J&J SNACK FOODS CORPORATION; *pg.* 865, *pg.* 1107
DAD'S OLD FASHIONED ROOT BEER - Soft Drink - THE MONARCH BEVERAGE COMPANY, INC.; *pg.* 257, *pg.* 514
DAF - Trucks - PACCAR INC.; *pg.* 187, *pg.* 1816
DAFFODIL - Wall Decor - ETHAN ALLEN INTERIORS INC.; *pg.* 924, *pg.* 343
DAFFODIL DAYS - Support Programs - AMERICAN CANCER SOCIETY, INC.; *pg.* 126, *pg.* 487
DAFINA - Publishing Imprint - KENSINGTON PUBLISHING CORP.; *pg.* 1656, *pg.* 1248
DAGMAR - Lamp - ASHLEY FURNITURE INDUSTRIES, INC.; *pg.* 914, *pg.* 1852
DAHL - Diesel Filters/Separators - BALDWIN FILTERS; *pg.* 1316, *pg.* 1011

First page reference indicates Business Class Edition
Second page reference indicates Geographic Edition

DAHLE - Art, Photo & Office Products - DAHLE USA; *pg.* 382, *pg.* 1038
DAHLIA - Lamp - ASHLEY FURNITURE INDUSTRIES, INC.; *pg.* 914, *pg.* 1852
DAHLOF - Footwear - K-SWISS; *pg.* 1837, *pg.* 306
DAI DAY - Bottled Food Product - ALLIED OLD ENGLISH, INC.; *pg.* 836, *pg.* 1110
DAILY 3 - Lottery Tickets - CALIFORNIA LOTTERY; *pg.* 990, *pg.* 196
DAILY 3 - Game - MICHIGAN STATE LOTTERY BUREAU; *pg.* 999, *pg.* 895
DAILY 3 - Lottery Game - MINNESOTA STATE LOTTERY; *pg.* 999, *pg.* 956
DAILY 3 - Game - THE STATE LOTTERY COMMISSION OF INDIANA; *pg.* 1006, *pg.* 690
DAILY 4 - Game - MICHIGAN STATE LOTTERY BUREAU; *pg.* 999, *pg.* 895
DAILY 4 - Game - THE STATE LOTTERY COMMISSION OF INDIANA; *pg.* 1006, *pg.* 690
DAILY 4 - Lottery Game - TEXAS LOTTERY COMMISSION; *pg.* 1007, *pg.* 1666
THE DAILY BEAST - Online Services - IAC/INTERACTIVECORP; *pg.* 292, *pg.* 1242
DAILY BIOBASICS - Nutritional Care Product - LIFEPLUS INTERNATIONAL; *pg.* 1556, *pg.* 29
DAILY BREAD - Fresh Prepared Foods - THE HAIN CELESTIAL GROUP, INC.; *pg.* 860, *pg.* 1172
THE DAILY BREEZE - Publisher - THE DAILY BREEZE; *pg.* 1632, *pg.* 293
DAILY CAMERA (BOULDER) - Newspaper - THE E.W. SCRIPPS COMPANY; *pg.* 1639, *pg.* 1412
DAILY DEMOCRAT - Publisher - THE DEMOCRAT CO.; *pg.* 1634, *pg.* 708
DAILY DERBY - Lottery Tickets - CALIFORNIA LOTTERY; *pg.* 990, *pg.* 196
THE DAILY FIX - Book - RODALE, INC.; *pg.* 1681, *pg.* 1530
DAILY GATE CITY - Newspaper - THE DEMOCRAT CO.; *pg.* 1634, *pg.* 708
DAILY GRANITE - Polish Refill - METHOD PRODUCTS INC.; *pg.* 332, *pg.* 223
DAILY HERALD - Newspaper - PADDOCK PUBLICATIONS, INC.; *pg.* 1674, *pg.* 554
DAILY LABOR REPORT - Publisher - BLOOMBERG BNA; *pg.* 1621, *pg.* 1772
DAILY LIFE - Fuel Processing - KOCH INDUSTRIES, INC.; *pg.* 1463, *pg.* 724
DAILY MOISTURE - Skin Care - AVON PRODUCTS, INC.; *pg.* 500, *pg.* 1198
THE DAILY NEWS - North Carolina Newspaper - FREEDOM COMMUNICATIONS, INC.; *pg.* 1643, *pg.* 110
THE DAILY NEWS - Newspaper - LOS ANGELES DAILY NEWS PUBLISHING COMPANY; *pg.* 1660, *pg.* 308
DAILY NEWS RECORD - Business Publication - FAIRCHILD FASHION GROUP; *pg.* 1640, *pg.* 1230
THE DAILY NUMBER - Daily 3-Digit Drawing - PENNSYLVANIA STATE LOTTERY; *pg.* 1003, *pg.* 1552
DAILY PILOT - Newspaper - LOS ANGELES TIMES COMMUNICATIONS, LLC; *pg.* 1660, *pg.* 135
DAILY PRESS - California Newspaper - FREEDOM COMMUNICATIONS, INC.; *pg.* 1643, *pg.* 110
DAILY PURE - Bathroom Cleaner - S.C. JOHNSON & SON, INC.; *pg.* 334, *pg.* 1889
DAILY RACING FORM - Thoroughbred Horse Racing Industry Newspaper - DAILY RACING FORM, LLC; *pg.* 1632, *pg.* 1221
DAILY RECORD - Newspaper - DAILY RECORD; *pg.* 1633, *pg.* 1103
DAILY REPORTS FOR EXECUTIVES - Publisher - BLOOMBERG BNA; *pg.* 1621, *pg.* 1772
DAILY SHOWER - Spray - METHOD PRODUCTS INC.; *pg.* 332, *pg.* 223
DAILY TAX REPORT - Publisher - BLOOMBERG BNA; *pg.* 1621, *pg.* 1772
DAILY TIMES LEADER - Newspaper - DAILY TIMES LEADER; *pg.* 1633, *pg.* 972
DAILY VITAMIN - Boost - JAMBA, INC.; *pg.* 1024, *pg.* 84
DAILY VITS - Nutritional Product - NOW HEALTH GROUP, INC.; *pg.* 1576, *pg.* 557
DAILYBURN - Online Fitness Video Service - IAC/INTERACTIVECORP; *pg.* 292, *pg.* 1242
DAILYKIND - Hair Care Product - NU SKIN ENTERPRISES, INC.; *pg.* 518, *pg.* 1755
DAINE SCREEN - Pharmaceutical Product - ALERE INC.; *pg.* 1488, *pg.* 849
DAINTY DAISIES - Embroidered Tees - HABAND COMPANY, INC.; *pg.* 1772, *pg.* 1099
DAIRY BAKE - Bakery Ingredient - FOREMOST FARMS USA COOPERATIVE; *pg.* 856, *pg.* 1854
THE DAIRY BEST - Slogan - OAK FARMS DAIRY; *pg.* 887, *pg.* 1685
DAIRY FOCUS - Animal Nutrition - CARGILL LIMITED; *pg.* 1475, *pg.* 1914
DAIRY FORTIFIER PLUS YEAST - Nutritional Supplements - KENT NUTRITION GROUP; *pg.* 1477, *pg.* 710
DAIRY FRESH - Dairy Product - DEAN FOODS COMPANY; *pg.* 852, *pg.* 1679
DAIRY HERD MANAGEMENT - Magazine - VANCE PUBLISHING CORPORATION; *pg.* 1699, *pg.* 627
DAIRY MART - Convenience Store & Gas Station - ALIMENTATION COUCHE-TARD INC.; *pg.* 1013, *pg.* 1951
DAIRY MILK - Chocolates - THE HERSHEY CO.; *pg.* 1855, *pg.* 1538
DAIRY QUEEN - Soft Service Ice Milk Product - INTERNATIONAL DAIRY QUEEN, INC.; *pg.* 1732, *pg.* 938
DAIRY SEE - Animal Treatment - KENT NUTRITION GROUP; *pg.* 1477, *pg.* 710
DAIRYLAND - Seeds - DOW AGROSCIENCES LLC; *pg.* 1156, *pg.* 684
DAIRYLAND - Dairy Products - SAPUTO, INC.; *pg.* 893, *pg.* 1956
DAIRYLANE - Dairy Products - BROUGHTON FOODS COMPANY; *pg.* 842, *pg.* 1458
DAIRYPLAN C21 - Software - GEA FARM TECHNOLOGIES; *pg.* 704, *pg.* 636
DAIRYPURE - Milk - DEAN FOODS COMPANY; *pg.* 852, *pg.* 1679
DAISY - Lamp - ASHLEY FURNITURE INDUSTRIES, INC.; *pg.* 914, *pg.* 1852
DAISY - Footwear - CAPEZIO BALLET MAKERS INC.; *pg.* 1805, *pg.* 1125
DAISY - Mattress Pad - CARPENTER CO.; *pg.* 920, *pg.* 1801
DAISY - Footwear - COBIAN CORP.; *pg.* 1806, *pg.* 253
DAISY - Youthline Air Rifles - DAISY MANUFACTURING COMPANY; *pg.* 1831, *pg.* 35
DAISY - Disposable Lady's Shaver - THE GILLETTE COMPANY; *pg.* 509, *pg.* 795
DAISY - Apparel - HERITAGE LACE INC.; *pg.* 694, *pg.* 711
DAISY CUTTER - Footwear - OAKLEY, INC.; *pg.* 1840, *pg.* 86
DAISY FLAPPER - Women's Clothing & Accessories - WOODEN SHIPS OF HOBOKEN; *pg.* 35, *pg.* 1315
DAISY FUENTES - Fragrance - THE ESTEE LAUDER COMPANIES INC.; *pg.* 508, *pg.* 1229
DAISY KINGDOM - Home Sewing - SPRINGS GLOBAL, INC.; *pg.* 698, *pg.* 1616
DAISY MART - Convenience Store Banner - ALIMENTATION COUCHE-TARD INC.; *pg.* 1013, *pg.* 1951
DAISY PLUS - Disposable Shaver - THE GILLETTE COMPANY, *pg.* 509, *pg.* 795
DAISY TRO - Pillow and Throw - HERITAGE LACE INC.; *pg.* 694, *pg.* 711
DAISYFRESH - Apparel - HANESBRANDS INC.; *pg.* 26, *pg.* 1394
DAIWA - Fishing Rods & Reels - DAIWA CORPORATION; *pg.* 1832, *pg.* 75
DAIWA SS-II - Freshwater Spinning Reels - DAIWA CORPORATION; *pg.* 1832, *pg.* 75
DAIWATCH - Computer Software - LOCKHEED MARTIN CORPORATION; *pg.* 229, *pg.* 762
DAIZU NO SUSUME - Beverages - THE COCA-COLA COMPANY; *pg.* 240, *pg.* 493
DAKAR - Bicycles - G. JOANNOU CYCLE CO. INC.; *pg.* 1707, *pg.* 1098
DAKAR SPORT - Bicycles - G. JOANNOU CYCLE CO. INC.; *pg.* 1707, *pg.* 1098
DAKAR XC COMP - Bicycles - G. JOANNOU CYCLE CO. INC.; *pg.* 1707, *pg.* 1098
DAKAR XC EXPERT - Bicycles - G. JOANNOU CYCLE CO. INC.; *pg.* 1707, *pg.* 1098
DAKAR XC PRO - Bicycles - G. JOANNOU CYCLE CO. INC.; *pg.* 1707, *pg.* 1098
DAKAR XLT 1.0 - Bicycles - G. JOANNOU CYCLE CO. INC.; *pg.* 1707, *pg.* 1098
DAKAR XLT 2.0 - Bicycles - G. JOANNOU CYCLE CO. INC.; *pg.* 1707, *pg.* 1098
DAKAR XLT 3.0 - Bicycles - G. JOANNOU CYCLE CO. INC.; *pg.* 1707, *pg.* 1098
DAKOTA - 3-Tab Roofing Shingles - BUILDING PRODUCTS OF CANADA CORP.; *pg.* 72, *pg.* 1951
DAKOTA - Footwear - EASTLAND SHOE CORPORATION; *pg.* 1808, *pg.* 750
DAKOTA - Lighting - LSI INDUSTRIES INC.; *pg.* 58, *pg.* 1416
DAKOTA - Footwear - MARKS WORK WEARHOUSE LTD.; *pg.* 44, *pg.* 1903
DAKOTA - Vinyl - TRANSILWRAP COMPANY, INC.; *pg.* 1470, *pg.* 613
DAKOTA - Kitchenware - THE VOLLRATH COMPANY LLC; *pg.* 1139, *pg.* 1894
DAKOTA AL - Bicycles - G. JOANNOU CYCLE CO. INC.; *pg.* 1707, *pg.* 1098
DAKOTA BOOK - Paper Products - BOISE CASCADE HOLDINGS, L.L.C.; *pg.* 1453, *pg.* 546
DAKOTA BRAVE - Flour - NORTH DAKOTA MILL & ELEVATOR ASSOCIATION; *pg.* 833, *pg.* 1398
DAKOTA CASH - Lotto Game - SOUTH DAKOTA LOTTERY; *pg.* 1006, *pg.* 1624
DAKOTA CHAMPION - Flour - NORTH DAKOTA MILL & ELEVATOR ASSOCIATION; *pg.* 833, *pg.* 1398
DAKOTA DIAMOND - Flour - NORTH DAKOTA MILL & ELEVATOR ASSOCIATION; *pg.* 833, *pg.* 1398
DAKOTA DIGITAL BOOK - Paper Products - BOISE CASCADE HOLDINGS, L.L.C.; *pg.* 1453, *pg.* 546
DAKOTA MAID - Bakery Flour - NORTH DAKOTA MILL & ELEVATOR ASSOCIATION; *pg.* 833, *pg.* 1398
DAKOTA PRIDE - Flour - NORTH DAKOTA MILL & ELEVATOR ASSOCIATION; *pg.* 833, *pg.* 1398
DAKOTA THUNDER - Video Game - INTERNATIONAL GAME TECHNOLOGY; *pg.* 957, *pg.* 1024
DAKOTA XC - Bicycles - G. JOANNOU CYCLE CO. INC.; *pg.* 1707, *pg.* 1098
DAKSTATS - Sports Results & Statistics Software - DAKTRONICS, INC.; *pg.* 633, *pg.* 1624
DAKTENNIS - Software - DAKTRONICS, INC.; *pg.* 633, *pg.* 1624
DAKTICKER - Electronic Message System - DAKTRONICS, INC.; *pg.* 633, *pg.* 1624
DAL RACCOLTO - Oil, Pasta & Vegetables - COLAVITA USA, INC.; *pg.* 849, *pg.* 1056
DAL-TILE - Ceramic Tile - MOHAWK INDUSTRIES, INC.; *pg.* 935, *pg.* 527
DALIA - Furniture - AMISCO INDUSTRIES LTD.; *pg.* 913, *pg.* 1958
DALL-MILES - Orthopaedic Product - STRYKER CORPORATION; *pg.* 1598, *pg.* 894
DALLAS - Quality Chafers - CARLISLE FOODSERVICE PRODUCTS INCORPORATED; *pg.* 1455, *pg.* 1485
DALLAS COWBOYS OFFICIAL WEEKLY - Tabloid Newspaper Printed 32 Times A Year - DALLAS COWBOYS FOOTBALL CLUB, LTD.; *pg.* 543, *pg.* 1718
DALLASNEWS.COM - Website - THE DALLAS MORNING NEWS CO.; *pg.* 1633, *pg.* 1679
DALLASTAT - Potentiometer - MAXIM INTEGRATED PRODUCTS, INC.; *pg.* 653, *pg.* 247
DALMANE - Pharmaceutical Product - VALEANT PHARMACEUTICALS INTERNATIONAL; *pg.* 1605, *pg.* 1047
THE DALMORE - Single Malt Scotch - JIM BEAM BRANDS CO.; *pg.* 1965, *pg.* 601
DALPAD - Coalescing Agent - THE DOW CHEMICAL COMPANY; *pg.* 1157, *pg.* 898
DALTILE - Ceramic Tile - DAL-TILE CORPORATION; *pg.* 78, *pg.* 1678
DALTON - Furniture - ASHLEY FURNITURE INDUSTRIES, INC.; *pg.* 914, *pg.* 1852
DALTON - Furniture - HOOKER FURNITURE CORPORATION; *pg.* 928, *pg.* 1788
DAM - Led Drivers - MICREL, INC.; *pg.* 654, *pg.* 247
DAM LUMBERJACK BEAVERS - Video Game - INTERNATIONAL GAME TECHNOLOGY; *pg.* 957, *pg.* 1024
DAMA - Chemical Product - ALBEMARLE CORPORATION; *pg.* 1146, *pg.* 741
DAMAR - Varnish - MARTIN/F. WEBER COMPANY; *pg.* 962, *pg.* 1567
DAMARA - Lamp - ASHLEY FURNITURE INDUSTRIES, INC.; *pg.* 914, *pg.* 1852
DAMASCUS - Carpet - BEAULIEU GROUP, LLC; *pg.* 917, *pg.* 529
DAME GAME - Shoe - AEROGROUP INTERNATIONAL, INC.; *pg.* 1803, *pg.* 1055
DAME ROOM - Sandals - AEROGROUP INTERNATIONAL, INC.; *pg.* 1803, *pg.* 1055

DAME TIME - Sandals - AEROGROUP INTERNATIONAL, INC.; *pg.* 1803, *pg.* 1055
DAMIXA - Faucet - MASCO CORPORATION; *pg.* 96, *pg.* 909
DAMLA - Beverages - THE COCA-COLA COMPANY; *pg.* 240, *pg.* 493
DAMON - Recreation Vehicle - THOR INDUSTRIES, INC.; *pg.* 1711, *pg.* 1456
DAMP-SHRINK - Heat Shrink - PANDUIT CORP.; *pg.* 661, *pg.* 663
DAMRAQ - Gin - REMY COINTREAU USA INC.; *pg.* 1969, *pg.* 1285
DANA - Clothing - ABERCROMBIE & FITCH CO.; *pg.* 37, *pg.* 1466
DANA - Furniture - AMISCO INDUSTRIES LTD.; *pg.* 913, *pg.* 1958
DANA - Truck Component - EATON CORPORATION; *pg.* 1331, *pg.* 1429
DANA - Educational Materials - RENAISSANCE LEARNING, INC.; *pg.* 607, *pg.* 1899
DANA SPICER - Truck Component - EATON CORPORATION; *pg.* 1331, *pg.* 1429
DANAHER CONTROLS - Sensing And Control Product - DANAHER CORPORATION; *pg.* 1044, *pg.* 397
DANALITE - Showcase Lighting Fixtures - JUNO LIGHTING, INC.; *pg.* 1300, *pg.* 606
DANAZOL - Pharmaceutical Product - LANNETT COMPANY, INC.; *pg.* 1555, *pg.* 1566
DANBURY - Furniture - ASHLEY FURNITURE INDUSTRIES, INC.; *pg.* 914, *pg.* 1852
DANBURY - Furniture - FLEXSTEEL INDUSTRIES, INC.; *pg.* 925, *pg.* 707
DANBURY MINT - Heirloom - MBI INC.; *pg.* 1778, *pg.* 363
DANCE - DVD - GAIAM, INC.; *pg.* 1532, *pg.* 334
DANCE CAM - Toy & Game - HASBRO, INC.; *pg.* 954, *pg.* 1603
DANCE MAGAZINE - Publication - MACFADDEN COMMUNICATIONS GROUP, LLC; *pg.* 1660, *pg.* 1254
DANCE MAGAZINE COLLEGE GUIDE - Publication - MACFADDEN COMMUNICATIONS GROUP, LLC; *pg.* 1660, *pg.* 1254
DANCE MAGAZINE STERN'S DIRECTORY - Publication - MACFADDEN COMMUNICATIONS GROUP, LLC; *pg.* 1660, *pg.* 1254
DANCE SNEAKER - Jazz Dance Shoes - CAPEZIO BALLET MAKERS INC.; *pg.* 1805, *pg.* 1125
DANCE SPORT - Ballroom Dance Shoes - CAPEZIO BALLET MAKERS INC.; *pg.* 1805, *pg.* 1125
DANCER - Footwear - P.W. MINOR & SON, INC.; *pg.* 1816, *pg.* 1140
DANCESTEP - Flooring Product - STAGESTEP INC.; *pg.* 1688, *pg.* 1570
DANCIE - Dolls - THE GOLDBERGER COMPANY, LLC; *pg.* 954, *pg.* 1235
DANCING BULL - Wine - E&J GALLO WINERY; *pg.* 1962, *pg.* 149
DANCING DOLPHINS - Game - WMS INDUSTRIES INC.; *pg.* 593, *pg.* 666
DANCING IN THE ISLES - Nail Care Product - OPI PRODUCTS INC.; *pg.* 518, *pg.* 167
DANCING THROUGH TIME: AN AMERICAN GIRLS EVENT - Games - AMERICAN GIRL LLC; *pg.* 949, *pg.* 1871
DANCING WATERS - Sprinklers - RAIN BIRD CORPORATION; *pg.* 707, *pg.* 44
DANDUX - Handling Product - C.R. DANIELS, INC.; *pg.* 1456, *pg.* 769
DANDY - Food Product - A. DUDA & SONS INC.; *pg.* 835, *pg.* 457
DANETTE - Lamp - ASHLEY FURNITURE INDUSTRIES, INC.; *pg.* 914, *pg.* 1852
D'ANGELO - Sandwich Shop Chain - PAPA GINOS-DEANGELO HOLDING CORPORATION, INC.; *pg.* 1743, *pg.* 817
DANGEROUS - Apparel - OAKLEY, INC.; *pg.* 1840, *pg.* 86
DANGEROUS BEAUTY - Video Game - INTERNATIONAL GAME TECHNOLOGY; *pg.* 957, *pg.* 1024
DANIBLACK - Footwear - SCHWARTZ & BENJAMIN, INC.; *pg.* 1818, *pg.* 1290
DANIEL BOONE - Knife - BUCK KNIVES, INC.; *pg.* 1828, *pg.* 550
DANIEL WOODHEAD - Electronic Components - MOLEX INCORPORATED; *pg.* 655, *pg.* 628
DANIELA - Lighting - ETHAN ALLEN INTERIORS INC.; *pg.* 924, *pg.* 343
DANIELLE - Clothing - ABERCROMBIE & FITCH CO.; *pg.* 37, *pg.* 1466
DANIELLE - Lamp - ASHLEY FURNITURE INDUSTRIES, INC.; *pg.* 914, *pg.* 1852
DANIMALS - Yogurt - THE DANNON COMPANY, INC.; *pg.* 851, *pg.* 1351
DANISH - Corner Bead - USG CORPORATION; *pg.* 118, *pg.* 594
DANKERSITE - Lens - DANKER LABORATORIES INC.; *pg.* 1408, *pg.* 465
DANNER - Footwear - LACROSSE FOOTWEAR, INC.; *pg.* 1811, *pg.* 1503
DANNON - Soft Drink - THE COCA-COLA COMPANY; *pg.* 240, *pg.* 493
DANNON - Yogurt - THE DANNON COMPANY, INC.; *pg.* 851, *pg.* 1351
DANSCORELLA - Cheese - SAPUTO, INC.; *pg.* 893, *pg.* 1956
DANSK - Tableware, Glassware & Flatware Products - LENOX CORPORATION; *pg.* 1126, *pg.* 1518
DANSKIN - Apparel - ICONIX BRAND GROUP, INC.; *pg.* 26, *pg.* 1243
DANSNEAKER - Footwear - CAPEZIO BALLET MAKERS INC.; *pg.* 1805, *pg.* 1125
DANTE'S INFERNO - Video Game - ELECTRONIC ARTS INC.; *pg.* 951, *pg.* 189
DANTOBROM - Water Treatment Chemicals - LONZA INC.; *pg.* 1171, *pg.* 1041
DANTOCHLOR - Water Treatment Chemicals - LONZA INC.; *pg.* 1171, *pg.* 1041
DANTOGARD - Preservatives for Microbiological Control - LONZA INC.; *pg.* 1171, *pg.* 1041
DANTOGARD PLUS - Preservatives for Microbiological Control & HI+I - LONZA INC.; *pg.* 1171, *pg.* 1041
DANTOGARD PLUS LIQUID - Liquid Preservatives for Microbiological Control - LONZA INC.; *pg.* 1171, *pg.* 1041
DANTRIUM - Pharmaceutical Product - IMPAX LABORATORIES, INC.; *pg.* 1544, *pg.* 101
DANTZ - Software System - EMC CORPORATION; *pg.* 391, *pg.* 825
DANUBE - Flatware - ONEIDA LTD; *pg.* 1129, *pg.* 1318
DANVERN - Paint Nozzle - SHERWIN-WILLIAMS DIVERSIFIED BRANDS DIVISION; *pg.* 1448, *pg.* 1435
DANVERS - Footwear - EASTLAND SHOE CORPORATION; *pg.* 1808, *pg.* 750
DANYL - Lamp - ASHLEY FURNITURE INDUSTRIES, INC.; *pg.* 914, *pg.* 1852
DAOTAN - Waterborne - CYTEC INDUSTRIES, INC.; *pg.* 1155, *pg.* 1131
DAP - Caulks & Sealants - DAP PRODUCTS, INC.; *pg.* 1441, *pg.* 756
DAP - Coating And Sealant - RPM INTERNATIONAL INC.; *pg.* 1447, *pg.* 1464
DAP ALEX PLUS - Caulk And Sealant - DAP PRODUCTS, INC.; *pg.* 1441, *pg.* 756
DAP CAP - Caulk And Sealant - DAP PRODUCTS, INC.; *pg.* 1441, *pg.* 756
DAPCO - Chemical Product - CYTEC INDUSTRIES, INC.; *pg.* 1155, *pg.* 1131
DAPOXYL - Molecular Probe Product - THERMO FISHER SCIENTIFIC INC.; *pg.* 1602, *pg.* 61
DAPTACEL - Medication for Diphtheria, Tetanus and Pertussis - SANOFI PASTEUR, INC; *pg.* 1591, *pg.* 1588
DAPTEX - Caulk And Sealant - DAP PRODUCTS, INC.; *pg.* 1441, *pg.* 756
DAR - Medical Device - MALLINCKRODT PHARMACEUTICALS; *pg.* 1557, *pg.* 978
DAR - Breathing Systems & Respiratory Supplies - MEDTRONIC; *pg.* 1563, *pg.* 183
DARA MICHELLE - Women's Fashion Accessories Stores - CLAIRE'S STORES, INC.; *pg.* 1764, *pg.* 617
DARACLEAN - Micro-Lubricant System - ITW FLUIDS NORTH AMERICA; *pg.* 980, *pg.* 614
DARACLEAN - Aqueous Cleaners - ITW MAGNAFLUX; *pg.* 1418, *pg.* 615
DARAMAX - Fermentation Process Aids - GE WATER & PROCESS TECHNOLOGIES; *pg.* 1339, *pg.* 1588
DARASPRAY - Paper Making Aids - GE WATER & PROCESS TECHNOLOGIES; *pg.* 1339, *pg.* 1588
DARC - Optoelectronic Product - BREWER SCIENCE, INC.; *pg.* 1150, *pg.* 989
DARCY - Clothing - ABERCROMBIE & FITCH CO.; *pg.* 37, *pg.* 1466
DARCY - Footwear - PHOENIX FOOTWEAR GROUP, INC.; *pg.* 1815, *pg.* 60
DARDA - Racing Cars & Sets - LIFOAM INDUSTRIES INC.; *pg.* 961, *pg.* 772
DARDEN RESTAURANTS - Restaurants - DARDEN RESTAURANTS, INC.; *pg.* 1724, *pg.* 453
DARDEVLE - Fishing Lures - EPPINGER MANUFACTURING CO.; *pg.* 1833, *pg.* 876
D.A.R.E. - Software - CLEARONE COMMUNICATIONS, INC.; *pg.* 629, *pg.* 1756
DAREDEVIL - Video Game - INTERNATIONAL GAME TECHNOLOGY; *pg.* 957, *pg.* 1024
DAREDEVIL FOOTBAGS - Pellet Filled Synthetic Leather Covers for All-Around Play - DUNCAN TOYS COMPANY; *pg.* 951, *pg.* 1465
DARFRESH - Vacuum-Skin Packaging Films & Equipment - SEALED AIR CORPORATION; *pg.* 1468, *pg.* 1058
DARI-KOOL FALLING - Milk Cooler - BOUMATIC LLC; *pg.* 701, *pg.* 1865
DARI-KOOL GLACIER - Milk Cooler - BOUMATIC LLC; *pg.* 701, *pg.* 1865
DARI-KOOL INSTA-KOOL - Milk Cooler - BOUMATIC LLC; *pg.* 701, *pg.* 1865
DARI-KOOL PLATE COOLER - Milk Cooler - BOUMATIC LLC; *pg.* 701, *pg.* 1865
DARIEN - Furniture - FLEXSTEEL INDUSTRIES, INC.; *pg.* 925, *pg.* 707
DARIGOLD - Dairy Products - DARIGOLD, INC.; *pg.* 852, *pg.* 1835
DARITEEN - Flavors - SYMRISE, INC.; *pg.* 1183, *pg.* 1125
DARITEK - Food Ingredient - FOREMOST FARMS USA COOPERATIVE; *pg.* 856, *pg.* 1854
DARK ALLEY - Books - HARPERCOLLINS PUBLISHERS INC.; *pg.* 1647, *pg.* 1237
DARK EYES - Vodka - JIM BEAM BRANDS CO.; *pg.* 1965, *pg.* 601
DARK FALLS - Educational Materials - SCHOLASTIC INC.; *pg.* 1683, *pg.* 1288
DARK HORSE COMICS - Comic-Book Publisher - DARK HORSE COMICS, INC.; *pg.* 1633, *pg.* 1500
DARK IRON - Web Applications - EOLAS TECHNOLOGIES, INC.; *pg.* 1243, *pg.* 573
DARK MAGIC - Coffee - KEURIG GREEN MOUNTAIN, INC.; *pg.* 868, *pg.* 1768
DARK MATTER - Nutritional Supplement - MAXIMUM HUMAN PERFORMANCE, INC.; *pg.* 1559, *pg.* 1065
DARK RAGE - Nutritional Supplement - MAXIMUM HUMAN PERFORMANCE, INC.; *pg.* 1559, *pg.* 1065
DARK-SKY - Security Lighting - JUNO LIGHTING, INC.; *pg.* 1300, *pg.* 606
DARK VANILLA - Women's Fragrance - COTY, INC.; *pg.* 506, *pg.* 1219
DARKNESS - Game - ACTIVISION BLIZZARD, INC.; *pg.* 948, *pg.* 271
DARKWING DUCK - Cartoon Character - THE WALT DISNEY COMPANY; *pg.* 317, *pg.* 52
DARLINGTON RACEWAY - Motorsports Facility - INTERNATIONAL SPEEDWAY CORPORATION; *pg.* 553, *pg.* 420
DARNELL-ROSE - Casters & Wheels - DARNELL-ROSE; *pg.* 1045, *pg.* 67
DARPHIN - Cosmetics & Fragrances - THE ESTEE LAUDER COMPANIES INC.; *pg.* 508, *pg.* 1229
DARRYL'S - Restaurants - HOULIHAN'S RESTAURANTS, INC.; *pg.* 1731, *pg.* 716
DARS - Criminal Justice & Rehabilitation Services - MEDTOX SCIENTIFIC, INC.; *pg.* 1422, *pg.* 962
DART - Digital Marketing Product - DOUBLECLICK, INC.; *pg.* 1239, *pg.* 1225
DART - Dick Test Card - STERIS CORPORATION; *pg.* 1597, *pg.* 1464
DART - Medical System - VARIAN MEDICAL SYSTEMS, INC.; *pg.* 1434, *pg.* 178
DART ENTERPRISE - Digital Marketing Product - DOUBLECLICK, INC.; *pg.* 1239, *pg.* 1225
DART FOR ADVERTISERS - Digital Marketing Product - DOUBLECLICK, INC.; *pg.* 1239, *pg.* 1225
DART FOR PUBLISHERS - Digital Marketing Product - DOUBLECLICK, INC.; *pg.* 1239, *pg.* 1225
DART SALES MANAGER - Digital Marketing Product - DOUBLECLICK, INC.; *pg.* 1239, *pg.* 1225
DART SEARCH - Digital Marketing Product - DOUBLECLICK, INC.; *pg.* 1239, *pg.* 1225
THE DART THROWER - Golf Products - FEEL GOLF CO., INC.; *pg.* 1834, *pg.* 465
DARTBOARD - Eyewear - OAKLEY, INC.; *pg.* 1840, *pg.* 86
DARVAN - Surfactants - R.T. VANDERBILT COMPANY, INC.; *pg.* 1180, *pg.* 364

First page reference indicates Business Class Edition
Second page reference indicates Geographic Edition

444, *pg.* 287

DARVON - Pharmaceutical Product - ELI LILLY AND COMPANY; *pg.* 1527, *pg.* 684
DARWIN CALIBRATOR - Software - BENTLEY SYSTEMS, INC.; *pg.* 361, *pg.* 1531
DARWIN DESIGNER - Software - BENTLEY SYSTEMS, INC.; *pg.* 361, *pg.* 1531
DAS RAD - Educational Materials - SCHOLASTIC INC.; *pg.* 1683, *pg.* 1288
DASANI - Bottled Water - THE COCA-COLA COMPANY; *pg.* 240, *pg.* 493
DASANI ACTIVE - Beverages - THE COCA-COLA COMPANY; *pg.* 240, *pg.* 493
DASANI BALANCE - Beverages - THE COCA-COLA COMPANY; *pg.* 240, *pg.* 493
DASANI FLAVORS - Beverages - THE COCA-COLA COMPANY; *pg.* 240, *pg.* 493
DASANI NUTRIWATER - Beverages - THE COCA-COLA COMPANY; *pg.* 240, *pg.* 493
DASANI PLUS - Beverages - THE COCA-COLA COMPANY; *pg.* 240, *pg.* 493
DASCARD - Electronic Instrument - KEITHLEY INSTRUMENTS, INC.; *pg.* 1418, *pg.* 1473
DASD MANAGER PLUS - Software - BMC SOFTWARE, INC.; *pg.* 362, *pg.* 1701
DASH - Data Acquisition Recorder - ASTRO-MED, INC.; *pg.* 619, *pg.* 1609
DASH - Aircraft - THE BOEING COMPANY; *pg.* 225, *pg.* 567
DASH - Fire Chassis - PIERCE MANUFACTURING, INC.; *pg.* 188, *pg.* 1852
DASH - Laundry Product - THE PROCTER & GAMBLE COMPANY; *pg.* 1129, *pg.* 1418
DASH - Bike - TREK BICYCLE CORPORATION; *pg.* 1847, *pg.* 1896
DASH-IN GRILL - Restaurants - KWIK TRIP INC.; *pg.* 1026, *pg.* 1864
DASH PRO - Bicycle - TREK BICYCLE CORPORATION; *pg.* 1847, *pg.* 1896
DASL - Assay - ILLUMINA, INC.; *pg.* 412, *pg.* 203
DASR - Defense System - RAYTHEON COMPANY; *pg.* 233, *pg.* 854
DAT DDS - Drive - QUANTUM CORPORATION; *pg.* 458, *pg.* 250
DATA ACCELERATOR COMPRESSION - Software - BMC SOFTWARE, INC.; *pg.* 362, *pg.* 1701
DATA ADAPTER - Software - EGAIN COMMUNICATIONS CORPORATION; *pg.* 1242, *pg.* 284
DATA ANSWERS - Wireless Communication System - AT&T SOUTHEAST; *pg.* 1868, *pg.* 489
DATA CENTER OUTSOURCING - Software - SUNGARD DATA SYSTEMS INC.; *pg.* 477, *pg.* 1592
DATA DOMAIN - Deduplication Storage Systems - EMC CORPORATION; *pg.* 391, *pg.* 825
DATA-FENCE - Network Security - WIREMOLD/LEGRAND; *pg.* 689, *pg.* 383
DATA FIRE - Computer Peripheral Equipment - DIGI INTERNATIONAL INC.; *pg.* 387, *pg.* 948
DATA-FLEX - Conduit - SOUTHWIRE COMPANY; *pg.* 1063, *pg.* 527
DATA-FRAME - CRT Display Format - EASTMAN KODAK COMPANY; *pg.* 1408, *pg.* 1333
DATA HIGHWAY II - Software - ROCKWELL AUTOMATION, INC.; *pg.* 668, *pg.* 1880
DATA HIGHWAY PLUS - Software - ROCKWELL AUTOMATION, INC.; *pg.* 668, *pg.* 1880
DATA I/O - Automated Device Programming System - DATA I/O CORPORATION; *pg.* 382, *pg.* 1824
THE DATA INTEGRATION COMPANY - Slogan - INFORMATICA CORPORATION; *pg.* 414, *pg.* 190
DATA LIFEGUARD - Software - WESTERN DIGITAL CORPORATION; *pg.* 492, *pg.* 118
DATA LIFEGUARD TOOLS - Software - WESTERN DIGITAL CORPORATION; *pg.* 492, *pg.* 118
DATA MANAGEMENT MODULE - Software - INTERNATIONAL GAME TECHNOLOGY; *pg.* 957, *pg.* 1024
DATA MEDIA - Filing Cabinets - TAB PRODUCTS CO. LLC; *pg.* 481, *pg.* 1869
DATA ONHAND - Software - WESTERN DIGITAL CORPORATION; *pg.* 492, *pg.* 118
DATA ONTAP - Software - NETAPP, INC.; *pg.* 444, *pg.* 287
DATA ONTAP 7G - Software - NETAPP, INC.; *pg.* 444, *pg.* 287
DATA ONTAP GX - Software - NETAPP, INC.; *pg.* 444, *pg.* 287
DATA ONTAP GX SYSTEM - Software - NETAPP, INC.; *pg.* 444, *pg.* 287
DATA PACKER - DASD Data Compression - BMC SOFTWARE, INC.; *pg.* 362, *pg.* 1701
DATA-PAK - Filing System - FELLOWES, INC.; *pg.* 397, *pg.* 620
DATA-PATCH - Copper Product - PANDUIT CORP.; *pg.* 661, *pg.* 663
DATA SOLVENT - Software System - MENTOR GRAPHICS CORPORATION; *pg.* 432, *pg.* 1510
DATA TAGS SOLUTION KIT - Software - BOTTOMLINE TECHNOLOGIES INC.; *pg.* 363, *pg.* 483
DATAARCHITECT - Software - DATATRAK INTERNATIONAL, INC.; *pg.* 383, *pg.* 1462
DATABASE INTEGRITY PLUS - Software - BMC SOFTWARE, INC.; *pg.* 362, *pg.* 1701
DATABASE PERFORMANCE - Software - BMC SOFTWARE, INC.; *pg.* 362, *pg.* 1701
DATABASEXTENDER - Software System - EMC CORPORATION; *pg.* 391, *pg.* 825
DATABRIDGE - Software - ATTACHMATE CORPORATION; *pg.* 356, *pg.* 1833
DATACARD - Desktop Card System - DATACARD CORPORATION; *pg.* 382, *pg.* 948
DATACARD GROUP - Card - DATACARD CORPORATION; *pg.* 382, *pg.* 948
DATACASTING XD - Software - INTERNATIONAL DATACASTING CORPORATION; *pg.* 419, *pg.* 1921
DATACENTRIC MODEL - Software System - MENTOR GRAPHICS CORPORATION; *pg.* 432, *pg.* 1510
DATADIRECT CONNECT - Software - PROGRESS DATADIRECT; *pg.* 457, *pg.* 1385
DATADIRECT CONNECT64 - Software - PROGRESS SOFTWARE CORPORATION; *pg.* 457, *pg.* 786
DATADIRECT OPENACCESS - Software - PROGRESS SOFTWARE CORPORATION; *pg.* 457, *pg.* 786
DATADIRECT SEQUELINK - Software - PROGRESS SOFTWARE CORPORATION; *pg.* 457, *pg.* 786
DATADIRECT SHADOW - Software - PROGRESS SOFTWARE CORPORATION; *pg.* 457, *pg.* 786
DATADIRECT SHADOW INTERFACE - Software - PROGRESS SOFTWARE CORPORATION; *pg.* 457, *pg.* 786
DATADIRECT TECHNOLOGIES - Software - PROGRESS SOFTWARE CORPORATION; *pg.* 457, *pg.* 786
DATADIRECT XML CONVERTERS - Software - PROGRESS SOFTWARE CORPORATION; *pg.* 457, *pg.* 786
DATADIRECT XQUERY - Software - PROGRESS SOFTWARE CORPORATION; *pg.* 457, *pg.* 786
DATADISC - Software - ROCKWELL AUTOMATION, INC.; *pg.* 668, *pg.* 1880
DATAEXCHANGE - Business Management Solutions - ADVENT SOFTWARE, INC.; *pg.* 345, *pg.* 211
DATAFABRIC - Software - NETAPP, INC.; *pg.* 444, *pg.* 287
DATAFACTORY - Software - DELL SOFTWARE; *pg.* 385, *pg.* 40
DATAFAX - Software - ENCORIUM GROUP, INC.; *pg.* 1528, *pg.* 1591
DATAFILE - Folders - TAB PRODUCTS CO. LLC; *pg.* 481, *pg.* 1869
DATAFINDER - Software - CERC; *pg.* 990, *pg.* 369
DATAFIRE - Computer Peripheral Equipment - DIGI INTERNATIONAL INC.; *pg.* 387, *pg.* 948
DATAFLASH - Memory Product - ATMEL CORPORATION; *pg.* 621, *pg.* 238
DATAFLASH - Lighting Product - HIGH END SYSTEMS, INC.; *pg.* 1299, *pg.* 1663
DATAFLEX - Thermal Transfer Imaging System - VIDEOJET TECHNOLOGIES INC.; *pg.* 489, *pg.* 671
DATAFLO - Software - EPICOR SOFTWARE CORPORATION; *pg.* 393, *pg.* 110
DATAFORCE - Network Storage System - CANDELIS, INC.; *pg.* 368, *pg.* 165
DATAFORT - Software - NETAPP, INC.; *pg.* 444, *pg.* 287
DATAFUSION - Software System - MENTOR GRAPHICS CORPORATION; *pg.* 432, *pg.* 1510
DATAGATE - Electronic Components - MOLEX INCORPORATED; *pg.* 655, *pg.* 628
DATAGATE PLUS - Electronic Components - MOLEX INCORPORATED; *pg.* 655, *pg.* 628
DATAGRAPHIC - Chart & Marking System - GRAPHIC CONTROLS LLC; *pg.* 401, *pg.* 1148
DATAGRAPHIX - Duplicate Film - ANACOMP, INC.; *pg.* 350, *pg.* 1777
DATAGRIP - Paper Products - BOISE CASCADE HOLDINGS, L.L.C.; *pg.* 1453, *pg.* 546
DATAGUARD - Software - F5 NETWORKS, INC.; *pg.* 396, *pg.* 1835
DATAGUARD - Communications-Grade Wire - HOUSTON WIRE & CABLE COMPANY; *pg.* 643, *pg.* 1708
DATAGUARD - Transport & Storage Case - IMATION CORP.; *pg.* 413, *pg.* 952
DATAGUIDE - Informational & Instructional Guides - EASTMAN KODAK COMPANY; *pg.* 1408, *pg.* 1333
DATAGYR 1000 - Meter Translation System - SIEMENS BUILDING TECHNOLOGIES, INC.; *pg.* 1376, *pg.* 560
DATALINK - Storage Solutions - DATALINK CORPORATION; *pg.* 382, *pg.* 922
DATALINK - Mobile Messaging Software - IPMOBILENET, LLC; *pg.* 648, *pg.* 261
DATALINK.COM - Storage Solutions Website - DATALINK CORPORATION; *pg.* 382, *pg.* 922
DATAMAN - Machine Vision System - COGNEX CORPORATION; *pg.* 1406, *pg.* 834
DATAMAPPER - Semiconductor Product - AVAGO TECHNOLOGIES; *pg.* 358, *pg.* 238
DATAMASTER - Imaging System - ANACOMP, INC.; *pg.* 350, *pg.* 1777
DATAMASTER - Electronic Message System - DAKTRONICS, INC.; *pg.* 633, *pg.* 1624
DATAMATIC - Meter Reading System - BADGER METER, INC.; *pg.* 1401, *pg.* 1873
DATAPAK - Photo Film - EASTMAN KODAK COMPANY; *pg.* 1408, *pg.* 1333
DATAPATH - Software System - MENTOR GRAPHICS CORPORATION; *pg.* 432, *pg.* 1510
DATAPORT - Medical Product - HOLOGIC, INC.; *pg.* 1416, *pg.* 784
DATAPULT - Information Sensor - COMVERGE, INC.; *pg.* 1325, *pg.* 536
DATARAM - Mini-Computer Related Products - DATARAM CORPORATION; *pg.* 383, *pg.* 1111
DATARIBBON - Printer Ribbon - RICOH PRINTING SYSTEMS AMERICA, INC.; *pg.* 462, *pg.* 279
DATASAFE - Reserve Power Batteries - ENERSYS INC.; *pg.* 1334, *pg.* 1584
DATASCOPE - Satellite Communication Product - KVH INDUSTRIES INC; *pg.* 650, *pg.* 1602
DATASCOPE - Medical Apparatus & Supplies - MAQUET; *pg.* 1558, *pg.* 1082
DATASELECT - Software - R.R. DONNELLEY & SONS COMPANY; *pg.* 1682, *pg.* 589
DATASERVER ELS - Software Product - DAEGIS INC; *pg.* 381, *pg.* 195
DATASONICS - Oceanographic Product - TELEDYNE BENTHOS, INC.; *pg.* 1431, *pg.* 838
DATASPEED - Paper - INTERNATIONAL PAPER COMPANY; *pg.* 1460, *pg.* 1644
DATASTREAM - Financial Publications - THOMSON REUTERS CORPORATION; *pg.* 1693, *pg.* 1944
DATASTREAMER - Software - DAKTRONICS, INC.; *pg.* 633, *pg.* 1624
DATASURE - Wireless Data Collection - THE L.S. STARRETT COMPANY; *pg.* 1421, *pg.* 783
DATATIME - Electronic Message System - DAKTRONICS, INC.; *pg.* 633, *pg.* 1624
DATATRAC - Electronic Message System - DAKTRONICS, INC.; *pg.* 633, *pg.* 1624
DATATRACE - Electronic Measurement Instrument - MESA LABORATORIES, INC.; *pg.* 1567, *pg.* 333
DATATRACKER - Software - SILVON SOFTWARE INC.; *pg.* 470, *pg.* 669
DATATRAK - Software - DATATRAK INTERNATIONAL, INC.; *pg.* 383, *pg.* 1462
DATATRAK ECLINICAL - Software Suite - DATATRAK INTERNATIONAL, INC.; *pg.* 383, *pg.* 1462
DATATRAK MEDICAL CODING SYSTEM - Medical Coding System - DATATRAK INTERNATIONAL, INC.; *pg.* 383, *pg.* 1462
DATATRAK PORTAL - Web-Enabled Self-Directed Workgroups - DATATRAK INTERNATIONAL, INC.; *pg.* 383, *pg.* 1462
DATATRAVELER - USB Flash Memory Drives - KINGSTON TECHNOLOGY COMPANY, INC.; *pg.* 425, *pg.* 90
DATATWIST - Wire & Cable Products - BELDEN, INC.; *pg.* 624, *pg.* 993
DATAVAC - Thermal Processing Equipment - SURFACE COMBUSTION, INC.; *pg.* 1077, *pg.* 1462
DATAVIEW - Software System - IMS HEALTH, INC.; *pg.* 1544, *pg.* 344
DATAVIEW - Software - NEWAGE TESTING INSTRUMENTS,

First page reference indicates Business Class Edition
Second page reference indicates Geographic Edition

INC.; *pg.* 1058, *pg.* 1532
DATAWALL - Electronic Display System - TRANS-LUX CORPORATION; *pg.* 681, *pg.* 365
DATAWATCH BDS - Content Management Product - DATAWATCH CORPORATION; *pg.* 383, *pg.* 813
DATAWATCH ES - Business Intelligence Product - DATAWATCH CORPORATION; *pg.* 383, *pg.* 813
DATAWATCH MAIL MANAGER - Content Management Product - DATAWATCH CORPORATION; *pg.* 383, *pg.* 813
DATAWINDOW - Data Access - SAP; *pg.* 465, *pg.* 78
DATAXTEND - Software - PROGRESS SOFTWARE CORPORATION; *pg.* 457, *pg.* 786
DATE NIGHT - Underwear - HABAND COMPANY, INC.; *pg.* 1772, *pg.* 1099
DATE.CA - Online Dating Service - SPARK NETWORKS, INC.; *pg.* 472, *pg.* 140
DATEL - Innerspace - STANLEY BLACK & DECKER, INC.; *pg.* 1063, *pg.* 358
DATEWORKS - Calendars - AMERICAN GREETINGS CORPORATION; *pg.* 1615, *pg.* 1428
DAUB GENIE ON - Video Game - INTERNATIONAL GAME TECHNOLOGY; *pg.* 957, *pg.* 1024
DAUBOND - Adhesive - DAUBERT INDUSTRIES, INC.; *pg.* 1155, *pg.* 561
DAUBRITE - Devices - DAUBERT INDUSTRIES, INC.; *pg.* 1155, *pg.* 561
DAUPHIN - Model Helicopter - AIRBUS HELICOPTERS, INC.; *pg.* 223, *pg.* 1698
DAVEY THE DOG - Stuffed Animal - 1-800-FLOWERS.COM, INC.; *pg.* 1758, *pg.* 1151
DAVEY TREE - Tree & Lawn Care Services - THE DAVEY TREE EXPERT COMPANY; *pg.* 1794, *pg.* 1456
DAVID - Food Product - CONAGRA FOODS, INC.; *pg.* 826, *pg.* 1014
DAVID BROOKS - Misses' & Petite's Clothing - KELLWOOD COMPANY; *pg.* 28, *pg.* 975
DAVID DART - Bridge Casualwear & Dresses - KELLWOOD COMPANY; *pg.* 28, *pg.* 975
DAVID MEISTER - Contemporary Eveningwear - KELLWOOD COMPANY; *pg.* 28, *pg.* 975
DAVID RODRIGUEZ - Fabrics - CHEROKEE GLOBAL BRANDS; *pg.* 21, *pg.* 278
DAVID WHITE - Electronic Measuring Tools - STANLEY BLACK & DECKER, INC.; *pg.* 1063, *pg.* 358
DAVID YURMAN - Jewelry And Watch - YURMAN DESIGN, INC.; *pg.* 15, *pg.* 1316
DAVID3 - Endoscopic System - AESCULAP, INC.; *pg.* 1487, *pg.* 1521
DAVIES - Seating Product - IRWIN SEATING COMPANY INC.; *pg.* 929, *pg.* 887
DAVINCI - Hearing Instrument - STARKEY LABORATORIES, INC.; *pg.* 1597, *pg.* 923
DAVINCI - Semiconductors - TEXAS INSTRUMENTS INCORPORATED; *pg.* 679, *pg.* 1688
DAVINCI COLOR NATURAL - Bath Accessory - CROSCILL, INC.; *pg.* 1122, *pg.* 1220
DAVIN'S DREAM TEAM - Ticket Program - BUCCANEERS LIMITED PARTNERSHIP; *pg.* 534, *pg.* 471
DAVIS - Waterproof Coating - DAVIS PAINT COMPANY; *pg.* 1441, *pg.* 982
DAVIS & SANFORD - Support System - THE TIFFEN COMPANY LLC; *pg.* 1432, *pg.* 1165
DAVIS INDUSTRIAL - Coating - DAVIS PAINT COMPANY; *pg.* 1441, *pg.* 982
DAVISIL - Chemical Product - SPECTRUM CHEMICALS & LABORATORY PRODUCTS, INC.; *pg.* 1181, *pg.* 94
DAVOL - Fabric Line - VICTOR INNOVATIVE TEXTILES; *pg.* 699, *pg.* 819
DAVOL RELIA VAC - Wound Drain & Closed Wound Suction Evacuator - C.R. BARD, INC.; *pg.* 1519, *pg.* 1094
DAVOL SYSTEM 5000 - Electro Surgical Generator - C.R. BARD, INC.; *pg.* 1519, *pg.* 1094
DAVSON - In/Out Personnel System - RUBBERMAID HOME PRODUCTS; *pg.* 1138, *pg.* 1453
DAVY CROCKETT - Knife - BUCK KNIVES, INC.; *pg.* 1828, *pg.* 550
DAW - Lamp - ASHLEY FURNITURE INDUSTRIES, INC.; *pg.* 914, *pg.* 1852
DAWN - Dishwashing Product - THE PROCTER & GAMBLE COMPANY; *pg.* 1129, *pg.* 1418
DAWN BOTANICALS - Dishwashing Detergent - THE PROCTER & GAMBLE COMPANY; *pg.* 1129, *pg.* 1418
DAWN DIRECT FOAM - Dishwashing Product - THE PROCTER & GAMBLE COMPANY; *pg.* 1129, *pg.* 1418
DAWN OF ACES - Online Game - IENTERTAINMENT NETWORK, INC.; *pg.* 1258, *pg.* 1360
DAWN PATROL - Glove - CALLAWAY GOLF COMPANY; *pg.* 1829, *pg.* 58
DAWN PLUS ODOR ERASER - Dishwashing Product - THE PROCTER & GAMBLE COMPANY; *pg.* 1129, *pg.* 1418
DAWN PLUS POWER SCRUBBERS - Dishwashing Product - THE PROCTER & GAMBLE COMPANY; *pg.* 1129, *pg.* 1418
DAWN POWER DISSOLVER - Cleaning Product - THE PROCTER & GAMBLE COMPANY; *pg.* 1129, *pg.* 1418
DAWN SIMPLE PLEASURES - Dishwashing Product - THE PROCTER & GAMBLE COMPANY; *pg.* 1129, *pg.* 1418
DAWN ULTRA - Dishwashing Detergent - THE PROCTER & GAMBLE COMPANY; *pg.* 1129, *pg.* 1418
DAWSON - Furniture - AMERICAN LEATHER LP; *pg.* 912, *pg.* 1673
DAWSON - Furniture - ETHAN ALLEN INTERIORS INC.; *pg.* 924, *pg.* 343
DAWSON - Bear - GUND, INC.; *pg.* 954, *pg.* 1056
DAXAD - Dispersing Agent - THE DOW CHEMICAL COMPANY; *pg.* 1157, *pg.* 898
DAXAS - Pulmonary Disease Treatment - PFIZER INC.; *pg.* 1581, *pg.* 1278
DAXBOURNE INTERNATIONAL - Extensions, Wigs, & Hairpiece Supplier - SPECIALTY CATALOG CORPORATION; *pg.* 1786, *pg.* 856
DAY AT THE FAIR - Lottery Game - ILLINOIS STATE LOTTERY; *pg.* 995, *pg.* 578
DAY-BRITE - Lighting Fixture & Control - PHILIPS LIGHTING; *pg.* 1303, *pg.* 806
DAY-END SYNC - Software - SYMANTEC CORPORATION; *pg.* 478, *pg.* 161
DAY FIT - DVD - GAIAM, INC.; *pg.* 1532, *pg.* 334
DAY-GLO - Fluorescent Colors - DAY-GLO COLOR CORP.; *pg.* 1441, *pg.* 1429
DAY MATT - Mattress Specifically for Day Bed Use - KINGSDOWN, INC.; *pg.* 932, *pg.* 1383
DAY NAUTA - Conical Mixers - LITTLEFORD DAY INC.; *pg.* 1356, *pg.* 728
DAY OF DEFEAT - Game - ACTIVISION BLIZZARD, INC.; *pg.* 948, *pg.* 271
DAY RUNNER - Office & School Supplies - WESTROCK COMPANY; *pg.* 1472, *pg.* 1805
DAY-TIMER - Time Management Systems - ACCO BRANDS CORPORATION; *pg.* 340, *pg.* 626
DAY TO DAY - Monthly Calendar - GUARDSMARK, LLC; *pg.* 401, *pg.* 1237
DAYAMINERAL - Pharmaceutical Products - ABBOTT LABORATORIES; *pg.* 1484, *pg.* 551
DAYHIKER - Safety Product - WISCONSIN PHARMACAL COMPANY, LLC; *pg.* 1610, *pg.* 1861
DAYLINK - Pharmaceutical Product - ALERE INC.; *pg.* 1488, *pg.* 849
DAYMAX - High-Shear Dispersion Blenders - LITTLEFORD DAY INC.; *pg.* 1356, *pg.* 728
DAYPRO - Medicine - PFIZER INC.; *pg.* 1581, *pg.* 1278
DAYPRO ALTA - Pharmaceutical Product - PFIZER INC.; *pg.* 1581, *pg.* 1278
DAYQUIL - Cold Medication - THE PROCTER & GAMBLE COMPANY; *pg.* 1129, *pg.* 1418
DAYQUIL PLUS VITAMIN C - Health Care Product - THE PROCTER & GAMBLE COMPANY; *pg.* 1129, *pg.* 1418
DAYS BUSINESS PLACE - Hotel, Motel & Restaurant Services - DAYS INNS WORLDWIDE, INC.; *pg.* 1089, *pg.* 1103
DAYS HOTELS - Hotels - DAYS INNS WORLDWIDE, INC.; *pg.* 1089, *pg.* 1103
DAYS INN - Motels & Hotels - DAYS INNS WORLDWIDE, INC.; *pg.* 1089, *pg.* 1103
DAYS INN - Hotels - WYNDHAM WORLDWIDE CORPORATION; *pg.* 1119, *pg.* 1107
DAYS SUITES - Suite Hotels - DAYS INNS WORLDWIDE, INC.; *pg.* 1089, *pg.* 1103
DAYSTAR - Information Display - INDUSTRIAL ELECTRONIC ENGINEERS, INC.; *pg.* 644, *pg.* 300
DAYSTAR NOVA - LCD Display Modules - INDUSTRIAL ELECTRONIC ENGINEERS, INC.; *pg.* 644, *pg.* 300
DAYSTOP - Motels - DAYS INNS WORLDWIDE, INC.; *pg.* 1089, *pg.* 1103
DAYTON - Tires - BRIDGESTONE AMERICAS, INC.; *pg.* 1879, *pg.* 1648
DAYTON - Metal Stamping Tools - FEDERAL SIGNAL CORPORATION; *pg.* 638, *pg.* 645
DAYTON - Electric Motors, HVAC & Pumps - W.W. GRAINGER, INC.; *pg.* 1390, *pg.* 625
DAYTONA 500 - Competitive Motorsport Event - INTERNATIONAL SPEEDWAY CORPORATION; *pg.* 553, *pg.* 420
DAYTONA 500 EXPERIENCE - Motorsports Event - INTERNATIONAL SPEEDWAY CORPORATION; *pg.* 553, *pg.* 420
DAYTONA DREAM LAPS - Motorsports Event - INTERNATIONAL SPEEDWAY CORPORATION; *pg.* 553, *pg.* 420
DAYTONA INTERNATIONAL SPEEDWAY - Motorsports Facility - INTERNATIONAL SPEEDWAY CORPORATION; *pg.* 553, *pg.* 420
DAYTONA USA - Motorsport - INTERNATIONAL SPEEDWAY CORPORATION; *pg.* 553, *pg.* 420
DAYTRANA - Estradiol Transdermal System - NOVEN PHARMACEUTICALS, INC.; *pg.* 1576, *pg.* 445
DAYTRIPPER - Golfing Accessories - CALLAWAY GOLF COMPANY; *pg.* 1829, *pg.* 58
DAZ - Laundry Product - THE PROCTER & GAMBLE COMPANY; *pg.* 1129, *pg.* 1418
DAZEY - Personal Care Electrical Product - HELEN OF TROY L.P.; *pg.* 511, *pg.* 1692
DAZZLE - Software - CITRIX SYSTEMS, INC.; *pg.* 375, *pg.* 424
DAZZLE - Window Treatment - CROSCILL, INC.; *pg.* 1122, *pg.* 1220
THE DAZZLER - Baby & Toddler Cups - EVENFLO COMPANY, INC.; *pg.* 924, *pg.* 1470
DAZZLING DIAMONDS - Video Game - INTERNATIONAL GAME TECHNOLOGY; *pg.* 957, *pg.* 1024
DAZZLING DOLLARS - Video Game - INTERNATIONAL GAME TECHNOLOGY; *pg.* 957, *pg.* 1024
DBA PRODUCTS - Bowling Equipment - BRUNSWICK BOWLING & BILLIARDS CORP.; *pg.* 1828, *pg.* 622
DBC - Brewer - BUNN-O-MATIC CORPORATION; *pg.* 53, *pg.* 661
DBC CAPS - Software - SS&C TECHNOLOGIES HOLDINGS, INC.; *pg.* 473, *pg.* 386
DBC DEBT MANAGER - Software - SS&C TECHNOLOGIES HOLDINGS, INC.; *pg.* 473, *pg.* 386
DBC FINANCE - Software - SS&C TECHNOLOGIES HOLDINGS, INC.; *pg.* 473, *pg.* 386
DBC FINLITE - Software - SS&C TECHNOLOGIES HOLDINGS, INC.; *pg.* 473, *pg.* 386
DBC HOUSING - Software - SS&C TECHNOLOGIES HOLDINGS, INC.; *pg.* 473, *pg.* 386
DBC MULTI-FAMILY - Software - SS&C TECHNOLOGIES HOLDINGS, INC.; *pg.* 473, *pg.* 386
DBC MULTI-FAMILY/HEALTH CARE - Software - SS&C TECHNOLOGIES HOLDINGS, INC.; *pg.* 473, *pg.* 386
DBC PORTOPT - Software - SS&C TECHNOLOGIES HOLDINGS, INC.; *pg.* 473, *pg.* 386
DBC STUDENT LOAN - Software - SS&C TECHNOLOGIES HOLDINGS, INC.; *pg.* 473, *pg.* 386
DBCHECK - Laser Measurement Instrument - COHERENT, INC.; *pg.* 1406, *pg.* 265
DBCORE - Automotive Thermal & Acoustical Barrier - LYDALL, INC.; *pg.* 1357, *pg.* 354
DBLYTE - Acoustical Barrier - LYDALL, INC.; *pg.* 1357, *pg.* 354
DBQDO - Vulcanizing Agents - LORD CORPORATION; *pg.* 1357, *pg.* 1360
DBUG - Software System - MENTOR GRAPHICS CORPORATION; *pg.* 432, *pg.* 1510
DBX - Medical Device - DEPUY SYNTHES; *pg.* 1523, *pg.* 1593
DBX - Compressors & Limiters - HARMAN INTERNATIONAL INDUSTRIES, INCORPORATED; *pg.* 641, *pg.* 374
DBXRAY - Software - BMC SOFTWARE, INC.; *pg.* 362, *pg.* 1701
DBY - Dresses & Career Apparel - KELLWOOD COMPANY; *pg.* 28, *pg.* 975
DBYII - Dresses & Career Apparel - KELLWOOD COMPANY; *pg.* 28, *pg.* 975
DC - Steel - A. FINKL & SONS CO.; *pg.* 1309, *pg.* 563
DC - Software - BIO-RAD LABORATORIES, INC.; *pg.* 1504, *pg.* 101
DC - Action Sports Footwear - QUIKSILVER, INC.; *pg.* 31, *pg.* 104
DC-210 PLUS - Zoom Digital Camera - EASTMAN KODAK COMPANY; *pg.* 1408, *pg.* 1333
DC-240 - Zoom Digital Camera - EASTMAN KODAK COMPANY; *pg.* 1408, *pg.* 1333
DC-3200 - Digital Camera - EASTMAN KODAK COMPANY;

First page reference indicates Business Class Edition
Second page reference indicates Geographic Edition

pg. 1408, pg. 1333

DC-4 - Lottery Game - D.C. LOTTERY & CHARITABLE GAMES CONTROL BOARD; pg. 991, pg. 398

DC ANALYZER - Software System - MENTOR GRAPHICS CORPORATION; pg. 432, pg. 1510

DC COMICS - Comic Books - DC COMICS, INC.; pg. 1633, pg. 1221

D.C. CURRENT - Financial Products - DOW JONES & COMPANY, INC.; pg. 1637, pg. 1225

DC EPIC - Fan - CRAFTMADE INTERNATIONAL, INC.; pg. 1295, pg. 1670

DC EXPERT - Software - SYNOPSYS, INC.; pg. 480, pg. 162

DC KENO - Lottery - D.C. LOTTERY & CHARITABLE GAMES CONTROL BOARD; pg. 991, pg. 398

DC PROFESSIONAL - Software - SYNOPSYS, INC.; pg. 480, pg. 162

DC SLAB - Laser System - ROFIN-SINAR TECHNOLOGIES, INC.; pg. 668, pg. 904

DC SUPER FRIENDS - Action Toys - FISHER-PRICE, INC.; pg. 953, pg. 1156

DC ULTRA - Software - SYNOPSYS, INC.; pg. 480, pg. 162

DC (VAD) - Steel - A. FINKL & SONS CO.; pg. 1309, pg. 563

DC VISTAR - 12V & 24V DC Flood Light (Metal Halide) - THE WILL-BURT CO., INC.; pg. 1437, pg. 1469

DC XCELLERATOR - Computer Software - PARAGON TECHNOLOGIES, INC.; pg. 1367, pg. 1528

DC-XTRA - Steel Product - A. FINKL & SONS CO.; pg. 1309, pg. 563

DC25 - Staples - ARROW FASTENER COMPANY, INC.; pg. 1042, pg. 1118

DC66 - Staples - ARROW FASTENER COMPANY, INC.; pg. 1042, pg. 1118

DCE - Computer Hardware - CISCO SYSTEMS, INC.; pg. 372, pg. 240

DCE - Apparels - UNDER ARMOUR, INC.; pg. 49, pg. 759

DCF - Steel - A. FINKL & SONS CO.; pg. 1309, pg. 563

DCL TRANSLATING - Lens - DANKER LABORATORIES INC.; pg. 1408, pg. 465

DCM - Glass & Ceramic Material - CORNING INCORPORATED; pg. 1122, pg. 1154

DCNL - Personal Care Electronic Product - HELEN OF TROY L.P.; pg. 511, pg. 1692

DCODE - Software - BIO-RAD LABORATORIES, INC.; pg. 1504, pg. 101

DCPC - Coupler - OPLINK COMMUNICATIONS, INC.; pg. 660, pg. 91

DCR - Transceiver - SKYWORKS SOLUTIONS, INC.; pg. 674, pg. 862

DCS-1800 - Security Software - ITUS CORPORATION; pg. 422, pg. 1180

DCS "THE BAG" - Alternate Delivery - THE DISPATCH PRINTING COMPANY; pg. 1636, pg. 1439

DCT - Lip Regimen - BLISTEX, INC.; pg. 502, pg. 644

DCX - Network Switch - BROCADE COMMUNICATIONS SYSTEMS, INC.; pg. 365, pg. 239

DDA - Banking Software - JACK HENRY & ASSOCIATES, INC.; pg. 422, pg. 988

DDDPLUS - Device to Simulate In Vitro Dissolution & Disintegration of Dosage Forms - SIMULATIONS PLUS, INC.; pg. 470, pg. 121

DDF - Personal & Household Product - THE PROCTER & GAMBLE COMPANY; pg. 1129, pg. 1418

DDI - Liquid Aliphatic Diisocyanate - HENKEL CORPORATION; pg. 1165, pg. 1535

DDI - Software - WIND RIVER SYSTEMS, INC.; pg. 493, pg. 38

DDL - Pumps - IDEX CORPORATION; pg. 1347, pg. 623

DDR - Memory Interfaces Controller Systems - RAMBUS INC.; pg. 459, pg. 288

DDS - Pumps - IDEX CORPORATION; pg. 1347, pg. 623

DD'S DISCOUNTS - Stores - ROSS STORES, INC.; pg. 1783, pg. 78

DDV - Fluid Handling System - GRACO, INC.; pg. 1342, pg. 935

DD(X) - Defense System - RAYTHEON COMPANY; pg. 233, pg. 854

DE-83R - Flame Retardants - CHEMTURA CORPORATION; pg. 1152, pg. 355

DE-AIREX - Defoamers - HERCULES INCORPORATED; pg. 1166, pg. 392

DE/CL-100 - Degreaser/Cleaner - HILLYARD, INC.; pg. 331, pg. 990

DE-EXPOSE - Software - BIO-RAD LABORATORIES, INC.; pg. 1504, pg. 101

DE-FLEX - Medical Product - W.L. GORE & ASSOCIATES, INC.; pg. 122, pg. 388

DE-GEL SUPREME - Lubricant - TEXAS REFINERY CORP.; pg. 986, pg. 1696

DE HAGO - Jewelry - DE HAGO, INC.; pg. 4, pg. 1222

DE LA RITZ - Hair Spray - BLUE CROSS LABORATORIES; pg. 326, pg. 277

DE-MOL DRY - Sweetener - ARCHER-DANIELS-MIDLAND COMPANY; pg. 825, pg. 565

DE-MOL FLAKE - Sweetener - ARCHER-DANIELS-MIDLAND COMPANY; pg. 825, pg. 565

DE NOBILI - Cigar - AVANTI CIGAR CORPORATION; pg. 1894, pg. 1527

DE NOIR - Wine - BILTMORE ESTATE WINE COMPANY; pg. 1958, pg. 1358

DE RUITER - Vegetable Seeds - MONSANTO COMPANY; pg. 1173, pg. 999

DE-STA-CO - Industrial & Production Hardware; Blower Housings - DE-STA-CO INDUSTRIES; pg. 1045, pg. 867

DE-STAIN - Clinging Liquid - DELTA FOREMOST CHEMICAL CORPORATION; pg. 1155, pg. 1642

DE-STRESS - Nutritional Supplement - WHITEWING LABS, INC.; pg. 1610, pg. 99

DE-TONE - Hearing Protection - SELLSTROM MANUFACTURING CO.; pg. 1428, pg. 659

DE-VO-KO - Alkyd & Latex Finishes - AKZONOBEL DECORATIVE PAINTS U.S.; pg. 1439, pg. 1474

DE-VO-LAC - Lacquers - AKZONOBEL DECORATIVE PAINTS U.S.; pg. 1439, pg. 1474

DE-VO-PRO - Contractor Product Line of Paints - AKZONOBEL DECORATIVE PAINTS U.S.; pg. 1439, pg. 1474

DE-VO-TEX - Texture Coating - AKZONOBEL DECORATIVE PAINTS U.S.; pg. 1439, pg. 1474

DE WITT - Beauty Product - FLEET LABORATORIES; pg. 1531, pg. 1787

DE ZAAN - Cocoa Powders - ARCHER-DANIELS-MIDLAND COMPANY; pg. 825, pg. 565

DEA - Footwear - PHOENIX FOOTWEAR GROUP, INC.; pg. 1815, pg. 60

DEACON - Shoes - COACH, INC.; pg. 3, pg. 1214

DEAD HEAT HOT SAUCE - Backyard Grill - BARBEQUES GALORE, INC.; pg. 51, pg. 173

DEAD-LENGTH - Spindle Tooling - HARDINGE INC.; pg. 1344, pg. 1157

DEAD-ON - Gaming Product - GLD PRODUCTS, INC.; pg. 1835, pg. 1862

DEAD SPACE - Video Game - ELECTRONIC ARTS INC.; pg. 951, pg. 189

DEADSPIN - Sports Media Site - GAWKER MEDIA LLC; pg. 1248, pg. 1234

DEAE - Chromatography Product - PALL CORPORATION; pg. 232, pg. 1323

DEAL - Apparel - OAKLEY, INC.; pg. 1840, pg. 86

DEAL - Computer Software - TECK RESOURCES LIMITED; pg. 1183, pg. 1912

DEAL OR NO DEAL - Lottery Game - OHIO LOTTERY COMMISSION; pg. 1002, pg. 1433

DEAL WITH THE DEVIL - Video Game - INTERNATIONAL GAME TECHNOLOGY; pg. 957, pg. 1024

DEALER & APPLICATOR - Magazine - VANCE PUBLISHING CORPORATION; pg. 1699, pg. 627

DEALER-PAK - Fasteners - DORMAN PRODUCTS, INC.; pg. 204, pg. 1522

DEALER SPECIALTIES - Advertising Publication - DOMINION ENTERPRISES; pg. 1636, pg. 1796

DEALERAXESS - Online Trading Services - MARKETAXESS HOLDINGS INC.; pg. 778, pg. 1256

DEALERSCOPE MERCHANDISING - Magazine - NORTH AMERICAN PUBLISHING COMPANY; pg. 1671, pg. 1567

DEALERSKINS - Advertising Publication - DOMINION ENTERPRISES; pg. 1636, pg. 1796

DEALTIME - Magazine - SHOPPING.COM, LTD.; pg. 1280, pg. 50

DEAN - Tires - COOPER TIRE & RUBBER COMPANY; pg. 1881, pg. 1453

DEAN - Kosher Poultry - EMPIRE KOSHER POULTRY, INC.; pg. 854, pg. 1553

DEAN & DELUCA - Food And Kitchenware - DEAN & DELUCA, INC.; pg. 1018, pg. 723

DEANNA - Furniture - J. ROBERT SCOTT INC.; pg. 930, pg. 105

DEAN'S - Dairy Product - DEAN FOODS COMPANY; pg. 852, pg. 1679

DEAR AMERICA - Educational Materials - SCHOLASTIC INC.; pg. 1683, pg. 1288

DEARBORN - Office Furniture - STEELCASE INC.; pg. 475, pg. 889

DEARFOAMS - Footwear - R.G. BARRY CORPORATION; pg. 1818, pg. 1470

THE DEARFOAMS COMPANY - Tagline - R.G. BARRY CORPORATION; pg. 1818, pg. 1470

DEARTEK - Detackification Products - GE WATER & PROCESS TECHNOLOGIES; pg. 1339, pg. 1588

DEB PLUS - Fashions - DEB SHOPS, INC.; pg. 23, pg. 1563

DEBBIE - Clothing - ABERCROMBIE & FITCH CO.; pg. 37, pg. 1466

DEBICA - Tire And Rubber Product - THE GOODYEAR TIRE & RUBBER COMPANY; pg. 1883, pg. 1401

DEBIT TALK - Telephone Service - IDT CORPORATION; pg. 643, pg. 1096

DEBLISTER - Packaging Device - MTS MEDICATION TECHNOLOGIES, INC.; pg. 442, pg. 463

DEBOLES - Food Product - THE HAIN CELESTIAL GROUP, INC.; pg. 860, pg. 1172

DEBONAIR - Medical Equipment - INVACARE CORPORATION; pg. 1546, pg. 1451

DEBORAH - Clothing - ABERCROMBIE & FITCH CO.; pg. 37, pg. 1466

DEBORAH - Lamp - ASHLEY FURNITURE INDUSTRIES, INC.; pg. 914, pg. 1852

DEBORAH LEWIS - Collectibles - ENESCO, LLC; pg. 1124, pg. 620

DEBRI-SHIELD - Vinyl Rainwater System - GENOVA PRODUCTS, INC.; pg. 83, pg. 875

DEBT AND DERIVATIVES - Software - SS&C TECHNOLOGIES HOLDINGS, INC.; pg. 473, pg. 386

DEBT MANAGER - Collection & Recovery Solutions - FAIR ISAAC CORPORATION; pg. 1247, pg. 955

DEBUG DETECTIVE - Software System - MENTOR GRAPHICS CORPORATION; pg. 432, pg. 1510

DEBUT - Shoe - AEROGROUP INTERNATIONAL, INC.; pg. 1803, pg. 1055

DEBUT - Furniture - JASPER GROUP; pg. 930, pg. 691

DEC-RANGER - Decade Resistance Selector - OHMITE MANUFACTURING COMPANY; pg. 660, pg. 553

DECADE - Boots - AEROGROUP INTERNATIONAL, INC.; pg. 1803, pg. 1055

DECADE PLUS - Dental Chair - A-DEC, INC.; pg. 1483, pg. 1500

DECADE SHOWCASE WITH ENDURACOTE - Two sided steel door with painted hardware - RAYNOR GARAGE DOORS; pg. 106, pg. 607

DECAF CAFFE VERONA - Coffee - STARBUCKS CORPORATION; pg. 897, pg. 1840

DECAF ESPRESSO ROAST - Coffee - STARBUCKS CORPORATION; pg. 897, pg. 1840

DECAF FRENCH ROAST - Coffee - PEET'S COFFEE & TEA, INC.; pg. 1029, pg. 85

DECAF HOUSE BLEND - Coffee - PEET'S COFFEE & TEA, INC.; pg. 1029, pg. 85

DECAF KOMODO DRAGON BLEND - Coffee - STARBUCKS CORPORATION; pg. 897, pg. 1840

DECAF LIGHTNOTE BLEND - Coffee - STARBUCKS CORPORATION; pg. 897, pg. 1840

DECAF MAJOR DICKASON'S BLEND - Coffee - PEET'S COFFEE & TEA, INC.; pg. 1029, pg. 85

DECAF MINT GREEN TEA - Tea Product - CELESTIAL SEASONINGS, INC.; pg. 846, pg. 310

DECAF MOCHA JAVA - Coffee - PEET'S COFFEE & TEA, INC.; pg. 1029, pg. 85

DECAF PIKE PLACE ROAST - Coffee - STARBUCKS CORPORATION; pg. 897, pg. 1840

DECAF SIERRA DORADA - Coffee - PEET'S COFFEE & TEA, INC.; pg. 1029, pg. 85

DECAF SPECIAL BLEND - Coffee - PEET'S COFFEE & TEA, INC.; pg. 1029, pg. 85

DECAF SUMATRA - Coffee - PEET'S COFFEE & TEA, INC.; pg. 1029, pg. 85

DECAF SUMATRA - Coffee - STARBUCKS CORPORATION; pg. 897, pg. 1840

DECALOG - Software - SUNGARD DATA SYSTEMS INC.; pg. 477, pg. 1592

DECAMIRED - Filter - THE TIFFEN COMPANY LLC; pg. 1432, pg. 1165

DECANOX - Feed Ingredients - ARCHER-DANIELS-MIDLAND COMPANY; pg. 825, pg. 565

DECANOX MTS-30 - Feed Ingredient - ARCHER-DANIELS-MIDLAND COMPANY; pg. 825, pg. 565

DECANOX MTS-50 - Feed Ingredient - ARCHER-DANIELS-MIDLAND COMPANY; pg. 825, pg. 565

DECANOX MTS-70 - Feed Ingredients - ARCHER-DANIELS-MIDLAND COMPANY; *pg.* 825, *pg.* 565
DECANOX MTS-90 - Feed Ingredient - ARCHER-DANIELS-MIDLAND COMPANY; *pg.* 825, *pg.* 565
DECARBONIZER - Soak Tank Kitchenware - ECOLAB INC.; *pg.* 329, *pg.* 960
DECARBONIZER MXP - Soaking Solution - ECOLAB INC.; *pg.* 329, *pg.* 960
DECATHLON - Medical Device - SPIRE CORPORATION; *pg.* 1378, *pg.* 786
DECATHLON - Zipper - YKK CORPORATION OF AMERICA; *pg.* 699, *pg.* 536
DECCA - Sonar Fish Finder - SPERRY MARINE INC.; *pg.* 1430, *pg.* 1778
DECCK - Footwear - STEVEN MADDEN, LTD.; *pg.* 1819, *pg.* 1176
DECCOX - Animal Nutrition Product - MANNA PRO CORPORATION; *pg.* 1478, *pg.* 975
DECDRIVER - Semiconductor Devices - ANALOG DEVICES, INC.; *pg.* 617, *pg.* 839
DECHLORANE - Flame Retardant - OCCIDENTAL CHEMICAL CORPORATION; *pg.* 1175, *pg.* 1685
DECIDE! - Software - SCHLUMBERGER LIMITED; *pg.* 801, *pg.* 1714
DECIDE WITH CONFIDENCE - Tagline - THE DUN & BRADSTREET CORP.; *pg.* 1637, *pg.* 1120
DECILAB - Software - BIO-RAD LABORATORIES, INC.; *pg.* 1504, *pg.* 101
DECIMAL - Fabric - MOMENTUM TEXTILES INC.; *pg.* 697, *pg.* 114
DECIPHER - Software - TRIZETTO CORPORATION; *pg.* 485, *pg.* 327
DECISCAN - Software - BIO-RAD LABORATORIES, INC.; *pg.* 1504, *pg.* 101
DECISION ANALYZER - Software - ASPEN TECHNOLOGY, INC.; *pg.* 354, *pg.* 804
DECISION POWER - Health Care Insurance - HEALTH NET, INC.; *pg.* 1540, *pg.* 308
DECISIONCENTER - Medical Service - OMNICELL INC.; *pg.* 1578, *pg.* 161
DECISIONS, DECISIONS - Educational Materials - SCHOLASTIC INC.; *pg.* 1683, *pg.* 1288
DECISPLIT - Fiber Optic Splitter - COMMUNICATIONS SPECIALTIES, INC.; *pg.* 377, *pg.* 1338
DECITABINE - Pharmaceutical Product - ASTEX PHARMACEUTICALS, INC; *pg.* 1497, *pg.* 77
DECK - Office Furniture - STEELCASE INC.; *pg.* 475, *pg.* 889
DECK FRAME - Roof System - VARCO PRUDEN BUILDINGS, INC.; *pg.* 118, *pg.* 1647
THE DECK OF A LIFETIME - Slogan - TREX COMPANY, INC.; *pg.* 116, *pg.* 1812
DECK SCREWS - Roofing Fastener - POWERS FASTENERS INC.; *pg.* 1059, *pg.* 1143
DECK THE HALLS - Lottery Game - MASSACHUSETTS STATE LOTTERY; *pg.* 998, *pg.* 802
DECK THE WALLS - Art & Picture Frame Stores - FRANCHISE CONCEPTS, INC.; *pg.* 1769, *pg.* 1005
DECKER - Fluid Handling System - GRACO, INC.; *pg.* 1342, *pg.* 935
DECKER - Dress Shoes - JOHNSTON & MURPHY CO.; *pg.* 1810, *pg.* 1651
DECKER INDUSTRIES - Fluid Handling System - GRACO, INC.; *pg.* 1342, *pg.* 935
DECKERS - Footwear Product - DECKERS OUTDOOR CORPORATION; *pg.* 1807, *pg.* 100
DECKHOG - Industrial Cleaning System - FLOW INTERNATIONAL CORPORATION; *pg.* 1337, *pg.* 1821
DECKMASTER - Monitor - AKRON BRASS COMPANY; *pg.* 1311, *pg.* 1482
DECKPRO - Nailable Base Sheet - JOHNS MANVILLE CORPORATION; *pg.* 89, *pg.* 320
DECKSCAPES - Stain - THE SHERWIN-WILLIAMS COMPANY; *pg.* 1447, *pg.* 1435
DECKWORKS - Coating & Paint - AKZO NOBEL DECORATIVE PAINTS, USA; *pg.* 1439, *pg.* 1474
DECLAR - Chemical Product - CYTEC INDUSTRIES, INC.; *pg.* 1155, *pg.* 1131
DECLOMYCIN - Pharmaceutical Product - IMPAX LABORATORIES, INC.; *pg.* 1544, *pg.* 101
DECO - Furniture - ASHLEY FURNITURE INDUSTRIES, INC.; *pg.* 914, *pg.* 1852
DECO - Carpet - INTERFACE, INC.; *pg.* 695, *pg.* 512
DECO - Jewelry - YURMAN DESIGN, INC.; *pg.* 15, *pg.* 1316
DECO TURF - Tennis Court System - CALIFORNIA PRODUCTS CORPORATION; *pg.* 1441, *pg.* 781
DECOGLAZE - Epoxy Enamel - JONES-BLAIR COMPANY; *pg.* 1443, *pg.* 1682
DECOGLO - Interior Acrylic Semi-Gloss Enamel - DUNN-EDWARDS CORPORATION; *pg.* 1442, *pg.* 129
DECOLAC - Lacquer - DUNN-EDWARDS CORPORATION; *pg.* 1442, *pg.* 129
DECOLAC II - Lacquer Stain - DUNN-EDWARDS CORPORATION; *pg.* 1442, *pg.* 129
DECOLITE - Mailer Product - POLYAIR INTER PACK INC.; *pg.* 1467, *pg.* 1941
DECOLLETE - Cosmetic Product - MERLE NORMAN COSMETICS, INC.; *pg.* 517, *pg.* 136
DECOMA - Automotive System - MAGNA INTERNATIONAL INC.; *pg.* 211, *pg.* 1918
DECONSAL - Pharmaceutical Product - CHIESI USA, INC.; *pg.* 1515, *pg.* 1359
DECOPUFFS - Pre-cut Tissue Squares - PACON CORPORATION; *pg.* 1466, *pg.* 1852
DECOR - Carpet - BEAULIEU GROUP, LLC; *pg.* 917, *pg.* 529
DECOR - Antique Reproduction Mirrors - OMEGA NATIONAL PRODUCTS; *pg.* 939, *pg.* 737
DECOR - Garage Door - WAYNE-DALTON CORP.; *pg.* 120, *pg.* 1465
DECOR WALL - Covering - AMERICAN FELT & FILTER COMPANY; *pg.* 1312, *pg.* 1184
DECORA - Hardware - FORTUNE BRANDS HOME & SECURITY, INC.; *pg.* 55, *pg.* 600
DECORA - Electronic Component - LEVITON MANUFACTURING COMPANY, INC.; *pg.* 1301, *pg.* 1180
DECORA - Cabinetry - MASTERBRAND CABINETS, INC.; *pg.* 96, *pg.* 692
DECORA - Accessories - MIDDLE ATLANTIC PRODUCTS INC.; *pg.* 1360, *pg.* 1065
DECORA - Electronic Components - MOLEX INCORPORATED; *pg.* 655, *pg.* 628
DECORATIFS - Decorative Pieces - GUITTARD CHOCOLATE COMPANY; *pg.* 1855, *pg.* 55
DECORATING - Magazine - MEREDITH CORPORATION; *pg.* 1663, *pg.* 705
DECORATOR - Paint - JONES-BLAIR COMPANY; *pg.* 1443, *pg.* 1682
DECORATOR SERIES - Switches & Receptacles - PASS & SEYMOUR/LEGRAND; *pg.* 1303, *pg.* 1344
DECORATOR WALL LIGHT - Commercial Lighting - SWIVELIER CO., INC.; *pg.* 1307, *pg.* 1142
DECORE - Keypad - CRESTRON ELECTRONICS INC.; *pg.* 631, *pg.* 1116
DECOREX - Vehicle System - MACLEAN-FOGG COMPANY INC.; *pg.* 1358, *pg.* 635
DECORLITE - Lighting Product - WESTINGHOUSE LIGHTING CORPORATION; *pg.* 687, *pg.* 1571
DECORUM - Office Furniture - STEELCASE INC.; *pg.* 475, *pg.* 889
DECORUM - Software - WIND RIVER SYSTEMS, INC.; *pg.* 493, *pg.* 38
DECOSHEEN - Interior Acrylic Eggshell Paint - DUNN-EDWARDS CORPORATION; *pg.* 1442, *pg.* 129
DECOSTA - Processed Food - KAYEM FOODS, INC.; *pg.* 867, *pg.* 814
DECOVEL - Interior Velvet Flat Finish - DUNN-EDWARDS CORPORATION; *pg.* 1442, *pg.* 129
DECT - Baby Monitor - PHILIPS ELECTRONICS NORTH AMERICA; *pg.* 662, *pg.* 782
DECTOMAX - Pharmaceutical Product - PFIZER INC.; *pg.* 1581, *pg.* 1278
DECTOR - Carie Detector - DEN-MAT CORPORATION; *pg.* 1522, *pg.* 271
DEDICATED TO BUILDING YOUR PET CARE BUSINESS - Slogan - PETEDGE; *pg.* 1481, *pg.* 787
DEDICATED TO SERVICE AND QUALITY - Tagline - MENARD, INC.; *pg.* 1055, *pg.* 1857
DEDICATED TO THE PURE JOY OF BAKING - Tagline - THE KING ARTHUR FLOUR COMPANY, INC.; *pg.* 833, *pg.* 1767
DEDICATED TO YOUR SUCCESS - Computer Services - AVNET, INC.; *pg.* 622, *pg.* 15
DEDUCTIBLE SAVINGS BENEFIT - Insurance Service - METLIFE, INC.; *pg.* 1208, *pg.* 1258
DEDUCTIONS@WORK - Computer Software - JACKSON HEWITT TAX SERVICE INC.; *pg.* 771, *pg.* 1103
DEDUPLICATION - Software - NETAPP, INC.; *pg.* 444, *pg.* 287
DEE - Furniture - AMISCO INDUSTRIES LTD.; *pg.* 913, *pg.* 1958
DEE ZEE - Automotive Running Boards - LANCASTER COLONY CORPORATION; *pg.* 873, *pg.* 1441
DEEANNA DENTON - Doll - TONNER DOLL COMPANY, INC.; *pg.* 968, *pg.* 1171
DEEP ACTION - Cleaning Product - HILLYARD, INC.; *pg.* 331, *pg.* 990
DEEP BLUE - Tuna - CAMERICAN INTERNATIONAL; *pg.* 844, *pg.* 1101
DEEP CLEANING BOOSTER - Cleaning Formula Additive - BISSELL HOMECARE, INC.; *pg.* 52, *pg.* 887
DEEP CONTENT CONTROL - Software - WEBSENSE, INC.; *pg.* 491, *pg.* 210
DEEP FREEZE - Ice Cream - UNITED DAIRY FARMERS, INC.; *pg.* 906, *pg.* 1426
DEEP HEATING - Pain relieving rub - THE MENTHOLATUM COMPANY; *pg.* 1565, *pg.* 1320
DEEP INK - Educational Materials - SCHOLASTIC INC.; *pg.* 1683, *pg.* 1288
DEEP LAKE - T-Shirts - ABERCROMBIE & FITCH CO.; *pg.* 37, *pg.* 1466
DEEP MAGIC - Cleansing Lotions & Moisturizers - THE GILLETTE COMPANY; *pg.* 509, *pg.* 795
DEEP POCKETS - Video Slots - INTERNATIONAL GAME TECHNOLOGY; *pg.* 957, *pg.* 1024
DEEP PROTEOME - Software - BIO-RAD LABORATORIES, INC.; *pg.* 1504, *pg.* 101
DEEP RENEWAL - Lip Care Product - BLISTEX, INC.; *pg.* 502, *pg.* 644
DEEP ROASTING - Coffee Roasting Method - PEET'S COFFEE & TEA, INC.; *pg.* 1029, *pg.* 85
DEEP SEA - Canned Fish - OCEAN BEAUTY SEAFOODS, INC.; *pg.* 1028, *pg.* 1838
DEEP SEAL - Sealing Compound - WALTER G. LEGGE COMPANY, INC.; *pg.* 337, *pg.* 1321
DEEP SKY IMAGER - Telescope - MEADE INSTRUMENTS CORPORATION; *pg.* 1422, *pg.* 113
DEEP SKY IMAGER II - Astrophotographer - MEADE INSTRUMENTS CORPORATION; *pg.* 1422, *pg.* 113
DEEP SKY IMAGER III - Astrophotographer - MEADE INSTRUMENTS CORPORATION; *pg.* 1422, *pg.* 113
DEEP SKY IMAGER PRO - Telescope - MEADE INSTRUMENTS CORPORATION; *pg.* 1422, *pg.* 113
DEEP SLEEP - Mattress - SIMMONS COMPANY; *pg.* 943, *pg.* 520
DEEP SYNC - Semiconductor Solution - CYPRESS SEMICONDUCTOR CORPORATION; *pg.* 1326, *pg.* 243
DEEP SYNC 36 - Semiconductor Solution - CYPRESS SEMICONDUCTOR CORPORATION; *pg.* 1326, *pg.* 243
DEEP SYNC II - Semiconductor Solution - CYPRESS SEMICONDUCTOR CORPORATION; *pg.* 1326, *pg.* 243
DEEP THAW - Snow & Ice Melter - MORGRO, INC.; *pg.* 1798, *pg.* 1759
DEEP V TANK - Clothing - K-SWISS; *pg.* 1837, *pg.* 306
DEEP WOODS OFF! - Insect Repellents - S.C. JOHNSON & SON, INC.; *pg.* 334, *pg.* 1889
DEEPSEE - Autonomous Underwater Vehicle - RAYTHEON APPLIED SIGNAL TECHNOLOGY, INC.; *pg.* 667, *pg.* 288
DEEPSIGHT - Security System - SYMANTEC CORPORATION; *pg.* 479, *pg.* 1753
DEEPSITE - Lighting System - STERIS CORPORATION; *pg.* 1597, *pg.* 1464
DEER BROOK - T-Shirts - ABERCROMBIE & FITCH CO.; *pg.* 37, *pg.* 1466
DEER NETTING - Plant Protection Products - E.I. DU PONT DE NEMOURS & COMPANY; *pg.* 1159, *pg.* 390
DEER OFF - Deer Repellant - GARDENS ALIVE!, INC.; *pg.* 1796, *pg.* 693
DEER PARK - Water - NESTLE WATERS NORTH AMERICA INC.; *pg.* 257, *pg.* 375
DEER STAGS - Slippers - HABAND COMPANY, INC.; *pg.* 1772, *pg.* 1099
DEER VALLEY - Carpet - BEAULIEU GROUP, LLC; *pg.* 917, *pg.* 529
DEER VALLEY SPICE - Nail Care Product - OPI PRODUCTS INC.; *pg.* 518, *pg.* 167
DEERFIELD - Shoes - ALLEN-EDMONDS SHOE CORP.; *pg.* 1804, *pg.* 1887
DEERFIELD - Kitchen Product - KOHLER CO.; *pg.* 91, *pg.* 1862
DEERSTALKER RIFLE - Black Powder Rifle - LYMAN PRODUCTS CORPORATION; *pg.* 1839, *pg.* 356
DEFAULT FILTER - Standard Credit Analysis Tool - STANDARD & POOR'S RATINGS SERVICES; *pg.* 805, *pg.* 1296

First page reference indicates Business Class Edition
Second page reference indicates Geographic Edition

DEFECT ANALYZER - Electron Microscope - FEI COMPANY; *pg.* 1413, *pg.* 1498
DEFEND - Pharmaceutical - MERCK & CO., INC.; *pg.* 1566, *pg.* 1077
DEFENDER - Waterproof Outerwear - BLAUER MANUFACTURING COMPANY, INC.; *pg.* 20, *pg.* 789
DEFENDER - Software - DELL SOFTWARE; *pg.* 385, *pg.* 40
DEFENDER - Portable Room Air Cleaners - HMI INDUSTRIES INC.; *pg.* 56, *pg.* 1475
DEFENDER - Faceshield Frame - MINE SAFETY APPLIANCES COMPANY; *pg.* 1361, *pg.* 1525
DEFENDER ENERGY SAVER - Water Heater - BRADFORD-WHITE CORPORATION; *pg.* 1069, *pg.* 1514
DEFENSE - Sports Drink - ENERGY BRANDS, INC.; *pg.* 854, *pg.* 1227
DEFENSE - Beverage - MONSTER BEVERAGE CORPORATION; *pg.* 257, *pg.* 69
DEFENSE ID - Access Control - INTELLICHECK MOBILISA, INC.; *pg.* 416, *pg.* 1823
DEFENSE TECHNOLOGY - Anti-Riot & Crowd Control Products - BAE SYSTEMS PRODUCTS GROUP; *pg.* 359, *pg.* 432
DEFIANCE - Orthopedic Product - DJO INCORPORATED; *pg.* 1524, *pg.* 302
DEFIANT - Security System - NORTEK, INC.; *pg.* 100, *pg.* 1607
DEFIER - Footwear - K-SWISS; *pg.* 1837, *pg.* 306
DEFIER II - Athletic Shoes - K-SWISS; *pg.* 1837, *pg.* 306
DEFIER MISOUL TECH - Footwear - K-SWISS; *pg.* 1837, *pg.* 306
DEFIER RS - Footwear - K-SWISS; *pg.* 1837, *pg.* 306
DEFINING EFFECTS - Cosmetic Product - NU SKIN ENTERPRISES, INC.; *pg.* 518, *pg.* 1755
DEFINING MOMENTS - Systems Integration & Aeronautics - LOCKHEED MARTIN CORPORATION; *pg.* 229, *pg.* 762
DEFINING POMADE - Hair Care Product - JOHN PAUL MITCHELL SYSTEMS; *pg.* 512, *pg.* 133
DEFINING THE STANDARD OF CARE IN WOMEN'S HEALTH - Tagline - HOLOGIC, INC.; *pg.* 1416, *pg.* 784
THE DEFINITION OF QUALITY - Service Mark - PLANAR SYSTEMS, INC.; *pg.* 455, *pg.* 1495
DEFINITIVE - Cosmetic Product - MERLE NORMAN COSMETICS, INC.; *pg.* 517, *pg.* 136
DEFINITIVE TECHNOLOGY - Loudspeakers - DEI HOLDINGS, INC.; *pg.* 633, *pg.* 302
DEFINITV - Light Engine - VIAVI SOLUTIONS INC.; *pg.* 1435, *pg.* 148
DEFINITY - Telecommunication Product - AVAYA INC.; *pg.* 621, *pg.* 264
DEFINITY SEATING - Church Pew With Individual Seat Cushions - SAUDER MANUFACTURING COMPANY; *pg.* 941, *pg.* 1403
DEFLECTA-SHIELD - Truck Styling Products - LUND INTERNATIONAL, INC.; *pg.* 211, *pg.* 526
DEFLOX - Pharmaceutical Products - ABBOTT LABORATORIES; *pg.* 1484, *pg.* 551
DEFLUX - Pharmaceutical Product - SALIX PHARMACEUTICALS, INC.; *pg.* 1591, *pg.* 1388
DEFOAMER - Defoamer - HUNTSMAN CORPORATION; *pg.* 1167, *pg.* 1758
DEFOR - Corrugated Packaging System - INTERNATIONAL PAPER COMPANY; *pg.* 1460, *pg.* 1644
DEFRAME - Computer Software - NOVELL INC.; *pg.* 446, *pg.* 852
DEFT CLEAR WOOD FINISH - Brushable Lacquer - PPG AEROSPACE DEFT FACILITY; *pg.* 1445, *pg.* 115
DEFT INTERIOR POLYURETHANE - Polyurethane Varnish - PPG AEROSPACE DEFT FACILITY; *pg.* 1445, *pg.* 115
DEFT RESPONSE - Tachycardia Products - ST. JUDE MEDICAL, INC.; *pg.* 1596, *pg.* 963
DEFTHANE - Wood Finishing Products - PPG AEROSPACE DEFT FACILITY; *pg.* 1445, *pg.* 115
DEFTOIL DANISH OIL FINISH - Stain & Oil Finish - PPG AEROSPACE DEFT FACILITY; *pg.* 1445, *pg.* 115
DEFY THE ELEMENTS. - Slogan - PELICAN PRODUCTS; *pg.* 1467, *pg.* 843
DEGREE - Herbicide - MONSANTO COMPANY; *pg.* 1173, *pg.* 999
DEGREE - Deodorant - UNILEVER UNITED STATES, INC.; *pg.* 904, *pg.* 1061
DEGREES OF READING POWER - Educational Test - QUESTAR ASSESSMENT, INC.; *pg.* 1679, *pg.* 1143
DEGREEWORKS - Software - SUNGARD DATA SYSTEMS INC.; *pg.* 477, *pg.* 1592
D.E.H. - Epoxy Curing Agents & Intermediates - THE DOW CHEMICAL COMPANY; *pg.* 1157, *pg.* 898
DEHSCOFIX - Sulphonic Acid Salt - HUNTSMAN CORPORATION; *pg.* 1167, *pg.* 1758
DEHSCOTEX - Chemical - HUNTSMAN CORPORATION; *pg.* 1167, *pg.* 1758
DEHYBOR - Medicine And Agricultural Product - RIO TINTO BORAX; *pg.* 334, *pg.* 331
DEIDRA - Lamp - ASHLEY FURNITURE INDUSTRIES, INC.; *pg.* 914, *pg.* 1852
DEIRDRE - Women's Clothing & Accessories - WOODEN SHIPS OF HOBOKEN; *pg.* 35, *pg.* 1315
DEJA BLUE - Non-Carbonated Soft Drink - DR PEPPER SNAPPLE GROUP, INC.; *pg.* 250, *pg.* 1729
DEJA VU DIAMONDS - Game - WMS INDUSTRIES INC.; *pg.* 593, *pg.* 666
DEKALB - Seeds - MONSANTO COMPANY; *pg.* 1173, *pg.* 999
DEKALB CHOICE GENETICS - Genetics - MONSANTO COMPANY; *pg.* 1173, *pg.* 999
DEKFAST - Fastening System - SFS INTEC, INC.; *pg.* 1061, *pg.* 1596
DEKLENE - Biotechnology Product - GENZYME CORPORATION; *pg.* 1534, *pg.* 808
DEKOMPRESSOR - Interventional Pain Instrument - STRYKER CORPORATION; *pg.* 1598, *pg.* 894
DEKOWE - Fabric Product - BELTON INDUSTRIES, INC.; *pg.* 691, *pg.* 1612
DEKS OLJE - Coating & Paint - AKZO NOBEL DECORATIVE PAINTS, USA; *pg.* 1439, *pg.* 1474
DEKSWOOD - Coating & Paint - AKZO NOBEL DECORATIVE PAINTS, USA; *pg.* 1439, *pg.* 1474
DEKTAK - Metrology Systems - VEECO INSTRUMENTS INC.; *pg.* 1434, *pg.* 1322
DEKTAK 6M - Bench-top Stylus Profiler - VEECO INSTRUMENTS INC.; *pg.* 1434, *pg.* 1322
DEKTAK 8 - Surface Profiler - VEECO INSTRUMENTS INC.; *pg.* 1434, *pg.* 1322
DEKTOL - Photo Developer - EASTMAN KODAK COMPANY; *pg.* 1408, *pg.* 1333
DEKTOMATIC - Photographic Chemicals - EASTMAN KODAK COMPANY; *pg.* 1408, *pg.* 1333
DEKUYPER - Cordial - JIM BEAM BRANDS CO.; *pg.* 1965, *pg.* 601
DEL CARIBE - Food Product - V&V SUPREMO FOODS, INC.; *pg.* 907, *pg.* 595
DEL DESTINO - Olive Oil - ATALANTA CORPORATION; *pg.* 838, *pg.* 1057
DEL FRISCO'S DOUBLE EAGLE STEAK HOUSE - Steak Houses - LONE STAR STEAKHOUSE & SALOON, INC.; *pg.* 1736, *pg.* 1733
DEL-GUARD - Fabric Protector - DELTA FOREMOST CHEMICAL CORPORATION; *pg.* 1155, *pg.* 1642
DEL HIGH VOLTAGE - High Voltage Power Supplies - DGT HOLDINGS; *pg.* 634, *pg.* 1223
DEL MEDICAL - Medical Imaging Supplies - DGT HOLDINGS; *pg.* 634, *pg.* 1223
DEL MONTE - Canned Vegetables, Tomatoes & Fruits - DEL MONTE FOODS, INC.; *pg.* 852, *pg.* 304
DEL MONTE GOLD - Pineapples - FRESH DEL MONTE PRODUCE INC.; *pg.* 856, *pg.* 418
DEL-SEAL - Acrylic Automotive Coatings - PPG INDUSTRIES, INC.; *pg.* 1445, *pg.* 1579
DEL VALLE - Beverages - THE COCA-COLA COMPANY; *pg.* 240, *pg.* 493
DELAC - Polymer Product - CHEMTURA CORPORATION; *pg.* 1152, *pg.* 355
DELACORTE PRESS BOOKS - Books for Young Readers - PENGUIN RANDOM HOUSE CHILDREN'S BOOKS; *pg.* 1676, *pg.* 1277
DELAFIELD - Furniture - ASHLEY FURNITURE INDUSTRIES, INC.; *pg.* 914, *pg.* 1852
DELAFIELD - Kitchen Product - KOHLER CO.; *pg.* 91, *pg.* 1862
DELAGIL - Pharmaceutical Product - VALEANT PHARMACEUTICALS INTERNATIONAL; *pg.* 1605, *pg.* 1047
DELANEY - Furniture - AMISCO INDUSTRIES LTD.; *pg.* 913, *pg.* 1958
DELANEY - Guest Chairs - BERNHARDT DESIGN; *pg.* 918, *pg.* 1381
DELANEY - Sunglasses - COACH, INC.; *pg.* 3, *pg.* 1214
DELASTIC - Bridge Product - THE D.S. BROWN COMPANY; *pg.* 79, *pg.* 1468
DELAUNAY - Fabric - NEMSCHOFF, INC.; *pg.* 936, *pg.* 1890
DELAWARE - Titling Equipment - EASTMAN KODAK COMPANY; *pg.* 1408, *pg.* 1333
DELAWARE MICROSHORT - Apparels - UNDER ARMOUR, INC.; *pg.* 49, *pg.* 759
DELAWARE PUNCH - Soft Drink - THE COCA-COLA COMPANY; *pg.* 240, *pg.* 493
DELCLEAR - Acrylic Urethane Coatings - PPG INDUSTRIES, INC.; *pg.* 1445, *pg.* 1579
DELCO - Generator Controls Rebuilding Services - FLIGHT SYSTEMS, INC.; *pg.* 1337, *pg.* 1548
DELCO - Stainless Steel Hollowware - ONEIDA LTD; *pg.* 1129, *pg.* 1318
DELCO/BOSE - Audio System - DELPHI ELECTRONICS & SAFETY; *pg.* 633, *pg.* 692
DELCO ETR - Electronically Tuned Receiver - DELPHI ELECTRONICS & SAFETY; *pg.* 633, *pg.* 692
DELCO LOC - Radio Theft Deterrent - DELPHI ELECTRONICS & SAFETY; *pg.* 633, *pg.* 692
DELCRETE - Bridge Product - THE D.S. BROWN COMPANY; *pg.* 79, *pg.* 1468
DELEGATE - Insecticide - DOW AGROSCIENCES LLC; *pg.* 1156, *pg.* 684
DELFIA - Assay & Reagent - PERKINELMER, INC.; *pg.* 1426, *pg.* 853
DELFLOC - Cationic & Anionic Polymers - HERCULES INCORPORATED; *pg.* 1166, *pg.* 392
DELGARD - Aluminum Fencing - DELAIR GROUP, LLC; *pg.* 78, *pg.* 1053
DELGLO - Acrylic Automotive Coatings - PPG INDUSTRIES, INC.; *pg.* 1445, *pg.* 1579
DELI BITES - Snack Sausage - JOHNSONVILLE SAUSAGE, LLC; *pg.* 867, *pg.* 1894
DELI BREAK - Food Product - ADVANCEPIERRE FOODS, INC.; *pg.* 1714, *pg.* 1409
DELI CAT - Cat Food - NESTLE PURINA PETCARE COMPANY; *pg.* 1479, *pg.* 1000
DELI CUTS - Ultra Thin Deli Meats - CARL BUDDIG & COMPANY; *pg.* 846, *pg.* 619
DELI LINE - Bread - KLOSTERMAN BAKING COMPANY, INC.; *pg.* 869, *pg.* 1415
DELI-TRAY - Packaging Product - CASCADES, INC.; *pg.* 73, *pg.* 1950
DELIBERATELY INNOVATIVE - Software - INTERACTIVE INTELLIGENCE, INC.; *pg.* 417, *pg.* 687
DELICATO FAMILY VINEYARDS - Premium Wines - DELICATO FAMILY VINEYARDS; *pg.* 1961, *pg.* 163
DELICATO SHIRAZ - Wine - DELICATO FAMILY VINEYARDS; *pg.* 1961, *pg.* 163
DELICE DE FRANCE - Brie & Camembert Cheese - BONGRAIN NORTH AMERICA; *pg.* 841, *pg.* 1556
DELICIA - Lamp - ASHLEY FURNITURE INDUSTRIES, INC.; *pg.* 914, *pg.* 1852
DELICIOUS CELEBRATION - Fruit Arrangements - EDIBLE ARRANGEMENTS INTERNATIONAL, INC.; *pg.* 1768, *pg.* 382
DELICIOUS FRUIT DESIGN - Fruit Arrangements - EDIBLE ARRANGEMENTS INTERNATIONAL, INC.; *pg.* 1768, *pg.* 382
DELICIOUS PARTY - Fruit Arrangements - EDIBLE ARRANGEMENTS INTERNATIONAL, INC.; *pg.* 1768, *pg.* 382
DELICIOUSLY TWISTED. DELICIOUSLY CHEESY. - Tag Line - FRITO-LAY NORTH AMERICA, INC.; *pg.* 1853, *pg.* 1730
DELICO - Baby Swiss, Smoked Baby Swiss, Feta Cheese - BONGRAIN NORTH AMERICA; *pg.* 841, *pg.* 1556
DELIGHT - Fabric - NEMSCHOFF, INC.; *pg.* 936, *pg.* 1890
DELIGHT - Footwear - PHOENIX FOOTWEAR GROUP, INC.; *pg.* 1815, *pg.* 60
DELIGHT - Nutritional Supplement - RELIV INTERNATIONAL, INC.; *pg.* 1589, *pg.* 975
DELIGHT - Fastening System - TEXTRON INC.; *pg.* 235, *pg.* 1607
DELIGHT BITES - Food Product - ADVANCEPIERRE FOODS, INC.; *pg.* 1714, *pg.* 1409
DELIGHTS - Pharmaceutical Product - PURETEK CORPORATION; *pg.* 1587, *pg.* 211
DELILAH - Footwear - PHOENIX FOOTWEAR GROUP, INC.; *pg.* 1815, *pg.* 60
DELINAISE - Mustard/Mayo Sandwich Spread - CAINS FOODS, L.P.; *pg.* 843, *pg.* 784
DELINK - Catalyst - BASF CATALYSTS LLC; *pg.* 1148, *pg.* 1074
DELIVERABILITY - Software - PITNEY BOWES INC.; *pg.* 454, *pg.* 376
DELIVERING EVERYTHING, THE BEST FROM

ANYWHERE. - Tagline - QUAKER CHEMICAL CORP.; *pg.* 1178, *pg.* 1524
DELIVERING EXPERIENCE - Tag Line - BLUCORA; *pg.* 1232, *pg.* 1813
DELIVERING MORE THAN POWER - Slogan - SALT RIVER PROJECT; *pg.* 707, *pg.* 26
DELIVERING PERFORMANCE - Tagline - IDEX CORPORATION; *pg.* 1347, *pg.* 623
DELIVERING POWER - Slogan - AMERICAN AXLE & MANUFACTURING HOLDINGS, INC.; *pg.* 198, *pg.* 879
DELIVERING SATISFACTION. IT.S WHAT WE DO. - Slogan - SHAMROCK FOODS COMPANY; *pg.* 895, *pg.* 20
DELIVERING SOLUTIONS FOR DERMATOLOGY - Slogan - DUSA PHARMACEUTICALS, INC.; *pg.* 1525, *pg.* 860
DELIVERING SOLUTIONS YOU TRUST - Slogan - COLE-PARMER INSTRUMENT COMPANY; *pg.* 1406, *pg.* 664
DELIVERING THE WORLD'S BEST IDEA IN SILICON - Tagline - DATA I/O CORPORATION; *pg.* 382, *pg.* 1824
DELIVERS MORE - Tagline - AT&T SOUTHEAST; *pg.* 1868, *pg.* 489
DELIVERS NOW - Tagline - INTEGRATED BIOPHARMA, INC.; *pg.* 1546, *pg.* 1073
DELIVERY CONFIRMATION - Postal Services - UNITED STATES POSTAL SERVICE; *pg.* 1009, *pg.* 406
DELIVERY DELIGHT - Fruit Arrangements - EDIBLE ARRANGEMENTS INTERNATIONAL, INC.; *pg.* 1768, *pg.* 382
DELIVERYONE - Wireless Capabilities - QUALCOMM INCORPORATED; *pg.* 1873, *pg.* 207
DELIWARE - Deli Displayware - CARLISLE FOODSERVICE PRODUCTS INCORPORATED; *pg.* 1455, *pg.* 1485
DELL - Switch - BROCADE CORPORATION; *pg.* 365, *pg.* 312
DELL DIMENSION - Computer Peripherals - DELL INC.; *pg.* 383, *pg.* 1737
DELL DOLLARS - Coupons - DELL INC.; *pg.* 383, *pg.* 1737
DELL INK MANAGEMENT SYSTEM - Printing & Imaging System - DELL INC.; *pg.* 383, *pg.* 1737
DELL OPENMANAGE - Systems Management - DELL INC.; *pg.* 383, *pg.* 1737
DELL PRECISION - Workstations - DELL INC.; *pg.* 383, *pg.* 1737
DELL SONICWALL - IT Security Software - DELL INC.; *pg.* 383, *pg.* 1737
DELL TALK - Community Forum - DELL INC.; *pg.* 383, *pg.* 1737
DELL THEFT - Recovery Software - DELL INC.; *pg.* 383, *pg.* 1737
DELL TONER MANAGEMENT SYSTEM - Printing & Imaging System - DELL INC.; *pg.* 383, *pg.* 1737
DELL XPS ONE - Computer - DELL INC.; *pg.* 383, *pg.* 1737
DELLA MANO - Hardwood Floor - ANDERSON HARDWOOD FLOORS; *pg.* 67, *pg.* 1613
DELLA SUPREMA - Pizza - RICH PRODUCTS CORPORATION; *pg.* 892, *pg.* 1150
DELLA VITA - Food Service - FOOD SERVICES OF AMERICA, INC.; *pg.* 856, *pg.* 21
DELLGUARD - Notebook Computers Services - DELL INC.; *pg.* 383, *pg.* 1737
DELLWARE - Custom Factory Integration Product - DELL INC.; *pg.* 383, *pg.* 1737
DELLWARE FACTS LINE - Notebook Computers Services - DELL INC.; *pg.* 383, *pg.* 1737
DELMAR - Educational Publications - THOMSON REUTERS CORPORATION; *pg.* 1693, *pg.* 1944
DELMONICO - Fabric - NEMSCHOFF, INC.; *pg.* 936, *pg.* 1890
DELMONICO - Cutlery - ONEIDA LTD; *pg.* 1129, *pg.* 1318
DELNET - Geometric Apertured Film - DELSTAR TECHNOLOGIES, INC.; *pg.* 1881, *pg.* 387
DELO - Oil Fuel - CHEVRON CORPORATION; *pg.* 974, *pg.* 259
DELOITTE REVIEW - Biannual Periodical - DELOITTE & TOUCHE USA LLP; *pg.* 743, *pg.* 1222
DELORE - Nail Care - AMERICAN INTERNATIONAL INDUSTRIES COMPANY; *pg.* 498, *pg.* 126
DELORES - Footwear - PHOENIX FOOTWEAR GROUP, INC.; *pg.* 1815, *pg.* 60
DELORMY - Furniture - ASHLEY FURNITURE INDUSTRIES, INC.; *pg.* 914, *pg.* 1852
DELPATCH - Bridge Product - THE D.S. BROWN COMPANY; *pg.* 79, *pg.* 1468
DELPHI - Medical Test System - HOLOGIC, INC.; *pg.* 1416, *pg.* 784
DELPHOS - Fabric - NEMSCHOFF, INC.; *pg.* 936, *pg.* 1890
DELPORE - Melt Blown Non Woven Fabrics - DELSTAR TECHNOLOGIES, INC.; *pg.* 1881, *pg.* 387
DELRAY - Lighting Product - QUOIZEL INC.; *pg.* 1304, *pg.* 1616
DELRIN - Plastic Ball - ABBOTT BALL COMPANY; *pg.* 1040, *pg.* 383
DELRIN - Plastic - ACRISON, INC.; *pg.* 1310, *pg.* 1087
DELRIN - Acetal Resins - E.I. DU PONT DE NEMOURS & COMPANY; *pg.* 1159, *pg.* 390
DELRIN - Ball Bearing - HAMILTON CASTER & MFG. CO.; *pg.* 206, *pg.* 1454
DELRIN - Buckle - MCNETT CORPORATION; *pg.* 1839, *pg.* 1817
DELSA - Testing Instrument System - BECKMAN COULTER, INC.; *pg.* 1402, *pg.* 48
DELSETTE - Resins - HERCULES INCORPORATED; *pg.* 1166, *pg.* 392
DELSTAR - Resin-Based Finishes - PPG INDUSTRIES, INC.; *pg.* 1445, *pg.* 1579
DELSYM - Cough Medicine - RECKITT BENCKISER INC.; *pg.* 1136, *pg.* 1105
DELTA - Abrasive Cutters - BUEHLER, LTD.; *pg.* 1403, *pg.* 622
DELTA - Metal Building System - BUTLER MANUFACTURING COMPANY; *pg.* 72, *pg.* 981
DELTA - Dumpblock - ESCO CORPORATION; *pg.* 1335, *pg.* 1502
DELTA - Furniture - J. ROBERT SCOTT INC.; *pg.* 930, *pg.* 105
DELTA - Faucets - MASCO CORPORATION; *pg.* 96, *pg.* 909
DELTA - Device - MEDTRONIC, INC.; *pg.* 1564, *pg.* 939
DELTA - Mass Flow Control - MKS INSTRUMENTS, INC.; *pg.* 1362, *pg.* 781
DELTA - Industrial Automotive Coating - PPG INDUSTRIES, INC.; *pg.* 1445, *pg.* 1579
DELTA - Fog Product - ROSCO LABORATORIES, INC.; *pg.* 1782, *pg.* 378
DELTA - Liquid Chromatography Instrument - WATERS CORPORATION; *pg.* 1436, *pg.* 834
DELTA ALBAPLEX - Hormonal & Antibiotic Veterinary Preparation - PFIZER INC.; *pg.* 1581, *pg.* 1278
DELTA BLOCK - Software - IRON MOUNTAIN INCORPORATED; *pg.* 421, *pg.* 796
DELTA BLUES - Musical Instrument - PEAVEY ELECTRONICS CORPORATION; *pg.* 662, *pg.* 970
DELTA-CAL - Blood Pressure Monitoring Accessories - UTAH MEDICAL PRODUCTS, INC.; *pg.* 1605, *pg.* 1752
DELTA CONNECTION - Air Transportation Service - DELTA AIR LINES, INC.; *pg.* 1905, *pg.* 503
DELTA CONSOLIDATED INDUSTRIES - Tool Storage Product - DANAHER CORPORATION; *pg.* 1044, *pg.* 397
DELTA DOWNS RACE TRACK & CASINO - Race Track & Casino - BOYD GAMING CORPORATION; *pg.* 1082, *pg.* 1022
DELTA EDUCATION - Educational Resources - SCHOOL SPECIALTY, INC.; *pg.* 467, *pg.* 1860
DELTA EIGHT - Household Insect Control - BONIDE PRODUCTS, INC.; *pg.* 1794, *pg.* 1320
DELTA-FAB - Cored Welding System - MILLER ELECTRIC MANUFACTURING CO.; *pg.* 1361, *pg.* 1852
DELTA FAUCET - Plumbing Fixtures - MASCO CORPORATION; *pg.* 96, *pg.* 909
DELTA-FLOW - Blood Pressure Monitoring Accessories - UTAH MEDICAL PRODUCTS, INC.; *pg.* 1605, *pg.* 1752
DELTA HOTELS - Hotels & Resorts - FAIRMONT HOTELS & RESORTS INC.; *pg.* 1091, *pg.* 1938
DELTA III - Running Boards - LUND INTERNATIONAL, INC.; *pg.* 211, *pg.* 526
DELTA-PAK - Analytical Column - WATERS CORPORATION; *pg.* 1436, *pg.* 834
DELTA PLUS VIRTUAL TERMINAL - Software - BMC SOFTWARE, INC.; *pg.* 362, *pg.* 1701
DELTA PRIME - Catfish Filets - CONSOLIDATED CATFISH COMPANIES, LLC; *pg.* 850, *pg.* 969
DELTA PRO - Truck Equipment - AMERICAN VAN EQUIPMENT INC.; *pg.* 199, *pg.* 1078
DELTA SELECT - Faucets - DELTA FAUCET COMPANY; *pg.* 78, *pg.* 684
DELTA SHUTTLE - Air Transportation - DELTA AIR LINES, INC.; *pg.* 1905, *pg.* 503
DELTA SKY CLUB - Air Transportation - DELTA AIR LINES, INC.; *pg.* 1905, *pg.* 503
DELTA SPRAY - Spray Guns - GRACO, INC.; *pg.* 1342, *pg.* 935
DELTA SPRAY II - Fluid Handling System - GRACO, INC.; *pg.* 1342, *pg.* 935
DELTA SPRAY XT - Fluid Handling System - GRACO, INC.; *pg.* 1342, *pg.* 935
DELTA STAR - Rice - RICELAND FOODS, INC.; *pg.* 892, *pg.* 36
DELTA T - Cell & Tissue Manipulation - STOELTING CO.; *pg.* 1430, *pg.* 671
DELTA-TE - Burner - MAXON CORPORATION; *pg.* 1359, *pg.* 695
DELTA THERM - Polyurethane Foam Dispensing Equipment - THE DOW CHEMICAL COMPANY; *pg.* 1157, *pg.* 898
DELTA3 - Radio Frequency Components - NORTEK SECURITY & CONTROL LLC; *pg.* 659, *pg.* 59
DELTA39K - Software - CYPRESS SEMICONDUCTOR CORPORATION; *pg.* 1326, *pg.* 243
DELTABASS - Musical Instrument - PEAVEY ELECTRONICS CORPORATION; *pg.* 662, *pg.* 970
DELTADYNE - Filter Monitor - PALL CORPORATION; *pg.* 232, *pg.* 1323
DELTAFEX - Musical Instrument - PEAVEY ELECTRONICS CORPORATION; *pg.* 662, *pg.* 970
DELTAGRIP - Writing Instrument - SHEAFFER PEN CORPORATION; *pg.* 469, *pg.* 371
DELTALINX - Musical Instrument - PEAVEY ELECTRONICS CORPORATION; *pg.* 662, *pg.* 970
DELTAMAT - Chair Mat - RUBBERMAID HOME PRODUCTS; *pg.* 1138, *pg.* 1453
DELTANET 6.0 - Software System - MENTOR GRAPHICS CORPORATION; *pg.* 432, *pg.* 1510
DELTAPINE - Seeds - MONSANTO; *pg.* 1798, *pg.* 971
DELTAPINE - Row Crop Seeds - MONSANTO COMPANY; *pg.* 1173, *pg.* 999
DELTAV - Process Control System - EMERSON PROCESS MANAGEMENT ROSEMOUNT INC.; *pg.* 1334, *pg.* 920
DELTAV - Software System - MENTOR GRAPHICS CORPORATION; *pg.* 432, *pg.* 1510
DELTAWELD - Welding & Cutting Equip. - MILLER ELECTRIC MANUFACTURING CO.; *pg.* 1361, *pg.* 1852
DELTEC - Cable Support System - THOMAS & BETTS CORPORATION; *pg.* 680, *pg.* 1646
DELTEC COZMO - Insulin Pump - SMITHS MEDICAL MD, INC.; *pg.* 1594, *pg.* 963
DELTEK VISION - Computer Applications - DELTEK, INC.; *pg.* 386, *pg.* 1784
DELTEK WINSIGHT - Computer Applications - DELTEK, INC.; *pg.* 386, *pg.* 1784
DELTHANE - Catalytic Additives for Automotive Paint - PPG INDUSTRIES, INC.; *pg.* 1445, *pg.* 1579
DELTIO - Titanium Dioxide Pigments - HUNTSMAN CORPORATION; *pg.* 1167, *pg.* 1758
DELTON - Dental Product - DENTSPLY INTERNATIONAL INC.; *pg.* 1522, *pg.* 1596
DELTONA - Builder of Major Planned Communities - THE DELTONA CORPORATION; *pg.* 1089, *pg.* 452
DELTRAN - Blood Pressure Monitor/Transducer - UTAH MEDICAL PRODUCTS, INC.; *pg.* 1605, *pg.* 1752
DELTRON - Coating Product - PPG INDUSTRIES, INC.; *pg.* 1445, *pg.* 1579
DELUCEMINE - Pharmaceutical - NPS PHARMACEUTICALS, INC.; *pg.* 1576, *pg.* 1043
DELUXE - Fruit Cakes - COLLIN STREET BAKERY; *pg.* 1851, *pg.* 1672
DELUXE - Bag - DATREK GOLF; *pg.* 1832, *pg.* 1801
DELUXE - Sinks - MOEN INCORPORATED; *pg.* 1056, *pg.* 1468
DELUXE - Lighting Product - QUOIZEL INC.; *pg.* 1304, *pg.* 1616
DELUXE - Lawn Fertilizer - THE SCOTTS MIRACLE-GRO COMPANY; *pg.* 1799, *pg.* 1459
DELUXE 900 - Guitar Amplifier - FENDER MUSICAL INSTRUMENTS CORPORATION; *pg.* 547, *pg.* 21
DELUXE ACTIVE JAZZ BASS - Electric Bass - FENDER MUSICAL INSTRUMENTS CORPORATION; *pg.* 547, *pg.* 21
DELUXE ACTIVE JAZZ BASS V - Electric Bass - FENDER MUSICAL INSTRUMENTS CORPORATION; *pg.* 547, *pg.* 21
DELUXE BUSINESS ADVANTAGE - Newsletter - DELUXE CORPORATION; *pg.* 1634, *pg.* 964
DELUXE CANASTA CALIENTE - Game - WINNING MOVES GAMES, INC.; *pg.* 970, *pg.* 816
DELUXE DETECT - Software - DELUXE CORPORATION; *pg.* 1634, *pg.* 964
DELUXE DONUT - Orthopedic Product - DJO INCORPORATED; *pg.* 1524, *pg.* 302

First page reference indicates Business Class Edition
Second page reference indicates Geographic Edition

DELUXE DOODLEBUG - Bike - TREK BICYCLE CORPORATION; *pg.* 1847, *pg.* 1896
DELUXE ELECTROL - Electric Screen - DA-LITE SCREEN COMPANY; *pg.* 632, *pg.* 698
DELUXE EUROPA - Soccer Shinguards - FRANKLIN SPORTS, INC.; *pg.* 1834, *pg.* 847
DELUXE ID THEFTBLOCK - Software - DELUXE CORPORATION; *pg.* 1634, *pg.* 964
DELUXE INSTA-THEATER - Screen - DA-LITE SCREEN COMPANY; *pg.* 632, *pg.* 698
DELUXE KNOWLEDGE EXCHANGE - Customer Solution - DELUXE CORPORATION; *pg.* 1634, *pg.* 964
DELUXE MODEL B - Screen - DA-LITE SCREEN COMPANY; *pg.* 632, *pg.* 698
DELUXE PASS THE PIG - Game - WINNING MOVES GAMES, INC.; *pg.* 970, *pg.* 816
DELUXE PIT - Game - WINNING MOVES GAMES, INC.; *pg.* 970, *pg.* 816
DELUXE PLAYERS STRAT - Electric Guitar - FENDER MUSICAL INSTRUMENTS CORPORATION; *pg.* 547, *pg.* 21
DELUXE ROOK - Game - WINNING MOVES GAMES, INC.; *pg.* 970, *pg.* 816
DELUXE RX - Microfiber Cart - GEERPRES INC.; *pg.* 1339, *pg.* 901
DELUXE SECUREMAIL - Software - DELUXE CORPORATION; *pg.* 1634, *pg.* 964
DELUXE SNO-THROS - Lawn Product - ARIENS COMPANY INC.; *pg.* 700, *pg.* 1855
DELUXE STRAT HSS - Electric Guitar - FENDER MUSICAL INSTRUMENTS CORPORATION; *pg.* 547, *pg.* 21
DELUXE TEMPTROL - Bathroom Accessories - SYMMONS INDUSTRIES, INC.; *pg.* 114, *pg.* 803
DELUXE UNO - Card Game - MATTEL, INC.; *pg.* 962, *pg.* 81
DELUXE WHIZ BANG - Pop Corn Machine - GOLD MEDAL PRODUCTS CO.; *pg.* 55, *pg.* 1414
DELUXE ZONE BASS - Electric Bass - FENDER MUSICAL INSTRUMENTS CORPORATION; *pg.* 547, *pg.* 21
DELUXECALLING - Calling Program - DELUXE CORPORATION; *pg.* 1634, *pg.* 964
DELUXECARD - Gift Card - DELUXE CORPORATION; *pg.* 1634, *pg.* 964
DELUXEDBED - Mattress System - TEMPUR SEALY INTERNATIONAL, INC.; *pg.* 944, *pg.* 731
DELUXESELECT - Software - DELUXE CORPORATION; *pg.* 1634, *pg.* 964
DELVE - Qualitative & Quantitative Research Data Collection Network - MARITZ INC.; *pg.* 1914, *pg.* 977
DEM-KOTE - Spray Paints - W.W. GRAINGER, INC.; *pg.* 1390, *pg.* 625
DEMADEX - Pharmaceutical Product - HOFFMANN-LA ROCHE INC.; *pg.* 1542, *pg.* 1099
DEMAG - Crane - TEREX CORPORATION; *pg.* 1381, *pg.* 384
DEMAK'UP - Beauty Product - GEORGIA-PACIFIC LLC; *pg.* 1458, *pg.* 507
DEMAND - Apparel - OAKLEY, INC.; *pg.* 1840, *pg.* 86
DEMAND BETTER & EXPECT MORE - Slogan - GENERAL CABLE CORPORATION; *pg.* 83, *pg.* 729
DEMAND CLASSIFICATION - Software - JDA SOFTWARE GROUP, INC.; *pg.* 423, *pg.* 22
DEMAND DECOMPOSITION - Software - JDA SOFTWARE GROUP, INC.; *pg.* 423, *pg.* 22
DEMAND DELIVERY - Fluid Handling System - GRACO, INC.; *pg.* 1342, *pg.* 935
DEMANDSELECT - Software - R.R. DONNELLEY & SONS COMPANY; *pg.* 1682, *pg.* 589
DEMASE - Boot - ALDO GROUP; *pg.* 1804, *pg.* 1959
DEMASTATS - Laser Delivery Device - AMERICAN MEDICAL SYSTEMS, INC.; *pg.* 1399, *pg.* 238
DEMBE - Lamp - ASHLEY FURNITURE INDUSTRIES, INC.; *pg.* 914, *pg.* 1852
DEMCO-BOUND - Book Binding - DEMCO INC.; *pg.* 386, *pg.* 1865
DEMCOTE - Adhesive - DEMCO INC.; *pg.* 386, *pg.* 1865
DEMETRIUS - Lamp - ASHLEY FURNITURE INDUSTRIES, INC.; *pg.* 914, *pg.* 1852
DEMI - Lamp - ASHLEY FURNITURE INDUSTRIES, INC.; *pg.* 914, *pg.* 1852
DEMI-LOAF - Frozen Bread - BRIDGFORD FOODS CORPORATION; *pg.* 842, *pg.* 42
DEMI SOFT - Footwear - CAPEZIO BALLET MAKERS INC.; *pg.* 1805, *pg.* 1125
DEMILAV - Bath Product - KOHLER CO.; *pg.* 91, *pg.* 1862
DEMILUNE - Furniture - ETHAN ALLEN INTERIORS INC.; *pg.* 924, *pg.* 343
DEMILUNE - Furniture - HOOKER FURNITURE CORPORATION; *pg.* 928, *pg.* 1788
DEMING'S - Canned Salmon - PETER PAN SEAFOODS, INC.; *pg.* 889, *pg.* 1838
DEMITRI - Lighting Product - QUOIZEL INC.; *pg.* 1304, *pg.* 1616
DEMOCRACY - Misses' Apparel - KELLWOOD COMPANY; *pg.* 28, *pg.* 975
DEMOLETTER - Software - CLEARONE COMMUNICATIONS, INC.; *pg.* 629, *pg.* 1756
DEMOLITION - Blade - LENOX; *pg.* 1053, *pg.* 817
DEMON - Plastic Refractory - PLIBRICO CO. LLC; *pg.* 104, *pg.* 587
DEMONSTRABLY SUPERIOR & PLEASINGLY DIFFERENT - Slogan - CALLAWAY GOLF COMPANY; *pg.* 1829, *pg.* 58
DEMOSHIELD - Software - FLEXERA SOFTWARE INC.; *pg.* 398, *pg.* 658
DEMPSEY - Furniture - ASHLEY FURNITURE INDUSTRIES, INC.; *pg.* 914, *pg.* 1852
DEMPSTER'S - Food Product - MAPLE LEAF FOODS INC.; *pg.* 875, *pg.* 1927
DEMS - Chemical Product - AIR PRODUCTS AND CHEMICALS, INC.; *pg.* 1145, *pg.* 1513
DEMTROL - Demulsifier - THE DOW CHEMICAL COMPANY; *pg.* 1157, *pg.* 898
D.E.N. - Epoxy Novolac Resins - THE DOW CHEMICAL COMPANY; *pg.* 1157, *pg.* 898
DENAKA IMPORTED VODKA - Vodka - SAZERAC COMPANY, INC.; *pg.* 1969, *pg.* 745
DENALI - Furniture - ASHLEY FURNITURE INDUSTRIES, INC.; *pg.* 914, *pg.* 1852
DENALI - Furniture - BUSH INDUSTRIES INC.; *pg.* 919, *pg.* 1170
DENALI PRINCESS LODGE - Hotel - PRINCESS TOURS; *pg.* 1920, *pg.* 1838
DENATURANT G - Chemical Product - BIRKO CORPORATION; *pg.* 1149, *pg.* 332
DENDHUR - Furniture - HAWORTH, INC.; *pg.* 402, *pg.* 891
DENDOH - Power Assist Fishing Reel - DAIWA CORPORATION; *pg.* 1832, *pg.* 75
DENEVE - Lounge Chairs - BERNHARDT DESIGN; *pg.* 918, *pg.* 1381
DENISE - Clothing - ABERCROMBIE & FITCH CO.; *pg.* 37, *pg.* 1466
DENNISON'S - Food Product - CONAGRA FOODS, INC.; *pg.* 826, *pg.* 1014
DENOMINATOR - Fabric - NEMSCHOFF, INC.; *pg.* 936, *pg.* 1890
DENSARMOR - Building Product - GEORGIA-PACIFIC LLC; *pg.* 1458, *pg.* 507
DENSDECK - Roof Board - G-P GYPSUM CORPORATION; *pg.* 978, *pg.* 505
DENSDECK - Gypsum Board - GEORGIA-PACIFIC LLC; *pg* 1458, *pg.* 507
DENSEPAK - Glass & Ceramic Material - CORNING INCORPORATED; *pg.* 1122, *pg.* 1154
DENSGLASS - Fiberglass-Faced Gypsum Sheathing - GEORGIA-PACIFIC LLC; *pg.* 1458, *pg.* 507
DENSGLASS GOLD - Gypsum Wallboard Product - G-P GYPSUM CORPORATION; *pg.* 978, *pg.* 505
DENSGLASS GOLD - Exterior Sheathing - GEORGIA-PACIFIC LLC; *pg.* 1458, *pg.* 507
DENSGLASS SILVER - Residential Sheathing - GEORGIA-PACIFIC LLC; *pg.* 1458, *pg.* 507
DENSGUARD - Building Product - GEORGIA-PACIFIC LLC; *pg.* 1458, *pg.* 507
DENSIEYE - Densitometer - X-RITE, INCORPORATED; *pg.* 1437, *pg.* 891
DENSIL - Silicone Adhesive - FLEXCON CORPORATION; *pg.* 1457, *pg.* 844
DENSKA - Office Furniture - STEELCASE INC.; *pg.* 475, *pg.* 889
DENSSHIELD - Tile Backer - G-P GYPSUM CORPORATION; *pg.* 978, *pg.* 505
DENSSHIELD - Gypsum Board - GEORGIA-PACIFIC LLC; *pg.* 1458, *pg.* 507
DENT-X - Dental X-Ray Equipment - IMAGEWORKS; *pg.* 1544, *pg.* 1158
DENT-X PROIMAGE - Software - IMAGEWORKS; *pg.* 1544, *pg.* 1158
DENTABURST - Teeth Cleaners - KIMBERLY-CLARK CORPORATION; *pg.* 1461, *pg.* 1720
DENTAL - Tobacco Product - AMERICAN SNUFF COMPANY; *pg.* 1893, *pg.* 1641
DENTAL - Dog Toy - THE HARTZ MOUNTAIN CORP.; *pg.* 1476, *pg.* 1120
DENTAL CENTER - Dental Tools - THE GILLETTE COMPANY; *pg.* 509, *pg.* 795
DENTAL DIRECT - Dental Coverage Service - BLUE CROSS & BLUE SHIELD OF RHODE ISLAND; *pg.* 1195, *pg.* 1606
DENTAL EXPLORER - Health Plan & Publication - MEDICA, INC.; *pg.* 1208, *pg.* 949
DENTAL REFERRAL SERVICE - Dental Marketing Service - FUTUREDONTICS, INC.; *pg.* 1532, *pg.* 131
DENTALBLUE - Health Product - ANTHEM BLUE CROSS BLUE SHIELD; *pg.* 1192, *pg.* 1886
DENTALVISION - Dental Software - HENRY SCHEIN, INC.; *pg.* 1541, *pg.* 1180
DENTEMP - Temporary Dental Cement - MAJESTIC DRUG COMPANY, INC.; *pg.* 516, *pg.* 1343
DENTEMP OS - Over-the-Counter Dental Cement - MAJESTIC DRUG COMPANY, INC.; *pg.* 516, *pg.* 1343
DENTISTRY.COM - Dental Information - FUTUREDONTICS, INC.; *pg.* 1532, *pg.* 131
DENTLEY'S CHEWRITE - Pet Chew Treats - PETSMART, INC.; *pg.* 1481, *pg.* 18
DENTON CHEWING GUM - Chewing Gum Company - TONNER DOLL COMPANY, INC.; *pg.* 968, *pg.* 1171
THE DENTON RECORD CHRONICLE - Publisher Company - DENTON PUBLISHING COMPANY; *pg.* 1634, *pg.* 1691
DENTOOL - Dental Product - MAJESTIC DRUG COMPANY, INC.; *pg.* 516, *pg.* 1343
DENTOOL JR. - Dental Product - MAJESTIC DRUG COMPANY, INC.; *pg.* 516, *pg.* 1343
DENTRIX - Software - HENRY SCHEIN, INC.; *pg.* 1541, *pg.* 1180
DENT'S - Ear Wax Drops & Dental Aids - GRANDPA BRANDS COMPANY; *pg.* 1538, *pg.* 727
DENTS AWAY...SAME DAY - Tag Line - DENT WIZARD INTERNATIONAL CORP.; *pg.* 204, *pg.* 973
DENT`S EAR WAX DROPS - Ear Wax Drop - GRANDPA BRANDS COMPANY; *pg.* 1538, *pg.* 727
DENT`S EXTRA STRENGTH - Toothache Gum - GRANDPA BRANDS COMPANY; *pg.* 1538, *pg.* 727
DENT`S MAXI-STRENGTH - Toothache Drops Treatment - GRANDPA BRANDS COMPANY; *pg.* 1538, *pg.* 727
DENTSPLY - Dental Product - DENTSPLY INTERNATIONAL INC.; *pg.* 1522, *pg.* 1596
DENTSULATE - Dental Product - DENTSPLY INTERNATIONAL INC.; *pg.* 1522, *pg.* 1596
DENTURITE - Health & Beauty Product - COMBE INCORPORATED; *pg.* 1516, *pg.* 1351
DENTYNE - Chewing Gum - MONDELEZ INTERNATIONAL, INC.; *pg.* 878, *pg.* 601
DENVER - Densitometers, Film Editing Equipment - EASTMAN KODAK COMPANY; *pg.* 1408, *pg.* 1333
DENVER DUCK & THE QUEST FOR THE GOLDEN EGG - Video Game - INTERNATIONAL GAME TECHNOLOGY; *pg.* 957, *pg.* 1024
DENVER DUCK SLOTS - Video Game - INTERNATIONAL GAME TECHNOLOGY; *pg.* 957, *pg.* 1024
DENVER HAYES - Apparel - MARKS WORK WEARHOUSE LTD.; *pg.* 44, *pg.* 1903
DENVER JEANS - Men's Jeans - KELLWOOD COMPANY; *pg.* 28, *pg.* 975
DENVER NUGGETS - Basketball Team - THE DENVER NUGGETS LIMITED PARTNERSHIP; *pg.* 544, *pg.* 319
THE DENVER POST - Newspaper - THE DENVER NEWSPAPER AGENCY; *pg.* 1634, *pg.* 318
DENVER ROCKY MOUNTAIN NEWS - Newspaper - THE E.W. SCRIPPS COMPANY; *pg.* 1639, *pg.* 1412
DENVER TASTE - Communication Product - CENTURYLINK, INC; *pg.* 1870, *pg.* 317
DEO-MIST - Dispenser - DELTA FOREMOST CHEMICAL CORPORATION; *pg.* 1155, *pg.* 1642
DEON - Lamp - ASHLEY FURNITURE INDUSTRIES, INC.; *pg.* 914, *pg.* 1852
DEOXIDE - Metal Finishing Product - HEATBATH CORPORATION; *pg.* 1165, *pg.* 826
DEOXIDINE - Metalworking Chemical - HENKEL CORPORATION; *pg.* 1166, *pg.* 897
DEOXO - Catalyst - BASF CATALYSTS LLC; *pg.* 1148, *pg.* 1074
DEPACON IV - Pharmaceutical - ABBOTT LABORATORIES; *pg.* 1484, *pg.* 551
DEPADE - Pharmaceutical Product - MALLINCKRODT PHARMACEUTICALS; *pg.* 1557, *pg.* 978
DEPAKOTE - Tablet - ABBOTT LABORATORIES; *pg.* 1484,

pg. 551
DEPAKOTE - Estradiol Transdermal System - NOVEN PHARMACEUTICALS, INC.; *pg.* 1576, *pg.* 445
DEPAKOTE ER - Pharmaceutical Product - IMPAX LABORATORIES, INC.; *pg.* 1544, *pg.* 101
DEPAKOTE ER - Estradiol Transdermal System - NOVEN PHARMACEUTICALS, INC.; *pg.* 1576, *pg.* 445
DEPARTURES - Magazine - AMERICAN EXPRESS COMPANY; *pg.* 712, *pg.* 1190
DEPARTURES - Media Publication - TIME INC.; *pg.* 1693, *pg.* 1300
DEPEND - Incontinence Product - KIMBERLY-CLARK CORPORATION; *pg.* 1461, *pg.* 1720
DEPEND-O-LOK - Piping System - VICTAULIC COMPANY; *pg.* 1066, *pg.* 1529
DEPLOY - Apparel - OAKLEY, INC.; *pg.* 1840, *pg.* 86
DEPLOYDIRECTOR - Software - DELL SOFTWARE; *pg.* 385, *pg.* 40
DEPO - Medicine - PFIZER INC.; *pg.* 1581, *pg.* 1278
DEPO-ESTRADIOL - Pharmaceutical Product - PFIZER INC.; *pg.* 1581, *pg.* 1278
DEPO-MEDROL - Prescription Pharmaceutical - PFIZER INC.; *pg.* 1581, *pg.* 1278
DEPO-PROVERA - Contraceptive - PFIZER INC.; *pg.* 1581, *pg.* 1278
DEPO-SUBQ PROVERA 104 - Pharmaceutical Product - PFIZER INC.; *pg.* 1581, *pg.* 1278
DEPO-TESTOSTERONE - Pharmaceutical Product - PFIZER INC.; *pg.* 1581, *pg.* 1278
DEPOBUPIVACAINE - Analgesic - PACIRA PHARMACEUTICALS, INC.; *pg.* 1579, *pg.* 1104
DEPOCYT - Chemotherapeutic Agent - PACIRA PHARMACEUTICALS, INC.; *pg.* 1579, *pg.* 1104
DEPOCYTE - Pharmaceutical Product - PACIRA PHARMACEUTICALS, INC.; *pg.* 1579, *pg.* 1104
DEPODUR - Pharmaceutical Product - ENDO PHARMACEUTICALS HOLDINGS, INC.; *pg.* 1528, *pg.* 1549
DEPODUR - Analgesic - PACIRA PHARMACEUTICALS, INC.; *pg.* 1579, *pg.* 1104
DEPOFOAM - Pharmaceutical Product - PACIRA PHARMACEUTICALS, INC.; *pg.* 1579, *pg.* 1104
DEPOLARIZED - Alloy Product - SPECIAL METALS CORPORATION; *pg.* 1377, *pg.* 1850
DEPTHMASTER - Trolling Rod - CABELA'S INCORPORATED; *pg.* 535, *pg.* 1019
DEPUY - Orthopedic Products - DEPUYSYNTHES; *pg.* 1523, *pg.* 699
DEQUORUM - Power Portals - WIREMOLD/LEGRAND; *pg.* 689, *pg.* 383
D.E.R. - Epoxy Resins - THE DOW CHEMICAL COMPANY; *pg.* 1157, *pg.* 898
DERAKANE - Trade Bulletin - ASHLAND INC.; *pg.* 972, *pg.* 726
DERAMAXX - Pet Medication - PETMED EXPRESS, INC.; *pg.* 1781, *pg.* 460
DERBY - Office Furniture - STEELCASE INC.; *pg.* 475, *pg.* 889
DEREK - Furniture - AMISCO INDUSTRIES LTD.; *pg.* 913, *pg.* 1958
DEREK - Lamp - ASHLEY FURNITURE INDUSTRIES, INC.; *pg.* 914, *pg.* 1852
DEREK - Beer - COASTAL EXTREME BREWING COMPANY; *pg.* 240, *pg.* 1602
DEREK JETER DRIVEN - Fragrance - AVON PRODUCTS, INC.; *pg.* 500, *pg.* 1198
DERICA - Lamp - ASHLEY FURNITURE INDUSTRIES, INC.; *pg.* 914, *pg.* 1852
DERIFIL - Medical Device - INTEGRA LIFESCIENCES HOLDINGS CORPORATION; *pg.* 1545, *pg.* 1109
DERIPHAT - Amphoteric Surfactants - HENKEL CORPORATION; *pg.* 1165, *pg.* 1535
DERMA CARE - Health & Beauty Product - BLUE CROSS LABORATORIES; *pg.* 326, *pg.* 277
DERMA CLEAN - Antibacterial Dish Liquid - BLUE CROSS LABORATORIES; *pg.* 326, *pg.* 277
DERMA-CLENS - Veterinary Cleansing Cream - PFIZER INC.; *pg.* 1581, *pg.* 1278
DERMA E - Beauty Care Products - STEARNS PRODUCTS INC.; *pg.* 523, *pg.* 279
DERMA-GEL - Medical Product - MEDLINE INDUSTRIES, INC.; *pg.* 1562, *pg.* 635
DERMA PRO ANTIMICROBIAL - Soap - SWISHER HYGIENE INC.; *pg.* 336, *pg.* 1507
DERMA PRO LOTION - Skin Cleanser - SWISHER HYGIENE INC.; *pg.* 336, *pg.* 1507
DERMA-SURE SKIN BARRIER - Protective Skin Lotion - UNITED-GUARDIAN, INC.; *pg.* 1184, *pg.* 1165
DERMABLEND - Cosmetics - L'OREAL USA; *pg.* 514, *pg.* 1252
DERMABOND - Healthcare Product - JOHNSON & JOHNSON; *pg.* 1549, *pg.* 1091
DERMADRATE - Pharmaceutical Product - VALEANT PHARMACEUTICALS INTERNATIONAL; *pg.* 1605, *pg.* 1047
DERMAGENETICS - Neutraceutical Product - GENELINK, INC.; *pg.* 1533, *pg.* 438
DERMAGLIDE - Oculoplastic Sutures - SURGICAL SPECIALTIES CORPORATION; *pg.* 1600, *pg.* 1912
DERMAGRAN - Wound Dressing - DERMA SCIENCES, INC.; *pg.* 1523, *pg.* 1111
DERMAKLENZ - Cleaning Chemical Product - KYZEN CORPORATION; *pg.* 331, *pg.* 1652
DERMAL C - Health & Beauty Product - DIXIE HEALTH, INC.; *pg.* 1524, *pg.* 535
DERMAL-E - Vitamin E Anti-aging Cream - DIXIE HEALTH, INC.; *pg.* 1524, *pg.* 535
DERMAL GLOVES - Cotton Gloves - GEORGE GLOVE CO., INC.; *pg.* 5, *pg.* 1084
DERMAL H3 - Health & Beauty Product - DIXIE HEALTH, INC.; *pg.* 1524, *pg.* 535
DERMAL K - Health & Beauty Product - DIXIE HEALTH, INC.; *pg.* 1524, *pg.* 535
DERMAL XL - Health & Beauty Product - DIXIE HEALTH, INC.; *pg.* 1524, *pg.* 535
DERMAMITT - Wound Care Products - ALIMED, INC.; *pg.* 1490, *pg.* 816
DERMAQUIL - Nutritional Product - NUTRACEUTICAL INTERNATIONAL CORPORATION; *pg.* 1576, *pg.* 1753
DERMASAVER - Skin Care Product - ALIMED, INC.; *pg.* 1490, *pg.* 816
DERMASAVER RELEVATOR - Wound Care Products - ALIMED, INC.; *pg.* 1490, *pg.* 816
DERMASITE - Semi-solid SITE RELEASE Configuration for Topical Applications to the Skin - LUMARA HEALTH INC.; *pg.* 1557, *pg.* 973
DERMASSAGE - Dishwashing Liquid - COLGATE-PALMOLIVE COMPANY; *pg.* 504, *pg.* 1215
DERMASTAT - Tracing Instruments Used in Teating Small Cutaneous Surface Lesions - AMERICAN MEDICAL SYSTEMS, INC.; *pg.* 1399, *pg.* 238
DERMATEMP - Thermometer System - EXERGEN CORPORATION; *pg.* 1412, *pg.* 855
DERMATIC EFFECTS - Skin Care Product - NU SKIN ENTERPRISES, INC.; *pg.* 518, *pg.* 1755
DERMATIX - Pharmaceutical Product - VALEANT PHARMACEUTICALS INTERNATIONAL; *pg.* 1605, *pg.* 1047
DERMATOLOGICA - Skin Care Products - DERMALOGICA, INC.; *pg.* 1523, *pg.* 63
DERMAVEEN - Pharmaceutical Product - VALEANT PHARMACEUTICALS INTERNATIONAL; *pg.* 1605, *pg.* 1047
DERMAWRAP - Wound Care Products - ALIMED, INC.; *pg.* 1490, *pg.* 816
DERMED - Medicated Shampoo - PETEDGE; *pg.* 1481, *pg.* 787
DERMULSENE - Resin Dispersion - NEVILLE CHEMICAL COMPANY; *pg.* 1174, *pg.* 1578
DERRYDALE - Publishing Imprint - PENGUIN RANDOM HOUSE; *pg.* 1675, *pg.* 1276
DERUSTAL - Metal Finishing Product - HEATBATH CORPORATION; *pg.* 1165, *pg.* 826
DERUSTO - Rust Preventative Paint - DAP PRODUCTS, INC.; *pg.* 1441, *pg.* 756
DERUTA - Ceramic Tile, Hand Painted - WALKER & ZANGER, INC.; *pg.* 119, *pg.* 281
DERVOS - Apparels - UNDER ARMOUR, INC.; *pg.* 49, *pg.* 759
DES OWEN - Pharmaceutical Products - GALDERMA LABORATORIES, L.P.; *pg.* 1532, *pg.* 1695
DESAL - Membranes - GE WATER & PROCESS TECHNOLOGIES; *pg.* 1339, *pg.* 1588
DESANA - Lamp - ASHLEY FURNITURE INDUSTRIES, INC.; *pg.* 914, *pg.* 1852
DESCHAUX BRANDY - Spirits - LEONARD KREUSCH, INC.; *pg.* 254, *pg.* 1099
DESCOGLAS - Wall Coating - THE VALSPAR CORPORATION; *pg.* 1449, *pg.* 945
DESCOGLAZE - Wall Coating - THE VALSPAR CORPORATION; *pg.* 1449, *pg.* 945
DESCOTE - Microencapsulated Vitamin, Mineral & Active Pharmaceutical Raw Matls. - LUMARA HEALTH INC.; *pg.* 1557, *pg.* 973
DESDEMON - Lamp - ASHLEY FURNITURE INDUSTRIES, INC.; *pg.* 914, *pg.* 1852
DESDEMONA - Furniture - J. ROBERT SCOTT INC.; *pg.* 930, *pg.* 105
DESERT - Car Dealerships - AUTONATION, INC.; *pg.* 165, *pg.* 423
DESERT BREEZE - Ethnobotanical Product - NU SKIN ENTERPRISES, INC.; *pg.* 518, *pg.* 1755
DESERT DISPATCH - California Newspaper - FREEDOM COMMUNICATIONS, INC.; *pg.* 1643, *pg.* 110
DESERT FOX - Hose - THE GOODYEAR TIRE & RUBBER COMPANY; *pg.* 1883, *pg.* 1401
DESERT GOLD - Lottery Game - RHODE ISLAND LOTTERY; *pg.* 1004, *pg.* 1600
DESERT MOON - Video Game - INTERNATIONAL GAME TECHNOLOGY; *pg.* 957, *pg.* 1024
DESERT REFLECTIONS - Pigment - BASF CATALYSTS LLC; *pg.* 1148, *pg.* 1074
DESERT SPIRIT - Video Game - INTERNATIONAL GAME TECHNOLOGY; *pg.* 957, *pg.* 1024
DESERT TIMES - Newsletter - NEWS MEDIA CORPORATION; *pg.* 1670, *pg.* 654
DESERT WASH - Apparel - BRODER BROS., CO.; *pg.* 1828, *pg.* 1588
DESERT WINDS - Dinnerware - THE HOMER LAUGHLIN CHINA COMPANY; *pg.* 1125, *pg.* 1850
DESERTCAT 8 PLATESETTER - Eight Up Thermal Platesetter - ECRM IMAGING SYSTEMS, INC.; *pg.* 1410, *pg.* 848
DESERTCAT 88 - Eight Page Thermal Platesetter & Proofer - ECRM IMAGING SYSTEMS, INC.; *pg.* 1410, *pg.* 848
DESERTHOG - Battery - ENERSYS INC.; *pg.* 1334, *pg.* 1584
DESI-DRI - Gas Dehydration System - CAMERON INTERNATIONAL; *pg.* 1151, *pg.* 1702
DESICAP - Desiccant Cap - MULTISORB TECHNOLOGIES, INC.; *pg.* 1570, *pg.* 1150
DESICCITE - Adsorbent - BASF CATALYSTS LLC; *pg.* 1148, *pg.* 1074
DESIFORM - Packaging Product - MULTISORB TECHNOLOGIES, INC.; *pg.* 1570, *pg.* 1150
DESIGN - Fragrance - ELIZABETH ARDEN, INC.; *pg.* 507, *pg.* 448
DESIGN-A-ROUND - Balloon - CONTINENTAL AMERICAN CORP.; *pg.* 1880, *pg.* 723
DESIGN-A-SET - Medical Device - HOSPIRA, INC.; *pg.* 1542, *pg.* 623
DESIGN ANALYZER - Software - SYNOPSYS, INC.; *pg.* 480, *pg.* 162
DESIGN ARCHITECT - Software System - MENTOR GRAPHICS CORPORATION; *pg.* 432, *pg.* 1510
DESIGN ARCHITECT ELITE - Software System - MENTOR GRAPHICS CORPORATION; *pg.* 432, *pg.* 1510
DESIGN ARCHITECT-IC - Software System - MENTOR GRAPHICS CORPORATION; *pg.* 432, *pg.* 1510
DESIGN BASICS - Wood Blinds - SPRINGS WINDOW FASHIONS LLC; *pg.* 943, *pg.* 1872
DESIGN CAPTURE - Software System - MENTOR GRAPHICS CORPORATION; *pg.* 432, *pg.* 1510
DESIGN COMPILER - Software - SYNOPSYS, INC.; *pg.* 480, *pg.* 162
DESIGN DOCTOR - Software - AUTODESK INC.; *pg.* 356, *pg.* 257
DESIGN EXCHANGE - Software System - MENTOR GRAPHICS CORPORATION; *pg.* 432, *pg.* 1510
DESIGN FOR SIGNAL - P-wave Vibrator - ION GEOPHYSICAL CORPORATION; *pg.* 1350, *pg.* 1708
DESIGN FREEDOM - Perm Shampoo Styling Aids & Conditioners - ZOTOS INTERNATIONAL, INC.; *pg.* 524, *pg.* 345
DESIGN. ILLUMINATE. ENJOY - Tagline - HINKLEY LIGHTING INC.; *pg.* 1299, *pg.* 1404
DESIGN MANAGER - Software - GE ENERGY; *pg.* 1338, *pg.* 506
DESIGN MANAGER - Software System - MENTOR GRAPHICS CORPORATION; *pg.* 432, *pg.* 1510
DESIGN SERVER - Software - AUTODESK INC.; *pg.* 356, *pg.* 257
DESIGN STATION - Software System - MENTOR GRAPHICS CORPORATION; *pg.* 432, *pg.* 1510
DESIGN VIEW - Curtain Wall & Wall Framing Products - KAWNEER COMPANY, INC.; *pg.* 90, *pg.* 537

DESIGN VISION - Software - SYNOPSYS, INC.; *pg.* 480, *pg.* 162
DESIGN WEB FORMAT - Software - AUTODESK INC.; *pg.* 356, *pg.* 257
DESIGN4 - Laminates - OMNOVA SOLUTIONS INC; *pg.* 1176, *pg.* 1453
DESIGNACOLOR - Color Display Accessories - PPG INDUSTRIES, INC.; *pg.* 1445, *pg.* 1579
DESIGNANALYST - Software System - MENTOR GRAPHICS CORPORATION; *pg.* 432, *pg.* 1510
DESIGNARE - Plybent Wood Chair - SAUDER MANUFACTURING COMPANY; *pg.* 941, *pg.* 1403
DESIGNBOOK - Software System - MENTOR GRAPHICS CORPORATION; *pg.* 432, *pg.* 1510
DESIGNCENTER - Software - AUTODESK INC.; *pg.* 356, *pg.* 257
DESIGNED PERFORMANCE - Office Product - HAWORTH, INC.; *pg.* 402, *pg.* 891
DESIGNED TO PERFORM. DESIGNED TO LAST. - Tag Line - INTERPHASE CORPORATION; *pg.* 420, *pg.* 1732
DESIGNER - Recreational Vehicles - JAYCO INC.; *pg.* 1708, *pg.* 695
DESIGNER - Floor Cleaning Product - NSS ENTERPRISES, INC.; *pg.* 59, *pg.* 1476
DESIGNER CAREFREE - Vinyl Tile - CONGOLEUM CORPORATION; *pg.* 921, *pg.* 1084
DESIGNER CONTOUR - Screen - DA-LITE SCREEN COMPANY; *pg.* 632, *pg.* 698
DESIGNER DA-TAB ELECTROL - Screen - DA-LITE SCREEN COMPANY; *pg.* 632, *pg.* 698
THE DESIGNER DIAMOND COLLECTION - Jewlery - HELZBERG'S DIAMOND SHOPS, INC.; *pg.* 6, *pg.* 984
DESIGNER DRY - Carpet Vacuum - NSS ENTERPRISES, INC.; *pg.* 59, *pg.* 1476
DESIGNER ELECTROL - Electric Screen - DA-LITE SCREEN COMPANY; *pg.* 632, *pg.* 698
DESIGNER IMPOSTERS - Women's Body Sprays & Fragrances - PARFUMS DE COEUR LTD.; *pg.* 519, *pg.* 376
DESIGNER INLAID - Flooring Product - CONGOLEUM CORPORATION; *pg.* 921, *pg.* 1084
DESIGNER LINE - Air Filters, Regulators & Lubricators - NORGREN, INC.; *pg.* 231, *pg.* 333
DESIGNER MANUAL - Portable Projection Screen - DA-LITE SCREEN COMPANY; *pg.* 632, *pg.* 698
DESIGNER MODEL B - Portable Projection Screen - DA-LITE SCREEN COMPANY; *pg.* 632, *pg.* 698
DESIGNER PROTEIN THERAPEUTICS - Technology Platforms - REGENERON PHARMACEUTICALS, INC.; *pg.* 1588, *pg.* 1345
DESIGNER QUALITY FRAGRANCES, NOT DESIGNER PRICES - Slogan - PARFUMS DE COEUR LTD.; *pg.* 519, *pg.* 376
DESIGNER SERIES - Toilet Partitions - BOBRICK WASHROOM EQUIPMENT, INC.; *pg.* 1043, *pg.* 166
DESIGNER SERIES - EnduraClad Wood Windows & Patio Doors - PELLA CORPORATION; *pg.* 104, *pg.* 711
DESIGNER SERIES - Cabinets - TAB PRODUCTS CO. LLC; *pg.* 481, *pg.* 1869
DESIGNER SOLARIAN - Wood Flooring Product - ARMSTRONG WORLD INDUSTRIES, INC.; *pg.* 914, *pg.* 1545
DESIGNER STOCK SIGNATURE SERIES - Stock Framed Cabinetry - NORCRAFT HOLDINGS, LP; *pg.* 100, *pg.* 921
DESIGNER SURFACE - Pushbuttons - CRAFTMADE INTERNATIONAL, INC.; *pg.* 1295, *pg.* 1670
DESIGNER TOUCH - Hair Care Products - LUSTER PRODUCTS INC.; *pg.* 515, *pg.* 581
DESIGNER WALL - Steel Wall Panel - CLESTRA HAUSERMAN, INC.; *pg.* 76, *pg.* 1526
DESIGNER WEDGES - Golf Products - FEEL GOLF CO., INC.; *pg.* 1834, *pg.* 465
DESIGNERHDL - Software - SYNOPSYS, INC.; *pg.* 480, *pg.* 162
DESIGNER'S CHOICE - Ceiling Fan - HUNTER FAN COMPANY; *pg.* 57, *pg.* 1631
DESIGNER'S CHOICE COLLECTION - Ceiling Fans - HUNTER FAN COMPANY; *pg.* 57, *pg.* 1631
DESIGNERS' COLLECTION - Stationery - AMERICAN GREETINGS CORPORATION; *pg.* 1615, *pg.* 1428
DESIGNERS ORIGINALS - Sweaters - HAMPSHIRE GROUP LIMITED; *pg.* 25, *pg.* 1237
DESIGNER'S WORLD - Toy & Game - HASBRO, INC.; *pg.* 954, *pg.* 1603
DESIGNKIDS - Software - AUTODESK INC.; *pg.* 356, *pg.* 257
DESIGNPOWER - Software - SYNOPSYS, INC.; *pg.* 480, *pg.* 162
DESIGNPROF - Software - AUTODESK INC.; *pg.* 356, *pg.* 257
DESIGNS FOR DANCE - Tagline - WEISSMAN THEATRICAL SUPPLY, INC.; *pg.* 35, *pg.* 1004
DESIGNSTUDIO - Software - AUTODESK INC.; *pg.* 356, *pg.* 257
DESIGNSTUDIO - Software - BOTTOMLINE TECHNOLOGIES INC.; *pg.* 363, *pg.* 483
DESIGNTEX - Office Furniture - STEELCASE INC.; *pg.* 475, *pg.* 889
DESIGNVIEW - Software System - MENTOR GRAPHICS CORPORATION; *pg.* 432, *pg.* 1510
DESIGNWALL - Interior Panels - HOMASOTE COMPANY; *pg.* 87, *pg.* 1126
DESIGNWARE - Party Goods - AMERICAN GREETINGS CORPORATION; *pg.* 1615, *pg.* 1428
DESIGNWARE - Software - SYNOPSYS, INC.; *pg.* 480, *pg.* 162
DESIMAX - Desiccant Label - MULTISORB TECHNOLOGIES, INC.; *pg.* 1570, *pg.* 1150
DESIMAX SLF - Desiccant In Tape Form - MULTISORB TECHNOLOGIES, INC.; *pg.* 1570, *pg.* 1150
DESINGLINE - Cooler - SEELEY INTERNATIONAL AMERICAS; *pg.* 1076, *pg.* 19
DESIRED EFFECTS - Cosmetic Product - NU SKIN ENTERPRISES, INC.; *pg.* 518, *pg.* 1755
DESITIN - Diaper Rash Relief - JOHNSON & JOHNSON; *pg.* 1549, *pg.* 1091
DESK-LINK - Glass & Ceramic Material - CORNING INCORPORATED; *pg.* 1122, *pg.* 1154
DESKDOCK - Adapter - DELL INC.; *pg.* 383, *pg.* 1737
DESKTOP - Software - MICROSTRATEGY, INC.; *pg.* 1266, *pg.* 1809
DESKTOP AUTHORITY - Software - DELL SOFTWARE; *pg.* 385, *pg.* 40
DESKTOP EXPRESS - Software - PITNEY BOWES INC.; *pg.* 454, *pg.* 376
DESKTOP FIREWALL - Software - WEBROOT SOFTWARE, INC.; *pg.* 1289, *pg.* 313
DESKTOP PUBLISHING - Document Creation - PITNEY BOWES INC.; *pg.* 454, *pg.* 376
DESKTOP SECURITY - Management Platform - IMAGEWARE SYSTEMS, INC.; *pg.* 412, *pg.* 203
DESKTOP TO GO - Software - DATAVIZ, INC.; *pg.* 383, *pg.* 356
DESKTOPASIC - Software System - MENTOR GRAPHICS CORPORATION; *pg.* 432, *pg.* 1510
DESKTOPSTREAMING - Software - CITRIX SYSTEMS, INC.; *pg.* 375, *pg.* 424
DESMOND & DUFF SCOTCH - Spirits - LEONARD KREUSCH, INC.; *pg.* 254, *pg.* 1099
DESOBOND - Coating Product - PPG INDUSTRIES, INC.; *pg.* 1445, *pg.* 1579
DESOCLEAN - Coating Product - PPG INDUSTRIES, INC.; *pg.* 1445, *pg.* 1579
DESOFILL - Coating Product - PPG INDUSTRIES, INC.; *pg.* 1445, *pg.* 1579
DESOPRIME - Coating Product - PPG INDUSTRIES, INC.; *pg.* 1445, *pg.* 1579
DESOTHANE - Coating Product - PPG INDUSTRIES, INC.; *pg.* 1445, *pg.* 1579
DESOTO - Coating Product - PPG INDUSTRIES, INC.; *pg.* 1445, *pg.* 1579
DESPARD - Interchangeable Switches, Receptacles & Pilot Lights - PASS & SEYMOUR/LEGRAND; *pg.* 1303, *pg.* 1344
DESPERADO - Agricultural Product - WILBUR-ELLIS COMPANY; *pg.* 1185, *pg.* 234
DESPERADOS - Beer - HEINEKEN USA INC.; *pg.* 252, *pg.* 1352
DESPRO - Glove - LAKELAND INDUSTRIES, INC.; *pg.* 1354, *pg.* 1338
DESSA - Clothing - ABERCROMBIE & FITCH CO.; *pg.* 37, *pg.* 1466
DESSANGE PARIS - Hair Salon - DESSANGE INTERNATIONAL, INC.; *pg.* 506, *pg.* 787
DESSERT CUPS - Bakery Product - ALFRED NICKLES BAKERY, INC.; *pg.* 836, *pg.* 1466
DESTAB - Direct Compression Products - LUMARA HEALTH INC.; *pg.* 1557, *pg.* 973
DESTINATION - Fragrance & Personal Care Products - ANN INC.; *pg.* 18, *pg.* 1195
DESTINATION - Motor Homes - WINNEBAGO INDUSTRIES, INC.; *pg.* 1712, *pg.* 707
DESTINATION MATERNITY - Maternity Clothing & Retail Stores - DESTINATION MATERNITY CORPORATION; *pg.* 23, *pg.* 1563
DESTINATION PCB - Software System - MENTOR GRAPHICS CORPORATION; *pg.* 432, *pg.* 1510
DESTINATION WEDDINGS & HONEYMOONS - Magazine - BONNIER CORPORATION; *pg.* 1622, *pg.* 480
DESTINATIONHUB - Advertising Services - LIVE CURRENT MEDIA INC.; *pg.* 1263, *pg.* 1911
DESTINY - Bridal Wear - ALFRED ANGELO, INC.; *pg.* 17, *pg.* 1532
DESTINY - Women's Fragrance - MARILYN MIGLIN, L.P.; *pg.* 516, *pg.* 581
DESTINY - High-end Frameless Stock & Semi-custom Cabinets - NORCRAFT HOLDINGS, LP; *pg.* 100, *pg.* 921
DESTINY - Hearing Instrument - STARKEY LABORATORIES, INC.; *pg.* 1597, *pg.* 923
DESTINY RE - Software System - MENTOR GRAPHICS CORPORATION; *pg.* 432, *pg.* 1510
DESYRE - Footwear - STEVEN MADDEN, LTD.; *pg.* 1819, *pg.* 1176
DET-O-JET - Cleaning Detergent - ALCONOX, INC.; *pg.* 325, *pg.* 1351
DETA - Battery - EXIDE TECHNOLOGIES; *pg.* 204, *pg.* 483
DETAC - Pitch Control Technology - GE WATER & PROCESS TECHNOLOGIES; *pg.* 1339, *pg.* 1588
DETACHABLE PLUS - Hair Clipper - ANDIS COMPANY; *pg.* 498, *pg.* 1895
DETACHATIP - Medical Equipment - CONMED CORPORATION; *pg.* 1517, *pg.* 1347
DETAILS - Magazine - CONDE NAST PUBLICATIONS, INC.; *pg.* 1629, *pg.* 1217
DETAILS - Office Furniture - STEELCASE INC.; *pg.* 475, *pg.* 889
THE DETANGLER - Hair Care Product - JOHN PAUL MITCHELL SYSTEMS; *pg.* 512, *pg.* 133
DETECT COMPARE IMAGING DIAGNOSTICS - Sensor - NAPCO SECURITY SYSTEMS, INC.; *pg.* 658, *pg.* 1138
DETECTA-DUCT - Special Loop Cable - STANDARD WIRE & CABLE CO.; *pg.* 1306, *pg.* 187
DETECTABLE NEEDLES - Animal Safety Product - NEOGEN CORPORATION; *pg.* 883, *pg.* 896
DETECTAGAS - Air Cleaner - RESEARCH PRODUCTS CORPORATION; *pg.* 1075, *pg.* 1867
DETECTAGENE - Molecular Probe Product - THERMO FISHER SCIENTIFIC INC.; *pg.* 1602, *pg.* 61
DETECTIVE ACADEMY - Educational Materials - SCHOLASTIC INC.; *pg.* 1683, *pg.* 1288
DETECTO - Portable Wheelchair Scale - ALIMED, INC.; *pg.* 1490, *pg.* 816
THE DETECTOR - Lighting Product - HUBBELL INCORPORATED; *pg.* 1299, *pg.* 370
DETENTE - Steel Office Desk - INVINCIBLE OFFICE FURNITURE; *pg.* 420, *pg.* 1868
DETER - Family Toiletries - AMWAY CORPORATION; *pg.* 326, *pg.* 864
DETERGENT 101 - Liquid Detergent - ECOLAB INC.; *pg.* 329, *pg.* 960
DETERGENT 8 - Detergent - ALCONOX, INC.; *pg.* 325, *pg.* 1351
DETERMINE - Rapid Membrane Test Products - ALERE INC.; *pg.* 1488, *pg.* 849
DETONATOR - Apparel - OAKLEY, INC.; *pg.* 1840, *pg.* 86
DETOUR - Salon Product - GREAT CLIPS, INC.; *pg.* 510, *pg.* 937
DETOUR - Fabric - NEMSCHOFF, INC.; *pg.* 936, *pg.* 1890
DETOUR - Office Furniture - STEELCASE INC.; *pg.* 475, *pg.* 889
DETOUR DOUBLER - Lottery Game - ILLINOIS STATE LOTTERY; *pg.* 995, *pg.* 578
DETOX AM TEA - Tea Product - CELESTIAL SEASONINGS, INC.; *pg.* 846, *pg.* 310
DETOX SUPPORT - Dietary Supplement - NOW HEALTH GROUP, INC.; *pg.* 1576, *pg.* 557
DETOXIFIBER - Health Supplement - GARDEN OF LIFE, INC.; *pg.* 1532, *pg.* 478
DETOXYGEN - Nutritional Supplement - NATURAL ORGANICS, INC.; *pg.* 1571, *pg.* 1181
DETREY - Dental Instrument - DENTSPLY INTERNATIONAL INC.; *pg.* 1522, *pg.* 1596
DETROIT - Stoker - DETROIT STOKER CO.; *pg.* 1070, *pg.* 900
DETROIT FREE PRESS - Newspaper - MICHIGAN.COM; *pg.*

1665, *pg.* 884

DETROIT LIONS L.E.A.D.ERS FOR LIFE - School Assembly Program - THE DETROIT LIONS, INC.; *pg.* 544, *pg.* 864

DETROIT LIONS SKILL DEVELOPMENT SESSIONS - Development Program - THE DETROIT LIONS, INC.; *pg.* 544, *pg.* 864

DETROIT LIONS YOUTH FOOTBALL - Initiative - THE DETROIT LIONS, INC.; *pg.* 544, *pg.* 864

DETROIT LIONS YOUTH FOOTBALL FORUM - Forum - THE DETROIT LIONS, INC.; *pg.* 544, *pg.* 864

DETROIT NEWS - Newspaper - MICHIGAN.COM; *pg.* 1665, *pg.* 884

DETROIT PISTONS - Professional Basketball Team - DETROIT PISTONS BASKETBALL COMPANY; *pg.* 544, *pg.* 868

DETROIT RED WINGS CLOTHING - Hockey Team - DETROIT RED WINGS, INC.; *pg.* 544, *pg.* 880

DETROIT TIGERS STADIUM - Baseball Club - DETROIT TIGERS BASEBALL CLUB, INC.; *pg.* 545, *pg.* 880

DETROL Overactive Bladder Medication - PFIZER INC.; *pg.* 1581, *pg.* 1278

DETROL LA - Pharmaceutical Product - IMPAX LABORATORIES, INC.; *pg.* 1544, *pg.* 101

DETROL LA - Pharmaceutical Product - PFIZER INC.; *pg.* 1581, *pg.* 1278

DETTOL - Cleaning Products & Disinfectants - RECKITT BENCKISER INC.; *pg.* 1136, *pg.* 1105

DETUINEN - Nutritional Supplements - NBTY, INC.; *pg.* 1572, *pg.* 1338

DEUCE - Golf Equipment - CALLAWAY GOLF COMPANY; *pg.* 1829, *pg.* 58

DEUCE - Video Scaler - COMMUNICATIONS SPECIALTIES, INC.; *pg.* 377, *pg.* 1338

DEUCE - Motorcycle - HARLEY-DAVIDSON, INC.; *pg.* 178, *pg.* 1874

DEUCE - Baseball Bat - HILLERICH & BRADSBY CO., INC.; *pg.* 1836, *pg.* 576

DEUCES WILD - Game - MISSOURI LOTTERY; *pg.* 999, *pg.* 979

DEUCES WILD BONUS POKER - Video Game - INTERNATIONAL GAME TECHNOLOGY; *pg.* 957, *pg.* 1024

DEUTSCH - High-Precision Oil & Air Filters (Automotive) - AUTOZONE, INC.; *pg.* 200, *pg.* 1641

DEUTSCHMACHER - Processed Food - KAYEM FOODS, INC.; *pg.* 867, *pg.* 814

DEV KIT OMAP2530 - Development Platform - BSQUARE CORPORATION; *pg.* 366, *pg.* 1813

DEV KIT OMAP3530 - Development Platform - BSQUARE CORPORATION; *pg.* 366, *pg.* 1813

DEV KIT PXA255 - Development Platform - BSQUARE CORPORATION; *pg.* 366, *pg.* 1813

DEV KIT PXA270 - Development Platform - BSQUARE CORPORATION; *pg.* 366, *pg.* 1813

DEV KITPXA255 - Development Platform - BSQUARE CORPORATION; *pg.* 366, *pg.* 1813

DEVA - Industrial Bearings - FEDERAL-MOGUL HOLDINGS CORPORATION; *pg.* 205, *pg.* 907

DEVACENTRAL - Software - F5 NETWORKS, INC.; *pg.* 396, *pg.* 1835

DEVAR - Process Control Instrument - DEVAR, INC.; *pg.* 633, *pg.* 339

DEVASTATOR - Stripper - HILLYARD, INC.; *pg.* 331, *pg.* 990

DEVCHEM - Coatings - AKZONOBEL DECORATIVE PAINTS U.S.; *pg.* 1439, *pg.* 1474

DEVCHLOR - Chlorinated Rubber Coating - AKZONOBEL DECORATIVE PAINTS U.S.; *pg.* 1439, *pg.* 1474

DEVELOMAX - Claflin Filling - BOLTON-EMERSON AMERICAS, INC.; *pg.* 1318, *pg.* 827

DEVELOPERNET - Computer Software - NOVELL INC.; *pg.* 446, *pg.* 852

DEVEN - Lamp - ASHLEY FURNITURE INDUSTRIES, INC.; *pg.* 914, *pg.* 1852

DEVERAUX - Furniture - JASPER GROUP; *pg.* 930, *pg.* 691

DEVEREAUX - Lighting Product - QUOIZEL INC.; *pg.* 1304, *pg.* 1616

THE DEVEREAUX SISTERS - Doll - TONNER DOLL COMPANY, INC.; *pg.* 968, *pg.* 1171

DEVICE CENTRAL - Software - ADOBE SYSTEMS INCORPORATED; *pg.* 342, *pg.* 235

DEVICE-CENTRIC-SERVICES - Manual - XEROX CORPORATION; *pg.* 494, *pg.* 365

DEVICE CERTIFICATE SERVICES - Online Transaction Security Product - VERISIGN, INC.; *pg.* 488, *pg.* 1799

DEVICE VALIDATION TESTSUITE - Software Application - BSQUARE CORPORATION; *pg.* 366, *pg.* 1813

DEVICECARE - Packaging Product - ENTEGRIS, INC.; *pg.* 1882, *pg.* 788

DEVICECONNECT - Two-factor Network Protection Solution - PHOENIX TECHNOLOGIES LTD.; *pg.* 454, *pg.* 147

DEVICELOGIX - Software - ROCKWELL AUTOMATION, INC.; *pg.* 668, *pg.* 1880

DEVICENET - Thermal Mass Flow Controller - MKS INSTRUMENTS, INC.; *pg.* 1362, *pg.* 781

DEVIL'S SPIT - BBQ Sauce - FAMOUS DAVE'S OF AMERICA, INC.; *pg.* 1728, *pg.* 926

DEVINE - Lighting Product - HUBBELL INCORPORATED; *pg.* 1299, *pg.* 370

DEVINNE - Footwear - STEVEN MADDEN, LTD.; *pg.* 1819, *pg.* 1176

DEVLIEG - Machine Tool Product - BOURN & KOCH MACHINE TOOL COMPANY; *pg.* 1319, *pg.* 654

DEVNET - Software - VERIFONE SYSTEMS, INC.; *pg.* 487, *pg.* 251

DEVOE - Trade Sales Paint - AKZONOBEL DECORATIVE PAINTS U.S.; *pg.* 1439, *pg.* 1474

DEVON - Furniture - BASSETT FURNITURE INDUSTRIES, INCORPORATED; *pg.* 916, *pg.* 1776

DEVON - Restaurant - HOULIHAN'S RESTAURANTS, INC.; *pg.* 1731, *pg.* 716

DEVON - Lighting Product - QUOIZEL INC.; *pg.* 1304, *pg.* 1616

DEVON - Software - SUNGARD DATA SYSTEMS INC.; *pg.* 477, *pg.* 1592

DEVON - Women's Clothing & Accessories - WOODEN SHIPS OF HOBOKEN; *pg.* 35, *pg.* 1315

DEVON'S SHANDY - Shandy - ANHEUSER-BUSCH COMPANIES, LLC; *pg.* 237, *pg.* 991

DEVONSHIRE - Furniture - ETHAN ALLEN INTERIORS INC.; *pg.* 924, *pg.* 343

DEVONSHIRE - Bath Product - KOHLER CO.; *pg.* 91, *pg.* 1862

DEVOTO - Shoe - ALDO GROUP; *pg.* 1804, *pg.* 1959

DEVO'ZINE - Devotional Magazine for Teens - THE UPPER ROOM; *pg.* 1698, *pg.* 1655

DEVPARTNER - Software - COMPUWARE CORPORATION; *pg.* 379, *pg.* 879

DEVRAN - Coating - AKZONOBEL DECORATIVE PAINTS U.S.; *pg.* 1439, *pg.* 1474

DEVRY - Providing Job Placements - DEVRY EDUCATION GROUP INC.; *pg.* 600, *pg.* 607

DEVRY INSTITUTE OF TECHNOLOGY - Education Center - DEVRY EDUCATION GROUP INC.; *pg.* 600, *pg.* 607

DEVYN - Sunglasses - COACH, INC.; *pg.* 3, *pg.* 1214

DEWALT - Tools - STANLEY BLACK & DECKER, INC.; *pg.* 1063, *pg.* 358

DEWEZE - Bale Chopper - HARPER INDUSTRIES, INC.; *pg.* 704, *pg.* 715

DEWITTS - Anagesics - MONTICELLO DRUG CO.; *pg.* 1569, *pg.* 434

DEX - Communication Product - CENTURYLINK, INC; *pg.* 1870, *pg.* 317

DEX - Advertising Products - DEX ONE CORPORATION; *pg.* 1635, *pg.* 1360

DEX ONE - Advertising Products - DEX ONE CORPORATION; *pg.* 1635, *pg.* 1360

DEXATRIM - Diet Aid - CHATTEM, INC.; *pg.* 1515, *pg.* 1628

DEXCOM DATA MANAGER - Software - DEXCOM INC; *pg.* 1524, *pg.* 202

DEXCOM DM - Software - DEXCOM INC; *pg.* 1524, *pg.* 202

DEXFERRUM - Intravenous Iron Preparation - LUITPOLD PHARMACEUTICALS, INC.; *pg.* 1557, *pg.* 1342

DEXKNOW.COM - Online Business Listings - DEX MEDIA INC; *pg.* 1635, *pg.* 1680

DEXRON - Automatic Transmission Fluid - GENERAL MOTORS COMPANY; *pg.* 175, *pg.* 881

DEXTER - Cutlery - DEXTER-RUSSELL INC.; *pg.* 1123, *pg.* 844

DEXTER - Door Hardware - INGERSOLL-RAND COMPANY; *pg.* 1349, *pg.* 1370

DEXTER - Furniture - JASPER GROUP; *pg.* 930, *pg.* 691

DEXTER/RUSSELL - Professional Cutlery - DEXTER-RUSSELL INC.; *pg.* 1123, *pg.* 844

DEXTER'S LABORATORY - Animated Series - THE CARTOON NETWORK; *pg.* 273, *pg.* 492

DEXTRA - Lamp - ASHLEY FURNITURE INDUSTRIES, INC.; *pg.* 914, *pg.* 1852

DEXTRA-LITE - Industrial Lighting - SWIVELIER CO., INC.; *pg.* 1307, *pg.* 1142

DEXTRAGARD - Glove - LAKELAND INDUSTRIES, INC.; *pg.* 1354, *pg.* 1338

DEXTRO-PAK - Cartridge - WATERS CORPORATION; *pg.* 1436, *pg.* 834

DEXTRUS - Medical Device - BOSTON SCIENTIFIC CORPORATION; *pg.* 1508, *pg.* 831

DEZIGNRITE - Paint & Paint Sundries Retailers - PRO GROUP, INC.; *pg.* 1782, *pg.* 331

DF - Slipper - R.G. BARRY CORPORATION; *pg.* 1818, *pg.* 1470

DFT - Systems Integration & Aeronautics - LOCKHEED MARTIN CORPORATION; *pg.* 229, *pg.* 762

DFT CLASSIC - Filter Cartridge - PALL CORPORATION; *pg.* 232, *pg.* 1323

DFTA - Microphone Technology - ANDREA ELECTRONICS CORPORATION; *pg.* 617, *pg.* 1143

DFTADVISOR - Software System - MENTOR GRAPHICS CORPORATION; *pg.* 432, *pg.* 1510

DFTARCHITECT - Software System - MENTOR GRAPHICS CORPORATION; *pg.* 432, *pg.* 1510

DFTINSIGHT - Software System - MENTOR GRAPHICS CORPORATION; *pg.* 432, *pg.* 1510

DFTMAX - Software - SYNOPSYS, INC.; *pg.* 480, *pg.* 162

DFWORKS - Print Finishing & Production Management - PITNEY BOWES INC.; *pg.* 454, *pg.* 376

DFX - Golf Equipment - CALLAWAY GOLF COMPANY; *pg.* 1829, *pg.* 58

DFX - Filter - CAMERON INTERNATIONAL; *pg.* 1151, *pg.* 1702

DFX - Glass & Ceramic Material - CORNING INCORPORATED; *pg.* 1122, *pg.* 1154

DFX - Software - THE TIFFEN COMPANY LLC; *pg.* 1432, *pg.* 1165

DFX-5000+ - Dot Matrix Printer - EPSON AMERICA INC.; *pg.* 394, *pg.* 122

DFX-8000 - Dot Matrix Printer - EPSON AMERICA INC.; *pg.* 394, *pg.* 122

DGA AWARD - Award - DIRECTORS GUILD OF AMERICA, INC.; *pg.* 139, *pg.* 129

DGAUSS - Supercomputing System - CRAY INC.; *pg.* 380, *pg.* 1834

DGPS MAX - Wireless Product - HEMISPHERE GPS INC.; *pg.* 642, *pg.* 1903

DH, DHS & DL SERIES GATE VALVES - Gate Valves - DRIL-QUIP, INC.; *pg.* 1330, *pg.* 1704

DH+ - Software - ROCKWELL AUTOMATION, INC.; *pg.* 668, *pg.* 1880

DH10BAC - Molecular Biology Product - THERMO FISHER SCIENTIFIC INC.; *pg.* 1602, *pg.* 61

DH12S - Molecular Biology Product - THERMO FISHER SCIENTIFIC INC.; *pg.* 1602, *pg.* 61

DH5A - Molecular Biology Product - THERMO FISHER SCIENTIFIC INC.; *pg.* 1602, *pg.* 61

DHA CHEWABLES - Health Supplement - GARDEN OF LIFE, INC.; *pg.* 1532, *pg.* 478

DHA NEUROMINS - Vitamin & Dietary Supplement - NATROL, INC.; *pg.* 1570, *pg.* 64

DHEA - Health Care Product - HEALTH PRODUCTS CORPORATION; *pg.* 1540, *pg.* 1356

DHEA - Nutritional Supplement - NATURAL ORGANICS, INC.; *pg.* 1571, *pg.* 1181

DHF SERIES FIRE-RESISTANT GATE VALVES - Gate Valves - DRIL-QUIP, INC.; *pg.* 1330, *pg.* 1704

DHII - Software - ROCKWELL AUTOMATION, INC.; *pg.* 668, *pg.* 1880

DHL - International Air Express - DHL HOLDINGS (USA), INC.; *pg.* 1906, *pg.* 459

DHL CONNECT - Customer Shipping Software - DHL HOLDINGS (USA), INC.; *pg.* 1906, *pg.* 459

DHP - Shipping Purpose - UNIVERSAL FOREST PRODUCTS, INC.; *pg.* 117, *pg.* 890

DI - Crane - COLUMBUS MCKINNON CORPORATION; *pg.* 1325, *pg.* 1138

DI - Direct Imaging Systems - PRESSTEK LLC; *pg.* 1678, *pg.* 1034

DI CASE - Healthcare Product - MEDICOOL, INC.; *pg.* 1562, *pg.* 294

DI-ELYTE - Non-Metallic Wire - ROCHLING GLASTIC COMPOSITES; *pg.* 1889, *pg.* 1435

DI-FENDER - Animal Safety Product - NEOGEN CORPORATION; *pg.* 883, *pg.* 896

DI LUSSO - Deli Food Products - HORMEL FOODS CORPORATION; *pg.* 863, *pg.* 915

DI LUSSO - Deli Meat - HY-VEE, INC.; *pg.* 1023, *pg.* 713

DI-MAX - Steel Product - AK STEEL HOLDING

CORPORATION; *pg.* 1311, *pg.* 1479

DI-NA-CAL - Packaging Product - GRAPHIC PACKAGING HOLDING COMPANY; *pg.* 1459, *pg.* 509

DI PESCARA - Italian Steak & Seafood Restaurant - LETTUCE ENTERTAIN YOU ENTERPRISES, INC.; *pg.* 1735, *pg.* 580

DI-PIP - Piperidyl - VERTELLUS SPECIALTIES INC.; *pg.* 1185, *pg.* 690

DI-PYR - Piperidyl - VERTELLUS SPECIALTIES INC.; *pg.* 1185, *pg.* 690

DI VINCI - Crystal - ONEIDA LTD; *pg.* 1129, *pg.* 1318

DIA-FILTROPLAST - Filter Cartridge - PALL CORPORATION; *pg.* 232, *pg.* 1323

DIA-PAK - Carrying Case - MEDICOOL, INC.; *pg.* 1562, *pg.* 294

DIA-PAK CLASSIC - Healthcare Product - MEDICOOL, INC.; *pg.* 1562, *pg.* 294

DIA-PAK DAYMATE - Healthcare Product - MEDICOOL, INC.; *pg.* 1562, *pg.* 294

DIA-PAK DELUXE - Healthcare Product - MEDICOOL, INC.; *pg.* 1562, *pg.* 294

DIA-PRO - Paint & Coating - DIAMOND VOGEL PAINT, INC.; *pg.* 1441, *pg.* 710

DIA-SCAN - Self-Diagnostic System - A.O. SMITH CORPORATION; *pg.* 1313, *pg.* 1872

DIA-SCHUMALITH - Filter Cartridge - PALL CORPORATION; *pg.* 232, *pg.* 1323

DIABETES ESSENTIALS - Nutritional Product - NUTRITION 21, INC.; *pg.* 1577, *pg.* 1327

DIABETES ESSENTIALS NUTRITION TO GO - Nutritional Product - NUTRITION 21, INC.; *pg.* 1577, *pg.* 1327

DIABETES HEALTHWAYS - Disease Management - HEALTHWAYS, INC.; *pg.* 1540, *pg.* 1632

DIABETIC LIVING - Magazine - MEREDITH CORPORATION; *pg.* 1663, *pg.* 705

DIABETIC TUSSIN - Diabetic Cough Suppressant & Expectorant Products - AKORN; *pg.* 1488, *pg.* 1138

DIABETICARE - Foot Cream - ALIMED, INC.; *pg.* 1490, *pg.* 816

DIABETICARE - Foot Cream - THE SALK COMPANY; *pg.* 1591, *pg.* 800

DIABETIDERM - Diabetic Epidermal Products - AKORN; *pg.* 1488, *pg.* 1138

DIABETISWEET - Diabetic Sugar Substitute - AKORN; *pg.* 1488, *pg.* 1138

DIABINESE - Medicine - PFIZER INC.; *pg.* 1581, *pg.* 1278

DIABLITOS UNDERWOOD - Food Product - GENERAL MILLS, INC.; *pg.* 828, *pg.* 933

DIABLO - Manual - XEROX CORPORATION; *pg.* 494, *pg.* 365

DIABLO DIAMOND - Video Game - INTERNATIONAL GAME TECHNOLOGY; *pg.* 957, *pg.* 1024

DIABOLO - Container Grown Plant - MONROVIA GROWERS; *pg.* 1797, *pg.* 44

DIACHROME - Nutritional Product - NUTRITION 21, INC.; *pg.* 1577, *pg.* 1327

DIACID - Chemical Product - WESTROCK COMPANY; *pg.* 1472, *pg.* 1805

DIACTOLATE - Food Grade Acid - BIRKO CORPORATION; *pg.* 1149, *pg.* 332

DIADEM - Educational Materials - SCHOLASTIC INC.; *pg.* 1683, *pg.* 1288

DIAGNOSTIC EDGE - Online Newsletter - IDEXX LABORATORIES, INC.; *pg.* 1543, *pg.* 753

DIAGNOSTIC HYSTEROSCOPY REDI-KIT - Surgical Preparatory Kits - THE COOPER COMPANIES, INC.; *pg.* 1518, *pg.* 183

DIAGNOSTIC IMAGING STAFF - Healthcare Service - ON ASSIGNMENT, INC.; *pg.* 449, *pg.* 56

DIAGNOSTIC NAVIGATOR - Manual - XEROX CORPORATION; *pg.* 494, *pg.* 365

DIAGONAL DASH - Dresses & Sets - HABAND COMPANY, INC.; *pg.* 1772, *pg.* 1099

DIAGONAL ROLLBAR - Apparel Technology - BROOKS SPORTS INC.; *pg.* 1805, *pg.* 1818

DIAGRAPH - Label Equipment - DIAGRAPH; *pg.* 387, *pg.* 989

DIAGRID - Pad Conditioner - DOW CHEMICAL; *pg.* 1156, *pg.* 1563

DIAK - Crosslinking Agents - R.T. VANDERBILT COMPANY, INC.; *pg.* 1180, *pg.* 364

DIAL - Personal Cleansing Products - HENKEL CONSUMER GOODS; *pg.* 511, *pg.* 22

DIAL - Children's Hardcover Books - PENGUIN RANDOM HOUSE; *pg.* 1675, *pg.* 1276

DIAL A DIAMOND - Jewelry - EMPIRE DIAMOND CORPORATION; *pg.* 4, *pg.* 1227

DIAL ANTIOXIDANT BODY WASH - Anti-Aging Shower Product - HENKEL CONSUMER GOODS; *pg.* 511, *pg.* 22

DIAL-DATA - Electronic Daily & Historical Price Data on World-Wide Exchanges - TRACK DATA CORPORATION; *pg.* 1284, *pg.* 1147

DIAL FOR MEN BLUE GRIT - Soap - HENKEL CONSUMER GOODS; *pg.* 511, *pg.* 22

DIAL SET - Adjustable Boring Bars - KENNAMETAL INC.; *pg.* 1052, *pg.* 1547

DIAL WITH STYLE - Educational Materials - SCHOLASTIC INC.; *pg.* 1683, *pg.* 1288

DIAL YOGURT - Yogurt-Based Soap - HENKEL CONSUMER GOODS; *pg.* 511, *pg.* 22

DIALARC - Welding Machine - MILLER ELECTRIC MANUFACTURING CO.; *pg.* 1361, *pg.* 1852

DIALECT - Modern Occasional Tables - BERNHARDT DESIGN; *pg.* 918, *pg.* 1381

DIALGRADE - Precision Navigation Aid - TRIMBLE NAVIGATION LIMITED; *pg.* 1384, *pg.* 288

DIALLO - Lamp - ASHLEY FURNITURE INDUSTRIES, INC.; *pg.* 914, *pg.* 1852

DIAL'N SPRAY - Garden Pest Control - THE SCOTTS MIRACLE-GRO COMPANY; *pg.* 1799, *pg.* 1459

DIALOG - Meter Reading System - BADGER METER, INC.; *pg.* 1401, *pg.* 1873

DIALOG - Legal Publications - THOMSON REUTERS CORPORATION; *pg.* 1693, *pg.* 1944

DIALOG HELPER - Software - WIPRO GALLAGHER SOLUTIONS; *pg.* 823, *pg.* 447

DIALOGUE - Software - SKILLSOFT PLC; *pg.* 470, *pg.* 1037

DIALUX - Software - ENERGY FOCUS, INC.; *pg.* 1411, *pg.* 1472

DIALY-NATE - Neonatal & Pediatric Disposable Peritoneal Dialysis System - UTAH MEDICAL PRODUCTS, INC.; *pg.* 1605, *pg.* 1752

DIAM - Fatty Diamines - HENKEL CORPORATION; *pg.* 1165, *pg.* 1535

DIAMANTA - Lamp - ASHLEY FURNITURE INDUSTRIES, INC.; *pg.* 914, *pg.* 1852

DIAMAT - Software - BIO-RAD LABORATORIES, INC.; *pg.* 1504, *pg.* 101

DIAMIN - Pharmaceutical Product - VALEANT PHARMACEUTICALS INTERNATIONAL; *pg.* 1605, *pg.* 1047

DIAMON DEB - Eye Care Product - THE W.E. BASSETT COMPANY; *pg.* 524, *pg.* 371

DIAMOND - DC Power System - ADVANCED ENERGY INDUSTRIES, INC.; *pg.* 613, *pg.* 328

DIAMOND - Server & Storage Device - BLACK BOX CORPORATION; *pg.* 361, *pg.* 1547

DIAMOND - Laser & Laser System - COHERENT, INC.; *pg.* 1406, *pg.* 265

DIAMOND - Canvas Products - DIAMOND BRAND CANVAS PRODUCTS CO., INC.; *pg.* 1832, *pg.* 1372

DIAMOND - Roller & Conveyor Chains - DIAMOND CHAIN COMPANY; *pg.* 1328, *pg.* 684

DIAMOND - Hardware - FORTUNE BRANDS HOME & SECURITY, INC.; *pg.* 55, *pg.* 600

DIAMOND - Kitchen Products - JARDEN CORPORATION; *pg.* 1885, *pg.* 412

DIAMOND - Matches, Toothpicks, Clothes Pins & Plastic Cutlery - JARDEN HOME BRANDS; *pg.* 1126, *pg.* 920

DIAMOND - Cabinetry - MASTERBRAND CABINETS, INC.; *pg.* 96, *pg.* 692

DIAMOND - Tableware - PACTIV CORPORATION; *pg.* 1466, *pg.* 624

DIAMOND - Aluminum Foil - REYNOLDS CONSUMER PRODUCTS; *pg.* 1138, *pg.* 625

DIAMOND - Hardware Product - THOMAS & BETTS CORPORATION; *pg.* 680, *pg.* 1646

DIAMOND - Petcare - TRACTOR SUPPLY COMPANY; *pg.* 708, *pg.* 1627

DIAMOND - Sport Apparel - UNDER ARMOUR, INC.; *pg.* 49, *pg.* 759

DIAMOND - Interior Finish - USG CORPORATION; *pg.* 118, *pg.* 594

DIAMOND - Paint Protection - ZIEBART INTERNATIONAL CORPORATION; *pg.* 222, *pg.* 912

DIAMOND A - Canned Vegetables - SENECA FOODS CORPORATION; *pg.* 895, *pg.* 1177

DIAMOND BACK - Carpet - BEAULIEU GROUP, LLC; *pg.* 917, *pg.* 529

DIAMOND-BACK - Mirror Back Coatings - PPG INDUSTRIES, INC.; *pg.* 1445, *pg.* 1579

DIAMOND BINGO - Game - MISSOURI LOTTERY; *pg.* 999, *pg.* 979

DIAMOND BLAST - Video Game - INTERNATIONAL GAME TECHNOLOGY; *pg.* 957, *pg.* 1024

DIAMOND CAPITAL MANAGEMENT - Management Services - NATIONAL BANK OF INDIANAPOLIS CORPORATION; *pg.* 785, *pg.* 688

DIAMOND CHAIN STORE AGE - Industry Publication - LEBHAR-FRIEDMAN INC.; *pg.* 1658, *pg.* 1250

DIAMOND CINEMA - Game - INTERNATIONAL GAME TECHNOLOGY; *pg.* 957, *pg.* 1024

DIAMOND COAT - Film Lamination - THE COLAD GROUP, INC.; *pg.* 377, *pg.* 1147

DIAMOND COAT - Protective & Decorative Coatings - PPG INDUSTRIES, INC.; *pg.* 1445, *pg.* 1579

DIAMOND CRYSTAL - Salt - CARGILL, INC.; *pg.* 845, *pg.* 965

DIAMOND CRYSTAL - Sugar & Seasoning Products - HORMEL FOODS CORPORATION; *pg.* 863, *pg.* 915

DIAMOND CUT - Utility Shears - THE FULLER BRUSH COMPANY; *pg.* 330, *pg.* 715

DIAMOND DASH - Lottery Game - LOUISIANA LOTTERY CORPORATION; *pg.* 997, *pg.* 742

DIAMOND DAZZLER - Lottery Game - CALIFORNIA LOTTERY; *pg.* 990, *pg.* 196

DIAMOND DOLLARS - Game - MISSOURI LOTTERY; *pg.* 999, *pg.* 979

DIAMOND DUO - Spread/Blanket - MEDLINE INDUSTRIES, INC.; *pg.* 1562, *pg.* 635

DIAMOND ELITE - Glove - NIKE, INC.; *pg.* 1812, *pg.* 1492

DIAMOND FIRE - Video Game - INTERNATIONAL GAME TECHNOLOGY; *pg.* 957, *pg.* 1024

DIAMOND FIVES - Slots - INTERNATIONAL GAME TECHNOLOGY; *pg.* 957, *pg.* 1024

DIAMOND-FLEX - Pharmaceutical Product - GENZYME CORPORATION; *pg.* 1534, *pg.* 808

DIAMOND FLEX - Protective & Decorative Coatings - PPG INDUSTRIES, INC.; *pg.* 1445, *pg.* 1579

DIAMOND GALAXY - Video Game - INTERNATIONAL GAME TECHNOLOGY; *pg.* 957, *pg.* 1024

DIAMOND GRADE - Tape - 3M COMPANY; *pg.* 1142, *pg.* 956

DIAMOND-GRIP - Safety Grating - ALABAMA METAL INDUSTRIES CORPORATION; *pg.* 65, *pg.* 1

DIAMOND HOME CENTER - Industry Publication - LEBHAR-FRIEDMAN INC.; *pg.* 1658, *pg.* 1250

DIAMOND HUNT - Game - WMS INDUSTRIES INC.; *pg.* 593, *pg.* 666

DIAMOND ICE - Video Game - INTERNATIONAL GAME TECHNOLOGY; *pg.* 957, *pg.* 1024

DIAMOND JACKPOTS - Video Game - INTERNATIONAL GAME TECHNOLOGY; *pg.* 957, *pg.* 1024

DIAMOND KOOL - Water-Soluble Coolant - UNIVERSAL PHOTONICS, INC.; *pg.* 1433, *pg.* 1167

DIAMOND-LINE - Pharmaceutical Product - GENZYME CORPORATION; *pg.* 1534, *pg.* 808

DIAMOND LINE 775 - Slot Machine - BALLY TECHNOLOGIES, INC.; *pg.* 531, *pg.* 1022

DIAMOND MINE - Lottery Game - CALIFORNIA LOTTERY; *pg.* 990, *pg.* 196

DIAMOND NIGHTS - Video Game - INTERNATIONAL GAME TECHNOLOGY; *pg.* 957, *pg.* 1024

DIAMOND OF CALIFORNIA - Snack Nuts - DIAMOND FOODS, INC.; *pg.* 1851, *pg.* 216

DIAMOND PENDANT - Diamond Product - BLUE NILE, INC.; *pg.* 2, *pg.* 1834

DIAMOND QUEEN - Video Game - INTERNATIONAL GAME TECHNOLOGY; *pg.* 957, *pg.* 1024

DIAMOND RETAILTECHNOLOGY - Industry Publication - LEBHAR-FRIEDMAN INC.; *pg.* 1658, *pg.* 1250

DIAMOND RIDGE - Game - WMS INDUSTRIES INC.; *pg.* 593, *pg.* 666

DIAMOND RING - Game - WMS INDUSTRIES INC.; *pg.* 593, *pg.* 666

DIAMOND SERIES - Microphone - PEAVEY ELECTRONICS CORPORATION; *pg.* 662, *pg.* 970

DIAMOND SHAMROCK - Gasoline Retail Outlets - VALERO ENERGY CORPORATION; *pg.* 986, *pg.* 1743

DIAMOND SPURS - Video Game - INTERNATIONAL GAME TECHNOLOGY; *pg.* 957, *pg.* 1024

DIAMOND STAR - Apparel - ENNIS, INC.; *pg.* 393, *pg.* 1727

DIAMOND STARS - Slots - INTERNATIONAL GAME TECHNOLOGY; *pg.* 957, *pg.* 1024

DIAMOND THIEF - Slots - INTERNATIONAL GAME

TECHNOLOGY; *pg.* 957, *pg.* 1024
DIAMOND-TOUCH - Pharmaceutical Product - GENZYME CORPORATION; *pg.* 1534, *pg.* 808
DIAMOND V - Yeast Culture - MANNA PRO CORPORATION; *pg.* 1478, *pg.* 975
DIAMOND VAULT - Video Game - INTERNATIONAL GAME TECHNOLOGY; *pg.* 957, *pg.* 1024
DIAMOND VOGEL - Paint Company - DIAMOND VOGEL PAINT, INC.; *pg.* 1441, *pg.* 710
DIAMONDBACK - Gaming Product - GLD PRODUCTS, INC.; *pg.* 1835, *pg.* 1882
DIAMONDBACK GUIDE - Knife - BUCK KNIVES, INC.; *pg.* 1828, *pg.* 550
DIAMONDBACK OUTFITTER - Knife - BUCK KNIVES, INC.; *pg.* 1828, *pg.* 550
DIAMONDCELL - Cellular Shades - SPRINGS WINDOW FASHIONS LLC; *pg.* 943, *pg.* 1872
DIAMONDCOAT - Deluxe Nonstick Finish - NATIONAL PRESTO INDUSTRIES, INC; *pg.* 1128, *pg.* 1857
DIAMONDGUARD - Glass Product - GUARDIAN INDUSTRIES CORP.; *pg.* 85, *pg.* 869
DIAMONDHEAD - Gaming Product - GLD PRODUCTS, INC.; *pg.* 1835, *pg.* 1882
DIAMONDHEAD BEACH RESORT - Resort - SUNSTREAM, INC.; *pg.* 1116, *pg.* 428
DIAMONDS & DEVILS - Slot Machine - BALLY TECHNOLOGIES, INC.; *pg.* 531, *pg.* 1022
DIAMONDS IN THE ROUGH - Game - WMS INDUSTRIES INC.; *pg.* 593, *pg.* 666
DIAMONDS OF DUBLIN - Game - WMS INDUSTRIES INC.; *pg.* 593, *pg.* 666
DIAMONDS THAT MAKE A DIFFERENCE - Tag Line - HARRY KOTLAR & CO., INC.; *pg.* 6, *pg.* 132
DIANA - Footwear - PHOENIX FOOTWEAR GROUP, INC.; *pg.* 1815, *pg.* 60
THE DIANA PRINCESS OF WALES BOUQUET - Flower Arrangement - FTD GROUP, INC.; *pg.* 1795, *pg.* 608
DIANDRA - Beauty Product - COSMETIQUE, INC.; *pg.* 1765, *pg.* 664
DIANE - Lamp - ASHLEY FURNITURE INDUSTRIES, INC.; *pg.* 914, *pg.* 1852
DIANE - Magazine - CURVES INTERNATIONAL INC.; *pg.* 542, *pg.* 1748
DIANE - Furniture - NEMSCHOFF, INC.; *pg.* 936, *pg.* 1890
DIANE BISH SERIES - Organs - ALLEN ORGAN COMPANY; *pg.* 527, *pg.* 1549
DIANE BISH SIGNATURE SERIES - Organs - ALLEN ORGAN COMPANY; *pg.* 527, *pg.* 1549
DIANE VON FURSTENBERG - Luxury Women's Fashion Brand - D.V.F. STUDIOS; *pg.* 24, *pg.* 1226
DIANODIC - Scale Inhibitor - GE WATER & PROCESS TECHNOLOGIES; *pg.* 1339, *pg.* 1588
DIANTOL - Fungicide - THE DOW CHEMICAL COMPANY; *pg.* 1157, *pg.* 898
DIAPASON - Spinal System - STRYKER CORPORATION; *pg.* 1598, *pg.* 894
DIAPER DUCK - Baby Care Product - MUNCHKIN, INC.; *pg.* 964, *pg.* 300
DIAPER GENIE - Infant Care - EDGEWELL PERSONAL CARE; *pg.* 1526, *pg.* 995
DIAPERS.COM - Baby Products - QUIDSI, INC.; *pg.* 1276, *pg.* 1076
DIARYVISIION - Trend Analysis Program - HOLSTEIN ASSOCIATION USA, INC.; *pg.* 143, *pg.* 1764
DIAS PLUS - High Volume Microplate Processor - IMMUCOR, INC.; *pg.* 1544, *pg.* 537
DIASOX - Sock for Diabetics - MEDICOOL, INC.; *pg.* 1562, *pg.* 294
DIASTAT - Clinical Diagnostic Product - BIO-RAD LABORATORIES, INC.; *pg.* 1504, *pg.* 101
DIAVITE - Healthcare Product - MEDICOOL, INC.; *pg.* 1562, *pg.* 294
DIAZOOM - Microscope - UNITRON INC.; *pg.* 1433, *pg.* 1153
DIBOND - Pressed & Monolithic Refractory - RESCO PRODUCTS, INC.; *pg.* 107, *pg.* 1581
DIBS - Ice Cream - DREYER'S GRAND ICE CREAM HOLDINGS, INC.; *pg.* 1852, *pg.* 171
DICE - Furniture - NEUTRAL POSTURE, INC.; *pg.* 939, *pg.* 1669
DICE HOLDINGS - Specialized Career Websites - DHI GROUP, INC.; *pg.* 1238, *pg.* 1223
DICEA - Hemodialysis Dialyzer - BAXTER INTERNATIONAL INC.; *pg.* 1499, *pg.* 599
DICE.COM - Job Board - DHI GROUP, INC.; *pg.* 1238, *pg.* 1223
DICE.COM - Job Search Service - DICE.COM; *pg.* 1238, *pg.* 712
DICK CLARK'S NEW YEAR'S ROCKIN' EVE - Music Television Program - DICK CLARK PRODUCTIONS, INC.; *pg.* 281, *pg.* 273
DICK GRAYSON - Character - DC COMICS, INC.; *pg.* 1633, *pg.* 1221
DICKASON'S BLEND - Coffee - PEET'S COFFEE & TEA, INC.; *pg.* 1029, *pg.* 85
DICKIES - Work Clothing - WILLIAMSON-DICKIE MANUFACTURING COMPANY; *pg.* 50, *pg.* 1696
DICKINSON - Kitchen Product - KOHLER CO.; *pg.* 91, *pg.* 1862
DICKINSON - Flatware - ONEIDA LTD; *pg.* 1129, *pg.* 1318
DICKINSON'S - Preserves - THE J.M. SMUCKER COMPANY; *pg.* 865, *pg.* 1468
DICKSON - Custom Fabrics - GLEN RAVEN, INC.; *pg.* 693, *pg.* 1373
DICKSON - Fabric - NATIONAL SPINNING COMPANY, INC.; *pg.* 697, *pg.* 1265
DICOM - Educational Programs - EASTMAN KODAK COMPANY; *pg.* 1408, *pg.* 1333
DICTIONARY.COM - Reference Service - IAC/INTERACTIVECORP; *pg.* 292, *pg.* 1242
DICURAL - Veterinary Antibacterial Preparation - BOEHRINGER INGELHEIM VETMEDICA, INC.; *pg.* 1474, *pg.* 989
DICYANEX - Chemical Products - AIR PRODUCTS AND CHEMICALS, INC.; *pg.* 1145, *pg.* 1513
DICYCLOMINE HCL - Pharmaceutical Product - LANNETT COMPANY, INC.; *pg.* 1555, *pg.* 1566
DID - Communication Product - CENTURYLINK, INC; *pg.* 1870, *pg.* 317
DIDI - Puppet - GUND, INC.; *pg.* 954, *pg.* 1056
DIDJ - Toys - LEAPFROG ENTERPRISES, INC.; *pg.* 961, *pg.* 84
DIDREX - Pharmaceutical Product - IMPAX LABORATORIES, INC.; *pg.* 1544, *pg.* 101
DIDREX - Medicine - PFIZER INC.; *pg.* 1581, *pg.* 1278
DIE BRITE - Brite Dip - HUBBARD-HALL, INC.; *pg.* 1167, *pg.* 382
DIE HARD - Sports Energy Drink - LEADING BRANDS, INC.; *pg.* 1026, *pg.* 1911
DIEBAND - Metal Cutting Saw Blade - SIMONDS INTERNATIONAL CORPORATION; *pg.* 1376, *pg.* 819
DIEBOLD - Corporate Name - DIEBOLD, INCORPORATED; *pg.* 387, *pg.* 1407
DIECI - Telehandler - DEGELMAN INDUSTRIES LTD.; *pg.* 703, *pg.* 1962
DIEDRA - Footwear - PHOENIX FOOTWEAR GROUP, INC.; *pg.* 1815, *pg.* 60
DIEDRICH - Coffee - KEURIG GREEN MOUNTAIN, INC.; *pg.* 868, *pg.* 1768
DIEHARD - Battery - SEARS HOLDINGS CORPORATION; *pg.* 1784, *pg.* 618
DIEKMAN - Office Furniture - STEELCASE INC.; *pg.* 475, *pg.* 889
DIELUX - Compression Molded Product - WESTLAKE PLASTICS COMPANY; *pg.* 1892, *pg.* 1548
DIEMASTER - Blade - LENOX; *pg.* 1053, *pg.* 817
DIENE-O-LEAN - Nutritional Supplement - NU SKIN ENTERPRISES, INC.; *pg.* 518, *pg.* 1755
DIESEL 40- THE ENGINE CONDITIONER - Motorsports Entertainment - SPEEDWAY MOTORSPORTS, INC.; *pg.* 584, *pg.* 1370
DIESEL 911 - Diesel Fuel - POWER SERVICE PRODUCTS, INC.; *pg.* 983, *pg.* 1749
DIESEL ADDITIVES - Slogan - POWER SERVICE PRODUCTS, INC.; *pg.* 983, *pg.* 1749
DIESEL EAGLE - Pump - FLOW INTERNATIONAL CORPORATION; *pg.* 1337, *pg.* 1821
DIESEL FUEL SUPPLEMENT - Diesel Fuel - POWER SERVICE PRODUCTS, INC.; *pg.* 983, *pg.* 1749
DIESEL KLEEN - Diesel Fuel - POWER SERVICE PRODUCTS, INC.; *pg.* 983, *pg.* 1749
DIESEL LUBE - Diesel Additive - POWER SERVICE PRODUCTS, INC.; *pg.* 983, *pg.* 1749
DIESEL-TONE - Fuel Conditioner - RADIATOR SPECIALTY COMPANY; *pg.* 215, *pg.* 1380
DIESELKARE - Fuel System - SNAP-ON INCORPORATED; *pg.* 1062, *pg.* 1862
DIESELPOWER - Diesel Additives - GOLD EAGLE COMPANY; *pg.* 206, *pg.* 575
DIET 5 - Nutritional Product - NUTRACEUTICAL INTERNATIONAL CORPORATION; *pg.* 1576, *pg.* 1753
DIET A&W - Beverages - THE COCA-COLA COMPANY; *pg.* 240, *pg.* 493
DIET ANDINA FRUT - Beverages - THE COCA-COLA COMPANY; *pg.* 240, *pg.* 493
DIET ANDINA NECTAR - Beverages - THE COCA-COLA COMPANY; *pg.* 240, *pg.* 493
DIET BARQ'S - Root Beer - THE COCA-COLA COMPANY; *pg.* 240, *pg.* 493
DIET CANADA DRY - Beverages - THE COCA-COLA COMPANY; *pg.* 240, *pg.* 493
DIET CENTER - Weight Loss Centers - DIET CENTER WORLDWIDE, INC.; *pg.* 1524, *pg.* 1400
DIET CHASER - Soft Drink - DOUBLE-COLA CO.-USA; *pg.* 249, *pg.* 1629
DIET CHERRY COKE - Diet Soft Drink - THE COCA-COLA COMPANY; *pg.* 240, *pg.* 493
DIET COKE - Diet Soft Drink - THE COCA-COLA COMPANY; *pg.* 240, *pg.* 493
DIET COKE BLACK CHERRY VANILLA - Beverages - THE COCA-COLA COMPANY; *pg.* 240, *pg.* 493
DIET COKE CITRA - Beverages - THE COCA-COLA COMPANY; *pg.* 240, *pg.* 493
DIET COKE PLUS - Beverages - THE COCA-COLA COMPANY; *pg.* 240, *pg.* 493
DIET COKE SWEETENED WITH SPLENDA - Beverages - THE COCA-COLA COMPANY; *pg.* 240, *pg.* 493
DIET COKE WITH LEMON - Beverages - THE COCA-COLA COMPANY; *pg.* 240, *pg.* 493
DIET COKE WITH LIME - Beverages - THE COCA-COLA COMPANY; *pg.* 240, *pg.* 493
DIET COKE WITH RASPBERRY - Beverages - THE COCA-COLA COMPANY; *pg.* 240, *pg.* 493
DIET CRUSH - Beverages - THE COCA-COLA COMPANY; *pg.* 240, *pg.* 493
DIET DOUBLE-COLA - Soft Drink - DOUBLE-COLA CO.-USA; *pg.* 249, *pg.* 1629
DIET DR PEPPER - Beverages - THE COCA-COLA COMPANY; *pg.* 240, *pg.* 493
DIET FANTA - Beverages - THE COCA-COLA COMPANY; *pg.* 240, *pg.* 493
DIET FRESKYTA - Beverages - THE COCA-COLA COMPANY; *pg.* 240, *pg.* 493
DIET INCA KOLA - Beverages - THE COCA-COLA COMPANY; *pg.* 240, *pg.* 493
DIET KIA ORA - Beverages - THE COCA-COLA COMPANY; *pg.* 240, *pg.* 493
DIET KREST - Beverages - THE COCA-COLA COMPANY; *pg.* 240, *pg.* 493
DIET LIFT - Beverages - THE COCA-COLA COMPANY; *pg.* 240, *pg.* 493
DIET LILT - Beverages - THE COCA-COLA COMPANY; *pg.* 240, *pg.* 493
DIET MASTER POUR - Beverages - THE COCA-COLA COMPANY; *pg.* 240, *pg.* 493
DIET MELLO YELLO - Diet Soft Drink - THE COCA-COLA COMPANY; *pg.* 240, *pg.* 493
DIET MOUNTAIN DEW - Soft Drink - PEPSICO, INC.; *pg.* 259, *pg.* 1327
DIET MOUNTAIN DEW CODE RED - Soft Drink - PEPSICO, INC.; *pg.* 259, *pg.* 1327
DIET MOUNTAIN DEW ULTRAVIOLET - Soft Drink - PEPSICO, INC.; *pg.* 259, *pg.* 1327
DIET MR. PIBB - Soft Drink - THE COCA-COLA COMPANY; *pg.* 240, *pg.* 493
DIET NESTEA - Soft Drink - THE COCA-COLA COMPANY; *pg.* 240, *pg.* 493
DIET NORTHERN NECK - Beverages - THE COCA-COLA COMPANY; *pg.* 240, *pg.* 493
DIET NUTRITION PACK - Nutritional Supplement - PHARMAVITE LLC; *pg.* 1584, *pg.* 167
DIET OASIS - Beverages - THE COCA-COLA COMPANY; *pg.* 240, *pg.* 493
DIET OCEAN SPRAY - Juice - OCEAN SPRAY CRANBERRIES, INC.; *pg.* 887, *pg.* 827
DIET PEPSI - Soft Drink - PEPSICO, INC.; *pg.* 259, *pg.* 1327
DIET PEPSI FREE - Caffeine Free Diet Cola - PEPSICO, INC.; *pg.* 259, *pg.* 1327
DIET PEPSI LIME - Soft Drink - PEPSICO, INC.; *pg.* 259, *pg.* 1327
DIET PEPSI MAX - Soft Drink - PEPSICO, INC.; *pg.* 259, *pg.* 1327
DIET PEPSI TWIST - Soft Drink - PEPSICO, INC.; *pg.* 259, *pg.* 1327
DIET PEPSI VANILLA - Soft Drink - PEPSICO, INC.; *pg.* 259, *pg.* 1327

DIET QUATRO - Beverages - THE COCA-COLA COMPANY; *pg.* 240, *pg.* 493
DIET RED ENERGY - Beverage - MONSTER BEVERAGE CORPORATION; *pg.* 257, *pg.* 69
DIET SCHWEPPES - Beverages - THE COCA-COLA COMPANY; *pg.* 240, *pg.* 493
DIET SIERRA MIST - Diet Carbonated Beverage - PEPSICO, INC.; *pg.* 259, *pg.* 1327
DIET SKI - Soft Drink - DOUBLE-COLA CO.-USA; *pg.* 249, *pg.* 1629
DIET SLICE - Lemon-Lime Caffeine Free Soft Drink - PEPSICO, INC.; *pg.* 259, *pg.* 1327
DIET SPRITE - Diet Soft Drink - THE COCA-COLA COMPANY; *pg.* 240, *pg.* 493
DIET SPRITE ZERO - Soft Drink - THE COCA-COLA COMPANY; *pg.* 240, *pg.* 493
DIET SQUIRT - Beverages - THE COCA-COLA COMPANY; *pg.* 240, *pg.* 493
DIET TAI - Beverages - THE COCA-COLA COMPANY; *pg.* 240, *pg.* 493
DIET VANILLA COKE - Soft Drink - THE COCA-COLA COMPANY; *pg.* 240, *pg.* 493
DIETZCO - Paper Converting Machinery - THE ENTWISTLE CO.; *pg.* 637, *pg.* 826
DIF - Sundry - KELLY-MOORE PAINT COMPANY, INC.; *pg.* 1443, *pg.* 198
DIFFERENCE - Design Software - H.E. WILLIAMS, INC.; *pg.* 1299, *pg.* 974
THE DIFFERENCE, DEMONSTRATED - Tagline - NU SKIN ENTERPRISES, INC.; *pg.* 518, *pg.* 1755
THE DIFFERENCE IN DISTRIBUTION - Slogan - TECH DATA CORPORATION; *pg.* 482, *pg.* 416
THE DIFFERENCES INSIDE - Tagline - THE ROCKPORT GROUP; *pg.* 1818, *pg.* 812
DIFFERENT BY DESIGN - Games - PENN NATIONAL GAMING, INC.; *pg.* 574, *pg.* 1595
DIFFERIN CREAM - Rx Products - GALDERMA LABORATORIES, L.P.; *pg.* 1532, *pg.* 1695
DIFFERIN GEL - Pharmaceutical Products - GALDERMA LABORATORIES, L.P.; *pg.* 1532, *pg.* 1695
DIFFERIN SOLUTION - Rx Products - GALDERMA LABORATORIES, L.P.; *pg.* 1532, *pg.* 1695
DIFFRACTIONS - Material - ROSCO LABORATORIES, INC.; *pg.* 1782, *pg.* 378
DIFFRIENT - Tables - HOWE FURNITURE CORPORATION; *pg.* 928, *pg.* 998
DIFFSPIN - Diagnostic Urinalysis System - IRIS INTERNATIONAL, INC.; *pg.* 1547, *pg.* 64
DIFFUSION - Apparel - OAKLEY, INC.; *pg.* 1840, *pg.* 86
DIFFUSION - Horizontal Blinds - SPRINGS WINDOW FASHIONS LLC; *pg.* 943, *pg.* 1872
DIFFUSION-FX - Filter & Lens - THE TIFFEN COMPANY LLC; *pg.* 1432, *pg.* 1165
DIFLUCAN - Medicine - PFIZER INC.; *pg.* 1581, *pg.* 1278
DIGESDAHL - Digestion Module - HACH COMPANY; *pg.* 1415, *pg.* 334
THE DIGEST - Magazine - THE READER'S DIGEST ASSOCIATION, INC.; *pg.* 1679, *pg.* 1322
DIGESTION FORMULA - Nutritional Product - RBC LIFE SCIENCES, INC.; *pg.* 1588, *pg.* 1723
DIGESTIVE ADVANTAGE - Irritable Bowel Syndrome - GANEDEN BIOTECH, INC.; *pg.* 1532, *pg.* 1463
DIGESTIVE ADVANTAGE - Digestive Pain Relief - RECKITT BENCKISER INC.; *pg.* 1136, *pg.* 1105
DIGGIN' FOR DOLLARS - Lottery Game - KENTUCKY LOTTERY CORPORATION; *pg.* 996, *pg.* 735
DIGGING FOR GOLD - Game - WMS INDUSTRIES INC.; *pg.* 593, *pg.* 666
DIGI CM - Computer Peripheral Equipment - DIGI INTERNATIONAL INC.; *pg.* 387, *pg.* 948
DIGI CONNECT - Computer Peripheral Equipment - DIGI INTERNATIONAL INC.; *pg.* 387, *pg.* 948
DIGI CORE - Card Stock - TRANSILWRAP COMPANY, INC.; *pg.* 1470, *pg.* 613
DIGI-FLEX - Medical & Aesthetic Product - DYNATRONICS CORPORATION; *pg.* 1526, *pg.* 1757
DIGI-INK - Ink - VAN SON HOLLAND INK CORPORATION OF AMERICA; *pg.* 487, *pg.* 1169
DIGI INTERNATIONAL - Communications & Networking Products - DIGI INTERNATIONAL INC.; *pg.* 387, *pg.* 948
DIGI NEO - Computer Peripheral Equipment - DIGI INTERNATIONAL INC.; *pg.* 387, *pg.* 948
DIGI ONE - Computer Peripheral Equipment - DIGI INTERNATIONAL INC.; *pg.* 387, *pg.* 948
DIGI PASSPORT - Computer Peripheral Equipment - DIGI INTERNATIONAL INC.; *pg.* 387, *pg.* 948
DIGI-PHY - Wireless Technology - BROADCOM CORPORATION; *pg.* 364, *pg.* 108
DIGI SHOWBOX - Remote Display Connectivity - DIGI INTERNATIONAL INC.; *pg.* 387, *pg.* 948
DIGI-SPAN - Digital Temp/Setpoint Control - HEAT-TIMER CORPORATION; *pg.* 1072, *pg.* 1065
DIGI-TEL - Fluid Handling System - GRACO, INC.; *pg.* 1342, *pg.* 935
DIGI TRANSPORT - Protocol Support - DIGI INTERNATIONAL INC.; *pg.* 387, *pg.* 948
DIGIBIRD - Maintenance & Operation - ION GEOPHYSICAL CORPORATION; *pg.* 1350, *pg.* 1708
DIGIBOX CODI - Software System - CHYRONHEGO; *pg.* 371, *pg.* 1179
DIGICAL - Calibrator - MINE SAFETY APPLIANCES COMPANY; *pg.* 1361, *pg.* 1525
DIGICATESSAN - Food Product - BOAR'S HEAD PROVISIONS CO., INC.; *pg.* 841, *pg.* 465
DIGICEPT - Voice Processing Platform - ELECTRONIC TELE-COMMUNICATIONS, INC.; *pg.* 390, *pg.* 1897
DIGICEPT EMCEE - Announcement System - ELECTRONIC TELE-COMMUNICATIONS, INC.; *pg.* 390, *pg.* 1897
DIGICOMP - Paint - ROSCO LABORATORIES, INC.; *pg.* 1782, *pg.* 378
DIGICON - Cable - ARRIS GROUP, INC.; *pg.* 353, *pg.* 541
DIGICOURSE - Data Library - ION GEOPHYSICAL CORPORATION; *pg.* 1350, *pg.* 1708
DIGIDESIGN PRO TOOLS - Digital Audio Workstation - AVID TECHNOLOGY, INC.; *pg.* 622, *pg.* 804
DIGIDOC-IT - Ultraviolet Product - UVP, INC.; *pg.* 1434, *pg.* 298
DIGIFIN - Streamer Steering - ION GEOPHYSICAL CORPORATION; *pg.* 1350, *pg.* 1708
DIGIFINISH - Manual - XEROX CORPORATION; *pg.* 494, *pg.* 365
DIGIGLOSS - Adhesive Coated Paper - SPINNAKER COATING, LLC; *pg.* 1470, *pg.* 1477
DIGIHELIC - Differential Pressure Controller - DWYER INSTRUMENTS INC.; *pg.* 1330, *pg.* 694
DIGIKOTE - Thermal Laminating Film - TRANSILWRAP COMPANY, INC.; *pg.* 1470, *pg.* 613
DIGILINK - Telecommunications Services - SPRINT CORPORATION; *pg.* 1874, *pg.* 719
DIGIMAG - Software - R.R. DONNELLEY & SONS COMPANY; *pg.* 1682, *pg.* 589
DIGIMASTER - High Volume Digital Printers - EASTMAN KODAK COMPANY; *pg.* 1408, *pg.* 1333
DIGIMATTE - Adhesive Coated Paper - SPINNAKER COATING, LLC; *pg.* 1470, *pg.* 1477
DIGIMEDICS - Pharmacy Information System - MEDIWARE INFORMATION SYSTEMS, INC.; *pg.* 431, *pg.* 716
DIGIMESH - Computer Peripheral Equipment - DIGI INTERNATIONAL INC.; *pg.* 387, *pg.* 948
DIGIONE - Imaging Service - DIGIRAD CORPORATION; *pg.* 1524, *pg.* 185
DIGIORNO - Pizza - NESTLE USA, INC.; *pg.* 883, *pg.* 96
DIGIPAK - Paperboard Packaging Product - WESTROCK COMPANY; *pg.* 1472, *pg.* 1805
DIGIPATH - Scanner - XEROX CORPORATION; *pg.* 494, *pg.* 365
DIGIPRO - Floor Care Product - BISSELL HOMECARE, INC.; *pg.* 52, *pg.* 887
DIGIPRO - Adhesive-Backed Plastic Film - FLEXCON CORPORATION; *pg.* 1457, *pg.* 844
DIGIRAD IMAGINIG SOLUTIONS - Digital Gamma Camera - DIGIRAD CORPORATION; *pg.* 1524, *pg.* 185
DIGIRENT - Imaging Service - DIGIRAD CORPORATION; *pg.* 1524, *pg.* 185
DIGISCALE - Home Products - HABAND COMPANY, INC.; *pg.* 1772, *pg.* 1099
DIGISCOPE - Imaging System - NEUROMETRIX, INC.; *pg.* 1572, *pg.* 852
DIGISHAKER - Software - BIO-RAD LABORATORIES, INC.; *pg.* 1504, *pg.* 101
DIGISIM - Software - BIOANALYTICAL SYSTEMS, INC.; *pg.* 1402, *pg.* 700
DIGISINE - Sensor Technology - CUSTOM SENSORS & TECHNOLOGIES; *pg.* 1407, *pg.* 152
DIGISNAP - Clamp Meter - IDEAL INDUSTRIES, INC.; *pg.* 1051, *pg.* 662
DIGISPOT - Medical Product - HOLOGIC, INC.; *pg.* 1416, *pg.* 784
DIGISTAK - Paperboard Packaging Product - WESTROCK COMPANY; *pg.* 1472, *pg.* 1805
DIGISTAR - Software & Hardware - EVANS & SUTHERLAND COMPUTER CORPORATION; *pg.* 638, *pg.* 1757
DIGISTREAMER - Marine Imaging - ION GEOPHYSICAL CORPORATION; *pg.* 1350, *pg.* 1708
DIGITAIR - End-of-Train System - ANSALDO STS; *pg.* 618, *pg.* 1573
DIGITAL - Sport Product - FRANKLIN SPORTS, INC.; *pg.* 1834, *pg.* 847
DIGITAL ANGEL - Personal Tracking & Recovery System - VERITEQ; *pg.* 488, *pg.* 422
DIGITAL BOOKMARK - Copier - XEROX CORPORATION; *pg.* 494, *pg.* 365
DIGITAL BREWER CONTROL - Coffee Grinder - BUNN-O-MATIC CORPORATION; *pg.* 53, *pg.* 661
DIGITAL CERTIFICATE - Online Transaction Security Product - VERISIGN, INC.; *pg.* 488, *pg.* 1799
DIGITAL COLOR ELITE SILK - Manual - XEROX CORPORATION; *pg.* 494, *pg.* 365
DIGITAL COLOR GLOSS - Printer - XEROX CORPORATION; *pg.* 494, *pg.* 365
DIGITAL CONFERENCE - Computer Equipment - VIEWSONIC CORPORATION; *pg.* 489, *pg.* 303
DIGITAL COSMOLIGHT - Flexo CTP System - ANDERSON & VREELAND, INC.; *pg.* 1616, *pg.* 1064
DIGITAL DISPLAY - Computer Equipment - VIEWSONIC CORPORATION; *pg.* 489, *pg.* 303
DIGITAL DIVIDE NETWORK - Online Public Policy Initiative - BENTON FOUNDATION; *pg.* 134, *pg.* 396
DIGITAL DNA - Communications Product - MOTOROLA SOLUTIONS, INC.; *pg.* 657, *pg.* 659
DIGITAL DOWNLOAD ESSENTIALS - Software - RENTRAK CORPORATION; *pg.* 306, *pg.* 1506
DIGITAL DRIVE - Room Correction Software - VELODYNE ACOUSTICS, INC.; *pg.* 685, *pg.* 152
DIGITAL DYLUX - Ink Jet Proofing Media - E.I. DU PONT DE NEMOURS & COMPANY; *pg.* 1159, *pg.* 390
DIGITAL EDITIONS - Software - ADOBE SYSTEMS INCORPORATED; *pg.* 342, *pg.* 235
DIGITAL ESSX - Wireless Communication System - AT&T SOUTHEAST; *pg.* 1868, *pg.* 489
DIGITAL ETCH A SKETCH - Toy - THE OHIO ART COMPANY, INC.; *pg.* 965, *pg.* 1406
DIGITAL EVOLUTION ALERT MANAGER - Software - AKANA; *pg.* 346, *pg.* 125
DIGITAL EVOLUTION CONSOLE - Software - AKANA; *pg.* 346, *pg.* 125
DIGITAL EVOLUTION GATEWAY - Software - AKANA; *pg.* 346, *pg.* 125
DIGITAL EVOLUTION MANAGEMENT POINT - Software - AKANA; *pg.* 346, *pg.* 125
DIGITAL EVOLUTION POLICY MANAGER - Software - AKANA; *pg.* 346, *pg.* 125
DIGITAL EVOLUTION REGISTRY - Software - AKANA; *pg.* 346, *pg.* 125
DIGITAL EVOLUTION SERVICE MANAGER - Software - AKANA; *pg.* 346, *pg.* 125
DIGITAL EVOLUTION XML VPN - Software - AKANA; *pg.* 346, *pg.* 125
THE DIGITAL EVOLUTION XML VPN - Software - AKANA; *pg.* 346, *pg.* 125
DIGITAL GEM - Computer Software - EASTMAN KODAK COMPANY; *pg.* 1408, *pg.* 1333
DIGITAL HOME - Computer Hardware & Software - ECHELON CORPORATION; *pg.* 389, *pg.* 245
DIGITAL ID - Online Transaction Security Product - VERISIGN, INC.; *pg.* 488, *pg.* 1799
DIGITAL IMMUNE SYSTEM - Software - SYMANTEC CORPORATION; *pg.* 478, *pg.* 161
DIGITAL INSIGHT - Online Banking Services - INTUIT INC.; *pg.* 769, *pg.* 158
DIGITAL INTERPLOT - Software - BENTLEY SYSTEMS, INC.; *pg.* 361, *pg.* 1531
DIGITAL IVISION - Display Technology - KOPIN CORPORATION; *pg.* 425, *pg.* 847
DIGITAL LAB STANDARD - Stereotaxic Equipment - STOELTING CO.; *pg.* 1430, *pg.* 671
DIGITAL LASER OPAQUE - Manual - XEROX CORPORATION; *pg.* 494, *pg.* 365
DIGITAL LIGHT PROCESSING - Semiconductors - TEXAS INSTRUMENTS INCORPORATED; *pg.* 679, *pg.* 1688
DIGITAL MACROVIEW - Veterinary Otoscope - WELCH ALLYN INC.; *pg.* 1436, *pg.* 1342
DIGITAL MAGIC - Elevation Sensor - WINEGARD COMPANY; *pg.* 688, *pg.* 702
DIGITAL MAILROOM - Software - EMC CORPORATION; *pg.*

391, *pg.* 825
DIGITAL MEDIA TRANSMISSION - Process Technology - ACACIA RESEARCH CORPORATION; *pg.* 1398, *pg.* 165
DIGITAL MINIPORTRAIT (DMP) - All-in-one Digital Camera & Thermal Printing System - POLAROID CORPORATION; *pg.* 1426, *pg.* 815
DIGITAL OPPORTUNITY CHANNEL - Online Public Policy Initiative - BENTON FOUNDATION; *pg.* 134, *pg.* 396
DIGITAL PAD - Medical & Aesthetic Product - DYNATRONICS CORPORATION; *pg.* 1526, *pg.* 1757
DIGITAL PALETTE HR 6000 - High Resolution Professional Camera - POLAROID CORPORATION; *pg.* 1426, *pg.* 815
DIGITAL RECORD CENTER - Software System - IRON MOUNTAIN INCORPORATED; *pg.* 421, *pg.* 796
DIGITAL RIGHTS MANAGEMENT - Software - CERTICOM CORP.; *pg.* 371, *pg.* 1925
DIGITAL ROC - Computer Software - EASTMAN KODAK COMPANY; *pg.* 1408, *pg.* 1333
DIGITAL SAFE - Software - AUTONOMY PLEASANTON; *pg.* 358, *pg.* 183
DIGITAL SHO - Computer Software - EASTMAN KODAK COMPANY; *pg.* 1408, *pg.* 1333
DIGITAL STOREFRONT - Printing Product - ELECTRONICS FOR IMAGING, INC.; *pg.* 390, *pg.* 88
DIGITAL SWATCH MATCH - Online Services - R.R. DONNELLEY & SONS COMPANY; *pg.* 1682, *pg.* 589
DIGITAL SYRINGE - Robotic Product - HAMILTON CO., INC.; *pg.* 1415, *pg.* 1031
DIGITAL THUNDER - Software & Integrated Circuits - TEXAS INSTRUMENTS INCORPORATED; *pg.* 679, *pg.* 1688
DIGITAL TRACKING SYSTEM - Hydraulic Sprayer - GRACO, INC.; *pg.* 1342, *pg.* 935
DIGITAL VETTEK - Veterinary X-Ray Apparatus - IMAGEWORKS; *pg.* 1544, *pg.* 1158
DIGITAL VIBRANCE CONTROL - Software - NVIDIA CORPORATION; *pg.* 447, *pg.* 268
DIGITAL VISIONS - Printer - XEROX CORPORATION; *pg.* 494, *pg.* 365
DIGITAL VOLTAGE INDICATOR - Electrical Test & Measurement - HD ELECTRIC COMPANY; *pg.* 1299, *pg.* 666
DIGITALBACKPACK - Educational Service - KNOVATION; *pg.* 1261, *pg.* 1415
DIGITALCHOICE - Paper - DOMTAR CORPORATION; *pg.* 1456, *pg.* 1954
DIGITALIFT - Floor Trays - MACNEIL AUTOMOTIVE PRODUCTS, LTD.; *pg.* 211, *pg.* 559
DIGITALME - Computer Software - NOVELL INC.; *pg.* 446, *pg.* 852
DIGITALNOW - Film Digitizing - HOLOGIC, INC.; *pg.* 1416, *pg.* 784
DIGITALOPS - Service Delivery Platform - VERIZON TERREMARK; *pg.* 685, *pg.* 447
DIGITECH - Imaging Service - DIGIRAD CORPORATION; *pg.* 1524, *pg.* 185
DIGITECH - Audio & Video Product - HARMAN INTERNATIONAL INDUSTRIES, INCORPORATED; *pg.* 641, *pg.* 374
DIGITEK - Pharmaceutical Product - MYLAN, INC.; *pg.* 1570, *pg.* 1520
DIGITEK - Digital Motion Detectors - VICON INDUSTRIES, INC.; *pg.* 685, *pg.* 1166
DIGITENN - Test Equipment - SPX THERMAL PRODUCT SOLUTIONS; *pg.* 1378, *pg.* 1555
DIGITEX - Pigment - BASF CATALYSTS LLC; *pg.* 1148, *pg.* 1074
DIGITRAC - Train Location System - ANSALDO STS; *pg.* 618, *pg.* 1573
DIGITRAPPER MKIII - Synectics Product - MEDTRONIC, INC.; *pg.* 1564, *pg.* 939
DIGITRONIC - Solid State Temperature Controller - DESPATCH INDUSTRIES; *pg.* 1070, *pg.* 927
DIGIVET-1417CR - Veterinary Imaging System - IMAGEWORKS; *pg.* 1544, *pg.* 1158
DIGIVIEW - Visual Displays - COBRA ELECTRONICS CORPORATION; *pg.* 629, *pg.* 572
DIGIVOLT - Electrical Test & Measurement - HD ELECTRIC COMPANY; *pg.* 1299, *pg.* 666
DIGOXIN - Pharmaceutical Product - LANNETT COMPANY, INC.; *pg.* 1555, *pg.* 1566
DIH-PRO-SLR DIGITAL - Photo Equipment - NIKON INC.; *pg.* 1424, *pg.* 1181
DIKMAN - Lamp - ASHLEY FURNITURE INDUSTRIES, INC.; *pg.* 914, *pg.* 1852
DILACOR - Pharmaceutical Product - ALLERGAN; *pg.* 1490, *pg.* 1101
DILANTIN - Medicine - PFIZER INC.; *pg.* 1581, *pg.* 1278
DILANTIN-125 - Pharmaceutical Product - PFIZER INC.; *pg.* 1581, *pg.* 1278
DILANTIN INFATABS - Pharmaceutical Product - PFIZER INC.; *pg.* 1581, *pg.* 1278
DILANTIN KAPSEALS - Pharmaceutical Product - PFIZER INC.; *pg.* 1581, *pg.* 1278
DILAUDID - Pharmaceutical Product - LANNETT COMPANY, INC.; *pg.* 1555, *pg.* 1566
DILLEN - Plastic Product - MYERS INDUSTRIES, INC.; *pg.* 1887, *pg.* 1402
DILLIAN - Lamp - ASHLEY FURNITURE INDUSTRIES, INC.; *pg.* 914, *pg.* 1852
DILLON - Furniture - AMERICAN LEATHER LP; *pg.* 912, *pg.* 1673
DILLON - Guest Chairs - BERNHARDT DESIGN; *pg.* 918, *pg.* 1381
DILLON - Supermarket - THE KROGER CO.; *pg.* 1025, *pg.* 1416
DILLY BAR - Frozen Novelties - INTERNATIONAL DAIRY QUEEN, INC.; *pg.* 1732, *pg.* 938
DILLYWICH - Frozen Novelties - INTERNATIONAL DAIRY QUEEN, INC.; *pg.* 1732, *pg.* 938
DILUCO - Metal Casting Product - HILL & GRIFFITH COMPANY; *pg.* 1167, *pg.* 1414
DIM WITT - Apparel - VANS, INC.; *pg.* 1821, *pg.* 76
DIMCOGRIP - Knob & Handle - DIMCO-GRAY COMPANY; *pg.* 1881, *pg.* 1409
DIMENSION - Desktop Computers - DELL INC.; *pg.* 383, *pg.* 1737
DIMENSION - Chemical Coating - ENTHONE INC.; *pg.* 1161, *pg.* 381
DIMENSION - Delivery Body or Trailer - HACKNEY INTERNATIONAL; *pg.* 178, *pg.* 1392
DIMENSION - Technical Furniture - IAC INDUSTRIES, INC.; *pg.* 929, *pg.* 48
DIMENSION - Furniture - JASPER GROUP; *pg.* 930, *pg.* 691
DIMENSION - Canoes & Kayaks - JOHNSON OUTDOORS INC.; *pg.* 1837, *pg.* 1888
DIMENSION - Welding & Cutting Equipment - MILLER ELECTRIC MANUFACTURING CO.; *pg.* 1361, *pg.* 1852
DIMENSION - Components - QUALITY BICYCLE PRODUCTS; *pg.* 1710, *pg.* 918
DIMENSION - Diagnostic Product - SIEMENS HEALTHCARE DIAGNOSTICS; *pg.* 673, *pg.* 604
DIMENSION - 3D Printer - STRATASYS, INC.; *pg.* 476, *pg.* 923
DIMENSION - Scanning Probe Microscope - VEECO INSTRUMENTS INC.; *pg.* 1434, *pg.* 1322
DIMENSION 3 - Stretch Backs - WELLS LAMONT CORPORATION; *pg.* 15, *pg.* 638
DIMENSION 3100 - Scanning Probe Microscope - VEECO INSTRUMENTS INC.; *pg.* 1434, *pg.* 1322
DIMENSION 4 - Workstations - IAC INDUSTRIES, INC.; *pg.* 929, *pg.* 48
DIMENSION 5000 - Scanning Probe Microscope - VEECO INSTRUMENTS INC.; *pg.* 1434, *pg.* 1322
DIMENSION BASS - Electric Bass - FENDER MUSICAL INSTRUMENTS CORPORATION; *pg.* 547, *pg.* 21
DIMENSION EXCEL - CTP Imaging System - PRESSTEK LLC; *pg.* 1678, *pg.* 1034
DIMENSION PRO 800 - CTP Imaging System - PRESSTEK LLC; *pg.* 1678, *pg.* 1034
DIMENSION SERIES - Metal Building Product - CENTRIA, INC.; *pg.* 74, *pg.* 1554
DIMENSION SERIES - Platesetter - PRESSTEK LLC; *pg.* 1678, *pg.* 1034
DIMENSION VX 210 - Atomic Force Profiler - VEECO INSTRUMENTS INC.; *pg.* 1434, *pg.* 1322
DIMENSION VX 330 - Atomic Force Profiler - VEECO INSTRUMENTS INC.; *pg.* 1434, *pg.* 1322
DIMENSION X - Atomic Force Microscope for Etch Depth at 90nm & Below - VEECO INSTRUMENTS INC.; *pg.* 1434, *pg.* 1322
DIMENSIONAIR - Balloon - CONTINENTAL AMERICAN CORP.; *pg.* 1880, *pg.* 723
DIMENSIONS - Paper & Nonwoven Material - FIBERMARK INC.; *pg.* 1457, *pg.* 1764
DIMENSIONS - Medical Product - HOLOGIC, INC.; *pg.* 1416, *pg.* 784
DIMENSIONS - Electronic Component - LEVITON MANUFACTURING COMPANY, INC.; *pg.* 1301, *pg.* 1180
DIMENSIONS - Wall System - MARLITE, INC.; *pg.* 95, *pg.* 1448
DIMENSIONS - Manufacturing Automotive Software - UNIVERSAL INSTRUMENTS CORPORATION; *pg.* 683, *pg.* 1154
DIMETALLIC - Metals Passivators for Refining - GE WATER & PROCESS TECHNOLOGIES; *pg.* 1339, *pg.* 1588
DIMETAPP - Cold & Allergy Relief - PFIZER INC.; *pg.* 1581, *pg.* 1278
DIMETCOTE - Coating & Finish - NOV AMERON; *pg.* 100, *pg.* 187
DIMETRA - Communications Product - MOTOROLA SOLUTIONS, INC.; *pg.* 657, *pg.* 659
DIMEZONE - Photo Developing Agent - EASTMAN KODAK COMPANY; *pg.* 1408, *pg.* 1333
DIMFAB - Pad - FABREEKA INTERNATIONAL, INC.; *pg.* 1882, *pg.* 847
DIMLIN - Polymer Product - CHEMTURA CORPORATION; *pg.* 1152, *pg.* 355
DIMMER SWITCH - Disk Storage Control Software - AVAGO TECHNOLOGIES; *pg.* 358, *pg.* 238
DIMPLEX - Electrical Heating Product - DIMPLEX NORTH AMERICA LIMITED; *pg.* 54, *pg.* 1920
DIN-A-MITE - Power Controller - WATLOW ELECTRIC MANUFACTURING COMPANY; *pg.* 1078, *pg.* 1004
DINAH - Footwear - PHOENIX FOOTWEAR GROUP, INC.; *pg.* 1815, *pg.* 60
DINE-A-WIPE - Foodservice Wipes - GEORGIA-PACIFIC LLC; *pg.* 1458, *pg.* 507
DINEEQUITY - Restaurant Services - DINEEQUITY, INC.; *pg.* 1725, *pg.* 95
DINE'N WITH - Food Product - ADVANCEPIERRE FOODS, INC.; *pg.* 1714, *pg.* 1409
DINERS' CHOICE - Refrigerated Potato Products - MICHAEL FOODS, INC.; *pg.* 877, *pg.* 949
DINERS CLUB - Credit Card - DISCOVER FINANCIAL SERVICES; *pg.* 744, *pg.* 653
DING DONGS - Snack Cakes - HOSTESS BRANDS LLC; *pg.* 1856, *pg.* 984
DINGLEE - Pumps - IDEX CORPORATION; *pg.* 1347, *pg.* 623
DINNER BELL - Meat Products - JOHN MORRELL & CO.; *pg.* 866, *pg.* 1415
DINOFOURS - Educational Materials - SCHOLASTIC INC.; *pg.* 1683, *pg.* 1288
DINOHYDE - Glove - LAKELAND INDUSTRIES, INC.; *pg.* 1354, *pg.* 1338
DINOSAURS - Nutritional Product - NUTRACEUTICAL INTERNATIONAL CORPORATION; *pg.* 1576, *pg.* 1753
DINOSITOS - Educational Materials - SCHOLASTIC INC.; *pg.* 1683, *pg.* 1288
DINTY MOORE - Food Products - HORMEL FOODS CORPORATION; *pg.* 863, *pg.* 915
DIODE-CC - Switch - POWER INTEGRATIONS, INC.; *pg.* 1369, *pg.* 249
DIOLASEPLUS - Dental Laser Product - BIOLASE TECHNOLOGY, INC.; *pg.* 1506, *pg.* 107
DIOLITE - Medical Laser System - IRIDEX CORPORATION; *pg.* 648, *pg.* 160
DIOPEEL - Plastics Product - AEP INDUSTRIES INC.; *pg.* 1878, *pg.* 1085
DIOPEXY - Medical Laser System - IRIDEX CORPORATION; *pg.* 648, *pg.* 160
DIOPSIS - DSP Platform - ATMEL CORPORATION; *pg.* 621, *pg.* 238
DIOR - Make-Up Products - PARFUMS CHRISTIAN DIOR, INC; *pg.* 519, *pg.* 1276
DIOR ADDICT EDITION LIMITEE - Women's Fragrance - PARFUMS CHRISTIAN DIOR, INC; *pg.* 519, *pg.* 1276
DIOR ADDICT PERFUMED BODY LINE - Women's Fragrance - PARFUMS CHRISTIAN DIOR, INC; *pg.* 519, *pg.* 1276
DIOR RALEXANDTE - Women's Fragrance - PARFUMS CHRISTIAN DIOR, INC; *pg.* 519, *pg.* 1276
DIORAMA DESIGNER - Educational Materials - SCHOLASTIC INC.; *pg.* 1683, *pg.* 1288
DIORELLA - Women's Fragrance - PARFUMS CHRISTIAN DIOR, INC; *pg.* 519, *pg.* 1276
DIORESSENCE - Women's Fragrance - PARFUMS CHRISTIAN DIOR, INC; *pg.* 519, *pg.* 1276
DIORISSIMO - Women's Fragrance - PARFUMS CHRISTIAN DIOR, INC; *pg.* 519, *pg.* 1276
DIOSIN - Nutritional Product - RBC LIFE SCIENCES, INC.; *pg.* 1588, *pg.* 1723
DIOVOL - Pharmaceutical Product - CHURCH & DWIGHT CANADA CORP.; *pg.* 503, *pg.* 1925
DIOXOR - Gas Analyzer - BACHARACH INC.; *pg.* 1400, *pg.*

1556
DIP - Instant Silver Cleaner - L&R MANUFACTURING COMPANY; *pg.* 1419, *pg.* 1076
DIP-ALARM - Indicators - PROJECTS UNLIMITED, INC.; *pg.* 665, *pg.* 1446
DIP-FLASH - Indicators - PROJECTS UNLIMITED, INC.; *pg.* 665, *pg.* 1446
DIP-IT - Food & Beverage Stain Remover - RECKITT BENCKISER INC.; *pg.* 1136, *pg.* 1105
DIP/LOC - Electronic Equipment - EVERETT CHARLES TECHNOLOGIES; *pg.* 638, *pg.* 185
DIP QUIK - Icing And Base - DAWN FOOD PRODUCTS, INC.; *pg.* 1018, *pg.* 893
DIPCRAFT - Tradename - DIPCRAFT MANUFACTURING COMPANY; *pg.* 79, *pg.* 1518
DIPEB - Diisopropenylbenzene - CYTEC INDUSTRIES, INC.; *pg.* 1155, *pg.* 1131
DIPHENHIST - Pharmaceutical Product - ALLERGAN; *pg.* 1490, *pg.* 1101
DIPHENOXYLATE - Pharmaceutical Product - LANNETT COMPANY, INC.; *pg.* 1555, *pg.* 1566
DIPLAST - Plasticizers - HUNTSMAN CORPORATION; *pg.* 1167, *pg.* 1758
DIPLOMACY - Game - HASBRO, INC.; *pg.* 954, *pg.* 1603
DIPLOMAT - Framed Decorator Switch - PASS & SEYMOUR/LEGRAND; *pg.* 1303, *pg.* 1344
DIPLOMAT - Footwear - P.W. MINOR & SON, INC.; *pg.* 1816, *pg.* 1140
DIPLOMATIC EXPO - Telephone Service - IDT CORPORATION; *pg.* 643, *pg.* 1096
THE DIPPED FRUIT BOUQUET - Chocolate Dipped Fruit Arrangements - EDIBLE ARRANGEMENTS INTERNATIONAL, INC.; *pg.* 1768, *pg.* 382
DIPPIN DOTS - Logo - DIPPIN' DOTS LLC; *pg.* 853, *pg.* 739
DIPPIN' ZONE - Starters & Desserts - MAZZIO'S CORPORATION; *pg.* 1737, *pg.* 1490
DIPRO - Drill-In Fluid - M-I SWACO; *pg.* 980, *pg.* 1710
DIPROLENE - Medicine - MERCK & CO., INC.; *pg.* 1566, *pg.* 1077
DIPSTICK - Biomolecule Product - THERMO FISHER SCIENTIFIC INC.; *pg.* 1602, *pg.* 61
DIRECT - Telecommunication System - EQUINIX, INC.; *pg.* 394, *pg.* 190
DIRECT - Lottery System - INTERNATIONAL GAME TECHNOLOGY; *pg.* 420, *pg.* 1606
DIRECT BITE - Oncology Product - C.R. BARD, INC.; *pg.* 1519, *pg.* 1094
DIRECT CONNECT - Software - BIO-RAD LABORATORIES, INC.; *pg.* 1504, *pg.* 101
DIRECT DEPOSIT - Software - COMPUTER PROGRAMS & SYSTEMS, INC.; *pg.* 378, *pg.* 7
DIRECT EVENT - Conferencing Service - INTERCALL, INC.; *pg.* 417, *pg.* 578
DIRECT FIT - Catalytic Converter - AP EXHAUST PRODUCTS, INC.; *pg.* 199, *pg.* 1373
DIRECT-GRIP - Glove Insert - W.L. GORE & ASSOCIATES, INC.; *pg.* 122, *pg.* 388
DIRECT LIGHT - Lighting System - PHILIPS SOLID-STATE LIGHTING SOLUTIONS; *pg.* 1303, *pg.* 806
DIRECT LIGHT PLAYER - Lighting System - PHILIPS SOLID-STATE LIGHTING SOLUTIONS; *pg.* 1303, *pg.* 806
DIRECT-LINK - Electronic Components - MOLEX INCORPORATED; *pg.* 655, *pg.* 628
DIRECT LYRICS - Music Lyrics, Tracks & Videos Site - SPINMEDIA; *pg.* 1282, *pg.* 104
DIRECT MAIL - Direct Mail - VALASSIS COMMUNICATIONS, INC.; *pg.* 1287, *pg.* 897
DIRECT MATRIX - Software - EMC CORPORATION; *pg.* 391, *pg.* 825
DIRECT MATRIX ARCHITECTURE - Software - EMC CORPORATION; *pg.* 391, *pg.* 825
DIRECT PRINT - Ink Jet Label - AVERY DENNISON CORPORATION; *pg.* 1452, *pg.* 95
DIRECT RADIOGRAPHY - Medical Product - HOLOGIC, INC.; *pg.* 1416, *pg.* 784
DIRECT RAMBUS - Clock & Buffer Product - CYPRESS SEMICONDUCTOR CORPORATION; *pg.* 1326, *pg.* 243
DIRECT/REFLECTING - Audio Product - BOSE CORPORATION; *pg.* 626, *pg.* 820
DIRECT RESPONSE INDEX - Marketing Database - MARKET DATA RETRIEVAL; *pg.* 1661, *pg.* 370
DIRECT SILICON ACCESS - Software - SYNOPSYS, INC.; *pg.* 480, *pg.* 162
DIRECT SYSTEM VERIFICATION - Software System - MENTOR GRAPHICS CORPORATION; *pg.* 432, *pg.* 1510
DIRECT-TO-DOOR - Door Delivered Promotion - VALASSIS COMMUNICATIONS, INC.; *pg.* 1287, *pg.* 897
DIRECT TO TARGET - Catheter - ST. JUDE MEDICAL, INC.; *pg.* 1596, *pg.* 963
DIRECT2DATA - Wireless Product - PARKERVISION, INC.; *pg.* 1426, *pg.* 434
DIRECT2POWER - Transmitter/Power Amplifier Technology - PARKERVISION, INC.; *pg.* 1426, *pg.* 434
DIRECTAC - Removable Inner Cartridge - LAVI INDUSTRIES INC.; *pg.* 93, *pg.* 299
DIRECTALERTS - Patient Care - ST. JUDE MEDICAL, INC.; *pg.* 1596, *pg.* 963
DIRECTBANKING.COM - Online Banking Services - SALEM FIVE CENTS SAVINGS BANK; *pg.* 800, *pg.* 843
DIRECTBLOG - Weblog Technology - IMAKENEWS, INC.; *pg.* 413, *pg.* 851
DIRECTCALL - Patient Care - ST. JUDE MEDICAL, INC.; *pg.* 1596, *pg.* 963
DIRECTCONNECTSM - Software System - MENTOR GRAPHICS CORPORATION; *pg.* 432, *pg.* 1510
DIRECTDRIVE - Amplifiers - MAXIM INTEGRATED PRODUCTS, INC.; *pg.* 653, *pg.* 247
DIRECTED - Mobile Video Equipment - DEI HOLDINGS, INC.; *pg.* 633, *pg.* 302
DIRECTEDACOUSTICS - Electronic Product - LRAD CORPORATION; *pg.* 652, *pg.* 204
DIRECTEDSOUND - Electronic Product - LRAD CORPORATION; *pg.* 652, *pg.* 204
DIRECTFET - Power Semiconductor Device - INTERNATIONAL RECTIFIER CORPORATION; *pg.* 647, *pg.* 80
DIRECTFETKY - Power Semiconductor Device - INTERNATIONAL RECTIFIER CORPORATION; *pg.* 647, *pg.* 80
DIRECTFILL - Tungsten Deposition System - LAM RESEARCH CORPORATION; *pg.* 1354, *pg.* 246
DIRECTIVITY - Electronic Product - LRAD CORPORATION; *pg.* 652, *pg.* 204
DIRECTLINE - Software Support - DELL INC.; *pg.* 383, *pg.* 1737
DIRECTLINK - Software - TRIZETTO CORPORATION; *pg.* 485, *pg.* 327
DIRECTOIRE - Furniture - J. ROBERT SCOTT INC.; *pg.* 930, *pg.* 105
DIRECTOR - Software - ADOBE SYSTEMS INCORPORATED; *pg.* 342, *pg.* 235
DIRECTOR - Medical Equipment - CONMED CORPORATION; *pg.* 1517, *pg.* 1347
DIRECTOR - Financial Product - LINCOLN NATIONAL CORPORATION; *pg.* 776, *pg.* 1567
DIRECTOR - Furniture - TELESCOPE CASUAL FURNITURE INC.; *pg.* 944, *pg.* 1162
DIRECTOR ELECTROL - Screen - DA-LITE SCREEN COMPANY; *pg.* 632, *pg.* 698
DIRECTOR II - School Communication Systems - RAULAND-BORG CORPORATION; *pg.* 666, *pg.* 634
DIRECTORY - Book - MANUFACTURERS' NEWS, INC.; *pg.* 1661, *pg.* 612
DIRECTORY OF DOLLARS & C-STORE DIRECTORY - Directory - SUMNER COMMUNICATIONS INC.; *pg.* 1690, *pg.* 338
DIRECTORY OF IMPORTERS & EXPORTERS - Trade Publication - JOC GROUP INC.; *pg.* 1654, *pg.* 1096
DIRECTORY OF WHOLESALERS, IMPORTERS & LIQUIDATORS - Directory - SUMNER COMMUNICATIONS INC.; *pg.* 1690, *pg.* 338
THE DIRECTORY STORE - Global Directory Bookstore - DEX MEDIA INC.; *pg.* 1635, *pg.* 1680
DIRECTORYANALYZER - Software - DELL SOFTWARE; *pg.* 385, *pg.* 40
DIRECTORYTROUBLESHOOTER - Software - DELL SOFTWARE; *pg.* 385, *pg.* 40
DIRECTOVALVE - Control Valve - SPRAYING SYSTEMS CO.; *pg.* 1063, *pg.* 670
DIRECTRAC - Free Standing Sign Stand - LAVI INDUSTRIES INC.; *pg.* 93, *pg.* 299
DIRECTRAY - Medical Test System - HOLOGIC, INC.; *pg.* 1416, *pg.* 784
DIRECTV - Management Services - CENTURYLINK, INC; *pg.* 1870, *pg.* 317
DIRECTV - Satellite Television Services - DIRECTV GROUP HOLDINGS, LLC; *pg.* 281, *pg.* 79
DIRECTV - Wireless Communications - VERIZON COMMUNICATIONS INC.; *pg.* 1875, *pg.* 1309
DIRECTVIEW - Software - EASTMAN KODAK COMPANY; *pg.* 1408, *pg.* 1333
DIRECTX - Software - NVIDIA CORPORATION; *pg.* 447, *pg.* 268
DIREX - Herbicide - E.I. DU PONT DE NEMOURS & COMPANY; *pg.* 1159, *pg.* 390
DIRK - Furniture - AMISCO INDUSTRIES LTD.; *pg.* 913, *pg.* 1958
DIROL - Chewing Gum - MONDELEZ INTERNATIONAL, INC.; *pg.* 878, *pg.* 601
DIRT BAG - Bicycle Accessories - SPECIALIZED BICYCLE COMPONENTS, INC.; *pg.* 1711, *pg.* 152
DIRT BALDY - Bicycle Accessories - SPECIALIZED BICYCLE COMPONENTS, INC.; *pg.* 1711, *pg.* 152
DIRT CONTROL - Bicycle Accessories - SPECIALIZED BICYCLE COMPONENTS, INC.; *pg.* 1711, *pg.* 152
DIRT ERASER - Mobile Dust Collection Unit - THE SPENCER TURBINE CO.; *pg.* 1378, *pg.* 386
DIRT-FUSE - Filter Cartridge - PALL CORPORATION; *pg.* 232, *pg.* 1323
DIRT MASTER - Bicycle Accessories - SPECIALIZED BICYCLE COMPONENTS, INC.; *pg.* 1711, *pg.* 152
DIRT PIC - Automotive Surface Cleaner - ITW - EVERCOAT; *pg.* 1443, *pg.* 1415
DIRT RIDER - Magazine - RENTPATH, INC.; *pg.* 1680, *pg.* 538
DIRT RODZ - Bicycle Accessories - SPECIALIZED BICYCLE COMPONENTS, INC.; *pg.* 1711, *pg.* 152
DIRT-TERGENT - Fluid Handling System - GRACO, INC.; *pg.* 1342, *pg.* 935
DIRT WORM - Bicycle Accessories - SPECIALIZED BICYCLE COMPONENTS, INC.; *pg.* 1711, *pg.* 152
DIRTEX - Cleaner - THE SAVOGRAN COMPANY; *pg.* 1447, *pg.* 840
DIRTLIFTER - PowerBrush - BISSELL HOMECARE, INC.; *pg.* 52, *pg.* 887
DIRTY DANCING - Motion Pictures - LIONS GATE ENTERTAINMENT CORP.; *pg.* 296, *pg.* 274
DIRTY DUTY - Electric Motors - BALDOR ELECTRIC COMPANY; *pg.* 1316, *pg.* 32
DIRXML - Computer Software - NOVELL INC.; *pg.* 446, *pg.* 852
DISAL - Furosemide Injection & Tablets - BOEHRINGER INGELHEIM VETMEDICA, INC.; *pg.* 1474, *pg.* 989
DISASTER SCIENCE - Educational Materials - SCHOLASTIC INC.; *pg.* 1683, *pg.* 1288
DISC - Farm Tools - AG-MEIER INDUSTRIES LLC; *pg.* 700, *pg.* 1668
DISC STAKKA - Automated CD & DVD Manager - IMATION CORP.; *pg.* 413, *pg.* 952
DISC TAKER - Shoe - AEROGROUP INTERNATIONAL, INC.; *pg.* 1803, *pg.* 1055
DISCAL YEAR - Sandals - AEROGROUP INTERNATIONAL, INC.; *pg.* 1803, *pg.* 1055
DISCCOVER - Olfactory Sampling System - ARCADE MARKETING, INC.; *pg.* 352, *pg.* 1196
DISCERN - Care Solutions - CERNER CORPORATION; *pg.* 1514, *pg.* 981
DISCERN EXPERT - Automated Alert Solution for Healthcare Professionals - CERNER CORPORATION; *pg.* 1514, *pg.* 981
DISCERN EXPLORER - HNA & Client-developed Database Maintenance & Extraction Application - CERNER CORPORATION; *pg.* 1514, *pg.* 981
DISCIDE - Disinfectant - ALIMED, INC.; *pg.* 1490, *pg.* 816
DISCIDE - Medical & Aesthetic Product - DYNATRONICS CORPORATION; *pg.* 1526, *pg.* 1757
DISCIPLE DESKTOP - Software - BIO-RAD LABORATORIES, INC.; *pg.* 1504, *pg.* 101
DISCIPLINED BY OUR OPERATING MODEL - Tagline - IDEX CORPORATION; *pg.* 1347, *pg.* 623
DISCJET - Spray Product - SPRAYING SYSTEMS CO.; *pg.* 1063, *pg.* 670
DISCKETTE - Sandals - AEROGROUP INTERNATIONAL, INC.; *pg.* 1803, *pg.* 1055
DISCKIT - Kit Used to Perform LDD Procedures with the KTP/532 - AMERICAN MEDICAL SYSTEMS, INC.; *pg.* 1399, *pg.* 238
DISCLOSE - Plaque Disclosing Solution - BEUTLICH PHARMACEUTICALS LP; *pg.* 1503, *pg.* 665
DISCLOSURE - Software Tool And Application - THOMSON REUTERS MARKETS; *pg.* 810, *pg.* 1299
DISCLOSURE DIRECTORY - Bond Market Data - STANDARD & POOR'S RATINGS SERVICES; *pg.* 805, *pg.* 1296
DISCO - Terminal Reel Fed - PANDUIT CORP.; *pg.* 661, *pg.*

663
DISCO DANCE - Shoe - AEROGROUP INTERNATIONAL, INC.; *pg.* 1803, *pg.* 1055
DISCO-GRIP - Standard Disconnect - PANDUIT CORP.; *pg.* 661, *pg.* 663
DISCO-LOK - Terminal Loose Piece - PANDUIT CORP.; *pg.* 661, *pg.* 663
DISCO TUB LIGHTS - Baby Care Product - MUNCHKIN, INC.; *pg.* 964, *pg.* 300
DISCOGRIP - Terminal Loose Piece - PANDUIT CORP.; *pg.* 661, *pg.* 663
DISCONEX - Switch - HUBBELL INCORPORATED; *pg.* 1299, *pg.* 370
DISCOUNT FOOD MART - Retail Fuel & Convenience Stores - DELEK US HOLDINGS, INC.; *pg.* 975, *pg.* 1627
DISCOVATOR - Tillage Product - GREAT PLAINS MANUFACTURING, INCORPORATED; *pg.* 704, *pg.* 721
DISCOVER - Computer-Based Career Planning Program - ACT INC.; *pg.* 597, *pg.* 708
DISCOVER - Dry Cleaning & Laundry Product - ADCO, INC.; *pg.* 325, *pg.* 482
DISCOVER - Microwave Synthesis System - CEM CORPORATION; *pg.* 1405, *pg.* 1382
DISCOVER - Credit Cards - DISCOVER FINANCIAL SERVICES; *pg.* 744, *pg.* 653
DISCOVER BOATING - Public Awareness & Information Program - NATIONAL MARINE MANUFACTURERS ASSOCIATION; *pg.* 149, *pg.* 584
DISCOVER CARD - Credit Cards - DISCOVER FINANCIAL SERVICES; *pg.* 744, *pg.* 653
DISCOVER CLASSIC CARD - Credit Cards - DISCOVER FINANCIAL SERVICES; *pg.* 744, *pg.* 653
DISCOVER GOLD CARD - Credit Cards - DISCOVER FINANCIAL SERVICES; *pg.* 744, *pg.* 653
DISCOVER GREAT NEW WRITERS - Awards Program - BARNES & NOBLE, INC.; *pg.* 1619, *pg.* 1201
DISCOVER-IE - Knowledge Discovery - RAYTHEON APPLIED SIGNAL TECHNOLOGY, INC.; *pg.* 667, *pg.* 288
DISCOVER MUSIC! - Music - SEATTLE SYMPHONY ORCHESTRA; *pg.* 582, *pg.* 1840
DISCOVER PLATINUM CARD - Credit Cards - DISCOVER FINANCIAL SERVICES; *pg.* 744, *pg.* 653
DISCOVER SOMETHING - Tagline - SARATOGA CASINO & RACEWAY; *pg.* 581, *pg.* 1340
DISCOVER THE DESIGNER IN YOU - Tagline - HANCOCK FABRICS, INC.; *pg.* 693, *pg.* 968
DISCOVER WHAT YOUR LIPS ARE MISSING. - Slogan - BLISTEX, INC.; *pg.* 502, *pg.* 644
DISCOVERASE - Molecular Biology Product - THERMO FISHER SCIENTIFIC INC.; *pg.* 1602, *pg.* 61
DISCOVERER - Binocular - BUSHNELL OUTDOOR PRODUCTS, INC.; *pg.* 1403, *pg.* 718
DISCOVERIES - Market Trends Magazine for Collectible CD's, Records & Memorabilia - KRAUSE PUBLICATIONS, INC.; *pg.* 1657, *pg.* 1861
DISCOVERNOW - Networking Software - OPENCONNECT SYSTEMS, INC.; *pg.* 449, *pg.* 1685
DISCOVERY - Infant Car Seat - EVENFLO COMPANY, INC.; *pg.* 924, *pg.* 1470
DISCOVERY - QDR Bone Densitometer - HOLOGIC, INC.; *pg.* 1416, *pg.* 784
DISCOVERY - Steel Laboratory Cabinets - KEWAUNEE SCIENTIFIC CORPORATION; *pg.* 931, *pg.* 1391
DISCOVERY - Imaging System - MOLECULAR DEVICES CORPORATION; *pg.* 1568, *pg.* 287
DISCOVERY - Software - SYMANTEC CORPORATION; *pg.* 479, *pg.* 1753
DISCOVERY - Software - SYNOPSYS, INC.; *pg.* 480, *pg.* 162
DISCOVERY - Implant System - ZIMMER BIOMET HOLDINGS, INC.; *pg.* 1611, *pg.* 699
DISCOVERY 2000 - Ultra High Speed Polish - HILLYARD, INC.; *pg.* 331, *pg.* 990
DISCOVERY CHANNEL - Television Station - DISCOVERY COMMUNICATIONS, INC.; *pg.* 282, *pg.* 777
DISCOVERY HEALTH CHANNEL - Television Station - DISCOVERY COMMUNICATIONS, INC.; *pg.* 282, *pg.* 777
DISCOVERY KIDS SCANOPEDIA - Electronic Leisure Product - JAKKS PACIFIC, INC.; *pg.* 960, *pg.* 142
THE DISCOVERY SERIES - Software - BIO-RAD LABORATORIES, INC.; *pg.* 1504, *pg.* 101
DISCOVERY SERVICES - Software - BMC SOFTWARE, INC.; *pg.* 362, *pg.* 1701
DISCOVERY ST - Medical Device - GE HEALTHCARE TECHNOLOGIES; *pg.* 1533, *pg.* 1897
DISCOVERY STARTS WITH SAMPLE PREPARATION - Slogan - PRESSURE BIOSCIENCES, INC.; *pg.* 1586, *pg.* 844
DISCOVERY TIMES CHANNEL - Television Station - DISCOVERY COMMUNICATIONS, INC.; *pg.* 282, *pg.* 777
DISCOVERY WIZARD FOR SHAREPOINT - Software - DELL SOFTWARE; *pg.* 385, *pg.* 40
DISCOVERY WIZARD FOR SQL SERVER - Software - DELL SOFTWARE; *pg.* 385, *pg.* 40
DISCREET - Modeling Solutions - AUTODESK INC.; *pg.* 356, *pg.* 257
DISCRETION - Nursing Pads - EVENFLO COMPANY, INC.; *pg.* 924, *pg.* 1470
DISH DROPS - Dish Washing Products - AMWAY CORPORATION; *pg.* 326, *pg.* 864
DISK TOOL SHARPENING STONE - Disc Sharpener - GERBER LEGENDARY BLADES; *pg.* 1834, *pg.* 1503
DISK-VAC - Software - BIO-RAD LABORATORIES, INC.; *pg.* 1504, *pg.* 101
DISKDOUBLER - Software - SYMANTEC CORPORATION; *pg.* 478, *pg.* 161
DISKEEPER - Software - CONDUSIV TECHNOLOGIES; *pg.* 379, *pg.* 51
DISKIT - Respiratory Protection - MCR SAFETY; *pg.* 1422, *pg.* 1630
DISKLOCK - Software - SYMANTEC CORPORATION; *pg.* 478, *pg.* 161
DISKOS - Commercial Lighting - SWIVELIER CO., INC.; *pg.* 1307, *pg.* 1142
DISKSTATE - Software Product - RAXCO SOFTWARE, INC.; *pg.* 459, *pg.* 770
DISKXTENDER - Software System - EMC CORPORATION; *pg.* 391, *pg.* 825
DISKXTENDER 2000 - Software - EMC CORPORATION; *pg.* 391, *pg.* 825
DISNEY - Toy & Game - HASBRO, INC.; *pg.* 954, *pg.* 1603
DISNEY & PIXAR'S STORY - Toy - MATTEL, INC.; *pg.* 962, *pg.* 81
THE DISNEY CHANNEL - Television Channel - THE WALT DISNEY COMPANY; *pg.* 317, *pg.* 52
DISNEY CRUISE LINE - Cruise Line - THE WALT DISNEY COMPANY; *pg.* 317, *pg.* 52
DISNEY INFINITY - Video Game - DISNEY INTERACTIVE MEDIA GROUP; *pg.* 1239, *pg.* 95
DISNEY ON ICE - Ice Shows - FELD ENTERTAINMENT, INC.; *pg.* 547, *pg.* 458
DISNEY PRESS - Newspaper - THE WALT DISNEY COMPANY; *pg.* 317, *pg.* 52
DISNEY PRINCESSES - Toy - MATTEL, INC.; *pg.* 962, *pg.* 81
DISNEY.COM - Kids Entertainment Destination - DISNEY INTERACTIVE MEDIA GROUP; *pg.* 1239, *pg.* 95
DISNEYLAND - Amusement Park - THE WALT DISNEY COMPANY; *pg.* 317, *pg.* 52
DISNEY'S ACTIVITY CENTER - Playhouse - THE WALT DISNEY COMPANY; *pg.* 317, *pg.* 52
DISNEY'S ATLANTIS - Toy - MATTEL, INC.; *pg.* 962, *pg.* 81
DISNEY'S TARZAN - Game - ACTIVISION BLIZZARD, INC.; *pg.* 948, *pg.* 271
DISOGRIN - Rubber Seal - FREUDENBERG-NOK; *pg.* 1882, *pg.* 904
DISPARLON - Chemical Product - KING INDUSTRIES, INC.; *pg.* 1443, *pg.* 363
DISPATCH CONSUMER SERVICES - Commercial Printing - THE DISPATCH PRINTING COMPANY; *pg.* 1636, *pg.* 1439
DISPEN-SI-MATIC - Order Selection System - PARAGON TECHNOLOGIES, INC.; *pg.* 1367, *pg.* 1528
DISPENSE-A-LINER - Vinyl Liners - WITT INDUSTRIES, INC.; *pg.* 1140, *pg.* 1461
DISPENSING SOLUTIONS - Slogan - JAMES ALEXANDER CORPORATION; *pg.* 1461, *pg.* 1044
DISPENSIT - Fluid Handling System - GRACO, INC.; *pg.* 1342, *pg.* 935
DISPENTECH - Fluid Handling System - GRACO, INC.; *pg.* 1342, *pg.* 935
DISPERSA - Paper Towels - GEORGIA-PACIFIC LLC; *pg.* 1458, *pg.* 507
DISPERSALLOY - Dental Product - DENTSPLY INTERNATIONAL INC.; *pg.* 1522, *pg.* 1596
DISPLACER SERIES SNOWPLOWS - Snowplow - HIGHWAY EQUIPMENT COMPANY; *pg.* 704, *pg.* 702
DISPLAWALL - Wall System - MARLITE, INC.; *pg.* 95, *pg.* 1448
DISPLAWALL DIMENSIONS - Retail Merchandising System - MARLITE, INC.; *pg.* 95, *pg.* 1448
DISPLAWALL FL - Retail Merchandising System - MARLITE, INC.; *pg.* 95, *pg.* 1448
DISPLAY BROKER - Systems Integration & Aeronautics - LOCKHEED MARTIN CORPORATION; *pg.* 229, *pg.* 762
DISPLAYINSPECT - Machine Vision System - COGNEX CORPORATION; *pg.* 1406, *pg.* 834
DISPLAYLINK - Projector - INFOCUS CORPORATION; *pg.* 644, *pg.* 1503
DISPODIALYZER - Lab Dialysis Product - SPECTRUM LABORATORIES INC.; *pg.* 1595, *pg.* 69
DISPOSA-COVERS - Disposable Cover for Hyperthermia Blankets - CINCINNATI SUB-ZERO PRODUCTS, INC.; *pg.* 1070, *pg.* 1411
DISPOSA-HOOD - Newborn Environmental Control Device - UTAH MEDICAL PRODUCTS, INC.; *pg.* 1605, *pg.* 1752
DISPOSA-SHIELD - Dental Product - DENTSPLY INTERNATIONAL INC.; *pg.* 1522, *pg.* 1596
DISPOSA-VIEW - Disposable Head Positioning Device - VITAL SIGNS, INC.; *pg.* 1607, *pg.* 1126
DISPOSORB - Carbon Adsorption System - CALGON CARBON CORPORATION; *pg.* 1151, *pg.* 1574
DISPURSA - Polyurethane Dispersion Services - THE DOW CHEMICAL COMPANY; *pg.* 1157, *pg.* 898
DISRIBUTECH - Magazine - RENTPATH, INC.; *pg.* 1680, *pg.* 538
DISSECTRON - Medical Device - INTEGRA LIFESCIENCES HOLDINGS CORPORATION; *pg.* 1545, *pg.* 1109
DISSOLVOSACK - Water Soluble Laundry Bag - MONOSOL, LLC; *pg.* 59, *pg.* 694
DISTANCE DOESN'T HAVE TO BE HARD - Tag Line - ACUSHNET COMPANY; *pg.* 1824, *pg.* 818
DISTANT HORIZONS - Wall Decor - ETHAN ALLEN INTERIORS INC.; *pg.* 924, *pg.* 343
DISTAVIEW - Scoreboard & Sports Product - DAKTRONICS, INC.; *pg.* 633, *pg.* 1624
DISTILLERS' MASTERPIECE - Bourbon - JIM BEAM BRANDS CO.; *pg.* 1965, *pg.* 601
DISTINCTIVE HOMES - Advertising Publication - DOMINION ENTERPRISES; *pg.* 1636, *pg.* 1796
DISTINCTIVELY BETTER - Slogan - MONROVIA GROWERS; *pg.* 1797, *pg.* 44
DISTINCTIVELY DIFFERENT - Tag Line - CRAIGER DRAKE DESIGNS; *pg.* 4, *pg.* 1562
DISTINGUISHED HOSPITAL AWARD - Healthcare Product - HEALTH GRADES, INC.; *pg.* 1256, *pg.* 319
DISTRESS O.S - Day Visual Distress Signal - ACR ELECTRONICS, INC.; *pg.* 612, *pg.* 422
DISTRIBOJET - Spray Product - SPRAYING SYSTEMS CO.; *pg.* 1063, *pg.* 670
DISTRIBUTED MEDIA APPLICATION - Conferencing Solution - POLYCOM, INC.; *pg.* 664, *pg.* 249
DISTRIBUTION SYSTEM OPTIMIZER - Computer Software - PARAGON TECHNOLOGIES, INC.; *pg.* 1367, *pg.* 1528
DISTRICT - Bicycle - TREK BICYCLE CORPORATION; *pg.* 1847, *pg.* 1896
DITHANE - Fungicide - DOW AGROSCIENCES LLC; *pg.* 1156, *pg.* 684
DITO - Fruit Equipment - CHESHER EQUIPMENT LTD.; *pg.* 1323, *pg.* 1925
DITROPAN XL - Pharmaceutical Product - IMPAX LABORATORIES, INC.; *pg.* 1544, *pg.* 101
DITROPAN XL - Healthcare Product - JOHNSON & JOHNSON; *pg.* 1549, *pg.* 1091
DITZ-LAC - Automobile Finishes - PPG INDUSTRIES, INC.; *pg.* 1445, *pg.* 1579
DITZ-O - Wax & Grease Remover - PPG INDUSTRIES, INC.; *pg.* 1445, *pg.* 1579
DITZCO - Liquid Paints & Paint Enamels - PPG INDUSTRIES, INC.; *pg.* 1445, *pg.* 1579
DITZLER - Decorative & Protective Coatings - PPG INDUSTRIES, INC.; *pg.* 1445, *pg.* 1579
DIUREX - Pharmaceutical Product - ALVA/AMCO PHARMACAL COMPANIES, INC.; *pg.* 1492, *pg.* 637
DIURIL - Pharmaceutical Product - SALIX PHARMACEUTICALS, INC.; *pg.* 1591, *pg.* 1388
DIVA - Beverages - THE COCA-COLA COMPANY; *pg.* 240, *pg.* 493
DIVA - Women's Shoe - JACK SCHWARTZ SHOES, INC.; *pg.* 1810, *pg.* 1245
DIVA - Fabric - NEMSCHOFF, INC.; *pg.* 936, *pg.* 1890
DIVA - Seating - STEELCASE INC.; *pg.* 475, *pg.* 889
DIVA - Acoustical Shell System - WENGER CORPORATION; *pg.* 1307, *pg.* 952
DIVA - Cosmetics - WESTROCK COMPANY; *pg.* 1472, *pg.*

First page reference indicates Business Class Edition
Second page reference indicates Geographic Edition

1805
DIVA STARZ - Toy - MATTEL, INC.; *pg.* 962, *pg.* 81
DIVACOMPLETE - Digital Archive System - PRESILIENT, LLC; *pg.* 456, *pg.* 313
DIVADIRECTOR - Web-Based Content Management Application - PRESILIENT, LLC; *pg.* 456, *pg.* 313
DIVAMONITOR - Computer Application System - PRESILIENT, LLC; *pg.* 456, *pg.* 313
DIVARCHIVE - Software - PRESILIENT, LLC; *pg.* 456, *pg.* 313
DIVAWORKS - Archive Management Appliance - PRESILIENT, LLC; *pg.* 456, *pg.* 313
DIVER DAVE - Pool Cleaner - HAYWARD POOL PRODUCTS; *pg.* 1049, *pg.* 1057
DIVERSACUT - Dicer - URSCHEL LABORATORIES INCORPORATED; *pg.* 1386, *pg.* 698
DIVERSACUT 2110 - Food Cutting Equipment - URSCHEL LABORATORIES INCORPORATED; *pg.* 1386, *pg.* 698
DIVERSIFLEX - Hose - THE GOODYEAR TIRE & RUBBER COMPANY; *pg.* 1883, *pg.* 1401
DIVERSIPHASE - Wireless Electronics - SHURE INCORPORATED; *pg.* 672, *pg.* 638
DIVERSIPRINT - Adhesive Coated Paper - SPINNAKER COATING, LLC; *pg.* 1470, *pg.* 1477
DIVERSITY DATABASE - Software - BIO-RAD LABORATORIES, INC.; *pg.* 1504, *pg.* 101
DIVERSIWALL - Wall System - OMNOVA SOLUTIONS INC; *pg.* 1176, *pg.* 1453
DIVERTER SYSTEMS - Riser Systems - DRIL-QUIP, INC.; *pg.* 1330, *pg.* 1704
DIVICOM - Digital Video Product - HARMONIC, INC.; *pg.* 402, *pg.* 246
DIVIDABLE MULTIPLE-ACTION DELIVERY SYSTEM - Proprietary Drug Delivery Technology - IMPAX LABORATORIES, INC.; *pg.* 1544, *pg.* 101
DIVIDEND CARD - Banking Service - CANADIAN IMPERIAL BANK OF COMMERCE; *pg.* 729, *pg.* 1935
DIVIDEND PLATINUM - Banking Service - CANADIAN IMPERIAL BANK OF COMMERCE; *pg.* 729, *pg.* 1935
DIVIDEND RECORD - Dividend Payment Tracking - STANDARD & POOR'S RATINGS SERVICES; *pg.* 805, *pg.* 1296
DIVIDENDS - Office Furniture - KNOLL, INC.; *pg.* 425, *pg.* 1527
DIVIDENDS - Skin Care Product - NU SKIN ENTERPRISES, INC.; *pg.* 518, *pg.* 1755
DIVIDENDS HORIZON - Office Furniture - KNOLL, INC.; *pg.* 425, *pg.* 1527
DIVIDOHM - Vitreous Enamel Power Resistor - OHMITE MANUFACTURING COMPANY; *pg.* 660, *pg.* 553
DIVINE NINE - Golfing Product - CALLAWAY GOLF COMPANY; *pg.* 1829, *pg.* 58
DIVINER - Position Indicator - HENRY PRATT COMPANY; *pg.* 1049, *pg.* 555
DIVINO - Texture - USG CORPORATION; *pg.* 118, *pg.* 594
DIVISION - Software - PARAMETRIC TECHNOLOGY CORPORATION; *pg.* 452, *pg.* 835
DIVISIONS - High Performance Fabric - MILLIKEN & COMPANY; *pg.* 696, *pg.* 1622
DIVITRACKIP - Digital Video Product - HARMONIC, INC.; *pg.* 402, *pg.* 246
DIVITRACKXE - Digital Video Product - HARMONIC, INC.; *pg.* 402, *pg.* 246
DIVOT DIGGER - Video Game - INTERNATIONAL GAME TECHNOLOGY; *pg.* 957, *pg.* 1024
DIVOT FIX - Golf Product - FAIRMOUNT SANTROL; *pg.* 1162, *pg.* 1409
DIWATEX - Chemical Product - WESTROCK COMPANY; *pg.* 1472, *pg.* 1805
DIX-PRO-SLR DIGITAL - Photo Equipment - NIKON INC.; *pg.* 1424, *pg.* 1181
DIXECON - Solid Carbide Rotary File - REGAL BELOIT CORPORATION; *pg.* 106, *pg.* 1854
DIXIE - Food Service - GEORGIA-PACIFIC LLC; *pg.* 1458, *pg.* 507
DIXIE - Candied Fruit - PARADISE, INC.; *pg.* 888, *pg.* 458
DIXIE CARBIDE - Sold Under Regal Cutting Tools & National - REGAL BELOIT CORPORATION; *pg.* 106, *pg.* 1854
DIXIE CRYSTALS - Sugar & Sweetener Product - IMPERIAL SUGAR COMPANY; *pg.* 864, *pg.* 1746
DIXIE DYNA-DRILLS - Solid Carbide Drills - REGAL BELOIT CORPORATION; *pg.* 106, *pg.* 1854
DIXIE DYNA-MILLS - Square End Ball End Mills - REGAL BELOIT CORPORATION; *pg.* 106, *pg.* 1854
DIXIE DYNA-REAMERS - Solid Carbide Reamers - REGAL BELOIT CORPORATION; *pg.* 106, *pg.* 1854
DIXIE STAMPEDE - Entertainment Product - HERSCHEND FAMILY ENTERTAINMENT CORP.; *pg.* 552, *pg.* 973
DIXIEWARE - Containers - GEORGIA-PACIFIC LLC; *pg.* 1458, *pg.* 507
DIXON - Writing Instruments - DIXON TICONDEROGA COMPANY; *pg.* 388, *pg.* 430
DIXX BLU - Golf Product - TAYLORMADE-ADIDAS GOLF; *pg.* 1847, *pg.* 60
DIZZY - Pillow - AMERICAN LEATHER LP; *pg.* 912, *pg.* 1673
DJD II - External Fixation System - STRYKER CORPORATION; *pg.* 1598, *pg.* 894
DJIA - Business News & Information Services - DOW JONES & COMPANY, INC.; *pg.* 1637, *pg.* 1225
DJK RESIDENTIAL - Relocation & Management Services - SIRVA, INC.; *pg.* 1923, *pg.* 669
DK-50 - Photographic Developers - EASTMAN KODAK COMPANY; *pg.* 1408, *pg.* 1333
DK-50R - Photographic Developers - EASTMAN KODAK COMPANY; *pg.* 1408, *pg.* 1333
DKNY - Designer Fashions - THE DONNA KARAN COMPANY LLC; *pg.* 23, *pg.* 1225
DL-50 - Electronic Components - MOLEX INCORPORATED; *pg.* 655, *pg.* 628
DL SERIES GATE VALVES & DLH ACTUATORS - Gate Valves - DRIL-QUIP, INC.; *pg.* 1330, *pg.* 1704
DL.1 - Lighting - HIGH END SYSTEMS, INC.; *pg.* 1299, *pg.* 1663
DLP - Signage - ANC SPORTS ENTERPRISES, LLC; *pg.* 1825, *pg.* 1325
DLP - Subsidiary - MEDTRONIC, INC.; *pg.* 1564, *pg.* 939
DLP - Digital Light Processing Optical Semiconductor - TEXAS INSTRUMENTS INCORPORATED; *pg.* 679, *pg.* 1688
DLP CINEMA - Digital Image Controller - TEXAS INSTRUMENTS INCORPORATED; *pg.* 679, *pg.* 1688
DLP COMPOSER - Software - TEXAS INSTRUMENTS INCORPORATED; *pg.* 679, *pg.* 1688
DLRO - Digital Low Resistance Ohmmeters - MEGGER INC.; *pg.* 1422, *pg.* 1557
DLS - Absorbent Pads for Food Packaging - SEALED AIR CORPORATION; *pg.* 1468, *pg.* 1058
DLS-2 - Lighting Systems - REVOLUTION LIGHTING TECHNOLOGIES, INC.; *pg.* 1304, *pg.* 377
DLT - Digital Linear Tape - QUANTUM CORPORATION; *pg.* 458, *pg.* 250
DLT VS - Tape Drives - QUANTUM CORPORATION; *pg.* 458, *pg.* 250
DLTICE - Archival Functionality - QUANTUM CORPORATION; *pg.* 458, *pg.* 250
DLTSAGE - Diagnostic Technology - QUANTUM CORPORATION; *pg.* 458, *pg.* 250
DLTTAPE - 80 Gig Backup Cartridges for Servers - IMATION CORP.; *pg.* 413, *pg.* 952
DLTTAPE - Data Storage Products - QUANTUM CORPORATION; *pg.* 458, *pg.* 250
DLW - Resilient Flooring Products - ARMSTRONG WORLD INDUSTRIES, INC.; *pg.* 914, *pg.* 1545
DM 1100 - Digital Mailing System - PITNEY BOWES INC.; *pg.* 454, *pg.* 376
DM 200 - Digital Mailing System - PITNEY BOWES INC.; *pg.* 454, *pg.* 376
DM 300 - Digital Mailing System - PITNEY BOWES INC.; *pg.* 454, *pg.* 376
DM 400 - Digital Mailing System - PITNEY BOWES INC.; *pg.* 454, *pg.* 376
DM 525 - Digital Mailing System - PITNEY BOWES INC.; *pg.* 454, *pg.* 376
DM 575 - Digital Mailing System - PITNEY BOWES INC.; *pg.* 454, *pg.* 376
DM 875 - Digital Mailing System - PITNEY BOWES INC.; *pg.* 454, *pg.* 376
DM 925 - Digital Mailing System - PITNEY BOWES INC.; *pg.* 454, *pg.* 376
DM-BODIPY - Molecular Probe Product - THERMO FISHER SCIENTIFIC INC.; *pg.* 1602, *pg.* 61
DM CHOICE - Flavorings - DAVID MICHAEL & CO. INC.; *pg.* 852, *pg.* 1563
D.M. FERRY'S - Garden Seeds - FERRY-MORSE SEED COMPANY; *pg.* 1795, *pg.* 728
DM INFINITY SERIES - Digital Mailing System - PITNEY BOWES INC.; *pg.* 454, *pg.* 376
DMAIL - Mailer - PITNEY BOWES INC.; *pg.* 454, *pg.* 376
DMAMP-80 - Amino Alcohol - THE DOW CHEMICAL COMPANY; *pg.* 1157, *pg.* 898
D'MAND - Circulators - TACO INCORPORATED; *pg.* 1077, *pg.* 1601
DMC PLUS - Logistics Software - ASPEN TECHNOLOGY, INC.; *pg.* 354, *pg.* 804
DMET - Array - AFFYMETRIX, INC.; *pg.* 1487, *pg.* 263
DMI - Agricultural Equipment - CNH AMERICA LLC; *pg.* 702, *pg.* 560
DMI - Institute - ENVIRONMENTAL TECTONICS CORPORATION; *pg.* 1411, *pg.* 1587
DMI OFFICE FURNITURE - Furniture - DMI FURNITURE, INC.; *pg.* 923, *pg.* 733
DMS - Software System - MENTOR GRAPHICS CORPORATION; *pg.* 432, *pg.* 1510
DMS-59 - Monitor System Interface - MOLEX INCORPORATED; *pg.* 655, *pg.* 628
DMS DECISION - Software - RUDOLPH TECHNOLOGIES, INC.; *pg.* 669, *pg.* 918
DMS XCHANGE - Software System - MENTOR GRAPHICS CORPORATION; *pg.* 432, *pg.* 1510
DMSVISION - Software - RUDOLPH TECHNOLOGIES, INC.; *pg.* 669, *pg.* 918
DMWD - Retrievable, Directional Measurement While Drilling - BAKER HUGHES INTEQ; *pg.* 1316, *pg.* 1700
DMX - Footwear Cushioning Technology - REEBOK INTERNATIONAL LTD.; *pg.* 1817, *pg.* 811
DMX REFLEX - Running Shoes - REEBOK INTERNATIONAL LTD.; *pg.* 1817, *pg.* 811
DNA-BIND - Glass & Ceramic Material - CORNING INCORPORATED; *pg.* 1122, *pg.* 1154
DNA ENGINE - Software - BIO-RAD LABORATORIES, INC.; *pg.* 1504, *pg.* 101
DNA ENGINE DYAD - Software - BIO-RAD LABORATORIES, INC.; *pg.* 1504, *pg.* 101
DNA ENGINE OPTICON - Software - BIO-RAD LABORATORIES, INC.; *pg.* 1504, *pg.* 101
DNA ENGINE TETRAD - Software - BIO-RAD LABORATORIES, INC.; *pg.* 1504, *pg.* 101
DNA INTEGRITY ASSAY - Stool DNA Test - EXACT SCIENCES CORPORATION; *pg.* 1529, *pg.* 1865
DNA MASS - Molecular Biology Product - THERMO FISHER SCIENTIFIC INC.; *pg.* 1602, *pg.* 61
DNA PREP - Workstation & DNA Unit - BECKMAN COULTER, INC.; *pg.* 1402, *pg.* 48
DNA ULTRACUSTOM - Non-medicated Skincare - GENELINK, INC.; *pg.* 1533, *pg.* 438
DNACODE - Software - BIO-RAD LABORATORIES, INC.; *pg.* 1504, *pg.* 101
DNAWITHPAP - Molecular Diagnostic Test - QIAGEN GAITHERSBURG INC.; *pg.* 1587, *pg.* 771
DNAZ.NET - Radio & Multimedia Service - BRS MEDIA INC.; *pg.* 1233, *pg.* 214
DNAZOL - Molecular Biology Product - THERMO FISHER SCIENTIFIC INC.; *pg.* 1602, *pg.* 61
D'NEALIAN - Chart Tablets & Pads - PACON CORPORATION; *pg.* 1466, *pg.* 1852
DNS@DOT - Radio & Multimedia Service - BRS MEDIA INC.; *pg.* 1233, *pg.* 214
DNT - High Speed Washer/Thickener - KADANT BLACK CLAWSON INC.; *pg.* 1352, *pg.* 1460
DO-IT-ALL - Wiring Devices - SWIVELIER CO., INC.; *pg.* 1307, *pg.* 1142
DO IT CENTER - Hardware - DO IT BEST CORP.; *pg.* 1045, *pg.* 680
DO IT ONCE. DO IT RIGHT. - Slogan - TACO INCORPORATED; *pg.* 1077, *pg.* 1601
DO IT YOURSELF - Game - FORTUNET, INC.; *pg.* 953, *pg.* 1024
DO-IT-YOURSELF - Tag Line - OLD WORLD INDUSTRIES, INC.; *pg.* 1175, *pg.* 641
DO IT YOURSELF NETWORK - Cable Network - THE E.W. SCRIPPS COMPANY; *pg.* 1639, *pg.* 1412
DO SOMETHING AMAZING - Slogan - AKZO NOBEL DECORATIVE PAINTS, USA; *pg.* 1439, *pg.* 1474
DO THE RIGHT THING.DO WHATEVER IT TAKES.HAVE FUN - Tagline - JACK HENRY & ASSOCIATES, INC.; *pg.* 422, *pg.* 988
DO WHAT YOU DO BETTER - Slogan - STEELCASE INC.; *pg.* 475, *pg.* 889
DOBBS - Car Dealerships - AUTONATION, INC.; *pg.* 165, *pg.* 423
DOBBY - Shirt - SIMMS FISHING PRODUCTS CORP.; *pg.* 1845, *pg.* 1008
DOBEL TEQUILA - Spirits - PROXIMO SPIRITS, INC.; *pg.* 1969, *pg.* 1076
DOBER - Industrial Chemicals - DOBER CHEMICAL CORP.; *pg.* 1156, *pg.* 671

DOBIE - Cleaning Pad - 3M COMPANY; *pg.* 1142, *pg.* 956
DOBRA - Vodka - SAZERAC COMPANY, INC.; *pg.* 1969, *pg.* 745
DOBRIY - Beverages - THE COCA-COLA COMPANY; *pg.* 240, *pg.* 493
DOBRO - Musical Instrument - GIBSON GUITAR CORP.; *pg.* 550, *pg.* 1650
DOBUTREX - Pharmaceutical Product - ELI LILLY AND COMPANY; *pg.* 1527, *pg.* 684
DOC - Guide Wire Extension - ABBOTT LABORATORIES; *pg.* 1484, *pg.* 551
D.O.C. - Dental Product - MAJESTIC DRUG COMPANY, INC.; *pg.* 516, *pg.* 1343
DOC-IT LS - Image Analysis Software - UVP, INC.; *pg.* 1434, *pg.* 298
DOC-IT LS 1D - Software - UVP, INC.; *pg.* 1434, *pg.* 298
DOC OTIS' - Lemon-Flavored Malt Beverage - ANHEUSER-BUSCH COMPANIES, LLC; *pg.* 237, *pg.* 991
DOC1 SUITE - Direct Marketing & Campaign Management - PITNEY BOWES INC.; *pg.* 454, *pg.* 376
DOCALERT - Medical News Alerts - EPOCRATES, INC.; *pg.* 1529, *pg.* 254
DOCCAM - Software - CLEARONE COMMUNICATIONS, INC.; *pg.* 629, *pg.* 1756
DOCCAM PRO - Audio Conferencing System - CLEARONE COMMUNICATIONS, INC.; *pg.* 629, *pg.* 1756
DOCFIND - Physician Search Tool - AETNA INC.; *pg.* 1187, *pg.* 351
DOCHARBOR - Software System - ANACOMP, INC.; *pg.* 350, *pg.* 1777
DOCKERS - Apparel - LEVI STRAUSS & CO.; *pg.* 43, *pg.* 220
DOCKLITE - Lighting Fixture - PHOENIX PRODUCTS COMPANY; *pg.* 1304, *pg.* 1879
DOCKMASTER - Bulk Delivery Trailer or Body - HACKNEY INTERNATIONAL; *pg.* 178, *pg.* 1392
DOCKSIDE - Bath Product - KOHLER CO.; *pg.* 91, *pg.* 1862
DOCMATCHER - Software - SRA INTERNATIONAL, INC.; *pg.* 473, *pg.* 1780
DOCMEMO - Medical News Alerts - EPOCRATES, INC.; *pg.* 1529, *pg.* 254
DOCSIS - Cable - BROADCOM CORPORATION; *pg.* 364, *pg.* 108
DOCSIS 1.1 - Cable - BROADCOM CORPORATION; *pg.* 364, *pg.* 108
DOCSIS 2.0 - Cable - BROADCOM CORPORATION; *pg.* 364, *pg.* 108
DOCSTAR - Software - AUTHENTIDATE HOLDING CORP.; *pg.* 356, *pg.* 1044
DOCSTREAM - Printing Products - ELECTRONICS FOR IMAGING, INC.; *pg.* 390, *pg.* 88
DOCTOR DESIGN - Software - WIND RIVER SYSTEMS, INC.; *pg.* 493, *pg.* 38
DOCTOR GUN - Fluid Handling System - GRACO, INC.; *pg.* 1342, *pg.* 935
DOCTOR STAIN - Stain Remover - NILODOR, INC.; *pg.* 332, *pg.* 1406
THE DOCTOR'S BRUSHPICK - Toothpick - PRESTIGE BRANDS HOLDINGS, INC.; *pg.* 520, *pg.* 1345
DOCTOR'S HOUSE CALL - Snacks Bag - 1-800-FLOWERS.COM, INC.; *pg.* 1758, *pg.* 1151
THE DOCTOR'S NITE GUARD - Mouth Guard - PRESTIGE BRANDS HOLDINGS, INC.; *pg.* 520, *pg.* 1345
DOCTOR'S VALUVISION - Eye Care Centers - VISIONWORKS OF AMERICA, INC.; *pg.* 1436, *pg.* 1744
DOCTOR'S VISIONWORKS - Eye Care Centers - VISIONWORKS OF AMERICA, INC.; *pg.* 1436, *pg.* 1744
DOCTUS - Software - MITEK SYSTEMS, INC.; *pg.* 440, *pg.* 204
DOCU-COVER - Paper & Nonwoven Material - FIBERMARK INC.; *pg.* 1457, *pg.* 1764
DOCUCARD - Manual - XEROX CORPORATION; *pg.* 494, *pg.* 365
DOCUCREASE - Creaser - STANDARD DUPLICATING MACHINES CORPORATION; *pg.* 473, *pg.* 783
DOCUFOLD - Folder - STANDARD DUPLICATING MACHINES CORPORATION; *pg.* 473, *pg.* 783
DOCUGLOSSCARD - ID Card - XEROX CORPORATION; *pg.* 494, *pg.* 365
DOCUIMAGE - Printer - XEROX CORPORATION; *pg.* 494, *pg.* 365
DOCUJOB - Software - XEROX CORPORATION; *pg.* 494, *pg.* 365
DOCULAN - Software - XEROX CORPORATION; *pg.* 494, *pg.* 365
DOCULIFE - Software - XEROX CORPORATION; *pg.* 494, *pg.* 365
DOCULINK - Software - XEROX CORPORATION; *pg.* 494, *pg.* 365
DOCULOCK - Manual - XEROX CORPORATION; *pg.* 494, *pg.* 365
DOCUMAGIX - Communication Product - J2 GLOBAL COMMUNICATIONS, INC.; *pg.* 1260, *pg.* 133
DOCUMATCH - Integrated Mail System - PITNEY BOWES INC.; *pg.* 454, *pg.* 376
DOCUMATE - Scanner - XEROX CORPORATION; *pg.* 494, *pg.* 365
DOCUMENT ADVISOR OFFICE - Manual - XEROX CORPORATION; *pg.* 494, *pg.* 365
DOCUMENT APPLIANCE - Copier - XEROX CORPORATION; *pg.* 494, *pg.* 365
DOCUMENT CENTER - Software - ADOBE SYSTEMS INCORPORATED; *pg.* 342, *pg.* 235
DOCUMENT CENTRE IMAGE RETRIEVER - Manual - XEROX CORPORATION; *pg.* 494, *pg.* 365
DOCUMENT CHANNEL - Manual - XEROX CORPORATION; *pg.* 494, *pg.* 365
THE DOCUMENT COMPANY - Manual - XEROX CORPORATION; *pg.* 494, *pg.* 365
DOCUMENT EFFICIENCY AT WORK - Slogan - RICOH AMERICA; *pg.* 461, *pg.* 1550
THE DOCUMENT EXPERTS - Tagline - MICROSYSTEMS; *pg.* 440, *pg.* 608
DOCUMENT HOME CENTRE - Manual - XEROX CORPORATION; *pg.* 494, *pg.* 365
DOCUMENT INTENSIVE BUSINESS PROCESSES - Manual - XEROX CORPORATION; *pg.* 494, *pg.* 365
DOCUMENT PATHWAYS - Proprietary System - R.R. DONNELLEY & SONS COMPANY; *pg.* 1682, *pg.* 589
DOCUMENT SCIENCES - Software - EMC CORPORATION; *pg.* 391, *pg.* 825
DOCUMENT SOULS - Printer - XEROX CORPORATION; *pg.* 494, *pg.* 365
THE DOCUMENT SOURCE - Manual - XEROX CORPORATION; *pg.* 494, *pg.* 365
DOCUMENT WORKCENTRE - Software - XEROX CORPORATION; *pg.* 494, *pg.* 365
DOCUMENTATION STATION - Software System - MENTOR GRAPHICS CORPORATION; *pg.* 432, *pg.* 1510
DOCUMENTDIRECTOR - Software - R.R. DONNELLEY & SONS COMPANY; *pg.* 1682, *pg.* 589
DOCUMENTING DREAMS - Manual - XEROX CORPORATION; *pg.* 494, *pg.* 365
DOCUMENTING DREAMS WRITING WEEK - Manual - XEROX CORPORATION; *pg.* 494, *pg.* 365
DOCUMENTMALL - Video - RICOH AMERICAS CORPORATION; *pg.* 461, *pg.* 1131
DOCUMENTS DIRECT - Manual - XEROX CORPORATION; *pg.* 494, *pg.* 365
DOCUMENTS ON DEMAND - Software - XEROX CORPORATION; *pg.* 494, *pg.* 365
DOCUMENTS TO GO TOTAL OFFICE - Software - DATAVIZ, INC.; *pg.* 383, *pg.* 356
DOCUMENTSERVER PRO - Software - RICOH AMERICAS CORPORATION; *pg.* 461, *pg.* 1131
DOCUMENTUM - Software - EMC CORPORATION; *pg.* 391, *pg.* 825
DOCUPAC - Printer - XEROX CORPORATION; *pg.* 494, *pg.* 365
DOCUPATH - Manual - XEROX CORPORATION; *pg.* 494, *pg.* 365
DOCUPM - Software - XEROX CORPORATION; *pg.* 494, *pg.* 365
DOCUPRINT 6135 - Printer - XEROX CORPORATION; *pg.* 494, *pg.* 365
DOCUPRINT NC60 - Printer - XEROX CORPORATION; *pg.* 494, *pg.* 365
DOCUPRINT P12 - Printer - XEROX CORPORATION; *pg.* 494, *pg.* 365
DOCUPRINT P8 - Printer - XEROX CORPORATION; *pg.* 494, *pg.* 365
DOCUPRINTSERVER - Manual - XEROX CORPORATION; *pg.* 494, *pg.* 365
DOCURIGHT - Software Product - XEROX CORPORATION; *pg.* 494, *pg.* 365
DOCUSHARE - Software - XEROX CORPORATION; *pg.* 494, *pg.* 365
DOCUSOFT S - Pharmaceutical Product - G&W LABORATORIES INC.; *pg.* 1532, *pg.* 1123
DOCUSP - Software - XEROX CORPORATION; *pg.* 494, *pg.* 365
DOCUSTACK - Management Solution - HTC GLOBAL SERVICES INC.; *pg.* 409, *pg.* 911
DOCUSTAMP - Manual - XEROX CORPORATION; *pg.* 494, *pg.* 365
DOCUSTORE - Software - HEALTHPORT, INC.; *pg.* 403, *pg.* 484
DOCUTECH - Office Product - XEROX CORPORATION; *pg.* 494, *pg.* 365
DOCUTECH NETWORK PUBLISHER - Manual - XEROX CORPORATION; *pg.* 494, *pg.* 365
DOCVIEW - Supercomputing System - CRAY INC.; *pg.* 380, *pg.* 1834
DOCWISE - Software - SCAN-OPTICS, LLC; *pg.* 467, *pg.* 354
DOCXAMINE - Document Drafting Software - MICROSYSTEMS; *pg.* 440, *pg.* 608
DOCXCHANGE - Document Conversion Software - MICROSYSTEMS; *pg.* 440, *pg.* 608
DOCXPRESS - Paper - XEROX CORPORATION; *pg.* 494, *pg.* 365
DOCXTOOLS - Document Drafting Software - MICROSYSTEMS; *pg.* 440, *pg.* 608
DOD - Professional Electronics - HARMAN INTERNATIONAL INDUSTRIES, INCORPORATED; *pg.* 641, *pg.* 374
DODECA - Software - BIO-RAD LABORATORIES, INC.; *pg.* 1504, *pg.* 101
DODGE - Automobiles - FCA US LLC; *pg.* 170, *pg.* 868
DODGE AVENGER - Automobile - FCA US LLC; *pg.* 170, *pg.* 868
DODGE CALIBER SRT4 - Automobile - FCA US LLC; *pg.* 170, *pg.* 868
DODGE CARAVAN - Minivan - FCA US LLC; *pg.* 170, *pg.* 868
DODGE CHALLENGER - Automobile - FCA US LLC; *pg.* 170, *pg.* 868
DODGE CHARGER - Automobile - FCA US LLC; *pg.* 170, *pg.* 868
DODGE DAKOTA - Pickup Truck - FCA US LLC; *pg.* 170, *pg.* 868
DODGE DURANGO - Sport Utility - FCA US LLC; *pg.* 170, *pg.* 868
DODGE GRAND CARAVAN - Truck & Minivan - FCA US LLC; *pg.* 170, *pg.* 868
DODGE INTREPID - Car - FCA US LLC; *pg.* 170, *pg.* 868
DODGE JOURNEY - Crossover Vehicle - FCA US LLC; *pg.* 170, *pg.* 868
DODGE NEON - Car - FCA US LLC; *pg.* 170, *pg.* 868
DODGE RAM - Pickup Truck - FCA US LLC; *pg.* 170, *pg.* 868
DODGE RAM WAGON & VAN - Truck - FCA US LLC; *pg.* 170, *pg.* 868
DODGE STRATUS - Car - FCA US LLC; *pg.* 170, *pg.* 868
DODGE VIPER - High-Performance Automobile - FCA US LLC; *pg.* 170, *pg.* 868
DODGER - Furniture - ASHLEY FURNITURE INDUSTRIES, INC.; *pg.* 914, *pg.* 1852
DODOT - Personal & Household Product - THE PROCTER & GAMBLE COMPANY; *pg.* 1129, *pg.* 1418
DOG - Drilling Product - SMITH INTERNATIONAL, INC.; *pg.* 1377, *pg.* 1715
DOG CHOW - Dog Food - NESTLE PURINA PETCARE COMPANY; *pg.* 1479, *pg.* 1000
DOG DICE - Game - GAMEWRIGHT; *pg.* 953, *pg.* 836
DOG FANCY - Magazine - I-5 PUBLISHING LLC; *pg.* 1651, *pg.* 133
DOG LEG POLO - Apparels - UNDER ARMOUR, INC.; *pg.* 49, *pg.* 759
DOG MAGIC - Power-and Free Trolley Systems - DAIFUKU WEBB; *pg.* 1327, *pg.* 885
DOGADAN - Beverages - THE COCA-COLA COMPANY; *pg.* 240, *pg.* 493
DOGEROO - Hot Dog Machine - GOLD MEDAL PRODUCTS CO.; *pg.* 55, *pg.* 1414
D.O.G.G. - Outdoor Equipment Cleaner & Protector - GOLD EAGLE COMPANY; *pg.* 206, *pg.* 575
DOGGIE DAY CAMP - Pet Supplies - PETSMART, INC.; *pg.* 1481, *pg.* 18
DOGGIE DOUGH DOUBLER - Lottery Game - MINNESOTA STATE LOTTERY; *pg.* 999, *pg.* 956
DOGHOUSE - Apparel - VANS, INC.; *pg.* 1821, *pg.* 76
DOGNY - Public Art Initiative - AMERICAN KENNEL CLUB, INC.; *pg.* 129, *pg.* 1193
DOGPILE - Internet Search Engine - BLUCORA; *pg.* 1232, *pg.* 1813
DOGPILE.COM - Website - BLUCORA; *pg.* 1232, *pg.* 1813

First page reference indicates Business Class Edition
Second page reference indicates Geographic Edition

DOGS USA - Magazine - I-5 PUBLISHING LLC; pg. 1651, pg. 133
DOGSTERS - Pet Product - J&J SNACK FOODS CORPORATION; pg. 865, pg. 1107
DOGWATCH - Newsletter - BELVOIR MEDIA GROUP, LLC; pg. 1620, pg. 360
DOGWOOD - Window Treatment - HERITAGE LACE INC.; pg. 694, pg. 711
DOGWOOD - Golf Shoes - JOHNSTON & MURPHY CO.; pg. 1810, pg. 1651
DOH DOH'S ISLAND BEACH BUGGY - Toy & Game - HASBRO, INC.; pg. 954, pg. 1603
DOHVILLE - Toy & Game - HASBRO, INC.; pg. 954, pg. 1603
DOING BUSINESS WITH THE PRINCIPAL - Management Services - PRINCIPAL FINANCIAL GROUP, INC.; pg. 796, pg. 706
DOING THE RIGHT THING FOR EYE CARE - Tag Line - ALIMERA SCIENCES, INC.; pg. 1490, pg. 482
DOING THE RIGHT THING IS SMART BUSINESS. - Slogan - PROTECTIVE LIFE CORPORATION; pg. 1215, pg. 4
DOING THE RIGHT THING IS SMART BUSINESS - Slogan - PROTECTIVE LIFE INSURANCE COMPANY; pg. 1215, pg. 4
DOING WHAT'S RIGHT! - Tag Line - TYSON FOODS, INC.; pg. 902, pg. 35
DOK-COMMANDER - Control System - RITE-HITE HOLDING CORPORATION; pg. 1372, pg. 1880
DOK-DOR - Roll-Up Door - RITE-HITE HOLDING CORPORATION; pg. 1372, pg. 1880
DOK-LOK - Vehicle Restraints - RITE-HITE HOLDING CORPORATION; pg. 1372, pg. 1880
DOK-LOKS - Vehicle Restraint - RITE-HITE HOLDING CORPORATION; pg. 1372, pg. 1880
DOLBY - Software - NVIDIA CORPORATION; pg. 447, pg. 268
DOLCE - Fabric - NEMSCHOFF, INC.; pg. 936, pg. 1890
DOLCE & GABBANA - Men's & Women's Apparel - DOLCE & GABBANA USA, INC.; pg. 23, pg. 1225
DOLCE VITA - Bath Product - KOHLER CO.; pg. 91, pg. 1862
DOLCO - Egg Carton - TEKNI-PLEX, INC.; pg. 1470, pg. 1122
DOLE - Fresh & Canned Produce, Citrus, Fruit & Flowers - DOLE FOOD COMPANY, INC.; pg. 853, pg. 306
DOLE - Food Product - ELLENBEE-LEGGETT COMPANY INC.; pg. 854, pg. 1452
DOLE - Food Product - NESTLE USA, INC.; pg. 883, pg. 96
DOLFIN SWIM WEAR - Swimwear, Warm-Ups & Track Suits - DOLFIN INTERNATIONAL CORPORATION; pg. 23, pg. 1553
DOLL HOSPITAL - Educational Materials - SCHOLASTIC INC.; pg. 1683, pg. 1288
DOLLAR - Guest Chairs - BERNHARDT DESIGN; pg. 918, pg. 1381
DOLLAR GENERAL STORES - Discount Retail Stores - DOLLAR GENERAL CORPORATION; pg. 1767, pg. 1635
DOLLARS & SCENTS - Cash Rebate Program - FTD GROUP, INC.; pg. 1795, pg. 608
DOLLE - Footwear - STEVEN MADDEN, LTD.; pg. 1819, pg. 1176
DOLLHOUSE MINIATURES - Magazine - KALMBACH PUBLISHING CO.; pg. 1656, pg. 1898
DOLLY - Lamp - ASHLEY FURNITURE INDUSTRIES, INC.; pg. 914, pg. 1852
DOLLY DIAPERS - Dolls - THE GOLDBERGER COMPANY, LLC; pg. 954, pg. 1235
DOLMIO - Food Products - MARS, INCORPORATED; pg. 1858, pg. 1792
DOLORES - Lamp - ASHLEY FURNITURE INDUSTRIES, INC.; pg. 914, pg. 1852
DOLORMIN - Healthcare Product - JOHNSON & JOHNSON; pg. 1549, pg. 1091
DOLPHIN - Pulse Oximetry - CONMED CORPORATION; pg. 1517, pg. 1347
DOLPHIN - Fabric - NEMSCHOFF, INC.; pg. 936, pg. 1890
DOLPHIN - Packaging Materials - SEALED AIR CORPORATION; pg. 1468, pg. 1058
DOLPHIN - Plumbing Product - SLOAN VALVE COMPANY; pg. 1062, pg. 613
DOLPHIN - Fabric - UNIROYAL ENGINEERED PRODUCTS; pg. 699, pg. 467
DOLPHIN - Extraction System - VON SCHRADER COMPANY; pg. 62, pg. 1890
DOLPHIN BAY - Game - WMS INDUSTRIES INC.; pg. 593, pg. 666
DOLPHIN PAD - Foam Laminate Wrap - SEALED AIR CORPORATION; pg. 1468, pg. 1058
DOLPHINS - Protective Eyewear - SELLSTROM MANUFACTURING CO.; pg. 1428, pg. 659
DOM PERIGNON - Champagne - MOET HENNESSY; pg. 1966, pg. 1260
DOM SUPER-SAFE - Stick Game - SCHOOL-TECH, INC.; pg. 1844, pg. 866
DOMAIN - Fabric - NEMSCHOFF, INC.; pg. 936, pg. 1890
DOMAIN CHANDON - Champagne - DOMAINE CHANDON, INC.; pg. 1962, pg. 308
DOMAIN MIGRATION WIZARD - Software - DELL SOFTWARE; pg. 385, pg. 40
DOMAIN STATISTICS WIZARD - Software - DELL SOFTWARE; pg. 385, pg. 40
DOMAINE CHANDON - Wine - MOET HENNESSY; pg. 1966, pg. 1260
DOMAINE D'OR - Wine - ANDREW PELLER LIMITED; pg. 1956, pg. 1920
DOMAINS BY PROXY - Software - GO DADDY INC.; pg. 1249, pg. 21
DOMAMATE - Thermal Insulation - THE DOW CHEMICAL COMPANY; pg. 1157, pg. 898
DOMANIA - Real Estate Broker - IAC/INTERACTIVECORP; pg. 292, pg. 1242
DOME - Lid for Home Canning Jars - JARDEN CORPORATION; pg. 1885, pg. 412
DOME - Nozzle - NORDSON CORPORATION; pg. 1365, pg. 1480
DOME CXTRA QX EDITION - Software System - PLANAR SYSTEMS, INC.; pg. 455, pg. 1495
DOME DASHBOARD - Software System - PLANAR SYSTEMS, INC.; pg. 455, pg. 1495
DOME-LITES - Commercial & Display Lighting - SWIVELIER CO., INC.; pg. 1307, pg. 1142
DOME-TOP - Cable Tie - PANDUIT CORP.; pg. 661, pg. 663
DOME-TRIM - Designed toothbrush - SUNSTAR AMERICAS INC.; pg. 1599, pg. 591
DOMEA - Software - OPENTEXT CORPORATION; pg. 450, pg. 1948
DOMEBORO - Medicine - BAYER HEALTHCARE CONSUMER CARE DIVISION; pg. 1500, pg. 1087
DOMESTIC PUMP - Condensate Handling Equipment, Boiler Feed Units & Centrifugal Pumps - XYLEM INC.; pg. 1078, pg. 1339
DOMESTICATIONS - Specialty Home Textiles Catalog - HANOVER DIRECT, INC.; pg. 1772, pg. 1130
DOMINATOR - Aluminum Boat - ALUMACRAFT BOAT COMPANY; pg. 1705, pg. 964
DOMINATOR - Saw Blade - SIMONDS INTERNATIONAL CORPORATION; pg. 1376, pg. 819
DOMINICALL - Telephone Service - IDT CORPORATION; pg. 643, pg. 1096
DOMINICK'S - Bakery Products - ALPHA BAKING COMPANY; pg. 836, pg. 564
DOMINION - Table - BLATT BOWLING & BILLIARD CORP.; pg. 1827, pg. 1203
DOMINION - Bowling Equipment - BRUNSWICK BOWLING & BILLIARDS CORP.; pg. 1828, pg. 622
DOMINION - Database Solutions - ONVIA, INC.; pg. 1272, pg. 1838
DOMINION LIFE - Excess Interest Whole Life Product - GENWORTH LIFE AND ANNUITY INSURANCE COMPANY; pg. 1201, pg. 1802
DOMINIQUE - Bedcovering - ETHAN ALLEN INTERIORS INC.; pg. 924, pg. 343
DOMINIQUE - Furniture - HOOKER FURNITURE CORPORATION; pg. 928, pg. 1788
DOMINIQUE - Lighting Product - QUOIZEL INC.; pg. 1304, pg. 1616
DOMINO - Magazine - CONDE NAST PUBLICATIONS, INC.; pg. 1629, pg. 1217
DOMINO - Fabric - NEMSCHOFF, INC.; pg. 936, pg. 1890
DOMINO - Surface Material - STEELCASE INC.; pg. 475, pg. 889
DOMINO DINERO - Video Game - INTERNATIONAL GAME TECHNOLOGY; pg. 957, pg. 1024
DOMINOES - Fabric - NEMSCHOFF, INC.; pg. 936, pg. 1890
DOMINO'S AMERICAN LEGENDS - Premium Products Line - DOMINO'S PIZZA, INC.; pg. 1726, pg. 865
DOMINO'S PIZZA - Pizza - DOMINO'S PIZZA, INC.; pg. 1726, pg. 865
DOMITOR - Veterinary Sedative - PFIZER INC.; pg. 1581, pg. 1278
DOMIX - Water Mixing Meters - BELSHAW ADAMATIC BAKERY GROUP; pg. 1317, pg. 1813
DOMKE - Filter & Lens - THE TIFFEN COMPANY LLC; pg. 1432, pg. 1165
DOMORE - Office Seating - MITY ENTERPRISES, INC.; pg. 935, pg. 1753
DOMTAR COLORS - Paper - DOMTAR CORPORATION; pg. 1456, pg. 1954
DOMTAR CORNWALL - Paper - DOMTAR CORPORATION; pg. 1456, pg. 1954
DON & CHARLIE'S - Casual Dining Restaurant - LETTUCE ENTERTAIN YOU ENTERPRISES, INC.; pg. 1735, pg. 580
DON CAMILO - Handmade Cigar - ALTADIS USA, INC.; pg. 1893, pg. 423
DON D CIDE - Liquid Disinfecting Cleaner - EDWARD DON & COMPANY; pg. 54, pg. 672
DON DE DIEU - Beer - SLEEMAN UNIBROUE QUEBEC; pg. 265, pg. 1950
DON DIEGO - Premium Cigars - ALTADIS USA, INC.; pg. 1893, pg. 423
DON EDUARDO - Tequilas - BROWN-FORMAN CORPORATION; pg. 1958, pg. 732
DON JULIO - Tequila - DIAGEO NORTH AMERICA, INC.; pg. 1961, pg. 361
DON JULIO - Tortillas, Chips & Salsa - TYSON FOODS, INC.; pg. 902, pg. 35
DON MANUEL - Coffee Product - COFFEE HOLDING CO., INC.; pg. 849, pg. 1343
DON MARIO - Container Grown Plant - MONROVIA GROWERS; pg. 1797, pg. 44
DON MATEO - Premium Cigars - ALTADIS USA, INC.; pg. 1893, pg. 423
DON MELO CENTENARIO - Handmade Cigar - ALTADIS USA, INC.; pg. 1893, pg. 423
DON MIGUEL - Cigars - ALTADIS USA, INC.; pg. 1893, pg. 423
DON O MITE - Cleaning Product - EDWARD DON & COMPANY; pg. 54, pg. 672
DON PINK - Liquid Detergent - EDWARD DON & COMPANY; pg. 54, pg. 672
DONA MARIA - Mexican Food Products - HORMEL FOODS CORPORATION; pg. 863, pg. 915
DONACLONE - Air Cleaner - DONALDSON COMPANY, INC.; pg. 1329, pg. 917
DONALD DUCK - Cartoon Character - THE WALT DISNEY COMPANY; pg. 317, pg. 52
DONASONIC - Gas Turbine Intake Silencer - DONALDSON COMPANY, INC.; pg. 1329, pg. 917
DONATA - Lamp - ASHLEY FURNITURE INDUSTRIES, INC.; pg. 914, pg. 1852
DONATOS - Pizza - DONATOS PIZZERIA CORPORATION; pg. 1727, pg. 1439
DONETTES - Mini Doughnuts - HOSTESS BRANDS LLC; pg. 1856, pg. 984
DONIZETTI - Flatware - ONEIDA LTD; pg. 1129, pg. 1318
DONJOY - Orthopedic Product - DJO INCORPORATED; pg. 1524, pg. 302
DONJOY VISTA - Orthopedic Product - DJO INCORPORATED; pg. 1524, pg. 302
DONN - Suspension Systems - CGC INC.; pg. 75, pg. 1925
DONNA - Lamp - ASHLEY FURNITURE INDUSTRIES, INC.; pg. 914, pg. 1852
DONNA KARAN - Designer Fashions - THE DONNA KARAN COMPANY LLC; pg. 23, pg. 1225
DONNA KARAN - Beauty Product - THE ESTEE LAUDER COMPANIES INC.; pg. 508, pg. 1229
DONNA LAWRENCE - Shoes - SHOE CARNIVAL, INC.; pg. 1819, pg. 679
DONNELLY - Medical Stool - BLICKMAN HEALTH INDUSTRIES, INC.; pg. 1506, pg. 1051
DONNIELI - Bath & Plumbing Product - JACUZZI BRANDS CORPORATION; pg. 554, pg. 65
DONOVAN - Office Furniture - STEELCASE INC.; pg. 475, pg. 889
DON'T BE KOI WITH ME - Nail Care Product - OPI PRODUCTS INC.; pg. 518, pg. 167
DON'T BORROW TROUBLE - Financial Services - FEDERAL HOME LOAN MORTGAGE CORPORATION; pg. 751, pg. 1790
DON'T BREAK THE ICE - Toy & Game - HASBRO, INC.; pg. 954, pg. 1603
DON'T EAT PETE - Educational Materials - SCHOLASTIC INC.; pg. 1683, pg. 1288
DON.T JUST LIVE. SHINE. - Tagline - MARSHFIELD CLINIC;

pg. 1558, *pg.* 1869
DON'T LEAVE HOME WITHOUT IT - Slogan - AMERICAN EXPRESS COMPANY; *pg.* 712, *pg.* 1190
DON'T LEAVE HOME WITHOUT THEM - Card Services - AMERICAN EXPRESS COMPANY; *pg.* 712, *pg.* 1190
DON'T LEAVE HOMEPAGES WITHOUT IT - Card Services - AMERICAN EXPRESS COMPANY; *pg.* 712, *pg.* 1190
DON'T LET THE NAME FOOL YOU! - Slogan - RENT-A-WRECK OF AMERICA, INC.; *pg.* 1921, *pg.* 773
DON'T SOCRA-TEASE ME - Nail Care Product - OPI PRODUCTS INC.; *pg.* 518, *pg.* 167
DON'T SPILL THE BEANS - Toy & Game - HASBRO, INC.; *pg.* 954, *pg.* 1603
DON'T WIN YUKON DO IT - Nail Care Product - OPI PRODUCTS INC.; *pg.* 518, *pg.* 167
DONUT FAIRS - Donuts - ALFRED NICKLES BAKERY, INC.; *pg.* 836, *pg.* 1466
DONUT ROBOT - Commercial Donut Frying Equipment - BELSHAW ADAMATIC BAKERY GROUP; *pg.* 1317, *pg.* 1813
DOO-Z - Brush - THE WOOSTER BRUSH COMPANY; *pg.* 1450, *pg.* 1482
DOODLE PRO - Drawing Toy - FISHER-PRICE, INC.; *pg.* 953, *pg.* 1156
DOODLE SKETCH - Toy - THE OHIO ART COMPANY, INC.; *pg.* 965, *pg.* 1406
DOODLEBUG - Cleaning System - 3M COMPANY; *pg.* 1142, *pg.* 956
DOODLEBUG - Bicycle - TREK BICYCLE CORPORATION; *pg.* 1847, *pg.* 1896
DOOM - Video Game - ID SOFTWARE, INC.; *pg.* 956, *pg.* 1727
DOOM PATROL - Character - DC COMICS, INC.; *pg.* 1633, *pg.* 1221
THE DOOR CLUB - Home Security System - WINNER INTERNATIONAL, LLC; *pg.* 222, *pg.* 1586
DOOR-EASE - Lubricants - AMERICAN GREASE STICK CO.; *pg.* 971, *pg.* 902
DOORKEEPERS - Door Accessory - SOUTHCO, INC.; *pg.* 1063, *pg.* 1522
DOORMASTER - Header Mounted Garage Door Opener - WAYNE-DALTON CORP.; *pg.* 120, *pg.* 1465
DOORS OF A LIFETIME - Slogan - SIMPSON DOOR COMPANY; *pg.* 110, *pg.* 1823
DOPHILUS - Nutritional Supplement - NATURAL ORGANICS, INC.; *pg.* 1571, *pg.* 1181
DOPP - Case - BROWN & BIGELOW, INC.; *pg.* 1624, *pg.* 959
DOPP - Travel Kits & Business Cases - BUXTON ACQUISITION CO., LLC; *pg.* 2, *pg.* 845
DOPP KIT - Bag - OAKLEY, INC.; *pg.* 1840, *pg.* 86
DOPPLE BOCK - Beverage - SPRECHER BREWING COMPANY; *pg.* 265, *pg.* 1858
DOR-KOR - Transit Protection Product - GREIF INC.; *pg.* 1459, *pg.* 1447
DOR-O-MATIC - Door Hardware - INGERSOLL-RAND COMPANY; *pg.* 1349, *pg.* 1370
DORA AND FRIENDS - Dolls - FISHER-PRICE, INC.; *pg.* 953, *pg.* 1156
DORA THE EXPLORER - Dolls & Toys - FISHER-PRICE, INC.; *pg.* 953, *pg.* 1156
DORA THE EXPLORER - Toy & Game - HASBRO, INC.; *pg.* 954, *pg.* 1603
DORADO - Lighting Product - QUOIZEL INC.; *pg.* 1304, *pg.* 1616
DORAL - Lighting - LSI INDUSTRIES INC.; *pg.* 58, *pg.* 1416
DORBY - Women's Apparel - KELLWOOD COMPANY; *pg.* 28, *pg.* 975
DORCHESTER - Furniture - J. ROBERT SCOTT INC.; *pg.* 930, *pg.* 105
DORCY - Flash Light - DORCY INTERNATIONAL INC.; *pg.* 1046, *pg.* 1439
DOREEN - Footwear - PHOENIX FOOTWEAR GROUP, INC.; *pg.* 1815, *pg.* 60
DORIAN - Toilet Partition - METPAR CORP.; *pg.* 97, *pg.* 1350
DORIBAX - Abdominal Infection Medication - JOHNSON & JOHNSON; *pg.* 1549, *pg.* 1091
DORIS - Lamp - ASHLEY FURNITURE INDUSTRIES, INC.; *pg.* 914, *pg.* 1852
DORIS - Footwear - PHOENIX FOOTWEAR GROUP, INC.; *pg.* 1815, *pg.* 60
DORITOS - Tortilla Chips - FRITO-LAY NORTH AMERICA, INC.; *pg.* 1853, *pg.* 1730
DORITOS - Snack Food - PEPSICO, INC.; *pg.* 259, *pg.* 1327
DORITOS A LA TURCA - Snack - FRITO-LAY NORTH AMERICA, INC.; *pg.* 1853, *pg.* 1730
DORITOS COLLISIONS - Chips - FRITO-LAY NORTH AMERICA, INC.; *pg.* 1853, *pg.* 1730
DORITOS DIPPAS - Snack - FRITO-LAY NORTH AMERICA, INC.; *pg.* 1853, *pg.* 1730
DORITOS LOCOS - Tacos - TACO BELL CORP.; *pg.* 1752, *pg.* 117
DORITOS LOCOS TACO SUPREME - Tacos - TACO BELL CORP.; *pg.* 1752, *pg.* 117
DORITOS ROLLITOS - Snack - FRITO-LAY NORTH AMERICA, INC.; *pg.* 1853, *pg.* 1730
DORMAN - Fasteners - DORMAN PRODUCTS, INC.; *pg.* 204, *pg.* 1522
DORMANT - Home & Farm Product - PBI/GORDON CORPORATION; *pg.* 1176, *pg.* 985
DORNA - Beverages - THE COCA-COLA COMPANY; *pg.* 240, *pg.* 493
DORNE & MARGOLIN - Antennas & Electronic Reserve Equipment - METAL TEXTILES CORPORATION; *pg.* 654, *pg.* 1057
DORNEY PARK - Amusement Park - CEDAR FAIR, L.P.; *pg.* 537, *pg.* 1471
DORNEY PARK & WILDWATER KINGDOM - Amusement Park - CEDAR FAIR, L.P.; *pg.* 537, *pg.* 1471
DOROTHY'S KIDS SERIES - Custom Imprinted Packet Seeds for Advertising Specialty - THE PAGE SEED CO.; *pg.* 1798, *pg.* 1163
DORPAK - Rigid Paper Containers - SONOCO PRODUCTS COMPANY; *pg.* 1469, *pg.* 1619
D'ORSAY - Lamp - J. ROBERT SCOTT INC.; *pg.* 930, *pg.* 105
DORSET - Lamp - ASHLEY FURNITURE INDUSTRIES, INC.; *pg.* 914, *pg.* 1852
DORSET - Paper & Nonwoven Material - FIBERMARK INC.; *pg.* 1457, *pg.* 1764
DORSET - Fabric - NEMSCHOFF, INC.; *pg.* 936, *pg.* 1890
DORYX - Pharmaceutical Product - IMPAX LABORATORIES, INC.; *pg.* 1544, *pg.* 101
DOS EQUIS - Beer - HEINEKEN USA INC.; *pg.* 252, *pg.* 1352
DOS HERMANOS - Mexican Restaurant & Cantina - LEVY RESTAURANTS, INC.; *pg.* 1736, *pg.* 580
DOSE-A-DAY - Software - DATAVIZ, INC.; *pg.* 383, *pg.* 356
DOSEPAK - Paperboard Packaging Product - WESTROCK COMPANY; *pg.* 1472, *pg.* 1805
DOSEPAK EXPRESS - Adherence Packaging - WESTROCK COMPANY; *pg.* 1472, *pg.* 1805
DOSKOCIL - Pet Product - PETSMART, INC.; *pg.* 1481, *pg.* 18
DOSTINEX - Medicine - PFIZER INC.; *pg.* 1581, *pg.* 1278
DOT - Directional Orientation Tool - BAKER HUGHES INTEQ; *pg.* 1316, *pg.* 1700
DOT CAKE - Cake - DIPPIN' DOTS LLC; *pg.* 853, *pg.* 739
DOT DELICACIES - Desserts - DIPPIN' DOTS LLC; *pg.* 853, *pg.* 739
DOT MATRIX - Apparel - OAKLEY, INC.; *pg.* 1840, *pg.* 86
DOT QUAKE - Sundae & Shake - DIPPIN' DOTS LLC; *pg.* 853, *pg.* 739
DOTAM - Radio & Multimedia Service - BRS MEDIA INC.; *pg.* 1233, *pg.* 214
DOTCOAT - Medical Device - OLIVER PRODUCTS COMPANY INC.; *pg.* 1367, *pg.* 888
DOTFM - Radio & Multimedia Service - BRS MEDIA INC.; *pg.* 1233, *pg.* 214
DOTMATION - Game - WMS INDUSTRIES INC.; *pg.* 593, *pg.* 666
DOTRADIO - Radio & Multimedia Service - BRS MEDIA INC.; *pg.* 1233, *pg.* 214
DOTS & CROWS - Candy - TOOTSIE ROLL INDUSTRIES, INC.; *pg.* 1863, *pg.* 591
DOTS IN MOTION - Solid Ink - RICOH PRINTING SYSTEMS AMERICA, INC.; *pg.* 462, *pg.* 279
DOTS N CREAM - Cream - DIPPIN' DOTS LLC; *pg.* 853, *pg.* 739
DOTS WITH DASH - Slacks & Shorts - HABAND COMPANY, INC.; *pg.* 1772, *pg.* 1099
DOTSPY - Artwork System - ANDERSON & VREELAND, INC.; *pg.* 1616, *pg.* 1064
DOTTI - Cover Ups & Resortwear - KELLWOOD COMPANY; *pg.* 28, *pg.* 975
DOTTY - Footwear - COBIAN CORP.; *pg.* 1806, *pg.* 253
DOTWICH - Food Product - DIPPIN' DOTS LLC; *pg.* 853, *pg.* 739
DOTZCD - Radio & Multimedia Service - BRS MEDIA INC.; *pg.* 1233, *pg.* 214
DOTZDJ - Radio & Multimedia Service - BRS MEDIA INC.; *pg.* 1233, *pg.* 214
DOTZLA - Radio & Multimedia Service - BRS MEDIA INC.; *pg.* 1233, *pg.* 214
DOTZ.MD - Radio & Multimedia Service - BRS MEDIA INC.; *pg.* 1233, *pg.* 214
DOTZTV - Radio & Multimedia Service - BRS MEDIA INC.; *pg.* 1233, *pg.* 214
DOUBBLE - Footwear - STEVEN MADDEN, LTD.; *pg.* 1819, *pg.* 1176
DOUBLE - Bolt & Shield Anchor - POWERS FASTENERS INC.; *pg.* 1059, *pg.* 1143
DOUBLE 3X4X5X DYNAMITE - Video Game - INTERNATIONAL GAME TECHNOLOGY; *pg.* 957, *pg.* 1024
DOUBLE 3X4X5X HAYWIRE - Video Game - INTERNATIONAL GAME TECHNOLOGY; *pg.* 957, *pg.* 1024
DOUBLE 3X4X5X ICE DIAMONDS - Video Game - INTERNATIONAL GAME TECHNOLOGY; *pg.* 957, *pg.* 1024
DOUBLE 3X4X5X RED HOT 7S - Video Game - INTERNATIONAL GAME TECHNOLOGY; *pg.* 957, *pg.* 1024
DOUBLE 3X4X5X TIMES PAY - Video Game - INTERNATIONAL GAME TECHNOLOGY; *pg.* 957, *pg.* 1024
DOUBLE 4X BULLS-EYE - Video Game - INTERNATIONAL GAME TECHNOLOGY; *pg.* 957, *pg.* 1024
DOUBLE 4X PAY - Video Game - INTERNATIONAL GAME TECHNOLOGY; *pg.* 957, *pg.* 1024
DOUBLE 4X VOODOO 7S - Video Game - INTERNATIONAL GAME TECHNOLOGY; *pg.* 957, *pg.* 1024
DOUBLE 4X WILD CHERRY - Video Game - INTERNATIONAL GAME TECHNOLOGY; *pg.* 957, *pg.* 1024
DOUBLE-A ZONE - Trademark - NATIONAL COLLEGIATE ATHLETIC ASSOCIATION; *pg.* 567, *pg.* 688
DOUBLE AGENT - Apparel - OAKLEY, INC.; *pg.* 1840, *pg.* 86
DOUBLE AMERICAN BEAUTY - Slots - INTERNATIONAL GAME TECHNOLOGY; *pg.* 957, *pg.* 1024
DOUBLE ARM - High-Torque Mixer - LITTLEFORD DAY INC.; *pg.* 1356, *pg.* 728
DOUBLE BALL - Guitar Strings - GIBSON GUITAR CORP.; *pg.* 550, *pg.* 1650
DOUBLE BARREL - Combination Aggregate Dryer/Mixer Center - ASTEC INDUSTRIES, INC.; *pg.* 69, *pg.* 1628
DOUBLE BARREL - Flashlight - ENERGIZER HOLDINGS, INC.; *pg.* 637, *pg.* 996
DOUBLE BARREL - Apparel - OAKLEY, INC.; *pg.* 1840, *pg.* 86
DOUBLE BLACK - Fragrance - RALPH LAUREN CORPORATION; *pg.* 46, *pg.* 1284
DOUBLE BONUS CROSSWORD - Lottery Game - MINNESOTA STATE LOTTERY; *pg.* 999, *pg.* 956
DOUBLE BONUS POKER - Video Game - INTERNATIONAL GAME TECHNOLOGY; *pg.* 957, *pg.* 1024
DOUBLE BRIGHT - Flashlight - ENERGIZER HOLDINGS, INC.; *pg.* 637, *pg.* 996
DOUBLE BUCKS - Slots - INTERNATIONAL GAME TECHNOLOGY; *pg.* 957, *pg.* 1024
DOUBLE CASKED - Distilled Spirits - JIM BEAM BRANDS CO.; *pg.* 1965, *pg.* 601
DOUBLE CHECK - Security System - NORTEK, INC.; *pg.* 100, *pg.* 1607
DOUBLE CHERRY BELLS - Pulltab Game - IDAHO LOTTERY; *pg.* 995, *pg.* 547
DOUBLE CLEAN - Fuel System Cleaner - MOC PRODUCTS COMPANY, INC.; *pg.* 332, *pg.* 174
DOUBLE-COLA - Soft Drink - DOUBLE-COLA CO.-USA; *pg.* 249, *pg.* 1629
DOUBLE CORE - Medical & Aesthetic Product - DYNATRONICS CORPORATION; *pg.* 1526, *pg.* 1757
DOUBLE COVER - Liquid & Paste Paints - PPG INDUSTRIES, INC.; *pg.* 1445, *pg.* 1579
DOUBLE CROISSAN'WICH - Sandwich - BURGER KING CORPORATION; *pg.* 1719, *pg.* 440
DOUBLE DEAL! - Outerwear - HABAND COMPANY, INC.; *pg.* 1772, *pg.* 1099
DOUBLE-DECKER - Peanut Butter - CHATTANOOGA BAKERY INC.; *pg.* 847, *pg.* 1628
DOUBLE DECKER RED - Nail Care Product - OPI PRODUCTS INC.; *pg.* 518, *pg.* 167

DOUBLE DELIGHT - Blouses - HABAND COMPANY, INC.; *pg.* 1772, *pg.* 1099
DOUBLE DESIRE - Slots - INTERNATIONAL GAME TECHNOLOGY; *pg.* 957, *pg.* 1024
DOUBLE DIAMOND - Game - INTERNATIONAL GAME TECHNOLOGY; *pg.* 957, *pg.* 1024
DOUBLE DIAMOND - Combo Tool - SMITH INTERNATIONAL, INC.; *pg.* 1377, *pg.* 1715
DOUBLE DIAMOND 2000 - Video Slots - INTERNATIONAL GAME TECHNOLOGY; *pg.* 957, *pg.* 1024
DOUBLE DIAMOND DELUXE - Slots - INTERNATIONAL GAME TECHNOLOGY; *pg.* 957, *pg.* 1024
DOUBLE DIAMOND DELUXE BONUS WHEEL - Slots - INTERNATIONAL GAME TECHNOLOGY; *pg.* 957, *pg.* 1024
DOUBLE DIAMOND FAST HIT - Video Slots - INTERNATIONAL GAME TECHNOLOGY; *pg.* 957, *pg.* 1024
DOUBLE DIAMOND MINE - Slots - INTERNATIONAL GAME TECHNOLOGY; *pg.* 957, *pg.* 1024
DOUBLE DIPPED PEANUTS - Chocolate Coated Nuts - NEW ENGLAND CONFECTIONERY COMPANY INC.; *pg.* 1860, *pg.* 842
DOUBLE DISH - Kitchen Appliance - HAMILTON BEACH BRANDS, INC.; *pg.* 56, *pg.* 1783
DOUBLE DOLLARS - Slots - INTERNATIONAL GAME TECHNOLOGY; *pg.* 957, *pg.* 1024
DOUBLE DOLLARS - Game - MISSOURI LOTTERY; *pg.* 999, *pg.* 979
DOUBLE DOLLARS - Lottery Game - NEW YORK STATE LOTTERY; *pg.* 1001, *pg.* 1340
DOUBLE-DOUBLE - Burger - IN-N-OUT BURGERS, INC.; *pg.* 1732, *pg.* 111
DOUBLE DOUBLER - Lottery Game - OHIO LOTTERY COMMISSION; *pg.* 1002, *pg.* 1433
DOUBLE DOWN STUD - Video Poker - INTERNATIONAL GAME TECHNOLOGY; *pg.* 957, *pg.* 1024
DOUBLE DRUM - Pulley - VAN GORP CORPORATION; *pg.* 1387, *pg.* 711
DOUBLE-DRY - Soft Drink - DOUBLE-COLA CO.-USA; *pg.* 249, *pg.* 1629
DOUBLE DUTY - Flashlight - ENERGIZER HOLDINGS, INC.; *pg.* 637, *pg.* 996
DOUBLE DUTY - Hammer - VAUGHAN & BUSHNELL MANUFACTURING COMPANY, INC.; *pg.* 1066, *pg.* 616
DOUBLE EAGLE - Tires - THE GOODYEAR TIRE & RUBBER COMPANY; *pg.* 1883, *pg.* 1401
DOUBLE EASY MONEY - Game - WMS INDUSTRIES INC.; *pg.* 593, *pg.* 666
DOUBLE FLUSH - Robotic Product - HAMILTON CO., INC.; *pg.* 1415, *pg.* 1031
DOUBLE FRUIT - Jams & Jellies - THE J.M. SMUCKER COMPANY; *pg.* 865, *pg.* 1468
DOUBLE FUDGE FRENZY - Friazos - WELLS ENTERPRISES, INC.; *pg.* 909, *pg.* 709
DOUBLE GARD V - Vinyl-Window Systems - NORTEK, INC.; *pg.* 100, *pg.* 1607
DOUBLE GOLD - Slots - INTERNATIONAL GAME TECHNOLOGY; *pg.* 957, *pg.* 1024
DOUBLE HEARTS - Slots - INTERNATIONAL GAME TECHNOLOGY; *pg.* 957, *pg.* 1024
DOUBLE IT - Lottery Game - NEW JERSEY STATE LOTTERY; *pg.* 1000, *pg.* 1126
DOUBLE KENO BLASTER - Game - WMS INDUSTRIES INC.; *pg.* 593, *pg.* 666
DOUBLE KNOCK OUT - Garden Roses - THE CONARD-PYLE COMPANY; *pg.* 1794, *pg.* 1594
DOUBLE LIFE OF LUXURY - Game - WMS INDUSTRIES INC.; *pg.* 593, *pg.* 666
DOUBLE MYSTICAL MERMAID - Slots - INTERNATIONAL GAME TECHNOLOGY; *pg.* 957, *pg.* 1024
DOUBLE PAY SPIN POKER - Video Game - INTERNATIONAL GAME TECHNOLOGY; *pg.* 957, *pg.* 1024
DOUBLE PLAY DAILY - Lottery Game - IDAHO LOTTERY; *pg.* 995, *pg.* 547
DOUBLE PLUS - Free Flow Chain - U.S. TSUBAKI, INC.; *pg.* 221, *pg.* 670
DOUBLE PORE - Robotic Product - HAMILTON CO., INC.; *pg.* 1415, *pg.* 1031
DOUBLE Q - Canned Salmon - PETER PAN SEAFOODS, INC.; *pg.* 889, *pg.* 1838
DOUBLE RED WHITE & BLUE - Slots - INTERNATIONAL GAME TECHNOLOGY; *pg.* 957, *pg.* 1024
DOUBLE RL - Apparel & Accessories - RALPH LAUREN CORPORATION; *pg.* 46, *pg.* 1284
DOUBLE SENSOR - Smoke Detector - BRK BRANDS, INC.; *pg.* 627, *pg.* 554
DOUBLE SHOOTOUT - Basketball Game - SCHOOL-TECH, INC.; *pg.* 1844, *pg.* 866
DOUBLE SHOT - Arcade-Type Basketball - LIFETIME PRODUCTS INC.; *pg.* 933, *pg.* 1751
DOUBLE SHOT - Container Grown Plant - MONROVIA GROWERS; *pg.* 1797, *pg.* 44
DOUBLE STAMPEDE DELUXE - Game - WMS INDUSTRIES INC.; *pg.* 593, *pg.* 666
DOUBLE STRAWBERRY - Ice Cream - WELLS ENTERPRISES, INC.; *pg.* 909, *pg.* 709
DOUBLE STRIKE - Slots - INTERNATIONAL GAME TECHNOLOGY; *pg.* 957, *pg.* 1024
DOUBLE TAKE! - Slacks & Shorts - HABAND COMPANY, INC.; *pg.* 1772, *pg.* 1099
DOUBLE TEN TIMES PAY - Slots - INTERNATIONAL GAME TECHNOLOGY; *pg.* 957, *pg.* 1024
DOUBLE-TIME SHINE - Nail Buffer - ORLY INTERNATIONAL, INC.; *pg.* 518, *pg.* 137
DOUBLE TOP DOLLAR - Slots - INTERNATIONAL GAME TECHNOLOGY; *pg.* 957, *pg.* 1024
DOUBLE TRIPLE DIAMOND DELUXE WITH CHEESE - Slots - INTERNATIONAL GAME TECHNOLOGY; *pg.* 957, *pg.* 1024
DOUBLE-WALL - Cylinder - BIMBA MANUFACTURING COMPANY; *pg.* 1317, *pg.* 633
DOUBLE WALL - Steel Wall Panel - CLESTRA HAUSERMAN, INC.; *pg.* 76, *pg.* 1526
DOUBLE WHAMMY - Lottery Game - MICHIGAN STATE LOTTERY BUREAU; *pg.* 999, *pg.* 895
DOUBLE WHOPPER - Sandwich - BURGER KING CORPORATION; *pg.* 1719, *pg.* 440
DOUBLE WILD - Slots - INTERNATIONAL GAME TECHNOLOGY; *pg.* 957, *pg.* 1024
DOUBLE WILD CHERRY BONUS WHEEL - Slots - INTERNATIONAL GAME TECHNOLOGY; *pg.* 957, *pg.* 1024
DOUBLE-X - Photo Film - EASTMAN KODAK COMPANY; *pg.* 1408, *pg.* 1333
DOUBLE X LON - Laundry Product - BIRKO CORPORATION; *pg.* 1149, *pg.* 332
DOUBLE X-TENZ - Sleeper & Recliner Seating - STEELCASE INC.; *pg.* 475, *pg.* 889
DOUBLECHECK - Central Station Security Monitoring Service - THE ADT CORPORATION; *pg.* 612, *pg.* 409
DOUBLECHECKGOLD - Pharmaceutical Product - ALERE INC.; *pg.* 1488, *pg.* 849
DOUBLECLICK - Digital Marketing Services - DOUBLECLICK, INC.; *pg.* 1239, *pg.* 1225
DOUBLECLICK - Ad Management Solution - GOOGLE INC.; *pg.* 1249, *pg.* 153
DOUBLEDAY - Book Stores - BARNES & NOBLE, INC.; *pg.* 1619, *pg.* 1201
DOUBLEDAY - Publishing Imprint - THE KNOPF DOUBLEDAY GROUP; *pg.* 1657, *pg.* 1249
DOUBLEFLY - Rescue Strobe Light - ACR ELECTRONICS, INC.; *pg.* 612, *pg.* 422
DOUBLEMINT - Gum - WM. WRIGLEY JR. COMPANY; *pg.* 1863, *pg.* 596
DOUBLEPULSE - Laser Device - TRIMEDYNE, INC.; *pg.* 1432, *pg.* 121
DOUBLES - Ice Cream - WELLS ENTERPRISES, INC.; *pg.* 909, *pg.* 709
DOUBLESHOT - Espresso Drink - STARBUCKS CORPORATION; *pg.* 897, *pg.* 1840
DOUBLETAKE 2 - Software - MELISSA DATA CORP.; *pg.* 432, *pg.* 188
DOUBLETALK - Bandwidth Compression System - RAYTHEON APPLIED SIGNAL TECHNOLOGY, INC.; *pg.* 667, *pg.* 288
DOUBLETREE - Upscale Full-Service Hotel & Resort - HILTON WORLDWIDE, INC.; *pg.* 1094, *pg.* 1791
DOUBLETREE GUEST SUITES - Hotels - HILTON WORLDWIDE, INC.; *pg.* 1094, *pg.* 1791
DOUBLING 8'S - Game - MISSOURI LOTTERY; *pg.* 999, *pg.* 979
DOUBLING DOLLARS - Lottery Game - OHIO LOTTERY COMMISSION; *pg.* 1002, *pg.* 1433
DOUBLING STAR CASHWORD - Lottery Game - OHIO LOTTERY COMMISSION; *pg.* 1002, *pg.* 1433
DOUGLAS-COOKER - High Shear Cooker Corn Starches - PENFORD CORPORATION; *pg.* 1177, *pg.* 314
DOUGLAS-ENZYME - Enzyme-Converting Corn Starches - PENFORD CORPORATION; *pg.* 1177, *pg.* 314
DOUGLASS - Door & Wood Product - CONESTOGA WOOD SPECIALTIES CORP.; *pg.* 921, *pg.* 1527
DOVE - Guitars - GIBSON GUITAR CORP.; *pg.* 550, *pg.* 1650
DOVE - Bookmark - HERITAGE LACE INC.; *pg.* 694, *pg.* 711
DOVE - Candy - MARS, INCORPORATED; *pg.* 1858, *pg.* 1792
DOVE - Beauty and Hair Care Products - UNILEVER UNITED STATES, INC.; *pg.* 904, *pg.* 1061
DOVEBARS - Ice Cream Bars - MARS, INCORPORATED; *pg.* 1858, *pg.* 1792
DOVER - Furniture - ASHLEY FURNITURE INDUSTRIES, INC.; *pg.* 914, *pg.* 1852
THE DOVER - Ready-to-assemble Swing Set - CREATIVE PLAYTHINGS LTD.; *pg.* 1831, *pg.* 820
DOVER - Air Bearing Stages & Precision Mechanical Stages - DANAHER MOTION; *pg.* 1327, *pg.* 1593
DOVER - Automobile Races - DOVER MOTORSPORTS, INC.; *pg.* 545, *pg.* 387
DOVER - Flatware - ONEIDA LTD; *pg.* 1129, *pg.* 1318
DOVER - Grill Scraper - ZEPHYR MANUFACTURING COMPANY INC.; *pg.* 1141, *pg.* 1006
DOVER DOWNS RACEWAY - Race Track - DOVER DOWNS GAMING & ENTERTAINMENT, INC.; *pg.* 545, *pg.* 387
DOVER DOWNS SLOTS - Casino Complex - DOVER DOWNS GAMING & ENTERTAINMENT, INC.; *pg.* 545, *pg.* 387
DOVER INTERNATIONAL SPEEDWAY - Motor & Horse Racetrack - DOVER MOTORSPORTS, INC.; *pg.* 545, *pg.* 387
DOVERLUBE - Chemical Product - DOVER CHEMICAL CORPORATION; *pg.* 1156, *pg.* 1447
DOVERNOX - Chemical Product - DOVER CHEMICAL CORPORATION; *pg.* 1156, *pg.* 1447
DOVERPHOS - Chemical Product - DOVER CHEMICAL CORPORATION; *pg.* 1156, *pg.* 1447
DOVERSPERSE - Chemical Product - DOVER CHEMICAL CORPORATION; *pg.* 1156, *pg.* 1447
DOVETAIL - Sunglass - 180S, LLC; *pg.* 1824, *pg.* 754
DOVETAIL - Seal & Thermoplastic Component - GREENE, TWEED & CO.; *pg.* 1344, *pg.* 1544
THE DOW - Investment Fund Services - DOW JONES & COMPANY, INC.; *pg.* 1637, *pg.* 1225
DOW CORNING - Silicone & Other Chemicals - DOW CORNING CORPORATION; *pg.* 1159, *pg.* 900
DOW JONES - Business News & Information Services - DOW JONES & COMPANY, INC.; *pg.* 1637, *pg.* 1225
THE DOW JONES AVERAGES - Stock Indices - DOW JONES & COMPANY, INC.; *pg.* 1637, *pg.* 1225
DOW JONES INDEXES - Electronic Publishing - DOW JONES & COMPANY, INC.; *pg.* 1637, *pg.* 1225
DOW JONES INDUSTRY GROUPS - Financial Products - DOW JONES & COMPANY, INC.; *pg.* 1637, *pg.* 1225
DOW JONES NEWSWIRES - Electronic Publishing - DOW JONES & COMPANY, INC.; *pg.* 1637, *pg.* 1225
DOW XLA - Elastic Fiber - THE DOW CHEMICAL COMPANY; *pg.* 1157, *pg.* 898
DOWANOL - Oxygenated Solvent - THE DOW CHEMICAL COMPANY; *pg.* 1157, *pg.* 898
DOWCAL - Heat Transfer Agent - THE DOW CHEMICAL COMPANY; *pg.* 1157, *pg.* 898
DOWCLENE - Degreasing Agents - THE DOW CHEMICAL COMPANY; *pg.* 1157, *pg.* 898
DOWCLOR - Dry Cleaning Solvent - THE DOW CHEMICAL COMPANY; *pg.* 1157, *pg.* 898
DOWDEN CUSTOM MEDIA - Industry Publication - LEBHAR-FRIEDMAN INC.; *pg.* 1658, *pg.* 1250
DOWEX - Ion Exchange Resins - THE DOW CHEMICAL COMPANY; *pg.* 1157, *pg.* 898
DOWEX OPTIPORE - Adsorbents - THE DOW CHEMICAL COMPANY; *pg.* 1157, *pg.* 898
DOWEX QCAT - Catalyst - THE DOW CHEMICAL COMPANY; *pg.* 1157, *pg.* 898
DOWFAX - Nonionic Surfactant - THE DOW CHEMICAL COMPANY; *pg.* 1157, *pg.* 898
DOWFLAKE - Calcium Chloride - THE DOW CHEMICAL COMPANY; *pg.* 1157, *pg.* 898
DOWFROST - Heat Transfer Fluid - THE DOW CHEMICAL COMPANY; *pg.* 1157, *pg.* 898
DOWICIDE - Antimicrobial Bactericides & Fungicides - THE DOW CHEMICAL COMPANY; *pg.* 1157, *pg.* 898
DOWLEX - Resin - THE DOW CHEMICAL COMPANY; *pg.* 1157, *pg.* 898
DOWN-HOLE - Air Gun - BOLT TECHNOLOGY

CORPORATION; *pg.* 1318, *pg.* 360
DOWN ON THE FARM - Restaurant Services - BOB EVANS FARMS, LLC; *pg.* 841, *pg.* 1467
DOWN-RIGHT - Deposition Management Agent - UNIVERSAL COOPERATIVES, INC.; *pg.* 1482, *pg.* 922
DOWN TO EARTH - Online Services - IAC/INTERACTIVECORP; *pg.* 292, *pg.* 1242
DOWNEY UNSTOPABLES - Wash Scent Booster - THE PROCTER & GAMBLE COMPANY; *pg.* 1129, *pg.* 1418
DOWNFLO - Air Filtration & Contaminant Collection System - DONALDSON COMPANY, INC.; *pg.* 1329, *pg.* 917
DOWNLIGHT REINVENTED - LED - CREE INC.; *pg.* 631, *pg.* 1371
DOWNLOAD CONFIGURATION MANAGER - Video Game - BALLY TECHNOLOGIES, INC.; *pg.* 531, *pg.* 1022
DOWNLOADS2GO - Educational Materials - SCHOLASTIC INC.; *pg.* 1683, *pg.* 1288
DOWNS - Lifting Equipment - DOWNS CRANE & HOIST CO, INC.; *pg.* 1330, *pg.* 129
DOWNTIME ELIMINATOR - Fluid Handling System - GRACO, INC.; *pg.* 1342, *pg.* 935
DOWNTOWN WIRELESS - Video Game - ELECTRONIC ARTS INC.; *pg.* 951, *pg.* 189
DOWNY - Laundry Product - THE PROCTER & GAMBLE COMPANY; *pg.* 1129, *pg.* 1418
DOWNY TROPICAL BLOOM - Fabric Softener - THE PROCTER & GAMBLE COMPANY; *pg.* 1129, *pg.* 1418
DOWPER - Solvent - THE DOW CHEMICAL COMPANY; *pg.* 1157, *pg.* 898
DOWPHARMA - Manufacturer Services - THE DOW CHEMICAL COMPANY; *pg.* 1157, *pg.* 898
DOWTHERM - Heat Transfer Fluid - THE DOW CHEMICAL COMPANY; *pg.* 1157, *pg.* 898
DOX - Office Products - ACCO BRANDS CORPORATION; *pg.* 340, *pg.* 626
DOX - Clean-up System - CAMERON INTERNATIONAL; *pg.* 1151, *pg.* 1702
DOX - Patient Monitoring System - CRITICARE SYSTEMS, INC.; *pg.* 1520, *pg.* 1897
DOXIDAN - Medicine - MCNEIL-PPC, INC.; *pg.* 1560, *pg.* 1533
DOXIL - Healthcare Product - JOHNSON & JOHNSON; *pg.* 1549, *pg.* 1091
DOXIMER - Water Soluble Resin - THE DOW CHEMICAL COMPANY; *pg.* 1157, *pg.* 898
DOZENS OF DIAMONDS - Slots - INTERNATIONAL GAME TECHNOLOGY; *pg.* 957, *pg.* 1024
DP 1011 - Projector - XEROX CORPORATION; *pg.* 494, *pg.* 365
DP-2000 - Digital Projector - EASTMAN KODAK COMPANY; *pg.* 1408, *pg.* 1333
DP-45 - Flame Retardants - CHEMTURA CORPORATION; *pg.* 1152, *pg.* 355
DP-CALC - Micromanometer - TSI INCORPORATED; *pg.* 1432, *pg.* 965
DP4 - Multi-Purpose Faceshield - SELLSTROM MANUFACTURING CO.; *pg.* 1428, *pg.* 659
DPA-SWITCH - Analog Integrated Circuits & Switches - POWER INTEGRATIONS, INC.; *pg.* 1369, *pg.* 249
DPC III - Dynamic Process Controller Version Three - DUKANE CORPORATION; *pg.* 634, *pg.* 658
DPF FORMULA - Automated Side Loader - HEIL ENVIRONMENTAL INDUSTRIES, LTD.; *pg.* 207, *pg.* 1629
DPJ - Medical Equipment - INVACARE CORPORATION; *pg.* 1546, *pg.* 1451
DPOE - Power Patch Panel - PANDUIT CORP.; *pg.* 661, *pg.* 663
DPX - Soot Filter - BASF CATALYSTS LLC; *pg.* 1148, *pg.* 1074
DPX - Sport Performance Sterndrive - VOLVO PENTA OF THE AMERICAS, INC.; *pg.* 1712, *pg.* 1778
DPX-1000 - Digital Cinema Projector - YAMAHA ELECTRONICS CORPORATION USA; *pg.* 689, *pg.* 51
DQ - Dairy Queen Products - AMERICAN DAIRY QUEEN CORPORATION; *pg.* 1714, *pg.* 930
DQ - Molecular Probe Product - THERMO FISHER SCIENTIFIC INC.; *pg.* 1602, *pg.* 61
DQ CHIPPER SANDWICH - Frozen Novelties - INTERNATIONAL DAIRY QUEEN, INC.; *pg.* 1732, *pg.* 938
DQ HOMESTYLE ULTIMATE BURGER - Bacon Cheeseburger - INTERNATIONAL DAIRY QUEEN, INC.; *pg.* 1732, *pg.* 938
DQWICH - Frozen Novelties - INTERNATIONAL DAIRY QUEEN, INC.; *pg.* 1732, *pg.* 938
DR - Casters & Wheels - DARNELL-ROSE; *pg.* 1045, *pg.* 67
DR. BARNHOUSE & THE BIBLE - Radio Broadcast - ALLIANCE OF CONFESSING EVANGELICALS, INC.; *pg.* 126, *pg.* 1545
DR. BIZER'S VISIONWORLD - Eye Care Centers - VISIONWORKS OF AMERICA, INC.; *pg.* 1436, *pg.* 1744
DR. BIZER'S VALUVISION - Eye Care Centers - VISIONWORKS OF AMERICA, INC.; *pg.* 1436, *pg.* 1744
DR. BREW - Printed Educational Materials - BUNN-O-MATIC CORPORATION; *pg.* 53, *pg.* 661
DR. BROWN'S NATURAL FLOW - Baby Bottle - HANDI-CRAFT COMPANY; *pg.* 954, *pg.* 998
DR BUCK - Footwear - STEVEN MADDEN, LTD.; *pg.* 1819, *pg.* 1176
DR. CACHE - Computer Software - NOVELL INC.; *pg.* 446, *pg.* 852
DR. FEEL - Golf Products - FEEL GOLF CO., INC.; *pg.* 1834, *pg.* 465
DR. FOOT - Foot Powder - BLUE CROSS LABORATORIES; *pg.* 326, *pg.* 277
DR. FRANKS - Animal Safety Product - NEOGEN CORPORATION; *pg.* 883, *pg.* 896
DR. FULLER - Mattresses - RESTONIC MATTRESS CORPORATION; *pg.* 941, *pg.* 553
DR. G JUST FOR TEENS - Mattresses & Box Springs for Teenagers - KINGSDOWN, INC.; *pg.* 932, *pg.* 1383
DR. GOODBONES - Juvenile Mattress & Box Springs - KINGSDOWN, INC.; *pg.* 932, *pg.* 1383
DR. JACKPOT & MR. WILD - Game - WMS INDUSTRIES INC.; *pg.* 593, *pg.* 666
DR. MCGILLICUDDY'S - Mentholmint Schnapps - SAZERAC COMPANY, INC.; *pg.* 1969, *pg.* 745
DR. NAYLORS - Veterinary Products - H.W. NAYLOR COMPANY, INC.; *pg.* 1477, *pg.* 1183
DR. NICK'S TRANSMISSION - Automotive Repair Service - MORAN INDUSTRIES, INC.; *pg.* 213, *pg.* 632
DR PEPPER - Beverages - THE COCA-COLA COMPANY; *pg.* 240, *pg.* 493
DR PEPPER - Carbonated Soft Drink - DR PEPPER SNAPPLE GROUP, INC.; *pg.* 250, *pg.* 1729
DR PEPPER ZERO - Beverages - THE COCA-COLA COMPANY; *pg.* 240, *pg.* 493
DR. SCHOLL'S - Foot Care Products - BAYER HEALTHCARE CONSUMER CARE DIVISION; *pg.* 1500, *pg.* 1087
DR. SCHOLL'S - Leather Loafers - HABAND COMPANY, INC.; *pg.* 1772, *pg.* 1099
DR. TEAL'S - Therapeutic Bath & Body Products - ADVANCED BEAUTY SYSTEMS INC.; *pg.* 498, *pg.* 1672
DR. TELEWORK - Communication Product - CENTURYLINK, INC; *pg.* 1870, *pg.* 317
DR. WELLS - Beverage - THE MONARCH BEVERAGE COMPANY, INC.; *pg.* 257, *pg.* 514
DRACIEL - Toy & Game - HASBRO, INC.; *pg.* 954, *pg.* 1603
DRACIEL FORTRESS - Toy & Game - HASBRO, INC.; *pg.* 954, *pg.* 1603
DRAFT BUSTERS - Door Insulators - HENKEL CONSUMER ADHESIVES, INC.; *pg.* 403, *pg.* 1480
DRAFTRITE - Gauge - BACHARACH INC.; *pg.* 1400, *pg.* 1556
DRAG - Tire - THE GOODYEAR TIRE & RUBBER COMPANY; *pg.* 1883, *pg.* 1401
DRAGNET - Vehicle Arresting Barriers - THE ENTWISTLE CO.; *pg.* 637, *pg.* 826
DRAGNET - Pest Control Product - FMC CORPORATION; *pg.* 1163, *pg.* 1564
DRAGON - Rice - AMERICAN RICE, INC.; *pg.* 837, *pg.* 1700
DRAGON - Cutterhead Dredge - ELLICOTT DREDGES, LLC; *pg.* 1333, *pg.* 757
DRAGON - Bicycles - G. JOANNOU CYCLE CO. INC.; *pg.* 1707, *pg.* 1098
DRAGON - Gaming Product - GLD PRODUCTS, INC.; *pg.* 1835, *pg.* 1882
DRAGON - Speech Recognition Software - NUANCE COMMUNICATIONS, INC.; *pg.* 447, *pg.* 806
DRAGON - Apparel - VANS, INC.; *pg.* 1821, *pg.* 76
DRAGON - Magazine - WIZARDS OF THE COAST, INC.; *pg.* 970, *pg.* 1830
DRAGON BACCARAT - Video Game - INTERNATIONAL GAME TECHNOLOGY; *pg.* 957, *pg.* 1024
DRAGON BURN - Software - NTI CORPORATION; *pg.* 446, *pg.* 114
DRAGON DANCE - Video Game - INTERNATIONAL GAME TECHNOLOGY; *pg.* 957, *pg.* 1024
DRAGON DRYER - Biosolids Dryer - EVOQUA WATER TECHNOLOGIES; *pg.* 1162, *pg.* 541
DRAGON EYE - Unmanned Air Vehicle - AEROVIRONMENT, INC.; *pg.* 223, *pg.* 150
DRAGON FIRE - Roller Coaster - CANADA'S WONDERLAND COMPANY; *pg.* 536, *pg.* 1947
DRAGON FIRE - Game - WMS INDUSTRIES INC.; *pg.* 593, *pg.* 666
DRAGON NATURALLY SPEAKING - Voice Enabled Software - NUANCE COMMUNICATIONS, INC.; *pg.* 447, *pg.* 806
DRAGON PHOENIX - Video Game - INTERNATIONAL GAME TECHNOLOGY; *pg.* 957, *pg.* 1024
DRAGON SKIN - Liquid Rubber - SMOOTH-ON INC.; *pg.* 111, *pg.* 1528
DRAGON SKIN Q - Liquid Rubber - SMOOTH-ON INC.; *pg.* 111, *pg.* 1528
DRAGON STRIKE - Toy & Game - HASBRO, INC.; *pg.* 954, *pg.* 1603
DRAGON TOOTH - Connector - THOMAS & BETTS CORPORATION; *pg.* 680, *pg.* 1646
DRAGON WORLD - Game - WMS INDUSTRIES INC.; *pg.* 593, *pg.* 666
DRAGONBALL - Semiconductor Product - FREESCALE SEMICONDUCTOR, INC.; *pg.* 398, *pg.* 1662
DRAGONFLY - Video Game - INTERNATIONAL GAME TECHNOLOGY; *pg.* 957, *pg.* 1024
DRAGONFLY - Publishing Imprint - PENGUIN RANDOM HOUSE CHILDREN'S BOOKS; *pg.* 1676, *pg.* 1277
DRAGONFLY 7S - Video Game - INTERNATIONAL GAME TECHNOLOGY; *pg.* 957, *pg.* 1024
DRAGON'S GATE - Video Game - INTERNATIONAL GAME TECHNOLOGY; *pg.* 957, *pg.* 1024
DRAGONS GOLD - Video Slots - INTERNATIONAL GAME TECHNOLOGY; *pg.* 957, *pg.* 1024
DRAGOON - Toy & Game - HASBRO, INC.; *pg.* 954, *pg.* 1603
DRAIN OPENER - Drain Cleaner - BLUE CROSS LABORATORIES; *pg.* 326, *pg.* 277
DRAIN TITAN - Pump - FLOWSERVE CORPORATION; *pg.* 82, *pg.* 1719
DRAIN VALVE LUBRICANT - Holding Tank Lubricant - THETFORD CORPORATION; *pg.* 337, *pg.* 867
DRAINGUARD - Cleaner - ROCHESTER MIDLAND CORPORATION; *pg.* 334, *pg.* 1337
DRAINO - Footwear - COBIAN CORP.; *pg.* 1806, *pg.* 253
DRAINRAM - Drain Cleaner - GOODWAY TECHNOLOGIES CORPORATION; *pg.* 1341, *pg.* 374
DRAINTAINER - Oil Recycling Pan - RUBBERMAID HOME PRODUCTS; *pg.* 1138, *pg.* 1453
DRAKE - Furniture - ASHLEY FURNITURE INDUSTRIES, INC.; *pg.* 914, *pg.* 1852
DRAKE - Furniture - ETHAN ALLEN INTERIORS INC.; *pg.* 924, *pg.* 343
DRAKE WATERFOWL - Handling Product - C.R. DANIELS, INC.; *pg.* 1456, *pg.* 769
DRAKENFELD - Pigments - FERRO CORPORATION; *pg.* 1162, *pg.* 1462
DRAKES BEACH - Bike - MARIN BIKES; *pg.* 1708, *pg.* 168
DRAKOTHERM - Decorative Coatings - FERRO CORPORATION; *pg.* 1162, *pg.* 1462
DRALION - Show And Ticket - CIRQUE DU SOLEIL INC.; *pg.* 540, *pg.* 1954
DRAM - Wafer Test Product - FORMFACTOR, INC.; *pg.* 1882, *pg.* 122
DRAMA TONE - Colorants - AKZONOBEL DECORATIVE PAINTS U.S.; *pg.* 1439, *pg.* 1474
DRAMAMINE - Medicine - MCNEIL-PPC, INC.; *pg.* 1560, *pg.* 1533
DRANO - Drain Clearing Product - S.C. JOHNSON & SON, INC.; *pg.* 334, *pg.* 1889
DRANO BUILD-UP - Clog Remover - S.C. JOHNSON & SON, INC.; *pg.* 334, *pg.* 1889
DRANO CRYSTAL - Clog Remover - S.C. JOHNSON & SON, INC.; *pg.* 334, *pg.* 1889
DRANO LIQUID - Clog Remover - S.C. JOHNSON & SON, INC.; *pg.* 334, *pg.* 1889
DRANO MAX GEL - Clog Remover - S.C. JOHNSON & SON, INC.; *pg.* 334, *pg.* 1889
DRANO PROFESSIONAL STRENGTH - Clog Remover - S.C. JOHNSON & SON, INC.; *pg.* 334, *pg.* 1889
DRAPE SHADES - Lace - HERITAGE LACE INC.; *pg.* 694, *pg.* 711
DRAPER KING COLE - Food Product - HANOVER FOODS CORPORATION; *pg.* 861, *pg.* 1535
DRAPEX - Polymer Product - CHEMTURA CORPORATION; *pg.* 1152, *pg.* 355
DRAW 6 POKER - Video Game - INTERNATIONAL GAME

TECHNOLOGY; *pg.* 957, *pg.* 1024
DRAW BLACK - Cleaning And Descaling Salt - HEATBATH CORPORATION; *pg.* 1165, *pg.* 826
DRAW WRITE NOW - Educational Product - BARKER CREEK PUBLISHING INC.; *pg.* 1619, *pg.* 1818
DRAWBREAKERS - Educational Materials - SCHOLASTIC INC.; *pg.* 1683, *pg.* 1288
DRAWCORD - Cover & Pad - HOME PRODUCTS INTERNATIONAL, INC.; *pg.* 1125, *pg.* 577
DRAWER/GANIZERS - Labware Storage System - SPECTRUM LABORATORIES INC.; *pg.* 1595, *pg.* 69
DRAWING - Trade Publication - THE NIELSEN COMPANY B.V.; *pg.* 1671, *pg.* 1272
DRAWIT - Software - BIO-RAD LABORATORIES, INC.; *pg.* 1504, *pg.* 101
DRAXXIN - Pharmaceutical Product - PFIZER INC.; *pg.* 1581, *pg.* 1278
DRC - Axial Field Technology - PERKINELMER, INC.; *pg.* 1426, *pg.* 853
DREAM - Vehicle - AEROVIRONMENT, INC.; *pg.* 223, *pg.* 150
DREAM - Integrated Circuit - ATMEL CORPORATION; *pg.* 621, *pg.* 238
DREAM - Wood & Wood Finished Decking Products - THERMAL INDUSTRIES, INC.; *pg.* 115, *pg.* 1555
DREAM BARS - Candy - SORBEE INTERNATIONAL, LLC; *pg.* 1862, *pg.* 1570
DREAM BIG. WIN BIG - Video Game - INTERNATIONAL GAME TECHNOLOGY; *pg.* 957, *pg.* 1024
DREAM CANDY - Low-Fat & Low-Calorie Chocolate Bars - SORBEE INTERNATIONAL, LLC; *pg.* 1862, *pg.* 1570
DREAM CARD - Video Game - INTERNATIONAL GAME TECHNOLOGY; *pg.* 957, *pg.* 1024
DREAM COIL - Mattress Pad - CARPENTER CO.; *pg.* 920, *pg.* 1801
DREAM DECKS & PATIOS - Magazine - MEREDITH CORPORATION; *pg.* 1663, *pg.* 705
DREAM-EZE - Solid Carbide Drill/Reamer Combination - REGAL BELOIT CORPORATION; *pg.* 106, *pg.* 1854
DREAM IN COLOR - Bridal Wear - ALFRED ANGELO, INC.; *pg.* 17, *pg.* 1532
DREAM MOUSSE - Blush & Bronzer Products - MAYBELLINE LLC; *pg.* 516, *pg.* 1257
DREAM PUFFS - Pajamas - HABAND COMPANY, INC.; *pg.* 1772, *pg.* 1099
DREAM RIDE - Infant Car Bed/Car Seat - DOREL JUVENILE GROUP, INC.; *pg.* 923, *pg.* 676
DREAM SMOOTH - Foundation - MAYBELLINE LLC; *pg.* 516, *pg.* 1257
DREAM STAKES - Game - MISSOURI LOTTERY; *pg.* 999, *pg.* 979
DREAM WORKS SHARK TALE - Game - ACTIVISION BLIZZARD, INC.; *pg.* 948, *pg.* 271
DREAMA - Lamp - ASHLEY FURNITURE INDUSTRIES, INC.; *pg.* 914, *pg.* 1852
DREAMFIT - Bedding - SELECT COMFORT CORPORATION; *pg.* 942, *pg.* 942
DREAMGIRL - Sleep Mask - MCKEON PRODUCTS, INC.; *pg.* 1559, *pg.* 912
DREAMGLAS GALLERY COLLECTION - Custom-Made Replacement Windows - THERMAL INDUSTRIES, INC.; *pg.* 115, *pg.* 1555
DREAMIN' FOR DOLLARS - Lottery Game - KENTUCKY LOTTERY CORPORATION; *pg.* 996, *pg.* 735
DREAMLIFE - Beauty Product - AVON PRODUCTS, INC.; *pg.* 500, *pg.* 1198
DREAMLINER - Airplane - THE BOEING COMPANY; *pg.* 225, *pg.* 567
DREAMMAKER BATH & KITCHEN - Remodeling & Refinishing Businesses - THE DWYER GROUP, INC.; *pg.* 79, *pg.* 1748
DREAMPLUG - Earplug - MCKEON PRODUCTS, INC.; *pg.* 1559, *pg.* 912
DREAMPORT - Business Unit - INTERNATIONAL GAME TECHNOLOGY; *pg.* 420, *pg.* 1606
DREAMSCAPE - Vinyl Wall Covering - COOLEY GROUP, INC.; *pg.* 691, *pg.* 1603
DREAMSCAPE - Pillows - HOLLANDER SLEEP PRODUCTS; *pg.* 927, *pg.* 411
DREAMSCAPES - Baby Toy - LEAPFROG ENTERPRISES, INC.; *pg.* 961, *pg.* 84
DREAMSPACE - Patio Enclosures - THERMAL INDUSTRIES, INC.; *pg.* 115, *pg.* 1555
DREAMTOWN - Toy & Game - HASBRO, INC.; *pg.* 954, *pg.* 1603
DREAMWEAVER - Software - ADOBE SYSTEMS INCORPORATED; *pg.* 342, *pg.* 235
DREAMWEAVER - Sleep Mask - MCKEON PRODUCTS, INC.; *pg.* 1559, *pg.* 912
DREAMWELL - Mattress - SIMMONS COMPANY; *pg.* 943, *pg.* 520
DREAMWORKS - Children Product - TUPPERWARE BRANDS CORPORATION; *pg.* 1139, *pg.* 456
DREAMY - Fabric - NEMSCHOFF, INC.; *pg.* 936, *pg.* 1890
DREEMM - Footwear - STEVEN MADDEN, LTD.; *pg.* 1819, *pg.* 1176
DREFT - Laundry Product - THE PROCTER & GAMBLE COMPANY; *pg.* 1129, *pg.* 1418
DREMEL - Flex-Shaft Drill - STOELTING CO.; *pg.* 1430, *pg.* 671
DREMEL MOTO-TOOL - Stereotaxic Equipment - STOELTING CO.; *pg.* 1430, *pg.* 671
DREN - Nutritional Supplement - MAXIMUM HUMAN PERFORMANCE, INC.; *pg.* 1559, *pg.* 1065
DRESINATE - Rosin Soaps - EASTMAN CHEMICAL COMPANY; *pg.* 1159, *pg.* 1636
DRESINATE - Additive - HERCULES INCORPORATED; *pg.* 1166, *pg.* 392
DRESS ALL - Cooking Oil - VENTURA FOODS, LLC; *pg.* 908, *pg.* 49
DRESS BARN - Women's Clothing Stores - THE DRESS BARN, INC.; *pg.* 1767, *pg.* 1343
DRESS LIKE YOUR DOLL - Doll And Toy - AMERICAN GIRL LLC; *pg.* 949, *pg.* 1871
DRESS TO EMPRESS - Nail Care Product - OPI PRODUCTS INC.; *pg.* 518, *pg.* 167
DRESS TO IMPRESS - Pant Set - HABAND COMPANY, INC.; *pg.* 1772, *pg.* 1099
DRESSABOUT - Shoes - MASON COMPANIES, INC.; *pg.* 1811, *pg.* 1856
DRESSER-RAND - Gas Turbine - INGERSOLL-RAND COMPANY; *pg.* 1349, *pg.* 1370
DRESSLER - Power System - ADVANCED ENERGY INDUSTRIES, INC.; *pg.* 613, *pg.* 328
DRESSY DAISY - Toy & Game - HASBRO, INC.; *pg.* 954, *pg.* 1603
DREW - Alkaline-Base Degreaser - ASHLAND INC.; *pg.* 972, *pg.* 726
DREWCLEAN - Cleaning Preparations - ASHLAND INC.; *pg.* 972, *pg.* 726
DREWFAX - Surface Active Agent - ASHLAND INC.; *pg.* 972, *pg.* 726
DREWFLOC - Water Treatment - ASHLAND INC.; *pg.* 972, *pg.* 726
DREWGARD - Chemicals - ASHLAND INC.; *pg.* 972, *pg.* 726
DREWMULSE - Chemical Product - STEPAN COMPANY; *pg.* 1182, *pg.* 643
DREWPLAST - Chemical Product - STEPAN COMPANY; *pg.* 1182, *pg.* 643
DREWPLUS - Chemicals - ASHLAND INC.; *pg.* 972, *pg.* 726
DREWPOL - Chemical Product - STEPAN COMPANY; *pg.* 1182, *pg.* 643
DREWRAD - Synthetic Resins - ASHLAND INC.; *pg.* 972, *pg.* 726
DREWSPERSE - Antifoulants - ASHLAND INC.; *pg.* 972, *pg.* 726
DREWZYME - Chemicals - ASHLAND INC.; *pg.* 972, *pg.* 726
DREXEL HERITAGE - Furniture - HERITAGE HOME GROUP; *pg.* 926, *pg.* 1379
DREYER'S - Ice Cream - DREYER'S GRAND ICE CREAM HOLDINGS, INC.; *pg.* 1852, *pg.* 171
DREYER'S - Food Product - NESTLE USA, INC.; *pg.* 883, *pg.* 96
DREYER'S GRAND ICE CREAM - Food Product - NESTLE USA, INC.; *pg.* 883, *pg.* 96
DREYFUS - Bear - GUND, INC.; *pg.* 954, *pg.* 1056
DRF.COM - Thoroughbred Horse Racing Internet Site - DAILY RACING FORM, LLC; *pg.* 1632, *pg.* 1221
DRGFINDER - Medical Computer Program - 3M COMPANY; *pg.* 1142, *pg.* 956
DRGPS - Navigation Aid - TRIMBLE NAVIGATION LIMITED; *pg.* 1384, *pg.* 288
DRI - Nonionic Surfactant - KALO, INC.; *pg.* 1796, *pg.* 719
DRI-CAN - Desiccating Containers - MULTISORB TECHNOLOGIES, INC.; *pg.* 1570, *pg.* 1150
DRI-CHEM - Veterinary Chemistry Analyzer - HESKA CORPORATION; *pg.* 1542, *pg.* 335
DRI-CONTROL - Valves - VALCOR ENGINEERING CORPORATION; *pg.* 1386, *pg.* 1123
DRI COTE - Woodworking Machinery Lubricant - BOSTIK INC.; *pg.* 1150, *pg.* 833
DRI-FIT - Apparel - NIKE, INC.; *pg.* 1812, *pg.* 1492
DRI-FLO - Automatic Continuous Flow System for Grain Bins - SHIVVERS INC.; *pg.* 707, *pg.* 704
DRI-KOOL - Coolant - UNIVERSAL PHOTONICS, INC.; *pg.* 1433, *pg.* 1167
DRI-LITES - Men's & Women's Golf Shoes - ETONIC WORLDWIDE LLC; *pg.* 1808, *pg.* 857
DRI-LOC - Meat, Fish & Poultry Absorbent Pads - SEALED AIR CORPORATION; *pg.* 1468, *pg.* 1058
DRI-MOL 60 - Sweetener - ARCHER-DANIELS-MIDLAND COMPANY; *pg.* 825, *pg.* 565
DRI-MOL 604 - Sweetener - ARCHER-DANIELS-MIDLAND COMPANY; *pg.* 825, *pg.* 565
DRI-MOL DRY - Sweetener - ARCHER-DANIELS-MIDLAND COMPANY; *pg.* 825, *pg.* 565
DRI-MOL FLAKE - Sweetener - ARCHER-DANIELS-MIDLAND COMPANY; *pg.* 825, *pg.* 565
DRI-MOL R - Sweetener - ARCHER-DANIELS-MIDLAND COMPANY; *pg.* 825, *pg.* 565
DRI-MOP - Towels - ORCHIDS PAPER PRODUCTS COMPANY; *pg.* 1465, *pg.* 1488
DRI 'N LUBE - Dispersant - DELTA FOREMOST CHEMICAL CORPORATION; *pg.* 1155, *pg.* 1642
DRI POP - Popcorn Oil - VENTURA FOODS, LLC; *pg.* 908, *pg.* 49
DRI-Q - Moisture Transport Fabrics - GUILFORD PERFORMANCE TEXTILES; *pg.* 693, *pg.* 1393
DRI-RELEASE - Fiber - 180S, LLC; *pg.* 1824, *pg.* 754
DRI-SATE - Dry Acid System - ROCKWELL MEDICAL TECHNOLOGIES, INC.; *pg.* 1590, *pg.* 913
DRI-SEAL - Vehicle Safety System - GROTE INDUSTRIES, INC.; *pg.* 206, *pg.* 693
DRI-SOLONOID - Valves - VALCOR ENGINEERING CORPORATION; *pg.* 1386, *pg.* 1123
DRI WALK - Ice Remover - SWISHER HYGIENE INC.; *pg.* 336, *pg.* 1507
DRI-Y - Boxer Brief - JOCKEY INTERNATIONAL, INC.; *pg.* 27, *pg.* 1861
DRIBBLEHAPPY - Bib - CARTER'S, INC.; *pg.* 21, *pg.* 491
DRICAP - Desiccant Cartridge - MULTISORB TECHNOLOGIES, INC.; *pg.* 1570, *pg.* 1150
DRICORE - Rain Resistant Paperboard - SONOCO PRODUCTS COMPANY; *pg.* 1469, *pg.* 1619
DRIED FRUIT TENDERS - Backyard Birding - GARDENS ALIVE!, INC.; *pg.* 1796, *pg.* 693
DRIERITE - Chemical Product - SPECTRUM CHEMICALS & LABORATORY PRODUCTS, INC.; *pg.* 1181, *pg.* 94
DRIFAST - Foam - FXI; *pg.* 1163, *pg.* 1552
DRIFT - Sampling Module - BRUKER CORPORATION; *pg.* 1511, *pg.* 788
DRIFT - Garden Roses - THE CONARD-PYLE COMPANY; *pg.* 1794, *pg.* 1594
DRIFT - Bicycle - TREK BICYCLE CORPORATION; *pg.* 1847, *pg.* 1896
DRIFTER - Furniture - ASHLEY FURNITURE INDUSTRIES, INC.; *pg.* 914, *pg.* 1852
DRIFTER - Footwear - COBIAN CORP.; *pg.* 1806, *pg.* 253
DRIFTER - Men's Boot - JACK SCHWARTZ SHOES, INC.; *pg.* 1810, *pg.* 1245
DRIFTER LO - Men's Shoe - JACK SCHWARTZ SHOES, INC.; *pg.* 1810, *pg.* 1245
DRIFTWOOD - Bath Accessory - CROSCILL, INC.; *pg.* 1122, *pg.* 1220
DRIFZ - Custom Wheels - AMERICAN TIRE DISTRIBUTORS HOLDINGS, INC.; *pg.* 199, *pg.* 1379
DRIGER - Toy & Game - HASBRO, INC.; *pg.* 954, *pg.* 1603
DRIKETTE - Desiccant Paper - MULTISORB TECHNOLOGIES, INC.; *pg.* 1570, *pg.* 1150
DRIL-THRU - Mudline Suspension System - DRIL-QUIP, INC.; *pg.* 1330, *pg.* 1704
DRIL-THRU COMPLETION SYSTEMS - Mudline Equipment - DRIL-QUIP, INC.; *pg.* 1330, *pg.* 1704
DRILL AROUND - Data Access & Analysis Technology - INFOR LAWSON; *pg.* 414, *pg.* 961
DRILL-EASE - Lubricant - AMERICAN GREASE STICK CO.; *pg.* 971, *pg.* 902
DRILL GEL - Minerals - MINERALS TECHNOLOGIES INC.; *pg.* 1173, *pg.* 617
DRILL PRESS - Roll Covering - VAIL RUBBER WORKS, INC.; *pg.* 1891, *pg.* 906
DRILL PRESS II - Premium Roll Covers - VAIL RUBBER WORKS, INC.; *pg.* 1891, *pg.* 906
DRILL PRESS X - Premium Roll Covers - VAIL RUBBER WORKS, INC.; *pg.* 1891, *pg.* 906

DRILLCRETE - Concrete Screws - ROBERTSON INC.; pg. 1372, pg. 1924
DRILLER'S CHOICE - Salt - CARGILL LIMITED; pg. 1475, pg. 1914
DRILLING DYNAMICS - Drilling System - BAKER HUGHES INTEQ; pg. 1316, pg. 1700
DRILLSTAR - Microvia Laser Drilling System - GSI GROUP INC.; pg. 1415, pg. 784
DRILPLEX - Mixed Metal Oxide Fluid - M-I SWACO; pg. 980, pg. 1710
DRIMOP - Liquid Absorber - MULTISORB TECHNOLOGIES, INC.; pg. 1570, pg. 1150
DRINA - Lamp - ASHLEY FURNITURE INDUSTRIES, INC.; pg. 914, pg. 1852
DRINK IT. ITS GOOD - Tagline - NEW ENGLAND BREWING COMPANY; pg. 1967, pg. 386
DRINK SMART - Tag Line - JIM BEAM BRANDS CO.; pg. 1965, pg. 601
DRINK STOP - Food Product - SONIC CORP.; pg. 1750, pg. 1487
DRINKMASTER - Kitchen Appliance - HAMILTON BEACH BRANDS, INC.; pg. 56, pg. 1783
DRIP FREE - Spray Product - SPRAYING SYSTEMS CO.; pg. 1063, pg. 670
DRIP-O-MATIC - Drip Dispenser - SURCO PRODUCTS, INC.; pg. 336, pg. 1581
DRIPDRY - Nail Care Product - OPI PRODUCTS INC.; pg. 518, pg. 167
DRIPLESS - Fluid Handling System - GRACO, INC.; pg. 1342, pg. 935
DRITZ - Sewing Notions & Art Needlework - PRYM CONSUMER USA; pg. 698, pg. 1622
DRIVE - Anti-Perspirants & After Shave - THE GILLETTE COMPANY; pg. 509, pg. 795
DRIVE - Expansion Bolt - POWERS FASTENERS INC.; pg. 1059, pg. 1143
DRIVE - Office Furniture - STEELCASE INC.; pg. 475, pg. 889
DRIVE ARCHITECTURE - Hearing Technology - STARKEY LABORATORIES, INC.; pg. 1597, pg. 923
DRIVE EASY - Slogan - AMERICA'S CAR-MART, INC.; pg. 164, pg. 29
DRIVE FOR LIFE - Awareness Program - MOTHERS AGAINST DRUNK DRIVING (MADD); pg. 147, pg. 1723
DRIVE IMAGE - Software - SYMANTEC CORPORATION; pg. 478, pg. 161
DRIVE-IN - Rack - SPEEDRACK PRODUCTS GROUP, LTD.; pg. 112, pg. 908
DRIVE-IN DEALS - Restaurant Type - SONIC CORP.; pg. 1750, pg. 1487
DRIVE-IN FOR A CHANGE - Slogan - SONIC CORP.; pg. 1750, pg. 1487
DRIVE-IN TO SUMMER - Food Service - SONIC CORP.; pg. 1750, pg. 1487
THE DRIVE TO DISCOVER. THE EXPERIENCE TO DELIVER. - Tagline - INCYTE CORPORATION; pg. 1545, pg. 392
DRIVE VALUE. DELIVER SUCCESS. - Tagline - THE CASEY GROUP; pg. 369, pg. 1102
DRIVEBACKUP - Software - NTI CORPORATION; pg. 446, pg. 114
DRIVECARE - Warranty Provider - DRIVETIME AUTOMOTIVE GROUP, INC.; pg. 169, pg. 16
DRIVELINK - Storage System - HGST; pg. 406, pg. 260
DRIVEN - Publication - MOTHERS AGAINST DRUNK DRIVING (MADD); pg. 147, pg. 1723
DRIVEN BY INNOVATION - Tagline - IDEX CORPORATION; pg. 1347, pg. 623
DRIVEN BY NATURE - Tagline - UNITED NATURAL FOODS, INC.; pg. 907, pg. 1608
DRIVEN TO BE THE BEST - Slogan - AUTONATION, INC.; pg. 165, pg. 423
DRIVER - Video Game - UBISOFT INC.; pg. 589, pg. 229
DRIVER MANAGEMENT ONLINE - Online Fleet Management Application - J.J. KELLER & ASSOCIATES, INC.; pg. 1654, pg. 1883
DRIVERAGENT - PC Scan & Update Software - PHOENIX TECHNOLOGIES LTD.; pg. 454, pg. 147
DRIVERLINX - Software - KEITHLEY INSTRUMENTS, INC.; pg. 1418, pg. 1473
DRIVERSTUDIO - Software - COMPUWARE CORPORATION; pg. 379, pg. 879
DRIVESAFE - Resource Management - TRIMBLE NAVIGATION LIMITED; pg. 1384, pg. 288
DRIVESAVER - Vibration Dampening System - GLOBE COMPOSITE SOLUTIONS, LTD.; pg. 1883, pg. 842
DRIVEWEAR - Lens - YOUNGER OPTICS; pg. 1437, pg. 297
DRIVING FOR EXCELLENCE - Tagline - THOR INDUSTRIES, INC.; pg. 1711, pg. 1456
DRIVING SUCCESS - Slogan - CAREY INTERNATIONAL, INC.; pg. 1902, pg. 397
DRIVING YOUR INFORMATION ROUTE - Slogan - OMTOOL, LTD.; pg. 449, pg. 782
DRIXORAL - Medicine - MERCK & CO., INC.; pg. 1566, pg. 1077
DRIZZLE BOOTS - Rain & Snow Boots - PRINCIPLE PLASTICS, INC.; pg. 1816, pg. 94
DRJAYS.COM - Internet Store - DR. JAY'S INC.; pg. 40, pg. 1085
DRO GO - Chemical Cleanser - A.L. WILSON CHEMICAL CO.; pg. 325, pg. 1076
DROID - Smart Phone - MOTOROLA SOLUTIONS, INC.; pg. 657, pg. 659
DROID PRO - Smart Phone - MOTOROLA SOLUTIONS, INC.; pg. 657, pg. 659
DROP - Ear Rings - COACH, INC.; pg. 3, pg. 1214
DROP-INS - Flashlight - ENERGIZER HOLDINGS, INC.; pg. 637, pg. 996
DROP ON DEMAND - Ink - ELECTRONICS FOR IMAGING, INC.; pg. 390, pg. 88
DROP POPZ - Toy - SPIN MASTER LTD.; pg. 967, pg. 1943
DROP TOP AMBER ALE - Beer - CRAFT BREWERS ALLIANCE, INC; pg. 247, pg. 1502
DROP ZONE - Thrill Ride - CANADA'S WONDERLAND COMPANY; pg. 536, pg. 1947
DROPCURE - Graphic Art UV System - NORDSON CORPORATION; pg. 1365, pg. 1480
DROPIN - Bolt & Shield Anchor - POWERS FASTENERS INC.; pg. 1059, pg. 1143
DROPLETS ON CIRCLE - Fluid Handling System - GRACO, INC.; pg. 1342, pg. 935
DROP'N GO EMMA - Toy - THE OHIO ART COMPANY, INC.; pg. 965, pg. 1406
THE DROPPER CREW - Apparels - UNDER ARMOUR, INC.; pg. 49, pg. 759
DROPSTUFF - Software - SMITH MICRO SOFTWARE, INC.; pg. 471, pg. 41
DROPTAR - Software - SMITH MICRO SOFTWARE, INC.; pg. 471, pg. 41
DROPZIP - Software - SMITH MICRO SOFTWARE, INC.; pg. 471, pg. 41
DROTT - Bulk Material Handling - ANVIL ATTACHMENTS, LLC; pg. 1313, pg. 748
DROUHIN - Burgundy Wines - DREYFUS ASHBY INC.; pg. 1962, pg. 1226
DROVERS - Magazine - VANCE PUBLISHING CORPORATION; pg. 1699, pg. 627
DROXIA - Atrial Fibrillation Medication - BRISTOL-MYERS SQUIBB COMPANY; pg. 1509, pg. 1206
DRP - Shroud - ESCO CORPORATION; pg. 1335, pg. 1502
DRP-BOOKLINK - Software - QUESTAR ASSESSMENT, INC.; pg. 1679, pg. 1143
DRP EZCONVERTER - Software - QUESTAR ASSESSMENT, INC.; pg. 1679, pg. 1143
DRUG DIGEST - Drugs & Health Information - EXPRESS SCRIPTS, INC.; pg. 1530, pg. 997
DRUG DISCOVERY & DEVELOPMENT - Trade Magazine - ADVANTAGE BUSINESS MEDIA; pg. 1613, pg. 1116
DRUG INFORMATION FRAMEWORK - Software - FIRST DATABANK, INC.; pg. 397, pg. 217
DRUG INFORMATION FRAMEWORK TRANSACTION OBJECTS - Software - FIRST DATABANK, INC.; pg. 397, pg. 217
DRUG STORE NEWS - Industry Publication - LEBHAR-FRIEDMAN INC.; pg. 1658, pg. 1250
DRUG TOPICS - Pharmacy Publication - TRUVEN HEALTH ANALYTICS; pg. 1696, pg. 867
DRUG TOPICS RED BOOK - Pharmacy Publication - TRUVEN HEALTH ANALYTICS; pg. 1696, pg. 867
DRUGDEX - Medical Information - TRUVEN HEALTH ANALYTICS; pg. 486, pg. 331
DRUGMATRIX - Chemogenomics Reference Database - INCYTE CORPORATION; pg. 1545, pg. 392
DRUGSTORE.COM - On-line Pharmacy Service - CIGNA TEL-DRUG, INC.; pg. 1515, pg. 1625
DRUM - Furniture - THE COMMERCIAL FURNITURE GROUP; pg. 920, pg. 994
DRUM - Rotary Designs - GARDNER DENVER, INC.; pg. 1338, pg. 1592
DRUM - Furniture - J. ROBERT SCOTT INC.; pg. 930, pg. 105
DRUM BOGIE - Dolly For Carrying A Drum - EAGLE MANUFACTURING COMPANY; pg. 79, pg. 1851
DRUM HEAD - Nozzle - NORDSON CORPORATION; pg. 1365, pg. 1480
DRUM-KOR - Drum Separator - GREIF INC.; pg. 1459, pg. 1447
DRUMCAL - Sensitive Film & Adhesive - FLEXCON CORPORATION; pg. 1457, pg. 844
DRUMCAP - Dispensers - UNETTE CORPORATION; pg. 1184, pg. 1114
DRUMMER - Interactive Drum Pattern Sequencer - GIBSON GUITAR CORP.; pg. 550, pg. 1650
DRUMMOND MCCALL - Metal Products - RUSSEL METALS INC.; pg. 1180, pg. 1928
DRUMS OF FIRE - Processed Chicken - TYSON FOODS, INC.; pg. 902, pg. 35
DRUMSTICK - Food Product - NESTLE USA, INC.; pg. 883, pg. 96
DRX - Steel - A. FINKL & SONS CO.; pg. 1309, pg. 563
DRX - Bar Code Data Reconstruction Software - DATALOGIC; pg. 382, pg. 1588
DRY-CHROMA COLOR - Colorant & Additive System - CHROMA CORPORATION; pg. 1441, pg. 632
DRY CREEK - Fishing Gear Product - SIMMS FISHING PRODUCTS CORP.; pg. 1845, pg. 1008
DRY FLOATATION - Customizable Flotation Cushions - THE ROHO GROUP; pg. 1591, pg. 556
DRY FOG - Paint - KELLY-MOORE PAINT COMPANY, INC.; pg. 1443, pg. 198
DRY FOOT - Socks & Knitted Headwear - WIGWAM MILLS, INC.; pg. 15, pg. 1894
DRY HANDS - Lotion For Improving An Athlete's Grip; Drying Agent for Wet Hands - TENDER CORPORATION; pg. 1601, pg. 1035
DRY IDEA - Anti-Perspirant Deodorants - HENKEL CONSUMER GOODS; pg. 511, pg. 22
DRY MICRO - Anti Fog Coating - MCNETT CORPORATION; pg. 1839, pg. 1817
DRY-N-CLEAR - Ear Drying Aid - MCKEON PRODUCTS, INC.; pg. 1559, pg. 912
DRY 'N STRAIGHT - Hair Straightener - CONAIR CORPORATION; pg. 505, pg. 1055
DRY-PAK - Absorbent Cushioned Pads - SEALED AIR CORPORATION; pg. 1468, pg. 1058
DRY-PLUS - Guidewear - CABELA'S INCORPORATED; pg. 535, pg. 1019
DRY-PLUS PRO SERIES - Guidewear - CABELA'S INCORPORATED; pg. 535, pg. 1019
DRY-PRO - Dry Pump - GARDNER DENVER NASH; pg. 1338, pg. 381
DRY PROCESS DICING - Dicing Equipment - DYNATEX INTERNATIONAL; pg. 635, pg. 277
DRY PYROCIDE - Pesticide - MCLAUGHLIN GORMLEY KING COMPANY; pg. 1797, pg. 939
DRY-SHRINK - Heat Shrink - PANDUIT CORP.; pg. 661, pg. 663
DRY-TOUCH - Paper Product - KIMBERLY-CLARK CORPORATION; pg. 1461, pg. 1720
DRY-UR-FLY - Fishing Line - CORTLAND LINE COMPANY; pg. 1831, pg. 1155
DRY WAX - Hair Care Product - JOHN PAUL MITCHELL SYSTEMS; pg. 512, pg. 133
DRY WIPES - Baby Care Product - MUNCHKIN, INC.; pg. 964, pg. 300
DRYCOLUBE - Metal Casting Product - HILL & GRIFFITH COMPANY; pg. 1167, pg. 1414
DRYDEX - Repair Product - DAP PRODUCTS, INC.; pg. 1441, pg. 756
DRYEASE - Molecular Biology Product - THERMO FISHER SCIENTIFIC INC.; pg. 1602, pg. 61
DRYFLEX - Colorite Polymer - TEKNI-PLEX, INC.; pg. 1470, pg. 1122
DRYFLO - Cartridge Collectors - DONALDSON COMPANY, INC.; pg. 1329, pg. 917
DRYGUARD - Desiccant - BASF CATALYSTS LLC; pg. 1148, pg. 1074
DRYIR - Radiant Infrared Heater - PRECISION CONTROL SYSTEMS, INC./ RESEARCH INC.; pg. 1427, pg. 923
DRYJOYS - Shoes - ACUSHNET COMPANY; pg. 1824, pg. 818
DRYJOYS PERFORMANCE COLLECTION - Shoes - ACUSHNET COMPANY; pg. 1824, pg. 818
DRYJOYS PERFORMANCE FLEECE - Golf Shoe -

First page reference indicates Business Class Edition
Second page reference indicates Geographic Edition

ACUSHNET COMPANY; *pg.* 1824, *pg.* 818
DRYJOYS PERFORMANCE LIGHT - Shoes - ACUSHNET COMPANY; *pg.* 1824, *pg.* 818
DRYLIFE - Filter - W.L. GORE & ASSOCIATES, INC.; *pg.* 122, *pg.* 388
DRYLOFT - All-Weather Fabric - W.L. GORE & ASSOCIATES, INC.; *pg.* 122, *pg.* 388
DRYLOK - Masonry Product - UNITED GILSONITE LABORATORIES; *pg.* 1449, *pg.* 1527
DRYLOX - Cover Glass - E.I. DU PONT DE NEMOURS & COMPANY; *pg.* 1159, *pg.* 390
DRYLUBE - Soap Lubricant - HEATBATH CORPORATION; *pg.* 1165, *pg.* 826
DRYPERS - Baby Diaper - ASSOCIATED HYGIENIC PRODUCTS LLC; *pg.* 1496, *pg.* 531
DRYPIX1000 - Dry Imager - FUJIFILM MEDICAL SYSTEMS USA, INC.; *pg.* 1531, *pg.* 374
DRYPIX3000 - Dry Imager - FUJIFILM MEDICAL SYSTEMS USA, INC.; *pg.* 1531, *pg.* 374
DRYPIX5000 - Dry Imager - FUJIFILM MEDICAL SYSTEMS USA, INC.; *pg.* 1531, *pg.* 374
DRYPIX7000 - Dry Imager - FUJIFILM MEDICAL SYSTEMS USA, INC.; *pg.* 1531, *pg.* 374
DRYROD - Welding Rod Oven - PHOENIX PRODUCTS COMPANY; *pg.* 1304, *pg.* 1879
DRYSAFE - Battery - EXIDE TECHNOLOGIES; *pg.* 204, *pg.* 483
DRYSDALES - Apparel - DRYSDALES INC.; *pg.* 1767, *pg.* 1489
DRYSPORT - Golfing Product - CALLAWAY GOLF COMPANY; *pg.* 1829, *pg.* 58
DRYSTONE - Gypsum Cement - USG CORPORATION; *pg.* 118, *pg.* 594
DRYTECH - Polymer - THE DOW CHEMICAL COMPANY; *pg.* 1157, *pg.* 898
DRYTEX - Orthopedic Product - DJO INCORPORATED; *pg.* 1524, *pg.* 302
DRYVIEW - Computer Software - EASTMAN KODAK COMPANY; *pg.* 1408, *pg.* 1333
DRYWALL VAC - Industrial Vacuum for Drywall Cleaning - SHOP-VAC CORPORATION; *pg.* 1375, *pg.* 1595
DRYWIRE - Welding Rod Oven - PHOENIX PRODUCTS COMPANY; *pg.* 1304, *pg.* 1879
DRYZ - Insoles - JOHNSTON & MURPHY CO.; *pg.* 1810, *pg.* 1651
DS-105TR - Electronic Component - EMCORE CORPORATION; *pg.* 636, *pg.* 39
DS-108TR - Electronic Component - EMCORE CORPORATION; *pg.* 636, *pg.* 39
DS-109TR - Electronic Component - EMCORE CORPORATION; *pg.* 636, *pg.* 39
DS-120MDR - Electronic Component - EMCORE CORPORATION; *pg.* 636, *pg.* 39
DS-150 - Electronic Component - EMCORE CORPORATION; *pg.* 636, *pg.* 39
DS-2OOO - Beginning & Intermediate Telescopes - MEADE INSTRUMENTS CORPORATION; *pg.* 1422, *pg.* 113
DS-50 - Electronic Components - MOLEX INCORPORATED; *pg.* 655, *pg.* 628
DS-726/T3/E3 - Electronic Component - EMCORE CORPORATION; *pg.* 636, *pg.* 39
DS-DENIM - Footwear - STEVEN MADDEN, LTD.; *pg.* 1819, *pg.* 1176
DS-DITSY - Dress - STEVEN MADDEN, LTD.; *pg.* 1819, *pg.* 1176
DS EXPERT - Software - DELL SOFTWARE; *pg.* 385, *pg.* 40
DS-LACEY - Dress - STEVEN MADDEN, LTD.; *pg.* 1819, *pg.* 1176
DS-TUXEDO - Dress - STEVEN MADDEN, LTD.; *pg.* 1819, *pg.* 1176
DS230 - Heat Detector - BOSCH SECURITY SYSTEMS, INC.; *pg.* 626, *pg.* 1158
DS230F - Heat Detector - BOSCH SECURITY SYSTEMS, INC.; *pg.* 626, *pg.* 1158
DS233F - Heat Detector - BOSCH SECURITY SYSTEMS, INC.; *pg.* 626, *pg.* 1158
DS240 - Smoke Detector - BOSCH SECURITY SYSTEMS, INC.; *pg.* 626, *pg.* 1158
DS241 - Smoke Detector - BOSCH SECURITY SYSTEMS, INC.; *pg.* 626, *pg.* 1158
DS250 - Smoke Detector - BOSCH SECURITY SYSTEMS, INC.; *pg.* 626, *pg.* 1158
DS260 - Smoke Detectors - BOSCH SECURITY SYSTEMS, INC.; *pg.* 626, *pg.* 1158
DS280 - Smoke Detectors - BOSCH SECURITY SYSTEMS, INC.; *pg.* 626, *pg.* 1158
DS6 - Culture for Grade - CHR. HANSEN; *pg.* 847, *pg.* 1873
DS9484 - Power Supply - BOSCH SECURITY SYSTEMS, INC.; *pg.* 626, *pg.* 1158
DSB - Barrier Screw - DAVIS-STANDARD LLC; *pg.* 1328, *pg.* 368
DSBM-T - Feed Screw - DAVIS-STANDARD LLC; *pg.* 1328, *pg.* 368
DSC NEXOS - Computer Programs - ALCATEL-LUCENT USA, INC.; *pg.* 615, *pg.* 1728
DSD - Drives - MAGNETEK, INC.; *pg.* 1301, *pg.* 1870
DSDA - Microphone Technology - ANDREA ELECTRONICS CORPORATION; *pg.* 617, *pg.* 1143
DSDM - Digital System Development Methodology Handbook - COMPUTER SCIENCES CORPORATION; *pg.* 378, *pg.* 1780
DSI ADAPTOR DEVELOPMENT - Network Solutions - SONUS NETWORKS INC.; *pg.* 1281, *pg.* 858
DSL - Copper Connectivity - CHANNELL COMMERCIAL CORP.; *pg.* 1870, *pg.* 291
DSLC - Digital Synchronizer - WOODWARD, INC.; *pg.* 122, *pg.* 329
DSM - Navigation Aid - TRIMBLE NAVIGATION LIMITED; *pg.* 1384, *pg.* 288
DSMAC - Systems Integration & Aeronautics - LOCKHEED MARTIN CORPORATION; *pg.* 229, *pg.* 762
DSP/BIOS - Software Kernel Foundation - TEXAS INSTRUMENTS INCORPORATED; *pg.* 679, *pg.* 1688
DSP BUILDER - Software - ALTERA CORPORATION; *pg.* 348, *pg.* 237
DSP-SYNC - Memory Products - TEXAS INSTRUMENTS INCORPORATED; *pg.* 679, *pg.* 1688
DSPLL - Frequency Synthesis - SILICON LABORATORIES INC.; *pg.* 674, *pg.* 1666
DSS BROADCASTER - Software - MICROSTRATEGY, INC.; *pg.* 1266, *pg.* 1809
DSS BROADCASTER SERVER - Software - MICROSTRATEGY, INC.; *pg.* 1266, *pg.* 1809
DSS (DECISION SUPPORT SYSTEM) - Software System - MENTOR GRAPHICS CORPORATION; *pg.* 432, *pg.* 1510
DSS OFFICE - Software - MICROSTRATEGY, INC.; *pg.* 1266, *pg.* 1809
DSS SUBSCRIBER - Software - MICROSTRATEGY, INC.; *pg.* 1266, *pg.* 1809
DSS TELECASTER - Software - MICROSTRATEGY, INC.; *pg.* 1266, *pg.* 1809
DSSARCHITECT - Software - MICROSTRATEGY, INC.; *pg.* 1266, *pg.* 1809
DSSSERVER - Software - MICROSTRATEGY, INC.; *pg.* 1266, *pg.* 1809
DSSWEB - Software - MICROSTRATEGY, INC.; *pg.* 1266, *pg.* 1809
DST - Software - DST SYSTEMS, INC.; *pg.* 388, *pg.* 982
DST - Defined Substrate Technology - IDEXX LABORATORIES, INC.; *pg.* 1543, *pg.* 753
DST SYSTEMS - Software - DST SYSTEMS, INC.; *pg.* 388, *pg.* 982
DSTAR - Deployable System for Training & Readiness - CUBIC CORPORATION; *pg.* 632, *pg.* 201
DSU - Network Accessing Product - ADTRAN, INC.; *pg.* 344, *pg.* 6
DSU 56/64 - Automatic Dial Backup - ADTRAN, INC.; *pg.* 344, *pg.* 6
DSU 5600 - Automatic Dial Backup - ADTRAN, INC.; *pg.* 344, *pg.* 6
DSU III AR - Automatic Dial Backup - ADTRAN, INC.; *pg.* 344, *pg.* 6
DSU III S2W - Network Accessing Product - ADTRAN, INC.; *pg.* 344, *pg.* 6
DSU III S4W - Network Accessing Product - ADTRAN, INC.; *pg.* 344, *pg.* 6
DSU III TDM - Network Accessing Product - ADTRAN, INC.; *pg.* 344, *pg.* 6
DSU IQ - Network Accessing Product - ADTRAN, INC.; *pg.* 344, *pg.* 6
DSU IV ESP - Network Accessing Product - ADTRAN, INC.; *pg.* 344, *pg.* 6
DSV - Software System - MENTOR GRAPHICS CORPORATION; *pg.* 432, *pg.* 1510
DSVIEW - Software - NER HOLDINGS INC.; *pg.* 444, *pg.* 1071
DT - Golf Equipment - ACUSHNET COMPANY; *pg.* 1824, *pg.* 818
DT - Fluid Handling System - GRACO, INC.; *pg.* 1342, *pg.* 935
DT - Medication for Diphtheria, Tetanus and Pertussis for Children - SANOFI PASTEUR, INC; *pg.* 1591, *pg.* 1588
DT CHAMP - Upgrade Program - DRIVETIME AUTOMOTIVE GROUP, INC.; *pg.* 169, *pg.* 16
DT SOLO - Golf Equipment - ACUSHNET COMPANY; *pg.* 1824, *pg.* 818
DT3 - Automatic Chromatic Tuner - KORG USA, INC.; *pg.* 556, *pg.* 1180
DT7 - Guitar & Bass Tuner - KORG USA, INC.; *pg.* 556, *pg.* 1180
DT700 - Glue Gun - ARROW FASTENER COMPANY, INC.; *pg.* 1042, *pg.* 1118
DTM - Coating & Enamel - KELLY-MOORE PAINT COMPANY, INC.; *pg.* 1443, *pg.* 198
DTP - Gene Expression Analysis - RESPONSE GENETICS, INC.; *pg.* 1590, *pg.* 139
DTR-1000 - Digital Rack Mount Tuner - KORG USA, INC.; *pg.* 556, *pg.* 1180
DTR-2000 - Digital Rack Mount Tuner - KORG USA, INC.; *pg.* 556, *pg.* 1180
DTR410 - Two Way Radios - MOTOROLA SOLUTIONS, INC.; *pg.* 657, *pg.* 659
DTR510 - Two Way Radios - MOTOROLA SOLUTIONS, INC.; *pg.* 657, *pg.* 659
DTR550 - Two Way Radios - MOTOROLA SOLUTIONS, INC.; *pg.* 657, *pg.* 659
DTR610 - Two Way Radios - MOTOROLA SOLUTIONS, INC.; *pg.* 657, *pg.* 659
DTR650 - Two Way Radios - MOTOROLA SOLUTIONS, INC.; *pg.* 657, *pg.* 659
DTS - Orthopedic Device - DJO SURGICAL; *pg.* 1525, *pg.* 1661
DTS - Sedan - GENERAL MOTORS COMPANY; *pg.* 175, *pg.* 881
DTS-HD ENCODER - Encoder - DTS, INC.; *pg.* 634, *pg.* 55
DTS-HD HIGH RESOLUTION AUDIO - Audio Entertainment - DTS, INC.; *pg.* 634, *pg.* 55
DTS-HD MASTER AUDIO SUITE - Audio Entertainment - DTS, INC.; *pg.* 634, *pg.* 55
DTS-HD STREAMPLAYER - Decoder - DTS, INC.; *pg.* 634, *pg.* 55
DTS-HD STREAMTOOLS - Encoder Tool - DTS, INC.; *pg.* 634, *pg.* 55
DTS MASTER AUDIO - Audio Entertainment - DTS, INC.; *pg.* 634, *pg.* 55
DTS SURROUND SENSATION ULTRAPAC - Audio Entertainment - DTS, INC.; *pg.* 634, *pg.* 55
DTS SURROUND SENSATION ULTRAPC - Audio Entertainment - DTS, INC.; *pg.* 634, *pg.* 55
DTX - Fluid Handling System - GRACO, INC.; *pg.* 1342, *pg.* 935
DTX - Herbal Formula - SHAKLEE CORPORATION; *pg.* 1593, *pg.* 184
DU - Spectrophotometer - BECKMAN COULTER, INC.; *pg.* 1402, *pg.* 48
DU ALL - Antifreeze Drainage System - WYNN OIL COMPANY; *pg.* 987, *pg.* 173
DU-SOM - Drum Upender - LIFTOMATIC MATERIAL HANDLING INC.; *pg.* 94, *pg.* 560
DUA-PULL - Pulling Grip - HUBBELL INCORPORATED; *pg.* 1299, *pg.* 370
DUAL - Specialty Paper - APPVION INC.; *pg.* 1451, *pg.* 1852
DUAL-8 - Ablation Catheter - ST. JUDE MEDICAL, INC.; *pg.* 1596, *pg.* 963
DUAL-824 - Security System - NORTEK SECURITY & CONTROL LLC; *pg.* 659, *pg.* 59
DUAL ALPHA - Software - BIO-RAD LABORATORIES, INC.; *pg.* 1504, *pg.* 101
DUAL BASE MINUS OIL - Beauty Product - AVEDA CORPORATION; *pg.* 499, *pg.* 917
DUAL BORE PRODUCTION SYSTEM - Subsea Equipment - DRIL-QUIP, INC.; *pg.* 1330, *pg.* 1704
DUAL CLIMATE - Shoes - ACUSHNET COMPANY; *pg.* 1824, *pg.* 818
DUAL-COOL - Climate Control Device - E.D. BULLARD COMPANY; *pg.* 1332, *pg.* 727
DUAL DELTAFEX - Musical Instrument - PEAVEY ELECTRONICS CORPORATION; *pg.* 662, *pg.* 970
DUAL-DOKLIFT/LEVELER - Combination Hydraulic Scissors Lift & Hydraulic Dock Leveler - RITE-HITE HOLDING CORPORATION; *pg.* 1372, *pg.* 1880
DUAL DOVETAIL - Optical Product - LEUPOLD & STEVENS, INC.; *pg.* 1420, *pg.* 1492
DUAL DUROMETER - Grip - EATON CORPORATION; *pg.* 1331, *pg.* 1429

DUAL DUTY PLUS - Home Sewing Thread - MAKE IT COATS; *pg.* 696, *pg.* 1367
DUAL FORCE - Golf Equipment - CALLAWAY GOLF COMPANY; *pg.* 1829, *pg.* 58
DUAL FORCE - Analog Controller - MAD CATZ INTERACTIVE INC.; *pg.* 429, *pg.* 204
DUAL FORCE 2 - Video Game Controller - MAD CATZ INTERACTIVE INC.; *pg.* 429, *pg.* 204
DUAL FORCE 2 CONTROLLER - Video Game Controller - MAD CATZ INTERACTIVE INC.; *pg.* 429, *pg.* 204
DUAL FORCE PRO - Video Game Controller - MAD CATZ INTERACTIVE INC.; *pg.* 429, *pg.* 204
DUAL FREQUENCY - Oil Treater Product - CAMERON INTERNATIONAL; *pg.* 1151, *pg.* 1702
DUAL FREQUENCY CONFINED - Plasma Technology Used to Extend Dielectric Etch Capability - LAM RESEARCH CORPORATION; *pg.* 1354, *pg.* 91
DUAL HIP - Medical Test System - HOLOGIC, INC.; *pg.* 1416, *pg.* 784
DUAL LANE - Wrapper - CAMPBELL WRAPPER CORPORATION; *pg.* 1454, *pg.* 1856
DUAL-LITE - Lighting - HUBBELL INCORPORATED; *pg.* 1299, *pg.* 370
DUAL LOCK - Fastening System - 3M COMPANY; *pg.* 1142, *pg.* 956
DUAL LOCK - Quick Disconnects Designed for Hose Assemblies Used on Pneumatic Air Tools - DIXON VALVE & COUPLING COMPANY; *pg.* 1045, *pg.* 766
DUAL-LOFT - Pillow - SELECT COMFORT CORPORATION; *pg.* 942, *pg.* 942
DUAL-LOK - Fastener - LONG-LOK FASTENERS CORP.; *pg.* 1053, *pg.* 1416
DUAL MASKING ELECTROL - Screen - DA-LITE SCREEN COMPANY; *pg.* 632, *pg.* 698
DUAL MODE - Programmable Micropower Voltage Regulators - MAXIM INTEGRATED PRODUCTS, INC.; *pg.* 653, *pg.* 247
DUAL-OPTION - Hard Drive - WESTERN DIGITAL CORPORATION; *pg.* 492, *pg.* 118
DUAL OVAL - Vacuum Cleaner For Carwash Systems - D&S CAR WASH EQUIPMENT CO.; *pg.* 1327, *pg.* 979
DUAL PEAK - Chargers - HOBBICO, INC.; *pg.* 956, *pg.* 562
DUAL PHY - Ethernet Transceiver - BROADCOM CORPORATION; *pg.* 364, *pg.* 108
DUAL POLARITY - Oil Treater Product - CAMERON INTERNATIONAL; *pg.* 1151, *pg.* 1702
DUAL-RAIL - Electronic Sound Pickups for Guitars - GIBSON GUITAR CORP.; *pg.* 550, *pg.* 1650
DUAL-RANGE - Manometer - DWYER INSTRUMENTS INC.; *pg.* 1330, *pg.* 694
DUAL RIDER - Void Filler - GREIF INC.; *pg.* 1459, *pg.* 1447
DUAL SOFT HEAT - Beverage - BUNN-O-MATIC CORPORATION; *pg.* 53, *pg.* 661
DUAL SPECTRUM - Cosmetic Product - MERLE NORMAN COSMETICS, INC.; *pg.* 517, *pg.* 136
DUAL SPEED - Straight Knife - THE WOLF MACHINE CO.; *pg.* 1389, *pg.* 1427
DUAL-TAC - Blade - 3M COMPANY; *pg.* 1142, *pg.* 956
DUAL-THERM - Discrete Process Controller - DAVIS-STANDARD LLC; *pg.* 1328, *pg.* 368
DUAL TORQUE - Drilling Product - SMITH INTERNATIONAL, INC.; *pg.* 1377, *pg.* 1715
DUAL TOUCH - Integrated Circuit - ATMEL CORPORATION; *pg.* 621, *pg.* 238
DUAL TRACK - Trailer - HINIKER COMPANY; *pg.* 704, *pg.* 927
DUAL VISION - Slot Product - BALLY TECHNOLOGIES, INC.; *pg.* 531, *pg.* 1022
DUAL WHEEL EXCAVATOR - Underwater Bucketwheel Cutter - ELLICOTT DREDGES, LLC; *pg.* 1333, *pg.* 757
DUAL-ZONE - Pressure Controller - MKS INSTRUMENTS, INC.; *pg.* 1362, *pg.* 781
DUALBEAM - Electron Microscope - FEI COMPANY; *pg.* 1413, *pg.* 1498
DUALCOM - Glass & Ceramic Material - CORNING INCORPORATED; *pg.* 1122, *pg.* 1154
DUALCON - Electronic Components - MOLEX INCORPORATED; *pg.* 655, *pg.* 628
DUALDADDY - Electrical Appliance & Housewares - NATIONAL PRESTO INDUSTRIES, INC; *pg.* 1128, *pg.* 1857
DUALFLEX - Wheelchair Back - INVACARE CORPORATION; *pg.* 1546, *pg.* 1451
DUALFLEX SPRING SYSTEM - Furniture - FLEXSTEEL INDUSTRIES, INC.; *pg.* 925, *pg.* 707
DUALINE - Dental Product - DENTSPLY INTERNATIONAL INC.; *pg.* 1522, *pg.* 1596
DUALITE - Signs - DUALITE SALES & SERVICE, INC.; *pg.* 1296, *pg.* 1482
DUALMESH - Surgical Product - W.L. GORE & ASSOCIATES, INC.; *pg.* 122, *pg.* 388
DUALNET - Computer Hardware - NVIDIA CORPORATION; *pg.* 447, *pg.* 268
DUALOY - Fiberglass Pipe Product - NOV AMERON; *pg.* 100, *pg.* 187
DUALSHARP - Ink Jet Label - AVERY DENNISON CORPORATION; *pg.* 1452, *pg.* 95
DUALSPEED/BILEVEL - Fault Protection - MAXIM INTEGRATED PRODUCTS, INC.; *pg.* 653, *pg.* 247
DUALTOUCH - Software - CRESTRON ELECTRONICS INC.; *pg.* 631, *pg.* 1116
DUALTRANS - Vacuum Transducer - MKS INSTRUMENTS, INC.; *pg.* 1362, *pg.* 781
DUALTRONIC - Transmission System - BORGWARNER INC.; *pg.* 167, *pg.* 867
DUBALL - Valves - FLOWSERVE CORPORATION; *pg.* 82, *pg.* 1719
DUBAN - Bandage - DERMA SCIENCES, INC.; *pg.* 1523, *pg.* 1111
DUBBLE BUBBLE - Lottery Game - IOWA LOTTERY; *pg.* 996, *pg.* 705
DUBBLE BUBBLE - Chewing Gum - TOOTSIE ROLL INDUSTRIES, INC.; *pg.* 1863, *pg.* 591
DUBBLEGUM - Shoe - AEROGROUP INTERNATIONAL, INC.; *pg.* 1803, *pg.* 1055
DUBL DUCK - Pet Grooming Product - MILLERS FORGE INC.; *pg.* 1056, *pg.* 1733
DUBL-PANL - Stressed-Skin Building Systems - BEHLEN MFG. CO.; *pg.* 701, *pg.* 1010
DUBL-SERV - Towel Dispenser - WAUSAU PAPER BAY WEST; *pg.* 1471, *pg.* 1465
DUBL-TOUGH - Wipers - WAUSAU PAPER BAY WEST; *pg.* 1471, *pg.* 1465
DUBLE TIME - Boots - AEROGROUP INTERNATIONAL, INC.; *pg.* 1803, *pg.* 1055
DUBLE TROUBLE - Boots - AEROGROUP INTERNATIONAL, INC.; *pg.* 1803, *pg.* 1055
DUBLIN - Fabric - NEMSCHOFF, INC.; *pg.* 936, *pg.* 1890
DUBLIN DOLLARS - Lottery Game - MASSACHUSETTS STATE LOTTERY; *pg.* 998, *pg.* 802
DUBLSOFT - Towels & Tissues - WAUSAU PAPER BAY WEST; *pg.* 1471, *pg.* 1465
DUBOT - Furniture - ASHLEY FURNITURE INDUSTRIES, INC.; *pg.* 914, *pg.* 1852
DUCANE - Heating & Cooling Product - LENNOX INTERNATIONAL INC.; *pg.* 1073, *pg.* 1736
DUCARE - Wound Dressing - DERMA SCIENCES, INC.; *pg.* 1523, *pg.* 1111
DUCAROSSO CHIANTI RESERVA - Wine - SHAW ROSS INTERNATIONAL IMPORTERS; *pg.* 1970, *pg.* 449
DUCATI JULIET - Sunglasses - OAKLEY, INC.; *pg.* 1840, *pg.* 86
DUCATI MONSTER DOG - Sunglasses - OAKLEY, INC.; *pg.* 1840, *pg.* 86
DUCATI ZERO - Sunglasses - OAKLEY, INC.; *pg.* 1840, *pg.* 86
DUCERAGOLD - Dental Product - DENTSPLY INTERNATIONAL INC.; *pg.* 1522, *pg.* 1596
DUCERAM - Dental Product - DENTSPLY INTERNATIONAL INC.; *pg.* 1522, *pg.* 1596
DUCHESS - Lighting Product - QUOIZEL INC.; *pg.* 1304, *pg.* 1616
DUCHESS - Theater Glasses - SWIFT OPTICAL INSTRUMENTS, INC.; *pg.* 1430, *pg.* 1744
DUCHESSA BRECCIA - Tile - ARTISTIC TILE INC.; *pg.* 914, *pg.* 1119
DUCHESSA SEMPLICE - Tile - ARTISTIC TILE INC.; *pg.* 914, *pg.* 1119
DUCK BILLS - Lottery Game - KENTUCKY LOTTERY CORPORATION; *pg.* 996, *pg.* 735
DUCK BOOTS - Footwear - L.L. BEAN, INC.; *pg.* 1777, *pg.* 750
DUCK STAMPS - Video Game - INTERNATIONAL GAME TECHNOLOGY; *pg.* 957, *pg.* 1024
DUCK TAPE - Adhesive - HENKEL CONSUMER ADHESIVES, INC.; *pg.* 403, *pg.* 1480
DUCKBILL - Valve - VERNAY LABORATORIES, INC.; *pg.* 1891, *pg.* 1482
THE DUCKS - Cartoon Character - THE WALT DISNEY COMPANY; *pg.* 317, *pg.* 52
DUCKSBACK - Roofing Underlayment System - MINERALS TECHNOLOGIES INC.; *pg.* 1173, *pg.* 617
DUCROS - Seasonings - MCCORMICK & COMPANY, INCORPORATED; *pg.* 1027, *pg.* 779
DUDE - Food - WESTERN SIZZLIN CORPORATION; *pg.* 1755, *pg.* 1806
DUDLEY - Softball - SPALDING; *pg.* 1845, *pg.* 846
DUDRESS - Wound Dressing - DERMA SCIENCES, INC.; *pg.* 1523, *pg.* 1111
DUE DATE - Maternity Wear - KELLWOOD COMPANY; *pg.* 28, *pg.* 975
DUEL MASTERS - Toy & Game - HASBRO, INC.; *pg.* 954, *pg.* 1603
DUELER - Passenger Tires - BRIDGESTONE AMERICAS, INC.; *pg.* 201, *pg.* 1649
DUET - Guest Chairs - BERNHARDT DESIGN; *pg.* 918, *pg.* 1381
DUET - Generator - CHYRONHEGO; *pg.* 371, *pg.* 1179
DUET - Mattress - ETHAN ALLEN INTERIORS INC.; *pg.* 924, *pg.* 343
DUET - Fabric - NEMSCHOFF, INC.; *pg.* 936, *pg.* 1890
DUET - Hearing Instrument - SEMTECH CORPORATION GENNUM PRODUCTS; *pg.* 671, *pg.* 1919
DUET - Home Appliance Product - WHIRLPOOL CORPORATION; *pg.* 62, *pg.* 872
DUETT - Medical Device - VASCULAR SOLUTIONS, INC.; *pg.* 1434, *pg.* 946
DUETTA - Bath & Plumbing Product - JACUZZI BRANDS CORPORATION; *pg.* 554, *pg.* 65
DUETTE - Triple Honeycomb Shades for Maximum Energy Efficiency - HUNTER DOUGLAS, INC.; *pg.* 928, *pg.* 1320
DUEX - Film Cassettes - EASTMAN KODAK COMPANY; *pg.* 1408, *pg.* 1333
DUFF - Hot Roll Mixes - GILSTER-MARY LEE CORPORATION; *pg.* 858, *pg.* 563
DUFF-NORTON - Crane - COLUMBUS MCKINNON CORPORATION; *pg.* 1325, *pg.* 1138
DUFF-NORTON - Jacks - DUFF-NORTON; *pg.* 204, *pg.* 1365
DUFFEL COOL - Cooler - IGLOO PRODUCTS CORPORATION; *pg.* 1126, *pg.* 1724
DUGOUT - Utility Tool - RAYTHEON APPLIED SIGNAL TECHNOLOGY, INC.; *pg.* 667, *pg.* 288
DUKE - Knife - COAST CUTLERY COMPANY; *pg.* 1121, *pg.* 1501
DUKE - Fluid Handling System - GRACO, INC.; *pg.* 1342, *pg.* 935
DUKE - Eyewear - MAUI JIM, INC.; *pg.* 9, *pg.* 651
DUKE - Footwear - P.W. MINOR & SON, INC.; *pg.* 1816, *pg.* 1140
DUKE 301 - Jacket - HABAND COMPANY, INC.; *pg.* 1772, *pg.* 1099
DUKE OF WELLINGTON - Beer - GRANITE CITY FOOD & BREWERY LTD; *pg.* 1730, *pg.* 937
DUKE'S - Mayonnaise, Salad Products & Oils - THE C.F. SAUER COMPANY; *pg.* 847, *pg.* 1801
DULAMEL - Interior Solvent Enamel - BENJAMIN MOORE & CO.; *pg.* 1440, *pg.* 1085
DULCE - Apparel - VANS, INC.; *pg.* 1821, *pg.* 76
DULCE DE LECHE - Pudding - KOZY SHACK INC.; *pg.* 869, *pg.* 1167
DULCE DE LECHE - Nail Care Product - OPI PRODUCTS INC.; *pg.* 518, *pg.* 167
DULCE DE LECHE - Candy - SWEET CANDY COMPANY; *pg.* 1862, *pg.* 1761
DULCET - Sweetening Ingredient - MERISANT COMPANY; *pg.* 876, *pg.* 581
DULCET - Graphic Art Paper - MONADNOCK PAPER MILLS, INC.; *pg.* 1464, *pg.* 1033
DULCETTE - Fabric - NEMSCHOFF, INC.; *pg.* 936, *pg.* 1890
DULCINYL - Fragrance Ingredient - INTERNATIONAL FLAVORS & FRAGRANCES INC.; *pg.* 512, *pg.* 1244
DULEX - Medical Device - C.R. BARD, INC.; *pg.* 1519, *pg.* 1094
DULUX - Paint - AKZONOBEL DECORATIVE PAINTS U.S.; *pg.* 1439, *pg.* 1474
DULUX - Fluorescent Lamps - SIEMENS CORPORATION; *pg.* 803, *pg.* 1291
DULUX ENDURANCE - Paint - AKZONOBEL DECORATIVE PAINTS U.S.; *pg.* 1439, *pg.* 1474
DULUX INSPIRATIONS - Paint - AKZONOBEL DECORATIVE PAINTS U.S.; *pg.* 1439, *pg.* 1474
DUM DUM - Candy Cane - SPANGLER CANDY COMPANY; *pg.* 1862, *pg.* 1407
DUM DUM CHEWY POPS - Lollipop - SPANGLER CANDY COMPANY; *pg.* 1862, *pg.* 1407

First page reference indicates Business Class Edition
Second page reference indicates Geographic Edition

DUM DUM GUM POPS - Gum Filled Lollipop - SPANGLER CANDY COMPANY; *pg.* 1862, *pg.* 1407
DUM-DUMS - Suckers - SPANGLER CANDY COMPANY; *pg.* 1862, *pg.* 1407
DUMMIES - Educational & Technical Resource Books - JOHN WILEY & SONS, INC.; *pg.* 1655, *pg.* 1073
DUMONT - Forceps - STOELTING CO.; *pg.* 1430, *pg.* 671
DUMOR - Animal Feeds - TRACTOR SUPPLY COMPANY; *pg.* 708, *pg.* 1627
DUMOR NUTRISOURCE - Health Product - TRACTOR SUPPLY COMPANY; *pg.* 708, *pg.* 1627
DUMORE - Motor - DUMORE CORPORATION; *pg.* 1330, *pg.* 1869
DUN-AURA - Film - DUNMORE CORPORATION; *pg.* 1456, *pg.* 1518
DUN-BRITE - Laminating Films - DUNMORE CORPORATION; *pg.* 1456, *pg.* 1518
DUN-CHROME - Metallized Films - DUNMORE CORPORATION; *pg.* 1456, *pg.* 1518
DUN-DIGITAL - Coating - DUNMORE CORPORATION; *pg.* 1456, *pg.* 1518
DUN-GUARD - Film - DUNMORE CORPORATION; *pg.* 1456, *pg.* 1518
DUN-KOTE - Special Coatings on Films - DUNMORE CORPORATION; *pg.* 1456, *pg.* 1518
DUN-LAM - Laminations for Industry - DUNMORE CORPORATION; *pg.* 1456, *pg.* 1518
DUN-MET - Metallized Films for Aerospace - DUNMORE CORPORATION; *pg.* 1456, *pg.* 1518
DUN-NOVEL - Metallized PVC - DUNMORE CORPORATION; *pg.* 1456, *pg.* 1518
DUN-ORO - Gold Colored Films - DUNMORE CORPORATION; *pg.* 1456, *pg.* 1518
DUN-PRINT - Print Patterns, Custom Designs - DUNMORE CORPORATION; *pg.* 1456, *pg.* 1518
DUN-QUICK - Customer Service Program - DUNMORE CORPORATION; *pg.* 1456, *pg.* 1518
DUN-SHIELD - Film - DUNMORE CORPORATION; *pg.* 1456, *pg.* 1518
DUN-SOLAR - Backsheet - DUNMORE CORPORATION; *pg.* 1456, *pg.* 1518
DUN-STRIPE - Metallic Stripe Patterns - DUNMORE CORPORATION; *pg.* 1456, *pg.* 1518
DUN-TRAN - Metallic Transfers - DUNMORE CORPORATION; *pg.* 1456, *pg.* 1518
DUNBAR - Furniture - ASHLEY FURNITURE INDUSTRIES, INC.; *pg.* 914, *pg.* 1852
DUNBAR - Footwear - VANS, INC.; *pg.* 1821, *pg.* 76
DUNBARS ROASTED RED PEPPERS - Food - MOODY DUNBAR INC.; *pg.* 1028, *pg.* 1635
DUNCAN - Towing Products - BLUE OX; *pg.* 701, *pg.* 1019
DUNCAN - Toy - FLAMBEAU, INC.; *pg.* 1336, *pg.* 1854
DUNCAN - Electricity Meters - SIEMENS BUILDING TECHNOLOGIES, INC.; *pg.* 1376, *pg.* 560
DUNCAN BUTTERFLY - Classic Yo-Yo - DUNCAN TOYS COMPANY; *pg.* 951, *pg.* 1465
DUNCAN HINES - Frosting, Cake, Brownie, & Cookie Mixes - PINNACLE FOODS GROUP LLC; *pg.* 889, *pg.* 1104
DUNCAN SENSOR - Sensors - CUSTOM SENSORS & TECHNOLOGIES; *pg.* 1407, *pg.* 152
DUNCAN TETRA TOPS - Tops Designed to Spin on Multiple Axes - DUNCAN TOYS COMPANY; *pg.* 951, *pg.* 1465
DUNDEE - Home Designing Product - SPRINGS GLOBAL, INC.; *pg.* 698, *pg.* 1616
DUNE - Wood Flooring Product - ARMSTRONG WORLD INDUSTRIES, INC.; *pg.* 914, *pg.* 1545
DUNE - Bedding - CROSCILL, INC.; *pg.* 1122, *pg.* 1220
DUNE - Deodorant - THE GILLETTE COMPANY; *pg.* 509, *pg.* 795
DUNE - Fabric - NEMSCHOFF, INC.; *pg.* 936, *pg.* 1890
DUNE - Women's Fragrance - PARFUMS CHRISTIAN DIOR, INC; *pg.* 519, *pg.* 1276
DUNE - Tables - STEELCASE INC.; *pg.* 475, *pg.* 889
DUNE MEN - Men's Fragrance - PARFUMS CHRISTIAN DIOR, INC; *pg.* 519, *pg.* 1276
DUNE SUN - Women's Fragrance - PARFUMS CHRISTIAN DIOR, INC; *pg.* 519, *pg.* 1276
DUNGAREE - Fabric - NEMSCHOFF, INC.; *pg.* 936, *pg.* 1890
DUNGEONS & DRAGONS - Toy & Game - HASBRO, INC.; *pg.* 954, *pg.* 1603
DUNGEONS & DRAGONS - Game - WIZARDS OF THE COAST, INC.; *pg.* 970, *pg.* 1830
DUNGEONS & DRAGONS MINIATURES - Toy & Game - HASBRO, INC.; *pg.* 954, *pg.* 1603
DUNHAM - Boots - HITCHCOCK SHOES, INC.; *pg.* 1810, *pg.* 824
DUNHAM - Athletic Shoes - NEW BALANCE ATHLETIC SHOE, INC.; *pg.* 1811, *pg.* 798
DUNHAM - Footwear - THE ROCKPORT GROUP; *pg.* 1818, *pg.* 812
DUNHEATH SCOTCH - Scotch - LAIRD & COMPANY, INC.; *pg.* 1966, *pg.* 1119
DUNHILL - Lounge Chairs - BERNHARDT DESIGN; *pg.* 918, *pg.* 1381
DUNIXI - Lamp - ASHLEY FURNITURE INDUSTRIES, INC.; *pg.* 914, *pg.* 1852
DUNJA - Lamp - ASHLEY FURNITURE INDUSTRIES, INC.; *pg.* 914, *pg.* 1852
DUNK HIGH - Footwear - NIKE, INC.; *pg.* 1812, *pg.* 1492
DUNK HIGH BE TRUE - Footwear - NIKE, INC.; *pg.* 1812, *pg.* 1492
DUNK LOW BE TRUE - Footwear - NIKE, INC.; *pg.* 1812, *pg.* 1492
DUNK LOW PREMIUM - Footwear - NIKE, INC.; *pg.* 1812, *pg.* 1492
DUNK ZONE - Portable Basketball Standards - LIFETIME PRODUCTS INC.; *pg.* 933, *pg.* 1751
DUNKIN' DONUTS - Donuts - DUNKIN' BRANDS GROUP, INC.; *pg.* 1727, *pg.* 810
DUNLOP - Tires - THE GOODYEAR TIRE & RUBBER COMPANY; *pg.* 1883, *pg.* 1401
DUNNE - Lamp - ASHLEY FURNITURE INDUSTRIES, INC.; *pg.* 914, *pg.* 1852
DUNNEWOOD - Wine - CONSTELLATION BRANDS, INC.; *pg.* 1960, *pg.* 1348
DUNSRIGHT - Quality Process - THE DUN & BRADSTREET CORP.; *pg.* 1637, *pg.* 1120
DUO - Shampoo - DELTA FOREMOST CHEMICAL CORPORATION; *pg.* 1155, *pg.* 1642
DUO - Security Systems - THE EASTERN COMPANY; *pg.* 1331, *pg.* 357
DUO - Paper Products - INTERNATIONAL PAPER COMPANY; *pg.* 1460, *pg.* 1644
DUO - Patient Monitoring Device - MAQUET; *pg.* 1558, *pg.* 1082
DUO - Office Furniture - STEELCASE INC.; *pg.* 475, *pg.* 889
DUO 638 - Herbicide - UNIVERSAL COOPERATIVES, INC.; *pg.* 1482, *pg.* 922
DUO CLEAN - Hair Care Product - ZOTOS INTERNATIONAL, INC.; *pg.* 524, *pg.* 345
DUO-FINE - Filter Cartridge - PALL CORPORATION; *pg.* 232, *pg.* 1323
DUO-FLASH - Sterilization Product - PROPPER MANUFACTURING COMPANY, INC.; *pg.* 1586, *pg.* 1175
DUO-FLO - Mechanical Proportioners - GRACO, INC.; *pg.* 1342, *pg.* 935
DUO-GLASS - Coated Abrasive Belt - 3M COMPANY; *pg.* 1142, *pg.* 956
DUO-GRIP - Aluminum Plank - ALABAMA METAL INDUSTRIES CORPORATION; *pg.* 65, *pg.* 1
DUO-LIGHT - Hospital Lighting - SWIVELIER CO., INC.; *pg.* 1307, *pg.* 1142
DUO-LOCK - Piping System - VICTAULIC COMPANY; *pg.* 1066, *pg.* 1529
DUO-MATIC - Automated Lubrication Systems - LINCOLN INDUSTRIAL CORP.; *pg.* 1355, *pg.* 999
DUO-MIX - Fluid Handling System - GRACO, INC.; *pg.* 1342, *pg.* 935
DUO RECORD - Sterilization Product - PROPPER MANUFACTURING COMPANY, INC.; *pg.* 1586, *pg.* 1175
DUO SPIN-ON - Electronic Material - HONEYWELL INTERNATIONAL INC.; *pg.* 407, *pg.* 1088
DUO-SPORE - Sterilization Product - PROPPER MANUFACTURING COMPANY, INC.; *pg.* 1586, *pg.* 1175
DUO SURE GRIP - Gaming Product - GLD PRODUCTS, INC.; *pg.* 1835, *pg.* 1882
DUO-TWIN - Respirator - MINE SAFETY APPLIANCES COMPANY; *pg.* 1361, *pg.* 1525
DUO WEAVE - Woven Rugs - MOHAWK HOME; *pg.* 935, *pg.* 541
DUO FACE-PLUS - Seal - THE TIMKEN COMPANY; *pg.* 218, *pg.* 1408
DUOBOND - Coaxial Cable - BELDEN, INC.; *pg.* 624, *pg.* 993
DUOBOND - Fluid Handling System - GRACO, INC.; *pg.* 1342, *pg.* 935
DUOBOX - Electrical Cranes & Hoists - AMERICAN CRANE & EQUIPMENT CORPORATION; *pg.* 1312, *pg.* 1526
DUOCOR - Metamorphic Wire - LIQUIDMETAL TECHNOLOGIES, INC.; *pg.* 1356, *pg.* 188
DUODERM - Wound Care Product - CONVATEC LTD.; *pg.* 1518, *pg.* 1121
DUODOZEN - Paperboard Packaging Product - WESTROCK COMPANY; *pg.* 1472, *pg.* 1805
DUOFILM - Liquid Wart Remover - MERCK & CO., INC.; *pg.* 1566, *pg.* 1077
DUOFOLD - Outdoor Apparel - HANESBRANDS INC.; *pg.* 26, *pg.* 1394
DUOFOLD - Visual Packaging - WESTROCK COMPANY; *pg.* 1472, *pg.* 1805
DUOLEAN - Nutritional Supplement - NU SKIN ENTERPRISES, INC.; *pg.* 518, *pg.* 1755
DUOLITE - Resin - DOW CHEMICAL; *pg.* 1156, *pg.* 1563
DUOMATRIX - Polymer Additive System - SMOOTH-ON INC.; *pg.* 111, *pg.* 1528
DUOMATRIX-C - Concrete Additive - SMOOTH-ON INC.; *pg.* 111, *pg.* 1528
DUOMATRIX-G - Concrete Additive - SMOOTH-ON INC.; *pg.* 111, *pg.* 1528
DUOMATRIX NEO - Resin - SMOOTH-ON INC.; *pg.* 111, *pg.* 1528
DUOMET - Belt Surfacer - BUEHLER, LTD.; *pg.* 1403, *pg.* 622
DUOMIX - Conveying System - MOTAN, INC.; *pg.* 1886, *pg.* 903
DUOMO - Fabric - NEMSCHOFF, INC.; *pg.* 936, *pg.* 1890
DUOPLY - Paper Product - WESTROCK COMPANY; *pg.* 1472, *pg.* 1805
DUOPORT - Pressure Relief Valve Manifold for Small Storage Containers - ENGINEERED CONTROLS INTERNATIONAL LLC; *pg.* 1334, *pg.* 1372
DUOPRO - Headset - PLANTRONICS, INC.; *pg.* 663, *pg.* 270
DUOPROP - Sterndrive - VOLVO PENTA OF THE AMERICAS, INC.; *pg.* 1712, *pg.* 1778
DUOSAFE - Light Curtain Controller - OMRON SCIENTIFIC TECHNOLOGIES INCORPORATED; *pg.* 1425, *pg.* 91
DUOSEAL - Fluid Sealing Product - A.W. CHESTERTON COMPANY; *pg.* 1315, *pg.* 861
DUOSET - Headset - PLANTRONICS, INC.; *pg.* 663, *pg.* 270
DUOSET - Biological Product - TECHNE CORPORATION; *pg.* 1601, *pg.* 944
DUOSTAT - Rotating Hemostatic Valve - ABBOTT LABORATORIES; *pg.* 1484, *pg.* 551
DUOTECT - Pressure Switch - DWYER INSTRUMENTS INC.; *pg.* 1330, *pg.* 694
DUOTEX - Textured Metals - RIGIDIZED METALS CORP.; *pg.* 108, *pg.* 1151
DUOTOME SIDELITE - Medical Device - BOSTON SCIENTIFIC CORPORATION; *pg.* 1508, *pg.* 831
DUPAD - Wound Dressing Pad - DERMA SCIENCES, INC.; *pg.* 1523, *pg.* 1111
DUPAQUE - Wound Dressing - DERMA SCIENCES, INC.; *pg.* 1523, *pg.* 1111
DUPEN - Catheter - C.R. BARD, INC.; *pg.* 1519, *pg.* 1094
DUPLATE - Flat Glass - PPG INDUSTRIES, INC.; *pg.* 1445, *pg.* 1579
DUPLI-COLOR - Aerosol - THE SHERWIN-WILLIAMS COMPANY; *pg.* 1447, *pg.* 1435
DUPLI-COLOR - Spray & Touch Up Paints - SHERWIN-WILLIAMS DIVERSIFIED BRANDS DIVISION; *pg.* 1448, *pg.* 1435
DUPLO - Burster - AUTOMATION MAILING AND SHIPPING SOLUTIONS, INC.; *pg.* 358, *pg.* 1428
DUPLOCATH - Biopharmaceutical Product - BAXTER INTERNATIONAL INC.; *pg.* 1499, *pg.* 599
DUPLOTIP - Biopharmaceutical Product - BAXTER INTERNATIONAL INC.; *pg.* 1499, *pg.* 599
DUPONT - Chemical Products - E.I. DU PONT DE NEMOURS & COMPANY; *pg.* 1159, *pg.* 390
DUPONT REGISTRY - Magazine - DUPONT PUBLISHING, INC.; *pg.* 1637, *pg.* 462
DUPONT REGISTRY TAMPA BAY - Magazine - DUPONT PUBLISHING, INC.; *pg.* 1637, *pg.* 462
DUPONT TEIJIN FILMS - Polyester Films - E.I. DU PONT DE NEMOURS & COMPANY; *pg.* 1159, *pg.* 390
DUPONTREGISTRY.COM - Magazine Website - DUPONT PUBLISHING, INC.; *pg.* 1637, *pg.* 462
DUPRESS - Burn Dressing - DERMA SCIENCES, INC.; *pg.* 1523, *pg.* 1111
DUR-A-BEAD - Corner Bead - USG CORPORATION; *pg.* 118, *pg.* 594
DUR NI - Chemical Coating - ENTHONE INC.; *pg.* 1161, *pg.* 381
DURA - Homebuilding Services - KB HOME; *pg.* 90, *pg.* 134

DURA-BALL - Counter Display - LA-CO INDUSTRIES MARKAL CO., INC.; *pg.* 1170, *pg.* 610
DURA BUILDERS - Homebuilding Services - KB HOME; *pg.* 90, *pg.* 134
DURA-CAGE - CageLayer System or Cages - CTB INTERNATIONAL CORP.; *pg.* 850, *pg.* 695
DURA-CHROME STEEL - Bath Organizer - HOME PRODUCTS INTERNATIONAL, INC.; *pg.* 1125, *pg.* 577
DURA-COATED STEEL - Bath Organizer - HOME PRODUCTS INTERNATIONAL, INC.; *pg.* 1125, *pg.* 577
DURA-CRYSTAL - Watch & Clock - BULOVA CORPORATION; *pg.* 2, *pg.* 1356
DURA-CUBE - Salt - CARGILL LIMITED; *pg.* 1475, *pg.* 1914
DURA-CUBE - Water Softener Salt - CARGILL SALT; *pg.* 846, *pg.* 926
DURA-CYL - Cryogenic Product - CHART INDUSTRIES, INC.; *pg.* 1405, *pg.* 1454
DURA-CYL - Cylinder Operator - HENRY PRATT COMPANY; *pg.* 1049, *pg.* 555
DURA DC Fluid Handling System - GRACO, INC.; *pg.* 1342, *pg.* 935
DURA-DOMES - Welding Electrode - ELECTRON BEAM TECHNOLOGIES, INC.; *pg.* 1046, *pg.* 621
DURA-DRIVE - Corrugator Belt - ALBANY INTERNATIONAL CORP.; *pg.* 691, *pg.* 1038
DURA-DRY - Corrugator Belt - ALBANY INTERNATIONAL CORP.; *pg.* 691, *pg.* 1038
DURA-DUST - Homeowner Product - PBI/GORDON CORPORATION; *pg.* 1176, *pg.* 985
DURA-FLO - Air Operated Pumps - GRACO, INC.; *pg.* 1342, *pg.* 935
DURA-FLOW - Electrosurgical Devices - ANGIODYNAMICS, INC.; *pg.* 1495, *pg.* 1173
DURA-GO - Plastic Film - TEKRA CORPORATION; *pg.* 1184, *pg.* 1884
DURA-INK - Counter Display - LA-CO INDUSTRIES MARKAL CO., INC.; *pg.* 1170, *pg.* 610
DURA KOLD - Orthopedic Product - DJO INCORPORATED; *pg.* 1524, *pg.* 302
DURA-KOOL - Sleeves for Handles - CARLISLE FOODSERVICE PRODUCTS INCORPORATED; *pg.* 1455, *pg.* 1485
DURA-LIFE - Baghouse Collectors - DONALDSON COMPANY, INC.; *pg.* 1329, *pg.* 917
DURA-LINE - Electric Coreless Induction Furnaces - INDUCTOTHERM CORP.; *pg.* 1348, *pg.* 1114
DURA-MARK - Printer - PANDUIT CORP.; *pg.* 661, *pg.* 663
DURA MAX - Boiler - A.O. SMITH CORPORATION; *pg.* 1313, *pg.* 1872
DURA-NAP - Blankets - MEDLINE INDUSTRIES, INC.; *pg.* 1562, *pg.* 635
DURA-POWER - Standard Electric Water Heaters - A.O. SMITH CORPORATION; *pg.* 1313, *pg.* 1872
DURA-POXY - Paint - KELLY-MOORE PAINT COMPANY, INC.; *pg.* 1443, *pg.* 198
DURA-PRIME - Coating Product - PPG INDUSTRIES, INC.; *pg.* 1445, *pg.* 1579
DURA-RED - Hose - HBD INDUSTRIES, INC.; *pg.* 207, *pg.* 1449
DURA-SCREEN - Vibratory Sieve - NORDSON CORPORATION; *pg.* 1365, *pg.* 1480
DURA-SKRIM - Laminate - RAVEN INDUSTRIES, INC.; *pg.* 1888, *pg.* 1625
DURA-SMOOTH - Plastic Packaging Product - POLY PAK AMERICA, INC.; *pg.* 1467, *pg.* 138
DURA SOFT - Orthopedic Product - DJO INCORPORATED; *pg.* 1524, *pg.* 302
DURA-SON 3.5 MM - Laminate Wood Cushions - DURA UNDERCUSHIONS LTD.; *pg.* 923, *pg.* 1954
DURA-SPRAY - Homeowner Product - PBI/GORDON CORPORATION; *pg.* 1176, *pg.* 985
DURA-STICK - Orthopedic Device - DJO SURGICAL; *pg.* 1525, *pg.* 1661
DURA-STIM - Orthopedic Device - DJO SURGICAL; *pg.* 1525, *pg.* 1661
DURA-TAB - Pressed & Monolithic Refractory - RESCO PRODUCTS, INC.; *pg.* 107, *pg.* 1581
DURA-TABLE - Table - LIFETIME PRODUCTS INC.; *pg.* 933, *pg.* 1751
DURA-TEC - Sampler Kit - THE HILSINGER CO.; *pg.* 1416, *pg.* 841
DURA-TILT - Exterior Masonry Finish - DUNN-EDWARDS CORPORATION; *pg.* 1442, *pg.* 129
DURA-TY - Cable Tie - PANDUIT CORP.; *pg.* 661, *pg.* 663
DURA-Z - Ceramic & Plastic Product - COORSTEK, INC.; *pg.* 77, *pg.* 330
DURABAKE - Switchgear Enclosure Finish - S&C ELECTRIC COMPANY; *pg.* 1305, *pg.* 589
DURABASE - Shower Floor - E.L. MUSTEE & SONS, INC.; *pg.* 1124, *pg.* 1430
DURABEAM - Flashlight - DURACELL; *pg.* 635, *pg.* 337
DURABELT - Process Belt - ALBANY INTERNATIONAL CORP.; *pg.* 691, *pg.* 1038
DURABILT - Storage Product - HOME PRODUCTS INTERNATIONAL, INC.; *pg.* 1125, *pg.* 577
DURABILT - Safety Wear - HONEYWELL NORTH SAFETY PRODUCTS; *pg.* 42, *pg.* 1600
DURABLE PRODUCT MARKING - Pressure-Sensitive Film - FLEXCON CORPORATION; *pg.* 1457, *pg.* 844
DURABLE TRFLON - Nitrous System - EDELBROCK CORPORATION; *pg.* 204, *pg.* 293
DURABLEND - Engine Gear Oil - ASHLAND INC.; *pg.* 972, *pg.* 726
DURABLOCK - Solid Plastic Portable Gage - DWYER INSTRUMENTS INC.; *pg.* 1330, *pg.* 694
DURABLOCK - Pallet Blocks - SONOCO PRODUCTS COMPANY; *pg.* 1469, *pg.* 1619
DURABLUE - Melter - NORDSON CORPORATION; *pg.* 1365, *pg.* 1480
DURABOND - Epoxies - HENKEL CORPORATION; *pg.* 1049, *pg.* 369
DURABOND - Durabubble Product - POLYAIR INTER PACK INC.; *pg.* 1467, *pg.* 1941
DURABOND - Mortars, Mastics & Grouts - USG CORPORATION; *pg.* 118, *pg.* 594
DURABOOT - Walker Attachment - ALIMED, INC.; *pg.* 1490, *pg.* 816
DURABRITE - Clear & Metallic Coatings - PPG INDUSTRIES, INC.; *pg.* 1445, *pg.* 1579
DURABUBBLE - Durabubble Product - POLYAIR INTER PACK INC.; *pg.* 1467, *pg.* 1941
DURABULL - Wheel Rake - VERMEER MANUFACTURING COMPANY; *pg.* 708, *pg.* 711
DURACAL - Buffer - HAMILTON CO., INC.; *pg.* 1415, *pg.* 1031
DURACAL - Cement - USG CORPORATION; *pg.* 118, *pg.* 594
DURACAM - Cam Locks - MEDECO HIGH SECURITY LOCKS, INC.; *pg.* 1055, *pg.* 1806
DURACAM II R/C - Removable Core Cam Locks - MEDECO HIGH SECURITY LOCKS, INC.; *pg.* 1055, *pg.* 1806
DURACAP - Vinyl Compound - POLYONE CORPORATION; *pg.* 1177, *pg.* 1404
DURACARB - Hydroxyl Terminated Polycarbonate - PPG INDUSTRIES, INC.; *pg.* 1445, *pg.* 1579
DURACARB - Carbon Brake - UTC AEROSPACE SYSTEMS; *pg.* 236, *pg.* 1369
DURACAST - Metal Building Product - CENTRIA, INC.; *pg.* 74, *pg.* 1554
DURACAST - Building Material - PELLA CORPORATION; *pg.* 104, *pg.* 711
DURACAT - Catalyst - BASF CATALYSTS LLC; *pg.* 1148, *pg.* 1074
DURACELL - Batteries - DURACELL; *pg.* 635, *pg.* 337
DURACELL - Battery - THE GILLETTE COMPANY; *pg.* 509, *pg.* 795
DURACELL - Batteries - THE PROCTER & GAMBLE COMPANY; *pg.* 1129, *pg.* 1418
DURACELL ULTRA - Batteries - DURACELL; *pg.* 635, *pg.* 337
DURACELL ULTRA - Battery - THE GILLETTE COMPANY; *pg.* 509, *pg.* 795
DURACERAMIC - Ceramic Floor Tile - CONGOLEUM CORPORATION; *pg.* 921, *pg.* 1084
DURACLAD - Cable - SOUTHWIRE COMPANY; *pg.* 1063, *pg.* 527
DURACLEAN - Cleaning System - DURACLEAN INTERNATIONAL, INC.; *pg.* 329, *pg.* 553
DURACLEAR - Material - AUTOMATED PACKAGING SYSTEMS INC.; *pg.* 1452, *pg.* 1474
DURACLEAR - Display Material - EASTMAN KODAK COMPANY; *pg.* 1408, *pg.* 1333
DURACLEAR 2000 - Bag & Pouch Material - AUTOMATED PACKAGING SYSTEMS INC.; *pg.* 1452, *pg.* 1474
DURACLIK - Electronic Components - MOLEX INCORPORATED; *pg.* 655, *pg.* 628
DURACOAT - Metal Finishing Product - HEATBATH CORPORATION; *pg.* 1165, *pg.* 826
DURACOAT - Pre-Catalyzed System - MOHAWK FINISHING PRODUCTS, INC.; *pg.* 1173, *pg.* 1378
DURACOLOR - Interior & Exterior Latex House, Wall & Trim Paint - PPG INDUSTRIES, INC.; *pg.* 1445, *pg.* 1579
DURACOMFORT - Pant - WILLIAMSON-DICKIE MANUFACTURING COMPANY; *pg.* 50, *pg.* 1696
DURACON - Orthopaedic Product - STRYKER CORPORATION; *pg.* 1598, *pg.* 894
DURACORD - Furniture - ASHLEY FURNITURE INDUSTRIES, INC.; *pg.* 914, *pg.* 1852
DURACOUSTIC - Acoustical Underpadding - DURA UNDERCUSHIONS LTD.; *pg.* 923, *pg.* 1954
DURACRON - Coating Product - PPG INDUSTRIES, INC.; *pg.* 1445, *pg.* 1579
DURACRYL - Acrylic Coatings, Thinners & Sealers - PPG INDUSTRIES, INC.; *pg.* 1445, *pg.* 1579
DURACUSHION - Carpet Cushion - DURA UNDERCUSHIONS LTD.; *pg.* 923, *pg.* 1954
DURACYN - Elastomer - FERRO CORPORATION; *pg.* 1162, *pg.* 1462
DURADIANT - Burner - SELAS HEAT TECHNOLOGY COMPANY LLC; *pg.* 1076, *pg.* 1553
DURADIG - Excavator Parts - THE FROG, SWITCH & MANUFACTURING COMPANY; *pg.* 1338, *pg.* 1520
DURADRUM - Bulk Delivery System - NORDSON CORPORATION; *pg.* 1365, *pg.* 1480
DURAFAXX - Engine Filter/Fluid Testing - DONALDSON COMPANY, INC.; *pg.* 1329, *pg.* 917
DURAFILM - Composite Films - MONOSOL, LLC; *pg.* 59, *pg.* 694
DURAFLAKE - Wood & Building Material - WEYERHAEUSER COMPANY; *pg.* 121, *pg.* 1820
DURAFLAME - Firelog - DURAFLAME, INC.; *pg.* 1123, *pg.* 280
DURAFLEX - Processing Trays, Photographic Film - EASTMAN KODAK COMPANY; *pg.* 1408, *pg.* 1333
DURAFLEX - Airless Paint Hose - GRACO, INC.; *pg.* 1342, *pg.* 935
DURAFLEX - Fastener - NATIONAL MOLDING, LLC; *pg.* 1887, *pg.* 430
DURAFLEX - Insulating System - OWENS CORNING; *pg.* 102, *pg.* 1476
DURAFLEX - Interactive Product - RADIX WIRE COMPANY; *pg.* 1304, *pg.* 1434
DURAFLEX 360 - Wall System - SMITH-MIDLAND CORPORATION; *pg.* 111, *pg.* 1795
DURAFLO - Alkyd Gloss Enamel - DUNN-EDWARDS CORPORATION; *pg.* 1442, *pg.* 129
DURAFLO - Photographic Chemicals - EASTMAN KODAK COMPANY; *pg.* 1408, *pg.* 1333
DURAFO - Orthopedic Product - DJO INCORPORATED; *pg.* 1524, *pg.* 302
DURAFOAM - Roof Insulation - JOHNS MANVILLE CORPORATION; *pg.* 89, *pg.* 320
DURAFORM - Solid Imaging Material - 3D SYSTEMS CORPORATION; *pg.* 339, *pg.* 1621
DURAFORM - Paper - NEENAH PAPER, INC.; *pg.* 1465, *pg.* 484
DURAFORM - Adhesive Coated Paper - SPINNAKER COATING, LLC; *pg.* 1470, *pg.* 1477
DURAFUSION - Printer - PRINTRONIX, INC.; *pg.* 456, *pg.* 115
DURAGARD - Coating System - CENTRIA, INC.; *pg.* 74, *pg.* 1554
DURAGARD - Protective Polyester - DATACARD CORPORATION; *pg.* 382, *pg.* 948
DURAGEN - Off Grid Solar Power System - CARMANAH TECHNOLOGIES CORPORATION; *pg.* 628, *pg.* 1913
DURAGEN - Medical Device - INTEGRA LIFESCIENCES HOLDINGS CORPORATION; *pg.* 1545, *pg.* 1109
DURAGEN PLUS - Medical Device - INTEGRA LIFESCIENCES HOLDINGS CORPORATION; *pg.* 1545, *pg.* 1109
DURAGESIC - Pain Reliever - JANSSEN PHARMACEUTICA PRODUCTS, L.P.; *pg.* 1548, *pg.* 1125
DURAGESIC - Healthcare Product - JOHNSON & JOHNSON; *pg.* 1549, *pg.* 1091
DURAGLAS - Glass Containers - OWENS-ILLINOIS, INC.; *pg.* 1466, *pg.* 1470
DURAGLIDE - Medical Equipment - CONMED CORPORATION; *pg.* 1517, *pg.* 1347
DURAGLOW - Cheimical Additive - DOW CHEMICAL; *pg.* 1156, *pg.* 1563
DURAGRAPHIC - Printing Process - AVERY DENNISON CORPORATION; *pg.* 1452, *pg.* 95
DURAGRAPHIC - Decorative Coatings - PPG INDUSTRIES, INC.; *pg.* 1445, *pg.* 1579

DURAGRIP - Corrugator Belt - ALBANY INTERNATIONAL CORP.; pg. 691, pg. 1038
DURAGRIP - Molding & Extrusion - FERRO CORPORATION; pg. 1162, pg. 1462
DURAGRIP - Finishing Process - LSI INDUSTRIES INC.; pg. 58, pg. 1416
DURAGRIP-S - Corrugator Belt - ALBANY INTERNATIONAL CORP.; pg. 691, pg. 1038
DURAGUARD - Corrugator Belt - ALBANY INTERNATIONAL CORP.; pg. 691, pg. 1038
DURAGUARD - Wall Guard - E.L. MUSTEE & SONS, INC.; pg. 1124, pg. 1430
DURAGUARD - Insecticide - W.F. YOUNG, INC.; pg. 1610, pg. 817
DURAGUARD-S - Corrugator Belt - ALBANY INTERNATIONAL CORP.; pg. 691, pg. 1038
DURAHESIVE - Ostomy Skin Barriers - ALIMED, INC.; pg. 1490, pg. 816
DURAHESIVE - Ostomy Care Product - CONVATEC LTD.; pg. 1518, pg. 1121
DURAHIDE - Furniture - ASHLEY FURNITURE INDUSTRIES, INC.; pg. 914, pg. 1852
DURAHIDE - Head Gear - SCHOOL-TECH, INC.; pg. 1844, pg. 866
DURAKOTA - Semolina - NORTH DAKOTA MILL & ELEVATOR ASSOCIATION; pg. 833, pg. 1398
DURAKOTE - Plastic Film - TEKRA CORPORATION; pg. 1184, pg. 1884
DURAKRAFT - Durabubble Product - POLYAIR INTER PACK INC.; pg. 1467, pg. 1941
DURAL-REACH - Bi Directional Deflection - ST. JUDE MEDICAL, INC.; pg. 1596, pg. 963
DURALAST - Automotive Hard Parts Including Starters, Alternators & Batteries - AUTOZONE, INC.; pg. 200, pg. 1641
DURALAST - Polyurethane System - THE DOW CHEMICAL COMPANY; pg. 1157, pg. 898
DURALAST - Wheel - HAMILTON CASTER & MFG. CO.; pg. 206, pg. 1454
DURALAST GOLD - Batteries - AUTOZONE, INC.; pg. 200, pg. 1641
DURALEE - Fabric - NEMSCHOFF, INC.; pg. 936, pg. 1890
DURALENS - Premium Grade Acrylic - PLASKOLITE, INC.; pg. 1888, pg. 1443
DURALIFE - Pump Product - IDEX CORPORATION; pg. 1347, pg. 623
DURALINE - Floor Care - NILFISK-ADVANCE, INC.; pg. 332, pg. 953
DURALINE - Paper Product - WESTROCK COMPANY; pg. 1472, pg. 1805
DURALINE SERIES - Toilet Partitions - BOBRICK WASHROOM EQUIPMENT, INC.; pg. 1043, pg. 166
DURALINK - Pin Material - FLEXIBLE STEEL LACING COMPANY; pg. 1337, pg. 608
DURALITE - Air Cleaner - DONALDSON COMPANY, INC.; pg. 1329, pg. 917
DURALITE - Plastic Packaging Product - POLY PAK AMERICA, INC.; pg. 1467, pg. 138
DURALITE - Pressed & Monolithic Refractory - RESCO PRODUCTS, INC.; pg. 107, pg. 1581
DURALITE ENVELOPES - Flexible Packaging Product - POLY PAK AMERICA, INC.; pg. 1467, pg. 138
DURALLURE - Coating System - CENTRIA, INC.; pg. 74, pg. 1554
DURALOADER - Folding Aluminum Loading Ramp - LUND INTERNATIONAL, INC.; pg. 211, pg. 526
DURALOBE - Pump Product - IDEX CORPORATION; pg. 1347, pg. 623
DURALUBE - Special Lubricated Chain - DIAMOND CHAIN COMPANY; pg. 1328, pg. 684
DURALUME - Commercial Retail Lighting - JUNO LIGHTING, INC.; pg. 1300, pg. 606
DURALUX - Carpet Cushion - DURA UNDERCUSHIONS LTD.; pg. 923, pg. 1954
DURALYTE - Light Fixtures - JUNO LIGHTING, INC.; pg. 1300, pg. 606
DURAMAL - Special Treated Iron - WEBSTER INDUSTRIES INC.; pg. 1388, pg. 1475
DURAMASK - Durabubble Product - POLYAIR INTER PACK INC.; pg. 1467, pg. 1941
DURAMATE - Insulated Sheathing - THE DOW CHEMICAL COMPANY; pg. 1157, pg. 898
DURAMATIC - Fluid Handling System - GRACO, INC.; pg. 1342, pg. 935
DURAMATRIX - Biomaterial - STRYKER CORPORATION; pg. 1598, pg. 894
DURAMAX - Shoes - ACUSHNET COMPANY; pg. 1824, pg. 818
DURAMAX - Corrugator Belt - ALBANY INTERNATIONAL CORP.; pg. 691, pg. 1038
DURAMAX - Lube Filter - DONALDSON COMPANY, INC.; pg. 1329, pg. 917
DURAMETALLIC - Seal - FLOWSERVE CORPORATION; pg. 82, pg. 1719
DURAMIC - Nonstick Coating System - AMWAY CORPORATION; pg. 326, pg. 864
DURAMIC - Diaphragms - ELSTER AMERICAN METER COMPANY; pg. 1411, pg. 1387
DURAMID - Cage Layer System or Cages - CTB INTERNATIONAL CORP.; pg. 850, pg. 695
DURAMINE - Decorative Melamine - GEORGIA-PACIFIC LLC; pg. 1458, pg. 507
DURAMIX - Heating Coil Control - ARMSTRONG INTERNATIONAL, INC.; pg. 1069, pg. 909
DURAMOLD - Vehicle Safety System - GROTE INDUSTRIES, INC.; pg. 206, pg. 693
DURAMOLD - Pottery Plaster - USG CORPORATION; pg. 118, pg. 594
DURAMOULD - Polyurethane System - THE DOW CHEMICAL COMPANY; pg. 1157, pg. 898
DURAMUNE - Canine Vaccine - BOEHRINGER INGELHEIM VETMEDICA, INC.; pg. 1474, pg. 989
DURAN ANCORE - Annuloplasty Ring & Band - MEDTRONIC, INC.; pg. 1564, pg. 939
DURAN BLACK - Fabric - UNIROYAL ENGINEERED PRODUCTS; pg. 699, pg. 467
DURANAR - Coating Product - PPG INDUSTRIES, INC.; pg. 1445, pg. 1579
DURANGO - Furniture - ASHLEY FURNITURE INDUSTRIES, INC.; pg. 914, pg. 1852
DURANGO - Carpet - BEAULIEU GROUP, LLC; pg. 917, pg. 529
THE DURANGO - Naturaline Swing Set - CREATIVE PLAYTHINGS LTD.; pg. 1831, pg. 820
DURANGO - Paper & Nonwoven Material - FIBERMARK INC.; pg. 1457, pg. 1764
DURANGO - Fabric - NEMSCHOFF, INC.; pg. 936, pg. 1890
DURANGO - Footwear - ROCKY BRANDS, INC.; pg. 1818, pg. 1466
DURANGO ANCIENT - Ceramic, Glass, Stone Tiles & Slabs - WALKER & ZANGER, INC.; pg. 119, pg. 281
DURANGO SPORT - Bicycles - G. JOANNOU CYCLE CO. INC.; pg. 1707, pg. 1098
DURANGO SX - Bicycles - G. JOANNOU CYCLE CO. INC.; pg. 1707, pg. 1098
DURANICKEL - Alloy Product - SPECIAL METALS CORPORATION; pg. 1377, pg. 1850
DURANT - Electrical Product - EATON CORPORATION; pg. 1331, pg. 1429
DURANT - Footwear - K-SWISS; pg. 1837, pg. 306
DURANT LAKE - Clothing - ABERCROMBIE & FITCH CO.; pg. 37, pg. 1466
DURAPACK - Refuse Bodies - HEIL ENVIRONMENTAL INDUSTRIES, LTD.; pg. 207, pg. 1629
DURAPAIL - Bulk Delivery System - NORDSON CORPORATION; pg. 1365, pg. 1480
DURAPAN - Heater - E.L. MUSTEE & SONS, INC.; pg. 1124, pg. 1430
DURAPAPER - Manual - XEROX CORPORATION; pg. 494, pg. 365
DURAPELLA - Furniture - ASHLEY FURNITURE INDUSTRIES, INC.; pg. 914, pg. 1852
DURAPLANK - Decking - SAFWAY SERVICES, LLC; pg. 109, pg. 1898
DURAPLEX - Impact Modified Acrylic Sheet - PLASKOLITE, INC.; pg. 1888, pg. 1443
DURAPLUS - Probe Card - KULICKE & SOFFA INDUSTRIES, INC.; pg. 650, pg. 1533
DURAPLUS - Chemicals - VOLVO PENTA OF THE AMERICAS, INC.; pg. 1712, pg. 1778
DURAPLUSH - Furniture - ASHLEY FURNITURE INDUSTRIES, INC.; pg. 914, pg. 1852
DURAPOSIT - Electroless Nickel Process - THE DOW CHEMICAL COMPANY; pg. 1157, pg. 898
DURAPREP - Surgical Solution - 3M COMPANY; pg. 1142, pg. 956
DURAPREP - Ancillary Process Product - DOW CHEMICAL; pg. 1156, pg. 1563
DURAPRESS - Paper & Nonwoven Material - FIBERMARK INC.; pg. 1457, pg. 1764
DURAPRO - Fluid Handling System - GRACO, INC.; pg. 1342, pg. 935
DURAPROOF - Mildewcide Services - DURACLEAN INTERNATIONAL, INC.; pg. 329, pg. 553
DURASEAL - Mechanical Seals - FLOWSERVE CORPORATION; pg. 82, pg. 1719
DURASEAL - Tire - THE GOODYEAR TIRE & RUBBER COMPANY; pg. 1883, pg. 1401
DURASEAL - Pharmaceutical Product - NEKTAR THERAPEUTICS; pg. 1572, pg. 224
DURASEAL - Hardwood Floors Coating Products - THE SHERWIN-WILLIAMS COMPANY; pg. 1447, pg. 1435
DURASECT - Livestock Insecticide - PFIZER INC.; pg. 1581, pg. 1278
DURASENSE - Ceramic & Plastic Product - COORSTEK, INC.; pg. 77, pg. 330
DURASHADE SERIES - Retractable Solar Shades - DURASOL AWNINGS, INC.; pg. 79, pg. 1153
DURASHEATH - Cable - GENERAL CABLE CORPORATION; pg. 83, pg. 729
DURASHEILD - Wiring Products - PASS & SEYMOUR/LEGRAND; pg. 1303, pg. 1344
DURASHIELD PLUS - Stain Repellant Services - DURACLEAN INTERNATIONAL, INC.; pg. 329, pg. 553
DURASHOCKS - Comfort System for Workboots - WOLVERINE WORLD WIDE, INC.; pg. 1822, pg. 905
DURASKIN - Backboard Padding - SCHOOL-TECH, INC.; pg. 1844, pg. 866
DURASLOT - Pipe - ADVANCED DRAINAGE SYSTEMS, INC.; pg. 1878, pg. 1455
DURASOX - Healthcare Product - MEDICOOL, INC.; pg. 1562, pg. 294
DURASPEXX - Bearing - THE TIMKEN COMPANY; pg. 218, pg. 1408
DURASTALL - Shower Stall - E.L. MUSTEE & SONS, INC.; pg. 1124, pg. 1430
DURASTAR - Polymer - EASTMAN CHEMICAL COMPANY; pg. 1159, pg. 1636
DURASTAR - Coating Product - PPG INDUSTRIES, INC.; pg. 1445, pg. 1579
DURASTAT - Industrial Manufacturing Chemicals - PPG INDUSTRIES, INC.; pg. 1445, pg. 1579
DURASTEP - Vinyl Flooring - AMERICAN BILTRITE INC.; pg. 1878, pg. 856
DURASTEP RAMP - Hard Drive - WESTERN DIGITAL CORPORATION; pg. 492, pg. 118
DURASTONE - Flooring - CONGOLEUM CORPORATION; pg. 921, pg. 1084
DURASTONE - Tub & Sink - E.L. MUSTEE & SONS, INC.; pg. 1124, pg. 1430
DURASTONE CLASSIC - Flooring - CONGOLEUM CORPORATION; pg. 921, pg. 1084
DURASTONE HPF - Flooring Product - CONGOLEUM CORPORATION; pg. 921, pg. 1084
DURASTRATE - Ceramic & Plastic Product - COORSTEK, INC.; pg. 77, pg. 330
DURASTRIP - Metal Finishing Product - HEATBATH CORPORATION; pg. 1165, pg. 826
DURASUEDE - Fabric - NEMSCHOFF, INC.; pg. 936, pg. 1890
DURATA - Tachycardia Products - ST. JUDE MEDICAL, INC.; pg. 1596, pg. 963
DURATABLE UTILITY - Portable Picnic Tables - LIFETIME PRODUCTS INC.; pg. 933, pg. 1751
DURATEC - Band Saw Blades - THE L.S. STARRETT COMPANY; pg. 1421, pg. 783
DURATECH - Control Stations - KILLARK ELECTRIC; pg. 1300, pg. 998
DURATEK - Air Filters - DONALDSON COMPANY, INC.; pg. 1329, pg. 917
DURATHANE - Medical Apparatus - MAQUET; pg. 1558, pg. 1082
DURATHANE - Two-Part Urethane Paint - PETTIT PAINT COMPANY; pg. 1444, pg. 1116
DURATHERM - Electro-Thermal Deicing - UTC AEROSPACE SYSTEMS; pg. 236, pg. 1369
DURATHON - Dock Seal Fabric - RITE-HITE HOLDING CORPORATION; pg. 1372, pg. 1880
DURATION - Rolled Rubber Sheet - ROBBINS, INC.; pg. 108, pg. 1425
DURATION - Paint - THE SHERWIN-WILLIAMS COMPANY; pg. 1447, pg. 1435
DURATION HOME - Paint - THE SHERWIN-WILLIAMS COMPANY; pg. 1447, pg. 1435
DURATION PLUS - Rolled Rubber Sheet Over Pad -

ROBBINS, INC.; *pg.* 108, *pg.* 1425
DURATITE - Lift Table Cover - DYNATECT MANUFACTURING INC.; *pg.* 1330, *pg.* 1883
DURATOOL - Chemical Product - CYTEC INDUSTRIES, INC.; *pg.* 1155, *pg.* 1131
DURATRAC - Floor Care - NILFISK-ADVANCE, INC.; *pg.* 332, *pg.* 953
DURATRANS - Photo Film - EASTMAN KODAK COMPANY; *pg.* 1408, *pg.* 1333
DURATRAP - Glass & Ceramic Material - CORNING INCORPORATED; *pg.* 1122, *pg.* 1154
DURATRIM - Bathtub Wall - E.L. MUSTEE & SONS, INC.; *pg.* 1124, *pg.* 1430
DURATUB - Tub & Sink - E.L. MUSTEE & SONS, INC.; *pg.* 1124, *pg.* 1430
DURATUF - Composites - CRANE CO.; *pg.* 227, *pg.* 373
DURAVAC - Floor Care - NILFISK-ADVANCE, INC.; *pg.* 332, *pg.* 953
DURAVELLE - Plastic Film - THE DOW CHEMICAL COMPANY; *pg.* 1157, *pg.* 898
DURAVIEW - Solvent Inkjet Products - TEKRA CORPORATION; *pg.* 1184, *pg.* 1884
DURAVINYL - Vinyl Tile - AMERICAN BILTRITE INC.; *pg.* 1878, *pg.* 856
DURAWALL - Bathtub Wall - E.L. MUSTEE & SONS, INC.; *pg.* 1124, *pg.* 1430
DURAWEAVE - Fabric - NEMSCHOFF, INC.; *pg.* 936, *pg.* 1890
DURAWELD - Tables - LUXOR CORP.; *pg.* 428, *pg.* 666
DURAWIPE XTRA - Wipe - POLYMER GROUP, INC.; *pg.* 698, *pg.* 1368
DURAYAG - Optic Module - LIGHTPATH TECHNOLOGIES INC; *pg.* 1420, *pg.* 454
DURAZONE - Polymer Product - CHEMTURA CORPORATION; *pg.* 1152, *pg.* 355
DURBAN - Footwear - COBIAN CORP.; *pg.* 1806, *pg.* 253
DURCO - Valve - FLOWSERVE CORPORATION; *pg.* 82, *pg.* 1719
DURCO-CAST - Equipment - FLOWSERVE CORPORATION; *pg.* 82, *pg.* 1719
DURCO-D - Equipment - FLOWSERVE CORPORATION; *pg.* 82, *pg.* 1719
DURCOMETER - Metering Pumps - FLOWSERVE CORPORATION; *pg.* 82, *pg.* 1719
DURCON - Alloys - FLOWSERVE CORPORATION; *pg.* 82, *pg.* 1719
DURCOPUMP - Pumps - FLOWSERVE CORPORATION; *pg.* 82, *pg.* 1719
DUREL - Lighting System - ROGERS CORPORATION; *pg.* 1305, *pg.* 369
DURELAST - Medical & Aesthetic Product - DYNATRONICS CORPORATION; *pg.* 1526, *pg.* 1757
DURELON - Polycarboxylate Luting Cement - 3M COMPANY; *pg.* 1142, *pg.* 956
DURETHANE - Coating Product - PPG INDUSTRIES, INC.; *pg.* 1445, *pg.* 1579
DUREX - Contraceptives - RECKITT BENCKISER INC.; *pg.* 1136, *pg.* 1105
DURICHLOR - Alloys - FLOWSERVE CORPORATION; *pg.* 82, *pg.* 1719
DURIRON - Equipment - FLOWSERVE CORPORATION; *pg.* 82, *pg.* 1719
DURLEX - Plastic & Rubber - TEKNOR APEX COMPANY; *pg.* 1889, *pg.* 1605
DURO - Paper & Paperboard - SONOCO PRODUCTS COMPANY; *pg.* 1469, *pg.* 1619
DURO - Slicer - UNIVEX CORPORATION; *pg.* 1386, *pg.* 1039
DURO-CORES - Wound Paper Tubes - SONOCO PRODUCTS COMPANY; *pg.* 1469, *pg.* 1619
DUROBOARD - Roof Insulation - JOHNS MANVILLE CORPORATION; *pg.* 89, *pg.* 320
DUROCHOLOR - Chemical Products - HAVILAND ENTERPRISES INC.; *pg.* 1165, *pg.* 887
DUROCK - Cement Board - USG CORPORATION; *pg.* 118, *pg.* 594
DURODI - Steel Product - A. FINKL & SONS CO.; *pg.* 1309, *pg.* 563
DUROFLOW - Blower - GARDNER DENVER, INC.; *pg.* 1338, *pg.* 1592
DUROFTALT - Solventborne - CYTEC INDUSTRIES, INC.; *pg.* 1155, *pg.* 1131
DUROLENE - Paper, Paperboard & Wound Paper Tubes - SONOCO PRODUCTS COMPANY; *pg.* 1469, *pg.* 1619
DURON - Friction Products - FEDERAL-MOGUL HOLDINGS CORPORATION; *pg.* 205, *pg.* 907
DURON - Treated Surfaces Tubes - SONOCO PRODUCTS COMPANY; *pg.* 1469, *pg.* 1619
DUROX - Paper & Paperboard - SONOCO PRODUCTS COMPANY; *pg.* 1469, *pg.* 1619
DUROXYN - Solventborne - CYTEC INDUSTRIES, INC.; *pg.* 1155, *pg.* 1131
DURRIYA - Lamp - ASHLEY FURNITURE INDUSTRIES, INC.; *pg.* 914, *pg.* 1852
DURSBAN - Insecticide - SOUTHERN AGRICULTURAL INSECTICIDES, INC.; *pg.* 1181, *pg.* 458
DURST - Farm Irrigation Drives - REGAL BELOIT CORPORATION; *pg.* 106, *pg.* 1854
DURUS - Dinnerware - CARLISLE FOODSERVICE PRODUCTS INCORPORATED; *pg.* 1455, *pg.* 1485
DURWARD ANKL WEIGHTS - Buckle - MCNETT CORPORATION; *pg.* 1839, *pg.* 1817
DUSK - Fabric - NEMSCHOFF, INC.; *pg.* 936, *pg.* 1890
DUSK AND DAWN - Riflescope - BUSHNELL OUTDOOR PRODUCTS, INC.; *pg.* 1403, *pg.* 718
DUSK OVER CAIRO - Nail Care Product - OPI PRODUCTS INC.; *pg.* 518, *pg.* 167
DUSKGLO - Cosmetic Product - MERLE NORMAN COSMETICS, INC.; *pg.* 517, *pg.* 136
DUSOFT - Wound Dressing - DERMA SCIENCES, INC.; *pg.* 1523, *pg.* 1111
DUSOR - Bandage - DERMA SCIENCES, INC.; *pg.* 1523, *pg.* 1111
DUST-A-WAY - Cleaner - DELTA FOREMOST CHEMICAL CORPORATION; *pg.* 1155, *pg.* 1642
DUST COMMAND - Cleaner - DELTA FOREMOST CHEMICAL CORPORATION; *pg.* 1155, *pg.* 1642
DUST FORCE - Premium Dust Mop - RUBBERMAID HOME PRODUCTS; *pg.* 1138, *pg.* 1453
DUST MASTER - Dustless FD&C Dye - SENSIENT COLORS INC.; *pg.* 1180, *pg.* 1003
DUST-N-CLEAN - Special Application Wipers - GEORGIA-PACIFIC LLC; *pg.* 1458, *pg.* 507
DUST-OFF - Chemical Compounds - CARGILL, INC.; *pg.* 845, *pg.* 965
DUSTAIR - Dust & Airborne - AERVOE INDUSTRIES INCORPORATED; *pg.* 1439, *pg.* 1021
DUSTER - Aerosol Dust Removal System - CRC INDUSTRIES, INC.; *pg.* 329, *pg.* 1590
DUSTER - Pressurized Air - HOBBICO, INC.; *pg.* 956, *pg.* 562
DUSTER PLUS - Wax-Free Cleaner - S.C. JOHNSON & SON, INC.; *pg.* 334, *pg.* 1889
DUSTTRAK - Aerosol Monitor - TSI INCORPORATED; *pg.* 1432, *pg.* 965
DUTAILIER - Rocking Chair - GROUPE DUTAILIER INC.; *pg.* 926, *pg.* 1960
DUTCH BOY - Paints & Coatings - THE SHERWIN-WILLIAMS COMPANY; *pg.* 1447, *pg.* 1435
DUTCH BOY - Paint - SHERWIN-WILLIAMS DIVERSIFIED BRANDS DIVISION; *pg.* 1448, *pg.* 1435
DUTCH CRUNCH - Food Product - OLD DUTCH FOODS, INC.; *pg.* 888, *pg.* 956
DUTCH GIRL - Apple Butter & Jellies - THE J.M. SMUCKER COMPANY; *pg.* 865, *pg.* 1468
DUTCH GOLD HONEY - Honey - DUTCH GOLD HONEY INC.; *pg.* 854, *pg.* 1546
DUTCH HARBOR - Seafood Products - UNISEA FOODS, INC.; *pg.* 906, *pg.* 1829
DUTCH MASTERS - Domestic Cigars - ALTADIS USA, INC.; *pg.* 1893, *pg.* 423
DUTCH MILL - Bakery Goods - TASTY BAKING COMPANY; *pg.* 1862, *pg.* 1571
DUTCH OAK - Aluminum Siding - PLY GEM SIDING GROUP; *pg.* 105, *pg.* 986
DUTCH TREATS - Domestic Cigars - ALTADIS USA, INC.; *pg.* 1893, *pg.* 423
DUTCH TREATS - Drink - AUNTIE ANNE'S INC.; *pg.* 1715, *pg.* 1546
DUTCH TULIPS - Nail Care Product - OPI PRODUCTS INC.; *pg.* 518, *pg.* 167
DUTCH TWIST - Soft Pretzels - J&J SNACK FOODS CORPORATION; *pg.* 865, *pg.* 1107
DUTCHESS - Footwear - P.W. MINOR & SON, INC.; *pg.* 1816, *pg.* 1140
DUTCHMEN - Recreation Vehicle - THOR INDUSTRIES, INC.; *pg.* 1711, *pg.* 1456
DUTCHTECH - Vacuum Bag - ORECK CORPORATION; *pg.* 59, *pg.* 1653
DUTEX - Bandage - DERMA SCIENCES, INC.; *pg.* 1523, *pg.* 1111
DUTOP - Wound Dressing - DERMA SCIENCES, INC.; *pg.* 1523, *pg.* 1111
DUTTON & NAL - Adult Hardcover Books - PENGUIN RANDOM HOUSE; *pg.* 1675, *pg.* 1276
DUTTON CHILDREN'S - Children's Hardcover Books - PENGUIN RANDOM HOUSE; *pg.* 1675, *pg.* 1276
DUTY GEAR - Safety Holster, Belts & Related Accessories - BAE SYSTEMS PRODUCTS GROUP; *pg.* 359, *pg.* 432
DUTYMAX - Shirts - ELBECO INCORPORATED; *pg.* 40, *pg.* 1584
DUTYMAXX - Shirts - ELBECO INCORPORATED; *pg.* 40, *pg.* 1584
DUZ IT ALL II - Cleaner - SWISHER HYGIENE INC.; *pg.* 336, *pg.* 1507
DV CAMCORDERS - Camera - ALAN GORDON ENTERPRISES, INC.; *pg.* 1399, *pg.* 125
DV DEMON - Loudspeaker Systems - GIBSON GUITAR CORP.; *pg.* 550, *pg.* 1650
DV-E - Low Cost Digital Viscometer - BROOKFIELD ENGINEERING LABORATORIES, INC.; *pg.* 1403, *pg.* 833
DV-I+ - Digital Viscometer - BROOKFIELD ENGINEERING LABORATORIES, INC.; *pg.* 1403, *pg.* 833
DV-II+ PRO - Digital Viscometer - BROOKFIELD ENGINEERING LABORATORIES, INC.; *pg.* 1403, *pg.* 833
DV-III ULTRA - Laboratory Rheometer - BROOKFIELD ENGINEERING LABORATORIES, INC.; *pg.* 1403, *pg.* 833
DV-III+ - Digital Rheometer - BROOKFIELD ENGINEERING LABORATORIES, INC.; *pg.* 1403, *pg.* 833
DV-LOADER - Software - BROOKFIELD ENGINEERING LABORATORIES, INC.; *pg.* 1403, *pg.* 833
DV-PRIME - Single-Wafer Clean - LAM RESEARCH CORPORATION; *pg.* 1354, *pg.* 91
DV-WIZARD - Digital Video Product - HAUPPAUGE DIGITAL, INC.; *pg.* 402, *pg.* 1164
DV-WIZARD PRO - Video Editing - HAUPPAUGE DIGITAL, INC.; *pg.* 402, *pg.* 1164
DVD CARBON EDGE PRO - Laser Lens Cleaner - ALLSOP, INC.; *pg.* 347, *pg.* 1817
DVD ON DEMAND - Personalized Application - SEACHANGE INTERNATIONAL, INC.; *pg.* 1279, *pg.* 781
DVD STUDIO PRO - Application Program - APPLE INC.; *pg.* 350, *pg.* 73
D'VERSIBIT - Flexible Bit System - GREENLEE TEXTRON INC.; *pg.* 1048, *pg.* 655
DVP - Imaging System - UVP, INC.; *pg.* 1434, *pg.* 298
DVS - Golf Club Shafts - ALDILA, INC.; *pg.* 1825, *pg.* 185
DVS - Diary Product - CHR. HANSEN; *pg.* 847, *pg.* 1873
DVS - Footwear Brand - SEQUENTIAL BRANDS GROUP, INC.; *pg.* 1395, *pg.* 1290
DVS-1200 - Security System - NORTEK SECURITY & CONTROL LLC; *pg.* 659, *pg.* 59
DVS-2400 - Security System - NORTEK SECURITY & CONTROL LLC; *pg.* 659, *pg.* 59
DVT - Vision System - COGNEX CORPORATION; *pg.* 1406, *pg.* 834
DVT - Polyphase Processors - LITTLEFORD DAY INC.; *pg.* 1356, *pg.* 728
DWAN - Footwear - K-SWISS; *pg.* 1837, *pg.* 306
DWDMG 100GHZ 4/8CH - Fiber Optic Component - OPLINK COMMUNICATIONS, INC.; *pg.* 660, *pg.* 91
DWDMG 200GHZ 4/8 CH - Fiber Optic Component - OPLINK COMMUNICATIONS, INC.; *pg.* 660, *pg.* 91
DWELL - Fabric - NEMSCHOFF, INC.; *pg.* 936, *pg.* 1890
DWFC 1X2 - Coupler - OPLINK COMMUNICATIONS, INC.; *pg.* 660, *pg.* 91
DWFC 1X3 - Coupler - OPLINK COMMUNICATIONS, INC.; *pg.* 660, *pg.* 91
DWFC 2X2 - Coupler - OPLINK COMMUNICATIONS, INC.; *pg.* 660, *pg.* 91
DWG - Software - AUTODESK INC.; *pg.* 356, *pg.* 257
DWG TRUECONVERT - Software - AUTODESK INC.; *pg.* 356, *pg.* 257
DWG TRUEVIEW - Software - AUTODESK INC.; *pg.* 356, *pg.* 257
DWTC - Splitter - OPLINK COMMUNICATIONS, INC.; *pg.* 660, *pg.* 91
DX - Fluid Handling System - GRACO, INC.; *pg.* 1342, *pg.* 935
DX - Exothermic Atmosphere Gas Generators - SURFACE COMBUSTION, INC.; *pg.* 1077, *pg.* 1462
DX DESIGN - Photographic Films - EASTMAN KODAK COMPANY; *pg.* 1408, *pg.* 1333
DX-SERIES - Disk-Based Backup - QUANTUM CORPORATION; *pg.* 458, *pg.* 250

First page reference indicates Business Class Edition
Second page reference indicates Geographic Edition

DX WELLHEAD CONNECTORS - Subsea Equipment - DRIL-QUIP, INC.; *pg.* 1330, *pg.* 1704
DXA - Medical Test System - HOLOGIC, INC.; *pg.* 1416, *pg.* 784
DXANALOG - Software System - MENTOR GRAPHICS CORPORATION; *pg.* 432, *pg.* 1510
DXB - Wafer Bonder - DYNATEX INTERNATIONAL; *pg.* 635, *pg.* 277
DXCART - E-Commerce Solution - DXSTORM.COM INC.; *pg.* 1239, *pg.* 1930
DXCUSTOM - E-Commerce Solution - DXSTORM.COM INC.; *pg.* 1239, *pg.* 1930
DXDATABOOK - Software System - MENTOR GRAPHICS CORPORATION; *pg.* 432, *pg.* 1510
DXDATAMANAGER - Software System - MENTOR GRAPHICS CORPORATION; *pg.* 432, *pg.* 1510
DXDESIGNER - Software System - MENTOR GRAPHICS CORPORATION; *pg.* 432, *pg.* 1510
DXE - Wafer Expander - DYNATEX INTERNATIONAL; *pg.* 635, *pg.* 277
DXENTERPRISE FOR AGILE - Software System - MENTOR GRAPHICS CORPORATION; *pg.* 432, *pg.* 1510
DXF - File Format - AUTODESK INC.; *pg.* 356, *pg.* 257
DXI - Immunoassay System - BECKMAN COULTER, INC.; *pg.* 1402, *pg.* 48
DXI-SERIES - Disk Backup - QUANTUM CORPORATION; *pg.* 458, *pg.* 250
DXL - Lubricant Injector - DYNATEX INTERNATIONAL; *pg.* 635, *pg.* 277
DXLIBRARYSTUDIO - Software System - MENTOR GRAPHICS CORPORATION; *pg.* 432, *pg.* 1510
DXMATRIX - Software System - MENTOR GRAPHICS CORPORATION; *pg.* 432, *pg.* 1510
DXNOW - Online Services - DYNAMEX, INC.; *pg.* 1906, *pg.* 1680
DXNOW - Online Services - INTEGRATED BIOPHARMA, INC.; *pg.* 1546, *pg.* 1073
DXPARTS - Software System - MENTOR GRAPHICS CORPORATION; *pg.* 432, *pg.* 1510
DXPDF - Software System - MENTOR GRAPHICS CORPORATION; *pg.* 432, *pg.* 1510
DXR-701 - DX Receiver - NORTEK SECURITY & CONTROL LLC; *pg.* 659, *pg.* 59
DXSHOP - E-Commerce Solution - DXSTORM.COM INC.; *pg.* 1239, *pg.* 1930
DXSIM - Software System - MENTOR GRAPHICS CORPORATION; *pg.* 432, *pg.* 1510
DXSTORM.COM - Website - DXSTORM.COM INC.; *pg.* 1239, *pg.* 1930
DXTVENT - Footwear - LACROSSE FOOTWEAR, INC.; *pg.* 1811, *pg.* 1503
DXVARIANTMANAGER - Software System - MENTOR GRAPHICS CORPORATION; *pg.* 432, *pg.* 1510
DXVIEWDRAW - Software System - MENTOR GRAPHICS CORPORATION; *pg.* 432, *pg.* 1510
DXVIEWONLY - Software System - MENTOR GRAPHICS CORPORATION; *pg.* 432, *pg.* 1510
DXWEB - E-Commerce Solution - DXSTORM.COM INC.; *pg.* 1239, *pg.* 1930
DY-O-DERM - Pharmaceutical Products - GALDERMA LABORATORIES, L.P.; *pg.* 1532, *pg.* 1695
DYAD - Software - BIO-RAD LABORATORIES, INC.; *pg.* 1504, *pg.* 101
DYAD DISCIPLE - Software - BIO-RAD LABORATORIES, INC.; *pg.* 1504, *pg.* 101
DYANI - Lamp - ASHLEY FURNITURE INDUSTRIES, INC.; *pg.* 914, *pg.* 1852
DYANITE - Dry Cleaning & Laundry Product - ADCO, INC.; *pg.* 325, *pg.* 482
DYANITE - Cemented Tungsten Carbide - MULTI-METALS; *pg.* 1363, *pg.* 737
DYANITE 2000 - Charge Soap - ADCO, INC.; *pg.* 325, *pg.* 482
DYANITE DOUBLE - Charge Soap - ADCO, INC.; *pg.* 325, *pg.* 482
DYCAL - Dental Product - DENTSPLY INTERNATIONAL INC.; *pg.* 1522, *pg.* 1596
DYCEM - Anti-Fatigue Mat - ALIMED, INC.; *pg.* 1490, *pg.* 816
DYECHROME - Molecular Probe Product - THERMO FISHER SCIENTIFIC INC.; *pg.* 1602, *pg.* 61
DYECYCLE - Molecular Probe Product - THERMO FISHER SCIENTIFIC INC.; *pg.* 1602, *pg.* 61
DYEMER - Molecular Probe Product - THERMO FISHER SCIENTIFIC INC.; *pg.* 1602, *pg.* 61
DYFORM - Wire Rope Process - BRIDON AMERICAN CORP.; *pg.* 1319, *pg.* 1594
DYKOR - Fluoropolymer Coating System - WHITFORD WORLDWIDE COMPANY; *pg.* 1185, *pg.* 1529
DYLAN - Lamp - ASHLEY FURNITURE INDUSTRIES, INC.; *pg.* 914, *pg.* 1852
DYLARK - High Performance Styrenics - NOVA CHEMICALS CORPORATION; *pg.* 1175, *pg.* 1904
DYLENE - Expandable Polystyrene - NOVA CHEMICALS CORPORATION; *pg.* 1175, *pg.* 1904
DYLITE - Expandable Polystyrene - NOVA CHEMICALS CORPORATION; *pg.* 1175, *pg.* 1904
DYLUX - Image Proofing System - E.I. DU PONT DE NEMOURS & COMPANY; *pg.* 1159, *pg.* 390
DYMASIL - Dimethylsiloxane Fluid - DOW CORNING CORPORATION; *pg.* 1159, *pg.* 900
DYMEC - Turf Product - PBI/GORDON CORPORATION; *pg.* 1176, *pg.* 985
DYMEL - Industrial Propellants - E.I. DU PONT DE NEMOURS & COMPANY; *pg.* 1159, *pg.* 390
DYMENSION - Manifolds - ENTEGRIS, INC.; *pg.* 1882, *pg.* 788
DYMEREX - Rosins - EASTMAN CHEMICAL COMPANY; *pg.* 1159, *pg.* 1636
DYMETROL - Suspension Fabric - E.I. DU PONT DE NEMOURS & COMPANY; *pg.* 1159, *pg.* 390
DYMO - Electronic and Embossing Labeling Systems - ESSELTE BUSINESS CORP; *pg.* 395, *pg.* 1179
DYMO - Office Products - NEWELL RUBBERMAID INC.; *pg.* 1128, *pg.* 515
DYMONDWOOD - Box - BROWN & BIGELOW, INC.; *pg.* 1624, *pg.* 959
DYMONIC - Roofing Material - TREMCO INCORPORATED; *pg.* 116, *pg.* 1405
DYMORIG - Power Tools - MILWAUKEE ELECTRIC TOOL CORP.; *pg.* 1056, *pg.* 1855
DYN-O MELT - Salt - CARGILL LIMITED; *pg.* 1475, *pg.* 1914
DYNA - Motorcycle - HARLEY-DAVIDSON, INC.; *pg.* 178, *pg.* 1874
DYNA - Actuator - WOODWARD, INC.; *pg.* 122, *pg.* 329
DYNA-AIR - Turbine Engine - ALLEN AIRCRAFT PRODUCTS, INC.; *pg.* 223, *pg.* 1471
DYNA-BRAKE - Fall Protection Equipment - MINE SAFETY APPLIANCES COMPANY; *pg.* 1361, *pg.* 1525
DYNA-DECK - Screening - TELSMITH, INC.; *pg.* 1381, *pg.* 1871
DYNA DEFENDER - Motorcycles - HARLEY-DAVIDSON, INC.; *pg.* 178, *pg.* 1874
DYNA-FLEX - Healthcare Product - JOHNSON & JOHNSON; *pg.* 1549, *pg.* 1091
DYNA GLIDE - Motorcycles - HARLEY-DAVIDSON, INC.; *pg.* 178, *pg.* 1874
DYNA-GLIDE - Fall Protection Equipment - MINE SAFETY APPLIANCES COMPANY; *pg.* 1361, *pg.* 1525
DYNA-KLEEN - Alkaline Product - DELTA FOREMOST CHEMICAL CORPORATION; *pg.* 1155, *pg.* 1642
DYNA-LINE - Rescue Equipment - MINE SAFETY APPLIANCES COMPANY; *pg.* 1361, *pg.* 1525
DYNA-LOCK - Self-Retracting Lanyard - MINE SAFETY APPLIANCES COMPANY; *pg.* 1361, *pg.* 1525
DYNA-MIGHT - Energy-Absorbing Lanyard - MINE SAFETY APPLIANCES COMPANY; *pg.* 1361, *pg.* 1525
DYNA-STAR - Pump & Reciprocator - GRACO, INC.; *pg.* 1342, *pg.* 935
DYNA STOP - Electronic Brake - REULAND ELECTRIC COMPANY; *pg.* 1304, *pg.* 68
DYNA-THRED - Fastener - LONG-LOK FASTENERS CORP.; *pg.* 1053, *pg.* 1416
DYNA-THRED II - Self-Locking Fasteners - LONG-LOK FASTENERS CORP.; *pg.* 1053, *pg.* 1416
DYNA-TOUCH - Amplifier - FENDER MUSICAL INSTRUMENTS CORPORATION; *pg.* 547, *pg.* 21
DYNA/TRACE - Medical Equipment - CONMED CORPORATION; *pg.* 1517, *pg.* 1347
DYNA-TRIM - Tuning Device - JOHANSON MANUFACTURING CORPORATION; *pg.* 648, *pg.* 1045
DYNABEADS - Molecular Biology Product - THERMO FISHER SCIENTIFIC INC.; *pg.* 1602, *pg.* 61
DYNABLAST - Surgical Implant - LIFECORE BIOMEDICAL, LLC; *pg.* 1556, *pg.* 920
DYNACHARGE - Accu Rechargeable Batteries - DURACELL; *pg.* 635, *pg.* 337
DYNACHUFF - Toy Train - LIONEL LLC; *pg.* 961, *pg.* 875
DYNACLAD - Modified Bitumen Membrane - JOHNS MANVILLE CORPORATION; *pg.* 89, *pg.* 320
DYNACLEAN - Automatic Sediment Cleaning System - A.O. SMITH CORPORATION; *pg.* 1313, *pg.* 1872
DYNACLONE - Dust Filter - SLY, INC.; *pg.* 1376, *pg.* 1475
DYNACOLOR - Pigment - BASF CATALYSTS LLC; *pg.* 1148, *pg.* 1074
DYNACON - String Connector - ION GEOPHYSICAL CORPORATION; *pg.* 1350, *pg.* 1708
DYNACON GEO - String Connector - ION GEOPHYSICAL CORPORATION; *pg.* 1350, *pg.* 1708
DYNACOR - Disposable Hospital Supplies - MEDLINE INDUSTRIES, INC.; *pg.* 1562, *pg.* 635
DYNACORE - Gasket - W.L. GORE & ASSOCIATES, INC.; *pg.* 122, *pg.* 388
DYNACRAFT - Trucks - PACCAR INC.; *pg.* 187, *pg.* 1816
DYNACRAWL - Crawl - CHYRONHEGO; *pg.* 371, *pg.* 1179
DYNAFIBRE - Filtration System - SPECTRUM LABORATORIES INC.; *pg.* 1595, *pg.* 69
DYNAFILTER - Air-Cleaning Cartridge - KAZ, INC.; *pg.* 58, *pg.* 844
DYNAFIND - Software - MITEK SYSTEMS, INC.; *pg.* 440, *pg.* 204
DYNAFLEX - Medical & Aesthetic Product - DYNATRONICS CORPORATION; *pg.* 1526, *pg.* 1757
DYNAFLEX - Modified Bitumen Sheet - JOHNS MANVILLE CORPORATION; *pg.* 89, *pg.* 320
DYNAFLEX - Coupling - LORD CORPORATION; *pg.* 1357, *pg.* 1360
DYNAFLEX 230 - Caulk And Sealant - DAP PRODUCTS, INC.; *pg.* 1441, *pg.* 756
DYNAFOCAL - Aircraft Engine Mounts & Access. - LORD CORPORATION; *pg.* 1357, *pg.* 1360
DYNAFORCE - HVAC Equipment - MESTEK, INC.; *pg.* 1074, *pg.* 857
DYNAGARD - Filtration System - SPECTRUM LABORATORIES INC.; *pg.* 1595, *pg.* 69
DYNAGEL - Medical & Aesthetic Product - DYNATRONICS CORPORATION; *pg.* 1526, *pg.* 1757
DYNAGLAS - Modified Bitumen Sheet - JOHNS MANVILLE CORPORATION; *pg.* 89, *pg.* 320
DYNAGLAS 30 FR - Modified Bitumen Sheet - JOHNS MANVILLE CORPORATION; *pg.* 89, *pg.* 320
DYNAGLAS FR - Modified Bitumen Sheet - JOHNS MANVILLE CORPORATION; *pg.* 89, *pg.* 320
DYNAGLIDE - Medical Device - BOSTON SCIENTIFIC CORPORATION; *pg.* 1508, *pg.* 831
DYNAGRAFT-D - Surgical Implant - LIFECORE BIOMEDICAL, LLC; *pg.* 1556, *pg.* 920
DYNAGRIP - Self-Adhering Roofing Membrane - JOHNS MANVILLE CORPORATION; *pg.* 89, *pg.* 320
DYNAGRIP - Utility Knives - STANLEY BLACK & DECKER, INC.; *pg.* 1063, *pg.* 358
DYNAHEAT - Medical & Aesthetic Product - DYNATRONICS CORPORATION; *pg.* 1526, *pg.* 1757
DYNAKAP - Modified Bitumen Roofing - JOHNS MANVILLE CORPORATION; *pg.* 89, *pg.* 320
DYNAKEY - Point-of-Service Computer Product - NCR CORPORATION; *pg.* 443, *pg.* 531
DYNAL - Molecular Biology Product - THERMO FISHER SCIENTIFIC INC.; *pg.* 1602, *pg.* 61
DYNALASTIC 180 - SBS Modified Bitumen Sheet - JOHNS MANVILLE CORPORATION; *pg.* 89, *pg.* 320
DYNALASTIC 250 - Modified Bitumen Sheet - JOHNS MANVILLE CORPORATION; *pg.* 89, *pg.* 320
DYNALIFT - Telescopic Handler - GEHL COMPANY; *pg.* 1339, *pg.* 1899
DYNALINK - Self-Expanding Stent System - ABBOTT LABORATORIES; *pg.* 1484, *pg.* 551
DYNALITE - Golf Shaft - TRUE TEMPER SPORTS, INC.; *pg.* 1847, *pg.* 1647
DYNALOOP - Software - BIO-RAD LABORATORIES, INC.; *pg.* 1504, *pg.* 101
DYNALOY - Coating - GENERAL MAGNAPLATE CORPORATION; *pg.* 1164, *pg.* 1079
DYNAMAIL - Software - R.R. DONNELLEY & SONS COMPANY; *pg.* 1682, *pg.* 589
DYNAMATCH - Credit Scoring Service - FAIR ISAAC CORPORATION; *pg.* 1247, *pg.* 955
DYNAMATE - Mop Handles - GEERPRES INC.; *pg.* 1339, *pg.* 901
DYNAMATH - Educational Materials - SCHOLASTIC INC.; *pg.* 1683, *pg.* 1288
DYNAMAX - Wiper And Cleaning Cloth - GEORGIA-PACIFIC LLC; *pg.* 1458, *pg.* 507
DYNAMELT - Fluid Handling System - GRACO, INC.; *pg.* 1342, *pg.* 935
DYNAMEX DELIVERS NOW - Slogan - DYNAMEX, INC.; *pg.*

1906, *pg.* 1680
DYNAMIC - Medical Device - BOSTON SCIENTIFIC CORPORATION; *pg.* 1508, *pg.* 831
DYNAMIC - Golf Shaft - TRUE TEMPER SPORTS, INC.; *pg.* 1847, *pg.* 1647
DYNAMIC ANALOG - Automatic Test Equipment - NEXTEST SYSTEMS CORPORATION; *pg.* 445, *pg.* 248
DYNAMIC BARRIER - Fume Hood - KEWAUNEE SCIENTIFIC CORPORATION; *pg.* 931, *pg.* 1391
DYNAMIC DEMAND RESPONSE - Software - JDA SOFTWARE GROUP, INC.; *pg.* 423, *pg.* 22
DYNAMIC DESIGNER - Motion Simulation Software - MSC SOFTWARE CORPORATION; *pg.* 441, *pg.* 262
DYNAMIC DIGITAL SIGNAGE - Tag Line - WIRELESS RONIN TECHNOLOGIES INC.; *pg.* 689, *pg.* 951
DYNAMIC DISK - Separation Chamber - HAEMONETICS CORPORATION; *pg.* 1538, *pg.* 802
DYNAMIC DOCUMENT SERVER - Software - QUARK, INC.; *pg.* 458, *pg.* 322
DYNAMIC DOLLARS - Video Game - INTERNATIONAL GAME TECHNOLOGY; *pg.* 957, *pg.* 1024
DYNAMIC FLOW - Electrosurgical Devices - ANGIODYNAMICS, INC.; *pg.* 1495, *pg.* 1173
DYNAMIC IMMERSION - Language Learning Solutions - ROSETTA STONE INC.; *pg.* 462, *pg.* 1774
DYNAMIC JOINT DISTRACTOR II - Surgical & Medical Product - STRYKER CORPORATION; *pg.* 1598, *pg.* 894
DYNAMIC LINK - Software - ADOBE SYSTEMS INCORPORATED; *pg.* 342, *pg.* 235
DYNAMIC OFFICE BALANCER - Electronic Echo Canceler for use with Telephone Systems - ALCATEL-LUCENT USA, INC.; *pg.* 615, *pg.* 1728
DYNAMIC PATH FAILOVER - Software - CAMBEX CORPORATION; *pg.* 368, *pg.* 844
DYNAMIC POWERDOWN - Tape Drive - QUANTUM CORPORATION; *pg.* 458, *pg.* 250
DYNAMIC PROCESS CONTROLLER - Ultrasonic Welder - DUKANE CORPORATION; *pg.* 634, *pg.* 658
DYNAMIC PROTOCOL MANAGEMENT - Software - WEBSENSE, INC.; *pg.* 491, *pg.* 210
DYNAMIC ROUTING ARCHITECTURE - Software - PROGRESS SOFTWARE CORPORATION; *pg.* 457, *pg.* 786
DYNAMIC SIM ALLOCATION - Software - EVOLVING SYSTEMS, INC.; *pg.* 395, *pg.* 326
DYNAMIC TCP OFFLOAD - Network Technology - ALACRITECH, INC.; *pg.* 346, *pg.* 237
DYNAMIC-TENSION - Training Method - CHARLES ATLAS, LTD.; *pg.* 538, *pg.* 1211
DYNAMIC-VID - Switch - INTERSIL CORPORATION; *pg.* 647, *pg.* 146
DYNAMIC VIRTUAL TAPE - Technology - OVERLAND STORAGE, INC.; *pg.* 451, *pg.* 205
DYNAMIC WATERJET - Cutting Process - FLOW INTERNATIONAL CORPORATION; *pg.* 1337, *pg.* 1821
DYNAMICBLACK - Video Monitoring System - TEXAS INSTRUMENTS INCORPORATED; *pg.* 679, *pg.* 1688
DYNAMICS - Software - ASPEN TECHNOLOGY, INC.; *pg.* 354, *pg.* 804
DYNAMICS - Dinnerware - THE HOMER LAUGHLIN CHINA COMPANY; *pg.* 1125, *pg.* 1850
DYNAMIGHT - Fatigue Testing Machine - INSTRON CORPORATION; *pg.* 1349, *pg.* 839
DYNAMIKE - Electrical Circuit - COBRA ELECTRONICS CORPORATION; *pg.* 629, *pg.* 572
DYNAMINI - Fluid Handling System - GRACO, INC.; *pg.* 1342, *pg.* 935
DYNAMITE - String - ASHAWAY LINE & TWINE MFG. CO.; *pg.* 1826, *pg.* 1600
DYNAMITE - Air Operated Pumps & Valves - GRACO, INC.; *pg.* 1342, *pg.* 935
DYNAMITE BLAST - Video Game - INTERNATIONAL GAME TECHNOLOGY; *pg.* 957, *pg.* 1024
DYNAMITE ENERGY SHAKE - Energy Drink - HAYDENERGY, INC.; *pg.* 861, *pg.* 1238
DYNAMITE VITES - Vitamins - HAYDENERGY, INC.; *pg.* 861, *pg.* 1238
DYNAMIX - Shower Systems - BRADLEY CORPORATION; *pg.* 71, *pg.* 1870
DYNAMO - Software - AMX CORPORATION; *pg.* 349, *pg.* 1735
DYNAMO - Bowling Equipment - BRUNSWICK BOWLING & BILLIARDS CORP.; *pg.* 1828, *pg.* 622
DYNAMO - Communication Devices - DYNAVOX INC.; *pg.* 635, *pg.* 1574
DYNAMYX - Air Bearing Stage System - NEWPORT CORPORATION; *pg.* 1424, *pg.* 114
DYNAMYX 300 - Air Bearing System - NEWPORT CORPORATION; *pg.* 1424, *pg.* 114
DYNAPAC - Block Machine - BESSER COMPANY; *pg.* 1317, *pg.* 865
DYNAPAR - Encoder - DYNAPAR; *pg.* 1408, *pg.* 616
DYNAPATH - Software - FALCONSTOR SOFTWARE, INC.; *pg.* 396, *pg.* 1179
DYNAPLY - Modified Bitumen Sheet - JOHNS MANVILLE CORPORATION; *pg.* 89, *pg.* 320
DYNAPPLY - Fluid Handling System - GRACO, INC.; *pg.* 1342, *pg.* 935
DYNAPRO - Fluid Handling System - GRACO, INC.; *pg.* 1342, *pg.* 935
DYNAPULSE - Clinical Bedding Control System - KINETIC CONCEPTS, INC.; *pg.* 1553, *pg.* 1741
DYNARAD - High Voltage Power Supplies - DGT HOLDINGS; *pg.* 634, *pg.* 1223
DYNASPERSE - Chemical Product - WESTROCK COMPANY; *pg.* 1472, *pg.* 1805
DYNASTAT - Painkiller - PFIZER INC.; *pg.* 1581, *pg.* 1278
DYNASTY - Apparel - HERITAGE LACE INC.; *pg.* 694, *pg.* 711
DYNASTY - Horse Feeds - KENT NUTRITION GROUP; *pg.* 1477, *pg.* 710
DYNASTY - Cabinetry - MASTERBRAND CABINETS, INC.; *pg.* 96, *pg.* 692
DYNASTY - Welding Machine - MILLER ELECTRIC MANUFACTURING CO.; *pg.* 1361, *pg.* 1852
DYNATEL - Cable Materials - 3M COMPANY; *pg.* 1142, *pg.* 956
DYNATHANE - Polyurethane System - THE DOW CHEMICAL COMPANY; *pg.* 1157, *pg.* 898
DYNATRAC - Tires - AMERICAN TIRE DISTRIBUTORS HOLDINGS, INC.; *pg.* 199, *pg.* 1379
DYNATRED - Roof Walkway - JOHNS MANVILLE CORPORATION; *pg.* 89, *pg.* 320
DYNATRON - Medical Device - DYNATRONICS CORPORATION; *pg.* 1526, *pg.* 1757
DYNATRON T3 - Specialty Tables - DYNATRONICS CORPORATION; *pg.* 1526, *pg.* 1757
DYNATRON T4 - Specialty Tables - DYNATRONICS CORPORATION; *pg.* 1526, *pg.* 1757
DYNATRON T4X - Specialty Tables - DYNATRONICS CORPORATION; *pg.* 1526, *pg.* 1757
DYNATRON X3 - Light Therapy Unit - DYNATRONICS CORPORATION; *pg.* 1526, *pg.* 1757
DYNATRON X5 - Light Therapy Unit - DYNATRONICS CORPORATION; *pg.* 1526, *pg.* 1757
DYNATUP - Impact Testing Instrument - INSTRON CORPORATION; *pg.* 1349, *pg.* 839
DYNATUP IMPULSE - Software - INSTRON CORPORATION; *pg.* 1349, *pg.* 839
DYNAVOX - Language, Speech & Learning Impaired Devices - DYNAVOX INC.; *pg.* 635, *pg.* 1574
DYNAWALL - Electronic Display System - TRANS-LUX CORPORATION; *pg.* 681, *pg.* 365
DYNAWRITE - Keyboard-Based Communication Device - DYNAVOX INC.; *pg.* 635, *pg.* 1574
DYNAX - Sensors, Treadles, & Interfaces - INTERNATIONAL ROAD DYNAMICS INC.; *pg.* 1912, *pg.* 1962
DYNE-BRAKE - Energy-Absorbing Lanyard - MINE SAFETY APPLIANCES COMPANY; *pg.* 1361, *pg.* 1525
DYNEEMA - Gloves & Sleeves - LAKELAND INDUSTRIES, INC.; *pg.* 1354, *pg.* 1338
DYNEEMA - Polyethylene Fiber - SAMSON ROPE TECHNOLOGIES; *pg.* 1468, *pg.* 1820
DYNESCAPE - Rescue Equipment - MINE SAFETY APPLIANCES COMPANY; *pg.* 1361, *pg.* 1525
DYNETIC - Phonograph Cartridges - SHURE INCORPORATED; *pg.* 672, *pg.* 638
DYNETICS - Deburring And Finishing System - KENNAMETAL EXTRUDE HONE; *pg.* 1352, *pg.* 1542
DYNEVAC - Rescue Equipment - MINE SAFETY APPLIANCES COMPANY; *pg.* 1361, *pg.* 1525
DYNEX - Lcd Hdtv - BEST BUY CO., INC.; *pg.* 1761, *pg.* 954
DYNIPAK - Pressure Transducer - DYNISCO INSTRUMENTS LLC; *pg.* 1526, *pg.* 823
DYNO BRITE - Liquid Detergent - EDWARD DON & COMPANY; *pg.* 54, *pg.* 672
DYNO-MINS - Nutritional Supplement - NATURAL ORGANICS, INC.; *pg.* 1571, *pg.* 1181
DYNO-MITES - Protective Eyewear - SELLSTROM MANUFACTURING CO.; *pg.* 1428, *pg.* 659
DYNO-VITES - Nutritional Supplement - NATURAL ORGANICS, INC.; *pg.* 1571, *pg.* 1181
DYNOL - Chemical Products - AIR PRODUCTS AND CHEMICALS, INC.; *pg.* 1145, *pg.* 1513
DYNOMAX - Exhaust Product - TENNECO, INC.; *pg.* 985, *pg.* 625
DYNTEK - Dynamic Technology Solutions - DYNTEK, INC.; *pg.* 389, *pg.* 165
DYRA TORQUE - Tractor Tires - THE GOODYEAR TIRE & RUBBER COMPANY; *pg.* 1883, *pg.* 1401
DYRACT - Dental Product - DENTSPLY INTERNATIONAL INC.; *pg.* 1522, *pg.* 1596
DYTEK - Pharmaceutical Reagents & Construction/Lubricants Applications - INVISTA B.V.; *pg.* 1168, *pg.* 723
DYTRAN - Software - MSC SOFTWARE CORPORATION; *pg.* 441, *pg.* 262
DZL-LENE XL/10 - High Performance Diesel Gasoline Additive - TEXAS REFINERY CORP.; *pg.* 986, *pg.* 1696
DZL-PEP ARCTIC - Fuel Treatment - TEXAS REFINERY CORP.; *pg.* 986, *pg.* 1696

E

E - Value Code Savings - DELL INC.; *pg.* 383, *pg.* 1737
E-12 SUPER ENZYMES - Supplement & Food Product - NEW EARTH LIFE SCIENCES, INC.; *pg.* 1573, *pg.* 1499
E-6 ECK - Design Mark for Photographic Technical Advice - EASTMAN KODAK COMPANY; *pg.* 1408, *pg.* 1333
E-ACCELERATION - Electronic Enabling Services - CIBER, INC.; *pg.* 372, *pg.* 330
E&J BRANDY - Brandy - E&J GALLO WINERY; *pg.* 1962, *pg.* 149
E&S - Laser Projector - EVANS & SUTHERLAND COMPUTER CORPORATION; *pg.* 638, *pg.* 1757
E-BARATRON - Capacitance Manometer - MKS INSTRUMENTS, INC.; *pg.* 1362, *pg.* 781
E-BARRIER - Paint - THE SHERWIN-WILLIAMS COMPANY; *pg.* 1447, *pg.* 1435
E-BASE - Molecular Biology Product - THERMO FISHER SCIENTIFIC INC.; *pg.* 1602, *pg.* 61
E-BILLING PLUS - Online Billing Software - ATC HEALTHCARE, INC.; *pg.* 1497, *pg.* 1184
E-BIOLOGY - Biopharmaceutical Product - LEXICON PHARMACEUTICALS, INC.; *pg.* 1555, *pg.* 1747
E-BRITE - Material & Alloy - ALLEGHENY TECHNOLOGIES INCORPORATED; *pg.* 66, *pg.* 1572
E-BULK FOODS - E-Commerce System - JOHN B. SANFILIPPO & SON, INC.; *pg.* 1024, *pg.* 610
E-BUSINESS FOR EVERYONE - Tagline - BROADVISION, INC.; *pg.* 365, *pg.* 189
E CAGE - Bicycle Accessories - SPECIALIZED BICYCLE COMPONENTS, INC.; *pg.* 1711, *pg.* 152
E-CBU - Security Locker - AMERICAN LOCKER GROUP INCORPORATED; *pg.* 1041, *pg.* 1674
E-CBU - Security Locker - AMERICAN LOCKER SECURITY SYSTEMS, INC.; *pg.* 1042, *pg.* 1674
E-CELL - Electrodeionization Equipment - GE WATER & PROCESS TECHNOLOGIES; *pg.* 1339, *pg.* 1588
E-CLASS - Bar Code System - DATAMAX CORPORATION; *pg.* 1633, *pg.* 453
E-CLASS - Skylighting Product - WASCO PRODUCTS, INC.; *pg.* 120, *pg.* 752
E. COLI PULSER - Software - BIO-RAD LABORATORIES, INC.; *pg.* 1504, *pg.* 101
E-COLOUR - Filter - ROSCO LABORATORIES, INC.; *pg.* 1782, *pg.* 378
E-CONTROL - Software - CRESTRON ELECTRONICS INC.; *pg.* 631, *pg.* 1116
E-CORE - Fiber Optic Product - KVH INDUSTRIES INC; *pg.* 650, *pg.* 1602
E CUSTOMERDIRECT - Computerized Ordering & Billing Services - KAWNEER COMPANY, INC.; *pg.* 90, *pg.* 537
E-DART - Gaming Product - GLD PRODUCTS, INC.; *pg.* 1835, *pg.* 1882
E-DATALOG - Software - CRESTRON ELECTRONICS INC.; *pg.* 631, *pg.* 1116
E-DIAL - Software - CRESTRON ELECTRONICS INC.; *pg.* 631, *pg.* 1116
E-DIF - Wireless Product - HEMISPHERE GPS INC.; *pg.* 642, *pg.* 1903
E-DISCOVERY MANAGER - Software - DELL SOFTWARE; *pg.* 385, *pg.* 40
E-EDITOR - Software - THERMO FISHER SCIENTIFIC INC.; *pg.* 1602, *pg.* 61

First page reference indicates Business Class Edition
Second page reference indicates Geographic Edition

E-FACTOR - Apparel - AMC, INC.; *pg.* 1759, *pg.* 487
E-FAQ KNOWLEDGE MANAGER - Software - INTERACTIVE INTELLIGENCE, INC.; *pg.* 417, *pg.* 687
E FAX BROADCAST - Software - EFAX.COM INC.; *pg.* 1242, *pg.* 129
E FAX CORPORATE - Software - EFAX.COM INC.; *pg.* 1242, *pg.* 129
E FAX FREE - Software - EFAX.COM INC.; *pg.* 1242, *pg.* 129
E FAX PLUS - Software - EFAX.COM INC.; *pg.* 1242, *pg.* 129
E-FLO - Fluid Handling System - GRACO, INC.; *pg.* 1342, *pg.* 935
E-FLOOD - Flashlight - STREAMLIGHT INC.; *pg.* 1306, *pg.* 1527
E-FORM - Software - THOMSON REUTERS TAX & ACCOUNTING; *pg.* 1693, *pg.* 1299
E-FUSION - Resiliency & Shock Absorption Components - BROOKS SPORTS INC.; *pg.* 1805, *pg.* 1818
E-GEL - Molecular Biology Product - THERMO FISHER SCIENTIFIC INC.; *pg.* 1602, *pg.* 61
E-HOLDER - Cell Culture Product - THERMO FISHER SCIENTIFIC INC.; *pg.* 1602, *pg.* 61
E-HOME WONDER - Graphics Driver - ADVANCED MICRO DEVICES, INC.; *pg.* 613, *pg.* 282
E-HOME WONDER - Computer Enhancement - ADVANCED MICRO DEVICES, INC.-MARKHAM; *pg.* 345, *pg.* 1922
E-INTELLIPRISE - Software System - AMERICAN SOFTWARE, INC.; *pg.* 349, *pg.* 488
E-ISSUES - Software - MAC-GRAY CORPORATION; *pg.* 58, *pg.* 852
E-KITS DIRECT - Manual - XEROX CORPORATION; *pg.* 494, *pg.* 365
E-KLIPS - Electrical & Mechanical Fixing System - THOMAS & BETTS CORPORATION; *pg.* 680, *pg.* 1646
E-LAB - Software - EMC CORPORATION; *pg.* 391, *pg.* 825
E-LINK - Seating Product - IRWIN SEATING COMPANY INC.; *pg.* 929, *pg.* 887
E-LOK - Seating System - HENRY PRATT COMPANY; *pg.* 1049, *pg.* 555
E-MAIL SECURITY SAAS - Software - WEBROOT SOFTWARE, INC.; *pg.* 1289, *pg.* 313
E-MAT - Excelsior Fiber - AMERICAN EXCELSIOR COMPANY; *pg.* 1451, *pg.* 1659
E-MAXMC - Payment Software - LANDACORP, INC.; *pg.* 426, *pg.* 65
E-MEDIA PLAYER - Software - CRESTRON ELECTRONICS INC.; *pg.* 631, *pg.* 1116
E-MERGE - Online Services - R.R. DONNELLEY & SONS COMPANY; *pg.* 1682, *pg.* 589
E-MMEDIATE GIFT - Retail Store Services - 1-800-FLOWERS.COM, INC.; *pg.* 1758, *pg.* 1151
E-MMEDIATE GIFTS - Emailed Gift Notices - THE POPCORN FACTORY; *pg.* 1861, *pg.* 625
E-MOVE - Trailer - U-HAUL INTERNATIONAL, INC.; *pg.* 1926, *pg.* 20
E-ONE - Fire & Rescue Vehicles - FEDERAL SIGNAL CORPORATION; *pg.* 638, *pg.* 645
E-OUTLOOK - Software - CRESTRON ELECTRONICS INC.; *pg.* 631, *pg.* 1116
E-P PLUS - Commercial Washers - PELLERIN MILNOR CORPORATION; *pg.* 1368, *pg.* 744
E-PACKAGE - Software - UNITED PARCEL SERVICE, INC.; *pg.* 1928, *pg.* 522
E-PAGE - Molecular Biology Product - THERMO FISHER SCIENTIFIC INC.; *pg.* 1602, *pg.* 61
E-PLEX 5000 - Electronic Pushbutton Lock - KABA ILCO CORP.; *pg.* 1052, *pg.* 1390
E PLUS HIGH C - Hair & Skin Product - AUBREY ORGANICS INC.; *pg.* 499, *pg.* 470
E-PORT - Software - USA TECHNOLOGIES, INC.; *pg.* 815, *pg.* 1550
E-POWERPOINT - Software - CRESTRON ELECTRONICS INC.; *pg.* 631, *pg.* 1116
E-PRIME - Nutritional Supplement - USANA HEALTH SCIENCES, INC.; *pg.* 1605, *pg.* 1761
E-PRO - Education Program - NATIONAL ASSOCIATION OF REALTORS; *pg.* 1666, *pg.* 584
E-PROPOSALS - Software - QVIDIAN; *pg.* 458, *pg.* 829
E-QOE - Software - AVAGO TECHNOLOGIES; *pg.* 358, *pg.* 238
E-RACE AWAY - Educational Product - BARKER CREEK PUBLISHING INC.; *pg.* 1619, *pg.* 1818
E-RESULTS - Web Based Application - LABORATORY CORPORATION OF AMERICA HOLDINGS; *pg.* 1554, *pg.* 1359
E-SAFE - Hybrid Power Switch - WATLOW ELECTRIC MANUFACTURING COMPANY; *pg.* 1078, *pg.* 1004
E-SATCENTRAL - Satellite-Based Communications Networks Software - LOCKHEED MARTIN CORPORATION; *pg.* 229, *pg.* 762
E-SCREEN - Allergy Testing - HESKA CORPORATION; *pg.* 1542, *pg.* 335
E-SCRIPT - Software - CRESTRON ELECTRONICS INC.; *pg.* 631, *pg.* 1116
E-SELECT - Extranet Product & Rating Information - SELECTIVE INSURANCE GROUP, INC.; *pg.* 1216, *pg.* 1045
E-SERIES - Truck - FORD MOTOR COMPANY OF CANADA, LIMITED; *pg.* 174, *pg.* 1930
E-SERIES OZONE - Standard Ozone Equipment - GE WATER & PROCESS TECHNOLOGIES; *pg.* 1339, *pg.* 1588
E-SERIES RO - Standard Reverse Osmosis Equipment - GE WATER & PROCESS TECHNOLOGIES; *pg.* 1339, *pg.* 1588
E-SHIELD - Switch - POWER INTEGRATIONS, INC.; *pg.* 1369, *pg.* 249
E-SNAPS - Connector - BOMAR INTERCONNECT PRODUCTS, INC.; *pg.* 1318, *pg.* 1079
E SQUARED - Computer Equipment - VIEWSONIC CORPORATION; *pg.* 489, *pg.* 303
E-STAR - Refrigeration Units - PAUL MUELLER COMPANY; *pg.* 706, *pg.* 1007
E-STAR - Turf Maintenance Machinery - SMITHCO, INC.; *pg.* 1377, *pg.* 1592
E-START - Software - CRESTRON ELECTRONICS INC.; *pg.* 631, *pg.* 1116
E-STROKE - Electronic Stroke Alert - INDIAN HEAD INDUSTRIES, INC.; *pg.* 208, *pg.* 1367
E-SUDS - Software - USA TECHNOLOGIES, INC.; *pg.* 815, *pg.* 1550
E-TABLE - Tables - STEELCASE INC.; *pg.* 475, *pg.* 889
E-TEGRITY - Medical Product - HOLOGIC, INC.; *pg.* 1416, *pg.* 784
E-THREE - Energy Services - NV ENERGY, INC.; *pg.* 1948, *pg.* 1028
E-TORQ - Electric Motor - BODINE ELECTRIC COMPANY; *pg.* 1318, *pg.* 641
E-TRONIC - Electronic Wipe - WEIMAN PRODUCTS, LLC; *pg.* 337, *pg.* 616
E TRUDE - Drilling Product - SMITH INTERNATIONAL, INC.; *pg.* 1377, *pg.* 1715
E-US COLD - Internet Customer Service - UNITED STATES COLD STORAGE, INC.; *pg.* 61, *pg.* 1051
E-VALET - Software - CRESTRON ELECTRONICS INC.; *pg.* 631, *pg.* 1116
E-VANTAGE - Host Access Server for Unisys Mainframe Customers - ATTACHMATE CORPORATION; *pg.* 356, *pg.* 1833
E-VISION - Gas Analyzer - MKS INSTRUMENTS, INC.; *pg.* 1362, *pg.* 781
E-Z BOND - Animal Safety Product - NEOGEN CORPORATION; *pg.* 883, *pg.* 896
E-Z BOOT - Pressure Eliminator - ALIMED, INC.; *pg.* 1490, *pg.* 816
E-Z BOWMAKER - Bow Maker - E-Z BOWZ, LLC; *pg.* 692, *pg.* 1635
E-Z BOWZ - Bows - E-Z BOWZ, LLC; *pg.* 692, *pg.* 1635
E-Z BRAZE - Steel Product - RUSSEL METALS INC.; *pg.* 1180, *pg.* 1928
E-Z BREAK - Anti-Seize Compound - LA-CO INDUSTRIES MARKAL CO., INC.; *pg.* 1170, *pg.* 610
E-Z CATCH - Animal Safety Product - NEOGEN CORPORATION; *pg.* 883, *pg.* 896
E-Z CHECK - Electrical Tester - IDEAL INDUSTRIES, INC.; *pg.* 1051, *pg.* 662
E-Z CLOR - Pool Water Treatment Product - POOL CORPORATION; *pg.* 1843, *pg.* 743
E-Z COAT - Food Product - BUNGE LIMITED; *pg.* 842, *pg.* 1351
E-Z CODE - Identification Product - THOMAS & BETTS CORPORATION; *pg.* 680, *pg.* 1646
E-Z COMMAND - Model Train Control System - BACHMANN INDUSTRIES, INC.; *pg.* 950, *pg.* 1559
E-Z EDIT - Educational Product - BARKER CREEK PUBLISHING INC.; *pg.* 1619, *pg.* 1818
E-Z-EST COIN CLEANER - Cleaning Preparation - AERVOE INDUSTRIES INCORPORATED; *pg.* 1439, *pg.* 1021
E-Z-EST SPEED DIP - Cleaning Preparation - AERVOE INDUSTRIES INCORPORATED; *pg.* 1439, *pg.* 1021
E-Z-GO - Golf, Turf & Specialty Products - TEXTRON INC.; *pg.* 235, *pg.* 1607
E-Z-GROUND - Compression Connector - THOMAS & BETTS CORPORATION; *pg.* 680, *pg.* 1646
E-Z KARE - Paint - TRUE VALUE COMPANY; *pg.* 1065, *pg.* 592
E-Z LUBE - Lubricating Oil - BACHMANN INDUSTRIES, INC.; *pg.* 950, *pg.* 1559
E-Z LUX - Electric Lamps - GENERAL ELECTRIC COMPANY; *pg.* 1297, *pg.* 347
E-Z MATE - Couplers - BACHMANN INDUSTRIES, INC.; *pg.* 950, *pg.* 1559
E-Z OUT - Utility Knife - GERBER LEGENDARY BLADES; *pg.* 1834, *pg.* 1503
E-Z PEEL - Plastic Casing - VISKASE COMPANIES, INC.; *pg.* 1471, *pg.* 599
E-Z PRIME - Exterior Acrylic Wood Primer - DUNN-EDWARDS CORPORATION; *pg.* 1442, *pg.* 129
E-Z ROSE & FLOWER MAKER - Rose Maker - E-Z BOWZ, LLC; *pg.* 692, *pg.* 1635
E-Z SMOKE - Plastic Casing - VISKASE COMPANIES, INC.; *pg.* 1471, *pg.* 599
E-Z SPLIT KEY - Pharmaceutical Product - ALERE INC.; *pg.* 1488, *pg.* 849
E-Z SWING - Tools - VAUGHAN & BUSHNELL MANUFACTURING COMPANY, INC.; *pg.* 1066, *pg.* 616
E-Z TRACK SYSTEM - Lock-In Tracks - BACHMANN INDUSTRIES, INC.; *pg.* 950, *pg.* 1559
E-Z VIEW - Bulk Spout - SLY, INC.; *pg.* 1376, *pg.* 1475
E-Z VINYL - White Primer - MOHAWK FINISHING PRODUCTS, INC.; *pg.* 1173, *pg.* 1378
E-ZEE - Case Gauge - LYMAN PRODUCTS CORPORATION; *pg.* 1839, *pg.* 356
E-ZEE FLO - Universal Powder Trickler - LYMAN PRODUCTS CORPORATION; *pg.* 1839, *pg.* 356
E-ZPASS - Electronic Toll Collection for North, Middle Atlantic & South East States - METROPOLITAN TRANSPORTATION AUTHORITY; *pg.* 1915, *pg.* 1260
E-Z CUT - Food Product - JOHN MORRELL & CO.; *pg.* 866, *pg.* 1415
E2 - Beverages - THE COCA-COLA COMPANY; *pg.* 240, *pg.* 493
E2 - Computer Equipment - VIEWSONIC CORPORATION; *pg.* 489, *pg.* 303
E2CMOS - Proprietary Process Technology for CPLD Products - LATTICE SEMICONDUCTOR CORPORATION; *pg.* 651, *pg.* 1498
E3 - Clean Air - AGCO CORPORATION; *pg.* 700, *pg.* 530
E3 - Hard Facing Application - ESCO CORPORATION; *pg.* 1335, *pg.* 1502
E3LCABLE - Software System - MENTOR GRAPHICS CORPORATION; *pg.* 432, *pg.* 1510
E86 - Embedded Processor - ADVANCED MICRO DEVICES, INC.; *pg.* 613, *pg.* 282
E86MON - Software - ADVANCED MICRO DEVICES, INC.; *pg.* 613, *pg.* 282
EA-40 - Epoxy Adhesive - SMOOTH-ON INC.; *pg.* 111, *pg.* 1528
EA GAMES - Game - ELECTRONIC ARTS INC.; *pg.* 951, *pg.* 189
EA SPORTS - Computer & Video Games - ELECTRONIC ARTS INC.; *pg.* 951, *pg.* 189
EA SPORTS ACTIVE - Video Game - ELECTRONIC ARTS INC.; *pg.* 951, *pg.* 189
EA SPORTS BIG - Computer & Video Games - ELECTRONIC ARTS INC.; *pg.* 951, *pg.* 189
EAA - Diagnostic Test Product - SPECTRAL DIAGNOSTICS INC.; *pg.* 1430, *pg.* 1943
EAC - MIDI Products - ALLEN ORGAN COMPANY; *pg.* 527, *pg.* 1549
EAD - Custom Designed Motors, Fans & Blowers - ELECTROCRAFT, INC; *pg.* 1333, *pg.* 1033
EADIE'S KITCHEN & MARKET - Restaurant - LEVY RESTAURANTS, INC.; *pg.* 1736, *pg.* 580
EAGLE - Glass - CORNING INCORPORATED; *pg.* 1122, *pg.* 1154
EAGLE - Cutting Room Equipment - EASTMAN MACHINE COMPANY; *pg.* 1331, *pg.* 1148
EAGLE - Ice Cream - GIANT EAGLE AMERICAN SEAWAY FOODS; *pg.* 1020, *pg.* 1405
EAGLE - High-Performance Tires - THE GOODYEAR TIRE & RUBBER COMPANY; *pg.* 1883, *pg.* 1401
EAGLE - Air-Operated Piston Pumps - GRACO, INC.; *pg.* 1342, *pg.* 935

EAGLE - Recreational Vehicles - JAYCO INC.; *pg.* 1708, *pg.* 695
EAGLE - Golf Shoes - JOHNSTON & MURPHY CO.; *pg.* 1810, *pg.* 1651
EAGLE - Lighting - LSI INDUSTRIES INC.; *pg.* 58, *pg.* 1416
EAGLE - Towing & Recovery Equipment - MILLER INDUSTRIES, INC.; *pg.* 185, *pg.* 1655
EAGLE - Power Tool - MILWAUKEE ELECTRIC TOOL CORP.; *pg.* 1056, *pg.* 1855
EAGLE - Electronic Components - MOLEX INCORPORATED; *pg.* 655, *pg.* 628
EAGLE - Apparel - PVH CORP.; *pg.* 46, *pg.* 1283
EAGLE - Pressed & Monolithic Refractory - RESCO PRODUCTS, INC.; *pg.* 107, *pg.* 1581
EAGLE - Hammer - VAUGHAN & BUSHNELL MANUFACTURING COMPANY, INC.; *pg.* 1066, *pg.* 616
EAGLE 2000 - Glass Substrate - CORNING INCORPORATED; *pg.* 1122, *pg.* 1154
EAGLE 9 - Insurance - CORELOGIC, INC.; *pg.* 1198, *pg.* 109
EAGLE BRAND - Condensed Milk Products - THE J.M. SMUCKER COMPANY; *pg.* 865, *pg.* 1468
EAGLE-CAT - Fluid Handling System - GRACO, INC.; *pg.* 1342, *pg.* 935
EAGLE CLAW BASS - Specie Hook - WRIGHT & MCGILL CO.; *pg.* 1848, *pg.* 324
EAGLE CLAW CATFISH - Specie Hook - WRIGHT & MCGILL CO.; *pg.* 1848, *pg.* 324
EAGLE CLAW PANFISH - Specie Hook - WRIGHT & MCGILL CO.; *pg.* 1848, *pg.* 324
EAGLE CLAW TROUT - Specie Hook - WRIGHT & MCGILL CO.; *pg.* 1848, *pg.* 324
EAGLE CLAW WALLEYE - Specie Hook - WRIGHT & MCGILL CO.; *pg.* 1848, *pg.* 324
EAGLE CREEK - Case - BROWN & BIGELOW, INC.; *pg.* 1624, *pg.* 959
EAGLE CREEK - Luggage, Packs & Travel Accessories - V.F. CORPORATION; *pg.* 34, *pg.* 1376
EAGLE EDGE - Ten-step Customer Care Program - JOHN EAGLE HONDA OF HOUSTON; *pg.* 180, *pg.* 1709
EAGLE EYE - Unmanned Aerial Vehicle - BELL HELICOPTER TEXTRON, INC.; *pg.* 224, *pg.* 1693
EAGLE EYE - Electronic Faucets - THE CHICAGO FAUCET COMPANY; *pg.* 1044, *pg.* 606
EAGLE MASTER TRAK - Storage System - MEDLINE INDUSTRIES, INC.; *pg.* 1562, *pg.* 635
EAGLE MILLS - Food Product - CONTINENTAL MILLS, INC.; *pg.* 827, *pg.* 1845
EAGLE #1 - Tire And Rubber Product - THE GOODYEAR TIRE & RUBBER COMPANY; *pg.* 1883, *pg.* 1401
EAGLE ONE - Automobile Grill Emblems, Hitch Covers & Hitch Cover Locks - ASHLAND INC.; *pg.* 972, *pg.* 726
EAGLE PD - Tire And Rubber Product - THE GOODYEAR TIRE & RUBBER COMPANY; *pg.* 1883, *pg.* 1401
EAGLE PEST - Poly Pesticide Storage Cabinet - EAGLE MANUFACTURING COMPANY; *pg.* 79, *pg.* 1851
EAGLE RARE - Bourbon - SAZERAC COMPANY, INC.; *pg.* 1969, *pg.* 745
EAGLE SELECT - Camping Trailer - JAYCO INC.; *pg.* 1708, *pg.* 695
EAGLE SIGNAL - Control System - DYNAPAR; *pg.* 1408, *pg.* 616
EAGLE SPEED - Systems Integration & Aeronautics - LOCKHEED MARTIN CORPORATION; *pg.* 229, *pg.* 762
EAGLE-VISION - Visual Performance/Procedures Trainer - ENVIRONMENTAL TECTONICS CORPORATION; *pg.* 1411, *pg.* 1587
EAGLEEYE - Camera - POLYCOM, INC.; *pg.* 664, *pg.* 249
EAGLEPAC - Heat Seal Pouch - STERIS CORPORATION; *pg.* 1597, *pg.* 1464
EAGLE'S NEST - Child Care Activity - GIANT EAGLE, INC.; *pg.* 1020, *pg.* 1575
EAGLE'S TRACE - Retirement Community - ERICKSON LIVING; *pg.* 1090, *pg.* 766
EAI-530 - Video Switch - ADTRAN, INC.; *pg.* 344, *pg.* 6
EAMES - Chairs - HERMAN MILLER, INC.; *pg.* 926, *pg.* 913
EAMES - Paper - NEENAH PAPER, INC.; *pg.* 1465, *pg.* 484
E.ANALYSIS - Web Content Analysis Service - ACTUATE CORPORATION; *pg.* 342, *pg.* 253
EAR - Banking Software - JACK HENRY & ASSOCIATES, INC.; *pg.* 422, *pg.* 988
EAR CARE ANTISEPTIC - Ear Piercing Product - INVERNESS CORPORATION; *pg.* 512, *pg.* 783
EAR COUPLERS - Medical Device - NATUS MEDICAL INCORPORATED; *pg.* 1572, *pg.* 199
EAR-LOKT - Pump Product - IDEX CORPORATION; *pg.* 1347, *pg.* 623
EAR PLUG - Headphone Amplifiers - GIBSON GUITAR CORP.; *pg.* 550, *pg.* 1650
EAR REPLACEABLES - Jewelry - ROMAN RESEARCH, INC.; *pg.* 11, *pg.* 824
EAR SEALS - Soft Flanged Earplugs - MCKEON PRODUCTS, INC.; *pg.* 1559, *pg.* 912
EARACHE RELIEF - Medicine Product - SIMILASAN CORPORATION; *pg.* 1594, *pg.* 332
EARDRYER - Healthcare Product - MCKEON PRODUCTS, INC.; *pg.* 1559, *pg.* 912
EARL - Knife - COAST CUTLERY COMPANY; *pg.* 1121, *pg.* 1501
EARL JEAN - Knitwear - V.F. CORPORATION; *pg.* 34, *pg.* 1376
EARL MAY SEED & NURSERY - Flower Seed, Vegetable Seed & Nursery Stock - EARL MAY SEED & NURSERY L.C.; *pg.* 1795, *pg.* 712
EARLIER. SIMPLER. BETTER - Slogan - HOLOGIC, INC.; *pg.* 1416, *pg.* 784
EARLUSION - Earring - STULLER, INC.; *pg.* 13, *pg.* 745
EARLY A.M. - Software - UNITED PARCEL SERVICE, INC.; *pg.* 1928, *pg.* 522
EARLY BIRDIE - Women's Clothing & Accessories - WOODEN SHIPS OF HOBOKEN; *pg.* 35, *pg.* 1315
EARLY CALIFORNIA - Olives - MUSCO FAMILY OLIVE COMPANY; *pg.* 882, *pg.* 297
EARLY EXPOSURE - Floor Underlayment - USG CORPORATION; *pg.* 118, *pg.* 594
EARLY FALL - Fabric - NEMSCHOFF, INC.; *pg.* 936, *pg.* 1890
EARLY INSIGHT - Software System - IMS HEALTH, INC.; *pg.* 1544, *pg.* 344
EARLY PLANT - Hybrid Corn - LANDEC CORPORATION; *pg.* 1419, *pg.* 145
EARLY RECOGNITION. EARLY DECISIONS. - Slogan - ALERE INC.; *pg.* 1488, *pg.* 849
EARLY TIMES BOURBON - Kentucky Whiskey - BROWN-FORMAN CORPORATION; *pg.* 1958, *pg.* 732
EARLYVIEW - Software System - IMS HEALTH, INC.; *pg.* 1544, *pg.* 344
EARNINGS.COM - Financial Information Software - THOMSON REUTERS MARKETS; *pg.* 810, *pg.* 1299
EAROBICS LITERACY LAUNCH - Literacy Instruction - HOUGHTON MIFFLIN HARCOURT PUBLISHING COMPANY; *pg.* 1651, *pg.* 796
EARPHONE ANCHORS - Earplug - MCKEON PRODUCTS, INC.; *pg.* 1559, *pg.* 912
EARPLANES - Flight Ear Protection - MCNETT CORPORATION; *pg.* 1839, *pg.* 1817
EARSAVER - Earplug - MCKEON PRODUCTS, INC.; *pg.* 1559, *pg.* 912
EARTH - Carpet - INTERFACE, INC.; *pg.* 695, *pg.* 512
EARTH & SKY - Beverages - THE COCA-COLA COMPANY; *pg.* 240, *pg.* 493
EARTH ANSWER - Microbial Deodorizer - GARDENS ALIVE!, INC.; *pg.* 1796, *pg.* 693
EARTH AWARE - Hair & Skin Product - AUBREY ORGANICS INC.; *pg.* 499, *pg.* 470
EARTH BALANCE - Plant-Based Diet - BOULDER BRANDS, INC.; *pg.* 1016, *pg.* 310
EARTH BORN - Shampoo - THE GILLETTE COMPANY; *pg.* 509, *pg.* 795
EARTH CRUISER 1 - Bicycles - G. JOANNOU CYCLE CO. INC.; *pg.* 1707, *pg.* 1098
EARTH CRUISER 4 - Bicycles - G. JOANNOU CYCLE CO. INC.; *pg.* 1707, *pg.* 1098
EARTH ELEMENTS - Yoga Mat - HUGGER MUGGER YOGA PRODUCTS LLC; *pg.* 1836, *pg.* 1758
EARTH-FRIENDLY - Coffee Filters - KEURIG GREEN MOUNTAIN, INC.; *pg.* 868, *pg.* 1768
EARTH QUAKE - Textiles - BERNHARDT DESIGN; *pg.* 918, *pg.* 1381
EARTH QUAKER - Video Game - INTERNATIONAL GAME TECHNOLOGY; *pg.* 957, *pg.* 1024
EARTH SCENTS - Candles & Potpourri - BRIGHT OF AMERICA, INC.; *pg.* 1121, *pg.* 1851
EARTH SECRETS - Hair Lotion - LUSTER PRODUCTS INC.; *pg.* 515, *pg.* 581
EARTH STOVE - Stoves - LENNOX HEARTH PRODUCTS; *pg.* 93, *pg.* 1652
EARTHAWARE - Bag & Pouch Material - AUTOMATED PACKAGING SYSTEMS INC.; *pg.* 1452, *pg.* 1474
EARTHCHOICE - Paper - DOMTAR CORPORATION; *pg.* 1456, *pg.* 1954
EARTHCHOICE - Disposable Tableware - PACTIV CORPORATION; *pg.* 1466, *pg.* 624
EARTHFIRST - Plastic Product - PLASTIC SUPPLIERS, INC.; *pg.* 1888, *pg.* 1443
EARTHGRO - Soil Product - THE SCOTTS MIRACLE-GRO COMPANY; *pg.* 1799, *pg.* 1459
EARTHKEEPERS - Boots - THE TIMBERLAND COMPANY; *pg.* 1821, *pg.* 1039
EARTHLINE - Laboratory Product - KEWAUNEE SCIENTIFIC CORPORATION; *pg.* 931, *pg.* 1391
EARTHLINK - Internet Service - EARTHLINK HOLDINGS CORP.; *pg.* 1240, *pg.* 504
EARTHLINK DSL - DSL Internet Service - EARTHLINK HOLDINGS CORP.; *pg.* 1240, *pg.* 504
EARTHLINK PROTECTIONBLOG - Online Blog - EARTHLINK HOLDINGS CORP.; *pg.* 1240, *pg.* 504
EARTHLINK REVOLVES AROUND YOU - Slogan - EARTHLINK HOLDINGS CORP.; *pg.* 1240, *pg.* 504
EARTHLINKS - Toy - MUNCHKIN, INC.; *pg.* 964, *pg.* 300
EARTHMOMENT.COM - Web Site - OGDEN PUBLICATIONS, INC.; *pg.* 1672, *pg.* 722
EARTH'S BEST - Food Product - THE HAIN CELESTIAL GROUP, INC.; *pg.* 860, *pg.* 1172
EARTHSEARCH - Educational Materials - SCHOLASTIC INC.; *pg.* 1683, *pg.* 1288
EARTHWISE - Toner Cartridge - IMATION CORP.; *pg.* 413, *pg.* 952
EARTHWOOD - Guitar - ERNIE BALL INC.; *pg.* 1768, *pg.* 68
EAS - Software - AUTONOMY PLEASANTON; *pg.* 358, *pg.* 183
EAS-HD - Alert System - CHYRONHEGO; *pg.* 371, *pg.* 1179
EASE SPORT - Misses' & Junior Apparel - KELLWOOD COMPANY; *pg.* 28, *pg.* 975
EASEBETWEEN - Floss - RANIR LLC; *pg.* 520, *pg.* 888
EASEL MONEY - Video Game - INTERNATIONAL GAME TECHNOLOGY; *pg.* 957, *pg.* 1024
EASI-BRICK - Wall System - SMITH-MIDLAND CORPORATION; *pg.* 111, *pg.* 1795
EASI-SET - Wall System - SMITH-MIDLAND CORPORATION; *pg.* 111, *pg.* 1795
EASI-SLI - Shipper Instructor - UNZ & COMPANY, INC.; *pg.* 1698, *pg.* 1084
EASI SOLUTIONS - Computer Software - COMPUTER SCIENCES CORPORATION; *pg.* 378, *pg.* 1780
EASI-SPAN - Wall System - SMITH-MIDLAND CORPORATION; *pg.* 111, *pg.* 1795
EASICUT - Software - EASTMAN MACHINE COMPANY; *pg.* 1331, *pg.* 1148
EASIDNA - Software - EASTMAN MACHINE COMPANY; *pg.* 1331, *pg.* 1148
EASIDOCK - Power Adapter - IGO, INC.; *pg.* 644, *pg.* 22
EASIEST - Software & Hardware - EVANS & SUTHERLAND COMPUTER CORPORATION; *pg.* 638, *pg.* 1757
EASIHOLD - Cutting System - EASTMAN MACHINE COMPANY; *pg.* 1331, *pg.* 1148
EASILABEL - Cutting Room Equipment - EASTMAN MACHINE COMPANY; *pg.* 1331, *pg.* 1148
EASIMARK - Cutting Room Equipment - EASTMAN MACHINE COMPANY; *pg.* 1331, *pg.* 1148
EASIPULL - Spreader - EASTMAN MACHINE COMPANY; *pg.* 1331, *pg.* 1148
EASISELECT - Software - EASTMAN MACHINE COMPANY; *pg.* 1331, *pg.* 1148
EASISTAR - Extranet Computer Services - LOCKHEED MARTIN CORPORATION; *pg.* 229, *pg.* 762
E!ASSIST - Logistics Software - ASPEN TECHNOLOGY, INC.; *pg.* 354, *pg.* 804
EAST & WEST - Video Game - INTERNATIONAL GAME TECHNOLOGY; *pg.* 957, *pg.* 1024
EAST COAST - Retail Fuel & Convenience Stores - DELEK US HOLDINGS, INC.; *pg.* 975, *pg.* 1627
EAST COAST MERCHANDISER - Magazine - SUMNER COMMUNICATIONS INC.; *pg.* 1690, *pg.* 338
EAST DAWNING - China Restaurant Chain - YUM! BRANDS, INC.; *pg.* 1756, *pg.* 738
EAST EUROPEAN MONOGRAPHS - Publisher - COLUMBIA UNIVERSITY PRESS; *pg.* 1628, *pg.* 1216
EAST INDIA PALE ALE - Seasonal Beer - THE BROOKLYN BREWERY; *pg.* 239, *pg.* 1145
EAST ISLAND - Men's Clothing - BLOOMINGDALE'S, INC.; *pg.* 1763, *pg.* 1204
EAST PAK - Backpacks - JANSPORT; *pg.* 1837, *pg.* 38
EAST PEAK - Bike - MARIN BIKES; *pg.* 1708, *pg.* 168
EAST SIDE MARIO'S - Restaurants - PRIME RESTAURANTS INC.; *pg.* 1746, *pg.* 1947

First page reference indicates Business Class Edition
Second page reference indicates Geographic Edition

EAST VALLEY TRIBUNE - Newspaper - EAST VALLEY TRIBUNE; *pg.* 1638, *pg.* 25
EAST VALLEY TRIBUNE - Arizona Newspaper - FREEDOM COMMUNICATIONS, INC.; *pg.* 1643, *pg.* 110
EASTACRYL - Acrylic Polymer - EASTMAN CHEMICAL COMPANY; *pg.* 1159, *pg.* 1636
EASTALLOY - Polymers - EASTMAN CHEMICAL COMPANY; *pg.* 1159, *pg.* 1636
EASTAPURE - Electronic Chemicals - EASTMAN CHEMICAL COMPANY; *pg.* 1159, *pg.* 1636
EASTAR - Copolyester - EASTMAN CHEMICAL COMPANY; *pg.* 1159, *pg.* 1636
EASTBAY - Direct Marketer - FOOT LOCKER, INC.; *pg.* 1808, *pg.* 1231
EASTBORNE - Carpet - BEAULIEU GROUP, LLC; *pg.* 917, *pg.* 529
EASTER GARDEN BOUQUET - Floral Bouquet - FTD GROUP, INC.; *pg.* 1795, *pg.* 608
EASTER SENTIMENTS - Plant - 1-800-FLOWERS.COM, INC.; *pg.* 1758, *pg.* 1151
EASTERN - Pump Product - IDEX CORPORATION; *pg.* 1347, *pg.* 623
EASTERN SUN - Video Game - INTERNATIONAL GAME TECHNOLOGY; *pg.* 957, *pg.* 1024
EASTERN TREASURES - Video Game - INTERNATIONAL GAME TECHNOLOGY; *pg.* 957, *pg.* 1024
EASTGATE - Lighting Product - WESTINGHOUSE LIGHTING CORPORATION; *pg.* 687, *pg.* 1571
EASTLIGHT - Office Products - ACCO BRANDS CORPORATION; *pg.* 340, *pg.* 626
EASTMAN - Cellulose Esters - EASTMAN CHEMICAL COMPANY; *pg.* 1159, *pg.* 1636
EASTMAN - Film - EASTMAN KODAK COMPANY; *pg.* 1408, *pg.* 1333
EASTMAN AQ - Polymers - EASTMAN CHEMICAL COMPANY; *pg.* 1159, *pg.* 1636
EASTMAN AQUA PET - Polymer - EASTMAN CHEMICAL COMPANY; *pg.* 1159, *pg.* 1636
EASTMAN G - Polymers - EASTMAN CHEMICAL COMPANY; *pg.* 1159, *pg.* 1636
EASTMAN NPG - Glycol - EASTMAN CHEMICAL COMPANY; *pg.* 1159, *pg.* 1636
EASTMAN PET - Polymers - EASTMAN CHEMICAL COMPANY; *pg.* 1159, *pg.* 1636
EASTMAN TXIB - Formulation Additive - EASTMAN CHEMICAL COMPANY; *pg.* 1159, *pg.* 1636
EASTOBRITE - Optical Brightener - EASTMAN CHEMICAL COMPANY; *pg.* 1159, *pg.* 1636
EASTOFLEX - Amorphous Polyolefins - EASTMAN CHEMICAL COMPANY; *pg.* 1159, *pg.* 1636
EASTON - Furniture - BASSETT FURNITURE INDUSTRIES, INCORPORATED; *pg.* 916, *pg.* 1776
EASTON - Bats & Ice Hockey Sticks, Football & Hockey Protective Pads & Sport Bags - EASTON SPORTS, INC.; *pg.* 1833, *pg.* 299
EASTON - Flatware - ONEIDA LTD; *pg.* 1129, *pg.* 1318
EASTONE - Copolyester - EASTMAN CHEMICAL COMPANY; *pg.* 1159, *pg.* 1636
EASTOTAC - Resin - EASTMAN CHEMICAL COMPANY; *pg.* 1159, *pg.* 1636
EASTPAK - Backpacks & Book Bags - V.F. CORPORATION; *pg.* 34, *pg.* 1376
EASTRIDGE - Furniture - ASHLEY FURNITURE INDUSTRIES, INC.; *pg.* 914, *pg.* 1852
EASY - Furniture - NEMSCHOFF, INC.; *pg.* 936, *pg.* 1890
EASY - Spreader - THE SCOTTS MIRACLE-GRO COMPANY; *pg.* 1799, *pg.* 1459
EASY-2-DRAW - Educational Product - BARKER CREEK PUBLISHING INC.; *pg.* 1619, *pg.* 1818
EASY ACCESS - Plumbing Wall Panel - SLOAN VALVE COMPANY; *pg.* 1062, *pg.* 613
EASY AIR - Polyurethane Foam - SPAN-AMERICA MEDICAL SYSTEMS, INC.; *pg.* 1595, *pg.* 1618
EASY-AIRE - Vehicle Seat - COMMERCIAL VEHICLE GROUP, INC.; *pg.* 203, *pg.* 1467
EASY APPLY RS - Film - AVERY DENNISON CORPORATION; *pg.* 1452, *pg.* 95
EASY AS PIE - Carpet - BEAULIEU GROUP, LLC; *pg.* 917, *pg.* 529
EASY-BAKE OVEN - Kenner Products - HASBRO, INC.; *pg.* 954, *pg.* 1603
EASY CAP - Software - BIO-RAD LABORATORIES, INC.; *pg.* 1504, *pg.* 101
EASY CAP - CO2 Detectors - MEDTRONIC; *pg.* 1563, *pg.* 183
EASY CARE - Nursing Home Bed - MEDLINE INDUSTRIES, INC.; *pg.* 1562, *pg.* 635
EASY CARE - Paints - PPG INDUSTRIES, INC.; *pg.* 1445, *pg.* 1579
EASY CARE - First Aid Kit - TENDER CORPORATION; *pg.* 1601, *pg.* 1035
EASY CLEAN - Chamber - BALTIMORE AIRCOIL COMPANY; *pg.* 1069, *pg.* 773
EASY-CLEAN - Baby Carrier Fabric - EVENFLO COMPANY, INC.; *pg.* 924, *pg.* 1470
EASY CLEAN - Conveyor - SHUTTLEWORTH, INC.; *pg.* 1375, *pg.* 682
EASY CLEANSE - Digestive Cleansing Program - NOW HEALTH GROUP, INC.; *pg.* 1576, *pg.* 557
EASY CLEAR - Coffee & Beverage Equipment - BUNN-O-MATIC CORPORATION; *pg.* 53, *pg.* 661
EASY COLOR - Paint - TRUE VALUE COMPANY; *pg.* 1065, *pg.* 592
EASY CONNECT - Piping - BALTIMORE AIRCOIL COMPANY; *pg.* 1069, *pg.* 773
EASY CONNECTION - Adapter Kit - LANTRONIX, INC.; *pg.* 426, *pg.* 112
EASY CORE - Medical Device - BOSTON SCIENTIFIC CORPORATION; *pg.* 1508, *pg.* 831
EASY DENTAL - Software - HENRY SCHEIN, INC.; *pg.* 1541, *pg.* 1180
EASY DESIGN - Speaker - BOGEN COMMUNICATIONS INTERNATIONAL INC.; *pg.* 625, *pg.* 1113
EASY-DNA - Molecular Biology Product - THERMO FISHER SCIENTIFIC INC.; *pg.* 1602, *pg.* 61
EASY-EDGE - Lawn Edging - FLEX-O-GLASS, INC.; *pg.* 1457, *pg.* 574
EASY ENTREES - Poultry Products - PILGRIM'S PRIDE CORPORATION; *pg.* 889, *pg.* 330
EASY ENTRY - Seat Folding System - LEAR CORPORATION; *pg.* 229, *pg.* 907
EASY- EXIT CREEPER - Baby Dress - CARTER'S, INC.; *pg.* 21, *pg.* 491
EASY FAMILY FOOD - Magazine - MEREDITH CORPORATION; *pg.* 1663, *pg.* 705
EASY FAXING ANYWHERE - Slogan - EFAX.COM INC.; *pg.* 1242, *pg.* 129
EASY FAXING ANYWHERE - Slogan - J2 GLOBAL COMMUNICATIONS, INC.; *pg.* 1260, *pg.* 133
EASY FILL - Kitchen Appliance - HAMILTON BEACH BRANDS, INC.; *pg.* 56, *pg.* 1783
EASY FLAPS - Bag - PACTIV CORPORATION; *pg.* 1466, *pg.* 624
EASY-FLEX - Eyewear - MINE SAFETY APPLIANCES COMPANY; *pg.* 1361, *pg.* 1525
EASY-FLO - Dimethylaminopyridine - VERTELLUS SPECIALTIES INC.; *pg.* 1185, *pg.* 690
EASY FLOW - Dispensing Closure - OWENS-ILLINOIS, INC.; *pg.* 1466, *pg.* 1470
EASY-GLIDE - Kitchen Appliance - VIKING RANGE CORPORATION; *pg.* 61, *pg.* 968
EASY GRIP - Cups - PACTIV CORPORATION; *pg.* 1466, *pg.* 624
EASY-GROW - Plastic Garden Mulch - WARP BROTHERS; *pg.* 1471, *pg.* 595
EASY HEAT - Electrical Products - EMERSON INDUSTRIAL AUTOMATION; *pg.* 1296, *pg.* 657
EASY HOLD - Nail Care Product - THE W.E. BASSETT COMPANY; *pg.* 524, *pg.* 371
EASY HOLD - Game - WMS INDUSTRIES INC.; *pg.* 593, *pg.* 666
EASY ID - Animal Identification Software - HOLSTEIN ASSOCIATION USA, INC.; *pg.* 143, *pg.* 1764
EASY LIFT - Height-Adjustable Basketball Standards - LIFETIME PRODUCTS INC.; *pg.* 933, *pg.* 1751
EASY LINER - Shelf Liner - HENKEL CONSUMER ADHESIVES, INC.; *pg.* 403, *pg.* 1480
EASY LITE - Lens - YOUNGER OPTICS; *pg.* 1437, *pg.* 297
EASY LIVING - Paints - SEARS HOLDINGS CORPORATION; *pg.* 1784, *pg.* 618
EASY LIVING RADIO - Radio - LIVE365, INC.; *pg.* 1264, *pg.* 89
EASY LOADER - Lifting Devise - GENERAL ENGINES COMPANY INC.; *pg.* 174, *pg.* 437
EASY-MARK - Software - PANDUIT CORP.; *pg.* 661, *pg.* 663
EASY-OFF - Oven Cleaning Products - RECKITT BENCKISER INC.; *pg.* 1136, *pg.* 1105
EASY ON - Children's Winter Gloves - KOMBI, LTD.; *pg.* 1838, *pg.* 1766
EASY-ON - Stone & Bug Deflectors - MACNEIL AUTOMOTIVE PRODUCTS, LTD.; *pg.* 211, *pg.* 559
EASY-ON - Electronic Components - MOLEX INCORPORATED; *pg.* 655, *pg.* 628
EASY ON - Spray Starch - RECKITT BENCKISER INC.; *pg.* 1136, *pg.* 1105
EASY-ON - Storm Window Kit - WARP BROTHERS; *pg.* 1471, *pg.* 595
EASY OPTION ACCOUNT - Insurance Product - SBLI USA LIFE INSURANCE COMPANY, INC.; *pg.* 1216, *pg.* 1288
EASY-OUT - Dry Cleaning & Laundry Product - ADCO, INC.; *pg.* 325, *pg.* 482
EASY OUT - Fluid Handling System - GRACO, INC.; *pg.* 1342, *pg.* 935
EASY PATH - Circuit Board - XILINX, INC.; *pg.* 496, *pg.* 252
EASY-PLY - Building Product - HOMASOTE COMPANY; *pg.* 87, *pg.* 1126
EASY POUR - Coffee & Beverage Equipment - BUNN-O-MATIC CORPORATION; *pg.* 53, *pg.* 661
EASY-PULL - Tooling System - KENNAMETAL INC.; *pg.* 1052, *pg.* 1547
EASY-PUSH - Metering Faucets - SPEAKMAN COMPANY; *pg.* 112, *pg.* 388
EASY QUOTE - Software - AETNA INC.; *pg.* 1187, *pg.* 351
EASY READER - Educational Kit - LEAPFROG ENTERPRISES, INC.; *pg.* 961, *pg.* 84
EASY REBOOK - Airline Service - UNITED CONTINENTAL HOLDINGS, INC.; *pg.* 1927, *pg.* 593
EASY RIDER - Lawn Cart - RUBBERMAID HOME PRODUCTS; *pg.* 1138, *pg.* 1453
EASY RISER - Stair Stringer System - UNIVERSAL FOREST PRODUCTS, INC.; *pg.* 117, *pg.* 890
EASY RISER - Swing Check Valve - THE VIKING GROUP; *pg.* 119, *pg.* 891
EASY ROUTE - Software - UNITED PARCEL SERVICE, INC.; *pg.* 1928, *pg.* 522
EASY SAND - Polyester Finishing & Glazing Putty - ITW - EVERCOAT; *pg.* 1443, *pg.* 1415
EASY SAND - Joint Compound - USG CORPORATION; *pg.* 118, *pg.* 594
EASY SCHEDULE - Airline Service - UNITED CONTINENTAL HOLDINGS, INC.; *pg.* 1927, *pg.* 593
EASY SEAT - Wheel Chair Cushion - DYNATRONICS CORPORATION; *pg.* 1526, *pg.* 1757
EASY SET - Trap - THE WOODSTREAM CORPORATION; *pg.* 1801, *pg.* 1549
THE EASY SNAP - Henley - HABAND COMPANY, INC.; *pg.* 1772, *pg.* 1099
EASY SOLUTIONS - Caulk And Sealant - DAP PRODUCTS, INC.; *pg.* 1441, *pg.* 756
EASY SPIRIT - Women's Shoes - NINE WEST HOLDINGS, INC.; *pg.* 1815, *pg.* 1272
EASY START - Hair Care Product - CONAIR CORPORATION; *pg.* 505, *pg.* 1055
EASY-STOMP - Zipper - ZIP-PAK; *pg.* 1473, *pg.* 631
EASY STREET - Manual - XEROX CORPORATION; *pg.* 494, *pg.* 365
EASY SURFACE PREP - Coating & Paint - AKZO NOBEL DECORATIVE PAINTS, USA; *pg.* 1439, *pg.* 1474
EASY-SWEEP - Vinyl Matting - THE BILTRITE CORPORATION; *pg.* 1879, *pg.* 850
EASY TUGGER - Puller - GREENLEE TEXTRON INC.; *pg.* 1048, *pg.* 655
EASY VAC - Vacuum - BISSELL HOMECARE, INC.; *pg.* 52, *pg.* 887
EASY-VI - Manual - XEROX CORPORATION; *pg.* 494, *pg.* 365
EASY WATCH - Security & Law Enforcement Products - MACE SECURITY INTERNATIONAL, INC.; *pg.* 1172, *pg.* 1541
THE EASY WAY TO BETTER HEALTH - Slogan - PHARMAVITE LLC; *pg.* 1584, *pg.* 167
EASY5 - Software - MSC SOFTWARE CORPORATION; *pg.* 441, *pg.* 262
EASYACCESS - Fluid Handling System - GRACO, INC.; *pg.* 1342, *pg.* 935
EASYACCT - Software - INTUIT INC.; *pg.* 769, *pg.* 158
EASYAIRE - Pneumatic Conveyor System - DIEBOLD, INCORPORATED; *pg.* 387, *pg.* 1407
EASYASK - Software - PROGRESS SOFTWARE CORPORATION; *pg.* 457, *pg.* 786
EASYBID - Electronic Sealed Bidding Solution - ESM SOLUTIONS CORPORATION; *pg.* 1243, *pg.* 1591
EASYBOARD - Ironing Board - HOME PRODUCTS INTERNATIONAL, INC.; *pg.* 1125, *pg.* 577

EASYBUILDER - Machine Vision System - COGNEX CORPORATION; *pg.* 1406, *pg.* 834
EASYCARE - Laptop Bag - DELL INC.; *pg.* 383, *pg.* 1737
EASYCARE - Laboratory Product - EPPENDORF NORTH AMERICA; *pg.* 1412, *pg.* 1164
EASYCOMP - Biomolecule Product - THERMO FISHER SCIENTIFIC INC.; *pg.* 1602, *pg.* 61
EASYCONTROL - Robotic Product - HAMILTON CO., INC.; *pg.* 1415, *pg.* 1031
EASYCREASEPRO - Creaser - STANDARD DUPLICATING MACHINES CORPORATION; *pg.* 473, *pg.* 783
EASYEDGE - Data Services - UNITED STATES CELLULAR CORPORATION; *pg.* 1875, *pg.* 594
EASYEST AG - Electronic Instrument - KEITHLEY INSTRUMENTS, INC.; *pg.* 1418, *pg.* 1473
EASYFERM - Robotic Product - HAMILTON CO., INC.; *pg.* 1415, *pg.* 1031
EASYFINDER - Laboratory Product - METTLER-TOLEDO INTERNATIONAL INC.; *pg.* 1423, *pg.* 1441
EASYFIT - Adaptor IRIDEX CORPORATION; *pg.* 648, *pg.* 160
EASYFIT - Fiber Glass Insulation - JOHNS MANVILLE CORPORATION; *pg.* 89, *pg.* 320
EASYFIX - Flush Valve Repair Kit - LAVELLE INDUSTRIES INC.; *pg.* 1053, *pg.* 1856
EASYFLEX - Toothbrush - RANIR LLC; *pg.* 520, *pg.* 888
EASYFLEX - Miniature Condenser Microphone - SHURE INCORPORATED; *pg.* 672, *pg.* 638
EASYFORMS - Electronic Tool for Form Management - ESM SOLUTIONS CORPORATION; *pg.* 1243, *pg.* 1591
EASYGARD - Plastic Attachments - BUNN-O-MATIC CORPORATION; *pg.* 53, *pg.* 661
EASYGEN - Genset Control - WOODWARD, INC.; *pg.* 122, *pg.* 329
EASYGLIDE - Swivel - GRACO, INC.; *pg.* 1342, *pg.* 935
EASYGRAF - Chart & Marking System - GRAPHIC CONTROLS LLC; *pg.* 401, *pg.* 1148
EASYGREEN - Lawn Fertilizer - THE SCOTTS MIRACLE-GRO COMPANY; *pg.* 1799, *pg.* 1459
EASYJEWEL - Laser Marking Device - ROFIN-SINAR TECHNOLOGIES, INC.; *pg.* 668, *pg.* 904
EASYKEY - Fluid Handling System - GRACO, INC.; *pg.* 1342, *pg.* 935
EASYLANGUAGE - Proprietary Programming Language - TRADESTATION GROUP, INC.; *pg.* 811, *pg.* 459
EASYLINK - Software - WESTERN DIGITAL CORPORATION; *pg.* 492, *pg.* 118
EASYMACRO - Computer Hardware - AVAGO TECHNOLOGIES; *pg.* 358, *pg.* 238
EASYMARK - Laser Product - ROFIN-SINAR TECHNOLOGIES, INC.; *pg.* 668, *pg.* 904
EASYMARK II - Laser Marking Device - ROFIN-SINAR TECHNOLOGIES, INC.; *pg.* 668, *pg.* 904
EASYMATE - Vacuum - BISSELL HOMECARE, INC.; *pg.* 52, *pg.* 887
EASYMAX - Calorimeter - METTLER-TOLEDO INTERNATIONAL INC.; *pg.* 1423, *pg.* 1441
EASYMENU - Electronic Port - ADTRAN, INC.; *pg.* 344, *pg.* 6
EASYNAP - Napkin Dispensing System - GEORGIA-PACIFIC LLC; *pg.* 1458, *pg.* 507
EASYON - Hot Melt Pneumatic Gun Mounting Module - NORDSON CORPORATION; *pg.* 1365, *pg.* 1480
EASYPACK - Software - BIO-RAD LABORATORIES, INC.; *pg.* 1504, *pg.* 101
EASYPAY - Payment Solution - ESM SOLUTIONS CORPORATION; *pg.* 1243, *pg.* 1591
EASYPOINT - ATM & Kiosk Hardware & Software Products - NCR CORPORATION; *pg.* 443, *pg.* 531
EASYPOWER - Computer Peripheral Equipment - DIGI INTERNATIONAL INC.; *pg.* 387, *pg.* 948
EASYPOXY - Chemical Product - CYTEC INDUSTRIES, INC.; *pg.* 1155, *pg.* 1131
EASYPOXY - Gloss Enamel - PETTIT PAINT COMPANY; *pg.* 1444, *pg.* 1116
EASYPRINT - Printer and Coder - BELL-MARK CORPORATION; *pg.* 1620, *pg.* 1108
EASYPRINT - Desktop Inkjet Inks - VAN SON HOLLAND INK CORPORATION OF AMERICA; *pg.* 487, *pg.* 1169
EASYPROBE - Meter Reading Device - BADGER METER, INC.; *pg.* 1401, *pg.* 1873
EASYPROJECT - Electronic Tool For Managing Requests - ESM SOLUTIONS CORPORATION; *pg.* 1243, *pg.* 1591
EASYPURCHASE - Software - ESM SOLUTIONS CORPORATION; *pg.* 1243, *pg.* 1591
EASYPURCHASE WAREHOUSE - Web Commerce Solution - ESM SOLUTIONS CORPORATION; *pg.* 1243, *pg.* 1591
EASYQUOTE - Electronic Sourcing Tool - ESM SOLUTIONS CORPORATION; *pg.* 1243, *pg.* 1591
EASYRF - Software Tools - TEXAS INSTRUMENTS INCORPORATED; *pg.* 679, *pg.* 1688
EASYRIDER - Infant Carrier - INFANTINO, LLC; *pg.* 957, *pg.* 203
EASYRIDERS - Magazine - PAISANO PUBLICATIONS, LLC; *pg.* 1674, *pg.* 38
EASYSAVER - Catalog - WALGREEN CO.; *pg.* 1608, *pg.* 605
EASYSCALE - Interface - TEXAS INSTRUMENTS INCORPORATED; *pg.* 679, *pg.* 1688
EASYSCAN - Editor - WORDEN BROTHERS, INC.; *pg.* 823, *pg.* 1372
EASYSEAL - Tamper-Evident Closure - OWENS-ILLINOIS, INC.; *pg.* 1466, *pg.* 1470
EASYSET - Software - COBRA ELECTRONICS CORPORATION; *pg.* 629, *pg.* 572
EASYSHADE - Solar Screen - SUNSETTER PRODUCTS, LP; *pg.* 113, *pg.* 830
EASYSHARE - Digital Cameras - EASTMAN KODAK COMPANY; *pg.* 1408, *pg.* 1333
EASYSHOCK - Software - BIO-RAD LABORATORIES, INC.; *pg.* 1504, *pg.* 101
EASYSORT - Faucet Washer - LAVELLE INDUSTRIES INC.; *pg.* 1053, *pg.* 1856
EASYST - Wireless Network Product - AIRSPAN NETWORKS INC.; *pg.* 346, *pg.* 410
EASYST-WI-FI - Wireless Network Product - AIRSPAN NETWORKS INC.; *pg.* 346, *pg.* 410
EASYSTEPS - Software - NTI CORPORATION; *pg.* 446, *pg.* 114
EASYSTREET - Suspension Systems - AIR LIFT COMPANY; *pg.* 198, *pg.* 895
EASYSTREET - Software - MELISSA DATA CORP.; *pg.* 432, *pg.* 188
EASYTIME - Firelog - DURAFLAME, INC.; *pg.* 1123, *pg.* 280
EASYTRAK - Medical Device - BOSTON SCIENTIFIC CORPORATION; *pg.* 1508, *pg.* 831
EASYTURN - Fluid Handling System - GRACO, INC.; *pg.* 1342, *pg.* 935
EASYVAC POWERBRUSH - Bare Floor Vacuum - BISSELL HOMECARE, INC.; *pg.* 52, *pg.* 887
EASYVENT - Hot Air Balloon Deflation System - CAMERON BALLOONS U.S.; *pg.* 1829, *pg.* 884
EASYVIEW - Binoculars - MEADE INSTRUMENTS CORPORATION; *pg.* 1422, *pg.* 113
EASYVIEW - Software - MKS INSTRUMENTS, INC.; *pg.* 1362, *pg.* 781
EASYVUE - Copy Holder - RUBBERMAID HOME PRODUCTS; *pg.* 1138, *pg.* 1453
EASYWEAR - Lens - EMERGING VISION, INC.; *pg.* 1411, *pg.* 1227
EAT BETTER - Fresh Sandwich - PORT OF SUBS INC.; *pg.* 1746, *pg.* 1032
EAT-MORE - Candy - THE HERSHEY CO.; *pg.* 1855, *pg.* 1538
EAT 'N PARK - Restaurants - EAT'N PARK HOSPITALITY GROUP; *pg.* 1728, *pg.* 1539
EAT SMART - Food Product - LANDEC CORPORATION; *pg.* 1419, *pg.* 145
EAT THIS, NOT THAT! - Book - RODALE, INC.; *pg.* 1681, *pg.* 1530
EAT WELL - Tagline - PILGRIM'S PRIDE CORPORATION; *pg.* 889, *pg.* 330
EAT WELL. DO GOOD. - Tagline - NATURE'S PATH FOODS INC.; *pg.* 833, *pg.* 1908
EAT WELL LIVE WELL - Slogan - WEGMANS FOOD MARKETS, INC.; *pg.* 1037, *pg.* 1337
EAT WELL STAY HEALTHY - Poultry Product - PILGRIM'S PRIDE CORPORATION; *pg.* 889, *pg.* 330
EATIN' GOOD IN THE NEIGHBORHOOD - Tagline - APPLEBEE'S INTERNATIONAL, INC.; *pg.* 1715, *pg.* 980
EATIN' RIGHT NEVER TASTED SO GOOD - Tagline - APPLEBEE'S INTERNATIONAL, INC.; *pg.* 1715, *pg.* 980
EATING RIGHT KIDS - Healthy Food Products for Children - SAFEWAY INC.; *pg.* 1032, *pg.* 184
EATON - Electrical Products - EATON CORPORATION; *pg.* 1331, *pg.* 1429
EATON - Mechanical & Electrical System - JOHNSON CONTROLS, INC.; *pg.* 209, *pg.* 1876
EATONCARE - Customer Care - EATON CORPORATION; *pg.* 1331, *pg.* 1429
EATSMART - Snack Food Product - SNYDER'S OF HANOVER, INC.; *pg.* 1862, *pg.* 1536
EAU BENITE - Beer - SLEEMAN UNIBROUE QUEBEC; *pg.* 265, *pg.* 1950
EAU DE DIOR ENERGISANTE - Women's Fragrance - PARFUMS CHRISTIAN DIOR, INC; *pg.* 519, *pg.* 1276
EAU DE DIOR RALEXANTE - Women's Fragrance - PARFUMS CHRISTIAN DIOR, INC; *pg.* 519, *pg.* 1276
EAU DE DOLCE VITA - Women's Fragrance - PARFUMS CHRISTIAN DIOR, INC; *pg.* 519, *pg.* 1276
EAU FRAICHE - Perfume - ELIZABETH ARDEN, INC.; *pg.* 507, *pg.* 448
EAU FRAICHE - Women's Fragrance - PARFUMS CHRISTIAN DIOR, INC; *pg.* 519, *pg.* 1276
EAU SAUVAGE - Men's Fragrance - PARFUMS CHRISTIAN DIOR, INC; *pg.* 519, *pg.* 1276
EAU SAUVAGE EXTREME - Men's Fragrance - PARFUMS CHRISTIAN DIOR, INC; *pg.* 519, *pg.* 1276
EAW - Loudspeakers - LOUD TECHNOLOGIES INC.; *pg.* 652, *pg.* 1847
EAZEO DVR1B1161 - Video Surveillance Unit - BOSCH SECURITY SYSTEMS, INC.; *pg.* 626, *pg.* 1158
EAZEO OBSERVATION SYSTEM - Video Surveillance - BOSCH SECURITY SYSTEMS, INC.; *pg.* 626, *pg.* 1158
EAZI-BREED - Pharmaceutical Product - PFIZER INC.; *pg.* 1581, *pg.* 1278
EAZYCONNECT - Software - ADVANCED MICRO DEVICES, INC.; *pg.* 613, *pg.* 282
EAZYLAUNCH - Software - ADVANCED MICRO DEVICES, INC.; *pg.* 613, *pg.* 282
EAZYLOOK - Software - ADVANCED MICRO DEVICES, INC.; *pg.* 613, *pg.* 282
EAZYTYME - Web Based Electronic Time System - THE JUDGE GROUP, INC.; *pg.* 424, *pg.* 1594
EB GAMES - Games - GAMESTOP CORP.; *pg.* 399, *pg.* 1699
EB900 - Lighting Systems - REVOLUTION LIGHTING TECHNOLOGIES, INC.; *pg.* 1304, *pg.* 377
EB901 - Lighting Systems - REVOLUTION LIGHTING TECHNOLOGIES, INC.; *pg.* 1304, *pg.* 377
EB902 - Lighting Systems - REVOLUTION LIGHTING TECHNOLOGIES, INC.; *pg.* 1304, *pg.* 377
EB903 - Lighting Systems - REVOLUTION LIGHTING TECHNOLOGIES, INC.; *pg.* 1304, *pg.* 377
EBAP - Software - HTC GLOBAL SERVICES INC.; *pg.* 409, *pg.* 911
EBAY LIVE AUCTIONS - Live, Real-Time Online Bidding - EBAY INC.; *pg.* 1240, *pg.* 243
EBAY MOBILE - Online Services - EBAY INC.; *pg.* 1240, *pg.* 243
EBAY MOTORS - Online Automotive Auction Marketplace - EBAY INC.; *pg.* 1240, *pg.* 243
EBAY PROFESSIONAL SERVICES - Small Business Marketplace - EBAY INC.; *pg.* 1240, *pg.* 243
THE EBAY SHOP - Online Services - EBAY INC.; *pg.* 1240, *pg.* 243
EBAY STORE - Customized Shopping Marketplace - EBAY INC.; *pg.* 1240, *pg.* 243
EBAY TOOLBAR - Web Application - EBAY INC.; *pg.* 1240, *pg.* 243
EBBA - Lamp - ASHLEY FURNITURE INDUSTRIES, INC.; *pg.* 914, *pg.* 1852
EBBI - Electronic Components - MOLEX INCORPORATED; *pg.* 655, *pg.* 628
EBECRYL - Radiation-Curing Resins - CYTEC INDUSTRIES, INC.; *pg.* 1155, *pg.* 1131
EBEL - Watch - MOVADO GROUP, INC.; *pg.* 10, *pg.* 1101
EBERHARD - Locking Devices - THE EASTERN COMPANY; *pg.* 1331, *pg.* 357
EBERHARD - Truck & Trailer Hardware - EBERHARD MANUFACTURING DIVISION; *pg.* 1046, *pg.* 1475
EBERRON - Game Setting - WIZARDS OF THE COAST, INC.; *pg.* 970, *pg.* 1830
EBET USA - Games - PENN NATIONAL GAMING, INC.; *pg.* 574, *pg.* 1595
EBI - Diagnostic Testing - IDEXX LABORATORIES, INC.; *pg.* 1543, *pg.* 753
EBI TOOL - Software - BOMBARDIER INC.; *pg.* 1318, *pg.* 1953
EBILL COMPANION - Communication Product - CENTURYLINK, INC; *pg.* 1870, *pg.* 317
EBILL-PAY - Electronic Bill Payment - UNITED STATES POSTAL SERVICE; *pg.* 1009, *pg.* 406
EBIX - Software - EBIX INC.; *pg.* 1241, *pg.* 504
EBIX ASP - Software - EBIX INC.; *pg.* 1241, *pg.* 504
EBIX.COM - Software - EBIX INC.; *pg.* 1241, *pg.* 504

First page reference indicates Business Class Edition
Second page reference indicates Geographic Edition

EBLASTER - Software - SPECTORSOFT CORPORATION; *pg.* 1281, *pg.* 478
EBLASTER MAC - Software - SPECTORSOFT CORPORATION; *pg.* 1281, *pg.* 478
EBLY - Food Product - MARS, INCORPORATED; *pg.* 1858, *pg.* 1792
EBMRV CYCLOMAX LOW NOX - Gas Burner - MAXON CORPORATION; *pg.* 1359, *pg.* 695
EBONE - Cosmetics - FASHION FAIR COSMETICS, LLC; *pg.* 509, *pg.* 573
EBONE - Cosmetics - JOHNSON PUBLISHING COMPANY, INC.; *pg.* 1655, *pg.* 579
EBONITE - Hose - HBD INDUSTRIES, INC.; *pg.* 207, *pg.* 1449
EBONITE - Standard Roll Covers - VAIL RUBBER WORKS, INC.; *pg.* 1891, *pg.* 906
EBONOL - Salts for Blackening & Coloring Metals - ENTHONE INC.; *pg.* 1161, *pg.* 381
EBONY - Magazine - JOHNSON PUBLISHING COMPANY, INC.; *pg.* 1655, *pg.* 579
EBONY - Black PVC Fabric - STANDARD SAFETY EQUIPMENT CO.; *pg.* 1379, *pg.* 632
EBONY FASHION FAIR - Fashion Show - JOHNSON PUBLISHING COMPANY, INC.; *pg.* 1655, *pg.* 579
EBONY RICH - Hosiery & Related Apparel - MAYER/BERKSHIRE CORPORATION; *pg.* 29, *pg.* 1129
EBONY SUPREME - Hosiery & Related Apparel - MAYER/BERKSHIRE CORPORATION; *pg.* 29, *pg.* 1129
EBOOKERS - Travel Website - ORBITZ WORLDWIDE, INC.; *pg.* 1918, *pg.* 586
EBOOKMAN - Publication - FRANKLIN ELECTRONIC PUBLISHERS, INC.; *pg.* 398, *pg.* 1048
EBREZA - Pharmaceutical Preparation - PFIZER INC.; *pg.* 1581, *pg.* 1278
EBROADCASTER - Software - MICROSTRATEGY, INC.; *pg.* 1266, *pg.* 1809
EBT721 ELECTRONIC BALANCING TOOL - Balometer - TSI INCORPORATED; *pg.* 1432, *pg.* 965
EBUSINESS CONFERENCE & EXPO - Publisher - UNITED BUSINESS MEDIA LLC; *pg.* 1697, *pg.* 1177
EBUSINESS IT'S WORKING - Drilling Product - SMITH INTERNATIONAL, INC.; *pg.* 1377, *pg.* 1715
EBYT - Footwear - STEVEN MADDEN, LTD.; *pg.* 1819, *pg.* 1176
EC - Interface - IMAGINATION TECHNOLOGIES; *pg.* 412, *pg.* 285
EC - Clear Wheel - REVOLUTION LIGHTING TECHNOLOGIES, INC.; *pg.* 1304, *pg.* 377
EC-2 - Lighting Product - HIGH END SYSTEMS, INC.; *pg.* 1299, *pg.* 1663
EC-400 - Electronic Condensate Pump - LITTLE GIANT PUMP COMPANY; *pg.* 1356, *pg.* 1486
EC-H2O - Water Technology - TENNANT COMPANY; *pg.* 1381, *pg.* 944
EC-NAPROSYN - Pharmaceutical Product - HOFFMANN-LA ROCHE INC.; *pg.* 1542, *pg.* 1099
EC120 - Model Helicopter - AIRBUS HELICOPTERS, INC.; *pg.* 223, *pg.* 1698
EC135 - Model Helicopter - AIRBUS HELICOPTERS, INC.; *pg.* 223, *pg.* 1698
EC155 - Model Helicopter - AIRBUS HELICOPTERS, INC.; *pg.* 223, *pg.* 1698
EC3 - Conveyorized Cutting System - EASTMAN MACHINE COMPANY; *pg.* 1331, *pg.* 1148
EC3 - Imaging System - UVP, INC.; *pg.* 1434, *pg.* 298
ECA CERTIFICATE - Internet Site Security Product - VERISIGN, INC.; *pg.* 488, *pg.* 1799
ECAE - Electronic Material - HONEYWELL INTERNATIONAL INC.; *pg.* 407, *pg.* 1088
ECALLANTIDE - Pharmaceutical Product - CUBIST PHARMACEUTICALS, INC.; *pg.* 1521, *pg.* 828
ECARO-25 - Halon Replacement - FIKE CORPORATION; *pg.* 1047, *pg.* 973
ECAS - Call Accounting System - CALERO SOFTWARE, LLC; *pg.* 368, *pg.* 1333
ECASEMANAGER - Electronic Case Management - HDI SOLUTIONS, INC.; *pg.* 403, *pg.* 1
ECASTER - Software - MICROSTRATEGY, INC.; *pg.* 1266, *pg.* 1809
ECAT - Position Emission Tomography - SIEMENS CORPORATION; *pg.* 803, *pg.* 1291
ECC0H - Non-Halogenated Compound - POLYONE CORPORATION; *pg.* 1177, *pg.* 1404
THE ECCENTRIC - Newspaper - HOMETOWN COMMUNICATIONS NETWORK, INC.; *pg.* 1650, *pg.* 904
ECCO - Books - HARPERCOLLINS PUBLISHERS INC.; *pg.* 1647, *pg.* 1237
ECCO DOMANI - Wine - E&J GALLO WINERY; *pg.* 1962, *pg.* 149
ECCONDO - Chemicals - HUNTSMAN CORPORATION; *pg.* 1167, *pg.* 1758
ECD TECHNOLOGY - Industrial Production Machines - APPLIED MATERIALS, INC; *pg.* 618, *pg.* 1009
ECDEL - Elastomer - EASTMAN CHEMICAL COMPANY; *pg.* 1159, *pg.* 1636
ECDEL - Elastomer, Copolyester, Flexible Polyester, Flexible CoPolyester, Elastomer - EASTMAN KODAK COMPANY; *pg.* 1408, *pg.* 1333
E!CEMS - Logistics Software - ASPEN TECHNOLOGY, INC.; *pg.* 354, *pg.* 804
ECENERGY - Computer Software - CENVEO INC.; *pg.* 1626, *pg.* 372
ECG ANALYZER - Vetronic Product - BIOANALYTICAL SYSTEMS, INC.; *pg.* 1402, *pg.* 700
ECHART - Software - ELEKTA; *pg.* 391, *pg.* 284
ECHECKSECURE - Software - TROY GROUP INC.; *pg.* 485, *pg.* 71
ECHELON - Polyurethane Prepolymer - THE DOW CHEMICAL COMPANY; *pg.* 1157, *pg.* 898
ECHELON - Lighting System - LITECONTROL CORPORATION; *pg.* 1301, *pg.* 841
ECHELON - Plaster Wall System - USG CORPORATION; *pg.* 118, *pg.* 594
ECHELON - Zipper - YKK CORPORATION OF AMERICA; *pg.* 699, *pg.* 536
ECHINACEA COMPLETE CARE - Wellness Tea - CELESTIAL SEASONINGS, INC.; *pg.* 846, *pg.* 310
ECHINACEA WELLNESS TEA - Herb Tea - CELESTIAL SEASONINGS, INC.; *pg.* 846, *pg.* 310
ECHO - Apparel - THE ECHO DESIGN GROUP, INC.; *pg.* 4, *pg.* 1226
ECHO - Furniture - ETHAN ALLEN INTERIORS INC.; *pg.* 924, *pg.* 343
ECHO - Sweeper - HI-VAC CORPORATION; *pg.* 56, *pg.* 1458
ECHO - Telecommunications Products - INCONTACT, INC.; *pg.* 413, *pg.* 1752
ECHO - Golf Club - KARSTEN MANUFACTURING CORPORATION; *pg.* 1838, *pg.* 17
ECHO - Cost Management Software - LAVASTORM ANALYTICS; *pg.* 427, *pg.* 797
ECHO - Electronic Measurement Instrument - MESA LABORATORIES, INC.; *pg.* 1567, *pg.* 333
ECHO - Fabric - NEMSCHOFF, INC.; *pg.* 936, *pg.* 1890
ECHO - Biomolecule Product - THERMO FISHER SCIENTIFIC INC.; *pg.* 1602, *pg.* 61
ECHO - Furniture - TROPITONE FURNITURE CO., INC.; *pg.* 945, *pg.* 118
ECHO DESIGN LAB - Designing Service - THE ECHO DESIGN GROUP, INC.; *pg.* 4, *pg.* 1226
ECHO-SCREEN - Hearing Screener - NATUS MEDICAL INCORPORATED; *pg.* 1572, *pg.* 199
ECHOCORE - Firmware - MERCURY COMPUTER SYSTEMS, INC.; *pg.* 434, *pg.* 813
ECHOFON - Twitter Application - UBERMEDIA, INC.; *pg.* 1286, *pg.* 181
ECHOLDX - Navigation Aid - TRIMBLE NAVIGATION LIMITED; *pg.* 1384, *pg.* 288
ECHOLINK - Medical Device - NATUS MEDICAL INCORPORATED; *pg.* 1572, *pg.* 199
ECHOMAC - Nondestructive Testing - MAGNETIC ANALYSIS CORPORATION; *pg.* 1421, *pg.* 1158
ECHOMUSIC - Entertainment News - IAC/INTERACTIVECORP; *pg.* 292, *pg.* 1242
ECHOPLEX - Musical Instrument - GIBSON GUITAR CORP.; *pg.* 550, *pg.* 1650
ECHORTX - Navigation Aid - TRIMBLE NAVIGATION LIMITED; *pg.* 1384, *pg.* 288
ECHOSONIX - Ultrasonic Transmitter - SOR, INC.; *pg.* 1306, *pg.* 716
ECHOSTOP - Desktop System - ANDREA ELECTRONICS CORPORATION; *pg.* 617, *pg.* 1143
ECHOTEK - Digital Receivers - MERCURY COMPUTER SYSTEMS, INC.; *pg.* 434, *pg.* 813
ECHOTIP - Medical Device - COOK GROUP, INC.; *pg.* 1518, *pg.* 674
ECHOVST - Navigation Aid - TRIMBLE NAVIGATION LIMITED; *pg.* 1384, *pg.* 288
ECII - Gas Product - ENGINEERED CONTROLS INTERNATIONAL LLC; *pg.* 1334, *pg.* 1372
ECKERD - Pharmacies - RITE AID CORPORATION; *pg.* 1590, *pg.* 1519
ECKRICH - Meat Products - JOHN MORRELL FOOD GROUP; *pg.* 866, *pg.* 628
ECKRICH - Food Products - SMITHFIELD FOODS, INC.; *pg.* 896, *pg.* 1806
ECKRICH READY CRISP - Food Product - CONAGRA FOODS, INC.; *pg.* 826, *pg.* 1014
ECL PRO - Integrated Circuits - MICREL, INC.; *pg.* 654, *pg.* 247
ECLAIRS GOLD - Confectionery - THE HERSHEY CO.; *pg.* 1855, *pg.* 1538
ECLECTIC REMEDIES - Pure Essential Oils - ANNIE OAKLEY ENTERPRISES, INC.; *pg.* 499, *pg.* 693
ECLECTRICS - Kitchen Appliance - HAMILTON BEACH BRANDS, INC.; *pg.* 56, *pg.* 1783
ECLICK - Software - XEROX CORPORATION; *pg.* 494, *pg.* 365
ECLINICAL - Computer Software - OMNICOMM SYSTEMS, INC.; *pg.* 1272, *pg.* 426
ECLIPSE - Tent Fabric - ANCHOR INDUSTRIES, INC.; *pg.* 1825, *pg.* 678
ECLIPSE - Furniture - ASHLEY FURNITURE INDUSTRIES, INC.; *pg.* 914, *pg.* 1852
ECLIPSE - Pigment - BASF CATALYSTS LLC; *pg.* 1148, *pg.* 1074
ECLIPSE - Hand Dryer - BOBRICK WASHROOM EQUIPMENT, INC.; *pg.* 1043, *pg.* 166
ECLIPSE - Range Hoods - BROAN-NUTONE LLC; *pg.* 1069, *pg.* 1860
ECLIPSE - Switch - BROCADE CORPORATION; *pg.* 365, *pg.* 312
ECLIPSE - Building Material - BUILDING PRODUCTS OF CANADA CORP.; *pg.* 72, *pg.* 1951
ECLIPSE - Compact Electrocardiograph - CARDIAC SCIENCE CORPORATION; *pg.* 1512, *pg.* 1897
ECLIPSE - Glass & Ceramic Material - CORNING INCORPORATED; *pg.* 1122, *pg.* 1154
ECLIPSE - Dental Product - DENTSPLY INTERNATIONAL INC.; *pg.* 1522, *pg.* 1596
ECLIPSE - Indus. Latches - THE EASTERN COMPANY; *pg.* 1331, *pg.* 357
ECLIPSE - Fire Service - E.D. BULLARD COMPANY; *pg.* 1332, *pg.* 727
ECLIPSE - Pigments - FERRO CORPORATION; *pg.* 1162, *pg.* 1462
ECLIPSE - Bicycle - G. JOANNOU CYCLE CO. INC.; *pg.* 1707, *pg.* 1098
ECLIPSE - Gaming Product - GLD PRODUCTS, INC.; *pg.* 1835, *pg.* 1882
ECLIPSE - Engine Management System - IMPCO TECHNOLOGIES, INC.; *pg.* 208, *pg.* 261
ECLIPSE - Software - INTUIT INC.; *pg.* 769, *pg.* 158
ECLIPSE - Contour Cutters - KENNAMETAL IPG; *pg.* 1353, *pg.* 1615
ECLIPSE - Styling Covers - LUND INTERNATIONAL, INC.; *pg.* 211, *pg.* 526
ECLIPSE - Disposable Surgical Gowns - MEDLINE INDUSTRIES, INC.; *pg.* 1562, *pg.* 635
ECLIPSE - Feline Vaccine - MERCK & CO., INC.; *pg.* 1566, *pg.* 1077
ECLIPSE - Fabric - NEMSCHOFF, INC.; *pg.* 936, *pg.* 1890
ECLIPSE - Biological Microscopes - NIKON INC.; *pg.* 1424, *pg.* 1181
ECLIPSE - Control & Detection System - NORDSON CORPORATION; *pg.* 1365, *pg.* 1480
ECLIPSE - Tray - PACTIV CORPORATION; *pg.* 1466, *pg.* 624
ECLIPSE - Satellite Command & Control Software - RAYTHEON COMPANY; *pg.* 233, *pg.* 854
ECLIPSE - Engineering Software - SCHLUMBERGER LIMITED; *pg.* 801, *pg.* 1714
ECLIPSE - Label Printing System - WEBER PACKAGING SOLUTIONS, INC.; *pg.* 491, *pg.* 554
ECLIPSE - Fluoropolymer Coating System - WHITFORD WORLDWIDE COMPANY; *pg.* 1185, *pg.* 1529
ECLIPSE - Sugar Free Gum - WM. WRIGLEY JR. COMPANY; *pg.* 1863, *pg.* 596
ECLIPSE 550 TWIN-ENGINE LIGHT JET - Aircraft - ONE AVIATION CORPORATION; *pg.* 232, *pg.* 1135
ECLIPSE BAYONET - Ultra Recuperator - ECLIPSE INC.; *pg.* 1332, *pg.* 655
ECLIPSE BI-FLAME - Internal Testing Machine - ECLIPSE INC.; *pg.* 1332, *pg.* 655
ECLIPSE EXTENSOJET - Burner - ECLIPSE INC.; *pg.* 1332,

pg. 655
ECLIPSE II - Illuminator - REVOLUTION LIGHTING TECHNOLOGIES, INC.; *pg.* 1304, *pg.* 377
ECLIPSE OEM BOARD - Wireless Product - HEMISPHERE GPS INC.; *pg.* 642, *pg.* 1903
ECLIPSE PN03 - Nonmetallic Raceway - WIREMOLD/LEGRAND; *pg.* 689, *pg.* 383
ECLIPSE PN03L - Nonmetallic Raceway - WIREMOLD/LEGRAND; *pg.* 689, *pg.* 383
ECLIPSE PN05 - Nonmetallic Raceway - WIREMOLD/LEGRAND; *pg.* 689, *pg.* 383
ECLIPSE PN10 - Nonmetallic Raceway - WIREMOLD/LEGRAND; *pg.* 689, *pg.* 383
ECLIPSE PREMIER - Electrocardiograph - CARDIAC SCIENCE CORPORATION; *pg.* 1512, *pg.* 1897
ECLIPSE RATIOMATIC - Burner - ECLIPSE INC.; *pg.* 1332, *pg.* 655
ECLIPSE SIMOPT - Model Calibration Software - SCHLUMBERGER LIMITED; *pg.* 801, *pg.* 1714
ECLIPSE SPIRAL FLAME - Burner - ECLIPSE INC.; *pg.* 1332, *pg.* 655
ECLIPSE SURFACE BLOCKER - Digital Lens Layout Blocking System - GERBER SCIENTIFIC, INC.; *pg.* 1414, *pg.* 380
ECLIPSE T 100 - Biological Microscope - NIKON INC.; *pg.* 1424, *pg.* 1181
ECLIPSE THERMJET - Burner - ECLIPSE INC.; *pg.* 1332, *pg.* 655
ECLIPSE THERMTHIEF - Nozzle Mixing - ECLIPSE INC.; *pg.* 1332, *pg.* 655
ECLIPSE VERI-FLAME - Monitoring System - ECLIPSE INC.; *pg.* 1332, *pg.* 655
ECLIPSE VORTOMETRIC - Burner - ECLIPSE INC.; *pg.* 1332, *pg.* 655
ECLISSE - Paper & Nonwoven Material - FIBERMARK INC.; *pg.* 1457, *pg.* 1764
ECLYPSE - Software - SYNOPSYS, INC.; *pg.* 480, *pg.* 162
ECM GROUP - Deburring And Finishing System - KENNAMETAL EXTRUDE HONE; *pg.* 1352, *pg.* 1542
ECMO - Heater - CINCINNATI SUB-ZERO PRODUCTS, INC.; *pg.* 1070, *pg.* 1411
ECO - Pump Product - IDEX CORPORATION; *pg.* 1347, *pg.* 623
ECO-ADVANTAGE - Sweepers - TENNANT COMPANY; *pg.* 1381, *pg.* 944
ECO-BAK - Crusher Backing - ESCO CORPORATION; *pg.* 1335, *pg.* 1502
ECO-CRYL - Chemical - MILLER-STEPHENSON CHEMICAL COMPANY, INC.; *pg.* 1172, *pg.* 344
ECO-DFS - Coatings - TENNANT COMPANY; *pg.* 1381, *pg.* 944
ECO-DQS - Coatings - TENNANT COMPANY; *pg.* 1381, *pg.* 944
ECO-ECT - Floor Coating System - TENNANT COMPANY; *pg.* 1381, *pg.* 944
ECO-FLOW - Packaging Product - AMERICAN EXCELSIOR COMPANY; *pg.* 1451, *pg.* 1659
ECO-HARD-N-SEAL - Concrete Hardener & Sealer - TENNANT COMPANY; *pg.* 1381, *pg.* 944
ECO-HPS - Coatings - TENNANT COMPANY; *pg.* 1381, *pg.* 944
ECO IMMUNITYSM - Software System - MENTOR GRAPHICS CORPORATION; *pg.* 432, *pg.* 1510
ECO PAC - Breakfast Cereals - NATURE'S PATH FOODS INC.; *pg.* 833, *pg.* 1908
ECO PILE - Fabric - DRAPER KNITTING CO., INC.; *pg.* 692, *pg.* 810
ECO-PJS - Coatings - TENNANT COMPANY; *pg.* 1381, *pg.* 944
ECO-PRIME - Coating Product - PPG INDUSTRIES, INC.; *pg.* 1445, *pg.* 1579
ECO-PROTEKT - Overlay System - TENNANT COMPANY; *pg.* 1381, *pg.* 944
ECO-SEEKER - Lab Science Material - CAROLINA BIOLOGICAL SUPPLY COMPANY; *pg.* 1513, *pg.* 1359
ECO-SHOPFLOOR - Shop Floor System - TENNANT COMPANY; *pg.* 1381, *pg.* 944
ECO-SOLVENT PLUS - Ink for the Falcon II Outdoor & Falcon Outdoor Inkjet Printers - MUTOH AMERICA INC.; *pg.* 443, *pg.* 18
ECO SPEC - Paint And Stain Product - BENJAMIN MOORE & CO.; *pg.* 1440, *pg.* 1085
ECO-STAR - Low-emission Burners - HAUCK MANUFACTURING COMPANY, INC.; *pg.* 1345, *pg.* 1522
ECO TEC - Ear Warmer - 180S, LLC; *pg.* 1824, *pg.* 754
ECO-TEMP - Low-Temperature Warewashing Rental & Service Program - ECOLAB INC.; *pg.* 329, *pg.* 960
ECO TRU - Aircraft Disinfectant - MCGEAN-ROHCO, INC.; *pg.* 1172, *pg.* 1432
ECO TURN - Rail Seals - THE TIMKEN COMPANY; *pg.* 218, *pg.* 1408
ECO2 - Lasers - GSI GROUP INC.; *pg.* 1415, *pg.* 784
ECO2000 - Awareness Program - ECOLAB INC.; *pg.* 329, *pg.* 960
ECO2FUME - Chemical Product - CYTEC INDUSTRIES, INC.; *pg.* 1155, *pg.* 1131
ECOANALYTIX - Biofuel Solution - PERKINELMER, INC.; *pg.* 1426, *pg.* 853
ECOAT - Paint - KELLY-MOORE PAINT COMPANY, INC.; *pg.* 1443, *pg.* 198
ECOBAY - Cabinet - SANMINA-SCI CORPORATION; *pg.* 671, *pg.* 250
ECOBLACK - Carbon Black - CABOT CORPORATION; *pg.* 1151, *pg.* 792
ECOBOOST - Engine - FORD MOTOR COMPANY; *pg.* 172, *pg.* 876
ECOBRIGHT - Compostable Film - HAZEN PAPER COMPANY; *pg.* 1459, *pg.* 825
ECOBRITE - Forest Product - CANFOR CORPORATION; *pg.* 1454, *pg.* 1910
ECOBRITE - Coating Product - PPG INDUSTRIES, INC.; *pg.* 1445, *pg.* 1579
ECODRY - Hair Dryer - CONAIR CORPORATION; *pg.* 505, *pg.* 1055
ECODRY - Compound Dryer - NORDSON CORPORATION; *pg.* 1365, *pg.* 1480
ECOETHERNET - Ethernet Network Equipment - VITESSE SEMICONDUCTOR CORPORATION; *pg.* 686, *pg.* 57
ECOFLEX - Liquid Rubber - SMOOTH-ON INC.; *pg.* 111, *pg.* 1528
ECOFLUX - Filter Cartridge - PALL CORPORATION; *pg.* 232, *pg.* 1323
ECOGUARD - Glass Product - GUARDIAN INDUSTRIES CORP.; *pg.* 85, *pg.* 869
ECOHEAT - Gun - MASTER APPLIANCE CORP.; *pg.* 1055, *pg.* 1888
ECOLINE - Pump Product - IDEX CORPORATION; *pg.* 1347, *pg.* 623
ECOLINE - Glassware Washer - STERIS CORPORATION; *pg.* 1597, *pg.* 1464
ECOLINE - Chemical Cleaner Product - TECH SPRAY, L.P.; *pg.* 1183, *pg.* 1659
ECOLINER - Compound Gun - NORDSON CORPORATION; *pg.* 1365, *pg.* 1480
ECOLITE - Mailer Product - POLYAIR INTER PACK INC.; *pg.* 1467, *pg.* 1941
ECOLUBE - Chemical Cleaner Product - TECH SPRAY, L.P.; *pg.* 1183, *pg.* 1659
ECOLUBE-ENDURAMET - Coatings - CARPENTER TECHNOLOGY CORPORATION; *pg.* 73, *pg.* 1584
ECOMASS - Polymer-Metal - POLYONE CORPORATION; *pg.* 1177, *pg.* 1404
ECOMAX - Lighting Product - WESTINGHOUSE LIGHTING CORPORATION; *pg.* 687, *pg.* 1571
ECOMET - Low-Price Polishing & Grinding Machine - BUEHLER, LTD.; *pg.* 1403, *pg.* 622
ECOMFORT - Shoes - ACUSHNET COMPANY; *pg.* 1824, *pg.* 818
E.COMINTEGRATE - Software - BOTTOMLINE TECHNOLOGIES INC.; *pg.* 363, *pg.* 483
ECOMIX - Fluid Handling System - GRACO, INC.; *pg.* 1342, *pg.* 935
E.COMPRESENT - Software - BOTTOMLINE TECHNOLOGIES INC.; *pg.* 363, *pg.* 483
ECON LINER - Truck-Mounted Pavement Striper - M-B COMPANIES, INC.; *pg.* 1357, *pg.* 1884
ECON-O-MITE - Electronic Components - MOLEX INCORPORATED; *pg.* 655, *pg.* 628
ECONLINE - Cleaning Product - TECH SPRAY, L.P.; *pg.* 1183, *pg.* 1659
ECONO - Paint & Coating - AERVOE INDUSTRIES INCORPORATED; *pg.* 1439, *pg.* 1021
ECONO - Software - BIO-RAD LABORATORIES, INC.; *pg.* 1504, *pg.* 101
ECONO-CAL - Calibration Cylinders - MINE SAFETY APPLIANCES COMPANY; *pg.* 1361, *pg.* 1525
ECONO CARD - Loyalty Card System that Gathers Customer Purchase Information - SPARTANNASH CO.; *pg.* 1034, *pg.* 925
ECONO-COLUMN - Software - BIO-RAD LABORATORIES, INC.; *pg.* 1504, *pg.* 101
ECONO-COOL - Payment System - COIN ACCEPTORS, INC.; *pg.* 1324, *pg.* 994
ECONO-FLO - Water Conserving Spout Outlet - THE CHICAGO FAUCET COMPANY; *pg.* 1044, *pg.* 606
ECONO LODGE - Hotels - CHOICE HOTELS INTERNATIONAL, INC.; *pg.* 1086, *pg.* 775
ECONO-MOX - Thick Film High Voltage Resistors - OHMITE MANUFACTURING COMPANY; *pg.* 660, *pg.* 553
ECONO-PAC - Software - BIO-RAD LABORATORIES, INC.; *pg.* 1504, *pg.* 101
ECONO-POP - Popcorn Machine - GOLD MEDAL PRODUCTS CO.; *pg.* 55, *pg.* 1414
ECONO-STOCK - Drilling Product - SMITH INTERNATIONAL, INC.; *pg.* 1377, *pg.* 1715
ECONO-TAPE - Contact Materials - BASF CATALYSTS LLC; *pg.* 1148, *pg.* 1074
ECONOBACK - Towel - CROSSTEX INTERNATIONAL INC.; *pg.* 1520, *pg.* 1164
ECONOBAKE - Bakery Ingredient - FOREMOST FARMS USA COOPERATIVE; *pg.* 856, *pg.* 1854
ECONOBAY - Light Fixtures - JUNO LIGHTING, INC.; *pg.* 1300, *pg.* 606
ECONOFOODS - Retail Grocery Stores - SPARTANNASH CO.; *pg.* 1034, *pg.* 925
ECONOGREEN - Plastic Bags & Drop Cloths - JIG-A-WORLD; *pg.* 980, *pg.* 1951
ECONOIRON - Hot Knife - MASTER APPLIANCE CORP.; *pg.* 1055, *pg.* 1888
ECONOLAP - Metal Building Product - CENTRIA, INC.; *pg.* 74, *pg.* 1554
ECONOLINE - Janitor Cart - GEERPRES INC.; *pg.* 1339, *pg.* 901
ECONOLITE - Vehicle Safety System - GROTE INDUSTRIES, INC.; *pg.* 206, *pg.* 693
ECONOLRON - Soldering Iron & Heat Tool - MASTER APPLIANCE CORP.; *pg.* 1055, *pg.* 1888
ECONOMATE - Buffet Equipment & Salad Bars - DUKE MANUFACTURING COMPANY, INC.; *pg.* 54, *pg.* 995
ECONOMATE - Mop Handles - GEERPRES INC.; *pg.* 1339, *pg.* 901
ECONOMATIC - Thermal Processing Equipment - SURFACE COMBUSTION, INC.; *pg.* 1077, *pg.* 1462
ECONOMIE - Home, Health, & Beauty Products - THE JEAN COUTU GROUP (PJC) INC.; *pg.* 1548, *pg.* 1952
ECONOMIST - Mold Release - SLIDE PRODUCTS, INC.; *pg.* 1181, *pg.* 670
ECONOMUFF - Hearing System - MINE SAFETY APPLIANCES COMPANY; *pg.* 1361, *pg.* 1525
ECONOMY - Fibre Drum - GREIF INC.; *pg.* 1459, *pg.* 1447
ECONOMY - Protective Goggle - SELLSTROM MANUFACTURING CO.; *pg.* 1428, *pg.* 659
ECONOMY HEAT-SHRINKABLE END CAPS - Heat Shrink - CHANNELL COMMERCIAL CORP.; *pg.* 1870, *pg.* 291
ECONOPOUR - Integral Paperboard Pour Spout - CARAUSTAR INDUSTRIES, INC.; *pg.* 1455, *pg.* 525
ECONOSAL - Salt Bath System - AJAX ELECTRIC CO.; *pg.* 1068, *pg.* 1541
ECONOSCILLATOR - Semiconductor - MAXIM INTEGRATED PRODUCTS, INC.; *pg.* 653, *pg.* 247
ECONOSHOT - Fluid Handling System - GRACO, INC.; *pg.* 1342, *pg.* 935
ECONOSPRAY - Cleaning Product - SLIDE PRODUCTS, INC.; *pg.* 1181, *pg.* 670
ECONOTIG - Welding & Cutting Equip. - MILLER ELECTRIC MANUFACTURING CO.; *pg.* 1361, *pg.* 1852
ECONOX - Chemical Product - CARUS CORPORATION; *pg.* 1152, *pg.* 652
ECOPANE - Plastic Foam - THE DOW CHEMICAL COMPANY; *pg.* 1157, *pg.* 898
ECOPIA - Passenger Tires - BRIDGESTONE AMERICAS, INC.; *pg.* 201, *pg.* 1649
ECOPLATE - Metallic Coating - PARKER CHOMERICS; *pg.* 662, *pg.* 862
ECOPY - Software - NUANCE DOCUMENT IMAGING SOLUTIONS; *pg.* 1271, *pg.* 1037
ECOR - Biomolecule Product - THERMO FISHER SCIENTIFIC INC.; *pg.* 1602, *pg.* 61
ECORA ENTERPRISE AUDITOR - Software - ECORA SOFTWARE CORPORATION; *pg.* 389, *pg.* 1662
ECORAD - Resin - SI GROUP, INC.; *pg.* 1181, *pg.* 1341
ECORE - Wallcovering - OMNOVA SOLUTIONS INC; *pg.* 1176, *pg.* 1453
ECOSAFE - Battery - ENERSYS INC.; *pg.* 1334, *pg.* 1584
ECOSAVR - Pool Chemical Disposable Dispenser - FLEXIBLE

First page reference indicates Business Class Edition
Second page reference indicates Geographic Edition

SOLUTIONS INTERNATIONAL, INC.; *pg.* 1163, *pg.* 1913
ECOSMART - Catering Warmer - ALTO-SHAAM INC.; *pg.* 836, *pg.* 1869
ECOSMART - Technology - POWER INTEGRATIONS, INC.; *pg.* 1369, *pg.* 249
ECOSOFT - Solvent - THE DOW CHEMICAL COMPANY; *pg.* 1157, *pg.* 898
ECOSOFT - Recycled Towel & Tissue Products - WASAU PAPER CORP.; *pg.* 1471, *pg.* 1882
ECOSPRAY - Fitment - TRICORBRAUN; *pg.* 1471, *pg.* 1004
ECOSTAR - Power Converter - BALLARD POWER SYSTEMS, INC.; *pg.* 70, *pg.* 1907
ECOSTONE - Coaster - BROWN & BIGELOW, INC.; *pg.* 1624, *pg.* 959
ECOSTOR - Storage System - DOT HILL SYSTEMS CORP.; *pg.* 388, *pg.* 333
ECOSTYLE - Washing Machine - WHIRLPOOL CORPORATION; *pg.* 62, *pg.* 872
ECOSURE - Quality Assurance System - ECOLAB INC.; *pg.* 329, *pg.* 960
ECOSURF - Biodegradable Surfactants - THE DOW CHEMICAL COMPANY; *pg.* 1157, *pg.* 898
ECOTAINER - Packaging - INTERNATIONAL PAPER COMPANY; *pg.* 1460, *pg.* 1644
ECOTECT - Software - AUTODESK INC.; *pg.* 356, *pg.* 257
ECOTERIC - Surfactant - HUNTSMAN CORPORATION; *pg.* 1167, *pg.* 1758
ECOTONE - Pigment - ARCHER-DANIELS-MIDLAND COMPANY; *pg.* 825, *pg.* 565
ECOTRACE - Parallel Heating Cables - THERMON AMERICAS INC.; *pg.* 1077, *pg.* 1744
ECOTRITION - Pet Product - PETSMART, INC.; *pg.* 1481, *pg.* 18
ECOTRU - Disinfectant & Cleaner - CROSSTEX INTERNATIONAL INC.; *pg.* 1520, *pg.* 1164
ECOUSTIC - Musical Instrument - PEAVEY ELECTRONICS CORPORATION; *pg.* 662, *pg.* 970
ECOWORX - Manual - XEROX CORPORATION; *pg.* 494, *pg.* 365
ECOWORX DESIGN - Software - XEROX CORPORATION; *pg.* 494, *pg.* 365
ECP - Profiling System - WATERS CORPORATION; *pg.* 1436, *pg.* 834
ECROMIUM - Laminations - HAZEN PAPER COMPANY; *pg.* 1459, *pg.* 825
ECRU - Pillow - ETHAN ALLEN INTERIORS INC.; *pg.* 924, *pg.* 343
ECS - Automotive Refinish Coatings - PPG INDUSTRIES, INC.; *pg.* 1445, *pg.* 1579
ECSTASY - Personal Care Electronic Product - HELEN OF TROY L.P.; *pg.* 511, *pg.* 1692
ECSTASY - Mattress & Box Spring Sets - KINGSDOWN, INC.; *pg.* 932, *pg.* 1383
ECT - Database Generation System - EVANS & SUTHERLAND COMPUTER CORPORATION; *pg.* 638, *pg.* 1757
ECTIVA - Embolic Protection System - ABBOTT LABORATORIES; *pg.* 1484, *pg.* 551
ECUSTOMIZE - Software Tool - IRON MOUNTAIN INCORPORATED; *pg.* 421, *pg.* 796
ECWMS - Effects Wheel - REVOLUTION LIGHTING TECHNOLOGIES, INC.; *pg.* 1304, *pg.* 377
ECX-7700-XEN - Electronic Component - EMCORE CORPORATION; *pg.* 636, *pg.* 39
ECX-7700-XFP - Electronic Component - EMCORE CORPORATION; *pg.* 636, *pg.* 39
ED - Post Hole Diggers - AG-MEIER INDUSTRIES LLC; *pg.* 700, *pg.* 1668
ED, EDD 'N EDDY - Animated Series - THE CARTOON NETWORK; *pg.* 273, *pg.* 492
E.D. SMITH - Jams & Sauces - TREEHOUSE FOODS, INC.; *pg.* 901, *pg.* 649
ED-U-SCOPE - Microscope - UNITRON INC.; *pg.* 1433, *pg.* 1153
EDA/SQL - Data Access Products - INFORMATION BUILDERS INC.; *pg.* 415, *pg.* 1243
EDA TECH FORUM - Software System - MENTOR GRAPHICS CORPORATION; *pg.* 432, *pg.* 1510
EDACONNECT - Computer Software - CIMETRIX INCORPORATED; *pg.* 372, *pg.* 1756
EDAMAME - Maternity Spa - DESTINATION MATERNITY CORPORATION; *pg.* 23, *pg.* 1563
EDATA ENTRY - Software - ERESEARCH TECHNOLOGY INC.; *pg.* 1243, *pg.* 1564
EDATA MANAGEMENT - Software - ERESEARCH TECHNOLOGY INC.; *pg.* 1243, *pg.* 1564
EDD ELECTRO-DYNAMIC - Desalter - CAMERON INTERNATIONAL; *pg.* 1151, *pg.* 1702
EDDY - Clothing - ABERCROMBIE & FITCH CO.; *pg.* 37, *pg.* 1466
EDE - Generation, Transmission & Distribution of Electricity - THE EMPIRE DISTRICT ELECTRIC COMPANY; *pg.* 1941, *pg.* 980
EDELMANN - Power Steering Hoses; Automotive Fittings & Brake Lines - PLEWS/EDELMANN; *pg.* 215, *pg.* 607
EDEN - Footwear - COBIAN CORP.; *pg.* 1806, *pg.* 253
EDEN - Lace - HERITAGE LACE INC.; *pg.* 694, *pg.* 711
EDEN - Fabric - NEMSCHOFF, INC.; *pg.* 936, *pg.* 1890
EDEN - Musical Instrument - U.S. MUSIC CORPORATION; *pg.* 315, *pg.* 560
EDEN BIFA 15 - Food Supplement - EDEN FOODS INC.; *pg.* 1019, *pg.* 875
EDEN ORGANIC - Food Product - EDEN FOODS INC.; *pg.* 1019, *pg.* 875
EDEN RANCH - Food Supplement - EDEN FOODS INC.; *pg.* 1019, *pg.* 875
EDEN SPRINGS - Artesian Water - EDEN FOODS INC.; *pg.* 1019, *pg.* 875
EDENAIRE - Air Conditioning - NORTEK, INC.; *pg.* 100, *pg.* 1607
EDENBALANCE - Food Supplement - EDEN FOODS INC.; *pg.* 1019, *pg.* 875
EDENBLEND - Beverage - EDEN FOODS INC.; *pg.* 1019, *pg.* 875
EDENSOY - Beverage - EDEN FOODS INC.; *pg.* 1019, *pg.* 875
EDENTEC ASSURANCE - Monitor - CAS MEDICAL SYSTEMS, INC.; *pg.* 1513, *pg.* 339
EDENTREND - Software CAS MEDICAL SYSTEMS, INC.; *pg.* 1513, *pg.* 339
EDG - Electronic Components - MOLEX INCORPORATED; *pg.* 655, *pg.* 628
EDG-PREP - Tools - AGI-VR/WESSON INC; *pg.* 1041, *pg.* 415
EDGE - All Purpose Cleaning Preparation - ASHLAND INC.; *pg.* 972, *pg.* 726
EDGE - Cymbals - AVEDIS ZILDJIAN COMPANY; *pg.* 531, *pg.* 839
EDGE - Software Program - BEHLEN MFG. CO.; *pg.* 701, *pg.* 1010
EDGE - Hearing Device - BELTONE ELECTRONICS LLC; *pg.* 1503, *pg.* 614
EDGE - Flicker Noise Measurement System - CASCADE MICROTECH, INC.; *pg.* 1405, *pg.* 1492
EDGE - Bath Accessory - CROSCILL, INC.; *pg.* 1122, *pg.* 1220
EDGE - Shaving Products - EDGEWELL PERSONAL CARE; *pg.* 1526, *pg.* 995
EDGE - Switching Products - EXTREME NETWORKS INC; *pg* 287, *pg.* 245
EDGE - Crossover SUV - FORD MOTOR COMPANY; *pg.* 172, *pg.* 876
EDGE - Fluid Handling System - GRACO, INC.; *pg.* 1342, *pg.* 935
EDGE - Cryostat & Microtome - HACKER INSTRUMENTS & INDUSTRIES INC.; *pg.* 1415, *pg.* 1623
EDGE - Cutter - HOUGEN MANUFACTURING INC.; *pg.* 1347, *pg.* 908
EDGE - Interface Device - ITERIS, INC.; *pg.* 293, *pg.* 261
EDGE - Software System - MENTOR GRAPHICS CORPORATION; *pg.* 432, *pg.* 1510
THE EDGE - Servo Roll Feed - P/A INDUSTRIES, INC.; *pg.* 1367, *pg.* 339
THE EDGE - Ecofriendly Pan - POLAR WARE COMPANY; *pg.* 1129, *pg.* 1862
EDGE - On-Line Workforce Management System - SELECTREMEDY; *pg.* 468, *pg.* 263
EDGE - Semi Finished Product - STANBEE COMPANY, INC.; *pg.* 1819, *pg.* 1050
EDGE - Glazing System - SUPER SKY PRODUCTS, INC.; *pg.* 113, *pg.* 1871
THE EDGE - Grill - W.C. BRADLEY CO.; *pg.* 62, *pg.* 528
EDGE - Ladder Product - WERNER HOLDING CO.; *pg.* 121, *pg.* 1534
EDGE ALERT II - Workhorse Inspection System - PRESSCO TECHNOLOGY INC.; *pg.* 1370, *pg.* 1434
EDGE DEBUGGER - Software System - MENTOR GRAPHICS CORPORATION; *pg.* 432, *pg.* 1510
EDGE FACTORY - Computer Software Design - LOCKHEED MARTIN CORPORATION; *pg.* 229, *pg.* 762
EDGE FOAM - Packaging Product - PACTIV CORPORATION; *pg.* 1466, *pg.* 624
EDGE-FX - Software - F5 NETWORKS, INC.; *pg.* 396, *pg.* 1835
EDGE FX - Printer - GERBER SCIENTIFIC, INC.; *pg.* 1414, *pg.* 380
EDGE MAX - Glazing System - SUPER SKY PRODUCTS, INC.; *pg.* 113, *pg.* 1871
EDGE PROFILER - Software System - MENTOR GRAPHICS CORPORATION; *pg.* 432, *pg.* 1510
EDGE2X - Knife - BUCK KNIVES, INC.; *pg.* 1828, *pg.* 550
EDGECOMPUTING - Computer Applications - AKAMAI TECHNOLOGIES, INC.; *pg.* 1226, *pg.* 807
EDGECONTROL - Network Tools - AKAMAI TECHNOLOGIES, INC.; *pg.* 1226, *pg.* 807
EDGEGLO - Colorant - POLYONE CORPORATION; *pg.* 1177, *pg.* 1404
EDGEGUARD - Spreader - THE SCOTTS MIRACLE-GRO COMPANY; *pg.* 1799, *pg.* 1459
EDGELINE - Electronic Components - MOLEX INCORPORATED; *pg.* 655, *pg.* 628
EDGELOK - Apparel Interlining - HARODITE INDUSTRIES, INC.; *pg.* 693, *pg.* 847
EDGEMATE - Optical Product - UNIVERSAL PHOTONICS, INC.; *pg.* 1433, *pg.* 1167
EDGENET - Internet-Based Trading & Information Gathering System - FEDERATED INVESTORS, INC.; *pg.* 752, *pg.* 1575
EDGEPLATFORM - Network Tools - AKAMAI TECHNOLOGIES, INC.; *pg.* 1226, *pg.* 807
EDGEPORT - Computer Peripheral Equipment - DIGI INTERNATIONAL INC.; *pg.* 387, *pg.* 948
EDGESCAPE - Internet Marketing Tool - AKAMAI TECHNOLOGIES, INC.; *pg.* 1226, *pg.* 807
EDGESEAL - Glass Sealant - PPG INDUSTRIES, INC.; *pg.* 1445, *pg.* 1579
EDGESIGHT - Software - CITRIX SYSTEMS, INC.; *pg.* 375, *pg.* 424
EDGESUITE - Internet Tool - AKAMAI TECHNOLOGIES, INC.; *pg.* 1226, *pg.* 807
EDGETEK - Engineered Compound & Composite - POLYONE CORPORATION; *pg.* 1177, *pg.* 1404
EDGETEK XT - Polyester Compounds - POLYONE CORPORATION; *pg.* 1177, *pg.* 1404
EDGEUSB - Software - DIGI INTERNATIONAL INC.; *pg.* 387, *pg.* 948
EDGEWATER BEACH HOTEL & CLUB - Magazine - PALM BEACH MEDIA GROUP INC.; *pg.* 1674, *pg.* 457
EDGEWOOD - Bronze Grave Markers - MATTHEWS INTERNATIONAL CORPORATION; *pg.* 1662, *pg.* 1578
EDI CONVERSATION SERVICES - Software - INFOACCESS.NET LLC; *pg.* 1258, *pg.* 1456
EDI EXPRESS SM - Communication System - OPENTEXT GXS; *pg.* 1272, *pg.* 770
EDICIONES Y ESTUDIOS - Spanish Language Industry Publication - LEBHAR-FRIEDMAN INC.; *pg.* 1658, *pg.* 1250
EDICTIONARY - Software - ERESEARCH TECHNOLOGY INC.; *pg.* 1243, *pg.* 1564
EDIGEL - Wheat Starch - ARCHER-DANIELS-MIDLAND COMPANY; *pg.* 825, *pg.* 565
EDIN BURGUNDY - Nail Care Product - OPI PRODUCTS INC.; *pg.* 518, *pg.* 167
EDINBURGH UNIVERSITY PRESS - Publisher - COLUMBIA UNIVERSITY PRESS; *pg.* 1628, *pg.* 1216
EDIRECTORY - Software - NOVELL INC.; *pg.* 446, *pg.* 852
EDISCLOSE - Software - HEALTHPORT, INC.; *pg.* 403, *pg.* 484
EDIT ELITE - Video Editing Software Suite - STRYKER CORPORATION; *pg.* 1598, *pg.* 894
EDITH - Transaction Processing System - EVERI HOLDINGS INC.; *pg.* 749, *pg.* 1023
EDITION - Hotels - MARRIOTT INTERNATIONAL, INC.; *pg.* 1102, *pg.* 764
EDITOR & PUBLISHER - Trade Publication - THE NIELSEN COMPANY B.V.; *pg.* 1671, *pg.* 1272
EDKO 76 - Coconut Oil - ARCHER-DANIELS-MIDLAND COMPANY; *pg.* 825, *pg.* 565
EDL - Carbon Brake - UTC AEROSPACE SYSTEMS; *pg.* 236, *pg.* 1369
EDLP - Medical Equipment - INVACARE CORPORATION; *pg.* 1546, *pg.* 1451
EDM - Software - EMC CORPORATION; *pg.* 391, *pg.* 825
EDMUND - Scientific Equipment - EDMUND INDUSTRIAL OPTICS INC.; *pg.* 1411, *pg.* 1041

EDMUNDS AUTOOBSERVER - Automotive Information - EDMUNDS, INC.; *pg.* 1241, *pg.* 273
EDMUNDS CARSPACE - Automotive Information - EDMUNDS, INC.; *pg.* 1241, *pg.* 273
EDMUNDS DATA SERVICES - Data Services - EDMUNDS, INC.; *pg.* 1241, *pg.* 273
EDMUNDS INSIDE LINE - Automotive Information - EDMUNDS, INC.; *pg.* 1241, *pg.* 273
EDMUNDS.COM - Automotive Website - EDMUNDS, INC.; *pg.* 1241, *pg.* 273
EDNA - Lamp - ASHLEY FURNITURE INDUSTRIES, INC.; *pg.* 914, *pg.* 1852
EDNA - Flight Test System - BAE SYSTEMS-INFORMATION WARFARE; *pg.* 623, *pg.* 1036
EDNA'S PLACE - Nursing Care - SUNRISE SENIOR LIVING, INC.; *pg.* 1599, *pg.* 1795
EDNOTES - Medium Term Notes Program - SLM CORPORATION; *pg.* 804, *pg.* 388
EDOLIE - Lamp - ASHLEY FURNITURE INDUSTRIES, INC.; *pg.* 914, *pg.* 1852
E.DOT - Electric Gun - NORDSON CORPORATION; *pg.* 1365, *pg.* 1480
EDOX - Printing Products - ELECTRONICS FOR IMAGING, INC.; *pg.* 390, *pg.* 88
EDS - Electronic Display Systems - CHIEF INDUSTRIES, INC.; *pg.* 1323, *pg.* 1010
EDT - Software System - MENTOR GRAPHICS CORPORATION; *pg.* 432, *pg.* 1510
EDTN - Publisher - UNITED BUSINESS MEDIA LLC; *pg.* 1697, *pg.* 1177
EDTRAK - Human Resources Software - API HEALTHCARE CORP.; *pg.* 350, *pg.* 1860
EDUCARD - Education Services - DEVRY EDUCATION GROUP INC.; *pg.* 600, *pg.* 607
THE EDUCATION EDGE - Student Information Management Software - BLACKBAUD, INC.; *pg.* 361, *pg.* 1613
EDUCATION ESSENTIALS - Retail Store Catalog - SCHOOL SPECIALTY, INC.; *pg.* 467, *pg.* 1860
EDUCATION FOR REAL LIFE - Slogan - PROFESSIONAL EDUCATION INSTITUTE; *pg.* 457, *pg.* 561
EDUCATION LEADS US - Tagline - SLM CORPORATION; *pg.* 804, *pg.* 388
EDUCATION PLACE - Website - HOUGHTON MIFFLIN HARCOURT PUBLISHING COMPANY; *pg.* 1651, *pg.* 796
EDUCATION SALES PLUS - Sales Program Suite - RAINMAKER SYSTEMS INC.; *pg.* 458, *pg.* 58
EDUCATIONDEGREESOURCE.COM - Website for Higher Education Prospecting - LENDINGTREE, LLC; *pg.* 775, *pg.* 1367
EDUCATOR ADVANTAGE - Retirement Benefit Plan - HORACE MANN COMPANIES; *pg.* 1203, *pg.* 662
EDUCATORS EDGE - Manual - XEROX CORPORATION; *pg.* 494, *pg.* 365
EDUMATION - Magazine And Newsletter - SAS INSTITUTE INC.; *pg.* 466, *pg.* 1361
EDUPASS - Software - SAS INSTITUTE INC.; *pg.* 466, *pg.* 1361
EDUSOFT - Web-Based Assessment - HOUGHTON MIFFLIN HARCOURT PUBLISHING COMPANY; *pg.* 1651, *pg.* 796
EDUSPACE - Course Management Tool - HOUGHTON MIFFLIN HARCOURT PUBLISHING COMPANY; *pg.* 1651, *pg.* 796
EDUTRADES - Education Group - TIGRENT INC.; *pg.* 608, *pg.* 415
EDWARD - Furniture - AMISCO INDUSTRIES LTD.; *pg.* 913, *pg.* 1958
EDWARD - Valve - FLOWSERVE CORPORATION; *pg.* 82, *pg.* 1719
EDWARD DON - Food Service Equipment, Furnishings & Supplies - EDWARD DON & COMPANY; *pg.* 54, *pg.* 672
EDWARD G. ROBINSON - Pipe Tobaccos - ALTADIS USA, INC.; *pg.* 1893, *pg.* 423
EDWARDIAN - Fan - WESTINGHOUSE LIGHTING CORPORATION; *pg.* 687, *pg.* 1571
EDWARD'S - Frozen Desserts - THE SCHWAN FOOD COMPANY; *pg.* 894, *pg.* 928
EDWIN - Furniture - AMISCO INDUSTRIES LTD.; *pg.* 913, *pg.* 1958
EDWINA - Lamp - ASHLEY FURNITURE INDUSTRIES, INC.; *pg.* 914, *pg.* 1852
EDWIN'S - Fabric - SCALAMANDRE, INC.; *pg.* 941, *pg.* 1058
EDX-P - Packet Switching Systems - SIEMENS CORPORATION; *pg.* 803, *pg.* 1291
EDY'S - Ice Cream - DREYER'S GRAND ICE CREAM HOLDINGS, INC.; *pg.* 1852, *pg.* 171
EDY'S - Ice Cream - NESTLE USA, INC.; *pg.* 883, *pg.* 96
EE-MAIL - Software - MAXIM INTEGRATED PRODUCTS, INC.; *pg.* 653, *pg.* 247
EE TIMES - Newspaper - UNITED BUSINESS MEDIA LLC; *pg.* 1697, *pg.* 1177
EE-ZEE ADE - Imitation Fruit-Like Drinks - GOLD MEDAL PRODUCTS CO.; *pg.* 55, *pg.* 1414
EE-ZEE SNO-KONE CONCENTRATE - Premeasured Concentrate - GOLD MEDAL PRODUCTS CO.; *pg.* 55, *pg.* 1414
EECO - Switch - TRANSICO INCORPORATED; *pg.* 682, *pg.* 49
EECO KEYPAD - Switch - TRANSICO INCORPORATED; *pg.* 682, *pg.* 49
EECO SWITCH - Switch - TRANSICO INCORPORATED; *pg.* 682, *pg.* 49
EELCAM - Pipeline Inspection Systems - ELECTRIC EEL MANUFACTURING CO., INC.; *pg.* 80, *pg.* 1473
EEZ-THRU - Dental Floss - SUNSTAR AMERICAS INC.; *pg.* 1599, *pg.* 591
EEZE OFF - Waffle Mold - GOLD MEDAL PRODUCTS CO.; *pg.* 55, *pg.* 1414
EEZEE-GRIP - Digital Sensor Holder - DENTSPLY INTERNATIONAL INC.; *pg.* 1522, *pg.* 1596
EF-1 - Nailcare Product - MEDICOOL, INC.; *pg.* 1562, *pg.* 294
EFAPROXYN - Biopharmaceutical Product - ALLOS THERAPEUTICS, INC.; *pg.* 1492, *pg.* 336
EFAS - Healthcare Product - SWANSON HEALTH PRODUCTS INC.; *pg.* 1600, *pg.* 1397
EFAX - Communication Product - J2 GLOBAL COMMUNICATIONS, INC.; *pg.* 1260, *pg.* 133
EFAX BROADCAST - Communication Product - J2 GLOBAL COMMUNICATIONS, INC.; *pg.* 1260, *pg.* 133
EFAX CORPORATE - Communication Product - J2 GLOBAL COMMUNICATIONS, INC.; *pg.* 1260, *pg.* 133
EFAX FREE - Fax Messaging Solution - J2 GLOBAL COMMUNICATIONS, INC.; *pg.* 1260, *pg.* 133
EFAX MESSANGER - Communication Product - J2 GLOBAL COMMUNICATIONS, INC.; *pg.* 1260, *pg.* 133
EFEEL - Software - IMMERSION CORPORATION; *pg.* 413, *pg.* 246
EFF-STOP - Acrylic Masonry Primer/Sealer - DUNN-EDWARDS CORPORATION; *pg.* 1442, *pg.* 129
EFFECTIONS - Chemical Product - THE DOW CHEMICAL COMPANY; *pg.* 1157, *pg.* 898
EFFECTONE - Undercoater - JONES-BLAIR COMPANY; *pg.* 1443, *pg.* 1682
EFFEN VODKA - Vodka - JIM BEAM BRANDS CO.; *pg.* 1965, *pg.* 601
EFFER-C - Nutritional Product - NOW HEALTH GROUP, INC.; *pg.* 1576, *pg.* 557
EFFERDENT - Denture Cleanser - MCNEIL-PPC, INC.; *pg.* 1560, *pg.* 1533
EFFERGRIP - Denture Adhesive - MCNEIL-PPC, INC.; *pg.* 1560, *pg.* 1533
EFFERVESCENCE - Tile - ARTISTIC TILE INC.; *pg.* 914, *pg.* 1119
EFFERVESCENCE - Bedding - CROSCILL, INC.; *pg.* 1122, *pg.* 1220
EFFERZYME - Cleaning Solution - CROSSTEX INTERNATIONAL INC.; *pg.* 1520, *pg.* 1164
EFFEXOR - Anti-Depressant - PFIZER INC.; *pg.* 1581, *pg.* 1278
EFFEXOR XR - Pharmaceutical Product - IMPAX LABORATORIES, INC.; *pg.* 1544, *pg.* 101
EFFEXOR XR - Anti-Depressant - PFIZER INC.; *pg.* 1581, *pg.* 1278
EFFICIENCY - Kitchen Product - KOHLER CO.; *pg.* 91, *pg.* 1862
EFFICIENCY - Water Heater - LOCHINVAR CORPORATION; *pg.* 1073, *pg.* 1640
EFFICIENCY + - Residential & Light Commercial Water Heaters & Boilers - LOCHINVAR CORPORATION; *pg.* 1073, *pg.* 1640
EFFICIENCY-PAC - Water Heater - LOCHINVAR CORPORATION; *pg.* 1073, *pg.* 1640
EFFICIENCY THROUGH TECHNOLOGY - Tagline - IXYS CORPORATION; *pg.* 422, *pg.* 146
EFFICIENCYMAPE - Software - GE ENERGY; *pg.* 1338, *pg.* 506
EFFICIENT FIBER OPTICS - Fiber Optic Lighting System - ENERGY FOCUS, INC.; *pg.* 1411, *pg.* 1472
EFFIPURE - Stool DNA Test - EXACT SCIENCES CORPORATION; *pg.* 1529, *pg.* 1865
EFG - Glazing Systems - PPG INDUSTRIES, INC.; *pg.* 1445, *pg.* 1579
EFINANCIALCAREERS - Recruiting & Career Development Website - DHI GROUP, INC.; *pg.* 1238, *pg.* 1223
EFLEX - Software - BIO-RAD LABORATORIES, INC.; *pg.* 1504, *pg.* 101
EFO-ICE - Fiber Optic Lighting System - ENERGY FOCUS, INC.; *pg.* 1411, *pg.* 1472
EFS - Extruded Flexible Sheet Heat Transfer Cement - THERMON AMERICAS INC.; *pg.* 1077, *pg.* 1744
EFT SERVER - Software - GLOBALSCAPE INC.; *pg.* 401, *pg.* 1740
EFUDEX - Treatment for Skin Cancer - VALEANT PHARMACEUTICALS INTERNATIONAL; *pg.* 1605, *pg.* 1047
EFX - Elliptical Fitness Crosstrainers - PRECOR, INC.; *pg.* 1843, *pg.* 1847
EGAIN ADMINISTRATOR - Processing Services - EGAIN COMMUNICATIONS CORPORATION; *pg.* 1242, *pg.* 284
EGAIN ADVISOR - Knowledge Management Product - EGAIN COMMUNICATIONS CORPORATION; *pg.* 1242, *pg.* 284
EGAIN AUTOCLASSIFY - Platform - EGAIN COMMUNICATIONS CORPORATION; *pg.* 1242, *pg.* 284
EGAIN AUTOWORKFLOW - Platform Services - EGAIN COMMUNICATIONS CORPORATION; *pg.* 1242, *pg.* 284
EGAIN CALL TRACK - Call Tracking Software - EGAIN COMMUNICATIONS CORPORATION; *pg.* 1242, *pg.* 284
EGAIN CAMPAIGN - Software - EGAIN COMMUNICATIONS CORPORATION; *pg.* 1242, *pg.* 284
EGAIN CASEBASE - Data Services - EGAIN COMMUNICATIONS CORPORATION; *pg.* 1242, *pg.* 284
EGAIN CHAT - Chat Assistance to Website Visitors - EGAIN COMMUNICATIONS CORPORATION; *pg.* 1242, *pg.* 284
EGAIN CHATBOT - Web Self-Service Product - EGAIN COMMUNICATIONS CORPORATION; *pg.* 1242, *pg.* 284
EGAIN CIH - Platform Services - EGAIN COMMUNICATIONS CORPORATION; *pg.* 1242, *pg.* 284
EGAIN COBROWSE - Software - EGAIN COMMUNICATIONS CORPORATION; *pg.* 1242, *pg.* 284
EGAIN CONSOLES - Processing Services - EGAIN COMMUNICATIONS CORPORATION; *pg.* 1242, *pg.* 284
EGAIN CTI ADAPTER - Platform Services - EGAIN COMMUNICATIONS CORPORATION; *pg.* 1242, *pg.* 284
EGAIN CUSTOMERS - Data Services - EGAIN COMMUNICATIONS CORPORATION; *pg.* 1242, *pg.* 284
EGAIN DASHBOARD - Analytic Service - EGAIN COMMUNICATIONS CORPORATION; *pg.* 1242, *pg.* 284
EGAIN EMAIL ADAPTER - Platform Services - EGAIN COMMUNICATIONS CORPORATION; *pg.* 1242, *pg.* 284
EGAIN FAX - Software - EGAIN COMMUNICATIONS CORPORATION; *pg.* 1242, *pg.* 284
EGAIN INFERENCE ENGINE - Processing Services - EGAIN COMMUNICATIONS CORPORATION; *pg.* 1242, *pg.* 284
EGAIN INFORM - Web FAQ Self-Service - EGAIN COMMUNICATIONS CORPORATION; *pg.* 1242, *pg.* 284
EGAIN INTERACTIONS - Data Services - EGAIN COMMUNICATIONS CORPORATION; *pg.* 1242, *pg.* 284
EGAIN IVR - Phone Self Services - EGAIN COMMUNICATIONS CORPORATION; *pg.* 1242, *pg.* 284
EGAIN KNOWLEDGEAGENT - Software - EGAIN COMMUNICATIONS CORPORATION; *pg.* 1242, *pg.* 284
EGAIN KNOWLEDGEBASE - Data Services - EGAIN COMMUNICATIONS CORPORATION; *pg.* 1242, *pg.* 284
EGAIN LIVE - Software - EGAIN COMMUNICATIONS CORPORATION; *pg.* 1242, *pg.* 284
EGAIN LIVEWEB - Software - EGAIN COMMUNICATIONS CORPORATION; *pg.* 1242, *pg.* 284
EGAIN MAIL - Software - EGAIN COMMUNICATIONS CORPORATION; *pg.* 1242, *pg.* 284
EGAIN MESSAGE CENTER - Web Self-Service Product - EGAIN COMMUNICATIONS CORPORATION; *pg.* 1242, *pg.* 284
EGAIN MONITOR - Analytic Service - EGAIN COMMUNICATIONS CORPORATION; *pg.* 1242, *pg.* 284
EGAIN NOTIFY - Platform Services - EGAIN COMMUNICATIONS CORPORATION; *pg.* 1242, *pg.* 284
EGAIN ON-DEMAND - Software - EGAIN COMMUNICATIONS CORPORATION; *pg.* 1242, *pg.* 284
EGAIN REPORTS - Analytic Service - EGAIN COMMUNICATIONS CORPORATION; *pg.* 1242, *pg.* 284
EGAIN SECURE MAIL - Software - EGAIN COMMUNICATIONS CORPORATION; *pg.* 1242, *pg.* 284
EGAIN SELF SERVICE - Software - EGAIN COMMUNICATIONS CORPORATION; *pg.* 1242, *pg.* 284
EGAIN SERVICE - Software - EGAIN COMMUNICATIONS

First page reference indicates Business Class Edition
Second page reference indicates Geographic Edition

CORPORATION; *pg.* 1242, *pg.* 284
EGAIN SERVICEEXPRESS - Software - EGAIN COMMUNICATIONS CORPORATION; *pg.* 1242, *pg.* 284
EGAIN SME - Knowledge Management Product - EGAIN COMMUNICATIONS CORPORATION; *pg.* 1242, *pg.* 284
EGAIN SMS - SMS Customer Interaction System - EGAIN COMMUNICATIONS CORPORATION; *pg.* 1242, *pg.* 284
EGAIN SURVEY - Platform Services - EGAIN COMMUNICATIONS CORPORATION; *pg.* 1242, *pg.* 284
EGAIN USERS - Data Services - EGAIN COMMUNICATIONS CORPORATION; *pg.* 1242, *pg.* 284
EGAIN WEBFORMS - Software - EGAIN COMMUNICATIONS CORPORATION; *pg.* 1242, *pg.* 284
EGAIN WORKFLOW ENGINE - Processing Services - EGAIN COMMUNICATIONS CORPORATION; *pg.* 1242, *pg.* 284
EGAIN WORKFLOWS - Data Services - EGAIN COMMUNICATIONS CORPORATION; *pg.* 1242, *pg.* 284
EGCG BOOST - Nutritional Product - NUTRACEUTICAL INTERNATIONAL CORPORATION; *pg.* 1576, *pg.* 1753
EGENCIA - Travel Information - EXPEDIA, INC.; *pg.* 1244, *pg.* 1814
EGERMEIER'S - Bible Story Book - WARNER PRESS, INC.; *pg.* 1701, *pg.* 673
EGG BEATERS - Food Product - CONAGRA FOODS, INC.; *pg.* 826, *pg.* 1014
EGG INDUSTRY - Global Magazine for Egg Producers - WATT PUBLISHING COMPANY; *pg.* 1701, *pg.* 655
EGG-LAND'S BEST - Eggs - CAL-MAINE FOODS, INC.; *pg.* 843, *pg.* 969
EGG MCMUFFIN - Sandwich - MCDONALD'S CORPORATION; *pg.* 1737, *pg.* 645
EGG ROLE - Shoe - AEROGROUP INTERNATIONAL, INC.; *pg.* 1803, *pg.* 1055
EGGBEATER - Bladed PDC - BAKER HUGHES INTEQ; *pg.* 1316, *pg.* 1700
EGGBERT - Candy - R.M. PALMER COMPANY; *pg.* 1861, *pg.* 1585
EGGGENIE - Cookware - HABAND COMPANY, INC.; *pg.* 1772, *pg.* 1099
EGGLAND'S BEST - Eggs - EGGLAND'S BEST, INC.; *pg.* 854, *pg.* 1542
EGGO - Food Product - KELLOGG COMPANY; *pg.* 831, *pg.* 870
EGGO APPLE CINNAMON WAFFLES - Snacks - KELLOGG COMPANY; *pg.* 831, *pg.* 870
EGGO BANANA BREAD WAFFLES - Snacks - KELLOGG COMPANY; *pg.* 831, *pg.* 870
EGGO BUTTERMILK PANCAKES - Snacks - KELLOGG COMPANY; *pg.* 831, *pg.* 870
EGGO NUTRI-GRAIN WHOLE GRAIN WAFFLES - Snacks - KELLOGG COMPANY; *pg.* 831, *pg.* 870
EGGO NUTRI-GRAIN WHOLE WHEAT WAFFLES - Snacks - KELLOGG COMPANY; *pg.* 831, *pg.* 870
EGGO SPECIAL K WAFFLES - Snacks - KELLOGG COMPANY; *pg.* 831, *pg.* 870
EGGO TOASTER SWIRLZ - Food Product - KELLOGG COMPANY; *pg.* 831, *pg.* 870
EGGREP PRO - Food Product - LEPRINO FOODS COMPANY; *pg.* 874, *pg.* 320
EGGSPLUS - Table Eggs - PILGRIM'S PRIDE CORPORATION; *pg.* 889, *pg.* 330
EGGXPERT - Online Community - NEWEGG INC.; *pg.* 1271, *pg.* 67
EGIL - Breaker Analyzer - GE ENERGY; *pg.* 1338, *pg.* 506
EGO - Wireless Product - TRANSCORE HOLDINGS INC.; *pg.* 485, *pg.* 1541
EGOPARKS - Publication - NATIONAL PARK FOUNDATION; *pg.* 1000, *pg.* 402
EGOTASTIC - News & Gossip Site - SPINMEDIA; *pg.* 1282, *pg.* 104
EGOVERNMENT - Software - THOMSON REUTERS TAX & ACCOUNTING; *pg.* 484, *pg.* 905
EGRAMS - Software - HTC GLOBAL SERVICES INC.; *pg.* 409, *pg.* 911
EGUIDE - Computer Operations - NOVELL INC.; *pg.* 446, *pg.* 852
EGYPT - Game - WMS INDUSTRIES INC.; *pg.* 593, *pg.* 666
EGYPTIAN - Linens Fabrics - TEMPUR SEALY INTERNATIONAL, INC.; *pg.* 944, *pg.* 731
EGYPTIAN HENNA - Beauty Product - AMERICAN INTERNATIONAL INDUSTRIES COMPANY; *pg.* 498, *pg.* 126
EGYPTIAN RICHES - Game - WMS INDUSTRIES INC.; *pg.* 593, *pg.* 666
EH 3C - Paper Drill - THE CHALLENGE MACHINERY COMPANY; *pg.* 1322, *pg.* 902
EHCM - Electronic Human Capital Management - THE JUDGE GROUP, INC.; *pg.* 424, *pg.* 1594
EHEALTH EDUCATION - Software - ERESEARCH TECHNOLOGY INC.; *pg.* 1243, *pg.* 1564
EHOB WAFFLE - Mattress Overlay - ALIMED, INC.; *pg.* 1490, *pg.* 816
EHSD - Connector - AMPHENOL CORPORATION; *pg.* 616, *pg.* 381
EIBD - Online Newspaper - INVESTORS BUSINESS DAILY, INC.; *pg.* 1653, *pg.* 133
EICU - Remote Monitoring Interface - SENTARA HEALTHCARE; *pg.* 1593, *pg.* 1797
EID PRODUCTS - Electronic Identification Devices for Cattle - MIDWEST MICROSYSTEMS, LLC; *pg.* 1267, *pg.* 1012
EIFFEL TOWER - French Restaurant - LETTUCE ENTERTAIN YOU ENTERPRISES, INC.; *pg.* 1735, *pg.* 580
EIGHT AT THE PLATE - Trademark (Div. I Baseball) - NATIONAL COLLEGIATE ATHLETIC ASSOCIATION; *pg.* 567, *pg.* 688
EIGHT HOUR CREAM - Skin Care Products - ELIZABETH ARDEN, INC.; *pg.* 507, *pg.* 448
EIGHT O'CLOCK - Soft Drink - THE COCA-COLA COMPANY; *pg.* 240, *pg.* 493
EIGHT O'CLOCK - Coffee - EIGHT O'CLOCK COFFEE; *pg.* 250, *pg.* 1086
EIGHT O'CLOCK FUNCHUM - Beverages - THE COCA-COLA COMPANY; *pg.* 240, *pg.* 493
EILEEN WEST - Apparel - SAN FRANCISCO MERCANTILE COMPANY, INC.; *pg.* 32, *pg.* 227
EILIS - Lamp - ASHLEY FURNITURE INDUSTRIES, INC.; *pg.* 914, *pg.* 1852
EINPUT - Software - EMC CORPORATION; *pg.* 391, *pg.* 825
EINSTEIN BROS - Bakery Product - EINSTEIN NOAH RESTAURANT GROUP, INC.; *pg.* 1019, *pg.* 332
EIRE - Forging Product - SUPERIOR DIE SET CORP.; *pg.* 1379, *pg.* 1885
EIRENE - Lamp.- ASHLEY FURNITURE INDUSTRIES, INC.; *pg.* 914, *pg.* 1852
EISTREAM - Software - OPENTEXT; *pg.* 450, *pg.* 1665
EITD - Trade Directory - ADVANTAGE BUSINESS MEDIA; *pg.* 1613, *pg.* 1116
EIUS - Medical Product - STRYKER CORPORATION; *pg.* 1598, *pg.* 894
EJA - Tensile Tester - THWING-ALBERT INSTRUMENT COMPANY; *pg.* 1432, *pg.* 1131
EK - Particle Board Blenders - LITTLEFORD DAY INC.; *pg.* 1356, *pg.* 728
EK-10 - Electrocardiograph - CARDIAC SCIENCE CORPORATION; *pg.* 1512, *pg.* 1897
EK-AWAY - Molecular Biology Product - THERMO FISHER SCIENTIFIC INC.; *pg.* 1602, *pg.* 61
E.K. CAMPBELL - Heaters - THOMAS & BETTS CORPORATION; *pg.* 680, *pg.* 1646
EKEY - Video Game - INTERNATIONAL GAME TECHNOLOGY; *pg.* 957, *pg.* 1024
EKMAX - Molecular Biology Product - THERMO FISHER SCIENTIFIC INC.; *pg.* 1602, *pg.* 61
EKTACHROME - Film - EASTMAN KODAK COMPANY; *pg.* 1408, *pg.* 1333
EKTACHROME-X - Color Photographic Film - EASTMAN KODAK COMPANY; *pg.* 1408, *pg.* 1333
EKTACOLOR - Color Photo Film, Paper, Apparatus & Chemicals - EASTMAN KODAK COMPANY; *pg.* 1408, *pg.* 1333
EKTAFICHE - Microfilm Duplicator - EASTMAN KODAK COMPANY; *pg.* 1408, *pg.* 1333
EKTAFLO - Photo Processing Chemicals - EASTMAN KODAK COMPANY; *pg.* 1408, *pg.* 1333
EKTAGRAPHIC - Motion Picture, Slide Projectors & Other Audiovisual Apparatus - EASTMAN KODAK COMPANY; *pg.* 1408, *pg.* 1333
EKTALITH - Copying Equipment, Photo Paper, Copy Paper Chemicals - EASTMAN KODAK COMPANY; *pg.* 1408, *pg.* 1333
EKTALURE - Photo Paper - EASTMAN KODAK COMPANY; *pg.* 1408, *pg.* 1333
EKTALUX - Light Filters - EASTMAN KODAK COMPANY; *pg.* 1408, *pg.* 1333
EKTAMARK - Photographic Film & Chemicals - EASTMAN KODAK COMPANY; *pg.* 1408, *pg.* 1333
EKTAMAT - Radiographic Film - EASTMAN KODAK COMPANY; *pg.* 1408, *pg.* 1333
EKTAMATE - Photo Paper, Lenses, Microfilm Equipment - EASTMAN KODAK COMPANY; *pg.* 1408, *pg.* 1333
EKTAMATIC - Photo Paper & Chemicals, Processing Apparatus - EASTMAN KODAK COMPANY; *pg.* 1408, *pg.* 1333
EKTAMITE - Flash Lighting Apparatus - EASTMAN KODAK COMPANY; *pg.* 1408, *pg.* 1333
EKTANAR - Photo Lenses - EASTMAN KODAK COMPANY; *pg.* 1408, *pg.* 1333
EKTANON - Photo Lenses - EASTMAN KODAK COMPANY; *pg.* 1408, *pg.* 1333
EKTAPAN - Photo Film - EASTMAN KODAK COMPANY; *pg.* 1408, *pg.* 1333
EKTAPRESS - Photographic Film - EASTMAN KODAK COMPANY; *pg.* 1408, *pg.* 1333
EKTAPRINT - Xerographic Copier - EASTMAN KODAK COMPANY; *pg.* 1408, *pg.* 1333
EKTAPRO - Cassettes, Lenses, Motion Analyzers, Processors, Slide Projectors - EASTMAN KODAK COMPANY; *pg.* 1408, *pg.* 1333
EKTAR - Synthetic Resins, Photographic Lenses & Film - EASTMAN KODAK COMPANY; *pg.* 1408, *pg.* 1333
EKTASCAN - Imaging Scanning Equipment, Film & Software - EASTMAN KODAK COMPANY; *pg.* 1408, *pg.* 1333
EKTASPEED - X-ray Film - EASTMAN KODAK COMPANY; *pg.* 1408, *pg.* 1333
EKTATHERM - Video Print Cartridges, Paper, Etc. - EASTMAN KODAK COMPANY; *pg.* 1408, *pg.* 1333
EKTAVISION - Film - EASTMAN KODAK COMPANY; *pg.* 1408, *pg.* 1333
EKTAVOLT - Photographic Film & Chemicals - EASTMAN KODAK COMPANY; *pg.* 1408, *pg.* 1333
EKTAWRITE - Film Folios - EASTMAN KODAK COMPANY; *pg.* 1408, *pg.* 1333
EKTON - Photo Lenses - EASTMAN KODAK COMPANY; *pg.* 1408, *pg.* 1333
EKTONOL - Photo Developer - EASTMAN KODAK COMPANY; *pg.* 1408, *pg.* 1333
EKTRA - Cameras - EASTMAN KODAK COMPANY; *pg.* 1408, *pg.* 1333
EKTRALITE - Cameras - EASTMAN KODAK COMPANY; *pg.* 1408, *pg.* 1333
EL AL ISRAEL AIRLINES - Airline Service Company - EL AL ISRAEL AIRLINES, LTD.; *pg.* 1906, *pg.* 1226
EL APOSENTO ALTO - Daily Devotional Guide in Spanish - THE UPPER ROOM; *pg.* 1698, *pg.* 1655
EL AUTOBUS MAGICO - Educational Materials - SCHOLASTIC INC.; *pg.* 1683, *pg.* 1288
EL CAPITAN - Acoustic Bass Guitars - GIBSON GUITAR CORP.; *pg.* 550, *pg.* 1650
EL CHARRO - Tequila - MCCORMICK DISTILLING CO., INC.; *pg.* 1966, *pg.* 1007
EL CID BRAZILIAN - Premium Cigars - ALTADIS USA, INC.; *pg.* 1893, *pg.* 423
EL CONDOR - Tequila - MONTEBELLO BRANDS INC.; *pg.* 1967, *pg.* 758
EL CONQUISTADOR - Tequila - HEAVEN HILL DISTILLERIES, INC.; *pg.* 1964, *pg.* 725
EL DORADO - Area Rugs - COURISTAN INC.; *pg.* 921, *pg.* 1067
EL DORADO GOLD RESERVE - Premium Cigars - ALTADIS USA, INC.; *pg.* 1893, *pg.* 423
EL GUAPO - Food Product - MCCORMICK & COMPANY, INCORPORATED; *pg.* 1027, *pg.* 779
EL-ISE - Testing Instrument System - BECKMAN COULTER, INC.; *pg.* 1402, *pg.* 48
EL JIMADOR - Tequila - BROWN-FORMAN CORPORATION; *pg.* 1958, *pg.* 732
EL MERO MERO DRYWALERO - Entertainment Services - USG CORPORATION; *pg.* 118, *pg.* 594
EL MONTEREY - Frozen Mexican Food - RUIZ FOOD PRODUCTS, INC.; *pg.* 893, *pg.* 77
EL NACHO GRANDE - Snacks - GOLD MEDAL PRODUCTS CO.; *pg.* 55, *pg.* 1414
EL NUEVO HERALD - Newspaper - THE MIAMI HERALD; *pg.* 1665, *pg.* 444
EL PASO CANTINA - Mexican Restaurants - REAL MEX RESTAURANTS, INC.; *pg.* 1746, *pg.* 75
EL PICO - Removers - W.M. BARR & COMPANY, INC.; *pg.* 338, *pg.* 1647
EL POLLO LOCO - Restaurants - EL POLLO LOCO, INC.; *pg.* 1728, *pg.* 70
EL PORTO - Footwear - VANS, INC.; *pg.* 1821, *pg.* 76
EL PRODUCTO - Domestic Cigars - ALTADIS USA, INC.; *pg.* 1893, *pg.* 423
EL PUESTO DE PEDRO - Food Product - ADVANCEPIERRE

FOODS, INC.; pg. 1714, pg. 1409
EL RAYEK - Beverages - THE COCA-COLA COMPANY; pg. 240, pg. 493
EL RIO GRANDE - Restaurant - ARK RESTAURANTS CORP.; pg. 1715, pg. 1196
EL SOL - Educational Materials - SCHOLASTIC INC.; pg. 1683, pg. 1288
EL TESORO DE DON FELIPE - Tequila - JIM BEAM BRANDS CO.; pg. 1965, pg. 601
EL TIEMPO LATINO - Weekly Newspaper - GRAHAM HOLDINGS COMPANY; pg. 1645, pg. 1773
EL TORITO - Mexican Food Products - HORMEL FOODS CORPORATION; pg. 863, pg. 915
EL TORITO - Mexican Restaurants - REAL MEX RESTAURANTS, INC.; pg. 1746, pg. 75
EL TORITO GRILL - Mexican Restaurants - REAL MEX RESTAURANTS, INC.; pg. 1746, pg. 75
EL TORO - Video Game - INTERNATIONAL GAME TECHNOLOGY; pg. 957, pg. 1024
EL TRELLIS - Cigars - SWISHER INTERNATIONAL, INC.; pg. 1895, pg. 345
EL ZOL 95.7 FM - Radio Station - SPANISH BROADCASTING SYSTEM INC.; pg. 310, pg. 446
ELA - Footwear - STEVEN MADDEN, LTD.; pg. 1819, pg. 1176
ELAB - Software - WATERS CORPORATION; pg. 1436, pg. 834
ELABCORP - Software - LABORATORY CORPORATION OF AMERICA HOLDINGS; pg. 1554, pg. 1359
ELABNOTEBOOK - Testing Instrument System - BECKMAN COULTER, INC.; pg. 1402, pg. 48
ELAINE - Lamp - ASHLEY FURNITURE INDUSTRIES, INC.; pg. 914, pg. 1852
ELAN - Ethernet Driver - ADVANCED MICRO DEVICES, INC.; pg. 613, pg. 282
ELAN - Lamp - ASHLEY FURNITURE INDUSTRIES, INC.; pg. 914, pg. 1852
ELAN - Polycarbonate Pitchers - CARLISLE FOODSERVICE PRODUCTS INCORPORATED; pg. 1455, pg. 1485
ELAN - Fabric - NEMSCHOFF, INC.; pg. 936, pg. 1890
ELAN - Inorganic Analyser - NORDION INC.; pg. 1573, pg. 1932
ELAN - ICP Spectrometer - PERKINELMER, INC.; pg. 1426, pg. 853
ELAN SERIES - Medical Equipment - INVACARE CORPORATION; pg. 1546, pg. 1451
ELAN VITAL - Vitamin & Herbal Supplement - SOURCE NATURALS; pg. 1595, pg. 278
ELANCE - Bikini - JOCKEY INTERNATIONAL, INC.; pg. 27, pg. 1861
ELANNIE - Footwear - STEVEN MADDEN, LTD.; pg. 1819, pg. 1176
ELANPLUS - Analysis Program - SCHLUMBERGER LIMITED; pg. 801, pg. 1714
ELANTEC - Semiconductor - INTERSIL CORPORATION; pg. 647, pg. 146
ELANTRA - Automobile - HYUNDAI MOTOR AMERICA; pg. 179, pg. 89
ELAPRIN - Biopharmaceutical Product - EMISPHERE TECHNOLOGIES, INC.; pg. 1528, pg. 1118
ELAPSE - Fabric - NEMSCHOFF, INC.; pg. 936, pg. 1890
ELARA - Bath & Plumbing Product - JACUZZI BRANDS CORPORATION; pg. 554, pg. 65
ELAST - Amplification System - PERKINELMER, INC.; pg. 1426, pg. 853
ELASTAKOTE - Paint Product - KELLY-MOORE PAINT COMPANY, INC.; pg. 1443, pg. 198
ELASTAMAX - Thermoplastic Elastomer Compound - POLYONE CORPORATION; pg. 1177, pg. 1404
ELASTENE - Polymer - DOW CHEMICAL; pg. 1156, pg. 1563
ELASTENE - Acrylics - THE DOW CHEMICAL COMPANY; pg. 1157, pg. 898
ELASTI TAG - Vegetable Tags - BEDFORD INDUSTRIES, INC.; pg. 1453, pg. 967
ELASTIC CLASSIC - Footwear - K-SWISS; pg. 1837, pg. 306
ELASTIMIDE - Lens - STAAR SURGICAL COMPANY; pg. 1597, pg. 151
ELASTIMOLD - Fuse - THOMAS & BETTS CORPORATION; pg. 680, pg. 1646
ELASTITAG - Twist Tie Closure - BEDFORD INDUSTRIES, INC.; pg. 1453, pg. 967
ELASTIVE - Bandage - DERMA SCIENCES, INC.; pg. 1523, pg. 1111
ELASTO-GEL - Medical & Aesthetic Product - DYNATRONICS CORPORATION; pg. 1526, pg. 1757
ELASTO-PREENE - Ankle Support - BECTON, DICKINSON & COMPANY; pg. 1501, pg. 1068
ELASTOMAG - Salt - DOW CHEMICAL; pg. 1156, pg. 1563
ELASTOMER KEYPADS - Switch - TRANSICO INCORPORATED; pg. 682, pg. 49
ELASTOMERIC TECHNOLOGIES - Electronic Component Product - TE CONNECTIVITY LTD.; pg. 677, pg. 1515
ELASTOMULL - Medical & Aesthetic Product - DYNATRONICS CORPORATION; pg. 1526, pg. 1757
ELASTOPATCH - Repair Product - DAP PRODUCTS, INC.; pg. 1441, pg. 756
ELASTOREZ - Chemical Product - WESTROCK COMPANY; pg. 1472, pg. 1805
ELASTOTHANE - Synthetic Polymer - AMERITYRE CORPORATION; pg. 1879, pg. 1021
ELATIONS - Glucosamine & Chondroitin Supplement - SUNNY DELIGHT BEVERAGES CO.; pg. 899, pg. 1426
ELAVIA - Software - BIO-RAD LABORATORIES, INC.; pg. 1504, pg. 101
ELBA - Broadloom - COURISTAN INC.; pg. 921, pg. 1067
ELBECO - Shirt - ELBECO INCORPORATED; pg. 40, pg. 1584
ELBECO CLASSIC - Uniforms - ELBECO INCORPORATED; pg. 40, pg. 1584
ELBERON RAIN - Jacket - I. SPIEWAK & SONS, INC.; pg. 42, pg. 1242
ELBERTINE - Lamp - ASHLEY FURNITURE INDUSTRIES, INC.; pg. 914, pg. 1852
ELCA - Excimer Laser System - THE SPECTRANETICS CORPORATION; pg. 1595, pg. 315
ELCAR FENCE - Fencing Contractor - ELCAR FENCE & SUPPLY CO.; pg. 80, pg. 319
ELCO - Fastening Systems - TEXTRON INC.; pg. 235, pg. 1607
ELCOM - Brushless Motor - PENN ENGINEERING & MANUFACTURING CORP.; pg. 1059, pg. 1525
ELCOM II - High Performance Brushless DC Motors & Gearmotors - PENN ENGINEERING & MANUFACTURING CORP.; pg. 1059, pg. 1525
ELCOTT - Furniture - ASHLEY FURNITURE INDUSTRIES, INC.; pg. 914, pg. 1852
ELDER & JENKS - Paint - THE MURALO COMPANY; pg. 1444, pg. 1042
ELDER WEAR - Apparel - ELDER MANUFACTURING COMPANY, INC.; pg. 40, pg. 996
ELDIM - Engineered Product And System - SULZER METCO (WESTBURY) INC.; pg. 1064, pg. 1350
ELDO - Analog & Mixed Signal Simulation Software - MENTOR GRAPHICS CORPORATION; pg. 432, pg. 1510
ELDON CRESTMONT - Desktop Accessories Line - RUBBERMAID HOME PRODUCTS; pg. 1138, pg. 1453
ELDOQUIN - Pharmaceutical Product - VALEANT PHARMACEUTICALS INTERNATIONAL; pg. 1605, pg. 1047
ELDORADO - Vinyl Matting - THE BILTRITE CORPORATION; pg. 1879, pg. 850
ELDORADO - Carpet Cushion - HSM SOLUTIONS; pg. 1884, pg. 1378
ELDORADO CASINO - Casino - BOYD GAMING CORPORATION; pg. 1082, pg. 1022
ELDORADO NATIONAL - Commercial Bus - THOR INDUSTRIES, INC.; pg. 1711, pg. 1456
ELDORADO RESORT CASINO - Resort Casino - ELDORADO RESORTS, INC.; pg. 546, pg. 1031
ELDRIDGE - Furniture - ASHLEY FURNITURE INDUSTRIES, INC.; pg. 914, pg. 1852
ELDRIDGE GRADE - Bike - MARIN BIKES; pg. 1708, pg. 168
ELE - Material Testing Instrument - DANAHER CORPORATION; pg. 1044, pg. 397
ELEANOR - Furniture - AMISCO INDUSTRIES LTD.; pg. 913, pg. 1958
ELEARNING SUITE - Software - ADOBE SYSTEMS INCORPORATED; pg. 342, pg. 235
ELECARE - Embolic Protection System - ABBOTT LABORATORIES; pg. 1484, pg. 551
ELECROGATOR - Irrigation Equipment Center Pivot - REINKE MANUFACTURING COMPANY, INC.; pg. 707, pg. 1010
ELECTA - Lamp - ASHLEY FURNITURE INDUSTRIES, INC.; pg. 914, pg. 1852
ELECTAR - Musical Instrument - GIBSON GUITAR CORP.; pg. 550, pg. 1650
ELECTECH - Online Training - PASS & SEYMOUR/LEGRAND; pg. 1303, pg. 1344
ELECTIVE ELEMENTS - Office Furniture - STEELCASE INC.; pg. 475, pg. 889
ELECTONE - Home Organ - YAMAHA CORPORATION OF AMERICA; pg. 595, pg. 51
ELECTRA - Testing Instrument System - BECKMAN COULTER, INC.; pg. 1402, pg. 48
ELECTRA - Bath Accessory - CROSCILL, INC.; pg. 1122, pg. 1220
ELECTRA - Digital Video Product - HARMONIC, INC.; pg. 402, pg. 246
ELECTRA - Systems Integration & Aeronautics - LOCKHEED MARTIN CORPORATION; pg. 229, pg. 762
ELECTRA - Lighting Product - QUOIZEL INC.; pg. 1304, pg. 1616
ELECTRA-GEAR - Gear Drives & Motors - REGAL BELOIT CORPORATION; pg. 106, pg. 1854
ELECTRA GLIDE - Motorcycle - HARLEY-DAVIDSON, INC.; pg. 178, pg. 1874
ELECTRA-GLO - Light Pod Kit - HARLEY-DAVIDSON, INC.; pg. 178, pg. 1874
ELECTRA MAGIC - Recirculating Toilet - THETFORD CORPORATION; pg. 337, pg. 867
ELECTRA-VITA - Electrolyte - TROUW NUTRITION USA; pg. 1482, pg. 616
ELECTRACK - Monorail Gearbox - REGAL BELOIT CORPORATION; pg. 106, pg. 1854
ELECTRAFLAME - Electrical Heating Product - DIMPLEX NORTH AMERICA LIMITED; pg. 54, pg. 1920
ELECTRASMOOTH - Steel Product - AK STEEL HOLDING CORPORATION; pg. 1311, pg. 1479
ELECTRI-COOL - Medical Product - CINCINNATI SUB-ZERO PRODUCTS, INC.; pg. 1070, pg. 1411
ELECTRIBE A - Analog Modeling Synthesizer - KORG USA, INC.; pg. 556, pg. 1180
ELECTRIBE AMKII - Analog Modeling Synthesizer - KORG USA, INC.; pg. 556, pg. 1180
ELECTRIBE M - Music Production Station - KORG USA, INC.; pg. 556, pg. 1180
ELECTRIBE MX - Music Production Station - KORG USA, INC.; pg. 556, pg. 1180
ELECTRIBE S - Rhythm Production Sampler - KORG USA, INC.; pg. 556, pg. 1180
ELECTRIC 7'S - Pulltab Game - IDAHO LOTTERY; pg. 995, pg. 547
ELECTRIC CITY - Footwear - PHOENIX FOOTWEAR GROUP, INC.; pg. 1815, pg. 60
ELECTRIC GIRL - Doll And Toy - AMERICAN GIRL LLC; pg. 949, pg. 1871
ELECTRIC GLIDE - Home Appliance - DACOR; pg. 54, pg. 67
ELECTRIC MAIL - Communication Product - J2 GLOBAL COMMUNICATIONS, INC.; pg. 1260, pg. 133
ELECTRIC TILT II - Transformer Tester - HD ELECTRIC COMPANY; pg. 1299, pg. 666
ELECTRIKBROOM - Cleaning Product - ORECK CORPORATION; pg. 59, pg. 1653
ELECTRO-4 DISC REFINER - Disc Refiner Machine - BOLTON-EMERSON AMERICAS, INC.; pg. 1318, pg. 827
ELECTRO AIR - Electronic Products Distribution Services - AVNET, INC.; pg. 622, pg. 15
ELECTRO-CHECK - Pump Check Control System - HENRY PRATT COMPANY; pg. 1049, pg. 555
ELECTRO-FAST - Molecular Biology Product - THERMO FISHER SCIENTIFIC INC.; pg. 1602, pg. 61
ELECTRO IMAGE - Electrodepositable Photoresist Coating - PPG INDUSTRIES, INC.; pg. 1445, pg. 1579
ELECTRO-KINETICS - Alternator & Generator System - DANAHER CORPORATION; pg. 1044, pg. 397
ELECTRO-KLEEN - Metal Cleaner - HEATBATH CORPORATION; pg. 1165, pg. 826
ELECTRO-PLASMA - Engineered Product And System - SULZER METCO (WESTBURY) INC.; pg. 1064, pg. 1350
ELECTRO PRO - Dietary Supplement - NOW HEALTH GROUP, INC.; pg. 1576, pg. 557
ELECTRO-SENTRY - Monitoring System - ELECTRO-SENSORS, INC.; pg. 1333, pg. 948
ELECTRO-STEAM - Valve - HAYS FLUID CONTROLS; pg. 1049, pg. 1370
ELECTRO-TEK - Meter - CUSTOM ACCESSORIES INC.; pg. 203, pg. 653
ELECTROCOMP - Molecular Biology Product - THERMO FISHER SCIENTIFIC INC.; pg. 1602, pg. 61
ELECTROCOUPLER - Toy Train - LIONEL LLC; pg. 961, pg.

875
ELECTROCUT - Film - 3M COMPANY; *pg.* 1142, *pg.* 956
ELECTRODE - Apparel - OAKLEY, INC.; *pg.* 1840, *pg.* 86
ELECTROFLO - Valve - HAYS FLUID CONTROLS; *pg.* 1049, *pg.* 1370
ELECTROFORCE - Test Instruments - BOSE CORPORATION; *pg.* 626, *pg.* 820
ELECTROGEN - Electron Generator Array - PHOTONIS USA PENNSYLVANIA; *pg.* 663, *pg.* 1547
ELECTROGUARD - Software - ROCKWELL AUTOMATION, INC.; *pg.* 668, *pg.* 1880
ELECTROJAC - Animal Safety Product - NEOGEN CORPORATION; *pg.* 883, *pg.* 896
ELECTROL - Screen - DA-LITE SCREEN COMPANY; *pg.* 632, *pg.* 698
ELECTROLET - Electric Projection Screen - DA-LITE SCREEN COMPANY; *pg.* 632, *pg.* 698
ELECTROLUX - Chef's Power Tool - CHESHER EQUIPMENT LTD.; *pg.* 1323, *pg.* 1925
ELECTROMAGNETIC CV - Vacuum Valve - MKS INSTRUMENTS, INC.; *pg.* 1362, *pg.* 781
ELECTROMAX - Oil Treater Product - CAMERON INTERNATIONAL; *pg.* 1151, *pg.* 1702
ELECTROMAX - Molecular Biology Product - THERMO FISHER SCIENTIFIC INC.; *pg.* 1602, *pg.* 61
ELECTROMET - Electrolytic Polisher & Etcher - BUEHLER, LTD.; *pg.* 1403, *pg.* 622
ELECTROMITE - Valve - HAYS FLUID CONTROLS; *pg.* 1049, *pg.* 1370
ELECTROMODE - Electrical Heating Product - DIMPLEX NORTH AMERICA LIMITED; *pg.* 54, *pg.* 1920
ELECTRON - Fabric - NEMSCHOFF, INC.; *pg.* 936, *pg.* 1890
ELECTRONIC BATTLESHIP - Toy & Game - HASBRO, INC.; *pg.* 954, *pg.* 1603
ELECTRONIC BUYERS' NEWS - Newspaper - UNITED BUSINESS MEDIA LLC; *pg.* 1697, *pg.* 1177
ELECTRONIC CATCH PHRASE - Toy & Game - HASBRO, INC.; *pg.* 954, *pg.* 1603
ELECTRONIC DEVICE FAILURE ANALYSIS - Trade Publication - ASM INTERNATIONAL; *pg.* 132, *pg.* 1461
ELECTRONIC DYNAMIC AGREEMANT - Software - JDA SOFTWARE GROUP, INC.; *pg.* 423, *pg.* 22
ELECTRONIC ENCYCLOPEDIA - Electronic Encyclopedia - FRANKLIN ELECTRONIC PUBLISHERS, INC.; *pg.* 398, *pg.* 1048
ELECTRONIC FLASH MAGIC - Educational Toys - LEAPFROG ENTERPRISES, INC.; *pg.* 961, *pg.* 84
ELECTRONIC FUNCTION SELECTION - Color Select Function - X-RITE, INCORPORATED; *pg.* 1437, *pg.* 891
ELECTRONIC HOLY BIBLE - King James & Revised Standard Versions - FRANKLIN ELECTRONIC PUBLISHERS, INC.; *pg.* 398, *pg.* 1048
ELECTRONIC LEARNING - Educational Materials - SCHOLASTIC INC.; *pg.* 1683, *pg.* 1288
ELECTRONIC MATERIALS HANDBOOK - Reference Book Series - ASM INTERNATIONAL; *pg.* 132, *pg.* 1461
ELECTRONIC.COM - Advertising Website - LIVE CURRENT MEDIA INC.; *pg.* 1263, *pg.* 1911
ELECTRONICS BOUTIQUE - Games - GAMESTOP CORP.; *pg.* 399, *pg.* 1699
ELECTRONICS ETO - Toy - THE OHIO ART COMPANY, INC.; *pg.* 965, *pg.* 1406
ELECTRONICS MANUFACTURING SERVICES - Tagline - SANMINA-SCI CORPORATION; *pg.* 671, *pg.* 250
ELECTRONMETER - Nutritional Product - RBC LIFE SCIENCES, INC.; *pg.* 1588, *pg.* 1723
ELECTROPHORESISTUTOR - Testing Instrument System - BECKMAN COULTER, INC.; *pg.* 1402, *pg.* 48
ELECTROPOLISH - Brite Dip - HUBBARD-HALL, INC.; *pg.* 1167, *pg.* 382
ELECTROSHIELD - Electrical Surgical Apparatus - ENCISION INC.; *pg.* 1528, *pg.* 310
ELECTROSILVER - Photographic Processing Chemicals - EASTMAN KODAK COMPANY; *pg.* 1408, *pg.* 1333
ELECTROSTITCH - Sealing Technology - MULTISORB TECHNOLOGIES, INC.; *pg.* 1570, *pg.* 1150
ELECTROTORK - Wrench - SNAP-ON INCORPORATED; *pg.* 1062, *pg.* 1862
ELECTROVERT - Soldering & Cleaning Equipment - SPEEDLINE TECHNOLOGIES, INC.; *pg.* 1378, *pg.* 823
ELEGANCE - Bra & Shapewear - GLAMORISE FOUNDATIONS, INC.; *pg.* 25, *pg.* 1235
ELEGANCE - Door - LARSON MANUFACTURING COMPANY; *pg.* 93, *pg.* 1624
ELEGANCE - Lotion Soap - SWISHER HYGIENE INC.; *pg.* 336, *pg.* 1507
ELEGANT - Sturdilite Floodlight - PHOENIX PRODUCTS COMPANY; *pg.* 1304, *pg.* 1879
ELEGANT ADDITIONS - Wood - WHITE RIVER HARDWOODS-WOODWORKS, INC.; *pg.* 121, *pg.* 31
ELEGANT BEVEL SERIES - Collection - ODL INCORPORATED; *pg.* 101, *pg.* 914
ELEGANT BRIDE - Magazine - CONDE NAST PUBLICATIONS, INC.; *pg.* 1629, *pg.* 1217
ELEGANT REFLECTIONS - Kitchenware - THE VOLLRATH COMPANY LLC; *pg.* 1139, *pg.* 1894
ELEGANT WISHES - Floral Arrangement - 1-800-FLOWERS.COM, INC.; *pg.* 1758, *pg.* 1151
ELEGANTWARE - Disposable Dishes - PACTIV CORPORATION; *pg.* 1466, *pg.* 624
ELEGUARD - Explosion Vent - FIKE CORPORATION; *pg.* 1047, *pg.* 973
ELEK - Electrical Systems - EATON CORPORATION; *pg.* 1331, *pg.* 1429
ELEKTRA - Record Label - WARNER MUSIC GROUP CORP.; *pg.* 590, *pg.* 1313
ELEKTROTOM - Medical Device - INTEGRA LIFESCIENCES HOLDINGS CORPORATION; *pg.* 1545, *pg.* 1109
ELEKTROTOM HITT - Medical Device - INTEGRA LIFESCIENCES HOLDINGS CORPORATION; *pg.* 1545, *pg.* 1109
ELEMENT - Battery - EXIDE TECHNOLOGIES; *pg.* 204, *pg.* 483
ELEMENT - Medical Equipment - INVACARE CORPORATION; *pg.* 1546, *pg.* 1451
ELEMENT - Hotels - STARWOOD HOTELS & RESORTS WORLDWIDE, INC.; *pg.* 1114, *pg.* 378
ELEMENT 5 - Beverage Bottle & Coolers - THERMOS L.L.C.; *pg.* 61, *pg.* 660
ELEMENT C1 - Medical Equipment - INVACARE CORPORATION; *pg.* 1546, *pg.* 1451
ELEMENT R1 - Medical Equipment - INVACARE CORPORATION; *pg.* 1546, *pg.* 1451
ELEMENTAL - Fabric - NEUTRAL POSTURE, INC.; *pg.* 939, *pg.* 1669
ELEMENTARY ELECTRICAL DIAGRAMS - Software - BENTLEY SYSTEMS, INC.; *pg.* 361, *pg.* 1531
ELEMENTARY/SECONDARY SERVICE - Instructional Programming & Resources; Professional Development Programming - PUBLIC BROADCASTING SERVICE; *pg* 305, *pg.* 1774
ELEMENTS - Fabric - NEMSCHOFF, INC.; *pg.* 936, *pg.* 1890
THE ELEMENTS OF LIFE - Tagline - BORGHESE, INC.; *pg.* 502, *pg.* 1205
ELEMENTSESSENTIELSFRANCAIS - Software - SKILLSOFT PLC; *pg.* 470, *pg.* 1037
ELEMICA BUYER DIRECT - Software - ELEMICA, INC.; *pg.* 1242, *pg.* 1591
ELEMICA SELLER DIRECT - Software - ELEMICA, INC.; *pg.* 1242, *pg.* 1591
ELEMICA SUPPLY CHAIN HOSTED SOLUTION - Software - ELEMICA, INC.; *pg.* 1242, *pg.* 1591
ELEMIX - Concrete Additive - NOVA CHEMICALS CORPORATION; *pg.* 1175, *pg.* 1904
ELEPHANT - Dental Product - DENTSPLY INTERNATIONAL INC.; *pg.* 1522, *pg.* 1596
ELEPHANT - Pillow - ETHAN ALLEN INTERIORS INC.; *pg.* 924, *pg.* 343
ELEPHANT - Fabric - NEMSCHOFF, INC.; *pg.* 936, *pg.* 1890
ELEPHANT BUBBALS - Apparel - VANS, INC.; *pg.* 1821, *pg.* 76
ELEPHANT KING - Video Slots - INTERNATIONAL GAME TECHNOLOGY; *pg.* 957, *pg.* 1024
ELEPHANT STAMPEDE - Ice Cream - WELLS ENTERPRISES, INC.; *pg.* 909, *pg.* 709
ELEQUENCH - Flameless Explosion Venting - FIKE CORPORATION; *pg.* 1047, *pg.* 973
ELESTAT - Eye Care Product - ALLERGAN, INC.; *pg.* 1491, *pg.* 106
ELETCTRIBE MKII - Rhythm Synthesizer - KORG USA, INC.; *pg.* 556, *pg.* 1180
ELEVATE - Lightweight Hair Dryer - ANDIS COMPANY; *pg.* 498, *pg.* 1895
ELEVATE - Furniture - ANTHRO CORPORATION; *pg.* 913, *pg.* 1509
ELEVATIONS - Carpet - BEAULIEU GROUP, LLC; *pg.* 917, *pg.* 529
ELEVATORS - Shoes - RICHLEE SHOE COMPANY; *pg.* 1818, *pg.* 769
ELEVEN TONGUES - Wines - BROWN-FORMAN CORPORATION; *pg.* 1958, *pg.* 732
ELEVETTE - Elevator - INCLINATOR COMPANY OF AMERICA; *pg.* 88, *pg.* 1536
ELEVONIC - Elevator Product - OTIS ELEVATOR COMPANY; *pg.* 102, *pg.* 349
ELEXA - Sexual Health Products - CHURCH & DWIGHT CO., INC.; *pg.* 1153, *pg.* 1063
ELEXAR - Plastic & Rubber - TEKNOR APEX COMPANY; *pg.* 1889, *pg.* 1605
ELF - Fish Products - VITA FOOD PRODUCTS, INC.; *pg.* 909, *pg.* 595
ELFRIEDA - Lamp - ASHLEY FURNITURE INDUSTRIES, INC.; *pg.* 914, *pg.* 1852
ELFTEX - Carbon Black - CABOT CORPORATION; *pg.* 1151, *pg.* 792
ELFTEX 3 - Chemical Product - CABOT CORPORATION; *pg.* 1151, *pg.* 792
ELGA - Water Treatment Products - CULLIGAN INTERNATIONAL COMPANY; *pg.* 54, *pg.* 656
ELGIN - Sweeper Vehicles - FEDERAL SIGNAL CORPORATION; *pg.* 638, *pg.* 645
ELGIN - Watch - M.Z. BERGER & CO., INC.; *pg.* 10, *pg.* 1175
ELI - Hearing Instrument - STARKEY LABORATORIES, INC.; *pg.* 1597, *pg.* 923
ELI WEATHERBY - Wood Stain - DAVIS PAINT COMPANY; *pg.* 1441, *pg.* 982
ELIGEN - Drug Delivery Platform - EMISPHERE TECHNOLOGIES, INC.; *pg.* 1528, *pg.* 1118
ELIMA-MATIC - Pump Product - IDEX CORPORATION; *pg.* 1347, *pg.* 623
ELIMINATE MPZ - Apparels - UNDER ARMOUR, INC.; *pg.* 49, *pg.* 759
ELIMINATOR - Connector - BOMAR INTERCONNECT PRODUCTS, INC.; *pg.* 1318, *pg.* 1079
ELIMINATOR - Medical Equipment - CONMED CORPORATION; *pg.* 1517, *pg.* 1347
ELIMINATOR - Dispensing Equipment - THE DOW CHEMICAL COMPANY; *pg.* 1157, *pg.* 898
ELIMINATOR - Test Product - EVERETT CHARLES TECHNOLOGIES; *pg.* 638, *pg.* 185
ELIMINATOR - Belt Cleaning Systems - FLEXIBLE STEEL LACING COMPANY; *pg.* 1337, *pg.* 608
ELIMINATOR - Surface Preparation System - FLOW INTERNATIONAL CORPORATION; *pg.* 1337, *pg.* 1821
ELIMINATOR - Gauge Wheel Kit - GREAT PLAINS MANUFACTURING, INCORPORATED; *pg.* 704, *pg.* 721
ELIMINATOR - Medical Equipment - INVACARE CORPORATION; *pg.* 1546, *pg.* 1451
ELIMINATOR - Effluent, Wastewater & Sewage Pumps - LITTLE GIANT PUMP COMPANY; *pg.* 1356, *pg.* 1486
ELIMINATOR - Solder Stripper - MACDERMID, INC.; *pg.* 1172, *pg.* 321
ELIMINATOR - Brace System - MITEK, INC.; *pg.* 1056, *pg.* 975
THE ELIMINATOR - Outlet Box - OATEY SUPPLY CHAIN SERVICES; *pg.* 30, *pg.* 1433
ELIMINATOR SERIES - Fly Reels - DAIWA CORPORATION; *pg.* 1832, *pg.* 75
ELIMSTAPH NO. 2 - Cleaning Preparation - WALTER G. LEGGE COMPANY, INC.; *pg.* 337, *pg.* 1321
ELIMSTAT - Non-Conductive Floor Cleaner - WALTER G. LEGGE COMPANY, INC.; *pg.* 337, *pg.* 1321
ELIMSTAT ATS - Non-Conductive Floor Cleaner - WALTER G. LEGGE COMPANY, INC.; *pg.* 337, *pg.* 1321
ELIMSTAT LX - Non-Conductive Floor Cleaner - WALTER G. LEGGE COMPANY, INC.; *pg.* 337, *pg.* 1321
ELIMSTAT SD - Non-Conductive Floor Cleaner - WALTER G. LEGGE COMPANY, INC.; *pg.* 337, *pg.* 1321
ELIMSTAT SDEC - Non-Conductive Floor Cleaner - WALTER G. LEGGE COMPANY, INC.; *pg.* 337, *pg.* 1321
ELIMSTAT SDSC - Non-Conductive Floor Cleaner - WALTER G. LEGGE COMPANY, INC.; *pg.* 337, *pg.* 1321
ELIMSTAT UXM-60P - Non-Conductive Floor Cleaner - WALTER G. LEGGE COMPANY, INC.; *pg.* 337, *pg.* 1321
ELIMSTATX SDSC - Non-Conductive Floor Cleaner - WALTER G. LEGGE COMPANY, INC.; *pg.* 337, *pg.* 1321
ELINA - Doll - MATTEL, INC.; *pg.* 962, *pg.* 81
ELIORA - Lamp - ASHLEY FURNITURE INDUSTRIES, INC.; *pg.* 914, *pg.* 1852
ELIPAR - FreeLight Curing Light - 3M COMPANY; *pg.* 1142, *pg.* 956
ELIS APPLE CRANBERRY TART - Cranberry Tart - ELI'S CHEESECAKE COMPANY; *pg.* 1852, *pg.* 572
ELIS GLAMOUR CAKES - Cheesecakes - ELI'S

CHEESECAKE COMPANY; *pg.* 1852, *pg.* 572
ELIS NO SUGAR ADDED ORIGINAL CHEESECAKE - Cheesecake - ELI'S CHEESECAKE COMPANY; *pg.* 1852, *pg.* 572
ELIS ORIGINAL PLAIN CHEESECAKE - Cheesecake - ELI'S CHEESECAKE COMPANY; *pg.* 1852, *pg.* 572
ELIS PECAN PIE - Pecan Pie - ELI'S CHEESECAKE COMPANY; *pg.* 1852, *pg.* 572
ELISA - Biomolecule Product - THERMO FISHER SCIENTIFIC INC.; *pg.* 1602, *pg.* 61
ELISA ILANA - Jewelry - ELISA ILANA CUSTOM DESIGNS; *pg.* 4, *pg.* 1015
ELISA IMMUNO EXPLORER - Software - BIO-RAD LABORATORIES, INC.; *pg.* 1504, *pg.* 101
ELISE - Footwear - VANS, INC.; *pg.* 1821, *pg.* 76
ELISEE - Ventilator - RESMED INC.; *pg.* 1589, *pg.* 207
ELISSA - Furniture - THE COMMERCIAL FURNITURE GROUP; *pg.* 920, *pg.* 994
ELISTEN - Software - SCANTRON CORPORATION; *pg.* 467, *pg.* 922
ELITA - Lamp - ASHLEY FURNITURE INDUSTRIES, INC.; *pg.* 914, *pg.* 1852
ELITE - Software - BIO-RAD LABORATORIES, INC.; *pg.* 1504, *pg.* 101
ELITE - Vaccines - BOEHRINGER INGELHEIM VETMEDICA, INC.; *pg.* 1474, *pg.* 989
ELITE - Bag - BROWN & BIGELOW, INC.; *pg.* 1624, *pg.* 959
ELITE - Food Product - BUNGE LIMITED; *pg.* 842, *pg.* 1351
ELITE - Binocular - BUSHNELL OUTDOOR PRODUCTS, INC.; *pg.* 1403, *pg.* 718
ELITE - Ladies' Wallets - BUXTON ACQUISITION CO., LLC; *pg.* 2, *pg.* 845
ELITE - Classic Chafers - CARLISLE FOODSERVICE PRODUCTS INCORPORATED; *pg.* 1455, *pg.* 1485
ELITE - Probe Station - CASCADE MICROTECH, INC.; *pg.* 1405, *pg.* 1492
ELITE - Residential & Commercial Gate Openers - THE CHAMBERLAIN GROUP, INC.; *pg.* 75, *pg.* 611
ELITE - Resin - THE DOW CHEMICAL COMPANY; *pg.* 1157, *pg.* 898
ELITE - Photographic Paper - EASTMAN KODAK COMPANY; *pg.* 1408, *pg.* 1333
ELITE - Air Cleaner - EDELBROCK CORPORATION; *pg.* 204, *pg.* 293
ELITE - Sink - ELKAY MANUFACTURING COMPANY; *pg.* 80, *pg.* 645
ELITE - Food Service - FOOD SERVICES OF AMERICA, INC.; *pg.* 856, *pg.* 21
ELITE - Gaming Product - GLD PRODUCTS, INC.; *pg.* 1835, *pg.* 1882
ELITE - Turning Machine - HARDINGE INC.; *pg.* 1344, *pg.* 1157
ELITE - Lighting Product - HAYWARD POOL PRODUCTS; *pg.* 1049, *pg.* 1057
ELITE - Medical Equipment - INVACARE CORPORATION; *pg.* 1546, *pg.* 1451
ELITE - Furniture - JASPER GROUP; *pg.* 930, *pg.* 691
ELITE - Gas Fireplace Inserts - LENNOX HEARTH PRODUCTS; *pg.* 93, *pg.* 1652
ELITE - Heating & Cooling Product - LENNOX INTERNATIONAL INC.; *pg.* 1073, *pg.* 1736
ELITE - Medical Apparatus - MAQUET; *pg.* 1558, *pg.* 1082
ELITE - Pacemaker - MEDTRONIC, INC.; *pg.* 1564, *pg.* 939
ELITE - Folding Leg Training/Conference Table - MITY ENTERPRISES, INC.; *pg.* 935, *pg.* 1753
ELITE - Lighting Product - QUOIZEL INC.; *pg.* 1304, *pg.* 1616
ELITE - Toothbrush - RANIR LLC; *pg.* 520, *pg.* 888
ELITE - Software - SRA INTERNATIONAL, INC.; *pg.* 473, *pg.* 1780
ELITE - Legal Publications - THOMSON REUTERS CORPORATION; *pg.* 1693, *pg.* 1944
ELITE - Bicycle - TREK BICYCLE CORPORATION; *pg.* 1847, *pg.* 1896
ELITE - Stethoscope - WELCH ALLYN INC.; *pg.* 1436, *pg.* 1342
ELITE - Ceiling Fan - WESTINGHOUSE LIGHTING CORPORATION; *pg.* 687, *pg.* 1571
ELITE 3 - Isolator - NEWPORT CORPORATION; *pg.* 1424, *pg.* 114
ELITE APEX - Client Relationship Management & Business Development Application - THOMSON ELITE; *pg.* 484, *pg.* 72
ELITE BRASS - Gaming Product - GLD PRODUCTS, INC.; *pg.* 1835, *pg.* 1882
ELITE BY ELKAY - Sink - ELKAY MANUFACTURING COMPANY; *pg.* 80, *pg.* 645
ELITE EIGHT - Trademark - NATIONAL COLLEGIATE ATHLETIC ASSOCIATION; *pg.* 567, *pg.* 688
ELITE GOLD - Drawers & Storage Units - HOME PRODUCTS INTERNATIONAL, INC.; *pg.* 1125, *pg.* 577
ELITE GOURMET - Sink - ELKAY MANUFACTURING COMPANY; *pg.* 80, *pg.* 645
ELITE II - Electrocardiograph - CARDIAC SCIENCE CORPORATION; *pg.* 1512, *pg.* 1897
ELITE II - Pacemaker - MEDTRONIC, INC.; *pg.* 1564, *pg.* 939
ELITE IMAGE - Office Products - GENUINE PARTS COMPANY; *pg.* 206, *pg.* 506
ELITE MPX - Hair Removal System - CYNOSURE, INC.; *pg.* 1521, *pg.* 858
THE ELITE POOL - In-Ground Vinyl Pools - POOL CORPORATION; *pg.* 1843, *pg.* 743
ELITE SECURE - Software - SRA INTERNATIONAL, INC.; *pg.* 473, *pg.* 1780
ELITE TEX - Scrubwear - MEDLINE INDUSTRIES, INC.; *pg.* 1562, *pg.* 635
ELITE8 - Trademark - NATIONAL COLLEGIATE ATHLETIC ASSOCIATION; *pg.* 567, *pg.* 688
ELITYS - X-ray System - EASTMAN KODAK COMPANY; *pg.* 1408, *pg.* 1333
ELIXIR - Cables & Strings - W.L. GORE & ASSOCIATES, INC.; *pg.* 122, *pg.* 388
ELIXIR - Chewing Gum Flavor - WM. WRIGLEY JR. COMPANY; *pg.* 1863, *pg.* 596
ELIZA - Lamp - ASHLEY FURNITURE INDUSTRIES, INC.; *pg.* 914, *pg.* 1852
ELIZA J - Apparel - G-III APPAREL GROUP, LTD.; *pg.* 41, *pg.* 1233
ELIZABETH - Clothing - ABERCROMBIE & FITCH CO.; *pg.* 37, *pg.* 1466
ELIZABETH - Lamp - ASHLEY FURNITURE INDUSTRIES, INC.; *pg.* 914, *pg.* 1852
ELIZABETH ARDEN GREEN TEA - Perfume - ELIZABETH ARDEN, INC.; *pg.* 507, *pg.* 448
ELIZABETH ARDEN'S PROVOCATIVE WOMAN - Fragrance - ELIZABETH ARDEN, INC.; *pg.* 507, *pg.* 448
ELIZABETH ARDEN'S RED DOOR - Fragrance - ELIZABETH ARDEN, INC.; *pg.* 507, *pg.* 448
ELIZABETH TAYLOR'S WHITE DIAMONDS - Fragrance - ELIZABETH ARDEN, INC.; *pg.* 507, *pg.* 448
ELKAY STARLITE - DuPont Corian Sink - ELKAY MANUFACTURING COMPANY; *pg.* 80, *pg.* 645
ELKWARE - Mobile Game - BLUCORA; *pg.* 1232, *pg.* 1813
ELLA - Furniture - AMISCO INDUSTRIES LTD.; *pg.* 913, *pg.* 1958
ELLA - Office Furniture - STEELCASE INC.; *pg.* 475, *pg.* 889
ELLA MOSS - Apparel - V.F. CORPORATION; *pg.* 34, *pg.* 1376
ELLANAR - Jewelry Cleaner - L&R MANUFACTURING COMPANY; *pg.* 1419, *pg.* 1076
ELLE - Beer - COASTAL EXTREME BREWING COMPANY; *pg.* 240, *pg.* 1602
ELLE - Magazine - THE HEARST CORPORATION; *pg.* 1649, *pg.* 1239
ELLE CANADA - Newspaper - TRANSCONTINENTAL INC.; *pg.* 1695, *pg.* 1957
ELLE.COM - Magazine - ELLE.COM; *pg.* 1242, *pg.* 1227
ELLEMA - Lamp - ASHLEY FURNITURE INDUSTRIES, INC.; *pg.* 914, *pg.* 1852
ELLEN BETRIX - Detergent - THE PROCTER & GAMBLE COMPANY; *pg.* 1129, *pg.* 1418
ELLEN TRACY - Apparel - G-III APPAREL GROUP, LTD.; *pg.* 41, *pg.* 1233
ELLEN TRACY - Fashion Lifestyle Brand - SEQUENTIAL BRANDS GROUP, INC.; *pg.* 1395, *pg.* 1290
ELLENCE - Breast Cancer Medication - PFIZER INC.; *pg.* 1581, *pg.* 1278
ELLERBEE - Lighting Product - QUOIZEL INC.; *pg.* 1304, *pg.* 1616
ELLERY - Bath Product - KOHLER CO.; *pg.* 91, *pg.* 1862
ELLI - Footwear - CAPEZIO BALLET MAKERS INC.; *pg.* 1805, *pg.* 1125
ELLICOTT - Dredges - ELLICOTT DREDGES, LLC; *pg.* 1333, *pg.* 757
ELLIE - Clothing - ABERCROMBIE & FITCH CO.; *pg.* 37, *pg.* 1466
ELLIE - Women's Clothing & Accessories - WOODEN SHIPS OF HOBOKEN; *pg.* 35, *pg.* 1315
ELLIE MAE NETWORK - Electronic Mortgage Network - ELLIE MAE, INC.; *pg.* 1243, *pg.* 183
ELLINGTON - Fabric - NEMSCHOFF, INC.; *pg.* 936, *pg.* 1890
ELLIOTT - Women's Clothing & Accessories - WOODEN SHIPS OF HOBOKEN; *pg.* 35, *pg.* 1315
ELLIPSA - Stroller - EVENFLO COMPANY, INC.; *pg.* 924, *pg.* 1470
ELLIPSE - Bathroom Fan - HUNTER FAN COMPANY; *pg.* 57, *pg.* 1631
ELLIPSE - Furniture - JASPER GROUP; *pg.* 930, *pg.* 691
ELLIPSE - Bath Product - KOHLER CO.; *pg.* 91, *pg.* 1862
ELLIPSE - Beanie - OAKLEY, INC.; *pg.* 1840, *pg.* 86
ELLIPSE - Office Furniture - STEELCASE INC.; *pg.* 475, *pg.* 889
ELLIPSE - Lighting Product - WESTINGHOUSE LIGHTING CORPORATION; *pg.* 687, *pg.* 1571
ELLIPSE - Motor Homes - WINNEBAGO INDUSTRIES, INC.; *pg.* 1712, *pg.* 707
ELLIPSO - Portion Cups - PACTIV CORPORATION; *pg.* 1466, *pg.* 624
ELLIPTICAL RIB - Fabric - NEMSCHOFF, INC.; *pg.* 936, *pg.* 1890
ELLIS - Lighting Product - QUOIZEL INC.; *pg.* 1304, *pg.* 1616
ELLO - Toy - MATTEL, INC.; *pg.* 962, *pg.* 81
ELLOWYNE WILDE - Doll - TONNER DOLL COMPANY, INC.; *pg.* 968, *pg.* 1171
ELLZEY CRIB - Footwear - K-SWISS; *pg.* 1837, *pg.* 306
ELM CITY LAGER - Beer - NEW ENGLAND BREWING COMPANY; *pg.* 1967, *pg.* 386
ELMA - Lamp - ASHLEY FURNITURE INDUSTRIES, INC.; *pg.* 914, *pg.* 1852
ELMA CHIPS - Food & Beverage - PEPSICO, INC.; *pg.* 259, *pg.* 1327
ELMER'S - Glue - ELMER'S PRODUCTS, INC.; *pg.* 1442, *pg.* 1479
ELMIRON - Healthcare Product - JOHNSON & JOHNSON; *pg.* 1549, *pg.* 1091
ELMO RIETSCHLE - Blowers & Compressors - GARDNER DENVER, INC.; *pg.* 1338, *pg.* 1592
ELNUEVOHERALD.COM - Web Site - THE MIAMI HERALD; *pg.* 1665, *pg.* 444
ELO TOUCHSYSTEMS - Touchscreen Products - TE CONNECTIVITY LTD.; *pg.* 677, *pg.* 1515
ELOCON - Medicine - MERCK & CO., INC.; *pg.* 1566, *pg.* 1077
ELOISE - Lamp - ASHLEY FURNITURE INDUSTRIES, INC.; *pg.* 914, *pg.* 1852
ELON - Photo Developing Agent - EASTMAN KODAK COMPANY; *pg.* 1408, *pg.* 1333
ELON-O-LOCK - Security Devices - HIGHFIELD MANUFACTURING CO.; *pg.* 1346, *pg.* 339
ELONGASE - Molecular Biology Product - THERMO FISHER SCIENTIFIC INC.; *pg.* 1602, *pg.* 61
ELOT - Software - MELISSA DATA CORP.; *pg.* 432, *pg.* 188
ELOXATIN - Oxaliplatin For Injection - SANOFI US; *pg.* 1592, *pg.* 1046
ELPAC POWER SYSTEMS - Power Systems - INTERNATIONAL COMPONENTS CORPORATION; *pg.* 647, *pg.* 669
ELPELYT - Chemical Coating - ENTHONE INC.; *pg.* 1161, *pg.* 381
ELPHA - Electromedical Device - ZYNEX, INC.; *pg.* 690, *pg.* 333
ELSA - Lighting - STEELCASE INC.; *pg.* 475, *pg.* 889
ELSIE - Clothing - ABERCROMBIE & FITCH CO.; *pg.* 37, *pg.* 1466
ELSIE - Dairy Product - DAIRY FARMERS OF AMERICA, INC.; *pg.* 851, *pg.* 982
ELSTREE - Ethernet Product - VITESSE SEMICONDUCTOR CORPORATION; *pg.* 686, *pg.* 57
ELTA - Lamp - ASHLEY FURNITURE INDUSTRIES, INC.; *pg.* 914, *pg.* 1852
ELTA - Software - TRIMBLE NAVIGATION LIMITED; *pg.* 1384, *pg.* 288
ELTESOL - Sulphonic Acid - HUNTSMAN CORPORATION; *pg.* 1167, *pg.* 1758
ELTRON - Electric Shavers - THE ELTRON COMPANY; *pg.* 507, *pg.* 103
ELUM - Trademark - REVOLUTION LIGHTING TECHNOLOGIES, INC.; *pg.* 1304, *pg.* 377
ELUM COVE RGB - Lighting Systems - REVOLUTION LIGHTING TECHNOLOGIES, INC.; *pg.* 1304, *pg.* 377
ELUMINA - Sink - ELKAY MANUFACTURING COMPANY; *pg.* 80, *pg.* 645

ELUTATUBE - Molecular Probe Product - THERMO FISHER SCIENTIFIC INC.; *pg.* 1602, *pg.* 61
ELVALOY - Resin - E.I. DU PONT DE NEMOURS & COMPANY; *pg.* 1159, *pg.* 390
ELVAMIDE - Nylon Multipolymer Resins - E.I. DU PONT DE NEMOURS & COMPANY; *pg.* 1159, *pg.* 390
ELVANOL - Polyvinyl Alcohol Resins - E.I. DU PONT DE NEMOURS & COMPANY; *pg.* 1159, *pg.* 390
ELVAX - Ethylene Vinyl Acetate Resins - E.I. DU PONT DE NEMOURS & COMPANY; *pg.* 1159, *pg.* 390
ELVIRA - Game - INTERNATIONAL GAME TECHNOLOGY; *pg.* 957, *pg.* 1024
ELVIRA - Signals Analysis Workstation - RAYTHEON APPLIED SIGNAL TECHNOLOGY, INC.; *pg.* 667, *pg.* 288
ELVIRA - Fabric - SCALAMANDRE, INC.; *pg.* 941, *pg.* 1058
ELVIS PRESLEY'S MEMPHIS - Restaurant - ELVIS PRESLEY ENTERPRISES, INC.; *pg.* 1090, *pg.* 1642
ELX-7100-X2M - Electronic Component - EMCORE CORPORATION; *pg.* 636, *pg.* 39
ELX-7100-XEN - Electronic Component - EMCORE CORPORATION; *pg.* 636, *pg.* 39
ELY AND WALKER - Label Apparel - OXFORD INDUSTRIES, INC.; *pg.* 30, *pg.* 517
ELY PLAINS - Apparel - OXFORD INDUSTRIES, INC.; *pg.* 30, *pg.* 517
ELY WOULD - Golfing Product - CALLAWAY GOLF COMPANY; *pg.* 1829, *pg.* 58
ELYSEES - Cameras - EASTMAN KODAK COMPANY; *pg.* 1408, *pg.* 1333
ELYSIA - Lamp - ASHLEY FURNITURE INDUSTRIES, INC.; *pg.* 914, *pg.* 1852
ELYSIAN FIELDS - Hair & Skin Product - AUBREY ORGANICS INC.; *pg.* 499, *pg.* 470
ELYX - Luxury Vodka - PERNOD RICARD USA, INC.; *pg.* 1968, *pg.* 1332
EM-PACT - Medical Device - MANNATECH, INCORPORATED; *pg.* 1558, *pg.* 1671
EMA - Lamp - ASHLEY FURNITURE INDUSTRIES, INC.; *pg.* 914, *pg.* 1852
EMABOND - Specialty Electromagnetic Adhesive Compounds, Equipment & Technology - ASHLAND INC.; *pg.* 972, *pg.* 726
EMAC - Computer - APPLE INC.; *pg.* 350, *pg.* 73
EMAC DIGITAL - Consulting Services - MCDONALD'S CORPORATION; *pg.* 1737, *pg.* 645
EMAIL AND DESIGN - Manual - XEROX CORPORATION; *pg.* 494, *pg.* 365
EMAIL DESIGN - Software - XEROX CORPORATION; *pg.* 494, *pg.* 365
EMAIL SERIES - Address Book - BROWN & BIGELOW, INC.; *pg.* 1624, *pg.* 959
EMAILXAMINER - Software System - EMC CORPORATION; *pg.* 391, *pg.* 825
EMAILXTENDER - Software System - EMC CORPORATION; *pg.* 391, *pg.* 825
EMAKI - Carpet - INTERFACE, INC.; *pg.* 605, *pg.* 512
EMANUELLE - Footwear - PHOENIX FOOTWEAR GROUP, INC.; *pg.* 1815, *pg.* 60
EMATRIX - Software - DASSAULT SYSTEMS ENOVIA; *pg.* 382, *pg.* 851
EMAX - Software - MOLECULAR DEVICES CORPORATION; *pg.* 1568, *pg.* 287
EMBARK - Turf Product - PBI/GORDON CORPORATION; *pg.* 1176, *pg.* 985
EMBASA - Mexican Food - MEGAMEX FOODS, LLC; *pg.* 833, *pg.* 66
EMBASSY - Leather Product - COACH, INC.; *pg.* 3, *pg.* 1214
EMBASSY - Commercial Locksets - MEDECO HIGH SECURITY LOCKS, INC.; *pg.* 1055, *pg.* 1806
EMBASSY CHEFS - International Cuisine Program - YOUTOO TECHNOLOGIES; *pg.* 324, *pg.* 1724
EMBASSY SUITES - Upscale All-Suites - HILTON WORLDWIDE, INC.; *pg.* 1094, *pg.* 1791
EMBEDDED DESKTOP - Software - WIND RIVER SYSTEMS, INC.; *pg.* 493, *pg.* 38
EMBEDDED EDGE - Magazine & Information Services - TEXAS INSTRUMENTS INCORPORATED; *pg.* 679, *pg.* 1688
EMBEDDED IN LIFE - Tagline - ZILOG INC.; *pg.* 497, *pg.* 252
EMBEDDED PROCESS VERIFICATION - Sensing Technology - CYBEROPTICS CORPORATION; *pg.* 1408, *pg.* 925
EMBEDDED TIMES - Software - WIND RIVER SYSTEMS, INC.; *pg.* 493, *pg.* 38
EMBEDDED TRUST SERVICES - Software - CERTICOM CORP.; *pg.* 371, *pg.* 1925
EMBEDHEAD - Software - INTERVALZERO INC.; *pg.* 420, *pg.* 851
EMBER CHROME - Metallic Finishes - STEELCASE INC.; *pg.* 475, *pg.* 889
EMBLA - Liquid Handling System - MOLECULAR DEVICES CORPORATION; *pg.* 1568, *pg.* 287
EMBLA - Diagnostic Device - RESMED INC.; *pg.* 1589, *pg.* 207
EMBLEM - Reels - DAIWA CORPORATION; *pg.* 1832, *pg.* 75
EMBLEM X-A - Saltwater Spinning Reels - DAIWA CORPORATION; *pg.* 1832, *pg.* 75
EMBLEM X-T - Saltwater Spinning Reels - DAIWA CORPORATION; *pg.* 1832, *pg.* 75
EMBLEM Z-A - Saltwater Spinning Reels - DAIWA CORPORATION; *pg.* 1832, *pg.* 75
EMBLETTA - Diagnostic Device - RESMED INC.; *pg.* 1589, *pg.* 207
EMBO - Bathroom Tissue - GEORGIA-PACIFIC LLC; *pg.* 1458, *pg.* 507
EMBOSAFE - Electrosurgical Devices - ANGIODYNAMICS, INC.; *pg.* 1495, *pg.* 1173
EMBOSHIELD - Embolic Protection System - ABBOTT LABORATORIES; *pg.* 1484, *pg.* 551
EMBOSHIELD BAREWIRE - Embolic Protection System - ABBOTT LABORATORIES; *pg.* 1484, *pg.* 551
EMBOSSED - Wallcovering - YORK WALLCOVERINGS INC.; *pg.* 947, *pg.* 1598
EMBRACE - Enteral Pump - ABBOTT LABORATORIES; *pg.* 1484, *pg.* 551
EMBRACE - Shrink Film Resins - EASTMAN CHEMICAL COMPANY; *pg.* 1159, *pg.* 1636
EMBRACE - Infant Car Seat - EVENFLO COMPANY, INC.; *pg.* 924, *pg.* 1470
EMBRACE - Furniture - NEUTRAL POSTURE, INC.; *pg.* 939, *pg.* 1669
EMBRACE MOTION - Furniture - NEUTRAL POSTURE, INC.; *pg.* 939, *pg.* 1669
EMBRACE SPACE - Space Science & Technology Educational Materials - LOCKHEED MARTIN CORPORATION; *pg.* 229, *pg.* 762
EMBRACE YOUR SPACE - Slogan - ART.COM; *pg.* 1229, *pg.* 83
EMBRACEABLE YOU - Carpet - BEAULIEU GROUP, LLC; *pg.* 917, *pg.* 529
EMBRACO - Home Appliance Product - WHIRLPOOL CORPORATION; *pg.* 62, *pg.* 872
EMBRASURE - Surface Material - STEELCASE INC.; *pg.* 475, *pg.* 889
EMC AUTOMATED NETWORKED STORAGE - Software - EMC CORPORATION; *pg.* 391, *pg.* 825
EMC CENTERA - Software - EMC CORPORATION; *pg.* 391, *pg.* 825
EMC CONTROLCENTER - Software - EMC CORPORATION; *pg.* 391, *pg.* 825
EMC DEVELOPERS PROGRAM - Software - EMC CORPORATION; *pg.* 391, *pg.* 825
EMC ENTERPRISE STORAGE - Software - EMC CORPORATION; *pg.* 391, *pg.* 825
EMC ENTERPRISE STORAGE NETWORK - Software - EMC CORPORATION; *pg.* 391, *pg.* 825
EMC LIFELINE - Software - EMC CORPORATION; *pg.* 391, *pg.* 825
EMC ONCOURSE - Software - EMC CORPORATION; *pg.* 391, *pg.* 825
EMC PROVEN - Software - EMC CORPORATION; *pg.* 391, *pg.* 825
EMC RECOVERPOINT - Software - EMC CORPORATION; *pg.* 391, *pg.* 825
EMC SNAP - Software - EMC CORPORATION; *pg.* 391, *pg.* 825
EMC SOURCEONE - Software - EMC CORPORATION; *pg.* 391, *pg.* 825
EMC STORAGE ADMINISTRATOR - Software - EMC CORPORATION; *pg.* 391, *pg.* 825
EMCAP - Maize Starch Line - CARGILL, INC.; *pg.* 845, *pg.* 965
EMCAST - Spinning Reel - DAIWA CORPORATION; *pg.* 1832, *pg.* 75
EMCAT-30 - Moving Bed Cracking Catalysts - BASF CATALYSTS LLC; *pg.* 1148, *pg.* 1074
EMCO - Industrial Flow Meter - ADVANCED ENERGY INDUSTRIES, INC.; *pg.* 613, *pg.* 328
EMCO - Lighting Fixture & Control - PHILIPS LIGHTING; *pg.* 1303, *pg.* 806
EMCO WHEATON - Fuel Handling Equipment - GARDNER DENVER, INC.; *pg.* 1338, *pg.* 1592
EMCOR - Additive - BASF CATALYSTS LLC; *pg.* 1148, *pg.* 1074
EMCORE - Electronic Components - EMCORE CORPORATION; *pg.* 636, *pg.* 39
EMCORE MICROWAVE DLS - Electronic Component - EMCORE CORPORATION; *pg.* 636, *pg.* 39
EMCOSOY - Soy Fiber Disintegrant - PENFORD CORPORATION; *pg.* 1177, *pg.* 314
EMCYT - Medicine - PFIZER INC.; *pg.* 1581, *pg.* 1278
EMDS - Supercomputing System - CRAY INC.; *pg.* 380, *pg.* 1834
EMEDICA - Health Plan & Publication - MEDICA, INC.; *pg.* 1208, *pg.* 949
EMEDICINE.COM - Diseases & Disorders Web Site - WEBMD HEALTH CORPORATION; *pg.* 1288, *pg.* 1313
EMEDICINEHEALTH.COM - Health Information Web Site - WEBMD HEALTH CORPORATION; *pg.* 1288, *pg.* 1313
EMELIA - Lamp - ASHLEY FURNITURE INDUSTRIES, INC.; *pg.* 914, *pg.* 1852
EMERALD - Hand Soap - BIRKO CORPORATION; *pg.* 1149, *pg.* 332
EMERALD - Area Rug - COURISTAN INC.; *pg.* 921, *pg.* 1067
EMERALD - Snack Nuts - DIAMOND FOODS, INC.; *pg.* 1851, *pg.* 216
EMERALD - Electronic Power Supply Enclosure - NORDSON CORPORATION; *pg.* 1365, *pg.* 1480
EMERALD - Medical System - VARIAN MEDICAL SYSTEMS, INC.; *pg.* 1434, *pg.* 178
EMERALD 7S - Video Game - INTERNATIONAL GAME TECHNOLOGY; *pg.* 957, *pg.* 1024
EMERALD CARPET - Container Grown Plant - MONROVIA GROWERS; *pg.* 1797, *pg.* 44
EMERALD EXCELLENCE - Flower Arrangement - 1-800-FLOWERS.COM, INC.; *pg.* 1758, *pg.* 1151
EMERALD EYES - Game - WMS INDUSTRIES INC.; *pg.* 593, *pg.* 666
EMERALD FOUNTAIN - Container Grown Plant - MONROVIA GROWERS; *pg.* 1797, *pg.* 44
EMERALD GARDENS GREEN TEA - Tea Product - CELESTIAL SEASONINGS, INC.; *pg.* 846, *pg.* 310
EMERALD GREEN 8'S - Lottery Card - MISSOURI LOTTERY; *pg.* 999, *pg.* 979
EMERALD ISLE - Container Grown Plant - MONROVIA GROWERS; *pg.* 1797, *pg.* 44
EMERALD KING - Container Grown Plant - MONROVIA GROWERS; *pg.* 1797, *pg.* 44
EMERALD RING - Game - WMS INDUSTRIES INC.; *pg.* 593, *pg.* 666
EMERALD ROSE - Video Game - INTERNATIONAL GAME TECHNOLOGY; *pg.* 957, *pg.* 1024
EMERALD SPREADER - Container Grown Plant - MONROVIA GROWERS; *pg.* 1797, *pg.* 44
EMERALD STONE - Roller Cover - VAIL RUBBER WORKS, INC.; *pg.* 1891, *pg.* 906
EMERALD STONE II - Premium Roll Covers - VAIL RUBBER WORKS, INC.; *pg.* 1891, *pg.* 906
EMERALD STONE X - Premium Roll Covers - VAIL RUBBER WORKS, INC.; *pg.* 1891, *pg.* 906
EMERALD TEAL - Fabric - NEMSCHOFF, INC.; *pg.* 936, *pg.* 1890
EMERALD VALLEY KITCHEN - Food Products - MONTEREY GOURMET FOODS, INC.; *pg.* 881, *pg.* 94
EMERALD WAVE - Container Grown Plant - MONROVIA GROWERS; *pg.* 1797, *pg.* 44
EMERALDS & RUBIES - Video Game - INTERNATIONAL GAME TECHNOLOGY; *pg.* 957, *pg.* 1024
EMERCHROME - Concrete System - L.M. SCOFIELD COMPANY; *pg.* 94, *pg.* 134
EMERGE - Resin - THE DOW CHEMICAL COMPANY; *pg.* 1157, *pg.* 898
EMERGE - Office Furniture - STEELCASE INC.; *pg.* 475, *pg.* 889
EMERGENCY BACKOUT SUB - Surface Equipment - DRIL-QUIP, INC.; *pg.* 1330, *pg.* 1704
EMERGI-LITE - Emergency Lighting System - THOMAS & BETTS CORPORATION; *pg.* 680, *pg.* 1646
EMERIL'S - Dressings, Seasonings & Sauces - B&G FOODS, INC.; *pg.* 838, *pg.* 1102
EMERIL'S & BAM! - Television Program - MARTHA STEWART LIVING OMNIMEDIA, INC.; *pg.* 1661, *pg.* 1256

EMERSON - Refiner Machines - BOLTON-EMERSON AMERICAS, INC.; *pg.* 1318, *pg.* 827
EMERSON - Seating Product - IRWIN SEATING COMPANY INC.; *pg.* 929, *pg.* 887
EMERSON - Furniture - JASPER GROUP; *pg.* 930, *pg.* 691
EMERY - Flatware - ONEIDA LTD; *pg.* 1129, *pg.* 1318
EMERY - Lighting Product - QUOIZEL INC.; *pg.* 1304, *pg.* 1616
EMETROL - Nausea Medicine - MCNEIL-PPC, INC.; *pg.* 1560, *pg.* 1533
EMF BROADCASTING - Christian Music Station - EDUCATIONAL MEDIA FOUNDATION; *pg.* 284, *pg.* 194
EMFLON - Filter Cartridge - PALL CORPORATION; *pg.* 232, *pg.* 1323
EMG RETRAINER - Orthopedic Device - DJO SURGICAL; *pg.* 1525, *pg.* 1661
EMHART - Fasteners - STANLEY BLACK & DECKER, INC.; *pg.* 1063, *pg.* 358
EMICLARE - Shielded Windows - PARKER CHOMERICS; *pg.* 662, *pg* 862
EMIGENT - Biopharmaceutical Product - EMISPHERE TECHNOLOGIES, INC.; *pg.* 1528, *pg.* 1118
EMILY - Adapter - MOLEX INCORPORATED; *pg.* 655, *pg.* 628
EMILY - Lighting Product - QUOIZEL INC.; *pg.* 1304, *pg.* 1616
EMISPHERE - Biopharmaceutical Product - EMISPHERE TECHNOLOGIES, INC.; *pg.* 1528, *pg.* 1118
EMKADIXOL - Glycol Ether Brake Fluids - THE DOW CHEMICAL COMPANY; *pg.* 1157, *pg.* 898
EMMA - Furniture - ETHAN ALLEN INTERIORS INC.; *pg.* 924, *pg.* 343
EMMA - Stuffed Animals - GUND, INC.; *pg.* 954, *pg.* 1056
EMMA - Footwear - PHOENIX FOOTWEAR GROUP, INC.; *pg.* 1815, *pg.* 60
EMMA BOOT - Clothing - ABERCROMBIE & FITCH CO.; *pg.* 37, *pg.* 1466
EMMA JAMES - Apparel - KATE SPADE & COMPANY; *pg.* 27, *pg.* 1248
EMMA-YARN CAP - Women's Clothing & Accessories - WOODEN SHIPS OF HOBOKEN; *pg.* 35, *pg.* 1315
EMMALINE - Clothing - ABERCROMBIE & FITCH CO.; *pg.* 37, *pg.* 1466
EMME - Misses & Women's Separates for Full Sized Women - KELLWOOD COMPANY; *pg.* 28, *pg.* 975
EMPART - Software - ARI NETWORK SERVICES, INC.; *pg.* 353, *pg.* 1873
EMPART PUBLISHER - Software - ARI NETWORK SERVICES, INC.; *pg.* 353, *pg.* 1873
EMPART VIEWER - Software - ARI NETWORK SERVICES, INC.; *pg.* 353, *pg.* 1873
EMPART WEB - Software - ARI NETWORK SERVICES, INC.; *pg.* 353, *pg.* 1873
EMPARTPUBLISHER - Software - ARI NETWORK SERVICES, INC.; *pg.* 353, *pg.* 1873
EMPARTVIEWER - Software - ARI NETWORK SERVICES, INC.; *pg.* 353, *pg.* 1873
EMPARTWEB - Software - ARI NETWORK SERVICES, INC.; *pg.* 353, *pg.* 1873
EMPERATRIZ - Waxes - THE CLOROX COMPANY; *pg.* 327, *pg.* 169
EMPEROR - Carbon Black - CABOT CORPORATION; *pg.* 1151, *pg.* 792
EMPEROR - Refrigerated Truck Trailer - KIDRON, INC.; *pg.* 181, *pg.* 1457
EMPEROR OF ANTARCTICA - Video Game - INTERNATIONAL GAME TECHNOLOGY; *pg.* 957, *pg.* 1024
EMPERORS CHOICE - Herb Tea - CELESTIAL SEASONINGS, INC.; *pg.* 846, *pg.* 310
EMPEROR'S CHOICE - Video Game - INTERNATIONAL GAME TECHNOLOGY; *pg.* 957, *pg.* 1024
EMPEROR'S PALACE - Video Game - INTERNATIONAL GAME TECHNOLOGY; *pg.* 957, *pg.* 1024
EMPHASIZE - Medical Product - HOLOGIC, INC.; *pg.* 1416, *pg.* 784
EMPI - Orthopedic Implant Product - DJO SURGICAL; *pg.* 1525, *pg.* 1661
EMPICOL - Alcohol Sulphate - HUNTSMAN CORPORATION; *pg.* 1167, *pg.* 1758
EMPIGEN - Alkyl Ampho - HUNTSMAN CORPORATION; *pg.* 1167, *pg.* 1758
EMPIMIN - Sulphosuccinamates - HUNTSMAN CORPORATION; *pg.* 1167, *pg.* 1758
EMPIPHOS - Phosphate Esters - HUNTSMAN CORPORATION; *pg.* 1167, *pg.* 1758
EMPIRE - Jewelry - EMPIRE DIAMOND CORPORATION; *pg.* 4, *pg.* 1227
EMPIRE - Kosher Poultry - EMPIRE KOSHER POULTRY, INC.; *pg.* 854, *pg.* 1553
EMPIRE - Seating Product - IRWIN SEATING COMPANY INC.; *pg.* 929, *pg.* 887
EMPIRE - Lighting Product - QUOIZEL INC.; *pg.* 1304, *pg.* 1616
EMPIRE DESK - Furniture - J. ROBERT SCOTT INC.; *pg.* 930, *pg.* 105
EMPIRE RESORTS - Gaming Service - EMPIRE RESORTS, INC.; *pg.* 1090, *pg.* 1183
EMPIRE SEAM TOP - Clothing - K-SWISS; *pg.* 1837, *pg.* 306
EMPIRES - Game - ACTIVISION BLIZZARD, INC.; *pg.* 948, *pg.* 271
EMPIRES TREASURE - Seafood - PERFORMANCE FOOD GROUP COMPANY, LLC; *pg.* 1030, *pg.* 1803
EMPIRIC - Organosilicone Surfactant - KALO, INC.; *pg.* 1796, *pg.* 719
EMPIWAX - Emulsifying Waxes - HUNTSMAN CORPORATION; *pg.* 1167, *pg.* 1758
EMPLOYEE BENEFITS LIBRARY - Publisher - BLOOMBERG BNA; *pg.* 1621, *pg.* 1772
EMPLOYEE OWNED | CUSTOMER DRIVEN - Tagline - LITECONTROL CORPORATION; *pg.* 1301, *pg.* 841
EMPLOYEE SERVICE CENTER - Online Service Access - INSPERITY, INC.; *pg.* 416, *pg.* 1725
THE EMPLOYMENT GUIDE - Advertising Publication - DOMINION ENTERPRISES; *pg.* 1636, *pg.* 1796
EMPORE - Reactive Membrane Technology - 3M COMPANY; *pg.* 1142, *pg.* 956
EMPORIO ARMANI - Apparel & Fragrance - GIORGIO ARMANI CORPORATION; *pg.* 25, *pg.* 1234
EMPORIO ARMANI DIAMONDS - Perfume - GIORGIO ARMANI CORPORATION; *pg.* 25, *pg.* 1234
EMPOWER - Software - WATERS CORPORATION; *pg.* 1436, *pg.* 834
EMPOWER WITH LIGHT - Slogan - EMCORE CORPORATION; *pg.* 636, *pg.* 39
EMPOWERED - Mobile Broadband Connector - SIERRA WIRELESS INCORPORATED; *pg.* 673, *pg.* 1909
EMPOWERED EDUCATION - Computer Services - SPRINT CORPORATION; *pg.* 1874, *pg.* 719
EMPOWERING EXTRAORDINARY HEALTH - Slogan - GARDEN OF LIFE, INC.; *pg.* 1532, *pg.* 478
EMPOWERING HEALTHCARE - Tagline - MCKESSON CORPORATION; *pg.* 1560, *pg.* 222
EMPOWERING SOLUTION PROVIDERS - Slogan - SCANSOURCE, INC.; *pg.* 671, *pg.* 1618
EMPOWERING SOLUTIONS - Software System - MENTOR GRAPHICS CORPORATION; *pg.* 432, *pg.* 1510
EMPOWR - Copper & Aluminum Cable - GENERAL CABLE CORPORATION; *pg.* 83, *pg.* 729
EMPRESS - Vacuum Cleaner - HMI INDUSTRIES INC.; *pg.* 56, *pg.* 1475
EMPRESS - Canned Food Products - MITSUI FOODS, INC.; *pg.* 877, *pg.* 1099
EMPRESS CLUB - International Business Class - AIR CANADA; *pg.* 1896, *pg.* 1902
EMPRESS OF THE SEAS - Cruise Ship - ROYAL CARIBBEAN CRUISES LTD; *pg.* 1921, *pg.* 446
EMPRESS ZOYSIA - Food Product - A. DUDA & SONS INC.; *pg.* 835, *pg.* 457
EMPRIZONE - Skin Care Product - MANNATECH, INCORPORATED; *pg.* 1558, *pg.* 1671
EMPULSE - Software - CTI GROUP HOLDINGS INC.; *pg.* 381, *pg.* 684
EMRWEB - Software - HEALTHPORT, INC.; *pg.* 403, *pg.* 484
EMS - Enhanced Mobility System - AM GENERAL, LLC; *pg.* 163, *pg.* 697
EMS - Elastic Stockings for Medical & Therapeutic Use - MEDLINE INDUSTRIES, INC.; *pg.* 1562, *pg.* 635
EMS-ENABLE - Adapter - MOLEX INCORPORATED; *pg.* 655, *pg.* 628
EMS PANORAMA - Web-Based Elevator Management System - OTIS ELEVATOR COMPANY; *pg.* 102, *pg.* 349
EMSWORLDWIDE - Printed Circuit Boards - CTS CORPORATION; *pg.* 631, *pg.* 677
EMT - Emergency Medicine Tube - MEDTRONIC; *pg.* 1563, *pg.* 183
EMT - Homeowner Product - PBI/GORDON CORPORATION; *pg.* 1176, *pg.* 985
EMTRIVA - Biopharmaceutical Product - GILEAD SCIENCES, INC.; *pg.* 1535, *pg.* 88
EMU - Battery Management Circuits - TEXAS INSTRUMENTS INCORPORATED; *pg.* 679, *pg.* 1688
EMULLO - Nitrocellulose Lacquer Emulsions For Leather - HENKEL CORPORATION; *pg.* 1165, *pg.* 1535
EMULPHOPAL - Chemical Product - STEPAN COMPANY; *pg.* 1182, *pg.* 643
EMULPHOR - Chemical Product - STEPAN COMPANY; *pg.* 1182, *pg.* 643
EMULSA-BOND - Coating & Paint - AKZO NOBEL DECORATIVE PAINTS, USA; *pg.* 1439, *pg.* 1474
EMULUS - Software - SAS INSTITUTE INC.; *pg.* 466, *pg.* 1361
EMVELOP - Wax Matrix for Controlled-Release Tablets - PENFORD CORPORATION; *pg.* 1177, *pg.* 314
EMVISION360 - Software - OPENTEXT; *pg.* 450, *pg.* 1665
EMXXX - Fluid Handling System - GRACO, INC.; *pg.* 1342, *pg.* 935
EN3HANCE - Autoradiography Enhancer - PERKINELMER, INC.; *pg.* 1426, *pg.* 853
ENABLING CONVERGENT TECHNOLOGICS - Slogan - TELECOMMUNICATION SYSTEMS INC.; *pg.* 483, *pg.* 754
ENABLING SUPPLY CHAIN EXCELLENCE - Slogan - TECSYS, INC.; *pg.* 482, *pg.* 1956
ENABLING TECHNOLOGY - Slogan - GSI GROUP INC.; *pg.* 1415, *pg.* 784
ENABLING YIELD - Services - ENTEGRIS, INC.; *pg.* 1882, *pg.* 788
ENBOND - Metal Cleaner - ENTHONE INC.; *pg.* 1161, *pg.* 381
ENBREL - Medicine - AMGEN INC.; *pg.* 1493, *pg.* 291
ENBRITE - Plating Process - A BRITE COMPANY; *pg.* 1144, *pg.* 1697
ENCANTO - Publishing Imprint - KENSINGTON PUBLISHING CORP.; *pg.* 1656, *pg.* 1248
ENCAP - Potting & Encapsulating Compounds - HENKEL CORPORATION; *pg.* 1049, *pg.* 369
ENCAPSO K - Display Rubber - SMOOTH-ON INC.; *pg.* 111, *pg.* 1528
ENCAUSTIC - Fabric - NEMSCHOFF, INC.; *pg.* 936, *pg.* 1890
ENCHANT - Life Science Kit - PALL CORPORATION; *pg.* 232, *pg.* 1323
ENCHANTE - Lighting Product - WESTINGHOUSE LIGHTING CORPORATION; *pg.* 687, *pg.* 1571
ENCHANTED - Fabric - NEMSCHOFF, INC.; *pg.* 936, *pg.* 1890
ENCHANTED EGYPT - Video Game - INTERNATIONAL GAME TECHNOLOGY; *pg.* 957, *pg.* 1024
ENCHANTED GARDEN - Rug - COURISTAN INC.; *pg.* 921, *pg.* 1067
ENCHANTED GARDEN - Video Game - INTERNATIONAL GAME TECHNOLOGY; *pg.* 957, *pg.* 1024
ENCHANTED ISLAND - Video Game - INTERNATIONAL GAME TECHNOLOGY; *pg.* 957, *pg.* 1024
ENCHANTED KINGDOM - Game - WMS INDUSTRIES INC.; *pg.* 593, *pg.* 666
ENCHANTED TREE TREASURES - Educational Materials - SCHOLASTIC INC.; *pg.* 1683, *pg.* 1288
ENCHANTED UNICORN - Slots - INTERNATIONAL GAME TECHNOLOGY; *pg.* 957, *pg.* 1024
ENCHANTED UNIVERSE - Deluxe Cards - LEANIN' TREE, INC.; *pg.* 1658, *pg.* 311
ENCHANTMENT OF THE SEAS - Cruise Ship - ROYAL CARIBBEAN CRUISES LTD; *pg.* 1921, *pg.* 446
ENCHANTRESS - Container Grown Plant - MONROVIA GROWERS; *pg.* 1797, *pg.* 44
ENCHILADAS - Mexican Food - RUIZ FOOD PRODUCTS, INC.; *pg.* 893, *pg.* 77
ENCHORD - Furniture - HERMAN MILLER, INC.; *pg.* 926, *pg.* 913
ENCLAD - Cable & Thermocouple - BASF CATALYSTS LLC; *pg.* 1148, *pg.* 1074
ENCLAVE - Magazine - NETWORK COMMUNICATIONS INC.; *pg.* 1271, *pg.* 534
ENCLOSE - Office Product - HAWORTH, INC.; *pg.* 402, *pg.* 891
ENCO - Chemical Product - HURST CHEMICAL COMPANY; *pg.* 1168, *pg.* 174
ENCOMPASS - Diagnostic Product - ALERE SAN DIEGO; *pg.* 1489, *pg.* 199
ENCOMPASS - Work Flow Analysis Service - EASTMAN KODAK COMPANY; *pg.* 1408, *pg.* 1333
ENCOMPASS - Safety & Protective Equipment - ENCON SAFETY PRODUCTS; *pg.* 1334, *pg.* 1705

First page reference indicates Business Class Edition
Second page reference indicates Geographic Edition

ENCOMPASS - Dispense System - ENTEGRIS, INC.; *pg.* 1882, *pg.* 788
ENCOMPASS - Document Management Solution - THOMSON ELITE; *pg.* 484, *pg.* 72
ENCOMPASS BY PELLA - Vinyl Windows & Patio Doors - PELLA CORPORATION; *pg.* 104, *pg.* 711
ENCOMPASS PRO - Software - VIQ SOLUTIONS INC.; *pg.* 490, *pg.* 1905
ENCOMPASS360 - Software - ELLIE MAE, INC.; *pg.* 1243, *pg.* 183
ENCON - Company Name - ENCON SAFETY PRODUCTS; *pg.* 1334, *pg.* 1705
ENCORE - Software - ADOBE SYSTEMS INCORPORATED; *pg.* 342, *pg.* 235
ENCORE - Cannister Vacuum Cleaner - AERUS LLC; *pg.* 51, *pg.* 1673
ENCORE - Video Bridging & Recording - APPLIED GLOBAL TECHNOLOGIES; *pg.* 352, *pg.* 460
ENCORE - Tile - ARTISTIC TILE INC.; *pg.* 914, *pg.* 1119
ENCORE - Furniture - ASHLEY FURNITURE INDUSTRIES, INC.; *pg.* 914, *pg.* 1852
ENCORE - Coating, Fats & Confections - CARGILL LIMITED; *pg.* 1475, *pg.* 1914
ENCORE - Beverage Service & Stainless Steel Pitcher - CARLISLE FOODSERVICE PRODUCTS INCORPORATED; *pg.* 1455, *pg.* 1485
ENCORE - On-Chip Controller - CYPRESS SEMICONDUCTOR CORPORATION; *pg.* 1326, *pg.* 243
ENCORE - Facility Control System - GRASS VALLEY, INC.; *pg.* 641, *pg.* 164
ENCORE - Scarf - HERITAGE LACE INC.; *pg.* 694, *pg.* 711
ENCORE - Conferencing Service - INTERCALL, INC.; *pg.* 417, *pg.* 578
ENCORE - Furniture - JASPER GROUP; *pg.* 930, *pg.* 691
ENCORE - Thermal Framing System - KAWNEER COMPANY, INC.; *pg.* 90, *pg.* 537
ENCORE - Lighting - LSI INDUSTRIES INC.; *pg.* 58, *pg.* 1416
ENCORE - Healthcare Product - MEDICOOL, INC.; *pg.* 1562, *pg.* 294
ENCORE - Telecommunications Products - MITEL NETWORKS, INC.; *pg.* 1872, *pg.* 13
ENCORE - Filter Cartridge - PALL CORPORATION; *pg.* 232, *pg.* 1323
ENCORE - Pet Product - PETSMART, INC.; *pg.* 1481, *pg.* 18
ENCORE - Headset - PLANTRONICS, INC.; *pg.* 663, *pg.* 270
ENCORE - Commercial CD Jukebox - ROWE INTERNATIONAL CORP; *pg.* 669, *pg.* 889
ENCORE - Door - SIMPSON DOOR COMPANY; *pg.* 110, *pg.* 1823
ENCORE - Flooring Product - STAGESTEP INC.; *pg.* 1688, *pg.* 1570
ENCORE - Drug Delivery System - SURMODICS, INC.; *pg.* 1600, *pg.* 924
ENCORE - Software - SYNOPSYS, INC.; *pg.* 480, *pg.* 162
ENCORE - Casino - WYNN RESORTS LIMITED; *pg.* 1119, *pg.* 1030
ENCORE! - Micrologic Semiconductor Device - ZILOG INC.; *pg.* 497, *pg.* 252
ENCORE EDGE - Cable Television Channel - STARZ ENTERTAINMENT, LLC; *pg.* 310, *pg.* 327
ENCORE ELITE - Flooring Product - STAGESTEP INC.; *pg.* 1688, *pg.* 1570
ENCORE GRIP - Roller Ball Pens - PENTEL OF AMERICA, LTD.; *pg.* 453, *pg.* 295
ENCORE HD - Cable Television - STARZ ENTERTAINMENT, LLC; *pg.* 310, *pg.* 327
ENCORE RECYCLED APPLIANCES - Appliance Retail Store - APPLIANCE RECYCLING CENTERS OF AMERICA, INC.; *pg.* 51, *pg.* 930
ENCORE! XP - Micrologic Semiconductor Device - ZILOG INC.; *pg.* 497, *pg.* 252
ENCORECX - Communication System - MITEL NETWORKS, INC.; *pg.* 1872, *pg.* 13
ENCORR - Software - DST SYSTEMS, INC.; *pg.* 388, *pg.* 982
ENCOTE - Safety & Protective Equipment - ENCON SAFETY PRODUCTS; *pg.* 1334, *pg.* 1705
ENCOUNTER - Software - CADENCE DESIGN SYSTEMS, INC.; *pg.* 367, *pg.* 239
ENCOUNTER - Server - EZENIA! INC.; *pg.* 396, *pg.* 1039
...ENCOURAGING NEW DISCOVERY - Tagline - KEWAUNEE SCIENTIFIC CORPORATION; *pg.* 931, *pg.* 1391
ENCRYPTION - Remedy Software - BMC SOFTWARE, INC.; *pg.* 362, *pg.* 1701
ENCUENTROS - Spanish Cards - LEANIN' TREE, INC.; *pg.* 1658, *pg.* 311
ENCYCLOPEDIA AMERICA - Educational Materials - SCHOLASTIC INC.; *pg.* 1683, *pg.* 1288
ENCYCLOPEDIA OF ORGANIC GARDENING - Book - RODALE, INC.; *pg.* 1681, *pg.* 1530
END-CAP - Test Cap - OATEY SUPPLY CHAIN SERVICES; *pg.* 30, *pg.* 1433
END-MATE - Chalk Product - C.H. HANSON COMPANY; *pg.* 1322, *pg.* 636
THE END OF OVEREATING - Book - RODALE, INC.; *pg.* 1681, *pg.* 1530
END OF THE RAINBOW - Video Game - INTERNATIONAL GAME TECHNOLOGY; *pg.* 957, *pg.* 1024
END SMOKE - Smoke Odor Removal System - SURCO PRODUCTS, INC.; *pg.* 336, *pg.* 1581
END-TO-END ENERGY INTELLIGENCE - Slogan - COMVERGE, INC.; *pg.* 1325, *pg.* 536
END2END - Video Game - INTERNATIONAL GAME TECHNOLOGY; *pg.* 957, *pg.* 1024
ENDA-BUG - Insecticide - ENESCO, LLC; *pg.* 1124, *pg.* 620
ENDEAVOR - Furniture - ASHLEY FURNITURE INDUSTRIES, INC.; *pg.* 914, *pg.* 1852
ENDEAVOR - Disc Publisher - MICROBOARDS TECHNOLOGY, LLC; *pg.* 434, *pg.* 920
ENDEAVOUR - Cleaning Product - HILLYARD, INC.; *pg.* 331, *pg.* 990
ENDEX - Hydrocarbon Resins - EASTMAN CHEMICAL COMPANY; *pg.* 1159, *pg.* 1636
ENDGLOW - Fiber Optic Cable - REVOLUTION LIGHTING TECHNOLOGIES, INC.; *pg.* 1304, *pg.* 377
ENDICIA - Internet Postage - NEWELL RUBBERMAID INC.; *pg.* 1128, *pg.* 515
ENDIMAL - Room Deodorant - E.I. DU PONT DE NEMOURS & COMPANY; *pg.* 1159, *pg.* 390
ENDLESS - Shoe - AEROGROUP INTERNATIONAL, INC.; *pg.* 1803, *pg.* 1055
ENDLESS SUMMER COMFORT - Patio Heater - BLUE RHINO CORPORATION; *pg.* 1318, *pg.* 1393
ENDO - Implant Product - ZIMMER BIOMET HOLDINGS, INC.; *pg.* 1611, *pg.* 699
ENDO-FLO - Medical Device - C.R. BARD, INC.; *pg.* 1519, *pg.* 1094
ENDO-SUCTION SINUS MICROSTATS - Surgical Instrument - AMERICAN MEDICAL SYSTEMS, INC.; *pg.* 1399, *pg.* 238
ENDOCABG - Pharmaceutical Product - GENZYME CORPORATION; *pg.* 1534, *pg.* 808
ENDOCET - Pharmaceutical Product - ENDO PHARMACEUTICALS HOLDINGS, INC.; *pg.* 1528, *pg.* 1549
ENDOCHECK - Medical Product - HOLOGIC, INC.; *pg.* 1416, *pg.* 784
ENDOCURETTE - Endometrial Suction Curette - UTAH MEDICAL PRODUCTS, INC.; *pg.* 1605, *pg.* 1752
ENDODAN - Pharmaceutical Product - ENDO PHARMACEUTICALS HOLDINGS, INC.; *pg.* 1528, *pg.* 1549
ENDOFIT - Thoracic Endovascular Products - LEMAITRE VASCULAR, INC.; *pg.* 1555, *pg.* 805
ENDOGAS - Heat Treating Equipment - SECO/WARWICK CORPORATION; *pg.* 1076, *pg.* 1552
ENDOHELIX - Medical Device - LEMAITRE VASCULAR, INC.; *pg.* 1555, *pg.* 805
ENDOLOGIX - Medical Treatment - ENDOLOGIX, INC.; *pg.* 1528, *pg.* 109
ENDONURSE - Publication - INFORMA EXHIBITIONS LLC; *pg.* 1653, *pg.* 17
ENDOPROBE - Medical Laser System - IRIDEX CORPORATION; *pg.* 648, *pg.* 160
ENDOQUENCH - Thermal Processing Equipment - SURFACE COMBUSTION, INC.; *pg.* 1077, *pg.* 1462
ENDORE - Remote Endarterectomy Instrumentation - LEMAITRE VASCULAR, INC.; *pg.* 1555, *pg.* 805
ENDORPHIN SPIKE - Footwear - SAUCONY, INC.; *pg.* 1818, *pg.* 828
ENDOS - Dental X-Ray Machines - IMAGEWORKS; *pg.* 1544, *pg.* 1158
ENDOSONIC - Dental Product - DENTSPLY INTERNATIONAL INC.; *pg.* 1522, *pg.* 1596
ENDOSTAIN - Biomolecule Product - THERMO FISHER SCIENTIFIC INC.; *pg.* 1602, *pg.* 61
ENDOSTAT - Medical Laser Product - AMERICAN MEDICAL SYSTEMS, INC.; *pg.* 1399, *pg.* 238
ENDOSTATIN - Molecular Probe Product - THERMO FISHER SCIENTIFIC INC.; *pg.* 1602, *pg.* 61
ENDOSUITE - Integrated Operating Room - STRYKER CORPORATION; *pg.* 1598, *pg.* 894
ENDOTAK RELIANCE - Medical Device - BOSTON SCIENTIFIC CORPORATION; *pg.* 1508, *pg.* 831
ENDOTROL - Tracheal Tube - MEDTRONIC; *pg.* 1563, *pg.* 183
ENDOVIVE - Medical Device - BOSTON SCIENTIFIC CORPORATION; *pg.* 1508, *pg.* 831
ENDOWRIST - Instrument System - INTUITIVE SURGICAL, INC.; *pg.* 1546, *pg.* 286
ENDREM - Cams - GLEASON CORPORATION; *pg.* 1340, *pg.* 1335
ENDSEAL - Grooved Pipe Coupling Gasket For Lined Pipe End Preparation - VICTAULIC COMPANY; *pg.* 1066, *pg.* 1529
ENDUR - Material - ROGERS CORPORATION; *pg.* 1305, *pg.* 369
ENDUR-IC - Semiconductor Device - MICRON TECHNOLOGY, INC.; *pg.* 435, *pg.* 547
ENDURA - Physical Vapor Deposition System - APPLIED MATERIALS, INC.; *pg.* 618, *pg.* 264
ENDURA - Rubber Flooring - THE BILTRITE CORPORATION; *pg.* 1879, *pg.* 850
ENDURA - Paper & Nonwoven Material - FIBERMARK INC.; *pg.* 1457, *pg.* 1764
ENDURA - Medical Device - INTEGRA LIFESCIENCES HOLDINGS CORPORATION; *pg.* 1545, *pg.* 1109
ENDURA - Power Management - INTERSIL CORPORATION; *pg.* 647, *pg.* 146
ENDURA - High Density Plastic Carts - LUXOR CORP.; *pg.* 428, *pg.* 666
ENDURA - Plate - MULBERRY METAL PRODUCTS, INC.; *pg.* 1302, *pg.* 1127
ENDURA - Industrial Flame Retardant Composition - PPG INDUSTRIES, INC.; *pg.* 1445, *pg.* 1579
ENDURA - Embedded Computer System - RADISYS CORPORATION; *pg.* 458, *pg.* 1498
ENDURA-CLASSIC - Wood - PACIFIC COLUMNS, INC.; *pg.* 103, *pg.* 49
ENDURA-COAT - Exterior Flat - DUNN-EDWARDS CORPORATION; *pg.* 1442, *pg.* 129
ENDURA-CRAFT - Wood - PACIFIC COLUMNS, INC.; *pg.* 103, *pg.* 49
ENDURA-LUM - Wood - PACIFIC COLUMNS, INC.; *pg.* 103, *pg.* 49
ENDURA-SERIES - Architectural Columns - PACIFIC COLUMNS, INC.; *pg.* 103, *pg.* 49
ENDURA-STONE - Wood - PACIFIC COLUMNS, INC.; *pg.* 103, *pg.* 49
ENDURA-TEK - Cartridge - DONALDSON COMPANY, INC.; *pg.* 1329, *pg.* 917
ENDURA-TRAC - Slip Rings - MOOG INC.; *pg.* 231, *pg.* 1156
ENDURACAST - Gypsum Matrix - USG CORPORATION; *pg.* 118, *pg.* 594
ENDURACLAD - Windows - PELLA CORPORATION; *pg.* 104, *pg.* 711
ENDURACRYL - Exterior Low Sheen Paint - DUNN-EDWARDS CORPORATION; *pg.* 1442, *pg.* 129
ENDURAGLOSS - Alkyd Gloss Sealer - DUNN-EDWARDS CORPORATION; *pg.* 1442, *pg.* 129
ENDURAGOLD - Fiber Glass Duct Product - OWENS CORNING; *pg.* 102, *pg.* 1476
ENDURAMET - Steel Rebar - CARPENTER TECHNOLOGY CORPORATION; *pg.* 73, *pg.* 1584
ENDURANCE - Paint & Stain - AKZONOBEL DECORATIVE PAINTS U.S.; *pg.* 1439, *pg.* 1474
ENDURANCE - Filter - DONALDSON COMPANY, INC.; *pg.* 1329, *pg.* 917
ENDURANCE - Polyurethane Dispersions - THE DOW CHEMICAL COMPANY; *pg.* 1157, *pg.* 898
ENDURANCE - Sports Drink - ENERGY BRANDS, INC.; *pg.* 854, *pg.* 1227
ENDURANCE - Piston Pump - GRACO, INC.; *pg.* 1342, *pg.* 935
ENDURANCE - Casters - HAMILTON CASTER & MFG. CO.; *pg.* 206, *pg.* 1454
ENDURANCE - Power Tool - MILWAUKEE ELECTRIC TOOL CORP.; *pg.* 1056, *pg.* 1855
ENDURANCE ADVANTAGE - Fluid Handling System - GRACO, INC.; *pg.* 1342, *pg.* 935
ENDURANCE E - Piston Pump - GRACO, INC.; *pg.* 1342, *pg.* 935

ENDURANCE PISTON PUMP - Piston Pump - GRACO, INC.; pg. 1342, pg. 935
ENDURAPATCH - Elastomeric Sealer - DUNN-EDWARDS CORPORATION; pg. 1442, pg. 129
ENDURASEAL - Acrylic Masonry Seal - DUNN-EDWARDS CORPORATION; pg. 1442, pg. 129
ENDURASHINE - Valve Cover - EDELBROCK CORPORATION; pg. 204, pg. 293
ENDURATEC - Alkyd Gloss Enamel - DUNN-EDWARDS CORPORATION; pg. 1442, pg. 129
ENDURAWALL - Elastomeric Wall Coating - DUNN-EDWARDS CORPORATION; pg. 1442, pg. 129
ENDURE - Valves - GRACO, INC.; pg. 1342, pg. 935
ENDURION - Wallcovering - OMNOVA SOLUTIONS INC; pg. 1176, pg. 1453
ENDURO - Furniture - ASHLEY FURNITURE INDUSTRIES, INC.; pg. 914, pg. 1852
ENDURO - Dicing Blade - KULICKE & SOFFA INDUSTRIES, INC.; pg. 650, pg. 1533
ENDURO - Flashlight - STREAMLIGHT INC.; pg. 1306, pg. 1527
ENDURO-FLITE - Formed Piano Hinge Conveyor - WEBSTER INDUSTRIES INC.; pg. 1388, pg. 1475
ENDURO-FLO - Drag Conveyor - SCREW CONVEYOR INDUSTRIES; pg. 1374, pg. 682
ENDURO-STS - Sorter System - GLOBE COMPOSITE SOLUTIONS, LTD.; pg. 1883, pg. 842
ENDUROFLEX - Furniture - HSM SOLUTIONS; pg. 1884, pg. 1378
ENDUROFOAM - Foam Product - HSM SOLUTIONS; pg. 1884, pg. 1378
ENDUROLOFT - Fiber Product - HSM SOLUTIONS; pg. 1884, pg. 1378
ENDUROPAD - Fiber Product - HSM SOLUTIONS; pg. 1884, pg. 1378
ENDUROPOWER - Open Plant Cleaning Chemical - DIVERSEY, INC.; pg. 1123, pg. 1896
ENDUROX EXCEL - Supplement - PACIFICHEALTH LABORATORIES, INC.; pg. 1579, pg. 1083
ENDUROX R4 - Health Care Product - PACIFICHEALTH LABORATORIES, INC.; pg. 1579, pg. 1083
ENDUROX RESTORE - Recovery Drink - PACIFICHEALTH LABORATORIES, INC.; pg. 1579, pg. 1083
ENEA - Office Furniture - STEELCASE INC.; pg. 475, pg. 889
ENEA BARSTOOL - Office Furniture - STEELCASE INC.; pg. 475, pg. 889
ENEA CAFE TABLE - Tables - STEELCASE INC.; pg. 475, pg. 889
ENER-CAP - Seal & Thermoplastic Component - GREENE, TWEED & CO.; pg. 1344, pg. 1544
ENERBOND - Adhesive - THE DOW CHEMICAL COMPANY; pg. 1157, pg. 898
ENERBOND BA - Polyurethane Foam Adhesive - THE DOW CHEMICAL COMPANY; pg. 1157, pg. 898
ENERBOND DW - Polyurethane Foam Adhesive - THE DOW CHEMICAL COMPANY; pg. 1157, pg. 898
ENERBOND SF - Polyurethane Foam Adhesive - THE DOW CHEMICAL COMPANY; pg. 1157, pg. 898
ENERFOAM - Sealant - THE DOW CHEMICAL COMPANY; pg. 1157, pg. 898
ENERG - Health System Product - LANELABS USA INC.; pg. 1554, pg. 1128
ENERG-EYES - Nutritional Supplement - WHITEWING LABS, INC.; pg. 1610, pg. 99
ENERG-V - Health Care Product - NATURE'S SUNSHINE PRODUCTS, INC.; pg. 1571, pg. 1754
ENERGADE - Beverage - MONSTER BEVERAGE CORPORATION; pg. 257, pg. 69
ENERGAIN - Energy Efficient Materials - E.I. DU PONT DE NEMOURS & COMPANY; pg. 1159, pg. 390
ENERGAIRE - Air Purifier - MICRON CORPORATION; pg. 654, pg. 840
ENERGEN - Energy Holding Company - ENERGEN CORPORATION; pg. 1941, pg. 2
ENERGETIC MATERIALS - Energetic Device - DANAHER CORPORATION; pg. 1044, pg. 397
ENERGIA - Battery - ENERSYS INC.; pg. 1334, pg. 1584
ENERGIA - Foam Product - FXI; pg. 1163, pg. 1552
ENERGILASS - Sheep Product - KENT NUTRITION GROUP; pg. 1477, pg. 710
ENERGIZE, MAXIMIZE, CHIQUITA-TIZE - Fruit & Vegetable Product - CHIQUITA BRANDS INTERNATIONAL, INC.; pg. 847, pg. 1365
ENERGIZER - Software - BMC SOFTWARE, INC.; pg. 362, pg. 1701
ENERGIZER ADVANCED FORMULA - Alkaline Battery - ENERGIZER HOLDINGS, INC.; pg. 637, pg. 996
ENERGIZER BUNNY - Product Icon - ENERGIZER HOLDINGS, INC.; pg. 637, pg. 996
ENERGIZER E2 - Batteries - ENERGIZER HOLDINGS, INC.; pg. 637, pg. 996
ENERGIZER MAX - Batteries - ENERGIZER HOLDINGS, INC.; pg. 637, pg. 996
ENERGIZER ULTRAPLUS - Flashlight - ENERGIZER HOLDINGS, INC.; pg. 637, pg. 996
ENERGIZING FRAGRANCE - Cosmetic Product - SHISEIDO COSMETICS AMERICA OF SAC; pg. 522, pg. 1291
ENERGY - Sports Drink - ENERGY BRANDS, INC.; pg. 854, pg. 1227
ENERGY - Dinnerware - THE HOMER LAUGHLIN CHINA COMPANY; pg. 1125, pg. 1850
ENERGY - Beverage - MONSTER BEVERAGE CORPORATION; pg. 257, pg. 69
ENERGY - Nutritional Product - NUTRACEUTICAL INTERNATIONAL CORPORATION; pg 1576, pg. 1753
ENERGY BOOST - Boost - JAMBA, INC.; pg. 1024, pg. 84
ENERGY CONNECTION - Newsletter - CPS ENERGY; pg. 1939, pg. 1739
ENERGY EFFICIENT - Machine Tools - SENECA FALLS MACHINES; pg. 1374, pg. 1341
ENERGY ELIXIR - Nutritional Supplement - NATURAL ORGANICS, INC.; pg. 1571, pg. 1181
ENERGY FOR LIFE - Slogan - NEW EARTH LIFE SCIENCES, INC.; pg. 1573, pg. 1499
ENERGY FOR PEOPLE - Tagline - ENCANA CORP.; pg. 976, pg. 1903
ENERGY FOR THE COMMUNITY - Program - EXELON CORPORATION; pg. 1942, pg. 573
ENERGY FOR TOMORROW - Tagline - CONOCOPHILLIPS; pg. 975, pg. 1703
ENERGY INNOVATIONS - Software - IDEALAB, INC.; pg. 1258, pg. 180
ENERGY KNIGHT - Terminal Air Conditioner - HEAT CONTROLLER, INC.; pg. 1072, pg. 893
ENERGY MAKEOVER - Public Awareness - XCEL ENERGY INC.; pg. 1955, pg. 946
ENERGY MISER - Fan System - BALTIMORE AIRCOIL COMPANY; pg. 1069, pg. 773
ENERGY MISER - Water Heater - RHEEM MANUFACTURING COMPANY; pg. 1075, pg. 519
ENERGY PLUS - Battery - ENERSYS INC.; pg. 1334, pg. 1584
ENERGY RADIANT TUBE - Thermal Processing Equipment - SURFACE COMBUSTION, INC.; pg. 1077, pg. 1462
ENERGY SAVER - Window & Door - JELD-WEN, INC.; pg. 1051, pg. 1499
ENERGY SAVER HOME - Energy-efficient Homes - DOMINION VIRGINIA POWER; pg. 1939, pg. 1802
ENERGY SAVERS - Pet Product - PETSMART, INC.; pg. 1481, pg. 18
ENERGY SERIES - Power Transmission Product - U.S. TSUBAKI, INC.; pg. 221, pg. 670
ENERGY SIGNAL PROCESSING - Wireless Technology - PARKERVISION, INC.; pg. 1426, pg. 434
ENERGY SMART - Fluorescent Lighting Package - GENERAL ELECTRIC COMPANY; pg. 1297, pg. 347
ENERGY SMART SERVICES - Financial Incentive - SEATTLE CITY LIGHT; pg. 1951, pg. 1839
ENERGY STAR - Window & Door - HARVEY INDUSTRIES, INC.; pg. 86, pg. 851
ENERGY STAR - Software - MAC-GRAY CORPORATION; pg. 58, pg. 852
ENERGY STAR - Energy Efficiency - ODL INCORPORATED; pg. 101, pg. 914
ENERGY STAR - Lighting Product - WESTINGHOUSE LIGHTING CORPORATION; pg. 687, pg. 1571
THE ENERGY SUPPLEMENTS - Slogan - NATURAL ORGANICS, INC.; pg. 1571, pg. 1181
ENERGY WATER - Beverage - MONSTER BEVERAGE CORPORATION; pg. 257, pg. 69
THE ENERGY WITHIN - Tagline - PIEDMONT NATURAL GAS COMPANY, INC.; pg. 1949, pg. 1368
ENERGYAXIS - Water Metering Tool - ELSTER AMCO WATER, INC.; pg. 1411, pg. 452
ENERGYLINE - Automatic Switch Control - S&C ELECTRIC COMPANY; pg. 1305, pg. 589
ENERGYLINE 5800 - Automatic Switch Control - S&C ELECTRIC COMPANY; pg. 1305, pg. 589
ENERGYMISER - Software - USA TECHNOLOGIES, INC.; pg. 815, pg. 1550
ENERGYRITE - Pool Heater - LOCHINVAR CORPORATION; pg. 1073, pg. 1640
ENERGYSAVER - Lighting Control System - SYNACOR, INC.; pg. 479, pg. 1380
ENERGYSCOPE - Software - SUNGARD DATA SYSTEMS INC.; pg. 477, pg. 1592
ENERGYSERVER - Software - SUNGARD DATA SYSTEMS INC.; pg. 477, pg. 1592
ENERLIP - Seal & Thermoplastic Component - GREENE, TWEED & CO.; pg. 1344, pg. 1544
ENERMAX - Premium Wall Panels - BUILDING PRODUCTS OF CANADA CORP.; pg. 72, pg. 1951
ENERSOL-X - Minerals - MINERALS TECHNOLOGIES INC.; pg. 1173, pg. 617
ENERSYS IRONCLAD - Battery - ENERSYS INC.; pg. 1334, pg. 1584
ENERTEC - Batteries & Feedthroughs - MEDTRONIC, INC.; pg. 1564, pg. 939
ENERTIA - Fat Bypass Products - ARCHER-DANIELS-MIDLAND COMPANY; pg. 825, pg. 565
ENERXAN - Personal Care Product - LIFEPLUS INTERNATIONAL; pg. 1556, pg. 29
ENETMETER - Electronic Components - MOLEX INCORPORATED; pg. 655, pg. 628
ENFAMAMA A+ - Infant Health Care Product - MEAD JOHNSON NUTRITION COMPANY; pg. 1561, pg. 615
ENFAMIL - Infant Formula - MEAD JOHNSON NUTRITION COMPANY; pg. 1561, pg. 615
ENFAMIL HUMAN MILK FORTIFIER - Powdered Supplement Added to Preterm Human Milk fed to Premature Infants - MEAD JOHNSON NUTRITION COMPANY; pg. 1561, pg. 615
ENFINITY - Chemical Coating - ENTHONE INC.; pg. 1161, pg. 381
ENFLOW - Blood Warmer - VITAL SIGNS, INC.; pg. 1607, pg. 1126
ENFOG - Safety & Protective Equipment - ENCON SAFETY PRODUCTS; pg. 1334, pg. 1705
ENFORCER - Chemical Product - ACUITY BRANDS, INC.; pg. 1294, pg. 487
ENFORCER - Muffler - AP EXHAUST PRODUCTS, INC.; pg. 199, pg. 1373
ENFORCER - Carpet Backing - THE DOW CHEMICAL COMPANY; pg. 1157, pg. 898
ENFORCER - Fire Chassis - PIERCE MANUFACTURING, INC.; pg. 188, pg. 1852
ENFORCER - Insecticides, Herbicides & Rodenticides - ZEP INC.; pg. 338, pg. 524
ENFORCER II - Universal Fit Muffler - AP EXHAUST PRODUCTS, INC.; pg. 199, pg. 1373
ENFORM CONSULTING - Software - SUNGARD DATA SYSTEMS INC.; pg. 477, pg. 1592
ENFUSELLE - Skin Care System - SHAKLEE CORPORATION; pg. 1593, pg. 184
ENFUSION - Labels, Cards & Decals - ENNIS, INC.; pg. 393, pg. 1727
ENFUTOX - Firming Serum - SHAKLEE CORPORATION; pg. 1593, pg. 184
ENGAGE - Chemical Product - THE DOW CHEMICAL COMPANY; pg. 1157, pg. 898
ENGAGE. CULTIVATE. CONNECT. - Tagline - GOVDELIVERY, INC.; pg. 1255, pg. 961
ENGAGE. EMPOWER. EVOLVE - Slogan - HYLAND SOFTWARE, INC.; pg. 409, pg. 1480
ENGAGING COMMUNICATION - Tagline - ON24, INC.; pg. 1272, pg. 224
ENGALOY - Brazing Alloys - BASF CATALYSTS LLC; pg. 1148, pg. 1074
ENGARDE - Fluid Handling System - GRACO, INC.; pg. 1342, pg. 935
ENGENIO - Data Mining Software - AVAGO TECHNOLOGIES; pg. 358, pg. 238
ENGINE BRITE - Degreaser/Cleaner - RADIATOR SPECIALTY COMPANY; pg. 215, pg. 1380
ENGINE DRIVER - Software - BIO-RAD LABORATORIES, INC.; pg. 1504, pg. 101
ENGINE EXHAUST PARTICLE SIZER - Spectrometer - TSI INCORPORATED; pg. 1432, pg. 965
ENGINE GEAR - Toy & Game - HASBRO, INC.; pg. 954, pg. 1603
ENGINE GUARD II - Automotive Filters - MIGHTY DISTRIBUTING SYSTEM OF AMERICA; pg. 213, pg. 538
ENGINE SAVER - Engine Protection Equipment - FLIGHT SYSTEMS, INC.; pg. 1337, pg. 1548

ENGINEERED ENERGY - Power Conversion Product - MAGNETEK, INC.; *pg.* 1301, *pg.* 1870
ENGINEERED FOR LIFE - Tagline - ITT CORPORATION; *pg.* 1351, *pg.* 1354
ENGINEERED MATERIALS HANDBOOK - Reference Book Series - ASM INTERNATIONAL; *pg.* 132, *pg.* 1461
ENGINEERED PRODUCTS FOR GLOBAL PARTNERS - Slogan - BREEZE-EASTERN CORPORATION; *pg.* 1319, *pg.* 1132
ENGINEERING-E.COM - Software - MSC SOFTWARE CORPORATION; *pg.* 441, *pg.* 262
ENGINEERING EXCHANGE - Software - MSC SOFTWARE CORPORATION; *pg.* 441, *pg.* 262
ENGINEERING, FURNISHING & INSTALLATION - Global Services - SONUS NETWORKS INC.; *pg.* 1281, *pg.* 858
ENGINEERING THE FLOW OF COMMUNICATION - Slogan - PITNEY BOWES INC.; *pg.* 454, *pg.* 376
ENGINEERINGPRO - Software - SKILLSOFT PLC; *pg.* 470, *pg.* 1037
ENGINEER'S DESKTOP - Software System - MENTOR GRAPHICS CORPORATION; *pg.* 432, *pg.* 1510
ENGINEER'S TOOLSET - Computer Product - SOLARWINDS, INC.; *pg.* 471, *pg.* 1666
ENGINEERVIEW - Software System - MENTOR GRAPHICS CORPORATION; *pg.* 432, *pg.* 1510
ENGINOMICS - Cost-Effective Program to Enhance Current Designs & Products - DRIV-LOK, INC.; *pg.* 1046, *pg.* 662
ENGINUITY - Software - EMC CORPORATION; *pg.* 391, *pg.* 825
ENGLAND - Office Furniture - STEELCASE INC.; *pg.* 475, *pg.* 889
ENGLASS - Packaging Systems - TRIMAS CORPORATION; *pg.* 1383, *pg.* 874
ENGLEWOOD - Lighting Product - QUOIZEL INC.; *pg.* 1304, *pg.* 1616
ENGLISH - Clock - ETHAN ALLEN INTERIORS INC.; *pg.* 924, *pg.* 343
ENGLISH COTTAGE - Plant Growing Kit - AEROGROW INTERNATIONAL, INC.; *pg.* 1393, *pg.* 310
ENGLISH COUNTRY ROSE - Scarf - HERITAGE LACE INC.; *pg.* 694, *pg.* 711
ENGLISH IN A FLASH - Educational Materials - RENAISSANCE LEARNING, INC.; *pg.* 607, *pg.* 1899
ENGLISH IVY - Carpet - BEAULIEU GROUP, LLC; *pg.* 917, *pg.* 529
ENGLISH IVY - Lace - HERITAGE LACE INC.; *pg.* 694, *pg.* 711
ENGLISH LIBRARY - Lighting Product - QUOIZEL INC.; *pg.* 1304, *pg.* 1616
ENGLISH OVALS - Cigarettes - PHILIP MORRIS USA INC.; *pg.* 1894, *pg.* 1803
ENGLISH PUB - Fabric - UNIROYAL ENGINEERED PRODUCTS; *pg.* 699, *pg.* 467
ENGLISH TEATIME - Tea - R.C. BIGELOW, INC.; *pg.* 891, *pg.* 348
ENGRAVOGRAPH - Engraving Machines - GRAVOGRAPH-NEW HERMES; *pg.* 1344, *pg.* 531
ENGUARD - Synthetic Resins - ASHLAND INC.; *pg.* 972, *pg.* 726
ENHANCE - Furniture - ASHLEY FURNITURE INDUSTRIES, INC.; *pg.* 914, *pg.* 1852
ENHANCE - Paint And Stain Product - BENJAMIN MOORE & CO.; *pg.* 1440, *pg.* 1085
ENHANCE - Dental Product - DENTSPLY INTERNATIONAL INC.; *pg.* 1522, *pg.* 1596
ENHANCE - Fabric - NEMSCHOFF, INC.; *pg.* 936, *pg.* 1890
ENHANCED ENERGY - Nutritional Product - NUTRACEUTICAL INTERNATIONAL CORPORATION; *pg.* 1576, *pg.* 1753
ENHANCED PAYROLL - Software - INTUIT INC.; *pg.* 769, *pg.* 158
ENHANCER - Carpet Backing - THE DOW CHEMICAL COMPANY; *pg.* 1157, *pg.* 898
THE ENHANCER - Carpet Backing - THE DOW CHEMICAL COMPANY; *pg.* 1157, *pg.* 898
ENHANCER - Seat Cushion - THE ROHO GROUP; *pg.* 1591, *pg.* 556
ENHANCER - Chemical Reagent - WATERS CORPORATION; *pg.* 1436, *pg.* 834
ENHANCING - Filter - THE TIFFEN COMPANY LLC; *pg.* 1432, *pg.* 1165
ENHANCING FOAM - Hair Care Product - JOHN PAUL MITCHELL SYSTEMS; *pg.* 512, *pg.* 133
ENHANCING IMAGE & SAFETY THROUGH INNOVATION - Slogan - G&K SERVICES INC.; *pg.* 693, *pg.* 949
ENHANCING PHARMACEUTICALS ENHANCING LIVES - Tagline - DEPOMED, INC.; *pg.* 1523, *pg.* 143
ENHANCYT - Medical Product - HOLOGIC, INC.; *pg.* 1416, *pg.* 784
ENI - Software - MKS INSTRUMENTS, INC.; *pg.* 1362, *pg.* 781
ENI - Pharmaceutical Product - VALEANT PHARMACEUTICALS INTERNATIONAL; *pg.* 1605, *pg.* 1047
ENI DEVELOPMENT SYSTEM - Software - MKS INSTRUMENTS, INC.; *pg.* 1362, *pg.* 781
ENID - Lamp - ASHLEY FURNITURE INDUSTRIES, INC.; *pg.* 914, *pg.* 1852
ENIGMA - Fabric - NEMSCHOFF, INC.; *pg.* 936, *pg.* 1890
ENIMAC - Software - GE ENERGY; *pg.* 1338, *pg.* 506
ENJOY LIFE IN HD - Slogan - OTTLITE; *pg.* 1303, *pg.* 475
ENJOY THE LOCAL FLAVOR - Slogan - HONEY DEW ASSOCIATES, INC.; *pg.* 1731, *pg.* 841
ENLABEL - Labeling Software - INTEGRATED SOFTWARE DESIGN, INC.; *pg.* 416, *pg.* 830
ENLACE - Spanish-Language Publication - THE SAN DIEGO UNION-TRIBUNE, LLC; *pg.* 1682, *pg.* 208
ENLIGHT - Photovoltaic Manufacturing Products - THE DOW CHEMICAL COMPANY; *pg.* 1157, *pg.* 898
ENLIGHTENED SMOOTHIES - Smoothie - JAMBA, INC.; *pg.* 1024, *pg.* 84
ENLITE - Polyolefin Elastomer - THE DOW CHEMICAL COMPANY; *pg.* 1157, *pg.* 898
ENLITE - Herbicide - E.I. DU PONT DE NEMOURS & COMPANY; *pg.* 1159, *pg.* 390
ENLIVE - Nutritional Products - ABBOTT LABORATORIES; *pg.* 1484, *pg.* 551
ENLOY - Chemical Coating - ENTHONE INC.; *pg.* 1161, *pg.* 381
ENMOTION - Towel Dispenser - GEORGIA-PACIFIC LLC; *pg.* 1458, *pg.* 507
ENNIS - Lamp - ASHLEY FURNITURE INDUSTRIES, INC.; *pg.* 914, *pg.* 1852
ENOGEX - Gas Transportation Service - OGE ENERGY CORP.; *pg.* 1948, *pg.* 1486
ENONOMOUNT - TV & VCR Mounting Systems - LUXOR CORP.; *pg.* 428, *pg.* 666
ENOOK - Furniture - ANTHRO CORPORATION; *pg.* 913, *pg.* 1509
ENOVATE - Blowing Agent - HONEYWELL INTERNATIONAL INC.; *pg.* 407, *pg.* 1088
ENOZ - Moth Preventives - WILLERT HOME PRODUCTS, INC.; *pg.* 1140, *pg.* 1005
ENPLATE - Chemical Coating - ENTHONE INC.; *pg.* 1161, *pg.* 381
ENPLOT - Engineering Software - ASM INTERNATIONAL; *pg.* 132, *pg.* 1461
ENPREP - Chemical Coating - ENTHONE INC.; *pg.* 1161, *pg.* 381
ENREAD - Software System - MENTOR GRAPHICS CORPORATION; *pg.* 432, *pg.* 1510
ENRGY - Digital Video Product - HARMONIC, INC.; *pg.* 402, *pg.* 246
ENRGY 3 - Roof Insulation Board - JOHNS MANVILLE CORPORATION; *pg.* 89, *pg.* 320
ENRICH-O COBS - Pet Litter - THE ANDERSONS INCORPORATED; *pg.* 1793, *pg.* 1461
ENRICH PLUS - Nutritional Products - ABBOTT LABORATORIES; *pg.* 1484, *pg.* 551
ENRICHING LIVES THROUGH INNOVATION - Tagline - HUNTSMAN CORPORATION; *pg.* 1167, *pg.* 1758
ENRICHING LIVES THROUGH INNOVATON - Tagline - HUNTSMAN CORPORATION; *pg.* 1167, *pg.* 1758
ENROLLMENT - Online Financial Services - ACI WORLDWIDE; *pg.* 710, *pg.* 1777
ENROUTE - In-Flight Magazine - ACE AVIATION HOLDINGS INC.; *pg.* 1896, *pg.* 1953
ENSEAL - Chemical Coating - ENTHONE INC.; *pg.* 1161, *pg.* 381
ENSEMBLE - Musical Instrument - ALLEN ORGAN COMPANY; *pg.* 527, *pg.* 1549
ENSEMBLE - Speaker - CAMBRIDGE SOUNDWORKS, INC.; *pg.* 1234, *pg.* 781
ENSEMBLE - Dielectric Coating - THE DOW CHEMICAL COMPANY; *pg.* 1157, *pg.* 898
ENSEMBLE - Visual System - EVANS & SUTHERLAND COMPUTER CORPORATION; *pg.* 638, *pg.* 1757
ENSEMBLE - Telecommunication Equipment - MERCURY COMPUTER SYSTEMS, INC.; *pg.* 434, *pg.* 813
ENSEMBLE - Fabric - NEMSCHOFF, INC.; *pg.* 936, *pg.* 1890
ENSEMBLE - Office Furniture - STEELCASE INC.; *pg.* 475, *pg.* 889
ENSEMBLE2 - Hardware & Software Integration - MERCURY COMPUTER SYSTEMS, INC.; *pg.* 434, *pg.* 813
ENSIGN DOCK BOX - Lighting Product - THE WILL-BURT CO., INC.; *pg.* 1437, *pg.* 1469
ENSITE ARRAY - Electrophysiology Products - ST. JUDE MEDICAL, INC.; *pg.* 1596, *pg.* 963
ENSITE CONNECT - Network Connection - ST. JUDE MEDICAL, INC.; *pg.* 1596, *pg.* 963
ENSITE FUSION - Electrophysiology Product - ST. JUDE MEDICAL, INC.; *pg.* 1596, *pg.* 963
ENSITE NAVX - Electrophysiology Products - ST. JUDE MEDICAL, INC.; *pg.* 1596, *pg.* 963
ENSITE SYSTEM - Electrophysiology Products - ST. JUDE MEDICAL, INC.; *pg.* 1596, *pg.* 963
ENSITE VERISMO - Electrophysiology Products - ST. JUDE MEDICAL, INC.; *pg.* 1596, *pg.* 963
ENSPIRE - Instrument - PERKINELMER, INC.; *pg.* 1426, *pg.* 853
ENSTRIP - Selective Stripping for Plated Metal Coatings - ENTHONE INC.; *pg.* 1161, *pg.* 381
ENSTRON - Particleboard - POTLATCH CORPORATION; *pg.* 1467, *pg.* 1844
ENSURE - Nutritional Supplement - ABBOTT LABORATORIES; *pg.* 1484, *pg.* 551
ENSURE - Liquid Nutrition - ABBOTT NUTRITION; *pg.* 1485, *pg.* 1437
ENSURE HIGH PROTEIN - Nutritional Beverage - ABBOTT LABORATORIES; *pg.* 1484, *pg.* 551
ENSURE PLUS - Nutritional Beverage - ABBOTT LABORATORIES; *pg.* 1484, *pg.* 551
ENSURE SMART - Vehicle Insurance - HDI SOLUTIONS, INC.; *pg.* 403, *pg.* 1
ENSUREDMAIL - E-Mail Security Solutions - CICERO INC.; *pg.* 372, *pg.* 1360
ENTAKE - Medical Equipment - CONMED CORPORATION; *pg.* 1517, *pg.* 1347
ENTARA - Swing Entrance - KAWNEER COMPANY, INC.; *pg.* 90, *pg.* 537
ENTEGRATE - Software - SUNGARD DATA SYSTEMS INC.; *pg.* 477, *pg.* 1592
ENTEGRIS RINGS DESIGN - Integrity Management Material - ENTEGRIS, INC.; *pg.* 1882, *pg.* 788
ENTEK - Chemical Coating - ENTHONE INC.; *pg.* 1161, *pg.* 381
ENTEK - Software - ROCKWELL AUTOMATION, INC.; *pg.* 668, *pg.* 1880
ENTELLISYS - Medium Voltage Switchgear - GENERAL ELECTRIC COMPANY; *pg.* 1297, *pg.* 347
ENTENDRE - Carpet - INTERFACE, INC.; *pg.* 695, *pg.* 512
ENTENTE SUITE - Software - PFSWEB, INC.; *pg.* 1275, *pg.* 1733
ENTER ELECTRO - Game - ACTIVISION BLIZZARD, INC.; *pg.* 948, *pg.* 271
ENTEREX - Nutritional Product - VICTUS, INC.; *pg.* 1606, *pg.* 447
ENTEREX DIABETIC - Nutritional Product - VICTUS, INC.; *pg.* 1606, *pg.* 447
ENTEREX RENAL - Nutritional Product - VICTUS, INC.; *pg.* 1606, *pg.* 447
ENTERGY IMAX THEATRE - Trademark & Theatre - AUDUBON NATURE INSTITUTE; *pg.* 531, *pg.* 746
ENTERION - Chemicals - HUNTSMAN CORPORATION; *pg.* 1167, *pg.* 1758
ENTEROLERT - Reagent - IDEXX LABORATORIES, INC.; *pg.* 1543, *pg.* 753
ENTERPRISE - Laser & Laser System - COHERENT, INC.; *pg.* 1406, *pg.* 265
ENTERPRISE - Footwear - EASTLAND SHOE CORPORATION; *pg.* 1808, *pg.* 750
ENTERPRISE - Messaging Software - MITEL NETWORKS, INC.; *pg.* 1872, *pg.* 13
ENTERPRISE ADVANTAGE PROGRAM - IT Consulting Services - COMPUTER SCIENCES CORPORATION; *pg.* 378, *pg.* 1780
ENTERPRISE DATA ACCESS/SQL - A Client/Server Family of Products for Heterogeneous Data Access - INFORMATION BUILDERS INC.; *pg.* 415, *pg.* 1243
ENTERPRISE GUIDE - Software - SAS INSTITUTE INC.; *pg.* 466, *pg.* 1361
ENTERPRISE LIBRARIAN - Software System - MENTOR GRAPHICS CORPORATION; *pg.* 432, *pg.* 1510
ENTERPRISE MINER - Software - SAS INSTITUTE INC.; *pg.* 466, *pg.* 1361

THE ENTERPRISE MOBILITY COMPANY - Slogan - MOTOROLA ENTERPRISE MOBILITY; *pg.* 441, *pg.* 1167
ENTERPRISE REPORTER - Software - SAS INSTITUTE INC.; *pg.* 466, *pg.* 1361
ENTERPRISE SDK - Software - AXEDA SYSTEMS INC.; *pg.* 359, *pg.* 819
ENTERPRISE SEAMLESS MOBILITY - Communications Product - MOTOROLA SOLUTIONS, INC.; *pg.* 657, *pg.* 659
ENTERPRISE SECURITY MANAGER - Software - SYMANTEC CORPORATION; *pg.* 478, *pg.* 161
ENTERPRISE SECURITY REPORTER - Software - DELL SOFTWARE; *pg.* 385, *pg.* 40
ENTERPRISE SERIES - Lottery System - INTERNATIONAL GAME TECHNOLOGY; *pg.* 420, *pg.* 1606
ENTERPRISE SINGLE SIGN-ON - Software - DELL SOFTWARE; *pg.* 385, *pg.* 40
ENTERPRISE SOLUTIONS - Software - AVNET TECHNOLOGY SOLUTIONS; *pg.* 359, *pg.* 25
ENTERPRISE SUITE - Software - ATEX MEDIA COMMAND, INC.; *pg.* 355, *pg.* 848
ENTERPRISE VALUE ARCHIVES ARCHITECTURE - Software - IRON MOUNTAIN INCORPORATED; *pg.* 421, *pg.* 796
ENTERPRISE VAULT - Software - SYMANTEC CORPORATION; *pg.* 478, *pg.* 161
ENTERPRISECONNECT - Software - ASPEN TECHNOLOGY, INC.; *pg.* 354, *pg.* 804
ENTERPRISEXPRESS - Enterprise Tape Library - OVERLAND STORAGE, INC.; *pg.* 451, *pg.* 205
ENTERRA - Chronic Nausea & Vomiting Treatment - MEDTRONIC, INC.; *pg.* 1564, *pg.* 939
ENTERTAIN WITH PIZAZZ FROM OMAHA STEAKS - Mail Order Catalog - OMAHA STEAKS INTERNATIONAL, INC.; *pg.* 1780, *pg.* 1017
ENTERTAINER - Kitchen Product - KOHLER CO.; *pg.* 91, *pg.* 1862
ENTERTAINMENT - Coupon Books - ENTERTAINMENT PUBLICATIONS, INC.; *pg.* 1639, *pg.* 910
ENTERTAINMENT - Benefit Program - NATIONAL ASSOCIATION OF REALTORS; *pg.* 1666, *pg.* 584
ENTERTAINMENT - Media Publication - TIME INC.; *pg.* 1693, *pg.* 1300
ENTERTAINMENT ESSENTIALS - Software - RENTRAK CORPORATION; *pg.* 306, *pg.* 1506
ENTERTAINMENT EXTRA! - Newspaper - TAMPA BAY NEWSPAPERS, INC.; *pg.* 1691, *pg.* 468
ENTERTAINMENT PREVIEW - Magazine - INGRAM ENTERTAINMENT INC.; *pg.* 292, *pg.* 1639
ENTERTAINMENT TECHNOLOGY - Lighting Fixture & Control - PHILIPS LIGHTING; *pg.* 1303, *pg.* 806
ENTERTAINMENT UPDATE - Magazine - INGRAM ENTERTAINMENT INC.; *pg.* 292, *pg.* 1639
ENTERTAINMENT WEEKLY - Magazine - TIME WARNER INC.; *pg.* 312, *pg.* 1302
ENTERYX - Medical Device - BOSTON SCIENTIFIC CORPORATION; *pg.* 1508, *pg.* 831
ENTHOBRITE - Zinc Cadmium & Copper Brightener - ENTHONE INC.; *pg.* 1161, *pg.* 381
ENTHOX - Conversion Coatings - ENTHONE INC.; *pg.* 1161, *pg.* 381
ENTICE WITH SPICE - Spice & Seasoning Blends - FUCHS NORTH AMERICA.; *pg.* 857, *pg.* 774
ENTICEMINT - Lip Gloss - THE BONNE BELL COMPANY; *pg.* 502, *pg.* 1480
ENTIRA - Resin Modifiers & Additives - E.I. DU PONT DE NEMOURS & COMPANY; *pg.* 1159, *pg.* 390
ENTITY - Pacemakers - ST. JUDE MEDICAL, INC.; *pg.* 1596, *pg.* 963
ENTOUCH - Medical & Surgical Instruments - ENCISION INC.; *pg.* 1528, *pg.* 310
ENTOURAGE - Fabric - NEMSCHOFF, INC.; *pg.* 936, *pg.* 1890
ENTRADA-Y-SALIDA - French Fried Potatoes - IN-N-OUT BURGERS, INC.; *pg.* 1732, *pg.* 111
ENTRALUX - Lighting Product - HUBBELL INCORPORATED; *pg.* 1299, *pg.* 370
ENTRAN - Sensor System - MEASUREMENT SPECIALTIES INC.; *pg.* 1360, *pg.* 1783
ENTREE - Kitchen Product - KOHLER CO.; *pg.* 91, *pg.* 1862
ENTREE - Low-priced Frameless Stock & Semi-custom Cabinets - NORCRAFT HOLDINGS, LP; *pg.* 100, *pg.* 921
ENTRENCHED WITH EXPERIENCE, ARMED WITH TECHNOLOGY - Tag Line - EN POINTE TECHNOLOGIES, INC.; *pg.* 1243, *pg.* 94
ENTREPRENEUR CONNECT - Social Network - ENTREPRENEUR MEDIA, INC.; *pg.* 1639, *pg.* 110
ENTREPRENEUR MAGAZINE - Magazine - ENTREPRENEUR MEDIA, INC.; *pg.* 1639, *pg.* 110
ENTREPRENEUR.COM - Website - ENTREPRENEUR MEDIA, INC.; *pg.* 1639, *pg.* 110
ENTREPRENEUR'S STARTUPS - Magazine - ENTREPRENEUR MEDIA, INC.; *pg.* 1639, *pg.* 110
ENTRO - Spray Adjuvant - KALO, INC.; *pg.* 1796, *pg.* 719
ENTROBEAN - Carpet - INTERFACE, INC.; *pg.* 695, *pg.* 512
ENTROLYTE - Veterinary Electrolyte Nutrient Supplement - PFIZER INC.; *pg.* 1581, *pg.* 1278
ENTROPY - Furniture - HAWORTH, INC.; *pg.* 402, *pg.* 891
ENTROPY - Carpet - INTERFACE, INC.; *pg.* 695, *pg.* 512
ENTROPY - Fabric - NEMSCHOFF, INC.; *pg.* 936, *pg.* 1890
ENTROPY - Door Glass - ODL INCORPORATED; *pg.* 101, *pg.* 914
ENTRUST AUTHORITY - Software - ENTRUST, INC.; *pg.* 393, *pg.* 1680
ENTRUST AUTHORITY PKCS - Security Toolkit - ENTRUST, INC.; *pg.* 393, *pg.* 1680
ENTRUST CERTIFICATE SERVICES - Software - ENTRUST, INC.; *pg.* 393, *pg.* 1680
ENTRUST ENTELLIGENCE - Software - ENTRUST, INC.; *pg.* 393, *pg.* 1680
ENTRUST GETACCESS - Software - ENTRUST, INC.; *pg.* 393, *pg.* 1680
ENTRUST READY - Software - ENTRUST, INC.; *pg.* 393, *pg.* 1680
ENTRUST SECURE TRANSACTION PLATFORM - Software - ENTRUST, INC.; *pg.* 393, *pg.* 1680
ENTRUST TRUEPASS - Software - ENTRUST, INC.; *pg.* 393, *pg.* 1680
ENTRUST USB TOKENS - Software - ENTRUST, INC.; *pg.* 393, *pg.* 1680
ENTRY LEVEL - Carpet - INTERFACE, INC.; *pg.* 695, *pg.* 512
ENTRYPOINT - Door Treatments - ODL INCORPORATED; *pg.* 101, *pg.* 914
ENTRYSLIDE - Motorhome - REXHALL INDUSTRIES, INC.; *pg.* 1710, *pg.* 121
ENTUNE - Software - MKS INSTRUMENTS, INC.; *pg.* 1362, *pg.* 781
ENVELON - Thermal Coating Resins - THE DOW CHEMICAL COMPANY; *pg.* 1157, *pg.* 898
ENVELOPE WINDOW FILM - Plastic Film - MULTI-PLASTICS, INC.; *pg.* 1886, *pg.* 1457
ENVI MAG - Magnetic Mapping System - SCINTREX LTD.; *pg.* 1374, *pg.* 1920
ENVI PRO - Magnetic System - SCINTREX LTD.; *pg.* 1374, *pg.* 1920
ENVI-RO-TECH - Chemical Cleaner Product - TECH SPRAY, L.P.; *pg.* 1183, *pg.* 1659
ENVIGA - Beverage - THE COCA-COLA COMPANY; *pg.* 240, *pg.* 493
ENVIRA-POXY - Primer - KELLY-MOORE PAINT COMPANY, INC.; *pg.* 1443, *pg.* 198
ENVIRACAIRE - Air Purifier - KAZ, INC.; *pg.* 58, *pg.* 844
ENVIRACRYL - Powder Coating Composition - PPG INDUSTRIES, INC.; *pg.* 1445, *pg.* 1579
ENVIREZ - Resins - ASHLAND INC.; *pg.* 972, *pg.* 726
ENVIRO - Tissue Paper - CASCADES, INC.; *pg.* 73, *pg.* 1950
ENVIRO - Fabric - NEMSCHOFF, INC.; *pg.* 936, *pg.* 1890
ENVIRO AID - Cleaner - SWISHER HYGIENE INC.; *pg.* 336, *pg.* 1507
ENVIRO-BAG - Plastic Bags - SONOCO PRODUCTS COMPANY; *pg.* 1469, *pg.* 1619
ENVIRO CARE - Disinfectant Preparation - ROCHESTER MIDLAND CORPORATION; *pg.* 334, *pg.* 1337
ENVIRO-CHEM - Engineering & Construction Management Services - MONSANTO COMPANY; *pg.* 1173, *pg.* 999
ENVIRO-COAT - Paint - KELLY-MOORE PAINT COMPANY, INC.; *pg.* 1443, *pg.* 198
ENVIRO-GUARD - Freeze Resistant Valve System for Drinking Fountains - HAWS CORPORATION; *pg.* 56, *pg.* 1032
ENVIRO-MATE - Leather-Like Book Binding Material - HOLLISTON LLC; *pg.* 1460, *pg.* 1630
ENVIRO-MATE - Recycled Content Bags - SONOCO PRODUCTS COMPANY; *pg.* 1469, *pg.* 1619
ENVIRO-PRIME - Coating Product - PPG INDUSTRIES, INC.; *pg.* 1445, *pg.* 1579
ENVIRO-SCRUB - Chemical Product - QUAKER CHEMICAL CORP.; *pg.* 1178, *pg.* 1524
ENVIRO-SHIELD - Erosion Control - USG CORPORATION; *pg.* 118, *pg.* 594
ENVIRO-TEK - Chemical Product - QUAKER CHEMICAL CORP.; *pg.* 1178, *pg.* 1524
ENVIRO-TUFF - Plastic Packaging Product - POLY PAK AMERICA, INC.; *pg.* 1467, *pg.* 138
ENVIROALERT - Environmental Security Product - WINLAND ELECTRONICS, INC.; *pg.* 688, *pg.* 928
ENVIROBASE - Paints - PPG INDUSTRIES, INC.; *pg.* 1445, *pg.* 1579
SAFETY.BLR.COM - Website - BUSINESS & LEGAL REPORTS INC.; *pg.* 1624, *pg.* 367
ENVIROBOX - Breakfast Cereals - NATURE'S PATH FOODS INC.; *pg.* 833, *pg.* 1908
ENVIROBRITE - Waste Water Treatment - A BRITE COMPANY; *pg.* 1144, *pg.* 1697
ENVIROCAM - Seal & Thermoplastic Component - GREENE, TWEED & CO.; *pg.* 1344, *pg.* 1544
ENVIROCARE - Solvent Cleaner - ASHLAND INC.; *pg.* 972, *pg.* 726
ENVIROCASTER - Animal Safety Product - NEOGEN CORPORATION; *pg.* 883, *pg.* 896
ENVIROCENTER - Fluid Decontamination Facility - M-I SWACO; *pg.* 980, *pg.* 1710
ENVIROCHECK - Filtering Product - PALL CORPORATION; *pg.* 232, *pg.* 1323
ENVIROCRON - Electrodeposition Coatings - PPG INDUSTRIES, INC.; *pg.* 1445, *pg.* 1579
ENVIRODOME CAMERA SYSTEMS - Surveillance Camera - BOSCH SECURITY SYSTEMS, INC.; *pg.* 626, *pg.* 1158
ENVIROEDGE - Vehicle Wash Products - ZEP INC.; *pg.* 338, *pg.* 524
ENVIROFLEX - Eco-Friendly Digital Printing Products - COOLEY GROUP, INC.; *pg.* 691, *pg.* 1603
ENVIROFOIL - Laminations - HAZEN PAPER COMPANY; *pg.* 1459, *pg.* 825
ENVIROGEM - Chemical Products - AIR PRODUCTS AND CHEMICALS, INC.; *pg.* 1145, *pg.* 1513
ENVIROGRAPHIC - Recycled Papers - BPM INC.; *pg.* 1454, *pg.* 1886
ENVIROKIDZ - Organic Children's Cereal - NATURE'S PATH FOODS INC.; *pg.* 833, *pg.* 1908
ENVIROLINK - Battery - ENERSYS INC.; *pg.* 1334, *pg.* 1584
ENVIROLLOY - Plating Process - A BRITE COMPANY; *pg.* 1144, *pg.* 1697
ENVIROMAX - Robotics Chambers - HEMCO CORPORATION; *pg.* 1416, *pg.* 979
ENVIROMULCH - Plastic Film for Use as Agricultural Mulch - SONOCO PRODUCTS COMPANY; *pg.* 1469, *pg.* 1619
ENVIRON - Software - CINCOM SYSTEMS, INC.; *pg.* 372, *pg.* 1411
ENVIRON - Coating Product - PPG INDUSTRIES, INC.; *pg.* 1445, *pg.* 1579
ENVIRONMENT - Paper - NEENAH PAPER, INC.; *pg.* 1465, *pg.* 484
ENVIRONMENT CREATION TOOL - Database Generation System - EVANS & SUTHERLAND COMPUTER CORPORATION; *pg.* 638, *pg.* 1757
ENVIRONMENT PROCESSOR - Image Generator - EVANS & SUTHERLAND COMPUTER CORPORATION; *pg.* 638, *pg.* 1757
ENVIRONMENTAL COLOR-2 - Lighting Product - HIGH END SYSTEMS, INC.; *pg.* 1299, *pg.* 1663
ENVIRONMENTAL CONTROL THROUGH IRRIGATION - Tag Line - WEATHERTEC CORPORATION; *pg.* 708, *pg.* 93
ENVIRONMENTAL NEWS DIGEST - Periodical of Environmental Pollution Information - AMERICAN AUTOMOBILE ASSOCIATION; *pg.* 1190, *pg.* 429
ENVIRONMENTAL PROTECTOR PLAN - Insurance Package Program - BROWN & BROWN, INC.; *pg.* 1196, *pg.* 419
ENVIRONMENTALLY BOUND - Recycling Program for Used Binders - AMERICAN THERMOPLASTIC COMPANY; *pg.* 349, *pg.* 1573
ENVIRONMENTALLY FRIENDLY COMPOSITE DECKING - Tagline - ADVANCED ENVIRONMENTAL RECYCLING TECHNOLOGIES, INC.; *pg.* 1310, *pg.* 35
ENVIRONMENTALLY RESPONSIBLE PRODUCTS THAT WORK! - Slogan - GARDENS ALIVE!, INC.; *pg.* 1796, *pg.* 693
ENVIRONMENTS FOR LIVING - Building Science Program - TOPBUILD CORPORATION; *pg.* 116, *pg.* 421
ENVIRONMET - Filtering & Recirculating Systems - BUEHLER, LTD.; *pg.* 1403, *pg.* 622
ENVIRONS - Fabric - NEMSCHOFF, INC.; *pg.* 936, *pg.* 1890
ENVIROPAK - Software - BIO-RAD LABORATORIES, INC.;

First page reference indicates Business Class Edition
Second page reference indicates Geographic Edition

pg. 1504, *pg.* 101
ENVIROPLUS - Water Treatment Chemicals - ASHLAND INC.; *pg.* 972, *pg.* 726
ENVIROPURE - Filter Cones & Cartridges - HMI INDUSTRIES INC.; *pg.* 56, *pg.* 1475
ENVIROPURGE - Cleaning System - WYNN OIL COMPANY; *pg.* 987, *pg.* 173
ENVIROSOLV - Chemical Product - FINE ORGANICS CORPORATION; *pg.* 330, *pg.* 1052
ENVIROSTONE - Transportation - NORFOLK SOUTHERN CORPORATION; *pg.* 1917, *pg.* 1797
ENVIROSTONE - Recycled Bulk Gypsum Product - USG CORPORATION; *pg.* 118, *pg.* 594
ENVIROSTRIP - Solvent - ARCHER-DANIELS-MIDLAND COMPANY; *pg.* 825, *pg.* 565
ENVIROSYSTEMS - Sterilant - STERIS CORPORATION; *pg.* 1597, *pg.* 1464
ENVIROTEMP - Silicone Fluid - NIAGARA TRANSFORMER CORP.; *pg.* 1302, *pg.* 1150
ENVIROTIGHT - Seal & Thermoplastic Component - GREENE, TWEED & CO.; *pg.* 1344, *pg.* 1544
ENVIROZONE AIR ENTRANCE - Air Door Systems - DAW TECHNOLOGIES, INC.; *pg.* 78, *pg.* 1756
ENVISION - Custom Foam Laminates - THE DOW CHEMICAL COMPANY; *pg.* 1157, *pg.* 898
ENVISION - High Chair - EVENFLO COMPANY, INC.; *pg.* 924, *pg.* 1470
ENVISION - Dinner & Luncheon Napkins - GEORGIA-PACIFIC LLC; *pg.* 1458, *pg.* 507
ENVISION - Plotter - GERBER SCIENTIFIC, INC.; *pg.* 1414, *pg.* 380
ENVISION - Plate Reader & Imager - PERKINELMER, INC.; *pg.* 1426, *pg.* 853
ENVISION - Syringe Plungers & Stoppers - WEST PHARMACEUTICAL SERVICES, INC.; *pg.* 1472, *pg.* 1532
ENVISION BUSINESS INTELLIGENCE - Software - ENVISION; *pg.* 393, *pg.* 1835
ENVISION CT - Injection Systems - MEDRAD, INC.; *pg.* 1563, *pg.* 1591
ENVISION ELEARNING - Software - ENVISION; *pg.* 393, *pg.* 1835
ENVISION FULL-TIME RECORDING - Software - ENVISION; *pg.* 393, *pg.* 1835
ENVISION PERFORMANCE SUITE - Software - ENVISION; *pg.* 393, *pg.* 1835
ENVISION QUALITY MONITORING - Software - ENVISION; *pg.* 393, *pg.* 1835
ENVISION QUIZTEST - Software - ENVISION; *pg.* 393, *pg.* 1835
ENVISION REPORT SERVER - Software - ENVISION; *pg.* 393, *pg.* 1835
ENVISION WORKFORCE MANAGEMENT - Software - ENVISION; *pg.* 393, *pg.* 1835
ENVISION XD - Surgical Instrument - OSTEOMED CORPORATION; *pg.* 1425, *pg.* 1658
ENVISYS - Noise & Vibration Control - COOPER-STANDARD AUTOMOTIVE INC.; *pg.* 1880, *pg.* 903
ENVIVE - Herbicide - E.I. DU PONT DE NEMOURS & COMPANY; *pg.* 1159, *pg.* 390
ENVIVIO - MPEG4 System - NEXAGE, INC.; *pg.* 1271, *pg.* 799
ENVOY - Security Locker - AMERICAN LOCKER GROUP INCORPORATED; *pg.* 1041, *pg.* 1674
ENVOY - Dinnerware - CARLISLE FOODSERVICE PRODUCTS INCORPORATED; *pg.* 1455, *pg.* 1485
ENVOY - Sport Utility Vehicle - GENERAL MOTORS COMPANY; *pg.* 175, *pg.* 881
ENVOY - Converting Papers - INTERNATIONAL PAPER COMPANY; *pg.* 1460, *pg.* 1644
ENVOY - Aerosol Compressor - INVACARE CORPORATION; *pg.* 1546, *pg.* 1451
ENVOY - Desk Stand - LAPWORKS, INC.; *pg.* 426, *pg.* 187
ENVOY - Marketing Research Services - MARITZ INC.; *pg.* 1914, *pg.* 977
ENVOY - Wireless Communicator - MOTOROLA SOLUTIONS, INC.; *pg.* 657, *pg.* 659
ENVOY - Windows & Doors - NORTEK, INC.; *pg.* 100, *pg.* 1607
ENVOY - Software - WIND RIVER SYSTEMS, INC.; *pg.* 493, *pg.* 38
ENVOY DENALI - Sport Utility Vehicle - GENERAL MOTORS COMPANY; *pg.* 175, *pg.* 881
ENVOY JR. - Aerosol Compressor - INVACARE CORPORATION; *pg.* 1546, *pg.* 1451
ENVOY XL - Sport Utility Vehicle - GENERAL MOTORS COMPANY; *pg.* 175, *pg.* 881
ENVOY XL DENALI - Sport Utility Vehicle - GENERAL MOTORS COMPANY; *pg.* 175, *pg.* 881
ENVURE - Chemical Product - SACHEM INC.; *pg.* 1180, *pg.* 1665
ENVY - Shoe - AEROGROUP INTERNATIONAL, INC.; *pg.* 1803, *pg.* 1055
ENVY - Catheter - COOK GROUP, INC.; *pg.* 1518, *pg.* 674
ENVYWORKS - Furniture - KIMBALL INTERNATIONAL, INC.; *pg.* 931, *pg.* 692
ENWRITE - Software System - MENTOR GRAPHICS CORPORATION; *pg.* 432, *pg.* 1510
ENYCE - Men's Apparel - KATE SPADE & COMPANY; *pg.* 27, *pg.* 1248
ENZ-ROT - Soil Care Product - GARDENS ALIVE!, INC.; *pg.* 1796, *pg.* 693
ENZAPLEX - Nutritional Product - NUTRACEUTICAL INTERNATIONAL CORPORATION; *pg.* 1576, *pg.* 1753
ENZCHEK - Molecular Probe Product - THERMO FISHER SCIENTIFIC INC.; *pg.* 1602, *pg.* 61
ENZIO - Furniture - BASSETT FURNITURE INDUSTRIES, INCORPORATED; *pg.* 916, *pg.* 1776
ENZODIRECT - Computer Software - ENZO BIOCHEM INC.; *pg.* 1529, *pg.* 1228
ENZYBATE - Chemical Compositions - ASHLAND INC.; *pg.* 972, *pg.* 726
ENZYCARE - Detergent - STERIS CORPORATION; *pg.* 1597, *pg.* 1464
ENZYME UNIVERSITY - Education about Product - NATIONAL ENZYME COMPANY; *pg.* 882, *pg.* 978
ENZYMES - Nutritional Product - NEW EARTH LIFE SCIENCES, INC.; *pg.* 1573, *pg.* 1499
EO EASY READ - Sterilization Product - PROPPER MANUFACTURING COMPANY, INC.; *pg.* 1586, *pg.* 1175
EO STEL SCAN - Monitoring System - STERIS CORPORATION; *pg.* 1597, *pg.* 1464
EOLAS - IT Solutions - EOLAS TECHNOLOGIES, INC.; *pg.* 1243, *pg.* 573
EOLE - Medical Device - RESMED INC.; *pg.* 1589, *pg.* 207
EOMS AND DESIGN - Manual - XEROX CORPORATION; *pg.* 494, *pg.* 365
EON TECHNOLOGY - Battery - ENERSYS INC.; *pg.* 1334, *pg.* 1584
EOS - Lighting Control System - ELECTRONIC THEATRE CONTROLS, INC.; *pg.* 1296, *pg.* 1872
EOS - Books - HARPERCOLLINS PUBLISHERS INC.; *pg.* 1647, *pg.* 1237
EOS-6000 - Switch - EMCORE CORPORATION; *pg.* 636, *pg.* 39
EP - Software - EVANS & SUTHERLAND COMPUTER CORPORATION; *pg.* 638, *pg.* 1757
EP-4 - Computerized Stimulator - ST. JUDE MEDICAL, INC.; *pg.* 1596, *pg.* 963
EP-MAX - Software - BIO-RAD LABORATORIES, INC.; *pg.* 1504, *pg.* 101
EP SERIES COPIERS - Copiers - KONICA MINOLTA BUSINESS SOLUTIONS USA, INC.; *pg.* 1419, *pg.* 1113
EP-WORKMATE - Lab Recording System - ST. JUDE MEDICAL, INC.; *pg.* 1596, *pg.* 963
EP21HT - Epoxy Adhesive - MASTER BOND INC.; *pg.* 1172, *pg.* 1072
EP31 - Adhesive - MASTER BOND INC.; *pg.* 1172, *pg.* 1072
EPAC - Variable Speed Drive - WEATHERFORD PRODUCTION OPTIMIZATION; *pg.* 987, *pg.* 1725
EPACO - Explosion Detection System - FIKE CORPORATION; *pg.* 1047, *pg.* 973
EPARTNERS - Software System - MENTOR GRAPHICS CORPORATION; *pg.* 432, *pg.* 1510
EPARTS - Software System - MENTOR GRAPHICS CORPORATION; *pg.* 432, *pg.* 1510
EPAS - Educational Achievement Monitoring System - ACT INC.; *pg.* 597, *pg.* 708
EPAYABLES - Software - INFOACCESS.NET LLC; *pg.* 1258, *pg.* 1456
EPAYROLL - Electronic Paystub - EQUIFAX WORKFORCE SOLUTIONS; *pg.* 394, *pg.* 997
EPC - Engine Pressure Controller - ENVIRONMENTAL TECTONICS CORPORATION; *pg.* 1411, *pg.* 1587
EPDS - Software - EASTMAN MACHINE COMPANY; *pg.* 1331, *pg.* 1148
EPEC - Paint & Coating - DIAMOND VOGEL PAINT, INC.; *pg.* 1441, *pg.* 710
EPERNAY - Bath Product - KOHLER CO.; *pg.* 91, *pg.* 1862
EPEX - General Radiography System - HOLOGIC, INC.; *pg.* 1416, *pg.* 784
EPEX ER - Medical Product - HOLOGIC, INC.; *pg.* 1416, *pg.* 784
EPEX SYMPHONY - Medical Product - HOLOGIC, INC.; *pg.* 1416, *pg.* 784
EPHARMA - Software - TIGERLOGIC CORPORATION; *pg.* 484, *pg.* 117
EPHEMERE - Beer - SLEEMAN UNIBROUE QUEBEC; *pg.* 265, *pg.* 1950
EPHPOD - Software - DATAVIZ, INC.; *pg.* 383, *pg.* 356
EPI-CURE - Chemical - MILLER-STEPHENSON CHEMICAL COMPANY, INC.; *pg.* 1172, *pg.* 344
EPI-LOCK - Medical & Aesthetic Product - DYNATRONICS CORPORATION; *pg.* 1526, *pg.* 1757
EPI-REZ - Chemical - MILLER-STEPHENSON CHEMICAL COMPANY, INC.; *pg.* 1172, *pg.* 344
EPI SUITE - Identification Solutions - IMAGEWARE SYSTEMS, INC.; *pg.* 412, *pg.* 203
EPIBOND - Adhesives - HUNTSMAN CORPORATION; *pg.* 1167, *pg.* 1758
EPIBROWSER - Diagnostic Tool - SEQUENOM, INC.; *pg.* 1593, *pg.* 209
EPIC - Glass & Ceramic Material - CORNING INCORPORATED; *pg.* 1122, *pg.* 1154
EPIC - Immersion Photoresists - THE DOW CHEMICAL COMPANY; *pg.* 1157, *pg.* 898
EPIC - Toiletries - THE GILLETTE COMPANY; *pg.* 509, *pg.* 795
EPIC - Fitness Equipment - ICON HEALTH & FITNESS, INC.; *pg.* 1837, *pg.* 1752
EPIC - Sturdilite Floodlight - PHOENIX PRODUCTS COMPANY; *pg.* 1304, *pg.* 1879
EPIC - Metal Cutting Saw Blade - SIMONDS INTERNATIONAL CORPORATION; *pg.* 1376, *pg.* 819
EPIC - Records Group - SONY MUSIC ENTERTAINMENT; *pg.* 309, *pg.* 1294
EPIC - Tissue Heart Valves - ST. JUDE MEDICAL, INC.; *pg.* 1596, *pg.* 963
EPIC - Patient Handling Equipment - STRYKER CORPORATION; *pg.* 1598, *pg.* 894
EPIC - Software - SYNOPSYS, INC.; *pg.* 480, *pg.* 162
EPIC - Printer - TRANSACT TECHNOLOGIES INCORPORATED; *pg.* 484, *pg.* 351
EPIC - Rod Pump Controller - WEATHERFORD PRODUCTION OPTIMIZATION; *pg.* 987, *pg.* 1725
EPIC 330 - Electric Airless Paint Sprayer - TITAN TOOL, INC.; *pg.* 1383, *pg.* 1100
EPIC DUELS - Toy & Game - HASBRO, INC.; *pg.* 954, *pg.* 1603
EPIC III - Supervisory Temperature Control System - DAVIS-STANDARD LLC; *pg.* 1328, *pg.* 368
EPIC SERIES - Upright Vacuum Cleaner - AERUS LLC; *pg.* 51, *pg.* 1673
EPIC SI-CLONE - Metal Cutting Saw Blade - SIMONDS INTERNATIONAL CORPORATION; *pg.* 1376, *pg.* 819
EPIC Z - Laundry Machines - WHIRLPOOL CORPORATION; *pg.* 62, *pg.* 872
EPICA - Vehicle - GENERAL MOTORS COMPANY; *pg.* 175, *pg.* 881
EPICEL - Biosurgical Product - GENZYME CORPORATION; *pg.* 1534, *pg.* 808
EPICENTER - Software - EXTREME NETWORKS INC; *pg.* 287, *pg.* 245
EPICENTER V6.0 - Software - EXTREME NETWORKS INC; *pg.* 287, *pg.* 245
EPICOR - Cardiac Ablation System - ST. JUDE MEDICAL, INC.; *pg.* 1596, *pg.* 963
EPICOR ENTERPRISE - Software - EPICOR SOFTWARE CORPORATION; *pg.* 393, *pg.* 110
EPICOR FOR SERVICE ENTERPRISES - Software - EPICOR SOFTWARE CORPORATION; *pg.* 393, *pg.* 110
EPICOR ITSM - Software - EPICOR SOFTWARE CORPORATION; *pg.* 393, *pg.* 110
EPICOR RETAIL - Software - EPICOR SOFTWARE CORPORATION; *pg.* 393, *pg.* 110
EPICS - Testing Instrument System - BECKMAN COULTER, INC.; *pg.* 1402, *pg.* 48
EPICURE - Home Appliance - DACOR; *pg.* 54, *pg.* 67
EPICUREAN - Kitchen Product - KOHLER CO.; *pg.* 91, *pg.* 1862
EPICURIOUS.COM - Gourmet Site - CONDE NAST DIGITAL; *pg.* 1237, *pg.* 1217
EPICURIOUS.COM - Website - CONDE NAST PUBLICATIONS, INC.; *pg.* 1629, *pg.* 1217
EPICUT - Surgical Instrument - MICROAIRE SURGICAL INSTRUMENTS INC.; *pg.* 1423, *pg.* 1778

EPIDESIGNER - Software - SEQUENOM, INC.; *pg.* 1593, *pg.* 209
EPIK - Orthopedic Implant Product - DJO SURGICAL; *pg.* 1525, *pg.* 1661
EPIKOTE - Epoxy Resin - HEXION; *pg.* 1166, *pg.* 1440
EPIKURE - Epoxy Curatives - HEXION; *pg.* 1166, *pg.* 1440
EPIL-STOP - Personal Care Electrical Product - HELEN OF TROY L.P.; *pg.* 511, *pg.* 1692
EPILINK - Chemical Products - AIR PRODUCTS AND CHEMICALS, INC.; *pg.* 1145, *pg.* 1513
EPINIONS - Magazine - SHOPPING.COM, LTD.; *pg.* 1280, *pg.* 50
EPINIONS.COM - Magazine - SHOPPING.COM, LTD.; *pg.* 1280, *pg.* 50
EPIPHONE - Musical Instrument - GIBSON GUITAR CORP.; *pg.* 550, *pg.* 1650
EPIR - Development Tool - ZILOG INC.; *pg.* 497, *pg.* 252
EPIREADY - Substrates - II-VI INCORPORATED; *pg.* 1417, *pg.* 1585
EPISCOPE - Skin Surface Microscope - WELCH ALLYN INC.; *pg.* 1436, *pg.* 1342
EPISERF - Biomolecule Product - THERMO FISHER SCIENTIFIC INC.; *pg.* 1602, *pg.* 61
EPISODE - Fabric - NEMSCHOFF, INC.; *pg.* 936, *pg.* 1890
EPISODE PROFILER - Pharmaceutical Supply Management System - MCKESSON CORPORATION; *pg.* 1560, *pg.* 222
EPITOME - Electrosurgical Scalpel with Ceramic Core - UTAH MEDICAL PRODUCTS, INC.; *pg.* 1605, *pg.* 1752
EPITYPER - Diagnostic Tool - SEQUENOM, INC.; *pg.* 1593, *pg.* 209
EPIVAL - Pharmaceutical Product - ABBOTT LABORATORIES; *pg.* 1484, *pg.* 551
EPKI - Software - CERTICOM CORP.; *pg.* 371, *pg.* 1925
EPLANNER - Software System - MENTOR GRAPHICS CORPORATION; *pg.* 432, *pg.* 1510
EPLOCK - Multichannel Synchronization - EVANS & SUTHERLAND COMPUTER CORPORATION; *pg.* 638, *pg.* 1757
EPM - Software - AUTHENTIDATE HOLDING CORP.; *pg.* 356, *pg.* 1044
EPMAR - Sealants, Encapsulants & Adhesives - QUAKER CHEMICAL CORP.; *pg.* 1178, *pg.* 1524
EPO-EASE - Epoxy Dispensing Systems - BUEHLER, LTD.; *pg.* 1403, *pg.* 622
EPO-ROK - Flooring System - THE VALSPAR CORPORATION; *pg.* 1449, *pg.* 945
EPOCAST - Epoxy Syntactic - HUNTSMAN CORPORATION; *pg.* 1167, *pg.* 1758
EPOCEL - Filter Cartridge - PALL CORPORATION; *pg.* 232, *pg.* 1323
EPOCH - Musical Instrument - GIBSON GUITAR CORP.; *pg.* 550, *pg.* 1650
EPOCH - Software - INTEGRAL SYSTEMS, INC.; *pg.* 416, *pg.* 767
EPOCH - Cosmetics - NU SKIN ENTERPRISES, INC.; *pg.* 518, *pg.* 1755
EPOCH BABY - Ethnobotanical Product - NU SKIN ENTERPRISES, INC.; *pg.* 518, *pg.* 1755
EPOCH CLIENT - Software - INTEGRAL SYSTEMS, INC.; *pg.* 416, *pg.* 767
EPOCH T&C - Software - INTEGRAL SYSTEMS, INC.; *pg.* 416, *pg.* 767
EPOCH TRIGGERS - Software - INTEGRAL SYSTEMS, INC.; *pg.* 416, *pg.* 767
EPOCH TRIGGERS SERVICE - Software - INTEGRAL SYSTEMS, INC.; *pg.* 416, *pg.* 767
EPOCH VERSION 4 - Software - INTEGRAL SYSTEMS, INC.; *pg.* 416, *pg.* 767
EPOCH WEB SERVER - Software - INTEGRAL SYSTEMS, INC.; *pg.* 416, *pg.* 767
EPOCRATES DX - Diagnosis Reference - EPOCRATES, INC.; *pg.* 1529, *pg.* 254
EPOCRATES ESSENTIALS - Drug & Disease Reference - EPOCRATES, INC.; *pg.* 1529, *pg.* 254
EPOCRATES ESSENTIALS DELUXE - Clinical Practice Suite - EPOCRATES, INC.; *pg.* 1529, *pg.* 254
EPOCRATES HONORS - Research Program - EPOCRATES, INC.; *pg.* 1529, *pg.* 254
EPOCRATES ID - Infectious Disease Guide - EPOCRATES, INC.; *pg.* 1529, *pg.* 254
EPOCRATES LAB - Diagnostic Reference - EPOCRATES, INC.; *pg.* 1529, *pg.* 254
EPOCRATES MEDINSIGHT - Research Reference - EPOCRATES, INC.; *pg.* 1529, *pg.* 254
EPOCRATES MEDTOOLS - Clinical Application - EPOCRATES, INC.; *pg.* 1529, *pg.* 254
EPOCRATES ONLINE PLUS AHFS - Hosting Service - EPOCRATES, INC.; *pg.* 1529, *pg.* 254
EPOCRATES QUICKQUAL - Medical Service - EPOCRATES, INC.; *pg.* 1529, *pg.* 254
EPOCRATES QUICKRECRUIT - Medical Service - EPOCRATES, INC.; *pg.* 1529, *pg.* 254
EPOCRATES QUICKSURVEY - Medical Service - EPOCRATES, INC.; *pg.* 1529, *pg.* 254
EPOCRATES RX - Drug Reference - EPOCRATES, INC.; *pg.* 1529, *pg.* 254
EPOCRATES RX FORMULARY - Clinical Reference - EPOCRATES, INC.; *pg.* 1529, *pg.* 254
EPOCRATES RX PRO - Enhanced Drug Reference - EPOCRATES, INC.; *pg.* 1529, *pg.* 254
EPOCRATES SXDX - Disease Reference - EPOCRATES, INC.; *pg.* 1529, *pg.* 254
EPODIL - Chemical Products - AIR PRODUCTS AND CHEMICALS, INC.; *pg.* 1145, *pg.* 1513
EPOGEN - Medicine - AMGEN INC.; *pg.* 1493, *pg.* 291
EPOLENE - Waxes - EASTMAN CHEMICAL COMPANY; *pg.* 1159, *pg.* 1636
EPON - Chemical Product - HEXION; *pg.* 1166, *pg.* 1440
EPONEX - Chemical - MILLER-STEPHENSON CHEMICAL COMPANY, INC.; *pg.* 1172, *pg.* 344
EPONOL - Chemical - MILLER-STEPHENSON CHEMICAL COMPANY, INC.; *pg.* 1172, *pg.* 344
EPORT CONNECT - Software - USA TECHNOLOGIES, INC.; *pg.* 815, *pg.* 1550
EPOSERT - Aerospace Cured Syntactic Inserts - HUNTSMAN CORPORATION; *pg.* 1167, *pg.* 1758
EPOWERMHS - Computer Program - COMPUTER SCIENCES CORPORATION; *pg.* 378, *pg.* 1780
EPOX - Encapsulated Current Limiting Fuse - G&W ELECTRIC COMPANY; *pg.* 1338, *pg.* 558
EPOX-E-SEAL - Polyamide Resins - HUNTSMAN CORPORATION; *pg.* 1167, *pg.* 1758
EPOXI GRIP - Floor Coating - REVERE PRODUCTS; *pg.* 107, *pg.* 1435
EPOXOBOND - Coating - YENKIN-MAJESTIC PAINT CORPORATION; *pg.* 1450, *pg.* 1445
EPOXY - Apparel - OAKLEY, INC.; *pg.* 1840, *pg.* 86
EPOXY - Resin - S&C ELECTRIC COMPANY; *pg.* 1305, *pg.* 589
EPOXY 350 - Waterborne Coating for Concrete - HILLYARD, INC.; *pg.* 331, *pg.* 990
EPOXY BOND - Epoxy Putties, Glues & Pastes - ATLAS MINERALS & CHEMICALS, INC.; *pg.* 69, *pg.* 1552
EPOXY II - Mop Wringers - GEERPRES INC.; *pg.* 1339, *pg.* 901
EPOXY-STIK - Repair Sealants - LA-CO INDUSTRIES MARKAL CO., INC.; *pg.* 1170, *pg.* 610
EPOXY-TAB - Repair Sealants - LA-CO INDUSTRIES MARKAL CO., INC.; *pg.* 1170, *pg.* 610
EPOXYSHIELD - Masking Product - KELLY-MOORE PAINT COMPANY, INC.; *pg.* 1443, *pg.* 198
EPPINGER - Fishing Lures - EPPINGER MANUFACTURING CO.; *pg.* 1833, *pg.* 876
EPR - Medical Device - RESMED INC.; *pg.* 1589, *pg.* 207
EPREX - Healthcare Product - JOHNSON & JOHNSON; *pg.* 1549, *pg.* 1091
EPRISM - Software - EDGEWAVE INC; *pg.* 390, *pg.* 202
EPRO - Software - DATATRAK INTERNATIONAL, INC.; *pg.* 383, *pg.* 1462
EPRODUCT DESIGNER - Software System - MENTOR GRAPHICS CORPORATION; *pg.* 432, *pg.* 1510
EPRODUCT SERVICES - Software System - MENTOR GRAPHICS CORPORATION; *pg.* 432, *pg.* 1510
EPS - Inserters - PITNEY BOWES INC.; *pg.* 454, *pg.* 376
EPS - Educational Resources - SCHOOL SPECIALTY, INC.; *pg.* 467, *pg.* 1860
EPS SILVER - High Performance Styrenics - NOVA CHEMICALS CORPORATION; *pg.* 1175, *pg.* 1904
THE EPS WAY - Energy Management Solutions - ENERGY & POWER SOLUTIONS, INC.; *pg.* 392, *pg.* 71
EPSON - Scanner - HURST CHEMICAL COMPANY; *pg.* 1168, *pg.* 174
E.P.T - Pregnancy Test - MCNEIL-PPC, INC.; *pg.* 1560, *pg.* 1533
EPT-1000 - Medical Device - BOSTON SCIENTIFIC CORPORATION; *pg.* 1508, *pg.* 831
EPTFE - Expanded PTFE Dialectric - CARLISLE INTERCONNECT TECHNOLOGIES; *pg.* 1294, *pg.* 461
EPV - Optical Based Measurement Devices - CYBEROPTICS CORPORATION; *pg.* 1408, *pg.* 925
EPX - Software - EVANS & SUTHERLAND COMPUTER CORPORATION; *pg.* 638, *pg.* 1757
EQ - Wash System - WHIRLPOOL CORPORATION; *pg.* 62, *pg.* 872
EQ TECHNOLOGY - Ethernet Network - VITESSE SEMICONDUCTOR CORPORATION; *pg.* 686, *pg.* 57
EQ TRAQ - Asset Management and Tracking System - AESCULAP, INC.; *pg.* 1487, *pg.* 1521
EQAS - Software - BIO-RAD LABORATORIES, INC.; *pg.* 1504, *pg.* 101
EQPYTIAN QUEST - Game - INTERNATIONAL GAME TECHNOLOGY; *pg.* 420, *pg.* 1606
EQSTIM - Immunostimulant - NEOGEN CORPORATION; *pg.* 883, *pg.* 896
EQUA - Chairs - HERMAN MILLER, INC.; *pg.* 926, *pg.* 913
EQUA CHAIR - Furniture - HERMAN MILLER, INC.; *pg.* 926, *pg.* 913
EQUABIN - Packaging - INTERNATIONAL PAPER COMPANY; *pg.* 1460, *pg.* 1644
EQUAL - Sweetener - MERISANT COMPANY; *pg.* 876, *pg.* 581
EQUAL SPACE - Carpet - INTERFACE, INC.; *pg.* 695, *pg.* 512
EQUALENS - Lens Material - BAUSCH & LOMB INCORPORATED; *pg.* 1401, *pg.* 1045
EQUALITY - Software - VERINT WITNESS ACTIONABLE SOLUTIONS; *pg.* 488, *pg.* 539
EQUALITY ANALYSIS - Software - VERINT WITNESS ACTIONABLE SOLUTIONS; *pg.* 488, *pg.* 539
EQUALITY BALANCE - Software - VERINT WITNESS ACTIONABLE SOLUTIONS; *pg.* 488, *pg.* 539
EQUALITY CALLMINER - Software - VERINT WITNESS ACTIONABLE SOLUTIONS; *pg.* 488, *pg.* 539
EQUALITY CONTACTSTORE - Software - VERINT WITNESS ACTIONABLE SOLUTIONS; *pg.* 488, *pg.* 539
EQUALITY COURSEWARE - Software - VERINT WITNESS ACTIONABLE SOLUTIONS; *pg.* 488, *pg.* 539
EQUALITY EVALUATION - Software - VERINT WITNESS ACTIONABLE SOLUTIONS; *pg.* 488, *pg.* 539
EQUALITY FOCUS - Software - VERINT WITNESS ACTIONABLE SOLUTIONS; *pg.* 488, *pg.* 539
EQUALITY NOW - Software - VERINT WITNESS ACTIONABLE SOLUTIONS; *pg.* 488, *pg.* 539
EQUALITY OFFICE - Software - VERINT WITNESS ACTIONABLE SOLUTIONS; *pg.* 488, *pg.* 539
EQUALITY PRODUCER - Software - VERINT WITNESS ACTIONABLE SOLUTIONS; *pg.* 488, *pg.* 539
EQUALITY VISION - Software - VERINT WITNESS ACTIONABLE SOLUTIONS; *pg.* 488, *pg.* 539
EQUALIZER - Software - BIO-RAD LABORATORIES, INC.; *pg.* 1504, *pg.* 101
EQUALIZER - Medical Device - BOSTON SCIENTIFIC CORPORATION; *pg.* 1508, *pg.* 831
EQUALIZER - Massage Product - HUMAN TOUCH; *pg.* 928, *pg.* 123
EQUALIZER - Bedding - JAMISON BEDDING, INC.; *pg.* 930, *pg.* 1651
EQUALIZER - Automatic Load Balancing Truck - MAGLINE, INC.; *pg.* 1358, *pg.* 908
THE EQUALIZER - Polyurethane Foam - SPAN-AMERICA MEDICAL SYSTEMS, INC.; *pg.* 1595, *pg.* 1618
EQUALIZER - Blower - TUTHILL CORPORATION; *pg.* 1385, *pg.* 561
EQUALIZER PRO - Massage Product - RELAX THE BACK CORPORATION; *pg.* 940, *pg.* 120
EQUALLOGIC - Computer Systems - DELL INC.; *pg.* 383, *pg.* 1737
EQUATE - Health & Beauty Aids - WAL-MART STORES, INC.; *pg.* 1790, *pg.* 29
EQUATION - Carpet - INTERFACE, INC.; *pg.* 695, *pg.* 512
EQUATOR - Carpet - INTERFACE, INC.; *pg.* 695, *pg.* 512
EQUATOR - Flatware - ONEIDA LTD; *pg.* 1129, *pg.* 1318
EQUATOR - Fastener - UNIVERSAL FOREST PRODUCTS, INC.; *pg.* 117, *pg.* 890
EQUESTRIAN - Table - BLATT BOWLING & BILLIARD CORP.; *pg.* 1827, *pg.* 1203
EQUI-FLOW - Medical Device - INTEGRA LIFESCIENCES HOLDINGS CORPORATION; *pg.* 1545, *pg.* 1109
EQUI PILE - Fabric - DRAPER KNITTING CO., INC.; *pg.* 692, *pg.* 810
EQUI-PLETE - Animal Nutrition Product - MANNA PRO CORPORATION; *pg.* 1478, *pg.* 975
EQUIBIT - Electronic Products & Components - TEXAS INSTRUMENTS INCORPORATED; *pg.* 679, *pg.* 1688
EQUICURV - Cutting Method - GLEASON CORPORATION;

pg. 1340, pg. 1335
EQUIFOAM - Plastic Foam - THE DOW CHEMICAL COMPANY; pg. 1157, pg. 898
EQUIGEST - Natural Progesterone Cream - AT LAST NATURALS, INC.; pg. 499, pg. 1347
EQUIGIZER - Horse Feeds - KENT NUTRITION GROUP; pg. 1477, pg. 710
EQUILIBRIUM - Carpet - INTERFACE, INC.; pg. 695, pg. 512
EQUILIBRIUM - Computer Keyboard Supports - STEELCASE INC.; pg. 475, pg. 889
EQUIMAX - Animal Safety Product - NEOGEN CORPORATION; pg. 883, pg. 896
EQUINE - Horse Food - DESIGNING HEALTH, INC.; pg. 1523, pg. 299
EQUINE - Horse Products - KENT NUTRITION GROUP; pg. 1477, pg. 710
EQUINE BASE - Horse Products - KENT NUTRITION GROUP; pg. 1477, pg. 710
EQUINE CHOICE - Horse Products - KENT NUTRITION GROUP; pg. 1477, pg. 710
EQUINE FORTIFIER - Horse Products - KENT NUTRITION GROUP; pg. 1477, pg. 710
EQUINIX EXCHANGE - Telecommunication System - EQUINIX, INC.; pg. 394, pg. 190
EQUINOX - Semiconductor Device - APPLIED MATERIALS, INC; pg. 618, pg. 1009
EQUINOX - Sport Utility Vehicle - GENERAL MOTORS COMPANY; pg. 175, pg. 881
EQUINOX - Thermal Blanket - MEDLINE INDUSTRIES, INC.; pg. 1562, pg. 635
EQUINOX - Silicone Rubber - SMOOTH-ON INC.; pg. 111, pg. 1528
EQUINOX - Bicycle - TREK BICYCLE CORPORATION; pg. 1847, pg. 1896
EQUINOX TTX - Bicycle - TREK BICYCLE CORPORATION; pg. 1847, pg. 1896
EQUINOXE - Shoulder System - EXACTECH, INC.; pg. 1529, pg. 428
EQUIPHEN - Veterinary Joint Disease Medicine - LUITPOLD PHARMACEUTICALS, INC.; pg. 1557, pg. 1342
EQUIPMENT CONNECTION - Publication - IOWA FARMER TODAY; pg. 1653, pg. 702
EQUIPMENT TRADER - Advertising Publication - DOMINION ENTERPRISES; pg. 1636, pg. 1796
EQUISLEEVE - Animal Safety Product - NEOGEN CORPORATION; pg. 883, pg. 896
EQUISPORT - Equine Support Bandage - 3M COMPANY; pg. 1142, pg. 956
EQUISTAT - Personal Care Material - BASF CATALYSTS LLC; pg. 1148, pg. 1074
EQUITE - Cleansing Line - PARFUMS CHRISTIAN DIOR, INC; pg. 519, pg. 1276
EQUITY - Office Furniture - KNOLL, INC.; pg. 425, pg. 1527
EQUITY - Pharmaceutical Product - PFIZER INC.; pg. 1581, pg. 1278
EQUITY*BUILDER - Brand Health Information System - IPSOS-ASI, INC.; pg. 421, pg. 363
EQUIVIEW - Software - IDEXX LABORATORIES, INC.; pg. 1543, pg. 753
EQUIWEDGE - Valves - FLOWSERVE CORPORATION; pg. 82, pg. 1719
EQULINE - Non-Thermal Windows - KAWNEER COMPANY, INC.; pg. 90, pg. 537
EQUUSSOURCE - Magazine - SOUTHERN STATES COOPERATIVE, INC.; pg. 1482, pg. 1804
EQYPTAIN HENNA - Hair & Skin Product - AUBREY ORGANICS INC.; pg. 499, pg. 470
ER BAC - Pharmaceutical Product - PFIZER INC.; pg. 1581, pg. 1278
ER BAC PLUS - Veterinary Vaccine - PFIZER INC.; pg. 1581, pg. 1278
ER-TRACKER - Molecular Probe Product - THERMO FISHER SCIENTIFIC INC.; pg. 1602, pg. 61
ERA - Laundry Product - THE PROCTER & GAMBLE COMPANY; pg. 1129, pg. 1418
ERA - Residential Real Estate Brokerage - REALOGY CORPORATION; pg. 1109, pg. 1081
ERA - Footwear - VANS, INC.; pg. 1821, pg. 76
ERA - Motor Homes - WINNEBAGO INDUSTRIES, INC.; pg. 1712, pg. 707
ERA-1 - Furniture - HAWORTH, INC.; pg. 402, pg. 891
ERADI-LITE - Awning Fabric - GLEN RAVEN, INC.; pg. 693, pg. 1373
ERAMS - Business Intelligence Product - DATAWATCH CORPORATION; pg. 383, pg. 813
ERASCO - Soups - CAMPBELL SOUP COMPANY; pg. 844, pg. 1048
ERASE-ITT - Sewage Odor Counteractant - SURCO PRODUCTS, INC.; pg. 336, pg. 1581
ERASERDISK - Hardware System - MICRO 2000, INC.; pg. 434, pg. 96
ERAXIS - Medicine - PFIZER INC.; pg. 1581, pg. 1278
ERBITUX - Cancer Medication - BRISTOL-MYERS SQUIBB COMPANY; pg. 1509, pg. 1206
ERBITUX - Therapeutic Product - IDERA PHARMACEUTICALS, INC.; pg. 1543, pg. 808
ERBITUX - Drug - INCYTE CORPORATION; pg. 1545, pg. 392
ERC - Gold Club Irons - CALLAWAY GOLF COMPANY; pg. 1829, pg. 58
ERC - Conduit - ELECTRON BEAM TECHNOLOGIES, INC.; pg. 1046, pg. 621
E.R.D.-HEALTHSCREEN - Urine Test - HESKA CORPORATION; pg. 1542, pg. 335
ERDISK - Software - DELL SOFTWARE; pg. 385, pg. 40
E.REPORT DESIGNER - Software - ACTUATE CORPORATION; pg. 342, pg. 253
E.REPORT OPTION - Software - ACTUATE CORPORATION; pg. 342, pg. 253
E.REPORTS - Software - ACTUATE CORPORATION; pg. 342, pg. 253
ERESEARCH COMMUNITY - Software - ERESEARCH TECHNOLOGY INC.; pg. 1243, pg. 1564
ERESNET - Software - ERESEARCH TECHNOLOGY INC.; pg. 1243, pg. 1564
ERGO - Laptop Riser - LAPWORKS, INC.; pg. 426, pg. 187
ERGO-ELITE - Hand Tool - IDEAL INDUSTRIES, INC.; pg. 1051, pg. 662
ERGO-FLEX - Leveling Arm System - FLEXSTEEL INDUSTRIES, INC.; pg. 925, pg. 707
ERGO GRIP - Hose - TEKNOR APEX COMPANY; pg. 1889, pg. 1605
ERGO LEG - Casters - TEMPUR SEALY INTERNATIONAL, INC.; pg. 944, pg. 731
ERGO-MATIC - Drum Handling Equipment - LIFTOMATIC MATERIAL HANDLING INC.; pg. 94, pg. 560
ERGOBASIC - Orthopedic Device - DJO SURGICAL; pg. 1525, pg. 1661
ERGODYNE - Rescue Gear Bag - ALIMED, INC.; pg. 1490, pg. 816
ERGOGRIP - Ladles - THE VOLLRATH COMPANY LLC; pg. 1139, pg. 1894
ERGOHUNTER - Knife - BUCK KNIVES, INC.; pg. 1828, pg. 550
ERGOHUNTER SMALL GAME - Knife - BUCK KNIVES, INC.; pg. 1828, pg. 550
ERGON - Furniture - HERMAN MILLER, INC.; pg. 926, pg. 913
ERGONOMIC HOSE PACKAGE - Hose Reel - STRAHMAN VALVES, INC.; pg. 1379, pg. 1517
ERGONOMIC INTRODUCER - Tagline - ANGIODYNAMICS, INC.; pg. 1495, pg. 1173
ERGOPRO - Frame Adjusting Plier - THE HILSINGER CO.; pg. 1416, pg. 841
ERGOSPEED - Adaptive Tool Interface Applications - BROOKS AUTOMATION, INC.; pg. 1320, pg. 813
ERGOSTYLE - Orthopedic Device - DJO SURGICAL; pg. 1525, pg. 1661
ERGOWAVE - Orthopedic Device - DJO SURGICAL; pg. 1525, pg. 1661
ERIC - Tester - MAGNETIC ANALYSIS CORPORATION; pg. 1421, pg. 1158
ERIC CLAPTON STRATOCASTER - Electric Guitar - FENDER MUSICAL INSTRUMENTS CORPORATION; pg. 547, pg. 21
ERIC GROSSBARDT COLLECTION - Fine Inlaid Gold & Silver Jewelry - ASCH/GROSSBARDT, INC.; pg. 1, pg. 1197
ERIC MORGAN - Furniture - BUSH INDUSTRIES INC.; pg. 919, pg. 1170
ERICA - Lamp - ASHLEY FURNITURE INDUSTRIES, INC.; pg. 914, pg. 1852
ERICA ABC - Furniture - NEMSCHOFF, INC.; pg. 936, pg. 1890
ERICA JR - Furniture - NEMSCHOFF, INC.; pg. 936, pg. 1890
ERICK - Shoes - COACH, INC.; pg. 3, pg. 1214
ERICKSON - Toolholding & Workholding Devices - KENNAMETAL INC.; pg. 1052, pg. 1547
ERICKSON ADVANTAGE - Health Insurance Plan - ERICKSON LIVING; pg. 1090, pg. 766
ERICKSON HEALTH - Health Care Program - ERICKSON LIVING; pg. 1090, pg. 766
ERIDEN - Microbicides & Bactericides for Eradicating Algae - DOW CHEMICAL; pg. 1156, pg. 1563
ERIE PRESS - Forging Product - SUPERIOR DIE SET CORP.; pg. 1379, pg. 1885
ERIEZ - Vibratory Feeder - ERIEZ MANUFACTURING CO. INC.; pg. 1335, pg. 1530
ERIFLEX - Electrical Panel - ERICO INTERNATIONAL CORPORATION; pg. 1335, pg. 1472
ERIK - Domestic Cigars - ALTADIS USA, INC.; pg. 1893, pg. 423
ERIK - Furniture - AMISCO INDUSTRIES LTD.; pg. 913, pg. 1958
ERIKA - Footwear - P.W. MINOR & SON, INC.; pg. 1816, pg. 1140
ERIN - Lamp - ASHLEY FURNITURE INDUSTRIES, INC.; pg. 914, pg. 1852
ERIS - Lamp - ASHLEY FURNITURE INDUSTRIES, INC.; pg. 914, pg. 1852
ERISA COMPLIANCE & ENFORCEMENT LIBRARY - Publisher - BLOOMBERG BNA; pg. 1621, pg. 1772
ERISTRUT - Fastener - ERICO INTERNATIONAL CORPORATION; pg. 1335, pg. 1472
ERITECH - Lightning Protection Products - ERICO INTERNATIONAL CORPORATION; pg. 1335, pg. 1472
ERIUM - Permanent Magnetic Power Source - ERIEZ MANUFACTURING CO. INC.; pg. 1335, pg. 1530
ERNIE BALL - Guitar - ERNIE BALL INC.; pg. 1768, pg. 68
ERNIE KEEBLER - Product Icon - KELLOGG COMPANY; pg. 831, pg. 870
EROOM - Software - EMC CORPORATION, pg. 391, pg. 825
EROSIONLAB - Erosion Control Product - AMERICAN EXCELSIOR COMPANY; pg. 1451, pg. 1659
EROSIONWORKS - Erosion Control Product - AMERICAN EXCELSIOR COMPANY; pg. 1451, pg. 1659
ERR - Systems Integration & Aeronautics - LOCKHEED MARTIN CORPORATION; pg. 229, pg. 762
ERROR AWARENESS - Educational Program - NEGOTIATION INSTITUTE, INC.; pg. 151, pg. 1268
ERS - Automatic Conveyor System - PARAGON TECHNOLOGIES, INC.; pg. 1367, pg. 1528
ERT - Dual Energy (Gas/Electric) Radiant Tube Heating System - SURFACE COMBUSTION, INC.; pg. 1077, pg. 1462
ERTHROCIN - Erythromycin - ABBOTT LABORATORIES; pg. 1484, pg. 551
ERTK - Navigation Aid - TRIMBLE NAVIGATION LIMITED; pg. 1384, pg. 288
ERY-PED - Pharmaceutical Product - ABBOTT LABORATORIES; pg. 1484, pg. 551
ERY-TAB - Pharmaceutical Product - ABBOTT LABORATORIES; pg. 1484, pg. 551
ERYTHROMYCIN, PCE - Genetic & Polymer Coated Antibiotic - ABBOTT LABORATORIES; pg. 1484, pg. 551
ES - Musical Instrument - GIBSON GUITAR CORP.; pg. 550, pg. 1650
ES - Coatings - TENNANT COMPANY; pg. 1381, pg. 944
ES-1000 - Measurement Device - ELECTRONICS FOR IMAGING, INC.; pg. 390, pg. 88
ES 2000 - Orthopedic Device - DJO SURGICAL; pg. 1525, pg. 1661
ES-KEY - Fire Suppression Product - IDEX CORPORATION; pg. 1347, pg. 623
ES1 RAIN SYSTEM - Rainwear - CABELA'S INCORPORATED; pg. 535, pg. 1019
ES1000 - Graphics Driver - ADVANCED MICRO DEVICES, INC.; pg. 613, pg. 282
ESA - Medical Product - CONMED CORPORATION; pg. 1517, pg. 1347
ESA - Thermal Processing Equipment - SURFACE COMBUSTION, INC.; pg. 1077, pg. 1462
ESA60 - Automatic Conveyor System - PARAGON TECHNOLOGIES, INC.; pg. 1367, pg. 1528
ESAFETY NET - Software - ERESEARCH TECHNOLOGY INC.; pg. 1243, pg. 1564
ESAR - Systems Integration & Aeronautics - LOCKHEED MARTIN CORPORATION; pg. 229, pg. 762
ESAT - Software - DATATRAK INTERNATIONAL, INC.; pg. 383, pg. 1462
ESBIOL - Pesticide - MCLAUGHLIN GORMLEY KING COMPANY; pg. 1797, pg. 939
ESCALADE - Sport Utility Vehicle - GENERAL MOTORS

COMPANY; *pg.* 175, *pg.* 881
ESCALADE ESV - Sport Utility Vehicle - GENERAL MOTORS COMPANY; *pg.* 175, *pg.* 881
ESCALADE EXT - Sport Utility Vehicle - GENERAL MOTORS COMPANY; *pg.* 175, *pg.* 881
ESCAN - Show Control - ELECTROSONIC SYSTEMS, INC.; *pg.* 635, *pg.* 949
ESCAPADE - Carpet - BEAULIEU GROUP, LLC; *pg.* 917, *pg.* 529
ESCAPADE - Motorhome - JAYCO INC.; *pg.* 1708, *pg.* 695
ESCAPADE - Office Furniture - STEELCASE INC.; *pg.* 475, *pg.* 889
ESCAPADE VACATIONS - Tour Packages - ISRAM WHOLESALE TOURS & TRAVEL LTD.; *pg.* 1913, *pg.* 1244
ESCAPADES - Door Glass - ODL INCORPORATED; *pg.* 101, *pg.* 914
ESCAPE - Medical Device - BOSTON SCIENTIFIC CORPORATION; *pg.* 1508, *pg.* 831
ESCAPE - Car & Van - FORD MOTOR COMPANY OF CANADA, LIMITED; *pg.* 174, *pg.* 1930
ESCAPE - Fiberglass Boat Product - GRADY-WHITE BOATS, INC.; *pg.* 1707, *pg.* 1377
ESCAPE - Sailboats - JOHNSON OUTDOORS INC.; *pg.* 1837, *pg.* 1888
ESCAPE - Medical Device - RESMED INC.; *pg.* 1589, *pg.* 207
ESCAPE FROM THE ORDINARY - Tag Line - NORM THOMPSON OUTFITTERS INC.; *pg.* 1780, *pg.* 1498
ESCAPE FROM ZIRCON - Film - MUSEUM OF SCIENCE AND INDUSTRY; *pg.* 565, *pg.* 583
ESCAPE LIGHT - Smoke Alarm Light - BRK BRANDS, INC.; *pg.* 627, *pg.* 554
THE ESCAPIST - Gaming Website - DEFYMEDIA; *pg.* 1237, *pg.* 1222
ESCAR-GO! - Slug & Snail Control - GARDENS ALIVE!, INC.; *pg.* 1796, *pg.* 693
ESCAT - Catalyst - BASF CATALYSTS LLC; *pg.* 1148, *pg.* 1074
ESCENTIALS - Apparel - RELIABLE OF MILWAUKEE; *pg.* 698, *pg.* 1879
ESCHOLASTIC - Educational Materials - SCHOLASTIC INC.; *pg.* 1683, *pg.* 1288
ESCO POSILOK - Tooth System - ESCO CORPORATION; *pg.* 1335, *pg.* 1502
ESCO SUPER V - Tooth System - ESCO CORPORATION; *pg.* 1335, *pg.* 1502
ESCO ZIPPER LIP - System - ESCO CORPORATION; *pg.* 1335, *pg.* 1502
ESCOALLOY - Plate - ESCO CORPORATION; *pg.* 1335, *pg.* 1502
ESCOBAK - Crusher Backing - ESCO CORPORATION; *pg.* 1335, *pg.* 1502
ESCOBAR - Footwear - VANS, INC.; *pg.* 1821, *pg.* 76
ESCORT - Herbicide - E.I. DU PONT DE NEMOURS & COMPANY; *pg.* 1159, *pg.* 390
ESCORT - Cleaning Equipment Cart - GEERPRES INC.; *pg.* 1339, *pg.* 901
ESCORT - Pump - MINE SAFETY APPLIANCES COMPANY; *pg.* 1361, *pg.* 1525
ESCORT - Musical Instrument - PEAVEY ELECTRONICS CORPORATION; *pg.* 662, *pg.* 970
ESCORT BALLOONS - Medical Device - COOK GROUP, INC.; *pg.* 1518, *pg.* 674
ESCORT RX - Hospital Housekeeping Cart - GEERPRES INC.; *pg.* 1339, *pg.* 901
ESCP - Displays & Projectors - EVANS & SUTHERLAND COMPUTER CORPORATION; *pg.* 638, *pg.* 1757
ESCRIBE - Web-based Report Generator & Viewer - INTEGRAL SYSTEMS, INC.; *pg.* 416, *pg.* 767
ESCRIPTION - Medical Transcription Software - NUANCE COMMUNICATIONS, INC.; *pg.* 447, *pg.* 806
ESCUIS - Beverages - THE COCA-COLA COMPANY; *pg.* 240, *pg.* 493
ESEK - Briefcase - JANDD MOUNTAINEERING, INC.; *pg.* 1837, *pg.* 204
ESEND - Software System - BOTTOMLINE TECHNOLOGIES (DE), INC.; *pg.* 727, *pg.* 1038
ESERVICE - Software - EGAIN COMMUNICATIONS CORPORATION; *pg.* 1242, *pg.* 284
ESG - Filter - REVOLUTION LIGHTING TECHNOLOGIES, INC.; *pg.* 1304, *pg.* 377
ESHE - Lamp - ASHLEY FURNITURE INDUSTRIES, INC.; *pg.* 914, *pg.* 1852
ESIG - Image Generators - EVANS & SUTHERLAND COMPUTER CORPORATION; *pg.* 638, *pg.* 1757
ESIGHT - Software System - MENTOR GRAPHICS CORPORATION; *pg.* 432, *pg.* 1510
ESIM - Software System - MENTOR GRAPHICS CORPORATION; *pg.* 432, *pg.* 1510
ESIP - Package Technique - POWER INTEGRATIONS, INC.; *pg.* 1369, *pg.* 249
ESITE MONITOR - Software - ERESEARCH TECHNOLOGY INC.; *pg.* 1243, *pg.* 1564
ESL - Refrigerated Egg Products - CARGILL LIMITED; *pg.* 1475, *pg.* 1914
ESL MIX BNB - Egg Substitute - MICHAEL FOODS, INC.; *pg.* 877, *pg.* 949
ESL MIX CARTON - Egg Substitute - MICHAEL FOODS, INC.; *pg.* 877, *pg.* 949
ESL WHITE BNB - Egg Substitute - MICHAEL FOODS, INC.; *pg.* 877, *pg.* 949
ESL WHITE CARTON - Egg Substitute - MICHAEL FOODS, INC.; *pg.* 877, *pg.* 949
ESL WHOLE BNB - Egg Substitute - MICHAEL FOODS, INC.; *pg.* 877, *pg.* 949
ESL WHOLE CARTON - Egg Substitute - MICHAEL FOODS, INC.; *pg.* 877, *pg.* 949
ESL YOLK BNB - Egg Substitute - MICHAEL FOODS, INC.; *pg.* 877, *pg.* 949
ESL YOLK CARTON - Egg Substitute - MICHAEL FOODS, INC.; *pg.* 877, *pg.* 949
ESLABON DE LUJO - Home Appliance Product - WHIRLPOOL CORPORATION; *pg.* 62, *pg.* 872
ESLINX - Show Control - ELECTROSONIC SYSTEMS, INC.; *pg.* 635, *pg.* 949
ESLP - Laser Projector - EVANS & SUTHERLAND COMPUTER CORPORATION; *pg.* 638, *pg.* 1757
ESLTEST - Material Tensile Testing - ELECTRO STANDARDS LABORATORIES INC.; *pg.* 390, *pg.* 1600
ESMARTLOG - Software - HEALTHPORT, INC.; *pg.* 403, *pg.* 484
ESN - Sculptured Nails Kits - AMERICAN INTERNATIONAL INDUSTRIES COMPANY; *pg.* 498, *pg.* 126
ESOTERIC - Electronic Equipment - TEAC AMERICA, INC.; *pg.* 678, *pg.* 151
E.SOURCE - Software - R.R. DONNELLEY & SONS COMPANY; *pg.* 1682, *pg.* 589
ESP - Stretch Polyester Fabrics - INVISTA B.V.; *pg.* 1168, *pg.* 723
ESP - Hair Care Product - JOHN PAUL MITCHELL SYSTEMS; *pg.* 512, *pg.* 133
ESP & DESIGN - Software - WIND RIVER SYSTEMS, INC.; *pg.* 493, *pg.* 38
ESP EASY SURFACE PREP - Wipe On/Wipe Off Surface Cleaner - AKZO NOBEL DECORATIVE PAINTS, USA; *pg.* 1439, *pg.* 1474
ESP-PARTS - Ordering Software - XYLEM INC.; *pg.* 1078, *pg.* 1339
ESP-PLUS - Ordering Software - XYLEM INC.; *pg.* 1078, *pg.* 1339
ESPACE - Fabric - NEMSCHOFF, INC.; *pg.* 936, *pg.* 1890
ESPE - Dental Adhesive - 3M COMPANY; *pg.* 1142, *pg.* 956
ESPECIALLY FOR DAD BOUQUET - Floral Bouquet - FTD GROUP, INC.; *pg.* 1795, *pg.* 608
ESPECIALLY YOURS - Nutritional Supplement for Women - NATURAL ORGANICS, INC.; *pg.* 1571, *pg.* 1181
ESPECIALLY YOURS - Wigs, Hair Pieces, & Apparel Catalog - SPECIALTY CATALOG CORPORATION; *pg.* 1786, *pg.* 856
ESPERA - Spanish-Language Parenting Magazine - MEREDITH CORPORATION; *pg.* 1663, *pg.* 705
ESPERAL - Polymer Product - CHEMTURA CORPORATION; *pg.* 1152, *pg.* 355
ESPERANZA - Watch - MOVADO GROUP, INC.; *pg.* 10, *pg.* 1101
ESPERANZA - Furniture - NEMSCHOFF, INC.; *pg.* 936, *pg.* 1890
ESPEROX - Polymer Product - CHEMTURA CORPORATION; *pg.* 1152, *pg.* 355
ESPLANADE - Fabric - NEMSCHOFF, INC.; *pg.* 936, *pg.* 1890
ESPN CLASSIC - Classic Sports Cable Network - ESPN, INC.; *pg.* 285, *pg.* 340
ESPN DEPORTES - Spanish-Language Sports Entertainment Multimedia - ESPN, INC.; *pg.* 285, *pg.* 340
ESPN FANTASY BASEBALL IS FREE. AND IT ROCKS. - Tagline - ESPN, INC.; *pg.* 285, *pg.* 340
ESPN NEWS - Sports News Cable Network - ESPN, INC.; *pg.* 285, *pg.* 340
ESPN RADIO - Radio Network - ESPN, INC.; *pg.* 285, *pg.* 340
ESPN THE MAGAZINE - Magazine - ESPN, INC.; *pg.* 285, *pg.* 340
ESPN ZONE - Sports Entertainment Bar & Restaurant Franchises - ESPN, INC.; *pg.* 285, *pg.* 340
ESPN ZONE - Sports Facilities - THE WALT DISNEY COMPANY; *pg.* 317, *pg.* 52
ESPN360.COM - Sports Broadband Network - ESPN, INC.; *pg.* 285, *pg.* 340
E.SPREADSHEET - Report Design & Delivery - ACTUATE CORPORATION; *pg.* 342, *pg.* 253
ESPRESSIMO - Espresso Machines & Grinders - GRINDMASTER CORPORATION; *pg.* 56, *pg.* 734
ESPRESSO FORTE - Coffee - PEET'S COFFEE & TEA, INC.; *pg.* 1029, *pg.* 85
ESPRESSO PERFECTO - Coffee - THE COFFEE BEANERY LTD.; *pg.* 849, *pg.* 886
ESPRESSO ROAST - Coffee - STARBUCKS CORPORATION; *pg.* 897, *pg.* 1840
ESPRING - Water Treatment System - AMWAY CORPORATION; *pg.* 326, *pg.* 864
ESPRIT - Furniture - ASHLEY FURNITURE INDUSTRIES, INC.; *pg.* 914, *pg.* 1852
ESPRIT - Cleaning System - VON SCHRADER COMPANY; *pg.* 62, *pg.* 1890
ESPY - Sensing Product - ENTEGRIS, INC.; *pg.* 1882, *pg.* 788
ESPYS - Sports Awards - ESPN, INC.; *pg.* 285, *pg.* 340
ESQ SWISS - Watches - MOVADO GROUP, INC.; *pg.* 10, *pg.* 1101
ESQUIRE - Case - BROWN & BIGELOW, INC.; *pg.* 1624, *pg.* 959
ESQUIRE - Magazine - THE HEARST CORPORATION; *pg.* 1649, *pg.* 1239
ESQUIRE - Coffee Server - THE VOLLRATH COMPANY LLC; *pg.* 1139, *pg.* 1894
ESRI DEVELOPER NETWORK - Software - ENVIRONMENTAL SYSTEMS RESEARCH INSTITUTE INC.; *pg.* 393, *pg.* 188
ESRI IMAGE SERVER - Software - ENVIRONMENTAL SYSTEMS RESEARCH INSTITUTE INC.; *pg.* 393, *pg.* 188
ESSEM - Processed Food - KAYEM FOODS, INC.; *pg.* 867, *pg.* 814
ESSENCE - Rug - COURISTAN INC.; *pg.* 921, *pg.* 1067
ESSENCE - Magazine - ESSENCE MAGAZINE; *pg.* 1639, *pg.* 1229
ESSENCE - Napkins - GEORGIA-PACIFIC LLC; *pg.* 1458, *pg.* 507
ESSENCE - Media Publication - TIME INC.; *pg.* 1693, *pg.* 1300
ESSENCE - Magazine - TIME WARNER INC.; *pg.* 312, *pg.* 1302
ESSENCE BRINGS YOU GREAT COOKING - Publication - ESSENCE MAGAZINE; *pg.* 1639, *pg.* 1229
ESSENCE IMPRESSIONS - Napkins & Towels - GEORGIA-PACIFIC LLC; *pg.* 1458, *pg.* 507
THE ESSENCE OF WELL-BEING - Slogan - AROMALAND INC.; *pg.* 499, *pg.* 1135
ESSENTIA - Fabric - NEMSCHOFF, INC.; *pg.* 936, *pg.* 1890
ESSENTIAL - Bag - BROWN & BIGELOW, INC.; *pg.* 1624, *pg.* 959
ESSENTIAL - Sports Drink - ENERGY BRANDS, INC.; *pg.* 854, *pg.* 1227
ESSENTIAL - Cushion - INVACARE CORPORATION; *pg.* 1546, *pg.* 1451
ESSENTIAL - Shampoo - KAO BRANDS CO. INC.; *pg.* 513, *pg.* 1415
ESSENTIAL - Hard Drive - WESTERN DIGITAL CORPORATION; *pg.* 492, *pg.* 118
ESSENTIAL BALANCED OMEGA 3/6 - Nutritional Supplement - PHARMAVITE LLC; *pg.* 1584, *pg.* 167
ESSENTIAL ENZYMES - Vitamin & Herbal Supplement - SOURCE NATURALS; *pg.* 1595, *pg.* 278
ESSENTIAL INFORMATION PROTECTION - Tag Line - WEBSENSE, INC.; *pg.* 491, *pg.* 210
ESSENTIAL MATRIX - Skin & Haircare Product - NEW EARTH LIFE SCIENCES, INC.; *pg.* 1573, *pg.* 1499
ESSENTIAL SERIES - Drumsticks - AVEDIS ZILDJIAN COMPANY; *pg.* 531, *pg.* 839
ESSENTIALBALANCED ENERGY PACK FOR WOMEN - Nutritional Supplement - PHARMAVITE LLC; *pg.* 1584, *pg.* 167
ESSENTIALLY PURE INGREDIENTS - Raw Materials -

NATROL, INC.; *pg.* 1570, *pg.* 64
ESSENTIALPOINTS - Detailing Program - EPOCRATES, INC.; *pg.* 1529, *pg.* 254
ESSENTIALS - Paint & Coating - AERVOE INDUSTRIES INCORPORATED; *pg.* 1439, *pg.* 1021
ESSENTIALS - Chairs - KNOLL, INC.; *pg.* 425, *pg.* 1527
ESSENTIALS - Supplement And Food - NEW EARTH LIFE SCIENCES, INC.; *pg.* 1573, *pg.* 1499
ESSENTIALS - Vinyl Siding - OWENS CORNING; *pg.* 102, *pg.* 1476
ESSENTIALS - Software - RENTRAK CORPORATION; *pg.* 306, *pg.* 1506
ESSENTIALS - Hair Care - SHAKLEE CORPORATION; *pg.* 1593, *pg.* 184
ESSENTIALS - Health Care Product - USANA HEALTH SCIENCES, INC.; *pg.* 1605, *pg.* 1761
ESSENTIALS FOR ADVENTURE - Catalog - MCNETT CORPORATION; *pg.* 1839, *pg.* 1817
ESSEX - Lighting - ETHAN ALLEN INTERIORS INC.; *pg.* 924, *pg.* 343
ESSEX - Furniture - HAWORTH, INC.; *pg.* 402, *pg.* 891
ESSEX - Wallcovering - OMNOVA SOLUTIONS INC; *pg.* 1176, *pg.* 1453
ESSEX - Mid-Priced Art-Deco Pianos - STEINWAY & SONS; *pg.* 586, *pg.* 1176
ESSEX ARGOSY - Newsletters - THE DOW CHEMICAL COMPANY; *pg.* 1157, *pg.* 898
ESSEXPAK - Adhesive Containers - THE DOW CHEMICAL COMPANY; *pg.* 1157, *pg.* 898
ESSLINGER PREMIUM - Beer - THE LION BREWERY, INC.; *pg.* 254, *pg.* 1594
ESSO - Fleet Card - IMPERIAL OIL LIMITED; *pg.* 979, *pg.* 1903
ESSURE - Birth Control Procedure - BAYER CORPORATION; *pg.* 1499, *pg.* 1573
ESSX - Wireless Communication System - AT&T SOUTHEAST; *pg.* 1868, *pg.* 489
EST 2000 - Combat Training System - CUBIC CORPORATION; *pg.* 632, *pg.* 201
ESTALIS - Estradiol Transdermal System - NOVEN PHARMACEUTICALS, INC.; *pg.* 1576, *pg.* 445
ESTANCIA - Wine - CONSTELLATION BRANDS, INC.; *pg.* 1960, *pg.* 1348
ESTANE - Engineered Polymers - THE LUBRIZOL CORPORATION; *pg.* 1171, *pg.* 1481
ESTAR - Film Base - EASTMAN KODAK COMPANY; *pg.* 1408, *pg.* 1333
ESTAR-AH - Film Base - EASTMAN KODAK COMPANY; *pg.* 1408, *pg.* 1333
ESTARS - Web-Based Software - LOCKHEED MARTIN CORPORATION; *pg.* 229, *pg.* 762
ESTASOL - Fatty Acid Ester - THE DOW CHEMICAL COMPANY; *pg.* 1157, *pg.* 898
ESTATE - Wall Panel - BLUELINX HOLDINGS, INC.; *pg.* 70, *pg.* 491
ESTATE - Fabric - NEMSCHOFF, INC.; *pg.* 936, *pg.* 1890
ESTATE - Home Appliance Product - WHIRLPOOL CORPORATION; *pg.* 62, *pg.* 872
ESTATE COLLECTION - Furniture - STANLEY FURNITURE CO., INC.; *pg.* 943, *pg.* 1379
ESTATE STRATEGIES GROUP - Fee Based & Business Succession Planning - THE NORTHWESTERN MUTUAL LIFE INSURANCE COMPANY; *pg.* 1212, *pg.* 1879
ESTATES - Rug - COURISTAN INC.; *pg.* 921, *pg.* 1067
ESTDC - Color Wheel - REVOLUTION LIGHTING TECHNOLOGIES, INC.; *pg.* 1304, *pg.* 377
ESTDS - Color Wheel - REVOLUTION LIGHTING TECHNOLOGIES, INC.; *pg.* 1304, *pg.* 377
ESTEE - Food Product - THE HAIN CELESTIAL GROUP, INC.; *pg.* 860, *pg.* 1172
ESTEE LAUDER - Beauty Products - THE ESTEE LAUDER COMPANIES INC.; *pg.* 508, *pg.* 1229
ESTEEM - Hearing Implant - ENVOY MEDICAL CORPORATION; *pg.* 1529, *pg.* 960
ESTEEM SYNERGY - Ostomy Care Product - CONVATEC LTD.; *pg.* 1518, *pg.* 1121
ESTER-C - Nutritional Product - NATROL, INC.; *pg.* 1570, *pg.* 64
ESTER-C - Vitamin - NBTY, INC.; *pg.* 1572, *pg.* 1338
ESTERA - Nutritional Supplement - NU SKIN ENTERPRISES, INC.; *pg.* 518, *pg.* 1755
ESTEREOTEMPO - Radio Station - SPANISH BROADCASTING SYSTEM INC.; *pg.* 310, *pg.* 446
ESTHER - Lamp - ASHLEY FURNITURE INDUSTRIES, INC.; *pg.* 914, *pg.* 1852
ESTHER WILLIAMS - Swimming Pools - DELAIR GROUP, LLC; *pg.* 78, *pg.* 1053
ESTHET X - Dental Product - DENTSPLY INTERNATIONAL INC.; *pg.* 1522, *pg.* 1596
ESTICLEAN - Ester Oil - THE DOW CHEMICAL COMPANY; *pg.* 1157, *pg.* 898
ESTILO - Footwear - VANS, INC.; *pg.* 1821, *pg.* 76
ESTILUBE - Multi-Functional Estar - THE DOW CHEMICAL COMPANY; *pg.* 1157, *pg.* 898
ESTIMOL - Multi-Functional Estar - THE DOW CHEMICAL COMPANY; *pg.* 1157, *pg.* 898
ESTRACELL - Sponges - ARMALY BRANDS; *pg.* 326, *pg.* 912
ESTRADOT - Estradiol Transdermal System - NOVEN PHARMACEUTICALS, INC.; *pg.* 1576, *pg.* 445
ESTRATEGY - Software - MICROSTRATEGY, INC.; *pg.* 1266, *pg.* 1809
ESTRATEGY SOLUTIONS - Agent/Broker Online Marketing & Consulting - HOMES.COM, INC.; *pg.* 1256, *pg.* 203
ESTRELLA DAMM - Beer - UNITED STATES BEVERAGE LLC; *pg.* 266, *pg.* 379
ESTRELLA TV - Spanish Language Network - LIBERMAN BROADCASTING CORPORATION; *pg.* 296, *pg.* 52
ESTRIE - Flooring - AMERICAN BILTRITE INC.; *pg.* 1878, *pg.* 856
ESTRING - Medicine - PFIZER INC.; *pg.* 1581, *pg.* 1278
ESTRIP - Solvent - ARCHER-DANIELS-MIDLAND COMPANY; *pg.* 825, *pg.* 565
ESTRO-GYNE - Natural Hormone Balancing Gel - DIXIE HEALTH, INC.; *pg.* 1524, *pg.* 535
ESTROBOND - Triacetin Plasticizers - EASTMAN CHEMICAL COMPANY; *pg.* 1159, *pg.* 1636
ESTROGYN - Health & Beauty Product - DIXIE HEALTH, INC.; *pg.* 1524, *pg.* 535
ESTROHEALTH - Pharmaceutical Product - ALERE INC.; *pg.* 1488, *pg.* 849
ESTRON - Acetate Yarn - EASTMAN CHEMICAL COMPANY; *pg.* 1159, *pg.* 1636
ESTROSUPPORT - Pharmaceutical Product - ALERE INC.; *pg.* 1488, *pg.* 849
ESTUDY CONDUCT - Software - ERESEARCH TECHNOLOGY INC.; *pg.* 1243, *pg.* 1564
ESU - Networking Product - ADTRAN, INC.; *pg.* 344, *pg.* 6
ESU 120E - Networking Product - ADTRAN, INC.; *pg.* 344, *pg.* 6
ESUE - Networking Product - ADTRAN, INC.; *pg.* 344, *pg.* 6
ET100 - Staples - ARROW FASTENER COMPANY, INC.; *pg.* 1042, *pg.* 1118
ET125 - Staples - ARROW FASTENER COMPANY, INC.; *pg.* 1042, *pg.* 1118
ET150 - Staples - ARROW FASTENER COMPANY, INC.; *pg.* 1042, *pg.* 1118
ET200 - Brad Nails - ARROW FASTENER COMPANY, INC.; *pg.* 1042, *pg.* 1118
ET2025 - Staples - ARROW FASTENER COMPANY, INC.; *pg.* 1042, *pg.* 1118
ET50 - Staples - ARROW FASTENER COMPANY, INC.; *pg.* 1042, *pg.* 1118
ETA-PROCESS - PLC Control Technology - MOTAN, INC.; *pg.* 1886, *pg.* 903
ETACOL - Apparel Interlining - HARODITE INDUSTRIES, INC.; *pg.* 693, *pg.* 847
ETADS - Software - EASTMAN MACHINE COMPANY; *pg.* 1331, *pg.* 1148
ETAG - Healthcare Product - MONOGRAM BIOSCIENCES, INC.; *pg.* 1569, *pg.* 280
ETAG PERFORMER - Software - MONOGRAM BIOSCIENCES, INC.; *pg.* 1569, *pg.* 280
ETAGE - Modern Occasional Tables - BERNHARDT DESIGN; *pg.* 918, *pg.* 1381
ETAGE - Stainless Steel Flatware - ONEIDA LTD; *pg.* 1129, *pg.* 1318
ETAGMANAGER - License Plate Processing - HDI SOLUTIONS, INC.; *pg.* 403, *pg.* 1
ETANA - Lamp - ASHLEY FURNITURE INDUSTRIES, INC.; *pg.* 914, *pg.* 1852
ETAPESTRY - Fundraising Software - BLACKBAUD, INC.; *pg.* 361, *pg.* 1613
ETC - LED - CREE INC.; *pg.* 631, *pg.* 1371
ETC50 - Staples - ARROW FASTENER COMPANY, INC.; *pg.* 1042, *pg.* 1118
ETCH-A-SKETCH - Sketching Toy - THE OHIO ART COMPANY, INC.; *pg.* 965, *pg.* 1406
ETCH A SKETCH FOR IPHONE & IPOD - Toy - THE OHIO ART COMPANY, INC.; *pg.* 965, *pg.* 1406
ETCH MANOMETER - Temperature Controller - MKS INSTRUMENTS, INC.; *pg.* 1362, *pg.* 781
ETCHED AND SILK SERIES - Collection - ODL INCORPORATED; *pg.* 101, *pg.* 914
ETCHED METALS - Fabric - NEMSCHOFF, INC.; *pg.* 936, *pg.* 1890
ETCHING - Fabric - NEMSCHOFF, INC.; *pg.* 936, *pg.* 1890
ETCSP - Packaging System - AMKOR TECHNOLOGY, INC.; *pg.* 67, *pg.* 25
ETELECASTER - Software - MICROSTRATEGY, INC.; *pg.* 1266, *pg.* 1809
ETERM.COM - Insurance Service - CIGI DIRECT INSURANCE SERVICES, INC.; *pg.* 1197, *pg.* 335
ETERNA - Semiconductor Processing Equipment - AXCELIS TECHNOLOGIES, INC.; *pg.* 1400, *pg.* 787
ETERNABRITE - Coating - SILBERLINE MANUFACTURING CO., INC.; *pg.* 110, *pg.* 1588
ETERNAL GRAPHICS - Display Products - RICHARDSON ELECTRONICS, LTD.; *pg.* 667, *pg.* 622
ETERNITY - Fabric - NEMSCHOFF, INC.; *pg.* 936, *pg.* 1890
ETF50 - Cordless Tacker - ARROW FASTENER COMPANY, INC.; *pg.* 1042, *pg.* 1118
ETF50BN - Staples - ARROW FASTENER COMPANY, INC.; *pg.* 1042, *pg.* 1118
ETF50PBN - Staples - ARROW FASTENER COMPANY, INC.; *pg.* 1042, *pg.* 1118
ETHACALC - Software - THE DOW CHEMICAL COMPANY; *pg.* 1157, *pg.* 898
ETHACURE - Chemical Product - ALBEMARLE CORPORATION; *pg.* 1146, *pg.* 741
ETHACURE - Polymer Product - CHEMTURA CORPORATION; *pg.* 1152, *pg.* 355
ETHAFOAM - Plastic Foam - THE DOW CHEMICAL COMPANY; *pg.* 1157, *pg.* 898
ETHAN - Furniture - AMERICAN LEATHER LP; *pg.* 912, *pg.* 1673
ETHAN - Furniture - HOOKER FURNITURE CORPORATION; *pg.* 928, *pg.* 1788
ETHANOX - Chemical Product - ALBEMARLE CORPORATION; *pg.* 1146, *pg.* 741
ETHAPHOS - Chemical Product - ALBEMARLE CORPORATION; *pg.* 1146, *pg.* 741
ETHARCY - Chemical Product - LYONDELLBASELL INDUSTRIES; *pg.* 980, *pg.* 1710
ETHAZATE - Polymer Product - CHEMTURA CORPORATION; *pg.* 1152, *pg.* 355
ETHEL - Lamp - ASHLEY FURNITURE INDUSTRIES, INC.; *pg.* 914, *pg.* 1852
ETHEL-M - Chocolate Candy - MARS, INCORPORATED; *pg.* 1858, *pg.* 1792
ETHERFAST - Adapter - CISCO SYSTEMS, INC.; *pg.* 372, *pg.* 240
ETHERLINK - Software - ACRISON, INC.; *pg.* 1310, *pg.* 1087
ETHERLITE - Computer Peripheral Equipment - DIGI INTERNATIONAL INC.; *pg.* 387, *pg.* 948
ETHERSWITCH - Multi-Port Switching - CISCO SYSTEMS, INC.; *pg.* 372, *pg.* 240
ETHERSYNC - PC Adapter - TROY GROUP INC.; *pg.* 485, *pg.* 71
ETHERTALK - Interface Card & Network - APPLE INC.; *pg.* 350, *pg.* 73
ETHERWIND - OEM Connectivity Module - TROY GROUP INC.; *pg.* 485, *pg.* 71
ETHIBOND EXCEL - Healthcare Product - JOHNSON & JOHNSON; *pg.* 1549, *pg.* 1091
ETHINK - Software - KEPNER-TREGOE, INC.; *pg.* 424, *pg.* 1112
ETHIOPIA SIDAMO - Coffee - CARIBOU COFFEE COMPANY, INC.; *pg.* 1764, *pg.* 932
ETHIOPIA SIDAMO - Coffee - STARBUCKS CORPORATION; *pg.* 897, *pg.* 1840
ETHIOPIAN FANCY - Coffee - PEET'S COFFEE & TEA, INC.; *pg.* 1029, *pg.* 85
ETHIOPIAN ORGANIC YIRGACHEFFE - Coffee - CARIBOU COFFEE COMPANY, INC.; *pg.* 1764, *pg.* 932
ETHNIC GOURMET - Food Product - THE HAIN CELESTIAL GROUP, INC.; *pg.* 860, *pg.* 1172
ETHOCEL - Polymer - THE DOW CHEMICAL COMPANY; *pg.* 1157, *pg.* 898
ETHOS - Diagnostic Tool - SNAP-ON INCORPORATED; *pg.* 1062, *pg.* 1862
ETHOS - Bottled Water - STARBUCKS CORPORATION; *pg.* 897, *pg.* 1840
ETHYL TRIFLUOROACETATE - Flurochemical -

HALOCARBON PRODUCTS CORPORATION; *pg.* 978, *pg.* 1116
ETHYL TUADS - Accelerators - R.T. VANDERBILT COMPANY, INC.; *pg.* 1180, *pg.* 364
ETHYLBLOC - Industrial Material - DOW CHEMICAL; *pg.* 1156, *pg.* 1563
ETHYOL - Medicine - MEDIMMUNE LLC; *pg.* 1562, *pg.* 770
ETL - Data Migrator - INFORMATION BUILDERS INC.; *pg.* 415, *pg.* 1243
ETN50 - Staples - ARROW FASTENER COMPANY, INC.; *pg.* 1042, *pg.* 1118
ETNA - Convenience Stores - THE PANTRY, INC.; *pg.* 1029, *pg.* 1360
ETO-ABATOR - Ethylene Oxide Removal Device - DONALDSON COMPANY, INC.; *pg.* 1329, *pg.* 917
ETO CONTAINER-STERISET - Container - MEDLINE INDUSTRIES, INC.; *pg.* 1562, *pg.* 635
ETOC - Systems Integration & Aeronautics - LOCKHEED MARTIN CORPORATION; *pg.* 229, *pg.* 762
ETOC - Pesticide - MCLAUGHLIN GORMLEY KING COMPANY; *pg.* 1797, *pg.* 939
ETOGESIC - Veterinary Anti-Inflammatory Preparation - PFIZER INC.; *pg.* 1581, *pg.* 1278
ETOILE - Wine - DOMAINE CHANDON, INC.; *pg.* 1962, *pg.* 308
ETOILE ROSE - Wine - DOMAINE CHANDON, INC.; *pg.* 1962, *pg.* 308
ETON - Furniture - HAWORTH, INC.; *pg.* 402, *pg.* 891
ETON - Fabric - NEMSCHOFF, INC.; *pg.* 936, *pg.* 1890
ETONIC - Shoes - MASON COMPANIES, INC.; *pg.* 1811, *pg.* 1856
ETOPOPHOS - Health Care Product - BRISTOL-MYERS SQUIBB COMPANY; *pg.* 1509, *pg.* 1206
ETOPPS - On-Line Ordering for Trading Cards & Sports Collectibles - THE TOPPS COMPANY, INC.; *pg.* 588, *pg.* 1302
ETOYS.COM - Online Toy Store - TOYS "R" US, INC.; *pg.* 968, *pg.* 1130
ETP - Shaft Bushings - ZERO-MAX, INC.; *pg.* 222, *pg.* 954
ETRAC - Satellite Communication Product - KVH INDUSTRIES INC; *pg.* 650, *pg.* 1602
ETRACK IT - Systems Integration & Aeronautics - LOCKHEED MARTIN CORPORATION; *pg.* 229, *pg.* 762
ETS - Software - INTERVALZERO INC.; *pg.* 420, *pg.* 851
ETUDE - Office Furniture - STEELCASE INC.; *pg.* 475, *pg.* 889
ETV - Towline Vehicles - PARAGON TECHNOLOGIES, INC.; *pg.* 1367, *pg.* 1528
ETX - diesel engine rebuild system - BASF CATALYSTS LLC; *pg.* 1148, *pg.* 1074
ETX - Telescope - MEADE INSTRUMENTS CORPORATION; *pg.* 1422, *pg.* 113
ETX-70AT - Optical Telescope - MEADE INSTRUMENTS CORPORATION; *pg.* 1422, *pg.* 113
ETX PREMIER - Telescope - MEADE INSTRUMENTS CORPORATION; *pg.* 1422, *pg.* 113
ETX SPOTTING SCOPE - Telescope - MEADE INSTRUMENTS CORPORATION; *pg.* 1422, *pg.* 113
EUCALYPTUS BLOSSOM - Honey - MILLER'S HONEY COMPANY; *pg.* 1860, *pg.* 1759
EUCERIN - Medical & Aesthetic Product - DYNATRONICS CORPORATION; *pg.* 1526, *pg.* 1757
EUCLID - Switch - HUBBELL INCORPORATED; *pg.* 1299, *pg.* 370
THE EUCLID CHEMICAL COMPANY - Coating And Sealant - RPM INTERNATIONAL INC.; *pg.* 1447, *pg.* 1464
EUCLID MEGA - Brake Repair Kits - MERITOR, INC.; *pg.* 212, *pg.* 911
EUCLID STOP MATE - Brake Repair Kits - MERITOR, INC.; *pg.* 212, *pg.* 911
EUDERMIC - Medical Product - MEDLINE INDUSTRIES, INC.; *pg.* 1562, *pg.* 635
EUDORA - Lamp - ASHLEY FURNITURE INDUSTRIES, INC.; *pg.* 914, *pg.* 1852
EUGENIA - Lamp - ASHLEY FURNITURE INDUSTRIES, INC.; *pg.* 914, *pg.* 1852
EUKANUBA - Pet Food & Veterinary Diets - IAMS COMPANY; *pg.* 1477, *pg.* 1633
EUKANUBA - Dog Food - MARS, INCORPORATED; *pg.* 1858, *pg.* 1792
EUKANUBA HEALTHY EXTRAS - Dog Food - IAMS COMPANY; *pg.* 1477, *pg.* 1633
EUKANUBA NATURAL LAMB & RICE - Dog Food - IAMS COMPANY; *pg.* 1477, *pg.* 1633
EUKANUBA VETERINARY DIETS - Veterinary Food - IAMS COMPANY; *pg.* 1477, *pg.* 1633
EULALIE - Lamp - ASHLEY FURNITURE INDUSTRIES, INC.; *pg.* 914, *pg.* 1852
EULEXIN - Advanced Prostate Cancer Treatment - MERCK & CO., INC.; *pg.* 1566, *pg.* 1077
EUNICE - Lamp - ASHLEY FURNITURE INDUSTRIES, INC.; *pg.* 914, *pg.* 1852
EUPEN - Corrugated Cable Connector - RF INDUSTRIES, LTD.; *pg.* 461, *pg.* 208
EUPHRATES - Carpet - WOVEN LEGENDS INC.; *pg.* 947, *pg.* 1572
EURECEN - Polymer Product - CHEMTURA CORPORATION; *pg.* 1152, *pg.* 355
EUREKA - Fatliquor & Chemical Auxiliary - ATLAS REFINERY, INC.; *pg.* 1148, *pg.* 1095
EUREKA! - Printing Paper - GEORGIA-PACIFIC LLC; *pg.* 1458, *pg.* 507
EUREKA - Video Game - INTERNATIONAL GAME TECHNOLOGY; *pg.* 957, *pg.* 1024
EUREKA! - Tents, Backpacks & Accessories - JOHNSON OUTDOORS INC.; *pg.* 1837, *pg.* 1888
EUREKA - Drug Delivery System - SURMODICS, INC.; *pg.* 1600, *pg.* 924
EURELON - Binders - HUNTSMAN CORPORATION; *pg.* 1167, *pg.* 1758
EUREMELT - Industrial Adhesives - HUNTSMAN CORPORATION; *pg.* 1167, *pg.* 1758
EURENOR - Polymer Product - CHEMTURA CORPORATION; *pg.* 1152, *pg.* 355
EURETEK - Adhesion Promoters - HUNTSMAN CORPORATION; *pg.* 1167, *pg.* 1758
EURO - Footwear - P.W. MINOR & SON, INC.; *pg.* 1816, *pg.* 1140
EURO-35 - Cameras - EASTMAN KODAK COMPANY; *pg.* 1408, *pg.* 1333
EURO-C - Circular Industrial Cordset - MOLEX INCORPORATED; *pg.* 655, *pg.* 628
EURO-DOCSIS - Cable - BROADCOM CORPORATION; *pg.* 364, *pg.* 108
EURO-FLO - Shower Head - SYMMONS INDUSTRIES, INC.; *pg.* 114, *pg.* 803
EURO M - Plastics Product - AEP INDUSTRIES INC.; *pg.* 1878, *pg.* 1085
EURO-SOFT - Polyester Glazing Putty - ITW - EVERCOAT; *pg.* 1443, *pg.* 1415
EURO STYLE - Hair Care Product - CONAIR CORPORATION; *pg.* 505, *pg.* 1055
EURO-STYLE - Lighting Product - WESTINGHOUSE LIGHTING CORPORATION; *pg.* 687, *pg.* 1571
EURO SWIRL - Ceiling Fan - WESTINGHOUSE LIGHTING CORPORATION; *pg.* 687, *pg.* 1571
EUROCLEAN - Floor Care - NILFISK-ADVANCE, INC.; *pg.* 332, *pg.* 953
EUROCOMBI - Dispensing Equipment - IDEX CORPORATION; *pg.* 1347, *pg.* 623
EUROFLEX - Servo Drive - BALDOR ELECTRIC COMPANY; *pg.* 1316, *pg.* 32
EUROLOFT - Pillow - SELECT COMFORT CORPORATION; *pg.* 942, *pg.* 942
EUROMASTER - Professional Hair Dryer - ANDIS COMPANY; *pg.* 498, *pg.* 1895
EUROMATE - Barrier Strip - MOLEX INCORPORATED; *pg.* 655, *pg.* 628
EUROMAX - Connector - MOLEX INCORPORATED; *pg.* 655, *pg.* 628
EUROMOD - Electronic Components - MOLEX INCORPORATED; *pg.* 655, *pg.* 628
EUROPA - Ceiling Fan - BROAN-NUTONE LLC; *pg.* 1069, *pg.* 1860
EUROPA - Architectural Roofing Shingles - BUILDING PRODUCTS OF CANADA CORP.; *pg.* 72, *pg.* 1951
EUROPA - Gloves - FRANKLIN SPORTS, INC.; *pg.* 1834, *pg.* 847
EUROPA - Furniture - HAWORTH, INC.; *pg.* 402, *pg.* 891
EUROPAC 600 - Valves - FLOWSERVE CORPORATION; *pg.* 82, *pg.* 1719
EUROPAK - Receiver - NOVATEL INC.; *pg.* 1424, *pg.* 1904
EUROPANEL - Data Supplier - IRI GROUP; *pg.* 421, *pg.* 579
EUROPEAN - Pudding - KOZY SHACK INC.; *pg.* 869, *pg.* 1167
EUROPEAN BAKERS - Food Product - FLOWERS FOODS, INC.; *pg.* 855, *pg.* 541
EUROPEAN HARVEST SIGNATURE - Bread - KLOSTERMAN BAKING COMPANY, INC.; *pg.* 869, *pg.* 1415
EUROPEAN MARKETSCOPE - Live Market Commentary - STANDARD & POOR'S RATINGS SERVICES; *pg.* 805, *pg.* 1296
EUROPEAN RUBBER JOURNAL - Trade Magazine - CRAIN COMMUNICATIONS, INC.; *pg.* 1631, *pg.* 879
EUROPEAN SECRETS - Bodycare & Skincare - AMERICAN INTERNATIONAL INDUSTRIES COMPANY; *pg.* 498, *pg.* 126
EUROPEAN STYLE - Food & Beverage Product - NESTLE USA, INC.; *pg.* 883, *pg.* 96
EUROPEAN SYMPATHY DISH GARDEN - Flower Basket - 1-800-FLOWERS.COM, INC.; *pg.* 1758, *pg.* 1151
EUROPE'S BEST - Food Products - THE J.M. SMUCKER COMPANY; *pg.* 865, *pg.* 1468
EUROPHOTONICS - European Photonics Industry Magazine - LAURIN PUBLISHING CO., INC.; *pg.* 1658, *pg.* 841
EUROPLEX - Plastic Film - EVONIK CYRO LLC; *pg.* 1162, *pg.* 1103
EUROPRINT/IGI - Business Unit - INTERNATIONAL GAME TECHNOLOGY; *pg.* 420, *pg.* 1606
EUROPRO - Fluid Handling System - GRACO, INC.; *pg.* 1342, *pg.* 935
EURORIDER - Infant Carrier - INFANTINO, LLC; *pg.* 957, *pg.* 203
EUROS RX - Compression Socks - ALIMED, INC.; *pg.* 1490, *pg.* 816
EUROSPAN - Acoustic System - OWENS CORNING; *pg.* 102, *pg.* 1476
EUROSTYLE - Terminal Block - MOLEX INCORPORATED; *pg.* 655, *pg.* 628
EUROTAPE - Sports Product - MUELLER SPORTS MEDICINE, INC.; *pg.* 1570, *pg.* 1887
EUROTEC - Trade Publication - THE NIELSEN COMPANY B.V.; *pg.* 1671, *pg.* 1272
EUROTECH - Sturdilite Floodlight - PHOENIX PRODUCTS COMPANY; *pg.* 1304, *pg.* 1879
EUROTHESYS LIFE & NON LIFE - Insurance Analysis - STANDARD & POOR'S RATINGS SERVICES; *pg.* 805, *pg.* 1296
EUROTINTER - Dispensing Equipment - IDEX CORPORATION; *pg.* 1347, *pg.* 623
EUSEBI - Fabric - NEMSCHOFF, INC.; *pg.* 936, *pg.* 1890
EUSTACIA - Lamp - ASHLEY FURNITURE INDUSTRIES, INC.; *pg.* 914, *pg.* 1852
EUTECTROL - Thermal Processing Equipment - SURFACE COMBUSTION, INC.; *pg.* 1077, *pg.* 1462
EUV - Energy Saving UV Control System - NORDSON CORPORATION; *pg.* 1365, *pg.* 1480
EV-2 - Sorter/Verifier - OPEX CORPORATION; *pg.* 450, *pg.* 1087
EV PRODUCTS - X-Ray Detector - II-VI INCORPORATED; *pg.* 1417, *pg.* 1585
EVA - Lamp - ASHLEY FURNITURE INDUSTRIES, INC.; *pg.* 914, *pg.* 1852
EVA - Digital Sensor - IMAGEWORKS; *pg.* 1544, *pg.* 1158
EVA - Furniture - LA-Z-BOY INCORPORATED; *pg.* 932, *pg.* 901
EVA - Faucets - MOEN INCORPORATED; *pg.* 1056, *pg.* 1468
EVA-POX - Coating Product - CHASE CORPORATION; *pg.* 1152, *pg.* 803
EVA-VET - Veterinary Dental Film - IMAGEWORKS; *pg.* 1544, *pg.* 1158
EVA WATER - Beverages - THE COCA-COLA COMPANY; *pg.* 240, *pg.* 493
EVAA - Software System - IRON MOUNTAIN INCORPORATED; *pg.* 421, *pg.* 796
EVAAS - Educational Service - SAS INSTITUTE INC.; *pg.* 466, *pg.* 1361
EVACTOR - Vacuum Pumps - CROLL-REYNOLDS COMPANY, INC.; *pg.* 1326, *pg.* 1103
EVACUATOR - Vacuum Cleaner - PULLMAN-HOLT CORPORATION; *pg.* 333, *pg.* 475
EVACUATOR - Construction Equipment - VERMEER MANUFACTURING COMPANY; *pg.* 708, *pg.* 711
EVAILABILITY - Software - BMC SOFTWARE, INC.; *pg.* 362, *pg.* 1701
EVALUATIONS OF DRUG INTERACTIONS - Software - FIRST DATABANK, INC.; *pg.* 397, *pg.* 217
EVALUATOR - Electrophysiology Catheters - ST. JUDE MEDICAL, INC.; *pg.* 1596, *pg.* 963
EVAN WILLIAMS - Kentucky Straight Bourbon Whisky, Egg Nog & Single Barrel Vintage Bourbon - HEAVEN HILL DISTILLERIES, INC.; *pg.* 1964, *pg.* 725
EVANACID - Acid - THE DOW CHEMICAL COMPANY; *pg.*

First page reference indicates Business Class Edition
Second page reference indicates Geographic Edition

1157, *pg.* 898
EVANEAU - Office Furniture - STEELCASE INC.; *pg.* 475, *pg.* 889
EVANGELINE GHASTLY - Doll - TONNER DOLL COMPANY, INC.; *pg.* 968, *pg.* 1171
EVANOHM - Alloy - CARPENTER TECHNOLOGY CORPORATION; *pg.* 73, *pg.* 1584
THE EVANSVILLE COURIER & PRESS - Newspaper - THE E.W. SCRIPPS COMPANY; *pg.* 1639, *pg.* 1412
EVAPO-RUST - Rust Removing Solution - DAUBERT INDUSTRIES, INC.; *pg.* 1155, *pg.* 561
EVARO - Athletic Shoes - K-SWISS; *pg.* 1837, *pg.* 306
EVELINA - Lamp - ASHLEY FURNITURE INDUSTRIES, INC.; *pg.* 914, *pg.* 1852
EVELINA - Footwear - STEVEN MADDEN, LTD.; *pg.* 1819, *pg.* 1176
EVELYN - Lighting Product - QUOIZEL INC.; *pg.* 1304, *pg.* 1616
EVEN COMPLEXION - Nutritional Supplement - PHARMAVITE LLC; *pg.* 1584, *pg.* 167
EVEN-FLO - Applicator - TRICO MFG. CORP.; *pg.* 219, *pg.* 1886
EVEN HOTELS - Hotels with Complete Wellness Experience - INTERCONTINENTAL HOTELS CORPORATION; *pg.* 1097, *pg.* 511
EVEN MORE FUN TODAY THAN WHEN WE WERE KIDS! - Tag Line - UNIVERSITY GAMES CORPORATION; *pg.* 969, *pg.* 230
EVENAIR - Duct Boosters - FIELD CONTROLS LLC; *pg.* 1071, *pg.* 1380
EVENCOOK - Processed Chicken - TYSON FOODS, INC.; *pg.* 902, *pg.* 35
EVENFLO - Baby Equipment - EVENFLO COMPANY, INC.; *pg.* 924, *pg.* 1470
EVENFLO - Automatic Pressure Control - GRACO, INC.; *pg* 1342, *pg.* 935
EVENFLOW - Fluid Handling System - GRACO, INC.; *pg.* 1342, *pg.* 935
EVENING GLOW - Nutritional Supplement - WHITEWING LABS, INC.; *pg.* 1610, *pg.* 99
EVENING LAVENDER - Natural Spray - ANNIE OAKLEY ENTERPRISES, INC.; *pg.* 499, *pg.* 693
EVENING PRIMROSE - Hair & Skin Product - AUBREY ORGANICS INC.; *pg.* 499, *pg.* 470
EVENLIT - Light Panel - CARMANAH TECHNOLOGIES CORPORATION; *pg.* 628, *pg.* 1913
EVENMIST - Humidifiers - FIELD CONTROLS LLC; *pg.* 1071, *pg.* 1380
EVENMORE - Electrosurgical Devices - ANGIODYNAMICS, INC.; *pg.* 1495, *pg.* 1173
EVENRUN - Abrasive Bands - 3M COMPANY; *pg.* 1142, *pg.* 956
EVENT CENTER - Teleconferencing Service - CISCO SYSTEMS, INC.; *pg.* 372, *pg.* 240
EVENT CENTER - Software - WEBEX COMMUNICATIONS, INC.; *pg.* 491, *pg.* 270
EVENT EXPLORER - Software - EMC CORPORATION; *pg.* 391, *pg.* 825
EVENT-LINK - Monitoring System - CAS MEDICAL SYSTEMS, INC.; *pg.* 1513, *pg.* 339
EVENT MANAGER - Software - BMC SOFTWARE, INC.; *pg.* 362, *pg.* 1701
EVENT MANAGER BASE - Software - BMC SOFTWARE, INC.; *pg.* 362, *pg.* 1701
EVENT MANAGER - ENTERPRISE BASE - Software - BMC SOFTWARE, INC.; *pg.* 362, *pg.* 1701
EVENTSECURE - Software Product - MAXIMUS, INC.; *pg.* 780, *pg.* 1799
EVENTSPOTTER - Software - XEROX CORPORATION; *pg.* 494, *pg.* 365
EVER - Food Product - SHAMROCK FOODS COMPANY; *pg.* 895, *pg.* 20
EVER CLEAN - Cat Litter - THE CLOROX COMPANY; *pg.* 327, *pg.* 169
EVER-FLEX - Innerspring Assemblies for Mattresses - LEGGETT & PLATT, INCORPORATED; *pg.* 933, *pg.* 974
EVER FRESH - Carpet Cleaning, Upholstery & General Household Cleaning Products - RUG DOCTOR, LP; *pg.* 1373, *pg.* 1734
EVER GREEN BECAUSE IT'S OUR WORLD TOO - Slogan - DJO SURGICAL; *pg.* 1525, *pg.* 1661
EVER GRIP - Golf Glove Technology - ETONIC WORLDWIDE LLC; *pg.* 1808, *pg.* 857
EVER-LAST - Applicator - TRICO MFG. CORP.; *pg.* 219, *pg.* 1886
EVER-LOK - Locking Device - TRIENDA, LLC; *pg.* 1890, *pg.* 1887
EVER-STAY - Engine Mount - GLOBE COMPOSITE SOLUTIONS, LTD.; *pg.* 1883, *pg.* 842
EVER-TITE - Coupling - MORRIS COUPLING COMPANY; *pg.* 1057, *pg.* 1530
EVER VIGILANT - Tagline - CACI INTERNATIONAL INC.; *pg.* 367, *pg.* 1773
EVERCARE - Master Brand - THE EVERCARE COMPANY; *pg.* 1124, *pg.* 483
EVERCARE PET - Pet Line - THE EVERCARE COMPANY; *pg.* 1124, *pg.* 483
EVERCARE PROFESSIONAL - Drycleaning Line - THE EVERCARE COMPANY; *pg.* 1124, *pg.* 483
EVERCARE VETERINARIAN - Vet Line - THE EVERCARE COMPANY; *pg.* 1124, *pg.* 483
EVERCIDE - Pesticide - MCLAUGHLIN GORMLEY KING COMPANY; *pg.* 1797, *pg.* 939
EVERCLEAN - Clumping Litter, Pans & Liners - THE CLOROX COMPANY; *pg.* 327, *pg.* 169
EVERCLING - High-Density Polyurethane Plastic Sheeting - ITW - EVERCOAT; *pg.* 1443, *pg.* 1415
EVERCOAT - Repair Products - ITW - EVERCOAT; *pg.* 1443, *pg.* 1415
EVERDREAM - IT Desktop Management Services - DELL INC.; *pg.* 383, *pg.* 1737
EVERDURE - Rubber Sole - MASON COMPANIES, INC.; *pg.* 1811, *pg.* 1856
EVEREADY - Battery - ENERGIZER HOLDINGS, INC.; *pg.* 637, *pg.* 996
EVEREF - Robotic Product - HAMILTON CO., INC.; *pg.* 1415, *pg.* 1031
EVEREST - Laminated Roofing Shingles - BUILDING PRODUCTS OF CANADA CORP.; *pg.* 72, *pg.* 1951
EVEREST - Rug - COURISTAN INC.; *pg.* 921, *pg.* 1067
EVEREST - Car Booster Seat - EVENFLO COMPANY, INC.; *pg.* 924, *pg.* 1470
EVEREST - Packaging - INTERNATIONAL PAPER COMPANY; *pg.* 1460, *pg.* 1644
EVEREST - Fine Dining Restaurant - LETTUCE ENTERTAIN YOU ENTERPRISES, INC.; *pg.* 1735, *pg.* 580
EVEREST - Navigation Aid - TRIMBLE NAVIGATION LIMITED; *pg.* 1384, *pg.* 288
EVEREST 3D - Stage Simulation Software - ROSCO LABORATORIES, INC.; *pg.* 1782, *pg.* 378
EVEREST & JENNINGS - Wheelchairs - GF HEALTH PRODUCTS, INC.; *pg.* 1535, *pg.* 508
EVEREST ELITE - Sleeping Bags - KELLWOOD COMPANY; *pg.* 28, *pg.* 975
EVERESTPLUS - Payment Terminal - VERIFONE SYSTEMS, INC.; *pg.* 487, *pg.* 251
EVERFLAT - Papers - XEROX CORPORATION; *pg.* 494, *pg.* 365
EVERFLAT IMAGE SOLUTIONS PAPER - Papers - XEROX CORPORATION; *pg.* 494, *pg.* 365
EVERFLEX - Health Care Product - NATURE'S SUNSHINE PRODUCTS, INC.; *pg.* 1571, *pg.* 1754
EVERFLO - Optical Product - UNIVERSAL PHOTONICS, INC.; *pg.* 1433, *pg.* 1167
EVERFRESH - Cat Litter - THE CLOROX COMPANY; *pg.* 327, *pg.* 169
EVERFRESH - Foundation, Pressed Powder & Concealer - MAYBELLINE LLC; *pg.* 516, *pg.* 1257
EVERFRESH - Soft Drink - NATIONAL BEVERAGE CORP.; *pg.* 257, *pg.* 425
EVERFRESH WATER CARE SYSTEM - Water Care System - WATKINS MANUFACTURING CORPORATION; *pg.* 120, *pg.* 303
EVERGEN - Lighting Product - CARMANAH TECHNOLOGIES CORPORATION; *pg.* 628, *pg.* 1913
EVERGLASS - Fiberglass Reinforced Body Filler - ITW - EVERCOAT; *pg.* 1443, *pg.* 1415
EVERGLIDE - Ethnobotanical Product - NU SKIN ENTERPRISES, INC.; *pg.* 518, *pg.* 1755
EVERGREEN - Bedding - CROSCILL, INC.; *pg.* 1122, *pg.* 1220
EVERGREEN - Pesticide - MCLAUGHLIN GORMLEY KING COMPANY; *pg.* 1797, *pg.* 939
EVERGREEN - Rubber - SMOOTH-ON INC.; *pg.* 111, *pg.* 1528
EVERGREEN - Lawn & Garden Care - TRACTOR SUPPLY COMPANY; *pg.* 708, *pg.* 1627
EVERITE - Glaze Powder - MALLET & COMPANY, INC.; *pg.* 875, *pg.* 1521
EVERLAST - Quilt Foam - KING KOIL LICENSING COMPANY INC.; *pg.* 932, *pg.* 671
EVERLASTING LOVE - Flower Arrangement - 1-800-FLOWERS.COM, INC.; *pg.* 1758, *pg.* 1151
EVERMATE - Electronic Components - MOLEX INCORPORATED; *pg.* 655, *pg.* 628
EVERNU - Cover - NATIONAL PRESTO INDUSTRIES, INC; *pg.* 1128, *pg.* 1857
EVERON - Electroless Nickel Product - DOW CHEMICAL; *pg.* 1156, *pg.* 1563
EVERPURE - Water Treatment Products - CULLIGAN INTERNATIONAL COMPANY; *pg.* 54, *pg.* 656
EVERSHARP - Lip System - ESCO CORPORATION; *pg.* 1335, *pg.* 1502
EVERSHARP - Electrical Appliance & Housewares - NATIONAL PRESTO INDUSTRIES, INC; *pg.* 1128, *pg.* 1857
EVERSHIELD - Exterior Wood & Masonry Flat Paint - DUNN-EDWARDS CORPORATION; *pg.* 1442, *pg.* 129
EVERTON FALLS - T-Shirts - ABERCROMBIE & FITCH CO.; *pg.* 37, *pg.* 1466
EVERWATCH - Fume Hood Monitor - TSI INCORPORATED; *pg.* 1432, *pg.* 965
EVERY BUTT ON A BIKE - Tagline - QUALITY BICYCLE PRODUCTS; *pg.* 1710, *pg.* 918
EVERY DAY COUNTS - Math Aid - HOUGHTON MIFFLIN HARCOURT PUBLISHING COMPANY; *pg.* 1651, *pg.* 796
EVERY DAY MATTERS - Slogan - ALEXION PHARMACEUTICALS, INC.; *pg.* 1489, *pg.* 341
EVERY DAY MATTERS - Slogan - J.C. PENNEY COMPANY, INC.; *pg.* 1774, *pg.* 1732
EVERY DAY WITH RACHAEL RAY - Food & Recipe Magazine - MEREDITH CORPORATION; *pg.* 1663, *pg.* 705
EVERY INGREDIENT COUNTS - Slogan - DEL MONTE FOODS, INC.; *pg.* 852, *pg.* 304
EVERY LAST WORD - Bible-Study Program - ALLIANCE OF CONFESSING EVANGELICALS, INC.; *pg.* 126, *pg.* 1545
EVERY WHERE EVERY DAY - Tagline - CTS CORPORATION; *pg.* 631, *pg.* 677
EVERY WOMAN EVERY DAY - Slogan - JACQUES MORET, INC.; *pg.* 27, *pg.* 1245
EVERYBODY WINS - Educational Program - NEGOTIATION INSTITUTE, INC.; *pg.* 151, *pg.* 1268
EVERYBODY'S CONNECTING - Slogan - NETGEAR, INC.; *pg.* 444, *pg.* 247
EVERYDAY - Stone & Tile Cleaner - H.B. FULLER COMPANY; *pg.* 1165, *pg.* 961
EVERYDAY BASICS - Bra - PLAYTEX APPAREL, INC.; *pg.* 31, *pg.* 1395
EVERYDAY CREDIT CARD - Credit Card - AMERICAN EXPRESS COMPANY; *pg.* 712, *pg.* 1190
EVERYDAY FOOD - Magazine & Television Program - MARTHA STEWART LIVING OMNIMEDIA, INC.; *pg.* 1661, *pg.* 1256
EVERYDAY GREATNESS - Publication - FRANKLIN COVEY CO.; *pg.* 1642, *pg.* 1758
EVERYDAY WE HELP PEOPLE - Tag Line - CORELOGIC, INC.; *pg.* 1198, *pg.* 109
EVERYJOE.COM - Website - DEFYMEDIA; *pg.* 1237, *pg.* 1222
EVERYMAN LIBRARY - Publishing Imprint for Classic Books - ALFRED A. KNOPF, INC.; *pg.* 1614, *pg.* 1189
EVERYONE BENEFITS - Slogan - MEDICA, INC.; *pg.* 1208, *pg.* 949
EVERYONE RESPECTS A BEAR - Tag Line - BEAR & SON CUTLERY, INC.; *pg.* 1827, *pg.* 7
EVERYTHING ABOUT THE MUSIC - Slogan - HOT TOPIC, INC.; *pg.* 42, *pg.* 67
EVERYTHING AUTOMOTIVE - Tagline - J.C. WHITNEY & CO.; *pg.* 209, *pg.* 621
EVERYTHING CUPCAKE - Cupcake - 1-800-FLOWERS.COM, INC.; *pg.* 1758, *pg.* 1151
EVERYTHING FOR THE GAME - Slogan - GOLF GALAXY, INC.; *pg.* 1835, *pg.* 1525
EVERYTHING IS EITHER GROWN OR MINED - Slogan - JOY GLOBAL, INC.; *pg.* 1351, *pg.* 1876
EVERYTHING MATERIAL - Slogan - ASM INTERNATIONAL; *pg.* 132, *pg.* 1461
EVERYTHING NICE - Carpet - BEAULIEU GROUP, LLC; *pg.* 917, *pg.* 529
EVERYTHING. RIGHT WHERE YOU NEED IT. - Tag Line - HILTON WORLDWIDE, INC.; *pg.* 1094, *pg.* 1791
EVERYTHING RUBBERMAID - Laboratory Store (Research & Retail) - RUBBERMAID HOME PRODUCTS; *pg.* 1138, *pg.* 1453

EVERYTHING RUNS BETTER WITH BARDAHL - Tagline - BARDAHL MANUFACTURING CORPORATION; pg. 972, pg. 1833
EVERYTHING THAT MAKES GIRLS CLICK - Doll And Toy - AMERICAN GIRL LLC; pg. 949, pg. 1871
EVERYTHING YOU IMAGINE - Tag Line - EAGLE COMMUNICATIONS INC.; pg. 284, pg. 715
EVERYTHING YOU WANT.EVERYTHING YOU NEED - Slogan - LENNAR CORPORATION; pg. 1100, pg. 443
EVERYTHING'S INCLUDED - Plastic Model Kits - REVELL; pg. 966, pg. 611
EVERYTHING'S RIGHT ABOUT THAT - Insurance Product - SBLI USA LIFE INSURANCE COMPANY, INC.; pg. 1216, pg. 1288
EVERYWHERE - Software - LAPLINK SOFTWARE, INC.; pg. 426, pg. 1815
EVERYWHERE YOU ARE - Slogan - ATMEL CORPORATION; pg. 621, pg. 238
EVETTE - Clothing - ABERCROMBIE & FITCH CO.; pg. 37, pg. 1466
EVETTE - Furniture - ETHAN ALLEN INTERIORS INC.; pg. 924, pg. 343
EVI-PAQ - Security Product - BAE SYSTEMS PRODUCTS GROUP; pg. 359, pg. 432
EVIDENCE - Plastic Food Trays - THE DOW CHEMICAL COMPANY; pg. 1157, pg. 898
EVIDENT - Software - EVOLVING SYSTEMS, INC.; pg. 395, pg. 326
EVIL - Game - ACTIVISION BLIZZARD, INC.; pg. 948, pg. 271
EVIL TWIN - Bicycle Accessories - SPECIALIZED BICYCLE COMPONENTS, INC.; pg. 1711, pg. 152
EVINRUDE - Outboard Engines - BOMBARDIER RECREATIONAL PRODUCTS, INC.; pg. 201, pg. 1960
EVINRUDE E TEC - Engine Technology - BOMBARDIER RECREATIONAL PRODUCTS, INC.; pg. 201, pg. 1960
EVIROCRON - Coating Product - PPG INDUSTRIES, INC.; pg. 1445, pg. 1579
EVIS - Laser Equipment - NEWPORT CORPORATION; pg. 1424, pg. 114
EVISTA - Pharmaceutical Product - ELI LILLY AND COMPANY; pg. 1527, pg. 684
EVITA - Furniture - NEMSCHOFF, INC.; pg. 936, pg. 1890
EVITE - Online Services - IAC/INTERACTIVECORP; pg. 292, pg. 1242
EVIVA - Paper & Nonwoven Material - FIBERMARK INC.; pg. 1457, pg. 1764
EVIVA - Breast Biopsy Device - HOLOGIC, INC.; pg. 1416, pg. 784
EVO WOVEN COLLECTION - Furniture - TROPITONE FURNITURE CO., INC.; pg. 945, pg. 118
EVOA T2 - Attenuator - OPLINK COMMUNICATIONS, INC.; pg. 660, pg. 91
EVOA T3 - Attenuator - OPLINK COMMUNICATIONS, INC.; pg. 660, pg. 91
EVOCAR - Vinyl Acetate Ethylene - THE DOW CHEMICAL COMPANY; pg. 1157, pg. 898
EVOCLEAR - High Index Ophthalmic Lenses - SIGNET ARMORLITE, INC.; pg. 1429, pg. 60
EVOICE - Communication Product - J2 GLOBAL COMMUNICATIONS, INC.; pg. 1260, pg. 133
EVOLANT - Solutions for Broadband Networks - CORNING CABLE SYSTEMS LLC; pg. 1407, pg. 1378
EVOLANT - Glass & Ceramic Material - CORNING INCORPORATED; pg. 1122, pg. 1154
EVOLIS - Clinical Diagnostic Product - BIO-RAD LABORATORIES, INC.; pg. 1504, pg. 101
EVOLTRA - Clofarabine - GENZYME CORPORATION; pg. 1534, pg. 808
EVOLUTION - Laser & Laser System - COHERENT, INC.; pg. 1406, pg. 265
EVOLUTION - Luxury Vinyl Tile - CONGOLEUM CORPORATION; pg. 921, pg. 1084
EVOLUTION - Building Product - COOLEY GROUP, INC.; pg. 691, pg. 1603
EVOLUTION - Implantable Medical Devices - DOW CORNING CORPORATION; pg. 1159, pg. 900
EVOLUTION - Performance Enamel - FERRO CORPORATION; pg. 1162, pg. 1462
EVOLUTION - Locomotives - GENERAL ELECTRIC COMPANY; pg. 1297, pg. 347
EVOLUTION - Engine - HARLEY-DAVIDSON, INC.; pg. 178, pg. 1874
EVOLUTION - Modular Workstation - KEWAUNEE SCIENTIFIC CORPORATION; pg. 931, pg. 1391
EVOLUTION - Thermal Imaging Camera - MINE SAFETY APPLIANCES COMPANY; pg. 1361, pg. 1525
EVOLUTION - Computer Software - NOVELL INC.; pg. 446, pg. 852
EVOLUTION - Set-up Boxes - WESTROCK COMPANY; pg. 1472, pg. 1805
EVOLUTION - Wiring Products - WIREMOLD/LEGRAND; pg. 689, pg. 383
EVOLUTION 5000 - Thermal Imaging Camera - MINE SAFETY APPLIANCES COMPANY; pg. 1361, pg. 1525
EVOLUTION CHEMICALS - Agricultural Products - ARCHER-DANIELS-MIDLAND COMPANY; pg. 825, pg. 565
THE EVOLUTION OF ANALOG - Slogan - INTERSIL CORPORATION; pg. 647, pg. 146
EVOLUTION OS - Software - LANTRONIX, INC.; pg. 426, pg. 112
EVOLUTION ROBOTICS - Software - IDEALAB, INC.; pg. 1258, pg. 180
EVOLVE - Fabric - NEMSCHOFF, INC.; pg. 936, pg. 1890
EVON'S - Food Product - JOHN B. SANFILIPPO & SON, INC.; pg. 1024, pg. 610
EVOPRO - Protein Supplement - CYTOSPORT, INC.; pg. 1018, pg. 45
EVOQUEST - Molecular Biology Product - THERMO FISHER SCIENTIFIC INC.; pg. 1602, pg. 61
EVOTRACK - Molecular Biology Product - THERMO FISHER SCIENTIFIC INC.; pg. 1602, pg. 61
EVUE - Digital Imaging System - CASCADE MICROTECH, INC.; pg. 1405, pg. 1492
EW-SIGINT - Defense Communication System - ROCKWELL COLLINS, INC.; pg. 234, pg. 702
E.W. STUDIO - Apparel - SAN FRANCISCO MERCANTILE COMPANY, INC.; pg. 32, pg. 227
EWATCH - Newspaper - PR NEWSWIRE ASSOCIATION LLC; pg. 1678, pg. 1283
EWAVE - Power Supply System - ADVANCED ENERGY INDUSTRIES, INC.; pg. 613, pg. 328
EWENICE - Lamb Puppet - GUND, INC.; pg. 954, pg. 1056
EWS - Lexan Wheel - REVOLUTION LIGHTING TECHNOLOGIES, INC.; pg. 1304, pg. 377
EWS EXTENDED WORKPLACE SOLUTIONS - Communication Product - CENTURYLINK, INC; pg. 1870, pg. 317
EWX100 - Automatic Conveyor System - PARAGON TECHNOLOGIES, INC.; pg. 1367, pg. 1528
EX - Medical Equipment - INVACARE CORPORATION; pg. 1546, pg. 1451
EX - Campaign Against Smoking - TRUTH INITIATIVE; pg. 158, pg. 405
EX LIGHT - Low Calorie Beer - MOLSON COORS CANADA INC.; pg. 256, pg. 1955
EX-O-FIT - Footwear - REEBOK INTERNATIONAL LTD.; pg. 1817, pg. 811
EX SERIES - Padlock - MASTER LOCK COMPANY LLC; pg. 1055, pg. 1884
EXA LUB - Oils & Greases - MALLET & COMPANY, INC.; pg. 875, pg. 1521
EXABYTE - Data Storage - TANDBERG DATA; pg. 481, pg. 311
EXACT - Security System - ANALOGIC CORPORATION; pg. 1399, pg. 840
EXACT - Culture - CHR. HANSEN; pg. 847, pg. 1873
EXACT - Dental Software - HENRY SCHEIN, INC.; pg. 1541, pg. 1180
EXACT - Pet Product - PETSMART, INC.; pg. 1481, pg. 18
EXACT - Paper Product - WASAU PAPER CORP.; pg. 1471, pg. 1882
EXACT EXPRESS - New Accelerated & Time Definite Delivery Service - YRC WORLDWIDE INC.; pg. 1931, pg. 720
EXACT FIT - Windshield Wiper - TRICO PRODUCTS CORPORATION; pg. 220, pg. 905
EXACT HIP INSTRUMENTATION - Hip Product - ZIMMER BIOMET HOLDINGS, INC.; pg. 1611, pg. 699
EXACT SEQUENCE SORT - Software - OPEX CORPORATION; pg. 450, pg. 1087
EXACTA - Flashlight - ENERGIZER HOLDINGS, INC.; pg. 637, pg. 996
EXACTA - Hardness Tester - NEWAGE TESTING INSTRUMENTS, INC.; pg. 1058, pg. 1532
EXACTLY THE WAY YOU WANT IT - Tagline - BIGLARI HOLDINGS INC.; pg. 1015, pg. 1739
EXACTOMER - Vinyl Ether Resins - HUNTSMAN CORPORATION; pg. 1167, pg. 1758
EXACTPHASE - Digital Detection Technology - MERCURY COMPUTER SYSTEMS, INC.; pg. 434, pg. 813
EXACTUNE - Fiber Connectorization System - JOHANSON MANUFACTURING CORPORATION; pg. 648, pg. 1045
EXACTUNE PM - Fiber Connectorization System - JOHANSON MANUFACTURING CORPORATION; pg. 648, pg. 1045
EXACTUS - Optical Thermometer - BASF CATALYSTS LLC; pg. 1148, pg. 1074
EXAM COACH - Medical Product - HOLOGIC, INC.; pg. 1416, pg. 784
EXAM LIGHT III - Exam Light - WELCH ALLYN INC.; pg. 1436, pg. 1342
EXAM STOOL - Multi-purpose Seating - STEELCASE INC.; pg. 475, pg. 889
THE EXAMINER - Newspaper - THE EXAMINER; pg. 1640, pg. 979
THE EXAMINER - Weekly Publication - GREATER MEDIA NEWSPAPERS, INC.; pg. 1646, pg. 1071
EXAMINER - Lighting System - STERIS CORPORATION; pg. 1597, pg. 1464
EXAMINER 3DX - Systems Integration & Aeronautics - LOCKHEED MARTIN CORPORATION; pg. 229, pg. 762
EXAMINERT - Software - MERCURY COMPUTER SYSTEMS, INC.; pg. 434, pg. 813
EXAMVIEW TEST GENERATOR - Educational Software - PEARSON ASSESSMENTS; pg. 1674, pg. 918
EXATRON - Epoxy Casting - HUNTSMAN CORPORATION; pg. 1167, pg. 1758
EXBG - Diabetes Treatment Products - ANIMAS CORPORATION; pg. 1495, pg. 1593
EXCALIBER - Pigment - BASF CATALYSTS LLC; pg. 1148, pg. 1074
EXCALIBUR - Embedded Processor Solution - ALTERA CORPORATION; pg. 348, pg. 237
EXCALIBUR - Calcium Removal - BAKER PETROLITE CORPORATION; pg. 1148, pg. 1745
EXCALIBUR - Gaming Product - GLD PRODUCTS, INC.; pg. 1835, pg. 1882
EXCALIBUR - Hose - HBD INDUSTRIES, INC.; pg. 207, pg. 1449
EXCALIBUR - Apparel - I. SPIEWAK & SONS, INC.; pg. 42, pg. 1242
EXCALIBUR - Resort & Casino - MGM RESORTS INTERNATIONAL; pg. 1105, pg. 1028
EXCALIBUR - Fabric - NEMSCHOFF, INC.; pg. 936, pg. 1890
EXCALIBUR - Hand Tools - NUPLA CORPORATION; pg. 101, pg. 281
EXCALIBUR - Pen & Pencils - PENTEL OF AMERICA, LTD.; pg. 453, pg. 295
EXCALIBUR - Switching Regulators & DC Converters - TEXAS INSTRUMENTS INCORPORATED; pg. 679, pg. 1688
EXCALIBUR - Coating System - WHITFORD WORLDWIDE COMPANY; pg. 1185, pg. 1529
EXCALIBUR COLLECTION - World Premiere Recordings of Classic Film Scores - INTRADA INC.; pg. 1773, pg. 171
EXCALIBURPLUS PC - Medical Equipment - CONMED CORPORATION; pg. 1517, pg. 1347
EXCEDRIN - Aspirin - NOVARTIS CORPORATION; pg. 1574, pg. 1273
EXCEED - Computer Program - COMPUTER SCIENCES CORPORATION; pg. 378, pg. 1780
EXCEED - Clothing Line - G&K SERVICES INC.; pg. 693, pg. 949
EXCEED - Software - OPENTEXT CORPORATION; pg. 450, pg. 1948
EXCEED - Solutions Process - SCHNELLER, INC.; pg. 234, pg. 1456
EXCEED FREEDOM - Software - OPENTEXT CORPORATION; pg. 450, pg. 1948
EXCEED ONDEMAND - Software - OPENTEXT CORPORATION; pg. 450, pg. 1948
EXCEED POLICY - Computer Program - COMPUTER SCIENCES CORPORATION; pg. 378, pg. 1780
EXCEED POWERSUITE - Software - OPENTEXT CORPORATION; pg. 450, pg. 1948
EXCEED XDK - Software - OPENTEXT CORPORATION; pg. 450, pg. 1948
EXCEL - Bagger - AUTOMATED PACKAGING SYSTEMS INC.; pg. 1452, pg. 1474
EXCEL - Panel - BEHLEN MFG. CO.; pg. 701, pg. 1010
EXCEL - Rugged Outerwear - BLAUER MANUFACTURING COMPANY, INC.; pg. 20, pg. 789
EXCEL - Beef - CARGILL, INC.; pg. 845, pg. 965
EXCEL - Book - CHARISMA MEDIA; pg. 1627, pg. 436

First page reference indicates Business Class Edition
Second page reference indicates Geographic Edition

EXCEL - Labeling - FLEXCON CORPORATION; *pg.* 1457, *pg.* 844
EXCEL - Front Wheel Drive Automobile - HYUNDAI MOTOR AMERICA; *pg.* 179, *pg.* 89
EXCEL - Medical Equipment - INVACARE CORPORATION; *pg.* 1546, *pg.* 1451
EXCEL - Powder Spray Booth - NORDSON CORPORATION; *pg.* 1365, *pg.* 1480
EXCEL - Gum - WM. WRIGLEY JR. COMPANY; *pg.* 1863, *pg.* 596
EXCEL - Turbine Control System - WOODWARD, INC.; *pg.* 122, *pg.* 329
EXCEL 2100 - Small Character Ink Jet Printer - VIDEOJET TECHNOLOGIES INC.; *pg.* 489, *pg.* 671
EXCEL ADD IN - Online Trading Services - MARKETAXESS HOLDINGS INC.; *pg.* 778, *pg.* 1256
EXCEL II - Premium Wall Panels - BUILDING PRODUCTS OF CANADA CORP.; *pg.* 72, *pg.* 1951
EXCEL PLUS CIP CLEANER - Powder - BOUMATIC LLC; *pg.* 701, *pg.* 1865
EXCELAIR - Broadband Wireless Equipment - AXXCELERA BROADBAND WIRELESS INC.; *pg.* 623, *pg.* 263
EXCELBOND - Pressed & Monolithic Refractory - RESCO PRODUCTS, INC.; *pg.* 107, *pg.* 1581
EXCELERATOR - Graphite Golf Shaft - ALDILA, INC.; *pg.* 1825, *pg.* 185
EXCELERATOR - Medical Equipment - INVACARE CORPORATION; *pg.* 1546, *pg.* 1451
EXCELERATOR - Computer Software - NOVELL INC.; *pg.* 446, *pg.* 852
EXCELFRAX - Microporous Insulation - UNIFRAX CORPORATION; *pg.* 220, *pg.* 1317
EXCELINE - Lighting Fixture & Control - PHILIPS LIGHTING; *pg.* 1303, *pg.* 806
EXCELINE - Pressed & Monolithic Refractory - RESCO PRODUCTS, INC.; *pg.* 107, *pg.* 1581
EXCELINX - Software - KEITHLEY INSTRUMENTS, INC.; *pg.* 1418, *pg.* 1473
EXCELIS - Mortgage Loan Servicing Systems - CORELOGIC, INC.; *pg.* 1198, *pg.* 109
EXCELL - Aluminum Flashlights - DORCY INTERNATIONAL INC.; *pg.* 1046, *pg.* 1439
EXCELLENCE - Delivery System - A-DEC, INC.; *pg.* 1483, *pg.* 1500
EXCELLENCE IN PRECAST CONCRETE - Tagline - SMITH-MIDLAND CORPORATION; *pg.* 111, *pg.* 1795
EXCELLENCE IN RESEARCH - Tagline - WESTAT INC.; *pg.* 161, *pg.* 776
EXCELLENCE IN SCIENCE & TECHNOLOGY - Tagline - UES, INC.; *pg.* 1449, *pg.* 1447
EXCELLENCE IN SECURITY SOLUTIONS - Tag Line - GUARDSMARK, LLC; *pg.* 401, *pg.* 1237
EXCELLENCE THROUGH INNOVATION - Slogan - S&C ELECTRIC COMPANY; *pg.* 1305, *pg.* 589
EXCELLENCE THROUGH SENIOR ADVOCACY - Slogan - ALMOST FAMILY, INC.; *pg.* 1492, *pg.* 731
EXCELLERATOR - Battery and Capacitor - W.L. GORE & ASSOCIATES, INC.; *pg.* 122, *pg.* 388
EXCELO - Architectural & Industrial Coatings - THE SHERWIN-WILLIAMS COMPANY; *pg.* 1447, *pg.* 1435
EXCELON - Wood Flooring Product - ARMSTRONG WORLD INDUSTRIES, INC.; *pg.* 914, *pg.* 1545
EXCELON - Medical Device - BOSTON SCIENTIFIC CORPORATION; *pg.* 1508, *pg.* 831
EXCELON - Compressed Air Filters, Regulators & Lubricators - NORGREN, INC.; *pg.* 231, *pg.* 333
EXCELSIOR - Banking Service - THE BANK OF NOVA SCOTIA; *pg.* 721, *pg.* 1935
EXCELSIOR - Medical Device - BOSTON SCIENTIFIC CORPORATION; *pg.* 1508, *pg.* 831
EXCELSIOR - Dental Product - DENTSPLY INTERNATIONAL INC.; *pg.* 1522, *pg.* 1596
EXCELSIOR - Fabric - NEMSCHOFF, INC.; *pg.* 936, *pg.* 1890
EXCELSIOR - Laser - NEWPORT CORPORATION; *pg.* 1424, *pg.* 114
EXCELSIOR - Industrial Safety Eyewear - UVEX SAFETY; *pg.* 1433, *pg.* 1608
EXCELSIOR 1018 - Medical Device - BOSTON SCIENTIFIC CORPORATION; *pg.* 1508, *pg.* 831
EXCENEL - Pharmaceutical Product - PFIZER INC.; *pg.* 1581, *pg.* 1278
EXCEPTION - Golf Equipment - ACUSHNET COMPANY; *pg.* 1824, *pg.* 818
EXCEPTION MANAGER - Software - VITRIA TECHNOLOGY, INC.; *pg.* 490, *pg.* 289
EXCEPTIONAL - Color - ELIZABETH ARDEN, INC.; *pg.* 507, *pg.* 448
EXCHANGE - Fabric - NEMSCHOFF, INC.; *pg.* 936, *pg.* 1890
EXCHANGE - Tables - STEELCASE INC.; *pg.* 475, *pg.* 889
EXCHANGE. KNOW. ACT - Slogan - HEALTHTRIO INC.; *pg.* 403, *pg.* 320
EXCHANGE MIGRATION WIZARD - Software - DELL SOFTWARE; *pg.* 385, *pg.* 40
EXCHANGEINFO - Telecommunications Infrastructure Map Database - PITNEY BOWES SOFTWARE INC.; *pg.* 455, *pg.* 1468
EXCISTAR - Laser & Laser System - COHERENT, INC.; *pg.* 1406, *pg.* 265
EXCITE - Online Services - IAC/INTERACTIVECORP; *pg.* 292, *pg.* 1242
EXCITE - Web Portal - IAC SEARCH & MEDIA, INC.; *pg.* 1257, *pg.* 171
EXCITING THE PLANET - Tagline - GLOBAL GEOPHYSICAL SERVICES, INC.; *pg.* 1414, *pg.* 1727
EXCLAMATION - Fragrance - COTY, INC.; *pg.* 506, *pg.* 1219
EXCLUDER - Medical Product - W.L. GORE & ASSOCIATES, INC.; *pg.* 122, *pg.* 388
EXCLUSIVELY A&B - Bra & Shapewear - GLAMORISE FOUNDATIONS, INC.; *pg.* 25, *pg.* 1235
EXCLUSIVELY YOU - Weight Management Program - DIET CENTER WORLDWIDE, INC.; *pg.* 1524, *pg.* 1400
EXCURSION - Binocular - BUSHNELL OUTDOOR PRODUCTS, INC.; *pg.* 1403, *pg.* 718
EXCURSION - Car & Van - FORD MOTOR COMPANY OF CANADA, LIMITED; *pg.* 174, *pg.* 1930
EXCURSIONS - Furniture Collection - LANE VENTURE, INC.; *pg.* 933, *pg.* 1379
EXEC SOLUTIONS - Magazine - SAS INSTITUTE INC.; *pg.* 466, *pg.* 1361
EXECBLUEPRINTS - Software - SKILLSOFT PLC; *pg.* 470, *pg.* 1037
EXECSUITE - Software - SKILLSOFT PLC; *pg.* 470, *pg.* 1037
EXECSUMMARIES - Software - SKILLSOFT PLC; *pg.* 470, *pg.* 1037
EXECTTEMP - Valve - MOEN INCORPORATED; *pg.* 1056, *pg.* 1468
EXECUCOMP - Executive Compensation Data - STANDARD & POOR'S RATINGS SERVICES; *pg.* 805, *pg.* 1296
EXECUSTAY - Executive Extended-Stay Services - MARRIOTT INTERNATIONAL, INC.; *pg.* 1102, *pg.* 764
EXECUTE360 - Software - OPENTEXT; *pg.* 450, *pg.* 1665
EXECUTIVE - Screen - DA-LITE SCREEN COMPANY; *pg.* 632, *pg.* 698
EXECUTIVE - Footwear - EASTLAND SHOE CORPORATION; *pg.* 1808, *pg.* 750
EXECUTIVE - Bathroom Tissue & Dispensers - GEORGIA-PACIFIC LLC; *pg.* 1458, *pg.* 507
EXECUTIVE - Lighting Product - H.E. WILLIAMS, INC.; *pg.* 1299, *pg.* 974
EXECUTIVE 3000 - Bath Tissue Dispenser - GEORGIA-PACIFIC LLC; *pg.* 1458, *pg.* 507
EXECUTIVE BENEFIT RESTORATION SERVICE - Administration of Employee & Executive Benefit Plans - MARSH & MCLENNAN COMPANIES INC.; *pg.* 1207, *pg.* 1256
EXECUTIVE CHEF - Kitchen Product - KOHLER CO.; *pg.* 91, *pg.* 1862
EXECUTIVE DASHBOARD - Software - ECORA SOFTWARE CORPORATION; *pg.* 389, *pg.* 1662
EXECUTIVE ELECTROL - Electric Screen - DA-LITE SCREEN COMPANY; *pg.* 632, *pg.* 698
EXECUTIVE FLAP - Briefcase - SANTA FE LEATHER CORPORATION; *pg.* 12, *pg.* 1059
EXECUTIVE LAPTOP - Briefcase - SANTA FE LEATHER CORPORATION; *pg.* 12, *pg.* 1059
EXECUTIVE MEMBER - Travel Agency - COSTCO WHOLESALE CORPORATION; *pg.* 1765, *pg.* 1820
EXECUTIVE MONEY MASTER - Banking Service - THE BANK OF NOVA SCOTIA; *pg.* 721, *pg.* 1935
EXECUTIVE PORTHOLE FLAP - Briefcase - SANTA FE LEATHER CORPORATION; *pg.* 12, *pg.* 1059
EXECUTIVE SERVICE PLAN - Hotel & Awards Program for Business Travelers & Business Travel Planners - OMNI HOTELS & RESORTS; *pg.* 1107, *pg.* 1685
EXELAN - Dielectric Etch System - LAM RESEARCH CORPORATION; *pg.* 1354, *pg.* 91
EXELON 2020 - Reduce Greenhouse Gas Emissions - EXELON CORPORATION; *pg.* 1942, *pg.* 573
EXELPET - Pet Accessories - MARS, INCORPORATED; *pg.* 1858, *pg.* 1792
EXELTRA - Hemodialysis Dialyzer - BAXTER INTERNATIONAL INC.; *pg.* 1499, *pg.* 599
EXEMPLAR - Software System - MENTOR GRAPHICS CORPORATION; *pg.* 432, *pg.* 1510
EXEMPLARLOGIC - Software System - MENTOR GRAPHICS CORPORATION; *pg.* 432, *pg.* 1510
EXERCHIZER - Healthcare Product - MEDICOOL, INC.; *pg.* 1562, *pg.* 294
EXERCISE AND EAT RIGHT - Slogan - SOLOFLEX, INC.; *pg.* 1845, *pg.* 1498
EXERCISES BODY & MIND - Slogan - EVENFLO COMPANY, INC.; *pg.* 924, *pg.* 1470
EXERCYCLE - Exercise Equipment - EXERCYCLE CORPORATION; *pg.* 1833, *pg.* 823
EXERGEN D-SERIES - Thermometer System - EXERGEN CORPORATION; *pg.* 1412, *pg.* 855
EXERGEN DX-SERIES - Thermometer System - EXERGEN CORPORATION; *pg.* 1412, *pg.* 855
EXERGEN E-SERIES - Thermometer System - EXERGEN CORPORATION; *pg.* 1412, *pg.* 855
EXERSAUCER - Activity Center - EVENFLO COMPANY, INC.; *pg.* 924, *pg.* 1470
EXERTHERM - Thermometer System - EXERGEN CORPORATION; *pg.* 1412, *pg.* 855
EXETER - Furniture - ASHLEY FURNITURE INDUSTRIES, INC.; *pg.* 914, *pg.* 1852
EXETER - Carpet - BEAULIEU GROUP, LLC; *pg.* 917, *pg.* 529
EXETER - Commercial Retail Lighting - JUNO LIGHTING, INC.; *pg.* 1300, *pg.* 606
EXETER - Medical Product - STRYKER CORPORATION; *pg.* 1598, *pg.* 894
EXFLEX PROGRAMMING - Diabetes Treatment Products - ANIMAS CORPORATION; *pg.* 1495, *pg.* 1593
EXFLIP - Diabetes Treatment Products - ANIMAS CORPORATION; *pg.* 1495, *pg.* 1593
EXHALE - Heating System - 180S, LLC; *pg.* 1824, *pg.* 754
EXHALE HEATING SYSTEM - Glove - 180S, LLC; *pg.* 1824, *pg.* 754
EXHUBERANCE - Carpet - BEAULIEU GROUP, LLC; *pg.* 917, *pg.* 529
EXICOR - Measurement System - HINDS INSTRUMENTS, INC.; *pg.* 1416, *pg.* 1498
EXIDE - Motive Power Batteries - ENERSYS INC.; *pg.* 1334, *pg.* 1584
EXILE - Bicycle - G. JOANNOU CYCLE CO. INC.; *pg.* 1707, *pg.* 1098
EXIT STRATEGIES - Power Service - TRC COMPANIES, INC.; *pg.* 1383, *pg.* 386
EXL - Motor Oil - BEL-RAY COMPANY, INC.; *pg.* 972, *pg.* 1128
EXL - Medical Equipment - CONMED CORPORATION; *pg.* 1517, *pg.* 1347
EXMARK - Irrigation Products - THE TORO COMPANY; *pg.* 1065, *pg.* 918
EXO - Heat Exchangers & Recuperators - ECLIPSE INC.; *pg.* 1332, *pg.* 655
EXO ALUMINUM AIR - Heat Exchanger - ECLIPSE INC.; *pg.* 1332, *pg.* 655
EXO HEATPAK - Burner - ECLIPSE INC.; *pg.* 1332, *pg.* 655
EXO RED-RAY - Burner - ECLIPSE INC.; *pg.* 1332, *pg.* 655
EXO RIELLO - Burner - ECLIPSE INC.; *pg.* 1332, *pg.* 655
EXO-SET UNO - Plastic Refractory - PLIBRICO CO. LLC; *pg.* 104, *pg.* 587
EXOAIR - Roofing Material - TREMCO INCORPORATED; *pg.* 116, *pg.* 1405
EXODERMIC - Bridge Product - THE D.S. BROWN COMPANY; *pg.* 79, *pg.* 1468
EXOGAS - Heat Treating Equipment - SECO/WARWICK CORPORATION; *pg.* 1076, *pg.* 1552
EXOLITE - Ear Warmer - 180S, LLC; *pg.* 1824, *pg.* 754
EXOLITE ACOUSTIC - Ear Warmer - 180S, LLC; *pg.* 1824, *pg.* 754
EXOLITE NITE TEC ACOUSTIC - Ear Warmer - 180S, LLC; *pg.* 1824, *pg.* 754
EXOLITE PATROL - Ear Warmer - 180S, LLC; *pg.* 1824, *pg.* 754
EXOLITE ULTRALITE - Ear Warmer - 180S, LLC; *pg.* 1824, *pg.* 754
EXOSKELETON - Fuel Cell System - AEROVIRONMENT, INC.; *pg.* 223, *pg.* 150
EXOSKELETON - Electronic Control Device - TASER INTERNATIONAL, INC.; *pg.* 677, *pg.* 24

EXOTECH - Security Product - BAE SYSTEMS PRODUCTS GROUP; *pg.* 359, *pg.* 432

EXOTHERMIC - Bicycle Tire - SPECIALIZED BICYCLE COMPONENTS, INC.; *pg.* 1711, *pg.* 152

EXOTHERMICS - Burner System - ECLIPSE INC.; *pg.* 1332, *pg.* 655

EXOTIC - Carpet - BEAULIEU GROUP, LLC; *pg.* 917, *pg.* 529

EXOTIC BREEZE - Flower Arrangement - 1-800-FLOWERS.COM, INC.; *pg.* 1758, *pg.* 1151

EXOTIC COLLECTION - Hardwood Floor - ANDERSON HARDWOOD FLOORS; *pg.* 67, *pg.* 1613

EXP6000 - Software - XEROX CORPORATION; *pg.* 494, *pg.* 365

EXPAND-A-MAILER - Envelope - CALUMET CARTON COMPANY; *pg.* 1454, *pg.* 661

EXPAND-TITE - Engine Expansion Plugs - DORMAN PRODUCTS, INC.; *pg.* 204, *pg.* 1522

EXPAND YOUR VISION - Video Communication System - GLOWPOINT, INC.; *pg.* 401, *pg.* 1094

EXPANDABLE - Spreader - EASTMAN MACHINE COMPANY; *pg.* 1331, *pg.* 1148

EXPANDABLE - Briefcase - SANTA FE LEATHER CORPORATION; *pg.* 12, *pg.* 1059

EXPANDABLE LEMAITRE VALVULOTOME - Vascular Device - LEMAITRE VASCULAR, INC.; *pg.* 1555, *pg.* 805

EXPANDABLE WHEELABOARD - Rolling Luggage - VERA BRADLEY, INC.; *pg.* 15, *pg.* 697

EXPANDABLE X-TREME - Briefcase - SANTA FE LEATHER CORPORATION; *pg.* 12, *pg.* 1059

EXPANDED COVERAGE - Communication Product - CENTURYLINK, INC; *pg.* 1870, *pg.* 317

EXPANDED QUEEN - Mattress - SELECT COMFORT CORPORATION; *pg.* 942, *pg.* 942

EXPANDER - Oil & Fat Extracting Device - ANDERSON INTERNATIONAL CORP.; *pg.* 1313, *pg.* 1474

EXPANDER-DRYER - Extracting Device - ANDERSON INTERNATIONAL CORP.; *pg.* 1313, *pg.* 1474

EXPANDER-EXTRUDER-COOKER - Food Extracting Device - ANDERSON INTERNATIONAL CORP.; *pg.* 1313, *pg.* 1474

EXPANDEX - Polymer Product - CHEMTURA CORPORATION; *pg.* 1152, *pg.* 355

EXPANDING - Dental Floss - SUNSTAR AMERICAS INC.; *pg.* 1599, *pg.* 591

EXPANDING YOUR UNIVERSE - Slogan - POTTERS INDUSTRIES, INC.; *pg.* 105, *pg.* 1515

EXPANDO SEAL - Seals - TRICORBRAUN; *pg.* 1471, *pg.* 1004

EXPANDOMATIC - Pants - HAGGAR CORPORATION; *pg.* 41, *pg.* 1682

EXPANLIN - Paper & Nonwoven Material - FIBERMARK INC.; *pg.* 1457, *pg.* 1764

EXPANSION - Scoring Solutions - FAIR ISAAC CORPORATION; *pg.* 1247, *pg.* 955

EXPANSION SWING - Baby Gate - EVENFLO COMPANY, INC.; *pg.* 924, *pg.* 1470

EXPANYARD - Energy-Absorbing Lanyard - MINE SAFETY APPLIANCES COMPANY; *pg.* 1361, *pg.* 1525

EXPAREL - Pharmaceutical Product - PACIRA PHARMACEUTICALS, INC.; *pg.* 1579, *pg.* 1104

EXPECT GREAT THINGS - Slogan - KOHL'S CORPORATION; *pg.* 1775, *pg.* 1870

EXPECT LOW PRICES EVERY DAY - Slogan - DESTINATION MATERNITY CORPORATION; *pg.* 23, *pg.* 1563

EXPECT MORE, PAY LESS - Tag Line - TARGET CORPORATION; *pg.* 1786, *pg.* 942

EXPECT SOMETHING EXTRA - Tag Line - CVS HEALTH CORPORATION; *pg.* 1765, *pg.* 1610

EXPECTANT MOMENTS - Maternity Bra - PLAYTEX APPAREL, INC.; *pg.* 31, *pg.* 1395

EXPEDATA - Digital Pen & Paper - THE STANDARD REGISTER COMPANY; *pg.* 473, *pg.* 1446

EXPEDIAL - Medical Device - LEMAITRE VASCULAR, INC.; *pg.* 1555, *pg.* 805

EXPEDITE - Fleet Service - DYNAMEX, INC.; *pg.* 1906, *pg.* 1680

EXPEDITER - Cleaning Product - HILLYARD, INC.; *pg.* 331, *pg.* 990

EXPEDITION - Furniture - ASHLEY FURNITURE INDUSTRIES, INC.; *pg.* 914, *pg.* 1852

EXPEDITION - Travel System - BABY TREND, INC.; *pg.* 916, *pg.* 173

EXPEDITION - Car & Van - FORD MOTOR COMPANY OF CANADA, LIMITED; *pg.* 174, *pg.* 1930

EXPEDITION - Software System - MENTOR GRAPHICS CORPORATION; *pg.* 432, *pg.* 1510

EXPEDITION - Bicycle Tire - SPECIALIZED BICYCLE COMPONENTS, INC.; *pg.* 1711, *pg.* 152

EXPEDITION - Outdoor Watch Line - TIMEX CORPORATION; *pg.* 14, *pg.* 355

EXPEDITION - Safety Product - WISCONSIN PHARMACAL COMPANY, LLC; *pg.* 1610, *pg.* 1861

EXPEDITION SERIES - Software System - MENTOR GRAPHICS CORPORATION; *pg.* 432, *pg.* 1510

EXPEDITOR - Data Management System - SCHLUMBERGER LIMITED; *pg.* 801, *pg.* 1714

EXPELL - Chemical Product - SACHEM INC.; *pg.* 1180, *pg.* 1665

EXPELLER - Mechanical Oil & Fat Extracting Device - ANDERSON INTERNATIONAL CORP.; *pg.* 1313, *pg.* 1474

EXPERIENCE - Software - AMX CORPORATION; *pg.* 349, *pg.* 1735

EXPERIENCE A NEW WORLD OF INTERACTION - Tagline - NCR CORPORATION; *pg.* 443, *pg.* 531

EXPERIENCE IN MOTION - Tagline - FLOWSERVE CORPORATION; *pg.* 82, *pg.* 1719

THE EXPERIENCE IS EVERYTHING - Slogan - WCI COMMUNITIES, INC.; *pg.* 1118, *pg.* 414

EXPERIENCE LIFE - Magazine - LIFE TIME FITNESS, INC.; *pg.* 1556, *pg.* 920

EXPERIENCE MORE - Tagline - ST. PETERSBURG AREA CHAMBER OF COMMERCE; *pg.* 157, *pg.* 464

THE EXPERIENCE OF AUTHENTIC LUXURY - Tag Line - ROHL LLC; *pg.* 1061, *pg.* 116

EXPERIENCE ONBOARD - Tagline - VETJOBS, INC.; *pg.* 1287, *pg.* 535

EXPERIENCE OUR CONNECTIVITY - Slogan - EXAR CORPORATION; *pg.* 395, *pg.* 91

EXPERIENCE. REDEFINED. - Slogan - HURON CONSULTING GROUP INC.; *pg.* 768, *pg.* 577

THE EXPERIENCE SPEAKS FOR ITSELF - Slogan - NUANCE COMMUNICATIONS, INC.; *pg.* 447, *pg.* 806

EXPERIENCE SUCCESS - Slogan - SALESFORCE.COM, INC.; *pg.* 1278, *pg.* 226

EXPERIENCE THE DIFFERENCE - Slogan - AMC ENTERTAINMENT INC.; *pg.* 527, *pg.* 716

EXPERIENCE THE DIFFERENCE - Tag Line - GRACO, INC.; *pg.* 1342, *pg.* 935

EXPERIENCE THE LIFESTYLE - Tagline - BOYNE USA RESORTS INC.; *pg.* 1082, *pg.* 874

THE EXPERIENCE TO HANDLE IT RIGHT - Slogan - SCREW CONVEYOR INDUSTRIES; *pg.* 1374, *pg.* 682

EXPERIMENT - Apparel - OAKLEY, INC.; *pg.* 1840, *pg.* 86

EXPERION - Software - BIO-RAD LABORATORIES, INC.; *pg.* 1504, *pg.* 101

EXPERION - Control System - HONEYWELL INTERNATIONAL INC.; *pg.* 407, *pg.* 1088

EXPERT - Software - ERESEARCH TECHNOLOGY INC.; *pg.* 1243, *pg.* 1564

EXPERT - Printer - XEROX CORPORATION; *pg.* 494, *pg.* 365

EXPERT DIRECT - Software - ERESEARCH TECHNOLOGY INC.; *pg.* 1243, *pg.* 1564

EXPERT EPRO - Software - ERESEARCH TECHNOLOGY INC.; *pg.* 1243, *pg.* 1564

EXPERT EVIDENCE REPORT - Publisher - BLOOMBERG BNA; *pg.* 1621, *pg.* 1772

EXPERT EYES - Eyeliners, Shadows, Mascaras - MAYBELLINE LLC; *pg.* 516, *pg.* 1257

EXPERT2000SM - Software System - MENTOR GRAPHICS CORPORATION; *pg.* 432, *pg.* 1510

EXPERTCITY - Software - CITRIX SYSTEMS, INC.; *pg.* 375, *pg.* 424

EXPERTDESIGNER - Software - BENTLEY SYSTEMS, INC.; *pg.* 361, *pg.* 1531

EXPERTEAM - Promotional Programs - EASTMAN KODAK COMPANY; *pg.* 1408, *pg.* 1333

EXPERTISE APPLIED ANSWERS DELIVERED - Tagline - LITTELFUSE, INC.; *pg.* 1301, *pg.* 580

EXPERTISE THAT MAKES THE DIFFERENCE - Slogan - PAREXEL INTERNATIONAL CORPORATION; *pg.* 1580, *pg.* 853

THE EXPERT'S CHOICE - Software - WIND RIVER SYSTEMS, INC.; *pg.* 493, *pg.* 38

EXPERTS CHOOSE ADTRAN - Slogan - ADTRAN, INC.; *pg.* 344, *pg.* 6

EXPERTS IN SPRAY TECHNOLOGY - Tagline - SPRAYING SYSTEMS CO.; *pg.* 1063, *pg.* 670

EXPERXT ADVISOR - Web-based Tool - EXPRESS SCRIPTS; *pg.* 1530, *pg.* 1070

EXPIDA - Electron Microscope - FEI COMPANY; *pg.* 1413, *pg.* 1498

EXPLODING WILD - Video Game - INTERNATIONAL GAME TECHNOLOGY; *pg.* 957, *pg.* 1024

EXPLORABOOK - Educational Materials - SCHOLASTIC INC.; *pg.* 1683, *pg.* 1288

EXPLORATION - Suitcase - SAMSONITE CORPORATION; *pg.* 11, *pg.* 830

EXPLORE - Careers & Planning System - ACT INC.; *pg.* 597, *pg.* 708

EXPLORE: BLUE PLANET RED PLANET - Museum Exhibition Services - MUSEUM OF SCIENCE AND INDUSTRY; *pg.* 565, *pg.* 583

EXPLORE MOVIES - Digital Directory - ROVI CORPORATION; *pg.* 463, *pg.* 269

EXPLORE MUSIC - Digital Directory - ROVI CORPORATION; *pg.* 463, *pg.* 269

EXPLORE NEW WORLDS - Game - WMS INDUSTRIES INC.; *pg.* 593, *pg.* 866

EXPLORE THE ARTS - Art Performance Service - JOHN F. KENNEDY CENTER FOR THE PERFORMING ARTS; *pg.* 555, *pg.* 401

EXPLORE THE POSSIBILITIES - Tagline - JARCO/U.S. CASTINGS; *pg.* 1051, *pg.* 1127

EXPLORER - Furniture - ASHLEY FURNITURE INDUSTRIES, INC.; *pg.* 914, *pg.* 1852

EXPLORER - Software - BMC SOFTWARE, INC.; *pg.* 362, *pg.* 1701

EXPLORER - Microwave Synthesis Product - CEM CORPORATION; *pg.* 1405, *pg.* 1382

EXPLORER - Online Assessment Tool - COMPASSLEARNING, INC.; *pg.* 1628, *pg.* 1661

EXPLORER - Auto Booster Seat for Older Child - DOREL JUVENILE GROUP, INC.; *pg.* 923, *pg.* 676

EXPLORER - Cameras - EASTMAN KODAK COMPANY; *pg.* 1408, *pg.* 1333

EXPLORER - Musical Instrument - GIBSON GUITAR CORP.; *pg.* 550, *pg.* 1650

EXPLORER - Mobile Earth Stations - GLOBECOMM SYSTEMS INC.; *pg.* 640, *pg.* 1164

EXPLORER - Cleaning Product - HILLYARD, INC.; *pg.* 331, *pg.* 990

EXPLORER - Medical Test System - HOLOGIC, INC.; *pg.* 1416, *pg.* 784

EXPLORER - Steel Laboratory Cabinets - KEWAUNEE SCIENTIFIC CORPORATION; *pg.* 931, *pg.* 1391

EXPLORER - Systems Integration & Aeronautics - LOCKHEED MARTIN CORPORATION; *pg.* 229, *pg.* 762

EXPLORER - Fragrance - RALPH LAUREN CORPORATION; *pg.* 46, *pg.* 1284

EXPLORER - Investment Product - THE VANGUARD GROUP, INC.; *pg.* 816, *pg.* 1550

EXPLORER - Scanning Probe Microscope - VEECO INSTRUMENTS INC.; *pg.* 1434, *pg.* 1322

EXPLORER 1.0 - Bicycles - G. JOANNOU CYCLE CO. INC.; *pg.* 1707, *pg.* 1098

EXPLORER 2.0 - Bicycles - G. JOANNOU CYCLE CO. INC.; *pg.* 1707, *pg.* 1098

EXPLORER 3.0 - Bicycles - G. JOANNOU CYCLE CO. INC.; *pg.* 1707, *pg.* 1098

EXPLORER 360 - Medical Device - BOSTON SCIENTIFIC CORPORATION; *pg.* 1508, *pg.* 831

EXPLORER 360 JR - Medical Device - BOSTON SCIENTIFIC CORPORATION; *pg.* 1508, *pg.* 831

EXPLORER 4.0 - Bicycles - G. JOANNOU CYCLE CO. INC.; *pg.* 1707, *pg.* 1098

EXPLORER CAECO LAYOUT - Software System - MENTOR GRAPHICS CORPORATION; *pg.* 432, *pg.* 1510

EXPLORER CHECKMATE - Software System - MENTOR GRAPHICS CORPORATION; *pg.* 432, *pg.* 1510

EXPLORER DATAPATH - Software System - MENTOR GRAPHICS CORPORATION; *pg.* 432, *pg.* 1510

EXPLORER LSIM - Software System - MENTOR GRAPHICS CORPORATION; *pg.* 432, *pg.* 1510

EXPLORER LSIM-C - Software System - MENTOR GRAPHICS CORPORATION; *pg.* 432, *pg.* 1510

EXPLORER LSIM-S - Software System - MENTOR GRAPHICS CORPORATION; *pg.* 432, *pg.* 1510

EXPLORER LTIME - Software System - MENTOR GRAPHICS CORPORATION; *pg.* 432, *pg.* 1510

EXPLORER OF THE SEAS - Cruise Ship - ROYAL CARIBBEAN CRUISES LTD; *pg.* 1921, *pg.* 446

EXPLORER SCHEMATIC - Software System - MENTOR GRAPHICS CORPORATION; *pg.* 432, *pg.* 1510
EXPLORER SPORT TRAC - Car & Van - FORD MOTOR COMPANY OF CANADA, LIMITED; *pg.* 174, *pg.* 1930
EXPLORER ST - Medical Device - BOSTON SCIENTIFIC CORPORATION; *pg.* 1508, *pg.* 831
EXPLORER VHDLSIM - Software System - MENTOR GRAPHICS CORPORATION; *pg.* 432, *pg.* 1510
EXPLOSIMETER - Combustible Gas Indicator - MINE SAFETY APPLIANCES COMPANY; *pg.* 1361, *pg.* 1525
EXPO - Fertilizer - LEBANON SEABOARD CORPORATION; *pg.* 1797, *pg.* 1547
EXPO - Office Products - NEWELL RUBBERMAID INC.; *pg.* 1128, *pg.* 515
EXPO 32 - Flow Cytometry Software - BECKMAN COULTER, INC.; *pg.* 1402, *pg.* 48
EXPORT - Beer - MOLSON COORS CANADA INC.; *pg.* 256, *pg.* 1955
EXPORTSS - Software - SLM CORPORATION; *pg.* 804, *pg.* 388
EXPOSE - Computer Software - APPLE INC.; *pg.* 350, *pg.* 73
EXPOSE - Medical Equipment - CONMED CORPORATION; *pg.* 1517, *pg.* 1347
EXPOSEDPAD - Packaging System - AMKOR TECHNOLOGY, INC.; *pg.* 67, *pg.* 25
EXPOSITION - Table - BLATT BOWLING & BILLIARD CORP.; *pg.* 1827, *pg.* 1203
EXPOSURES - Mail Order - SILVER STAR BRANDS; *pg.* 1785, *pg.* 1886
EXPREE SERIES - Towing & Recovery Equipment - MILLER INDUSTRIES, INC.; *pg.* 185, *pg.* 1655
EXPRESS - Dental Registration Material, Vinyl Polysiloxane - 3M COMPANY; *pg.* 1142, *pg.* 956
EXPRESS - Credit Card - AMERICAN EXPRESS COMPANY; *pg.* 712, *pg.* 1190
EXPRESS - Vaccines - BOEHRINGER INGELHEIM VETMEDICA, INC.; *pg.* 1474, *pg.* 989
EXPRESS - Medical Device - BOSTON SCIENTIFIC CORPORATION; *pg.* 1508, *pg.* 831
EXPRESS - Lavatory System - BRADLEY CORPORATION; *pg.* 71, *pg.* 1870
EXPRESS - Herbicide - E.I. DU PONT DE NEMOURS & COMPANY; *pg.* 1159, *pg.* 390
EXPRESS - Shirts - ELBECO INCORPORATED; *pg.* 40, *pg.* 1584
EXPRESS - Battery - ENERSYS INC.; *pg.* 1334, *pg.* 1584
EXPRESS - Fiberglass Boat Product - GRADY-WHITE BOATS, INC.; *pg.* 1707, *pg.* 1377
EXPRESS - Heater - KAZ, INC.; *pg.* 58, *pg.* 844
EXPRESS - Nail Color, Foundation & Blush - MAYBELLINE LLC; *pg.* 516, *pg.* 1257
EXPRESS - Shotgun - REMINGTON ARMS COMPANY, LLC; *pg.* 1844, *pg.* 1382
EXPRESS 3000 SERIES - ISDN Modems - ADTRAN, INC.; *pg.* 344, *pg.* 6
EXPRESS 3010 - Connecting Router - ADTRAN, INC.; *pg.* 344, *pg.* 6
EXPRESS 3100 - Connecting Router - ADTRAN, INC.; *pg.* 344, *pg.* 6
EXPRESS 3110 - Connecting Router - ADTRAN, INC.; *pg.* 344, *pg.* 6
EXPRESS 5000 SERIES - Frame Relay Access Devices - ADTRAN, INC.; *pg.* 344, *pg.* 6
EXPRESS 5100 - Connecting Router - ADTRAN, INC.; *pg.* 344, *pg.* 6
EXPRESS 5200 - Connecting Router - ADTRAN, INC.; *pg.* 344, *pg.* 6
EXPRESS 5210 - Connecting Router - ADTRAN, INC.; *pg.* 344, *pg.* 6
EXPRESS 6000 SERIES - xDSL Access - ADTRAN, INC.; *pg.* 344, *pg.* 6
EXPRESS 6200 - Connecting Router - ADTRAN, INC.; *pg.* 344, *pg.* 6
EXPRESS 6500 - Connecting Router - ADTRAN, INC.; *pg.* 344, *pg.* 6
EXPRESS 6503 - Connecting Router - ADTRAN, INC.; *pg.* 344, *pg.* 6
EXPRESS 6530 - Connecting Router - ADTRAN, INC.; *pg.* 344, *pg.* 6
EXPRESS 6531 - Connecting Router - ADTRAN, INC.; *pg.* 344, *pg.* 6
EXPRESS APPROVAL - Credit Card Charges - AMERICAN EXPRESS COMPANY; *pg.* 712, *pg.* 1190
EXPRESS BMD - Medical Product - HOLOGIC, INC.; *pg.* 1416, *pg.* 784
EXPRESS BOOK FREIGHT - Intl. Shipping Service - TRANSACTION PUBLISHERS, INC.; *pg.* 1695, *pg.* 1109
EXPRESS CARE - Automotive Service - ASHLAND INC.; *pg.* 972, *pg.* 726
EXPRESS CARGO - Van - GENERAL MOTORS COMPANY; *pg.* 175, *pg.* 881
EXPRESS CINEMA - Wireless Communication System - AT&T SOUTHEAST; *pg.* 1868, *pg.* 489
EXPRESS CRUISERS - Cruisers - CHRIS-CRAFT CORPORATION; *pg.* 1706, *pg.* 465
EXPRESS DELIVERY - Software - DIEBOLD, INCORPORATED; *pg.* 387, *pg.* 1407
EXPRESS DELIVERY XT - Transaction Product - DIEBOLD, INCORPORATED; *pg.* 387, *pg.* 1407
EXPRESS EXAM - Medical Test System - HOLOGIC, INC.; *pg.* 1416, *pg.* 784
EXPRESS EXCHANGE - Service Package - VIEWSONIC CORPORATION; *pg.* 489, *pg.* 303
EXPRESS FIVE - Biomolecule Product - THERMO FISHER SCIENTIFIC INC.; *pg.* 1602, *pg.* 61
EXPRESS GUIDE - Software - SKILLSOFT PLC; *pg.* 470, *pg.* 1037
EXPRESS INSERT - One Page Insert - VALASSIS COMMUNICATIONS, INC.; *pg.* 1287, *pg.* 897
EXPRESS INSTALL - Installation Service - PELLA CORPORATION; *pg.* 104, *pg.* 711
EXPRESS LOCKDOWN - Software - WEBSENSE, INC.; *pg.* 491, *pg.* 210
EXPRESS MAIL - Overnight Shipping - UNITED STATES POSTAL SERVICE; *pg.* 1009, *pg.* 406
EXPRESS MAIL INTERNATIONAL - Postal Services - UNITED STATES POSTAL SERVICE; *pg.* 1009, *pg.* 406
EXPRESS MODE DESIGN - Software - XEROX CORPORATION; *pg.* 494, *pg.* 365
EXPRESS PAK - Dispenser Cartridges - NESTLE PROFESSIONAL BEVERAGES; *pg.* 257, *pg.* 474
EXPRESS PASSENGER - Van - GENERAL MOTORS COMPANY; *pg.* 175, *pg.* 881
EXPRESS SAVER - Shipping Service - FEDEX CORPORATION; *pg.* 1907, *pg.* 1642
EXPRESS STYLE - Hair Care Product - JOHN PAUL MITCHELL SYSTEMS; *pg.* 512, *pg.* 133
EXPRESS TEST - Pharmaceutical Product - ALERE INC.; *pg.* 1488, *pg.* 849
EXPRESS TRACK - Drug Discovery Program - COMBIMATRIX CORPORATION; *pg.* 1407, *pg.* 109
EXPRESS TRAY - Cable Management System - THOMAS & BETTS CORPORATION; *pg.* 680, *pg.* 1646
EXPRESS YOURSELF - Game - HASBRO, INC.; *pg.* 954, *pg.* 1603
EXPRESS YOURSELF - Manual - XEROX CORPORATION; *pg.* 494, *pg.* 365
EXPRESS2 - Medical Device - BOSTON SCIENTIFIC CORPORATION; *pg.* 1508, *pg.* 831
EXPRESSALIGN - Alignment System Software - HUNTER ENGINEERING COMPANY; *pg.* 208, *pg.* 973
EXPRESSCARD - Test Electronic Device - TELEDYNE LECROY; *pg.* 1431, *pg.* 1153
EXPRESSCHARGE - Battery Recharge - DELL INC.; *pg.* 383, *pg.* 1737
EXPRESSDSP - Software & Development Tools - TEXAS INSTRUMENTS INCORPORATED; *pg.* 679, *pg.* 1688
EXPRESSI/O - Software System - MENTOR GRAPHICS CORPORATION; *pg.* 432, *pg.* 1510
EXPRESSION - Lighting Control Console - ELECTRONIC THEATRE CONTROLS, INC.; *pg.* 1296, *pg.* 1872
EXPRESSION 636 - Color Scanner - EPSON AMERICA INC.; *pg.* 394, *pg.* 122
EXPRESSION 836XL COLOR SCANNER - Color Scanner - EPSON AMERICA INC.; *pg.* 394, *pg.* 122
EXPRESSIONIST - Speaker - ALTEC LANSING LLC; *pg.* 348, *pg.* 1553
EXPRESSIONIST - Fabric - NEMSCHOFF, INC.; *pg.* 936, *pg.* 1890
EXPRESSIONS - Decorative Faucets - THE CHICAGO FAUCET COMPANY; *pg.* 1044, *pg.* 606
EXPRESSIONS - Greeting Card - HALLMARK CARDS, INC.; *pg.* 1646, *pg.* 983
EXPRESSIONS - Dinnerware - THE HOMER LAUGHLIN CHINA COMPANY; *pg.* 1125, *pg.* 1850
EXPRESSIONS - Decorative Architectural Product - MASCO CORPORATION; *pg.* 96, *pg.* 909
EXPRESSIONS - Fabric - NEMSCHOFF, INC.; *pg.* 936, *pg.* 1890
EXPRESSIONS - Door Glass - ODL INCORPORATED; *pg.* 101, *pg.* 914
EXPRESSIONS - Indoor Planters - RUBBERMAID HOME PRODUCTS; *pg.* 1138, *pg.* 1453
EXPRESSIONS - Fabric - UNIROYAL ENGINEERED PRODUCTS; *pg.* 699, *pg.* 467
EXPRESSIONS EXCHANGE - Communication Services - 1-800-FLOWERS.COM, INC.; *pg.* 1758, *pg.* 1151
EXPRESSIONS OF LIFE - Casket Personalization - AURORA CASKET COMPANY, INC.; *pg.* 1393, *pg.* 673
EXPRESSIONS OF PINK - Flower Arrangement - 1-800-FLOWERS.COM, INC.; *pg.* 1758, *pg.* 1151
EXPRESSLOCKS - Vacuum Process Tool - BROOKS AUTOMATION, INC.; *pg.* 1320, *pg.* 813
EXPRESSPARC - Exit Pay Credit Card System - AMANO CINCINNATI, INC.; *pg.* 348, *pg.* 1117
EXPRESSPAYMENT - Financial Payment Service - MONEYGRAM INTERNATIONAL, INC.; *pg.* 783, *pg.* 1684
EXPRESSPRINT - Label Technology - THE PENN COMPANIES; *pg.* 10, *pg.* 1568
EXPRESSWAY - Molecular Biology Product - THERMO FISHER SCIENTIFIC INC.; *pg.* 1602, *pg.* 61
EXPRO ELITE SNARE - Snare - VASCULAR SOLUTIONS, INC.; *pg.* 1434, *pg.* 946
EXQUEST - Software - BIO-RAD LABORATORIES, INC.; *pg.* 1504, *pg.* 101
EXQUISICAT - Cat Care - PETSMART, INC.; *pg.* 1481, *pg.* 18
EXR - Motion Picture Films - EASTMAN KODAK COMPANY; *pg.* 1408, *pg.* 1333
EXSILON - Pigment - BASF CATALYSTS LLC; *pg.* 1148, *pg.* 1074
EXSPEECH - Medical Dictation Software - NUANCE COMMUNICATIONS, INC.; *pg.* 447, *pg.* 806
EXSTREAM - Fishing Gear Product - SIMMS FISHING PRODUCTS CORP.; *pg.* 1845, *pg.* 1008
EXT-EXTREME HAIR THERAPY - Hair Care Product - HAIR CLUB FOR MEN, LTD., INC.; *pg.* 511, *pg.* 411
EXTEK - Duplicators - HF GROUP INC.; *pg.* 1346, *pg.* 68
EXTEND - software - INSTRON CORPORATION; *pg.* 1349, *pg.* 839
EXTEND - Computer Operations - NOVELL INC.; *pg.* 446, *pg.* 852
EXTEND - Liquid Frying Shortening - VENTURA FOODS, LLC; *pg.* 908, *pg.* 49
EXTEND-A-LIFE - Blade Rinse - PETEDGE; *pg.* 1481, *pg.* 787
EXTEND-R - Donut Mixes - DAWN FOOD PRODUCTS, INC.; *pg.* 1018, *pg.* 893
EXTENDBAR - Healthcare Product - MEDICOOL, INC.; *pg.* 1562, *pg.* 294
EXTENDED & ENHANCED - tagline - MORTON'S RESTAURANT GROUP, INC.; *pg.* 1741, *pg.* 583
EXTENDED BUFFER MANAGER - Software - BMC SOFTWARE, INC.; *pg.* 362, *pg.* 1701
EXTENDED DAY READING - Educational Materials - SCHOLASTIC INC.; *pg.* 1683, *pg.* 1288
EXTENDED DYNAMIC RANGE - Microchannel Plate - PHOTONIS USA PENNSYLVANIA; *pg.* 663, *pg.* 1547
EXTENDED REACH - Thermal Processing Equipment - SURFACE COMBUSTION, INC.; *pg.* 1077, *pg.* 1462
EXTENDED REACH BLOW-IN - Newspaper Insert - VALASSIS COMMUNICATIONS, INC.; *pg.* 1287, *pg.* 897
EXTENDED REACH INSERT - Mailed Promotional Tool - VALASSIS COMMUNICATIONS, INC.; *pg.* 1287, *pg.* 897
EXTENDED SURFACE - Cold Plate - LYTRON INCORPORATED; *pg.* 1074, *pg.* 861
EXTENDED SURFACE I - Cold Plate - LYTRON INCORPORATED; *pg.* 1074, *pg.* 861
EXTENDED SURFACE II - Cold Plate - LYTRON INCORPORATED; *pg.* 1074, *pg.* 861
EXTENDER - Commercial Lighting - SWIVELIER CO., INC.; *pg.* 1307, *pg.* 1142
EXTENDING THE LIMITS - Tagline - BRION TECHNOLOGIES INC.; *pg.* 1319, *pg.* 265
EXTENDING YOUR REACH - Tag Line - ASPYRA, INC.; *pg.* 355, *pg.* 306
THE EXTENDO - Advertising & Promotional Brochure Design - STRUCTURAL GRAPHICS, LLC; *pg.* 1689, *pg.* 346
EXTENDO-DIE - Die Steels - CARPENTER TECHNOLOGY CORPORATION; *pg.* 73, *pg.* 1584
EXTENSA - Kitchen Faucet - MOEN INCORPORATED; *pg.* 1056, *pg.* 1468
EXTENSIS - Seal & Thermoplastic Component - GREENE, TWEED & CO.; *pg.* 1344, *pg.* 1544
EXTENSURE - Consulting Services - AVNET, INC.; *pg.* 622,

First page reference indicates Business Class Edition
Second page reference indicates Geographic Edition

pg. 15
EXTERIOR BODY SOLVENT - Automotive Reconditioning Product - MOC PRODUCTS COMPANY, INC.; *pg.* 332, *pg.* 174
EXTERN-A-THERM - Recuperator - ECLIPSE INC.; *pg.* 1332, *pg.* 655
EXTERNO - Ice Hockey Skates - REEBOK-CCM HOCKEY, INC.; *pg.* 1844, *pg.* 1960
EXTHERO - Pharmaceutical Preparation - PFIZER INC.; *pg.* 1581, *pg.* 1278
EXTINGUISHER - Candy Product - AMERICAN LICORICE CO. INC.; *pg.* 1850, *pg.* 692
EXTON - Furniture - ASHLEY FURNITURE INDUSTRIES, INC.; *pg.* 914, *pg.* 1852
EXTRA! - Software - ATTACHMATE CORPORATION; *pg.* 356, *pg.* 1833
EXTRA - Sugar Free Gum & Bubble Gum - WM. WRIGLEY JR. COMPANY; *pg.* 1863, *pg.* 596
EXTRA BODY - Hair Care Product - JOHN PAUL MITCHELL SYSTEMS; *pg.* 512, *pg.* 133
EXTRA BUCKS - Store Program - CVS HEALTH CORPORATION; *pg.* 1765, *pg.* 1610
EXTRA/BUILD - Mastics - ROYAL ADHESIVES & SEALANTS LLC; *pg.* 1179, *pg.* 697
EXTRA CHUNKY - Salsa - GOLD PURE FOOD PRODUCTS CO., INC.; *pg.* 858, *pg.* 1166
EXTRA CRISPY - Fried Chicken - KFC CORPORATION; *pg.* 1733, *pg.* 735
EXTRA DRAW KENO - Video Game - INTERNATIONAL GAME TECHNOLOGY; *pg.* 957, *pg.* 1024
EXTRA EXTRA LUCK - Game - WMS INDUSTRIES INC.; *pg.* 593, *pg.* 666
EXTRA-FINE - Art Product - DANIEL SMITH INC.; *pg.* 1766, *pg.* 1835
EXTRA POINT - Game - WMS INDUSTRIES INC.; *pg.* 593, *pg.* 666
EXTRA REWARDS - Frequent Shoppers Program - GIANT FOOD STORES, LLC; *pg.* 1021, *pg.* 1520
EXTRA SENSORY DETECTION - Laser Detectors - COBRA ELECTRONICS CORPORATION; *pg.* 629, *pg.* 572
EXTRA VALUE MEAL - Sandwich, Fries & Drink - MCDONALD'S CORPORATION; *pg.* 1737, *pg.* 645
EXTRA VIRGIN COCONUT OIL - Health Supplement - GARDEN OF LIFE, INC.; *pg.* 1532, *pg.* 478
EXTRA WIDE KEVLAR - Sleeves - LAKELAND INDUSTRIES, INC.; *pg.* 1354, *pg.* 1338
EXTRACARE - Store Program - CVS HEALTH CORPORATION; *pg.* 1765, *pg.* 1610
EXTRACLEAR - Glass Product - GUARDIAN INDUSTRIES CORP.; *pg.* 85, *pg.* 869
EXTRACT - Specimen Bags - CONMED CORPORATION; *pg.* 1517, *pg.* 1347
EXTRACTOR - Software - AUTONOMY, INC.; *pg.* 358, *pg.* 212
EXTRACTOR - Medical Device - BOSTON SCIENTIFIC CORPORATION; *pg.* 1508, *pg.* 831
EXTRACTOVATOR - Foam Extraction Cleaning Equipment - DURACLEAN INTERNATIONAL, INC.; *pg.* 329, *pg.* 553
EXTRAGAL - Exposed Hot Dip Galvanized Coated Steel - ARCELORMITTAL DOFASCO INC.; *pg.* 68, *pg.* 1921
EXTRAMATE - Extruded Polystyrene Foam - THE DOW CHEMICAL COMPANY; *pg.* 1157, *pg.* 898
EXTRAMILE - Retail Convenience Store - CHEVRON CORPORATION; *pg.* 974, *pg.* 259
EXTRANEAL - Peritoneal Dialyzer - BAXTER INTERNATIONAL INC.; *pg.* 1499, *pg.* 599
EXTRAORDINARY - Fragrance - AVON PRODUCTS, INC.; *pg.* 500, *pg.* 1198
EXTRAORDINARY RESORTS.EXCEPTIONAL EXPERIENCES. - Slogan - VAIL RESORTS, INC.; *pg.* 1117, *pg.* 313
EXTRAPURE - Service Instrument - BAXTER INTERNATIONAL INC.; *pg.* 1499, *pg.* 599
EXTRAS - Extendable Rate Adjustable Securities - THE ZIEGLER COMPANIES, INC.; *pg.* 824, *pg.* 597
EXTRASMOOTH - Steel Product - AK STEEL HOLDING CORPORATION; *pg.* 1311, *pg.* 1479
EXTRASPORT - Vests & Accessories - JOHNSON OUTDOORS INC.; *pg.* 1837, *pg.* 1888
EXTRATERRORESTRIAL ALIEN ENCOUNTER - Amusement Park - THE WALT DISNEY COMPANY; *pg.* 317, *pg.* 52
EXTRAVAGANT - Carpet - BEAULIEU GROUP, LLC; *pg.* 917, *pg.* 529
EXTRAVIDIN - Reagent - SIGMA-ALDRICH CORPORATION; *pg.* 1181, *pg.* 1003
EXTREEMM - Footwear - STEVEN MADDEN, LTD.; *pg.* 1819, *pg.* 1176
EXTREL - Film Product - TREDEGAR CORPORATION; *pg.* 1890, *pg.* 1804
EXTREMA - Chemical Products - AIR PRODUCTS AND CHEMICALS, INC.; *pg.* 1145, *pg.* 1513
EXTREME - Software - ADOBE SYSTEMS INCORPORATED; *pg.* 342, *pg.* 235
EXTREME - Glove - KOMBI, LTD.; *pg.* 1838, *pg.* 1766
EXTREME - Portable Basketball Standards - LIFETIME PRODUCTS INC.; *pg.* 933, *pg.* 1751
EXTREME - Fabric - NEMSCHOFF, INC.; *pg.* 936, *pg.* 1890
EXTREME - Excimer Laser System - THE SPECTRANETICS CORPORATION; *pg.* 1595, *pg.* 315
EXTREME ATS - Footwear - LACROSSE FOOTWEAR, INC.; *pg.* 1811, *pg.* 1503
EXTREME BRIGHT DATAGRAFIX - Laser Detectors - COBRA ELECTRONICS CORPORATION; *pg.* 629, *pg.* 572
EXTREME COMBO - Reward Scheme - MAVERIK COUNTRY STORES, INC.; *pg.* 1027, *pg.* 1752
EXTREME CONTROL - Bicycle Accessories - SPECIALIZED BICYCLE COMPONENTS, INC.; *pg.* 1711, *pg.* 152
EXTREME CZPOWER - Electronic Components - MOLEX INCORPORATED; *pg.* 655, *pg.* 628
EXTREME FROSTY - Lottery Game - D.C. LOTTERY & CHARITABLE GAMES CONTROL BOARD; *pg.* 991, *pg.* 398
EXTREME GREEN - Lottery Game - OHIO LOTTERY COMMISSION; *pg.* 1002, *pg.* 1433
EXTREME HEAT - Deoderant - BLUE CROSS LABORATORIES; *pg.* 326, *pg.* 277
EXTREME HIGHCPOWER - Electronic Components - MOLEX INCORPORATED; *pg.* 655, *pg.* 628
EXTREME LAPTOP - Briefcase - SANTA FE LEATHER CORPORATION; *pg.* 12, *pg.* 1059
EXTREME LIGHT - Flashlight - STREAMLIGHT INC.; *pg.* 1306, *pg.* 1527
EXTREME LPHPOWER - Electronic Components - MOLEX INCORPORATED; *pg.* 655, *pg.* 628
EXTREME MASTER - Bicycle Accessories - SPECIALIZED BICYCLE COMPONENTS, INC.; *pg.* 1711, *pg.* 152
EXTREME MICROPOWER - Electronic Components - MOLEX INCORPORATED; *pg.* 655, *pg.* 628
EXTREME PARKER - Glove - KOMBI, LTD.; *pg.* 1838, *pg.* 1766
EXTREME PERFORMANCE - Integrated Circuits - LATTICE SEMICONDUCTOR CORPORATION; *pg.* 651, *pg.* 1498
EXTREME POWERBBC - Electronic Components - MOLEX INCORPORATED; *pg.* 655, *pg.* 628
EXTREME POWERDOCK - Electronic Components - MOLEX INCORPORATED; *pg.* 655, *pg.* 628
EXTREME POWEREDGE - Electronic Components - MOLEX INCORPORATED; *pg.* 655, *pg.* 628
EXTREME POWERMASS - Electronic Components - MOLEX INCORPORATED; *pg.* 655, *pg.* 628
EXTREME POWERPLUS - Electronic Components - MOLEX INCORPORATED; *pg.* 655, *pg.* 628
EXTREME SAUSAGE - Sausage Sandwiches - JACK IN THE BOX INC.; *pg.* 1732, *pg.* 204
EXTREME SERVICE - Shipping Service - FEDEX CORPORATION; *pg.* 1907, *pg.* 1642
EXTREME SERVICE - Software - XEROX CORPORATION; *pg.* 494, *pg.* 365
EXTREME SPORT - Deodorant - THE GILLETTE COMPANY; *pg.* 509, *pg.* 795
EXTREME SUPREME - Guacamole - J.R. SIMPLOT COMPANY; *pg.* 867, *pg.* 547
EXTREME TEN50POWER - Electronic Components - MOLEX INCORPORATED; *pg.* 655, *pg.* 628
EXTREME TEN60POWER - Electronic Components - MOLEX INCORPORATED; *pg.* 655, *pg.* 628
EXTREME VOLUME - Beauty Product - AVON PRODUCTS, INC.; *pg.* 500, *pg.* 1198
EXTREME WINS - Video Game - INTERNATIONAL GAME TECHNOLOGY; *pg.* 957, *pg.* 1024
EXTREME ZPOWER - Electronic Components - MOLEX INCORPORATED; *pg.* 655, *pg.* 628
EXTREMEDGE TITANIUM - Scissors - ACME UNITED CORPORATION; *pg.* 1040, *pg.* 346
EXTREMEFLEX - Cable Product - COMMSCOPE, INC.; *pg.* 278, *pg.* 1378
EXTREMELY GENTLE SOFTLINER - Eye Pencils - COVER GIRL COSMETICS; *pg.* 506, *pg.* 772
EXTREMERAID - Large Storage Subsystems - AVAGO TECHNOLOGIES; *pg.* 358, *pg.* 238
EXTREMES - Coat - CARHARTT, INC.; *pg.* 39, *pg.* 875
EXTREMETECH.COM - Publication - ZIFF DAVIS, LLC; *pg.* 1703, *pg.* 1316
EXTREMEWARE - Network Operating System - EXTREME NETWORKS INC; *pg.* 287, *pg.* 245
EXTREMEWARE EDGE - Switch - EXTREME NETWORKS INC; *pg.* 287, *pg.* 245
EXTREMEXOS - Operating System - EXTREME NETWORKS INC; *pg.* 287, *pg.* 245
EXTREMFIX - Surgical Screws - OSTEOMED CORPORATION; *pg.* 1425, *pg.* 1658
EXTRUCLEAN - Dustless FD&C Dyes - SENSIENT COLORS INC.; *pg.* 1180, *pg.* 1003
EXTRUDE-TITE - Screw - SFS INTEC, INC.; *pg.* 1061, *pg.* 1596
EXUBERA - Pharmaceutical Product - NEKTAR THERAPEUTICS; *pg.* 1572, *pg.* 224
EXUMA - Hat - CORTLAND LINE COMPANY; *pg.* 1831, *pg.* 1155
EXV - Pants - CABELA'S INCORPORATED; *pg.* 535, *pg.* 1019
EXWRAP - Diabetes Treatment Products - ANIMAS CORPORATION; *pg.* 1495, *pg.* 1593
EXXCEL - Medical Device - BOSTON SCIENTIFIC CORPORATION; *pg.* 1508, *pg.* 831
EXXON - Petroleum Products - EXXON MOBIL CORPORATION; *pg.* 977, *pg.* 1718
EXXON CLEAR LITE - Synthetic Heater Fuel - W.M. BARR & COMPANY, INC.; *pg.* 338, *pg.* 1647
EXXONMOBIL - Petroleum Products - EXXON MOBIL CORPORATION; *pg.* 977, *pg.* 1718
EXXONMOBIL PERSONAL CARD - Cash Card - CITIGROUP INC.; *pg.* 735, *pg.* 1212
EXXUS - Furniture - J. ROBERT SCOTT INC.; *pg.* 930, *pg.* 105
EXYTE - Footwear - STEVEN MADDEN, LTD.; *pg.* 1819, *pg.* 1176
EXZHELLENT - Cable - GENERAL CABLE CORPORATION; *pg.* 83, *pg.* 729
EYE CONNECT - Techniques & Technology - POLYCOM, INC.; *pg.* 664, *pg.* 249
EYE DEFENSE - Nutritional Supplement - PHARMAVITE LLC; *pg.* 1584, *pg.* 167
EYE DEVICE - Electrical & Scientific Apparatus - THE COOPER COMPANIES, INC.; *pg.* 1518, *pg.* 183
EYE DRX - Eye Care Centers - VISIONWORKS OF AMERICA, INC.; *pg.* 1436, *pg.* 1744
EYE DUETS - Eyeliner & Shadow - MAYBELLINE LLC; *pg.* 516, *pg.* 1257
EYE ESSENTIALS - Nutritional Supplement - PHARMAVITE LLC; *pg.* 1584, *pg.* 167
EYE EXPRESS - Eyeliner - MAYBELLINE LLC; *pg.* 516, *pg.* 1257
EYE, HI & GOODBYE! - Games - PENN NATIONAL GAMING, INC.; *pg.* 574, *pg.* 1595
EYE, HI & GOODBYE ARGOSY & DESIGN - Games - PENN NATIONAL GAMING, INC.; *pg.* 574, *pg.* 1595
EYE LINE MINUS PETRO WAXES - Eye Liner - AVEDA CORPORATION; *pg.* 499, *pg.* 917
THE EYE OF HORUS - Game - WMS INDUSTRIES INC.; *pg.* 593, *pg.* 666
THE EYE OF JUDGEMENT - Toy & Game - HASBRO, INC.; *pg.* 954, *pg.* 1603
EYE OF THE DRAGON - Game - WMS INDUSTRIES INC.; *pg.* 593, *pg.* 666
EYE OF THE HAWK - Ale - MENDOCINO BREWING COMPANY; *pg.* 254, *pg.* 298
EYE OF THE STORM - Real-Time Project Monitoring System - MAXONS RESTORATIONS; *pg.* 332, *pg.* 1257
EYE-OPENER - Cable Assembly - W.L. GORE & ASSOCIATES, INC.; *pg.* 122, *pg.* 388
EYE SAVER - Lighting Product - WESTINGHOUSE LIGHTING CORPORATION; *pg.* 687, *pg.* 1571
EYE-SHAPED DESIGN - Opthalmic Apparatus, Accessories & Preparations - THE COOPER COMPANIES, INC.; *pg.* 1518, *pg.* 183
EYE STYLE - Mascara - THE BONNE BELL COMPANY; *pg.* 502, *pg.* 1480
EYEBALL FIXTURE - Fiber Optic Fixtures - REVOLUTION LIGHTING TECHNOLOGIES, INC.; *pg.* 1304, *pg.* 377
EYEBROW & LINER PENCIL - Eye Pencils - COVER GIRL COSMETICS; *pg.* 506, *pg.* 772
EYECATCHERS - Hosiery & Related Apparel -

MAYER/BERKSHIRE CORPORATION; *pg.* 29, *pg.* 1129

EYECLOPS - Night Vision Infrared Product - JAKKS PACIFIC, INC.; *pg.* 960, *pg.* 142

EYEFINDER - Semiconductor Implementation - AVAGO TECHNOLOGIES; *pg.* 358, *pg.* 238

EYELIT - Footwear - STEVEN MADDEN, LTD.; *pg.* 1819, *pg.* 1176

EYEMASTERS - Eye Care Centers - VISIONWORKS OF AMERICA, INC.; *pg.* 1436, *pg.* 1744

EYEOPENER - Computer Products - BROADCOM CORPORATION; *pg.* 364, *pg.* 108

EYES BY DESIGN - Cosmetics & Fragrances - THE ESTEE LAUDER COMPANIES INC.; *pg.* 508, *pg.* 1229

EYESAVER - Safety Eye Wash Faucet - SPEAKMAN COMPANY; *pg.* 112, *pg.* 388

EYESHADOW TRIO - Beauty Product - AVON PRODUCTS, INC.; *pg.* 500, *pg.* 1198

EYESTYLE SHADOW BOX - Eye Shadow - THE BONNE BELL COMPANY; *pg.* 502, *pg.* 1480

EYEWEAR FOR THE OUTDOORS - Tagline - FGX INTERNATIONAL, INC.; *pg.* 5, *pg.* 1608

EYEWITNESS BOOKS - Children's Series of Non-Fiction Books - DK PUBLISHING; *pg.* 1636, *pg.* 1224

EYEWITNESS TRAVEL - Travel Guides - DK PUBLISHING; *pg.* 1636, *pg.* 1224

EZ - LED - CREE INC.; *pg.* 631, *pg.* 1371

EZ-12 - LED - CREE INC.; *pg.* 631, *pg.* 1371

EZ-16 - LED - CREE INC.; *pg.* 631, *pg.* 1371

EZ-18 - LED - CREE INC.; *pg.* 631, *pg.* 1371

EZ-21 - LED - CREE INC.; *pg.* 631, *pg.* 1371

EZ-24 - LED - CREE INC.; *pg.* 631, *pg.* 1371

EZ-7 - LED - CREE INC.; *pg.* 631, *pg.* 1371

EZ-8.5 - LED - CREE INC.; *pg.* 631, *pg.* 1371

EZ-APN - Software - USA TECHNOLOGIES, INC.; *pg.* 815, *pg.* 1550

EZ-BANNER - Pump Product - IDEX CORPORATION; *pg.* 1347, *pg.* 623

EZ BAR - Electronic Components - MOLEX INCORPORATED; *pg.* 655, *pg.* 628

EZ BASE - Form Equipment - BESSER COMPANY; *pg.* 1317, *pg.* 865

EZ BEAD - Glass Bead Application System - GRACO, INC.; *pg.* 1342, *pg.* 935

EZ BOSS LOCK - Cam & Groove Couplings - DIXON VALVE & COUPLING COMPANY; *pg.* 1045, *pg.* 766

EZ BOX - Form Equipment - BESSER COMPANY; *pg.* 1317, *pg.* 865

EZ BRACKET - Custom Fit Mounting Bracket - LUND INTERNATIONAL, INC.; *pg.* 211, *pg.* 526

EZ-BREAK - Anti-Seize Compound - LA-CO INDUSTRIES MARKAL CO., INC.; *pg.* 1170, *pg.* 610

EZ CAST - Pressed & Monolithic Refractory - RESCO PRODUCTS, INC.; *pg.* 107, *pg.* 1581

EZ CHANGE - Battery - ENERGIZER HOLDINGS, INC.; *pg.* 637, *pg.* 996

EZ-CHANGE - Watchstrap - STULLER, INC.; *pg.* 13, *pg.* 745

EZ CLIP - Wound Closing Kit - STOELTING CO.; *pg.* 1430, *pg.* 671

EZ COIL - Binding Product - SOUTHWEST BINDING & LAMINATING; *pg.* 1377, *pg.* 988

EZ-COLOR - LED Controllers - CYPRESS SEMICONDUCTOR CORPORATION; *pg.* 1326, *pg.* 243

EZ-CONN - Connector - MOLEX INCORPORATED; *pg.* 655, *pg.* 628

EZ COOLERS - ADA Compliant Water Cooler - ELKAY MANUFACTURING COMPANY; *pg.* 80, *pg.* 645

EZ-CREASE - Apparel Interlining - HARODITE INDUSTRIES, INC.; *pg.* 693, *pg.* 847

EZ CUBE - Modular Furniture - SAUDER WOODWORKING CO.; *pg.* 941, *pg.* 1403

EZ CUBED - Pressed & Monolithic Refractory - RESCO PRODUCTS, INC.; *pg.* 107, *pg.* 1581

EZ DETECT - Medical Test Product - BIOMERICA, INC.; *pg.* 1506, *pg.* 107

EZ-DISH - Polyurethane Foam - SPAN-AMERICA MEDICAL SYSTEMS, INC.; *pg.* 1595, *pg.* 1618

EZ DRY - Rinse Additive - ECOLAB INC.; *pg.* 329, *pg.* 960

EZ FILL - Starch - CARGILL, INC.; *pg.* 845, *pg.* 965

EZ-FIRE - Heating System for Aluminum, Non-Ferrous Metals - AIR PRODUCTS AND CHEMICALS, INC.; *pg.* 1145, *pg.* 1513

EZ FLEX-LOC - Car Seats - BABY TREND, INC.; *pg.* 916, *pg.* 173

EZ-FLOW - Nail Care - AMERICAN INTERNATIONAL INDUSTRIES COMPANY; *pg.* 498, *pg.* 126

EZ FLOW - Additive - BASF CATALYSTS LLC; *pg.* 1148, *pg.* 1074

EZ-FLOW - Medical Apparatus - MAQUET; *pg.* 1558, *pg.* 1082

EZ-FLOW - Welded Steel Pipe - NORTHWEST PIPE COMPANY; *pg.* 100, *pg.* 1846

EZ FOIL - Disposable Cookware - PACTIV CORPORATION; *pg.* 1466, *pg.* 624

EZ GRAND - Lottery Game - IOWA LOTTERY; *pg.* 996, *pg.* 705

EZ GRASP - Puzzle - HASBRO, INC.; *pg.* 954, *pg.* 1603

EZ GREASER - Fluid Handling System - GRACO, INC.; *pg.* 1342, *pg.* 935

EZ GRIP - Canister - THE COFFEE BEANERY LTD.; *pg.* 849, *pg.* 886

EZ-GUIDE - Navigation Aid - TRIMBLE NAVIGATION LIMITED; *pg.* 1384, *pg.* 288

EZ-HCG - Medical Test Product - BIOMERICA, INC.; *pg.* 1506, *pg.* 107

EZ HEALTHCHECK - Dry Chemistry System - HESKA CORPORATION; *pg.* 1542, *pg.* 335

EZ-HP - Medical Test Product - BIOMERICA, INC.; *pg.* 1506, *pg.* 107

EZ INVOICE - Software - OPENAIR, INC.; *pg.* 1272, *pg.* 800

EZ KLEEN - Furnace Filter - RESEARCH PRODUCTS CORPORATION; *pg.* 1075, *pg.* 1867

EZ-LH - Medical Test Product - BIOMERICA, INC.; *pg.* 1506, *pg.* 107

EZ LIFT - Patient Lift - KINETIC CONCEPTS, INC.; *pg.* 1553, *pg.* 1741

EZ-LINK - Evaluation & Development Kit - CYPRESS SEMICONDUCTOR CORPORATION; *pg.* 1326, *pg.* 243

EZ LOAD - Software - BIO-RAD LABORATORIES, INC.; *pg.* 1504, *pg.* 101

EZ MICRO - Software - BIO-RAD LABORATORIES, INC.; *pg.* 1504, *pg.* 101

EZ-MIX - Urethane Liquid Rubber - SMOOTH-ON INC.; *pg.* 111, *pg.* 1528

EZ MONEY - Lottery Game - OHIO LOTTERY COMMISSION; *pg.* 1002, *pg.* 1433

EZ MOVES PRO - Foam Rubber Pads Used to Facilitate the Movement of Furniture - STANLEY STEEMER INTERNATIONAL, INC.; *pg.* 944, *pg.* 1450

EZ OPEN - Cake Container - INLINE PLASTICS CORP.; *pg.* 1460, *pg.* 370

EZ-OTG - Development Kit - CYPRESS SEMICONDUCTOR CORPORATION; *pg.* 1326, *pg.* 243

EZ OZONEWARE - Disposable Cookware - PACTIV CORPORATION; *pg.* 1466, *pg.* 624

EZ-PALM - Truck Equipment - AMERICAN VAN EQUIPMENT INC.; *pg.* 199, *pg.* 1078

EZ-PASS - Tray - COOK GROUP, INC.; *pg.* 1518, *pg.* 674

EZ PAY - Casino Ticket System - INTERNATIONAL GAME TECHNOLOGY; *pg.* 957, *pg.* 1024

EZ-PSA - Medical Test Product - BIOMERICA, INC.; *pg.* 1506, *pg.* 107

EZ-QC - Quality Control Kit - IDEXX LABORATORIES, INC.; *pg.* 1543, *pg.* 753

EZ RIDER - Coatings - TENNANT COMPANY; *pg.* 1381, *pg.* 944

EZ-RJ - Connector - BOMAR INTERCONNECT PRODUCTS, INC.; *pg.* 1318, *pg.* 1079

EZ ROAD - Telephone Service - IDT CORPORATION; *pg.* 643, *pg.* 1096

EZ ROLLER - Retrofit Radius Component - INTRALOX LLC; *pg.* 1350, *pg.* 744

EZ ROLLER RETROFIT - Plastic Conveyor Belt - THE LAITRAM LLC; *pg.* 1354, *pg.* 744

EZ ROUTE - Game - INTERNATIONAL GAME TECHNOLOGY; *pg.* 957, *pg.* 1024

EZ RULES - Software - BIO-RAD LABORATORIES, INC.; *pg.* 1504, *pg.* 101

EZ RUNS - Software - BIO-RAD LABORATORIES, INC.; *pg.* 1504, *pg.* 101

EZ SAFE - Game - INTERNATIONAL GAME TECHNOLOGY; *pg.* 957, *pg.* 1024

EZ-SCP - Easy Mount Bracket Assembly - ELECTRO-SENSORS, INC.; *pg.* 1333, *pg.* 948

EZ-SCREEN - Diagnostic Product - MEDTOX SCIENTIFIC, INC.; *pg.* 1422, *pg.* 962

EZ-SEAL - Adhesives - AMERICAN GREASE STICK CO.; *pg.* 971, *pg.* 902

EZ SEED - Seeding Mix - THE SCOTTS MIRACLE-GRO COMPANY; *pg.* 1799, *pg.* 1459

EZ SET - Package Conveying Machinery - INTELLIGRATED SYSTEMS LLC; *pg.* 1350, *pg.* 998

EZ SHOT - Battery Operated Grease Gun - GRACO, INC.; *pg.* 1342, *pg.* 935

EZ SPAN - Furniture - TROPITONE FURNITURE CO., INC.; *pg.* 945, *pg.* 118

EZ-SPRAY - Silicone Rubber - SMOOTH-ON INC.; *pg.* 111, *pg.* 1528

EZ-SPRAY JR. - Spray Gun - SMOOTH-ON INC.; *pg.* 111, *pg.* 1528

EZ SQUEEGEE - Squeegee - NUPLA CORPORATION; *pg.* 101, *pg.* 281

EZ STA K - Cable Product - COMMSCOPE, INC.; *pg.* 278, *pg.* 1378

EZ STACKING - Medical Stool - BLICKMAN HEALTH INDUSTRIES, INC.; *pg.* 1506, *pg.* 1051

EZ-STEER - Navigation Aid - TRIMBLE NAVIGATION LIMITED; *pg.* 1384, *pg.* 288

EZ-TEAR - Perforation - AUTOMATED PACKAGING SYSTEMS INC.; *pg.* 1452, *pg.* 1474

EZ-TERM - Glass & Ceramic Material - CORNING INCORPORATED; *pg.* 1122, *pg.* 1154

EZ TICKET - Video Game - INTERNATIONAL GAME TECHNOLOGY; *pg.* 957, *pg.* 1024

EZ-TOUCH - Touchpad - INTERNATIONAL GAME TECHNOLOGY; *pg.* 957, *pg.* 1024

EZ TRACK - Plastic Conveyor Belt - THE LAITRAM LLC; *pg.* 1354, *pg.* 744

E.Z. TRAINER - Educational Publication - ISSA; *pg.* 145, *pg.* 640

EZ-USB AT2LPTM L8 - Low-Speed USB - CYPRESS SEMICONDUCTOR CORPORATION; *pg.* 1326, *pg.* 243

EZ-USB AT2S - Low-Speed USB - CYPRESS SEMICONDUCTOR CORPORATION; *pg.* 1326, *pg.* 243

EZ-USB FX - Low-Speed USB - CYPRESS SEMICONDUCTOR CORPORATION; *pg.* 1326, *pg.* 243

EZ-USB FX2 - Low-Speed USB - CYPRESS SEMICONDUCTOR CORPORATION; *pg.* 1326, *pg.* 243

EZ-USB FX2LP - Low-Speed USB - CYPRESS SEMICONDUCTOR CORPORATION; *pg.* 1326, *pg.* 243

EZ-USB HX2 - Low-Speed USB - CYPRESS SEMICONDUCTOR CORPORATION; *pg.* 1326, *pg.* 243

EZ-USB HX2LP - Low-Speed USB - CYPRESS SEMICONDUCTOR CORPORATION; *pg.* 1326, *pg.* 243

EZ-USB MX2 - Low-Speed USB - CYPRESS SEMICONDUCTOR CORPORATION; *pg.* 1326, *pg.* 243

EZ-USB SX2 - Low-Speed USB - CYPRESS SEMICONDUCTOR CORPORATION; *pg.* 1326, *pg.* 243

EZ-USB SX2LP - Low-Speed USB - CYPRESS SEMICONDUCTOR CORPORATION; *pg.* 1326, *pg.* 243

EZ-USB SX2LPTM L8 - Low-Speed USB - CYPRESS SEMICONDUCTOR CORPORATION; *pg.* 1326, *pg.* 243

EZ-USB TX2 - Low-Speed USB - CYPRESS SEMICONDUCTOR CORPORATION; *pg.* 1326, *pg.* 243

EZ-VIEW - Dental Product - DENTSPLY INTERNATIONAL INC.; *pg.* 1522, *pg.* 1596

EZ-YIELD - Software - BROOKFIELD ENGINEERING LABORATORIES, INC.; *pg.* 1403, *pg.* 833

EZ-ZONE - Controllers - WATLOW ELECTRIC MANUFACTURING COMPANY; *pg.* 1078, *pg.* 1004

EZ290 - LED - CREE INC.; *pg.* 631, *pg.* 1371

EZ80 - Micrologic Semiconductor Device - ZILOG INC.; *pg.* 497, *pg.* 252

EZ80ACCLAIM - Micrologic Semiconductor Device - ZILOG INC.; *pg.* 497, *pg.* 252

EZ80ACCLAIMPLUS! - Software - ZILOG INC.; *pg.* 497, *pg.* 252

EZA - Zeolite-A Detergent Builders - ALBEMARLE CORPORATION; *pg.* 1146, *pg.* 741

EZAIR - Terminal Reel Fed - PANDUIT CORP.; *pg.* 661, *pg.* 663

EZANALOG - Integrated Circuits - MICREL, INC.; *pg.* 654, *pg.* 247

EZBOLUS - Diabetes Treatment Products - ANIMAS CORPORATION; *pg.* 1495, *pg.* 1593

EZBRIGHT - LED - CREE INC.; *pg.* 631, *pg.* 1371

EZBRIGHT1000 - LED - CREE INC.; *pg.* 631, *pg.* 1371

EZBRIGHT290 - LED - CREE INC.; *pg.* 631, *pg.* 1371

EZCASCADE - Interface Simplifies Multiple Driver - MAXIM INTEGRATED PRODUCTS, INC.; *pg.* 653, *pg.* 247

EZCOLOR - Software - X-RITE, INCORPORATED; *pg.* 1437, *pg.* 891

EZDATA - Educational Software - PEARSON ASSESSMENTS; *pg.* 1674, *pg.* 918

EZE-BREEZE - Sliding Panel - PGT, INC.; *pg.* 104, *pg.* 452

EZE-LOK - Medical Product - GF HEALTH PRODUCTS, INC.;

pg. 1535, *pg.* 508
EZE WORKMASTER - Workbenches - IAC INDUSTRIES, INC.; *pg.* 929, *pg.* 48
EZI-ACTION - Pump - TRICO MFG. CORP.; *pg.* 219, *pg.* 1886
EZLASE - Dental Laser Product - BIOLASE TECHNOLOGY, INC.; *pg.* 1506, *pg.* 107
EZLOGIC - Software - BIO-RAD LABORATORIES, INC.; *pg.* 1504, *pg.* 101
EZMANAGER - Health Care System - ANIMAS CORPORATION; *pg.* 1495, *pg.* 1593
EZMANAGER PLUS - Software - ANIMAS CORPORATION; *pg.* 1495, *pg.* 1593
EZMONEY - Credit Services - EZCORP, INC.; *pg.* 750, *pg.* 1662
EZPAWN - Credit Services - EZCORP, INC.; *pg.* 750, *pg.* 1662
EZPC - LED - CREE INC.; *pg.* 631, *pg.* 1371
EZQ - Molecular Biology Product - THERMO FISHER SCIENTIFIC INC.; *pg.* 1602, *pg.* 61
EZR - LED - CREE INC.; *pg.* 631, *pg.* 1371
EZREADER - Book Light - ULTRAOPTIX, INC.; *pg.* 1433, *pg.* 346
EZSET - Health Care System - ANIMAS CORPORATION; *pg.* 1495, *pg.* 1593
EZSET INSERTER - Health Care System - ANIMAS CORPORATION; *pg.* 1495, *pg.* 1593
EZSMOKER - Vaporizer - VAPOR CORP.; *pg.* 61, *pg.* 427
EZTRAK - Mowers - DEERE & COMPANY; *pg.* 703, *pg.* 632
EZVIEW - Diabetes Treatment Products - ANIMAS CORPORATION; *pg.* 1495, *pg.* 1593
EZVIEW - Fluid Handling System - GRACO, INC.; *pg.* 1342, *pg.* 935
EZWAVE - Software System - MENTOR GRAPHICS CORPORATION; *pg.* 432, *pg.* 1510
EZY - Sock Helper - ALIMED, INC.; *pg.* 1490, *pg.* 816
EZY CLEANER - Detergent - DELTA FOREMOST CHEMICAL CORPORATION; *pg.* 1155, *pg.* 1642

F

F-100 - Fog Generator - HIGH END SYSTEMS, INC.; *pg.* 1299, *pg.* 1663
F-104 - Military Aircraft - LOCKHEED MARTIN CORPORATION; *pg.* 229, *pg.* 762
F-117 - Military Aircraft - LOCKHEED MARTIN CORPORATION; *pg.* 229, *pg.* 762
F-150 - Truck - FORD MOTOR COMPANY OF CANADA, LIMITED; *pg.* 174, *pg.* 1930
F-16 - Jet Aircraft - LOCKHEED MARTIN CORPORATION; *pg.* 229, *pg.* 762
F-16 FIGHTING FALCON - Jet Aircraft - LOCKHEED MARTIN CORPORATION; *pg.* 229, *pg.* 762
F-22 - Systems Integration & Aeronautics - LOCKHEED MARTIN CORPORATION; *pg.* 229, *pg.* 762
F-250 SUPER DUTY - Truck - FORD MOTOR COMPANY OF CANADA, LIMITED; *pg.* 174, *pg.* 1930
F-35 - Systems Integration & Aeronautics - LOCKHEED MARTIN CORPORATION; *pg.* 229, *pg.* 762
F-350 SUPER DUTY - Truck - FORD MOTOR COMPANY OF CANADA, LIMITED; *pg.* 174, *pg.* 1930
F-80 - Systems Integration & Aeronautics - LOCKHEED MARTIN CORPORATION; *pg.* 229, *pg.* 762
F-94 - Systems Integration & Aeronautics - LOCKHEED MARTIN CORPORATION; *pg.* 229, *pg.* 762
F/A-22 RAPTOR - Jet Aircraft & Structural Parts - LOCKHEED MARTIN CORPORATION; *pg.* 229, *pg.* 762
F-I-T SYSTEM - Foam Liner for Ice Hockey Skates & Helmets - REEBOK-CCM HOCKEY, INC.; *pg.* 1844, *pg.* 1960
F/O - Laryngoscope - PROPPER MANUFACTURING COMPANY, INC.; *pg.* 1586, *pg.* 1175
F-O-F - Plastics Product - AEP INDUSTRIES INC.; *pg.* 1878, *pg.* 1085
F SERIES - Snowmobile - ARCTIC CAT INC.; *pg.* 1705, *pg.* 953
F-SERIES - Cage Mill/Pulverizer - STEDMAN MACHINE COMPANY; *pg.* 1379, *pg.* 673
F10 EVO - Disk Shipper - ENTEGRIS, INC.; *pg.* 1882, *pg.* 788
F2 - Watch - FOSSIL GROUP, INC.; *pg.* 5, *pg.* 1735
F2 YOUTH - Baseball Bat - WILSON SPORTING GOODS CO.; *pg.* 1848, *pg.* 596
F21 - Polish & Cleanser - TURTLE WAX, INC.; *pg.* 220, *pg.* 671
F220 - Heat Detector - BOSCH SECURITY SYSTEMS, INC.; *pg.* 626, *pg.* 1158
F220-P - Smoke Detector - BOSCH SECURITY SYSTEMS, INC.; *pg.* 626, *pg.* 1158
F220-PTH - Smoke Detector - BOSCH SECURITY SYSTEMS, INC.; *pg.* 626, *pg.* 1158
F220-PTHC - Smoke Detector - BOSCH SECURITY SYSTEMS, INC.; *pg.* 626, *pg.* 1158
F3 - Shoes - ACUSHNET COMPANY; *pg.* 1824, *pg.* 818
F3 - Carotid Shunt - LEMAITRE VASCULAR, INC.; *pg.* 1555, *pg.* 805
F4 - Trademark (Div. I Men's & Women's Basketball) - NATIONAL COLLEGIATE ATHLETIC ASSOCIATION; *pg.* 567, *pg.* 688
F5 ACOPIA - Data Solutions Product - F5 NETWORKS, INC.; *pg.* 396, *pg.* 1835
F5 MANAGEMENT PACK - Software - F5 NETWORKS, INC.; *pg.* 396, *pg.* 1835
F5 NETWORKS - Delivery Network Devices - F5 NETWORKS, INC.; *pg.* 396, *pg.* 1835
FA-2000 - Fan Tray - EMCORE CORPORATION; *pg.* 636, *pg.* 39
FA-SET - Storefront Window Framing System - KAWNEER COMPANY, INC.; *pg.* 90, *pg.* 537
FAB - Laundry Detergent - THE PROCTER & GAMBLE COMPANY; *pg.* 1129, *pg.* 1418
FAB FACE - Acne Pads - BLUE CROSS LABORATORIES; *pg.* 326, *pg.* 277
FAB WRAP - Plastics Product - AEP INDUSTRIES INC.; *pg.* 1878, *pg.* 1085
FABBACK - Polycarbonate Mirror Sheet - PLASKOLITE, INC.; *pg.* 1888, *pg.* 1443
FABCEL - Pad - FABREEKA INTERNATIONAL, INC.; *pg.* 1882, *pg.* 847
FABCEL LEV-L MOUNT - Machinery Mounts - FABREEKA INTERNATIONAL, INC.; *pg.* 1882, *pg.* 847
FABCO - Belting & Railway Tie Pads - FABREEKA INTERNATIONAL, INC.; *pg.* 1882, *pg.* 847
FABEXPRESS - Hardware Product - BROOKS AUTOMATION, INC.; *pg.* 1320, *pg.* 813
FABFACTORY - Software System - MENTOR GRAPHICS CORPORATION; *pg.* 432, *pg.* 1510
FABFLOOR - Equipment Pedestal - NEWPORT CORPORATION; *pg.* 1424, *pg.* 114
FABGUARD - Plastics Product - AEP INDUSTRIES INC.; *pg.* 1878, *pg.* 1085
FABKIDS - Children's Clothes - JUSTFAB, INC.; *pg.* 27, *pg.* 80
FABLENE - Conveyor Belting - FABREEKA INTERNATIONAL, INC.; *pg.* 1882, *pg.* 847
FABLES AND FLOWERS - Bath Product - KOHLER CO.; *pg.* 91, *pg.* 1862
FABLETICS - Active Wear - JUSTFAB, INC.; *pg.* 27, *pg.* 80
FABLINK - Software System - MENTOR GRAPHICS CORPORATION; *pg.* 432, *pg.* 1510
FABLON - Heavy-Duty Conveyor Belting - FABREEKA INTERNATIONAL, INC.; *pg.* 1882, *pg.* 847
FABPROTEX - Car Care Product - STONER INC.; *pg.* 985, *pg.* 1583
FABRAZYME - Lysosomal Storage Disorder - GENZYME CORPORATION; *pg.* 1534, *pg.* 808
FABRI FAST - Fabric Attachment - HSM SOLUTIONS; *pg.* 1884, *pg.* 1378
FABRI FAST II - Fabric Attachment - HSM SOLUTIONS; *pg.* 1884, *pg.* 1378
FABRI-FIT - Electronic Components - MOLEX INCORPORATED; *pg.* 655, *pg.* 628
FABRIC FUN - Art Supplies - PENTEL OF AMERICA, LTD.; *pg.* 453, *pg.* 295
FABRIC MATE - Markers - YASUTOMO & CO.; *pg.* 497, *pg.* 280
THE FABRIC OF SECURE COMMUNICATIONS - Tagline - LATTICE INC.; *pg.* 1872, *pg.* 1108
THE FABRIC OF YOUR SUCCESS - Slogan - HIRSCH INTERNATIONAL CORP.; *pg.* 694, *pg.* 1164
FABRIC OS - Software - BROCADE COMMUNICATIONS SYSTEMS, INC.; *pg.* 365, *pg.* 239
FABRIC REFRESHER - Cleaning Preparation - BLUE CROSS LABORATORIES; *pg.* 326, *pg.* 277
FABRIC SEAL - Automotive Reconditioning Product - MOC PRODUCTS COMPANY, INC.; *pg.* 332, *pg.* 174
FABRIC-SHIELD - Storm Panel - WAYNE-DALTON CORP.; *pg.* 120, *pg.* 1465
FABRICA - Carpet - THE DIXIE GROUP, INC.; *pg.* 692, *pg.* 1629
FABRICENTER - Cabinet - BROCADE CORPORATION; *pg.* 365, *pg.* 312
FABRICRAFT - Peel & Stick Fabrics - RUBBERMAID HOME PRODUCTS; *pg.* 1138, *pg.* 1453
FABRICRAFTER - Drapery & Upholstery Cleaning Equipment - DURACLEAN INTERNATIONAL, INC.; *pg.* 329, *pg.* 553
FABRICUT - Openmesh Web Coated Abrasives - 3M COMPANY; *pg.* 1142, *pg.* 956
FABRIFLEX - Film Product - TREDEGAR CORPORATION; *pg.* 1890, *pg.* 1804
FABRIQUE - Dinnerware - THE HOMER LAUGHLIN CHINA COMPANY; *pg.* 1125, *pg.* 1850
FABRISOFT - Dry Cleaning & Laundry Product - ADCO, INC.; *pg.* 325, *pg.* 482
FABRY PEROT LRM TOSA - Electronic Components - EMCORE CORPORATION; *pg.* 636, *pg.* 39
FABSORB - Foundation Isolation - FABREEKA INTERNATIONAL, INC.; *pg.* 1882, *pg.* 847
FABSYN - Food Conveyor Belting - FABREEKA INTERNATIONAL, INC.; *pg.* 1882, *pg.* 847
FABTEK - Timber Harvesting Equipment - BLOUNT INTERNATIONAL, INC.; *pg.* 1043, *pg.* 1501
FABU-LAS - Adhesive - H.B. FULLER COMPANY; *pg.* 1165, *pg.* 961
FABULON - Paints & Coatings - THE SHERWIN-WILLIAMS COMPANY; *pg.* 1447, *pg.* 1435
FABULOUS FASHION. FIERCE PRICES - Tagline - BLUEFLY, INC.; *pg.* 1232, *pg.* 1205
FABULOUS FORTUNE - Lottery Game - KENTUCKY LOTTERY CORPORATION; *pg.* 996, *pg.* 735
FABVISION - Inspection System - KLA-TENCOR CORPORATION; *pg.* 1353, *pg.* 146
FACE LIFT - Skin Care Product - NU SKIN ENTERPRISES, INC.; *pg.* 518, *pg.* 1755
FACE ROBOT - Software - AUTODESK INC.; *pg.* 356, *pg.* 257
FACEBOOK HOME - Android App - FACEBOOK, INC.; *pg.* 1245, *pg.* 143
FACELINK.COM - Online Personal Service - SPARK NETWORKS, INC.; *pg.* 472, *pg.* 140
FACER - Paper Product - WESTROCK COMPANY; *pg.* 1472, *pg.* 1805
FACES - Electronic Components - MOLEX INCORPORATED; *pg.* 655, *pg.* 628
FACET - Frequency Assignment & Certification Engineering Tool - ALION SCIENCE AND TECHNOLOGY CORPORATION; *pg.* 615, *pg.* 1788
FACET - Office Furniture - JOFCO INC.; *pg.* 931, *pg.* 691
FACETIME - Video Calling - APPLE INC.; *pg.* 350, *pg.* 73
FACETS - Fabric - NEMSCHOFF, INC.; *pg.* 936, *pg.* 1890
FACETS - Software - TRIZETTO CORPORATION; *pg.* 485, *pg.* 327
FACETS EXTENDED ENTERPRISE - Software - TRIZETTO CORPORATION; *pg.* 485, *pg.* 327
FACIL - Camera - EASTMAN KODAK COMPANY; *pg.* 1408, *pg.* 1333
FACILITATOR - Pharmaceutical Product - IDEXX LABORATORIES, INC.; *pg.* 1543, *pg.* 753
THE FACILITATOR - Multi-Funded Annuity - NEW YORK LIFE INSURANCE COMPANY; *pg.* 1211, *pg.* 1268
FACILITE - Home Appliance Product - WHIRLPOOL CORPORATION; *pg.* 62, *pg.* 872
FACILITY WALL - Steel Wall Panel - CLESTRA HAUSERMAN, INC.; *pg.* 76, *pg.* 1526
FACILITYFOCUS - Software Product - MAXIMUS, INC.; *pg.* 780, *pg.* 1799
FACOM - Hand Tools - SK HAND TOOL CORPORATION; *pg.* 1062, *pg.* 663
FACOM - Facom Tools - STANLEY BLACK & DECKER, INC.; *pg.* 1063, *pg.* 358
FACSIMILE - Plastic Dimensional Transfer Material - FLEXBAR MACHINE CORP.; *pg.* 1337, *pg.* 1169
FACSPREP - System to Automate Preparation of Tissue Samples - BECTON, DICKINSON & COMPANY; *pg.* 1501, *pg.* 1068
FACT - Value-Added Services - AVNET, INC.; *pg.* 622, *pg.* 15
FACT PLUS - Diagnostic Product - ABBOTT LABORATORIES; *pg.* 1484, *pg.* 551
FACT PLUS - Diagnostic Product - ALERE INC.; *pg.* 1488, *pg.* 849
FACTIVA - Magazine - DOW JONES & COMPANY, INC.; *pg.* 1637, *pg.* 1225
FACTNET - Software - R.R. DONNELLEY & SONS COMPANY; *pg.* 1682, *pg.* 589

FACTORY AIR - Motor Product - STANDARD MOTOR PRODUCTS, INC.; *pg.* 218, *pg.* 1176

FACTORY AUTOMATION SOLUTIONS - Automative Service - ATS AUTOMATION TOOLING SYSTEMS INC.; *pg.* 355, *pg.* 1919

FACTORYSOFT OPC - Software - AXEDA SYSTEMS INC.; *pg.* 359, *pg.* 819

FACTORYTALK - Software - ROCKWELL AUTOMATION, INC.; *pg.* 668, *pg.* 1880

FACTS COMPLETE - Conferencing Service - INTERCALL, INC.; *pg.* 417, *pg.* 578

FACTSPOTTER - Software - XEROX CORPORATION; *pg.* 494, *pg.* 365

FACULTYONLINE - Publications for Colleges & Universities - R.R. BOWKER LLC; *pg.* 1682, *pg.* 1095

FADE - Apparel - OAKLEY, INC.; *pg.* 1840, *pg.* 86

FADE BLADE - Special Clipper Blade For Cutting Fade - ANDIS COMPANY; *pg.* 498, *pg.* 1895

FADED - Musical Instrument - GIBSON GUITAR CORP.; *pg.* 550, *pg.* 1650

FADED - Apparel - VANS, INC.; *pg.* 1821, *pg.* 76

FADED GLORY - T-Shirts - WAL-MART STORES, INC.; *pg.* 1790, *pg.* 29

FADELESS - Bulletin Board Paper - PACON CORPORATION; *pg.* 1466, *pg.* 1852

FAFNIR - Bearing Product - THE TIMKEN COMPANY; *pg.* 218, *pg.* 1408

FAHRENHEIT - Hats - CENTURY 21 PROMOTIONS, INC.; *pg.* 2, *pg.* 1834

FAHRENHEIT - Men's Fragrance - PARFUMS CHRISTIAN DIOR, INC; *pg.* 519, *pg.* 1276

FAHRENHEIT 0 DEGREE - Men's Fragrance - PARFUMS CHRISTIAN DIOR, INC; *pg.* 519, *pg.* 1276

FAIADE - Fabric - NEMSCHOFF, INC.; *pg.* 936, *pg.* 1890

FAIL-SAFE - Fan Clutch - BORGWARNER INC.; *pg.* 167, *pg.* 867

FAILING - Rotary Drilling Rigs - THE GEORGE E. FAILING COMPANY; *pg.* 1340, *pg.* 1484

FAILSAFE - Clock & Buffer Product - CYPRESS SEMICONDUCTOR CORPORATION; *pg.* 1326, *pg.* 243

FAILSAFE - Rechargeable Lanterns - DORCY INTERNATIONAL INC.; *pg.* 1046, *pg.* 1439

FAILSAFE - Escalator Safety Device - ELECTROID CO; *pg.* 1333, *pg.* 1123

FAILSAFE - Surge Protector - TII NETWORK TECHNOLOGIES, INC.; *pg.* 680, *pg.* 1157

FAIR CHASE - Knife - BUCK KNIVES, INC.; *pg.* 1828, *pg.* 550

FAIR GROUNDS RACE COURSE - Thoroughbred Horse Racing Track - FAIR GROUNDS CORPORATION; *pg.* 547, *pg.* 747

FAIR ISAAC BLAZE ADVISOR - Business Rules Management System - FAIR ISAAC CORPORATION; *pg.* 1247, *pg.* 955

FAIR PLAY - Fly Line - CORTLAND LINE COMPANY; *pg.* 1831, *pg.* 1155

FAIR-PLAY - Electronic Scoreboard - TRANS-LUX CORPORATION; *pg.* 681, *pg.* 365

FAIR TRADE BLEND - Coffee - STARBUCKS CORPORATION; *pg.* 897, *pg.* 1840

FAIR TRADE CERTIFIED - Flower Arrangement - 1-800-FLOWERS.COM, INC.; *pg.* 1758, *pg.* 1151

FAIRBANKS - Games - PENN NATIONAL GAMING, INC.; *pg.* 574, *pg.* 1595

FAIRBANKS PRINCESS LODGE - Hotel - PRINCESS TOURS; *pg.* 1920, *pg.* 1838

FAIRCHILD - Publications - FAIRCHILD FASHION GROUP; *pg.* 1640, *pg.* 1230

FAIRCHILD - Designer Fragrance - PARFUMS DE COEUR LTD.; *pg.* 519, *pg.* 376

FAIRFAX - Shoes - ALLEN-EDMONDS SHOE CORP.; *pg.* 1804, *pg.* 1887

THE FAIRFAX - Ready-to-assemble Swing Set - CREATIVE PLAYTHINGS LTD.; *pg.* 1831, *pg.* 820

FAIRFAX - Upholstery - ETHAN ALLEN INTERIORS INC.; *pg.* 924, *pg.* 343

FAIRFAX - Kitchen Product - KOHLER CO.; *pg.* 91, *pg.* 1862

FAIRFAX - Bike - MARIN BIKES; *pg.* 1708, *pg.* 168

FAIRFIELD - Furniture - JASPER GROUP; *pg.* 930, *pg.* 691

FAIRFIELD - Fabric - NEMSCHOFF, INC.; *pg.* 936, *pg.* 1890

FAIRFIELD INN - Hotel Chain - MARRIOTT INTERNATIONAL, INC.; *pg.* 1102, *pg.* 764

FAIRFORM FLYER - Yacht & Vessels - HUCKINS YACHT CORPORATION; *pg.* 1708, *pg.* 433

FAIRIEES - Toys - MGA ENTERTAINMENT, INC.; *pg.* 964, *pg.* 300

FAIRLIFE - High-End Milk - THE COCA-COLA COMPANY; *pg.* 240, *pg.* 493

FAIRMONT - Furniture - JASPER GROUP; *pg.* 930, *pg.* 691

FAIRMONT - Lighting Product - QUOIZEL INC.; *pg.* 1304, *pg.* 1616

FAIRMONT HOTELS & RESORTS - Hotels & Resorts - FAIRMONT HOTELS & RESORTS INC.; *pg.* 1091, *pg.* 1938

FAIROAKS - Ethernet Product - VITESSE SEMICONDUCTOR CORPORATION; *pg.* 686, *pg.* 57

FAIRPLAY - Software Technology - APPLE INC.; *pg.* 350, *pg.* 73

FAIRPLAY - Tapered Leader - CORTLAND LINE COMPANY; *pg.* 1831, *pg.* 1155

FAIRVIEW - Furniture - BUSH INDUSTRIES INC.; *pg.* 919, *pg.* 1170

FAIRVIEW - Footwear - EASTLAND SHOE CORPORATION; *pg.* 1808, *pg.* 750

FAIRVIEW - Dinnerware - THE HOMER LAUGHLIN CHINA COMPANY; *pg.* 1125, *pg.* 1850

FAIRWAY - Trademark & Golf Cart Tires - CARLISLE TIRE & WHEEL COMPANY; *pg.* 1880, *pg.* 1612

FAIRY - Dishwashing Products - THE PROCTER & GAMBLE COMPANY; *pg.* 1129, *pg.* 1418

FAIRY BOWZ - Bow Kit - E-Z BOWZ, LLC; *pg.* 692, *pg.* 1635

FAIRY'S FORTUNE - Game - WMS INDUSTRIES INC.; *pg.* 593, *pg.* 666

FAITH - Furniture - AMISCO INDUSTRIES LTD.; *pg.* 913, *pg.* 1958

FAITH - Pillow and Throw - HERITAGE LACE INC.; *pg.* 694, *pg.* 711

FAITH - Fabric - NEMSCHOFF, INC.; *pg.* 936, *pg.* 1890

FAITH KIDZ - Books, Toys & Games - DAVID C. COOK; *pg.* 1633, *pg.* 315

FAJITA BREAST STRIPS - Poultry Product - PILGRIM'S PRIDE CORPORATION; *pg.* 889, *pg.* 330

FALCO - Cheese - CANADIAN FISH EXPORTERS, INC.; *pg.* 845, *pg.* 784

FALCON - Binocular - BUSHNELL OUTDOOR PRODUCTS, INC.; *pg.* 1403, *pg.* 718

FALCON - Cutting Room Equipment - EASTMAN MACHINE COMPANY; *pg.* 1331, *pg.* 1148

FALCON - Fraud Manager Systems - FAIR ISAAC CORPORATION; *pg.* 1247, *pg.* 955

FALCON - Gaming Product - GLD PRODUCTS, INC.; *pg.* 1835, *pg.* 1882

FALCON - Air-Operated Piston Pumps - GRACO, INC.; *pg.* 1342, *pg.* 935

FALCON - Door Hardware - INGERSOLL-RAND COMPANY; *pg.* 1349, *pg.* 1370

FALCON - Software System - MENTOR GRAPHICS CORPORATION; *pg.* 432, *pg.* 1510

FALCON - Apparel - OAKLEY, INC.; *pg.* 1840, *pg.* 86

FALCON - Filter Cartridge - PALL CORPORATION; *pg.* 232, *pg.* 1323

FALCON - Rotors - RAIN BIRD CORPORATION; *pg.* 707, *pg.* 44

FALCON 2000 - Executive Jet Aircraft - DASSAULT FALCON JET CORP.; *pg.* 227, *pg.* 1122

FALCON 2000 EX - Executive Jet Aircraft - DASSAULT FALCON JET CORP.; *pg.* 227, *pg.* 1122

FALCON 50EX - Executive Jet Aircraft - DASSAULT FALCON JET CORP.; *pg.* 227, *pg.* 1122

FALCON 900C - Executive Jet Aircraft - DASSAULT FALCON JET CORP.; *pg.* 227, *pg.* 1122

FALCON 900EX - Executive Jet Aircraft - DASSAULT FALCON JET CORP.; *pg.* 227, *pg.* 1122

FALCON FRAMEWORK - Software System - MENTOR GRAPHICS CORPORATION; *pg.* 432, *pg.* 1510

FALCON GUIDES - Outdoor/Recreation Publishing Imprint - THE GLOBE PEQUOT PRESS, INC.; *pg.* 1645, *pg.* 350

FALCON II - Application Control System - AGCO CORPORATION; *pg.* 700, *pg.* 530

FALCON II - Eight-color Variable Dot Color Inkjet Printer - MUTOH AMERICA INC.; *pg.* 443, *pg.* 18

FALCON II OUTDOOR - Outdoor Commercial Grade Printer - MUTOH AMERICA INC.; *pg.* 443, *pg.* 18

FALCON OUTDOOR - Large Format Outdoor Color Printers - MUTOH AMERICA INC.; *pg.* 443, *pg.* 18

FALCON PLUS - Large Format Printers - MUTOH AMERICA INC.; *pg.* 443, *pg.* 18

FALCONSAR - Systems Integration & Aeronautics - LOCKHEED MARTIN CORPORATION; *pg.* 229, *pg.* 762

FALK'S - Healthcare Product - SWANSON HEALTH PRODUCTS INC.; *pg.* 1600, *pg.* 1397

FALL - Pillow - AMERICAN LEATHER LP; *pg.* 912, *pg.* 1673

FALL HARVEST - Lettuce - DOLE FRESH VEGETABLES; *pg.* 854, *pg.* 198

FALL LAWNS ALIVE! - Lawn Care Product - GARDENS ALIVE!, INC.; *pg.* 1796, *pg.* 693

FALL TOY PREVIEW - Annual Event - TOY INDUSTRY ASSOCIATION, INC.; *pg.* 158, *pg.* 1303

FALLING WATER - Carpet - INTERFACE, INC.; *pg.* 695, *pg.* 512

FALLING WATER - Bath Product - KOHLER CO.; *pg.* 91, *pg.* 1862

FALSTAFF - Beer - PABST BREWING COMPANY; *pg.* 258, *pg.* 137

FAM - Family Channel - ABC FAMILY CHANNEL; *pg.* 268, *pg.* 51

FAMB - Respiratory Product - E.D. BULLARD COMPANY; *pg.* 1332, *pg.* 727

FAME - Ophthalmic Product - ALIMERA SCIENCES, INC.; *pg.* 1490, *pg.* 482

FAME - Software - SUNGARD DATA SYSTEMS INC.; *pg.* 477, *pg.* 1592

FAME & FORTUNE - Video Game - INTERNATIONAL GAME TECHNOLOGY; *pg.* 957, *pg.* 1024

FAMILIES IN ACTION - Educational Program - ACTIVE PARENTING PUBLISHERS; *pg.* 1613, *pg.* 535

FAMILY - Dish Detergent - KAO BRANDS CO. INC.; *pg.* 513, *pg.* 1415

FAMILY - Safety Product - WISCONSIN PHARMACAL COMPANY, LLC; *pg.* 1610, *pg.* 1861

FAMILY CARE - Rabbit Food - KENT NUTRITION GROUP; *pg.* 1477, *pg.* 710

FAMILY CIRCLE - Magazine - THE FAMILY CIRCLE, INC.; *pg.* 1640, *pg.* 1230

FAMILY CIRCLE - Magazine - MEREDITH CORPORATION; *pg.* 1663, *pg.* 705

FAMILY DIGNITY PLAN - Insurance - PAN-AMERICAN LIFE INSURANCE COMPANY; *pg.* 1213, *pg.* 747

FAMILY DOLLAR STORES - Real Variety Store - FAMILY DOLLAR STORES, INC.; *pg.* 1768, *pg.* 1382

FAMILY FEUD - Game - INTERNATIONAL GAME TECHNOLOGY; *pg.* 957, *pg.* 1024

FAMILY FOODS - Food Store - URM STORES, INC.; *pg.* 1036, *pg.* 1844

FAMILY FRESH MARKET - Retail Grocery Stores - SPARTANNASH CO.; *pg.* 1034, *pg.* 925

FAMILY GAME NIGHT - Toy & Game - HASBRO, INC.; *pg.* 954, *pg.* 1603

THE FAMILY HANDYMAN - Magazine - THE READER'S DIGEST ASSOCIATION, INC.; *pg.* 1679, *pg.* 1322

FAMILY LAW REPORTER - Publisher - BLOOMBERG BNA; *pg.* 1621, *pg.* 1772

FAMILY OF FARMS - Tagline - COOPERATIVE REGIONS OF ORGANIC PRODUCER POOLS; *pg.* 850, *pg.* 1864

FAMILY OF FINE FOODS - Tag Line - MURRY'S, INC.; *pg.* 882, *pg.* 780

FAMILY OF FLAVORS - Condiments - MCILHENNY COMPANY; *pg.* 876, *pg.* 741

FAMILY PHARMACY - Private Label Vitamins, Health & Beauty Products - AMERISOURCEBERGEN CORPORATION; *pg.* 1493, *pg.* 1522

FAMILY THRIFT CENTER - Retail Grocery Stores - SPARTANNASH CO.; *pg.* 1034, *pg.* 925

FAMILY TREE - Carpet - INTERFACE, INC.; *pg.* 695, *pg.* 512

FAMILYHISTORY.COM - Website - ANCESTRY.COM LLC; *pg.* 1228, *pg.* 1754

FAMILYMOONS - Travel Agency Services - SANDALS RESORTS INTERNATIONAL; *pg.* 1111, *pg.* 446

FAMILYTALK - Cellular Phone Plan Feature - AT&T MOBILITY LLC; *pg.* 619, *pg.* 488

FAMOUS - Footwear - FAMOUS FOOTWEAR; *pg.* 1808, *pg.* 997

FAMOUS AMOS - Food Product - KELLOGG COMPANY; *pg.* 831, *pg.* 870

THE FAMOUS DELI - Food Product - GIANT EAGLE, INC.; *pg.* 1020, *pg.* 1575

FAMOUS FAMIGLIA - Pizza Restaurant - FAMIGLIA - DEBARTOLO, LLC; *pg.* 1728, *pg.* 1352

FAMOUS GAMES - Video Game - INTERNATIONAL GAME TECHNOLOGY; *pg.* 957, *pg.* 1024

FAMOUS HAIR - Hair Salons - REGIS CORPORATION; *pg.* 521, *pg.* 941

FAMOUS SQWISH CANDY FISH - Candies - PROMOTION IN MOTION, INC.; *pg.* 1861, *pg.* 1052

FAN - Software - DST SYSTEMS, INC.; *pg.* 388, *pg.* 982
FAN - Wall System - SMITH-MIDLAND CORPORATION; *pg.* 111, *pg.* 1795
FAN FACE - Sport Product - FRANKLIN SPORTS, INC.; *pg.* 1834, *pg.* 847
FAN MAIL - Software - DST SYSTEMS, INC.; *pg.* 388, *pg.* 982
FAN MASTER - Brace & Box - WESTINGHOUSE LIGHTING CORPORATION; *pg.* 687, *pg.* 1571
FAN-OUT FAILOVER - Computer Software - NOVELL INC.; *pg.* 446, *pg.* 852
FAN WEB - Software - DST SYSTEMS, INC.; *pg.* 388, *pg.* 982
FANATICAL SUPPORT - Customer Services - RACKSPACE HOSTING, INC.; *pg.* 1277, *pg.* 1742
FANCOM - Poultry System - CTB INTERNATIONAL CORP.; *pg.* 850, *pg.* 695
FANCY - Fabric - NEMSCHOFF, INC.; *pg.* 936, *pg.* 1890
FANCY FEAST - Pet Care Product - NESTLE PURINA PETCARE COMPANY; *pg.* 1479, *pg.* 1000
FANDANGO - Bedding - CROSCILL, INC.; *pg.* 1122, *pg.* 1220
FANDANGOS - Corn Snack - FRITO-LAY NORTH AMERICA, INC.; *pg.* 1853, *pg.* 1730
FANDANGOS - Corn Snacks - PEPSICO, INC.; *pg.* 259, *pg.* 1327
FANFARE - Workforce Motivation Strategies Product - CX ACT, INC.; *pg.* 1394, *pg.* 1773
FANFARE - Food Product - MARS, INCORPORATED; *pg.* 1858, *pg.* 1792
FANFARE - Dynamic Video - SANDISK CORPORATION; *pg.* 465, *pg.* 147
FANFARES - Shoes - CALERES, INC.; *pg.* 1805, *pg.* 993
FANG - Footwear - LACROSSE FOOTWEAR, INC.; *pg.* 1811, *pg.* 1503
FANGORIA - Magazine - STARLOG GROUP, INC.; *pg.* 1689, *pg.* 1296
FANNIE MAY - Confections - 1-800-FLOWERS.COM, INC.; *pg.* 1758, *pg.* 1151
FANPOP - Pop Cultural Site - SPINMEDIA; *pg.* 1282, *pg.* 104
FANS FIRST - Motorsports Entertainment - SPEEDWAY MOTORSPORTS, INC.; *pg.* 584, *pg.* 1370
FANSPRAY - Paint Nozzle Pattern - SHERWIN-WILLIAMS DIVERSIFIED BRANDS DIVISION; *pg.* 1448, *pg.* 1435
FANTA - Soft Drink - THE COCA-COLA COMPANY; *pg.* 240, *pg.* 493
FANTA FREE - Beverages - THE COCA-COLA COMPANY; *pg.* 240, *pg.* 493
FANTA LIGHT - Beverages - THE COCA-COLA COMPANY; *pg.* 240, *pg.* 493
FANTA VERDIA - Beverages - THE COCA-COLA COMPANY; *pg.* 240, *pg.* 493
FANTA ZERO - Beverages - THE COCA-COLA COMPANY; *pg.* 240, *pg.* 493
FANTACY - Footwear - STEVEN MADDEN, LTD.; *pg.* 1819, *pg.* 1176
FANTASIA - Fabric - NEMSCHOFF, INC.; *pg.* 936, *pg.* 1890
FANTASIE - Color - FERRO CORPORATION; *pg.* 1162, *pg.* 1462
FANTASTIC 4 - Toy & Game - HASBRO, INC.; *pg.* 954, *pg.* 1603
FANTASTIC FORTUNES - Lottery Game - IOWA LOTTERY; *pg.* 996, *pg.* 705
FANTASTIC FOUR - Game - ACTIVISION BLIZZARD, INC.; *pg.* 948, *pg.* 271
FANTASTIC FOUR - Toy & Game - HASBRO, INC.; *pg.* 954, *pg.* 1603
FANTASTIC SAM'S - Hair Salon Franchisor - DESSANGE INTERNATIONAL, INC.; *pg.* 506, *pg.* 787
FANTASTIK - Cleaning Product - S.C. JOHNSON & SON, INC.; *pg.* 334, *pg.* 1889
FANTASTIK ALL-PURPOSE - Cleaner - S.C. JOHNSON & SON, INC.; *pg.* 334, *pg.* 1889
FANTASTIK BLEACH - Cleaner - S.C. JOHNSON & SON, INC.; *pg.* 334, *pg.* 1889
FANTASTIK LEMON POWER - Cleaner - S.C. JOHNSON & SON, INC.; *pg.* 334, *pg.* 1889
FANTASTIK MULTI-SURFACE WIPE - Cleaner - S.C. JOHNSON & SON, INC.; *pg.* 334, *pg.* 1889
FANTASTIK ORANGE ACTION - Cleaner - S.C. JOHNSON & SON, INC.; *pg.* 334, *pg.* 1889
FANTASTIK ORANGE WIPE - Cleaner - S.C. JOHNSON & SON, INC.; *pg.* 334, *pg.* 1889
FANTASTIK OXY POWER - Cleaner - S.C. JOHNSON & SON, INC.; *pg.* 334, *pg.* 1889
FANTASY 5 - Lottery Game - ARIZONA LOTTERY; *pg.* 988, *pg.* 14
FANTASY 5 - Lottery Tickets - CALIFORNIA LOTTERY; *pg.* 990, *pg.* 196
FANTASY 5 - Lottery Game - THE FLORIDA LOTTERY; *pg.* 992, *pg.* 469
FANTASY 5 - Lottery Game - GEORGIA LOTTERY CORPORATION; *pg.* 993, *pg.* 506
FANTASY 5 - Game - MICHIGAN STATE LOTTERY BUREAU; *pg.* 999, *pg.* 895
FANTASYLAND - Amusement Park - THE WALT DISNEY COMPANY; *pg.* 317, *pg.* 52
FANUC - Robotic - WELDON SOLUTIONS; *pg.* 1388, *pg.* 1598
FANUC ROBOTICS - Automated Grinding Process - WELDON SOLUTIONS; *pg.* 1388, *pg.* 1598
FAO SCHWARZ - Retail Toy Stores - TOYS "R" US, INC.; *pg.* 968, *pg.* 1130
FAR AWAY - Beauty Product - AVON PRODUCTS, INC.; *pg.* 500, *pg.* 1198
FAR COAST - Beverages - THE COCA-COLA COMPANY; *pg.* 240, *pg.* 493
FAR CRY - Video Game - UBISOFT INC.; *pg.* 589, *pg.* 229
FAR EAST FORTUNES - Game - WMS INDUSTRIES INC.; *pg.* 593, *pg.* 666
FAR EASTERN ECONOMIC REVIEW - Magazine - DOW JONES & COMPANY, INC.; *pg.* 1637, *pg.* 1225
FAR-PUL - Light-Duty Belt Clamp - FLEXIBLE STEEL LACING COMPANY; *pg.* 1337, *pg.* 608
FARADAY - Fire Alarm Systems - FARADAY; *pg.* 638, *pg.* 1066
FARADAY - Monitoring Instrument - GE ENERGY; *pg.* 1338, *pg.* 506
FARADFLEX - Buried Capacitance Material - SANMINA-SCI CORPORATION; *pg.* 671, *pg.* 250
FARAH - Apparel - PERRY ELLIS INTERNATIONAL, INC.; *pg.* 45, *pg.* 445
FARBERWARE - Cutlery, Kitchen Tools & Gadgets & Cutting Boardss - LIFETIME BRANDS, INC.; *pg.* 1127, *pg.* 1161
FARGO - Power Systems - HUBBELL INCORPORATED; *pg.* 1299, *pg.* 370
FARM - Filter - VICOR CORPORATION; *pg.* 1435, *pg.* 783
FARM & RANCH - Pet Food - INTERMOUNTAIN FARMERS ASSOCIATION; *pg.* 705, *pg.* 1759
FARM COLLECTOR - Monthly Magazine - OGDEN PUBLICATIONS, INC.; *pg.* 1672, *pg.* 722
FARM FRESH - Grocery Store - FARM FRESH INC.; *pg.* 1019, *pg.* 1810
FARM FRESH - Food Product - SUPERVALU, INC.; *pg.* 1035, *pg.* 924
FARM FRESH FOODS - Food Service Product - MICHAEL FOODS, INC.; *pg.* 877, *pg.* 949
FARM MART - Farm Supply Distributors/Retailers - PRO GROUP, INC.; *pg.* 1782, *pg.* 331
FARM PLUS - Hobby & Part-time Farmer Farm Supply Store - SOUTHERN STATES COOPERATIVE, INC.; *pg.* 1482, *pg.* 1804
FARM RICH - Non-Dairy Creamer - RICH PRODUCTS CORPORATION; *pg.* 892, *pg.* 1150
FARM SPECIALIST - Trademark & Agricultural Wheels & Tires - CARLISLE TIRE & WHEEL COMPANY; *pg.* 1880, *pg.* 1612
FARM-TASTIC - Educational Product - BARKER CREEK PUBLISHING INC.; *pg.* 1619, *pg.* 1818
FARMAN'S - Pickles - TREEHOUSE FOODS, INC.; *pg.* 901, *pg.* 649
FARMASTER - Gates; S&K Tanks; Feeders - BEHLEN MFG. CO.; *pg.* 701, *pg.* 1010
FARMATIC - On-Farm Feed Processing - A.T. FERRELL COMPANY, INC.; *pg.* 701, *pg.* 674
FARMER BOY - Meat Products - WORLDWIDE FOOD PRODUCTS INC.; *pg.* 910, *pg.* 1170
FARMER JOHN - Meats - CLOUGHERTY PACKING COMPANY; *pg.* 848, *pg.* 128
FARMERS CHOICE BRAND FOOD PRODUCTS - Food Product - PROMOTION IN MOTION, INC.; *pg.* 1861, *pg.* 1052
FARMERS MARKET - Vegetable Salad - UNITED DAIRY FARMERS, INC.; *pg.* 906, *pg.* 1426
FARMER'S MARKET FRESH - Gardening Seed Kits - AEROGROW INTERNATIONAL, INC.; *pg.* 1393, *pg.* 310
FARMER'S PRIDE - Natural Chicken - FARMERS PRIDE, INC.; *pg.* 855, *pg.* 1534
FARMETRICS - Educational Program - BUNGE LIMITED; *pg.* 842, *pg.* 1351
FARMFLEX - Credit Card Financing Program - MONSANTO; *pg.* 1798, *pg.* 1399
FARMHAND - Loaders - AGCO CORPORATION; *pg.* 700, *pg.* 530
FARMHOUSE - Eggs - CAL-MAINE FOODS, INC.; *pg.* 843, *pg.* 969
FARMHOUSE - Bread - PEPPERIDGE FARM, INC.; *pg.* 888, *pg.* 363
FARMINGTON - Bath Product - KOHLER CO.; *pg.* 91, *pg.* 1862
FARMLAND - Food Products - SMITHFIELD FOODS, INC.; *pg.* 896, *pg.* 1806
FARMSTED - Metal Building System - BUTLER MANUFACTURING COMPANY; *pg.* 72, *pg.* 981
FARMVILLE - Online Game - ZYNGA INC.; *pg.* 1292, *pg.* 235
FARPOINT - Software - EMC CORPORATION; *pg.* 391, *pg.* 825
FARRAR, STRAUS & GIROUX - Books - FARRAR, STRAUS & GIROUX, INC.; *pg.* 1640, *pg.* 1231
FARRIS - Dress Shoes - JOHNSTON & MURPHY CO.; *pg.* 1810, *pg.* 1651
FARROWSURE - Swine Vaccine - PFIZER INC.; *pg.* 1581, *pg.* 1278
FAS - Bagging Machine - AUTOMATED PACKAGING SYSTEMS INC.; *pg.* 1452, *pg.* 1474
FAS - Banking Software - JACK HENRY & ASSOCIATES, INC.; *pg.* 422, *pg.* 988
FAS GAS - Retail Automotive Fuel & Convenience Products - PARKLAND FUEL CORPORATION; *pg.* 983, *pg.* 1906
FAS-PIK - Hair Accessories - STA-RITE GINNIE LOU, INC.; *pg.* 523, *pg.* 660
FAS TRAK - Mower Tractor - EXCEL INDUSTRIES, INC.; *pg.* 1795, *pg.* 715
FAS2000 SERIES SOFTWARE PACKS - Software - NETAPP, INC.; *pg.* 444, *pg.* 287
FAS3100 SERIES - Software - NETAPP, INC.; *pg.* 444, *pg.* 287
FAS6000 SERIES - Software - NETAPP, INC.; *pg.* 444, *pg.* 287
FASCAL - Cast Vinyls - AVERY DENNISON CORPORATION; *pg.* 1452, *pg.* 95
FASCIASOFT - Software - ANC SPORTS ENTERPRISES, LLC; *pg.* 1825, *pg.* 1325
FASCLEAR - Label Film - AVERY DENNISON CORPORATION; *pg.* 1452, *pg.* 95
FASCOPY - High Quality Self Adhesive for use in Copy Machines - AVERY DENNISON CORPORATION; *pg.* 1452, *pg.* 95
FASHION - Footwear - P.W. MINOR & SON, INC.; *pg.* 1816, *pg.* 1140
FASHION AVENUE - Toy - MATTEL, INC.; *pg.* 962, *pg.* 81
FASHION BUG - Junior, Misses Apparel & Large Size Apparel - ASCENA RETAIL GROUP, INC.; *pg.* 18, *pg.* 1081
FASHION BUG PLUS - Large Size Women's Apparel - ASCENA RETAIL GROUP, INC.; *pg.* 18, *pg.* 1081
FASHION FAIR - Cosmetics - JOHNSON PUBLISHING COMPANY, INC.; *pg.* 1655, *pg.* 579
FASHION FAIR COSMETICS - Cosmetics - JOHNSON PUBLISHING COMPANY, INC.; *pg.* 1655, *pg.* 579
FASHION FINISH - Dry Cleaning & Laundry Product - ADCO, INC.; *pg.* 325, *pg.* 482
FASHION FLAKES - Dry Cleaning & Laundry Product - ADCO, INC.; *pg.* 325, *pg.* 482
FASHION FLEECE - Ear Warmer - 180S, LLC; *pg.* 1824, *pg.* 754
FASHION NAUTIQUE - Clothing Line - CORRECT CRAFT, INC.; *pg.* 1706, *pg.* 452
FASHION PLEAT - Window Shades - SPRINGS GLOBAL, INC.; *pg.* 698, *pg.* 1616
FASHION SEAL - Apparel - SUPERIOR UNIFORM GROUP, INC.; *pg.* 33, *pg.* 468
FASHION SEAL HEALTHCARE - Apparel - SUPERIOR UNIFORM GROUP, INC.; *pg.* 33, *pg.* 468
FASHUN - Laundry Product - BIRKO CORPORATION; *pg.* 1149, *pg.* 332
FASKURE FT - General Purpose Resin Coated Sand - HEXION; *pg.* 1166, *pg.* 1440
FASKUT - Dental Product - DENTSPLY INTERNATIONAL INC.; *pg.* 1522, *pg.* 1596
FASS - Computer Software - ASTRO-MED, INC.; *pg.* 619, *pg.* 1609
FASS-DRI - Coating - MAINTENANCE, INC.; *pg.* 95, *pg.* 1482
FASSON - Adhesives - AVERY DENNISON CORPORATION;

First page reference indicates Business Class Edition
Second page reference indicates Geographic Edition

pg. 1452, *pg.* 95
FAST - Flux - LA-CO INDUSTRIES MARKAL CO., INC.; *pg.* 1170, *pg.* 610
FAST - Sealer - THE SAVOGRAN COMPANY; *pg.* 1447, *pg.* 840
FAST - Foam Scrubbing System - TENNANT COMPANY; *pg.* 1381, *pg.* 944
FAST ACCESS - Semiconductor Solution - CYPRESS SEMICONDUCTOR CORPORATION; *pg.* 1326, *pg.* 243
FAST ACTION DRAW POKER - Video Poker - INTERNATIONAL GAME TECHNOLOGY; *pg.* 957, *pg.* 1024
FAST AND FRIENDLY! - Tagline - ANTHRO CORPORATION; *pg.* 913, *pg.* 1509
FAST APPLICATION PROXY - Software - F5 NETWORKS, INC.; *pg.* 396, *pg.* 1835
FAST-BALL - Lubrication Transfer Pumps - GRACO, INC.; *pg.* 1342, *pg.* 935
FAST BITES - Food Product - ADVANCEPIERRE FOODS, INC.; *pg.* 1714, *pg.* 1409
FAST BLAST - Jar Adaptor - BADGER AIR BRUSH COMPANY; *pg.* 359, *pg.* 612
FAST BLAST - Software - BIO-RAD LABORATORIES, INC.; *pg.* 1504, *pg.* 101
FAST BREAK - Candy Bars - THE HERSHEY CO.; *pg.* 1855, *pg.* 1538
FAST CACHE - Software - F5 NETWORKS, INC.; *pg.* 396, *pg.* 1835
FAST CASH - Game - MISSOURI LOTTERY; *pg.* 999, *pg.* 979
FAST CASH - Lottery Game - OHIO LOTTERY COMMISSION; *pg.* 1002, *pg.* 1433
FAST CAST - Gypsum Cement - USG CORPORATION; *pg.* 118, *pg.* 594
FAST CAT - Cure Accelerator - SMOOTH-ON INC.; *pg.* 111, *pg.* 1528
FAST CAT - Molecular Probe Product - THERMO FISHER SCIENTIFIC INC.; *pg.* 1602, *pg.* 61
FAST-CATH - Cardiology & Vascular Access Products - ST. JUDE MEDICAL, INC.; *pg.* 1596, *pg.* 963
FAST CHART - Charts - CHYRONHEGO; *pg.* 371, *pg.* 1179
FAST CHOICE - Food Product - ADVANCEPIERRE FOODS, INC.; *pg.* 1714, *pg.* 1409
FAST COMPANY - Business Magazine - MANSUETO VENTURES LLC; *pg.* 1661, *pg.* 1256
FAST DRYING SCULPTING SPRAY - Hair Care Product - JOHN PAUL MITCHELL SYSTEMS; *pg.* 512, *pg.* 133
FAST FARE - Convenience Stores - CROWN CENTRAL LLC; *pg.* 975, *pg.* 756
FAST FINISH - Food Product - TYSON FOODS, INC.; *pg.* 902, *pg.* 35
FAST-FIRE'D - Pizza Franchise - BLAZE PIZZA LLC; *pg.* 1716, *pg.* 179
FAST-FLAP - Surgical Instrument - OSTEOMED CORPORATION; *pg.* 1425, *pg.* 1658
FAST/FLEX - Baseboard Connectors - SLANT/FIN CORPORATION; *pg.* 1076, *pg.* 1163
FAST-FLO - Pumps - GRACO, INC.; *pg.* 1342, *pg.* 935
FAST FLUID MANAGEMENT - Fluid Dispensing, Metering & Mixing Equipment - IDEX CORPORATION; *pg.* 1347, *pg.* 623
FAST-FOLD - Screen - DA-LITE SCREEN COMPANY; *pg.* 632, *pg.* 698
FAST-FOLD DELUXE - Portable Folding Screen - DA-LITE SCREEN COMPANY; *pg.* 632, *pg.* 698
FAST-FOLD TRUSS - Portable Folding Screen - DA-LITE SCREEN COMPANY; *pg.* 632, *pg.* 698
FAST FOOD & FUEL - Retail Fuel & Convenience Stores - DELEK US HOLDINGS, INC.; *pg.* 975, *pg.* 1627
FAST FORWARD ICE - Refrigerator Ice Dispensing System - WHIRLPOOL CORPORATION; *pg.* 62, *pg.* 872
FAST FORWARD INVENTING THE FUTURE - Multimedia Exploration - MUSEUM OF SCIENCE AND INDUSTRY; *pg.* 565, *pg.* 583
FAST FORWORD - Software - SCIENTIFIC LEARNING CORPORATION; *pg.* 607, *pg.* 172
FAST FORWORD BASICS - Software - SCIENTIFIC LEARNING CORPORATION; *pg.* 607, *pg.* 172
FAST FORWORD BOOKSHELF - Software - SCIENTIFIC LEARNING CORPORATION; *pg.* 607, *pg.* 172
FAST FORWORD LANGUAGE - Software - SCIENTIFIC LEARNING CORPORATION; *pg.* 607, *pg.* 172
FAST FRAME - Adjustable Frame - MARTIN/F. WEBER COMPANY; *pg.* 962, *pg.* 1567
FAST HULL - Systems Integration & Aeronautics - LOCKHEED MARTIN CORPORATION; *pg.* 229, *pg.* 762
FAST JACKS - Lottery Game - LOUISIANA LOTTERY CORPORATION; *pg.* 997, *pg.* 742
FAST-KILL - Rodent Control - THE WOODSTREAM CORPORATION; *pg.* 1801, *pg.* 1549
FAST LANE - Convenience Stores - THE PANTRY, INC.; *pg.* 1029, *pg.* 1360
FAST MAPS - Mapping Service - CHYRONHEGO; *pg.* 371, *pg.* 1179
FAST MARK - Colorant - POLYONE CORPORATION; *pg.* 1177, *pg.* 1404
FAST MOBILITY PARTICLE SIZER - Spectrometer - TSI INCORPORATED; *pg.* 1432, *pg.* 965
FAST MONEY - Video Game - INTERNATIONAL GAME TECHNOLOGY; *pg.* 957, *pg.* 1024
FAST 'N EASY - Wire Feeder - ELECTRON BEAM TECHNOLOGIES, INC.; *pg.* 1046, *pg.* 621
FAST 'N FIRM - Seam Sealer - 3M COMPANY; *pg.* 1142, *pg.* 956
FAST PACK - Crushing System - ASTEC INDUSTRIES, INC.; *pg.* 69, *pg.* 1628
FAST PACK - Portable Crushing-Screening-Stockpiling Plant - KPI-JCI; *pg.* 1354, *pg.* 1626
FAST PADDLE - Fully Automatic Selfadjusting Tilt - HOLOGIC, INC.; *pg.* 1416, *pg.* 784
FAST-PAK - Bag - PACTIV CORPORATION; *pg.* 1466, *pg.* 624
FAST-PAK - Equipped Scrubbers - TENNANT COMPANY; *pg.* 1381, *pg.* 944
FAST-PASS - Insulation Product - ST. JUDE MEDICAL, INC.; *pg.* 1596, *pg.* 963
FAST PATH - Software - BMC SOFTWARE, INC.; *pg.* 362, *pg.* 1701
FAST PLAY - Lottery Game - ARIZONA LOTTERY; *pg.* 988, *pg.* 14
FAST POWER LEARNING - Software - SCIENTIFIC LEARNING CORPORATION; *pg.* 607, *pg.* 172
FAST QUOTE - Stock Exchange Service - CHYRONHEGO; *pg.* 371, *pg.* 1179
FAST READ - Medical Apparatus - WALGREEN CO.; *pg.* 1608, *pg.* 605
FAST ROOF - Computer Software System - BUTLER MANUFACTURING COMPANY; *pg.* 72, *pg.* 981
FAST-SPEC - Hand Held Information System - THEXTON MANUFACTURING COMPANY, INC.; *pg.* 218, *pg.* 925
FAST TO MARKET - Plastic Processing Technology - WENTWORTH TECHNOLOGIES CO. LTD.; *pg.* 1891, *pg.* 1919
FAST TRACK - Fluid Handling System - GRACO, INC.; *pg.* 1342, *pg.* 935
FAST TRACK - Candy - LIFETIME PRODUCTS INC.; *pg.* 933, *pg.* 1751
FAST-TRACK - Steel - THE TIMKEN COMPANY; *pg.* 218, *pg.* 1408
FAST TRAX - Crushers - ASTEC INDUSTRIES, INC.; *pg.* 69, *pg.* 1628
FAST TWITCH - Energy Drink - CYTOSPORT, INC.; *pg.* 1018, *pg.* 45
FAST WX - Online Integrated Graphics Tools - CHYRONHEGO; *pg.* 371, *pg.* 1179
FASTACCESS - DSL Service - AT&T SOUTHEAST; *pg.* 1868, *pg.* 489
FASTACK - Rivet - ALLFAST FASTENING SYSTEMS, INC.; *pg.* 1041, *pg.* 66
FASTACK RIVET - Blind Rivet - ALLFAST FASTENING SYSTEMS, INC.; *pg.* 1041, *pg.* 66
FASTAGGER - Tagging Tool - WEBER PACKAGING SOLUTIONS, INC.; *pg.* 491, *pg.* 554
FASTAPE - Tape - DEMCO INC.; *pg.* 386, *pg.* 1865
FASTBACK - Cab Fairing - LUND INTERNATIONAL, INC.; *pg.* 211, *pg.* 526
FASTBATT - Insulating System - OWENS CORNING; *pg.* 102, *pg.* 1476
FASTBEAM - Software - BLUELINX HOLDINGS, INC.; *pg.* 70, *pg.* 491
FASTBINDERS - Binder - BROWN & BIGELOW, INC.; *pg.* 1624, *pg.* 959
FASTBLOCK - Insulation - ESTERLINE TECHNOLOGIES CORPORATION; *pg.* 1412, *pg.* 1814
FASTBOND - Contact Cements - 3M COMPANY; *pg.* 1142, *pg.* 956
FASTBOY - Bicycle Accessories - SPECIALIZED BICYCLE COMPONENTS, INC.; *pg.* 1711, *pg.* 152
FASTCAT - Rubber - SMOOTH-ON INC.; *pg.* 111, *pg.* 1528
FASTCOMPANY.COM - Business Site - MANSUETO VENTURES LLC; *pg.* 1661, *pg.* 1256
FASTDRAW - Games - PENN NATIONAL GAMING, INC.; *pg.* 574, *pg.* 1595
FASTEDGE - Clock & Buffer Product - CYPRESS SEMICONDUCTOR CORPORATION; *pg.* 1326, *pg.* 243
FASTEEL - Furnace - TENOVA; *pg.* 114, *pg.* 1525
FASTEN MATES - Plastic Buckles - YKK CORPORATION OF AMERICA; *pg.* 699, *pg.* 536
FASTENMASTER - Fasteners - OMG, INC.; *pg.* 1367, *pg.* 781
FASTER START, FINER FINISH - Tagline - FOAMPRO MANUFACTURING, INC.; *pg.* 1442, *pg.* 110
FASTERCASTER - Alignment System Software - HUNTER ENGINEERING COMPANY; *pg.* 208, *pg.* 973
FASTEX - Premixed Texture - USG CORPORATION; *pg.* 118, *pg.* 594
FASTEYE - Software System - MENTOR GRAPHICS CORPORATION; *pg.* 432, *pg.* 1510
FASTFIND - Computer Software - WAIGLOBAL; *pg.* 221, *pg.* 1585
FASTFIT - Interior Wood Door - MASONITE INTERNATIONAL CORPORATION; *pg.* 1054, *pg.* 1920
FASTIME - Time Capture & Reporting - EQUIFAX WORKFORCE SOLUTIONS; *pg.* 394, *pg.* 997
FASTIPS - Dental Product - DENTSPLY INTERNATIONAL INC.; *pg.* 1522, *pg.* 1596
FASTJUNCTION - Electronic Components - MOLEX INCORPORATED; *pg.* 655, *pg.* 628
FASTLAB - Laboratory Equipment - GENERAL ELECTRIC COMPANY; *pg.* 1297, *pg.* 347
FASTMATH - Educational Materials - SCHOLASTIC INC.; *pg.* 1683, *pg.* 1288
FASTMELT - Furnace - TENOVA; *pg.* 114, *pg.* 1525
FASTMESH - Optical Switch System - CIENA CORPORATION; *pg.* 628, *pg.* 771
FASTMIPS - Semiconductor Device - IMAGINATION TECHNOLOGIES; *pg.* 412, *pg.* 285
FAST'N FINAL - Repair Product - DAP PRODUCTS, INC.; *pg.* 1441, *pg.* 756
FASTNET - Catalyst - BASF CATALYSTS LLC; *pg.* 1148, *pg.* 1074
FASTPAC - Inserting System - PITNEY BOWES INC.; *pg.* 454, *pg.* 376
FASTPAK - Mailer Product - POLYAIR INTER PACK INC.; *pg.* 1467, *pg.* 1941
FASTPLAN - Medical System - VARIAN MEDICAL SYSTEMS, INC.; *pg.* 1434, *pg.* 178
FASTPROP - De-Icing Technology - UTC AEROSPACE SYSTEMS; *pg.* 236, *pg.* 1369
FASTRAC - Shower - BRADLEY CORPORATION; *pg.* 71, *pg.* 1870
FASTRACE - Medical Equipment - CONMED CORPORATION; *pg.* 1517, *pg.* 1347
FASTRACK - Snowmobile - ARCTIC CAT INC.; *pg.* 1705, *pg.* 953
FASTRAK - Self-propelled Lawn Mower - EXCEL INDUSTRIES, INC.; *pg.* 1795, *pg.* 715
FASTRAK - Systems Integration & Aeronautics - LOCKHEED MARTIN CORPORATION; *pg.* 229, *pg.* 762
FASTRAX - High Performance Door - RITE-HITE HOLDING CORPORATION; *pg.* 1372, *pg.* 1880
FASTREE - Software - MICROWAY, INC.; *pg.* 1267, *pg.* 841
FASTRING - Geophone Land Case System - ION GEOPHYSICAL CORPORATION; *pg.* 1350, *pg.* 1708
FASTRIP - Brush Cleaner - UNITED GILSONITE LABORATORIES; *pg.* 1449, *pg.* 1527
FASTSCAN - Software System - MENTOR GRAPHICS CORPORATION; *pg.* 432, *pg.* 1510
FASTSCAN - Scanner - OMRON SCIENTIFIC TECHNOLOGIES INCORPORATED; *pg.* 1425, *pg.* 91
FASTSENSE - Tape Drive - QUANTUM CORPORATION; *pg.* 458, *pg.* 250
FASTSET - Adhesive - H.B. FULLER COMPANY; *pg.* 1165, *pg.* 961
FASTSET - Concrete Product - QUIKRETE COMPANIES; *pg.* 106, *pg.* 519
FASTSTART - Software System - MENTOR GRAPHICS CORPORATION; *pg.* 432, *pg.* 1510
FASTTRACK - Interconnect Routing Structure - ALTERA CORPORATION; *pg.* 348, *pg.* 237
FASTTRACK - Software - INSTRON CORPORATION; *pg.* 1349, *pg.* 839
FASTTRACK - Communication Product - NUMEREX CORP.; *pg.* 660, *pg.* 517
FASTTRACK - Molecular Biology Product - THERMO FISHER

SCIENTIFIC INC.; *pg.* 1602, *pg.* 61
FASTTRACK CONSULTING - Software System - MENTOR GRAPHICS CORPORATION; *pg.* 432, *pg.* 1510
FAT BOY - Motorcycle - HARLEY-DAVIDSON, INC.; *pg.* 178, *pg.* 1874
FAT BURNER - Weight Control Product - NATROL, INC.; *pg.* 1570, *pg.* 64
FAT CAT - Table Soccer Tables - GLD PRODUCTS, INC.; *pg.* 1835, *pg.* 1882
FAT CAT TRIPLER - Lottery Game - OHIO LOTTERY COMMISSION; *pg.* 1002, *pg.* 1433
FAT CAT TRIPLER - Lottery Game - WEST VIRGINIA LOTTERY; *pg.* 1011, *pg.* 1849
FAT CHECK - Food Product - ADVANCEPIERRE FOODS, INC.; *pg.* 1714, *pg.* 1409
FAT FREDDIE - Meat Snacks - CARL BUDDIG & COMPANY; *pg.* 846, *pg.* 619
FAT GRABBERS - Health Care Product - NATURE'S SUNSHINE PRODUCTS, INC.; *pg.* 1571, *pg.* 1754
FAT MAGNET - Nutritional Product - NUTRACEUTICAL INTERNATIONAL CORPORATION; *pg.* 1576, *pg.* 1753
FAT PACK - Power Tool - MILWAUKEE ELECTRIC TOOL CORP.; *pg.* 1056, *pg.* 1855
FAT PAYDAY - Pulltab Game - IDAHO LOTTERY; *pg.* 995, *pg.* 547
FAT-STACK - Seating - HUSSEY SEATING CO.; *pg.* 929, *pg.* 751
FAT TIRE AMBER ALE - Beer - NEW BELGIUM BREWING COMPANY, INC.; *pg.* 258, *pg.* 328
FAT-X - Nutritional Product - NUTRACEUTICAL INTERNATIONAL CORPORATION; *pg.* 1576, *pg.* 1753
FATBOY - Toy Train - LIONEL LLC; *pg.* 961, *pg.* 875
FATBOY - Bicycle - SPECIALIZED BICYCLE COMPONENTS, INC.; *pg.* 1711, *pg.* 152
FATE MAGAZINE - Magazine - LLEWELLYN WORLDWIDE LIMITED; *pg.* 1660, *pg.* 967
FATE: THE CARNIVALE GAME - Game - HOME BOX OFFICE, INC.; *pg.* 290, *pg.* 1240
FATGIRL - Bicycle Accessories - SPECIALIZED BICYCLE COMPONENTS, INC.; *pg.* 1711, *pg.* 152
FATHOM - IP Network Analysis Tool to Measure Video Performance - APPLIED GLOBAL TECHNOLOGIES; *pg.* 352, *pg.* 460
FATHOM - Medical Device - BOSTON SCIENTIFIC CORPORATION; *pg.* 1508, *pg.* 831
FATHOM - Social Impact Travel - CARNIVAL CRUISE LINES; *pg.* 1902, *pg.* 441
FATHOM - Filtration Product - KIMBERLY-CLARK CORPORATION; *pg.* 1461, *pg.* 1720
FATHOM - Fabric - NEMSCHOFF, INC.; *pg.* 936, *pg.* 1890
FATHOM - Software - PROGRESS SOFTWARE CORPORATION; *pg.* 457, *pg.* 786
FATMAX - Hand Tools - STANLEY BLACK & DECKER, INC.; *pg.* 1063, *pg.* 358
FAUCHEUX - Loader - ALAMO GROUP INC.; *pg.* 1311, *pg.* 1745
FAULKNER - Reading Glass - A. T. CROSS COMPANY; *pg.* 339, *pg.* 1602
FAULT EVALUATOR - Computer Software - COMPUTER SCIENCES CORPORATION; *pg.* 378, *pg.* 1780
FAULT TAMER - Fuse Limiter - S&C ELECTRIC COMPANY; *pg.* 1305, *pg.* 589
FAUST - Seafood - TRIDENT SEAFOODS CORPORATION; *pg.* 902, *pg.* 1842
FAUVISM - Fabric - NEMSCHOFF, INC.; *pg.* 936, *pg.* 1890
FAUX FINESSE - Paint And Stain Product - BENJAMIN MOORE & CO.; *pg.* 1440, *pg.* 1085
FAUX FUR - Glove - KOMBI, LTD.; *pg.* 1838, *pg.* 1766
FAUX SUEDE - Bath Accessory - CROSCILL, INC.; *pg.* 1122, *pg.* 1220
FAUX TIN - Mirror - ETHAN ALLEN INTERIORS INC.; *pg.* 924, *pg.* 343
FAVERSHAM HALL - Furniture - BASSETT FURNITURE INDUSTRIES, INCORPORATED; *pg.* 916, *pg.* 1776
FAVES AND CRAVES - Food Product - SONIC CORP.; *pg.* 1750, *pg.* 1487
FAVOR - Furniture Polish - S.C. JOHNSON & SON, INC.; *pg.* 334, *pg.* 1889
FAVORITE - Bird Seed - INTERMOUNTAIN FARMERS ASSOCIATION; *pg.* 705, *pg.* 1759
FAVORITE MARKETS - Retail Fuel & Convenience Stores - DELEK US HOLDINGS, INC.; *pg.* 975, *pg.* 1627
FAVORITES - Mail Order Catalog - LILLIAN VERNON CORPORATION; *pg.* 1776, *pg.* 315
FAWICK - Clutch & Brake - EATON CORPORATION; *pg.* 1331, *pg.* 1429
FAX OF LIFE - Shoe - AEROGROUP INTERNATIONAL, INC.; *pg.* 1803, *pg.* 1055
FAX2MAIL (STYLIZED) - Telecom Product - PREMIERE GLOBAL SERVICES, INC.; *pg.* 1275, *pg.* 518
FAXASAK - Ordering Form - BIGLARI HOLDINGS INC.; *pg.* 1015, *pg.* 1739
FAXCENTRE - Printer - XEROX CORPORATION; *pg.* 494, *pg.* 365
FAXENABLE - Connector - MOLEX INCORPORATED; *pg.* 655, *pg.* 628
FAXES - Camera - KONICA MINOLTA BUSINESS SOLUTIONS USA, INC.; *pg.* 1419, *pg.* 1113
FAXFINDER - Communication Product - MULTI-TECH SYSTEMS INC.; *pg.* 442, *pg.* 951
FAXREACH - Telecom Product - PREMIERE GLOBAL SERVICES, INC.; *pg.* 1275, *pg.* 518
FAXSONIC - Computer Equipment - VIEWSONIC CORPORATION; *pg.* 489, *pg.* 303
FAXSTF - Software - SMITH MICRO SOFTWARE, INC.; *pg.* 471, *pg.* 41
FAYE - Clothing - ABERCROMBIE & FITCH CO.; *pg.* 37, *pg.* 1466
FAYETTEVILLE ONLINE - Website - FAYETTEVILLE PUBLISHING CO.; *pg.* 1641, *pg.* 1372
FAYGO - Soft Drink - NATIONAL BEVERAGE CORP.; *pg.* 257, *pg.* 425
FAZACLO - Pharmaceutical Preparations - AVANIR PHARMACEUTICALS; *pg.* 1498, *pg.* 40
FAZEPRO - Drill-In Fluid - M-I SWACO; *pg.* 980, *pg.* 1710
FAZOLI'S - Italian Restaurant - FAZOLI'S MANAGEMENT INC.; *pg.* 1728, *pg.* 729
FAZOR - Polymer Product - CHEMTURA CORPORATION; *pg.* 1152, *pg.* 355
FBC - Building Solutions - THE LUBRIZOL CORPORATION; *pg.* 1171, *pg.* 1481
FBRM - Particle System - METTLER-TOLEDO INTERNATIONAL INC.; *pg.* 1423, *pg.* 1441
FBX - Software - AUTODESK INC.; *pg.* 356, *pg.* 257
FC FEMALE CONDOM - Health Care Product - THE FEMALE HEALTH COMPANY; *pg.* 1530, *pg.* 573
FC HOST PLATFORMS - Software - NETAPP, INC.; *pg.* 444, *pg.* 287
FC SAN - Software - NETAPP, INC.; *pg.* 444, *pg.* 287
FC SWITCHES & DIRECTORS - Software - NETAPP, INC.; *pg.* 444, *pg.* 287
FC VELOCITY - Heavy Duty Product - BALLARD POWER SYSTEMS, INC.; *pg.* 70, *pg.* 1907
FCA - Vapor Phase Activated Carbons - CALGON CARBON CORPORATION; *pg.* 1151, *pg.* 1574
FCCSP - Packaging Technology - AMKOR TECHNOLOGY, INC.; *pg.* 67, *pg.* 25
FCM - Continuous Mixer - FARREL CORPORATION; *pg.* 1336, *pg.* 337
FCMBGA - Packaging Technology - AMKOR TECHNOLOGY, INC.; *pg.* 67, *pg.* 25
FCOE - Software - NETAPP, INC.; *pg.* 444, *pg.* 287
FCOJ-A - Agriculture Exchange - INTERCONTINENTALEXCHANGE, INC.; *pg.* 769, *pg.* 512
FCP-500 - Smoke Detector - BOSCH SECURITY SYSTEMS, INC.; *pg.* 626, *pg.* 1158
FCS MULE - Unmanned Military Vehicle - LOCKHEED MARTIN CORPORATION; *pg.* 229, *pg.* 762
FCTRACER - Analyzer - TELEDYNE LECROY; *pg.* 1431, *pg.* 1153
FD&C RED CONCENTRATE - Chemical Product - BIRKO CORPORATION; *pg.* 1149, *pg.* 332
FD100 - Payment Processing Hardware - FIRST DATA CORPORATION; *pg.* 754, *pg.* 505
FD300 - Payment Processing Hardware - FIRST DATA CORPORATION; *pg.* 754, *pg.* 505
FD50 - Payment Processing Hardware - FIRST DATA CORPORATION; *pg.* 754, *pg.* 505
FD700SC - Lighting Systems - REVOLUTION LIGHTING TECHNOLOGIES, INC.; *pg.* 1304, *pg.* 377
FD700SP - Lighting Systems - REVOLUTION LIGHTING TECHNOLOGIES, INC.; *pg.* 1304, *pg.* 377
FD701SC - Lighting Systems - REVOLUTION LIGHTING TECHNOLOGIES, INC.; *pg.* 1304, *pg.* 377
FD701SP - Lighting Systems - REVOLUTION LIGHTING TECHNOLOGIES, INC.; *pg.* 1304, *pg.* 377
FD702SC - Lighting Systems - REVOLUTION LIGHTING TECHNOLOGIES, INC.; *pg.* 1304, *pg.* 377
FD702SP - Lighting Systems - REVOLUTION LIGHTING TECHNOLOGIES, INC.; *pg.* 1304, *pg.* 377
FD703SC - Lighting Systems - REVOLUTION LIGHTING TECHNOLOGIES, INC.; *pg.* 1304, *pg.* 377
FD703SP - Lighting Systems - REVOLUTION LIGHTING TECHNOLOGIES, INC.; *pg.* 1304, *pg.* 377
FDC - Fiber Distribution Center - CORNING CABLE SYSTEMS LLC; *pg.* 1407, *pg.* 1378
FDC - Glass & Ceramic Material - CORNING INCORPORATED; *pg.* 1122, *pg.* 1154
FDL (FLOW DEFINITION LANGUAGE) - Software System - MENTOR GRAPHICS CORPORATION; *pg.* 432, *pg.* 1510
FDM - Modeling Technology - STRATASYS, INC.; *pg.* 476, *pg.* 923
FDM MAXUM - Rapid Prototyping System - STRATASYS, INC.; *pg.* 476, *pg.* 923
FDM PROCESS - Begins with Creation of Conceptual Geometric Model on CAD Workstation - STRATASYS, INC.; *pg.* 476, *pg.* 923
FDM TEAM - Software - STRATASYS, INC.; *pg.* 476, *pg.* 923
FDM TITAN - Rapid Prototyping System - STRATASYS, INC.; *pg.* 476, *pg.* 923
FDM VANTAGE - Rapid Prototyping System - STRATASYS, INC.; *pg.* 476, *pg.* 923
FDS - Feminine Spray & Baby Powder - UNILEVER UNITED STATES, INC.; *pg.* 904, *pg.* 1061
FDV SERIES - Electronic Component - EMCORE CORPORATION; *pg.* 636, *pg.* 39
FE-CAP - Electrode Design - KEMET CORPORATION; *pg.* 649, *pg.* 1621
FEAR FANG - Game - HASBRO, INC.; *pg.* 954, *pg.* 1603
FEARN - Baking Goods, Cake Mixes, Misc. Health Food - MODERN PRODUCTS, INC.; *pg.* 1568, *pg.* 1871
FEAST!MAGAZINE - Food Lovers Magazine - GREAT LAKES PUBLISHING COMPANY; *pg.* 1646, *pg.* 1431
FEATHER - Healthcare Product - GF HEALTH PRODUCTS, INC.; *pg.* 1535, *pg.* 508
FEATHER FILL - Polyester Primer Surfacer - ITW - EVERCOAT; *pg.* 1443, *pg.* 1415
FEATHER-FLO - Eye & Face-Wash Fountains & Showers - HAWS CORPORATION; *pg.* 56, *pg.* 1032
FEATHER LITE - Liquid Plastic - SMOOTH-ON INC.; *pg.* 111, *pg.* 1528
FEATHERLIGHT - Fishing Equipment - WRIGHT & MCGILL CO.; *pg.* 1848, *pg.* 324
FEATHERLITE - Scissors - ACME UNITED CORPORATION; *pg.* 1040, *pg.* 346
FEATHERLITE - Lenses - ICARE INDUSTRIES, INC.; *pg.* 1417, *pg.* 463
FEATHERLITE - Rolling Steel Service Door - RAYNOR GARAGE DOORS; *pg.* 106, *pg.* 607
FEATHEROCK - Natural Stone Mining - U.S. PUMICE COMPANY; *pg.* 1185, *pg.* 65
FEATHERWEIGHT - Floor Care Product - BISSELL HOMECARE, INC.; *pg.* 52, *pg.* 887
FEATHERWEIGHT - Mop Handles - GEERPRES INC.; *pg.* 1339, *pg.* 901
FEATHERWEIGHT - Sugar-Free Fructose-Sweetened & Low-Sodium Product - THE HAIN CELESTIAL GROUP, INC.; *pg.* 860, *pg.* 1172
FEBREZE - Room Deodorizers, Sprays & Candles - THE PROCTER & GAMBLE COMPANY; *pg.* 1129, *pg.* 1418
FEBREZE AIR FRESHENERS - Personal & Household Product - THE PROCTER & GAMBLE COMPANY; *pg.* 1129, *pg.* 1418
FEBREZE REFRESHERS - Personal & Household Product - THE PROCTER & GAMBLE COMPANY; *pg.* 1129, *pg.* 1418
FEC - Dryer And Cooler - BUHLER AEROGLIDE; *pg.* 1069, *pg.* 1359
FECTIN - Biomolecule Product - THERMO FISHER SCIENTIFIC INC.; *pg.* 1602, *pg.* 61
FEDERAL - Sporting Ammunition - FEDERAL PREMIUM AMMUNITION; *pg.* 1834, *pg.* 915
FEDERAL APD - Parking & Ground Transportation Systems - FEDERAL SIGNAL CORPORATION; *pg.* 638, *pg.* 645
FEDERAL LABORATORIES - Anti-Riot & Crowd Control Products - BAE SYSTEMS PRODUCTS GROUP; *pg.* 359, *pg.* 432
FEDERAL-MOGUL - Engine Bearings - FEDERAL-MOGUL HOLDINGS CORPORATION; *pg.* 205, *pg.* 907
FEDERATED CLICK 2 PAY - Insurance Service - FEDERATED MUTUAL INSURANCE COMPANY; *pg.* 1200, *pg.* 952
FEDERATED DIRECT - Insurance Service - FEDERATED MUTUAL INSURANCE COMPANY; *pg.* 1200, *pg.* 952
FEDERATED HEALTH CHOICE - Insurance Plan -

First page reference indicates Business Class Edition
Second page reference indicates Geographic Edition

FEDERATED MUTUAL INSURANCE COMPANY; pg. 1200, pg. 952
FEDERATOR - Software - AUTONOMY, INC.; pg. 358, pg. 212
FEDEX 1DAY - Shipping Service - FEDEX CORPORATION; pg. 1907, pg. 1642
FEDEX 2DAY - Shipping Service - FEDEX CORPORATION; pg. 1907, pg. 1642
FEDEX 3DAY - Shipping Service - FEDEX CORPORATION; pg. 1907, pg. 1642
FEDEX ASIAONE - Shipping Service - FEDEX CORPORATION; pg. 1907, pg. 1642
FEDEX ASSOCIATION ADVANTAGE - Shipping Service - FEDEX CORPORATION; pg. 1907, pg. 1642
FEDEX AUTHORIZED SHIPCENTER - Shipping Service - FEDEX CORPORATION; pg. 1907, pg. 1642
FEDEX BUSINESS BONUS - Shipping Service - FEDEX CORPORATION; pg. 1907, pg. 1642
FEDEX CHAMPIONSHIP SERIES - Shipping Service - FEDEX CORPORATION; pg. 1907, pg. 1642
FEDEX CHARTERS - Shipping Service - FEDEX CORPORATION; pg. 1907, pg. 1642
FEDEX COLLECT ON DELIVERY - Shipping Service - FEDEX CORPORATION; pg. 1907, pg. 1642
FEDEX COLLECTION - Shipping Service - FEDEX CORPORATION; pg. 1907, pg. 1642
FEDEX COMMERCE SERVER - Shipping Service - FEDEX CORPORATION; pg. 1907, pg. 1642
FEDEX COSMOS - Shipping Service - FEDEX CORPORATION; pg. 1907, pg. 1642
FEDEX CUSTOM CRITICAL - Shipping Services - FEDEX CORPORATION; pg. 1907, pg. 1642
FEDEX CUSTOMER RESOURCE CENTER - Shipping Service - FEDEX CORPORATION; pg. 1907, pg. 1642
FEDEX DIRECTLINK - Shipping Service - FEDEX CORPORATION; pg. 1907, pg. 1642
FEDEX E-LABEL - Shipping Service - FEDEX CORPORATION; pg. 1907, pg. 1642
FEDEX EDI INVOICE - Shipping Service - FEDEX CORPORATION; pg. 1907, pg. 1642
FEDEX EXPRESS - Shipping Service - FEDEX CORPORATION; pg. 1907, pg. 1642
FEDEX EXPRESS CLEAR - Shipping Service - FEDEX CORPORATION; pg. 1907, pg. 1642
FEDEX FREIGHT - Shipping Service - FEDEX CORPORATION; pg. 1907, pg. 1642
FEDEX GROUND - Shipping Service - FEDEX CORPORATION; pg. 1907, pg. 1642
FEDEX HOME DELIVERY - Shipping Service - FEDEX CORPORATION; pg. 1907, pg. 1642
FEDEX INSIGHT - Shipping Service - FEDEX CORPORATION; pg. 1907, pg. 1642
FEDEX INTERNATIONAL PRIORITY DIRECT DISTRIBUTION - Shipping Service - FEDEX CORPORATION; pg. 1907, pg. 1642
FEDEX SERVICES - Shipping Service - FEDEX CORPORATION; pg. 1907, pg. 1642
FEDEX SERVICES GUIDE - Guide - FEDEX CORPORATION; pg. 1907, pg. 1642
FEDEX SUPPLY CHAIN SERVICES - Shipping Service - FEDEX CORPORATION; pg. 1907, pg. 1642
FEDEX TRADE NETWORKS - Shipping Service - FEDEX CORPORATION; pg. 1907, pg. 1642
FEDMET TUBULARS - Oil Country Tubular Products - RUSSEL METALS INC.; pg. 1180, pg. 1928
FEDSELECT - Database Program - CACI INTERNATIONAL INC.; pg. 367, pg. 1773
FEED GRADE - Soybean Oil - ARCHER-DANIELS-MIDLAND COMPANY; pg. 825, pg. 565
FEED INT'L - Eastern Hemisphere Magazine for Feed Manufacturing - WATT PUBLISHING COMPANY; pg. 1701, pg. 655
FEED MANAGEMENT - North American Magazine for Food Manufacturers - WATT PUBLISHING COMPANY; pg. 1701, pg. 655
FEED THE PIG - Advertising Public Services - AMERICAN INSTITUTE OF CERTIFIED PUBLIC ACCOUNTANTS INC.; pg. 129, pg. 1192
FEEDBACK FERRET - Musical Instrument - PEAVEY ELECTRONICS CORPORATION; pg. 662, pg. 970
FEEDBURNER - Services - GOOGLE INC.; pg. 1249, pg. 153
FEEDCLIP - Feed Capture System - GRASS VALLEY, INC.; pg. 641, pg. 164
FEEDFLARE - Services - GOOGLE INC.; pg. 1249, pg. 153
FEEDMASTER - Offset Printing Blanket - ROTADYNE; pg. 1681, pg. 529
FEEL - Golf Products - FEEL GOLF CO., INC.; pg. 1834, pg. 465
FEEL BEAUTIFUL - Apparel - PLAYTEX APPAREL, INC.; pg. 31, pg. 1395
FEEL FREE - Deodorant - THE GILLETTE COMPANY; pg. 509, pg. 795
FEEL GOLF - Golf Products - FEEL GOLF CO., INC.; pg. 1834, pg. 465
FEEL THE GAME - Software - IMMERSION CORPORATION; pg. 413, pg. 246
FEELANEW - Vitamin & Dietary Supplement - NATROL, INC.; pg. 1570, pg. 64
FEELIN FRESH - Beauty Product - AVON PRODUCTS, INC.; pg. 500, pg. 1198
THE FEELING NEVER ENDS - Trade Mark - FTD GROUP, INC.; pg. 1795, pg. 608
FEELS LIKE HOME - Sheet Set - MEDLINE INDUSTRIES, INC.; pg. 1562, pg. 635
FEELS SO LIVELY - Perm - ZOTOS INTERNATIONAL, INC.; pg. 524, pg. 345
FEELTHEWEB - Software - IMMERSION CORPORATION; pg. 413, pg. 246
FEELTITE - Heavy Closures - WELLS LAMONT CORPORATION; pg. 15, pg. 638
FEESST - Fiberoptic Endoscopic Evaluation - PENTAX MEDICAL COMPANY; pg. 1580, pg. 1086
FEET RELIEF - Hair & Skin Product - AUBREY ORGANICS INC.; pg. 499, pg. 470
FEETFIX - Medical Device - GAMMEX RMI INC.; pg. 1532, pg. 1872
FEI - Synchronization Product - FREQUENCY ELECTRONICS, INC.; pg. 639, pg. 1182
FEIBA VH - Biopharmaceutical Product - BAXTER INTERNATIONAL INC.; pg. 1499, pg. 599
FEISTY FETA - Cheese Spread - GRECIAN DELIGHT FOODS INC.; pg. 859, pg. 610
FEKKAI - Personal & Household Product - THE PROCTER & GAMBLE COMPANY; pg. 1129, pg. 1418
FEL-O-VAX - Feline Distemper Vaccine - BOEHRINGER INGELHEIM VETMEDICA, INC.; pg. 1474, pg. 989
FEL-PRO - Gaskets - FEDERAL-MOGUL HOLDINGS CORPORATION; pg. 205, pg. 907
FELDENE - Medicine - PFIZER INC.; pg. 1581, pg. 1278
FELICE - Lighting Product - QUOIZEL INC.; pg. 1304, pg. 1616
FELICIA - Lighting - ETHAN ALLEN INTERIORS INC.; pg. 924, pg. 343
FELICITY - Clothing - ABERCROMBIE & FITCH CO.; pg. 37, pg. 1466
FELICITY - Doll And Toy - AMERICAN GIRL LLC; pg. 949, pg. 1871
FELICITY - Kitchen & Bath Products - MOEN INCORPORATED; pg. 1056, pg. 1468
FELICITY MERRIMAN - Doll And Toy - AMERICAN GIRL LLC; pg. 949, pg. 1871
FELICITY'S COLLECTION - Doll And Toy - AMERICAN GIRL LLC; pg. 949, pg. 1871
FELIN MIGNON - Cat Food - PETSMART, INC.; pg. 1481, pg. 18
FELINE - Cat Food - DESIGNING HEALTH, INC.; pg. 1523, pg. 299
FELINE FRIENDS - Pillow and Throw - HERITAGE LACE INC.; pg. 694, pg. 711
FELINE TRIPLE - Test Kit - IDEXX LABORATORIES, INC.; pg. 1543, pg. 753
FELINE ULTRANASAL - Vaccine - HESKA CORPORATION; pg. 1542, pg. 335
FELIX - Asset Visibility Software - NUMEREX CORP.; pg. 660, pg. 517
FELIZ - Fabric - NEMSCHOFF, INC.; pg. 936, pg. 1890
FELLECIA - Footwear - STEVEN MADDEN, LTD.; pg. 1819, pg. 1176
FELLOWS - Machine Tool Product - BOURN & KOCH MACHINE TOOL COMPANY; pg. 1319, pg. 654
FELOCELL - Feline Vaccine - PFIZER INC.; pg. 1581, pg. 1278
FELTAN - Felt - AMERICAN FELT & FILTER COMPANY; pg. 1312, pg. 1184
FELTASTIC - Felt - AMERICAN FELT & FILTER COMPANY; pg. 1312, pg. 1184
FELXIPAC - Plastics Product - AEP INDUSTRIES INC.; pg. 1878, pg. 1085
FEM AID - Healthcare Product - MEDICOOL, INC.; pg. 1562, pg. 294
FEMALE FOURCE - Orthopedic Product - DJO INCORPORATED; pg. 1524, pg. 302
FEMME BOOST - Boost - JAMBA, INC.; pg. 1024, pg. 84
FEMPRO - Software - AUTODESK INC.; pg. 356, pg. 257
FEMSTAT - Gynecological Pharmaceutical Preparation - BAYER HEALTHCARE CONSUMER CARE DIVISION; pg. 1500, pg. 1087
FEMTOGUARD - Wafer Probing System - CASCADE MICROTECH, INC.; pg. 1405, pg. 1492
FEMYSTIQUE - Dental Product - MAJESTIC DRUG COMPANY, INC.; pg. 516, pg. 1343
FENATRAK - Power Transmission Belting - FENNER DRIVES; pg. 1336, pg. 1551
FEND FOR YOURSELF - Tag Line - GERBER LEGENDARY BLADES; pg. 1834, pg. 1503
FENDER BASSMAN - Electric Guitar - FENDER MUSICAL INSTRUMENTS CORPORATION; pg. 547, pg. 21
FENDORA - Footwear - STEVEN MADDEN, LTD.; pg. 1819, pg. 1176
FENESHIELD - Fiber Glass Yarn - PPG INDUSTRIES, INC.; pg. 1445, pg. 1579
FENG SHUI - Video Game - INTERNATIONAL GAME TECHNOLOGY; pg. 957, pg. 1024
FENIMORE - Fabric - NEMSCHOFF, INC.; pg. 936, pg. 1890
FENN - Precision Metal Parts - SPX PRECISION COMPONENTS - FENN DIVISION; pg. 1378, pg. 360
FENNER DRIVES - Machine Parts - FENNER DRIVES; pg. 1336, pg. 1551
FENTON - Motor Vehicle Components - SPEEDWAY MOTORS INC.; pg. 218, pg. 1012
FENTON ART GLASS - Art Glass - THE FENTON ART GLASS COMPANY; pg. 1124, pg. 1851
FENWICK - Furniture - HOOKER FURNITURE CORPORATION; pg. 928, pg. 1788
FEORA - Paper & Nonwoven Material - FIBERMARK INC.; pg. 1457, pg. 1764
FER-IN-SOL - Iron Supplement for Prevention & Treatment of Iron Deficiency Anemia - MEAD JOHNSON NUTRITION COMPANY; pg. 1561, pg. 615
FERAHEME - Ferumoxytol Injection - AMAG PHARMACEUTICALS, INC.; pg. 1492, pg. 827
FERGON - Iron Tonic - BAYER HEALTHCARE CONSUMER CARE DIVISION; pg. 1500, pg. 1087
FERIDEX I.V - Nanoparticle Product - AMAG PHARMACEUTICALS, INC.; pg. 1492, pg. 827
FERMASURE - Ethanol Additive - E.I. DU PONT DE NEMOURS & COMPANY; pg. 1159, pg. 390
FERMEC - Compact Equipment - TEREX CORPORATION; pg. 1381, pg. 384
FERMENTOL - Pharmaceutical Product - CHURCH & DWIGHT CANADA CORP.; pg. 503, pg. 1925
FERMENTUS INTERRUPTUS - Beer - GRANITE CITY FOOD & BREWERY LTD; pg. 1730, pg. 937
FERMOTRODE Electrode - HAMILTON CO., INC.; pg. 1415, pg. 1031
FERN - Pillow and Throw - HERITAGE LACE INC.; pg. 694, pg. 711
FERN - Fabric - SCALAMANDRE, INC.; pg. 941, pg. 1058
FERN TOSS - Wallcovering - YORK WALLCOVERINGS INC.; pg. 947, pg. 1598
FERNANDA - Women's Clothing & Accessories - WOODEN SHIPS OF HOBOKEN; pg. 35, pg. 1315
FERNANDEZ - Fabric - NEMSCHOFF, INC.; pg. 936, pg. 1890
FERNANDO'S - Food Product - CONAGRA FOODS, INC.; pg. 826, pg. 1014
FERNWOOD - Rug - COURISTAN INC.; pg. 921, pg. 1067
FERODO - Brake & Friction Product - FEDERAL-MOGUL HOLDINGS CORPORATION; pg. 205, pg. 907
FERRARA - Faucet - ELKAY MANUFACTURING COMPANY; pg. 80, pg. 645
FERRELL NORTH AMERICA - Wholesale - FERRELLGAS PARTNERS, L.P.; pg. 977, pg. 718
FERRELL-ROSS - Material Processing and Recovery - A.T. FERRELL COMPANY, INC.; pg. 701, pg. 674
FERRELLGAS - Bottled Gas - FERRELLGAS PARTNERS, L.P.; pg. 977, pg. 718
FERRENE - Electronic Thermoplastic Compound - FERRO CORPORATION; pg. 1162, pg. 1462
FERRETS - Magazine - I-5 PUBLISHING LLC; pg. 1651, pg. 133
FERRETS USA - Magazine - I-5 PUBLISHING LLC; pg. 1651, pg. 133
FERRETTI - Furniture - ASHLEY FURNITURE INDUSTRIES,

INC.; *pg.* 914, *pg.* 1852
FERREX - High Gloss Mineral-Filled Polypropylene - FERRO CORPORATION; *pg.* 1162, *pg.* 1462
FERRLECIT - Pharmaceutical Product - ALLERGAN; *pg.* 1490, *pg.* 1101
FERRO - Performance Materials - FERRO CORPORATION; *pg.* 1162, *pg.* 1462
FERRO-FILM - Films - DAUBERT INDUSTRIES, INC.; *pg.* 1155, *pg.* 561
FERRO FIVE - Battery - C&D TECHNOLOGIES, INC.; *pg.* 627, *pg.* 1517
FERRO-GALV - Papers - DAUBERT INDUSTRIES, INC.; *pg.* 1155, *pg.* 561
FERRO-PERC - Powder Enamel - FERRO CORPORATION; *pg.* 1162, *pg.* 1462
FERRO-SEQUELS - Iron Supplement Product - ALERE INC.; *pg.* 1488, *pg.* 849
FERROCON - Conductive Thermoplastic - FERRO CORPORATION; *pg.* 1162, *pg.* 1462
FERROCOTE - Corrosion Preventive - QUAKER CHEMICAL CORP.; *pg.* 1178, *pg.* 1524
FERROFLEX - Thermoplastic Olefin-Based Elastomers - FERRO CORPORATION; *pg.* 1162, *pg.* 1462
FERROFLO - Thermoplastic Lubricated Compound - FERRO CORPORATION; *pg.* 1162, *pg.* 1462
FERROMEC - Turf Product - PBI/GORDON CORPORATION; *pg.* 1176, *pg.* 985
FERROPAK - Thermoplastic Packaging Compounds - FERRO CORPORATION; *pg.* 1162, *pg.* 1462
FERROPHOS - Pigment - OCCIDENTAL CHEMICAL CORPORATION; *pg.* 1175, *pg.* 1685
FERROVER - Chemical Reagent - HACH COMPANY; *pg.* 1415, *pg.* 334
FERROWELD - Electrode - LINCOLN ELECTRIC HOLDINGS, INC.; *pg.* 1355, *pg.* 1432
FERROX X - Pressed & Monolithic Refractory - RESCO PRODUCTS, INC.; *pg.* 107, *pg.* 1581
FERROZINE - Chemical Reagent - HACH COMPANY; *pg.* 1415, *pg.* 334
FERROZINE - Chemical Product - SPECTRUM CHEMICALS & LABORATORY PRODUCTS, INC.; *pg.* 1181, *pg.* 94
FERRULE-PAK - Plastic Tube - SWAGELOK COMPANY; *pg.* 1064, *pg.* 1473
FERRY - Alloy Product - SPECIAL METALS CORPORATION; *pg.* 1377, *pg.* 1850
FERTIL MALE - Health System Product - LANELABS USA INC.; *pg.* 1554, *pg.* 1128
THE FERTILITY COMPANY - Slogan - INTEGRAMED AMERICA, INC.; *pg.* 1546, *pg.* 1325
FERTILITYDIRECT - Software - INTEGRAMED AMERICA, INC.; *pg.* 1546, *pg.* 1325
FERTILITYMARKIT - Software - INTEGRAMED AMERICA, INC.; *pg.* 1546, *pg.* 1325
FERTILO-PAK - Medical Product - GF HEALTH PRODUCTS, INC.; *pg.* 1535, *pg.* 508
FERUMOXYTOL - Nanoparticle Product - AMAG PHARMACEUTICALS, INC.; *pg.* 1492, *pg.* 827
FESCANT PLUS - Cant Strip - JOHNS MANVILLE CORPORATION; *pg.* 89, *pg.* 320
FESCO BOARD - Insulation Board - JOHNS MANVILLE CORPORATION; *pg.* 89, *pg.* 320
FESCO FOAM - Roof Insulations - JOHNS MANVILLE CORPORATION; *pg.* 89, *pg.* 320
FESTAL - Canned Foods - SENECA FOODS CORPORATION; *pg.* 895, *pg.* 1177
FESTER - Bicycle - G. JOANNOU CYCLE CO. INC.; *pg.* 1707, *pg.* 1098
FESTINO - Network Processors - AVAGO TECHNOLOGIES; *pg.* 358, *pg.* 238
FESTIVA - Area Rugs - COURISTAN INC.; *pg.* 921, *pg.* 1067
FESTIVAL - Cleaning Product - ALEN AMERICAS INC.; *pg.* 325, *pg.* 1699
FESTIVAL - Fabric - NEMSCHOFF, INC.; *pg.* 936, *pg.* 1890
FESTIVAL - Furniture - TELESCOPE CASUAL FURNITURE INC.; *pg.* 944, *pg.* 1162
FESTIVAL FANTASTICO - Video Game - INTERNATIONAL GAME TECHNOLOGY; *pg.* 957, *pg.* 1024
FESTIVAL TRAYS - Buffetware & Food Trays - CARLISLE FOODSERVICE PRODUCTS INCORPORATED; *pg.* 1455, *pg.* 1485
FESTO - Sunglass - 180S, LLC; *pg.* 1824, *pg.* 754
FETALGARD - Monitoring System - ANALOGIC CORPORATION; *pg.* 1399, *pg.* 840
FETALGARDLITE - Fetal Monitor - ANALOGIC CORPORATION; *pg.* 1399, *pg.* 840
FETKY - Power Semiconductor Device - INTERNATIONAL RECTIFIER CORPORATION; *pg.* 647, *pg.* 80
FETZER - California Wines - BROWN-FORMAN CORPORATION; *pg.* 1958, *pg.* 732
FEUTRON - Felt Filter Media - AMERICAN FELT & FILTER COMPANY; *pg.* 1312, *pg.* 1184
FEVERGUARD - Animal Treatment - KENT NUTRITION GROUP; *pg.* 1477, *pg.* 710
FEY - Bumper - WESTIN AUTOMOTIVE PRODUCTS, INC.; *pg.* 222, *pg.* 211
FF - Tips for Paint Spray Guns - GRACO, INC.; *pg.* 1342, *pg.* 935
FF-680 - Flame Retardants - CHEMTURA CORPORATION; *pg.* 1152, *pg.* 355
FF DESIGN - Software - XEROX CORPORATION; *pg.* 494, *pg.* 365
FFA NEW HORIZONS - Magazines - NATIONAL FFA ORGANIZATION; *pg.* 149, *pg.* 688
FFS - Federal Financial System; Accounting System for Federal Government Agencies - CGI TECHNOLOGIES & SOLUTIONS INC.; *pg.* 371, *pg.* 1779
FGA - Voltage Reference - INTERSIL CORPORATION; *pg.* 647, *pg.* 146
FHT - Power Transmission Belting - FENNER DRIVES; *pg.* 1336, *pg.* 1551
FI MAGAZINE: FISHER ISLAND - Magazine - PALM BEACH MEDIA GROUP INC.; *pg.* 1674, *pg.* 457
FIAMMA - Fabric - NEMSCHOFF, INC.; *pg.* 936, *pg.* 1890
FIANO - Bathroom Accessories - SYMMONS INDUSTRIES, INC.; *pg.* 114, *pg.* 803
FIAP S.P.A. DEVICE - Plastics Product - AEP INDUSTRIES INC.; *pg.* 1878, *pg.* 1085
FIASCO DIS - Apparel - VANS, INC.; *pg.* 1821, *pg.* 76
FIATALLIS - Agricultural Equipment - CNH AMERICA LLC; *pg.* 702, *pg.* 560
FIBER-AIRE - Roof Ventilator - SWARTWOUT DIVISION; *pg.* 114, *pg.* 978
FIBER ARRAY PACKAGE - Diode Bar - COHERENT, INC.; *pg.* 1406, *pg.* 265
FIBER-ART - Gypsum Cement - USG CORPORATION; *pg.* 118, *pg.* 594
FIBER BOOST - Boost - JAMBA, INC.; *pg.* 1024, *pg.* 84
FIBER-CLASSIC - Insulated Fiberglass Exterior Doors - THERMA-TRU CORP.; *pg.* 115, *pg.* 1462
FIBER CRAFT - Doors - THERMA-TRU CORP.; *pg.* 115, *pg.* 1462
FIBER-DUCT - Fiber Cable Routing - PANDUIT CORP.; *pg.* 661, *pg.* 663
FIBER GREENS - Food Supplement - ORANGE PEEL ENTERPRISES, INC.; *pg.* 1028, *pg.* 477
FIBER GREENS+ - Vitamins - ORANGE PEEL ENTERPRISES, INC.; *pg.* 1028, *pg.* 477
FIBER KRUNCH - Starch Systems - CARGILL, INC.; *pg.* 845, *pg.* 965
FIBER LITE - Fiber Optic Illuminator - STOELTING CO.; *pg.* 1430, *pg.* 671
FIBER-LITE - Mazes & Video Tracking Accessories - STOELTING CO.; *pg.* 1430, *pg.* 671
FIBER ONE - Cereal - GENERAL MILLS, INC.; *pg.* 828, *pg.* 933
FIBER ONE BROWNIES - 90 Calorie Brownies - GENERAL MILLS, INC.; *pg.* 828, *pg.* 933
FIBER OPTIC STEP LIGHT - Fiber Optic Fixtures - REVOLUTION LIGHTING TECHNOLOGIES, INC.; *pg.* 1304, *pg.* 377
FIBER OPTIMA FIBER OPTICS BY COMMSCOPE - Optical Fiber Product - COMMSCOPE, INC.; *pg.* 278, *pg.* 1378
FIBER-PROTEC - Seal & Thermoplastic Component - GREENE, TWEED & CO.; *pg.* 1344, *pg.* 1544
FIBER-SERT - Fasteners - YARDLEY PRODUCTS CORPORATION; *pg.* 1391, *pg.* 1596
FIBER TECH - Repair Compound - ITW - EVERCOAT; *pg.* 1443, *pg.* 1415
FIBER-WEB - Industrial Filter - DONALDSON COMPANY, INC.; *pg.* 1329, *pg.* 917
FIBERAID - Weight Management System - WATKINS INCORPORATED; *pg.* 909, *pg.* 967
FIBERBOND - Bridge Product - THE D.S. BROWN COMPANY; *pg.* 79, *pg.* 1468
FIBERCHECK - Laser Delivery Verification - IRIDEX CORPORATION; *pg.* 648, *pg.* 160
FIBERCLEAR...CLEARLY BETTER - Nutritional Supplement - PHARMAVITE LLC; *pg.* 1584, *pg.* 167
FIBERCON - Bulk Forming Fiber Therapy - PFIZER INC.; *pg.* 1581, *pg.* 1278
FIBERDIRECT - Software - TELLABS, INC.; *pg.* 678, *pg.* 637
FIBERESSENCE - Fiber - BEAULIEU GROUP, LLC; *pg.* 917, *pg.* 529
FIBEREX - Excelsior Fiber - AMERICAN EXCELSIOR COMPANY; *pg.* 1451, *pg.* 1659
FIBERFRAX - Alumino-Silicate Fibers - UNIFRAX CORPORATION; *pg.* 220, *pg.* 1317
FIBERGLAS - Fiber Glass Duct Product - OWENS CORNING; *pg.* 102, *pg.* 1476
FIBERGY - Health Care Product - USANA HEALTH SCIENCES, INC.; *pg.* 1605, *pg.* 1761
FIBERGY BARS - Health Care Product - USANA HEALTH SCIENCES, INC.; *pg.* 1605, *pg.* 1761
FIBERIFIC - Nutritional Supplement - NATURAL ORGANICS, INC.; *pg.* 1571, *pg.* 1181
FIBERINSPECT - Machine Vision System - COGNEX CORPORATION; *pg.* 1406, *pg.* 834
FIBERIZATION - Meltblown, Bead & Dot Adhesive Applicators - NORDSON CORPORATION; *pg.* 1365, *pg.* 1480
FIBERJACKS - Fiber Optic Lighting System - ENERGY FOCUS, INC.; *pg.* 1411, *pg.* 1472
FIBERLINK - Fiber Optic Transmission System - COMMUNICATIONS SPECIALTIES, INC.; *pg.* 377, *pg.* 1338
FIBERLOC - Vinyl Compound - POLYONE CORPORATION; *pg.* 1177, *pg.* 1404
FIBERMARK - Rifle - WEATHERBY, INC.; *pg.* 1848, *pg.* 181
FIBERMARK 1 - Large Capacity Fiber Optic Splice Enclosure - CHANNELL COMMERCIAL CORP.; *pg.* 1870, *pg.* 291
FIBERMULCH - Erosion Control Product - AMERICAN EXCELSIOR COMPANY; *pg.* 1451, *pg.* 1659
FIBEROCK - Gypsum Panel - USG CORPORATION; *pg.* 118, *pg.* 594
FIBERPLUG - Wall Anchor - POWERS FASTENERS INC.; *pg.* 1059, *pg.* 1143
FIBERPLUS - Antioxidant Bars - KELLOGG COMPANY; *pg.* 831, *pg.* 870
FIBERPRO - Illuminator - REVOLUTION LIGHTING TECHNOLOGIES, INC.; *pg.* 1304, *pg.* 377
FIBERRUNNER - Fiber Cable Routing - PANDUIT CORP.; *pg.* 661, *pg.* 663
FIBERSHELF - Rack-Mount Shelf - VIAVI SOLUTIONS INC.; *pg.* 1435, *pg.* 148
FIBERSOF - Shoes - ACUSHNET COMPANY; *pg.* 1824, *pg.* 818
FIBERSOFT - Bleached Cotton - BARNHARDT MANUFACTURING COMPANY; *pg.* 1498, *pg.* 1364
FIBERSOL-2 - Soluble Fibers for Reduced-Calorie Products - ARCHER-DANIELS-MIDLAND COMPANY; *pg.* 825, *pg.* 565
FIBERSPOTS - Fiber Optic Lighting System - ENERGY FOCUS, INC.; *pg.* 1411, *pg.* 1472
FIBERSTARS EFO - Fiber Optic Lighting - ENERGY FOCUS, INC.; *pg.* 1411, *pg.* 1472
FIBERSTRONG - Building Product - BLUELINX HOLDINGS, INC.; *pg.* 70, *pg.* 491
FIBERSTRONG - Rim Board - GEORGIA-PACIFIC LLC; *pg.* 1458, *pg.* 507
FIBERSTRUCT - Fibrous Engineering Constructions - AMERICAN FELT & FILTER COMPANY; *pg.* 1312, *pg.* 1184
FIBERSYM - Food Product - MGP INGREDIENTS, INC.; *pg.* 877, *pg.* 714
FIBERVISIONS - Thermal Bond Polypropylene Staple Fiber - HERCULES INCORPORATED; *pg.* 1166, *pg.* 392
FIBERWRAP - Flashlight - STREAMLIGHT INC.; *pg.* 1306, *pg.* 1527
FIBRACOL - Healthcare Product - JOHNSON & JOHNSON; *pg.* 1549, *pg.* 1091
FIBRANCE - Fiber Enhancing Polymers - THE DOW CHEMICAL COMPANY; *pg.* 1157, *pg.* 898
FIBRE-U - Fibre Partitions - SONOCO PRODUCTS COMPANY; *pg.* 1469, *pg.* 1619
FIBREFORM - Equipment Enclosure - THERMON AMERICAS INC.; *pg.* 1077, *pg.* 1744
FIBRELAM - Core Material - HEXCEL CORPORATION; *pg.* 1884, *pg.* 375
FIBRELIFT - Fibre Sheet - INTERNATIONAL PAPER COMPANY; *pg.* 1460, *pg.* 1644
FIBRENE - Nonmetallic Material - WEBSTER INDUSTRIES INC.; *pg.* 1388, *pg.* 1475
FIBRENET - Nutritional Supplement - NU SKIN ENTERPRISES, INC.; *pg.* 518, *pg.* 1755
FIBREQUIK - Data Storage Product - CAMBEX CORPORATION; *pg.* 368, *pg.* 844

FIBRESPY - Switches - EMULEX CORPORATION; *pg.* 392, *pg.* 70
FIBRESTORE - Nutritional Product - RELIV INTERNATIONAL, INC.; *pg.* 1589, *pg.* 975
FIBRETIMER - Repeater - VITESSE SEMICONDUCTOR CORPORATION; *pg.* 686, *pg.* 57
FIBREX - Fiber Product - INTERNATIONAL FIBER CORP.; *pg.* 865, *pg.* 1317
FIBREX - Decking & Railing - TREX COMPANY, INC.; *pg.* 116, *pg.* 1812
FIBRILLA - Hostess Trays - MOLDED FIBER GLASS COMPANIES; *pg.* 1886, *pg.* 1403
FIBRILLEX - AA Amyloidosis Treatment - BELLUS HEALTH INC.; *pg.* 1503, *pg.* 1951
FIBRLOK - Splicing Trays & Tools - 3M COMPANY; *pg.* 1142, *pg.* 956
FIBRMET - Optical Fiber Polisher - BUEHLER, LTD.; *pg.* 1403, *pg.* 622
FIBRO-DEK - Asphalt Roof Coating - REVERE PRODUCTS; *pg.* 107, *pg.* 1435
FIBRO-RESPONSE - Vitamin & Herbal Supplement - SOURCE NATURALS; *pg.* 1595, *pg.* 278
FIBROSPECT - Therapy System - PROMETHEUS LABORATORIES, INC.; *pg.* 1586, *pg.* 206
FIBROSURE - Medical Research - LABORATORY CORPORATION OF AMERICA HOLDINGS; *pg.* 1554, *pg.* 1359
FIBRSKOPE - Microscope - BUEHLER, LTD.; *pg.* 1403, *pg.* 622
FIBRX - Light Activated Fibrinogen/Thrombin Surgical Sealant - CRYOLIFE, INC.; *pg.* 1520, *pg.* 534
FICO - Software - EQUIFAX INC.; *pg.* 748, *pg.* 504
FICO - Software System - FAIR ISAAC CORPORATION; *pg.* 1247, *pg.* 955
FICO SCORE SIMULATOR - Credit Scoring Service - FAIR ISAAC CORPORATION; *pg.* 1247, *pg.* 955
FICON - Converter - BROCADE CORPORATION; *pg.* 365, *pg.* 312
FICTION CONNECTION - Online Fiction Titles Search Engine - R.R. BOWKER LLC; *pg.* 1682, *pg.* 1095
FIDDLE FADDLE - Food Product - CONAGRA FOODS, INC.; *pg.* 826, *pg.* 1014
FIDDLER'S GREEN - Video Game - INTERNATIONAL GAME TECHNOLOGY; *pg.* 957, *pg.* 1024
FIDELIO - Property Management Systems - MICROS SYSTEMS, INC.; *pg.* 435, *pg.* 768
FIDELITY - Intra-Aortic Balloon Catheter - MAQUET; *pg.* 1558, *pg.* 1082
FIDELITY ADVISOR FUNDS - Investment Product - FMR LLC (FIDELITY INVESTMENTS); *pg.* 759, *pg.* 794
FIDELITY ANYWHERE - Wireless Service - FMR LLC (FIDELITY INVESTMENTS); *pg.* 759, *pg.* 794
FIDELITY E-LEARNING - Online Workshops & Live Web-Based Sessions - FMR LLC (FIDELITY INVESTMENTS); *pg.* 759, *pg.* 794
FIDELITY NETBENEFITS - Online Account Access & Planning Tools - FMR LLC (FIDELITY INVESTMENTS); *pg.* 759, *pg.* 794
FIDELITYENGINE - Image Processing Product - SEMTECH CORPORATION GENNUM PRODUCTS; *pg.* 671, *pg.* 1919
FIDRA - Men's Golf Apparel - QUIKSILVER, INC.; *pg.* 31, *pg.* 104
FIDUCIARY TRUST - Mutual Funds - FRANKLIN RESOURCES, INC.; *pg.* 760, *pg.* 254
FIELD - Apparel - OAKLEY, INC.; *pg.* 1840, *pg.* 86
FIELD - Processed Meat - SPECIALTY FOODS GROUP-FIELD PACKING DIV.; *pg.* 897, *pg.* 739
FIELD & STREAM - Sports Equipment - ALLIANCE SPORTS GROUP, L.P.; *pg.* 1825, *pg.* 1698
FIELD & STREAM - Sporting Goods Stores - AMERICAN SPORTS LICENSING, INC.; *pg.* 1825, *pg.* 1524
FIELD & STREAM - Magazine - BONNIER ACTIVE MEDIA, INC.; *pg.* 1622, *pg.* 1205
FIELD & STREAM - Magazine - BONNIER CORPORATION; *pg.* 1622, *pg.* 480
FIELD & STREAM - Sunglasses - FGX INTERNATIONAL, INC.; *pg.* 5, *pg.* 1608
FIELD & STREAM - Knife - GERBER LEGENDARY BLADES; *pg.* 1834, *pg.* 1503
FIELD BOXES - Storage Product - PLANO MOLDING COMPANY; *pg.* 1887, *pg.* 652
FIELD-FLANGE 350 - Fittings - UNITED STATES PIPE & FOUNDRY COMPANY, INC.; *pg.* 117, *pg.* 5
FIELD LOK 350 - Gaskets - UNITED STATES PIPE & FOUNDRY COMPANY, INC.; *pg.* 117, *pg.* 5
FIELD RECORDER - Data Recording Apparatus - ASTRO-MED, INC.; *pg.* 619, *pg.* 1609
FIELDANDSTREAM.COM - Web Site - BONNIER ACTIVE MEDIA, INC.; *pg.* 1622, *pg.* 1205
FIELDBREEZE - Air Refreshner - BLUE CROSS LABORATORIES; *pg.* 326, *pg.* 277
FIELDCALC - Construction Equipment - VERMEER MANUFACTURING COMPANY; *pg.* 708, *pg.* 711
FIELDCLEER - Ingredient System - PENFORD CORPORATION; *pg.* 1177, *pg.* 314
FIELDCREST - Apparel - ICONIX BRAND GROUP, INC.; *pg.* 26, *pg.* 1243
FIELDFRESH - Pet Litter - THE ANDERSONS INCORPORATED; *pg.* 1793, *pg.* 1461
FIELDLAZER - Fluid Handling System - GRACO, INC.; *pg.* 1342, *pg.* 935
FIELDMASTER - Laser Measurement Instrument - COHERENT, INC.; *pg.* 1406, *pg.* 265
FIELDMASTER - Drift Tube - PHOTONIS USA PENNSYLVANIA; *pg.* 663, *pg.* 1547
FIELDMASTER - Firearms - REMINGTON ARMS COMPANY, LLC; *pg.* 1844, *pg.* 1382
FIELDMATE - Laser Measurement Instrument - COHERENT, INC.; *pg.* 1406, *pg.* 265
FIELDMAX - Laser Measurement Instrument - COHERENT, INC.; *pg.* 1406, *pg.* 265
FIELDNET - Irrigation Management System - LINDSAY CORPORATION; *pg.* 1356, *pg.* 1016
FIELDPLUS - Articulated Pivot Irrigation System - LINDSAY CORPORATION; *pg.* 1356, *pg.* 1016
FIELDS - Fabric - NEMSCHOFF, INC.; *pg.* 936, *pg.* 1890
FIELDS OF ECUADOR - Flower Arrangement - 1-800-FLOWERS.COM, INC.; *pg.* 1758, *pg.* 1151
FIELDS OF EUROPE - Flower Arrangement - 1-800-FLOWERS.COM, INC.; *pg.* 1758, *pg.* 1151
FIELDS OF GERMANY - Flower Arrangement - 1-800-FLOWERS.COM, INC.; *pg.* 1758, *pg.* 1151
FIELDS OF JAPAN - Flower Arrangement - 1-800-FLOWERS.COM, INC.; *pg.* 1758, *pg.* 1151
FIELDS OF MEXICO - Flower Arrangement - 1-800-FLOWERS.COM, INC.; *pg.* 1758, *pg.* 1151
FIELDS OF NATURE - Pharmaceutical Product - ALERE INC.; *pg.* 1488, *pg.* 849
FIELDS OF THE NETHERLANDS - Flower Arrangement - 1-800-FLOWERS.COM, INC.; *pg.* 1758, *pg.* 1151
FIELDS OF THE WORLD - Retail Store Services - 1-800-FLOWERS.COM, INC.; *pg.* 1758, *pg.* 1151
FIELDSENTRY - Monitoring System - LINDSAY CORPORATION; *pg.* 1356, *pg.* 1016
FIELDSTONE - Kitchen & Bath Cabinetry - MASCO CORPORATION; *pg.* 96, *pg.* 909
FIELDSTONE - Snacks & Cereals - MCKEE FOODS CORPORATION; *pg.* 1860, *pg.* 1630
FIELDSTONE CABINETRY - Semi-custom Cabinetry - NORCRAFT HOLDINGS, LP; *pg.* 100, *pg.* 921
FIELDWARE - Plastic Cutlery - PACTIV CORPORATION; *pg.* 1466, *pg.* 624
FIERY - Printing Products - ELECTRONICS FOR IMAGING, INC.; *pg.* 390, *pg.* 88
FIERY CENTRAL - Printing Product - ELECTRONICS FOR IMAGING, INC.; *pg.* 390, *pg.* 88
FIERY SEVENS - Game - WMS INDUSTRIES INC.; *pg.* 593, *pg.* 666
FIERY SYSTEM 8E - Multifunction Embedded Print Server - ELECTRONICS FOR IMAGING, INC.; *pg.* 390, *pg.* 88
FIESSTAA - Footwear - STEVEN MADDEN, LTD.; *pg.* 1819, *pg.* 1176
FIESTA - Patio Canopy - ANCHOR INDUSTRIES, INC.; *pg.* 1825, *pg.* 678
FIESTA - Table - BLATT BOWLING & BILLIARD CORP.; *pg.* 1827, *pg.* 1203
FIESTA - Footwear - COBIAN CORP.; *pg.* 1806, *pg.* 253
FIESTA - Camera - EASTMAN KODAK COMPANY; *pg.* 1408, *pg.* 1333
FIESTA - Color - FERRO CORPORATION; *pg.* 1162, *pg.* 1462
FIESTA - Rice Mix - GOYA FOODS, INC.; *pg.* 859, *pg.* 1075
FIESTA - Dinnerware - THE HOMER LAUGHLIN CHINA COMPANY; *pg.* 1125, *pg.* 1850
FIESTA - Fabric - NEMSCHOFF, INC.; *pg.* 936, *pg.* 1890
FIESTA - Pet Product - PETSMART, INC.; *pg.* 1481, *pg.* 18
FIESTA HAIR - Hair Salons - REGIS CORPORATION; *pg.* 521, *pg.* 941
FIESTA HENDERSON HOTEL & CASINO - Hotel & Casino - STATION CASINOS, INC.; *pg.* 585, *pg.* 1030
FIESTA RANCHO CASINO & HOTEL - Hotel & Casino - STATION CASINOS, INC.; *pg.* 585, *pg.* 1030
FIEXOMER - Resin - THE DOW CHEMICAL COMPANY; *pg.* 1157, *pg.* 898
FIFTH AVENUE PLANK - Laminated 3-5-7" Plank-Beveled - ROBBINS, INC.; *pg.* 108, *pg.* 1425
FIFTH PARTY - Video Game - INTERNATIONAL GAME TECHNOLOGY; *pg.* 957, *pg.* 1024
FIFTH PARTY LEVEL - Video Game - INTERNATIONAL GAME TECHNOLOGY; *pg.* 957, *pg.* 1024
FIFTY-FOUR - Bags - FOSSIL GROUP, INC.; *pg.* 5, *pg.* 1735
FIFTY-ONE - Electronic Cigarette - VAPOR CORP.; *pg.* 61, *pg.* 427
FIG-ARO - Tile - ARTISTIC TILE INC.; *pg.* 914, *pg.* 1119
FIGARINO - Cable Storage Device - SHERMAN & REILLY, INC.; *pg.* 1062, *pg.* 1629
FIGARO - Bedding - CROSCILL, INC.; *pg.* 1122, *pg.* 1220
FIGARO - Video Game - INTERNATIONAL GAME TECHNOLOGY; *pg.* 957, *pg.* 1024
FIGARO - Cable Storage Device - SHERMAN & REILLY, INC.; *pg.* 1062, *pg.* 1629
FIGARONE - Cable Storage Device - SHERMAN & REILLY, INC.; *pg.* 1062, *pg.* 1629
FIGE MAPPER - Software - BIO-RAD LABORATORIES, INC.; *pg.* 1504, *pg.* 101
FIGHTER - Additive - CARGILL LIMITED; *pg.* 1475, *pg.* 1914
THE FIGHTER ENTERPRISE - Engineering, Technical Consulting & Advisory Services - LOCKHEED MARTIN CORPORATION; *pg.* 229, *pg.* 762
FIGHTING FALCON - Jet Aircraft - LOCKHEED MARTIN CORPORATION; *pg.* 229, *pg.* 762
FIGI'S - Food Gift Baskets - MASON COMPANIES, INC.; *pg.* 1811, *pg.* 1856
FIGMENT - Fabric - NEMSCHOFF, INC.; *pg.* 936, *pg.* 1890
FIGURES - Fabric - NEMSCHOFF, INC.; *pg.* 936, *pg.* 1890
FIGURFIT - Sleepwear & Lingerie - INDERA MILLS COMPANY; *pg.* 26, *pg.* 1396
FIHR - Software - ASPEN TECHNOLOGY, INC.; *pg.* 354, *pg.* 804
FIJI - Carpet - BEAULIEU GROUP, LLC; *pg.* 917, *pg.* 529
FIJI - Footwear - COBIAN CORP.; *pg.* 1806, *pg.* 253
FIJI WEEJEE FAWN - Nail Care Product - OPI PRODUCTS INC.; *pg.* 518, *pg.* 167
FIKEGUARD - Fire Protection System - FIKE CORPORATION; *pg.* 1047, *pg.* 973
FIL-KOTE - Paint & Coating - DIAMOND VOGEL PAINT, INC.; *pg.* 1441, *pg.* 710
FILA - Footwear, Apparel & Accessories - FILA USA; *pg.* 1808, *pg.* 779
FILE-AID - Software - COMPUWARE CORPORATION; *pg.* 379, *pg.* 879
FILE LIFECYCLE MANAGER - Software - BROCADE COMMUNICATIONS SYSTEMS, INC.; *pg.* 365, *pg.* 239
FILE MIGRATOR FOR SHAREPOINT - Software - DELL SOFTWARE; *pg.* 385, *pg.* 40
FILE SPRAY - Podiatry Machine - MEDICOOL, INC.; *pg.* 1562, *pg.* 294
FILE STORAGE RESOURCE MANAGER - Software - NETAPP, INC.; *pg.* 444, *pg.* 287
FILE STREAM - Podiatry Machine - MEDICOOL, INC.; *pg.* 1562, *pg.* 294
FILE SYSTEM AUDITOR - Software - DELL SOFTWARE; *pg.* 385, *pg.* 40
FILE TRACKER - Barcode Systems - TAB PRODUCTS CO. LLC; *pg.* 481, *pg.* 1869
FILE360 - Software - OPENTEXT; *pg.* 450, *pg.* 1665
FILECD - Software - NTI CORPORATION; *pg.* 446, *pg.* 114
FILEMAKER PRO - Database Software - APPLE INC.; *pg.* 350, *pg.* 73
FILEMAKER PRO - Computer Software - FILEMAKER, INC.; *pg.* 639, *pg.* 265
FILEMAKER SERVER - Software - FILEMAKER, INC.; *pg.* 639, *pg.* 265
FILEMASTER 520 - Nailcare Product - MEDICOOL, INC.; *pg.* 1562, *pg.* 294
FILEMOVER - Software - LAPLINK SOFTWARE, INC.; *pg.* 426, *pg.* 1815
FILEPAK - Customizable Labels - TAB PRODUCTS CO. LLC; *pg.* 481, *pg.* 1869
FILERVIEW - Software - NETAPP, INC.; *pg.* 444, *pg.* 287
FILESENDER - Software - LAPLINK SOFTWARE, INC.; *pg.* 426, *pg.* 1815
FILET-O-FISH - Sandwich - MCDONALD'S CORPORATION; *pg.* 1737, *pg.* 645

FILEVAULT - Application Program - APPLE INC.; *pg.* 350, *pg.* 73
FILEXPRESS-XST - Desktop & Host-initiated, High-speed File Transfer Automation Software - ATTACHMATE CORPORATION; *pg.* 356, *pg.* 1833
FILIFE - Online Services - IAC/INTERACTIVECORP; *pg.* 292, *pg.* 1242
FILIGREE - Bath Accessory - CROSCILL, INC.; *pg.* 1122, *pg.* 1220
FILIGREE - Fabric - NEMSCHOFF, INC.; *pg.* 936, *pg.* 1890
FILL-AIR - Packaging Product - SEALED AIR CORPORATION; *pg.* 1468, *pg.* 1058
FILL-AIR ELITE - Inflatable Packaging System - SEALED AIR CORPORATION; *pg.* 1468, *pg.* 1058
FILL & FLY - Guarantee Fuel Pricing Program - SIGNATURE FLIGHT SUPPORT CORP.; *pg.* 234, *pg.* 456
FILL & SEAL - Expanding Foam Sealant - THE DOW CHEMICAL COMPANY; *pg.* 1157, *pg.* 898
FILL BOND - Paint - THE SHERWIN-WILLIAMS COMPANY; *pg.* 1447, *pg.* 1435
FILL SENTRY - Auxiliary Equipment - NORDSON CORPORATION; *pg.* 1365, *pg.* 1480
FILLEASY - Auxiliary Equipment - NORDSON CORPORATION; *pg.* 1365, *pg.* 1480
FILLERUP - Automotive Body Filler - PPG INDUSTRIES, INC.; *pg.* 1445, *pg.* 1579
FILLMASTER - Auxiliary Equipment - NORDSON CORPORATION; *pg.* 1365, *pg.* 1480
FILM - Wall Decor - ETHAN ALLEN INTERIORS INC.; *pg.* 924, *pg.* 343
FILM COMPOSER - Editing System - AVID TECHNOLOGY, INC.; *pg.* 622, *pg.* 804
FILM/FLASH - Newsletter - EASTMAN KODAK COMPANY; *pg.* 1408, *pg.* 1333
THE FILM IN THE FAMILIAR YELLOW BOX - Photographic film - EASTMAN KODAK COMPANY; *pg.* 1408, *pg.* 1333
FILM JOURNAL INTERNATIONAL - Trade Publication - THE NIELSEN COMPANY B.V.; *pg.* 1671, *pg.* 1272
FILM ON FILM - Plastics Product - AEP INDUSTRIES INC.; *pg.* 1878, *pg.* 1085
FILM SCORE MONTHLY - Magazine - FILM SCORE MONTHLY; *pg.* 1641, *pg.* 103
THE FILM THAT'S A CAMERA - Photo Film/Camera Combination - EASTMAN KODAK COMPANY; *pg.* 1408, *pg.* 1333
FILMBOX - Software - AUTODESK INC.; *pg.* 356, *pg.* 257
FILMSTAR - Fluid Handling System - GRACO, INC.; *pg.* 1342, *pg.* 935
FILMSTRIP - Fabric - NEMSCHOFF, INC.; *pg.* 936, *pg.* 1890
FILMTEC - Membrane Module - THE DOW CHEMICAL COMPANY; *pg.* 1157, *pg.* 898
FILON - Composites - CRANE CO.; *pg.* 227, *pg.* 373
FILPRO - Filtration Products - U.S. SILICA COMPANY; *pg.* 1185, *pg.* 1849
FILTA-MAX - Technology Services - IDEXX LABORATORIES, INC.; *pg.* 1543, *pg.* 753
FILTA-MAX XPRESS - Technology Services - IDEXX LABORATORIES, INC.; *pg.* 1543, *pg.* 753
FILTAIRE - Oil Demister - ALGAS-SDI; *pg.* 1311, *pg.* 1831
FILTEK - Supreme Universal Restorative - 3M COMPANY; *pg.* 1142, *pg.* 956
FILTER - Apparel - OAKLEY, INC.; *pg.* 1840, *pg.* 86
FILTER QUEEN - Vacuum Cleaners - HMI INDUSTRIES INC.; *pg.* 56, *pg.* 1475
FILTER QUEEN INDOOR AIR QUALITY SYSTEM - Air Filter System - HMI INDUSTRIES INC.; *pg.* 56, *pg.* 1475
FILTER SELECT - Cigarettes - PHILIP MORRIS USA INC.; *pg.* 1894, *pg.* 1803
FILTERCHARGER - Filter System - K&N ENGINEERING INC.; *pg.* 210, *pg.* 194
FILTEREDFLO - Medical Product - CINCINNATI SUB-ZERO PRODUCTS, INC.; *pg.* 1070, *pg.* 1411
FILTERFUSE - Switch - POWER INTEGRATIONS, INC.; *pg.* 1369, *pg.* 249
FILTERIZE - Apparel - OAKLEY, INC.; *pg.* 1840, *pg.* 86
FILTERPRO - Software - TEXAS INSTRUMENTS INCORPORATED; *pg.* 679, *pg.* 1688
FILTERSKILLS - Training Program - GE ENERGY; *pg.* 1338, *pg.* 506
FILTERSPUN ACCUWOUND - Wound Filter Media - SERFILCO, LTD.; *pg.* 1375, *pg.* 641
FILTERWIRE EZ - Medical Device - BOSTON SCIENTIFIC CORPORATION; *pg.* 1508, *pg.* 831
FILTHY RICH - Game - MULTIMEDIA GAMES INC.; *pg.* 442, *pg.* 1664
FILTRASORB - Activated Carbon Product - CALGON CARBON CORPORATION; *pg.* 1151, *pg.* 1574
FILTRESSE - Surgical Smoker Handler & Filter - UTAH MEDICAL PRODUCTS, INC.; *pg.* 1605, *pg.* 1752
FILTRETE - Filters - 3M COMPANY; *pg.* 1142, *pg.* 956
FILTREX - Specialty Smoke Detector - SYSTEM SENSOR; *pg.* 676, *pg.* 658
FILTRODE - Photodiode Chip - ADVANCED PHOTONIX, INC.; *pg.* 1398, *pg.* 865
FILTRON - Surgical Mask - 3M COMPANY; *pg.* 1142, *pg.* 956
FILTRON - Interference Filters - DGT HOLDINGS; *pg.* 634, *pg.* 1223
FIN DU MONDE - Beer - SLEEMAN UNIBROUE QUEBEC; *pg.* 265, *pg.* 1950
FINA - Faucet - MOEN INCORPORATED; *pg.* 1056, *pg.* 1468
FINAL 4 - Trademark (Div. I Men's & Women's Basketball) - NATIONAL COLLEGIATE ATHLETIC ASSOCIATION; *pg.* 567, *pg.* 688
FINAL CUT - Application Program - APPLE INC.; *pg.* 350, *pg.* 73
FINAL CUT PRO - Application Program - APPLE INC.; *pg.* 350, *pg.* 73
FINAL DOOM - Video Game - ID SOFTWARE, INC.; *pg.* 956, *pg.* 1727
FINAL EXAM - Shoe - AEROGROUP INTERNATIONAL, INC.; *pg.* 1803, *pg.* 1055
FINAL FOUR - Trademark (Div. I Men's & Women's Basketball) - NATIONAL COLLEGIATE ATHLETIC ASSOCIATION; *pg.* 567, *pg.* 688
FINAL FOUR FRIDAY - Trademark (Div. I Men's & Women's Basketball) - NATIONAL COLLEGIATE ATHLETIC ASSOCIATION; *pg.* 567, *pg.* 688
FINAL NET - Personal Care Electrical Product - HELEN OF TROY L.P.; *pg.* 511, *pg.* 1692
FINAL SECOND - Basketball Equipment - LIFETIME PRODUCTS INC.; *pg.* 933, *pg.* 1751
FINALCUT STUDIO - Application Program - APPLE INC.; *pg.* 350, *pg.* 73
FINALIST - Software - PITNEY BOWES INC.; *pg.* 454, *pg.* 376
FINALSTOPP - Plugging - T.D. WILLIAMSON, INC.; *pg.* 1380, *pg.* 1490
FINANCEPRO - Software - SKILLSOFT PLC; *pg.* 470, *pg.* 1037
FINANCIAL ACCESS NETWORK - Software - DST SYSTEMS, INC.; *pg.* 388, *pg.* 982
THE FINANCIAL ADVISOR SYMPOSIUM - Tradeshow - INVESTMENT SEMINARS, INC.; *pg.* 420, *pg.* 466
FINANCIAL ADVISORS - Tag Line - WADDELL & REED FINANCIAL, INC.; *pg.* 818, *pg.* 721
THE FINANCIAL EDGE - Financial Management Software - BLACKBAUD, INC.; *pg.* 361, *pg.* 1613
FINANCIAL FUSION - Server - SAP; *pg.* 465, *pg.* 78
FINANCIAL PLANNER - Financial Planning Services - THE VANGUARD GROUP, INC.; *pg.* 816, *pg.* 1550
FINANCIAL SERVICES FOR THE GREATER GOOD - Slogan - TEACHERS INSURANCE & ANNUITY ASSOCIATION - COLLEGE RETIREMENT EQUITIES FUND; *pg.* 1219, *pg.* 1297
FINANCIAL WEEK - Newspaper - CRAIN COMMUNICATIONS, INC.; *pg.* 1631, *pg.* 879
FINANCING RURAL AMERICA - Tagline - FEDERAL AGRICULTURAL MORTGAGE CORPORATION; *pg.* 751, *pg.* 399
FINCH - Paper - FINCH PAPER LLC; *pg.* 1457, *pg.* 1161
FINCH DELIGHT - Bird Seed - INTERMOUNTAIN FARMERS ASSOCIATION; *pg.* 705, *pg.* 1759
FINCK BRANDS SAMPLER - Cigars - FINCK CIGAR CO.; *pg.* 1894, *pg.* 1740
FINCK'S 1893 - Cigars - FINCK CIGAR CO.; *pg.* 1894, *pg.* 1740
FINCK'S COMMERCE - Cigars - FINCK CIGAR CO.; *pg.* 1894, *pg.* 1740
FINCK'S RESAGOS SABOR NUEVO - Cigars - FINCK CIGAR CO.; *pg.* 1894, *pg.* 1740
FIND - Track & Find Bluetooth Tag - SENSEGIZ INC.; *pg.* 110, *pg.* 227
FIND-A-BEAR - Bear Projects - BUILD-A-BEAR WORKSHOP, INC.; *pg.* 950, *pg.* 993
FIND A WORKSHOP - Location - BUILD-A-BEAR WORKSHOP, INC.; *pg.* 950, *pg.* 993
FIND-FLIGHT - Software - PASSUR AEROSPACE, INC.; *pg.* 233, *pg.* 376
FIND ME - Flashlight - ENERGIZER HOLDINGS, INC.; *pg.* 637, *pg.* 996
FIND NEW ROADS - Chevrolet Tagline - GENERAL MOTORS COMPANY; *pg.* 175, *pg.* 881
FIND YOUR SIGNATURE FIT - Tagline - FGX INTERNATIONAL, INC.; *pg.* 5, *pg.* 1608
FINDD - Footwear - STEVEN MADDEN, LTD.; *pg.* 1819, *pg.* 1176
FINDER - Operating System Software - APPLE INC.; *pg.* 350, *pg.* 73
FINDING NEW WAYS - Slogan - CONCUR TECHNOLOGIES; *pg.* 1903, *pg.* 501
FINDLAW.COM - Web Search - FINDLAW; *pg.* 1641, *pg.* 285
FINDME - Communication Product - CENTURYLINK, INC; *pg.* 1870, *pg.* 317
FINDMRO - Sourcing Service - W.W. GRAINGER, INC.; *pg.* 1390, *pg.* 625
FINDVIAMOTO - Software - MOTOROLA SOLUTIONS, INC.; *pg.* 657, *pg.* 659
FINE EDGE - Diamond Sharpening Pad - GERBER LEGENDARY BLADES; *pg.* 1834, *pg.* 1503
FINE FISSURED - Ceilings & Walls - ARMSTRONG WORLD INDUSTRIES, INC.; *pg.* 914, *pg.* 1545
FINE KNIT - Beanie - OAKLEY, INC.; *pg.* 1840, *pg.* 86
FINE-L-KOTE - Chemical Cleaner Product - TECH SPRAY, L.P.; *pg.* 1183, *pg.* 1659
FINE/LINE - Hydronic Baseboard - SLANT/FIN CORPORATION; *pg.* 1076, *pg.* 1163
FINEADJUST - Electronic Components - MOLEX INCORPORATED; *pg.* 655, *pg.* 628
FINECARB - Vacuum Furance System - SECO/WARWICK CORPORATION; *pg.* 1076, *pg.* 1552
FINEEDGE - Image Processing Product - SEMTECH CORPORATION GENNUM PRODUCTS; *pg.* 671, *pg.* 1919
FINELINE BGA - Packaging Technology - ALTERA CORPORATION; *pg.* 348, *pg.* 237
FINENG - Investment Products & Services - FINANCIAL ENGINES, INC.; *pg.* 753, *pg.* 285
FINEPOINT - Printer - XEROX CORPORATION; *pg.* 494, *pg.* 365
FINER THINGS - Carpet - INTERFACE, INC.; *pg.* 695, *pg.* 512
FINESCALE MODELER - Magazine - KALMBACH PUBLISHING CO.; *pg.* 1656, *pg.* 1898
FINESSE - Textiles - BERNHARDT DESIGN; *pg.* 918, *pg.* 1381
FINESSE - Broadloom - COURISTAN INC.; *pg.* 921, *pg.* 1067
FINESSE - Dental Product - DENTSPLY INTERNATIONAL INC.; *pg.* 1522, *pg.* 1596
FINESSE - Herbicide - E.I. DU PONT DE NEMOURS & COMPANY; *pg.* 1159, *pg.* 390
FINESSE - Range Hood - NORTEK, INC.; *pg.* 100, *pg.* 1607
FINESSE - Footwear - P.W. MINOR & SON, INC.; *pg.* 1816, *pg.* 1140
FINESSE - Electrosurgical Generator With Integrated Smoke Evacuator - UTAH MEDICAL PRODUCTS, INC.; *pg.* 1605, *pg.* 1752
FINESSE HD - Software - SS&C TECHNOLOGIES HOLDINGS, INC.; *pg.* 473, *pg.* 386
FINESSE-IT - Automotive Paint Repair System - 3M COMPANY; *pg.* 1142, *pg.* 956
THE FINEST BERRIES IN THE WORLD - Slogan - DRISCOLL STRAWBERRY ASSOCIATES INC.; *pg.* 854, *pg.* 305
FINEST HOUR - Game - ACTIVISION BLIZZARD, INC.; *pg.* 948, *pg.* 271
FINEST IN THE FIELD - Athletic Equipment & Sporting Goods - RAWLINGS SPORTING GOODS CO., INC.; *pg.* 1843, *pg.* 1002
FINETUNE DATA - Data Quality & Postal Presorting - PITNEY BOWES INC.; *pg.* 454, *pg.* 376
FINEWELD - Copper Alloy - OLIN CORPORATION; *pg.* 1176, *pg.* 976
FINEX - Fluid Handling System - GRACO, INC.; *pg.* 1342, *pg.* 935
FINGER PINKIES - Hand Cleaners - THE GILLETTE COMPANY; *pg.* 509, *pg.* 795
FINGER SHIELD - Garage Door System that Helps Prevent Severed Fingers in Section Joints - MARTIN DOOR MANUFACTURING, INC.; *pg.* 96, *pg.* 1759
FINGER TRAC - Rubber Mat - THE BILTRITE CORPORATION; *pg.* 1879, *pg.* 850
FINGERCHIP - Sensor - ATMEL CORPORATION; *pg.* 621,

First page reference indicates Business Class Edition
Second page reference indicates Geographic Edition

pg. 238
FINGERHUT - E-Commerce Retailer - BLUESTEM BRANDS, INC.; *pg.* 1763, *pg.* 922
FINGERMAJIG - Toys - 1-800-FLOWERS.COM, INC.; *pg.* 1758, *pg.* 1151
FINGERPRINTING - Software - BIO-RAD LABORATORIES, INC.; *pg.* 1504, *pg.* 101
FINGERPRINTING II INFORMATIX - Software - BIO-RAD LABORATORIES, INC.; *pg.* 1504, *pg.* 101
FINGERPRINTING PLUS - Software - BIO-RAD LABORATORIES, INC.; *pg.* 1504, *pg.* 101
FINIAL - Kitchen Product - KOHLER CO.; *pg.* 91, *pg.* 1862
FINIAN'S FORTUNE - Video Game - INTERNATIONAL GAME TECHNOLOGY; *pg.* 957, *pg.* 1024
FINISH - Dishwashing Products - RECKITT BENCKISER INC.; *pg.* 1136, *pg.* 1105
FINISH LINE - Textiles - BERNHARDT DESIGN; *pg.* 918, *pg.* 1381
FINISH LINE BLUE LABEL - Sportswear - THE FINISH LINE, INC.; *pg.* 1769, *pg.* 686
FINISH LYNX - Scoreboard & Sports Product - DAKTRONICS, INC.; *pg.* 633, *pg.* 1624
FINISH PLUS - Automotive Reconditioning Product - MOC PRODUCTS COMPANY, INC.; *pg.* 332, *pg.* 174
FINISHIELD - Window & Door - JELD-WEN, INC.; *pg.* 1051, *pg.* 1499
FINISHING ELEMENTS - Accent Piece - OWENS CORNING; *pg.* 102, *pg.* 1476
FINISHING PRODUCTS FOR THE IMAGING INDUSTRY - Tagline - CODA INC.; *pg.* 1406, *pg.* 1081
FINISHING SPRAY - Hair Care Product - JOHN PAUL MITCHELL SYSTEMS; *pg.* 512, *pg.* 133
FINISHING TOUCH - Fluid Handling System - GRACO, INC.; *pg.* 1342, *pg.* 935
FINISHPRO - Fluid Handling System - GRACO, INC.; *pg.* 1342, *pg.* 935
FINIUM - Paint & Coating - DIAMOND VOGEL PAINT, INC.; *pg.* 1441, *pg.* 710
FINLAND - Footwear - EASTLAND SHOE CORPORATION; *pg.* 1808, *pg.* 750
FINLANDIA - Vodka - BROWN-FORMAN CORPORATION; *pg.* 1958, *pg.* 732
FINLAY - Crushing & Screening Equipment - TEREX CORPORATION; *pg.* 1381, *pg.* 384
FINLEY - Beverages - THE COCA-COLA COMPANY; *pg.* 240, *pg.* 493
FINLEY - Furniture - JASPER GROUP; *pg.* 930, *pg.* 691
FINN-AQUA - Water Still - STERIS CORPORATION; *pg.* 1597, *pg.* 1464
FINNALINE - Pigmented Powdered Leather Finish Concentrate - HENKEL CORPORATION; *pg.* 1165, *pg.* 1535
FINNIGAN - Women's Clothing & Accessories - WOODEN SHIPS OF HOBOKEN; *pg.* 35, *pg.* 1315
FINPRO - Insurance Brokerage Services - MARSH & MCLENNAN COMPANIES INC.; *pg.* 1207, *pg.* 1256
FINSEAL - Weatherstripping - SCHLEGEL SYSTEMS, INC.; *pg.* 109, *pg.* 1337
FINYL RAIL - Vinyl Railing - NORTEK, INC.; *pg.* 100, *pg.* 1607
FIONA - Bath Accessory - CROSCILL, INC.; *pg.* 1122, *pg.* 1220
FIONA - Furniture - ETHAN ALLEN INTERIORS INC.; *pg.* 924, *pg.* 343
FIONA - Furniture - HOOKER FURNITURE CORPORATION; *pg.* 928, *pg.* 1788
FIORAVANTI - Soft Drink - THE COCA-COLA COMPANY; *pg.* 240, *pg.* 493
FIORD - Fabric - NEMSCHOFF, INC.; *pg.* 936, *pg.* 1890
FIORE - Window Treatment - CROSCILL, INC.; *pg.* 1122, *pg.* 1220
FIORE - Bath & Plumbing Product - JACUZZI BRANDS CORPORATION; *pg.* 554, *pg.* 65
FIORI - Fan - CRAFTMADE INTERNATIONAL, INC.; *pg.* 1295, *pg.* 1670
FIORINAL - Pharmaceutical Product - LANNETT COMPANY, INC.; *pg.* 1555, *pg.* 1566
FIOS - Fiber Optic Network for Broadband Communication - VERIZON COMMUNICATIONS INC.; *pg.* 1875, *pg.* 1309
FIP - Semiconductor Product - RENESAS ELECTRONICS AMERICA INC.; *pg.* 667, *pg.* 269
FIPROFLAX - Nutritional Product - NUTRACEUTICAL INTERNATIONAL CORPORATION; *pg.* 1576, *pg.* 1753
FIRE - Software - AUTODESK INC.; *pg.* 356, *pg.* 257
FIRE - Beverages - THE COCA-COLA COMPANY; *pg.* 240, *pg.* 493
FIRE ALARM/CONTROL CABLE - Fire Alarm & Control Wiring Cable - AFC CABLE SYSTEMS, INC.; *pg.* 1294, *pg.* 835
FIRE & ICE - Desserts - FRISCH'S RESTAURANTS, INC.; *pg.* 1729, *pg.* 1413
FIRE & ICE - Perfume - REVLON, INC.; *pg.* 521, *pg.* 1286
FIRE-BALL - Pumps - GRACO, INC.; *pg.* 1342, *pg.* 935
FIRE BELLS - Video Game - INTERNATIONAL GAME TECHNOLOGY; *pg.* 957, *pg.* 1024
FIRE CHECK - Waste Receptacles - THE PROTECTOSEAL COMPANY; *pg.* 1370, *pg.* 556
FIRE DIAMONDS - Video Game - INTERNATIONAL GAME TECHNOLOGY; *pg.* 957, *pg.* 1024
FIRE-GARD - Poke-Thru Service Fittings - SCHNEIDER ELECTRIC USA, INC.; *pg.* 1306, *pg.* 650
FIRE GODDESS - Video Game - INTERNATIONAL GAME TECHNOLOGY; *pg.* 957, *pg.* 1024
FIRE HORSE - Video Game - INTERNATIONAL GAME TECHNOLOGY; *pg.* 957, *pg.* 1024
FIRE ISLAND - Game - WMS INDUSTRIES INC.; *pg.* 593, *pg.* 666
FIRE IT UP - Video Game - INTERNATIONAL GAME TECHNOLOGY; *pg.* 957, *pg.* 1024
FIRE LITE - Metal Building System - BUTLER MANUFACTURING COMPANY; *pg.* 72, *pg.* 981
FIRE LITE - Alarms - NOTIFIER CO.; *pg.* 659, *pg.* 360
FIRE MOUNTAIN - Restaurants - OVATION BRANDS; *pg.* 1743, *pg.* 921
FIRE-N-ICE - Lottery Game - OHIO LOTTERY COMMISSION; *pg.* 1002, *pg.* 1433
FIRE OPALS - Video Game - INTERNATIONAL GAME TECHNOLOGY; *pg.* 957, *pg.* 1024
FIRE PHONE - Smart Phone - AMAZON.COM, INC.; *pg.* 1226, *pg.* 1831
FIRE PLEX - Fire Alarm System - RAULAND-BORG CORPORATION; *pg.* 666, *pg.* 634
FIRE POWER - Shoe - AEROGROUP INTERNATIONAL, INC.; *pg.* 1803, *pg.* 1055
FIRE POWER - Gaming Product - GLD PRODUCTS, INC.; *pg.* 1835, *pg.* 1882
FIRE-R - Fire Retardant Gasket - VICTAULIC COMPANY; *pg.* 1066, *pg.* 1529
FIRE-SAFE - Security File - SENTRY GROUP, INC.; *pg.* 468, *pg.* 1337
FIRE SMART - Fire Detection Equipment - FARADAY; *pg.* 638, *pg.* 1066
FIRE STAR - Skate - ROLLER DERBY SKATE CORP.; *pg.* 966, *pg.* 630
FIRE VULCAN - Flashlight - STREAMLIGHT INC.; *pg.* 1306, *pg.* 1527
FIRE WATCH - Product Series - FARADAY; *pg.* 638, *pg.* 1066
FIREBALL - Cinnamon Whisky - SAZERAC COMPANY, INC.; *pg.* 1969, *pg.* 745
FIREBALL - Valve Series 727, Grooved End Ball Valve - VICTAULIC COMPANY; *pg.* 1066, *pg.* 1529
FIREBALL KENO - Game - INTERNATIONAL GAME TECHNOLOGY; *pg.* 420, *pg.* 1606
FIREBAR - Heater - WATLOW ELECTRIC MANUFACTURING COMPANY; *pg.* 1078, *pg.* 1004
FIREBIRDS - Protective Eyewear - SELLSTROM MANUFACTURING CO.; *pg.* 1428, *pg.* 659
FIREBLOCKER - System - SERTA, INC.; *pg.* 942, *pg.* 619
FIREBOX - Recessed Downlighting Fixtures with UL Fire Rating - HUBBELL LIGHTING - PROGRESS LIGHTING DIVISION; *pg.* 1300, *pg.* 1617
FIREBOX - Flashlight - STREAMLIGHT INC.; *pg.* 1306, *pg.* 1527
FIREBOX - Hardware - WATCHGUARD TECHNOLOGIES, INC.; *pg.* 491, *pg.* 1842
FIREBOX EDGE - Software - WATCHGUARD TECHNOLOGIES, INC.; *pg.* 491, *pg.* 1842
FIREBOX X - Software - WATCHGUARD TECHNOLOGIES, INC.; *pg.* 491, *pg.* 1842
FIRECAT - Snowmobile - ARCTIC CAT INC.; *pg.* 1705, *pg.* 953
FIRECODE - Firestop Sealant - USG CORPORATION; *pg.* 118, *pg.* 594
FIRECON - Flame Retardant Compounds - POLYONE CORPORATION; *pg.* 1177, *pg.* 1404
FIRECRACKER - Food Product - CONAGRA FOODS, INC.; *pg.* 826, *pg.* 1014
FIRECYCLE - System - THE VIKING GROUP; *pg.* 119, *pg.* 891
FIRED EARTH - Fabrics - LEE JOFA, INC.; *pg.* 933, *pg.* 1142
FIREDAM - Endothermic Fire Protection Caulk - 3M COMPANY; *pg.* 1142, *pg.* 956
FIREDEFENDER - Building Product - GEORGIA-PACIFIC LLC; *pg.* 1458, *pg.* 507
FIREDOME - Fire Helmet - E.D. BULLARD COMPANY; *pg.* 1332, *pg.* 727
FIREFLIR - Thermal Imaging System - FLIR SYSTEMS, INC.; *pg.* 1413, *pg.* 1510
FIREFLY - Rescue Strobe Light - ACR ELECTRONICS, INC.; *pg.* 612, *pg.* 422
FIREFLY - Riflescope - BUSHNELL OUTDOOR PRODUCTS, INC.; *pg.* 1403, *pg.* 718
FIREFLY - LAND RECORDING - ION GEOPHYSICAL CORPORATION; *pg.* 1350, *pg.* 1708
FIREFLY - Educational Materials - SCHOLASTIC INC.; *pg.* 1683, *pg.* 1288
FIREFLY - Illuminated Reader & Illuminated Opera Glass - SWIFT OPTICAL INSTRUMENTS, INC.; *pg.* 1430, *pg.* 1744
FIREFLY - Detonation Detection - WOODWARD, INC.; *pg.* 122, *pg.* 329
FIREFLY 2 - Rescue Strobe Light - ACR ELECTRONICS, INC.; *pg.* 612, *pg.* 422
FIREFLY PLUS - Recreational Strobe - ACR ELECTRONICS, INC.; *pg.* 612, *pg.* 422
FIREFOX - Nozzle - AKRON BRASS COMPANY; *pg.* 1311, *pg.* 1482
FIREGL - 3D Graphical Technology - ADVANCED MICRO DEVICES, INC.-MARKHAM; *pg.* 345, *pg.* 1922
FIREGLOW - Container Grown Plant - MONROVIA GROWERS; *pg.* 1797, *pg.* 44
FIREGUARD - Electrical Product - EATON CORPORATION; *pg.* 1331, *pg.* 1429
FIREGUARD - Aboveground Storage Tank - MODERN WELDING COMPANY, INC.; *pg.* 1363, *pg.* 739
FIREGUARD - Plastic & Rubber - TEKNOR APEX COMPANY; *pg.* 1889, *pg.* 1605
FIREGUARD LSZH - Cable Compound - TEKNOR APEX COMPANY; *pg.* 1889, *pg.* 1605
FIREHAWK - Air Respirator - MINE SAFETY APPLIANCES COMPANY; *pg.* 1361, *pg.* 1525
FIREHOUSE SUBS - Restaurant Chain - FIREHOUSE SUBS; *pg.* 1728, *pg.* 433
FIREINSPECTOR - Analyzer - TELEDYNE LECROY; *pg.* 1431, *pg.* 1153
FIREJACKET - Fire Retardant Duct - DURA-LINE HOLDINGS; *pg.* 389, *pg.* 1636
FIRELOCK - Rigid Fire Protection Coupling - VICTAULIC COMPANY; *pg.* 1066, *pg.* 1529
FIRELOCK EZ - Rigid Coupling - VICTAULIC COMPANY; *pg.* 1066, *pg.* 1529
FIREMASTER - Flame Retardants - CHEMTURA CORPORATION; *pg.* 1152, *pg.* 355
FIREMIST - Pigment - BASF CATALYSTS LLC; *pg.* 1148, *pg.* 1074
FIRENZE - Surface Material - STEELCASE INC.; *pg.* 475, *pg.* 889
FIRENZE - Ceramic, Glass, Stone Tiles & Slabs - WALKER & ZANGER, INC.; *pg.* 119, *pg.* 281
FIRENZE GRAPE - Pillow - AMERICAN LEATHER LP; *pg.* 912, *pg.* 1673
FIREPASS - Software - F5 NETWORKS, INC.; *pg.* 396, *pg.* 1835
FIREPLACES - Ceramic, Glass, Stone Tiles & Slabs - WALKER & ZANGER, INC.; *pg.* 119, *pg.* 281
FIREPLI - Paper Product - WESTROCK COMPANY; *pg.* 1472, *pg.* 1805
FIRERANGE - Fireboot - WEINBRENNER SHOE COMPANY, INC.; *pg.* 1822, *pg.* 1871
FIRERASER - Fire Suppression System - FIKE CORPORATION; *pg.* 1047, *pg.* 973
FIREROD - Heater - WATLOW ELECTRIC MANUFACTURING COMPANY; *pg.* 1078, *pg.* 1004
FIRESHIELD - Flame Retardants - CHEMTURA CORPORATION; *pg.* 1152, *pg.* 355
FIRESIDE BOOKS - Paperback Books - SIMON & SCHUSTER, INC.; *pg.* 1687, *pg.* 1292
FIRESTALL - Building Product - HOMASOTE COMPANY; *pg.* 87, *pg.* 1126
FIRESTAR - Buffet Bars - CARLISLE FOODSERVICE PRODUCTS INCORPORATED; *pg.* 1455, *pg.* 1485
FIRESTART - Firestarter - DURAFLAME, INC.; *pg.* 1123, *pg.* 280

FIRESTICK - Construction Equipment - VERMEER MANUFACTURING COMPANY; *pg.* 708, *pg.* 711
FIRESTONE TRUCK TIRES - Commercial Tires - BRIDGESTONE AMERICAS, INC.; *pg.* 201, *pg.* 1649
FIRESTORM - Polymer Product - CHEMTURA CORPORATION; *pg.* 1152, *pg.* 355
FIRESTORM - Character - DC COMICS, INC.; *pg.* 1633, *pg.* 1221
FIRESTORM - Video Game - ELECTRONIC ARTS INC.; *pg.* 951, *pg.* 189
FIRESTORM - Knife - GERBER LEGENDARY BLADES; *pg.* 1834, *pg.* 1503
FIRETECH - Footwear - LACROSSE FOOTWEAR, INC.; *pg.* 1811, *pg.* 1503
FIRETROL - Fire Pump Controller - ASCO POWER TECHNOLOGIES, L.P.; *pg.* 1314, *pg.* 1066
FIREVUE - Electrical & Computer Cables, Cable Adapters, Connectors & Interface Boards - RELAX TECHNOLOGY, INC.; *pg.* 461, *pg.* 298
FIREWALKER - Ethnobotanical Product - NU SKIN ENTERPRISES, INC.; *pg.* 518, *pg.* 1755
FIREWALL - Burner - NAO, INC.; *pg.* 1074, *pg.* 1567
FIREWALL-FRIENDLY - Software - AXEDA SYSTEMS INC.; *pg.* 359, *pg.* 819
FIREWIRE - Serial Bus - APPLE INC.; *pg.* 350, *pg.* 73
FIREWIRE - Machine Vision System - COGNEX CORPORATION; *pg.* 1406, *pg.* 834
FIREWIRE - Thermal Imaging System - FLIR SYSTEMS, INC.; *pg.* 1413, *pg.* 1510
FIREWIRE - Camera - THORLABS INC.; *pg.* 1432, *pg.* 1098
FIREWIRE - Cable Card - TRIPPE MANUFACTURING COMPANY; *pg.* 220, *pg.* 592
FIREWIRE COMPACTFLASH - Digital Film Reader - LEXAR MEDIA, INC.; *pg.* 1262, *pg.* 146
FIREWIRE SYMBOL - Symbol - APPLE INC.; *pg.* 350, *pg.* 73
FIREWOLF - Conventional Trolling Reels - DAIWA CORPORATION; *pg.* 1832, *pg.* 75
FIREWOLF - Fire Product - NAPCO SECURITY SYSTEMS, INC.; *pg.* 658, *pg.* 1138
FIREWORKS - Software - ADOBE SYSTEMS INCORPORATED; *pg.* 342, *pg.* 235
FIREWORKS - Carpet - BEAULIEU GROUP, LLC; *pg.* 917, *pg.* 529
FIREWORKS - Jewelry Collection - TIFFANY & CO.; *pg.* 13, *pg.* 1299
FIREWORKS.COM - Fireworks Website - B.J. ALAN COMPANY; *pg.* 1150, *pg.* 1483
FIRM - Wire Guide - COOK GROUP, INC.; *pg.* 1518, *pg.* 674
THE FIRM - Fitness DVD - GAIAM, INC.; *pg.* 1532, *pg.* 334
FIRM FINISHING SPRAY - Hair Care Product - JOHN PAUL MITCHELL SYSTEMS; *pg.* 512, *pg.* 133
FIRM-O-PEDIC - Mattress & Box Spring Sets - KINGSDOWN, INC.; *pg.* 932, *pg.* 1383
FIRM WHERE YOU NEED IT - Slogan - TEMPUR SEALY INTERNATIONAL, INC.; *pg.* 944, *pg.* 731
FIRMFEEL - Golfing Product - CALLAWAY GOLF COMPANY; *pg.* 1829, *pg.* 58
FIRO-B - Technical Guide - CPP, INC.; *pg.* 1631, *pg.* 153
FIROMATIC - Valves & Security Products - HIGHFIELD MANUFACTURING CO.; *pg.* 1346, *pg.* 339
FIRST ALERT - Home Protection Products - BRK BRANDS, INC.; *pg.* 627, *pg.* 554
FIRST ALERT - Medical Equipment - INVACARE CORPORATION; *pg.* 1546, *pg.* 1451
FIRST ALERT ESCAPE - Light Smoke Alarm - TRACTOR SUPPLY COMPANY; *pg.* 708, *pg.* 1627
FIRST ALERT PLUG - Carbon Monoxide Alarm - TRACTOR SUPPLY COMPANY; *pg.* 708, *pg.* 1627
FIRST AVIATION - Aircraft Parts - FIRST AVIATION SERVICES INC.; *pg.* 227, *pg.* 384
FIRST BITE - Dental Product - DENTSPLY INTERNATIONAL INC.; *pg.* 1522, *pg.* 1596
FIRST CALL - Financial Publications - THOMSON REUTERS CORPORATION; *pg.* 1693, *pg.* 1944
FIRST CHECK - Drug Abuse & Disease Test Products - ALERE INC.; *pg.* 1488, *pg.* 849
FIRST CHOICE - Paper - DOMTAR CORPORATION; *pg.* 1456, *pg.* 1954
FIRST CHOICE - Paper Product - WEYERHAEUSER COMPANY; *pg.* 121, *pg.* 1820
THE FIRST CHOICE FOR NEW HOMES - Slogan - MOVE, INC.; *pg.* 1268, *pg.* 247
FIRST CHOICE HAIRCUTTERS - Hair Salons - REGIS CORPORATION; *pg.* 521, *pg.* 941
FIRST CHOICE WHEN QUALITY COUNTS - Tag Line - GRACO, INC.; *pg.* 1342, *pg.* 935
FIRST CLASS - Carpet - BEAULIEU GROUP, LLC; *pg.* 917, *pg.* 529
FIRST-CLASS MAIL - Postal Services - UNITED STATES POSTAL SERVICE; *pg.* 1009, *pg.* 406
FIRST CONNECTIONS - Utility Service - CPS ENERGY; *pg.* 1939, *pg.* 1739
FIRST DATABANK - Pharmaceutical Data - THE HEARST CORPORATION; *pg.* 1649, *pg.* 1239
FIRST DEFENSE - Pepper Sprays - BAE SYSTEMS PRODUCTS GROUP; *pg.* 359, *pg.* 432
FIRST DRAFT - Educational Materials - SCHOLASTIC INC.; *pg.* 1683, *pg.* 1288
FIRST ENCOUNTER - Virtual Prototyping Application - CADENCE DESIGN SYSTEMS, INC.; *pg.* 367, *pg.* 239
FIRST FILE - Office Furniture - STEELCASE INC.; *pg.* 475, *pg.* 889
FIRST FILL - Pharmaceutical Product - PROGRESSIVE MEDICAL, INC.; *pg.* 1586, *pg.* 1480
FIRST GRADE FRIENDS - Educational Materials - SCHOLASTIC INC.; *pg.* 1683, *pg.* 1288
FIRST IN CLEAN AIR - Slogan - PURAFIL, INC.; *pg.* 333, *pg.* 530
THE FIRST IN SYNTHETICS - Slogan - AMSOIL INC.; *pg.* 971, *pg.* 1896
FIRST ISSUE - Business Casual Apparel - KATE SPADE & COMPANY; *pg.* 27, *pg.* 1248
FIRST LADY - Beauty Salon & Barber Shop Furniture - BELVEDERE USA CORPORATION; *pg.* 917, *pg.* 556
FIRST LOOK - Systems Integration & Aeronautics - LOCKHEED MARTIN CORPORATION; *pg.* 229, *pg.* 762
FIRST LOVE - Carpet - BEAULIEU GROUP, LLC; *pg.* 917, *pg.* 529
FIRST LOVE - Container Grown Plant - MONROVIA GROWERS; *pg.* 1797, *pg.* 44
FIRST MARK - Non-Food Disposable Products - PERFORMANCE FOOD GROUP COMPANY, LLC; *pg.* 1030, *pg.* 1803
FIRST NAME FIRST CHOICE - Tagline - GRACO, INC.; *pg.* 1342, *pg.* 935
THE FIRST NAME IN AVOCADOS - Slogan - CALAVO GROWERS, INC.; *pg.* 843, *pg.* 276
THE FIRST NAME IN ELECTROSURGERY. - Tagline - BOVIE MEDICAL CORPORATION; *pg.* 1402, *pg.* 1178
THE FIRST NAME IN VEHICLE SAFETY SYSTEMS - Tag Line - GROTE INDUSTRIES, INC.; *pg.* 206, *pg.* 693
FIRST NATURE - Pet Product - PETSMART, INC.; *pg.* 1481, *pg.* 18
FIRST-PASS DESIGN SUCCESS - Software System - MENTOR GRAPHICS CORPORATION; *pg.* 432, *pg.* 1510
FIRST-PASS SUCCESS - Software System - MENTOR GRAPHICS CORPORATION; *pg.* 432, *pg.* 1510
FIRST PRIZE - Buckwheat Flour - THE BIRKETT MILLS; *pg.* 826, *pg.* 1321
FIRST RATE - Show Feeds for Cattle - KENT NUTRITION GROUP; *pg.* 1477, *pg.* 710
FIRST RESPONSE - Pregnancy Test - CHURCH & DWIGHT CO., INC.; *pg.* 1153, *pg.* 1063
FIRST ROAD - Road Simulator - MTS SYSTEMS CORPORATION; *pg.* 442, *pg.* 923
FIRST SENIORITY FREEDOM - Medical Service - HARVARD PILGRIM HEALTH CARE, INC.; *pg.* 1539, *pg.* 856
FIRST SIGNAL - Pharmaceutical Product - ALERE INC.; *pg.* 1488, *pg.* 849
FIRST SILICON SYSTEM - Timing System - CADENCE DESIGN SYSTEMS, INC.; *pg.* 367, *pg.* 239
FIRST SNOW - Container Grown Plant - MONROVIA GROWERS; *pg.* 1797, *pg.* 44
FIRST SOLAR & DESIGN - Solar Module - FIRST SOLAR, INC.; *pg.* 639, *pg.* 26
FIRST SOLAR PV - Solar Module - FIRST SOLAR, INC.; *pg.* 639, *pg.* 26
FIRST STEP SELECT - Mattress - KINETIC CONCEPTS, INC.; *pg.* 1553, *pg.* 1741
FIRST STOP - Brake & Clutch - DORMAN PRODUCTS, INC.; *pg.* 204, *pg.* 1522
FIRST THINGS FIRST - Publication - FRANKLIN COVEY CO.; *pg.* 1642, *pg.* 1758
FIRST WATCH - Spray Bottle - KALO, INC.; *pg.* 1796, *pg.* 719
FIRST WITH AID, COMFORT AND QUALITY - Tagline - A-T SURGICAL MFG. CO., INC.; *pg.* 1483, *pg.* 825
FIRST WRAP - Plastics Product - AEP INDUSTRIES INC.; *pg.* 1878, *pg.* 1085
FIRSTAR - Financial Institutions - U.S. BANCORP; *pg.* 815, *pg.* 945
FIRSTBIOS - Software - PHOENIX TECHNOLOGIES LTD.; *pg.* 454, *pg.* 147
FIRSTCHOICE - Pharmaceutical Product - HOSPIRA, INC.; *pg.* 1542, *pg.* 623
FIRSTCLASS - Software - OPENTEXT CORPORATION; *pg.* 450, *pg.* 1948
FIRSTCURE - Chemical Product - ALBEMARLE CORPORATION; *pg.* 1146, *pg.* 741
FIRSTCYTYC - Medical Product - HOLOGIC, INC.; *pg.* 1416, *pg.* 784
FIRSTDEFENSE-ISR - Software Product - RAXCO SOFTWARE, INC.; *pg.* 459, *pg.* 770
FIRSTEP - Safety & Protective Equipment - ENCON SAFETY PRODUCTS; *pg.* 1334, *pg.* 1705
FIRSTFLUSH - Safety & Protective Equipment - ENCON SAFETY PRODUCTS; *pg.* 1334, *pg.* 1705
FIRSTFOOD - Nutritional Product - RBC LIFE SCIENCES, INC.; *pg.* 1588, *pg.* 1723
FIRSTGPS - Navigation Aid - TRIMBLE NAVIGATION LIMITED; *pg.* 1384, *pg.* 288
FIRSTJOYS - Shoes - ACUSHNET COMPANY; *pg.* 1824, *pg.* 818
FIRSTLIGHT - UV Illuminator - UVP, INC.; *pg.* 1434, *pg.* 298
FIRSTLINE - Pest Control Product - FMC CORPORATION; *pg.* 1163, *pg.* 1564
FIRSTNET - Emergency Medicine Information System - CERNER CORPORATION; *pg.* 1514, *pg.* 981
FIRSTPASS - Software - EMC CORPORATION; *pg.* 391, *pg.* 825
FIRSTPAY - Internet Bill Payment System - FIRSTRUST SAVINGS BANK; *pg.* 758, *pg.* 1523
FIRSTSAVE - Automated External Defibrillator - CARDIAC SCIENCE CORPORATION; *pg.* 1512, *pg.* 1897
FIRSTSAVER - Passbook Service - FIRSTRUST SAVINGS BANK; *pg.* 758, *pg.* 1523
FIRSTSHOT - Herbicide - E.I. DU PONT DE NEMOURS & COMPANY; *pg.* 1159, *pg.* 390
FIRSTSITE - Web-Based Resource - FIRSTRUST SAVINGS BANK; *pg.* 758, *pg.* 1523
FIRSTSTEP - Clinical Bedding - KINETIC CONCEPTS, INC.; *pg.* 1553, *pg.* 1741
FIRSTSTREET - Catalog & Website - TECHNOBRANDS, INC.; *pg.* 1788, *pg.* 1778
FIRSTTOUCH - Semiconductor Solution - CYPRESS SEMICONDUCTOR CORPORATION; *pg.* 1326, *pg.* 243
FIRSTVANTAGE - Term Insurance - CATHOLIC ORDER OF FORESTERS; *pg.* 1196, *pg.* 635
FIRSTVANTAGE/PATHWAYS PROGRAM - Fraternal Benefits - CATHOLIC ORDER OF FORESTERS; *pg.* 1196, *pg.* 635
FIRSTWARE - Business Software - PHOENIX TECHNOLOGIES LTD.; *pg.* 454, *pg.* 147
FISCHER'S - Deli Meats - SPECIALTY FOODS GROUP-FIELD PACKING DIV.; *pg.* 897, *pg.* 739
FISH & HOOK - Hand Tools - SNAP-ON INCORPORATED; *pg.* 1062, *pg.* 1862
FISH EAGLE - Fishing Rods - CABELA'S INCORPORATED; *pg.* 535, *pg.* 1019
FISH FRY - Video Game - INTERNATIONAL GAME TECHNOLOGY; *pg.* 957, *pg.* 1024
FISH HAWK - Video Viewing System - SWORDFISH FINANCIAL, INC.; *pg.* 1430, *pg.* 1737
FISH IN A BARREL - Video Game - INTERNATIONAL GAME TECHNOLOGY; *pg.* 957, *pg.* 1024
FISH TV - Video Viewing System - SWORDFISH FINANCIAL, INC.; *pg.* 1430, *pg.* 1737
FISHAMAJIG - Fish Sandwich - FRIENDLY ICE CREAM, LLC; *pg.* 1853, *pg.* 859
FISHER - Food Product - JOHN B. SANFILIPPO & SON, INC.; *pg.* 1024, *pg.* 610
FISHER - Peanut - PROMOTION IN MOTION, INC.; *pg.* 1861, *pg.* 1052
FISHER BOY - Frozen Fish Fillets-United States - HIGH LINER FOODS INCORPORATED; *pg.* 862, *pg.* 1917
FISHER MILK CHOCOLATE PEANUTS - Food Product - PROMOTION IN MOTION, INC.; *pg.* 1861, *pg.* 1052
FISHER PIERCE - Lighting & Control System - DANAHER CORPORATION; *pg.* 1044, *pg.* 397
FISHER-PRICE - Toys - MATTEL, INC.; *pg.* 962, *pg.* 81
FISHER SCIENTIFIC - Laboratory Equipment & Chemicals - THERMO FISHER SCIENTIFIC INC.; *pg.* 1431, *pg.* 854
FISHERINGS - Frozen Seafood - HIGH LINER FOODS INCORPORATED; *pg.* 862, *pg.* 1917
FISHERMAN - Aluminum Boat - ALUMACRAFT BOAT

First page reference indicates Business Class Edition
Second page reference indicates Geographic Edition

COMPANY; *pg.* 1705, *pg.* 964

FISHERMAN - Fiberglass Boat Product - GRADY-WHITE BOATS, INC.; *pg.* 1707, *pg.* 1377

FISHERMEN'S WOOL - Yarn - LION BRAND YARN COMPANY; *pg.* 696, *pg.* 1050

FISHIN FOR CASH - Slots - INTERNATIONAL GAME TECHNOLOGY; *pg.* 957, *pg.* 1024

FISHIN' FOR FORTUNE - Lottery Game - MINNESOTA STATE LOTTERY; *pg.* 999, *pg.* 956

FISHING CAMP - Belt - PHOENIX FOOTWEAR GROUP, INC.; *pg.* 1815, *pg.* 60

FISHING GAME - Video Game - INTERNATIONAL GAME TECHNOLOGY; *pg.* 957, *pg.* 1024

FISHING TACKLE RETAILER - Magazine - B.A.S.S., L.L.C.; *pg.* 270, *pg.* 1

FISHMATE - Fish Tank Filters & Accessories - LILYPONS WATER GARDENS INC.; *pg.* 1797, *pg.* 766

FISK - Tires - MICHELIN NORTH AMERICA INC.; *pg.* 1886, *pg.* 1618

FISTFUL OF $50S - Game - MISSOURI LOTTERY; *pg.* 999, *pg.* 979

FISTFUL OF DOLLARS - Game - MISSOURI LOTTERY; *pg.* 999, *pg.* 979

FIT - Software - KEMET CORPORATION; *pg.* 649, *pg.* 1621

FIT - Fast Installation Technique - VICTAULIC COMPANY; *pg.* 1066, *pg.* 1529

FIT-AL - Saw Blades - KENNAMETAL IPG; *pg.* 1353, *pg.* 1615

FIT-BED - Shoes - ACUSHNET COMPANY; *pg.* 1824, *pg.* 818

FIT CHOICES BY MEDICA - Health Plan & Publication - MEDICA, INC.; *pg.* 1208, *pg.* 949

FIT, FEEL & APPEAL. - Slogan - WELLS LAMONT CORPORATION; *pg.* 15, *pg.* 638

FIT FLEX - Circles - BALANCED BODY, INC.; *pg.* 1826, *pg.* 195

FIT FOR DUTY FIT FOR YOU - Slogan - ELBECO INCORPORATED; *pg.* 40, *pg.* 1584

FIT-FOREVER - Slacks - HABAND COMPANY, INC.; *pg.* 1772, *pg.* 1099

FIT LAB - Hard Drive - WESTERN DIGITAL CORPORATION; *pg.* 492, *pg.* 118

FIT 'N EASY - Skinless & Boneless Poultry - PERDUE FARMS INCORPORATED; *pg.* 889, *pg.* 777

FIT 'N FRUITFUL - Fruit Drink - JAMBA, INC.; *pg.* 1024, *pg.* 84

FIT 'N TRIM - Dog Food - NESTLE PURINA PETCARE COMPANY; *pg.* 1479, *pg.* 1000

FIT POKE-THRU - Wiring Products - WIREMOLD/LEGRAND; *pg.* 689, *pg.* 383

FIT PREGNANCY - Magazine - AMERICAN MEDIA, INC.; *pg.* 1615, *pg.* 410

FIT STRIP - Resistance Exercise - SCHOOL-TECH, INC.; *pg.* 1844, *pg.* 866

FIT SYSTEM - Furniture - ANTHRO CORPORATION; *pg.* 913, *pg.* 1509

FITFORUMS - Internet Health Information - PFIZER INC.; *pg.* 1581, *pg.* 1278

FITNESS - Magazine - MEREDITH CORPORATION; *pg.* 1663, *pg.* 705

FITNESS FORMULA - Fitness Product - BALLY TOTAL FITNESS HOLDINGS CORPORATION; *pg.* 532, *pg.* 1200

FITNESS HOODIE - Clothing - K-SWISS; *pg.* 1837, *pg.* 306

FITNESS ON DEMAND - Fitness Kiosk & Platform - LIFT BRANDS; *pg.* 557, *pg.* 920

FITNESS RX FOR MEN - Magazine - FITNESS RX; *pg.* 1641, *pg.* 1342

FITNESS RX FOR WOMEN - Magazine - FITNESS RX; *pg.* 1641, *pg.* 1342

FITS-ALL - Paint Can - FOAMPRO MANUFACTURING, INC.; *pg.* 1442, *pg.* 110

FITS OVER - SLOGAN - FGX INTERNATIONAL, INC.; *pg.* 5, *pg.* 1608

FITTI - Baby Diaper - ASSOCIATED HYGIENIC PRODUCTS LLC; *pg.* 1496, *pg.* 531

FITTING WORKS - Golf Equipment - ACUSHNET COMPANY; *pg.* 1824, *pg.* 818

FITWOMAN MULTI - Nutritional Product - NUTRACEUTICAL INTERNATIONAL CORPORATION; *pg.* 1576, *pg.* 1753

FIVE ACES POKER - Video Poker - INTERNATIONAL GAME TECHNOLOGY; *pg.* 957, *pg.* 1024

FIVE ALIVE - Chilled, Aseptic & Frozen Concentrated Refreshment Beverages - THE COCA-COLA COMPANY; *pg.* 240, *pg.* 493

FIVE & DIME - Slot Machine - BALLY TECHNOLOGIES, INC.; *pg.* 531, *pg.* 1022

FIVE CARD INSTANT BINGO - Video Slots - INTERNATIONAL GAME TECHNOLOGY; *pg.* 957, *pg.* 1024

FIVE CROWNS - Restaurant - LAWRY'S RESTAURANTS, INC.; *pg.* 1735, *pg.* 180

FIVE DIAMOND - Credit Card Services - AMERICAN AUTOMOBILE ASSOCIATION; *pg.* 1190, *pg.* 429

FIVE O'CLOCK - Gin & Vodka - LAIRD & COMPANY, INC.; *pg.* 1966, *pg.* 1119

FIVE RIVERS - Wine - BROWN-FORMAN CORPORATION; *pg.* 1958, *pg.* 732

FIVE ROSES - Food Products - THE J.M. SMUCKER COMPANY; *pg.* 865, *pg.* 1468

FIVE STAR - Publisher - GALE CENGAGE LEARNING; *pg.* 1643, *pg.* 885

FIVE STAR - Slots - INTERNATIONAL GAME TECHNOLOGY; *pg.* 957, *pg.* 1024

FIVE STAR - Office Product - WESTROCK COMPANY; *pg.* 1472, *pg.* 1805

FIVE STAR AMERICAN - Blended Whiskey - LAIRD & COMPANY, INC.; *pg.* 1966, *pg.* 1119

FIVE STAR SEAL - Seal - FLOWSERVE CORPORATION; *pg.* 82, *pg.* 1719

FIVE STARSM - Applicator Program - USG CORPORATION; *pg.* 118, *pg.* 594

FIVE-STONE RING - Diamond Product - BLUE NILE, INC.; *pg.* 2, *pg.* 1834

FIVE TEN - Footwear Product - DECKERS OUTDOOR CORPORATION; *pg.* 1807, *pg.* 100

FIVE TIMES GOLD - Slots - INTERNATIONAL GAME TECHNOLOGY; *pg.* 957, *pg.* 1024

FIVE TIMES PAY - Slots - INTERNATIONAL GAME TECHNOLOGY; *pg.* 957, *pg.* 1024

FIVE TIMES PAY BONUS WHEEL - Slots - INTERNATIONAL GAME TECHNOLOGY; *pg.* 957, *pg.* 1024

FIVE TIMES PAY DELUXE - Slots - INTERNATIONAL GAME TECHNOLOGY; *pg.* 957, *pg.* 1024

FIVES - Eyewear - OAKLEY, INC.; *pg.* 1840, *pg.* 86

FIVESTAR - Gas Monitor - MINE SAFETY APPLIANCES COMPANY; *pg.* 1361, *pg.* 1525

FIX-A-FLAT - Tire Inflator - SHELL LUBRICANTS; *pg.* 217, *pg.* 1714

FIX-A-THRED - Thread Repair Kit - TRACTOR SUPPLY COMPANY; *pg.* 708, *pg.* 1627

FIX MESSAGING - Online Trading Services - MARKETAXESS HOLDINGS INC.; *pg.* 778, *pg.* 1256

FIX QUIX - Food Product - CARL BUDDIG & COMPANY; *pg.* 846, *pg.* 619

FIX THE MIXI - Games - LEAPFROG ENTERPRISES, INC.; *pg.* 961, *pg.* 84

FIXATION - Tissue Treatment - MEDTRONIC, INC.; *pg.* 1564, *pg.* 939

FIXED DOWNLIGHTS - Fiber Optic Fixtures - REVOLUTION LIGHTING TECHNOLOGIES, INC.; *pg.* 1304, *pg.* 377

FIXED RATE ULTRA - Wireless Communication System - AT&T SOUTHEAST; *pg.* 1868, *pg.* 489

FIXEDMATCH - Network Technology - ADVANCED ENERGY INDUSTRIES, INC.; *pg.* 613, *pg.* 328

FIXLOAD - Hardware Product - BROOKS AUTOMATION, INC.; *pg.* 1320, *pg.* 813

FIXMASTER - Epoxies - HENKEL CORPORATION; *pg.* 1049, *pg.* 369

FIXODENT - Oral Care Product - THE PROCTER & GAMBLE COMPANY; *pg.* 1129, *pg.* 1418

FIXXERS - Flashlight - BROWN & BIGELOW, INC.; *pg.* 1624, *pg.* 959

FIZZ - Educational Materials - SCHOLASTIC INC.; *pg.* 1683, *pg.* 1288

FIZZ C - Nutritional Product - NUTRACEUTICAL INTERNATIONAL CORPORATION; *pg.* 1576, *pg.* 1753

FIZZ-ITS - Home Cleaner - S.C. JOHNSON & SON, INC.; *pg.* 334, *pg.* 1889

FJ - Shoes - ACUSHNET COMPANY; *pg.* 1824, *pg.* 818

FJ CRUISER - Sports Utility Vehicle - TOYOTA MOTOR NORTH AMERICA, INC.; *pg.* 192, *pg.* 1303

FKI SECURITY GROUP - Fire Proof File Cabinet - FIRE KING SECURITY GROUP; *pg.* 1336, *pg.* 696

FKM - Batch Mixers - LITTLEFORD DAY INC.; *pg.* 1356, *pg.* 728

FLA-VOR-ICE - Frozen Confection - THE JEL SERT COMPANY; *pg.* 865, *pg.* 668

FLABBERGASTED - Shoe - AEROGROUP INTERNATIONAL, INC.; *pg.* 1803, *pg.* 1055

FLAG-A-TAG - Game Apparatus - SPORT SUPPLY GROUP, INC.; *pg.* 1846, *pg.* 1687

FLAGSHIP - Service - THE VANGUARD GROUP, INC.; *pg.* 816, *pg.* 1550

FLAGSTONE - Shoe - AEROGROUP INTERNATIONAL, INC.; *pg.* 1803, *pg.* 1055

FLAGYL - Medicine - PFIZER INC.; *pg.* 1581, *pg.* 1278

FLAIR - Cutting Tool - LEATHERMAN TOOL GROUP, INC.; *pg.* 1053, *pg.* 1504

FLAIR - Ventilation Systems - NORTEK, INC.; *pg.* 100, *pg.* 1607

FLAIR - Residential Lighting - SWIVELIER CO., INC.; *pg.* 1307, *pg.* 1142

FLAKE - Chocolate Bar - MONDELEZ INTERNATIONAL, INC.; *pg.* 878, *pg.* 601

FLAKEGLAS - Foliated Glass - OWENS CORNING; *pg.* 102, *pg.* 1476

FLAMARREST - Wire & Cable Products - BELDEN, INC.; *pg.* 624, *pg.* 993

FLAME - On-Line Visual Effects System - AUTODESK INC.; *pg.* 356, *pg.* 257

FLAME - Vanity Lights - CRAFTMADE INTERNATIONAL, INC.; *pg.* 1295, *pg.* 1670

FLAME - Container Grown Plant - MONROVIA GROWERS; *pg.* 1797, *pg.* 44

FLAME KING - Home Products - HABAND COMPANY, INC.; *pg.* 1772, *pg.* 1099

FLAME-OUT - Welded Steel Pipe - NORTHWEST PIPE COMPANY; *pg.* 100, *pg.* 1846

FLAME OUT - Foam - SMOOTH-ON INC.; *pg.* 111, *pg.* 1528

FLAMEGARD - Gas Sensor - MINE SAFETY APPLIANCES COMPANY; *pg.* 1361, *pg.* 1525

FLAMEKIST - Steaks - WESTERN SIZZLIN CORPORATION; *pg.* 1755, *pg.* 1806

FLAMELESS - Flame Retardant Paper - PACON CORPORATION; *pg.* 1466, *pg.* 1852

FLAMEMASTEER - Burner - GE ENERGY; *pg.* 1338, *pg.* 506

FLAMEMASTIC 77 - Fire Protection Coating - THE FLAMEMASTER CORPORATION; *pg.* 1162, *pg.* 174

FLAMENCO - Premium Cigars - ALTADIS USA, INC.; *pg.* 1893, *pg.* 423

FLAMERESIST - Blanket - E.I. DU PONT DE NEMOURS & COMPANY; *pg.* 1159, *pg.* 390

FLAMESHIELD - Aboveground Storage Tank - MODERN WELDING COMPANY, INC.; *pg.* 1363, *pg.* 739

FLAMESTOPPER - Fittings - WIREMOLD/LEGRAND; *pg.* 689, *pg.* 383

FLAMINGO - Integrated Circuit - ATMEL CORPORATION; *pg.* 621, *pg.* 238

FLAMINGO - Software - BIO-RAD LABORATORIES, INC.; *pg.* 1504, *pg.* 101

FLAMINGO - Casino - CAESARS ENTERTAINMENT CORPORATION; *pg.* 1083, *pg.* 1023

FLAMMA - Fabric - NEMSCHOFF, INC.; *pg.* 936, *pg.* 1890

FLAMQUENCH - Flameless Explosion Venting - FIKE CORPORATION; *pg.* 1047, *pg.* 973

FLAMQUENCH II - Fameless Explosion Venting Device for Use in Industrial Facilities - FIKE CORPORATION; *pg.* 1047, *pg.* 973

FLANGE-ADAPTER - Armature - HAMILTON CO., INC.; *pg.* 1415, *pg.* 1031

FLANGE-TYTE - Gaskets - UNITED STATES PIPE & FOUNDRY COMPANY, INC.; *pg.* 117, *pg.* 5

FLANGEMOUNT - Case - PELICAN PRODUCTS; *pg.* 1467, *pg.* 843

FLANK DRIVE - Wrenches - SNAP-ON INCORPORATED; *pg.* 1062, *pg.* 1862

THE FLANNELETTE - Healthcare Apparel - THE SALK COMPANY; *pg.* 1591, *pg.* 800

FLANNELETTE PLUS - Healthcare Apparel - THE SALK COMPANY; *pg.* 1591, *pg.* 800

FLAPFIX - Medical Device - DEPUY SYNTHES; *pg.* 1523, *pg.* 1593

FLAPJACK - Monkey Puppet - GUND, INC.; *pg.* 954, *pg.* 1056

FLAPPER - Print System - STRUCTURAL GRAPHICS, LLC; *pg.* 1689, *pg.* 346

THE FLAPPER - Advertising & Promotional Brochure Design - STRUCTURAL GRAPHICS, LLC; *pg.* 1689, *pg.* 346

FLAPPER - Women's Clothing & Accessories - WOODEN SHIPS OF HOBOKEN; *pg.* 35, *pg.* 1315

FLARE - Form Equipment - BESSER COMPANY; *pg.* 1317, *pg.* 865

FLARE - Software - EMC CORPORATION; *pg.* 391, *pg.* 825

FLARE - Chewing Gum Flavor - WM. WRIGLEY JR.

COMPANY; *pg.* 1863, *pg.* 596
FLARE 542 - Jean - LEVI STRAUSS & CO.; *pg.* 43, *pg.* 220
FLASH - Software - ADOBE SYSTEMS INCORPORATED; *pg.* 342, *pg.* 235
THE FLASH - Character - DC COMICS, INC.; *pg.* 1633, *pg.* 1221
FLASH - Magazine - PAISANO PUBLICATIONS, LLC; *pg.* 1674, *pg.* 38
FLASH 21 - Game - MULTIMEDIA GAMES INC.; *pg.* 442, *pg.* 1664
FLASH BOARDS - Game - FORTUNET, INC.; *pg.* 953, *pg.* 1024
FLASH-FAR - Commercial Lighting - SWIVELIER CO., INC.; *pg.* 1307, *pg.* 1142
FLASH GUARD - Regulator And Torch - THE HARRIS PRODUCTS GROUP; *pg.* 1345, *pg.* 533
FLASH LITE - Software - ADOBE SYSTEMS INCORPORATED; *pg.* 342, *pg.* 235
FLASH LITE IIP - Patient ID, QA & Image Processing Station - FUJIFILM MEDICAL SYSTEMS USA, INC.; *pg.* 1531, *pg.* 374
FLASH MEDIA - Server - ADOBE SYSTEMS INCORPORATED; *pg.* 342, *pg.* 235
FLASH-ON 441 - Cement - KOPPERS HOLDINGS INC.; *pg.* 1170, *pg.* 1577
FLASH PLAYER - Software - ADOBE SYSTEMS INCORPORATED; *pg.* 342, *pg.* 235
FLASH PLUS IIP - Patient ID, QA & Image Processing Workstation - FUJIFILM MEDICAL SYSTEMS USA, INC.; *pg.* 1531, *pg.* 374
FLASH REMOTING - Software - ADOBE SYSTEMS INCORPORATED; *pg.* 342, *pg.* 235
FLASH UI EXTENDER - Software - BSQUARE CORPORATION; *pg.* 366, *pg.* 1813
FLASH VIDEO STREAMING SERVICE - Software - ADOBE SYSTEMS INCORPORATED; *pg.* 342, *pg.* 235
FLASH370 - CPLDs - CYPRESS SEMICONDUCTOR CORPORATION; *pg.* 1326, *pg.* 243
FLASH370I - CPLDs - CYPRESS SEMICONDUCTOR CORPORATION; *pg.* 1326, *pg.* 243
FLASHBACK - Telescope - MEADE INSTRUMENTS CORPORATION; *pg.* 1422, *pg.* 113
FLASHBACK - Bicycle Accessories - SPECIALIZED BICYCLE COMPONENTS, INC.; *pg.* 1711, *pg.* 152
FLASHBACK - Industrial Safety Eyewear - UVEX SAFETY; *pg.* 1433, *pg.* 1608
FLASHBAK - Chipset - LATTICE SEMICONDUCTOR CORPORATION; *pg.* 651, *pg.* 1498
FLASHCALL - Signaling Protocol - EF JOHNSON TECHNOLOGIES, INC.; *pg.* 390, *pg.* 1718
FLASHCAST - Software - ADOBE SYSTEMS INCORPORATED; *pg.* 342, *pg.* 235
FLASHCONNECT - Software - TIGERLOGIC CORPORATION; *pg.* 484, *pg.* 117
FLASHCORE - Automated Device Programming System - DATA I/O CORPORATION; *pg.* 382, *pg.* 1824
FLASHCP - Memory Card - SANDISK CORPORATION; *pg.* 465, *pg.* 147
FLASHCREDIT - Customized Datacard Software Solutions - DATACARD CORPORATION; *pg.* 382, *pg.* 948
FLASHCURE - Light Curing Adhesives - HENKEL CORPORATION; *pg.* 1049, *pg.* 369
FLASHES PUBLISHERS - Printing Publication - FLASHES PUBLISHERS; *pg.* 1641, *pg.* 864
FLASHFORMULA - Software - BRUKER CORPORATION; *pg.* 1511, *pg.* 788
FLASHISR - CPLDs - CYPRESS SEMICONDUCTOR CORPORATION; *pg.* 1326, *pg.* 243
FLASHLIGHT READERS - Educational Materials - SCHOLASTIC INC.; *pg.* 1683, *pg.* 1288
FLASHLINK - Memory Card - HGST; *pg.* 406, *pg.* 260
FLASHLOGIC - Programmable Logic Devices - ALTERA CORPORATION; *pg.* 348, *pg.* 237
FLASHMASTER - Sliding Protection - BENJAMIN OBDYKE, INC.; *pg.* 70, *pg.* 1540
FLASHMASTER - Plug - PHOTOGENIC PROFESSIONAL LIGHTING; *pg.* 1426, *pg.* 556
FLASHMASTER - Aluminized Oversuit for Flash Protection - STANDARD SAFETY EQUIPMENT CO.; *pg.* 1379, *pg.* 632
FLASHMITE - Camera - EASTMAN KODAK COMPANY; *pg.* 1408, *pg.* 1333
FLASHPAK - Flash Memory Device - DATA I/O CORPORATION; *pg.* 382, *pg.* 1824
FLASHPAPER - Software - ADOBE SYSTEMS INCORPORATED; *pg.* 342, *pg.* 235
FLASHPAY - Financial Payment Service - MONEYGRAM INTERNATIONAL, INC.; *pg.* 783, *pg.* 1684
FLASHPLATE - White Polystyrene Microplate - PERKINELMER, INC.; *pg.* 1426, *pg.* 853
FLASHPOINT - Electronic Newsletter - THE INDEPENDENT LUBRICANT MANUFACTURERS ASSOCIATION; *pg.* 144, *pg.* 1770
FLASHPRO - Software - PHOENIX TECHNOLOGIES LTD.; *pg.* 454, *pg.* 147
FLASHSIGHT - Thermal Imaging System - FLIR SYSTEMS, INC.; *pg.* 1413, *pg.* 1510
FLASHSNAP - Software - SYMANTEC CORPORATION; *pg.* 478, *pg.* 161
FLASTCLIP - Mounting Plate System - PELICAN PRODUCTS; *pg.* 1467, *pg.* 843
FLAT - Bath Bars - CRAFTMADE INTERNATIONAL, INC.; *pg.* 1295, *pg.* 1670
FLAT BACK - Lighting - SWIVELIER CO., INC.; *pg.* 1307, *pg.* 1142
FLAT BELLY DIET! - Book - RODALE, INC.; *pg.* 1681, *pg.* 1530
FLAT BLOCK - Software - BIO-RAD LABORATORIES, INC.; *pg.* 1504, *pg.* 101
FLAT EARTH - Fruit & Vegetable Crisps - FRITO-LAY NORTH AMERICA, INC.; *pg.* 1853, *pg.* 1730
FLAT FOOT TECHNOLOGY - Bike - ELECTRA BICYCLE COMPANY; *pg.* 1706, *pg.* 303
FLAT-I - Cylinders - BIMBA MANUFACTURING COMPANY; *pg.* 1317, *pg.* 633
FLAT PAN-POST - Rack & Cable - PANDUIT CORP.; *pg.* 661, *pg.* 663
FLAT PANEL FOCUS - Display - ADVANCED ENERGY INDUSTRIES, INC.; *pg.* 613, *pg.* 328
FLAT TOP - Conveyor Chain - DIAMOND CHAIN COMPANY; *pg.* 1328, *pg.* 684
FLAT TOP - Office Furniture - STEELCASE INC.; *pg.* 475, *pg.* 889
FLAT-TRAC - Roadway Test System - MTS SYSTEMS CORPORATION; *pg.* 442, *pg.* 923
FLATFREE - Tires - AMERITYRE CORPORATION; *pg.* 1879, *pg.* 1021
FLATIRON - Stringed Instruments - GIBSON GUITAR CORP.; *pg.* 550, *pg.* 1650
FLATJET - Spray Product - SPRAYING SYSTEMS CO.; *pg.* 1063, *pg.* 670
FLATLINK - Low-Voltage Differential Signal Transmitter - TEXAS INSTRUMENTS INCORPORATED; *pg.* 679, *pg.* 1688
FLATOUT - Kitchenware - TUPPERWARE BRANDS CORPORATION; *pg.* 1139, *pg.* 456
FLATPAC - Power Supply System - VICOR CORPORATION; *pg.* 1435, *pg.* 783
FLATPAK - Insulated Tubing - O'BRIEN CORPORATION; *pg.* 1366, *pg.* 1001
FLATS SNEAKER - Footwear - SIMMS FISHING PRODUCTS CORP.; *pg.* 1845, *pg.* 1008
FLAUNT - Apparel - LANE BRYANT; *pg.* 1776, *pg.* 1441
FLAUNT - Fabric - NEMSCHOFF, INC.; *pg.* 936, *pg.* 1890
FLAVACOL - Seasoning Salt - GOLD MEDAL PRODUCTS CO.; *pg.* 55, *pg.* 1414
FLAVIA - Drinks & Beverage Systems - MARS, INCORPORATED; *pg.* 1858, *pg.* 1792
FLAVOR ACTION - Floss - RANIR LLC; *pg.* 520, *pg.* 888
FLAVOR-AID - Soft Drink Powder - THE JEL SERT COMPANY; *pg.* 865, *pg.* 668
FLAVOR BLASTED - Food Product - PEPPERIDGE FARM, INC.; *pg.* 888, *pg.* 363
FLAVOR-CRISP - Restaurant Equipment - BALLANTYNE STRONG, INC.; *pg.* 623, *pg.* 1013
FLAVOR DUO - Frozen Yogurt Ice-cream Maker - CUISINART INC.; *pg.* 1123, *pg.* 373
FLAVOR KIST - Baked Goods - SCHULZE & BURCH BISCUIT COMPANY; *pg.* 894, *pg.* 589
FLAVOR PAC - Food Product - ELLENBEE-LEGGETT COMPANY INC.; *pg.* 854, *pg.* 1452
FLAVOR RAGE - Beverages - THE COCA-COLA COMPANY; *pg.* 240, *pg.* 493
FLAVOR-REDI - Food Product - TYSON FOODS, INC.; *pg.* 902, *pg.* 35
FLAVOR TIME - Food Product - SUBCO FOODS, INC.; *pg.* 899, *pg.* 668
FLAVOR TREE - Food Product - JOHN B. SANFILIPPO & SON, INC.; *pg.* 1024, *pg.* 610
FLAVORBEST - Apples - MICHIGAN APPLE COMMITTEE; *pg.* 147, *pg.* 895
FLAVORCELL - Food Processor Product - MCCORMICK & COMPANY, INCORPORATED; *pg.* 1027, *pg.* 779
FLAVORE - Food Products - SMITHFIELD FOODS, INC.; *pg.* 896, *pg.* 1806
FLAVORGARD - Coffee Dispensers - BUNN-O-MATIC CORPORATION; *pg.* 53, *pg.* 661
FLAVORIZER - Gas Grill - WEBER-STEPHEN PRODUCTS LLC; *pg.* 62, *pg.* 650
FLAVORPLUS - Kitchen Appliance - HAMILTON BEACH BRANDS, INC.; *pg.* 56, *pg.* 1783
FLAVORSHURE - Nutrition & Food Product - BALCHEM CORPORATION; *pg.* 839, *pg.* 1183
FLAVORTECH - Pharmaceutical Product - LUMARA HEALTH INC.; *pg.* 1557, *pg.* 973
FLAVORTRAK - Flavor Tracking Service - NEWLY WEDS FOODS, INC.; *pg.* 886, *pg.* 585
FLAVOURED CRUST - Pizza - HUNGRY HOWIE'S PIZZA & SUBS INC.; *pg.* 1023, *pg.* 897
FLAWLESS FINISH - Color - ELIZABETH ARDEN, INC.; *pg.* 507, *pg.* 448
FLAX - Patterned Glass - AGC GLASS NORTH AMERICA, INC.; *pg.* 65, *pg.* 482
FLAX PLUS - Cereal - NATURE'S PATH FOODS INC.; *pg.* 833, *pg.* 1908
FLAXSNAX - Non-Medicated Animal Feed - MANNA PRO CORPORATION; *pg.* 1478, *pg.* 975
FLEA BEACON - Pet Supplies - HAPPY JACK INC.; *pg.* 1476, *pg.* 1390
FLEA BEATER 210 - Household Insect Control - BONIDE PRODUCTS, INC.; *pg.* 1794, *pg.* 1320
FLEA GARD - Pet Supplies - HAPPY JACK INC.; *pg.* 1476, *pg.* 1390
FLEA MARKET MANIA - Antiques & Collectibles Program - YOUTOO TECHNOLOGIES; *pg.* 324, *pg.* 1724
FLEA SECURE - Insect Pest Control Product - GARDENS ALIVE!, INC.; *pg.* 1796, *pg.* 693
FLEAKER - Beaker Spacer - SPECTRUM LABORATORIES INC.; *pg.* 1595, *pg.* 69
FLEAPOT - Digital Potentiometers - MAXIM INTEGRATED PRODUCTS, INC.; *pg.* 653, *pg.* 247
FLEECE FLIP - Glove - KOMBI, LTD.; *pg.* 1838, *pg.* 1766
FLEECY FRIENDS - Pet Supplies - PETSMART, INC.; *pg.* 1481, *pg.* 18
FLEES AWAY - Pet Shampoo - BLUE CROSS LABORATORIES; *pg.* 326, *pg.* 277
FLEET BY NETJETS - Tagline - MARQUIS JET PARTNERS INC.; *pg.* 1915, *pg.* 1256
THE FLEET CARD THAT'S DRIVING AMERICA'S BUSINESS - Slogan - WRIGHT EXPRESS CORPORATION; *pg.* 493, *pg.* 753
FLEET CHARGE - Antifreeze Solution - OLD WORLD INDUSTRIES, INC.; *pg.* 1175, *pg.* 641
FLEET DRY - Paint & Coating - DIAMOND VOGEL PAINT, INC.; *pg.* 1441, *pg.* 710
FLEET FINANCIALS - Magazine - BOBIT BUSINESS MEDIA; *pg.* 1622, *pg.* 293
FLEET-LINK - Wireless Product - HEMISPHERE GPS INC.; *pg.* 642, *pg.* 1903
FLEET LOADER - Software - UNITED PARCEL SERVICE, INC.; *pg.* 1928, *pg.* 522
FLEET PHOSPHO-SODA - Laxative Product - FLEET LABORATORIES; *pg.* 1531, *pg.* 1787
FLEET TEAM - Commercial Aviation Service - THE BOEING COMPANY; *pg.* 225, *pg.* 567
FLEETCARE - Truck Maintenance & Repair Services - FLEETPRIDE, INC.; *pg.* 205, *pg.* 1747
FLEETFOCUS - Software Product - MAXIMUS, INC.; *pg.* 780, *pg.* 1799
FLEETGUARD/NELSON - Filters - CUMMINS INC.; *pg.* 1326, *pg.* 676
FLEETVISION - Software - TRIMBLE NAVIGATION LIMITED; *pg.* 1384, *pg.* 288
FLEETWELD - Electrode - LINCOLN ELECTRIC HOLDINGS, INC.; *pg.* 1355, *pg.* 1432
FLEETWOOD - Furniture - JASPER GROUP; *pg.* 930, *pg.* 691
FLEISCHMANN'S - Food Product - CONAGRA FOODS, INC.; *pg.* 826, *pg.* 1014
FLEISCHMANN'S - Spreads and Cooking Oil - UNILEVER CANADA INC.; *pg.* 903, *pg.* 1946
FLEMING'S PRIME STEAKHOUSE & WINE BAR - Restaurant - BLOOMIN' BRANDS, INC.; *pg.* 1716, *pg.* 471
FLETCHER - Weaving Loom - FLETCHER INDUSTRIES, INC.; *pg.* 1337, *pg.* 1390

First page reference indicates Business Class Edition
Second page reference indicates Geographic Edition

FLETCHERS CASTORIA - Laxative - THE MENTHOLATUM COMPANY; *pg.* 1565, *pg.* 1320
FLEUR - Carpet Cleaners - THE CLOROX COMPANY; *pg.* 327, *pg.* 169
FLEUR - Bath Product - KOHLER CO.; *pg.* 91, *pg.* 1862
FLEUR - Fabric - NEMSCHOFF, INC.; *pg.* 936, *pg.* 1890
FLEUR DE LAIT - Cream Cheese Based Products - BONGRAIN NORTH AMERICA; *pg.* 841, *pg.* 1556
FLEUR DE LAIT LIGHT - Light Cream Cheese Based Products - BONGRAIN NORTH AMERICA; *pg.* 841, *pg.* 1556
FLEUR DE LYS - Women's Clothing & Accessories - WOODEN SHIPS OF HOBOKEN; *pg.* 35, *pg.* 1315
FLEURETTE - Decorative Hook - HERITAGE LACE INC.; *pg.* 694, *pg.* 711
FLEURETTES BY YODER - Flower Grower - ARIS HORTICULTURE, INC.; *pg.* 1793, *pg.* 1404
FLEX - Feed Tubes - ABBOTT LABORATORIES; *pg.* 1484, *pg.* 551
FLEX - Software - ADOBE SYSTEMS INCORPORATED; *pg.* 342, *pg.* 235
FLEX - FPGA Device - ALTERA CORPORATION; *pg.* 348, *pg.* 237
FLEX - Muscle Fitness Magazine - AMERICAN MEDIA, INC.; *pg.* 1615, *pg.* 410
FLEX - Crossover SUV - FORD MOTOR COMPANY; *pg.* 172, *pg.* 876
FLEX - Dielectric Etch - LAM RESEARCH CORPORATION; *pg.* 1354, *pg.* 91
FLEX - Steel Wheels - MAXION WHEELS; *pg.* 212, *pg.* 903
FLEX - Software - ROCKWELL AUTOMATION, INC.; *pg.* 668, *pg.* 1880
FLEX - Software - UNITED PARCEL SERVICE, INC.; *pg.* 1928, *pg.* 522
FLEX 10K Mid-Density Field-Programmable Gate Array - ALTERA CORPORATION; *pg.* 348, *pg.* 237
FLEX 10KA - Mid-density Field-programmable Gate Arrays - ALTERA CORPORATION; *pg.* 348, *pg.* 237
FLEX 10KE - Mid-density Field-programmable Gate Arrays - ALTERA CORPORATION; *pg.* 348, *pg.* 237
FLEX 21 - String - ASHAWAY LINE & TWINE MFG. CO.; *pg.* 1826, *pg.* 1600
FLEX 21 MICRO - String - ASHAWAY LINE & TWINE MFG. CO.; *pg.* 1826, *pg.* 1600
FLEX 6000 - Mature Device - ALTERA CORPORATION; *pg.* 348, *pg.* 237
FLEX 6000A - Mature Device - ALTERA CORPORATION; *pg.* 348, *pg.* 237
FLEX 8000 - Mature Device - ALTERA CORPORATION; *pg.* 348, *pg.* 237
FLEX-A-DRIVE - Double Input Center Pivot Irrigation Final Drive - REGAL BELOIT CORPORATION; *pg.* 106, *pg.* 1854
FLEX A FLO - Fertilizer - THE BIRKETT MILLS; *pg.* 826, *pg.* 1321
FLEX-A-MOUNT Center Pivot Irrigation Center Drive - REGAL BELOIT CORPORATION; *pg.* 106, *pg.* 1854
FLEX-ALL - Handle Adaptors - CARLISLE FOODSERVICE PRODUCTS INCORPORATED; *pg.* 1455, *pg.* 1485
FLEX-AUGER - Feed Delivery System or Conveying System - CTB INTERNATIONAL CORP.; *pg.* 850, *pg.* 695
FLEX BACK - Blade - LENOX; *pg.* 1053, *pg.* 817
FLEX-BAND - Closures - OWENS-ILLINOIS, INC.; *pg.* 1466, *pg.* 1470
FLEX BED - Healthcare Product - GF HEALTH PRODUCTS, INC.; *pg.* 1535, *pg.* 508
FLEX-BOLT - Coupling - LORD CORPORATION; *pg.* 1357, *pg.* 1360
FLEX CONTROL - Electric Shaver - THE GILLETTE COMPANY; *pg.* 509, *pg.* 795
FLEX-CUF - Disposable Restraints - BAE SYSTEMS PRODUCTS GROUP; *pg.* 359, *pg.* 432
FLEX CUP - Vacuum Delivery Cups - UTAH MEDICAL PRODUCTS, INC.; *pg.* 1605, *pg.* 1752
FLEX DRIVE II - Servo Drive - BALDOR ELECTRIC COMPANY; *pg.* 1316, *pg.* 32
FLEX-EDGE - Furniture - HERMAN MILLER, INC.; *pg.* 926, *pg.* 913
FLEX EX - Software - ROCKWELL AUTOMATION, INC.; *pg.* 668, *pg.* 1880
FLEX FASHION - Hanger - MCNETT CORPORATION; *pg.* 1839, *pg.* 1817
FLEX-FLASH - Roof Flashing - OATEY SUPPLY CHAIN SERVICES; *pg.* 30, *pg.* 1433
FLEX FORKS - Mower Tractor - EXCEL INDUSTRIES, INC.; *pg.* 1795, *pg.* 715
FLEX FORM - Dog Toy - THE HARTZ MOUNTAIN CORP.; *pg.* 1476, *pg.* 1120
FLEX-GEAR - Ratchet Suspension System - E.D. BULLARD COMPANY; *pg.* 1332, *pg.* 727
FLEX-GUIDE - Metal Building System - BUTLER MANUFACTURING COMPANY; *pg.* 72, *pg.* 981
FLEX HR - Automated Optical Inspection - CYBEROPTICS CORPORATION; *pg.* 1408, *pg.* 925
FLEX-I-DRAIN - Flexible Roof Drains - JOHNS MANVILLE CORPORATION; *pg.* 89, *pg.* 320
FLEX I/O - Integrated Circuits Software - AVAGO TECHNOLOGIES; *pg.* 358, *pg.* 238
FLEX-I-VISION - Hanging Folders - SMEAD MANUFACTURING COMPANY; *pg.* 470, *pg.* 926
FLEX-IN-LINE - Concentric Shart Helical Gear Speedreducers - REGAL BELOIT CORPORATION; *pg.* 106, *pg.* 1854
FLEX-LAG - Rubber - FLEXIBLE STEEL LACING COMPANY; *pg.* 1337, *pg.* 608
FLEX-LITE - Fiber Optic Cable Assembly - W.L. GORE & ASSOCIATES, INC.; *pg.* 122, *pg.* 388
FLEX-LOC - Car Seats - BABY TREND, INC.; *pg.* 916, *pg.* 173
FLEX-LOC - Hose - HBD INDUSTRIES, INC.; *pg.* 207, *pg.* 1449
FLEX-LOC - Tamper-Evident Closure - OWENS-ILLINOIS, INC.; *pg.* 1466, *pg.* 1470
FLEX-LOCK - Bed - FLEXSTEEL INDUSTRIES, INC.; *pg.* 925, *pg.* 707
FLEX MOBILITY - Nutritional Product - NOW HEALTH GROUP, INC.; *pg.* 1576, *pg.* 557
FLEX-O-BAG - Plastic Bags - FLEX-O-GLASS, INC.; *pg.* 1457, *pg.* 574
FLEX-O-COAT - Gravure & Transfer Applicator - NORDSON CORPORATION; *pg.* 1365, *pg.* 1480
FLEX-O-CRYLIC - Polyethylene Film - FLEX-O-GLASS, INC.; *pg.* 1457, *pg.* 574
FLEX-O-FILM - Plastic Packaging Film - FLEX-O-GLASS, INC.; *pg.* 1457, *pg.* 574
FLEX-O-GLASS - Window Material - FLEX-O-GLASS, INC.; *pg.* 1457, *pg.* 574
FLEX-O-GLASS - Window Material - WARP BROTHERS; *pg.* 1471, *pg.* 595
FLEX-O-GLAZE - Rigid Plastic Glazing - FLEX-O-GLASS, INC.; *pg.* 1457, *pg.* 574
FLEX-O-LATORS, INC. - Automotive Seating Systems - LEGGETT & PLATT, INCORPORATED; *pg.* 933, *pg.* 974
FLEX-O-PANE - Window Material - WARP BROTHERS; *pg.* 1471, *pg.* 595
FLEX-PAK - Media Cart & Pack - NER HOLDINGS INC.; *pg.* 444, *pg.* 1071
FLEX PAY - Computer Software - JACKSON HEWITT TAX SERVICE INC.; *pg.* 771, *pg.* 1103
FLEX PLAY POKER - Video Poker - INTERNATIONAL GAME TECHNOLOGY; *pg.* 957, *pg.* 1024
FLEX PLUS - Spray Guns - GRACO, INC.; *pg.* 1342, *pg.* 935
FLEX-PRIME - Flexible Alkali-Resistant Primer - DUNN-EDWARDS CORPORATION; *pg.* 1442, *pg.* 129
FLEX PRO - Gloves - FRANKLIN SPORTS, INC.; *pg.* 1834, *pg.* 847
FLEX RING TONER - Accessories - BALANCED BODY, INC.; *pg.* 1826, *pg.* 195
FLEX RX - Pharmacy System - LOZIER CORPORATION; *pg.* 94, *pg.* 1016
FLEX RX SYSTEM - Pharmacy Shelving - LOZIER CORPORATION; *pg.* 94, *pg.* 1016
FLEX SPLITTER - BX Cutter - GREENLEE TEXTRON INC.; *pg.* 1048, *pg.* 655
FLEX-TEC - Catalyst - BASF CATALYSTS LLC; *pg.* 1148, *pg.* 1074
FLEX-TEX - Texture Coating - DUNN-EDWARDS CORPORATION; *pg.* 1442, *pg.* 129
FLEX-TRUNK - Fume Exhauster - DONALDSON COMPANY, INC.; *pg.* 1329, *pg.* 917
FLEX-TUBE - Manometer - DWYER INSTRUMENTS INC.; *pg.* 1330, *pg.* 694
FLEX-VENT - Piston Rings - HASTINGS MANUFACTURING COMPANY, LLC; *pg.* 207, *pg.* 891
FLEX-X - Wire Rope - WIRECO WORLDGROUP; *pg.* 1389, *pg.* 987
FLEX XP - Shaving System - BRAUN NORTH AMERICA; *pg.* 52, *pg.* 792
FLEX+ - Dietary Joint Supplement - W.F. YOUNG, INC.; *pg.* 1610, *pg.* 817
FLEX36 - Synchronous Dual-Port RAM - CYPRESS SEMICONDUCTOR CORPORATION; *pg.* 1326, *pg.* 243
FLEX45 - Dielectric Etch System - LAM RESEARCH CORPORATION; *pg.* 1354, *pg.* 91
FLEX72 - Synchronous Dual-Port RAM - CYPRESS SEMICONDUCTOR CORPORATION; *pg.* 1326, *pg.* 243
FLEX72-E - Synchronous Dual-Port RAM - CYPRESS SEMICONDUCTOR CORPORATION; *pg.* 1326, *pg.* 243
FLEXA FOAM - Dog Toy - THE HARTZ MOUNTAIN CORP.; *pg.* 1476, *pg.* 1120
FLEXA-SWITCH - Gravity Conveyor - METZGAR CONVEYOR COMPANY; *pg.* 1360, *pg.* 875
FLEXABLES - Label - BROWN & BIGELOW, INC.; *pg.* 1624, *pg.* 959
FLEXACLEAN - Food Industry Gearbox - REGAL BELOIT CORPORATION; *pg.* 106, *pg.* 1854
FLEXACRON - Coating Product - PPG INDUSTRIES, INC.; *pg.* 1445, *pg.* 1579
FLEXALINE - Standard Gearbox with Modular Design/Applications - REGAL BELOIT CORPORATION; *pg.* 106, *pg.* 1854
FLEXALL - Health & Beauty Product - CHATTEM, INC.; *pg.* 1515, *pg.* 1628
FLEXALL - Medical & Aesthetic Product - DYNATRONICS CORPORATION; *pg.* 1526, *pg.* 1757
FLEXALLOY - Plastic & Rubber - TEKNOR APEX COMPANY; *pg.* 1889, *pg.* 1605
FLEXAMINE - Polymer Product - CHEMTURA CORPORATION; *pg.* 1152, *pg.* 355
FLEXANAR - Flexible Coating for Metal & Plastic Surfaces - PPG INDUSTRIES, INC.; *pg.* 1445, *pg.* 1579
FLEXAR - LC Analysis - PERKINELMER, INC.; *pg.* 1426, *pg.* 853
FLEXATION - Shoe - AEROGROUP INTERNATIONAL, INC.; *pg.* 1803, *pg.* 1055
FLEXATIVE - Elastomeric Coating Additive - PPG INDUSTRIES, INC.; *pg.* 1445, *pg.* 1579
FLEXATRON - Insulating/Padding Material - KINGSDOWN, INC.; *pg.* 932, *pg.* 1383
FLEXBEAM - Fluid Handling System - GRACO, INC.; *pg.* 1342, *pg.* 935
FLEXBEAM - Electronic Components - MOLEX INCORPORATED; *pg.* 655, *pg.* 628
FLEXBGA - Packaging System - AMKOR TECHNOLOGY, INC.; *pg.* 67, *pg.* 25
FLEXBOND - Polyvinyl Acetate Copolymer Emulsions - AIR PRODUCTS AND CHEMICALS, INC.; *pg.* 1145, *pg.* 1513
FLEXBOND - Coating - ROSCO LABORATORIES, INC.; *pg.* 1782, *pg.* 378
FLEXBUMIN - Healthcare Product - BAXTER INTERNATIONAL INC.; *pg.* 1499, *pg.* 599
FLEXCACHE - Software - NETAPP, INC.; *pg.* 444, *pg.* 287
FLEXCAM - Audio Conferencing System - CLEARONE COMMUNICATIONS, INC.; *pg.* 629, *pg.* 1756
FLEXCARE - Software - DYNTEK, INC.; *pg.* 389, *pg.* 165
FLEXCEL - Printing Plates - EASTMAN KODAK COMPANY; *pg.* 1408, *pg.* 1333
FLEXCENTER - Line of Multi-Axis Machine Modules - SETCO SALES COMPANY; *pg.* 1061, *pg.* 1426
FLEXCLEAN - Equipped Scrubbers - TENNANT COMPANY; *pg.* 1381, *pg.* 944
FLEXCLOCKING - Chip Interface System - RAMBUS INC.; *pg.* 459, *pg.* 288
FLEXCLONE - Software - NETAPP, INC.; *pg.* 444, *pg.* 287
FLEXCO - Rubber Covered Top Plate - FLEXIBLE STEEL LACING COMPANY; *pg.* 1337, *pg.* 608
FLEXCOAT - Coating - ROSCO LABORATORIES, INC.; *pg.* 1782, *pg.* 378
FLEXCOMM - In-Flight Direct Communication System - HONEYWELL AEROSPACE ELECTRONIC SYSTEMS; *pg.* 228, *pg.* 17
FLEXCOR - Flexible Wire Mesh Grips - PASS & SEYMOUR/LEGRAND; *pg.* 1303, *pg.* 1344
FLEXCORD - Paper Covered Wire - LEGGETT & PLATT, INCORPORATED; *pg.* 933, *pg.* 974
FLEXCREME - Nutritional Supplement - NU SKIN ENTERPRISES, INC.; *pg.* 518, *pg.* 1755
FLEXCRYL - Acrylic Emulsions - AIR PRODUCTS AND CHEMICALS, INC.; *pg.* 1145, *pg.* 1513
FLEXDOCK - Hose - THE GOODYEAR TIRE & RUBBER COMPANY; *pg.* 1883, *pg.* 1401
FLEXDROP - Liquid Handling Dispenser - PERKINELMER, INC.; *pg.* 1426, *pg.* 853
FLEXEES - Intimate Apparel - HANESBRANDS INC.; *pg.* 26, *pg.* 1394
FLEXERIL - Healthcare Product - JOHNSON & JOHNSON;

pg. 1549, *pg.* 1091
FLEXFIT - Chipset - ADVANCED MICRO DEVICES, INC.; *pg.* 613, *pg.* 282
FLEXFIT - Medical Product - ST. JUDE MEDICAL, INC.; *pg.* 1596, *pg.* 963
FLEXFLO - Bicycle Accessories - SPECIALIZED BICYCLE COMPONENTS, INC.; *pg.* 1711, *pg.* 152
FLEXFOAM-IT! - Foam - SMOOTH-ON INC.; *pg.* 111, *pg.* 1528
FLEXFOIL - Durabubble Product - POLYAIR INTER PACK INC.; *pg.* 1467, *pg.* 1941
FLEXFRONT - Furniture - HERMAN MILLER, INC.; *pg.* 926, *pg.* 913
FLEXHEAD - Pole Spray Gun - GRACO, INC.; *pg.* 1342, *pg.* 935
FLEXI-COIL - Agricultural Equipment - CNH AMERICA LLC; *pg.* 702, *pg.* 560
FLEXI-DUSTER - Overhead Dusting Tools - HILLYARD, INC.; *pg.* 331, *pg.* 990
FLEXI-FILTER - Pad - MINE SAFETY APPLIANCES COMPANY; *pg.* 1361, *pg.* 1525
FLEXI FLO - Bulk Commodity Service - CONSOLIDATED RAIL CORPORATION; *pg.* 1903, *pg.* 1562
FLEXI-FLOR - Adhesive - R.C.A. RUBBER COMPANY; *pg.* 1888, *pg.* 1402
FLEXI-MONITOR - Fluid Handling System - GRACO, INC.; *pg.* 1342, *pg.* 935
FLEXI-SEAL - Fecal Management Product - CONVATEC LTD.; *pg.* 1518, *pg.* 1121
FLEXI-SPOT - Software - BIO-RAD LABORATORIES, INC.; *pg.* 1504, *pg.* 101
FLEXIBAR - Lightning Protection - ERICO INTERNATIONAL CORPORATION; *pg.* 1335, *pg.* 1472
FLEXIBLE CLEAR - Tape - 3M COMPANY; *pg.* 1142, *pg.* 956
FLEXIBLE CONCATENATION - Optical Networking System - CIENA CORPORATION; *pg.* 628, *pg.* 771
FLEXIBLE FEEDER - Low Loss Drop Feeder Cable - TIMES FIBER COMMUNICATIONS, INC.; *pg.* 681, *pg.* 382
FLEXIBLE PANCAKE - Wiring System - WIREMOLD/LEGRAND; *pg.* 689, *pg.* 383
FLEXIBLE SEAL - Roofing Sealants - QUAKER CHEMICAL CORP.; *pg.* 1178, *pg.* 1524
FLEXIBLE SPENDING ACCOUNT - Employee Benefits - PAYCHEX, INC.; *pg.* 792, *pg.* 1336
FLEXICHANGE - Dental Product - DENTSPLY INTERNATIONAL INC.; *pg.* 1522, *pg.* 1596
FLEXICLEAR - Auto Body Seam Sealer - 3M COMPANY; *pg.* 1142, *pg.* 956
FLEXICOAT - Powder Coating Booth - NORDSON CORPORATION; *pg.* 1365, *pg.* 1480
FLEXICOLOR - Photo Processing Chemicals - EASTMAN KODAK COMPANY; *pg.* 1408, *pg.* 1333
FLEXICORE - Spinal System - STRYKER CORPORATION; *pg.* 1598, *pg.* 894
FLEXIDOME I - Camera - BOSCH SECURITY SYSTEMS, INC.; *pg.* 626, *pg.* 1158
FLEXIDOME II - Camera - BOSCH SECURITY SYSTEMS, INC.; *pg.* 626, *pg.* 1158
FLEXIDOMEXT LTC 136X - Camera - BOSCH SECURITY SYSTEMS, INC.; *pg.* 626, *pg.* 1158
FLEXIDOMEXTLTC 146X - Camera - BOSCH SECURITY SYSTEMS, INC.; *pg.* 626, *pg.* 1158
FLEXIFIT - Armature - HAMILTON CO., INC.; *pg.* 1415, *pg.* 1031
FLEXIFLANGE - Armature - HAMILTON CO., INC.; *pg.* 1415, *pg.* 1031
FLEXIFLASH - Chipset - LATTICE SEMICONDUCTOR CORPORATION; *pg.* 651, *pg.* 1498
FLEXIFLO - Feed Tubes - ABBOTT LABORATORIES; *pg.* 1484, *pg.* 551
FLEXIFLO - Felt - AMERICAN FELT & FILTER COMPANY; *pg.* 1312, *pg.* 1184
FLEXIFLO II - Enteral Feeding System - ABBOTT LABORATORIES; *pg.* 1484, *pg.* 551
FLEXIFRAME - Window - ANDERSEN CORPORATION; *pg.* 67, *pg.* 916
FLEXIGAS - Piper - SIMPSON TECHNOLOGIES CORPORATION; *pg.* 111, *pg.* 555
FLEXIGNAL - Distribution Board - MKS INSTRUMENTS, INC.; *pg.* 1362, *pg.* 781
FLEXIGRIP - Medical & Aesthetic Product - DYNATRONICS CORPORATION; *pg.* 1526, *pg.* 1757
FLEXIJOINT - Flexible - ROMAC INDUSTRIES, INC.; *pg.* 1061, *pg.* 1818
FLEXIMAC - Ethernet - LATTICE SEMICONDUCTOR CORPORATION; *pg.* 651, *pg.* 1498
FLEXIMAGING - Digital Gamma Camera - DIGIRAD CORPORATION; *pg.* 1524, *pg.* 185
FLEXIMINT - Mint Oil Technology - INTERNATIONAL FLAVORS & FRAGRANCES INC.; *pg.* 512, *pg.* 1244
FLEXIO - Chip Interface System - RAMBUS INC.; *pg.* 459, *pg.* 288
FLEXIPAC - Plastics Product - AEP INDUSTRIES INC.; *pg.* 1878, *pg.* 1085
FLEXIPAC - Orthopedic Device - DJO SURGICAL; *pg.* 1525, *pg.* 1661
FLEXIPANEL - Electric Tank Heating Pads - THERMON AMERICAS INC.; *pg.* 1077, *pg.* 1744
FLEXIPCS - DeSerializer - LATTICE SEMICONDUCTOR CORPORATION; *pg.* 651, *pg.* 1498
FLEXISENSOR - Pulse Oximetry Sensor - MAQUET; *pg.* 1558, *pg.* 1082
FLEXISOFT - Electric Toothbrush Head - THE GILLETTE COMPANY; *pg.* 509, *pg.* 795
FLEXITECH - Paperboard Packaging Product - WESTROCK COMPANY; *pg.* 1472, *pg.* 1805
FLEXITIP - Medical Equipment - CONMED CORPORATION; *pg.* 1517, *pg.* 1347
FLEXIUM - Medical Device - MEMRY CORPORATION; *pg.* 1565, *pg.* 337
FLEXIVENT - Window - ANDERSEN CORPORATION; *pg.* 67, *pg.* 916
FLEXJET - Jet - BOMBARDIER INC.; *pg.* 1318, *pg.* 1953
FLEXJET - Placement Head - UNIVERSAL INSTRUMENTS CORPORATION; *pg.* 683, *pg.* 1154
FLEXJOINT - Caulking Compound - ARKEMA INC.; *pg.* 1147, *pg.* 1543
FLEXJUMPER - Electronic Components - MOLEX INCORPORATED; *pg.* 655, *pg.* 628
FLEXKING - Hose - HBD INDUSTRIES, INC.; *pg.* 207, *pg.* 1449
FLEXKLEER - Paint Booth Coating Composition - PPG INDUSTRIES, INC.; *pg.* 1445, *pg.* 1579
FLEXLED - Lighting System - REVOLUTION LIGHTING TECHNOLOGIES, INC.; *pg.* 1304, *pg.* 377
FLEXLIFE - Cable Assembly - W.L. GORE & ASSOCIATES, INC.; *pg.* 122, *pg.* 388
FLEXLINK - Storage System - QUANTUM CORPORATION; *pg.* 458, *pg.* 250
FLEXLINK - Chip Interface System - RAMBUS INC.; *pg.* 459, *pg.* 288
FLEXLOCK - Wall System - BESSER COMPANY; *pg.* 1317, *pg.* 865
FLEXMAP - Mappers - AVAGO TECHNOLOGIES; *pg.* 358, *pg.* 238
FLEXMAP - Microsphere - LUMINEX CORPORATION; *pg.* 1421, *pg.* 1664
FLEXMAP 3D - Multiplexing System - LUMINEX CORPORATION; *pg.* 1421, *pg.* 1664
FLEXMARK - Polyester Film - FLEXCON CORPORATION; *pg.* 1457, *pg.* 844
FLEXMASTER F1 - Coronary Stent System - ABBOTT LABORATORIES; *pg.* 1484, *pg.* 551
FLEXMATIC - Scrub Station - STERIS CORPORATION; *pg.* 1597, *pg.* 1464
FLEXMESH - Gabions - MACCAFERRI, INC.; *pg.* 95, *pg.* 780
FLEXMIR - Custom Array Builder - LUMINEX CORPORATION; *pg.* 1421, *pg.* 1664
FLEXMIR MICRORNA - Analytical Device - LUMINEX CORPORATION; *pg.* 1421, *pg.* 1664
FLEXMIR SELECT - Analytical Device - LUMINEX CORPORATION; *pg.* 1421, *pg.* 1664
FLEXMOUNT - Graphic Attachment & Mounting - FLEXCON CORPORATION; *pg.* 1457, *pg.* 844
FLEXNET - Wireless Network Product - AIRSPAN NETWORKS INC.; *pg.* 346, *pg.* 410
FLEXNET - Software - FLEXERA SOFTWARE INC.; *pg.* 398, *pg.* 658
FLEXO - Printer and Coder - BELL-MARK CORPORATION; *pg.* 1620, *pg.* 1108
FLEXO - Synchronous Dual-Port RAM - CYPRESS SEMICONDUCTOR CORPORATION; *pg.* 1326, *pg.* 243
FLEXO - Film Clips - EASTMAN KODAK COMPANY; *pg.* 1408, *pg.* 1333
FLEXOCHOISE - Paper Products - BOISE CASCADE HOLDINGS, L.L.C.; *pg.* 1453, *pg.* 546
FLEXOFOLD - Paper Product - BOISE CASCADE HOLDINGS, L.L.C.; *pg.* 1453, *pg.* 546
FLEXOGLOSS - Paper Product - BOISE CASCADE HOLDINGS, L.L.C.; *pg.* 1453, *pg.* 546
FLEXOL - Plasticizer - THE DOW CHEMICAL COMPANY; *pg.* 1157, *pg.* 898
FLEXOMER - Chemical Product - THE DOW CHEMICAL COMPANY; *pg.* 1157, *pg.* 898
FLEXOMOUNT - Tape - 3M COMPANY; *pg.* 1142, *pg.* 956
FLEXON - Eyewear - MARCHON EYEWEAR, INC.; *pg.* 1421, *pg.* 1180
FLEXONEWS - Paper Products - BOISE CASCADE HOLDINGS, L.L.C.; *pg.* 1453, *pg.* 546
FLEXONICS - Expansion Joints, Compensator, Flexible Metal Hose, Ducting & Connectors - SENIOR FLEXONICS INC.; *pg.* 1375, *pg.* 556
FLEXOPLAST - Bandages - DERMA SCIENCES, INC.; *pg.* 1523, *pg.* 1111
FLEXOPRENE - Cable - STANDARD WIRE & CABLE CO.; *pg.* 1306, *pg.* 187
FLEXOR - Introducer Set - COOK GROUP, INC.; *pg.* 1518, *pg.* 674
FLEXPAK - Receiver - NOVATEL INC.; *pg.* 1424, *pg.* 1904
FLEXPAK - Enclosure System - O'BRIEN CORPORATION; *pg.* 1366, *pg.* 1001
FLEXPHASE - Chip Interface System - RAMBUS INC.; *pg.* 459, *pg.* 288
FLEXPLANE - Connector - MOLEX INCORPORATED; *pg.* 655, *pg.* 628
FLEXPOWER - Connector - WESTERN DIGITAL CORPORATION; *pg.* 492, *pg.* 118
FLEXPRINT - Printer and Coder - BELL-MARK CORPORATION; *pg.* 1620, *pg.* 1108
FLEXPRO - Fluid Handling System - GRACO, INC.; *pg.* 1342, *pg.* 935
FLEXPULL - Cable - ARRIS GROUP, INC.; *pg.* 353, *pg.* 541
FLEXPULSE - Hose - THE GOODYEAR TIRE & RUBBER COMPANY; *pg.* 1883, *pg.* 1401
FLEXROUTE - Satellite Broadcast System - INTERNATIONAL DATACASTING CORPORATION; *pg.* 419, *pg.* 1921
FLEXSAND - Rubber Coated Sand - FAIRMOUNT SANTROL; *pg.* 1162, *pg.* 1409
FLEXSEAL - Hose - HBD INDUSTRIES, INC.; *pg.* 207, *pg.* 1449
FLEXSEAL - Laminated Safety Glass - PPG INDUSTRIES, INC.; *pg.* 1445, *pg.* 1579
FLEXSEAL - Safety Goggles - UVEX SAFETY; *pg.* 1433, *pg.* 1608
FLEXSELECT - Multiplexing System - CIENA CORPORATION; *pg.* 628, *pg.* 771
FLEXSERV - Business Service - AT&T SOUTHEAST; *pg.* 1868, *pg.* 489
FLEXSHARE - Software - NETAPP, INC.; *pg.* 444, *pg.* 287
FLEXSHELL - Closure - THOMAS & BETTS CORPORATION; *pg.* 680, *pg.* 1646
FLEXSIDE - Press Side Systems - MOTAN, INC.; *pg.* 1886, *pg.* 903
FLEXSIM - Software System - MENTOR GRAPHICS CORPORATION; *pg.* 432, *pg.* 1510
FLEXSPACE - Home Design - DAVID WEEKLEY HOMES, LP; *pg.* 78, *pg.* 1704
FLEXSTAT - Graphic Film - FLEXCON CORPORATION; *pg.* 1457, *pg.* 844
FLEXSTATION - Software - MOLECULAR DEVICES CORPORATION; *pg.* 1568, *pg.* 287
FLEXSTEEL - Upholstered Furniture - FLEXSTEEL INDUSTRIES, INC.; *pg.* 925, *pg.* 707
FLEXSTEEL - Mattress - RESTONIC MATTRESS CORPORATION; *pg.* 941, *pg.* 553
FLEXSTREAM - Storage Semiconductor - AVAGO TECHNOLOGIES; *pg.* 358, *pg.* 238
FLEXSTRENGTH - Hose - HBD INDUSTRIES, INC.; *pg.* 207, *pg.* 1449
FLEXSURE - Testing Instrument System - BECKMAN COULTER, INC.; *pg.* 1402, *pg.* 48
FLEXSYS - Machining System - ATS AUTOMATION TOOLING SYSTEMS INC.; *pg.* 355, *pg.* 1919
FLEXSYSPAK - Packaging Solution - ATS AUTOMATION TOOLING SYSTEMS INC.; *pg.* 355, *pg.* 1919
FLEXTECH - Modular Furniture System - KEWAUNEE SCIENTIFIC CORPORATION; *pg.* 931, *pg.* 1391
FLEXTEST - Renal Panel - IDEXX LABORATORIES, INC.; *pg.* 1543, *pg.* 753
FLEXTEST - Software System - MENTOR GRAPHICS CORPORATION; *pg.* 432, *pg.* 1510
FLEXTEST - Clutch Test System - MTS SYSTEMS CORPORATION; *pg.* 442, *pg.* 923
FLEXTEST GT - Digital Servocontroller - MTS SYSTEMS

CORPORATION; pg. 442, pg. 923
FLEXTEST SE - Digital Servocontroller - MTS SYSTEMS CORPORATION; pg. 442, pg. 923
FLEXTEST SE BASIC - Digital Servocontroller - MTS SYSTEMS CORPORATION; pg. 442, pg. 923
FLEXTEST SE PLUS - Digital Servocontroller - MTS SYSTEMS CORPORATION; pg. 442, pg. 923
FLEXTHANE - Acrylic/Urethane Dispersions - AIR PRODUCTS AND CHEMICALS, INC.; pg. 1145, pg. 1513
FLEXTILT - Antennas - AMPHENOL CORPORATION; pg. 616, pg. 381
FLEXTRA - Sealant - H.B. FULLER COMPANY; pg. 1165, pg. 961
FLEXTRACT - Development Platform - MKS INSTRUMENTS, INC.; pg. 1362, pg. 781
FLEXTRAK - Vibratory Plow - VERMEER MANUFACTURING COMPANY; pg. 708, pg. 711
FLEXTRAN - Electronic Components - MOLEX INCORPORATED; pg. 655, pg. 628
FLEXTROLLEY - Machining System - ATS AUTOMATION TOOLING SYSTEMS INC.; pg. 355, pg. 1919
FLEXTUFF - Drum Labelling Material - WEBER PACKAGING SOLUTIONS, INC.; pg. 491, pg. 554
FLEXTWIN - Graphic Film - FLEXCON CORPORATION; pg. 1457, pg. 844
FLEXUNITS - Software - BENTLEY SYSTEMS, INC.; pg. 361, pg. 1531
FLEXVISION - Flexible Ureteroscope - STRYKER CORPORATION; pg. 1598, pg. 894
FLEXVOL - Software - NETAPP, INC.; pg. 444, pg. 287
FLEXWAIST - Pant - WILLIAMSON-DICKIE MANUFACTURING COMPANY; pg. 50, pg. 1696
FLEXWEAR - Industrial Uniform Shirts - UNIFIRST CORPORATION; pg. 50, pg. 860
FLEXWELL - Cable & Antenna System - RADIO FREQUENCY SYSTEMS, INC.; pg. 666, pg. 354
FLEXWORKS - Workbench Accessory System - LISTA INTERNATIONAL CORPORATION; pg. 934, pg. 825
FLEXWRAP - Olefin Wrap - E.I. DU PONT DE NEMOURS & COMPANY; pg. 1159, pg. 390
FLEXX - Apparel - BARCO UNIFORMS, INC.; pg. 19, pg. 94
FLEXXUS - Medical Equipment - CONMED CORPORATION; pg. 1517, pg. 1347
FLEXZONE - Polymer Product - CHEMTURA CORPORATION; pg. 1152, pg. 355
FLEXZORB - Tarnish Prevention Cloth - CALGON CARBON CORPORATION; pg. 1151, pg. 1574
FLICK TRIX - Toy - SPIN MASTER LTD.; pg. 967, pg. 1943
FLICKER - Fabric - NEMSCHOFF, INC.; pg. 936, pg. 1890
FLICKLOCK - Outdoor Products - BLACK DIAMOND, INC.; pg. 1827, pg. 1756
FLICKR - Photo Sharing Application - YAHOO! INC.; pg. 1289, pg. 289
FLIGHT - Flatware - ONEIDA LTD; pg. 1129, pg. 1318
FLIGHT CUSTOM II - Aviation Tires - THE GOODYEAR TIRE & RUBBER COMPANY; pg. 1883, pg. 1401
FLIGHT DECK U.S.A. - Outerwear for Men & Boys - I. SPIEWAK & SONS, INC.; pg. 42, pg. 1242
FLIGHT EAGLE - Aviation Tires - THE GOODYEAR TIRE & RUBBER COMPANY; pg. 1883, pg. 1401
FLIGHT GUARD - Travel Insurance - TRAVEL GUARD GROUP, INC.; pg. 1925, pg. 1895
FLIGHT LEADER - Aviation Tires - THE GOODYEAR TIRE & RUBBER COMPANY; pg. 1883, pg. 1401
FLIGHT OF FANCY - Bath Product - KOHLER CO.; pg. 91, pg. 1862
FLIGHT RADIAL - Aviation Tires - THE GOODYEAR TIRE & RUBBER COMPANY; pg. 1883, pg. 1401
FLIGHT SERIES - Sports Apparel - THE NORTH FACE, INC.; pg. 1840, pg. 252
FLIGHT SPECIAL II - Aviation Tires - THE GOODYEAR TIRE & RUBBER COMPANY; pg. 1883, pg. 1401
FLIGHTBAR - Navigation Aid - TRIMBLE NAVIGATION LIMITED; pg. 1384, pg. 288
FLIGHTFLEX - Electronic Components - MOLEX INCORPORATED; pg. 655, pg. 628
FLIGHTGRATITUDE - Air Transportation Service - JETBLUE AIRWAYS CORPORATION; pg. 1913, pg. 1174
FLIGHTLINK - Bus Transportation Service - GREYHOUND LINES, INC.; pg. 1910, pg. 1681
FLIGHTLINK - Software - PASSUR AEROSPACE, INC.; pg. 233, pg. 376
FLIGHTLOADS - Software - MSC SOFTWARE CORPORATION; pg. 441, pg. 262
FLIGHTMASTER - Hose - HBD INDUSTRIES, INC.; pg. 207, pg. 1449
FLIGHTNEWS LIVE - Software - PASSUR AEROSPACE, INC.; pg. 233, pg. 376
FLIGHTPERFORM - Software - PASSUR AEROSPACE, INC.; pg. 233, pg. 376
FLIGHTSURE - Software - PASSUR AEROSPACE, INC.; pg. 233, pg. 376
FLINCH - Footwear - OAKLEY, INC.; pg. 1840, pg. 86
FLINCH - Game - WINNING MOVES GAMES, INC.; pg. 970, pg. 816
FLING - Combined Film and Camera - EASTMAN KODAK COMPANY; pg. 1408, pg. 1333
FLING - Candy Bar - MARS, INCORPORATED; pg. 1858, pg. 1792
FLINT CREEK - Furniture - ASHLEY FURNITURE INDUSTRIES, INC.; pg. 914, pg. 1852
THE FLINT JOURNAL - Newspaper - MLIVE MEDIA GROUP; pg. 1665, pg. 888
FLINTSTONES MULTIVITAMINS - Vitamins - BAYER HEALTHCARE CONSUMER CARE DIVISION; pg. 1500, pg. 1087
FLIP - Floor Care Product - BISSELL HOMECARE, INC.; pg. 52, pg. 887
FLIP - Footwear - COBIAN CORP.; pg. 1806, pg. 253
FLIP - Vacuum Fluorescent Display Modules - INDUSTRIAL ELECTRONIC ENGINEERS, INC.; pg. 644, pg. 300
FLIP FLOP - Footwear - VANS, INC.; pg. 1821, pg. 76
FLIP FLOPS - Footwear Product - DECKERS OUTDOOR CORPORATION; pg. 1807, pg. 100
FLIP FOCALS - Magnifier - EDROY PRODUCTS CO., INC.; pg. 1411, pg. 1318
FLIP-FRAME - Transparency Protector - 3M COMPANY; pg. 1142, pg. 956
FLIP-IT - Hard Floor Cleaner - BISSELL HOMECARE, INC.; pg. 52, pg. 887
FLIP LID - Weatherproof Cover - PASS & SEYMOUR/LEGRAND; pg. 1303, pg. 1344
FLIP-LOC - Seating System - NEMSCHOFF, INC.; pg. 936, pg. 1890
FLIP 'N FLUFF - Kitchen Appliance - HAMILTON BEACH BRANDS, INC.; pg. 56, pg. 1783
FLIP 'N FRESH - Food Storage Products - HOME PRODUCTS INTERNATIONAL, INC.; pg. 1125, pg. 577
FLIP-OFF - Seal - WEST PHARMACEUTICAL SERVICES, INC.; pg. 1472, pg. 1532
FLIP-TOP - Lid (on feed bin) - CTB INTERNATIONAL CORP.; pg. 850, pg. 695
FLIP-TOP - Bottle Seal - WEST PHARMACEUTICAL SERVICES, INC.; pg. 1472, pg. 1532
FLIPCHART - Appliances - STEELCASE INC.; pg. 475, pg. 889
FLIP.COM - Teenager Focused Site - CONDE NAST DIGITAL; pg. 1237, pg. 1217
FLIPFAZE - Game - UNIVERSITY GAMES CORPORATION; pg. 969, pg. 230
FLIPFET - Power Semiconductor Device - INTERNATIONAL RECTIFIER CORPORATION; pg. 647, pg. 80
FLIPFORMS - Riser Platform - WENGER CORPORATION; pg. 1307, pg. 952
FLIPKY - Power Semiconductor Device - INTERNATIONAL RECTIFIER CORPORATION; pg. 647, pg. 80
FLIPPER - Embolization - COOK GROUP, INC.; pg. 1518, pg. 674
FLIPR - Screening System - MOLECULAR DEVICES CORPORATION; pg. 1568, pg. 287
FLIPR 384 - Fluorometric Imaging Plate Reader - MOLECULAR DEVICES CORPORATION; pg. 1568, pg. 287
FLIPRTETRA - Plate Reader - MOLECULAR DEVICES CORPORATION; pg. 1568, pg. 287
FLIPS - Software - SCANTRON CORPORATION; pg. 467, pg. 922
FLIP'S SQUAD - Ticket Program - BUCCANEERS LIMITED PARTNERSHIP; pg. 534, pg. 471
FLIPSOLE - Footwear Product - DECKERS OUTDOOR CORPORATION; pg. 1807, pg. 100
FLIPSTER - Gaming Product - GLD PRODUCTS, INC.; pg. 1835, pg. 1882
FLIPTOP - Plastic Houseware Product - STERILITE CORPORATION; pg. 1138, pg. 848
FLIPTOP CONTOUR - Dispensing Closure - OWENS-ILLINOIS, INC.; pg. 1466, pg. 1470
FLIR QUICKPLOT & FLIR RESEARCHIR - Software - FLIR SYSTEMS, INC.; pg. 1413, pg. 1510
FLIR QUICKREPORT - Software - FLIR SYSTEMS, INC.; pg. 1413, pg. 1510
FLIR REPORTER BUILDING - Software - FLIR SYSTEMS, INC.; pg. 1413, pg. 1510
FLIR REPORTER STANDARD / PRO - Software - FLIR SYSTEMS, INC.; pg. 1413, pg. 1510
FLIR RTOOLS - Software - FLIR SYSTEMS, INC.; pg. 1413, pg. 1510
FLIRT! - Makeup Products - THE ESTEE LAUDER COMPANIES INC.; pg. 508, pg. 1229
FLIRT - Women's Shoe - JACK SCHWARTZ SHOES, INC.; pg. 1810, pg. 1245
FLIRTATION - Nightgowns - HABAND COMPANY, INC.; pg. 1772, pg. 1099
FLIRTATIOUS - Fabric - NEMSCHOFF, INC.; pg. 936, pg. 1890
FLITE-FLOW - Valves - FLOWSERVE CORPORATION; pg. 82, pg. 1719
FLITE STAR - Residential Garage Door Opener - RAYNOR GARAGE DOORS; pg. 106, pg. 607
FLITECOMM - Voice Communications for Air Traffic Control - HONEYWELL AEROSPACE ELECTRONIC SYSTEMS; pg. 228, pg. 17
FLITEFONE - In-Flight Air-to-Ground Communication System - HONEYWELL AEROSPACE ELECTRONIC SYSTEMS; pg. 228, pg. 17
FLITRX - Molecular Biology Product - THERMO FISHER SCIENTIFIC INC.; pg. 1602, pg. 61
FLO-CARB - Minerals - MINERALS TECHNOLOGIES INC.; pg. 1173, pg. 617
FLO-CLEAN - Coated Filter Media - AMERICAN FELT & FILTER COMPANY; pg. 1312, pg. 1184
FLO CONTROL PLATFORM - Route Optimization System - INTERNAP NETWORK SERVICES CORPORATION; pg. 417, pg. 513
FLO-COTE - Paint - KELLY-MOORE PAINT COMPANY, INC.; pg. 1443, pg. 198
FLO-CUT - Food Cutting Machine - URSCHEL LABORATORIES INCORPORATED; pg. 1386, pg. 698
FLO-DIRECT - Direct-Fired Water Heater - ARMSTRONG INTERNATIONAL, INC.; pg. 1069, pg. 909
FLO-EVER - Salt - CARGILL LIMITED; pg. 1475, pg. 1914
FLO-GARD - Infusion Pump - BAXTER INTERNATIONAL INC.; pg. 1499, pg. 599
FLO-GARD - Synthetic Precipitated Silica Flow Conditioner & Anticaking Agent for Salt - PPG INDUSTRIES, INC.; pg. 1445, pg. 1579
FLO GLAZE - Floor Coating - REVERE PRODUCTS; pg. 107, pg. 1435
FLO GLO - Paint & Coating - AERVOE INDUSTRIES INCORPORATED; pg. 1439, pg. 1021
FLO-MANAGER - Control System - RAIN BIRD CORPORATION; pg. 707, pg. 44
FLO-MATIC - Cosmetics; Mascara - MERLE NORMAN COSMETICS, INC.; pg. 517, pg. 136
FLO-RITE-TEMP - Heat Exchanger - ARMSTRONG INTERNATIONAL, INC.; pg. 1069, pg. 909
FLO-SCINT - Classical Flow Cocktail - PERKINELMER, INC.; pg. 1426, pg. 853
FLO-SCOPE - Flow Meter - SELAS HEAT TECHNOLOGY COMPANY LLC; pg. 1076, pg. 1553
FLO-SEPTOR - Floor Sink - JOSAM COMPANY; pg. 89, pg. 695
FLO-SET - Roof Drain - JOSAM COMPANY; pg. 89, pg. 695
FLO SMART - Detection System - MOCON, INC.; pg. 1363, pg. 940
FLO-SOAR - Milking Claw - BOUMATIC LLC; pg. 701, pg. 1865
FLO-STAR LINEAR - Patented Fluted Barrel - BOUMATIC LLC; pg. 701, pg. 1865
FLO-STAR SUPREME CLAW - Shutoff Valve - BOUMATIC LLC; pg. 701, pg. 1865
FLO-TECH - Valve - WOODWARD, INC.; pg. 122, pg. 329
FLO-TEMP - Shampoo Bowl Fixture - BELVEDERE USA CORPORATION; pg. 917, pg. 556
FLO-TRAC - Profiler File - BADGER METER, INC.; pg. 1401, pg. 1873
FLOAM - Orthopedic Product - DJO INCORPORATED; pg. 1524, pg. 302
FLOAM - Fiber Product - INTERNATIONAL FIBER CORP.; pg. 865, pg. 1317
FLOAT-A-LYZER - Lab Dialysis Product - SPECTRUM LABORATORIES INC.; pg. 1595, pg. 69
FLOAT NOTE - Balloon - CONTINENTAL AMERICAN CORP.; pg. 1880, pg. 723
FLOAT-R - Inflatable Game - SCHOOL-TECH, INC.; pg.

1844, *pg.* 866
FLOATER - Footwear - COBIAN CORP.; *pg.* 1806, *pg.* 253
FLOATING SEAL - Valves - VALCOR ENGINEERING CORPORATION; *pg.* 1386, *pg.* 1123
FLOCKCHEK - Antibody Test Kit - IDEXX LABORATORIES, INC.; *pg.* 1543, *pg.* 753
FLOCKLOK - Adhesive - LORD CORPORATION; *pg.* 1357, *pg.* 1360
FLOCONTROL - Fluid Handling System - GRACO, INC.; *pg.* 1342, *pg.* 935
FLODS - Tamper-Evident Closure - OWENS-ILLINOIS, INC.; *pg.* 1466, *pg.* 1470
FLOEFD - Software System - MENTOR GRAPHICS CORPORATION; *pg.* 432, *pg.* 1510
FLOEFD MECHANICA BRIDGE - Software System - MENTOR GRAPHICS CORPORATION; *pg.* 432, *pg.* 1510
FLOEFD PATRAN BRIDGE - Software System - MENTOR GRAPHICS CORPORATION; *pg.* 432, *pg.* 1510
FLOEFDPRO - Software System - MENTOR GRAPHICS CORPORATION; *pg.* 432, *pg.* 1510
FLOEFDV5 - Software System - MENTOR GRAPHICS CORPORATION; *pg.* 432, *pg.* 1510
FLOETROL - Coating & Paint - AKZO NOBEL DECORATIVE PAINTS, USA; *pg.* 1439, *pg.* 1474
FLOGRID - Software - SCHLUMBERGER LIMITED; *pg.* 801, *pg.* 1714
FLOMASTER - Flexible Metal Hose - FEDERAL HOSE MANUFACTURING INC.; *pg.* 1047, *pg.* 1469
FLOMATIC - Photo Processing Chemicals - EASTMAN KODAK COMPANY; *pg.* 1408, *pg.* 1333
FLOMATIC - Designed for UP-Gas & Annydrous Ammonia Liquid Withdrawl - ENGINEERED CONTROLS INTERNATIONAL LLC; *pg.* 1334, *pg.* 1372
FLOMAX - Pharmaceutical Product - IMPAX LABORATORIES, INC.; *pg.* 1544, *pg.* 101
FLOMAX - Spray Product - SPRAYING SYSTEMS CO.; *pg.* 1063, *pg.* 670
FLOMAX - Medical Device - UROLOGIX, INC.; *pg.* 1604, *pg.* 945
FLOMCAD BRIDGE CATIA V5 READER - Software System - MENTOR GRAPHICS CORPORATION; *pg.* 432, *pg.* 1510
FLONASE - Nasal Spray - AIR PRODUCTS AND CHEMICALS, INC.; *pg.* 1145, *pg.* 1513
FLOOD-LUX - Flood Lighting - JUNO LIGHTING, INC.; *pg.* 1300, *pg.* 606
FLOOD STRIP II - Lighting System - REVOLUTION LIGHTING TECHNOLOGIES, INC.; *pg.* 1304, *pg.* 377
FLOODJET - Spray Product - SPRAYING SYSTEMS CO.; *pg.* 1063, *pg.* 670
FLOODPRO - Coating & Paint - AKZO NOBEL DECORATIVE PAINTS, USA; *pg.* 1439, *pg.* 1474
FLOODWOOD POND - Clothing - ABERCROMBIE & FITCH CO.; *pg.* 37, *pg.* 1466
FLOODXPERT - Internet Based Flood Services - THE SEIBELS BRUCE GROUP, INC.; *pg.* 1216, *pg.* 1614
FLOOR MODEL C - Screen - DA-LITE SCREEN COMPANY; *pg.* 632, *pg.* 698
FLOOR PRO - Floor Shampoo Machine - AERUS LLC; *pg.* 51, *pg.* 1673
FLOORGRIP - Silent Coil Nails - PASLODE; *pg.* 1059, *pg.* 664
FLOORGUARD - Cleaner - ROCHESTER MIDLAND CORPORATION; *pg.* 334, *pg.* 1337
FLOORKEEPERS - Automatic Scrubbers - TORNADO INDUSTRIES, INC.; *pg.* 1383, *pg.* 591
FLOORLEVEL - HVAC Equipment - MESTEK, INC.; *pg.* 1074, *pg.* 857
FLOORLINER - Floor Trays - MACNEIL AUTOMOTIVE PRODUCTS, LTD.; *pg.* 211, *pg.* 559
FLOORMACHINES - Vacuum Cleaners - TORNADO INDUSTRIES, INC.; *pg.* 1383, *pg.* 591
FLOORMASTER - Wet/dry Vacuum - SHOP-VAC CORPORATION; *pg.* 1375, *pg.* 1595
FLOORMATE - Insulation - THE DOW CHEMICAL COMPANY; *pg.* 1157, *pg.* 898
FLOORPORT - Service Covers - WIREMOLD/LEGRAND; *pg.* 689, *pg.* 383
FLOORSHINE R20 - Cleaning Preparation - WALTER G. LEGGE COMPANY, INC.; *pg.* 337, *pg.* 1321
FLOORSMART - Equipped Scrubbers - TENNANT COMPANY; *pg.* 1381, *pg.* 944
FLOORVAC - Vacuum Cleaning Inlet Valve - H-P PRODUCTS, INC.; *pg.* 85, *pg.* 1458
FLOP - Footwear - COBIAN CORP.; *pg.* 1806, *pg.* 253
FLOP - Furniture - NEMSCHOFF, INC.; *pg.* 936, *pg.* 1890
FLOP-SOCKS - Socks - REEBOK INTERNATIONAL LTD.; *pg.* 1817, *pg.* 811
FLOQUIL - Hobby Paint - THE TESTOR CORPORATION; *pg.* 968, *pg.* 655
FLOR - Carpet - INTERFACE, INC.; *pg.* 695, *pg.* 512
FLOR-COTE - Paint & Coating - DIAMOND VOGEL PAINT, INC.; *pg.* 1441, *pg.* 710
FLOR DE COPAN - Premium Cigars - ALTADIS USA, INC.; *pg.* 1893, *pg.* 423
FLOR-EVER - Sheet Vinyl Flooring - CONGOLEUM CORPORATION; *pg.* 921, *pg.* 1084
FLORA - Basket - THE LONGABERGER COMPANY; *pg.* 1127, *pg.* 1467
FLORA - Fabric - NEMSCHOFF, INC.; *pg.* 936, *pg.* 1890
FLORA ROYALE - Ceiling Fan - WESTINGHOUSE LIGHTING CORPORATION; *pg.* 687, *pg.* 1571
FLORAFIBER - Acidophilus & Fiber Tablets - HERBALIFE INTERNATIONAL OF AMERICA, INC.; *pg.* 1541, *pg.* 132
FLORAH - Footwear - STEVEN MADDEN, LTD.; *pg.* 1819, *pg.* 1176
FLORAL - Wall Decor - HERITAGE LACE INC.; *pg.* 694, *pg.* 711
FLORAL - Door Panel - MASONITE INTERNATIONAL CORPORATION; *pg.* 1054, *pg.* 1920
FLORAL - Washing Machine - WHIRLPOOL CORPORATION; *pg.* 62, *pg.* 872
FLORAL BOUQUET - Table Textile - HERITAGE LACE INC.; *pg.* 694, *pg.* 711
FLORAL EMBRACE - Flower Arrangement - 1-800-FLOWERS.COM, INC.; *pg.* 1758, *pg.* 1151
FLORAL INK - Apparel - OAKLEY, INC.; *pg.* 1840, *pg.* 86
FLORAL KNIT - Women's Clothing & Accessories - WOODEN SHIPS OF HOBOKEN; *pg.* 35, *pg.* 1315
FLORAL MAJESTIC - Rug - COURISTAN INC.; *pg.* 921, *pg.* 1067
FLORAL STRETCH - Apparel - OAKLEY, INC.; *pg.* 1840, *pg.* 86
FLORAL TRELLIS - Scarf - HERITAGE LACE INC.; *pg.* 694, *pg.* 711
FLORAL URN - Wall Decor - HERITAGE LACE INC.; *pg.* 694, *pg.* 711
FLORAMITE - Polymer Product - CHEMTURA CORPORATION; *pg.* 1152, *pg.* 355
FLORATAM - Food Product - A. DUDA & SONS INC.; *pg.* 835, *pg.* 457
FLORAVERSITY - Educational Services - 1-800-FLOWERS.COM, INC.; *pg.* 1758, *pg.* 1151
FLORECITA - Footwear - COBIAN CORP.; *pg.* 1806, *pg.* 253
FLORENAMEL - Enamel - AKZONOBEL DECORATIVE PAINTS U.S.; *pg.* 1439, *pg.* 1474
FLORENCE - Textiles - BERNHARDT DESIGN; *pg.* 918, *pg.* 1381
FLORENCE - Lighting - ETHAN ALLEN INTERIORS INC.; *pg.* 924, *pg.* 343
FLORENCE - Flatware - ONEIDA LTD; *pg.* 1129, *pg.* 1318
FLORENTINA - Dresses & Sets - HABAND COMPANY, INC.; *pg.* 1772, *pg.* 1099
FLORENTINE - Footwear - CLARKS COMPANIES; *pg.* 1806, *pg.* 836
FLORENTINE - Bath Accessory - CROSCILL, INC.; *pg.* 1122, *pg.* 1220
FLORENTINE - Mirror - ETHAN ALLEN INTERIORS INC.; *pg.* 924, *pg.* 343
FLORENTINO - Ladies' Wallets, Made from Mock Crocodile & Cowhide - BUXTON ACQUISITION CO., LLC; *pg.* 2, *pg.* 845
FLORESTA - Frozen Pasta - HIGH LINER FOODS INCORPORATED; *pg.* 862, *pg.* 1917
FLORET - Gas Analyzer - BACHARACH INC.; *pg.* 1400, *pg.* 1556
FLORET - Fabric - NEMSCHOFF, INC.; *pg.* 936, *pg.* 1890
FLORETTE - Area Rugs - COURISTAN INC.; *pg.* 921, *pg.* 1067
FLOREX - Patterned Glass - AGC GLASS NORTH AMERICA, INC.; *pg.* 65, *pg.* 482
FLORHIDE - Ready-Mixed Liquid Paint - PPG INDUSTRIES, INC.; *pg.* 1445, *pg.* 1579
FLORI ROBERTS - Ethnic Color Cosmetics - COLOR ME BEAUTIFUL, INC.; *pg.* 505, *pg.* 1787
FLORIADE - Scarf - HERITAGE LACE INC.; *pg.* 694, *pg.* 711
FLORIAN - Furniture - ASHLEY FURNITURE INDUSTRIES, INC.; *pg.* 914, *pg.* 1852
FLORIDA GIFT SHOW - Gift Show - AMC, INC.; *pg.* 1759, *pg.* 487
FLORIDA INTERNATIONAL MAGAZINE - Magazine - QUANTURO PUBLISHING, INC.; *pg.* 1679, *pg.* 445
FLORIDA LIFE, YOUR STYLE - Slogan - WCI COMMUNITIES, INC.; *pg.* 1118, *pg.* 414
FLORIDA LOTTERY - Lottery - THE FLORIDA LOTTERY; *pg.* 992, *pg.* 469
THE FLORIDA SHIPPER - Shipping Publication - JOC GROUP INC.; *pg.* 1654, *pg.* 1096
FLORIDA TRAVEL & LIFE - Magazine - BONNIER CORPORATION; *pg.* 1622, *pg.* 480
FLORIDA TREND - Monthly Business Magazine - THE TIMES PUBLISHING CO.; *pg.* 1695, *pg.* 464
FLORIDA VACATION GUIDE - Information Magazine - VISIT FLORIDA INC.; *pg.* 1010, *pg.* 470
FLORIDA WATER - Toilet Water - LANMAN & KEMP-BARCLAY CO., INC.; *pg.* 514, *pg.* 1132
FLORIDA WATER AEROSOL - Air Freshener - LANMAN & KEMP-BARCLAY CO., INC.; *pg.* 514, *pg.* 1132
FLORIDA'S CULTURAL COAST - Tag Line - SARASOTA CONVENTION & VISITORS BUREAU; *pg.* 1005, *pg.* 467
FLORIDA'S NATURAL - Orange Juice - FLORIDA'S NATURAL GROWERS; *pg.* 855, *pg.* 437
FLORIDA'S NATURAL GROWERS' PRIDE - Orange Juice - FLORIDA'S NATURAL GROWERS; *pg.* 855, *pg.* 437
FLORINEF - Pharmaceutical Product - IMPAX LABORATORIES, INC.; *pg.* 1544, *pg.* 101
FLORINEF - Pharmaceutical Product - KING PHARMACEUTICALS, INC.; *pg.* 1553, *pg.* 1627
FLORISIL - Magnesium Silicate Adsorbent - U.S. SILICA COMPANY; *pg.* 1185, *pg.* 1849
FLORIST IN A BOX - Hydroponic Garden Kit - AEROGROW INTERNATIONAL, INC.; *pg.* 1393, *pg.* 310
FLORITE - Air Velocity Instrument - BACHARACH INC.; *pg.* 1400, *pg.* 1556
FLORITE 500 - Rotating Vane Air Velocity Instrument - BACHARACH INC.; *pg.* 1400, *pg.* 1556
FLORITE 600 - Rotating Vane Air Velocity Instrument - BACHARACH INC.; *pg.* 1400, *pg.* 1556
FLORITE 700 - Electronic Air Velocity Instrument - BACHARACH INC.; *pg.* 1400, *pg.* 1556
FLORITE 800 - Electronic Air Velocity Instrument - BACHARACH INC.; *pg.* 1400, *pg.* 1556
FLORONE - Medicine - PFIZER INC.; *pg.* 1581, *pg.* 1278
FLORSHEIM - Footwear - WEYCO GROUP, INC.; *pg.* 1822, *pg.* 1858
FLOSBRUSH - Handled Floss - SUNSTAR AMERICAS INC.; *pg.* 1599, *pg.* 591
FLOSPLITTER - Water Separation Product - CAMERON INTERNATIONAL; *pg.* 1151, *pg.* 1702
FLOSS N TOSS - Disposable Flosser - 3M COMPANY; *pg.* 1142, *pg.* 956
FLOSSMATE - Floss Holder - SUNSTAR AMERICAS INC.; *pg.* 1599, *pg.* 591
FLOSSRX - Medicated Dental Floss - 3M COMPANY; *pg.* 1142, *pg.* 956
FLOSSUGAR - Ready Mix Extra Coarse Sugar - GOLD MEDAL PRODUCTS CO.; *pg.* 55, *pg.* 1414
FLOTECT - Liquid Level Switch - DWYER INSTRUMENTS INC.; *pg.* 1330, *pg.* 694
FLOTHERM - Software System - MENTOR GRAPHICS CORPORATION; *pg.* 432, *pg.* 1510
FLOTHERMPCB - Software System - MENTOR GRAPHICS CORPORATION; *pg.* 432, *pg.* 1510
FLOTREX - Pleated Microfiber Filters - GE WATER & PROCESS TECHNOLOGIES; *pg.* 1339, *pg.* 1588
FLOURISH - Fabric - NEMSCHOFF, INC.; *pg.* 936, *pg.* 1890
FLOVAC - Medical Equipment - CONMED CORPORATION; *pg.* 1517, *pg.* 1347
FLOVAIR - Medical Equipment - INVACARE CORPORATION; *pg.* 1546, *pg.* 1451
FLOVENT - Software System - MENTOR GRAPHICS CORPORATION; *pg.* 432, *pg.* 1510
FLOVIZ - Software System - MENTOR GRAPHICS CORPORATION; *pg.* 432, *pg.* 1510
FLOW - Apparel - OAKLEY, INC.; *pg.* 1840, *pg.* 86
FLOW AWAY - Cleaner - DELTA FOREMOST CHEMICAL CORPORATION; *pg.* 1155, *pg.* 1642
FLOW BED - Carton Flow Product - UNEX MANUFACTURING, INC.; *pg.* 1385, *pg.* 1075
FLOW CELL - Track & Rack Unit - UNEX MANUFACTURING, INC.; *pg.* 1385, *pg.* 1075
FLOW CONTROL XCELERATOR - Route Optimization System - INTERNAP NETWORK SERVICES CORPORATION; *pg.* 417, *pg.* 513
FLOW KOTE - Ready-Mixed Paints - PPG INDUSTRIES, INC.; *pg.* 1445, *pg.* 1579

First page reference indicates Business Class Edition
Second page reference indicates Geographic Edition

FLOW MANUFACTURING - Software System - AMERICAN SOFTWARE, INC.; *pg.* 349, *pg.* 488
THE FLOW OF GOOD IDEAS - Tagline - TI AUTOMOTIVE LIMITED; *pg.* 191, *pg.* 869
FLOW RITE - Packaging Foam - SEALED AIR CORPORATION; *pg.* 1468, *pg.* 1058
FLOW-RITE - Dispensing Cartridge - SONOCO PRODUCTS COMPANY; *pg.* 1469, *pg.* 1619
FLOW-TROL - Valve - VITAL SIGNS, INC.; *pg.* 1607, *pg.* 1126
FLOWCAST - Software - GE HEALTHCARE; *pg.* 399, *pg.* 1765
FLOWCHASER - Software - SYMANTEC CORPORATION; *pg.* 478, *pg.* 161
FLOWER COUNTRY - Retail Store Services - 1-800-FLOWERS.COM, INC.; *pg.* 1758, *pg.* 1151
FLOWER COUNTRY USA - Retail Store Services - 1-800-FLOWERS.COM, INC.; *pg.* 1758, *pg.* 1151
FLOWER-DRI - Garden Chemicals - PLANTABBS PRODUCTS COMPANY; *pg.* 1799, *pg.* 758
FLOWER FIELDS - Flower Grower - ARIS HORTICULTURE, INC.; *pg.* 1793, *pg.* 1404
FLOWER FRESH - Slogan - DURACLEAN INTERNATIONAL, INC.; *pg.* 329, *pg.* 553
FLOWER GARDEN - Carpet - BEAULIEU GROUP, LLC; *pg.* 917, *pg.* 529
FLOWER POTS - Lace Flag - HERITAGE LACE INC.; *pg.* 694, *pg.* 711
FLOWER POWER - Pillow - AMERICAN LEATHER LP; *pg.* 912, *pg.* 1673
FLOWER TRUG - Flower Arrangement - 1-800-FLOWERS.COM, INC.; *pg.* 1758, *pg.* 1151
FLOWERING VINE - Carpet - BEAULIEU GROUP, LLC; *pg.* 917, *pg.* 529
FLOWERS ALIVE - Flower Gardening - GARDENS ALIVE!, INC.; *pg.* 1796, *pg.* 693
FLOWGUARD - Plumbing Products - THE LUBRIZOL CORPORATION; *pg.* 1171, *pg.* 1481
FLOWGUARD - Cement & Primer - OATEY SUPPLY CHAIN SERVICES; *pg.* 30, *pg.* 1433
FLOWGUARD GOLD - Copper Tube - CHARLOTTE PIPE & FOUNDRY COMPANY; *pg.* 1044, *pg.* 1365
FLOWGUARD GOLD - Tubing And Fitting - GENOVA PRODUCTS, INC.; *pg.* 83, *pg.* 875
FLOWGUARD GOLD - Pipe & Fittings - THE LUBRIZOL CORPORATION; *pg.* 1171, *pg.* 1481
FLOWGUARD GOLD - Cement & Primer - OATEY SUPPLY CHAIN SERVICES; *pg.* 30, *pg.* 1433
FLOWMASTEER - Balancing Damper - GE ENERGY; *pg.* 1338, *pg.* 506
FLOWMASTER - Software - BENTLEY SYSTEMS, INC.; *pg.* 361, *pg.* 1531
FLOWMASTER - Software - FLOW INTERNATIONAL CORPORATION; *pg.* 1337, *pg.* 1821
FLOWMASTER - Pump Product - IDEX CORPORATION; *pg.* 1347, *pg.* 623
FLOWMASTER - Inserting System - PITNEY BOWES INC.; *pg.* 454, *pg.* 376
FLOWMASTER - Explosive Grade Ammonium Nitrate - POTASHCORP; *pg.* 1799, *pg.* 641
FLOWMETRIX - Analytical Device - LUMINEX CORPORATION; *pg.* 1421, *pg.* 1664
FLOWPORT - Software - XEROX CORPORATION; *pg.* 494, *pg.* 365
FLOWPRO - Material Handling Agents - GE WATER & PROCESS TECHNOLOGIES; *pg.* 1339, *pg.* 1588
FLOWSORB - Carbon Adsorption System - CALGON CARBON CORPORATION; *pg.* 1151, *pg.* 1574
FLOWTABS - Software System - MENTOR GRAPHICS CORPORATION; *pg.* 432, *pg.* 1510
FLOWVIEW PLATFORM - Route Optimization System - INTERNAP NETWORK SERVICES CORPORATION; *pg.* 417, *pg.* 513
FLOWXPERT - Software System - MENTOR GRAPHICS CORPORATION; *pg.* 432, *pg.* 1510
FLOXIN - Healthcare Product - JOHNSON & JOHNSON; *pg.* 1549, *pg.* 1091
FLOXIN OTIC - Ear Infection Medicine - MCNEIL-PPC, INC.; *pg.* 1560, *pg.* 1533
FLP-IN - Molecular Biology Product - THERMO FISHER SCIENTIFIC INC.; *pg.* 1602, *pg.* 61
FLT4 - Electronic Components - MOLEX INCORPORATED; *pg.* 655, *pg.* 628
FLUCATISONE - Pharmaceutical Product - G&W LABORATORIES INC.; *pg.* 1532, *pg.* 1123
FLUCTUATE - Fabric - NEMSCHOFF, INC.; *pg.* 936, *pg.* 1890
FLUE-RENEW - Firelog - DURAFLAME, INC.; *pg.* 1123, *pg.* 280
FLUENCE - Noise Reduction & Echo Cancellation Technology - QUALCOMM INCORPORATED; *pg.* 1873, *pg.* 207
FLUENCY FORMULA - Educational Materials - SCHOLASTIC INC.; *pg.* 1683, *pg.* 1288
FLUENT-BRAKE - Polyglycol - THE DOW CHEMICAL COMPANY; *pg.* 1157, *pg.* 898
FLUENT-CANE - Polyglycol - THE DOW CHEMICAL COMPANY; *pg.* 1157, *pg.* 898
FLUENT-FAX - Polyglycol - THE DOW CHEMICAL COMPANY; *pg.* 1157, *pg.* 898
FLUENT-LUB - Polyglycol - THE DOW CHEMICAL COMPANY; *pg.* 1157, *pg.* 898
FLUENT-MAT - Polyglycol - THE DOW CHEMICAL COMPANY; *pg.* 1157, *pg.* 898
FLUENT READER - Educational Materials - RENAISSANCE LEARNING, INC.; *pg.* 607, *pg.* 1899
FLUEPAC - Vapor Phase Activated Carbons - CALGON CARBON CORPORATION; *pg.* 1151, *pg.* 1574
FLUFFY STUFF - Candy - TOOTSIE ROLL INDUSTRIES, INC.; *pg.* 1863, *pg.* 591
FLUFFY THE CLASSROOM GUINEA PIG - Educational Materials - SCHOLASTIC INC.; *pg.* 1683, *pg.* 1288
FLUID CHEMISTRY - Refrigerant Service - HUDSON TECHNOLOGIES, INC.; *pg.* 1073, *pg.* 1320
FLUID COMMANDER - Fluid Management Systems - GRACO, INC.; *pg.* 1342, *pg.* 935
FLUID FILM - Corrosion Preventative, Lubricant & Rust Inhibitor - EUREKA CHEMICAL COMPANY; *pg.* 1161, *pg.* 279
FLUID METAL SUNGLASSES - Sunglasses - COSTA DEL MAR SUNGLASSES, INC.; *pg.* 1407, *pg.* 419
FLUID MISER - Underground Construction Equipment - CHARLES MACHINE WORKS, INC.; *pg.* 1322, *pg.* 1488
FLUID POWER INSTITUTE - Research Center - MILWAUKEE SCHOOL OF ENGINEERING; *pg.* 605, *pg.* 1878
FLUID-SHAFT - Electric Motors - REULAND ELECTRIC COMPANY; *pg.* 1304, *pg.* 68
FLUIDAIR - Wound Care Surface - KINETIC CONCEPTS, INC.; *pg.* 1553, *pg.* 1741
FLUIDFILE - Software - THE DOW CHEMICAL COMPANY; *pg.* 1157, *pg.* 898
FLUIDFILM - Video Motion Effects - AVID TECHNOLOGY, INC.; *pg.* 622, *pg.* 804
FLUIDIC SEAL - Vent Tip - NAO, INC.; *pg.* 1074, *pg.* 1567
FLUIDIC VENT TIP - Vent Tip - NAO, INC.; *pg.* 1074, *pg.* 1567
FLUIDKEEN - Bath Filtration System - SAFETY-KLEEN HOLDCO, INC.; *pg.* 1180, *pg.* 1734
FLUIDLASTIC - Rubber - LORD CORPORATION; *pg.* 1357, *pg.* 1360
FLUIDMOTION - Video Motion Effects - AVID TECHNOLOGY, INC.; *pg.* 622, *pg.* 804
FLUIDO - Orthopedic Device - DJO SURGICAL; *pg.* 1525, *pg.* 1661
FLUIDOTHERAPY - Orthopedic Device - DJO SURGICAL; *pg.* 1525, *pg.* 1661
FLUIDSEP - Filter - CAMERON INTERNATIONAL; *pg.* 1151, *pg.* 1702
FLUKA - Specialty Chemicals & Analytical Reagents for Research - SIGMA-ALDRICH CORPORATION; *pg.* 1181, *pg.* 1003
FLUKE - Electronic Test Tool - DANAHER CORPORATION; *pg.* 1044, *pg.* 397
FLUKE NETWORKS - Electronic Test Tool - DANAHER CORPORATION; *pg.* 1044, *pg.* 397
FLUKER FARMS - Pet Product - PETSMART, INC.; *pg.* 1481, *pg.* 18
FLUMADINE - Pharmaceutical Product - IMPAX LABORATORIES, INC.; *pg.* 1544, *pg.* 101
FLUMIST - Medicine - MEDIMMUNE LLC; *pg.* 1562, *pg.* 770
FLUOCELLS - Molecular Probe Product - THERMO FISHER SCIENTIFIC INC.; *pg.* 1602, *pg.* 61
FLUOPLATE - Software - BIO-RAD LABORATORIES, INC.; *pg.* 1504, *pg.* 101
FLUOR DANIEL - Construction Product - FLUOR CORPORATION; *pg.* 82, *pg.* 1719
FLUOR FEDERAL SERVICES - Operation & Environmental Remediation of Government Facilities - FLUOR CORPORATION; *pg.* 82, *pg.* 1719
FLUOR GLOBAL SERVICES - Telecommunication Service - FLUOR CORPORATION; *pg.* 82, *pg.* 1719
FLUOR-S - Software - BIO-RAD LABORATORIES, INC.; *pg.* 1504, *pg.* 101
FLUOR-S MAX - Software - BIO-RAD LABORATORIES, INC.; *pg.* 1504, *pg.* 101
FLUOR-S MAX2 - Software - BIO-RAD LABORATORIES, INC.; *pg.* 1504, *pg.* 101
FLUORACE - Software - BIO-RAD LABORATORIES, INC.; *pg.* 1504, *pg.* 101
FLUORAD - Fluorochemical Surfactants - 3M COMPANY; *pg.* 1142, *pg.* 956
FLUORAPTOR - Laser Sorter - KEY TECHNOLOGY, INC.; *pg.* 868, *pg.* 1847
FLUORAZ - Seal & Thermoplastic Component - GREENE, TWEED & CO.; *pg.* 1344, *pg.* 1544
FLUOREPORTER - Molecular Probe Product - THERMO FISHER SCIENTIFIC INC.; *pg.* 1602, *pg.* 61
FLUORESCENT - Filter - ROSCO LABORATORIES, INC.; *pg.* 1782, *pg.* 378
FLUORGUARD - Pest Control Product - FMC CORPORATION; *pg.* 1163, *pg.* 1564
FLUORINERT - Electronic Liquids - 3M COMPANY; *pg.* 1142, *pg.* 956
FLUORIVER - Chemical Reagent - HACH COMPANY; *pg.* 1415, *pg.* 334
FLUORO-PLUS - Filter Housing - PALL CORPORATION; *pg.* 232, *pg.* 1323
FLUOROCILLIN - Molecular Probe Product - THERMO FISHER SCIENTIFIC INC.; *pg.* 1602, *pg.* 61
FLUOROCORE - Dental Product - DENTSPLY INTERNATIONAL INC.; *pg.* 1522, *pg.* 1596
FLUOROETCH - Pre-Bonding Etchant - ACTON TECHNOLOGIES, INC.; *pg.* 1145, *pg.* 1582
FLUOROFINISH - Coating System - CENTRIA, INC.; *pg.* 74, *pg.* 1554
FLUOROFLEX - Rigid, Gas-Permeable Daily Wear Contact Lens - THE COOPER COMPANIES, INC.; *pg.* 1518, *pg.* 183
FLUOROFLEX UV - Contact Lenses - THE COOPER COMPANIES, INC.; *pg.* 1518, *pg.* 183
FLUOROGARD - Filters - ENTEGRIS, INC.; *pg.* 1882, *pg.* 788
FLUOROGUARD - Software - BIO-RAD LABORATORIES, INC.; *pg.* 1504, *pg.* 101
FLUOROGUARD - Polymer Additive - E.I. DU PONT DE NEMOURS & COMPANY; *pg.* 1159, *pg.* 390
FLUOROKINE - Biological Product - TECHNE CORPORATION; *pg.* 1601, *pg.* 944
FLUOROLINE - Tubing - ENTEGRIS, INC.; *pg.* 1882, *pg.* 788
FLUOROLUBES - Lubricants - OCCIDENTAL CHEMICAL CORPORATION; *pg.* 1175, *pg.* 1685
FLUOROMER - Seal & Thermoplastic Component - GREENE, TWEED & CO.; *pg.* 1344, *pg.* 1544
FLUOROMYELIN - Molecular Probe Product - THERMO FISHER SCIENTIFIC INC.; *pg.* 1602, *pg.* 61
FLUORONAV - Spinal Navigation Tool - MEDTRONIC, INC.; *pg.* 1564, *pg.* 939
FLUOROPLEX - Skin Care Product - ALLERGAN, INC.; *pg.* 1491, *pg.* 106
FLUOROPURE - Chemical Container - ENTEGRIS, INC.; *pg.* 1882, *pg.* 788
FLUOROPURE - Molecular Probe Product - THERMO FISHER SCIENTIFIC INC.; *pg.* 1602, *pg.* 61
FLUOROSCAN - Medical Test System - HOLOGIC, INC.; *pg.* 1416, *pg.* 784
FLUOROSCRIPT - Molecular Biology Product - THERMO FISHER SCIENTIFIC INC.; *pg.* 1602, *pg.* 61
FLUOROTAG - FITC Conjugation Kit - SIGMA-ALDRICH CORPORATION; *pg.* 1181, *pg.* 1003
FLUORYTE - Filter Cartridge - PALL CORPORATION; *pg.* 232, *pg.* 1323
FLUOSPHERES - Molecular Probe Product - THERMO FISHER SCIENTIFIC INC.; *pg.* 1602, *pg.* 61
FLUOZIN - Molecular Probe Product - THERMO FISHER SCIENTIFIC INC.; *pg.* 1602, *pg.* 61
FLUPRO - Polymer Product - CHEMTURA CORPORATION; *pg.* 1152, *pg.* 355
FLURESS - Ophthalmic Pharmaceutical Product - AKORN, INC.; *pg.* 1488, *pg.* 622
FLURODYNE - Filter Cartridge - PALL CORPORATION; *pg.* 232, *pg.* 1323
FLUROSHIELD - Dental Product - DENTSPLY INTERNATIONAL INC.; *pg.* 1522, *pg.* 1596
FLUROTEC - Barrier Coating - WEST PHARMACEUTICAL SERVICES, INC.; *pg.* 1472, *pg.* 1532
FLUSH - Door Lock - SOUTHCO, INC.; *pg.* 1063, *pg.* 1522

FLUSH FORTUNE POKER - Game - WMS INDUSTRIES INC.; *pg.* 593, *pg.* 666
FLUSHDUCT - Infloor Wiring System - WIREMOLD/LEGRAND; *pg.* 689, *pg.* 383
FLUSHLINE - Doorway Entrances - KAWNEER COMPANY, INC.; *pg.* 90, *pg.* 537
FLUSHLINE - Garage Door - MARTIN DOOR MANUFACTURING, INC.; *pg.* 96, *pg.* 1759
FLUSHLOK - Insulated Sash & Division Bar Window Units - PPG INDUSTRIES, INC.; *pg.* 1445, *pg.* 1579
FLUSHNUT - Pumps - IDEX CORPORATION; *pg.* 1347, *pg.* 623
FLUSHSEAL - Grooved Pipe Coupling Gasket - VICTAULIC COMPANY; *pg.* 1066, *pg.* 1529
FLUSHTRODE - Robotic Product - HAMILTON CO., INC.; *pg.* 1415, *pg.* 1031
FLUSS - Toilet Bowl Cleaners - THE CLOROX COMPANY; *pg.* 327, *pg.* 169
FLUSURE - Pharmaceutical Product - PFIZER INC.; *pg.* 1581, *pg.* 1278
FLUTE - Furniture - HERMAN MILLER, INC.; *pg.* 926, *pg.* 913
FLUTE - Waiting Seating - STEELCASE INC.; *pg.* 475, *pg.* 889
FLUTEX - Patterned Glass - AGC GLASS NORTH AMERICA, INC.; *pg.* 65, *pg.* 482
FLUTTERBUG - Toy - INFANTINO, LLC; *pg.* 957, *pg.* 203
FLUVAC - Equine Vaccine - PFIZER INC.; *pg.* 1581, *pg.* 1278
FLUVAC INNOVATOR - Equine Vaccine - PFIZER INC.; *pg.* 1581, *pg.* 1278
FLUVIRIN - Pharmaceutical Product - NOVARTIS VACCINES & DIAGNOSTICS, INC.; *pg.* 1575, *pg.* 809
FLUX REMOVER - Aerosol Cleaner - TECH SPRAY, L.P.; *pg.* 1183, *pg.* 1659
FLUX-RITE - Flux - LA-CO INDUSTRIES MARKAL CO., INC.; *pg.* 1170, *pg.* 610
FLUX-RITE 90 - Soldering Flux - LA-CO INDUSTRIES MARKAL CO., INC.; *pg.* 1170, *pg.* 610
FLUX TUBE - Electronic Equipment - KLIPSCH GROUP, INC.; *pg.* 649, *pg.* 688
FLUZONE - Influenza Virus Vaccine - SANOFI PASTEUR, INC; *pg.* 1591, *pg.* 1588
FLXLINK - Optical Networking Product - HARMONIC, INC.; *pg.* 402, *pg.* 246
FLXTITE - Film - AEP INDUSTRIES INC.; *pg.* 1878, *pg.* 1085
FLY-BY - Chip Interface System - RAMBUS INC.; *pg.* 459, *pg.* 288
FLY FISHING IN SALT WATERS - Magazine - BONNIER CORPORATION; *pg.* 1622, *pg.* 480
FLY FUSION - Toys - LEAPFROG ENTERPRISES, INC.; *pg.* 961, *pg.* 84
FLY MAGNET - Fly Bait Spray - THE WOODSTREAM CORPORATION; *pg.* 1801, *pg.* 1549
FLY TOP - Fly Floatant - MCNETT CORPORATION; *pg.* 1839, *pg.* 1817
FLY WITH ME - Designer Fragrance - PARFUMS DE COEUR LTD.; *pg.* 519, *pg.* 376
FLYER - Medical Equipment - INVACARE CORPORATION; *pg.* 1546, *pg.* 1451
FLYERFIT - Jewelry Collection - MARTIN FLYER INC.; *pg.* 9, *pg.* 1257
FLYERS' CHOICE - Bird Seed - INTERMOUNTAIN FARMERS ASSOCIATION; *pg.* 705, *pg.* 1759
FLYFORWARD - Switch - POWER INTEGRATIONS, INC.; *pg.* 1369, *pg.* 249
FLYGT - Fluid Technology - ITT CORPORATION; *pg.* 1351, *pg.* 1354
FLYING ALONE - Brochures For Parents of Children Traveling Alone - AMERICAN AUTOMOBILE ASSOCIATION; *pg.* 1190, *pg.* 429
FLYING COASTER - Coaster - BROWN & BIGELOW, INC.; *pg.* 1624, *pg.* 959
FLYING COLORS - Crafting Product - JAKKS PACIFIC, INC.; *pg.* 960, *pg.* 142
FLYING CROSS BY FECHHEIMER - Complete Line of Shirts, Trousers & Outerwear - THE FECHHEIMER BROTHERS COMPANY; *pg.* 41, *pg.* 1412
FLYING FLAG FISH HOUSE - Food Service - FOOD SERVICES OF AMERICA, INC.; *pg.* 856, *pg.* 21
FLYING PAGES - Educational Materials - SCHOLASTIC INC.; *pg.* 1683, *pg.* 1288
FLYING SPOT - X-ray Screening System - AMERICAN SCIENCE AND ENGINEERING, INC.; *pg.* 1399, *pg.* 787
FLYING TIGER - Jacket - L.L. BEAN, INC.; *pg.* 1777, *pg.* 750
FLYNAP - Biological Product - CAROLINA BIOLOGICAL SUPPLY COMPANY; *pg.* 1513, *pg.* 1359
FLYPAPER - Online Store - BLUEFLY, INC.; *pg.* 1232, *pg.* 1205
FLYS-X - Fly Control Product - W.F. YOUNG, INC.; *pg.* 1610, *pg.* 817
FLYSECURE - Software Product - MAXIMUS, INC.; *pg.* 780, *pg.* 1799
FLYTE - Food Product - MARS, INCORPORATED; *pg.* 1858, *pg.* 1792
FM - Engineered Materials - CYTEC INDUSTRIES, INC.; *pg.* 1155, *pg.* 1131
FM - Pilot Mixers - LITTLEFORD DAY INC.; *pg.* 1356, *pg.* 728
FM-200 - Fire Suppressant - E.I. DU PONT DE NEMOURS & COMPANY; *pg.* 1159, *pg.* 390
FM BROWNS - Pet Product - PETSMART, INC.; *pg.* 1481, *pg.* 18
FM-ON-DEMAND - Chipset - ADVANCED MICRO DEVICES, INC.; *pg.* 613, *pg.* 282
FM3A MANUAL - Photo Equipment - NIKON INC.; *pg.* 1424, *pg.* 1181
FMALERT - Software - KEY TECHNOLOGY, INC.; *pg.* 868, *pg.* 1847
FMC - Polysulfide Rubber - SMOOTH-ON INC.; *pg.* 111, *pg.* 1528
FMCNET - Software - SS&C TECHNOLOGIES HOLDINGS, INC.; *pg.* 473, *pg.* 386
FMDESKTOP - Software - AUTODESK INC.; *pg.* 356, *pg.* 257
FMN ONLINE - Continuing Educations Services for Accountants - SMARTPROS LTD.; *pg.* 1281, *pg.* 1166
FMP3 - Electronic Components - MOLEX INCORPORATED; *pg.* 655, *pg.* 628
FMS 300 - Marine Fuel Management - BENMAR MARINE ELECTRONICS, INC.; *pg.* 624, *pg.* 105
FMV-100K - Electronic Component - EMCORE CORPORATION; *pg.* 636, *pg.* 39
FMV-563 - Electronic Component - EMCORE CORPORATION; *pg.* 636, *pg.* 39
FMV-564 - Electronic Component - EMCORE CORPORATION; *pg.* 636, *pg.* 39
FMV-567 - Electronic Component - EMCORE CORPORATION; *pg.* 636, *pg.* 39
FMV-574 - Electronic Component - EMCORE CORPORATION; *pg.* 636, *pg.* 39
FMV-574D2 - Electronic Component - EMCORE CORPORATION; *pg.* 636, *pg.* 39
FMV-586 - Electronic Component - EMCORE CORPORATION; *pg.* 636, *pg.* 39
FMV-593 - Electronic Component - EMCORE CORPORATION; *pg.* 636, *pg.* 39
FMV-595 - Electronic Component - EMCORE CORPORATION; *pg.* 636, *pg.* 39
FMV-603 - Electronic Component - EMCORE CORPORATION; *pg.* 636, *pg.* 39
FN - Footwear News - FAIRCHILD FASHION GROUP; *pg.* 1640, *pg.* 1230
FO - Fine Organics - FINE ORGANICS CORPORATION; *pg.* 330, *pg.* 1052
FOAM - Footwear - COBIAN CORP.; *pg.* 1806, *pg.* 253
FOAM 140 - Alkaline Cleaner - STERIS CORPORATION; *pg.* 1597, *pg.* 1464
FOAM BREAKER - Antifoam-Defoaming Agent - UNIVERSAL COOPERATIVES, INC.; *pg.* 1482, *pg.* 922
FOAM CALC - Software - THE DOW CHEMICAL COMPANY; *pg.* 1157, *pg.* 898
FOAM CAST - Process that Utilizes Foam Patterns to Produce Castings - WAUKESHA FOUNDRY INC.; *pg.* 1388, *pg.* 1898
FOAM CAT - Systems for Spraying Insulating Foam - GRACO, INC.; *pg.* 1342, *pg.* 935
FOAM CRETE - Expanded Cellular Urethane - THE DOW CHEMICAL COMPANY; *pg.* 1157, *pg.* 898
FOAM-DYE - Visibility Foam - KALO, INC.; *pg.* 1796, *pg.* 719
FOAM-END - Cleaning Preparation - WALTER G. LEGGE COMPANY, INC.; *pg.* 337, *pg.* 1321
FOAM-IT! - Foam - SMOOTH-ON INC.; *pg.* 111, *pg.* 1528
FOAM KLEAN - Cleaner Product - AERVOE INDUSTRIES INCORPORATED; *pg.* 1439, *pg.* 1021
FOAM-N-KLEEN - Cleaner - DELTA FOREMOST CHEMICAL CORPORATION; *pg.* 1155, *pg.* 1642
FOAM PLUS - Expanding Foam - THE DOW CHEMICAL COMPANY; *pg.* 1157, *pg.* 898
FOAM SULATE - Expanding Foam Sealant - THE DOW CHEMICAL COMPANY; *pg.* 1157, *pg.* 898
FOAM-TROL - Antifoaming Agents - GE WATER & PROCESS TECHNOLOGIES; *pg.* 1339, *pg.* 1588
FOAM WORKS - Personal Care Product - COLGATE-PALMOLIVE COMPANY; *pg.* 504, *pg.* 1215
FOAMA-BAG - Colorant & Additive System - CHROMA CORPORATION; *pg.* 1441, *pg.* 632
FOAMA-SPHERES - Colorant & Additive System - CHROMA CORPORATION; *pg.* 1441, *pg.* 632
FOAMAWAY - Reagent - THERMO FISHER SCIENTIFIC INC.; *pg.* 1602, *pg.* 61
FOAMCOAT - Coating - ROSCO LABORATORIES, INC.; *pg.* 1782, *pg.* 378
FOAMCORE - Door - WAYNE-DALTON CORP.; *pg.* 120, *pg.* 1465
FOAMFAST - Fasteners - MOORE PUSH PIN CO.; *pg.* 441, *pg.* 1595
FOAMFIGHTER - Medical & Aesthetic Product - DYNATRONICS CORPORATION; *pg.* 1526, *pg.* 1757
FOAMFRAX - Foaming Insulation - UNIFRAX CORPORATION; *pg.* 220, *pg.* 1317
FOAMING POMMADE - Hair Care Product - JOHN PAUL MITCHELL SYSTEMS; *pg.* 512, *pg.* 133
FOAMLOGIX - Fire Pumps - IDEX CORPORATION; *pg.* 1347, *pg.* 623
FOAMMELT - Systems - NORDSON CORPORATION; *pg.* 1365, *pg.* 1480
FOAMPRO - Automatic Foam Proportioner - HYPRO; *pg.* 705, *pg.* 951
FOAMSEALR - Insulating System - OWENS CORNING; *pg.* 102, *pg.* 1476
FOAMULAR - Insulating System - OWENS CORNING; *pg.* 102, *pg.* 1476
FOAMY - Shave Preparations - THE GILLETTE COMPANY; *pg.* 509, *pg.* 795
FOBA - Laser Engraving Solution - VIRTEK VISION INTERNATIONAL, INC.; *pg.* 1435, *pg.* 1948
FOBCARE - Pharmaceutical Product - ALERE INC.; *pg.* 1488, *pg.* 849
FOCAL - Software - ELEKTA; *pg.* 391, *pg.* 987
FOCAL 4D - Software - ELEKTA; *pg.* 391, *pg.* 987
FOCAL DVS - Software - ELEKTA; *pg.* 391, *pg.* 987
FOCAL POINTS - Clustering System - IHS AUTOMOTIVE DRIVEN BY POLK; *pg.* 1652, *pg.* 907
FOCALCHECK - Molecular Probe Product - THERMO FISHER SCIENTIFIC INC.; *pg.* 1602, *pg.* 61
FOCALPOINT - Diagnostic Product - BD DIAGNOSTICS - TRIPATH; *pg.* 1402, *pg.* 1358
FOCAUDIT - An Auditing System - INFORMATION BUILDERS INC.; *pg.* 415, *pg.* 1243
FOCMAN - Project Management System - INFORMATION BUILDERS INC.; *pg.* 415, *pg.* 1243
FOCUS - Sports Drink - ENERGY BRANDS, INC.; *pg.* 854, *pg.* 1227
FOCUS - 4 GL for Developing Information Management Applications - INFORMATION BUILDERS INC.; *pg.* 415, *pg.* 1243
FOCUS - Office Furniture - KIMBALL INTERNATIONAL, INC.; *pg.* 931, *pg.* 692
FOCUS - Fabric - NEMSCHOFF, INC.; *pg.* 936, *pg.* 1890
FOCUS - Apparel - OAKLEY, INC.; *pg.* 1840, *pg.* 86
FOCUS - Turf Product - PBI/GORDON CORPORATION; *pg.* 1176, *pg.* 985
FOCUS - Suitcase - SAMSONITE CORPORATION; *pg.* 11, *pg.* 830
FOCUS - Remote Control Device - UNIVERSAL ELECTRONICS, INC.; *pg.* 683, *pg.* 262
FOCUS: ACHIEVING YOUR HIGHEST PRIORITIES - Book & Workshop - FRANKLIN COVEY CO.; *pg.* 1642, *pg.* 1758
FOCUS DAILIES - Lenses - ALCON; *pg.* 1399, *pg.* 530
FOCUS/ELS - Executive Information Systems - INFORMATION BUILDERS INC.; *pg.* 415, *pg.* 1243
FOCUS. EXECUTION. CONTINUITY. CONFIDENTIALITY. - Tagline - PRIVATEBANCORP INC.; *pg.* 796, *pg.* 587
FOCUS FOR WINDOWS - 4 GL PC Based Application Development System for Database Management - INFORMATION BUILDERS INC.; *pg.* 415, *pg.* 1243
FOCUS FUSION - Multi-Dimensional Data Base - INFORMATION BUILDERS INC.; *pg.* 415, *pg.* 1243
FOCUS HOPE - Human Right Organization - FOCUS: HOPE; *pg.* 141, *pg.* 881
FOCUS ON HEALTH - Health Plan & Publication - MEDICA, INC.; *pg.* 1208, *pg.* 949
THE FOCUS ON PROCESS - Tagline - PERCEPTRON, INC.; *pg.* 215, *pg.* 904

First page reference indicates Business Class Edition
Second page reference indicates Geographic Edition

FOCUS PROGRESSIVES - Lenses - ALCON; *pg.* 1399, *pg.* 530
FOCUS SYSTEMS - Software - ELEKTA; *pg.* 391, *pg.* 987
FOCUS16 - Semiconductor Solution - VITESSE SEMICONDUCTOR CORPORATION; *pg.* 686, *pg.* 57
FOCUSCONNECT - Network Product - VITESSE SEMICONDUCTOR CORPORATION; *pg.* 686, *pg.* 57
FOCUSED SYNTHESIS - Microwave Synthesis Product - CEM CORPORATION; *pg.* 1405, *pg.* 1382
FOCUSPRO - Thermostat - HONEYWELL INTERNATIONAL INC.; *pg.* 407, *pg.* 1088
FOCUSSED-INNOVATIVE-EFFECTIVE - Tagline - APTOSE BIOSCIENCES; *pg.* 1495, *pg.* 1934
FODEL - Film - E.I. DU PONT DE NEMOURS & COMPANY; *pg.* 1159, *pg.* 390
FODEN - Trucks - PACCAR INC.; *pg.* 187, *pg.* 1816
FOG FREE - Face Mask - CROSSTEX INTERNATIONAL INC.; *pg.* 1520, *pg.* 1164
FOG-GARD - Coating - PACTIV CORPORATION; *pg.* 1466, *pg.* 624
FOGJET - Spray Nozzle - SPRAYING SYSTEMS CO.; *pg.* 1063, *pg.* 670
FOGLIA - Carpet - INTERFACE, INC.; *pg.* 695, *pg.* 512
FOGLIGHT - Software - DELL SOFTWARE; *pg.* 385, *pg.* 40
FOGLIGHT PERFORMANCE ANALYSIS FOR SQL SERVER - Software - DELL SOFTWARE; *pg.* 385, *pg.* 40
FOGO SPORTS - Toy - SPIN MASTER LTD.; *pg.* 967, *pg.* 1943
FOHO FOR OILY HAIR ONLY - Shampoo & Rinse - THE GILLETTE COMPANY; *pg.* 509, *pg.* 795
FOIL-FAST - Adhesive Anchor - POWERS FASTENERS INC.; *pg.* 1059, *pg.* 1143
FOILGARD - Self-Expanding Fasteners - PENN ENGINEERING & MANUFACTURING CORP.; *pg.* 1059, *pg.* 1525
FOILLE - First Aid Spray - BLISTEX, INC.; *pg.* 502, *pg.* 644
FOLD 2 GO - Trikes - RADIO FLYER INC.; *pg.* 966, *pg.* 588
FOLD-FLAT - Laundry And Cleaning Product - FAULTLESS STARCH/BON AMI COMPANY; *pg.* 330, *pg.* 982
FOLD-FLAT CART - Gardening & Hardware Product - FAULTLESS STARCH/BON AMI COMPANY; *pg.* 330, *pg.* 982
FOLD-FORM - Insulating System - OWENS CORNING; *pg.* 102, *pg.* 1476
FOLD 'N GO - Carts - CARLISLE FOODSERVICE PRODUCTS INCORPORATED; *pg.* 1455, *pg.* 1485
FOLD 'N GO - Playard - GRACO CHILDREN'S PRODUCTS INC.; *pg.* 954, *pg.* 1531
FOLD 'N GO - Baby Care Product - MUNCHKIN, INC.; *pg.* 964, *pg.* 300
FOLDAWAY - Audio And Video Cable - CYBERRESEARCH INC.; *pg.* 381, *pg.* 339
FOLDBACK MODE - Integrated Circuits - MAXIM INTEGRATED PRODUCTS, INC.; *pg.* 653, *pg.* 247
FOLDBAK - TVS Diode for Telecommunications - LITTELFUSE, INC.; *pg.* 1301, *pg.* 580
FOLDIN' ART - Toy & Game - HASBRO, INC.; *pg.* 954, *pg.* 1603
FOLDING ALPHA HUNTER - Knife - BUCK KNIVES, INC.; *pg.* 1828, *pg.* 550
FOLDING BUCKLITE MAX - Knife - BUCK KNIVES, INC.; *pg.* 1828, *pg.* 550
FOLDING HUNTER - Cutlery - BUCK KNIVES, INC.; *pg.* 1828, *pg.* 550
FOLDING INNERNET - Sport Product - FRANKLIN SPORTS, INC.; *pg.* 1834, *pg.* 847
FOLDING KALINGA PRO - Knife - BUCK KNIVES, INC.; *pg.* 1828, *pg.* 550
FOLDING KALINGA PRO EAGLE - Knife - BUCK KNIVES, INC.; *pg.* 1828, *pg.* 550
FOLDING LED - Flashlight - ENERGIZER HOLDINGS, INC.; *pg.* 637, *pg.* 996
FOLDING OMNI HUNTER - Knife - BUCK KNIVES, INC.; *pg.* 1828, *pg.* 550
FOLD'N GO - Toy - THE OHIO ART COMPANY, INC.; *pg.* 965, *pg.* 1406
FOLED - Organic Light Emitting Device - UNIVERSAL DISPLAY CORPORATION; *pg.* 683, *pg.* 1064
FOLGERS - Coffee - THE J.M. SMUCKER COMPANY; *pg.* 865, *pg.* 1468
FOLIE A DEUX - Beverage - TRINCHERO FAMILY ESTATES; *pg.* 1971, *pg.* 197
FOLIO - Bath Product - KOHLER CO.; *pg.* 91, *pg.* 1862
FOLIO - Bag Liner - MCNETT CORPORATION; *pg.* 1839, *pg.* 1817
FOLIO - Fabric - NEMSCHOFF, INC.; *pg.* 936, *pg.* 1890
FOLIOTRONIC - Computerized Security Document Finishing System - DELPHAX TECHNOLOGIES INC.; *pg.* 386, *pg.* 917
FOLK ANGELS - Scarf - HERITAGE LACE INC.; *pg.* 694, *pg.* 711
FOLKLORE - Sandals - AEROGROUP INTERNATIONAL, INC.; *pg.* 1803, *pg.* 1055
FOLKMANIS - Puppet - FOLKMANIS, INC.; *pg.* 953, *pg.* 83
FOLLIDERM - Nutritional Supplement - NATURAL ORGANICS, INC.; *pg.* 1571, *pg.* 1181
FOLLISTIM - Pharmaceutical Preparation - MERCK & CO., INC.; *pg.* 1566, *pg.* 1077
FOLLOW ME ROAMING PLUS - Call Delivery System - SYNIVERSE HOLDINGS, INC.; *pg.* 479, *pg.* 475
FOLYSIL - Medical Device - MENTOR CORPORATION; *pg.* 1565, *pg.* 263
FOM-BLOC - Antifoam - BIRKO CORPORATION; *pg.* 1149, *pg.* 332
FOMACID - Acid Cleaner - BIRKO CORPORATION; *pg.* 1149, *pg.* 332
FOMADS - Business Forms Mngmt. & Distr. System - THE STANDARD REGISTER COMPANY; *pg.* 473, *pg.* 1446
FOMARK - Foam Marking Agent - KALO, INC.; *pg.* 1796, *pg.* 719
FOMREZ - Polymer Product - CHEMTURA CORPORATION; *pg.* 1152, *pg.* 355
FONAR 360 - Magnetic Resonance Scanning Room - FONAR CORPORATION; *pg.* 1413, *pg.* 1179
FONDO - Acrylic Leather Finish - HENKEL CORPORATION; *pg.* 1165, *pg.* 1535
FONGISCREEN - Software - BIO-RAD LABORATORIES, INC.; *pg.* 1504, *pg.* 101
FONIX - Hearing Aid Analyzer - FRYE ELECTRONICS, INC.; *pg.* 1413, *pg.* 1509
FONOS - Exhaust Product - TENNECO, INC.; *pg.* 985, *pg.* 625
FONT FOLIO - Software - ADOBE SYSTEMS INCORPORATED; *pg.* 342, *pg.* 235
FONTAIN - Furniture - J. ROBERT SCOTT INC.; *pg.* 930, *pg.* 105
FONTANA - Beverages - THE COCA-COLA COMPANY; *pg.* 240, *pg.* 493
FONTANA - Bath & Plumbing Product - JACUZZI BRANDS CORPORATION; *pg.* 554, *pg.* 65
FONTANA CANDIDA - Italian Wines - BROWN-FORMAN CORPORATION; *pg.* 1958, *pg.* 732
FONTANE - Fabric - SCALAMANDRE, INC.; *pg.* 941, *pg.* 1058
FONTENAY - Rug - COURISTAN INC.; *pg.* 921, *pg.* 1067
FONTEVECCHIA - Italian Wine - LAIRD & COMPANY, INC.; *pg.* 1966, *pg.* 1119
FONTVISION - Font Management Software - LEXMARK INTERNATIONAL, INC.; *pg.* 427, *pg.* 730
FOOD 4 LESS - Supermarket - THE KROGER CO.; *pg.* 1025, *pg.* 1416
FOOD ACTIVITIES - Toy - SPIN MASTER LTD.; *pg.* 967, *pg.* 1943
FOOD & BREWERY - Slogan - GRANITE CITY FOOD & BREWERY LTD; *pg.* 1730, *pg.* 937
FOOD & WINE - Media Publication - TIME INC.; *pg.* 1693, *pg.* 1300
FOOD BASICS - Food Stores - THE GREAT ATLANTIC & PACIFIC TEA COMPANY, INC.; *pg.* 1021, *pg.* 1086
FOOD BROKERAGE SYSTEM - Software Application - INFOACCESS.NET LLC; *pg.* 1258, *pg.* 1456
FOOD CHIEF - Convenience Stores - THE PANTRY, INC.; *pg.* 1029, *pg.* 1360
FOOD CITY - Supermarkets - K-VA-T FOOD STORES, INC.; *pg.* 1025, *pg.* 1770
FOOD CLUB - Food Products - BASHAS' SUPERMARKETS; *pg.* 1015, *pg.* 12
FOOD CLUB - Food Product - HAGGEN, INC.; *pg.* 1022, *pg.* 1817
FOOD CLUB - Foods - TOPCO HOLDINGS INC.; *pg.* 901, *pg.* 661
FOOD CONTAINMENT - AIRLITE PLASTICS COMPANY; *pg.* 1451, *pg.* 1013
FOOD EMPORIUM - Food Stores - THE GREAT ATLANTIC & PACIFIC TEA COMPANY, INC.; *pg.* 1021, *pg.* 1086
FOOD ENZYMES - Health Care Product - NATURE'S SUNSHINE PRODUCTS, INC.; *pg.* 1571, *pg.* 1754
FOOD FOLKS & FUN - Advertising Slogan - MCDONALD'S CORPORATION; *pg.* 1737, *pg.* 645
FOOD FOR THE FUN OF IT - Tag Line - FRITO-LAY NORTH AMERICA, INC.; *pg.* 1853, *pg.* 1730
FOOD LION - Grocery Stores - FOOD LION, LLC; *pg.* 1019, *pg.* 1390
FOOD MANUFACTURING - Trade Magazine - ADVANTAGE BUSINESS MEDIA; *pg.* 1613, *pg.* 1116
THE FOOD NETWORK - Cable Network - THE E.W. SCRIPPS COMPANY; *pg.* 1639, *pg.* 1412
FOOD NETWORK MAGAZINE - Magazine - FOOD NETWORK; *pg.* 287, *pg.* 1231
FOOD NETWORK MAGAZINE - Magazine - THE HEARST CORPORATION; *pg.* 1649, *pg.* 1239
FOOD PRIDE - Retail Grocery Stores - SPARTANNASH CO.; *pg.* 1034, *pg.* 925
FOOD PRODUCT DESIGN - Publication - INFORMA EXHIBITIONS LLC; *pg.* 1653, *pg.* 17
FOOD SAVER - Home Vacuum Packaging Systems - JARDEN CONSUMER SOLUTIONS; *pg.* 57, *pg.* 412
FOOD SERVICE - Recipes - B&G FOODS, INC.; *pg.* 838, *pg.* 1102
FOODLIFE - Casual Dining Restaurant - LETTUCE ENTERTAIN YOU ENTERPRISES, INC.; *pg.* 1735, *pg.* 580
FOODS CO. - Supermarket - THE KROGER CO.; *pg.* 1025, *pg.* 1416
FOODWISE - Food Safety Practices Info - TYSON FOODS, INC.; *pg.* 902, *pg.* 35
FOOGO - Beverage Bottle & Coolers - THERMOS L.L.C.; *pg.* 61, *pg.* 660
FOOL PRO - Investing Service - THE MOTLEY FOOL, INC.; *pg.* 784, *pg.* 1771
FOOLISH FOUR - Mechanical Strategy - THE MOTLEY FOOL, INC.; *pg.* 784, *pg.* 1771
FOOLMART - Books - THE MOTLEY FOOL, INC.; *pg.* 784, *pg.* 1771
FOOL'S GOLD - Ice Cream Product - PERRY'S ICE CREAM CO., INC.; *pg.* 1861, *pg.* 1137
FOOL'S SCHOOL - School - THE MOTLEY FOOL, INC.; *pg.* 784, *pg.* 1771
FOOT GUARD - Deodorant - THE GILLETTE COMPANY; *pg.* 509, *pg.* 795
FOOT-LITES - Apparel - RELIABLE OF MILWAUKEE; *pg.* 698, *pg.* 1879
FOOT LOCKER - Athletic Footwear & Apparel - FOOT LOCKER, INC.; *pg.* 1808, *pg.* 1231
FOOT MIRACLE - Personal Care Product - STRAIGHT ARROW PRODUCTS, INC.; *pg.* 523, *pg.* 1517
FOOT SOOTHER - Massage Product - HUMAN TOUCH; *pg.* 928, *pg.* 123
FOOT WORKS - Beauty Product - AVON PRODUCTS, INC.; *pg.* 500, *pg.* 1198
FOOTACTION USA - Athletic Wear & Shoes - FOOT LOCKER, INC.; *pg.* 1808, *pg.* 1231
FOOTBALL FEVER - Lottery Game - OHIO LOTTERY COMMISSION; *pg.* 1002, *pg.* 1433
FOOTE-JONES - Electrical Product - REGAL BELOIT CORPORATION; *pg.* 106, *pg.* 1854
FOOTER - Socks - WIGWAM MILLS, INC.; *pg.* 15, *pg.* 1894
FOOTHERAPY - Footcare Products - THE HAIN CELESTIAL GROUP, INC.; *pg.* 860, *pg.* 1172
FOOTICE - External Analgesic - ALVA/AMCO PHARMACAL COMPANIES, INC.; *pg.* 1492, *pg.* 637
FOOTJOY - Shoes - ACUSHNET COMPANY; *pg.* 1824, *pg.* 818
FOOTJOY CAPE COD COLLECTION - Shoes - ACUSHNET COMPANY; *pg.* 1824, *pg.* 818
FOOTJOY EUROPA COLLECTION - Shoes - ACUSHNET COMPANY; *pg.* 1824, *pg.* 818
FOOTLOCKER.COM - E-commerce - FOOT LOCKER, INC.; *pg.* 1808, *pg.* 1231
FOOTNOTES - Hosiery & Related Apparel - MAYER/BERKSHIRE CORPORATION; *pg.* 29, *pg.* 1129
FOOTNOTES - Annual Performing Arts Magazine - STAGESTEP INC.; *pg.* 1688, *pg.* 1570
FOOTNOTES - Music Rug - WENGER CORPORATION; *pg.* 1307, *pg.* 952
FOOTONIC ULTRA - Shoes - MASON COMPANIES, INC.; *pg.* 1811, *pg.* 1856
FOOTREST - Computer Support Worktools - STEELCASE INC.; *pg.* 475, *pg.* 889
FOOTSAVER - Plastic & Rubber - TEKNOR APEX COMPANY; *pg.* 1889, *pg.* 1605
FOOTUNDEEZ - Footwear - CAPEZIO BALLET MAKERS INC.; *pg.* 1805, *pg.* 1125
FOOTWELL - Jet - WATKINS MANUFACTURING CORPORATION; *pg.* 120, *pg.* 303

FOR A BETTER FINISH, START WITH HYDE. - Slogan - HYDE TOOLS, INC.; *pg.* 1125, *pg.* 844
FOR A BETTER WAY OF LIFE. - Slogan - GATE CITY BANK; *pg.* 761, *pg.* 1397
FOR A GOOD LOOK - Photographic Papers - EASTMAN KODAK COMPANY; *pg.* 1408, *pg.* 1333
FOR BETTER DENTISTRY - Tagline - DENTSPLY INTERNATIONAL INC.; *pg.* 1522, *pg.* 1596
FOR BOOMERS AND BEYOND - Slogan - TECHNOBRANDS, INC.; *pg.* 1788, *pg.* 1778
FOR DAYS LIKE TODAY - Slogan - CANADIAN TIRE CORPORATION LIMITED; *pg.* 202, *pg.* 1936
FOR EVER - Floor Wax - AKZONOBEL DECORATIVE PAINTS U.S.; *pg.* 1439, *pg.* 1474
FOR EVERY HEALTH DECISION - Slogan - HEALTHWISE, INCORPORATED; *pg.* 143, *pg.* 546
FOR EVERY LIFE & BREATH SITUATION - Slogan - CAS MEDICAL SYSTEMS, INC.; *pg.* 1513, *pg.* 339
FOR FEET WITH A LIFE - Slogan - EASTLAND SHOE CORPORATION; *pg.* 1808, *pg.* 750
FOR GENERATIONS - Tagline - B.C. HYDRO; *pg.* 1936, *pg.* 1909
FOR MY SWEETHEART BOUQUET - Floral Bouquet - FTD GROUP, INC.; *pg.* 1795, *pg.* 608
FOR PEOPLE GOING PLACES - Slogan - A-1 LIMOUSINE INC.; *pg.* 163, *pg.* 1110
FOR PEOPLE WHO CAN SIT WHEREVER THEY WANT - Slogan - INVACARE CORPORATION; *pg.* 1546, *pg.* 1451
FOR PEOPLE WHO LIKE TO WATCH - Tagline - NEW FRONTIER MEDIA, INC.; *pg.* 302, *pg.* 311
FOR PEOPLE WHO MAKE AMERICA WORK - Slogan - SBLI USA LIFE INSURANCE COMPANY, INC.; *pg.* 1216, *pg.* 1288
FOR RENT - Advertising Publication - DOMINION ENTERPRISES; *pg.* 1636, *pg.* 1796
FOR SURGERY. FOR LIFE. - Company Slogan - MICROAIRE SURGICAL INSTRUMENTS INC.; *pg.* 1423, *pg.* 1778
FOR THE ANARCHIST IN ALL OF US - Tagline - FGX INTERNATIONAL, INC.; *pg.* 5, *pg.* 1608
FOR THE BETTER - Tagline - PERKINELMER, INC.; *pg.* 1426, *pg.* 853
FOR THE CURVY YOU - Tagline - ALWAYS FOR ME INC.; *pg.* 17, *pg.* 1163
FOR THE FUN OF IT - Tagline - MONTANA LOTTERY; *pg.* 1000, *pg.* 1008
FOR THE LOVE OF COOKING - Slogan - WHIRLPOOL CORPORATION; *pg.* 62, *pg.* 872
FOR THE ONES WHO GET IT DONE - Tagline - W.W. GRAINGER, INC.; *pg.* 1390, *pg.* 625
FOR THE QUALITY OF LIFE - Slogan - GF HEALTH PRODUCTS, INC.; *pg.* 1535, *pg.* 508
FOR THE TIMES OF YOUR LIFE - Photographic Films & Paper - EASTMAN KODAK COMPANY; *pg.* 1408, *pg.* 1333
FOR THE TOUGHEST JOBS ON PLANET EARTH - Slogan - GORILLA GLUE CO.; *pg.* 1048, *pg.* 1414
FOR THE WAY IT'S MADE - Slogan - WHIRLPOOL CORPORATION; *pg.* 62, *pg.* 872
FOR THE WAY YOU LIVE. - Tag Line - LIFETIME PRODUCTS INC.; *pg.* 933, *pg.* 1751
FOR THOSE WHO LIVE THEIR CRAFT - Slogan - ACME UNITED CORPORATION; *pg.* 1040, *pg.* 346
FOR WHAT MATTERS. - Tagline - CANADIAN IMPERIAL BANK OF COMMERCE; *pg.* 729, *pg.* 1935
FOR WHAT'S VITAL - Slogan - CAS MEDICAL SYSTEMS, INC.; *pg.* 1513, *pg.* 339
FOR YOUR LIFE - Slogan - NEWS & RECORD; *pg.* 1669, *pg.* 1375
FORADIL - Medicine - MERCK & CO., INC.; *pg.* 1566, *pg.* 1077
FORAFAC - Fire Fighting Foams - E.I. DU PONT DE NEMOURS & COMPANY; *pg.* 1159, *pg.* 390
FORAGE MAX - Forage Harvest System - GEHL COMPANY; *pg.* 1339, *pg.* 1899
FORAL-E - Hydrogenated Rosins - EASTMAN CHEMICAL COMPANY; *pg.* 1159, *pg.* 1636
FORALYN - Hydrogenated Rosin Esters - EASTMAN CHEMICAL COMPANY; *pg.* 1159, *pg.* 1636
FORANE - Refrigerants & Foaming Agents & Amines - ARKEMA INC.; *pg.* 1147, *pg.* 1543
FORANE - Pharmaceutical Product - BAXTER INTERNATIONAL INC.; *pg.* 1499, *pg.* 599
FORAY - Dry Chemical Agent - ANSUL, INCORPORATED; *pg.* 1147, *pg.* 1869
FORAY - Furniture - HERMAN MILLER, INC.; *pg.* 926, *pg.* 913
FORAY - Fabric - MOMENTUM TEXTILES INC.; *pg.* 697, *pg.* 114
FORBES - Magazine - FORBES, INC.; *pg.* 1641, *pg.* 1232
FORBES ASIA - Magazine - FORBES, INC.; *pg.* 1641, *pg.* 1232
FORBESLIFE - Magazine - FORBES, INC.; *pg.* 1641, *pg.* 1232
FORBESTRAVELER.COM - Website - FORBES.COM LLC; *pg.* 1247, *pg.* 1232
FORBESWOMAN - Magazine - FORBES, INC.; *pg.* 1641, *pg.* 1232
FORBIDDEN - Game - WINNING MOVES GAMES, INC.; *pg.* 970, *pg.* 816
FORC-404 - Connectors - EMCORE CORPORATION; *pg.* 636, *pg.* 39
FORC-AIRE - Thermal Processing Equipment - SURFACE COMBUSTION, INC.; *pg.* 1077, *pg.* 1462
FORCE - Medical Equipment - INVACARE CORPORATION; *pg.* 1546, *pg.* 1451
FORCE - Navigation Aid - TRIMBLE NAVIGATION LIMITED; *pg.* 1384, *pg.* 288
THE FORCE - Apparel - V.F. CORPORATION; *pg.* 34, *pg.* 1376
FORCE 5 - Detergent - ECOLAB INC.; *pg.* 329, *pg.* 960
FORCE FIELD - Surface Protection - TREDEGAR CORPORATION; *pg.* 1890, *pg.* 1804
FORCE GPS - Software - TRIMBLE NAVIGATION LIMITED; *pg.* 1384, *pg.* 288
FORCE MOUSE - Software - IMMERSION CORPORATION; *pg.* 413, *pg.* 246
FORCE STICK - Software - IMMERSION CORPORATION; *pg.* 413, *pg.* 246
FORCEFIELD - Advanced Combat Helmet - MINE SAFETY APPLIANCES COMPANY; *pg.* 1361, *pg.* 1525
FORCEFIELD - Film Product - TREDEGAR CORPORATION; *pg.* 1890, *pg.* 1804
FORCEWARE - Software - NVIDIA CORPORATION; *pg.* 447, *pg.* 268
FORD BRASS - Meter Couplings & Fittings - THE FORD METER BOX COMPANY, INC.; *pg.* 1047, *pg.* 698
FORD E-SERIES - Vehicles - FORD MOTOR COMPANY; *pg.* 172, *pg.* 876
FORD ECONOLINE - Van - FORD MOTOR COMPANY; *pg.* 172, *pg.* 876
FORD ESCAPE - Sport Utility Vehicle - FORD MOTOR COMPANY; *pg.* 172, *pg.* 876
FORD ESCAPE HYBRID - Hybrid Sport Utility Vehicle - FORD MOTOR COMPANY; *pg.* 172, *pg.* 876
FORD EXCURSION - Sport Utility Vehicle - FORD MOTOR COMPANY; *pg.* 172, *pg.* 876
FORD EXPEDITION - Truck - FORD MOTOR COMPANY; *pg.* 172, *pg.* 876
FORD EXPLORER - Sport Utility Vehicle - FORD MOTOR COMPANY; *pg.* 172, *pg.* 876
FORD EXPLORER SPORT - Sport Utility Vehicle - FORD MOTOR COMPANY; *pg.* 172, *pg.* 876
FORD EXPLORER SPORT TRAC - Sport Utility Vehicle - FORD MOTOR COMPANY; *pg.* 172, *pg.* 876
FORD F-150 - Truck - FORD MOTOR COMPANY; *pg.* 172, *pg.* 876
FORD F-150 SVT - Truck - FORD MOTOR COMPANY; *pg.* 172, *pg.* 876
FORD F-150 SVT LIGHTNING - Truck - FORD MOTOR COMPANY; *pg.* 172, *pg.* 876
FORD F-150 SVT RAPTOR - Truck - FORD MOTOR COMPANY; *pg.* 172, *pg.* 876
FORD F-250 - Truck - FORD MOTOR COMPANY; *pg.* 172, *pg.* 876
FORD F-350 - Truck - FORD MOTOR COMPANY; *pg.* 172, *pg.* 876
FORD F-450 - Vehicles - FORD MOTOR COMPANY; *pg.* 172, *pg.* 876
FORD FIESTA - Automobile - FORD MOTOR COMPANY; *pg.* 172, *pg.* 876
FORD FIVE HUNDRED - Automobile - FORD MOTOR COMPANY; *pg.* 172, *pg.* 876
FORD FOCUS - Automobile - FORD MOTOR COMPANY; *pg.* 172, *pg.* 876
FORD FOCUS SE WAGON - Automobile - FORD MOTOR COMPANY; *pg.* 172, *pg.* 876
FORD FREESTYLE - Crossover Sport Utility Vehicle - FORD MOTOR COMPANY; *pg.* 172, *pg.* 876
FORD FUSION - Sedan - FORD MOTOR COMPANY; *pg.* 172, *pg.* 876
FORD FUSION HYBRID - Vehicles - FORD MOTOR COMPANY; *pg.* 172, *pg.* 876
FORD GT - Automobile - FORD MOTOR COMPANY; *pg.* 172, *pg.* 876
FORD MUSTANG CONVERTIBLE - Automobile - FORD MOTOR COMPANY; *pg.* 172, *pg.* 876
FORD MUSTANG COUPE - Automobile - FORD MOTOR COMPANY; *pg.* 172, *pg.* 876
FORD MUSTANG GT - Automobile - FORD MOTOR COMPANY; *pg.* 172, *pg.* 876
FORD RANGER - Truck - FORD MOTOR COMPANY; *pg.* 172, *pg.* 876
FORD SUPER DUTY - Truck - FORD MOTOR COMPANY; *pg.* 172, *pg.* 876
FORD SVT MUSTANG COBRA - Automobile - FORD MOTOR COMPANY; *pg.* 172, *pg.* 876
FORD TAURUS - Passenger Car - FORD MOTOR COMPANY; *pg.* 172, *pg.* 876
FORD TAURUS WAGON - Automobile - FORD MOTOR COMPANY; *pg.* 172, *pg.* 876
FORD TAURUS-X - Vehicles - FORD MOTOR COMPANY; *pg.* 172, *pg.* 876
FORD THUNDERBIRD - Automobile - FORD MOTOR COMPANY; *pg.* 172, *pg.* 876
FORD WINDSTAR - Mini-Van - FORD MOTOR COMPANY; *pg.* 172, *pg.* 876
FORDHOOK - Vegetable - W. ATLEE BURPEE & CO.; *pg.* 1801, *pg.* 1590
FORE-SIGHT - Absolute Cerebral Oximeter - CAS MEDICAL SYSTEMS, INC.; *pg.* 1513, *pg.* 339
FOREARM - Bicycle Accessories - SPECIALIZED BICYCLE COMPONENTS, INC.; *pg.* 1711, *pg.* 152
FORECAST - Fabric - NEMSCHOFF, INC.; *pg.* 936, *pg.* 1890
FORECAST - Lighting Fixture & Control - PHILIPS LIGHTING; *pg.* 1303, *pg.* 806
FORECAST - Hair Care Product - ZOTOS INTERNATIONAL, INC.; *pg.* 524, *pg.* 345
FORECASTER - Investment Products & Services - FINANCIAL ENGINES, INC.; *pg.* 753, *pg.* 285
FORECASTER - Online Budgeting & Planning Program - MICROSOFT CORP.; *pg.* 440, *pg.* 321
FORECASTER ROI TOOL - Investment Evaluation Program - MICROSOFT CORP.; *pg.* 440, *pg.* 321
FORECOURT - Footwear - K-SWISS; *pg.* 1837, *pg.* 306
FOREGROUND MUSIC ONE - Satellite Delivered Original Artist Music - MOOD MEDIA; *pg.* 298, *pg.* 1616
FOREIGN AFFAIRS - Magazine - COUNCIL ON FOREIGN RELATIONS; *pg.* 138, *pg.* 1219
FOREIGN TRADERS - Gifts & Housewares - FOREIGN TRADERS, INC.; *pg.* 1769, *pg.* 1135
FOREMAN WELLINGTON - Footwear - LACROSSE FOOTWEAR, INC.; *pg.* 1811, *pg.* 1503
FOREMOST IN AIR FILTRATION - Tagline - FLANDERS CORPORATION; *pg.* 1336, *pg.* 1392
FORENZE - Furniture - HAWORTH, INC.; *pg.* 402, *pg.* 891
FORESIGHT - Paper Mill Packaging - FORTIFIBER CORPORATION; *pg.* 83, *pg.* 1021
FOREST - Seating Product - IRWIN SEATING COMPANY INC.; *pg.* 929, *pg.* 887
FOREST GREEN (HA 26) - Tinted Glass - AGC GLASS NORTH AMERICA, INC.; *pg.* 65, *pg.* 482
FOREST PRO - Measurement Tool - LASER TECHNOLOGY, INC.; *pg.* 1419, *pg.* 314
FORESTBYTES - Newsletter - AMERICAN FORESTS; *pg.* 128, *pg.* 394
FORESTER - Car - SUBARU OF AMERICA, INC.; *pg.* 191, *pg.* 1050
FORESTER FLEX - Annuity Plans - CATHOLIC ORDER OF FORESTERS; *pg.* 1196, *pg.* 635
FORESTER GUARDIAN - Term Insurance - CATHOLIC ORDER OF FORESTERS; *pg.* 1196, *pg.* 635
FORESTER GUARDIAN PLUS - Term Insurance - CATHOLIC ORDER OF FORESTERS; *pg.* 1196, *pg.* 635
FORESTER HERITAGE - Whole Life Insurance - CATHOLIC ORDER OF FORESTERS; *pg.* 1196, *pg.* 635
FORESTER HERITAGE PLUS - Whole Life Insurance - CATHOLIC ORDER OF FORESTERS; *pg.* 1196, *pg.* 635
FORESTER LEGACY - Whole Life Insurance - CATHOLIC ORDER OF FORESTERS; *pg.* 1196, *pg.* 635
FORESTER LEVEL TERM TO AGE 35 - Term Insurance - CATHOLIC ORDER OF FORESTERS; *pg.* 1196, *pg.* 635
FORESTER LIFE - Whole Life Insurance - CATHOLIC ORDER OF FORESTERS; *pg.* 1196, *pg.* 635
FORESTER MEMBERSHIP AND TRAVEL CARE - Term Insurance - CATHOLIC ORDER OF FORESTERS; *pg.*

First page reference indicates Business Class Edition
Second page reference indicates Geographic Edition

1196, *pg.* 635
FORESTER OPTIMIZER - Annuity Plans - CATHOLIC ORDER OF FORESTERS; *pg.* 1196, *pg.* 635
FORESTER TRAVEL CARE - Term Insurance - CATHOLIC ORDER OF FORESTERS; *pg.* 1196, *pg.* 635
FORESTERBASIC - Whole Life Insurance - CATHOLIC ORDER OF FORESTERS; *pg.* 1196, *pg.* 635
FORESTERBASIC 10 - Whole Life Insurance - CATHOLIC ORDER OF FORESTERS; *pg.* 1196, *pg.* 635
FORESTERBASIC 15 - Whole Life Insurance - CATHOLIC ORDER OF FORESTERS; *pg.* 1196, *pg.* 635
FOREVER - Plastic Frames - FOSSIL GROUP, INC.; *pg.* 5, *pg.* 1735
FOREVER - Lip Color - MAYBELLINE LLC; *pg.* 516, *pg.* 1257
FOREVER 21 - Apparel - FOREVER 21, INC.; *pg.* 24, *pg.* 130
FOREVER AND EVER - Carpet - BEAULIEU GROUP, LLC; *pg.* 917, *pg.* 529
FOREVER ELIZABETH - Fragrance - ELIZABETH ARDEN, INC.; *pg.* 507, *pg.* 448
FOREVER GREEN - Magazine - TEMBEC INC.; *pg.* 114, *pg.* 1957
FOREVER ORGANIZED - Handbag - HABAND COMPANY, INC.; *pg.* 1772, *pg.* 1099
FOREVER SEVENS - Game - WMS INDUSTRIES INC.; *pg.* 593, *pg.* 666
FOREVER YOUNG - Nutritional Care Product - LIFEPLUS INTERNATIONAL; *pg.* 1556, *pg.* 29
FOREVERNEW - Casual Pants - HAGGAR CORPORATION; *pg.* 41, *pg.* 1682
THE FOREX TRADING EXPO - Tradeshow - INVESTMENT SEMINARS, INC.; *pg.* 420, *pg.* 466
FORGE - Apparel - OAKLEY, INC.; *pg.* 1840, *pg.* 86
FORGE - Books - ST. MARTINS PRESS, INC.; *pg.* 1688, *pg.* 1295
FORGE POND - Clothing - ABERCROMBIE & FITCH CO.; *pg.* 37, *pg.* 1466
FORGE-RITE - Forging Product - SUPERIOR DIE SET CORP.; *pg.* 1379, *pg.* 1885
FORGE TEMP - Steel Plate - ESCO CORPORATION; *pg.* 1335, *pg.* 1502
FORGED - Golf Product - CALLAWAY GOLF COMPANY; *pg.* 1829, *pg.* 58
FORGEMASTER - Casters - HAMILTON CASTER & MFG. CO.; *pg.* 206, *pg.* 1454
FORGES GORCE - Shackles - ALAMO GROUP INC.; *pg.* 1311, *pg.* 1745
FORGET ME NOT - Bath Collection - CROSCILL, INC.; *pg.* 1122, *pg.* 1220
FORGETEMP - Steel Plate - ESCO CORPORATION; *pg.* 1335, *pg.* 1502
FORGING - Cast Tooling - WAUKESHA FOUNDRY INC.; *pg.* 1388, *pg.* 1898
FORGOTTEN REALMS - Toy & Game - HASBRO, INC.; *pg.* 954, *pg.* 1603
FORGOTTEN REALMS - Game Setting - WIZARDS OF THE COAST, INC.; *pg.* 970, *pg.* 1830
FORK RHINO - Hitch Attachment - AUTOMATION DEVICES, INC.; *pg.* 1315, *pg.* 1532
FORLI - Ceiling Fan - WESTINGHOUSE LIGHTING CORPORATION; *pg.* 687, *pg.* 1571
FORM-FIT - Face Mask - CROSSTEX INTERNATIONAL INC.; *pg.* 1520, *pg.* 1164
FORM-FIT - Medical & Aesthetic Product - DYNATRONICS CORPORATION; *pg.* 1526, *pg.* 1757
FORM YOU FAST - Weight Reduction System - FORM YOU 3 INTERNATIONAL, INC.; *pg.* 1531, *pg.* 1400
FORMA - Office Furniture - JOFCO INC.; *pg.* 931, *pg.* 691
FORMA - Software System - MENTOR GRAPHICS CORPORATION; *pg.* 432, *pg.* 1510
FORMA KRISTALL - Office Furniture - JOFCO INC.; *pg.* 931, *pg.* 691
FORMABLE - Steel Product - AK STEEL HOLDING CORPORATION; *pg.* 1311, *pg.* 1479
FORMABOND - Building Product - CENTRIA, INC.; *pg.* 74, *pg.* 1554
FORMACEL - Foam Expansion Agents - E.I. DU PONT DE NEMOURS & COMPANY; *pg.* 1159, *pg.* 390
FORMALITY - Software - SYNOPSYS, INC.; *pg.* 480, *pg.* 162
FORMALPRO - Software System - MENTOR GRAPHICS CORPORATION; *pg.* 432, *pg.* 1510
FORMANCE - Nutritional Product - ABBOTT LABORATORIES; *pg.* 1484, *pg.* 551
FORMASORB - Vapor Phase Activated Carbons - CALGON CARBON CORPORATION; *pg.* 1151, *pg.* 1574
FORMATE - Cutting Method - GLEASON CORPORATION; *pg.* 1340, *pg.* 1335
FORMATIV - Skin Care Products - ULTA SALON, COSMETICS & FRAGRANCE, INC.; *pg.* 524, *pg.* 559
FORMAVUE - Building Product - CENTRIA, INC.; *pg.* 74, *pg.* 1554
FORMAWALL - Metal Building Product - CENTRIA, INC.; *pg.* 74, *pg.* 1554
FORMAX - Machinery - NATIONAL MACHINERY LLC; *pg.* 1363, *pg.* 1475
FORMAX - Plastic & Rubber - TEKNOR APEX COMPANY; *pg.* 1889, *pg.* 1605
FORMAX PLUS - Machinery - NATIONAL MACHINERY LLC; *pg.* 1363, *pg.* 1475
FORMBY'S - Furniture Refinishing Products - THE SHERWIN-WILLIAMS COMPANY; *pg.* 1447, *pg.* 1435
FORMEC - Turf Product - PBI/GORDON CORPORATION; *pg.* 1176, *pg.* 985
FORMED HUB - Bearing - THE TIMKEN COMPANY; *pg.* 218, *pg.* 1408
FORMER JOHN - Food Product - HORMEL FOODS CORPORATION; *pg.* 863, *pg.* 915
FORMFIT - Hearing System - MINE SAFETY APPLIANCES COMPANY; *pg.* 1361, *pg.* 1525
FORMFIT ANKLE - Medical & Aesthetic Product - DYNATRONICS CORPORATION; *pg.* 1526, *pg.* 1757
FORMFLOW - Registers - THE STANDARD REGISTER COMPANY; *pg.* 473, *pg.* 1446
FORMIC - Business Forms Mngmt. Service - THE STANDARD REGISTER COMPANY; *pg.* 473, *pg.* 1446
FORMION - Plastic Compound & Resin - A. SCHULMAN, INC.; *pg.* 1144, *pg.* 1452
FORMIX - Air Oil Separators - DONALDSON COMPANY, INC.; *pg.* 1329, *pg.* 917
FORMOL - Business Forms Mngmt. System - THE STANDARD REGISTER COMPANY; *pg.* 473, *pg.* 1446
FORMOSAT - Satellite - ORBITAL ATK; *pg.* 1425, *pg.* 1779
FORMS - Furniture - J. ROBERT SCOTT INC.; *pg.* 930, *pg.* 105
FORMSCAPE - Software - BOTTOMLINE TECHNOLOGIES (DE), INC.; *pg.* 727, *pg.* 1038
FORMSHARE - Computer Programs - CISCO SYSTEMS, INC.; *pg.* 372, *pg.* 240
FORMSMART - Level of Management Over the Forms & Supplies Needed for Bank Operations - JACK HENRY & ASSOCIATES, INC.; *pg.* 422, *pg.* 988
FORMS.MD - Electronic Forms Module - ALLSCRIPTS HEALTHCARE SOLUTIONS, INC.; *pg.* 1492, *pg.* 563
FORMSPRAG - Overrunning Clutches - WARNER ELECTRIC, INC.; *pg.* 221, *pg.* 661
FORMU-3 - Weight Reduction System - FORM YOU 3 INTERNATIONAL, INC.; *pg.* 1531, *pg.* 1400
FORMULA - Consumer Products - AKZO NOBEL; *pg.* 1439, *pg.* 1952
FORMULA - Floor Care Product - BISSELL HOMECARE, INC.; *pg.* 52, *pg.* 887
FORMULA - Sports Drink - ENERGY BRANDS, INC.; *pg.* 854, *pg.* 1227
FORMULA - Refuse Disposal Bodies - HEIL ENVIRONMENTAL INDUSTRIES, LTD.; *pg.* 207, *pg.* 1629
FORMULA - Medical Equipment - INVACARE CORPORATION; *pg.* 1546, *pg.* 1451
FORMULA - Automotive Reconditioning Product - MOC PRODUCTS COMPANY, INC.; *pg.* 332, *pg.* 174
FORMULA - Computer Software - NOVELL INC.; *pg.* 446, *pg.* 852
FORMULA - Arthroscopic Shaver System - STRYKER CORPORATION; *pg.* 1598, *pg.* 894
FORMULA 1 - Car Wax - NORTHERN LABS, INC.; *pg.* 517, *pg.* 1869
FORMULA 2000 - Floor Cleaner Concentrate - MOC PRODUCTS COMPANY, INC.; *pg.* 332, *pg.* 174
FORMULA 21 - Spot Removers, Grease Stain Removers & Odor Removers - THE FULLER BRUSH COMPANY; *pg.* 330, *pg.* 715
FORMULA 2533 - Chemical Reagent - HACH COMPANY; *pg.* 1415, *pg.* 334
FORMULA 2589 - Chemical Reagent - HACH COMPANY; *pg.* 1415, *pg.* 334
FORMULA 4-24 - Biological Product - CAROLINA BIOLOGICAL SUPPLY COMPANY; *pg.* 1513, *pg.* 1359
FORMULA-4-ALL - Glass & Surface Cleaner - BLUE CROSS LABORATORIES; *pg.* 326, *pg.* 277
FORMULA 409 - All Purpose Spray Cleaner & Carpet Cleaner - THE CLOROX COMPANY; *pg.* 327, *pg.* 169
FORMULA 510 - Cleanser - SWISHER HYGIENE INC.; *pg.* 336, *pg.* 1507
FORMULA 79 - Liquid Plastic - SMOOTH-ON INC.; *pg.* 111, *pg.* 1528
FORMULA 990 - Rust & Scale Remover - PENETONE CORPORATION; *pg.* 333, *pg.* 1050
FORMULA 991 - Cleaner - PENETONE CORPORATION; *pg.* 333, *pg.* 1050
FORMULA FORTE - Pharmaceutical Product - ALERE INC.; *pg.* 1488, *pg.* 849
FORMULA I - Nutritional Products - SHAKLEE CORPORATION; *pg.* 1593, *pg.* 184
FORMULA SI - Pipeline Pigging Product - T.D. WILLIAMSON, INC.; *pg.* 1380, *pg.* 1490
FORMULA Z 7 - Skate - ROLLER DERBY SKATE CORP.; *pg.* 966, *pg.* 630
FORMULA Z 90 - Skate - ROLLER DERBY SKATE CORP.; *pg.* 966, *pg.* 630
FORMULATION R - Ointment - G&W LABORATORIES INC.; *pg.* 1532, *pg.* 1123
FORMVELOPE - Envelopes - TENSION ENVELOPE CORPORATION; *pg.* 483, *pg.* 986
FORMWARE - Software - EMC CORPORATION; *pg.* 391, *pg.* 825
FORMWORK - Software - SUNGARD DATA SYSTEMS INC.; *pg.* 477, *pg.* 1592
FORNO DE MINAS - Food Product - GENERAL MILLS, INC.; *pg.* 828, *pg.* 933
FORPAN - Decorative Paper Overlay - UNIBOARD CANADA INC.; *pg.* 117, *pg.* 1952
FORPRENE - Thermoplastic Elastomer Compound - POLYONE CORPORATION; *pg.* 1177, *pg.* 1404
FORRESTER - Technology Research Report - FORRESTER RESEARCH, INC.; *pg.* 1642, *pg.* 807
FORRESTER OVAL PROGRAM - Technology Research Report - FORRESTER RESEARCH, INC.; *pg.* 1642, *pg.* 807
FORRESTER WAVE - Technology Research Report - FORRESTER RESEARCH, INC.; *pg.* 1642, *pg.* 807
FORRTEL - Online Service - FORRESTER RESEARCH, INC.; *pg.* 1642, *pg.* 807
FORSTER - Craft & Household Products - JARDEN HOME BRANDS; *pg.* 1126, *pg.* 920
FORSYTHIA - Fabric - NEMSCHOFF, INC.; *pg.* 936, *pg.* 1890
FORTACRETE - Structural Panel - USG CORPORATION; *pg.* 118, *pg.* 594
FORTAFIL - Carbon Fibers - TOHO TENAX AMERICA, INC.; *pg.* 1184, *pg.* 1655
FORTAL - Mold Base & Component - SUPERIOR DIE SET CORP.; *pg.* 1379, *pg.* 1885
FORTAY - Footwear - STEVEN MADDEN, LTD.; *pg.* 1819, *pg.* 1176
FORTE - Medical Device - BOSTON SCIENTIFIC CORPORATION; *pg.* 1508, *pg.* 831
FORTE - Process Automation System - KEY TECHNOLOGY, INC.; *pg.* 868, *pg.* 1847
FORTE - Kitchen Product - KOHLER CO.; *pg.* 91, *pg.* 1862
FORTE - Fabric - NEMSCHOFF, INC.; *pg.* 936, *pg.* 1890
FORTE - Flatware - ONEIDA LTD; *pg.* 1129, *pg.* 1318
FORTE - Automatic Drafting Pencil - PENTEL OF AMERICA, LTD.; *pg.* 453, *pg.* 295
FORTE - Acoustical Shell - WENGER CORPORATION; *pg.* 1307, *pg.* 952
FORTEFIBER - Soluble Dietary Fiber - THE DOW CHEMICAL COMPANY; *pg.* 1157, *pg.* 898
FORTEGRA - Epoxy Tougheners - THE DOW CHEMICAL COMPANY; *pg.* 1157, *pg.* 898
FORTEL - Medical Test Product - BIOMERICA, INC.; *pg.* 1506, *pg.* 107
FORTEO - Teriparatide - ELI LILLY AND COMPANY; *pg.* 1527, *pg.* 684
FORTERA - Tire - THE GOODYEAR TIRE & RUBBER COMPANY; *pg.* 1883, *pg.* 1401
FORTESSE - Paper & Nonwoven Material - FIBERMARK INC.; *pg.* 1457, *pg.* 1764
FORTGUARD - Towel And Wiper System - GEORGIA-PACIFIC LLC; *pg.* 1458, *pg.* 507
FORTGUARD VISTA - Dispensers - GEORGIA-PACIFIC LLC; *pg.* 1458, *pg.* 507
FORTI-DIET - Pet Product - PETSMART, INC.; *pg.* 1481, *pg.* 18
FORTIFILE - Eternafilm Reinforced Folders - TAB PRODUCTS CO. LLC; *pg.* 481, *pg.* 1869

FORTIFLASH - Flashing System - FORTIFIBER CORPORATION; *pg.* 83, *pg.* 1021
FORTIFY - Barrier - FORTIFIBER CORPORATION; *pg.* 83, *pg.* 1021
FORTIS - Fabric - NEMSCHOFF, INC.; *pg.* 936, *pg.* 1890
FORTIS - Furniture - TELESCOPE CASUAL FURNITURE INC.; *pg.* 944, *pg.* 1162
FORTOVASE - Pharmaceutical Product - HOFFMANN-LA ROCHE INC.; *pg.* 1542, *pg.* 1099
FORTRESS - Fungicide - DOW AGROSCIENCES LLC; *pg.* 1156, *pg.* 684
FORTRESS - Padlocks - MASTER LOCK COMPANY LLC; *pg.* 1055, *pg.* 1884
FORTRESS - Cattle Vaccines - PFIZER INC.; *pg.* 1581, *pg.* 1278
FORTRESS - Film - RAVEN INDUSTRIES, INC.; *pg.* 1888, *pg.* 1625
FORTUNE - Media Publication - TIME INC.; *pg.* 1693, *pg.* 1300
FORTUNE COOKIE - Video Slots - INTERNATIONAL GAME TECHNOLOGY; *pg.* 957, *pg.* 1024
FORTUNE COOKIE - Lottery Game - NEW YORK STATE LOTTERY; *pg.* 1001, *pg.* 1340
FORTUNE SEEKER - Game - WMS INDUSTRIES INC.; *pg.* 593, *pg.* 666
FORTUNE.COM - Business Information Site - FORTUNE; *pg.* 1642, *pg.* 1232
FORTUNES OF THE CARIBBEAN - Game - WMS INDUSTRIES INC.; *pg.* 593, *pg.* 666
FORTUNET - Game - FORTUNET, INC.; *pg.* 953, *pg.* 1024
FORTUS - Prototyping & Manufacturing System - STRATASYS, INC.; *pg.* 476, *pg.* 923
FORTUS 200MC - Build-Envelope System - STRATASYS, INC.; *pg.* 476, *pg.* 923
FORTUS 360MC - Build-Envelope System - STRATASYS, INC.; *pg.* 476, *pg.* 923
FORTUS 400MC - Build-Envelope System - STRATASYS, INC.; *pg.* 476, *pg.* 923
FORTUS 900MC - Build-Envelope System - STRATASYS, INC.; *pg.* 476, *pg.* 923
FORTY - Furniture - NEMSCHOFF, INC.; *pg.* 936, *pg.* 1890
FORUM - Magazine - FRIENDFINDER NETWORKS INC.; *pg.* 1643, *pg.* 411
FORUM - Toilet Partition - METPAR CORP.; *pg.* 97, *pg.* 1350
FORUM - Fabric - NEMSCHOFF, INC.; *pg.* 936, *pg.* 1890
FORUM PLANK - Flooring Product - CONGOLEUM CORPORATION; *pg.* 921, *pg.* 1084
FORUM SOLIDS - Flooring Product - CONGOLEUM CORPORATION; *pg.* 921, *pg.* 1084
FORWARD - Apparel - OAKLEY, INC.; *pg.* 1840, *pg.* 86
FORWARD THINKING. REAL RESULTS. - Tagline - NATIONAL BULK EQUIPMENT, INC.; *pg.* 1479, *pg.* 892
THE FORWARDERS LIST OF ATTORNEYS - Directory - JOC GROUP INC.; *pg.* 1654, *pg.* 1096
FORWARDTRAK - Software - PITNEY BOWES INC.; *pg.* 454, *pg.* 376
FORWARDTRAK NET - Postal Presorting - PITNEY BOWES INC.; *pg.* 454, *pg.* 376
FORWAY - Machine Bolt Expansion Shield - MKT FASTENING, LLC; *pg.* 1056, *pg.* 34
FORZA - Bathroom Accessories - SYMMONS INDUSTRIES, INC.; *pg.* 114, *pg.* 803
FORZA - Remote Control Device - UNIVERSAL ELECTRONICS, INC.; *pg.* 683, *pg.* 262
FORZE GPS - Sport Drink - PACIFICHEALTH LABORATORIES, INC.; *pg.* 1579, *pg.* 1083
FOSFREE - Supplement - MISSION PHARMACAL COMPANY INC.; *pg.* 1568, *pg.* 1742
FOSTER - Adhesive Materials & Coatings - H.B. FULLER COMPANY; *pg.* 1165, *pg.* 961
FOSTER - Pump Product - IDEX CORPORATION; *pg.* 1347, *pg.* 623
FOSTER GRANT - Sunglasses - FGX INTERNATIONAL, INC.; *pg.* 5, *pg.* 1608
FOSTERGE - Organic Phosphate Esters - HENKEL CORPORATION; *pg.* 1165, *pg.* 1535
FOSTER'S HOME FOR IMAGINARY FRIENDS - Game & TV Show - THE CARTOON NETWORK; *pg.* 273, *pg.* 492
FOSTER'S LAGER - Beer - MILLERCOORS; *pg.* 254, *pg.* 1877
FOSTER'S SPECIAL BITTER - Beer - MILLERCOORS; *pg.* 254, *pg.* 1877
FOSTEX - Alkylphosphonic Acids & Salts - HENKEL CORPORATION; *pg.* 1165, *pg.* 1535
FOSTORIA - Glassware - LANCASTER COLONY CORPORATION; *pg.* 873, *pg.* 1441
FOTO - Stencil Cutting Knife - BADGER AIR BRUSH COMPANY; *pg.* 359, *pg.* 612
FOTOANGELO - Software - ACD SYSTEMS INTERNATIONAL INC.; *pg.* 340, *pg.* 1913
FOTOCANVAS - Software - ACD SYSTEMS INTERNATIONAL INC.; *pg.* 340, *pg.* 1913
FOTONIC - Sensor - MECHANICAL TECHNOLOGY, INCORPORATED; *pg.* 1422, *pg.* 1137
FOTONIC - Fiber Optic Sensor Systems - MTI INSTRUMENTS INC.; *pg.* 658, *pg.* 1137
FOTOSLATE - Software - ACD SYSTEMS INTERNATIONAL INC.; *pg.* 340, *pg.* 1913
FOTOVAC - Software - ACD SYSTEMS INTERNATIONAL INC.; *pg.* 340, *pg.* 1913
FOUNDATION - Orthopedic Implant Product - DJO SURGICAL; *pg.* 1525, *pg.* 1661
FOUNDATION - Hearing Instrument - SEMTECH CORPORATION GENNUM PRODUCTS; *pg.* 671, *pg.* 1919
FOUNDATION DISCOVERY - Detection Software - BMC SOFTWARE, INC.; *pg.* 362, *pg.* 1701
THE FOUNDATION FOR INTELLIGENT E-BUSINESS - Slogan - MICROSTRATEGY, INC.; *pg.* 1266, *pg.* 1809
FOUNDATION STOCK SERVICE - Dog Owner Association - AMERICAN KENNEL CLUB, INC.; *pg.* 129, *pg.* 1193
FOUNDATIONS - Latex - THE DOW CHEMICAL COMPANY; *pg.* 1157, *pg.* 898
FOUNDATIONS - Figurines - ENESCO, LLC; *pg.* 1124, *pg.* 620
FOUNDED BY EDUCATORS FOR EDUCATORS - Slogan - HORACE MANN COMPANIES; *pg.* 1203, *pg.* 662
FOUNDER'S FAVORITE - Pizza - DONATOS PIZZERIA CORPORATION; *pg.* 1727, *pg.* 1439
FOUNDRY - Bicycle - QUALITY BICYCLE PRODUCTS; *pg.* 1710, *pg.* 918
FOUNTAIN FAVORITES - Drink - SONIC CORP.; *pg.* 1750, *pg.* 1487
FOUNTAIN PENTEL - Pens - PENTEL OF AMERICA, LTD.; *pg.* 453, *pg.* 295
THE FOUNTAINS - Services - SUNRISE SENIOR LIVING, INC.; *pg.* 1599, *pg.* 1795
FOUNTAINS OF CASH & DESIGN - Games - PENN NATIONAL GAMING, INC.; *pg.* 574, *pg.* 1595
FOUR BY FOUR - Cheeseburger - IN-N-OUT BURGERS, INC.; *pg.* 1732, *pg.* 111
FOUR-DUCTOR - Electronic Components - MOLEX INCORPORATED; *pg.* 655, *pg.* 628
FOUR EMUS - Premium Wine - CONSTELLATION BRANDS, INC.; *pg.* 1960, *pg.* 1348
FOUR KIT - Eye Shadows - COVER GIRL COSMETICS; *pg.* 506, *pg.* 772
FOUR N' ONE DRY - Food Storage Product - HOME PRODUCTS INTERNATIONAL, INC.; *pg.* 1125, *pg.* 577
FOUR POINTS - Hotels - STARWOOD HOTELS & RESORTS WORLDWIDE, INC.; *pg.* 1114, *pg.* 378
FOUR POINTS BY SHERATON - Hotel Chain - STARWOOD HOTELS & RESORTS WORLDWIDE, INC.; *pg.* 1114, *pg.* 378
FOUR QUEENS BLEND - Whiskey - LAIRD & COMPANY, INC.; *pg.* 1966, *pg.* 1119
FOUR ROSES - Whisky - DIAGEO CANADA, INC.; *pg.* 1961, *pg.* 1937
FOUR-S - Restaurant & Institutional Breads - BIMBO BAKERIES USA; *pg.* 840, *pg.* 151
FOUR SEASONS - Solariums & Glass Structures - FOUR SEASONS SUNROOM; *pg.* 83, *pg.* 1167
FOUR SEASONS - Distilled Spirits - HOOD RIVER DISTILLERS INC.; *pg.* 1964, *pg.* 1498
FOUR SEASONS - Auto Air Conditioning - STANDARD MOTOR PRODUCTS, INC.; *pg.* 218, *pg.* 1176
FOUR TIMES DIAMOND - Slots - INTERNATIONAL GAME TECHNOLOGY; *pg.* 957, *pg.* 1024
FOUR TIMES PAY - Slots - INTERNATIONAL GAME TECHNOLOGY; *pg.* 957, *pg.* 1024
FOUR-WAY - Cleaner - PENETONE CORPORATION; *pg.* 333, *pg.* 1050
FOUR WHEELER - Magazine - RENTPATH, INC.; *pg.* 1680, *pg.* 538
FOUR WINDS - Recreation Vehicle - THOR INDUSTRIES, INC.; *pg.* 1711, *pg.* 1456
FOURCE POINT - Orthopedic Product - DJO INCORPORATED; *pg.* 1524, *pg.* 302
FOURTH ESTATE - Books - HARPERCOLLINS PUBLISHERS INC.; *pg.* 1647, *pg.* 1237
FOWL PLAY - Game - GAMEWRIGHT; *pg.* 953, *pg.* 836
FOX - Car Dealerships - AUTONATION, INC.; *pg.* 165, *pg.* 423
FOX - Diagnostic System - BECTON, DICKINSON & COMPANY; *pg.* 1501, *pg.* 1068
FOX - Floor System - CHECKPOINT SYSTEMS, INC.; *pg.* 628, *pg.* 1559
FOX - Chemicals - DOW CORNING CORPORATION; *pg.* 1159, *pg.* 900
FOX - Television Network - FOX BROADCASTING COMPANY; *pg.* 287, *pg.* 130
FOX & HOUND - Restaurant - FOX & HOUND RESTAURANT GROUP; *pg.* 1729, *pg.* 723
FOX & HOUND ENGLISH PUB AND GRILLE - Restaurant - FOX & HOUND RESTAURANT GROUP; *pg.* 1729, *pg.* 723
FOX & HOUND SMOKEHOUSE AND TAVERN - Restaurant - FOX & HOUND RESTAURANT GROUP; *pg.* 1729, *pg.* 723
FOX BRADY - Road Sanding Equipment, Tailgates, Body Sanders & Cup Sanders - HINIKER COMPANY; *pg.* 704, *pg.* 927
FOX CRYSTALS AND OSCILLATORS - Electronic Equipment - FOX ELECTRONICS; *pg.* 639, *pg.* 428
FOX 'N' HOUND - Slots - INTERNATIONAL GAME TECHNOLOGY; *pg.* 957, *pg.* 1024
FOX PLUS - Catheter - ABBOTT LABORATORIES; *pg.* 1484, *pg.* 551
FOX RIDGE - Wine - GEYSER PEAK WINERY; *pg.* 1964, *pg.* 101
FOX RUN - Retirement Community - ERICKSON LIVING; *pg.* 1090, *pg.* 766
FOX SPORTS - TV Sport - FOX SPORTS NET; *pg.* 288, *pg.* 131
FOXBOX - Security & Access Device - NETWOLVES CORPORATION; *pg.* 1271, *pg.* 474
FOXHORN VINEYARDS - Varietal Wines - THE WINE GROUP, INC.; *pg.* 1972, *pg.* 234
FOXTAIL - Educational Materials - SCHOLASTIC INC.; *pg.* 1683, *pg.* 1288
FOXTROT - Surface Material - STEELCASE INC.; *pg.* 475, *pg.* 889
FOXWOODS - Hotel & Casino - FOXWOODS RESORT CASINO; *pg.* 549, *pg.* 353
FOYER - Furniture - IMPERIAL WOODWORKS, INC.; *pg.* 929, *pg.* 1749
FOZZY - Fabric - NEMSCHOFF, INC.; *pg.* 936, *pg.* 1890
FP - Food Product - MGP INGREDIENTS, INC.; *pg.* 877, *pg.* 714
FP - Flow Pencil Design - PAASCHE AIRBRUSH COMPANY; *pg.* 1444, *pg.* 587
FP DIAMOND - Fall Protection Equipment - MINE SAFETY APPLIANCES COMPANY; *pg.* 1361, *pg.* 1525
FP PRO - Body Harness - MINE SAFETY APPLIANCES COMPANY; *pg.* 1361, *pg.* 1525
FP STRYDER - Fall Protection Equipment - MINE SAFETY APPLIANCES COMPANY; *pg.* 1361, *pg.* 1525
FPA-FLEXIBLE PREMIUM ANNUITY - Fixed Annuity - NATIONAL LIFE INSURANCE COMPANY; *pg.* 1210, *pg.* 1766
FPDIESEL - Engine Parts - FEDERAL-MOGUL HOLDINGS CORPORATION; *pg.* 205, *pg.* 907
FPGA ADVANTAGE - Software System - MENTOR GRAPHICS CORPORATION; *pg.* 432, *pg.* 1510
FPGA BOARDLINK - Software System - MENTOR GRAPHICS CORPORATION; *pg.* 432, *pg.* 1510
FPGA BUILDER - Software System - MENTOR GRAPHICS CORPORATION; *pg.* 432, *pg.* 1510
FPGA STATION - Software System - MENTOR GRAPHICS CORPORATION; *pg.* 432, *pg.* 1510
FPGA XCHANGE - Software System - MENTOR GRAPHICS CORPORATION; *pg.* 432, *pg.* 1510
FPGADVISOR - Software System - MENTOR GRAPHICS CORPORATION; *pg.* 432, *pg.* 1510
FPGASIM - Software System - MENTOR GRAPHICS CORPORATION; *pg.* 432, *pg.* 1510
FPGAVIEW - Software - IMAGINATION TECHNOLOGIES; *pg.* 412, *pg.* 285
FPI - Frozen Seafood - HIGH LINER FOODS INCORPORATED; *pg.* 862, *pg.* 1917
FPOA - Semiconductor Chips - SAJAN, INC.; *pg.* 1278, *pg.* 1890
FPQUEST - Software - BIO-RAD LABORATORIES, INC.; *pg.* 1504, *pg.* 101
FPS - Inserters - PITNEY BOWES INC.; *pg.* 454, *pg.* 376

First page reference indicates Business Class Edition
Second page reference indicates Geographic Edition

FPSK - Shock Absorbing Lanyards - MINE SAFETY APPLIANCES COMPANY; *pg.* 1361, *pg.* 1525
FPSLIC - Gate Array - ATMEL CORPORATION; *pg.* 621, *pg.* 238
FR3 - Liquid Material - NIAGARA TRANSFORMER CORP.; *pg.* 1302, *pg.* 1150
FRACTIOLYNX - Software - WATERS CORPORATION; *pg.* 1436, *pg.* 834
FRACTION - Herbicide Spray - KALO, INC.; *pg.* 1796, *pg.* 719
FRACTIONLYNX - Software - WATERS CORPORATION; *pg.* 1436, *pg.* 834
FRAGMIN - Medicine - PFIZER INC.; *pg.* 1581, *pg.* 1278
FRAGONARD - Fabric - SCALAMANDRE, INC.; *pg.* 941, *pg.* 1058
FRAGPACK - Software - BIO-RAD LABORATORIES, INC.; *pg.* 1504, *pg.* 101
FRAGRANCE - Oil & Spray - AROMATIQUE INC.; *pg.* 499, *pg.* 32
FRAGRANCES OF LIFE - Scent Extraction Technology - INTERNATIONAL FLAVORS & FRAGRANCES INC.; *pg.* 512, *pg.* 1244
FRAGSHIELD - Software - CONDUSIV TECHNOLOGIES; *pg.* 379, *pg.* 51
FRAM - Oil & Air Filters - HONEYWELL CONSUMER PRODUCTS GROUP; *pg.* 208, *pg.* 344
FRAM - Refrigerants - HONEYWELL INTERNATIONAL INC.; *pg.* 407, *pg.* 1088
FRAMBOZEN - Seasonal Beer - NEW BELGIUM BREWING COMPANY, INC.; *pg.* 258, *pg.* 328
FRAME - Apparel - OAKLEY, INC.; *pg.* 1840, *pg.* 86
FRAME CHASE - Editing Tool - AVID TECHNOLOGY, INC.; *pg.* 622, *pg.* 804
FRAME-SEAL - Software - BIO-RAD LABORATORIES, INC.; *pg.* 1504, *pg.* 101
FRAMECONNECT - Software System - MENTOR GRAPHICS CORPORATION; *pg.* 432, *pg.* 1510
FRAMELINK - Neurosurgery Navigation Tool - MEDTRONIC, INC.; *pg.* 1564, *pg.* 939
FRAMELOK - Frame Screws - ROBERTSON INC.; *pg.* 1372, *pg.* 1924
FRAMEMAKER - Software - ADOBE SYSTEMS INCORPORATED; *pg.* 342, *pg.* 235
FRAMESTACK - Connector - MOLEX INCORPORATED; *pg.* 655, *pg.* 628
FRAMEWORKS - Tile - ARTISTIC TILE INC.; *pg.* 914, *pg.* 1119
FRAMEWORX - Bowling Equipment - BRUNSWICK BOWLING & BILLIARDS CORP.; *pg.* 1828, *pg.* 622
FRAMING & ART CENTER - Art & Picture Framing Stores - FRANCHISE CONCEPTS, INC.; *pg.* 1769, *pg.* 1005
FRAN - Software - ASPEN TECHNOLOGY, INC.; *pg.* 354, *pg.* 804
FRANCES DENNEY - Beauty Products - THE STEPHAN COMPANY; *pg.* 1597, *pg.* 426
FRANCESCA - Sweaters - ABERCROMBIE & FITCH CO.; *pg.* 37, *pg.* 1466
FRANCESCA - Furniture - AMISCO INDUSTRIES LTD.; *pg.* 913, *pg.* 1958
FRANCESCA - Furniture - ETHAN ALLEN INTERIORS INC.; *pg.* 924, *pg.* 343
FRANCHI - Firearm - BENELLI USA CORPORATION; *pg.* 1827, *pg.* 754
FRANCHISE 500 - Advertising Service - ENTREPRENEUR MEDIA, INC.; *pg.* 1639, *pg.* 110
THE FRANCHISER OF CHOICE - Tagline - POPEYES LOUISIANA KITCHEN, INC.; *pg.* 1745, *pg.* 517
FRANCIE - Footwear - PHOENIX FOOTWEAR GROUP, INC.; *pg.* 1815, *pg.* 60
FRANCIS - Turbine - GE ENERGY; *pg.* 1338, *pg.* 506
FRANCO - Furniture - ASHLEY FURNITURE INDUSTRIES, INC.; *pg.* 914, *pg.* 1852
FRANCOIS LABET - French Wine - LAIRD & COMPANY, INC.; *pg.* 1966, *pg.* 1119
FRANCOTYP-POSTALIA - Burster - AUTOMATION MAILING AND SHIPPING SOLUTIONS, INC.; *pg.* 358, *pg.* 1428
FRANK - Beer - COASTAL EXTREME BREWING COMPANY; *pg.* 240, *pg.* 1602
FRANK - Fabric - NEMSCHOFF, INC.; *pg.* 936, *pg.* 1890
FRANK LEWIS - Fruit Gift Packages - STANDEX INTERNATIONAL CORPORATION; *pg.* 60, *pg.* 1039
FRANK RUSSELL COMPANY - Money Management - THE NORTHWESTERN MUTUAL LIFE INSURANCE COMPANY; *pg.* 1212, *pg.* 1879
FRANK SCHAFFER - Educational Resources - SCHOOL SPECIALTY, INC.; *pg.* 467, *pg.* 1860
FRANKEN BERRY - Cereal - GENERAL MILLS, INC.; *pg.* 828, *pg.* 933
FRANKIES 5TH FLOOR PIZZERIA - Casual Dining Restaurant - LETTUCE ENTERTAIN YOU ENTERPRISES, INC.; *pg.* 1735, *pg.* 580
FRANKIE'S ITALIAN GRILLE - Italian Restaurants - LONE STAR STEAKHOUSE & SALOON, INC.; *pg.* 1736, *pg.* 1733
FRANKIES SCALOPPINE - Italian Restaurant - LETTUCE ENTERTAIN YOU ENTERPRISES, INC.; *pg.* 1735, *pg.* 580
FRANKLIN - Door & Wood Product - CONESTOGA WOOD SPECIALTIES CORP.; *pg.* 921, *pg.* 1527
FRANKLIN - Footwear - EASTLAND SHOE CORPORATION; *pg.* 1808, *pg.* 750
FRANKLIN - Furniture - ETHAN ALLEN INTERIORS INC.; *pg.* 924, *pg.* 343
FRANKLIN - Publisher - FRANKLIN ELECTRONIC PUBLISHERS, INC.; *pg.* 398, *pg.* 1048
FRANKLIN - Mutual Funds - FRANKLIN RESOURCES, INC.; *pg.* 760, *pg.* 254
FRANKLIN - Air Handler - GOODMAN GROUP, INC.; *pg.* 1072, *pg.* 1706
FRANKLIN - Furniture - NEMSCHOFF, INC.; *pg.* 936, *pg.* 1890
FRANKLIN BRASS - Decorative Architectural Product - MASCO CORPORATION; *pg.* 96, *pg.* 909
FRANKLIN ELECTRIC - Motor - FRANKLIN ELECTRIC CO., INC.; *pg.* 1337, *pg.* 680
THE FRANKLIN MINT - Collectibles - THE FRANKLIN MINT, LLC; *pg.* 1769, *pg.* 1533
THE FRANKLIN MINT - Collectible Gift Giving Products - SEQUENTIAL BRANDS GROUP, INC.; *pg.* 1395, *pg.* 1290
FRANKLIN PLANNER - Paper-based Planning System With a Variety of Sectioned Management Aids - FRANKLIN COVEY CO.; *pg.* 1642, *pg.* 1758
FRANKLIN SQUARE HOSPITAL CENTER - Hospital - MEDSTAR HEALTH INC.; *pg.* 1563, *pg.* 767
FRANKLIN WATTS - Educational Materials - SCHOLASTIC INC.; *pg.* 1683, *pg.* 1288
FRANK'S - Canned Foods - THE FREMONT COMPANY; *pg.* 856, *pg.* 1454
FRANNA - Crane - TEREX CORPORATION; *pg.* 1381, *pg.* 384
FRANZ - Breads - UNITED STATES BAKERY; *pg.* 907, *pg.* 1507
FRANZIA WINETAPS - Table Wines - THE WINE GROUP, INC.; *pg.* 1972, *pg.* 234
FRAPPUCCINO - Coffee Drink - STARBUCKS CORPORATION; *pg.* 897, *pg.* 1840
FRATERNAL BENEFIT POLICY - Whole Life Insurance - CATHOLIC ORDER OF FORESTERS; *pg.* 1196, *pg.* 635
FRATERNAL FINANCIAL - Service - MODERN WOODMEN OF AMERICA; *pg.* 1209, *pg.* 654
FRAUD EVALUATOR - Computer Software - COMPUTER SCIENCES CORPORATION; *pg.* 378, *pg.* 1780
FRAUDINTERCEPTOR - Wireless Telecommunication Product - SYNIVERSE HOLDINGS, INC.; *pg.* 479, *pg.* 475
FRAUDMANAGER - Pre-Call Validation Services - SYNIVERSE HOLDINGS, INC.; *pg.* 479, *pg.* 475
FRAUDPROTECT - Software - MITEK SYSTEMS, INC.; *pg.* 440, *pg.* 204
FRAUDVISION - Computer Program - COMPUTER SCIENCES CORPORATION; *pg.* 378, *pg.* 1780
FRAUDX - Wireless Telecommunication Product - SYNIVERSE HOLDINGS, INC.; *pg.* 479, *pg.* 475
FRE - Beverage - TRINCHERO FAMILY ESTATES; *pg.* 1971, *pg.* 197
FRE-HEATER - Hot Water Heating System - PAUL MUELLER COMPANY; *pg.* 706, *pg.* 1007
FRE-LINE - Fishing Reels - WRIGHT & MCGILL CO.; *pg.* 1848, *pg.* 324
FREAKFLEX - Paint - BADGER AIR BRUSH COMPANY; *pg.* 359, *pg.* 612
FRED - Laser & Laser System - COHERENT, INC.; *pg.* 1406, *pg.* 265
FRED BEAR - Sporting Good Product - ESCALADE INC.; *pg.* 1833, *pg.* 678
FRED MEYER - Supermarket - THE KROGER CO.; *pg.* 1025, *pg.* 1416
FRED MEYER JEWELERS - Jewelry Store - THE KROGER CO.; *pg.* 1025, *pg.* 1416
FREDDIE SUBS - Financial Services - FEDERAL HOME LOAN MORTGAGE CORPORATION; *pg.* 751, *pg.* 1790
FREDONIA - Lower Cost Flower & Vegetable Seeds - PLANTATION PRODUCTS INC; *pg.* 1799, *pg.* 839
FREDRICK MILLER CLASSIC CHOCOLATE LAGER - Seasonal Beer - MILLERCOORS; *pg.* 254, *pg.* 1877
FRED'S - Apparel - FRED'S INC.; *pg.* 1769, *pg.* 1644
FRED'S KIDS - Apparel - FRED'S INC.; *pg.* 1769, *pg.* 1644
FREE AIR - Pump - E.D. BULLARD COMPANY; *pg.* 1332, *pg.* 727
FREE-AIR - Pump - E.D. BULLARD COMPANY; *pg.* 1332, *pg.* 727
FREE & CLEAR - Smoking Cessation Program - MOLINA HEALTHCARE, INC.; *pg.* 1569, *pg.* 123
FREE-CUT INVAR - Alloys - CARPENTER TECHNOLOGY CORPORATION; *pg.* 73, *pg.* 1584
FREE EXTRAS - Store Program - CVS HEALTH CORPORATION; *pg.* 1765, *pg.* 1610
FREE KICK - Sport Product - FRANKLIN SPORTS, INC.; *pg.* 1834, *pg.* 847
FREE N EASY - Carpet - BEAULIEU GROUP, LLC; *pg.* 917, *pg.* 529
FREE 'N EASY - Shampoo - THE GILLETTE COMPANY; *pg.* 509, *pg.* 795
FREE PARKING - Game - WMS INDUSTRIES INC.; *pg.* 593, *pg.* 666
FREE PEOPLE - Apparel - URBAN OUTFITTERS, INC.; *pg.* 1789, *pg.* 1571
THE FREE PRESS - North Carolina Newspaper - FREEDOM COMMUNICATIONS, INC.; *pg.* 1643, *pg.* 110
THE FREE PRESS - Adult Publishing Imprint - SIMON & SCHUSTER, INC.; *pg.* 1687, *pg.* 1292
FREE SPACE - Audio Product - BOSE CORPORATION; *pg.* 626, *pg.* 820
FREE SPIN BONANZA - Game - WMS INDUSTRIES INC.; *pg.* 593, *pg.* 666
FREE SPIN FRENZY - Game - WMS INDUSTRIES INC.; *pg.* 593, *pg.* 666
FREE SPIN MAXIMUS - Game - WMS INDUSTRIES INC.; *pg.* 593, *pg.* 666
FREE SPIN PLUNDER - Game - WMS INDUSTRIES INC.; *pg.* 593, *pg.* 666
FREE SPIRIT - Online Service - SPIRIT AIRLINES, INC.; *pg.* 234, *pg.* 449
FREE THE HORSES: A CHARACTER EDUCATION ADVENTURE - Educational Program - ACTIVE PARENTING PUBLISHERS; *pg.* 1613, *pg.* 535
FREEATLAST - Telephone Service - IDT CORPORATION; *pg.* 643, *pg.* 1096
FREEBIRD - Food Product - THE HAIN CELESTIAL GROUP, INC.; *pg.* 860, *pg.* 1172
FREEDENT - Gum - WM. WRIGLEY JR. COMPANY; *pg.* 1863, *pg.* 596
FREEDM - Glass & Ceramic Material - CORNING INCORPORATED; *pg.* 1122, *pg.* 1154
FREEDOM - Table Width Extender - ALIMED, INC.; *pg.* 1490, *pg.* 816
FREEDOM - Hardwood Floor - ANDERSON HARDWOOD FLOORS; *pg.* 67, *pg.* 1613
FREEDOM - Electrical Product - EATON CORPORATION; *pg.* 1331, *pg.* 1429
FREEDOM - Solution for Processing Unstructured & Semi-Structured Forms - SCAN-OPTICS, LLC; *pg.* 467, *pg.* 354
FREEDOM - No-Rinse Floor Cleaner - SWISHER HYGIENE INC.; *pg.* 336, *pg.* 1507
THE FREEDOM FIBER - Agricultural Product - THE DOW CHEMICAL COMPANY; *pg.* 1157, *pg.* 898
FREEDOM FLANGES - Flange - TACO INCORPORATED; *pg.* 1077, *pg.* 1601
FREEDOM FROM SMOKING - Educational Activities - AMERICAN LUNG ASSOCIATION; *pg.* 129, *pg.* 395
FREEDOM HIP SYSTEM - Hip Product - ZIMMER BIOMET HOLDINGS, INC.; *pg.* 1611, *pg.* 699
FREEDOM HITCH - Quick Hitch Coupler - MIDWEST INDUSTRIES, INC.; *pg.* 185, *pg.* 708
FREEDOM KHAKI - Pants - HAGGAR CORPORATION; *pg.* 41, *pg.* 1682
FREEDOM LINE - Barrier-Free and Assisted-Care Bath Fixtures - AQUATIC; *pg.* 68, *pg.* 42
FREEDOM OF CHOICE - Printer - XEROX CORPORATION; *pg.* 494, *pg.* 365
FREEDOM OF CONNECTIVITY - Slogan - VERIZON TERREMARK; *pg.* 685, *pg.* 447
FREEDOM OF THE SEAS - Cruise Ship - ROYAL CARIBBEAN CRUISES LTD; *pg.* 1921, *pg.* 446
FREEDOM QUEUE - Computer Product - DELL INC.; *pg.*

383, *pg.* 1737
THE FREEDOM ROCK - Lottery Game - IOWA LOTTERY; *pg.* 996, *pg.* 705
FREEDOM SERIES - Headwear - MINE SAFETY APPLIANCES COMPANY; *pg.* 1361, *pg.* 1525
FREEDOM STARS - Slots - INTERNATIONAL GAME TECHNOLOGY; *pg.* 957, *pg.* 1024
FREEDOMCHIP - Cost Reduction Methodology - LATTICE SEMICONDUCTOR CORPORATION; *pg.* 651, *pg.* 1498
FREEDOMFABRIC - Software - F5 NETWORKS, INC.; *pg.* 396, *pg.* 1835
FREEDOMLYNX - Banking Services - MERCHANTS BANCSHARES, INC.; *pg.* 782, *pg.* 1768
FREEDOMPORT - Game - WMS INDUSTRIES INC.; *pg.* 593, *pg.* 666
FREEFALL - Hair Care Product - NU SKIN ENTERPRISES, INC.; *pg.* 518, *pg.* 1755
FREEFLEX - Flexible Heated Tubing - WATLOW ELECTRIC MANUFACTURING COMPANY; *pg.* 1078, *pg.* 1004
FREEFLO - Suitcase - SAMSONITE CORPORATION; *pg.* 11, *pg.* 830
FREEFLOW - Scanner - XEROX CORPORATION; *pg.* 494, *pg.* 365
FREEFLOW MAKEREADY - Software - XEROX CORPORATION; *pg.* 494, *pg.* 365
FREEFLOW OFFICE - Software - XEROX CORPORATION; *pg.* 494, *pg.* 365
FREEFLOW OUTPUT MANAGER - Software - XEROX CORPORATION; *pg.* 494, *pg.* 365
FREEFLOW PREPRESS SUITE - Manual - XEROX CORPORATION; *pg.* 494, *pg.* 365
FREEFLOW PROCESS MANAGER - Software - XEROX CORPORATION; *pg.* 494, *pg.* 365
FREEFLOW PRODUCTION HUB - Software - XEROX CORPORATION; *pg.* 494, *pg.* 365
FREEFOAM - Foam Extrusion Process - ROYLE SYSTEMS GROUP; *pg.* 1373, *pg.* 1100
FREEFORM - Glove - KOMBI, LTD.; *pg.* 1838, *pg.* 1766
FREEFORM - Machine Product - PRECITECH, INC.; *pg.* 1427, *pg.* 1035
FREEGLIDER - Shaving System - BRAUN NORTH AMERICA; *pg.* 52, *pg.* 792
FREEHAND - Software - ADOBE SYSTEMS INCORPORATED; *pg.* 342, *pg.* 235
FREEHAND - Communication Headset Product - PLANTRONICS, INC.; *pg.* 663, *pg.* 270
FREELINE - Fly Line Treatment - MCNETT CORPORATION; *pg.* 1839, *pg.* 1817
FREEMAN - Knife - GERBER LEGENDARY BLADES; *pg.* 1834, *pg.* 1503
FREEMAN HUNTER - Hunting Knife - GERBER LEGENDARY BLADES; *pg.* 1834, *pg.* 1503
FREEMOTION FITNESS - Health & Fitness Product - ICON HEALTH & FITNESS, INC.; *pg.* 1837, *pg.* 1752
FREEPLAY REPLAY - Lottery Game - IOWA LOTTERY; *pg.* 996, *pg.* 705
FREEPORT - Cigarette - PHILIP MORRIS USA INC.; *pg.* 1894, *pg.* 1803
FREESCALE - Board-Level Product - MERCURY COMPUTER SYSTEMS, INC.; *pg.* 434, *pg.* 813
FREESIA FANTASY - Fragrance - PARFUMS DE COEUR LTD.; *pg.* 519, *pg.* 376
FREESOLE - Adhesive & Seam Sealer - MCNETT CORPORATION; *pg.* 1839, *pg.* 1817
FREESTANDING PALM REST - Computer Support Worktools - STEELCASE INC.; *pg.* 475, *pg.* 889
FREESTAR - Car & Van - FORD MOTOR COMPANY OF CANADA, LIMITED; *pg.* 174, *pg.* 1930
FREESTONE - Fishing Gear Product - SIMMS FISHING PRODUCTS CORP.; *pg.* 1845, *pg.* 1008
FREESTYLE - Blood Glucose Monitoring System - ABBOTT DIABETES CARE, INC.; *pg.* 1483, *pg.* 38
FREESTYLE - Blood Glucose Monitoring System - ABBOTT LABORATORIES; *pg.* 1484, *pg.* 551
FREESTYLE - Table - LIFETIME PRODUCTS INC.; *pg.* 933, *pg.* 1751
FREESTYLE - Valve - MEDTRONIC, INC.; *pg.* 1564, *pg.* 939
FREESTYLE - Molecular Biology Product - THERMO FISHER SCIENTIFIC INC.; *pg.* 1602, *pg.* 61
FREESTYLE - Toy - WHAM-O, INC.; *pg.* 969, *pg.* 308
FREESTYLE FLASH - Blood Glucose Monitoring System - ABBOTT LABORATORIES; *pg.* 1484, *pg.* 551
FREESTYLE FREEDOM - Blood Glucose Monitoring System - ABBOTT LABORATORIES; *pg.* 1484, *pg.* 551
FREESTYLE FREEDOM LITE - Blood Glucose Monitoring System - ABBOTT LABORATORIES; *pg.* 1484, *pg.* 551
FREESTYLE LITE - Blood Glucose Monitoring System - ABBOTT LABORATORIES; *pg.* 1484, *pg.* 551
FREESTYLE MINI - Blood Glucose Monitoring System - ABBOTT LABORATORIES; *pg.* 1484, *pg.* 551
FREESTYLE NAVIGATOR - Blood Glucose Monitoring System - ABBOTT LABORATORIES; *pg.* 1484, *pg.* 551
FREETRAC - Software - HEMISPHERE GPS INC.; *pg.* 642, *pg.* 1903
FREEWAY - Flanged Radial Bearing - FREEWAY CORPORATION; *pg.* 1338, *pg.* 1431
FREEWAY - Software - LIONBRIDGE TECHNOLOGIES INC.; *pg.* 428, *pg.* 851
FREEWHEEL - Software - AUTODESK INC.; *pg.* 356, *pg.* 257
FREEWILL - Bath Product - KOHLER CO.; *pg.* 91, *pg.* 1862
FREEZE - Magazine - BONNIER ACTIVE MEDIA, INC.; *pg.* 1622, *pg.* 1205
FREEZE AND SHINE - Hair Care System - JOHN PAUL MITCHELL SYSTEMS; *pg.* 512, *pg.* 133
FREEZE AND SHINE SUPER SPRAY - Hair Care Product - JOHN PAUL MITCHELL SYSTEMS; *pg.* 512, *pg.* 133
FREEZE 'N CLEAR SKIN CLINIC - Wart Remover - ORASURE TECHNOLOGIES INC; *pg.* 1578, *pg.* 1516
FREEZE 'N SQUEEZE - Software - BIO-RAD LABORATORIES, INC.; *pg.* 1504, *pg.* 101
FREEZE WATCH - Indicator - 3M COMPANY; *pg.* 1142, *pg.* 956
FREEZEFLEX - Film - PLASTIC SUPPLIERS, INC.; *pg.* 1888, *pg.* 1443
FREEZEONLINE.COM - Web Site - BONNIER ACTIVE MEDIA, INC.; *pg.* 1622, *pg.* 1205
FREEZERATOR - Refrigerators & Freezers - WHIRLPOOL CORPORATION; *pg.* 62, *pg.* 872
FREEZERFRIGE - Potatoes - J.R. SIMPLOT COMPANY; *pg.* 867, *pg.* 547
FREEZETRODE - Robotic Product - HAMILTON CO., INC.; *pg.* 1415, *pg.* 1031
FREI BROTHERS - Wine - E&J GALLO WINERY; *pg.* 1962, *pg.* 149
FREIGHTLINER - Diesel Trucks & Tractors - FREIGHTLINER TRUCKS; *pg.* 174, *pg.* 1502
FREIGHTLINER CENTURY AMERICAN JOURNEY TRUCK - Toys - TRACTOR SUPPLY COMPANY; *pg.* 708, *pg.* 1627
FREJA - Relay Testing System - GE ENERGY; *pg.* 1338, *pg.* 506
FREMONT HOTEL & CASINO - Hotel & Casino - BOYD GAMING CORPORATION; *pg.* 1082, *pg.* 1022
FRENCH - Furniture - J. ROBERT SCOTT INC.; *pg.* 930, *pg.* 105
FRENCH 77 - Shoes & Apparel - PUMA NORTH AMERICA, INC.; *pg.* 1816, *pg.* 858
FRENCH COUNTRYSIDE - Flower Arrangement - 1-800-FLOWERS.COM, INC.; *pg.* 1758, *pg.* 1151
FRENCH CURVE - Bath Product - KOHLER CO.; *pg.* 91, *pg.* 1862
FRENCH KISS - Furniture - AMERICAN LEATHER LP; *pg.* 912, *pg.* 1673
FRENCH KISS - Vanilla Liqueur - SAZERAC COMPANY, INC.; *pg.* 1969, *pg.* 745
FRENCH QUARTER - Furniture - HOOKER FURNITURE CORPORATION; *pg.* 928, *pg.* 1788
FRENCH QUARTER - Fan - HUNTER FAN COMPANY; *pg.* 57, *pg.* 1631
FRENCH QUARTER - Ceiling Fan - WESTINGHOUSE LIGHTING CORPORATION; *pg.* 687, *pg.* 1571
FRENCH RIVIERA - Carpet - BEAULIEU GROUP, LLC; *pg.* 917, *pg.* 529
FRENCH ROAST - Coffee - PEET'S COFFEE & TEA, INC.; *pg.* 1029, *pg.* 85
FRENCH STRIPE - Women's Clothing & Accessories - WOODEN SHIPS OF HOBOKEN; *pg.* 35, *pg.* 1315
FRENCH TOAST - Children's Sportwear Apparel - LT APPAREL GROUP; *pg.* 29, *pg.* 1254
FRENCH TOAST OFFICIAL SCHOOL WEAR - School Uniforms - LT APPAREL GROUP; *pg.* 29, *pg.* 1254
FRENCH VANILLA BLEND - Food Product - MCCORMICK & COMPANY, INCORPORATED; *pg.* 1027, *pg.* 779
FRENCH VIOLETS - Dinnerware - THE HOMER LAUGHLIN CHINA COMPANY; *pg.* 1125, *pg.* 1850
FRENCHI - Apparels - NORDSTROM, INC.; *pg.* 1779, *pg.* 1837
FRENCHWOOD - Door - ANDERSEN CORPORATION; *pg.* 67, *pg.* 916
FRENZY - Apparel - OAKLEY, INC.; *pg.* 1840, *pg.* 86
FREP - Industrial Cables - GENERAL CABLE CORPORATION; *pg.* 83, *pg.* 729
FREQUENCY - Washroom Accessory - BRADLEY CORPORATION; *pg.* 71, *pg.* 1870
FREQUENCY - Carpet - INTERFACE, INC.; *pg.* 695, *pg.* 512
FREQUENT FLYER - Video Slots - INTERNATIONAL GAME TECHNOLOGY; *pg.* 957, *pg.* 1024
FREQUENT FLYERS - Coaster - BROWN & BIGELOW, INC.; *pg.* 1624, *pg.* 959
FREQUENT FUELER - Loyalty Card - FJ MANAGEMENT, INC.; *pg.* 978, *pg.* 1758
FREQUENT TRYER MILES - Points Program - STARTSAMPLING, INC.; *pg.* 1283, *pg.* 561
FREQUENT VALUES - Coupon Books - ENTERTAINMENT PUBLICATIONS, INC.; *pg.* 1639, *pg.* 910
FREQUENTTRAVELER.COM - Travel Website - LIVE CURRENT MEDIA INC.; *pg.* 1263, *pg.* 1911
FRESCA - Soft Drink Flavors - THE COCA-COLA COMPANY; *pg.* 240, *pg.* 493
FRESCA - Apparel - VANS, INC.; *pg.* 1821, *pg.* 76
FRESCA 1 - Beverages - THE COCA-COLA COMPANY; *pg.* 240, *pg.* 493
FRESCARINI - Food Product - GENERAL MILLS, INC.; *pg.* 828, *pg.* 933
FRESCAVENA - Beverage Powder - PEPSICO, INC.; *pg.* 259, *pg.* 1327
FRESCAVENA - Beverage Powder - THE QUAKER OATS COMPANY; *pg.* 834, *pg.* 588
FRESCHETTA - Frozen Pizza Products - THE SCHWAN FOOD COMPANY; *pg.* 894, *pg.* 928
FRESCO - Cleaning Product - BRONDOW, INC.; *pg.* 327, *pg.* 1346
FRESCO - Fan - CRAFTMADE INTERNATIONAL, INC.; *pg.* 1295, *pg.* 1670
FRESCO - Bath & Plumbing Product - JACUZZI BRANDS CORPORATION; *pg.* 554, *pg.* 65
FRESCO - Surface Material - STEELCASE INC.; *pg.* 475, *pg.* 889
FRESCOLAT - Fragrance - SYMRISE, INC.; *pg.* 1183, *pg.* 1125
FRESCOLITA - Beverages - THE COCA-COLA COMPANY; *pg.* 240, *pg.* 493
FRESH - Educational Services - 1-800-FLOWERS.COM, INC.; *pg.* 1758, *pg.* 1151
FRESH - Plumbing Product - MASCO CORPORATION; *pg.* 96, *pg.* 909
FRESH - Flooring Tool - Q.E.P. CO., INC.; *pg.* 1371, *pg.* 413
FRESH AIR - Oil & Spray - AROMATIQUE INC.; *pg.* 499, *pg.* 32
FRESH AIR - Ventilation - CRAFTMADE INTERNATIONAL, INC.; *pg.* 1295, *pg.* 1670
FRESH & SMOOTH - Skin Care - AVON PRODUCTS, INC.; *pg.* 500, *pg.* 1198
FRESH-AS-A-BABY - Odor Neutralizer - SURCO PRODUCTS, INC.; *pg.* 336, *pg.* 1581
THE FRESH BAKED IDEA COMPANY - Slogan - BRIDGFORD FOODS CORPORATION; *pg.* 842, *pg.* 42
FRESH BLUE MUSK - Fragrance - PARFUMS DE COEUR LTD.; *pg.* 519, *pg.* 376
FRESH BREAD MAKES FRIENDS - Slogan - PANERA BREAD COMPANY; *pg.* 1029, *pg.* 1001
FRESH BREATH - Breath Freshener Spray - WALGREEN CO.; *pg.* 1608, *pg.* 605
FRESH COMFORT - Detachable Mattress Pillow Top - KINGSDOWN, INC.; *pg.* 932, *pg.* 1383
FRESH COMFORT - Candle - THE YANKEE CANDLE COMPANY, INC.; *pg.* 1792, *pg.* 843
FRESH CONNECTION - Computer Workstation - 1-800-FLOWERS.COM, INC.; *pg.* 1758, *pg.* 1151
FRESH DECK - Deck Cleaning Preparation - PPG INDUSTRIES, INC.; *pg.* 1445, *pg.* 1579
FRESH EXPRESS - Salad Mix - CHIQUITA BRANDS INTERNATIONAL, INC.; *pg.* 847, *pg.* 1365
FRESH EXPRESS - Produce - PERFORMANCE FOOD GROUP COMPANY, LLC; *pg.* 1030, *pg.* 1803
FRESH EXTEND - Produce Storage Bags - PACTIV CORPORATION; *pg.* 1466, *pg.* 624
FRESH FLOWER HAPPY HOUR - Retail Store Services - 1-800-FLOWERS.COM, INC.; *pg.* 1758, *pg.* 1151
FRESH FOR YOU - Tagline - RESTAURANT DEVELOPERS CORP.; *pg.* 1747, *pg.* 1464
FRESH FORUM - Educational Services - 1-800-FLOWERS.COM, INC.; *pg.* 1758, *pg.* 1151
FRESH FUSION - Personal Care Product - COLGATE-PALMOLIVE COMPANY; *pg.* 504, *pg.* 1215

First page reference indicates Business Class Edition
Second page reference indicates Geographic Edition

FRESH HOME & GARDEN - Retail Store Services - 1-800-FLOWERS.COM, INC.; *pg.* 1758, *pg.* 1151

FRESH IDEAS FOR INDOOR AIR - Slogan - RESEARCH PRODUCTS CORPORATION; *pg.* 1075, *pg.* 1867

FRESH LIGHT - Charcoal Lighter - DURAFLAME, INC.; *pg.* 1123, *pg.* 280

FRESH LOCK - Package Closures - REYNOLDS CONSUMER PRODUCTS; *pg.* 1138, *pg.* 625

FRESH LOOK RADIANCE - Lenses - ALCON; *pg.* 1399, *pg.* 530

FRESH MEAT.NET - Website - GEEKNET, INC.; *pg.* 1248, *pg.* 1780

FRESH MEXICAN GRILL - Slogan - RUBIO'S RESTAURANTS, INC.; *pg.* 1748, *pg.* 60

FRESH MIXERS - Lunch Meals - CONAGRA FOODS, INC.; *pg.* 826, *pg.* 1014

FRESH 'N BRITE - Denture Toothpaste - MCNEIL-PPC, INC.; *pg.* 1560, *pg.* 1533

FRESH 'N FAIR - Skincare Product - MERLE NORMAN COSMETICS, INC.; *pg.* 517, *pg.* 136

FRESH-N-QUICK - Primer - SEYMOUR OF SYCAMORE, INC.; *pg.* 1447, *pg.* 663

FRESH-O-MATIC - Food Steamers - LINCOLN FOODSERVICE PRODUCTS, LLC; *pg.* 1127, *pg.* 1432

FRESH PANTRY - Meat Product - HORMEL FOODS CORPORATION; *pg.* 863, *pg.* 915

FRESH PEEL - Personal Care Product - TREDEGAR CORPORATION; *pg.* 1890, *pg.* 1804

FRESH PET - Shampoo - PETEDGE; *pg.* 1481, *pg.* 787

FRESH PLACE - Retail Grocery Stores - SPARTANNASH CO.; *pg.* 1034, *pg.* 925

FRESH PLUS - Mouthwash - BLUE CROSS LABORATORIES; *pg.* 326, *pg.* 277

FRESH-R - Tongue Cleaner - SUNSTAR AMERICAS INC.; *pg.* 1599, *pg.* 591

FRESH REWARDS - Retail Store Services - 1-800-FLOWERS.COM, INC.; *pg.* 1758, *pg.* 1151

FRESH RUSH - Personal Care Product - COLGATE-PALMOLIVE COMPANY; *pg.* 504, *pg.* 1215

FRESH SCENT CLOROX - Disinfecting Wipes - THE CLOROX COMPANY; *pg.* 327, *pg.* 169

FRESH SCENT TILEX - Daily Shower Cleaner - THE CLOROX COMPANY; *pg.* 327, *pg.* 169

FRESH SELECT - Food Product - SKYLINE CHILI, INC.; *pg.* 1033, *pg.* 1452

FRESH SERVICE - Foam Insulated Carafe - THERMOS L.L.C.; *pg.* 61, *pg.* 660

FRESH STEP - Cat Litter - THE CLOROX COMPANY; *pg.* 327, *pg.* 169

FRESH STEP PLUS DUAL ACTION CRYSTALS - Pet Care - THE CLOROX COMPANY; *pg.* 327, *pg.* 169

FRESH STRIPE - Toothpaste - COLGATE-PALMOLIVE COMPANY; *pg.* 504, *pg.* 1215

FRESH TALK - Newsletter - 1-800-FLOWERS.COM, INC.; *pg.* 1758, *pg.* 1151

THE FRESH TASTE OF WEST-MEX - Tagline - TACO JOHN'S INTERNATIONAL, INC.; *pg.* 1753, *pg.* 1901

FRESH THOUGHTS - Newsletter - 1-800-FLOWERS.COM, INC.; *pg.* 1758, *pg.* 1151

FRESH UNIVERSITY - Educational Services - 1-800-FLOWERS.COM, INC.; *pg.* 1758, *pg.* 1151

FRESH VALUE MEALS - Sandwich Combination Meal - SUBWAY RESTAURANTS; *pg.* 1751, *pg.* 356

FRESH VEGY - Subs - DONATOS PIZZERIA CORPORATION; *pg.* 1727, *pg.* 1439

FRESH WASH - Concentrate or Spray Wash for Vegetables & Fruits - WATKINS INCORPORATED; *pg.* 909, *pg.* 967

FRESH WHITE MUSK - Fragrance - PARFUMS DE COEUR LTD.; *pg.* 519, *pg.* 376

FRESH WHITE MUSK FANTASY - Fragrance - PARFUMS DE COEUR LTD.; *pg.* 519, *pg.* 376

FRESH XTREME - Designer Fragrance - PARFUMS DE COEUR LTD.; *pg.* 519, *pg.* 376

FRESH. YOUNG. CHICKEN - Tagline - FARMERS PRIDE, INC.; *pg.* 855, *pg.* 1534

FRESHCARD - Absorbing Cards - MULTISORB TECHNOLOGIES, INC.; *pg.* 1570, *pg.* 1150

FRESHCHOP - Kitchen Appliance - HAMILTON BEACH BRANDS, INC.; *pg.* 56, *pg.* 1783

FRESHER UNDER PRESSURE - Pressure Processing System - FLOW INTERNATIONAL CORPORATION; *pg.* 1337, *pg.* 1821

THE FRESHEST FOR YOUR FAMILY. GUARANTEED. - Tag Line - HATFIELD QUALITY MEATS, INC.; *pg.* 861, *pg.* 1537

THE FRESHEST IDEAS IN ITALIAN COOKING - Slogan - DEL MONTE FOODS, INC.; *pg.* 852, *pg.* 304

FRESHGUARD - Fabric - 180S, LLC; *pg.* 1824, *pg.* 754

FRESHGUARD - Clock - BROWN & BIGELOW, INC.; *pg.* 1624, *pg.* 959

FRESHLIKE - Canned & Frozen Vegetables - PINNACLE FOODS GROUP LLC; *pg.* 889, *pg.* 1104

FRESHLOOK COLOR STUDIO - Color Contacts - ALCON; *pg.* 1399, *pg.* 530

FRESHMAN RECORD - Yearbooks - HERFF JONES, INC.; *pg.* 7, *pg.* 686

FRESHMAX - Oxygen Absorbing Label - MULTISORB TECHNOLOGIES, INC.; *pg.* 1570, *pg.* 1150

FRESHMIST 90 - Humidifier - FIELD CONTROLS LLC; *pg.* 1071, *pg.* 1380

FRESHNESS CARE SYSTEM - Retail Store Services - 1-800-FLOWERS.COM, INC.; *pg.* 1758, *pg.* 1151

FRESHPAK - Gas Blends for Food Packaging - AIR PRODUCTS AND CHEMICALS, INC.; *pg.* 1145, *pg.* 1513

FRESHPAX - Oxygen Absorbing Packet - MULTISORB TECHNOLOGIES, INC.; *pg.* 1570, *pg.* 1150

FRESHRAP - Food Wrapping Paper - BPM INC.; *pg.* 1454, *pg.* 1886

FRESHZONE - Encapsulation Technology - CARGILL, INC.; *pg.* 845, *pg.* 965

FRESKYTA - Beverages - THE COCA-COLA COMPANY; *pg.* 240, *pg.* 493

FRESNO - Vanity Lights - CRAFTMADE INTERNATIONAL, INC.; *pg.* 1295, *pg.* 1670

FRESQUINHA - Beverages - THE COCA-COLA COMPANY; *pg.* 240, *pg.* 493

FRESS - Beverages - THE COCA-COLA COMPANY; *pg.* 240, *pg.* 493

FRETWORK - Fabric - NEMSCHOFF, INC.; *pg.* 936, *pg.* 1890

FREY SCIENTIFIC - Educational Resources - SCHOOL SPECIALTY, INC.; *pg.* 467, *pg.* 1860

FRIALIT - Dental Product - DENTSPLY INTERNATIONAL INC.; *pg.* 1522, *pg.* 1596

FRIAR BRIGGS - Table - BLATT BOWLING & BILLIARD CORP.; *pg.* 1827, *pg.* 1203

FRIAR FRIAR PANTS ON FIRE - Nail Care Product - OPI PRODUCTS INC.; *pg.* 518, *pg.* 167

FRIAR TUCK SHIRTS - Clergy Shirts - AUGSBURG FORTRESS; *pg.* 1618, *pg.* 931

FRIBBLE - Ice Milk Drink - FRIENDLY ICE CREAM, LLC; *pg.* 1853, *pg.* 859

FRIC-ROT - Shock Absorber & Strut - TENNECO, INC.; *pg.* 985, *pg.* 625

FRICO - Coal Testing Equipment - PREISER SCIENTIFIC, INC.; *pg.* 1427, *pg.* 1851

FRICTION - Metal Cutting Saw Blade - SIMONDS INTERNATIONAL CORPORATION; *pg.* 1376, *pg.* 819

FRICTION MANAGEMENT SOLUTIONS - Repairing Bearings - THE TIMKEN COMPANY; *pg.* 218, *pg.* 1408

FRIDA - Fabric - NEMSCHOFF, INC.; *pg.* 936, *pg.* 1890

FRIDAY NIGHT POKER - Video Game - INTERNATIONAL GAME TECHNOLOGY; *pg.* 957, *pg.* 1024

FRIDGE DJ - Toys - LEAPFROG ENTERPRISES, INC.; *pg.* 961, *pg.* 84

FRIDGE FARM - Magnetic Animal Set - LEAPFROG ENTERPRISES, INC.; *pg.* 961, *pg.* 84

FRIDGE PHONICS - Magnetic Set - LEAPFROG ENTERPRISES, INC.; *pg.* 961, *pg.* 84

FRIDGE TALK - Wordplay Recorder - LEAPFROG ENTERPRISES, INC.; *pg.* 961, *pg.* 84

FRIDGE VENDOR - Packaging Product - GRAPHIC PACKAGING HOLDING COMPANY; *pg.* 1459, *pg.* 509

FRIDGE WASH & GO - Toys - LEAPFROG ENTERPRISES, INC.; *pg.* 961, *pg.* 84

FRIDGE WORDS - Games - LEAPFROG ENTERPRISES, INC.; *pg.* 961, *pg.* 84

FRIDGEMASTER - Paperboard Packaging Product - WESTROCK COMPANY; *pg.* 1472, *pg.* 1805

FRIDGESMART - Kitchenware - TUPPERWARE BRANDS CORPORATION; *pg.* 1139, *pg.* 456

FRIED WITH PRIDE - Slogan - KFC CORPORATION; *pg.* 1733, *pg.* 735

THE FRIENDLIEST STORES IN TOWN - Tagline - SCHNUCK MARKETS, INC.; *pg.* 1033, *pg.* 1002

FRIENDLY - Ice Cream, Restaurants, Sherbet - FRIENDLY ICE CREAM, LLC; *pg.* 1853, *pg.* 859

FRIENDLY E-SAVERS - Bus Transportation Service - GREYHOUND LINES, INC.; *pg.* 1910, *pg.* 1681

FRIENDLYNET - Switch - ASANTE TECHNOLOGIES, INC.; *pg.* 619, *pg.* 238

FRIENDS - Movie Sharing - NETFLIX, INC.; *pg.* 1269, *pg.* 141

FRIENDSHIP - Dairy Products - FRIENDSHIP DAIRIES, INC.; *pg.* 857, *pg.* 1171

FRIENDS'N SUCH BOUQUET - Floral Bouquet - FTD GROUP, INC.; *pg.* 1795, *pg.* 608

FRIESEN - Bulk Seed Tender - CARGILL LIMITED; *pg.* 1475, *pg.* 1914

FRIEZE - Fabric - NEMSCHOFF, INC.; *pg.* 936, *pg.* 1890

FRIFRI - Cooking Equipment - THE MIDDLEBY CORPORATION; *pg.* 1361, *pg.* 610

FRIGA-BOHN - Refrigerators - LENNOX INTERNATIONAL INC.; *pg.* 1073, *pg.* 1736

FRIGHT NIGHT - Bodycare & Skincare - AMERICAN INTERNATIONAL INDUSTRIES COMPANY; *pg.* 498, *pg.* 126

FRIGIDAIRE - Air Conditioners & Furnaces - NORTEK GLOBAL HVAC; *pg.* 1075, *pg.* 989

FRIGITRON - Climate Control Device - E.D. BULLARD COMPANY; *pg.* 1332, *pg.* 727

FRIGITRONICS - Freon & Nitrous Oxide Cryosurgical Equipment - THE COOPER COMPANIES, INC.; *pg.* 1518, *pg.* 183

FRIGO - Cheese - SAPUTO, INC.; *pg.* 893, *pg.* 1956

FRIGO CHEESE HEADS - Food Product - SAPUTO CHEESE USA INC.; *pg.* 893, *pg.* 627

FRING - Footrest - NEUTRAL POSTURE, INC.; *pg.* 939, *pg.* 1669

FRINGANTE - Beer - SLEEMAN UNIBROUE QUEBEC; *pg.* 265, *pg.* 1950

FRINGYY - Slipper - STEVEN MADDEN, LTD.; *pg.* 1819, *pg.* 1176

FRIO - Healthcare Product - MEDICOOL, INC.; *pg.* 1562, *pg.* 294

FRIO GRANDE - Fried Ice Cream Scoops - WELLS ENTERPRISES, INC.; *pg.* 909, *pg.* 709

FRIOS - Dental Product - DENTSPLY INTERNATIONAL INC.; *pg.* 1522, *pg.* 1596

FRISBEE - Fabric - NEMSCHOFF, INC.; *pg.* 936, *pg.* 1890

FRISBEE - Toy - WHAM-O, INC.; *pg.* 969, *pg.* 308

FRISCH-LY MADE - Desserts - FRISCH'S RESTAURANTS, INC.; *pg.* 1729, *pg.* 1413

FRISCH'S BIG BOY - Restaurants - FRISCH'S RESTAURANTS, INC.; *pg.* 1729, *pg.* 1413

FRISCO - Furniture - ASHLEY FURNITURE INDUSTRIES, INC.; *pg.* 914, *pg.* 1852

FRISCO - Soft Drink - THE COCA-COLA COMPANY; *pg.* 240, *pg.* 493

FRISCO - Footwear - EASTLAND SHOE CORPORATION; *pg.* 1808, *pg.* 750

FRISCO - Actuator - PRECISION VALVE CORPORATION; *pg.* 1060, *pg.* 1357

FRISCO BAY - Security Systems - STANLEY BLACK & DECKER, INC.; *pg.* 1063, *pg.* 358

FRISCO BREAKFAST - Sandwich - HARDEES FOOD SYSTEMS, INC.; *pg.* 1731, *pg.* 998

FRISCO BURGER - Hamburger Sandwich - HARDEES FOOD SYSTEMS, INC.; *pg.* 1731, *pg.* 998

FRISK PLUS - Liquid Detergent - EDWARD DON & COMPANY; *pg.* 54, *pg.* 672

FRISKET - Stencil Cutting Knife - BADGER AIR BRUSH COMPANY; *pg.* 359, *pg.* 612

FRISKIES CANNED - Food & Beverage Product - NESTLE USA, INC.; *pg.* 883, *pg.* 96

FRISKIES CHEF'S BLEND - Food Product - NESTLE USA, INC.; *pg.* 883, *pg.* 96

FRISKIES COME 'N GET IT - Food Product - NESTLE USA, INC.; *pg.* 883, *pg.* 96

FRISKIES DRY - Food Product - NESTLE USA, INC.; *pg.* 883, *pg.* 96

FRISKIES FANCY FEAST - Food & Beverage Product - NESTLE USA, INC.; *pg.* 883, *pg.* 96

FRISKIES GOURMET - Food Product - NESTLE USA, INC.; *pg.* 883, *pg.* 96

FRISKIES KITTEN - Food Product - NESTLE USA, INC.; *pg.* 883, *pg.* 96

FRISKIES MASTER'S CHOICE - Food Product - NESTLE USA, INC.; *pg.* 883, *pg.* 96

FRISKIES MIGHTY DOG - Food Product - NESTLE USA, INC.; *pg.* 883, *pg.* 96

FRISKIES MIGHTY DOG SENIOR - Food Product - NESTLE USA, INC.; *pg.* 883, *pg.* 96

FRISKIES PRIME STEAKS - Food Product - NESTLE USA, INC.; *pg.* 883, *pg.* 96

FRISKIES PRIME STRIPS - Food Product - NESTLE USA, INC.; pg. 883, pg. 96
FRISKIES SENIOR - Food Product - NESTLE USA, INC.; pg. 883, pg. 96
FRISKIES SPECIAL DIET - Food Product - NESTLE USA, INC.; pg. 883, pg. 96
FRISKMASTER - Security Product - BAE SYSTEMS PRODUCTS GROUP; pg. 359, pg. 432
FRISKY - Carpet - BEAULIEU GROUP, LLC; pg. 917, pg. 529
THE FRISKY - Celebrity News Site - SPINMEDIA; pg. 1282, pg. 104
FRIT-IN-A-FERRULE - Pumps - IDEX CORPORATION; pg. 1347, pg. 623
FRITO-LAY - Food & Beverage - PEPSICO, INC.; pg. 259, pg. 1327
FRITOS - Corn Chips - FRITO-LAY NORTH AMERICA, INC.; pg. 1853, pg. 1730
FRITOS - Snack Food - PEPSICO, INC.; pg. 259, pg. 1327
FRITZTV - Educational Materials - SCHOLASTIC INC.; pg 1683, pg. 1288
FRIZZ CALMPLEX - Hair Care Product - JOHN PAUL MITCHELL SYSTEMS; pg. 512, pg. 133
FRIZZ DEFENSE - Hair Dryer - CONAIR CORPORATION; pg. 505, pg. 1055
FRM CRETE - Bridge Product - THE D.S. BROWN COMPANY; pg. 79, pg. 1468
FROG JUICE - Game - GAMEWRIGHT; pg. 953, pg. 836
FROG PRINCESS - Video Game - INTERNATIONAL GAME TECHNOLOGY; pg. 957, pg. 1024
FROGHAIR - Golf Shoes - JOHNSTON & MURPHY CO.; pg. 1810, pg. 1651
FROGHIDE - Cable - GENERAL CABLE CORPORATION; pg. 83, pg. 729
FROGLEG - Vacuum Process Tool - BROOKS AUTOMATION, INC.; pg. 1320, pg. 813
FROLIC - Boots - AEROGROUP INTERNATIONAL, INC.; pg. 1803, pg. 1055
FROLIC - Dog Food - MARS, INCORPORATED; pg. 1858, pg. 1792
FROLIC - Fabric - NEMSCHOFF, INC.; pg. 936, pg. 1890
FROM HERE TO SECURITY - Management Services - PRINCIPAL FINANCIAL GROUP, INC.; pg. 796, pg. 706
FROM INSIGHT TO RESULTS - Slogan - NEWMARK GRUBB KNIGHT FRANK; pg. 1106, pg. 1271
FROM LABORATORY TO LIFE - Tagline - G&W LABORATORIES INC.; pg. 1532, pg. 1123
FROM OUR FORSTS TO YOUR HOME - Tagline - HARDEN FURNITURE INC.; pg. 926, pg. 1177
FROM THE HEART OF BEEF COUNTRY, U.S.A. - Mail Order Service - OMAHA STEAKS INTERNATIONAL, INC.; pg. 1780, pg. 1017
FROM THE SOURCE TO THE PLATE - Slogan - TRIDENT SEAFOODS CORPORATION; pg. 902, pg. 1842
FROM THE VALLEYS OF CALIFORNIA - Almonds - BLUE DIAMOND GROWERS; pg. 840, pg. 195
FROM THE WORLD LEADER IN HOME CARE - Slogan - INVACARE CORPORATION; pg. 1546, pg. 1451
FROMA-DAR - Cheese - SAPUTO, INC.; pg. 893, pg. 1956
FROMM FOUR-STAR NUTRITIONALS - Dog Food - FROMM FAMILY PET FOODS, INC.; pg. 1476, pg. 1870
FROMMER'S - Travel Guides - JOHN WILEY & SONS, INC.; pg. 1655, pg. 1073
FRONT & CENTER - Blouses - HABAND COMPANY, INC.; pg. 1772, pg. 1099
FRONT ARENA - Software - SUNGARD DATA SYSTEMS INC.; pg. 477, pg. 1592
FRONT PORCH - Digital Video Archive Management Solutions - PRESILIENT, LLC; pg. 456, pg. 313
FRONT RUNNER - Hood Shield - LUND INTERNATIONAL, INC.; pg. 211, pg. 526
FRONT SURFACE - Lens - DANKER LABORATORIES INC.; pg. 1408, pg. 465
FRONTIER - Furniture - ASHLEY FURNITURE INDUSTRIES, INC.; pg. 914, pg. 1852
FRONTIER - Fan - CRAFTMADE INTERNATIONAL, INC.; pg. 1295, pg. 1670
FRONTIER - Telecommunication Services - FRONTIER COMMUNICATIONS CORPORATION; pg. 1871, pg. 362
FRONTIER - Clothing - LAKELAND INDUSTRIES, INC.; pg. 1354, pg. 1338
FRONTIER - Water Filter System - MCNETT CORPORATION; pg. 1839, pg. 1817
FRONTIER - Fabric - NEMSCHOFF, INC.; pg. 936, pg. 1890
FRONTIER - Bi-Ventricular Stimulation Devices - ST. JUDE MEDICAL, INC.; pg. 1596, pg. 963
FRONTIER CITY - Park - SIX FLAGS ENTERTAINMENT CORPORATION; pg. 583, pg. 1698
FRONTIER INSURANCE - Software - SUNGARD DATA SYSTEMS INC.; pg. 477, pg. 1592
FRONTIER LITE - Medical Equipment - INVACARE CORPORATION; pg. 1546, pg. 1451
FRONTIERLAND - Amusement Park - THE WALT DISNEY COMPANY; pg. 317, pg. 52
FRONTLINE - Book - CHARISMA MEDIA; pg. 1627, pg. 436
FRONTVIEW - Wireless Networking Product - NETGEAR, INC.; pg. 444, pg. 247
FRONTWAVE - Multi-Microphone System - SEMTECH CORPORATION GENNUM PRODUCTS; pg. 671, pg. 1919
FROOT LOOPS - Cereal - KELLOGG COMPANY; pg. 831, pg. 870
FROOTIES - Candy - TOOTSIE ROLL INDUSTRIES, INC.; pg. 1863, pg. 591
FROST - Software - AUTODESK INC.; pg. 356, pg. 257
FROST - Flatware - ONEIDA LTD; pg. 1129, pg. 1318
FROST - Footwear - PHOENIX FOOTWEAR GROUP, INC.; pg. 1815, pg. 60
FROST - Ceiling Panel - USG CORPORATION; pg. 118, pg. 594
FROST AND FIRE - Game - INTERNATIONAL GAME TECHNOLOGY; pg. 420, pg. 1606
FROST & GLOW - Hair Highlighter - REVLON, INC.; pg. 521, pg. 1286
FROST & TIP - Hair Coloring - P&G-CLAIROL, INC.; pg. 519, pg. 1418
FROST BLANKET - Crop Protection System - E.I. DU PONT DE NEMOURS & COMPANY; pg. 1159, pg. 390
FROST BRITE - Flashlights - DORCY INTERNATIONAL INC.; pg. 1046, pg. 1439
FROST KING - Weatherseal Product - THERMWELL PRODUCTS CO., INC.; pg. 1065, pg. 1082
FROSTBITE - Adhesive Coated Paper - SPINNAKER COATING, LLC; pg. 1470, pg. 1477
FROSTED FLAKES - Food Product - KELLOGG COMPANY; pg. 831, pg. 870
FROSTED FLAKES - Cereal - POST CONSUMER BRANDS; pg. 833, pg. 927
FROSTED IMAGES - Doors - THERMA-TRU CORP.; pg. 115, pg. 1462
FROSTED KRISPIES - Ready-Sweetened Rice Cereal - KELLOGG COMPANY; pg. 831, pg. 870
FROSTED MINI SPOONERS - Cereal - POST CONSUMER BRANDS; pg. 833, pg. 927
FROSTED MINI-WHEATS - Food Product - KELLOGG COMPANY; pg. 831, pg. 870
FROSTED WHEATIES - Cereal - GENERAL MILLS, INC.; pg. 828, pg. 933
FROSTER - Carbonated Beverages - ALIMENTATION COUCHE-TARD INC.; pg. 1013, pg. 1951
FROSTER SOAKCITY - Coolest Venue - ONTARIO PLACE CORPORATION; pg. 572, pg. 1941
FROSTLITE - Mattress & Pillow Cover - MEDLINE INDUSTRIES, INC.; pg. 1562, pg. 635
FROSTONE - Textured Metals - RIGIDIZED METALS CORP.; pg. 108, pg. 1151
FROSTY - Container Grown Plant - MONROVIA GROWERS; pg. 1797, pg. 44
FROSTY - Milk Shakes - THE WENDY'S COMPANY; pg. 1755, pg. 1450
FROSTY - Ice Cream Drink - WENDY'S INTERNATIONAL, INC.; pg. 1755, pg. 1451
FROSTY PAWS - Pet Treats - NESTLE USA, INC.; pg. 883, pg. 96
FROSTY SEAS - Food Prods. - FROSTY ACRES BRANDS, INC.; pg. 1020, pg. 484
FROSTY THE DOUGHMAN - Lottery Game - MASSACHUSETTS STATE LOTTERY; pg. 998, pg. 802
FROSTY WHIP - Food Prods. - FROSTY ACRES BRANDS, INC.; pg. 1020, pg. 484
FROSTY'S FORTUNE - Lottery Game - MASSACHUSETTS STATE LOTTERY; pg. 998, pg. 802
FROTH-PAK - Polyurethane Spray Foam - THE DOW CHEMICAL COMPANY; pg. 1157, pg. 898
FROVA - Pharmaceutical Product - ENDO PHARMACEUTICALS HOLDINGS, INC.; pg. 1528, pg. 1549
FROZEN FAVORITES - Drink - SONIC CORP.; pg. 1750, pg. 1487
FROZEN FOUR - Trademark (Div. I Men's & Women's Ice Hockey) - NATIONAL COLLEGIATE ATHLETIC ASSOCIATION; pg. 567, pg. 688
FROZEN-FROM-THE-INSIDE-OUT - Ice Cream - DIPPIN' DOTS LLC; pg. 853, pg. 739
FROZEN YOGURT - Ice Cream - BLUE BELL CREAMERIES, L.P.; pg. 1851, pg. 1668
FROZFRIUT - Ice Cream - WELLS ENTERPRISES, INC.; pg. 909, pg. 709
FRP - Fiberglass Tanks - AG-MEIER INDUSTRIES LLC; pg. 700, pg. 1668
FRP SERIES - Toilet Partitions - BOBRICK WASHROOM EQUIPMENT, INC.; pg. 1043, pg. 166
FRRROZEN HOT CHOCOLATE - Chilled Beverage - THE SECOND CUP LTD.; pg. 1749, pg. 1928
FRS - Bike - MARIN BIKES; pg. 1708, pg. 168
FRUEHAUF - Vehicle Safety System - GROTE INDUSTRIES, INC.; pg. 206, pg. 693
FRUGELI - Candy - SORBEE INTERNATIONAL, LLC; pg. 1862, pg. 1570
FRUGOS - Beverages - THE COCA-COLA COMPANY; pg. 240, pg. 493
FRUGOS FRESH - Beverages - THE COCA-COLA COMPANY; pg. 240, pg. 493
FRUIT-A-FREEZE - Iced Fruit Smoothies - J&J SNACK FOODS CORPORATION; pg. 865, pg. 1107
FRUIT & NUT - Chocolates - THE HERSHEY CO.; pg. 1855, pg. 1538
FRUIT BASKET - Scarf - HERITAGE LACE INC.; pg. 694, pg. 711
FRUIT BUZZ - Fast Food - MCDONALD'S CORPORATION; pg. 1737, pg. 645
FRUIT BY THE FOOT - Fruit Snack - GENERAL MILLS, INC.; pg. 828, pg. 933
FRUIT CHILLERS - Food Product - DEL MONTE FOODS, INC.; pg. 852, pg. 304
FRUIT CHOCOLATES - Candies - LIBERTY ORCHARDS CO., INC.; pg. 1857, pg. 1819
FRUIT DELIGHTS - Gift Box - LIBERTY ORCHARDS CO., INC.; pg. 1857, pg. 1819
FRUIT FIESTA - Fruit Arrangements - EDIBLE ARRANGEMENTS INTERNATIONAL, INC.; pg. 1768, pg. 382
FRUIT FLY TRAP - Fly Control Product - SENORET CHEMICAL COMPANY; pg. 335, pg. 1548
FRUIT GUSHERS - Snack - GENERAL MILLS, INC.; pg. 828, pg. 933
FRUIT HARVEST - Food Product - KELLOGG COMPANY; pg. 831, pg. 870
FRUIT JELL - Jelling Agent - JARDEN CORPORATION; pg. 1885, pg. 412
FRUIT NATURALS - Food Product - DEL MONTE FOODS, INC.; pg. 852, pg. 304
FRUIT OF THE LOOM - Underwear, Activewear & Socks - FRUIT OF THE LOOM, INC.; pg. 41, pg. 725
FRUIT-OF-THE-MONTH CLUB - Mail Order Fruit - HARRY & DAVID HOLDINGS, INC.; pg. 1022, pg. 1499
FRUIT PARADE - Fruit Snack - PROMOTION IN MOTION, INC.; pg. 1861, pg. 1052
FRUIT PARADE FRUIT ROLLS & FRUIT SNACKS - Food Product - PROMOTION IN MOTION, INC.; pg. 1861, pg. 1052
FRUIT PIE - Snack Cake - HOSTESS BRANDS LLC; pg. 1856, pg. 984
FRUIT PLUS - Food Product - SUN-RYPE PRODUCTS LTD.; pg. 899, pg. 1908
FRUIT ROLL-UPS - Snacks - GENERAL MILLS, INC.; pg. 828, pg. 933
FRUIT ROLLS - Candy - TOOTSIE ROLL INDUSTRIES, INC.; pg. 1863, pg. 591
FRUIT SHAPES - Food Product - GENERAL MILLS, INC.; pg. 828, pg. 933
FRUIT SLICES WILD-TILES - Video Game - INTERNATIONAL GAME TECHNOLOGY; pg. 957, pg. 1024
FRUIT SMOOTHIES - Lip Balm - BLISTEX, INC.; pg. 502, pg. 644
FRUIT SNACKS - Food Product - GENERAL MILLS, INC.; pg. 828, pg. 933
FRUIT SOLUTIONS - Beverages - THE COCA-COLA COMPANY; pg. 240, pg. 493
FRUIT STAND - Game - MULTIMEDIA GAMES INC.; pg. 442, pg. 1664
FRUIT-TASTIC - Video Game - INTERNATIONAL GAME TECHNOLOGY; pg. 957, pg. 1024
FRUIT TO GO - Food Product - SUN-RYPE PRODUCTS

LTD.; *pg.* 899, *pg.* 1908
FRUIT TREES ALIVE! - Home Orchard - GARDENS ALIVE!, INC.; *pg.* 1796, *pg.* 693
FRUIT2O - Fruit Drink - SUNNY DELIGHT BEVERAGES CO.; *pg.* 899, *pg.* 1426
FRUITEIN - Nutritional Supplement - NATURAL ORGANICS, INC.; *pg.* 1571, *pg.* 1181
FRUITIA - Beverages - THE COCA-COLA COMPANY; *pg.* 240, *pg.* 493
FRUITLAND - Fruit Juices - KRIER FOODS, INC.; *pg.* 253, *pg.* 1890
FRUITMASTER - Tray - PACTIV CORPORATION; *pg.* 1466, *pg.* 624
FRUITOPIA - Fruit Juice Drinks - THE COCA-COLA COMPANY; *pg.* 240, *pg.* 493
FRUITQUAKE - Prepackaged Fruit Smoothies - YOCREAM INTERNATIONAL INC.; *pg.* 1039, *pg.* 1508
FRUITS OF LIFE - Antioxidant Fruit Matrix - GARDEN OF LIFE, INC.; *pg.* 1532, *pg.* 478
FRUITSOURCE - Food Product - SUN-RYPE PRODUCTS LTD.; *pg.* 899, *pg.* 1908
FRUITWATER - Fruit Flavored Bottled Water - ENERGY BRANDS, INC.; *pg.* 854, *pg.* 1227
FRUITWORKS - Juice Drink - PEPSICO, INC.; *pg.* 259, *pg.* 1327
FRUITY DINO-BYTES - Cereal - POST CONSUMER BRANDS; *pg.* 833, *pg.* 927
FRUITY PEBBLES - Cereal - POST HOLDINGS, INC.; *pg.* 833, *pg.* 1002
FRUIVITA - Juices - PEPSICO, INC.; *pg.* 259, *pg.* 1327
FRUI'VITA - Juice - TROPICANA PRODUCTS, INC.; *pg.* 902, *pg.* 592
FRUIZZI - Chilled Beverage - THE SECOND CUP LTD.; *pg.* 1749, *pg.* 1928
FRUKTIME - Beverages - THE COCA-COLA COMPANY; *pg.* 240, *pg.* 493
FRUPAC - Fresh Fruits - CHIQUITA BRANDS INTERNATIONAL, INC.; *pg.* 847, *pg.* 1365
FRUSHEEZ - Food Equipment - GOLD MEDAL PRODUCTS CO.; *pg.* 55, *pg.* 1414
FRUSION - Low Fat Yogurt & Fruit - THE DANNON COMPANY, INC.; *pg.* 851, *pg.* 1351
FRUTATION - Fresh Fruit Snack Stores - EDIBLE ARRANGEMENTS INTERNATIONAL, INC.; *pg.* 1768, *pg.* 382
FRUTINA - Beverages - THE COCA-COLA COMPANY; *pg.* 240, *pg.* 493
FRUTISTA FREEZE - Frozen Beverage - TACO BELL CORP.; *pg.* 1752, *pg.* 117
FRUTONIC - Soft Drink - THE COCA-COLA COMPANY; *pg.* 240, *pg.* 493
FRUTTARE - Frozen Fruit Bars - UNILEVER UNITED STATES, INC.; *pg.* 904, *pg.* 1061
FRX - Financial Reporting & Analysis Software - MICROSOFT CORP.; *pg.* 440, *pg.* 321
FRY KRISP - Corn Dog & Hush Puppy Batter Mixes - FRY KRISP COMPANY; *pg.* 857, *pg.* 893
FRYBABY - Electric Deep Fryer - NATIONAL PRESTO INDUSTRIES, INC; *pg.* 1128, *pg.* 1857
FRYDADDY - Electrical Appliance & Housewares - NATIONAL PRESTO INDUSTRIES, INC; *pg.* 1128, *pg.* 1857
FRYE - Hearing Aid Analyzer - FRYE ELECTRONICS, INC.; *pg.* 1413, *pg.* 1509
FRYE - Footwear - JIMLAR CORPORATION; *pg.* 1810, *pg.* 1246
FRYING SAUCER - Rolling Machines - GOLD MEDAL PRODUCTS CO.; *pg.* 55, *pg.* 1414
FRYITE PRO - Combustion Gas Analyzer - BACHARACH INC.; *pg.* 1400, *pg.* 1556
FRY'S - Supermarket - THE KROGER CO.; *pg.* 1025, *pg.* 1416
FRZ BLEND CARTON - Egg Substitute - MICHAEL FOODS, INC.; *pg.* 877, *pg.* 949
FRZ EGGS D'LITE - Egg Substitute - MICHAEL FOODS, INC.; *pg.* 877, *pg.* 949
FRZ MIX BNB - Egg Substitute - MICHAEL FOODS, INC.; *pg.* 877, *pg.* 949
FRZ MIX CARTON - Egg Substitute - MICHAEL FOODS, INC.; *pg.* 877, *pg.* 949
FRZ WHITE CARTON - Egg Substitute - MICHAEL FOODS, INC.; *pg.* 877, *pg.* 949
FRZ WHOLE BNB - Egg Substitute - MICHAEL FOODS, INC.; *pg.* 877, *pg.* 949
FRZ WHOLE CARTON - Egg Substitute - MICHAEL FOODS, INC.; *pg.* 877, *pg.* 949
FRZ YOLK CARTON - Egg Substitute - MICHAEL FOODS, INC.; *pg.* 877, *pg.* 949
FS2 - Debug Technology - IMAGINATION TECHNOLOGIES; *pg.* 412, *pg.* 285
FS2 NAVIGATOR - Debug Technology - IMAGINATION TECHNOLOGIES; *pg.* 412, *pg.* 285
FSA GROUP - Foodservice Publication - LEBHAR-FRIEDMAN INC.; *pg.* 1658, *pg.* 1250
FSDS - Electrosurgery Generator - BOVIE MEDICAL CORPORATION; *pg.* 1402, *pg.* 1178
FT-1 - Radio Frequency Tester - NORTEK SECURITY & CONTROL LLC; *pg.* 659, *pg.* 59
FT-3 - Driver - CALLAWAY GOLF COMPANY; *pg.* 1829, *pg.* 58
FT-5 - Driver - CALLAWAY GOLF COMPANY; *pg.* 1829, *pg.* 58
FT-I - Driver - CALLAWAY GOLF COMPANY; *pg.* 1829, *pg.* 58
FT. PIERCE NEWS - Newspaper - THE E.W. SCRIPPS COMPANY; *pg.* 1639, *pg.* 1412
FT TUNES - Eye Wear - CALLAWAY GOLF COMPANY; *pg.* 1829, *pg.* 58
FTD - Florist Delivery Assn. - FTD GROUP, INC.; *pg.* 1795, *pg.* 608
FTD - Internet Service - UNITED ONLINE, INC.; *pg.* 1286, *pg.* 308
FTD YOUR DAY BOUQUET - Flower - FTD GROUP, INC.; *pg.* 1795, *pg.* 608
FTI-BRID - Driver - CALLAWAY GOLF COMPANY; *pg.* 1829, *pg.* 58
FTP - Software - LAPLINK SOFTWARE, INC.; *pg.* 426, *pg.* 1815
FT.PIERCE JAI-ALAI - Jai-Alai & Pocker Game Center - FLORIDA GAMING CORPORATION; *pg.* 548, *pg.* 442
FTSERVER - Computer Servers - STRATUS TECHNOLOGIES, INC.; *pg.* 477, *pg.* 832
FTTP - Fiber Optics - CHANNELL COMMERCIAL CORP.; *pg.* 1870, *pg.* 291
FTX - Twin Screw Extruder - FARREL CORPORATION; *pg.* 1336, *pg.* 337
FTX - Airless Spray Gun - GRACO, INC.; *pg.* 1342, *pg.* 935
FUBAR - Tools - STANLEY BLACK & DECKER, INC.; *pg.* 1063, *pg.* 358
FUBU THE COLLECTION - Sportswear - GTFM LLC; *pg.* 41, *pg.* 1236
FUCHS - Loading Machine - TEREX CORPORATION; *pg.* 1381, *pg.* 384
FUCOPROTEIN - Health Supplement - GARDEN OF LIFE, INC.; *pg.* 1532, *pg.* 478
FUCOTHIN - Health Supplement - GARDEN OF LIFE, INC.; *pg.* 1532, *pg.* 478
FUDDRUCKERS - Restaurants - LUBY'S FUDDRUCKERS RESTAURANTS, LLC; *pg.* 1736, *pg.* 1710
FUDGE SHOPPE - Food Product - THE JEL SERT COMPANY; *pg.* 865, *pg.* 668
FUDGE SHOPPE - Snacks - KELLOGG COMPANY; *pg.* 831, *pg.* 870
FUDGSICLE - Ice Cream and Frozen Novelties - UNILEVER CANADA INC.; *pg.* 903, *pg.* 1946
FUDGSICLE CANDY TWISTS - Food Product - PROMOTION IN MOTION, INC.; *pg.* 1861, *pg.* 1052
FUEL - Bags - FOSSIL GROUP, INC.; *pg.* 5, *pg.* 1735
FUEL - Bike - TREK BICYCLE CORPORATION; *pg.* 1847, *pg.* 1896
FUEL EX - Bicycle - TREK BICYCLE CORPORATION; *pg.* 1847, *pg.* 1896
FUEL-SOLV - Fireside Additive - GE WATER & PROCESS TECHNOLOGIES; *pg.* 1339, *pg.* 1588
FUEL TAX MASTER - Fuel Tax Reporting Software - J.J. KELLER & ASSOCIATES, INC.; *pg.* 1654, *pg.* 1883
FUEL TV - Extreme Sports Channel - FOX SPORTS NET; *pg.* 288, *pg.* 131
FUELCAST - Software - DAKTRONICS, INC.; *pg.* 633, *pg.* 1624
FUELFOCUS - Software Product - MAXIMUS, INC.; *pg.* 780, *pg.* 1799
FUELIGHT - Software - DAKTRONICS, INC.; *pg.* 633, *pg.* 1624
FUELPACK - Software - MAXIM INTEGRATED PRODUCTS, INC.; *pg.* 653, *pg.* 247
FUELSAVER - Fuel Preservative - THE DOW CHEMICAL COMPANY; *pg.* 1157, *pg.* 898
FUGITIVE - Marker - AERVOE INDUSTRIES INCORPORATED; *pg.* 1439, *pg.* 1021
FUGUE - Tables - HOWE FURNITURE CORPORATION; *pg.* 928, *pg.* 998
FUJI - Bath Accessory - CROSCILL, INC.; *pg.* 1122, *pg.* 1220
FUJI - Chemical Product - HURST CHEMICAL COMPANY; *pg.* 1168, *pg.* 174
FUL-GLO - Ophthalmic Pharmaceutical Product - AKORN, INC.; *pg.* 1488, *pg.* 622
FULCRUM - Computer Products - BROADCOM CORPORATION; *pg.* 364, *pg.* 108
FULCRUM - Mammography Film Digitizer - ICAD, INC.; *pg.* 643, *pg.* 1037
FULCRUM - Fabric - NEMSCHOFF, INC.; *pg.* 936, *pg.* 1890
FULDA - Tire And Rubber Product - THE GOODYEAR TIRE & RUBBER COMPANY; *pg.* 1883, *pg.* 1401
FULDA - Tires - TBC CORPORATION; *pg.* 1889, *pg.* 457
FULFILL-RX - Software - MCKESSON CORPORATION; *pg.* 1560, *pg.* 222
FULFLO SPECIALTIES - Valves - GUSHER PUMPS, INC.; *pg.* 1344, *pg.* 727
FULL ACCESS - Flashlight - ENERGIZER HOLDINGS, INC.; *pg.* 637, *pg.* 996
FULL ASSAULT - Apparel - OAKLEY, INC.; *pg.* 1840, *pg.* 86
FULL BLOOM - Cleaning Product - ORECK CORPORATION; *pg.* 59, *pg.* 1653
FULL CIRCLE - Natural & Organic Foods - BASHAS' SUPERMARKETS; *pg.* 1015, *pg.* 12
FULL CIRCLE - Food Product - HAGGEN, INC.; *pg.* 1022, *pg.* 1817
FULL CIRCLE - Food Product - HY-VEE, INC.; *pg.* 1023, *pg.* 713
FULL CIRCLE - Organic Foods - RALEY'S INC.; *pg.* 1031, *pg.* 305
FULL CIRCLE - Organic Products - SPARTANNASH CO; *pg.* 1034, *pg.* 889
FULL CIRCLE - Natural & Organic Foods - TOPCO HOLDINGS INC.; *pg.* 901, *pg.* 661
FULL CIRCUIT - Electronic Report - SLM CORPORATION; *pg.* 804, *pg.* 388
FULL HOUSE - Video Game - INTERNATIONAL GAME TECHNOLOGY; *pg.* 957, *pg.* 1024
FULL MEAL DEAL - Combination Meal - INTERNATIONAL DAIRY QUEEN, INC.; *pg.* 1732, *pg.* 938
FULL OF LIFE - Mail Order Catalog - JOHNSON SMITH COMPANY; *pg.* 1774, *pg.* 414
FULL-POUR - Polymer - H.B. FULLER COMPANY; *pg.* 1165, *pg.* 961
FULL-PROOF - Adhesive - H.B. FULLER COMPANY; *pg.* 1165, *pg.* 961
FULL RELEASE - Golf Products - FEEL GOLF CO., INC.; *pg.* 1834, *pg.* 465
FULL SERVICE DIRECTORY - Computer Software - NOVELL INC.; *pg.* 446, *pg.* 852
FULL THROTTLE - Energy Drink - THE COCA-COLA COMPANY; *pg.* 240, *pg.* 493
FULL THROTTLE BLUE DEMON - Beverages - THE COCA COLA COMPANY; *pg.* 240, *pg.* 493
FULL THROTTLE COFFEE - Coffee - THE COCA-COLA COMPANY; *pg.* 240, *pg.* 493
FULL THROTTLE SUGAR FREE - Beverages - THE COCA-COLA COMPANY; *pg.* 240, *pg.* 493
FULL VIEW - Control Measurement - BROOKS INSTRUMENT, LLC; *pg.* 1403, *pg.* 1537
FULL VOLUME - Skin Care Product - NEUTROGENA CORPORATION; *pg.* 517, *pg.* 137
FULLBOR - Adhesive - H.B. FULLER COMPANY; *pg.* 1165, *pg.* 961
FULLER - Truck Components - EATON CORPORATION; *pg.* 1331, *pg.* 1429
FULLER - Beauty Product - TUPPERWARE BRANDS CORPORATION; *pg.* 1139, *pg.* 456
FULLER-O'BRIEN - Coating - AKZONOBEL DECORATIVE PAINTS U.S.; *pg.* 1439, *pg.* 1474
FULLJET - Spray Product - SPRAYING SYSTEMS CO.; *pg.* 1063, *pg.* 670
FULLMOON - Container Grown Plant - MONROVIA GROWERS; *pg.* 1797, *pg.* 44
FULLPOWER - Shoe Cleaning Brush - THE FULLER BRUSH COMPANY; *pg.* 330, *pg.* 715
FULLSTREAM - Graphics Card - ADVANCED MICRO DEVICES, INC.; *pg.* 613, *pg.* 282
FULLTERM - Medical Product - HOLOGIC, INC.; *pg.* 1416, *pg.* 784
FULMEN - Battery - EXIDE TECHNOLOGIES; *pg.* 204, *pg.* 483
FULSCOPE - Chart & Marking System - GRAPHIC CONTROLS LLC; *pg.* 401, *pg.* 1148

FULTON - Shoes - ALLEN-EDMONDS SHOE CORP.; *pg.* 1804, *pg.* 1887
FULTON STREET - Textiles - BERNHARDT DESIGN; *pg.* 918, *pg.* 1381
FULTON'S CRABHOUSE - Restaurant - LEVY RESTAURANTS, INC.; *pg.* 1736, *pg.* 580
FULYZAQ - Pharmaceutical Product - SALIX PHARMACEUTICALS, INC.; *pg.* 1591, *pg.* 1388
FUMAGALLI - Steel Wheel - MERITOR, INC.; *pg.* 212, *pg.* 911
FUME BLANC - Wine - ROBERT MONDAVI WINERY; *pg.* 1969, *pg.* 173
FUME ERASER - Mobile Welding Fume Extractions Unit - THE SPENCER TURBINE CO.; *pg.* 1378, *pg.* 386
FUME INCINERATION - Burner - ECLIPSE INC.; *pg.* 1332, *pg.* 655
FUN - Molecular Probe Product - THERMO FISHER SCIENTIFIC INC.; *pg.* 1602, *pg.* 61
FUN & LEARN - Educational Toys - LEAPFROG ENTERPRISES, INC.; *pg.* 961, *pg.* 84
FUN & SUN - Dresses & Sets - HABAND COMPANY, INC.; *pg.* 1772, *pg.* 1099
FUN DIP - Food Product - NESTLE USA, INC.; *pg.* 883, *pg.* 96
FUN FRESH FOOD - Nutritional Product - NUTRACEUTICAL INTERNATIONAL CORPORATION; *pg.* 1576, *pg.* 1753
FUN FUNKY FINGERNAILS - Toy & Game - HASBRO, INC.; *pg.* 954, *pg.* 1603
FUN FUR - Yarn - LION BRAND YARN COMPANY; *pg.* 696, *pg.* 1050
FUN GRIPPER - Parachute - SCHOOL-TECH, INC.; *pg.* 1844, *pg.* 866
FUN HOUSE - Game - WMS INDUSTRIES INC.; *pg.* 593, *pg.* 666
FUN ICE - Baby Care Product - MUNCHKIN, INC.; *pg.* 964, *pg.* 300
FUN IN THE SUN - Toy guns - IMPERIAL TOY CORPORATION; *pg.* 957, *pg.* 166
FUN 'N FASHION - Stereophones - KOSS CORPORATION; *pg.* 649, *pg.* 1877
FUN ON THE RUN - Dresses & Sets - HABAND COMPANY, INC.; *pg.* 1772, *pg.* 1099
FUN SAVER - Motion Picture Camera - EASTMAN KODAK COMPANY; *pg.* 1408, *pg.* 1333
FUN SHAPES - Fully Cooked Chicken Nuggets - PERDUE FARMS INCORPORATED; *pg.* 889, *pg.* 777
THE FUN SHIPS - Cruise Line - CARNIVAL CRUISE LINES; *pg.* 1902, *pg.* 441
FUN WITH A PURPOSE - Descriptive Phrase - HIGHLIGHTS FOR CHILDREN, INC.; *pg.* 1650, *pg.* 1440
THE FUN ZONE - Magazine - HIGHLIGHTS FOR CHILDREN, INC.; *pg.* 1650, *pg.* 1440
FUNBITES - Fruit Snack - SUN-RYPE PRODUCTS LTD.; *pg.* 899, *pg.* 1908
FUNBRELLA - 20' Diameter Umbrella - ANCHOR INDUSTRIES, INC.; *pg.* 1825, *pg.* 678
FUNCAP - Cap - BROWN & BIGELOW, INC.; *pg.* 1624, *pg.* 959
FUNCOLAND - Book - BARNES & NOBLE, INC.; *pg.* 1619, *pg.* 1201
FUNCOLAND - Retailer - GAMESTOP CORP.; *pg.* 399, *pg.* 1699
FUNCTIONAL - Educational Product - BARKER CREEK PUBLISHING INC.; *pg.* 1619, *pg.* 1818
FUND OF INFORMATION - Financial Products - DOW JONES & COMPANY, INC.; *pg.* 1637, *pg.* 1225
FUND RAISIN'S - Chocolate Product - WORLD'S FINEST CHOCOLATE, INC.; *pg.* 1864, *pg.* 597
FUNDADOR - Brandy - JIM BEAM BRANDS CO.; *pg.* 1965, *pg.* 601
FUNDAMENTALS - Wood Flooring Product - ARMSTRONG WORLD INDUSTRIES, INC.; *pg.* 914, *pg.* 1545
FUNDAYS - Toys for Preschool Children - BANDAI AMERICA INCORPORATED; *pg.* 950, *pg.* 75
FUNDEMENTAL - Textiles - BERNHARDT DESIGN; *pg.* 918, *pg.* 1381
FUNDRUNNER - Software - SS&C TECHNOLOGIES HOLDINGS, INC.; *pg.* 473, *pg.* 386
FUNDRUNNER INVESTORSITE - Software - SS&C TECHNOLOGIES HOLDINGS, INC.; *pg.* 473, *pg.* 386
FUNDRUNNER MARATHON - Software - SS&C TECHNOLOGIES HOLDINGS, INC.; *pg.* 473, *pg.* 386
FUNERALPLAN.COM - Website - AURORA CASKET COMPANY, INC.; *pg.* 1393, *pg.* 673
FUNFLIP - Papers - XEROX CORPORATION; *pg.* 494, *pg.* 365
FUNFONE FUNSATIONAL - Balloon - CONTINENTAL AMERICAN CORP.; *pg.* 1880, *pg.* 723
FUNG-ONIL - Household Insect Control - BONIDE PRODUCTS, INC.; *pg.* 1794, *pg.* 1320
FUNGAL DEFENSE - Dietary Food Supplements - GARDEN OF LIFE, INC.; *pg.* 1532, *pg.* 478
FUNGALIGHT - Molecular Probe Product - THERMO FISHER SCIENTIFIC INC.; *pg.* 1602, *pg.* 61
FUNGALS - Girls' Underwear - FRUIT OF THE LOOM, INC.; *pg.* 41, *pg.* 725
FUNGI-BLOCK - Fungicidal Agent - THE DOW CHEMICAL COMPANY; *pg.* 1157, *pg.* 898
FUNGICURE - Pharmaceutical Product - ALVA/AMCO PHARMACAL COMPANIES, INC.; *pg.* 1492, *pg.* 637
FUNGISCREEN - Software - BIO-RAD LABORATORIES, INC.; *pg.* 1504, *pg.* 101
FUNGITEST - Software - BIO-RAD LABORATORIES, INC.; *pg.* 1504, *pg.* 101
FUNGIZONE - Cell Culture Product - THERMO FISHER SCIENTIFIC INC.; *pg.* 1602, *pg.* 61
FUNGO - Baseball Bat - HILLERICH & BRADSBY CO., INC.; *pg.* 1836, *pg.* 576
FUNGUS MD - Nail Product - ORLY INTERNATIONAL, INC.; *pg.* 518, *pg.* 137
FUNHOUSE TREATS - Candy - COSTCO WHOLESALE CORPORATION; *pg.* 1765, *pg.* 1820
FUNITOS - Tortilla Chips in Five Flavors - BARREL O'FUN SNACK FOODS CO.; *pg.* 1850, *pg.* 952
FUNK - Powershift Transmission - JOHN DEERE COFFEYVILLE WORKS INC; *pg.* 1351, *pg.* 714
FUNKY 5'S - Lottery Game - D.C. LOTTERY & CHARITABLE GAMES CONTROL BOARD; *pg.* 991, *pg.* 398
THE FUNKYLINE - Clip - BROWN & BIGELOW, INC.; *pg.* 1624, *pg.* 959
FUNMATE - Ice Chest - IGLOO PRODUCTS CORPORATION; *pg.* 1126, *pg.* 1724
FUNNBAR - Protein Snack - BPI SPORTS, LLC; *pg.* 842, *pg.* 430
FUNNEL - Cake Insert Pan - GOLD MEDAL PRODUCTS CO.; *pg.* 55, *pg.* 1414
THE FUNNEL CAKE FACTORY - Food Product - J&J SNACK FOODS CORPORATION; *pg.* 865, *pg.* 1107
FUNNEL CAKE FRIES - Food Product - J&J SNACK FOODS CORPORATION; *pg.* 865, *pg.* 1107
FUNNOODLE - Toy - JAKKS PACIFIC, INC.; *pg.* 960, *pg.* 142
FUNNY BONE BOOKS - Educational Materials - SCHOLASTIC INC.; *pg.* 1683, *pg.* 1288
FUNNY CHEW CHEWS - Childrens Vitamin - HEALTH PRODUCTS CORPORATION; *pg.* 1540, *pg.* 1356
FUNNY FRUITS - Video Game - INTERNATIONAL GAME TECHNOLOGY; *pg.* 957, *pg.* 1024
FUNNYFACE - Bag - SAMSONITE CORPORATION; *pg.* 11, *pg.* 830
FUNPALS - Boys' Underwear - FRUIT OF THE LOOM, INC.; *pg.* 41, *pg.* 725
FUNSAVER - Disposable Camera - EASTMAN KODAK COMPANY; *pg.* 1408, *pg.* 1333
FUNTAINER - Beverage Bottle - THERMOS L.L.C.; *pg.* 61, *pg.* 660
FUNTANK - Branded Games Developer & Publisher - PUBLISHERS CLEARING HOUSE; *pg.* 1782, *pg.* 1324
FUNTENSILS - Knives - PACTIV CORPORATION; *pg.* 1466, *pg.* 624
FUNTIME - Cameras - EASTMAN KODAK COMPANY; *pg.* 1408, *pg.* 1333
FUNYUNS - Onion Flavored Snack Rings - FRITO-LAY NORTH AMERICA, INC.; *pg.* 1853, *pg.* 1730
FUR BURRIES - Toy - SPIN MASTER LTD.; *pg.* 967, *pg.* 1943
FUR FIGHTER - Hair Remover Product - 3M COMPANY; *pg.* 1142, *pg.* 956
FURA RED - Molecular Probe Product - THERMO FISHER SCIENTIFIC INC.; *pg.* 1602, *pg.* 61
FURADAN - Insecticide - FMC CORPORATION; *pg.* 1163, *pg.* 1564
FURADAN 4F - Insecticides & Miticides - FMC CORPORATION; *pg.* 1163, *pg.* 1564
FURALAC - Corrosion-Resistant Mortar - ARKEMA INC.; *pg.* 1147, *pg.* 1543
FURAZIN - Molecular Probe Product - THERMO FISHER SCIENTIFIC INC.; *pg.* 1602, *pg.* 61
FURAZONE - Animal Safety Product - NEOGEN CORPORATION; *pg.* 883, *pg.* 896
FURL - Software - LOOKSMART, LTD.; *pg.* 1265, *pg.* 221
FURN-A-RAM - Pressed & Monolithic Refractory - RESCO PRODUCTS, INC.; *pg.* 107, *pg.* 1581
FURN-I-FRAME - Wood & Building Material - WEYERHAEUSER COMPANY; *pg.* 121, *pg.* 1820
FURN-WOOD - Metal Cutting Saw Blade - SIMONDS INTERNATIONAL CORPORATION; *pg.* 1376, *pg.* 819
FURNACON - Pressed & Monolithic Refractory - RESCO PRODUCTS, INC.; *pg.* 107, *pg.* 1581
FURNACUBED - Pressed & Monolithic Refractory - RESCO PRODUCTS, INC.; *pg.* 107, *pg.* 1581
FURNAL - Pressed & Monolithic Refractory - RESCO PRODUCTS, INC.; *pg.* 107, *pg.* 1581
FURNALITE - Pressed & Monolithic Refractory - RESCO PRODUCTS, INC.; *pg.* 107, *pg.* 1581
FURNANCE SYSTEM - Slogan - TENOVA; *pg.* 114, *pg.* 1525
FURNAS - Industrial Controls - SIEMENS PROCESS INDUSTRIES AND DRIVES; *pg.* 673, *pg.* 485
FURNASCRETE - Refractory Product - RESCO PRODUCTS, INC.; *pg.* 107, *pg.* 1581
FURNISHING YOUR STYLE - Slogan - RAYMOUR & FLANIGAN FURNITURE CO.; *pg.* 940, *pg.* 1174
FURNITURE BRANDS - Home Furnishings - HERITAGE HOME GROUP; *pg.* 926, *pg.* 1379
FURNITURE GUARD - Protective Packaging Material - PACTIV CORPORATION; *pg.* 1466, *pg.* 624
FURNITURE GUARD LITE - Protective Packaging Material - PACTIV CORPORATION; *pg.* 1466, *pg.* 624
FURNITURE MEDIC - On-Site Furniture Repair & Restoration - THE SERVICEMASTER COMPANY, LLC; *pg.* 335, *pg.* 1646
FURNITURE STYLE - Magazine - VANCE PUBLISHING CORPORATION; *pg.* 1699, *pg.* 627
FURNITUREONLINE.COM - Website - NATIONAL BUSINESS FURNITURE INC; *pg.* 1269, *pg.* 1879
FURREAL FRIENDS - Toy & Game - HASBRO, INC.; *pg.* 954, *pg.* 1603
FURROWS - Carpet - INTERFACE, INC.; *pg.* 695, *pg.* 512
FURROWS - Surface Material - STEELCASE INC.; *pg.* 475, *pg.* 889
FURRYTALE FRIENDS - Educational Materials - SCHOLASTIC INC.; *pg.* 1683, *pg.* 1288
FURSE - Wall Chart - THOMAS & BETTS CORPORATION; *pg.* 680, *pg.* 1646
FURSEWELD - Exothermic Grounding Product - THOMAS & BETTS CORPORATION; *pg.* 680, *pg.* 1646
FURUNO - Radiotelephones; Direction Finders; Marine Electronic Equipment - FURUNO USA, INC.; *pg.* 640, *pg.* 1819
FURUSATO DAYORI - Beverages - THE COCA-COLA COMPANY; *pg.* 240, *pg.* 493
FURY OF THE NILE - Amusement & Water Park - CEDAR FAIR, L.P.; *pg.* 537, *pg.* 1471
FUSABOND - Resins & Coatings - E.I. DU PONT DE NEMOURS & COMPANY; *pg.* 1159, *pg.* 390
FUSE - Cutting Tool - LEATHERMAN TOOL GROUP, INC.; *pg.* 1053, *pg.* 1504
FUSE - Services Framework - PROGRESS SOFTWARE CORPORATION; *pg.* 457, *pg.* 786
FUSED-LOCK - Fiber Coupler - ALLIANCE FIBER OPTIC PRODUCTS, INC.; *pg.* 1399, *pg.* 283
FUSELITE - Glass & Ceramic Material - CORNING INCORPORATED; *pg.* 1122, *pg.* 1154
FUSEWELDER - Coating System - WALL COLMONOY CORPORATION; *pg.* 1185, *pg.* 898
FUSIO CHIP - Component Module - SEQUENOM, INC.; *pg.* 1593, *pg.* 209
FUSION - Clear Overlay Binder - AMERICAN THERMOPLASTIC COMPANY; *pg.* 349, *pg.* 1573
FUSION - Furniture - ASHLEY FURNITURE INDUSTRIES, INC.; *pg.* 914, *pg.* 1852
FUSION - Automation Control Solution - BROOKS AUTOMATION, INC.; *pg.* 1320, *pg.* 813
FUSION - Valves - GRACO, INC.; *pg.* 1342, *pg.* 935
FUSION - Healthcare Fabric - HERCULITE PRODUCTS, INC.; *pg.* 694, *pg.* 1529
FUSION - Adhesives - HUNTSMAN CORPORATION; *pg.* 1167, *pg.* 1758
FUSION - Basketball Equipment - LIFETIME PRODUCTS INC.; *pg.* 933, *pg.* 1751
FUSION - Fiber Optic Collimators - LIGHTPATH TECHNOLOGIES INC; *pg.* 1420, *pg.* 454
FUSION - Software System - MENTOR GRAPHICS CORPORATION; *pg.* 432, *pg.* 1510
FUSION - Computer Workstation Product - STINGER

First page reference indicates Business Class Edition
Second page reference indicates Geographic Edition

MEDICAL LLC; *pg.* 476, *pg.* 1648
FUSION - Cleaning Product - VON SCHRADER COMPANY; *pg.* 62, *pg.* 1890
FUSION - Glass Tile - WALKER & ZANGER, INC.; *pg.* 119, *pg.* 281
FUSION - Home & Garden Product - WESTROCK COMPANY; *pg.* 1472, *pg.* 1805
FUSION BOND - Coating Products - RUSSEL METALS INC.; *pg.* 1180, *pg.* 1928
FUSION CHROME COLLECTION - Shaving Instruments - THE GILLETTE COMPANY; *pg.* 509, *pg.* 795
FUSION DIGITAL POWER - Semiconductor Devices - TEXAS INSTRUMENTS INCORPORATED; *pg.* 679, *pg.* 1688
FUSION DRIVERS - Golf Equipment - CALLAWAY GOLF COMPANY; *pg.* 1829, *pg.* 58
FUSION GLASS - Glass Tile - WALKER & ZANGER, INC.; *pg.* 119, *pg.* 281
FUSION-MPT - Input Output Interfaces - AVAGO TECHNOLOGIES; *pg.* 358, *pg.* 238
FUSION TELECOM - Communications Solutions - FUSION TELECOMMUNICATIONS INTERNATIONAL, INC.; *pg.* 1248, *pg.* 1233
FUSION TOOLS - Personal Care Electrical Product - HELEN OF TROY L.P.; *pg.* 511, *pg.* 1692
FUSION7D - Software - VITAL IMAGES, INC.; *pg.* 1607, *pg.* 950
FUSIONBOT - Internet Service - LOGIKA CORPORATION; *pg.* 1264, *pg.* 581
FUSIONI - Tile - ARTISTIC TILE INC.; *pg.* 914, *pg.* 1119
FUSIONQUAD - Packaging System - AMKOR TECHNOLOGY, INC.; *pg.* 67, *pg.* 25
FUSISTOR - Indoor Power Fuse - S&C ELECTRIC COMPANY; *pg.* 1305, *pg.* 589
FUSOR - Adhesive - LORD CORPORATION; *pg.* 1357, *pg.* 1360
FUTURA - Golf Equipment - ACUSHNET COMPANY; *pg.* 1824, *pg.* 818
FUTURA - Laptop Desk - LAPWORKS, INC.; *pg.* 426, *pg.* 187
FUTURA - Portable Electric Heater - SLANT/FIN CORPORATION; *pg.* 1076, *pg.* 1163
FUTURA - Industrial Goggles - UVEX SAFETY; *pg.* 1433, *pg.* 1608
FUTURA PHANTOM - Golf Equipment - ACUSHNET COMPANY; *pg.* 1824, *pg.* 818
FUTURAPAD - Animal Safety Product - NEOGEN CORPORATION; *pg.* 883, *pg.* 896
FUTURE - Floor Polish - S.C. JOHNSON & SON, INC.; *pg.* 334, *pg.* 1889
FUTURE ACCESS - Furniture - VIRCO MANUFACTURING CORPORATION; *pg.* 946, *pg.* 297
THE FUTURE ARRIVED EARLY - Tagline - EXTREME NETWORKS INC; *pg.* 287, *pg.* 245
THE FUTURE BELONGS TO YOU - Slogan - AMERICAN EQUITY MORTGAGE INC.; *pg.* 712, *pg.* 991
FUTURE FIRST - Computer Program - COMPUTER SCIENCES CORPORATION; *pg.* 378, *pg.* 1780
FUTURE GLUE - Glue - SUPER GLUE CORPORATION; *pg.* 1183, *pg.* 187
THE FUTURE IS FRIENDLY - Slogan - TELUS CORPORATION; *pg.* 1952, *pg.* 1912
THE FUTURE IS FUSION - Tagline - ADVANCED MICRO DEVICES, INC.; *pg.* 613, *pg.* 282
THE FUTURE OF MEMORY - Tag Line - RAMBUS INC.; *pg.* 459, *pg.* 288
THE FUTURE OF MUSIC AND SOUND - Tag Line - YAMAHA ELECTRONICS CORPORATION USA; *pg.* 689, *pg.* 51
THE FUTURE OF STORAGE ...TODAY - Slogan - WESTERN DIGITAL CORPORATION; *pg.* 492, *pg.* 118
THE FUTURE OF YOUR BUSINESS. STARTING NOW. - Slogan - TELLABS, INC.; *pg.* 678, *pg.* 637
THE FUTURE POWERED BY STRONG - Tagline - BALLANTYNE STRONG, INC.; *pg.* 623, *pg.* 1013
FUTURE SOLUTIONS: TODAY - Tagline - GLOBE COMPOSITE SOLUTIONS, LTD.; *pg.* 1883, *pg.* 842
FUTURE TILE - Carpet - INTERFACE, INC.; *pg.* 695, *pg.* 512
FUTUREMILL - Machine Tool Product - BOURN & KOCH MACHINE TOOL COMPANY; *pg.* 1319, *pg.* 654
FUTUREPOINT - Business Consulting Services - LOCKHEED MARTIN CORPORATION; *pg.* 229, *pg.* 762
FUTURES - Magazine - SCHOLASTIC INC.; *pg.* 1683, *pg.* 1288
FUTURETRUST - Maternity Apparel - DESTINATION MATERNITY CORPORATION; *pg.* 23, *pg.* 1563
FUTUREWAY - Glass & Ceramic Material - CORNING INCORPORATED; *pg.* 1122, *pg.* 1154
FUTURO - Support Bandages - 3M COMPANY; *pg.* 1142, *pg.* 956
FUZE - Bowling Equipment - BRUNSWICK BOWLING & BILLIARDS CORP.; *pg.* 1828, *pg.* 622
FUZE - Iced Tea Beverage - THE COCA-COLA COMPANY; *pg.* 240, *pg.* 493
FUZE HEALTHY INFUSIONS - Beverages - THE COCA-COLA COMPANY; *pg.* 240, *pg.* 493
FUZEON - Pharmaceutical Product - HOFFMANN-LA ROCHE INC.; *pg.* 1542, *pg.* 1099
FUZZY FLEECE BABY - Dolls - THE GOLDBERGER COMPANY, LLC; *pg.* 954, *pg.* 1235
FUZZY PARSER - Software - WIND RIVER SYSTEMS, INC.; *pg.* 493, *pg.* 38
FV - Musical Instrument - GIBSON GUITAR CORP.; *pg.* 550, *pg.* 1650
FVR - Substation Circuit Breaker - S&C ELECTRIC COMPANY; *pg.* 1305, *pg.* 589
FWX - Media Website - TIME INC.; *pg.* 1693, *pg.* 1300
FX - Television Network - FOX BROADCASTING COMPANY; *pg.* 287, *pg.* 130
FX - Apparel - LANDAU UNIFORMS INCORPORATED; *pg.* 28, *pg.* 971
FX-1170 - Dot Matrix Printer - EPSON AMERICA INC.; *pg.* 394, *pg.* 122
FX-880 - Dot Matrix Printer - EPSON AMERICA INC.; *pg.* 394, *pg.* 122
FX LIGHT - Fiber Optic Lighting System - ENERGY FOCUS, INC.; *pg.* 1411, *pg.* 1472
FX SPA LIGHT - Fiber Optic Lighting System - ENERGY FOCUS, INC.; *pg.* 1411, *pg.* 1472
FXRG - Apparel - HARLEY-DAVIDSON, INC.; *pg.* 178, *pg.* 1874
FXWIRE - Medical Equipment - CONMED CORPORATION; *pg.* 1517, *pg.* 1347
FYE - Retail Music & Video Stores - TRANS WORLD ENTERTAINMENT CORPORATION; *pg.* 313, *pg.* 1137
FYI - Health Supplement - GARDEN OF LIFE, INC.; *pg.* 1532, *pg.* 478
FYI - Computer Support Worktools - STEELCASE INC.; *pg.* 475, *pg.* 889
FYPON - Hardware - FORTUNE BRANDS HOME & SECURITY, INC.; *pg.* 55, *pg.* 600
FYREBLOC - Flame Retardants - CHEMTURA CORPORATION; *pg.* 1152, *pg.* 355
FYREPEL - Fire Fighting Apparel - LAKELAND INDUSTRIES, INC.; *pg.* 1354, *pg.* 1338
FYRETRED - Clothing - LAKELAND INDUSTRIES, INC.; *pg.* 1354, *pg.* 1338
FYREWRAP - Fire Protection Insulation - UNIFRAX CORPORATION; *pg.* 220, *pg.* 1317
FYRITE - Gas Analyzer - BACHARACH INC.; *pg.* 1400, *pg.* 1556
FYRITE TECH - Residential Combustion Analyzer - BACHARACH INC.; *pg.* 1400, *pg.* 1556
FYRIZER - Gas Analyzer - BACHARACH INC.; *pg.* 1400, *pg.* 1556

G

G - Fluid Handling System - GRACO, INC.; *pg.* 1342, *pg.* 935
G-15 - Fluid Handling System - GRACO, INC.; *pg.* 1342, *pg.* 935
G-3300 - Chemical Product - STEPAN COMPANY; *pg.* 1182, *pg.* 643
G-4 - Egg Spreader - HIGHWAY EQUIPMENT COMPANY; *pg.* 704, *pg.* 702
G-40 - Fluid Handling System - GRACO, INC.; *pg.* 1342, *pg.* 935
G-50 - AG Sprinklers - WEATHERTEC CORPORATION; *pg.* 708, *pg.* 93
G-AGE - Cutting And Grinding Machine - GLEASON CORPORATION; *pg.* 1340, *pg.* 1335
G-BLADES - Gallium Blades - DYNATEX INTERNATIONAL; *pg.* 635, *pg.* 277
G BY GUESS - Apparel - GUESS?, INC.; *pg.* 25, *pg.* 132
G-CLEAN - Cleaning Product - GREEN EARTH TECHNOLOGIES, INC.; *pg.* 704, *pg.* 1352
G-CODE - Video Recording System - ROVI CORPORATION; *pg.* 463, *pg.* 269
G-CRYL - Acrylic Resin - HENKEL CORPORATION; *pg.* 1165, *pg.* 1535
G-CURE - Acrylic Resin - HENKEL CORPORATION; *pg.* 1165, *pg.* 1535
G DESIGN - Fluid Handling System - GRACO, INC.; *pg.* 1342, *pg.* 935
G-DISPOSOIL - Lawn Care Product - GREEN EARTH TECHNOLOGIES, INC.; *pg.* 704, *pg.* 1352
G FORCE - Pressure Washers - GRACO, INC.; *pg.* 1342, *pg.* 935
G-GLASS - Cleaning Product - GREEN EARTH TECHNOLOGIES, INC.; *pg.* 704, *pg.* 1352
G-GUIDE - Digital Directory - ROVI CORPORATION; *pg.* 463, *pg.* 269
G HYDRA-MIX - Fluid Handling System - GRACO, INC.; *pg.* 1342, *pg.* 935
G-III - Apparel - G-III APPAREL GROUP, LTD.; *pg.* 41, *pg.* 1233
G-III SPORTS - Apparel - G-III APPAREL GROUP, LTD.; *pg.* 41, *pg.* 1233
G-III WOMEN - Apparel - G-III APPAREL GROUP, LTD.; *pg.* 41, *pg.* 1233
G-LAB - Software - GLEASON CORPORATION; *pg.* 1340, *pg.* 1335
G-MAXX - Machines for Gear Manufacture - GLEASON CORPORATION; *pg.* 1340, *pg.* 1335
G-METRIC - Tires - THE GOODYEAR TIRE & RUBBER COMPANY; *pg.* 1883, *pg.* 1401
G-NET - Control & Detection System - NORDSON CORPORATION; *pg.* 1365, *pg.* 1480
G-OIL - Cleaning Product - GREEN EARTH TECHNOLOGIES, INC.; *pg.* 704, *pg.* 1352
G-P LAM - Building Product - BLUELINX HOLDINGS, INC.; *pg.* 70, *pg.* 491
G-P LAM - Laminated Veneer Lumber - GEORGIA-PACIFIC LLC; *pg.* 1458, *pg.* 507
G-PLETE - Gear Cutting Machines - GLEASON CORPORATION; *pg.* 1340, *pg.* 1335
G-POINTING - Simulator - ENVIRONMENTAL TECTONICS CORPORATION; *pg.* 1411, *pg.* 1587
G-PROBE - Medical Laser System - IRIDEX CORPORATION; *pg.* 648, *pg.* 160
G-RFID - RFID Solution - NUMEREX CORP.; *pg.* 660, *pg.* 517
G-ROCX - Ethernet Network Equipment - VITESSE SEMICONDUCTOR CORPORATION; *pg.* 686, *pg.* 57
G-SCENT - Cleaning Product - GREEN EARTH TECHNOLOGIES, INC.; *pg.* 704, *pg.* 1352
G-SERIES - Cage Mill/Pulverizer - STEDMAN MACHINE COMPANY; *pg.* 1379, *pg.* 673
G-SOK - Shoe - ETONIC WORLDWIDE LLC; *pg.* 1808, *pg.* 857
G-STAR - Economical Bunker Rake - SMITHCO, INC.; *pg.* 1377, *pg.* 1592
G-T - Ring Seal - GREENE, TWEED & CO.; *pg.* 1344, *pg.* 1544
G-TECH - Gear Cutting Machines & Parts - GLEASON CORPORATION; *pg.* 1340, *pg.* 1335
G-TILE - Cleaning Product - GREEN EARTH TECHNOLOGIES, INC.; *pg.* 704, *pg.* 1352
G-TIRE - Automotive Cleaning Product - GREEN EARTH TECHNOLOGIES, INC.; *pg.* 704, *pg.* 1352
G-TRAC - Gear Manufacturing Machines & Parts - GLEASON CORPORATION; *pg.* 1340, *pg.* 1335
G-TRAC - Medical Equipment - INVACARE CORPORATION; *pg.* 1546, *pg.* 1451
G-U-M - Oral Hygiene Aids - SUNSTAR AMERICAS INC.; *pg.* 1599, *pg.* 591
G-WARE - Software - CLEARONE COMMUNICATIONS, INC.; *pg.* 629, *pg.* 1756
G-WASH - Cleaning Product - GREEN EARTH TECHNOLOGIES, INC.; *pg.* 704, *pg.* 1352
G-WHEEL - Automotive Cleaning Product - GREEN EARTH TECHNOLOGIES, INC.; *pg.* 704, *pg.* 1352
G. WIZ - Shoes - MASON COMPANIES, INC.; *pg.* 1811, *pg.* 1856
G+ - Game - WMS INDUSTRIES INC.; *pg.* 593, *pg.* 666
G2 - Glass & Ceramic Material - CORNING INCORPORATED; *pg.* 1122, *pg.* 1154
G2 DIGITAL - Monitor - HESKA CORPORATION; *pg.* 1542, *pg.* 335
G2 DOUBLE GLAZED - Chicken Wings - TYSON FOODS, INC.; *pg.* 902, *pg.* 35
G2 OPTIMA PLUS - Flushometer - SLOAN VALVE COMPANY; *pg.* 1062, *pg.* 613
G20 - Automobile - NISSAN NORTH AMERICA, INC.; *pg.* 186, *pg.* 1633
G2A - Software - CITRIX SYSTEMS, INC.; *pg.* 375, *pg.* 424

G2AX - Software - CITRIX SYSTEMS, INC.; *pg.* 375, *pg.* 424
G2L - Golf Club - KARSTEN MANUFACTURING CORPORATION; *pg.* 1838, *pg.* 17
G2M - Software - CITRIX SYSTEMS, INC.; *pg.* 375, *pg.* 424
G2T - Software - CITRIX SYSTEMS, INC.; *pg.* 375, *pg.* 424
G2W - Software - CITRIX SYSTEMS, INC.; *pg.* 375, *pg.* 424
G3 - Nutritional Supplement - NU SKIN ENTERPRISES, INC.; *pg.* 518, *pg.* 1755
G3 - Cleaning Product - TECH SPRAY, L.P.; *pg.* 1183, *pg.* 1659
G3 GUIDE - Fishing Gear Product - SIMMS FISHING PRODUCTS CORP.; *pg.* 1845, *pg.* 1008
G3 PRO - Defibrillator - CARDIAC SCIENCE CORPORATION; *pg.* 1512, *pg.* 1897
G35 - Automobile - NISSAN NORTH AMERICA, INC.; *pg.* 186, *pg.* 1633
G3504 - Pop Culture Smoothe Vol. 1 - THE SINGING MACHINE COMPANY, INC.; *pg.* 674, *pg.* 426
G3521 - Male Rock Vol. 1 - THE SINGING MACHINE COMPANY, INC.; *pg.* 674, *pg.* 426
G3523 - Male Rock Vol. 2 - THE SINGING MACHINE COMPANY, INC.; *pg.* 674, *pg.* 426
G3531 - Hip Hop/R&B Pop Culture Vol. 1 - THE SINGING MACHINE COMPANY, INC.; *pg.* 674, *pg.* 426
G3601 - Top Hits Vol. 2 - THE SINGING MACHINE COMPANY, INC.; *pg.* 674, *pg.* 426
G3603 - Top Hits Vol.3 - THE SINGING MACHINE COMPANY, INC.; *pg.* 674, *pg.* 426
G3631 - Hip Hop/R&B Vol. 2 - THE SINGING MACHINE COMPANY, INC.; *pg.* 674, *pg.* 426
G4 PRO - Outerwear - SIMMS FISHING PRODUCTS CORP.; *pg.* 1845, *pg.* 1008
G400 - Photoresist Strip System - LAM RESEARCH CORPORATION; *pg.* 1354, *pg.* 246
G4448 - Traditional Folk Songs - THE SINGING MACHINE COMPANY, INC.; *pg.* 674, *pg.* 426
G4Z - Stocking Foot - SIMMS FISHING PRODUCTS CORP.; *pg.* 1845, *pg.* 1008
G8 - Sedan - GENERAL MOTORS COMPANY; *pg.* 175, *pg.* 881
G8856 - Motown's Stop! In the Name of Love - THE SINGING MACHINE COMPANY, INC.; *pg.* 674, *pg.* 426
G8858 - Original Artist-Heatwave - THE SINGING MACHINE COMPANY, INC.; *pg.* 674, *pg.* 426
G8862 - It Takes Two: The Duets Collection - THE SINGING MACHINE COMPANY, INC.; *pg.* 674, *pg.* 426
GA500 - Process Gas Calorimeter - ALGAS-SDI; *pg.* 1311, *pg.* 1831
GA500 PLUS - Refrigerant Analyzer - BACHARACH INC.; *pg.* 1400, *pg.* 1556
GAB MED GMBH - Pharmaceutical Product - ALERE INC.; *pg.* 1488, *pg.* 849
GABAPENTIN GR - Pharmaceutical Product - DEPOMED, INC.; *pg.* 1523, *pg.* 143
GABCONTROL - Pharmaceutical Product - ALERE INC.; *pg.* 1488, *pg.* 849
GABCONTROL -AIRCHECK - Pharmaceutical Product - ALERE INC.; *pg.* 1488, *pg.* 849
GABE - Fabric - NEMSCHOFF, INC.; *pg.* 936, *pg.* 1890
GABOKKULT - Pharmaceutical Product - ALERE INC.; *pg.* 1488, *pg.* 849
GABRIEL - Furniture - AMISCO INDUSTRIES LTD.; *pg.* 913, *pg.* 1958
GABRIEL - Messenger Bags - JANDD MOUNTAINEERING, INC.; *pg.* 1837, *pg.* 204
GABRIEL - Shock Absorbers - MERITOR, INC.; *pg.* 212, *pg.* 911
GABRIELLE - Clothing - ABERCROMBIE & FITCH CO.; *pg.* 37, *pg.* 1466
GABRIELLE - Bath Product - KOHLER CO.; *pg.* 91, *pg.* 1862
GABRIELLE PLAID - Pillow and Throw - HERITAGE LACE INC.; *pg.* 694, *pg.* 711
GAC - Dental Product - DENTSPLY INTERNATIONAL INC.; *pg.* 1522, *pg.* 1596
GAC-1700 - Charger - GLOBALSTAR, INC.; *pg.* 401, *pg.* 743
GAD - Valve Trim - SPX PROCESS EQUIPMENT; *pg.* 1378, *pg.* 1551
GADGET - Shoe - AEROGROUP INTERNATIONAL, INC.; *pg.* 1803, *pg.* 1055
GADGET - Fabric - NEMSCHOFF, INC.; *pg.* 936, *pg.* 1890
GAETANO - Liqueurs - SHAW ROSS INTERNATIONAL IMPORTERS; *pg.* 1970, *pg.* 449
GAGECASE - Enclosure - THERMON AMERICAS INC.; *pg.* 1077, *pg.* 1744
GAGEPAK - Enclosure System - O'BRIEN CORPORATION; *pg.* 1366, *pg.* 1001
GAGGENAU - Household Appliances - BSH HOME APPLIANCES CORPORATION; *pg.* 53, *pg.* 108
GAI-TRONICS - Industrial Technology - HUBBELL INCORPORATED; *pg.* 1299, *pg.* 370
GAIA ORGANIC BLEND - Coffee - PEET'S COFFEE & TEA, INC.; *pg.* 1029, *pg.* 85
GAIN - Infant & Toddler Milk Products - ABBOTT NUTRITION; *pg.* 1485, *pg.* 1437
GAIN - Laundry Product - THE PROCTER & GAMBLE COMPANY; *pg.* 1129, *pg.* 1418
GAIN FROM OUR PERSPECTIVE - Slogan - FRANKLIN RESOURCES, INC.; *pg.* 760, *pg.* 254
GAIN HBT - Transistor Wafer - KOPIN CORPORATION; *pg.* 425, *pg.* 847
GAIN-HBT - Semiconductor Material - KOPIN CORPORATION; *pg.* 425, *pg.* 847
GAIN WHITE WATER FRESH - Detergent - THE PROCTER & GAMBLE COMPANY; *pg.* 1129, *pg.* 1418
GAINES' GANG - Ticket Program - BUCCANEERS LIMITED PARTNERSHIP; *pg.* 534, *pg.* 471
GAIRO - Handbag - ALDO GROUP; *pg.* 1804, *pg.* 1959
GAISER - Ceramic & Plastic Product - COORSTEK, INC.; *pg.* 77, *pg.* 330
GALA - Textiles - BERNHARDT DESIGN; *pg.* 918, *pg.* 1381
GALA - Dinnerware - THE HOMER LAUGHLIN CHINA COMPANY; *pg.* 1125, *pg.* 1850
GALA - Furniture - JASPER GROUP; *pg.* 930, *pg.* 691
GALA - Home Care - THE PROCTER & GAMBLE COMPANY; *pg.* 1129, *pg.* 1418
GALA ROUGE - Wine - BROWN-FORMAN CORPORATION; *pg.* 1958, *pg.* 732
GALACTASOL - Polymer - HERCULES INCORPORATED; *pg.* 1166, *pg.* 392
GALACTIC - Cameras - EASTMAN KODAK COMPANY; *pg.* 1408, *pg.* 1333
GALACTIC BLUE - Granite - ROCK OF AGES CORPORATION; *pg.* 108, *pg.* 1766
GALACTIC PAYBACK - Game - WMS INDUSTRIES INC.; *pg.* 593, *pg.* 666
GALARIO - Computer Software - VARITRONICS, LLC; *pg.* 487, *pg.* 954
GALAXIE - Plating Process - A BRITE COMPANY; *pg.* 1144, *pg.* 1697
GALAXOLIDE - Fragrance Ingredient - INTERNATIONAL FLAVORS & FRAGRANCES INC.; *pg.* 512, *pg.* 1244
GALAXY - Automated Meter Reading System - BADGER METER, INC.; *pg.* 1401, *pg.* 1873
GALAXY - Medical Device - BOSTON SCIENTIFIC CORPORATION; *pg.* 1508, *pg.* 831
GALAXY - Software Solutions - COMMVAULT SYSTEMS, INC.; *pg.* 377, *pg.* 1125
GALAXY - Scoreboard & Sports Product - DAKTRONICS, INC.; *pg.* 633, *pg.* 1624
GALAXY - Hose - THE GOODYEAR TIRE & RUBBER COMPANY; *pg.* 1883, *pg.* 1401
GALAXY - Flame-Resistant Vinyl Sign Material - HOLLISTON LLC; *pg.* 1460, *pg.* 1630
GALAXY - Top & Base Program - HOWE FURNITURE CORPORATION; *pg.* 928, *pg.* 998
GALAXY - Seating Product - IRWIN SEATING COMPANY INC.; *pg.* 929, *pg.* 887
GALAXY - Internet Service - LOGIKA CORPORATION; *pg.* 1264, *pg.* 581
GALAXY - Confectionery - MARS, INCORPORATED; *pg.* 1858, *pg.* 1792
GALAXY - Canine Vaccine - MERCK & CO., INC.; *pg.* 1566, *pg.* 1077
GALAXY - Automated Test System - MINE SAFETY APPLIANCES COMPANY; *pg.* 1361, *pg.* 1525
GALAXY - Fabric - NEMSCHOFF, INC.; *pg.* 936, *pg.* 1890
GALAXY - Floor Cleaning Product - NSS ENTERPRISES, INC.; *pg.* 59, *pg.* 1476
GALAXY - Mailing Systems - PITNEY BOWES INC.; *pg.* 454, *pg.* 376
GALAXY - Cruise Ship - ROYAL CARIBBEAN CRUISES LTD; *pg.* 1921, *pg.* 446
GALAXY - Cast Iron Gas Boiler - SLANT/FIN CORPORATION; *pg.* 1076, *pg.* 1163
GALAXY - Cold Cup - SOLO CUP COMPANY; *pg.* 1469, *pg.* 625
GALAXY - Software - SYNOPSYS, INC.; *pg.* 480, *pg.* 162
GALAXY - Communication System - TRIMBLE NAVIGATION LIMITED; *pg.* 1384, *pg.* 288
GALAXY COURIER - Navigation Aid - TRIMBLE NAVIGATION LIMITED; *pg.* 1384, *pg.* 288
GALAXY CUSTOM DESIGNER - Software - SYNOPSYS, INC.; *pg.* 480, *pg.* 162
GALAXY DS - Floor Cleaning Product - NSS ENTERPRISES, INC.; *pg.* 59, *pg.* 1476
GALAXY/GH - Property Management System - GALAXY HOTEL SYSTEMS LLC; *pg.* 1092, *pg.* 297
GALAXY III - Preamplifiers - BLONDER TONGUE LABORATORIES, INC.; *pg.* 625, *pg.* 1100
GALAXY INMARSAT-C/GPS - Navigation Aid - TRIMBLE NAVIGATION LIMITED; *pg.* 1384, *pg.* 288
GALAXY LIGHTSPEED - Property Management System - GALAXY HOTEL SYSTEMS LLC; *pg.* 1092, *pg.* 297
GALAXY POOL LIGHTS - Lighting Systems - REVOLUTION LIGHTING TECHNOLOGIES, INC.; *pg.* 1304, *pg.* 377
GALAXY SENTINEL - Navigation Aid - TRIMBLE NAVIGATION LIMITED; *pg.* 1384, *pg.* 288
GALAXY SUPER STIX - Snack Stick - GALAXY NUTRITIONAL FOODS, INC.; *pg.* 857, *pg.* 1603
GALAXY TAB - Tablet Computer - SAMSUNG ELECTRONICS AMERICA, INC.; *pg.* 669, *pg.* 1115
GALAXY/UX - Property Management System - GALAXY HOTEL SYSTEMS LLC; *pg.* 1092, *pg.* 297
GALAXYPLUS - Software System - FISERV, INC.; *pg.* 397, *pg.* 1855
GALAXYPRO - Software - DAKTRONICS, INC.; *pg.* 633, *pg.* 1624
GALBANI - Cheese - LACTALIS AMERICAN GROUP; *pg.* 873, *pg.* 1149
GALBRAITH-PILOT MARINE - Communication Equipment - MARINE ELECTRIC SYSTEMS, INC.; *pg.* 652, *pg.* 1123
GALE - Educational Publications - THOMSON REUTERS CORPORATION; *pg.* 1693, *pg.* 1944
GALE HAYMAN - Fragrance & Skin Care - COLOR ME BEAUTIFUL, INC.; *pg.* 505, *pg.* 1787
GALE INDUSTRIES - Installation of Insulation, Residential & Commercial - MASCO CORPORATION; *pg.* 96, *pg.* 909
GALERIE - Furniture - HAWORTH, INC.; *pg.* 402, *pg.* 891
GALEX - Satellite - ORBITAL ATK; *pg.* 1425, *pg.* 1779
GALFLEX - Conduit - SOUTHWIRE COMPANY; *pg.* 1063, *pg.* 527
GALIL - Kosher Poultry - EMPIRE KOSHER POULTRY, INC.; *pg.* 854, *pg.* 1553
GALILEI - Office Furniture - STEELCASE INC.; *pg.* 475, *pg.* 889
GALILEO - Thermometer - ACCUWEATHER, INC.; *pg.* 268, *pg.* 1587
GALILEO - Dispensing Equipment - IDEX CORPORATION; *pg.* 1347, *pg.* 623
GALILEO - Blood Bank Automation System - IMMUCOR, INC.; *pg.* 1544, *pg.* 537
GALILEO - Video Measurement System - THE L.S. STARRETT COMPANY; *pg.* 1421, *pg.* 783
GALILEO - Software System - MENTOR GRAPHICS CORPORATION; *pg.* 432, *pg.* 1510
GALILEO - Data Software - TELECOMMUNICATION SYSTEMS INC.; *pg.* 483, *pg.* 754
GALILEO - Global Travel Distribution System - TRAVELPORT LIMITED; *pg.* 1925, *pg.* 521
GALILEO-ECHO - Blood Bank Automation System - IMMUCOR, INC.; *pg.* 1544, *pg.* 537
GALILEOS - Imaging System - SIRONA DENTAL SYSTEMS, INC.; *pg.* 1429, *pg.* 1175
GALL-TOUGH - Stainless Steel Product - CARPENTER TECHNOLOGY CORPORATION; *pg.* 73, *pg.* 1584
GALL-TOUGH - Cast Alloy - WAUKESHA FOUNDRY INC.; *pg.* 1388, *pg.* 1898
GALLAGHER MILLENNIUM - Financial Services Software - WIPRO GALLAGHER SOLUTIONS; *pg.* 823, *pg.* 447
GALLAGHER'S - Restaurant - ARK RESTAURANTS CORP.; *pg.* 1715, *pg.* 1196
GALLAGHER'S BURGER BAR - Food Service - ARK RESTAURANTS CORP.; *pg.* 1715, *pg.* 1196
GALLAGHER'S STEAKHOUSE - Food Service - ARK RESTAURANTS CORP.; *pg.* 1715, *pg.* 1196
GALLANT - Lighting - LSI INDUSTRIES INC.; *pg.* 58, *pg.* 1416
GALLATIN - Footwear - PHOENIX FOOTWEAR GROUP, INC.; *pg.* 1815, *pg.* 60
GALLEON - Kitchen Product - KOHLER CO.; *pg.* 91, *pg.* 1862
GALLERIA - Scissors - ACME UNITED CORPORATION; *pg.* 1040, *pg.* 346
GALLERY - Guest Chairs, Conference & Modern Occasional Tables - BERNHARDT DESIGN; *pg.* 918, *pg.* 1381

GALLERY - Photo Albums - EASTMAN KODAK COMPANY; *pg.* 1408, *pg.* 1333
GALLERY - Beauty Care Product - HELEN OF TROY L.P.; *pg.* 511, *pg.* 1692
GALLERY - Bath & Plumbing Product - JACUZZI BRANDS CORPORATION; *pg.* 554, *pg.* 65
GALLERY - Furniture - JASPER GROUP; *pg.* 930, *pg.* 691
GALLERY EDITION - Ceiling Fan - HUNTER FAN COMPANY; *pg.* 57, *pg.* 1631
GALLERY EIGHT KIT - Eye Shadows - COVER GIRL COSMETICS; *pg.* 506, *pg.* 772
GALLERY OF HORSES - Deluxe Cards - LEANIN' TREE, INC.; *pg.* 1658, *pg.* 311
GALLERY OF THE WEST - Deluxe Cards - LEANIN' TREE, INC.; *pg.* 1658, *pg.* 311
GALLERY SERIES - Personal Care Electronic Product - HELEN OF TROY L.P.; *pg.* 511, *pg.* 1692
GALLIANO LIQUEUR - Spirits - REMY COINTREAU USA INC.; *pg.* 1969, *pg.* 1285
GALLIARD - Fabric - NEMSCHOFF, INC.; *pg.* 936, *pg.* 1890
GALLIOS - Flow Cytometer - BECKMAN COULTER, INC.; *pg.* 1402, *pg.* 48
GALLO OF SONOMA - Wine - E&J GALLO WINERY; *pg.* 1962, *pg.* 149
GALLO SALAME - Salame - TYSON FOODS, INC.; *pg.* 902, *pg.* 35
GALLON RHINO - Bulk Unloader - NORDSON CORPORATION; *pg.* 1365, *pg.* 1480
GALLUPS-HEALTHWAY WELL-BEING INDEX - Health Measurement - HEALTHWAYS, INC.; *pg.* 1540, *pg.* 1632
GALMAN - Toy & Game - HASBRO, INC.; *pg.* 954, *pg.* 1603
GALTEK - Valve - ENTEGRIS, INC.; *pg.* 1882, *pg.* 788
GALUCHET - Wallcovering - YORK WALLCOVERINGS INC.; *pg.* 947, *pg.* 1598
GALV-A-WELD - Cages - CTB INTERNATIONAL CORP.; *pg.* 850, *pg.* 695
GALV-ALUM - Galvanized Aluminum Metal Primer - DUNN-EDWARDS CORPORATION; *pg.* 1442, *pg.* 129
GALVA BRIGHT - Paint & Coating - AERVOE INDUSTRIES INCORPORATED; *pg.* 1439, *pg.* 1021
GALVA-GUARD - Solder - TECK RESOURCES LIMITED; *pg.* 1183, *pg.* 1912
GALVAFLEX - Lined Metal Hose/Galv. - FEDERAL HOSE MANUFACTURING INC.; *pg.* 1047, *pg.* 1469
GALVALUME - Aluminum & Zinc Coating Alloy - ARCELORMITTAL DOFASCO INC.; *pg.* 68, *pg.* 1921
GALVALUME PLUS - Aluminum & Zinc Coating Alloy - ARCELORMITTAL DOFASCO INC.; *pg.* 68, *pg.* 1921
GALVANIC SPA - Skin Care Product - NU SKIN ENTERPRISES, INC.; *pg.* 518, *pg.* 1755
GAMA SOLAR - Semiconductor Batch-Immersion System - AKRION, INC.; *pg.* 1311, *pg.* 1513
GAMBERDINE - Fabric - NEMSCHOFF, INC.; *pg.* 936, *pg.* 1890
GAMBLE - Fabric - NEMSCHOFF, INC.; *pg.* 936, *pg.* 1890
THE GAMBLER - Casino Game - INTERNATIONAL GAME TECHNOLOGY; *pg.* 957, *pg.* 1024
GAMBOOZLE.COM - Website - INTELIMAX MEDIA INC.; *pg.* 1259, *pg.* 1911
GAMCO - Chrome Plated Zinc Coatings - MASCO CORPORATION; *pg.* 96, *pg.* 909
GAME BOY ADVANCED - Video Game System - NINTENDO OF AMERICA, INC.; *pg.* 965, *pg.* 1829
GAME BOY COLOR - Video Game System - NINTENDO OF AMERICA, INC.; *pg.* 965, *pg.* 1829
GAME BOY POCKET - Portable Video Game - NINTENDO OF AMERICA, INC.; *pg.* 965, *pg.* 1829
GAME DAY - Fertilizer - SIMPLOT PARTNERS INC.; *pg.* 1800, *pg.* 548
GAME INFORMER - Games - GAMESTOP CORP.; *pg.* 399, *pg.* 1699
GAME KING - Game - INTERNATIONAL GAME TECHNOLOGY; *pg.* 957, *pg.* 1024
GAME KING PLUS - Casino Game - INTERNATIONAL GAME TECHNOLOGY; *pg.* 957, *pg.* 1024
GAME NOW - Personalized Application - SEACHANGE INTERNATIONAL, INC.; *pg.* 1279, *pg.* 781
GAME OF DRAGONS - Game - WMS INDUSTRIES INC.; *pg.* 593, *pg.* 666
GAME OF LIFE - Game - HASBRO, INC.; *pg.* 954, *pg.* 1603
THE GAME OF PERFECTION - Toy & Game - HASBRO, INC.; *pg.* 954, *pg.* 1603
THE GAME OF SCATTERGORIES - Toy & Game - HASBRO, INC.; *pg.* 954, *pg.* 1603
GAME OF THE STATES - Game - WINNING MOVES GAMES, INC.; *pg.* 970, *pg.* 816
THE GAME OF THINGS... - Toy & Game - HASBRO, INC.; *pg.* 954, *pg.* 1603
GAME ON - Advertising & Promotional Brochure Design - STRUCTURAL GRAPHICS, LLC; *pg.* 1689, *pg.* 346
GAME PRO - Hunting Knife - GERBER LEGENDARY BLADES; *pg.* 1834, *pg.* 1503
GAME SERIES - Glove - CALLAWAY GOLF COMPANY; *pg.* 1829, *pg.* 58
GAMECAST - Sporting News - ESPN, INC.; *pg.* 285, *pg.* 340
GAMECRAFT - Disc Toss Games - SPORT SUPPLY GROUP, INC.; *pg.* 1846, *pg.* 1687
GAMEFAQS - Video Gaming Information Website - CBS INTERACTIVE, INC.; *pg.* 369, *pg.* 215
GAMEGUARD - Lottery System - INTERNATIONAL GAME TECHNOLOGY; *pg.* 420, *pg.* 1606
GAMEMASTER - Footwear - LACROSSE FOOTWEAR, INC.; *pg.* 1811, *pg.* 1503
GAMEPOINT - Lottery System - INTERNATIONAL GAME TECHNOLOGY; *pg.* 420, *pg.* 1606
GAMEPRO - Technology Magazine - INTERNATIONAL DATA GROUP; *pg.* 1653, *pg.* 796
GAMER - Graphite Golf Shaft - ALDILA, INC.; *pg.* 1825, *pg.* 185
GAMER - Baseball Glove - HILLERICH & BRADSBY CO., INC.; *pg.* 1836, *pg.* 576
GAMER - Wireless Control Product - UNIVERSAL ELECTRONICS, INC.; *pg.* 683, *pg.* 262
GAMES GALORE - Lottery Game - MICHIGAN STATE LOTTERY BUREAU; *pg.* 999, *pg.* 895
GAMESA - Cookies - PEPSICO, INC.; *pg.* 259, *pg.* 1327
GAMESCAPE - Business Unit - INTERNATIONAL GAME TECHNOLOGY; *pg.* 420, *pg.* 1606
GAMESHARK - Game Code - MAD CATZ INTERACTIVE INC.; *pg.* 429, *pg.* 204
GAMESPOT - Video Gaming Website - CBS INTERACTIVE, INC.; *pg.* 369, *pg.* 215
GAMING ZONE - Game - WMS INDUSTRIES INC.; *pg.* 593, *pg.* 666
GAMMA - Footwear - EASTLAND SHOE CORPORATION; *pg.* 1808, *pg.* 750
GAMMA - Automated Wafer Fabrication System - LAM RESEARCH CORPORATION; *pg.* 1354, *pg.* 246
GAMMA - Barrier Containers - REXAM BEVERAGE CAN NORTH AMERICA; *pg.* 1468, *pg.* 588
GAMMA - Surgical & Medical Product - STRYKER CORPORATION; *pg.* 1598, *pg.* 894
GAMMAGARD - Biopharmaceutical Product - BAXTER INTERNATIONAL INC.; *pg.* 1499, *pg.* 599
GAMMAMEDPLUS - Medical System - VARIAN MEDICAL SYSTEMS, INC.; *pg.* 1434, *pg.* 178
GAMMARP - Immune Globulin Intravenous (Human Lyophilized) - CSL BEHRING LLC; *pg.* 1520, *pg.* 1543
GAMMEX LASERS - Medical Device - GAMMEX RMI INC.; *pg.* 1532, *pg.* 1872
GAMULIN RH - Immune Globulin Human - CSL BEHRING LLC; *pg.* 1520, *pg.* 1543
GAMUT - Knife - BUCK KNIVES, INC.; *pg.* 1828, *pg.* 550
GAN FETS - Electronic Material - EMCORE CORPORATION; *pg.* 636, *pg.* 39
GANDRAS - Catheter - VASCULAR SOLUTIONS, INC.; *pg.* 1434, *pg.* 946
GANDY'S - Milk - DEAN FOODS COMPANY; *pg.* 852, *pg.* 1679
GANG-LAM - Laminated Veneer Lumber - LOUISIANA-PACIFIC CORPORATION; *pg.* 94, *pg.* 1652
GANGNET - Software - SRA INTERNATIONAL, INC.; *pg.* 473, *pg.* 1780
GANIZERS - Disposable & Labware - SPECTRUM LABORATORIES INC.; *pg.* 1595, *pg.* 69
GANTRISIN - Pharmaceutical Product - HOFFMANN-LA ROCHE INC.; *pg.* 1542, *pg.* 1099
GAP - Software - BIO-RAD LABORATORIES, INC.; *pg.* 1504, *pg.* 101
GAP - Ulcer Test - BIOMERICA, INC.; *pg.* 1506, *pg.* 107
GAP - Retail Clothing Store - THE GAP, INC.; *pg.* 1770, *pg.* 218
GAP - Software Product - WOODWARD, INC.; *pg.* 122, *pg.* 329
GAP DESIGN EDITIONS - Apparel - THE GAP, INC.; *pg.* 1770, *pg.* 218
GAPEX - Polymer Blends - FERRO CORPORATION; *pg.* 1162, *pg.* 1462
GAPEX HT - Polypropylene Alloys - FERRO CORPORATION; *pg.* 1162, *pg.* 1462
GAR-KENYON - Hydraulic Valves - AMATOM ELECTRONIC HARDWARE, INC.; *pg.* 1041, *pg.* 342
GARAGE GAMES - Online Services - IAC/INTERACTIVECORP; *pg.* 292, *pg.* 1242
GARAGEBAND - Music Creation Application - APPLE INC.; *pg.* 350, *pg.* 73
GARAMOND - Bath Product - KOHLER CO.; *pg.* 91, *pg.* 1862
GARANIMALS - Color Related Tops & Bottoms for Children - GARAN, INCORPORATED; *pg.* 24, *pg.* 1234
GARANT - Impression Material - 3M COMPANY; *pg.* 1142, *pg.* 956
GARB-O-FLAKES - Garbage Pail Deodorant - SURCO PRODUCTS, INC.; *pg.* 336, *pg.* 1581
GARBO SETTEE - Furniture - J. ROBERT SCOTT INC.; *pg.* 930, *pg.* 105
GARDASIL - Medicine - MERCK & CO., INC.; *pg.* 1566, *pg.* 1077
GARDCO - Lighting Fixture & Control - PHILIPS LIGHTING; *pg.* 1303, *pg.* 806
GARDEN - Table - BLATT BOWLING & BILLIARD CORP.; *pg.* 1827, *pg.* 1203
GARDEN - Above-Ground Pool Kit - POOL CORPORATION; *pg.* 1843, *pg.* 743
GARDEN 7 - Nutritional Supplement - HERBALIFE INTERNATIONAL OF AMERICA, INC.; *pg.* 1541, *pg.* 132
GARDEN BANDANA - Bath Product - KOHLER CO.; *pg.* 91, *pg.* 1862
GARDEN BASKET - Basket - FTD GROUP, INC.; *pg.* 1795, *pg.* 608
GARDEN BOUQUET - Area Rug - COURISTAN INC.; *pg.* 921, *pg.* 1067
GARDEN CLAW - Gardening & Hardware Product - FAULTLESS STARCH/BON AMI COMPANY; *pg.* 330, *pg.* 982
GARDEN CLAW GOLD - Gardening & Hardware Product - FAULTLESS STARCH/BON AMI COMPANY; *pg.* 330, *pg.* 982
GARDEN, DECK, & LANDSCAPE - Magazine - MEREDITH CORPORATION; *pg.* 1663, *pg.* 705
GARDEN DELIGHT - Food Products - FROSTY ACRES BRANDS, INC.; *pg.* 1020, *pg.* 484
GARDEN DESIGN - Magazine - BONNIER CORPORATION; *pg.* 1622, *pg.* 480
GARDEN GLORY - Table Textile - HERITAGE LACE INC.; *pg.* 694, *pg.* 711
GARDEN GUARD - Homeowner Product - PBI/GORDON CORPORATION; *pg.* 1176, *pg.* 985
GARDEN MASTER - Lawn & Garden Distributors/Retailers - PRO GROUP, INC.; *pg.* 1782, *pg.* 331
GARDEN MATE - Hose - TEKNOR APEX COMPANY; *pg.* 1889, *pg.* 1605
GARDEN OF EATIN' - Mini Tortilla Chips - THE HAIN CELESTIAL GROUP, INC.; *pg.* 860, *pg.* 1172
GARDEN OF GRANDEUR - Flower Arrangement - 1-800-FLOWERS.COM, INC.; *pg.* 1758, *pg.* 1151
GARDEN OUTFITTERS - Slogan - PRINCIPLE PLASTICS, INC.; *pg.* 1816, *pg.* 94
GARDEN PARTY - Video Game - INTERNATIONAL GAME TECHNOLOGY; *pg.* 957, *pg.* 1024
GARDEN PARTY - Glove - WELLS LAMONT CORPORATION; *pg.* 15, *pg.* 638
GARDEN PATCH - Carpet - INTERFACE, INC.; *pg.* 695, *pg.* 512
GARDEN PATHWAY - Flower Arrangement - 1-800-FLOWERS.COM, INC.; *pg.* 1758, *pg.* 1151
GARDEN PLENTY - Plant Based Fertilizer - GARDENS ALIVE!, INC.; *pg.* 1796, *pg.* 693
GARDEN PRODUCTS - Gardening Solutions - E.I. DU PONT DE NEMOURS & COMPANY; *pg.* 1159, *pg.* 390
GARDEN PUPPETS BOUQUET - Floral Bouquet - FTD GROUP, INC.; *pg.* 1795, *pg.* 608
GARDEN RAILWAYS - Magazine - KALMBACH PUBLISHING CO.; *pg.* 1656, *pg.* 1898
GARDEN READY - Container Grown Plant - MONROVIA GROWERS; *pg.* 1797, *pg.* 44
GARDEN SENSATIONS - Salads - THE WENDY'S COMPANY; *pg.* 1755, *pg.* 1450
GARDEN SLEEP SYSTEM - Bed - HILTON WORLDWIDE, INC.; *pg.* 1094, *pg.* 1791
GARDEN SOLUTIONS - Wasp Trap - GARDENS ALIVE!, INC.; *pg.* 1796, *pg.* 693
GARDEN TREASURES - Flower Arrangement - 1-800-FLOWERS.COM, INC.; *pg.* 1758, *pg.* 1151
GARDEN WEASEL - Gardening & Hardware Product -

FAULTLESS STARCH/BON AMI COMPANY; *pg.* 330, *pg.* 982
GARDEN WEASEL EDGER - Garden Tool - FAULTLESS STARCH/BON AMI COMPANY; *pg.* 330, *pg.* 982
GARDENBURGER - Vegetarian Burger - KELLOGG COMPANY; *pg.* 831, *pg.* 870
GARDENCAST - Gypsum Cement - USG CORPORATION; *pg.* 118, *pg.* 594
GARDENELLA - Furniture - TELESCOPE CASUAL FURNITURE INC.; *pg.* 944, *pg.* 1162
GARDENER - Fabric - NEMSCHOFF, INC.; *pg.* 936, *pg.* 1890
GARDENER'S CHOICE - Gloves - WELLS LAMONT CORPORATION; *pg.* 15, *pg.* 638
GARDENERS GOLD - Soil Care Product - GARDENS ALIVE!, INC.; *pg.* 1796, *pg.* 693
GARDENER'S GUIDE - Book Series - DIRECT HOLDINGS AMERICAS INC.; *pg.* 1636, *pg.* 1780
GARDENIA - Decorative Fragrance - AROMATIQUE INC.; *pg.* 499, *pg.* 32
GARDENIA - Fragrance - ELIZABETH ARDEN, INC.; *pg.* 507, *pg.* 448
GARDENIA - Fragrance - NATURAL DECORATIONS, INC.; *pg.* 936, *pg.* 5
GARDENIA - Cheese - SAPUTO, INC.; *pg.* 893, *pg.* 1956
GARDENIA WHITE - Granite - ROCK OF AGES CORPORATION; *pg.* 108, *pg.* 1766
GARDENNAY - Food Product - CAMPBELL COMPANY OF CANADA LTD; *pg.* 844, *pg.* 1935
GARDENPOINT.COM - Software - ARI NETWORK SERVICES, INC.; *pg.* 353, *pg.* 1873
GARDENWORKS - Retail Store Services - 1-800-FLOWERS.COM, INC.; *pg.* 1758, *pg.* 1151
GARDETTO'S - Food Product - GENERAL MILLS, INC.; *pg.* 828, *pg.* 933
GARDIAN - Capsule Filter - PALL CORPORATION; *pg.* 232, *pg.* 1323
GARDS - Feminine Pads - HILLYARD, INC.; *pg.* 331, *pg.* 990
GARDZ - Sundry - KELLY-MOORE PAINT COMPANY, INC.; *pg.* 1443, *pg.* 198
GARELICK FARMS - Dairy Product - DEAN FOODS COMPANY; *pg.* 852, *pg.* 1679
GARELICK FARMS - Dairy Products & Juice - GARELICK FARMS, LLC; *pg.* 858, *pg.* 823
GARG - Endoscopic Technologies - CONMED CORPORATION; *pg.* 1517, *pg.* 1347
GARGOYLES - Sunglasses - FGX INTERNATIONAL, INC.; *pg.* 5, *pg.* 1608
GARLAND - Bath Product - KOHLER CO.; *pg.* 91, *pg.* 1862
GARLAND - Office Furniture - STEELCASE INC.; *pg.* 475, *pg.* 889
GARLIC - Herbal Formula - SHAKLEE CORPORATION; *pg.* 1593, *pg.* 184
GARLIC PLUS - Food Products - MODERN PRODUCTS, INC.; *pg.* 1568, *pg.* 1871
GARLIC ZING - Food Product - ARMANINO FOODS OF DISTINCTION, INC.; *pg.* 837, *pg.* 100
GARLIFE - Nutritional Supplement - PHARMAVITE LLC; *pg.* 1584, *pg.* 167
GARLIQUE - Health & Beauty Product - CHATTEM, INC.; *pg.* 1515, *pg.* 1628
GARLITE - Nutritional Supplement - NATURAL ORGANICS, INC.; *pg.* 1571, *pg.* 1181
GARLON - Herbicide - DOW AGROSCIENCES LLC; *pg.* 1156, *pg.* 684
GARMENT SELECT - Labeling - FLEXCON CORPORATION; *pg.* 1457, *pg.* 844
GARMIN - GPS Tracking Devices - GARMIN INTERNATIONAL, INC.; *pg.* 1414, *pg.* 717
GARNER - Shoes - ALLEN-EDMONDS SHOE CORP.; *pg.* 1804, *pg.* 1887
GARNET - Flat Panel Display - EPSILON SYSTEMS SOLUTIONS; *pg.* 1412, *pg.* 202
GARNET - Video Game - INTERNATIONAL GAME TECHNOLOGY; *pg.* 957, *pg.* 1024
GARNET - Fabric - NEMSCHOFF, INC.; *pg.* 936, *pg.* 1890
GARNEY HILL - Online Gift Store - IAC/INTERACTIVECORP; *pg.* 292, *pg.* 1242
GARNIER - Hair Care Products - L'OREAL USA; *pg.* 514, *pg.* 1252
GAROFOLI - Italian Wine - LAIRD & COMPANY, INC.; *pg.* 1966, *pg.* 1119
GARRCIA - Footwear - STEVEN MADDEN, LTD.; *pg.* 1819, *pg.* 1176
GARRETT - Snuff Tobacco - AMERICAN SNUFF COMPANY; *pg.* 1893, *pg.* 1641
GARRETT - Products for Commercial & Military Aircraft & Applications - HONEYWELL AEROSPACE; *pg.* 228, *pg.* 16
GARRETT SWEET - Snuff Tobacco - AMERICAN SNUFF COMPANY; *pg.* 1893, *pg.* 1641
GARRISON - Bag - BROWN & BIGELOW, INC.; *pg.* 1624, *pg.* 959
GARRISON - Footwear - LACROSSE FOOTWEAR, INC.; *pg.* 1811, *pg.* 1503
GARRY ELECTRONICS - I C Sockets & Connectors - COOPER INTERCONNECT; *pg.* 630, *pg.* 1118
GART SPORTS - Sporting Goods - THE SPORTS AUTHORITY, INC.; *pg.* 1846, *pg.* 326
GARTNER - Software - ANACOMP, INC.; *pg.* 350, *pg.* 1777
GARUDA BLEND - Coffee - PEET'S COFFEE & TEA, INC.; *pg.* 1029, *pg.* 85
GARY - Safe & Security Product - FIRE KING SECURITY GROUP; *pg.* 1336, *pg.* 696
GARY FARRELL - Wine - JIM BEAM BRANDS CO.; *pg.* 1965, *pg.* 601
GARY FISHER - Mountain Bike - TREK BICYCLE CORPORATION; *pg.* 1847, *pg.* 1896
GAS - Electronic Product - LRAD CORPORATION; *pg.* 652, *pg.* 204
G.A.S. - General Anesthesia Systems - VITAL SIGNS, INC.; *pg.* 1607, *pg.* 1126
GAS-CHEX - Sterilization Product - PROPPER MANUFACTURING COMPANY, INC.; *pg.* 1586, *pg.* 1175
GAS ENGINE MAGAZINE - Publication - OGDEN PUBLICATIONS, INC.; *pg.* 1672, *pg.* 722
GAS HUNTER - Gas Leak Detector - BACHARACH INC.; *pg.* 1400, *pg.* 1556
GAS MISER - Demand Regulator - MINE SAFETY APPLIANCES COMPANY; *pg.* 1361, *pg.* 1525
GAS MODULE SE - Gas Monitoring & Analysis - MAQUET; *pg.* 1558, *pg.* 1082
GAS-POINTER - Gas Detector - BACHARACH INC.; *pg.* 1400, *pg.* 1556
GAS POINTER II - Multi-Purpose Methane (or Propane) Detector - BACHARACH INC.; *pg.* 1400, *pg.* 1556
GAS PROCESSING SYSTEM - Thermal Processing Equipment - SURFACE COMBUSTION, INC.; *pg.* 1077, *pg.* 1462
GAS PUP - Gas Leak Detector - BACHARACH INC.; *pg.* 1400, *pg.* 1556
GAS-TESTER - Detector Tube Pumps - MINE SAFETY APPLIANCES COMPANY; *pg.* 1361, *pg.* 1525
GAS WATCHERS - Association Services - AMERICAN AUTOMOBILE ASSOCIATION; *pg.* 1190, *pg.* 429
GASCAN - Eyewear - OAKLEY, INC.; *pg.* 1840, *pg.* 86
GASCO - Gas Utility - THE GAS COMPANY LLC; *pg.* 1943, *pg.* 543
GASCOPE - Combustible Gas Indicator - MINE SAFETY APPLIANCES COMPANY; *pg.* 1361, *pg.* 1525
GASGUARD - Gas Cabinets for Electronic Industry - AIR PRODUCTS AND CHEMICALS, INC.; *pg.* 1145, *pg.* 1513
GASKET - Footwear - OAKLEY, INC.; *pg.* 1840, *pg.* 86
GASKET-SERT - Filter Assembly - PALL CORPORATION; *pg.* 232, *pg.* 1323
GASKLEEN - Filter Assembly - PALL CORPORATION; *pg.* 232, *pg.* 1323
GASPAC - Seal - FLOWSERVE CORPORATION; *pg.* 82, *pg.* 1719
GAST - Vacuum Pumps & Compressors - IDEX CORPORATION; *pg.* 1347, *pg.* 623
GAST - Spray Product - SPRAYING SYSTEMS CO.; *pg.* 1063, *pg.* 670
GASTAPE - Indicator Tape - STERIS CORPORATION; *pg.* 1597, *pg.* 1464
GASTIGHT - Syringe - HAMILTON CO., INC.; *pg.* 1415, *pg.* 1031
GASTOBAC - Tobacco Curing System - GAS-FIRED PRODUCTS, INC.; *pg.* 1338, *pg.* 1367
THE GASTON GAZETTE - North Carolina Newspaper - FREEDOM COMMUNICATIONS, INC.; *pg.* 1643, *pg.* 110
GASTROCCULT - Testing Instrument System - BECKMAN COULTER, INC.; *pg.* 1402, *pg.* 48
GASTROMARK - Nanoparticle Product - AMAG PHARMACEUTICALS, INC.; *pg.* 1492, *pg.* 827
GASTROPLUS - Drug Absorption Modeling Software - SIMULATIONS PLUS, INC.; *pg.* 470, *pg.* 121
GATE STATION - Software System - MENTOR GRAPHICS CORPORATION; *pg.* 432, *pg.* 1510
GATECYCLE - Software - GE ENERGY; *pg.* 1338, *pg.* 506
GATEGRAPH - Software System - MENTOR GRAPHICS CORPORATION; *pg.* 432, *pg.* 1510
GATEKEEPER - Purifier - ENTEGRIS, INC.; *pg.* 1882, *pg.* 788
GATEKEEPER - Software System - KRONOS INCORPORATED; *pg.* 425, *pg.* 813
GATEKEEPER - Tailgate Protector - LUND INTERNATIONAL, INC.; *pg.* 211, *pg.* 526
GATEPLACE - Software System - MENTOR GRAPHICS CORPORATION; *pg.* 432, *pg.* 1510
GATEROUTE - Software System - MENTOR GRAPHICS CORPORATION; *pg.* 432, *pg.* 1510
GATES - Belts & Hoses - THE GATES CORPORATION; *pg.* 205, *pg.* 319
GATES-MACGINITIE READING TESTS - Testing Tools - HOUGHTON MIFFLIN HARCOURT PUBLISHING COMPANY; *pg.* 1651, *pg.* 796
GATEWAY - Hardware Product - INTERPHASE CORPORATION; *pg.* 420, *pg.* 1732
GATEWAY - Molecular Biology Product - THERMO FISHER SCIENTIFIC INC.; *pg.* 1602, *pg.* 61
GATEWAY - Community Name - WCI COMMUNITIES, INC.; *pg.* 1118, *pg.* 414
GATEWAY GUY - Motor Racetrack - DOVER MOTORSPORTS, INC.; *pg.* 545, *pg.* 387
GATEWAY INTERNATIONAL RACEWAY - Motor Racetrack - DOVER MOTORSPORTS, INC.; *pg.* 545, *pg.* 387
GATEWAY MOTORSPORTS CLUB - Motor Racetrack - DOVER MOTORSPORTS, INC.; *pg.* 545, *pg.* 387
GATEWAY MSC - Mobile Solutions - SONUS NETWORKS INC.; *pg.* 1281, *pg.* 858
GATHER ROUND - Boots - AEROGROUP INTERNATIONAL, INC.; *pg.* 1803, *pg.* 1055
GATHERING - Kitchen Product - KOHLER CO.; *pg.* 91, *pg.* 1862
GATHERNET - Laundry & Utility Bag - MCNETT CORPORATION; *pg.* 1839, *pg.* 1817
GATO - Wine - SHAW ROSS INTERNATIONAL IMPORTERS; *pg.* 1970, *pg.* 449
GATOR - Utility Vehicle - DEERE & COMPANY; *pg.* 703, *pg.* 632
GATOR - Hunting & Fishing Knives - GERBER LEGENDARY BLADES; *pg.* 1834, *pg.* 1503
GATOR - Battery Operated Crimper - GREENLEE TEXTRON INC.; *pg.* 1048, *pg.* 655
GATOR - Multi-Vessel Navigation - ION GEOPHYSICAL CORPORATION; *pg.* 1350, *pg.* 1708
GATOR - Cleaning Product - THE LIBMAN COMPANY; *pg.* 331, *pg.* 553
GATOR-DECK - Fiberglass Pultruded Grating - ALABAMA METAL INDUSTRIES CORPORATION; *pg.* 65, *pg.* 1
GATOR EXCHANGE-A-BLADE - Bone Saw - GERBER LEGENDARY BLADES; *pg.* 1834, *pg.* 1503
GATOR GOLF - Toy & Game - HASBRO, INC.; *pg.* 954, *pg.* 1603
GATOR WIRE - Screen Material - BUFFALO WIRE WORKS CO., INC.; *pg.* 72, *pg.* 1147
GATORADE - Sports Beverage - PEPSICO, INC.; *pg.* 259, *pg.* 1327
GATORADE FIERCE - Sports Beverage - PEPSICO, INC.; *pg.* 259, *pg.* 1327
GATORADE FROST - Sports Drink - THE GATORADE COMPANY; *pg.* 251, *pg.* 574
GATORADE FROST - Sports Beverage - PEPSICO, INC.; *pg.* 259, *pg.* 1327
GATORADE G2 - Low-Calorie Sports Drink - PEPSICO, INC.; *pg.* 259, *pg.* 1327
GATORADE ICE - Sports Drink - THE GATORADE COMPANY; *pg.* 251, *pg.* 574
GATORADE ICE - Sports Beverage - PEPSICO, INC.; *pg.* 259, *pg.* 1327
GATORADE ICE THIRST - Drinks - PEPSICO, INC.; *pg.* 259, *pg.* 1327
GATORADE THIRST - Drinks - PEPSICO, INC.; *pg.* 259, *pg.* 1327
GATORADE X-FACTOR - Sports Drink - THE GATORADE COMPANY; *pg.* 251, *pg.* 574
GATORADE X-FACTOR - Sports Beverage - PEPSICO, INC.; *pg.* 259, *pg.* 1327
GATORADE XTREMO - Sports Drink - THE GATORADE COMPANY; *pg.* 251, *pg.* 574
GATORADE XTREMO - Sports Beverage - PEPSICO, INC.; *pg.* 259, *pg.* 1327
GATORBACK - Tire And Rubber Product - THE GOODYEAR TIRE & RUBBER COMPANY; *pg.* 1883, *pg.* 1401

First page reference indicates Business Class Edition
Second page reference indicates Geographic Edition

GATORGRATE - Open Molded Grating - ALABAMA METAL INDUSTRIES CORPORATION; *pg.* 65, *pg.* 1
GATORPRO - Fire Alarm - FIKE CORPORATION; *pg.* 1047, *pg.* 973
GATTEX - Pharmaceutical Product - NPS PHARMACEUTICALS, INC.; *pg.* 1576, *pg.* 1043
GATTILAND - Pizza Restaurants Featuring Arcade Entertainment - MR. GATTI'S, LP; *pg.* 1741, *pg.* 1664
GATTI'S-TO-GO - Restaurants - MR. GATTI'S, LP; *pg.* 1741, *pg.* 1664
GATTITOWN - Pizza Restaurants Featuring Arcade Entertainment - MR. GATTI'S, LP; *pg.* 1741, *pg.* 1664
GATWICK - Ethernet Product - VITESSE SEMICONDUCTOR CORPORATION; *pg.* 686, *pg.* 57
GAUNTLET - Herbicide for Soybeans - FMC CORPORATION; *pg.* 1163, *pg.* 1564
GAUSSOPT_IK - Software Used to Determine the Parameters for Lenses - SCHNEIDER OPTICS INC.; *pg.* 1428, *pg.* 1165
GAVIN - Sunglasses - COACH, INC.; *pg.* 3, *pg.* 1214
GAWKER - News & Gossip Site - GAWKER MEDIA LLC; *pg.* 1248, *pg.* 1234
GAY 90'S - Popcorn Machine - GOLD MEDAL PRODUCTS CO.; *pg.* 55, *pg.* 1414
GAY LEA - Dairy Products - GAY LEA FOODS CO-OPERATIVE LIMITED; *pg.* 858, *pg.* 1926
GAYLORD HAUSER - Food Products - MODERN PRODUCTS, INC.; *pg.* 1568, *pg.* 1871
GAYLORD HOTELS - Hotels - MARRIOTT INTERNATIONAL, INC.; *pg.* 1102, *pg.* 764
GAZE OF STONE - Game - WMS INDUSTRIES INC.; *pg.* 593, *pg.* 666
GAZEBO - Furniture - ETHAN ALLEN INTERIORS INC.; *pg.* 924, *pg.* 343
GAZEBO BLEND - Coffee - STARBUCKS CORPORATION; *pg.* 897, *pg.* 1840
GAZETEX - Wound Dressing - DERMA SCIENCES, INC.; *pg.* 1523, *pg.* 1111
THE GAZETTE - Newspaper - GAZETTE COMMUNICATIONS, INC.; *pg.* 1644, *pg.* 702
GAZETTEONLINE.COM - Online News Source - GAZETTE COMMUNICATIONS, INC.; *pg.* 1644, *pg.* 702
GAZIANI - Apparel - ENNIS, INC.; *pg.* 393, *pg.* 1727
GAZILLION BUBBLES - Toys - FUNRISE TOY CORP.; *pg.* 549, *pg.* 300
GAZOCAL - Calibration Bench - T.D. WILLIAMSON, INC.; *pg.* 1380, *pg.* 1490
GAZOMAT - Calibration Bench - T.D. WILLIAMSON, INC.; *pg.* 1380, *pg.* 1490
GB - Medical Equipment - INVACARE CORPORATION; *pg.* 1546, *pg.* 1451
GBC - Office Product - ACCO BRANDS CORPORATION; *pg.* 340, *pg.* 626
GBC JAM FREE - Shredder - ACCO BRANDS CORPORATION; *pg.* 340, *pg.* 626
GBC SHREDMASTER - Shredder - ACCO BRANDS CORPORATION; *pg.* 340, *pg.* 626
GBIC - Transceiver - FINISAR CORPORATION; *pg.* 639, *pg.* 285
GBP PLUS - Building Product - GUARDIAN INDUSTRIES CORP.; *pg.* 85, *pg.* 869
GBROR - Mass Flow Control - MKS INSTRUMENTS, INC.; *pg.* 1362, *pg.* 781
GBS - Defense System - RAYTHEON COMPANY; *pg.* 233, *pg.* 854
GBT-1700 - Module - GLOBALSTAR, INC.; *pg.* 401, *pg.* 743
GBX - Connector - AMPHENOL CORPORATION; *pg.* 616, *pg.* 381
GBX - Gigabit Ethernet Extender - VIAVI SOLUTIONS INC.; *pg.* 1435, *pg.* 148
GBX I-TRAC - Electronic Components - MOLEX INCORPORATED; *pg.* 655, *pg.* 628
GC-161 - Chemical Product - BIRKO CORPORATION; *pg.* 1149, *pg.* 332
GC SAKONITE - Pressed & Monolithic Refractory - RESCO PRODUCTS, INC.; *pg.* 107, *pg.* 1581
GC WIRELINE - Chart & Marking System - GRAPHIC CONTROLS LLC; *pg.* 401, *pg.* 1148
GCK-1410 - Satellite Phone Car Kit - GLOBALSTAR, INC.; *pg.* 401, *pg.* 743
GCP SERIES - Paint Spray Booth Additives - GE WATER & PROCESS TECHNOLOGIES; *pg.* 1339, *pg.* 1588
GCS - Logistics Software - ASPEN TECHNOLOGY, INC.; *pg.* 354, *pg.* 804
GCS PREMIER - Computer Applications - DELTEK, INC.; *pg.* 386, *pg.* 1784
GCSOLV - Chemical Product - SPECTRUM CHEMICALS & LABORATORY PRODUCTS, INC.; *pg.* 1181, *pg.* 94
GCSOLY - Chemical Product - SPECTRUM CHEMICALS & LABORATORY PRODUCTS, INC.; *pg.* 1181, *pg.* 94
GD2A - Gas Detector - BOSCH SECURITY SYSTEMS, INC.; *pg.* 626, *pg.* 1158
GDC - Networking Service - GENERAL DATACOMM INDUSTRIES, INC.; *pg.* 400, *pg.* 357
GDT - Software System - MENTOR GRAPHICS CORPORATION; *pg.* 432, *pg.* 1510
GDT-1700 - Data Kit - GLOBALSTAR, INC.; *pg.* 401, *pg.* 743
GDT CORE - Software System - MENTOR GRAPHICS CORPORATION; *pg.* 432, *pg.* 1510
GDT DESIGNER - Software System - MENTOR GRAPHICS CORPORATION; *pg.* 432, *pg.* 1510
GDT DEVELOPER - Software System - MENTOR GRAPHICS CORPORATION; *pg.* 432, *pg.* 1510
GDX - Programmable Component - LATTICE SEMICONDUCTOR CORPORATION; *pg.* 651, *pg.* 1498
GE CAFE - Home Appliances - GENERAL ELECTRIC COMPANY; *pg.* 1297, *pg.* 347
GE EDISON - Electric Lamps - GENERAL ELECTRIC COMPANY; *pg.* 1297, *pg.* 347
GE ENTRYSCAN - Electrical Product - GENERAL ELECTRIC COMPANY; *pg.* 1297, *pg.* 347
GE INNOVA - All Digital Cardiovascular Imaging System - GENERAL ELECTRIC COMPANY; *pg.* 1297, *pg.* 347
GE MONOGRAM - Major Appliances - GE CONSUMER & INDUSTRIAL; *pg.* 55, *pg.* 733
GE OP MAC - Fast Food - MCDONALD'S CORPORATION; *pg.* 1737, *pg.* 645
GE PROFILE - Home Appliance - GENERAL ELECTRIC COMPANY; *pg.* 1297, *pg.* 347
GE PROFILE ARCTICA - Refrigerators - GE CONSUMER & INDUSTRIAL; *pg.* 55, *pg.* 733
GE PROFILE CUSTOMSTYLE - Refrigerator - GE CONSUMER & INDUSTRIAL; *pg.* 55, *pg.* 733
GE PROFILE HARMONY - Washer & Dryer - GE CONSUMER & INDUSTRIAL; *pg.* 55, *pg.* 733
GE SMARTWATER - Water System - GE CONSUMER & INDUSTRIAL; *pg.* 55, *pg.* 733
GEAR - Drives, Bearings - BLOUNT INTERNATIONAL, INC.; *pg.* 1043, *pg.* 1501
GEAR FOR GOLF - Golf Clothing - GOLFSMITH INTERNATIONAL HOLDINGS, INC.; *pg.* 1835, *pg.* 1662
GEAR GUARD - Drive Line Product - MOC PRODUCTS COMPANY, INC.; *pg.* 332, *pg.* 174
GEAR GUY - Wireless Networking Product - NETGEAR, INC.; *pg.* 444, *pg.* 247
GEAR METERS - Meters - GRACO, INC.; *pg.* 1342, *pg.* 935
GEAREX - Pump - FLOWSERVE CORPORATION; *pg.* 82, *pg.* 1719
GEARLOGIC - Extended Warranty - PHILADELPHIA GEAR CORPORATION; *pg.* 1368, *pg.* 1544
GEARMATIC - Winches - PACCAR INC.; *pg.* 187, *pg.* 1816
GEAUGA LAKE - Amusement & Water Park - CEDAR FAIR, L.P.; *pg.* 537, *pg.* 1471
GEB-4800-IC - Electronic Component - EMCORE CORPORATION; *pg.* 636, *pg.* 39
GEBHARDT - Food Product - CONAGRA FOODS, INC.; *pg.* 826, *pg.* 1014
GECKO - Signal Processing System - GRASS VALLEY, INC.; *pg.* 641, *pg.* 164
GECO - Fuel Ratio Control - WOODWARD, INC.; *pg.* 122, *pg.* 329
GEDI - Web-Based Distributor Services - GRACO, INC.; *pg.* 1342, *pg.* 935
GEEK SQUAD - Computer Repair Service - BEST BUY CO., INC.; *pg.* 1761, *pg.* 954
GEEK.COM - Publication - ZIFF DAVIS, LLC; *pg.* 1703, *pg.* 1316
GEENEN - Medical Device - COOK GROUP, INC.; *pg.* 1518, *pg.* 674
GEERLINGS & WADE - Beverages - PHOENIX VINTNERS, LLC; *pg.* 1968, *pg.* 182
GEERPRES - Wringers & Buckets - GEERPRES INC.; *pg.* 1339, *pg.* 901
GEESINK - Truck Product - OSHKOSH CORPORATION; *pg.* 187, *pg.* 1885
GEFORCE - Software - NVIDIA CORPORATION; *pg.* 447, *pg.* 268
GEFORCE 6600 - Software - NVIDIA CORPORATION; *pg.* 447, *pg.* 268
GEFORCE 6600 GT - Software - NVIDIA CORPORATION; *pg.* 447, *pg.* 268
GEICO - Insurance - GEICO CORPORATION; *pg.* 1200, *pg.* 399
GEIGER - Furniture - HERMAN MILLER, INC.; *pg.* 926, *pg.* 913
GEKKEIKAN PLUM WINES & SAKE - Beverage - SIDNEY FRANK IMPORTING CO., INC.; *pg.* 1970, *pg.* 1184
GEL BLASTS - Ice Cream - WELLS ENTERPRISES, INC.; *pg.* 909, *pg.* 709
GEL BRONZE - Face & Body Product - THE BONNE BELL COMPANY; *pg.* 502, *pg.* 1480
GEL CADDY - Robotic Product - HAMILTON CO., INC.; *pg.* 1415, *pg.* 1031
GEL DOC - Software - BIO-RAD LABORATORIES, INC.; *pg.* 1504, *pg.* 101
GEL GRIPS - Hair Dryer - CONAIR CORPORATION; *pg.* 505, *pg.* 1055
GEL-PLAST - Robotic Product - HAMILTON CO., INC.; *pg.* 1415, *pg.* 1031
GEL PRO - Food Product - LEPRINO FOODS COMPANY; *pg.* 874, *pg.* 320
GEL-T - Polyurethane Foam - SPAN-AMERICA MEDICAL SYSTEMS, INC.; *pg.* 1595, *pg.* 1618
GELAIR - Software - BIO-RAD LABORATORIES, INC.; *pg.* 1504, *pg.* 101
GELATO - Graphic System - NVIDIA CORPORATION; *pg.* 447, *pg.* 268
GELCARIN - Food Ingredient - FMC CORPORATION; *pg.* 1163, *pg.* 1564
GELCLAIR - Operatory Products - SUNSTAR AMERICAS INC.; *pg.* 1599, *pg.* 591
GELCOLLAR - Visco-Elastic Gel - ACUSHNET COMPANY; *pg.* 1824, *pg.* 818
GELCORE - Lighting Product - EMCORE CORPORATION; *pg.* 636, *pg.* 39
GELDOC-IT - Imaging System - UVP, INC.; *pg.* 1434, *pg.* 298
GELEASE - Adhesive - LORD CORPORATION; *pg.* 1357, *pg.* 1360
GELEX - Turbidity Standard - HACH COMPANY; *pg.* 1415, *pg.* 334
GELFILM - Medicine - PFIZER INC.; *pg.* 1581, *pg.* 1278
GELFOAM - Medicine - PFIZER INC.; *pg.* 1581, *pg.* 1278
GELFOM - Antivibration Glove - ALIMED, INC.; *pg.* 1490, *pg.* 816
GELFUSION - Golf Shoe - ACUSHNET COMPANY; *pg.* 1824, *pg.* 818
GELLATIN - Modern Occasional Tables - BERNHARDT DESIGN; *pg.* 918, *pg.* 1381
GELLI-ROLL - Medical Product - CINCINNATI SUB-ZERO PRODUCTS, INC.; *pg.* 1070, *pg.* 1411
GELLY BAND - Educational Materials - SCHOLASTIC INC.; *pg.* 1683, *pg.* 1288
GEL'N - Moisturizer - LUSTER PRODUCTS INC.; *pg.* 515, *pg.* 501
GELNIQUE - Pharmaceutical Product - ALLERGAN; *pg.* 1490, *pg.* 1101
GELRIDE - Shock Absorbing Gel - ACUSHNET COMPANY; *pg.* 1824, *pg.* 818
GELSONS - Supermarkets - ARDEN GROUP, INC.; *pg.* 1014, *pg.* 68
GELSTAR - Food Ingredient - FMC CORPORATION; *pg.* 1163, *pg.* 1564
GELTEC - Software - BIO-RAD LABORATORIES, INC.; *pg.* 1504, *pg.* 101
GELTREX - Biomolecule Product - THERMO FISHER SCIENTIFIC INC.; *pg.* 1602, *pg.* 61
GELUCAPS - Pharmaceutical Product - ALERE INC.; *pg.* 1488, *pg.* 849
GELUSIL - Antacid - MCNEIL-PPC, INC.; *pg.* 1560, *pg.* 1533
GELVA - Multipolymer Emulsions - CYTEC INDUSTRIES, INC.; *pg.* 1155, *pg.* 1131
GELWORKS - Software - UVP, INC.; *pg.* 1434, *pg.* 298
GEM - Laser & Laser System - COHERENT, INC.; *pg.* 1406, *pg.* 265
GEM - Rug - COURISTAN INC.; *pg.* 921, *pg.* 1067
GEM - Electric Automobiles - FCA US LLC; *pg.* 170, *pg.* 868
GEM - Flushometer - SLOAN VALVE COMPANY; *pg.* 1062, *pg.* 613
GEM DR - Implantable defibrillators - MEDTRONIC, INC.; *pg.* 1564, *pg.* 939
GEM GRIP - Toothbrush - RANIR LLC; *pg.* 520, *pg.* 888
GEM HUNTER - Game - WMS INDUSTRIES INC.; *pg.* 593, *pg.* 666
GEM II DR - Implantable Defibrillators - MEDTRONIC, INC.;

pg. 1564, *pg.* 939
GEM III - Implantable Cardiac Defibrillator - MEDTRONIC, INC.; *pg.* 1564, *pg.* 939
GEMELLI - Food Product - ANNIE'S INC.; *pg.* 1760, *pg.* 45
GEMFIRE - Data Management Platform - GEMSTONE SYSTEMS, INC.; *pg.* 400, *pg.* 1492
GEMFIRE ENTERPRISE - Data Fabric solution - GEMSTONE SYSTEMS, INC.; *pg.* 400, *pg.* 1492
GEMFIRE REAL-TIME EVENTS - Event Processing Solution - GEMSTONE SYSTEMS, INC.; *pg.* 400, *pg.* 1492
GEMINI - Monitors - AKRON BRASS COMPANY; *pg.* 1311, *pg.* 1482
GEMINI - Laser System - AMERICAN MEDICAL SYSTEMS, INC.; *pg.* 1399, *pg.* 238
GEMINI - Detection Technology - AMERICAN SCIENCE AND ENGINEERING, INC.; *pg.* 1399, *pg.* 787
GEMINI - Furniture - ASHLEY FURNITURE INDUSTRIES, INC.; *pg.* 914, *pg.* 1852
GEMINI - Medical Device - BOSTON SCIENTIFIC CORPORATION; *pg.* 1508, *pg.* 831
GEMINI - Bio-Scrubber - CALGON CARBON CORPORATION; *pg.* 1151, *pg.* 1574
GEMINI - Footwear - EASTLAND SHOE CORPORATION; *pg.* 1808, *pg.* 750
GEMINI - Hose - THE GOODYEAR TIRE & RUBBER COMPANY; *pg.* 1883, *pg.* 1401
GEMINI - Video Game - INTERNATIONAL GAME TECHNOLOGY; *pg.* 957, *pg.* 1024
GEMINI - Medical Laser System - IRIDEX CORPORATION; *pg.* 648, *pg.* 160
GEMINI - Light Fixtures - JUNO LIGHTING, INC.; *pg.* 1300, *pg.* 606
GEMINI - Convertible Hand Truck - MAGLINE, INC.; *pg.* 1358, *pg.* 908
GEMINI - Blanket - MEDLINE INDUSTRIES, INC.; *pg.* 1562, *pg.* 635
GEMINI - Disc Publisher - MICROBOARDS TECHNOLOGY, LLC; *pg.* 434, *pg.* 920
GEMINI - Sealer - MTS MEDICATION TECHNOLOGIES, INC.; *pg.* 442, *pg.* 463
GEMINI - Control Panels, Keypads & Wireless Peripherals - NAPCO SECURITY SYSTEMS, INC.; *pg.* 658, *pg.* 1138
GEMINI - Fabric - NEMSCHOFF, INC.; *pg.* 936, *pg.* 1890
GEMINI - Seal Rock Bit - SMITH INTERNATIONAL, INC.; *pg.* 1377, *pg.* 1715
GEMINI - Range - WHIRLPOOL CORPORATION; *pg.* 62, *pg.* 872
GEMINI AUTOMOTIVE CARE - Automotive Care - THE GOODYEAR TIRE & RUBBER COMPANY; *pg.* 1883, *pg.* 1401
GEMINI EXPRESS - Vacuum Process Tool - BROOKS AUTOMATION, INC.; *pg.* 1320, *pg.* 813
GEMINI IN-MOLD DECORATING - Decorating Technology - SERIGRAPH, INC.; *pg.* 1686, *pg.* 1899
GEMMA - Intimate Apparel - V.F. CORPORATION; *pg.* 34, *pg.* 1376
GEMS - Golf Accessories - CALLAWAY GOLF COMPANY; *pg.* 1829, *pg.* 58
GEMS - Lab Science Material - CAROLINA BIOLOGICAL SUPPLY COMPANY; *pg.* 1513, *pg.* 1359
GEMS - Global Election Management Software - DIEBOLD, INCORPORATED; *pg.* 387, *pg.* 1407
GEMS, GEMS, GEMS - Game - WMS INDUSTRIES INC.; *pg.* 593, *pg.* 666
GEMS SENSORS - Flow & Pressure Sensor - DANAHER CORPORATION; *pg.* 1044, *pg.* 397
GEMS WILD-TILES - Video Game - INTERNATIONAL GAME TECHNOLOGY; *pg.* 957, *pg.* 1024
GEMSTAR - Medical Device - HOSPIRA, INC.; *pg.* 1542, *pg.* 623
GEMSTAR - Digital Directory - ROVI CORPORATION; *pg.* 463, *pg.* 269
GEMSTONE - Thermoset Polyester Microwave Cook & Bakeware - NORTHLAND ALUMINUM PRODUCTS INC.; *pg.* 1129, *pg.* 941
GEMSTONE 7S - Video Game - INTERNATIONAL GAME TECHNOLOGY; *pg.* 957, *pg.* 1024
GEMSTONE FACETS - Object Database - GEMSTONE SYSTEMS, INC.; *pg.* 400, *pg.* 1492
GEMSTONE/S - Object Server - GEMSTONE SYSTEMS, INC.; *pg.* 400, *pg.* 1492
GEMTECH - Cast Aluminum Wheels - MAXION WHEELS; *pg.* 212, *pg.* 903
GEMZAR - Pharmaceutical Product - ELI LILLY AND COMPANY; *pg.* 1527, *pg.* 684
GEN - Catalyst - BASF CATALYSTS LLC; *pg.* 1148, *pg.* 1074
GEN-5 - Knife - BUCK KNIVES, INC.; *pg.* 1828, *pg.* 550
GEN-GUARD - Paper & Nonwoven Material - FIBERMARK INC.; *pg.* 1457, *pg.* 1764
GEN-O - Organic Service - COOPERATIVE REGIONS OF ORGANIC PRODUCER POOLS; *pg.* 850, *pg.* 1864
GEN-PAK - Column - WATERS CORPORATION; *pg.* 1436, *pg.* 834
GEN2 - Elevator Product - OTIS ELEVATOR COMPANY; *pg.* 102, *pg.* 349
GEN3 - Radio Frequency - CHECKPOINT SYSTEMS, INC.; *pg.* 628, *pg.* 1559
GENA - Bodycare & Skincare - AMERICAN INTERNATIONAL INDUSTRIES COMPANY; *pg.* 498, *pg.* 126
GENAMID - Epoxy Coreactants - HENKEL CORPORATION; *pg.* 1165, *pg.* 1535
GENBLUE - Bluetooth Module - SEMTECH CORPORATION GENNUM PRODUCTS; *pg.* 671, *pg.* 1919
GENCAL - Radio Frequency Instrumentation - ADVANCED ENERGY INDUSTRIES, INC.; *pg.* 613, *pg.* 328
GENCAL - Chemical Product - OMNOVA SOLUTIONS INC; *pg.* 1176, *pg.* 1453
GENCEAL - Chemical Product - OMNOVA SOLUTIONS INC; *pg.* 1176, *pg.* 1453
GENCRYL - Chemical Product - OMNOVA SOLUTIONS INC; *pg.* 1176, *pg.* 1453
GENCRYL PT - Carpet Chemicals - OMNOVA SOLUTIONS INC; *pg.* 1176, *pg.* 1453
GENDEX - Dental Product - DANAHER CORPORATION; *pg.* 1044, *pg.* 397
GENE CYCLER - Thermal Cycler - BIO-RAD LABORATORIES, INC.; *pg.* 1504, *pg.* 101
GENE-LITE - Software - BIO-RAD LABORATORIES, INC.; *pg.* 1504, *pg.* 101
GENE POOL - Molecular Biology Product - THERMO FISHER SCIENTIFIC INC.; *pg.* 1602, *pg.* 61
GENE PULSER - Software - BIO-RAD LABORATORIES, INC.; *pg.* 1504, *pg.* 101
GENE PULSER MXCELL - Software - BIO-RAD LABORATORIES, INC.; *pg.* 1504, *pg.* 101
GENE PULSER XCELL - Software - BIO-RAD LABORATORIES, INC.; *pg.* 1504, *pg.* 101
GENE-TRAK - Food Safety Product - NEOGEN CORPORATION; *pg.* 883, *pg.* 896
GENEALOGICAL COMPUTING MAGAZINE - Magazine - ANCESTRY.COM LLC; *pg.* 1228, *pg.* 1754
GENEALOGY - Software - ASPEN TECHNOLOGY, INC.; *pg.* 354, *pg.* 804
GENEBEAM - Fluorescent Labeling System - ENZO BIOCHEM INC.; *pg.* 1529, *pg.* 1228
GENECATCHER - Molecular Biology Product - THERMO FISHER SCIENTIFIC INC.; *pg.* 1602, *pg.* 61
GENECHIP - Array - AFFYMETRIX, INC.; *pg.* 1487, *pg.* 263
GENECHIP-COMPATIBLE - Software - AFFYMETRIX, INC.; *pg.* 1487, *pg.* 263
GENECHIP CUSTOMSEQ - Resequencing Array - AFFYMETRIX, INC.; *pg.* 1487, *pg.* 263
GENECOMB - Software - BIO-RAD LABORATORIES, INC.; *pg.* 1504, *pg.* 101
GENED - Software - EDUPOINT EDUCATIONAL SYSTEMS, LLC; *pg.* 390, *pg.* 109
GENEDIA - Software - BIO-RAD LABORATORIES, INC.; *pg.* 1504, *pg.* 101
GENEDIA MIXT - Software - BIO-RAD LABORATORIES, INC.; *pg.* 1504, *pg.* 101
GENEGAZER - Software - BIO-RAD LABORATORIES, INC.; *pg.* 1504, *pg.* 101
GENEHOGS - Molecular Biology Product - THERMO FISHER SCIENTIFIC INC.; *pg.* 1602, *pg.* 61
GENEJUMPER - Molecular Biology Product - THERMO FISHER SCIENTIFIC INC.; *pg.* 1602, *pg.* 61
GENELAVIA - Software - BIO-RAD LABORATORIES, INC.; *pg.* 1504, *pg.* 101
GENELINK - Genomic Testing Services - GENELINK, INC.; *pg.* 1533, *pg.* 438
GENELINK HEALTHY AGING ASSESSMENT - Educational Publications - GENELINK, INC.; *pg.* 1533, *pg.* 438
GENELINK NUTRAGENETIC PROFILE - Genomic Testing Services - GENELINK, INC.; *pg.* 1533, *pg.* 438
GENELUTE - RNA Kit - SIGMA-ALDRICH CORPORATION; *pg.* 1181, *pg.* 1003
GENEPATH - Clinical Diagnostic Product - BIO-RAD LABORATORIES, INC.; *pg.* 1504, *pg.* 101
GENEPIX PRO - Software - MOLECULAR DEVICES CORPORATION; *pg.* 1568, *pg.* 287
GENEQUENCE - Food Safety Product - NEOGEN CORPORATION; *pg.* 883, *pg.* 896
GENERAC - Controls Rebuilding Service - FLIGHT SYSTEMS, INC.; *pg.* 1337, *pg.* 1548
GENERACER - Molecular Biology Product - THERMO FISHER SCIENTIFIC INC.; *pg.* 1602, *pg.* 61
GENERAL AIRE - Air Filter - GENERAL FILTERS, INC.; *pg.* 1072, *pg.* 903
GENERAL BATTERY - Motive Power Batteries - ENERSYS INC.; *pg.* 1334, *pg.* 1584
GENERAL COACH - Recreation Vehicle - THOR INDUSTRIES, INC.; *pg.* 1711, *pg.* 1456
GENERAL CONNECTOR - Connectors - COOPER INTERCONNECT; *pg.* 630, *pg.* 1118
GENERAL CONTROLS - Combustion Products - ASCO VALVE CANADA; *pg.* 619, *pg.* 1919
GENERAL DYNAMICS - Aviation Services - GENERAL DYNAMICS CORPORATION; *pg.* 228, *pg.* 1781
GENERAL EMPLOYMENT ENTERPRISES - Staffing Firm - GENERAL EMPLOYMENT ENTERPRISES, INC.; *pg.* 400, *pg.* 636
GENERAL FORMULA - Dry Cleaning & Laundry Product - ADCO, INC.; *pg.* 325, *pg.* 482
GENERAL HONE - Abrasive - SUNNEN PRODUCTS COMPANY; *pg.* 1379, *pg.* 1004
GENERAL OPTICS - Precision Motion System - GSI GROUP INC.; *pg.* 1415, *pg.* 784
GENERAL REVENUE CORP. - Magazine - SLM CORPORATION; *pg.* 804, *pg.* 388
GENERAL SCANNING - Precision Motion System - GSI GROUP INC.; *pg.* 1415, *pg.* 784
GENERALS - Cigarettes - PHILIP MORRIS USA INC.; *pg.* 1894, *pg.* 1803
GENERATION - Graphic Film - FLEXCON CORPORATION; *pg.* 1457, *pg.* 844
GENERATION - Musical Instrument - PEAVEY ELECTRONICS CORPORATION; *pg.* 662, *pg.* 970
GENERATION 2000 - Sensitive Film & Adhesive - FLEXCON CORPORATION; *pg.* 1457, *pg.* 844
GENERATION 3 - Bearing - THE TIMKEN COMPANY; *pg.* 218, *pg.* 1408
GENERATION 3000 - Sensitive Film & Adhesive - FLEXCON CORPORATION; *pg.* 1457, *pg.* 844
GENERATION 9-ELITE - Digital TV System - CSR; *pg.* 280, *pg.* 284
GENERATION EXP - Guitar - PEAVEY ELECTRONICS CORPORATION; *pg.* 662, *pg.* 970
GENERATION FLEX - Soft Toe - WEINBRENNER SHOE COMPANY, INC.; *pg.* 1822, *pg.* 1871
GENERATION JETS - Kids Clinic - NEW YORK JETS FOOTBALL CLUB, INC.; *pg.* 570, *pg.* 1067
GENERATION PORTER - Beverage - SPRECHER BREWING COMPANY; *pg.* 265, *pg.* 1858
GENERATION TECHNOLOGIES, INC. - Contract Services Firm - GENERAL EMPLOYMENT ENTERPRISES, INC.; *pg.* 400, *pg.* 636
GENERATIONS - Vinyl Siding & Vinyl Windows - OWENS CORNING; *pg.* 102, *pg.* 1476
GENERESSENCE - Flavor Analysis Technology - INTERNATIONAL FLAVORS & FRAGRANCES INC.; *pg.* 512, *pg.* 1244
GENERIC ARRAY LOGIC - Programmable Component - LATTICE SEMICONDUCTOR CORPORATION; *pg.* 651, *pg.* 1498
GENERICS FIRST - Health & Wellness Product - EXPRESS SCRIPTS; *pg.* 1530, *pg.* 1070
GENEROL - Phytosterols - HENKEL CORPORATION; *pg.* 1165, *pg.* 1535
GENES IN A BOTTLE - Software - BIO-RAD LABORATORIES, INC.; *pg.* 1504, *pg.* 101
GENESCO - Headwear & Shoes - GENESCO INC.; *pg.* 1809, *pg.* 1650
GENESEA - Software - EDUPOINT EDUCATIONAL SYSTEMS, LLC; *pg.* 390, *pg.* 109
GENESEQ - Healthcare Product - MONOGRAM BIOSCIENCES, INC.; *pg.* 1569, *pg.* 280
GENESHOT - Software - BIO-RAD LABORATORIES, INC.; *pg.* 1504, *pg.* 101
GENESIS - Furniture - BUSH INDUSTRIES INC.; *pg.* 919, *pg.* 1170
GENESIS - Surgical Instrumentation - CARDINAL HEALTH, INC.; *pg.* 1512, *pg.* 1448
GENESIS - Truck - CLARK MATERIAL HANDLING COMPANY; *pg.* 1323, *pg.* 729
GENESIS - Software - EDUPOINT EDUCATIONAL

First page reference indicates Business Class Edition
Second page reference indicates Geographic Edition

SYSTEMS, LLC; *pg.* 390, *pg.* 109
GENESIS - Reserve Power Batteries - ENERSYS INC.; *pg.* 1334, *pg.* 1584
GENESIS - Bed Covers - LUND INTERNATIONAL, INC.; *pg.* 211, *pg.* 526
GENESIS - Software - MKS INSTRUMENTS, INC.; *pg.* 1362, *pg.* 781
GENESIS - Blast Wheel Maintenance - PANGBORN CORPORATION; *pg.* 1367, *pg.* 532
GENESIS - Bag - SAMSONITE CORPORATION; *pg.* 11, *pg.* 830
GENESIS - Safety Eyewear - UVEX SAFETY; *pg.* 1433, *pg.* 1608
GENESIS - Gas Grill - WEBER-STEPHEN PRODUCTS LLC; *pg.* 62, *pg.* 650
GENESOLV - Solvent - HONEYWELL INTERNATIONAL INC.; *pg.* 407, *pg.* 1088
GENESOLV - Chemical Cleaner Product - TECH SPRAY, L.P.; *pg.* 1183, *pg.* 1659
GENESTORM - Molecular Biology Product - THERMO FISHER SCIENTIFIC INC.; *pg.* 1602, *pg.* 61
GENESYS - Track - COILCRAFT, INC.; *pg.* 1324, *pg.* 562
GENESYS - Multiplexers - VICON INDUSTRIES, INC.; *pg.* 685, *pg.* 1166
GENETAILOR - Molecular Biology Product - THERMO FISHER SCIENTIFIC INC.; *pg.* 1602, *pg.* 61
GENETIC SYSTEMS - Software - BIO-RAD LABORATORIES, INC.; *pg.* 1504, *pg.* 101
GENETICIN - Cell Culture Product - THERMO FISHER SCIENTIFIC INC.; *pg.* 1602, *pg.* 61
GENETITAN - Array Plate System - AFFYMETRIX, INC.; *pg.* 1487, *pg.* 263
GENETOWN - Pharmaceutical Product - BIOSPACE, INC.; *pg.* 1231, *pg.* 1082
GENETRAPPER - Molecular Biology Product - THERMO FISHER SCIENTIFIC INC.; *pg.* 1602, *pg.* 61
GENETRON - Fluorocarbon - HONEYWELL INTERNATIONAL INC.; *pg.* 407, *pg.* 1088
GENEVA - Software - ADVENT SOFTWARE, INC.; *pg.* 345, *pg.* 211
GENEVA - Computer Font - APPLE INC.; *pg.* 350, *pg.* 73
GENEVA - Furniture - FLEXSTEEL INDUSTRIES, INC.; *pg.* 925, *pg.* 707
GENEVA - Watch - GENEVA WATCH GROUP; *pg.* 5, *pg.* 1174
GENEVA - Cookies - PEPPERIDGE FARM, INC.; *pg.* 888, *pg.* 363
GENEVA INTEGRATION BROKER - Transport-Independent Message Broker - CICERO INC.; *pg.* 372, *pg.* 1360
GENEVA PRESS - Religious Books - PRESBYTERIAN PUBLISHING CORPORATION; *pg.* 1678, *pg.* 737
GENEVIVA - Footwear - STEVEN MADDEN, LTD.; *pg.* 1819, *pg.* 1176
GENEXPERT - Genetic Testing System - CEPHEID; *pg.* 1514, *pg.* 284
GENFLEX - Array - AFFYMETRIX, INC.; *pg.* 1487, *pg.* 263
GENFLEX - Roofing System - OMNOVA SOLUTIONS INC; *pg.* 1176, *pg.* 1453
GENFLO - Chemical Product - OMNOVA SOLUTIONS INC; *pg.* 1176, *pg.* 1453
GENFORMS - Labels - ENNIS, INC.; *pg.* 393, *pg.* 1727
GENGAUGE - Software - GE ENERGY; *pg.* 1338, *pg.* 506
GENGLAZE - Chemical Product - OMNOVA SOLUTIONS INC; *pg.* 1176, *pg.* 1453
GENGRAF - Prophylaxis of Organ Rejection - ABBOTT LABORATORIES; *pg.* 1484, *pg.* 551
GENICON - Molecular Biology Product - THERMO FISHER SCIENTIFIC INC.; *pg.* 1602, *pg.* 61
GENIDOCS - Software - OMTOOL, LTD.; *pg.* 449, *pg.* 782
GENIE - Software - BIO-RAD LABORATORIES, INC.; *pg.* 1504, *pg.* 101
GENIE - Dental Product - DENTSPLY INTERNATIONAL INC.; *pg.* 1522, *pg.* 1596
GENIE - Gate Opener & Wet/Dry Shop Vacuum - THE GENIE COMPANY; *pg.* 55, *pg.* 1403
GENIE - Telephone Service - IDT CORPORATION; *pg.* 643, *pg.* 1096
GENIE - Software System - MENTOR GRAPHICS CORPORATION; *pg.* 432, *pg.* 1510
GENIE - Door Operator Systems - OVERHEAD DOOR CORPORATION; *pg.* 102, *pg.* 1725
GENIE - Aerial Device - TEREX CORPORATION; *pg.* 1381, *pg.* 384
GENIE - Automatic Reversible Sheeter - UNIVEX CORPORATION; *pg.* 1386, *pg.* 1039
GENIE & THE SULTAN'S JEWELS - Game - WMS INDUSTRIES INC.; *pg.* 593, *pg.* 666
GENIE II - Major Surgery Light - MEDLINE INDUSTRIES, INC.; *pg.* 1562, *pg.* 635
GENIFAX - Fax System - OMTOOL, LTD.; *pg.* 449, *pg.* 782
GENIOUS - Footwear - STEVEN MADDEN, LTD.; *pg.* 1819, *pg.* 1176
GENISYS - Programmable Controller - ANSALDO STS; *pg.* 618, *pg.* 1573
GENIUS BAR - Service & Support Program - APPLE INC.; *pg.* 350, *pg.* 73
THE GENIUS IS IN THE DETAILS - Photographic Film - EASTMAN KODAK COMPANY; *pg.* 1408, *pg.* 1333
GENLECO - Leather Pastes And Non Resinated Pigments - HENKEL CORPORATION; *pg.* 1165, *pg.* 1535
GENLINK - Software - GENERAC POWER SYSTEMS INC.; *pg.* 1340, *pg.* 1898
GENMAGRAIN - Hardwood Flooring - NYDREE FLOORING; *pg.* 939, *pg.* 1782
GENNET M - Software - GULF PUBLISHING COMPANY; *pg.* 1646, *pg.* 1707
GENOA - Sausage - KAYEM FOODS, INC.; *pg.* 867, *pg.* 814
GENOGRIP - Adapter - GENOVA PRODUCTS, INC.; *pg.* 83, *pg.* 875
GENOME5000 - Biopharmaceutical Product - LEXICON PHARMACEUTICALS, INC.; *pg.* 1555, *pg.* 1747
GENOMELAB - Testing Instrument System - BECKMAN COULTER, INC.; *pg.* 1402, *pg.* 48
GENOMICS & PROTEOMICS - Trade Magazine - ADVANTAGE BUSINESS MEDIA; *pg.* 1613, *pg.* 1116
GENON - Wallcovering - OMNOVA SOLUTIONS INC; *pg.* 1176, *pg.* 1453
GENOSURE - Medical Research - LABORATORY CORPORATION OF AMERICA HOLDINGS; *pg.* 1554, *pg.* 1359
GENOTROPIN - Human Growth Hormone - PFIZER INC.; *pg.* 1581, *pg.* 1278
GENOTROPIN MIXER - Medicine - PFIZER INC.; *pg.* 1581, *pg.* 1278
GENOTYPING CONSOLE - Software - AFFYMETRIX, INC.; *pg.* 1487, *pg.* 263
GENOVA - Lighting Product - QUOIZEL INC.; *pg.* 1304, *pg.* 1616
GENOX - Polymer Product - CHEMTURA CORPORATION; *pg.* 1152, *pg.* 355
GENPAD - Software - VISTEON CORPORATION; *pg.* 221, *pg.* 912
GENPOWR - Industrial Cables - GENERAL CABLE CORPORATION; *pg.* 83, *pg.* 729
GENPRO - Protective Apparel - ALPHA PRO TECH, LTD.; *pg.* 1492, *pg.* 1922
GEN*S - Instrument & Computer Workstation - BECKMAN COULTER, INC.; *pg.* 1402, *pg.* 48
GENSCREEN - Software - BIO-RAD LABORATORIES, INC.; *pg.* 1504, *pg.* 101
GENSONA - Genetic Tests - INTERLEUKIN GENETICS, INC.; *pg.* 1546, *pg.* 851
GENSPEED - Data Communication Product - GENERAL CABLE CORPORATION; *pg.* 83, *pg.* 729
GENSTART - Battery-Free Power Product - ACTIVE POWER, INC.; *pg.* 1310, *pg.* 1660
GENT - Knife - BUCK KNIVES, INC.; *pg.* 1828, *pg.* 550
GENTAC - Chemical Product - OMNOVA SOLUTIONS INC; *pg.* 1176, *pg.* 1453
GENTAK - Ophthalmic Pharmaceutical Product - AKORN, INC.; *pg.* 1488, *pg.* 622
GENTEK - Building Product - ASSOCIATED MATERIALS LLC; *pg.* 69, *pg.* 1445
GENTEX - Automotive Components - GENTEX CORPORATION; *pg.* 206, *pg.* 913
GENTLE CARESS - Carpet - BEAULIEU GROUP, LLC; *pg.* 917, *pg.* 529
GENTLE DRAW - Lancing Device - NIPRO DIAGNOSTICS, INC.; *pg.* 1573, *pg.* 426
GENTLE-FLO - Suction Catheter - MEDTRONIC; *pg.* 1563, *pg.* 183
GENTLE GIANT - Cutting System - EASTMAN MACHINE COMPANY; *pg.* 1331, *pg.* 1148
GENTLE PAPER - Tape - 3M COMPANY; *pg.* 1142, *pg.* 956
GENTLE RAIN - Spray Wands - MELNOR, INC.; *pg.* 1055, *pg.* 1811
GENTLE SENSE - Lip Care Product - BLISTEX, INC.; *pg.* 502, *pg.* 644
GENTLE SOFT - Fabric Softener - HENKEL CONSUMER GOODS; *pg.* 511, *pg.* 22
GENTLE TOUCH - Soap - KAO BRANDS CO. INC.; *pg.* 513, *pg.* 1415
GENTLELASE - Aesthetic Treatment Lasers - CANDELA CORPORATION; *pg.* 1404, *pg.* 855
GENTLEMAN JACK - Tennessee Whiskey - BROWN-FORMAN CORPORATION; *pg.* 1958, *pg.* 732
GENTLEMAN JACK - Whiskey - JACK DANIEL'S DISTILLERY; *pg.* 1964, *pg.* 1640
GENTLEMAX - Multi-Wavelength Aesthetic Treatment Workstation - CANDELA CORPORATION; *pg.* 1404, *pg.* 855
GENTLEMEN'S QUARTERLY - Magazine - CONDE NAST PUBLICATIONS, INC.; *pg.* 1629, *pg.* 1217
GENTLETOUCH - Magnetic Catheter - STEREOTAXIS, INC.; *pg.* 1597, *pg.* 1004
GENTLEYAG - Aesthetic Treatment Lasers - CANDELA CORPORATION; *pg.* 1404, *pg.* 855
GENTNER - Software - CLEARONE COMMUNICATIONS, INC.; *pg.* 629, *pg.* 1756
GENTRY - Lighting Product - QUOIZEL INC.; *pg.* 1304, *pg.* 1616
GENTRY - Office Furniture - STEELCASE INC.; *pg.* 475, *pg.* 889
GENUINE BEAM - Whiskey - JIM BEAM BRANDS CO.; *pg.* 1965, *pg.* 601
GENUINE CALIFORNIA PIZZA - Slogan - STRAW HAT COOPERATIVE CORPORATION; *pg.* 1751, *pg.* 260
GENUINE FIESTA ACCESSORIES - Accessories for Chinaware - THE HOMER LAUGHLIN CHINA COMPANY; *pg.* 1125, *pg.* 1850
GENUINE INDIA STAG BONE - Knife - BEAR & SON CUTLERY, INC.; *pg.* 1827, *pg.* 7
GENUINE INGENUITY - Tagline - BRUNSWICK CORPORATION; *pg.* 1828, *pg.* 623
GENUINE KIDS - Children's Clothing - CARTER'S, INC.; *pg.* 21, *pg.* 491
GENUINE LEATHER CARRIERS - Jewelry Organizer - CONNOISSEURS PRODUCTS CORPORATION; *pg.* 329, *pg.* 861
GENUINE PRESSBOARD - Paper & Nonwoven Material - FIBERMARK INC.; *pg.* 1457, *pg.* 1764
GENUWOOD - Hardwood Flooring Product - NYDREE FLOORING; *pg.* 939, *pg.* 1782
GENUWOOD II - Flooring - NYDREE FLOORING; *pg.* 939, *pg.* 1782
GENVAKODE II - Track Circuit/Communications Systems - ALSTOM SIGNALING, INC.; *pg.* 1312, *pg.* 1350
GENWARE - Software System - MENTOR GRAPHICS CORPORATION; *pg.* 432, *pg.* 1510
GENWORTH FINANCIAL - Financial Services - GENWORTH FINANCIAL, INC.; *pg.* 761, *pg.* 1802
GENWRAP - Cable - GENERAL CABLE CORPORATION; *pg.* 83, *pg.* 729
GENZ STIX - Ice Fishing Equipment - SWORDFISH FINANCIAL, INC.; *pg.* 1430, *pg.* 1737
GENZYME-OPCAB ELITE DEEP STERNAL BLADES - Medical Product - GENZYME CORPORATION; *pg.* 1534, *pg.* 808
GENZYME-OPCAB ELITE SUTURE STOPS - Pharmaceutical Product - GENZYME CORPORATION; *pg.* 1534, *pg.* 808
GEO - Balloon - CONTINENTAL AMERICAN CORP.; *pg.* 1880, *pg.* 723
GEO 2000 - Pig Tracking - T.D. WILLIAMSON, INC.; *pg.* 1380, *pg.* 1490
GEO BLOSSOM - Balloon - CONTINENTAL AMERICAN CORP.; *pg.* 1880, *pg.* 723
GEO-BREAK - Software - NIELSEN AUDIO; *pg.* 446, *pg.* 768
GEO DONUT - Balloon - CONTINENTAL AMERICAN CORP.; *pg.* 1880, *pg.* 723
GEO-MATT - Polyurethane Foam - SPAN-AMERICA MEDICAL SYSTEMS, INC.; *pg.* 1595, *pg.* 1618
GEO-MATTRESS - Polyurethane Foam - SPAN-AMERICA MEDICAL SYSTEMS, INC.; *pg.* 1595, *pg.* 1618
GEO TREK - Lunch Sack - THERMOS L.L.C.; *pg.* 61, *pg.* 660
GEO-WAVE - Polyurethane Foam - SPAN-AMERICA MEDICAL SYSTEMS, INC.; *pg.* 1595, *pg.* 1618
GEO WEB - Software - BENTLEY SYSTEMS, INC.; *pg.* 361, *pg.* 1531
GEOBEACON - Navigation Aid - TRIMBLE NAVIGATION LIMITED; *pg.* 1384, *pg.* 288
GEOCILLIN - Medicine - PFIZER INC.; *pg.* 1581, *pg.* 1278
GEOCODER - Software - MELISSA DATA CORP.; *pg.* 432, *pg.* 188
GEOCOIR - Fabric Product - BELTON INDUSTRIES, INC.;

pg. 691, *pg.* 1612
GEODATABASE TOOLSET - Software - ENVIRONMENTAL SYSTEMS RESEARCH INSTITUTE INC.; *pg.* 393, *pg.* 188
GEODE - Complex Inorganic Color Pigments - FERRO CORPORATION; *pg.* 1162, *pg.* 1462
GEODE ORIGAMI - Mobile Communicator - ADVANCED MICRO DEVICES, INC.; *pg.* 613, *pg.* 282
GEODELINK - Chipset - ADVANCED MICRO DEVICES, INC.; *pg.* 613, *pg.* 282
GEODETIC SYSTEM SURVEYOR - Receiver - TRIMBLE NAVIGATION LIMITED; *pg.* 1384, *pg.* 288
GEODIAMOND - Drilling Product - SMITH INTERNATIONAL, INC.; *pg.* 1377, *pg.* 1715
GEODIMETER - Navigation Aid - TRIMBLE NAVIGATION LIMITED; *pg.* 1384, *pg.* 288
GEODON - Schizophrenia Medication - PFIZER INC.; *pg.* 1581, *pg.* 1278
GEOEXPLORER - Receiver - TRIMBLE NAVIGATION LIMITED; *pg.* 1384, *pg.* 288
GEOFRAME - Geo Science Solution - SCHLUMBERGER LIMITED; *pg.* 801, *pg.* 1714
GEOGENIUS - Navigation Aid - TRIMBLE NAVIGATION LIMITED; *pg.* 1384, *pg.* 288
GEOGRAPHY SEARCH - Educational Materials - SCHOLASTIC INC.; *pg.* 1683, *pg.* 1288
GEOGUARD - Construction Material - CRANE PLASTICS HOLDING COMPANY; *pg.* 1881, *pg.* 1439
GEOJUTE - Fabric Product - BELTON INDUSTRIES, INC.; *pg.* 691, *pg.* 1612
GEOLASPRO - UV Optical System - COHERENT, INC.; *pg.* 1406, *pg.* 265
GEOLLECT - Software - SRA INTERNATIONAL, INC.; *pg.* 473, *pg.* 1780
GEOLOGY - Fabric - NEMSCHOFF, INC.; *pg.* 936, *pg.* 1890
GEOM GENIE - Software System - MENTOR GRAPHICS CORPORATION; *pg.* 432, *pg.* 1510
GEOMACAO - Software - BENTLEY SYSTEMS, INC.; *pg.* 361, *pg.* 1531
GEOMAN - Press - MANROLAND INC.; *pg.* 430, *pg.* 669
GEOMATE - Foam - THE DOW CHEMICAL COMPANY; *pg.* 1157, *pg.* 898
GEOMELT - De-Icer - GRAIN PROCESSING CORPORATION; *pg.* 859, *pg.* 709
GEOMETRI - Fabric - NEMSCHOFF, INC.; *pg.* 936, *pg.* 1890
GEOMETRIC PIGMENT - Powder Coating - SILBERLINE MANUFACTURING CO., INC.; *pg.* 110, *pg.* 1588
GEOMETRIX - Ceiling Panel - USG CORPORATION; *pg.* 118, *pg.* 594
GEOMETRY - Carpet - INTERFACE, INC.; *pg.* 695, *pg.* 512
GEON 120 - Vinyl Compound - POLYONE CORPORATION; *pg.* 1177, *pg.* 1404
GEON 130 - Resin - POLYONE CORPORATION; *pg.* 1177, *pg.* 1404
GEON 140 - Resin - POLYONE CORPORATION; *pg.* 1177, *pg.* 1404
GEON 170 - Resin - POLYONE CORPORATION; *pg.* 1177, *pg.* 1404
GEON 180 - Resin - POLYONE CORPORATION; *pg.* 1177, *pg.* 1404
GEON 210 - Resin - POLYONE CORPORATION; *pg.* 1177, *pg.* 1404
GEON CPVC - Resin - POLYONE CORPORATION; *pg.* 1177, *pg.* 1404
GEON DURACAP - Vinyl Capstock Compounds - POLYONE CORPORATION; *pg.* 1177, *pg.* 1404
GEON FIBERLOC - Vinyl Glass Composites - POLYONE CORPORATION; *pg.* 1177, *pg.* 1404
GEON HC - Vinyl Healthcare Compounds - POLYONE CORPORATION; *pg.* 1177, *pg.* 1404
GEON HTX - Vinyl Rigid Compounds - POLYONE CORPORATION; *pg.* 1177, *pg.* 1404
GEON HTX ULTRA - Higher Heat Vinyl Alloys - POLYONE CORPORATION; *pg.* 1177, *pg.* 1404
GEON SPECIALTY SUSPENSION - Vinyl Wire & Cable Compounds - POLYONE CORPORATION; *pg.* 1177, *pg.* 1404
GEON VINYL CELLULAR - Rigid Extrusion Compounds - POLYONE CORPORATION; *pg.* 1177, *pg.* 1404
GEON VINYL DRY BLEND - Wire & Cable Compounds - POLYONE CORPORATION; *pg.* 1177, *pg.* 1404
GEON VINYL FITTINGS - Vinyl Compounds - POLYONE CORPORATION; *pg.* 1177, *pg.* 1404
GEON VINYL FLEXIBLE - Vinyl Compounds - POLYONE CORPORATION; *pg.* 1177, *pg.* 1404
GEON VINYL PACKAGING - Vinyl Compounds - POLYONE CORPORATION; *pg.* 1177, *pg.* 1404
GEON VINYL RIGID EXTRUSION - Vinyl Compounds - POLYONE CORPORATION; *pg.* 1177, *pg.* 1404
GEON VINYL RIGID MOLDING - Vinyl Compounds - POLYONE CORPORATION; *pg.* 1177, *pg.* 1404
GEON VINYL WIRE & CABLE - Vinyl Compounds - POLYONE CORPORATION; *pg.* 1177, *pg.* 1404
GEOPAK - Software - BENTLEY SYSTEMS, INC.; *pg.* 361, *pg.* 1531
GEOPLAT - 3D Software - SCHLUMBERGER LIMITED; *pg.* 801, *pg.* 1714
GEORGE - Guest Chairs - BERNHARDT DESIGN; *pg.* 918, *pg.* 1381
GEORGE - Merchandise - WAL-MART STORES, INC.; *pg.* 1790, *pg.* 29
GEORGE BURNS VINTAGE - Premium Cigars - ALTADIS USA, INC.; *pg.* 1893, *pg.* 423
GEORGE KILLIAN'S IRISH RED - Beverages - MOLSON COORS BREWING COMPANY; *pg.* 256, *pg.* 321
GEORGE LUCAS' SUPER LIVE ADVERNTURE - Family Entertainment - FELD ENTERTAINMENT, INC.; *pg.* 547, *pg.* 458
GEORGE WRIGHT - Organ - ALLEN ORGAN COMPANY; *pg.* 527, *pg.* 1549
GEORGES - Furniture - J. ROBERT SCOTT INC.; *pg.* 930, *pg.* 105
GEORGES BRASS - Bath Product - KOHLER CO.; *pg.* 91, *pg.* 1862
GEORGETOWN - Cabinetry - MASTERBRAND CABINETS, INC.; *pg.* 96, *pg.* 692
GEORGETOWN UNIVERSITY HOSPITAL - Hospital - MEDSTAR HEALTH INC.; *pg.* 1563, *pg.* 767
GEORGIA - Soft Drink - THE COCA-COLA COMPANY; *pg.* 240, *pg.* 493
GEORGIA - Footwear - PHOENIX FOOTWEAR GROUP, INC.; *pg.* 1815, *pg.* 60
GEORGIA BOOT - Footwear - ROCKY BRANDS, INC.; *pg.* 1818, *pg.* 1466
GEORGIA CLUB - Beverages - THE COCA-COLA COMPANY; *pg.* 240, *pg.* 493
GEORGIA COFFEE - Canned Iced Coffee - THE COCA-COLA COMPANY; *pg.* 240, *pg.* 493
GEORGIA GOLD - Beverages - THE COCA-COLA COMPANY; *pg.* 240, *pg.* 493
GEORGIA GRANDE - Beverages - THE COCA-COLA COMPANY; *pg.* 240, *pg.* 493
GEORGIA MUSTARD - BBQ Sauce - FAMOUS DAVE'S OF AMERICA, INC.; *pg.* 1728, *pg.* 926
GEORGIA-PACIFIC - Paper Towels, Bath Tissue, Soap & Dispensers, Building Products - GEORGIA-PACIFIC LLC; *pg.* 1458, *pg.* 507
GEORGIAN - Furniture - J. ROBERT SCOTT INC.; *pg.* 930, *pg.* 105
GEORGIAN - Fan - WESTINGHOUSE LIGHTING CORPORATION; *pg.* 687, *pg.* 1571
GEORGIAN MAROON - Brick & Tile Product - CHEROKEE BRICK & TILE COMPANY; *pg.* 75, *pg.* 535
GEOSAFARI - Electronic Learning Aid - EDUCATIONAL INSIGHTS, INC.; *pg.* 951, *pg.* 187
GEOSAFARI PHONICS LAB - Electronic Learning Aid - EDUCATIONAL INSIGHTS, INC.; *pg.* 951, *pg.* 187
GEOSAFARI PHONICS PAD - Electronic Learning Aid - EDUCATIONAL INSIGHTS, INC.; *pg.* 951, *pg.* 187
GEOSERVER - Software - RAYTHEON COMPANY; *pg.* 233, *pg.* 854
GEOSPERSE - Fluid Handling System - GRACO, INC.; *pg.* 1342, *pg.* 935
GEOSTAR - Survey Control System - TRIMBLE NAVIGATION LIMITED; *pg.* 1384, *pg.* 288
GEOSYNCHRONY - Software - EMC CORPORATION; *pg.* 391, *pg.* 825
GEOSYSTEMS - Soil Stabilization Solutions - REYNOLDS CONSUMER PRODUCTS; *pg.* 1138, *pg.* 625
GEOTEX - Pipe - ADVANCED DRAINAGE SYSTEMS, INC.; *pg.* 1878, *pg.* 1455
GEOTRACER - Navigation Aid - TRIMBLE NAVIGATION LIMITED; *pg.* 1384, *pg.* 288
GEOVIZ - 3D Software - SCHLUMBERGER LIMITED; *pg.* 801, *pg.* 1714
GEOVOR - Tooth System - ESCO CORPORATION; *pg.* 1335, *pg.* 1502
GEOXM - Navigation Aid - TRIMBLE NAVIGATION LIMITED; *pg.* 1384, *pg.* 288
GEOXT - Navigation Aid - TRIMBLE NAVIGATION LIMITED; *pg.* 1384, *pg.* 288
GEPON APD TIA IN TO-CAN - Electronic Components - EMCORE CORPORATION; *pg.* 636, *pg.* 39
GEPON DFB LASERS IN TO-CAN - Electronic Components - EMCORE CORPORATION; *pg.* 636, *pg.* 39
GERANIUMS - Lace - HERITAGE LACE INC.; *pg.* 694, *pg.* 711
GERARD - Furniture - HOOKER FURNITURE CORPORATION; *pg.* 928, *pg.* 1788
GERARD - Roof System Mfr - METALS USA, INC.; *pg.* 97, *pg.* 425
GERBER EDGE - Digital Printing System - GERBER SCIENTIFIC, INC.; *pg.* 1414, *pg.* 380
GERBER EMERSON ALLIANCE - Knife - GERBER LEGENDARY BLADES; *pg.* 1834, *pg.* 1503
GERBER HARDWATER - Faucets & Fittings with Ceramic Disc Valving - GERBER PLUMBING FIXTURES CORPORATION; *pg.* 84, *pg.* 672
GERBER NORTHSTAR - Lighting Signage - GERBER SCIENTIFIC, INC.; *pg.* 1414, *pg.* 380
GERBER ORGANIC - Cereal - GERBER PRODUCTS COMPANY; *pg.* 858, *pg.* 1067
GERBERCOLOR - Foil - GERBER SCIENTIFIC, INC.; *pg.* 1414, *pg.* 380
GERBERCUTTER - High-Ply Fabric Cutter - GERBER SCIENTIFIC, INC.; *pg.* 1414, *pg.* 380
GERBERGAUGE - Foil Measuring System - GERBER SCIENTIFIC, INC.; *pg.* 1414, *pg.* 380
GERBERNET - Software - GERBER SCIENTIFIC, INC.; *pg.* 1414, *pg.* 380
GERBERSAVER - Flaw Management System - GERBER SCIENTIFIC, INC.; *pg.* 1414, *pg.* 380
GERBERSPREADER - Fabric Spreading Systems - GERBER SCIENTIFIC, INC.; *pg.* 1414, *pg.* 380
GERBES - Supermarket - THE KROGER CO.; *pg.* 1025, *pg.* 1416
GERHARD SCHULZ - Wine & Spirits - LEONARD KREUSCH, INC.; *pg.* 254, *pg.* 1099
GERISTORE - Hybrid Ionomer Resin - DEN-MAT CORPORATION; *pg.* 1522, *pg.* 271
GERKENS - Cocoa - CARGILL, INC.; *pg.* 845, *pg.* 965
GERKENS CACAO - Cocoa Powders - CARGILL LIMITED; *pg.* 1475, *pg.* 1914
GERM - Air Purifier - LOWE'S COMPANIES, INC.; *pg.* 1053, *pg.* 1383
GERMAINE MONTEIL - Cosmetics - REVLON, INC.; *pg.* 521, *pg.* 1286
GERMAZIDE - Personal Care Material - BASF CATALYSTS LLC; *pg.* 1148, *pg.* 1074
GERMBUSTER - Hand Sanitizer - TWEEZERMAN INTERNATIONAL; *pg.* 524, *pg.* 1324
GERMINATOR - Frame - ANCHOR INDUSTRIES, INC.; *pg.* 1825, *pg.* 678
GERRY - Baby Equipment - EVENFLO COMPANY, INC.; *pg.* 924, *pg.* 1470
GERTRUDE - Fabric - NEMSCHOFF, INC.; *pg.* 936, *pg.* 1890
GES - Golf Accessories - CALLAWAY GOLF COMPANY; *pg.* 1829, *pg.* 58
GESAR - Footwear - STEVEN MADDEN, LTD.; *pg.* 1819, *pg.* 1176
GESCAN - Software - SAS INSTITUTE INC.; *pg.* 466, *pg.* 1361
GESCO - Catheters - UTAH MEDICAL PRODUCTS, INC.; *pg.* 1605, *pg.* 1752
GESSNER - Paper - NEENAH PAPER, INC.; *pg.* 1465, *pg.* 484
GESTRA - Valve - FLOWSERVE CORPORATION; *pg.* 82, *pg.* 1719
GET A GREAT SOUNDING WEB ADDRESS! - Slogan - BRS MEDIA INC.; *pg.* 1233, *pg.* 214
GET-A-WAY - Chair - HUMAN TOUCH; *pg.* 928, *pg.* 123
GET BACK TO BASICS - Slogan - FIRST NIAGARA FINANCIAL GROUP, INC.; *pg.* 757, *pg.* 1148
GET BACK TO YOUR DAY - Slogan - PFIZER INC.; *pg.* 1581, *pg.* 1278
GET DRESSED - Tagline - DR. JAY'S INC.; *pg.* 40, *pg.* 1085
GET EGGCITED - Video Game - INTERNATIONAL GAME TECHNOLOGY; *pg.* 957, *pg.* 1024
GET FRESH - Fruit Arrangements - EDIBLE ARRANGEMENTS INTERNATIONAL, INC.; *pg.* 1768, *pg.* 382
GET FRESH WITH KAYEM - Slogan - KAYEM FOODS, INC.; *pg.* 867, *pg.* 814
GET HOOKED - Game - WMS INDUSTRIES INC.; *pg.* 593,

pg. 666
GET IT TO GO - Tagline - BUFFALO WILD WINGS, INC.; *pg.* 1718, *pg.* 931
GET MORE IN RETURN - Slogan - JACKSON HEWITT TAX SERVICE INC.; *pg.* 771, *pg.* 1103
GET MOVING - Tag Line - SEGWAY INC.; *pg.* 1923, *pg.* 1033
GET NUTS - Video Game - INTERNATIONAL GAME TECHNOLOGY; *pg.* 957, *pg.* 1024
GET OUT AND STAY OUT - Fabric - W.L. GORE & ASSOCIATES, INC.; *pg.* 122, *pg.* 388
GET OUT THERE - Slogan - ROYAL CARIBBEAN CRUISES LTD; *pg.* 1921, *pg.* 446
GET READY FOR KINDERGARTEN! - Toy And Game - INNOVATIVE USA, INC.; *pg.* 957, *pg.* 363
GET REAL GET COTTON - Slogan - BARNHARDT MANUFACTURING COMPANY; *pg.* 1498, *pg.* 1364
GET SET, GO - Dresses & Sets - HABAND COMPANY, INC.; *pg.* 1772, *pg.* 1099
GET THE EDGE - Life Coaching Program - GUTHY-RENKER LLC; *pg.* 289, *pg.* 273
GET THE GARDEN - Gardening Appliance Systems - AEROGROW INTERNATIONAL, INC.; *pg.* 1393, *pg.* 310
GET THE POWER OF BLUE WORKING FOR YOU. - Slogan - ANTHEM BLUE CROSS BLUE SHIELD; *pg.* 1192, *pg.* 1886
GET TO A BETTER STATE - Tagline - STATE FARM MUTUAL AUTOMOBILE INSURANCE CO.; *pg.* 1218, *pg.* 557
GET TO THE ROUGE - Games - PENN NATIONAL GAMING, INC.; *pg.* 574, *pg.* 1595
GET TOGETHER AT RED LOBSTER - Slogan - RED LOBSTER; *pg.* 1747, *pg.* 455
GET TOGETHER GAMES - Toy & Game - HASBRO, INC.; *pg.* 954, *pg.* 1603
GET-U-UP - Medical Equipment - INVACARE CORPORATION; *pg.* 1546, *pg.* 1451
GET WEALTH SOON - Video Game - INTERNATIONAL GAME TECHNOLOGY; *pg.* 957, *pg.* 1024
GET YOUR HOME & AUTO COVERAGE ALL IN ONE PLACE - Tagline - THE PROGRESSIVE CORPORATION; *pg.* 1214, *pg.* 1463
GETGO - Food Product - GIANT EAGLE, INC.; *pg.* 1020, *pg.* 1575
GETGREEN ! - Cleaning Product - GREEN EARTH TECHNOLOGIES, INC.; *pg.* 704, *pg.* 1352
GETTA HAIRCUT - Home Hair Clipper Kit - ANDIS COMPANY; *pg.* 498, *pg.* 1895
GETTHERE - Traveling Service - SABRE HOLDINGS CORPORATION; *pg.* 1922, *pg.* 1745
GETTIN' LUCKY - Game - WMS INDUSTRIES INC.; *pg.* 593, *pg.* 666
GETTING BETTER ALL THE TIME - Slogan - MAGELLAN HEALTH SERVICES, INC.; *pg.* 1557, *pg.* 337
GETTING BETTER ALL THE TIME - Tagline - WINN DIXIE STORES, INC.; *pg.* 1038, *pg.* 435
GETTING FIT JUST GOT EASIER - Health Plan & Publication - MEDICA, INC.; *pg.* 1208, *pg.* 949
GETTING IT DONE. RIGHT. - Tagline - ERESEARCH TECHNOLOGY INC.; *pg.* 1243, *pg.* 1564
GETTING OFF THE BEATEN PATH - Tag Line - NORM THOMPSON OUTFITTERS INC.; *pg.* 1780, *pg.* 1498
GETTING THERE SAVINGS PROGRAM - Banking Service - THE BANK OF NOVA SCOTIA; *pg.* 721, *pg.* 1935
GETTING TO KNOW...NATURE'S CHILDREN - Educational Materials - SCHOLASTIC INC.; *pg.* 1683, *pg.* 1288
GETTINGTON.COM - E-Commerce Retailer - BLUESTEM BRANDS, INC.; *pg.* 1763, *pg.* 922
GETTY - Fabric - NEMSCHOFF, INC.; *pg.* 936, *pg.* 1890
GETVIAMOTO - Software - MOTOROLA SOLUTIONS, INC.; *pg.* 657, *pg.* 659
GEVALIA - Coffees - THE KRAFT HEINZ COMPANY; *pg.* 870, *pg.* 1577
GEVALIA - Coffee - MONDELEZ INTERNATIONAL, INC.; *pg.* 878, *pg.* 601
GEVRABON - Pharmaceutical Product - ALERE INC.; *pg.* 1488, *pg.* 849
GEYSER - Furniture - JASPER GROUP; *pg.* 930, *pg.* 691
GEYSER PEAK - Table Wines - GEYSER PEAK WINERY; *pg.* 1964, *pg.* 101
GEYSER PEAK WINERY - Winery - GEYSER PEAK WINERY; *pg.* 1964, *pg.* 101
GFFM - Electronic Component - OPLINK COMMUNICATIONS, INC.; *pg.* 660, *pg.* 91
GFLEX - Packaging Foam - SEALED AIR CORPORATION; *pg.* 1468, *pg.* 1058
GFO - Sealant - W.L. GORE & ASSOCIATES, INC.; *pg.* 122, *pg.* 388
GFS - Financial Forms - ENNIS, INC.; *pg.* 393, *pg.* 1727
GFS EXECUTIVE INFORMATION SYSTEM - Software - WIPRO GALLAGHER SOLUTIONS; *pg.* 823, *pg.* 447
GFS EXPERIENCE - Online Resource Food Service - GORDON FOOD SERVICE INC.; *pg.* 1021, *pg.* 913
GFS NAVIGATOR - Software - WIPRO GALLAGHER SOLUTIONS; *pg.* 823, *pg.* 447
GFSELECT - Chemical Product - GFS CHEMICALS, INC.; *pg.* 1164, *pg.* 1471
GG-100K PORTAPRO - Glue Gun - MASTER APPLIANCE CORP.; *pg.* 1055, *pg.* 1888
GG GOLDEN GUERNSEY DAIRY - Dairy Products - FOREMOST FARMS USA COOPERATIVE; *pg.* 856, *pg.* 1854
GH - Gas-Hydraulic Airless Sprayer - GRACO, INC.; *pg.* 1342, *pg.* 935
GH BASS & CO - Apparel - PVH CORP.; *pg.* 46, *pg.* 1283
GHB-1700 - Headset - GLOBALSTAR, INC.; *pg.* 401, *pg.* 743
GHH-RAND - Oil-Free Rotary Screw - INGERSOLL-RAND COMPANY; *pg.* 1349, *pg.* 1370
GHIL-LEAF - Apparel - CABELA'S INCORPORATED; *pg.* 535, *pg.* 1019
GHIRARDELLI - Food Product - CONTINENTAL MILLS, INC.; *pg.* 827, *pg.* 1845
GHIRARDELLI CHOCOLATE - Chocolate - GHIRARDELLI CHOCOLATE COMPANY; *pg.* 1854, *pg.* 252
GHIRARDELLI CHOCOLATE BAR COLLECTION - Chocolate - GHIRARDELLI CHOCOLATE COMPANY; *pg.* 1854, *pg.* 252
GHIRARDELLI CHOCOLATE SQUARES - Chocolate - GHIRARDELLI CHOCOLATE COMPANY; *pg.* 1854, *pg.* 252
GHIRARDELLI PREMIUM BAKING CHOCOLATE - Baking Chocolate - GHIRARDELLI CHOCOLATE COMPANY; *pg.* 1854, *pg.* 252
GHIRARDELLI SODA FOUNTAIN AND CHOCOLATE SHOPS - Eating Establishments - GHIRARDELLI CHOCOLATE COMPANY; *pg.* 1854, *pg.* 252
GHOST - Software - SYMANTEC CORPORATION; *pg.* 478, *pg.* 161
GHOST - Software - SYMANTEC CORPORATION; *pg.* 479, *pg.* 1753
GHOST ISLAND - Video Slots - INTERNATIONAL GAME TECHNOLOGY; *pg.* 957, *pg.* 1024
GHOST RIDER - Knife - BUCK KNIVES, INC.; *pg.* 1828, *pg.* 550
GHOST RIDER - Toy & Game - HASBRO, INC.; *pg.* 954, *pg.* 1603
GHOST WALKER - Software - SYMANTEC CORPORATION; *pg.* 478, *pg.* 161
GHOST WILDS - Video Game - INTERNATIONAL GAME TECHNOLOGY; *pg.* 957, *pg.* 1024
GHOSTKILLER - VHF/UHF FM Antenna - WINEGARD COMPANY; *pg.* 688, *pg.* 702
GHOSTLY GOODIES - Candy - R.M. PALMER COMPANY; *pg.* 1861, *pg.* 1585
GHOSTLY TREATS - Candy - R.M. PALMER COMPANY; *pg.* 1861, *pg.* 1585
GHOSTRIDER - Amusement & Water Park - CEDAR FAIR, L.P.; *pg.* 537, *pg.* 1471
GHOSTVILLE ELEMENTARY - Educational Materials - SCHOLASTIC INC.; *pg.* 1683, *pg.* 1288
G.I. JOE - Action Figures - HASBRO, INC.; *pg.* 954, *pg.* 1603
GI-PRO - Medical Device - MANNATECH, INCORPORATED; *pg.* 1558, *pg.* 1671
GI-ZYME - Medical Device - MANNATECH, INCORPORATED; *pg.* 1558, *pg.* 1671
GI48 - Health System Product - LANELABS USA INC.; *pg.* 1554, *pg.* 1128
GIA - Footwear - VANS, INC.; *pg.* 1821, *pg.* 76
GIANNA - Footwear - CAPEZIO BALLET MAKERS INC.; *pg.* 1805, *pg.* 1125
GIANT - Tires - THE HERCULES TIRE & RUBBER COMPANY; *pg.* 1884, *pg.* 1454
GIANT - Bread - KLOSTERMAN BAKING COMPANY, INC.; *pg.* 869, *pg.* 1415
GIANT FOOD - Grocery Stores - GIANT OF MARYLAND LLC; *pg.* 1021, *pg.* 773
GIANT GLASS - Vehicle Glass Repair - SAFELITE SOLUTIONS LLC; *pg.* 109, *pg.* 1443
GIANT KISS - Chocolate - THE HERSHEY CO.; *pg.* 1855, *pg.* 1538
GIANTS - Professional Football Team - THE NEW YORK GIANTS; *pg.* 570, *pg.* 1055
GIARDIAVAX - Canine Vaccine - PFIZER INC.; *pg.* 1581, *pg.* 1278
GIARDINO - Fabric - NEMSCHOFF, INC.; *pg.* 936, *pg.* 1890
GIBBO - Apparel - VANS, INC.; *pg.* 1821, *pg.* 76
GIBBONS - Premium Beer & Ale - THE LION BREWERY, INC.; *pg.* 254, *pg.* 1594
GIBBS - Processed Food - HANOVER FOODS CORPORATION; *pg.* 861, *pg.* 1535
GIBCO - Cell Culture Product - THERMO FISHER SCIENTIFIC INC.; *pg.* 1602, *pg.* 61
GIBCO FOAMAWAY - Reagent - THERMO FISHER SCIENTIFIC INC.; *pg.* 1602, *pg.* 61
GIBRALTAR - Flour - CARGILL LIMITED; *pg.* 1475, *pg.* 1914
GIBRALTER - Drums - KAMAN CORPORATION; *pg.* 229, *pg.* 338
GIBSON - Greeting Cards - AMERICAN GREETINGS CORPORATION; *pg.* 1615, *pg.* 1428
GIBSON - Table - BLATT BOWLING & BILLIARD CORP.; *pg.* 1827, *pg.* 1203
GIBSON - Air Conditioners & Furnaces - NORTEK GLOBAL HVAC; *pg.* 1075, *pg.* 989
GIBSON FALLS - Footwear - PHOENIX FOOTWEAR GROUP, INC.; *pg.* 1815, *pg.* 60
GIBSON PURE - Musical Instrument - GIBSON GUITAR CORP.; *pg.* 550, *pg.* 1650
GICS DIRECT - Reference Tool - STANDARD & POOR'S RATINGS SERVICES; *pg.* 805, *pg.* 1296
GICS HISTORY - Reference Tool - STANDARD & POOR'S RATINGS SERVICES; *pg.* 805, *pg.* 1296
GICS WITH GUTS - Banking Service - THE BANK OF NOVA SCOTIA; *pg.* 721, *pg.* 1935
GIFT BOOKS FROM HALLMARK - Gift Product - HALLMARK CARDS, INC.; *pg.* 1646, *pg.* 983
GIFT CONCIERGE SERVICE - Retail Store Services - 1-800-FLOWERS.COM, INC.; *pg.* 1758, *pg.* 1151
THE GIFT GARDEN - Flower Store - GIANT EAGLE, INC.; *pg.* 1020, *pg.* 1575
GIFT OF EAR PIERCING - Ear Piercing Product - INVERNESS CORPORATION; *pg.* 512, *pg.* 783
GIFT OF IMMORTALITY - Video Game - INTERNATIONAL GAME TECHNOLOGY; *pg.* 957, *pg.* 1024
GIFT POINTS - Video Game - INTERNATIONAL GAME TECHNOLOGY; *pg.* 957, *pg.* 1024
GIFT WELL LIVE WELL - Retail Store Services - 1-800-FLOWERS.COM, INC.; *pg.* 1758, *pg.* 1151
GIFTS FOR GAB - Telephone Service - IDT CORPORATION; *pg.* 643, *pg.* 1096
GIFTS FOR GOLF - Golf Gifts - GOLFSMITH INTERNATIONAL HOLDINGS, INC.; *pg.* 1835, *pg.* 1662
GIFTS.COM - Online Services - IAC/INTERACTIVECORP; *pg.* 292, *pg.* 1242
GIG STAND - Stand Product - WENGER CORPORATION; *pg.* 1307, *pg.* 952
GIGA - Cooking Equipment - THE MIDDLEBY CORPORATION; *pg.* 1361, *pg.* 610
GIGA PETS - Toy & Game - HASBRO, INC.; *pg.* 954, *pg.* 1603
GIGA-PUNCH - Copper Product - PANDUIT CORP.; *pg.* 661, *pg.* 663
GIGA-TRIM - Capacitor - JOHANSON MANUFACTURING CORPORATION; *pg.* 648, *pg.* 1045
GIGA-TX - Copper Product - PANDUIT CORP.; *pg.* 661, *pg.* 663
GIGABLAZE - Semiconductor Device - AVAGO TECHNOLOGIES; *pg.* 358, *pg.* 238
GIGACUBE - Software - MICROWAY, INC.; *pg.* 1267, *pg.* 841
GIGADRIVE - Storage Drive - CISCO SYSTEMS, INC.; *pg.* 372, *pg.* 240
GIGALIGHT - Optical Networking Product - HARMONIC, INC.; *pg.* 402, *pg.* 246
GIGANTE - Frozen Mexican Food - RUIZ FOOD PRODUCTS, INC.; *pg.* 893, *pg.* 77
GIGASIL - Precision Abrasive Product - SAINT-GOBAIN ABRASIVES, INC. - PHILADELPHIA; *pg.* 1180, *pg.* 1553
GIGASTREAM - Network Product - VITESSE SEMICONDUCTOR CORPORATION; *pg.* 686, *pg.* 57
GIGAWAVE TECHNOLOGIES - Wireless Local Area Network - TESSCO TECHNOLOGIES, INC.; *pg.* 679, *pg.* 773
GIGE EXCHANGE - Telecommunication System - EQUINIX, INC.; *pg.* 394, *pg.* 190
GIGGLE BALL - Toy - INFANTINO, LLC; *pg.* 957, *pg.* 203
GIGI - Male Grooming Product - AMERICAN

INTERNATIONAL INDUSTRIES COMPANY; *pg.* 498, *pg.* 126

GIGX - Data Communication Network - AVAGO TECHNOLOGIES; *pg.* 358, *pg.* 238

GIK-1700 - Satellite Phone - GLOBALSTAR, INC.; *pg.* 401, *pg.* 743

GIL-CHEM - Metal Shop Primers - JONES-BLAIR COMPANY; *pg.* 1443, *pg.* 1682

GILARDI FOODS - Food Product - CONAGRA FOODS, INC.; *pg.* 826, *pg.* 1014

GILASITE - Medical Product - HOLOGIC, INC.; *pg.* 1416, *pg.* 784

GILBANE - Construction Management - GILBANE BUILDING COMPANY; *pg.* 84, *pg.* 1606

GILBARCO - Fuel Dispensing Equipment - DANAHER CORPORATION; *pg.* 1044, *pg.* 397

GILBERT - Paper - NEENAH PAPER, INC.; *pg.* 1465, *pg.* 484

GILBERT H. WILD - Plants - GILBERT H. WILD & SON, LLC; *pg.* 1796, *pg.* 1005

GILBERT-ULTRASEAL - Hand Tool - IDEAL INDUSTRIES, INC.; *pg.* 1051, *pg.* 662

GILBEY DE LOUDENNE - Bordeaux Wines - DREYFUS ASHBY INC.; *pg.* 1962, *pg.* 1226

GILBEY'S - Gin & Vodka - JIM BEAM BRANDS CO.; *pg.* 1965, *pg.* 601

GILCOTE - Coating Product - PPG INDUSTRIES, INC.; *pg.* 1445, *pg.* 1579

GILDON - Clock - BROWN & BIGELOW, INC.; *pg.* 1624, *pg.* 959

GILEAD SCIENCES - Biopharmaceutical Product - GILEAD SCIENCES, INC.; *pg.* 1535, *pg.* 88

GILES - Furniture - ETHAN ALLEN INTERIORS INC.; *pg.* 924, *pg.* 343

GILFORD - Kitchen Product - KOHLER CO.; *pg.* 91, *pg.* 1862

GILIA PINOT GRIGIO - Wine - SHAW ROSS INTERNATIONAL IMPORTERS; *pg.* 1970, *pg.* 449

GILL - Cross Country Equipment - GILL ATHLETICS, INC.; *pg.* 1835, *pg.* 562

GILLESPIE - Paint - W.M. BARR & COMPANY, INC.; *pg.* 338, *pg.* 1647

GILLET - Exhaust System - TENNECO, INC.; *pg.* 985, *pg.* 625

GILLETTE - Shave Creams, Blades, Razors - THE GILLETTE COMPANY; *pg.* 509, *pg.* 795

GILLETTE - Shaving Creams, Razors & Blades - THE PROCTER & GAMBLE COMPANY; *pg.* 1129, *pg.* 1418

GILLETTE ANTI-PERSPIRANT - Anti-perspirant - THE GILLETTE COMPANY; *pg.* 509, *pg.* 795

GILLETTE BLUE BLADES - Blades - THE GILLETTE COMPANY; *pg.* 509, *pg.* 795

GILLETTE COMPLETE SKINCARE - Personal & Household Product - THE PROCTER & GAMBLE COMPANY; *pg.* 1129, *pg.* 1418

GILLETTE FOR WOMEN - Women's Razors - THE GILLETTE COMPANY; *pg.* 509, *pg.* 795

GILLETTE FUSION - Personal & Household Product - THE PROCTER & GAMBLE COMPANY; *pg.* 1129, *pg.* 1418

GILLETTE FUSION POWER - Razor - THE PROCTER & GAMBLE COMPANY; *pg.* 1129, *pg.* 1418

GILLETTE M3POWER - Personal & Household Product - THE PROCTER & GAMBLE COMPANY; *pg.* 1129, *pg.* 1418

GILLETTE M3POWER NITRO - Personal & Household Product - THE PROCTER & GAMBLE COMPANY; *pg.* 1129, *pg.* 1418

GILLETTE MACH3 - Personal & Household Product - THE PROCTER & GAMBLE COMPANY; *pg.* 1129, *pg.* 1418

GILLETTE MACH3 TURBO - Personal & Household Product - THE PROCTER & GAMBLE COMPANY; *pg.* 1129, *pg.* 1418

GILLETTE SATINCARE - Personal & Household Product - THE PROCTER & GAMBLE COMPANY; *pg.* 1129, *pg.* 1418

GILLETTE SENSOR - Blade And Razor - THE GILLETTE COMPANY; *pg.* 509, *pg.* 795

GILLETTE SERIES - Gel - THE GILLETTE COMPANY; *pg.* 509, *pg.* 795

GILLETTE SERIES COOL WAVE - Men's Grooming Products - THE GILLETTE COMPANY; *pg.* 509, *pg.* 795

GILLETTE SERIES WILD RAIN - Men's Grooming Products - THE GILLETTE COMPANY; *pg.* 509, *pg.* 795

GILLETTE SUPER BLUE BLADES - Blades - THE GILLETTE COMPANY; *pg.* 509, *pg.* 795

GILLETTE SUPER-SPEED - Razor - THE GILLETTE COMPANY; *pg.* 509, *pg.* 795

GILLETTE VENUS - Personal & Household Product - THE PROCTER & GAMBLE COMPANY; *pg.* 1129, *pg.* 1418

GILLIARD - Swiss Wines - DREYFUS ASHBY INC.; *pg.* 1962, *pg.* 1226

GILLITE - Coating Product - PPG INDUSTRIES, INC.; *pg.* 1445, *pg.* 1579

GILLNETTERS BEST - Canned Salmon - PETER PAN SEAFOODS, INC.; *pg.* 889, *pg.* 1838

GILLY HICKS - Clothing - ABERCROMBIE & FITCH CO.; *pg.* 37, *pg.* 1466

GILROY - Food Product - CONAGRA FOODS, INC.; *pg.* 826, *pg.* 1014

GIMBAL - Footwear - STEVEN MADDEN, LTD.; *pg.* 1819, *pg.* 1176

GIMINI - Cameras - EASTMAN KODAK COMPANY; *pg.* 1408, *pg.* 1333

GIMLET - Kitchen Product - KOHLER CO.; *pg.* 91, *pg.* 1862

GIN BABY - Nebulizer - VITAL SIGNS, INC.; *pg.* 1607, *pg.* 1126

GIN RICKEY - Shoe - AEROGROUP INTERNATIONAL, INC.; *pg.* 1803, *pg.* 1055

GIN RUMMY - Shoe - AEROGROUP INTERNATIONAL, INC.; *pg.* 1803, *pg.* 1055

GINA ITALIAN VILLAGE - Frozen Pasta - HIGH LINER FOODS INCORPORATED; *pg.* 862, *pg.* 1917

GINEVA - Shoe - AEROGROUP INTERNATIONAL, INC.; *pg.* 1803, *pg.* 1055

GINGER - Furniture - AMISCO INDUSTRIES LTD.; *pg.* 913, *pg.* 1958

GINGER - Plumbing Product - MASCO CORPORATION; *pg.* 96, *pg.* 909

GINGER - Fabric - NEMSCHOFF, INC.; *pg.* 936, *pg.* 1890

GINGER - Tables - STEELCASE INC.; *pg.* 475, *pg.* 889

GINGER ALE - Beverage - SPRECHER BREWING COMPANY; *pg.* 265, *pg.* 1858

GINGER LOTUS - Fragrance - PARFUMS DE COEUR LTD.; *pg.* 519, *pg.* 376

GINGER ZING - Organic Granola - NATURE'S PATH FOODS INC.; *pg.* 833, *pg.* 1908

GINGERBREAD SPICE - Holiday Tea - CELESTIAL SEASONINGS, INC.; *pg.* 846, *pg.* 310

GINGEREASE TEA - Tea Product - CELESTIAL SEASONINGS, INC.; *pg.* 846, *pg.* 310

GINGERWOOD - Carpet - BEAULIEU GROUP, LLC; *pg.* 917, *pg.* 529

GINGSENG ENERGY - Herb Tea - CELESTIAL SEASONINGS, INC.; *pg.* 846, *pg.* 310

GINI - Beverages - THE COCA-COLA COMPANY; *pg.* 240, *pg.* 493

GINKGO - Fabric - NEMSCHOFF, INC.; *pg.* 936, *pg.* 1890

GINKGO BILOBA - Office Furniture - STEELCASE INC.; *pg.* 475, *pg.* 889

GINKGO-COMBO - Nutritional Supplement - NATURAL ORGANICS, INC.; *pg.* 1571, *pg.* 1181

GINKGO LEAF - Carpet - INTERFACE, INC.; *pg.* 695, *pg.* 512

GINKGOSHARP - Wellness Tea - CELESTIAL SEASONINGS, INC.; *pg.* 846, *pg.* 310

GINKO-PS - Nutritional Supplement - USANA HEALTH SCIENCES, INC.; *pg.* 1605, *pg.* 1761

GINSENG - Hair & Skin Product - AUBREY ORGANICS INC.; *pg.* 499, *pg.* 470

GINSENG POWERMAX - Nutritional Product - NUTRACEUTICAL INTERNATIONAL CORPORATION; *pg.* 1576, *pg.* 1753

GINTY - Golf Accessories - CALLAWAY GOLF COMPANY; *pg.* 1829, *pg.* 58

GINZA - Carpet - INTERFACE, INC.; *pg.* 695, *pg.* 512

GINZA - Fabric - NEMSCHOFF, INC.; *pg.* 936, *pg.* 1890

GIORGIO - Fabric - NEMSCHOFF, INC.; *pg.* 936, *pg.* 1890

GIORGIO BEVERLY HILLS - Personal & Beauty Product - THE PROCTER & GAMBLE COMPANY; *pg.* 1129, *pg.* 1418

GIOTTO - Dispensing Equipment - IDEX CORPORATION; *pg.* 1347, *pg.* 623

GIOVANNI - Fabric - NEMSCHOFF, INC.; *pg.* 936, *pg.* 1890

GIRAFEE LIGHT - Residential Lighting - SWIVELIER CO., INC.; *pg.* 1307, *pg.* 1142

GIRARD'S - Salad Dressings & Sauces - LANCASTER COLONY CORPORATION; *pg.* 873, *pg.* 1441

GIRIOS GIRA - Beverages - THE COCA-COLA COMPANY; *pg.* 240, *pg.* 493

GIRL CRUSH - Toy - SPIN MASTER LTD.; *pg.* 967, *pg.* 1943

GIRL GOURMET - Ice Cream Maker - JAKKS PACIFIC, INC.; *pg.* 960, *pg.* 142

GIRL SCOUT COOKIES - Cookies - GIRL SCOUTS OF THE UNITED STATES OF AMERICA; *pg.* 142, *pg.* 1235

GIRL SCOUT GOLD AWARD - Award - GIRL SCOUTS OF THE UNITED STATES OF AMERICA; *pg.* 142, *pg.* 1235

GIRL STAR - Apparel - PERRY ELLIS INTERNATIONAL, INC.; *pg.* 45, *pg.* 445

GIRL TALK - Toy & Game - HASBRO, INC.; *pg.* 954, *pg.* 1603

GIRLS EXPRESS - Doll And Toy - AMERICAN GIRL LLC; *pg.* 949, *pg.* 1871

THE GIRLS OF CANBY HALL - Educational Materials - SCHOLASTIC INC.; *pg.* 1683, *pg.* 1288

GIRLS OF MANY LANDS - Doll And Toy - AMERICAN GIRL LLC; *pg.* 949, *pg.* 1871

GIRLS OF PENTHOUSE - Magazine - FRIENDFINDER NETWORKS INC.; *pg.* 1643, *pg.* 411

GIRLSENSE - Online Services - IAC/INTERACTIVECORP; *pg.* 292, *pg.* 1242

GIRLY - Belt - VANS, INC.; *pg.* 1821, *pg.* 76

GIS DATA REVIEWER - Software - ENVIRONMENTAL SYSTEMS RESEARCH INSTITUTE INC.; *pg.* 393, *pg.* 188

GIS PORTAL TOOLKIT - Software - ENVIRONMENTAL SYSTEMS RESEARCH INSTITUTE INC.; *pg.* 393, *pg.* 188

GIS WEB SERVICES - Software - ENVIRONMENTAL SYSTEMS RESEARCH INSTITUTE INC.; *pg.* 393, *pg.* 188

GISCONNECT - Software - BENTLEY SYSTEMS, INC.; *pg.* 361, *pg.* 1531

GISELLE - Furniture - HOOKER FURNITURE CORPORATION; *pg.* 928, *pg.* 1788

GISPERT - Handmade Cigar - ALTADIS USA, INC.; *pg.* 1893, *pg.* 423

GIST - Carpet - INTERFACE, INC.; *pg.* 695, *pg.* 512

GISTIT - Software - SRA INTERNATIONAL, INC.; *pg.* 473, *pg.* 1780

GITANO - Apparel - V.F. CORPORATION; *pg.* 34, *pg.* 1376

GIVE. SAVOR. CELEBRATE - Slogan - OMAHA STEAKS INTERNATIONAL, INC.; *pg.* 1780, *pg.* 1017

GIVE SOMETHING BACK NETWORK - Prepaid Card - HEARTLAND PAYMENT SYSTEMS, INC.; *pg.* 765, *pg.* 1111

GIVE THANKS - Pillow and Throw - HERITAGE LACE INC.; *pg.* 694, *pg.* 711

GIVE YOUR CHILD AN ADVANTAGE FOR LIFE - Service Mark - GERBER LIFE INSURANCE COMPANY; *pg.* 1201, *pg.* 1352

GIVE YOUR DREAMS A CHANCE - Slogan - NEW JERSEY STATE LOTTERY; *pg.* 1000, *pg.* 1126

GIVE YOURSELF AN INSTITUTIONAL ADVANTAGE - Tagline - QUODD FINANCIAL INFORMATION SERVICES; *pg.* 1276, *pg.* 1076

GIVEALA - Fund-Raising Program - AMERICAN LIBRARY ASSOCIATION; *pg.* 1615, *pg.* 564

GIVERNY - Fabric - SCALAMANDRE, INC.; *pg.* 941, *pg.* 1058

GIVING BUSINESS THE CREDIT IT DESERVES - Slogan - MICROFINANCIAL INCORPORATED; *pg.* 782, *pg.* 805

GIZA - Dinnerware - THE HOMER LAUGHLIN CHINA COMPANY; *pg.* 1125, *pg.* 1850

GIZA - Fabric - NEMSCHOFF, INC.; *pg.* 936, *pg.* 1890

GIZMO! - Flash Memory USB Drive - CRUCIAL TECHNOLOGY DIV OF MICRON; *pg.* 1237, *pg.* 550

GIZMO - Hardware - MICRON TECHNOLOGY, INC.; *pg.* 435, *pg.* 547

GIZMO - Ball Point Pens & Auto Pencils - PENTEL OF AMERICA, LTD.; *pg.* 453, *pg.* 295

GIZMODO - Online Gadgets - GAWKER MEDIA LLC; *pg.* 1248, *pg.* 1234

GL-3000-P - Laser Guidance System - M-B COMPANIES, INC.; *pg.* 1357, *pg.* 1884

GLACEAU FRUITWATER - Beverages - THE COCA-COLA COMPANY; *pg.* 240, *pg.* 493

GLACEAU SMARTWATER - Beverages - THE COCA-COLA COMPANY; *pg.* 240, *pg.* 493

GLACEAU VITAMINENERGY - Beverages - THE COCA-COLA COMPANY; *pg.* 240, *pg.* 493

GLACEAU VITAMINWATER - Beverages - THE COCA-COLA COMPANY; *pg.* 240, *pg.* 493

GLACEAU WATER+ - Bottled Water - ENERGY BRANDS, INC.; *pg.* 854, *pg.* 1227

GLACIAL ACETIC ACID - Chemical Product - BIRKO CORPORATION; *pg.* 1149, *pg.* 332

GLACIAL MARINE MUD - Skin Care Product - NU SKIN

First page reference indicates Business Class Edition
Second page reference indicates Geographic Edition

ENTERPRISES, INC.; *pg.* 518, *pg.* 1755
GLACIATOR - Athletic Shoes - K-SWISS; *pg.* 1837, *pg.* 306
GLACIER - Ice Cream Coating - CARGILL, INC.; *pg.* 845, *pg.* 965
GLACIER - Hose - HBD INDUSTRIES, INC.; *pg.* 207, *pg.* 1449
GLACIER - Jewelry - LAGOS INC.; *pg.* 8, *pg.* 1566
GLACIER - Binoculars - MEADE INSTRUMENTS CORPORATION; *pg.* 1422, *pg.* 113
GLACIER - Plow Kit - POLARIS INDUSTRIES INC.; *pg.* 1709, *pg.* 928
GLACIER - Ceiling Panel - USG CORPORATION; *pg.* 118, *pg.* 594
GLACIER BAY - Outerwear - HABAND COMPANY, INC.; *pg.* 1772, *pg.* 1099
GLACIER CLEAR - Building Material - PLUM CREEK TIMBER COMPANY, INC.; *pg.* 105, *pg.* 1838
GLACIER COMFORT TI-AC - Glass - AGC GLASS NORTH AMERICA, INC.; *pg.* 65, *pg.* 482
GLACIER GREEN - Building Material - PLUM CREEK TIMBER COMPANY, INC.; *pg.* 105, *pg.* 1838
GLACIER MELT - Salt - CARGILL LIMITED; *pg.* 1475, *pg.* 1914
GLACIER RAIN - Bottled Water - MAVERIK COUNTRY STORES, INC.; *pg.* 1027, *pg.* 1752
GLACIER VALLEY - Water - COUNTRY PURE FOODS, INC.; *pg.* 247, *pg.* 1400
GLACIER VANDERVELL - Bearings - DANA HOLDING CORPORATION; *pg.* 203, *pg.* 1461
GLACIERVAN - Refrigerated Truck Body - KIDRON, INC.; *pg.* 181, *pg.* 1457
GLACIERVAN PLUS - Refrigerated Truck Body - KIDRON, INC.; *pg.* 181, *pg.* 1457
GLACIERVAN QS - Refrigerated Truck Trailer - KIDRON, INC.; *pg.* 181, *pg.* 1457
GLAD - Plastic Products - THE CLOROX COMPANY; *pg.* 327, *pg.* 169
GLAD-LOCK - Reclosable Bags - THE CLOROX COMPANY; *pg.* 327, *pg.* 169
GLADE - Air Freshener - S.C. JOHNSON & SON, INC.; *pg.* 334, *pg.* 1889
GLADE PLUGINS - Air Care - S.C. JOHNSON & SON, INC.; *pg.* 334, *pg.* 1889
THE GLADES - Television Show - A&E TELEVISION NETWORKS, LLC; *pg.* 267, *pg.* 1185
GLADIATOR - Entertainment Lighting Product - BALLANTYNE STRONG, INC.; *pg.* 623, *pg.* 1013
GLADIATOR - Beverages - THE COCA-COLA COMPANY; *pg.* 240, *pg.* 493
GLADIATOR - Window & Door - JELD-WEN, INC.; *pg.* 1051, *pg.* 1499
GLADIATOR - Firefighting Nozzel - KIDDE FIRE FIGHTING; *pg.* 1170, *pg.* 1531
GLADIATOR - Home Appliance Product - WHIRLPOOL CORPORATION; *pg.* 62, *pg.* 872
GLADIATOR CLAW - Storage Device - WHIRLPOOL CORPORATION; *pg.* 62, *pg.* 872
GLADIATORS - Footwear - STEVEN MADDEN, LTD.; *pg.* 1819, *pg.* 1176
GLADWARE - Tight Sealing Containers - THE CLOROX COMPANY; *pg.* 327, *pg.* 169
GLAM - Fabric - NEMSCHOFF, INC.; *pg.* 936, *pg.* 1890
GLAM - Fabric - ROSCO LABORATORIES, INC.; *pg.* 1782, *pg.* 378
GLAMA - Outerwear - HABAND COMPANY, INC.; *pg.* 1772, *pg.* 1099
GLAME - Fabric - ROSCO LABORATORIES, INC.; *pg.* 1782, *pg.* 378
GLAMINATE - Multilayer Tubes - REXAM BEVERAGE CAN NORTH AMERICA; *pg.* 1468, *pg.* 588
GLAMOR - Paint - JONES-BLAIR COMPANY; *pg.* 1443, *pg.* 1682
GLAMORGLAZE - Epoxy Coating - PETTIT PAINT COMPANY; *pg.* 1444, *pg.* 1116
GLAMORISE SPORT - Bra & Shapewear - GLAMORISE FOUNDATIONS, INC.; *pg.* 25, *pg.* 1235
GLAMORTEX - Alkyd Enamel - PETTIT PAINT COMPANY; *pg.* 1444, *pg.* 1116
GLAMORUS - Footwear - STEVEN MADDEN, LTD.; *pg.* 1819, *pg.* 1176
GLAMOUR - Magazine - CONDE NAST PUBLICATIONS, INC.; *pg.* 1629, *pg.* 1217
GLAMOUR - Watch - GEVRIL USA; *pg.* 6, *pg.* 1348
GLAMOUR SHOTS - Photography - CANDID COLOR SYSTEMS, INC.; *pg.* 1404, *pg.* 1485
GLAMOURESQUE - Carpet - BEAULIEU GROUP, LLC; *pg.* 917, *pg.* 529
GLAS-WEB - Patching Material - TEXAS REFINERY CORP.; *pg.* 986, *pg.* 1696
GLASBAC - Carpet - INTERFACE, INC.; *pg.* 695, *pg.* 512
GLASBASE PLUS - Base Sheet - JOHNS MANVILLE CORPORATION; *pg.* 89, *pg.* 320
GLASBORD - Composites - CRANE CO.; *pg.* 227, *pg.* 373
GLASCOTE - Water Heaters - A.O. SMITH CORPORATION; *pg.* 1313, *pg.* 1872
GLASCRAFT - Fluid Handling System - GRACO, INC.; *pg.* 1342, *pg.* 935
GLASFAB - Fabric - KOPPERS HOLDINGS INC.; *pg.* 1170, *pg.* 1577
GLASGOW - Shoes - ALLEN-EDMONDS SHOE CORP.; *pg.* 1804, *pg.* 1887
GLASKAP - Cap Sheet - JOHNS MANVILLE CORPORATION; *pg.* 89, *pg.* 320
GLASKAP PLUS - Cap Sheet - JOHNS MANVILLE CORPORATION; *pg.* 89, *pg.* 320
GLASLOCK - Roofing Shingles - OWENS CORNING; *pg.* 102, *pg.* 1476
GLASMARK - Laser Engraving Solution - VIRTEK VISION INTERNATIONAL, INC.; *pg.* 1435, *pg.* 1948
GLASPLY - Fiberglass Relt - JOHNS MANVILLE CORPORATION; *pg.* 89, *pg.* 320
GLASPLY IV - Ply Felt - JOHNS MANVILLE CORPORATION; *pg.* 89, *pg.* 320
GLASPLY PREMIER - Ply Felt - JOHNS MANVILLE CORPORATION; *pg.* 89, *pg.* 320
GLASROD - Pultruded Rod - ROCHLING GLASTIC COMPOSITES; *pg.* 1889, *pg.* 1435
GLASS - Panel - LARSON MANUFACTURING COMPANY; *pg.* 93, *pg.* 1624
GLASS DOCTOR - Glass Repair & Installation Businesses - THE DWYER GROUP, INC.; *pg.* 79, *pg.* 1748
GLASS-KLENZ - Detergent - STERIS CORPORATION; *pg.* 1597, *pg.* 1464
GLASS-LITE - Reinforced Lightweight Filler - ITW - EVERCOAT; *pg.* 1443, *pg.* 1415
GLASS LOCK - Paint & Coating - DIAMOND VOGEL PAINT, INC.; *pg.* 1441, *pg.* 710
GLASS MARK - Ladder Product - WERNER HOLDING CO.; *pg.* 121, *pg.* 1534
GLASS-O-NET - Reinforced Window Material - WARP BROTHERS; *pg.* 1471, *pg.* 595
GLASS PLUS - Glass Cleaning Products - RECKITT BENCKISER INC.; *pg.* 1136, *pg.* 1105
THE GLASS POLYMER - Copolyesters - EASTMAN CHEMICAL COMPANY; *pg.* 1159, *pg.* 1636
GLASS QUICKLE - Cleaning Kit - KAO BRANDS CO. INC.; *pg.* 513, *pg.* 1415
GLASS RIDGE - Beverage - PHOENIX VINTNERS, LLC; *pg.* 1968, *pg.* 182
GLASSCLOTH - Target Face - SCHOOL-TECH, INC.; *pg.* 1844, *pg.* 866
GLASSCOAT - Fabric - KOPPERS HOLDINGS INC.; *pg.* 1170, *pg.* 1577
GLASSFAB - Fabric - KOPPERS HOLDINGS INC.; *pg.* 1170, *pg.* 1577
GLASSFLEX - Target Face - SCHOOL-TECH, INC.; *pg.* 1844, *pg.* 866
GLASSFYRE - Glass Firescreen Enclosures - PORTLAND WILLAMETTE; *pg.* 1129, *pg.* 1505
GLASSINE - Envelope Window Film - PLASTIC SUPPLIERS, INC.; *pg.* 1888, *pg.* 1443
GLASSMASTER - Monofilaments, Flexible & Electronic Controls & Composites - HAHL INC.; *pg.* 1299, *pg.* 1620
GLASSROOT - Fiber Glass Rovings for Soil Stabilization & Erosion Control - PPG INDUSTRIES, INC.; *pg.* 1445, *pg.* 1579
GLASSTEX - V-Belts - HBD INDUSTRIES, INC.; *pg.* 207, *pg.* 1449
GLASSVENT - Concealed Vents - KAWNEER COMPANY, INC.; *pg.* 90, *pg.* 537
GLASTEEL - Underground Storage Tank - MODERN WELDING COMPANY, INC.; *pg.* 1363, *pg.* 739
GLASTEEL II - Underground Storage Tank - MODERN WELDING COMPANY, INC.; *pg.* 1363, *pg.* 739
GLASTHERM - Thermal Insulating Sheet - ROCHLING GLASTIC COMPOSITES; *pg.* 1889, *pg.* 1435
GLASTIC - Fiberglass Reinforced Plastics - ROCHLING GLASTIC COMPOSITES; *pg.* 1889, *pg.* 1435
GLASTITE - Flexible Base Flashing - JOHNS MANVILLE CORPORATION; *pg.* 89, *pg.* 320
GLASTONE - Dental Product - DENTSPLY INTERNATIONAL INC.; *pg.* 1522, *pg.* 1596
GLASTRAC - Electronic Information Display Systems - PPG INDUSTRIES, INC.; *pg.* 1445, *pg.* 1579
GLASWORKS - Coating & Paint - AKZO NOBEL DECORATIVE PAINTS, USA; *pg.* 1439, *pg.* 1474
GLAZER - Ultra High Speed Glazer - TORNADO INDUSTRIES, INC.; *pg.* 1383, *pg.* 591
GLAZERS - Doughnuts - KWIK TRIP INC.; *pg.* 1026, *pg.* 1864
GLAZETITE - Wall Coating - THE VALSPAR CORPORATION; *pg.* 1449, *pg.* 945
GLAZEWEAR - Beauty Product - AVON PRODUCTS, INC.; *pg.* 500, *pg.* 1198
GLAZOL - Glazing Compound - UNITED GILSONITE LABORATORIES; *pg.* 1449, *pg.* 1527
GLB - Grade Level Box - CHANNELL COMMERCIAL CORP.; *pg.* 1870, *pg.* 291
GLEAMCLEAN - Glove - LAKELAND INDUSTRIES, INC.; *pg.* 1354, *pg.* 1338
GLEAMER - Halogen Task Light - MEDLINE INDUSTRIES, INC.; *pg.* 1562, *pg.* 635
GLEAN - Herbicide - E.I. DU PONT DE NEMOURS & COMPANY; *pg.* 1159, *pg.* 390
THE GLEANER - Newspaper - THE E.W. SCRIPPS COMPANY; *pg.* 1639, *pg.* 1412
GLEANINGS - Fabric - NEMSCHOFF, INC.; *pg.* 936, *pg.* 1890
GLEASON - Gearing Product - GLEASON CORPORATION; *pg.* 1340, *pg.* 1335
GLEASON BPG - CNC Cutter Sharpening Machine - GLEASON CORPORATION; *pg.* 1340, *pg.* 1335
GLEASON-HURTH - Machines for Producing Gears & Tooling & Spare Parts - GLEASON CORPORATION; *pg.* 1340, *pg.* 1335
GLEASON REEL - Industrial Technology - HUBBELL INCORPORATED; *pg.* 1299, *pg.* 370
GLEEM - Furniture Polish - SWISHER HYGIENE INC.; *pg.* 336, *pg.* 1507
GLEID - Home Cleaner - S.C. JOHNSON & SON, INC.; *pg.* 334, *pg.* 1889
GLEN - Footwear - DEER STAGS INC.; *pg.* 1807, *pg.* 1222
THE GLEN - Motorsport Race - INTERNATIONAL SPEEDWAY CORPORATION; *pg.* 553, *pg.* 420
GLEN ABBEY - Furniture - ASHLEY FURNITURE INDUSTRIES, INC.; *pg.* 914, *pg.* 1852
GLEN BURDINE - Malt - LEONARD KREUSCH, INC.; *pg.* 254, *pg.* 1099
GLEN EAGLE - Furniture - ASHLEY FURNITURE INDUSTRIES, INC.; *pg.* 914, *pg.* 1852
GLEN ELLEN WINES - Wine - DIAGEO NORTH AMERICA, INC.; *pg.* 1961, *pg.* 361
GLEN FALLS - Kitchen Product - KOHLER CO.; *pg.* 91, *pg.* 1862
GLEN-GERY - Face & Paving Brick - GLEN-GERY CORPORATION; *pg.* 84, *pg.* 1595
GLEN RAVEN - Canvas Fabrics - GLEN RAVEN, INC.; *pg.* 693, *pg.* 1373
GLEN SALEN - Pure Maly Scotch Whisky - HEAVEN HILL DISTILLERIES, INC.; *pg.* 1964, *pg.* 725
GLEN-SLEEVE - Protective Product - DERMA SCIENCES, INC.; *pg.* 1523, *pg.* 1111
GLENBARD REAMERS - Presicion Cutting Tools - REGAL BELOIT CORPORATION; *pg.* 106, *pg.* 1854
GLENBROOK LIFE - Life Insurance & Savings - THE ALLSTATE CORPORATION; *pg.* 1189, *pg.* 639
GLENBURY - Bath Product - KOHLER CO.; *pg.* 91, *pg.* 1862
GLENCO - Syringe - SPECTRUM LABORATORIES INC.; *pg.* 1595, *pg.* 69
GLENCOE - Tillage Equipment, Planters - AGCO CORPORATION; *pg.* 700, *pg.* 530
GLENDALE-NEWS PRESS - Newspaper - LOS ANGELES TIMES COMMUNICATIONS, LLC; *pg.* 1660, *pg.* 135
GLENDOWER - Fabric - NEMSCHOFF, INC.; *pg.* 936, *pg.* 1890
GLENDROSTAN SCOTCH - Spirits - LEONARD KREUSCH, INC.; *pg.* 254, *pg.* 1099
GLENFIELD - Shoes - ALLEN-EDMONDS SHOE CORP.; *pg.* 1804, *pg.* 1887
GLENGOYNE SINGLE MALT SCOTCH - Scotch Whiskey - SHAW ROSS INTERNATIONAL IMPORTERS; *pg.* 1970, *pg.* 449
THE GLENLIVET - Scotch - DIAGEO CANADA, INC.; *pg.* 1961, *pg.* 1937
THE GLENLIVET - Single Malt Scotch Whiskey - PERNOD

RICARD USA, INC.; *pg.* 1968, *pg.* 1332
GLENLO ABBEY - Carpet - BEAULIEU GROUP, LLC; *pg.* 917, *pg.* 529
GLENMORANGIE - Scotch Whiskey - BROWN-FORMAN CORPORATION; *pg.* 1958, *pg.* 732
GLENMORANGIE - Scotch - MOET HENNESSY; *pg.* 1966, *pg.* 1260
GLENTROMIE HIGHLAND MALT SCOTCH - Scotch - SAZERAC COMPANY, INC.; *pg.* 1969, *pg.* 745
GLI - Sensor & Analyzer - DANAHER CORPORATION; *pg.* 1044, *pg.* 397
GLIADEL - Pharmaceutical - EISAI INC.; *pg.* 1526, *pg.* 1133
GLID - Paint - AKZONOBEL DECORATIVE PAINTS U.S.; *pg.* 1439, *pg.* 1474
GLID-GUARD - Coating - AKZONOBEL DECORATIVE PAINTS U.S.; *pg.* 1439, *pg.* 1474
GLID-SHIELD - Paint - AKZONOBEL DECORATIVE PAINTS U.S.; *pg.* 1439, *pg.* 1474
GLID-THANE - Coating - AKZONOBEL DECORATIVE PAINTS U.S.; *pg.* 1439, *pg.* 1474
GLID-TILE - Paint - AKZONOBEL DECORATIVE PAINTS U.S.; *pg.* 1439, *pg.* 1474
GLID-TONE - Stain - AKZONOBEL DECORATIVE PAINTS U.S.; *pg.* 1439, *pg.* 1474
GLID-ZINC - Paint - AKZONOBEL DECORATIVE PAINTS U.S.; *pg.* 1439, *pg.* 1474
GLIDDEN - Paint - PPG INDUSTRIES, INC.; *pg.* 1445, *pg.* 1579
GLIDE - Footwear - CAPEZIO BALLET MAKERS INC.; *pg.* 1805, *pg.* 1125
GLIDE 2 RIDE BIKE - Toy & Game - HASBRO, INC.; *pg.* 954, *pg.* 1603
GLIDE-ON - Paint - AKZONOBEL DECORATIVE PAINTS U.S.; *pg.* 1439, *pg.* 1474
GLIDE PINS - Mold Base & Component - SUPERIOR DIE SET CORP.; *pg.* 1379, *pg.* 1885
GLIDE-R-MOTION - Gliding Technology - GROUPE DUTAILIER INC.; *pg.* 926, *pg.* 1960
GLIDE RITE - Ejector Component - SUPERIOR DIE SET CORP.; *pg.* 1379, *pg.* 1885
GLIDE SLEEVE - Ejector Component - SUPERIOR DIE SET CORP.; *pg.* 1379, *pg.* 1885
GLIDE SLEEVES - Ejector Component - SUPERIOR DIE SET CORP.; *pg.* 1379, *pg.* 1885
GLIDEAWAY - Cabinet Door System - NER HOLDINGS INC.; *pg.* 444, *pg.* 1071
GLIDETEC - Seal & Thermoplastic Component - GREENE, TWEED & CO.; *pg.* 1344, *pg.* 1544
GLIDEWIRE - Medical Device - BOSTON SCIENTIFIC CORPORATION; *pg.* 1508, *pg.* 831
GLIMMER - Fabric - NEMSCHOFF, INC.; *pg.* 936, *pg.* 1890
GLIMMER BRONZE - Face & Body Product - THE BONNE BELL COMPANY; *pg.* 502, *pg.* 1480
GLIMMER LIGHTS - Face & Body Product - THE BONNE BELL COMPANY; *pg.* 502, *pg.* 1480
GLIMMERGLASS - Filter & Lens - THE TIFFEN COMPANY LLC; *pg.* 1432, *pg.* 1165
GLIMMERSTICKS - Beauty Product - AVON PRODUCTS, INC.; *pg.* 500, *pg.* 1198
GLIMPSE - Skin Care Product - XANGO, LLC; *pg.* 1610, *pg.* 1751
GLISS - Footwear - CAPEZIO BALLET MAKERS INC.; *pg.* 1805, *pg.* 1125
GLISS PRO - Footwear - CAPEZIO BALLET MAKERS INC.; *pg.* 1805, *pg.* 1125
GLISTER - Oral Care Products - AMWAY CORPORATION; *pg.* 326, *pg.* 864
GLITCHCATHER - Current Boost Circuit - MAXIM INTEGRATED PRODUCTS, INC.; *pg.* 653, *pg.* 247
GLITTER & GOLD - Video Game - INTERNATIONAL GAME TECHNOLOGY; *pg.* 957, *pg.* 1024
GLITTERPRINT - Balloon - CONTINENTAL AMERICAN CORP.; *pg.* 1880, *pg.* 723
GLITTERSPUN - Yarn - LION BRAND YARN COMPANY; *pg.* 696, *pg.* 1050
GLITZ - Fabric - NEMSCHOFF, INC.; *pg.* 936, *pg.* 1890
GLNLIVET - Footwear - STEVEN MADDEN, LTD.; *pg.* 1819, *pg.* 1176
GLO BAY - HID Industrial Lighting - CRESCENT/STONCO SUPPLY DIVISION; *pg.* 1295, *pg.* 1121
GLO-COAT - Floor Polish - S.C. JOHNSON & SON, INC.; *pg.* 334, *pg.* 1889
GLO-PLUG - Extension Cord - SOUTHWIRE COMPANY; *pg.* 1063, *pg.* 527
GLO-STRIP - Rubber Stair Tread - R.C.A. RUBBER COMPANY; *pg.* 1888, *pg.* 1402
GLO-TECH - Valve - WOODWARD, INC.; *pg.* 122, *pg.* 329
GLOBAL - Fabric - NEMSCHOFF, INC.; *pg.* 936, *pg.* 1890
GLOBAL - Relocation Services - SIRVA, INC.; *pg.* 1923, *pg.* 669
GLOBAL 360 IMAGING FOR WINDOWS - Software - OPENTEXT; *pg.* 450, *pg.* 1665
GLOBAL 360 SCAN MANAGER - Software - OPENTEXT; *pg.* 450, *pg.* 1665
GLOBAL AMERICA - Telephone Service - IDT CORPORATION; *pg.* 643, *pg.* 1096
GLOBAL ARRAY MANAGER - Computer Network Software - AVAGO TECHNOLOGIES; *pg.* 358, *pg.* 238
GLOBAL ASSIST - Personal Card - AMERICAN EXPRESS COMPANY; *pg.* 712, *pg.* 1190
GLOBAL BOOKS IN PRINT - Publication - R.R. BOWKER LLC; *pg.* 1682, *pg.* 1095
GLOBAL CALL - Telephone Service - IDT CORPORATION; *pg.* 643, *pg.* 1096
GLOBAL DEBT MANAGER - Software - SS&C TECHNOLOGIES HOLDINGS, INC.; *pg.* 473, *pg.* 386
GLOBAL EXPRESS GUARANTEED - Postal Services - UNITED STATES POSTAL SERVICE; *pg.* 1009, *pg.* 406
GLOBAL FILE VIRTUALIZATION - Software - EMC CORPORATION; *pg.* 391, *pg.* 825
THE GLOBAL FLEET CARD COMPANY - Tagline - FLEETCOR TECHNOLOGIES, INC.; *pg.* 758, *pg.* 537
GLOBAL FUSION - Bath Accessory - CROSCILL, INC.; *pg.* 1122, *pg.* 1220
GLOBAL GRILL - Food Product - ADVANCEPIERRE FOODS, INC.; *pg.* 1714, *pg.* 1409
THE GLOBAL LEADER IN BLOOD MANAGEMENT SOLUTIONS - Tagline - HAEMONETICS CORPORATION; *pg.* 1538, *pg.* 802
GLOBAL LEADER IN STORED ELECTRICAL ENERGY - Tagline - EXIDE TECHNOLOGIES; *pg.* 204, *pg.* 483
GLOBAL MANAGEMENT SYSTEM - Web Based Management Software - POLYCOM, INC.; *pg.* 664, *pg.* 249
GLOBAL MANUFACTURING SOLUTIONS - Services & Solutions - ROCKWELL AUTOMATION, INC.; *pg.* 668, *pg.* 1880
GLOBAL MHS - Computer Software - NOVELL INC.; *pg.* 446, *pg.* 852
GLOBAL ONE - Software - SUNGARD DATA SYSTEMS INC.; *pg.* 477, *pg.* 1592
GLOBAL PLUS - Software - SUNGARD DATA SYSTEMS INC.; *pg.* 477, *pg.* 1592
GLOBAL PORTFOLIO II - Investment Fund - SUNGARD DATA SYSTEMS INC.; *pg.* 477, *pg.* 1592
GLOBAL PORTFOLIO SYSTEM - Software - DST SYSTEMS, INC.; *pg.* 388, *pg.* 982
GLOBAL PRESENCE WITH LOCAL SUPPORT! - Tagline - ESSENTRA COMPONENTS; *pg.* 1047, *pg.* 612
GLOBAL PRINT DRIVER - Software - XEROX CORPORATION; *pg.* 494, *pg.* 365
GLOBAL PRIORITY MAIL - International Shipping - UNITED STATES POSTAL SERVICE; *pg.* 1009, *pg.* 406
GLOBAL RATINGS HANDBOOK - Taxable Issues - STANDARD & POOR'S RATINGS SERVICES; *pg.* 805, *pg.* 1296
GLOBAL RELEAF - Education & Action Program - AMERICAN FORESTS; *pg.* 128, *pg.* 394
GLOBAL SERIES - Cylinder - FABCO-AIR, INC.; *pg.* 1336, *pg.* 429
GLOBAL-SITE - Software - F5 NETWORKS, INC.; *pg.* 396, *pg.* 1835
GLOBAL SOLUTIONS, LOCAL SERVICE. - Tag Line - A.W. CHESTERTON COMPANY; *pg.* 1315, *pg.* 861
THE GLOBAL SUPPLIER OF EFFECT PIGMENTS - Slogan - SILBERLINE MANUFACTURING CO., INC.; *pg.* 110, *pg.* 1588
GLOBAL SUPPLY CHAIN - Magazine - AVNET, INC.; *pg.* 622, *pg.* 15
THE GLOBAL SYMBOL FOR GREAT ITALIAN FOOD - Slogan - SBARRO, INC.; *pg.* 1749, *pg.* 1182
GLOBAL TERRAIN - Digital Terrain Elevation - INTERMAP TECHNOLOGIES CORPORATION; *pg.* 417, *pg.* 1903
GLOBAL TEXTURE - Software - EVANS & SUTHERLAND COMPUTER CORPORATION; *pg.* 638, *pg.* 1757
GLOBAL TOTAL SHOULDER SYSTEM - Orthopedic Product - DEPUYSYNTHES; *pg.* 1523, *pg.* 699
GLOBAL TRADE ACCESS - Computer Database - HUNTINGTON BANCSHARES INCORPORATED; *pg.* 767, *pg.* 1440
GLOBAL TRADEBOOK - Securites Trading Network - BLOOMBERG L.P.; *pg.* 725, *pg.* 1204
GLOBAL VILLAGE - VoIP Product - ZOOM TECHNOLOGIES, INC.; *pg.* 497, *pg.* 1317
GLOBAL VR - Vertical Vacuum Furnace - IPSEN INTERNATIONAL, INC.; *pg.* 1073, *pg.* 562
GLOBALACCESSSERVER - Software - AXEDA SYSTEMS INC.; *pg.* 359, *pg.* 819
GLOBALBOOKSINPRINT.COM - Online Database - R.R. BOWKER LLC; *pg.* 1682, *pg.* 1095
GLOBALFIX - Bracket - ACR ELECTRONICS, INC.; *pg.* 612, *pg.* 422
GLOBALGEAR - Pump - TUTHILL CORPORATION; *pg.* 1385, *pg.* 561
GLOBALIZATION-AT-SOURCE - Content Development & Localization Methodology - LIONBRIDGE TECHNOLOGIES INC.; *pg.* 428, *pg.* 851
GLOBALLOGIC VELOCITY - Software - GLOBALLOGIC, INC.; *pg.* 400, *pg.* 1791
GLOBALMEET - Conferencing Tool - PREMIERE GLOBAL SERVICES, INC.; *pg.* 1275, *pg.* 518
GLOBALSCAN - Software - RICOH AMERICAS CORPORATION; *pg.* 461, *pg.* 1131
GLOBALSCAPE CDP - Software - GLOBALSCAPE INC.; *pg.* 401, *pg.* 1740
GLOBALSCAPE EFT - Server - GLOBALSCAPE INC.; *pg.* 401, *pg.* 1740
GLOBALSCAPE SECURE FTP - Server - GLOBALSCAPE INC.; *pg.* 401, *pg.* 1740
GLOBALSCAPE WAFS - Software - GLOBALSCAPE INC.; *pg.* 401, *pg.* 1740
GLOBALSTAR - Satellite Phone - QUALCOMM INCORPORATED; *pg.* 1873, *pg.* 207
GLOBALTRACS - Wireless Data - QUALCOMM INCORPORATED; *pg.* 1873, *pg.* 207
GLOBALWAVE - Wireless Product - TRANSCORE HOLDINGS INC.; *pg.* 485, *pg.* 1541
GLOBE - Newspaper - AMERICAN MEDIA, INC.; *pg.* 1615, *pg.* 410
GLOBE - Rubber Works - GLOBE COMPOSITE SOLUTIONS, LTD.; *pg.* 1883, *pg.* 842
GLOBE - Bicycle - SPECIALIZED BICYCLE COMPONENTS, INC.; *pg.* 1711, *pg.* 152
GLOBE PEQUOT - Travel Books - THE GLOBE PEQUOT PRESS, INC.; *pg.* 1645, *pg.* 350
GLOBECOMM - Design Satellite - GLOBECOMM SYSTEMS INC.; *pg.* 640, *pg.* 1164
GLOBEL MODEL - Track - COILCRAFT, INC.; *pg.* 1324, *pg.* 562
GLOBEMASTER - Mass Merchandiser Type Globe - REPLOGLE GLOBES, INC.; *pg.* 461, *pg.* 559
GLOBEST.COM - Website - AMERICAN LAWYER MEDIA, INC.; *pg.* 1615, *pg.* 1193
GLOBO - Paints - THE SHERWIN-WILLIAMS COMPANY; *pg.* 1447, *pg.* 1435
GLOCOAT - Conditioner - PETEDGE; *pg.* 1481, *pg.* 787
GLOPRINT - Balloon - CONTINENTAL AMERICAN CORP.; *pg.* 1880, *pg.* 723
GLORIA - Beer - COASTAL EXTREME BREWING COMPANY; *pg.* 240, *pg.* 1602
GLORIA - Footwear - EASTLAND SHOE CORPORATION; *pg.* 1808, *pg.* 750
GLORIA - Fabric - NEMSCHOFF, INC.; *pg.* 936, *pg.* 1890
GLORIA - Footwear - PHOENIX FOOTWEAR GROUP, INC.; *pg.* 1815, *pg.* 60
GLORY - Rug Cleaner - S.C. JOHNSON & SON, INC.; *pg.* 334, *pg.* 1889
GLORY 7'S - Game - MULTIMEDIA GAMES INC.; *pg.* 442, *pg.* 1664
GLORY DAZE - Trivia Game Focused on Baby Boomer Topics - NTN BUZZTIME, INC.; *pg.* 659, *pg.* 60
GLOSETTE - Peanuts & Raisins - THE HERSHEY CO.; *pg.* 1855, *pg.* 1538
GLOSS - Dental Product - DENTSPLY INTERNATIONAL INC.; *pg.* 1522, *pg.* 1596
GLOSS BOSS - Mini Scrubber - PULLMAN-HOLT CORPORATION; *pg.* 333, *pg.* 475
GLOSS DROPS - Hair Care Product - JOHN PAUL MITCHELL SYSTEMS; *pg.* 512, *pg.* 133
GLOSS-N-SEAL - Dental Bonding System - DEN-MAT CORPORATION; *pg.* 1522, *pg.* 271
GLOSSAMER - Personal Care Product - TRI-K INDUSTRIES, INC.; *pg.* 523, *pg.* 1099
GLOSSBELT - Belting Product - ALBANY INTERNATIONAL CORP.; *pg.* 691, *pg.* 1038

GLOSSER - Topcoats - ORLY INTERNATIONAL, INC.; *pg.* 518, *pg.* 137
GLOSSMARK - Printer - XEROX CORPORATION; *pg.* 494, *pg.* 365
GLOTIP ERCP - Medical Device - COOK GROUP, INC.; *pg.* 1518, *pg.* 674
GLOVE COMPARTMENT GAMES - Educational Materials - SCHOLASTIC INC.; *pg.* 1683, *pg.* 1288
GLOVER'S - Dandruff Control Products - J. STRICKLAND & COMPANY; *pg.* 512, *pg.* 970
GLOW - Fabric - NEMSCHOFF, INC.; *pg.* 936, *pg.* 1890
GLOW CUBE - Reflected Light Displays - DAKTRONICS, INC.; *pg.* 633, *pg.* 1624
GLOW IMPERIAL - Glow-in-the-Dark Plastic Yo-Yo - DUNCAN TOYS COMPANY; *pg.* 951, *pg.* 1465
GLOW 'N' MOTION - 3-D Designs for Cups - EVENFLO COMPANY, INC.; *pg.* 924, *pg.* 1470
GLOW 'N TELL - Medical Tape - LEMAITRE VASCULAR, INC.; *pg.* 1555, *pg.* 805
GLOWALL - Burner - NAO, INC.; *pg.* 1074, *pg.* 1567
GLOWORM - Toy & Game - HASBRO, INC.; *pg.* 954, *pg.* 1603
GLOWZONE - Gloves - WELLS LAMONT CORPORATION; *pg.* 15, *pg.* 638
GLUCAFFECT - Nutritional Supplement - RELIV INTERNATIONAL, INC.; *pg.* 1589, *pg.* 975
GLUCAGON - Pharmaceutical Product - ELI LILLY AND COMPANY; *pg.* 1527, *pg.* 684
GLUCERNA - Nutritional Supplement - ABBOTT LABORATORIES; *pg.* 1484, *pg.* 551
GLUCERNA - Nutrition Shakes & Bars for Diabetics - ABBOTT NUTRITION; *pg.* 1485, *pg.* 1437
GLUCO-SCIENCE - Vitamin & Herbal Supplement - SOURCE NATURALS; *pg.* 1595, *pg.* 278
GLUCOBREAK - Appetite Suppressant - GENEREX BIOTECHNOLOGY CORPORATION; *pg.* 1534, *pg.* 1938
GLUCOLET 2 - Automatic Lancing Device - MEDLINE INDUSTRIES, INC.; *pg.* 1562, *pg.* 635
GLUCOPHAGE - Health Care Product - BRISTOL-MYERS SQUIBB COMPANY; *pg.* 1509, *pg.* 1206
GLUCOPHAGE XR - Health Care Product - BRISTOL-MYERS SQUIBB COMPANY; *pg.* 1509, *pg.* 1206
GLUCOPHAGE XR - Pharmaceutical Product - IMPAX LABORATORIES, INC.; *pg.* 1544, *pg.* 101
GLUCOSAMEND - Vitamin & Herbal Supplement - SOURCE NATURALS; *pg.* 1595, *pg.* 278
GLUCOSE - Reagent - BECKMAN COULTER, INC.; *pg.* 1402, *pg.* 48
GLUCOSUPPORT - Weight Control Product - NATROL, INC.; *pg.* 1570, *pg.* 64
GLUCOTRIM - Nutritional Supplement - NATURAL ORGANICS, INC.; *pg.* 1571, *pg.* 1181
GLUCOTROL - Medicine - PFIZER INC.; *pg.* 1581, *pg.* 1278
GLUCOTROL XL - Glipizide GITS - PFIZER INC.; *pg.* 1581, *pg.* 1278
GLUCOVANCE - Health Care Product - BRISTOL-MYERS SQUIBB COMPANY; *pg.* 1509, *pg.* 1206
GLUE DOTS - Glue & Adhesive - GLUEFAST COMPANY, INC.; *pg.* 1459, *pg.* 1090
GLUEAWAY - Dry Cleaning & Laundry Product - ADCO, INC.; *pg.* 325, *pg.* 482
GLUEFAST - Machine Glues - GLUEFAST COMPANY, INC.; *pg.* 1459, *pg.* 1090
GLUEFAST DUOS - Glue & Adhesive - GLUEFAST COMPANY, INC.; *pg.* 1459, *pg.* 1090
GLULAM - Laminated Timber - APA-THE ENGINEERED WOOD ASSOCIATION; *pg.* 132, *pg.* 1844
GLUMETZA - Pharmaceutical Product - DEPOMED, INC.; *pg.* 1523, *pg.* 143
GLUMETZA - Pharmaceutical Product - SALIX PHARMACEUTICALS, INC.; *pg.* 1591, *pg.* 1388
GLUMETZA - Pharmaceutical Product - VALEANT PHARMACEUTICALS INTERNATIONAL, INC.; *pg.* 1605, *pg.* 1957
GLUTAMAX - Cell Culture Product - THERMO FISHER SCIENTIFIC INC.; *pg.* 1602, *pg.* 61
GLUTAPAK - Nutritional Product - VICTUS, INC.; *pg.* 1606, *pg.* 447
GLUTAPAK-10 - Nutritional Product - VICTUS, INC.; *pg.* 1606, *pg.* 447
GLUTAREX-1 - Pharmaceutical Product - ABBOTT LABORATORIES; *pg.* 1484, *pg.* 551
GLUTEN FREE - Food Product - BOB'S RED MILL NATURAL FOODS, INC.; *pg.* 841, *pg.* 1500
GLUTINO - Gluten-Free Products - BOULDER BRANDS, INC.; *pg.* 1016, *pg.* 310
GLUTTON - Plastic Trash Can - HILLYARD, INC.; *pg.* 331, *pg.* 990
GLX - Light Source - CYMER, INC.; *pg.* 1296, *pg.* 202
GLY 4 - Herbicide - UNIVERSAL COOPERATIVES, INC.; *pg.* 1482, *pg.* 922
GLY 4 PLUS - Herbicide - UNIVERSAL COOPERATIVES, INC.; *pg.* 1482, *pg.* 922
GLYCENTIALS - Nutritional Product - MANNATECH, INCORPORATED; *pg.* 1558, *pg.* 1671
GLYCINE - Chemical Product - JARCHEM INDUSTRIES, INC.; *pg.* 1169, *pg.* 1096
GLYCO BEARS - Nutritional Product - MANNATECH, INCORPORATED; *pg.* 1558, *pg.* 1671
GLYCO DOC - Software - BIO-RAD LABORATORIES, INC.; *pg.* 1504, *pg.* 101
GLYCO-PAK - Column - WATERS CORPORATION; *pg.* 1436, *pg.* 834
GLYCOBLOT - Software - BIO-RAD LABORATORIES, INC.; *pg.* 1504, *pg.* 101
GLYCOCHROM - Software - BIO-RAD LABORATORIES, INC.; *pg.* 1504, *pg.* 101
GLYCODUR - Industrial Bearings - FEDERAL-MOGUL HOLDINGS CORPORATION; *pg.* 205, *pg.* 907
GLYCOLEAN - Medical Device - MANNATECH, INCORPORATED; *pg.* 1558, *pg.* 1671
GLYCOLUBE - Textile Chemicals - LONZA INC.; *pg.* 1171, *pg.* 1041
GLYCON - Glycerin, Sorbital for Humectancy In Food, Tobacco, Toothpaste - LONZA INC.; *pg.* 1171, *pg.* 1041
GLYCONITRIC - Nutritional Product - NUTRACEUTICAL INTERNATIONAL CORPORATION; *pg.* 1576, *pg.* 1753
GLYCOSAL - Software - BIO-RAD LABORATORIES, INC.; *pg.* 1504, *pg.* 101
GLYCOSLIM - Nutritional Product - MANNATECH, INCORPORATED; *pg.* 1558, *pg.* 1671
GLYCOSPERSE - Emulsifier & Water Treatment Chemical - LONZA INC.; *pg.* 1171, *pg.* 1041
GLYCOSTAT - Plastic Additives - LONZA INC.; *pg.* 1171, *pg.* 1041
GLYCOWAX - Defoamer Wax For Water Treatment - LONZA INC.; *pg.* 1171, *pg.* 1041
GLYDANT - Preservatives for Microbiological Control & Personal Care - LONZA INC.; *pg.* 1171, *pg.* 1041
GLYDANT PLUS - Preservatives for Microbiological Control - LONZA INC.; *pg.* 1171, *pg.* 1041
GLYDANT PLUS LIQUID - Liquid Preservatives for Microbiological Control - LONZA INC.; *pg.* 1171, *pg.* 1041
GLYDASEAL - Sluice Gate - RODNEY HUNT COMPANY; *pg.* 1372, *pg.* 840
GLYMINE - Gas Treating System - CAMERON INTERNATIONAL; *pg.* 1151, *pg.* 1702
GLYNASE - Medicine - PFIZER INC.; *pg.* 1581, *pg.* 1278
GLYNN-JOHNSON - Door Hardware - INGERSOLL-RAND COMPANY; *pg.* 1349, *pg.* 1370
GLYPHOMATE - Turf Product - PBI/GORDON CORPORATION; *pg.* 1176, *pg.* 985
GLYPHOMAX - Herbicide - DOW AGROSCIENCES LLC; *pg.* 1156, *pg.* 684
GLYPRO - Diagnostic Product - GENZYME CORPORATION; *pg.* 1534, *pg.* 808
GLYPTEX - Coating Product - PPG INDUSTRIES, INC.; *pg.* 1445, *pg.* 1579
GLYPURE - High Purity Glycolic Acid - E.I. DU PONT DE NEMOURS & COMPANY; *pg.* 1159, *pg.* 390
GLYQUIN - Pharmaceutical Product - VALEANT PHARMACEUTICALS INTERNATIONAL; *pg.* 1605, *pg.* 1047
GLYSET - Medicine - PFIZER INC.; *pg.* 1581, *pg.* 1278
GLYSOMED - Hand Care Product - BLISTEX, INC.; *pg.* 502, *pg.* 644
GLYTEX - Textile Chemicals - LONZA INC.; *pg.* 1171, *pg.* 1041
GLYTROL - Nutrition Supplement - NESTLE USA, INC.; *pg.* 883, *pg.* 96
GM PROTECTOR - Concentrated Nutrients for Internal Parasites - KENT NUTRITION GROUP; *pg.* 1477, *pg.* 710
GMAC - Financial Services - ALLY FINANCIAL INC.; *pg.* 711, *pg.* 878
GMAIL - Internet Application - GOOGLE INC.; *pg.* 1249, *pg.* 153
GMAX - Software - AUTODESK INC.; *pg.* 356, *pg.* 257
GMAX - Fluid Handling System - GRACO, INC.; *pg.* 1342, *pg.* 935
GMAX - Precision Subsystem & Module - GSI GROUP INC.; *pg.* 1415, *pg.* 784
GMC - Vehicle - GENERAL MOTORS COMPANY; *pg.* 175, *pg.* 881
GML - Onion Soup Mixes - GILSTER-MARY LEE CORPORATION; *pg.* 858, *pg.* 563
GML COMMANDER - Software - ROCKWELL AUTOMATION, INC.; *pg.* 668, *pg.* 1880
GML ULTRA - Software - ROCKWELL AUTOMATION, INC.; *pg.* 668, *pg.* 1880
GMLRS - Systems Integration & Aeronautics - LOCKHEED MARTIN CORPORATION; *pg.* 229, *pg.* 762
GMO INVESTIGATOR - Software - BIO-RAD LABORATORIES, INC.; *pg.* 1504, *pg.* 101
GMR SWITCH - Sensor - NVE CORPORATION; *pg.* 447, *pg.* 923
GMS - Glass & Ceramic Material - CORNING INCORPORATED; *pg.* 1122, *pg.* 1154
GMT - Watch - OAKLEY, INC.; *pg.* 1840, *pg.* 86
GMT - Metal Detector - WHITE'S ELECTRONICS; *pg.* 688, *pg.* 1509
GMX 200 - Navigational Systems - GARMIN INTERNATIONAL, INC.; *pg.* 1414, *pg.* 717
GMXXX - Fluid Handling System - GRACO, INC.; *pg.* 1342, *pg.* 935
GNAT-AWAY - Animal Safety Product - NEOGEN CORPORATION; *pg.* 883, *pg.* 896
GNATURAL - Animal Safety Product - NEOGEN CORPORATION; *pg.* 883, *pg.* 896
GNB - Battery - EXIDE TECHNOLOGIES; *pg.* 204, *pg.* 483
GNB FUSION - Battery - EXIDE TECHNOLOGIES; *pg.* 204, *pg.* 483
GNC-1700 - Case - GLOBALSTAR, INC.; *pg.* 401, *pg.* 743
GNP-1700 - Case - GLOBALSTAR, INC.; *pg.* 401, *pg.* 743
GNU - Snowboards - QUIKSILVER, INC.; *pg.* 31, *pg.* 104
GO - Guest Chairs & Conference Tables - BERNHARDT DESIGN; *pg.* 918, *pg.* 1381
GO ACTIVE - Slogan - MCDONALD'S CORPORATION; *pg.* 1737, *pg.* 645
GO-ANYWHERE - Gas Grill - WEBER-STEPHEN PRODUCTS LLC; *pg.* 62, *pg.* 650
GO AWAY MONSTER! - Game - GAMEWRIGHT; *pg.* 953, *pg.* 836
GO-BETWEENS - Tooth Cleaners - SUNSTAR AMERICAS INC.; *pg.* 1599, *pg.* 591
GO-BOTS - Toy & Game - HASBRO, INC.; *pg.* 954, *pg.* 1603
GO CARD - Mass Transit Card System - CUBIC CORPORATION; *pg.* 632, *pg.* 201
GO COLLECTIONS - Brief - JOCKEY INTERNATIONAL, INC.; *pg.* 27, *pg.* 1861
GO DIEGO GO! - Toy & Game - HASBRO, INC.; *pg.* 954, *pg.* 1603
GO DIEGO GO - Baby Care Product - MUNCHKIN, INC.; *pg.* 964, *pg.* 300
GO FLY A KITE - Sport & Leisure Product - JAKKS PACIFIC, INC.; *pg.* 960, *pg.* 142
GO FOR THE GREEN - Lottery Game - OHIO LOTTERY COMMISSION; *pg.* 1002, *pg.* 1433
GO FUG YOURSELF - Fashion Site - SPINMEDIA; *pg.* 1282, *pg.* 104
GO FURTHER. DO MORE. - Tagline - GLOBALSTAR, INC.; *pg.* 401, *pg.* 743
GO-GIRL - Shaver - THE ELTRON COMPANY; *pg.* 507, *pg.* 103
GO GO MY WALKING PUP - Toy & Game - HASBRO, INC.; *pg.* 954, *pg.* 1603
GO-GO TAQUITO - Snack - 7-ELEVEN, INC.; *pg.* 1012, *pg.* 1672
GO-GURT - Yogurt - GENERAL MILLS, INC.; *pg.* 828, *pg.* 933
GO-GURT - Yogurt - YOPLAIT USA, INC.; *pg.* 910, *pg.* 947
GO-LINE - Stain Remover - A.L. WILSON CHEMICAL CO.; *pg.* 325, *pg.* 1076
GO/NO GO - Gage Kits - HORNADY MANUFACTURING COMPANY; *pg.* 1836, *pg.* 1010
GO PHONE - Telephone Services - AT&T INC.; *pg.* 1867, *pg.* 1674
GO RVING - Vehicle - RECREATION VEHICLE INDUSTRY ASSOCIATION; *pg.* 155, *pg.* 1799
GO SLIM - Nutritional Supplement - PHARMAVITE LLC; *pg.* 1584, *pg.* 167
GO SNACKS - Snacks - FRITO-LAY NORTH AMERICA, INC.; *pg.* 1853, *pg.* 1730
GO SNACKS - Food & Beverage - PEPSICO, INC.; *pg.* 259, *pg.* 1327
GO SOLVE - Educational Materials - SCHOLASTIC INC.; *pg.*

1683, *pg.* 1288
GO THE DISTANCE - Tagline - FGX INTERNATIONAL, INC.; *pg.* 5, *pg.* 1608
THE GO-TO-GUYS FOR CARS AND CREDIT. - Slogan - DRIVETIME AUTOMOTIVE GROUP, INC.; *pg.* 169, *pg.* 16
GO-TO-IT - Blouses - HABAND COMPANY, INC.; *pg.* 1772, *pg.* 1099
THE GO-TO PLACE FOR THE NEXT GREAT IDEA - Tagline - CHF INDUSTRIES, INC.; *pg.* 920, *pg.* 1211
GO TO THE HEAD OF THE CLASS - Game - WINNING MOVES GAMES, INC.; *pg.* 970, *pg.* 816
GO-ULTRA - Catalyst - ALBEMARLE CORPORATION; *pg.* 1146, *pg.* 741
GO WITH CONFIDENCE - Tagline - EXPEDIA, INC.; *pg.* 1244, *pg.* 1814
GO WITH THE FLOW - Slogan - LIFEWAY FOODS, INC.; *pg.* 874, *pg.* 634
GOALIATH - Sporting Good Product - ESCALADE INC.; *pg.* 1833, *pg.* 678
GOALRILLA - Sporting Good Product - ESCALADE INC.; *pg.* 1833, *pg.* 678
GOASKFRED.COM - Dental Marketing Service - FUTUREDONTICS, INC.; *pg.* 1532, *pg.* 131
GOATEIN - Health Supplement - GARDEN OF LIFE, INC.; *pg.* 1532, *pg.* 478
GOBACK - Software - SYMANTEC CORPORATION; *pg.* 478, *pg.* 161
GOBAR - Software - SMITH MICRO SOFTWARE, INC.; *pg.* 471, *pg.* 41
GOBSTOPPERS - Candy - NESTLE USA, INC.; *pg.* 883, *pg.* 96
GOBUG - Bicycle - TREK BICYCLE CORPORATION; *pg.* 1847, *pg.* 1896
GOD BLESS AMERICA - Pillow and Throw - HERITAGE LACE INC.; *pg.* 694, *pg.* 711
GODDESS - Beauty Product - AVON PRODUCTS, INC.; *pg.* 500, *pg.* 1198
GODIVA - Chocolates - GODIVA CHOCOLATIER, INC.; *pg.* 1854, *pg.* 1235
GODIVA - Fire Pumps - IDEX CORPORATION; *pg.* 1347, *pg.* 623
GODIVA CHOCOISTE - Miniature Chocolates - GODIVA CHOCOLATIER, INC.; *pg.* 1854, *pg.* 1235
GODIVA LIQUEUR - Alcohol - DIAGEO CANADA, INC.; *pg.* 1961, *pg.* 1937
GOD'S PROMISES - Pillow and Throw - HERITAGE LACE INC.; *pg.* 694, *pg.* 711
GOD'S WORD TODAY - Daily Devotional Magazine - ALLIANCE OF CONFESSING EVANGELICALS, INC.; *pg.* 126, *pg.* 1545
GODS WORD TODAY - Magazine - BAYARD INC.; *pg.* 1620, *pg.* 359
GOETZ - Furniture - HERMAN MILLER, INC.; *pg.* 926, *pg.* 913
GOETZE - Pistons - FEDERAL-MOGUL HOLDINGS CORPORATION; *pg.* 205, *pg.* 907
GOFORCE - Wireless System - NVIDIA CORPORATION; *pg.* 447, *pg.* 268
GOGGLE BRIGHT - Anti-Fog Product - MCNETT CORPORATION; *pg.* 1839, *pg.* 1817
GOGORIDER - Infant Carrier - INFANTINO, LLC; *pg.* 957, *pg.* 203
GOIN' GREEN - Lottery Game - IDAHO LOTTERY; *pg.* 995, *pg.* 547
GOING FOR FOURS - Video Game - INTERNATIONAL GAME TECHNOLOGY; *pg.* 957, *pg.* 1024
GOING GREEN - Awareness Program - COYOTES HOCKEY, LLC; *pg.* 542, *pg.* 13
GOING PLACES - Auto Club Magazine - AMERICAN AUTOMOBILE ASSOCIATION; *pg.* 1190, *pg.* 429
GOING TO GRANDMA'S - Children's Luggage - MERCURY LUGGAGE/SEWARD TRUNK; *pg.* 9, *pg.* 434
GOING YOUR WAY - Slogan - METROPOLITAN TRANSPORTATION AUTHORITY; *pg.* 1915, *pg.* 1260
GOKEY - Snakeproof Boots - THE ORVIS COMPANY, INC.; *pg.* 1781, *pg.* 1764
GOLD - Scoreboard & Sports Product - DAKTRONICS, INC.; *pg.* 633, *pg.* 1624
GOLD - Photographic Film - EASTMAN KODAK COMPANY; *pg.* 1408, *pg.* 1333
GOLD - Software - LAPLINK SOFTWARE, INC.; *pg.* 426, *pg.* 1815
GOLD - Premixed Joint Compound - USG CORPORATION; *pg.* 118, *pg.* 594
GOLD - Cylindrical Grinder - WELDON SOLUTIONS; *pg.* 1388, *pg.* 1598
GOLD - Home Appliance Product - WHIRLPOOL CORPORATION; *pg.* 62, *pg.* 872
GOLD ANCHOR SERVICE - Cruise Ship - ROYAL CARIBBEAN CRUISES LTD; *pg.* 1921, *pg.* 446
GOLD BAR 7'S - Video Game - INTERNATIONAL GAME TECHNOLOGY; *pg.* 957, *pg.* 1024
GOLD BAR BINGO - Lottery Game - IDAHO LOTTERY; *pg.* 995, *pg.* 547
GOLD BAR BONANZA - Lottery Game - KENTUCKY LOTTERY CORPORATION; *pg.* 996, *pg.* 735
GOLD BARS - Video Game - INTERNATIONAL GAME TECHNOLOGY; *pg.* 957, *pg.* 1024
GOLD BOND - Health & Beauty Product - CHATTEM, INC.; *pg.* 1515, *pg.* 1628
GOLD BOND - Bedding - THE STANDARD MATTRESS COMPANY; *pg.* 943, *pg.* 352
GOLD BOND ULTIMATE - Health & Beauty Product - CHATTEM, INC.; *pg.* 1515, *pg.* 1628
GOLD C - Coupon Books - ENTERTAINMENT PUBLICATIONS, INC.; *pg.* 1639, *pg.* 910
GOLD CAP - Cabin Cleaning Service - SIGNATURE FLIGHT SUPPORT CORP.; *pg.* 234, *pg.* 456
GOLD CASH - Financial Services - FEDERAL HOME LOAN MORTGAGE CORPORATION; *pg.* 751, *pg.* 1790
GOLD CASH XTRA - Financial Services - FEDERAL HOME LOAN MORTGAGE CORPORATION; *pg.* 751, *pg.* 1790
GOLD CHECKER BONUS - Video Game - INTERNATIONAL GAME TECHNOLOGY; *pg.* 957, *pg.* 1024
GOLD-CLAD - Chemicals for Electro Plating - TECHNIC INCORPORATED; *pg.* 1183, *pg.* 1601
GOLD CLASSIC CARRY-OUT - Steamtable Pan - PACTIV CORPORATION; *pg.* 1466, *pg.* 624
GOLD COAST - Rug - COURISTAN INC.; *pg.* 921, *pg.* 1067
GOLD COAST - Container Grown Plant - MONROVIA GROWERS; *pg.* 1797, *pg.* 44
GOLD COAST BLEND - Coffee - STARBUCKS CORPORATION; *pg.* 897, *pg.* 1840
GOLD COINS OF THE WORLD - Gold Bullion Coin Set - MONEX DEPOSIT COMPANY; *pg.* 10, *pg.* 165
GOLD CONNECTION - Financial Services - FEDERAL HOME LOAN MORTGAGE CORPORATION; *pg.* 751, *pg.* 1790
GOLD CROWN - Table - BLATT BOWLING & BILLIARD CORP.; *pg.* 1827, *pg.* 1203
GOLD DIFFUSION/FX - Filter & Lens - THE TIFFEN COMPANY LLC; *pg.* 1432, *pg.* 1165
GOLD DISTANCE - Golf Equipment - ACUSHNET COMPANY; *pg.* 1824, *pg.* 818
THE GOLD FASHIONED GIRLS - Gold Promotion - WORLD GOLD COUNCIL; *pg.* 162, *pg.* 1315
GOLD FISH - Tape - IDEAL INDUSTRIES, INC.; *pg.* 1051, *pg.* 662
GOLD FISH - Game - WMS INDUSTRIES INC.; *pg.* 593, *pg.* 666
THE GOLD GLOVE AWARD - Award - RAWLINGS SPORTING GOODS CO., INC.; *pg.* 1843, *pg.* 1002
GOLD GOLD GOLD - Game - WMS INDUSTRIES INC.; *pg.* 593, *pg.* 666
GOLD K BILD - Manufacturer of Photographic Prints - EASTMAN KODAK COMPANY; *pg.* 1408, *pg.* 1333
GOLD KIST - Poultry - PILGRIM'S PRIDE CORPORATION; *pg.* 889, *pg.* 330
GOLD LABEL - Fishing Equipment - CABELA'S INCORPORATED; *pg.* 535, *pg.* 1019
GOLD LABEL - Non-Dairy Whipped Topping - RICH PRODUCTS CORPORATION; *pg.* 892, *pg.* 1150
GOLD LABEL - Shotgun - STURM, RUGER & COMPANY, INC.; *pg.* 1846, *pg.* 371
GOLD LANCE - Class Rings - JOSTENS, INC.; *pg.* 7, *pg.* 938
GOLD LEAF - Video Game - INTERNATIONAL GAME TECHNOLOGY; *pg.* 957, *pg.* 1024
GOLD LINE - Bracket - E.D. BULLARD COMPANY; *pg.* 1332, *pg.* 727
GOLD LINE - Registration Certificate - SETCO SALES COMPANY; *pg.* 1061, *pg.* 1426
GOLD MASTERCARD - Credit Card - MASTERCARD INCORPORATED; *pg.* 779, *pg.* 1325
GOLD MAXIMUM VELOCITY - Golf Equipment - ACUSHNET COMPANY; *pg.* 1824, *pg.* 818
GOLD MEASURE - Financial Services - FEDERAL HOME LOAN MORTGAGE CORPORATION; *pg.* 751, *pg.* 1790
GOLD MEDAL - Gold-Tone Electric Curling Irons - ANDIS COMPANY; *pg.* 498, *pg.* 1895
GOLD MEDAL - Food Product - THE C.F. SAUER COMPANY; *pg.* 847, *pg.* 1801
GOLD MEDAL - Food Product - GENERAL MILLS, INC.; *pg.* 828, *pg.* 933
GOLD MEDALIST - Cleaning Product - HILLYARD, INC.; *pg.* 331, *pg.* 990
GOLD MOUNTAIN - Video Game - INTERNATIONAL GAME TECHNOLOGY; *pg.* 957, *pg.* 1024
GOLD N CHEES - Food Product - SNYDER'S-LANCE, INC.; *pg.* 896, *pg.* 1368
GOLD' N HONEY - Poultry Frozen - TYSON FOODS, INC.; *pg.* 902, *pg.* 35
GOLD 'N NATURAL - Turbinado Sugar - IMPERIAL SUGAR COMPANY; *pg.* 864, *pg.* 1746
GOLD-N-SOFT - Cooking Product - VENTURA FOODS, LLC; *pg.* 908, *pg.* 49
GOLD-N-SWEET - Pan Coating - VENTURA FOODS, LLC; *pg.* 908, *pg.* 49
GOLD N'HOT - Personal Care Electrical Product - HELEN OF TROY L.P.; *pg.* 511, *pg.* 1692
GOLD NUGGET - Animal Safety Product - NEOGEN CORPORATION; *pg.* 883, *pg.* 896
GOLD NUTRITIONALS - Dog Food - FROMM FAMILY PET FOODS, INC.; *pg.* 1476, *pg.* 1870
GOLD PEAK - Iced Tea - THE COCA-COLA COMPANY; *pg.* 240, *pg.* 493
GOLD PERSPECTIVE - Financial Services - FEDERAL HOME LOAN MORTGAGE CORPORATION; *pg.* 751, *pg.* 1790
GOLD PLUS - Software - DAKTRONICS, INC.; *pg.* 633, *pg.* 1624
GOLD POINTS REWARD NETWORK - Visa Card - CARLSON COMPANIES INC.; *pg.* 1084, *pg.* 947
GOLD PROBE - Medical Device - BOSTON SCIENTIFIC CORPORATION; *pg.* 1508, *pg.* 831
GOLD RIBBON - Hams - HATFIELD QUALITY MEATS, INC.; *pg.* 861, *pg.* 1537
GOLD RIVER - Moist Snuff Smokeless Tobacco - SWISHER INTERNATIONAL, INC.; *pg.* 1895, *pg.* 345
GOLD RUSH - Financial Services - FEDERAL HOME LOAN MORTGAGE CORPORATION; *pg.* 751, *pg.* 1790
GOLD RUSH - Lottery Game - IDAHO LOTTERY; *pg.* 995, *pg.* 547
GOLD RUSH - Container Grown Plant - MONROVIA GROWERS; *pg.* 1797, *pg.* 44
GOLD SERIES - Reels - DAIWA CORPORATION; *pg.* 1832, *pg.* 75
GOLD SILVER BRONZE - Video Game - INTERNATIONAL GAME TECHNOLOGY; *pg.* 957, *pg.* 1024
GOLD SPOT - Beverages - THE COCA-COLA COMPANY; *pg.* 240, *pg.* 493
THE GOLD STANDARD OF QUALITY & CRAFTSMANSHIP - Slogan - MATTHEWS INTERNATIONAL CORPORATION; *pg.* 1662, *pg.* 1578
GOLD STAR - Cash Card - COSTCO WHOLESALE CORPORATION; *pg.* 1765, *pg.* 1820
GOLD STAR - Welding & Cutting Equip. - MILLER ELECTRIC MANUFACTURING CO.; *pg.* 1361, *pg.* 1852
GOLD STAR CHECKING - Account - SALEM FIVE CENTS SAVINGS BANK; *pg.* 800, *pg.* 843
GOLD STAR SAVER - Savings Account - SALEM FIVE CENTS SAVINGS BANK; *pg.* 800, *pg.* 843
GOLD STRIKE - Resort & Casino - MGM RESORTS INTERNATIONAL; *pg.* 1105, *pg.* 1028
GOLD STRIKE - Footwear - PHOENIX FOOTWEAR GROUP, INC.; *pg.* 1815, *pg.* 60
GOLD STRIKE RESORT - Resort & Casino - MGM RESORTS INTERNATIONAL; *pg.* 1105, *pg.* 1028
GOLD TAG 7S - Game - WMS INDUSTRIES INC.; *pg.* 593, *pg.* 666
GOLD TOE - Slippers - HABAND COMPANY, INC.; *pg.* 1772, *pg.* 1099
GOLD VALUE NOW CHECKING ACCOUNT - Personal Checking Account - APPLE BANK FOR SAVINGS; *pg.* 716, *pg.* 1196
GOLD WRAP - Animal Safety Product - NEOGEN CORPORATION; *pg.* 883, *pg.* 896
GOLDA - Furniture - NEMSCHOFF, INC.; *pg.* 936, *pg.* 1890
GOLDBERGER - Dolls - THE GOLDBERGER COMPANY, LLC; *pg.* 954, *pg.* 1235
GOLDBLATT - Hand Tools - STANLEY BLACK & DECKER, INC.; *pg.* 1063, *pg.* 358
GOLDCAST - Spinning Reels - DAIWA CORPORATION; *pg.* 1832, *pg.* 75
GOLDCHOICE - Banking Service - THE BANK OF NOVA

First page reference indicates Business Class Edition
Second page reference indicates Geographic Edition

SCOTIA; *pg.* 721, *pg.* 1935
GOLDCOAT - Software - BIO-RAD LABORATORIES, INC.; *pg.* 1504, *pg.* 101
GOLDDIGGERS - Food Product - ADVANCEPIERRE FOODS, INC.; *pg.* 1714, *pg.* 1409
GOLDE 50 - Life Insurance - OLD AMERICAN INSURANCE COMPANY; *pg.* 1213, *pg.* 985
GOLDEN ALMOND - Chocolate Bar - THE HERSHEY CO.; *pg.* 1855, *pg.* 1538
GOLDEN ALMOND NUGGETS - Chocolates - THE HERSHEY CO.; *pg.* 1855, *pg.* 1538
GOLDEN ALMOND SOLITAIRES - Chocolate Covered Almonds - THE HERSHEY CO.; *pg.* 1855, *pg.* 1538
GOLDEN ANNIVERSARY - Carpet - BEAULIEU GROUP, LLC; *pg.* 917, *pg.* 529
GOLDEN AWARD - Food Product - BUNGE LIMITED; *pg.* 842, *pg.* 1351
GOLDEN BACCARAT - Video Game - INTERNATIONAL GAME TECHNOLOGY; *pg.* 957, *pg.* 1024
GOLDEN BEAR - Cable - LOOS & COMPANY, INC.; *pg.* 1356, *pg.* 368
GOLDEN BLOSSOM - Video Game - INTERNATIONAL GAME TECHNOLOGY; *pg.* 957, *pg.* 1024
GOLDEN BLOSSOM HONEY - Honey Processor - JOHN PATON INC; *pg.* 866, *pg.* 1526
GOLDEN BOOKS - Publishing Imprint - PENGUIN RANDOM HOUSE CHILDREN'S BOOKS; *pg.* 1676, *pg.* 1277
GOLDEN BROWN - Sausage - JONES DAIRY FARM; *pg.* 867, *pg.* 1858
GOLDEN CANILLA - Rice - GOYA FOODS, INC.; *pg.* 859, *pg.* 1075
GOLDEN CANOLA - Canola Oil - MALLET & COMPANY, INC.; *pg.* 875, *pg.* 1521
GOLDEN CHARIOTS - Game - WMS INDUSTRIES INC.; *pg.* 593, *pg.* 666
GOLDEN CHERRIES - Game - WMS INDUSTRIES INC.; *pg.* 593, *pg.* 666
GOLDEN CHOICE BUFFET - Buffet And Grill - GOLDEN CORRAL CORPORATION; *pg.* 1730, *pg.* 1387
GOLDEN CIRCLE - Food Products - THE KRAFT HEINZ COMPANY; *pg.* 870, *pg.* 1577
GOLDEN COB - Food Product - MARS, INCORPORATED; *pg.* 1858, *pg.* 1792
GOLDEN CORRAL - Grill-Buffet Restaurant - FRISCH'S RESTAURANTS, INC.; *pg.* 1729, *pg.* 1413
GOLDEN CORRAL - Restaurants - GOLDEN CORRAL CORPORATION; *pg.* 1730, *pg.* 1387
GOLDEN CREME - Dairy & Bakery Items - UNIFIED GROCERS, INC.; *pg.* 1036, *pg.* 66
GOLDEN CRISP - Food Product - PATRICK CUDAHY INC.; *pg.* 888, *pg.* 1856
GOLDEN CRISP - Cereal - POST HOLDINGS, INC.; *pg.* 833, *pg.* 1002
GOLDEN CRUSH - Beverages - THE COCA-COLA COMPANY; *pg.* 240, *pg.* 493
GOLDEN CUISINE - Food Product - CONAGRA FOODS, INC.; *pg.* 826, *pg.* 1014
GOLDEN DIPT - Food Product - MCCORMICK & COMPANY, INCORPORATED; *pg.* 1027, *pg.* 779
GOLDEN DRAGON - Video Game - INTERNATIONAL GAME TECHNOLOGY; *pg.* 957, *pg.* 1024
GOLDEN EAGLE - Video Game - INTERNATIONAL GAME TECHNOLOGY; *pg.* 957, *pg.* 1024
GOLDEN EMPEROR - Game - WMS INDUSTRIES INC.; *pg.* 593, *pg.* 666
GOLDEN FIRE - Video Game - INTERNATIONAL GAME TECHNOLOGY; *pg.* 957, *pg.* 1024
GOLDEN FLAKE - Snack Foods - GOLDEN FLAKE SNACK FOODS, INC.; *pg.* 1854, *pg.* 3
GOLDEN FLO - Brush - THE WOOSTER BRUSH COMPANY; *pg.* 1450, *pg.* 1482
GOLDEN GALLON - Convenience Stores - THE PANTRY, INC.; *pg.* 1029, *pg.* 1360
GOLDEN GLO - Brush - THE WOOSTER BRUSH COMPANY; *pg.* 1450, *pg.* 1482
GOLDEN GLOW - Oil - MALLET & COMPANY, INC.; *pg.* 875, *pg.* 1521
GOLDEN GLUTEN - Wet Corn Gluten Feed - ARCHER-DANIELS-MIDLAND COMPANY; *pg.* 825, *pg.* 565
GOLDEN GODDESS - Video Game - INTERNATIONAL GAME TECHNOLOGY; *pg.* 957, *pg.* 1024
GOLDEN GRAHAMS - Cereal - GENERAL MILLS, INC.; *pg.* 828, *pg.* 933
GOLDEN GRAIN - Pasta - AMERICAN ITALIAN PASTA COMPANY; *pg.* 837, *pg.* 980
GOLDEN GRIDDLE FRY - Food Product - BUNGE LIMITED; *pg.* 842, *pg.* 1351
GOLDEN GRILL - Potato Pancake Mix - BASIC AMERICAN FOODS, INC.; *pg.* 839, *pg.* 303
GOLDEN GRIP - Corrugating & Bag - GRAIN PROCESSING CORPORATION; *pg.* 859, *pg.* 709
GOLDEN HAMMER - Game - WMS INDUSTRIES INC.; *pg.* 593, *pg.* 666
GOLDEN HEARTH - Bakery Products - ALPHA BAKING COMPANY; *pg.* 836, *pg.* 564
GOLDEN JACKPOT - Container Grown Plant - MONROVIA GROWERS; *pg.* 1797, *pg.* 44
GOLDEN KINGDOM - Video Game - INTERNATIONAL GAME TECHNOLOGY; *pg.* 957, *pg.* 1024
GOLDEN KNIGHT - Video Game - INTERNATIONAL GAME TECHNOLOGY; *pg.* 957, *pg.* 1024
GOLDEN LAYERS - Biscuits - GENERAL MILLS, INC.; *pg.* 828, *pg.* 933
GOLDEN LILY - Skin & Haircare Product - NEW EARTH LIFE SCIENCES, INC.; *pg.* 1573, *pg.* 1499
GOLDEN MEADOW - Honey - MILLER'S HONEY COMPANY; *pg.* 1860, *pg.* 1759
GOLDEN MOAI - Game - WMS INDUSTRIES INC.; *pg.* 593, *pg.* 666
GOLDEN NUGGET - Entertainment Product - MIRAGE RESORTS INCORPORATED; *pg.* 1105, *pg.* 1028
GOLDEN NUGGET - Container Grown Plant - MONROVIA GROWERS; *pg.* 1797, *pg.* 44
GOLDEN OPPORTUNITY - Video Game - INTERNATIONAL GAME TECHNOLOGY; *pg.* 957, *pg.* 1024
GOLDEN PEARL - Game - WMS INDUSTRIES INC.; *pg.* 593, *pg.* 666
THE GOLDEN PIG - Packaged Foods - ATALANTA CORPORATION; *pg.* 838, *pg.* 1057
GOLDEN PLAINS FOODS - Food - OMAHA STEAKS INTERNATIONAL, INC.; *pg.* 1780, *pg.* 1017
GOLDEN PRAIRIE - Processed Pork Products - AMERICAN FOODS GROUP, LLC; *pg.* 837, *pg.* 1859
GOLDEN PRINCE - Container Grown Plant - MONROVIA GROWERS; *pg.* 1797, *pg.* 44
GOLDEN PUFFS - Cereal - POST CONSUMER BRANDS; *pg.* 833, *pg.* 927
GOLDEN RING - Optical Product - LEUPOLD & STEVENS, INC.; *pg.* 1420, *pg.* 1492
GOLDEN STATE - Almonds - BLUE DIAMOND GROWERS; *pg.* 840, *pg.* 195
GOLDEN STATE WARRIORS - Basketball Team - GOLDEN STATE WARRIORS, LLC; *pg.* 550, *pg.* 171
GOLDEN STRATOCASTER - Electric Guitar - FENDER MUSICAL INSTRUMENTS CORPORATION; *pg.* 547, *pg.* 21
GOLDEN SUNRISE - Container Grown Plant - MONROVIA GROWERS; *pg.* 1797, *pg.* 44
GOLDEN SUPERB - Processed Pork Products - AMERICAN FOODS GROUP, LLC; *pg.* 837, *pg.* 1859
GOLDEN TEMPLE - Video Game - INTERNATIONAL GAME TECHNOLOGY; *pg.* 957, *pg.* 1024
GOLDEN TIG - Food Product - ELLENBEE-LEGGETT COMPANY INC.; *pg.* 854, *pg.* 1452
GOLDEN TIGER - Food Product - WINDSOR QUALITY FOOD CO., LTD.; *pg.* 910, *pg.* 1717
GOLDEN TIGER ETERNAL DRAGON - Video Game - INTERNATIONAL GAME TECHNOLOGY; *pg.* 957, *pg.* 1024
GOLDEN TOP - Popcorn Topping - VENTURA FOODS, LLC; *pg.* 908, *pg.* 49
GOLDEN TOUCH - Automotive Additive - GOLD EAGLE COMPANY; *pg.* 206, *pg.* 575
GOLDEN TWIST - Food Product - PEPPERIDGE FARM, INC.; *pg.* 888, *pg.* 363
GOLDEN WEST - Manufactured Homes - CLAYTON HOMES, INC.; *pg.* 1086, *pg.* 1640
GOLDEN YEARS - Nutritional Supplement - NATURAL ORGANICS, INC.; *pg.* 1571, *pg.* 1181
GOLDEN ZEBRA - Container Grown Plant - MONROVIA GROWERS; *pg.* 1797, *pg.* 44
GOLDENAIR - Hose - HBD INDUSTRIES, INC.; *pg.* 207, *pg.* 1449
GOLDENBERG'S PEANUT CHEWS - Candy - JUST BORN, INC.; *pg.* 1857, *pg.* 1516
GOLDEND - Fluid Sealing Product - A.W. CHESTERTON COMPANY; *pg.* 1315, *pg.* 861
GOLDENEDGE - Coating - GENERAL MAGNAPLATE CORPORATION; *pg.* 1164, *pg.* 1079
GOLDENGARD - Insulation Product - ALPHA ASSOCIATES, INC.; *pg.* 691, *pg.* 1078
GOLDENGATE - Assay - ILLUMINA, INC.; *pg.* 412, *pg.* 203
GOLDFINGER - Semiconductor Batch-Immersion System - AKRION, INC.; *pg.* 1311, *pg.* 1513
GOLDFISH - Crackers - CAMPBELL SOUP COMPANY; *pg.* 844, *pg.* 1048
GOLDFISH - Crackers - PEPPERIDGE FARM, INC.; *pg.* 888, *pg.* 363
GOLDFISH PREMIUM FLAKES - Fish Food - THE HARTZ MOUNTAIN CORP.; *pg.* 1476, *pg.* 1120
GOLDFISH SANDWICH SNACKERS - Snack - PEPPERIDGE FARM, INC.; *pg.* 888, *pg.* 363
GOLDILOCKS - Cable - LOOS & COMPANY, INC.; *pg.* 1356, *pg.* 368
GOLDLEAF - Clothing - LAKELAND INDUSTRIES, INC.; *pg.* 1354, *pg.* 1338
GOLDLINE - Valve Actuator - HAYWARD POOL PRODUCTS; *pg.* 1049, *pg.* 1057
GOLDMINE - Collectible Magazine for CD's, Records & Memorabilia - KRAUSE PUBLICATIONS, INC.; *pg.* 1657, *pg.* 1861
GOLD'N GRO - Fertilizer Products - ITRONICS INC.; *pg.* 1169, *pg.* 1031
GOLD'N PLUMP - Chicken, Fish & Marinades - GOLD'N PLUMP POULTRY, INC.; *pg.* 858, *pg.* 956
GOLD'N PLUMP PREMIUM SELECTS - Chicken Dinner - GOLD'N PLUMP POULTRY, INC.; *pg.* 858, *pg.* 956
GOLD'S - Horseradish, Borscht, Condiments - GOLD PURE FOOD PRODUCTS CO., INC.; *pg.* 858, *pg.* 1166
GOLD'S GYM - Health & Fitness Product - ICON HEALTH & FITNESS, INC.; *pg.* 1837, *pg.* 1752
GOLDSENSOR - Test Results - NIPRO DIAGNOSTICS, INC.; *pg.* 1573, *pg.* 426
GOLDSTAR - Digital Electronic Product Company - LG ELECTRONICS CANADA, INC.; *pg.* 651, *pg.* 1927
GOLDTONE - Amplifiers - GIBSON GUITAR CORP.; *pg.* 550, *pg.* 1650
GOLDWORKS - Financial Services - FEDERAL HOME LOAN MORTGAGE CORPORATION; *pg.* 751, *pg.* 1790
GOLEAN - High Protein/Fiber Foods - KASHI COMPANY; *pg.* 830, *pg.* 119
GOLEAN BARS - Food Product - KASHI COMPANY; *pg.* 830, *pg.* 119
GOLEAN CEREAL - High Protein/Fiber Bars - KASHI COMPANY; *pg.* 830, *pg.* 119
GOLEAN CRUNCH - Breakfast Cereal - KASHI COMPANY; *pg.* 830, *pg.* 119
GOLEAN HOT CEREAL - Cereal - KASHI COMPANY; *pg.* 830, *pg.* 119
GOLEAN SHAKES - Shakes - KASHI COMPANY; *pg.* 830, *pg.* 119
GOLEAN WAFFLES - Waffles - KASHI COMPANY; *pg.* 830, *pg.* 119
GOLF - Sock - OAKLEY, INC.; *pg.* 1840, *pg.* 86
GOLF CLUB - Mobile Game - BLUCORA; *pg.* 1232, *pg.* 1813
GOLF DIGEST - Magazine - CONDE NAST PUBLICATIONS, INC.; *pg.* 1629, *pg.* 1217
GOLF MAGAZINE - Magazine - BONNIER ACTIVE MEDIA, INC.; *pg.* 1622, *pg.* 1205
GOLF MAGAZINE.COM - Web Site - BONNIER ACTIVE MEDIA, INC.; *pg.* 1622, *pg.* 1205
GOLF PRIDE - Golf Club Grips - EATON CORPORATION; *pg.* 1331, *pg.* 1429
GOLF PRIVILEGE CARD - Discount Card - AMERICAN LUNG ASSOCIATION; *pg.* 129, *pg.* 395
GOLF SPIKE - Rubber Matting - THE BILTRITE CORPORATION; *pg.* 1879, *pg.* 850
GOLF WORLD - Magazine - CONDE NAST PUBLICATIONS, INC.; *pg.* 1629, *pg.* 1217
GOLFNOW.COM - Golfing Information & Tee Times - GOLF CHANNEL; *pg.* 551, *pg.* 454
GOLFONLINE.COM - Web Site - BONNIER ACTIVE MEDIA, INC.; *pg.* 1622, *pg.* 1205
GOLF'S SYMBOL OF EXCELLENCE - Tag Line - ACUSHNET COMPANY; *pg.* 1824, *pg.* 818
GOLFSMITH - Golf Equipment - GOLFSMITH INTERNATIONAL HOLDINGS, INC.; *pg.* 1835, *pg.* 1662
THE GOLFSMITH CREDIT CARD - Credit Card - GOLFSMITH INTERNATIONAL HOLDINGS, INC.; *pg.* 1835, *pg.* 1662
GOLIGHT - Truck Equipment - AMERICAN VAN EQUIPMENT INC.; *pg.* 199, *pg.* 1078
GOLIVE - Software - ADOBE SYSTEMS INCORPORATED; *pg.* 342, *pg.* 235
GOMCO - Suction Equipment - ALLIED HEALTHCARE

PRODUCTS, INC.; *pg.* 1491, *pg.* 990
GOMD - Software - NUANCE COMMUNICATIONS, INC.; *pg.* 447, *pg.* 806
GONAK - Ophthalmic Demulcent - AKORN, INC.; *pg.* 1488, *pg.* 622
GONE - Hair & Skin Product - AUBREY ORGANICS INC.; *pg.* 499, *pg.* 470
GONNELLA - French Bread & Rolls - GONNELLA BAKING COMPANY; *pg.* 859, *pg.* 575
GONOPROBE - Software - BIO-RAD LABORATORIES, INC.; *pg.* 1504, *pg.* 101
GONZALEZ-BYASS - Wine - REMY COINTREAU USA INC.; *pg.* 1969, *pg.* 1285
GONZALEZ Y GONZALEZ - Restaurant - ARK RESTAURANTS CORP.; *pg.* 1715, *pg.* 1196
GONZO - Household Cleaners - HOMAX PRODUCTS INC.; *pg.* 1442, *pg.* 1817
GONZO - Muppet - THE WALT DISNEY COMPANY; *pg.* 317, *pg.* 52
GOO - Puncture Seal - RADIATOR SPECIALTY COMPANY; *pg.* 215, *pg.* 1380
GOO GONE - Household Cleaner - HOMAX PRODUCTS INC.; *pg.* 1442, *pg.* 1817
GOO GOO CLUSTER - Chocolate Bar - STANDARD FUNCTIONAL FOODS GROUP(SFFG); *pg.* 1862, *pg.* 1654
GOOBER - Peanut Butter & Jelly Combination - THE J.M. SMUCKER COMPANY; *pg.* 865, *pg.* 1468
GOOBERS - Candy - NESTLE USA, INC.; *pg.* 883, *pg.* 96
GOOD & PLENTY - Candy - THE HERSHEY CO.; *pg.* 1855, *pg.* 1538
GOOD CENTS HOME - Program to Certify Energy Efficiency of Residential Dwellings - GEORGIA POWER COMPANY; *pg.* 1943, *pg.* 508
GOOD CHEER - Carpet - BEAULIEU GROUP, LLC; *pg.* 917, *pg.* 529
GOOD. CLEAN. FUN - Tagline - VERMONT LOTTERY COMMISSION; *pg.* 1010, *pg.* 1764
THE GOOD DOG - Snack Food Product - THE HAIN CELESTIAL GROUP, INC.; *pg.* 860, *pg.* 1172
GOOD DOG. GREAT RESULTS. - Slogan - BLUCORA; *pg.* 1232, *pg.* 1813
GOOD EQUIPMENT, PROPERLY SOLD & SERVICED - Tagline - A.J. JERSEY INC.; *pg.* 1310, *pg.* 1123
GOOD FOOD. BETTER LIFE. - Tagline - MCCAIN FOODS LIMITED; *pg.* 876, *pg.* 1915
GOOD FOOD GOOD REASON HEALTH AND HAPPINESS - Slogan - EDEN FOODS INC.; *pg.* 1019, *pg.* 875
GOOD FOOD.RESPONSIBLY. - Slogan - SMITHFIELD FOODS, INC.; *pg.* 896, *pg.* 1806
GOOD FOR LIFE - Slogan - PENDLETON WOOLEN MILLS, INC.; *pg.* 697, *pg.* 1505
GOOD FOR SMALL BUSINESS - Tag Line - INSPERITY, INC.; *pg.* 416, *pg.* 1725
GOOD FOR TODAY...GOOD FOR LIFE - Tag Line - IAMS COMPANY; *pg.* 1477, *pg.* 1633
GOOD FORTUNE - Birthday Gifts - 1-800-FLOWERS.COM, INC.; *pg.* 1758, *pg.* 1151
GOOD FRIENDS - Breakfast Cereal - KASHI COMPANY; *pg.* 830, *pg.* 119
GOOD FRIENDS CINNA-RAISIN CRUNCH - Cereal - KASHI COMPANY; *pg.* 830, *pg.* 119
GOOD GRIPS - Personal Care Electrical Product - HELEN OF TROY L.P.; *pg.* 511, *pg.* 1692
GOOD GRIPS - Kitchen Tools - OXO; *pg.* 1058, *pg.* 1275
GOOD HOUSEKEEPING - Magazine - THE HEARST CORPORATION; *pg.* 1649, *pg.* 1239
GOOD HUMOR - Ice Cream - UNILEVER UNITED STATES, INC.; *pg.* 904, *pg.* 1061
THE GOOD LIFE AT A GREAT PRICE. GUARANTEED. - Slogan - SEARS HOLDINGS CORPORATION; *pg.* 1784, *pg.* 618
GOOD LOOK - Photographic Papers - EASTMAN KODAK COMPANY; *pg.* 1408, *pg.* 1333
GOOD NEIGHBOR PHARMACY - Pharmaceutical Services - AMERISOURCEBERGEN CORPORATION; *pg.* 1493, *pg.* 1522
GOOD NEWS - Twin Blade Disposable Razors & Toiletries - THE GILLETTE COMPANY; *pg.* 509, *pg.* 795
GOOD NEWS PIVOT PLUS - Disposable Shavers - THE GILLETTE COMPANY; *pg.* 509, *pg.* 795
GOOD-O - Food Product - MARS, INCORPORATED; *pg.* 1858, *pg.* 1792
GOOD OLD DAYS - Nostalgia Magazine - ANNIE'S; *pg.* 1617, *pg.* 673
GOOD OLD DAYS SPECIAL ISSUES - Nostalgia Magazine - ANNIE'S; *pg.* 1617, *pg.* 673
GOOD PEOPLE MAKE BETTER PRODUCTS - Tagline - SMITHCO, INC.; *pg.* 1377, *pg.* 1592
GOOD PEOPLE TO KNOW - Slogan - NATIONWIDE MUTUAL INSURANCE COMPANY; *pg.* 1211, *pg.* 1536
GOOD SAMARITAN HOSPITAL - Hospital - MEDSTAR HEALTH INC.; *pg.* 1563, *pg.* 767
GOOD SKIN - Dermatologist Formulated, Fragrance-Free Skin Care Products - THE ESTEE LAUDER COMPANIES INC.; *pg.* 508, *pg.* 1229
THE GOOD SLICE - Snack Food Product - THE HAIN CELESTIAL GROUP, INC.; *pg.* 860, *pg.* 1172
GOOD START ESSENTIALS - Food & Beverage Product - NESTLE USA, INC.; *pg.* 883, *pg.* 96
GOOD START SUPREME - Infant Formula - NESTLE USA, INC.; *pg.* 883, *pg.* 96
GOOD THINGS COME FROM SYSCO - Slogan - SYSCO CORPORATION; *pg.* 1035, *pg.* 1716
GOOD THINGS COME IN OUR PACKAGES - Slogan - INLINE PLASTICS CORP.; *pg.* 1460, *pg.* 370
GOOD THINGS TO EAT - Publication - OGDEN PUBLICATIONS, INC.; *pg.* 1672, *pg.* 722
GOOD TIMES - Slots - INTERNATIONAL GAME TECHNOLOGY; *pg.* 957, *pg.* 1024
GOOD TIMES - Fast Food - MCDONALD'S CORPORATION; *pg.* 1737, *pg.* 645
GOOD TIMES - Newspaper - TRANSCONTINENTAL INC.; *pg.* 1695, *pg.* 1957
GOOD VALUE. FRIENDLY PEOPLE. - Slogan - VAGABOND FRANCHISE SYSTEM, INC.; *pg.* 1117, *pg.* 141
GOOD WEIGHING PRACTICE - Weighing Instrument - METTLER-TOLEDO INTERNATIONAL INC.; *pg.* 1423, *pg.* 1441
GOODCLEANTECH.COM - Web Site - PC MAGAZINE; *pg.* 1674, *pg.* 1276
GOODLIFE - Premium Dog & Cat Food - MARS, INCORPORATED; *pg.* 1858, *pg.* 1792
THE GOODLIFE RECIPE - Pet Food - MARS, INCORPORATED; *pg.* 1858, *pg.* 1792
THE GOODLIFE RECIPE - Pet Food - MARS PETCARE; *pg.* 1478, *pg.* 1633
GOODLOOK - Software - BIO-RAD LABORATORIES, INC.; *pg.* 1504, *pg.* 101
GOODMAN - Food Product - NEW WORLD PASTA COMPANY; *pg.* 885, *pg.* 1537
GOODMAN'S - Food Products - MANISCHEWITZ COMPANY; *pg.* 875, *pg.* 1097
GOODNESSKNOWS - Snack Products - MARS, INCORPORATED; *pg.* 1858, *pg.* 1792
GOODNITES - Training Pant - KIMBERLY-CLARK CORPORATION; *pg.* 1461, *pg.* 1720
GOODY - Hair Accessories - NEWELL RUBBERMAID INC.; *pg.* 1128, *pg.* 515
GOODYEAR - Tire - THE GOODYEAR TIRE & RUBBER COMPANY; *pg.* 1883, *pg.* 1401
GOODYEAR AUTO SERVICE CENTERS - Tire And Rubber Product - THE GOODYEAR TIRE & RUBBER COMPANY; *pg.* 1883, *pg.* 1401
GOODYEAR BLIMP LOGO - Blimp - THE GOODYEAR TIRE & RUBBER COMPANY; *pg.* 1883, *pg.* 1401
GOODYEAR CERTIFIED AUTO SERVICE - Auto Service - THE GOODYEAR TIRE & RUBBER COMPANY; *pg.* 1883, *pg.* 1401
GOOF OFF - Paint Remover - THE VALSPAR CORPORATION; *pg.* 1449, *pg.* 945
GOOFY - Cartoon Character - THE WALT DISNEY COMPANY; *pg.* 317, *pg.* 52
GOOGLE - Search Engine - ALPHABET INC.; *pg.* 347, *pg.* 153
GOOGLE ANALYTICS - Web Analytics Service - GOOGLE INC.; *pg.* 1249, *pg.* 153
GOOGLE APPS - Internet Application - GOOGLE INC.; *pg.* 1249, *pg.* 153
GOOGLE BOOKS - Web Application - GOOGLE INC.; *pg.* 1249, *pg.* 153
GOOGLE CALENDAR - Internet Application - GOOGLE INC.; *pg.* 1249, *pg.* 153
GOOGLE CHROME - Internet Browser - GOOGLE INC.; *pg.* 1249, *pg.* 153
GOOGLE CLOUD PRINT - Cloud Printing - GOOGLE INC.; *pg.* 1249, *pg.* 153
GOOGLE CO-OP - Custom Search Engine - GOOGLE INC.; *pg.* 1249, *pg.* 153
GOOGLE CODE - Web Developer Tools - GOOGLE INC.; *pg.* 1249, *pg.* 153
GOOGLE COMPUTE - Cloud Platform - GOOGLE INC.; *pg.* 1249, *pg.* 153
GOOGLE CRISIS RESPONSE - Tool to Collect & Share Emergency Information - GOOGLE INC.; *pg.* 1249, *pg.* 153
GOOGLE CUSTOM SEARCH ENGINE - Custom Search Engine - GOOGLE INC.; *pg.* 1249, *pg.* 153
GOOGLE DASHBOARD WIDGETS - Application - GOOGLE INC.; *pg.* 1249, *pg.* 153
GOOGLE DOCS - Program - GOOGLE INC.; *pg.* 1249, *pg.* 153
GOOGLE DRIVE - File Storage - GOOGLE INC.; *pg.* 1249, *pg.* 153
GOOGLE EARTH - Internet Application - GOOGLE INC.; *pg.* 1249, *pg.* 153
GOOGLE ENTERPRISE - Business Tools - GOOGLE INC.; *pg.* 1249, *pg.* 153
GOOGLE FUSION TABLES - Data Visualization Web App - GOOGLE INC.; *pg.* 1249, *pg.* 153
GOOGLE GREEN - Environmental Initiative - GOOGLE INC.; *pg.* 1249, *pg.* 153
GOOGLE GROUPS - Discussion Forums - GOOGLE INC.; *pg.* 1249, *pg.* 153
GOOGLE HANGOUTS - Chat Software - GOOGLE INC.; *pg.* 1249, *pg.* 153
GOOGLE IMAGE SEARCH - Image Search Application - GOOGLE INC.; *pg.* 1249, *pg.* 153
GOOGLE IMAGES - Internet Application - GOOGLE INC.; *pg.* 1249, *pg.* 153
GOOGLE KEEP - Note-taking App - GOOGLE INC.; *pg.* 1249, *pg.* 153
GOOGLE MAPS - Internet Application - GOOGLE INC.; *pg.* 1249, *pg.* 153
GOOGLE MOBILE - Service - GOOGLE INC.; *pg.* 1249, *pg.* 153
GOOGLE NEWS - Internet Application - GOOGLE INC.; *pg.* 1249, *pg.* 153
GOOGLE PLAY - Music, Movie and Book Android Apps - GOOGLE INC.; *pg.* 1249, *pg.* 153
GOOGLE PLUS - Social Networking Service - GOOGLE INC.; *pg.* 1249, *pg.* 153
GOOGLE POLITICS & ELECTIONS - Political & Elections News Resource - GOOGLE INC.; *pg.* 1249, *pg.* 153
GOOGLE SCHOLAR - Internet Application - GOOGLE INC.; *pg.* 1249, *pg.* 153
GOOGLE SEARCH - Internet Application - GOOGLE INC.; *pg.* 1249, *pg.* 153
GOOGLE VENTURES - Independent Venture Capital Fund - GOOGLE INC.; *pg.* 1249, *pg.* 153
GOOGLE WALLET - Virtual Wallet - GOOGLE INC.; *pg.* 1249, *pg.* 153
GOOGLE+ - Social Networking Service - GOOGLE INC.; *pg.* 1249, *pg.* 153
GOOGLE.ORG - Technology for Social Impact - GOOGLE INC.; *pg.* 1249, *pg.* 153
GOOGLY EYES - Educational Materials - SCHOLASTIC INC.; *pg.* 1683, *pg.* 1288
GOOP - Soap & Cleaner - CRITZAS INDUSTRIES, INC.; *pg.* 329, *pg.* 995
GOOP FIRST CHOICE - Hand Soap - CRITZAS INDUSTRIES, INC.; *pg.* 329, *pg.* 995
GOOP ORIGINAL FORMULA - Hand Soap - CRITZAS INDUSTRIES, INC.; *pg.* 329, *pg.* 995
GOOP PRINTER'S FRIEND - Pumice Hand Cleaner - CRITZAS INDUSTRIES, INC.; *pg.* 329, *pg.* 995
GOOP PUM-X - Pumice Soap - CRITZAS INDUSTRIES, INC.; *pg.* 329, *pg.* 995
GOOSE BRAND - Food Product - JOHN MORRELL & CO.; *pg.* 866, *pg.* 1415
GOOSEBUMPS - Family Entertainment - FELD ENTERTAINMENT, INC.; *pg.* 547, *pg.* 458
GOOSIN' AROUND - Game - WMS INDUSTRIES INC.; *pg.* 593, *pg.* 666
GOOSSEN - Agricultural Equipment - HARPER INDUSTRIES, INC.; *pg.* 704, *pg.* 715
GOPHER - Catheter - VASCULAR SOLUTIONS, INC.; *pg.* 1434, *pg.* 946
GOPHER 5 - Lottery Game - MINNESOTA STATE LOTTERY; *pg.* 999, *pg.* 956
GOPHER POKER - Video Game - INTERNATIONAL GAME TECHNOLOGY; *pg.* 957, *pg.* 1024
GOPHERTOX - Household Insect Control - BONIDE PRODUCTS, INC.; *pg.* 1794, *pg.* 1320
GOPHONE - Prepaid Cellular Phone Plan - AT&T MOBILITY

LLC; *pg.* 619, *pg.* 488
GOPOD - Locker - AMERICAN LOCKER GROUP INCORPORATED; *pg.* 1041, *pg.* 1674
GOPRO - Wearable Digital Camera - GOPRO; *pg.* 1414, *pg.* 255
GOPTEN - Pharmaceutical Product - ABBOTT LABORATORIES; *pg.* 1484, *pg.* 551
GORAG - Heavy Duty Wipers - GEORGIA-PACIFIC LLC; *pg.* 1458, *pg.* 507
GORDON FOOD SERVICE - Food Distribution - GORDON FOOD SERVICE INC.; *pg.* 1021, *pg.* 913
GORDON SIGNATURE - Food Product - GORDON FOOD SERVICE INC.; *pg.* 1021, *pg.* 913
GORDONGLO - Heater - ROBERTS-GORDON INC.; *pg.* 1076, *pg.* 1151
GORDONRAY - Heater - ROBERTS-GORDON INC.; *pg.* 1076, *pg.* 1151
GORE - Fabric - W.L. GORE & ASSOCIATES, INC.; *pg.* 122, *pg.* 388
GORE ALL-WEATHER - Membrane Vent - W.L. GORE & ASSOCIATES, INC.; *pg.* 122, *pg.* 388
GORE ARMACOR - Fabric - W.L. GORE & ASSOCIATES, INC.; *pg.* 122, *pg.* 388
GORE BIKE WEAR - Athletic Apparel - W.L. GORE & ASSOCIATES, INC.; *pg.* 122, *pg.* 388
GORE EZE-SIT - Vascular Surgeon - W.L. GORE & ASSOCIATES, INC.; *pg.* 122, *pg.* 388
GORE-FLEX - Fiber Optic Cable - W.L. GORE & ASSOCIATES, INC.; *pg.* 122, *pg.* 388
GORE-FLIGHT - Microwave Assembly - W.L. GORE & ASSOCIATES, INC.; *pg.* 122, *pg.* 388
GORE-MATE - Wafer Contactor - W.L. GORE & ASSOCIATES, INC.; *pg.* 122, *pg.* 388
GORE-NO STAT - Conductive Fiber - W.L. GORE & ASSOCIATES, INC.; *pg.* 122, *pg.* 388
GORE OSSEOQUEST - Medical Product - W.L. GORE & ASSOCIATES, INC.; *pg.* 122, *pg.* 388
GORE RESOLUT ADAPT - Medical Product - W.L. GORE & ASSOCIATES, INC.; *pg.* 122, *pg.* 388
GORE-SEAM - Tape - W.L. GORE & ASSOCIATES, INC.; *pg.* 122, *pg.* 388
GORE-SELECT - Composite Membrane - W.L. GORE & ASSOCIATES, INC.; *pg.* 122, *pg.* 388
GORE-SHIELD - EMI Shielding - W.L. GORE & ASSOCIATES, INC.; *pg.* 122, *pg.* 388
GORE SMOOTHER - Orthopedic Product - W.L. GORE & ASSOCIATES, INC.; *pg.* 122, *pg.* 388
GORE-SORBER - Exploration Survey Product - W.L. GORE & ASSOCIATES, INC.; *pg.* 122, *pg.* 388
GORE-TEX - Rainwear - CABELA'S INCORPORATED; *pg.* 535, *pg.* 1019
GORE-TEX - Adhesive Tape & Patch - MCNETT CORPORATION; *pg.* 1839, *pg.* 1817
GORE-TEX - Fabric - W.L. GORE & ASSOCIATES, INC.; *pg.* 122, *pg.* 388
GORE-TEX BEST DEFENSE - Fabric - W.L. GORE & ASSOCIATES, INC.; *pg.* 122, *pg.* 388
GORE-TEX COMFORT COOL - Fabric - W.L. GORE & ASSOCIATES, INC.; *pg.* 122, *pg.* 388
GORE-TEX EXACTGRIP - Glove - W.L. GORE & ASSOCIATES, INC.; *pg.* 122, *pg.* 388
GORE-TEX GR - Sheet Gasketing - W.L. GORE & ASSOCIATES, INC.; *pg.* 122, *pg.* 388
GORE-TEX GUARANTEED TO KEEP YOU DRY - Fabric - W.L. GORE & ASSOCIATES, INC.; *pg.* 122, *pg.* 388
GORE-TEX HEAVYWEIGHT - Filter Cartridge - W.L. GORE & ASSOCIATES, INC.; *pg.* 122, *pg.* 388
GORE-TEX PARTNERS IN PERFORMANCE - Fabric - W.L. GORE & ASSOCIATES, INC.; *pg.* 122, *pg.* 388
GORE-TEX XCR - Fabric - W.L. GORE & ASSOCIATES, INC.; *pg.* 122, *pg.* 388
GORFRAME - Bellow - DYNATECT MANUFACTURING INC.; *pg.* 1330, *pg.* 1883
GORGON - Gaming Product - GLD PRODUCTS, INC.; *pg.* 1835, *pg.* 1882
GORGONIAN EXTRACT - Chemical Ingredient - LIPO CHEMICALS INC.; *pg.* 1171, *pg.* 1107
GORGONZ BASIC FLEECE - Ear Warmer - 180S, LLC; *pg.* 1824, *pg.* 754
GORGONZ BROWN DUCK - Ear Warmer - 180S, LLC; *pg.* 1824, *pg.* 754
GORGONZ HIGH-VIS REFLECTIVE - Ear Warmer - 180S, LLC; *pg.* 1824, *pg.* 754
GORHAM - Silver Flatware & Giftware, Fine China, Crystal & Tableware Products - LENOX CORPORATION; *pg.* 1126, *pg.* 1518
GORHAM BRONZE - Bronze Products for the Death Care Industries - MATTHEWS INTERNATIONAL CORPORATION; *pg.* 1662, *pg.* 1578
GORILLA - Hose - THE GOODYEAR TIRE & RUBBER COMPANY; *pg.* 1883, *pg.* 1401
GORILLA GLUE - Heavy-Duty Glue - GORILLA GLUE CO.; *pg.* 1048, *pg.* 1414
GORILLA GRAPE - Fruit Juice Cocktail - NEWMAN'S OWN, INC.; *pg.* 886, *pg.* 384
GORILLA MUNCH - Breakfast Cereals - NATURE'S PATH FOODS INC.; *pg.* 833, *pg.* 1908
GORILLA VS BEAR - Music Blog - SPINMEDIA; *pg.* 1282, *pg.* 104
GORTIFLEX - Molded Bellow - DYNATECT MANUFACTURING INC.; *pg.* 1330, *pg.* 1883
GORTITE - Flexible Protective Cover - DYNATECT MANUFACTURING INC.; *pg.* 1330, *pg.* 1883
GORTITE - Mold Base & Component - SUPERIOR DIE SET CORP.; *pg.* 1379, *pg.* 1885
GORTON'S - Prepared Frozen Seafood - THE GORTON GROUP; *pg.* 859, *pg.* 823
GORTRAC - Cable & Hose System - DYNATECT MANUFACTURING INC.; *pg.* 1330, *pg.* 1883
GORTUBE - Cable & Hose System - DYNATECT MANUFACTURING INC.; *pg.* 1330, *pg.* 1883
GORZELL - Footwear - K-SWISS; *pg.* 1837, *pg.* 306
GORZELL ULTRA - Athletic Shoes - K-SWISS; *pg.* 1837, *pg.* 306
GOSLING'S - Rum - CASTLE BRANDS INC.; *pg.* 239, *pg.* 1209
GOSPELFEST - Fast Food - MCDONALD'S CORPORATION; *pg.* 1737, *pg.* 645
GOSSAMER - Fabric - NEMSCHOFF, INC.; *pg.* 936, *pg.* 1890
GOSSAMER - Women's Clothing & Accessories - WOODEN SHIPS OF HOBOKEN; *pg.* 35, *pg.* 1315
GOSSAMER BAY - Wine - E&J GALLO WINERY; *pg.* 1962, *pg.* 149
GOSYSTEM - Software - THOMSON REUTERS TAX & ACCOUNTING; *pg.* 1693, *pg.* 1299
GOT FUN FEVER - Games - PENN NATIONAL GAMING, INC.; *pg.* 574, *pg.* 1595
GOT PROTEIN? - Software - BIO-RAD LABORATORIES, INC.; *pg.* 1504, *pg.* 101
GOT THE BLUES FOR RED - Nail Care Product - OPI PRODUCTS INC.; *pg.* 518, *pg.* 167
GOT WHEEL - Video Game - INTERNATIONAL GAME TECHNOLOGY; *pg.* 957, *pg.* 1024
GOTCHA - Cord Connector - HUBBELL INCORPORATED; *pg.* 1299, *pg.* 370
GOTCHA - Apparel - PERRY ELLIS INTERNATIONAL, INC.; *pg.* 45, *pg.* 445
GOTCHA - Casual Apparel - QUIKSILVER, INC.; *pg.* 31, *pg.* 104
GOTHAM - Lighting Fixture Product - ACUITY BRANDS, INC.; *pg.* 1294, *pg.* 487
GOTHAM - Fabric - NEMSCHOFF, INC.; *pg.* 936, *pg.* 1890
THE GOTHAM COLLECTION - Deluxe Chafers - CARLISLE FOODSERVICE PRODUCTS INCORPORATED; *pg.* 1455, *pg.* 1485
GOTHIC - Table - BLATT BOWLING & BILLIARD CORP.; *pg.* 1827, *pg.* 1203
GOTHIC - Gaming Product - GLD PRODUCTS, INC.; *pg.* 1835, *pg.* 1882
GOTHIC - Dinnerware - THE HOMER LAUGHLIN CHINA COMPANY; *pg.* 1125, *pg.* 1850
GOTHICS MOUNTAIN - T-Shirts - ABERCROMBIE & FITCH CO.; *pg.* 37, *pg.* 1466
GOTOASSIST - Software - CITRIX ONLINE LLC; *pg.* 1235, *pg.* 99
GOTOASSIST CORPORATE - Software - CITRIX SYSTEMS, INC.; *pg.* 375, *pg.* 424
GOTOASSIST EXPRESS - Software - CITRIX SYSTEMS, INC.; *pg.* 375, *pg.* 424
GOTOMEETING - Software - CITRIX ONLINE LLC; *pg.* 1235, *pg.* 99
GOTOMYPC - Software - CITRIX ONLINE LLC; *pg.* 1235, *pg.* 99
GOTOMYPC - Software - VIEWSONIC CORPORATION; *pg.* 489, *pg.* 303
GOTOMYPC POCKETVIEW - Software - CITRIX SYSTEMS, INC.; *pg.* 375, *pg.* 424
GOTOTRAINING - Software - CITRIX SYSTEMS, INC.; *pg.* 375, *pg.* 424
GOTOWEBINAR - Software - CITRIX ONLINE LLC; *pg.* 1235, *pg.* 99
GOTOWEBINAR - Software - CITRIX SYSTEMS, INC.; *pg.* 375, *pg.* 424
GOTTA GETTA GUND - Tag Line - GUND, INC.; *pg.* 954, *pg.* 1056
GOTTA GO POTTY - Toilet Trainer - GRACO CHILDREN'S PRODUCTS INC.; *pg.* 954, *pg.* 1531
GOTTA GO TO MO'S - Tag Line - HENRY MODELL & COMPANY, INC.; *pg.* 1836, *pg.* 1240
GOUACHE - Fabric - NEMSCHOFF, INC.; *pg.* 936, *pg.* 1890
GOULBURN VALLEY - Beverages - THE COCA-COLA COMPANY; *pg.* 240, *pg.* 493
GOULD PUMPS - Fluid Technology - ITT CORPORATION; *pg.* 1351, *pg.* 1354
GOULDS PUMPS - Metal Pump - GOULDS PUMPS, INCORPORATED; *pg.* 1342, *pg.* 1341
GOUNDREY - Wine - CONSTELLATION BRANDS CANADA; *pg.* 1960, *pg.* 1925
GOURMET - Magazine - CONDE NAST PUBLICATIONS, INC.; *pg.* 1629, *pg.* 1217
GOURMET - Sink - ELKAY MANUFACTURING COMPANY; *pg.* 80, *pg.* 645
GOURMET - Food Processing Equipment - HOLLYMATIC CORPORATION; *pg.* 1346, *pg.* 598
GOURMET CHOICE - Tuna - STARKIST FOODS INC.; *pg.* 898, *pg.* 1581
GOURMET COLLECTION - Spices - MCCORMICK & COMPANY, INCORPORATED; *pg.* 1027, *pg.* 779
GOURMET-GLO - Kitchen Appliance - VIKING RANGE CORPORATION; *pg.* 61, *pg.* 968
GOURMET HOUSE - Wild Rice - RIVIANA FOODS INC.; *pg.* 892, *pg.* 1713
GOURMET ICE - Beverage - BUNN-O-MATIC CORPORATION; *pg.* 53, *pg.* 661
GOURMET JUICE - Coffee & Beverage Equipment - BUNN-O-MATIC CORPORATION; *pg.* 53, *pg.* 661
GOURMET LITE - Food Product - DIETZ & WATSON INC.; *pg.* 853, *pg.* 1563
GOURMET REWARDS - Gift Item - HICKORY FARMS, INC.; *pg.* 862, *pg.* 1462
GOURMET SELECTION - Fresh Poultry - TYSON FOODS, INC.; *pg.* 902, *pg.* 35
GOURMET TABLE - Condiments & Sauces - PERFORMANCE FOOD GROUP COMPANY, LLC; *pg.* 1030, *pg.* 1803
GOURMET TWISTS - Topped Soft Pretzels - J&J SNACK FOODS CORPORATION; *pg.* 865, *pg.* 1107
GOVAC - Sweeper/Vacuum - BISSELL HOMECARE, INC.; *pg.* 52, *pg.* 887
GOVAULT - Data Protection Solution - QUANTUM CORPORATION; *pg.* 458, *pg.* 250
GOVERNAIR - Air Conditioners - NORTEK, INC.; *pg.* 100, *pg.* 1607
GOVERNALE - Radiators - BURNHAM HOLDINGS, INC.; *pg.* 1069, *pg.* 1546
GOVERNING MAGAZINE - Monthly Publication on Trends in Government - THE TIMES PUBLISHING CO.; *pg.* 1695, *pg.* 464
GOVERNMENT FLEET - Magazine - BOBIT BUSINESS MEDIA; *pg.* 1622, *pg.* 293
GOVERNMENT REVENUE MANAGEMENT - Software - THOMSON REUTERS TAX & ACCOUNTING; *pg.* 484, *pg.* 905
GOVERNMENT SOLUTIONS - Government Video Tools - AVID TECHNOLOGY, INC.; *pg.* 622, *pg.* 804
GOVERNOR - Growth Regulator - THE ANDERSONS INCORPORATED; *pg.* 1793, *pg.* 1461
GOVESSENTIALS - Software - SKILLSOFT PLC; *pg.* 470, *pg.* 1037
GOVIEW - Software - CITRIX SYSTEMS, INC.; *pg.* 375, *pg.* 424
GOVOLS.COM - Web Site - KNOXVILLE NEWS-SENTINEL COMPANY; *pg.* 1657, *pg.* 1637
GOWBURY - Footwear - K-SWISS; *pg.* 1837, *pg.* 306
GOWBURY CANVAS - Footwear - K-SWISS; *pg.* 1837, *pg.* 306
GOWEAR - Fit Armband - NU SKIN ENTERPRISES, INC.; *pg.* 518, *pg.* 1755
GO.WEB - Software - PURPLE COMMUNICATIONS, INC.; *pg.* 457, *pg.* 194
GOWLLANDS - Healthcare Product - GF HEALTH PRODUCTS, INC.; *pg.* 1535, *pg.* 508
GOWMET CANVAS - Footwear - K-SWISS; *pg.* 1837, *pg.* 306

GOWMET LOW - Footwear - K-SWISS; *pg.* 1837, *pg.* 306
GOWMET LOW VNZ - Footwear - K-SWISS; *pg.* 1837, *pg.* 306
GOYA - Various Latino Foods - GOYA FOODS, INC.; *pg.* 859, *pg.* 1075
GP ADVANTAGE - Copier Paper - GEORGIA-PACIFIC LLC; *pg.* 1458, *pg.* 507
GP COLORS! - Colored Papers - GEORGIA-PACIFIC LLC; *pg.* 1458, *pg.* 507
GP EUREKA! - Copier Paper - GEORGIA-PACIFIC LLC; *pg.* 1458, *pg.* 507
GP GEOCYCLE - Copier Paper - GEORGIA-PACIFIC LLC; *pg.* 1458, *pg.* 507
GP HOTS! - Colored Papers - GEORGIA-PACIFIC LLC; *pg.* 1458, *pg.* 507
GP IMAGE PLUS - Copier Paper - GEORGIA-PACIFIC LLC; *pg.* 1458, *pg.* 507
GP PASTELS! - Colored Papers - GEORGIA-PACIFIC LLC; *pg.* 1458, *pg.* 507
GP PREMIUM LASER & COLOR COPIER COVER STOCK - Cover Stock - GEORGIA-PACIFIC LLC; *pg.* 1458, *pg.* 507
GP PREMIUM LASER & COLOR COPIER PAPER - Copier Paper - GEORGIA-PACIFIC LLC; *pg.* 1458, *pg.* 507
GP100 - Double-Action Revolver - STURM, RUGER & COMPANY, INC.; *pg.* 1846, *pg.* 371
GP400 - Navigation Aid - TRIMBLE NAVIGATION LIMITED; *pg.* 1384, *pg.* 288
GP94 - Parallel Twin-Screw Extruder - DAVIS-STANDARD LLC; *pg.* 1328, *pg.* 368
GPB-1700 - Battery - GLOBALSTAR, INC.; *pg.* 401, *pg.* 743
GPC - Corn-Based Product - GRAIN PROCESSING CORPORATION; *pg.* 859, *pg.* 709
GPD - Drives - MAGNETEK, INC.; *pg.* 1301, *pg.* 1870
GPDK-1410 - Satellite Phone Car Kit - GLOBALSTAR, INC.; *pg.* 401, *pg.* 743
GPEXPRESS - Board-Level Product - MERCURY COMPUTER SYSTEMS, INC.; *pg.* 434, *pg.* 813
GPHONE - Gravimeter - SCINTREX LTD.; *pg.* 1374, *pg.* 1920
GPLOAD - Analyst - TRIMBLE NAVIGATION LIMITED; *pg.* 1384, *pg.* 288
GPLYNX - Interface Integrated Circuits - TEXAS INSTRUMENTS INCORPORATED; *pg.* 679, *pg.* 1688
GPO - Glass & Ceramic Material - CORNING INCORPORATED; *pg.* 1122, *pg.* 1154
GPOADMIN - Software - DELL SOFTWARE; *pg.* 385, *pg.* 40
GPON APD TIA IN TO-CAN - Electronic Components - EMCORE CORPORATION; *pg.* 636, *pg.* 39
GPON DFB - Electronic Component - EMCORE CORPORATION; *pg.* 636, *pg.* 39
GPON DFB LASERS IN TO-CAN - Electronic Components - EMCORE CORPORATION; *pg.* 636, *pg.* 39
GPPO - Glass & Ceramic Material - CORNING INCORPORATED; *pg.* 1122, *pg.* 1154
GPR - Adhesive - SPINNAKER COATING, LLC; *pg.* 1470, *pg.* 1477
GPRI - Coatings - GEORGIA-PACIFIC LLC; *pg.* 1458, *pg.* 507
GPRSXPRESS - Cellular Service - NUMEREX CORP.; *pg.* 660, *pg.* 517
GPS - Software - DST SYSTEMS, INC.; *pg.* 388, *pg.* 982
GPS - Mop Handle - GEERPRES INC.; *pg.* 1339, *pg.* 901
GPS - Gas Processing System - SURFACE COMBUSTION, INC.; *pg.* 1077, *pg.* 1462
GPS ANALYST - Navigation Aid - TRIMBLE NAVIGATION LIMITED; *pg.* 1384, *pg.* 288
GPS PATHFINDER - Navigation Aid - TRIMBLE NAVIGATION LIMITED; *pg.* 1384, *pg.* 288
GPS TOTAL STATION - Navigation Aid - TRIMBLE NAVIGATION LIMITED; *pg.* 1384, *pg.* 288
GPSCORRECT - Navigation Aid - TRIMBLE NAVIGATION LIMITED; *pg.* 1384, *pg.* 288
GPSDREDGER - Global Positioning System Equipment - NOVATEL INC.; *pg.* 1424, *pg.* 1904
GPSNET - Software - TRIMBLE NAVIGATION LIMITED; *pg.* 1384, *pg.* 288
GPSOLUTION - Graphical User Interface Software - NOVATEL INC.; *pg.* 1424, *pg.* 1904
GPSONE - Computer Hardware - QUALCOMM INCORPORATED; *pg.* 1873, *pg.* 207
GPSTATION - Global Positioning System Equipment - NOVATEL INC.; *pg.* 1424, *pg.* 1904
GPSTEER - Wireless Product - HEMISPHERE GPS INC.; *pg.* 642, *pg.* 1903
GPSURVEY - Navigation Aid - TRIMBLE NAVIGATION LIMITED; *pg.* 1384, *pg.* 288
GPX - Gear Pump - FARREL CORPORATION; *pg.* 1336, *pg.* 337
GPX - Bus Transportation Service - GREYHOUND LINES, INC.; *pg.* 1910, *pg.* 1681
GQ - Magazine - CONDE NAST PUBLICATIONS, INC.; *pg.* 1629, *pg.* 1217
GR - Pumps - THE GORMAN-RUPP COMPANY; *pg.* 1341, *pg.* 1458
GR8-DOPHILUS - Dietary Supplement - NOW HEALTH GROUP, INC.; *pg.* 1576, *pg.* 557
GRAB-IT - Floor Wipes - S.C. JOHNSON & SON, INC.; *pg.* 334, *pg.* 1889
GRAB-IT CLOTHS - Cleaner - S.C. JOHNSON & SON, INC.; *pg.* 334, *pg.* 1889
GRAB-IT MATTS - Cleaner - S.C. JOHNSON & SON, INC.; *pg.* 334, *pg.* 1889
GRAB-IT MOP - Cleaner - S.C. JOHNSON & SON, INC.; *pg.* 334, *pg.* 1889
GRAB-IT SWEEPER - Cleaner - S.C. JOHNSON & SON, INC.; *pg.* 334, *pg.* 1889
GRAB-IT WIPE - Cleaner - S.C. JOHNSON & SON, INC.; *pg.* 334, *pg.* 1889
GRAB-N-GO - Iced Tea & Lemonades - NEWMAN'S OWN, INC.; *pg.* 886, *pg.* 384
GRABBER - Latch - SOUTHCO, INC.; *pg.* 1063, *pg.* 1522
GRABER - Window - SPRINGS GLOBAL, INC.; *pg.* 698, *pg.* 1616
GRABER - Window Blinds & Shades - SPRINGS WINDOW FASHIONS LLC; *pg.* 943, *pg.* 1872
GRABER SLIDE-VUE - Window System - SPRINGS WINDOW FASHIONS LLC; *pg.* 943, *pg.* 1872
GRABMASTER - Lifting Equipment - DOWNS CRANE & HOIST CO, INC.; *pg.* 1330, *pg.* 129
GRABS-ALL - Household Product - BLUE CROSS LABORATORIES; *pg.* 326, *pg.* 277
GRACE - Furniture - JASPER GROUP; *pg.* 930, *pg.* 691
GRACE - Footwear - P.W. MINOR & SON, INC.; *pg.* 1816, *pg.* 1140
GRACE COLLECTION - Fragrance - LUZIER PERSONALIZED COSMETICS, INC.; *pg.* 515, *pg.* 978
GRACE ELEGANCE - Furniture - ASHLEY FURNITURE INDUSTRIES, INC.; *pg.* 914, *pg.* 1852
GRACE IN ACTION - Newsletter - OUR SUNDAY VISITOR, INC.; *pg.* 1673, *pg.* 682
GRACEFUL FLIGHT - Squirrel Guard - PETSMART, INC.; *pg.* 1481, *pg.* 18
GRACELAND - Tour Site - ELVIS PRESLEY ENTERPRISES, INC.; *pg.* 1090, *pg.* 1642
GRACIA - Fabric - NEMSCHOFF, INC.; *pg.* 936, *pg.* 1890
GRACO - Sundry - KELLY-MOORE PAINT COMPANY, INC.; *pg.* 1443, *pg.* 198
GRACO - Children's Equipment - NEWELL RUBBERMAID INC.; *pg.* 1128, *pg.* 515
GRAD PHOTO NETWORK - Website - CANDID COLOR SYSTEMS, INC.; *pg.* 1404, *pg.* 1485
GRADAL - Ophthalmic Product - CARL ZEISS OPTICAL, INC.; *pg.* 1405, *pg.* 1778
GRADALL - Mowers - ALAMO GROUP INC.; *pg.* 1311, *pg.* 1745
GRADALL - Telehandler - JLG INDUSTRIES, INC.; *pg.* 1351, *pg.* 1551
GRADDOST - Cheese - A.V. OLSSON TRADING CO. INC.; *pg.* 838, *pg.* 372
GRADE - Trading Services - BLOOMBERG L.P.; *pg.* 725, *pg.* 1204
GRADEEYE - Receiver - TRIMBLE NAVIGATION LIMITED; *pg.* 1384, *pg.* 288
GRADEPRO - Navigation Aid - TRIMBLE NAVIGATION LIMITED; *pg.* 1384, *pg.* 288
GRADEXCEL - Student Loan Program - SLM CORPORATION; *pg.* 804, *pg.* 388
GRADIENT - Carpet - INTERFACE, INC.; *pg.* 695, *pg.* 512
GRADIENT - Fabric - NEMSCHOFF, INC.; *pg.* 936, *pg.* 1890
GRADIO - Receiver - TRIMBLE NAVIGATION LIMITED; *pg.* 1384, *pg.* 288
GRADIUM - Lens - LIGHTPATH TECHNOLOGIES INC; *pg.* 1420, *pg.* 454
GRADMA - Pillow and Throw - HERITAGE LACE INC.; *pg.* 694, *pg.* 711
GRADMAS ROCK - Pillow and Throw - HERITAGE LACE INC.; *pg.* 694, *pg.* 711
GRADUATE - Wire Guide - COOK GROUP, INC.; *pg.* 1518, *pg.* 674
GRADUATES - Lens Treatment Product - EMERGING VISION, INC.; *pg.* 1411, *pg.* 1227
GRAFCO - Healthcare Product - GF HEALTH PRODUCTS, INC.; *pg.* 1535, *pg.* 508
GRAFFITI - Cameras - EASTMAN KODAK COMPANY; *pg.* 1408, *pg.* 1333
GRAFFITI - Fabric - NEMSCHOFF, INC.; *pg.* 936, *pg.* 1890
GRAFFITI II - Glove - KOMBI, LTD.; *pg.* 1838, *pg.* 1766
GRAFFITI REMOVER - Coating Remover - THE SAVOGRAN COMPANY; *pg.* 1447, *pg.* 840
GRAFIK EYE - Interface - CRESTRON ELECTRONICS INC.; *pg.* 631, *pg.* 1116
GRAFIT - Protective Eyewear - SELLSTROM MANUFACTURING CO.; *pg.* 1428, *pg.* 659
GRAFKETTE - Healthcare Product - GF HEALTH PRODUCTS, INC.; *pg.* 1535, *pg.* 508
GRAFOIL & LAVA - Sealants - CONAX TECHNOLOGIES LLC; *pg.* 1325, *pg.* 1148
GRAFTMASTER - Coronary Stent Graft System - ABBOTT LABORATORIES; *pg.* 1484, *pg.* 551
GRAFTON - Paper & Nonwoven Material - FIBERMARK INC.; *pg.* 1457, *pg.* 1764
GRAHAM - Furniture - AMISCO INDUSTRIES LTD.; *pg.* 913, *pg.* 1958
GRAHAM - Motor & Control Drives - GRAHAM MOTORS AND CONTROLS; *pg.* 177, *pg.* 1692
GRAHAM & WHITESIDE - Publisher - GALE CENGAGE LEARNING; *pg.* 1643, *pg.* 885
GRAHAM COLLECTION - Office Furniture - KNOLL, INC.; *pg.* 425, *pg.* 1527
GRAIL - Genetic Research Computer Software - LOCKHEED MARTIN CORPORATION; *pg.* 229, *pg.* 762
GRAIN - Apparel - OAKLEY, INC.; *pg.* 1840, *pg.* 86
GRAIN FLOW FORGING - Manufacturing Process - MIZUNO USA, INC.; *pg.* 1839, *pg.* 538
GRAIN GOURMET - Cracked Wheat Bulgur - CONTINENTAL MILLS, INC.; *pg.* 827, *pg.* 1845
GRAINGER - Electric Motor - W.W. GRAINGER, INC.; *pg.* 1390, *pg.* 625
GRAINGER INTEGRATED SUPPLY - Automated Dispensing System - W.W. GRAINGER, INC.; *pg.* 1390, *pg.* 625
GRAINGER.COM - Material Handling Equipment - W.W. GRAINGER, INC.; *pg.* 1390, *pg.* 625
GRAINS NOIRS - Food Product - THE HAIN CELESTIAL GROUP, INC.; *pg.* 860, *pg.* 1172
GRAINWISE - Processed Wheat - CARGILL, INC.; *pg.* 845, *pg.* 965
GRALITE - Chemical Protective Clothing - STANDARD SAFETY EQUIPMENT CO.; *pg.* 1379, *pg.* 632
GRALITE-20 - Gray PVC Fabric - STANDARD SAFETY EQUIPMENT CO.; *pg.* 1379, *pg.* 632
GRAM CENTRAL - Shoe - AEROGROUP INTERNATIONAL, INC.; *pg.* 1803, *pg.* 1055
GRAMERCY - Fabric - F. SCHUMACHER & CO.; *pg.* 925, *pg.* 1230
GRAMERCY - Watch - GEVRIL USA; *pg.* 6, *pg.* 1348
GRAMERCY - Fabric - NEMSCHOFF, INC.; *pg.* 936, *pg.* 1890
GRAMERCY BOOKS - Publishing Imprint - PENGUIN RANDOM HOUSE; *pg.* 1675, *pg.* 1276
GRAMERCY PARK - Table - BLATT BOWLING & BILLIARD CORP.; *pg.* 1827, *pg.* 1203
GRAMERCY PARK - Ceramic Tile - WALKER & ZANGER, INC.; *pg.* 119, *pg.* 281
GRAMPS - Apparel - OAKLEY, INC.; *pg.* 1840, *pg.* 86
GRAN CENTENARIO TEQUILA - Spirits - PROXIMO SPIRITS, INC.; *pg.* 1969, *pg.* 1076
GRAN PATRON BURDEOS - Tequila - THE PATRON SPIRITS COMPANY; *pg.* 1967, *pg.* 1029
GRAN PATRON PLATINUM - Tequila - THE PATRON SPIRITS COMPANY; *pg.* 1967, *pg.* 1029
GRAN SAZON - Traditional Food - GORDON FOOD SERVICE INC.; *pg.* 1021, *pg.* 913
GRANADA - Paper & Nonwoven Material - FIBERMARK INC.; *pg.* 1457, *pg.* 1764
GRANADA - Lighting Product - QUOIZEL INC.; *pg.* 1304, *pg.* 1616
GRANCOURT - Footwear - K-SWISS; *pg.* 1837, *pg.* 306
GRAND - Quality Chafers - CARLISLE FOODSERVICE PRODUCTS INCORPORATED; *pg.* 1455, *pg.* 1485
GRAND AMERICA - Hotels - SINCLAIR OIL CORPORATION; *pg.* 984, *pg.* 1760
GRAND CANYON SUNSET - Nail Care Product - OPI PRODUCTS INC.; *pg.* 518, *pg.* 167
GRAND CARDINAL SPARKLING - Spirits - LEONARD KREUSCH, INC.; *pg.* 254, *pg.* 1099

GRAND CASINO - Casino - CAESARS ENTERTAINMENT CORPORATION; *pg.* 1083, *pg.* 1023
GRAND CAYMAN - Carpet - BEAULIEU GROUP, LLC; *pg.* 917, *pg.* 529
GRAND CAYMAN - Bedding - CROSCILL, INC.; *pg.* 1122, *pg.* 1220
GRAND CENTRAL CARNATION - Nail Care Product - OPI PRODUCTS INC.; *pg.* 518, *pg.* 167
GRAND CHAMPION - Chip - BROADCOM CORPORATION; *pg.* 364, *pg.* 108
GRAND CHAMPION - Turkey Product - HORMEL FOODS CORPORATION; *pg.* 863, *pg.* 915
GRAND CHAMPION - Food Product - JENNIE-O TURKEY STORE, LLC; *pg.* 865, *pg.* 966
GRAND DUKE - Bar Stool - BLATT BOWLING & BILLIARD CORP.; *pg.* 1827, *pg.* 1203
GRAND GARDENIA - Gardenia Plant - 1-800-FLOWERS.COM, INC.; *pg.* 1758, *pg.* 1151
GRAND GIVEAWAY - Lottery Game - MICHIGAN STATE LOTTERY BUREAU; *pg.* 999, *pg.* 895
GRAND HOTEL - Game - WMS INDUSTRIES INC.; *pg.* 593, *pg.* 666
GRAND ILLUSIONS - Carpet - BEAULIEU GROUP, LLC; *pg.* 917, *pg.* 529
THE GRAND ISLAND - Home Floor Plan - JACOBSEN MANUFACTURING, INC.; *pg.* 1098, *pg.* 460
GRAND ISLE - Food Products - VITA FOOD PRODUCTS, INC.; *pg.* 909, *pg.* 595
GRAND KING - Bed - SELECT COMFORT CORPORATION; *pg.* 942, *pg.* 942
GRAND LIGHT - Food & Beverage Product - NESTLE USA, INC.; *pg.* 883, *pg.* 96
GRAND LUX CAFE - Restaurant Concepts - CHEESECAKE FACTORY INCORPORATED; *pg.* 1017, *pg.* 56
GRAND MAJESTY - Flatware - ONEIDA LTD; *pg.* 1129, *pg.* 1318
GRAND MARINER - Cognac - MOET HENNESSY; *pg.* 1966, *pg.* 1260
GRAND MARNIER MOUSSE CAKE - Cake - ELI'S CHEESECAKE COMPANY; *pg.* 1852, *pg.* 572
GRAND MARQUIS - Lamp - J. ROBERT SCOTT INC.; *pg.* 930, *pg.* 105
GRAND MERE - Coffee - MONDELEZ INTERNATIONAL, INC.; *pg.* 878, *pg.* 601
GRAND MONARCH - Video Game - INTERNATIONAL GAME TECHNOLOGY; *pg.* 957, *pg.* 1024
GRAND OLE OPRY - Live Music Venue - GRAND OLE OPRY; *pg.* 289, *pg.* 1651
GRAND PARTY - Video Game - INTERNATIONAL GAME TECHNOLOGY; *pg.* 957, *pg.* 1024
GRAND PARTY LEVEL - Video Game - INTERNATIONAL GAME TECHNOLOGY; *pg.* 957, *pg.* 1024
GRAND PRIX - No Buff Wax - S.C. JOHNSON & SON, INC.; *pg.* 334, *pg.* 1889
GRAND PRIZE KENO - Video Game - INTERNATIONAL GAME TECHNOLOGY; *pg.* 957, *pg.* 1024
GRAND RAPIDS - Seating Product - IRWIN SEATING COMPANY INC.; *pg.* 929, *pg.* 887
THE GRAND RAPIDS PRESS - Newspaper - MLIVE MEDIA GROUP; *pg.* 1665, *pg.* 888
GRAND RESERVE - Beverage - KENDALL-JACKSON WINE ESTATES, LTD.; *pg.* 1965, *pg.* 277
GRAND RESIDENCES - Hotels - MARRIOTT INTERNATIONAL, INC.; *pg.* 1102, *pg.* 764
GRAND RIVER LODGE - Beds - CABELA'S INCORPORATED; *pg.* 535, *pg.* 1019
GRAND SIERRA - Vinyl Siding - PLY GEM SIDING GROUP; *pg.* 105, *pg.* 986
GRAND SLAM - Golf Clothing - PERRY ELLIS INTERNATIONAL, INC.; *pg.* 45, *pg.* 445
GRAND SLAM - Impactor - STEDMAN MACHINE COMPANY; *pg.* 1379, *pg.* 673
GRAND SLAM BREAKFAST - Breakfast - DENNY'S CORPORATION; *pg.* 1725, *pg.* 1622
GRAND TETON LODGE COMPANY - Resort - VAIL RESORTS, INC.; *pg.* 1117, *pg.* 313
GRAND TURBO - Gas Grill - BARBEQUES GALORE, INC.; *pg.* 51, *pg.* 173
GRAND VALLEY - French Fries - J.R. SIMPLOT COMPANY; *pg.* 867, *pg.* 547
THE GRAND VILLAGE - Theme Park - HERSCHEND FAMILY ENTERTAINMENT CORP.; *pg.* 552, *pg.* 973
GRAND WAVE - Saltwater Spinning Reels - DAIWA CORPORATION; *pg.* 1832, *pg.* 75
GRAND WAVE Z - Conventional Trolling Reels - DAIWA CORPORATION; *pg.* 1832, *pg.* 75
GRANDBED - Mattress System - TEMPUR SEALY INTERNATIONAL, INC.; *pg.* 944, *pg.* 731
GRANDE - Larger-Sized Baked Goods - AWREY BAKERIES, INC.; *pg.* 1015, *pg.* 896
GRANDE DENTURE - Brush - RANIR LLC; *pg.* 520, *pg.* 888
GRANDE GOURMET - Food Product - HORMEL FOODS CORPORATION; *pg.* 863, *pg.* 915
GRANDEUR OF THE SEAS - Cruise Ship - ROYAL CARIBBEAN CRUISES LTD; *pg.* 1921, *pg.* 446
GRANDEURA - Rug - COURISTAN INC.; *pg.* 921, *pg.* 1067
GRANDI GROOM - Carpet Brush - STANLEY STEEMER INTERNATIONAL, INC.; *pg.* 944, *pg.* 1450
GRANDIN ROAD - Online Gift Store - IAC/INTERACTIVECORP; *pg.* 292, *pg.* 1242
GRANDIOSO - Pan Spray - VENTURA FOODS, LLC; *pg.* 908, *pg.* 49
GRANDMA - Bookmark - HERITAGE LACE INC.; *pg.* 694, *pg.* 711
GRANDMA UTZ - Potato Chips - UTZ QUALITY FOODS, INC.; *pg.* 907, *pg.* 1536
GRANDMA'S - Molasses - B&G FOODS, INC.; *pg.* 838, *pg.* 1102
GRANDMA'S - Cookies - FRITO-LAY NORTH AMERICA, INC.; *pg.* 1853, *pg.* 1730
GRANDMA'S - Cookies - PEPSICO, INC.; *pg.* 259, *pg.* 1327
GRANDMA'S COOKIE JAR - Video Game - INTERNATIONAL GAME TECHNOLOGY; *pg.* 957, *pg.* 1024
GRANDMA'S MOLASSES - Health Product - B&G FOODS, INC.; *pg.* 838, *pg.* 1102
GRANDMOTHER'S - Bottled Food Product - ALLIED OLD ENGLISH, INC.; *pg.* 836, *pg.* 1110
GRANDOE - Gloves - TOTES ISOTONER CORPORATION; *pg.* 14, *pg.* 1426
GRANDPA - Knife - COAST CUTLERY COMPANY; *pg.* 1121, *pg.* 1501
GRANDPA ALGOLI SAVON - Soap - GRANDPA BRANDS COMPANY; *pg.* 1538, *pg.* 727
GRANDPA ARGILE BLANCHE SAVON - Soap - GRANDPA BRANDS COMPANY; *pg.* 1538, *pg.* 727
GRANDPA ARGIMIEL SAVON - Soap - GRANDPA BRANDS COMPANY; *pg.* 1538, *pg.* 727
GRANDPA JOHN'S - Snack Food Product - RUDOLPH FOODS COMPANY; *pg.* 892, *pg.* 1458
GRANDPA LE STICK - Deodorant - GRANDPA BRANDS COMPANY; *pg.* 1538, *pg.* 727
GRANDPA LOVE-MY-LOOFAH - Soap - GRANDPA BRANDS COMPANY; *pg.* 1538, *pg.* 727
GRANDPA OATMEAL - Soap - GRANDPA BRANDS COMPANY; *pg.* 1538, *pg.* 727
GRANDPA ORANGE ESSENCE - Soap - GRANDPA BRANDS COMPANY; *pg.* 1538, *pg.* 727
GRANDPA PATCHOULI - Soap - GRANDPA BRANDS COMPANY; *pg.* 1538, *pg.* 727
GRANDPA PINE TAR - Shampoo - GRANDPA BRANDS COMPANY; *pg.* 1538, *pg.* 727
GRANDPA SHEA BUTTER - Soap - GRANDPA BRANDS COMPANY; *pg.* 1538, *pg.* 727
GRANDPA'S - Soaps, Dental Aids, Ear Wax Drops & Silver Plating - GRANDPA BRANDS COMPANY; *pg.* 1538, *pg.* 727
GRANDPA'S GARDENS - Packet Seeds - THE PAGE SEED CO.; *pg.* 1798, *pg.* 1163
GRANDPILLOW - Pillow - TEMPUR SEALY INTERNATIONAL, INC.; *pg.* 944, *pg.* 731
GRANDPROTECT - Insurance - METLIFE, INC.; *pg.* 1208, *pg.* 1258
GRANDS! - Biscuits - GENERAL MILLS, INC.; *pg.* 828, *pg.* 933
GRANDSTAND - Fabric - NEMSCHOFF, INC.; *pg.* 936, *pg.* 1890
GRANGE - Footwear - LACROSSE FOOTWEAR, INC.; *pg.* 1811, *pg.* 1503
GRANIT BRONZ - Bronze & Granite Products for the Memorial Industry - COLD SPRING GRANITE COMPANY; *pg.* 76, *pg.* 920
GRANITE - Herbicide - DOW AGROSCIENCES LLC; *pg.* 1156, *pg.* 684
GRANITE - Trucks - MACK TRUCKS, INC.; *pg.* 183, *pg.* 1375
GRANITE - Software - PARAMETRIC TECHNOLOGY CORPORATION; *pg.* 452, *pg.* 835
GRANITE - Floor Color - R.C.A. RUBBER COMPANY; *pg.* 1888, *pg.* 1402
GRANITE - Ceramic, Glass, Stone Tiles & Slabs - WALKER & ZANGER, INC.; *pg.* 119, *pg.* 281
GRANITE CITY FOOD & BREWERY - Restaurant & Bar Services - GRANITE CITY FOOD & BREWERY LTD; *pg.* 1730, *pg.* 937
GRANITE DIGITAL - Storage Products - RELAX TECHNOLOGY, INC.; *pg.* 461, *pg.* 298
GRANITE ONE - Software - PARAMETRIC TECHNOLOGY CORPORATION; *pg.* 452, *pg.* 835
GRANITE RIDGE - Motorhome - JAYCO INC.; *pg.* 1708, *pg.* 695
GRANITEX - Concrete Floor Sealer - AKZONOBEL DECORATIVE PAINTS U.S.; *pg.* 1439, *pg.* 1474
GRANNY'S - Cheese - SAPUTO, INC.; *pg.* 893, *pg.* 1956
GRANNY'S - Tarts - VACHON BAKERY INC.; *pg.* 907, *pg.* 1959
GRANODINE - Metalworking Chemical - HENKEL CORPORATION; *pg.* 1166, *pg.* 897
GRANOSE - Meat-Free Frozen Product - THE HAIN CELESTIAL GROUP, INC.; *pg.* 860, *pg.* 1172
GRANPAPPY - Electrical Appliance & Housewares - NATIONAL PRESTO INDUSTRIES, INC; *pg.* 1128, *pg.* 1857
GRANSTAND - Medical & Aesthetic Product - DYNATRONICS CORPORATION; *pg.* 1526, *pg.* 1757
GRANT - Furniture - AMISCO INDUSTRIES LTD.; *pg.* 913, *pg.* 1958
GRANT - Fan - CRAFTMADE INTERNATIONAL, INC.; *pg.* 1295, *pg.* 1670
GRANT - Casual Shoes - JOHNSTON & MURPHY CO.; *pg.* 1810, *pg.* 1651
GRANTHAM - Carpet - BEAULIEU GROUP, LLC; *pg.* 917, *pg.* 529
GRANTLAND - Sports News - ESPN, INC.; *pg.* 285, *pg.* 340
GRANUFLO - Polymer Product - CHEMTURA CORPORATION; *pg.* 1152, *pg.* 355
GRANUFLO 1000 - Dry Acid Concentrate - FRESENIUS MEDICAL CARE NORTH AMERICA; *pg.* 1531, *pg.* 851
THE GRANULAR APPLICATOR PEOPLE - Tag Line - GANDY COMPANY; *pg.* 703, *pg.* 952
GRANULATED WOW! - Lawn Care Product - GARDENS ALIVE!, INC.; *pg.* 1796, *pg.* 693
GRANULATOR - Size Reduction Machine - S. HOWES, INC.; *pg.* 1373, *pg.* 1342
GRANULITE - Fertilizer Product - SYNAGRO TECHNOLOGIES, INC.; *pg.* 1800, *pg.* 759
GRANVILLE-PHILLIPS - Vacuum Gauges - BROOKS AUTOMATION, INC.; *pg.* 1320, *pg.* 813
GRAP- MO - Steel - THE TIMKEN COMPANY; *pg.* 218, *pg.* 1408
GRAPE KING - Table Grape Label - GIUMARRA VINEYARDS CORPORATION; *pg.* 1964, *pg.* 45
THE GRAPE LAKES - Nail Care Product - OPI PRODUCTS INC.; *pg.* 518, *pg.* 167
GRAPE-NUTS - Cereal - POST HOLDINGS, INC.; *pg.* 833, *pg.* 1002
GRAPE SYNERGY - Supplement & Food Product - NEW EARTH LIFE SCIENCES, INC.; *pg.* 1573, *pg.* 1499
GRAPEFRUIT DIET TABS - Natural Vitamin Pill - HEALTH PRODUCTS CORPORATION; *pg.* 1540, *pg.* 1356
GRAPELETS - Confections - LIBERTY ORCHARDS CO., INC.; *pg.* 1857, *pg.* 1819
GRAPETTE - Beverages - THE COCA-COLA COMPANY; *pg.* 240, *pg.* 493
GRAPEVINE - Bookmark - HERITAGE LACE INC.; *pg.* 694, *pg.* 711
GRAPH ACTION! - Educational Materials - SCHOLASTIC INC.; *pg.* 1683, *pg.* 1288
GRAPH-AIR - Low Temperature Air-Hardened Tool Steel - THE TIMKEN COMPANY; *pg.* 218, *pg.* 1408
THE GRAPH CLUB - Educational Materials - SCHOLASTIC INC.; *pg.* 1683, *pg.* 1288
GRAPHALLOY - Bearing & Bushing - GRAPHITE METALLIZING CORPORATION; *pg.* 1343, *pg.* 1356
GRAPHIC - Fabric - NEMSCHOFF, INC.; *pg.* 936, *pg.* 1890
GRAPHIC VISUALIZATION - Software - EMC CORPORATION; *pg.* 391, *pg.* 825
GRAPHICA - Lounge Chairs - BERNHARDT DESIGN; *pg.* 918, *pg.* 1381
GRAPHICAL ACCESS FOR JHA PLATFORM SYSTEM - Banking Software - JACK HENRY & ASSOCIATES, INC.; *pg.* 422, *pg.* 988
GRAPHICAL CONSOLE SYSTEM - Software - ASPEN TECHNOLOGY, INC.; *pg.* 354, *pg.* 804
GRAPHICS DOOR - Full Color Images on Rolling & Counter

Doors - CORNELL IRON WORKS, INC.; *pg.* 77, *pg.* 1554
GRAPHICS SERVER - Server - ADOBE SYSTEMS INCORPORATED; *pg.* 342, *pg.* 235
GRAPHICS.COM - Online Network - MEDIABISTRO, INC.; *pg.* 1266, *pg.* 1258
GRAPHITE EXTREME - Lubricant - JIG-A-WORLD; *pg.* 980, *pg.* 1951
GRAPHIX - Educational Materials - SCHOLASTIC INC.; *pg.* 1683, *pg.* 1288
GRAPHIXMAX - Electronic Display System - TRANS-LUX CORPORATION; *pg.* 681, *pg.* 365
GRAPHIXWALL - Electronic Display System - TRANS-LUX CORPORATION; *pg.* 681, *pg.* 365
GRAPHTALK - Computer Program - COMPUTER SCIENCES CORPORATION; *pg.* 378, *pg.* 1780
GRAPHTALK AIA - Computer Program - COMPUTER SCIENCES CORPORATION; *pg.* 378, *pg.* 1780
GRAPOLATOR - Glove - LAKELAND INDUSTRIES, INC.; *pg.* 1354, *pg.* 1338
GRAPPLER - Power-Fuse Handling Fitting - S&C ELECTRIC COMPANY; *pg.* 1305, *pg.* 589
GRASPIT - Medical Device - BOSTON SCIENTIFIC CORPORATION; *pg.* 1508, *pg.* 831
GRASPPACK - Backpack - IMMERSION CORPORATION; *pg.* 413, *pg.* 246
GRASS - Fabric - NEMSCHOFF, INC.; *pg.* 936, *pg.* 1890
GRASS-B-GON - Lawn & Garden Product - THE SCOTTS MIRACLE-GRO COMPANY; *pg.* 1799, *pg.* 1459
GRASS PATCH - Spray - THE WOODSTREAM CORPORATION; *pg.* 1801, *pg.* 1549
GRASS TELEFACTOR - Neurophysiological Recording Instrumentation - ASTRO-MED, INC.; *pg.* 619, *pg.* 1609
GRASSCLOTH - Wallcovering - YORK WALLCOVERINGS INC.; *pg.* 947, *pg.* 1598
GRASSHOPPER - Wheat Ale - BIG ROCK BREWERY INCOME TRUST; *pg.* 239, *pg.* 1902
GRASSHOPPERS - Women's Casual Footwear - THE STRIDE RITE CORPORATION; *pg.* 1820, *pg.* 828
GRASSLAND - Fabric - NEMSCHOFF, INC.; *pg.* 936, *pg.* 1890
GRASSROOTS - Skin Care Product - THE ESTEE LAUDER COMPANIES INC.; *pg.* 508, *pg.* 1229
GRASSROOTS - Software - GRASSROOTS ENTERPRISE, INC.; *pg.* 1255, *pg.* 400
GRASSROOTS MULTIPLIER - Software - GRASSROOTS ENTERPRISE, INC.; *pg.* 1255, *pg.* 400
GRATE - Apparel - OAKLEY, INC.; *pg.* 1840, *pg.* 86
GRATESTRIP - Caustic-Type Paint Stripper for Impolymerized Paint - PPG INDUSTRIES, INC.; *pg.* 1445, *pg.* 1579
GRAVEL GUARDS - Footwear - SIMMS FISHING PRODUCTS CORP.; *pg.* 1845, *pg.* 1008
GRAVI-TECH - Engineered Compound & Composite - POLYONE CORPORATION; *pg.* 1177, *pg.* 1404
GRAVICOLOR 100 - Modular Gravimetric Blender - MOTAN, INC.; *pg.* 1886, *pg.* 903
GRAVICOLOR 1000 - Modular Gravimetric Blender - MOTAN, INC.; *pg.* 1886, *pg.* 903
GRAVICOLOR 30 - Modular Gravimetric Blender - MOTAN, INC.; *pg.* 1886, *pg.* 903
GRAVICOLOR 300 - Modular Gravimetric Blender - MOTAN, INC.; *pg.* 1886, *pg.* 903
GRAVIFUFF - Scrap Recycling System - PROCESS CONTROL CORPORATION; *pg.* 1370, *pg.* 518
GRAVILOG - Gravity Tool - SCINTREX LTD.; *pg.* 1374, *pg.* 1920
GRAVIS - Footwear - BURTON SNOWBOARD COMPANY; *pg.* 1829, *pg.* 1765
GRAVIT-EYE - Eye Wash & Shower - SELLSTROM MANUFACTURING CO.; *pg.* 1428, *pg.* 659
GRAVITROL - Line Speed Device - PROCESS CONTROL CORPORATION; *pg.* 1370, *pg.* 518
GRAVITY - Fragrance - COTY, INC.; *pg.* 506, *pg.* 1219
GRAVITY - Fall Protection Equipment - MINE SAFETY APPLIANCES COMPANY; *pg.* 1361, *pg.* 1525
GRAVITY - Fabric - NEMSCHOFF, INC.; *pg.* 936, *pg.* 1890
GRAVITY - Apparel - OAKLEY, INC.; *pg.* 1840, *pg.* 86
GRAVITY CONVEYOR - Carton Flow Product - UNEX MANUFACTURING, INC.; *pg.* 1385, *pg.* 1075
GRAVOFLEX - Laminated Engravable Plastic - GRAVOGRAPH-NEW HERMES; *pg.* 1344, *pg.* 531
GRAVOL - Pharmaceutical Product - CHURCH & DWIGHT CANADA CORP.; *pg.* 503, *pg.* 1925
GRAVOPLY - Laminated Engravable Plastic - GRAVOGRAPH-NEW HERMES; *pg.* 1344, *pg.* 531
GRAVY TRAIN - Pet Food - BIG HEART PET BRANDS; *pg.* 1474, *pg.* 213
GRAY SHADOW - Hose - HBD INDUSTRIES, INC.; *pg.* 207, *pg.* 1449
GRAYHOUND - Capital Equipment - TEREX CORPORATION; *pg.* 1381, *pg.* 384
GRAYLITE - Glass Product - PPG INDUSTRIES, INC.; *pg.* 1445, *pg.* 1579
GRAYSON - Shoes - ALLEN-EDMONDS SHOE CORP.; *pg.* 1804, *pg.* 1887
GRAYSON - Furniture - AMERICAN LEATHER LP; *pg.* 912, *pg.* 1673
GRAYSON - Furniture - BASSETT FURNITURE INDUSTRIES, INCORPORATED; *pg.* 916, *pg.* 1776
GRAYWOLF - Computer Program - COMPUTER SCIENCES CORPORATION; *pg.* 378, *pg.* 1780
GRAZIOSI - Wine - LEONARD KREUSCH, INC.; *pg.* 254, *pg.* 1099
GRC-1700 - Case - GLOBALSTAR, INC.; *pg.* 401, *pg.* 743
GRE - Subject Test - EDUCATIONAL TESTING SERVICE INC.; *pg.* 1394, *pg.* 1111
GREASE-A-BEARING - Wheel Bearing - AMERICAN GREASE STICK CO.; *pg.* 971, *pg.* 902
GREASE-A-WAY - Oil & Grease Solvent - DELTA FOREMOST CHEMICAL CORPORATION; *pg.* 1155, *pg.* 1642
GREASE GOBBLER - Industrial Cleaner - TEXAS REFINERY CORP.; *pg.* 986, *pg.* 1696
GREASE JOCKEY - Fluid Handling System - GRACO, INC.; *pg.* 1342, *pg.* 935
GREASE LOCK - Cleaning Product - ORECK CORPORATION; *pg.* 59, *pg.* 1653
GREASE MAGNET - Concrete, Stone, Asphalt Cleaner (Removes Grease, Oil & Tar) - JELMAR COMPANY; *pg.* 331, *pg.* 660
GREAT AMERICAN BOOK FAIRS - Educational Materials - SCHOLASTIC INC.; *pg.* 1683, *pg.* 1288
GREAT AMERICAN COUNTRY - Cable Network - THE E.W. SCRIPPS COMPANY; *pg.* 1639, *pg.* 1412
GREAT AMERICAN HAMBURGERS - Hamburgers & Other Ground Meat Products - AMERICAN FOODS GROUP, LLC; *pg.* 837, *pg.* 1859
THE GREAT AMERICAN RACE - Motorsports Event - INTERNATIONAL SPEEDWAY CORPORATION; *pg.* 553, *pg.* 420
GREAT AMERICAN STEAK & BUFFET - Restaurants - WESTERN SIZZLIN CORPORATION; *pg.* 1755, *pg.* 1806
GREAT AMERICAN STEAKS - Steaks - AMERICAN FOODS GROUP, LLC; *pg.* 837, *pg.* 1859
GREAT BIG BERTHA - Golf Equipment - CALLAWAY GOLF COMPANY; *pg.* 1829, *pg.* 58
GREAT BLUE - Pipe Joint Compound - OATEY SUPPLY CHAIN SERVICES; *pg.* 30, *pg.* 1433
GREAT BOOKS OF THE WESTERN WORLD - Books - ENCYCLOPAEDIA BRITANNICA, INC.; *pg.* 1638, *pg.* 573
GREAT BREAKS - Fast Food - MCDONALD'S CORPORATION; *pg.* 1737, *pg.* 645
GREAT COFFEE MADE EASY - Coffee Service - KEURIG GREEN MOUNTAIN, INC.; *pg.* 868, *pg.* 1768
GREAT COFFEE MAKES A WORLD OF DIFFERENCE - Coffee - KEURIG GREEN MOUNTAIN, INC.; *pg.* 868, *pg.* 1768
GREAT DANE - Trailers - GREAT DANE TRAILERS; *pg.* 1707, *pg.* 539
GREAT EAGLE - Game - WMS INDUSTRIES INC.; *pg.* 593, *pg.* 666
THE GREAT ESCAPE - Games - PENN NATIONAL GAMING, INC.; *pg.* 574, *pg.* 1595
GREAT ESCAPE - Park - SIX FLAGS ENTERTAINMENT CORPORATION; *pg.* 583, *pg.* 1698
GREAT ESTATES - Wine - KENDALL-JACKSON WINE ESTATES, LTD.; *pg.* 1965, *pg.* 277
GREAT EXPECTATIONS - Hair Service Center - REGIS CORPORATION; *pg.* 521, *pg.* 941
GREAT EXPLORATIONS - Game - UNIVERSITY GAMES CORPORATION; *pg.* 969, *pg.* 230
GREAT FACES. GREAT PLACES. - Tagline - SOUTH DAKOTA'S DEPARTMENT OF TOURISM; *pg.* 1006, *pg.* 1624
GREAT FEELING - Soap - SWISHER HYGIENE INC.; *pg.* 336, *pg.* 1507
THE GREAT FRAME UP - Picture Frame Stores - FRANCHISE CONCEPTS, INC.; *pg.* 1769, *pg.* 1005
GREAT FRANCHISEES. GREAT BRAND. - Slogan - DINEEQUITY, INC.; *pg.* 1725, *pg.* 95
GREAT FUN - Discount Consumer Services - AFFINION GROUP, INC.; *pg.* 1225, *pg.* 372
GREAT GOOFS - Hunting Product - GERBER LEGENDARY BLADES; *pg.* 1834, *pg.* 1503
GREAT GRIP - Liquid Latex - THE DOW CHEMICAL COMPANY; *pg.* 1157, *pg.* 898
GREAT HEALTHCARE HAS COME HOME - Tag Line - GENTIVA HEALTH SERVICES, INC.; *pg.* 1534, *pg.* 506
THE GREAT INDOORS - Home Remodeling & Decorating Products - SEARS HOLDINGS CORPORATION; *pg.* 1784, *pg.* 618
GREAT LAKES ANGLER - Magazine - O'MEARA-BROWN PUBLICATIONS, INC.; *pg.* 1673, *pg.* 586
GREAT LAKES GOLD - Vinyl Windows & Patio Doors - NORTEK, INC.; *pg.* 100, *pg.* 1607
GREAT LAKES, GREAT FLAVORS. - Tagline - MICHIGAN APPLE COMMITTEE; *pg.* 147, *pg.* 895
GREAT LIFE - Designer Fragrance - PARFUMS DE COEUR LTD.; *pg.* 519, *pg.* 376
GREAT LIFE - Paints - SHERWIN WILLIAMS; *pg.* 1448, *pg.* 1436
GREAT OCEAN - Canned Goods - CAMERICAN INTERNATIONAL; *pg.* 844, *pg.* 1101
THE GREAT OCEAN RESCUE - Educational Materials - SCHOLASTIC INC.; *pg.* 1683, *pg.* 1288
GREAT OUTDOORSMAN - Jacket - HABAND COMPANY, INC.; *pg.* 1772, *pg.* 1099
THE GREAT OUTDOORS...PASS IT ON - Slogan - BASS PRO SHOPS, INC.; *pg.* 1826, *pg.* 1006
GREAT PEOPLE GREAT PRODUCTS - Slogan - EAGLE MANUFACTURING COMPANY; *pg.* 79, *pg.* 1851
GREAT PLAINS - Furniture - ASHLEY FURNITURE INDUSTRIES, INC.; *pg.* 914, *pg.* 1852
GREAT PLAINS - Video Game - INTERNATIONAL GAME TECHNOLOGY; *pg.* 957, *pg.* 1024
GREAT PLAINS - Fabric - NEMSCHOFF, INC.; *pg.* 936, *pg.* 1890
GREAT PLAINS HUNTER - Black Powder Rifle - LYMAN PRODUCTS CORPORATION; *pg.* 1839, *pg.* 356
GREAT PLAINS RIFLE - Black Powder Rifle - LYMAN PRODUCTS CORPORATION; *pg.* 1839, *pg.* 356
GREAT RANGE - T-Shirts - ABERCROMBIE & FITCH CO.; *pg.* 37, *pg.* 1466
GREAT REPUBLIC - Apparel - BRODER BROS., CO.; *pg.* 1828, *pg.* 1588
GREAT REWARDS - Servicing - SLM CORPORATION; *pg.* 804, *pg.* 388
GREAT SCOT! - Game - WMS INDUSTRIES INC.; *pg.* 593, *pg.* 666
GREAT SHAPES - Hosiery - KAYSER-ROTH CORPORATION; *pg.* 28, *pg.* 1374
THE GREAT SOLAR SYSTEM RESCUE - Educational Materials - SCHOLASTIC INC.; *pg.* 1683, *pg.* 1288
GREAT SOUTHERN - Banking Services - GREAT SOUTHERN BANCORP, INC.; *pg.* 763, *pg.* 1006
GREAT STEAKS! - Slogan - QUANTUM FOODS, INC.; *pg.* 891, *pg.* 559
GREAT STRIDES - Polyurethane Product - TEXTILE RUBBER & CHEMICAL COMPANY; *pg.* 1890, *pg.* 530
GREAT STUFF - Polyurethane Foam Sealant - THE DOW CHEMICAL COMPANY; *pg.* 1157, *pg.* 898
GREAT TASTE - Fast Food - MCDONALD'S CORPORATION; *pg.* 1737, *pg.* 645
GREAT TASTE HAS ITS BENEFITS - Tagline - THE COCA-COLA COMPANY; *pg.* 240, *pg.* 493
GREAT TASTE IS A FAMILY TRADITION - Tagline - FURMANO FOODS, INC.; *pg.* 857, *pg.* 1557
GREAT TASTE SIMPLY AND PURE - Slogan - PURITY DAIRIES, LLC; *pg.* 891, *pg.* 1653
GREAT TASTES FROM THE INSIDE OUT! - Tagline - SOKOL & COMPANY; *pg.* 1862, *pg.* 598
GREAT TEACHING IN THE ONE COMPUTER CLASSROOM - Educational Materials - SCHOLASTIC INC.; *pg.* 1683, *pg.* 1288
GREAT THINGS FOR CANADA - Slogan - HUDSON'S BAY COMPANY; *pg.* 1773, *pg.* 1938
GREAT VALUE - Grocery Items-Private Label Brand - WAL-MART STORES, INC.; *pg.* 1790, *pg.* 29
GREAT WALL - Game - WMS INDUSTRIES INC.; *pg.* 593, *pg.* 666
GREAT WEAR - Eyeliner & Concealer - MAYBELLINE LLC; *pg.* 516, *pg.* 1257
GREAT WHITE - Pizza - BJ'S RESTAURANTS, INC.; *pg.* 1716, *pg.* 104
GREAT WHITE - Paper - INTERNATIONAL PAPER COMPANY; *pg.* 1460, *pg.* 1644

First page reference indicates Business Class Edition
Second page reference indicates Geographic Edition

GREAT WHITE - Pipe Joint Compound - OATEY SUPPLY CHAIN SERVICES; *pg.* 30, *pg.* 1433
GREAT X - Game - UNIVERSITY GAMES CORPORATION; *pg.* 969, *pg.* 230
GREATBRITAIN.COM - Travel Website - LIVE CURRENT MEDIA INC.; *pg.* 1263, *pg.* 1911
GREATCOLOR - Four-Color Digital Process Printing for Loose-Leaf Products - AMERICAN THERMOPLASTIC COMPANY; *pg.* 349, *pg.* 1573
GREATEST GIFT - Pillow and Throw - HERITAGE LACE INC.; *pg.* 694, *pg.* 711
GREATEST SHOW ON EARTH - Entertainment Advertisement - FELD ENTERTAINMENT, INC.; *pg.* 547, *pg.* 458
GREATFOOD - Confections - 1-800-FLOWERS.COM, INC.; *pg.* 1758, *pg.* 1151
GREATFOOD.COM - Website - 1-800-FLOWERS.COM, INC.; *pg.* 1758, *pg.* 1151
GRECIAN - Apparel - BEBE STORES, INC.; *pg.* 19, *pg.* 49
GRECIAN 5 - Hair Coloring - COMBE INCORPORATED; *pg.* 1516, *pg.* 1351
GRECIAN FORMULA 16 - Hair Coloring Product - COMBE INCORPORATED; *pg.* 1516, *pg.* 1351
GRECIAN GOLD - Game - WMS INDUSTRIES INC.; *pg.* 593, *pg.* 666
GRECO - Lighting Product - WESTINGHOUSE LIGHTING CORPORATION; *pg.* 687, *pg.* 1571
GREED IS GOOD - Video Game - INTERNATIONAL GAME TECHNOLOGY; *pg.* 957, *pg.* 1024
GREEFF - Fabric - F. SCHUMACHER & CO.; *pg.* 925, *pg.* 1230
GREEK - Bath Product - KOHLER CO.; *pg.* 91, *pg.* 1862
GREEK MASTERPIZZA - Pizza - STRAW HAT COOPERATIVE CORPORATION; *pg.* 1751, *pg.* 260
GREEN & BLACK'S - Chocolate - MONDELEZ INTERNATIONAL, INC.; *pg.* 878, *pg.* 601
GREEN AND GOLD - Lottery Game - NEW YORK STATE LOTTERY; *pg.* 1001, *pg.* 1340
GREEN ARROW - Character - DC COMICS, INC.; *pg.* 1633, *pg.* 1221
GREEN BAY PACKERS - Professional Football Team - GREEN BAY PACKERS, INC.; *pg.* 551, *pg.* 1859
GREEN BUILDING STUDIO - Energy Analysis Tool - AUTODESK INC.; *pg.* 356, *pg.* 257
GREEN BURRITO - Quick Service Restaurant - CKE RESTAURANTS INC.; *pg.* 1723, *pg.* 63
GREEN BY NATURE - Slogan - CASCADES, INC.; *pg.* 73, *pg.* 1950
GREEN CAFFEINE BOOST - Fruit Drink - JAMBA, INC.; *pg.* 1024, *pg.* 84
GREEN CHARGER - Fertilizer - SOUTHERN STATES COOPERATIVE, INC.; *pg.* 1482, *pg.* 1804
GREEN CORPS - Abrasive Discs & Sheets - 3M COMPANY; *pg.* 1142, *pg.* 956
GREEN DAY - Guitar Concert - MAVERIK COUNTRY STORES, INC.; *pg.* 1027, *pg.* 1752
GREEN DOT - Credit Cards - GREEN DOT CORPORATION; *pg.* 763, *pg.* 180
GREEN EASE - Suede Booties - HABAND COMPANY, INC.; *pg.* 1772, *pg.* 1099
GREEN FOREST - Paper Product - GEORGIA-PACIFIC LLC; *pg.* 1458, *pg.* 507
GREEN GABIONS - Bank Protection - MACCAFERRI, INC.; *pg.* 95, *pg.* 780
GREEN GARDAN - Bedding - CROSCILL, INC.; *pg.* 1122, *pg.* 1220
GREEN GIANT - Food Product - GENERAL MILLS, INC.; *pg.* 828, *pg.* 933
GREEN-GO - Power Transmission Belting - FENNER DRIVES; *pg.* 1336, *pg.* 1551
GREEN GUARD - Plastics Product - AEP INDUSTRIES INC.; *pg.* 1878, *pg.* 1085
GREEN GUARD - Soil Care Product - GARDENS ALIVE!, INC.; *pg.* 1796, *pg.* 693
GREEN HORNET - Coating - HILL & GRIFFITH COMPANY; *pg.* 1167, *pg.* 1414
GREEN ICE - Container Grown Plant - MONROVIA GROWERS; *pg.* 1797, *pg.* 44
GREEN INTELLIGENCE - Sensor Monitors - WHIRLPOOL CORPORATION; *pg.* 62, *pg.* 872
GREEN LANTERN - Character - DC COMICS, INC.; *pg.* 1633, *pg.* 1221
GREEN LEAF PERENNIALS - Flower Grower - ARIS HORTICULTURE, INC.; *pg.* 1793, *pg.* 1404
GREEN LIGHTING - Nutritional Supplement - NATURAL ORGANICS, INC.; *pg.* 1571, *pg.* 1181
GREEN LIST - Environmentally Friendly Products Classifying System - S.C. JOHNSON & SON, INC.; *pg.* 334, *pg.* 1889
GREEN MACHINE - Bicycle - HUFFY CORPORATION; *pg.* 1836, *pg.* 1409
GREEN MACHINE - Lottery Game - NEW YORK STATE LOTTERY; *pg.* 1001, *pg.* 1340
GREEN MOUNTAIN - Coffee - KEURIG GREEN MOUNTAIN, INC.; *pg.* 868, *pg.* 1768
GREEN MOUNTAIN ANNUITY SERIES - Fixed Annuity - NATIONAL LIFE INSURANCE COMPANY; *pg.* 1210, *pg.* 1766
GREEN MOUNTAIN COFFEE - Coffee Service - KEURIG GREEN MOUNTAIN, INC.; *pg.* 868, *pg.* 1768
GREEN MOUNTAIN COFFEE ROASTERS - Coffee Service - KEURIG GREEN MOUNTAIN, INC.; *pg.* 868, *pg.* 1768
GREEN MOUNTAIN COFFEE ROASTERS & DESIGN - Coffee - KEURIG GREEN MOUNTAIN, INC.; *pg.* 868, *pg.* 1768
GREEN MOUNTAIN HERITAGE - Fixed Annuity - NATIONAL LIFE INSURANCE COMPANY; *pg.* 1210, *pg.* 1766
GREEN MOUNTAIN LIBERTY - Fixed Annuity - NATIONAL LIFE INSURANCE COMPANY; *pg.* 1210, *pg.* 1766
GREEN MOUNTAIN NATURALS - Fruit-Based Beverages - KEURIG GREEN MOUNTAIN, INC.; *pg.* 868, *pg.* 1768
GREEN MOUNTAIN PRIVILEGE - Fixed Annuity - NATIONAL LIFE INSURANCE COMPANY; *pg.* 1210, *pg.* 1766
GREEN MOUNTAIN SECURITY 3 - Fixed Annuity - NATIONAL LIFE INSURANCE COMPANY; *pg.* 1210, *pg.* 1766
GREEN MOUNTAIN SECURITY 5 - Fixed Annuity - NATIONAL LIFE INSURANCE COMPANY; *pg.* 1210, *pg.* 1766
GREEN PEACOCK - Rice - AMERICAN RICE, INC.; *pg.* 837, *pg.* 1700
GREEN PHYTO POWER - Nutritional Product - RBC LIFE SCIENCES, INC.; *pg.* 1588, *pg.* 1723
GREEN PUFFER - Vaporizer - VAPOR CORP.; *pg.* 61, *pg.* 427
GREEN REVERSIBLE - Pillow and Throw - HERITAGE LACE INC.; *pg.* 694, *pg.* 711
GREEN ROUTINE - Food Program - PUBLIX SUPER MARKETS, INC.; *pg.* 1031, *pg.* 437
GREEN SEASONS - Lawn & Garden Care - TRACTOR SUPPLY COMPANY; *pg.* 708, *pg.* 1627
GREEN SELECT - Cleaning Product - HILLYARD, INC.; *pg.* 331, *pg.* 990
GREEN SPOT - Fruit Drinks - GREEN SPOT, INC.; *pg.* 251, *pg.* 68
GREEN SQUAD - Recycling & Waste Treatment - WASTE MANAGEMENT, INC.; *pg.* 1954, *pg.* 1716
GREEN STAR - Turf Maintenance Machinery - SMITHCO, INC.; *pg.* 1377, *pg.* 1592
GREEN STEP - Insect Pest Control Product - GARDENS ALIVE!, INC.; *pg.* 1796, *pg.* 693
GREEN STUFF - Wax - MOC PRODUCTS COMPANY, INC.; *pg.* 332, *pg.* 174
GREEN TAPE - Materials & Parts - E.I. DU PONT DE NEMOURS & COMPANY; *pg.* 1159, *pg.* 390
GREEN TEA - Hair & Skin Product - AUBREY ORGANICS INC.; *pg.* 499, *pg.* 470
GREEN TEA - Perfume - ELIZABETH ARDEN, INC.; *pg.* 507, *pg.* 448
GREEN TEA REVITALIZE - Fragrance - ELIZABETH ARDEN, INC.; *pg.* 507, *pg.* 448
GREEN THUMB - Registered Art - LAWN DOCTOR INC.; *pg.* 1796, *pg.* 1074
GREEN TOE - Footwear Product - DECKERS OUTDOOR CORPORATION; *pg.* 1807, *pg.* 100
GREEN TOWER - Container Grown Plant - MONROVIA GROWERS; *pg.* 1797, *pg.* 44
GREEN TRIDENT - Flashlight - STREAMLIGHT INC.; *pg.* 1306, *pg.* 1527
GREEN WORKS - Eco-Friendly Household Cleaners - THE CLOROX COMPANY; *pg.* 327, *pg.* 169
GREEN WORLD ALLIANCE - Recycling Program - XEROX CORPORATION; *pg.* 494, *pg.* 365
GREENBACK ATTACK - Video Game - INTERNATIONAL GAME TECHNOLOGY; *pg.* 957, *pg.* 1024
GREENBRIAR - Table - BLATT BOWLING & BILLIARD CORP.; *pg.* 1827, *pg.* 1203
GREENBRIAR - Jacket - I. SPIEWAK & SONS, INC.; *pg.* 42, *pg.* 1242
GREENBRIAR - Lighting - LSI INDUSTRIES INC.; *pg.* 58, *pg.* 1416
GREENBRIAR - Fabric - NEMSCHOFF, INC.; *pg.* 936, *pg.* 1890
GREENBRIER - Lace Placemats, Doilies & Mantel Scarves - HERITAGE LACE INC.; *pg.* 694, *pg.* 711
GREEN.COM - Online Services - IAC/INTERACTIVECORP; *pg.* 292, *pg.* 1242
GREENE VALLEY - Promotional Packet Seeds - THE PAGE SEED CO.; *pg.* 1798, *pg.* 1163
GREENER - Molecular Probe Product - THERMO FISHER SCIENTIFIC INC.; *pg.* 1602, *pg.* 61
GREENER SELECTIONS - Lettuce - DOLE FRESH VEGETABLES; *pg.* 854, *pg.* 198
GREENFIELD - Tools - KENNAMETAL INC.; *pg.* 1052, *pg.* 1547
GREENFIELD - Taps & Dies - KENNAMETAL IPG; *pg.* 1353, *pg.* 1615
GREENFIELD - Mini-Lateral Machine - LINDSAY CORPORATION; *pg.* 1356, *pg.* 1016
GREENFIELD GAGE - Gages - KENNAMETAL IPG; *pg.* 1353, *pg.* 1615
GREENFOODS FORMULAS - Healthcare Product - SWANSON HEALTH PRODUCTS INC.; *pg.* 1600, *pg.* 1397
GREENFREE - Pressed & Monolithic Refractory - RESCO PRODUCTS, INC.; *pg.* 107, *pg.* 1581
GREENGERNOMICS - Furniture - HERMAN MILLER, INC.; *pg.* 926, *pg.* 913
GREENGUARD - Building Product - PACTIV CORPORATION; *pg.* 1466, *pg.* 624
GREENHAVEN PRESS - Publisher - GALE CENGAGE LEARNING; *pg.* 1643, *pg.* 885
GREENHOUSE - Fabric - NEMSCHOFF, INC.; *pg.* 936, *pg.* 1890
GREENIE - Screw-On-Connector - IDEAL INDUSTRIES, INC.; *pg.* 1051, *pg.* 662
GREENIE - Educational Materials - SCHOLASTIC INC.; *pg.* 1683, *pg.* 1288
GREENIES - Pet Food - MARS, INCORPORATED; *pg.* 1858, *pg.* 1792
GREENIES - Pet Food - MARS PETCARE; *pg.* 1478, *pg.* 1633
GREENJOYS - Shoes - ACUSHNET COMPANY; *pg.* 1824, *pg.* 818
GREENLEAF - Packaged Foods - ATALANTA CORPORATION; *pg.* 838, *pg.* 1057
GREENLEE - BX Cutter - GREENLEE TEXTRON INC.; *pg.* 1048, *pg.* 655
GREENLEE - Lighting - LSI INDUSTRIES INC.; *pg.* 58, *pg.* 1416
GREENLIGHT - Laser Therapy - AMERICAN MEDICAL SYSTEMS HOLDINGS, INC.; *pg.* 1493, *pg.* 947
GREENLIGHT - Fiberoptic Laryngoscope System - VITAL SIGNS, INC.; *pg.* 1607, *pg.* 1126
GREENLIGHT HPS - Medical Device - AMERICAN MEDICAL SYSTEMS HOLDINGS, INC.; *pg.* 1493, *pg.* 947
GREENLIGHT II - Laryngoscope System - VITAL SIGNS, INC.; *pg.* 1607, *pg.* 1126
GREENLIGHT PV SYSTEM - Surgical Laser System for Use in Prostate Surgery - AMERICAN MEDICAL SYSTEMS, INC.; *pg.* 1399, *pg.* 238
GREENLIMS - Software - PERKINELMER, INC.; *pg.* 1426, *pg.* 853
GREENLINE - Tape - CHASE CORPORATION; *pg.* 1152, *pg.* 803
GREENLINE - Animal Feed - TROUW NUTRITION USA; *pg.* 1482, *pg.* 616
GREENLINE - Environment Program - ZEP INC.; *pg.* 338, *pg.* 524
GREENLINK - Chemistry & Cleaning Processes - ZEP INC.; *pg.* 338, *pg.* 524
GREENLINKS GOLF RESORT - Resort - SUNSTREAM, INC.; *pg.* 1116, *pg.* 428
GREENPATH - Environmental Management System - DELAWARE NORTH COMPANIES, INC.; *pg.* 1089, *pg.* 1148
GREENRIDE - Web Based Ride Share - ECOLOGY AND ENVIRONMENT, INC.; *pg.* 1410, *pg.* 1173
GREENS - Food Supplement - ORANGE PEEL ENTERPRISES, INC.; *pg.* 1028, *pg.* 477
GREENS+ - Vitamins - ORANGE PEEL ENTERPRISES, INC.; *pg.* 1028, *pg.* 477
GREENS+ ENERGY BAR - Energy Bar - ORANGE PEEL ENTERPRISES, INC.; *pg.* 1028, *pg.* 477
GREENSKEEPER - Fertilizer - LEBANON SEABOARD CORPORATION; *pg.* 1797, *pg.* 1547

GREENSPRING - Retirement Community - ERICKSON LIVING; *pg.* 1090, *pg.* 766
GREENSTAR - Precision Farming - DEERE & COMPANY; *pg.* 703, *pg.* 632
GREENTANK - Tank - ZCL COMPOSITES INC.; *pg.* 1892, *pg.* 1906
GREENVIEW - Fertilizer - LEBANON SEABOARD CORPORATION; *pg.* 1797, *pg.* 1547
GREENVISTA - Garden Products - E.I. DU PONT DE NEMOURS & COMPANY; *pg.* 1159, *pg.* 390
GREENWILLOW BOOKS - Books - HARPERCOLLINS PUBLISHERS INC.; *pg.* 1647, *pg.* 1237
GREETING CANS - Gift Canisters of Popcorn - THE POPCORN FACTORY; *pg.* 1861, *pg.* 625
GREGORY - Security Product - BAE SYSTEMS PRODUCTS GROUP; *pg.* 359, *pg.* 432
GREGORY - Outdoor Products - BLACK DIAMOND, INC.; *pg.* 1827, *pg.* 1756
GRENADA - Footwear - EASTLAND SHOE CORPORATION; *pg.* 1808, *pg.* 750
GREPTILE - Gripping Material - 3M COMPANY; *pg.* 1142, *pg.* 956
GRETA - Clothing - ABERCROMBIE & FITCH CO.; *pg.* 37, *pg.* 1466
GRETAG - Ink-Jet Printer - COOLEY GROUP, INC.; *pg.* 691, *pg.* 1603
GRETCHAN - Footwear - STEVEN MADDEN, LTD.; *pg.* 1819, *pg.* 1176
GRETCHEN - Clothing - ABERCROMBIE & FITCH CO.; *pg.* 37, *pg.* 1466
GRETSCH - Guitar - FENDER MUSICAL INSTRUMENTS CORPORATION; *pg.* 547, *pg.* 21
GRETSCH - Drumset - KAMAN CORPORATION; *pg.* 229, *pg.* 338
GREY FLANNEL - Perfume - ELIZABETH ARDEN, INC.; *pg.* 507, *pg.* 448
GREY POUPON - Mustards - THE KRAFT HEINZ COMPANY; *pg.* 870, *pg.* 1577
GREY WATER ODOR CONTROL - Grey Water Holding Tank Deodorant - THETFORD CORPORATION; *pg.* 337, *pg.* 867
GREYHAWK - Motorhome - JAYCO INC.; *pg.* 1708, *pg.* 695
GREYHAWK - Game Setting - WIZARDS OF THE COAST, INC.; *pg.* 970, *pg.* 1830
GREYHOUND - Intercity Bus Transportation - GREYHOUND LINES, INC.; *pg.* 1910, *pg.* 1681
GREYHOUND PACKAGEXPRESS - Bus Transportation Service - GREYHOUND LINES, INC.; *pg.* 1910, *pg.* 1681
GREYHOUND TRAVEL SERVICES - Bus Transportation Service - GREYHOUND LINES, INC.; *pg.* 1910, *pg.* 1681
GREYSTONE - Steel Product - AK STEEL HOLDING CORPORATION; *pg.* 1311, *pg.* 1479
GREYSTONE BRIGHT - Steel Product - AK STEEL HOLDING CORPORATION; *pg.* 1311, *pg.* 1479
GREYSTONE DULL - Steel Product - AK STEEL HOLDING CORPORATION; *pg.* 1311, *pg.* 1479
GRF-1000 - Fly Rod - CORTLAND LINE COMPANY; *pg.* 1831, *pg.* 1155
GRI SECURITY PRODUCTS - Custom Security Products - GEORGE RISK INDUSTRIES, INC.; *pg.* 1298, *pg.* 1011
GRIBETZ - Quilting & Cutting Machinery - LEGGETT & PLATT, INCORPORATED; *pg.* 933, *pg.* 974
GRID - Footwear - SAUCONY, INC.; *pg.* 1818, *pg.* 828
GRID ADVANCE TR - Men's & Women's Trail Shoe - SAUCONY, INC.; *pg.* 1818, *pg.* 828
GRID AURA LX - Footwear - SAUCONY, INC.; *pg.* 1818, *pg.* 828
GRID AURA TR 5 - Men's & Women's Trail Shoe - SAUCONY, INC.; *pg.* 1818, *pg.* 828
GRID AZURA I - Men's & Women's Training Shoe - SAUCONY, INC.; *pg.* 1818, *pg.* 828
GRID AZURA LC - Footwear - SAUCONY, INC.; *pg.* 1818, *pg.* 828
GRID CHEBACCO - Footwear - SAUCONY, INC.; *pg.* 1818, *pg.* 828
GRID ENERGY - Women's Walking Shoe - SAUCONY, INC.; *pg.* 1818, *pg.* 828
GRID FASTWITCH - Footwear - SAUCONY, INC.; *pg.* 1818, *pg.* 828
GRID HURRICANE - Footwear - SAUCONY, INC.; *pg.* 1818, *pg.* 828
GRID INSTEP - Footwear - SAUCONY, INC.; *pg.* 1818, *pg.* 828
GRID INSTEP 600 - Women's Walking Shoe - SAUCONY, INC.; *pg.* 1818, *pg.* 828
GRID INTEGRITY - Footwear - SAUCONY, INC.; *pg.* 1818, *pg.* 828
GRID IRON - Apparel - OAKLEY, INC.; *pg.* 1840, *pg.* 86
GRID JAZZ 9 - Men's & Women's Training Shoe - SAUCONY, INC.; *pg.* 1818, *pg.* 828
GRID JAZZ X - Footwear - SAUCONY, INC.; *pg.* 1818, *pg.* 828
GRID-LOCK - Aerostructures - UTC AEROSPACE SYSTEMS; *pg.* 236, *pg.* 1369
GRID MOTION - Footwear - SAUCONY, INC.; *pg.* 1818, *pg.* 828
GRID MOTION 4 - Men's & Women's Walking Shoe - SAUCONY, INC.; *pg.* 1818, *pg.* 828
GRID OMNI - Footwear - SAUCONY, INC.; *pg.* 1818, *pg.* 828
GRID OMNI 3 - Men's & Women's Training Shoe - SAUCONY, INC.; *pg.* 1818, *pg.* 828
GRID ONE - Software - NIELSEN AUDIO; *pg.* 446, *pg.* 768
GRID REGULATE - Footwear - SAUCONY, INC.; *pg.* 1818, *pg.* 828
GRID RW 2 - Women's Walking Shoe - SAUCONY, INC.; *pg.* 1818, *pg.* 828
GRID SHADOW - Footwear - SAUCONY, INC.; *pg.* 1818, *pg.* 828
GRID SHADOW 8 - Men's & Women's Training Shoe - SAUCONY, INC.; *pg.* 1818, *pg.* 828
GRID SHADOW 8 TR - Men's & Women's Trail Shoe - SAUCONY, INC.; *pg.* 1818, *pg.* 828
GRID SMART - Electric Meter - AMERICAN ELECTRIC POWER COMPANY, INC.; *pg.* 1934, *pg.* 1437
GRID STABIL LE 2 - Men's & Women's Walking Shoe - SAUCONY, INC.; *pg.* 1818, *pg.* 828
GRID STABIL MC - Footwear - SAUCONY, INC.; *pg.* 1818, *pg.* 828
GRID SWERVE LS - Men's & Women's Training Shoe - SAUCONY, INC.; *pg.* 1818, *pg.* 828
GRID T4 - Men's & Women's Training Shoe - SAUCONY, INC.; *pg.* 1818, *pg.* 828
GRID TANGENT - Footwear - SAUCONY, INC.; *pg.* 1818, *pg.* 828
GRID TRAINER - Footwear - SAUCONY, INC.; *pg.* 1818, *pg.* 828
GRID TRIGON - Footwear - SAUCONY, INC.; *pg.* 1818, *pg.* 828
GRID TRIGON 2 - Men's & Women's Training Shoe - SAUCONY, INC.; *pg.* 1818, *pg.* 828
GRID TRIUMPH - Footwear - SAUCONY, INC.; *pg.* 1818, *pg.* 828
GRID UNITY - Footwear - SAUCONY, INC.; *pg.* 1818, *pg.* 828
GRIDSTOR - Software - COMMVAULT SYSTEMS, INC.; *pg.* 377, *pg.* 1125
GRIDZONE - Pillow - SELECT COMFORT CORPORATION; *pg.* 942, *pg.* 942
GRIEVE - Oven - THE GRIEVE CORPORATION; *pg.* 1072, *pg.* 657
GRIFCOTE - Concrete Industry Product - HILL & GRIFFITH COMPANY; *pg.* 1167, *pg.* 1414
GRIFFIN - Furniture - LA-Z-BOY INCORPORATED; *pg.* 932, *pg.* 901
GRIFFIN CREEK - Wine - WILLAMETTE VALLEY VINEYARDS, INC.; *pg.* 1972, *pg.* 1510
GRIFFIN SYRUP - Food Company - GRIFFIN FOOD COMPANY; *pg.* 860, *pg.* 1484
GRIFFIN'S GATE - Game - WMS INDUSTRIES INC.; *pg.* 593, *pg.* 666
GRIFFITH - Table - BLATT BOWLING & BILLIARD CORP.; *pg.* 1827, *pg.* 1203
GRIFFITH - Furniture - J. ROBERT SCOTT INC.; *pg.* 930, *pg.* 105
GRIFLUBE - Metal Casting Product - HILL & GRIFFITH COMPANY; *pg.* 1167, *pg.* 1414
GRIGIO E SABBIA - Tile - ARTISTIC TILE INC.; *pg.* 914, *pg.* 1119
THE GRILL AT TWO TREES - Food Service - ARK RESTAURANTS CORP.; *pg.* 1715, *pg.* 1196
GRILL BITS - Pet Foods - HEINZ NORTH AMERICA; *pg.* 861, *pg.* 1576
GRILL BRITE - Cleaner - DELTA FOREMOST CHEMICAL CORPORATION; *pg.* 1155, *pg.* 1642
GRILL MATES - Food Product - MCCORMICK & COMPANY, INCORPORATED; *pg.* 1027, *pg.* 779
GRILL-N-LITE - Electrical Appliance & Housewares - NATIONAL PRESTO INDUSTRIES, INC; *pg.* 1128, *pg.* 1857
GRILL ON THE ALLEY - Restaurant - GRILL CONCEPTS, INC.; *pg.* 1730, *pg.* 308
THE GRILL ROOM - Restaurant - ARK RESTAURANTS CORP.; *pg.* 1715, *pg.* 1196
GRILL TENDER - Grill Cleaner - LINCOLN FOODSERVICE PRODUCTS, LLC; *pg.* 1127, *pg.* 1432
GRILLE MARX - Beverages & Merchandise - DELEK US HOLDINGS, INC.; *pg.* 975, *pg.* 1627
GRILLED CHICKEN SALAD DELUXE - Salad - MCDONALD'S CORPORATION; *pg.* 1737, *pg.* 645
GRILLED HAM WITH BRIE AND APPLE - Food Product - GAY LEA FOODS CO-OPERATIVE LIMITED; *pg.* 858, *pg.* 1926
GRILLERS PRIME - Veggie Burgers - KELLOGG COMPANY; *pg.* 831, *pg.* 870
GRILLEWORK - Fabric - NEMSCHOFF, INC.; *pg.* 936, *pg.* 1890
GRILLMASTER - Grill Cleaner - U.S. PUMICE COMPANY; *pg.* 1185, *pg.* 65
GRILLWORK - Carpet - INTERFACE, INC.; *pg.* 695, *pg.* 512
GRIM REAPER - Gaming Product - GLD PRODUCTS, INC.; *pg.* 1835, *pg.* 1882
GRIME BOSS - Cleanser - NICE-PAK PRODUCTS, INC.; *pg.* 1465, *pg.* 1319
GRIME-X - Cleaning Agent - DELTA FOREMOST CHEMICAL CORPORATION; *pg.* 1155, *pg.* 1642
GRIMES - Dress Shoes - JOHNSTON & MURPHY CO.; *pg.* 1810, *pg.* 1651
GRIND - Musical Instrument - PEAVEY ELECTRONICS CORPORATION; *pg.* 662, *pg.* 970
GRIND IT - Kitchen Tools - OXO; *pg.* 1058, *pg.* 1275
GRINDMASTER - Coffee Grinders & Brewers - GRINDMASTER CORPORATION; *pg.* 56, *pg.* 734
GRIP - Footwear - COBIAN CORP.; *pg.* 1806, *pg.* 253
GRIP - Tables - STEELCASE INC.; *pg.* 475, *pg.* 889
GRIP - Mechanical Pencils - YASUTOMO & CO.; *pg.* 497, *pg.* 280
GRIP & RIP - Tearing Ruler - ACME UNITED CORPORATION; *pg.* 1040, *pg.* 346
GRIP IT - Screwdriver - KLEIN TOOLS INC.; *pg.* 1052, *pg.* 627
GRIP-LOK - Power Tool - MILWAUKEE ELECTRIC TOOL CORP.; *pg.* 1056, *pg.* 1855
GRIP-LUG - Grouser Bar - ALLIED CONSTRUCTION PRODUCTS, LLC; *pg.* 1311, *pg.* 1427
GRIP-MAT - Non-Slip Liner - WARP BROTHERS; *pg.* 1471, *pg.* 595
GRIP-N-LIFT - Cookware - POLAR WARE COMPANY; *pg.* 1129, *pg.* 1862
GRIP N SERV - Utensil - THE VOLLRATH COMPANY LLC; *pg.* 1139, *pg.* 1894
GRIP-N-STRIP - Wire Stripper - IDEAL INDUSTRIES, INC.; *pg.* 1051, *pg.* 662
GRIP N'SERV SPOODLE II - Plastic Portion Control Server - THE VOLLRATH COMPANY LLC; *pg.* 1139, *pg.* 1894
GRIP-RITE - Metal Rivet - ALCOA INC.; *pg.* 65, *pg.* 1188
GRIP-RITE - Smashminton Set - FRANKLIN SPORTS, INC.; *pg.* 1834, *pg.* 847
GRIP STRETCHFIT - Accessories - UNDER ARMOUR, INC.; *pg.* 49, *pg.* 759
GRIP-TEC - Footwear - RED WING SHOE COMPANY, INC.; *pg.* 1817, *pg.* 954
GRIP TO TIP - Golf Shaft - TRUE TEMPER SPORTS, INC.; *pg.* 1847, *pg.* 1647
GRIP TRUE - Plastic & Rubber - TEKNOR APEX COMPANY; *pg.* 1889, *pg.* 1605
GRIPIT - Tool Holder - GEERPRES INC.; *pg.* 1339, *pg.* 901
GRIPLITE - Medical Instrument - INTEGRA MILTEX, INC.; *pg.* 1546, *pg.* 1597
GRIPLOCK - Plier - CHANNELLOCK, INC.; *pg.* 1044, *pg.* 1551
GRIPPER - Shoe & Boot Covers - E.I. DU PONT DE NEMOURS & COMPANY; *pg.* 1159, *pg.* 390
GRIPPER - Mop Handle - HILLYARD, INC.; *pg.* 331, *pg.* 990
GRIPPER - Coupling - MORRIS COUPLING COMPANY; *pg.* 1057, *pg.* 1530
THE GRIPPER - Waste Bags - PACTIV CORPORATION; *pg.* 1466, *pg.* 624
GRIPPER - Residential Lighting - SWIVELIER CO., INC.; *pg.* 1307, *pg.* 1142
GRIPPLUS - Protective Glove Design - LAKELAND INDUSTRIES, INC.; *pg.* 1354, *pg.* 1338
GRIPRING - Pipe Restraint Product - ROMAC INDUSTRIES, INC.; *pg.* 1061, *pg.* 1818
GRIPSHIELD - Building Products - BOISE CASCADE HOLDINGS, L.L.C.; *pg.* 1453, *pg.* 546

First page reference indicates Business Class Edition
Second page reference indicates Geographic Edition

GRIPSTAY - Specialty Nails - W.H. MAZE COMPANY; *pg.* 1389, *pg.* 652
GRIPTEX - Cleaning Preparation - WALTER G. LEGGE COMPANY, INC.; *pg.* 337, *pg.* 1321
GRIPTITE - Trays - CARLISLE FOODSERVICE PRODUCTS INCORPORATED; *pg.* 1455, *pg.* 1485
GRIPTITE - Conveyor Belting - HBD INDUSTRIES, INC.; *pg.* 207, *pg.* 1449
GRIPTOP - Conveyor Belting - HBD INDUSTRIES, INC.; *pg.* 207, *pg.* 1449
GRIPZ - Cookies & Crackers - KELLOGG COMPANY; *pg.* 831, *pg.* 870
GRIT - Bi-Weekly Magazine - OGDEN PUBLICATIONS, INC.; *pg.* 1672, *pg.* 722
GRIT BLITZ - Hand Cleaner - DELTA FOREMOST CHEMICAL CORPORATION; *pg.* 1155, *pg.* 1642
GRIT GUARD - Filtering Unit - SUNNEN PRODUCTS COMPANY; *pg.* 1379, *pg.* 1004
GRIXXER - Grinder Mixer - ART'S-WAY MANUFACTURING CO., INC.; *pg.* 701, *pg.* 701
GRIZZLIES AUCTIONS - Online Auction - MEMPHIS GRIZZLIES; *pg.* 561, *pg.* 1645
GRIZZLY - Construction Tools - KLEIN TOOLS INC.; *pg.* 1052, *pg.* 627
GRIZZLY - Towel Dispensers - WAUSAU PAPER BAY WEST; *pg.* 1471, *pg.* 1465
GROEN - Foodservice - UNIFIED BRANDS INC.; *pg.* 1385, *pg.* 970
GROENTEBURGER - Fast Food - MCDONALD'S CORPORATION; *pg.* 1737, *pg.* 645
GROLIER - Educational Materials - SCHOLASTIC INC.; *pg.* 1683, *pg.* 1288
GROLSCH - Beverages - MOLSON COORS BREWING COMPANY; *pg.* 256, *pg.* 321
GROLSCH PREMIUM DUTCH - Beer - DIAGEO CANADA, INC.; *pg.* 1961, *pg.* 1937
GROLSCH WEIZEN - Beverages - MOLSON COORS BREWING COMPANY; *pg.* 256, *pg.* 321
GROMMET - Bicycle - TREK BICYCLE CORPORATION; *pg.* 1847, *pg.* 1896
GROOMAX - Pet Grooming Supplies - PETSMART, INC.; *pg.* 1481, *pg.* 18
GROOMER'S GOOP - Cleaning Preparation - CRITZAS INDUSTRIES, INC.; *pg.* 329, *pg.* 995
GROOMIN - Bath Accessory - CROSCILL, INC.; *pg.* 1122, *pg.* 1220
GROOMSMAN - Bread and Mustache Trimmer - WAHL CLIPPER CORPORATION; *pg.* 524, *pg.* 662
GROOVE - Fabric - NEMSCHOFF, INC.; *pg.* 936, *pg.* 1890
GROOVE - Office Furniture - STEELCASE INC.; *pg.* 475, *pg.* 889
GROOVE - Ceramic, Glass, Stone Tiles & Slabs - WALKER & ZANGER, INC.; *pg.* 119, *pg.* 281
GROOVE IT - Game - HASBRO, INC.; *pg.* 954, *pg.* 1603
GROOVE PAK - Accessories - SAM ASH MUSIC CORPORATION; *pg.* 669, *pg.* 1167
GROOVE PERCUSSION - Drums - SAM ASH MUSIC CORPORATION; *pg.* 669, *pg.* 1167
GROOVY - Beverages - THE COCA-COLA COMPANY; *pg.* 240, *pg.* 493
GROOVY - Potato Chips - MIKE-SELL'S POTATO CHIP COMPANY; *pg.* 1860, *pg.* 1446
GROOVY - Fabric - NEMSCHOFF, INC.; *pg.* 936, *pg.* 1890
GROOVY VAC - Floor Care Product - BISSELL HOMECARE, INC.; *pg.* 52, *pg.* 887
GROTAN - Metalworking Fluid Additive - TROY CORPORATION; *pg.* 1184, *pg.* 1067
GROTE - Vehicular Safety Lighting Products - GROTE INDUSTRIES, INC.; *pg.* 206, *pg.* 693
GROTE SELECT - LED Lighting System - GROTE INDUSTRIES, INC.; *pg.* 206, *pg.* 693
GROUND BEEF - Meat - CARGILL LIMITED; *pg.* 1475, *pg.* 1914
GROUND CONTROL - Bicycle Tire - SPECIALIZED BICYCLE COMPONENTS, INC.; *pg.* 1711, *pg.* 152
THE GROUND FLOOR - Financial Products - DOW JONES & COMPANY, INC.; *pg.* 1637, *pg.* 1225
GROUND FORCE - Bicycle Accessories - SPECIALIZED BICYCLE COMPONENTS, INC.; *pg.* 1711, *pg.* 152
GROUND FORCE GSE - Trademark & Industrial Tires - CARLISLE TIRE & WHEEL COMPANY; *pg.* 1880, *pg.* 1612
GROUND ISLAND CONTRACT CARRIER - Transportation - CHIEF INDUSTRIES, INC.; *pg.* 1323, *pg.* 1010
GROUNDBREAKERS - Landscaping - VAUGHAN & BUSHNELL MANUFACTURING COMPANY, INC.; *pg.* 1066, *pg.* 616
GROUNDED IN THE PAST, FOCUSED ON THE FUTURE - Tagline - THE CARLYLE JOHNSON MACHINE COMPANY, L.L.C.; *pg.* 1321, *pg.* 339
GROUNDFORCE - Pest Elimination System - ECOLAB INC.; *pg.* 329, *pg.* 960
GROUNDHOG - Butterfly Valve - HENRY PRATT COMPANY; *pg.* 1049, *pg.* 555
GROUNDSAVER - Software - UNITED PARCEL SERVICE, INC.; *pg.* 1928, *pg.* 522
GROUNDTRAC - Software - UNITED PARCEL SERVICE, INC.; *pg.* 1928, *pg.* 522
GROUNDWORKS - Windows, Walls & Weaves - LEE JOFA, INC.; *pg.* 933, *pg.* 1142
GROUNDWORKS - Lawn & Garden Supplies - TRACTOR SUPPLY COMPANY; *pg.* 708, *pg.* 1627
GROUP POLICY EXTENSIONS - Software - DELL SOFTWARE; *pg.* 385, *pg.* 40
GROUP POLICY MANAGER - Software - DELL SOFTWARE; *pg.* 385, *pg.* 40
GROUP RESOURCE - Newsletter Containing Insurance/Reinsurance Articles - LINCOLN NATIONAL CORPORATION; *pg.* 776, *pg.* 1567
GROUPCAST - Software - GE HEALTHCARE; *pg.* 399, *pg.* 1765
GROUPFACTS - Software - TRIZETTO CORPORATION; *pg.* 485, *pg.* 327
GROUPLINK - Software - PASSKEY INTERNATIONAL, INC.; *pg.* 1274, *pg.* 853
GROUPON - Social Buying, Groupon Now Smartphone Application - GROUPON, INC.; *pg.* 1255, *pg.* 575
GROUPONLIVE - Online Ticketing Deals Channel - GROUPON, INC.; *pg.* 1255, *pg.* 575
GROUPTRAK - Software - IRON MOUNTAIN INCORPORATED; *pg.* 421, *pg.* 796
GROUPWISE - Software - NOVELL INC.; *pg.* 446, *pg.* 852
GROUPWISE MIGRATOR - Software - DELL SOFTWARE; *pg.* 385, *pg.* 40
GROUPWORK - Office Furniture - STEELCASE INC.; *pg.* 475, *pg.* 889
GROUT SEALER - Sealer - THE SAVOGRAN COMPANY; *pg.* 1447, *pg.* 840
GROVE GEAR - Standard & Custom Industrial Gear Reducers - REGAL BELOIT CORPORATION; *pg.* 106, *pg.* 1854
GROW ANYTHING, ANYTIME, ANYWHERE - Slogan - AEROGROW INTERNATIONAL, INC.; *pg.* 1393, *pg.* 310
GROW 'N GO BIKE - Trikes - RADIO FLYER INC.; *pg.* 966, *pg.* 588
GROW TO PRO - Toy - MATTEL, INC.; *pg.* 962, *pg.* 81
GROW-UP PLAN - Life Insurance Policy - GERBER LIFE INSURANCE COMPANY; *pg.* 1201, *pg.* 1352
GROW WITH LOVE - Pillow and Throw - HERITAGE LACE INC.; *pg.* 694, *pg.* 711
GROW WITH ME - Baby & Toddler Cups - EVENFLO COMPANY, INC.; *pg.* 924, *pg.* 1470
GROW YOUR VINE - Video Communication System - GLOWPOINT, INC.; *pg.* 401, *pg.* 1094
THE GROWER - Magazine - VANCE PUBLISHING CORPORATION; *pg.* 1699, *pg.* 627
GROWING AND PROTECTING YOUR WEALTH - Slogan - PUBLIC SERVICE COMPANY OF OKLAHOMA; *pg.* 1950, *pg.* 1443
GROWING EXPRESSIONS - Seeds Cards - LEANIN' TREE, INC.; *pg.* 1658, *pg.* 311
GROWING FORESTS FOR OUR FUTURE? - Tagline - SIERRA PACIFIC INDUSTRIES; *pg.* 110, *pg.* 43
GROWING SUCCESS THROUGHOUT THE WORLD - Tagline - MICHIGAN BLUEBERRY GROWERS ASSOCIATION; *pg.* 147, *pg.* 886
GROWING UP GIRLS - Figurines - ENESCO, LLC; *pg.* 1124, *pg.* 620
GROWING VALUE FROM EXCEPTIONAL RESOURCES - Tagline - PLUM CREEK TIMBER COMPANY, INC.; *pg.* 105, *pg.* 1838
GROWMASTER - Hybrid & Varietal Seeds & Fertilizer - SOUTHERN STATES COOPERATIVE, INC.; *pg.* 1482, *pg.* 1804
GROWN IN IDAHO - Seal - IDAHO POTATO COMMISSION; *pg.* 144, *pg.* 549
GROWNOW - Gardening Appliance Systems - AEROGROW INTERNATIONAL, INC.; *pg.* 1393, *pg.* 310
GROWSMART - Irrigation Control Technology - LINDSAY CORPORATION; *pg.* 1356, *pg.* 1016
GROWTH THROUGH CUSTOMER SERVICE - Slogan - FASTENAL COMPANY; *pg.* 396, *pg.* 966
GROWTHLEADER.COM - Website - MARKET LEADER, INC.; *pg.* 1102, *pg.* 1822
GROWTHPACK - Fertilizer - SIMPLOT PARTNERS INC.; *pg.* 1800, *pg.* 548
GROWTTH - Get Rid of Waste Through Team Harmony - FREUDENBERG-NOK; *pg.* 1882, *pg.* 904
GRT - Apparel - COLUMBIA SPORTSWEAR COMPANY; *pg.* 1830, *pg.* 1501
GRUB-AWAY - Lawn Care Product - GARDENS ALIVE!, INC.; *pg.* 1796, *pg.* 693
GRUB-NO-MORE - Home & Farm Product - PBI/GORDON CORPORATION; *pg.* 1176, *pg.* 985
GRUBEX - Lawn Insect Control - THE SCOTTS MIRACLE-GRO COMPANY; *pg.* 1799, *pg.* 1459
GRUCCI - Firework Product - B.J. ALAN COMPANY; *pg.* 1150, *pg.* 1483
GRUEN - Watch - M.Z. BERGER & CO., INC.; *pg.* 10, *pg.* 1175
GRUMBACHER - Art Product - DANIEL SMITH INC.; *pg.* 1766, *pg.* 1835
GRUNGE ATTACK - Cleaning Product - ORECK CORPORATION; *pg.* 59, *pg.* 1653
GRUNTLINE - Braided Utility Cord - MCNETT CORPORATION; *pg.* 1839, *pg.* 1817
GRUNTLY & IGGY - Game - BIG IDEA, INC.; *pg.* 271, *pg.* 1632
GRUPO NELSON - Spanish-Language Bibles - THOMAS NELSON INC.; *pg.* 1692, *pg.* 1654
GRUVI - Flash Memory Card - SANDISK CORPORATION; *pg.* 465, *pg.* 147
GS 3000 - Skate - ROLLER DERBY SKATE CORP.; *pg.* 966, *pg.* 630
GS-5 - Beverage - GREEN SPOT, INC.; *pg.* 251, *pg.* 68
GS-700 - General Service Control Valves - SPX PROCESS EQUIPMENT; *pg.* 1378, *pg.* 1551
GS-800 - Software - BIO-RAD LABORATORIES, INC.; *pg.* 1504, *pg.* 101
GS GENE LINKER - Software - BIO-RAD LABORATORIES, INC.; *pg.* 1504, *pg.* 101
GS GENE PREP - Software - BIO-RAD LABORATORIES, INC.; *pg.* 1504, *pg.* 101
GSA - Software - INTEGRAL SYSTEMS, INC.; *pg.* 416, *pg.* 767
GSAP - Cameras - ALAN GORDON ENTERPRISES, INC.; *pg.* 1399, *pg.* 125
GSC - Gymnastic Wall Mats - SPORT SUPPLY GROUP, INC.; *pg.* 1846, *pg.* 1687
GSC ECARE - Online Customer Support System - GSC ENTERPRISES, INC.; *pg.* 1021, *pg.* 1746
GSE WHITE CONDUCTIVE - Geomembrane Liners - GSE LINING TECHNOLOGY, INC.; *pg.* 1164, *pg.* 1706
GSIC - Semiconductor Product - CREE INC.; *pg.* 631, *pg.* 1371
GSM - Surface Mount Assembly Machine - UNIVERSAL INSTRUMENTS CORPORATION; *pg.* 683, *pg.* 1154
GSM (CONSUMER) - Mobile Solutions - SONUS NETWORKS INC.; *pg.* 1281, *pg.* 858
GSM (ENTERPRISE) - Mobile Solutions - SONUS NETWORKS INC.; *pg.* 1281, *pg.* 858
GSM GENESIS PLATFORM - Electric Instrument - UNIVERSAL INSTRUMENTS CORPORATION; *pg.* 683, *pg.* 1154
GSMX - Electric Instrument - UNIVERSAL INSTRUMENTS CORPORATION; *pg.* 683, *pg.* 1154
GSMXS - Electric Instrument - UNIVERSAL INSTRUMENTS CORPORATION; *pg.* 683, *pg.* 1154
GSP-2900 - Satellite Phone - GLOBALSTAR, INC.; *pg.* 401, *pg.* 743
GSSMOKE - Cigarettes - ROCK CREEK PHARMACEUTICALS, INC.; *pg.* 1895, *pg.* 466
GST 100 MM SCRIBER BREAKER - Wafer Dicing Equipment - DYNATEX INTERNATIONAL; *pg.* 635, *pg.* 277
GST 150 MM SCRIBER BREAKER - Wafer Dicing Equipment - DYNATEX INTERNATIONAL; *pg.* 635, *pg.* 277
GSX - Recreational Vehicle - BOMBARDIER RECREATIONAL PRODUCTS, INC.; *pg.* 201, *pg.* 1960
GSX4000 - Low- To Medium-Density Media Gateway - SONUS NETWORKS INC.; *pg.* 1281, *pg.* 858
GSX9000 - Open Services Switch - SONUS NETWORKS INC.; *pg.* 1281, *pg.* 858
GT - Medical Equipment - INVACARE CORPORATION; *pg.* 1546, *pg.* 1451
GT FORM - Film Laminate - SCHNELLER, INC.; *pg.* 234, *pg.* 1456

GT SENSOR - Sensor - NVE CORPORATION; *pg.* 447, *pg.* 923
GT3 - Automatic Guitar & Bass Tuner - KORG USA, INC.; *pg.* 556, *pg.* 1180
GTA - Software - CITRIX SYSTEMS, INC.; *pg.* 375, *pg.* 424
GTA PLUS - Herbal Formula - SHAKLEE CORPORATION; *pg.* 1593, *pg.* 184
GTAX - Software - CITRIX SYSTEMS, INC.; *pg.* 375, *pg.* 424
GTB - Seal - GREENE, TWEED & CO.; *pg.* 1344, *pg.* 1544
GTL - Ring Seal - GREENE, TWEED & CO.; *pg.* 1344, *pg.* 1544
GTM - Software - CITRIX SYSTEMS, INC.; *pg.* 375, *pg.* 424
GTM - Software - F5 NETWORKS, INC.; *pg.* 396, *pg.* 1835
GT.M - Software - FIDELITY NATIONAL INFORMATION SERVICES; *pg.* 397, *pg.* 1549
GTO - Sporting Goods - BRUNSWICK BOWLING & BILLIARDS CORP.; *pg.* 1828, *pg.* 622
GTS - Footwear - COBIAN CORP.; *pg.* 1806, *pg.* 253
GTS-980 - Fluid Handling System - GRACO, INC.; *pg.* 1342, *pg.* 935
GTT - Software - CITRIX SYSTEMS, INC.; *pg.* 375, *pg.* 424
GTU - Urethane Seal - GREENE, TWEED & CO.; *pg.* 1344, *pg.* 1544
GTW - Software - CITRIX SYSTEMS, INC.; *pg.* 375, *pg.* 424
GTX - Outerwear Made with GORE-TEX Fabric - BLAUER MANUFACTURING COMPANY, INC.; *pg.* 20, *pg.* 789
GUADALAHARRY'S - Mexican Restaurants - REAL MEX RESTAURANTS, INC.; *pg.* 1746, *pg.* 75
GUAPA - Apparel - VANS, INC.; *pg.* 1821, *pg.* 76
GUARANA KUAT LIGHT - Beverages - THE COCA-COLA COMPANY; *pg.* 240, *pg.* 493
GUARANA KUAT ZERO - Beverages - THE COCA-COLA COMPANY; *pg.* 240, *pg.* 493
GUARANTEED TO KEEP YOU DRY - Tag Line - W.L. GORE & ASSOCIATES, INC.; *pg.* 122, *pg.* 388
GUARANTEED YOU HAVE OUR WORD - Slogan - L.L. BEAN, INC.; *pg.* 1777, *pg.* 750
GUARD - Wallcovering - OMNOVA SOLUTIONS INC; *pg.* 1176, *pg.* 1453
GUARD DOG - Industrial Tires - CARLISLE TIRE & WHEEL COMPANY; *pg.* 1880, *pg.* 1612
GUARD MASTER - Storage & Security Products - JUSTRITE MANUFACTURING COMPANY, LLC; *pg.* 1394, *pg.* 606
GUARD-PAK - Holder - WATERS CORPORATION; *pg.* 1436, *pg.* 834
GUARD-RITE - Protective Railing System - RITE-HITE HOLDING CORPORATION; *pg.* 1372, *pg.* 1880
GUARDIAN - Cannister Vacuum - AERUS LLC; *pg.* 51, *pg.* 1673
GUARDIAN - Amalgam Collector - AIR TECHNIQUES, INC.; *pg.* 1487, *pg.* 1178
GUARDIAN - Truck Equipment - AMERICAN VAN EQUIPMENT INC.; *pg.* 199, *pg.* 1078
GUARDIAN - Combustion Scrubber - ATMI, INC.; *pg.* 1314, *pg.* 342
GUARDIAN - Carpet - BEAULIEU GROUP, LLC; *pg.* 917, *pg.* 529
GUARDIAN - Paper - DOMTAR CORPORATION; *pg.* 1456, *pg.* 1954
GUARDIAN - Pump - FLOWSERVE CORPORATION; *pg.* 82, *pg.* 1719
GUARDIAN - Lawn Care Product - GARDENS ALIVE!, INC.; *pg.* 1796, *pg.* 693
GUARDIAN - Towel Dispensing System - GEORGIA-PACIFIC LLC; *pg.* 1458, *pg.* 507
GUARDIAN - Video Game - INTERNATIONAL GAME TECHNOLOGY; *pg.* 957, *pg.* 1024
GUARDIAN - Bath Product - KOHLER CO.; *pg.* 91, *pg.* 1862
GUARDIAN - Batch Blender - PROCESS CONTROL CORPORATION; *pg.* 1370, *pg.* 518
GUARDIAN - Filtration System - SERFILCO, LTD.; *pg.* 1375, *pg.* 641
GUARDIAN - Inspection Lighting System - UNILUX, INC.; *pg.* 682, *pg.* 1118
GUARDIAN - Catheter - VASCULAR SOLUTIONS, INC.; *pg.* 1434, *pg.* 946
GUARDIAN GEAR - Animal Clothing - PETEDGE; *pg.* 1481, *pg.* 787
GUARDIAN LIONS - Video Game - INTERNATIONAL GAME TECHNOLOGY; *pg.* 957, *pg.* 1024
GUARDIAN SERIES - Electronic Process Controller - CORAL CHEMICAL COMPANY; *pg.* 1154, *pg.* 666
GUARDIAN VOTING SYSTEMS - Voting System - DANAHER CORPORATION; *pg.* 1044, *pg.* 397
GUARDIANOS - Storage Operating System Software - OVERLAND STORAGE, INC.; *pg.* 451, *pg.* 205
GUARDMASTER - Software - ROCKWELL AUTOMATION, INC.; *pg.* 668, *pg.* 1880
GUARDSMAN - Watchclock - DETEX CORPORATION; *pg.* 633, *pg.* 1728
GUARDWIRE - Circulatory Product - MEDTRONIC, INC.; *pg.* 1564, *pg.* 939
GUARTEC - Gum Products - HENKEL CORPORATION; *pg.* 1165, *pg.* 1535
GUATAMALAN FINCA DOS MARIAS - Coffee - KEURIG GREEN MOUNTAIN, INC.; *pg.* 868, *pg.* 1768
GUATEMALA - Coffee - PEET'S COFFEE & TEA, INC.; *pg.* 1029, *pg.* 85
GUATEMALA ANTIGUA - Coffee - STARBUCKS CORPORATION; *pg.* 897, *pg.* 1840
GUATEMALA CASI CIELO - Coffee - STARBUCKS CORPORATION; *pg.* 897, *pg.* 1840
GUCCI - Luxury Goods - GUCCI AMERICA INC.; *pg.* 6, *pg.* 1237
GUERNSEY - Milk Chocolate - CARGILL LIMITED; *pg.* 1475, *pg.* 1914
GUESS - Apparel - G-III APPAREL GROUP, LTD.; *pg.* 41, *pg.* 1233
GUESS? - Apparel - GUESS?, INC.; *pg.* 25, *pg.* 132
GUESS BY MARCIANO - Apparel - GUESS?, INC.; *pg.* 25, *pg.* 132
GUESS COLLECTION - Apparel & Watch - GUESS?, INC.; *pg.* 25, *pg.* 132
GUESS JEANS - Apparel - GUESS?, INC.; *pg.* 25, *pg.* 132
GUESS KIDS - Apparel - GUESS?, INC.; *pg.* 25, *pg.* 132
GUESS U.S.A. - Apparel - GUESS?, INC.; *pg.* 25, *pg.* 132
GUESS WHERE - Game - HASBRO, INC.; *pg.* 954, *pg.* 1603
GUESS WHO? - Toy & Game - HASBRO, INC.; *pg.* 954, *pg.* 1603
GUESSTURES - Game - HASBRO, INC.; *pg.* 954, *pg.* 1603
GUEST CONNECTION - Software - MICROS SYSTEMS, INC.; *pg.* 435, *pg.* 768
GUEST-GARD - Protective Eyewear - SELLSTROM MANUFACTURING CO.; *pg.* 1428, *pg.* 659
GUEST HOUSE - Teas & Cocoas - PERFORMANCE FOOD GROUP COMPANY, LLC; *pg.* 1030, *pg.* 1803
GUESTLIFE - Magazine - DESERT PUBLICATIONS INC.; *pg.* 1635, *pg.* 174
GUESTPATH - Customer Service - DELAWARE NORTH COMPANIES, INC.; *pg.* 1089, *pg.* 1148
GUESTWARE - Disposable Dishes - PACTIV CORPORATION; *pg.* 1466, *pg.* 624
GUGULIPID - Vitamin & Dietary Supplement - NATROL, INC.; *pg.* 1570, *pg.* 64
GUIDANCE WHEN YOU NEED IT MOST - Slogan - HUMANA, INC.; *pg.* 1204, *pg.* 734
GUIDE - Fishing Gear Product - SIMMS FISHING PRODUCTS CORP.; *pg.* 1845, *pg.* 1008
GUIDE-LINE - Foam Marker - UNIVERSAL COOPERATIVES, INC.; *pg.* 1482, *pg.* 922
GUIDE STRIPE - Medical Device - MENTOR CORPORATION; *pg.* 1565, *pg.* 263
GUIDE TO ACTIVE FLEAMARKETS & SWAP MEETS - Directory - SUMNER COMMUNICATIONS INC.; *pg.* 1690, *pg.* 338
GUIDELINE - Solder Paste - ALPHA; *pg.* 1146, *pg.* 1123
GUIDELINELESS SUBSEA PRODUCTION SYSTEMS - Subsea Equipment - DRIL-QUIP, INC.; *pg.* 1330, *pg.* 1704
GUIDELINES - Fiber - CORNING CABLE SYSTEMS LLC; *pg.* 1407, *pg.* 1378
GUIDELINES - Glass & Ceramic Material - CORNING INCORPORATED; *pg.* 1122, *pg.* 1154
GUIDEMASTER - Electric Hose Guide - HANNAY REELS INC.; *pg.* 1344, *pg.* 1351
GUIDEPLUS+ - Digital Directory - ROVI CORPORATION; *pg.* 463, *pg.* 269
GUIDER SOFTIP - Medical Device - BOSTON SCIENTIFIC CORPORATION; *pg.* 1508, *pg.* 831
GUIDERIGHT - Guidewires - ST. JUDE MEDICAL, INC.; *pg.* 1596, *pg.* 963
GUIDESTAR - Research Data - PHILANTHROPEDIA; *pg.* 153, *pg.* 1811
GUIDEWEAR - Apparel - CABELA'S INCORPORATED; *pg.* 535, *pg.* 1019
GUIDEX - Paper & Nonwoven Material - FIBERMARK INC.; *pg.* 1457, *pg.* 1764
GUIDING AMERICA TO BETTER HEALTHCARE - Slogan - HEALTH GRADES, INC.; *pg.* 1256, *pg.* 319
GUIDING YOU TO A BRIGHTER FINANCIAL FUTURE - Slogan - BAKER BOYER BANCORP; *pg.* 717, *pg.* 1846
GUIDON - Pressed & Monolithic Refractory - RESCO PRODUCTS, INC.; *pg.* 107, *pg.* 1581
GUILD - Guitar - FENDER MUSICAL INSTRUMENTS CORPORATION; *pg.* 547, *pg.* 21
GUILD - Furniture - JASPER GROUP; *pg.* 930, *pg.* 691
GUILD OPTICIANS - Lenses & Optical Products - OPTICIANS ASSOCIATION OF AMERICA; *pg.* 152, *pg.* 1639
GUILDCRAFT - Lens - DANKER LABORATORIES INC.; *pg.* 1408, *pg.* 465
GUILFAST - Automotive Fabrics - GUILFORD PERFORMANCE TEXTILES; *pg.* 693, *pg.* 1393
GUILFORD - Furniture - BASSETT FURNITURE INDUSTRIES, INCORPORATED; *pg.* 916, *pg.* 1776
GUILTLESS GOURMET - Food Products - MANISCHEWITZ COMPANY; *pg.* 875, *pg.* 1097
GUINEVERE - Furniture - HOOKER FURNITURE CORPORATION; *pg.* 928, *pg.* 1788
GUINNESS - Footwear - STEVEN MADDEN, LTD.; *pg.* 1819, *pg.* 1176
THE GUITAR GRIMOIRE - Music Publisher - CARL FISCHER, LLC; *pg.* 1625, *pg.* 1209
GUITAR GURU - Computer Software - MUSICNOTES, INC.; *pg.* 1268, *pg.* 1866
GUITAR HERO - Computer Game - ACTIVISION BLIZZARD, INC.; *pg.* 948, *pg.* 271
GUITAR STAGE PACK - Musical Instrument - PEAVEY ELECTRONICS CORPORATION; *pg.* 662, *pg.* 970
GULDEN'S - Food Product - CONAGRA FOODS, INC.; *pg.* 826, *pg.* 1014
GULF SHIPPER - Transportation Publication - JOC GROUP INC.; *pg.* 1654, *pg.* 1096
GULF SHORE BOAT AND BOIL - Salt - CARGILL LIMITED; *pg.* 1475, *pg.* 1914
GULFSHORE BUSINESS - Magazine - OPEN SKY MEDIA; *pg.* 1673, *pg.* 451
GULFSHORE HOMEBUYER - Magazine - OPEN SKY MEDIA; *pg.* 1673, *pg.* 451
GULFSHORE LIFE - Magazine - OPEN SKY MEDIA; *pg.* 1673, *pg.* 451
GULFSPAN - Streamer - ION GEOPHYSICAL CORPORATION; *pg.* 1350, *pg.* 1708
GULFSTREAM - Fiberglass Boat Product - GRADY-WHITE BOATS, INC.; *pg.* 1707, *pg.* 1377
GULFSTREAM G150 - Aircraft - GULFSTREAM AEROSPACE CORPORATION; *pg.* 228, *pg.* 540
GULFSTREAM G200 - Aircraft - GULFSTREAM AEROSPACE CORPORATION; *pg.* 228, *pg.* 540
GULFSTREAM G250 - Aircraft - GULFSTREAM AEROSPACE CORPORATION; *pg.* 228, *pg.* 540
GULFSTREAM G350 - Aircraft - GULFSTREAM AEROSPACE CORPORATION; *pg.* 228, *pg.* 540
GULFSTREAM G450 - Aircraft - GULFSTREAM AEROSPACE CORPORATION; *pg.* 228, *pg.* 540
GULFSTREAM G500 - Aircraft - GULFSTREAM AEROSPACE CORPORATION; *pg.* 228, *pg.* 540
GULFSTREAM G550 - Aircraft - GULFSTREAM AEROSPACE CORPORATION; *pg.* 228, *pg.* 540
GULFSTREAM G650 - Aircraft - GULFSTREAM AEROSPACE CORPORATION; *pg.* 228, *pg.* 540
GULFSTREAM SERVICE CARE - Hourly Cost Maintenance Program - GULFSTREAM AEROSPACE CORPORATION; *pg.* 228, *pg.* 540
GULFSTREAM SHARES - Fractional Ownership Program - GULFSTREAM AEROSPACE CORPORATION; *pg.* 228, *pg.* 540
GULKAND - Confectionery - THE HERSHEY CO.; *pg.* 1855, *pg.* 1538
GULLIVERS TRAVEL ASSOCIATES - Travel Products & Services - TRAVELPORT LIMITED; *pg.* 1925, *pg.* 521
GULLWING BEACH RESORT - Resort - SUNSTREAM, INC.; *pg.* 1116, *pg.* 428
GULOST - Cheese - A.V. OLSSON TRADING CO. INC.; *pg.* 838, *pg.* 372
GUM-CRITTERS - Children's Toothbrush - SUNSTAR AMERICAS INC.; *pg.* 1599, *pg.* 591
GUM-GO - Gum & Candle Wax Remover - HILLYARD, INC.; *pg.* 331, *pg.* 990
GUM POSTCARE - Implant Floss Aids - SUNSTAR AMERICAS INC.; *pg.* 1599, *pg.* 591
GUM PULSE - Powered Toothbrush - SUNSTAR AMERICAS INC.; *pg.* 1599, *pg.* 591
GUM RELIEF - Health System Product - LANELABS USA INC.; *pg.* 1554, *pg.* 1128
GUMBALLS - Fabric - NEMSCHOFF, INC.; *pg.* 936, *pg.* 1890

GUMMERS - Plumbing Product - MASCO CORPORATION; *pg.* 96, *pg.* 909
GUMMI BEARS - Fragrance - PARFUMS DE COEUR LTD.; *pg.* 519, *pg.* 376
GUMMIBURSTS - Candy - MARS, INCORPORATED; *pg.* 1858, *pg.* 1792
GUMOUT - Carburetor Cleaner - SHELL LUBRICANTS; *pg.* 217, *pg.* 1714
GUMP'S - Retail Specialty Gift Stores - GUMP'S CORP.; *pg.* 1772, *pg.* 219
GUMPTION - Cleaners - THE CLOROX COMPANY; *pg.* 327, *pg.* 169
GUMPTION - Fabric - NEMSCHOFF, INC.; *pg.* 936, *pg.* 1890
GUN - Taps for Through Holes - KENNAMETAL IPG; *pg.* 1353, *pg.* 1615
GUN CLUB - Target Load - REMINGTON ARMS COMPANY, LLC; *pg.* 1844, *pg.* 1382
GUN FLUSH BOX - Automated Flushing System - GRACO, INC.; *pg.* 1342, *pg.* 935
GUN-ITE - Mining Product - QUIKRETE COMPANIES; *pg.* 106, *pg.* 519
GUN-ITE MS - Mining Product - QUIKRETE COMPANIES; *pg.* 106, *pg.* 519
GUN LIST - Firearms Magazine - KRAUSE PUBLICATIONS, INC.; *pg.* 1657, *pg.* 1861
GUN-NAILER - Construction Equipment - PASLODE; *pg.* 1059, *pg.* 664
GUNBLOK - Combination Locks for Firearm Safety - THE EASTERN COMPANY; *pg.* 1331, *pg.* 357
GUNDRY - Retrograde Cannula - MEDTRONIC, INC.; *pg.* 1564, *pg.* 939
GUNDSEAL - Geomembrane Liners - GSE LINING TECHNOLOGY, INC.; *pg.* 1164, *pg.* 1706
GUNGA DIN - Fabric - SCALAMANDRE, INC.; *pg.* 941, *pg.* 1058
GUNJET - Spray Product - SPRAYING SYSTEMS CO.; *pg.* 1063, *pg.* 670
GUNK - Brake Cleaner - RADIATOR SPECIALTY COMPANY; *pg.* 215, *pg.* 1380
GUNLOCK - Metal Gun Lock - MASTER LOCK COMPANY LLC; *pg.* 1055, *pg.* 1884
GUNLOCKE - Office Furniture - HNI CORPORATION; *pg.* 927, *pg.* 709
GUNSLINGER - Video Game - INTERNATIONAL GAME TECHNOLOGY; *pg.* 957, *pg.* 1024
GUNSLINGER GRAB-N-GO - Storage Product - PLANO MOLDING COMPANY; *pg.* 1887, *pg.* 652
GUNSMOKE-CANYON - Furniture - ASHLEY FURNITURE INDUSTRIES, INC.; *pg.* 914, *pg.* 1852
GUNSTOCKOAK - Hardware Flooring - LUMBER LIQUIDATORS HOLDINGS, INC.; *pg.* 94, *pg.* 1808
GUNTHER MIRROR & MORE CLEANER - Cleaners - ROYAL ADHESIVES & SEALANTS LLC; *pg.* 1179, *pg.* 697
GUNTHER PREMIERE - Adhesives - ROYAL ADHESIVES & SEALANTS LLC; *pg.* 1179, *pg.* 697
GUNTHER PRIME-N-SEAL - Sealants - ROYAL ADHESIVES & SEALANTS LLC; *pg.* 1179, *pg.* 697
GUNTHER TULIP - Vena Cava Filter - COOK GROUP, INC.; *pg.* 1518, *pg.* 674
GURILLA - Envelope - POLY PAK AMERICA, INC.; *pg.* 1467, *pg.* 138
GURILLA-TUFF - Plastic Packaging Product - POLY PAK AMERICA, INC.; *pg.* 1467, *pg.* 138
GUSHER - Pumps - GUSHER PUMPS, INC.; *pg.* 1344, *pg.* 727
GUSHER - Game - WMS INDUSTRIES INC.; *pg.* 593, *pg.* 666
GUSMER - Fluid Handling System - GRACO, INC.; *pg.* 1342, *pg.* 935
GUST - Car Care Product - STONER INC.; *pg.* 985, *pg.* 1583
GUST JACKET - Sport Apparel - UNDER ARMOUR, INC.; *pg.* 49, *pg.* 759
GUSTAVE BANQUETTE - Furniture - J. ROBERT SCOTT INC.; *pg.* 930, *pg.* 105
GUTH - Lighting - PHILIPS LIGHTING; *pg.* 1303, *pg.* 806
GUTHRIE - Lighting Product - QUOIZEL INC.; *pg.* 1304, *pg.* 1616
GUTHY-RENKER - Television Company - GUTHY-RENKER LLC; *pg.* 289, *pg.* 273
GUTS - Warranty Program - OVERLAND STORAGE, INC.; *pg.* 451, *pg.* 205
GUY CARPENTER - Reinsurance Broking Services - MARSH & MCLENNAN COMPANIES INC.; *pg.* 1207, *pg.* 1256
GUY GARDNER - Character - DC COMICS, INC.; *pg.* 1633, *pg.* 1221
GUZZLER - Industrial Vacuum Vehicles - FEDERAL SIGNAL CORPORATION; *pg.* 638, *pg.* 645
GVC-1700 - Charger - GLOBALSTAR, INC.; *pg.* 401, *pg.* 743
GVEOUS - Digital Video Effects - GRASS VALLEY, INC.; *pg.* 641, *pg.* 164
GWALTNEY - Food Products - SMITHFIELD FOODS, INC.; *pg.* 896, *pg.* 1806
GWEN - Dolls - AMERICAN GIRL LLC; *pg.* 949, *pg.* 1871
GWENNETH - Furniture - HOOKER FURNITURE CORPORATION; *pg.* 928, *pg.* 1788
GWP ADVISOR - Software - SS&C TECHNOLOGIES HOLDINGS, INC.; *pg.* 473, *pg.* 386
GWP MODEL - Software - SS&C TECHNOLOGIES HOLDINGS, INC.; *pg.* 473, *pg.* 386
GWP TRADE - Software - SS&C TECHNOLOGIES HOLDINGS, INC.; *pg.* 473, *pg.* 386
GX 550 - Telecommunication Products - ALCATEL-LUCENT; *pg.* 615, *pg.* 1094
GXT - Photoresist Strip System - LAM RESEARCH CORPORATION; *pg.* 1354, *pg.* 246
GYM-I-NEE - Playground Equipment - SCHOOL-TECH, INC.; *pg.* 1844, *pg.* 866
GYM X - Footwear - CAPEZIO BALLET MAKERS INC.; *pg.* 1805, *pg.* 1125
GYMBOREE OUTLET - Clothes - THE GYMBOREE CORPORATION; *pg.* 25, *pg.* 77
GYMBOREE PLAY & MUSIC - Play & Music Program - THE GYMBOREE CORPORATION; *pg.* 25, *pg.* 77
GYMNASTIK - Ball - SCHOOL-TECH, INC.; *pg.* 1844, *pg.* 866
GYMSEAL - Floor Finish - THE VALSPAR CORPORATION; *pg.* 1449, *pg.* 945
GYNE-ELECTRODE - Uterus Resectioning Instruments - THE COOPER COMPANIES, INC.; *pg.* 1518, *pg.* 183
GYNE-LOTRIMIN - Vaginal Cream - MERCK & CO., INC.; *pg.* 1566, *pg.* 1077
GYNE-PRO - Medical Device - C.R. BARD, INC.; *pg.* 1519, *pg.* 1094
GYNE-RESECTOSCOPE - Uterus Resectioning Equipment - THE COOPER COMPANIES, INC.; *pg.* 1518, *pg.* 183
GYNECARE - Healthcare Product - JOHNSON & JOHNSON; *pg.* 1549, *pg.* 1091
GYNECARE VERISTAT - Healthcare Product - JOHNSON & JOHNSON; *pg.* 1549, *pg.* 1091
GYNECORT - Feminine Cream Medication - COMBE INCORPORATED; *pg.* 1516, *pg.* 1351
GYP-LAP - Sheathing - USG CORPORATION; *pg.* 118, *pg.* 594
GYPSI - Personal Locator Beacon - ACR ELECTRONICS, INC.; *pg.* 612, *pg.* 422
GYPSI 406 PLB - Personal Locator Beacon with GPS Interface - ACR ELECTRONICS, INC.; *pg.* 612, *pg.* 422
GYPSY - Lashes - AMERICAN INTERNATIONAL INDUSTRIES COMPANY; *pg.* 498, *pg.* 126
GYRA II - Women's Footwear - UNDER ARMOUR, INC.; *pg.* 49, *pg.* 759
GYRASPHERE - Crusher - ASTEC INDUSTRIES, INC.; *pg.* 69, *pg.* 1628
GYRASPHERE - Rock Crushers - TELSMITH, INC.; *pg.* 1381, *pg.* 1871
GYRICON - Manual - XEROX CORPORATION; *pg.* 494, *pg.* 365
GYRO - Shaving Cream - THE GILLETTE COMPANY; *pg.* 509, *pg.* 795
GYRO-LITE - Recessed Lighting - SWIVELIER CO., INC.; *pg.* 1307, *pg.* 1142
GYRO-LUX - Lighting - SWIVELIER CO., INC.; *pg.* 1307, *pg.* 1142
GYRO TECH - Automatic Door System - NABCO ENTRANCES, INC.; *pg.* 99, *pg.* 1882
GYROCHIP - Sensor - CUSTOM SENSORS & TECHNOLOGIES; *pg.* 1407, *pg.* 152
GYROKONES - Food Product - KRONOS PRODUCTS, INC.; *pg.* 872, *pg.* 614
GYROTRAC - Digital Compass Product - KVH INDUSTRIES INC; *pg.* 650, *pg.* 1602

H

H-2-O SIZE - Dry Cleaning & Laundry Product - ADCO, INC.; *pg.* 325, *pg.* 482
H AIRBRUSH - Airbrush Design - PAASCHE AIRBRUSH COMPANY; *pg.* 1444, *pg.* 587
H-ALLOY - Furniture - HERMAN MILLER, INC.; *pg.* 926, *pg.* 913
H&C PAINT & COATINGS - Concrete Stains & Sealers - THE SHERWIN-WILLIAMS COMPANY; *pg.* 1447, *pg.* 1435
H-BAR STEERING - Mower Tractor - EXCEL INDUSTRIES, INC.; *pg.* 1795, *pg.* 715
H-DAC 64 - Electronic Components - MOLEX INCORPORATED; *pg.* 655, *pg.* 628
H-JELLYB - Footwear - STEVEN MADDEN, LTD.; *pg.* 1819, *pg.* 1176
H. PYLORI GII - Diagnostic Test Product - QUIDEL CORPORATION; *pg.* 1588, *pg.* 207
H SALON - Collections - HABAND COMPANY, INC.; *pg.* 1772, *pg.* 1099
H-SERIES - Die/Mold Machining Center - MAKINO INC.; *pg.* 1358, *pg.* 1461
H-SERIES - Cage Mill - STEDMAN MACHINE COMPANY; *pg.* 1379, *pg.* 673
H SYSTEM - Combined Cycle System - GE ENERGY; *pg.* 1338, *pg.* 506
H2 OFF - Water Rinsing Paint Remover - THE SAVOGRAN COMPANY; *pg.* 1447, *pg.* 840
H2700 - Fluid Handling System - GRACO, INC.; *pg.* 1342, *pg.* 935
H2GO - Laxative - LANELABS USA INC.; *pg.* 1554, *pg.* 1128
H2O - Binocular - BUSHNELL OUTDOOR PRODUCTS, INC.; *pg.* 1403, *pg.* 718
H2O CONTROL - Hockey Skates - REEBOK-CCM HOCKEY, INC.; *pg.* 1844, *pg.* 1960
H2OK - Agricultural Product - WILBUR-ELLIS COMPANY; *pg.* 1185, *pg.* 234
H2OUT - Wall System - SMITH-MIDLAND CORPORATION; *pg.* 111, *pg.* 1795
H3700 - Fluid Handling System - GRACO, INC.; *pg.* 1342, *pg.* 935
H5LP - High Speed Laser Printer - PITNEY BOWES INC.; *pg.* 454, *pg.* 376
HA SYSTEM CONFIGURATION - Software - NETAPP, INC.; *pg.* 444, *pg.* 287
HAAGEN-DAZS - Ice Cream - GENERAL MILLS, INC.; *pg.* 828, *pg.* 933
HAAGEN-DAZS - Food Product - NESTLE USA, INC.; *pg.* 883, *pg.* 96
HABAND - Men's & Women's Wear - HABAND COMPANY, INC.; *pg.* 1772, *pg.* 1099
HABAND TRAVELERS - Slippers - HABAND COMPANY, INC.; *pg.* 1772, *pg.* 1099
HABARDINE - Slacks - HABAND COMPANY, INC.; *pg.* 1772, *pg.* 1099
HABIB - Electrosurgical Devices - ANGIODYNAMICS, INC.; *pg.* 1495, *pg.* 1173
HABITANT - Food Product - CAMPBELL COMPANY OF CANADA LTD; *pg.* 844, *pg.* 1935
HABITANT - Jams & Sauces - TREEHOUSE FOODS, INC.; *pg.* 901, *pg.* 649
HABITAT - Fabric - MOMENTUM TEXTILES INC.; *pg.* 697, *pg.* 114
HABITAT - Fabric - NEMSCHOFF, INC.; *pg.* 936, *pg.* 1890
HACCO - Animal Safety Product - NEOGEN CORPORATION; *pg.* 883, *pg.* 896
HACEL-NETWORK - Lighting System - LITECONTROL CORPORATION; *pg.* 1301, *pg.* 841
HACH - Analytical System - DANAHER CORPORATION; *pg.* 1044, *pg.* 397
HACH ONE - pH Electrode - HACH COMPANY; *pg.* 1415, *pg.* 334
HACKER - Histology & Pathology Laboratory - HACKER INSTRUMENTS & INDUSTRIES INC.; *pg.* 1415, *pg.* 1623
HACKER-MILESTONE - Laboratory Microwave System - HACKER INSTRUMENTS & INDUSTRIES INC.; *pg.* 1415, *pg.* 1623
HACKMASTER - Blade - LENOX; *pg.* 1053, *pg.* 817
HACKNEY CLASSIC - Refrigerated Truck Body - KIDRON, INC.; *pg.* 181, *pg.* 1457
HACKNEY DAIRY CLASSIC - Refrigerated Truck Body - KIDRON, INC.; *pg.* 181, *pg.* 1457
THE HACKS SERIES - Magazine - O'REILLY MEDIA, INC.; *pg.* 1673, *pg.* 278
HACKY SACK - Footbag - WHAM-O, INC.; *pg.* 969, *pg.* 308
HADAS - Kosher Poultry - EMPIRE KOSHER POULTRY, INC.; *pg.* 854, *pg.* 1553
HADCO - Lighting Fixture & Control - PHILIPS LIGHTING; *pg.* 1303, *pg.* 806
HADLEIGH - Furniture - NEMSCHOFF, INC.; *pg.* 936, *pg.* 1890
HADLEY - Fabric - NEMSCHOFF, INC.; *pg.* 936, *pg.* 1890

HAEFELY TEST - Industrial Technology - HUBBELL INCORPORATED; *pg.* 1299, *pg.* 370
HAELAN 951 - Nutritional Products - HAELAN PRODUCTS, INC.; *pg.* 860, *pg.* 1847
HAESTAD METHODS - Software - BENTLEY SYSTEMS, INC.; *pg.* 361, *pg.* 1531
HAGEN - Printing Product - ELECTRONICS FOR IMAGING, INC.; *pg.* 390, *pg.* 88
HAGGAR - Apparel - HAGGAR CORPORATION; *pg.* 41, *pg.* 1682
HAGGAR BLACK LABEL - Apparel - HAGGAR CORPORATION; *pg.* 41, *pg.* 1682
HAGGEN C.A.R.D. - Purchase Card - HAGGEN, INC.; *pg.* 1022, *pg.* 1817
HAGGLE-FREE BUYING.WORRY FREE OWNERSHIP - Slogan - ENTERPRISE HOLDINGS, INC.; *pg.* 1906, *pg.* 996
HAIKU - Beauty Product - AVON PRODUCTS, INC.; *pg.* 500, *pg.* 1198
HAIKU - Fabric - NEMSCHOFF, INC.; *pg.* 936, *pg.* 1890
HAIN PURE FOODS - Food Product - THE HAIN CELESTIAL GROUP, INC.; *pg.* 860, *pg.* 1172
HAIN PURE SNAX - Food Product - THE HAIN CELESTIAL GROUP, INC.; *pg.* 860, *pg.* 1172
HAIPE - Broadband Satellite Network - VIASAT, INC.; *pg.* 489, *pg.* 62
HAIR CLUB - Hair Care Product - HAIR CLUB FOR MEN, LTD., INC.; *pg.* 511, *pg.* 411
HAIR CLUB FOR KIDS - Hair Care Product - HAIR CLUB FOR MEN, LTD., INC.; *pg.* 511, *pg.* 411
HAIR CLUB FOR MEN - Hair Care Product - HAIR CLUB FOR MEN, LTD., INC.; *pg.* 511, *pg.* 411
HAIR CLUB FOR MEN AND WOMEN - Hair Restoration Centers & Services - REGIS CORPORATION; *pg.* 521, *pg.* 941
HAIR CLUB FOR WOMEN - Hair Care Product - HAIR CLUB FOR MEN, LTD., INC.; *pg.* 511, *pg.* 411
HAIR CUTTERY - Hair Care Salon - THE RATNER COMPANIES; *pg.* 520, *pg.* 1809
HAIR EXCITEMENT - Hair Salons - REGIS CORPORATION; *pg.* 521, *pg.* 941
HAIR EXPRESS - UK Salon Brand - REGIS CORPORATION; *pg.* 521, *pg.* 941
HAIR OFF - Depilatory Products - CCA INDUSTRIES, INC.; *pg.* 503, *pg.* 1114
HAIR REPAIR TREATMENT - Hair Care Product - JOHN PAUL MITCHELL SYSTEMS; *pg.* 512, *pg.* 133
HAIR SCULPTING - Hair Care System - JOHN PAUL MITCHELL SYSTEMS; *pg.* 512, *pg.* 133
HAIR SCULPTING LOTION - Hair Care Product - JOHN PAUL MITCHELL SYSTEMS; *pg.* 512, *pg.* 133
HAIR TRAPPER - Bath Organizer & Accessory - HOME PRODUCTS INTERNATIONAL, INC.; *pg.* 1125, *pg.* 577
HAIRCRAFTERS - Hair Service Center - REGIS CORPORATION; *pg.* 521, *pg.* 941
HAIRGUARDS - Protective Head & Hair Caps - STANDARD SAFETY EQUIPMENT CO.; *pg.* 1379, *pg.* 632
HAIRMASTERS - Hair Salons - REGIS CORPORATION; *pg.* 521, *pg.* 941
HAIRPAINTING - Hair Coloring - P&G-CLAIROL, INC.; *pg.* 519, *pg.* 1418
HAITER - Mold Remover - KAO BRANDS CO. INC.; *pg.* 513, *pg.* 1415
HAJIME - Beverages - THE COCA-COLA COMPANY; *pg.* 240, *pg.* 493
HAKIM - Medical Device - INTEGRA LIFESCIENCES HOLDINGS CORPORATION; *pg.* 1545, *pg.* 1109
HAKUTSURU - Sake - DREYFUS ASHBY INC.; *pg.* 1962, *pg.* 1226
HALAR - Cable Tie - PANDUIT CORP.; *pg.* 661, *pg.* 663
HALAR - Thermoplastic Product - WESTLAKE PLASTICS COMPANY; *pg.* 1892, *pg.* 1548
HALCION - Medicine - PFIZER INC.; *pg.* 1581, *pg.* 1278
HALCYON - Ceiling Panel - USG CORPORATION; *pg.* 118, *pg.* 594
HALDOL - Healthcare Product - JOHNSON & JOHNSON; *pg.* 1549, *pg.* 1091
HALE - Fire Pumps - IDEX CORPORATION; *pg.* 1347, *pg.* 623
HALE BOOK CASES - Bookcases - F.E. HALE MANUFACTURING COMPANY; *pg.* 925, *pg.* 1160
HALEY - Lighting - ETHAN ALLEN INTERIORS INC.; *pg.* 924, *pg.* 343
HALF CAB - Footwear - VANS, INC.; *pg.* 1821, *pg.* 76
HALF CHOCOLATELY, HALF CANDY, HALF CRAZY - Tagline - THE TOPPS COMPANY, INC.; *pg.* 588, *pg.* 1302
HALF CIRCLE - Door & Wood Product - CONESTOGA WOOD SPECIALTIES CORP.; *pg.* 921, *pg.* 1527
HALF-HONEY - Furniture - HERMAN MILLER, INC.; *pg.* 926, *pg.* 913
HALF JACKET - Eyewear - OAKLEY, INC.; *pg.* 1840, *pg.* 86
HALF/PACK - Refuse Bodies - HEIL ENVIRONMENTAL INDUSTRIES, LTD.; *pg.* 207, *pg.* 1629
HALF-SIZE STERISET - Container - MEDLINE INDUSTRIES, INC.; *pg.* 1562, *pg.* 635
HALF WIRE - Eyewear - OAKLEY, INC.; *pg.* 1840, *pg.* 86
HALF.COM - Online Marketplace - EBAY INC.; *pg.* 1240, *pg.* 243
HALFED - Apparel - OAKLEY, INC.; *pg.* 1840, *pg.* 86
HALFTONE - Apparel - OAKLEY, INC.; *pg.* 1840, *pg.* 86
HALFTOP - Partial Soft Top - BESTOP, INC.; *pg.* 200, *pg.* 312
HALIFAX - Furniture - ASHLEY FURNITURE INDUSTRIES, INC.; *pg.* 914, *pg.* 1852
HALITE - De-Icing Salt - CARGILL SALT; *pg.* 846, *pg.* 920
HALITE WINTER MELT - Crystals - CARGILL LIMITED; *pg.* 1475, *pg.* 1914
HALL - Furniture - J. ROBERT SCOTT INC.; *pg.* 930, *pg.* 105
HALL EASY-FIT - Mechanical Valve - MEDTRONIC, INC.; *pg.* 1564, *pg.* 939
HALL-MARK GLOBAL SOLUTIONS - Consulting Services - AVNET, INC.; *pg.* 622, *pg.* 15
HALL OF CHAMPIONS - Trademark - NATIONAL COLLEGIATE ATHLETIC ASSOCIATION; *pg.* 567, *pg.* 688
HALLCOMID - Chemical Product - STEPAN COMPANY; *pg.* 1182, *pg.* 643
HALLEY - Office Light - KNOLL, INC.; *pg.* 425, *pg.* 1527
HALLEY'S BIBLE HANDBOOK - Religious Reference Book - THE ZONDERVAN CORPORATION; *pg.* 1703, *pg.* 891
HALLIE - Clothing - ABERCROMBIE & FITCH CO.; *pg.* 37, *pg.* 1466
HALLIE - Dolls - AMERICAN GIRL LLC; *pg.* 949, *pg.* 1871
HALLKIRK - Dress Shoes - JOHNSTON & MURPHY CO.; *pg.* 1810, *pg.* 1651
HALLMARK - Furniture - BUSH INDUSTRIES INC.; *pg.* 919, *pg.* 1170
HALLMARK - Tire And Rubber Product - THE GOODYEAR TIRE & RUBBER COMPANY; *pg.* 1883, *pg.* 1401
HALLMARK - Greeting Cards & Related Products - HALLMARK CARDS, INC.; *pg.* 1646, *pg.* 983
HALLMARK - Toy & Game - HASBRO, INC.; *pg.* 954, *pg.* 1603
HALLMARK - Waiting Seating - STEELCASE INC.; *pg.* 475, *pg.* 889
HALLMARK - Cigar And Tobacco - SWISHER INTERNATIONAL, INC.; *pg.* 1895, *pg.* 345
HALLMARK CHANNEL - Cable TV Channel - CROWN MEDIA HOLDINGS INC.; *pg.* 280, *pg.* 281
HALLMARK GOLD CROWN - Card & Stationery - HALLMARK CARDS, INC.; *pg.* 1646, *pg.* 983
HALLO-WIN - Lottery Game - MASSACHUSETTS STATE LOTTERY; *pg.* 998, *pg.* 802
HALLOWEEKENDS - Amusement & Water Park - CEDAR FAIR, L.P.; *pg.* 537, *pg.* 1471
HALLOWEENONLY.COM - Web Site - JOHNSON SMITH COMPANY; *pg.* 1774, *pg.* 414
HALLS - Cough Drops - MONDELEZ INTERNATIONAL, INC.; *pg.* 878, *pg.* 601
HALLSTRIP - Stripper - HUBBARD-HALL, INC.; *pg.* 1167, *pg.* 382
HALLU - Medical Device - INTEGRA LIFESCIENCES HOLDINGS CORPORATION; *pg.* 1545, *pg.* 1109
HALLU-FIX - Medical Device - INTEGRA LIFESCIENCES HOLDINGS CORPORATION; *pg.* 1545, *pg.* 1109
HALO - Digital Ammeter - HD ELECTRIC COMPANY; *pg.* 1299, *pg.* 666
HALO - Foam Product - HSM SOLUTIONS; *pg.* 1884, *pg.* 1378
HALO HEAT - Cooking Technology - ALTO-SHAAM INC.; *pg.* 836, *pg.* 1869
HALO SHAMPOO - Personal Care Product - COLGATE-PALMOLIVE COMPANY; *pg.* 504, *pg.* 1215
HALO SHIELD - Disposable Underpad - THE SALK COMPANY; *pg.* 1591, *pg.* 800
HALOBETASOL - Pharmaceutical Product - G&W LABORATORIES INC.; *pg.* 1532, *pg.* 1123
HALOGEN - Apparels - NORDSTROM, INC.; *pg.* 1779, *pg.* 1837
HALOGEN FLEX - Flexible Halogen Light - DAZOR MANUFACTURING CORP.; *pg.* 1296, *pg.* 995
HALOGEN HALOMAX - Lighting Product - WESTINGHOUSE LIGHTING CORPORATION; *pg.* 687, *pg.* 1571
HALOGEN HPX - Otoscopes - WELCH ALLYN INC.; *pg.* 1436, *pg.* 1342
HALOMAX - Lighting Product - WESTINGHOUSE LIGHTING CORPORATION; *pg.* 687, *pg.* 1571
HALOTESTIN CIII - Medicine - PFIZER INC.; *pg.* 1581, *pg.* 1278
HALOTHANE - Anesthetic - HALOCARBON PRODUCTS CORPORATION; *pg.* 978, *pg.* 1116
HALOVAC - Inert Vacuum Pump Oil - HALOCARBON PRODUCTS CORPORATION; *pg.* 978, *pg.* 1116
HALPACLEAN - Solvent - THE DOW CHEMICAL COMPANY; *pg.* 1157, *pg.* 898
HALPANAL - Solvent - THE DOW CHEMICAL COMPANY; *pg.* 1157, *pg.* 898
HALPASOL - Solvent - THE DOW CHEMICAL COMPANY; *pg.* 1157, *pg.* 898
HALPER - Imported Ski & Apres Ski Headwear, Scarves, Fashion Gloves - RELIABLE OF MILWAUKEE; *pg.* 698, *pg.* 1879
HALSO - Solvent - OCCIDENTAL CHEMICAL CORPORATION; *pg.* 1175, *pg.* 1685
HALSTEAD - Vanity Lights - CRAFTMADE INTERNATIONAL, INC.; *pg.* 1295, *pg.* 1670
HALSTEAD - Furniture - LA-Z-BOY INCORPORATED; *pg.* 932, *pg.* 901
HALSTON - Perfume - ELIZABETH ARDEN, INC.; *pg.* 507, *pg.* 448
HALTEX - Mineral Product - TOR MINERALS INTERNATIONAL INC.; *pg.* 1184, *pg.* 1672
HALTS - Lawn Fertilizer - THE SCOTTS MIRACLE-GRO COMPANY; *pg.* 1799, *pg.* 1459
HAMBEEN BLACK BEAN SALSA - Soup - N.K. HURST CO., INC.; *pg.* 886, *pg.* 689
HAMBEENS - Dried Beans - N.K. HURST CO., INC.; *pg.* 886, *pg.* 689
HAMBURGER HELPER - Food Product - GENERAL MILLS, INC.; *pg.* 828, *pg.* 933
HAMBURGER UNIVERSITY - Management Training School for McDonalds - MCDONALD'S CORPORATION; *pg.* 1737, *pg.* 645
HAMER - Guitars - KAMAN CORPORATION; *pg.* 229, *pg.* 338
HAMILTON - Musical Instrument - GIBSON GUITAR CORP.; *pg.* 550, *pg.* 1650
HAMILTON - Bike - MARIN BIKES; *pg.* 1708, *pg.* 168
HAMILTON BEACH - Small Appliances - HAMILTON BEACH BRANDS, INC.; *pg.* 56, *pg.* 1783
HAMILTON EASY KARV - Meat Products - THE SMITHFIELD PACKING CO., INC.; *pg.* 896, *pg.* 1807
HAMILTON ESTATES - Beverage - PHOENIX VINTNERS, LLC; *pg.* 1968, *pg.* 182
HAMILTON SUNDSTRAND - Aerospace Products - UNITED TECHNOLOGIES CORPORATION; *pg.* 235, *pg.* 353
HAMKA - Snacks - PEPSICO, INC.; *pg.* 259, *pg.* 1327
HAMKA'S - Snack - FRITO-LAY NORTH AMERICA, INC.; *pg.* 1853, *pg.* 1730
HAMMARY - Furniture - LA-Z-BOY INCORPORATED; *pg.* 932, *pg.* 901
HAMMER - Software - BENTLEY SYSTEMS, INC.; *pg.* 361, *pg.* 1531
HAMMER-CAPSULE - Adhesive Anchor System - POWERS FASTENERS INC.; *pg.* 1059, *pg.* 1143
HAMMER HEAD - Drywall Tools - HYDE TOOLS, INC.; *pg.* 1125, *pg.* 844
HAMMER STRENGTH - Fitness Equipment - BRUNSWICK CORPORATION; *pg.* 1828, *pg.* 623
HAMMERED - Patterned Glass - AGC GLASS NORTH AMERICA, INC.; *pg.* 65, *pg.* 482
HAMMERHEAD - Piercing Tools - CHARLES MACHINE WORKS, INC.; *pg.* 1322, *pg.* 1488
HAMMERITE - Decorative Architectural Product - MASCO CORPORATION; *pg.* 96, *pg.* 909
HAMMERLOK - Chain - COLUMBUS MCKINNON CORPORATION; *pg.* 1325, *pg.* 1138
HAMMERMILL - Paper - INTERNATIONAL PAPER COMPANY; *pg.* 1460, *pg.* 1644
HAMMERTONE - Beverage Bottle - THERMOS L.L.C.; *pg.* 61, *pg.* 660
HAMMOND - Furniture - JASPER GROUP; *pg.* 930, *pg.* 691
HAMMOND - Elevating & Conveying Equip. - SCREW

First page reference indicates Business Class Edition
Second page reference indicates Geographic Edition

CONVEYOR INDUSTRIES; *pg.* 1374, *pg.* 682
HAMMOND & STEPHENS - Educational Resources - SCHOOL SPECIALTY, INC.; *pg.* 467, *pg.* 1860
HAMM'S - Beer - MILLERCOORS; *pg.* 254, *pg.* 1877
HAMM'S DRAFT - Beer - MILLERCOORS; *pg.* 254, *pg.* 1877
HAMM'S SPECIAL LIGHT - Beer - MILLERCOORS; *pg.* 254, *pg.* 1877
HAMNIK - Packaged Foods - ATALANTA CORPORATION; *pg.* 838, *pg.* 1057
HAMO - Detergent - STERIS CORPORATION; *pg.* 1597, *pg.* 1464
HAMPSHIRE - Products & Services - THE DOW CHEMICAL COMPANY; *pg.* 1157, *pg.* 898
HAMPSHIRE - Furniture - ETHAN ALLEN INTERIORS INC.; *pg.* 924, *pg.* 343
HAMPSTEAD - Fabric - NEMSCHOFF, INC.; *pg.* 936, *pg.* 1890
HAMPTON - Furniture - AMERICAN LEATHER LP; *pg.* 912, *pg.* 1673
HAMPTON - Watches - BAUME & MERCIER, INC.; *pg.* 1, *pg.* 1201
THE HAMPTON - Ready-to-assemble Swing Set - CREATIVE PLAYTHINGS LTD.; *pg.* 1831, *pg.* 820
HAMPTON - Furniture - ETHAN ALLEN INTERIORS INC.; *pg.* 924, *pg.* 343
HAMPTON - Mid-Market Inn - HILTON WORLDWIDE, INC.; *pg.* 1094, *pg.* 1791
HAMPTON - Furniture - JASPER GROUP; *pg.* 930, *pg.* 691
HAMPTON - Door Panel - MASONITE INTERNATIONAL CORPORATION; *pg.* 1054, *pg.* 1920
HAMPTON - Fabric - NEMSCHOFF, INC.; *pg.* 936, *pg.* 1890
HAMPTON - Footwear - P.W. MINOR & SON, INC.; *pg.* 1816, *pg.* 1140
HAMPTON INN - Hotels - HILTON WORLDWIDE, INC.; *pg.* 1094, *pg.* 1791
HAMPTON INNS & SUITES - Mid-Market Suites - HILTON WORLDWIDE, INC.; *pg.* 1094, *pg.* 1791
HAMPTON PLAID - Rug - COURISTAN INC.; *pg.* 921, *pg.* 1067
HAMPTONROADS.COM - Online Newspaper - PILOT MEDIA; *pg.* 1677, *pg.* 1797
HAMPTONS - Leather Product - COACH, INC.; *pg.* 3, *pg.* 1214
HAMPTONS BLEND - Tile - ARTISTIC TILE INC.; *pg.* 914, *pg.* 1119
HAMWORTHY - Fluid Handling System - MARINE & OFFSHORE CANADA; *pg.* 1359, *pg.* 1933
HAN-D-PAK - Bags - BROWN PAPER GOODS COMPANY; *pg.* 1454, *pg.* 665
HANA - Eyewear - MAUI JIM, INC.; *pg.* 9, *pg.* 651
HANAA - Footwear - STEVEN MADDEN, LTD.; *pg.* 1819, *pg.* 1176
HANALEI - Eyewear - MAUI JIM, INC.; *pg.* 9, *pg.* 651
HANAUMA SURF CO - Sweatshirts - OVERSTOCK.COM, INC.; *pg.* 1273, *pg.* 1760
HANCOCK - Shoes - ALLEN-EDMONDS SHOE CORP.; *pg.* 1804, *pg.* 1887
HANCOCK - Door & Wood Product - CONESTOGA WOOD SPECIALTIES CORP.; *pg.* 921, *pg.* 1527
HANCOCK - Heart Valves - MEDTRONIC, INC.; *pg.* 1564, *pg.* 939
HANCOCK COUNTY JOURNAL PILOT - Newspaper - THE DEMOCRAT CO.; *pg.* 1634, *pg.* 708
HANCOCK FABRICS - Fabric And Sewing Machine - HANCOCK FABRICS, INC.; *pg.* 693, *pg.* 968
HANCOCK II - Tissue Valve - MEDTRONIC, INC.; *pg.* 1564, *pg.* 939
HANCOCK M.O. II - Aortic Heart Valve - MEDTRONIC, INC.; *pg.* 1564, *pg.* 939
HAND DEFENSE - Cleaning Product - HILLYARD, INC.; *pg.* 331, *pg.* 990
HAND E BALM - Balm - SCHOOL-TECH, INC.; *pg.* 1844, *pg.* 866
HAND E SAN - Hand Soap - BIRKO CORPORATION; *pg.* 1149, *pg.* 332
HAND HELD IRON MASK - Welding Shield - SELLSTROM MANUFACTURING CO.; *pg.* 1428, *pg.* 659
HAND HELPER - Medical & Aesthetic Product - DYNATRONICS CORPORATION; *pg.* 1526, *pg.* 1757
HAND-LENS - Magnifier - ULTRAOPTIX, INC.; *pg.* 1433, *pg.* 346
HAND-MASKER - Painting Masker - 3M COMPANY; *pg.* 1142, *pg.* 956
HAND ME THE MONEY - Lottery Game - KENTUCKY LOTTERY CORPORATION; *pg.* 996, *pg.* 735
HAND RX - Health & Beauty Product - BLUE CROSS LABORATORIES; *pg.* 326, *pg.* 277
HAND SAVER - Microemulsion Pump - STOELTING CO.; *pg.* 1430, *pg.* 671
HAND-SPUN MILKSHAKES - Milkshakes - CHICK-FIL-A, INC.; *pg.* 1721, *pg.* 492
HAND-Y - Towels - AERVOE INDUSTRIES INCORPORATED; *pg.* 1439, *pg.* 1021
HAND-Y PRO - Towels - AERVOE INDUSTRIES INCORPORATED; *pg.* 1439, *pg.* 1021
HANDBUILT IN THE ROCKIES - Tagline - MOOTS CYCLES; *pg.* 1709, *pg.* 335
HANDE - Drain Cleaner - ELECTRIC EEL MANUFACTURING CO., INC.; *pg.* 80, *pg.* 1473
HANDGUARD - Cleaner - ROCHESTER MIDLAND CORPORATION; *pg.* 334, *pg.* 1337
HANDGUNS - Magazine - RENTPATH, INC.; *pg.* 1680, *pg.* 538
HANDI BRUSH - Carpet Cleaning Instrument - STANLEY STEEMER INTERNATIONAL, INC.; *pg.* 944, *pg.* 1450
HANDI-FRESH - Soap Dispensers - GEORGIA-PACIFIC LLC; *pg.* 1458, *pg.* 507
HANDI GROOM - Pile Conditioner - STANLEY STEEMER INTERNATIONAL, INC.; *pg.* 944, *pg.* 1450
HANDI-PAK - Durabubble Product - POLYAIR INTER PACK INC.; *pg.* 1467, *pg.* 1941
HANDI-SCRUBB - Solvent-Free Hand Cleaner - GEORGIA-PACIFIC LLC; *pg.* 1458, *pg.* 507
HANDI-STAND - Metal Rack - PECO, INC.; *pg.* 1368, *pg.* 1505
HANDI-WIPES - Cleaning Cloth - THE CLOROX COMPANY; *pg.* 327, *pg.* 169
HANDIFLO - Tub & Sink - E.L. MUSTEE & SONS, INC.; *pg.* 1124, *pg.* 1430
HANDIHALER - Medicine - PFIZER INC.; *pg.* 1581, *pg.* 1278
HANDIHOLDER - Board - WENGER CORPORATION; *pg.* 1307, *pg.* 952
HANDIMATCH - Portable Computer Color Matching System - AKZONOBEL DECORATIVE PAINTS U.S.; *pg.* 1439, *pg.* 1474
HANDIMET - Abrasive Strip Grinder - BUEHLER, LTD.; *pg.* 1403, *pg.* 622
HANDISHAPES - Threshold Product - RELIABLE AUTOMATIC SPRINKLER CO., INC.; *pg.* 1137, *pg.* 1158
HANDIWIRE - Extention Cords, Drop Lights - ESSEX GROUP, INC.; *pg.* 638, *pg.* 680
HANDKEY - Security & Safety Product - INGERSOLL-RAND COMPANY; *pg.* 1349, *pg.* 1370
HANDLAIR - Agricultural Pneumatic Conveying Systems - CHRISTIANSON SYSTEMS, INC.; *pg.* 1323, *pg.* 917
HANDLE - Apparel - OAKLEY, INC.; *pg.* 1840, *pg.* 86
HANDLE EEZ - Grip Handle - FOAMPRO MANUFACTURING, INC.; *pg.* 1442, *pg.* 110
HANDLE-IT - Office Mobile Storage Systems - TAB PRODUCTS CO. LLC; *pg.* 481, *pg.* 1869
HANDLE-O-METER - Precision Instrument - THWING-ALBERT INSTRUMENT COMPANY; *pg.* 1432, *pg.* 1131
HANDLELOCK - Container - HONEYWELL INTERNATIONAL INC.; *pg.* 407, *pg.* 1088
HANDLESAK - Bag - PACTIV CORPORATION; *pg.* 1466, *pg.* 624
HANDLIFT - Elevator - SAVARIA CONCORD LIFTS INC.; *pg.* 1592, *pg.* 1919
HANDPUNCH - Security & Safety Product - INGERSOLL-RAND COMPANY; *pg.* 1349, *pg.* 1370
HANDS DOWN - Toy & Game - HASBRO, INC.; *pg.* 954, *pg.* 1603
HANDS FREE QC - Software - BIO-RAD LABORATORIES, INC.; *pg.* 1504, *pg.* 101
HANDS OFF - Automobile Cleaning & Detergent Preparations - ASHLAND INC.; *pg.* 972, *pg.* 726
HANDS-OFF - Fall Protection Equipment - MINE SAFETY APPLIANCES COMPANY; *pg.* 1361, *pg.* 1525
HANDS-OFF - Washing System - PELLERIN MILNOR CORPORATION; *pg.* 1368, *pg.* 744
HANDSAVER - Flashlight - ENERGIZER HOLDINGS, INC.; *pg.* 637, *pg.* 996
HANDSFREE - Fixtures - ROCHESTER MIDLAND CORPORATION; *pg.* 334, *pg.* 1337
HANDSPUN - Bicycle Wheels - QUALITY BICYCLE PRODUCTS; *pg.* 1710, *pg.* 918
HANDTITE - Guard Seal - GRACO, INC.; *pg.* 1342, *pg.* 935
HANDY BULB - Home Products - HABAND COMPANY, INC.; *pg.* 1772, *pg.* 1099
HANDY FILL - Pepper Pouch - MCCORMICK & COMPANY, INCORPORATED; *pg.* 1027, *pg.* 779
HANDY FUEL - Portable Heating Fuel - BLYTH, INC.; *pg.* 502, *pg.* 349
HANDY HAULER - Multi-Purpose Yard & Garden Cart - FLOWTRON OUTDOOR PRODUCTS; *pg.* 639, *pg.* 830
HANDY HOLDER - Hose - TEKNOR APEX COMPANY; *pg.* 1889, *pg.* 1605
HANDY MAN'S CHOICE - Slogan - ENCORE WIRE CORPORATION; *pg.* 637, *pg.* 1726
HANDY PACKER - Tool - LISLE CORPORATION; *pg.* 1356, *pg.* 703
HANDY-SAN - Sanitizer - DELTA FOREMOST CHEMICAL CORPORATION; *pg.* 1155, *pg.* 1642
HANDYANDY - Cleaners - THE CLOROX COMPANY; *pg.* 327, *pg.* 169
HANDYBAR - Gardening & Hardware Product - FAULTLESS STARCH/BON AMI COMPANY; *pg.* 330, *pg.* 982
HANDYCALL - Telephone Banking System - HANCOCK BANK; *pg.* 765, *pg.* 968
HANDYGREEN - Spreader - THE SCOTTS MIRACLE-GRO COMPANY; *pg.* 1799, *pg.* 1459
HANDYLINK - Connector - MOLEX INCORPORATED; *pg.* 655, *pg.* 628
HANDYMATE - Commercial Lighting - SWIVELIER CO., INC.; *pg.* 1307, *pg.* 1142
HANES - Apparel - HANESBRANDS INC.; *pg.* 26, *pg.* 1394
HANES HOSIERY - Apparel - HANESBRANDS INC.; *pg.* 26, *pg.* 1394
HANEX - Software - SYNOPSYS, INC.; *pg.* 480, *pg.* 162
HANG-A-HAMPER - Hamper - HOME PRODUCTS INTERNATIONAL, INC.; *pg.* 1125, *pg.* 577
HANG-UP - Wall Mounted Hair Dryer - ANDIS COMPANY; *pg.* 498, *pg.* 1895
HANG-UP LIGHT - Residential Lighting Handymate - SWIVELIER CO., INC.; *pg.* 1307, *pg.* 1142
HANG UP MINI - Mini Vacuum - SHOP-VAC CORPORATION; *pg.* 1375, *pg.* 1595
HANGER ONE VODKA - Spirits - PROXIMO SPIRITS, INC.; *pg.* 1969, *pg.* 1076
HANGERS.COM - Website - THE GREAT AMERICAN HANGER COMPANY INC.; *pg.* 926, *pg.* 442
HANGMAN - Game - HASBRO, INC.; *pg.* 954, *pg.* 1603
HANGO - Health Care Product - HEALTH PRODUCTS CORPORATION; *pg.* 1540, *pg.* 1356
HANGTIGHT - Mounting System - DAZOR MANUFACTURING CORP.; *pg.* 1296, *pg.* 995
HANITA - Tools - KENNAMETAL INC.; *pg.* 1052, *pg.* 1547
HANITA - Cutting Tools - KENNAMETAL IPG; *pg.* 1353, *pg.* 1615
HANNA-BARBERA - Production Studio - TIME WARNER INC.; *pg.* 312, *pg.* 1302
HANNA-BARBERA - Motion Picture Films - WARNER BROS. ANIMATION INC.; *pg.* 319, *pg.* 54
HANNA FX - Haircare Product - POLYONE CORPORATION; *pg.* 1177, *pg.* 1404
HANNAFORD FOOD AND DRUG - Retail Food & Drug Stores - HANNAFORD BROTHERS CO.; *pg.* 1022, *pg.* 752
HANNAH - Lighting Product - QUOIZEL INC.; *pg.* 1304, *pg.* 1616
HANNAH MONTANA - Toy & Game - HASBRO, INC.; *pg.* 954, *pg.* 1603
HANNIBAL'S MARCH - Video Game - INTERNATIONAL GAME TECHNOLOGY; *pg.* 957, *pg.* 1024
HANOMAN - Pant - HUGGER MUGGER YOGA PRODUCTS LLC; *pg.* 1836, *pg.* 1758
HANOVER - Dinnerware - THE HOMER LAUGHLIN CHINA COMPANY; *pg.* 1125, *pg.* 1850
HANSATOME - Microkeratome - BAUSCH & LOMB INCORPORATED; *pg.* 1401, *pg.* 1045
HANSEN CHERRY - Furniture - BUSH INDUSTRIES INC.; *pg.* 919, *pg.* 1170
HANSEN ISLAND - Microwave Fudge Mix - REDCO FOODS, INC.; *pg.* 891, *pg.* 1174
HANSEN'S - Juices - MONSTER BEVERAGE CORPORATION; *pg.* 257, *pg.* 69
HANSEN'S BLASTS - Juices - MONSTER BEVERAGE CORPORATION; *pg.* 257, *pg.* 69
HANSEN'S DIET RED ENERGY - Juice - MONSTER BEVERAGE CORPORATION; *pg.* 257, *pg.* 69
HANSEN'S JR. JUICE - Juice - MONSTER BEVERAGE CORPORATION; *pg.* 257, *pg.* 69
HANSEN'S JUICE SLAM - Juice - MONSTER BEVERAGE CORPORATION; *pg.* 257, *pg.* 69
HANSEN'S NATURAL - Juices - MONSTER BEVERAGE CORPORATION; *pg.* 257, *pg.* 69

HANSEN'S NATURAL SODAS - Sodas Made of Natural Ingredients - MONSTER BEVERAGE CORPORATION; *pg.* 257, *pg.* 69
HANSEN'S STAMINA - Juice - MONSTER BEVERAGE CORPORATION; *pg.* 257, *pg.* 69
HANSGROHE - Faucet - MASCO CORPORATION; *pg.* 96, *pg.* 909
HANSVEDT - Electrical Discharge Machine - HARDINGE INC.; *pg.* 1344, *pg.* 1157
HAP - Alkylpyridine - VERTELLUS SPECIALTIES INC.; *pg.* 1185, *pg.* 690
HAP HAZARD - Shoe - AEROGROUP INTERNATIONAL, INC.; *pg.* 1803, *pg.* 1055
HAPMAN - Bulk Handling Conveyors & Systems - PRAB, INC.; *pg.* 1369, *pg.* 894
HAPPENING - Carpet - INTERFACE, INC.; *pg.* 695, *pg.* 512
HAPPILY EVER ACCURATE - Home Products - HABAND COMPANY, INC.; *pg.* 1772, *pg.* 1099
HAPPY - Designer Fragrance - PARFUMS DE COEUR LTD.; *pg.* 519, *pg.* 376
HAPPY BIRTHDAY - Lottery Game - OHIO LOTTERY COMMISSION; *pg.* 1002, *pg.* 1433
HAPPY CAMPER - Video Game - INTERNATIONAL GAME TECHNOLOGY; *pg.* 957, *pg.* 1024
HAPPY CAMPER - Printed Periodical - TRAVELHOST, INC.; *pg.* 1696, *pg.* 1689
HAPPY ENDING - Ice Cream Dessert - FRIENDLY ICE CREAM, LLC; *pg.* 1853, *pg.* 859
HAPPY FACE - Cleansing Lotion - THE GILLETTE COMPANY; *pg.* 509, *pg.* 795
HAPPY FAMILY - Toy - MATTEL, INC.; *pg.* 962, *pg.* 81
HAPPY FEET - Cleaning Product - HILLYARD, INC.; *pg.* 331, *pg.* 990
HAPPY GO LIGHTLY - Shoes - P.W. MINOR & SON, INC.; *pg.* 1816, *pg.* 1140
HAPPY GO LUCKY - Carpet - BEAULIEU GROUP, LLC; *pg.* 917, *pg.* 529
HAPPY GO LUCKY - Lottery Game - OHIO LOTTERY COMMISSION; *pg.* 1002, *pg.* 1433
HAPPY HANDWRITING - Educational Product - BARKER CREEK PUBLISHING INC.; *pg.* 1619, *pg.* 1818
HAPPY HIPPO GYM - Toy - INFANTINO, LLC; *pg.* 957, *pg.* 203
HAPPY HOUR BOUQUETS - Flower Arrangement - 1-800-FLOWERS.COM, INC.; *pg.* 1758, *pg.* 1151
HAPPY MEAL - Children's Combination Meal - MCDONALD'S CORPORATION; *pg.* 1737, *pg.* 645
HAPPY PLACE - Baby Product - THE BOPPY COMPANY, LLC; *pg.* 20, *pg.* 329
HAPPY TIME - Popcorn - AMERICAN POP CORN COMPANY; *pg.* 825, *pg.* 712
HAPPY TOTE - Children's Product - THE STEP2 COMPANY LLC; *pg.* 1889, *pg.* 1474
HAPPYVILAGERS - Toys - 1-800-FLOWERS.COM, INC.; *pg.* 1758, *pg.* 1151
HAPPYVILLE BLOCKS - Toys - 1-800-FLOWERS.COM, INC.; *pg.* 1758, *pg.* 1151
HAPS - Software - SYNOPSYS, INC.; *pg.* 480, *pg.* 162
HAPSTRAK - Software - SYNOPSYS, INC.; *pg.* 480, *pg.* 162
HAPTIC PROFILER - Hardware & Software - IMMERSION CORPORATION; *pg.* 413, *pg.* 246
HAPTICCAD - Hardware & Software - IMMERSION CORPORATION; *pg.* 413, *pg.* 246
HAPTOKKULT - Pharmaceutical Product - ALERE INC.; *pg.* 1488, *pg.* 849
HAPUNA - Eyewear - MAUI JIM, INC.; *pg.* 9, *pg.* 651
HAR-MATIC - Machinery - HARDINGE INC.; *pg.* 1344, *pg.* 1157
HARAS DE PIRQUE - Wine - REMY COINTREAU USA INC.; *pg.* 1969, *pg.* 1285
HARBIL - Fluid Mixing, Metering Equipment - IDEX CORPORATION; *pg.* 1347, *pg.* 623
HARBOR - Furniture - JASPER GROUP; *pg.* 930, *pg.* 691
HARBOR - Eyewear - MAUI JIM, INC.; *pg.* 9, *pg.* 651
HARBOR - Surface Material - STEELCASE INC.; *pg.* 475, *pg.* 889
HARBOR HOSPITAL - Hospital - MEDSTAR HEALTH INC.; *pg.* 1563, *pg.* 767
HARBOR NITES BY SAG HARBOR - Misses' Eveningwear - KELLWOOD COMPANY; *pg.* 28, *pg.* 975
HARBORMASTER - Telescope - BUSHNELL OUTDOOR PRODUCTS, INC.; *pg.* 1403, *pg.* 718
HARBORMASTER - Marine Propulsion & Steering System - HARBORMASTER MARINE, INC.; *pg.* 1707, *pg.* 896
HARBORVIEW - Kitchen Product - KOHLER CO.; *pg.* 91, *pg.* 1862
HARBOUR ISLES - Community Name - WCI COMMUNITIES, INC.; *pg.* 1118, *pg.* 414
HARCRETE - Machinery - HARDINGE INC.; *pg.* 1344, *pg.* 1157
HARD BOILED - Hard Hats - E.D. BULLARD COMPANY; *pg.* 1332, *pg.* 727
HARD EDGE - Metal Cutting Saw Blade - SIMONDS INTERNATIONAL CORPORATION; *pg.* 1376, *pg.* 819
HARD HAT - Antenna Product - PCTEL, INC.; *pg.* 452, *pg.* 557
HARD LAKE - Clothing - ABERCROMBIE & FITCH CO.; *pg.* 37, *pg.* 1466
HARD METAL SYSTEM - Toy & Game - HASBRO, INC.; *pg.* 954, *pg.* 1603
HARD ROCK CAFE - Restaurant - HARD ROCK CAFE INTERNATIONAL, INC.; *pg.* 1730, *pg.* 454
HARD SCALD LIQUID - Chemical Product - BIRKO CORPORATION; *pg.* 1149, *pg.* 332
HARD-SHELL - Software - BIO-RAD LABORATORIES, INC.; *pg.* 1504, *pg.* 101
HARD TOP - Mousepad - ALLSOP, INC.; *pg.* 347, *pg.* 1817
HARD-WORKING GLOVES FOR SERIOUS CONDITIONS. - Slogan - WELLS LAMONT CORPORATION; *pg.* 15, *pg.* 638
HARDAC - Bevel Product - GLEASON CORPORATION; *pg.* 1340, *pg.* 1335
HARDBOTTOM - Storage Product - PLANO MOLDING COMPANY; *pg.* 1887, *pg.* 652
HARDCASE - Flashlight - ENERGIZER HOLDINGS, INC.; *pg.* 637, *pg.* 996
HARDCOPY - ASIC Device - ALTERA CORPORATION; *pg.* 348, *pg.* 237
HARDCORE - Perforated Plate - BUFFALO WIRE WORKS CO., INC.; *pg.* 72, *pg.* 1147
HARDCORE CIDER COMPANY - Brewer - THE BOSTON BEER COMPANY, INC.; *pg.* 239, *pg.* 790
HARDEE'S - Quick Service Restaurant - CKE RESTAURANTS INC.; *pg.* 1723, *pg.* 63
HARDEN - Furniture - HARDEN FURNITURE INC.; *pg.* 926, *pg.* 1177
HARDENED LOK-DOWELS - Press Fit Fastener - DRIV-LOK, INC.; *pg.* 1046, *pg.* 662
HARDI-CUBE - Salt - CARGILL LIMITED; *pg.* 1475, *pg.* 1914
HARDIGG - Company Name - PELICAN PRODUCTS; *pg.* 1467, *pg.* 843
HARDINGE CHNC II SUPER-PRECISION - Machinery - HARDINGE INC.; *pg.* 1344, *pg.* 1157
HARDITRIM - Nail - W.H. MAZE COMPANY; *pg.* 1389, *pg.* 652
HARDLOCK - Metal Locks & Keys - SPECIALIZED BICYCLE COMPONENTS, INC.; *pg.* 1711, *pg.* 152
HARDLOCK RAPPER - Lock - SPECIALIZED BICYCLE COMPONENTS, INC.; *pg.* 1711, *pg.* 152
HARDROCK - Bicycle - SPECIALIZED BICYCLE COMPONENTS, INC.; *pg.* 1711, *pg.* 152
HARDROCK'R - Bicycle Accessories - SPECIALIZED BICYCLE COMPONENTS, INC.; *pg.* 1711, *pg.* 152
HARDTOP KOOZIE - Case - BROWN & BIGELOW, INC.; *pg.* 1624, *pg.* 959
HARDWARE EXPRESS - Hardware Products - INTERLINE BRANDS, INC.; *pg.* 1051, *pg.* 433
HARDWARE MODELING LIBRARY - Software System - MENTOR GRAPHICS CORPORATION; *pg.* 432, *pg.* 1510
HARDWEAR - Upholstery & Wall Coverings Fabric - STEELCASE INC.; *pg.* 475, *pg.* 889
HARDWOOD - Cap - BROWN & BIGELOW, INC.; *pg.* 1624, *pg.* 959
HARDWOOD CLASSICS - Cap - NEW ERA CAP COMPANY INC.; *pg.* 1840, *pg.* 1155
HARDWOOD GREEN - Cap - BROWN & BIGELOW, INC.; *pg.* 1624, *pg.* 959
HARDY - Salt - CARGILL LIMITED; *pg.* 1475, *pg.* 1914
HARGROVE - Furniture - ASHLEY FURNITURE INDUSTRIES, INC.; *pg.* 914, *pg.* 1852
HARK - Soundbites of Quotes Site - SPINMEDIA; *pg.* 1282, *pg.* 104
HARKLASE - Pressed & Monolithic Refractory - RESCO PRODUCTS, INC.; *pg.* 107, *pg.* 1581
HARLEQUIN - Publisher - HARLEQUIN ENTERPRISES LIMITED; *pg.* 1647, *pg.* 1938
HARLEQUIN - Orange Liqueur - HEAVEN HILL DISTILLERIES, INC.; *pg.* 1964, *pg.* 725
HARLEQUIN - Furniture - JASPER GROUP; *pg.* 930, *pg.* 691
HARLEQUIN - Manual - XEROX CORPORATION; *pg.* 494, *pg.* 365
HARLEQUIN HISTORICALS - Romance Paperbacks - HARLEQUIN MAGAZINES INC; *pg.* 1647, *pg.* 1237
HARLEY-DAVIDSON - Motorcycle - HARLEY-DAVIDSON, INC.; *pg.* 178, *pg.* 1874
HARLEY-DAVIDSON - Footwear - WOLVERINE WORLD WIDE, INC.; *pg.* 1822, *pg.* 905
HARLEY OWNERS GROUP - Enthusiast Club - HARLEY-DAVIDSON, INC.; *pg.* 178, *pg.* 1874
HARMAN KARDON - Components - HARMAN CONSUMER, INC.; *pg.* 641, *pg.* 1355
HARMAN/KARDON - Audio & Video Products - HARMAN INTERNATIONAL INDUSTRIES, INCORPORATED; *pg.* 641, *pg.* 374
HARMON - Building Glass - APOGEE ENTERPRISES, INC.; *pg.* 67, *pg.* 930
HARMON HOMES - Home Advertising Guide - DOMINION ENTERPRISES; *pg.* 1636, *pg.* 1796
HARMONHOMES.COM - House Search Website - DOMINION ENTERPRISES; *pg.* 1636, *pg.* 1796
HARMONIC SCALPEL - Healthcare Product - JOHNSON & JOHNSON; *pg.* 1549, *pg.* 1091
HARMONIX - Materials Mapping - VEECO INSTRUMENTS INC.; *pg.* 1434, *pg.* 1322
HARMONIZER - Scale Stabilizing Software - AVERY WEIGH-TRONIX, INC.; *pg.* 1315, *pg.* 925
HARMONIZER - Positive Pressure Ventilation Unit - CTB INTERNATIONAL CORP.; *pg.* 850, *pg.* 695
HARMONY - Laminated Roofing Shingles - BUILDING PRODUCTS OF CANADA CORP.; *pg.* 72, *pg.* 1951
HARMONY - Rug - COURISTAN INC.; *pg.* 921, *pg.* 1067
HARMONY - Contact Center Solutions - CX ACT, INC.; *pg.* 1394, *pg.* 1773
HARMONY - Snack Nuts - DIAMOND FOODS, INC.; *pg.* 1851, *pg.* 216
HARMONY - Herbicide - E.I. DU PONT DE NEMOURS & COMPANY; *pg.* 1159, *pg.* 390
HARMONY - Software & Hardware - EVANS & SUTHERLAND COMPUTER CORPORATION; *pg.* 638, *pg.* 1757
HARMONY - Wafer Probe Card - FORMFACTOR, INC.; *pg.* 1882, *pg.* 122
HARMONY - Video - GAIAM, INC.; *pg.* 1532, *pg.* 334
HARMONY - Blood Glucose Monitoring System - LIFESCAN INC; *pg.* 1556, *pg.* 146
HARMONY - Sequencer - LOCHINVAR CORPORATION; *pg.* 1073, *pg.* 1640
HARMONY - Fabric - NEUTRAL POSTURE, INC.; *pg.* 939, *pg.* 1669
HARMONY - Software - PARAMETRIC TECHNOLOGY CORPORATION; *pg.* 452, *pg.* 835
HARMONY - Footwear - P.W. MINOR & SON, INC.; *pg.* 1816, *pg.* 1140
HARMONY - Lighting Product - QUOIZEL INC.; *pg.* 1304, *pg.* 1616
HARMONY - Seat Cushion - THE ROHO GROUP; *pg.* 1591, *pg.* 556
HARMONY - Paint - THE SHERWIN-WILLIAMS COMPANY; *pg.* 1447, *pg.* 1435
HARMONY - Innerspace - STANLEY BLACK & DECKER, INC.; *pg.* 1063, *pg.* 358
HARMONY - Equipment Management System - STERIS CORPORATION; *pg.* 1597, *pg.* 1464
HARMONY - Personal Care Product - WESTROCK COMPANY; *pg.* 1472, *pg.* 1805
HARMONY ASR - Software - RUDOLPH TECHNOLOGIES, INC.; *pg.* 669, *pg.* 918
HARMONY COLLECTION - Wallcovering - OMNOVA SOLUTIONS INC; *pg.* 1176, *pg.* 1453
HARMSCO - Filter Wraps - LILYPONS WATER GARDENS INC.; *pg.* 1797, *pg.* 766
HARNESS - Herbicide - MONSANTO COMPANY; *pg.* 1173, *pg.* 999
HAROCOL - Apparel Interlining - HARODITE INDUSTRIES, INC.; *pg.* 693, *pg.* 847
HAROFILM - Apparel Interlining - HARODITE INDUSTRIES, INC.; *pg.* 693, *pg.* 847
HAROFIT - Apparel Interlining - HARODITE INDUSTRIES, INC.; *pg.* 693, *pg.* 847
HAROFORM - Apparel Interlining - HARODITE INDUSTRIES, INC.; *pg.* 693, *pg.* 847
HARONET - Apparel Interlining - HARODITE INDUSTRIES, INC.; *pg.* 693, *pg.* 847
HAROPRESS - Apparel Interlining - HARODITE INDUSTRIES, INC.; *pg.* 693, *pg.* 847
HAROSHAPE - Apparel Interlining - HARODITE

First page reference indicates Business Class Edition
Second page reference indicates Geographic Edition

INDUSTRIES, INC.; pg. 693, pg. 847
HAROSTRETCH - Apparel Interlining - HARODITE INDUSTRIES, INC.; pg. 693, pg. 847
HAROT - Kosher Poultry - EMPIRE KOSHER POULTRY, INC.; pg. 854, pg. 1553
HAROWE - Housed & Frameless Resolver - DANAHER CORPORATION; pg. 1044, pg. 397
HARPER - Women's Clothing & Accessories - WOODEN SHIPS OF HOBOKEN; pg. 35, pg. 1315
HARPER DESIGN INTERNATONAL - Books - HARPERCOLLINS PUBLISHERS INC.; pg. 1647, pg. 1237
HARPERAUDIO - Audio Books - HARPERCOLLINS PUBLISHERS INC.; pg. 1647, pg. 1237
HARPERBUSINESS - Books - HARPERCOLLINS PUBLISHERS INC.; pg. 1647, pg. 1237
HARPERCOLLINS - Books - HARPERCOLLINS PUBLISHERS INC.; pg. 1647, pg. 1237
HARPERENTERTAINMENT - Books - HARPERCOLLINS PUBLISHERS INC.; pg. 1647, pg. 1237
HARPERFESTIVAL - Books - HARPERCOLLINS PUBLISHERS INC.; pg. 1647, pg. 1237
HARPERLARGEPRINT - Books - HARPERCOLLINS PUBLISHERS INC.; pg. 1647, pg. 1237
HARPERRESOURCE - Books - HARPERCOLLINS PUBLISHERS INC.; pg. 1647, pg. 1237
HARPER'S BAZAAR - Magazine - THE HEARST CORPORATION; pg. 1649, pg. 1239
HARPER'S INDEX - Editorial Magazine Feature - HARPER'S MAGAZINE FOUNDATION; pg. 1648, pg. 1238
HARPER'S MAGAZINE - Magazine - HARPER'S MAGAZINE FOUNDATION; pg. 1648, pg. 1238
HARPERSANFRANCISCO - Books - HARPERCOLLINS PUBLISHERS INC.; pg. 1647, pg. 1237
HARPERTEMPEST - Books - HARPERCOLLINS PUBLISHERS INC.; pg. 1647, pg. 1237
HARPERTORCH - Books - HARPERCOLLINS PUBLISHERS INC.; pg. 1647, pg. 1237
HARPERTROPHY - Books - HARPERCOLLINS PUBLISHERS INC.; pg. 1647, pg. 1237
HARPIC - Toilet Cleaner - RECKITT BENCKISER INC.; pg. 1136, pg. 1105
HARPOON - Conveyor - PRAB, INC.; pg. 1369, pg. 894
HARP'S FOOD STORE - Retail Groceries - HARPS FOOD STORES, INC.; pg. 1022, pg. 35
HARRAH'S - Casino - CAESARS ENTERTAINMENT CORPORATION; pg. 1083, pg. 1023
HARRINGTON - Fabric - NEMSCHOFF, INC.; pg. 936, pg. 1890
HARRINGTON - Lighting Product - QUOIZEL INC.; pg. 1304, pg. 1616
HARRIS - Paint - AKZONOBEL DECORATIVE PAINTS U.S.; pg. 1439, pg. 1474
HARRIS - Furniture - ETHAN ALLEN INTERIORS INC.; pg. 924, pg. 343
HARRIS - Communications & Information Technology - HARRIS CORPORATION; pg. 642, pg. 439
HARRIS - Laser Gas Delivery System - THE HARRIS PRODUCTS GROUP; pg. 1345, pg. 533
HARRIS - Shear - HARRIS WASTE MANAGEMENT GROUP, INC.; pg. 1345, pg. 526
HARRIS ADVANTEDGE - Investment Service - BMO HARRIS BANK N.A.; pg. 725, pg. 567
HARRIS TEETER - Food Product - HARRIS TEETER, INC.; pg. 1022, pg. 1383
HARRIS TEETER NATURALS - Food Product - HARRIS TEETER, INC.; pg. 1022, pg. 1383
HARRISDIRECT - Investment Service - BMO HARRIS BANK N.A.; pg. 725, pg. 567
HARRISON - Shoes - ALLEN-EDMONDS SHOE CORP.; pg. 1804, pg. 1887
HARRISON - Leather Products - COACH, INC.; pg. 3, pg. 1214
THE HARRISON SHOPPER - Coverage Shopping Guide - CYNTHIANA PUBLISHING CO.; pg. 1632, pg. 726
HARRITON - Apparel - BRODER BROS., CO.; pg. 1828, pg. 1588
HARRY & DAVID - Wholesale Rose Producer - HARRY & DAVID HOLDINGS, INC.; pg. 1022, pg. 1499
HARRY LONDON - Confections - 1-800-FLOWERS.COM, INC.; pg. 1758, pg. 1151
HARRY WINSTON - Precious Jewelry - HARRY WINSTON, INC.; pg. 6, pg. 1238
HARRY'S CRESTVIEW GROVES - Food Products - STANDEX INTERNATIONAL CORPORATION; pg. 60, pg. 1039
HARRY'S PREMIUM SNACKS - Snack Food Products - THE HAIN CELESTIAL GROUP, INC.; pg. 860, pg. 1172
HARSH - Truck Hoist - HARSH INTERNATIONAL, INC.; pg. 1345, pg. 324
HART SCIENTIFIC - Calibrating Thermometer - DANAHER CORPORATION; pg. 1044, pg. 397
HARTASIST - Specialty Dispersants - HUNTSMAN CORPORATION; pg. 1167, pg. 1758
HARTCO - Wood Flooring Products - ARMSTRONG WORLD INDUSTRIES, INC.; pg. 914, pg. 1545
HARTCO - Pneumatic Tool - STANLEY BLACK & DECKER, INC.; pg. 1063, pg. 358
HARTELL - Fluid Control Product - MILTON ROY COMPANY; pg. 1361, pg. 1542
HARTFORD - Furniture - FLEXSTEEL INDUSTRIES, INC.; pg. 925, pg. 707
HARTLAND - Kitchen Product - KOHLER CO.; pg. 91, pg. 1862
HARTLEY - Furniture - HOOKER FURNITURE CORPORATION; pg. 928, pg. 1788
HARTLEY - Automatic Bond Determinator - SIMPSON TECHNOLOGIES CORPORATION; pg. 111, pg. 555
HARTMANN - Luggage, Business Cases & Personal Leather Goods - BROWN-FORMAN CORPORATION; pg. 1958, pg. 732
HARTMANN - Luggage - SAMSONITE CORPORATION; pg. 11, pg. 830
HARTNEY - Dress Shoes - JOHNSTON & MURPHY CO.; pg. 1810, pg. 1651
HARTON - Footwear - VANS, INC.; pg. 1821, pg. 76
HART'S - Turf Foods - THE CHAS. C. HART SEED CO.; pg. 1794, pg. 384
HART'S ATHLETIC CLUBS - Fitness Centers - 24 HOUR FITNESS WORLDWIDE INC.; pg. 526, pg. 258
HARTWELL - Upholstery - ETHAN ALLEN INTERIORS INC.; pg. 924, pg. 343
HARTZ - Pet Supplies - THE HARTZ MOUNTAIN CORP.; pg. 1476, pg. 1120
HARTZ - Branded Seeds - MONSANTO COMPANY; pg. 1173, pg. 999
HARTZ - Pet Product - PETSMART, INC.; pg. 1481, pg. 18
HARTZ AT PLAY - Pet Toys - THE HARTZ MOUNTAIN CORP.; pg. 1476, pg. 1120
HARTZ DENTAL - Dental Products for Dogs - THE HARTZ MOUNTAIN CORP.; pg. 1476, pg. 1120
HARTZ LIVING - Pet Accessories - THE HARTZ MOUNTAIN CORP.; pg. 1476, pg. 1120
HARTZ NUTRITION - Pet Nutritional Products - THE HARTZ MOUNTAIN CORP.; pg. 1476, pg. 1120
HARU - Restaurant - BENIHANA INC.; pg. 1716, pg. 409
HARU NO MINT SHUKAN - Beverages - THE COCA-COLA COMPANY; pg. 240, pg. 493
HARVADE - Polymer Product - CHEMTURA CORPORATION; pg. 1152, pg. 355
HARVARD - Sporting Good Product - ESCALADE INC.; pg. 1833, pg. 678
HARVARD UNIVERSITY PRESS - Book Publishers - HARVARD UNIVERSITY PRESS; pg. 1648, pg. 808
HARVEL PLASTICS - Pipe - DETREX CORPORATION; pg. 1156, pg. 906
HARVEST - Starch Modifiers - THE DOW CHEMICAL COMPANY; pg. 1157, pg. 898
HARVEST - Candle - THE YANKEE CANDLE COMPANY, INC.; pg. 1792, pg. 843
HARVEST CAMOMILE - Herb Tea - CELESTIAL SEASONINGS, INC.; pg. 846, pg. 310
HARVEST CRUNCH - Cereal - PEPSICO, INC.; pg. 259, pg. 1327
HARVEST CRUNCH - Cereal - THE QUAKER OATS COMPANY; pg. 834, pg. 588
HARVEST FOODS - Food Store - URM STORES, INC.; pg. 1036, pg. 1844
HARVEST GARDEN HOSE - Lawn & Garden Care - TRACTOR SUPPLY COMPANY; pg. 708, pg. 1627
HARVEST GROVE - Food & Gifts - COLLIN STREET BAKERY; pg. 1851, pg. 1672
HARVEST HEFEWEIZEN - Beer - BJ'S RESTAURANTS, INC.; pg. 1716, pg. 104
HARVEST KING - Tire - TBC CORPORATION; pg. 1889, pg. 457
HARVEST MOON - Foods - SENECA FOODS CORPORATION; pg. 895, pg. 1177
HARVEST RECIPE - Bread - ROMAN MEAL COMPANY; pg. 834, pg. 1845
HARVEST SUPREME - Agricultural Products - TRACTOR SUPPLY COMPANY; pg. 708, pg. 1627
HARVEST TAN - Furniture - BUSH INDUSTRIES INC.; pg. 919, pg. 1170
HARVEST VALLEY - Juices - GORDON FOOD SERVICE INC.; pg. 1021, pg. 913
HARVESTER PRO - Software - CHYRONHEGO; pg. 371, pg. 1179
HARVESTERS - Domestic Cigars - ALTADIS USA, INC.; pg. 1893, pg. 423
HARVESTLAB - Agricultural Equipment - DEERE & COMPANY; pg. 703, pg. 632
HARVESTPAK - Fibre Drum - GREIF INC.; pg. 1459, pg. 1447
HARVEY - Furniture - LA-Z-BOY INCORPORATED; pg. 932, pg. 901
HARVEY - Stethoscope - WELCH ALLYN INC.; pg. 1436, pg. 1342
HARVEY ELITE - Cardiology Stethoscope - MEDLINE INDUSTRIES, INC.; pg. 1562, pg. 635
HARVEY ELITE - Stethoscope - WELCH ALLYN INC.; pg. 1436, pg. 1342
HARVEY PENICK - Golf Equipment - GOLFSMITH INTERNATIONAL HOLDINGS, INC.; pg. 1835, pg. 1662
HARVEYS - Casino - CAESARS ENTERTAINMENT CORPORATION; pg. 1083, pg. 1023
HARVEY'S - Hamburger Restaurants - CARA OPERATIONS LIMITED; pg. 1720, pg. 1947
HARVEYS - Sherry - JIM BEAM BRANDS CO.; pg. 1965, pg. 601
HASBRO GAMES - Toy & Game - HASBRO, INC.; pg. 954, pg. 1603
HASH ROUNDS - Breakfast Potatoes - HARDEES FOOD SYSTEMS, INC.; pg. 1731, pg. 998
HASK - Hair Treatment Products - INSPIRED BEAUTY BRANDS; pg. 512, pg. 1244
HASKEL - Hydraulic & Pneumatic Systems - MILTON ROY COMPANY; pg. 1361, pg. 1542
HASKELL PLACE - Shirts - ABERCROMBIE & FITCH CO.; pg. 37, pg. 1466
HASLER - Electric & Electronic Communication Systems - HASLER, INC.; pg. 1459, pg. 356
HASSEL FREE BANKING FOR BUSY PEOPLE - Slogan - PROVIDENT FINANCIAL SERVICES, INC.; pg. 796, pg. 1075
HASSLE FREE - Footwear - RED WING SHOE COMPANY, INC.; pg. 1817, pg. 954
HASTELLOY - Heat Exchanger - LYTRON INCORPORATED; pg. 1074, pg. 861
HASTINGS - Filters - BALDWIN FILTERS; pg. 1316, pg. 1011
HASTINGS - Dinnerware - THE HOMER LAUGHLIN CHINA COMPANY; pg. 1125, pg. 1850
HAT TRICK - Textiles - BERNHARDT DESIGN; pg. 918, pg. 1381
HAT ZONE - Headwear - GENESCO INC.; pg. 1809, pg. 1650
HATBOX - Bath Product - KOHLER CO.; pg. 91, pg. 1862
HATCH - Security Product - BAE SYSTEMS PRODUCTS GROUP; pg. 359, pg. 432
THE HATCHET - Saw - MILWAUKEE ELECTRIC TOOL CORP.; pg. 1056, pg. 1855
HATCHET WIRE - Eyewear - OAKLEY, INC.; pg. 1840, pg. 86
HATFIELD - Fresh Pork, Hams, Bacon, Sausage - HATFIELD QUALITY MEATS, INC.; pg. 861, pg. 1537
HATS OFF TO OUR HEROES - Honoring Everyday Local Heroes Program - CLEVELAND BROWNS FOOTBALL COMPANY LLC; pg. 541, pg. 1406
HATTERAS - Yachts - HATTERAS YACHTS; pg. 1708, pg. 1386
HATWORLD - Headwear - GENESCO INC.; pg. 1809, pg. 1650
HAUCK PULSE FIRING SYSTEM - Burner Control & Management Combustion System - HAUCK MANUFACTURING COMPANY, INC.; pg. 1345, pg. 1522
HAUL ICE - Cooler - IGLOO PRODUCTS CORPORATION; pg. 1126, pg. 1724
HAUL N CASH - Video Game - INTERNATIONAL GAME TECHNOLOGY; pg. 957, pg. 1024
HAUSER - Grinding Machine - HARDINGE INC.; pg. 1344, pg. 1157
HAUSMANN - Clinical Furniture - ALIMED, INC.; pg. 1490, pg. 816
HAUSTED - Stretcher - STERIS CORPORATION; pg. 1597,

pg. 1464
HAUTE COTURE - Tile - ARTISTIC TILE INC.; *pg.* 914, *pg.* 1119
HAVABLACK - Chemical Products - HAVILAND ENTERPRISES INC.; *pg.* 1165, *pg.* 887
HAVABOND - Chemical Products - HAVILAND ENTERPRISES INC.; *pg.* 1165, *pg.* 887
HAVAHART - Pest Control - THE WOODSTREAM CORPORATION; *pg.* 1801, *pg.* 1549
HAVANA - Fabric - NEMSCHOFF, INC.; *pg.* 936, *pg.* 1890
HAVANA BLEND - Cigars - FINCK CIGAR CO.; *pg.* 1894, *pg.* 1740
HAVANERA CO. - Apparel - PERRY ELLIS INTERNATIONAL, INC.; *pg.* 45, *pg.* 445
HAVASOL - Chemical Products - HAVILAND ENTERPRISES INC.; *pg.* 1165, *pg.* 887
HAVASTRIP - Chemical Products - HAVILAND ENTERPRISES INC.; *pg.* 1165, *pg.* 887
HAVE A BALL! - Tagline - ILLINOIS STATE LOTTERY; *pg.* 995, *pg.* 578
HAVE A TEMPURA TAN-TRUM - Nail Care Product - OPI PRODUCTS INC.; *pg.* 518, *pg.* 167
HAVE IT YOUR WAY - Slogan - BURGER KING CORPORATION; *pg.* 1719, *pg.* 440
HAVE LITE - Systems Integration & Aeronautics - LOCKHEED MARTIN CORPORATION; *pg.* 229, *pg.* 762
HAVE YOU HAD YOUR PROTEIN TODAY - Tag Line - TYSON FOODS, INC.; *pg.* 902, *pg.* 35
HAVEITALL - Software - BIO-RAD LABORATORIES, INC.; *pg.* 1504, *pg.* 101
HAVELOCK NEWS - North Carolina Newspaper - FREEDOM COMMUNICATIONS, INC.; *pg.* 1643, *pg.* 110
HAVEN HOME MEDIA - Home Improvement Network - THE READER'S DIGEST ASSOCIATION, INC.; *pg.* 1679, *pg.* 1322
HAVERHILL - Furniture - ASHLEY FURNITURE INDUSTRIES, INC.; *pg.* 914, *pg.* 1852
HAVILAND - Chocolate - NEW ENGLAND CONFECTIONERY COMPANY INC.; *pg.* 1860, *pg.* 842
HAVOC - Insecticide - KENT NUTRITION GROUP; *pg.* 1477, *pg.* 710
HAVOLINE - Motor Oil - CHEVRON CORPORATION; *pg.* 974, *pg.* 259
HAVPRO - Personal Vibration Monitors - 3M DETECTION SOLUTIONS; *pg.* 1398, *pg.* 1885
HAWAI - Beverages - THE COCA-COLA COMPANY; *pg.* 240, *pg.* 493
HAWAII - Magazine - I-5 PUBLISHING LLC; *pg.* 1651, *pg.* 133
HAWAII - Eyewear - MAUI JIM, INC.; *pg.* 9, *pg.* 651
HAWAII ARMOUR - Apparels - UNDER ARMOUR, INC.; *pg.* 49, *pg.* 759
HAWAII, THE ISLANDS OF ALOHA - Tourism - HAWAII VISITORS & CONVENTION BUREAU; *pg.* 994, *pg.* 543
HAWAIIAN - Pizza - DONATOS PIZZERIA CORPORATION; *pg.* 1727, *pg.* 1439
HAWAIIAN AIRLINES - Air Carrier - HAWAIIAN HOLDINGS, INC.; *pg.* 1910, *pg.* 544
HAWAIIAN BAMBOO - Sea Salt - NUTRACEUTICAL INTERNATIONAL CORPORATION; *pg.* 1576, *pg.* 1753
HAWAIIAN BLOSSOM - Honey - MILLER'S HONEY COMPANY; *pg.* 1860, *pg.* 1759
HAWAIIAN FRUIT DELIGHTS - Confections - LIBERTY ORCHARDS CO., INC.; *pg.* 1857, *pg.* 1819
HAWAIIAN ISLANDS TEA - Tea - HAWAII COFFEE COMPANY; *pg.* 861, *pg.* 543
HAWAIIAN MILES - Frequent Flyer Program - HAWAIIAN HOLDINGS, INC.; *pg.* 1910, *pg.* 544
HAWAIIAN PUNCH - Non-Carbonated Soft Drink - DR PEPPER SNAPPLE GROUP, INC.; *pg.* 250, *pg.* 1729
HAWAIIAN SUNDAE - Sundae - UNITED DAIRY FARMERS, INC.; *pg.* 906, *pg.* 1426
HAWAIIAN SUNSET - Video Game - INTERNATIONAL GAME TECHNOLOGY; *pg.* 957, *pg.* 1024
HAWAIIAN TROPIC - Sun Care - EDGEWELL PERSONAL CARE; *pg.* 1526, *pg.* 995
HAWCO - Bulk Material Handling - ANVIL ATTACHMENTS, LLC; *pg.* 1313, *pg.* 748
HAWG WASH - Power Tool - MILWAUKEE ELECTRIC TOOL CORP.; *pg.* 1056, *pg.* 1855
HAWK - Musical Instrument - GIBSON GUITAR CORP.; *pg.* 550, *pg.* 1650
HAWK - Power Tool - MILWAUKEE ELECTRIC TOOL CORP.; *pg.* 1056, *pg.* 1855
HAWK - Electronic Components - MOLEX INCORPORATED; *pg.* 655, *pg.* 628
HAWK - Truck Product - OSHKOSH CORPORATION; *pg.* 187, *pg.* 1885
HAWK - Skateboarding Shoes - QUIKSILVER, INC.; *pg.* 31, *pg.* 104
HAWK - Computer Software - TIBCO SOFTWARE INC.; *pg.* 484, *pg.* 178
HAWK/AMRAAM - Defense System - RAYTHEON COMPANY; *pg.* 233, *pg.* 854
HAWK CLOTHING - Boys' Apparel - QUIKSILVER, INC.; *pg.* 31, *pg.* 104
HAWK EYE - Golf Equipment - CALLAWAY GOLF COMPANY; *pg.* 1829, *pg.* 58
HAWK HILL - Bike - MARIN BIKES; *pg.* 1708, *pg.* 168
HAWKE - Electrical Product - HUBBELL INCORPORATED; *pg.* 1299, *pg.* 370
HAWKEN - Tobacco Product - AMERICAN SNUFF COMPANY; *pg.* 1893, *pg.* 1641
HAWKEN WINTERGREEN - Moist Tobacco - AMERICAN SNUFF COMPANY; *pg.* 1893, *pg.* 1641
HAWKER - Motive Power Batteries - ENERSYS INC.; *pg.* 1334, *pg.* 1584
HAWKEYE - Medical Equipment - CONMED CORPORATION; *pg.* 1517, *pg.* 1347
HAWKEYE - Film - EASTMAN KODAK COMPANY; *pg.* 1408, *pg.* 1333
HAWKEYE - Borescope - EDMUND INDUSTRIAL OPTICS INC.; *pg.* 1411, *pg.* 1041
HAWKEYE - Electronic Targeting Apparatus - LOCKHEED MARTIN CORPORATION; *pg.* 229, *pg.* 762
HAWKEYE - Bolt Action Rifles - STURM, RUGER & COMPANY, INC.; *pg.* 1846, *pg.* 371
HAWORTH - Furniture - HAWORTH, INC.; *pg.* 402, *pg.* 891
HAWORTH ARCHITECTURAL INTERIORS - Office Furniture - HAWORTH, INC.; *pg.* 402, *pg.* 891
HAWORTH HELPS YOU DESIGN GREAT - Slogan - HAWORTH, INC.; *pg.* 402, *pg.* 891
HAWS COMFORT CONTROL - Tempered Water - HAWS CORPORATION; *pg.* 56, *pg.* 1032
HAWTHORN - Table - BLATT BOWLING & BILLIARD CORP.; *pg.* 1827, *pg.* 1203
HAWTHORN SUITES - Hotels - WYNDHAM WORLDWIDE CORPORATION; *pg.* 1119, *pg.* 1107
HAWTHORNE - Furniture - BASSETT FURNITURE INDUSTRIES, INCORPORATED; *pg.* 916, *pg.* 1776
HAWTHORNE MOUNTAIN - Wine - CONSTELLATION BRANDS CANADA; *pg.* 1960, *pg.* 1925
HAWX - Ethernet Product - VITESSE SEMICONDUCTOR CORPORATION; *pg.* 686, *pg.* 57
HAYDEN - Table - BLATT BOWLING & BILLIARD CORP.; *pg.* 1827, *pg.* 1203
HAYDEN - Motor Product - STANDARD MOTOR PRODUCTS, INC.; *pg.* 218, *pg.* 1176
HAYES - Home & Garden Product - WESTROCK COMPANY; *pg.* 1472, *pg.* 1805
HAYES - ADSL Modem - ZOOM TECHNOLOGIES, INC.; *pg.* 497, *pg.* 1317
HAYES LEMMERZ...WE KEEP THE WORLD ROLLING - Slogan - MAXION WHEELS; *pg.* 212, *pg.* 903
HAYLON - Eyewear - OAKLEY, INC.; *pg.* 1840, *pg.* 86
HAYWIRE DELUXE - Slots - INTERNATIONAL GAME TECHNOLOGY; *pg.* 957, *pg.* 1024
HAYWOOD ESTATE - Wine - JIM BEAM BRANDS CO.; *pg.* 1965, *pg.* 601
HAZ-LO - Flashlight - STREAMLIGHT INC.; *pg.* 1306, *pg.* 1527
HAZARDGARD - Air Conditioner - FRIEDRICH AIR CONDITIONING CO.; *pg.* 1072, *pg.* 1740
HAZCAT - Hazardous Materials Training for Law Enforcement - ECOLOGY AND ENVIRONMENT, INC.; *pg.* 1410, *pg.* 1173
HAZEMAKER - Fog Product - ROSCO LABORATORIES, INC.; *pg.* 1782, *pg.* 378
HAZEN - Air Preheater - ABB INC.; *pg.* 1309, *pg.* 1359
HAZLUX - Lighting Fixture - THOMAS & BETTS CORPORATION; *pg.* 680, *pg.* 1646
HAZMAT - Apparel - OAKLEY, INC.; *pg.* 1840, *pg.* 86
HAZMATCAD - Gas Detection System - MINE SAFETY APPLIANCES COMPANY; *pg.* 1361, *pg.* 1525
HAZMAX - Containment Enclosure - HEMCO CORPORATION; *pg.* 1416, *pg.* 979
HAZTEX - Electronic Components - MOLEX INCORPORATED; *pg.* 655, *pg.* 628
HAZWOPER - Hazardous Waste Operations & Emergency Response Law Enforcement Course - ECOLOGY AND ENVIRONMENT, INC.; *pg.* 1410, *pg.* 1173
HAZZARD - Footwear - STEVEN MADDEN, LTD.; *pg.* 1819, *pg.* 1176
HB - Steel - A. FINKL & SONS CO.; *pg.* 1309, *pg.* 563
HB ADVISOR - Software - BIO-RAD LABORATORIES, INC.; *pg.* 1504, *pg.* 101
H.B. SCOTT'S - Tobacco Product - AMERICAN SNUFF COMPANY; *pg.* 1893, *pg.* 1641
HBANYWARE - Software - EMULEX CORPORATION; *pg.* 392, *pg.* 70
HBC.COM - Merchandise Store - HUDSON'S BAY COMPANY; *pg.* 1773, *pg.* 1938
HBH - Pet Product - PETSMART, INC.; *pg.* 1481, *pg.* 18
HBK - Banking Software - JACK HENRY & ASSOCIATES, INC.; *pg.* 422, *pg.* 988
HBMT - Electronic Components - MOLEX INCORPORATED; *pg.* 655, *pg.* 628
HBO - Pay Television Service - HOME BOX OFFICE, INC.; *pg.* 290, *pg.* 1240
HBO - Entertainment Product - TIME WARNER INC.; *pg.* 312, *pg.* 1302
HBO COMEDY - Cable Television Station - HOME BOX OFFICE, INC.; *pg.* 290, *pg.* 1240
HBO EXPRESS - Cable Television Station - HOME BOX OFFICE, INC.; *pg.* 290, *pg.* 1240
HBO FAMILY - Cable Television Station - HOME BOX OFFICE, INC.; *pg.* 290, *pg.* 1240
HBO LATINO - Cable Television Station - HOME BOX OFFICE, INC.; *pg.* 290, *pg.* 1240
HBO/MAX PAK - Movie Channel - HOME BOX OFFICE, INC.; *pg.* 290, *pg.* 1240
HBO ON DEMAND - Cable Television Station - HOME BOX OFFICE, INC.; *pg.* 290, *pg.* 1240
HBO PPV - Cable Television Station - HOME BOX OFFICE, INC.; *pg.* 290, *pg.* 1240
HBO SIGNATURE - Cable Television Station - HOME BOX OFFICE, INC.; *pg.* 290, *pg.* 1240
HBO SPORTS - Cable Television Station - HOME BOX OFFICE, INC.; *pg.* 290, *pg.* 1240
HBO WORLD CHAMPIONSHIP BOXING - Cable Television Show - HOME BOX OFFICE, INC.; *pg.* 290, *pg.* 1240
HBO ZONE - Cable Television Station - HOME BOX OFFICE, INC.; *pg.* 290, *pg.* 1240
HBT - Transistor Wafers - KOPIN CORPORATION; *pg.* 425, *pg.* 847
HC-12 - Cosmetic Product - MERLE NORMAN COSMETICS, INC.; *pg.* 517, *pg.* 136
HC AIRFLO - Burner - MAXON CORPORATION; *pg.* 1359, *pg.* 695
HC&S - Sugar - ALEXANDER & BALDWIN, INC.; *pg.* 1079, *pg.* 543
HCF - Cable - AFC CABLE SYSTEMS, INC.; *pg.* 1294, *pg.* 835
HCF-90 - Health Care Facilities Cable - AFC CABLE SYSTEMS, INC.; *pg.* 1294, *pg.* 835
HCF-LITE - Health Care Facilities Cable - AFC CABLE SYSTEMS, INC.; *pg.* 1294, *pg.* 835
HCI - Host Command Interface Applications Package - MITEL NETWORKS CORPORATION; *pg.* 654, *pg.* 1921
HCL-145 - Bowl Cleaner - HILLYARD, INC.; *pg.* 331, *pg.* 990
HCLL - Transfusion Management System - MEDIWARE INFORMATION SYSTEMS, INC.; *pg.* 431, *pg.* 716
HCP - Sensor - HELWIG CARBON PRODUCTS, INC.; *pg.* 1346, *pg.* 1875
HCR - Steel Product - AK STEEL HOLDING CORPORATION; *pg.* 1311, *pg.* 1479
HCR MANOR CARE - Assisted Living Units - HCR MANORCARE, INC.; *pg.* 1539, *pg.* 1476
HD-3000 STL HYDRAULIC LEVELER - Fully-Hydraulic Dock Leveler with Automatic Safe-T-Lip Vehicle Barrier - RITE-HITE HOLDING CORPORATION; *pg.* 1372, *pg.* 1880
HD DIGITAL RADIO - Digital Satellite Radio - IBIQUITY DIGITAL CORPORATION; *pg.* 409, *pg.* 767
HD MEZZ - Electronic Components - MOLEX INCORPORATED; *pg.* 655, *pg.* 628
HD OIL - Chemical Product - BIRKO CORPORATION; *pg.* 1149, *pg.* 332
HD-OPTYX - Optical Connector - TERADYNE INC.; *pg.* 679, *pg.* 838
HD-OPTX - Connector - AMPHENOL CORPORATION; *pg.* 616, *pg.* 381
HD PVR - Digital Video Product - HAUPPAUGE DIGITAL, INC.; *pg.* 402, *pg.* 1164
HD RADIO - Satellite Radio - IBIQUITY DIGITAL CORPORATION; *pg.* 409, *pg.* 767

HDC - Heat Dissipation Cover - CHANNELL COMMERCIAL CORP.; *pg.* 1870, *pg.* 291
HDCONFERENCE - Software - CLEARONE COMMUNICATIONS, INC.; *pg.* 629, *pg.* 1756
HDI/ PULSEWAVE CR-2000 - Research Cardiovascular Profiling System - HYPERTENSION DIAGNOSTICS, INC.; *pg.* 1543, *pg.* 921
HDL - Bearing - THE TIMKEN COMPANY; *pg.* 218, *pg.* 1408
HDL ANALYST - Software - SYNOPSYS, INC.; *pg.* 480, *pg.* 162
HDL ARCHITECT - Software System - MENTOR GRAPHICS CORPORATION; *pg.* 432, *pg.* 1510
HDL ARCHITECT STATION - Software System - MENTOR GRAPHICS CORPORATION; *pg.* 432, *pg.* 1510
HDL ASSISTANT - Software System - MENTOR GRAPHICS CORPORATION; *pg.* 432, *pg.* 1510
HDL AUTHOR - Software System - MENTOR GRAPHICS CORPORATION; *pg.* 432, *pg.* 1510
HDL COMPILER - Software - SYNOPSYS, INC.; *pg.* 480, *pg.* 162
HDL DESIGNER - Software System - MENTOR GRAPHICS CORPORATION; *pg.* 432, *pg.* 1510
HDL DESIGNER SERIES - Software System - MENTOR GRAPHICS CORPORATION; *pg.* 432, *pg.* 1510
HDL DETECTIVE - Software System - MENTOR GRAPHICS CORPORATION; *pg.* 432, *pg.* 1510
HDL EXPLORER - Design Resources - LATTICE SEMICONDUCTOR CORPORATION; *pg.* 651, *pg.* 1498
HDL INVENTOR - Software System - MENTOR GRAPHICS CORPORATION; *pg.* 432, *pg.* 1510
HDL LINK - Software System - MENTOR GRAPHICS CORPORATION; *pg.* 432, *pg.* 1510
HDL PILOT - Software System - MENTOR GRAPHICS CORPORATION; *pg.* 432, *pg.* 1510
HDL PROCESSOR - Software System - MENTOR GRAPHICS CORPORATION; *pg.* 432, *pg.* 1510
HDL2GRAPHICS - Software System - MENTOR GRAPHICS CORPORATION; *pg.* 432, *pg.* 1510
HDLSCORE - Software System - MENTOR GRAPHICS CORPORATION; *pg.* 432, *pg.* 1510
HDLSIM - Software System - MENTOR GRAPHICS CORPORATION; *pg.* 432, *pg.* 1510
HDLWRITE - Software System - MENTOR GRAPHICS CORPORATION; *pg.* 432, *pg.* 1510
HDM - High-Density Metric - AMPHENOL CORPORATION; *pg.* 616, *pg.* 381
HDM - Power Module - TERADYNE INC.; *pg.* 679, *pg.* 838
HDM PLUS - High-Density Metric - AMPHENOL CORPORATION; *pg.* 616, *pg.* 381
HDMS - Mass Spectrometer - WATERS CORPORATION; *pg.* 1436, *pg.* 834
H.D.R - Conveyor Pulley - VAN GORP CORPORATION; *pg.* 1387, *pg.* 711
HDS - Drilling Product - SMITH INTERNATIONAL, INC.; *pg.* 1377, *pg.* 1715
HDSLX/T1 - Networking Product - ADTRAN, INC.; *pg.* 344, *pg.* 6
HDTV WONDER - Graphics Card - ADVANCED MICRO DEVICES, INC.; *pg.* 613, *pg.* 282
HDTV WONDER - PCI Card - ADVANCED MICRO DEVICES, INC.-MARKHAM; *pg.* 345, *pg.* 1922
HDX - Software - CITRIX SYSTEMS, INC.; *pg.* 375, *pg.* 424
HDX - Electronic Components - MOLEX INCORPORATED; *pg.* 655, *pg.* 628
HDX 4000 - Video Conferencing Product - POLYCOM, INC.; *pg.* 664, *pg.* 249
HDX 8000 - Video Conferencing Product - POLYCOM, INC.; *pg.* 664, *pg.* 249
HDX 9000 - Video Conferencing - POLYCOM, INC.; *pg.* 664, *pg.* 249
HE/SHE/THEY'RE COVERED IF YOU'RE COVERED - Slogan - SBLI USA LIFE INSURANCE COMPANY, INC.; *pg.* 1216, *pg.* 1288
HE950 - Proximity Sensor - ELECTRO-SENSORS, INC.; *pg.* 1333, *pg.* 948
HEAD & SHOULDERS - Shampoo - THE PROCTER & GAMBLE COMPANY; *pg.* 1129, *pg.* 1418
HEAD & SHOULDERS INTENSIVE TREATMENTS - Shampoo - THE PROCTER & GAMBLE COMPANY; *pg.* 1129, *pg.* 1418
HEAD FIRST - Bicycle Accessories - SPECIALIZED BICYCLE COMPONENTS, INC.; *pg.* 1711, *pg.* 152
HEAD START - Hair Salons - REGIS CORPORATION; *pg.* 521, *pg.* 941
HEADACHE - Pillow and Throw - HERITAGE LACE INC.; *pg.* 694, *pg.* 711
HEADER PAK - Plastic Bag - ELKAY PLASTICS COMPANY, INC.; *pg.* 1882, *pg.* 68
HEADLINER - Hair Trimmer - ANDIS COMPANY; *pg.* 498, *pg.* 1895
HEADMASTER - Vacuum - TORNADO INDUSTRIES, INC.; *pg.* 1383, *pg.* 591
HEADMASTERS/TASKFORCE - Wet/Dry Vacuums - TORNADO INDUSTRIES, INC.; *pg.* 1383, *pg.* 591
HEADS UP - Hair Grooms - THE GILLETTE COMPANY; *pg.* 509, *pg.* 795
HEADS UP - Toy & Game - HASBRO, INC.; *pg.* 954, *pg.* 1603
HEADSTART - Magnetic Nail Holder - VAUGHAN & BUSHNELL MANUFACTURING COMPANY, INC.; *pg.* 1066, *pg.* 616
HEADSUP LITE - Flashlight - PELICAN PRODUCTS, INC.; *pg.* 1842, *pg.* 295
HEADSWEATS - Cap - BROWN & BIGELOW, INC.; *pg.* 1624, *pg.* 959
HEADWATERS - Fishing Gear Product - SIMMS FISHING PRODUCTS CORP.; *pg.* 1845, *pg.* 1008
HEAL PAD - Cushion - THE ROHO GROUP; *pg.* 1591, *pg.* 556
HEALEY - Implant Product - ZIMMER BIOMET HOLDINGS, INC.; *pg.* 1611, *pg.* 699
HEALFLOAT - Support Surface Product - THE ROHO GROUP; *pg.* 1591, *pg.* 556
HEALINC - Telephone Service - IDT CORPORATION; *pg.* 643, *pg.* 1096
HEALING WITH LIGHT - Slogan - AMERICAN MEDICAL SYSTEMS, INC.; *pg.* 1399, *pg.* 238
HEALON - Medical Device - ABBOTT MEDICAL OPTICS, INC.; *pg.* 1485, *pg.* 260
HEALSPA - Healthcare Product - MEDICOOL, INC.; *pg.* 1562, *pg.* 294
HEALTH - Consumer Women's Healthy Lifestyle Publication - HEALTH MAGAZINE; *pg.* 1648, *pg.* 1238
HEALTH ADVANTAGE BY MEDICA - Health Plan & Publication - MEDICA, INC.; *pg.* 1208, *pg.* 949
HEALTH ALLWAYS - Hand Soap - BLUE CROSS LABORATORIES; *pg.* 326, *pg.* 277
HEALTH BIKE - Exerciser - BATTLE CREEK EQUIPMENT CO.; *pg.* 1499, *pg.* 870
HEALTH CARE IS OUR BUSINESS - Slogan - EXTENDICARE; *pg.* 1530, *pg.* 1923
HEALTH EPA - Health Care Product - HEALTH PRODUCTS CORPORATION; *pg.* 1540, *pg.* 1356
HEALTH ESSENTIALS - Pharmaceutical Product - ALERE INC.; *pg.* 1488, *pg.* 849
HEALTH FROM THE SUN - Nutritional Product - NUTRACEUTICAL INTERNATIONAL CORPORATION; *pg.* 1576, *pg.* 1753
HEALTH HAIR - Vitamins - HEALTH PRODUCTS CORPORATION; *pg.* 1540, *pg.* 1356
HEALTH INVESTMENT - Health Program - HEALTHPARTNERS, INC.; *pg.* 1203, *pg.* 918
HEALTH-KOTE - Paint & Coating - DIAMOND VOGEL PAINT, INC.; *pg.* 1441, *pg.* 710
HEALTH MART - Retail Network - MCKESSON CORPORATION; *pg.* 1560, *pg.* 222
HEALTH NET ELECT - Health Care Utilization - HEALTH NET, INC.; *pg.* 1540, *pg.* 308
HEALTH NET SELECT - Health Care Utilization - HEALTH NET, INC.; *pg.* 1540, *pg.* 308
HEALTH NET SENIORITY PLUS - Health Care - HEALTH NET, INC.; *pg.* 1540, *pg.* 308
HEALTH O METER - Digital Chair Scale - ALIMED, INC.; *pg.* 1490, *pg.* 816
HEALTH O METER - Massagers, Cushions & Foot Baths - HELEN OF TROY L.P.; *pg.* 511, *pg.* 1692
HEALTH-O-METER - Personal Health Products - JARDEN CONSUMER SOLUTIONS; *pg.* 57, *pg.* 412
HEALTH PRIDE - Personal Care Products - THE GREAT ATLANTIC & PACIFIC TEA COMPANY, INC.; *pg.* 1021, *pg.* 1086
HEALTH REST - Mattress - RESTONIC MATTRESS CORPORATION; *pg.* 941, *pg.* 553
HEALTH SMART - Soups, Chowders, Salad Dressings, Condiments - CAINS FOODS, L.P.; *pg.* 843, *pg.* 784
HEALTH SMART - Fat-free Stick - WELLS ENTERPRISES, INC.; *pg.* 909, *pg.* 709
HEALTH VALLEY - Food Product - THE HAIN CELESTIAL GROUP, INC.; *pg.* 860, *pg.* 1172
HEALTH WALKER - Treadmill - BATTLE CREEK EQUIPMENT CO.; *pg.* 1499, *pg.* 870
HEALTH WATCH - Emergency Response System - HEALTH WATCH INC.; *pg.* 1540, *pg.* 411
HEALTHCARE DOCUMENT CHECKUP & DESIGN - Manual - XEROX CORPORATION; *pg.* 494, *pg.* 365
THE HEALTHCARE QUALITY EXPERTS - Slogan - HEALTH GRADES, INC.; *pg.* 1256, *pg.* 319
THE HEALTHCARE RATINGS EXPERTS - Healthcare Product - HEALTH GRADES, INC.; *pg.* 1256, *pg.* 319
HEALTHCARE SERIES - Medical Information - TRUVEN HEALTH ANALYTICS; *pg.* 486, *pg.* 331
HEALTHCAREERWEB.COM - Advertising Website - DOMINION ENTERPRISES; *pg.* 1636, *pg.* 1796
HEALTHCONNECT - Health Plan & Publication - MEDICA, INC.; *pg.* 1208, *pg.* 949
HEALTHDRI - Diabetic Socks, Briefs & Panties - THE SALK COMPANY; *pg.* 1591, *pg.* 800
HEALTHDYNE - Pharmaceutical Product - ALERE INC.; *pg.* 1488, *pg.* 849
HEALTHEWARE - Application Software - TRIZETTO CORPORATION; *pg.* 485, *pg.* 327
HEALTHFLOW - Baby Care Product - MUNCHKIN, INC.; *pg.* 964, *pg.* 300
HEALTHGRADES.COM - Healthcare Product - HEALTH GRADES, INC.; *pg.* 1256, *pg.* 319
HEALTHIER, EASIER, SMARTER. - Slogan - ORECK CORPORATION; *pg.* 59, *pg.* 1653
HEALTHLINE - Shower Commode Chair - ALIMED, INC.; *pg.* 1490, *pg.* 816
HEALTHMARKET - Natural & Organic Product - HY-VEE, INC.; *pg.* 1023, *pg.* 713
HEALTHMATE COAST-TO-COAST - Health Product - BLUE CROSS & BLUE SHIELD OF RHODE ISLAND; *pg.* 1195, *pg.* 1606
HEALTHMINDER - Fragrance Dispenser - SLOAN VALVE COMPANY; *pg.* 1062, *pg.* 613
HEALTHMIST - Humidifier - KAZ, INC.; *pg.* 58, *pg.* 844
HEALTHPAK - Nutritional Supplement - USANA HEALTH SCIENCES, INC.; *pg.* 1605, *pg.* 1761
HEALTHPLEX - Sports Club - CROZER-KEYSTONE HEALTH SYSTEM INC.; *pg.* 1520, *pg.* 1587
HEALTHQUEST - Healthcare Information Technology System - MCKESSON CORPORATION; *pg.* 1560, *pg.* 222
HEALTHRIDER - Health & Fitness Product - ICON HEALTH & FITNESS, INC.; *pg.* 1837, *pg.* 1752
HEALTHRITE - Collections - HABAND COMPANY, INC.; *pg.* 1772, *pg.* 1099
HEALTHSAVER - Healthcare Savings Services - AFFINION GROUP, INC.; *pg.* 1225, *pg.* 372
HEALTHSHEETS - Health Literacy Library - GENTIVA HEALTH SERVICES, INC.; *pg.* 1534, *pg.* 506
HEALTHSMART - Revenue Cycle Integration Solution - CERNER CORPORATION; *pg.* 1514, *pg.* 981
HEALTHSMART - Kitchen Appliance - HAMILTON BEACH BRANDS, INC.; *pg.* 56, *pg.* 1783
HEALTHSTREAM - Software - NETSOL TECHNOLOGIES, INC.; *pg.* 1270, *pg.* 56
HEALTHSTREAM AUTHORING CENTER - Software - HEALTHSTREAM, INC.; *pg.* 1649, *pg.* 1651
HEALTHSTREAM EXPRESS - Software - HEALTHSTREAM, INC.; *pg.* 1649, *pg.* 1651
HEALTHTEAM - Healthcare Product - GF HEALTH PRODUCTS, INC.; *pg.* 1535, *pg.* 508
HEALTHTEX - Apparel - LT APPAREL GROUP; *pg.* 29, *pg.* 1254
HEALTHTRIO CONNECT - Software - HEALTHTRIO INC.; *pg.* 403, *pg.* 320
HEALTHTRIO XPRESS - Software - HEALTHTRIO INC.; *pg.* 403, *pg.* 320
HEALTHWATCH - Health & Safety Articles - JOHNSON MANUFACTURING COMPANY; *pg.* 1169, *pg.* 712
HEALTHWATCH - Software - SHOPPERS DRUG MART CORPORATION; *pg.* 1594, *pg.* 1943
HEALTHWEB - Software - TRIZETTO CORPORATION; *pg.* 485, *pg.* 327
HEALTHWISE HANDBOOK - Self Care Guide - HEALTHWISE, INCORPORATED; *pg.* 143, *pg.* 546
HEALTHWISE KNOWLEDGEBASE - Health Web Content - HEALTHWISE, INCORPORATED; *pg.* 143, *pg.* 546
HEALTHWORKS - Beverages - THE COCA-COLA COMPANY; *pg.* 240, *pg.* 493
HEALTHY ATTITUDES - Health Plan & Publication - MEDICA, INC.; *pg.* 1208, *pg.* 949
HEALTHY AVENUE - Health Plan & Publication - MEDICA, INC.; *pg.* 1208, *pg.* 949

HEALTHY BAKE - Frozen Seafood - HIGH LINER FOODS INCORPORATED; *pg.* 862, *pg.* 1917
HEALTHY BAKER - Dog Biscuit - PETEDGE; *pg.* 1481, *pg.* 787
HEALTHY BOOST - Beauty Product - AVON PRODUCTS, INC.; *pg.* 500, *pg.* 1198
HEALTHY CHOICE - Food Product - CONAGRA FOODS, INC.; *pg.* 826, *pg.* 1014
HEALTHY CLIPPINGS - Booklets - UNITED NATURAL FOODS, INC.; *pg.* 907, *pg.* 1608
HEALTHY DEFENSE - Skin Care Product - NEUTROGENA CORPORATION; *pg.* 517, *pg.* 137
HEALTHY FOODS, HEALTHY FAMILIES, HEALTHY BUSINESS. - Tagline - DEAN FOODS COMPANY; *pg.* 852, *pg.* 1679
HEALTHY GARDENS - Vegetable Gardening - GARDENS ALIVE!, INC.; *pg.* 1796, *pg.* 693
HEALTHY GROWING UP - Services - MCDONALD'S CORPORATION; *pg.* 1737, *pg.* 645
HEALTHY GUMS HEALTHY LIFE - Slogan - SUNSTAR AMERICAS INC.; *pg.* 1599, *pg.* 591
HEALTHY HOME - Healthcare Product - SWANSON HEALTH PRODUCTS INC.; *pg.* 1600, *pg.* 1397
HEALTHY KIDS EN ESPANOL - Spanish-Language Parenting Magazine - MEREDITH CORPORATION; *pg.* 1663, *pg.* 705
HEALTHY ONES - Meat Product - JOHN MORRELL FOOD GROUP; *pg.* 866, *pg.* 628
HEALTHY ONES - Food Products - SMITHFIELD FOODS, INC.; *pg.* 896, *pg.* 1806
HEALTHY PC - Software - SYMANTEC CORPORATION; *pg.* 478, *pg.* 161
HEALTHY POP - Microwave Pop Corn - AMERICAN POP CORN COMPANY; *pg.* 825, *pg.* 712
HEALTHY RELIEF - Medicine Product - SIMILASAN CORPORATION; *pg.* 1594, *pg.* 332
HEALTHY REQUEST - Soup - CAMPBELL SOUP COMPANY; *pg.* 844, *pg.* 1048
HEALTHY WAY - Bread - MAPLE LEAF FOODS INC.; *pg.* 875, *pg.* 1927
HEALTHY WOMAN - Healthcare Product - JOHNSON & JOHNSON; *pg.* 1549, *pg.* 1091
HEAR PLUGS - Earplug - MCKEON PRODUCTS, INC.; *pg.* 1559, *pg.* 912
HEARD ON THE STREET - Column Heading - DOW JONES & COMPANY, INC.; *pg.* 1637, *pg.* 1225
THE HEARING AIDER - Functional Communication - ALIMED, INC.; *pg.* 1490, *pg.* 816
HEARST ANIMATION PRODUCTIONS - T.V. Production - THE HEARST CORPORATION; *pg.* 1649, *pg.* 1239
HEARST ARGYLE TELEVISION PRODUCTIONS - Publisher - THE HEARST CORPORATION; *pg.* 1649, *pg.* 1239
HEARST BOOKS - Magazine - THE HEARST CORPORATION; *pg.* 1649, *pg.* 1239
HEARST EAGLE AWARDS - Newspaper - THE HEARST CORPORATION; *pg.* 1649, *pg.* 1239
HEARST ENTERTAINMENT DISTRIBUTION - T.V. Distribution - THE HEARST CORPORATION; *pg.* 1649, *pg.* 1239
HEARST ENTERTAINMENT PRODUCTIONS - T.V. Production - THE HEARST CORPORATION; *pg.* 1649, *pg.* 1239
HEARST INTERACTIVE MEDIA - Interactive Media - THE HEARST CORPORATION; *pg.* 1649, *pg.* 1239
HEARST NEWS SERVICE - News Wire Service - THE HEARST CORPORATION; *pg.* 1649, *pg.* 1239
HEART - Shampoo - THE GILLETTE COMPANY; *pg.* 509, *pg.* 795
HEART ADVISOR - Newsletter - BELVOIR MEDIA GROUP, LLC; *pg.* 1620, *pg.* 360
HEART & SOUL - Game - WMS INDUSTRIES INC.; *pg.* 593, *pg.* 666
HEART BREAKER - Slots - INTERNATIONAL GAME TECHNOLOGY; *pg.* 957, *pg.* 1024
THE HEART COLLECTION - Jewelry - LAGOS INC.; *pg.* 8, *pg.* 1566
HEART DEFENDER - Fruit Drink - JAMBA, INC.; *pg.* 1024, *pg.* 84
HEART-HEALTHY LIVING - Magazine - MEREDITH CORPORATION; *pg.* 1663, *pg.* 705
HEART N SOUL - Sandals - AEROGROUP INTERNATIONAL, INC.; *pg.* 1803, *pg.* 1055
HEART OF GOLD - Wholesale Wigs - SPECIALTY CATALOG CORPORATION; *pg.* 1786, *pg.* 856
HEART OF TEXAS - Video Game - INTERNATIONAL GAME TECHNOLOGY; *pg.* 957, *pg.* 1024
HEART OF THE HIDE - Baseball Gloves - RAWLINGS SPORTING GOODS CO., INC.; *pg.* 1843, *pg.* 1002
HEART OF THE WEST - Video Game - INTERNATIONAL GAME TECHNOLOGY; *pg.* 957, *pg.* 1024
HEART OF THE WIRELESS MACHINE - Slogan - SIERRA WIRELESS INCORPORATED; *pg.* 673, *pg.* 1909
HEART SCIENCE - Vitamin & Herbal Supplement - SOURCE NATURALS; *pg.* 1595, *pg.* 278
HEART SMART SOLUTIONS - Pharmaceutical Product - ALERE INC.; *pg.* 1488, *pg.* 849
HEART START - Defibrillator - PHILIPS HEALTHCARE; *pg.* 1585, *pg.* 783
HEART TO HEART - Scarf - HERITAGE LACE INC.; *pg.* 694, *pg.* 711
HEART TO HEART - Breakfast Cereal - KASHI COMPANY; *pg.* 830, *pg.* 119
HEART TO HEART OATMEAL - Oatmeal - KASHI COMPANY; *pg.* 830, *pg.* 119
HEART TO HEART WAFFLES - Waffles - KASHI COMPANY; *pg.* 830, *pg.* 119
HEARTBREAK HOTEL - Hotel - ELVIS PRESLEY ENTERPRISES, INC.; *pg.* 1090, *pg.* 1642
HEARTCENTRIX - Connectivity Solutions - CARDIAC SCIENCE CORPORATION; *pg.* 1512, *pg.* 1897
HEARTCODE - Software - HEALTHSTREAM, INC.; *pg.* 1649, *pg.* 1651
HEARTFELT - Carpet - INTERFACE, INC.; *pg.* 695, *pg.* 512
HEARTGARD PLUS - Pet Medication - PETMED EXPRESS, INC.; *pg.* 1781, *pg.* 460
HEARTH ESSENTIALS - Fireplace Tools & Accessories - DURAFLAME, INC.; *pg.* 1123, *pg.* 280
HEARTH HEADQUARTERS - Retail Store Services - 1-800-FLOWERS.COM, INC.; *pg.* 1758, *pg.* 1151
HEARTHSIDE SELECT - Food Product - ADVANCEPIERRE FOODS, INC.; *pg.* 1714, *pg.* 1409
HEARTHSONG - Toys - 1-800-FLOWERS.COM, INC.; *pg.* 1758, *pg.* 1151
HEARTHSOURCE - Retail Store Services - 1-800-FLOWERS.COM, INC.; *pg.* 1758, *pg.* 1151
HEARTHSTONE CLASSICS - Ready Made Food - GORDON FOOD SERVICE INC.; *pg.* 1021, *pg.* 913
HEARTLAND - Pasta - AMERICAN ITALIAN PASTA COMPANY; *pg.* 837, *pg.* 980
HEARTLAND - Rod - DAIWA CORPORATION; *pg.* 1832, *pg.* 75
HEARTLAND - Long Term Care Centers, Rehabilitation & Home Health Operations - HCR MANORCARE, INC.; *pg.* 1539, *pg.* 1476
HEARTLAND - Dinnerware - THE HOMER LAUGHLIN CHINA COMPANY; *pg.* 1125, *pg.* 1850
HEARTLAND CARD PROCESSING - Financial Services - HEARTLAND PAYMENT SYSTEMS, INC.; *pg.* 765, *pg.* 1111
HEARTLAND CHECK MANAGEMENT - Financial Services - HEARTLAND PAYMENT SYSTEMS, INC.; *pg.* 765, *pg.* 1111
HEARTLAND CONNECT - Financial Services - HEARTLAND PAYMENT SYSTEMS, INC.; *pg.* 765, *pg.* 1111
HEARTLAND EXPRESS FUNDS - Financial Services - HEARTLAND PAYMENT SYSTEMS, INC.; *pg.* 765, *pg.* 1111
HEARTLAND GIFT CARDS - Financial Services - HEARTLAND PAYMENT SYSTEMS, INC.; *pg.* 765, *pg.* 1111
HEARTLAND LAUNDRY SOLUTIONS - Financial Services - HEARTLAND PAYMENT SYSTEMS, INC.; *pg.* 765, *pg.* 1111
HEARTLAND LENDING SERVICES - Financial Services - HEARTLAND PAYMENT SYSTEMS, INC.; *pg.* 765, *pg.* 1111
HEARTLAND MICROPAYMENTS - Financial Services - HEARTLAND PAYMENT SYSTEMS, INC.; *pg.* 765, *pg.* 1111
HEARTLAND ONLINE MERCHANT CENTER - Financial Services - HEARTLAND PAYMENT SYSTEMS, INC.; *pg.* 765, *pg.* 1111
HEARTLAND ONLINE PAYMENT - Financial Services - HEARTLAND PAYMENT SYSTEMS, INC.; *pg.* 765, *pg.* 1111
HEARTLAND PAYMENT SYSTEMS - Financial Services - HEARTLAND PAYMENT SYSTEMS, INC.; *pg.* 765, *pg.* 1111
HEARTLAND PAYROLL SERVICES - Financial Services - HEARTLAND PAYMENT SYSTEMS, INC.; *pg.* 765, *pg.* 1111
HEARTLAND TABLE SIDE - Payment Processing - HEARTLAND PAYMENT SYSTEMS, INC.; *pg.* 765, *pg.* 1111
HEARTLAND WEB CONNECT - Financial Services - HEARTLAND PAYMENT SYSTEMS, INC.; *pg.* 765, *pg.* 1111
HEARTQUEST - Inspirational Romance Website - TYNDALE HOUSE PUBLISHERS, INC.; *pg.* 1697, *pg.* 561
HEARTS - Women's Clothing & Accessories - WOODEN SHIPS OF HOBOKEN; *pg.* 35, *pg.* 1315
HEARTS AND BERRIES - Fruit Arrangements - EDIBLE ARRANGEMENTS INTERNATIONAL, INC.; *pg.* 1768, *pg.* 382
HEARTS AND KISSES - Fruit Arrangements - EDIBLE ARRANGEMENTS INTERNATIONAL, INC.; *pg.* 1768, *pg.* 382
HEARTS & KISSES BOUQUET - Floral Bouquet - FTD GROUP, INC.; *pg.* 1795, *pg.* 608
HEARTS ARE WILD - Lottery Game - MASSACHUSETTS STATE LOTTERY; *pg.* 998, *pg.* 802
HEARTS DESIRE BEACH - Bike - MARIN BIKES; *pg.* 1708, *pg.* 168
HEARTS OF VENICE - Game - WMS INDUSTRIES INC.; *pg.* 593, *pg.* 666
HEARTSTART - Home Defibrillator - PHILIPS ELECTRONICS NORTH AMERICA; *pg.* 662, *pg.* 782
HEARTSTRIDE - Exercise Stress System - CARDIAC SCIENCE CORPORATION; *pg.* 1512, *pg.* 1897
HEARTWOOD CREEK BY JIM SHORE - Home & Garden Product - ENESCO, LLC; *pg.* 1124, *pg.* 620
HEARTWORKS - Diagnostic Workstation - CARDIAC SCIENCE CORPORATION; *pg.* 1512, *pg.* 1897
HEARTY - Animal Nutrition Product - MANNA PRO CORPORATION; *pg.* 1478, *pg.* 975
HEARTY BAVARIAN - Mustard - PLOCHMAN, INC.; *pg.* 890, *pg.* 631
HEARTY PERFORMANCE - Animal Nutrition Product - MANNA PRO CORPORATION; *pg.* 1478, *pg.* 975
HEARTY PLATTER - Restaurants - KWIK TRIP INC.; *pg.* 1026, *pg.* 1864
HEARUSA - Hearing Care Center - HEARUSA, INC.; *pg.* 1541, *pg.* 457
HEARX - Prescriptions for Better Hearing - HEARUSA, INC.; *pg.* 1541, *pg.* 457
HEAT - Apparel - OAKLEY, INC.; *pg.* 1840, *pg.* 86
HEAT CONTROLLER - Electronic Air Cleaner - HEAT CONTROLLER, INC.; *pg.* 1072, *pg.* 893
HEAT GIANT - Heater - KAZ, INC.; *pg.* 58, *pg.* 844
HEAT ON DEMAND - Induction Heat Process - ALADDIN TEMP-RITE, LLC; *pg.* 1013, *pg.* 1635
HEAT SEAL - Hair Care Product - JOHN PAUL MITCHELL SYSTEMS; *pg.* 512, *pg.* 133
HEAT-SEAL STIK - Epoxy - LA-CO INDUSTRIES MARKAL CO., INC.; *pg.* 1170, *pg.* 610
HEAT SEAT - Microcore Technology - BATTELLE MEMORIAL INSTITUTE; *pg.* 1401, *pg.* 1437
HEAT SHIELD - Data Sheet - AMERICAN FELT & FILTER COMPANY; *pg.* 1312, *pg.* 1184
HEAT-SHRINKABLE CABLE BREAKOUTS - Heat Shrink - CHANNELL COMMERCIAL CORP.; *pg.* 1870, *pg.* 291
HEAT-SHRINKABLE CABLE SEALING GLANDS - Heat Shrink - CHANNELL COMMERCIAL CORP.; *pg.* 1870, *pg.* 291
HEAT-SHRINKABLE END CAPS - Heat Shrink - CHANNELL COMMERCIAL CORP.; *pg.* 1870, *pg.* 291
HEAT-SHRINKABLE SLEEVES - Heat Shrink - CHANNELL COMMERCIAL CORP.; *pg.* 1870, *pg.* 291
HEAT-SHRINKABLE WRAPAROUND CLOSURES - Heat Shrink - CHANNELL COMMERCIAL CORP.; *pg.* 1870, *pg.* 291
HEAT-SHRINKABLE WRAPAROUND REPAIR KITS - Heat Shrink - CHANNELL COMMERCIAL CORP.; *pg.* 1870, *pg.* 291
THE HEAT TECHNOLOGY COMPANY - Slogan - SELAS HEAT TECHNOLOGY COMPANY LLC; *pg.* 1076, *pg.* 1553
HEAT-TIMER - Electronic Controls - HEAT-TIMER CORPORATION; *pg.* 1072, *pg.* 1065
THE HEAT TRACING SPECIALISTS - Slogan - THERMON AMERICAS INC.; *pg.* 1077, *pg.* 1744
HEAT TREAT MANAGEMENT - Thermal Processing Equipment - SURFACE COMBUSTION, INC.; *pg.* 1077, *pg.* 1462
HEAT TREATING PROGRESS - Business Magazine - ASM

INTERNATIONAL; pg. 132, pg. 1461
HEAT-TROL - Hot Water Control - HEAT-TIMER CORPORATION; pg. 1072, pg. 1065
HEAT VENT - Ventilation - CRAFTMADE INTERNATIONAL, INC.; pg. 1295, pg. 1670
HEAT WAVE - Game - WMS INDUSTRIES INC.; pg. 593, pg. 666
HEAT YOU CAN BANK ON - Tag Line - AERCO INTERNATIONAL INC.; pg. 1068, pg. 1142
HEATBAN - Roof Paint - JONES-BLAIR COMPANY; pg. 1443, pg. 1682
HEATBATH - Metal Finishing Product - HEATBATH CORPORATION; pg. 1165, pg. 826
HEATBUSTER - Optical Component - OPTOSIGMA CORP.; pg. 1425, pg. 262
HEATCRAFT - Refrigeration Product - LENNOX INTERNATIONAL INC.; pg. 1073, pg. 1736
HEATDISH - Parabolic Electric Heater - NATIONAL PRESTO INDUSTRIES, INC; pg. 1128, pg. 1857
HEATEC - Asphalt Equipment - ASTEC INDUSTRIES, INC.; pg. 69, pg. 1628
THE HEATER - Golf Products - FEEL GOLF CO., INC.; pg. 1834, pg. 465
HEATGEAR - Fabric - UNDER ARMOUR, INC.; pg. 49, pg. 759
HEATH - Candy - THE HERSHEY CO.; pg. 1855, pg. 1538
HEATH - Pet Product - PETSMART, INC.; pg. 1481, pg. 18
HEATH - Ice Cream Bar - WELLS ENTERPRISES, INC.; pg. 909, pg. 709
HEATH BITS 'O BRICKLE - Toffee Bits - THE HERSHEY CO.; pg. 1855, pg. 1538
HEATHER - Clothing - ABERCROMBIE & FITCH CO.; pg. 37, pg. 1466
HEATHER - Furniture - HOOKER FURNITURE CORPORATION; pg. 928, pg. 1788
HEATHER-GLO - Liqueur - MONTEBELLO BRANDS INC.; pg. 1967, pg. 758
HEATHER'S NATURALS - Food Product - THE HAIN CELESTIAL GROUP, INC.; pg. 860, pg. 1172
HEATHROW - Ethernet Product - VITESSE SEMICONDUCTOR CORPORATION; pg. 686, pg. 57
HEATILATOR - Fireplaces - HNI CORPORATION; pg. 927, pg. 709
HEATLHSTREAM LEARNING CENTER - Software - HEALTHSTREAM, INC.; pg. 1649, pg. 1651
HEATMAPS - Software - SS&C TECHNOLOGIES HOLDINGS, INC.; pg. 473, pg. 386
HEATON - Ice Hockey Goalie Equipment - REEBOK-CCM HOCKEY, INC.; pg. 1844, pg. 1960
HEATPAK - Enclosure System - O'BRIEN CORPORATION; pg. 1366, pg. 1001
HEATPAK II - Enclosure System - O'BRIEN CORPORATION; pg. 1366, pg. 1001
HEATPRO - Pump - HAYWARD POOL PRODUCTS; pg. 1049, pg. 1057
HEATRIM - HVAC Equipment - MESTEK, INC.; pg. 1074, pg. 857
HEATSAFE - Specialty Paper - APPVION INC.; pg. 1451, pg. 1852
HEATSAVR - Solar Pool Cover - FLEXIBLE SOLUTIONS INTERNATIONAL, INC.; pg. 1163, pg. 1913
HEATSHIELD - Protector Panel - RITE-HITE HOLDING CORPORATION; pg. 1372, pg. 1880
HEATWAVE - Medical Equipment - CONMED CORPORATION; pg. 1517, pg. 1347
HEATWAVE - Bag - DOMINO'S PIZZA, INC.; pg. 1726, pg. 865
HEATWAVE - Polymer - EASTMAN CHEMICAL COMPANY; pg. 1159, pg. 1636
HEATWAVE - Metal Matrix Composite - ROGERS CORPORATION; pg. 1305, pg. 369
HEAVEN - Window Accent - HERITAGE LACE INC.; pg. 694, pg. 711
HEAVEN & EARTH - Beverages - THE COCA-COLA COMPANY; pg. 240, pg. 493
HEAVEN SENT - Pillow and Throw - HERITAGE LACE INC.; pg. 694, pg. 711
HEAVENLY - Hotels - STARWOOD HOTELS & RESORTS WORLDWIDE, INC.; pg. 1114, pg. 378
HEAVENLY - Resort - VAIL RESORTS, INC.; pg. 1117, pg. 313
HEAVENWOOD - Golf Accessories - CALLAWAY GOLF COMPANY; pg. 1829, pg. 58
HEAVY BLEND - Apparel - GILDAN ACTIVEWEAR INC.; pg. 1835, pg. 1955
HEAVY DUTY C.V. WASH - Vehicle Wash - HILLYARD, INC.; pg. 331, pg. 990
HEAVY DUTY PORTABLE - Portable Heavy Duty Vacuum - SHOP-VAC CORPORATION; pg. 1375, pg. 1595
HEAVY-DUTY PREP SOLVENT - Automotive Reconditioning Product - MOC PRODUCTS COMPANY, INC.; pg. 332, pg. 174
HEAVY HITTERS - Hammer - VAUGHAN & BUSHNELL MANUFACTURING COMPANY, INC.; pg. 1066, pg. 616
HEAVY MAGNUM - Enhanced Velocity Ammunition - HORNADY MANUFACTURING COMPANY; pg. 1836, pg. 1010
HEAVY METAL - Gaming Product - GLD PRODUCTS, INC.; pg. 1835, pg. 1882
HEAVY TRUCK CARD - Diesel & Bulk Fuel Credit Card - WRIGHT EXPRESS CORPORATION; pg. 493, pg. 753
HEAVY-WIPES - Heavy Duty Cleaning Cloths - THE CLOROX COMPANY; pg. 327, pg. 169
HEAVYDUTY CARDINAL - Cutting System - EASTMAN MACHINE COMPANY; pg. 1331, pg. 1148
HEBREW NATIONAL - Kosher Food Products - CONAGRA FOODS, INC.; pg. 826, pg. 1014
HEC-PACK - Software - BENTLEY SYSTEMS, INC.; pg. 361, pg. 1531
HECCOLON - Turkish Emery - IMERYS FUSED MINERALS; pg. 1348, pg. 1317
HECHE - Dress Shoes - JOHNSTON & MURPHY CO.; pg. 1810, pg. 1651
HECKERS - Unbleached Naturally White Flour - THE UHLMANN CO.; pg. 834, pg. 986
HECO - Mobile & Consumer Electronics - VOXX INTERNATIONAL; pg. 686, pg. 1166
HECON - Printer - DANAHER CORPORATION; pg. 1044, pg. 397
HECTABRITE - Bentonite Clay - MINERALS TECHNOLOGIES INC.; pg. 1173, pg. 617
HECTALITE - Bentonite Clay - MINERALS TECHNOLOGIES INC.; pg. 1173, pg. 617
HECTOR - Furniture - AMISCO INDUSTRIES LTD.; pg. 913, pg. 1958
HECTOROL - Vitamin - GENZYME CORPORATION; pg. 1534, pg. 808
HEDCO - Snowmaking Machines - THE DEWEY ELECTRONICS CORPORATION; pg. 1328, pg. 1099
HEDGE FUND - Shoe - AEROGROUP INTERNATIONAL, INC.; pg. 1803, pg. 1055
HEDGE MAPLE - Shoe - AEROGROUP INTERNATIONAL, INC.; pg. 1803, pg. 1055
HEDGEROW - Carpet - BEAULIEU GROUP, LLC; pg. 917, pg. 529
HEDIS - Healthcare Service - MOLINA HEALTHCARE, INC.; pg. 1569, pg. 123
HEEL CAGE - Bicycle Accessories - SPECIALIZED BICYCLE COMPONENTS, INC.; pg. 1711, pg. 152
HEEL SLOPE - Polyurethane Foam - SPAN-AMERICA MEDICAL SYSTEMS, INC.; pg. 1595, pg. 1618
HEELBO - Elbow Protection - ALIMED, INC.; pg. 1490, pg. 816
HEELBO - Medical & Aesthetic Product - DYNATRONICS CORPORATION; pg. 1526, pg. 1757
HEELIFT - Suspension Boot - ALIMED, INC.; pg. 1490, pg. 816
HEELSTAT - Static Control Device - WALTER G. LEGGE COMPANY, INC.; pg. 337, pg. 1321
HEELYS - Roller Shoe - HEELYS, INC.; pg. 1809, pg. 1669
HEELYS - Kids' Active Lifestyle Brand - SEQUENTIAL BRANDS GROUP, INC.; pg. 1395, pg. 1290
HEET - Gas-Line Antifreeze - GOLD EAGLE COMPANY; pg. 206, pg. 575
HEETSHEET - Vessel Heating System - THERMON AMERICAS INC.; pg. 1077, pg. 1744
HEFE WEISS - Beverage - SPRECHER BREWING COMPANY; pg. 265, pg. 1858
HEFTY - Trash Bags - PACTIV CORPORATION; pg. 1466, pg. 624
HEFTY - Waste Bags - REYNOLDS CONSUMER PRODUCTS; pg. 1138, pg. 625
HEICO - Aircraft Components - HEICO CORPORATION; pg. 228, pg. 431
HEIDI - Development Kit - AUTODESK INC.; pg. 356, pg. 257
HEIDI'S GOURMET DESSERTS - Dessert Products - THE SCHWAN FOOD COMPANY; pg. 894, pg. 928
HEIL - Truck Bodies - HEIL ENVIRONMENTAL INDUSTRIES, LTD.; pg. 207, pg. 1629
HEIN-WERNER - Collision Repair Products - SNAP-ON INCORPORATED; pg. 1062, pg. 1862
HEINEKEN - Beer - HEINEKEN USA INC.; pg. 252, pg. 1352
HEINEKEN LIGHT - Beer - HEINEKEN USA INC.; pg. 252, pg. 1352
HEINEMANN - Electrical Product - EATON CORPORATION; pg. 1331, pg. 1429
HEINE'S BLEND - Pipe Tobaccos - ALTADIS USA, INC.; pg. 1893, pg. 423
HEINZ - Food Product - ELLENBEE-LEGGETT COMPANY INC.; pg. 854, pg. 1452
HEINZ - Food Products - THE KRAFT HEINZ COMPANY; pg. 870, pg. 1577
HEINZ 57 SAUCE - Sauces - THE KRAFT HEINZ COMPANY; pg. 870, pg. 1577
HEINZ CHILI SAUCE - Sauces - THE KRAFT HEINZ COMPANY; pg. 870, pg. 1577
HEINZ COCKTAIL SAUCE - Sauces - THE KRAFT HEINZ COMPANY; pg. 870, pg. 1577
HEINZ FOODSERVICE SOUPS - Frozen Soups - THE KRAFT HEINZ COMPANY; pg. 870, pg. 1577
HEINZ GRAVY - Gravy - THE KRAFT HEINZ COMPANY; pg. 870, pg. 1577
HEINZ KETCHUP - Ketchups - THE KRAFT HEINZ COMPANY; pg. 870, pg. 1577
HEINZ VINEGAR - Vinegars - THE KRAFT HEINZ COMPANY; pg. 870, pg. 1577
HEIR TO THE THRONE - Video Game - INTERNATIONAL GAME TECHNOLOGY; pg. 957, pg. 1024
HEIRESS - Ladies' Wallets - BUXTON ACQUISITION CO., LLC; pg. 2, pg. 845
HEIRLOOM - Furniture - ASHLEY FURNITURE INDUSTRIES, INC.; pg. 914, pg. 1852
HEIRLOOM - Bedding Accessory - HERITAGE LACE INC.; pg. 694, pg. 711
HEIRLOOM - Carpet - INTERFACE, INC.; pg. 695, pg. 512
HEIRLOOM - Paper - NEENAH PAPER, INC.; pg. 1465, pg. 484
HEIRLOOM TOOL - Gardening Hand Tools - SMITH & HAWKEN, LTD.; pg. 1786, pg. 168
HEIRLOOMS - Door Glass - ODL INCORPORATED; pg. 101, pg. 914
HEISSE TASSE - Food Product - CAMPBELL SOUP COMPANY; pg. 844, pg. 1048
THE HEIST - Video Game - BALLY TECHNOLOGIES, INC.; pg. 531, pg. 1022
HEITRIN - Pharmaceutical Product - ABBOTT LABORATORIES; pg. 1484, pg. 551
HEKFECTIN - Software - BIO-RAD LABORATORIES, INC.; pg. 1504, pg. 101
HEKMAN - Fine Furniture - HOWARD MILLER COMPANY; pg. 7, pg. 914
HELDOR - In-Ground Vinyl Pools - POOL CORPORATION; pg. 1843, pg. 743
HELEN - Clothing - ABERCROMBIE & FITCH CO.; pg. 37, pg. 1466
HELENA - Sitting Bench & Lounge Chairs - BERNHARDT DESIGN; pg. 918, pg. 1381
HELEX - Septal Occluder Device - W.L. GORE & ASSOCIATES, INC.; pg. 122, pg. 388
HELI-GROOVE - Tubing & Pipe - MORRIS COUPLING COMPANY; pg. 1057, pg. 1530
HELI-HOIST - Helicopter Transportable Drilling Rigs - PARKER DRILLING COMPANY; pg. 982, pg. 1712
HELI-PIN - Mechanical Anchor & Fastener - POWERS FASTENERS INC.; pg. 1059, pg. 1143
HELIA - Medical Device - RESMED INC.; pg. 1589, pg. 207
HELIAX - Cable Products - COMMSCOPE, INC.; pg. 278, pg. 1378
HELICAL PIER - Pole And Pipeline - HUBBELL INCORPORATED; pg. 1299, pg. 370
HELICLAR - Pharmaceutical Product - ABBOTT LABORATORIES; pg. 1484, pg. 551
HELIDAC - Therapy System - PROMETHEUS LABORATORIES, INC.; pg. 1586, pg. 206
HELIFLEX - Cable & Antenna System - RADIO FREQUENCY SYSTEMS, INC.; pg. 666, pg. 354
HELIFLOW - Blower - GARDNER DENVER, INC.; pg. 1338, pg. 1592
HELIGRAV - Gravity Meter - SCINTREX LTD.; pg. 1374, pg. 1920
HELILOK - Tooth Equipment - ESCO CORPORATION; pg. 1335, pg. 1502
HELIODENT - Dental Equipment - SIRONA DENTAL SYSTEMS, INC.; pg. 1429, pg. 1175
HELIONAL - Fragrance Ingredient - INTERNATIONAL

FLAVORS & FRAGRANCES INC.; *pg.* 512, *pg.* 1244
HELIOS - Software - BIO-RAD LABORATORIES, INC.; *pg.* 1504, *pg.* 101
HELIOS - Automated Lubrication Systems - LINCOLN INDUSTRIAL CORP.; *pg.* 1355, *pg.* 999
HELIOS - Edge RF Subsystem - SKYWORKS SOLUTIONS, INC.; *pg.* 674, *pg.* 862
HELIOS - Electrophysiology Ablation Catheter - STEREOTAXIS, INC.; *pg.* 1597, *pg.* 1004
HELIOS NANOLAB - Electron Microscope - FEI COMPANY; *pg.* 1413, *pg.* 1498
HELIPATH - Stand - BROOKFIELD ENGINEERING LABORATORIES, INC.; *pg.* 1403, *pg.* 833
HELISAL - Software - BIO-RAD LABORATORIES, INC.; *pg.* 1504, *pg.* 101
HELISTAT - Medical Device - INTEGRA LIFESCIENCES HOLDINGS CORPORATION; *pg.* 1545, *pg.* 1109
HELITENE - Medical Device - INTEGRA LIFESCIENCES HOLDINGS CORPORATION; *pg.* 1545, *pg.* 1109
HELIX - Data Communication Product - GENERAL CABLE CORPORATION; *pg.* 83, *pg.* 729
HELIX - Apparel - OAKLEY, INC.; *pg.* 1840, *pg.* 86
HELIX - Flexible Screw Conveyors - PRAB, INC.; *pg.* 1369, *pg.* 894
HELIX - Software System - REALNETWORKS, INC.; *pg.* 460, *pg.* 1839
HELIX - Remote Control Device - UNIVERSAL ELECTRONICS, INC.; *pg.* 683, *pg.* 262
HELIX - Ceiling Fan - WESTINGHOUSE LIGHTING CORPORATION; *pg.* 687, *pg.* 1571
HELIX 2000 - Helical Reducers & Gear Motors - REGAL BELOIT CORPORATION; *pg.* 106, *pg.* 1854
HELIX FUSION - Ceiling Fan - WESTINGHOUSE LIGHTING CORPORATION; *pg.* 687, *pg.* 1571
HELIX-XBOX - Game - ACTIVISION BLIZZARD, INC.; *pg.* 948, *pg.* 271
HELIXATE - Antihemophiliac Factor (Recombinant) - CSL BEHRING LLC; *pg.* 1520, *pg.* 1543
HELIXFORM - Bevel Product - GLEASON CORPORATION; *pg.* 1340, *pg.* 1335
HELLFIRE - Systems Integration & Aeronautics - LOCKHEED MARTIN CORPORATION; *pg.* 229, *pg.* 762
HELLMANN'S - Mayonnaise; Seasonings & Spices; Salad Dressings - UNILEVER UNITED STATES, INC.; *pg.* 904, *pg.* 1061
HELLMANN'S MAYONNAISE - Mayonnaise - UNILEVER CANADA INC.; *pg.* 903, *pg.* 1946
HELLO - Furniture - HAWORTH, INC.; *pg.* 402, *pg.* 891
HELLO BETTY - Beauty Products - LUZIER PERSONALIZED COSMETICS, INC.; *pg.* 515, *pg.* 978
HELLO FUTURE - Slogan - LINCOLN NATIONAL CORPORATION; *pg.* 776, *pg.* 1567
HELLO MATH READER - Educational Materials - SCHOLASTIC INC.; *pg.* 1683, *pg.* 1288
HELLO READER! - Educational Materials - SCHOLASTIC INC.; *pg.* 1683, *pg.* 1288
HELLO WRITER - Educational Materials - SCHOLASTIC INC.; *pg.* 1683, *pg.* 1288
HELLSTERN - Electronic Component Product - TE CONNECTIVITY LTD.; *pg.* 677, *pg.* 1515
HELLY-HANSEN - Outerwear - HELLY-HANSEN (US), INC.; *pg.* 26, *pg.* 1813
HELLY-TECH - Rainwear - HELLY-HANSEN (US), INC.; *pg.* 26, *pg.* 1813
HELMET HEROES - Toy & Game - HASBRO, INC.; *pg.* 954, *pg.* 1603
HELOXY - Chemical - MILLER-STEPHENSON CHEMICAL COMPANY, INC.; *pg.* 1172, *pg.* 344
HELP! - Specialty Parts - DORMAN PRODUCTS, INC.; *pg.* 204, *pg.* 1522
HELP A HERO - Dog Toys - THE HARTZ MOUNTAIN CORP.; *pg.* 1476, *pg.* 1120
HELP IS JUST AROUND THE CORNER - Slogan - TRUE VALUE COMPANY; *pg.* 1065, *pg.* 592
HELPER - Casseroles - GENERAL MILLS, INC.; *pg.* 828, *pg.* 933
THE HELPFUL HARDWARE FOLKS - Slogan - ACE HARDWARE CORPORATION; *pg.* 1040, *pg.* 644
HELPING CREATE THE WORLD'S GREATEST IMAGES - Tagline - THE TIFFEN COMPANY LLC; *pg.* 1432, *pg.* 1165
HELPING GOVERNMENT SERVE THE PEOPLE - Slogan - MAXIMUS, INC.; *pg.* 780, *pg.* 1799
HELPING PEOPLE LIVE HEALTHIER LIVES - Tagline - UNITEDHEALTH GROUP INCORPORATED; *pg.* 1221, *pg.* 950
HELPING TO GROW THE THINGS YOU LOVE. - Tagline - INTERMOUNTAIN FARMERS ASSOCIATION; *pg.* 705, *pg.* 1759
HELPING YOU DO MORE - Tag Line - BANKFINANCIAL CORPORATION; *pg.* 722, *pg.* 560
HELPINGPATIENTS - Pharmaceutical Product - PHARMACEUTICAL RESEARCH & MANUFACTURERS OF AMERICA; *pg.* 153, *pg.* 404
HELPMATE - Plastic Grocery Bags - SONOCO PRODUCTS COMPANY; *pg.* 1469, *pg.* 1619
HELPMATE 3000 - Plastic Grocery Bags - SONOCO PRODUCTS COMPANY; *pg.* 1469, *pg.* 1619
HELPMATE JR. - Plastic Grocery Bags - SONOCO PRODUCTS COMPANY; *pg.* 1469, *pg.* 1619
HELPOUTS - Expert Assistance - GOOGLE INC.; *pg.* 1249, *pg.* 153
HELSPOT - Pressed & Monolithic Refractory - RESCO PRODUCTS, INC.; *pg.* 107, *pg.* 1581
HELZBERG - Diamonds - HELZBERG'S DIAMOND SHOPS, INC.; *pg.* 6, *pg.* 984
HELZBERG DIAMOND MASTERPIECE - Jewelry - HELZBERG'S DIAMOND SHOPS, INC.; *pg.* 6, *pg.* 984
HELZBERG LIMITED EDITION - Jewelry - HELZBERG'S DIAMOND SHOPS, INC.; *pg.* 6, *pg.* 984
HEMA-PLEX - Nutritional Supplement - NATURAL ORGANICS, INC.; *pg.* 1571, *pg.* 1181
HEMABATE - Medicine - PFIZER INC.; *pg.* 1581, *pg.* 1278
HEMASHIELD - Medical Device - BOSTON SCIENTIFIC CORPORATION; *pg.* 1508, *pg.* 831
HEMATEX - Collagen Hemostatic Agent - MAQUET; *pg.* 1558, *pg.* 1082
HEMATIDE - Red Blood Cell Production Stimulant - AFFYMAX, INC.; *pg.* 1487, *pg.* 73
HEMATRUE - Veterinary Hematology Analyzer - HESKA CORPORATION; *pg.* 1542, *pg.* 335
HEMAVISION - Clinical Diagnostic Product - BIO-RAD LABORATORIES, INC.; *pg.* 1504, *pg.* 101
HEMI - Engine - FCA US LLC; *pg.* 170, *pg.* 868
HEMI - Surgical Instrument - OSTEOMED CORPORATION; *pg.* 1425, *pg.* 1658
HEMI - Bicycle Accessories - SPECIALIZED BICYCLE COMPONENTS, INC.; *pg.* 1711, *pg.* 152
HEMILIGHT - Personal Emergency Locator Light - ACR ELECTRONICS, INC.; *pg.* 612, *pg.* 422
HEMISPHERE - Fabric - NEMSCHOFF, INC.; *pg.* 936, *pg.* 1890
HEMO-NATE - Disposable Blood Filtration System - UTAH MEDICAL PRODUCTS, INC.; *pg.* 1605, *pg.* 1752
HEMO-TAP - Spike - UTAH MEDICAL PRODUCTS, INC.; *pg.* 1605, *pg.* 1752
HEMOBAHN - Medical Product - W.L. GORE & ASSOCIATES, INC.; *pg.* 122, *pg.* 388
HEMOCARE - Blood Bank Information System - MEDIWARE INFORMATION SYSTEMS, INC.; *pg.* 431, *pg.* 716
HEMOCCULT - Testing Instrument System - BECKMAN COULTER, INC.; *pg.* 1402, *pg.* 48
HEMOCCULT II - Fecal Occult Blood Test - BECKMAN COULTER, INC.; *pg.* 1402, *pg.* 48
HEMOFIL - Biopharmaceutical Product - BAXTER INTERNATIONAL INC.; *pg.* 1499, *pg.* 599
HEMOFIL M - Clotting Factor For Hemophiliacs - BAXTER INTERNATIONAL INC.; *pg.* 1499, *pg.* 599
HEMOPUMP - Circulatory Assist Pump - MEDTRONIC, INC.; *pg.* 1564, *pg.* 939
HEMORID - Hemorrhoid Cream - MCNEIL-PPC, INC.; *pg.* 1560, *pg.* 1533
HEMORRHOL - Nutritional Product - NUTRACEUTICAL INTERNATIONAL CORPORATION; *pg.* 1576, *pg.* 1753
HEMOS - Software - BIO-RAD LABORATORIES, INC.; *pg.* 1504, *pg.* 101
HEMOSENSE - Pharmaceutical Product - ALERE INC.; *pg.* 1488, *pg.* 849
HEMOSTASE - Hemostatic Product - CRYOLIFE, INC.; *pg.* 1520, *pg.* 534
HEMOTHERM - Medical Product - CINCINNATI SUB-ZERO PRODUCTS, INC.; *pg.* 1070, *pg.* 1411
HEMP PLUS - Waffles - NATURE'S PATH FOODS INC.; *pg.* 833, *pg.* 1908
HEMPTOWN - Cap - BROWN & BIGELOW, INC.; *pg.* 1624, *pg.* 959
HENDRICK'S - Gin - WILLIAM GRANT & SONS, INC.; *pg.* 1972, *pg.* 1057
HENGSTLER - Encoder - DYNAPAR; *pg.* 1408, *pg.* 616
HENGSTLER GMBH - Counting & Control Component - DANAHER CORPORATION; *pg.* 1044, *pg.* 397
HENKE - Snowplows - ALAMO GROUP INC.; *pg.* 1311, *pg.* 1745
HENKEL - Duct Tape - HENKEL CORPORATION; *pg.* 1049, *pg.* 369
HENNESSY - Cognac - MOET HENNESSY; *pg.* 1966, *pg.* 1260
HENNESSY INDUSTRIES - Wheel-Service Equipment - DANAHER CORPORATION; *pg.* 1044, *pg.* 397
HENREDON - Furniture - HERITAGE HOME GROUP; *pg.* 926, *pg.* 1379
HENRI SAVARD BLANC DE BLANCS - Beverage - SIDNEY FRANK IMPORTING CO., INC.; *pg.* 1970, *pg.* 1184
HENRY - Beer - COASTAL EXTREME BREWING COMPANY; *pg.* 240, *pg.* 1602
HENRY - Fabric - NEMSCHOFF, INC.; *pg.* 936, *pg.* 1890
HENRY CLAY - Premium Cigars - ALTADIS USA, INC.; *pg.* 1893, *pg.* 423
HENRY FORD VILLAGE - Retirement Community - ERICKSON LIVING; *pg.* 1090, *pg.* 766
HENRY MCKENNA - Bourbon & Single Barrel Straight Bourbon Whisky - HEAVEN HILL DISTILLERIES, INC.; *pg.* 1964, *pg.* 725
HENRY WEINHARD'S AMBER ALE - Beer - MILLERCOORS; *pg.* 254, *pg.* 1877
HENRY WEINHARD'S BLUE BOAR PALE ALE - Beer - MILLERCOORS; *pg.* 254, *pg.* 1877
HENRY WEINHARD'S CLASSIC DARK - Beer - MILLERCOORS; *pg.* 254, *pg.* 1877
HENRY WEINHARD'S HEFEWEIZEN - Beer - MILLERCOORS; *pg.* 254, *pg.* 1877
HENRY WEINHARD'S NORTHWEST TRAIL BLONDE LAGER - Beer - MILLERCOORS; *pg.* 254, *pg.* 1877
HENRY WEINHARD'S PRIVATE RESERVE - Beer - MILLERCOORS; *pg.* 254, *pg.* 1877
HENRY WEINHARD'S SUMMER WHEAT - Beer - MILLERCOORS; *pg.* 254, *pg.* 1877
HENRY'S HARD SODA - Hard Ginger Ale & Hard Orange Soda - MILLERCOORS; *pg.* 254, *pg.* 1877
HENSLEY - Ground Engaging Tools - HENSLEY INDUSTRIES, INC.; *pg.* 1166, *pg.* 1682
HENTHORN - Furniture - ASHLEY FURNITURE INDUSTRIES, INC.; *pg.* 914, *pg.* 1852
HENZA MEAL - Nutritional Product - NUTRACEUTICAL INTERNATIONAL CORPORATION; *pg.* 1576, *pg.* 1753
HEPA - Air Cleaner - HONEYWELL INTERNATIONAL INC.; *pg.* 407, *pg.* 1088
HEPA-CLEAR - Air Purifier - SLANT/FIN CORPORATION; *pg.* 1076, *pg.* 1163
HEPAGAM B - Drug - EMERGENT BIOSOLUTIONS; *pg.* 1528, *pg.* 1914
HEPAMATE - Extracorporeal Temporary Liver Support System - ALLIQUA, INC.; *pg.* 1492, *pg.* 1189
HEPARIN HYPERD - Chromatography Product - PALL CORPORATION; *pg.* 232, *pg.* 1323
HEPATECH - Air Purifier - HUNTER FAN COMPANY; *pg.* 57, *pg.* 1631
HEPBURN - Furniture - ETHAN ALLEN INTERIORS INC.; *pg.* 924, *pg.* 343
HEPCON HMS PLUS - Hemostasis Management Sys. - MEDTRONIC, INC.; *pg.* 1564, *pg.* 939
HEPEX-B - Biopharmaceutical Product - CUBIST PHARMACEUTICALS, INC.; *pg.* 1521, *pg.* 828
HEPPINGER - Beverages - THE COCA-COLA COMPANY; *pg.* 240, *pg.* 493
HEPSERA - Biopharmaceutical Product - GILEAD SCIENCES, INC.; *pg.* 1535, *pg.* 88
HEPTA - Software - BIO-RAD LABORATORIES, INC.; *pg.* 1504, *pg.* 101
HEPTEEN BASE - Polymer Product - CHEMTURA CORPORATION; *pg.* 1152, *pg.* 355
HEPTIMAX - Medical Test - QUEST DIAGNOSTICS INCORPORATED; *pg.* 1587, *pg.* 1080
HER OPTION - Medical Device - AMERICAN MEDICAL SYSTEMS HOLDINGS, INC.; *pg.* 1493, *pg.* 947
HERALD - Speaker Cabinet - ALLEN ORGAN COMPANY; *pg.* 527, *pg.* 1549
HERB & GARLIC SEASONED SPLASH! - Seafood - CLEAR SPRINGS FOODS, INC.; *pg.* 848, *pg.* 548
HERB APPEAL - Prerecorded Compact Discs - AEROGROW INTERNATIONAL, INC.; *pg.* 1393, *pg.* 310
HERB CHICKEN - Food Product - ANNIE'S INC.; *pg.* 1760, *pg.* 45
HERB COMPANION - Publication - OGDEN PUBLICATIONS, INC.; *pg.* 1672, *pg.* 722

HERB GARDEN - Carpet - BEAULIEU GROUP, LLC; *pg.* 917, *pg.* 529
HERB IT UP - Plant Growing Kit - AEROGROW INTERNATIONAL, INC.; *pg.* 1393, *pg.* 310
HERB 'N SERVE - Vinaigrette & Marinade Maker - AEROGROW INTERNATIONAL, INC.; *pg.* 1393, *pg.* 310
HERB-OX - Broths & Seasonings - HORMEL FOODS CORPORATION; *pg.* 863, *pg.* 915
HERBA-TEIN - Nutritional Supplement - NATURAL ORGANICS, INC.; *pg.* 1571, *pg.* 1181
HERBAL ABCS - Nutritional Supplement - PHARMAVITE LLC; *pg.* 1584, *pg.* 167
HERBAL ANSWER - Lip Balm - BLISTEX, INC.; *pg.* 502, *pg.* 644
HERBAL BOUQUET - Body Lotion - BLUE CROSS LABORATORIES; *pg.* 326, *pg.* 277
HERBAL BOUQUET - Food Product - MODERN PRODUCTS, INC.; *pg.* 1568, *pg.* 1871
HERBAL ESSENCES - Hair Care Products - P&G-CLAIROL, INC.; *pg.* 519, *pg.* 1418
HERBAL ESSENCES - Hair Care Products - THE PROCTER & GAMBLE COMPANY; *pg.* 1129, *pg.* 1418
HERBAL LIQUID - Hair & Skin Product - AUBREY ORGANICS INC.; *pg.* 499, *pg.* 470
HERBAL PLUS - Herbal Supplements - GENERAL NUTRITION CENTERS, INC.; *pg.* 1534, *pg.* 1575
HERBAL SPRINGS - Body Wash - HENKEL CONSUMER GOODS; *pg.* 511, *pg.* 22
HERBAL V - Health System Product - LANELABS USA INC.; *pg.* 1554, *pg.* 1128
HERBALIFELINE - Marine Source Liquid Complex Capsules - HERBALIFE INTERNATIONAL OF AMERICA, INC.; *pg.* 1541, *pg.* 132
HERBCRAFT - Cover Ups, Robes & Loungewear - KELLWOOD COMPANY; *pg.* 28, *pg.* 975
HERBCRAFT II - Dusters & Better Loungewear - KELLWOOD COMPANY; *pg.* 28, *pg.* 975
HERBESSENCE - Hair & Skin Product - AUBREY ORGANICS INC.; *pg.* 499, *pg.* 470
HERBS ALIVE - Plant Care Product - GARDENS ALIVE!, INC.; *pg.* 1796, *pg.* 693
HERBS FOR HEALTH - Publication - OGDEN PUBLICATIONS, INC.; *pg.* 1672, *pg.* 722
HERBS FOR KIDS - Nutritional Product - NUTRACEUTICAL INTERNATIONAL CORPORATION; *pg.* 1576, *pg.* 1753
HERBSAINT LIQUEUR D'ANIS - Liqueur - SAZERAC COMPANY, INC.; *pg.* 1969, *pg.* 745
HERC ALLOY - Grade 80 Chain - COLUMBUS MCKINNON CORPORATION; *pg.* 1325, *pg.* 1138
HERCEPTIN - Breast Cancer Treatment - GENENTECH, INC.; *pg.* 1533, *pg.* 279
HERCEPTIN - Drug - INCYTE CORPORATION; *pg.* 1545, *pg.* 392
HERCOBOND - Dry-Strength Resin - HERCULES INCORPORATED; *pg.* 1166, *pg.* 392
HERCOFLEX - Ester Plasticizer - HERCULES INCORPORATED; *pg.* 1166, *pg.* 392
HERCOLUBE - Oil - HERCULES INCORPORATED; *pg.* 1166, *pg.* 392
HERCON - Sizing Agent - HERCULES INCORPORATED; *pg.* 1166, *pg.* 392
HERCOSET - Resins - HERCULES INCORPORATED; *pg.* 1166, *pg.* 392
HERCUFLEX - Coated Glass Fiber & Yarn for Building & Industrial Use - PPG INDUSTRIES, INC.; *pg.* 1445, *pg.* 1579
HERCULES - Chemical Scrubber - CALGON CARBON CORPORATION; *pg.* 1151, *pg.* 1574
HERCULES - Sports Net - CARRON NET COMPANY, INC.; *pg.* 1830, *pg.* 1896
HERCULES - Amusement & Water Park - CEDAR FAIR, L.P.; *pg.* 537, *pg.* 1471
HERCULES - Hose - HBD INDUSTRIES, INC.; *pg.* 207, *pg.* 1449
HERCULES - Tires - THE HERCULES TIRE & RUBBER COMPANY; *pg.* 1884, *pg.* 1454
HERCULES - Lighting Product - HUBBELL INCORPORATED; *pg.* 1299, *pg.* 370
HERCULES - Dispensing Equipment - IDEX CORPORATION; *pg.* 1347, *pg.* 623
HERCULES - Systems Integration & Aeronautics - LOCKHEED MARTIN CORPORATION; *pg.* 229, *pg.* 762
HERCULES - Foam System - OSHKOSH CORPORATION; *pg.* 187, *pg.* 1885
HERCULES - Compressed Air Foam System - PIERCE MANUFACTURING, INC.; *pg.* 188, *pg.* 1852
HERCULES - Footwear - P.W. MINOR & SON, INC.; *pg.* 1816, *pg.* 1140
HERCULES - Chemical - SENSIENT COLORS INC.; *pg.* 1180, *pg.* 1003
HERCULES - Equipment Delivery System - STRYKER CORPORATION; *pg.* 1598, *pg.* 894
HERCULES - Software - SYNOPSYS, INC.; *pg.* 480, *pg.* 162
HERCULES - Plastic & Rubber - TEKNOR APEX COMPANY; *pg.* 1889, *pg.* 1605
HERCULES - Brace & Box - WESTINGHOUSE LIGHTING CORPORATION; *pg.* 687, *pg.* 1571
HERCULES 500 - Heavy-duty Air & Water Hose - HBD INDUSTRIES, INC.; *pg.* 207, *pg.* 1449
HERCULES EXPRESS - Vacuum Transport System - BROOKS AUTOMATION, INC.; *pg.* 1320, *pg.* 813
HERCULES ST - Footwear - P.W. MINOR & SON, INC.; *pg.* 1816, *pg.* 1140
HERCULEX - Insect Protection Products - DOW AGROSCIENCES LLC; *pg.* 1156, *pg.* 684
HERCULEX - Fabrics - HERCULITE PRODUCTS, INC.; *pg.* 694, *pg.* 1529
HERCULEX - Lighting - LSI INDUSTRIES INC.; *pg.* 58, *pg.* 1416
HERCULEX - Seed Corn - MOEWS SEED CO., INC.; *pg.* 1797, *pg.* 616
HERCULINE - Actuator - HONEYWELL INTERNATIONAL INC.; *pg.* 407, *pg.* 1088
HERCULINER - Bed Liner - OLD WORLD INDUSTRIES, INC.; *pg.* 1175, *pg.* 641
HERCULINK - Stent System - ABBOTT LABORATORIES; *pg.* 1484, *pg.* 551
HERCULITE - Fabrics - HERCULITE PRODUCTS, INC.; *pg.* 694, *pg.* 1529
HERCULITE - Tempered & Semitempered Sheet, Flat & Shaped Glass - PPG INDUSTRIES, INC.; *pg.* 1445, *pg.* 1579
HERCULITE AUSTENITIC PROTECTION FABRICS - Fabrics - HERCULITE PRODUCTS, INC.; *pg.* 694, *pg.* 1529
HERCUVIT - Glass-Based Crystalline Materials for Industrial Arts Applications - PPG INDUSTRIES, INC.; *pg.* 1445, *pg.* 1579
HERDCHEK - Test Kit - IDEXX LABORATORIES, INC.; *pg.* 1543, *pg.* 753
HERDEZ - Mexican Foods - HORMEL FOODS CORPORATION; *pg.* 863, *pg.* 915
HERDSECURE - Printed Materials Concerning Animal Health - PFIZER INC.; *pg.* 1581, *pg.* 1278
HERE EVERYTHING'S BETTER - Slogan - H-E-B; *pg.* 1022, *pg.* 1740
HERE TODAY...GONE TOMORROW - Slogan - ALERE INC.; *pg.* 1488, *pg.* 849
HERETIC - Video Game - ID SOFTWARE, INC.; *pg.* 956, *pg.* 1727
HERFF JONES - School & Graduation Products - HERFF JONES, INC.; *pg.* 7, *pg.* 686
HERITAGE - Organs - ALLEN ORGAN COMPANY; *pg.* 527, *pg.* 1549
HERITAGE - Furniture - ASHLEY FURNITURE INDUSTRIES, INC.; *pg.* 914, *pg.* 1852
HERITAGE - Wrapper - CAMPBELL WRAPPER CORPORATION; *pg.* 1454, *pg.* 1856
HERITAGE - Rug - COURISTAN INC.; *pg.* 921, *pg.* 1067
HERITAGE - Vanity Lights - CRAFTMADE INTERNATIONAL, INC.; *pg.* 1295, *pg.* 1670
HERITAGE - Donut Mixes - DAWN FOOD PRODUCTS, INC.; *pg.* 1018, *pg.* 893
HERITAGE - Food Product - DUKE MANUFACTURING COMPANY, INC.; *pg.* 54, *pg.* 995
HERITAGE - Apparel - HAGGAR CORPORATION; *pg.* 41, *pg.* 1682
HERITAGE - Furniture - JASPER GROUP; *pg.* 930, *pg.* 691
HERITAGE - Lighting - LSI INDUSTRIES INC.; *pg.* 58, *pg.* 1416
HERITAGE - Plumbing Products - MASCO CORPORATION; *pg.* 96, *pg.* 909
HERITAGE - Eye Protection Product - MINE SAFETY APPLIANCES COMPANY; *pg.* 1361, *pg.* 1525
HERITAGE - Breakfast Cereals - NATURE'S PATH FOODS INC.; *pg.* 833, *pg.* 1908
HERITAGE COLLECTION - Church Worship Bulletins for the Black Church - WARNER PRESS, INC.; *pg.* 1701, *pg.* 673
HERITAGE COMICS AUCTIONS - Auctioneer - HERITAGE GALLERIES & AUCTIONEER; *pg.* 143, *pg.* 1682
HERITAGE CREWEL - Bedding - CROSCILL, INC.; *pg.* 1122, *pg.* 1220
HERITAGE CURRENCY AUCTION OF AMERICA - Auctioneer - HERITAGE GALLERIES & AUCTIONEER; *pg.* 143, *pg.* 1682
HERITAGE FOODS - Cereal - KASHI COMPANY; *pg.* 830, *pg.* 119
HERITAGE OVENS - Bakery Goods - PERFORMANCE FOOD GROUP COMPANY, LLC; *pg.* 1030, *pg.* 1803
HERITANCE - Hardwood Shutters - HUNTER DOUGLAS, INC.; *pg.* 928, *pg.* 1320
HERKIMER LANDING - Clothing - ABERCROMBIE & FITCH CO.; *pg.* 37, *pg.* 1466
HERMACRIMP - Seal & Thermoplastic Component - GREENE, TWEED & CO.; *pg.* 1344, *pg.* 1544
HERMAN MILLER - Furniture - HERMAN MILLER, INC.; *pg.* 926, *pg.* 913
HERMARK - Healthcare Product - MONOGRAM BIOSCIENCES, INC.; *pg.* 1569, *pg.* 280
HERMATIC GAS - Booster - ECLIPSE INC.; *pg.* 1332, *pg.* 655
HERMES - Surgical Control System - INTUITIVE SURGICAL, INC.; *pg.* 1546, *pg.* 286
HERMES-READY - Surgical Table - STERIS CORPORATION; *pg.* 1597, *pg.* 1464
HERMETEK - Fiber or Cardboard Tubes for Cartridges for Sealants & Adhesives - SONOCO PRODUCTS COMPANY; *pg.* 1469, *pg.* 1619
HERMETIC - Medical Device - INTEGRA LIFESCIENCES HOLDINGS CORPORATION; *pg.* 1545, *pg.* 1109
HERMETIC BOOSTER - Booster - ECLIPSE INC.; *pg.* 1332, *pg.* 655
HERMETICOOL - Test Equipment - SPX THERMAL PRODUCT SOLUTIONS; *pg.* 1378, *pg.* 1555
HERMILT - Belt - VANS, INC.; *pg.* 1821, *pg.* 76
HERMITAGE - Fabric - NEMSCHOFF, INC.; *pg.* 936, *pg.* 1890
HERMOSA - Footwear - COBIAN CORP.; *pg.* 1806, *pg.* 253
HERMOSA - Fabric - NEMSCHOFF, INC.; *pg.* 936, *pg.* 1890
HERO - Beverages - THE COCA-COLA COMPANY; *pg.* 240, *pg.* 493
HERO - Insecticides & Miticides - FMC CORPORATION; *pg.* 1163, *pg.* 1564
HERO - Wearable Digital Camera - GOPRO; *pg.* 1414, *pg.* 255
HERO BY WRANGLER - Apparel - V.F. CORPORATION; *pg.* 34, *pg.* 1376
HERO EW - Insecticides & Miticides - FMC CORPORATION; *pg.* 1163, *pg.* 1564
HEROES TRUST STREAMLIGHT - Slogan - STREAMLIGHT INC.; *pg.* 1306, *pg.* 1527
HEROINE - Furniture - JASPER GROUP; *pg.* 930, *pg.* 691
HERON BAY - Community Name - WCI COMMUNITIES, INC.; *pg.* 1118, *pg.* 414
HERON ISLES - Community Name - WCI COMMUNITIES, INC.; *pg.* 1118, *pg.* 414
HEROSCAPE - Game - HASBRO, INC.; *pg.* 954, *pg.* 1603
HEROX - Nylon Toothbrush Filaments - E.I. DU PONT DE NEMOURS & COMPANY; *pg.* 1159, *pg.* 390
HERPECIN-L - Health & Beauty Product - CHATTEM, INC.; *pg.* 1515, *pg.* 1628
HERPESELECT - Medical Test - QUEST DIAGNOSTICS INCORPORATED; *pg.* 1587, *pg.* 1080
HERPETROL - Pharmaceutical Product - ALVA/AMCO PHARMACAL COMPANIES, INC.; *pg.* 1492, *pg.* 637
HERRADURA - Tequila - BROWN-FORMAN CORPORATION; *pg.* 1958, *pg.* 732
HERRADURA - Tequila - SAZERAC COMPANY, INC.; *pg.* 1969, *pg.* 745
HERREN - Office Furniture - STEELCASE INC.; *pg.* 475, *pg.* 889
HERRGARD - Cheese - A.V. OLSSON TRADING CO. INC.; *pg.* 838, *pg.* 372
HERRING/OAM - Footwear - COBIAN CORP.; *pg.* 1806, *pg.* 253
HERRINGBONE - Bedcovering - ETHAN ALLEN INTERIORS INC.; *pg.* 924, *pg.* 343
HERR'S BACON & HORSERADISH - Smokey Bacon & Spicy Horseradish Potato Chips - HERR FOODS INC.; *pg.* 861, *pg.* 1557
HERR'S CRUNCHY CHEESE STICKS - Cheese Flavored Snacks - HERR FOODS INC.; *pg.* 861, *pg.* 1557
HERR'S JALAPENO - Tortilla Chips - HERR FOODS INC.; *pg.* 861, *pg.* 1557
HERR'S KETTLE COOKED CHIPS - Buffalo Wings & Boardwalk Salt & Vinegar Flavored Chips - HERR FOODS

INC.; pg. 861, pg. 1557
HERR'S OLD FASHIONED - Original Handcooked Potato Chips - HERR FOODS INC.; pg. 861, pg. 1557
HERR'S PHILLY CHEESE STEAK - Kettle Cooked Flavored Potato Chips - HERR FOODS INC.; pg. 861, pg. 1557
HERR'S SOUR CREAM & ONION - Kettle Cooked Potato Chips - HERR FOODS INC.; pg. 861, pg. 1557
HERR'S STIX - Fat-Free Pretzels - HERR FOODS INC.; pg. 861, pg. 1557
HERR'S WHITE CHEDDAR RANCH - Popcorn - HERR FOODS INC.; pg. 861, pg. 1557
HERRSCHNERS - Needlework Hobbycrafts - HERRSCHNERS, INC.; pg. 694, pg. 1895
HERS - Fitness Magazine - AMERICAN MEDIA, INC.; pg. 1615, pg. 410
HERSCH - Measurement Devices - MOCON, INC.; pg. 1363, pg. 940
HERSCHEL - Mowing & Construction Equipment - ALAMO GROUP INC.; pg. 1311, pg. 1745
HERSHEY CLASSIC SPECIAL EDITION - Footwear - K-SWISS; pg. 1837, pg. 306
HERSHEY'S BITES - Candies - THE HERSHEY CO.; pg. 1855, pg. 1538
HERSHEY'S BLISS - Dark Chocolate - THE HERSHEY CO.; pg. 1855, pg. 1538
HERSHEY'S CHOCOLATE MILK - Chocolate Milk - THE HERSHEY CO.; pg. 1855, pg. 1538
HERSHEY'S CHOCOLATE SHOPPE - Fudge Toppings - THE HERSHEY CO.; pg. 1855, pg. 1538
HERSHEY'S CLASSIC CARAMELS - Candy - THE HERSHEY CO.; pg. 1855, pg. 1538
HERSHEY'S COOKIES - Snacks - THE HERSHEY CO.; pg. 1855, pg. 1538
HERSHEY'S COOKIES 'N' CREME - Candy Bar - THE HERSHEY CO.; pg. 1855, pg. 1538
HERSHEY'S COOKIES 'N' CREME NUGGETS - Candy Bar - THE HERSHEY CO.; pg. 1855, pg. 1538
HERSHEY'S EXTRA DARK - Chocolate Candy - THE HERSHEY CO.; pg. 1855, pg. 1538
HERSHEY'S GOODNIGHT HUGS - Hot Cocoa Mixes - THE HERSHEY CO.; pg. 1855, pg. 1538
HERSHEY'S GOODNIGHT KISSES - Hot Cocoa Mixes - THE HERSHEY CO.; pg. 1855, pg. 1538
HERSHEY'S HOT COCOA - Hot Cocoa Mix - THE HERSHEY CO.; pg. 1855, pg. 1538
HERSHEY'S HUGS - Candy - THE HERSHEY CO.; pg. 1855, pg. 1538
HERSHEY'S KISSES - Chocolates - THE HERSHEY CO.; pg. 1855, pg. 1538
HERSHEY'S KISSES WITH ALMONDS - Chocolates with Almonds - THE HERSHEY CO.; pg. 1855, pg. 1538
HERSHEY'S MINIATURES - Chocolate Bars - THE HERSHEY CO.; pg. 1855, pg. 1538
HERSHEY'S NUGGETS - Chocolates - THE HERSHEY CO.; pg. 1855, pg. 1538
HERSHEY'S POT OF GOLD - Boxed Chocolates - THE HERSHEY CO.; pg. 1855, pg. 1538
HERSHEY'S S'MORES - Candy - THE HERSHEY CO.; pg. 1855, pg. 1538
HERSHEY'S SUGAR FREE - Candy - THE HERSHEY CO.; pg. 1855, pg. 1538
HERSHEY'S SYMPHONY - Chocolate Candy - THE HERSHEY CO.; pg. 1855, pg. 1538
HERSHEY'S SYRUP - Syrup - THE HERSHEY CO.; pg. 1855, pg. 1538
HERSHEY'S TAKE 5 - Chocolate Candy - THE HERSHEY CO.; pg. 1855, pg. 1538
HERSHEY'S TOP SCOTCH - Butterscotch Syrup - THE HERSHEY CO.; pg. 1855, pg. 1538
HERSHEY'S.COM - Web Site - THE HERSHEY CO.; pg. 1855, pg. 1538
HERVE LEGER - Clothing & Accessories for Women - BCBG MAX AZRIA GROUP LLC; pg. 19, pg. 301
HESKAVIEW INTEGRATED SOFTWARE - Program - HESKA CORPORATION; pg. 1542, pg. 335
HESPERIA STAR - California Newspaper - FREEDOM COMMUNICATIONS, INC.; pg. 1643, pg. 110
HESS - Franchised Service Stations - HESS CORPORATION; pg. 979, pg. 1240
HESS EXPRESS - Convenience Stores - HESS CORPORATION; pg. 979, pg. 1240
HESS TOY TRUCK - Collectibles - HESS CORPORATION; pg. 979, pg. 1240
HESTRON - Heat Strengthened Glass - PPG INDUSTRIES, INC.; pg. 1445, pg. 1579
HETACIN-K - Veterinary Oral Antibiotic - BOEHRINGER INGELHEIM VETMEDICA, INC.; pg. 1474, pg. 989
HETERO CAVITY - Molding - NATIONAL MOLDING, LLC; pg. 1887, pg. 430
HETRON - Polyester Resins - ASHLAND INC.; pg. 972, pg. 726
HEUBLEIN COCKTAILS - Cocktails - DIAGEO NORTH AMERICA, INC.; pg. 1961, pg. 361
HEUGA - Carpeting - INTERFACE, INC.; pg. 695, pg. 512
HEVACOMP - Software - BENTLEY SYSTEMS, INC.; pg. 361, pg. 1531
HEVI-BAR - Safety Equipment - CONDUCTIX INC.; pg. 1295, pg. 1015
HEVI-BAR II - Safety Equipment - CONDUCTIX INC.; pg. 1295, pg. 1015
HEVI-HITTER - Mechanical Drilling Jar - BAKER HUGHES INTEQ; pg. 1316, pg. 1700
HEVI-SAND - Chromite Sand - MINERALS TECHNOLOGIES INC.; pg. 1173, pg. 617
HEVI SHOT - Shotshell - REMINGTON ARMS COMPANY, LLC; pg. 1844, pg. 1302
HEWLETT-PACKARD - Company Name - HEWLETT-PACKARD COMPANY; pg. 404, pg. 175
HEX - Skincare Product - MERLE NORMAN COSMETICS, INC.; pg. 517, pg. 136
HEX - Valve - RICHARDS INDUSTRIES VALVE GROUP; pg. 107, pg. 1425
HEX GRIP - Power Tool - MILWAUKEE ELECTRIC TOOL CORP.; pg. 1056, pg. 1855
HEX-PHY - Ethernet Transceiver - BROADCOM CORPORATION; pg. 364, pg. 108
HEX VALVE - Instrumentation Valves - RICHARDS INDUSTRIES VALVE GROUP; pg. 107, pg. 1425
HEXABLOK - Packaging - PACTIV CORPORATION; pg. 1466, pg. 624
HEXACOMB - Honeycomb Product - PACTIV CORPORATION; pg. 1466, pg. 624
HEXAD - Burner - NAO, INC.; pg. 1074, pg. 1567
HEXAFLEX - Medical Equipment - INVACARE CORPORATION; pg. 1546, pg. 1451
HEXAFLUOROISOPROPANOL - Flurochemical - HALOCARBON PRODUCTS CORPORATION; pg. 978, pg. 1116
HEXAGRAM - Meter Reading System - BADGER METER, INC.; pg. 1401, pg. 1873
HEXAKLEAN - Chemicals - ASHLAND INC.; pg. 972, pg. 726
HEXALEN - Pharmaceutical - EISAI INC.; pg. 1526, pg. 1133
HEXALITE - Cushioning System - REEBOK INTERNATIONAL LTD.; pg. 1817, pg. 811
HEXANICITE - Chemical Product - SPECTRUM CHEMICALS & LABORATORY PRODUCTS, INC.; pg. 1181, pg. 94
HEXAR - Supercomputing System - CRAY INC.; pg. 380, pg. 1834
HEXAVER - Chemical Reagent - HACH COMPANY; pg. 1415, pg. 334
HEXBREAKER - Video Slots - INTERNATIONAL GAME TECHNOLOGY; pg. 957, pg. 1024
HEXCOAT - Gel Coat - HEXCEL CORPORATION; pg. 1884, pg. 375
HEXEN - Video Game - ID SOFTWARE, INC.; pg. 956, pg. 1727
HEXEN II - Video Game - ID SOFTWARE, INC.; pg. 956, pg. 1727
HEXENTRIC - Outdoor Products - BLACK DIAMOND, INC.; pg. 1827, pg. 1756
HEXFET - Power Semiconductor Device - INTERNATIONAL RECTIFIER CORPORATION; pg. 647, pg. 80
HEXFIT - Film Infusion Technology - HEXCEL CORPORATION; pg. 1884, pg. 375
HEXFLOW - Resin Transfer Molding System - HEXCEL CORPORATION; pg. 1884, pg. 375
HEXFORCE - Fabric - HEXCEL CORPORATION; pg. 1884, pg. 375
HEXFRED - Power Semiconductor Device - INTERNATIONAL RECTIFIER CORPORATION; pg. 647, pg. 80
HEXFRED - Die & Wafer - VISHAY INTERTECHNOLOGY, INC.; pg. 1435, pg. 1551
HEXISPLIT - Fiber Optic Splitter - COMMUNICATIONS SPECIALTIES, INC.; pg. 377, pg. 1338
HEXLITE - Core Material - HEXCEL CORPORATION; pg. 1884, pg. 375
HEXMC - Sheet-Molding Compound - HEXCEL CORPORATION; pg. 1884, pg. 375
HEXPLY - Prepreg - HEXCEL CORPORATION; pg. 1884, pg. 375
HEXQUISITE - Bowl - PACTIV CORPORATION; pg. 1466, pg. 624
HEXSENSE - Power Semiconductor Device - INTERNATIONAL RECTIFIER CORPORATION; pg. 647, pg. 80
HEXSIGHT - Object Location System - ADEPT TECHNOLOGY, INC.; pg. 1310, pg. 182
HEXTEND - Medical Device - HOSPIRA, INC.; pg. 1542, pg. 623
HEXTOOL - Tooling Materials - HEXCEL CORPORATION; pg. 1884, pg. 375
HEXTOW - Fibers - HEXCEL CORPORATION; pg. 1884, pg. 375
HEXWARE - Bowl - PACTIV CORPORATION; pg. 1466, pg. 624
HEXWEB - Core Material - HEXCEL CORPORATION; pg. 1884, pg. 375
HEYER-SCHULTE - Medical Device - INTEGRA LIFESCIENCES HOLDINGS CORPORATION; pg. 1545, pg. 1109
HF MESSENGER - Software - ROCKWELL COLLINS, INC.; pg. 234, pg. 702
HFV - Power Generator - ADVANCED ENERGY INDUSTRIES, INC.; pg. 613, pg. 328
HFZ - Cracking Catalysts - BASF CATALYSTS LLC; pg. 1148, pg. 1074
HG-LINK - Molecular Probe Product - THERMO FISHER SCIENTIFIC INC.; pg. 1602, pg. 61
HGR - Activated Vapor Phase Carbons - CALGON CARBON CORPORATION; pg. 1151, pg. 1574
HGR LH - Activated Vapor Phase Carbon - CALGON CARBON CORPORATION; pg. 1151, pg. 1574
HGR-P - Activated Vapor Phase Carbon - CALGON CARBON CORPORATION; pg. 1151, pg. 1574
HGTV MAGAZINE - Magazine - THE HEARST CORPORATION; pg. 1649, pg. 1239
HGTV43 - Diagnostic Product - ENZO BIOCHEM INC.; pg. 1529, pg. 1228
HGX - Mercury Decontaminant Powder - ACTON TECHNOLOGIES, INC.; pg. 1145, pg. 1582
H.H. GREGG - Appliances & Electronics - HHGREGG, INC.; pg. 56, pg. 686
H.H. SCOTT - Electronic Components - EMERSON RADIO CORP.; pg. 636, pg. 1087
HHR - Sport Utility Vehicle - GENERAL MOTORS COMPANY; pg. 175, pg. 881
HI-ALMAX - Refractory Product - RESCO PRODUCTS, INC.; pg. 107, pg. 1581
HI-ALMAX DRY - Pressed & Monolithic Refractory - RESCO PRODUCTS, INC.; pg. 107, pg. 1581
HI-ARC - Faucet - ELKAY MANUFACTURING COMPANY; pg. 80, pg. 645
HI-BAR - Safety Screen - THE LEE COMPANY; pg. 1420, pg. 383
HI-BULK - Braided Fishing Line - CORTLAND LINE COMPANY; pg. 1831, pg. 1155
HI-C - Fruit Drinks - THE COCA-COLA COMPANY; pg. 240, pg. 493
HI COUNT - Economy LED Lighting - GROTE INDUSTRIES, INC.; pg. 206, pg. 693
HI-DEP - Agricultural Product - PBI/GORDON CORPORATION; pg. 1176, pg. 985
HI-DRI - Sterilization Product - PROPPER MANUFACTURING COMPANY, INC.; pg. 1586, pg. 1175
HI-DRY - Molecular Sieve - MULTISORB TECHNOLOGIES, INC.; pg. 1570, pg. 1150
HI-FLO - Hose - HBD INDUSTRIES, INC.; pg. 207, pg. 1449
HI-FLO - Air Cleaner - KEY TECHNOLOGY, INC.; pg. 868, pg. 1847
HI-FLO CO-AX - Hose - HBD INDUSTRIES, INC.; pg. 207, pg. 1449
HI-FLOW - Combustible Gas Leak Detector - BACHARACH INC.; pg. 1400, pg. 1556
HI FLOW - Gas Leak Detector - BACHARACH INC.; pg. 1400, pg. 1556
HI FLOW SAMPLER - Natural Gas Leak Rate Measurement System - BACHARACH INC.; pg. 1400, pg. 1556
HI GAIN - Systems Integration & Aeronautics - LOCKHEED MARTIN CORPORATION; pg. 229, pg. 762
HI GEAR - CB Accessories - COBRA ELECTRONICS CORPORATION; pg. 629, pg. 572
HI-GLO - Yellow PVC Fabric - STANDARD SAFETY EQUIPMENT CO.; pg. 1379, pg. 632
HI GREEN - Fertilizer - POTASH CORP.; pg. 1177, pg. 641

First page reference indicates Business Class Edition
Second page reference indicates Geographic Edition

HI-HARD - Steel Product - A. FINKL & SONS CO.; *pg.* 1309, *pg.* 563
HI-HARD P-20 - Steel - A. FINKL & SONS CO.; *pg.* 1309, *pg.* 563
HI-HAT - Tripods & Supports - ALAN GORDON ENTERPRISES, INC.; *pg.* 1399, *pg.* 125
HI-HEAT - Paint & Coating - AERVOE INDUSTRIES INCORPORATED; *pg.* 1439, *pg.* 1021
HI-HIDE - Coating Product - PPG INDUSTRIES, INC.; *pg.* 1445, *pg.* 1579
HI-HIDE PLEXICOLOR - Paint - CALIFORNIA PRODUCTS CORPORATION; *pg.* 1441, *pg.* 781
HI HO CHERRY-O - Game - HASBRO, INC.; *pg.* 954, *pg.* 1603
HI-LIFE - Alloy Product - ESCO CORPORATION; *pg.* 1335, *pg.* 1502
HI-LIFT - Jack - THE BLOOMFIELD MANUFACTURING CO., INC.; *pg.* 70, *pg.* 674
HI-LIGHTER - Lighting System - UNILUX, INC.; *pg.* 682, *pg.* 1118
HI-LITER - Highlighting Pen - AVERY DENNISON CORPORATION; *pg.* 1452, *pg.* 95
HI LO - Plastics Product - AEP INDUSTRIES INC.; *pg.* 1878, *pg.* 1085
HI-LO - Two-Level Swivel Casters - HAMILTON CASTER & MFG. CO.; *pg.* 206, *pg.* 1454
HI-LO - Tracheal Tube - MEDTRONIC; *pg.* 1563, *pg.* 183
HI-LUX - Light Fixtures - JUNO LIGHTING, INC.; *pg.* 1300, *pg.* 606
HI MILER - Bias Truck Tires - THE GOODYEAR TIRE & RUBBER COMPANY; *pg.* 1883, *pg.* 1401
HI-POLYMER - Lead - PENTEL OF AMERICA, LTD.; *pg.* 453, *pg.* 295
HI-PORE - Software - BIO-RAD LABORATORIES, INC.; *pg.* 1504, *pg.* 101
HI-POWER - Cylinder - FABCO-AIR, INC.; *pg.* 1336, *pg.* 429
HI-POWER - Water Heater - LOCHINVAR CORPORATION; *pg.* 1073, *pg.* 1640
HI-PRO - Dry Dog Food - NESTLE PURINA PETCARE COMPANY; *pg.* 1479, *pg.* 1000
HI-Q - Tire And Rubber Product - THE GOODYEAR TIRE & RUBBER COMPANY; *pg.* 1883, *pg.* 1401
HI-RAM - Pressed & Monolithic Refractory - RESCO PRODUCTS, INC.; *pg.* 107, *pg.* 1581
HI-RANGER - Cable Placer - TEREX CORPORATION; *pg.* 1381, *pg.* 384
HI-REL - Capacitors - KEMET CORPORATION; *pg.* 649, *pg.* 1621
HI-SIL - Silica Product - PPG INDUSTRIES, INC.; *pg.* 1445, *pg.* 1579
HI-SPACE - Computer System - BATTELLE MEMORIAL INSTITUTE; *pg.* 1401, *pg.* 1437
HI-SPAND - Chucks & Arbors - GLEASON CORPORATION; *pg.* 1340, *pg.* 1335
HI-SPEED - Sterilization Product - PROPPER MANUFACTURING COMPANY, INC.; *pg.* 1586, *pg.* 1175
HI-SPEEDPOWER - Spindle - BRYANT GRINDER; *pg.* 1320, *pg.* 1768
HI SPOT - Beverages - THE COCA-COLA COMPANY; *pg.* 240, *pg.* 493
HI STEP - Chemical Coating - ENTHONE INC.; *pg.* 1161, *pg.* 381
HI-STRENGTH - Pressed & Monolithic Refractory - RESCO PRODUCTS, INC.; *pg.* 107, *pg.* 1581
HI-T-LUBE - Coating - GENERAL MAGNAPLATE CORPORATION; *pg.* 1164, *pg.* 1079
HI-TECH - Floss - RANIR LLC; *pg.* 520, *pg.* 888
HI-TECH - Coatings - SEYMOUR OF SYCAMORE, INC.; *pg.* 1447, *pg.* 663
HI-TECK - Coolant - DELTA FOREMOST CHEMICAL CORPORATION; *pg.* 1155, *pg.* 1642
HI-TEMP - Catalyst - BASF CATALYSTS LLC; *pg.* 1148, *pg.* 1074
HI-TEMP - Data Communication Product - GENERAL CABLE CORPORATION; *pg.* 83, *pg.* 729
HI-TEMPIR - Radiant Heater Systems for High Temperature Applications - PRECISION CONTROL SYSTEMS, INC./ RESEARCH INC.; *pg.* 1427, *pg.* 923
HI-TENSIL - Garage Door - MARTIN DOOR MANUFACTURING, INC.; *pg.* 96, *pg.* 1759
HI-TEX - Salt - CARGILL LIMITED; *pg.* 1475, *pg.* 1914
HI-TORQUE BALANCE - Coronary Guide Wire - ABBOTT LABORATORIES; *pg.* 1484, *pg.* 551
HI-TORQUE BALANCE MIDDLEWEIGHT UNIVERSAL - Coronary Guide Wire - ABBOTT LABORATORIES; *pg.* 1484, *pg.* 551
HI-TORQUE CROSS-IT XT - Coronary Guide Wire - ABBOTT LABORATORIES; *pg.* 1484, *pg.* 551
HI-TORQUE PILOT - Coronary Guide Wire - ABBOTT LABORATORIES; *pg.* 1484, *pg.* 551
HI-TORQUE SPARTACORE - Guide Wire - ABBOTT LABORATORIES; *pg.* 1484, *pg.* 551
HI-TORQUE WHISPER - Coronary Guide Wire - ABBOTT LABORATORIES; *pg.* 1484, *pg.* 551
HI-TRI - Solvent - THE DOW CHEMICAL COMPANY; *pg.* 1157, *pg.* 898
HI-VAC - Hose - HBD INDUSTRIES, INC.; *pg.* 207, *pg.* 1449
HI-VISIBILITY - Rainwear - BLAUER MANUFACTURING COMPANY, INC.; *pg.* 20, *pg.* 789
HI-WAY - Dump Body - HIGHWAY EQUIPMENT COMPANY; *pg.* 704, *pg.* 702
HI-WAY AUTUMNMATE - Leaf Collection Unit - HIGHWAY EQUIPMENT COMPANY; *pg.* 704, *pg.* 702
HI-WHITE - Software - XEROX CORPORATION; *pg.* 494, *pg.* 365
HI-Y - Catalyst Additive - JOHNSON MATTHEY PROCESS TECHNOLOGIES; *pg.* 1169, *pg.* 1083
HI-YIELD - Food Processing Equipment - HOLLYMATIC CORPORATION; *pg.* 1346, *pg.* 598
HIAWATHA - Fabric - NEMSCHOFF, INC.; *pg.* 936, *pg.* 1890
HIBACHI - Food Product - BENIHANA INC.; *pg.* 1716, *pg.* 409
HIBACHI GRILL - Food Product - HORMEL FOODS CORPORATION; *pg.* 863, *pg.* 915
HIBACHI-SAN - Japanese Restaurants - PANDA RESTAURANT GROUP, INC.; *pg.* 1743, *pg.* 194
HIBEAMZ - Magazine - PAISANO PUBLICATIONS, LLC; *pg.* 1674, *pg.* 38
HIBICLENS - Medical Device - SPIRE CORPORATION; *pg.* 1378, *pg.* 786
HIBISCUS - Eyewear - MAUI JIM, INC.; *pg.* 9, *pg.* 651
HIBORE - Golf Club - ROGER CLEVELAND GOLF COMPANY, INC.; *pg.* 1844, *pg.* 105
HIBRITE - Medical Product - HOLOGIC, INC.; *pg.* 1416, *pg.* 784
HIBTITER - Vaccine - PFIZER INC.; *pg.* 1581, *pg.* 1278
HIC RULES - Software System - MENTOR GRAPHICS CORPORATION; *pg.* 432, *pg.* 1510
HICKORY - Sticks - PEPSICO, INC.; *pg.* 259, *pg.* 1327
HICKORY CHAIR - Furniture - HICKORY CHAIR COMPANY; *pg.* 927, *pg.* 1378
HICKORY CHASE - Retirement Plan - ERICKSON LIVING; *pg.* 1090, *pg.* 766
HICKORY NEWS - North Carolina Newspaper - FREEDOM COMMUNICATIONS, INC.; *pg.* 1643, *pg.* 110
HICKORY POINT - Furniture - ASHLEY FURNITURE INDUSTRIES, INC.; *pg.* 914, *pg.* 1852
HICKORY STICKS - Meat Snack - FRITO-LAY NORTH AMERICA, INC.; *pg.* 1853, *pg.* 1730
HICOM - Terminal - HARRIS CORP. RF COMMUNICATIONS DIVISION; *pg.* 642, *pg.* 1336
HID AND THE BEAM - Post-Mount Spotlight - UNITY MANUFACTURING COMPANY; *pg.* 221, *pg.* 594
HID-N-AIRE - Wall Blower - SWARTWOUT DIVISION; *pg.* 114, *pg.* 978
HIDA - Electronic Product - LRAD CORPORATION; *pg.* 652, *pg.* 204
HIDDEN AGENDA - Outerwear for Men & Boys - I. SPIEWAK & SONS, INC.; *pg.* 42, *pg.* 1242
HIDDEN ASSETS - Video Game - INTERNATIONAL GAME TECHNOLOGY; *pg.* 957, *pg.* 1024
HIDDEN BAY - Food Product - SHAMROCK FOODS COMPANY; *pg.* 895, *pg.* 20
HIDDEN CANYON - Bike - MARIN BIKES; *pg.* 1708, *pg.* 168
HIDDEN EDGE - Utility Knives - THE L.S. STARRETT COMPANY; *pg.* 1421, *pg.* 783
HIDDEN HAVEN - Game - WMS INDUSTRIES INC.; *pg.* 593, *pg.* 666
HIDDEN HITCH - Trailer Hitch Systems - TRIMAS CORPORATION; *pg.* 1383, *pg.* 874
HIDDEN PICTURE - Books & Magazine - HIGHLIGHTS FOR CHILDREN, INC.; *pg.* 1650, *pg.* 1440
HIDDEN POSTAGE - Postage - STAMPS.COM INC.; *pg.* 1282, *pg.* 82
HIDDEN TRACKS - Footwear - WOLVERINE WORLD WIDE, INC.; *pg.* 1822, *pg.* 905
HIDDEN TREASURE - Carpet - BEAULIEU GROUP, LLC; *pg.* 917, *pg.* 529
HIDDEN VALLEY - Bottled Salad Dressings - THE CLOROX COMPANY; *pg.* 327, *pg.* 169
HIDE-A-BED - Bedding Products - SIMMONS COMPANY; *pg.* 943, *pg.* 520
HIDE-A-DISC - Air Freshener - SURCO PRODUCTS, INC.; *pg.* 336, *pg.* 1581
HIDE-A-HOOK - Truck Cover - PENDA CORPORATION; *pg.* 214, *pg.* 1887
HIDE-A-VECTOR2 - Compact Hot Water Heaters - EMBASSY INDUSTRIES, INC.; *pg.* 1071, *pg.* 1164
HIDE & SLEEK - Clothing - SPANX INC.; *pg.* 32, *pg.* 520
HIDE 'N SNAK - Lunch Box - THERMOS L.L.C.; *pg.* 61, *pg.* 660
HIDEAWAY - Fabric - NEMSCHOFF, INC.; *pg.* 936, *pg.* 1890
HIDEAWAY - Economy Folding Bi-Directional - WINEGARD COMPANY; *pg.* 688, *pg.* 702
HIDEF CONFERENCING - Software - CITRIX SYSTEMS, INC.; *pg.* 375, *pg.* 424
HIDRA - Amplifier - COHERENT, INC.; *pg.* 1406, *pg.* 265
HIDUSTER - Overhead Dusting Tools - HILLYARD, INC.; *pg.* 331, *pg.* 990
HIERARCHIAL INJECTION - Software System - MENTOR GRAPHICS CORPORATION; *pg.* 432, *pg.* 1510
HIERARCHICAL OPTIMIZATION TECHNOLOGY - Software - SYNOPSYS, INC.; *pg.* 480, *pg.* 162
HIERARCHY INJECTION - Software System - MENTOR GRAPHICS CORPORATION; *pg.* 432, *pg.* 1510
HIFLEX - Icing Powders - MALLET & COMPANY, INC.; *pg.* 875, *pg.* 1521
HIGH DEFINITION - Slogan - AUDIO RESEARCH CORPORATION; *pg.* 621, *pg.* 953
HIGH DEFINITION MASS SPECTROMETRY - Spectrometry System - WATERS CORPORATION; *pg.* 1436, *pg.* 834
HIGH DEFINITION NATURAL LIGHTING - Lighting Product - OTTLITE; *pg.* 1303, *pg.* 475
HIGH DEFINITION NIGHT VISION - Tagline - XENONICS HOLDINGS, INC.; *pg.* 1308, *pg.* 62
HIGH-DEMAND - Medical Equipment - CONMED CORPORATION; *pg.* 1517, *pg.* 1347
HIGH DENSITY PLUS - Electronic Component - TERADYNE INC.; *pg.* 679, *pg.* 838
HIGH DENSITY PLUS - Board-to-Board Connectors - WINCHESTER ELECTRONICS CORP.; *pg.* 688, *pg.* 382
HIGH DIMENSION - Eyeliners & Mascara; Haircolor - REVLON, INC.; *pg.* 521, *pg.* 1286
HIGH DIVIDE - Cart Bag - DATREK GOLF; *pg.* 1832, *pg.* 1801
HIGH DOLLAR 7S - Game - WMS INDUSTRIES INC.; *pg.* 593, *pg.* 666
HIGH ENDURANCE - Cellular Phone Batteries - VARTA MICROBATTERY, INC.; *pg.* 221, *pg.* 1339
HIGH-FIDELITY - Mirrors & Specialty Flat & Curved Glass - PPG INDUSTRIES, INC.; *pg.* 1445, *pg.* 1579
HIGH FIVE - Cell Culture Product - THERMO FISHER SCIENTIFIC INC.; *pg.* 1602, *pg.* 61
HIGH-FLO - Pump - GRACO, INC.; *pg.* 1342, *pg.* 935
HIGH FLOW - Adsorber - CALGON CARBON CORPORATION; *pg.* 1151, *pg.* 1574
HIGH-FLOW VENTSORB - Activated Carbon Vapor Phase Adsorption System - CALGON CARBON CORPORATION; *pg.* 1151, *pg.* 1574
HIGH FLYER - Game Bird Product - KENT NUTRITION GROUP; *pg.* 1477, *pg.* 710
HIGH FLYER - Industrial Safety Eyewear - UVEX SAFETY; *pg.* 1433, *pg.* 1608
HIGH GRADE WESTERN WEAR - Men's Apparel - PENDLETON WOOLEN MILLS, INC.; *pg.* 697, *pg.* 1505
HIGH H BATCH - Cookware - TURBOCHEF TECHNOLOGIES, INC.; *pg.* 902, *pg.* 1670
HIGH H CONVEYOR 2020 - Cookware - TURBOCHEF TECHNOLOGIES, INC.; *pg.* 902, *pg.* 1670
HIGH H CONVEYOR 3240 - Cookware - TURBOCHEF TECHNOLOGIES, INC.; *pg.* 902, *pg.* 1670
HIGH IMPACT - Cart Bag - DATREK GOLF; *pg.* 1832, *pg.* 1801
HIGH IMPACT - Scented Oils - HENKEL CONSUMER GOODS; *pg.* 511, *pg.* 22
HIGH INTENSITY - Mixers - BUNN-O-MATIC CORPORATION; *pg.* 53, *pg.* 661
HIGH-K - Shell & Tube Heat Exchangers - BALTIMORE AIRCOIL COMPANY; *pg.* 1069, *pg.* 773
HIGH LINER - Frozen & Canned Seafood - HIGH LINER FOODS INCORPORATED; *pg.* 862, *pg.* 1917
HIGH ON THE HOG - Video Game - INTERNATIONAL GAME TECHNOLOGY; *pg.* 957, *pg.* 1024
HIGH PEAKS REGION - Clothing - ABERCROMBIE & FITCH CO.; *pg.* 37, *pg.* 1466

HIGH-PEN PRIMER 452 - Primers - KOPPERS HOLDINGS INC.; *pg.* 1170, *pg.* 1577
HIGH PERFORMANCE - Cold Plate - LYTRON INCORPORATED; *pg.* 1074, *pg.* 861
HIGH PERFORMANCE-10 - Steel Product - AK STEEL HOLDING CORPORATION; *pg.* 1311, *pg.* 1479
HIGH-PERFORMANCE ASIC PROTOTYPING SYSTEM - Software - SYNOPSYS, INC.; *pg.* 480, *pg.* 162
HIGH PLAINS - Carpet - INTERFACE, INC.; *pg.* 695, *pg.* 512
HIGH POWER ILLUMINATION - Tagline - XENONICS HOLDINGS, INC.; *pg.* 1308, *pg.* 62
HIGH PRODUCTIVITY DEVELOPMENT - Technology - ATMI, INC.; *pg.* 1314, *pg.* 342
HIGH PROFILE - Seat Cushion - THE ROHO GROUP; *pg.* 1591, *pg.* 556
HIGH RIDGE - Wall Panel - BLUELINX HOLDINGS, INC.; *pg.* 70, *pg.* 491
HIGH ROCK - T-Shirts - ABERCROMBIE & FITCH CO.; *pg.* 37, *pg.* 1466
HIGH SCHOOL MUSICAL - Toy & Game - HASBRO, INC.; *pg.* 954, *pg.* 1603
HIGH SPEED - Neutral Salt - HEATBATH CORPORATION; *pg.* 1165, *pg.* 826
HIGH-SPEED - Internet Service - SHAW COMMUNICATIONS INC.; *pg.* 307, *pg.* 1904
HIGH SPEED - Game - WMS INDUSTRIES INC.; *pg.* 593, *pg.* 666
HIGH-SPEED LITE - Internet Service - SHAW COMMUNICATIONS INC.; *pg.* 307, *pg.* 1904
HIGH-STAK - Filing System - FELLOWES, INC.; *pg.* 397, *pg.* 620
HIGH STAKES - Game - MISSOURI LOTTERY; *pg.* 999, *pg.* 979
HIGH-TAP - Office Product - HAWORTH, INC.; *pg.* 402, *pg.* 891
HIGH-TEMP - Grease Developed for High Temperature Applications - LUBRIPLATE LUBRICANTS; *pg.* 980, *pg.* 1097
HIGH TIDE - Computer Software - LOCKHEED MARTIN CORPORATION; *pg.* 229, *pg.* 762
HIGHER FACE & BODY COLLECTION - Men's Fragrance - PARFUMS CHRISTIAN DIOR, INC; *pg.* 519, *pg.* 1276
HIGHER MIND - Vitamin & Herbal Supplement - SOURCE NATURALS; *pg.* 1595, *pg.* 278
HIGHER POWER - Clothing - SPANX INC.; *pg.* 32, *pg.* 520
HIGHFIELD - Security Devices - HIGHFIELD MANUFACTURING CO.; *pg.* 1346, *pg.* 339
HIGHFLO - Vinyl Rainwater System - GENOVA PRODUCTS, INC.; *pg.* 83, *pg.* 875
HIGHLAND - Vinyl Plastic Electrical Tape, Pressure Sensitive Adhesive Tape - 3M COMPANY; *pg.* 1142, *pg.* 956
HIGHLAND - Rug - COURISTAN INC.; *pg.* 921, *pg.* 1067
HIGHLAND - Window Treatment - CROSCILL, INC.; *pg.* 1122, *pg.* 1220
HIGHLAND - Drive Truck - OSHKOSH CORPORATION; *pg.* 187, *pg.* 1885
HIGHLAND - Cargo Loading Systems - TRIMAS CORPORATION; *pg.* 1383, *pg.* 874
HIGHLAND - Lighting Product - WESTINGHOUSE LIGHTING CORPORATION; *pg.* 687, *pg.* 1571
HIGHLAND ESTATE - Beverage - KENDALL-JACKSON WINE ESTATES, LTD.; *pg.* 1965, *pg.* 277
HIGHLAND HOUSE - Mattress & Box Spring Sets - KINGSDOWN, INC.; *pg.* 932, *pg.* 1383
HIGHLAND PARK - Furniture - ASHLEY FURNITURE INDUSTRIES, INC.; *pg.* 914, *pg.* 1852
HIGHLAND PARK - Scotch - REMY COINTREAU USA INC.; *pg.* 1969, *pg.* 1285
HIGHLAND SPRINGS - Retirement Community - ERICKSON LIVING; *pg.* 1090, *pg.* 766
HIGHLANDER - Sports Utility Vehicle - TOYOTA MOTOR NORTH AMERICA, INC.; *pg.* 192, *pg.* 1303
HIGHLANDER HYBRID - Hybrid SUV - TOYOTA MOTOR NORTH AMERICA, INC.; *pg.* 192, *pg.* 1303
HIGHLANDS - Kitchen Product - KOHLER CO.; *pg.* 91, *pg.* 1862
HIGHLANDS - Fabric - NEMSCHOFF, INC.; *pg.* 936, *pg.* 1890
HIGHLIGHT - Direct Diode Industrial System - COHERENT, INC.; *pg.* 1406, *pg.* 265
HIGHLIGHT - Sheet Vinyl Flooring - CONGOLEUM CORPORATION; *pg.* 921, *pg.* 1084
HIGHLIGHTS FOR CHILDREN - Magazine - HIGHLIGHTS FOR CHILDREN, INC.; *pg.* 1650, *pg.* 1440
HIGHLIGHTSKIDS - Magazine - HIGHLIGHTS FOR CHILDREN, INC.; *pg.* 1650, *pg.* 1440
HIGHLINE - Bath Product - KOHLER CO.; *pg.* 91, *pg.* 1862
HIGHLINER - Video Game - INTERNATIONAL GAME TECHNOLOGY; *pg.* 957, *pg.* 1024
HIGHLITES - Lighting - PHILIPS LIGHTING; *pg.* 1303, *pg.* 806
HIGHLY MANAGED HOSTING - Hosting Service - VERIZON TERREMARK; *pg.* 685, *pg.* 447
HIGHMARK - Paper Products - BOISE CASCADE HOLDINGS, L.L.C.; *pg.* 1453, *pg.* 546
HIGHRISE - Roof Flashing - OATEY SUPPLY CHAIN SERVICES; *pg.* 30, *pg.* 1433
HIGHROAD - Software - EMC CORPORATION; *pg.* 391, *pg.* 825
HIGHSCHOOLPEOPLESEARCH.COM - Internet Service - UNITED ONLINE, INC.; *pg.* 1286, *pg.* 308
HIGHVIEW - Adaptable Workflow - CACI INTERNATIONAL INC.; *pg.* 367, *pg.* 1773
HIGHWAY 1 - Guitar - FENDER MUSICAL INSTRUMENTS CORPORATION; *pg.* 547, *pg.* 21
HIGHWAY HERO - Tire And Rubber Product - THE GOODYEAR TIRE & RUBBER COMPANY; *pg.* 1883, *pg.* 1401
HIGHWAY ONE - Bike - MARIN BIKES; *pg.* 1708, *pg.* 168
HIGHWIRE FAMILY - Compact PCI - NEONODE, INC.; *pg.* 659, *pg.* 268
HIGIG - Wireless Network - BROADCOM CORPORATION; *pg.* 364, *pg.* 108
HIGUERAL - Salami - PATRICK CUDAHY INC.; *pg.* 888, *pg.* 1856
HIKARI - Pet Product - PETSMART, INC.; *pg.* 1481, *pg.* 18
HIKER - Footwear - P.W. MINOR & SON, INC.; *pg.* 1816, *pg.* 1140
HIKER+ - Energy Bars - NATURE'S PATH FOODS INC.; *pg.* 833, *pg.* 1908
HIL-GLO - Cleaning Product - HILLYARD, INC.; *pg.* 331, *pg.* 990
HIL-MIST - Cleaning Product - HILLYARD, INC.; *pg.* 331, *pg.* 990
HIL-PAC - Cleaning Product - HILLYARD, INC.; *pg.* 331, *pg.* 990
HIL-PHENE - Cleaning Product - HILLYARD, INC.; *pg.* 331, *pg.* 990
HIL-SHEEN - Cleaning Product - HILLYARD, INC.; *pg.* 331, *pg.* 990
HIL-TEX - Sealer/Undercoater - HILLYARD, INC.; *pg.* 331, *pg.* 990
HIL-TREAT - Cleaner & Polish - HILLYARD, INC.; *pg.* 331, *pg.* 990
HILAN - High Speed Drill System - AESCULAP, INC.; *pg.* 1487, *pg.* 1521
HILAND - Dairy Food - HILAND DAIRY FOODS COMPANY; *pg.* 862, *pg.* 1006
HILANDER - Supermarket - THE KROGER CO.; *pg.* 1025, *pg.* 1416
HILARIE - Footwear - STEVEN MADDEN, LTD.; *pg.* 1819, *pg.* 1176
HILARIUM - Toy - MATTEL, INC.; *pg.* 962, *pg.* 81
HILIGHT - Generator - ADVANCED ENERGY INDUSTRIES, INC.; *pg.* 613, *pg.* 328
HILIGHT - Testing Instrument - NEWAGE TESTING INSTRUMENTS, INC.; *pg.* 1058, *pg.* 1532
HILL HOUSE - Furniture - ASHLEY FURNITURE INDUSTRIES, INC.; *pg.* 914, *pg.* 1852
HILLCREST - Shoes - ALLEN-EDMONDS SHOE CORP.; *pg.* 1804, *pg.* 1887
HILLCREST - Paper & Nonwoven Material - FIBERMARK INC.; *pg.* 1457, *pg.* 1764
HILLCREST - Outdoor Storage - LIFETIME PRODUCTS INC.; *pg.* 933, *pg.* 1751
HILLCREST - Lighting Product - QUOIZEL INC.; *pg.* 1304, *pg.* 1616
HILLEBRAND ESTATES - Wine - ANDREW PELLER LIMITED; *pg.* 1956, *pg.* 1920
HILL'S - Petcare - TRACTOR SUPPLY COMPANY; *pg.* 708, *pg.* 1627
HILLSHIRE FARMS - Lunchmeats & Smoked Sausages - TYSON FOODS, INC.; *pg.* 902, *pg.* 35
HILLYARD - Air Freshener - HILLYARD, INC.; *pg.* 331, *pg.* 990
HILLYARD - FIRST IN GYM FINISHES - Tag Line - HILLYARD, INC.; *pg.* 331, *pg.* 990
HILO - Eyewear - MAUI JIM, INC.; *pg.* 9, *pg.* 651
HILO-AL - Pressed & Monolithic Refractory - RESCO PRODUCTS, INC.; *pg.* 107, *pg.* 1581
HILOBOND - Refractory Product - RESCO PRODUCTS, INC.; *pg.* 107, *pg.* 1581
HILOY - Plastic Compound & Resin - A. SCHULMAN, INC.; *pg.* 1144, *pg.* 1452
HILROY - Office Product - WESTROCK COMPANY; *pg.* 1472, *pg.* 1805
HILTI - Construction Tool Company - HILTI, INC.; *pg.* 1346, *pg.* 1490
HILTON - Lighting - LSI INDUSTRIES INC.; *pg.* 58, *pg.* 1416
HILTON - Fabric - SCALAMANDRE, INC.; *pg.* 941, *pg.* 1058
HILTON GARDEN INN - Hotels - HILTON WORLDWIDE, INC.; *pg.* 1094, *pg.* 1791
HILTON GRAND VACATION CLUB - Vacationing Package - HILTON WORLDWIDE, INC.; *pg.* 1094, *pg.* 1791
HILTON GRAND VACATIONS COMPANY - Vacation Timeshare - HILTON WORLDWIDE, INC.; *pg.* 1094, *pg.* 1791
HILTON HAWAIIAN VILLAGE BEACH RESORT & SPA - Resort - HILTON WORLDWIDE, INC.; *pg.* 1094, *pg.* 1791
HILTON HHONORS - Cards - AMERICAN EXPRESS COMPANY; *pg.* 712, *pg.* 1190
HILTON HONORS - Hotel - HILTON WORLDWIDE, INC.; *pg.* 1094, *pg.* 1791
HILTON HOTELS - Hotel - HILTON WORLDWIDE, INC.; *pg.* 1094, *pg.* 1791
HILTON OVAL - Dispensing Closure - OWENS-ILLINOIS, INC.; *pg.* 1466, *pg.* 1470
HIMALAYA - Rug - COURISTAN INC.; *pg.* 921, *pg.* 1067
HIMARK - Molecular Biology Product - THERMO FISHER SCIENTIFIC INC.; *pg.* 1602, *pg.* 61
HIMARS - Mobile Guided Missile Systems - LOCKHEED MARTIN CORPORATION; *pg.* 229, *pg.* 762
HIND - Athletic Apparel - SAUCONY, INC.; *pg.* 1818, *pg.* 828
HINDS - Optical Head - HINDS INSTRUMENTS, INC.; *pg.* 1416, *pg.* 1498
HINDS I - Optical Head - HINDS INSTRUMENTS, INC.; *pg.* 1416, *pg.* 1498
HINDS II - Optical Head - HINDS INSTRUMENTS, INC.; *pg.* 1416, *pg.* 1498
HINGE-FREE - Lubricant - STERIS CORPORATION; *pg.* 1597, *pg.* 1464
HINIKER - Rowcrop & Field Cultivators, Seeders, Rear Blades & Shredders - HINIKER COMPANY; *pg.* 704, *pg.* 927
HINT - Fabric - NEMSCHOFF, INC.; *pg.* 936, *pg.* 1890
HINTEGRA - Medical Device - INTEGRA LIFESCIENCES HOLDINGS CORPORATION; *pg.* 1545, *pg.* 1109
HIP AA-SMART - Software - BOTTOMLINE TECHNOLOGIES INC.; *pg.* 363, *pg.* 483
HIP-AIR - Air Respirator - MINE SAFETY APPLIANCES COMPANY; *pg.* 1361, *pg.* 1525
HIP DIPPERS - Food Product - TYSON FOODS, INC.; *pg.* 902, *pg.* 35
HIP HOP - Furniture - AMERICAN LEATHER LP; *pg.* 912, *pg.* 1673
HIP HUGGER - Laundry Basket Contoured for Easy Carrying on the Hip - RUBBERMAID HOME PRODUCTS; *pg.* 1138, *pg.* 1453
HIPAA GATEWAY - Software - TRIZETTO CORPORATION; *pg.* 485, *pg.* 327
HIPAASUCCESS - Software - TRIZETTO CORPORATION; *pg.* 485, *pg.* 327
HIPEC - Semiconductor Protective Silicon-Based Coating - DOW CORNING CORPORATION; *pg.* 1159, *pg.* 900
HIPER - Integrated Circuits - POWER INTEGRATIONS, INC.; *pg.* 1369, *pg.* 249
HIPERBATCH - Computer Product - INTERNATIONAL BUSINESS MACHINES CORPORATION; *pg.* 418, *pg.* 1138
HIPERCO - Alloy - CARPENTER TECHNOLOGY CORPORATION; *pg.* 73, *pg.* 1584
HIPERDYN - Semiconductor Product - IXYS CORPORATION; *pg.* 422, *pg.* 146
HIPERFILTER - Filter - CAMERON INTERNATIONAL; *pg.* 1151, *pg.* 1702
HIPERFORM - Refrigeration System - PAUL MUELLER COMPANY; *pg.* 706, *pg.* 1007
HIPERFORM - Molecular Biology Product - THERMO FISHER SCIENTIFIC INC.; *pg.* 1602, *pg.* 61
HIPERFRED - Semiconductor Product - IXYS CORPORATION; *pg.* 422, *pg.* 146
HIPERMAX - Wireless Network Product - AIRSPAN NETWORKS INC.; *pg.* 346, *pg.* 410
HIPERNOM - Alloy - CARPENTER TECHNOLOGY CORPORATION; *pg.* 73, *pg.* 1584
HIPERPLC - Combined PFC & LLC Off-Line Controller -

First page reference indicates Business Class Edition
Second page reference indicates Geographic Edition

POWER INTEGRATIONS, INC.; *pg.* 1369, *pg.* 249
HIPERSCREEN - Strainer - CAMERON INTERNATIONAL; *pg.* 1151, *pg.* 1702
HIPERSTATION - Software - COMPUWARE CORPORATION; *pg.* 379, *pg.* 879
HIPERSTRIP - Deaerator - CAMERON INTERNATIONAL; *pg.* 1151, *pg.* 1702
HIPERVAC - Deaerator - CAMERON INTERNATIONAL; *pg.* 1151, *pg.* 1702
HIPNOTIC - Low Rise Footless Hosiery - SPANX INC.; *pg.* 32, *pg.* 520
HIPOTRONICS - Testing Equipment - HUBBELL INCORPORATED; *pg.* 1299, *pg.* 370
HIPPO GLO - Body Lotion - ORANGE PEEL ENTERPRISES, INC.; *pg.* 1028, *pg.* 477
HIPPO-VAC - Vacuum - SHOP-VAC CORPORATION; *pg.* 1375, *pg.* 1595
HIQNET - Software - HARMAN INTERNATIONAL INDUSTRIES, INCORPORATED; *pg.* 641, *pg.* 374
HIRATE - Battery - ULTRALIFE CORPORATION; *pg.* 1385, *pg.* 1317
HIRDA - Cathodic Protection - CORRPRO COMPANIES, INC.; *pg.* 631, *pg.* 1464
HIREXPRESS - Electronic Onboarding Service - EQUIFAX WORKFORCE SOLUTIONS; *pg.* 394, *pg.* 997
HIRI - Optical Product - PPG INDUSTRIES, INC.; *pg.* 1445, *pg.* 1579
HIRISE - Kitchen Product - KOHLER CO.; *pg.* 91, *pg.* 1862
HISAR - Airborne Surveillance System - RAYTHEON COMPANY; *pg.* 233, *pg.* 854
HISAT - Electrical Test & Measurement - HD ELECTRIC COMPANY; *pg.* 1299, *pg.* 666
HISIDE - Switch - POWER INTEGRATIONS, INC.; *pg.* 1369, *pg.* 249
HISIZE - Bag - SAMSONITE CORPORATION; *pg.* 11, *pg.* 830
HISONIC - Medical Device - MISONIX INC.; *pg.* 1568, *pg.* 1159
HISPANIC CO-OP INSERT - Mailed Promotional Insert - VALASSIS COMMUNICATIONS, INC.; *pg.* 1287, *pg.* 897
THE HISPANIC HEARTBEAT OF AMERICA - Tagline - UNIVISION COMMUNICATIONS INC.; *pg.* 683, *pg.* 1307
HISPEC - Connector - MOLEX INCORPORATED; *pg.* 655, *pg.* 628
HISPEC GS - Electronic Components - MOLEX INCORPORATED; *pg.* 655, *pg.* 628
HISSS - Game - GAMEWRIGHT; *pg.* 953, *pg.* 836
HISTABLOCK - Health Care Product - NATURE'S SUNSHINE PRODUCTS, INC.; *pg.* 1571, *pg.* 1754
HISTOFREEZER - Portable Cryosurgical System - ORASURE TECHNOLOGIES INC; *pg.* 1578, *pg.* 1516
HISTORY CHANNEL - Television Channel - A&E TELEVISION NETWORKS, LLC; *pg.* 267, *pg.* 1185
HISTORY MYSTERIES - Toys - AMERICAN GIRL LLC; *pg.* 949, *pg.* 1871
HISTORYCHANNEL.COM - Historical Information Web Site - THE HISTORY CHANNEL; *pg.* 290, *pg.* 1240
HIT - Beverages - THE COCA-COLA COMPANY; *pg.* 240, *pg.* 493
HIT IT AT THE BELLE! - Games - PENN NATIONAL GAMING, INC.; *pg.* 574, *pg.* 1595
HIT IT BELIEVE IT - Slogan - CALLAWAY GOLF COMPANY; *pg.* 1829, *pg.* 58
HIT IT LONG, HIT IT STRAIGHT - Tag Line - ACUSHNET COMPANY; *pg.* 1824, *pg.* 818
HIT THE JACKPOT - Lottery Game - MINNESOTA STATE LOTTERY; *pg.* 999, *pg.* 956
HIT YOUR FLAVOR TARGET FASTER - Slogan - DAVID MICHAEL & CO. INC.; *pg.* 852, *pg.* 1563
HITACHI - Data Storage System - HITACHI DATA SYSTEMS CORPORATION; *pg.* 407, *pg.* 265
HITCH HAND - Truck Bed Extender - LUND INTERNATIONAL, INC.; *pg.* 211, *pg.* 526
HITCH-HIKER - Portable Ground Fault Circuit Interrupter - PASS & SEYMOUR/LEGRAND; *pg.* 1303, *pg.* 1344
HITCH WORLD - Moving Aid - U-HAUL INTERNATIONAL, INC.; *pg.* 1926, *pg.* 20
HITCHCOCK UPSIZED - Shoe - HITCHCOCK SHOES, INC.; *pg.* 1810, *pg.* 824
HITCHSTEP - Cargo Access Step - LUND INTERNATIONAL, INC.; *pg.* 211, *pg.* 526
HITCLIPS - Toy & Game - HASBRO, INC.; *pg.* 954, *pg.* 1603
HITEC - Chemical Product - ALBEMARLE CORPORATION; *pg.* 1146, *pg.* 741
HITEC - Performance Additives - NEWMARKET CORPORATION; *pg.* 982, *pg.* 1803
HITOX - Mineral Product - TOR MINERALS INTERNATIONAL INC.; *pg.* 1184, *pg.* 1672
H.I.T.S. - Chemist Team - WILD FLAVORS, INC.; *pg.* 910, *pg.* 728
HIVEX - Expanders - ANDERSON INTERNATIONAL CORP.; *pg.* 1313, *pg.* 1474
HIVID - Pharmaceutical Product - HOFFMANN-LA ROCHE INC.; *pg.* 1542, *pg.* 1099
HIVIZ - Fiber Optic Sight - SMITH & WESSON HOLDING CORPORATION; *pg.* 1845, *pg.* 846
HIYIELD - Specialty Paper - APPVION INC.; *pg.* 1451, *pg.* 1852
HJ - School & Graduation Products - HERFF JONES, INC.; *pg.* 7, *pg.* 686
HL 5500 - Hall Effect Measurement System - NANOMETRICS INCORPORATED; *pg.* 1423, *pg.* 147
HLS SERIES - Heavy-Duty Lighting - PHOENIX PRODUCTS COMPANY; *pg.* 1304, *pg.* 1879
HLV - Machinery - HARDINGE INC.; *pg.* 1344, *pg.* 1157
HMC - High Momentum Burners - HAUCK MANUFACTURING COMPANY, INC.; *pg.* 1345, *pg.* 1522
HMC - Electronic Components - MOLEX INCORPORATED; *pg.* 655, *pg.* 628
HMF-02 - Fixed Displacement Motor - LINDE HYDRAULICS CORPORATION; *pg.* 1356, *pg.* 1407
HMF/VR-02 - Fixed Displacement Motor - LINDE HYDRAULICS CORPORATION; *pg.* 1356, *pg.* 1407
HMIC - Integrated Circuit - ONMOBILE LIVE, INC.; *pg.* 449, *pg.* 829
HMMWV - M998 Series Military Tactical Wheeled Vehicle - AM GENERAL, LLC; *pg.* 163, *pg.* 697
HMR-02 - Regulated Motor - LINDE HYDRAULICS CORPORATION; *pg.* 1356, *pg.* 1407
HMV-02 - Variable Motor - LINDE HYDRAULICS CORPORATION; *pg.* 1356, *pg.* 1407
HNK - Lighting - SWIVELIER CO., INC.; *pg.* 1307, *pg.* 1142
HNX - High Nitrogen Atmosphere Gas Generators - SURFACE COMBUSTION, INC.; *pg.* 1077, *pg.* 1462
HO-PAC - Vibratory Mounted Compactor & Driver - ALLIED CONSTRUCTION PRODUCTS, LLC; *pg.* 1311, *pg.* 1427
HOBART - Arc Welding Systems, Battery Chargers & Aircraft Ground Power Units - HOBART BROTHERS COMPANY; *pg.* 1346, *pg.* 1477
HOBBY - Cameras - EASTMAN KODAK COMPANY; *pg.* 1408, *pg.* 1333
HOBBY FARMS - Magazine - I-5 PUBLISHING LLC; *pg.* 1651, *pg.* 133
HOBBY-PAC - Photographic Chemicals - EASTMAN KODAK COMPANY; *pg.* 1408, *pg.* 1333
HOBBY PAL - Assembly Equipment - BADGER AIR BRUSH COMPANY; *pg.* 359, *pg.* 612
HOBBYLITE - Filter - HOBBICO, INC.; *pg.* 956, *pg.* 562
HOBBYPOXY - Specialty Products for Hobby Use - PETTIT PAINT COMPANY; *pg.* 1444, *pg.* 1116
HOBBYTEC - Knife - COAST CUTLERY COMPANY; *pg.* 1121, *pg.* 1501
HOBIE - Catamarans, Kayaks & Fishing Boats - HOBIE CAT COMPANY; *pg.* 1708, *pg.* 173
HOBIE CAT - Catamarans & Sailboats - HOBIE CAT COMPANY; *pg.* 1708, *pg.* 173
HOCHTALER - Wine - ANDREW PELLER LIMITED; *pg.* 1956, *pg.* 1920
THE HOCKEY NEWS - Newspaper - TRANSCONTINENTAL INC.; *pg.* 1695, *pg.* 1957
HOCUS FOCUS - Game - GAMEWRIGHT; *pg.* 953, *pg.* 836
HOCUT - Metal Cutting - HOUGHTON INTERNATIONAL INC.; *pg.* 1167, *pg.* 1589
HOFFMAN - Blower - GARDNER DENVER, INC.; *pg.* 1338, *pg.* 1592
HOFFMAN GROVE - Wine - GEYSER PEAK WINERY; *pg.* 1964, *pg.* 101
HOFFMAN HOUSE - Sauces & Syrups - TREEHOUSE FOODS, INC.; *pg.* 901, *pg.* 649
HOFFMAN II COMPACT - External Fixation System - STRYKER CORPORATION; *pg.* 1598, *pg.* 894
HOFFMAN MODULATION CONTRAST SYSTEM - Viewing System for Microscopes - SLANT/FIN CORPORATION; *pg.* 1076, *pg.* 1163
HOFFMAN MOUNTAIN - Shirts - ABERCROMBIE & FITCH CO.; *pg.* 37, *pg.* 1466
HOFFMAN SPECIALTY - Fluid Technology - ITT CORPORATION; *pg.* 1351, *pg.* 1354
HOFFMAN SPECIALTY - Steam Specialties - XYLEM INC.; *pg.* 1078, *pg.* 1339
HOFFMANN II - Surgical & Medical Product - STRYKER CORPORATION; *pg.* 1598, *pg.* 894
HOFFMEISTER - Lighting - PHILIPS LIGHTING; *pg.* 1303, *pg.* 806
HOFFRITZ - Cutlery, Kitchen Tools & Gadgets & Cutting Boards - LIFETIME BRANDS, INC.; *pg.* 1127, *pg.* 1161
HOFMANN - Wheel Balancers, Lifts, Tire Changers & Aligners - SNAP-ON INCORPORATED; *pg.* 1062, *pg.* 1862
H.O.G. - Enthusiast Club - HARLEY-DAVIDSON, INC.; *pg.* 178, *pg.* 1874
HOG - Software - HIGH END SYSTEMS, INC.; *pg.* 1299, *pg.* 1663
HOG IPC - Lighting Product - HIGH END SYSTEMS, INC.; *pg.* 1299, *pg.* 1663
HOG RING - Pliers - TRACTOR SUPPLY COMPANY; *pg.* 708, *pg.* 1627
HOG WILD - Game - WMS INDUSTRIES INC.; *pg.* 593, *pg.* 666
HOGAN - Computer Program - COMPUTER SCIENCES CORPORATION; *pg.* 378, *pg.* 1780
HOGUE - Wine - CONSTELLATION BRANDS CANADA; *pg.* 1960, *pg.* 1925
HOGUE - Dress Shoes - JOHNSTON & MURPHY CO.; *pg.* 1810, *pg.* 1651
HOHOS - Snack Cakes - HOSTESS BRANDS LLC; *pg.* 1856, *pg.* 984
HOISTALOY - Load Chain - COLUMBUS MCKINNON CORPORATION; *pg.* 1325, *pg.* 1138
HOKA ONE ONE - Running Shoes - DECKERS OUTDOOR CORPORATION; *pg.* 1807, *pg.* 100
HOKU - Eyewear - MAUI JIM, INC.; *pg.* 9, *pg.* 651
HOLA AMIGOS - Mexican Restaurants - REAL MEX RESTAURANTS, INC.; *pg.* 1746, *pg.* 75
HOLA, LECTOR! - Reading Program - SCHOLASTIC INC.; *pg.* 1683, *pg.* 1288
HOLAHOY.COM - Spanish-Language Website - CHICAGO TRIBUNE COMPANY; *pg.* 1627, *pg.* 570
HOLBROOK - Shoes - ALLEN-EDMONDS SHOE CORP.; *pg.* 1804, *pg.* 1887
HOLCUTTERS - Cutter - HOUGEN MANUFACTURING INC.; *pg.* 1347, *pg.* 908
HOLD-A-NOTES - Magazine Program - OLYMPIA SALES, INC.; *pg.* 1780, *pg.* 346
HOLD-A-PHONE - Headphone Display - KOSS CORPORATION; *pg.* 649, *pg.* 1877
HOLD & CLEAN - Hair Preparations - THE GILLETTE COMPANY; *pg.* 509, *pg.* 795
HOLD-E-ZEE - Screw Holding Screwdriver - CHANNELLOCK, INC.; *pg.* 1044, *pg.* 1551
HOLD 'EM CHALLENGE - Video Poker - INTERNATIONAL GAME TECHNOLOGY; *pg.* 957, *pg.* 1024
HOLD IT ALL - Denim Handbag - HABAND COMPANY, INC.; *pg.* 1772, *pg.* 1099
HOLD THAT THOUGHT - Book - BOOKS-A-MILLION, INC.; *pg.* 1623, *pg.* 2
HOLD-ZIT - Rubber Straps & Fasteners - RADIATOR SPECIALTY COMPANY; *pg.* 215, *pg.* 1380
HOLD'EM HIGH - Software - DATAVIZ, INC.; *pg.* 383, *pg.* 356
HOLDEN - Furniture - AMERICAN LEATHER LP; *pg.* 912, *pg.* 1673
HOLDEN - Vehicle - GENERAL MOTORS COMPANY; *pg.* 175, *pg.* 881
HOLDENS FOUNDATION SEEDS - Foundation Seeds - MONSANTO COMPANY; *pg.* 1173, *pg.* 999
HOLDFAST - Roll Gauze - 3M COMPANY; *pg.* 1142, *pg.* 956
HOLDINGPATTERN - Hair Care Product - NU SKIN ENTERPRISES, INC.; *pg.* 518, *pg.* 1755
HOLDRITE - Bracket - OATEY SUPPLY CHAIN SERVICES; *pg.* 30, *pg.* 1433
HOLE HAMMER - Pneumatic Tool - MCLAUGHLIN BORING SYSTEMS; *pg.* 1360, *pg.* 1617
HOLE HAWG - Power Tools - MILWAUKEE ELECTRIC TOOL CORP.; *pg.* 1056, *pg.* 1855
HOLE-HOG - Underground Piercing Tool - ALLIED CONSTRUCTION PRODUCTS, LLC; *pg.* 1311, *pg.* 1427
HOLE SHOOTERS - Power Tools - MILWAUKEE ELECTRIC TOOL CORP.; *pg.* 1056, *pg.* 1855
HOLE SHOT - Car Part Accessory - PRO-LINE, INC.; *pg.* 966, *pg.* 45
HOLEC - Electrical Products - EATON CORPORATION; *pg.* 1331, *pg.* 1429
HOLEY SMOKES - Video Game - INTERNATIONAL GAME TECHNOLOGY; *pg.* 957, *pg.* 1024
HOLGA - Office Furniture - HNI CORPORATION; *pg.* 927,

pg. 709
HOLIDAY BLEND - Coffee Blend - THE SECOND CUP LTD.; *pg.* 1749, *pg.* 1928
HOLIDAY CELEBRATIONS BOUQUET - Floral Bouquet - FTD GROUP, INC.; *pg.* 1795, *pg.* 608
HOLIDAY EMBROIDERED - Table Textile - HERITAGE LACE INC.; *pg.* 694, *pg.* 711
HOLIDAY EXPRESS LOAN PROGRAM - Temporary Loans - JACKSON HEWITT TAX SERVICE INC.; *pg.* 771, *pg.* 1103
HOLIDAY FLOWER TREE - Flower Arrangement - 1-800-FLOWERS.COM, INC.; *pg.* 1758, *pg.* 1151
HOLIDAY HAIR - Hair Salons - REGIS CORPORATION; *pg.* 521, *pg.* 941
HOLIDAY HOUSE - Restaurant - STAR BUFFET, INC.; *pg.* 1751, *pg.* 24
HOLIDAY HYSTERIA - Games - PENN NATIONAL GAMING, INC.; *pg.* 574, *pg.* 1595
HOLIDAY IN VENICE - Video Game - INTERNATIONAL GAME TECHNOLOGY; *pg.* 957, *pg.* 1024
HOLIDAY INN - Hotels for Business & Leisure Travelers - INTERCONTINENTAL HOTELS CORPORATION; *pg.* 1097, *pg.* 511
HOLIDAY INN EXPRESS - Hotels - INTERCONTINENTAL HOTELS CORPORATION; *pg.* 1097, *pg.* 511
HOLIDAY JACK - Game - MISSOURI LOTTERY; *pg.* 999, *pg.* 979
HOLIDAY JAZZ - Coffee - COMMUNITY COFFEE COMPANY LLC; *pg.* 849, *pg.* 741
HOLIDAY SAGE - Candle - THE YANKEE CANDLE COMPANY, INC.; *pg.* 1792, *pg.* 843
HOLIDAY TREATS - Lottery Game - KENTUCKY LOTTERY CORPORATION; *pg.* 996, *pg.* 735
HOLIDAYS NEWS SERVICE - Holiday Travel Information - AMERICAN AUTOMOBILE ASSOCIATION; *pg.* 1190, *pg.* 429
HOLLAND AMERICA - Passenger Cruises & Tours - CARNIVAL CORPORATION; *pg.* 1902, *pg.* 441
HOLLAND AMERICA LINE - Cruise Tour Operator - HOLLAND AMERICA LINE INC.; *pg.* 1911, *pg.* 1836
HOLLAND & BARRETT - Nutritional Products - NBTY, INC.; *pg.* 1572, *pg.* 1338
HOLLAND RAIN - Hat - WOODEN SHIPS OF HOBOKEN; *pg.* 35, *pg.* 1315
HOLLISTER - Lighting Product - QUOIZEL INC.; *pg.* 1304, *pg.* 1616
HOLLISTER CO. - Teen Clothing - ABERCROMBIE & FITCH CO.; *pg.* 37, *pg.* 1466
HOLLOW POINT - Footwear - OAKLEY, INC.; *pg.* 1840, *pg.* 86
HOLLOW-SET - Bolt & Shield Anchor - POWERS FASTENERS INC.; *pg.* 1059, *pg.* 1143
HOLLOWBODY - Guitar - PAUL REED SMITH GUITARS; *pg.* 574, *pg.* 779
HOLLOWJET - Spray Product - SPRAYING SYSTEMS CO.; *pg.* 1063, *pg.* 670
HOLLOWOOD STAR DISCUS - 2.0K, 1.6K & 1.0K Discus - GILL ATHLETICS, INC.; *pg.* 1835, *pg.* 562
HOLLY - Scarf - HERITAGE LACE INC.; *pg.* 694, *pg.* 711
HOLLY - Sugar & Sweetener Product - IMPERIAL SUGAR COMPANY; *pg.* 864, *pg.* 1746
HOLLY - Light Duty Anchor - MKT FASTENING, LLC; *pg.* 1056, *pg.* 34
HOLLY FARMS - Chicken Products - TYSON FOODS, INC.; *pg.* 902, *pg.* 35
HOLLY JOLLY - Lottery Game - MICHIGAN STATE LOTTERY BUREAU; *pg.* 999, *pg.* 895
HOLLY JOLLY CHRISTMAS - Scarf - HERITAGE LACE INC.; *pg.* 694, *pg.* 711
HOLLY MINI-MATIC - Food Processing Equipment - HOLLYMATIC CORPORATION; *pg.* 1346, *pg.* 598
HOLLY PINE - Fragrance - NATURAL DECORATIONS, INC.; *pg.* 936, *pg.* 5
HOLLY RIBBON - Pillow and Throw - HERITAGE LACE INC.; *pg.* 694, *pg.* 711
HOLLYTEX - Carpet - BEAULIEU GROUP, LLC; *pg.* 917, *pg.* 529
HOLLYWOOD - Food Product - THE HAIN CELESTIAL GROUP, INC.; *pg.* 860, *pg.* 1172
HOLLYWOOD - Gum - MONDELEZ INTERNATIONAL, INC.; *pg.* 878, *pg.* 601
HOLLYWOOD - Base - SCHOOL-TECH, INC.; *pg.* 1844, *pg.* 866
HOLLYWOOD - Filter - THE TIFFEN COMPANY LLC; *pg.* 1432, *pg.* 1165
HOLLYWOOD CLASSIC - Video Game - INTERNATIONAL GAME TECHNOLOGY; *pg.* 957, *pg.* 1024
HOLLYWOOD CONNECTION - Entertainment Center - CARMIKE CINEMAS, INC.; *pg.* 273, *pg.* 528
HOLLYWOOD-FX - Filter & Lens - THE TIFFEN COMPANY LLC; *pg.* 1432, *pg.* 1165
HOLLYWOOD HIGH - Educational Materials - SCHOLASTIC INC.; *pg.* 1683, *pg.* 1288
HOLLYWOOD HILLS - Carpet - BEAULIEU GROUP, LLC; *pg.* 917, *pg.* 529
HOLLYWOOD RECORDS - Record Label - THE WALT DISNEY COMPANY; *pg.* 317, *pg.* 52
THE HOLLYWOOD REPORTER - Trade Magazine - THE NIELSEN COMPANY B.V.; *pg.* 1671, *pg.* 1272
HOLMAN - Kitchen Equipment - THE MIDDLEBY CORPORATION; *pg.* 1361, *pg.* 610
HOLMATRO - Cutting And Pulling Tool - HOLMATRO, INC.; *pg.* 1346, *pg.* 771
HOLMES - Garage Doors - CLOPAY BUILDING PRODUCTS COMPANY; *pg.* 76, *pg.* 1459
HOLMES - Home Environment Products - JARDEN CONSUMER SOLUTIONS; *pg.* 57, *pg.* 412
HOLMES - Towing & Recovery Equipment - MILLER INDUSTRIES, INC.; *pg.* 185, *pg.* 1655
HOLMES & NARVER - Architects & Engineers - AECOM; *pg.* 64, *pg.* 173
HOLO-KROME - Mechanic Hand Tool - DANAHER CORPORATION; *pg.* 1044, *pg.* 397
HOLOFIBER - Diabetic Socks - ALIMED, INC.; *pg.* 1490, *pg.* 816
HOLOFIBER - Socks & Sleeves - THE SALK COMPANY; *pg.* 1591, *pg.* 800
HOLOFLAKE - Colorant - POLYONE CORPORATION; *pg.* 1177, *pg.* 1404
HOLOMEDIC - Sleep Liner - DRAPER KNITTING CO., INC.; *pg.* 692, *pg.* 810
HOLOPHANE - Lighting Fixture Product - ACUITY BRANDS, INC.; *pg.* 1294, *pg.* 487
HOLOSIGHT - Riflescope - BUSHNELL OUTDOOR PRODUCTS, INC.; *pg.* 1403, *pg.* 718
HOLOTEX - Paper & Nonwoven Material - FIBERMARK INC.; *pg.* 1457, *pg.* 1764
HOLOVISION - Installation Kit - CRESTRON ELECTRONICS INC.; *pg.* 631, *pg.* 1116
HOLOVISION - Integral Laser Sight System - M-B COMPANIES, INC.; *pg.* 1357, *pg.* 1884
HOLSET - Turbocharger - CUMMINS INC.; *pg.* 1326, *pg.* 676
HOLSTER-TOP - Ladder Product - WERNER HOLDING CO.; *pg.* 121, *pg.* 1534
HOLSUM - Bread - KLOSTERMAN BAKING COMPANY, INC.; *pg.* 869, *pg.* 1415
HOLTON - Shoes - ALLEN-EDMONDS SHOE CORP.; *pg.* 1804, *pg.* 1887
HOLTS - Car Care Product - HONEYWELL CONSUMER PRODUCTS GROUP; *pg.* 208, *pg.* 344
HOLTS - Turbocharger - HONEYWELL INTERNATIONAL INC.; *pg.* 407, *pg.* 1088
HOLY HEMP - Nutritional Product - NUTRACEUTICAL INTERNATIONAL CORPORATION; *pg.* 1576, *pg.* 1753
HOLY LANDS SUN TOURS - Tour Packages - ISRAM WHOLESALE TOURS & TRAVEL LTD.; *pg.* 1913, *pg.* 1244
HOLY PINK PAGODA - Nail Care Product - OPI PRODUCTS INC.; *pg.* 518, *pg.* 167
HOMAC - Cable Management System - THOMAS & BETTS CORPORATION; *pg.* 680, *pg.* 1646
HOMASOTE - Building Product - HOMASOTE COMPANY; *pg.* 87, *pg.* 1126
HOME - Crop Protectant - GARDENS ALIVE!, INC.; *pg.* 1796, *pg.* 693
HOME - Carpet - INTERFACE, INC.; *pg.* 695, *pg.* 512
HOME & GARDEN - Home & Garden Products - ENESCO, LLC; *pg.* 1124, *pg.* 620
HOME & GARDEN TELEVISION - Cable Network - THE E.W. SCRIPPS COMPANY; *pg.* 1639, *pg.* 1412
HOME BOOK PACK - Educational Materials - SCHOLASTIC INC.; *pg.* 1683, *pg.* 1288
HOME BOX OFFICE - Pay Television Service - HOME BOX OFFICE, INC.; *pg.* 290, *pg.* 1240
HOME CARE - Furniture - FLEXSTEEL INDUSTRIES, INC.; *pg.* 925, *pg.* 707
HOME CARE - Shower Faucets & Handles - MOEN INCORPORATED; *pg.* 1056, *pg.* 1468
HOME CHANNEL NEWS - Industry Publication - LEBHAR-FRIEDMAN INC.; *pg.* 1658, *pg.* 1250
HOME CHOICE PRO - Automated Peritoneal Dialysis - BAXTER INTERNATIONAL INC.; *pg.* 1499, *pg.* 599
HOME COOKING - Culinary Magazine - ANNIE'S; *pg.* 1617, *pg.* 673
HOME DECOR STAIR - Baby Gate - EVENFLO COMPANY, INC.; *pg.* 924, *pg.* 1470
HOME DECORATORS COLLECTION - Home Decorating Catalog - THE HOME DEPOT, INC.; *pg.* 1050, *pg.* 510
HOME DEFENSE MAX - Lawn & Garden Product - THE SCOTTS MIRACLE-GRO COMPANY; *pg.* 1799, *pg.* 1459
THE HOME DEPOT - Credit Card - CITIGROUP INC.; *pg.* 735, *pg.* 1212
THE HOME DIGITAL JUKEBOX - Digital Music Audio Recording & Playback System - GIBSON GUITAR CORP.; *pg.* 550, *pg.* 1650
HOME FT. LAUDERDALE - Magazine - BONNIER CORPORATION; *pg.* 1622, *pg.* 480
HOME HEALTH QUALITY GUIDE - Healthcare Product - HEALTH GRADES, INC.; *pg.* 1256, *pg.* 319
HOME HEALTH REPORT CARDS - Healthcare Product - HEALTH GRADES, INC.; *pg.* 1256, *pg.* 319
HOME HELPERS - Household Product - HY-VEE, INC., *pg.* 1023, *pg.* 713
HOME JUICE - Soft Drink - NATIONAL BEVERAGE CORP.; *pg.* 257, *pg.* 425
HOME MARKETPLACE - Catalog of Home Goods - SILVER STAR BRANDS; *pg.* 1785, *pg.* 1886
HOME MAT - Insecticides - THE CLOROX COMPANY; *pg.* 327, *pg.* 169
HOME MIAMI - Magazine - BONNIER CORPORATION; *pg.* 1622, *pg.* 480
HOME MOVIES - Carpet - INTERFACE, INC.; *pg.* 695, *pg.* 512
HOME NEWS TRIBUNE - Daily Newspaper - ASBURY PARK PRESS INC.; *pg.* 1617, *pg.* 1090
THE HOME OF HOMESTYLE - Tag Line - BOB EVANS FARMS, LLC; *pg.* 841, *pg.* 1467
HOME OF SELECTED OVEN DRESSED - Tagline - KAUFFMAN POULTRY FARMS, INC.; *pg.* 867, *pg.* 665
HOME OF THE BEST AGENTS - Slogan - RE/MAX INTERNATIONAL, INC.; *pg.* 1109, *pg.* 322
HOME OUTFITTERS - Merchandise Store - HUDSON'S BAY COMPANY; *pg.* 1773, *pg.* 1938
HOME PERFORMANCE REBATE - Public Utility Service - XCEL ENERGY INC.; *pg.* 1955, *pg.* 946
HOME PLANS - Magazine - GARLINGHOUSE COMPANY; *pg.* 1644, *pg.* 1612
HOME POSSIBLE - Financial Services - FEDERAL HOME LOAN MORTGAGE CORPORATION; *pg.* 751, *pg.* 1790
HOME RUN - Pastries - UNITED STATES BAKERY; *pg.* 907, *pg.* 1507
HOME RUN CABLE - Galvanized Steel Armored Cable - AFC CABLE SYSTEMS, INC.; *pg.* 1294, *pg.* 835
HOME RUN DERBY - Baseball Tournament - THE PHILLIES, L.P.; *pg.* 575, *pg.* 1569
HOME RUN READERS - Educational Program - OAKLAND ATHLETICS LIMITED PARTNERSHIP; *pg.* 571, *pg.* 172
HOME SALE MAXIMIZER - Real Estate Seller Advisory Solutions - HOMEGAIN.COM, INC.; *pg.* 1256, *pg.* 83
HOME SCIENCES - Prefabricated Non-Metal Walls - PULTEGROUP, INC.; *pg.* 1109, *pg.* 873
HOME SLICKER - Roofing Ventilation Product - BENJAMIN OBDYKE, INC.; *pg.* 70, *pg.* 1540
HOME SMILE COOKIN' - Entrees - EAT'N PARK HOSPITALITY GROUP; *pg.* 1728, *pg.* 1539
HOME SOLUTION - Allergy Control - AERUS LLC; *pg.* 51, *pg.* 1673
HOME SOLUTIONS - Advertising Publication - DOMINION ENTERPRISES; *pg.* 1636, *pg.* 1796
HOME STYLE - Potato Chips - UTZ QUALITY FOODS, INC.; *pg.* 907, *pg.* 1536
HOME STYLER - Primers - SHERWIN WILLIAMS; *pg.* 1448, *pg.* 1436
HOME SWEET HOME - Pillow and Throw - HERITAGE LACE INC.; *pg.* 694, *pg.* 711
HOME VALUATOR - Software - EQUIFAX INC.; *pg.* 748, *pg.* 504
HOME VIDEO ESSENTIALS - Software - RENTRAK CORPORATION; *pg.* 306, *pg.* 1506
HOME2SUITES - Extended Stay Hotel - HILTON WORLDWIDE, INC.; *pg.* 1094, *pg.* 1791
HOMEAGAIN - Microchip Identification System - MERCK & CO., INC.; *pg.* 1566, *pg.* 1077
HOMEBASE - Software - EMC CORPORATION; *pg.* 391, *pg.* 825

HOMEBIZ - Home Business Insurance - UTICA MUTUAL INSURANCE COMPANY; *pg.* 1222, *pg.* 1183
HOMEBUILDER.COM - Website - MOVE, INC.; *pg.* 1268, *pg.* 247
HOMEBUYER'S PREFERRED - Radon Detection Program - LANDAUER, INC.; *pg.* 1554, *pg.* 615
HOMECHOICE - Peritoneal Dialyzer - BAXTER INTERNATIONAL INC.; *pg.* 1499, *pg.* 599
HOMECHOICE - Wire & Cable Products - BELDEN, INC.; *pg.* 624, *pg.* 993
HOMECREST - Hardware - FORTUNE BRANDS HOME & SECURITY, INC.; *pg.* 55, *pg.* 600
HOMECREST - Cabinetry - MASTERBRAND CABINETS, INC.; *pg.* 96, *pg.* 692
HOMEFILL - Oxygen Compressor - INVACARE CORPORATION; *pg.* 1546, *pg.* 1451
HOMEFINDER.COM - Real Estate Business Website - CLASSIFIED VENTURES, LLC; *pg.* 1235, *pg.* 571
HOMEFREE - Telephone Service - NTELOS HOLDINGS CORP.; *pg.* 659, *pg.* 1811
HOMEGAIN - Real Estate Marketing Solutions - CLASSIFIED VENTURES, LLC; *pg.* 1235, *pg.* 571
HOMEKEEPER - Insecticides - THE CLOROX COMPANY; *pg.* 327, *pg.* 169
HOMELAND SECURITY BRIEFING - Publisher - BLOOMBERG BNA; *pg.* 1621, *pg.* 1772
HOMELINK - Computer Network Card - CISCO SYSTEMS, INC.; *pg.* 372, *pg.* 240
HOMELINK - Auto-Dimming Mirror Vehicle-Based Control Systems - GENTEX CORPORATION; *pg.* 206, *pg.* 913
HOMEMADE BRAND - Ice Cream - UNITED DAIRY FARMERS, INC.; *pg.* 906, *pg.* 1426
HOMEMARKETONLINE - Web Site - KNOXVILLE NEWS-SENTINEL COMPANY; *pg.* 1657, *pg.* 1637
HOMEOPATHY - Healthcare Product - SWANSON HEALTH PRODUCTS INC.; *pg.* 1600, *pg.* 1397
HOMEOWNER FOR LIFE - Slogan - PULTEGROUP, INC.; *pg.* 1109, *pg.* 873
HOMEPHY - Chipset - ADVANCED MICRO DEVICES, INC.; *pg.* 613, *pg.* 282
HOMEPLATE - Siding - BOISE CASCADE HOLDINGS, L.L.C.; *pg.* 1453, *pg.* 546
HOMEPLUG - Connector Modules - BEL FUSE INC.; *pg.* 624, *pg.* 1075
HOMEPRIDE - Sauces - CAMPBELL SOUP COMPANY; *pg.* 844, *pg.* 1048
HOMEPRO - Hair Cutting Kit - WAHL CLIPPER CORPORATION; *pg.* 524, *pg.* 662
HOMERECEPTIONIST - Communication Product - CENTURYLINK, INC; *pg.* 1870, *pg.* 317
HOMERWOOD - Wood Flooring Products - ARMSTRONG WORLD INDUSTRIES, INC.; *pg.* 914, *pg.* 1545
HOMESCAN - Consumer Information - ACNIELSEN CORPORATION; *pg.* 341, *pg.* 1187
HOMES.COM - Advertising Website - DOMINION ENTERPRISES; *pg.* 1636, *pg.* 1796
HOMESIGHT - Home Monitoring - MOTOROLA SOLUTIONS, INC.; *pg.* 657, *pg.* 659
HOMESITE - Software - ADOBE SYSTEMS INCORPORATED; *pg.* 342, *pg.* 235
HOMESMART - Retail Store Service - XCEL ENERGY INC.; *pg.* 1955, *pg.* 946
HOMESPUN - Scarf - HERITAGE LACE INC.; *pg.* 694, *pg.* 711
HOMESPUN - Yarn - LION BRAND YARN COMPANY; *pg.* 696, *pg.* 1050
THE HOMESTEAD - Hotel - THE OMNI HOMESTEAD RESORT; *pg.* 1106, *pg.* 1786
HOMESTEAD-MIAMI SPEEDWAY - Motorsports Facility - INTERNATIONAL SPEEDWAY CORPORATION; *pg.* 553, *pg.* 420
HOMESTEPS - Financial Services - FEDERAL HOME LOAN MORTGAGE CORPORATION; *pg.* 751, *pg.* 1790
HOMESTYLE - Food Product - 4C FOODS CORPORATION; *pg.* 835, *pg.* 1145
HOMESTYLE - Hamburger Sandwiches - INTERNATIONAL DAIRY QUEEN, INC.; *pg.* 1732, *pg.* 938
HOMESTYLE - Bread - KLOSTERMAN BAKING COMPANY, INC.; *pg.* 869, *pg.* 1415
HOMESTYLE - Pretzels - SNYDER'S OF HANOVER, INC.; *pg.* 1862, *pg.* 1536
HOMESTYLE BOWLS - Frozen Food - BELLISIO FOODS, INC.; *pg.* 840, *pg.* 931
HOMESTYLE DOUBLE BURGER - Hamburgers - INTERNATIONAL DAIRY QUEEN, INC.; *pg.* 1732, *pg.* 938
HOMESTYLES - All Products - DMI FURNITURE, INC.; *pg.* 923, *pg.* 733
HOMETOWN BUFFET - Restaurants - OVATION BRANDS; *pg.* 1743, *pg.* 921
THE HOMETOWN EXPERTS WITH A WORLD OF EXPERIENCE - Slogan - RE/MAX INTERNATIONAL, INC.; *pg.* 1109, *pg.* 322
HOMETOWN HEARTH AND GRILL - Fireplace Superstore - SUBURBAN PROPANE PARTNERS, L.P.; *pg.* 113, *pg.* 1132
HOMETOWN PROUD - IGA Image Advertising Program - IGA, INC.; *pg.* 1023, *pg.* 578
HOMETOWNANNAPOLIS.COM - Newspaper Website - CAPITAL GAZETTE COMMUNICATIONS INC.; *pg.* 1625, *pg.* 754
HOMEWAITER - Dumbwaiter - INCLINATOR COMPANY OF AMERICA; *pg.* 88, *pg.* 1536
HOMEWOOD SUITES BY HILTON - Extended-Stay Suites - HILTON WORLDWIDE, INC.; *pg.* 1094, *pg.* 1791
HOMEWORKS - Desk Top (Which Fits Over Two Twin-Drawer Filing Cabinets) - RUBBERMAID HOME PRODUCTS; *pg.* 1138, *pg.* 1453
HOMEX - Building Product - HOMASOTE COMPANY; *pg.* 87, *pg.* 1126
HOMINEX-1 - Pharmaceutical Product - ABBOTT LABORATORIES; *pg.* 1484, *pg.* 551
HOMMAGE - Suitcase - SAMSONITE CORPORATION; *pg.* 11, *pg.* 830
HON - Office Furniture - HNI CORPORATION; *pg.* 927, *pg.* 709
HONALL - Honing Tool - SUNNEN PRODUCTS COMPANY; *pg.* 1379, *pg* 1004
HONDURAN BUNDLES - Premium Cigars - ALTADIS USA, INC.; *pg.* 1893, *pg.* 423
HONEST - Tobacco Product - AMERICAN SNUFF COMPANY; *pg.* 1893, *pg.* 1641
HONESTY & SERVICE - Software - SRA INTERNATIONAL, INC.; *pg.* 473, *pg.* 1780
HONEY - Breakfast Cereals - NATURE'S PATH FOODS INC.; *pg.* 833, *pg.* 1908
HONEY BBQ SANDWICH - Barbeque Chicken Sandwich - KFC CORPORATION; *pg.* 1733, *pg.* 735
HONEY BEE - 90 Cleaner - MCGEAN-ROHCO, INC.; *pg.* 1172, *pg.* 1432
HONEY-BEE - Cleaner Product - MCGEAN-ROHCO, INC.; *pg.* 1172, *pg.* 1432
HONEY BROWN - Beer - BIG ROCK BREWERY INCOME TRUST; *pg.* 239, *pg.* 1902
HONEY BUNCHES OF OATS - Cereal - POST HOLDINGS, INC.; *pg.* 833, *pg.* 1002
HONEY BUTTER BISCUITS - Nutrition Product - CHURCH'S CHICKEN, INC.; *pg.* 1722, *pg.* 493
HONEY BUZZERS - Cereal - POST CONSUMER BRANDS; *pg.* 833, *pg.* 927
HONEY CRUNCH CORN FLAKES - Cereal - KELLOGG COMPANY; *pg.* 831, *pg.* 870
HONEY DEW DONUTS - Food Product - HONEY DEW ASSOCIATES, INC.; *pg.* 1731, *pg.* 841
HONEY DIJON - Mustard - PLOCHMAN, INC.; *pg.* 890, *pg.* 631
HONEY GRAHAM TOASTERS - Cereal - POST CONSUMER BRANDS; *pg.* 833, *pg.* 927
HONEY IN THE ROUGH - Honey - DUTCH GOLD HONEY INC.; *pg.* 854, *pg.* 1546
HONEY LOOPS - Cereal - KELLOGG COMPANY; *pg.* 831, *pg.* 870
HONEY MAID - Crackers, Cookies & Pie Crusts - MONDELEZ INTERNATIONAL, INC.; *pg.* 878, *pg.* 601
HONEY NUT CHEERIOS - Cereal - GENERAL MILLS, INC.; *pg.* 828, *pg.* 933
HONEY NUT CLUSTERS - Cereal - GENERAL MILLS, INC.; *pg.* 828, *pg.* 933
HONEY NUT TOASTY O'S - Cereal - POST CONSUMER BRANDS; *pg.* 833, *pg.* 927
HONEY SMACKS - Cereal - KELLOGG COMPANY; *pg.* 831, *pg.* 870
HONEY STUNG - Frozen Poultry - TYSON FOODS, INC.; *pg.* 902, *pg.* 35
HONEY WHEAT PRETZEL BRAIDS - Snack Food - INVENTURE FOODS, INC.; *pg.* 1023, *pg.* 17
HONEY WHEAT STICKS - Organic Snacks - SNYDER'S OF HANOVER, INC.; *pg.* 1862, *pg.* 1536
HONEYBEE - Educational Materials - SCHOLASTIC INC.; *pg.* 1683, *pg.* 1288
HONEYCOMB - Fraction Collector - BIOANALYTICAL SYSTEMS, INC.; *pg.* 1402, *pg.* 700
HONEYCOMB - Wall Decor - HERITAGE LACE INC.; *pg.* 694, *pg.* 711
HONEYCOMB - Fabric - NEMSCHOFF, INC.; *pg.* 936, *pg.* 1890
HONEYCOMB - Cereal - POST HOLDINGS, INC.; *pg.* 833, *pg.* 1002
HONEY'D - Breakfast Cereals - NATURE'S PATH FOODS INC.; *pg.* 833, *pg.* 1908
HONEYFAB - Confectionery - THE HERSHEY CO.; *pg.* 1855, *pg.* 1538
HONEYKISS - Lip Color - THE BONNE BELL COMPANY; *pg.* 502, *pg.* 1480
HONEYSOY - Food Product - CHS INC.; *pg.* 702, *pg.* 926
HONEYSUCKLE - Poultry - CARGILL, INC.; *pg.* 845, *pg.* 965
HONEYSUCKLE ROSE - Hair & Skin Product - AUBREY ORGANICS INC.; *pg.* 499, *pg.* 470
HONEYSUCKLE WHITE - Turkey Products - CARGILL, INC.; *pg.* 845, *pg.* 965
HONEYSUCKLE WHITE - Turkey - CARGILL LIMITED; *pg.* 1475, *pg.* 1914
HONEYWELL - Air Purifier - KAZ, INC.; *pg.* 58, *pg.* 844
HONG KONG SUNRISE - Nail Care Product - OPI PRODUCTS INC.; *pg.* 518, *pg.* 167
HONI-BAKE - Sweetener - ARCHER-DANIELS-MIDLAND COMPANY; *pg.* 825, *pg.* 565
HONI-BAKE 705 - Sweetener - ARCHER-DANIELS-MIDLAND COMPANY; *pg.* 825, *pg.* 565
HONI-BAKE DRY - Sweetener - ARCHER-DANIELS-MIDLAND COMPANY; *pg.* 825, *pg.* 565
HONI-BAKE HS DRY - Sweetener - ARCHER-DANIELS-MIDLAND COMPANY; *pg.* 825, *pg.* 565
HONI-BAKE MB DRY - Sweetener - ARCHER-DANIELS-MIDLAND COMPANY; *pg.* 825, *pg.* 565
HONI-FLAKE - Agricultural Product - ARCHER-DANIELS-MIDLAND COMPANY; *pg.* 825, *pg.* 565
HONI-FLAKE 705 - Sweetener - ARCHER-DANIELS-MIDLAND COMPANY; *pg.* 825, *pg.* 565
HONI-FLAKE DRY - Sweetener - ARCHER-DANIELS-MIDLAND COMPANY; *pg.* 825, *pg.* 565
HONIG - Pasta, Soups, Sauces & Baking Mixes - THE KRAFT HEINZ COMPANY; *pg.* 870, *pg.* 1577
HONING STEEL - Sharpening Tool - GERBER LEGENDARY BLADES; *pg.* 1834, *pg.* 1503
THE HONOLULU STAR-ADVERTISER - Newspaper - THE HONOLULU STAR-ADVERTISER; *pg.* 1650, *pg.* 544
HONOR - Inspirational Books - DAVID C. COOK; *pg.* 1633, *pg.* 315
HONOR OF THE SAMURAI - Game - GAMEWRIGHT; *pg.* 953, *pg.* 836
HONOR PLUS - Fabric - NEMSCHOFF, INC.; *pg.* 936, *pg.* 1890
HONOUR - Footwear - STEVEN MADDEN, LTD.; *pg.* 1819, *pg.* 1176
HOOD - Dairy Products - HP HOOD LLC; *pg.* 864, *pg.* 829
HOODOO VOODOO - Nail Care Product - OPI PRODUCTS INC.; *pg.* 518, *pg.* 167
HOOFLEX - Hoof Care Product - W.F. YOUNG, INC.; *pg.* 1610, *pg.* 817
HOOFLEX+ - Pelleted Hoof Supplement - W.F. YOUNG, INC.; *pg.* 1610, *pg.* 817
HOOFMAKER - Animal Care Product - STRAIGHT ARROW PRODUCTS, INC.; *pg.* 523, *pg.* 1517
HOOFSNAX - Non-Medicated Animal Feed - MANNA PRO CORPORATION; *pg.* 1478, *pg.* 975
HOOK, LINE & SINKER - Lottery Game - IDAHO LOTTERY; *pg.* 995, *pg.* 547
HO'OKIPA - Eyewear - MAUI JIM, INC.; *pg.* 9, *pg.* 651
HOOKIT - Automotive Refinishing Pads - 3M COMPANY; *pg.* 1142, *pg.* 956
HOOLA HOOP - Fabric - NEMSCHOFF, INC.; *pg.* 936, *pg.* 1890
HOOP CHUTE - Basketball Equipment - LIFETIME PRODUCTS INC.; *pg.* 933, *pg.* 1751
HOOP CITY - Trademark - NATIONAL COLLEGIATE ATHLETIC ASSOCIATION; *pg.* 567, *pg.* 688
HOOP TIME - Height-Adjustable Basketball Standards - LIFETIME PRODUCTS INC.; *pg.* 933, *pg.* 1751
HOOPS TO GO - Sport Product - FRANKLIN SPORTS, INC.; *pg.* 1834, *pg.* 847
HOOPSTER - Basketball Backboards - LIFETIME PRODUCTS INC.; *pg.* 933, *pg.* 1751
HOOSIER LOTTO - Numbers Game - THE STATE LOTTERY

COMMISSION OF INDIANA; *pg.* 1006, *pg.* 690
HOOT LOOT - Video Game - INTERNATIONAL GAME TECHNOLOGY; *pg.* 957, *pg.* 1024
HOOVER - Floor Care Products - TTI FLOOR CARE NORTH AMERICA; *pg.* 61, *pg.* 1473
HOP & GO - Bakery Products - SAPUTO, INC.; *pg.* 893, *pg.* 1956
HOP & GO! - Bakery Product - VACHON BAKERY INC.; *pg.* 907, *pg.* 1959
HOPE. HEALTH. OPPURTUNITY. - Tagline - MANNATECH, INCORPORATED; *pg.* 1558, *pg.* 1671
HOPPIN' WILD - Game - WMS INDUSTRIES INC.; *pg.* 593, *pg.* 666
HOPPIN'S JOHN - Rice Mix - GOYA FOODS, INC.; *pg.* 859, *pg.* 1075
HOPSACKERS - Potato Sack - SCHOOL-TECH, INC.; *pg.* 1844, *pg.* 866
HOPSCOTCH - Fabric - NEMSCHOFF, INC.; *pg.* 936, *pg.* 1890
HOPSCOTCH HILL SCHOOL - Doll And Toy - AMERICAN GIRL LLC; *pg.* 949, *pg.* 1871
HORA HISPANA - Newspaper - DAILY NEWS, L.P.; *pg.* 1632, *pg.* 1221
HORACE MANN - Insurance for America's Educational Community - HORACE MANN COMPANIES; *pg.* 1203, *pg.* 662
HORACE SMALL - Apparel - V.F. CORPORATION; *pg.* 34, *pg.* 1376
HORATIO'S - Restaurant - RESTAURANTS UNLIMITED, INC.; *pg.* 1748, *pg.* 1839
HORCHOW - Home Furnishings Catalog - NEIMAN MARCUS, INC.; *pg.* 30, *pg.* 1684
HORDARESIN - Chemical Product - DOVER CHEMICAL CORPORATION; *pg.* 1156, *pg.* 1447
HORIZON - Dry Cleaning & Laundry Product - ADCO, INC.; *pg.* 325, *pg.* 482
HORIZON - Beverages - THE COCA-COLA COMPANY; *pg.* 240, *pg.* 493
HORIZON - Hose - THE GOODYEAR TIRE & RUBBER COMPANY; *pg.* 1883, *pg.* 1401
HORIZON - Fluid Management Systems - GRACO, INC.; *pg.* 1342, *pg.* 935
HORIZON - Motion Conveyor - KEY TECHNOLOGY, INC.; *pg.* 868, *pg.* 1847
HORIZON - Eyewear - MAUI JIM, INC.; *pg.* 9, *pg.* 651
HORIZON - Rescue Equipment - MINE SAFETY APPLIANCES COMPANY; *pg.* 1361, *pg.* 1525
HORIZON - Carpet - MOHAWK INDUSTRIES, INC.; *pg.* 935, *pg.* 527
HORIZON - Spray Booth - NORDSON CORPORATION; *pg.* 1365, *pg.* 1480
HORIZON - Lighting Fixture & Control - PHILIPS LIGHTING; *pg.* 1303, *pg.* 806
HORIZON - Software - ROSCO LABORATORIES, INC.; *pg.* 1782, *pg.* 378
HORIZON - Machinery/Graphic - STANDARD DUPLICATING MACHINES CORPORATION; *pg.* 473, *pg.* 783
HORIZON - Flush Sprinkler - THE VIKING GROUP; *pg.* 119, *pg.* 891
HORIZON AIR - Air Transportation - HORIZON AIR INDUSTRIES; *pg.* 1912, *pg.* 1836
HORIZON COLLECTION - Aluminum Siding - PLY GEM SIDING GROUP; *pg.* 105, *pg.* 986
HORIZON DESIGNS - Bags & Purses - HORIZON DESIGNS, INC.; *pg.* 695, *pg.* 1011
HORIZON ELECTROL - Electric Screen - DA-LITE SCREEN COMPANY; *pg.* 632, *pg.* 698
HORIZON MEDCOMM-RX - Software - MCKESSON CORPORATION; *pg.* 1560, *pg.* 222
HORIZON PROPHECY POLLS - Manual - XEROX CORPORATION; *pg.* 494, *pg.* 365
HORIZON SHANGLE - Asphalt Roofing - CERTAINTEED CORPORATION; *pg.* 74, *pg.* 1589
HORIZONS 2 - Antifouling Paint-Multi Season - PETTIT PAINT COMPANY; *pg.* 1444, *pg.* 1116
HORIZONS STUDIO - Furniture - ETHAN ALLEN INTERIORS INC.; *pg.* 924, *pg.* 343
THE HORIZONTAL RED LINE - Coffee & Beverage Equipment - BUNN-O-MATIC CORPORATION; *pg.* 53, *pg.* 661
HORIZONTAL-VERTICAL - Medical Device - INTEGRA LIFESCIENCES HOLDINGS CORPORATION; *pg.* 1545, *pg.* 1109
HORMEL - Food Products - HORMEL FOODS CORPORATION; *pg.* 863, *pg.* 915
HORMONES - Health Supplement - GARDEN OF LIFE, INC.; *pg.* 1532, *pg.* 478
HORN LAKE - Shirts - ABERCROMBIE & FITCH CO.; *pg.* 37, *pg.* 1466
HORNER RAUSCH - Optical Retail Stores - HORNER RAUSCH OPTICAL COMPANY EAST, INC.; *pg.* 1417, *pg.* 1651
HORNET - Medical Equipment - CONMED CORPORATION; *pg.* 1517, *pg.* 1347
HORNET - Mobile Electronics Equipment - DEI HOLDINGS, INC.; *pg.* 633, *pg.* 302
HORNITOS - Tequila - JIM BEAM BRANDS CO.; *pg.* 1965, *pg.* 601
HORNSBY'S - Hard Cider - E&J GALLO WINERY; *pg.* 1962, *pg.* 149
HOROWITZ MARGARETEN - Food Products - MANISCHEWITZ COMPANY; *pg.* 875, *pg.* 1097
HORRIBLE HISTORIES - Educational Materials - SCHOLASTIC INC.; *pg.* 1683, *pg.* 1288
HORRIBLE SCIENCE - Educational Materials - SCHOLASTIC INC.; *pg.* 1683, *pg.* 1288
HORRORS - Educational Materials - SCHOLASTIC INC.; *pg.* 1683, *pg.* 1288
HORSE ILLUSTRATED - Magazine - I-5 PUBLISHING LLC; *pg.* 1651, *pg.* 133
HORSE LOVER'S BULLETIN - Newsletter - W.F. YOUNG, INC.; *pg.* 1610, *pg.* 817
HORSE SHOW - Game - GAMEWRIGHT; *pg.* 953, *pg.* 836
THE HORSE WORLD'S MOST TRUSTED NAME - Slogan - W.F. YOUNG, INC.; *pg.* 1610, *pg.* 817
HORSEGO - Horse Products - KENT NUTRITION GROUP; *pg.* 1477, *pg.* 710
HORSEMAN'S CHOICE - Horse Equipment - BEHLEN MFG. CO.; *pg.* 701, *pg.* 1010
HORSEMAN'S ONE STEP - Leather Care Product - W.F. YOUNG, INC.; *pg.* 1610, *pg.* 817
HORSEPOWER - Herbicide Product - NUFARM AMERICAS INC; *pg.* 1798, *pg.* 552
HORSES USA - Magazine - I-5 PUBLISHING LLC; *pg.* 1651, *pg.* 133
HORSESHOE - Casino - CAESARS ENTERTAINMENT CORPORATION; *pg.* 1083, *pg.* 1023
HORSESHOE PATELLA - Orthopedic Product - DJO INCORPORATED; *pg.* 1524, *pg.* 302
HORTON AUTOMATICS - Automatic Door Products - OVERHEAD DOOR CORPORATION; *pg.* 102, *pg.* 1725
HORTON CLASSIC STRAIGHT - Clothing - ABERCROMBIE & FITCH CO.; *pg.* 37, *pg.* 1466
HORTON CLASSIC STRAIGHT DESTROYED - Clothing - ABERCROMBIE & FITCH CO.; *pg.* 37, *pg.* 1466
HOSP - Engineered Product And System - SULZER METCO (WESTBURY) INC.; *pg.* 1064, *pg.* 1350
HOSPICE PREFERRED CHOICE - Health Service - GOLDEN LIVING; *pg.* 1538, *pg.* 32
HOSPICE REPORT CARDS - Healthcare Product - HEALTH GRADES, INC.; *pg.* 1256, *pg.* 319
HOSPIT ALL - Cleaner - SWISHER HYGIENE INC.; *pg.* 336, *pg.* 1507
HOSPIT ALL II - Cleaner - SWISHER HYGIENE INC.; *pg.* 336, *pg.* 1507
HOSPIT ALL III - Cleaner - SWISHER HYGIENE INC.; *pg.* 336, *pg.* 1507
HOSPITAL CLEAN - Cleaning Product - ORECK CORPORATION; *pg.* 59, *pg.* 1653
HOSPITAL PHARMACIST REPORT - Pharmacy Publication - TRUVEN HEALTH ANALYTICS; *pg.* 1696, *pg.* 867
HOSPITAL QUALITY GUIDE - Healthcare Product - HEALTH GRADES, INC.; *pg.* 1256, *pg.* 319
HOSPITAL REPORT CARDS - Healthcare Product - HEALTH GRADES, INC.; *pg.* 1256, *pg.* 319
HOSPITAL SUPPLY INDEX - Software System - IMS HEALTH, INC.; *pg.* 1544, *pg.* 344
HOSPITALAR - Event - ENTERPRISE FLORIDA, INC.; *pg.* 992, *pg.* 453
HOSPITALDIRECT - Software - HEALTHSTREAM, INC.; *pg.* 1649, *pg.* 1651
HOSPITALITY - Whipped Topping Mixes - GILSTER-MARY LEE CORPORATION; *pg.* 858, *pg.* 563
HOSPITALITYPRO - Software - SKILLSOFT PLC; *pg.* 470, *pg.* 1037
HOSS - Hard Top Organized Storage System - BESTOP, INC.; *pg.* 200, *pg.* 312
HOSTESS - Potato - PEPSICO, INC.; *pg.* 259, *pg.* 1327
HOSTESS - Bakery Product - SAPUTO, INC.; *pg.* 893, *pg.* 1956
HOSTEXPLORER - Software - OPENTEXT CORPORATION; *pg.* 450, *pg.* 1948
HOSTILE-LITE - Lighting Fixtures - KILLARK ELECTRIC; *pg.* 1300, *pg.* 998
HOSTMARK - Periodical Newsletter (Travel & Touring) - AMERICAN AUTOMOBILE ASSOCIATION; *pg.* 1190, *pg.* 429
HOSTPRINT SERVER - Mainframe Printing Server - ATTACHMATE CORPORATION; *pg.* 356, *pg.* 1833
HOSTROCK.NET - Radio & Multimedia Service - BRS MEDIA INC.; *pg.* 1233, *pg.* 214
HOT & SPICY - Spicy Fried Chicken - KFC CORPORATION; *pg.* 1733, *pg.* 735
HOT BONNET - Software - BIO-RAD LABORATORIES, INC.; *pg.* 1504, *pg.* 101
HOT BUTTERED CHEESESTEAK - Steaks - RESTAURANT DEVELOPERS CORP.; *pg.* 1747, *pg.* 1464
HOT DAWG - Garage Heaters - MODINE MANUFACTURING COMPANY; *pg.* 1074, *pg.* 1888
HOT DOG TIPS - Flare - NAO, INC.; *pg.* 1074, *pg.* 1567
HOT DOGGIES - Pet Foods - HEINZ NORTH AMERICA; *pg.* 861, *pg.* 1576
HOT DOT - Bicycle Accessories - SPECIALIZED BICYCLE COMPONENTS, INC.; *pg.* 1711, *pg.* 152
HOT FIVE - Lottery - D.C. LOTTERY & CHARITABLE GAMES CONTROL BOARD; *pg.* 991, *pg.* 398
HOT FIX - Computer Software - NOVELL INC.; *pg.* 446, *pg.* 852
HOT FLASHES - Video Game - INTERNATIONAL GAME TECHNOLOGY; *pg.* 957, *pg.* 1024
HOT FLASHEX - Nutritional Product - NATROL, INC.; *pg.* 1570, *pg.* 64
HOT-FLO - Fibre Drum - GREIF INC.; *pg.* 1459, *pg.* 1447
HOT FUDGE KAHLUA BROWNIES - Desert - FAMOUS DAVE'S OF AMERICA, INC.; *pg.* 1728, *pg.* 926
HOT HAM N CHEESE - Sandwich - HARDEES FOOD SYSTEMS, INC.; *pg.* 1731, *pg.* 998
HOT HAND - Game - MINNESOTA STATE LOTTERY; *pg.* 999, *pg.* 956
HOT-HATS - Stuffed Sandwiches - STRAW HAT COOPERATIVE CORPORATION; *pg.* 1751, *pg.* 260
HOT HOT 777 - Game - WMS INDUSTRIES INC.; *pg.* 593, *pg.* 666
HOT HOT ACTION - Game - WMS INDUSTRIES INC.; *pg.* 593, *pg.* 666
HOT HOT JACKPOTS - Game - WMS INDUSTRIES INC.; *pg.* 593, *pg.* 666
HOT HOT PENNY - Game - WMS INDUSTRIES INC.; *pg.* 593, *pg.* 666
HOT HOT PENNY DESIGN - Game - WMS INDUSTRIES INC.; *pg.* 593, *pg.* 666
HOT HOT SUPER JACKPOT - Game - WMS INDUSTRIES INC.; *pg.* 593, *pg.* 666
HOT HOT SUPER RESPIN - Game - WMS INDUSTRIES INC.; *pg.* 593, *pg.* 666
HOT HOT TOURNAMENT POWER - Game - WMS INDUSTRIES INC.; *pg.* 593, *pg.* 666
HOT/ICE - Therapy Pad - CINCINNATI SUB-ZERO PRODUCTS, INC.; *pg.* 1070, *pg.* 1411
HOT ICE - Video Game - INTERNATIONAL GAME TECHNOLOGY; *pg.* 957, *pg.* 1024
HOT IRON - Ironing & Cleaning Product - FAULTLESS STARCH/BON AMI COMPANY; *pg.* 330, *pg.* 982
HOT KRISPY KREME ORIGINAL GLAZED NOW - Doughnuts - KRISPY KREME DOUGHNUTS, INC.; *pg.* 1734, *pg.* 1394
HOT-LINE - Credit Card Protection Services - AFFINION GROUP, INC.; *pg.* 1225, *pg.* 372
HOT LISTINGS - Information Retrieval Services - CARFAX INC.; *pg.* 202, *pg.* 1777
HOT LOTTO - Lottery Game - MINNESOTA STATE LOTTERY; *pg.* 999, *pg.* 956
HOT LOTTO - Lottery Game - MONTANA LOTTERY; *pg.* 1000, *pg.* 1008
HOT LOTTO - Lottery Game - WEST VIRGINIA LOTTERY; *pg.* 1011, *pg.* 1849
HOT 'N COLD - Conveyor Belting - HBD INDUSTRIES, INC.; *pg.* 207, *pg.* 1449
HOT 'N' READY - Food Product - ADVANCEPIERRE FOODS, INC.; *pg.* 1714, *pg.* 1409
HOT N' SPICY - Food Product - JOHNSONVILLE SAUSAGE, LLC; *pg.* 867, *pg.* 1894
HOT NOTCHER - Drilling & Marking Machine - EASTMAN MACHINE COMPANY; *pg.* 1331, *pg.* 1148
HOT OAT - Crunch Cereal - PEPSICO, INC.; *pg.* 259, *pg.*

First page reference indicates Business Class Edition
Second page reference indicates Geographic Edition

1327
HOT OAT CRUNCH - Cereal - THE QUAKER OATS COMPANY; pg. 834, pg. 588
THE HOT ONE - Shave Cream - THE GILLETTE COMPANY; pg. 509, pg. 795
HOT PEPPER - Cheese - THE GREAT LAKES CHEESE CO., INC.; pg. 859, pg. 1455
HOT PEPPERS - Slots - INTERNATIONAL GAME TECHNOLOGY; pg. 957, pg. 1024
HOT PICKS - Game - WMS INDUSTRIES INC.; pg. 593, pg. 666
HOT PINK - Handbags - LUCKY BRAND DUNGAREES, INC.; pg. 29, pg. 301
HOT POCKETS - Food & Beverage Product - NESTLE USA, INC.; pg. 883, pg. 96
HOT POINT - Beverages - THE COCA-COLA COMPANY; pg. 240, pg. 493
HOT POTATO - Envelope - TENSION ENVELOPE CORPORATION; pg. 483, pg. 986
HOT PROPERTIES - Game - WMS INDUSTRIES INC.; pg. 593, pg. 666
HOT PURSUIT POKER - Video Game - INTERNATIONAL GAME TECHNOLOGY; pg. 957, pg. 1024
HOT ROD - Bicycle - G. JOANNOU CYCLE CO. INC.; pg. 1707, pg. 1098
HOT ROD - Video Game - INTERNATIONAL GAME TECHNOLOGY; pg. 957, pg. 1024
HOT ROD - Fabric - NEMSCHOFF, INC.; pg. 936, pg. 1890
HOT ROD GARAGE - Garage Storage Products - SAUDER WOODWORKING CO.; pg. 941, pg. 1403
HOT SCOOPS - Merchandising Program - BASIC AMERICAN FOODS, INC.; pg. 839, pg. 303
HOT SHOT - Signal Mirror - ACR ELECTRONICS, INC.; pg. 612, pg. 422
HOT SHOT - Fluid Handling System - GRACO, INC.; pg. 1342, pg. 935
HOT SHOT PROGRESSIVE - Video Game - BALLY TECHNOLOGIES, INC.; pg. 531, pg. 1022
HOT SLOTS - Game - MISSOURI LOTTERY; pg. 999, pg. 979
HOT SPA - Beauty Care Product - HELEN OF TROY L.P.; pg. 511, pg. 1692
HOT SPOT - Lottery Tickets - CALIFORNIA LOTTERY; pg. 990, pg. 196
HOT SPOT - Plumbing Product - MASCO CORPORATION; pg. 96, pg. 909
HOT SPOT SUMMER - Lottery Game - LOUISIANA LOTTERY CORPORATION; pg. 997, pg. 742
HOT SPOTZ - Hi-Temp Insulation - THE ZIPPERTUBING COMPANY; pg. 1892, pg. 12
HOT SPRING - Plumbing Product - MASCO CORPORATION; pg. 96, pg. 909
HOT SPRING - Portable Spa - WATKINS MANUFACTURING CORPORATION; pg. 120, pg. 303
HOT SPRING CLASSIC - Portable Spa Model - WATKINS MANUFACTURING CORPORATION; pg. 120, pg. 303
HOT SPRING GRANDEE - Portable Spa Model - WATKINS MANUFACTURING CORPORATION; pg. 120, pg. 303
HOT SPRING JETSETTER - Portable Spa Model - WATKINS MANUFACTURING CORPORATION; pg. 120, pg. 303
HOT SPRING PRODIGY - Portable Spa Model - WATKINS MANUFACTURING CORPORATION; pg. 120, pg. 303
HOT SPRING SOVEREIGN - Portable Spa Model - WATKINS MANUFACTURING CORPORATION; pg. 120, pg. 303
HOT SUBS - Frozen Food - BELLISIO FOODS, INC.; pg. 840, pg. 931
HOT SURFACE IGNITION - Furnace Controls for Heating - EMERSON WHITE-RODGERS; pg. 1071, pg. 996
HOT TAMALES - Candy - JUST BORN, INC.; pg. 1857, pg. 1516
HOT TO TROT - Game - WMS INDUSTRIES INC.; pg. 593, pg. 666
HOT TOOLS - Beauty Care Product - HELEN OF TROY L.P.; pg. 511, pg. 1692
HOT TOP DOLLAR - Video Game - INTERNATIONAL GAME TECHNOLOGY; pg. 957, pg. 1024
HOT TOPPINGS - Game - WMS INDUSTRIES INC.; pg. 593, pg. 666
HOT TRUCKIN' - Die Cast Replicas - REVELL; pg. 966, pg. 611
HOT TYPE - Column - CHICAGO READER, INC.; pg. 1627, pg. 570
HOT WATER ON DEMAND - Spray Adapter - THE COLEMAN COMPANY, INC.; pg. 1830, pg. 723
HOT WHEELS - Toy - MATTEL, INC.; pg. 962, pg. 81
HOT WHEELS COLLECTIBLES - Vehicles for Adult Collectors - MATTEL, INC.; pg. 962, pg. 81
HOT WINGS - Frozen Poultry - TYSON FOODS, INC.; pg. 902, pg. 35
HOT WIRE - Video Game - INTERNATIONAL GAME TECHNOLOGY; pg. 957, pg. 1024
HOT ZONE - Disk Shipper - ENTEGRIS, INC.; pg. 1882, pg. 788
HOTBISCUS - Hibiscus Plants - ARMSTRONG GARDEN CENTERS, INC.; pg. 1793, pg. 99
HOTEL BAR - Dairy Product - DAIRY FARMERS OF AMERICA, INC.; pg. 851, pg. 982
HOTEL BLEND - Coffee - COMMUNITY COFFEE COMPANY LLC; pg. 849, pg. 741
HOTEL INDIGO - Hotels - INTERCONTINENTAL HOTELS CORPORATION; pg. 1097, pg. 511
THE HOTEL NETWORKS - Hospitatlity Services - SONIFI SOLUTIONS; pg. 1281, pg. 1625
HOTELCLUB - Hotel Accommodations Website - ORBITZ WORLDWIDE, INC.; pg. 1918, pg. 586
HOTELCOUPONS.COM - Travel Website - DOMINION ENTERPRISES; pg. 1636, pg. 1796
HOTELDIRECT - Software - PASSKEY INTERNATIONAL, INC.; pg. 1274, pg. 853
HOTELS.COM - Travel Information - EXPEDIA, INC.; pg. 1244, pg. 1814
HOTFAX - Software - SMITH MICRO SOFTWARE, INC.; pg. 471, pg. 41
HOTHUES - Custom Finishes - E.I. DU PONT DE NEMOURS & COMPANY; pg. 1159, pg. 390
HOTLINE - Calendars - BROWN & BIGELOW, INC.; pg. 1624, pg. 959
HOTLINK - Physical Layer Device - CYPRESS SEMICONDUCTOR CORPORATION; pg. 1326, pg. 243
HOTLINK DX - Physical Layer Device - CYPRESS SEMICONDUCTOR CORPORATION; pg. 1326, pg. 243
HOTLINK II - Physical Layer Device - CYPRESS SEMICONDUCTOR CORPORATION; pg. 1326, pg. 243
HOTLINK II - Computer Product - RADIANCE TECHNOLOGIES, INC.; pg. 1277, pg. 6
HOTLINK III - Physical Layer Device - CYPRESS SEMICONDUCTOR CORPORATION; pg. 1326, pg. 243
HOTLINKDX - Physical Layer Device - CYPRESS SEMICONDUCTOR CORPORATION; pg. 1326, pg. 243
HOTLIST - Computer Software - NOVELL INC.; pg. 446, pg. 852
HOTPAC - Orthopedic Device - DJO SURGICAL; pg. 1525, pg. 1661
HOTPLOT - Software System - MENTOR GRAPHICS CORPORATION; pg. 432, pg. 1510
HOTPOINT - Home Appliance - GENERAL ELECTRIC COMPANY; pg. 1297, pg. 347
HOTROCK - Bicycle - SPECIALIZED BICYCLE COMPONENTS, INC.; pg. 1711, pg. 152
HOTS - Paper - DOMTAR CORPORATION; pg. 1456, pg. 1954
HOTSCALE - Drives Adding Software - AVAGO TECHNOLOGIES; pg. 358, pg. 238
HOTSHOT - Automatic Telephone Dialer - ZOOM TECHNOLOGIES, INC.; pg. 497, pg. 1317
HOTSHOTS - Protective Eyewear - SELLSTROM MANUFACTURING CO.; pg. 1428, pg. 659
HOTSPOTR - Software - NER HOLDINGS INC.; pg. 444, pg. 1071
HOTTER, COOLER, FRESHER THINKING - Slogan - THERMOS L.L.C.; pg. 61, pg. 660
HOTTER 'N HOT JALAPENO - Potato Chip Flavor - ZAPP'S POTATO CHIPS, INC.; pg. 1864, pg. 743
HOTTIME - Software - SMITH MICRO SOFTWARE, INC.; pg. 471, pg. 41
HOTWIRE.COM - Travel Information - EXPEDIA, INC.; pg. 1244, pg. 1814
HOTZ - Smoked Link Sausage with Jalapeno Peppers - BOB EVANS FARMS, LLC; pg. 841, pg. 1467
HOTZONE - Software - FALCONSTOR SOFTWARE, INC.; pg. 396, pg. 1179
HOTZONE - Pressed & Monolithic Refractory - RESCO PRODUCTS, INC.; pg. 107, pg. 1581
HOUDINI REELS OF MYSTERY - Game - WMS INDUSTRIES INC.; pg. 593, pg. 666
HOUGHTO-DRAW - Metal Forming - HOUGHTON INTERNATIONAL INC.; pg. 1167, pg. 1589
HOUGHTO-QUENCH - Heat Treating Product - HOUGHTON INTERNATIONAL INC.; pg. 1167, pg. 1589
HOUGHTO-SAFE - Fluid Power - HOUGHTON INTERNATIONAL INC.; pg. 1167, pg. 1589
HOUGHTON - Metal Forming Oil - HOUGHTON INTERNATIONAL INC.; pg. 1167, pg. 1589
HOUGHTON MIFFLIN - Publishing - HOUGHTON MIFFLIN HARCOURT PUBLISHING COMPANY; pg. 1651, pg. 796
HOUGHTON MIFFLIN MATH - Instruction Books - HOUGHTON MIFFLIN HARCOURT PUBLISHING COMPANY; pg. 1651, pg. 796
HOUND SURROUND - Fencing - MASTER HALCO; pg. 96, pg. 474
HOUNDSTOOTH - Pillow - AMERICAN LEATHER LP; pg. 912, pg. 1673
HOUNDSTOOTH - Hat - WOODEN SHIPS OF HOBOKEN; pg. 35, pg. 1315
HOUR EYES - Eye Care Centers - VISIONWORKS OF AMERICA, INC.; pg. 1436, pg. 1744
HOURGLASS - Bath Product - KOHLER CO.; pg. 91, pg. 1862
HOUSE - Wall Decor - HERITAGE LACE INC.; pg. 694, pg. 711
HOUSE BEAUTIFUL - Magazine - THE HEARST CORPORATION; pg. 1649, pg. 1239
HOUSE BLEND - Coffee - PEET'S COFFEE & TEA, INC.; pg. 1029, pg. 85
HOUSE CAT - Lace Flag - HERITAGE LACE INC.; pg. 694, pg. 711
HOUSE COLLECTIBLES - Publishing Imprint - PENGUIN RANDOM HOUSE; pg. 1675, pg. 1276
HOUSE OF 9 DRAGONS - Video Game - INTERNATIONAL GAME TECHNOLOGY; pg. 957, pg. 1024
HOUSE OF BARBIE - Barbie Store & Spa - MATTEL, INC.; pg. 962, pg. 81
HOUSE OF JEWELS - Video Game - INTERNATIONAL GAME TECHNOLOGY; pg. 957, pg. 1024
HOUSE OF TSANG - Asian Sauces & Oils - HORMEL FOODS CORPORATION; pg. 863, pg. 915
HOUSEBRITE - Chemical Company - W.M. BARR & COMPANY, INC.; pg. 338, pg. 1647
HOUSECALL - Retail Services such as Appliance Repair, CO Detection, Home Security - CONSUMERS ENERGY COMPANY; pg. 1938, pg. 893
HOUSECALL - Telemarketing - KB HOME; pg. 90, pg. 134
HOUSECALL PLUS - Remote Patient Monitoring System - ST. JUDE MEDICAL, INC.; pg. 1596, pg. 963
HOUSEHOLD BANK - Credit Card - CAPITAL ONE FINANCIAL CORPORATION; pg. 730, pg. 1789
HOUSEPLANTS ALIVE! - Fertilizer - GARDENS ALIVE!, INC.; pg. 1796, pg. 693
HOUSEWARMER - Candle - THE YANKEE CANDLE COMPANY, INC.; pg. 1792, pg. 843
HOUSTON - Women's Trousers - LANE BRYANT; pg. 1776, pg. 1441
HOUSTON - Fire Helmet - MINE SAFETY APPLIANCES COMPANY; pg. 1361, pg. 1525
HOUSTON ASTROS - Baseball Team - HOUSTON ASTROS BASEBALL CLUB; pg. 552, pg. 1707
HOUSTON CHRONICLE - Newspaper - THE HEARST CORPORATION; pg. 1649, pg. 1239
HOUSTON CHRONICLE - Newspaper - HOUSTON CHRONICLE; pg. 1651, pg. 1707
HOUSTON COMETS - WNBA Women's Pro Basketball - HOUSTON ROCKETS; pg. 552, pg. 1707
HOUSTON ROCKETS - Basketball Team - HOUSTON ROCKETS; pg. 552, pg. 1707
HOUWIRE - Low-Voltage Cable & Wire Products - HOUSTON WIRE & CABLE COMPANY; pg. 643, pg. 1708
HOVA-BATOR - Incubator Still Air Model - SCHOOL-TECH, INC.; pg. 1844, pg. 866
HOVAN'S HEROES - Ticket Program - BUCCANEERS LIMITED PARTNERSHIP; pg. 534, pg. 471
HOVCAT - Network Product - VITESSE SEMICONDUCTOR CORPORATION; pg. 686, pg. 57
HOVCAT192 - Semiconductor Solution - VITESSE SEMICONDUCTOR CORPORATION; pg. 686, pg. 57
HOVCAT48 - Semiconductor Solution - VITESSE SEMICONDUCTOR CORPORATION; pg. 686, pg. 57
HOVCAT48E - Semiconductor Solution - VITESSE SEMICONDUCTOR CORPORATION; pg. 686, pg. 57
HOVCATE - Semiconductor Solution - VITESSE SEMICONDUCTOR CORPORATION; pg. 686, pg. 57
HOVER - Web Hosting - TUCOWS, INC.; pg. 1285, pg. 1946
HOVEROUND - Personal Mobility Vehicle - HOVEROUND CORP.; pg. 1543, pg. 466
HOVERTANK 3D - Video Game - ID SOFTWARE, INC.; pg. 956, pg. 1727

HOW BUSINESS IS ONE - Tagline - NFI INDUSTRIES INC.; *pg.* 1917, *pg.* 1127
HOW DEW DOES DIET - Tagline - PEPSICO, INC.; *pg.* 259, *pg.* 1327
HOW GOLF SHOULD FEEL - Slogan - CALLAWAY GOLF COMPANY; *pg.* 1829, *pg.* 58
HOW INTELLIGENCE TRAVELS - Slogan - COMMSCOPE, INC.; *pg.* 278, *pg.* 1378
HOW LUCKY CAN YOU GET - Video Game - INTERNATIONAL GAME TECHNOLOGY; *pg.* 957, *pg.* 1024
HOW OUTDOOR LIVING SHOULD FEEL - Tagline - TREX COMPANY, INC.; *pg.* 116, *pg.* 1812
HOW SMART THINGS THINK - Software - WIND RIVER SYSTEMS, INC.; *pg.* 493, *pg.* 38
HOW SWEET IT IS - Lottery Game - WEST VIRGINIA LOTTERY; *pg.* 1011, *pg.* 1849
HOW TO PROTECT YOURSELF FROM CRIME - Book - GUARDSMARK, LLC; *pg.* 401, *pg.* 1237
HOW TO SURVIVE ANYTHING CLUB - Educational Materials - SCHOLASTIC INC.; *pg.* 1683, *pg.* 1288
HOWARD - Instrument Table - BLICKMAN HEALTH INDUSTRIES, INC.; *pg.* 1506, *pg.* 1051
HOWARD - Musical Instrument - GIBSON GUITAR CORP.; *pg.* 550, *pg.* 1650
HOWARD - Linen Papers - NEENAH PAPER, INC.; *pg.* 1465, *pg.* 484
HOWARD JOHNSON - Hotels - WYNDHAM WORLDWIDE CORPORATION; *pg.* 1119, *pg.* 1107
HOWARD MILLER - Clock - HOWARD MILLER COMPANY; *pg.* 7, *pg.* 914
HOWE FURNITURE - Furniture - THE COMMERCIAL FURNITURE GROUP; *pg.* 920, *pg.* 994
HOWELL BUNGER VALVE - Fixed Core Valve - RODNEY HUNT COMPANY; *pg.* 1372, *pg.* 840
HOWERMOWER - Garden Equipment - EASTMAN INDUSTRIES; *pg.* 1046, *pg.* 751
HOWIE WINGS - Chicken Wings - HUNGRY HOWIE'S PIZZA & SUBS INC.; *pg.* 1023, *pg.* 897
HOWMEDICA - Medical Product - STRYKER CORPORATION; *pg.* 1598, *pg.* 894
HOY CHICAGO - Spanish-Language Daily Newspaper - CHICAGO TRIBUNE COMPANY; *pg.* 1627, *pg.* 570
HOYLE - Playing Cards - THE UNITED STATES PLAYING CARD COMPANY; *pg.* 969, *pg.* 727
HOYT - Colognes & Perfumes - J. STRICKLAND & COMPANY; *pg.* 512, *pg.* 970
HP - Hydrogenated Shortening - CARGILL LIMITED; *pg.* 1475, *pg.* 1914
HP - Fluid Handling System - GRACO, INC.; *pg.* 1342, *pg.* 935
HP - Catheter - ST. JUDE MEDICAL, INC.; *pg.* 1596, *pg.* 963
HP - Fishhooks - WRIGHT & MCGILL CO.; *pg.* 1848, *pg.* 324
HP-80 - High Pressure Washer - CLAYTON INDUSTRIES CO.; *pg.* 1323, *pg.* 66
HP CAM DRIVE - Fluid Handling System - GRACO, INC.; *pg.* 1342, *pg.* 935
HP DESKJET - Printer - HEWLETT-PACKARD COMPANY; *pg.* 404, *pg.* 175
HP DESKJET PLUS - Printer - HEWLETT-PACKARD COMPANY; *pg.* 404, *pg.* 175
HP LASERJET - Printer - HEWLETT-PACKARD COMPANY; *pg.* 404, *pg.* 175
HP LEFTHAND P4000 SAN - Storage Area Network Technology - HEWLETT-PACKARD COMPANY; *pg.* 404, *pg.* 175
HP MINER - Hose - THE GOODYEAR TIRE & RUBBER COMPANY; *pg.* 1883, *pg.* 1401
HP OFFICEJET - Printer, Fax & Copier - HEWLETT-PACKARD COMPANY; *pg.* 404, *pg.* 175
HP OPENVIEW - Software Product - CLARY CORPORATION; *pg.* 226, *pg.* 150
HP P4000 SAN - Storage Area Network Technology - HEWLETT-PACKARD COMPANY; *pg.* 404, *pg.* 175
HP PAVILION - Desktops & Workstations - HEWLETT-PACKARD COMPANY; *pg.* 404, *pg.* 175
HP PRO - Plastic Window Frame - ODL INCORPORATED; *pg.* 101, *pg.* 914
HP SCANJET - Computer Scanner - HEWLETT-PACKARD COMPANY; *pg.* 404, *pg.* 175
HP SIGNATURE - Musical Instrument - PEAVEY ELECTRONICS CORPORATION; *pg.* 662, *pg.* 970
HP250II - Valve - HENRY PRATT COMPANY; *pg.* 1049, *pg.* 555
HPFS - Optical Fiber - CORNING INCORPORATED; *pg.* 1122, *pg.* 1154
HPG - Generator - ADVANCED ENERGY INDUSTRIES, INC.; *pg.* 613, *pg.* 328
HPHCONNECT - Web Based Transaction Service - HARVARD PILGRIM HEALTH CARE, INC.; *pg.* 1539, *pg.* 856
HPI CONSTRUCTION BOXSCORE - Trade Journal - GULF PUBLISHING COMPANY; *pg.* 1646, *pg.* 1707
HPL - Latex - THE DOW CHEMICAL COMPANY; *pg.* 1157, *pg.* 898
HPL INTEGRA - Wooden Bowling Lanes - BOWLMOR AMF; *pg.* 1828, *pg.* 1206
HPN - Hydrogenation Catalyst - BASF CATALYSTS LLC; *pg.* 1148, *pg.* 1074
HPS - Sliding Doors - KAWNEER COMPANY, INC.; *pg.* 90, *pg.* 537
HPS - Vacuum Components, Valves & Gauges - MKS INSTRUMENTS, INC.; *pg.* 1362, *pg.* 781
HPSA - Diagnostic Test Product - MERIDIAN BIOSCIENCE INC.; *pg.* 1422, *pg.* 1417
HPT - Human Resources Technology - SELECTREMEDY; *pg.* 468, *pg.* 263
HPV-02 - Variable Pump for Closed Loop Circuit - LINDE HYDRAULICS CORPORATION; *pg.* 1356, *pg.* 1407
HPV DNA TEST - Molecular Diagnostic Test - QIAGEN GAITHERSBURG INC.; *pg.* 1587, *pg.* 771
HPX - Resin - PELICAN PRODUCTS; *pg.* 1467, *pg.* 843
HPX HYDRATING GEL - Skin Care Product - NU SKIN ENTERPRISES, INC.; *pg.* 518, *pg.* 1755
HQ - Paper Mill Cores - SONOCO PRODUCTS COMPANY; *pg.* 1469, *pg.* 1619
HQ ACB - Paper Tubes & Cores - SONOCO PRODUCTS COMPANY; *pg.* 1469, *pg.* 1619
H.R. 2000 - Restorer - HILLYARD, INC.; *pg.* 331, *pg.* 990
HR VISION - H.R. Management Solution - SAS INSTITUTE INC.; *pg.* 466, *pg.* 1361
HRB - Baler - HARRIS WASTE MANAGEMENT GROUP, INC.; *pg.* 1345, *pg.* 526
COMPENSATION.BLR.COM - Website - BUSINESS & LEGAL REPORTS INC.; *pg.* 1624, *pg.* 367
HRD - Distilled Spirits - HOOD RIVER DISTILLERS INC.; *pg.* 1964, *pg.* 1498
HRI - Chemical Product - AIR PRODUCTS AND CHEMICALS, INC.; *pg.* 1145, *pg.* 1513
HRP - Photographic Developer - EASTMAN KODAK COMPANY; *pg.* 1408, *pg.* 1333
HS-75 - Stereo Headphones - ANDREA ELECTRONICS CORPORATION; *pg.* 617, *pg.* 1143
HS DOCK - Connector - MOLEX INCORPORATED; *pg.* 655, *pg.* 628
HS MEZZ - Connector - MOLEX INCORPORATED; *pg.* 655, *pg.* 628
HS TRASK - Footwear - PHOENIX FOOTWEAR GROUP, INC.; *pg.* 1815, *pg.* 60
HSAUTOLINK - Electronic Components - MOLEX INCORPORATED; *pg.* 655, *pg.* 628
HSB - Inspection And Insurance Company - HSB GROUP, INC.; *pg.* 1204, *pg.* 352
HSC - Polycrystalline Silicon & Silicon Source Chemicals - DOW CORNING CORPORATION; *pg.* 1159, *pg.* 900
HSIM - Software - SYNOPSYS, INC.; *pg.* 480, *pg.* 162
HSIMPLUS - Software - SYNOPSYS, INC.; *pg.* 480, *pg.* 162
HSPICE - Software - SYNOPSYS, INC.; *pg.* 480, *pg.* 162
HSRA - Rinse Additive - ECOLAB INC.; *pg.* 329, *pg.* 960
HSS - Hypersonic Sound Technology - LRAD CORPORATION; *pg.* 652, *pg.* 204
HT - Kaolin Pigment - BASF CATALYSTS LLC; *pg.* 1148, *pg.* 1074
HT TRADERS - Food Product - HARRIS TEETER, INC.; *pg.* 1022, *pg.* 1383
HTC - Medical Product - HOLOGIC, INC.; *pg.* 1416, *pg.* 784
HTC - Electronic Components - MOLEX INCORPORATED; *pg.* 655, *pg.* 628
HTFS RESEARCH NETWORK - Software - ASPEN TECHNOLOGY, INC.; *pg.* 354, *pg.* 804
HTM - Heat Treat Management System - SURFACE COMBUSTION, INC.; *pg.* 1077, *pg.* 1462
HTML WORKS - Software - WIND RIVER SYSTEMS, INC.; *pg.* 493, *pg.* 38
HTP-2 - Iron Oxide Dispersants - GE WATER & PROCESS TECHNOLOGIES; *pg.* 1339, *pg.* 1588
HTP COMPLEX - Nutritional Supplement - NU SKIN ENTERPRISES, INC.; *pg.* 518, *pg.* 1755
HTP THERMAL SOURCEBOOK - Trade Magazine - ASM INTERNATIONAL; *pg.* 132, *pg.* 1461
HTS - Surround Sound Decoders - SHURE INCORPORATED; *pg.* 672, *pg.* 638
HTS - Connectors - TE CONNECTIVITY LTD.; *pg.* 677, *pg.* 1515
HTT HUMAN TOUCH TEHCNOLOGY - Chair - HUMAN TOUCH; *pg.* 928, *pg.* 123
HTX - Adapter - ADVANCED MICRO DEVICES, INC.; *pg.* 613, *pg.* 282
HTX - Glass Fibers, Strands, Rovings & Mats - PPG INDUSTRIES, INC.; *pg.* 1445, *pg.* 1579
HUALUXE - Upscale Hotels for Chinese Travelers - INTERCONTINENTAL HOTELS CORPORATION; *pg.* 1097, *pg.* 511
HUANG - Beverages - THE COCA-COLA COMPANY; *pg.* 240, *pg.* 493
THE HUB - Weekly Publication - GREATER MEDIA NEWSPAPERS, INC.; *pg.* 1646, *pg.* 1071
HUB - Dicing Blade - KULICKE & SOFFA INDUSTRIES, INC.; *pg.* 650, *pg.* 1533
HUB - Apparel - OAKLEY, INC.; *pg.* 1840, *pg.* 86
HUB 51 - Restaurant - LETTUCE ENTERTAIN YOU ENTERPRISES, INC.; *pg.* 1735, *pg.* 580
HUB CITY - Gear drives, sub-FHP gearmotors, mounted bearings & accessories - REGAL BELOIT CORPORATION; *pg.* 106, *pg.* 1854
HUBBA BUBBA - Gum - WM. WRIGLEY JR. COMPANY; *pg.* 1863, *pg.* 596
HUBBARD - Television Broadcasting Stations - HUBBARD BROADCASTING, INC.; *pg.* 291, *pg.* 961
HUBBARD MILLING - Livestock Feed & Pet Food - HUBBARD FEEDS INC.; *pg.* 1477, *pg.* 928
HUBERCARB - Surface Treatment Product - J.M. HUBER CORPORATION; *pg.* 1169, *pg.* 1056
HUBPORT - Computer Peripheral Equipment - DIGI INTERNATIONAL INC.; *pg.* 387, *pg.* 948
HUCK - Bolt - TUTHILL CORPORATION; *pg.* 1385, *pg.* 561
HUCK-SPIN - Clamp - ALCOA INC.; *pg.* 65, *pg.* 1188
HUCKINS - Yachts - HUCKINS YACHT CORPORATION; *pg.* 1708, *pg.* 433
HUDDERSFIELD - Carpet - BEAULIEU GROUP, LLC; *pg.* 917, *pg.* 529
HUDSON - Furniture - ASHLEY FURNITURE INDUSTRIES, INC.; *pg.* 914, *pg.* 1852
HUDSON - Furniture - JASPER GROUP; *pg.* 930, *pg.* 691
HUDSON - Systems Integration & Aeronautics - LOCKHEED MARTIN CORPORATION; *pg.* 229, *pg.* 762
HUDSON - Footwear - VANS, INC.; *pg.* 1821, *pg.* 76
HUDSON STREET - Furniture - STANLEY FURNITURE CO., INC.; *pg.* 943, *pg.* 1379
HUDSON'S BAY SCOTCH - Beverage - SIDNEY FRANK IMPORTING CO., INC.; *pg.* 1970, *pg.* 1184
HUE - Legwear & Apparel - KAYSER-ROTH CORPORATION; *pg.* 28, *pg.* 1374
HUEBSCH - Commercial Washers, Dryers, Stack Dryers & Washer-Extractors - ALLIANCE LAUNDRY HOLDINGS LLC; *pg.* 51, *pg.* 1890
HUEGA - Flooring - INTERFACE, INC.; *pg.* 695, *pg.* 512
HUEY II - Military Helicopter - BELL HELICOPTER TEXTRON, INC.; *pg.* 224, *pg.* 1693
THE HUFFINGTON POST - Newspaper - THEHUFFINGTONPOST.COM, INC.; *pg.* 1692, *pg.* 1298
HUFFY - Bicycle - HUFFY CORPORATION; *pg.* 1836, *pg.* 1409
HUFFY BIKES - Bicycle - HUFFY CORPORATION; *pg.* 1836, *pg.* 1409
HUFFY SPORTS - Sports Related Equipment - HUFFY CORPORATION; *pg.* 1836, *pg.* 1409
HUFFY SPORTS - Sports Equipment - RUSSELL BRANDS LLC; *pg.* 698, *pg.* 726
HUFGUARD - Safety System - HUFCOR INCORPORATED; *pg.* 87, *pg.* 1861
HUG & LEARN - Educational Toys - LEAPFROG ENTERPRISES, INC.; *pg.* 961, *pg.* 84
HUGGABLES - Medical Equipment - CONMED CORPORATION; *pg.* 1517, *pg.* 1347
HUGGIES - Disposable Diapers & Baby Wipes - KIMBERLY-CLARK CORPORATION; *pg.* 1461, *pg.* 1720
HUGGY TUB - Bath Tub - GRACO CHILDREN'S PRODUCTS INC.; *pg.* 954, *pg.* 1531
HUGO - Personal & Household Product - THE PROCTER & GAMBLE COMPANY; *pg.* 1129, *pg.* 1418
HUGS N KISSES - Carpet - BEAULIEU GROUP, LLC; *pg.* 917, *pg.* 529
HULA - Eyewear - MAUI JIM, INC.; *pg.* 9, *pg.* 651
HULA MOOLAH - Video Game - INTERNATIONAL GAME

TECHNOLOGY; *pg.* 957, *pg.* 1024
HULLWORKS - Coating & Paint - AKZO NOBEL DECORATIVE PAINTS, USA; *pg.* 1439, *pg.* 1474
HUMALOG - Pharmaceutical Product - ELI LILLY AND COMPANY; *pg.* 1527, *pg.* 684
HUMAN BIOARMOR - Slogan - SIGA TECHNOLOGIES, INC.; *pg.* 1594, *pg.* 1292
HUMAN ENERGY - Slogan - CHEVRON CORPORATION; *pg.* 974, *pg.* 259
HUMAN ENGINEERING - Anti-Immune Technology - XOMA CORPORATION; *pg.* 1611, *pg.* 46
HUMAN NATURE - Carpet - INTERFACE, INC.; *pg.* 695, *pg.* 512
HUMAN RESOURCE TRAINING CUSTOMIZER - Training Program Design Software - J.J. KELLER & ASSOCIATES, INC.; *pg.* 1654, *pg.* 1883
HUMANAACCESS - Credit Card - HUMANA, INC.; *pg.* 1204, *pg.* 734
HUMANABEGINNINGS - Pregnancy Health Coverage - HUMANA, INC.; *pg.* 1204, *pg.* 734
HUMANAONE - Health Coverage - HUMANA, INC.; *pg.* 1204, *pg.* 734
HUMANE FUND - Fund-Raising Program - AMERICAN KENNEL CLUB, INC.; *pg.* 129, *pg.* 1193
HUMANELINES - Newsletter - THE HUMANE SOCIETY OF THE UNITED STATES; *pg.* 143, *pg.* 400
HUMANIK - Animation Middleware - AUTODESK INC.; *pg.* 356, *pg.* 257
HUMANTOUCH - Chair - HUMAN TOUCH; *pg.* 928, *pg.* 123
HUMAPEN - Insulin Injection Device - BATTELLE MEMORIAL INSTITUTE; *pg.* 1401, *pg.* 1437
HUMATE-P - Antihemophiliac Factor (Human) Pasteurized - CSL BEHRING LLC; *pg.* 1520, *pg.* 1543
HUMATROPE - Pharmaceutical Product - ELI LILLY AND COMPANY; *pg.* 1527, *pg.* 684
HUMERAL CUFF - Orthopedic Product - DJO INCORPORATED; *pg.* 1524, *pg.* 302
HUMID-A-WARE - Software - ARMSTRONG INTERNATIONAL, INC.; *pg.* 1069, *pg.* 909
HUMID-AIRE - Humidifiers - ADAMS MFG. CO.; *pg.* 51, *pg.* 1427
HUMIDAIRE - Humidifier - RESMED INC.; *pg.* 1589, *pg.* 207
HUMIDICLEAN - Gas-Fired Steam - ARMSTRONG INTERNATIONAL, INC.; *pg.* 1069, *pg.* 909
HUMIRA - Healthcare Product - ABBOTT LABORATORIES; *pg.* 1484, *pg.* 551
HUMISEAL - Moisture Protective Coating - CHASE CORPORATION; *pg.* 1152, *pg.* 803
HUMITEK - Moisture & Mold Resistant Gypsum Panels - USG CORPORATION; *pg.* 118, *pg.* 594
HUMITENN - Test Equipment - SPX THERMAL PRODUCT SOLUTIONS; *pg.* 1378, *pg.* 1555
HUMMER - Vehicle - AM GENERAL, LLC; *pg.* 163, *pg.* 697
HUMMER - Flour - CARGILL LIMITED; *pg.* 1475, *pg.* 1914
HUMMER - Micro Implant System - STRYKER CORPORATION; *pg.* 1598, *pg.* 894
HUMMINBIRD - Fishfinders - JOHNSON OUTDOORS INC.; *pg.* 1837, *pg.* 1888
HUMMING 1/3 - Softeners - KAO BRANDS CO. INC.; *pg.* 513, *pg.* 1415
HUMMING BIRD - Oral Product - THE GILLETTE COMPANY; *pg.* 509, *pg.* 795
HUMMINGBIRD - Guitars - GIBSON GUITAR CORP.; *pg.* 550, *pg.* 1650
HUMMINGBIRD - Game - WMS INDUSTRIES INC.; *pg.* 593, *pg.* 666
HUMONITOR - Humidity Indicator Card - MULTISORB TECHNOLOGIES, INC.; *pg.* 1570, *pg.* 1150
HUMPHREYS CORNER - Bed Linen - SPRINGS GLOBAL, INC.; *pg.* 698, *pg.* 1616
HUMPRHEY THE DINOSAUR - Children's Hamper - RUBBERMAID HOME PRODUCTS; *pg.* 1138, *pg.* 1453
HUMPTY DUMPTY - Canned Salmon - PETER PAN SEAFOODS, INC.; *pg.* 889, *pg.* 1838
HUMULIN - Pharmaceutical Product - ELI LILLY AND COMPANY; *pg.* 1527, *pg.* 684
HUMVEE - Military Vehicle - AM GENERAL, LLC; *pg.* 163, *pg.* 697
HUNDO - Apparels - UNDER ARMOUR, INC.; *pg.* 49, *pg.* 759
HUNDRED OR NOTHING - Video Game - INTERNATIONAL GAME TECHNOLOGY; *pg.* 957, *pg.* 1024
HUNDRED PLAY DRAW POKER - Video Poker - INTERNATIONAL GAME TECHNOLOGY; *pg.* 957, *pg.* 1024
HUNGRY HUNGRY HIPPOS - Toy & Game - HASBRO, INC.; *pg.* 954, *pg.* 1603
HUNGRY JACK - Food Products - THE J.M. SMUCKER COMPANY; *pg.* 865, *pg.* 1468
HUNGRY-MAN - Frozen Dinner - PINNACLE FOODS GROUP LLC; *pg.* 889, *pg.* 1104
THE HUNGRY PELICAN - Toy - THE OHIO ART COMPANY, INC.; *pg.* 965, *pg.* 1406
HUNTER - Gas Monitor - BACHARACH INC.; *pg.* 1400, *pg.* 1556
HUNTER - Alignment System - HUNTER ENGINEERING COMPANY; *pg.* 208, *pg.* 973
HUNTER - Meat Products - JOHN MORRELL & CO.; *pg.* 866, *pg.* 1415
HUNTER - Air Purifier - LOWE'S COMPANIES, INC.; *pg.* 1053, *pg.* 1383
HUNTER - Sail Boats - MARLOW-HUNTER LLC; *pg.* 1709, *pg.* 409
HUNTER - Fabric - NEMSCHOFF, INC.; *pg.* 936, *pg.* 1890
HUNTER FARMS - Food Product - HARRIS TEETER, INC.; *pg.* 1022, *pg.* 1383
HUNTERLOGIC - Storage Product - PLANO MOLDING COMPANY; *pg.* 1887, *pg.* 652
HUNTERPRO - Lathe Packages - HUNTER ENGINEERING COMPANY; *pg.* 208, *pg.* 973
HUNTER'S PAL - Knife - COAST CUTLERY COMPANY; *pg.* 1121, *pg.* 1501
HUNTER'S PERFORMANCE - Sport Apparel - UNDER ARMOUR, INC.; *pg.* 49, *pg.* 759
HUNTINGTON - Carpet - BEAULIEU GROUP, LLC; *pg.* 917, *pg.* 529
HUNTINGTON - Bar Stool - BLATT BOWLING & BILLIARD CORP.; *pg.* 1827, *pg.* 1203
HUNTINGTON - Cleaning Product - ECOLAB INC.; *pg.* 329, *pg.* 960
HUNTINGTON - Furniture - J. ROBERT SCOTT INC.; *pg.* 930, *pg.* 105
HUNTINGTON AT WORK - Banking Services - HUNTINGTON BANCSHARES INCORPORATED; *pg.* 767, *pg.* 1440
HUNTINGTON FUNDS - Financial Service - HUNTINGTON BANCSHARES INCORPORATED; *pg.* 767, *pg.* 1440
HUNTINGTON PARK - Financial Service - HUNTINGTON BANCSHARES INCORPORATED; *pg.* 767, *pg.* 1440
HUNTINGTON PAYMENT FREEDOM - Debt Cancellation - HUNTINGTON BANCSHARES INCORPORATED; *pg.* 767, *pg.* 1440
HUNTINGTON SMARTTAX - Tax Payments - HUNTINGTON BANCSHARES INCORPORATED; *pg.* 767, *pg.* 1440
HUNTINGTON VISUAL ARCHIVE - Financial Information - HUNTINGTON BANCSHARES INCORPORATED; *pg.* 767, *pg.* 1440
HUNT'S - Food Product - CONAGRA FOODS, INC.; *pg.* 826, *pg.* 1014
HUNTSMAN - Chemical Product - HUNTSMAN CORPORATION; *pg.* 1167, *pg.* 1758
HUONO - Kitchen Equipment - THE MIDDLEBY CORPORATION; *pg.* 1361, *pg.* 610
HUP - Battery - ENERSYS INC.; *pg.* 1334, *pg.* 1584
HUPERZINE - Nutritional Supplement - NATURAL ORGANICS, INC.; *pg.* 1571, *pg.* 1181
HURD - Windows & Patio Doors - HURD WINDOWS & DOORS INC; *pg.* 88, *pg.* 1869
HURD FEELSAFE - Windows & Doors - HURD WINDOWS & DOORS INC; *pg.* 88, *pg.* 1869
THE HURLER - Wooden Rollercoaster - CAROWINDS; *pg.* 537, *pg.* 1364
HURLETRON - Automated Control Systems - ALTAIR CORPORATION; *pg.* 1312, *pg.* 910
HURON - Dinnerware - THE HOMER LAUGHLIN CHINA COMPANY; *pg.* 1125, *pg.* 1850
HURON - Consulting Services - HURON CONSULTING GROUP INC.; *pg.* 768, *pg.* 577
HURON - Quick Connectors - TI AUTOMOTIVE LIMITED; *pg.* 191, *pg.* 869
HURON DAILY TRIBUNE - Newspaper - THE HEARST CORPORATION; *pg.* 1649, *pg.* 1239
HURRICANE - Topical Anesthetics-Liquid Gel & Aerosol - BEUTLICH PHARMACEUTICALS LP; *pg.* 1503, *pg.* 665
HURRICANE - Medical Device - BOSTON SCIENTIFIC CORPORATION; *pg.* 1508, *pg.* 831
HURRICANE - Footwear - EASTLAND SHOE CORPORATION; *pg.* 1808, *pg.* 750
HURRICANE - Fluid Handling System - GRACO, INC.; *pg.* 1342, *pg.* 935
HURRICANE AMBER ALE - Beer - COASTAL EXTREME BREWING COMPANY; *pg.* 240, *pg.* 1602
HURRICANE HIGH GRAVITY - Malt Liquor - ANHEUSER-BUSCH COMPANIES, LLC; *pg.* 237, *pg.* 991
HURRICANE ICE - Malt Liquor - ANHEUSER-BUSCH COMPANIES, LLC; *pg.* 237, *pg.* 991
HURRICANE MALT LIQUOR - Malt Liquor - ANHEUSER-BUSCH COMPANIES, LLC; *pg.* 237, *pg.* 991
HURRISEAL - Dentin Desensitizer - BEUTLICH PHARMACEUTICALS LP; *pg.* 1503, *pg.* 665
HURRIVIEW - Swabs - BEUTLICH PHARMACEUTICALS LP; *pg.* 1503, *pg.* 665
HURRYDATE.COM - Online Dating Service - SPARK NETWORKS, INC.; *pg.* 472, *pg.* 140
HURST - Rescue System - IDEX CORPORATION; *pg.* 1347, *pg.* 623
HURST GRAPHICS - Graphic Product - HURST CHEMICAL COMPANY; *pg.* 1168, *pg.* 174
HURTH - Tools & Machines for Milling & Gearings - GLEASON CORPORATION; *pg.* 1340, *pg.* 1335
HURTH SPHERIC - Gear Honing Machine - GLEASON CORPORATION; *pg.* 1340, *pg.* 1335
HUSH - Fabric - NEMSCHOFF, INC.; *pg.* 936, *pg.* 1890
HUSH - Valve Trim - SPX PROCESS EQUIPMENT; *pg.* 1378, *pg.* 1551
HUSH PUPPIES - Footwear - WOLVERINE WORLD WIDE, INC.; *pg.* 1822, *pg.* 905
HUSHALON - Acoustical Felt - AMERICAN FELT & FILTER COMPANY; *pg.* 1312, *pg.* 1184
HUSHBOARD - Sound Deadening Board - GEORGIA-PACIFIC LLC; *pg.* 1458, *pg.* 507
HUSKEE - Power Equipment - TRACTOR SUPPLY COMPANY; *pg.* 708, *pg.* 1627
HUSKIE - Motor Oil - ROCK VALLEY OIL & CHEMICAL COMPANY; *pg.* 1179, *pg.* 631
HUSKY - Paper - DOMTAR CORPORATION; *pg.* 1456, *pg.* 1954
HUSKY - Pump - FLOW INTERNATIONAL CORPORATION; *pg.* 1337, *pg.* 1821
HUSKY - Air Powered Double Diaphragm Pump - GRACO, INC.; *pg.* 1342, *pg.* 935
HUSKY - Automatic Door Closer - KAWNEER COMPANY, INC.; *pg.* 90, *pg.* 537
HUSKY - Foam System - OSHKOSH CORPORATION; *pg.* 187, *pg.* 1885
HUSKY - Foam System - PIERCE MANUFACTURING, INC.; *pg.* 188, *pg.* 1852
HUSKY - Consumer Mechanics Tools - STANLEY BLACK & DECKER, INC.; *pg.* 1063, *pg.* 358
HUSKY - Tobacco Product - U.S. SMOKELESS TOBACCO COMPANY; *pg.* 1895, *pg.* 1804
HUSKY - Paper Product - WEYERHAEUSER COMPANY; *pg.* 121, *pg.* 1820
HUSKY STACK - Toy Train - LIONEL LLC; *pg.* 961, *pg.* 875
HUSSEY - Seating Company - HUSSEY SEATING CO.; *pg.* 929, *pg.* 751
HUSSMANN - Refrigeration Equipment Company - HUSSMANN INTERNATIONAL, INC.; *pg.* 1347, *pg.* 973
HUSSMANN - Refrigeration Equipment - INGERSOLL-RAND COMPANY; *pg.* 1349, *pg.* 1370
HUSSONG'S - Tequila - MCCORMICK DISTILLING CO., INC.; *pg.* 1966, *pg.* 1007
HUSTLER - Mower Tractor - EXCEL INDUSTRIES, INC.; *pg.* 1795, *pg.* 715
HUSTLER ATZ - Mower Tractor - EXCEL INDUSTRIES, INC.; *pg.* 1795, *pg.* 715
HUSTLER Z - Self-propelled Lawn Mower - EXCEL INDUSTRIES, INC.; *pg.* 1795, *pg.* 715
HUTCH - Suspensions, Sliding Subframes & Lubricants - HUTCHENS INDUSTRIES INC.; *pg.* 208, *pg.* 1006
HUZAF - Antibody - PDL BIOPHARMA INC.; *pg.* 1580, *pg.* 1022
HVC - Golf Equipment - ACUSHNET COMPANY; *pg.* 1824, *pg.* 818
HVC SOFT FEEL - Golf Equipment - ACUSHNET COMPANY; *pg.* 1824, *pg.* 818
HVD - Personal Care Product - WESTROCK COMPANY; *pg.* 1472, *pg.* 1805
HVI - Motor Oil - BEL-RAY COMPANY, INC.; *pg.* 972, *pg.* 1128
HVL - Switchgear - SCHNEIDER ELECTRIC USA, INC.; *pg.* 1306, *pg.* 650
HVL/CC - Switchgear - SCHNEIDER ELECTRIC USA, INC.; *pg.* 1306, *pg.* 650
HVLP 2500 - Fluid Handling System - GRACO, INC.; *pg.* 1342, *pg.* 935

HVLP 3800 - Fluid Handling System - GRACO, INC.; *pg.* 1342, *pg.* 935
HVLP 4900 - Fluid Handling System - GRACO, INC.; *pg.* 1342, *pg.* 935
HWDMG1513/1315 - Fiber Optic Component - OPLINK COMMUNICATIONS, INC.; *pg.* 660, *pg.* 91
HWG 2009 - Food Product - MGP INGREDIENTS, INC.; *pg.* 877, *pg.* 714
HWI - Hardware Wholesaler - DO IT BEST CORP.; *pg.* 1045, *pg.* 680
HX - Golf Equipment - CALLAWAY GOLF COMPANY; *pg.* 1829, *pg.* 58
HX - Hydrogen Atmosphere Gas Generator - SURFACE COMBUSTION, INC.; *pg.* 1077, *pg.* 1462
HX HOT - Golf Product - CALLAWAY GOLF COMPANY; *pg.* 1829, *pg.* 58
HX HOT BITE - Golf Ball - CALLAWAY GOLF COMPANY; *pg.* 1829, *pg.* 58
HX PEARL - Golf Ball - CALLAWAY GOLF COMPANY; *pg.* 1829, *pg.* 58
HX SERIES - Loudspeakers - YAMAHA ELECTRONICS CORPORATION USA; *pg.* 689, *pg.* 51
HX TOUR - Golf Product - CALLAWAY GOLF COMPANY; *pg.* 1829, *pg.* 58
HY-FLEX - Hose - HBD INDUSTRIES, INC.; *pg.* 207, *pg.* 1449
HY-FLEX 200 - Composite/Rubber Dock & Barge Hose - HBD INDUSTRIES, INC.; *pg.* 207, *pg.* 1449
HY-LITE - Hardware - FORTUNE BRANDS HOME & SECURITY, INC.; *pg.* 55, *pg.* 600
HY N DRY - Impervious Stockinette - SPECTRUM LABORATORIES INC.; *pg.* 1595, *pg.* 69
HY-Q - Sluice Gates - RODNEY HUNT COMPANY; *pg.* 1372, *pg.* 840
HY-RA - Alloys - CARPENTER TECHNOLOGY CORPORATION; *pg.* 73, *pg.* 1584
HY-SPAN - Network Communications - AVAGO TECHNOLOGIES; *pg.* 358, *pg.* 238
HY-TEK - Scoreboard & Sports Product - DAKTRONICS, INC.; *pg.* 633, *pg.* 1624
HY-VENTS - Air Vent - TACO INCORPORATED; *pg.* 1077, *pg.* 1601
HYACINTH - Furniture - ETHAN ALLEN INTERIORS INC.; *pg.* 924, *pg.* 343
HYACINTH - Lighting Product - QUOIZEL INC.; *pg.* 1304, *pg.* 1616
HYACT - Chemical Product - WESTROCK COMPANY; *pg.* 1472, *pg.* 1805
HYAMINE 1622 - Topical Biocide - LONZA INC.; *pg.* 1171, *pg.* 1041
HYANNIS - Shoes - ALLEN-EDMONDS SHOE CORP.; *pg.* 1804, *pg.* 1887
HYANNIS - Flatware - ONEIDA LTD; *pg.* 1129, *pg.* 1318
HYANNIS PORT - Fan - WESTINGHOUSE LIGHTING CORPORATION; *pg.* 687, *pg.* 1571
HYATT - Bearing Product - GENERAL BEARING CORPORATION; *pg.* 205, *pg.* 1350
HYB-SEAL - Software - BIO-RAD LABORATORIES, INC.; *pg.* 1504, *pg.* 101
HYBASE - Polymer Product - CHEMTURA CORPORATION; *pg.* 1152, *pg.* 355
HYBON - Glass Fibers - PPG INDUSTRIES, INC.; *pg.* 1445, *pg.* 1579
HYBRICYCLER - Hybridisation Oven - UVP, INC.; *pg.* 1434, *pg.* 298
HYBRID - Air Brush - BADGER AIR BRUSH COMPANY; *pg.* 359, *pg.* 612
HYBRID - Apparel - OAKLEY, INC.; *pg.* 1840, *pg.* 86
HYBRID - Heat Exchanger - PAUL MUELLER COMPANY; *pg.* 706, *pg.* 1007
HYBRID - Panel Fastener Assemblies - PENN ENGINEERING & MANUFACTURING CORP.; *pg.* 1059, *pg.* 1525
HYBRID-2 - Ball Point Pen - PENTEL OF AMERICA, LTD.; *pg.* 453, *pg.* 295
HYBRID CAPTURE - Molecular Diagnostic - QIAGEN GAITHERSBURG INC.; *pg.* 1587, *pg.* 771
HYBRID COMMANDER - Fluid Handling System - GRACO, INC.; *pg.* 1342, *pg.* 935
HYBRID DESIGNER - Software System - MENTOR GRAPHICS CORPORATION; *pg.* 432, *pg.* 1510
HYBRID G800 - Skate - ROLLER DERBY SKATE CORP.; *pg.* 966, *pg.* 630
HYBRID G900 - Skate - ROLLER DERBY SKATE CORP.; *pg.* 966, *pg.* 630
HYBRID GEL GRIP - Pens - PENTEL OF AMERICA, LTD.; *pg.* 453, *pg.* 295
HYBRID GEL ROLLER - Pens - PENTEL OF AMERICA, LTD.; *pg.* 453, *pg.* 295
HYBRID HUNTER - Molecular Biology Product - THERMO FISHER SCIENTIFIC INC.; *pg.* 1602, *pg.* 61
HYBRID STATION - Software System - MENTOR GRAPHICS CORPORATION; *pg.* 432, *pg.* 1510
HYBRID TRACER - Medical Device - COOK GROUP, INC.; *pg.* 1518, *pg.* 674
HYBRIDSELECT - Bed Safety & Positioning - ALIMED, INC.; *pg.* 1490, *pg.* 816
HYBRIDSELECT - Support Surface Product - THE ROHO GROUP; *pg.* 1591, *pg.* 556
HYBRIDUR - Acrylic-Urethane Polymers - AIR PRODUCTS AND CHEMICALS, INC.; *pg.* 1145, *pg.* 1513
HYBRILINKER - Hybridization System - UVP, INC.; *pg.* 1434, *pg.* 298
HYBRISLIP - Molecular Probe Product - THERMO FISHER SCIENTIFIC INC.; *pg.* 1602, *pg.* 61
HYBRITECH - Testing Instrument System - BECKMAN COULTER, INC.; *pg.* 1402, *pg.* 48
HYBRITRON - Potentiometer - BOURNS, INC.; *pg.* 627, *pg.* 193
HYBRIWELL - Molecular Probe Product - THERMO FISHER SCIENTIFIC INC.; *pg.* 1602, *pg.* 61
HYBRYX - Hybrid Air Bearing Stage - NEWPORT CORPORATION; *pg.* 1424, *pg.* 114
HYCALOG - Diamond Bits - SCHLUMBERGER WELL COMPLETIONS; *pg.* 1373, *pg.* 1714
HYCODAN - Pharmaceutical Product - ENDO PHARMACEUTICALS HOLDINGS, INC.; *pg.* 1528, *pg.* 1549
HYCORE - Linear Motor Product - BALDOR ELECTRIC COMPANY; *pg.* 1316, *pg.* 32
HYCOTUSS - Pharmaceutical Product - ENDO PHARMACEUTICALS HOLDINGS, INC.; *pg.* 1528, *pg.* 1549
HYCYCLE UNICRACKING - Hydrocracking Technology Used in the Production of High-quality Diesel Fuel - UOP LLC; *pg.* 1386, *pg.* 606
HYDAPIPE - Exposed Pressure Balanced Safety Shower Systems - SYMMONS INDUSTRIES, INC.; *pg.* 114, *pg.* 803
HYDASE - Ophthalmic Pharmaceutical Product - AKORN, INC.; *pg.* 1488, *pg.* 622
HYDE - Furniture - ETHAN ALLEN INTERIORS INC.; *pg.* 924, *pg.* 343
HYDE - Fabric - NEMSCHOFF, INC.; *pg.* 936, *pg.* 1890
HYDE - Casual Footwear - SAUCONY, INC.; *pg.* 1818, *pg.* 828
HYDE PARK - Furniture - BASSETT FURNITURE INDUSTRIES, INCORPORATED; *pg.* 916, *pg.* 1776
HYDPRO - Software - GULF PUBLISHING COMPANY; *pg.* 1646, *pg.* 1707
HYDRA - Video Game - INTERNATIONAL GAME TECHNOLOGY; *pg.* 957, *pg.* 1024
HYDRA - Gasoline-powered Electric Airless Paint Sprayers - TITAN TOOL, INC.; *pg.* 1383, *pg.* 1100
HYDRA-CAT - Proportioning Pumps - GRACO, INC.; *pg.* 1342, *pg.* 935
HYDRA-CELL - Pump - LINDSAY CORPORATION; *pg.* 1356, *pg.* 1016
HYDRA-CLEAN - High Pressure Washers - GRACO, INC.; *pg.* 1342, *pg.* 935
HYDRA DIOR - Skin Care Products - PARFUMS CHRISTIAN DIOR, INC; *pg.* 519, *pg.* 1276
HYDRA-DRIVE - Drilling Product - SMITH INTERNATIONAL, INC.; *pg.* 1377, *pg.* 1715
HYDRA FAST-EN - Adhesives - ROYAL ADHESIVES & SEALANTS LLC; *pg.* 1179, *pg.* 697
HYDRA INJECT - Injection System - LINDSAY CORPORATION; *pg.* 1356, *pg.* 1016
HYDRA INJECT I - Displacement Pump - LINDSAY CORPORATION; *pg.* 1356, *pg.* 1016
HYDRA INJECT II - Displacement Pump - LINDSAY CORPORATION; *pg.* 1356, *pg.* 1016
HYDRA INJECT III - Displacement Pump - LINDSAY CORPORATION; *pg.* 1356, *pg.* 1016
HYDRA JAGWIRE - Medical Device - BOSTON SCIENTIFIC CORPORATION; *pg.* 1508, *pg.* 831
HYDRA-MATE - Mechanical Proportioners - GRACO, INC.; *pg.* 1342, *pg.* 935
HYDRA PRO - Gasoline-powered Airless Paint Sprayers - TITAN TOOL, INC.; *pg.* 1383, *pg.* 1100
HYDRA PRO SUPER - Gasoline-powered Airless Paint Sprayers - TITAN TOOL, INC.; *pg.* 1383, *pg.* 1100
HYDRA-RIB - Bearing Product - THE TIMKEN COMPANY; *pg.* 218, *pg.* 1408
HYDRA-SPRAY - Airless Spray Painting Equipment - GRACO, INC.; *pg.* 1342, *pg.* 935
HYDRA-STOP - Pumps - IDEX CORPORATION; *pg.* 1347, *pg.* 623
HYDRA-STOPPER - pump Product - IDEX CORPORATION; *pg.* 1347, *pg.* 623
HYDRA-TAPPER - Pump Product - IDEX CORPORATION; *pg.* 1347, *pg.* 623
HYDRA-TORAX - Drilling Product - SMITH INTERNATIONAL, INC.; *pg.* 1377, *pg.* 1715
HYDRA-TURN - Pump - IDEX CORPORATION; *pg.* 1347, *pg.* 623
HYDRA WATER QUALITY INSTRUMENT - Quality Service - MESA LABORATORIES, INC.; *pg.* 1567, *pg.* 333
HYDRACEL - Nutritional Supplement - RBC LIFE SCIENCES, INC.; *pg.* 1588, *pg.* 1723
HYDRAGEL - Starches - CARGILL LIMITED; *pg.* 1475, *pg.* 1914
HYDRAGLIDE - Ride Control System - GEHL COMPANY; *pg.* 1339, *pg.* 1899
HYDRAKIND - Hair Care Product - NU SKIN ENTERPRISES, INC.; *pg.* 518, *pg.* 1755
HYDRALIGN - Automatic Web Splicer - BUTLER AUTOMATIC, INC.; *pg.* 1320, *pg.* 833
HYDRALIGN - Web Guide Systems - HYDRALIGN; *pg.* 1257, *pg.* 833
HYDRALOC - Brakes - GEHL COMPANY; *pg.* 1339, *pg.* 1899
HYDRAMAX - Gas-Hydraulic Sprayers - GRACO, INC.; *pg.* 1342, *pg.* 935
HYDRAN - Monitoring Instrument - GE ENERGY; *pg.* 1338, *pg.* 506
HYDRANAL - Chemical Product - GFS CHEMICALS, INC.; *pg.* 1164, *pg.* 1471
HYDRANAL - Chemical Product - SPECTRUM CHEMICALS & LABORATORY PRODUCTS, INC.; *pg.* 1181, *pg.* 94
HYDRAPOL - Surfactant - HUNTSMAN CORPORATION; *pg.* 1167, *pg.* 1758
HYDRAPORT - Fluid Handling System - GRACO, INC.; *pg.* 1342, *pg.* 935
HYDRASAN - Vacuum Breaker - JOSAM COMPANY; *pg.* 89, *pg.* 695
HYDRATOME - Medical Device - BOSTON SCIENTIFIC CORPORATION; *pg.* 1508, *pg.* 831
HYDRAULIC DAWG UDH-70-T - Underground Puller - SHERMAN & REILLY, INC.; *pg.* 1062, *pg.* 1629
HYDRAULIC REGAL - Flushometer - SLOAN VALVE COMPANY; *pg.* 1062, *pg.* 613
HYDRAULIC SUPERJET - System for Installing Fiber Optic Cable - SHERMAN & REILLY, INC.; *pg.* 1062, *pg.* 1629
HYDRAVER - Chemical Reagent - HACH COMPANY; *pg.* 1415, *pg.* 334
HYDRAVISION - Graphics Card - ADVANCED MICRO DEVICES, INC.; *pg.* 613, *pg.* 282
HYDRAVISION - Software - ADVANCED MICRO DEVICES, INC.-MARKHAM; *pg.* 345, *pg.* 1922
HYDREA - Health Care Product - BRISTOL-MYERS SQUIBB COMPANY; *pg.* 1509, *pg.* 1206
HYDREL - Lighting Fixture Product - ACUITY BRANDS, INC.; *pg.* 1294, *pg.* 487
HYDREX - Valves - FLOWSERVE CORPORATION; *pg.* 82, *pg.* 1719
HYDREX - Cleaning Product - PETROFERM INC.; *pg.* 1177, *pg.* 616
HYDRHOLAC - Emulsion - DOW CHEMICAL; *pg.* 1156, *pg.* 1563
HYDRIENCE - Hair Coloring - P&G-CLAIROL, INC.; *pg.* 519, *pg.* 1418
HYDRION - Chemical Product - SPECTRUM CHEMICALS & LABORATORY PRODUCTS, INC.; *pg.* 1181, *pg.* 94
HYDRO - Rear Engine Rider - ARIENS COMPANY INC.; *pg.* 700, *pg.* 1855
HYDRO - Fabric - NEMSCHOFF, INC.; *pg.* 936, *pg.* 1890
HYDRO-AX - Feller Bunchers - BLOUNT INTERNATIONAL, INC.; *pg.* 1043, *pg.* 1501
HYDRO-CUSHION - Washer Suspension System - PELLERIN MILNOR CORPORATION; *pg.* 1368, *pg.* 744
HYDRO-FRACTIONATED - Soybean Oil - ARCHER-DANIELS-MIDLAND COMPANY; *pg.* 825, *pg.* 565
HYDRO-LIFT - Full Closure Core Catcher - BAKER HUGHES INTEQ; *pg.* 1316, *pg.* 1700
HYDRO-LINE - Hydraulic Components - EATON

First page reference indicates Business Class Edition
Second page reference indicates Geographic Edition

CORPORATION; *pg.* 1331, *pg.* 1429
HYDRO MELT - Liquid Deicer with Corrosion Inhibitor - CARGILL LIMITED; *pg.* 1475, *pg.* 1914
HYDRO MULCH - Mulch Fibers - RSI HOME PRODUCTS; *pg.* 108, *pg.* 1381
HYDRO PRO - Moisture Analyzer - ARIZONA INSTRUMENT LLC; *pg.* 1400, *pg.* 12
HYDRO-PRO - Spray Nozzle - STRAHMAN VALVES, INC.; *pg.* 1379, *pg.* 1517
HYDRO-PRO 150 - Spray Nozzle - STRAHMAN VALVES, INC.; *pg.* 1379, *pg.* 1517
HYDRO-RETRIEVER - Cleaning Product - HILLYARD, INC.; *pg.* 331, *pg.* 990
HYDRO-SHUR - Waterproofing Coatings - AKZONOBEL DECORATIVE PAINTS U.S.; *pg.* 1439, *pg.* 1474
HYDRO-SOFT - Healthcare Product - DERMA SCIENCES, INC.; *pg.* 1523, *pg.* 1111
HYDRO SONIC - Cleaning Concentrate with Ammonia - L&R MANUFACTURING COMPANY; *pg.* 1419, *pg.* 1076
HYDRO SPOT - Dry Cleaning & Laundry Product - ADCO, INC.; *pg.* 325, *pg.* 482
HYDRO-STONE - Gypsum Cement - USG CORPORATION; *pg.* 118, *pg.* 594
HYDRO STRIKE - Toy - MATTEL, INC.; *pg.* 962, *pg.* 81
HYDRO THERMABLATOR - Medical Device - BOSTON SCIENTIFIC CORPORATION; *pg.* 1508, *pg.* 831
HYDRO-TITE - Baseboard Expansion Joint - SLANT/FIN CORPORATION; *pg.* 1076, *pg.* 1163
HYDRO WALKBEHIND - Self-propelled Lawn Mower - EXCEL INDUSTRIES, INC.; *pg.* 1795, *pg.* 715
HYDRO-WET - Turf Wetting Agent - KALO, INC.; *pg.* 1796, *pg.* 719
HYDROBMS - Navigation Aid - TRIMBLE NAVIGATION LIMITED; *pg.* 1384, *pg.* 288
HYDROCAL - Plaster - USG CORPORATION; *pg.* 118, *pg.* 594
HYDROCARBON PROCESSING - Trade Journal - GULF PUBLISHING COMPANY; *pg.* 1646, *pg.* 1707
HYDROCAT - Surface Preparation System - FLOW INTERNATIONAL CORPORATION; *pg.* 1337, *pg.* 1821
HYDROCELL - Wound Foam Dressing - DERMA SCIENCES, INC.; *pg.* 1523, *pg.* 1111
HYDROCHLORIDE PIGMENT PROCESS - Pigment Production Process - ALTAIR NANOTECHNOLOGIES INC.; *pg.* 1147, *pg.* 1031
HYDROCOLLATOR - Orthopedic Device - DJO SURGICAL; *pg.* 1525, *pg.* 1661
HYDROCOLLATOR COLPAC - Orthopedic Device - DJO SURGICAL; *pg.* 1525, *pg.* 1661
HYDROCONTOUR - Navigation Aid - TRIMBLE NAVIGATION LIMITED; *pg.* 1384, *pg.* 288
HYDROCOOL - Burner - NAO, INC.; *pg.* 1074, *pg.* 1567
HYDROCRACKER - Software - ASPEN TECHNOLOGY, INC.; *pg.* 354, *pg.* 804
HYDRODERM - Elastomeric Coatings - AKZONOBEL DECORATIVE PAINTS U.S.; *pg.* 1439, *pg.* 1474
HYDRODREDGE - Navigation Aid - TRIMBLE NAVIGATION LIMITED; *pg.* 1384, *pg.* 288
HYDRODUCT - Medical Equipment - CONMED CORPORATION; *pg.* 1517, *pg.* 1347
HYDRODY - Blower Dryer - HILLYARD, INC.; *pg.* 331, *pg.* 990
HYDROEDIT - Software - TRIMBLE NAVIGATION LIMITED; *pg.* 1384, *pg.* 288
HYDROELASTIC - Bushing - TENNECO, INC.; *pg.* 985, *pg.* 625
HYDROEXAMINE - Navigation Aid - TRIMBLE NAVIGATION LIMITED; *pg.* 1384, *pg.* 288
HYDROFLEX - Elastomeric Coatings - AKZONOBEL DECORATIVE PAINTS U.S.; *pg.* 1439, *pg.* 1474
HYDROFLEX - Medical Device - C.R. BARD, INC.; *pg.* 1519, *pg.* 1094
HYDROFLEX - Waterborne Film Lamination Adhesive - H.B. FULLER COMPANY; *pg.* 1165, *pg.* 961
HYDROFLOW - Apparel Technology - BROOKS SPORTS INC.; *pg.* 1805, *pg.* 1818
HYDROFLX - Cushioning Technology - BROOKS SPORTS INC.; *pg.* 1805, *pg.* 1818
HYDROFORCE - Line of Water-Based Cleaners/Degreasers - CRC INDUSTRIES, INC.; *pg.* 329, *pg.* 1590
HYDROGARD - Special Application Filters - VITAL SIGNS, INC.; *pg.* 1607, *pg.* 1126
HYDROGEN - Textiles - BERNHARDT DESIGN; *pg.* 918, *pg.* 1381
HYDROGEN ATMOSPHERE - Thermal Processing Equipment - SURFACE COMBUSTION, INC.; *pg.* 1077, *pg.* 1462
HYDROGENATED - Soybean Oil - ARCHER-DANIELS-MIDLAND COMPANY; *pg.* 825, *pg.* 565
HYDROGLIDE - Machinery - HARDINGE INC.; *pg.* 1344, *pg.* 1157
HYDROGRAPHIC SURVEYOR - Surveying Equipment - NOVATEL INC.; *pg.* 1424, *pg.* 1904
HYDROGRATE - Stoker - DETROIT STOKER CO.; *pg.* 1070, *pg.* 900
HYDROKINETIC - Dental Laser Product - BIOLASE TECHNOLOGY, INC.; *pg.* 1506, *pg.* 107
HYDROL - Polyalkylene Glycol - HUNTSMAN CORPORATION; *pg.* 1167, *pg.* 1758
HYDROLAB - Multiparameter Water Monitoring Instrumentation - DANAHER CORPORATION; *pg.* 1044, *pg.* 397
HYDROLERT - Moisture Detection - TRICO MFG. CORP.; *pg.* 219, *pg.* 1886
HYDROLIFT - Medical & Aesthetic Product - DYNATRONICS CORPORATION; *pg.* 1526, *pg.* 1757
HYDROLIN - Chlorine & Caustic Soda - OLIN CORPORATION; *pg.* 1176, *pg.* 976
HYDROLOCK - Adhesive - H.B. FULLER COMPANY; *pg.* 1165, *pg.* 961
HYDROLOGY - Leather Tanning Products - E.I. DU PONT DE NEMOURS & COMPANY; *pg.* 1159, *pg.* 390
HYDROLOK - Seat Recline System - CRANE CO.; *pg.* 227, *pg.* 373
HYDROLUBE - Lubricant - BIRKO CORPORATION; *pg.* 1149, *pg.* 332
HYDROLUBRIC - Fluid Power - HOUGHTON INTERNATIONAL INC.; *pg.* 1167, *pg.* 1589
HYDROMASSAGE - Health Services - ETS, LLC; *pg.* 54, *pg.* 685
HYDROMESH - Apparel - SPORT OBERMEYER LTD.; *pg.* 1846, *pg.* 310
HYDROMINS - Nutritional Supplements - NATURAL ALTERNATIVES INTERNATIONAL, INC.; *pg.* 1571, *pg.* 253
HYDROMITE - Gypsum Cement - USG CORPORATION; *pg.* 118, *pg.* 594
HYDROMORPHONE HCL - Pharmaceutical Product - LANNETT COMPANY, INC.; *pg.* 1555, *pg.* 1566
HYDROMOVE - Shoe Liner - REEBOK INTERNATIONAL LTD.; *pg.* 1817, *pg.* 811
HYDRONEAL - Gas Generators - BASF CATALYSTS LLC; *pg.* 1148, *pg.* 1074
HYDROPAK - Concrete Pipe Machinery - BESSER COMPANY; *pg.* 1317, *pg.* 865
HYDROPATCH - Elastomeric Coatings - AKZONOBEL DECORATIVE PAINTS U.S.; *pg.* 1439, *pg.* 1474
HYDROPERM - Metal Casting Plaster - USG CORPORATION; *pg.* 118, *pg.* 594
HYDROPHOTONICS - Dental Laser Product - BIOLASE TECHNOLOGY, INC.; *pg.* 1506, *pg.* 107
HYDROPLAS - Water Borne Coating - RED SPOT PAINT & VARNISH CO., INC.; *pg.* 1446, *pg.* 679
HYDROPLASTIC - Elastomeric Coatings - AKZONOBEL DECORATIVE PAINTS U.S.; *pg.* 1439, *pg.* 1474
HYDROPRIME - Elastomeric Coatings - AKZONOBEL DECORATIVE PAINTS U.S.; *pg.* 1439, *pg.* 1474
HYDROPRO - Software - TRIMBLE NAVIGATION LIMITED; *pg.* 1384, *pg.* 288
HYDROPROCESSING - Technology - TRIMBLE NAVIGATION LIMITED; *pg.* 1384, *pg.* 288
HYDROPROFILE - Navigation Aid - TRIMBLE NAVIGATION LIMITED; *pg.* 1384, *pg.* 288
HYDRORIG - Software - TRIMBLE NAVIGATION LIMITED; *pg.* 1384, *pg.* 288
HYDROSEAL - Engine Degreaser - RADIATOR SPECIALTY COMPANY; *pg.* 215, *pg.* 1380
HYDROSEALER - Elastomeric Coatings - AKZONOBEL DECORATIVE PAINTS U.S.; *pg.* 1439, *pg.* 1474
HYDROSEISMIC - Navigation Aid - TRIMBLE NAVIGATION LIMITED; *pg.* 1384, *pg.* 288
HYDROSEP - Safety & Protective Equipment - ENCON SAFETY PRODUCTS; *pg.* 1334, *pg.* 1705
HYDROSET - Biomaterial - STRYKER CORPORATION; *pg.* 1598, *pg.* 894
HYDROSHIELD - Waterproofing System - MINERALS TECHNOLOGIES INC.; *pg.* 1173, *pg.* 617
HYDROSHIELD 451 - Mastic - KOPPERS HOLDINGS INC.; *pg.* 1170, *pg.* 1577
HYDROSIL - Dental Product - DENTSPLY INTERNATIONAL INC.; *pg.* 1522, *pg.* 1596
HYDROSKIN - Pharmaceutical Product - ALLERGAN; *pg.* 1490, *pg.* 1101
HYDROSMOOTH - Marine Transmissions - REGAL BELOIT CORPORATION; *pg.* 106, *pg.* 1854
HYDROSPIN - Shower Massage Kit - WAXMAN INDUSTRIES, INC.; *pg.* 120, *pg.* 1406
HYDROSTEER - Guidewires - ST. JUDE MEDICAL, INC.; *pg.* 1596, *pg.* 963
HYDROSTRIKE - Game - PRESSMAN TOY CORPORATION; *pg.* 965, *pg.* 1734
HYDROTECH - Software - BIO-RAD LABORATORIES, INC.; *pg.* 1504, *pg.* 101
HYDROTHERM - HVAC Equipment - MESTEK, INC.; *pg.* 1074, *pg.* 857
HYDROTIDE - Gauge - TRIMBLE NAVIGATION LIMITED; *pg.* 1384, *pg.* 288
HYDROTRANSFER - Navigation Aid - TRIMBLE NAVIGATION LIMITED; *pg.* 1384, *pg.* 288
HYDROTRUSS - Jordan Filling - BOLTON-EMERSON AMERICAS, INC.; *pg.* 1318, *pg.* 827
HYDROTUG - Management System - TRIMBLE NAVIGATION LIMITED; *pg.* 1384, *pg.* 288
HYDROVAR - Fluid Technology Product & Service - ITT CORPORATION; *pg.* 1351, *pg.* 1354
HYDROVSP - Navigation Aid - TRIMBLE NAVIGATION LIMITED; *pg.* 1384, *pg.* 288
HYDROX - Cookie - KELLOGG COMPANY; *pg.* 831, *pg.* 870
HYDROZONE - Semiconductor Device - APPLIED MATERIALS, INC; *pg.* 618, *pg.* 1009
HYFLEX - Paper & Nonwoven Material - FIBERMARK INC.; *pg.* 1457, *pg.* 1764
HYFRECATOR - Medical Equipment - CONMED CORPORATION; *pg.* 1517, *pg.* 1347
HYGEIA - Dairy Product - DEAN FOODS COMPANY; *pg.* 852, *pg.* 1679
HYGENIC - Floor Maintenance Equipment - TENNANT COMPANY; *pg.* 1381, *pg.* 944
HYGICULT - Food Safety Product - NEOGEN CORPORATION; *pg.* 883, *pg.* 896
HYGIEIA - Chalkboard Cleaner - DIXON TICONDEROGA COMPANY; *pg.* 388, *pg.* 430
HYGRADE - Hot Dogs & Sliced Meats - MAPLE LEAF FOODS INC.; *pg.* 875, *pg.* 1927
HYGRADE - Automotive Products - STANDARD MOTOR PRODUCTS, INC.; *pg.* 218, *pg.* 1176
HYGROCHRON - Data Loggers - MAXIM INTEGRATED PRODUCTS, INC.; *pg.* 653, *pg.* 247
HYLAFORM - Sodium Hyaluronate - GENZYME CORPORATION; *pg.* 1534, *pg.* 808
HYLAND - Apparel - ENNIS, INC.; *pg.* 393, *pg.* 1727
HYLARTIN - Pharmaceutical Product - PFIZER INC.; *pg.* 1581, *pg.* 1278
HYLENEX - Pharmaceutical Product - BAXTER INTERNATIONAL INC.; *pg.* 1499, *pg.* 599
HYLITE - Vehicle Safety System - GROTE INDUSTRIES, INC.; *pg.* 206, *pg.* 693
HYLITE 225RR - Canola Hybrids - MONSANTO; *pg.* 1798, *pg.* 1399
HYLITE 292 CL - Canola Hybrids - MONSANTO; *pg.* 1798, *pg.* 1399
HYLITE 618 CL - Canola Hybrids - MONSANTO; *pg.* 1798, *pg.* 1399
HYLUMED - Bulk Product - GENZYME CORPORATION; *pg.* 1534, *pg.* 808
HYMOR - Plastic Refractory - PLIBRICO CO. LLC; *pg.* 104, *pg.* 587
HYMU "77" - Alloys - CARPENTER TECHNOLOGY CORPORATION; *pg.* 73, *pg.* 1584
HYMU "800" - Alloys - CARPENTER TECHNOLOGY CORPORATION; *pg.* 73, *pg.* 1584
HYNAP - Dispenser Napkin - GEORGIA-PACIFIC LLC; *pg.* 1458, *pg.* 507
HYOLA 357 RR MAGNUM - Canola Hybrids - MONSANTO; *pg.* 1798, *pg.* 1399
HYOLA 420 - Canola Hybrids - MONSANTO; *pg.* 1798, *pg.* 1399
HYOLA 440 - Canola Hybrids - MONSANTO; *pg.* 1798, *pg.* 1399
HYOLA 505 RR - Canola Hybrids - MONSANTO; *pg.* 1798, *pg.* 1399
HYOLA 514 RR - Canola Hybrids - MONSANTO; *pg.* 1798, *pg.* 1399
HYOMAX - Pharmaceutical Product - CHIESI USA, INC.; *pg.* 1515, *pg.* 1359

HYP - Cap - BROWN & BIGELOW, INC.; *pg.* 1624, *pg.* 959
HYPAFIX - Medical & Aesthetic Product - DYNATRONICS CORPORATION; *pg.* 1526, *pg.* 1757
HYPAK - Prefillable Syringes - BECTON, DICKINSON & COMPANY; *pg.* 1501, *pg.* 1068
HYPALON - Insulation Product - ALPHA ASSOCIATES, INC.; *pg.* 691, *pg.* 1078
HYPALON - Coated Fabric - DYNATECT MANUFACTURING INC.; *pg.* 1330, *pg.* 1883
HYPALON - Tubing - E.I. DU PONT DE NEMOURS & COMPANY; *pg.* 1159, *pg.* 390
HYPALON - Shampoo - MCNETT CORPORATION; *pg.* 1839, *pg.* 1817
HYPALON - Wire & Cable - THE ZIPPERTUBING COMPANY; *pg.* 1892, *pg.* 12
HYPAN - Chemical Ingredient - LIPO CHEMICALS INC.; *pg.* 1171, *pg.* 1107
HYPE HAIR - Hair Straightener - CONAIR CORPORATION; *pg.* 505, *pg.* 1055
THE HYPE MACHINE - Music Aggregator - SPINMEDIA; *pg.* 1282, *pg.* 104
HYPER-BOX - Holographic Carton Packaging - HOLO-SOURCE CORPORATION; *pg.* 1416, *pg.* 896
HYPER-CARD - Holographic Blister Card - HOLO-SOURCE CORPORATION; *pg.* 1416, *pg.* 896
HYPER DIRECTIONAL - Electronic Product - LRAD CORPORATION; *pg.* 652, *pg.* 204
HYPER-DRI - Footwear - LACROSSE FOOTWEAR, INC.; *pg.* 1811, *pg.* 1503
HYPER-FLEX - Holographic Flexible Packaging - HOLO-SOURCE CORPORATION; *pg.* 1416, *pg.* 896
HYPER-FOLIC - Release Additive - SMOOTH-ON INC.; *pg.* 111, *pg.* 1528
HYPER-G - Pen - PENTEL OF AMERICA, LTD.; *pg.* 453, *pg.* 295
HYPER-LABEL - Holographic Labels - HOLO-SOURCE CORPORATION; *pg.* 1416, *pg.* 896
HYPER POWER - Flexible & Affordable Fuel Pricing Program - SIGNATURE FLIGHT SUPPORT CORP.; *pg.* 234, *pg.* 456
HYPER SLIDE - Toy & Game - HASBRO, INC.; *pg.* 954, *pg.* 1603
HYPER STEAM - Convection Steamer - UNIFIED BRANDS INC.; *pg.* 1385, *pg.* 970
HYPER X - Driver - CALLAWAY GOLF COMPANY; *pg.* 1829, *pg.* 58
HYPER-X - Rocket - ORBITAL ATK; *pg.* 1425, *pg.* 1779
HYPERASSEMBLY - Software - QVIDIAN; *pg.* 458, *pg.* 829
HYPERBUILD - Software - WIND RIVER SYSTEMS, INC.; *pg.* 493, *pg.* 38
HYPERCACHE - Physical Layer Device - CYPRESS SEMICONDUCTOR CORPORATION; *pg.* 1326, *pg.* 243
HYPERCACHE PLUS - Physical Layer Device - CYPRESS SEMICONDUCTOR CORPORATION; *pg.* 1326, *pg.* 243
HYPERCARD - Application Program - APPLE INC.; *pg.* 350, *pg.* 73
HYPERCEL - Chromatography Product - PALL CORPORATION; *pg.* 232, *pg.* 1323
HYPERCLIP - Video Tools - AVID TECHNOLOGY, INC.; *pg.* 622, *pg.* 804
HYPERCOOL - Thermal Management Technology - DELL INC.; *pg.* 383, *pg.* 1737
HYPERDEBUG - Debug Technology - IMAGINATION TECHNOLOGIES; *pg.* 412, *pg.* 285
HYPERDSC - Aluminum Sample Pan - PERKINELMER, INC.; *pg.* 1426, *pg.* 853
HYPERDUNK - Basketball Shoes - NIKE, INC.; *pg.* 1812, *pg.* 1492
HYPERFLASK - Glass & Ceramic Material - CORNING INCORPORATED; *pg.* 1122, *pg.* 1154
HYPERION - Analytical Device - BRUKER CORPORATION; *pg.* 1511, *pg.* 788
HYPERION - Carpet - INTERFACE, INC.; *pg.* 695, *pg.* 512
HYPERION 1000 - Analytical Device - BRUKER CORPORATION; *pg.* 1511, *pg.* 788
HYPERION 2000 - Analytical Device - BRUKER CORPORATION; *pg.* 1511, *pg.* 788
HYPERION 3000 - Analytical Device - BRUKER CORPORATION; *pg.* 1511, *pg.* 788
HYPERION AUDIOBOOKS - Books on Tape - HYPERION BOOKS; *pg.* 1651, *pg.* 1242
HYPERION EAST - Books with Asian Themes - HYPERION BOOKS; *pg.* 1651, *pg.* 1242
HYPERION R-LITE - Lighting Systems - REVOLUTION LIGHTING TECHNOLOGIES, INC.; *pg.* 1304, *pg.* 377
HYPERJACK - Magnetic Jack - MOLEX INCORPORATED; *pg.* 655, *pg.* 628
HYPERJTAG - Connection System - IMAGINATION TECHNOLOGIES; *pg.* 412, *pg.* 285
HYPERKOTE - Sprayable Polyurethane System - THE DOW CHEMICAL COMPANY; *pg.* 1157, *pg.* 898
HYPERLAST - Polyurethane System - THE DOW CHEMICAL COMPANY; *pg.* 1157, *pg.* 898
HYPERLINK - Gas Piping Systems - OMEGA FLEX, INC.; *pg.* 982, *pg.* 1532
HYPERLYNX - Software System - MENTOR GRAPHICS CORPORATION; *pg.* 432, *pg.* 1510
HYPERMAPPER - Integrated Circuits - AVAGO TECHNOLOGIES; *pg.* 358, *pg.* 238
HYPERPACS - Software - RADIANCE TECHNOLOGIES, INC.; *pg.* 1277, *pg.* 6
HYPERPHY - Integrated Circuits - AVAGO TECHNOLOGIES; *pg.* 358, *pg.* 238
HYPERSOFT - Bedding Foam - CARPENTER CO.; *pg.* 920, *pg.* 1801
HYPERSOFT - Quilting Foam - SELECT COMFORT CORPORATION; *pg.* 942, *pg.* 942
HYPERSONIC SOUND - Electronic Product - LRAD CORPORATION; *pg.* 652, *pg.* 204
HYPERSOUND - Audio Brand - HYPERSOUND; *pg.* 643, *pg.* 186
HYPERSPACE - Independent Application Installation Software - PHOENIX TECHNOLOGIES LTD.; *pg.* 454, *pg.* 147
HYPERSUITE - Software System - MENTOR GRAPHICS CORPORATION; *pg.* 432, *pg.* 1510
HYPERTALK - Application Program - APPLE INC.; *pg.* 350, *pg.* 73
HYPERTRANSPORT - Connectivity Product - ADVANCED MICRO DEVICES, INC.; *pg.* 613, *pg.* 282
HYPERTRANSPORT - Integrated Circuits - BROADCOM CORPORATION; *pg.* 364, *pg.* 108
HYPERTRANSPORT - Chip - CRAY INC.; *pg.* 380, *pg.* 1834
HYPERTRANSPORT - Interface System - NVIDIA CORPORATION; *pg.* 447, *pg.* 268
HYPERTROL - Nutritional Supplement - NATURAL ORGANICS, INC.; *pg.* 1571, *pg.* 1181
HYPERVENT - Musical Instrument - PEAVEY ELECTRONICS CORPORATION; *pg.* 662, *pg.* 970
HYPERX - Generator - CHYRONHEGO; *pg.* 371, *pg.* 1179
HYPERX - Memory - KINGSTON TECHNOLOGY COMPANY, INC.; *pg.* 425, *pg.* 90
HYPERZ - Graphics Card - ADVANCED MICRO DEVICES, INC.; *pg.* 613, *pg.* 282
HYPEX - Software - RAYTHEON COMPANY; *pg.* 233, *pg.* 854
HYPLEX - Pump - FLOW INTERNATIONAL CORPORATION; *pg.* 1337, *pg.* 1821
HYPNOTIC POISON - Women's Fragrance - PARFUMS CHRISTIAN DIOR, INC; *pg.* 519, *pg.* 1276
HYPOFLEX - Metal Tubing - SUPERIOR TUBE COMPANY INC.; *pg.* 113, *pg.* 1522
HYPOID 90 - Outboard Gear Lube - AMERICAN GREASE STICK CO.; *pg.* 971, *pg.* 902
HYPOL - Prepolymer - THE DOW CHEMICAL COMPANY; *pg.* 1157, *pg.* 898
HYPONEX - Soil Product - THE SCOTTS MIRACLE-GRO COMPANY; *pg.* 1799, *pg.* 1459
HYPOPUMP - Pumps - IDEX CORPORATION; *pg.* 1347, *pg.* 623
HYPOTPLUS - Electrical Test Instruments - ASSOCIATED RESEARCH INC.; *pg.* 1400, *pg.* 622
HYPRO - Pumps - HYPRO; *pg.* 705, *pg.* 951
HYPURE - Cartridge Filters - GE WATER & PROCESS TECHNOLOGIES; *pg.* 1339, *pg.* 1588
HYPURE - Imaging System - PERKINELMER, INC.; *pg.* 1426, *pg.* 853
HYRATE - Plastic Refractory - PLIBRICO CO. LLC; *pg.* 104, *pg.* 587
HYREZIST - Plastic Refractory - PLIBRICO CO. LLC; *pg.* 104, *pg.* 587
HYROTONE MAX - Pharmaceutical Product - VALEANT PHARMACEUTICALS INTERNATIONAL; *pg.* 1605, *pg.* 1047
HYSOC - Specialty Fats - CARGILL LIMITED; *pg.* 1475, *pg.* 1914
HYSON - Nitrogen Gas Springs - BARNES GROUP INC.; *pg.* 1317, *pg.* 340
HYSTER - Lift Truck - NACCO INDUSTRIES, INC.; *pg.* 1174, *pg.* 1433
HYSTER-YALE - Material Handling Equipment - HYSTER-YALE MATERIALS HANDLING; *pg.* 1347, *pg.* 1503
HYSTEROCATH - Cup - COOK GROUP, INC.; *pg.* 1518, *pg.* 674
HYSTEROSCOPY REDIKIT - Surgical Preparatory Kit - THE COOPER COMPANIES, INC.; *pg.* 1518, *pg.* 183
HYSTRENE - Polymer Product - CHEMTURA CORPORATION; *pg.* 1152, *pg.* 355
HYSUN - Sunflower Hybrids - MONSANTO; *pg.* 1798, *pg.* 1399
HYSUN525 - Sunflower Hybrids - MONSANTO; *pg.* 1798, *pg.* 1399
HYSYS - Logistics Software - ASPEN TECHNOLOGY, INC.; *pg.* 354, *pg.* 804
HYSYS - Software System - HONEYWELL INTERNATIONAL INC.; *pg.* 407, *pg.* 1088
HYSYS NEURAL NET - Software - ASPEN TECHNOLOGY, INC.; *pg.* 354, *pg.* 804
HYSYS OLI INTERFACE - Software - ASPEN TECHNOLOGY, INC.; *pg.* 354, *pg.* 804
HYSYS OPTIMIZER - Software - ASPEN TECHNOLOGY, INC.; *pg.* 354, *pg.* 804
HYSYS TACITE - Software - ASPEN TECHNOLOGY, INC.; *pg.* 354, *pg.* 804
HYTEC - Plumbing Fixtures - KOHLER CO.; *pg.* 91, *pg.* 1862
HYTEST - Footwear - WOLVERINE WORLD WIDE, INC.; *pg.* 1822, *pg.* 905
HYTOR - Pumps - GARDNER DENVER NASH; *pg.* 1338, *pg.* 381
HYTREL - Polyester Thermoplastic Elastomer - E.I. DU PONT DE NEMOURS & COMPANY; *pg.* 1159, *pg.* 390
HYTREX - Depth Filters - GE WATER & PROCESS TECHNOLOGIES; *pg.* 1339, *pg.* 1588
HYTRIN - Alpha-Blocking Drug - ABBOTT LABORATORIES; *pg.* 1484, *pg.* 551
HYUNDAI ADVANTAGE - Tag Line - HYUNDAI MOTOR AMERICA; *pg.* 179, *pg.* 89
HYVAR - Herbicide - E.I. DU PONT DE NEMOURS & COMPANY; *pg.* 1159, *pg.* 390
HYVEX - High Temperature Resin Compounds - FERRO CORPORATION; *pg.* 1162, *pg.* 1462
HYVISC - Hyaluronate Sodium - BOEHRINGER INGELHEIM VETMEDICA, INC.; *pg.* 1474, *pg.* 989
HYZEEN - Hydrzine Solution - GE WATER & PROCESS TECHNOLOGIES; *pg.* 1339, *pg.* 1588
HZ-1 - Catalyst & Catalyst Support - BASF CATALYSTS LLC; *pg.* 1148, *pg.* 1074
HZ-PLUS - Cracking Catalyst - BASF CATALYSTS LLC; *pg.* 1148, *pg.* 1074

I

I AM A PHOENIX - Slogan - THE UNIVERSITY OF PHOENIX, INC.; *pg.* 610, *pg.* 27
I AM LOVED - Jewelry - HELZBERG'S DIAMOND SHOPS, INC.; *pg.* 6, *pg.* 984
I/B/E/S - Software Tool And Application - THOMSON REUTERS MARKETS; *pg.* 810, *pg.* 1299
I-BARATRON - Capacitance Manometer - MKS INSTRUMENTS, INC.; *pg.* 1362, *pg.* 781
I-BEAM - Software - ELEKTA; *pg.* 391, *pg.* 987
I-BRAKE - Bicycle Component - SRAM CORPORATION; *pg.* 967, *pg.* 590
I BUTTON - Communications Product - MAXIM INTEGRATED PRODUCTS, INC.; *pg.* 653, *pg.* 247
I/C - Engine Type - BRIGGS & STRATTON CORPORATION; *pg.* 201, *pg.* 1899
I CAN COPE - Education & Support Programs - AMERICAN CANCER SOCIETY, INC.; *pg.* 126, *pg.* 487
I CAN'T BELIEVE IT'S NOT BUTTER! - Spreads and Cooking Oil - UNILEVER CANADA INC.; *pg.* 903, *pg.* 1946
I CAN'T BELIEVE IT'S NOT BUTTER - Soft Spread - UNILEVER UNITED STATES, INC.; *pg.* 904, *pg.* 1061
I-CEE DOUBLE - Video Game - INTERNATIONAL GAME TECHNOLOGY; *pg.* 957, *pg.* 1024
I-CHEM - Specialty Chemicals - ZEP INC.; *pg.* 338, *pg.* 524
I-CHING - Fabric - NEMSCHOFF, INC.; *pg.* 936, *pg.* 1890
I-CLASS - Bar Code System - DATAMAX CORPORATION; *pg.* 1633, *pg.* 453
I-CLASS - Transfer Bench - INVACARE CORPORATION; *pg.* 1546, *pg.* 1451
I-CLASS-RFID - Bar Code System - DATAMAX CORPORATION; *pg.* 1633, *pg.* 453
I-CONTROL - Feature - TIMEX CORPORATION; *pg.* 14, *pg.* 355
I-CU - Copper Anodes - ENTEGRIS, INC.; *pg.* 1882, *pg.* 788

First page reference indicates Business Class Edition
Second page reference indicates Geographic Edition

I-CUE - Intelligent Mirror - ROSCO LABORATORIES, INC.; *pg.* 1782, *pg.* 378
I-DEAS PRO - Noise & Vibration Test Data Analysis Software - MTS SYSTEMS CORPORATION; *pg.* 442, *pg.* 923
I-DOG - Toy & Game - HASBRO, INC.; *pg.* 954, *pg.* 1603
I-DROP - Software - AUTODESK INC.; *pg.* 356, *pg.* 257
I-F - Carbon Steel Product - AK STEEL HOLDING CORPORATION; *pg.* 1311, *pg.* 1479
I FEEL PRETTY - Dresses & Sets - HABAND COMPANY, INC.; *pg.* 1772, *pg.* 1099
I-FIT - Medical Equipment - INVACARE CORPORATION; *pg.* 1546, *pg.* 1451
I-FIT - Software - WATERS CORPORATION; *pg.* 1436, *pg.* 834
I-FORCE - Cleaning Product - HILLYARD, INC.; *pg.* 331, *pg.* 990
I-GEAR - Software - SYMANTEC CORPORATION; *pg.* 478, *pg.* 161
I-GUIDE - Digital Programming Directory - ROVI CORPORATION; *pg.* 463, *pg.* 269
I-GUIDE - Interactive TV Guide - SHAW COMMUNICATIONS INC.; *pg.* 307, *pg.* 1904
I-LINC - Multi-Function Aviation Display - L-3 AVIONICS SYSTEMS, INC.; *pg.* 650, *pg.* 888
I-LIST - Toy & Game - HASBRO, INC.; *pg.* 954, *pg.* 1603
I LOVE JACKPOTS - Video Game - BALLY TECHNOLOGIES, INC.; *pg.* 531, *pg.* 1022
I-LYNX - Diagnostic Product - SPECTRAL DIAGNOSTICS INC.; *pg.* 1430, *pg.* 1943
I-MAG - Vacuum Transducer - MKS INSTRUMENTS, INC.; *pg.* 1362, *pg.* 781
I-MIX - Golf Accessories - CALLAWAY GOLF COMPANY; *pg.* 1829, *pg.* 58
I/O DESIGNER - Software System - MENTOR GRAPHICS CORPORATION; *pg.* 432, *pg.* 1510
I/O EXPRESS - Disk Caching Software - CONDUSIV TECHNOLOGIES; *pg.* 379, *pg.* 51
I PATCH - Repair Patches - MCNETT CORPORATION; *pg.* 1839, *pg.* 1817
I-PLANT - Brachytherapy Seed - IMPLANT SCIENCES CORPORATION; *pg.* 1348, *pg.* 860
I-RIDE - Suspension Module - AMERICAN AXLE & MANUFACTURING HOLDINGS, INC.; *pg.* 198, *pg.* 879
I-SAGE - Molecular Biology Product - THERMO FISHER SCIENTIFIC INC.; *pg.* 1602, *pg.* 61
I/SEARCH - Staffing Software - SELECTREMEDY; *pg.* 468, *pg.* 263
I-SEED - Brachytherapy System - THERAGENICS CORPORATION; *pg.* 1431, *pg.* 527
I-SENSE - Ophthalmic Product - AKORN, INC.; *pg.* 1488, *pg.* 622
I SERIES - InterBold ATM Product Line - DIEBOLD, INCORPORATED; *pg.* 387, *pg.* 1407
I-SHELTER - Solar-Powered LED Lighting - CARMANAH TECHNOLOGIES CORPORATION; *pg.* 628, *pg.* 1913
I SKI - Sunglasses - SAFILO USA INC.; *pg.* 11, *pg.* 1106
I-SONIC - All-In-One Home Entertainment System - DEI HOLDINGS, INC.; *pg.* 633, *pg.* 302
I-STAT - Hand-Held Blood Analysis Tool - ABBOTT LABORATORIES; *pg.* 1484, *pg.* 551
I-STAT - Hand-Held Blood Analyzer - ABBOTT POINT OF CARE, INC.; *pg.* 1486, *pg.* 1110
I-STOP - Lighting Product - CARMANAH TECHNOLOGIES CORPORATION; *pg.* 628, *pg.* 1913
I-SUITE - Operating Room - STRYKER CORPORATION; *pg.* 1598, *pg.* 894
I SWIM - Electronic Payment System - ANTHONY & SYLVAN POOLS CORPORATION; *pg.* 1826, *pg.* 1428
I-TATOO - Toy - SPIN MASTER LTD.; *pg.* 967, *pg.* 1943
I-TONE - Printing Paper - MOHAWK FINE PAPERS, INC.; *pg.* 1464, *pg.* 1153
I-TRAC - Wheel Drive - BORGWARNER INC.; *pg.* 167, *pg.* 867
I-TRAX - Golf Product - CALLAWAY GOLF COMPANY; *pg.* 1829, *pg.* 58
I-VATION - Intravitreal Implant - SURMODICS, INC.; *pg.* 1600, *pg.* 924
I-VIRTUAL STEPPER - Software - SYNOPSYS, INC.; *pg.* 480, *pg.* 162
I-WATCH - Software - INTELLIGRATED, INC.; *pg.* 1349, *pg.* 1460
I-ZONE 300 & 550 - Instant Cameras & Films - POLAROID CORPORATION; *pg.* 1426, *pg.* 815
I2 CARGO - Personal Transporter - SEGWAY INC.; *pg.* 1923, *pg.* 1033
I2 COMMUTER - Personal Transporter - SEGWAY INC.; *pg.* 1923, *pg.* 1033
I2I - Office Furniture - STEELCASE INC.; *pg.* 475, *pg.* 889
I3 - Footwear - REEBOK INTERNATIONAL LTD.; *pg.* 1817, *pg.* 811
I3 - Software - SYMANTEC CORPORATION; *pg.* 478, *pg.* 161
I3 - Smoke Detector - SYSTEM SENSOR; *pg.* 676, *pg.* 658
I3 - Oven - TURBOCHEF TECHNOLOGIES, INC.; *pg.* 902, *pg.* 1670
I30 INFINITI - Automobile - NISSAN NORTH AMERICA, INC.; *pg.* 186, *pg.* 1633
I5 - Oven - TURBOCHEF TECHNOLOGIES, INC.; *pg.* 902, *pg.* 1670
I711.COM - Telecommunications Relay Service - PURPLE COMMUNICATIONS, INC.; *pg.* 457, *pg.* 194
IAC - Furniture - IAC INDUSTRIES, INC.; *pg.* 929, *pg.* 48
IAC ADVERTISING SOLUTIONS - Online Services - IAC/INTERACTIVECORP; *pg.* 292, *pg.* 1242
IACCESS - Metal Locks - MASTER LOCK COMPANY LLC; *pg.* 1055, *pg.* 1884
IAM THE BOSS - Toy - THE OHIO ART COMPANY, INC.; *pg.* 965, *pg.* 1406
IAMS - Pet Food - MARS, INCORPORATED; *pg.* 1858, *pg.* 1792
IAMS ACTIVE MATURITY - Dog & Cat Food - IAMS COMPANY; *pg.* 1477, *pg.* 1633
IAMS CHUNKS - Dog Food - IAMS COMPANY; *pg.* 1477, *pg.* 1633
IAMS HAIRBALL CARE - Cat Food - IAMS COMPANY; *pg.* 1477, *pg.* 1633
IAMS INDOOR HAIRBALL CARE - Cat Food - IAMS COMPANY; *pg.* 1477, *pg.* 1633
IAMS INDOOR WEIGHT & HAIRBALL CARE - Cat Food - IAMS COMPANY; *pg.* 1477, *pg.* 1633
IAMS KITTEN - Cat Food - IAMS COMPANY; *pg.* 1477, *pg.* 1633
IAMS LARGE BREED - Dog Food - IAMS COMPANY; *pg.* 1477, *pg.* 1633
IAMS MINICHUNKS - Dog Food - IAMS COMPANY; *pg.* 1477, *pg.* 1633
IAMS PUPPY SAVORY SAUCE - Dog Food - IAMS COMPANY; *pg.* 1477, *pg.* 1633
IAMS SMART PUPPY - Dog Food - IAMS COMPANY; *pg.* 1477, *pg.* 1633
IAMS WEIGHT CONTROL - Dog & Cat Food - IAMS COMPANY; *pg.* 1477, *pg.* 1633
IAN - Furniture - AMISCO INDUSTRIES LTD.; *pg.* 913, *pg.* 1958
IANYWHERE - Mobile Office - SAP; *pg.* 465, *pg.* 78
IANYWHERE SOLUTIONS - Solutions Developer Community - SAP; *pg.* 465, *pg.* 78
IAPMO - Tub & Sink - E.L. MUSTEE & SONS, INC.; *pg.* 1124, *pg.* 1430
IAQ-CALC - Air Quality Meter - TSI INCORPORATED; *pg.* 1432, *pg.* 965
IASAP - Global Positioning System - COBRA ELECTRONICS CORPORATION; *pg.* 629, *pg.* 572
IB - Software System - MENTOR GRAPHICS CORPORATION; *pg.* 432, *pg.* 1510
IBASE - Molecular Biology Product - THERMO FISHER SCIENTIFIC INC.; *pg.* 1602, *pg.* 61
IBD 100 - Stock Index - INVESTORS BUSINESS DAILY, INC.; *pg.* 1653, *pg.* 133
IBD 100 SMARTLINK - Online Stock Research Tool - INVESTORS BUSINESS DAILY, INC.; *pg.* 1653, *pg.* 133
IBD EXTRA! - Online Newsletter - INVESTORS BUSINESS DAILY, INC.; *pg.* 1653, *pg.* 133
IBD FIRST STEP - Therapy System - PROMETHEUS LABORATORIES, INC.; *pg.* 1586, *pg.* 206
IBD NUTRIVENT - Food Product - NESTLE USA, INC.; *pg.* 883, *pg.* 96
IBEAM - Rod Pump Controller - WEATHERFORD PRODUCTION OPTIMIZATION; *pg.* 987, *pg.* 1725
IBERO CRUISES - Passenger Cruises & Tours - CARNIVAL CORPORATION; *pg.* 1902, *pg.* 441
IBERVILLE - Roughing-In Product - THOMAS & BETTS CORPORATION; *pg.* 680, *pg.* 1646
IBIZA - Broadloom - COURISTAN INC.; *pg.* 921, *pg.* 1067
IBLOT - Molecular Biology Product - THERMO FISHER SCIENTIFIC INC.; *pg.* 1602, *pg.* 61
IBM COGNOS - Analysis Software - INTERNATIONAL BUSINESS MACHINES CORPORATION; *pg.* 418, *pg.* 1138
IBM DB2 - Software - INTERNATIONAL BUSINESS MACHINES CORPORATION; *pg.* 418, *pg.* 1138
IBM EXPERIENCEONE - Customer Engagement Solutions - INTERNATIONAL BUSINESS MACHINES CORPORATION; *pg.* 418, *pg.* 1138
IBM GPFS - General Parallel FIle Systems - INTERNATIONAL BUSINESS MACHINES CORPORATION; *pg.* 418, *pg.* 1138
IBM LOTUS - Software - INTERNATIONAL BUSINESS MACHINES CORPORATION; *pg.* 418, *pg.* 1138
IBM LTFS - Linear Tape FIle System - INTERNATIONAL BUSINESS MACHINES CORPORATION; *pg.* 418, *pg.* 1138
IBM OPENPAGES - Software - INTERNATIONAL BUSINESS MACHINES CORPORATION; *pg.* 418, *pg.* 1138
IBM OPENPAGES INTERNAL AUDIT MANAGEMENT - Management Software - INTERNATIONAL BUSINESS MACHINES CORPORATION; *pg.* 418, *pg.* 1138
IBM PUREDATA SYSTEM - Data Management Software - INTERNATIONAL BUSINESS MACHINES CORPORATION; *pg.* 418, *pg.* 1138
IBM SMARTCLOUD ORCHESTRATOR - Business Solution Software - INTERNATIONAL BUSINESS MACHINES CORPORATION; *pg.* 418, *pg.* 1138
IBM SPSS - Software - INTERNATIONAL BUSINESS MACHINES CORPORATION; *pg.* 418, *pg.* 1138
IBM STORWIZE - Storage System - INTERNATIONAL BUSINESS MACHINES CORPORATION; *pg.* 418, *pg.* 1138
IBM SYSTEM STORAGE - Storage System - INTERNATIONAL BUSINESS MACHINES CORPORATION; *pg.* 418, *pg.* 1138
IBM THREAT PROTECTION SYSTEM - Integrated System to Protect Against Cyber Attack - INTERNATIONAL BUSINESS MACHINES CORPORATION; *pg.* 418, *pg.* 1138
IBM TIVOLI - Storage Manager - INTERNATIONAL BUSINESS MACHINES CORPORATION; *pg.* 418, *pg.* 1138
IBM WEBSPHERE - Software - INTERNATIONAL BUSINESS MACHINES CORPORATION; *pg.* 418, *pg.* 1138
IBOOK - Computer - APPLE INC.; *pg.* 350, *pg.* 73
IBOOKS STORE - Online Store - APPLE INC.; *pg.* 350, *pg.* 73
IBOT - Healthcare Product - JOHNSON & JOHNSON; *pg.* 1549, *pg.* 1091
IBOX - Delivery Device - DYNATRONICS CORPORATION; *pg.* 1526, *pg.* 1757
IBOX - Imaging System - UVP, INC.; *pg.* 1434, *pg.* 298
IBP TRUSTED EXCELLENCE - Beef & Pork Products - TYSON FOODS, INC.; *pg.* 902, *pg.* 35
IBSEN - Lighting Product - QUOIZEL INC.; *pg.* 1304, *pg.* 1616
IBSS - Integrated Broadband Services Switch - ALCATEL-LUCENT USA, INC.; *pg.* 615, *pg.* 1728
IBTRACER - Analyzer - TELEDYNE LECROY; *pg.* 1431, *pg.* 1153
IBU-RELIEF 12 - Pain Relief Cream - HABAND COMPANY, INC.; *pg.* 1772, *pg.* 1099
IBUFEN - Pharmaceutical Product - ABBOTT LABORATORIES; *pg.* 1484, *pg.* 551
IBXFLEX - Telecommunication System - EQUINIX, INC.; *pg.* 394, *pg.* 190
IC - Protective Eyewear - CROSSTEX INTERNATIONAL INC.; *pg.* 1520, *pg.* 1164
IC-CAP - Software - KEITHLEY INSTRUMENTS, INC.; *pg.* 1418, *pg.* 1473
IC DESIGN STATION - Software System - MENTOR GRAPHICS CORPORATION; *pg.* 432, *pg.* 1510
IC DESIGNER - Software System - MENTOR GRAPHICS CORPORATION; *pg.* 432, *pg.* 1510
IC FBRM - Software - METTLER-TOLEDO INTERNATIONAL INC.; *pg.* 1423, *pg.* 1441
IC-GREEN - Ophthalmic Pharmaceutical Product - AKORN, INC.; *pg.* 1488, *pg.* 622
IC IR - Software - METTLER-TOLEDO INTERNATIONAL INC.; *pg.* 1423, *pg.* 1441
IC LAYOUT STATION - Software System - MENTOR GRAPHICS CORPORATION; *pg.* 432, *pg.* 1510
IC-PAK - Analytical Column - WATERS CORPORATION; *pg.* 1436, *pg.* 834
IC PROTECTIVE - Eyewear - CROSSTEX INTERNATIONAL INC.; *pg.* 1520, *pg.* 1164
IC RAMAN - Software - METTLER-TOLEDO INTERNATIONAL INC.; *pg.* 1423, *pg.* 1441
IC STATION - Software System - MENTOR GRAPHICS

First page reference indicates Business Class Edition
Second page reference indicates Geographic Edition

CORPORATION; *pg.* 432, *pg.* 1510
IC TOWER - Memory Chip Stacking Technology - HGST; *pg.* 406, *pg.* 260
ICAL - Software Product - APPLE INC.; *pg.* 350, *pg.* 73
ICAMP - Fun Program - NOBEL LEARNING COMMUNITIES, INC.; *pg.* 605, *pg.* 1593
ICANALYST - Software System - MENTOR GRAPHICS CORPORATION; *pg.* 432, *pg.* 1510
ICAT - Molecular Biology Product - THERMO FISHER SCIENTIFIC INC.; *pg.* 1602, *pg.* 61
ICBASIC - Software System - MENTOR GRAPHICS CORPORATION; *pg.* 432, *pg.* 1510
ICBLOCKS - Software System - MENTOR GRAPHICS CORPORATION; *pg.* 432, *pg.* 1510
ICCHECK - Software System - MENTOR GRAPHICS CORPORATION; *pg.* 432, *pg.* 1510
ICCOMPACT - Software System - MENTOR GRAPHICS CORPORATION; *pg.* 432, *pg.* 1510
ICDEVICE - Software System - MENTOR GRAPHICS CORPORATION; *pg.* 432, *pg.* 1510
ICE - Bag - BROWN & BIGELOW, INC.; *pg.* 1624, *pg.* 959
ICE - Clear Polish - TURTLE WAX, INC.; *pg.* 220, *pg.* 671
ICE ANGELS - Container Grown Plant - MONROVIA GROWERS; *pg.* 1797, *pg.* 44
ICE BREAKER - Material Handling Equipment - DEGELMAN INDUSTRIES LTD.; *pg.* 703, *pg.* 1962
ICE BREAKERS - Gum And Mints - THE HERSHEY CO.; *pg.* 1855, *pg.* 1538
ICE BREAKERS - Frozen Beverage - YOCREAM INTERNATIONAL INC.; *pg.* 1039, *pg.* 1508
ICE-CHASER - Automotive Cleaner - DELTA FOREMOST CHEMICAL CORPORATION; *pg.* 1155, *pg.* 1642
ICE CHILLER - Thermal Storage Unit - BALTIMORE AIRCOIL COMPANY; *pg.* 1069, *pg.* 773
ICE COLD CRYSTALS - Baby Care Product - MUNCHKIN, INC.; *pg.* 964, *pg.* 300
ICE DATA - Market Data Services - INTERCONTINENTALEXCHANGE, INC.; *pg.* 769, *pg.* 512
ICE DECK - Building Product - HOMASOTE COMPANY; *pg.* 87, *pg.* 1126
ICE DEW - Beverages - THE COCA-COLA COMPANY; *pg.* 240, *pg.* 493
ICE FIGHTER PLUS - Snow & Ice Melter - MORGRO, INC.; *pg.* 1798, *pg.* 1759
ICE FISHING - Video Viewing System - SWORDFISH FINANCIAL, INC.; *pg.* 1430, *pg.* 1737
ICE KING - Footwear - LACROSSE FOOTWEAR, INC.; *pg.* 1811, *pg.* 1503
ICE-LOGIC - Ice Thickness Controller - BALTIMORE AIRCOIL COMPANY; *pg.* 1069, *pg.* 773
ICE-OFF - Windshield Spray De-Icer - CRC INDUSTRIES, INC.; *pg.* 329, *pg.* 1590
ICE PALACE - Carpet - BEAULIEU GROUP, LLC; *pg.* 917, *pg.* 529
ICE SCHOOL - Community Foundation Program - EDMONTON OILERS HOCKEY CLUB; *pg.* 546, *pg.* 1906
ICE SCULPTURES - Decorative Ice Molds - CARLISLE FOODSERVICE PRODUCTS INCORPORATED; *pg.* 1455, *pg.* 1485
ICE WAND - Ice Machine Cleaner - APYRON TECHNOLOGIES, INC.; *pg.* 1495, *pg.* 488
ICE2O - Refrigerator - WHIRLPOOL CORPORATION; *pg.* 62, *pg.* 872
ICEBERG - Calcined Kaolin - BURGESS PIGMENT COMPANY; *pg.* 1150, *pg.* 535
ICEBLASTER - Fluid Handling System - GRACO, INC.; *pg.* 1342, *pg.* 935
ICEBOX - Micrologic Semiconductor Device - ZILOG INC.; *pg.* 497, *pg.* 252
ICECAP - Food Product - NESTLE USA, INC.; *pg.* 883, *pg.* 96
ICECORE - Computer Software - NOVELL INC.; *pg.* 446, *pg.* 852
ICECRUSHER - Software - TEXAS INSTRUMENTS INCORPORATED; *pg.* 679, *pg.* 1688
ICED FUDGE RIPPLE - Coffee - THE COFFEE BEANERY LTD.; *pg.* 849, *pg.* 886
ICEDANCER - Ethnobotanical Product - NU SKIN ENTERPRISES, INC.; *pg.* 518, *pg.* 1755
ICEE - Semi-Frozen Carbonated Beverage - J&J SNACK FOODS CORPORATION; *pg.* 865, *pg.* 1107
ICEE BLUE - Container Grown Plant - MONROVIA GROWERS; *pg.* 1797, *pg.* 44
ICEEBITS - Nutritional Snack Foods - J&J SNACK FOODS CORPORATION; *pg.* 865, *pg.* 1107
ICEFET - LED - CREE INC.; *pg.* 631, *pg.* 1371
ICEFLY - Coolants - AIR PRODUCTS AND CHEMICALS, INC.; *pg.* 1145, *pg.* 1513
ICEGARD - Underlayment - GAF MATERIALS CORP.; *pg.* 83, *pg.* 1681
ICEHOUSE 5.0 - Beer - MILLERCOORS; *pg.* 254, *pg.* 1877
ICEHOUSE 5.5 - Beer - MILLERCOORS; *pg.* 254, *pg.* 1877
ICEHOUSE LIGHT - Beer - MILLERCOORS; *pg.* 254, *pg.* 1877
ICELAND HEALTH - Nutritional Product - NUTRITION 21, INC.; *pg.* 1577, *pg.* 1327
ICELANDIC - Frozen Seafood - HIGH LINER FOODS; *pg.* 862, *pg.* 1796
ICEM - Software - PARAMETRIC TECHNOLOGY CORPORATION; *pg.* 452, *pg.* 835
ICEMAGIC - Ice Makers - WHIRLPOOL CORPORATION; *pg.* 62, *pg.* 872
ICEMAN - Orthopedic Product - DJO INCORPORATED; *pg.* 1524, *pg.* 302
ICEMAN - Footwear - LACROSSE FOOTWEAR, INC.; *pg.* 1811, *pg.* 1503
ICEPACK - Mounting Frame - WESTERN DIGITAL CORPORATION; *pg.* 492, *pg.* 118
ICEPRESSO CHILLER - Chilled Coffee Beverage - THE SECOND CUP LTD.; *pg.* 1749, *pg.* 1928
ICESTOR - Solar Pool Heating System - FAFCO INC.; *pg.* 1071, *pg.* 65
ICESTORM - Software - WIND RIVER SYSTEMS, INC.; *pg.* 493, *pg.* 38
ICEWEB - Data Storage Products - UNIFIEDONLINE, INC.; *pg.* 486, *pg.* 1780
ICEXTRACT - Software System - MENTOR GRAPHICS CORPORATION; *pg.* 432, *pg.* 1510
ICG - Extruded Film & Treated Textiles - HOLLISTON LLC; *pg.* 1460, *pg.* 1630
ICGEN - Software System - MENTOR GRAPHICS CORPORATION; *pg.* 432, *pg.* 1510
ICGRAPH - Software System - MENTOR GRAPHICS CORPORATION; *pg.* 432, *pg.* 1510
ICHAIN - Computer Operations - NOVELL INC.; *pg.* 446, *pg.* 852
ICHART - Medical Dictation Software - NUANCE COMMUNICATIONS, INC.; *pg.* 447, *pg.* 806
ICHAT - Software Product - APPLE INC.; *pg.* 350, *pg.* 73
ICHEM - Urinalysis Workstation - IRIS INTERNATIONAL, INC.; *pg.* 1547, *pg.* 64
ICI - Women's Fragrance - COTY, INC.; *pg.* 506, *pg.* 1219
ICI - Banking Software - JACK HENRY & ASSOCIATES, INC.; *pg.* 422, *pg.* 988
ICIMS - Logo - ICIMS, INC.; *pg.* 411, *pg.* 1083
ICING - Women's Retail Products - CLAIRE'S STORES, INC.; *pg.* 1764, *pg.* 617
ICKY POO - Educational Materials - SCHOLASTIC INC.; *pg.* 1683, *pg.* 1288
ICLEAN - Software - SMITH MICRO SOFTWARE, INC.; *pg.* 471, *pg.* 41
ICLINK - Software System - MENTOR GRAPHICS CORPORATION; *pg.* 432, *pg.* 1510
ICLISTER - Software System - MENTOR GRAPHICS CORPORATION; *pg.* 432, *pg.* 1510
ICLOUD - Cloud Service - APPLE INC.; *pg.* 350, *pg.* 73
ICM - Marketing Process - ACI WORLDWIDE; *pg.* 710, *pg.* 1777
ICMA - Institute of Certified Management Accountants - INSTITUTE OF MANAGEMENT ACCOUNTANTS, INC.; *pg.* 144, *pg.* 1086
ICNOTIFY - Software - INTERACTIVE INTELLIGENCE, INC.; *pg.* 417, *pg.* 687
ICOLOR - Lighting System - PHILIPS SOLID-STATE LIGHTING SOLUTIONS; *pg.* 1303, *pg.* 806
ICOLOR COVE - Lighting System - PHILIPS SOLID-STATE LIGHTING SOLUTIONS; *pg.* 1303, *pg.* 806
ICOM - Materials Compounding - MOLDED FIBER GLASS COMPANIES; *pg.* 1886, *pg.* 1403
ICOMMAND - Software - SYMANTEC CORPORATION; *pg.* 478, *pg.* 161
I.CO.S - Screw - INTEGRA LIFESCIENCES HOLDINGS CORPORATION; *pg.* 1545, *pg.* 1109
ICOMS - Billing Service - CONVERGYS CORPORATION; *pg.* 379, *pg.* 1412
ICON - Headsets - ALIPHCOM, INC.; *pg.* 616, *pg.* 212
ICON - Testing Instrument System - BECKMAN COULTER, INC.; *pg.* 1402, *pg.* 48
ICON - Fabric - MOMENTUM TEXTILES INC.; *pg.* 697, *pg.* 114
ICON - Beanie - OAKLEY, INC.; *pg.* 1840, *pg.* 86
ICON BARS - Apparel - OAKLEY, INC.; *pg.* 1840, *pg.* 86
ICON BEATER - Apparel - OAKLEY, INC.; *pg.* 1840, *pg.* 86
ICON SMALL - Watch - OAKLEY, INC.; *pg.* 1840, *pg.* 86
ICONE - Treatment - PARFUMS CHRISTIAN DIOR, INC; *pg.* 519, *pg.* 1276
ICONIC - Carpet - INTERFACE, INC.; *pg.* 695, *pg.* 512
ICONTROL - Software - F5 NETWORKS, INC.; *pg.* 396, *pg.* 1835
ICONTROL - Integrated Control System - NORDSON CORPORATION; *pg.* 1365, *pg.* 1480
ICOOK - Stainless Steel Cookware - AMWAY CORPORATION; *pg.* 326, *pg.* 864
ICOOL - Connector - MOLEX INCORPORATED; *pg.* 655, *pg.* 628
ICOUPLER - Isolator - ANALOG DEVICES, INC.; *pg.* 617, *pg.* 839
ICPLAN - Software System - MENTOR GRAPHICS CORPORATION; *pg.* 432, *pg.* 1510
ICPLATE2 - Portable Plate Platereader - X-RITE, INCORPORATED; *pg.* 1437, *pg.* 891
ICROSS - Medical Device - BOSTON SCIENTIFIC CORPORATION; *pg.* 1508, *pg.* 831
ICRT CONTROLLER LCOMPILER - Software System - MENTOR GRAPHICS CORPORATION; *pg.* 432, *pg.* 1510
ICRULES - Software System - MENTOR GRAPHICS CORPORATION; *pg.* 432, *pg.* 1510
ICSPYWARE - Software - SMITH MICRO SOFTWARE, INC.; *pg.* 471, *pg.* 41
ICSTUDIO - Software System - MENTOR GRAPHICS CORPORATION; *pg.* 432, *pg.* 1510
ICT - Golf Accessories - CALLAWAY GOLF COMPANY; *pg.* 1829, *pg.* 58
ICTRACE - Software System - MENTOR GRAPHICS CORPORATION; *pg.* 432, *pg.* 1510
ICU - Cap - BROWN & BIGELOW, INC.; *pg.* 1624, *pg.* 959
ICUE - Semiconductor Product - CABOT MICROELECTRONICS CORPORATION; *pg.* 1151, *pg.* 554
ICV - Vacuum Treatment - A-DEC, INC.; *pg.* 1483, *pg.* 1500
ICVERIFY - Software System - MENTOR GRAPHICS CORPORATION; *pg.* 432, *pg.* 1510
ICVIEW - Software System - MENTOR GRAPHICS CORPORATION; *pg.* 432, *pg.* 1510
ICW - Custom Wheels - AMERICAN TIRE DISTRIBUTORS HOLDINGS, INC.; *pg.* 199, *pg.* 1379
ICX - Waterline Treatment Tablet - A-DEC, INC.; *pg.* 1483, *pg.* 1500
ICX - Software System - MENTOR GRAPHICS CORPORATION; *pg.* 432, *pg.* 1510
ICX PRO - Software System - MENTOR GRAPHICS CORPORATION; *pg.* 432, *pg.* 1510
ICX PROJECT MODELING - Software System - MENTOR GRAPHICS CORPORATION; *pg.* 432, *pg.* 1510
ICX SENTRY - Software System - MENTOR GRAPHICS CORPORATION; *pg.* 432, *pg.* 1510
ICX STANDARD LIBRARY - Software System - MENTOR GRAPHICS CORPORATION; *pg.* 432, *pg.* 1510
ICX TAU - Software System - MENTOR GRAPHICS CORPORATION; *pg.* 432, *pg.* 1510
ICX VERIFY - Software System - MENTOR GRAPHICS CORPORATION; *pg.* 432, *pg.* 1510
ICX VISION - Software System - MENTOR GRAPHICS CORPORATION; *pg.* 432, *pg.* 1510
ICY BLAST - Personal Care Product - COLGATE-PALMOLIVE COMPANY; *pg.* 504, *pg.* 1215
ICY COLD TO GO! - Diary Product - ANDERSON ERICKSON DAIRY COMPANY; *pg.* 837, *pg.* 704
ICY HOT - Health & Beauty Product - CHATTEM, INC.; *pg.* 1515, *pg.* 1628
ICY HOT PRO THERAPY - Health & Beauty Product - CHATTEM, INC.; *pg.* 1515, *pg.* 1628
ICY POINT - Canned - OCEAN BEAUTY SEAFOODS, INC.; *pg.* 1028, *pg.* 1838
ICY SURGE - Personal Care Product - COLGATE-PALMOLIVE COMPANY; *pg.* 504, *pg.* 1215
ICYCLER - Software - BIO-RAD LABORATORIES, INC.; *pg.* 1504, *pg.* 101
ICYCLER IQ - Detection System - BIO-RAD LABORATORIES, INC.; *pg.* 1504, *pg.* 101
I.D. 200 - Degreaser - HILLYARD, INC.; *pg.* 331, *pg.* 990
ID CARD MAKER SOFTWARE - Software for Designing Custom Photo ID Cards - POLAROID CORPORATION; *pg.* 1426, *pg.* 815
ID-CHECK - Software - INTELLICHECK MOBILISA, INC.; *pg.*

416, *pg.* 1823

ID PAL - Labelling Tool - BRADY CORPORATION; *pg.* 363, *pg.* 1873

ID PATROL - Software - EQUIFAX INC.; *pg.* 748, *pg.* 504

ID VAULT - USB Security Device - WHITE SKY, INC.; *pg.* 492, *pg.* 256

ID WORKS - Software - DATACARD CORPORATION; *pg.* 382, *pg.* 948

IDA - Ink Dispersion Analyzer - KEVLIN CORPORATION; *pg.* 649, *pg.* 1034

IDAHO GOLD - Distilled Spirits - HOOD RIVER DISTILLERS INC.; *pg.* 1964, *pg.* 1498

IDAHO PICK 3 - Lottery Game - IDAHO LOTTERY; *pg.* 995, *pg.* 547

IDAHO SILVER - Distilled Spirits - HOOD RIVER DISTILLERS INC.; *pg.* 1964, *pg.* 1498

IDAHOAN - Potato Products - J.R. SIMPLOT COMPANY; *pg.* 867, *pg.* 547

IDAMYCIN - Medicine - PFIZER INC.; *pg.* 1581, *pg.* 1278

IDATAFAX - Software - ENCORIUM GROUP, INC.; *pg.* 1528, *pg.* 1591

IDATEN JUMP - Toy & Game - HASBRO, INC.; *pg.* 954, *pg.* 1603

IDCAM - Audio Conferencing System - CLEARONE COMMUNICATIONS, INC.; *pg.* 629, *pg.* 1756

IDDINGS - Brush - ROSCO LABORATORIES, INC.; *pg.* 1782, *pg.* 378

IDE FLASH MODULE - Storage System - HGST; *pg.* 406, *pg.* 260

IDE FLD - Storage System - HGST; *pg.* 406, *pg.* 260

IDEA - Health & Nutrition Product - NOVUS INTERNATIONAL, INC.; *pg.* 706, *pg.* 1001

IDEA - Golf Clubs - TAYLORMADE-ADIDAS GOLF; *pg.* 1847, *pg.* 60

IDEA @ WORK - Ergonomic Office Products - KNAPE & VOGT MANUFACTURING COMPANY; *pg.* 1052, *pg.* 913

IDEA CART - Furniture - ANTHRO CORPORATION; *pg.* 913, *pg.* 1509

IDEA NETWORKS - Online Community Solution - METRIXLAB; *pg.* 1266, *pg.* 223

IDEA SCAPES - Coating Product - PPG INDUSTRIES, INC.; *pg.* 1445, *pg.* 1579

IDEA SERIES - Software System - MENTOR GRAPHICS CORPORATION; *pg.* 432, *pg.* 1510

IDEA STATION - Software System - MENTOR GRAPHICS CORPORATION; *pg.* 432, *pg.* 1510

IDEA TO ACTION - Tagline - ITAGROUP, INC.; *pg.* 422, *pg.* 713

IDEAL - Animal Safety Product - NEOGEN CORPORATION; *pg.* 883, *pg.* 896

IDEAL - Educational Resources - SCHOOL SPECIALTY, INC.; *pg.* 467, *pg.* 1860

IDEAL DOOR - Garage Doors - CLOPAY BUILDING PRODUCTS COMPANY; *pg.* 76, *pg.* 1459

IDEALEYES - Skin Care Product - NU SKIN ENTERPRISES, INC.; *pg.* 518, *pg.* 1755

IDEAS - Software - JDA SOFTWARE GROUP, INC.; *pg.* 423, *pg.* 22

IDEAS TO GROW WITH - Agricultural Chemicals - WILBUR-ELLIS COMPANY; *pg.* 1185, *pg.* 234

IDEAS TO PROFITS - Tagline - AT&T SOUTHEAST; *pg.* 1868, *pg.* 489

IDEAS YOU CAN BUILD ON - Trend Bulletins - BASIC AMERICAN FOODS, INC.; *pg.* 839, *pg.* 303

IDEN - Communications Product - MOTOROLA SOLUTIONS, INC.; *pg.* 657, *pg.* 659

IDENTEON - Business Consulting Services - SYNTEL, INC.; *pg.* 480, *pg.* 911

IDENTICATOR - Security Product - BAE SYSTEMS PRODUCTS GROUP; *pg.* 359, *pg.* 432

IDENTIFY - Software - SYNOPSYS, INC.; *pg.* 480, *pg.* 162

IDENTIFY-X - Risk Management Solution - ACXIOM CORPORATION; *pg.* 342, *pg.* 33

IDENTITY - Software - BMC SOFTWARE, INC.; *pg.* 362, *pg.* 1701

IDENTITY - Furniture - NER HOLDINGS INC.; *pg.* 444, *pg.* 1071

IDENTITY - Apparel - OAKLEY, INC.; *pg.* 1840, *pg.* 86

IDENTITY - Pacemakers - ST. JUDE MEDICAL, INC.; *pg.* 1596, *pg.* 963

IDENTITY GUARD - Identity Theft Protection - INTERSECTIONS INC.; *pg.* 769, *pg.* 1777

IDESIGN - Window Treatment Selection Tool - 3 DAY BLINDS, INC.; *pg.* 912, *pg.* 105

IDEXX DIGITAL - Software - IDEXX LABORATORIES, INC.; *pg.* 1543, *pg.* 753

IDEXX-DIRECT - Clinical Testing - IDEXX LABORATORIES, INC.; *pg.* 1543, *pg.* 753

IDEXX SNAPSHOT DX - Analyzer - IDEXX LABORATORIES, INC.; *pg.* 1543, *pg.* 753

IDEXX VETVAULT - Online Backup Service - IDEXX LABORATORIES, INC.; *pg.* 1543, *pg.* 753

IDG.NET - Technology Magazine - INTERNATIONAL DATA GROUP; *pg.* 1653, *pg.* 796

IDI - Medical Surgical System - BECTON, DICKINSON & COMPANY; *pg.* 1501, *pg.* 1068

IDIC - Integrated Circuit - ATMEL CORPORATION; *pg.* 621, *pg.* 238

IDIGI - Computer Peripheral Equipment - DIGI INTERNATIONAL INC.; *pg.* 387, *pg.* 948

IDIOM - Fabric - NEMSCHOFF, INC.; *pg.* 936, *pg.* 1890

IDISK - Online Services - APPLE INC.; *pg.* 350, *pg.* 73

IDLE MODE - Technology - MAXIM INTEGRATED PRODUCTS, INC.; *pg.* 653, *pg.* 247

IDO - Inspection System - KLA-TENCOR CORPORATION; *pg.* 1353, *pg.* 146

IDOLATOR - Pop Music News Site - SPINMEDIA; *pg.* 1282, *pg.* 104

IDOTZ.NET - Radio & Multimedia Service - BRS MEDIA INC.; *pg.* 1233, *pg.* 214

IDP - Pump - FLOWSERVE CORPORATION; *pg.* 82, *pg.* 1719

IDP1600 - Imaging System - ANACOMP, INC.; *pg.* 350, *pg.* 1777

IDQUEST - Software - BIO-RAD LABORATORIES, INC.; *pg.* 1504, *pg.* 101

IDRA - Women's Clothing - URBAN OUTFITTERS, INC.; *pg.* 1789, *pg.* 1571

IDRIVE - Garage Door - WAYNE-DALTON CORP.; *pg.* 120, *pg.* 1465

IDS - Data System - ADVANCED ENERGY INDUSTRIES, INC.; *pg.* 613, *pg.* 328

IDS/MEDLEY - Telecommunications Products - MITEL NETWORKS, INC.; *pg.* 1872, *pg.* 13

IDSR INDICATOR - Indicating Power Guard Fuse - LITTELFUSE, INC.; *pg.* 1301, *pg.* 580

IDVD - Software Product - APPLE INC.; *pg.* 350, *pg.* 73

IDX PRO - Metal Detector - WHITE'S ELECTRONICS; *pg.* 688, *pg.* 1509

IDYLIS - Air Purifier - LOWE'S COMPANIES, INC.; *pg.* 1053, *pg.* 1383

IECHO - Internet Based Inventory Management Program - AMERISOURCEBERGEN CORPORATION; *pg.* 1493, *pg.* 1522

IEEEXPLORE - Digital Library - INSTITUTE OF ELECTRICAL AND ELECTRONICS ENGINEERS, INC.; *pg.* 144, *pg.* 1109

IENCODE - Video Webcasting Solution - ONSTREAM MEDIA CORPORATION; *pg.* 449, *pg.* 459

IEP-CAM - Systems Integration & Aeronautics - LOCKHEED MARTIN CORPORATION; *pg.* 229, *pg.* 762

IESP - Electrical Pump Controller - WEATHERFORD PRODUCTION OPTIMIZATION; *pg.* 987, *pg.* 1725

IESX - Seismic Interpretation - SCHLUMBERGER LIMITED; *pg.* 801, *pg.* 1714

IEWS - Vehicle Diagnostic Management System - BAE SYSTEMS-INFORMATION WARFARE; *pg.* 623, *pg.* 1036

IEXCHANGE - Web-Based Medical Authorization System - MEDECISION, INC.; *pg.* 431, *pg.* 1592

IF - Furniture - HAWORTH, INC.; *pg.* 402, *pg.* 891

IF IT ISN.T A SEA RAY, YOU.VE MISSED THE BOAT. - Slogan - SEA RAY BOATS, INC.; *pg.* 1710, *pg.* 1638

IF IT ISN'T FRESH IT ISN'T LEGAL! - Slogan - LEGAL SEA FOODS INC.; *pg.* 1735, *pg.* 797

IF IT'S GOYA IT HAS TO BE GOOD - Slogan - GOYA FOODS, INC.; *pg.* 859, *pg.* 1075

IF IT'S NOT ALLISON, IT'S NOT AUTOMATIC - Tagline - ALLISON TRANSMISSION, INC.; *pg.* 198, *pg.* 682

IF OBJECTS COULD TALK. - Slogan - PROGRESS SOFTWARE CORPORATION; *pg.* 457, *pg.* 786

IF YOU HAVE A BODY, YOU ARE AN ATHLETE - Tagline - NIKE, INC.; *pg.* 1812, *pg.* 1492

IF YOU SEE SOMETHING, SAY SOMETHING - Slogan - METROPOLITAN TRANSPORTATION AUTHORITY; *pg.* 1915, *pg.* 1260

K. HOVNANIAN'S FOUR SEASONS - Tagline - HOVNANIAN ENTERPRISES, INC.; *pg.* 1096, *pg.* 1114

IFAS - Software - SUNGARD DATA SYSTEMS INC.; *pg.* 477, *pg.* 1592

IFB - HVAC Equipment - MESTEK, INC.; *pg.* 1074, *pg.* 857

IFC - Television Network - AMC NETWORKS INC.; *pg.* 269, *pg.* 1189

IFC FILMS - Independent Films - AMC NETWORKS INC.; *pg.* 269, *pg.* 1189

IFIT - Fitness Product - ICON HEALTH & FITNESS, INC.; *pg.* 1837, *pg.* 1752

IFLOW - Precision Dispensing System - NORDSON CORPORATION; *pg.* 1365, *pg.* 1480

IFOLDER - Computer Operations - NOVELL INC.; *pg.* 446, *pg.* 852

IFR - Software Tool And Application - THOMSON REUTERS MARKETS; *pg.* 810, *pg.* 1299

IFX - Software System - MENTOR GRAPHICS CORPORATION; *pg.* 432, *pg.* 1510

IG-LO - Automotive Refrigerants - ASHLAND INC.; *pg.* 972, *pg.* 726

IGA - Grocery Stores - SUPERVALU, INC.; *pg.* 1035, *pg.* 924

IGAME-PLUS - Interactive Video Game - INTERNATIONAL GAME TECHNOLOGY; *pg.* 957, *pg.* 1024

IGEN - Class 5 Switch Offering Traditional & Next-Generation Services - ALCATEL-LUCENT; *pg.* 615, *pg.* 38

IGEN3 - Printer - XEROX CORPORATION; *pg.* 494, *pg.* 365

IGEN4 - Printer - XEROX CORPORATION; *pg.* 494, *pg.* 365

IGEPAL - Chemical Product - STEPAN COMPANY; *pg.* 1182, *pg.* 643

IGG BOOST - Nutritional Supplement - NU SKIN ENTERPRISES, INC.; *pg.* 518, *pg.* 1755

IGGLE VIDEO - Video Store - GIANT EAGLE, INC.; *pg.* 1020, *pg.* 1575

IGI EUROPRINT - Lottery System - INTERNATIONAL GAME TECHNOLOGY; *pg.* 420, *pg.* 1606

IGLOO - Ice Chest & Beverage Cooler - IGLOO PRODUCTS CORPORATION; *pg.* 1126, *pg.* 1724

IGLOO BEVERAGE CUBE - Beverage Cooler - IGLOO PRODUCTS CORPORATION; *pg.* 1126, *pg.* 1724

IGLOO LUNCH & MUNCH - Insulated Lunch Bag - IGLOO PRODUCTS CORPORATION; *pg.* 1126, *pg.* 1724

IGN INSIDER - Channel - IGN ENTERTAINMENT, INC.; *pg.* 1258, *pg.* 220

IGN.COM - Gaming And Entertainment Company - IGN ENTERTAINMENT, INC.; *pg.* 1258, *pg.* 220

IGNITE - Production System - GRASS VALLEY, INC.; *pg.* 641, *pg.* 164

IGNITE - Fluorescent Pigment - SMOOTH-ON INC.; *pg.* 111, *pg.* 1528

IGNITE-O - Fire Starters - JOSEPH ENTERPRISES, INC.; *pg.* 960, *pg.* 220

IGNITE SLIDE - Women's Footwear - UNDER ARMOUR, INC.; *pg.* 49, *pg.* 759

IGNITION - Apparel - OAKLEY, INC.; *pg.* 1840, *pg.* 86

IGNITION SERIES ATM - Automated Teller Machines - TIDEL ENGINEERING, L.P.; *pg.* 1382, *pg.* 1670

IGO - Mobile Electronic Device - IGO, INC.; *pg.* 644, *pg.* 22

IGO AUTOPOWER - Power Adapter - IGO, INC.; *pg.* 644, *pg.* 22

IGO AUTOPOWER 3000 SERIES - Portable Computer Solutions - IGO, INC.; *pg.* 644, *pg.* 22

IGO DUALPOWER - Power Adapter - IGO, INC.; *pg.* 644, *pg.* 22

IGO EVERYWHEREPOWER 3500 SERIES - Portable Computer Solutions - IGO, INC.; *pg.* 644, *pg.* 22

IGO INTERNATIONAL PLUG ADAPTER KIT - Adapter Kit - IGO, INC.; *pg.* 644, *pg.* 22

IGO INTERNATIONAL TRAVEL ADAPTER - Adapter - IGO, INC.; *pg.* 644, *pg.* 22

IGO MULTI-CARD READER - Multi-Card Reader - IGO, INC.; *pg.* 644, *pg.* 22

IGO NOTEBOOK CLEANING KIT - Cleaning Kit - IGO, INC.; *pg.* 644, *pg.* 22

IGO TIP WALLET - Wallet - IGO, INC.; *pg.* 644, *pg.* 22

IGO WALLPOWER - Power Adapter - IGO, INC.; *pg.* 644, *pg.* 22

IGPAP-PLUS - Patient Care - LABORATORY CORPORATION OF AMERICA HOLDINGS; *pg.* 1554, *pg.* 1359

IGR MINERALS - Mineral Feed - ARCHER-DANIELS-MIDLAND COMPANY; *pg.* 825, *pg.* 565

IGRID - Electronic Components - MOLEX INCORPORATED; *pg.* 655, *pg.* 628

IGT ADVANTAGE - Software - INTERNATIONAL GAME TECHNOLOGY; *pg.* 957, *pg.* 1024

IGT SLOTS - Lottery Game - OHIO LOTTERY COMMISSION; *pg.* 1002, *pg.* 1433

IGUANA - Fabric - NEMSCHOFF, INC.; *pg.* 936, *pg.* 1890

IGUIDE - Software - BROADVISION, INC.; *pg.* 365, *pg.* 189

IGUIDES - Computer Software - LOCKHEED MARTIN CORPORATION; *pg.* 229, *pg.* 762
IHAWK - Software - CONCURRENT COMPUTER CORPORATION; *pg.* 379, *pg.* 531
IHIFI - Wireless Transmitters & Receivers - ZOOM TECHNOLOGIES, INC.; *pg.* 497, *pg.* 1317
IHOME - Audio Entertainment Systems for iPod - SDI TECHNOLOGIES, INC.; *pg.* 671, *pg.* 1113
IICE - Software - SYNOPSYS, INC.; *pg.* 480, *pg.* 162
IJ/3000 - Large Character Ink Jet System - DIAGRAPH; *pg.* 387, *pg.* 989
IJ SERIES - Digital Mailing Machines - NEOPOST CANADA LIMITED; *pg.* 1364, *pg.* 1924
IJOY - Chair - HUMAN TOUCH; *pg.* 928, *pg.* 123
IKARIA - Pet Beauty Product - PETEDGE; *pg.* 1481, *pg.* 787
IKEA - Housewares & Furniture - IKEA NORTH AMERICA SERVICES LLC; *pg.* 929, *pg.* 1523
IKEGAMI - Electronics - IKEGAMI ELECTRONICS (U.S.A.), INC.; *pg.* 644, *pg.* 1083
IKONMETAL - Hybrid Metal Powder - IKONICS CORPORATION; *pg.* 1168, *pg.* 921
IKONOS - Satellite - DIGITALGLOBE; *pg.* 227, *pg.* 1785
IKOR - Converter - ADVANCED ENERGY INDUSTRIES, INC.; *pg.* 613, *pg.* 328
IKOS - Software System - MENTOR GRAPHICS CORPORATION; *pg.* 432, *pg.* 1510
IL - Protein Test - BECKMAN COULTER, INC.; *pg.* 1402, *pg.* 48
IL BACIO - Fragrance - BORGHESE, INC.; *pg.* 502, *pg.* 1205
IL BRUNONE - Wine - SHAW ROSS INTERNATIONAL IMPORTERS; *pg.* 1970, *pg.* 449
IL FORNAIO - Restaurants - IL FORNAIO (AMERICA) CORPORATION; *pg.* 1731, *pg.* 70
IL PRANZARE - Furniture - J. ROBERT SCOTT INC.; *pg.* 930, *pg.* 105
ILAB - Medical Device - BOSTON SCIENTIFIC CORPORATION; *pg.* 1508, *pg.* 831
ILEC - Reverse Osmosis Element - THE DOW CHEMICAL COMPANY; *pg.* 1157, *pg.* 898
ILEVEL - Wood & Building Material - WEYERHAEUSER COMPANY; *pg.* 121, *pg.* 1820
ILIAD - Fabric - NEMSCHOFF, INC.; *pg.* 936, *pg.* 1890
ILIFE - Software Products - APPLE INC.; *pg.* 350, *pg.* 73
ILLEGAL LENGTHS - Mascara - MAYBELLINE LLC; *pg.* 516, *pg.* 1257
ILLINOIS - Locks - THE EASTERN COMPANY; *pg.* 1331, *pg.* 357
ILLINOIS BRONZE - Spray Paints - SHERWIN-WILLIAMS DIVERSIFIED BRANDS DIVISION; *pg.* 1448, *pg.* 1435
ILLINOIS GEAR - Electrical Product - REGAL BELOIT CORPORATION; *pg.* 106, *pg.* 1854
THE ILLINOIS INSTITUTE OF ART - Art School - EDUCATION MANAGEMENT CORPORATION; *pg.* 601, *pg.* 1575
ILLUMATECH - Light Dimming & Ceiling Fan Control Switch - LEVITON MANUFACTURING COMPANY, INC.; *pg.* 1301, *pg.* 1180
ILLUMINA - Mirror - CONAIR CORPORATION; *pg.* 505, *pg.* 1055
ILLUMINATE. NAVIGATE. DOMINATE. - Slogan - STREAMLIGHT INC.; *pg.* 1306, *pg.* 1527
ILLUMINATING SHINE SPRAY - Hair Care Product - JOHN PAUL MITCHELL SYSTEMS; *pg.* 512, *pg.* 133
ILLUMINATIONS - Candles - THE YANKEE CANDLE COMPANY, INC.; *pg.* 1792, *pg.* 843
ILLUMINATOR - Geophysical Survey Design - ION GEOPHYSICAL CORPORATION; *pg.* 1350, *pg.* 1708
ILLUMINE - Dental Product - DENTSPLY INTERNATIONAL INC.; *pg.* 1522, *pg.* 1596
ILLUSION - Textiles - BERNHARDT DESIGN; *pg.* 918, *pg.* 1381
ILLUSION - Fabric - NEMSCHOFF, INC.; *pg.* 936, *pg.* 1890
ILLUSIONS - Decorative Faucets - THE CHICAGO FAUCET COMPANY; *pg.* 1044, *pg.* 606
ILLUSIONS - Building Product - COOLEY GROUP, INC.; *pg.* 691, *pg.* 1603
ILLUSIONS - Rug - COURISTAN INC.; *pg.* 921, *pg.* 1067
ILLUSIONS - Faux Finishing Product - THE SHERWIN-WILLIAMS COMPANY; *pg.* 1447, *pg.* 1435
ILLUSTRATOR - Software - ADOBE SYSTEMS INCORPORATED; *pg.* 342, *pg.* 235
ILLY CAFE - Beverages - THE COCA-COLA COMPANY; *pg.* 240, *pg.* 493
ILOCK - Electronic Components - MOLEX INCORPORATED; *pg.* 655, *pg.* 628
I.LON - Internet Servers - ECHELON CORPORATION; *pg.* 389, *pg.* 245
ILOOK - Ultrasound System - SONOSITE, INC.; *pg.* 1429, *pg.* 1818
ILOVECHEESE.COM - Web Site - AMERICAN DAIRY ASSOCIATION; *pg.* 127, *pg.* 656
ILS - Systems Integration & Aeronautics - LOCKHEED MARTIN CORPORATION; *pg.* 229, *pg.* 762
ILS SERIES - Linear Stage - NEWPORT CORPORATION; *pg.* 1424, *pg.* 114
ILUMINA - Interactive Bible & Encyclopedia Suite - TYNDALE HOUSE PUBLISHERS, INC.; *pg.* 1697, *pg.* 561
ILUVIEN - Ophthalmic Product - ALIMERA SCIENCES, INC.; *pg.* 1490, *pg.* 482
ILUX - Software - CRESTRON ELECTRONICS INC.; *pg.* 631, *pg.* 1116
ILX SYSTEMS - Software Tool And Application - THOMSON REUTERS MARKETS; *pg.* 810, *pg.* 1299
I'M A MADD DAD - Awareness Program - MOTHERS AGAINST DRUNK DRIVING (MADD); *pg.* 147, *pg.* 1723
IM ATTACHMENT MANAGER - Software - WEBSENSE, INC.; *pg.* 491, *pg.* 210
IM CONTROL - Software - WEBSENSE, INC.; *pg.* 491, *pg.* 210
I'M FEELING LUCKY - Internet Application - GOOGLE INC.; *pg.* 1249, *pg.* 153
I'M LOVIN' IT - Slogan - MCDONALD'S CORPORATION; *pg.* 1737, *pg.* 645
IM MINI - Portable Audio System - ALTEC LANSING LLC; *pg.* 348, *pg.* 1553
I'M NOT REALLY A WAITRESS - Nail Care Product - OPI PRODUCTS INC.; *pg.* 518, *pg.* 167
I.M. SAW - Surgical & Medical Product - STRYKER CORPORATION; *pg.* 1598, *pg.* 894
I'M SWEET FOR YOU BOUQUET - Floral Bouquet - FTD GROUP, INC.; *pg.* 1795, *pg.* 608
IMAC - Computer - APPLE INC.; *pg.* 350, *pg.* 73
IMAC - Resin - DOW CHEMICAL; *pg.* 1156, *pg.* 1563
IMAGE - Textiles - BERNHARDT DESIGN; *pg.* 918, *pg.* 1381
IMAGE - Health & Fitness Product - ICON HEALTH & FITNESS, INC.; *pg.* 1837, *pg.* 1752
IMAGE - Cinematographic Movie Film - RLJ ENTERTAINMENT, INC.; *pg.* 306, *pg.* 778
IMAGE - Lens - YOUNGER OPTICS; *pg.* 1437, *pg.* 297
IMAGE 1 - Produces Laminated Custom-Cover Folders or Counter Cards - VARITRONICS, LLC; *pg.* 487, *pg.* 954
IMAGE 300 - High Speed Camera - ALAN GORDON ENTERPRISES, INC.; *pg.* 1399, *pg.* 125
IMAGE-BEIGE - Burnishing Pad - AMERICO MANUFACTURING CO., INC.; *pg.* 325, *pg.* 482
IMAGE CARD - Card Printer - DATACARD CORPORATION; *pg.* 382, *pg.* 948
IMAGE CLIP - Heat Transfer Papers - NEENAH PAPER, INC.; *pg.* 1465, *pg.* 484
IMAGE COPY PLUS - Software - BMC SOFTWARE, INC.; *pg.* 362, *pg.* 1701
IMAGE DIRECT - Imaging System - ANACOMP, INC.; *pg.* 350, *pg.* 1777
IMAGE EMC++ - Solution for Maximizing the Auto-Adjudication of Health Insurance Claims - SCAN-OPTICS, LLC; *pg.* 467, *pg.* 354
IMAGE FIX - Printer - XEROX CORPORATION; *pg.* 494, *pg.* 365
IMAGE FOX - Software - ACD SYSTEMS INTERNATIONAL INC.; *pg.* 340, *pg.* 1913
IMAGE GLASS - Gobo Rotator - ROSCO LABORATORIES, INC.; *pg.* 1782, *pg.* 378
IMAGE GUARD - Microfilm Process Monitoring Service - EASTMAN KODAK COMPANY; *pg.* 1408, *pg.* 1333
IMAGE GUARD - Fabric Product - G&K SERVICES INC.; *pg.* 693, *pg.* 949
IMAGE-IT - Molecular Probe Product - THERMO FISHER SCIENTIFIC INC.; *pg.* 1602, *pg.* 61
IMAGE LAB - Software - BIO-RAD LABORATORIES, INC.; *pg.* 1504, *pg.* 101
IMAGE MASTER - Offset Printing Blanket - ROTADYNE; *pg.* 1681, *pg.* 529
IMAGE MUSIC GROUP - Music Compact Discs - RLJ ENTERTAINMENT, INC.; *pg.* 306, *pg.* 778
THE IMAGE OF UNDERSTANDING - Tagline - VITAL IMAGES, INC.; *pg.* 1607, *pg.* 950
IMAGE PAK - Computer Software - HERFF JONES, INC.; *pg.* 7, *pg.* 686
IMAGE PRO - Image-processing Software - HOLOGIC, INC.; *pg.* 1416, *pg.* 784
IMAGE RESCUE - Software - LEXAR MEDIA, INC.; *pg.* 1262, *pg.* 146
IMAGE RETRIEVER - Printer - XEROX CORPORATION; *pg.* 494, *pg.* 365
IMAGE STAR - Image Processor - ELECTROSONIC SYSTEMS, INC.; *pg.* 635, *pg.* 949
IMAGE VAULT - Digital Video Recorder - FIRE KING SECURITY GROUP; *pg.* 1336, *pg.* 696
IMAGE-VET 70 - Veterinary X-Ray System - IMAGEWORKS; *pg.* 1544, *pg.* 1158
IMAGE VIEW - Binocular - BUSHNELL OUTDOOR PRODUCTS, INC.; *pg.* 1403, *pg.* 718
IMAGEALERT - Mail Verification System - PITNEY BOWES INC.; *pg.* 454, *pg.* 376
IMAGEATLAS - Browser - DIGITALGLOBE, INC.; *pg.* 1408, *pg.* 333
IMAGEBUILDER - Software - DIGITALGLOBE, INC.; *pg.* 1408, *pg.* 333
IMAGECARD IV - Desktop Card System - DATACARD CORPORATION; *pg.* 382, *pg.* 948
IMAGECARE - Program - DELL INC.; *pg.* 383, *pg.* 1737
IMAGECAST - Software - GE HEALTHCARE; *pg.* 399, *pg.* 1765
IMAGECLIP - Heat Transfer Paper - NEENAH PAPER, INC.; *pg.* 1465, *pg.* 484
IMAGECONNECT - Software - DIGITALGLOBE, INC.; *pg.* 1408, *pg.* 333
IMAGEFOX - Software - ACD SYSTEMS INTERNATIONAL INC.; *pg.* 340, *pg.* 1913
IMAGEGRID - Network Storage System - CANDELIS, INC.; *pg.* 368, *pg.* 165
IMAGELINK - Software - COMPUTER PROGRAMS & SYSTEMS, INC.; *pg.* 378, *pg.* 7
IMAGELINK - Microfilm - EASTMAN KODAK COMPANY; *pg.* 1408, *pg.* 1333
IMAGELITE - Film - EASTMAN KODAK COMPANY; *pg.* 1408, *pg.* 1333
IMAGEMAG - Image Processor - ELECTROSONIC SYSTEMS, INC.; *pg.* 635, *pg.* 949
IMAGEMARK - Automatic Teller Machine - NCR CORPORATION; *pg.* 443, *pg.* 531
IMAGEMASTER - Video Cassettes - EASTMAN KODAK COMPANY; *pg.* 1408, *pg.* 1333
IMAGEMASTER - Phototooling System - E.I. DU PONT DE NEMOURS & COMPANY; *pg.* 1159, *pg.* 390
IMAGEMASTER - Digital Photographic Reproduction - HERFF JONES, INC.; *pg.* 7, *pg.* 686
IMAGEMATE - Photographic Paper & Chemicals for Micrographics Applications - EASTMAN KODAK COMPANY; *pg.* 1408, *pg.* 1333
IMAGEMATE - Reader - SANDISK CORPORATION; *pg.* 465, *pg.* 147
IMAGEMERCHANT - Software - R.R. DONNELLEY & SONS COMPANY; *pg.* 1682, *pg.* 589
IMAGEMODELER - Software - AUTODESK INC.; *pg.* 356, *pg.* 257
IMAGEN - Visual Server - CONCURRENT COMPUTER CORPORATION; *pg.* 379, *pg.* 531
IMAGENATION - Frame Grabbers - CYBEROPTICS CORPORATION; *pg.* 1408, *pg.* 925
IMAGENE GREEN - Molecular Biology Product - THERMO FISHER SCIENTIFIC INC.; *pg.* 1602, *pg.* 61
IMAGENE RED - Molecular Probe Product - THERMO FISHER SCIENTIFIC INC.; *pg.* 1602, *pg.* 61
IMAGENET - Software - MITEK SYSTEMS, INC.; *pg.* 440, *pg.* 204
IMAGENET DATA CAPTURE - Software - MITEK SYSTEMS, INC.; *pg.* 440, *pg.* 204
IMAGENET MOBILE DEPOSIT - Software - MITEK SYSTEMS, INC.; *pg.* 440, *pg.* 204
IMAGENET PAYMENTS - Software - MITEK SYSTEMS, INC.; *pg.* 440, *pg.* 204
IMAGENET PHOTO & VIDEO - Software - MITEK SYSTEMS, INC.; *pg.* 440, *pg.* 204
IMAGENET PREP & ID - Software - MITEK SYSTEMS, INC.; *pg.* 440, *pg.* 204
IMAGENET SIGNATURES - Software - MITEK SYSTEMS, INC.; *pg.* 440, *pg.* 204
IMAGEON - 3D Graphical Technology - ADVANCED MICRO DEVICES, INC.-MARKHAM; *pg.* 345, *pg.* 1922
IMAGEPRINT - Paper - DOMTAR CORPORATION; *pg.* 1456, *pg.* 1954
IMAGEPRINT - Paper Product - WEYERHAEUSER COMPANY; *pg.* 121, *pg.* 1820
IMAGEPRO - High Resolution Aerial Photography - PITNEY

BOWES SOFTWARE INC.; pg. 455, pg. 1346
IMAGEPRO - Gobo Rotator - ROSCO LABORATORIES, INC.; pg. 1782, pg. 378
IMAGER - Medical Device - BOSTON SCIENTIFIC CORPORATION; pg. 1508, pg. 831
IMAGER - Perfectly Flat, Permanent Wall-mounted Screen Ideal for Video Projection - DA-LITE SCREEN COMPANY; pg. 632, pg. 698
IMAGER - Digital Gamma Camera - DIGIRAD CORPORATION; pg. 1524, pg. 185
IMAGER - Systems Integration & Aeronautics - LOCKHEED MARTIN CORPORATION; pg. 229, pg. 762
IMAGESCAPE - Terrain Model Solution - DIGITALGLOBE, INC.; pg. 1408, pg. 333
IMAGESCORE - Software - MITEK SYSTEMS, INC.; pg. 440, pg. 204
IMAGESHARE - Data Sharing Cable - POLYCOM, INC.; pg. 664, pg. 249
IMAGESHARE II - Video Conferencing Product - POLYCOM, INC.; pg. 664, pg. 249
IMAGESHARK - Software - ACD SYSTEMS INTERNATIONAL INC.; pg. 340, pg. 1913
IMAGESITE - Software Product - XEROX CORPORATION; pg. 494, pg. 365
IMAGESOURCE - Printer - EASTMAN KODAK COMPANY; pg. 1408, pg. 1333
IMAGESTAR - Microfilm Readers, Reader-Printers - EASTMAN KODAK COMPANY; pg. 1408, pg. 1333
IMAGETRAX - Record Management System - SMEAD MANUFACTURING COMPANY; pg. 470, pg. 926
IMAGEWATCH - Computer Services - DELL INC.; pg. 383, pg. 1737
IMAGEWATCH - Film Processor Checklist - EASTMAN KODAK COMPANY; pg. 1408, pg. 1333
IMAGEWAY - Software - DIEBOLD, INCORPORATED; pg. 387, pg. 1407
IMAGEWEAR - Apparel - V.F. CORPORATION; pg. 34, pg. 1376
IMAGEWRITER - Printer - APPLE INC.; pg. 350, pg. 73
IMAGEXPRESS - Software - MOLECULAR DEVICES CORPORATION; pg. 1568, pg. 287
IMAGGIA II - Digital Printing System - DELPHAX TECHNOLOGIES INC.; pg. 386, pg. 917
IMAGI-PRINT - Software - DAKTRONICS, INC.; pg. 633, pg. 1624
IMAGIN - Medical Probe Cable Assembly - W.L. GORE & ASSOCIATES, INC.; pg. 122, pg. 388
IMAGINATION AT WORK - Slogan - GENERAL ELECTRIC COMPANY; pg. 1297, pg. 347
IMAGINATION CELEBRATON - Educational Programs for Children - JOHN F. KENNEDY CENTER FOR THE PERFORMING ARTS; pg. 555, pg. 401
IMAGINATION DESK - Learning System - LEAPFROG ENTERPRISES, INC.; pg. 961, pg. 84
IMAGINATION IN METALLURGY - Slogan - HITCHINER MANUFACTURING COMPANY INC.; pg. 87, pg. 1037
IMAGINE - Fragrance - ALOETTE COSMETICS, INC.; pg. 498, pg. 487
IMAGINE - Computer Software - HERFF JONES, INC.; pg. 7, pg. 686
IMAGINE - Tagline - MONSANTO COMPANY; pg. 1173, pg. 999
IMAGINE - Video Game - UBISOFT INC.; pg. 589, pg. 229
IMAGINE AIR - Paint - BADGER AIR BRUSH COMPANY; pg. 359, pg. 612
IMAGINE FOODS - Food Product - THE HAIN CELESTIAL GROUP, INC.; pg. 860, pg. 1172
IMAGINEERING - Amusement Park - THE WALT DISNEY COMPANY; pg. 317, pg. 52
IMAGINEXT - Toys - FISHER-PRICE, INC.; pg. 953, pg. 1156
IMAGINEXT - Toy - MATTEL, INC.; pg. 962, pg. 81
IMAGING KIOST SOLUTION - Manual - XEROX CORPORATION; pg. 494, pg. 365
IMAGING SOLUTIONS - Software - BOTTOMLINE TECHNOLOGIES INC.; pg. 363, pg. 483
IMAGING SOLUTIONS FOR EVERY MISSION - Tagline - FLIR SYSTEMS, INC.; pg. 1413, pg. 1510
IMAGINING LIFE'S POSSIBILITIES - Slogan - NPS PHARMACEUTICALS, INC.; pg. 1576, pg. 1043
IMAGINIT - Software - RAND A TECHNOLOGY CORPORATION; pg. 459, pg. 774
IMAKENEWS - E-Newsletter - IMAKENEWS, INC.; pg. 413, pg. 851
IMAN - Ethnic Skin Care & Color Cosmetics - COLOR ME BEAUTIFUL, INC.; pg. 505, pg. 1787
IMANUAL - Software System - ALION SCIENCE AND TECHNOLOGY CORPORATION; pg. 615, pg. 1788
IMAP - Telecommunication Installation, Maintenance & Testing - TEXTRON INC.; pg. 235, pg. 1607
IMARI - Beauty Product - AVON PRODUCTS, INC.; pg. 500, pg. 1198
IMARK - Software - BIO-RAD LABORATORIES, INC.; pg. 1504, pg. 101
IMASTER - Electronic Security Devices - MASTER LOCK COMPANY LLC; pg. 1055, pg. 1884
IMATERNITY.COM - Maternity Clothing Online - DESTINATION MATERNITY CORPORATION; pg. 23, pg. 1563
IMATION - Chemical Product - HURST CHEMICAL COMPANY; pg. 1168, pg. 174
IMAX 3D - Large Format Motion Picture Theaters - IMAX CORPORATION; pg. 1417, pg. 1926
IMAX DMR - Digital Re-Mastering Technology - IMAX CORPORATION; pg. 1417, pg. 1926
IMAX DOME - Large Format Motion Picture Theaters - IMAX CORPORATION; pg. 1417, pg. 1926
THE IMAX EXPERIENCE - Motion Picture Theatre - IMAX CORPORATION; pg. 1417, pg. 1926
IMD1 - Decorating Technology - SERIGRAPH, INC.; pg. 1686, pg. 1899
IMDUR - Oral Nitrate Drug for Treatment of Angina Pectoris - MERCK & CO., INC.; pg. 1566, pg. 1077
IMEDIA - Software - CRESTRON ELECTRONICS INC.; pg. 631, pg. 1116
IMEDICA - Health Plan & Publication - MEDICA, INC.; pg. 1208, pg. 949
IMEET - Telecom Product - PREMIERE GLOBAL SERVICES, INC.; pg. 1275, pg. 518
IMEGARAID - Hard Disk Control Software - AVAGO TECHNOLOGIES; pg. 358, pg. 238
IMEMS - Sensor - ANALOG DEVICES, INC.; pg. 617, pg. 839
IMICURE - Epoxy Curatives - AIR PRODUCTS AND CHEMICALS, INC.; pg. 1145, pg. 1513
IMIDIPRO - Turf & Ornamental - PBI/GORDON CORPORATION; pg. 1176, pg. 985
IMIJ - Adhesive Coated Paper - SPINNAKER COATING, LLC; pg. 1470, pg. 1477
IMIX - Coffee Dispensers - BUNN O-MATIC CORPORATION; pg. 53, pg. 661
IML - Software - SAS INSTITUTE INC.; pg. 466, pg. 1361
IMMAGE - Testing Instrument System - BECKMAN COULTER, INC.; pg. 1402, pg. 48
IMMEDIA - Molecular Biology Product - THERMO FISHER SCIENTIFIC INC.; pg. 1602, pg. 61
IMMEDIATE CARE BUSINESS - Publication - INFORMA EXHIBITIONS LLC; pg. 1653, pg. 17
IMMEDIATE RESPONSE - Claims Reporting Service - THE PROGRESSIVE CORPORATION; pg. 1214, pg. 1403
IMMERGE - Software - VARIAN MEDICAL SYSTEMS, INC.; pg. 1434, pg. 178
IMMERSION - Fabric - W.L. GORE & ASSOCIATES, INC.; pg. 122, pg. 388
IMMERSION STUDIO - Hardware & Software - IMMERSION CORPORATION; pg. 413, pg. 246
IMMERSION TOUCHSENSETECHNOLOGY - Technology - IMMERSION CORPORATION; pg. 413, pg. 246
IMMERSOJET - Burners - ECLIPSE INC.; pg. 1332, pg. 655
IMMERSOPAK - Burner - ECLIPSE INC.; pg. 1332, pg. 655
IMMOBILIZER - Biotechnology Product - GENZYME CORPORATION; pg. 1534, pg. 808
IMMORTAL FORTUNE - Video Game - INTERNATIONAL GAME TECHNOLOGY; pg. 957, pg. 1024
IMMORTAL JOURNEY - Video Game - INTERNATIONAL GAME TECHNOLOGY; pg. 957, pg. 1024
IMMORTAL MOUNTAIN - Video Game - INTERNATIONAL GAME TECHNOLOGY; pg. 957, pg. 1024
IMMORTAL POWERS - Video Game - INTERNATIONAL GAME TECHNOLOGY; pg. 957, pg. 1024
IMMORTAL WORDS - Trivia Game of Who Said What! - NTN BUZZTIME, INC.; pg. 659, pg. 60
IMMOTUS - Insulation Element - THE DOW CHEMICAL COMPANY; pg. 1157, pg. 898
IMMUCHECK - Veterinary Diagnostic Laboratories - HESKA CORPORATION; pg. 1542, pg. 335
IMMUN-BLOT - Software - BIO-RAD LABORATORIES, INC.; pg. 1504, pg. 101
IMMUN-LITE - Software - BIO-RAD LABORATORIES, INC.; pg. 1504, pg. 101
IMMUN-STAR WESTERNC - Software - BIO-RAD LABORATORIES, INC.; pg. 1504, pg. 101
IMMUNACE - Nutritional Supplement - NATURAL ORGANICS, INC.; pg. 1571, pg. 1181
IMMUNACTIN - Nutritional Supplement - NATURAL ORGANICS, INC.; pg. 1571, pg. 1181
IMMUNE - Nutritional Product - RBC LIFE SCIENCES, INC.; pg. 1588, pg. 1723
IMMUNE-ACTION - Nutritional Supplements for the Immune System - NATURAL ORGANICS, INC.; pg. 1571, pg. 1181
IMMUNE DEFENSE - Nutritional Supplement - WHITEWING LABS, INC.; pg. 1610, pg. 99
IMMUNE REVIEW - Dietary Supplement - NOW HEALTH GROUP, INC.; pg. 1576, pg. 557
IMMUNE360 - Nutritional Product - RBC LIFE SCIENCES, INC.; pg. 1588, pg. 1723
IMMUNECTAR - Nutritional Supplement - NATURAL ORGANICS, INC.; pg. 1571, pg. 1181
IMMUNEJUICE - Beverage - MONSTER BEVERAGE CORPORATION; pg. 257, pg. 69
IMMUNITY BOOST - Boost - JAMBA, INC.; pg. 1024, pg. 84
IMMUNIX - Computer Software - NOVELL INC.; pg. 446, pg. 852
IMMUNO-BRITE - Testing Instrument System - BECKMAN COULTER, INC.; pg. 1402, pg. 48
IMMUNO-TROL - Testing Instrument System - BECKMAN COULTER, INC.; pg. 1402, pg. 48
IMMUNOCAP - Blood Tests - QUEST DIAGNOSTICS INCORPORATED; pg. 1587, pg. 1080
IMMUNOCARD - Diagnostic Test Product - MERIDIAN BIOSCIENCE INC.; pg. 1422, pg. 1417
IMMUNOCARD STAT! - Rapid Membrane Assay for Detecting Infectious Diseases - MERIDIAN BIOSCIENCE INC.; pg. 1422, pg. 1417
IMMUNODYNE - Membrane - PALL CORPORATION; pg. 232, pg. 1323
IMMUNOFIN - Health System Product - LANELABS USA INC.; pg. 1554, pg. 1128
IMMUNOPREP - Testing Instrument System - BECKMAN COULTER, INC.; pg. 1402, pg. 48
IMMUNOPROBE - Biotinylation Kit - SIGMA-ALDRICH CORPORATION; pg. 1181, pg. 1003
IMMUNOREGULIN - Animal Safety Product - NEOGEN CORPORATION; pg. 883, pg. 896
IMMUNOSTART - Nutritional Product - MANNATECH, INCORPORATED; pg. 1558, pg. 1671
IMMUNOTECH - Testing Instrument System - BECKMAN COULTER, INC.; pg. 1402, pg. 48
IMMUNOVET - Animal Safety Product - NEOGEN CORPORATION; pg. 883, pg. 896
IMMUNOWASH - Software - BIO-RAD LABORATORIES, INC.; pg. 1504, pg. 101
IMMUNOX - Chemical Coating - ENTHONE INC.; pg. 1161, pg. 381
IMMUSTRIP - Antibody - IMMUNOMEDICS, INC.; pg. 1544, pg. 1087
IMMUSUN - Supplement & Food Product - NEW EARTH LIFE SCIENCES, INC.; pg. 1573, pg. 1499
IMO - Therapeutic Product - IDERA PHARMACEUTICALS, INC.; pg. 1543, pg. 808
IMODIUM - Healthcare Product - JOHNSON & JOHNSON; pg. 1549, pg. 1091
IMOGAM - Rabies Immune Globulin - SANOFI PASTEUR, INC; pg. 1591, pg. 1588
IMOM - Training Program - FAMILY FIRST; pg. 140, pg. 472
IMOTION - Power Semiconductor Device - INTERNATIONAL RECTIFIER CORPORATION; pg. 647, pg. 80
IMOUT - Software - AUTODESK INC.; pg. 356, pg. 257
IMOVAX - Rabies Vaccine - SANOFI PASTEUR, INC; pg. 1591, pg. 1588
IMOVE - Management & Relocation Services - SIRVA, INC.; pg. 1923, pg. 669
IMOVIE - Software Product - APPLE INC.; pg. 350, pg. 73
IMPAC - Standard Conveyor Controllers - DORNER MANUFACTURING CORP.; pg. 1329, pg. 1861
IMPACEL - Paper Products - INTERNATIONAL PAPER COMPANY; pg. 1460, pg. 1644
IMPACT - Alarm System - ALLIED HEALTHCARE PRODUCTS, INC.; pg. 1491, pg. 990
IMPACT - Filter & Manifolds - ENTEGRIS, INC.; pg. 1882, pg. 788
IMPACT - Laser System - GSI GROUP INC.; pg. 1415, pg. 784
IMPACT - Display Merchandise for Supermarkets - HUSSMANN INTERNATIONAL, INC.; pg. 1347, pg. 973

IMPACT - Furniture - JASPER GROUP; *pg.* 930, *pg.* 691
IMPACT - Basketball Equipment - LIFETIME PRODUCTS INC.; *pg.* 933, *pg.* 1751
IMPACT - Proprietary Travel Logistics Management System - MARITZ INC.; *pg.* 1914, *pg.* 977
IMPACT - Electronic Components - MOLEX INCORPORATED; *pg.* 655, *pg.* 628
IMPACT - Clinical Trial Management System - PAREXEL INTERNATIONAL CORPORATION; *pg.* 1580, *pg.* 853
IMPACT - Packaging Film - SEALED AIR CORPORATION; *pg.* 1468, *pg.* 1058
IMPACT - Office Furniture - STEELCASE INC.; *pg.* 475, *pg.* 889
IMPACT - Steel - THE TIMKEN COMPANY; *pg.* 218, *pg.* 1408
IMPACT - Implant Product - ZIMMER BIOMET HOLDINGS, INC.; *pg.* 1611, *pg.* 699
IMPACT DATABASE GATEWAY - Software - BMC SOFTWARE, INC.; *pg.* 362, *pg.* 1701
IMPACT EXPLORER - Software - BMC SOFTWARE, INC.; *pg.* 362, *pg.* 1701
IMPACT FOR MEN - Cologne - LUZIER PERSONALIZED COSMETICS, INC.; *pg.* 515, *pg.* 978
IMPACT INTEGRATION - Software - BMC SOFTWARE, INC.; *pg.* 362, *pg.* 1701
IMPACT PLUS - Co-operative Advertising Program - EASTMAN KODAK COMPANY; *pg.* 1408, *pg.* 1333
IMPACT-TOUGH - Glue Formula - GORILLA GLUE CO.; *pg.* 1048, *pg.* 1414
IMPACT-X - Campaign Management & Analytics Platform - ACXIOM CORPORATION; *pg.* 342, *pg.* 33
IMPACT ZERO - Magazine - TEMBEC INC.; *pg.* 114, *pg.* 1957
IMPACT.MD - Software - ALLSCRIPTS HEALTHCARE SOLUTIONS, INC.; *pg.* 1492, *pg.* 563
IMPACTNXT - Electronic Components - MOLEX INCORPORATED; *pg.* 655, *pg.* 628
IMPACTO - Air Glove - ALIMED, INC.; *pg.* 1490, *pg.* 816
IMPACTRT - Board-Level Product - MERCURY COMPUTER SYSTEMS, INC.; *pg.* 434, *pg.* 813
IMPACTVCB - Digital Video Product - HAUPPAUGE DIGITAL, INC.; *pg.* 402, *pg.* 1164
IMPAK - Electronic Components - GE ENERGY; *pg.* 1338, *pg.* 506
IMPALA - Sedan - GENERAL MOTORS COMPANY; *pg.* 175, *pg.* 881
IMPAQ - Chemical Product - SPECTRUM CHEMICALS & LABORATORY PRODUCTS, INC.; *pg.* 1181, *pg.* 94
IMPASTO - Fabric - NEMSCHOFF, INC.; *pg.* 936, *pg.* 1890
IMPAX - Hammer - NUPLA CORPORATION; *pg.* 101, *pg.* 281
IMPAX - Metal Building Self-Drill Fasteners - SFS INTEC, INC.; *pg.* 1061, *pg.* 1596
IMPCO GASEOUS FUEL ENGINES - Alternative Fuel Engines - IMPCO TECHNOLOGIES, INC.; *pg.* 208, *pg.* 261
IMPCTFILM - Labeling - FLEXCON CORPORATION; *pg.* 1457, *pg.* 844
IMPEDANCE TRACK - Integrated Circuits - TEXAS INSTRUMENTS INCORPORATED; *pg.* 679, *pg.* 1688
IMPERFECTS - Video Game - ELECTRONIC ARTS INC.; *pg.* 951, *pg.* 189
IMPERIA - Dinnerware - THE HOMER LAUGHLIN CHINA COMPANY; *pg.* 1125, *pg.* 1850
IMPERIAL - Diamond Coated Abrasives - 3M COMPANY; *pg.* 1142, *pg.* 956
IMPERIAL - Felt - AMERICAN FELT & FILTER COMPANY; *pg.* 1312, *pg.* 1184
IMPERIAL - Electric Pump - GRACO, INC.; *pg.* 1342, *pg.* 935
IMPERIAL - Seating Product - IRWIN SEATING COMPANY INC.; *pg.* 929, *pg.* 887
IMPERIAL - Motor Product - STANDARD MOTOR PRODUCTS, INC.; *pg.* 218, *pg.* 1176
IMPERIAL - Spreads and Cooking Oil - UNILEVER CANADA INC.; *pg.* 903, *pg.* 1946
IMPERIAL - Gypsum Base, Tape, Basecoat Plaster & Finish Plaster - USG CORPORATION; *pg.* 118, *pg.* 594
IMPERIAL - Ceiling Fan - WESTINGHOUSE LIGHTING CORPORATION; *pg.* 687, *pg.* 1571
IMPERIAL - Chocolate Product - WORLD'S FINEST CHOCOLATE, INC.; *pg.* 1864, *pg.* 597
IMPERIAL BLUE - Bath Product - KOHLER CO.; *pg.* 91, *pg.* 1862
IMPERIAL COMFORT - Mattress & Box Spring Sets - KINGSDOWN, INC.; *pg.* 932, *pg.* 1383
IMPERIAL DRAGON - Video Game - INTERNATIONAL GAME TECHNOLOGY; *pg.* 957, *pg.* 1024
IMPERIAL GOLD - Paint - AKZONOBEL DECORATIVE PAINTS U.S.; *pg.* 1439, *pg.* 1474
IMPERIAL PRINCESS - Container Grown Plant - MONROVIA GROWERS; *pg.* 1797, *pg.* 44
IMPERIAL QUEEN - Container Grown Plant - MONROVIA GROWERS; *pg.* 1797, *pg.* 44
IMPERIAL STOUT - Beverage - SPRECHER BREWING COMPANY; *pg.* 265, *pg.* 1858
IMPERIAL TELECARD - Prepaid Calling Cards - IDT CORPORATION; *pg.* 643, *pg.* 1096
IMPERIAL TOUCH - Paint - AKZONOBEL DECORATIVE PAINTS U.S.; *pg.* 1439, *pg.* 1474
IMPERIAL VALLEY - Beef Products - NATIONAL BEEF PACKING COMPANY, LLC; *pg.* 882, *pg.* 985
IMPERIAL VELOUR - Broadloom - COURISTAN INC.; *pg.* 921, *pg.* 1067
IMPERIUM - Ceramic, Glass, Stone Tiles & Slabs - WALKER & ZANGER, INC.; *pg.* 119, *pg.* 281
IMPERM - Minerals - MINERALS TECHNOLOGIES INC.; *pg.* 1173, *pg.* 617
IMPERVEX - Latex Gloss Enamel - BENJAMIN MOORE & CO.; *pg.* 1440, *pg.* 1085
IMPERVO - Solvent Enamels & Varnishes - BENJAMIN MOORE & CO.; *pg.* 1440, *pg.* 1085
IMPERVO WITH DESIGN - Paint And Stain Product - BENJAMIN MOORE & CO.; *pg.* 1440, *pg.* 1085
IMPINGER - Conveyor Ovens - LINCOLN FOODSERVICE PRODUCTS, LLC; *pg.* 1127, *pg.* 1432
IMPINJET - Wet Scrubber - SLY, INC.; *pg.* 1376, *pg.* 1475
IMPLANON - Non-Degradable Implant - MERCK & CO., INC.; *pg.* 1566, *pg.* 1077
IMPLANT 20:1 - Straight & Contra Angle Handpieces - SIRONA DENTAL SYSTEMS, INC.; *pg.* 1429, *pg.* 1175
IMPLEMENTATION ASSISTANCE - Software - BMC SOFTWARE, INC.; *pg.* 362, *pg.* 1701
IMPLUSE - Flatware - ONEIDA LTD; *pg.* 1129, *pg.* 1318
IMPO-AID - Healthcare Product - MEDICOOL, INC.; *pg.* 1562, *pg.* 294
IMPORT - Device - MEDTRONIC, INC.; *pg.* 1564, *pg.* 939
IMPORT - Hardware - TRANSACT TECHNOLOGIES INCORPORATED; *pg.* 484, *pg.* 351
IMPORT REFERENCE GUIDE - Publisher - BLOOMBERG BNA; *pg.* 1621, *pg.* 1772
IMPORTERS.COM - Business to Business Website - LIVE CURRENT MEDIA INC.; *pg.* 1263, *pg.* 1911
IMPOSSIBLE STOPS HERE - Medical Services - INVACARE CORPORATION; *pg.* 1546, *pg.* 1451
IMPOSTER - Apparel - OAKLEY, INC.; *pg.* 1840, *pg.* 86
IMPOWER - Software - SUNGARD DATA SYSTEMS INC.; *pg.* 477, *pg.* 1592
IMPOWER - Shipping Services - UNITED PARCEL SERVICE, INC.; *pg.* 1928, *pg.* 522
IMPREGUM - Dental Impression Material - 3M COMPANY; *pg.* 1142, *pg.* 956
IMPRELIS - Selective Herbicide - E.I. DU PONT DE NEMOURS & COMPANY; *pg.* 1159, *pg.* 390
IMPRESO - Specialty Paper - IMPRESO, INC.; *pg.* 413, *pg.* 1671
IMPRESS - Burnishing Pad - AMERICO MANUFACTURING CO., INC.; *pg.* 325, *pg.* 482
IMPRESS - Body Wash - BLUE CROSS LABORATORIES; *pg.* 326, *pg.* 277
IMPRESS - Chemical Product - LYONDELLBASELL INDUSTRIES; *pg.* 980, *pg.* 1710
IMPRESS II - Balloon - CONTINENTAL AMERICAN CORP.; *pg.* 1880, *pg.* 723
IMPRESS V - Balloon - CONTINENTAL AMERICAN CORP.; *pg.* 1880, *pg.* 723
IMPRESSION - Dies - BUNTING MAGNETICS CO.; *pg.* 1320, *pg.* 717
IMPRESSION - Eyewear - MINE SAFETY APPLIANCES COMPANY; *pg.* 1361, *pg.* 1525
IMPRESSION SERIES - Advertising Specialty Custom Imprinted Packet Seeds - THE PAGE SEED CO.; *pg.* 1798, *pg.* 1163
IMPRESSIONPLUS - Decoration Colors - FERRO CORPORATION; *pg.* 1162, *pg.* 1462
IMPRESSIONS - Hair Dryer - CONAIR CORPORATION; *pg.* 505, *pg.* 1055
IMPRESSIONS - Trade Publication - THE NIELSEN COMPANY B.V.; *pg.* 1671, *pg.* 1272
IMPRESSIONS - Door Glass - ODL INCORPORATED; *pg.* 101, *pg.* 914
IMPRESSIONS - Premium Wiring Devices - PASS & SEYMOUR/LEGRAND; *pg.* 1303, *pg.* 1344
IMPRESSIONS FROM ISOTONER - Gloves - TOTES ISOTONER CORPORATION; *pg.* 14, *pg.* 1426
IMPREZA 2.5I - Car - SUBARU OF AMERICA, INC.; *pg.* 191, *pg.* 1050
IMPREZA WRX - Car - SUBARU OF AMERICA, INC.; *pg.* 191, *pg.* 1050
IMPRINT - Dental Impression Material - 3M COMPANY; *pg.* 1142, *pg.* 956
IMPRINTING EPIPANEL - Diagnostic Tool - SEQUENOM, INC.; *pg.* 1593, *pg.* 209
IMPROCON - Controller Module - IMPULSE NC LLC; *pg.* 1051, *pg.* 1385
IMPROMPTU GOURMET - Prepared Meals & Frozen Products By Mail Order - THE SCHWAN FOOD COMPANY; *pg.* 894, *pg.* 928
IMPROV - Seating - HAWORTH, INC.; *pg.* 402, *pg.* 891
IMPROV - Building Product - LESTER BUILDING SYSTEMS, LLC; *pg.* 93, *pg.* 927
IMPROVED MXM - Synthetic Paper - TRANSILWRAP COMPANY, INC.; *pg.* 1470, *pg.* 613
IMPROVED TERRAZZINE - Cleaning Product - HILLYARD, INC.; *pg.* 331, *pg.* 990
IMPROVEMENTS - Online Gift Store - IAC/INTERACTIVECORP; *pg.* 292, *pg.* 1242
IMPROVING HEALTH THROUGH INNOVATION - Slogan - SUNOVION PHARMACEUTICALS INC.; *pg.* 1599, *pg.* 832
IMPROVING HOME IMPROVEMENT - Slogan - LOWE'S COMPANIES, INC.; *pg.* 1053, *pg.* 1383
IMPROVING QUALITY OF LIFE - Slogan - GANEDEN BIOTECH, INC.; *pg.* 1532, *pg.* 1463
IMPROVING THE WAY BUSINESS GETS DONE - Slogan - THE STANDARD REGISTER COMPANY; *pg.* 473, *pg.* 1446
IMPULSE - Knife - BUCK KNIVES, INC.; *pg.* 1828, *pg.* 550
IMPULSE - Fan - CRAFTMADE INTERNATIONAL, INC.; *pg.* 1295, *pg.* 1670
IMPULSE - Character - DC COMICS, INC.; *pg.* 1633, *pg.* 1221
IMPULSE - Electromagnetic Conveyor - KEY TECHNOLOGY, INC.; *pg.* 868, *pg.* 1847
IMPULSE - Integrated Metrology Tool - NANOMETRICS INCORPORATED; *pg.* 1423, *pg.* 147
IMPULSE - Fabric - NEMSCHOFF, INC.; *pg.* 936, *pg.* 1890
IMPULSE - Cordless Power Nailing System - PASLODE; *pg.* 1059, *pg.* 664
IMPULSE - Musical Instrument - PEAVEY ELECTRONICS CORPORATION; *pg.* 662, *pg.* 970
IMPULSE - Auto-Darkening Filter - SELLSTROM MANUFACTURING CO.; *pg.* 1428, *pg.* 659
IMPULSE - Motor Homes - WINNEBAGO INDUSTRIES, INC.; *pg.* 1712, *pg.* 707
IMPULSE ENGINE 2000 - Force Feedback Research Joystick - IMMERSION CORPORATION; *pg.* 413, *pg.* 246
IMPULSE STICK - Hardware & Software - IMMERSION CORPORATION; *pg.* 413, *pg.* 246
IMRON - Polyurethane Enamel - E.I. DU PONT DE NEMOURS & COMPANY; *pg.* 1159, *pg.* 390
IMRT - Software - ELEKTA; *pg.* 391, *pg.* 987
IMS - Computer Support Furniture - HOWE FURNITURE CORPORATION; *pg.* 928, *pg.* 998
IMS - Consulting Service - IMS HEALTH, INC.; *pg.* 1544, *pg.* 344
IMS ATU ADVANTAGE - Software Solution - IMS HEALTH, INC.; *pg.* 1544, *pg.* 344
IMS NPA - Market Dynamics - IMS HEALTH, INC.; *pg.* 1544, *pg.* 344
IMS/PC 2.0 - Architecture - SONUS NETWORKS INC.; *pg.* 1281, *pg.* 858
IMS/SIP CORE (CONSUMER) - Mobile Solutions - SONUS NETWORKS INC.; *pg.* 1281, *pg.* 858
IMS/SIP CORE (ENTERPRISE) - Mobile Solutions - SONUS NETWORKS INC.; *pg.* 1281, *pg.* 858
IMS/TISPAN - Architecture - SONUS NETWORKS INC.; *pg.* 1281, *pg.* 858
IMT - Micrographic Equipment - EASTMAN KODAK COMPANY; *pg.* 1408, *pg.* 1333
IMT - Furniture - HERMAN MILLER, INC.; *pg.* 926, *pg.* 913
IMTN - Telecommunications Switching Equipment - ALCATEL-LUCENT USA, INC.; *pg.* 615, *pg.* 1728
IMURAN - Therapy System - PROMETHEUS LABORATORIES, INC.; *pg.* 1586, *pg.* 206
IMUTABS - Vitamins - HEALTH PRODUCTS

First page reference indicates Business Class Edition
Second page reference indicates Geographic Edition

CORPORATION; *pg.* 1540, *pg.* 1356
IMUX - Oceanographic Product - TELEDYNE BENTHOS, INC.; *pg.* 1431, *pg.* 838
IMX - Diagnostic Products - ABBOTT LABORATORIES; *pg.* 1484, *pg.* 551
IMX - Chemical Technology - NOVA CHEMICALS CORPORATION; *pg.* 1175, *pg.* 1904
IMX 2.1 - Multimedia Application Platform - SONUS NETWORKS INC.; *pg.* 1281, *pg.* 858
IN - Furniture - TRENDWAY CORPORATION; *pg.* 945, *pg.* 892
IN A BOTTLE - Video Game - INTERNATIONAL GAME TECHNOLOGY; *pg.* 957, *pg.* 1024
THE "IN A NUTSHELL" SERIES - Magazine - O'REILLY MEDIA, INC.; *pg.* 1673, *pg.* 278
IN A SNAP - Nail Product - ORLY INTERNATIONAL, INC.; *pg.* 518, *pg.* 137
IN ALL THE RIGHT PLACES - Software System - MENTOR GRAPHICS CORPORATION; *pg.* 432, *pg.* 1510
IN & OUT - Release Agent - SMOOTH-ON INC.; *pg.* 111, *pg.* 1528
IN BETWEEN - Skin Cleanser - DERMA SCIENCES, INC.; *pg.* 1523, *pg.* 1111
IN BUSINESS TO WRITE BUSINESS - Business Insurance - AUTO-OWNERS INSURANCE GROUP; *pg.* 1194, *pg.* 895
IN-CABINET - Rack & Cable - PANDUIT CORP.; *pg.* 661, *pg.* 663
IN CONTROL - Hosiery & Related Apparel - MAYER/BERKSHIRE CORPORATION; *pg.* 29, *pg.* 1129
IN-DOOR-ICE - Home Appliance Product - WHIRLPOOL CORPORATION; *pg.* 62, *pg.* 872
IN-FAST - Healthcare System - AMERICAN MEDICAL SYSTEMS HOLDINGS, INC.; *pg.* 1493, *pg.* 947
IN-FISHERMAN - Magazine - RENTPATH, INC.; *pg.* 1680, *pg.* 538
IN-HAND SCAN CARD - Scanning Product - SOCKET MOBILE, INC.; *pg.* 471, *pg.* 164
IN-JERSEY - Online News - ASBURY PARK PRESS INC.; *pg.* 1617, *pg.* 1090
IN-LINE - Cable Tie - PANDUIT CORP.; *pg.* 661, *pg.* 663
IN-LINE - Diagnostic Test Product - QUIDEL CORPORATION; *pg.* 1588, *pg.* 207
IN-LINE - Circulator - TACO INCORPORATED; *pg.* 1077, *pg.* 1601
IN-LINE - Surge Protector - TII NETWORK TECHNOLOGIES, INC.; *pg.* 680, *pg.* 1157
IN LINE DOC SUPPORT - Computer Support Worktools - STEELCASE INC.; *pg.* 475, *pg.* 889
IN-N-OUT BURGER FOUNDATION - Foundation - IN-N-OUT BURGERS, INC.; *pg.* 1732, *pg.* 111
IN-OVATION - Dental Product - DENTSPLY INTERNATIONAL INC.; *pg.* 1522, *pg.* 1596
IN-PHASE - Software - SYNOPSYS, INC.; *pg.* 480, *pg.* 162
IN-PULSE - Fuel Injection System - WOODWARD, INC.; *pg.* 122, *pg.* 329
IN SERVICES - Wireline Solutions - SONUS NETWORKS INC.; *pg.* 1281, *pg.* 858
IN-SIGHT - Machine Vision System - COGNEX CORPORATION; *pg.* 1406, *pg.* 834
IN SIGHT IT MIGHT BE RIGHT - Tagline - BIGLARI HOLDINGS INC.; *pg.* 1015, *pg.* 1739
IN-SINK-ERATOR - Garbage Disposals & Trash Compactors - IN-SINK-ERATOR; *pg.* 57, *pg.* 1888
IN-SITU - Fluid Measurements - SCHLUMBERGER LIMITED; *pg.* 801, *pg.* 1714
IN-SPEC - Chemical Product - GFS CHEMICALS, INC.; *pg.* 1164, *pg.* 1471
IN-SPEC - Portable Tester - INSTRON CORPORATION; *pg.* 1349, *pg.* 839
IN STYLE - Magazine - IN STYLE MAGAZINE; *pg.* 1652, *pg.* 1243
IN-SURE - Push-In Connector - IDEAL INDUSTRIES, INC.; *pg.* 1051, *pg.* 662
IN-SYNC - Software - SYNOPSYS, INC.; *pg.* 480, *pg.* 162
IN-SYSTEM REPROGRAMMABLE - Software - CYPRESS SEMICONDUCTOR CORPORATION; *pg.* 1326, *pg.* 243
IN-TANDEM - Software - SYNOPSYS, INC.; *pg.* 480, *pg.* 162
IN THE CHIPS - Lottery Game - LOUISIANA LOTTERY CORPORATION; *pg.* 997, *pg.* 742
IN THE FACE OF PAIN - Online Advocacy Toolkit - PURDUE PHARMA LP; *pg.* 1587, *pg.* 377
IN THE LINE OF DUTY - Lottery Game - CALIFORNIA LOTTERY; *pg.* 990, *pg.* 196
IN THE MONEY - Lottery Game - KENTUCKY LOTTERY CORPORATION; *pg.* 996, *pg.* 735
IN THE SPIRIT - Publication - ESSENCE MAGAZINE; *pg.* 1639, *pg.* 1229
IN THE WIND - Magazine - PAISANO PUBLICATIONS, LLC; *pg.* 1674, *pg.* 38
IN THE ZONE - Portable Basketball Standards - LIFETIME PRODUCTS INC.; *pg.* 933, *pg.* 1751
IN VENT - Bicycle Accessories - SPECIALIZED BICYCLE COMPONENTS, INC.; *pg.* 1711, *pg.* 152
IN-VEST - Outerwear - SIMMS FISHING PRODUCTS CORP.; *pg.* 1845, *pg.* 1008
IN VITRO - Diagnostic Product - SURMODICS, INC.; *pg.* 1600, *pg.* 924
IN2IT - Software - BIO-RAD LABORATORIES, INC.; *pg.* 1504, *pg.* 101
INAHARA-PRUITT - Medical Device - LEMAITRE VASCULAR, INC.; *pg.* 1555, *pg.* 805
INAMED - Silicone Implants - ALLERGAN, INC.; *pg.* 1491, *pg.* 106
INAND - Flash Memory Card - SANDISK CORPORATION; *pg.* 465, *pg.* 147
INAV - Hardware Product - INTERPHASE CORPORATION; *pg.* 420, *pg.* 1732
INBAY - Automotive Lift Design - ROTARY LIFT; *pg.* 216, *pg.* 694
INBOX TO GO - Software - DATAVIZ, INC.; *pg.* 383, *pg.* 356
INBOX TO GO WIRELESS - Software - DATAVIZ, INC.; *pg.* 383, *pg.* 356
INCA - Signal Processing Computer Hardware & Software - TEXAS INSTRUMENTS INCORPORATED; *pg.* 679, *pg.* 1688
INCA KOLA - Soft Drink - THE COCA-COLA COMPANY; *pg.* 240, *pg.* 493
INCEILING - Speaker - TRIAD SPEAKERS, INC.; *pg.* 682, *pg.* 1507
INCENTIV - Footwear - STEVEN MADDEN, LTD.; *pg.* 1819, *pg.* 1176
INCENTIVE - Fabric - NEMSCHOFF, INC.; *pg.* 936, *pg.* 1890
INCENTIVE - Trade Publication - THE NIELSEN COMPANY B.V.; *pg.* 1671, *pg.* 1272
INCH NUTBUSTER - Plier - CHANNELLOCK, INC.; *pg.* 1044, *pg.* 1551
INCH WORM - Toy - THE OHIO ART COMPANY, INC.; *pg.* 965, *pg.* 1406
THE INCHWORM - Ride-ons - RADIO FLYER INC.; *pg.* 966, *pg.* 588
INCINERATOR - Master Station Software - AUTODESK INC.; *pg.* 356, *pg.* 257
INCINI-CONE - Burner - ECLIPSE INC.; *pg.* 1332, *pg.* 655
INCISIVE - Software - CADENCE DESIGN SYSTEMS, INC.; *pg.* 367, *pg.* 239
INCLINATOR - Elevator Drive System - INCLINATOR COMPANY OF AMERICA; *pg.* 88, *pg.* 1536
INCLINATOR VL - Vertical Wheelchair Lift - INCLINATOR COMPANY OF AMERICA; *pg.* 88, *pg.* 1536
INCLINETTE - Customized Stairway Lift - INCLINATOR COMPANY OF AMERICA; *pg.* 88, *pg.* 1536
INCLOSIA - Solution - THE DOW CHEMICAL COMPANY; *pg.* 1157, *pg.* 898
INCOBAR - Alloy Product - SPECIAL METALS CORPORATION; *pg.* 1377, *pg.* 1850
INCOGNITO - Perfume - COVER GIRL COSMETICS; *pg.* 506, *pg.* 772
INCOGNITO - Feminine Hygiene Products - FEMPRO CONSUMER PRODUCTS ULC.; *pg.* 1530, *pg.* 1950
INCOGNITO - Fabric - NEMSCHOFF, INC.; *pg.* 936, *pg.* 1890
INCOGNITO - Office Furniture - STEELCASE INC.; *pg.* 475, *pg.* 889
INCOLOY - Alloy Product - SPECIAL METALS CORPORATION; *pg.* 1377, *pg.* 1850
INCOLOY - Heater - WATLOW ELECTRIC MANUFACTURING COMPANY; *pg.* 1078, *pg.* 1004
INCOME/EXPENSE ANALYSIS - Publication - INSTITUTE OF REAL ESTATE MANAGEMENT; *pg.* 144, *pg.* 578
INCONCERT - Alliance Program - AMX CORPORATION; *pg.* 349, *pg.* 1735
INCONCERT - Computer Products - BROADCOM CORPORATION; *pg.* 364, *pg.* 108
INCONCERT - Computer Software - TIBCO SOFTWARE INC.; *pg.* 484, *pg.* 178
INCONEL - Knitted Mesh Product - ACS INDUSTRIES, INC.; *pg.* 1040, *pg.* 1602
INCONEL - Alloy Product - SPECIAL METALS CORPORATION; *pg.* 1377, *pg.* 1850
INCONEL - Heater - WATLOW ELECTRIC MANUFACTURING COMPANY; *pg.* 1078, *pg.* 1004
INCONEL 600 - Spring Wire - GIBBS WIRE & STEEL COMPANY, INC.; *pg.* 1048, *pg.* 371
INCONEL X750 - Spring Temper Wire - GIBBS WIRE & STEEL COMPANY, INC.; *pg.* 1048, *pg.* 371
INCONTACT - Telecommunications Products - INCONTACT, INC.; *pg.* 413, *pg.* 1752
INCONTEXT EDITING - Online Service - ADOBE SYSTEMS INCORPORATED; *pg.* 342, *pg.* 235
INCONTROL - Software System - IRON MOUNTAIN INCORPORATED; *pg.* 421, *pg.* 796
INCONTROLWARE - Conveyor Control System - INTELLIGRATED, INC.; *pg.* 1349, *pg.* 1460
INCOPY - Software - ADOBE SYSTEMS INCORPORATED; *pg.* 342, *pg.* 235
INCORNER - Speaker - TRIAD SPEAKERS, INC.; *pg.* 682, *pg.* 1507
INC. - Business Magazine - MANSUETO VENTURES LLC; *pg.* 1661, *pg.* 1256
INC.COM - Business Site - MANSUETO VENTURES LLC; *pg.* 1661, *pg.* 1256
INCOTHERM - Alloy Product - SPECIAL METALS CORPORATION; *pg.* 1377, *pg.* 1850
INCRALAC - Clearcoat for Bronze - STANCHEM, INC.; *pg.* 1449, *pg.* 345
INCREASE THE IMPACT. TRANSFORM THE EXPERIENCE. - Tagline - BLACKBOARD INC.; *pg.* 1232, *pg.* 396
INCREDIBALL - Safety Ball, Bat & Glove Line - EASTON SPORTS, INC.; *pg.* 1833, *pg.* 299
THE INCREDIBLE CLAY BOOK - Educational Materials - SCHOLASTIC INC.; *pg.* 1683, *pg.* 1288
THE INCREDIBLE EDIBLE EGG - Slogan - AMERICAN EGG BOARD; *pg.* 128, *pg.* 650
INCREDIBLE HULK - Toy & Game - HASBRO, INC.; *pg.* 954, *pg.* 1603
INCREDIBOW - Balloon - CONTINENTAL AMERICAN CORP.; *pg.* 1880, *pg.* 723
INCUTEMP - Temperature Probes - MEDTRONIC; *pg.* 1563, *pg.* 183
INCUTROL - Temperature Regulator - HACH COMPANY; *pg.* 1415, *pg.* 334
IND-X - Fire Suppression Systems - ANSUL, INCORPORATED; *pg.* 1147, *pg.* 1869
INDAG - Rubber - 3M COMPANY; *pg.* 1142, *pg.* 956
INDASH - Cellular Telephone Mount - PANAVISE PRODUCTS, INC.; *pg.* 1058, *pg.* 1032
INDE-PENDANTS - Lighting System - LITECONTROL CORPORATION; *pg.* 1301, *pg.* 841
INDEFLATOR - Inflating Device - ABBOTT LABORATORIES; *pg.* 1484, *pg.* 551
INDEFLATOR PLUS - Inflating Device - ABBOTT LABORATORIES; *pg.* 1484, *pg.* 551
INDENTRON - Hardness Tester - NEWAGE TESTING INSTRUMENTS, INC.; *pg.* 1058, *pg.* 1532
INDEPENDENCE - Healthcare Product - JOHNSON & JOHNSON; *pg.* 1549, *pg.* 1091
INDEPENDENCE HALL - Theme Park - KNOTT'S BERRY FARM; *pg.* 556, *pg.* 50
INDEPENDENCE SHANGLE - Shingle - CERTAINTEED CORPORATION; *pg.* 74, *pg.* 1589
INDEPENDENT - Weekly Publication - GREATER MEDIA NEWSPAPERS, INC.; *pg.* 1646, *pg.* 1071
THE INDEPENDENT LIVING - Long Term Insurance Care - PENN TREATY AMERICAN CORPORATION; *pg.* 793, *pg.* 1514
INDEPTH - Software - SYMANTEC CORPORATION; *pg.* 478, *pg.* 161
INDERA - Menswear - INDERA MILLS COMPANY; *pg.* 26, *pg.* 1396
INDERAL - Adrenergic Beta-Receptor Blocking Agent - PFIZER INC.; *pg.* 1581, *pg.* 1278
INDESIGN - Software - ADOBE SYSTEMS INCORPORATED; *pg.* 342, *pg.* 235
INDESIGN - Book Projects - CENVEO INC.; *pg.* 1626, *pg.* 372
INDEX - Interpolymers - THE DOW CHEMICAL COMPANY; *pg.* 1157, *pg.* 898
INDEX - Laser System - GSI GROUP INC.; *pg.* 1415, *pg.* 784
INDEX ALERT - Reference Tool - STANDARD & POOR'S RATINGS SERVICES; *pg.* 805, *pg.* 1296
INDEX ALERT-AUSTRALIA - Market Alerts - STANDARD & POOR'S RATINGS SERVICES; *pg.* 805, *pg.* 1296
INDGO - Medical Device - MALLINCKRODT PHARMACEUTICALS; *pg.* 1557, *pg.* 978

INDGO - Disposable Manual Resuscitator - MEDTRONIC; *pg.* 1563, *pg.* 183
INDIA PALE ALE - Beverage - CRAFT BREWERS ALLIANCE, INC; *pg.* 247, *pg.* 1502
INDIAN ARCHERY - Archery Equipment - ESCALADE INC.; *pg.* 1833, *pg.* 678
INDIAN BLANKET - Pillow - AMERICAN LEATHER LP; *pg.* 912, *pg.* 1673
INDIAN CORN - Soap - GRANDPA BRANDS COMPANY; *pg.* 1538, *pg.* 727
INDIAN FIRE TRAIL - Bike - MARIN BIKES; *pg.* 1708, *pg.* 168
INDIAN MUSK - Natural Spray - ANNIE OAKLEY ENTERPRISES, INC.; *pg.* 499, *pg.* 693
INDIAN PRINCESS - Container Grown Plant - MONROVIA GROWERS; *pg.* 1797, *pg.* 44
INDIANA GLASS - Glassware - LANCASTER COLONY CORPORATION; *pg.* 873, *pg.* 1441
INDIANA JONES - Toy & Game - HASBRO, INC.; *pg.* 954, *pg.* 1603
INDIANA JONES - Adventure Game - ZYNGA INC.; *pg.* 1292, *pg.* 235
INDIANA PACERS - Basketball Team - PACERS BASKETBALL, LLC; *pg.* 573, *pg.* 689
INDIANAPOLIS COLTS - Professional Football Team - INDIANAPOLIS COLTS, INC.; *pg.* 553, *pg.* 687
INDIASPAN - Data Library - ION GEOPHYSICAL CORPORATION; *pg.* 1350, *pg.* 1708
INDICARE - Internet Based Software Application - AMERISOURCEBERGEN CORPORATION; *pg.* 1493, *pg.* 1522
INDICATOR - Thermal - E.D. BULLARD COMPANY; *pg.* 1332, *pg.* 727
INDICATOR - Toothbrush - GILLETTE; *pg.* 1536, *pg.* 795
INDICATORPHIAL - Chemical Product - SPECTRUM CHEMICALS & LABORATORY PRODUCTS, INC.; *pg.* 1181, *pg.* 94
INDIGLO - Thermostat - HUNTER FAN COMPANY; *pg.* 57, *pg.* 1631
INDIGLO - Feature - TIMEX CORPORATION; *pg.* 14, *pg.* 355
INDIGO - Laser & Laser System - COHERENT, INC.; *pg.* 1406, *pg.* 265
INDIGO - Dinnerware - THE HOMER LAUGHLIN CHINA COMPANY; *pg.* 1125, *pg.* 1850
INDIGO - Healthcare Product - JOHNSON & JOHNSON; *pg.* 1549, *pg.* 1091
INDIGO CARMINE - Pharmaceutical Product - AKORN, INC.; *pg.* 1488, *pg.* 622
INDIGO HILLS - Champagne - E&J GALLO WINERY; *pg.* 1962, *pg.* 149
INDIGO PALMS - Label Apparel - OXFORD INDUSTRIES, INC.; *pg.* 30, *pg.* 517
INDIGO SWING - Video Slots - INTERNATIONAL GAME TECHNOLOGY; *pg.* 957, *pg.* 1024
INDIO - Color - FERRO CORPORATION; *pg.* 1162, *pg.* 1462
INDIO - Furniture - FLEXSTEEL INDUSTRIES, INC.; *pg.* 925, *pg.* 707
INDIUM - Fabric - NEMSCHOFF, INC.; *pg.* 936, *pg.* 1890
INDO - Food Products - MODERN PRODUCTS, INC.; *pg.* 1568, *pg.* 1871
INDO-NATURAL - Rug - COURISTAN INC.; *pg.* 921, *pg.* 1067
INDO-PERSIAN - Rugs - COURISTAN INC.; *pg.* 921, *pg.* 1067
INDOCOLLYRE - Anti-Inflammatory Solution - BAUSCH & LOMB INCORPORATED; *pg.* 1401, *pg.* 1045
INDONESIA.COM - Travel Website - LIVE CURRENT MEDIA INC.; *pg.* 1263, *pg.* 1911
INDOOR STYLE. OUTDOOR FURNITURE - Tagline - TROPITONE FURNITURE CO., INC.; *pg.* 945, *pg.* 118
INDOOR TRINECTOR - Extension Cord - COLEMAN CABLE, INC.; *pg.* 1324, *pg.* 665
INDOSTAR - Satellite - ORBITAL ATK; *pg.* 1425, *pg.* 1779
INDUC-E-COOL - Crawford Equipment - PLIBRICO CO. LLC; *pg.* 104, *pg.* 587
INDUCLOR - Calcium Hypochlorite Granules - PPG INDUSTRIES, INC.; *pg.* 1445, *pg.* 1579
INDUCT - Gas Analyzer - MKS INSTRUMENTS, INC.; *pg.* 1362, *pg.* 781
INDUCTO-POUR - Automatic Metal Pouring System for Foundries - INDUCTOTHERM CORP.; *pg.* 1348, *pg.* 1114
INDUFLEX - Laminate - ROGERS CORPORATION; *pg.* 1305, *pg.* 369
INDULIN - Chemical Product - WESTROCK COMPANY; *pg.* 1472, *pg.* 1805
INDUO - Blood Glucose Monitor & Insulin Delivery Device - LIFESCAN INC; *pg.* 1556, *pg.* 146
INDURA - Catheter for Drug Pump - MEDTRONIC, INC.; *pg.* 1564, *pg.* 939
INDURA - Film Laminate - SCHNELLER, INC.; *pg.* 234, *pg.* 1456
INDURA - Outerwear - UNIFIRST CORPORATION; *pg.* 50, *pg.* 860
INDUSTRAVAC - Vacuum Unit - THE SPENCER TURBINE CO.; *pg.* 1378, *pg.* 386
INDUSTRENE - Polymer Product - CHEMTURA CORPORATION; *pg.* 1152, *pg.* 355
INDUSTREX - Patterned Glass - AGC GLASS NORTH AMERICA, INC.; *pg.* 65, *pg.* 482
INDUSTREX - Film - EASTMAN KODAK COMPANY; *pg.* 1408, *pg.* 1333
INDUSTRIA AVICOLA - Latin American Poultry Magazine - WATT PUBLISHING COMPANY; *pg.* 1701, *pg.* 655
INDUSTRIAL - Paint & Coating - AERVOE INDUSTRIES INCORPORATED; *pg.* 1430, *pg.* 1021
INDUSTRIAL - Indoor/Outdoor Vacuums - SHOP-VAC CORPORATION; *pg.* 1375, *pg.* 1595
INDUSTRIAL COTTON - Apparel - G-III APPAREL GROUP, LTD.; *pg.* 41, *pg.* 1233
INDUSTRIAL INTERFACES - Electronic Components - MOLEX INCORPORATED; *pg.* 655, *pg.* 628
INDUSTRIAL MAINTENANCE & PLANT OPERATION - Trade Magazine - ADVANTAGE BUSINESS MEDIA; *pg.* 1613, *pg.* 1116
INDUSTRIAL PLUS - Engine Type - BRIGGS & STRATTON CORPORATION; *pg.* 201, *pg.* 1899
INDUSTRIAL-STRENGTH BUSINESS INTELLIGENCE - Software - MICROSTRATEGY, INC.; *pg.* 1266, *pg.* 1809
INDUSTRIAL STRENGTH SPAGHETTI SAUCE - Spaghetti Sauce - NEWMAN'S OWN, INC.; *pg.* 886, *pg.* 384
INDUSTRIAL VISION SOURCE - Security & Law Enforcement Products - MACE SECURITY INTERNATIONAL, INC.; *pg.* 1172, *pg.* 1541
INDUSTRIALNET - Copper Product - PANDUIT CORP.; *pg.* 661, *pg.* 663
INDUSTRIALTUFF - Industrial & Factory Floor Cables - BELDEN, INC.; *pg.* 624, *pg.* 993
INDUSTRY. ANSWERS. RESULTS. - Tag Line - THOMAS REGISTER OF AMERICAN MANUFACTURERS; *pg.* 1692, *pg.* 1299
INDUSTRY LEADING CUSTOMER FIRST - Slogan - PLANAR SYSTEMS, INC.; *pg.* 455, *pg.* 1495
THE INDUSTRY STANDARD - On Line Magazine Covering the Internet Economy - INTERNATIONAL DATA GROUP; *pg.* 1653, *pg.* 796
INDUSTRY SURVEYS (GLOBAL) - Reference Tool - STANDARD & POOR'S RATINGS SERVICES; *pg.* 805, *pg.* 1296
INDY - Office Furniture - STEELCASE INC.; *pg.* 475, *pg.* 889
INDY 500 - Long-Wear Soling Compound - THE GOODYEAR TIRE & RUBBER COMPANY; *pg.* 1883, *pg.* 1401
INDYSTAR - Heavy Duty Performance Laser - COHERENT, INC.; *pg.* 1406, *pg.* 265
INERGEN - Clean Extinguishing Agent - ANSUL, INCORPORATED; *pg.* 1147, *pg.* 1869
INERTOL - Bituminous Coating - PETTIT PAINT COMPANY; *pg.* 1444, *pg.* 1116
INERTRA - Containers - ENTEGRIS, INC.; *pg.* 1882, *pg.* 788
INEST - Real Estate Broker - IAC/INTERACTIVECORP; *pg.* 292, *pg.* 1242
INET - Patient Data Management Solution - CERNER CORPORATION; *pg.* 1514, *pg.* 981
INEXIA - Software System - MENTOR GRAPHICS CORPORATION; *pg.* 432, *pg.* 1510
INFAB - Foundation Isolation - FABREEKA INTERNATIONAL, INC.; *pg.* 1882, *pg.* 847
INFACT - Software System - MENTOR GRAPHICS CORPORATION; *pg.* 432, *pg.* 1510
INFANT TO TODDLER - Bath Tub - EVENFLO COMPANY, INC.; *pg.* 924, *pg.* 1470
INFANTOL - Pharmaceutical Product - CHURCH & DWIGHT CANADA CORP.; *pg.* 503, *pg.* 1925
INFECTION CONTROL TODAY - Publication - INFORMA EXHIBITIONS LLC; *pg.* 1653, *pg.* 17
INFED - Pharmaceutical Product - ALLERGAN; *pg.* 1490, *pg.* 1101
INFERGEN - Hepatitis C Treatment - AMGEN INC.; *pg.* 1493, *pg.* 291
INFERNO - On-Line Visual Effects System - AUTODESK INC.; *pg.* 356, *pg.* 257
INFERNO - Bowling Equipment - BRUNSWICK BOWLING & BILLIARDS CORP.; *pg.* 1828, *pg.* 622
INFERNO - IC Board - W.L. GORE & ASSOCIATES, INC.; *pg.* 122, *pg.* 388
INFIELDER - Groomer - SMITHCO, INC.; *pg.* 1377, *pg.* 1592
INFINEON RACEWAY - Entertainment Venue - SPEEDWAY MOTORSPORTS, INC.; *pg.* 584, *pg.* 1370
INFINET - Software - CRESTRON ELECTRONICS INC.; *pg.* 631, *pg.* 1116
INFINIBAND - Cables - SANMINA-SCI CORPORATION; *pg.* 671, *pg.* 250
INFINICOR - Fiber - CORNING CABLE SYSTEMS LLC; *pg.* 1407, *pg.* 1378
INFINICOR - Glass & Ceramic Material - CORNING INCORPORATED; *pg.* 1122, *pg.* 1154
INFINIFLEX - Software - EMC CORPORATION; *pg.* 391, *pg.* 825
INFINISTRUCTURE - Managed Storage - VERIZON TERREMARK; *pg.* 685, *pg.* 447
INFINIT - Software System - CHYRONHEGO; *pg.* 371, *pg.* 1179
INFINITA - Footwear - CAPEZIO BALLET MAKERS INC.; *pg.* 1805, *pg.* 1125
INFINITE HEALTH - Water - LEADING BRANDS, INC.; *pg.* 1026, *pg.* 1911
INFINITE RADIUS LOCK-IN - Fluid Handling System - GRACO, INC.; *pg.* 1342, *pg.* 935
INFINITE RIDER POSITIONING - Snowmobile - ARCTIC CAT INC.; *pg.* 1705, *pg.* 953
INFINITEYE - Binoculars - HABAND COMPANY, INC.; *pg.* 1772, *pg.* 1099
INFINITI - Hair Care Product - CONAIR CORPORATION; *pg.* 505, *pg.* 1055
INFINITI - Automobile - NISSAN NORTH AMERICA, INC.; *pg.* 186, *pg.* 1633
INFINITI CORD-KEEPER - Hair Dryer - CONAIR CORPORATION; *pg.* 505, *pg.* 1055
INFINITI NANO SILVER - Hair Dryer - CONAIR CORPORATION; *pg.* 505, *pg.* 1055
INFINITY - Air Conditioner - CARRIER CORPORATION; *pg.* 1070, *pg.* 349
INFINITY - Swimming Pools - DELAIR GROUP, LLC; *pg.* 78, *pg.* 1053
INFINITY - Hybrid Resin Ionomer Cement - DEN-MAT CORPORATION; *pg.* 1522, *pg.* 271
INFINITY - Chemical Coating - ENTHONE INC.; *pg.* 1161, *pg.* 381
INFINITY - Bimetallic Wear Product - ESCO CORPORATION; *pg.* 1335, *pg.* 1502
INFINITY - Plotter - GERBER SCIENTIFIC, INC.; *pg.* 1414, *pg.* 380
INFINITY - Recording & Storage Devices - GRASS VALLEY, INC.; *pg.* 641, *pg.* 164
INFINITY - Audio & Video Product - HARMAN INTERNATIONAL INDUSTRIES, INCORPORATED; *pg.* 641, *pg.* 374
INFINITY - Lighting Product - H.E. WILLIAMS, INC.; *pg.* 1299, *pg.* 974
INFINITY - Pulp Mill Technology - HERCULES INCORPORATED; *pg.* 1166, *pg.* 392
INFINITY - Contour - INVACARE CORPORATION; *pg.* 1546, *pg.* 1451
INFINITY - French Fries - J.R. SIMPLOT COMPANY; *pg.* 867, *pg.* 547
INFINITY - Spring Water - LEADING BRANDS, INC.; *pg.* 1026, *pg.* 1911
INFINITY - Cushion - MANNINGTON MILLS, INC.; *pg.* 934, *pg.* 1119
INFINITY - Gobo Animation Device - ROSCO LABORATORIES, INC.; *pg.* 1782, *pg.* 378
INFINITY - Elevator - SAVARIA CONCORD LIFTS INC.; *pg.* 1592, *pg.* 1919
INFINITY - Recreation Vehicle - THOR INDUSTRIES, INC.; *pg.* 1711, *pg.* 1456
INFINITY - Ink - VAN SON HOLLAND INK CORPORATION OF AMERICA; *pg.* 487, *pg.* 1169
INFINITY - Home & Garden Product - WESTROCK COMPANY; *pg.* 1472, *pg.* 1805
INFINITY ACHROVID - Microscope Objective - EDMUND INDUSTRIAL OPTICS INC.; *pg.* 1411, *pg.* 1041
INFINITY PROBE - Wafer Probing System - CASCADE MICROTECH, INC.; *pg.* 1405, *pg.* 1492
INFINITY SPC - Software Management - MCT WORLDWIDE LLC; *pg.* 653, *pg.* 939

First page reference indicates Business Class Edition
Second page reference indicates Geographic Edition

INFINITY SRE - Elevator - SAVARIA CONCORD LIFTS INC.; *pg.* 1592, *pg.* 1919
INFINITY ULTRA - Lighting Product - GERBER LEGENDARY BLADES; *pg.* 1834, *pg.* 1503
INFINIUM - Assay - ILLUMINA, INC.; *pg.* 412, *pg.* 203
INFLAMACTIN - Nutritional Supplement - NATURAL ORGANICS, INC.; *pg.* 1571, *pg.* 1181
INFLECTION - Fabric - NEMSCHOFF, INC.; *pg.* 936, *pg.* 1890
INFLEXION PLATFORM - Software System - MENTOR GRAPHICS CORPORATION; *pg.* 432, *pg.* 1510
INFLUENCE - Paper - INTERNATIONAL PAPER COMPANY; *pg.* 1460, *pg.* 1644
INFLUENCE - Fabric - NEMSCHOFF, INC.; *pg.* 936, *pg.* 1890
INFLUX - Molecular Probe Product - THERMO FISHER SCIENTIFIC INC.; *pg.* 1602, *pg.* 61
INFO EXPRESS - Trade Publication - THE NIELSEN COMPANY B.V.; *pg.* 1671, *pg.* 1272
INFO-LINK - Software Program for Computer Output Microfilmers - EASTMAN KODAK COMPANY; *pg.* 1408, *pg.* 1333
INFO-TEL - Product Information Service to Customers - EASTMAN KODAK COMPANY; *pg.* 1408, *pg.* 1333
INFOBASE - Enhancement Services - ACXIOM CORPORATION; *pg.* 342, *pg.* 33
INFOBASE-X - Data Product - ACXIOM CORPORATION; *pg.* 342, *pg.* 33
INFOBLEU - Information Services - THE DOW CHEMICAL COMPANY; *pg.* 1157, *pg.* 898
INFOCONNECT - Software - ATTACHMATE CORPORATION; *pg.* 356, *pg.* 1833
INFOCUS ENGINE - Technology - INFOCUS CORPORATION; *pg.* 644, *pg.* 1503
INFOLINK - Health Information - HOOPER HOLMES, INC.; *pg.* 1542, *pg.* 718
INFOMANAGER - Software - UNITED RENTALS, INC.; *pg.* 1386, *pg.* 350
INFOMARK - Printer - GERBER SCIENTIFIC, INC.; *pg.* 1414, *pg.* 380
INFOMEDIA - Digital Directory - ROVI CORPORATION; *pg.* 463, *pg.* 269
INFOMOVER - Software - EMC CORPORATION; *pg.* 391, *pg.* 825
INFONET - Electronic Message System - DAKTRONICS, INC.; *pg.* 633, *pg.* 1624
INFOQUEST - Software - BIO-RAD LABORATORIES, INC.; *pg.* 1504, *pg.* 101
INFOQUEST - Software - DST SYSTEMS, INC.; *pg.* 388, *pg.* 982
INFORM - Software System - MENTOR GRAPHICS CORPORATION; *pg.* 432, *pg.* 1510
INFORMANT - Gas Leak Detector - BACHARACH INC.; *pg.* 1400, *pg.* 1556
INFORMANT 2 - Refrigerant or Combustible Gas Leak Detector - BACHARACH INC.; *pg.* 1400, *pg.* 1556
INFORMATICA BUSINESS OPERATIONS ANALYTICS - Software - INFORMATICA CORPORATION; *pg.* 414, *pg.* 190
INFORMATICA CUSTOMER RELATIONSHIP ANALYTICS - Software - INFORMATICA CORPORATION; *pg.* 414, *pg.* 190
INFORMATICA DATA EXPLORER - Software - INFORMATICA CORPORATION; *pg.* 414, *pg.* 190
INFORMATICA DATA INTEGRATION PLATFORM - Software - INFORMATICA CORPORATION; *pg.* 414, *pg.* 190
INFORMATICA DATA QUALITY - Software - INFORMATICA CORPORATION; *pg.* 414, *pg.* 190
INFORMATICA FINANCIAL ANALYTICS - Software - INFORMATICA CORPORATION; *pg.* 414, *pg.* 190
INFORMATICA HUMAN RESOURCE ANALYTICS - Software - INFORMATICA CORPORATION; *pg.* 414, *pg.* 190
INFORMATICA IDENTITY SOLUTION - Software - INFORMATICA CORPORATION; *pg.* 414, *pg.* 190
INFORMATICA SUPERGLUE - Enterprise Metadata Management Software - INFORMATICA CORPORATION; *pg.* 414, *pg.* 190
INFORMATICA SUPPLY CHAIN ANALYTICS - Software - INFORMATICA CORPORATION; *pg.* 414, *pg.* 190
INFORMATICA WAREHOUSE - Software - INFORMATICA CORPORATION; *pg.* 414, *pg.* 190
INFORMATICA WEB CHANNEL ANALYTICS - Software - INFORMATICA CORPORATION; *pg.* 414, *pg.* 190
INFORMATION BUS - Computer Software - TIBCO SOFTWARE INC.; *pg.* 484, *pg.* 178
THE INFORMATION EDGE - Business Intelligence Software - BLACKBAUD, INC.; *pg.* 361, *pg.* 1613
INFORMATION FOUNDATION - Software - SYMANTEC CORPORATION; *pg.* 478, *pg.* 161
INFORMATION INTEGRITY - Software - INFOGIX INC.; *pg.* 414, *pg.* 636
INFORMATION INTEGRITY - Software - SYMANTEC CORPORATION; *pg.* 478, *pg.* 161
INFORMATION LIKE WATER - Software - MICROSTRATEGY, INC.; *pg.* 1266, *pg.* 1809
INFORMATION MADE EASY - Slogan - DATAWATCH CORPORATION; *pg.* 383, *pg.* 813
INFORMATION MANAGER - Software - SS&C TECHNOLOGIES HOLDINGS, INC.; *pg.* 473, *pg.* 386
INFORMATION PROTECTION & STORAGE - Tagline - IRON MOUNTAIN INCORPORATED; *pg.* 421, *pg.* 796
INFORMATION SERVER - Software - NETAPP, INC.; *pg.* 444, *pg.* 287
INFORMATIONAL INNOVATIONS - Educational Materials - SCHOLASTIC INC.; *pg.* 1683, *pg.* 1288
INFORMATIONWEEK - Magazine - UNITED BUSINESS MEDIA LLC; *pg.* 1697, *pg.* 1177
INFORMAX - Alarm Systems - NAPCO SECURITY SYSTEMS, INC.; *pg.* 658, *pg.* 1138
THE INFORMER - Service Indicator - DONALDSON COMPANY, INC.; *pg.* 1329, *pg.* 917
INFORMER - Fluid Meter - GRACO, INC.; *pg.* 1342, *pg.* 935
INFORM.INSPIRE.INVOLVE - Retirement Service - ERICKSON LIVING; *pg.* 1090, *pg.* 766
INFORUM - Technology Mart - AMC, INC.; *pg.* 1759, *pg.* 487
INFOSCAN - Syndication Market Research - IRI GROUP; *pg.* 421, *pg.* 579
INFOSCAPE - Software - EMC CORPORATION; *pg.* 391, *pg.* 825
INFOSCENT - Printer - XEROX CORPORATION; *pg.* 494, *pg.* 365
INFOSMART - Acconting Service - XCEL ENERGY INC.; *pg.* 1955, *pg.* 946
INFOSMART - Manual - XEROX CORPORATION; *pg.* 494, *pg.* 365
INFOSPACE MOBILE - Software - BLUCORA; *pg.* 1232, *pg.* 1813
INFOSPACE.COM - Website - BLUCORA; *pg.* 1232, *pg.* 1813
INFOSTEPP - Computer Software - COMPUTER SCIENCES CORPORATION; *pg.* 378, *pg.* 1780
INFOTAP - Software - SAS INSTITUTE INC.; *pg.* 466, *pg.* 1361
INFOVAULT - Software - SYMANTEC CORPORATION; *pg.* 478, *pg.* 161
INFOWALL - Electronic Display System - TRANS-LUX CORPORATION; *pg.* 681, *pg.* 365
INFOWEB - Secure Electronic Presentment Solution Products - ACTUATE CANADA; *pg.* 1225, *pg.* 1933
INFOWISE - Accounting Service - XCEL ENERGY INC.; *pg.* 1955, *pg.* 946
INFOWORKSPACE - Software - EZENIA! INC.; *pg.* 396, *pg.* 1039
INFOWORLD - Technology Magazine - INTERNATIONAL DATA GROUP; *pg.* 1653, *pg.* 796
INFRA - Software - EMC CORPORATION; *pg.* 391, *pg.* 825
INFRA-RED - Humidifiers - ADAMS MFG. CO.; *pg.* 51, *pg.* 1427
INFRADURA - Welding Lenses - UVEX SAFETY; *pg.* 1433, *pg.* 1608
INFRANOR - Lighting Fixture - HUBBELL INCORPORATED; *pg.* 1299, *pg.* 370
INFRAREADY OPTICS - Replacement Optics for Lasers - II-VI INCORPORATED; *pg.* 1417, *pg.* 1585
INFRASCAN - Software - BIO-RAD LABORATORIES, INC.; *pg.* 1504, *pg.* 101
INFRASHIELD - Computer Services - COMPUTER SCIENCES CORPORATION; *pg.* 378, *pg.* 1780
INFRASTRUCTURE INVESTMENT & POLICY REPORT - Publisher - BLOOMBERG BNA; *pg.* 1621, *pg.* 1772
INFRASTRUXURE - Software Tool - SCHNEIDER ELECTRIC; *pg.* 467, *pg.* 1609
INFRAVISION - Laparoscopy Imaging System - STRYKER CORPORATION; *pg.* 1598, *pg.* 894
INFUSABLE - Pressure Infusor - VITAL SIGNS, INC.; *pg.* 1607, *pg.* 1126
INFUSASCAN - Manual Pressure Infuser - VITAL SIGNS, INC.; *pg.* 1607, *pg.* 1126
INFUSE - Resins - THE DOW CHEMICAL COMPANY; *pg.* 1157, *pg.* 898
INFUSE - Bone Morphogenetic Protein Material - MEDTRONIC, INC.; *pg.* 1564, *pg.* 939
INFUSE-A-PORT - Electrosurgical Devices - ANGIODYNAMICS, INC.; *pg.* 1495, *pg.* 1173
INFUSION - Fabric - NEMSCHOFF, INC.; *pg.* 936, *pg.* 1890
INFUSION - Analyzer - TELEDYNE LECROY; *pg.* 1431, *pg.* 1153
INFUSION SERIES - Tea & Coffee Brewer - BUNN-O-MATIC CORPORATION; *pg.* 53, *pg.* 661
INFUSIONS - Ceilings & Walls - ARMSTRONG WORLD INDUSTRIES, INC.; *pg.* 914, *pg.* 1545
INFUSIUM 23 - Hair Care Products - HELEN OF TROY L.P.; *pg.* 511, *pg.* 1692
INFUSO.R - Syringe Pump - BAXTER INTERNATIONAL INC.; *pg.* 1499, *pg.* 599
INGAP HBT - Transistor Wafer - KOPIN CORPORATION; *pg.* 425, *pg.* 847
INGENIUS - Software - SKILLSOFT PLC; *pg.* 470, *pg.* 1037
INGENIUS - Sock - WIGWAM MILLS, INC.; *pg.* 15, *pg.* 1894
INGENIX - Health Data Management, Consulting & Pharmaceutical Development Services - UNITEDHEALTH GROUP INCORPORATED; *pg.* 1221, *pg.* 950
INGENUITY TAKES ENERGY - Slogan - THE WILLIAMS COMPANIES, INC.; *pg.* 987, *pg.* 1491
INGESTATION - Tape Digitalization System - GRASS VALLEY, INC.; *pg.* 641, *pg.* 164
INGLEBROOK - Furniture - ASHLEY FURNITURE INDUSTRIES, INC.; *pg.* 914, *pg.* 1852
INGLES - Grocery Stores - INGLES MARKETS, INCORPORATED; *pg.* 1023, *pg.* 1358
INGLES BEST - Grocery Products - INGLES MARKETS, INCORPORATED; *pg.* 1023, *pg.* 1358
INGLIS - Major Appliances - WHIRLPOOL CORPORATION; *pg.* 62, *pg.* 872
INGREDIENTS FOR LIFE. - Slogan - SAFEWAY INC.; *pg.* 1032, *pg.* 184
INGRID - Fabric - SCALAMANDRE, INC.; *pg.* 941, *pg.* 1058
INGRID - Women's Clothing & Accessories - WOODEN SHIPS OF HOBOKEN; *pg.* 35, *pg.* 1315
INHIBISOL OS - Cleaner - PENETONE CORPORATION; *pg.* 333, *pg.* 1050
INHIBITOR - Storage Product - PLANO MOLDING COMPANY; *pg.* 1887, *pg.* 652
INIKI - Messenger Bag - JANDD MOUNTAINEERING, INC.; *pg.* 1837, *pg.* 204
INION - Biomaterial - STRYKER CORPORATION; *pg.* 1598, *pg.* 894
INION CPS - Surgical Instruments - OSTEOMED CORPORATION; *pg.* 1425, *pg.* 1658
INISHKEA - Manual - XEROX CORPORATION; *pg.* 494, *pg.* 365
INITIALI - Initiator - FMC CORPORATION; *pg.* 1163, *pg.* 1564
INITIATOR - Clinical Trial Management System - PAREXEL INTERNATIONAL CORPORATION; *pg.* 1580, *pg.* 853
INJEC-TITE - Plastic Refractory - PLIBRICO CO. LLC; *pg.* 104, *pg.* 587
INJECTA COLOR - Colorant & Additive System - CHROMA CORPORATION; *pg.* 1441, *pg.* 632
INJECTAPAK - Adherence Packaging - WESTROCK COMPANY; *pg.* 1472, *pg.* 1805
INJECTO-FLO - Fluid Handling System - GRACO, INC.; *pg.* 1342, *pg.* 935
INJECTO-STIK - Animal Safety Product - NEOGEN CORPORATION; *pg.* 883, *pg.* 896
INK STICK CONFIGURATION(340/350/360-C) - Printer - XEROX CORPORATION; *pg.* 494, *pg.* 365
INK STICK CONFIGURATION(340/350/360-K - Printer - XEROX CORPORATION; *pg.* 494, *pg.* 365
INK STICK CONFIGURATION(340/350/360-M) - Printer - XEROX CORPORATION; *pg.* 494, *pg.* 365
INK STICK CONFIGURATION(340/350/360-Y) - Printer - XEROX CORPORATION; *pg.* 494, *pg.* 365
INK STICK DESIGN(340/350/360-C) - Printer - XEROX CORPORATION; *pg.* 494, *pg.* 365
INK STICK DESIGN(340/350/360-K) - Printer - XEROX CORPORATION; *pg.* 494, *pg.* 365
INK STICK DESIGN(340/350/360-M) - Printer - XEROX CORPORATION; *pg.* 494, *pg.* 365
INK STICK DESIGN(340/350/360-Y) - Printer - XEROX CORPORATION; *pg.* 494, *pg.* 365
INK STICK DESIGN(SWIFT-C) - Printer - XEROX CORPORATION; *pg.* 494, *pg.* 365
INKLINGS - Stickers - HIGHLIGHTS FOR CHILDREN, INC.; *pg.* 1650, *pg.* 1440

INKLOGIC - Manual - XEROX CORPORATION; *pg.* 494, *pg.* 365
INKOMETER - Graphic Testing Instrument - THWING-ALBERT INSTRUMENT COMPANY; *pg.* 1432, *pg.* 1131
INKO'S - Iced White Tea - INKO'S WHITE ICED TEA; *pg.* 1023, *pg.* 1243
INKPAK - Fiber Drums - SONOCO PRODUCTS COMPANY; *pg.* 1469, *pg.* 1619
INKSOURCE - Fluids & Supplies - VIDEOJET TECHNOLOGIES INC.; *pg.* 489, *pg.* 671
INKTANK - Pens & Markers - CRAYOLA LLC; *pg.* 951, *pg.* 1528
INKWELL - Application Program - APPLE INC.; *pg.* 350, *pg.* 73
INKWORKS - Hair Care Product - FORTIFIBER CORPORATION; *pg.* 83, *pg.* 1021
INKWORKS - Hair Care System - JOHN PAUL MITCHELL SYSTEMS; *pg.* 512, *pg.* 133
INLAB - Dental Equipment - SIRONA DENTAL SYSTEMS, INC.; *pg.* 1429, *pg.* 1175
INLAY - Fabric - NEMSCHOFF, INC.; *pg.* 936, *pg.* 1890
INLIGHT - Dosimetry Product - LANDAUER, INC.; *pg.* 1554, *pg.* 615
INLIGHTEN - Interior Light Shelf - KAWNEER COMPANY, INC.; *pg.* 90, *pg.* 537
INLIGHTEN - Window Screens - W.L. GORE & ASSOCIATES, INC.; *pg.* 122, *pg.* 388
INLIGNER - Hardware Product - BROOKS AUTOMATION, INC.; *pg.* 1320, *pg.* 813
INLINE EXPRESS - Vacuum Process Tool - BROOKS AUTOMATION, INC.; *pg.* 1320, *pg.* 813
INLINK - Control Module - LITTELFUSE, INC.; *pg.* 1301, *pg.* 580
INLINK - Wireless Telecommunication Product - SYNIVERSE HOLDINGS, INC.; *pg.* 479, *pg.* 475
INLYTA - Pharmaceutical Cancer Treatment Preparation - PFIZER INC.; *pg.* 1581, *pg.* 1278
INM - Inspection System - KLA-TENCOR CORPORATION; *pg.* 1353, *pg.* 146
INMARSAT - Satellite Communication Product - KVH INDUSTRIES INC; *pg.* 650, *pg.* 1602
INMOTION - Portable Audio System - ALTEC LANSING LLC; *pg.* 348, *pg.* 1553
INMOTION - Motion Control System - DANAHER CORPORATION; *pg.* 1044, *pg.* 397
INMUNEX - Nutritional Product - VICTUS, INC.; *pg.* 1606, *pg.* 447
INN MAID - Egg Noodles - LANCASTER COLONY CORPORATION; *pg.* 873, *pg.* 1441
INN MAID - Noodles - T. MARZETTI COMPANY; *pg.* 900, *pg.* 1444
INNDURA - Poly Product - SMEAD MANUFACTURING COMPANY; *pg.* 470, *pg.* 926
INNER CIRCLE - Membership Plan - BJ'S WHOLESALE CLUB, INC.; *pg.* 1762, *pg.* 857
INNER NUTRITION - Nutritional Supplement - HERBALIFE INTERNATIONAL OF AMERICA, INC.; *pg.* 1541, *pg.* 132
INNERACT - Bedding Product - HSM SOLUTIONS; *pg.* 1884, *pg.* 1378
INNERBODYWORKS - Educational Materials - SCHOLASTIC INC.; *pg.* 1683, *pg.* 1288
INNERCHANGE - Catheter - VASCULAR SOLUTIONS, INC.; *pg.* 1434, *pg.* 946
INNERCLEAN - Interior Clean - ZIEBART INTERNATIONAL CORPORATION; *pg.* 222, *pg.* 912
INNERGIZE - Nutritional Product - RELIV INTERNATIONAL, INC.; *pg.* 1589, *pg.* 975
INNERGUARD - Interior Detailing Plus Protection - ZIEBART INTERNATIONAL CORPORATION; *pg.* 222, *pg.* 912
INNERGY - Mattress - THERAPEDIC ASSOCIATES, INC.; *pg.* 945, *pg.* 1112
INNERLUBE - Fluid Sealing Product - A.W. CHESTERTON COMPANY; *pg.* 1315, *pg.* 861
INNERNET - Sport Product - FRANKLIN SPORTS, INC.; *pg.* 1834, *pg.* 847
INNERSPACE - Innerspace - STANLEY BLACK & DECKER, INC.; *pg.* 1063, *pg.* 358
INNERSTYLE - Vertical Blinds - HUNTER DOUGLAS, INC.; *pg.* 928, *pg.* 1320
INNERVAULT - Software - COMMVAULT SYSTEMS, INC.; *pg.* 377, *pg.* 1125
INNERVISION - Endoscope - MEDTRONIC, INC.; *pg.* 1564, *pg.* 939
INNISKILLIN - Wine - CONSTELLATION BRANDS CANADA; *pg.* 1960, *pg.* 1925
INNOCENCE - Shoes - SHOE CARNIVAL, INC.; *pg.* 1819, *pg.* 679
INNODATA - Consulting Services - INNODATA ISOGEN, INC.; *pg.* 1259, *pg.* 1072
INNOLAST - Composite Panel - NOVA CHEMICALS CORPORATION; *pg.* 1175, *pg.* 1904
INNORX - Sustained Release System - SURMODICS, INC.; *pg.* 1600, *pg.* 924
INNOTIDE - Tissue Protection Agent - AFFYMAX, INC.; *pg.* 1487, *pg.* 73
INNOVA - Laser & Laser System - COHERENT, INC.; *pg.* 1406, *pg.* 265
INNOVA - Food Flavorings - GRIFFITH LABORATORIES, INC.; *pg.* 860, *pg.* 552
INNOVACIONES - Educational Materials - SCHOLASTIC INC.; *pg.* 1683, *pg.* 1288
INNOVAIR - Duct Smoke Detector - SYSTEM SENSOR; *pg.* 676, *pg.* 658
INNOVATE PCB - Software System - MENTOR GRAPHICS CORPORATION; *pg.* 432, *pg.* 1510
INNOVATING FOR LIFE - Slogan - ROGERS COMMUNICATIONS INC.; *pg.* 668, *pg.* 1942
INNOVATING PROCESSING SOLUTIONS - Tagline - FARREL CORPORATION; *pg.* 1336, *pg.* 337
INNOVATING TEST TECHNOLOGIES - Slogan - CASCADE MICROTECH, INC.; *pg.* 1405, *pg.* 1492
INNOVATING WITH EXTREME - Slogan - EXTREME NETWORKS INC; *pg.* 287, *pg.* 245
INNOVATION CHANGES EVERYTHING - Manual - XEROX CORPORATION; *pg.* 494, *pg.* 365
INNOVATION DELIVERED - Slogan - DIEBOLD, INCORPORATED; *pg.* 387, *pg.* 1407
INNOVATION DELIVERED - Tagline - MAXIM INTEGRATED PRODUCTS, INC.; *pg.* 653, *pg.* 247
INNOVATION. EXPERIENCE. PERFORMANCE. - Slogan - CHART INDUSTRIES, INC.; *pg.* 1405, *pg.* 1454
INNOVATION FOR LIVING - Slogan - OWENS CORNING; *pg.* 102, *pg.* 1476
INNOVATION HUB OF THE AMERICAS - Slogan - ENTERPRISE FLORIDA, INC.; *pg.* 992, *pg.* 453
INNOVATION IN EVERY VALVE - Tagline - MILWAUKEE VALVE COMPANY, INC.; *pg.* 1361, *pg.* 1884
INNOVATION IN MINIATURE - Tag Line - THE LEE COMPANY; *pg.* 1420, *pg.* 383
INNOVATION IS PERSONAL - Tagline - ELI LILLY AND COMPANY; *pg.* 1527, *pg.* 684
INNOVATION. LEADERSHIP. VALUE DRIVEN. - Tagline - NER HOLDINGS INC.; *pg.* 444, *pg.* 1071
INNOVATION PUT TO THE TEST - Slogan - FORMFACTOR, INC.; *pg.* 1882, *pg.* 122
INNOVATION QUALITY CONVENIENCE - Tagline - LABORATORY CORPORATION OF AMERICA HOLDINGS; *pg.* 1554, *pg.* 1359
INNOVATION REDEFINED - Tagline - LEGGETT & PLATT, INCORPORATED; *pg.* 933, *pg.* 974
INNOVATION THROUGH TECHNOLOGY - Slogan - MICREL, INC.; *pg.* 654, *pg.* 247
INNOVATION TO GO - Slogan - SKYWORKS SOLUTIONS, INC.; *pg.* 674, *pg.* 862
INNOVATION YOU CAN COUNT ON - Slogan - ORBITAL ATK; *pg.* 1425, *pg.* 1779
INNOVATIONS - Lab Management Software - GERBER SCIENTIFIC, INC.; *pg.* 1414, *pg.* 380
INNOVATIONS EXPERIENCING LITERATURE - Educational Materials - SCHOLASTIC INC.; *pg.* 1683, *pg.* 1288
INNOVATIVE ACRYLIC SOLUTIONS - Tagline - PLASKOLITE, INC.; *pg.* 1888, *pg.* 1443
INNOVATIVE BRAKING AND CONTROLS WORLDWIDE - Tag Line - MICO, INCORPORATED; *pg.* 212, *pg.* 951
INNOVATIVE BULK RIBBON - Cheese - LEPRINO FOODS COMPANY; *pg.* 874, *pg.* 320
INNOVATIVE PRINTING AND CONVERTING SOLUTIONS - Slogan - TOPFLIGHT CORPORATION; *pg.* 681, *pg.* 1534
INNOVATIVE PYRAMID - Wafer Probing System - CASCADE MICROTECH, INC.; *pg.* 1405, *pg.* 1492
INNOVATIVE SOLUTIONS. - Tag Line - SPAN-AMERICA MEDICAL SYSTEMS, INC.; *pg.* 1595, *pg.* 1618
INNOVATIVE STEM CELL SOLUTIONS - Tagline - CRYO-CELL INTERNATIONAL, INC.; *pg.* 1520, *pg.* 452
INNOVATIVE TECHNOLOGY. TRUSTED PRODUCTIVITY. - Tag Line - LAM RESEARCH CORPORATION; *pg.* 1354, *pg.* 246
INNOVATIVE THERAPIES. NOVEL PRODUCTS - Tagline - VIVUS, INC.; *pg.* 1608, *pg.* 163
INNOVATIVE THERMAL SOLUTIONS WORLDWIDE - Tagline - ECLIPSE INC.; *pg.* 1332, *pg.* 655
INNOVATIVE WATER SOLUTIONS - Tagline - WATTS WATER TECHNOLOGIES, INC.; *pg.* 1078, *pg.* 837
INNOVATOR - Circuit Boards & Integrated Circuits - TEXAS INSTRUMENTS INCORPORATED; *pg.* 679, *pg.* 1688
INNOVAX ND-SB - Vaccine Against Newcastle Disease - MERCK & CO., INC.; *pg.* 1566, *pg.* 1077
INNOVEDA - Software System - MENTOR GRAPHICS CORPORATION; *pg.* 432, *pg.* 1510
INNOVENTIONS - Amusement Ride - THE WALT DISNEY COMPANY; *pg.* 317, *pg.* 52
INNOVOX - Conference Server - POLYCOM, INC.; *pg.* 664, *pg.* 249
INNOVX - Networking Quality - GENERAL DATACOMM INDUSTRIES, INC.; *pg.* 400, *pg.* 357
INNSBRUCK - Socks - WIGWAM MILLS, INC.; *pg.* 15, *pg.* 1894
INNSBRUCK BRONZE - Nail Care Product - OPI PRODUCTS INC.; *pg.* 518, *pg.* 167
INNSPECT BED BUG SERVICE - Awareness Program - ECOLAB INC.; *pg.* 329, *pg.* 960
INNSUITES - Hotels Operating in Arizona, New Mexico & Southern California - INNSUITES HOSPITALITY TRUST; *pg.* 1097, *pg.* 17
INNUENDO - Fabric - NEMSCHOFF, INC.; *pg.* 936, *pg.* 1890
INO - Baseball Caps - IN-N-OUT BURGERS, INC.; *pg.* 1732, *pg.* 111
INOVA - Automated Wafer Fabrication System - LAM RESEARCH CORPORATION; *pg.* 1354, *pg.* 246
INOVA SPORTSPLEX - Educational Service - INOVA HEALTH SYSTEM; *pg.* 1545, *pg.* 1781
INPACK - Wireless Telecommunication Product - SYNIVERSE HOLDINGS, INC.; *pg.* 479, *pg.* 475
INPLACE - Software - BIO-RAD LABORATORIES, INC.; *pg.* 1504, *pg.* 101
INPLANT GRAPHIC - Publisher - NORTH AMERICAN PUBLISHING COMPANY; *pg.* 1671, *pg.* 1567
INPLEX - Cystic Fibrosis Test - HOLOGIC, INC.; *pg.* 1416, *pg.* 784
INPOINT - Data Gathering & Management System - GE ENERGY; *pg.* 1338, *pg.* 506
INPORT - Wireless Telecommunication Product - SYNIVERSE HOLDINGS, INC.; *pg.* 479, *pg.* 475
INPOSITION - Wireless Telecommunication Product - SYNIVERSE HOLDINGS, INC.; *pg.* 479, *pg.* 475
INPOWER - PC-based Configuration Transfer Switches - CUMMINS POWER GENERATION; *pg.* 1326, *pg.* 932
INPUTACCEL - Software - EMC CORPORATION; *pg.* 391, *pg.* 825
INPUTACCEL EXPRESS - Software - EMC CORPORATION; *pg.* 391, *pg.* 825
INQUIRER & MIRROR - Newspaper - THE INQUIRER & MIRROR; *pg.* 1653, *pg.* 834
INQUIRY - Medical Device - BOSTON SCIENTIFIC CORPORATION; *pg.* 1508, *pg.* 831
INQUIRY - Diagnostic Catheter - ST. JUDE MEDICAL, INC.; *pg.* 1596, *pg.* 963
INQUIRY H-CURVE - Medical Device - BOSTON SCIENTIFIC CORPORATION; *pg.* 1508, *pg.* 831
INRAGEE - Footwear - STEVEN MADDEN, LTD.; *pg.* 1819, *pg.* 1176
INRAIL - Software - BENTLEY SYSTEMS, INC.; *pg.* 361, *pg.* 1531
INROADS - Software - BENTLEY SYSTEMS, INC.; *pg.* 361, *pg.* 1531
INROOM - Speaker - TRIAD SPEAKERS, INC.; *pg.* 682, *pg.* 1507
INS - Inspection System - KLA-TENCOR CORPORATION; *pg.* 1353, *pg.* 146
INSANELY DELICIOUS - Burgers - RED ROBIN GOURMET BURGERS, INC.; *pg.* 1747, *pg.* 331
INSCOSITY - Food Ingredient - GRAIN PROCESSING CORPORATION; *pg.* 859, *pg.* 709
INSCRYBE - Software - AUTHENTIDATE HOLDING CORP.; *pg.* 356, *pg.* 1044
INSECT-O-CUTOR - Insect Control Equip. - HARRIS HOLDINGS INC.; *pg.* 1345, *pg.* 541
INSECT-O-FOG - Insecticide - DELTA FOREMOST CHEMICAL CORPORATION; *pg.* 1155, *pg.* 1642
INSECT SHIELD - Trout Cap - THE ORVIS COMPANY, INC.; *pg.* 1781, *pg.* 1764
INSECTI-MIST - Insecticide - DELTA FOREMOST CHEMICAL CORPORATION; *pg.* 1155, *pg.* 1642
INSECTSELECT - Molecular Biology Product - THERMO FISHER SCIENTIFIC INC.; *pg.* 1602, *pg.* 61

First page reference indicates Business Class Edition
Second page reference indicates Geographic Edition

INSERTAVALVE - Valve Insertion - ROMAC INDUSTRIES, INC.; *pg.* 1061, *pg.* 1818
INSET - Infusion System - ANIMAS CORPORATION; *pg.* 1495, *pg.* 1593
INSHELL - Black Walnut - HAMMONS PRODUCTS COMPANY; *pg.* 1855, *pg.* 1007
THE INSIDE ADVANTAGE - Slogan - GREENE, TWEED & CO.; *pg.* 1344, *pg.* 1544
INSIDE BUSINESS - Magazine - INSIDE BUSINESS INC.; *pg.* 1653, *pg.* 1797
INSIDE BUSINESS MAGAZINE - Magazine - GREAT LAKES PUBLISHING COMPANY; *pg.* 1646, *pg.* 1431
INSIDE SELF-STORAGE - Publication - INFORMA EXHIBITIONS LLC; *pg.* 1653, *pg.* 17
INSIDE TRACK - Publication - MOTHERS AGAINST DRUNK DRIVING (MADD); *pg.* 147, *pg.* 1723
INSIDELINE - Computer Products - BROADCOM CORPORATION; *pg.* 364, *pg.* 108
INSIDEMETALS - Internet Website - ITRONICS INC.; *pg.* 1169, *pg.* 1031
INSIDER PAGES - Software - IDEALAB, INC.; *pg.* 1258, *pg.* 180
INSIDERPAGES - Online Services - IAC/INTERACTIVECORP; *pg.* 292, *pg.* 1242
INSIDER'S GUIDE - Travel Books - THE GLOBE PEQUOT PRESS, INC.; *pg.* 1645, *pg.* 350
INSIGHT - Film - EASTMAN KODAK COMPANY; *pg.* 1408, *pg.* 1333
INSIGHT - Power Control Solutions - EATON CORPORATION; *pg.* 1331, *pg.* 1429
INSIGHT - Biotechnology Product - GENZYME CORPORATION; *pg.* 1534, *pg.* 808
INSIGHT - Animal Safety Product - NEOGEN CORPORATION; *pg.* 883, *pg.* 896
INSIGHT - Software - SAS INSTITUTE INC.; *pg.* 466, *pg.* 1361
INSIGHT - Network Management System - SONUS NETWORKS INC.; *pg.* 1281, *pg.* 858
INSIGHT - Film - SPINNAKER COATING, LLC; *pg.* 1470, *pg.* 1477
INSIGHT - Software - STRATASYS, INC.; *pg.* 476, *pg.* 923
INSIGHT - Visual Packaging - WESTROCK COMPANY; *pg.* 1472, *pg.* 1805
INSIGHT 3G - Data Management Software - TSI INCORPORATED; *pg.* 1432, *pg.* 965
INSIGHT IS EVERYTHING - Software - MICROSTRATEGY, INC.; *pg.* 1266, *pg.* 1809
INSIGHT NETWORKS - Online Community Solution - METRIXLAB; *pg.* 1266, *pg.* 223
INSIGHT ONSITE - Customer Solution - HARSCO CORPORATION; *pg.* 86, *pg.* 1519
INSIGHT SLIDER - Visual Packaging - WESTROCK COMPANY; *pg.* 1472, *pg.* 1805
INSIGHT TECH - Golf Product - TAYLORMADE-ADIDAS GOLF; *pg.* 1847, *pg.* 60
INSIGHT XTD - Golf Product - TAYLORMADE-ADIDAS GOLF; *pg.* 1847, *pg.* 60
INSIGHT360 - Software - OPENTEXT; *pg.* 450, *pg.* 1665
INSIGNIA - Converters - BEST BUY CO., INC.; *pg.* 1761, *pg.* 954
INSIGNIA - Fabric - NEMSCHOFF, INC.; *pg.* 936, *pg.* 1890
INSIST ON CYMER - Laser - CYMER, INC.; *pg.* 1296, *pg.* 202
INSITE - Embedded Resistor - DOW CHEMICAL; *pg.* 1156, *pg.* 1563
INSITE - Catalyst - THE DOW CHEMICAL COMPANY; *pg.* 1157, *pg.* 898
INSITE - Surgical System - INTUITIVE SURGICAL, INC.; *pg.* 1546, *pg.* 286
INSITE - Wireless System - PCTEL, INC.; *pg.* 452, *pg.* 557
INSITE - Tracking System - PITNEY BOWES INC.; *pg.* 454, *pg.* 376
INSITUFORM - Cured in Place Pipe - INSITUFORM TECHNOLOGIES INC; *pg.* 88, *pg.* 974
INSITUFORM BLUE - Pipeline Repair - INSITUFORM TECHNOLOGIES INC; *pg.* 88, *pg.* 974
INSITUFORM CIPP - Sanitary Sewer - INSITUFORM TECHNOLOGIES INC; *pg.* 88, *pg.* 974
INSITUFORM CP - Fiber Composite - INSITUFORM TECHNOLOGIES INC; *pg.* 88, *pg.* 974
INSITUFORM PPL - Pressure Pipe - INSITUFORM TECHNOLOGIES INC; *pg.* 88, *pg.* 974
INSITUGUARD - Pressure Pipe System - INSITUFORM TECHNOLOGIES INC; *pg.* 88, *pg.* 974
INSITUMAIN - Pipe - INSITUFORM TECHNOLOGIES INC; *pg.* 88, *pg.* 974
INSL-WALL - Building Product - LESTER BUILDING SYSTEMS, LLC; *pg.* 93, *pg.* 927
INSOCAP - IV & Infusion Cap - WEST PHARMACEUTICAL SERVICES, INC.; *pg.* 1472, *pg.* 1532
INSOL-U-25 - Agricultural Urea Formaldehyde Concentrate - GEORGIA-PACIFIC LLC; *pg.* 1458, *pg.* 507
INSOLASE - Food Enzyme Product - NATIONAL ENZYME COMPANY; *pg.* 882, *pg.* 978
INSOURCE - Software - THOMSON REUTERS TAX & ACCOUNTING; *pg.* 1693, *pg.* 1299
INSPECK - Molecular Probe Product - THERMO FISHER SCIENTIFIC INC.; *pg.* 1602, *pg.* 61
INSPECT - Electron Microscope - FEI COMPANY; *pg.* 1413, *pg.* 1498
INSPECTION - Software - AMERICAN SCIENCE AND ENGINEERING, INC.; *pg.* 1399, *pg.* 787
INSPECTOR - Magnifiers - PROPHOTONIX LIMITED; *pg.* 1427, *pg.* 1039
INSPECTRA - Tissue Spectrometer - HUTCHINSON TECHNOLOGY INC.; *pg.* 409, *pg.* 926
INSPEED - Storage & Server OEMs - EMULEX CORPORATION; *pg.* 392, *pg.* 70
INSPIRATION - Shoe - AEROGROUP INTERNATIONAL, INC.; *pg.* 1803, *pg.* 1055
INSPIRATION - Educational Software Tools for 6-12th Grade Students - INSPIRATION SOFTWARE, INC.; *pg.* 1653, *pg.* 1503
INSPIRATIONAL GIFT TRENDS - Magazine - CHARISMA MEDIA; *pg.* 1627, *pg.* 436
INSPIRATIONAL ORCHARD - Wall Decor - ETHAN ALLEN INTERIORS INC.; *pg.* 924, *pg.* 343
INSPIRATIONS - Skincare Product - MERLE NORMAN COSMETICS, INC.; *pg.* 517, *pg.* 136
INSPIRATIONS - Bathroom Products - MOEN INCORPORATED; *pg.* 1056, *pg.* 1468
INSPIRE - Resin - THE DOW CHEMICAL COMPANY; *pg.* 1157, *pg.* 898
INSPIRED LEARNING COMMUNITY - Online Community - INSPIRATION SOFTWARE, INC.; *pg.* 1653, *pg.* 1503
INSPIRED SOLUTIONS FOR TEACHING & LEARNING - Slogan - EDMENTUM, INC.; *pg.* 390, *pg.* 917
INSPIREDATA - Software - INSPIRATION SOFTWARE, INC.; *pg.* 1653, *pg.* 1503
INSPIRING PEOPLE, ENRICHING LIVES - Slogan - DJO SURGICAL; *pg.* 1525, *pg.* 1661
INSPIRING PEOPLE TO GREATER PERFORMANCE - Tagline - MARKETING INNOVATORS INTERNATIONAL, INC.; *pg.* 430, *pg.* 657
INSPIRING PROGRESS - Slogan - INGERSOLL-RAND COMPANY; *pg.* 1349, *pg.* 1370
INSPIRITU - Perfume - AVEDA CORPORATION; *pg.* 499, *pg.* 917
INSPIRON - Notebook Computers - DELL INC.; *pg.* 383, *pg.* 1737
INSPRA - Medicine - PFIZER INC.; *pg.* 1581, *pg.* 1278
INSRKIT - Semiconductor Solution - CYPRESS SEMICONDUCTOR CORPORATION; *pg.* 1326, *pg.* 243
INSTA-BIN - Trash Containers - WASTE MANAGEMENT, INC.; *pg.* 1954, *pg.* 1716
INSTA-BLEND - Motorized blender - LINCOLN FOODSERVICE PRODUCTS, LLC; *pg.* 1127, *pg.* 1432
INSTA-BLOOM - Specialty cutters - LINCOLN FOODSERVICE PRODUCTS, LLC; *pg.* 1127, *pg.* 1432
INSTA DELIVERY - Internet Service - MIRROR IMAGE INTERNET, INC.; *pg.* 1267, *pg.* 848
INSTA FLO - Spray Gun - THE DOW CHEMICAL COMPANY; *pg.* 1157, *pg.* 898
INSTA GLUCOSE - Healthcare Product - MEDICOOL, INC.; *pg.* 1562, *pg.* 294
INSTA-GRIP - Adhesive - THE DOW CHEMICAL COMPANY; *pg.* 1157, *pg.* 898
INSTA-JECT - Injector - MEDICOOL, INC.; *pg.* 1562, *pg.* 294
INSTA-MATCH - Utility Lighter - DURAFLAME, INC.; *pg.* 1123, *pg.* 280
INSTA-PUMP - Footwear - REEBOK INTERNATIONAL LTD.; *pg.* 1817, *pg.* 811
INSTA SEAL - Polyurethane Foam Sealant - THE DOW CHEMICAL COMPANY; *pg.* 1157, *pg.* 898
INSTA-SLICE - Specialty cutters - LINCOLN FOODSERVICE PRODUCTS, LLC; *pg.* 1127, *pg.* 1432
INSTA-STIK - Roof Insulation Adhesive - THE DOW CHEMICAL COMPANY; *pg.* 1157, *pg.* 898
INSTACLEAN - Filter System - GRACO, INC.; *pg.* 1342, *pg.* 935
INSTACOUNT - Instrument Inventory Management System - AESCULAP, INC.; *pg.* 1487, *pg.* 1521
INSTACURE - Polymer Coating - TENNANT COMPANY; *pg.* 1381, *pg.* 944
INSTAFAX - Photographic Processing Chemicals - EASTMAN KODAK COMPANY; *pg.* 1408, *pg.* 1333
INSTAFILL - Packaging Foam - SEALED AIR CORPORATION; *pg.* 1468, *pg.* 1058
INSTAFLEX - Packaging Foam - SEALED AIR CORPORATION; *pg.* 1468, *pg.* 1058
INSTAGENE - Clinical Diagnostic Product - BIO-RAD LABORATORIES, INC.; *pg.* 1504, *pg.* 101
INSTAGRAM - Photo Sharing Service - FACEBOOK, INC.; *pg.* 1245, *pg.* 143
INSTAGRAPHIC - Film & Video Imaging Accessories - EASTMAN KODAK COMPANY; *pg.* 1408, *pg.* 1333
INSTALERT - Portable Message Sign - INTERNATIONAL ROAD DYNAMICS INC.; *pg.* 1912, *pg.* 1962
INSTALERT RAPID MESSENGER - Portable Message Sign - INTERNATIONAL ROAD DYNAMICS INC.; *pg.* 1912, *pg.* 1962
INSTALLATION MASTERS - Window & Door Installer Training Program - AMERICAN ARCHITECTURAL MANUFACTURERS ASSOCIATION; *pg.* 126, *pg.* 658
INSTALLEDGE.COM - Car Audio System - ROCKFORD CORPORATION; *pg.* 667, *pg.* 26
INSTALLER-PAK - Oil Drain Plugs - DORMAN PRODUCTS, INC.; *pg.* 204, *pg.* 1522
INSTALLERMAKER - Software - SMITH MICRO SOFTWARE, INC.; *pg.* 471, *pg.* 41
INSTALLSCAPE - Software - CADENCE DESIGN SYSTEMS, INC.; *pg.* 367, *pg.* 239
INSTALLSHIELD - Software - FLEXERA SOFTWARE INC.; *pg.* 398, *pg.* 658
INSTALOAD - Automatic Paperloading Device - TRANSACT TECHNOLOGIES INCORPORATED; *pg.* 484, *pg.* 351
INSTALOC - Ceiling Fan - WESTINGHOUSE LIGHTING CORPORATION; *pg.* 687, *pg.* 1571
INSTAMATE - Packaging Films - SEALED AIR CORPORATION; *pg.* 1468, *pg.* 1058
INSTAMATIC - Bed Frame - LEGGETT & PLATT, INCORPORATED; *pg.* 933, *pg.* 974
INSTAMOLDER - Automated Cushion-Molding System - SEALED AIR CORPORATION; *pg.* 1468, *pg.* 1058
INSTANT - Software - BIO-RAD LABORATORIES, INC.; *pg.* 1504, *pg.* 101
INSTANT - Fabric - NEMSCHOFF, INC.; *pg.* 936, *pg.* 1890
INSTANT ACCUGEL - High Performance, Cold Water Swelling, Modified Dent Cornstarches - CARGILL LIMITED; *pg.* 1475, *pg.* 1914
INSTANT ACTION - Online Services - IAC/INTERACTIVECORP; *pg.* 292, *pg.* 1242
INSTANT ACTIVATION - Pharmaceutical Product - PROGRESSIVE MEDICAL, INC.; *pg.* 1586, *pg.* 1480
INSTANT BED - Vehicle Seating - FLEXSTEEL INDUSTRIES, INC.; *pg.* 925, *pg.* 707
INSTANT BRONZE - Skin Care Product - NEUTROGENA CORPORATION; *pg.* 517, *pg.* 137
INSTANT COPY - Quick Printing Services - ALLEGRA NETWORK LLC; *pg.* 1614, *pg.* 904
INSTANT DESIGNER - Software - POLYCOM, INC.; *pg.* 664, *pg.* 249
INSTANT INCUBATION - Software - BIO-RAD LABORATORIES, INC.; *pg.* 1504, *pg.* 101
INSTANT INSANITY - Game - WINNING MOVES GAMES, INC.; *pg.* 970, *pg.* 816
INSTANT KENO - Lottery Game - OHIO LOTTERY COMMISSION; *pg.* 1002, *pg.* 1433
INSTANT LEGACY - Universal Life Insurance Policy - NEW YORK LIFE INSURANCE COMPANY; *pg.* 1211, *pg.* 1268
INSTANT MOISTURE - Hair Care Product - JOHN PAUL MITCHELL SYSTEMS; *pg.* 512, *pg.* 133
INSTANT MONOPOLY - Lottery Game - OHIO LOTTERY COMMISSION; *pg.* 1002, *pg.* 1433
INSTANT OFFICE - Telephony System - VERTICAL COMMUNICATIONS, INC.; *pg.* 488, *pg.* 270
INSTANT PAYDAY - Lottery Game - OHIO LOTTERY COMMISSION; *pg.* 1002, *pg.* 1433
INSTANT PURE-COAT - Pharmaceutical Ingredient - GRAIN PROCESSING CORPORATION; *pg.* 859, *pg.* 709
INSTANT REPLAY - Binocular - BUSHNELL OUTDOOR PRODUCTS, INC.; *pg.* 1403, *pg.* 718
INSTANT SHAPE UP - Diet Management Program - DIET CENTER WORLDWIDE, INC.; *pg.* 1524, *pg.* 1400
INSTANT TICKETS - Lottery Game - IOWA LOTTERY; *pg.*

996, *pg.* 705
INSTANT USB - Integrated Circuits - AVAGO TECHNOLOGIES; *pg.* 358, *pg.* 238
INSTANT VERTEBRAL ASSESSMENT - Medical Test System - HOLOGIC, INC.; *pg.* 1416, *pg.* 784
INSTANT VIDEO EVERYWHERE - Video Communication System - GLOWPOINT, INC.; *pg.* 401, *pg.* 1094
INSTANT WINNER - Game - WMS INDUSTRIES INC.; *pg.* 593, *pg.* 666
INSTANT WINNER & DESIGN - Game - WMS INDUSTRIES INC.; *pg.* 593, *pg.* 666
INSTANT X-RAY - Investment Portfolio Analysis Application - MORNINGSTAR, INC.; *pg.* 784, *pg.* 583
INSTANTCOLOR - Color Stains - FERRO CORPORATION; *pg.* 1162, *pg.* 1462
INSTANTQC - Software - BIO-RAD LABORATORIES, INC.; *pg.* 1504, *pg.* 101
INSTANTRON - Epilator Accessories - INSTANTRON CO., INC.; *pg.* 512, *pg.* 1608
INSTAPACKER - Packaging Film - SEALED AIR CORPORATION; *pg.* 1468, *pg.* 1058
INSTAPAD - Air Cellular Packaging Materials - SEALED AIR CORPORATION; *pg.* 1468, *pg.* 1058
INSTAPAK - Packaging Product - SEALED AIR CORPORATION; *pg.* 1468, *pg.* 1058
INSTAPAK QUICK - Foam-in-Pace Packaging Foam & Systems - SEALED AIR CORPORATION; *pg.* 1468, *pg.* 1058
INSTAPRICE - Calculator - PRINTINGFORLESS.COM, INC.; *pg.* 456, *pg.* 1009
INSTASHADES - Ophthalmic Lenses - SIGNET ARMORLITE, INC.; *pg.* 1429, *pg.* 60
INSTASHEETER - High Speed Converting System - SEALED AIR CORPORATION; *pg.* 1468, *pg.* 1058
INSTASLITTER - Roll Material Slitter - SEALED AIR CORPORATION; *pg.* 1468, *pg.* 1058
INSTASPEC - Spectroscopy Instrument - NEWPORT CORPORATION; *pg.* 1424, *pg.* 114
INSTATECH - Camera - EASTMAN KODAK COMPANY; *pg.* 1408, *pg.* 1333
INSTATRACE - Medical Equipment - CONMED CORPORATION; *pg.* 1517, *pg.* 1347
INSTEEMATIC - Cleaning Solution - CLAYTON INDUSTRIES CO.; *pg.* 1323, *pg.* 66
INSTEP - Polymer Enhancers - THE DOW CHEMICAL COMPANY; *pg.* 1157, *pg.* 898
INSTEX - Plastic & Rubber - TEKNOR APEX COMPANY; *pg.* 1889, *pg.* 1605
INSTILL - Vacuum Insulation Core - THE DOW CHEMICAL COMPANY; *pg.* 1157, *pg.* 898
INSTINCT - Beauty Product - AVON PRODUCTS, INC.; *pg.* 500, *pg.* 1198
INSTINT - Synthetic Resins - ASHLAND INC.; *pg.* 972, *pg.* 726
INSTRACRYL - Acrylamide Gel - EASTMAN KODAK COMPANY; *pg.* 1408, *pg.* 1333
INSTRON - Hardness Tester - NEWAGE TESTING INSTRUMENTS, INC.; *pg.* 1058, *pg.* 1532
INSTRUCALC - Software - GULF PUBLISHING COMPANY; *pg.* 1646, *pg.* 1707
INSTRUCTIONAL FAIR - Educational Resources - SCHOOL SPECIALTY, INC.; *pg.* 467, *pg.* 1860
INSTRUCTOR - Collaboration Appliance - POLYCOM, INC.; *pg.* 664, *pg.* 249
INSTRUCTOR - Magazine - SCHOLASTIC INC.; *pg.* 1683, *pg.* 1288
INSTRUCTOR'S GUIDE - Textbook - ACADEMIC INNOVATIONS; *pg.* 1613, *pg.* 262
INSTRUMENTS - Developer Software - APPLE INC.; *pg.* 350, *pg.* 73
INSTY-PRINTS - Quick Printing Services - ALLEGRA NETWORK LLC; *pg.* 1614, *pg.* 904
INSTYLE - Media Publication - TIME INC.; *pg.* 1693, *pg.* 1300
INSUL 250 - Premium Roll Covers - VAIL RUBBER WORKS, INC.; *pg.* 1891, *pg.* 906
INSUL-AID - Vapor Barrier Paint - AKZONOBEL DECORATIVE PAINTS U.S.; *pg.* 1439, *pg.* 1474
INSUL-BLAZE - Paint - AKZONOBEL DECORATIVE PAINTS U.S.; *pg.* 1439, *pg.* 1474
INSUL-DRI - Hot Melt Matrix - H.B. FULLER COMPANY; *pg.* 1165, *pg.* 961
INSUL-DRYER - Dehydration System - GE ENERGY; *pg.* 1338, *pg.* 506
INSUL-GUIDE - Healthcare Product - MEDICOOL, INC.; *pg.* 1562, *pg.* 294
INSUL-PLUS - Pellet System - ALADDIN TEMP-RITE, LLC; *pg.* 1013, *pg.* 1635
INSUL-QUICK - Glass Fiber Insulation - OWENS CORNING; *pg.* 102, *pg.* 1476
INSUL-RITE - Sectional Dock Door - RITE-HITE HOLDING CORPORATION; *pg.* 1372, *pg.* 1880
INSUL-SAFE - Fiberglass Insulation For Blown-In Application - CERTAINTEED CORPORATION; *pg.* 74, *pg.* 1589
INSUL SAFE III - Fiberglass Insulation - CERTAINTEED CORPORATION; *pg.* 74, *pg.* 1589
INSUL-TACKS - Fastener - GRIPNAIL CORPORATION; *pg.* 1048, *pg.* 1601
INSULATOR - Apparel - LACROSSE FOOTWEAR, INC.; *pg.* 1811, *pg.* 1503
INSULATOR - Dock Sealing System - RITE-HITE HOLDING CORPORATION; *pg.* 1372, *pg.* 1880
INSULATOR SPORT - Flashlight - ENERGIZER HOLDINGS, INC.; *pg.* 637, *pg.* 996
INSULCLAD - Door System - ALCOA INC.; *pg.* 65, *pg.* 1188
INSULCLAD - Thermal Entrances - KAWNEER COMPANY, INC.; *pg.* 90, *pg.* 537
INSULEDGE - Multiple Glazing Window Units - PPG INDUSTRIES, INC.; *pg.* 1445, *pg.* 1579
INSULFAB - Ventilation Ducting - FLEXFAB HORIZONS INTERNATIONAL, LLC; *pg.* 1072, *pg.* 891
INSULFRAX - Thermal Insulation Products - UNIFRAX CORPORATION; *pg.* 220, *pg.* 1317
INSULIN PROTECTOR - Carrying Case - MEDICOOL, INC.; *pg.* 1562, *pg.* 294
INSULKRIMP - Electronic Components - MOLEX INCORPORATED; *pg.* 655, *pg.* 628
INSULPINK - Insulating System - OWENS CORNING; *pg.* 102, *pg.* 1476
THE INSURANCE INFORMATION SOURCE - Tagline - A.M. BEST COMPANY; *pg.* 1614, *pg.* 1101
THE INSURANCE MARKETPLACE - Magazine - THE ROUGH NOTES COMPANY, INC.; *pg.* 1681, *pg.* 675
INSURANCE POLICY DATABASE - Software System - MAJESCO; *pg.* 429, *pg.* 1089
INSURANCE THAT STARTS WITH YOU - Slogan - UTICA MUTUAL INSURANCE COMPANY; *pg.* 1222, *pg.* 1183
INSURE - Nutritional Product - NUTRACEUTICAL INTERNATIONAL CORPORATION; *pg.* 1576, *pg.* 1753
INSURED MAIL - Postal Services - UNITED STATES POSTAL SERVICE; *pg.* 1009, *pg.* 406
INSYNC - Software - DELL SOFTWARE; *pg.* 385, *pg.* 40
INSYNC - Biventricular Stimulator - MEDTRONIC, INC.; *pg.* 1564, *pg.* 939
INSYNC.ICD - Biventricular Pacemaker Defibrillators - MEDTRONIC, INC.; *pg.* 1564, *pg.* 939
INSYTE-A - Arterial Catheter with Vialon - BECTON, DICKINSON & COMPANY; *pg.* 1501, *pg.* 1068
INSYTE-W - Intravenous Catheter Placement Unit with Vialon - BECTON, DICKINSON & COMPANY; *pg.* 1501, *pg.* 1068
INT64Y8W128M8L-A15LTU - Storage System - HGST; *pg.* 406, *pg.* 260
INT64Y8W256M8L-A15LTU - Storage System - HGST; *pg.* 406, *pg.* 260
INTACT - Packaging Films & Equipment - SEALED AIR CORPORATION; *pg.* 1468, *pg.* 1058
INTACTIX - Software - JDA SOFTWARE GROUP, INC.; *pg.* 423, *pg.* 22
INTACTIX KNOWLEDGE BASE - Software - JDA SOFTWARE GROUP, INC.; *pg.* 423, *pg.* 22
INTAGLIO - Fabric - MOMENTUM TEXTILES INC.; *pg.* 697, *pg.* 114
INTAK - Beverage Bottle - THERMOS L.L.C.; *pg.* 61, *pg.* 660
INTAL - Pharmaceutical Product - KING PHARMACEUTICALS, INC.; *pg.* 1553, *pg.* 1627
INTARSIO ROMANO - Ceramic, Glass, Stone Tiles & Slabs - WALKER & ZANGER, INC.; *pg.* 119, *pg.* 281
INTAS - Software - SUNGARD DATA SYSTEMS INC.; *pg.* 477, *pg.* 1592
INTECH - Investment Services - JANUS CAPITAL GROUP, INC.; *pg.* 772, *pg.* 320
INTEGRA - Software - BIO-RAD LABORATORIES, INC.; *pg.* 1504, *pg.* 101
INTEGRA - Healthcare Product - DERMA SCIENCES, INC.; *pg.* 1523, *pg.* 1111
INTEGRA - Valve - ENTEGRIS, INC.; *pg.* 1882, *pg.* 788
INTEGRA - Cleaning Product - HILLYARD, INC.; *pg.* 331, *pg.* 990
INTEGRA - Kitchen Faucet - MOEN INCORPORATED; *pg.* 1056, *pg.* 1468
INTEGRA - Software - NEWPORT CORPORATION; *pg.* 1424, *pg.* 114
INTEGRA - Semiconductor Test System - TERADYNE INC.; *pg.* 679, *pg.* 838
INTEGRA EPILEPSY - Medical Device - INTEGRA LIFESCIENCES HOLDINGS CORPORATION; *pg.* 1545, *pg.* 1109
INTEGRA MOTOR - Electric Motor - BODINE ELECTRIC COMPANY; *pg.* 1318, *pg.* 641
INTEGRA MOZAIK - Medical Device - INTEGRA LIFESCIENCES HOLDINGS CORPORATION; *pg.* 1545, *pg.* 1109
INTEGRA NEUROSUPPLIES - Medical Device - INTEGRA LIFESCIENCES HOLDINGS CORPORATION; *pg.* 1545, *pg.* 1109
INTEGRA RS - Dry Stripe Application Suite - AXCELIS TECHNOLOGIES, INC.; *pg.* 1400, *pg.* 787
INTEGRA SERIES - Mailing & Shipping Scales - PITNEY BOWES INC.; *pg.* 454, *pg.* 376
INTEGRA STATION - Software System - MENTOR GRAPHICS CORPORATION; *pg.* 432, *pg.* 1510
INTEGRAL - Sunglass - 180S, LLC; *pg.* 1824, *pg.* 754
INTEGRAL - Chemical Product - THE DOW CHEMICAL COMPANY; *pg.* 1157, *pg.* 898
INTEGRAL - Implant Product - ZIMMER BIOMET HOLDINGS, INC.; *pg.* 1611, *pg.* 699
INTEGRAL BLADE - Stabilizer - BAKER HUGHES INTEQ; *pg.* 1316, *pg.* 1700
INTEGRAL HIP SYSTEM - Hip Stem - ZIMMER BIOMET HOLDINGS, INC.; *pg.* 1611, *pg.* 699
INTEGRAPAK - Packaging Product - GRAPHIC PACKAGING HOLDING COMPANY; *pg.* 1459, *pg.* 509
INTEGRASYS - Software System - FISERV, INC.; *pg.* 397, *pg.* 1855
INTEGRATED ARCHITECTURE - Software - ROCKWELL AUTOMATION, INC.; *pg.* 668, *pg.* 1880
INTEGRATED LOGISTICS SOLUTIONS - Software - MANHATTAN ASSOCIATES, INC.; *pg.* 430, *pg.* 513
INTEGRATED PRODUCT DEVELOPMENT - Software System - MENTOR GRAPHICS CORPORATION; *pg.* 432, *pg.* 1510
INTEGRATED PROMOTIONAL SERVICES - Software Solution - IMS HEALTH, INC.; *pg.* 1544, *pg.* 344
INTEGRATED SURVEYING - Navigation Aid - TRIMBLE NAVIGATION LIMITED; *pg.* 1384, *pg.* 288
INTEGRATED WEDGE - Ice Hockey Skate Performance Enhancing Technology - REEBOK-CCM HOCKEY, INC.; *pg.* 1844, *pg.* 1960
INTEGRATING SCIENCE AND SOFTWARE - Slogan - SIMULATIONS PLUS, INC.; *pg.* 470, *pg.* 121
INTEGRATION PLUS - Wireless Communication System - AT&T SOUTHEAST; *pg.* 1868, *pg.* 489
INTEGRATION TOOL KIT - Software System - MENTOR GRAPHICS CORPORATION; *pg.* 432, *pg.* 1510
INTEGRATIONS - Educational Resources - SCHOOL SPECIALTY, INC.; *pg.* 467, *pg.* 1860
INTEGRATOR - Software & Hardware - EVANS & SUTHERLAND COMPUTER CORPORATION; *pg.* 638, *pg.* 1757
INTEGRATOR - Software - JDA SOFTWARE GROUP, INC.; *pg.* 423, *pg.* 22
INTEGREX - Technology - EASTMAN CHEMICAL COMPANY; *pg.* 1159, *pg.* 1636
INTEGRIFORM - Building Products - BOISE CASCADE HOLDINGS, L.L.C.; *pg.* 1453, *pg.* 546
INTEGRILIN - Medicine - MERCK & CO., INC.; *pg.* 1566, *pg.* 1077
INTEGRILIN - Pharmaceutical Product - MILLENNIUM: THE TAKEDA ONCOLOGY COMPANY; *pg.* 1568, *pg.* 809
INTEGRITI VITALS - Sensor - STINGER MEDICAL LLC; *pg.* 476, *pg.* 1648
INTEGRITY - Temporary Crown & Bridge Cement - DENTSPLY INTERNATIONAL INC.; *pg.* 1522, *pg.* 1596
INTEGRITY - Tires - THE GOODYEAR TIRE & RUBBER COMPANY; *pg.* 1883, *pg.* 1401
INTEGRITY - Pacemakers - ST. JUDE MEDICAL, INC.; *pg.* 1596, *pg.* 963
INTEGRITY - Books - THOMAS NELSON INC.; *pg.* 1692, *pg.* 1654
INTEGRITY - Wall Coating - THE VALSPAR CORPORATION; *pg.* 1449, *pg.* 945
INTEGRITY AT WORK. - Slogan - NSS ENTERPRISES, INC.; *pg.* 59, *pg.* 1476
INTEGRITY COACHING - Software - INTEGRITY SOLUTIONS; *pg.* 145, *pg.* 22

First page reference indicates Business Class Edition
Second page reference indicates Geographic Edition

INTEGRITY, DEDICATION, PERFORMANCE, PRIDE. - Tag Line - REGAL WARE, INC.; *pg.* 1137, *pg.* 1862
INTEGRITY SELLING - Software - INTEGRITY SOLUTIONS; *pg.* 145, *pg.* 22
INTEGRO - Generator - ADVANCED ENERGY INDUSTRIES, INC.; *pg.* 613, *pg.* 328
INTEGRON - Two-layer Surgical Glove - BECTON, DICKINSON & COMPANY; *pg.* 1501, *pg.* 1068
INTEK - Engine Type - BRIGGS & STRATTON CORPORATION; *pg.* 201, *pg.* 1899
INTEL - Cluster - MICROWAY, INC.; *pg.* 1267, *pg.* 841
INTEL ATOM - Microprocessor - INTEL CORPORATION; *pg.* 645, *pg.* 266
INTEL ATOM INSIDE - Microprocessor - INTEL CORPORATION; *pg.* 645, *pg.* 266
INTEL CORE - Microprocessor - INTEL CORPORATION; *pg.* 645, *pg.* 266
INTEL INSIDE - Program to Grow Businesses - INTEL CORPORATION; *pg.* 645, *pg.* 266
INTEL ITANIUM - Microprocessor - INTEL CORPORATION; *pg.* 645, *pg.* 266
INTEL XEON - Microprocessor - INTEL CORPORATION; *pg.* 645, *pg.* 266
INTEL XEON PHI - Coprocessor - INTEL CORPORATION; *pg.* 645, *pg.* 266
INTELECT - Orthopedic Device - DJO SURGICAL; *pg.* 1525, *pg.* 1661
INTELECT LEGEND - Orthopedic Device - DJO SURGICAL; *pg.* 1525, *pg.* 1661
INTELI-POWER 9100 - Power Converted/Battery Charger - PROGRESSIVE DYNAMICS, INC.; *pg.* 665, *pg.* 898
INTELIJET - Printer and Coder - BELL-MARK CORPORATION; *pg.* 1620, *pg.* 1108
INTELIJET - Computerized Aircraft Management Program - NETJETS INC.; *pg.* 1917, *pg.* 1442
INTELIMER - Polymers - LANDEC CORPORATION; *pg.* 1419, *pg.* 145
INTELITOUCH - Integrated Parcel Processing & Shipping Management System - HASLER, INC.; *pg.* 1459, *pg.* 356
INTELL-IGNITION - Ignition System - EMERSON WHITE-RODGERS; *pg.* 1071, *pg.* 996
INTELLECT - Software - JDA SOFTWARE GROUP, INC.; *pg.* 423, *pg.* 22
INTELLI-CLEAN - Programmable Logic Controller - GE ENERGY; *pg.* 1338, *pg.* 506
INTELLI-FIN - Water Heater - LOCHINVAR CORPORATION; *pg.* 1073, *pg.* 1640
INTELLI-PICK - Collation Technology - DELPHAX TECHNOLOGIES INC.; *pg.* 386, *pg.* 917
INTELLI-POWER - Floor Maintenance Equipment - TENNANT COMPANY; *pg.* 1381, *pg.* 944
INTELLI-TEAM - Interactive Sensing & Control - S&C ELECTRIC COMPANY; *pg.* 1305, *pg.* 589
INTELLI-TRONIC - Voice Articulation Technology - PLAYMATES TOYS INC.; *pg.* 965, *pg.* 82
INTELLIBASE - National Repository Line Level Database - INTRADO INC.; *pg.* 420, *pg.* 334
INTELLIBUCKET - Software - BIO-RAD LABORATORIES, INC.; *pg.* 1504, *pg.* 101
INTELLICAP - Capacitor Control - S&C ELECTRIC COMPANY; *pg.* 1305, *pg.* 589
INTELLICAP PLUS - Automatic Capacitor Control - S&C ELECTRIC COMPANY; *pg.* 1305, *pg.* 589
INTELLICAST - Target Notification Services - INTRADO INC.; *pg.* 420, *pg.* 334
INTELLICENTER - Software - ROCKWELL AUTOMATION, INC.; *pg.* 668, *pg.* 1880
INTELLICHECK - Air Purifier - KAZ, INC.; *pg.* 58, *pg.* 844
INTELLICOAT - Seed Coatings - LANDEC CORPORATION; *pg.* 1419, *pg.* 145
INTELLICODE - Access Security System - THE GENIE COMPANY; *pg.* 55, *pg.* 1403
INTELLICOR - Pharmaceutical Product - SALIX PHARMACEUTICALS, INC.; *pg.* 1591, *pg.* 1388
INTELLICORP - Web Products - INTELLICORP, INC.; *pg.* 417, *pg.* 268
INTELLICRYPT - Software - SYMANTEC CORPORATION; *pg.* 478, *pg.* 161
INTELLIFIND - Search Engine - BLUCORA; *pg.* 1232, *pg.* 1813
INTELLIGEL - Shoe And Glove - ACUSHNET COMPANY; *pg.* 1824, *pg.* 818
INTELLIGEN - Dispense System - ENTEGRIS, INC.; *pg.* 1882, *pg.* 788
INTELLIGENCE APPLIED - Tagline - IMS HEALTH, INC.; *pg.* 1544, *pg.* 344
INTELLIGENCE AT THE CORE - Tag Line - ENCORIUM GROUP, INC.; *pg.* 1528, *pg.* 1591
THE INTELLIGENCE COMPANY - Slogan - MICROSTRATEGY, INC.; *pg.* 1266, *pg.* 1809
INTELLIGENCE DRIVEN SOLUTIONS - Data Solution - ACXIOM CORPORATION; *pg.* 342, *pg.* 33
INTELLIGENCE EVERYWHERE - Slogan - MOTOROLA SOLUTIONS, INC.; *pg.* 657, *pg.* 659
INTELLIGENCE. INSIGHT. IMPACT. - Slogan - IHS AUTOMOTIVE DRIVEN BY POLK; *pg.* 1652, *pg.* 907
INTELLIGENCE SERVER - Software - MICROSTRATEGY, INC.; *pg.* 1266, *pg.* 1809
INTELLIGENT ASSISTANCE SUITE - Software - SUPPORT.COM, INC.; *pg.* 1283, *pg.* 192
INTELLIGENT CONTENT PROTECTION - Software - WEBSENSE, INC.; *pg.* 491, *pg.* 210
INTELLIGENT CUBES - Software - MICROSTRATEGY, INC.; *pg.* 1266, *pg.* 1809
INTELLIGENT DEPOSITORY MODULE - Consumer Interface Panel - DIEBOLD, INCORPORATED; *pg.* 387, *pg.* 1407
INTELLIGENT DESIGN & INNOVATION - Tagline - LINDSAY CORPORATION; *pg.* 1356, *pg.* 1016
INTELLIGENT DIVERSITY RECEPTION - Wireless Communications Technology - IPMOBILENET, LLC; *pg.* 648, *pg.* 261
INTELLIGENT DOCUMENT SOLUTIONS - Software - CINCOM SYSTEMS, INC.; *pg.* 372, *pg.* 1411
INTELLIGENT E-BUSINESS - Software - MICROSTRATEGY, INC.; *pg.* 1266, *pg.* 1809
INTELLIGENT EMERGENCY NETWORK - Telecommunication System - INTRADO INC.; *pg.* 420, *pg.* 334
INTELLIGENT LAUNDRY SOLUTIONS - Slogan - MAC-GRAY CORPORATION; *pg.* 58, *pg.* 852
INTELLIGENT LIBRARY SYSTEM - Photographic Image Processing Computer Software - LOCKHEED MARTIN CORPORATION; *pg.* 229, *pg.* 762
INTELLIGENT LOAN FOLDER - Manual - XEROX CORPORATION; *pg.* 494, *pg.* 365
INTELLIGENT MAIL - Software - PITNEY BOWES INC.; *pg.* 454, *pg.* 376
INTELLIGENT PROCESS CONTROL - Software - DUKANE CORPORATION; *pg.* 634, *pg.* 658
INTELLIGENT REVIEW TECHNOLOGY - Fraud Management Automation - CYBERSOURCE CORPORATION; *pg.* 381, *pg.* 216
INTELLIGENT SERIAL INTERFACE - Remote Access Product - MULTI-TECH SYSTEMS INC.; *pg.* 442, *pg.* 951
INTELLIGENT SERVO DRIVER - Optical Scanner - GSI GROUP INC.; *pg.* 1415, *pg.* 784
INTELLIGENT SPEED - Analytical Column - WATERS CORPORATION; *pg.* 1436, *pg.* 834
INTELLIGENT STAFFING. EXTRA-MILE SERVICE. - Slogan - SELECTREMEDY; *pg.* 468, *pg.* 263
INTELLIGENT SYSTEM SOLUTIONS - Slogan - ARMSTRONG INTERNATIONAL, INC.; *pg.* 1069, *pg.* 909
INTELLIGENT VRA - Hearing Diagnostic Equipment & Visual Reinforcement Audiometry - INTELLIGENT HEARING SYSTEMS CORP.; *pg.* 1546, *pg.* 443
THE INTELLIGENT WINDOW - Glass Panes - PPG INDUSTRIES, INC.; *pg.* 1445, *pg.* 1579
INTELLIJET - Plastic Nozzles - IRT, INC.; *pg.* 1169, *pg.* 771
INTELLILAB - Software - ELEKTA; *pg.* 391, *pg.* 284
INTELLILINK - Software - S&C ELECTRIC COMPANY; *pg.* 1305, *pg.* 589
INTELLIMASS - Workhorse Inspection System - PRESSCO TECHNOLOGY INC.; *pg.* 1370, *pg.* 1434
INTELLIMIX - Discussion System - SHURE INCORPORATED; *pg.* 672, *pg.* 638
INTELLIMUTE - Laser Detectors - COBRA ELECTRONICS CORPORATION; *pg.* 629, *pg.* 572
INTELLINEWS - Software - SMITH MICRO SOFTWARE, INC.; *pg.* 471, *pg.* 41
INTELLIPARK - Drive Technology - WESTERN DIGITAL CORPORATION; *pg.* 492, *pg.* 118
INTELLIPET - Pet Product - PETEDGE; *pg.* 1481, *pg.* 787
INTELLIPOWER - Drive Technology - WESTERN DIGITAL CORPORATION; *pg.* 492, *pg.* 118
INTELLIPRICING - Software Program - INTELLIGRATED, INC.; *pg.* 1349, *pg.* 1460
INTELLIQ - Zero Pressure Accumulation - INTELLIGRATED, INC.; *pg.* 1349, *pg.* 1460
INTELLIRIDE - Air Spring - FIRESTONE INDUSTRIAL PRODUCTS DIVISION; *pg.* 1882, *pg.* 686
INTELLIROL - Roller Conveyor - PARAGON TECHNOLOGIES, INC.; *pg.* 1367, *pg.* 1528
INTELLIROUTE - Routing Software for Truckers - RAND MCNALLY & COMPANY; *pg.* 1679, *pg.* 661
INTELLIRUPTER - PulseCloser - S&C ELECTRIC COMPANY; *pg.* 1305, *pg.* 589
INTELLISAMPLE - Graphic System - NVIDIA CORPORATION; *pg.* 447, *pg.* 268
INTELLISEEK - Drive Technology - WESTERN DIGITAL CORPORATION; *pg.* 492, *pg.* 118
INTELLISEND - Telecom Product - PREMIERE GLOBAL SERVICES, INC.; *pg.* 1275, *pg.* 518
INTELLISENSE - Battery Product - CARDIAC SCIENCE CORPORATION; *pg.* 1512, *pg.* 1897
INTELLISENSE - Workhorse Inspection System - PRESSCO TECHNOLOGY INC.; *pg.* 1370, *pg.* 1434
INTELLISHARE - Image Networking - IDEXX LABORATORIES, INC.; *pg.* 1543, *pg.* 753
INTELLISHIELD - Screening Feature - COBRA ELECTRONICS CORPORATION; *pg.* 629, *pg.* 572
INTELLISHIELD EXTREME - Membrane - ACUSHNET COMPANY; *pg.* 1824, *pg.* 818
INTELLISORT - Sorting Technology - KEY TECHNOLOGY, INC.; *pg.* 868, *pg.* 1847
INTELLISOURCING - Software Application - SYNTEL, INC.; *pg.* 480, *pg.* 911
INTELLISPEC - Workhorse Inspection System - PRESSCO TECHNOLOGY INC.; *pg.* 1370, *pg.* 1434
INTELLISTART - Software - WATERS CORPORATION; *pg.* 1436, *pg.* 834
INTELLISYNC - Medical Apparatus - MAQUET; *pg.* 1558, *pg.* 1082
INTELLITEAM II - Automated Restoration System - S&C ELECTRIC COMPANY; *pg.* 1305, *pg.* 589
INTELLITEST - Software System - MENTOR GRAPHICS CORPORATION; *pg.* 432, *pg.* 1510
INTELLITIRE - Tire Pressure Monitoring System - LEAR CORPORATION; *pg.* 229, *pg.* 907
INTELLITOOLS - Hand Tools - STANLEY BLACK & DECKER, INC.; *pg.* 1063, *pg.* 358
INTELLITRANSFER - Telecom Software - SYNTEL, INC.; *pg.* 480, *pg.* 911
INTELLITRAX - Auto Scanning System - X-RITE, INCORPORATED; *pg.* 1437, *pg.* 891
INTELLITRIP - Electronic Circuit Breaker - INTERSIL CORPORATION; *pg.* 647, *pg.* 146
INTELLIVECTOR - Wireless Network Transaction Services & Systems - INTRADO INC.; *pg.* 420, *pg.* 334
INTELLIVENT - Medical Apparatus - MAQUET; *pg.* 1558, *pg.* 1082
INTELLIVISOR - Software - SAS INSTITUTE INC.; *pg.* 466, *pg.* 1361
INTELLIWHITE - Lighting System - PHILIPS SOLID-STATE LIGHTING SOLUTIONS; *pg.* 1303, *pg.* 806
INTELLUME - Electrical Lighting Fixtures - STEELCASE INC.; *pg.* 475, *pg.* 889
INTEMPO - Adaptive Imaging System - ACCURAY INCORPORATED; *pg.* 1486, *pg.* 282
INTENSE MILKS - Dairy Product - UPSTATE NIAGARA COOPERATIVE, INC.; *pg.* 907, *pg.* 1151
INTENSELY DIFFERENT - Salted Snack Food - INVENTURE FOODS, INC.; *pg.* 1023, *pg.* 17
INTENSI-F - Wireless Network - BROADCOM CORPORATION; *pg.* 364, *pg.* 108
INTENSIFIED COFFEE STOUT - Seasonal Beer - THE BROOKLYN BREWERY; *pg.* 239, *pg.* 1145
INTENSS - Band Saw Blades - THE L.S. STARRETT COMPANY; *pg.* 1421, *pg.* 783
INTENT - Furniture - HERMAN MILLER, INC.; *pg.* 926, *pg.* 913
INTENTION - Necklaces - HUGGER MUGGER YOGA PRODUCTS LLC; *pg.* 1836, *pg.* 1758
INTEPRO - Large Pore Polypropylene Mesh - AMERICAN MEDICAL SYSTEMS HOLDINGS, INC.; *pg.* 1493, *pg.* 947
INTEQ - Medical Equipment - CONMED CORPORATION; *pg.* 1517, *pg.* 1347
INTER@CTIVE - Two-Way Radio Pager - BLACKBERRY LIMITED; *pg.* 625, *pg.* 1947
INTER FIX - Threaded Spinal Fusion Device - MEDTRONIC, INC.; *pg.* 1564, *pg.* 939
INTER-TEL AXXESS - Communication System - MITEL NETWORKS CORPORATION; *pg.* 654, *pg.* 1921
INTERA - Amplifiers - SKYWORKS SOLUTIONS, INC.; *pg.* 674, *pg.* 862
INTERACT - Data Manager - MEDTRONIC, INC.; *pg.* 1564,

pg. 939
INTERACTION - Office Furniture - KNOLL, INC.; *pg.* 425, *pg.* 1527
INTERACTION ADMINISTRATOR - Software - INTERACTIVE INTELLIGENCE, INC.; *pg.* 417, *pg.* 687
INTERACTION ATTENDANT - Software - INTERACTIVE INTELLIGENCE, INC.; *pg.* 417, *pg.* 687
INTERACTION CENTER PLATFORM - Software - INTERACTIVE INTELLIGENCE, INC.; *pg.* 417, *pg.* 687
INTERACTION CLIENT - Software - INTERACTIVE INTELLIGENCE, INC.; *pg.* 417, *pg.* 687
INTERACTION DESIGNER - Software - INTERACTIVE INTELLIGENCE, INC.; *pg.* 417, *pg.* 687
INTERACTION DESKTOP - Software - INTERACTIVE INTELLIGENCE, INC.; *pg.* 417, *pg.* 687
INTERACTION DIALER - Software - INTERACTIVE INTELLIGENCE, INC.; *pg.* 417, *pg.* 687
INTERACTION DIRECTOR - Software - INTERACTIVE INTELLIGENCE, INC.; *pg.* 417, *pg.* 687
INTERACTION EASYSCRIPTER - Software - INTERACTIVE INTELLIGENCE, INC.; *pg.* 417, *pg.* 687
INTERACTION FAQ - Software - INTERACTIVE INTELLIGENCE, INC.; *pg.* 417, *pg.* 687
INTERACTION FAX VIEWER - Software - INTERACTIVE INTELLIGENCE, INC.; *pg.* 417, *pg.* 687
INTERACTION FEEDBACK - Software - INTERACTIVE INTELLIGENCE, INC.; *pg.* 417, *pg.* 687
INTERACTION GATEWAY - Software - INTERACTIVE INTELLIGENCE, INC.; *pg.* 417, *pg.* 687
INTERACTION MARQUEE - Software - INTERACTIVE INTELLIGENCE, INC.; *pg.* 417, *pg.* 687
INTERACTION MEDIA SERVER - Media Server - INTERACTIVE INTELLIGENCE, INC.; *pg.* 417, *pg.* 687
INTERACTION MELDER - Software - INTERACTIVE INTELLIGENCE, INC.; *pg.* 417, *pg.* 687
INTERACTION MESSAGE INDICATOR - Software - INTERACTIVE INTELLIGENCE, INC.; *pg.* 417, *pg.* 687
INTERACTION MIGRATOR - Software - INTERACTIVE INTELLIGENCE, INC.; *pg.* 417, *pg.* 687
INTERACTION MOBILE OFFICE - Software - INTERACTIVE INTELLIGENCE, INC.; *pg.* 417, *pg.* 687
INTERACTION MONITOR - Software - INTERACTIVE INTELLIGENCE, INC.; *pg.* 417, *pg.* 687
INTERACTION OPTIMIZER - Software - INTERACTIVE INTELLIGENCE, INC.; *pg.* 417, *pg.* 687
INTERACTION RECORDER - Software - INTERACTIVE INTELLIGENCE, INC.; *pg.* 417, *pg.* 687
INTERACTION SCREEN RECORDER - Software - INTERACTIVE INTELLIGENCE, INC.; *pg.* 417, *pg.* 687
INTERACTION SCRIPTER - Software - INTERACTIVE INTELLIGENCE, INC.; *pg.* 417, *pg.* 687
INTERACTION SERVER - Software - INTERACTIVE INTELLIGENCE, INC.; *pg.* 417, *pg.* 687
INTERACTION SIP PROXY - Software - INTERACTIVE INTELLIGENCE, INC.; *pg.* 417, *pg.* 687
INTERACTION SUPERVISOR - Software - INTERACTIVE INTELLIGENCE, INC.; *pg.* 417, *pg.* 687
INTERACTION TRACKER - Software - INTERACTIVE INTELLIGENCE, INC.; *pg.* 417, *pg.* 687
INTERACTION VOICEMAIL PLAYER - Software - INTERACTIVE INTELLIGENCE, INC.; *pg.* 417, *pg.* 687
INTERACTION WEB PORTAL - Software - INTERACTIVE INTELLIGENCE, INC.; *pg.* 417, *pg.* 687
INTERACTIONCHECK - Drug Interaction Feature - EPOCRATES, INC.; *pg.* 1529, *pg.* 254
INTERACTIVE COMFORT TECHNOLOGY - Shoe And Glove - ACUSHNET COMPANY; *pg.* 1824, *pg.* 818
INTERACTIVE INTELLIGENCE LIVE CONFERENCE - Software - INTERACTIVE INTELLIGENCE, INC.; *pg.* 417, *pg.* 687
INTERACTIVE KIDS - Educational Materials - SCHOLASTIC INC.; *pg.* 1683, *pg.* 1288
INTERACTIVE LAYOUT - Software System - MENTOR GRAPHICS CORPORATION; *pg.* 432, *pg.* 1510
INTERACTIVE MYSTIQUE - Dental Product - DENTSPLY INTERNATIONAL INC.; *pg.* 1522, *pg.* 1596
INTERACTIVE PHONICS READERS - Educational Materials - SCHOLASTIC INC.; *pg.* 1683, *pg.* 1288
INTERACTIVE PHYSICS - Software - MSC SOFTWARE CORPORATION; *pg.* 441, *pg.* 262
INTERACTIVE UPDATE - Software - INTERACTIVE INTELLIGENCE, INC.; *pg.* 417, *pg.* 687
INTERACTIVELEASE - Software - INTERACTIVE INTELLIGENCE, INC.; *pg.* 417, *pg.* 687
INTERACTIVITY FOR THE WORLD - Tagline - ADVANCED TELECOM SERVICES; *pg.* 1865, *pg.* 1591
INTERART - Greeting Card - HALLMARK CARDS, INC.; *pg.* 1646, *pg.* 983
INTERCEED - Healthcare Product - JOHNSON & JOHNSON; *pg.* 1549, *pg.* 1091
INTERCELL - Carpet - INTERFACE, INC.; *pg.* 695, *pg.* 512
INTERCEPT - Filters - ENTEGRIS, INC.; *pg.* 1882, *pg.* 788
INTERCEPT - Window & Door - HARVEY INDUSTRIES, INC.; *pg.* 86, *pg.* 851
INTERCEPT - Oral Fluid Drug Test - ORASURE TECHNOLOGIES INC; *pg.* 1578, *pg.* 1516
INTERCEPT - Glass Product - PPG INDUSTRIES, INC.; *pg.* 1445, *pg.* 1579
INTERCEPTOR - Wrap Bug Shield - LUND INTERNATIONAL, INC.; *pg.* 211, *pg.* 526
INTERCEPTOR - Pet Medication - PETMED EXPRESS, INC.; *pg.* 1781, *pg.* 460
INTERCOMM - Software - PARAMETRIC TECHNOLOGY CORPORATION; *pg.* 452, *pg.* 835
INTERCONNECT TABLE - Software System - MENTOR GRAPHICS CORPORATION; *pg.* 432, *pg.* 1510
INTERCONTINENTAL - Hotels & Resorts - INTERCONTINENTAL HOTELS CORPORATION; *pg.* 1097, *pg.* 511
INTERCONTINENTALEXCHANGE - Software - INTERCONTINENTALEXCHANGE, INC.; *pg.* 769, *pg.* 512
INTERDENTAL FLOSSUPS - Floss - RANIR LLC; *pg.* 520, *pg.* 888
INTEREST.COM - Online Financial Information - BANKRATE, INC.; *pg.* 1231, *pg.* 451
INTERFACE - Floor Coverings - INTERFACE FLOORING SYSTEMS INC.; *pg.* 929, *pg.* 534
INTERFACE-BASED DESIGN - Software System - MENTOR GRAPHICS CORPORATION; *pg.* 432, *pg.* 1510
INTERFACE EXCEL - Shaving System - BRAUN NORTH AMERICA; *pg.* 52, *pg.* 792
INTERFACE FLOORING SYSTEMS - Fabric & Flooring - INTERFACE, INC.; *pg.* 695, *pg.* 512
INTERFACEFABRIC - Fabric & Flooring - INTERFACE, INC.; *pg.* 695, *pg.* 512
INTERFACEFLOR - Fabric & Flooring - INTERFACE, INC.; *pg.* 695, *pg.* 512
INTERFLEX - Electronic Access Control - INGERSOLL-RAND COMPANY; *pg.* 1349, *pg.* 1370
INTERFOLD - Carpet - INTERFACE, INC.; *pg.* 695, *pg.* 512
INTERFUSE - Technology - CHYRONHEGO; *pg.* 371, *pg.* 1179
INTERGRATEDMOBILE - Software - TELLABS, INC.; *pg.* 678, *pg.* 637
INTERIOR EXPRESSIONS - Collection of Drapery Accessories & Upholstery Supplies - PRYM CONSUMER USA; *pg.* 698, *pg.* 1622
INTERIORS - Magazine - NIELSEN BUSINESS MEDIA; *pg.* 1671, *pg.* 1272
INTERJECT - Medical Device - BOSTON SCIENTIFIC CORPORATION; *pg.* 1508, *pg.* 831
INTERLACE - Kitchen Product - KOHLER CO.; *pg.* 91, *pg.* 1862
INTERLINX - Reporting Software - AMERISOURCEBERGEN CORPORATION; *pg.* 1493, *pg.* 1522
INTERLOCHEN - Fabric - NEMSCHOFF, INC.; *pg.* 936, *pg.* 1890
INTERLOCK - Rifle Bullet - HORNADY MANUFACTURING COMPANY; *pg.* 1836, *pg.* 1010
INTERLOCKEN - Rug - COURISTAN INC.; *pg.* 921, *pg.* 1067
INTERLOCKEN - Acoustic System - OWENS CORNING; *pg.* 102, *pg.* 1476
INTERLOK - Metal Strip - PENFLEX, INC.; *pg.* 104, *pg.* 1534
INTERLOK - Implant Product - ZIMMER BIOMET HOLDINGS, INC.; *pg.* 1611, *pg.* 699
INTERLOTT - Lottery System - INTERNATIONAL GAME TECHNOLOGY; *pg.* 420, *pg.* 1606
INTERLOY - Polymer Product - CHEMTURA CORPORATION; *pg.* 1152, *pg.* 355
INTERMEDE - International Salon Brand - REGIS CORPORATION; *pg.* 521, *pg.* 941
INTERMEDIAIR - Trade Magazine - THE NIELSEN COMPANY B.V.; *pg.* 1671, *pg.* 1272
INTERMEDIATE HI-LO - Tracheal Tube - MEDTRONIC; *pg.* 1563, *pg.* 183
INTERMISSION - Carpet - BEAULIEU GROUP, LLC; *pg.* 917, *pg.* 529
INTERMIX - Batch Mixer - FARREL CORPORATION; *pg.* 1336, *pg.* 337
INTERMIX - Fabric - NEMSCHOFF, INC.; *pg.* 936, *pg.* 1890
INTERNAL HEALTH EXTERNAL BEAUTY - Nutritional Supplement - PHARMAVITE LLC; *pg.* 1584, *pg.* 167
INTERNATIONAL - Trucks - NAVISTAR INTERNATIONAL CORPORATION; *pg.* 186, *pg.* 630
INTERNATIONAL - Toys - TRACTOR SUPPLY COMPANY; *pg.* 708, *pg.* 1627
INTERNATIONAL AUTOBODY CONGRESS & EXPOSITION - Event - AUTOMOTIVE SERVICE ASSOCIATION; *pg.* 134, *pg.* 1670
INTERNATIONAL BOSTON SEAFOOD SHOW - Publication - DIVERSIFIED COMMUNICATIONS; *pg.* 284, *pg.* 751
INTERNATIONAL BUILDING CODE - Fire Safety Book - NATIONAL FIRE PROTECTION ASSOCIATION; *pg.* 149, *pg.* 842
INTERNATIONAL BUSINESS AWARDS - Award - STEVIE AWARDS, INC.; *pg.* 157, *pg.* 1780
INTERNATIONAL CHOICE - Packaged Foods - ATALANTA CORPORATION; *pg.* 838, *pg.* 1057
INTERNATIONAL DELIGHT - Nondairy Creamer - THE WHITEWAVE FOODS COMPANY; *pg.* 1037, *pg.* 324
INTERNATIONAL DOCUMENT SERVICE - International Document Delivery - DHL HOLDINGS (USA), INC.; *pg.* 1906, *pg.* 459
INTERNATIONAL GAME TECHNOLOGY - Video Game - INTERNATIONAL GAME TECHNOLOGY; *pg.* 957, *pg.* 1024
INTERNATIONAL GATEWAY - Wireline Solutions - SONUS NETWORKS INC.; *pg.* 1281, *pg.* 858
THE INTERNATIONAL HERALD TRIBUNE - Newspaper - THE NEW YORK TIMES COMPANY; *pg.* 1668, *pg.* 1270
INTERNATIONAL HOUSE OF PANCAKES - Restaurants - DINEEQUITY, INC.; *pg.* 1725, *pg.* 95
INTERNATIONAL INSPIRER - Educational Materials - SCHOLASTIC INC.; *pg.* 1683, *pg.* 1288
INTERNATIONAL MALE - Catalog Containing Unique Men's Apparel - HANOVER DIRECT, INC.; *pg.* 1772, *pg.* 1130
INTERNATIONAL MATERIALS REVIEWS - Trade Publication - ASM INTERNATIONAL; *pg.* 132, *pg.* 1461
INTERNATIONAL MECHANICAL CODE - Fire Safety Book - NATIONAL FIRE PROTECTION ASSOCIATION; *pg.* 149, *pg.* 842
INTERNATIONAL MEDIA GUIDE - Media Directory - SRDS, INC.; *pg.* 1688, *pg.* 657
INTERNATIONAL MUSIC & MEDIA CONFERENCE - Marketing Information Services - NIELSEN BUSINESS MEDIA; *pg.* 1671, *pg.* 1272
INTERNATIONAL PIZZA EXPO - Trade Show - MACFADDEN COMMUNICATIONS GROUP, LLC; *pg.* 1660, *pg.* 1254
INTERNATIONAL PLUMBING CODE - Fire Safety Book - NATIONAL FIRE PROTECTION ASSOCIATION; *pg.* 149, *pg.* 842
INTERNATIONAL RESIDENTIAL CODE - Fire Safety Book - NATIONAL FIRE PROTECTION ASSOCIATION; *pg.* 149, *pg.* 842
INTERNATIONAL SERIES - Drum - PEAVEY ELECTRONICS CORPORATION; *pg.* 662, *pg.* 970
INTERNATIONAL TRADE REPORTER DECISIONS - Publisher - BLOOMBERG BNA; *pg.* 1621, *pg.* 1772
INTERNATIONAL TRAVEL ASSOCIATES - Corporate Travel - ITAGROUP, INC.; *pg.* 422, *pg.* 713
INTERNATIONALE - Milk Chocolate - RUSSELL STOVER CANDIES, INC.; *pg.* 1861, *pg.* 986
INTERNET ADDRESS - Internet Registry - NEUSTAR, INC.; *pg.* 1872, *pg.* 1807
INTERNET ADVISORY TEAM - Provides Help with Internet Research, Training & Web Site Development - GUIDELINE, INC.; *pg.* 402, *pg.* 1237
INTERNET BRANDS - Software - IDEALAB, INC.; *pg.* 1258, *pg.* 180
INTERNET BUSINESS EXCHANGE - Telecommunication System - EQUINIX, INC.; *pg.* 394, *pg.* 190
INTERNET CLEANUP - Software - SMITH MICRO SOFTWARE, INC.; *pg.* 471, *pg.* 41
INTERNET CONTROL ARCHITECTURE - Software - F5 NETWORKS, INC.; *pg.* 396, *pg.* 1835
INTERNET HONEYGRID - Software - WEBSENSE, INC.; *pg.* 491, *pg.* 210
INTERNET INDUSTRY & DESIGN - Telephone Service - IDT CORPORATION; *pg.* 643, *pg.* 1096
INTERNET MESSENGER - Sport Watch - TIMEX CORPORATION; *pg.* 14, *pg.* 355
INTERNET OFFICE - Standby UPS Systems - TRIPPE MANUFACTURING COMPANY; *pg.* 220, *pg.* 592
INTERNET POSTAGE - Postage - STAMPS.COM INC.; *pg.* 1282, *pg.* 82

First page reference indicates Business Class Edition
Second page reference indicates Geographic Edition

INTERNET QUOTIENT - Computer Network - CISCO SYSTEMS, INC.; *pg.* 372, *pg.* 240
INTERNET TELEPHONY - Trade Publication - TECHNOLOGY MARKETING CORP.; *pg.* 1691, *pg.* 364
INTERNET UNIVERSAL - Biopharmaceutical Product - LEXICON PHARMACEUTICALS, INC.; *pg.* 1555, *pg.* 1747
INTERNET.COM - Online Network - MEDIABISTRO, INC.; *pg.* 1266, *pg.* 1258
INTERNETWEEK - Publisher - UNITED BUSINESS MEDIA LLC; *pg.* 1697, *pg.* 1177
INTERNODE - Prefabricated Electrical Conduits - STEELCASE INC.; *pg.* 475, *pg.* 889
INTERO - Power Semiconductor Device - INTERNATIONAL RECTIFIER CORPORATION; *pg.* 647, *pg.* 80
INTERPHLEX - Surgical Instrument - OSTEOMED CORPORATION; *pg.* 1425, *pg.* 1658
INTERPLAK - Oral Care - CONAIR CORPORATION; *pg.* 505, *pg.* 1055
INTERPLANT - Software - ELEKTA; *pg.* 391, *pg.* 987
INTERPLAY - Carpet - INTERFACE, INC.; *pg.* 695, *pg.* 512
INTERPOINT - Carpet - INTERFACE, INC.; *pg.* 695, *pg.* 512
INTERPOLATION - Textiles - BERNHARDT DESIGN; *pg.* 918, *pg.* 1381
INTERPOSE - Fabric - NEMSCHOFF, INC.; *pg.* 936, *pg.* 1890
INTERPRETATIONS - Area Rugs - COURISTAN INC.; *pg.* 921, *pg.* 1067
INTERPRETATIONS - Door Glass - ODL INCORPORATED; *pg.* 101, *pg.* 914
INTERPRISE - Digitized & Packetized Voice & Data Routers & Hubs - MITEL NETWORKS, INC.; *pg.* 1872, *pg.* 13
INTERPULSE - Pulse Irrigation System - STRYKER CORPORATION; *pg.* 1598, *pg.* 894
INTERRA - Polyester & Ceramic Products - E.I. DU PONT DE NEMOURS & COMPANY; *pg.* 1159, *pg.* 390
INTERRACIALSINGLES.NET - Online Dating Service - SPARK NETWORKS, INC.; *pg.* 472, *pg.* 140
INTERRAGATOR - Construction Equipment - VERMEER MANUFACTURING COMPANY; *pg.* 708, *pg.* 711
INTERSECT - Optical Networking Product - HARMONIC, INC.; *pg.* 402, *pg.* 246
INTERSECT - Carpet - INTERFACE, INC.; *pg.* 695, *pg.* 512
INTERSECT JEWEL - Rug - ETHAN ALLEN INTERIORS INC.; *pg.* 924, *pg.* 343
INTERSEPT - Carpet - INTERFACE, INC.; *pg.* 695, *pg.* 512
INTERSOURCING - Software - THE ULTIMATE SOFTWARE GROUP, INC.; *pg.* 486, *pg.* 479
INTERSPACE - Orthopaedic Implant Device - EXACTECH, INC.; *pg.* 1529, *pg.* 428
INTERSPACE - Brush Head - THE GILLETTE COMPANY; *pg.* 509, *pg.* 795
INTERSTAT - Matting - INTERFACE, INC.; *pg.* 695, *pg.* 512
INTERSTATE - Windshield Towels - GEORGIA-PACIFIC LLC; *pg.* 1458, *pg.* 507
INTERSTATER - Mower - ALAMO GROUP INC.; *pg.* 1311, *pg.* 1745
INTERSTIM - Therapy for Urinary Control - MEDTRONIC, INC.; *pg.* 1564, *pg.* 939
INTERTHERM - Heating & Cooling Products - NORTEK GLOBAL HVAC; *pg.* 1075, *pg.* 989
INTERTHERM - Air Conditioners & Furnaces - NORTEK, INC.; *pg.* 100, *pg.* 1607
INTERTRONICS - Seating System - LEAR CORPORATION; *pg.* 229, *pg.* 907
INTERTWINE - Fabric - NEMSCHOFF, INC.; *pg.* 936, *pg.* 1890
INTERTWIST - Carpet - INTERFACE, INC.; *pg.* 695, *pg.* 512
INTERVAL - Fabric - NEMSCHOFF, INC.; *pg.* 936, *pg.* 1890
INTERVASCULAR - Medical Apparatus - MAQUET; *pg.* 1558, *pg.* 1082
INTERVENE - Skin Care Product - ELIZABETH ARDEN, INC.; *pg.* 507, *pg.* 448
INTERVENE - Gas Barrier Filter - PALL CORPORATION; *pg.* 232, *pg.* 1323
INTERVENTION RX - Pharmaceutical Service - PROGRESSIVE MEDICAL, INC.; *pg.* 1586, *pg.* 1480
INTERVIA - Acid Copper - DOW CHEMICAL; *pg.* 1156, *pg.* 1563
INTERVIA - Advanced Packaging Photodielectrics - THE DOW CHEMICAL COMPANY; *pg.* 1157, *pg.* 898
INTERVIEW - Magazine - BRANT PUBLICATIONS, INC.; *pg.* 1623, *pg.* 1206
INTERVIEW - Carpet - INTERFACE, INC.; *pg.* 695, *pg.* 512
INTESYS - Fastening Systems - TEXTRON INC.; *pg.* 235, *pg.* 1607
INTEX - Cleaner Product - MCGEAN-ROHCO, INC.; *pg.* 1172, *pg.* 1432
INTIER AUTOMOTIVE - Automotive Parts for Interiors, Seating, & Closures - MAGNA INTERNATIONAL INC.; *pg.* 211, *pg.* 1918
INTIMATE - Skin Lotion - INTER PARFUMS, INC.; *pg.* 512, *pg.* 1244
INTIMATE APPEAL - Apparel - ASCENA RETAIL GROUP, INC.; *pg.* 18, *pg.* 1081
INTO THE STARS - Video Game - INTERNATIONAL GAME TECHNOLOGY; *pg.* 957, *pg.* 1024
INTOUCH - Telecommunications Products - INCONTACT, INC.; *pg.* 413, *pg.* 1752
INTOUCH VOICE RESPONSE - Fully-Automated Interactive Voice Response for Telephone-Based Banking - JACK HENRY & ASSOCIATES, INC.; *pg.* 422, *pg.* 988
INTOUCH ZONE - Medical Equipment - INVACARE CORPORATION; *pg.* 1546, *pg.* 1451
INTRA-KOOL - Thermal Processing Equipment - SURFACE COMBUSTION, INC.; *pg.* 1077, *pg.* 1462
INTRACORE - Switch - ASANTE TECHNOLOGIES, INC.; *pg.* 619, *pg.* 238
INTRADER - Software - SUNGARD DATA SYSTEMS INC.; *pg.* 477, *pg.* 1592
INTRAJECT - Pharmaceutical Product - ZOGENIX, INC.; *pg.* 1612, *pg.* 211
INTRALINKS COURIER - File Transfer Solution - INTRALINKS INC.; *pg.* 420, *pg.* 1244
INTRALINKS EXCHANGES - Workflow Management - INTRALINKS INC.; *pg.* 420, *pg.* 1244
INTRALON - Plastic Conveyor Belt - THE LAITRAM LLC; *pg.* 1354, *pg.* 744
INTRALOX - Plastic, Modular Construction Conveyor Belting - INTRALOX LLC; *pg.* 1350, *pg.* 744
INTRALOX - Plastic Conveyor Belt - THE LAITRAM LLC; *pg.* 1354, *pg.* 744
INTRALUS - Bed - SELECT COMFORT CORPORATION; *pg.* 942, *pg.* 942
INTRAN - Medical Product - UTAH MEDICAL PRODUCTS, INC.; *pg.* 1605, *pg.* 1752
INTRAPREP - Testing Instrument System - BECKMAN COULTER, INC.; *pg.* 1402, *pg.* 48
INTRASPECT ANALYTICS - Software System - KRONOS INCORPORATED; *pg.* 425, *pg.* 813
INTRASTEPSM - Software System - MENTOR GRAPHICS CORPORATION; *pg.* 432, *pg.* 1510
INTRAVIA - Injection - BAXTER INTERNATIONAL INC.; *pg.* 1499, *pg.* 599
INTREPID - Storage Networking System - BROCADE CORPORATION; *pg.* 365, *pg.* 312
INTREPID - Filtration Product - KIMBERLY-CLARK CORPORATION; *pg.* 1461, *pg.* 1720
INTREPID - Heating System - SLANT/FIN CORPORATION; *pg.* 1076, *pg.* 1163
INTRIGUE - Vinyl Tile - CONGOLEUM CORPORATION; *pg.* 921, *pg.* 1084
INTRIGUE - Lighting Fixture - PHOENIX PRODUCTS COMPANY; *pg.* 1304, *pg.* 1879
THE INTRIGUE - Writing Instrument - SHEAFFER PEN CORPORATION; *pg.* 469, *pg.* 371
INTRIGUE - Chafer - THE VOLLRATH COMPANY LLC; *pg.* 1139, *pg.* 1894
INTRINSIC - Furniture - ASHLEY FURNITURE INDUSTRIES, INC.; *pg.* 914, *pg.* 1852
INTRINSICS - Cotton Coil And Cushion - BARNHARDT MANUFACTURING COMPANY; *pg.* 1498, *pg.* 1364
INTRO-SERT - Fasteners - YARDLEY PRODUCTS CORPORATION; *pg.* 1391, *pg.* 1596
INTRO-TIP - Pneumothorax Set - COOK GROUP, INC.; *pg.* 1518, *pg.* 674
INTRO TO THE 7 HABITS FOR HEALTHCARE - Workshop - FRANKLIN COVEY CO.; *pg.* 1642, *pg.* 1758
INTRON - Medicine - MERCK & CO., INC.; *pg.* 1566, *pg.* 1077
!INTROS! - Food Product - SHAMROCK FOODS COMPANY; *pg.* 895, *pg.* 20
INTROSPECT - Software - AUTONOMY PLEASANTON; *pg.* 358, *pg.* 183
INTRUDER - Insecticide - E.I. DU PONT DE NEMOURS & COMPANY; *pg.* 1159, *pg.* 390
INTRUDER - Fire Helmet - MINE SAFETY APPLIANCES COMPANY; *pg.* 1361, *pg.* 1525
INTRUDER ALERT - Software - SYMANTEC CORPORATION; *pg.* 478, *pg.* 161
INTRUST - Software - DELL SOFTWARE; *pg.* 385, *pg.* 40
INTRUST PLUG-IN FOR ACTIVE DIRECTORY - Software - DELL SOFTWARE; *pg.* 385, *pg.* 40
INTRUST PLUG-IN FOR EXCHANGE - Software - DELL SOFTWARE; *pg.* 385, *pg.* 40
INTRUST PLUG-IN FOR FILE ACCESS - Software - DELL SOFTWARE; *pg.* 385, *pg.* 40
INTUIT PAYROLL - Software - INTUIT INC.; *pg.* 769, *pg.* 158
INTUIT REAL ESTATE SOLUTIONS - Software - INTUIT INC.; *pg.* 769, *pg.* 158
INTUITION - Fabric - NEMSCHOFF, INC.; *pg.* 936, *pg.* 1890
INTUITION - Eyewear - SIGNATURE EYEWEAR, INC.; *pg.* 1429, *pg.* 105
INTUITIVE - Surgical System - INTUITIVE SURGICAL, INC.; *pg.* 1546, *pg.* 286
INTUITRAK - Medical Delivery System - ENDOLOGIX, INC.; *pg.* 1528, *pg.* 109
INTUITY - Telecommunication Product - AVAYA INC.; *pg.* 621, *pg.* 264
INTUNE - Software - BMC SOFTWARE, INC.; *pg.* 362, *pg.* 1701
INTYCE - Footwear - STEVEN MADDEN, LTD.; *pg.* 1819, *pg.* 1176
INVACARE - Full-Electric Low Bed - ALIMED, INC.; *pg.* 1490, *pg.* 816
INVACARE VIRTUAL SERVICE - Medical Services - INVACARE CORPORATION; *pg.* 1546, *pg.* 1451
INVADER - Mop Handle - HILLYARD, INC.; *pg.* 331, *pg.* 990
INVADER - Fire Helmet - MINE SAFETY APPLIANCES COMPANY; *pg.* 1361, *pg.* 1525
INVADER-X - Saw Blade - THE DOALL COMPANY; *pg.* 1329, *pg.* 670
INVADER-XP - Saw Blade - THE DOALL COMPANY; *pg.* 1329, *pg.* 670
INVADERS FROM THE PLANET MOOLAH - Game - WMS INDUSTRIES INC.; *pg.* 593, *pg.* 666
INVANCE - Medical Device - AMERICAN MEDICAL SYSTEMS HOLDINGS, INC.; *pg.* 1493, *pg.* 947
INVAR - Cast Tooling - WAUKESHA FOUNDRY INC.; *pg.* 1388, *pg.* 1898
INVARIGON - Camera Lenses - CVI MELLES GRIOT; *pg.* 1407, *pg.* 59
INVAROX - Film - E.I. DU PONT DE NEMOURS & COMPANY; *pg.* 1159, *pg.* 390
INVASION - Game - ACTIVISION BLIZZARD, INC.; *pg.* 948, *pg.* 271
INVASION - Apparel - OAKLEY, INC.; *pg.* 1840, *pg.* 86
INVASION WILD - Game - WMS INDUSTRIES INC.; *pg.* 593, *pg.* 666
INVENTED HERE - Slogan - EOLAS TECHNOLOGIES, INC.; *pg.* 1243, *pg.* 573
INVENTIT - Software - LOCKHEED MARTIN CORPORATION; *pg.* 229, *pg.* 762
INVENTOR - Software - AUTODESK INC.; *pg.* 356, *pg.* 257
INVENTOR LT - Software - AUTODESK INC.; *pg.* 356, *pg.* 257
THE INVENTOR OF MR SCANNING - Slogan - FONAR CORPORATION; *pg.* 1413, *pg.* 1179
INVENTORY PLANNER - Software - ASPEN TECHNOLOGY, INC.; *pg.* 354, *pg.* 804
INVENTRA - Software System - MENTOR GRAPHICS CORPORATION; *pg.* 432, *pg.* 1510
INVERNESS - Dinnerware - THE HOMER LAUGHLIN CHINA COMPANY; *pg.* 1125, *pg.* 1850
INVERNESS 1000 - Ear Piercing Systems - INVERNESS CORPORATION; *pg.* 512, *pg.* 783
INVERNESS 2000 - Ear Piercing System - INVERNESS CORPORATION; *pg.* 512, *pg.* 783
INVERSINE - Hypertension Treatment - TARGACEPT, INC.; *pg.* 1601, *pg.* 1395
INVERT - Solvents - THE DOW CHEMICAL COMPANY; *pg.* 1157, *pg.* 898
INVERT-A-CAP - Paint & Coating - AERVOE INDUSTRIES INCORPORATED; *pg.* 1439, *pg.* 1021
INVERTA-VOLT - Inverter - LA MARCHE MANUFACTURING COMPANY; *pg.* 1300, *pg.* 606
INVERTEC - Power Source - LINCOLN ELECTRIC HOLDINGS, INC.; *pg.* 1355, *pg.* 1432
INVERTED CRESCENT - Lens - DANKER LABORATORIES INC.; *pg.* 1408, *pg.* 465
INVERTER DRIVE MOTOR - Industrial Electric Motors - BALDOR ELECTRIC COMPANY; *pg.* 1316, *pg.* 32
INVERTER SPIKE RESISTANT - Magnet Wire - BALDOR ELECTRIC COMPANY; *pg.* 1316, *pg.* 32
INVESCO PERPETUAL - Investment Management Products & Services - INVESCO LTD.; *pg.* 771, *pg.* 513

INVEST WITH CONFIDENCE - Slogan - T. ROWE PRICE GROUP INC.; pg. 808, pg. 759
INVESTAR - Software - SUNGARD DATA SYSTEMS INC.; pg. 477, pg. 1592
INVESTEXT - Software Tool And Application - THOMSON REUTERS MARKETS; pg. 810, pg. 1299
INVESTIER - Software - SUNGARD DATA SYSTEMS INC.; pg. 477, pg. 1592
INVESTIGATOR - Clinical Trial Management System - PAREXEL INTERNATIONAL CORPORATION; pg. 1580, pg. 853
INVESTING FOR THE LONG RUN - Slogan - W.P. CAREY & CO., LLC; pg. 823, pg. 1315
INVESTING IN THE FUTURE - Tagline - BURNHAM HOLDINGS, INC.; pg. 1069, pg. 1546
INVESTMENTNEWS - Newspaper - CRAIN COMMUNICATIONS, INC.; pg. 1631, pg. 879
INVESTONE - Software - SUNGARD DATA SYSTEMS INC.; pg. 477, pg. 1592
INVESTONE ENTERPRISE - Software - SUNGARD DATA SYSTEMS INC.; pg. 477, pg. 1592
INVESTORS BUSINESS DAILY - Newspaper - INVESTORS BUSINESS DAILY, INC.; pg. 1653, pg. 133
INVESTORS.COM - Website - INVESTORS BUSINESS DAILY, INC.; pg. 1653, pg. 133
INVESTRAN - Software - SUNGARD DATA SYSTEMS INC.; pg. 477, pg. 1592
INVICTA - Tires - THE GOODYEAR TIRE & RUBBER COMPANY; pg. 1883, pg. 1401
INVIEW - Image Fusion & Contouring Station - ACCURAY INCORPORATED; pg. 1486, pg. 282
INVIEW - Message Displayer - ROCKWELL AUTOMATION, INC.; pg. 668, pg. 1880
INVIEW AP - Software System - BOTTOMLINE TECHNOLOGIES (DE), INC.; pg. 727, pg. 1038
INVINCIBLE - Elastomeric Expansion Joints, Rubber Hose - THE MERCER RUBBER COMPANY; pg. 1886, pg. 1165
INVIRASE - Pharmaceutical Product - HOFFMANN-LA ROCHE INC.; pg. 1542, pg. 1099
INVISA - Hearing Aid - BELTONE ELECTRONICS LLC; pg. 1503, pg. 614
INVISALIGN - Orthodontic Device - ALIGN TECHNOLOGY, INC.; pg. 1489, pg. 237
INVISATRACE - Medical Product - CONMED CORPORATION; pg. 1517, pg. 1347
THE INVISIBLE CONCEALER - Blemish Concealer - COVER GIRL COSMETICS; pg. 506, pg. 772
INVISIBLE DRY - Personal Care Product - COLGATE-PALMOLIVE COMPANY; pg. 504, pg. 1215
INVISIBLE GLASS - Car Care Product - STONER INC.; pg. 985, pg. 1583
INVISIBLE SUPER LOW - Medical Equipment - INVACARE CORPORATION; pg. 1546, pg. 1451
INVISIBLESHIELD - Protective Coating - ZAGG INCORPORATED; pg. 690, pg. 1762
INVISIGRIP - Medical Device - LEMAITRE VASCULAR, INC.; pg. 1555, pg. 805
INVISION - Printer System - 3D SYSTEMS CORPORATION; pg. 339, pg. 1621
INVISION - Plastic Compound & Resin - A. SCHULMAN, INC.; pg. 1144, pg. 1452
INVISION - Welding & Cutting Equipment - MILLER ELECTRIC MANUFACTURING CO.; pg. 1361, pg. 1852
INVISION - Molecular Biology Product - THERMO FISHER SCIENTIFIC INC.; pg. 1602, pg. 61
INVISION 2000 - Cooler & Freezer Door - JAMISON DOOR COMPANY; pg. 89, pg. 771
INVISTA - Software - EMC CORPORATION; pg. 391, pg. 825
INVITATION - Almonds - BLUE DIAMOND GROWERS; pg. 840, pg. 195
INVITATION - Bath Product - KOHLER CO.; pg. 91, pg. 1862
INVITIUM - Medical Display System - PLANAR SYSTEMS, INC.; pg. 455, pg. 1495
INVITROLON - Molecular Biology Product - THERMO FISHER SCIENTIFIC INC.; pg. 1602, pg. 61
INVITROMASS - Molecular Biology Product - THERMO FISHER SCIENTIFIC INC.; pg. 1602, pg. 61
INVITROSOL - Molecular Biology Product - THERMO FISHER SCIENTIFIC INC.; pg. 1602, pg. 61
INVOLVE - Software - DIEBOLD, INCORPORATED; pg. 387, pg. 1407
INWALL - Speaker - TRIAD SPEAKERS, INC.; pg. 682, pg. 1507
INX - Ink And Coating Company - INX INTERNATIONAL INK CO.; pg. 421, pg. 658
INXCURE - Ink - INX INTERNATIONAL INK CO.; pg. 421, pg. 658
INXFLEX - Ink - INX INTERNATIONAL INK CO.; pg. 421, pg. 658
INXFRESH - Ink - INX INTERNATIONAL INK CO.; pg. 421, pg. 658
INXIGHT - Software - XEROX CORPORATION; pg. 494, pg. 365
INXWELL - Printing Paper - MOHAWK FINE PAPERS, INC.; pg. 1464, pg. 1153
IO-IO - Confectionery Products - THE HERSHEY CO.; pg. 1855, pg. 1538
IO9 - Technoculture Roundtable - GAWKER MEDIA LLC; pg. 1248, pg. 1234
IOA - Software - BMC SOFTWARE, INC.; pg. 362, pg. 1701
IOBI HOME - Telecommunications - VERIZON COMMUNICATIONS INC.; pg. 1875, pg. 1309
IOBIO - Bacteria, Slime and Algae Control - BALTIMORE AIRCOIL COMPANY; pg. 1069, pg. 773
IOC - Integrated Overflow Compartment - MODERN WELDING COMPANY, INC.; pg. 1363, pg. 739
IOLITE - Necklace - HUGGER MUGGER YOGA PRODUCTS LLC; pg. 1836, pg. 1758
ION - Buffered Electrodes - DYNATRONICS CORPORATION; pg. 1526, pg. 1757
ION - Lighting Control Console - ELECTRONIC THEATRE CONTROLS, INC.; pg. 1296, pg. 1872
ION - Software - INTERACTIVE INTELLIGENCE, INC.; pg. 417, pg. 687
ION-JOIN - Enhanced Bone Cement Adhesion - SPIRE CORPORATION; pg. 1378, pg. 786
ION SHINE - Hair Care Product - CONAIR CORPORATION; pg. 505, pg. 1055
ION SHINE CLEARPOWER - Hair Dryer - CONAIR CORPORATION; pg. 505, pg. 1055
ION-SIGHT - Medical Device - SPIRE CORPORATION; pg. 1378, pg. 786
ION SPORT - Sunglasses - SAFILO USA INC.; pg. 11, pg. 1106
IONA - Software - PROGRESS SOFTWARE CORPORATION; pg. 457, pg. 786
IONEDIT 2001 - Website Content Management Application - LCG TECHNOLOGIES CORPORATION; pg. 1261, pg. 779
IONGUARD - Orthopedic Device - SPIRE CORPORATION; pg. 1378, pg. 786
IONGUARD 3000 - Ion Implantation System - SPIRE CORPORATION; pg. 1378, pg. 786
IONIC CORD-KEEPER - Hair Dryer - CONAIR CORPORATION; pg. 505, pg. 1055
IONIC WHISPER - Room Ionizer - HABAND COMPANY, INC.; pg. 1772, pg. 1099
IONIS - Software - BIO-RAD LABORATORIES, INC.; pg. 1504, pg. 101
IONIX - Software - EMC CORPORATION; pg. 391, pg. 825
IONKLEEN - Purifier - PALL CORPORATION; pg. 232, pg. 1323
IONOMATIC 3000 - Home Products - HABAND COMPANY, INC.; pg. 1772, pg. 1099
IONOMATIC PLUS - Home Products - HABAND COMPANY, INC.; pg. 1772, pg. 1099
IONOTRODE - Robotic Product - HAMILTON CO., INC.; pg. 1415, pg. 1031
IONOX - Cleaning Chemical Product - KYZEN CORPORATION; pg. 331, pg. 1652
IONPRO - Thermal Processing Equipment - SURFACE COMBUSTION, INC.; pg. 1077, pg. 1462
IONWORKS - Electrophysiology System - MOLECULAR DEVICES CORPORATION; pg. 1568, pg. 287
IOPATH - Testing Instrument System - BECKMAN COULTER, INC.; pg. 1402, pg. 48
IOPE - Skin Care Products - AMOREPACIFIC US, INC.; pg. 498, pg. 1195
IOQ - Internet Services - IPASS, INC.; pg. 1259, pg. 193
IOS - Multi-Touch Operating System - APPLE INC.; pg. 350, pg. 73
IOS - Software - CISCO SYSTEMS, INC.; pg. 372, pg. 240
IOS - Lighting - STEELCASE INC.; pg. 475, pg. 889
IOSSO - Metal Processes System - SUPERIOR DIE SET CORP.; pg. 1379, pg. 1885
IOTA - Furniture - HERMAN MILLER, INC.; pg. 926, pg. 913
IOTEST - Testing Instrument System - BECKMAN COULTER, INC.; pg. 1402, pg. 48
IOUTSOURCE - Software - CINCOM SYSTEMS, INC.; pg. 372, pg. 1411
IOWA FARMER TODAY - Newspaper - IOWA FARMER TODAY; pg. 1653, pg. 702
IOWA TESTS OF BASIC SKILLS - School Testing System - HOUGHTON MIFFLIN HARCOURT PUBLISHING COMPANY; pg. 1651, pg. 796
IOWALIFECHANGING - Slogan - IOWA DEPARTMENT OF ECONOMIC DEVELOPMENT; pg. 995, pg. 705
IOWA'S $100,000 CASH GAME - Lottery Game - IOWA LOTTERY; pg. 996, pg. 705
IOWA'S POWERBALL - Lottery Game - IOWA LOTTERY; pg. 996, pg. 705
IP APPLICATION SWITCH - Software - F5 NETWORKS, INC.; pg. 396, pg. 1835
IP BUSINESS TRUNKS - Cable & Wireline Solutions - SONUS NETWORKS INC.; pg. 1281, pg. 858
IP CENTRAL OFFICE - Telephone Service - IDT CORPORATION; pg. 643, pg. 1096
IP CENTREX/VOBB - Wireline Solutions - SONUS NETWORKS INC.; pg. 1281, pg. 858
IP ENGINE - Software System - MENTOR GRAPHICS CORPORATION; pg. 432, pg. 1510
IP EVALUATION KIT - Software System - MENTOR GRAPHICS CORPORATION; pg. 432, pg. 1510
IP FACTORY - Software System - MENTOR GRAPHICS CORPORATION; pg. 432, pg. 1510
IP OASIS - Software - CYPRESS SEMICONDUCTOR CORPORATION; pg. 1326, pg. 243
IP-PCB - Software System - MENTOR GRAPHICS CORPORATION; pg. 432, pg. 1510
IP QUICKUSE - Software System - MENTOR GRAPHICS CORPORATION; pg. 432, pg. 1510
IP SAN (ISCSI) SOLUTIONS - Software - NETAPP, INC.; pg. 444, pg. 287
IP SERIES - Pump Product - IDEX CORPORATION; pg. 1347, pg. 623
IP SERIES - Wireless Communications Products - IPMOBILENET, LLC; pg. 648, pg. 261
IP2LOCATION - Software - MELISSA DATA CORP.; pg. 432, pg. 188
IPAC - Amplifier - SKYWORKS SOLUTIONS, INC.; pg. 674, pg. 862
IPAD - Electronic Tablet - APPLE INC.; pg. 350, pg. 73
IPANEMA POMEGRANITE - Beverage - BAI BRANDS; pg. 238, pg. 1073
IPAP MAX - Medical Device - RESMED INC.; pg. 1589, pg. 207
IPAP MIN - Medical Device - RESMED INC.; pg. 1589, pg. 207
IPAQ - Lighting Equipment - ELECTRONIC THEATRE CONTROLS, INC.; pg. 1296, pg. 1872
IPAQ - Pocket Computer - HEWLETT-PACKARD COMPANY; pg. 404, pg. 175
IPARTNER - Customer Support Programs Portfolio - KLA-TENCOR CORPORATION; pg. 1353, pg. 146
IPARTNER SOLUTIONS - Medical Services - INVACARE CORPORATION; pg. 1546, pg. 1451
IPASS - Electronic Components - MOLEX INCORPORATED; pg. 655, pg. 628
IPASS CONNECT - Software - IPASS, INC.; pg. 1259, pg. 193
IPASS CORPORATE ACCESS - Internet Services - IPASS, INC.; pg. 1259, pg. 193
IPASS MANAGED ACCESS - Internet Services - IPASS, INC.; pg. 1259, pg. 193
IPASS+ - Electronic Components - MOLEX INCORPORATED; pg. 655, pg. 628
IPC - Interface Process Control - DUKANE CORPORATION; pg. 634, pg. 658
IPEX - Laser System - GSI GROUP INC.; pg. 1415, pg. 784
IPEX - Lingerie - VICTORIA'S SECRET STORES, LLC; pg. 1789, pg. 1471
IPEXPRESS - Configurable IP Cores - LATTICE SEMICONDUCTOR CORPORATION; pg. 651, pg. 1498
IPFS - Freight Service - FEDEX CORPORATION; pg. 1907, pg. 1642
IPGRUNNER - Molecular Biology Product - THERMO FISHER SCIENTIFIC INC.; pg. 1602, pg. 61
IPHONE - Smartphone - APPLE INC.; pg. 350, pg. 73
IPHOTO - Software Product - APPLE INC.; pg. 350, pg. 73
IPL - Elevator - SAVARIA CONCORD LIFTS INC.; pg. 1592, pg. 1919
IPLAS - Filter - GE ENERGY; pg. 1338, pg. 506
IPLAYER - Lighting System - PHILIPS SOLID-STATE LIGHTING SOLUTIONS; pg. 1303, pg. 806

First page reference indicates Business Class Edition
Second page reference indicates Geographic Edition

IPLEX - Software - SEQUENOM, INC.; *pg.* 1593, *pg.* 209
IPLEX GOLD - Diagnostic System - SEQUENOM, INC.; *pg.* 1593, *pg.* 209
IPLOT - Ingredient Analysis Technology - INTERNATIONAL FLAVORS & FRAGRANCES INC.; *pg.* 512, *pg.* 1244
IPLUS COMPOSITE - Sanitary Sewer - INSITUFORM TECHNOLOGIES INC; *pg.* 88, *pg.* 974
IPLUS INFUSION - Sanitary Sewer - INSITUFORM TECHNOLOGIES INC; *pg.* 88, *pg.* 974
IPMONITOR - Computer Software - SOLARWINDS, INC.; *pg.* 471, *pg.* 1666
IPN - Latex - THE DOW CHEMICAL COMPANY; *pg.* 1157, *pg.* 898
IPNET - Intelligent Process Network - PERCEPTRON, INC.; *pg.* 215, *pg.* 904
IPOD - Portable Digital Music & Media Players - APPLE INC.; *pg.* 350, *pg.* 73
IPOD - Software - CRESTRON ELECTRONICS INC.; *pg.* 631, *pg.* 1116
IPOD CLASSIC - Portable Digital Music & Media Players - APPLE INC.; *pg.* 350, *pg.* 73
IPOD HI-FI - Speakers - APPLE INC.; *pg.* 350, *pg.* 73
IPOD NANO - Portable Digital Music & Media Players - APPLE INC.; *pg.* 350, *pg.* 73
IPOD SHUFFLE - Portable Digital Music & Media Players - APPLE INC.; *pg.* 350, *pg.* 73
IPOD SOCKS - Computer Hardware Holder - APPLE INC.; *pg.* 350, *pg.* 73
IPOD SYSTEMS - Audio Player - EMERSON RADIO CORP.; *pg.* 636, *pg.* 1087
IPOD TOUCH - Portable Digital Music & Media Players - APPLE INC.; *pg.* 350, *pg.* 73
IPOINT - Pencil Sharpener - ACME UNITED CORPORATION; *pg.* 1040, *pg.* 346
IPOL - Poliovirus Vaccine - SANOFI PASTEUR, INC; *pg.* 1591, *pg.* 1588
IPOWER - Financial Services - JACKSON HEWITT TAX SERVICE INC.; *pg.* 771, *pg.* 1103
IPOWER - Video Conferencing Product - POLYCOM, INC.; *pg.* 664, *pg.* 249
IPOWIR - Power Semiconductor Device - INTERNATIONAL RECTIFIER CORPORATION; *pg.* 647, *pg.* 80
IPR-3 - Foot Care Product - CCA INDUSTRIES, INC.; *pg.* 503, *pg.* 1114
IPRIORITY - QoS Feature Set - POLYCOM, INC.; *pg.* 664, *pg.* 249
IPRISM - Software - EDGEWAVE INC; *pg.* 390, *pg.* 202
IPRO - Imaging System - 3D SYSTEMS CORPORATION; *pg.* 339, *pg.* 1621
IPROOF - Reagent - BIO-RAD LABORATORIES, INC.; *pg.* 1504, *pg.* 101
IPROX - Electrical Product - EATON CORPORATION; *pg.* 1331, *pg.* 1429
IPSEC - Software - CERTICOM CORP.; *pg.* 371, *pg.* 1925
IPSEI - Beverages - THE COCA-COLA COMPANY; *pg.* 240, *pg.* 493
IPSIM - Software System - MENTOR GRAPHICS CORPORATION; *pg.* 432, *pg.* 1510
IPSTOR - Software - FALCONSTOR SOFTWARE, INC.; *pg.* 396, *pg.* 1179
IPTV - TV Service - SONUS NETWORKS INC.; *pg.* 1281, *pg.* 858
IPUMP - Pain Management Pump - BAXTER INTERNATIONAL INC.; *pg.* 1499, *pg.* 599
IPUMP - Media Server - WEGENER CORPORATION; *pg.* 687, *pg.* 533
IPURE - Software - BIO-RAD LABORATORIES, INC.; *pg.* 1504, *pg.* 101
IPX - Computer Software - NOVELL INC.; *pg.* 446, *pg.* 852
IQ - Frame Relay Traffic Management - ADTRAN, INC.; *pg.* 344, *pg.* 6
IQ - Software - BIO-RAD LABORATORIES, INC.; *pg.* 1504, *pg.* 101
IQ - Bowling Equipment - BRUNSWICK BOWLING & BILLIARDS CORP.; *pg.* 1828, *pg.* 622
IQ - Recreational Vehicle - CLUB CAR, INC.; *pg.* 1830, *pg.* 532
IQ - Pumps - IDEX CORPORATION; *pg.* 1347, *pg.* 623
IQ - Urinalysis Workstation - IRIS INTERNATIONAL, INC.; *pg.* 1547, *pg.* 64
IQ - Online Services - QSOUND LABS, INC.; *pg.* 666, *pg.* 1904
I.Q. - Nutritional Product - RBC LIFE SCIENCES, INC.; *pg.* 1588, *pg.* 1723
I.Q. - Chairs - VIRCO MANUFACTURING CORPORATION; *pg.* 946, *pg.* 297
IQ 577 - Laser - IRIDEX CORPORATION; *pg.* 648, *pg.* 160
IQ 710 - Connecting Router - ADTRAN, INC.; *pg.* 344, *pg.* 6
IQ 810 - Laser - IRIDEX CORPORATION; *pg.* 648, *pg.* 160
IQ-CHECK - Software - BIO-RAD LABORATORIES, INC.; *pg.* 1504, *pg.* 101
IQ GEOMETRY - Medical Knives - SURGICAL SPECIALTIES CORPORATION; *pg.* 1600, *pg.* 1912
IQ NETWORKING - Fiber-Optic Network System - CENTURYLINK, INC; *pg.* 1870, *pg.* 317
IQ PROFILER - Sensor - NAPCO SECURITY SYSTEMS, INC.; *pg.* 658, *pg.* 1138
IQ SORT - Sorter - OPEX CORPORATION; *pg.* 450, *pg.* 1087
IQ VIEW - Software - ADTRAN, INC.; *pg.* 344, *pg.* 6
IQ200 - Microscopic Analyzer - IRIS INTERNATIONAL, INC.; *pg.* 1547, *pg.* 64
IQ2200 - Semiconductor Solution - VITESSE SEMICONDUCTOR CORPORATION; *pg.* 686, *pg.* 57
IQC - Software - BIO-RAD LABORATORIES, INC.; *pg.* 1504, *pg.* 101
IQEPAL - Chemical Product - SPECTRUM CHEMICALS & LABORATORY PRODUCTS, INC.; *pg.* 1181, *pg.* 94
IQEVENT ENGINE - Firmware - TRIMBLE NAVIGATION LIMITED; *pg.* 1384, *pg.* 288
IQFX - Software - QSOUND LABS, INC.; *pg.* 666, *pg.* 1904
IQFX2 - Audio System - QSOUND LABS, INC.; *pg.* 666, *pg.* 1904
IQFX3 - Audio System - QSOUND LABS, INC.; *pg.* 666, *pg.* 1904
IQHEALTH - Consumer Relationship Management Solution for Healthcare Professionals - CERNER CORPORATION; *pg.* 1514, *pg.* 981
IQMODEL POWERTOOLS - Software - ASPEN TECHNOLOGY, INC.; *pg.* 354, *pg.* 804
IQMS - Software - QSOUND LABS, INC.; *pg.* 666, *pg.* 1904
IQMS2 - Software - QSOUND LABS, INC.; *pg.* 666, *pg.* 1904
IQSMART - Smart - EASTMAN KODAK COMPANY; *pg.* 1408, *pg.* 1333
IR BENDER - IR Equipment - UNIVERSAL ELECTRONICS, INC.; *pg.* 683, *pg.* 262
IR CHANNEL - Financial Information - THOMSON REUTERS CORPORATION; *pg.* 1693, *pg.* 1944
IR MENTOR PRO - Software - BIO-RAD LABORATORIES, INC.; *pg.* 1504, *pg.* 101
IRACORE - Pipe System - INDUSTRIAL RUBBER PRODUCTS, INC.; *pg.* 1349, *pg.* 926
IRADIO - Computer Program - MOTOROLA SOLUTIONS, INC.; *pg.* 657, *pg.* 659
IRATHANE - Elastomeric Protective Coating - INDUSTRIAL RUBBER PRODUCTS, INC.; *pg.* 1349, *pg.* 926
IRB - Software - CHYRONHEGO; *pg.* 371, *pg.* 1179
IRCO - Coating Product - PPG INDUSTRIES, INC.; *pg.* 1445, *pg.* 1579
IRCOGEL - Use with Metallo-Organic Thixotropic Agents - THE LUBRIZOL CORPORATION; *pg.* 1171, *pg.* 1481
IRDA - Software - ZILOG INC.; *pg.* 497, *pg.* 252
IREACH - Educational Materials - SCHOLASTIC INC.; *pg.* 1683, *pg.* 1288
IREACH READ ACHIEVE - Educational Materials - SCHOLASTIC INC.; *pg.* 1683, *pg.* 1288
IRECRUITER - Software - ICIMS, INC.; *pg.* 411, *pg.* 1083
IRENE - Clothing - ABERCROMBIE & FITCH CO.; *pg.* 37, *pg.* 1466
IRENE - Furniture - LA-Z-BOY INCORPORATED; *pg.* 932, *pg.* 901
IRGENT - Telecom Product - PREMIERE GLOBAL SERVICES, INC.; *pg.* 1275, *pg.* 518
IRICELL - Urinalysis Workstation - IRIS INTERNATIONAL, INC.; *pg.* 1547, *pg.* 64
IRIDESCENT TAFFETA - Bridal Wear - ALFRED ANGELO, INC.; *pg.* 17, *pg.* 1532
IRIDESCENTS - Paper & Nonwoven Material - FIBERMARK INC.; *pg.* 1457, *pg.* 1764
IRIDIUM - Tile - ARTISTIC TILE INC.; *pg.* 914, *pg.* 1119
IRIMO - Hand Tools - SNAP-ON INCORPORATED; *pg.* 1062, *pg.* 1862
IRINA - Furniture - AMISCO INDUSTRIES LTD.; *pg.* 913, *pg.* 1958
IRIS - Variable Aperture Collimator - ACCURAY INCORPORATED; *pg.* 1486, *pg.* 282
IRIS - Furniture - THE COMMERCIAL FURNITURE GROUP; *pg.* 920, *pg.* 994
IRIS - Medical Product - HOLOGIC, INC.; *pg.* 1416, *pg.* 784
IRIS - Diagnostic Urinalysis System - IRIS INTERNATIONAL, INC.; *pg.* 1547, *pg.* 64
IRIS - Furniture - NEMSCHOFF, INC.; *pg.* 936, *pg.* 1890
IRISH LINEN - Printing Paper - MOHAWK FINE PAPERS, INC.; *pg.* 1464, *pg.* 1153
IRISH O'GARLIC - Sausage - JOHNSONVILLE SAUSAGE, LLC; *pg.* 867, *pg.* 1894
IRISH SETTER - Outdoor Sport Boots - RED WING SHOE COMPANY, INC.; *pg.* 1817, *pg.* 954
IRISH SETTER SPORT BOOTS - Footwear - RED WING SHOE COMPANY, INC.; *pg.* 1817, *pg.* 954
IRISH SPRING - Personal Care Product - COLGATE-PALMOLIVE COMPANY; *pg.* 504, *pg.* 1215
IRISH STOUT - Beverage - SPRECHER BREWING COMPANY; *pg.* 265, *pg.* 1858
IRM - Dental Product - DENTSPLY INTERNATIONAL INC.; *pg.* 1522, *pg.* 1596
IROBOT - Robotic Equipment - IROBOT CORP.; *pg.* 1418, *pg.* 785
IROBOT CONNECTR - Communication Robots - IROBOT CORP.; *pg.* 1418, *pg.* 785
IROBOT CREATE - Programmable Robot - IROBOT CORP.; *pg.* 1418, *pg.* 785
IROBOT DIRT DOG - Shop Sweeping Robot - IROBOT CORP.; *pg.* 1418, *pg.* 785
IROBOT LOOJ - Gutter Cleaning Robot - IROBOT CORP.; *pg.* 1418, *pg.* 785
IROBOT NEGOTIATOR - Surveillance Robot - IROBOT CORP.; *pg.* 1418, *pg.* 785
IROBOT RANGER - Government & Industrial Robots - IROBOT CORP.; *pg.* 1418, *pg.* 785
IROBOT SEAGLIDER - Government & Industrial Robots - IROBOT CORP.; *pg.* 1418, *pg.* 785
IROBOT TRANSPHIBIAN - Government & Industrial Robots - IROBOT CORP.; *pg.* 1418, *pg.* 785
IROBOT WARRIOR - Government & Industrial Robots - IROBOT CORP.; *pg.* 1418, *pg.* 785
IROGRAN - Thermoplastic Polyurethanes - HUNTSMAN CORPORATION; *pg.* 1167, *pg.* 1758
IROM - Orthopedic Product - DJO INCORPORATED; *pg.* 1524, *pg.* 302
IRON CURTAIN - Bicycle Accessories - SPECIALIZED BICYCLE COMPONENTS, INC.; *pg.* 1711, *pg.* 152
IRON ETCHINGS - Bath Product - KOHLER CO.; *pg.* 91, *pg.* 1862
IRON-FRAME - Vertical-Field Magnet Design - FONAR CORPORATION; *pg.* 1413, *pg.* 1179
IRON GRILLED - Sandwich - INTERNATIONAL DAIRY QUEEN, INC.; *pg.* 1732, *pg.* 938
IRON MAN - Sunglasses - FGX INTERNATIONAL, INC.; *pg.* 5, *pg.* 1608
IRON MAN - Toy & Game - HASBRO, INC.; *pg.* 954, *pg.* 1603
IRON MAN - Heat Transfer Paper - NEENAH PAPER, INC.; *pg.* 1465, *pg.* 484
IRON MASK - Protective Welding Helmet - SELLSTROM MANUFACTURING CO.; *pg.* 1428, *pg.* 659
IRON MEND - Adhesive & Sealant - MCNETT CORPORATION; *pg.* 1839, *pg.* 1817
IRON MOUNTAIN CONNECT - Software System - IRON MOUNTAIN INCORPORATED; *pg.* 421, *pg.* 796
IRON WORKS - Bath Product - KOHLER CO.; *pg.* 91, *pg.* 1862
IRON WORKS HISTORIC - Bath Product - KOHLER CO.; *pg.* 91, *pg.* 1862
IRONCLAD - Cold Condition Glove - ALIMED, INC.; *pg.* 1490, *pg.* 816
IRONCLAD - Industrial Coatings - BENJAMIN MOORE & CO.; *pg.* 1440, *pg.* 1085
IRONCLAD - Performance Gloves - MACE SECURITY INTERNATIONAL, INC.; *pg.* 1172, *pg.* 1541
IRONINGPRO - Ironing Board - HOME PRODUCTS INTERNATIONAL, INC.; *pg.* 1125, *pg.* 577
IRONMAN ICONTROL - Watch - TIMEX CORPORATION; *pg.* 14, *pg.* 355
IRONMAN TRIATHLON - Licensee - TIMEX CORPORATION; *pg.* 14, *pg.* 355
IRONMATE - Ironing Board - HOME PRODUCTS INTERNATIONAL, INC.; *pg.* 1125, *pg.* 577
IRONPORT - Email & Web Security Product - CISCO SYSTEMS, INC.; *pg.* 372, *pg.* 240
IRONTUFF - Sub-Zero Clothing - REFRIGIWEAR, INC.; *pg.* 47, *pg.* 529
IRONWORKS - Tile - ARTISTIC TILE INC.; *pg.* 914, *pg.* 1119
IROOM - Intelligent Room - TELUS CORPORATION; *pg.* 1952, *pg.* 1912

IROPSNET - Software - PASSUR AEROSPACE, INC.; *pg.* 233, *pg.* 376
IRP - Snowmobile - ARCTIC CAT INC.; *pg.* 1705, *pg.* 953
IRRIGO - Medical Product - PROPPER MANUFACTURING COMPANY, INC.; *pg.* 1586, *pg.* 1175
IRRITROL SYSTEMS - Irrigation Product - THE TORO COMPANY; *pg.* 1065, *pg.* 918
IRRP.NET - Radio & Multimedia Service - BRS MEDIA INC.; *pg.* 1233, *pg.* 214
IRS - Software - NIELSEN AUDIO; *pg.* 446, *pg.* 768
IRT/C - Thermometer System - EXERGEN CORPORATION; *pg.* 1412, *pg.* 855
IRTRAN - Infrared Transmitting Materials & Optics - EASTMAN KODAK COMPANY; *pg.* 1408, *pg.* 1333
IRULES - Software - F5 NETWORKS, INC.; *pg.* 396, *pg.* 1835
IRVING THE VIKING - Video Game - INTERNATIONAL GAME TECHNOLOGY; *pg.* 957, *pg.* 1024
IRVISTA - Software - FLIR SYSTEMS, INC.; *pg.* 1413, *pg.* 1510
IRWINDOWS - Software - HEICO CORPORATION; *pg.* 228, *pg.* 431
IRX - Thermal Processing Equipment - SURFACE COMBUSTION, INC.; *pg.* 1077, *pg.* 1462
IS THIS THE YEAR? - Commercial Campaign - NATIONAL HOCKEY LEAGUE; *pg.* 568, *pg.* 1265
IS639 - Sunflower Hybrids - MONSANTO; *pg.* 1798, *pg.* 1399
ISABEL - Clothing - ABERCROMBIE & FITCH CO.; *pg.* 37, *pg.* 1466
ISABEL - Dolls - AMERICAN GIRL LLC; *pg.* 949, *pg.* 1871
ISABEL - Women's Clothing & Accessories - WOODEN SHIPS OF HOBOKEN; *pg.* 35, *pg.* 1315
ISABEL CRISTINA - Nailcare Product - MEDICOOL, INC.; *pg.* 1562, *pg.* 294
ISABELLA - Vanity Lights - CRAFTMADE INTERNATIONAL, INC.; *pg.* 1295, *pg.* 1670
ISABELLA - Video Game - INTERNATIONAL GAME TECHNOLOGY; *pg.* 957, *pg.* 1024
ISABELLA - Lighting Product - QUOIZEL INC.; *pg.* 1304, *pg.* 1616
ISABELLA BIRD - Online Gift Store - IAC/INTERACTIVECORP; *pg.* 292, *pg.* 1242
IS_ANALYZER - Software System - MENTOR GRAPHICS CORPORATION; *pg.* 432, *pg.* 1510
ISAP - Paper Products - BOISE CASCADE HOLDINGS, L.L.C.; *pg.* 1453, *pg.* 546
ISCALA - Software - EPICOR SOFTWARE CORPORATION; *pg.* 393, *pg.* 110
ISCAN - Scanner System - ILLUMINA, INC.; *pg.* 412, *pg.* 203
ISCD - Storage System - HGST; *pg.* 406, *pg.* 260
ISCEON - Refrigerants - E.I. DU PONT DE NEMOURS & COMPANY; *pg.* 1159, *pg.* 390
ISCH-DISH - Polyurethane Foam - SPAN-AMERICA MEDICAL SYSTEMS, INC.; *pg.* 1595, *pg.* 1618
ISCRIPT - Reagent - BIO-RAD LABORATORIES, INC.; *pg.* 1504, *pg.* 101
ISCSI - Software - OVERLAND STORAGE, INC.; *pg.* 451, *pg.* 205
ISD CREATIONSM - Software System - MENTOR GRAPHICS CORPORATION; *pg.* 432, *pg.* 1510
ISELI - Swiss Screw Machine - DANAHER CORPORATION; *pg.* 1044, *pg.* 397
ISENSOR - Integrated Circuits - ANALOG DEVICES, INC.; *pg.* 617, *pg.* 839
ISEP - Ion Exchange Resin - CALGON CARBON CORPORATION; *pg.* 1151, *pg.* 1574
ISEQ - Molecular Typing - SEQUENOM, INC.; *pg.* 1593, *pg.* 209
ISERIES CENTRAL - Software System - KRONOS INCORPORATED; *pg.* 425, *pg.* 813
ISERVER - Content Management Server - ACTUATE CORPORATION; *pg.* 342, *pg.* 253
ISEWRITE - Software - TRANS-LUX CORPORATION; *pg.* 681, *pg.* 365
ISFAHAN - Rug - ETHAN ALLEN INTERIORS INC.; *pg.* 924, *pg.* 343
IS_FLOORPLANNER - Software System - MENTOR GRAPHICS CORPORATION; *pg.* 432, *pg.* 1510
ISHIHARA - Healthcare Product - GF HEALTH PRODUCTS, INC.; *pg.* 1535, *pg.* 508
ISHIPDOCS - Digital Shipping Tool - AMERICAN REPROGRAPHICS COMPANY; *pg.* 1616, *pg.* 303
ISI - Software - WIND RIVER SYSTEMS, INC.; *pg.* 493, *pg.* 38
ISID-PLUS - Securities Identifiers - STANDARD & POOR'S RATINGS SERVICES; *pg.* 805, *pg.* 1296
ISIGHT - Camera - APPLE INC.; *pg.* 350, *pg.* 73
ISIM - Online Design Tool - INTERSIL CORPORATION; *pg.* 647, *pg.* 146
ISIS - Software - EMC CORPORATION; *pg.* 391, *pg.* 825
ISIS - Electrical System - LITTELFUSE, INC.; *pg.* 1301, *pg.* 580
ISIS - Footwear - VANS, INC.; *pg.* 1821, *pg.* 76
ISIS 2L - Women's Specific Hydration Pack - JANSPORT; *pg.* 1837, *pg.* 38
ISKILLS - Information & Communication Technology Literacy Test - EDUCATIONAL TESTING SERVICE INC.; *pg.* 1394, *pg.* 1111
ISLAND FARMS - Dairy Products - AGROPUR COOPERATIVE; *pg.* 836, *pg.* 1950
ISLAND FORTUNE - Game - WMS INDUSTRIES INC.; *pg.* 593, *pg.* 666
ISLAND GRAND - Resort - TRADEWINDS ISLANDS RESORTS ON SAINT PETE BEACH; *pg.* 1116, *pg.* 461
ISLAND MANGO - Candle - THE YANKEE CANDLE COMPANY, INC.; *pg.* 1792, *pg.* 843
ISLAND NATURALS - Hair & Skin Product - AUBREY ORGANICS INC.; *pg.* 499, *pg.* 470
ISLAND ORANGE SPICE - Spiced Tea - CELESTIAL SEASONINGS, INC.; *pg.* 846, *pg.* 310
ISLAND SOFT - Label Apparel - OXFORD INDUSTRIES, INC.; *pg.* 30, *pg.* 517
ISLAND STAGS - Slippers - HABAND COMPANY, INC.; *pg.* 1772, *pg.* 1099
ISLANDER - Weekly Newspaper - ASBURY PARK PRESS INC.; *pg.* 1617, *pg.* 1090
ISLANDS - Magazine - BONNIER CORPORATION; *pg.* 1622, *pg.* 480
ISLES SERIES - Workbenches - IAC INDUSTRIES, INC.; *pg.* 929, *pg.* 48
ISLET - Flatware - ONEIDA LTD; *pg.* 1129, *pg.* 1318
ISLETEST - Diabetes Prediction Test - BIOMERICA, INC.; *pg.* 1506, *pg.* 107
ISM 370 - iPod Docking with CD/CD+G Karaoke System - THE SINGING MACHINE COMPANY, INC.; *pg.* 674, *pg.* 426
ISMATEC - Pump Product - IDEX CORPORATION; *pg.* 1347, *pg.* 623
IS_MULTIBOARD - Software System - MENTOR GRAPHICS CORPORATION; *pg.* 432, *pg.* 1510
ISO 3 - Roof Insulation - JOHNS MANVILLE CORPORATION; *pg.* 89, *pg.* 320
ISO E SUPER - Fragrance Ingredient - INTERNATIONAL FLAVORS & FRAGRANCES INC.; *pg.* 512, *pg.* 1244
ISO-FAST - Catalysts & Synthetic Resins - ASHLAND INC.; *pg.* 972, *pg.* 726
ISO-FLO - Vibratory Conveyor - KEY TECHNOLOGY, INC.; *pg.* 868, *pg.* 1847
ISO-FLO - Voltage Block System - NORDSON CORPORATION; *pg.* 1365, *pg.* 1480
ISO FORCE - Golf Club - KARSTEN MANUFACTURING CORPORATION; *pg.* 1838, *pg.* 17
ISO-GRID - Food Safety Product - NEOGEN CORPORATION; *pg.* 883, *pg.* 896
ISO-GRIP - Mechanical Grip Controllers - ALTEC INDUSTRIES INC.; *pg.* 1312, *pg.* 1
ISO-HD - Whey Protein Isolate & Hydrolysate - BPI SPORTS, LLC; *pg.* 842, *pg.* 430
ISO-OHM - Dielectric Coatings & Films - FERRO CORPORATION; *pg.* 1162, *pg.* 1462
ISO-PRINE - Animal Safety Product - NEOGEN CORPORATION; *pg.* 883, *pg.* 896
ISO SEARCH - Image Simulator Software - AMERICAN SCIENCE AND ENGINEERING, INC.; *pg.* 1399, *pg.* 787
ISO-SPAND - Bevel Product - GLEASON CORPORATION; *pg.* 1340, *pg.* 1335
ISO TAB-L - Vibration Isolation Table - FABREEKA INTERNATIONAL, INC.; *pg.* 1882, *pg.* 847
ISO-TEK - Cold Storage Door System - RITE-HITE HOLDING CORPORATION; *pg.* 1372, *pg.* 1880
ISO-TIP - Cordless Soldering Iron - WAHL CLIPPER CORPORATION; *pg.* 524, *pg.* 662
ISOBAND - Medical & Aesthetic Product - DYNATRONICS CORPORATION; *pg.* 1526, *pg.* 1757
ISOBAR - Surge Suppressors; Premium - TRIPPE MANUFACTURING COMPANY; *pg.* 220, *pg.* 592
ISOBEL - Personal Care Electrical Product - HELEN OF TROY L.P.; *pg.* 511, *pg.* 1692
ISOBIND - Isocyanate Binders - THE DOW CHEMICAL COMPANY; *pg.* 1157, *pg.* 898
ISOBOND - Coating - YENKIN-MAJESTIC PAINT CORPORATION; *pg.* 1450, *pg.* 1445
ISOBUTYL NICLATE - Antioxidants - R.T. VANDERBILT COMPANY, INC.; *pg.* 1180, *pg.* 364
ISOCAL HCN - Liquid Diet for Tube Feeding - MEAD JOHNSON NUTRITION COMPANY; *pg.* 1561, *pg.* 615
ISOCAST - Insulation Panels - THE DOW CHEMICAL COMPANY; *pg.* 1157, *pg.* 898
ISOCAT - Catalyst Additive - JOHNSON MATTHEY PROCESS TECHNOLOGIES; *pg.* 1169, *pg.* 1083
ISOCAT HP - Enhancement Additive - JOHNSON MATTHEY PROCESS TECHNOLOGIES; *pg.* 1169, *pg.* 1083
ISOCATH - Endotracheal Tube Suctioning - VITAL SIGNS, INC.; *pg.* 1607, *pg.* 1126
ISOCENTER - Transformer - MIDDLE ATLANTIC PRODUCTS INC.; *pg.* 1360, *pg.* 1065
ISOCHEM - Pump Product - IDEX CORPORATION; *pg.* 1347, *pg.* 623
ISOCIL - Chemical Product - LONZA INC.; *pg.* 1171, *pg.* 1041
ISOCLASS - Bearing Product - THE TIMKEN COMPANY; *pg.* 218, *pg.* 1408
ISOCLEAN - Protective Clothing - E.I. DU PONT DE NEMOURS & COMPANY; *pg.* 1159, *pg.* 390
ISOCLEAR - High Fructose Corn Syrups - CARGILL LIMITED; *pg.* 1475, *pg.* 1914
ISOCOAT - Resin - SI GROUP, INC.; *pg.* 1181, *pg.* 1341
ISOCURE - Resin Binders - ASHLAND INC.; *pg.* 972, *pg.* 726
ISOFACE - Pharmaceutical Product - VALEANT PHARMACEUTICALS INTERNATIONAL; *pg.* 1605, *pg.* 1047
ISOFLAVONE - Nutritional Supplement - NATURAL ORGANICS, INC.; *pg.* 1571, *pg.* 1181
ISOFLEX - Passive-Fixation Leads - ST. JUDE MEDICAL, INC.; *pg.* 1596, *pg.* 963
ISOFLEX - Patient Handling Equipment - STRYKER CORPORATION; *pg.* 1598, *pg.* 894
ISOFLO - Inhalant Anesthetic - ABBOTT LABORATORIES; *pg.* 1484, *pg.* 551
ISOFLUID - Face Mask - CROSSTEX INTERNATIONAL INC.; *pg.* 1520, *pg.* 1164
ISOFLURANE - Anesthetic - HALOCARBON PRODUCTS CORPORATION; *pg.* 978, *pg.* 1116
ISOFORM - Isomerization Grade Perchloroethylene - THE DOW CHEMICAL COMPANY; *pg.* 1157, *pg.* 898
ISOFORM - Gear Shaper Cutters - GLEASON CORPORATION; *pg.* 1340, *pg.* 1335
ISOFRAX - Thermal Insulation Products - UNIFRAX CORPORATION; *pg.* 220, *pg.* 1317
ISOGRIP - Adhesives - ASHLAND INC.; *pg.* 972, *pg.* 726
ISOJECT - Medicine - PFIZER INC.; *pg.* 1581, *pg.* 1278
ISOLAGEN PROCESS - Cellular Processing - FIBROCELL SCIENCE, INC.; *pg.* 1530, *pg.* 1531
ISOLATIONWEAR - Medical Fabric - E.I. DU PONT DE NEMOURS & COMPANY; *pg.* 1159, *pg.* 390
ISOLATOR - Pipe - ADVANCED DRAINAGE SYSTEMS, INC.; *pg.* 1878, *pg.* 1455
ISOLATOR - Face Mask - CROSSTEX INTERNATIONAL INC.; *pg.* 1520, *pg.* 1164
ISOLEX - Magnetic Cell Selection System - BAXTER INTERNATIONAL INC.; *pg.* 1499, *pg.* 599
ISOLEX - Medical Product - MEDLINE INDUSTRIES, INC.; *pg.* 1562, *pg.* 635
ISOLEX 3001 - Magnetic Cell Separator System - BAXTER INTERNATIONAL INC.; *pg.* 1499, *pg.* 599
ISOLIS - Chemical Product - SACHEM INC.; *pg.* 1180, *pg.* 1665
ISOLITE - Face Mask - CROSSTEX INTERNATIONAL INC.; *pg.* 1520, *pg.* 1164
ISOLITE - Unsaturated Polyesters - SI GROUP, INC.; *pg.* 1181, *pg.* 1341
ISOLOCK - Non-Metal Thermal Barrier - KAWNEER COMPANY, INC.; *pg.* 90, *pg.* 537
ISOLOOP - Isolator - NVE CORPORATION; *pg.* 447, *pg.* 923
ISOLVE - Software System - MENTOR GRAPHICS CORPORATION; *pg.* 432, *pg.* 1510
ISOMALTIDEX - Food Additives - CARGILL, INC.; *pg.* 845, *pg.* 965
ISOMAR - Process Used to Maximize the Recovery of Certain Xylene Isomers - UOP LLC; *pg.* 1386, *pg.* 606
ISOMAX - Synthetic Resin Binders - ASHLAND INC.; *pg.* 972, *pg.* 726
ISOMED - Fixed-Rate Infusion Sys. - MEDTRONIC, INC.; *pg.* 1564, *pg.* 939
ISOMELT - Hot Melt Adhesives - ASHLAND INC.; *pg.* 972, *pg.* 726

First page reference indicates Business Class Edition
Second page reference indicates Geographic Edition

ISOMET - Low Speed Saw - BUEHLER, LTD.; *pg.* 1403, *pg.* 622
ISOMIL - Nutritional Supplement - ABBOTT LABORATORIES; *pg.* 1484, *pg.* 551
ISOMIL - Soy Infant Feeding - ABBOTT NUTRITION; *pg.* 1485, *pg.* 1437
ISOMIL ADVANCE - Infant Formula - ABBOTT NUTRITION; *pg.* 1485, *pg.* 1437
ISOMODEM - Integrated Circuit Product - SILICON LABORATORIES INC.; *pg.* 674, *pg.* 1666
ISONATE - Pure & Modified - THE DOW CHEMICAL COMPANY; *pg.* 1157, *pg.* 898
ISONOL - Polyether Polyols - THE DOW CHEMICAL COMPANY; *pg.* 1157, *pg.* 898
ISONOX - Chemical Product - SI GROUP, INC.; *pg.* 1181, *pg.* 1341
ISOPAC - Semiconductor Product - SEMTECH CORPORATION; *pg.* 671, *pg.* 57
ISOPACK - Chemical Product - NOVA CHEMICALS CORPORATION; *pg.* 1175, *pg.* 1904
ISOPACK PREMIUM - Chemical Product - NOVA CHEMICALS CORPORATION; *pg.* 1175, *pg.* 1904
ISOPLAST - Resin - THE DOW CHEMICAL COMPANY; *pg.* 1157, *pg.* 898
ISOPLAST - Resins - THE LUBRIZOL CORPORATION; *pg.* 1171, *pg.* 1481
ISOPLEX - Splines - KAWNEER COMPANY, INC.; *pg.* 90, *pg.* 537
ISOPLUS - Semiconductor Product - IXYS CORPORATION; *pg.* 422, *pg.* 146
ISOPLUS I4-PAC - Power Semiconductor & Module - IXYS CORPORATION; *pg.* 422, *pg.* 146
ISOPOL - Chemical Product - NOVA CHEMICALS CORPORATION; *pg.* 1175, *pg.* 1904
ISOPORT - Ribbon Window - ALCOA INC.; *pg.* 65, *pg.* 1188
ISOPORT - Ribbon Windows - KAWNEER COMPANY, INC.; *pg.* 90, *pg.* 537
IS_OPTIMIZER - Software System - MENTOR GRAPHICS CORPORATION; *pg.* 432, *pg.* 1510
ISOPTIN - Pharmaceutical Product - ABBOTT LABORATORIES; *pg.* 1484, *pg.* 551
ISORAD - Resin - SI GROUP, INC.; *pg.* 1181, *pg.* 1341
ISORDIL - Pharmaceutical Product - VALEANT PHARMACEUTICALS INTERNATIONAL, INC.; *pg.* 1605, *pg.* 1957
ISOSCAN - Imaging System - PERKINELMER, INC.; *pg.* 1426, *pg.* 853
ISOSEAL - Sand Additive - ASHLAND INC.; *pg.* 972, *pg.* 726
ISOSEARCH - Container X-Ray System - AMERICAN SCIENCE AND ENGINEERING, INC.; *pg.* 1399, *pg.* 787
ISOSET - Emulsion Urethane Adhesives - ASHLAND INC.; *pg.* 972, *pg.* 726
ISOSOURCE - Pharmaceutical Product - NESTLE HEALTHCARE NUTRITION; *pg.* 1572, *pg.* 941
ISOSTRUT - Nylon Separators - KAWNEER COMPANY, INC.; *pg.* 90, *pg.* 537
ISOTEC - Insulation - THERMOS L.L.C.; *pg.* 61, *pg.* 660
ISOTEK31 - Fertilizer - LEBANON SEABOARD CORPORATION; *pg.* 1797, *pg.* 1547
ISOTHERM - Climate Control Device - E.D. BULLARD COMPANY; *pg.* 1332, *pg.* 727
ISOTHERM - Thermistor - YSI INCORPORATED; *pg.* 1438, *pg.* 1483
ISOTHERMING - Medical Fabrics - E.I. DU PONT DE NEMOURS & COMPANY; *pg.* 1159, *pg.* 390
ISOTONER - Medical & Aesthetic Product - DYNATRONICS CORPORATION; *pg.* 1526, *pg.* 1757
ISOTONER - Umbrellas - TOTES ISOTONER CORPORATION; *pg.* 14, *pg.* 1426
ISOTONIC - Mattress Pad - CARPENTER CO.; *pg.* 920, *pg.* 1801
ISOTOP - Bipolar Transistor - MICROSEMI CORPORATION; *pg.* 435, *pg.* 41
ISOTUBE - Self-Cleaning Rubber Blow Tube - ASHLAND INC.; *pg.* 972, *pg.* 726
ISOVALERIMIDE - Pharmaceutical - NPS PHARMACEUTICALS, INC.; *pg.* 1576, *pg.* 1043
ISOWEB - Thermal Windows - ALCOA INC.; *pg.* 65, *pg.* 1188
ISPAN - Hardware Product - INTERPHASE CORPORATION; *pg.* 420, *pg.* 1732
ISPATE - Software - LATTICE SEMICONDUCTOR CORPORATION; *pg.* 651, *pg.* 1498
ISPGAL - Circuit Board - LATTICE SEMICONDUCTOR CORPORATION; *pg.* 651, *pg.* 1498
ISPLEVERCORE - Connection Program - LATTICE SEMICONDUCTOR CORPORATION; *pg.* 651, *pg.* 1498
ISPOT - Software - BIO-RAD LABORATORIES, INC.; *pg.* 1504, *pg.* 101
ISPRAY - Nozzle Selection Tool - SPRAYING SYSTEMS CO.; *pg.* 1063, *pg.* 670
ISPTRACY - Logic Analyzer - LATTICE SEMICONDUCTOR CORPORATION; *pg.* 651, *pg.* 1498
ISPVIRTUAL MACHINE - Computer Software - LATTICE SEMICONDUCTOR CORPORATION; *pg.* 651, *pg.* 1498
ISR - Security Products - STANLEY BLACK & DECKER, INC.; *pg.* 1063, *pg.* 358
ISSA/INTERCLEAN - Tradeshow Events - ISSA; *pg.* 145, *pg.* 640
ISSA MEMBER THE EXPERTS ON CLEANING & MAINTENANCE - Slogan - ISSA; *pg.* 145, *pg.* 640
ISSAALERT - Publication - ISSA; *pg.* 145, *pg.* 640
IS_SYNTHESIZER - Software System - MENTOR GRAPHICS CORPORATION; *pg.* 432, *pg.* 1510
ISTALOL - Ophthalmology Product - BAUSCH & LOMB INCORPORATED; *pg.* 1401, *pg.* 1045
ISTANBUL - Fabric - NEMSCHOFF, INC.; *pg.* 936, *pg.* 1890
ISU - ISDN Service Units & Inverse Multiplexers - ADTRAN, INC.; *pg.* 344, *pg.* 6
ISU 128 - Network Termination - ADTRAN, INC.; *pg.* 344, *pg.* 6
ISU 2X64 - Rackmount Module - ADTRAN, INC.; *pg.* 344, *pg.* 6
ISU 512 - Network Termination - ADTRAN, INC.; *pg.* 344, *pg.* 6
ISU 512E - Management Information Base - ADTRAN, INC.; *pg.* 344, *pg.* 6
ISUPPORT - Remote Assistance & Tool Maintenance Solution - KLA-TENCOR CORPORATION; *pg.* 1353, *pg.* 146
ISUPPORT - Software - SMITH MICRO SOFTWARE, INC.; *pg.* 471, *pg.* 41
ISUSPENSION - Outsole Technology - ACUSHNET COMPANY; *pg.* 1824, *pg.* 818
ISYS - Software - CRESTRON ELECTRONICS INC.; *pg.* 631, *pg.* 1116
ISYS - Point of Sale Terminal - INTERNATIONAL GAME TECHNOLOGY; *pg.* 420, *pg.* 1606
ISYS I/O - Software - CRESTRON ELECTRONICS INC.; *pg.* 631, *pg.* 1116
IT - Software System - MENTOR GRAPHICS CORPORATION; *pg.* 432, *pg.* 1510
IT-4 - Insulator Tester - HD ELECTRIC COMPANY; *pg.* 1299, *pg.* 666
IT AGILITY. YOUR WAY. - Tagline - F5 NETWORKS, INC.; *pg.* 396, *pg.* 1835
IT ALL BEGINS WITH PAPER - Slogan - DOMTAR CORPORATION; *pg.* 1456, *pg.* 1954
IT ALL STARTS WITH A SPARKLE - Slogan - CHARLES & COLVARD LTD; *pg.* 3, *pg.* 1384
IT ALL STARTS WITH CARE - Slogan - CAREMARK PHARMACY SERVICES; *pg.* 1513, *pg.* 1649
IT CAREERS MAGAZINE - Recruitment Advertising - COMPUTERWORLD, INC.; *pg.* 1629, *pg.* 820
IT CHARGE MANAGER - Software - SAS INSTITUTE INC.; *pg.* 466, *pg.* 1361
IT DOES GOOD THINGS - Slogan - OREGON STATE LOTTERY; *pg.* 1003, *pg.* 1508
IT DOESN.T SUCK. - Slogan - BARE BONES SOFTWARE, INC.; *pg.* 360, *pg.* 838
IT FITS, IT FITS! - Hosiery & Related Apparel - MAYER/BERKSHIRE CORPORATION; *pg.* 29, *pg.* 1129
IT GURU - Software Product & Module - RIVERBED PERFORMANCE MANAGEMENT; *pg.* 462, *pg.* 765
IT GURU NETWORK PLANNER - Software Product & Module - RIVERBED PERFORMANCE MANAGEMENT; *pg.* 462, *pg.* 765
IT GURU SYSTEMS PLANNER - Systems Capacity Management For Enterprises - RIVERBED PERFORMANCE MANAGEMENT; *pg.* 462, *pg.* 765
IT PAID FROM OUTER SPACE - Game - WMS INDUSTRIES INC.; *pg.* 593, *pg.* 666
IT PAYS TO BE PREFERRED - Games - PENN NATIONAL GAMING, INC.; *pg.* 574, *pg.* 1595
IT SENTINEL - Software Product & Module - RIVERBED PERFORMANCE MANAGEMENT; *pg.* 462, *pg.* 765
IT SERVICE MANAGEMENT SUITE - Software - BMC SOFTWARE, INC.; *pg.* 362, *pg.* 1701
IT SERVICE VISION - Software - SAS INSTITUTE INC.; *pg.* 466, *pg.* 1361
IT SOAKS INTO METAL - Motorsports Entertainment - SPEEDWAY MOTORSPORTS, INC.; *pg.* 584, *pg.* 1370
IT'S BETTER LIVE - Tagline - LIVE NATION WORLDWIDE - TIMES SQUARE OFFICE; *pg.* 558, *pg.* 1252
ITAG - MHC Tetramers - BECKMAN COULTER, INC.; *pg.* 1402, *pg.* 48
ITALIAN BMT - Genoa Salami, Pepperoni & Ham Sandwich - SUBWAY RESTAURANTS; *pg.* 1751, *pg.* 356
ITALIAN COLLECTION BY TREADEASY - Shoes - P.W. MINOR & SON, INC.; *pg.* 1816, *pg.* 1140
ITALIAN CRUST - Food Product - PIZZA INN, INC.; *pg.* 1745, *pg.* 1746
ITALIAN ESPRESS - Scoop N Clip - THE COFFEE BEANERY LTD.; *pg.* 849, *pg.* 886
ITALIAN HOLIDAY - Food - ARMANINO FOODS OF DISTINCTION, INC.; *pg.* 837, *pg.* 100
ITALIAN LOVE AFFAIR - Nail Care Product - OPI PRODUCTS INC.; *pg.* 518, *pg.* 167
ITALIAN ROAST - Coffee - PEET'S COFFEE & TEA, INC.; *pg.* 1029, *pg.* 85
ITALIAN ROCOCO - Mirror - ETHAN ALLEN INTERIORS INC.; *pg.* 924, *pg.* 343
ITALIAN VILLAGE - Frozen Pasta - HIGH LINER FOODS INCORPORATED; *pg.* 862, *pg.* 1917
ITALMACCHINE - Capital Equipment - TEREX CORPORATION; *pg.* 1381, *pg.* 384
ITANIUM - Cluster - MICROWAY, INC.; *pg.* 1267, *pg.* 841
ITAP - Pipe Service Reconnection - INSITUFORM TECHNOLOGIES INC; *pg.* 88, *pg.* 974
ITAQ - Reagent - BIO-RAD LABORATORIES, INC.; *pg.* 1504, *pg.* 101
ITASCA - Furniture - ASHLEY FURNITURE INDUSTRIES, INC.; *pg.* 914, *pg.* 1852
ITASCA - Recreation Vehicle - WINNEBAGO INDUSTRIES, INC.; *pg.* 1712, *pg.* 707
ITASCA HORIZON - Motor Homes - WINNEBAGO INDUSTRIES, INC.; *pg.* 1712, *pg.* 707
ITBBU - Battery Backup - AVAGO TECHNOLOGIES; *pg.* 358, *pg.* 238
ITCB INFUSION - Beverage - BUNN-O-MATIC CORPORATION; *pg.* 53, *pg.* 661
ITEACH - Educational Materials - SCHOLASTIC INC.; *pg.* 1683, *pg.* 1288
ITEACH.COM - Educational Materials - SCHOLASTIC INC.; *pg.* 1683, *pg.* 1288
ITEC - Equipment Control - DEERE & COMPANY; *pg.* 703, *pg.* 632
ITECHNOLOGY - Footwear - WOLVERINE WORLD WIDE, INC.; *pg.* 1822, *pg.* 905
ITEK - Chemical Product - HURST CHEMICAL COMPANY; *pg.* 1168, *pg.* 174
ITEK GRAPHIX - Pre-Press, Press & Post-Press Equipment & Supplies - PRESSTEK, INC.; *pg.* 456, *pg.* 606
ITHACA - Printer - TRANSACT TECHNOLOGIES INCORPORATED; *pg.* 484, *pg.* 351
ITHACOLOR - Ink Jet Paper - TRANSACT TECHNOLOGIES INCORPORATED; *pg.* 484, *pg.* 351
ITHERM - Thermal Printers - TRANSACT TECHNOLOGIES INCORPORATED; *pg.* 484, *pg.* 351
ITI - Ball Bearings - KAYDON CORPORATION; *pg.* 1352, *pg.* 866
ITIL - Software - SKILLSOFT PLC; *pg.* 470, *pg.* 1037
ITK - Molecular Probe Product - THERMO FISHER SCIENTIFIC INC.; *pg.* 1602, *pg.* 61
ITMA - Power Monitor - OPLINK COMMUNICATIONS, INC.; *pg.* 660, *pg.* 91
ITMOV - Thermally Protected Metal Oxide Varistors - LITTELFUSE, INC.; *pg.* 1301, *pg.* 580
ITMS - Power Monitor - OPLINK COMMUNICATIONS, INC.; *pg.* 660, *pg.* 91
ITOLL - Highway Toll Collection & Auditing System - INTERNATIONAL ROAD DYNAMICS INC.; *pg.* 1912, *pg.* 1962
ITONE - Wireless Network Product - AIRSPAN NETWORKS INC.; *pg.* 346, *pg.* 410
ITOPIA - Epitope Discovery System - BECKMAN COULTER, INC.; *pg.* 1402, *pg.* 48
THE ITOPIA ADVANTAGE - Business Intelligence Application - TECSYS, INC.; *pg.* 482, *pg.* 1956
ITPRO - Software - SKILLSOFT PLC; *pg.* 470, *pg.* 1037
ITRAN - Image Tracking - NCR CORPORATION; *pg.* 443, *pg.* 531
ITRAX - Spray Monitor System - NORDSON CORPORATION; *pg.* 1365, *pg.* 1480
ITREL - Neurostimulation System - MEDTRONIC, INC.; *pg.* 1564, *pg.* 939
ITREL EZ - Stimulator - MEDTRONIC, INC.; *pg.* 1564, *pg.*

939
ITREL II - Spinal Cord Stimulation Sys. - MEDTRONIC, INC.; *pg.* 1564, *pg.* 939
ITREND - Software - NORDSON CORPORATION; *pg.* 1365, *pg.* 1480
ITRIN - Pharmaceutical Product - ABBOTT LABORATORIES; *pg.* 1484, *pg.* 551
ITRON - Automated Meter Reading System - BADGER METER, INC.; *pg.* 1401, *pg.* 1873
ITS A BELIEF - Slogan - YOCREAM INTERNATIONAL INC.; *pg.* 1039, *pg.* 1508
IT'S A BOY - Lace Flag - HERITAGE LACE INC.; *pg.* 694, *pg.* 711
IT'S A CINCH - Tag Line - ACUSHNET COMPANY; *pg.* 1824, *pg.* 818
IT'S A GIRL - Lace Flag - HERITAGE LACE INC.; *pg.* 694, *pg.* 711
ITS A LIFESTYLE - Slogan - YOCREAM INTERNATIONAL INC.; *pg.* 1039, *pg.* 1508
IT'S A MADD HOUSE HERE - Publication - MOTHERS AGAINST DRUNK DRIVING (MADD); *pg.* 147, *pg.* 1723
IT'S A TRIP - Tag Line - ALBUQUERQUE CONVENTION & VISITORS BUREAU; *pg.* 988, *pg.* 1135
IT'S A TRUST THING - Tag Line - SOMERSET TIRE SERVICE, INC.; *pg.* 217, *pg.* 1047
IT'S A WONDERFUL LIFE - Lottery Game - NEW JERSEY STATE LOTTERY; *pg.* 1000, *pg.* 1126
IT'S ALL ABOUT THE TIRE - Slogan - COKER TIRE COMPANY; *pg.* 1880, *pg.* 1628
IT'S ALL ABOUT YOU - Flower Arrangement - 1-800-FLOWERS.COM, INC.; *pg.* 1758, *pg.* 1151
IT'S ALL ABOUT YOU - Tagline - TACO INCORPORATED; *pg.* 1077, *pg.* 1601
IT'S ALL GOOD - Tagline - MCCAIN FOODS LIMITED; *pg.* 876, *pg.* 1915
IT'S ALL GREEK TO ME - Nail Care Product - OPI PRODUCTS INC.; *pg.* 518, *pg.* 167
IT'S ALL HERE - Slogan - MASSACHUSETTS OFFICE OF TRAVEL & TOURISM; *pg.* 998, *pg.* 798
IT'S ALL IN THE DETAILS - Tagline - JHB INTERNATIONAL, INC.; *pg.* 696, *pg.* 320
IT'S ALWAYS A FIESTA WITH AZTECA - Slogan - AZTECA FOODS, INCORPORATED; *pg.* 838, *pg.* 566
IT'S AS CLOSE TO THE GROVE AS YOU CAN GET - Slogan - FLORIDA'S NATURAL GROWERS; *pg.* 855, *pg.* 437
ITS CLEAR WE CARE. - Slogan - HEARUSA, INC.; *pg.* 1541, *pg.* 457
IT'S COMPATIBLE - Printer - XEROX CORPORATION; *pg.* 494, *pg.* 365
IT'S FASHION - Apparel - THE CATO CORPORATION; *pg.* 21, *pg.* 1364
IT'S FOR YOU - Slogan - AT&T SOUTHEAST; *pg.* 1868, *pg.* 489
IT'S GOOD BEING FIRST - Slogan - DELAWARE TOURISM OFFICE; *pg.* 991, *pg.* 387
IT'S GOOD TO BE GREEN - Slogan - WCI COMMUNITIES, INC.; *pg.* 1118, *pg.* 414
IT'S GRO TIME - Tagline - THE SCOTTS MIRACLE-GRO COMPANY; *pg.* 1799, *pg.* 1459
IT'S JUST A SMARTER WAY TO DO BUSINESS - Slogan - FAIR ISAAC CORPORATION; *pg.* 1247, *pg.* 955
IT'S MADE FOR SLEEP - Slogan - SEALY CORPORATION; *pg.* 942, *pg.* 1391
IT.S MADE FOR SLEEP. IT.S A SEALY. - Slogan - SEALY CORPORATION; *pg.* 942, *pg.* 1391
IT'S MORE THAN A FLOOR - Tagline - MOHAWK INDUSTRIES, INC.; *pg.* 935, *pg.* 527
IT'S MORE THAN A GAME - Trademark - NATIONAL COLLEGIATE ATHLETIC ASSOCIATION; *pg.* 567, *pg.* 688
ITS MORE THAN A MAN ITS A PROMISE - Tag Line - ACCURATE CHEMICAL & SCIENTIFIC CORPORATION; *pg.* 1145, *pg.* 1350
IT'S MORE THAN JUST TOOLS - Slogan - MENTOR GRAPHICS CORPORATION; *pg.* 432, *pg.* 1510
IT.S NOT TV. IT.S HBO. - Tag Line - HOME BOX OFFICE, INC.; *pg.* 290, *pg.* 1240
IT'S OUR BUSINESS TO PROTECT YOURS - Slogan - FEDERATED MUTUAL INSURANCE COMPANY; *pg.* 1200, *pg.* 952
IT'S OUR NATURE - Slogan - NUCOR CORPORATION; *pg.* 101, *pg.* 1368
IT'S OUR PLEASURE - Slogan - PUBLIX SUPER MARKETS, INC.; *pg.* 1031, *pg.* 437
IT'S PUDDING - Dairy Food Product - LIFEWAY FOODS, INC.; *pg.* 874, *pg.* 634
IT'S SHEER LUCK - Nail Care Product - OPI PRODUCTS INC.; *pg.* 518, *pg.* 167
IT'S SKYLINE TIME - Slogan - SKYLINE CHILI, INC.; *pg.* 1033, *pg.* 1452
IT'S SO SIMPLE IT'S BRILLIANT - Printer - XEROX CORPORATION; *pg.* 494, *pg.* 365
IT'S THE BEST GAME IN TOWN - Slogan - PENN NATIONAL GAMING, INC.; *pg.* 574, *pg.* 1595
IT'S THE ICE CREAM-IEST - Slogan - PERRY'S ICE CREAM CO., INC.; *pg.* 1861, *pg.* 1137
IT'S THE JOURNEY - Trademark - NATIONAL COLLEGIATE ATHLETIC ASSOCIATION; *pg.* 567, *pg.* 688
IT'S THE LITTLE THINGS - Tagline - MUNCHKIN, INC.; *pg.* 964, *pg.* 300
IT'S TIME FOR SPEND MANAGEMENT - Slogan - ARIBA, INC.; *pg.* 353, *pg.* 283
IT'S TIME TO DISCOVER A HEALTHIER YOU - Publication - BJC HEALTHCARE; *pg.* 1506, *pg.* 993
IT'S TIME TO FEEL BETTER - Tagline - CIGNA CORPORATION; *pg.* 1197, *pg.* 338
IT'S WHAT YOUR FAMILY DESERVES - Tag Line - TYSON FOODS, INC.; *pg.* 902, *pg.* 35
IT'S WHERE AMERICA SWIMS - Slogan - ANTHONY & SYLVAN POOLS CORPORATION; *pg.* 1826, *pg.* 1428
IT'S YOUR DAY BOUQUET - Flower Arrangement - 1-800-FLOWERS.COM, INC.; *pg.* 1758, *pg.* 1151
IT'S YOUR HEALTH - Health Plan & Publication - MEDICA, INC.; *pg.* 1208, *pg.* 949
ITS YOUR HOME - Tagline - DOMINION HOMES, INC.; *pg.* 79, *pg.* 1449
IT'S YOUR LIFE AND YOU'RE WORTH IT - Slogan - E.D. BULLARD COMPANY; *pg.* 1332, *pg.* 727
IT'S YOUR SUNNY DAY - Flower Arrangement - 1-800-FLOWERS.COM, INC.; *pg.* 1758, *pg.* 1151
IT'S YOUR WORLD. BUILD IT. - Tagline - USG CORPORATION; *pg.* 118, *pg.* 594
ITSDEDUCTIBLE - Software - INTUIT INC.; *pg.* 769, *pg.* 158
ITSY BITSY - Container Grown Plant - MONROVIA GROWERS; *pg.* 1797, *pg.* 44
ITSY BITSY SPIDER - Game - HASBRO, INC.; *pg.* 954, *pg.* 1603
ITT STANDARD - Fluid Technology - ITT CORPORATION; *pg.* 1351, *pg.* 1354
ITTY-BITTY TEENY-TINY LEARNING BOOK - Educational Materials - SCHOLASTIC INC.; *pg.* 1683, *pg.* 1288
ITTYBITTY - Integrated Circuits - MICREL, INC.; *pg.* 654, *pg.* 247
ITUNES - Audio Application Program - APPLE INC.; *pg.* 350, *pg.* 73
ITUNES MUSIC STORE - Online Music Store - APPLE INC.; *pg.* 350, *pg.* 73
ITUNES PLUS - Online Store Features - APPLE INC.; *pg.* 350, *pg.* 73
ITUNES RADIO - Internet Streaming Service - APPLE INC.; *pg.* 350, *pg.* 73
ITUNES STORE - Online Store - APPLE INC.; *pg.* 350, *pg.* 73
ITUNES U - Sharing and Distribution Platform - APPLE INC.; *pg.* 350, *pg.* 73
ITV - Interactive Television - NAGRA USA; *pg.* 443, *pg.* 223
ITW RAMSET - Fastener - POWERS FASTENERS INC.; *pg.* 1059, *pg.* 1143
IV/700 - Large Character Ink Jet System - DIAGRAPH; *pg.* 387, *pg.* 989
THE I.V. GOWN - Healthcare Apparel - THE SALK COMPANY; *pg.* 1591, *pg.* 800
I.V. START PAK - Intravenous Start Kit - BECTON, DICKINSON & COMPANY; *pg.* 1501, *pg.* 1068
IVA - Medical Product - HOLOGIC, INC.; *pg.* 1416, *pg.* 784
IVA WORKS - Diagnostic Imaging Product - HOLOGIC, INC.; *pg.* 1416, *pg.* 784
IVAC - Patient Monitoring System - CRITICARE SYSTEMS, INC.; *pg.* 1520, *pg.* 1897
IVALOO - Fabric - NEMSCHOFF, INC.; *pg.* 936, *pg.* 1890
IVANA - Footwear - COBIAN CORP.; *pg.* 1806, *pg.* 253
IVAREST - Pain Relief - BLISTEX, INC.; *pg.* 502, *pg.* 644
IVASION - Software - WIND RIVER SYSTEMS, INC.; *pg.* 493, *pg.* 38
IVC - Medical Equipment - INVACARE CORPORATION; *pg.* 1546, *pg.* 1451
IVC 9000 XT - Lightweight Wheelchair - INVACARE CORPORATION; *pg.* 1546, *pg.* 1451
IVC TRACER IV - Wheelchair Designed for the Active Individual - INVACARE CORPORATION; *pg.* 1546, *pg.* 1451
IVC TRACER SX5 - Manual Wheelchair - INVACARE CORPORATION; *pg.* 1546, *pg.* 1451
IVEAGH - Fabric - SCALAMANDRE, INC.; *pg.* 941, *pg.* 1058
IVEEGAM - Biopharmaceutical Product - BAXTER INTERNATIONAL INC.; *pg.* 1499, *pg.* 599
IVERHART PLUS FLAVORED CHEWABLES - Veterinary Product - VIRBAC CORPORATION; *pg.* 1606, *pg.* 1696
IVERSON - Footwear - REEBOK INTERNATIONAL LTD.; *pg.* 1817, *pg.* 811
IVES - Door Hardware - INGERSOLL-RAND COMPANY; *pg.* 1349, *pg.* 1370
IVIEW DM - Video Game - BALLY TECHNOLOGIES, INC.; *pg.* 531, *pg.* 1022
IVIEWXT - Software - R.R. DONNELLEY & SONS COMPANY; *pg.* 1682, *pg.* 589
IV'LOCITY - Software System - MENTOR GRAPHICS CORPORATION; *pg.* 432, *pg.* 1510
IVOMEC IVERMECTIN - Injection - TRACTOR SUPPLY COMPANY; *pg.* 708, *pg.* 1627
IVORY - Coating - ARCHER-DANIELS-MIDLAND COMPANY; *pg.* 825, *pg.* 565
IVORY - Pillow and Throw - HERITAGE LACE INC.; *pg.* 694, *pg.* 711
IVORY - Personal & House Care Products - THE PROCTER & GAMBLE COMPANY; *pg.* 1129, *pg.* 1418
IVORY FEATHERS - Container Grown Plant - MONROVIA GROWERS; *pg.* 1797, *pg.* 44
IVRA - Hearing Diagnostic Equipment & Visual Reinforcement Audiometry - INTELLIGENT HEARING SYSTEMS CORP.; *pg.* 1546, *pg.* 443
IVS 185 - Metrology System - NANOMETRICS INCORPORATED; *pg.* 1423, *pg.* 147
IVS-CONNECT - Test Results - IDEXX LABORATORIES, INC.; *pg.* 1543, *pg.* 753
IVY - Dresses, Sportswear & Sweaters - KELLWOOD COMPANY; *pg.* 28, *pg.* 975
IVY BELLPULL - Wall Decor - HERITAGE LACE INC.; *pg.* 694, *pg.* 711
IWAPU - Software - MICROSTRATEGY, INC.; *pg.* 1266, *pg.* 1809
IWARE - Software - INTERPHASE CORPORATION; *pg.* 420, *pg.* 1732
IWEB - Application Program - APPLE INC.; *pg.* 350, *pg.* 73
IWMA - Power Monitor - OPLINK COMMUNICATIONS, INC.; *pg.* 660, *pg.* 91
IWON! - Online Services - IAC/INTERACTIVECORP; *pg.* 292, *pg.* 1242
IWON - Loyalty-Based Web Portal - IAC SEARCH & MEDIA, INC.; *pg.* 1257, *pg.* 171
IWORK - Software Product - APPLE INC.; *pg.* 350, *pg.* 73
IWORKS - Software - SUNGARD DATA SYSTEMS INC.; *pg.* 477, *pg.* 1592
IWP - Window & Door - JELD-WEN, INC.; *pg.* 1051, *pg.* 1499
IWS EPI BUILDER - Software - IMAGEWARE SYSTEMS, INC.; *pg.* 412, *pg.* 203
IWS EPI ID - Software - IMAGEWARE SYSTEMS, INC.; *pg.* 412, *pg.* 203
IWS EPI XPRESS - Software - IMAGEWARE SYSTEMS, INC.; *pg.* 412, *pg.* 203
IWS GREEN SCREEN - Digital Photography Software - IMAGEWARE SYSTEMS, INC.; *pg.* 412, *pg.* 203
IWS LAW ENFORCEMENT - Software - IMAGEWARE SYSTEMS, INC.; *pg.* 412, *pg.* 203
IWS PC EVENT - Software - IMAGEWARE SYSTEMS, INC.; *pg.* 412, *pg.* 203
IWS PC PRO - Software - IMAGEWARE SYSTEMS, INC.; *pg.* 412, *pg.* 203
IWS PROLAB - Software - IMAGEWARE SYSTEMS, INC.; *pg.* 412, *pg.* 203
IWS SCHOOL DAYS PLUS - Software - IMAGEWARE SYSTEMS, INC.; *pg.* 412, *pg.* 203
IWS STUDIO - Software - IMAGEWARE SYSTEMS, INC.; *pg.* 412, *pg.* 203
IX SERIES - Advanced Function ATM - DIEBOLD, INCORPORATED; *pg.* 387, *pg.* 1407
IXACCESS - Network Testing System - IXIA; *pg.* 422, *pg.* 56
IXADMIN - Asset Management - IXIA; *pg.* 422, *pg.* 56
IXANALYZE - Data Communications Equipment & Network Testing Application - IXIA; *pg.* 422, *pg.* 56
IXANVL - Network Testing System - IXIA; *pg.* 422, *pg.* 56
IXAUTHENTICATE - Network Testing System - IXIA; *pg.* 422, *pg.* 56
IXAUTOMATE - Network Testing System - IXIA; *pg.* 422, *pg.* 56

First page reference indicates Business Class Edition
Second page reference indicates Geographic Edition

IXCHARIOT - Network Testing System - IXIA; *pg.* 422, *pg.* 56
IXDEFEND - Network Testing System - IXIA; *pg.* 422, *pg.* 56
IXEMPRA - Cancer Medication - BRISTOL-MYERS SQUIBB COMPANY; *pg.* 1509, *pg.* 1206
IXEXPLORER - Network Testing System - IXIA; *pg.* 422, *pg.* 56
IXF - Freight Service - FEDEX CORPORATION; *pg.* 1907, *pg.* 1642
IXGREEN - Network Testing System - IXIA; *pg.* 422, *pg.* 56
IXI - Portable Wet/dry Vacuum - SHOP-VAC CORPORATION; *pg.* 1375, *pg.* 1595
IXIP - Connectivity Services - EQUINIX, INC.; *pg.* 394, *pg.* 190
IXLOAD - Network Testing System - IXIA; *pg.* 422, *pg.* 56
IXNETWORK - Network Testing System - IXIA; *pg.* 422, *pg.* 56
IXOLAR - Solar Cell - IXYS CORPORATION; *pg.* 422, *pg.* 146
IXRAVE - Network Testing System - IXIA; *pg.* 422, *pg.* 56
IXROUTER - Network Testing System - IXIA; *pg.* 422, *pg.* 56
IXSAN - Network Testing System - IXIA; *pg.* 422, *pg.* 56
IXSCRIPTMATE - Network Testing System - IXIA; *pg.* 422, *pg.* 56
IXVERIFY - Network Testing System - IXIA; *pg.* 422, *pg.* 56
IXVOICE - Network Testing System - IXIA; *pg.* 422, *pg.* 56
IXVPN - Network Testing System - IXIA; *pg.* 422, *pg.* 56
IXWLAN - Network Testing System - IXIA; *pg.* 422, *pg.* 56
IYEMON CHA - Bottled Green Tea - NESTLE WATERS NORTH AMERICA INC.; *pg.* 257, *pg.* 375
IZMIR - Rug - COURISTAN INC.; *pg.* 921, *pg.* 1067
IZOD - Sport Shirt - BROWN & BIGELOW, INC.; *pg.* 1624, *pg.* 959
IZOD - Apparel - PVH CORP.; *pg.* 46, *pg.* 1283
IZON - Optically Variable Devices - E.I. DU PONT DE NEMOURS & COMPANY; *pg.* 1159, *pg.* 390
IZONE - School Tools - ACME UNITED CORPORATION; *pg.* 1040, *pg.* 346
IZVORUL ALB - Beverages - THE COCA-COLA COMPANY; *pg.* 240, *pg.* 493

J

J-16 - Asphalt Sealer - MAINTENANCE, INC.; *pg.* 95, *pg.* 1482
J-45 - Musical Instrument - GIBSON GUITAR CORP.; *pg.* 550, *pg.* 1650
J-50 - Musical Instrument - GIBSON GUITAR CORP.; *pg.* 550, *pg.* 1650
J & J BAND-AID - Sheer Adhesive Bandages - ALIMED, INC.; *pg.* 1490, *pg.* 816
J & M - Shoe Trees - JOHNSTON & MURPHY CO.; *pg.* 1810, *pg.* 1651
J&P COATS - Needle Crafts - MAKE IT COATS; *pg.* 696, *pg.* 1367
J. BLUM: PRINTER & MERCHANT - Shop - OLD SALEM, INCORPORATED; *pg.* 572, *pg.* 1395
J. CHESTERFIELD STUDIO - Wallpaper - YORK WALLCOVERINGS INC.; *pg.* 947, *pg.* 1598
J. CHUCKLES - Women's Apparel - A&E STORES, INC.; *pg.* 17, *pg.* 1124
J. COUNTRYMAN - Inspirational Gift Books - THOMAS NELSON INC.; *pg.* 1692, *pg.* 1654
J CREW - Casual Clothing - J. CREW GROUP, INC.; *pg.* 1773, *pg.* 1245
J-FLEX - Dispenser - DIVERSEY, INC.; *pg.* 1123, *pg.* 1896
J. GARCIA - Wine - JIM BEAM BRANDS CO.; *pg.* 1965, *pg.* 601
J. GILBERTS WOOD-FIRED STEAKS - Restaurants - HOULIHAN'S RESTAURANTS, INC.; *pg.* 1731, *pg.* 716
J-HOOK - Hook - OATEY SUPPLY CHAIN SERVICES; *pg.* 30, *pg.* 1433
J-J HOOKS - Concrete Safety Barrier - SMITH-MIDLAND CORPORATION; *pg.* 111, *pg.* 1795
J.J. KELLER'S DRIVER FILE - Recordkeeping Software - J.J. KELLER & ASSOCIATES, INC.; *pg.* 1654, *pg.* 1883
J JILL - Women's Clothing - THE TALBOTS, INC.; *pg.* 34, *pg.* 824
J-LINE - Insulated Tubing - O'BRIEN CORPORATION; *pg.* 1366, *pg.* 1001
J-LINE - Bearing - THE TIMKEN COMPANY; *pg.* 218, *pg.* 1408
J. M. SEMANIER - Furniture - J. ROBERT SCOTT INC.; *pg.* 930, *pg.* 105
J. MCLAUGHLIN - Clothing - SEA ISLAND CLOTHIERS, LLC; *pg.* 32, *pg.* 1146
J-MOD - Wiring Accessory - PANDUIT CORP.; *pg.* 661, *pg.* 663
J MURPHY BLACKSMITH - Wall Decor - ETHAN ALLEN INTERIORS INC.; *pg.* 924, *pg.* 343
J-PRO - Wiring Accessory - PANDUIT CORP.; *pg.* 661, *pg.* 663
J RECORDS - Artist - SONY MUSIC ENTERTAINMENT; *pg.* 309, *pg.* 1294
J ROBERT SCOTT - Furniture & Textiles - J. ROBERT SCOTT INC.; *pg.* 930, *pg.* 105
J-TRACK - Air Filtration System - PURAFIL, INC.; *pg.* 333, *pg.* 530
J-WEB - Software - JUNIPER NETWORKS, INC.; *pg.* 1260, *pg.* 286
J2 - Communication Product - J2 GLOBAL COMMUNICATIONS, INC.; *pg.* 1260, *pg.* 133
J2 GLOBAL - Communication Product - J2 GLOBAL COMMUNICATIONS, INC.; *pg.* 1260, *pg.* 133
J30 - Automobile - NISSAN NORTH AMERICA, INC.; *pg.* 186, *pg.* 1633
J6-MI - High-Capacity Centrifuge - BECKMAN COULTER, INC.; *pg.* 1402, *pg.* 48
JAAPA - Medical Publication - TRUVEN HEALTH ANALYTICS; *pg.* 1696, *pg.* 867
JABRA - Headset & Speakerphone Solutions - GN NETCOM INC.; *pg.* 640, *pg.* 1037
JAC - Pharmaceutical Product - JAMES ALEXANDER CORPORATION; *pg.* 1461, *pg.* 1044
JAC - Pharmacy Stock Control System - MEDIWARE INFORMATION SYSTEMS, INC.; *pg.* 431, *pg.* 716
JACK - Sandwiches & Burritos - JACK IN THE BOX INC.; *pg.* 1732, *pg.* 204
JACK - Office Furniture - STEELCASE INC.; *pg.* 475, *pg.* 889
JACK - Bicycle - TREK BICYCLE CORPORATION; *pg.* 1847, *pg.* 1896
JACK & BERNIE'S BLOODY MARY MIX - Drink Mix - SHAW ROSS INTERNATIONAL IMPORTERS; *pg.* 1970, *pg.* 449
JACK BAKER'S LOBSTER SHANTY & WHARFSIDE - Restaurants - CHEF'S INTERNATIONAL, INC.; *pg.* 1721, *pg.* 1110
JACK CASH - Gift Cards - JACK IN THE BOX INC.; *pg.* 1732, *pg.* 204
JACK DANIEL - Musical Instrument - PEAVEY ELECTRONICS CORPORATION; *pg.* 662, *pg.* 970
JACK DANIEL'S - Tennessee Whiskey & Country Cocktails - BROWN-FORMAN CORPORATION; *pg.* 1958, *pg.* 732
JACK DANIEL'S COUNTRY COCKTAILS - Alcoholic Beverages - BROWN-FORMAN CORPORATION; *pg.* 1958, *pg.* 732
JACK DANIEL'S SAUCES - Sauces - THE KRAFT HEINZ COMPANY; *pg.* 870, *pg.* 1577
JACK DANIEL'S SINGLE BARREL TENNESSEE WHISKEY - Tennessee Whiskey - BROWN-FORMAN CORPORATION; *pg.* 1958, *pg.* 732
JACK DANIEL'S TENNESSEE HONEY - Whiskey - JACK DANIEL'S DISTILLERY; *pg.* 1964, *pg.* 1640
JACK DANIEL'S TENNESSEE WHISKEY - Whiskey - BROWN-FORMAN CORPORATION; *pg.* 1958, *pg.* 732
JACK FROST - Candle - THE YANKEE CANDLE COMPANY, INC.; *pg.* 1792, *pg.* 843
JACK JR. - Restaurant Services - JACK IN THE BOX INC.; *pg.* 1732, *pg.* 204
JACK LINKS - Meat Snack Product - LINK SNACKS, INC.; *pg.* 874, *pg.* 1881
JACK LINKS BEEF JERKY - Food Product - LINK SNACKS, INC.; *pg.* 874, *pg.* 1881
JACK PURCELL - Shoe - CONVERSE INC.; *pg.* 1831, *pg.* 793
JACK RABBIT - Paper Products - BOISE CASCADE HOLDINGS, L.L.C.; *pg.* 1453, *pg.* 546
JACK ROSE - Restaurant - ARK RESTAURANTS CORP.; *pg.* 1715, *pg.* 1196
JACKAL - Gaming Product - GLD PRODUCTS, INC.; *pg.* 1835, *pg.* 1882
JACKET - Office Furniture - STEELCASE INC.; *pg.* 475, *pg.* 889
JACKET ARRAY - Eyewear - OAKLEY, INC.; *pg.* 1840, *pg.* 86
JACKIE - Footwear - PHOENIX FOOTWEAR GROUP, INC.; *pg.* 1815, *pg.* 60
JACKLEY - Furniture - LA-Z-BOY INCORPORATED; *pg.* 932, *pg.* 901
JACKLITE - Task Lighting - PROPHOTONIX LIMITED; *pg.* 1427, *pg.* 1039
JACKPORT PARTY - Game - MULTIMEDIA GAMES INC.; *pg.* 442, *pg.* 1664
JACKPOT 7S - Video Game - INTERNATIONAL GAME TECHNOLOGY; *pg.* 957, *pg.* 1024
JACKPOT AEROSOL - Air Freshener - LANMAN & KEMP-BARCLAY CO., INC.; *pg.* 514, *pg.* 1132
JACKPOT BLOCK PARTY - Game - WMS INDUSTRIES INC.; *pg.* 593, *pg.* 666
JACKPOT BONANZA - Video Game - INTERNATIONAL GAME TECHNOLOGY; *pg.* 957, *pg.* 1024
JACKPOT CANYON - Game - WMS INDUSTRIES INC.; *pg.* 593, *pg.* 666
JACKPOT COMET - Game - WMS INDUSTRIES INC.; *pg.* 593, *pg.* 666
JACKPOT EXPLOSION - Game - WMS INDUSTRIES INC.; *pg.* 593, *pg.* 666
JACKPOT HUNTER - Video Game - INTERNATIONAL GAME TECHNOLOGY; *pg.* 957, *pg.* 1024
JACKPOT JAVA - Games - PENN NATIONAL GAMING, INC.; *pg.* 574, *pg.* 1595
JACKPOT JEWELS - Video Slots - INTERNATIONAL GAME TECHNOLOGY; *pg.* 957, *pg.* 1024
JACKPOT JUNGLE - Video Game - INTERNATIONAL GAME TECHNOLOGY; *pg.* 957, *pg.* 1024
JACKPOT PARTY - Game - WMS INDUSTRIES INC.; *pg.* 593, *pg.* 666
JACKPOT PARTY PROGRESSIVE - Game - WMS INDUSTRIES INC.; *pg.* 593, *pg.* 666
JACKPOT POKER - Video Game - INTERNATIONAL GAME TECHNOLOGY; *pg.* 957, *pg.* 1024
JACKPOT SEVENS - Video Game - INTERNATIONAL GAME TECHNOLOGY; *pg.* 957, *pg.* 1024
JACKPOT STAMPEDE - Game - WMS INDUSTRIES INC.; *pg.* 593, *pg.* 666
JACKPOT STATION - Game - WMS INDUSTRIES INC.; *pg.* 593, *pg.* 666
JACKPOTEERS - Video Game - INTERNATIONAL GAME TECHNOLOGY; *pg.* 957, *pg.* 1024
JACKRABBIT - Beer - BIG ROCK BREWERY INCOME TRUST; *pg.* 239, *pg.* 1902
JACKS - Pillow - AMERICAN LEATHER LP; *pg.* 912, *pg.* 1673
JACK'S - Cookies - KELLOGG COMPANY; *pg.* 831, *pg.* 870
JACK'S BACK - Restaurant Services - JACK IN THE BOX INC.; *pg.* 1732, *pg.* 204
JACK'S GEAR - Electronic & Mail Order - JACK IN THE BOX INC.; *pg.* 1732, *pg.* 204
JACK'S KID'S MEAL - Children's Meals - JACK IN THE BOX INC.; *pg.* 1732, *pg.* 204
JACK'S PIZZA - Pizza - NESTLE USA, INC.; *pg.* 883, *pg.* 96
JACK'S PUMPKIN SPICE ALE - Seasonal Beer - ANHEUSER-BUSCH COMPANIES, LLC; *pg.* 237, *pg.* 991
JACK'S SPICY CHICKEN - Chicken - JACK IN THE BOX INC.; *pg.* 1732, *pg.* 204
JACK'S WORLD - Providing General Information - JACK IN THE BOX INC.; *pg.* 1732, *pg.* 204
JACKSON - Shoes - COACH, INC.; *pg.* 3, *pg.* 1214
JACKSON - Guitar - FENDER MUSICAL INSTRUMENTS CORPORATION; *pg.* 547, *pg.* 21
JACKSON - Buffs - JASON INDUSTRIES, INC.; *pg.* 208, *pg.* 1875
JACKSON - Lighting Product - QUOIZEL INC.; *pg.* 1304, *pg.* 1616
THE JACKSON CITIZEN PATRIOT - Newspaper - MLIVE MEDIA GROUP; *pg.* 1665, *pg.* 888
JACKSON HEWITT CASHCARD - Debit Cards - JACKSON HEWITT TAX SERVICE INC.; *pg.* 771, *pg.* 1103
JACKSON-TRIGGS - Wine - CONSTELLATION BRANDS CANADA; *pg.* 1960, *pg.* 1925
JACKSONLEA - Buffing Wheel & Compound - JASON INDUSTRIES, INC.; *pg.* 208, *pg.* 1875
JACKSONN - Footwear - STEVEN MADDEN, LTD.; *pg.* 1819, *pg.* 1176
JACKSONS - Cookies - KELLOGG COMPANY; *pg.* 831, *pg.* 870
THE JACKSONVILLE DAILY NEWS - Newspaper - THE JACKSONVILLE DAILY NEWS CO.; *pg.* 1654, *pg.* 1380
JACKSONVILLE JOURNAL-COURIER - Illinois Newspaper - FREEDOM COMMUNICATIONS, INC.; *pg.* 1643, *pg.* 110
JACLYN SMITH HOME COLLECTION - Home Goods - KMART CORPORATION; *pg.* 1775, *pg.* 617
JACMAR - Restaurant Food - JACMAR COMPANIES, INC.; *pg.* 1733, *pg.* 67
JACOB DELAFON - Plumbing Fixtures - KOHLER CO.; *pg.* 91, *pg.* 1862

JACOBEAN - Furniture - HOOKER FURNITURE CORPORATION; *pg.* 928, *pg.* 1788
JACOBEAN - Wallcovering - YORK WALLCOVERINGS INC.; *pg.* 947, *pg.* 1598
JACOBI - Brandy - JIM BEAM BRANDS CO.; *pg.* 1965, *pg.* 601
JACOBS - Cutter - HOUGEN MANUFACTURING INC.; *pg.* 1347, *pg.* 908
JACOBS - Technical Services - JACOBS ENGINEERING GROUP, INC.; *pg.* 88, *pg.* 180
JACOBS - Coffee - MONDELEZ INTERNATIONAL, INC.; *pg.* 878, *pg.* 601
JACOBS BLEEDER BRAKE - Engine Retarder - JACOBS VEHICLE SYSTEMS; *pg.* 1351, *pg.* 338
JACOBS CHUCK MANUFACTURING - Drill Chuck - DANAHER CORPORATION; *pg.* 1044, *pg.* 397
JACOB'S CREEK - Wine - PERNOD RICARD USA, INC.; *pg.* 1968, *pg.* 1332
JACOBS EXHAUST BRAKE - Supplementary Braking System - JACOBS VEHICLE SYSTEMS; *pg.* 1351, *pg.* 338
JACOBS VEHICLE SYSTEMS - Jake Brake Retarder Product - DANAHER CORPORATION; *pg.* 1044, *pg.* 397
JACOBSEN - Golf, Turf & Specialty Products - TEXTRON INC.; *pg.* 235, *pg.* 1607
JACQUARD - Beanie - OAKLEY, INC.; *pg.* 1840, *pg.* 86
JACQUES CARDIN NAPOLEON VSOP BRANDY - Beverage - SIDNEY FRANK IMPORTING CO., INC.; *pg.* 1970, *pg.* 1184
JACQUES CARDIN XO BRANDY - Beverage - SIDNEY FRANK IMPORTING CO., INC.; *pg.* 1970, *pg.* 1184
JACQUES MORET KIDS - Children's Apparel - JACQUES MORET, INC.; *pg.* 27, *pg.* 1245
JACQUES PERGAY - Furniture Collection - LANE VENTURE, INC.; *pg.* 933, *pg.* 1379
JADA - Candle Stand - ETHAN ALLEN INTERIORS INC.; *pg.* 924, *pg.* 343
JADE - Dinnerware - THE HOMER LAUGHLIN CHINA COMPANY; *pg.* 1125, *pg.* 1850
JADE - Kitchen Equipment - THE MIDDLEBY CORPORATION; *pg.* 1361, *pg.* 610
JADE - Footwear - PHOENIX FOOTWEAR GROUP, INC.; *pg.* 1815, *pg.* 60
THE JADE ELEPHANT - Game - WMS INDUSTRIES INC.; *pg.* 593, *pg.* 666
JADE GATE - Video Game - INTERNATIONAL GAME TECHNOLOGY; *pg.* 957, *pg.* 1024
THE JADE MONKEY - Slot Machine - WMS INDUSTRIES INC.; *pg.* 593, *pg.* 666
JADE PALACE - Game - WMS INDUSTRIES INC.; *pg.* 593, *pg.* 666
JADEN - Candle Stand - ETHAN ALLEN INTERIORS INC.; *pg.* 924, *pg.* 343
J'ADORE EAU DE PARFUM - Women's Fragrance - PARFUMS CHRISTIAN DIOR, INC; *pg.* 519, *pg.* 1276
J'ADORE EAU DE TOLIETTE - Women's Fragrance - PARFUMS CHRISTIAN DIOR, INC; *pg.* 519, *pg.* 1276
J'ADORE PERFUMED BODY LINE - Women's Fragrance - PARFUMS CHRISTIAN DIOR, INC; *pg.* 519, *pg.* 1276
J'ADORE SUMMER - Women's Fragrance - PARFUMS CHRISTIAN DIOR, INC; *pg.* 519, *pg.* 1276
JAG - Apparel - PERRY ELLIS INTERNATIONAL, INC.; *pg.* 45, *pg.* 445
JAG-STANG - Electric Guitar - FENDER MUSICAL INSTRUMENTS CORPORATION; *pg.* 547, *pg.* 21
JAGER BUILDING SYSTEMS - Engineered Wood Product - TEMBEC INC.; *pg.* 114, *pg.* 1957
JAGERMEISTER - Beverage - SIDNEY FRANK IMPORTING CO., INC.; *pg.* 1970, *pg.* 1184
JAGGER - Furniture - BUSH INDUSTRIES INC.; *pg.* 919, *pg.* 1170
JAGGERR - Footwear - STEVEN MADDEN, LTD.; *pg.* 1819, *pg.* 1176
JAGUAR - Snowmobile - ARCTIC CAT INC.; *pg.* 1705, *pg.* 953
JAGUAR - Gaming Product - GLD PRODUCTS, INC.; *pg.* 1835, *pg.* 1882
JAGUAR! - Roller Coaster - KNOTT'S BERRY FARM; *pg.* 556, *pg.* 50
JAGUAR BARITONE CUSTOM - Electric Guitar - FENDER MUSICAL INSTRUMENTS CORPORATION; *pg.* 547, *pg.* 21
JAH MAGAZINE - Magazine - REEVES INTERNATIONAL, INC.; *pg.* 966, *pg.* 1108
JAILVIEW - Software Product - MAXIMUS, INC.; *pg.* 780, *pg.* 1799
JAKARTA - Carpet - INTERFACE, INC.; *pg.* 695, *pg.* 512
JAKARTA - Fabric - NEMSCHOFF, INC.; *pg.* 936, *pg.* 1890
JAKE - Footwear - EASTLAND SHOE CORPORATION; *pg.* 1808, *pg.* 750
JAKE BRAKE - Engine Retarders - JACOBS VEHICLE SYSTEMS; *pg.* 1351, *pg.* 338
JAKE ENGINE BRAKE - Engine Retarder - JACOBS VEHICLE SYSTEMS; *pg.* 1351, *pg.* 338
JAKES FAULT - Wine - JIM BEAM BRANDS CO.; *pg.* 1965, *pg.* 601
JAKKS INTERACTIVE - Software & Electronic Toys - JAKKS PACIFIC, INC.; *pg.* 960, *pg.* 142
JALAPENO - Barbecue Sauce - LOUIS MAULL COMPANY; *pg.* 875, *pg.* 999
JALAPENO - Potato Chips - SNYDER'S OF HANOVER, INC.; *pg.* 1862, *pg.* 1536
JALAPENO CHEESE BOMBERS - Nutrition Product - CHURCH'S CHICKEN, INC.; *pg.* 1722, *pg.* 493
JALAPENO LOPRO - Vacuum Valve - MKS INSTRUMENTS, INC.; *pg.* 1362, *pg.* 781
JALGO - Daughter Card - IMAGINATION TECHNOLOGIES; *pg.* 412, *pg.* 285
JALITOS - Breaded - LEON'S FINE FOODS, INC.; *pg.* 874, *pg.* 1727
JALOPNIK - Automotive News - GAWKER MEDIA LLC; *pg.* 1248, *pg.* 1234
JAM-BUSTER - Wrench - IN-SINK-ERATOR; *pg.* 57, *pg.* 1888
JAM-INATOR - Kitchen Appliance - VIKING RANGE CORPORATION; *pg.* 61, *pg.* 968
JAM PACK - Computer Software - APPLE INC.; *pg.* 350, *pg.* 73
JAMA: JOURNAL OF THE AMERICAN MEDICAL ASSOCIATION - Medical Journal - AMERICAN MEDICAL ASSOCIATION; *pg.* 130, *pg.* 564
JAMAICA - Furniture - ETHAN ALLEN INTERIORS INC.; *pg.* 924, *pg.* 343
JAMAICAN COWBOY - Alcoholic Beverages - TEXAS ROADHOUSE, INC.; *pg.* 1753, *pg.* 738
JAMBA FUNCTIONALS - Smoothie - JAMBA, INC.; *pg.* 1024, *pg.* 84
JAMBA JUICE - Fruit Drinks - JAMBA, INC.; *pg.* 1024, *pg.* 84
JAMBA MULTI-BOOST - Energy Drink - JAMBA, INC.; *pg.* 1024, *pg.* 84
JAMBA POWERBOOST - Smoothie - JAMBA, INC.; *pg.* 1024, *pg.* 84
JAMBOX - Wireless Speakers - ALIPHCOM, INC.; *pg.* 616, *pg.* 212
JAMES - Beer - COASTAL EXTREME BREWING COMPANY; *pg.* 240, *pg.* 1602
THE JAMES - Hotels - DENIHAN HOSPITALITY GROUP, LLC; *pg.* 1089, *pg.* 1223
JAMES - Furniture - HOOKER FURNITURE CORPORATION; *pg.* 928, *pg.* 1788
JAMES BURTON TELECASTER - Electric Guitar - FENDER MUSICAL INSTRUMENTS CORPORATION; *pg.* 547, *pg.* 21
JAMES FOXE - Canadian Whiskey - SAZERAC COMPANY, INC.; *pg.* 1969, *pg.* 745
JAMESON - Irish Whiskey - PERNOD RICARD USA, INC.; *pg.* 1968, *pg.* 1332
JAMESTOWN - Furniture - BUSH INDUSTRIES INC.; *pg.* 919, *pg.* 1170
JAMESTOWN - Fabric - NEMSCHOFF, INC.; *pg.* 936, *pg.* 1890
JAMESTOWN BRAND - Meat Products - THE SMITHFIELD PACKING CO., INC.; *pg.* 896, *pg.* 1807
JAMIE - Yarn - LION BRAND YARN COMPANY; *pg.* 696, *pg.* 1050
JAMIE - Footwear - PHOENIX FOOTWEAR GROUP, INC.; *pg.* 1815, *pg.* 60
JAMIE - Women's Clothing & Accessories - WOODEN SHIPS OF HOBOKEN; *pg.* 35, *pg.* 1315
JAMIE-CLASSIC - Yarn - LION BRAND YARN COMPANY; *pg.* 696, *pg.* 1050
JAMIE POMPADOUR - Yarn - LION BRAND YARN COMPANY; *pg.* 696, *pg.* 1050
JAMIS - Bicycles - G. JOANNOU CYCLE CO. INC.; *pg.* 1707, *pg.* 1098
JAMMERS - Home Protection - MACE SECURITY INTERNATIONAL, INC.; *pg.* 1172, *pg.* 1541
JAMMIN - Fabric - NEMSCHOFF, INC.; *pg.* 936, *pg.* 1890
JAMOCLEAR - Cold Storage Doors - JAMISON DOOR COMPANY; *pg.* 89, *pg.* 771
JAMOLITE II - Cold Storage Doors - JAMISON DOOR COMPANY; *pg.* 89, *pg.* 771
JAMOLITE III - Cold Storage Doors - JAMISON DOOR COMPANY; *pg.* 89, *pg.* 771
JAMOTUF - Cold Storage Doors - JAMISON DOOR COMPANY; *pg.* 89, *pg.* 771
JAN-PRO - Cleaning Services - PREMIUM FRANCHISE BRANDS LLC; *pg.* 333, *pg.* 485
JANDO - Footwear - K-SWISS; *pg.* 1837, *pg.* 306
JANE - Clothing - ABERCROMBIE & FITCH CO.; *pg.* 37, *pg.* 1466
JANE - Furniture - AMISCO INDUSTRIES LTD.; *pg.* 913, *pg.* 1958
JANE - Furniture - THE COMMERCIAL FURNITURE GROUP; *pg.* 920, *pg.* 994
JANESVILLE - Fiber Insulation - JANESVILLE ACOUSTICS; *pg.* 1885, *pg.* 907
JANESVILLE - Motor Vehicle Product - JASON INDUSTRIES, INC.; *pg.* 208, *pg.* 1875
JANICE'S - Leather Product - COACH, INC.; *pg.* 3, *pg.* 1214
JANIE & JACK - Crafted Clothing & Accessory - THE GYMBOREE CORPORATION; *pg.* 25, *pg.* 77
JANSPORT - Backpacks & Casual Wear - V.F. CORPORATION; *pg.* 34, *pg.* 1376
JANSPORT, INC. - Backpacks - JANSPORT; *pg.* 1837, *pg.* 38
JANTZEN - Sportswear - PERRY ELLIS INTERNATIONAL, INC.; *pg.* 45, *pg.* 445
JANUMET - Medicine - MERCK & CO., INC.; *pg.* 1566, *pg.* 1077
JANUS - Automated Workstation - PERKINELMER, INC.; *pg.* 1426, *pg.* 853
JAPAN AIRLINES - Airlines - JAPAN AIRLINES COMPANY, LTD.; *pg.* 1913, *pg.* 1245
JAPANESE FERN - Carpet - INTERFACE, INC.; *pg.* 695, *pg.* 512
JAPANESE ROSE GARDEN - Nail Care Product - OPI PRODUCTS INC.; *pg.* 518, *pg.* 167
JAQUES - Crushing & Screening Equipment - TEREX CORPORATION; *pg.* 1381, *pg.* 384
JAR KING - Hydraulic Drilling Jar - BAKER HUGHES INTEQ; *pg.* 1316, *pg.* 1700
JAR-PACT - Drilling Jar Product - SMITH INTERNATIONAL, INC.; *pg.* 1377, *pg.* 1715
JARBROM - Chemical Product - JARCHEM INDUSTRIES, INC.; *pg.* 1169, *pg.* 1096
JARBROM I-16 - Isocetyl Bromide - JARCHEM INDUSTRIES, INC.; *pg.* 1169, *pg.* 1096
JARCHLOR - Chemical Product - JARCHEM INDUSTRIES, INC.; *pg.* 1169, *pg.* 1096
JARCHLOR I-16 - Isocetyl Chloride - JARCHEM INDUSTRIES, INC.; *pg.* 1169, *pg.* 1096
JARCO - Desk Accessories - JARCO/U.S. CASTINGS; *pg.* 1051, *pg.* 1127
JARCOAL - Chemical Product - JARCHEM INDUSTRIES, INC.; *pg.* 1169, *pg.* 1096
JARCOL - Chemical Product - JARCHEM INDUSTRIES, INC.; *pg.* 1169, *pg.* 1096
JARED - Jewelers - STERLING JEWELERS INC.; *pg.* 13, *pg.* 1402
JARESTER - Chemical Product - JARCHEM INDUSTRIES, INC.; *pg.* 1169, *pg.* 1096
JARGRIP - Chemical Product - JARCHEM INDUSTRIES, INC.; *pg.* 1169, *pg.* 1096
JARIC 22U - Erucic Acid - JARCHEM INDUSTRIES, INC.; *pg.* 1169, *pg.* 1096
JARIC I-12 - Isolauric Acid - JARCHEM INDUSTRIES, INC.; *pg.* 1169, *pg.* 1096
JARIT - Medical Device - INTEGRA LIFESCIENCES HOLDINGS CORPORATION; *pg.* 1545, *pg.* 1109
JARLC - Chemical Product - JARCHEM INDUSTRIES, INC.; *pg.* 1169, *pg.* 1096
JARLSBERG - Premium Imported Cheese - NORSELAND, INC.; *pg.* 886, *pg.* 376
JARLSBERG LITE - Premium Imported Cheese - NORSELAND, INC.; *pg.* 886, *pg.* 376
JARMAN - Shoes - GENESCO INC.; *pg.* 1809, *pg.* 1650
JARPOL - Chemical Product - JARCHEM INDUSTRIES, INC.; *pg.* 1169, *pg.* 1096
JARRITOS - Frozen Beverage - YOCREAM INTERNATIONAL INC.; *pg.* 1039, *pg.* 1508
JARTHERM - Chemical Product - JARCHEM INDUSTRIES, INC.; *pg.* 1169, *pg.* 1096
JAS - Golf Club - KARSTEN MANUFACTURING CORPORATION; *pg.* 1838, *pg.* 17

JASMINE SHINE - Hair & Skin Product - AUBREY ORGANICS INC.; *pg.* 499, *pg.* 470
JASON - Furniture - AMISCO INDUSTRIES LTD.; *pg.* 913, *pg.* 1958
JASON - Personal Care - THE HAIN CELESTIAL GROUP, INC.; *pg.* 860, *pg.* 1172
JASON - Brush - JASON INDUSTRIES, INC.; *pg.* 208, *pg.* 1875
JASON - Spout - PRECISION VALVE CORPORATION; *pg.* 1060, *pg.* 1357
JASON PROJECT - Lab Science Material - CAROLINA BIOLOGICAL SUPPLY COMPANY; *pg.* 1513, *pg.* 1359
THE JASPER - Home Floor Plan - JACOBSEN MANUFACTURING, INC.; *pg.* 1098, *pg.* 460
JASPER - Engines & Transmissions - JASPER ENGINE & TRANSMISSION EXCHANGE; *pg.* 209, *pg.* 691
JASSM - Systems Integration & Aeronautics - LOCKHEED MARTIN CORPORATION; *pg.* 229, *pg.* 762
JAUNTY - Fabric - NEMSCHOFF, INC.; *pg.* 936, *pg.* 1890
JAVA - Commercial Lighting - SWIVELIER CO., INC.; *pg.* 1307, *pg.* 1142
JAVA MAUVE-A - Nail Care Product - OPI PRODUCTS INC.; *pg.* 518, *pg.* 167
JAVA SONATA CAFE - Coffee - GIANT EAGLE, INC.; *pg.* 1020, *pg.* 1575
JAVAWORKS - Insulated Plastic Drinkware - WHIRLEY INDUSTRIES, INC.; *pg.* 1892, *pg.* 1590
JAVELIN - Fabric - NEMSCHOFF, INC.; *pg.* 936, *pg.* 1890
JAVELIN - Defense System - RAYTHEON COMPANY; *pg.* 233, *pg.* 854
JAVELIN - Writing Instrument - SHEAFFER PEN CORPORATION; *pg.* 469, *pg.* 371
JAVELIN - Wood & Building Material - WEYERHAEUSER COMPANY; *pg.* 121, *pg.* 1820
JAWBONE ERA - Headsets - ALIPHCOM, INC.; *pg.* 616, *pg.* 212
JAWBUSTERS - Candy - FERRARA CANDY CO.; *pg.* 1852, *pg.* 612
JAWS - Dispensing Nozzles for Plastic Bags - SONOCO PRODUCTS COMPANY; *pg.* 1469, *pg.* 1619
JAWS OF LIFE - Hydraulic Equipment - IDEX CORPORATION; *pg.* 1347, *pg.* 623
JAX - Misses' Sportswear - KELLWOOD COMPANY; *pg.* 28, *pg.* 975
JAX COUNTRY - Misses' & Women's Casual & Career Sportswear - KELLWOOD COMPANY; *pg.* 28, *pg.* 975
JAY C - Supermarket - THE KROGER CO.; *pg.* 1025, *pg.* 1416
JAY FEATHER EXP - Expandable Travel Trailer - JAYCO INC.; *pg.* 1708, *pg.* 695
JAY FEATHER LGT - Lightweight Travel Trailer - JAYCO INC.; *pg.* 1708, *pg.* 695
JAY FEATHER SPORT - Lightweight Travel Trailer - JAYCO INC.; *pg.* 1708, *pg.* 695
JAY FLIGHT - Recreational Vehicles - JAYCO INC.; *pg.* 1708, *pg.* 695
JAYHAWK BOXES - Corrugated Boxes - LAWRENCE PAPER COMPANY; *pg.* 1463, *pg.* 715
JAYS SNACKS - Sanck Food - SNYDER'S-LANCE, INC.; *pg.* 896, *pg.* 1368
JAZ COLA - Soft Drink - THE COCA-COLA COMPANY; *pg.* 240, *pg.* 493
JAZZ - Carpet - BEAULIEU GROUP, LLC; *pg.* 917, *pg.* 529
JAZZ - Window Treatment - CROSCILL, INC.; *pg.* 1122, *pg.* 1220
JAZZ - Fabric - NEMSCHOFF, INC.; *pg.* 936, *pg.* 1890
JAZZ - Musical Instrument - PEAVEY ELECTRONICS CORPORATION; *pg.* 662, *pg.* 970
JAZZ ANKLE - Footwear - CAPEZIO BALLET MAKERS INC.; *pg.* 1805, *pg.* 1125
JAZZ AT LINCOLN CENTER - Performing Arts Program - LINCOLN CENTER FOR THE PERFORMING ARTS, INC.; *pg.* 557, *pg.* 1251
JAZZ LIGHT - Fiber Optic Lighting System - ENERGY FOCUS, INC.; *pg.* 1411, *pg.* 1472
JAZZERTOGS - Fitness Apparel & Accessories - JAZZERCISE, INC.; *pg.* 554, *pg.* 59
JAZZY - Footwear - PHOENIX FOOTWEAR GROUP, INC.; *pg.* 1815, *pg.* 60
JB - Enamel - JONES-BLAIR COMPANY; *pg.* 1443, *pg.* 1682
JB GUM - Chewing Gum - JELLY BELLY CANDY COMPANY; *pg.* 1857, *pg.* 86
JBL - Loudspeakers - HARMAN INTERNATIONAL INDUSTRIES, INCORPORATED; *pg.* 641, *pg.* 374
JBLAST - Communication Product - J2 GLOBAL COMMUNICATIONS, INC.; *pg.* 1260, *pg.* 133
JBROKER - Computer Software - NOVELL INC.; *pg.* 446, *pg.* 852
JBZ - Chocolate Candies - JELLY BELLY CANDY COMPANY; *pg.* 1857, *pg.* 86
JCASE - Cartridge Fuse - LITTELFUSE, INC.; *pg.* 1301, *pg.* 580
JCHARGE - Software - VERIFONE SYSTEMS, INC.; *pg.* 487, *pg.* 251
JCI - Cone Crusher - ASTEC INDUSTRIES, INC.; *pg.* 69, *pg.* 1628
JCLASS - Software - DELL SOFTWARE; *pg.* 385, *pg.* 40
JCLASS SERVERVIEWS - Software - DELL SOFTWARE; *pg.* 385, *pg.* 40
JCONNECT - Communication Product - J2 GLOBAL COMMUNICATIONS, INC.; *pg.* 1260, *pg.* 133
JCONNECT FREE - Fax Messaging Solution - J2 GLOBAL COMMUNICATIONS, INC.; *pg.* 1260, *pg.* 133
JCONNECT PREMIER - Fax & Voicemail Messaging Solution - J2 GLOBAL COMMUNICATIONS, INC.; *pg.* 1260, *pg.* 133
JD EDWARDS - Software - ORACLE CORPORATION; *pg.* 450, *pg.* 191
JDA AIRLINE REVENUE OPTIMIZER - Software - JDA SOFTWARE GROUP, INC.; *pg.* 423, *pg.* 22
JDA CARGO REVENUE OPTIMIZER - Software - JDA SOFTWARE GROUP, INC.; *pg.* 423, *pg.* 22
JDA CARRIER - Software - JDA SOFTWARE GROUP, INC.; *pg.* 423, *pg.* 22
JDA CHANNEL CLUSTERING - Software - JDA SOFTWARE GROUP, INC.; *pg.* 423, *pg.* 22
JDA CRUISE REVENUE OPTIMIZER - Software - JDA SOFTWARE GROUP, INC.; *pg.* 423, *pg.* 22
JDA FLOOR PLANNING - Software - JDA SOFTWARE GROUP, INC.; *pg.* 423, *pg.* 22
JDA FREIGHT PAY - Software - JDA SOFTWARE GROUP, INC.; *pg.* 423, *pg.* 22
JDA MARKDOWN OPTIMIZATION - Software - JDA SOFTWARE GROUP, INC.; *pg.* 423, *pg.* 22
JDA MARKETPLACE - Software - JDA SOFTWARE GROUP, INC.; *pg.* 423, *pg.* 22
JDA MASTER PLANNING - Software - JDA SOFTWARE GROUP, INC.; *pg.* 423, *pg.* 22
JDA PLANOGRAM GENERATOR - Software - JDA SOFTWARE GROUP, INC.; *pg.* 423, *pg.* 22
JDA PRICE OPTIMIZER - Software - JDA SOFTWARE GROUP, INC.; *pg.* 423, *pg.* 22
JDA PROMOTIONS OPTIMIZATION - Software - JDA SOFTWARE GROUP, INC.; *pg.* 423, *pg.* 22
JDA RAIL REVENUE OPTIMIZER - Software - JDA SOFTWARE GROUP, INC.; *pg.* 423, *pg.* 22
JDA ROUTING - Software - JDA SOFTWARE GROUP, INC.; *pg.* 423, *pg.* 22
JDA SEQUENCING - Software - JDA SOFTWARE GROUP, INC.; *pg.* 423, *pg.* 22
JDA SHELF ASSORTMENT - Software - JDA SOFTWARE GROUP, INC.; *pg.* 423, *pg.* 22
JDA SHELF PRICE OPTIMIZATION - Software - JDA SOFTWARE GROUP, INC.; *pg.* 423, *pg.* 22
JDA SPACE AUTOMATION - Software - JDA SOFTWARE GROUP, INC.; *pg.* 423, *pg.* 22
JDA STORE PORTAL - Software - JDA SOFTWARE GROUP, INC.; *pg.* 423, *pg.* 22
JDA SUPPLY - Software - JDA SOFTWARE GROUP, INC.; *pg.* 423, *pg.* 22
JDA TOUR REVENUE OPTIMIZER - Software - JDA SOFTWARE GROUP, INC.; *pg.* 423, *pg.* 22
JDA TRANSPORT RFQ - Software - JDA SOFTWARE GROUP, INC.; *pg.* 423, *pg.* 22
JDATE - Online Dating Service for Jewish Singles - SPARK NETWORKS, INC.; *pg.* 472, *pg.* 140
JDC - Precision Sample Cutter - THWING-ALBERT INSTRUMENT COMPANY; *pg.* 1432, *pg.* 1131
JDLINK - Management Products - DEERE & COMPANY; *pg.* 703, *pg.* 632
JDOFFICE - Management Products - DEERE & COMPANY; *pg.* 703, *pg.* 632
JE-VAX - Japanese Encephalitis Vaccine - SANOFI PASTEUR, INC; *pg.* 1591, *pg.* 1588
JEAN BAPTISTE - Brass & Woodwind Instruments - SAM ASH MUSIC CORPORATION; *pg.* 669, *pg.* 1167
JEAN LOUIS DAVID - Hair Salons - REGIS CORPORATION; *pg.* 521, *pg.* 941
JEAN-MICHELLE - Beauty Product - COSMETIQUE, INC.; *pg.* 1765, *pg.* 664
JEAN PHILIPPE - Fragrances - INTER PARFUMS, INC.; *pg.* 512, *pg.* 1244
JEANNE GATINEAU - Fragrance - REVLON, INC.; *pg.* 521, *pg.* 1286
JEANS MACHINE - Straight Knife - THE WOLF MACHINE CO.; *pg.* 1389, *pg.* 1427
JEDIT - Computer Software - NOVELL INC.; *pg.* 446, *pg.* 852
JEEP - Binocular Set - CITIZENS BANK & TRUST; *pg.* 737, *pg.* 976
JEEP - Automobiles - FCA US LLC; *pg.* 170, *pg.* 868
JEEP CHEROKEE - Sport Utility Vehicle - FCA US LLC; *pg.* 170, *pg.* 868
JEEP COMMANDER - Sport-Utility Vehicle - FCA US LLC; *pg.* 170, *pg.* 868
JEEP GRAND CHEROKEE - Sport Utility - FCA US LLC; *pg.* 170, *pg.* 868
JEEP GRAND CHEROKEE LAREDO - Sport Utility Vehicle - FCA US LLC; *pg.* 170, *pg.* 868
JEEP LIBERTY - Sport-Utility Vehicle - FCA US LLC; *pg.* 170, *pg.* 868
JEEP PATRIOT - Sport Utility Vehicle - FCA US LLC; *pg.* 170, *pg.* 868
JEEP WRANGLER - Sport Utility - FCA US LLC; *pg.* 170, *pg.* 868
JEEPERS CREEPER - Mechanic's Creeper - LISLE CORPORATION; *pg.* 1356, *pg.* 703
JEFF BANKS - Sunglasses - FGX INTERNATIONAL, INC.; *pg.* 5, *pg.* 1608
JEFF BECK STRATOCASTER - Electric Guitar - FENDER MUSICAL INSTRUMENTS CORPORATION; *pg.* 547, *pg.* 21
JEFFAMINE - Epoxy Curing Agent - HUNTSMAN CORPORATION; *pg.* 1167, *pg.* 1758
JEFFCAT - Urethane Catalysts - HUNTSMAN CORPORATION; *pg.* 1167, *pg.* 1758
JEFFCOOL - Industrial Coolant - HUNTSMAN CORPORATION; *pg.* 1167, *pg.* 1758
JEFFERSON - Decorative Accessory - ETHAN ALLEN INTERIORS INC.; *pg.* 924, *pg.* 343
JEFFERSON - Furniture - JASPER GROUP; *pg.* 930, *pg.* 691
JEFFERSON ISLAND - Salt - CARGILL LIMITED; *pg.* 1475, *pg.* 1914
JEFFERSON PILOT FINANCIAL - Covers all Companies That are Within The Jefferson-Pilot Corporation - LINCOLN FINANCIAL GROUP; *pg.* 1206, *pg.* 1375
JEFFERSON'S - Bourbon - CASTLE BRANDS INC.; *pg.* 239, *pg.* 1209
JEFFERSON'S RESERVE - Bourbon - CASTLE BRANDS INC.; *pg.* 239, *pg.* 1209
JEFFOL - Urethane Polyol - HUNTSMAN CORPORATION; *pg.* 1167, *pg.* 1758
JEFFRY - Furniture - J. ROBERT SCOTT INC.; *pg.* 930, *pg.* 105
JEFFSOL - Carbonates - HUNTSMAN CORPORATION; *pg.* 1167, *pg.* 1758
JEKEL - Vineyards - BROWN-FORMAN CORPORATION; *pg.* 1958, *pg.* 732
JEKEL VINEYARDS - California Wines - BROWN-FORMAN CORPORATION; *pg.* 1958, *pg.* 732
JEKYLL & HYDE - Video Game - INTERNATIONAL GAME TECHNOLOGY; *pg.* 957, *pg.* 1024
JELLO - Food Product - THE KRAFT HEINZ COMPANY; *pg.* 870, *pg.* 1577
JELLY BASLER BELLY - Candy Cane - SPANGLER CANDY COMPANY; *pg.* 1862, *pg.* 1407
JELLY BEAN - Nursing Cover - MUNCHKIN, INC.; *pg.* 964, *pg.* 300
JELLY BEANS - Candy - JELLY BELLY CANDY COMPANY; *pg.* 1857, *pg.* 86
JELLY LIGHTS - Fiber Optic Lighting System - ENERGY FOCUS, INC.; *pg.* 1411, *pg.* 1472
JELTEC - Starch - ARCHER-DANIELS-MIDLAND COMPANY; *pg.* 825, *pg.* 565
JELTRATE - Dental Product - DENTSPLY INTERNATIONAL INC.; *pg.* 1522, *pg.* 1596
J.E.MORGAN - Apparel - HANESBRANDS INC.; *pg.* 26, *pg.* 1394
JENGA - Game - HASBRO, INC.; *pg.* 954, *pg.* 1603
JENGA E XTREME - Toy & Game - HASBRO, INC.; *pg.* 954, *pg.* 1603
JENIUS - Insulation - THE DOW CHEMICAL COMPANY; *pg.* 1157, *pg.* 898
JENN-AIR - Stainless Appliances - WHIRLPOOL CORPORATION; *pg.* 62, *pg.* 872

JENNE - Shampoo - KAO BRANDS CO. INC.; *pg.* 513, *pg.* 1415
JENNIE-O TURKEY STORE - Turkey Products - HORMEL FOODS CORPORATION; *pg.* 863, *pg.* 915
JENNIFER - Furniture - HOOKER FURNITURE CORPORATION; *pg.* 928, *pg.* 1788
JENNINGS - Sporting Good Product - ESCALADE INC.; *pg.* 1833, *pg.* 678
JENNINGS TECHNOLOGY - Vacuum Technology - DANAHER CORPORATION; *pg.* 1044, *pg.* 397
JENNY - Cleaning Equipment & Cleaning Compounds - JENNY PRODUCTS, INC.; *pg.* 331, *pg.* 1586
JENNY - Office Furniture - STEELCASE INC.; *pg.* 475, *pg.* 889
JENNY CLUB - Office Furniture - STEELCASE INC.; *pg.* 475, *pg.* 889
JENNY CRAIG - Weight Loss Centers - JENNY CRAIG OPERATIONS, INC.; *pg.* 1548, *pg.* 59
JENNY CRAIG DIRECT - At-home Weight Loss Program - JENNY CRAIG OPERATIONS, INC.; *pg.* 1548, *pg.* 59
JENO'S - Food Product - GENERAL MILLS, INC.; *pg.* 828, *pg.* 933
JENSEN - Furniture - ETHAN ALLEN INTERIORS INC.; *pg.* 924, *pg.* 343
JENSEN - Fabric - NEMSCHOFF, INC.; *pg.* 936, *pg.* 1890
JENSEN - Electrician Tools - STANLEY BLACK & DECKER, INC.; *pg.* 1063, *pg.* 358
JENSEN - Mobile & Consumer Electronics - VOXX INTERNATIONAL; *pg.* 686, *pg.* 1166
JENSON - Packaging Product - CASCADES, INC.; *pg.* 73, *pg.* 1950
JERGEN - Mold Base & Component - SUPERIOR DIE SET CORP.; *pg.* 1379, *pg.* 1885
JERGENS - Face Cream, Hand & Body Lotion, Body Wash, Soap & Bath Products, - KAO BRANDS CO. INC.; *pg.* 513, *pg.* 1415
JERICHO - Beverages - THE COCA-COLA COMPANY; *pg.* 240, *pg.* 493
JERKY TREATS - Pet Food - BIG HEART PET BRANDS; *pg.* 1474, *pg.* 213
JEROME - Analyzer - ARIZONA INSTRUMENT LLC; *pg.* 1400, *pg.* 12
JERR-DAN - Truck Product - OSHKOSH CORPORATION; *pg.* 187, *pg.* 1885
JERRY'S FAMOUS DELI - Food Product - JERRY'S FAMOUS DELI, INC.; *pg.* 1733, *pg.* 281
JERSEY - Paper & Nonwoven Material - FIBERMARK INC.; *pg.* 1457, *pg.* 1764
JERSEY - Office Furniture - STEELCASE INC.; *pg.* 475, *pg.* 889
JERSEY CASH 5 - Five Digit Numbers Game Drawn Five Times Per Week - NEW JERSEY STATE LOTTERY; *pg.* 1000, *pg.* 1126
THE JERSEY JOURNAL - Online Business Center - JERSEY JOURNAL NEWSPAPER; *pg.* 1654, *pg.* 1120
JERUSALEM STONE - Ceramic, Glass, Stone Tiles & Slabs - WALKER & ZANGER, INC.; *pg.* 119, *pg.* 281
JERVISBWEBB - Automatic Guided Vehicle - DAIFUKU WEBB; *pg.* 1327, *pg.* 885
JERZEES - Apparel - RUSSELL BRANDS LLC; *pg.* 698, *pg.* 726
JESMASTER-PLUS - Software - ACTUATE CANADA; *pg.* 1225, *pg.* 1933
JESS - Footwear - PHOENIX FOOTWEAR GROUP, INC.; *pg.* 1815, *pg.* 60
JESSEMAL - Fragrance Ingredient - INTERNATIONAL FLAVORS & FRAGRANCES INC.; *pg.* 512, *pg.* 1244
JESSEN - Footwear - VANS, INC.; *pg.* 1821, *pg.* 76
JESSICA - Footwear - PHOENIX FOOTWEAR GROUP, INC.; *pg.* 1815, *pg.* 60
JESSICA - Fabric - SCALAMANDRE, INC.; *pg.* 941, *pg.* 1058
JESSICA HOWARD - Apparel - G-III APPAREL GROUP, LTD.; *pg.* 41, *pg.* 1233
JESSICA LONDON - Apparel - FULLBEAUTY BRANDS; *pg.* 1770, *pg.* 1233
JESTER - Video Game - INTERNATIONAL GAME TECHNOLOGY; *pg.* 957, *pg.* 1024
JESTER - Fabric - NEMSCHOFF, INC.; *pg.* 936, *pg.* 1890
JESTER'S WILD - Lottery Game - LOUISIANA LOTTERY CORPORATION; *pg.* 997, *pg.* 742
JET - Atmospheric Transport System - BROOKS AUTOMATION, INC.; *pg.* 1320, *pg.* 813
JET - Energy Product - CONOCOPHILLIPS; *pg.* 975, *pg.* 1703
JET - Magazine - JOHNSON PUBLISHING COMPANY, INC.; *pg.* 1655, *pg.* 579
JET - Instruments - L-3 AVIONICS SYSTEMS, INC.; *pg.* 650, *pg.* 888
JET - Bicycle - TREK BICYCLE CORPORATION; *pg.* 1847, *pg.* 1896
JET - Leath - ZIMMERMAN-MCDONALD MACHINERY, INC.; *pg.* 1391, *pg.* 1005
JET BEE - Wasp & Hornet Control - BONIDE PRODUCTS, INC.; *pg.* 1794, *pg.* 1320
JET-CLEAN - Jet Pulse Type Separator - THE SPENCER TURBINE CO.; *pg.* 1378, *pg.* 386
JET-CLUSTER - Jet - WATKINS MANUFACTURING CORPORATION; *pg.* 120, *pg.* 303
JET-FLECS - Electronic Components - MOLEX INCORPORATED; *pg.* 655, *pg.* 628
JET GLO - Paint - THE SHERWIN-WILLIAMS COMPANY; *pg.* 1447, *pg.* 1435
JET GLO EXPRESS - Paint - THE SHERWIN-WILLIAMS COMPANY; *pg.* 1447, *pg.* 1435
JET-LH - Electrode - LINCOLN ELECTRIC HOLDINGS, INC.; *pg.* 1355, *pg.* 1432
JET MIX - Burner - NAO, INC.; *pg.* 1074, *pg.* 1567
JET MIX VORTEX - Vent Tip - NAO, INC.; *pg.* 1074, *pg.* 1567
JET-OPAQUE - Heat Transfer Papers - NEENAH PAPER, INC.; *pg.* 1465, *pg.* 484
JET PACK - Solid Ink - RICOH PRINTING SYSTEMS AMERICA, INC.; *pg.* 462, *pg.* 279
JET-PAK - Spray System - SHERWIN-WILLIAMS DIVERSIFIED BRANDS DIVISION; *pg.* 1448, *pg.* 1435
JET PRINT PHOTO - Paper - INTERNATIONAL PAPER COMPANY; *pg.* 1460, *pg.* 1644
JET-PRO - Paper - NEENAH PAPER, INC.; *pg.* 1465, *pg.* 484
JET-PUFFED - Snacks - THE KRAFT HEINZ COMPANY; *pg.* 870, *pg.* 1577
JET SETTER - Video Game - INTERNATIONAL GAME TECHNOLOGY; *pg.* 957, *pg.* 1024
JET SKI - Water Sport Vehicle - KAWASAKI MOTORS CORP., U.S.A.; *pg.* 1708, *pg.* 111
JET SPRAY - Beverage Dispensing System - CORNELIUS INC.; *pg.* 54, *pg.* 614
JET SPRAY - Beverage Dispenser - CORNELIUS INC; *pg.* 1326, *pg.* 952
JET SPRAY CLEAN - Detergent - DELTA FOREMOST CHEMICAL CORPORATION; *pg.* 1155, *pg.* 1642
JET TONIC - Beverages - THE COCA-COLA COMPANY; *pg.* 240, *pg.* 493
JET TRAC - Underground Construction Equipment - CHARLES MACHINE WORKS, INC.; *pg.* 1322, *pg.* 1488
JET-TRANS - Heat Transfer Papers - NEENAH PAPER, INC.; *pg.* 1465, *pg.* 484
JET-TRON - Proximity Detectors - AUTOMATION DEVICES, INC.; *pg.* 1315, *pg.* 1532
JET-VENT - Air Vent - BOUMATIC LLC; *pg.* 701, *pg.* 1865
JET-WELD - Adhesive - 3M COMPANY; *pg.* 1142, *pg.* 956
JETANGER - Fastening System - TEXTRON INC.; *pg.* 235, *pg.* 1607
JETBLUE - Air Transportation Service - JETBLUE AIRWAYS CORPORATION; *pg.* 1913, *pg.* 1174
JETBLUE FEATURES - Entertainment Services - JETBLUE AIRWAYS CORPORATION; *pg.* 1913, *pg.* 1174
JETBOND - Graphic Film - FLEXCON CORPORATION; *pg.* 1457, *pg.* 844
JETBOX - Chemical Product - AIR PRODUCTS AND CHEMICALS, INC.; *pg.* 1145, *pg.* 1513
JETCAL - Analyzer - HOWELL INSTRUMENTS INC.; *pg.* 1417, *pg.* 1695
JETCAL2000 - Engine Analyzer - HOWELL INSTRUMENTS INC.; *pg.* 1417, *pg.* 1695
JETCAL2000 ANALYZER - Engine Test System - HOWELL INSTRUMENTS INC.; *pg.* 1417, *pg.* 1695
JETCLEAN - Dishwasher - WHIRLPOOL CORPORATION; *pg.* 62, *pg.* 872
JETCLEANER - Tube Cleaner - GOODWAY TECHNOLOGIES CORPORATION; *pg.* 1341, *pg.* 374
JETE - Footwear - CAPEZIO BALLET MAKERS INC.; *pg.* 1805, *pg.* 1125
JETFLEX - Paint - THE SHERWIN-WILLIAMS COMPANY; *pg.* 1447, *pg.* 1435
JETGLAS - Gas, Electric & Oil Powered Heaters - BRADFORD-WHITE CORPORATION; *pg.* 1069, *pg.* 1514
JETLOAD - Tube Cleaner - GOODWAY TECHNOLOGIES CORPORATION; *pg.* 1341, *pg.* 374
JETRION - Printing Product - ELECTRONICS FOR IMAGING, INC.; *pg.* 390, *pg.* 88
JETS - Steel Wool Soap Pads - THE CLOROX COMPANY; *pg.* 327, *pg.* 169
JETS - Computer Software - COMPUTER SCIENCES CORPORATION; *pg.* 378, *pg.* 1780
JETS TRAINING CAMP - Camp - NEW YORK JETS FOOTBALL CLUB, INC.; *pg.* 570, *pg.* 1067
JETSIE STRIPE CAMI - Apparel - VANS, INC.; *pg.* 1821, *pg.* 76
JETSON - Fabric - NEMSCHOFF, INC.; *pg.* 936, *pg.* 1890
JETSTAR - Systems Integration & Aeronautics - LOCKHEED MARTIN CORPORATION; *pg.* 229, *pg.* 762
JETSTREAM - Water Blasting Equipment - FEDERAL SIGNAL CORPORATION; *pg.* 638, *pg.* 645
JETSTREAM - Jet - WATKINS MANUFACTURING CORPORATION; *pg.* 120, *pg.* 303
JETSTREAM PRO - Back Support System - THE ROHO GROUP; *pg.* 1591, *pg.* 556
JETTIZO - Pharmaceutical Preparation - PFIZER INC.; *pg.* 1581, *pg.* 1278
JETWELD - Electrode - LINCOLN ELECTRIC HOLDINGS, INC.; *pg.* 1355, *pg.* 1432
JEUMONTSCHNEIDER - Pump - FLOWSERVE CORPORATION; *pg.* 82, *pg.* 1719
JEVITY - Medical Nutritional Tube-Feeding Product - ABBOTT LABORATORIES; *pg.* 1484, *pg.* 551
JEWEL - Food Product And Drug - ALBERTSON'S LLC; *pg.* 1013, *pg.* 546
JEWEL - Table - BLATT BOWLING & BILLIARD CORP.; *pg.* 1827, *pg.* 1203
JEWEL - Arrhythmia Management Device - MEDTRONIC, INC.; *pg.* 1564, *pg.* 939
JEWEL - Ceiling Fan - WESTINGHOUSE LIGHTING CORPORATION; *pg.* 687, *pg.* 1571
JEWEL CUT - Gaming Product - GLD PRODUCTS, INC.; *pg.* 1835, *pg.* 1882
JEWEL OF ARABIA - Video Game - INTERNATIONAL GAME TECHNOLOGY; *pg.* 957, *pg.* 1024
JEWEL OF INDIA - Nail Care Product - OPI PRODUCTS INC.; *pg.* 518, *pg.* 167
THE JEWEL OF PALM BEACH: THE MAR-A-LAGO CLUB - Magazine - PALM BEACH MEDIA GROUP INC.; *pg.* 1674, *pg.* 457
JEWEL OF THE SEAS - Cruise Ship - ROYAL CARIBBEAN CRUISES LTD; *pg.* 1921, *pg.* 446
JEWEL-OSCO - Bakery Products - ALPHA BAKING COMPANY; *pg.* 836, *pg.* 564
JEWEL-OSCO - Food Stores - JEWEL-OSCO; *pg.* 1024, *pg.* 620
JEWEL-OSCO - Store - SUPERVALU, INC.; *pg.* 1035, *pg.* 924
JEWEL PCD - Implantable Defibrillator - MEDTRONIC, INC.; *pg.* 1564, *pg.* 939
JEWEL PLUS - Implantable Cardioverter Defibrillator - MEDTRONIC, INC.; *pg.* 1564, *pg.* 939
JEWEL T - Recovery Tool - CAMERON INTERNATIONAL; *pg.* 1151, *pg.* 1702
JEWELL - Instruments - JEWELL INSTRUMENTS, LLC; *pg.* 1418, *pg.* 1036
JEWELRY SOAP - Jewelry Cleaner - CONNOISSEURS PRODUCTS CORPORATION; *pg.* 329, *pg.* 861
JEWELRY WIPES - Jewelry Cleaner - CONNOISSEURS PRODUCTS CORPORATION; *pg.* 329, *pg.* 861
JEWELS OF AFRICA - Game - WMS INDUSTRIES INC.; *pg.* 593, *pg.* 666
JEWELS OF ASIA - Video Game - INTERNATIONAL GAME TECHNOLOGY; *pg.* 957, *pg.* 1024
JEWELS OF INDIA - Video Game - INTERNATIONAL GAME TECHNOLOGY; *pg.* 957, *pg.* 1024
JEWELS OF ISIS - Game - WMS INDUSTRIES INC.; *pg.* 593, *pg.* 666
JEWELS OF THE NIGHT - Game - WMS INDUSTRIES INC.; *pg.* 593, *pg.* 666
JEWELS OF THE PHARAOH - Game - WMS INDUSTRIES INC.; *pg.* 593, *pg.* 666
JEWISH HERITAGE TOURS - Tour Packages - ISRAM WHOLESALE TOURS & TRAVEL LTD.; *pg.* 1913, *pg.* 1244
JEXPRESS - Software - WIND RIVER SYSTEMS, INC.; *pg.* 493, *pg.* 38
JEXTREME - Software - WIND RIVER SYSTEMS, INC.; *pg.* 493, *pg.* 38
JEZEBEL - Fashion & Gossip - GAWKER MEDIA LLC; *pg.* 1248, *pg.* 1234
JF - Paper Drill - THE CHALLENGE MACHINERY COMPANY;

First page reference indicates Business Class Edition
Second page reference indicates Geographic Edition

pg. 1322, *pg.* 902
JFAX - Communication Product - J2 GLOBAL COMMUNICATIONS, INC.; *pg.* 1260, *pg.* 133
JG SEATING - Auditorium Seating - MITY ENTERPRISES, INC.; *pg.* 935, *pg.* 1753
J.G.HOOK - Bedding Product - HOLLANDER SLEEP PRODUCTS; *pg.* 927, *pg.* 411
JGL TOOLKIT - Software - RECURSION SOFTWARE, INC.; *pg.* 460, *pg.* 1697
JH COLLECTIBLES - Casual Apparel - KATE SPADE & COMPANY; *pg.* 27, *pg.* 1248
JHERI REDDING - Hair Care Line - CONAIR CORPORATION; *pg.* 505, *pg.* 1055
J.HUNGERFORD SMITH - Food Product - CONAGRA FOODS, INC.; *pg.* 826, *pg.* 1014
JIBBITZ - Footwear - CROCS, INC.; *pg.* 1806, *pg.* 335
JIF - Peanut Butter - THE J.M. SMUCKER COMPANY; *pg.* 865, *pg.* 1468
JIFFY - Garden Seeds - FERRY-MORSE SEED COMPANY; *pg.* 1795, *pg.* 728
JIFFY - Yarn - LION BRAND YARN COMPANY; *pg.* 696, *pg.* 1050
JIFFY - Protective Packaging Material - PACTIV CORPORATION; *pg.* 1466, *pg.* 624
JIFFY - Mailers - SEALED AIR CORPORATION; *pg.* 1468, *pg.* 1058
JIFFY COVER - Plastic Drop Cloth - FLEX-O-GLASS, INC.; *pg.* 1457, *pg.* 574
JIFFY-COVER - Drop Cloths - WARP BROTHERS; *pg.* 1471, *pg.* 595
JIFFY DRY - Enamel & Stain - JONES-BLAIR COMPANY; *pg.* 1443, *pg.* 1682
JIFFY EXPRESS - Packaging Machinery - SEALED AIR CORPORATION; *pg.* 1468, *pg.* 1058
JIFFY LUBE - Oil Change Facilities - JIFFY LUBE INTERNATIONAL, INC.; *pg.* 209, *pg.* 1709
JIFFY MAILER - Packaging Product - SEALED AIR CORPORATION; *pg.* 1468, *pg.* 1058
JIFFY MELT - Deicing Crystals - CARGILL LIMITED; *pg.* 1475, *pg.* 1914
JIFFY PACKER - Paper Packaging System - SEALED AIR CORPORATION; *pg.* 1468, *pg.* 1058
JIFFY PADWRAP - Paper Cushioning Materials - SEALED AIR CORPORATION; *pg.* 1468, *pg.* 1058
JIFFY POP - Food Product - CONAGRA FOODS, INC.; *pg.* 826, *pg.* 1014
JIFFY PREMIUM PAD - Paper Cushioned Materials - SEALED AIR CORPORATION; *pg.* 1468, *pg.* 1058
JIFFY PREP - Paint Condition - JONES-BLAIR COMPANY; *pg.* 1443, *pg.* 1682
JIFFY RIGI BAG - Mailers - SEALED AIR CORPORATION; *pg.* 1468, *pg.* 1058
JIFFYLITE - Air Cellular Cushioned Mailers - SEALED AIR CORPORATION; *pg.* 1468, *pg.* 1058
JIFFYWRAP - Packaging Materials - SEALED AIR CORPORATION; *pg.* 1468, *pg.* 1058
JIG-A-CLEAN - Hand Cleaner - JIG-A-WORLD; *pg.* 980, *pg.* 1951
JIG-A-LOO - Lubricant - JIG-A-WORLD; *pg.* 980, *pg.* 1951
JIG-A-PATCH - Sprayable Spackling Drywall Filler - JIG-A-WORLD; *pg.* 980, *pg.* 1951
JIGE - Towing & Recovery Equipment - MILLER INDUSTRIES, INC.; *pg.* 185, *pg.* 1655
JIGSAW - Fabric - NEMSCHOFF, INC.; *pg.* 936, *pg.* 1890
JIGSAW JONES MYSTERY - Educational Materials - SCHOLASTIC INC.; *pg.* 1683, *pg.* 1288
JILL ROSE - Award - BREAST CANCER RESEARCH FOUNDATION; *pg.* 134, *pg.* 1206
JILLIAN - Clothing - ABERCROMBIE & FITCH CO.; *pg.* 37, *pg.* 1466
JIM BEAM - Bourbon - JIM BEAM BRANDS CO.; *pg.* 1965, *pg.* 601
JIM BEAM & COLA - Pre-Mixed Cocktail - JIM BEAM BRANDS CO.; *pg.* 1965, *pg.* 601
JIM BEAM BLACK - Bourbon - JIM BEAM BRANDS CO.; *pg.* 1965, *pg.* 601
JIM BEAM BLACK & COLA - Pre-Mixed Cocktail - JIM BEAM BRANDS CO.; *pg.* 1965, *pg.* 601
JIM BEAM CHOICE & DRY - Pre-Mixed Cocktail - JIM BEAM BRANDS CO.; *pg.* 1965, *pg.* 601
JIM BEAM KENTUCKY ROADHOUSE - Whiskey - JIM BEAM BRANDS CO.; *pg.* 1965, *pg.* 601
JIM BEAM MARINADE - Backyard Grill - BARBEQUES GALORE, INC.; *pg.* 51, *pg.* 173
JIM BEAM RYE - Bourbon - JIM BEAM BRANDS CO.; *pg.* 1965, *pg.* 601
JIM DANDY - Food Product - NESTLE USA, INC.; *pg.* 883, *pg.* 96
JIM GORDON - Character - DC COMICS, INC.; *pg.* 1633, *pg.* 1221
JIM HJELM COUTURE - Wedding Gowns - JLM COUTURE, INC.; *pg.* 27, *pg.* 1246
JIM HJELM OCCASIONS - Bridesmaids Gowns - JLM COUTURE, INC.; *pg.* 27, *pg.* 1246
JIM HJELM VISIONS - Wedding Gowns - JLM COUTURE, INC.; *pg.* 27, *pg.* 1246
JIMMIE VAUGHAN TEX-MEX STRAT - Electric Guitar - FENDER MUSICAL INSTRUMENTS CORPORATION; *pg.* 547, *pg.* 21
JIMMY - Fire Fighter Puppet - GUND, INC.; *pg.* 954, *pg.* 1056
JIMMY DEAN - Breakfast Sausages - TYSON FOODS, INC.; *pg.* 902, *pg.* 35
JIMMY NEUTRON BOY GENIUS - Toy - MATTEL, INC.; *pg.* 962, *pg.* 81
JIMMY OLSEN - Character - DC COMICS, INC.; *pg.* 1633, *pg.* 1221
JINGLE BELL BINGO - Game - MISSOURI LOTTERY; *pg.* 999, *pg.* 979
JINGLE BELL CASH - Lottery Game - MASSACHUSETTS STATE LOTTERY; *pg.* 998, *pg.* 802
JINGLE BELLS - Pillow and Throw - HERITAGE LACE INC.; *pg.* 694, *pg.* 711
JINGLE BUCKS - Lottery Game - CALIFORNIA LOTTERY; *pg.* 990, *pg.* 196
JINX - Fabric - NEMSCHOFF, INC.; *pg.* 936, *pg.* 1890
JITTERBUG - Cell Phone - TECHNOBRANDS, INC.; *pg.* 1788, *pg.* 1778
JIU JITSU - Footwear - COBIAN CORP.; *pg.* 1806, *pg.* 253
JIVANA - Clothing - HUGGER MUGGER YOGA PRODUCTS LLC; *pg.* 1836, *pg.* 1758
JIVE - Fabric - NEMSCHOFF, INC.; *pg.* 936, *pg.* 1890
JIVE POD - Toy & Game - HASBRO, INC.; *pg.* 954, *pg.* 1603
JJ JUMPER - Trademark (Collegiate Basketball) - NATIONAL COLLEGIATE ATHLETIC ASSOCIATION; *pg.* 567, *pg.* 688
JJ NORTH'S - Restaurant - STAR BUFFET, INC.; *pg.* 1751, *pg.* 24
JK - Lasers - GSI GROUP INC.; *pg.* 1415, *pg.* 784
JLA - Character - DC COMICS, INC.; *pg.* 1633, *pg.* 1221
JLGLIFT - Aerial Work Platforms - JLG INDUSTRIES, INC.; *pg.* 1351, *pg.* 1551
JM APP - Base Sheet - JOHNS MANVILLE CORPORATION; *pg.* 89, *pg.* 320
JM LYNNE - Wallcovering - DESIGNTEX GROUP INC.; *pg.* 692, *pg.* 1223
JM LYNNE - Cloth & Vinyl Wall Coverings - STEELCASE INC.; *pg.* 475, *pg.* 889
JMPER CABLE - Newsletter - SAS INSTITUTE INC.; *pg.* 466, *pg.* 1361
JO - Paper Drill - THE CHALLENGE MACHINERY COMPANY; *pg.* 1322, *pg.* 902
JO MALONE - Fragrance Products - THE ESTEE LAUDER COMPANIES INC.; *pg.* 508, *pg.* 1229
JO-PRO - Molecular Probe Product - THERMO FISHER SCIENTIFIC INC.; *pg.* 1602, *pg.* 61
JOAN OF ARC - Beans - B&G FOODS, INC.; *pg.* 838, *pg.* 1102
JOANNA COTLER BOOKS - Books - HARPERCOLLINS PUBLISHERS INC.; *pg.* 1647, *pg.* 1237
JOANN.COM - Web Site - JO-ANN STORES LLC; *pg.* 696, *pg.* 1455
JOB SMART - Hardware & Tools - TRACTOR SUPPLY COMPANY; *pg.* 708, *pg.* 1627
JOBALOT.COM - Advertising Website - DOMINION ENTERPRISES; *pg.* 1636, *pg.* 1796
JOBREADY - Software - ADOBE SYSTEMS INCORPORATED; *pg.* 342, *pg.* 235
JOBSINTHEMONEY - Recruiting & Career Development Website - DHI GROUP, INC.; *pg.* 1238, *pg.* 1223
JOBSKIN - Medical & Aesthetic Product - DYNATRONICS CORPORATION; *pg.* 1526, *pg.* 1757
JOBSPY - Software System - MENTOR GRAPHICS CORPORATION; *pg.* 432, *pg.* 1510
JOBST - Medical & Aesthetic Product - DYNATRONICS CORPORATION; *pg.* 1526, *pg.* 1757
JOBST SOCKS - Healthcare Product - MEDICOOL, INC.; *pg.* 1562, *pg.* 294
JOCATH MAESTRO - Catheter - ABBOTT LABORATORIES; *pg.* 1484, *pg.* 551
JOCATH MAESTRO X - Catheter - ABBOTT LABORATORIES; *pg.* 1484, *pg.* 551
JOCATH MERCURY - Catheter - ABBOTT LABORATORIES; *pg.* 1484, *pg.* 551
JOCATH O.P.E.R.A. - Catheter - ABBOTT LABORATORIES; *pg.* 1484, *pg.* 551
JOCKAMO I.P.A. - Beer - ABITA BREWING COMPANY; *pg.* 237, *pg.* 741
JOCKEY FOR HER - Underwear & Sleepwear - JOCKEY INTERNATIONAL, INC.; *pg.* 27, *pg.* 1861
JOCKEY-SILKS - Brief - JOCKEY INTERNATIONAL, INC.; *pg.* 27, *pg.* 1861
JOCO - Rotary Joint - KADANT JOHNSON INC.; *pg.* 1073, *pg.* 909
JOE - Furniture - AMERICAN LEATHER LP; *pg.* 912, *pg.* 1673
JOE BOXER - Intimates, Sleepwear, Loungewear, Sportswear, Socks & Yogawear - ICONIX BRAND GROUP, INC.; *pg.* 26, *pg.* 1243
JOE MUGGS - Coffee Bars - BOOKS-A-MILLION, INC.; *pg.* 1623, *pg.* 2
JOE'S - Seafood & Steak Restaurant - LETTUCE ENTERTAIN YOU ENTERPRISES, INC.; *pg.* 1735, *pg.* 580
JOE'S AMERICAN BAR & GRILL - Restaurants - TAVISTOCK RESTAURANT GROUP; *pg.* 1753, *pg.* 803
JOE'S CRAB SHACK - Restaurants - IGNITE RESTAURANT GROUP, INC.; *pg.* 1731, *pg.* 1708
JOE'S JEANS - Denim Brand - SEQUENTIAL BRANDS GROUP, INC.; *pg.* 1395, *pg.* 1290
JOE'S YARD GAMES - Casino Game - INTERNATIONAL GAME TECHNOLOGY; *pg.* 957, *pg.* 1024
JOFA - Ice Hockey Equipment - REEBOK-CCM HOCKEY, INC.; *pg.* 1844, *pg.* 1960
JOG-FAST - Paper Jogger - STANDARD DUPLICATING MACHINES CORPORATION; *pg.* 473, *pg.* 783
JOGLIDE - Catheter - ABBOTT LABORATORIES; *pg.* 1484, *pg.* 551
JOGRAPHY - Catheter - ABBOTT LABORATORIES; *pg.* 1484, *pg.* 551
JOGUIDE - Catheter - ABBOTT LABORATORIES; *pg.* 1484, *pg.* 551
JOHN 5 TELECASTER - Electric Guitar - FENDER MUSICAL INSTRUMENTS CORPORATION; *pg.* 547, *pg.* 21
JOHN BEAN - Under-Car & Other Service Equipment - SNAP-ON INCORPORATED; *pg.* 1062, *pg.* 1862
JOHN BUNN - Medical Product - GF HEALTH PRODUCTS, INC.; *pg.* 1535, *pg.* 508
JOHN DEERE - Farming Equipment - JOHN DEERE CONSUMER & COMMERCIAL EQUIPMENT, INC.; *pg.* 705, *pg.* 1360
JOHN DEERE - Basket - THE LONGABERGER COMPANY; *pg.* 1127, *pg.* 1467
JOHN HANCOCK - Insurance - JOHN HANCOCK FINANCIAL SERVICES; *pg.* 1205, *pg.* 796
JOHN HANDY - Scotch - SAZERAC COMPANY, INC.; *pg.* 1969, *pg.* 745
JOHN HASSALL - Special Cold Forged Products & Fasteners - JOHN HASSALL, INC.; *pg.* 1052, *pg.* 1350
JOHN HENRY - Dress & Casual Clothing - PERRY ELLIS INTERNATIONAL, INC.; *pg.* 45, *pg.* 445
JOHN LABATT CLASSIC - Beer - LABATT BREWING COMPANY LIMITED; *pg.* 253, *pg.* 1939
JOHN MORRELL - Meat Products - JOHN MORRELL & CO.; *pg.* 866, *pg.* 1415
JOHN MORRELL - Food Products - SMITHFIELD FOODS, INC.; *pg.* 896, *pg.* 1806
JOHN MORRELL TENDER N JUICY - Food Product - JOHN MORRELL & CO.; *pg.* 866, *pg.* 1415
JOHN STERLING - Shelving & Hardware Products - KNAPE & VOGT MANUFACTURING COMPANY; *pg.* 1052, *pg.* 913
JOHN VARVATOS - Men's Wear - V.F. CORPORATION; *pg.* 34, *pg.* 1376
JOHN W. NORDSTROM - Apparels - NORDSTROM, INC.; *pg.* 1779, *pg.* 1837
JOHNNIE WALKER - Scotch Whisky - DIAGEO NORTH AMERICA, INC.; *pg.* 1961, *pg.* 361
JOHNNY - Apparel - OAKLEY, INC.; *pg.* 1840, *pg.* 86
JOHNNY APPLESEED HARD APPLE CIDER - Hard Cider - ANHEUSER-BUSCH COMPANIES, LLC; *pg.* 237, *pg.* 991
JOHNNY BRAVO - Animated Series - THE CARTOON NETWORK; *pg.* 273, *pg.* 492
JOHNNY JUMP-UP - Exerciser - EVENFLO COMPANY, INC.; *pg.* 924, *pg.* 1470
JOHNNY WEISSMULLER - Swimming Pools - DELAIR GROUP, LLC; *pg.* 78, *pg.* 1053
JOHNSON - Outboard Engines - BOMBARDIER

RECREATIONAL PRODUCTS, INC.; *pg.* 201, *pg.* 1960
JOHNSON & JOHNSON BABY SHAMPOO - Baby Shampoo - JOHNSON & JOHNSON; *pg.* 1549, *pg.* 1091
JOHNSON DMS - Control Package - KADANT JOHNSON INC.; *pg.* 1073, *pg.* 909
JOHNSON-ROSS - Concrete Batch Plant - TEREX CORPORATION; *pg.* 1381, *pg.* 384
JOHNSON SYSTEM - Dryer Drainage System - KADANT JOHNSON INC.; *pg.* 1073, *pg.* 909
JOHNSON TABLES - Furniture - THE COMMERCIAL FURNITURE GROUP; *pg.* 920, *pg.* 994
JOHNSON'S FOOT SOAP - Foot Soap - COMBE INCORPORATED; *pg.* 1516, *pg.* 1351
JOHNSTON & MURPHY - Footwear - GENESCO INC.; *pg.* 1809, *pg.* 1650
JOHNSTONE - Dispensing System - INGERSOLL-RAND COMPANY; *pg.* 1349, *pg.* 1370
JOIN THE REVOLUTION - Tagline - HARRINGTON HOISTS, INC.; *pg.* 1345, *pg.* 1551
JOINT AIDE - Nutritional Supplement - WHITEWING LABS, INC.; *pg.* 1610, *pg.* 99
JOINT MATRIX - Joint Protection Supplement - CYTOSPORT, INC.; *pg.* 1018, *pg.* 45
JOINT STRIKE FIGHTER - Jet Aircraft & Structural Parts - LOCKHEED MARTIN CORPORATION; *pg.* 229, *pg.* 762
JOINT TACTICAL - Electric Vehicle - AEROVIRONMENT, INC.; *pg.* 223, *pg.* 150
JOIST JACKETS - Building Product - BLUELINX HOLDINGS, INC.; *pg.* 70, *pg.* 491
JOIST REWARDS & DESIGN - Building Products - BOISE CASCADE HOLDINGS, L.L.C.; *pg.* 1453, *pg.* 546
JOJO - Molecular Probe Product - THERMO FISHER SCIENTIFIC INC.; *pg.* 1602, *pg.* 61
JOJOBA AND ALOE - Hair & Skin Product - AUBREY ORGANICS INC.; *pg.* 499, *pg.* 470
JOKER - Character - DC COMICS, INC.; *pg.* 1633, *pg.* 1221
JOKER MAD ENERGY - Energy Drinks - MONSTER BEVERAGE CORPORATION; *pg.* 257, *pg.* 69
JOKER MANIA - Video Game - INTERNATIONAL GAME TECHNOLOGY; *pg.* 957, *pg.* 1024
JOKER'S GOLD - Video Game - INTERNATIONAL GAME TECHNOLOGY; *pg.* 957, *pg.* 1024
JOKERS WILD CASINO - Casino - BOYD GAMING CORPORATION; *pg.* 1082, *pg.* 1022
JOLEN - Cream Bleach for Unwanted Hair - JOLEN CREME BLEACH CORP.; *pg.* 513, *pg.* 348
JOLIVETTE - Pharmaceutical Product - ALLERGAN; *pg.* 1490, *pg.* 1101
JOLLIET HEIGHTS - Furniture - ASHLEY FURNITURE INDUSTRIES, INC.; *pg.* 914, *pg.* 1852
JOLLY GOOD - Soft Drinks - KRIER FOODS, INC.; *pg.* 253, *pg.* 1890
JOLLY JUICE - Beverages - THE COCA-COLA COMPANY; *pg.* 240, *pg.* 493
JOLLY RANCHER - Candy - THE HERSHEY CO.; *pg.* 1855, *pg.* 1538
JOLLY RANCHER - Ice Cream - WELLS ENTERPRISES, INC.; *pg.* 909, *pg.* 709
JOLLY RANCHER - Frozen Beverage - YOCREAM INTERNATIONAL INC.; *pg.* 1039, *pg.* 1508
JOLLY RANCHER JOLLY BEANS - Jelly Beans - THE HERSHEY CO.; *pg.* 1855, *pg.* 1538
JOLLY RANCHER JOLLY JELLIES - Candy - THE HERSHEY CO.; *pg.* 1855, *pg.* 1538
JOLLY ROGER - Video Game - INTERNATIONAL GAME TECHNOLOGY; *pg.* 957, *pg.* 1024
JOLT - Animal Safety Product - NEOGEN CORPORATION; *pg.* 883, *pg.* 896
JOLT - Solid Ink - RICOH PRINTING SYSTEMS AMERICA, INC.; *pg.* 462, *pg.* 279
JOLTSTICK - Software - IMMERSION CORPORATION; *pg.* 413, *pg.* 246
JOMAC - Gloves - WELLS LAMONT CORPORATION; *pg.* 15, *pg.* 638
JON DONAIRE - Food Products - RICH PRODUCTS CORPORATION; *pg.* 892, *pg.* 1150
JONATHAN - Dispensing Equipment - IDEX CORPORATION; *pg.* 1347, *pg.* 623
JONATHAN - Furniture - J. ROBERT SCOTT INC.; *pg.* 930, *pg.* 105
JONATHAN COREY - Shirt - BROWN & BIGELOW, INC.; *pg.* 1624, *pg.* 959
JONES & LAMSON - Machine Tool Product - BOURN & KOCH MACHINE TOOL COMPANY; *pg.* 1319, *pg.* 654
JONES DUTY - Jacket - I. SPIEWAK & SONS, INC.; *pg.* 42, *pg.* 1242
JONES ENERGY - Beverage - JONES SODA CO.; *pg.* 253, *pg.* 1836
JONES EYE INSTITUTE - Eye Disease Treatment & Research - UNIVERSITY OF ARKANSAS FOR MEDICAL SCIENCES; *pg.* 608, *pg.* 34
JONES GABA - Beverage - JONES SODA CO.; *pg.* 253, *pg.* 1836
JONES NATURALS - Beverage - JONES SODA CO.; *pg.* 253, *pg.* 1836
JONES NEW YORK - Apparel - G-III APPAREL GROUP, LTD.; *pg.* 41, *pg.* 1233
JONES NEW YORK CITY - Apparels - THE MEN'S WEARHOUSE, INC.; *pg.* 44, *pg.* 1711
JONES ORGANICS - Beverage - JONES SODA CO.; *pg.* 253, *pg.* 1836
JONES POST - North Carolina Newspaper - FREEDOM COMMUNICATIONS, INC.; *pg.* 1643, *pg.* 110
JONES PURE CANE SODA - Beverage - JONES SODA CO.; *pg.* 253, *pg.* 1836
JONKER DIAMOND - Jewelry - HARRY WINSTON, INC.; *pg.* 6, *pg.* 1238
JONNY CAT - Cat Litter & Liners - THE CLOROX COMPANY; *pg.* 327, *pg.* 169
JONNY CAT - Cat Litter - OIL-DRI CORPORATION OF AMERICA; *pg.* 1480, *pg.* 586
JONREZ - Chemical Product - WESTROCK COMPANY; *pg.* 1472, *pg.* 1805
JOOLZ - Lighting System - PHILIPS SOLID-STATE LIGHTING SOLUTIONS; *pg.* 1303, *pg.* 806
JORDAN - Furniture - ETHAN ALLEN INTERIORS INC.; *pg.* 924, *pg.* 343
JORDAN - Footwear - NIKE, INC.; *pg.* 1812, *pg.* 1492
JORDAN - Valve - RICHARDS INDUSTRIES VALVE GROUP; *pg.* 107, *pg.* 1425
JORDAN VALVE - Regulator & Control Valves - RICHARDS INDUSTRIES VALVE GROUP; *pg.* 107, *pg.* 1425
JORDAN'S - Processed Food - KAYEM FOODS, INC.; *pg.* 867, *pg.* 814
JOS. A. BANK - Men's Clothing - JOS. A. BANK CLOTHIERS, INC.; *pg.* 42, *pg.* 771
JOSE CUERVO PLATINO - Premium Silver Tequila - DIAGEO NORTH AMERICA, INC.; *pg.* 1961, *pg.* 361
JOSEF BRIGL - Wine - WILLIAM GRANT & SONS, INC.; *pg.* 1972, *pg.* 1057
JOSEFINA - Dolls - AMERICAN GIRL LLC; *pg.* 949, *pg.* 1871
JOSEFINA MONTOYA - Dolls - AMERICAN GIRL LLC; *pg.* 949, *pg.* 1871
JOSEFINA'S COLLECTION - Dolls - AMERICAN GIRL LLC; *pg.* 949, *pg.* 1871
JOSEL - Athletic Shoes - K-SWISS; *pg.* 1837, *pg.* 306
JOSEPH ABBOUD - Mattress - SIMMONS COMPANY; *pg.* 943, *pg.* 520
JOSEPH & FEISS - Apparels - THE MEN'S WEARHOUSE, INC.; *pg.* 44, *pg.* 1711
JOSEPHINE - Furniture - J. ROBERT SCOTT INC.; *pg.* 930, *pg.* 105
JOSHUA LIONEL COWEN - Toy Train - LIONEL LLC; *pg.* 961, *pg.* 875
JOSIE - Dinnerware - THE HOMER LAUGHLIN CHINA COMPANY; *pg.* 1125, *pg.* 1850
JOS.LOUIS - Bakery Product - SAPUTO, INC.; *pg.* 893, *pg.* 1956
JOS.LOUIS - Bakery Product - VACHON BAKERY INC.; *pg.* 907, *pg.* 1959
JOSLYN - Surge Protection - DANAHER CORPORATION; *pg.* 1044, *pg.* 397
JOSLYN - Surge Protection - THOMAS & BETTS CORPORATION; *pg.* 680, *pg.* 1646
JOSLYN CLARK - Electric Fire Pump Controller - DANAHER CORPORATION; *pg.* 1044, *pg.* 397
JOSLYN HI-VOLTAGE - Fault Protection Product - DANAHER CORPORATION; *pg.* 1044, *pg.* 397
JOSSEY-BASS - Trade Journals - JOHN WILEY & SONS, INC.; *pg.* 1655, *pg.* 1073
JOSTENT - Catheter - ABBOTT LABORATORIES; *pg.* 1484, *pg.* 551
JOT.TRON - Toy - IMPERIAL TOY CORPORATION; *pg.* 957, *pg.* 166
JOUCOMATIC - Air Controls - ASCO VALVE CANADA; *pg.* 619, *pg.* 1919
JOURDAN RIVER GRILLE - Games - PENN NATIONAL GAMING, INC.; *pg.* 574, *pg.* 1595
JOURNAL OF ACCOUNTANCY - Professional Publication - AMERICAN INSTITUTE OF CERTIFIED PUBLIC ACCOUNTANTS INC.; *pg.* 129, *pg.* 1192
JOURNAL OF COMMERCE - International Business Daily Newspaper - JOC GROUP INC.; *pg.* 1654, *pg.* 1096
JOURNAL OF COMMERCE ONLINE - Interactive Business Tool - JOC GROUP INC.; *pg.* 1654, *pg.* 1096
JOURNAL OF FAILURE ANALYSIS & PREVENTION - Trade Publication - ASM INTERNATIONAL; *pg.* 132, *pg.* 1461
THE JOURNAL OF FAMILY PRACTICE - Healthcare Publication - LEBHAR-FRIEDMAN INC.; *pg.* 1658, *pg.* 1250
JOURNAL OF MANUFACTURING PROCESSES - Journal & Research Publication - SOCIETY OF MANUFACTURING ENGINEERS; *pg.* 157, *pg.* 878
JOURNAL OF MANUFACTURING SYSTEMS - Journal & Research Publication - SOCIETY OF MANUFACTURING ENGINEERS; *pg.* 157, *pg.* 878
JOURNAL OF MATERIALS ENGINEERING & PERFORMANCE - Trade Publication - ASM INTERNATIONAL; *pg.* 132, *pg.* 1461
JOURNAL OF PHASE EQUILIBRIA & DIFFUSION - Trade Publication - ASM INTERNATIONAL; *pg.* 132, *pg.* 1461
JOURNAL OF THERMAL SPRAY TECHNOLOGY - Trade Publication - ASM INTERNATIONAL; *pg.* 132, *pg.* 1461
JOURNEY - Strollers - EVENFLO COMPANY, INC.; *pg.* 924, *pg.* 1470
JOURNEY - Crossover Vehicle - FCA US LLC; *pg.* 170, *pg.* 868
JOURNEY - Fiberglass Boat Product - GRADY-WHITE BOATS, INC.; *pg.* 1707, *pg.* 1377
JOURNEY - Kitchen Product - KOHLER CO.; *pg.* 91, *pg.* 1862
JOURNEY - Preschool Program - LA PETITE ACADEMY, INC.; *pg.* 603, *pg.* 903
JOURNEY - Motor Homes - WINNEBAGO INDUSTRIES, INC.; *pg.* 1712, *pg.* 707
JOURNEY OF HOPE - Computer Equipment - VIEWSONIC CORPORATION; *pg.* 489, *pg.* 303
JOURNEYS - Footwear - GENESCO INC.; *pg.* 1809, *pg.* 1650
JOURNEYS KIDZ - Footwear - GENESCO INC.; *pg.* 1809, *pg.* 1650
JOVAN MUSK - Men's & Women's Fragrance - COTY, INC.; *pg.* 506, *pg.* 1219
JOY - Beverages - THE COCA-COLA COMPANY; *pg.* 240, *pg.* 493
JOY - Mining Machinery - JOY GLOBAL, INC.; *pg.* 1351, *pg.* 1876
JOY - House Care Product - THE PROCTER & GAMBLE COMPANY; *pg.* 1129, *pg.* 1418
THE JOY OF HEALTHY LIFE - Slogan - D'ARRIGO BROS. COMPANY; *pg.* 852, *pg.* 197
JOYA - Beverages - THE COCA-COLA COMPANY; *pg.* 240, *pg.* 493
JOYCAM & 500 FILM - Instant Camera & Film for Pocket-Sized Photography - POLAROID CORPORATION; *pg.* 1426, *pg.* 815
JOYCE - Reading Glass - A. T. CROSS COMPANY; *pg.* 339, *pg.* 1602
JOYCE - Footwear - PHOENIX FOOTWEAR GROUP, INC.; *pg.* 1815, *pg.* 60
JOYFUL ANGEL - Mantel Scarf - HERITAGE LACE INC.; *pg.* 694, *pg.* 711
JOYWALKERS - Shoes - ACUSHNET COMPANY; *pg.* 1824, *pg.* 818
JP 8000 - Oxy-Fuel System - PRAXAIR-TAFA; *pg.* 1370, *pg.* 1033
JPA - Junior Putters of America - THE PROFESSIONAL PUTTERS ASSOCIATION; *pg.* 154, *pg.* 1735
JPC BOOK DIVISION - Latest Hardcover & Paperback Editions - JOHNSON PUBLISHING COMPANY, INC.; *pg.* 1655, *pg.* 579
JPI - Toys & Leisure Product - JAKKS PACIFIC, INC.; *pg.* 960, *pg.* 142
JPM - Publication - INSTITUTE OF REAL ESTATE MANAGEMENT; *pg.* 144, *pg.* 578
JPROBE - Software - DELL SOFTWARE; *pg.* 385, *pg.* 40
JR. - Pump Product - IDEX CORPORATION; *pg.* 1347, *pg.* 623
JR .EXEC - Footwear - COBIAN CORP.; *pg.* 1806, *pg.* 253
JR. JUMBO BUCKS - Lottery Game - D.C. LOTTERY & CHARITABLE GAMES CONTROL BOARD; *pg.* 991, *pg.* 398
JR. KRONOMATIC - Electric Gyros Broiler - KRONOS PRODUCTS, INC.; *pg.* 872, *pg.* 614
JR RESERVE BLEND - Coffee - PEET'S COFFEE & TEA,

INC.; *pg.* 1029, *pg.* 85
JR. TYETTE - Footwear - CAPEZIO BALLET MAKERS INC.; *pg.* 1805, *pg.* 1125
JRUN - Software - ADOBE SYSTEMS INCORPORATED; *pg.* 342, *pg.* 235
JSA - Character - DC COMICS, INC.; *pg.* 1633, *pg.* 1221
JSF - Systems Integration & Aeronautics - LOCKHEED MARTIN CORPORATION; *pg.* 229, *pg.* 762
JSOW - Defense System - RAYTHEON COMPANY; *pg.* 233, *pg.* 854
JSX - Musical Instrument - PEAVEY ELECTRONICS CORPORATION; *pg.* 662, *pg.* 970
JT15D - Aircraft Engine - PRATT & WHITNEY CANADA CORP.; *pg.* 1370, *pg.* 1952
JT21 - Staple Gun - ARROW FASTENER COMPANY, INC.; *pg.* 1042, *pg.* 1118
JTECH SOLUTIONS - Software - MICROS SYSTEMS, INC.; *pg.* 435, *pg.* 768
JUAN PABLO - Eyewear - OAKLEY, INC.; *pg.* 1840, *pg.* 86
JUBILANCE - Easily Operable Roman Shades - HUNTER DOUGLAS, INC.; *pg.* 928, *pg.* 1320
JUBILEE - Textiles - BERNHARDT DESIGN; *pg.* 918, *pg.* 1381
JUBILEE - Wall Panel - BLUELINX HOLDINGS, INC.; *pg.* 70, *pg.* 491
JUBILEE - Cameras - EASTMAN KODAK COMPANY; *pg.* 1408, *pg.* 1333
JUBILEE - Plastic Cutlery - MARYLAND PLASTICS, INC.; *pg.* 1885, *pg.* 769
JUBILEE - Furniture Polish - S.C. JOHNSON & SON, INC.; *pg.* 334, *pg.* 1889
JUDGE - Watch - OAKLEY, INC.; *pg.* 1840, *pg.* 86
THE JUDGE - Color Evaluation System - X-RITE, INCORPORATED; *pg.* 1437, *pg.* 891
JUDITH RIPKA - Jewelry - JUDITH RIPKA COMPANIES INC.; *pg.* 7, *pg.* 1247
JUDY BUSWELL - Deluxe Cards - LEANIN' TREE, INC.; *pg.* 1658, *pg.* 311
JUDY INSTRUCTO - Educational Resources - SCHOOL SPECIALTY, INC.; *pg.* 467, *pg.* 1860
JUGENDSTIL - Fabric - NEMSCHOFF, INC.; *pg.* 936, *pg.* 1890
JUGGLEBEANBALLS - Soft Plastic Ball - SCHOOL-TECH, INC.; *pg.* 1844, *pg.* 866
JUGGLING BALLS - Durable 4-Panel Vinyl Shell Filled with Plastic Beans - DUNCAN TOYS COMPANY; *pg.* 951, *pg.* 1465
JUGGLING FOR THE COMPLETE KLUTZ - Educational Materials - SCHOLASTIC INC.; *pg.* 1683, *pg.* 1288
JUGGLING SCARVES - Juggling Kit Includes CD-Rom & 3 Scarves - DUNCAN TOYS COMPANY; *pg.* 951, *pg.* 1465
JUICE - Cutting Tool - LEATHERMAN TOOL GROUP, INC.; *pg.* 1053, *pg.* 1504
JUICE BAR - Perfume - PARFUMS DE COEUR LTD.; *pg.* 519, *pg.* 376
JUICE JAM - Promotion for Juice Drink Flavors - OCEAN SPRAY CRANBERRIES, INC.; *pg.* 887, *pg.* 827
JUICE SQUEEZE - Natural Soda & Juice Product - CRYSTAL GEYSER WATER COMPANY; *pg.* 248, *pg.* 57
JUICEBOOST - Nutritional Supplements - GENELINK, INC.; *pg.* 1533, *pg.* 438
JUICEBOX - Toy - MATTEL, INC.; *pg.* 962, *pg.* 81
JUICECAN - Precipitator Power Maximizer - GE ENERGY; *pg.* 1338, *pg.* 506
JUICEOLOGY - Blended Juice Beverages - DAKLEN INC.; *pg.* 851, *pg.* 129
JUICIES - Fruit Drinks - JAMBA, INC.; *pg.* 1024, *pg.* 84
JUICY DROP POP - Candy & Gum - THE TOPPS COMPANY, INC.; *pg.* 588, *pg.* 1302
JUICY FRUIT - Gum - WM. WRIGLEY JR. COMPANY; *pg.* 1863, *pg.* 596
JUICY JUICE - Fruit Juices - HARVEST HILL BEVERAGE COMPANY; *pg.* 251, *pg.* 375
JUICY WISHES - Fruit Arrangements - EDIBLE ARRANGEMENTS INTERNATIONAL, INC.; *pg.* 1768, *pg.* 382
JUKE - Cell Phone - SAMSUNG TELECOMMUNICATIONS AMERICA, LLC; *pg.* 670, *pg.* 1736
JULEP CUP BOUQUET - Bouquet - 1-800-FLOWERS.COM, INC.; *pg.* 1758, *pg.* 1151
JULES - Furniture - LA-Z-BOY INCORPORATED; *pg.* 932, *pg.* 901
JULES - Computer Support Worktools - STEELCASE INC.; *pg.* 475, *pg.* 889
JULIA - Furniture - AMISCO INDUSTRIES LTD.; *pg.* 913, *pg.* 1958
JULIA MARIE - Cookie - A.V. OLSSON TRADING CO. INC.; *pg.* 838, *pg.* 372
JULIE LEAH - Diamonds - ICE.COM, INC.; *pg.* 1258, *pg.* 1955
JULIE UELAND - Home & Garden Products - ENESCO, LLC; *pg.* 1124, *pg.* 620
JULIET - Furniture - AMISCO INDUSTRIES LTD.; *pg.* 913, *pg.* 1958
JULIET - Footwear - CAPEZIO BALLET MAKERS INC.; *pg.* 1805, *pg.* 1125
JULIET - Eyewear - OAKLEY, INC.; *pg.* 1840, *pg.* 86
JULIET - Flatware - ONEIDA LTD; *pg.* 1129, *pg.* 1318
JULIETTE - Lighting - ETHAN ALLEN INTERIORS INC.; *pg.* 924, *pg.* 343
JULIUS - Footwear - STEVEN MADDEN, LTD.; *pg.* 1819, *pg.* 1176
JULIUS ES - Ceiling Fan - WESTINGHOUSE LIGHTING CORPORATION; *pg.* 687, *pg.* 1571
JUMBO - Soft Drink - DOUBLE-COLA CO.-USA; *pg.* 249, *pg.* 1629
JUMBO - Hydraulic Dock Leveler - RITE-HITE HOLDING CORPORATION; *pg.* 1372, *pg.* 1880
JUMBO BUCKS - Lottery Game - MASSACHUSETTS STATE LOTTERY; *pg.* 998, *pg.* 802
JUMBO GO GO GO - Toy - THE OHIO ART COMPANY, INC.; *pg.* 965, *pg.* 1406
JUMBO GRILLER - Hot Dogs - HATFIELD QUALITY MEATS, INC.; *pg.* 861, *pg.* 1537
JUMBO HONEY BUN - Snack Cakes - HOSTESS BRANDS LLC; *pg.* 1856, *pg.* 984
JUMBO JACK - Hamburger - JACK IN THE BOX INC.; *pg.* 1732, *pg.* 204
JUMBO-KOTER - Brush - THE WOOSTER BRUSH COMPANY; *pg.* 1450, *pg.* 1482
JUMBO MULTI-GRAIN KRISPIES - Multi-Grain Krispies - KELLOGG COMPANY; *pg.* 831, *pg.* 870
JUMBO SHAMSORB - Soaker Towels - HABAND COMPANY, INC.; *pg.* 1772, *pg.* 1099
JUMBO TEX - Roofing Ventilation Product - BENJAMIN OBDYKE, INC.; *pg.* 70, *pg.* 1540
JUMBO TEX - Barrier - FORTIFIBER CORPORATION; *pg.* 83, *pg.* 1021
JUMBO VACS - Large Capacity Industrial Vacs - TORNADO INDUSTRIES, INC.; *pg.* 1383, *pg.* 591
JUMBOSEP - Centrifugal Device - PALL CORPORATION; *pg.* 232, *pg.* 1323
JUMP - Wireless Communication Product - CRICKET WIRELESS LLC; *pg.* 381, *pg.* 483
JUMP - Desktop Tools - HAWORTH, INC.; *pg.* 402, *pg.* 891
JUMP - Remote Button - TIVO INC.; *pg.* 313, *pg.* 251
JUMP & GO - Baby Exerciser - EVENFLO COMPANY, INC.; *pg.* 924, *pg.* 1470
JUMP BREAK - Gaming Product - GLD PRODUCTS, INC.; *pg.* 1835, *pg.* 1882
JUMP JIVE & WIN - Game - WMS INDUSTRIES INC.; *pg.* 593, *pg.* 666
JUMP-N-CARRY - Battery Charging Product - CLORE AUTOMOTIVE LLC; *pg.* 202, *pg.* 716
JUMP-SHOT - Homeowner Product - PBI/GORDON CORPORATION; *pg.* 1176, *pg.* 985
JUMP-STARTPLUS - Microbial Gel - MANNA PRO CORPORATION; *pg.* 1478, *pg.* 975
JUMP STUDIO - Photography - CANDID COLOR SYSTEMS, INC.; *pg.* 1404, *pg.* 1485
JUMPDRIVE - Flash Drive - LEXAR MEDIA, INC.; *pg.* 1262, *pg.* 146
JUMPDRIVE LIGHTNING - Digital Film - LEXAR MEDIA, INC.; *pg.* 1262, *pg.* 146
JUMPDRIVE SECURE 2.0 - Security Oriented, Impact-resistant, Password-protected USB Flash Drive - LEXAR MEDIA, INC.; *pg.* 1262, *pg.* 146
JUMPDRIVE TRIO - Portable USB Storage Device - LEXAR MEDIA, INC.; *pg.* 1262, *pg.* 146
JUMPGEAR - MP3 Player - LEXAR MEDIA, INC.; *pg.* 1262, *pg.* 146
JUMPIN JUICE - Smoothies - THE SECOND CUP LTD.; *pg.* 1749, *pg.* 1928
JUMPIN' JUNGLE - Video Game - INTERNATIONAL GAME TECHNOLOGY; *pg.* 957, *pg.* 1024
JUMPIN' MONKEYS - Game - PRESSMAN TOY CORPORATION; *pg.* 965, *pg.* 1734
JUMPMAN TEAM PRO - Footwear - NIKE, INC.; *pg.* 1812, *pg.* 1492
JUMPSHOT READER - Reader Specifically Designed to Work with Lexar Media Compactflash Cards - LEXAR MEDIA, INC.; *pg.* 1262, *pg.* 146
JUNCTURE - Sitting Bench, Lounge Chairs & Modern Occasional Tables - BERNHARDT DESIGN; *pg.* 918, *pg.* 1381
JUNEAU - Footwear - STEVEN MADDEN, LTD.; *pg.* 1819, *pg.* 1176
JUNEAU COUNTY REMINDER - Newspaper - MADISON NEWSPAPERS, INC.; *pg.* 1661, *pg.* 1866
JUNEAU COUNTY STAR TIMES - Newspaper - MADISON NEWSPAPERS, INC.; *pg.* 1661, *pg.* 1866
JUNGAMALS - Nutritional Supplement - NU SKIN ENTERPRISES, INC.; *pg.* 518, *pg.* 1755
JUNGLE - Pet Product - PETSMART, INC.; *pg.* 1481, *pg.* 18
JUNGLE ADVENTURES - Ice Cream - WELLS ENTERPRISES, INC.; *pg.* 909, *pg.* 709
JUNGLE BEASTIES - Toys - 1-800-FLOWERS.COM, INC.; *pg.* 1758, *pg.* 1151
JUNGLE CATS - Game - WMS INDUSTRIES INC.; *pg.* 593, *pg.* 666
JUNGLE GREENS - Food Supplement - ORANGE PEEL ENTERPRISES, INC.; *pg.* 1028, *pg.* 477
JUNGLE GREENS+ - Vitamins - ORANGE PEEL ENTERPRISES, INC.; *pg.* 1028, *pg.* 477
JUNGLE JUICE - Game - MULTIMEDIA GAMES INC.; *pg.* 442, *pg.* 1664
JUNGLE MAGIC - Video Game - INTERNATIONAL GAME TECHNOLOGY; *pg.* 957, *pg.* 1024
JUNGLE MAJESTY - Game - WMS INDUSTRIES INC.; *pg.* 593, *pg.* 666
JUNGLE PRINCESS - Video Game - INTERNATIONAL GAME TECHNOLOGY; *pg.* 957, *pg.* 1024
JUNGLE WILD - Game - WMS INDUSTRIES INC.; *pg.* 593, *pg.* 666
JUNIOR - Puzzles - HASBRO, INC.; *pg.* 954, *pg.* 1603
JUNIOR - Clamping Systems - IDEX CORPORATION; *pg.* 1347, *pg.* 623
JUNIOR - Furniture - NEMSCHOFF, INC.; *pg.* 936, *pg.* 1890
JUNIOR - Hoagie Sandwich - WAWA, INC.; *pg.* 1037, *pg.* 1552
JUNIOR JUICE - Juice - MONSTER BEVERAGE CORPORATION; *pg.* 257, *pg.* 69
JUNIOR KMINTS - Candy - TOOTSIE ROLL INDUSTRIES, INC.; *pg.* 1863, *pg.* 591
JUNIOR MAX - Insurance Service - MODERN WOODMEN OF AMERICA; *pg.* 1209, *pg.* 654
JUNIOR MINTS - Chocolate Covered Mints - TOOTSIE ROLL INDUSTRIES, INC.; *pg.* 1863, *pg.* 591
JUNIOR SCHOLASTIC - Magazine - SCHOLASTIC INC.; *pg.* 1683, *pg.* 1288
JUNIORS - Bakery Product - TASTY BAKING COMPANY; *pg.* 1862, *pg.* 1571
JUNIOSCOPE - Software - JUNIPER NETWORKS, INC.; *pg.* 1260, *pg.* 286
JUNIPER - Fabric - NEMSCHOFF, INC.; *pg.* 936, *pg.* 1890
JUNIPER NETWORKS E-SERIES - Router Portfolio - ALCATEL-LUCENT; *pg.* 615, *pg.* 1094
JUNIPER NETWORKS M-SERIES - Router Portfolio - ALCATEL-LUCENT; *pg.* 615, *pg.* 1094
JUNIPER NETWORKS T-SERIES - Router Portfolio - ALCATEL-LUCENT; *pg.* 615, *pg.* 1094
JUNIPER TRAIL - Bike - MARIN BIKES; *pg.* 1708, *pg.* 168
JUNKET - Dessert Products - REDCO FOODS, INC.; *pg.* 891, *pg.* 1174
JUNO - Knife - BUCK KNIVES, INC.; *pg.* 1828, *pg.* 550
JUNO - Bath Accessory - CROSCILL, INC.; *pg.* 1122, *pg.* 1220
JUNO - Internet Service - UNITED ONLINE, INC.; *pg.* 1286, *pg.* 308
JUNOS - Software - JUNIPER NETWORKS, INC.; *pg.* 1260, *pg.* 286
JUNOSE - IP Infrastructure Software - JUNIPER NETWORKS, INC.; *pg.* 1260, *pg.* 286
JUNSEISET - Ceramic & Plastic Product - COORSTEK, INC.; *pg.* 77, *pg.* 330
JUNXION BOX - Wireless Modem - SIERRA WIRELESS INCORPORATED; *pg.* 673, *pg.* 1909
JUPITER - Furniture - FLEXSTEEL INDUSTRIES, INC.; *pg.* 925, *pg.* 707
JUPITER - Control System - GRASS VALLEY, INC.; *pg.* 641, *pg.* 164
JUPITER - Software - SYNOPSYS, INC.; *pg.* 480, *pg.* 162
JUPITER - Ceiling Fan - WESTINGHOUSE LIGHTING CORPORATION; *pg.* 687, *pg.* 1571
JUPITER ACCUSWITCH - Controller - GRASS VALLEY, INC.;

pg. 641, *pg.* 164
THE JUPITER COURIER - Newspaper - THE E.W. SCRIPPS COMPANY; *pg.* 1639, *pg.* 1412
JUPITER-DP - Software - SYNOPSYS, INC.; *pg.* 480, *pg.* 162
JUPITER S - Freshwater Spinning Reels - DAIWA CORPORATION; *pg.* 1832, *pg.* 75
JUPITER Z - Saltwater Spinning Reels - DAIWA CORPORATION; *pg.* 1832, *pg.* 75
JUPITERXT - Software - SYNOPSYS, INC.; *pg.* 480, *pg.* 162
JUPITERXT-ASIC - Software - SYNOPSYS, INC.; *pg.* 480, *pg.* 162
JURASSIPET - Pet Product - PETSMART, INC.; *pg.* 1481, *pg.* 18
JURID - Turbocharger - HONEYWELL INTERNATIONAL INC.; *pg.* 407, *pg.* 1088
JURY - Watch - OAKLEY, INC.; *pg.* 1840, *pg.* 86
JURYMAX - Payment Generation - MAXIMUS, INC.; *pg.* 780, *pg.* 1799
JURYVIEW - Software Product - MAXIMUS, INC.; *pg.* 780, *pg.* 1799
JUS-ROL - Food Product - GENERAL MILLS, INC.; *pg.* 828, *pg.* 933
JUST - Laundry & Cleaning Products - KAO BRANDS CO. INC.; *pg.* 513, *pg.* 1415
JUST 2 POINTS - Nutritional Snack Bar - WEIGHT WATCHERS INTERNATIONAL, INC.; *pg.* 1609, *pg.* 1313
JUST 3 POINTS - Breakfast Bar - WEIGHT WATCHERS INTERNATIONAL, INC.; *pg.* 1609, *pg.* 1313
JUST 5 - Hair Dye for Women - COMBE INCORPORATED; *pg.* 1516, *pg.* 1351
JUST A BUCK - Lottery Game - OHIO LOTTERY COMMISSION; *pg.* 1002, *pg.* 1433
JUST A BUCK, CHANGE THEIR LUCK - Pet Charity Tagline - PETSMART, INC.; *pg.* 1481, *pg.* 18
JUST AUTOMOTIVE - Advertising Publication - DOMINION ENTERPRISES; *pg.* 1636, *pg.* 1796
JUST BEGAUZE - Slacks & Shorts - HABAND COMPANY, INC.; *pg.* 1772, *pg.* 1099
JUST CALL OUR NAME - Retail Store Services - 1-800-FLOWERS.COM, INC.; *pg.* 1758, *pg.* 1151
JUST COTTON - Underwear - BLUE CANOE BODYWEAR; *pg.* 20, *pg.* 94
JUST DUCKY - Gift Set - 1-800-FLOWERS.COM, INC.; *pg.* 1758, *pg.* 1151
JUST FOR KIDS - Preventive Treatment Gel - 3M COMPANY; *pg.* 1142, *pg.* 956
JUST FOR KIDS - Fitness Equipment - THE WALT DISNEY COMPANY; *pg.* 317, *pg.* 52
JUST FOR ME - Children's Hair Care Products - UNILEVER UNITED STATES, INC.; *pg.* 904, *pg.* 1061
JUST FOR MEN - Health & Beauty Product - COMBE INCORPORATED; *pg.* 1516, *pg.* 1351
JUST FOR MEN/MUSTACHE, BEARD & SIDEBURNS - Health & Beauty Product - COMBE INCORPORATED; *pg.* 1516, *pg.* 1351
JUST FOR MICE - Stereotaxic Instrument - STOELTING CO.; *pg.* 1430, *pg.* 671
JUST FOR YOU - Hosiery & Related Apparel - MAYER/BERKSHIRE CORPORATION; *pg.* 29, *pg.* 1129
JUST FRESH FRUIT - Fresh Fruit Salads - CHIQUITA BRANDS INTERNATIONAL, INC.; *pg.* 847, *pg.* 1365
JUST JARED - Celebrity News Site - SPINMEDIA; *pg.* 1282, *pg.* 104
JUST JARED JR - Celebrity News Site - SPINMEDIA; *pg.* 1282, *pg.* 104
JUST JUICE - Beverages - THE COCA-COLA COMPANY; *pg.* 240, *pg.* 493
JUST LET GO - Tag Line - TRADEWINDS ISLANDS RESORTS ON SAINT PETE BEACH; *pg.* 1116, *pg.* 461
JUST LETTUCE - Lettuce - DOLE FRESH VEGETABLES; *pg.* 854, *pg.* 198
JUST LIKE WOOD - Tube - 3M COMPANY; *pg.* 1142, *pg.* 956
JUST LIKE YOU - Doll Collections - AMERICAN GIRL LLC; *pg.* 949, *pg.* 1871
JUST LIKE YOU LIKE IT - Slogan - WHATABURGER, INC.; *pg.* 1755, *pg.* 1744
JUST MY SIZE - Apparel - HANESBRANDS INC.; *pg.* 26, *pg.* 1394
JUST ONE YEAR - Baby & Toddler Apparel & Accessories - CARTER'S, INC.; *pg.* 21, *pg.* 491
JUST PEACHY - Premium Ice Cream - WELLS ENTERPRISES, INC.; *pg.* 909, *pg.* 709
JUST PERFECT - Turkey Products - BUTTERBALL, LLC; *pg.* 843, *pg.* 1385
JUST PIKT - Processed Fruit Products - NAKED JUICE COMPANY, INC.; *pg.* 882, *pg.* 150
JUST RIGHT - Slacks & Shorts - HABAND COMPANY, INC.; *pg.* 1772, *pg.* 1099
JUST RIGHT - Thermostat - HUNTER FAN COMPANY; *pg.* 57, *pg.* 1631
JUST ROCKS - Furniture - ASHLEY FURNITURE INDUSTRIES, INC.; *pg.* 914, *pg.* 1852
JUST SAY YO - Frozen Yogurt - YOCREAM INTERNATIONAL INC.; *pg.* 1039, *pg.* 1508
JUST SCHOOLIN' AROUND - Educational Materials - SCHOLASTIC INC.; *pg.* 1683, *pg.* 1288
JUST SO - Hair Products - J. STRICKLAND & COMPANY; *pg.* 512, *pg.* 970
JUST WHAT THE DOCTOR ORDERED - Flower Arrangement - 1-800-FLOWERS.COM, INC.; *pg.* 1758, *pg.* 1151
JUST WHISTLE - Twin Blade Self-Adjusting Razor - THE GILLETTE COMPANY; *pg.* 509, *pg.* 795
JUST WIPE'N SERVE - Dry Disposable Wipe - CONNOISSEURS PRODUCTS CORPORATION; *pg.* 329, *pg.* 861
JUST WRITE - Balloon - CONTINENTAL AMERICAN CORP.; *pg.* 1880, *pg.* 723
JUST YOUR STYLE - Advertising Campaign - LA-Z-BOY INCORPORATED; *pg.* 932, *pg.* 901
JUSTABURGER - Hamburger - WHATABURGER, INC.; *pg.* 1755, *pg.* 1744
JUSTFAB - Shoes, Clothes & Accessories - JUSTFAB, INC.; *pg.* 27, *pg.* 80
JUSTFIBER - Powdered Cellulose & Cottonseed Fiber - INTERNATIONAL FIBER CORP.; *pg.* 865, *pg.* 1317
JUSTICE - Girls' Apparel Stores - TWEEN BRANDS INC.; *pg.* 34, *pg.* 1467
JUSTICE LEAGUE - Game & TV Show - THE CARTOON NETWORK; *pg.* 273, *pg.* 492
JUSTICE LEAGUE OF AMERICA - Comic Book - DC COMICS, INC.; *pg.* 1633, *pg.* 1221
JUSTICE SOCIETY OF AMERICA - Character - DC COMICS, INC.; *pg.* 1633, *pg.* 1221
JUSTICEMAX - Software Product - MAXIMUS, INC.; *pg.* 780, *pg.* 1799
JUSTIFYY - Footwear - STEVEN MADDEN, LTD.; *pg.* 1819, *pg.* 1176
JUSTIN BOOTS - Cowboy Boots - JUSTIN BRANDS, INC.; *pg.* 1810, *pg.* 1695
JUSTIN ORIGINAL WORKBOOT - Workboots - JUSTIN BRANDS, INC.; *pg.* 1810, *pg.* 1695
JUSTINNA - Footwear - STEVEN MADDEN, LTD.; *pg.* 1819, *pg.* 1176
JUSTIN'S - Restaurants - BAD BOY WORLDWIDE ENTERTAINMENT GROUP; *pg.* 270, *pg.* 1199
JUSTLISTED.COM - Website - MARKET LEADER, INC.; *pg.* 1102, *pg.* 1822
JUSTTECHJOBS.COM - Online Network - MEDIABISTRO, INC.; *pg.* 1266, *pg.* 1258
JUSTTIRES - Tire And Rubber Product - THE GOODYEAR TIRE & RUBBER COMPANY; *pg.* 1883, *pg.* 1401
JUSTUS - Log Homes - LINDAL CEDAR HOMES, INC.; *pg.* 94, *pg.* 1837
JUTE - Fabric - KOPPERS HOLDINGS INC.; *pg.* 1170, *pg.* 1577
JUVEDERM - Dermal Filler - ALLERGAN, INC.; *pg.* 1491, *pg.* 106
JUVEN - Catheter - ABBOTT LABORATORIES; *pg.* 1484, *pg.* 551
J.VICTOR - Apparels - THE MEN'S WEARHOUSE, INC.; *pg.* 44, *pg.* 1711
JVP DOMES - Research Instruments - STOELTING CO.; *pg.* 1430, *pg.* 671
J.W. FOSTER - Track & Field Equipment - REEBOK INTERNATIONAL LTD.; *pg.* 1817, *pg.* 811
JW MARRIOTT - Hotels & Resorts - MARRIOTT INTERNATIONAL, INC.; *pg.* 1102, *pg.* 764
JW SERIES - Submersible Pump - THE GORMAN-RUPP COMPANY; *pg.* 1341, *pg.* 1458
JYMNI - Pediatric Wheelchair - INVACARE CORPORATION; *pg.* 1546, *pg.* 1451

K

K-12 FAMILY EDUCATION LOAN - Loan for K-12 Students - SLM CORPORATION; *pg.* 804, *pg.* 388
K-12 GEAR - Apparel - ELDER MANUFACTURING COMPANY, INC.; *pg.* 40, *pg.* 996
K-4 - Herbicide - E.I. DU PONT DE NEMOURS & COMPANY; *pg.* 1159, *pg.* 390
K-9 CAPERS - Game - GAMEWRIGHT; *pg.* 953, *pg.* 836
K&B - Paint And Stain Product - BENJAMIN MOORE & CO.; *pg.* 1440, *pg.* 1085
K-BEAM - Flashlight - ENERGIZER HOLDINGS, INC.; *pg.* 637, *pg.* 996
K-BLUE - Animal Safety Product - NEOGEN CORPORATION; *pg.* 883, *pg.* 896
K-BLUE SUBSTRATE - Easy Use Test Kits - NEOGEN CORPORATION; *pg.* 883, *pg.* 896
K-CHROME - Photographic Film - EASTMAN KODAK COMPANY; *pg.* 1408, *pg.* 1333
K-COLOR - Photographic Film - EASTMAN KODAK COMPANY; *pg.* 1408, *pg.* 1333
K-CORR - Chemical Product - KING INDUSTRIES, INC.; *pg.* 1443, *pg.* 363
K-CUP - Coffee Portion Packs - KEURIG GREEN MOUNTAIN, INC.; *pg.* 868, *pg.* 1768
K-CURE - Chemical Product - KING INDUSTRIES, INC.; *pg.* 1443, *pg.* 363
K-D TOOLS - Mechanic Hand Tool - DANAHER CORPORATION; *pg.* 1044, *pg.* 397
K-DUR - Medicine - MERCK & CO., INC.; *pg.* 1566, *pg.* 1077
K-FAST - Nuts - ALCOA INC.; *pg.* 65, *pg.* 1188
K-FIX - Medical Device - INTEGRA LIFESCIENCES HOLDINGS CORPORATION; *pg.* 1545, *pg.* 1109
K-FLEX - Chemical Product - KING INDUSTRIES, INC.; *pg.* 1443, *pg.* 363
K-FLEX - Cable, Galvanized & Stainless Steel & Resin for Terminations - LOOS & COMPANY, INC.; *pg.* 1356, *pg.* 368
K FORCE - Footwear - K-SWISS; *pg.* 1837, *pg.* 306
K-GOLD - Animal Safety Product - NEOGEN CORPORATION; *pg.* 883, *pg.* 896
K-GUARD - Fire Extinguishers - ANSUL, INCORPORATED; *pg.* 1147, *pg.* 1869
K. HOVNANIAN - Homebuilder of Residential Communities - HOVNANIAN ENTERPRISES, INC.; *pg.* 1096, *pg.* 1114
IF YOU'RE NOT 55 YEARS OLD...YOU'LL WISH YOU WERE - Active Adult Communities - HOVNANIAN ENTERPRISES, INC.; *pg.* 1096, *pg.* 1114
K-II - Photographic Film - EASTMAN KODAK COMPANY; *pg.* 1408, *pg.* 1333
K-KAT - Chemical Product - KING INDUSTRIES, INC.; *pg.* 1443, *pg.* 363
K-KLEAN - Equipment Cleaner - KALO, INC.; *pg.* 1796, *pg.* 719
K-KUT - Hobs for Cutting Gears & Splines - GLEASON CORPORATION; *pg.* 1340, *pg.* 1335
K-LITE - Joint Compound - USG CORPORATION; *pg.* 118, *pg.* 594
K-LOR - Potassium Supplement - ABBOTT LABORATORIES; *pg.* 1484, *pg.* 551
K LOVE - Christian Music Station - EDUCATIONAL MEDIA FOUNDATION; *pg.* 284, *pg.* 194
K LUBE - White Oils - MALLET & COMPANY, INC.; *pg.* 875, *pg.* 1521
K-MAX - External Lift Helicopter - KAMAN CORPORATION; *pg.* 229, *pg.* 338
K ONA S - Footwear - K-SWISS; *pg.* 1837, *pg.* 306
K-PAK - Nutritional Product - COUNTRY PURE FOODS, INC.; *pg.* 247, *pg.* 1400
K-PHOS M.F. - Pharmaceuticals - BEACH PRODUCTS, INC.; *pg.* 1501, *pg.* 471
K-PHOS NEUTRAL - Pharmaceuticals - BEACH PRODUCTS, INC.; *pg.* 1501, *pg.* 471
K-PHOS NO. 2 - Pharmaceuticals - BEACH PRODUCTS, INC.; *pg.* 1501, *pg.* 471
K-PHOS ORIGINAL - Pharmaceuticals - BEACH PRODUCTS, INC.; *pg.* 1501, *pg.* 471
K-PLUS - Chemical Product - CABOT CORPORATION; *pg.* 1151, *pg.* 792
K-RESIN - Energy Product - CONOCOPHILLIPS; *pg.* 975, *pg.* 1703
K-RING - Nozzle Heaters - WATLOW ELECTRIC MANUFACTURING COMPANY; *pg.* 1078, *pg.* 1004
K SERIES - Semiconductor Product - RENESAS ELECTRONICS AMERICA INC.; *pg.* 667, *pg.* 269
K-SPERSE - Chemical Product - KING INDUSTRIES, INC.; *pg.* 1443, *pg.* 363
K-STAY - Chemical Product - KING INDUSTRIES, INC.; *pg.* 1443, *pg.* 363

K-STAY 501 - Metal Sulfonate Rheology Control Agent - KING INDUSTRIES, INC.; *pg.* 1443, *pg.* 363
K-T ANALYZER - Inspection System - KLA-TENCOR CORPORATION; *pg.* 1353, *pg.* 146
K-TAB - Potassium Supplement - ABBOTT LABORATORIES; *pg.* 1484, *pg.* 551
K-TEL DRUG MART - Pharmaceutical Service - K-TEL INTERNATIONAL, INC.; *pg.* 1052, *pg.* 953
K-VAN - Services - UNITED PARCEL SERVICE, INC.; *pg.* 1928, *pg.* 522
K-Y BRAND - Personal Lubricants - JOHNSON & JOHNSON; *pg.* 1549, *pg.* 1091
K2 - Media Server - GRASS VALLEY, INC.; *pg.* 641, *pg.* 164
K2 - Medical Device - INTEGRA LIFESCIENCES HOLDINGS CORPORATION; *pg.* 1545, *pg.* 1109
K2 CATALOG - Software - AUTONOMY, INC.; *pg.* 358, *pg.* 212
K2 DEVELOPER - Software - AUTONOMY, INC.; *pg.* 358, *pg.* 212
K2 ENTERPRISE - Software - AUTONOMY, INC.; *pg.* 358, *pg.* 212
K2 SPIDER - Software - AUTONOMY, INC.; *pg.* 358, *pg.* 212
K2000 - Medical Equipment - INVACARE CORPORATION; *pg.* 1546, *pg.* 1451
K3000 - Medical Equipment - INVACARE CORPORATION; *pg.* 1546, *pg.* 1451
K4000 - Medical Equipment - INVACARE CORPORATION; *pg.* 1546, *pg.* 1451
K56 - Golf Bag - KARSTEN MANUFACTURING CORPORATION; *pg.* 1838, *pg.* 17
K7000 - Medical Equipment - INVACARE CORPORATION; *pg.* 1546, *pg.* 1451
K9 ADVANTIX - Pet Medication - PETMED EXPRESS, INC.; *pg.* 1781, *pg.* 460
KA - Theatrical Production - CIRQUE DU SOLEIL INC.; *pg.* 540, *pg.* 1954
KA - Degreaser - HILLYARD, INC.; *pg.* 331, *pg.* 990
KA-NB CLEANER/DEGREASER - Cleaner & Degreaser - HILLYARD, INC.; *pg.* 331, *pg.* 990
KA'ANAPALI - Eyewear - MAUI JIM, INC.; *pg.* 9, *pg.* 651
KABBIKILLER - Home Cleaner - S.C. JOHNSON & SON, INC.; *pg.* 334, *pg.* 1889
KABLE - Rug - COURISTAN INC.; *pg.* 921, *pg.* 1067
KABLE-EASE - Cable Lubricant - AMERICAN GREASE STICK CO.; *pg.* 971, *pg.* 902
KABOODLE - Social Shopping Network - THE HEARST CORPORATION; *pg.* 1649, *pg.* 1239
KABOOM - Bathroom Cleaner - CHURCH & DWIGHT CO., INC.; *pg.* 1153, *pg.* 1063
KABOOM - Game - WMS INDUSTRIES INC.; *pg.* 593, *pg.* 666
KABUKI - Carpet - INTERFACE, INC.; *pg.* 695, *pg.* 512
KABUKI - Fabric - NEMSCHOFF, INC.; *pg.* 936, *pg.* 1890
KADEN - Furniture - AMERICAN LEATHER LP; *pg.* 912, *pg.* 1673
K.A.F KIDS - Bakery Good Mixes - THE KING ARTHUR FLOUR COMPANY, INC.; *pg.* 833, *pg.* 1767
KAFE-LA-TE - Powder Mix - TRADER VIC'S GOURMET PRODUCTS, INC.; *pg.* 901, *pg.* 69
KAFLEX - Drive Shafts - KAMAN CORPORATION; *pg.* 229, *pg.* 338
KAHANA - Furniture - TROPITONE FURNITURE CO., INC.; *pg.* 945, *pg.* 118
KAHLUA - Liquor - PERNOD RICARD USA, INC.; *pg.* 1968, *pg.* 1332
KAHUNA - Eyewear - MAUI JIM, INC.; *pg.* 9, *pg.* 651
KAHUNA KASH - Game - WMS INDUSTRIES INC.; *pg.* 593, *pg.* 666
KAI - Furniture - AMISCO INDUSTRIES LTD.; *pg.* 913, *pg.* 1958
KAILEY - Dolls - AMERICAN GIRL LLC; *pg.* 949, *pg.* 1871
KAILUA - Eyewear - MAUI JIM, INC.; *pg.* 9, *pg.* 651
KAIMANA - Eyewear - MAUI JIM, INC.; *pg.* 9, *pg.* 651
KAISER PERMANENTE - Health Plan - KAISER FOUNDATION HEALTH PLAN OF THE MID-ATLANTIC STATES, INC.; *pg.* 1205, *pg.* 776
KAKE MATE - Cake Emulsifier - MALLET & COMPANY, INC.; *pg.* 875, *pg.* 1521
KAL - Nutritional Product - NUTRACEUTICAL INTERNATIONAL CORPORATION; *pg.* 1576, *pg.* 1753
KAL KAN - Pet Foods - MARS, INCORPORATED; *pg.* 1858, *pg.* 1792
KALAHARI - Rug - COURISTAN INC.; *pg.* 921, *pg.* 1067
KALAHARI - Dinnerware - THE HOMER LAUGHLIN CHINA COMPANY; *pg.* 1125, *pg.* 1850
KALAHARI - Fabric - NEMSCHOFF, INC.; *pg.* 936, *pg.* 1890
THE KALAMAZOO GAZETTE - Newspaper - MLIVE MEDIA GROUP; *pg.* 1665, *pg.* 888
KALEIDO - Watch - FOSSIL GROUP, INC.; *pg.* 5, *pg.* 1735
KALEIDOSCOPE - Software - BIO-RAD LABORATORIES, INC.; *pg.* 1504, *pg.* 101
KALEIDOSCOPE - Shoe - ETONIC WORLDWIDE LLC; *pg.* 1808, *pg.* 857
KALEIDOSCOPE - Game - WMS INDUSTRIES INC.; *pg.* 593, *pg.* 666
KALETRA - Protease Inhibitor - ABBOTT LABORATORIES; *pg.* 1484, *pg.* 551
KALIFORNIAKOLORS - Spray Paint - SHERWIN-WILLIAMS DIVERSIFIED BRANDS DIVISION; *pg.* 1448, *pg.* 1435
KALIHARI - Bedding - CROSCILL, INC.; *pg.* 1122, *pg.* 1220
KALINGA PRO - Knife - BUCK KNIVES, INC.; *pg.* 1828, *pg.* 550
KALIPER - Coupling Tool - T.D. WILLIAMSON, INC.; *pg.* 1380, *pg.* 1490
KALISTAA - Footwear - STEVEN MADDEN, LTD.; *pg.* 1819, *pg.* 1176
KALIX - Medical Device - INTEGRA LIFESCIENCES HOLDINGS CORPORATION; *pg.* 1545, *pg.* 1109
KALLASSY - Orthopedic Product - DJO SURGICAL; *pg.* 1525, *pg.* 1661
KALLER - Nitrogen Gas Springs - BARNES GROUP INC.; *pg.* 1317, *pg.* 340
KALLER - Mold Base & Component - SUPERIOR DIE SET CORP.; *pg.* 1379, *pg.* 1885
KALLESTAD - Clinical Diagnostic Product - BIO-RAD LABORATORIES, INC.; *pg.* 1504, *pg.* 101
KALLIMA - Paperboard - TEMBEC INC.; *pg.* 114, *pg.* 1957
KALLISTA - Bathroom Fixtures - KOHLER CO.; *pg.* 91, *pg.* 1862
KALLY - Furniture - JASPER GROUP; *pg.* 930, *pg.* 691
KALM-ASSURE - Nutritional Supplement - NATURAL ORGANICS, INC.; *pg.* 1571, *pg.* 1181
KALREZ - Dry Disconnect Coupling - DIXON VALVE & COUPLING COMPANY; *pg.* 1045, *pg.* 766
KALREZ - Sealing Products - E.I. DU PONT DE NEMOURS & COMPANY; *pg.* 1159, *pg.* 390
KALREZ - Seal - MKS INSTRUMENTS, INC.; *pg.* 1362, *pg.* 781
KALSITEX - Mica Additive - BASF CATALYSTS LLC; *pg.* 1148, *pg.* 1074
KALYPSO - Video Switchers - GRASS VALLEY, INC.; *pg.* 641, *pg.* 164
KAMAKAZI - Cocktail - MONTEBELLO BRANDS INC.; *pg.* 1967, *pg.* 758
KAMALA - Carpet - INTERFACE, INC.; *pg.* 695, *pg.* 512
KAMCHATKA - Vodka - JIM BEAM BRANDS CO.; *pg.* 1965, *pg.* 601
KAMELEON - Media Processing System - GRASS VALLEY, INC.; *pg.* 641, *pg.* 164
KAMELEON - Wireless Control Product - UNIVERSAL ELECTRONICS, INC.; *pg.* 683, *pg.* 262
KAMI - Waiting Seating - STEELCASE INC.; *pg.* 475, *pg.* 889
KAMIK - Shoes - GENFOOT INC.; *pg.* 1809, *pg.* 1951
KAMIKAZE - Fabric - NEMSCHOFF, INC.; *pg.* 936, *pg.* 1890
KAMMER - Valve - FLOWSERVE CORPORATION; *pg.* 82, *pg.* 1719
KAMORA - Cordial - JIM BEAM BRANDS CO.; *pg.* 1965, *pg.* 601
KAMPIDANO - Footwear - K-SWISS; *pg.* 1837, *pg.* 306
KAMPING KABINS - Rental Units - KAMPGROUNDS OF AMERICA, INC.; *pg.* 555, *pg.* 1008
KAMPING KOTTAGES - Rental Units - KAMPGROUNDS OF AMERICA, INC.; *pg.* 555, *pg.* 1008
KAMPING LODGES - Rental Units - KAMPGROUNDS OF AMERICA, INC.; *pg.* 555, *pg.* 1008
KAN TONG - Food Product - MARS, INCORPORATED; *pg.* 1858, *pg.* 1792
KANAHA - Eyewear - MAUI JIM, INC.; *pg.* 9, *pg.* 651
KANANGA WATER - Cologne - LANMAN & KEMP-BARCLAY CO., INC.; *pg.* 514, *pg.* 1132
KANDRAA - Footwear - STEVEN MADDEN, LTD.; *pg.* 1819, *pg.* 1176
KANDY KAKES - Bakery Product - TASTY BAKING COMPANY; *pg.* 1862, *pg.* 1571
KANGA ROCKA ROO - Carrier - GRACO CHILDREN'S PRODUCTS INC.; *pg.* 954, *pg.* 1531
KANGAROO - Enteral Feeding Pump - MEDLINE INDUSTRIES, INC.; *pg.* 1562, *pg.* 635
KANGAROO - Convenience Stores - THE PANTRY, INC.; *pg.* 1029, *pg.* 1360
KANGAROO CROSSING - Video Game - INTERNATIONAL GAME TECHNOLOGY; *pg.* 957, *pg.* 1024
KANGAROO ENTRIFLUSH - Feeding Pump - MEDLINE INDUSTRIES, INC.; *pg.* 1562, *pg.* 635
KANGAROO EXPRESS - Convenience Stores - THE PANTRY, INC.; *pg.* 1029, *pg.* 1360
KANGATAPE - Installation Tape for Carpet with Attached Polyurethane Cushion - TEXTILE RUBBER & CHEMICAL COMPANY; *pg.* 1890, *pg.* 530
KANGATOOLS - Carpet Installation Tools - TEXTILE RUBBER & CHEMICAL COMPANY; *pg.* 1890, *pg.* 530
KANJI - Fabric - SCALAMANDRE, INC.; *pg.* 941, *pg.* 1058
KANK-A - Mouth Pain Liquid - BLISTEX, INC.; *pg.* 502, *pg.* 644
KANSAS CITY CHIEFS - Football Club - KANSAS CITY CHIEFS FOOTBALL CLUB, INC.; *pg.* 555, *pg.* 984
KANSAS CITY HOMES & GARDENS - Magazine - NETWORK COMMUNICATIONS INC.; *pg.* 1271, *pg.* 534
KANSAS CITY SOUTHERN - Transportation Company - THE KANSAS CITY SOUTHERN RAILWAY COMPANY; *pg.* 1913, *pg.* 985
KANSAS DIAMOND - Flour - ARCHER-DANIELS-MIDLAND COMPANY; *pg.* 825, *pg.* 565
KANSAS SPEEDWAY - Motorsports Facility - INTERNATIONAL SPEEDWAY CORPORATION; *pg.* 553, *pg.* 420
KANT-SLIP - Pressure Sensitive Labels - THE STANDARD REGISTER COMPANY; *pg.* 473, *pg.* 1446
KAOLINER - Dental Product - DENTSPLY INTERNATIONAL INC.; *pg.* 1522, *pg.* 1596
KAOPECTATE - Diarrhea Relief Product - CHATTEM, INC.; *pg.* 1515, *pg.* 1628
KAOSS MIXER - Dynamic DJ Mixer - KORG USA, INC.; *pg.* 556, *pg.* 1180
KAOSS PAD ENTRANCER - Audio/Video Processor - KORG USA, INC.; *pg.* 556, *pg.* 1180
KAP - Paper Products - BOISE CASCADE HOLDINGS, L.L.C.; *pg.* 1453, *pg.* 546
KAP - Paper & Nonwoven Material - FIBERMARK INC.; *pg.* 1457, *pg.* 1764
KAPALUA - Eyewear - MAUI JIM, INC.; *pg.* 9, *pg.* 651
KAPEL - Starch Film-Coating - GRAIN PROCESSING CORPORATION; *pg.* 859, *pg.* 709
KAPENA - Eyewear - MAUI JIM, INC.; *pg.* 9, *pg.* 651
KAPLAN - Turbine - GE ENERGY; *pg.* 1338, *pg.* 506
KAPLAN - Adult Publishing Imprint - SIMON & SCHUSTER, INC.; *pg.* 1687, *pg.* 1292
KAPO - Beverages - THE COCA-COLA COMPANY; *pg.* 240, *pg.* 493
KAPRISE - Footwear - STEVEN MADDEN, LTD.; *pg.* 1819, *pg.* 1176
KAPTON - Voice Coil Former Material - ATLAS SOUND; *pg.* 621, *pg.* 1692
KAPTON - Film - E.I. DU PONT DE NEMOURS & COMPANY; *pg.* 1159, *pg.* 390
KAPTON - Heater - WATLOW ELECTRIC MANUFACTURING COMPANY; *pg.* 1078, *pg.* 1004
KARA - Furniture - AMISCO INDUSTRIES LTD.; *pg.* 913, *pg.* 1958
KARADA MEGURI-CHA - Beverages - THE COCA-COLA COMPANY; *pg.* 240, *pg.* 493
KARASTAN - Carpets & Rugs - MOHAWK INDUSTRIES, INC.; *pg.* 935, *pg.* 527
KARAT - Testing Instrument System - BECKMAN COULTER, INC.; *pg.* 1402, *pg.* 48
KARAT PLATINUM - Jewelry - KARAT PLATINUM LLC; *pg.* 7, *pg.* 1168
KARATE.COM - Advertising Website - LIVE CURRENT MEDIA INC.; *pg.* 1263, *pg.* 1911
KARBO-MATIC - Heating System - SELAS HEAT TECHNOLOGY COMPANY LLC; *pg.* 1076, *pg.* 1553
KARBONOFF - Cleaning Solution - CLAYTON INDUSTRIES CO.; *pg.* 1323, *pg.* 66
KARD-KARRIER - Envelope - TENSION ENVELOPE CORPORATION; *pg.* 483, *pg.* 986
KARDVELOPE - Envelope - TENSION ENVELOPE CORPORATION; *pg.* 483, *pg.* 986
KAREENA - Watch Set - HABAND COMPANY, INC.; *pg.* 1772, *pg.* 1099
KAREN - Clothing - ABERCROMBIE & FITCH CO.; *pg.* 37, *pg.* 1466
KAREN NEUBURGER - Bedding Product - HOLLANDER SLEEP PRODUCTS; *pg.* 927, *pg.* 411
KARGARD - Protective Shield for Autos - BLUE OX; *pg.* 701, *pg.* 1019

KARGES BY HAND - Wood Furniture - THE KARGES FURNITURE COMPANY, INC.; *pg.* 931, *pg.* 679
KARINA - Personal Care Electrical Product - HELEN OF TROY L.P.; *pg.* 511, *pg.* 1692
KARISMA - Furniture - NEMSCHOFF, INC.; *pg.* 936, *pg.* 1890
KARL - Furniture - AMISCO INDUSTRIES LTD.; *pg.* 913, *pg.* 1958
KARL MARX VODKA - Spirits - LEONARD KREUSCH, INC.; *pg.* 254, *pg.* 1099
KARLEX - Polycarbonate Compounds - FERRO CORPORATION; *pg.* 1162, *pg.* 1462
KARLY - Footwear - COBIAN CORP.; *pg.* 1806, *pg.* 253
KARMA - Sandals - AEROGROUP INTERNATIONAL, INC.; *pg.* 1803, *pg.* 1055
KARMA - Computer Application - FACEBOOK, INC.; *pg.* 1245, *pg.* 143
KAROLL - Footwear - STEVEN MADDEN, LTD.; *pg.* 1819, *pg.* 1176
KARON - Bearings - KAMAN CORPORATION; *pg.* 229, *pg.* 338
KARRY-ALL - Rack - FANCORT INDUSTRIES, INC.; *pg.* 1336, *pg.* 1131
KARSTEN 2 - Golf Club - KARSTEN MANUFACTURING CORPORATION; *pg.* 1838, *pg.* 17
KART - Furniture - STEELCASE INC.; *pg.* 475, *pg.* 889
KART STACK - Office Furniture - STEELCASE INC.; *pg.* 475, *pg.* 889
KARY KART - Luggage Cart System - AMERICAN LOCKER GROUP INCORPORATED; *pg.* 1041, *pg.* 1674
KARYNA - Furniture - AMISCO INDUSTRIES LTD.; *pg.* 913, *pg.* 1958
KARYOMAX - Cell Culture Product - THERMO FISHER SCIENTIFIC INC.; *pg.* 1602, *pg.* 61
KASARE - Ceramic, Glass, Stone Tiles & Slabs - WALKER & ZANGER, INC.; *pg.* 119, *pg.* 281
KASBAH - Fabric - NEMSCHOFF, INC.; *pg.* 936, *pg.* 1890
KASEY THE KINDERBOT - Toy - MATTEL, INC.; *pg.* 962, *pg.* 81
KASH N' KARRY - Promotion - FOOD LION, LLC; *pg.* 1019, *pg.* 1390
KASHAN - Rug - ETHAN ALLEN INTERIORS INC.; *pg.* 924, *pg.* 343
KASHI - Breakfast Cereal - KASHI COMPANY; *pg.* 830, *pg.* 119
KASHI - Cereal - KELLOGG COMPANY; *pg.* 831, *pg.* 870
KASHI 7 WHOLE GRAIN PILAF - Cereal - KASHI COMPANY; *pg.* 830, *pg.* 119
KASHI FLAKES - Cereal - KASHI COMPANY; *pg.* 830, *pg.* 119
KASHI HONEY ALMOND FLAX - Granola Bar - KASHI COMPANY; *pg.* 830, *pg.* 119
KASHI HONEY PUFFS - Breakfast Cereal - KASHI COMPANY; *pg.* 830, *pg.* 119
KASHI MEDLEY - Breakfast Cereal - KASHI COMPANY; *pg.* 830, *pg.* 119
KASHI MOUNTAIN MEDLEY - Granola - KASHI COMPANY; *pg.* 830, *pg.* 119
KASHI NUGGETS - Cereal - KASHI COMPANY; *pg.* 830, *pg.* 119
KASHI ORCHARD SPICE - Granola - KASHI COMPANY; *pg.* 830, *pg.* 119
KASHI PEANUT PEANUT BUTTER - Granola Bar - KASHI COMPANY; *pg.* 830, *pg.* 119
KASHI PILAF - Cereal - KASHI COMPANY; *pg.* 830, *pg.* 119
KASHI PUFFS - Cereal - KASHI COMPANY; *pg.* 830, *pg.* 119
KASHI TRAIL MIX - Granola Bar - KASHI COMPANY; *pg.* 830, *pg.* 119
KASHI VIVE - Cereal - KASHI COMPANY; *pg.* 830, *pg.* 119
KASHIMAR - Rug - COURISTAN INC.; *pg.* 921, *pg.* 1067
KASIDY - Footwear - STEVEN MADDEN, LTD.; *pg.* 1819, *pg.* 1176
KASIL - Potassium Silicate - PQ CORPORATION; *pg.* 1178, *pg.* 1515
KASIL SS - Potassium Silicate - PQ CORPORATION; *pg.* 1178, *pg.* 1515
KASOLV - Potassium Silicate - PQ CORPORATION; *pg.* 1178, *pg.* 1515
KASSER - Vodka - LAIRD & COMPANY, INC.; *pg.* 1966, *pg.* 1119
KASSERS '51' BLEND - Gin - LAIRD & COMPANY, INC.; *pg.* 1966, *pg.* 1119
KAST - Lighting - STEELCASE INC.; *pg.* 475, *pg.* 889
KASTEEL CRU - Beverages - MOLSON COORS BREWING COMPANY; *pg.* 256, *pg.* 321
KASTEL - Ion Exchange Agent - THE DOW CHEMICAL COMPANY; *pg.* 1157, *pg.* 898
KASTLE SYSTEMS - Office Building Security Systems - KASTLE SYSTEMS LLC; *pg.* 648, *pg.* 1773
KASTOR - Saltwater Spinning Reels - DAIWA CORPORATION; *pg.* 1832, *pg.* 75
KASTRO - Footwear - STEVEN MADDEN, LTD.; *pg.* 1819, *pg.* 1176
KAT KIT - Cat Litter - OIL-DRI CORPORATION OF AMERICA; *pg.* 1480, *pg.* 586
KATABAT - Advertising Publication - DOMINION ENTERPRISES; *pg.* 1636, *pg.* 1796
KATALYST - Medical Device - INTEGRA LIFESCIENCES HOLDINGS CORPORATION; *pg.* 1545, *pg.* 1109
KATAPULT - Shoe - AEROGROUP INTERNATIONAL, INC.; *pg.* 1803, *pg.* 1055
KATARINA - Clothing - ABERCROMBIE & FITCH CO.; *pg.* 37, *pg.* 1466
KATE SPADE - Accessories - KATE SPADE & COMPANY; *pg.* 27, *pg.* 1248
KATHERINE - Clothing - ABERCROMBIE & FITCH CO.; *pg.* 37, *pg.* 1466
KATHERINE TEGEN - Books - HARPERCOLLINS PUBLISHERS INC.; *pg.* 1647, *pg.* 1237
KATHIE LEE - Women's Dresses & Sportswear - KELLWOOD COMPANY; *pg.* 28, *pg.* 975
KATHLEEN - Clothing - ABERCROMBIE & FITCH CO.; *pg.* 37, *pg.* 1466
KATHLEEN - Dolls - AMERICAN GIRL LLC; *pg.* 949, *pg.* 1871
KATHMANDU - Rug - COURISTAN INC.; *pg.* 921, *pg.* 1067
KATHON - Biocide - DOW CHEMICAL; *pg.* 1156, *pg.* 1563
KATHRYN - Kitchen Product - KOHLER CO.; *pg.* 91, *pg.* 1862
KATHRYN - Office Furniture - STEELCASE INC.; *pg.* 475, *pg.* 889
KATIA - Furniture - HAWORTH, INC.; *pg.* 402, *pg.* 891
KATIE - Footwear - P.W. MINOR & SON, INC.; *pg.* 1816, *pg.* 1140
KATIE - Hat - WOODEN SHIPS OF HOBOKEN; *pg.* 35, *pg.* 1315
KATINA - Apparel - VANS, INC.; *pg.* 1821, *pg.* 76
KATMAI - Binocular - LEUPOLD & STEVENS, INC.; *pg.* 1420, *pg.* 1492
KATOSTAT - Wound Care Product - CONVATEC LTD.; *pg.* 1518, *pg.* 1121
KATT - Electronic Components - MOLEX INCORPORATED; *pg.* 655, *pg.* 628
KATT PDS - Electronic Components - MOLEX INCORPORATED; *pg.* 655, *pg.* 628
KATY - Industrial & Household Products - KATY INDUSTRIES, INC.; *pg.* 1126, *pg.* 973
KATY'S KITCHEN - Food Product - SHAMROCK FOODS COMPANY; *pg.* 895, *pg.* 20
KAUAI - Bedding - CROSCILL, INC.; *pg.* 1122, *pg.* 1220
KAUAI COFFEE - Estate-Grown Roasted Coffee - ALEXANDER & BALDWIN, INC.; *pg.* 1079, *pg.* 543
KAUFMAN & BROAD - Provider of Homebuilding Services - KB HOME; *pg.* 90, *pg.* 134
KAUFMANFLEX - Rotary Transfer Machines - KAUFMAN MFG. COMPANY; *pg.* 1352, *pg.* 1868
KAV - Home Theater & Home Stereo Components - KRELL INDUSTRIES, INC.; *pg.* 650, *pg.* 367
KAVATROK - Stress & Mood Relief Product - NATROL, INC.; *pg.* 1570, *pg.* 64
KAVATROL - Nutritional Product - NATROL, INC.; *pg.* 1570, *pg.* 64
KAVIR - Dinnerware - THE HOMER LAUGHLIN CHINA COMPANY; *pg.* 1125, *pg.* 1850
KAVO - Dental Instrument - DANAHER CORPORATION; *pg.* 1044, *pg.* 397
KAWASAKI MOUNTAIN BIKES - Recreation Vehicles - KAWASAKI MOTORS CORP., U.S.A.; *pg.* 1708, *pg.* 111
KAWNEER - Curtain Walls, Doors, Entrances, Storefronts & Window Framing Products - KAWNEER COMPANY, INC.; *pg.* 90, *pg.* 537
KAWNEER RUBBER & PLASTICS - Non-Metal Gaskets & Non-Metal Setting Blocks - KAWNEER COMPANY, INC.; *pg.* 90, *pg.* 537
KAY - Medical Cabinet - BLICKMAN HEALTH INDUSTRIES, INC.; *pg.* 1506, *pg.* 1051
KAY JEWELERS - Jewelers - STERLING JEWELERS INC.; *pg.* 13, *pg.* 1402
KAYA - Dolls - AMERICAN GIRL LLC; *pg.* 949, *pg.* 1871
KAYABU - Footwear - K-SWISS; *pg.* 1837, *pg.* 306
KAYAK - Digital Video Equipment - GRASS VALLEY, INC.; *pg.* 641, *pg.* 164
KAYAK - Moist Snuff - SWISHER INTERNATIONAL, INC.; *pg.* 1895, *pg.* 345
KAYAK.COM - Travel Website - KAYAK; *pg.* 1260, *pg.* 363
KAYDOL - Polymer Product - CHEMTURA CORPORATION; *pg.* 1152, *pg.* 355
KAYEM - Deli Meats - KAYEM FOODS, INC.; *pg.* 867, *pg.* 814
KAYESTEE - Footwear - K-SWISS; *pg.* 1837, *pg.* 306
KAYLA - Apparel - BEBE STORES, INC.; *pg.* 19, *pg.* 49
KAYLA - Wallcovering - YORK WALLCOVERINGS INC.; *pg.* 947, *pg.* 1598
KAYSTRIP - Cleaning Products - CLAYTON INDUSTRIES CO.; *pg.* 1323, *pg.* 66
KAYTEE - Pet Food - PETSMART, INC.; *pg.* 1481, *pg.* 18
KAZLER - Footwear - STEVEN MADDEN, LTD.; *pg.* 1819, *pg.* 1176
KAZOOZLES - Candy - NESTLE USA, INC.; *pg.* 883, *pg.* 96
KAZULAH - Online Services - IAC/INTERACTIVECORP; *pg.* 292, *pg.* 1242
KB - Homebuilding Services - KB HOME; *pg.* 90, *pg.* 134
KB - Lawn & Garden Products - THE SCOTTS MIRACLE-GRO COMPANY; *pg.* 1799, *pg.* 1459
KB URBAN - Homebuilding Services - KB HOME; *pg.* 90, *pg.* 134
KBB - Software - BIO-RAD LABORATORIES, INC.; *pg.* 1504, *pg.* 101
KC 1000 - Gas Fired Water Heater-Boiler Line - AERCO INTERNATIONAL INC.; *pg.* 1068, *pg.* 1142
K.C. MASTERPIECE - Barbecue Sauce - THE CLOROX COMPANY; *pg.* 327, *pg.* 169
KCI EXPRESS - Support System - KINETIC CONCEPTS, INC.; *pg.* 1553, *pg.* 1741
KC'S - Gaming Product - GLD PRODUCTS, INC.; *pg.* 1835, *pg.* 1882
KD CONTEXT - Metal Seating - THE COMMERCIAL FURNITURE GROUP; *pg.* 920, *pg.* 994
KDAT - Lumber & Panel - UNIVERSAL FOREST PRODUCTS, INC.; *pg.* 117, *pg.* 890
KDR - Bicycle - TREK BICYCLE CORPORATION; *pg.* 1847, *pg.* 1896
KDT800 - Radio Transceiver - MOTOROLA SOLUTIONS, INC.; *pg.* 657, *pg.* 659
KEA! X - PC X Server - ATTACHMATE CORPORATION; *pg.* 356, *pg.* 1833
KEAHOU - Footwear - K-SWISS; *pg.* 1837, *pg.* 306
KEAHOU C - Footwear - K-SWISS; *pg.* 1837, *pg.* 306
KEANE - Lighting Product - QUOIZEL INC.; *pg.* 1304, *pg.* 1616
KEATING - Lighting Product - QUOIZEL INC.; *pg.* 1304, *pg.* 1616
KEATON - Furniture - AMERICAN LEATHER LP; *pg.* 912, *pg.* 1673
KEDS - Footwear - WOLVERINE WORLD WIDE, INC.; *pg.* 1822, *pg.* 905
KEEBLER - Food Product - KELLOGG COMPANY; *pg.* 831, *pg.* 870
KEEBLER COOKIE CRUNCH - Cereal - KELLOGG COMPANY; *pg.* 831, *pg.* 870
KEEBLER EL FUDGE - Sandwich Cookies - KELLOGG COMPANY; *pg.* 831, *pg.* 870
KEENE VALLEY - Clothing - ABERCROMBIE & FITCH CO.; *pg.* 37, *pg.* 1466
THE KEENELAND LIBRARY - Library Services - KEENELAND ASSOCIATION INC.; *pg.* 1477, *pg.* 730
KEEP-AWAY - Pacifier Shield - EVENFLO COMPANY, INC.; *pg.* 924, *pg.* 1470
KEEP CRISP - Bag - CHIQUITA BRANDS INTERNATIONAL, INC.; *pg.* 847, *pg.* 1365
KEEP GOING - Slogan - ENERGIZER HOLDINGS, INC.; *pg.* 637, *pg.* 996
KEEP IT A SAFE SUMMER - Awareness Program - MOTHERS AGAINST DRUNK DRIVING (MADD); *pg.* 147, *pg.* 1723
KEEP-IT-COOL - Clip - BROWN & BIGELOW, INC.; *pg.* 1624, *pg.* 959
KEEP IT SIMPLE. CATCH IT EARLY - Slogan - EXACT SCIENCES CORPORATION; *pg.* 1529, *pg.* 1865
KEEP-ME-DRY - Burp Cloth - CARTER'S, INC.; *pg.* 21, *pg.* 491
KEEP/SAFE - Safe - SENTRY GROUP, INC.; *pg.* 468, *pg.* 1337
KEEP SAFER - Security System - NORTEK, INC.; *pg.* 100,

pg. 1607

KEEP THE WHEELS TURNING - Tagline - ADVANCE AUTO PARTS, INC.; pg. 197, pg. 1805

KEEP-TITE! - Specialty Fasteners - DORMAN PRODUCTS, INC.; pg. 204, pg. 1522

KEEP YOUR GARBAGE IN THE DARK - Tagline - PACTIV CORPORATION; pg. 1466, pg. 624

KEEP YOUR SAVINGS CLOSE TO HOME - Slogan - GUARANTY BANK; pg. 764, pg. 1006

KEEPCOLD - Cryogenic Fill Services Program - AIR PRODUCTS AND CHEMICALS, INC.; pg. 1145, pg. 1513

KEEPERS OF THE ARTS - Book - NOVICA UNITED, INC.; pg. 1271, pg. 137

KEEPIN' IT HOT - Video Game - INTERNATIONAL GAME TECHNOLOGY; pg. 957, pg. 1024

KEEPIN' UP WITH THE JONESES - Video Game - WMS INDUSTRIES INC.; pg. 593, pg. 666

KEEPING LAWNS HEALTHY FOR LIFE. - Slogan - LAWN DOCTOR INC.; pg. 1796, pg. 1074

KEEPING PACE - Orthopedic Footwear - MAURICE J. MARKELL SHOE CO., INC.; pg. 1811, pg. 1356

KEEPING THE WORLD IN MOTION - Slogan - GLEASON CORPORATION; pg. 1340, pg. 1335

KEEPING UP WITH YOU - Slogan - INVACARE CORPORATION; pg. 1546, pg. 1451

KEEPING YOU COMFORTABLE EVERYDAY - Tagline - THE SALK COMPANY; pg. 1591, pg. 800

KEEPING YOU ORGANIZED - Slogan - SMEAD MANUFACTURING COMPANY; pg. 470, pg. 926

KEEPSAFE - Tamper-Evident Bags - SEALED AIR CORPORATION; pg. 1468, pg. 1058

KEEPSAKE - Azalea - ARIS HORTICULTURE, INC.; pg. 1793, pg. 1404

KEEPSAKE - Cremation Urns - BATESVILLE CASKET COMPANY, INC.; pg. 1393, pg. 673

KEEPSAKE AZALEAS - Flower Grower - ARIS HORTICULTURE, INC.; pg. 1793, pg. 1404

KEEPSAKE ORNAMENTS - Gold Crown Card - HALLMARK CARDS, INC.; pg. 1646, pg. 983

KEEPSMART ENGINEERING - PDH Courses - SMARTPROS LTD.; pg. 1281, pg. 1166

KEFIR - Dairy Food Product - LIFEWAY FOODS, INC.; pg. 874, pg. 634

KEG MOVER - Additional Utility - MAGLINE, INC.; pg. 1358, pg. 908

KEI - Defense System - RAYTHEON COMPANY; pg. 233, pg. 854

KEIFER - Furniture - AMERICAN LEATHER LP; pg. 912, pg. 1673

KEIJE - Cabinet Organizers - CLOSETMAID CORPORATION; pg. 920, pg. 452

KEIKI - Eyewear - MAUI JIM, INC.; pg. 9, pg. 651

KEKE BEACH - Liqueur - MCCORMICK DISTILLING CO., INC.; pg. 1966, pg. 1007

KEL-AQUA - Undercoater - KELLY-MOORE PAINT COMPANY, INC.; pg. 1443, pg. 198

KEL-BOND - Paint - KELLY-MOORE PAINT COMPANY, INC.; pg. 1443, pg. 198

KEL-BOND II - Surface Conditioner - KELLY-MOORE PAINT COMPANY, INC.; pg. 1443, pg. 198

KEL-COTE - Paint - KELLY-MOORE PAINT COMPANY, INC.; pg. 1443, pg. 198

KEL-GUARD - Paint - KELLY-MOORE PAINT COMPANY, INC.; pg. 1443, pg. 198

KEL-PRO - Paint - KELLY-MOORE PAINT COMPANY, INC.; pg. 1443, pg. 198

KEL-SEAL - Paint Product - KELLY-MOORE PAINT COMPANY, INC.; pg. 1443, pg. 198

KEL-SEAL 77 - Masonry Water Repellent - KELLY-MOORE PAINT COMPANY, INC.; pg. 1443, pg. 198

KEL-TEX - Paint Product - KELLY-MOORE PAINT COMPANY, INC.; pg. 1443, pg. 198

KEL-THANE - Varnish - KELLY-MOORE PAINT COMPANY, INC.; pg. 1443, pg. 198

KEL-TONE - Stain - KELLY-MOORE PAINT COMPANY, INC.; pg. 1443, pg. 198

KEL-VARIA - Machinery - HARDINGE INC.; pg. 1344, pg. 1157

KEL-VISION - Machinery - HARDINGE INC.; pg. 1344, pg. 1157

KELDAX - Sound Barrier Resins - E.I. DU PONT DE NEMOURS & COMPANY; pg. 1159, pg. 390

KELLEMS - Wiring Systems - HUBBELL INCORPORATED; pg. 1299, pg. 370

KELLENBERGER - Grinding Machine - HARDINGE INC.; pg. 1344, pg. 1157

KELLER GRADUATE SCHOOL OF MANAGEMENT - Education Center - DEVRY EDUCATION GROUP INC.; pg. 600, pg. 607

KELLER-SOFT - Regulatory Software - J.J. KELLER & ASSOCIATES, INC.; pg. 1654, pg. 1883

KELLERONLINE - Online Safety Management Application - J.J. KELLER & ASSOCIATES, INC.; pg. 1654, pg. 1883

KELLER'S FOOD BIOTERRORISM INFORMATION CENTER - Regulatory Handbook - J.J. KELLER & ASSOCIATES, INC.; pg. 1654, pg. 1883

KELLER'S INCIDENT INVESTIGATOR - Recordkeeping Software - J.J. KELLER & ASSOCIATES, INC.; pg. 1654, pg. 1883

KELLER'S INFORMATION CENTERS - Online Safety & Regulatory Information Resource - J.J. KELLER & ASSOCIATES, INC.; pg. 1654, pg. 1883

KELLER'S JOB SAFETY ANALYZER - Recordkeeping Software - J.J. KELLER & ASSOCIATES, INC.; pg. 1654, pg. 1883

KELLER'S MAINTENANCE MANAGER - Recordkeeping Software - J.J. KELLER & ASSOCIATES, INC.; pg. 1654, pg. 1883

KELLER'S MSDS VIEWER - Recordkeeping Software - J.J. KELLER & ASSOCIATES, INC.; pg. 1654, pg. 1883

KELLER'S NAFTA RESOURCE CENTER - Regulatory Handbook - J.J. KELLER & ASSOCIATES, INC.; pg. 1654, pg. 1883

KELLER'S SECURITY RESOURCE CENTER - Regulatory Handbook - J.J. KELLER & ASSOCIATES, INC.; pg. 1654, pg. 1883

KELLERSCAN - Recordkeeping Software - J.J. KELLER & ASSOCIATES, INC.; pg. 1654, pg. 1883

KELLERSTAR - Recordkeeping Software - J.J. KELLER & ASSOCIATES, INC.; pg. 1654, pg. 1883

KELLOGG'S CORN FLAKES - Corn Flakes Cereal - KELLOGG COMPANY; pg. 831, pg. 870

KELLOGG'S CORNFLAKE CRUMBS - Cereal - KELLOGG COMPANY; pg. 831, pg. 870

KELLOGG'S CRUNCH - Cereal - KELLOGG COMPANY; pg. 831, pg. 870

KELLOGG'S FROSTED FLAKES - Frosted Flakes of Corn Cereal - KELLOGG COMPANY; pg. 831, pg. 870

KELLOGG'S KITCHEN - Test Kitchen - KELLOGG COMPANY; pg. 831, pg. 870

KELLOGG'S RACING - Product Promotion - KELLOGG COMPANY; pg. 831, pg. 870

KELLOGG'S STUFFING MIX - Stuffing - KELLOGG COMPANY; pg. 831, pg. 870

KELLY - Tire And Rubber Product - THE GOODYEAR TIRE & RUBBER COMPANY; pg. 1883, pg. 1401

KELLY - Dinnerware - THE HOMER LAUGHLIN CHINA COMPANY; pg. 1125, pg. 1850

KELLY - Toy - MATTEL, INC.; pg. 962, pg. 81

KELLY HOPPEN - Home Interior Design - CHEROKEE GLOBAL BRANDS; pg. 21, pg. 278

KELLY SERVICES - Staffing Services - KELLY SERVICES, INC.; pg. 424, pg. 911

KELLY SLATER'S PRO SURFER - Game - ACTIVISION BLIZZARD, INC.; pg. 948, pg. 271

KELLYS REVENGE - Premium Wine - CONSTELLATION BRANDS, INC.; pg. 1960, pg. 1348

KELOCO - Beverages - THE COCA-COLA COMPANY; pg. 240, pg. 493

KELSEY - Clothing - ABERCROMBIE & FITCH CO.; pg. 37, pg. 1466

KELSEY - Furniture - ASHLEY FURNITURE INDUSTRIES, INC.; pg. 914, pg. 1852

KELSEY'S - Casual Dining Restaurants - CARA OPERATIONS LIMITED; pg. 1720, pg. 1947

KELSO - Furniture - JASPER GROUP; pg. 930, pg. 691

KELTROL - Gum - J.M. HUBER CORPORATION; pg. 1169, pg. 1056

KELTY - Backpacks, Sleeping Bags & Tents - EXXEL OUTDOORS LLC; pg. 1833, pg. 311

KELVINATOR - Air Conditioners & Furnaces - NORTEK GLOBAL HVAC; pg. 1075, pg. 989

KELVX - Resin - EASTMAN CHEMICAL COMPANY; pg. 1159, pg. 1636

KEM - Playing Cards - THE UNITED STATES PLAYING CARD COMPANY; pg. 969, pg. 727

KEM LINK - Buffering Agent - UNIVERSAL COOPERATIVES, INC.; pg. 1482, pg. 922

KEMAH BOARDWALK - Entertainment Complex - LANDRY'S, INC.; pg. 1735, pg. 1709

KEMAMIDE - Polymer Product - CHEMTURA CORPORATION; pg. 1152, pg. 355

KEMAMINE - Polymer Product - CHEMTURA CORPORATION; pg. 1152, pg. 355

KEMESTER - Polymer Product - CHEMTURA CORPORATION; pg. 1152, pg. 355

KEMET CHARGED - Capacitors - KEMET CORPORATION; pg. 649, pg. 1621

KEMIKAL - Lime - USG CORPORATION; pg. 118, pg. 594

KEMIKO - Sealers & Wax Removers - QUAKER CHEMICAL CORP.; pg. 1178, pg. 1524

KEMLEX - Specialty Resin Compounds - FERRO CORPORATION; pg. 1162, pg. 1462

KEMLITE - Composites - CRANE CO.; pg. 227, pg. 373

KEMPER - Cabinetry - MASTERBRAND CABINETS, INC.; pg. 96, pg. 692

KEMPSMITH - File Folder Machine - KEMPSMITH MACHINE COMPANY; pg. 1352, pg. 1876

KEMRESIN - Epoxy Resin Worktop - KEWAUNEE SCIENTIFIC CORPORATION; pg. 931, pg. 1391

KEMSTRENE - Polymer Product - CHEMTURA CORPORATION; pg. 1152, pg. 355

KENAI PRINCESS LODGE - Hotel - PRINCESS TOURS; pg. 1920, pg. 1838

KENALOG-10 - Health Care Product - BRISTOL-MYERS SQUIBB COMPANY; pg. 1509, pg. 1206

KENBORE - Boring Bars - KENNAMETAL INC.; pg. 1052, pg. 1547

KENCAST - Tooling System - KENNAMETAL INC.; pg. 1052, pg. 1547

KENCLAW - Tooling System - KENNAMETAL INC.; pg. 1052, pg. 1547

KENCO - Coffee - MONDELEZ INTERNATIONAL, INC.; pg. 878, pg. 601

KENCOAT - Tooling System - KENNAMETAL INC.; pg. 1052, pg. 1547

KENDALL - Furniture - AMERICAN LEATHER LP; pg. 912, pg. 1673

KENDALL - Oil - CONOCOPHILLIPS; pg. 975, pg. 1703

KENDALL - Furniture - JASPER GROUP; pg. 930, pg. 691

KENDALL - Lighting Product - QUOIZEL INC.; pg. 1304, pg. 1616

KENDEX - Metal Cutting Tools - KENNAMETAL INC.; pg. 1052, pg. 1547

KENDO - Fabric - NEMSCHOFF, INC.; pg. 936, pg. 1890

KENDRA - Lighting Product - QUOIZEL INC.; pg. 1304, pg. 1616

KENEDIE - Footwear - STEVEN MADDEN, LTD.; pg. 1819, pg. 1176

KENETT - Hydraulic & Pneumatic Components - THE ENTWISTLE CO.; pg. 637, pg. 826

KENFACE - Tooling System - KENNAMETAL INC.; pg. 1052, pg. 1547

KENLOC - Metal Cutting Tools - KENNAMETAL INC.; pg. 1052, pg. 1547

KENMAC - Fluid System - SWAGELOK COMPANY; pg. 1064, pg. 1473

KENMAN - Candy - WM. WRIGLEY JR. COMPANY; pg. 1863, pg. 596

KENMORE - Fabric - SCALAMANDRE, INC.; pg. 941, pg. 1058

KENMORE - Home Appliance - SEARS HOLDINGS CORPORATION; pg. 1784, pg. 618

KENMORE ELITE - Home Appliance - SEARS HOLDINGS CORPORATION; pg. 1784, pg. 618

KENNA-LOK - Tooling System - KENNAMETAL INC.; pg. 1052, pg. 1547

KENNEBUNK-PORT - Nail Care Product - OPI PRODUCTS INC.; pg. 518, pg. 167

KENNEDY - Medical Cabinet - BLICKMAN HEALTH INDUSTRIES, INC.; pg. 1506, pg. 1051

KENNEDY - Furniture - JASPER GROUP; pg. 930, pg. 691

KENNEL WASH - All-Purpose Cleaner - NILODOR, INC.; pg. 332, pg. 1406

KENNETH COLE - Apparel - G-III APPAREL GROUP, LTD.; pg. 41, pg. 1233

KENNETT - Book Cloth - HOLLISTON LLC; pg. 1460, pg. 1630

KENNY ROGERS ROASTERS - Food Products - NATHAN'S FAMOUS INC.; pg. 1741, pg. 1171

KENNYBASE - Online Fixed-Income Database - STANDARD & POOR'S RATINGS SERVICES; pg. 805, pg. 1296

KENNYWEB - Web-Based Bond Data - STANDARD & POOR'S RATINGS SERVICES; pg. 805, pg. 1296

KENO - Lottery Game - GEORGIA LOTTERY

CORPORATION; *pg.* 993, *pg.* 506

KENO - Lottery Game - MASSACHUSETTS STATE LOTTERY; *pg.* 998, *pg.* 802

KENO - Game - MICHIGAN STATE LOTTERY BUREAU; *pg.* 999, *pg.* 895

KENO - Lottery Game - RHODE ISLAND LOTTERY; *pg.* 1004, *pg.* 1600

KENO BONUS - Lottery Game - WEST VIRGINIA LOTTERY; *pg.* 1011, *pg.* 1849

KENO BOOSTER - Game - WMS INDUSTRIES INC.; *pg.* 593, *pg.* 666

KENO BURST - Game - WMS INDUSTRIES INC.; *pg.* 593, *pg.* 666

KENO INVADERS - Video Game - INTERNATIONAL GAME TECHNOLOGY; *pg.* 957, *pg.* 1024

KENO PLUS - Lottery Game - RHODE ISLAND LOTTERY; *pg.* 1004, *pg.* 1600

KENSINGTON - Computer Bag - A. T. CROSS COMPANY; *pg.* 339, *pg.* 1602

KENSINGTON - Computer Accessories - ACCO BRANDS CORPORATION; *pg.* 340, *pg.* 626

KENSINGTON - Rug - COURISTAN INC.; *pg.* 921, *pg.* 1067

KENSINGTON - Furniture - ETHAN ALLEN INTERIORS INC.; *pg.* 924, *pg.* 343

KENSINGTON - Pottery - THE HOMER LAUGHLIN CHINA COMPANY; *pg.* 1125, *pg.* 1850

KENSINGTON - Furniture - JOFCO INC.; *pg.* 931, *pg.* 691

KENSINGTON - Publishing Imprint - KENSINGTON PUBLISHING CORP.; *pg.* 1656, *pg.* 1248

KENSINGTON - Fabric - NEMSCHOFF, INC.; *pg.* 936, *pg.* 1890

KENSINGTON - Flatware - ONEIDA LTD; *pg.* 1129, *pg.* 1318

KENSINGTON - LCD Display - VIEWSONIC CORPORATION; *pg.* 489, *pg.* 303

KENT - Medical Stool - BLICKMAN HEALTH INDUSTRIES, INC.; *pg.* 1506, *pg.* 1051

KENT - Handleset - INGERSOLL-RAND COMPANY; *pg.* 1349, *pg.* 1370

KENT - Livestock Feed - KENT NUTRITION GROUP; *pg.* 1477, *pg.* 710

KENT - Candy & Chocolate - MONDELEZ INTERNATIONAL, INC.; *pg.* 878, *pg.* 601

KENT MARINE - Pet Product - PETSMART, INC.; *pg.* 1481, *pg.* 18

KENTFIELD - Bike - MARIN BIKES; *pg.* 1708, *pg.* 168

KENTROL - Animal Treatment - KENT NUTRITION GROUP; *pg.* 1477, *pg.* 710

KENTUCKIAN GOLD - Deli Meats - SPECIALTY FOODS GROUP-FIELD PACKING DIV.; *pg.* 897, *pg.* 739

KENTUCKY - Tobacco Product - AMERICAN SNUFF COMPANY; *pg.* 1893, *pg.* 1641

KENTUCKY CASHBALL - Lottery Game - KENTUCKY LOTTERY CORPORATION; *pg.* 996, *pg.* 735

KENTUCKY CLUB - Motorsports Entertainment - SPEEDWAY MOTORSPORTS, INC.; *pg.* 584, *pg.* 1370

KENTUCKY DALE - Blended Whiskey - SAZERAC COMPANY, INC.; *pg.* 1969, *pg.* 745

KENTUCKY DERBY - Race - CHURCHILL DOWNS, INC.; *pg.* 540, *pg.* 733

KENTUCKY DERBY FESTIVAL - Festival Celebrating the Annual Kentucky Derby - KENTUCKY DERBY FESTIVAL, INC.; *pg.* 556, *pg.* 735

KENTUCKY FRIED CHICKEN - Fast Food Chicken Restaurants - YUM! BRANDS, INC.; *pg.* 1756, *pg.* 738

KENTUCKY KING - Twist Tobacco - AMERICAN SNUFF COMPANY; *pg.* 1893, *pg.* 1641

KENTUCKY LEGEND - Ham - SPECIALTY FOODS GROUP-FIELD PACKING DIV.; *pg.* 897, *pg.* 739

KENTUCKY SPEEDWAY - Entertainment Venue - SPEEDWAY MOTORSPORTS, INC.; *pg.* 584, *pg.* 1370

KENTWILLY - Carpet - WOVEN LEGENDS INC.; *pg.* 947, *pg.* 1572

KENWICK GARDENS - Rug - COURISTAN INC.; *pg.* 921, *pg.* 1067

KENWOOD - Flatware - ONEIDA LTD; *pg.* 1129, *pg.* 1318

KENWORTH - Trucks - PACCAR INC.; *pg.* 187, *pg.* 1816

KENWORTH - Toys - TRACTOR SUPPLY COMPANY; *pg.* 708, *pg.* 1627

KENYA - Furniture - ASHLEY FURNITURE INDUSTRIES, INC.; *pg.* 914, *pg.* 1852

KENYA - Coffee - PEET'S COFFEE & TEA, INC.; *pg.* 1029, *pg.* 85

KENYON - Furniture - ASHLEY FURNITURE INDUSTRIES, INC.; *pg.* 914, *pg.* 1852

KEO - Precision Cutting Tools - TRIMAS CORPORATION; *pg.* 1383, *pg.* 874

KEP-DRI - Leather Waterproofing Systems - HENKEL CORPORATION; *pg.* 1165, *pg.* 1535

KEP-TITE - Emulsion Leather Finish - HENKEL CORPORATION; *pg.* 1165, *pg.* 1535

KEPECO - Water Miscible Leather Finishes - HENKEL CORPORATION; *pg.* 1165, *pg.* 1535

KEPOLAC - Lacquer Leather Finishes - HENKEL CORPORATION; *pg.* 1165, *pg.* 1535

KERAJET - Inkjet Printing System - FERRO CORPORATION; *pg.* 1162, *pg.* 1462

KERAMOS - Orthopedic Implant Product - DJO SURGICAL; *pg.* 1525, *pg.* 1661

KERASTICK - Biopharmaceutical Product - DUSA PHARMACEUTICALS, INC.; *pg.* 1525, *pg.* 860

KERBOOM - Lead Core Fly Line - CORTLAND LINE COMPANY; *pg.* 1831, *pg.* 1155

KERF-AID - Dicing Saw Lubricant - DYNATEX INTERNATIONAL; *pg.* 635, *pg.* 277

KERFUL - Cleaning Solution - CLAYTON INDUSTRIES CO.; *pg.* 1323, *pg.* 66

KERI - Beverages - THE COCA-COLA COMPANY; *pg.* 240, *pg.* 493

KERIMID - Laminating Resins - HUNTSMAN CORPORATION; *pg.* 1167, *pg.* 1758

KERLITE - Cleaning Solution - CLAYTON INDUSTRIES CO.; *pg.* 1323, *pg.* 66

KERMEED - Cleaning Products - CLAYTON INDUSTRIES CO.; *pg.* 1323, *pg.* 66

KERMEL - Shirt and Trouser - BLAUER MANUFACTURING COMPANY, INC.; *pg.* 20, *pg.* 789

KERMEL - Fibre - STANFIELD'S LIMITED; *pg.* 48, *pg.* 1917

KERMIT THE FROG - Muppet - THE WALT DISNEY COMPANY; *pg.* 317, *pg.* 52

KERNEL - Fabric - NEMSCHOFF, INC.; *pg.* 936, *pg.* 1890

KERPLUNK - Premium Lead Core - CORTLAND LINE COMPANY; *pg.* 1831, *pg.* 1155

KERR - Plastic Closures - BERRY PLASTICS LANCASTER; *pg.* 1453, *pg.* 1546

KERR - Home Canning Products - JARDEN CORPORATION; *pg.* 1885, *pg.* 412

KERRICK KLEANERS - Cleaning Solution - CLAYTON INDUSTRIES CO.; *pg.* 1323, *pg.* 66

KERRMAPPER - Inspection System - KLA-TENCOR CORPORATION; *pg.* 1353, *pg.* 146

KERRY - Clothing - ABERCROMBIE & FITCH CO.; *pg.* 37, *pg.* 1466

KER'S WINGHOUSE - Bar & Grill - KER, INC.; *pg.* 1733, *pg.* 438

KESSLER - Whiskey - JIM BEAM BRANDS CO.; *pg.* 1965, *pg.* 601

KESTER LEAD-FREE SOLUTIONS - Lead-Free Soldering - KESTER, INC.; *pg.* 649, *pg.* 620

KESTREL - Telescope - MEADE INSTRUMENTS CORPORATION; *pg.* 1422, *pg.* 113

KESTREL K350 SINGLE-ENGINE TURBOPROP - Aircraft - ONE AVIATION CORPORATION; *pg.* 232, *pg.* 1135

KETAC - Conditioner Pretreatment Solution - 3M COMPANY; *pg.* 1142, *pg.* 956

KETAC-BOND - Glass Ionomer Base Cement - 3M COMPANY; *pg.* 1142, *pg.* 956

KETAC-FIL - Glass Ionomer Restorative - 3M COMPANY; *pg.* 1142, *pg.* 956

KETAC-SILVER - Ionomer Cement Restorative - 3M COMPANY; *pg.* 1142, *pg.* 956

KETASET - Anesthetic - PFIZER INC.; *pg.* 1581, *pg.* 1278

KETEL ONE CITROEN - Imported Lemon Flavored Vodka - NOLET SPIRITS USA INC.; *pg.* 1967, *pg.* 41

KETEL ONE VODKA - Vodka - DIAGEO NORTH AMERICA, INC.; *pg.* 1961, *pg.* 361

KETEL ONE VODKA - Imported Vodka - NOLET SPIRITS USA INC.; *pg.* 1967, *pg.* 41

KETOCHROME - Software - BIO-RAD LABORATORIES, INC.; *pg.* 1504, *pg.* 101

KETOJUICE - Nutritional Supplement - NATURAL ORGANICS, INC.; *pg.* 1571, *pg.* 1181

KETONE CARE - Test Strip - NIPRO DIAGNOSTICS, INC.; *pg.* 1573, *pg.* 426

KETONEX - Pharmaceutical Product - ABBOTT LABORATORIES; *pg.* 1484, *pg.* 551

KETOSLIM - Nutritional Supplement - NATURAL ORGANICS, INC.; *pg.* 1571, *pg.* 1181

KETOSNAX - Nutritional Supplement - NATURAL ORGANICS, INC.; *pg.* 1571, *pg.* 1181

KETOTROPIC - Nutritional Supplement - NATURAL ORGANICS, INC.; *pg.* 1571, *pg.* 1181

KETOZYME - Nutritional Supplement - NATURAL ORGANICS, INC.; *pg.* 1571, *pg.* 1181

KETTLE CLASSICS - Potato Chips - UTZ QUALITY FOODS, INC.; *pg.* 907, *pg.* 1536

KETTLE MANIA - Microwave Pop Corn - AMERICAN POP CORN COMPANY; *pg.* 825, *pg.* 712

KETTLECORN - Flavored Popcorn - THE POPCORN FACTORY; *pg.* 1861, *pg.* 625

KEURIG - Coffee Brewing System - KEURIG GREEN MOUNTAIN, INC.; *pg.* 868, *pg.* 1768

KEVIN - Furniture - AMISCO INDUSTRIES LTD.; *pg.* 913, *pg.* 1958

KEVLAR - Fiber - DRAPER KNITTING CO., INC.; *pg.* 692, *pg.* 810

KEVLAR - Fiber & Protective Clothing - E.I. DU PONT DE NEMOURS & COMPANY; *pg.* 1159, *pg.* 390

KEVLAR - Power Transmission Belt - HBD INDUSTRIES, INC.; *pg.* 207, *pg.* 1449

KEVLAR - Fabric - HEXCEL CORPORATION; *pg.* 1884, *pg.* 375

KEVLAR - Shears - NEWPORT CORPORATION; *pg.* 1424, *pg.* 114

KEVLAR - Apparel - OAKLEY, INC.; *pg.* 1840, *pg.* 86

KEVLAR - Polyethylene Fiber - SAMSON ROPE TECHNOLOGIES; *pg.* 1468, *pg.* 1820

KEVLAR XP - Bullet Stopping Fabric - E.I. DU PONT DE NEMOURS & COMPANY; *pg.* 1159, *pg.* 390

KEVLAST - Bicycle Accessories - SPECIALIZED BICYCLE COMPONENTS, INC.; *pg.* 1711, *pg.* 152

KEVLIN MICROWAVE - Microwave - KEVLIN CORPORATION; *pg.* 649, *pg.* 1034

KEWANEE - Truck Dumper - SCREW CONVEYOR INDUSTRIES; *pg.* 1374, *pg.* 682

KEWPIE - Doll - CHARISMA BRANDS, LLC; *pg.* 2, *pg.* 120

KEY - Bib Overalls - KEY INDUSTRIES, INC.; *pg.* 43, *pg.* 714

KEY BISCAYNE - Deep Seat Wicker Collection - TELESCOPE CASUAL FURNITURE INC.; *pg.* 944, *pg.* 1162

KEY-CUFF - Disposable Restraints - BAE SYSTEMS PRODUCTS GROUP; *pg.* 359, *pg.* 432

KEY LARGO - Shoes - ALLEN-EDMONDS SHOE CORP.; *pg.* 1804, *pg.* 1887

KEY-LOC - Plastics Product - AEP INDUSTRIES INC.; *pg.* 1878, *pg.* 1085

KEY-MATE - Flashlight - STREAMLIGHT INC.; *pg.* 1306, *pg.* 1527

KEY OF BABYLON - Video Game - INTERNATIONAL GAME TECHNOLOGY; *pg.* 957, *pg.* 1024

KEY-PRO - Software - MORSE WATCHMANS INC.; *pg.* 656, *pg.* 368

KEY-RING - Key Ring Device - MORSE WATCHMANS INC.; *pg.* 656, *pg.* 368

KEY-RINGS - Tamper-Proof Key Ring Device - MORSE WATCHMANS INC.; *pg.* 656, *pg.* 368

KEY-TAINER - Key Holders - BUXTON ACQUISITION CO., LLC; *pg.* 2, *pg.* 845

KEY TO MY HEART - Flower Arrangement - 1-800-FLOWERS.COM, INC.; *pg.* 1758, *pg.* 1151

KEY TRONIC - Computer Keyboards & Input Devices - KEY TRONIC CORPORATION; *pg.* 424, *pg.* 1844

KEYBANK - Software - MORSE WATCHMANS INC.; *pg.* 656, *pg.* 368

KEYCEL - Cellulose Fiber Product - INTERNATIONAL FIBER CORP.; *pg.* 865, *pg.* 1317

KEYCHAIN - Operating System Feature - APPLE INC.; *pg.* 350, *pg.* 73

KEYDECK - Wire Mesh - KEYSTONE STEEL & WIRE CO.; *pg.* 91, *pg.* 651

KEYED STEEL PADLOCK - Lock Protector - AMERICAN CASTING & MANUFACTURING CORPORATION; *pg.* 1312, *pg.* 1321

KEYENTRY - Software - SCAN-OPTICS, LLC; *pg.* 467, *pg.* 354

KEYFILE - Software - OPENTEXT; *pg.* 450, *pg.* 1665

KEYFLOW - Software - OPENTEXT; *pg.* 450, *pg.* 1665

KEYFRAME - Animation Production Services - DAKTRONICS, INC.; *pg.* 633, *pg.* 1624

KEYFREE - Keyless Entry - COMMERCIAL VEHICLE GROUP, INC.; *pg.* 203, *pg.* 1467

KEYINJECT - Computer Hardware - CERTICOM CORP.; *pg.* 371, *pg.* 1925

KEYKODE - Machine-Readable Numbers - EASTMAN KODAK COMPANY; *pg.* 1408, *pg.* 1333

KEYMARK - Interchangeable Core, Mortise, Rim & Knob

First page reference indicates Business Class Edition
Second page reference indicates Geographic Edition

Cylinders - MEDECO HIGH SECURITY LOCKS, INC.; *pg.* 1055, *pg.* 1806
KEYMESH - Stucco Netting - KEYSTONE STEEL & WIRE CO.; *pg.* 91, *pg.* 651
KEYNOTE - iWork App for Presentations - APPLE INC.; *pg.* 350, *pg.* 73
KEYNOTE - Fabric - NEMSCHOFF, INC.; *pg.* 936, *pg.* 1890
KEYPOINT - Portable Diagnostic Sys. - MEDTRONIC, INC.; *pg.* 1564, *pg.* 939
KEYSTONE - Cable - ARRIS GROUP, INC.; *pg.* 353, *pg.* 541
KEYSTONE - Orthopedic Product - DJO SURGICAL; *pg.* 1525, *pg.* 1661
KEYSTONE - Herbicide - DOW AGROSCIENCES LLC; *pg.* 1156, *pg.* 684
KEYSTONE - Furniture - JASPER GROUP; *pg.* 930, *pg.* 691
KEYSTONE - Machine Bolt Expansion - MKT FASTENING, LLC; *pg.* 1056, *pg.* 34
KEYSTONE - Footwear - P.W. MINOR & SON, INC.; *pg.* 1816, *pg.* 1140
KEYSTONE - Rack - SPEEDRACK PRODUCTS GROUP, LTD.; *pg.* 112, *pg.* 908
KEYSTONE - Recreation Vehicle - THOR INDUSTRIES, INC.; *pg.* 1711, *pg.* 1456
KEYSTONE - Ski Resort - VAIL RESORTS, INC.; *pg.* 1117, *pg.* 313
KEYSTONE GRILL - Mexican Restaurants - REAL MEX RESTAURANTS, INC.; *pg.* 1746, *pg.* 75
KEYSTONE ICE - Beer - MOLSON COORS BREWING COMPANY; *pg.* 256, *pg.* 321
KEYSTONE LG - Fencing Products - KEYSTONE STEEL & WIRE CO.; *pg.* 91, *pg.* 651
KEYSTONE LIGHT - Low-Calorie Beer - MOLSON COORS BREWING COMPANY; *pg.* 256, *pg.* 321
KEYSTONE PREMIUM - Beer - MOLSON COORS BREWING COMPANY; *pg.* 256, *pg.* 321
KEYSTROKE - Software - ROSCO LABORATORIES, INC.; *pg.* 1782, *pg.* 378
KEYTWIST - Nails - KEYSTONE STEEL & WIRE CO.; *pg.* 91, *pg.* 651
KEYVIEW - Software - AUTONOMY, INC.; *pg.* 358, *pg.* 212
KEYWARE - Software - KEY TECHNOLOGY, INC.; *pg.* 868, *pg.* 1847
KEYWATCHER - Software - MORSE WATCHMANS INC.; *pg.* 656, *pg.* 368
KEYWORD DNA - Indexing Technology - LOCAL.COM CORPORATION; *pg.* 1264, *pg.* 113
KEZIZ - Pressure Sintered Compositions - KENNAMETAL INC.; *pg.* 1052, *pg.* 1547
KF - Floor Protective Hardware - WAXMAN INDUSTRIES, INC.; *pg.* 120, *pg.* 1406
KF TELFORD - Valve & Fluid Product - CIRCOR INTERNATIONAL, INC.; *pg.* 76, *pg.* 805
KFC SNACKER - Chicken Filet Sandwich - KFC CORPORATION; *pg.* 1733, *pg.* 735
KFOAM - Carbon Foam Product - KOPPERS HOLDINGS INC.; *pg.* 1170, *pg.* 1577
KFORCE KNOWLEDGE STAFFING MODEL - Management Services - KFORCE INC.; *pg.* 1261, *pg.* 473
KFORCE ONSTAFF GROUP - Professional Staffing Services - KFORCE INC.; *pg.* 1261, *pg.* 473
KFX - All-Terrain Vehicle - KAWASAKI MOTORS CORP., U.S.A.; *pg.* 1708, *pg.* 111
K.G. SAUR - Publisher - GALE CENGAGE LEARNING; *pg.* 1643, *pg.* 885
KGTI - Medical Device - INTEGRA LIFESCIENCES HOLDINGS CORPORATION; *pg.* 1545, *pg.* 1109
KH3/GHQ10 - Natural Growth Hormone Precursor Cream - DIXIE HEALTH, INC.; *pg.* 1524, *pg.* 535
KHAMELEON SOFTWARE - E-Business Management Application Software - ASA INTERNATIONAL LTD.; *pg.* 353, *pg.* 1036
KHARISMAL - Fragrance Ingredient - INTERNATIONAL FLAVORS & FRAGRANCES INC.; *pg.* 512, *pg.* 1244
KHG-7 - Vitamin - HEALTH PRODUCTS CORPORATION; *pg.* 1540, *pg.* 1356
KHOU.COM - Media Service - KHOU-TV, INC.; *pg.* 294, *pg.* 1709
KHROMASORT - Sorter - KEY TECHNOLOGY, INC.; *pg.* 868, *pg.* 1847
KI-272 - Speaker System - KLIPSCH GROUP, INC.; *pg.* 649, *pg.* 688
KI-362 - Speaker System - KLIPSCH GROUP, INC.; *pg.* 649, *pg.* 688
KIA ORA - Beverages - THE COCA-COLA COMPANY; *pg.* 240, *pg.* 493
KIBBLES & CHUNKS - Dog Food - NESTLE PURINA PETCARE COMPANY; *pg.* 1479, *pg.* 1000
KIBBLES 'N BITS - Dog Treats - BIG HEART PET BRANDS; *pg.* 1474, *pg.* 213
KIC - Kitchen Appliance - WHIRLPOOL CORPORATION; *pg.* 62, *pg.* 872
KICK - Cutting Tool - LEATHERMAN TOOL GROUP, INC.; *pg.* 1053, *pg.* 1504
KICK - Office Furniture - STEELCASE INC.; *pg.* 475, *pg.* 889
KICK FREESTANDING - Office Furniture - STEELCASE INC.; *pg.* 475, *pg.* 889
KICK-IT - Cure Accelerator - SMOOTH-ON INC.; *pg.* 111, *pg.* 1528
KICKAPOO JOY JUICE - Beverage - THE MONARCH BEVERAGE COMPANY, INC.; *pg.* 257, *pg.* 514
KICKBOX - DVD - GAIAM, INC.; *pg.* 1532, *pg.* 334
THE KICKER - Lottery Game - OHIO LOTTERY COMMISSION; *pg.* 1002, *pg.* 1433
KICKIN' KENO - Video Game - INTERNATIONAL GAME TECHNOLOGY; *pg.* 957, *pg.* 1024
KICKITS - Doll - TONNER DOLL COMPANY, INC.; *pg.* 968, *pg.* 1171
KICKS - Hosiery & Related Apparel - MAYER/BERKSHIRE CORPORATION; *pg.* 29, *pg.* 1129
KICKSTART - Reality Show - MAVERIK COUNTRY STORES, INC.; *pg.* 1027, *pg.* 1752
KICNET - Telemarketing Services - EASTMAN KODAK COMPANY; *pg.* 1408, *pg.* 1333
KID BUILDERS - Gymnastic Playground Equipment - RUBBERMAID HOME PRODUCTS; *pg.* 1138, *pg.* 1453
KID CUISINE - Food Product - CONAGRA FOODS, INC.; *pg.* 826, *pg.* 1014
KID DEFENDER - Software - ACTIONTEC ELECTRONICS, INC.; *pg.* 342, *pg.* 282
KID KLEEN - Toy - SPIN MASTER LTD.; *pg.* 967, *pg.* 1943
KID MOTION - Toy & Game - HASBRO, INC.; *pg.* 954, *pg.* 1603
KID TESTED KID APPOVED - Tag Line - TYSON FOODS, INC.; *pg.* 902, *pg.* 35
KIDABC'S - Educational Product - BARKER CREEK PUBLISHING INC.; *pg.* 1619, *pg.* 1818
KIDDIE CHEESE - Food Product - ZAXBY'S FRANCHISING, INC.; *pg.* 1756, *pg.* 486
KIDDIE FINGER - Food Product - ZAXBY'S FRANCHISING, INC.; *pg.* 1756, *pg.* 486
KIDDIGEM - Jewelry - UNCAS MANUFACTURING COMPANY; *pg.* 15, *pg.* 1608
KIDHAVEN PRESS - Publisher - GALE CENGAGE LEARNING; *pg.* 1643, *pg.* 885
KIDKARE - Pharmaceutical Product - ALLERGAN; *pg.* 1490, *pg.* 1101
KIDMATH - Educational Product - BARKER CREEK PUBLISHING INC.; *pg.* 1619, *pg.* 1818
KIDPHONICS - Educational Product - BARKER CREEK PUBLISHING INC.; *pg.* 1619, *pg.* 1818
KIDREAD - Educational Product - BARKER CREEK PUBLISHING INC.; *pg.* 1619, *pg.* 1818
KIDS - Cameras - EASTMAN KODAK COMPANY; *pg.* 1408, *pg.* 1333
KIDS-A-MILLION - Book - BOOKS-A-MILLION, INC.; *pg.* 1623, *pg.* 2
KIDS ARE AUTHORS - Educational Materials - SCHOLASTIC INC.; *pg.* 1683, *pg.* 1288
KIDS ARE AUTHORS AWARD - Educational Materials - SCHOLASTIC INC.; *pg.* 1683, *pg.* 1288
KIDS CAPS AND CASH - Cash Redemption Program For Schools - FOREMOST FARMS USA COOPERATIVE; *pg.* 856, *pg.* 1854
KIDS' CHOICE - Modular Playsystem - MIRACLE RECREATION EQUIPMENT COMPANY; *pg.* 1839, *pg.* 988
KIDS CLUB - Children's Meals, Activities - BURGER KING CORPORATION; *pg.* 1719, *pg.* 440
KID'S COMPANION - Vitamin & Dietary Supplement - NATROL, INC.; *pg.* 1570, *pg.* 64
KID'S COURT - Basketball Court - LIFETIME PRODUCTS INC.; *pg.* 933, *pg.* 1751
KIDS FOOT LOCKER - Children's Athletic Footwear & Apparel - FOOT LOCKER, INC.; *pg.* 1808, *pg.* 1231
KIDS KITCHEN - Microwave Meals - HORMEL FOODS CORPORATION; *pg.* 863, *pg.* 915
KIDS MD - Syndicated Television Programming - CWK NETWORK, INC.; *pg.* 281, *pg.* 503
KIDS NEXT DOOR - Game & TV Show - THE CARTOON NETWORK; *pg.* 273, *pg.* 492
KIDS ON STAGE - Game - UNIVERSITY GAMES CORPORATION; *pg.* 969, *pg.* 230
KIDS TIME BUBBLE BATH - Bath Products - BLUE CROSS LABORATORIES; *pg.* 326, *pg.* 277
KIDS TRAVEL - Magazine - SCHOLASTIC INC.; *pg.* 1683, *pg.* 1288
KIDS WILDLIFE FLOSSUPS - Floss - RANIR LLC; *pg.* 520, *pg.* 888
KIDSCRAFT - Craft Sticks & Pipe Cleaners - HENKEL CONSUMER ADHESIVES, INC.; *pg.* 403, *pg.* 1480
KIDSEARS - Pharmaceutical Product - PFIZER INC.; *pg.* 1581, *pg.* 1278
KIDSEED - Seed - PLANTATION PRODUCTS INC; *pg.* 1799, *pg.* 839
KIDSHAPES - Educational Product - BARKER CREEK PUBLISHING INC.; *pg.* 1619, *pg.* 1818
KIDSKETCH - Educational Materials - SCHOLASTIC INC.; *pg.* 1683, *pg.* 1288
KIDSPIRATION - Software Tools for K-5 Learners - INSPIRATION SOFTWARE, INC.; *pg.* 1653, *pg.* 1503
KIDSSCAPE - Wall Designs & Borders, Self-Adhesive Vinyl Coverings for Children's Rooms - RUBBERMAID HOME PRODUCTS; *pg.* 1138, *pg.* 1453
KIDSTA - Medical Device - RESMED INC.; *pg.* 1589, *pg.* 207
KIDSWORLD - Superstore Encompassing All 3 "R" Us Concepts Under 1 Roof - TOYS "R" US, INC.; *pg.* 968, *pg.* 1130
KIDTIVITY - Children's Organization Products - HOME PRODUCTS INTERNATIONAL, INC.; *pg.* 1125, *pg.* 577
KIDUSA - Educational Product - BARKER CREEK PUBLISHING INC.; *pg.* 1619, *pg.* 1818
KIDVANTAGE - Retail Services - SEARS HOLDINGS CORPORATION; *pg.* 1784, *pg.* 618
KIDWICH - Ice Cream and Frozen Novelties - UNILEVER CANADA INC.; *pg.* 903, *pg.* 1946
KIDWORDS - Educational Product - BARKER CREEK PUBLISHING INC.; *pg.* 1619, *pg.* 1818
KIDWORKS - Beverage Ware - WHIRLEY INDUSTRIES, INC.; *pg.* 1892, *pg.* 1590
KIEHL'S - Cosmetics - L'OREAL USA; *pg.* 514, *pg.* 1252
KIENINGER - Clocks - HOWARD MILLER COMPANY; *pg.* 7, *pg.* 914
KIESZ - Medical Device - BOSTON SCIENTIFIC CORPORATION; *pg.* 1508, *pg.* 831
KIGGEN - Truck Product - OSHKOSH CORPORATION; *pg.* 187, *pg.* 1885
KILAUEA FREE SPIN ERUPTION - Game - WMS INDUSTRIES INC.; *pg.* 593, *pg.* 666
KILBURN BOOT - Clothing - ABERCROMBIE & FITCH CO.; *pg.* 37, *pg.* 1466
KILGORE FLARES - Flares - KILGORE FLARES; *pg.* 1170, *pg.* 1656
KILIM MOTIF - Carpet - INTERFACE, INC.; *pg.* 695, *pg.* 512
KILIMANJARO - Beverages - THE COCA-COLA COMPANY; *pg.* 240, *pg.* 493
KILIMANJARO - Video Game - INTERNATIONAL GAME TECHNOLOGY; *pg.* 957, *pg.* 1024
KILKENNY - Footwear - SAUCONY, INC.; *pg.* 1818, *pg.* 828
KILKENNY - Fabric - SCALAMANDRE, INC.; *pg.* 941, *pg.* 1058
KILL-A-WATT - Energy Saving Program - COMVERGE, INC.; *pg.* 1325, *pg.* 536
KILLARK - Electrical Product - HUBBELL INCORPORATED; *pg.* 1299, *pg.* 370
KILLARNEY - Furniture - FLEXSTEEL INDUSTRIES, INC.; *pg.* 925, *pg.* 707
KILLER - Television Reception Product - WINEGARD COMPANY; *pg.* 688, *pg.* 702
KILLER BEE - Gaming Product - GLD PRODUCTS, INC.; *pg.* 1835, *pg.* 1882
KILLER BEE - Golf Equipment - GOLFSMITH INTERNATIONAL HOLDINGS, INC.; *pg.* 1835, *pg.* 1662
KILLER CASH - Video Game - INTERNATIONAL GAME TECHNOLOGY; *pg.* 957, *pg.* 1024
KILLEX - Lawn & Garden Products - THE SCOTTS MIRACLE-GRO COMPANY; *pg.* 1799, *pg.* 1459
KILLFIRE - Hybrid String - ASHAWAY LINE & TWINE MFG. CO.; *pg.* 1826, *pg.* 1600
KILN - Salt - CARGILL LIMITED; *pg.* 1475, *pg.* 1914
KILO - Beverage - GREEN SPOT, INC.; *pg.* 251, *pg.* 68
KILOBASEPACK - Software - BIO-RAD LABORATORIES, INC.; *pg.* 1504, *pg.* 101
KILOHANA - Eyewear - MAUI JIM, INC.; *pg.* 9, *pg.* 651
KILSTAIN - Stain Killer - AKZONOBEL DECORATIVE PAINTS U.S.; *pg.* 1439, *pg.* 1474

KILSTAIN WB - Waterborne Primer-Sealer - AKZONOBEL DECORATIVE PAINTS U.S.; pg. 1439, pg. 1474
KILTER - Fabric - NEMSCHOFF, INC.; pg. 936, pg. 1890
KILZ - Decorative Architectural Product - MASCO CORPORATION; pg. 96, pg. 909
KIM - Lighting Product - HUBBELL INCORPORATED; pg. 1299, pg. 370
KIM CRAWFORD - Wine - CONSTELLATION BRANDS CANADA; pg. 1960, pg. 1925
KIM CRAWFORD - Wine - CONSTELLATION BRANDS, INC.; pg. 1960, pg. 1348
KIM POSSIBLE - Game - HASBRO, INC.; pg. 954, pg. 1603
KIMBALL HOSPITALITY - Hospitality Furniture - KIMBALL INTERNATIONAL, INC.; pg. 931, pg. 692
KIMBALL OFFICE - Office Furniture - KIMBALL INTERNATIONAL, INC.; pg. 931, pg. 692
KIMBERLY-CLARK - Wiper And Disposable Product - KIMBERLY-CLARK CORPORATION; pg. 1461, pg. 1720
KIMCO ACTUATOR - Actuators - CUSTOM SENSORS & TECHNOLOGIES; pg. 1407, pg. 152
KIMDURA - Paper - NEENAH PAPER, INC.; pg. 1465, pg. 484
KIMGUARD - Sterile Wrap - KIMBERLY-CLARK CORPORATION; pg. 1461, pg. 1720
KIMLON - Papers - NEENAH PAPER, INC.; pg. 1465, pg. 484
KIMONO - Fabric - NEMSCHOFF, INC.; pg. 936, pg. 1890
KIMTECH - Skin Care Product - KIMBERLY-CLARK CORPORATION; pg. 1461, pg. 1720
KIMWIPES - Towels - KIMBERLY-CLARK CORPORATION; pg. 1461, pg. 1720
KIN - Beverages - THE COCA-COLA COMPANY; pg. 240, pg. 493
KINAIR - Bed Therapy System - KINETIC CONCEPTS, INC.; pg. 1553, pg. 1741
KINCAID - Furniture - LA-Z-BOY INCORPORATED; pg. 932, pg. 901
KINCAID'S FISH, CHOP & STEAK HOUSE - Restaurant Chain - RESTAURANTS UNLIMITED, INC.; pg. 1748, pg. 1839
KIND NEWS - Newsletter - THE HUMANE SOCIETY OF THE UNITED STATES; pg. 143, pg. 400
KINDEL - Furniture - KINDEL FURNITURE COMPANY; pg. 931, pg. 887
KINDERGARD - Security & Law Enforcement Products - MACE SECURITY INTERNATIONAL, INC.; pg. 1172, pg. 1541
KINDERMINS - Vitamins for Infants & Children - HERBALIFE INTERNATIONAL OF AMERICA, INC.; pg. 1541, pg. 132
KINDEST KARE - Skin Care Product - STERIS CORPORATION; pg. 1597, pg. 1464
KINDLE - Electronic Reader Device - AMAZON.COM, INC.; pg. 1226, pg. 1831
KINDLE FIRE - Multimedia Device - AMAZON.COM, INC.; pg. 1226, pg. 1831
KINDORF - Metal Framing - THOMAS & BETTS CORPORATION; pg. 680, pg. 1646
KINEDIZER - Burner - MAXON CORPORATION; pg. 1359, pg. 695
KINEL - Polyimide - HUNTSMAN CORPORATION; pg. 1167, pg. 1758
KINEMA - Pump - GARDNER DENVER NASH; pg. 1338, pg. 381
KINEMAP - Topographical & Geological Computer Software - LOCKHEED MARTIN CORPORATION; pg. 229, pg. 762
KINEMAT - Furniture - HERMAN MILLER, INC.; pg. 926, pg. 913
KINEMAX - Glass Polishing Material - FERRO CORPORATION; pg. 1162, pg. 1462
KINEMAX - Burner - MAXON CORPORATION; pg. 1359, pg. 695
KINERASE - Pharmaceutical Product - VALEANT PHARMACEUTICALS INTERNATIONAL; pg. 1605, pg. 1047
KINERET - Food Product - THE HAIN CELESTIAL GROUP, INC.; pg. 860, pg. 1172
KINESIO - Medical & Aesthetic Product - DYNATRONICS CORPORATION; pg. 1526, pg. 1757
KINESIS - Software - BIO-RAD LABORATORIES, INC.; pg. 1504, pg. 101
KINESIS - Carpet - INTERFACE, INC.; pg. 695, pg. 512
KINETA WALK - Footwear - SAUCONY, INC.; pg. 1818, pg. 828
KINETIC - Ride Control Technology - TENNECO, INC.; pg. 985, pg. 625
KINETIC COLLECTOR - Software - BIO-RAD LABORATORIES, INC.; pg. 1504, pg. 101
KINETIC REFLEX - Wire Stripper - IDEAL INDUSTRIES, INC.; pg. 1051, pg. 662
KINETIC SUPER - Wire Stripper - IDEAL INDUSTRIES, INC.; pg. 1051, pg. 662
KINETIC THERAPHY - Therapy System - KINETIC CONCEPTS, INC.; pg. 1553, pg. 1741
KINETICS - Furniture - HAWORTH, INC.; pg. 402, pg. 891
KINETIX - Electrostatic Spray System - NORDSON CORPORATION; pg. 1365, pg. 1480
KINETIX - Software - ROCKWELL AUTOMATION, INC.; pg. 668, pg. 1880
KINETRA - Deep Brain Stimulator - MEDTRONIC, INC.; pg. 1564, pg. 939
KINFITSIM - Software - BIOANALYTICAL SYSTEMS, INC.; pg. 1402, pg. 700
KING - Sporting Goods - BRUNSWICK BOWLING & BILLIARDS CORP.; pg. 1828, pg. 622
KING CASH - Slots - INTERNATIONAL GAME TECHNOLOGY; pg. 957, pg. 1024
KING COBRA - Malt Liquor - ANHEUSER-BUSCH COMPANIES, LLC; pg. 237, pg. 991
KING COBRA - Bicycle Accessories - SPECIALIZED BICYCLE COMPONENTS, INC.; pg. 1711, pg. 152
KING COBRA - Heavy Duty Clamps - THOMAS & BETTS CORPORATION; pg. 680, pg. 1646
KING CUT - Power & Hand Tools - THE L.S. STARRETT COMPANY; pg. 1421, pg. 783
KING CUTTER - PDC Bits - BAKER HUGHES INTEQ; pg. 1316, pg. 1700
KING EDWARD - Cigar - SWISHER INTERNATIONAL, INC.; pg. 1895, pg. 345
KING JAMES - Flatware - ONEIDA LTD; pg. 1129, pg. 1318
KING KAT - Fishing Equipment - CABELA'S INCORPORATED; pg. 535, pg. 1019
KING KUTTER - Specialty cutters - LINCOLN FOODSERVICE PRODUCTS, LLC; pg. 1127, pg. 1432
KING MIDAS - Game - WMS INDUSTRIES INC.; pg. 593, pg. 666
KING NUT - Nuts - KANAN ENTERPRISES, INC.; pg. 1857, pg. 1473
KING-O-PEDIC - Mattresses - KINGSDOWN, INC.; pg. 932, pg. 1383
KING O SEAS - Seafood - BON SECOUR FISHERIES INC.; pg. 841, pg. 5
KING OF AFRICA - Game - WMS INDUSTRIES INC.; pg. 593, pg. 666
KING OF BEERS - Slogan - ANHEUSER-BUSCH COMPANIES, LLC; pg. 237, pg. 991
KING OF THE GRILL - Video Game - INTERNATIONAL GAME TECHNOLOGY; pg. 957, pg. 1024
KING OF THE ROAD - 5th Wheel & Travel Trailers - CHIEF INDUSTRIES, INC.; pg. 1323, pg. 1010
KING OF THE WILD - Game - WMS INDUSTRIES INC.; pg. 593, pg. 666
KING OSCAR - Seafood - BUMBLE BEE FOODS LLC; pg. 842, pg. 201
KING PANTRY - Canned Good - STROHMEYER & ARPE COMPANY; pg. 899, pg. 1042
KING PELICANLITE - Flashlight - PELICAN PRODUCTS, INC.; pg. 1842, pg. 295
KING PIN BOWLING - Video Game - INTERNATIONAL GAME TECHNOLOGY; pg. 957, pg. 1024
KING-SHROUD - Fluid Handling System - GRACO, INC.; pg. 1342, pg. 935
KING SOOPERS - Supermarket - THE KROGER CO.; pg. 1025, pg. 1416
KING VITAMIN - Cereal - THE QUAKER OATS COMPANY; pg. 834, pg. 588
KINGALEY - Shoes - ALLEN-EDMONDS SHOE CORP.; pg. 1804, pg. 1887
KINGDOM OF GOLD - Video Game - INTERNATIONAL GAME TECHNOLOGY; pg. 957, pg. 1024
KINGDOM OF THE DINOSAURS - Thrill Ride - KNOTT'S BERRY FARM; pg. 556, pg. 50
KINGDOM OF THE TITANS - Game - WMS INDUSTRIES INC.; pg. 593, pg. 666
KINGFIELD - Shoes - ALLEN-EDMONDS SHOE CORP.; pg. 1804, pg. 1887
KINGLINE - Dinnerware - CARLISLE FOODSERVICE PRODUCTS INCORPORATED; pg. 1455, pg. 1485
KINGS CRIBBAGE - Game - WINNING MOVES GAMES, INC.; pg. 970, pg. 816
KINGS CROWN - Scotch - MONTEBELLO BRANDS INC.; pg. 1967, pg. 758
KINGS DOMINION - Amusement Park - CEDAR FAIR, L.P.; pg. 537, pg. 1471
KINGS HAWAIIAN - Logo - KING'S HAWAIIAN BAKERY WEST, INC.; pg. 869, pg. 293
KINGS ISLAND - Amusement Park - CEDAR FAIR, L.P.; pg. 537, pg. 1471
KINGS ROAD - Carpet - INTERFACE, INC.; pg. 695, pg. 512
KINGSBURY - Beer - PABST BREWING COMPANY; pg. 258, pg. 137
KINGSDOWN POSTURE - Sleeping Sofa Mattress - KINGSDOWN, INC.; pg. 932, pg. 1383
KINGSDOWN TUFF GRIP - Mattress Handles - KINGSDOWN, INC.; pg. 932, pg. 1383
KINGSFORD - Charcoal Briquets & Lighter Fluid & Grill Cleaner - THE CLOROX COMPANY; pg. 327, pg. 169
KINGSFORD BBQ BAG - Single-Use, Lightable Bag of Charcoal Briquettes - THE CLOROX COMPANY; pg. 327, pg. 169
KINGSFORD MATCH LIGHT - Instant-Lighting Charcoal Briquets - THE CLOROX COMPANY; pg. 327, pg. 169
KINGSIZE - Apparel - FULLBEAUTY BRANDS; pg. 1770, pg. 1233
KINGSLEY - Bathroom Faucet - MOEN INCORPORATED; pg. 1056, pg. 1468
KINGSMEN - Plastic Cutlery - MARYLAND PLASTICS, INC.; pg. 1885, pg. 769
KINGSTON - Furniture - BUSH INDUSTRIES INC.; pg. 919, pg. 1170
KINIGHT DRANZER - Toy & Game - HASBRO, INC.; pg. 954, pg. 1603
KINKY - Footwear - STEVEN MADDEN, LTD.; pg. 1819, pg. 1176
KINLEY - Soft Drink - THE COCA-COLA COMPANY; pg. 240, pg. 493
KINNEY - Pump - TUTHILL CORPORATION; pg. 1385, pg. 561
KINO ON VIDEO - Video & DVD Catalog - KINO INTERNATIONAL CORP.; pg. 294, pg. 1249
KIODEX - Software - SUNGARD DATA SYSTEMS INC.; pg. 477, pg. 1592
KIOVIG - Healthcare Product - BAXTER INTERNATIONAL INC.; pg. 1499, pg. 599
KIPLING - Apparel - V.F. CORPORATION; pg. 34, pg. 1376
KIPLINGER AGRICULTURAL LETTER - Publication - THE KIPLINGER WASHINGTON EDITORS, INC.; pg. 1657, pg. 401
KIPLINGER CALIFORNIA LETTER - Publication - THE KIPLINGER WASHINGTON EDITORS, INC.; pg. 1657, pg. 401
THE KIPLINGER LETTER - Publication - THE KIPLINGER WASHINGTON EDITORS, INC.; pg. 1657, pg. 401
KIPLINGER PERSONAL FINANCE - Publication - THE KIPLINGER WASHINGTON EDITORS, INC.; pg. 1657, pg. 401
KIPLINGER TAX LETTER - Publication - THE KIPLINGER WASHINGTON EDITORS, INC.; pg. 1657, pg. 401
KIPLINGER TAXCUT - Software - THE KIPLINGER WASHINGTON EDITORS, INC.; pg. 1657, pg. 401
KIPLINGERFORCAST.COM - Subscription Based Website - THE KIPLINGER WASHINGTON EDITORS, INC.; pg. 1657, pg. 401
KIPLINGER'S HOME LEGAL ADVISOR - Software - THE KIPLINGER WASHINGTON EDITORS, INC.; pg. 1657, pg. 401
KIPLINGER'S MUTUAL FUNDS - Annual Magazine - THE KIPLINGER WASHINGTON EDITORS, INC.; pg. 1657, pg. 401
KIPLINGER'S PERSONAL FINANCE - Magazine - THE KIPLINGER WASHINGTON EDITORS, INC.; pg. 1657, pg. 401
KIPLINGER'S RETIREMENT REPORT - Magazine - THE KIPLINGER WASHINGTON EDITORS, INC.; pg. 1657, pg. 401
KIPLINGER'S SMALL BUSINESS ATTORNEY - Software - THE KIPLINGER WASHINGTON EDITORS, INC.; pg. 1657, pg. 401
KIRA - Fan - CRAFTMADE INTERNATIONAL, INC.; pg. 1295, pg. 1670
KIRK - Phone - POLYCOM, INC.; pg. 664, pg. 249
KIRKLAND SIGNATURE - Private Label Products - COSTCO WHOLESALE CORPORATION; pg. 1765, pg. 1820
KIRKLAND'S - Home Decor Retailers - KIRKLAND'S INC.; pg. 1126, pg. 1652
KIRKWOOD - Shoes - ALLEN-EDMONDS SHOE CORP.; pg.

1804, *pg.* 1887

KIRRA - Footwear - COBIAN CORP.; *pg.* 1806, *pg.* 253

KIRSCH - Window Blinds - NEWELL RUBBERMAID INC.; *pg.* 1128, *pg.* 515

KIRSCHNER - Processed Food - KAYEM FOODS, INC.; *pg.* 867, *pg.* 814

KIRSTEN - Dolls - AMERICAN GIRL LLC; *pg.* 949, *pg.* 1871

KIRSTEN LARSON - Dolls - AMERICAN GIRL LLC; *pg.* 949, *pg.* 1871

KIRSTEN'S BIRTHDAY TEA - Dolls - AMERICAN GIRL LLC; *pg.* 949, *pg.* 1871

KISMET - Textiles - BERNHARDT DESIGN; *pg.* 918, *pg.* 1381

KISS - Series of How-To-Guides - DK PUBLISHING; *pg.* 1636, *pg.* 1224

KISS THIS GLOSS - Lip Color - THE BONNE BELL COMPANY; *pg.* 502, *pg.* 1480

KISSBIND - Semiconductor Solution - CYPRESS SEMICONDUCTOR CORPORATION; *pg.* 1326, *pg.* 243

KISSIMEE - Bear - GUND, INC.; *pg.* 954, *pg.* 1056

KISTLER MORSE - Level Measurement Solution - DANAHER CORPORATION; *pg.* 1044, *pg.* 397

KIT - Dolls - AMERICAN GIRL LLC; *pg.* 949, *pg.* 1871

KIT - No Buff Wax - S.C. JOHNSON & SON, INC.; *pg.* 334, *pg.* 1889

KIT & CAT - Cat Food - KENT NUTRITION GROUP; *pg.* 1477, *pg.* 710

KIT CAR - Magazine - RENTPATH, INC.; *pg.* 1680, *pg.* 538

KIT E KAT - Cat Food - MARS, INCORPORATED; *pg.* 1858, *pg.* 1792

KIT KITTREDGE - Dolls - AMERICAN GIRL LLC; *pg.* 949, *pg.* 1871

KIT 'N KABOODLE - Cat Food - NESTLE PURINA PETCARE COMPANY; *pg.* 1479, *pg.* 1000

KITCHEN AND BATH IDEAS - Magazine - MEREDITH CORPORATION; *pg.* 1663, *pg.* 705

KITCHEN & COOK - Culinary Magazine - BELVOIR MEDIA GROUP, LLC; *pg.* 1620, *pg.* 360

KITCHEN BOUQUET - Browning & Seasoning Sauce & Gravy Aid - THE CLOROX COMPANY; *pg.* 327, *pg.* 169

KITCHEN CLASSICS - Soup - CAMPBELL SOUP COMPANY; *pg.* 844, *pg.* 1048

KITCHEN CLASSICS - Cabinetry - MASTERBRAND CABINETS, INC.; *pg.* 96, *pg.* 692

KITCHEN CRAFT - Hardware - FORTUNE BRANDS HOME & SECURITY, INC.; *pg.* 55, *pg.* 600

KITCHEN CRAFT - Cabinetry - MASTERBRAND CABINETS, INC.; *pg.* 96, *pg.* 692

KITCHEN CROP - Sprouter - PLANTATION PRODUCTS INC; *pg.* 1799, *pg.* 839

KITCHEN ESSENTIALS - Food Service - GORDON FOOD SERVICE INC.; *pg.* 1021, *pg.* 913

KITCHEN FRESH - Waste Bags - PACTIV CORPORATION; *pg.* 1466, *pg.* 624

KITCHEN HELPERS - Kitchen Gadget - HY-VEE, INC.; *pg.* 1023, *pg.* 713

KITCHEN KETTLE - Electrical Appliance & Housewares - NATIONAL PRESTO INDUSTRIES, INC; *pg.* 1128, *pg.* 1857

KITCHEN MASTER - Packaging Product - GRAPHIC PACKAGING HOLDING COMPANY; *pg.* 1459, *pg.* 509

KITCHEN RX - Kitchen Cleaner - BLUE CROSS LABORATORIES; *pg.* 326, *pg.* 277

KITCHENAID - Home Appliance Product - WHIRLPOOL CORPORATION; *pg.* 62, *pg.* 872

KITCHENJET - Computer Printers - TRANSACT TECHNOLOGIES INCORPORATED; *pg.* 484, *pg.* 351

KITCHENMATE - Cabinet Door Pantry Rack - OMEGA NATIONAL PRODUCTS; *pg.* 939, *pg.* 737

KITCHENS - Magazine - MEREDITH CORPORATION; *pg.* 1663, *pg.* 705

KITEBOARDING - Magazine - BONNIER CORPORATION; *pg.* 1622, *pg.* 480

THE KITSAP SUN - Newspaper - THE E.W. SCRIPPS COMPANY; *pg.* 1639, *pg.* 1412

KITTEN CHOW - Cat Food - NESTLE PURINA PETCARE COMPANY; *pg.* 1479, *pg.* 1000

KITTENS USA - Magazine - I-5 PUBLISHING LLC; *pg.* 1651, *pg.* 133

KITTENSOFT - Paper Towel - GEORGIA-PACIFIC LLC; *pg.* 1458, *pg.* 507

KITTY CORNERS - Game - GAMEWRIGHT; *pg.* 953, *pg.* 836

KITTY GLITTER - Video Game - INTERNATIONAL GAME TECHNOLOGY; *pg.* 957, *pg.* 1024

KITTY HAIR - Fiberglass Reinforced Filler - ITW - EVERCOAT; *pg.* 1443, *pg.* 1415

KITTY HAWK - Bath Product - KOHLER CO.; *pg.* 91, *pg.* 1862

KITVEYOR - Conveyor System - AUTOMATED PACKAGING SYSTEMS INC.; *pg.* 1452, *pg.* 1474

KIV-21 - Network System - VIASAT, INC.; *pg.* 489, *pg.* 62

KIVAR - Paper & Nonwoven Material - FIBERMARK INC.; *pg.* 1457, *pg.* 1764

KIVARFLEX - Paper & Nonwoven Material - FIBERMARK INC.; *pg.* 1457, *pg.* 1764

KIWAMI - Engine Oil - BARDAHL MANUFACTURING CORPORATION; *pg.* 972, *pg.* 1833

KIWI BERRY BURNER - Smoothie - JAMBA, INC.; *pg.* 1024, *pg.* 84

KIWI PEAR - Decorative Fragrance - AROMATIQUE INC.; *pg.* 499, *pg.* 32

KIWIBURGER - Fast Food - MCDONALD'S CORPORATION; *pg.* 1737, *pg.* 645

KIX - Cereal - GENERAL MILLS, INC.; *pg.* 828, *pg.* 933

KIYO - Conductor Etch System - LAM RESEARCH CORPORATION; *pg.* 1354, *pg.* 91

KIYO45 - Conductor Etch System - LAM RESEARCH CORPORATION; *pg.* 1354, *pg.* 91

KJRH, CHANNEL 2 (TULSA) - Television Broadcasting Station - THE E.W. SCRIPPS COMPANY; *pg.* 1639, *pg.* 1412

KL SERIES - Heavy-Duty Lighting - PHOENIX PRODUCTS COMPANY; *pg.* 1304, *pg.* 1879

KLA-TENCOR - Management Solutions - KLA-TENCOR CORPORATION; *pg.* 1353, *pg.* 146

KLACID - Macrolide Anti-Infective - ABBOTT LABORATORIES; *pg.* 1484, *pg.* 551

KLACIPED - Pharmaceutical Product - ABBOTT LABORATORIES; *pg.* 1484, *pg.* 551

KLAFOLD - Paperboard - WESTROCK COMPANY; *pg.* 1472, *pg.* 1805

KLARAID - Oily Waste Treatment - GE WATER & PROCESS TECHNOLOGIES; *pg.* 1339, *pg.* 1588

KLARICID - Pharmaceutical Product - ABBOTT LABORATORIES; *pg.* 1484, *pg.* 551

KLARITY - Medical & Aesthetic Product - DYNATRONICS CORPORATION; *pg.* 1526, *pg.* 1757

KLARITY - Bitmap Analysis - KLA-TENCOR CORPORATION; *pg.* 1353, *pg.* 146

KLARITY ACE XP - Correlation Engine - KLA-TENCOR CORPORATION; *pg.* 1353, *pg.* 146

KLARITY BITMAP - Bitmap Analysis for Yield Enhancement - KLA-TENCOR CORPORATION; *pg.* 1353, *pg.* 146

KLARITY DEFECT - Automated Defect Data Analysis Solution - KLA-TENCOR CORPORATION; *pg.* 1353, *pg.* 146

KLAUKE - Telecommunication Installation, Maintenance & Testing - TEXTRON INC.; *pg.* 235, *pg.* 1607

KLE DISHMACHINES - Pumps - IDEX CORPORATION; *pg.* 1347, *pg.* 623

KLEAN KUT - Dust Mop - HILLYARD, INC.; *pg.* 331, *pg.* 990

KLEAN STRIP - Paint - W.M. BARR & COMPANY, INC.; *pg.* 338, *pg.* 1647

KLEAN'N SHINE - Furniture Cleaner - S.C. JOHNSON & SON, INC.; *pg.* 334, *pg.* 1889

KLEAR - Cleaning Product - S.C. JOHNSON & SON, INC.; *pg.* 334, *pg.* 1889

KLEAR POR - Plastic Storage Products - HOME PRODUCTS INTERNATIONAL, INC.; *pg.* 1125, *pg.* 577

KLEAR STOR - Food Storage Product - HOME PRODUCTS INTERNATIONAL, INC.; *pg.* 1125, *pg.* 577

KLEAR-TRAC - Vinyl Matting - THE BILTRITE CORPORATION; *pg.* 1879, *pg.* 850

KLEAR-TRACE - Neonatal Product - CAS MEDICAL SYSTEMS, INC.; *pg.* 1513, *pg.* 339

KLEARFOLD - Paperboard Packaging Product - WESTROCK COMPANY; *pg.* 1472, *pg.* 1805

KLEBOSOL - Slurry - DOW CHEMICAL; *pg.* 1156, *pg.* 1563

KLEEN AND DRI - Wet Wipe - BOUMATIC LLC; *pg.* 701, *pg.* 1865

KLEEN BORE - Security Product - BAE SYSTEMS PRODUCTS GROUP; *pg.* 359, *pg.* 432

KLEEN-CHANGE - Filter Capsule - PALL CORPORATION; *pg.* 232, *pg.* 1323

KLEEN-GARD - Grease Filter - RESEARCH PRODUCTS CORPORATION; *pg.* 1075, *pg.* 1867

KLEEN-IT - Chemical Cleaner Product - TECH SPRAY, L.P.; *pg.* 1183, *pg.* 1659

KLEEN KING - Ironing & Cleaning Product - FAULTLESS STARCH/BON AMI COMPANY; *pg.* 330, *pg.* 982

KLEEN-KOIL - Cleaning Products - CLAYTON INDUSTRIES CO.; *pg.* 1323, *pg.* 66

KLEEN-KOOL - Cutting Fluid - THE DOALL COMPANY; *pg.* 1329, *pg.* 670

KLEEN POWER - Liquid Gel Cleaner - BLUE CROSS LABORATORIES; *pg.* 326, *pg.* 277

KLEEN-RITE - Rubber Matting - THE BILTRITE CORPORATION; *pg.* 1879, *pg.* 850

KLEEN SWEEPS - Cleaner - BROWN & BIGELOW, INC.; *pg.* 1624, *pg.* 959

KLEEN-TEAM - Automotive Scrub - 3M COMPANY; *pg.* 1142, *pg.* 956

KLEEN-UP SOLVENT - Cleaning Product - HILLYARD, INC.; *pg.* 331, *pg.* 990

KLEENALL - Filter - BARNES INTERNATIONAL INC.; *pg.* 1317, *pg.* 654

KLEENATRON - Drain Cleaning Products - JOSAM COMPANY; *pg.* 89, *pg.* 695

KLEENCUT - Scissors - ACME UNITED CORPORATION; *pg.* 1040, *pg.* 346

KLEENEARTH - Trimmers - ACME UNITED CORPORATION; *pg.* 1040, *pg.* 346

KLEENEX - Facial & Bathroom Tissue - KIMBERLY-CLARK CORPORATION; *pg.* 1461, *pg.* 1720

KLEENFAST - Cleaning Products - KATY INDUSTRIES, INC.; *pg.* 1126, *pg.* 973

KLEENGUARD - Disposable Garment - KIMBERLY-CLARK CORPORATION; *pg.* 1461, *pg.* 1720

KLEENPAK - Capsule Filter - PALL CORPORATION; *pg.* 232, *pg.* 1323

KLEENSEAL - Portable Lubrication System - LINCOLN INDUSTRIAL CORP.; *pg.* 1355, *pg.* 999

KLEENSPEC - Speculum Lighting System - WELCH ALLYN INC.; *pg.* 1436, *pg.* 1342

KLEENUP - Household Insect Control - BONIDE PRODUCTS, INC.; *pg.* 1794, *pg.* 1320

KLEER KOTE - Paint & Coating - AERVOE INDUSTRIES INCORPORATED; *pg.* 1439, *pg.* 1021

KLEER SEAL - Concrete Coating - DELTA FOREMOST CHEMICAL CORPORATION; *pg.* 1155, *pg.* 1642

KLEERMOUNT - Biological Supplies - CAROLINA BIOLOGICAL SUPPLY COMPANY; *pg.* 1513, *pg.* 1359

KLEERWATER - Oil Water Separator - MODERN WELDING COMPANY, INC.; *pg.* 1363, *pg.* 739

KLEIN - Road & Mountain Bike - TREK BICYCLE CORPORATION; *pg.* 1847, *pg.* 1896

KLEIN-BENFIELD - Conduit Benders - KLEIN TOOLS INC.; *pg.* 1052, *pg.* 627

KLEIN-FLEX - Fish Tape - KLEIN TOOLS INC.; *pg.* 1052, *pg.* 627

KLEIN HAVEN'S GRIP - Wire, Cable Pulling Grips - KLEIN TOOLS INC.; *pg.* 1052, *pg.* 627

KLEIN KLEANERS - Hand Cleaning Disposable Towels - KLEIN TOOLS INC.; *pg.* 1052, *pg.* 627

KLEIN-KURVE - Heavy-Duty Utility Knife - KLEIN TOOLS INC.; *pg.* 1052, *pg.* 627

KLEIN-LITE - Non-Metallic Fish Tapes - KLEIN TOOLS INC.; *pg.* 1052, *pg.* 627

KLENZ-GLIDE - Conveyor Sanitizer & Lubricant - ECOLAB INC.; *pg.* 329, *pg.* 960

KLENZYME - Enzyme - STERIS CORPORATION; *pg.* 1597, *pg.* 1464

KLF-30 - Loudspeaker - KLIPSCH GROUP, INC.; *pg.* 649, *pg.* 688

KLIKXX - Earrings - INVERNESS CORPORATION; *pg.* 512, *pg.* 783

KLIMATEPRO - Paperboard - CARAUSTAR INDUSTRIES, INC.; *pg.* 1455, *pg.* 525

KLING - Table - BLATT BOWLING & BILLIARD CORP.; *pg.* 1827, *pg.* 1203

KLINGONS - Wall Sticker - CANDID COLOR SYSTEMS, INC.; *pg.* 1404, *pg.* 1485

KLING'S - Theatrical Shoes - EL CHARRO LLC; *pg.* 1808, *pg.* 1691

KLIPMART - Digital Marketing Product - DOUBLECLICK, INC.; *pg.* 1239, *pg.* 1225

KLIPPER KING - Clipper - BROWN & BIGELOW, INC.; *pg.* 1624, *pg.* 959

KLIPSCHORN - Electronic Equipment - KLIPSCH GROUP, INC.; *pg.* 649, *pg.* 688

KLIX - Vending Machines - MARS, INCORPORATED; *pg.* 1858, *pg.* 1792

KLIXON - Temperature Controlled Electric Switches - TEXAS INSTRUMENTS INCORPORATED; *pg.* 679, *pg.* 1688

KLM BY ANDERSEN - Entrance Ways - ANDERSEN

CORPORATION; *pg.* 67, *pg.* 916
KLONDIKE - Ice Cream - UNILEVER UNITED STATES, INC.; *pg.* 904, *pg.* 1061
KLONDIKE TREASURE - Video Game - INTERNATIONAL GAME TECHNOLOGY; *pg.* 957, *pg.* 1024
KLONDIKERS - Plastic Blocks - PACON CORPORATION; *pg.* 1466, *pg.* 1852
KLONOPIN - Pharmaceutical Product - HOFFMANN-LA ROCHE INC.; *pg.* 1542, *pg.* 1099
KLP - Selective Hydrogenation Technology for Use in Butadiene Purification - UOP LLC; *pg.* 1386, *pg.* 606
KLUCEL - Polymer - HERCULES INCORPORATED; *pg.* 1166, *pg.* 392
KLUTZ - Educational Materials - SCHOLASTIC INC.; *pg.* 1683, *pg.* 1288
KLUTZ BOOK FACTORY - Educational Materials - SCHOLASTIC INC.; *pg.* 1683, *pg.* 1288
KLUTZ GALACTIC HEADQUARTERS - Educational Materials - SCHOLASTIC INC.; *pg.* 1683, *pg.* 1288
KLUTZ KWIZ - Educational Materials - SCHOLASTIC INC.; *pg.* 1683, *pg.* 1288
KLUTZ TO GO - Educational Materials - SCHOLASTIC INC.; *pg.* 1683, *pg.* 1288
KM - Metal Cutting Tools - KENNAMETAL INC.; *pg.* 1052, *pg.* 1547
KM - Continuous Mixers - LITTLEFORD DAY INC.; *pg.* 1356, *pg.* 728
KM-2 - Loudspeaker - KLIPSCH GROUP, INC.; *pg.* 649, *pg.* 688
KM PROFESSIONAL - Paint - KELLY-MOORE PAINT COMPANY, INC.; *pg.* 1443, *pg.* 198
THE KNACK - Razor - THE GILLETTE COMPANY; *pg.* 509, *pg.* 795
KNACK AND BACK - Food Product - GENERAL MILLS, INC.; *pg.* 828, *pg.* 933
KNAPPOGUE CASTLE WHISKEY - Whiskey - CASTLE BRANDS INC.; *pg.* 239, *pg.* 1209
KNEE-PRO ULTRA FLEX III - Knee Pad - SELLSTROM MANUFACTURING CO.; *pg.* 1428, *pg.* 659
KNEEFIX - Medical Device - GAMMEX RMI INC.; *pg.* 1532, *pg.* 1872
KNEEL-EZE - Knee Pad - SELLSTROM MANUFACTURING CO.; *pg.* 1428, *pg.* 659
KNEERELIEF - Pharmaceutical Product - ALVA/AMCO PHARMACAL COMPANIES, INC.; *pg.* 1492, *pg.* 637
KNET LT - Bonder Connectivity Product - KULICKE & SOFFA INDUSTRIES, INC.; *pg.* 650, *pg.* 1533
KNICKERBOCKER - Furniture - NEMSCHOFF, INC.; *pg.* 936, *pg.* 1890
KNICKERS IRISH CREAM WHISKY - Distilled Spirits - HOOD RIVER DISTILLERS INC.; *pg.* 1964, *pg.* 1498
KNIFELIGHT - Micro Implant System - STRYKER CORPORATION; *pg.* 1598, *pg.* 894
KNIGHT - Knife - BUCK KNIVES, INC.; *pg.* 1828, *pg.* 550
KNIGHT - Dispensing Equipment - IDEX CORPORATION; *pg.* 1347, *pg.* 623
KNIGHT & HALE - Game Calls - EBSCO INDUSTRIES, INC.; *pg.* 1638, *pg.* 2
KNIGHT MOVES - Video Game - INTERNATIONAL GAME TECHNOLOGY; *pg.* 957, *pg.* 1024
KNIGHTCOTE - Coating - CARPENTER TECHNOLOGY CORPORATION; *pg.* 73, *pg.* 1584
KNIGHTS & DRAGONS - Game - WMS INDUSTRIES INC.; *pg.* 593, *pg.* 666
KNIGHTS INN - Hotels - WYNDHAM WORLDWIDE CORPORATION; *pg.* 1119, *pg.* 1107
KNIGHT'S QUEST - Game - INTERNATIONAL GAME TECHNOLOGY; *pg.* 420, *pg.* 1606
KNIGHTSBRIDGE - Computer Bag - A. T. CROSS COMPANY; *pg.* 339, *pg.* 1602
KNIGHTSDALE PINOT NOIR - Wine - WEIBEL, INC.; *pg.* 1972, *pg.* 122
KNIT SHORT - Clothing - K-SWISS; *pg.* 1837, *pg.* 306
KNIT SPORT SHORT - Clothing - K-SWISS; *pg.* 1837, *pg.* 306
KNIT TO BE TRIED - Blouses - HABAND COMPANY, INC.; *pg.* 1772, *pg.* 1099
KNITTEX - Textile Finishes - HUNTSMAN CORPORATION; *pg.* 1167, *pg.* 1758
KNITTING DIGEST - Crafts Magazine - ANNIE'S; *pg.* 1617, *pg.* 673
KNOB CREEK - Bourbon - JIM BEAM BRANDS CO.; *pg.* 1965, *pg.* 601
KNOB HILL - Rug - COURISTAN INC.; *pg.* 921, *pg.* 1067
KNOBPOT - Electrical Apparatus - BOURNS, INC.; *pg.* 627, *pg.* 193
KNOCK DOWN - Slots - INTERNATIONAL GAME TECHNOLOGY; *pg.* 957, *pg.* 1024
KNOCK OUT - Dry Cleaning & Laundry Product - ADCO, INC.; *pg.* 325, *pg.* 482
KNOCK-OUT - Fuel - BARDAHL MANUFACTURING CORPORATION; *pg.* 972, *pg.* 1833
KNOCK OUT - Rose Plants - THE CONARD-PYLE COMPANY; *pg.* 1794, *pg.* 1594
KNOCK-OUT - Test Cap - OATEY SUPPLY CHAIN SERVICES; *pg.* 30, *pg.* 1433
KNOCK-OUT GNATS - Insect Pest Control Product - GARDENS ALIVE!, INC.; *pg.* 1796, *pg.* 693
KNOCKDOWN - Class A Firefighting Foam - KIDDE FIRE FIGHTING; *pg.* 1170, *pg.* 1531
KNOCKOUT - Coated Paper - BOISE CASCADE HOLDINGS, L.L.C.; *pg.* 1453, *pg.* 546
KNOCKOUT - Beanie - OAKLEY, INC.; *pg.* 1840, *pg.* 86
KNOCKOUT - Biomolecule Product - THERMO FISHER SCIENTIFIC INC.; *pg.* 1602, *pg.* 61
KNOCKOUT DRESSING - Automotive Reconditioning Product - MOC PRODUCTS COMPANY, INC.; *pg.* 332, *pg.* 174
KNOGLO - Electronic Article Surveillance System - SENTRY TECHNOLOGY CORPORATION; *pg.* 672, *pg.* 1339
KNOGO - Electronic Article Surveillance System - SENTRY TECHNOLOGY CORPORATION; *pg.* 672, *pg.* 1339
KNOLL - Fabric - NEMSCHOFF, INC.; *pg.* 936, *pg.* 1890
KNOLL SPACE - Sales Program - KNOLL, INC.; *pg.* 425, *pg.* 1527
KNOLL WAUBY CLESTRA HAUSERMAN - Steel Wall Panel - CLESTRA HAUSERMAN, INC.; *pg.* 76, *pg.* 1526
KNOLLEXTRA - Computer & Desk Accessories - KNOLL, INC.; *pg.* 425, *pg.* 1527
KNOLLSTUDIO - Office Furniture - KNOLL, INC.; *pg.* 425, *pg.* 1527
KNOLLTEXTILES - Fabric & Leather Upholstery - KNOLL, INC.; *pg.* 425, *pg.* 1527
KNOPF CHILDREN'S BOOKS - Publishing Imprint - PENGUIN RANDOM HOUSE CHILDREN'S BOOKS; *pg.* 1676, *pg.* 1277
KNORR - Soups, Bouillons, Sauces, Mealmakers, Seasonings, Spices, Potato Products - UNILEVER UNITED STATES, INC.; *pg.* 904, *pg.* 1061
KNOSCAPE - Electronic Article Surveillance System - SENTRY TECHNOLOGY CORPORATION; *pg.* 672, *pg.* 1339
KNOSSOS - Dinnerware - THE HOMER LAUGHLIN CHINA COMPANY; *pg.* 1125, *pg.* 1850
THE KNOT - Online Wedding Resource - XO GROUP INC.; *pg.* 1289, *pg.* 1316
KNOTTINGHAM - Furniture - HOOKER FURNITURE CORPORATION; *pg.* 928, *pg.* 1788
KNOTT'S BERRY FARM - Amusement Park - CEDAR FAIR, L.P.; *pg.* 537, *pg.* 1471
KNOTT'S BERRY FARM - Jam - THE J.M. SMUCKER COMPANY; *pg.* 865, *pg.* 1468
KNOW NOW - Slogan - PASSUR AEROSPACE, INC.; *pg.* 233, *pg.* 376
KNOW YOUR BUSINESS BETTER - Tagline - PAR TECHNOLOGY CORPORATION; *pg.* 452, *pg.* 1183
KNOW YOUR CONDITION - Pharmaceutical Product - PFIZER INC.; *pg.* 1581, *pg.* 1278
KNOWING MORE - Pharmaceutical Product - PFIZER INC.; *pg.* 1581, *pg.* 1278
KNOWITALL - Software - BIO-RAD LABORATORIES, INC.; *pg.* 1504, *pg.* 101
KNOWITALL ANYWARE - Software - BIO-RAD LABORATORIES, INC.; *pg.* 1504, *pg.* 101
KNOWITALL QUICKSEARCH - Software - BIO-RAD LABORATORIES, INC.; *pg.* 1504, *pg.* 101
KNOWLEDGE@WORK - Initiative - FLUOR CORPORATION; *pg.* 82, *pg.* 1719
KNOWLEDGE BEYOND DOUBT - Tag Line - HOUGHTON MIFFLIN HARCOURT PUBLISHING COMPANY; *pg.* 1651, *pg.* 796
KNOWLEDGE CENTER - Software System - MENTOR GRAPHICS CORPORATION; *pg.* 432, *pg.* 1510
KNOWLEDGE CENTER - Software - SUPPORT.COM, INC.; *pg.* 1283, *pg.* 192
KNOWLEDGE FOR GENERATIONS - Slogan - JOHN WILEY & SONS, INC.; *pg.* 1655, *pg.* 1073
KNOWLEDGE FOR PROFESSIONALS - Slogan - SMARTPROS LTD.; *pg.* 1281, *pg.* 1166
KNOWLEDGE IN ACTION - Slogan - EMCOR GROUP, INC.; *pg.* 80, *pg.* 361
THE KNOWLEDGE INSIDE - Tag Line - FIRST DATABANK, INC.; *pg.* 397, *pg.* 217
KNOWLEDGE LINK - Software System - IMS HEALTH, INC.; *pg.* 1544, *pg.* 344
KNOWLEDGE MANAGEMENT - Software - BMC SOFTWARE, INC.; *pg.* 362, *pg.* 1701
KNOWLEDGE MANAGEMENT EXPRESS - Software - BMC SOFTWARE, INC.; *pg.* 362, *pg.* 1701
KNOWLEDGE ON - Calculating Tool - INTEGRATED SOFTWARE DESIGN, INC.; *pg.* 416, *pg.* 830
KNOWLEDGE PORTAL - Software - DELL SOFTWARE; *pg.* 385, *pg.* 40
KNOWLEDGE PUMP - Manual - XEROX CORPORATION; *pg.* 494, *pg.* 365
KNOWLEDGE SHARING CENTRE - Manual - XEROX CORPORATION; *pg.* 494, *pg.* 365
KNOWLEDGE-SOURCING - Software System - MENTOR GRAPHICS CORPORATION; *pg.* 432, *pg.* 1510
KNOWLEDGE STREET - Software - XEROX CORPORATION; *pg.* 494, *pg.* 365
THE KNOWLEDGE THAT POWERS THE NETWORK - Slogan - LCC INTERNATIONAL, INC.; *pg.* 651, *pg.* 1792
KNOWLEDGE TRAIN - Manual - XEROX CORPORATION; *pg.* 494, *pg.* 365
KNOWLEDGE WORKER - Manual - XEROX CORPORATION; *pg.* 494, *pg.* 365
KNOWLEDGE XPERT - Software - DELL SOFTWARE; *pg.* 385, *pg.* 40
KNOWLEDGE XPERT FOR DB2 Z/OS - Software - DELL SOFTWARE; *pg.* 385, *pg.* 40
KNOWLEDGE XPERT FOR MYSQL - Software - DELL SOFTWARE; *pg.* 385, *pg.* 40
KNOWLEDGE XPERT FOR ORACLE ADMINISTRATION - Software - DELL SOFTWARE; *pg.* 385, *pg.* 40
KNOWLEDGE XPERT FOR PL/SQL - Software - DELL SOFTWARE; *pg.* 385, *pg.* 40
KNOWLEDGEAGENT - Software - EGAIN COMMUNICATIONS CORPORATION; *pg.* 1242, *pg.* 284
KNOWLEDGEBASE - Semiconductor Solution - CYPRESS SEMICONDUCTOR CORPORATION; *pg.* 1326, *pg.* 243
THE KNOWLEDGEFORCE - Professional Staffing Services - KFORCE INC.; *pg.* 1261, *pg.* 473
KNOWLEDGESHARE - Manual - XEROX CORPORATION; *pg.* 494, *pg.* 365
KNOXAPARTMENTS.COM - Web Site - KNOXVILLE NEWS-SENTINEL COMPANY; *pg.* 1657, *pg.* 1637
KNOXCARS.COM - Web Site - KNOXVILLE NEWS-SENTINEL COMPANY; *pg.* 1657, *pg.* 1637
KNOXNEWS.COM - Web Site - KNOXVILLE NEWS-SENTINEL COMPANY; *pg.* 1657, *pg.* 1637
THE KNOXVILLE NEWS-SENTINEL - Newspaper - THE E.W. SCRIPPS COMPANY; *pg.* 1639, *pg.* 1412
KNOXVILLE NEWS-SENTINEL - Newspaper - KNOXVILLE NEWS-SENTINEL COMPANY; *pg.* 1657, *pg.* 1637
KNUCKLE DOWN II - Glove - KOMBI, LTD.; *pg.* 1838, *pg.* 1766
KNUCKLEHEAD - Flashlight - STREAMLIGHT INC.; *pg.* 1306, *pg.* 1527
KNUCKLES - Car Part Accessory - PRO-LINE, INC.; *pg.* 966, *pg.* 45
KNUDSEN - Cottage Cheese & Sour Cream - THE KRAFT HEINZ COMPANY; *pg.* 870, *pg.* 1577
KNXV, ABC (PHOENIX) - Television Broadcasting Station - THE E.W. SCRIPPS COMPANY; *pg.* 1639, *pg.* 1412
KOA - Eyewear - MAUI JIM, INC.; *pg.* 9, *pg.* 651
KOA VALUE KARD - Discount Program - KAMPGROUNDS OF AMERICA, INC.; *pg.* 555, *pg.* 1008
KOALA CRISP - Cereal - NATURE'S PATH FOODS INC.; *pg.* 833, *pg.* 1908
KOALA KARE - Baby Changing Tables, High Chairs & Activity Products - BOBRICK WASHROOM EQUIPMENT, INC.; *pg.* 1043, *pg.* 166
KOAVONE - Fragrance Ingredient - INTERNATIONAL FLAVORS & FRAGRANCES INC.; *pg.* 512, *pg.* 1244
KOBELCO - Construction Equipment - CNH AMERICA LLC; *pg.* 702, *pg.* 560
KOBRAA - Footwear - STEVEN MADDEN, LTD.; *pg.* 1819, *pg.* 1176
KOBRAND - Wine - KOBRAND CORPORATION; *pg.* 1965, *pg.* 1325
KOBYGARD - Surgical Instrument - OSTEOMED CORPORATION; *pg.* 1425, *pg.* 1658
KOCH - Container - BUCKEYE CORRUGATED INC.; *pg.* 1454, *pg.* 1400
KOCHAKADEN - Soft Drink - THE COCA-COLA COMPANY;

First page reference indicates Business Class Edition
Second page reference indicates Geographic Edition

pg. 240, *pg.* 493
KOCIDE - Fungicide - E.I. DU PONT DE NEMOURS & COMPANY; *pg.* 1159, *pg.* 390
KODABROME - Photo Paper - EASTMAN KODAK COMPANY; *pg.* 1408, *pg.* 1333
KODABROMIDE - Photo Paper - EASTMAN KODAK COMPANY; *pg.* 1408, *pg.* 1333
KODACEL - Film - EASTMAN KODAK COMPANY; *pg.* 1408, *pg.* 1333
KODACHROME - Film - EASTMAN KODAK COMPANY; *pg.* 1408, *pg.* 1333
KODACHROME-X - Color Photographic Film - EASTMAN KODAK COMPANY; *pg.* 1408, *pg.* 1333
KODACOLOR - Color Photo Film & Prints - EASTMAN KODAK COMPANY; *pg.* 1408, *pg.* 1333
KODACOLOR VR - Photographic Film - EASTMAN KODAK COMPANY; *pg.* 1408, *pg.* 1333
KODACOLOR-X - Color Photographic Film - EASTMAN KODAK COMPANY; *pg.* 1408, *pg.* 1333
KODACRAFT - Photo Developing Equipment - EASTMAN KODAK COMPANY; *pg.* 1408, *pg.* 1333
KODAFIX - Photo Fixer - EASTMAN KODAK COMPANY; *pg.* 1408, *pg.* 1333
KODAFLEX - Radiographic Film - EASTMAN KODAK COMPANY; *pg.* 1408, *pg.* 1333
KODAGRAPH - Industrial Photo Film, Paper, Chemicals - EASTMAN KODAK COMPANY; *pg.* 1408, *pg.* 1333
KODAK - Camera - EASTMAN KODAK COMPANY; *pg.* 1408, *pg.* 1333
KODAK APPROVAL - Digital Color Proofing System - EASTMAN KODAK COMPANY; *pg.* 1408, *pg.* 1333
KODAK BEACON - Enlargers - EASTMAN KODAK COMPANY; *pg.* 1408, *pg.* 1333
KODAK BISNET - Business Assistance Network & Software - EASTMAN KODAK COMPANY; *pg.* 1408, *pg.* 1333
KODAK DIAPORAMA - Projector Dissolve Units, Cases - EASTMAN KODAK COMPANY; *pg.* 1408, *pg.* 1333
KODAK EXPRESS - Photofinishing Quality Control Services - EASTMAN KODAK COMPANY; *pg.* 1408, *pg.* 1333
KODAK PREVIEW - Computer Network, Terminals - EASTMAN KODAK COMPANY; *pg.* 1408, *pg.* 1333
KODAK PROFESSIONAL - Camera - EASTMAN KODAK COMPANY; *pg.* 1408, *pg.* 1333
KODAK SIGNATURE - Color Proofing Material, Apparatus, Chemicals - EASTMAN KODAK COMPANY; *pg.* 1408, *pg.* 1333
KODAK VISION - Film - EASTMAN KODAK COMPANY; *pg.* 1408, *pg.* 1333
KODAKERY - Newspaper - EASTMAN KODAK COMPANY; *pg.* 1408, *pg.* 1333
KODALINE - Photo Film - EASTMAN KODAK COMPANY; *pg.* 1408, *pg.* 1333
KODALITH - Photo Film, Chemicals, Developer & Fixer, Paper, Processing Equipment - EASTMAN KODAK COMPANY; *pg.* 1408, *pg.* 1333
KODALK - Balanced Alkali for Use in Developers & Other Solutions - EASTMAN KODAK COMPANY; *pg.* 1408, *pg.* 1333
KODALUX - Flash Unit - EASTMAN KODAK COMPANY; *pg.* 1408, *pg.* 1333
KODAMATIC - Processing Apparatus - EASTMAN KODAK COMPANY; *pg.* 1408, *pg.* 1333
KODARAMA - Display - EASTMAN KODAK COMPANY; *pg.* 1408, *pg.* 1333
KODASCAN - Photofinishing Equipment - EASTMAN KODAK COMPANY; *pg.* 1408, *pg.* 1333
KODASE - Industrial Enzymes - EASTMAN KODAK COMPANY; *pg.* 1408, *pg.* 1333
KODASLIDE - Slide Projectors, Viewers, Filing Containers - EASTMAN KODAK COMPANY; *pg.* 1408, *pg.* 1333
KODASTAR - Film - EASTMAN KODAK COMPANY; *pg.* 1408, *pg.* 1333
KODESTAR - Barcode Readers - EASTMAN KODAK COMPANY; *pg.* 1408, *pg.* 1333
KODIAK - Tobacco Product - AMERICAN SNUFF COMPANY; *pg.* 1893, *pg.* 1641
KODIAK - Cooling System - LYTRON INCORPORATED; *pg.* 1074, *pg.* 861
KODIAK ICE - Moist Tobacco - AMERICAN SNUFF COMPANY; *pg.* 1893, *pg.* 1641
KODIAK KRAFT - Paper Product - CANFOR CORPORATION; *pg.* 1454, *pg.* 1910
KODIAK STRAIGHT - Moist Tobacco - AMERICAN SNUFF COMPANY; *pg.* 1893, *pg.* 1641
KOEHRING - Capital Equipment - TEREX CORPORATION; *pg.* 1381, *pg.* 384
KOESTER KT - Furnace - TENOVA; *pg.* 114, *pg.* 1525
KOFRON - Pharmaceutical Product - ABBOTT LABORATORIES; *pg.* 1484, *pg.* 551
KOHINOOL - Fragrance Ingredient - INTERNATIONAL FLAVORS & FRAGRANCES INC.; *pg.* 512, *pg.* 1244
KOHLER - Generator Controls Rebuilding Service - FLIGHT SYSTEMS, INC.; *pg.* 1337, *pg.* 1548
KOHLER - Dairy Mixes - MICHAEL FOODS, INC.; *pg.* 877, *pg.* 949
KOHL'S - Department Stores - KOHL'S CORPORATION; *pg.* 1775, *pg.* 1870
KOHO - Ice Hockey Equipment - REEBOK-CCM HOCKEY, INC.; *pg.* 1844, *pg.* 1960
KOHOD SCHOOL OF BUSINESS - Educational Services - AMERICAN UNIVERSITY; *pg.* 597, *pg.* 395
KOI - Carpet - INTERFACE, INC.; *pg.* 695, *pg.* 512
KOI DANCE - Bath Product - KOHLER CO.; *pg.* 91, *pg.* 1862
KOI WORLD & WATER GARDENS - Magazine - I-5 PUBLISHING LLC; *pg.* 1651, *pg.* 133
KOIL BRITE - Alkaline Product - DELTA FOREMOST CHEMICAL CORPORATION; *pg.* 1155, *pg.* 1642
KOIL MASTER - Coil Cleaner - DELTA FOREMOST CHEMICAL CORPORATION; *pg.* 1155, *pg.* 1642
KOILED KORDS - Cable - WHITNEY BLAKE CO., INC.; *pg.* 1308, *pg.* 1764
KOKACHIN - Restaurant Services - OMNI HOTELS & RESORTS; *pg.* 1107, *pg.* 1685
KOKANAKA - Confectionery - THE HERSHEY CO.; *pg.* 1855, *pg.* 1538
KOKO GOLD COCONUT OIL - Coconut Oil - MALLET & COMPANY, INC.; *pg.* 875, *pg.* 1521
KOKOPELLIS - Dinnerware - THE HOMER LAUGHLIN CHINA COMPANY; *pg.* 1125, *pg.* 1850
KOLA INGLESA - Beverages - THE COCA-COLA COMPANY; *pg.* 240, *pg.* 493
KOLBERG - Processing Equipment - ASTEC INDUSTRIES, INC.; *pg.* 69, *pg.* 1628
KOLD GLACIER LAGER - Lager - BIG ROCK BREWERY INCOME TRUST; *pg.* 239, *pg.* 1902
KOLD KEEPER - Re-Usable Refrigerants - CRES-COR; *pg.* 1326, *pg.* 1464
KOLD-N-KLOSE - Sheath Repair System - THOMAS & BETTS CORPORATION; *pg.* 680, *pg.* 1646
KOLD PAK - Test Equipment - SPX THERMAL PRODUCT SOLUTIONS; *pg.* 1378, *pg.* 1555
KOLDWAVE - HVAC Equipment - MESTEK, INC.; *pg.* 1074, *pg.* 857
KOLINSKY BRUSHES - Nailcare Product - MEDICOOL, INC.; *pg.* 1562, *pg.* 294
KOLLECTOR - Digital Video Recording System - VICON INDUSTRIES, INC.; *pg.* 685, *pg.* 1166
KOLLECTOR ELITE - 16 Channel Digital Recorder - VICON INDUSTRIES, INC.; *pg.* 685, *pg.* 1166
KOLLECTOR PRO - 16 Channel Digital Recorder - VICON INDUSTRIES, INC.; *pg.* 685, *pg.* 1166
KOLLMORGEN - Motor And Drive Product - DANAHER CORPORATION; *pg.* 1044, *pg.* 397
KOLLMORGEN - Electric Products - DANAHER MOTION; *pg.* 1327, *pg.* 1593
KOLLMORGEN ELECTRO-OPTICAL - Electro-Optical Product - DANAHER CORPORATION; *pg.* 1044, *pg.* 397
KOLOR FAST - Colored Wrapping Tissue - PACON CORPORATION; *pg.* 1466, *pg.* 1852
KOLORKINS - Cameras & Stuffed Toys - EASTMAN KODAK COMPANY; *pg.* 1408, *pg.* 1333
KOLUMN FORM - Construction Tubes - CARAUSTAR INDUSTRIES, INC.; *pg.* 1455, *pg.* 525
KOMODO DRAGON BLEND - Coffee - STARBUCKS CORPORATION; *pg.* 897, *pg.* 1840
KOMODO FX - Bicycles - G. JOANNOU CYCLE CO. INC.; *pg.* 1707, *pg.* 1098
KOMPRESSOR - Medical Device - INTEGRA LIFESCIENCES HOLDINGS CORPORATION; *pg.* 1545, *pg.* 1109
KOMPREX - Medical & Aesthetic Product - DYNATRONICS CORPORATION; *pg.* 1526, *pg.* 1757
KOMSTAR - Microimage Processors & Lenses - EASTMAN KODAK COMPANY; *pg.* 1408, *pg.* 1333
KONA - Eyewear - MAUI JIM, INC.; *pg.* 9, *pg.* 651
KONA - Coffee - PEET'S COFFEE & TEA, INC.; *pg.* 1029, *pg.* 85
KONA BAY - Fan - CRAFTMADE INTERNATIONAL, INC.; *pg.* 1295, *pg.* 1670
KONA BREWING COMPANY - Craft Brewery - CRAFT BREWERS ALLIANCE, INC; *pg.* 247, *pg.* 1502
KONA SEA SALT - Biological Products - MERA PHARMACEUTICALS, INC.; *pg.* 1566, *pg.* 545
KONADERM - Pharmaceutical Product - VALEANT PHARMACEUTICALS INTERNATIONAL; *pg.* 1605, *pg.* 1047
KONDAR - Acrylic Automotive Coating Composition - PPG INDUSTRIES, INC.; *pg.* 1445, *pg.* 1579
KONEJO - Footwear - K-SWISS; *pg.* 1837, *pg.* 306
KONEPAC - Air Cleaner - DONALDSON COMPANY, INC.; *pg.* 1329, *pg.* 917
KONETA - Truck Accessories - LANCASTER COLONY CORPORATION; *pg.* 873, *pg.* 1441
KONI - Shock Absorbers - ITT CORPORATION; *pg.* 1351, *pg.* 1354
KONIG - Medical Product - MEDLINE INDUSTRIES, INC.; *pg.* 1562, *pg.* 635
KONJAC - Food Ingredient - FMC CORPORATION; *pg.* 1163, *pg.* 1564
KONTAX - Optical Product - UNIVERSAL PHOTONICS, INC.; *pg.* 1433, *pg.* 1167
KONTOUR - Actuator - PRECISION VALVE CORPORATION; *pg.* 1060, *pg.* 1357
KONVA-KORE - Paperboard Product - CARAUSTAR INDUSTRIES, INC.; *pg.* 1455, *pg.* 525
KOOKY KREATURES - Puppets - GUND, INC.; *pg.* 954, *pg.* 1056
KOOL-AID - Beverages - THE KRAFT HEINZ COMPANY; *pg.* 870, *pg.* 1577
KOOL-ALL - Cutting Fluid - THE DOALL COMPANY; *pg.* 1329, *pg.* 670
KOOL KAT - Slots - INTERNATIONAL GAME TECHNOLOGY; *pg.* 957, *pg.* 1024
KOOL KIDS - Mattress - KING KOIL LICENSING COMPANY INC.; *pg.* 932, *pg.* 671
KOOL-KIT - Medical Product - CINCINNATI SUB-ZERO PRODUCTS, INC.; *pg.* 1070, *pg.* 1411
KOOL KIT - Insulated Lunch Bag - IGLOO PRODUCTS CORPORATION; *pg.* 1126, *pg.* 1724
KOOL KLASSIC - Insulated Lunch Bag - IGLOO PRODUCTS CORPORATION; *pg.* 1126, *pg.* 1724
KOOL MATE - Thermoelectric Cooler/Warmer - IGLOO PRODUCTS CORPORATION; *pg.* 1126, *pg.* 1724
KOOL SIPPER - Lunch Kit - IGLOO PRODUCTS CORPORATION; *pg.* 1126, *pg.* 1724
KOOL-TOUCH - Buffetware - THE VOLLRATH COMPANY LLC; *pg.* 1139, *pg.* 1894
KOOL-TOUCH COVERS - Food Service Inset Covers - THE VOLLRATH COMPANY LLC; *pg.* 1139, *pg.* 1894
KOOL-TOUCH LADLES - Coated S.S. Ladles - THE VOLLRATH COMPANY LLC; *pg.* 1139, *pg.* 1894
KOOLERZ - Chewing Gum - THE HERSHEY CO.; *pg.* 1855, *pg.* 1538
KOOLFOAM - Pillows - HOLLANDER SLEEP PRODUCTS; *pg.* 927, *pg.* 411
KOOL'N KLEEN - Antiseptic Moist Towelettes - MEDLINE INDUSTRIES, INC.; *pg.* 1562, *pg.* 635
KOOLPADS - Cellulose Sponge Sweatbands - STANDARD SAFETY EQUIPMENT CO.; *pg.* 1379, *pg.* 632
KOOLVUE BRONZE - Float Glass - AGC GLASS NORTH AMERICA, INC.; *pg.* 65, *pg.* 482
KOOTENAY - Brewery - LABATT BREWING COMPANY LIMITED; *pg.* 253, *pg.* 1939
KOOZIE - Stadium Cushion - BROWN & BIGELOW, INC.; *pg.* 1624, *pg.* 959
KOP-COAT - Coatings - KOP-COAT, INC.; *pg.* 1444, *pg.* 1576
KOP-KLAD - Roof System - KOPPERS HOLDINGS INC.; *pg.* 1170, *pg.* 1577
KOP-R - Roof Insulation - KOPPERS HOLDINGS INC.; *pg.* 1170, *pg.* 1577
KOPIRA - Medicine - PFIZER INC.; *pg.* 1581, *pg.* 1278
KORBEL - California Champagnes, Wines & Brandy - BROWN-FORMAN CORPORATION; *pg.* 1958, *pg.* 732
KORBEL - Champagne - F. KORBEL BROS. INC.; *pg.* 1963, *pg.* 100
KORBEL BLANC DE NOIRS - Champagne - F. KORBEL BROS. INC.; *pg.* 1963, *pg.* 100
KORBEL BRUT - Champagne - F. KORBEL BROS. INC.; *pg.* 1963, *pg.* 100
KORBEL BRUT ROSE - Champagne - F. KORBEL BROS. INC.; *pg.* 1963, *pg.* 100
KORBEL CHARDONNAY - Champagne - F. KORBEL BROS. INC.; *pg.* 1963, *pg.* 100
KORBEL EXTRA DRY - Champagne - F. KORBEL BROS. INC.; *pg.* 1963, *pg.* 100

KORBEL MOSCATO FRIZZANTE - Champagne - F. KORBEL BROS. INC.; *pg.* 1963, *pg.* 100
KORBEL SEC - Champagne - F. KORBEL BROS. INC.; *pg.* 1963, *pg.* 100
KORDEK - Compression-Molded Grating - ALABAMA METAL INDUSTRIES CORPORATION; *pg.* 65, *pg.* 1
KORDEK II - Compression Molded Grating - ALABAMA METAL INDUSTRIES CORPORATION; *pg.* 65, *pg.* 1
KORDITE - Food Product - PACTIV CORPORATION; *pg.* 1466, *pg.* 624
KORET - Misses' & Women's Coordinates - KELLWOOD COMPANY; *pg.* 28, *pg.* 975
KORFUND DYNAMICS - Shock & Vibration - AEROFLEX INCORPORATED; *pg.* 614, *pg.* 1321
KORKY - Plumbing Products - LAVELLE INDUSTRIES INC.; *pg.* 1053, *pg.* 1856
KORKY PLUS - Toilet Flappers - LAVELLE INDUSTRIES INC.; *pg.* 1053, *pg.* 1856
KORKY QUIETFILL - Toilet Tank Fill Valve - LAVELLE INDUSTRIES INC.; *pg.* 1053, *pg.* 1856
KOROFLEX - Coating Product - PPG INDUSTRIES, INC.; *pg.* 1445, *pg.* 1579
KOROPON - Coating Product - PPG INDUSTRIES, INC.; *pg.* 1445, *pg.* 1579
KOROWHITE - Conveyor Belting - HBD INDUSTRIES, INC.; *pg.* 207, *pg.* 1449
KORRVU - Packaging Product - SEALED AIR CORPORATION; *pg.* 1468, *pg.* 1058
KOSCIUSKO - Mustard - PLOCHMAN, INC.; *pg.* 890, *pg.* 631
KOSHER DILL - Potato Chips - SNYDER'S OF HANOVER, INC.; *pg.* 1862, *pg.* 1536
KOSMOS - Musical Instrument - PEAVEY ELECTRONICS CORPORATION; *pg.* 662, *pg.* 970
KOSMOS - Button - PRECISION VALVE CORPORATION; *pg.* 1060, *pg.* 1357
KOSMOS - Oven & Microwave - WHIRLPOOL CORPORATION; *pg.* 62, *pg.* 872
KOSSACKS KASH - Video Game - INTERNATIONAL GAME TECHNOLOGY; *pg.* 957, *pg.* 1024
KOTAKU - Video Game News - GAWKER MEDIA LLC; *pg.* 1248, *pg.* 1234
KOTEX - Sanitary Napkin - KIMBERLY-CLARK CORPORATION; *pg.* 1461, *pg.* 1720
KOTLAR CUSHION - Cut Diamonds - HARRY KOTLAR & CO., INC.; *pg.* 6, *pg.* 132
KOVEL'S - Antiques Guide to Collecting - PENGUIN RANDOM HOUSE; *pg.* 1675, *pg.* 1276
KOWET - Chemical - SENSIENT COLORS INC.; *pg.* 1180, *pg.* 1003
KOWTOWL - Special Application Wipers - GEORGIA-PACIFIC LLC; *pg.* 1458, *pg.* 507
KOXKA - Refrigeration Equipment - INGERSOLL-RAND COMPANY; *pg.* 1349, *pg.* 1370
KOZAK - Waterless Automotive Cleaners - SUMMIT INDUSTRIES, INC.; *pg.* 1599, *pg.* 535
KOZY KITTEN - Canned - HEINZ NORTH AMERICA; *pg.* 861, *pg.* 1576
KOZY SHACK - Rice Pudding - KOZY SHACK INC.; *pg.* 869, *pg.* 1167
KP - Room Air Conditioners - FRIEDRICH AIR CONDITIONING CO.; *pg.* 1072, *pg.* 1740
KP-110 - Speaker System - KLIPSCH GROUP, INC.; *pg.* 649, *pg.* 688
KP-250 - Speaker System - KLIPSCH GROUP, INC.; *pg.* 649, *pg.* 688
KP-262 - Speaker System - KLIPSCH GROUP, INC.; *pg.* 649, *pg.* 688
KP PUMPS - Pump Product - IDEX CORPORATION; *pg.* 1347, *pg.* 623
KP1H - Pumps - IDEX CORPORATION; *pg.* 1347, *pg.* 623
KP2 KAOSS PAD - Dynamic Effect/Controller - KORG USA, INC.; *pg.* 556, *pg.* 1180
KPL - Photosensitive Lacquer - EASTMAN KODAK COMPANY; *pg.* 1408, *pg.* 1333
KPT-684 - Subwoofer - KLIPSCH GROUP, INC.; *pg.* 649, *pg.* 688
KPT-8001 - Loudspeaker System - KLIPSCH GROUP, INC.; *pg.* 649, *pg.* 688
KRACK - Refrigeration Equipment - INGERSOLL-RAND COMPANY; *pg.* 1349, *pg.* 1370
KRACKEL - Chocolate Candy - THE HERSHEY CO.; *pg.* 1855, *pg.* 1538
KRAFT - Food Products - THE KRAFT HEINZ COMPANY; *pg.* 870, *pg.* 1577
KRAFT BARBEQUE SAUCE - Sauces - THE KRAFT HEINZ COMPANY; *pg.* 870, *pg.* 1577
KRAFT FOODSERVICE - Informational Services - THE KRAFT HEINZ COMPANY; *pg.* 870, *pg.* 1577
KRAFT MACARONI & CHEESE - Food Product - THE KRAFT HEINZ COMPANY; *pg.* 870, *pg.* 1577
KRAFT NATURAL CHEESE - Cheeses - THE KRAFT HEINZ COMPANY; *pg.* 870, *pg.* 1577
KRAFT SALAD DRESSINGS - Dressings - THE KRAFT HEINZ COMPANY; *pg.* 870, *pg.* 1577
KRAFT SINGLES - Cheese Products - THE KRAFT HEINZ COMPANY; *pg.* 870, *pg.* 1577
KRAFTEX - Paperboard - CARAUSTAR INDUSTRIES, INC.; *pg.* 1455, *pg.* 525
KRAFTMAID - Furniture And Cabinetry Company - KRAFTMAID CABINETRY, INC.; *pg.* 1053, *pg.* 1465
KRAFTMAID - Kitchen & Bath Cabinetry - MASCO CORPORATION; *pg.* 96, *pg.* 909
KRAFTPAK - Paperboard Packaging Product - WESTROCK COMPANY; *pg.* 1472, *pg.* 1805
KRAFTPLEX - Chemical Product - WESTROCK COMPANY; *pg.* 1472, *pg.* 1805
KRAFTSPERSE - Chemical Product - WESTROCK COMPANY; *pg.* 1472, *pg.* 1805
KRAK STIK - Repair Sealants - LA-CO INDUSTRIES MARKAL CO., INC.; *pg.* 1170, *pg.* 610
KRAKATOA EAST OF JAVA - Game - WMS INDUSTRIES INC.; *pg.* 593, *pg.* 666
KRAKEN RUM - Spirits - PROXIMO SPIRITS, INC.; *pg.* 1969, *pg.* 1076
KRAMER - Musical Instrument - GIBSON GUITAR CORP.; *pg.* 550, *pg.* 1650
KRANIOS - Medical Device - INTEGRA LIFESCIENCES HOLDINGS CORPORATION; *pg.* 1545, *pg.* 1109
KRAVE - Food Product - KELLOGG COMPANY; *pg.* 831, *pg.* 870
KRAVE - Vaporizer - VAPOR CORP.; *pg.* 61, *pg.* 427
KRAVET - Fabric - NEMSCHOFF, INC.; *pg.* 936, *pg.* 1890
KRAVET BASICS - Fabric - KRAVET FABRICS INC.; *pg.* 932, *pg.* 1142
KRAVET COLLECTIONS - Fabric - KRAVET FABRICS INC.; *pg.* 932, *pg.* 1142
KRAVET CONTRACT - Fabric - KRAVET FABRICS INC.; *pg.* 932, *pg.* 1142
KRAVET DESIGN - Fabric - KRAVET FABRICS INC.; *pg.* 932, *pg.* 1142
KRAVET SOLEIL - Fabric - KRAVET FABRICS INC.; *pg.* 932, *pg.* 1142
KRAVETCOUTURE - Fabric - KRAVET FABRICS INC.; *pg.* 932, *pg.* 1142
KRAYTON - Knife - COAST CUTLERY COMPANY; *pg.* 1121, *pg.* 1501
KRAZY GLUE - Glue & Adhesive - ELMER'S PRODUCTS, INC.; *pg.* 1442, *pg.* 1479
KRAZY KREAMS - Ice Cream - UNITED DAIRY FARMERS, INC.; *pg.* 906, *pg.* 1426
KRAZY KRITTERS - Cups & Plates - GEORGIA-PACIFIC LLC; *pg.* 1458, *pg.* 507
KREAMIES - Bakery Product - TASTY BAKING COMPANY; *pg.* 1862, *pg.* 1571
KREAMO - Bakery Products - ALPHA BAKING COMPANY; *pg.* 836, *pg.* 564
KRELL - Electronic Product Company - KRELL INDUSTRIES, INC.; *pg.* 650, *pg.* 367
KREME N KLEEN - Cream Cleaner - SWISHER HYGIENE INC.; *pg.* 336, *pg.* 1507
KRENITE - Herbicide - E.I. DU PONT DE NEMOURS & COMPANY; *pg.* 1159, *pg.* 390
KREST - Beverages - THE COCA-COLA COMPANY; *pg.* 240, *pg.* 493
KRETSCHMAR - Meat Products - JOHN MORRELL & CO.; *pg.* 866, *pg.* 1415
KRETSCHMAR - Food Products - SMITHFIELD FOODS, INC.; *pg.* 896, *pg.* 1806
KRIAL - Pressed & Monolithic Refractory - RESCO PRODUCTS, INC.; *pg.* 107, *pg.* 1581
KRICON - Pressed & Monolithic Refractory - RESCO PRODUCTS, INC.; *pg.* 107, *pg.* 1581
KRICOR - Pressed & Monolithic Refractory - RESCO PRODUCTS, INC.; *pg.* 107, *pg.* 1581
KRILEX - Pressed & Monolithic Refractory - RESCO PRODUCTS, INC.; *pg.* 107, *pg.* 1581
KRILINE - Pressed & Monolithic Refractory - RESCO PRODUCTS, INC.; *pg.* 107, *pg.* 1581
KRIMPETS - Bakery Product - TASTY BAKING COMPANY; *pg.* 1862, *pg.* 1571
KRIMPTITE - Electronic Components - MOLEX INCORPORATED; *pg.* 655, *pg.* 628
KRIMUL - Pressed & Monolithic Refractory - RESCO PRODUCTS, INC.; *pg.* 107, *pg.* 1581
KRIS - Furniture - AMISCO INDUSTRIES LTD.; *pg.* 913, *pg.* 1958
KRISPY - Saltine Crackers - KELLOGG COMPANY; *pg.* 831, *pg.* 870
KRISPY KREME - Doughnuts - KRISPY KREME DOUGHNUTS, INC.; *pg.* 1734, *pg.* 1394
KRISPY KREME ORIGINAL GLAZED - Doughnuts - KRISPY KREME DOUGHNUTS, INC.; *pg.* 1734, *pg.* 1394
KRISTA - Clothing - ABERCROMBIE & FITCH CO.; *pg.* 37, *pg.* 1466
KRISTA - Footwear - P.W. MINOR & SON, INC.; *pg.* 1816, *pg.* 1140
KRISTALEX - Hydrocarbon Resins - EASTMAN CHEMICAL COMPANY; *pg.* 1159, *pg.* 1636
KRISTALOSE - Pharmaceutical Product - MYLAN, INC.; *pg.* 1570, *pg.* 1520
KRITAB - Pressed & Monolithic Refractory - RESCO PRODUCTS, INC.; *pg.* 107, *pg.* 1581
KROGER FRESH FARE - Super Market - THE KROGER CO.; *pg.* 1025, *pg.* 1416
KROGER'S ACTIVE LIFESTYLE - Cholesterol Managing Foods - THE KROGER CO.; *pg.* 1025, *pg.* 1416
KROMAG - Pressed & Monolithic Refractory - RESCO PRODUCTS, INC.; *pg.* 107, *pg.* 1581
KRONITOX - Flame Retardants - CHEMTURA CORPORATION; *pg.* 1152, *pg.* 355
KRONOMATIC - Food Product - KRONOS PRODUCTS, INC.; *pg.* 872, *pg.* 614
KRONOS 4500 - Badge Terminals - KRONOS INCORPORATED; *pg.* 425, *pg.* 813
KRONOS 4500 TOUCH ID - Badge Terminal Featuring Biometric Verification Technology - KRONOS INCORPORATED; *pg.* 425, *pg.* 813
KRONOS E-CENTRAL - Internet-Based Employee Time & Labor Tracking Application - KRONOS INCORPORATED; *pg.* 425, *pg.* 813
KRONOS ISERIES CENTRAL - Time & Labor Solutions - KRONOS INCORPORATED; *pg.* 425, *pg.* 813
THE KRONOS PERFECT PORTION CONTROL SYSTEM - Serving Options for Makers of Gyros - KRONOS PRODUCTS, INC.; *pg.* 872, *pg.* 614
KROPLA BESKIDU - Beverages - THE COCA-COLA COMPANY; *pg.* 240, *pg.* 493
KROSFLO - Fluid Purification System - SPECTRUM LABORATORIES INC.; *pg.* 1595, *pg.* 69
KROSSGRINDING - Honing Tool - SUNNEN PRODUCTS COMPANY; *pg.* 1379, *pg.* 1004
KROVAR - Herbicide - E.I. DU PONT DE NEMOURS & COMPANY; *pg.* 1159, *pg.* 390
KROY - Vinyl Fencing, Railing & Decking - NORTEK, INC.; *pg.* 100, *pg.* 1607
KRRRRISPKRAUT - Food Product - GLK FOODS, LLC; *pg.* 858, *pg.* 1852
KRUG - Champagne - MOET HENNESSY; *pg.* 1966, *pg.* 1260
KRUM - Horticultural Perlite - SILBRICO CORPORATION; *pg.* 110, *pg.* 617
KRUSTEAZ - Food Product - CONTINENTAL MILLS, INC.; *pg.* 827, *pg.* 1845
KRUSTEAZ CARBSIMPLE - Food Product - CONTINENTAL MILLS, INC.; *pg.* 827, *pg.* 1845
KRYLINER - Marking System - SHERWIN-WILLIAMS DIVERSIFIED BRANDS DIVISION; *pg.* 1448, *pg.* 1435
KRYLON - Aerosol - THE SHERWIN-WILLIAMS COMPANY; *pg.* 1447, *pg.* 1435
KRYLON - Interior & Exterior Enamel - SHERWIN-WILLIAMS DIVERSIFIED BRANDS DIVISION; *pg.* 1448, *pg.* 1435
KRYOCIDE - Chemical - ARKEMA INC.; *pg.* 1147, *pg.* 1543
KRYPTO - Character - DC COMICS, INC.; *pg.* 1633, *pg.* 1221
KRYPTONITE - Locking System - INGERSOLL-RAND COMPANY; *pg.* 1349, *pg.* 1370
KRYSTAL FLUTES - Patterned Glass - AGC GLASS NORTH AMERICA, INC.; *pg.* 65, *pg.* 482
KRYSTAL-KLEAN - Minerals - MINERALS TECHNOLOGIES INC.; *pg.* 1173, *pg.* 617
KRYSTAL KLEAR - Low Iron Float Glass - AGC GLASS NORTH AMERICA, INC.; *pg.* 65, *pg.* 482
KRYSTALFLEX - Thermoplastic Polyurethanes - HUNTSMAN CORPORATION; *pg.* 1167, *pg.* 1758

First page reference indicates Business Class Edition
Second page reference indicates Geographic Edition

KRYSTALGRAN - Thermoplastic Polyurethanes - HUNTSMAN CORPORATION; *pg.* 1167, *pg.* 1758
KRZR - Cellular Telephone - MOTOROLA SOLUTIONS, INC.; *pg.* 657, *pg.* 659
K'S KIDS - Toy - THE OHIO ART COMPANY, INC.; *pg.* 965, *pg.* 1406
KSH - Lighting Lens - PLASKOLITE, INC.; *pg.* 1888, *pg.* 1443
KSHB, NBC (KANSAS CITY) - Television Broadcasting Station - THE E.W. SCRIPPS COMPANY; *pg.* 1639, *pg.* 1412
KSM-12 - Stage Monitor - KLIPSCH GROUP, INC.; *pg.* 649, *pg.* 688
KSM-15 - Stage Monitor - KLIPSCH GROUP, INC.; *pg.* 649, *pg.* 688
KSM-8 - Stage Monitor - KLIPSCH GROUP, INC.; *pg.* 649, *pg.* 688
KSW-12 - Subwoofer - KLIPSCH GROUP, INC.; *pg.* 649, *pg.* 688
KSW-15 - Subwoofer - KLIPSCH GROUP, INC.; *pg.* 649, *pg.* 688
KT WAY - Solution - KEPNER-TREGOE, INC.; *pg.* 424, *pg.* 1112
KTP/532 - Surgical Laser System - AMERICAN MEDICAL SYSTEMS, INC.; *pg.* 1399, *pg.* 238
KTP/YAG - Surgical Laser System Designed Hospital Use - AMERICAN MEDICAL SYSTEMS, INC.; *pg.* 1399, *pg.* 238
KU-1+ - Krebs Units Digital Viscometer - BROOKFIELD ENGINEERING LABORATORIES, INC.; *pg.* 1403, *pg.* 833
KUAT - Beverages - THE COCA-COLA COMPANY; *pg.* 240, *pg.* 493
KUAT GUARANA - Beverages - THE COCA-COLA COMPANY; *pg.* 240, *pg.* 493
KUAT LIGHT - Beverages - THE COCA-COLA COMPANY; *pg.* 240, *pg.* 493
KUDOS - Snack Food - MARS, INCORPORATED; *pg.* 1858, *pg.* 1792
KUDOS BOUQUET - Flower Arrangement - 1-800-FLOWERS.COM, INC.; *pg.* 1758, *pg.* 1151
KUEMMERLING - Cordial - JIM BEAM BRANDS CO.; *pg.* 1965, *pg.* 601
KUKUNA - Eyewear - MAUI JIM, INC.; *pg.* 9, *pg.* 651
KULA - Eyewear - MAUI JIM, INC.; *pg.* 9, *pg.* 651
KULER - Web-Hosted Application - ADOBE SYSTEMS INCORPORATED; *pg.* 342, *pg.* 235
KULI - Beverages - THE COCA-COLA COMPANY; *pg.* 240, *pg.* 493
KULICKE & SOFFA - Semiconductor Assembly Equipment - KULICKE & SOFFA INDUSTRIES, INC.; *pg.* 650, *pg.* 1533
KULJIAN - Engineering & Architectural Services - THE KULJIAN CORPORATION; *pg.* 92, *pg.* 1566
KUMARONE - Flavor Ingredient - INTERNATIONAL FLAVORS & FRAGRANCES INC.; *pg.* 512, *pg.* 1244
KUMFY-GRIP - Scissors - ACME UNITED CORPORATION; *pg.* 1040, *pg.* 346
KUNG-FU PANDA - Children Product - TUPPERWARE BRANDS CORPORATION; *pg.* 1139, *pg.* 456
KURKURE - Chips - PEPSICO, INC.; *pg.* 259, *pg.* 1327
KURL - Video Effect Equipment - GRASS VALLEY, INC.; *pg.* 641, *pg.* 164
KURLASH - Eye Care Product - THE W.E. BASSETT COMPANY; *pg.* 524, *pg.* 371
KURTIS MSD - Suction Device - VITAL SIGNS, INC.; *pg.* 1607, *pg.* 1126
KURZWEIL - Synthesizers & Keyboards - YOUNG CHANG NORTH AMERICA; *pg.* 595, *pg.* 77
KUSHION KRAFT - Packaging Product - SEALED AIR CORPORATION; *pg.* 1468, *pg.* 1058
KUSS - Filtration System - CUMMINS INC.; *pg.* 1326, *pg.* 676
KUT-A-WAY - Dust Mop - HILLYARD, INC.; *pg.* 331, *pg.* 990
KUTBUSTER - Glove - LAKELAND INDUSTRIES, INC.; *pg.* 1354, *pg.* 1338
KUTKIT - Styptic Swabs - MAJESTIC DRUG COMPANY, INC.; *pg.* 516, *pg.* 1343
KUTTER - Agricultural Product - WILBUR-ELLIS COMPANY; *pg.* 1185, *pg.* 234
KUTZIT - Coating Remover - THE SAVOGRAN COMPANY; *pg.* 1447, *pg.* 840
KV - Drawer Slides - KNAPE & VOGT MANUFACTURING COMPANY; *pg.* 1052, *pg.* 913
KV/24 - Once-Daily Dosing for Tablets or Capsules - LUMARA HEALTH INC.; *pg.* 1557, *pg.* 973
KVM SERVSWITCH - USB Micro Extender Kit - BLACK BOX CORPORATION; *pg.* 361, *pg.* 1547
KVUE.COM - Website - KVUE-TV; *pg.* 295, *pg.* 1663
KW-120-THX - Subwoofer - KLIPSCH GROUP, INC.; *pg.* 649, *pg.* 688
KWAIT BLOOMS - Jewelry - KWIAT INC.; *pg.* 8, *pg.* 1249
KWAIT STAR - Jewelry - KWIAT INC.; *pg.* 8, *pg.* 1249
KWAIT TIARA - Jewelry - KWIAT INC.; *pg.* 8, *pg.* 1249
KWANDO - Fitness Product - BALLY TOTAL FITNESS HOLDINGS CORPORATION; *pg.* 532, *pg.* 1200
KWIK - Paint - W.M. BARR & COMPANY, INC.; *pg.* 338, *pg.* 1647
KWIK-BLAK - Metal Finishing Product - HEATBATH CORPORATION; *pg.* 1165, *pg.* 826
KWIK-BOLT - Anchors - HILTI, INC.; *pg.* 1346, *pg.* 1490
KWIK-CLEAN - Spray Nozzle - STRAHMAN VALVES, INC.; *pg.* 1379, *pg.* 1517
KWIK CYCLE - Crimper - GREENLEE TEXTRON INC.; *pg.* 1048, *pg.* 655
KWIK-DRAW - Detector Tube Pumps - MINE SAFETY APPLIANCES COMPANY; *pg.* 1361, *pg.* 1525
KWIK-EDGE - Scraper Blade - ESCO CORPORATION; *pg.* 1335, *pg.* 1502
KWIK-FILL - Plastic Bag - ELKAY PLASTICS COMPANY, INC.; *pg.* 1882, *pg.* 68
KWIK FIND - Handle Wraps - LAPWORKS, INC.; *pg.* 426, *pg.* 187
KWIK FOAM - Caulk And Sealant - DAP PRODUCTS, INC.; *pg.* 1441, *pg.* 756
KWIK KIK - Soccer Trainer - SCHOOL-TECH, INC.; *pg.* 1844, *pg.* 866
KWIK-LOK - Wear Protection - ESCO CORPORATION; *pg.* 1335, *pg.* 1502
KWIK-LOK II - Mechanical Locking System - ESCO CORPORATION; *pg.* 1335, *pg.* 1502
KWIK MULL - Organic Polymer - HILL & GRIFFITH COMPANY; *pg.* 1167, *pg.* 1414
KWIK SEAL - Caulk And Sealant - DAP PRODUCTS, INC.; *pg.* 1441, *pg.* 756
KWIK SEAL PLUS - Caulk And Sealant - DAP PRODUCTS, INC.; *pg.* 1441, *pg.* 756
KWIK-SKRENE - Transformer Test Kit - GE ENERGY; *pg.* 1338, *pg.* 506
KWIK-SLEEVE - Components - THE TIMKEN COMPANY; *pg.* 218, *pg.* 1408
KWIK STAR - Convenience Stores - KWIK TRIP INC.; *pg.* 1026, *pg.* 1864
KWIK STEPPER - Bits - GREENLEE TEXTRON INC.; *pg.* 1048, *pg.* 655
KWIK STRIPPER - Wire Stripper - GREENLEE TEXTRON INC.; *pg.* 1048, *pg.* 655
KWIK-TIP - Tips for Airless Spray Machines - DUNN-EDWARDS CORPORATION; *pg.* 1442, *pg.* 129
KWIK-TIP - Tooth Equipment - ESCO CORPORATION; *pg.* 1335, *pg.* 1502
KWIK-TIP - Fluid Handling System - GRACO, INC.; *pg.* 1342, *pg.* 935
KWIK-TOG - Anchors - HILTI, INC.; *pg.* 1346, *pg.* 1490
KWIK TRIP - Convenience Stores - KWIK TRIP INC.; *pg.* 1026, *pg.* 1864
KWIKDEK - Decking - BENJAMIN OBDYKE, INC.; *pg.* 70, *pg.* 1540
KWIKEE - Internet Images - MULTI-AD, INC.; *pg.* 1666, *pg.* 652
KWIKEE - Sprayer - SMOOTH-ON INC.; *pg.* 111, *pg.* 1528
KWIKEE KOLOR - Product Illustration System - MULTI-AD, INC.; *pg.* 1666, *pg.* 652
KWIKEE RECAS - Coop Information System - MULTI-AD, INC.; *pg.* 1666, *pg.* 652
KWIKEE SYSTEMS - Product Illustration System - MULTI-AD, INC.; *pg.* 1666, *pg.* 652
KWIKEEZE - Cleaner - THE SAVOGRAN COMPANY; *pg.* 1447, *pg.* 840
KWIKERY BAKERY - Bakery - KWIK TRIP INC.; *pg.* 1026, *pg.* 1864
KWIKLOK - Printer and Coder - BELL-MARK CORPORATION; *pg.* 1620, *pg.* 1108
KWIKPAY - Electronic Payment Mode - NELNET, INC.; *pg.* 786, *pg.* 1012
KWIKPULL - Fingerless Glove Removal - WELLS LAMONT CORPORATION; *pg.* 15, *pg.* 638
KWIKSET - Door Locks & Hardware - STANLEY BLACK & DECKER, INC.; *pg.* 1063, *pg.* 358
KWIKWRAP - Weather Protectant Wrap - GAF MATERIALS CORP.; *pg.* 83, *pg.* 1681
KWIXIN - Wood Screws - ROBERTSON INC.; *pg.* 1372, *pg.* 1924
KWK - Minerals - MINERALS TECHNOLOGIES INC.; *pg.* 1173, *pg.* 617
KWW - Filler Clay - BASF CATALYSTS LLC; *pg.* 1148, *pg.* 1074
KYBREAK - Repulping Aids - HERCULES INCORPORATED; *pg.* 1166, *pg.* 392
KYLE - Furniture - AMISCO INDUSTRIES LTD.; *pg.* 913, *pg.* 1958
KYLE RAYNER - Character - DC COMICS, INC.; *pg.* 1633, *pg.* 1221
KYMENE - Wet-Strength Resin - HERCULES INCORPORATED; *pg.* 1166, *pg.* 392
KYNAPSE - Middleware - AUTODESK INC.; *pg.* 356, *pg.* 257
KYNAR - Compression Molded Product - WESTLAKE PLASTICS COMPANY; *pg.* 1892, *pg.* 1548
KYON - Metal Cutting Tools - KENNAMETAL INC.; *pg.* 1052, *pg.* 1547
KYOTO BRAND - Healthcare Product - SWANSON HEALTH PRODUCTS INC.; *pg.* 1600, *pg.* 1397
KYPOST.COM - Online Newspaper - THE E.W. SCRIPPS COMPANY; *pg.* 1639, *pg.* 1412
KYSOR - Fan Drive - BORGWARNER INC.; *pg.* 167, *pg.* 867
KYTAMER - Chitosan Derivative - THE DOW CHEMICAL COMPANY; *pg.* 1157, *pg.* 898
KYTRIL - Pharmaceutical Product - HOFFMANN-LA ROCHE INC.; *pg.* 1542, *pg.* 1099
KYUN - Beverages - THE COCA-COLA COMPANY; *pg.* 240, *pg.* 493
KYZEN - Cleaning Chemical Product - KYZEN CORPORATION; *pg.* 331, *pg.* 1652

L

L-1011 - Systems Integration & Aeronautics - LOCKHEED MARTIN CORPORATION; *pg.* 229, *pg.* 762
L-20(A) - Water Activated Exterior/Interior Raft Light - ACR ELECTRONICS, INC.; *pg.* 612, *pg.* 422
L&M - Cigarettes - PHILIP MORRIS USA INC.; *pg.* 1894, *pg.* 1803
L & P - Bed Springs - LEGGETT & PLATT, INCORPORATED; *pg.* 933, *pg.* 974
L & R - Instrument Delivery Cassette System - L&R MANUFACTURING COMPANY; *pg.* 1419, *pg.* 1076
L-ARGININE - Nutritional Supplement - NATURAL ORGANICS, INC.; *pg.* 1571, *pg.* 1181
L-B-C - Lead Barrier Compound (Lead Paint Encapsulant) - CALIFORNIA PRODUCTS CORPORATION; *pg.* 1441, *pg.* 781
L-CARNITINE - Pharmaceutical Product - ALLERGAN; *pg.* 1490, *pg.* 1101
L-GLUTAMINE - Nutritional Supplement - NATURAL ORGANICS, INC.; *pg.* 1571, *pg.* 1181
L-LYSINE - Nutritional Supplement - NATURAL ORGANICS, INC.; *pg.* 1571, *pg.* 1181
L/M ANIMAL FARMS - Pet Products - THE HARTZ MOUNTAIN CORP.; *pg.* 1476, *pg.* 1120
L-METHIONINE - Nutritional Supplement - NATURAL ORGANICS, INC.; *pg.* 1571, *pg.* 1181
L-ORNITHINE - Nutritional Supplement - NATURAL ORGANICS, INC.; *pg.* 1571, *pg.* 1181
L-R WALL - Curtain Wall System - ALCOA INC.; *pg.* 65, *pg.* 1188
L SERIES - Microphone System - SHURE INCORPORATED; *pg.* 672, *pg.* 638
L-TYROSINE - Nutritional Supplement - NATURAL ORGANICS, INC.; *pg.* 1571, *pg.* 1181
L. WOODS - Casual Dining Restaurant - LETTUCE ENTERTAIN YOU ENTERPRISES, INC.; *pg.* 1735, *pg.* 580
L1900 - Fluid Handling System - GRACO, INC.; *pg.* 1342, *pg.* 935
L2O - Seafood Restaurant - LETTUCE ENTERTAIN YOU ENTERPRISES, INC.; *pg.* 1735, *pg.* 580
L8-1(A) - Water Activated Survivor Locator Light - ACR ELECTRONICS, INC.; *pg.* 612, *pg.* 422
L8-3 - Water Activated Personal Rescue Light - ACR ELECTRONICS, INC.; *pg.* 612, *pg.* 422
LA - Monthly Magazine - LOS ANGELES TIMES COMMUNICATIONS, LLC; *pg.* 1660, *pg.* 135
LA/1000 - Label Applicator - DIAGRAPH; *pg.* 387, *pg.* 989
LA ABUELITA - Food Product - PATRICK CUDAHY INC.; *pg.* 888, *pg.* 1856
L.A. BLUES - Apparel - ASCENA RETAIL GROUP, INC.; *pg.*

18, *pg.* 1081
LA BOLA EXPLORADORA - Toys - LEAPFROG ENTERPRISES, INC.; *pg.* 961, *pg.* 84
LA BOLDUE - Beer - SLEEMAN UNIBROUE QUEBEC; *pg.* 265, *pg.* 1950
LA BOULANGE - Bakery Products - STARBUCKS CORPORATION; *pg.* 897, *pg.* 1840
LA CANADA VALLEY SUN - Newspaper - LOS ANGELES TIMES COMMUNICATIONS, LLC; *pg.* 1660, *pg.* 135
LA CHIARA GAVI DI GAVI - Wine - SHAW ROSS INTERNATIONAL IMPORTERS; *pg.* 1970, *pg.* 449
LA CHOY - Food Product - CONAGRA FOODS, INC.; *pg.* 826, *pg.* 1014
LA-CO BRITE - Flux - LA-CO INDUSTRIES MARKAL CO., INC.; *pg.* 1170, *pg.* 610
LA COCINA MEXICANA - Publication - MACFADDEN COMMUNICATIONS GROUP, LLC; *pg.* 1660, *pg.* 1254
LA CORONA - Domestic Cigars - ALTADIS USA, INC.; *pg.* 1893, *pg.* 423
LA COSTA - Dinnerware - THE HOMER LAUGHLIN CHINA COMPANY; *pg.* 1125, *pg.* 1850
LA COSTA - Office Furniture - STEELCASE INC.; *pg.* 475, *pg.* 889
LA COUR PAVILLON - Bordeaux Wines - DREYFUS ASHBY INC.; *pg.* 1962, *pg.* 1226
LA CRESCENTA VALLEY SUN - Newspaper - LOS ANGELES TIMES COMMUNICATIONS, LLC; *pg.* 1660, *pg.* 135
LA CRYSTA - Lighting Product - QUOIZEL INC.; *pg.* 1304, *pg.* 1616
LA ESPANOLA - Olive Oil - CARGILL LIMITED; *pg.* 1475, *pg.* 1914
LA FOLIE - Beer - NEW BELGIUM BREWING COMPANY, INC.; *pg.* 258, *pg.* 328
LA FRUTA - Dairy Food Product - LIFEWAY FOODS, INC.; *pg.* 874, *pg.* 634
LA GAILLARDE - Beer - SLEEMAN UNIBROUE QUEBEC; *pg.* 265, *pg.* 1950
LA GEAR - Activewear - L.A. GEAR, INC.; *pg.* 1811, *pg.* 134
LA GRANDE ORANGE - Restaurant - LETTUCE ENTERTAIN YOU ENTERPRISES, INC.; *pg.* 1735, *pg.* 580
L.A. INTIMATES - Sleepwear - KELLWOOD COMPANY; *pg.* 28, *pg.* 975
LA INTIMIDAD - Cigar And Tobacco - SWISHER INTERNATIONAL, INC.; *pg.* 1895, *pg.* 345
LA JOLLA - Carpet - BEAULIEU GROUP, LLC; *pg.* 917, *pg.* 529
LA JOLLA - Beverages - THE COCA-COLA COMPANY; *pg.* 240, *pg.* 493
LA JOLLA - Rug - COURISTAN INC.; *pg.* 921, *pg.* 1067
LA JOLLA - Pharmaceutical Product - LA JOLLA PHARMACEUTICAL COMPANY; *pg.* 1554, *pg.* 204
LA LEAF - Tile - ARTISTIC TILE INC.; *pg.* 914, *pg.* 1119
LA LECHERA - Food & Beverage Product - NESTLE USA, INC.; *pg.* 883, *pg.* 96
LA LEY 107.9 FM - Radio Station - SPANISH BROADCASTING SYSTEM INC.; *pg.* 310, *pg.* 446
LA LIGHTS - Children - L.A. GEAR, INC.; *pg.* 1811, *pg.* 134
LA LINEA LATINA - Telephone Service - IDT CORPORATION; *pg.* 643, *pg.* 1096
LA LOVING - Cap - BROWN & BIGELOW, INC.; *pg.* 1624, *pg.* 959
LA MEGA - Radio Station - SPANISH BROADCASTING SYSTEM INC.; *pg.* 310, *pg.* 446
LA MER - Luxurious Skin Treatments - THE ESTEE LAUDER COMPANIES INC.; *pg.* 508, *pg.* 1229
LA MINITA - Estate Coffee - THE SECOND CUP LTD.; *pg.* 1749, *pg.* 1928
LA NOUBA - Show And Ticket - CIRQUE DU SOLEIL INC.; *pg.* 540, *pg.* 1954
LA PALMA - Carpet - BEAULIEU GROUP, LLC; *pg.* 917, *pg.* 529
LA PARRA - Lighting Product - QUOIZEL INC.; *pg.* 1304, *pg.* 1616
LA PAULINA - Cheese & Dairy Products - SAPUTO, INC.; *pg.* 893, *pg.* 1956
LA PAZ-ITIVELY HOT - Nail Care Product - OPI PRODUCTS INC.; *pg.* 518, *pg.* 167
LA POMMERAIE CALVADOS - Liquor - WILLIAM GRANT & SONS, INC.; *pg.* 1972, *pg.* 1057
LA PRADA - Carpet - BEAULIEU GROUP, LLC; *pg.* 917, *pg.* 529
LA QUINTA INN & SUITES - Hotel Chain - LA QUINTA CORPORATION; *pg.* 1099, *pg.* 1722
LA QUINTA INNS - Hotel Chain - LA QUINTA CORPORATION; *pg.* 1099, *pg.* 1722
LA RAMBLA - Restaurant - ARK RESTAURANTS CORP.; *pg.* 1715, *pg.* 1196
LA RAZA 93.3 FM - Radio Station - SPANISH BROADCASTING SYSTEM INC.; *pg.* 310, *pg.* 446
LA RAZA 97.9 FM - Radio Station - SPANISH BROADCASTING SYSTEM INC.; *pg.* 310, *pg.* 446
LA REDOUTE - Apparel - FULLBEAUTY BRANDS; *pg.* 1770, *pg.* 1233
LA ROCHE - Wine - REMY COINTREAU USA INC.; *pg.* 1969, *pg.* 1285
LA SALLE - Fabric - NEMSCHOFF, INC.; *pg.* 936, *pg.* 1890
LA SALSA FRESH MEXICAN GRILL - Restaurant - CKE RESTAURANTS INC.; *pg.* 1723, *pg.* 63
LA SALTENA - Food Product - GENERAL MILLS, INC.; *pg.* 828, *pg.* 933
LA SCALA - Loudspeaker - KLIPSCH GROUP, INC.; *pg.* 649, *pg.* 688
LA SCALA - Furniture - TROPITONE FURNITURE CO., INC.; *pg.* 945, *pg.* 118
LA SCALA - Community Name - WCI COMMUNITIES, INC.; *pg.* 1118, *pg.* 414
LA SENORITA - Restaurant - MEXICAN RESTAURANTS, INC.; *pg.* 1741, *pg.* 1711
LA SONIC - Jewelry Cleaner - CONNOISSEURS PRODUCTS CORPORATION; *pg.* 329, *pg.* 861
L.A. T SPORT - Men's & Boy's Coordinated Knits - L.A. T SPORTSWEAR, LLC; *pg.* 1838, *pg.* 526
L.A. T SPORTSWEAR - Ladies & Unisex Products - L.A. T SPORTSWEAR, LLC; *pg.* 1838, *pg.* 526
LA TOUR - Fan - CRAFTMADE INTERNATIONAL, INC.; *pg.* 1295, *pg.* 1670
LA UNIVERSAL - Telephone Service - IDT CORPORATION; *pg.* 643, *pg.* 1096
LA VELA - Fan - CRAFTMADE INTERNATIONAL, INC.; *pg.* 1295, *pg.* 1670
LA VICTORIA - Salsa & Sauces - MEGAMEX FOODS, LLC; *pg.* 833, *pg.* 66
LA YOGURT - Yogurt - JOHANNA FOODS INC.; *pg.* 866, *pg.* 1066
LA-Z-BOY - Furniture - LA-Z-BOY INCORPORATED; *pg.* 932, *pg.* 901
LA-Z-BOY COMFORT STUDIOS - Slogan - LA-Z-BOY INCORPORATED; *pg.* 932, *pg.* 901
LA-Z-BOY DESIGNER'S CHOICE - Furniture - LA-Z-BOY INCORPORATED; *pg.* 932, *pg.* 901
LA-Z-BOY KIDZ - In-Store Gallery Program - LA-Z-BOY INCORPORATED; *pg.* 932, *pg.* 901
LA-Z-COIL - Furniture - LA-Z-BOY INCORPORATED; *pg.* 932, *pg.* 901
LA-Z-TOUCH - Furniture - LA-Z-BOY INCORPORATED; *pg.* 932, *pg.* 901
LA ZETA - Radio Station - SPANISH BROADCASTING SYSTEM INC.; *pg.* 310, *pg.* 446
LAB - Hair Care Product - JOHN PAUL MITCHELL SYSTEMS; *pg.* 512, *pg.* 133
LAB CLIPBOARD - Robotic Product - HAMILTON CO., INC.; *pg.* 1415, *pg.* 1031
LAB FLO - Lab Faucets & Fittings - T&S BRASS & BRONZE WORKS, INC.; *pg.* 114, *pg.* 1623
LAB-IN-A-BOX - Software - BIO-RAD LABORATORIES, INC.; *pg.* 1504, *pg.* 101
LAB-LOC - Plastic Bag - ELKAY PLASTICS COMPANY, INC.; *pg.* 1882, *pg.* 68
LAB PAK - Moisture Proof Tamper-Evident Mailers - SEALED AIR CORPORATION; *pg.* 1468, *pg.* 1058
LAB REPORTING SYSTEM - Hardware And Software - HESKA CORPORATION; *pg.* 1542, *pg.* 335
LAB SERIES - Men's Skin Care Products - THE ESTEE LAUDER COMPANIES INC.; *pg.* 508, *pg.* 1229
LAB STANDARD - Ear Bar - STOELTING CO.; *pg.* 1430, *pg.* 671
LAB SUPPORT - Healthcare Service - ON ASSIGNMENT, INC.; *pg.* 449, *pg.* 56
LABAC - Medical Product - GF HEALTH PRODUCTS, INC.; *pg.* 1535, *pg.* 508
LABADEE - Cruise Ship - ROYAL CARIBBEAN CRUISES LTD; *pg.* 1921, *pg.* 446
LABARGE - Furniture - HERITAGE HOME GROUP; *pg.* 926, *pg.* 1379
LABASIX - Lenses - NEWPORT CORPORATION; *pg.* 1424, *pg.* 114
LABATT - Beer - LABATT BREWING COMPANY LIMITED; *pg.* 253, *pg.* 1939
LABATT 50 - Ale - LABATT BREWING COMPANY LIMITED; *pg.* 253, *pg.* 1939
LABATT LITE - Beer - LABATT BREWING COMPANY LIMITED; *pg.* 253, *pg.* 1939
LABATT STERLING - Brewery - LABATT BREWING COMPANY LIMITED; *pg.* 253, *pg.* 1939
LABDIRECT - Medical Research - LABORATORY CORPORATION OF AMERICA HOLDINGS; *pg.* 1554, *pg.* 1359
LABEDA - Wheel - ROLLER DERBY SKATE CORP.; *pg.* 966, *pg.* 630
LABEL-AIRE - Automatic Labeling Equip. - LABEL-AIRE, INC.; *pg.* 426, *pg.* 93
LABEL-LYTE - Film - SPINNAKER COATING, LLC; *pg.* 1470, *pg.* 1477
LABEL PRO - Glue & Adhesive - GLUEFAST COMPANY, INC.; *pg.* 1459, *pg.* 1090
LABEL SECURE - Program - TOPFLIGHT CORPORATION; *pg.* 681, *pg.* 1534
LABELCORE - Labeling Product - PANDUIT CORP.; *pg.* 661, *pg.* 663
LABELFLEX - Plastic Product - PLASTIC SUPPLIERS, INC.; *pg.* 1888, *pg.* 1443
LABELLOK - Packaging Materials & Equipment - SEALED AIR CORPORATION; *pg.* 1468, *pg.* 1058
LABELMARK - Label Printer - BRADY CORPORATION; *pg.* 363, *pg.* 1873
LABELS FOR EDUCATION - School Program - CAMPBELL SOUP COMPANY; *pg.* 844, *pg.* 1048
LABELZON - Security Label - AMERICAN CASTING & MANUFACTURING CORPORATION; *pg.* 1312, *pg.* 1321
LABET - French Wine - LAIRD & COMPANY, INC.; *pg.* 1966, *pg.* 1119
LABKLENZ - Alkaline Detergent - STERIS CORPORATION; *pg.* 1597, *pg.* 1464
LABLEGS - Stabilizer Pneumatic Isolators - NEWPORT CORPORATION; *pg.* 1424, *pg.* 114
LABMASTER - Filtration System - SERFILCO, LTD.; *pg.* 1375, *pg.* 641
LABMAX - Monitor Laser Output - COHERENT, INC.; *pg.* 1406, *pg.* 265
LABMAX - Calorimeter - METTLER-TOLEDO INTERNATIONAL INC.; *pg.* 1423, *pg.* 1441
LABMICE.NET - Website - TECHTARGET, INC.; *pg.* 482, *pg.* 837
LABOR - Kitchen Product - KOHLER CO.; *pg.* 91, *pg.* 1862
LABOR READY - General Labor Staffing - TRUEBLUE, INC.; *pg.* 485, *pg.* 1845
LABOR RELATIONS REPORTER - Publisher - BLOOMBERG BNA; *pg.* 1621, *pg.* 1772
LABORATORY EQUIPMENT - Trade Magazine - ADVANTAGE BUSINESS MEDIA; *pg.* 1613, *pg.* 1116
LABORATORY WORKBENCH - Software - CONCURRENT COMPUTER CORPORATION; *pg.* 379, *pg.* 531
LABORCARE - Health Plan & Publication - MEDICA, INC.; *pg.* 1208, *pg.* 949
LABORPLUS - Publisher - BLOOMBERG BNA; *pg.* 1621, *pg.* 1772
LABOUNTY - Hydraulic Tool - STANLEY BLACK & DECKER, INC.; *pg.* 1063, *pg.* 358
LABPRO - Pump Product - IDEX CORPORATION; *pg.* 1347, *pg.* 623
LABREXX - Electronic Tests - IDEXX LABORATORIES, INC.; *pg.* 1543, *pg.* 753
LABSHARE - Molecular Biology Product - THERMO FISHER SCIENTIFIC INC.; *pg.* 1602, *pg.* 61
LABSTAR - Healthcare Product - GF HEALTH PRODUCTS, INC.; *pg.* 1535, *pg.* 508
LABTAP - Laboratory Fixtures - BRADLEY CORPORATION; *pg.* 71, *pg.* 1870
LABTOOLS - Software - BIO-RAD LABORATORIES, INC.; *pg.* 1504, *pg.* 101
LABTRON - Medical Product - GF HEALTH PRODUCTS, INC.; *pg.* 1535, *pg.* 508
LABVIEW - Software - CASCADE MICROTECH, INC.; *pg.* 1405, *pg.* 1492
LABWORKS - Software - PERKINELMER, INC.; *pg.* 1426, *pg.* 853
LABYRINTH - Rug - COURISTAN INC.; *pg.* 921, *pg.* 1067
LABYRINTH - Fabric - NEMSCHOFF, INC.; *pg.* 936, *pg.* 1890
LAC - Liquid Alkaline Cleaner - ASHLAND INC.; *pg.* 972, *pg.* 726
LACE AND GROMMET - Screen Surface - DA-LITE SCREEN COMPANY; *pg.* 632, *pg.* 698
LACE BITE PROTECTOR - Hockey Ice Skate Lace Pressure

First page reference indicates Business Class Edition
Second page reference indicates Geographic Edition

Distribution Technology - REEBOK-CCM HOCKEY, INC.; *pg.* 1844, *pg.* 1960
LACE GEORGIA - Women's Clothing & Accessories - WOODEN SHIPS OF HOBOKEN; *pg.* 35, *pg.* 1315
LACE HOODIE - Women's Clothing & Accessories - WOODEN SHIPS OF HOBOKEN; *pg.* 35, *pg.* 1315
LACE TO TOE - Footwear - P.W. MINOR & SON, INC.; *pg.* 1816, *pg.* 1140
LACE WITH GRAC - Blazer - HABAND COMPANY, INC.; *pg.* 1772, *pg.* 1099
LACERTE - Tax Preparation Software - INTUIT INC.; *pg.* 769, *pg.* 158
LACHAT INSTRUMENTS - Flow Injection Analyzer - DANAHER CORPORATION; *pg.* 1044, *pg.* 397
LACI LAXATIV-A-TEA - Laxative Tea - NATROL, INC.; *pg.* 1570, *pg.* 64
LACI LE BEAU - Nutritional Product - NATROL, INC.; *pg.* 1570, *pg.* 64
LACLEDE - Natural Gas - THE LACLEDE GROUP, INC.; *pg.* 980, *pg.* 999
LACQUER-STIK - Paint Marker - LA-CO INDUSTRIES MARKAL CO., INC.; *pg.* 1170, *pg.* 610
LACROIX - Spring & Carbonated Water Products - NATIONAL BEVERAGE CORP.; *pg.* 257, *pg.* 425
LACROSSE - Sedan - GENERAL MOTORS COMPANY; *pg.* 175, *pg.* 881
LACROSSE - Footwear - LACROSSE FOOTWEAR, INC.; *pg.* 1811, *pg.* 1503
LACTA - Chocolate - MONDELEZ INTERNATIONAL, INC.; *pg.* 878, *pg.* 601
LACTAID - Healthcare Product - JOHNSON & JOHNSON; *pg.* 1549, *pg.* 1091
LACTALINS - Pharmaceuticals - HEALTH PRODUCTS CORPORATION; *pg.* 1540, *pg.* 1356
LACTARIN - Food Ingredient - FMC CORPORATION; *pg.* 1163, *pg.* 1564
LACTEEZE - Lactose-Reduced Milk - GAY LEA FOODS CO-OPERATIVE LIMITED; *pg.* 858, *pg.* 1926
LACTO BONBON - Confectionery - THE HERSHEY CO.; *pg.* 1855, *pg.* 1538
LACTOFERON - Nutritional Supplement - NATURAL ORGANICS, INC.; *pg.* 1571, *pg.* 1181
LACTOFREE - Lactose-Free Infant Formula - MEAD JOHNSON NUTRITION COMPANY; *pg.* 1561, *pg.* 615
LACTOSE - Food Ingredient - FOREMOST FARMS USA COOPERATIVE; *pg.* 856, *pg.* 1854
LACY - Wall Decor - HERITAGE LACE INC.; *pg.* 694, *pg.* 711
LADDER - Fabric - NEMSCHOFF, INC.; *pg.* 936, *pg.* 1890
LADDER UP - Extension Safety Post for Fixed Ladders - THE BILCO COMPANY; *pg.* 70, *pg.* 383
LADDERUP - Safety Post - THE BILCO COMPANY; *pg.* 70, *pg.* 383
LADDERY TICKET - Shoe - AEROGROUP INTERNATIONAL, INC.; *pg.* 1803, *pg.* 1055
LADDIE - Golf Balls - BRIDGESTONE GOLF, INC.; *pg.* 1828, *pg.* 528
LADEN - Kitchen Appliance - WHIRLPOOL CORPORATION; *pg.* 62, *pg.* 872
LADERA - Furniture - JOFCO INC.; *pg.* 931, *pg.* 691
LADIES CHOICE - Pants - ELBECO INCORPORATED; *pg.* 40, *pg.* 1584
LADIES DAY - Deodorant - BLUE CROSS LABORATORIES; *pg.* 326, *pg.* 277
LADIES' HOME JOURNAL - Magazine - MEREDITH CORPORATION; *pg.* 1663, *pg.* 705
LADLELINE - Pressed & Monolithic Refractory - RESCO PRODUCTS, INC.; *pg.* 107, *pg.* 1581
LADLEMAX - Pressed & Monolithic Refractory - RESCO PRODUCTS, INC.; *pg.* 107, *pg.* 1581
LADY ASTER - Mexican & Tortilla Products - TYSON FOODS, INC.; *pg.* 902, *pg.* 35
LADY ATTACHE - USB Flash Drive - PNY TECHNOLOGIES, INC.; *pg.* 455, *pg.* 1105
LADY BUG - Bicycle - G. JOANNOU CYCLE CO. INC.; *pg.* 1707, *pg.* 1098
LADY DORBY - Dresses & Career Apparel - KELLWOOD COMPANY; *pg.* 28, *pg.* 975
LADY FOOT LOCKER - Women's Athletic Footwear & Apparel - FOOT LOCKER, INC.; *pg.* 1808, *pg.* 1231
LADY HARDWICK - Clothing - HARDWICK CLOTHES INC.; *pg.* 42, *pg.* 1630
LADY OF SPAIN - Game - WMS INDUSTRIES INC.; *pg.* 593, *pg.* 666
LADY OF THE LAKE - Video Game - INTERNATIONAL GAME TECHNOLOGY; *pg.* 957, *pg.* 1024
LADY PILLOW BACK - Footwear - P.W. MINOR & SON, INC.; *pg.* 1816, *pg.* 1140
LADY SPEED STICK - Personal Care Product - COLGATE-PALMOLIVE COMPANY; *pg.* 504, *pg.* 1215
LADY SUPREME - Hosiery & Related Apparel - MAYER/BERKSHIRE CORPORATION; *pg.* 29, *pg.* 1129
LADY VANITY - Bath Product - KOHLER CO.; *pg.* 91, *pg.* 1862
LADY WAHL - Shaver - WAHL CLIPPER CORPORATION; *pg.* 524, *pg.* 662
LADYBUG - Footwear - COBIAN CORP.; *pg.* 1806, *pg.* 253
LADYFAIRE - Cotton Shorts - HABAND COMPANY, INC.; *pg.* 1772, *pg.* 1099
LADYLACE - Healthcare Apparel - THE SALK COMPANY; *pg.* 1591, *pg.* 800
LADY'S AIDE - Cleaning Bar - U.S. PUMICE COMPANY; *pg.* 1185, *pg.* 65
LADY'S CHOICE - Deodorant - CHURCH & DWIGHT CO., INC.; *pg.* 1153, *pg.* 1063
LADYSMITH - Pistol - SMITH & WESSON HOLDING CORPORATION; *pg.* 1845, *pg.* 846
LADYSPORT - Footwear - P.W. MINOR & SON, INC.; *pg.* 1816, *pg.* 1140
LAFACE RECORDS - Artist - SONY MUSIC ENTERTAINMENT; *pg.* 309, *pg.* 1294
LAFARGE - Cement, Concrete & Related Products - LAFARGE NORTH AMERICA INC.; *pg.* 93, *pg.* 579
LAFAYETTE - Polycarbonate Tumbler - CARLISLE FOODSERVICE PRODUCTS INCORPORATED; *pg.* 1455, *pg.* 1485
LAFAYETTE - Door & Wood Product - CONESTOGA WOOD SPECIALTIES CORP.; *pg.* 921, *pg.* 1527
LAFAYETTE - Watch - GEVRIL USA; *pg.* 6, *pg.* 1348
LAFAYETTE - Women's Trousers - LANE BRYANT; *pg.* 1776, *pg.* 1441
LAFAYETTE - Ceiling Fan - WESTINGHOUSE LIGHTING CORPORATION; *pg.* 687, *pg.* 1571
LAFEBER - Pet Product - PETSMART, INC.; *pg.* 1481, *pg.* 18
LAFERIA - Cheese - SCHREIBER FOODS, INC.; *pg.* 894, *pg.* 1859
LAG SHIELD - Bolt & Shield Anchor - POWERS FASTENERS INC.; *pg.* 1059, *pg.* 1143
LAGO - Cap - PRECISION VALVE CORPORATION; *pg.* 1060, *pg.* 1357
LAGOON - Fabric - NEMSCHOFF, INC.; *pg.* 936, *pg.* 1890
LAGRANGE - Shoes - ALLEN-EDMONDS SHOE CORP.; *pg.* 1804, *pg.* 1887
LAGUNA - Golf Equipment - ACUSHNET COMPANY; *pg.* 1824, *pg.* 818
LAGUNA - Bar Stool - BLATT BOWLING & BILLIARD CORP.; *pg.* 1827, *pg.* 1203
LAGUNA - Footwear - PHOENIX FOOTWEAR GROUP, INC.; *pg.* 1815, *pg.* 60
LAGUNA - Boat - SEA RAY BOATS, INC.; *pg.* 1710, *pg.* 1638
LAGUNA - Ceramic Tile - WALKER & ZANGER, INC.; *pg.* 119, *pg.* 281
LAGUNA BEACH COASTLINE PILOT - Newspaper - LOS ANGELES TIMES COMMUNICATIONS, LLC; *pg.* 1660, *pg.* 135
LAGUNITAS - Bike - MARIN BIKES; *pg.* 1708, *pg.* 168
LAHAINA - Eyewear - MAUI JIM, INC.; *pg.* 9, *pg.* 651
LAHORE - Rug - COURISTAN INC.; *pg.* 921, *pg.* 1067
LAHORE - Rug - ETHAN ALLEN INTERIORS INC.; *pg.* 924, *pg.* 343
LAILA - Footwear - EASTLAND SHOE CORPORATION; *pg.* 1808, *pg.* 750
LAILA ALI - Sporting Goods & Accessories - CHEROKEE GLOBAL BRANDS; *pg.* 21, *pg.* 278
LAINY - Footwear - STEVEN MADDEN, LTD.; *pg.* 1819, *pg.* 1176
LAIRD'S - Vodka & Gin - LAIRD & COMPANY, INC.; *pg.* 1966, *pg.* 1119
LAIRD'S APPLEJACK - Brandy - LAIRD & COMPANY, INC.; *pg.* 1966, *pg.* 1119
LAIRD'S BOTTLED IN BOND APPLE BRANDY - Apple Brandy - LAIRD & COMPANY, INC.; *pg.* 1966, *pg.* 1119
LAIRD'S RARE OLD BRANDY - Brandy - LAIRD & COMPANY, INC.; *pg.* 1966, *pg.* 1119
LAITS GO - Dairy Products - SAPUTO, INC.; *pg.* 893, *pg.* 1956
LAKE - Fabric - NEMSCHOFF, INC.; *pg.* 936, *pg.* 1890
LAKE & LODGE - Coffee Service - KEURIG GREEN MOUNTAIN, INC.; *pg.* 868, *pg.* 1768
LAKE BUENA VISTA - Golf Course - THE WALT DISNEY COMPANY; *pg.* 317, *pg.* 52
LAKE CHAMPLAIN - Clothing - ABERCROMBIE & FITCH CO.; *pg.* 37, *pg.* 1466
LAKE CITY - Newspaper - LAKE CITY REPORTER; *pg.* 1657, *pg.* 436
LAKE EFFECT - Enclosure - GREAT LAKES CASE & CABINET CO., INC.; *pg.* 401, *pg.* 1529
LAKE HURON - Lakeland Boating Ports O'Call Cruise Guides - O'MEARA-BROWN PUBLICATIONS, INC.; *pg.* 1673, *pg.* 586
LAKE MICHIGAN - Lakeland Boating Ports O'Call Cruise Guides - O'MEARA-BROWN PUBLICATIONS, INC.; *pg.* 1673, *pg.* 586
LAKE ONTARIO - Lakeland Boating Ports O'Call Cruise Guide - O'MEARA-BROWN PUBLICATIONS, INC.; *pg.* 1673, *pg.* 586
LAKE SUPERIOR - Lakeland Boating Ports O'Call Cruise Guide - O'MEARA-BROWN PUBLICATIONS, INC.; *pg.* 1673, *pg.* 586
LAKEFIELD - Kitchen Product - KOHLER CO.; *pg.* 91, *pg.* 1862
LAKELAND - Furniture - ASHLEY FURNITURE INDUSTRIES, INC.; *pg.* 914, *pg.* 1852
LAKELAND BOATING - Regional Yachting Magazine - O'MEARA-BROWN PUBLICATIONS, INC.; *pg.* 1673, *pg.* 586
LAKELAND SHOPPER - Newspaper - NEWS CHIEF; *pg.* 1669, *pg.* 480
LAKESIDE - Furniture - TROPITONE FURNITURE CO., INC.; *pg.* 945, *pg.* 118
LAKESIDE ERGO-ONE - System Utility Cart - MEDLINE INDUSTRIES, INC.; *pg.* 1562, *pg.* 635
LAKEWOOD - Furniture - FLEXSTEEL INDUSTRIES, INC.; *pg.* 925, *pg.* 707
LAKEWOOD - Bath Product - KOHLER CO.; *pg.* 91, *pg.* 1862
LAKEWOOD - Lighting Product - QUOIZEL INC.; *pg.* 1304, *pg.* 1616
LAKEWOOD PLANTATION - Processed Turkey - HOUSE OF RAEFORD FARMS, INC.; *pg.* 864, *pg.* 1386
LAKOLENE - FD&C Lake - SENSIENT COLORS INC.; *pg.* 1180, *pg.* 1003
LAL - Cap - BROWN & BIGELOW, INC.; *pg.* 1624, *pg.* 959
LALA - Glove - KOMBI, LTD.; *pg.* 1838, *pg.* 1766
LALIQUE - Fabric - NEMSCHOFF, INC.; *pg.* 936, *pg.* 1890
LAM LIGHTING SYSTEMS - Lighting - PHILIPS LIGHTING; *pg.* 1303, *pg.* 806
LAMA - Lamb Feed - MANNA PRO CORPORATION; *pg.* 1478, *pg.* 975
LAMAL - Adhesive & Sealant - DOW CHEMICAL; *pg.* 1156, *pg.* 1563
LAMB - Food Product - ELLENBEE-LEGGETT COMPANY INC.; *pg.* 854, *pg.* 1452
LAMB WESTON - Food Product - CONAGRA FOODS, INC.; *pg.* 826, *pg.* 1014
LAMB WESTON INLAND VALLEY - Food Product - CONAGRA FOODS, INC.; *pg.* 826, *pg.* 1014
LAMBDA - Laser - COHERENT, INC.; *pg.* 1406, *pg.* 265
LAMBDA - Spectrometer - PERKINELMER, INC.; *pg.* 1426, *pg.* 853
LAMBDA - Lube-Free Roller Chain - U.S. TSUBAKI, INC.; *pg.* 221, *pg.* 670
LAMBDAUNITE - Software System - ALCATEL-LUCENT; *pg.* 615, *pg.* 1094
LAMBDAUNITE - MultiService Switch (MSS) - ALCATEL-LUCENT; *pg.* 615, *pg.* 38
LAMBDAXTREME - Software System - ALCATEL-LUCENT; *pg.* 615, *pg.* 1094
LAMBEAU FIELD - Football Stadium - GREEN BAY PACKERS, INC.; *pg.* 551, *pg.* 1859
LAMBENT - Raw Material - PETROFERM INC.; *pg.* 1177, *pg.* 616
LAMBERT - Furniture - ASHLEY FURNITURE INDUSTRIES, INC.; *pg.* 914, *pg.* 1852
LAMBERT KAY - Pet Product - CHURCH & DWIGHT CO., INC.; *pg.* 1153, *pg.* 1063
LAMBRITE - In-Home Furniture & Drapery Cleaning - STEAMATIC INC.; *pg.* 60, *pg.* 1696
LAMB'S CLUB - Cigars - FINCK CIGAR CO.; *pg.* 1894, *pg.* 1740
LAMB'S NAVY - Rum - CORBY DISTILLERIES LTD.; *pg.* 1961, *pg.* 1937
LAMB'S PALM BREEZE - Rum - CORBY DISTILLERIES

LTD.; *pg.* 1961, *pg.* 1937
LAMB'S WHITE - Rum - CORBY DISTILLERIES LTD.; *pg.* 1961, *pg.* 1937
LAMDEX - Plastic Foam - THE DOW CHEMICAL COMPANY; *pg.* 1157, *pg.* 898
LAME - Dinnerware - THE HOMER LAUGHLIN CHINA COMPANY; *pg.* 1125, *pg.* 1850
LAMIALL - Laminate - INX INTERNATIONAL INK CO.; *pg.* 421, *pg.* 658
LAMIBAG - Lamifoam Pouch - POLYAIR INTER PACK INC.; *pg.* 1467, *pg.* 1941
LAMIFILM - Foam Product - POLYAIR INTER PACK INC.; *pg.* 1467, *pg.* 1941
LAMIFOAM - Foam Product - POLYAIR INTER PACK INC.; *pg.* 1467, *pg.* 1941
LAMIGLASS - Flat Glass - PPG INDUSTRIES, INC.; *pg.* 1445, *pg.* 1579
LAMILUX - Corrugated Carton Stock - GEORGIA-PACIFIC LLC; *pg.* 1458, *pg.* 507
LAMIN8 - Solventless Film Laminating Adhesive - H B FULLER COMPANY; *pg.* 1165, *pg.* 961
LAMINATE MODELER - Software - MSC SOFTWARE CORPORATION; *pg.* 441, *pg.* 262
LAMINATING & CONVERTING FILMS - Plastic Film - MULTI-PLASTICS, INC.; *pg.* 1886, *pg.* 1457
LAMINITE - Wear-Resistant Material - HENSLEY INDUSTRIES, INC.; *pg.* 1166, *pg.* 1682
LAMONS - Gasket Company - TRIMAS CORPORATION; *pg.* 1383, *pg.* 874
LAMORINDA - Bath & Plumbing Product - JACUZZI BRANDS CORPORATION; *pg.* 554, *pg.* 65
LAMOTTE - Lab Science Material - CAROLINA BIOLOGICAL SUPPLY COMPANY; *pg.* 1513, *pg.* 1359
LAMPERT LEGEND - Windows - LAMPERT YARDS, INC.; *pg.* 1053, *pg.* 962
LAMPGARD - Car Headlight Covers - MACNEIL AUTOMOTIVE PRODUCTS, LTD.; *pg.* 211, *pg.* 559
LAMPHUGGER - Wiring Devices - SWIVELIER CO., INC.; *pg.* 1307, *pg.* 1142
LAMPLIGHT - Oil Lamp & Candle - W.C. BRADLEY CO.; *pg.* 62, *pg.* 528
LAMS - Petcare - TRACTOR SUPPLY COMPANY; *pg.* 708, *pg.* 1627
LAMSON - Blower - GARDNER DENVER, INC.; *pg.* 1338, *pg.* 1592
LAN WORKGROUP - Computer Software - NOVELL INC.; *pg.* 446, *pg.* 852
LAN WORKPLACE - Computer Software - NOVELL INC.; *pg.* 446, *pg.* 852
LAN2LAN - Software - CISCO SYSTEMS, INC.; *pg.* 372, *pg.* 240
LANA - Footwear - PHOENIX FOOTWEAR GROUP, INC.; *pg.* 1815, *pg.* 60
LANA-LOTION - Liquid Soap - ADCO, INC.; *pg.* 325, *pg.* 482
LANABIOTIC - Triple Antibiotic Creme - COMBE INCORPORATED; *pg.* 1516, *pg.* 1351
LANACANE - Cream Medication - COMBE INCORPORATED; *pg.* 1516, *pg.* 1351
LANACANE - Anti-Itch Cream - RECKITT BENCKISER INC.; *pg.* 1136, *pg.* 1105
LANACORT - Health & Beauty Product - COMBE INCORPORATED; *pg.* 1516, *pg.* 1351
LANACRON - Complex Dyes - HUNTSMAN CORPORATION; *pg.* 1167, *pg.* 1758
LANAI - Kayaks - HOBIE CAT COMPANY; *pg.* 1708, *pg.* 173
LANAI - Eyewear - MAUI JIM, INC.; *pg.* 9, *pg.* 651
LANALIN OIL - Dry Cleaning & Laundry Product - ADCO, INC.; *pg.* 325, *pg.* 482
LANARK - Wallcovering - OMNOVA SOLUTIONS INC; *pg.* 1176, *pg.* 1453
LANASET - Dyeing System - HUNTSMAN CORPORATION; *pg.* 1167, *pg.* 1758
LANASOL - Reactive Dyes - HUNTSMAN CORPORATION; *pg.* 1167, *pg.* 1758
LANBOY - Case - ANTEC INCORPORATED; *pg.* 350, *pg.* 90
LANCASTER - Furniture - ASHLEY FURNITURE INDUSTRIES, INC.; *pg.* 914, *pg.* 1852
LANCASTER - Furniture - BASSETT FURNITURE INDUSTRIES, INCORPORATED; *pg.* 916, *pg.* 1776
LANCASTER - Milk Candy - THE HERSHEY CO.; *pg.* 1855, *pg.* 1538
LANCASTER - Fan - HUNTER FAN COMPANY; *pg.* 57, *pg.* 1631
THE LANCASTER - Ceiling Fan - HUNTER FAN COMPANY; *pg.* 57, *pg.* 1631
LANCASTER - Fabric - NEMSCHOFF, INC.; *pg.* 936, *pg.* 1890
LANCASTER - Chewing Tobacco - SWISHER INTERNATIONAL, INC.; *pg.* 1895, *pg.* 345
LANCE - Truck Product - OSHKOSH CORPORATION; *pg.* 187, *pg.* 1885
LANCE - Assay Platform - PERKINELMER, INC.; *pg.* 1426, *pg.* 853
LANCE - Fire Chassis - PIERCE MANUFACTURING, INC.; *pg.* 188, *pg.* 1852
LANCE - Packaged Snack Food Products - SNYDER'S-LANCE, INC.; *pg.* 896, *pg.* 1368
LANCE ARMSTRONG - Eyewear - OAKLEY, INC.; *pg.* 1840, *pg.* 86
LANCE-N-LOC - Metal Joining System - BTM CORPORATION; *pg.* 1320, *pg.* 898
LANCELOT - Shoe - AEROGROUP INTERNATIONAL, INC.; *pg.* 1803, *pg.* 1055
LANCELOT - Furniture - JASPER GROUP; *pg.* 930, *pg.* 691
LANCELOT - Mold Inhibitor - MALLET & COMPANY, INC.; *pg.* 875, *pg.* 1521
LANCELOT - Stainless Steel Sinks - MOEN INCORPORATED; *pg.* 1056, *pg.* 1468
LANCELOT - Pen - PENTEL OF AMERICA, LTD.; *pg.* 453, *pg.* 295
LANCELOT - Game - WMS INDUSTRIES INC.; *pg.* 593, *pg.* 666
LANCER - Knife - BUCK KNIVES, INC.; *pg.* 1828, *pg.* 550
LANCER - Fire Helmet - E.D. BULLARD COMPANY; *pg.* 1332, *pg.* 727
LANCERS WINES - Wines - DIAGEO NORTH AMERICA, INC.; *pg.* 1961, *pg.* 361
LANCET - Fastening System - TEXTRON INC.; *pg.* 235, *pg.* 1607
LANCIA - Food Product - NEW WORLD PASTA COMPANY; *pg.* 885, *pg.* 1537
LANCOME - Cosmetics & Perfumes - L'OREAL USA; *pg.* 514, *pg.* 1252
LAND CRUISER - Sports Utility Vehicle - TOYOTA MOTOR NORTH AMERICA, INC.; *pg.* 192, *pg.* 1303
LAND O' LAKES - Consumer Dairy Products - LAND O'LAKES, INC.; *pg.* 873, *pg.* 915
LAND OF ENCHANTMENT - Tagline - NEW MEXICO TOURISM DEPARTMENT; *pg.* 1001, *pg.* 1136
LAND OF LIBERTY - Lottery Game - IOWA LOTTERY; *pg.* 996, *pg.* 705
LAND PRIDE - Implements for Tractors up to 65 hp. - GREAT PLAINS MANUFACTURING, INCORPORATED; *pg.* 704, *pg.* 721
LAND ROVER - Sport Utility Vehicle - JAGUAR LAND ROVER NORTH AMERICA LLC; *pg.* 180, *pg.* 1081
LAND YACHT - Recreation Vehicle - THOR INDUSTRIES, INC.; *pg.* 1711, *pg.* 1456
LANDACORP - Company Name - LANDACORP, INC.; *pg.* 426, *pg.* 65
LANDAU E - Apparel - LANDAU UNIFORMS INCORPORATED; *pg.* 28, *pg.* 971
LANDAU FOR HER - Apparel - LANDAU UNIFORMS INCORPORATED; *pg.* 28, *pg.* 971
LANDAUER - Radiation Measurement Services - LANDAUER, INC.; *pg.* 1554, *pg.* 615
LANDCADD - Software - EAGLE POINT SOFTWARE CORPORATION; *pg.* 389, *pg.* 707
LANDLOK - Pipe - ADVANCED DRAINAGE SYSTEMS, INC.; *pg.* 1878, *pg.* 1455
LANDMARK - Furniture - ASHLEY FURNITURE INDUSTRIES, INC.; *pg.* 914, *pg.* 1852
LANDMARK - Customer Service Research Product - CX ACT, INC.; *pg.* 1394, *pg.* 1773
LANDMARK - Herbicide - E.I. DU PONT DE NEMOURS & COMPANY; *pg.* 1159, *pg.* 390
LANDMARK - Terrain Awareness & Warning System - L-3 AVIONICS SYSTEMS, INC.; *pg.* 650, *pg.* 888
LANDMARK - Outdoor Storage - LIFETIME PRODUCTS INC.; *pg.* 933, *pg.* 1751
LANDMARK - Fabric - NEMSCHOFF, INC.; *pg.* 936, *pg.* 1890
LANDMARK - Office Furniture - STEELCASE INC.; *pg.* 475, *pg.* 889
LANDMARK - Ceramic Tile - SUMMITVILLE TILES, INC.; *pg.* 113, *pg.* 1475
LANDMARK 2000 - Structural System - BUTLER MANUFACTURING COMPANY; *pg.* 72, *pg.* 981
LANDMARK FEEDS - Livestock Feeds - MAPLE LEAF FOODS INC.; *pg.* 875, *pg.* 1927
LANDMARX - Surgical Navigation System - MEDTRONIC, INC.; *pg.* 1564, *pg.* 939
LANDRY'S SEAFOOD HOUSE - Restaurant Chain - LANDRY'S, INC.; *pg.* 1735, *pg.* 1709
LANDSCO LIGHT - Visual Inspection System - DOYLE SYSTEMS; *pg.* 1330, *pg.* 1404
LANDSTAR GEMINI - Security Programs - LANDSTAR SYSTEM, INC.; *pg.* 1914, *pg.* 434
LANDSTAR INWAY - Security Programs - LANDSTAR SYSTEM, INC.; *pg.* 1914, *pg.* 434
LANDSTAR LIGON - Security Programs - LANDSTAR SYSTEM, INC.; *pg.* 1914, *pg.* 434
LANDSTAR RANGER - Security Programs - LANDSTAR SYSTEM, INC.; *pg.* 1914, *pg.* 434
LANDSTAR SYSTEM INC. - Security Programs - LANDSTAR SYSTEM, INC.; *pg.* 1914, *pg.* 434
LANDSTARBROKER.COM - Security Programs Website - LANDSTAR SYSTEM, INC.; *pg.* 1914, *pg.* 434
LANDSTAR.COM - Security Programs Website - LANDSTAR SYSTEM, INC.; *pg.* 1914, *pg.* 434
LANDSTARCOMPANYSTORE.COM - Security Programs - LANDSTAR SYSTEM, INC.; *pg.* 1914, *pg.* 434
LANDSTARONLINE.COM - Security Programs Website - LANDSTAR SYSTEM, INC.; *pg.* 1914, *pg.* 434
LANDXML - Software - EAGLE POINT SOFTWARE CORPORATION; *pg.* 389, *pg.* 707
LANDXPLORER - Software - AUTODESK INC.; *pg.* 356, *pg.* 257
LANE - Furniture - HERITAGE HOME GROUP; *pg.* 926, *pg.* 1379
LANE BRYANT - Apparel - ASCENA RETAIL GROUP, INC.; *pg.* 18, *pg.* 1081
LANE BRYANT OUTLET - Apparel Store - ASCENA RETAIL GROUP, INC.; *pg.* 18, *pg.* 1081
LANE SHIELD - Bowling Equipment - BRUNSWICK BOWLING & BILLIARDS CORP.; *pg.* 1828, *pg.* 622
LANEIGE - Skin Care Products - AMOREPACIFIC US, INC.; *pg.* 498, *pg.* 1195
LANELINK - Connector - MOLEX INCORPORATED; *pg.* 655, *pg.* 628
LANEX - Screen - EASTMAN KODAK COMPANY; *pg.* 1408, *pg.* 1333
LANG - Kitchen Equipment - THE MIDDLEBY CORPORATION; *pg.* 1361, *pg.* 610
LANGLADE - Kitchen Product - KOHLER CO.; *pg.* 91, *pg.* 1862
LANGSTON - Fabric - SCALAMANDRE, INC.; *pg.* 941, *pg.* 1058
LANGSTON - Medical Device - VASCULAR SOLUTIONS, INC.; *pg.* 1434, *pg.* 946
LANGUAGE ACQUISITION - Educational Materials - RENAISSANCE LEARNING, INC.; *pg.* 607, *pg.* 1899
LANGUAGE LINE - Language Interpretation Service - LANGUAGE LINE SERVICES HOLDINGS, INC.; *pg.* 426, *pg.* 151
LANGUAGE LINE OVER THE PHONE - Language Interpretation Service - LANGUAGE LINE SERVICES HOLDINGS, INC.; *pg.* 426, *pg.* 151
LANGUAGE MASTER - Electronic Dictionary - FRANKLIN ELECTRONIC PUBLISHERS, INC.; *pg.* 398, *pg.* 1048
LANGUAGE NEUTRAL LICENSING - Software System - MENTOR GRAPHICS CORPORATION; *pg.* 432, *pg.* 1510
LANIER CLOTHES - Men's Suits & Sportscoats - OXFORD INDUSTRIES, INC.; *pg.* 30, *pg.* 517
LANNATE - Insecticide - E.I. DU PONT DE NEMOURS & COMPANY; *pg.* 1159, *pg.* 390
LANSCAPE - Fiber Optic Computer Network Solutions - CORNING CABLE SYSTEMS LLC; *pg.* 1407, *pg.* 1378
LANSCAPE - Cable System - CORNING INCORPORATED; *pg.* 1122, *pg.* 1154
LANSDOWNE - Weather Instrument - SWIFT OPTICAL INSTRUMENTS, INC.; *pg.* 1430, *pg.* 1744
LANSING - Furniture - AMERICAN LEATHER LP; *pg.* 912, *pg.* 1673
LANSING - Ethernet Product - VITESSE SEMICONDUCTOR CORPORATION; *pg.* 686, *pg.* 57
LANSOLVE - Notebook Computers Services - DELL INC.; *pg.* 383, *pg.* 1737
LANSURVEYOR - Computer Software - SOLARWINDS, INC.; *pg.* 471, *pg.* 1666
LANTANA - Jewelry - YURMAN DESIGN, INC.; *pg.* 15, *pg.* 1316
LANTERN LOGO (ARTHUR A. LEVINE BOOKS) - Educational Materials - SCHOLASTIC INC.; *pg.* 1683, *pg.* 1288

First page reference indicates Business Class Edition
Second page reference indicates Geographic Edition

LANTHASCREEN - Molecular Biology Product - THERMO FISHER SCIENTIFIC INC.; *pg.* 1602, *pg.* 61
LANTIRN - Systems Integration & Aeronautics - LOCKHEED MARTIN CORPORATION; *pg.* 229, *pg.* 762
LANTISEPTIC - Therapeutic Skin Protectants - SUMMIT INDUSTRIES, INC.; *pg.* 1599, *pg.* 535
LANTUS - Insulin Glargine Injection - SANOFI US; *pg.* 1592, *pg.* 1046
LANVIN - Perfume - INTER PARFUMS, INC.; *pg.* 512, *pg.* 1244
LANZ - Pressure Regulating Valve - MEDTRONIC; *pg.* 1563, *pg.* 183
LAP-BAND - Adjustable Gastric Banding System - ALLERGAN, INC.; *pg.* 1491, *pg.* 106
LAP OF LUXURY - Carpet - BEAULIEU GROUP, LLC; *pg.* 917, *pg.* 529
LAPAROSCOPY SIMULATOR - Virtual Laparoscopic Interface or Laparoscopic Surgical Workstation - IMMERSION CORPORATION; *pg.* 413, *pg.* 246
LAPHROAIG - Malt Whiskey - JIM BEAM BRANDS CO.; *pg.* 1965, *pg.* 601
LAPJACK - Laptop Computer Support - KNOLL, INC.; *pg.* 425, *pg.* 1527
LAPLINK CONTROLLER - File Transfer Software for Mobile Devices - LAPLINK SOFTWARE, INC.; *pg.* 426, *pg.* 1815
LAPLINK EVERYWHERE - Online File Transfer Application - LAPLINK SOFTWARE, INC.; *pg.* 426, *pg.* 1815
LAPLINK GOLD 11.5 - File Transfer Software - LAPLINK SOFTWARE, INC.; *pg.* 426, *pg.* 1815
LAPLINK GOLD CORPORATE - File Transfer Software - LAPLINK SOFTWARE, INC.; *pg.* 426, *pg.* 1815
LAPLINK V FOR DOS - File Transfer Software - LAPLINK SOFTWARE, INC.; *pg.* 426, *pg.* 1815
LAPOLLA - Foam, Coatings, Paints & Sealants - LAPOLLA INDUSTRIES, INC.; *pg.* 1444, *pg.* 1710
LAPROSCOPIC INSTRUMENTS - Tag Line - ENCISION INC.; *pg.* 1528, *pg.* 310
LAPROSTAT - Handsets for Use with Laserscope Surgical Laser Systems - AMERICAN MEDICAL SYSTEMS, INC.; *pg.* 1399, *pg.* 238
LAPSYNC - Software - WIPRO GALLAGHER SOLUTIONS; *pg.* 823, *pg.* 447
LAPTOP LEGS - Laptop Riser - LAPWORKS, INC.; *pg.* 426, *pg.* 187
LAPTOP MAILBAG - Briefcase - SANTA FE LEATHER CORPORATION; *pg.* 12, *pg.* 1059
LAPTOP PROP - Furniture - NEUTRAL POSTURE, INC.; *pg.* 939, *pg.* 1669
LAPULEUCEL-T - Cancer Treatment - DENDREON CORPORATION; *pg.* 1522, *pg.* 1835
LARABAR - Energy Bar - GENERAL MILLS, INC.; *pg.* 828, *pg.* 933
LARCHMONT - Fabric - NEMSCHOFF, INC.; *pg.* 936, *pg.* 1890
LARCOBOND - Pressed & Monolithic Refractory - RESCO PRODUCTS, INC.; *pg.* 107, *pg.* 1581
LAREDO - Fungicide - DOW AGROSCIENCES LLC; *pg.* 1156, *pg.* 684
LAREDO - Film Cleaning Equipment - EASTMAN KODAK COMPANY; *pg.* 1408, *pg.* 1333
LAREDO - Furniture - JASPER GROUP; *pg.* 930, *pg.* 691
LAREDO MORNING TIMES - Newspaper - THE HEARST CORPORATION; *pg.* 1649, *pg.* 1239
LARENSTAN - Area Rug - COURISTAN INC.; *pg.* 921, *pg.* 1067
LARGE BOARDWALK - Basket - THE LONGABERGER COMPANY; *pg.* 1127, *pg.* 1467
LARGE BRA SAVER - Bra - BARE NECESSITIES, INC.; *pg.* 19, *pg.* 1056
LARGE CONCORD - Sturdilite Floodlight - PHOENIX PRODUCTS COMPANY; *pg.* 1304, *pg.* 1879
LARGE COVE - Door & Wood Product - CONESTOGA WOOD SPECIALTIES CORP.; *pg.* 921, *pg.* 1527
LARGE DESKTOP - Basket - THE LONGABERGER COMPANY; *pg.* 1127, *pg.* 1467
LARGE LAPTOP BACKPACK - Briefcase - SANTA FE LEATHER CORPORATION; *pg.* 12, *pg.* 1059
LARGE PRINT PRESS - Publisher - GALE CENGAGE LEARNING; *pg.* 1643, *pg.* 885
LARGE RECIPE - Basket - THE LONGABERGER COMPANY; *pg.* 1127, *pg.* 1467
LARGE TEAM DUFFEL - Footwear - NIKE, INC.; *pg.* 1812, *pg.* 1492
LARGE TRAPPER - Knife - BUCK KNIVES, INC.; *pg.* 1828, *pg.* 550
LARGO - Guest Chairs - BERNHARDT DESIGN; *pg.* 918, *pg.* 1381
LARGO BAY - Embroidered Capri Set - HABAND COMPANY, INC.; *pg.* 1772, *pg.* 1099
LARGO LEADER - Newspaper - TAMPA BAY NEWSPAPERS, INC.; *pg.* 1691, *pg.* 468
LARIAT - Window Treatment - CROSCILL, INC.; *pg.* 1122, *pg.* 1220
LARIAT - Fabric - NEMSCHOFF, INC.; *pg.* 936, *pg.* 1890
LARIOS - Gin - JIM BEAM BRANDS CO.; *pg.* 1965, *pg.* 601
LARIUM - Pharmaceutical Product - HOFFMANN-LA ROCHE INC.; *pg.* 1542, *pg.* 1099
LARK - Cigarettes - PHILIP MORRIS USA INC.; *pg.* 1894, *pg.* 1803
LARK - Luggage - SAMSONITE CORPORATION; *pg.* 11, *pg.* 830
LARK - Theater Glasses - SWIFT OPTICAL INSTRUMENTS, INC.; *pg.* 1430, *pg.* 1744
LARKSPUR - Bath Product - KOHLER CO.; *pg.* 91, *pg.* 1862
LARKSPUR - Bike - MARIN BIKES; *pg.* 1708, *pg.* 168
LAROSA - Stemware Rack - LAVI INDUSTRIES INC.; *pg.* 93, *pg.* 299
LAROSTAT - Antistatic Agent for use in Synthetic Fibers, Fiberglass & Plastics - PPG INDUSTRIES, INC.; *pg.* 1445, *pg.* 1579
LARROWE'S - Buckwheat Food Product - THE BIRKETT MILLS; *pg.* 826, *pg.* 1321
LARRY-BOY - Video - BIG IDEA, INC.; *pg.* 271, *pg.* 1632
LARRY'S - Prepared Side Dishes - THE SCHWAN FOOD COMPANY; *pg.* 894, *pg.* 928
LARSON-JUHL CLASSIC COLLECTION - Wood Framing Products - LARSON-JUHL US LLC; *pg.* 933, *pg.* 537
LARYNGOSEAL - Laryngeal Mask - MEDTRONIC; *pg.* 1563, *pg.* 183
LAS BRISAS - Mexican Restaurants - REAL MEX RESTAURANTS, INC.; *pg.* 1746, *pg.* 75
LAS CABRILLAS - Premium Cigars - ALTADIS USA, INC.; *pg.* 1893, *pg.* 423
LAS CRUCES - Furniture - FLEXSTEEL INDUSTRIES, INC.; *pg.* 925, *pg.* 707
LAS PALMAS - Sauces - B&G FOODS, INC.; *pg.* 838, *pg.* 1102
LAS VEGAS MOTOR SPEEDWAY - Entertainment Venue - SPEEDWAY MOTORSPORTS, INC.; *pg.* 584, *pg.* 1370
LAS VEGAS SUN - Newspaper - LAS VEGAS SUN, INC.; *pg.* 1657, *pg.* 1021
LASAR - Mill-Wide Connectivity - PERCEPTRON, INC.; *pg.* 215, *pg.* 904
LASCO - Pipe Fittings, Bath Fixtures, Tubs & Showers - AQUATIC; *pg.* 68, *pg.* 42
LASCO - Forging Product - SUPERIOR DIE SET CORP.; *pg.* 1379, *pg.* 1885
LASCO STEAM - Steam Showers & Tub/Showers - AQUATIC; *pg.* 68, *pg.* 42
LASCOAT - Bathware Product Material - AQUATIC; *pg.* 68, *pg.* 42
LASCOLITE - Fiberglass Building Panels - AQUATIC; *pg.* 68, *pg.* 42
LASER - Bicycle - G. JOANNOU CYCLE CO. INC.; *pg.* 1707, *pg.* 1098
LASER - Baseball Bat - HILLERICH & BRADSBY CO., INC.; *pg.* 1836, *pg.* 576
LASER - Brite Dip - HUBBARD-HALL, INC.; *pg.* 1167, *pg.* 382
LASER - Apparel - OAKLEY, INC.; *pg.* 1840, *pg.* 86
LASER 1 OPAQUE - Heat Transfer Paper - NEENAH PAPER, INC.; *pg.* 1465, *pg.* 484
LASER 7.9 MX - Skate - ROLLER DERBY SKATE CORP.; *pg.* 966, *pg.* 630
LASER ALIGN - Sensor - CYBEROPTICS CORPORATION; *pg.* 1408, *pg.* 925
LASER BRAND - Toothpaste - COLGATE-PALMOLIVE COMPANY; *pg.* 504, *pg.* 1215
LASER CHALLENGE - Sport & Leisure Product - JAKKS PACIFIC, INC.; *pg.* 960, *pg.* 142
LASER-CYL - Cryogenic Product - CHART INDUSTRIES, INC.; *pg.* 1405, *pg.* 1454
LASER DIODE INC. - Electronic Component Product - TE CONNECTIVITY LTD.; *pg.* 677, *pg.* 1515
LASER-FLEX - Tracheal Tube - MALLINCKRODT PHARMACEUTICALS; *pg.* 1557, *pg.* 978
LASER-FLEX - Tracheal Tube - MEDTRONIC; *pg.* 1563, *pg.* 183
LASER GENESIS - Skin Treatment - CUTERA, INC.; *pg.* 1521, *pg.* 49
LASER MOUSE VCSELS - Electronic Component - EMCORE CORPORATION; *pg.* 636, *pg.* 39
LASER SERIES - Electric Rider Forklifts - NISSAN FORKLIFT CORPORATION, NORTH AMERICA; *pg.* 186, *pg.* 631
LASER-SIGHT - Optical Technology - CAS MEDICAL SYSTEMS, INC.; *pg.* 1513, *pg.* 339
LASER SIGHTS - Light - SUREFIRE, LLC; *pg.* 1307, *pg.* 90
LASER-TEC - Cryogenic Product - CHART INDUSTRIES, INC.; *pg.* 1405, *pg.* 1454
LASER UT - Aircraft Testing Instrumentation - LOCKHEED MARTIN CORPORATION; *pg.* 229, *pg.* 762
LASERBODYSCULPTING - Workstations - CYNOSURE, INC.; *pg.* 1521, *pg.* 858
LASERCAM - Camera - COHERENT, INC.; *pg.* 1406, *pg.* 265
LASERCHECK - Laser Measurement Instrument - COHERENT, INC.; *pg.* 1406, *pg.* 265
LASERCNC - Laser Engraving Solution - VIRTEK VISION INTERNATIONAL, INC.; *pg.* 1435, *pg.* 1948
LASERCOMPACT - Air Monitoring Equipment - FIKE CORPORATION; *pg.* 1047, *pg.* 973
LASERCYTE - Analyzer - IDEXX LABORATORIES, INC.; *pg.* 1543, *pg.* 753
LASERDYNE - Laser System - GSI GROUP INC.; *pg.* 1415, *pg.* 784
LASERED TITAN GOLD - Chain - STULLER, INC.; *pg.* 13, *pg.* 745
LASEREYE - Laser Detectors - COBRA ELECTRONICS CORPORATION; *pg.* 629, *pg.* 572
LASERFORM - Solid Imaging Material - 3D SYSTEMS CORPORATION; *pg.* 339, *pg.* 1621
LASERGAGE - Laser Power Meter - COHERENT, INC.; *pg.* 1406, *pg.* 265
LASERGUARD - Medical System - VARIAN MEDICAL SYSTEMS, INC.; *pg.* 1434, *pg.* 178
LASERLEVEL - Leveling System - TRIMBLE NAVIGATION LIMITED; *pg.* 1384, *pg.* 288
LASERMARK - Laser System - GSI GROUP INC.; *pg.* 1415, *pg.* 784
LASERMATE - Laser Measurement Instrument - COHERENT, INC.; *pg.* 1406, *pg.* 265
LASERMILL - Micro-Milling Machine - NEW WAVE RESEARCH INCORPORATED; *pg.* 1423, *pg.* 91
LASERNET FINES - Optical Oil Debris Analyzer - LOCKHEED MARTIN CORPORATION; *pg.* 229, *pg.* 762
LASERPAD - Laser Measurement Instrument - COHERENT, INC.; *pg.* 1406, *pg.* 265
LASERPLANE - Navigation Aid - TRIMBLE NAVIGATION LIMITED; *pg.* 1384, *pg.* 288
LASERPLUS - Air Monitoring Equipment - FIKE CORPORATION; *pg.* 1047, *pg.* 973
LASERPRO - Flashlight - PELICAN PRODUCTS, INC.; *pg.* 1842, *pg.* 295
LASERQC - Laser Engraving Solution - VIRTEK VISION INTERNATIONAL, INC.; *pg.* 1435, *pg.* 1948
LASERS & LIGHT - Slogan - CUTERA, INC.; *pg.* 1521, *pg.* 49
LASER'S EDGE - Computer Wheel Aligner - BEE LINE COMPANY; *pg.* 200, *pg.* 701
LASERSAFE - Safeguarding System - OMRON SCIENTIFIC TECHNOLOGIES INCORPORATED; *pg.* 1425, *pg.* 91
LASERSELECT - Computer Paper - NCR CORPORATION; *pg.* 443, *pg.* 531
LASERSMILE - Dental Laser Product - BIOLASE TECHNOLOGY, INC.; *pg.* 1506, *pg.* 107
LASERSTAR NOSTALGIA - CD Jukebox - ROWE INTERNATIONAL CORP; *pg.* 669, *pg.* 889
LASERSTATION - Navigation Aid - TRIMBLE NAVIGATION LIMITED; *pg.* 1384, *pg.* 288
LASERSTREAM - Electronic Components - MOLEX INCORPORATED; *pg.* 655, *pg.* 628
LASERTUBES - Metal Telescopic Cover - DYNATECT MANUFACTURING INC.; *pg.* 1330, *pg.* 1883
LASERWELD - Fiber Attachment System - NEWPORT CORPORATION; *pg.* 1424, *pg.* 114
LASERWIDE - Projector - EVANS & SUTHERLAND COMPUTER CORPORATION; *pg.* 638, *pg.* 1757
LASERWRITER - Laser Printer - APPLE INC.; *pg.* 350, *pg.* 73
LASH DISCOVERY - Mascara - MAYBELLINE LLC; *pg.* 516, *pg.* 1257
LASH EXPANSION - Mascara - MAYBELLINE LLC; *pg.* 516, *pg.* 1257
LASH FANTASY - Cosmetic - REVLON, INC.; *pg.* 521, *pg.* 1286

LASH GLOSS - Mascara - THE BONNE BELL COMPANY; *pg.* 502, *pg.* 1480
LASH PROFESSIONAL - Beauty Product - AVON PRODUCTS, INC.; *pg.* 500, *pg.* 1198
LASIKPLUS - Fixed-Site Laser Vision Correction Centers - LCA-VISION INC.; *pg.* 1419, *pg.* 1416
LASIRIS - Diode Laser Module - PROPHOTONIX LIMITED; *pg.* 1427, *pg.* 1039
LASOO - Footwear - STEVEN MADDEN, LTD.; *pg.* 1819, *pg.* 1176
LASSALE - Watches - SEIKO CORPORATION OF AMERICA; *pg.* 12, *pg.* 1082
LASSEN - Navigation Aid - TRIMBLE NAVIGATION LIMITED; *pg.* 1384, *pg.* 288
LASSO - Carpet - INTERFACE, INC.; *pg.* 695, *pg.* 512
LASSO - Herbicide - MONSANTO COMPANY; *pg.* 1173, *pg.* 999
LASSO - Fabric - NEMSCHOFF, INC.; *pg.* 936, *pg.* 1890
LASSO - Music Management Software - ROVI CORPORATION; *pg.* 463, *pg.* 260
LASSO YOUR LOVER - Restaurant & Bar Services - TEXAS ROADHOUSE, INC.; *pg.* 1753, *pg.* 738
THE LAST HURRAH - Restaurant, Tavern & Hotel - OMNI HOTELS & RESORTS; *pg.* 1107, *pg.* 1685
LASTEK - Crack/Joint Sealants - MAINTENANCE, INC.; *pg.* 95, *pg.* 1482
LASTICAULK - Caulk - UNITED GILSONITE LABORATORIES; *pg.* 1449, *pg.* 1527
LASTICITY - Boots - AEROGROUP INTERNATIONAL, INC.; *pg.* 1803, *pg.* 1055
LASTIGLAS - Steel Lined Containers - ENERFAB, INC.; *pg.* 81, *pg.* 1412
LASTING PERFORMANCE - Mascara - COVER GIRL COSMETICS; *pg.* 506, *pg.* 772
LASTING ROMANCE BOUQUET - Floral Bouquet - FTD GROUP, INC.; *pg.* 1795, *pg.* 608
LASTING TOUCH - Liquid Polish - DENTSPLY INTERNATIONAL INC.; *pg.* 1522, *pg.* 1596
LASTINGLESSONS - Educational Product - BARKER CREEK PUBLISHING INC.; *pg.* 1619, *pg.* 1818
LASTMINUTE.COM - Travel Website - EXPEDIA, INC.; *pg.* 1244, *pg.* 1814
LASTOFLEX - Elastomeric Laminated Bearings - LORD CORPORATION; *pg.* 1357, *pg.* 1360
LASTOSPHERE - Shock Absorbing Access. - LORD CORPORATION; *pg.* 1357, *pg.* 1360
LAT - Home Stereo Loudspeakers - KRELL INDUSTRIES, INC.; *pg.* 650, *pg.* 367
LATAINFO - Local Access Transport Area Maps - PITNEY BOWES SOFTWARE INC.; *pg.* 455, *pg.* 1346
LATALINKS - Wireless Telecommunication Product - SYNIVERSE HOLDINGS, INC.; *pg.* 479, *pg.* 475
LATCH-LOCK - Bin Door - CTB INTERNATIONAL CORP.; *pg.* 850, *pg.* 695
LATE HARVEST - Beverage - CRAFT BREWERS ALLIANCE, INC; *pg.* 247, *pg.* 1502
LATE NIGHT & DESIGN - Restaurant Services - JACK IN THE BOX INC.; *pg.* 1732, *pg.* 204
LATE NIGHT TV - Carpet - INTERFACE, INC.; *pg.* 695, *pg.* 512
LATE SEASON - Apparel - CABELA'S INCORPORATED; *pg.* 535, *pg.* 1019
LATE SPORT - Sportswear - L.A. T SPORTSWEAR, LLC; *pg.* 1838, *pg.* 526
LATERAL - Orthopedic Product - DJO INCORPORATED; *pg.* 1524, *pg.* 302
LATEST-TO-LEGACY - Computer Software Development - SYNTEL, INC.; *pg.* 480, *pg.* 911
LATEX - Apparel - OAKLEY, INC.; *pg.* 1840, *pg.* 86
LATEX ZONE - Marking Paint - JONES-BLAIR COMPANY; *pg.* 1443, *pg.* 1682
LATEXFREE - Medical Product - MEDLINE INDUSTRIES, INC.; *pg.* 1562, *pg.* 635
LATHANOL - Chemical Product - STEPAN COMPANY; *pg.* 1182, *pg.* 643
LATHERGUARD - Safety Shield - FLEXBAR MACHINE CORP.; *pg.* 1337, *pg.* 1169
LATIMES.COM - Online Newspaper - LOS ANGELES TIMES COMMUNICATIONS, LLC; *pg.* 1660, *pg.* 135
LATIN PERCUSSION - Drums - KAMAN CORPORATION; *pg.* 229, *pg.* 338
LATINA - Footwear - CAPEZIO BALLET MAKERS INC.; *pg.* 1805, *pg.* 1125
LATINA - Food Product - GENERAL MILLS, INC.; *pg.* 828, *pg.* 933
LATINA - Magazine - LATINA MEDIA VENTURES, LLC; *pg.* 1657, *pg.* 1250
LATINO 96.3 FM - Radio Station - SPANISH BROADCASTING SYSTEM INC.; *pg.* 310, *pg.* 446
LATINO MACHINO - Video Game - INTERNATIONAL GAME TECHNOLOGY; *pg.* 957, *pg.* 1024
LATISSE - Eyelash Lengthener - ALLERGAN, INC.; *pg.* 1491, *pg.* 106
LATITUDE - Drug - 3M COMPANY; *pg.* 1142, *pg.* 956
LATITUDE - Medical Device - BOSTON SCIENTIFIC CORPORATION; *pg.* 1508, *pg.* 831
LATITUDE - Notebook Computers - DELL INC.; *pg.* 383, *pg.* 1737
LATITUDE - Fabrication Systems - DOW CHEMICAL; *pg.* 1156, *pg.* 1563
LATITUDE - Lighting System - LITECONTROL CORPORATION; *pg.* 1301, *pg.* 841
LATITUDE - Fabric - NEMSCHOFF, INC.; *pg.* 936, *pg.* 1890
LATITUDE - Motor Homes - WINNEBAGO INDUSTRIES, INC.; *pg.* 1712, *pg.* 707
LATITUDE GP - Lens - DANKER LABORATORIES INC.; *pg.* 1408, *pg.* 465
LATITUDE SOFT - Lens - DANKER LABORATORIES INC.; *pg.* 1408, *pg.* 465
LATITUDES - Pharmaceutical Product - ALERE INC.; *pg.* 1488, *pg.* 849
LATITUDES - Furniture - FLEXSTEEL INDUSTRIES, INC.; *pg.* 925, *pg.* 707
LATITUDES - Mattress - SIMMONS COMPANY; *pg.* 943, *pg.* 520
LATITUDES - Composite Decking - UNIVERSAL FOREST PRODUCTS, INC.; *pg.* 117, *pg.* 890
LATIUM - Software System - MENTOR GRAPHICS CORPORATION; *pg.* 432, *pg.* 1510
LATOUR - Tour Packages - ISRAM WHOLESALE TOURS & TRAVEL LTD.; *pg.* 1913, *pg.* 1244
LATTICE - Furniture - ASHLEY FURNITURE INDUSTRIES, INC.; *pg.* 914, *pg.* 1852
LATTICE - Furniture - THE COMMERCIAL FURNITURE GROUP; *pg.* 920, *pg.* 994
LATTICE - Food Ingredient - FMC CORPORATION; *pg.* 1163, *pg.* 1564
LATTICEECP2M - Integrated Circuits - LATTICE SEMICONDUCTOR CORPORATION; *pg.* 651, *pg.* 1498
LATTICEMICO32 - Microcontroller - LATTICE SEMICONDUCTOR CORPORATION; *pg.* 651, *pg.* 1498
LATTITUDE EXECUTIVE - Office Furniture - STEELCASE INC.; *pg.* 475, *pg.* 889
L'AUBERGE - Casino & Hotel - PINNACLE ENTERTAINMENT, INC.; *pg.* 576, *pg.* 1029
LAUDERDALE - Shoes - ALLEN-EDMONDS SHOE CORP.; *pg.* 1804, *pg.* 1887
LAUGH & LEARN - Educational Toys - FISHER-PRICE, INC.; *pg.* 953, *pg.* 1156
LAUNCH - Racing Boat - CHRIS-CRAFT CORPORATION; *pg.* 1706, *pg.* 465
LAUNCH - Turf Product - PBI/GORDON CORPORATION; *pg.* 1176, *pg.* 985
LAUNCH PAD - Media Control System - AVID TECHNOLOGY, INC.; *pg.* 622, *pg.* 804
LAUNCHFAX.COM - Fax Service Provider - LAUNCHFAX.COM INC.; *pg.* 1261, *pg.* 1064
LAUNCHPAD - Software - QUALCOMM INCORPORATED; *pg.* 1873, *pg.* 207
LAUNDRY - Software - MAC-GRAY CORPORATION; *pg.* 58, *pg.* 852
LAUNDRY BY SHELLI SEGAL - Apparel - KATE SPADE & COMPANY; *pg.* 27, *pg.* 1248
LAUNDRY BY SHELLI SEGAL - Apparel - PERRY ELLIS INTERNATIONAL, INC.; *pg.* 45, *pg.* 445
LAUNDRY-MATE - In Wall Washing Machine Supply & Drain Fixture - SYMMONS INDUSTRIES, INC.; *pg.* 114, *pg.* 803
LAUNDRY PLUS - Clothing - KAZOO, INC.; *pg.* 43, *pg.* 894
LAUNDRYLINK - Software - MAC-GRAY CORPORATION; *pg.* 58, *pg.* 852
LAUNDRYVIEW - Software - MAC-GRAY CORPORATION; *pg.* 58, *pg.* 852
LAURA - Furniture - HAWORTH, INC.; *pg.* 402, *pg.* 891
LAURA ASHLEY - Bedding Product - HOLLANDER SLEEP PRODUCTS; *pg.* 927, *pg.* 411
LAURA CREEK - Cookware Set - OVERSTOCK.COM, INC.; *pg.* 1273, *pg.* 1760
LAURA GERINGER BOOKS - Books - HARPERCOLLINS PUBLISHERS INC.; *pg.* 1647, *pg.* 1237
LAURA INGRAHAM - Radio Program - TALK RADIO NETWORK; *pg.* 311, *pg.* 1497
LAURA LYNN - Store Brand - INGLES MARKETS, INCORPORATED; *pg.* 1023, *pg.* 1358
LAURA SCUDDER'S - Peanut Butter - THE J.M. SMUCKER COMPANY; *pg.* 865, *pg.* 1468
LAUREATE - Bath Product - KOHLER CO.; *pg.* 91, *pg.* 1862
LAUREATE EDUCATION - Education Servicer Provider - LAUREATE EDUCATION, INC.; *pg.* 603, *pg.* 757
LAUREATE INTERNATIONAL UNIVERSITY - Education Servicer Provider - LAUREATE EDUCATION, INC.; *pg.* 603, *pg.* 757
LAUREL - Furniture - JASPER GROUP; *pg.* 930, *pg.* 691
LAUREL-LEAF - Publishing Imprint - PENGUIN RANDOM HOUSE CHILDREN'S BOOKS; *pg.* 1676, *pg.* 1277
LAUREL WOODS - Ceiling Fan - WESTINGHOUSE LIGHTING CORPORATION; *pg.* 687, *pg.* 1571
LAUREN - Women's Fragrance - RALPH LAUREN CORPORATION; *pg.* 46, *pg.* 1284
LAUREN BY RALPH LAUREN - Women's Apparel - RALPH LAUREN CORPORATION; *pg.* 46, *pg.* 1284
LAUREN FOR MEN - Men's Apparel - RALPH LAUREN CORPORATION; *pg.* 46, *pg.* 1284
LAUREN HANCOCK COLLECTION - Fabric - HANCOCK FABRICS, INC.; *pg.* 693, *pg.* 968
LAUREN JEANS CO. - Denim Apparel - RALPH LAUREN CORPORATION; *pg.* 46, *pg.* 1284
LAUREN PETITE - Apparel - RALPH LAUREN CORPORATION; *pg.* 46, *pg.* 1284
LAUREN SPA - Organic Bedding & Bath Accessories - RALPH LAUREN CORPORATION; *pg.* 46, *pg.* 1284
LAUREX - Polymer Product - CHEMTURA CORPORATION; *pg.* 1152, *pg.* 355
LAUREX - Fatty Alcohol - HUNTSMAN CORPORATION; *pg.* 1167, *pg.* 1758
LAURS - Footwear - VANS, INC.; *pg.* 1821, *pg.* 76
LAVA - Ceram Overlay Porcelain - 3M COMPANY; *pg.* 1142, *pg.* 956
LAVA - Record Label - WARNER MUSIC GROUP CORP.; *pg.* 590, *pg.* 1313
LAVA - Hand Cleaner - WD-40 COMPANY; *pg.* 337, *pg.* 210
LAVACOL - Antiseptic - MCNEIL-PPC, INC.; *pg.* 1560, *pg.* 1533
LAVACUATOR - Gastrointestinal Tube - MEDTRONIC; *pg.* 1563, *pg.* 183
LAVAR - Rug - COURISTAN INC.; *pg.* 921, *pg.* 1067
LAVATZA DELUXE - Footwear - K-SWISS; *pg.* 1837, *pg.* 306
LAVAX - Paint Enamels, Varnishes & Ready-Mixed Paints - PPG INDUSTRIES, INC.; *pg.* 1445, *pg.* 1579
LAVAZZA - Coffee - LAVAZZA PREMIUM COFFEES CORP.; *pg.* 874, *pg.* 1250
LAVCARE - Patient Care Units - BRADLEY CORPORATION; *pg.* 71, *pg.* 1870
LAVELLE - Fabric - NEMSCHOFF, INC.; *pg.* 936, *pg.* 1890
LAVENDER CLEAN PINE-SOL - All Purpose Cleaner - THE CLOROX COMPANY; *pg.* 327, *pg.* 169
LAVENDER JOY - Flower Arrangement - 1-800-FLOWERS.COM, INC.; *pg.* 1758, *pg.* 1151
LAVENDER SWIRL - Container Grown Plant - MONROVIA GROWERS; *pg.* 1797, *pg.* 44
LAVENUS - Hair Care - KAO BRANDS CO. INC.; *pg.* 513, *pg.* 1415
LAVISH - Window Treatment - CROSCILL, INC.; *pg.* 1122, *pg.* 1220
LAW.COM - Website - AMERICAN LAWYER MEDIA, INC.; *pg.* 1615, *pg.* 1193
LAWN-BOY - Irrigation Products - THE TORO COMPANY; *pg.* 1065, *pg.* 918
LAWN-CLAW - Gardening & Hardware Product - FAULTLESS STARCH/BON AMI COMPANY; *pg.* 330, *pg.* 982
LAWN-GARD - Lawn Care Product - GARDENS ALIVE!, INC.; *pg.* 1796, *pg.* 693
LAWN GENIE - Irrigation Products - THE TORO COMPANY; *pg.* 1065, *pg.* 918
LAWN PRO - Lawn Fertilizer - THE SCOTTS MIRACLE-GRO COMPANY; *pg.* 1799, *pg.* 1459
LAWNSERVICE - Lawn & Garden Product - THE SCOTTS MIRACLE-GRO COMPANY; *pg.* 1799, *pg.* 1459
LAWRENCE - Furniture - LA-Z-BOY INCORPORATED; *pg.* 932, *pg.* 901
LAWRENCE TECHNOLOGY - Electric Cable - SCHLUMBERGER WELL COMPLETIONS; *pg.* 1373, *pg.* 1714
LAWRY 'S CRAVERY - Restaurant - LAWRY'S RESTAURANTS, INC.; *pg.* 1735, *pg.* 180

First page reference indicates Business Class Edition
Second page reference indicates Geographic Edition

LAWRY'S - Marinades & Seasoning Blends - MCCORMICK & COMPANY, INCORPORATED; *pg.* 1027, *pg.* 779
LAWRY'S THE PRIME RIB - Restaurant - LAWRY'S RESTAURANTS, INC.; *pg.* 1735, *pg.* 180
LAWSON INSIGHT - Computer Software - INFOR LAWSON; *pg.* 414, *pg.* 961
LAWSON PORTAL - User Interface - INFOR LAWSON; *pg.* 414, *pg.* 961
LAWTER - Inks - HEXION; *pg.* 1166, *pg.* 1440
LAWYERS PROTECTOR PLAN - Insurance Package Program - BROWN & BROWN, INC.; *pg.* 1196, *pg.* 419
THE LAWYERS PROTECTOR PLAN - Insurance Package Program - BROWN & BROWN, INC.; *pg.* 1196, *pg.* 419
LAWYERS USA - Newspaper - MASSACHUSETTS LAWYERS WEEKLY, INC.; *pg.* 1662, *pg.* 798
LAXATIV-A-TEA - Vitamin & Dietary Supplement - NATROL, INC.; *pg.* 1570, *pg.* 64
LAY-IN - Brush - ROSCO LABORATORIES, INC.; *pg.* 1782, *pg.* 378
LAYBY - Herbicide - E.I. DU PONT DE NEMOURS & COMPANY; *pg.* 1159, *pg.* 390
LAYERED RACERBACK TANK - Clothing - K-SWISS; *pg.* 1837, *pg.* 306
LAYOUT - Software System - MENTOR GRAPHICS CORPORATION; *pg.* 432, *pg.* 1510
LAY'S - Potato Chips - FRITO-LAY NORTH AMERICA, INC.; *pg.* 1853, *pg.* 1730
LAY'S - Potato Chips - PEPSICO, INC.; *pg.* 259, *pg.* 1327
LAY'S FRIES - Snack - FRITO-LAY NORTH AMERICA, INC.; *pg.* 1853, *pg.* 1730
LAY'S KETTLE - Potato Chips - PEPSICO, INC.; *pg.* 259, *pg.* 1327
LAY'S KETTLE COOKED - Potato Chips - FRITO-LAY NORTH AMERICA, INC.; *pg.* 1853, *pg.* 1730
LAY'S MEDITERANNEAS - Potato Chips - FRITO-LAY NORTH AMERICA, INC.; *pg.* 1853, *pg.* 1730
LAY'S STAX - Potato Chips - FRITO-LAY NORTH AMERICA, INC.; *pg.* 1853, *pg.* 1730
LAYTON - Towable Recreational Vehicle - SKYLINE CORPORATION; *pg.* 1711, *pg.* 677
LAYYLAA - Footwear - STEVEN MADDEN, LTD.; *pg.* 1819, *pg.* 1176
LAZARO - Wedding Gowns - JLM COUTURE, INC.; *pg.* 27, *pg.* 1246
LAZARO BRIDESMAID - Bridesmaids Gowns - JLM COUTURE, INC.; *pg.* 27, *pg.* 1246
LAZER - Blade - LENOX; *pg.* 1053, *pg.* 817
LAZER - Apparel - OAKLEY, INC.; *pg.* 1840, *pg.* 86
LAZER BOND - Specialty Paper - IMPRESO, INC.; *pg.* 413, *pg.* 1671
LAZER CUT SHEETS - Specialty Paper - IMPRESO, INC.; *pg.* 413, *pg.* 1671
LAZER LINE - Fishing Tackle - WRIGHT & MCGILL CO.; *pg.* 1848, *pg.* 324
LAZER SHARP - Fishing Equipment Hooks - WRIGHT & MCGILL CO.; *pg.* 1848, *pg.* 324
LAZER TAG - Toy & Game - HASBRO, INC.; *pg.* 954, *pg.* 1603
LAZER-TEC - Ink Jet - CHROMA CORPORATION; *pg.* 1441, *pg.* 632
LAZERMARK - Rifle - WEATHERBY, INC.; *pg.* 1848, *pg.* 181
LAZLO - Office Furniture - STEELCASE INC.; *pg.* 475, *pg.* 889
LAZRFILM - Labeling - FLEXCON CORPORATION; *pg.* 1457, *pg.* 844
LAZY SUSAN - Office & Industrial Lighting - SWIVELIER CO., INC.; *pg.* 1307, *pg.* 1142
LAZZARONI - Amaretto - HEAVEN HILL DISTILLERIES, INC.; *pg.* 1964, *pg.* 725
LAZZURIL - Automotive Finishes - THE SHERWIN-WILLIAMS COMPANY; *pg.* 1447, *pg.* 1435
LB SERIES - Line Printers - RICOH PRINTING SYSTEMS AMERICA, INC.; *pg.* 462, *pg.* 279
LBIST - Software System - MENTOR GRAPHICS CORPORATION; *pg.* 432, *pg.* 1510
LBISTARCHITECT - Software System - MENTOR GRAPHICS CORPORATION; *pg.* 432, *pg.* 1510
LC - Pumps - IDEX CORPORATION; *pg.* 1347, *pg.* 623
LC - Software System - MENTOR GRAPHICS CORPORATION; *pg.* 432, *pg.* 1510
LC-EURO - Lighting System - LITECONTROL CORPORATION; *pg.* 1301, *pg.* 841
LC-PAD - Adapter - LORD CORPORATION; *pg.* 1357, *pg.* 1360
LCAPP - Landstar Contractors' Advantage Purchasing Program - LANDSTAR SYSTEM, INC.; *pg.* 1914, *pg.* 434
LCAPP.COM - Security Programs Website - LANDSTAR SYSTEM, INC.; *pg.* 1914, *pg.* 434
LCC/DISPENSIT - Fluid Handling System - GRACO, INC.; *pg.* 1342, *pg.* 935
LCC PUMPS - Slurry Pump - GIW INDUSTRIES, INC.; *pg.* 1340, *pg.* 533
LCEC - Flowcells - BIOANALYTICAL SYSTEMS, INC.; *pg.* 1402, *pg.* 700
LCF-2310 - Inclinometer - JEWELL INSTRUMENTS, LLC; *pg.* 1418, *pg.* 1036
LCG - Glass & Ceramic Material - CORNING INCORPORATED; *pg.* 1122, *pg.* 1154
LCG - Banking Software - JACK HENRY & ASSOCIATES, INC.; *pg.* 422, *pg.* 988
LCGX - Glass & Ceramic Material - CORNING INCORPORATED; *pg.* 1122, *pg.* 1154
LCM-100 - Accelerometer - JEWELL INSTRUMENTS, LLC; *pg.* 1418, *pg.* 1036
LCMAG - Pumps - IDEX CORPORATION; *pg.* 1347, *pg.* 623
LCMASS - Pumps - IDEX CORPORATION; *pg.* 1347, *pg.* 623
LCN - Door Closer - INGERSOLL-RAND COMPANY; *pg.* 1349, *pg.* 1370
LCORE - Software System - MENTOR GRAPHICS CORPORATION; *pg.* 432, *pg.* 1510
LCP - Centerfire Pistols - STURM, RUGER & COMPANY, INC.; *pg.* 1846, *pg.* 371
LCR - Pumps - IDEX CORPORATION; *pg.* 1347, *pg.* 623
LCR - Revolver - STURM, RUGER & COMPANY, INC.; *pg.* 1846, *pg.* 371
LCRII - Pumps - IDEX CORPORATION; *pg.* 1347, *pg.* 623
LCS 2000 - Radio Transceiver - MOTOROLA SOLUTIONS, INC.; *pg.* 657, *pg.* 659
LCS PRO - Reactivator - SENTRY TECHNOLOGY CORPORATION; *pg.* 672, *pg.* 1339
LCS TOTAL KNEE SYSTEM - Orthopedic Product - DEPUYSYNTHES; *pg.* 1523, *pg.* 699
LCT - Mass Spectrometer - WATERS CORPORATION; *pg.* 1436, *pg.* 834
LCX - Diagnostic System - ABBOTT LABORATORIES; *pg.* 1484, *pg.* 551
LDLA - Polyethylene Resins - THE DOW CHEMICAL COMPANY; *pg.* 1157, *pg.* 898
LDP LEAN DOCUMENT PRODUCTION & DESIGN - Printer - XEROX CORPORATION; *pg.* 494, *pg.* 365
LDS - Inspection System - KLA-TENCOR CORPORATION; *pg.* 1353, *pg.* 146
LDS MINGLE - Online Dating Service & Chat Room - SPARK NETWORKS, INC.; *pg.* 472, *pg.* 140
LDX - Low Pressure Dry Pipe Systems - RELIABLE AUTOMATIC SPRINKLER CO., INC.; *pg.* 1137, *pg.* 1158
LE - Truck Seating - SEATS INCORPORATED; *pg.* 217, *pg.* 1890
LE-9000SX Edger - SANTINELLI INTERNATIONAL INC.; *pg.* 1395, *pg.* 1165
LE CTRQUE - Fabric - SCALAMANDRE, INC.; *pg.* 941, *pg.* 1058
LE JARDIN - Rug - COURISTAN INC.; *pg.* 921, *pg.* 1067
LE MARCHE DU - Window - BLINDS TO GO INC.; *pg.* 918, *pg.* 1101
LE MERIDIEN - Hotels - STARWOOD HOTELS & RESORTS WORLDWIDE, INC.; *pg.* 1114, *pg.* 378
LE MIDI - Lamp - J. ROBERT SCOTT INC.; *pg.* 930, *pg.* 105
LE-PRO - Food Product - LEPRINO FOODS COMPANY; *pg.* 874, *pg.* 320
LE SCRUB - Bathroom Cleaner - METHOD PRODUCTS INC.; *pg.* 332, *pg.* 223
LE STICK - Beauty Product - GRANDPA BRANDS COMPANY; *pg.* 1538, *pg.* 727
LE TECHNIQ - Soap - HY-VEE, INC.; *pg.* 1023, *pg.* 713
LE TONG - Plastic Serving Tongs - THE VOLLRATH COMPANY LLC; *pg.* 1139, *pg.* 1894
LEA&PERRINS - Worcestershire Sauces - THE KRAFT HEINZ COMPANY; *pg.* 870, *pg.* 1577
LEACH - Relay - ESTERLINE TECHNOLOGIES CORPORATION; *pg.* 1412, *pg.* 1814
LEAD FRAME MODULE - Packaging Technology - RF MICRO DEVICES, INC.; *pg.* 667, *pg.* 1376
LEAD-GASKET - Specialty Nails - W.H. MAZE COMPANY; *pg.* 1389, *pg.* 652
LEAD LOCKING DEVICE - Cardiac Lead Removal Device - THE SPECTRANETICS CORPORATION; *pg.* 1595, *pg.* 315
LEAD PACK - X-Ray Film Pack - EASTMAN KODAK COMPANY; *pg.* 1408, *pg.* 1333
LEAD THE FIELD - Recordings On Tapes - NIGHTINGALE-CONANT CORPORATION; *pg.* 152, *pg.* 670
LEADER - Carpet - INTERFACE, INC.; *pg.* 695, *pg.* 512
LEADER - Selective Herbicide - MONSANTO COMPANY; *pg.* 1173, *pg.* 999
LEADER BY DESIGN - Tag Line - HARDINGE INC.; *pg.* 1344, *pg.* 1157
LEADER DRUGSTORES - Pharmaceutical - CARDINAL HEALTH, INC.; *pg.* 1512, *pg.* 1448
THE LEADER IN BLUE-COLLAR STAFFING - Tagline - TRUEBLUE, INC.; *pg.* 485, *pg.* 1845
THE LEADER IN ENTERPRISE INFORMATION APPLICATIONS - Tagline - ACTUATE CORPORATION; *pg.* 342, *pg.* 253
THE LEADER IN FOOTWEAR - Slogan - CALERES, INC.; *pg.* 1805, *pg.* 993
THE LEADER IN HOME KARAOKE & BEYOND - Slogan - THE SINGING MACHINE COMPANY, INC.; *pg.* 674, *pg.* 426
THE LEADER IN PEST CONTROL - Tagline - ROLLINS, INC.; *pg.* 1179, *pg.* 519
THE LEADER IN VISUAL THINKING AND LEARNING - Slogan - INSPIRATION SOFTWARE, INC.; *pg.* 1653, *pg.* 1503
LEADER OF THE THREE WORLD - Tag Line - LEHMAN TRIKES INC.; *pg.* 1708, *pg.* 1626
LEADER-VIEW - Conferencing Service - INTERCALL, INC.; *pg.* 417, *pg.* 578
LEADERS IN DIGITAL AUDIO INNOVATION - Tagline - QSOUND LABS, INC.; *pg.* 666, *pg.* 1904
LEADERSHIP - Magazine - CHRISTIANITY TODAY INTERNATIONAL; *pg.* 1627, *pg.* 561
LEADERSHIP BRANDS HELPING CUSTOMERS GROW! - Tagline - MYERS INDUSTRIES, INC.; *pg.* 1887, *pg.* 1402
LEADING EDGE - Horse Feed - MANNA PRO CORPORATION; *pg.* 1478, *pg.* 975
LEADING EDGE - Heated Air Curtain - MARLEY ENGINEERED PRODUCTS; *pg.* 1074, *pg.* 1612
THE LEADING IMAGE - Surface Coil - MEDRAD, INC.; *pg.* 1563, *pg.* 1591
LEADING THE DIGITAL ENTERTAINMENT REVOLUTION - Slogan - CIRRUS LOGIC, INC.; *pg.* 629, *pg.* 1661
LEADING THE WAY - Tagline - THE PNC FINANCIAL SERVICES GROUP, INC.; *pg.* 795, *pg.* 1579
LEADING THE WAY - Tagline - PORTLAND BUSINESS ALLIANCE; *pg.* 1004, *pg.* 1505
LEADING THE WAY IN BIOSEPARATION - Tagline - SPECTRUM LABORATORIES INC.; *pg.* 1595, *pg.* 69
LEADING THE WAY IN ELECTRICITY - Slogan - EDISON INTERNATIONAL; *pg.* 1941, *pg.* 194
LEADING THE WAY IN QUALITY BEEF - Slogan - NATIONAL BEEF PACKING COMPANY, LLC; *pg.* 882, *pg.* 985
LEADING THE WAY IN THE SEARCH FOR CURES - Slogan - PHARMACEUTICAL RESEARCH & MANUFACTURERS OF AMERICA; *pg.* 153, *pg.* 404
LEADING/THINKING/PERFORMING - Tagline - AMERICAN APPRAISAL ASSOCIATES, INC.; *pg.* 349, *pg.* 1872
LEADS - Security Programs - LANDSTAR SYSTEM, INC.; *pg.* 1914, *pg.* 434
LEADTRAK - Test Kit - HACH COMPANY; *pg.* 1415, *pg.* 334
LEAF - Fiber - CORNING CABLE SYSTEMS LLC; *pg.* 1407, *pg.* 1378
LEAF - Optical Fiber - CORNING INCORPORATED; *pg.* 1122, *pg.* 1154
LEAF - Furniture - HERMAN MILLER, INC.; *pg.* 926, *pg.* 913
LEAF & LADLE - Food Product - GIANT EAGLE, INC.; *pg.* 1020, *pg.* 1575
LEAF BERRY - Decorative Accessory - ETHAN ALLEN INTERIORS INC.; *pg.* 924, *pg.* 343
LEAF CELL TOOLKIT - Software System - MENTOR GRAPHICS CORPORATION; *pg.* 432, *pg.* 1510
LEAF EATER - Electric Leaf Mulching Machine - FLOWTRON OUTDOOR PRODUCTS; *pg.* 639, *pg.* 830
LEAF RELIEF - Home Exterior Product - ALCOA INC.; *pg.* 65, *pg.* 1188
LEAF RELIEF - Gutter Protection System - PLY GEM SIDING GROUP; *pg.* 105, *pg.* 986
LEAFAGE - Fabric - NEMSCHOFF, INC.; *pg.* 936, *pg.* 1890
LEAFETTE - Fabric - NEMSCHOFF, INC.; *pg.* 936, *pg.* 1890
LEAFLESS - Polymer Product - CHEMTURA CORPORATION; *pg.* 1152, *pg.* 355
LEAFLET - Fabric - NEMSCHOFF, INC.; *pg.* 936, *pg.* 1890
LEAFS TV - Television Channel - MAPLE LEAF SPORTS &

ENTERTAINMENT LTD.; pg. 560, pg. 1940

LEAH - Clothing - ABERCROMBIE & FITCH CO.; pg. 37, pg. 1466

LEAK SEEKER - Filter - MIDWESCO FILTER RESOURCES INC.; pg. 1464, pg. 1811

LEAK-TITE - Thread Sealant - LA-CO INDUSTRIES MARKAL CO., INC.; pg. 1170, pg. 610

LEAKATOR - Gas Leak Detector - BACHARACH INC.; pg. 1400, pg. 1556

LEAKATOR 10 - Combustible Gas Leak Detector - BACHARACH INC.; pg. 1400, pg. 1556

LEAKGUARD - Masking Product - KELLY-MOORE PAINT COMPANY, INC.; pg. 1443, pg. 198

LEAM - Melting Product - AIR PRODUCTS AND CHEMICALS, INC.; pg. 1145, pg. 1513

LEAN ADVANTAGE - Nutritional Supplement - PHARMAVITE LLC; pg. 1584, pg. 167

LEAN & MEAN - Food Product - WHATABURGER, INC.; pg. 1755, pg. 1744

LEAN CELL - Color Change Powder - NORDSON CORPORATION; pg. 1365, pg. 1480

LEAN CUISINE - Frozen Food - NESTLE USA, INC.; pg. 883, pg. 96

LEAN GOURMET - Frozen Food - BELLISIO FOODS, INC.; pg. 840, pg. 931

LEAN LINKS - Food Product - MAPLE LEAF CONSUMER FOODS; pg. 875, pg. 1922

LEAN POCKETS - Frozen Food - NESTLE USA, INC.; pg. 883, pg. 96

LEAN VALUE - Animal Nutritional Supplement - HUBBARD FEEDS INC.; pg. 1477, pg. 928

LEANING TOWER OF PISA - Video Game - INTERNATIONAL GAME TECHNOLOGY; pg. 957, pg. 1024

LEANIN'TREE - Greeting Cards - LEANIN' TREE, INC.; pg. 1658, pg. 311

LEANNA - Apparel - VANS, INC.; pg. 1821, pg. 76

LEANNE - Sunglasses - COACH, INC.; pg. 3, pg. 1214

LEANSTUFFS - Food Product - MAPLE LEAF CONSUMER FOODS; pg. 875, pg. 1922

LEAO GREEN TEA - Beverages - THE COCA-COLA COMPANY; pg. 240, pg. 493

LEAO GUARANA POWER - Beverages - THE COCA-COLA COMPANY; pg. 240, pg. 493

LEAO ICED TEA - Beverages - THE COCA-COLA COMPANY; pg. 240, pg. 493

LEAP - Blocking Pad - 3M COMPANY; pg. 1142, pg. 956

LEAP - Office Furniture - STEELCASE INC.; pg. 475, pg. 889

LEAP BRIDGE - Software - BENTLEY SYSTEMS, INC.; pg. 361, pg. 1531

LEAP FROG - Infant Books & Toys - LEAPFROG ENTERPRISES, INC.; pg. 961, pg. 84

LEAP PC-HELP - Software - BENTLEY SYSTEMS, INC.; pg. 361, pg. 1531

LEAP PRESTO - Software - BENTLEY SYSTEMS, INC.; pg. 361, pg. 1531

LEAP VERTEX - Software - BENTLEY SYSTEMS, INC.; pg. 361, pg. 1531

LEAPFROG - Vacuum Process Tool - BROOKS AUTOMATION, INC.; pg. 1320, pg. 813

LEAPFROG SCHOOLHOUSE - Multisensory PreK-8 Curriculum - LEAPFROG ENTERPRISES, INC.; pg. 961, pg. 84

LEAPPAD - Learning System - LEAPFROG ENTERPRISES, INC.; pg. 961, pg. 84

LEAP'S PHONICS - Educational Toys - LEAPFROG ENTERPRISES, INC.; pg. 961, pg. 84

LEAPSTART - Educational Toys - LEAPFROG ENTERPRISES, INC.; pg. 961, pg. 84

LEAPSTER - Multimedia Learning System - LEAPFROG ENTERPRISES, INC.; pg. 961, pg. 84

LEAPSTER L-MAX - Toys - LEAPFROG ENTERPRISES, INC.; pg. 961, pg. 84

LEAPTRACK - K-5 Assessment & Instruction System Using LeapPad Technology - LEAPFROG ENTERPRISES, INC.; pg. 961, pg. 84

LEARJET - Jet - BOMBARDIER INC.; pg. 1318, pg. 1953

LEARN-ALONG - Educational Toys - LEAPFROG ENTERPRISES, INC.; pg. 961, pg. 84

LEARN & GROOVE - Educational Toys - LEAPFROG ENTERPRISES, INC.; pg. 961, pg. 84

LEARN BIG - Projector - INFOCUS CORPORATION; pg. 644, pg. 1503

LEARN NOT TO BURN - Firesafety Education - NATIONAL FIRE PROTECTION ASSOCIATION; pg. 149, pg. 842

LEARN TO PLAY - Sport Product - FRANKLIN SPORTS, INC.; pg. 1834, pg. 847

LEARNING ABOUT SEX - Book - CONCORDIA PUBLISHING HOUSE; pg. 1629, pg. 995

LEARNING BABY TAD - Toys - LEAPFROG ENTERPRISES, INC.; pg. 961, pg. 84

LEARNING BAND - Educational Toys - LEAPFROG ENTERPRISES, INC.; pg. 961, pg. 84

LEARNING EDGE - Game - WMS INDUSTRIES INC.; pg. 593, pg. 666

LEARNING FRIEND - Educational Toys - LEAPFROG ENTERPRISES, INC.; pg. 961, pg. 84

THE LEARNING LIGHT - Lighting Product - OTTLITE; pg. 1303, pg. 475

THE LEARNING LINE - Bed Linen - SPRINGS GLOBAL, INC.; pg. 698, pg. 1616

LEARNING MAGNETS - Educational Product - BARKER CREEK PUBLISHING INC.; pg. 1619, pg. 1818

LEARNING MAPS - Software - SCIENTIFIC LEARNING CORPORATION; pg. 607, pg. 172

LEARNING PATTERNS - Toy - MATTEL, INC.; pg. 962, pg. 81

LEARNING WALLS - Educational Murals - PACON CORPORATION; pg. 1466, pg. 1852

LEASEMANAGER - Software - WINMARK CORPORATION; pg. 1792, pg. 946

LEASEPAK - Software - NETSOL TECHNOLOGIES, INC.; pg. 1270, pg. 56

LEASESOFT - Software - NETSOL TECHNOLOGIES, INC.; pg. 1270, pg. 56

LEASESOFT ASSET - Software - NETSOL TECHNOLOGIES, INC.; pg. 1270, pg. 56

LEASESOFT EVOLVE - Software - NETSOL TECHNOLOGIES, INC.; pg. 1270, pg. 56

LEASESOFT INSURANCE PREMIUM - Software - NETSOL TECHNOLOGIES, INC.; pg. 1270, pg. 56

LEASESOFT.CAP - Software - NETSOL TECHNOLOGIES, INC.; pg. 1270, pg. 56

LEASESOFT.CMS - Software - NETSOL TECHNOLOGIES, INC.; pg. 1270, pg. 56

LEASESOFT.WFS - Software - NETSOL TECHNOLOGIES, INC.; pg. 1270, pg. 56

LEASH - Apparel - OAKLEY, INC.; pg. 1840, pg. 86

LEATHER FOLDING HUNTER - Knife - BUCK KNIVES, INC.; pg. 1828, pg. 550

LEATHER LIFECASE - Briefcase - HABAND COMPANY, INC.; pg. 1772, pg. 1099

LEATHER SHEEN - Dry Cleaning & Laundry Product - ADCO, INC.; pg. 325, pg. 482

LEATHER SHEEN II - Detergent - ADCO, INC.; pg. 325, pg. 482

LEATHER ZIP & GO! - Jacket - HABAND COMPANY, INC.; pg. 1772, pg. 1099

LEATHERETTE - Envelope - TENSION ENVELOPE CORPORATION; pg. 483, pg. 986

LEATHERETTE CARRYALLS - Jewelry Organizer - CONNOISSEURS PRODUCTS CORPORATION; pg. 329, pg. 861

LEATHERMAN - Tools - TRACTOR SUPPLY COMPANY; pg. 708, pg. 1627

LEAVE NOTHING TO CHANCE - Slogan - NETJETS INC.; pg. 1917, pg. 1442

LEAVES - Window Accent - HERITAGE LACE INC.; pg. 694, pg. 711

LEBANONTURF - Lawn Products - LEBANON SEABOARD CORPORATION; pg. 1797, pg. 1547

LEBRA - Footwear - STEVEN MADDEN, LTD.; pg. 1819, pg. 1176

LECI-CHOLINE - Food Additives - CARGILL, INC.; pg. 845, pg. 965

LECINFO - Local Exchange Carrier Database - PITNEY BOWES SOFTWARE INC.; pg. 455, pg. 1346

LECTRA-CON - Conductants - SCHLEGEL SYSTEMS, INC.; pg. 109, pg. 1337

LECTRA HAUL - Capital Equipment - TEREX CORPORATION; pg. 1381, pg. 384

LECTRABOND - Silicone Septa - WATERS CORPORATION; pg. 1436, pg. 834

LECTRAFORM - Grinder - BRYANT GRINDER; pg. 1320, pg. 1768

LECTRALINE - Grinder - BRYANT GRINDER; pg. 1320, pg. 1768

LECTRIC SHAVE - Health & Beauty Product - COMBE INCORPORATED; pg. 1516, pg. 1351

LECTRO - Salt - FMC CORPORATION; pg. 1163, pg. 1564

LECTRO-LOK - Box Springs - LEGGETT & PLATT, INCORPORATED; pg. 933, pg. 974

LECTRO-SOLV - Safety Solvent - DELTA FOREMOST CHEMICAL CORPORATION; pg. 1155, pg. 1642

LECTROCOUNT - Pump Product - IDEX CORPORATION; pg. 1347, pg. 623

LECTROCOUNT LCR-II - Electronic Register & Flow Computer - LIQUID CONTROLS, INC.; pg. 1356, pg. 622

LECTROFLUOR - Coating - GENERAL MAGNAPLATE CORPORATION; pg. 1164, pg. 1079

LECTROLITE - Fabrics - HERCULITE PRODUCTS, INC.; pg. 694, pg. 1529

LECTROLITE COMFORT - Fabrics - HERCULITE PRODUCTS, INC.; pg. 694, pg. 1529

LED - Software System - MENTOR GRAPHICS CORPORATION; pg. 432, pg. 1510

LED CITY - LED - CREE INC.; pg. 631, pg. 1371

LED HOME - LED - CREE INC.; pg. 631, pg. 1371

LED JET - Electronic Display System - TRANS-LUX CORPORATION; pg. 681, pg. 365

LED LAYOUT - Software System - MENTOR GRAPHICS CORPORATION; pg. 432, pg. 1510

LED NEWSJET - Electronic Display System - TRANS-LUX CORPORATION; pg. 681, pg. 365

LED UNIVERSITY - Initiative Program - CREE INC.; pg. 631, pg. 1371

LED WORKPLACE - Initiative Program - CREE INC.; pg. 631, pg. 1371

LEDA - Software - SYNOPSYS, INC.; pg. 480, pg. 162

LEDALITE - Lighting Fixture & Control - PHILIPS LIGHTING; pg. 1303, pg. 806

LEDERA - Bath Accessory - CROSCILL, INC.; pg. 1122, pg. 1220

LEDGER - Fabric - NEMSCHOFF, INC.; pg. 936, pg. 1890

LEDGER JACKETS - Building Product - BLUELINX HOLDINGS, INC.; pg. 70, pg. 491

LEE - Clock - BROWN & BIGELOW, INC.; pg. 1624, pg. 959

LEE - Furniture - ETHAN ALLEN INTERIORS INC.; pg. 924, pg. 343

LEE - Tires - THE GOODYEAR TIRE & RUBBER COMPANY; pg. 1883, pg. 1401

LEE - Jeanswear - V.F. CORPORATION; pg. 34, pg. 1376

LEE CHEK - MicroHydraulic Product - THE LEE COMPANY; pg. 1420, pg. 383

LEE FLOSERT - Flow Control - THE LEE COMPANY; pg. 1420, pg. 383

LEE FLOW CONTROL - Flow Control - THE LEE COMPANY; pg. 1420, pg. 383

LEE HYDAMP - Damper - THE LEE COMPANY; pg. 1420, pg. 383

LEE JELA - Nozzle - THE LEE COMPANY; pg. 1420, pg. 383

LEE JET - MicroHydraulic Product - THE LEE COMPANY; pg. 1420, pg. 383

LEE JOFA - Fabrics, Furniture, Wallcoverings & Trimmings - LEE JOFA, INC.; pg. 933, pg. 1142

LEE KIPSTER - Recorder - THE LEE COMPANY; pg. 1420, pg. 383

LEE MICRO DAMP - MicroHydraulic Product - THE LEE COMPANY; pg. 1420, pg. 383

LEE MINSTAC - Tubing & Connectors - THE LEE COMPANY; pg. 1420, pg. 383

LEE NATIONAL DENIM DAY - Fund-Raising Tag Line - V.F. CORPORATION; pg. 34, pg. 1376

LEE PLUG - MicroHydraulic Product - THE LEE COMPANY; pg. 1420, pg. 383

LEE RESTRICTOR CHEK - Flow Control - THE LEE COMPANY; pg. 1420, pg. 383

LEE ROY SELMON'S - Southern-Style Restaurant - BLOOMIN' BRANDS, INC.; pg. 1716, pg. 471

LEE SCHOOL - School Uniforms - LT APPAREL GROUP; pg. 29, pg. 1254

LEE SPIN JET - Nozzle - THE LEE COMPANY; pg. 1420, pg. 383

LEE SPORT - Knitwear - V.F. CORPORATION; pg. 34, pg. 1376

LEE SWANSON SIGNATURE LINE - Healthcare Product - SWANSON HEALTH PRODUCTS INC.; pg. 1600, pg. 1397

LEE TRI - Valve - THE LEE COMPANY; pg. 1420, pg. 383

LEE Y SERAS - Educational Materials - SCHOLASTIC INC.; pg. 1683, pg. 1288

LEEDS - Shoes - ALLEN-EDMONDS SHOE CORP.; pg. 1804, pg. 1887

LEEGEN - Plasticizers - R.T. VANDERBILT COMPANY, INC.;

First page reference indicates Business Class Edition
Second page reference indicates Geographic Edition

pg. 1180, *pg.* 364
LEENA - Pharmaceutical Product - ALLERGAN; *pg.* 1490, *pg.* 1101
LEEP - Medical Apparatus - THE COOPER COMPANIES, INC.; *pg.* 1518, *pg.* 183
LEEP ELECTRODE - Uterus Surgical Instruments - THE COOPER COMPANIES, INC.; *pg.* 1518, *pg.* 183
LEEP REDIKIT - Surgical Preparatory Kits - THE COOPER COMPANIES, INC.; *pg.* 1518, *pg.* 183
LEEP SYSTEM 6000 - Loop Electrosurgical Excision Equipment - THE COOPER COMPANIES, INC.; *pg.* 1518, *pg.* 183
LEEP VAC - Smoke Evacuator Equipment - THE COOPER COMPANIES, INC.; *pg.* 1518, *pg.* 183
LEEPRI - Valve - THE LEE COMPANY; *pg.* 1420, *pg.* 383
LEESON ELECTRIC - AC Motors - REGAL BELOIT CORPORATION; *pg.* 106, *pg.* 1854
LEFT BEHIND - Christian Fiction Series - TYNDALE HOUSE PUBLISHERS, INC.; *pg.* 1697, *pg.* 561
LEGACY - Binocular - BUSHNELL OUTDOOR PRODUCTS, INC.; *pg.* 1403, *pg.* 718
LEGACY - Golf Accessories - CALLAWAY GOLF COMPANY; *pg.* 1829, *pg.* 58
LEGACY - Wrapper - CAMPBELL WRAPPER CORPORATION; *pg.* 1454, *pg.* 1856
LEGACY - Decorative Faucet - THE CHICAGO FAUCET COMPANY; *pg.* 1044, *pg.* 606
LEGACY - Mattress - CHILD CRAFT INDUSTRIES, INC.; *pg.* 920, *pg.* 1463
LEGACY - Leather Product - COACH, INC.; *pg.* 3, *pg.* 1214
LEGACY - Rug - COURISTAN INC.; *pg.* 921, *pg.* 1067
LEGACY - Motion Picture Series - EASTMAN KODAK COMPANY; *pg.* 1408, *pg.* 1333
LEGACY - Furniture - JASPER GROUP; *pg.* 930, *pg.* 691
LEGACY - Recreational Vehicles - JAYCO INC.; *pg.* 1708, *pg.* 695
LEGACY - Control System - LIONEL LLC; *pg.* 961, *pg.* 875
LEGACY - Vitatron Pacemaker - MEDTRONIC, INC.; *pg.* 1564, *pg.* 939
LEGACY - Fabric - NEMSCHOFF, INC.; *pg.* 936, *pg.* 1890
LEGACY - Scotch - SAZERAC COMPANY, INC.; *pg.* 1969, *pg.* 745
LEGACY - Acoustical Shell System - WENGER CORPORATION; *pg.* 1307, *pg.* 952
LEGACY AUDIO - Audio Equipment - ALLEN ORGAN COMPANY; *pg.* 527, *pg.* 1549
LEGACY MASTER - Door Glass - ODL INCORPORATED; *pg.* 101, *pg.* 914
LEGACY: PONTE VEDRA INN & CLUB - Magazine - PALM BEACH MEDIA GROUP INC.; *pg.* 1674, *pg.* 457
LEGACY RECORDINGS - Artist - SONY MUSIC ENTERTAINMENT; *pg.* 309, *pg.* 1294
LEGAL - Briefcase - SANTA FE LEATHER CORPORATION; *pg.* 12, *pg.* 1059
LEGAL EBILL - Computer Program - COMPUTER SCIENCES CORPORATION; *pg.* 378, *pg.* 1780
LEGAL EXCHANGE - Software - BOTTOMLINE TECHNOLOGIES (DE), INC.; *pg.* 727, *pg.* 1038
LEGAL SOLUTIONS SUITE - Computer Program - COMPUTER SCIENCES CORPORATION; *pg.* 378, *pg.* 1780
LEGAL TEMPLATESPLUS - Document Drafting - MICROSYSTEMS; *pg.* 440, *pg.* 608
LEGATO - Software - EMC CORPORATION; *pg.* 391, *pg.* 825
LEGCIDE .5 - Cleaning Preparation - WALTER G. LEGGE COMPANY, INC.; *pg.* 337, *pg.* 1321
LEGCIDE HB PLUS - Cleaning Preparation - WALTER G. LEGGE COMPANY, INC.; *pg.* 337, *pg.* 1321
LEGCLEAN - Cleaning Compound - WALTER G. LEGGE COMPANY, INC.; *pg.* 337, *pg.* 1321
LEGEND - Shoe - AEROGROUP INTERNATIONAL, INC.; *pg.* 1803, *pg.* 1055
LEGEND - Mink - AMERICAN LEGEND COOPERATIVE; *pg.* 18, *pg.* 1833
LEGEND - Binocular - BUSHNELL OUTDOOR PRODUCTS, INC.; *pg.* 1403, *pg.* 718
LEGEND - Amplifier - COHERENT, INC.; *pg.* 1406, *pg.* 265
LEGEND - Orthopedic Product - DJO INCORPORATED; *pg.* 1524, *pg.* 302
LEGEND - Cameras - EASTMAN KODAK COMPANY; *pg.* 1408, *pg.* 1333
LEGEND - Fluid Handling System - GRACO, INC.; *pg.* 1342, *pg.* 935
LEGEND - Seating Product - HUSSEY SEATING CO.; *pg.* 929, *pg.* 751
LEGEND - Beverage Cooler & Ice Chest - IGLOO PRODUCTS CORPORATION; *pg.* 1126, *pg.* 1724
LEGEND - Sail Boats - MARLOW-HUNTER LLC; *pg.* 1709, *pg.* 409
LEGEND - Fencing - MASTER HALCO; *pg.* 96, *pg.* 474
LEGEND - Goggles - MCR SAFETY; *pg.* 1422, *pg.* 1630
LEGEND - Kitchen Faucets - MOEN INCORPORATED; *pg.* 1056, *pg.* 1468
LEGEND - Fabric - NEMSCHOFF, INC.; *pg.* 936, *pg.* 1890
LEGEND 2000 - Boiler - A.O. SMITH CORPORATION; *pg.* 1313, *pg.* 1872
THE LEGEND OF LANDLOCK - Game - GAMEWRIGHT; *pg.* 953, *pg.* 836
LEGEND OF THE FIREBIRD - Video Game - INTERNATIONAL GAME TECHNOLOGY; *pg.* 957, *pg.* 1024
LEGEND OF THE PHOENIX - Video Game - INTERNATIONAL GAME TECHNOLOGY; *pg.* 957, *pg.* 1024
LEGEND OF THE SEAS - Cruise Ship - ROYAL CARIBBEAN CRUISES LTD; *pg.* 1921, *pg.* 446
LEGEND PLUS - Pacemaker - MEDTRONIC, INC.; *pg.* 1564, *pg.* 939
LEGEND SIX-PACKER - Ice Chest - IGLOO PRODUCTS CORPORATION; *pg.* 1126, *pg.* 1724
LEGENDARY BAKING - Bakeries - AMERICAN BLUE RIBBON HOLDINGS; *pg.* 1714, *pg.* 1648
LEGENDARY FOOD, LEGENDARY SERVICE - Slogan - TEXAS ROADHOUSE, INC.; *pg.* 1753, *pg.* 738
LEGENDARY FOR QUALITY - Slogan - BUNN-O-MATIC CORPORATION; *pg.* 53, *pg.* 661
LEGENDARY PIT BAR-B-QUE - Slogan - FAMOUS DAVE'S OF AMERICA, INC.; *pg.* 1728, *pg.* 926
LEGENDARY RELIABILITY - Slogan - SCHNEIDER ELECTRIC; *pg.* 467, *pg.* 1609
LEGENDARY STRENGTH - Tagline - SCHAEFER MARINE INC.; *pg.* 1373, *pg.* 835
LEGENDS - Horse Feed - SOUTHERN STATES COOPERATIVE, INC.; *pg.* 1482, *pg.* 1804
LEGENDS CARE - Motorsports Entertainment - SPEEDWAY MOTORSPORTS, INC.; *pg.* 584, *pg.* 1370
LEGENDS OF OLYMPIA - Video Game - INTERNATIONAL GAME TECHNOLOGY; *pg.* 957, *pg.* 1024
LEGGE - Construction Service - INGERSOLL-RAND COMPANY; *pg.* 1349, *pg.* 1370
LEGGE-ACY - Floor Finishes - WALTER G. LEGGE COMPANY, INC.; *pg.* 337, *pg.* 1321
L'EGGS - Hosiery - HANESBRANDS INC.; *pg.* 26, *pg.* 1394
LEGIJET - Ink Jet Coding System - WEBER PACKAGING SOLUTIONS, INC.; *pg.* 491, *pg.* 554
LEGION - Vanity Lights - CRAFTMADE INTERNATIONAL, INC.; *pg.* 1295, *pg.* 1670
LEGION POINT - Furniture - ASHLEY FURNITURE INDUSTRIES, INC.; *pg.* 914, *pg.* 1852
LEGITRONIC - Electronic Label Printer - WEBER PACKAGING SOLUTIONS, INC.; *pg.* 491, *pg.* 554
LEGPHENE - Cleaning Preparation - WALTER G. LEGGE COMPANY, INC.; *pg.* 337, *pg.* 1321
LEGRAND - Guitars - GIBSON GUITAR CORP.; *pg.* 550, *pg.* 1650
LEGS - Wall Anchor - POWERS FASTENERS INC.; *pg.* 1059, *pg.* 1143
LEGSOLVE - Cleaning Preparation - WALTER G. LEGGE COMPANY, INC.; *pg.* 337, *pg.* 1321
LEGSOLVE-IT - Cleaning Preparation - WALTER G. LEGGE COMPANY, INC.; *pg.* 337, *pg.* 1321
LEGSTAT - Anti-Static Device - WALTER G. LEGGE COMPANY, INC.; *pg.* 337, *pg.* 1321
LEHIGH - Footwear - ROCKY BRANDS, INC.; *pg.* 1818, *pg.* 1466
LEHIGH VALLEY - Dairy Product - DEAN FOODS COMPANY; *pg.* 852, *pg.* 1679
LEHUA - Eyewear - MAUI JIM, INC.; *pg.* 9, *pg.* 651
LEIBINGER - Medical Product - STRYKER CORPORATION; *pg.* 1598, *pg.* 894
LEICA M7 - Camera - LEICA CAMERA, INC.; *pg.* 1420, *pg.* 1041
LEIF - Software - CHYRONHEGO; *pg.* 371, *pg.* 1179
LEIFSDOTTIR - Apparel - URBAN OUTFITTERS, INC.; *pg.* 1789, *pg.* 1571
LEIGHTON - Bath Product - KOHLER CO.; *pg.* 91, *pg.* 1862
LEILANI - Women's Swimwear - QUIKSILVER, INC.; *pg.* 31, *pg.* 104
LEINENKUGEL - Premium Beer - JACOB LEINENKUGEL BREWING CO.; *pg.* 253, *pg.* 1856
LEINENKUGEL'S APPLE SPICE - Seasonal Beer - MILLERCOORS; *pg.* 254, *pg.* 1877
LEINENKUGEL'S BALLYARD BREWERY - Beverage - MILLERCOORS; *pg.* 254, *pg.* 1877
LEINENKUGEL'S BERRY WEISS - Seasonal Beer - MILLERCOORS; *pg.* 254, *pg.* 1877
LEINENKUGEL'S BIG BUTT DOPPELBOCK - Beer - MILLERCOORS; *pg.* 254, *pg.* 1877
LEINENKUGEL'S CREAMY DARK - Beer - MILLERCOORS; *pg.* 254, *pg.* 1877
LEINENKUGEL'S HONEY WEISS - Beer - MILLERCOORS; *pg.* 254, *pg.* 1877
LEINENKUGEL'S LEINIE'S RED - Beer - MILLERCOORS; *pg.* 254, *pg.* 1877
LEINENKUGEL'S LIGHT - Beer - MILLERCOORS; *pg.* 254, *pg.* 1877
LEINENKUGEL'S ORIGINAL PREMIUM - Beer - MILLERCOORS; *pg.* 254, *pg.* 1877
LEINENKUGEL'S RED LAGER - Beer - MILLERCOORS; *pg.* 254, *pg.* 1877
LEINENKUGEL'S SUNSET WHEAT - Beer - MILLERCOORS; *pg.* 254, *pg.* 1877
LEINGANG - Replacement Window & Door - TRUE HOME VALUE, INC.; *pg.* 117, *pg.* 738
LEISURE - Footwear - P.W. MINOR & SON, INC.; *pg.* 1816, *pg.* 1140
LEISURE LIFE - Canoes, Paddle Boats, Deck Boats & Tenders - JOHNSON OUTDOORS INC.; *pg.* 1837, *pg.* 1888
LEISURE TAN - Tanning Solution - PAASCHE AIRBRUSH COMPANY; *pg.* 1444, *pg.* 587
LEISURE TIME - Footwear - P.W. MINOR & SON, INC.; *pg.* 1816, *pg.* 1140
LEISURE TIME - Apparel - VANS, INC.; *pg.* 1821, *pg.* 76
LEISURE.COM - Advertising Website - LIVE CURRENT MEDIA INC.; *pg.* 1263, *pg.* 1911
LEJON - Vermouth - THE WINE GROUP, INC.; *pg.* 1972, *pg.* 234
LEKSAND - Cracker - A.V. OLSSON TRADING CO. INC.; *pg.* 838, *pg.* 372
LEM - Commercial Lighting - SWIVELIER CO., INC.; *pg.* 1307, *pg.* 1142
LEM-O-LUNCH - Snack Food - SNYDER'S-LANCE, INC.; *pg.* 896, *pg.* 1368
LEMAITRE - Medical Device - LEMAITRE VASCULAR, INC.; *pg.* 1555, *pg.* 805
LEMON - Cream Polish - SWISHER HYGIENE INC.; *pg.* 336, *pg.* 1507
LEMON AND PEPPER - Food Product - MCCORMICK & COMPANY, INCORPORATED; *pg.* 1027, *pg.* 779
LEMON BLOSSOM - Hair & Skin Product - AUBREY ORGANICS INC.; *pg.* 499, *pg.* 470
LEMON CHECK - Information Retrieval Services - CARFAX INC.; *pg.* 202, *pg.* 1777
LEMON CRUSH - Cleaner - SWISHER HYGIENE INC.; *pg.* 336, *pg.* 1507
LEMON DROP - Compartment Rack - THE VOLLRATH COMPANY LLC; *pg.* 1139, *pg.* 1894
LEMON DROP PRESS - Educational Materials - SCHOLASTIC INC.; *pg.* 1683, *pg.* 1288
LEMON FRESH CLOROX - Disinfecting Wipes - THE CLOROX COMPANY; *pg.* 327, *pg.* 169
LEMON FRESH PINE-SOL - All Purpose Cleaner - THE CLOROX COMPANY; *pg.* 327, *pg.* 169
LEMON LIFT - Tea - R.C. BIGELOW, INC.; *pg.* 891, *pg.* 348
LEMON LIME TWIST - Game - WMS INDUSTRIES INC.; *pg.* 593, *pg.* 666
LEMON MILDEW ROOT - Penetrator & Remover - THE CLOROX COMPANY; *pg.* 327, *pg.* 169
LEMON PEPPER - Food Product - MODERN PRODUCTS, INC.; *pg.* 1568, *pg.* 1871
LEMON SQUEEZE - Cleaner - SWISHER HYGIENE INC.; *pg.* 336, *pg.* 1507
LEMON SWIRL - Container Grown Plant - MONROVIA GROWERS; *pg.* 1797, *pg.* 44
LEMON THYME DISHWASH LIQUID - Cleaning Product - BI-O-KLEEN INDUSTRIES, INC.; *pg.* 326, *pg.* 1845
LEMON TWIST - Lottery Game - CALIFORNIA LOTTERY; *pg.* 990, *pg.* 196
LEMON TWIST - Lottery Game - LOUISIANA LOTTERY CORPORATION; *pg.* 997, *pg.* 742
LEMON UP - Shampoo & Creme Rinse - THE GILLETTE COMPANY; *pg.* 509, *pg.* 795
LEMOND - Road Bike - TREK BICYCLE CORPORATION; *pg.*

1847, *pg.* 1896
LEMONHEADS - Candy - FERRARA CANDY CO.; *pg.* 1852, *pg.* 612
LENATURISTE - Nutritional Supplements - NBTY, INC.; *pg.* 1572, *pg.* 1338
LENCKITE - Motorsports Entertainment - SPEEDWAY MOTORSPORTS, INC.; *pg.* 584, *pg.* 1370
LENDEL - Paddles - JOHNSON OUTDOORS INC.; *pg.* 1837, *pg.* 1888
LENDER'S - Frozen & Shelf Stable Bagels - PINNACLE FOODS GROUP LLC; *pg.* 889, *pg.* 1104
LENDER'S BAGELS - Bagels - PINNACLE FOODS GROUP LLC; *pg.* 889, *pg.* 1104
LENDING NATURE A HAND - Health & Beauty Product - DIXIE HEALTH, INC.; *pg.* 1524, *pg.* 535
LENGTH-TRAC - Machinery/Accessories - REEL-O-MATIC, INC.; *pg.* 1371, *pg.* 1487
LENIUM - Cleaning Product - PETROFERM INC.; *pg.* 1177, *pg.* 616
LENNIN - Footwear - STEVEN MADDEN, LTD.; *pg.* 1819, *pg.* 1176
LENNITE - Compression Molded Product - WESTLAKE PLASTICS COMPANY; *pg.* 1892, *pg.* 1548
LENNOX - Heating & Cooling Product - LENNOX INTERNATIONAL INC.; *pg.* 1073, *pg.* 1736
LENOR - Fabric Conditioner - THE PROCTER & GAMBLE COMPANY; *pg.* 1129, *pg.* 1418
LENORAH - Footwear - STEVEN MADDEN, LTD.; *pg.* 1819, *pg.* 1176
LENOX - Saw Blades & Tools - NEWELL RUBBERMAID INC.; *pg.* 1128, *pg.* 515
LENOX SETTEE - Fabric - SCALAMANDRE, INC.; *pg.* 941, *pg.* 1058
LENS 1ST - Contact Lenses - 1-800 CONTACTS, INC.; *pg.* 1758, *pg.* 1753
LENS EXPRESS - Contact Lenses - 1-800 CONTACTS, INC.; *pg.* 1758, *pg.* 1753
LENSCRAFTERS - Eyeglass Retailer - LUXOTTICA RETAIL; *pg.* 8, *pg.* 1460
LENSI - Pasta - AMERICAN ITALIAN PASTA COMPANY; *pg.* 837, *pg.* 980
LENSTAR - Software System - FAIR ISAAC CORPORATION; *pg.* 1247, *pg.* 955
LENTICULAR - Printing Technology - SERIGRAPH, INC.; *pg.* 1686, *pg.* 1899
LENTON - Concrete Reinforcing Product - ERICO INTERNATIONAL CORPORATION; *pg.* 1335, *pg.* 1472
LENZING - Fibre - STANFIELD'S LIMITED; *pg.* 48, *pg.* 1917
LENZING-FR - Fiber - DRAPER KNITTING CO., INC.; *pg.* 692, *pg.* 810
LEO - Furniture - AMISCO INDUSTRIES LTD.; *pg.* 913, *pg.* 1958
LEO THE LETTER LOVING LOBSTER - Educational Materials - SCHOLASTIC INC.; *pg.* 1683, *pg.* 1288
LEOLUX - Dispensing Equipment - IDEX CORPORATION; *pg.* 1347, *pg.* 623
LEONA - Fan - CRAFTMADE INTERNATIONAL, INC.; *pg.* 1295, *pg.* 1670
LEONARD - Furniture - NEMSCHOFF, INC.; *pg.* 936, *pg.* 1890
LEONARD KREUSCH - Wine - LEONARD KREUSCH, INC.; *pg.* 254, *pg.* 1099
LEONARDINI - Wine - LEONARD KREUSCH, INC.; *pg.* 254, *pg.* 1099
LEONARDO - Dispensing Equipment - IDEX CORPORATION; *pg.* 1347, *pg.* 623
LEONARDO - Software System - MENTOR GRAPHICS CORPORATION; *pg.* 432, *pg.* 1510
LEONARDOINSIGHT - Software System - MENTOR GRAPHICS CORPORATION; *pg.* 432, *pg.* 1510
LEONARDOSPECTRUM - Software System - MENTOR GRAPHICS CORPORATION; *pg.* 432, *pg.* 1510
LEOPARD - Spotting Scope - SWIFT OPTICAL INSTRUMENTS, INC.; *pg.* 1430, *pg.* 1744
LEOPARD CLAW - Video Game - INTERNATIONAL GAME TECHNOLOGY; *pg.* 957, *pg.* 1024
LEOPARD SPOTS - Video Slots - INTERNATIONAL GAME TECHNOLOGY; *pg.* 957, *pg.* 1024
LEPAGE - Adhesive - HENKEL CONSUMER ADHESIVES, INC.; *pg.* 403, *pg.* 1480
LEPRECHAUN LUCK - Game - MISSOURI LOTTERY; *pg.* 999, *pg.* 979
LEPRECHAUN'S GOLD - Game - WMS INDUSTRIES INC.; *pg.* 593, *pg.* 666
LEPTYNE - Turpentine Substitute - PPG INDUSTRIES, INC.; *pg.* 1445, *pg.* 1579
LEPTOFERM-5 - Veterinary Vaccine - PFIZER INC.; *pg.* 1581, *pg.* 1278
LEPTOS - Pharmaceutical Product - ABBOTT LABORATORIES; *pg.* 1484, *pg.* 551
LEPTOVAX - Canine Veterinary Vaccine - BOEHRINGER INGELHEIM VETMEDICA, INC.; *pg.* 1474, *pg.* 989
LEQ A SEA - Seafood - TRIDENT SEAFOODS CORPORATION; *pg.* 902, *pg.* 1842
LERAN - Propane Installation & Appliance Products - INTERLINE BRANDS, INC.; *pg.* 1051, *pg.* 433
LERNER - Apparel - FULLBEAUTY BRANDS; *pg.* 1770, *pg.* 1233
LEROUX - Cordial - JIM BEAM BRANDS CO.; *pg.* 1965, *pg.* 601
LES AFFAIRES - Newspaper - TRANSCONTINENTAL INC.; *pg.* 1695, *pg.* 1957
LES CAFES ORIENT EXPRESS - Coffee - VAN HOUTTE, INC.; *pg.* 908, *pg.* 1957
LES FLEURS - Scarf - HERITAGE LACE INC.; *pg.* 694, *pg.* 711
LES PAUL - Musical Instrument - GIBSON GUITAR CORP.; *pg.* 550, *pg.* 1650
LES PETITS - Toys - LEAPFROG ENTERPRISES, INC.; *pg.* 961, *pg.* 84
LESBETH - Sunglasses - COACH, INC.; *pg.* 3, *pg.* 1214
LESIEUR - Mayonnaise - CAMPBELL SOUP COMPANY; *pg.* 844, *pg.* 1048
LESLEY - Clothing - ABERCROMBIE & FITCH CO.; *pg.* 37, *pg.* 1466
LESLIE - All Purpose Table Salt - CARGILL LIMITED; *pg.* 1475, *pg.* 1914
LESLIE'S - Pool Supplies - LESLIE'S POOLMART, INC.; *pg.* 1838, *pg.* 17
LESS IS MORE - Tagline - SYNACOR, INC.; *pg.* 479, *pg.* 1380
LESSONWORKS - Dry-Erase Board System - WENGER CORPORATION; *pg.* 1307, *pg.* 952
LESTER NET - Building Product - LESTER BUILDING SYSTEMS, LLC; *pg.* 93, *pg.* 927
LESTER QUOTE - Building Product - LESTER BUILDING SYSTEMS, LLC; *pg.* 93, *pg.* 927
LESTOIL - Heavy Duty Cleaner - THE CLOROX COMPANY; *pg.* 327, *pg.* 169
LET-GO - Penetrating Oil - SHERWIN-WILLIAMS DIVERSIFIED BRANDS DIVISION; *pg.* 1448, *pg.* 1435
LET GO. CATCH LIFE. - Slogan - WCI COMMUNITIES, INC.; *pg.* 1118, *pg.* 414
LET HEAVEN - Pillow and Throw - HERITAGE LACE INC.; *pg.* 694, *pg.* 711
LET HORIZON DESIGN FOR YOU - Tagline - HORIZON DESIGNS, INC.; *pg.* 695, *pg.* 1011
LET IT SNOW - Pillow and Throw - HERITAGE LACE INC.; *pg.* 694, *pg.* 711
LET THE FRESH AIR IN - Wind & Rain Deflectors - MACNEIL AUTOMOTIVE PRODUCTS, LTD.; *pg.* 211, *pg.* 559
LET THE GOOD TIMES ROLL - Tagline - KAWASAKI MOTORS CORP., U.S.A.; *pg.* 1708, *pg.* 111
LET THEM EAT RICE CAKE - Nail Care Product - OPI PRODUCTS INC.; *pg.* 518, *pg.* 167
LET US POWER YOU - Slogan - UNIVERSAL POWER GROUP, INC.; *pg.* 683, *pg.* 1671
LET YOUR FINGER DO THE WALKING - Slogan - AT&T SOUTHEAST; *pg.* 1868, *pg.* 489
LET YOURSELF GO - Games - PENN NATIONAL GAMING, INC.; *pg.* 574, *pg.* 1595
LETAIRIS - Biopharmaceutical Product - GILEAD SCIENCES, INC.; *pg.* 1535, *pg.* 88
LET'S B - Office Furniture - STEELCASE INC.; *pg.* 475, *pg.* 889
LET'S BUILD SOMETHING TOGETHER - Slogan - LOWE'S COMPANIES, INC.; *pg.* 1053, *pg.* 1383
LET'S FIND OUT - Educational Materials - SCHOLASTIC INC.; *pg.* 1683, *pg.* 1288
LET'S GO - Nailcare Product - MEDICOOL, INC.; *pg.* 1562, *pg.* 294
LET'S GO FISHING - Game - PRESSMAN TOY CORPORATION; *pg.* 965, *pg.* 1734
LET'S PARTY! - Dresses & Sets - HABAND COMPANY, INC.; *pg.* 1772, *pg.* 1099
LETS PLAY - Online Games - DEL MONTE FOODS, INC.; *pg.* 852, *pg.* 304
LET'S SAY THANKS - Slogan - XEROX CORPORATION; *pg.* 494, *pg.* 365
LET'S START - Educational Materials - SCHOLASTIC INC.; *pg.* 1683, *pg.* 1288
LETS STEAM OUT. KEEP SPLATTERS IN. - Tag Line - GEORGIA-PACIFIC LLC; *pg.* 1458, *pg.* 507
LET'S TALK COLORADO - Tagline - COLORADO TOURISM OFFICE; *pg.* 991, *pg.* 318
LET'S THRIVE - Slogan - THRIVENT FINANCIAL FOR LUTHERANS; *pg.* 1219, *pg.* 944
LET'S TOUCH - Nailcare Product - MEDICOOL, INC.; *pg.* 1562, *pg.* 294
LETTER CRAZY - Games - LEAPFROG ENTERPRISES, INC.; *pg.* 961, *pg.* 84
LETTER FACTORY - Educational Toys - LEAPFROG ENTERPRISES, INC.; *pg.* 961, *pg.* 84
LETTERS - Fabric - NEMSCHOFF, INC.; *pg.* 936, *pg.* 1890
LETTERS WITH LULU - Toys - LEAPFROG ENTERPRISES, INC.; *pg.* 961, *pg.* 84
LETTRA - Letterpress Paper Products - CRANE & CO., INC.; *pg.* 1456, *pg.* 816
LETTUCE ENTERTAIN YOU - Restaurants & Night Clubs - LETTUCE ENTERTAIN YOU ENTERPRISES, INC.; *pg.* 1735, *pg.* 580
LETTUCE KING I - Vegetable slicer - LINCOLN FOODSERVICE PRODUCTS, LLC; *pg.* 1127, *pg.* 1432
LETTUCE KING IV - Vegetable slicer - LINCOLN FOODSERVICE PRODUCTS, LLC; *pg.* 1127, *pg.* 1432
LETZ - Loop Excision of the Transformation Zone Procedure - UTAH MEDICAL PRODUCTS, INC.; *pg.* 1605, *pg.* 1752
LEUCOTROPIN - Drug - EMERGENT BIOSOLUTIONS; *pg.* 1528, *pg.* 1914
LEUKOCELL - Feline Leukemia Vaccine - PFIZER INC.; *pg.* 1581, *pg.* 1278
LEUKOGUARD - Filter - PALL CORPORATION; *pg.* 232, *pg.* 1323
LEUKOSCAN - Antibody - IMMUNOMEDICS, INC.; *pg.* 1544, *pg.* 1087
LEUKOTAN - Acrylic Syntan - DOW CHEMICAL; *pg.* 1156, *pg.* 1563
LEUKOTAPE - Medical & Aesthetic Product - DYNATRONICS CORPORATION; *pg.* 1526, *pg.* 1757
LEUMETA - Plasma Based Testing - QUEST DIAGNOSTICS INCORPORATED; *pg.* 1587, *pg.* 1080
LEUSTATIN - Healthcare Product - JOHNSON & JOHNSON; *pg.* 1549, *pg.* 1091
LEV-L - Mount - FABREEKA INTERNATIONAL, INC.; *pg.* 1882, *pg.* 847
LEVAQUIN - Healthcare Product - JOHNSON & JOHNSON; *pg.* 1549, *pg.* 1091
LEVEEN - Medical Device - BOSTON SCIENTIFIC CORPORATION; *pg.* 1508, *pg.* 831
LEVEEN COACCESS - Medical Device - BOSTON SCIENTIFIC CORPORATION; *pg.* 1508, *pg.* 831
LEVEL - Fabric - NEMSCHOFF, INC.; *pg.* 936, *pg.* 1890
LEVEL 5 OBJECT - Export System Object-Oriented System for Microsoft Windows - INFORMATION BUILDERS INC.; *pg.* 415, *pg.* 1243
LEVEL-BEST - Floor Leveler & Spackling Compound - THE SAVOGRAN COMPANY; *pg.* 1447, *pg.* 840
LEVEL GAGECASE - Enclosure - THERMON AMERICAS INC.; *pg.* 1077, *pg.* 1744
LEVEL GAUGE CLEANER - Holding Tank Probe Cleaner - THETFORD CORPORATION; *pg.* 337, *pg.* 867
LEVEL II VIEWER - Software - MONEY.NET, INC.; *pg.* 1268, *pg.* 1261
LEVEL IV - Design & Implementation - COMPUTER SCIENCES CORPORATION; *pg.* 378, *pg.* 1780
LEVEL PLUS - Liquid Level Sensors - MTS SYSTEMS CORPORATION; *pg.* 442, *pg.* 923
LEVEL REMINDER - Sensor - HUNTER ENGINEERING COMPANY; *pg.* 208, *pg.* 973
LEVEL TWO - Photography - CANDID COLOR SYSTEMS, INC.; *pg.* 1404, *pg.* 1485
LEVELER-VU - Light - RITE-HITE HOLDING CORPORATION; *pg.* 1372, *pg.* 1880
LEVELROCK - Underlayment - USG CORPORATION; *pg.* 118, *pg.* 594
LEVELS - Risk Analysis - STANDARD & POOR'S RATINGS SERVICES; *pg.* 805, *pg.* 1296
LEVELTONE - Resinated-Pigment Finish For Leather - HENKEL CORPORATION; *pg.* 1165, *pg.* 1535
LEVENTA - Pharmaceutical Preparations - MERCK & CO., INC.; *pg.* 1566, *pg.* 1077
LEVER 1500 - Automatic, Single Knife Roll Slitter - LEVER MANUFACTURING CORP.; *pg.* 1355, *pg.* 1082
LEVER 2000 - Soap - UNILEVER UNITED STATES, INC.; *pg.* 904, *pg.* 1061

First page reference indicates Business Class Edition
Second page reference indicates Geographic Edition

LEVER 300 - Semi-Automatic Single Knife Roll Slitter - LEVER MANUFACTURING CORP.; *pg.* 1355, *pg.* 1082
LEVER 6200 - Automatic, Single Knife Roll Slitter - LEVER MANUFACTURING CORP.; *pg.* 1355, *pg.* 1082
LEVEREDGE - Medical Device - LEMAITRE VASCULAR, INC.; *pg.* 1555, *pg.* 805
LEVI EXTRA - Loose Leaf Tobacco - AMERICAN SNUFF COMPANY; *pg.* 1893, *pg.* 1641
LEVI GARRETT - Tobacco Product - AMERICAN SNUFF COMPANY; *pg.* 1893, *pg.* 1641
LEVI STRAUSS SIGNATURE - Apparel - LEVI STRAUSS & CO.; *pg.* 43, *pg.* 220
LEVINGTON - Lawn & Garden Products - THE SCOTTS MIRACLE-GRO COMPANY; *pg.* 1799, *pg.* 1459
LEVI'S - Apparel - LEVI STRAUSS & CO.; *pg.* 43, *pg.* 220
LEVI'S 513 - Jean - LEVI STRAUSS & CO.; *pg.* 43, *pg.* 220
LEVI'S 517 - Jean - LEVI STRAUSS & CO.; *pg.* 43, *pg.* 220
LEVI'S 524 - Jean - LEVI STRAUSS & CO.; *pg.* 43, *pg.* 220
LEVI'S 560 - Jean - LEVI STRAUSS & CO.; *pg.* 43, *pg.* 220
LEVI'S ECO - Jean - LEVI STRAUSS & CO.; *pg.* 43, *pg.* 220
LEVITATOR - Computer Workstation Product - STINGER MEDICAL LLC; *pg.* 476, *pg.* 1648
LEVITON - Electronic Component - LEVITON MANUFACTURING COMPANY, INC.; *pg.* 1301, *pg.* 1180
LEVITON INTEGRATED NETWORKS - Wiring Product - LEVITON MANUFACTURING COMPANY, INC.; *pg.* 1301, *pg.* 1180
LEVITRA - Medicine - MERCK & CO., INC.; *pg.* 1566, *pg.* 1077
LEVOLOR - Window Blinds - NEWELL RUBBERMAID INC.; *pg.* 1128, *pg.* 515
LEVOTHYROXINE SODIUM - Pharmaceutical Product - LANNETT COMPANY, INC.; *pg.* 1555, *pg.* 1566
LEVOXYL - Pharmaceutical Product - KING PHARMACEUTICALS, INC.; *pg.* 1553, *pg.* 1627
LEVOXYL - Pharmaceutical Product - LANNETT COMPANY, INC.; *pg.* 1555, *pg.* 1566
LEVULAN - Biopharmaceutical Product - DUSA PHARMACEUTICALS, INC.; *pg.* 1525, *pg.* 860
LEW MAGRAM - Apparel - ASCENA RETAIL GROUP, INC.; *pg.* 18, *pg.* 1081
LEW-TEX - Mousepads - LEWTAN INDUSTRIES CORP.; *pg.* 1658, *pg.* 352
LEWIS - Furniture - ETHAN ALLEN INTERIORS INC.; *pg.* 924, *pg.* 343
LEWIS - Furniture - JOFCO INC.; *pg.* 931, *pg.* 691
LEWIS & CLARK - Distilled Spirits - HOOD RIVER DISTILLERS INC.; *pg.* 1964, *pg.* 1498
LEW'S - Fishing Reels - ZEBCO; *pg.* 1848, *pg.* 1491
LEX - Graphic Engine - CHYRONHEGO; *pg.* 371, *pg.* 1179
L.E.X. - Texturized Fiber Glass Yarns for Cloth Manufacturing Applications - PPG INDUSTRIES, INC.; *pg.* 1445, *pg.* 1579
LEX 1000 - Lens Edger - SANTINELLI INTERNATIONAL INC.; *pg.* 1395, *pg.* 1165
LEX-C - Polycarbonate Crossing Signals - ALSTOM SIGNALING, INC.; *pg.* 1312, *pg.* 1350
LEX LUTHOR - Character - DC COMICS, INC.; *pg.* 1633, *pg.* 1221
LEX2 - Graphics System Software - CHYRONHEGO; *pg.* 371, *pg.* 1179
LEXAMINE - Cosmetic Ingredient - INOLEX GROUP INC.; *pg.* 1168, *pg.* 1566
LEXAN - Plastic Bottled Water & Beverage Containers - GENERAL ELECTRIC COMPANY; *pg.* 1297, *pg.* 347
LEXAN - Enclosure - THERMON AMERICAS INC.; *pg.* 1077, *pg.* 1744
LEXAPRO - Pharmaceutical Product - ABBOTT LABORATORIES; *pg.* 1484, *pg.* 551
LEXATE - Cosmetic Ingredient - INOLEX GROUP INC.; *pg.* 1168, *pg.* 1566
LEXEXPRESS - Repair Services - LEXMARK INTERNATIONAL, INC.; *pg.* 427, *pg.* 730
LEXFEEL - Cosmetic Ingredient - INOLEX GROUP INC.; *pg.* 1168, *pg.* 1566
LEXGARD - Cosmetic Ingredient - INOLEX GROUP INC.; *pg.* 1168, *pg.* 1566
LEXGEN.COM - Biopharmaceutical Product Website - LEXICON PHARMACEUTICALS, INC.; *pg.* 1555, *pg.* 1747
LEXGENE - Biopharmaceutical Product - LEXICON PHARMACEUTICALS, INC.; *pg.* 1555, *pg.* 1747
LEXICON - Tool for Assessing Business Systems - CARTESIAN; *pg.* 369, *pg.* 718
LEXICON - Audio & Video Product - HARMAN INTERNATIONAL INDUSTRIES, INCORPORATED; *pg.* 641, *pg.* 374
LEXIDE - Paper & Nonwoven Material - FIBERMARK INC.; *pg.* 1457, *pg.* 1764
LEXIE - Footwear - COBIAN CORP.; *pg.* 1806, *pg.* 253
LEXINGTON - Polycarbonate Mugs - CARLISLE FOODSERVICE PRODUCTS INCORPORATED; *pg.* 1455, *pg.* 1485
LEXINGTON - Watch - COACH, INC.; *pg.* 3, *pg.* 1214
THE LEXINGTON - Natural Pine Swing Set - CREATIVE PLAYTHINGS LTD.; *pg.* 1831, *pg.* 820
LEXINGTON - Dinnerware - THE HOMER LAUGHLIN CHINA COMPANY; *pg.* 1125, *pg.* 1850
LEXINGTON - Women's Trousers - LANE BRYANT; *pg.* 1776, *pg.* 1441
LEXINGTON - Footwear - P.W. MINOR & SON, INC.; *pg.* 1816, *pg.* 1140
LEXINGTON - Weather Instrument - SWIFT OPTICAL INSTRUMENTS, INC.; *pg.* 1430, *pg.* 1744
LEXINGTON KIDS - Furniture - LEXINGTON HOME BRANDS; *pg.* 933, *pg.* 1391
LEXIS - Hearing Instrument - STARKEY LABORATORIES, INC.; *pg.* 1597, *pg.* 923
LEXIVA - Pharmaceutical Product - VERTEX PHARMACEUTICALS INCORPORATED; *pg.* 1606, *pg.* 801
LEXOL - Leather Care Products - SUMMIT INDUSTRIES, INC.; *pg.* 1599, *pg.* 535
LEXONSITE - Repair Services - LEXMARK INTERNATIONAL, INC.; *pg.* 427, *pg.* 730
LEXOREZ - Cosmetic Ingredient - INOLEX GROUP INC.; *pg.* 1168, *pg.* 1566
LEXOTONE - Paper & Nonwoven Material - FIBERMARK INC.; *pg.* 1457, *pg.* 1764
LEXQUAT - Cosmetic Ingredient - INOLEX GROUP INC.; *pg.* 1168, *pg.* 1566
L'EXTRA - Cheese - AGROPUR COOPERATIVE; *pg.* 836, *pg.* 1950
LEXVISION - Biopharmaceutical Product - LEXICON PHARMACEUTICALS, INC.; *pg.* 1555, *pg.* 1747
LEYLA - Dolls - AMERICAN GIRL LLC; *pg.* 949, *pg.* 1871
LFFB - Limiter Fuse Block - LITTELFUSE, INC.; *pg.* 1301, *pg.* 580
LFH - Electronic Components - MOLEX INCORPORATED; *pg.* 655, *pg.* 628
LGS - Reduction Additive - JOHNSON MATTHEY PROCESS TECHNOLOGIES; *pg.* 1169, *pg.* 1083
LGX - Multiplexer - VIAVI SOLUTIONS INC.; *pg.* 1435, *pg.* 148
LH - Hematology Analyzer - BECKMAN COULTER, INC.; *pg.* 1402, *pg.* 48
L'HERMITAGE - Lamp - J. ROBERT SCOTT INC.; *pg.* 930, *pg.* 105
LHERMITE - Trade Automatic Equipment - STANDEX INTERNATIONAL CORPORATION; *pg.* 60, *pg.* 1039
LHR - Reflective Glass - PPG INDUSTRIES, INC.; *pg.* 1445, *pg.* 1579
LI-24 - Electronic Components - MOLEX INCORPORATED; *pg.* 655, *pg.* 628
LI MING - Cooking Oil - CARGILL LIMITED; *pg.* 1475, *pg.* 1914
LIA - Laboratory Information Access; Data Management Service - FRESENIUS MEDICAL CARE NORTH AMERICA; *pg.* 1531, *pg.* 851
LIAISON - Computer Services - AVNET, INC.; *pg.* 622, *pg.* 15
LIASON - Software - WIND RIVER SYSTEMS, INC.; *pg.* 493, *pg.* 38
LIB TECHNOLOGIES - Snowboards - QUIKSILVER, INC.; *pg.* 31, *pg.* 104
LIBBIEE - Footwear - STEVEN MADDEN, LTD.; *pg.* 1819, *pg.* 1176
LIBBY'S - Food Product - CONAGRA FOODS, INC.; *pg.* 826, *pg.* 1014
LIBBY'S - Foods - SENECA FOODS CORPORATION; *pg.* 895, *pg.* 1177
LIBBY'S JUICE BLAST - Food & Beverage Product - NESTLE USA, INC.; *pg.* 883, *pg.* 96
LIBBY'S KERNS - Food & Beverage Product - NESTLE USA, INC.; *pg.* 883, *pg.* 96
LIBBY'S KERNS NECTARS - Hispanic Food - NESTLE USA, INC.; *pg.* 883, *pg.* 96
LIBBY'S PUMPKIN - Food & Beverage Product - NESTLE USA, INC.; *pg.* 883, *pg.* 96
LIBERATOR - Battery - EXIDE TECHNOLOGIES; *pg.* 204, *pg.* 483
LIBERATOR - Systems Integration & Aeronautics - LOCKHEED MARTIN CORPORATION; *pg.* 229, *pg.* 762
LIBERATOR - Optical Product - UNIVERSAL PHOTONICS, INC.; *pg.* 1433, *pg.* 1167
LIBERTE - Medical Device - BOSTON SCIENTIFIC CORPORATION; *pg.* 1508, *pg.* 831
LIBERTY - Oxygen Therapy Equipment - ALLIED HEALTHCARE PRODUCTS, INC.; *pg.* 1491, *pg.* 990
LIBERTY - String - ASHAWAY LINE & TWINE MFG. CO.; *pg.* 1826, *pg.* 1600
LIBERTY - Material Handling Equipment - C&D TECHNOLOGIES, INC.; *pg.* 627, *pg.* 1517
LIBERTY - Milk Chocolate - CARGILL, INC.; *pg.* 845, *pg.* 965
LIBERTY - Flavour - CARGILL LIMITED; *pg.* 1475, *pg.* 1914
LIBERTY - Digital RF System - CHECKPOINT SYSTEMS, INC.; *pg.* 628, *pg.* 1559
LIBERTY - Donut Mixes - DAWN FOOD PRODUCTS, INC.; *pg.* 1018, *pg.* 893
LIBERTY - Filing System - FELLOWES, INC.; *pg.* 397, *pg.* 620
LIBERTY - Water-Soluble Polymer Suspension - HERCULES INCORPORATED; *pg.* 1166, *pg.* 392
LIBERTY - Paper - INTERNATIONAL PAPER COMPANY; *pg.* 1460, *pg.* 1644
LIBERTY - Banking Software - JACK HENRY & ASSOCIATES, INC.; *pg.* 422, *pg.* 988
LIBERTY - Sailboat - MARLOW-HUNTER LLC; *pg.* 1709, *pg.* 409
LIBERTY - Decorative Architectural Product - MASCO CORPORATION; *pg.* 96, *pg.* 909
LIBERTY - Fabric - NEMSCHOFF, INC.; *pg.* 936, *pg.* 1890
LIBERTY - Fabric - NEUTRAL POSTURE, INC.; *pg.* 939, *pg.* 1669
LIBERTY - Cast Iron Oil Boiler - SLANT/FIN CORPORATION; *pg.* 1076, *pg.* 1163
LIBERTY - Software - SYNOPSYS, INC.; *pg.* 480, *pg.* 162
LIBERTY - Electrostimulation Device to Treat Female Urinary Incontinence - UTAH MEDICAL PRODUCTS, INC.; *pg.* 1605, *pg.* 1752
LIBERTY 2000 MAX - Value-Regulated, Lead Acid Battery - C&D TECHNOLOGIES, INC.; *pg.* 627, *pg.* 1517
LIBERTY BANK - Banking & Financial Services - LIBERTY BANK INC.; *pg.* 776, *pg.* 356
LIBERTY BARS - Pulltab Game - IDAHO LOTTERY; *pg.* 995, *pg.* 547
LIBERTY COAT - Porcelain Enamel Frits - FERRO CORPORATION; *pg.* 1162, *pg.* 1462
LIBERTY ELITE - Vinyl Siding - PLY GEM SIDING GROUP; *pg.* 105, *pg.* 986
LIBERTY HARDWARE - Decorative Hardware - MASCO CORPORATION; *pg.* 96, *pg.* 909
LIBERTY LINK - Seed Corn - MOEWS SEED CO., INC.; *pg.* 1797, *pg.* 616
LIBERTY OF THE SEAS - Cruise Ship - ROYAL CARIBBEAN CRUISES LTD; *pg.* 1921, *pg.* 446
LIBERTY SERIES 1000 - Value-Regulated, Lead Acid Battery - C&D TECHNOLOGIES, INC.; *pg.* 627, *pg.* 1517
LIBRA - Amplifier - COHERENT, INC.; *pg.* 1406, *pg.* 265
LIBRA - Carpet - INTERFACE, INC.; *pg.* 695, *pg.* 512
LIBRA-PASSPORT - Software - SYNOPSYS, INC.; *pg.* 480, *pg.* 162
LIBRA TASK - Lamp - J. ROBERT SCOTT INC.; *pg.* 930, *pg.* 105
LIBRARIAN - Software System - MENTOR GRAPHICS CORPORATION; *pg.* 432, *pg.* 1510
LIBRARY - Track - COILCRAFT, INC.; *pg.* 1324, *pg.* 562
LIBRARY BUILDER - Software System - MENTOR GRAPHICS CORPORATION; *pg.* 432, *pg.* 1510
LIBRARY COMPILER - Software - SYNOPSYS, INC.; *pg.* 480, *pg.* 162
LIBRARY EFFICIENCY - Molecular Biology Product - THERMO FISHER SCIENTIFIC INC.; *pg.* 1602, *pg.* 61
LIBRARY MAIL - Postal Services - UNITED STATES POSTAL SERVICE; *pg.* 1009, *pg.* 406
LIBRARY MANAGER - Software System - MENTOR GRAPHICS CORPORATION; *pg.* 432, *pg.* 1510
LIBRARY SYSTEM - Software - CHECKPOINT SYSTEMS, INC.; *pg.* 628, *pg.* 1559
LIBRARYPRO - Enterprise Tape Library - OVERLAND STORAGE, INC.; *pg.* 451, *pg.* 205
LIBRARYXPRESS - Enterprise Tape Library - OVERLAND STORAGE, INC.; *pg.* 451, *pg.* 205
LIBRAX - Pharmaceutical Product - VALEANT PHARMACEUTICALS INTERNATIONAL; *pg.* 1605, *pg.* 1047

LICA - Digital Camera Company - LEICA CAMERA, INC.; *pg.* 1420, *pg.* 1041
LICE-NO-MORE - Farm & Ranch Product - PBI/GORDON CORPORATION; *pg.* 1176, *pg.* 985
LICEMD - Head Lice Treatment - RECKITT BENCKISER INC.; *pg.* 1136, *pg.* 1105
LICENSE-TITE! - License Plate Fasteners - DORMAN PRODUCTS, INC.; *pg.* 204, *pg.* 1522
LICOR 43 - Liqueur - WILLIAM GRANT & SONS, INC.; *pg.* 1972, *pg.* 1057
LICORICE - Dolls - AMERICAN GIRL LLC; *pg.* 949, *pg.* 1871
LICOX - Medical Device - INTEGRA LIFESCIENCES HOLDINGS CORPORATION; *pg.* 1545, *pg.* 1109
LICRON - Chemical Cleaner Product - TECH SPRAY, L.P.; *pg.* 1183, *pg.* 1659
LID EASE - Pump Product - IDEX CORPORATION; *pg.* 1347, *pg.* 623
LID LASSO - Caps - SONOCO PRODUCTS COMPANY; *pg.* 1469, *pg.* 1619
LID-SYSTEM - Glass & Ceramic Material - CORNING INCORPORATED; *pg.* 1122, *pg.* 1154
LIDDLE GRIDDLE - Electrical Appliance & Housewares - NATIONAL PRESTO INDUSTRIES, INC; *pg.* 1128, *pg.* 1857
LIDO - Cookies - PEPPERIDGE FARM, INC.; *pg.* 888, *pg.* 363
LIDO - Outdoor Lighting - SWIVELIER CO., INC.; *pg.* 1307, *pg.* 1142
LIDO-LUSTER - Metal Polish Cream - LAVI INDUSTRIES INC.; *pg.* 93, *pg.* 299
LIDO RAIL - Product Sold Through Home Centers - LAVI INDUSTRIES INC.; *pg.* 93, *pg.* 299
LIDO-TONE - Powder Coating - LAVI INDUSTRIES INC.; *pg.* 93, *pg.* 299
LIDO-WELD - Metal Contact Cement - LAVI INDUSTRIES INC.; *pg.* 93, *pg.* 299
LIDOCORT - Pharmaceutical Product - CHIESI USA, INC.; *pg.* 1515, *pg.* 1359
LIDODERM - Pharmaceutical Product - ENDO PHARMACEUTICALS HOLDINGS, INC.; *pg.* 1528, *pg.* 1549
LIDS - Headwear - GENESCO INC.; *pg.* 1809, *pg.* 1650
LIDSYS - Packaging Systems & Materials - SEALED AIR CORPORATION; *pg.* 1468, *pg.* 1058
LIDTENDER - Stacking Robot - WELDON SOLUTIONS; *pg.* 1388, *pg.* 1598
LIEBERMAN'S - Loose Leaf Tobacco - AMERICAN SNUFF COMPANY; *pg.* 1893, *pg.* 1641
LIEBIG - Soups - CAMPBELL SOUP COMPANY; *pg.* 844, *pg.* 1048
LIEBOTSCHONER - Cream Ale - THE LION BREWERY, INC.; *pg.* 254, *pg.* 1594
LIENA - Footwear - STEVEN MADDEN, LTD.; *pg.* 1819, *pg.* 1176
LIENWATCH - Early Distress Notification Services - CORELOGIC, INC.; *pg.* 1198, *pg.* 109
LIESE - Hair Care - KAO BRANDS CO. INC.; *pg.* 513, *pg.* 1415
LIF-O-GEN - Filled Disposable Oxygen Cylinders - ALLIED HEALTHCARE PRODUCTS, INC.; *pg.* 1491, *pg.* 990
LIFA - Polypropylene Bodywear - HELLY-HANSEN (US), INC.; *pg.* 26, *pg.* 1813
LIFE - Ergonomic Seating - KNOLL, INC.; *pg.* 425, *pg.* 1527
LIFE - Cereal - PEPSICO, INC.; *pg.* 259, *pg.* 1327
LIFE - Cereal - THE QUAKER OATS COMPANY; *pg.* 834, *pg.* 588
LIFE ACCELERATOR - Tag Line - UNITED STATES NAVY RECRUITING COMMAND; *pg.* 1009, *pg.* 1648
LIFE ADVICE - Consumer Education Program - METLIFE, INC.; *pg.* 1208, *pg.* 1258
LIFE-AIR - Blower - PROGRESSIVE DYNAMICS, INC.; *pg.* 665, *pg.* 898
LIFE CHECK - Pharmacy Services - RITE AID CORPORATION; *pg.* 1590, *pg.* 1519
LIFE COMES AT YOU FAST - Insurance Service - NATIONWIDE MUTUAL INSURANCE COMPANY; *pg.* 1210, *pg.* 1442
LIFE-CORE - Door - LARSON MANUFACTURING COMPANY; *pg.* 93, *pg.* 1624
LIFE DOESN.T WAIT. - Tag Line - IBERIABANK CORPORATION; *pg.* 768, *pg.* 744
LIFE ENGINE - Internet Services - YAHOO! INC.; *pg.* 1289, *pg.* 289
LIFE ESSENTIALS - Nutritional Supplement - NU SKIN ENTERPRISES, INC.; *pg.* 518, *pg.* 1755
LIFE EVENTS LEGAL PLAN - Pre-Paid Legal Services - LEGAL SHIELD; *pg.* 775, *pg.* 1484
LIFE FITNESS - Fitness Equipment - BRUNSWICK CORPORATION; *pg.* 1828, *pg.* 623
LIFE-FOAM - Seat Cushion - RELAX THE BACK CORPORATION; *pg.* 940, *pg.* 120
LIFE FORCE - Vitamin & Herbal Supplement - SOURCE NATURALS; *pg.* 1595, *pg.* 278
LIFE IN BALANCE - Slogan - MIRAVAL RESORT; *pg.* 1105, *pg.* 12
LIFE IN THE COUNTRY - Kitchen Product - KOHLER CO.; *pg.* 91, *pg.* 1862
LIFE INSURANCE FOR PEOPLE THAT MAKE AMERICA WORK - Insurance Product - SBLI USA LIFE INSURANCE COMPANY, INC.; *pg.* 1216, *pg.* 1288
LIFE IS A RIDE - Tagline - AMERICAN QUARTER HORSE ASSOCIATION; *pg.* 130, *pg.* 1658
LIFE IS CRAP - Classic Cards - LEANIN' TREE, INC.; *pg.* 1658, *pg.* 311
LIFE IS ENTERTAINING. ENTERTAINMENT IS OUR LIFE. - Tagline - A&E TELEVISION NETWORKS, LLC; *pg.* 267, *pg.* 1185
LIVE IS FULL OF FLAVOR. BUMBLE BEE. YUM - Tagline - BUMBLE BEE FOODS LLC; *pg.* 842, *pg.* 201
LIFE IS GOOD POMPEIAN MAKES IT BETTER. - Tagline - POMPEIAN, INC.; *pg.* 890, *pg.* 759
LIFE IS TICKING - Slogan - TIMEX CORPORATION; *pg.* 14, *pg.* 355
LIFE JOURNEY - Christian Books about Every Day Living - DAVID C. COOK; *pg.* 1633, *pg.* 315
LIFE, LIBERTY & THE PURSUIT OF ALL WHO THREATEN IT - Tag Line - UNITED STATES NAVY RECRUITING COMMAND; *pg.* 1009, *pg.* 1648
LIFE-LIKE - Track System - LIFOAM INDUSTRIES INC.; *pg.* 961, *pg.* 772
LIFE-LIKE RACING - Slot Cars & Sets - LIFOAM INDUSTRIES INC.; *pg.* 961, *pg.* 772
LIFE-LIKE TRAINS - Model Trains & Sets - LIFOAM INDUSTRIES INC.; *pg.* 961, *pg.* 772
LIFE LINE - Textiles - BERNHARDT DESIGN; *pg.* 918, *pg.* 1381
LIFE NEEDS FROSTING - Slogan - CINNABON, INC.; *pg.* 1723, *pg.* 493
LIFE OF LUXURY - Game - WMS INDUSTRIES INC.; *pg.* 593, *pg.* 666
THE LIFE OF THE KITCHEN - Slogan - DACOR; *pg.* 54, *pg.* 67
LIFE SAFETY CODE - Fire Safety Book - NATIONAL FIRE PROTECTION ASSOCIATION; *pg.* 149, *pg.* 842
LIFE SAVERS - Candy - WM. WRIGLEY JR. COMPANY; *pg.* 1863, *pg.* 596
LIFE SPEED - Battery - ENERSYS INC.; *pg.* 1334, *pg.* 1584
LIFE STORY - Textiles - BERNHARDT DESIGN; *pg.* 918, *pg.* 1381
LIFE STRIDE - Shoes - CALERES, INC.; *pg.* 1805, *pg.* 993
LIFE SUPPORT PRODUCTS ADVANTAGE - Portable Suction Unit - ALLIED HEALTHCARE PRODUCTS, INC.; *pg.* 1491, *pg.* 990
LIFE TASTES BETTER WITH KFC - Slogan - KFC CORPORATION; *pg.* 1733, *pg.* 735
LIFE WATCH - Product Series - FARADAY; *pg.* 638, *pg.* 1066
LIFE WELL SPENT - Tagline - SEARS HOLDINGS CORPORATION; *pg.* 1784, *pg.* 618
LIFE123 - Online Services - IAC/INTERACTIVECORP; *pg.* 292, *pg.* 1242
LIFECARE - Medical Device - HOSPIRA, INC.; *pg.* 1542, *pg.* 623
LIFECARE PCA - Infusion System - HOSPIRA, INC.; *pg.* 1542, *pg.* 623
LIFECYCLE - Building Material - ADVANCED ENVIRONMENTAL RECYCLING TECHNOLOGIES, INC.; *pg.* 1310, *pg.* 35
LIFECYCLE - Software - PERKINELMER, INC.; *pg.* 1426, *pg.* 853
LIFEDESIGN - Floorplan - DAVID WEEKLEY HOMES, LP; *pg.* 78, *pg.* 1704
LIFEEST - Calculation Methodology - WESTERN DIGITAL CORPORATION; *pg.* 492, *pg.* 118
LIFEFLO - Nutritional Product - NUTRACEUTICAL INTERNATIONAL CORPORATION; *pg.* 1576, *pg.* 1753
LIFEGARD - Monitoring System - ANALOGIC CORPORATION; *pg.* 1399, *pg.* 840
LIFEGUARD - Battery - ENERSYS INC.; *pg.* 1334, *pg.* 1584
LIFEGUARD - Flame-Retardant Cable - HOUSTON WIRE & CABLE COMPANY; *pg.* 643, *pg.* 1708
LIFEGUARD - Medical Apparatus - MAQUET; *pg.* 1558, *pg.* 1082
LIFEHACKER - Digital Productivity News - GAWKER MEDIA LLC; *pg.* 1248, *pg.* 1234
LIFEJET F-16 - Electrosurgical Devices - ANGIODYNAMICS, INC.; *pg.* 1495, *pg.* 1173
LIFELINE - Electric Hair Clipper - ANDIS COMPANY; *pg.* 498, *pg.* 1895
LIFELINE - Computer Services - KEYNOTE SYSTEMS INCORPORATED; *pg.* 425, *pg.* 255
LIFELINE - Blood Bank Software - MEDIWARE INFORMATION SYSTEMS, INC.; *pg.* 431, *pg.* 716
LIFELINER - Shelf Liner - WARP BROTHERS; *pg.* 1471, *pg.* 595
LIFELINER SYSTEM - Corrosion Resistant System - ZCL COMPOSITES INC.; *pg.* 1892, *pg.* 1906
LIFELINES - Wallcovering - OMNOVA SOLUTIONS INC; *pg.* 1176, *pg.* 1453
LIFEMAP - Planning Service - THRIVENT FINANCIAL FOR LUTHERANS; *pg.* 1219, *pg.* 944
LIFEMAP CUSTOM - Nutritional Supplements - GENELINK, INC.; *pg.* 1533, *pg.* 438
LIFEMAP ESSENTIALS - Nutritional Supplements - GENELINK, INC.; *pg.* 1533, *pg.* 438
LIFEMAP NUTRITION - Nutritional Supplements - GENELINK, INC.; *pg.* 1533, *pg.* 438
LIFEMAP SKIN CARE - Cosmetic Preparations - GENELINK, INC.; *pg.* 1533, *pg.* 438
LIFEMAP WEALTH SYSTEM - Distributorship Services - GENELINK, INC.; *pg.* 1533, *pg.* 438
LIFEMASTER - Paint - AKZONOBEL DECORATIVE PAINTS U.S.; *pg.* 1439, *pg.* 1474
LIFEMASTER 2000 - No-Voc Paint - AKZONOBEL DECORATIVE PAINTS U.S.; *pg.* 1439, *pg.* 1474
LIFEMASTER-PRO - Paint - AKZONOBEL DECORATIVE PAINTS U.S.; *pg.* 1439, *pg.* 1474
LIFEPAK - Defibrillator & Monitors - MEDTRONIC, INC.; *pg.* 1564, *pg.* 939
LIFEPAK - Nutritional Supplement - NU SKIN ENTERPRISES, INC.; *pg.* 518, *pg.* 1755
LIFEPAK 500 - Automated External Defibrillator - MEDTRONIC, INC.; *pg.* 1564, *pg.* 939
LIFEPLUS - Battery - ENERSYS INC.; *pg.* 1334, *pg.* 1584
LIFEPORT - Electrosurgical Devices - ANGIODYNAMICS, INC.; *pg.* 1495, *pg.* 1173
LIFEREACH - Wireless Communication System - AT&T SOUTHEAST; *pg.* 1868, *pg.* 489
LIFE'S BETTER WHEN IT FITS - Slogan - DESTINATION XL GROUP, INC.; *pg.* 40, *pg.* 810
LIFE'S BRIGHTER - Slogan - REVOLUTION LIGHTING TECHNOLOGIES, INC.; *pg.* 1304, *pg.* 377
LIFE'S CHOICE - Delight Bites Snacks - CONAGRA FOODS, INC.; *pg.* 826, *pg.* 1014
LIFE'S TRIBUTE - Flower Arrangement - 1-800-FLOWERS.COM, INC.; *pg.* 1758, *pg.* 1151
LIFESCAPE - Eyewear - SIGNATURE EYEWEAR, INC.; *pg.* 1429, *pg.* 105
LIFESCAPES - Plastic Product - THE STEP2 COMPANY LLC; *pg.* 1889, *pg.* 1474
LIFESEP - Magnetic Product - DEXTER MAGNETIC TECHNOLOGIES, INC.; *pg.* 634, *pg.* 610
LIFESEQ - Human Gene Sequence Database - INCYTE CORPORATION; *pg.* 1545, *pg.* 392
LIFESHIELD - Medical Device - HOSPIRA, INC.; *pg.* 1542, *pg.* 623
LIFESMART - Care Protocol - GENTIVA HEALTH SERVICES, INC.; *pg.* 1534, *pg.* 506
LIFESPAN - Carpet Backing - THE DOW CHEMICAL COMPANY; *pg.* 1157, *pg.* 898
LIFESTREAM - Natural Waffles - NATURE'S PATH FOODS INC.; *pg.* 833, *pg.* 1908
LIFESTYLE - Line of PC Cases - ANTEC INCORPORATED; *pg.* 350, *pg.* 90
LIFESTYLE - Audio Product - BOSE CORPORATION; *pg.* 626, *pg.* 820
LIFESTYLE - Door - LARSON MANUFACTURING COMPANY; *pg.* 93, *pg.* 1624
LIFESTYLE - Children's Product - THE STEP2 COMPANY LLC; *pg.* 1889, *pg.* 1474
LIFESTYLE FORMULAS - Nutritional Product - NUTRACEUTICAL INTERNATIONAL CORPORATION; *pg.* 1576, *pg.* 1753
LIFESTYLE MARKET ANALYST - Media Directory - SRDS, INC.; *pg.* 1688, *pg.* 657

First page reference indicates Business Class Edition
Second page reference indicates Geographic Edition

LIFESTYLE MATH - Textbook - ACADEMIC INNOVATIONS; *pg.* 1613, *pg.* 262

LIFESTYLEBLUE - Health And Wellness Product - ANTHEM BLUE CROSS BLUE SHIELD; *pg.* 1192, *pg.* 1886

LIFESTYLEMATH.COM - Web-Based Curriculum - ACADEMIC INNOVATIONS; *pg.* 1613, *pg.* 262

LIFETECH - Admixture - FMC CORPORATION; *pg.* 1163, *pg.* 1564

LIFETIME - Admixture - FMC CORPORATION; *pg.* 1163, *pg.* 1564

LIFETIME - Entertainment Channel - LIFETIME ENTERTAINMENT SERVICES LLC; *pg.* 296, *pg.* 1251

LIFETIME - Wiring Devices - PASS & SEYMOUR/LEGRAND; *pg.* 1303, *pg.* 1344

LIFETIME ACCENT - Table - LIFETIME PRODUCTS INC.; *pg.* 933, *pg.* 1751

LIFETIME ADVANTAGE - Picnic Tables - LIFETIME PRODUCTS INC.; *pg.* 933, *pg.* 1751

LIFETIME COMPETITION POWERLIFT - Basketball Equipment - LIFETIME PRODUCTS INC.; *pg.* 933, *pg.* 1751

LIFETIME KEY MANAGEMENT - Software - NETAPP, INC.; *pg.* 444, *pg.* 287

LIFETIME PLUS - Electrical Extension Cords, Spark Plug Wire Sets - GENERAL CABLE CORPORATION; *pg.* 83, *pg.* 729

LIFETIME RICHES - Lottery Card - MISSOURI LOTTERY; *pg.* 999, *pg.* 979

LIFETIME RICHES - Lottery Game - OHIO LOTTERY COMMISSION; *pg.* 1002, *pg.* 1433

LIFETOUCH - Pumps - IDEX CORPORATION; *pg.* 1347, *pg.* 623

LIFETRAK - Blood Bank System - MEDIWARE INFORMATION SYSTEMS, INC.; *pg.* 431, *pg.* 716

LIFETRAX - Pharmaceutical Product - ALERE INC.; *pg.* 1488, *pg.* 849

LIFEVALVE - Electrosurgical Devices - ANGIODYNAMICS, INC.; *pg.* 1495, *pg.* 1173

LIFEVEST - Wearable Defibrillator - ZOLL MEDICAL CORPORATION; *pg.* 1612, *pg.* 814

LIFEWORK - Furniture - HERMAN MILLER, INC.; *pg.* 926, *pg.* 913

LIFEX - Bag & Pouch Material - AUTOMATED PACKAGING SYSTEMS INC.; *pg.* 1452, *pg.* 1474

LIFE.YOURS - Jewelry Collection - DANECRAFT INC.; *pg.* 4, *pg.* 1606

LIFFAROME - Fragrance Ingredient - INTERNATIONAL FLAVORS & FRAGRANCES INC.; *pg.* 512, *pg.* 1244

LIFMIOR - Pharmaceutical Preparation - PFIZER INC.; *pg.* 1581, *pg.* 1278

LIFOAM - Polystyrene Foam - LIFOAM INDUSTRIES INC.; *pg.* 961, *pg.* 772

LIFT - Soft Drink - THE COCA-COLA COMPANY; *pg.* 240, *pg.* 493

LIFT-AND-RELEASE - Wall System - SMITH-MIDLAND CORPORATION; *pg.* 111, *pg.* 1795

LIFT AND TURN - Compression Latch - SOUTHCO, INC.; *pg.* 1063, *pg.* 1522

THE LIFT BUYER'S BIBLE - Automotive Manual - ROTARY LIFT; *pg.* 216, *pg.* 694

LIFT LIGHT - Beverages - THE COCA-COLA COMPANY; *pg.* 240, *pg.* 493

LIFT MATES - Carton Grip - THE PROTECTOSEAL COMPANY; *pg.* 1370, *pg.* 556

LIFT-OFF - Floor Care Product - BISSELL HOMECARE, INC.; *pg.* 52, *pg.* 887

LIFT-PAK - Passenger Bridge Power Cable Storage & Retrieval Device - DAIFUKU WEBB; *pg.* 1327, *pg.* 885

LIFT PLUS - Beverages - THE COCA-COLA COMPANY; *pg.* 240, *pg.* 493

LIFT PLUS LIGHT - Beverages - THE COCA-COLA COMPANY; *pg.* 240, *pg.* 493

LIFT SAFE - Winch - BLOOM MANUFACTURING, INC.; *pg.* 701, *pg.* 708

LIFTER - Hand Cleaner - LA-CO INDUSTRIES MARKAL CO., INC.; *pg.* 1170, *pg.* 610

LIFTMASTER - Residential & Commercial Garage Door & Gate Openers - THE CHAMBERLAIN GROUP, INC.; *pg.* 75, *pg.* 611

LIFT'N TOSS - Wastebaskets - RUBBERMAID HOME PRODUCTS; *pg.* 1138, *pg.* 1453

LIGER LOOT - Video Game - INTERNATIONAL GAME TECHNOLOGY; *pg.* 957, *pg.* 1024

LIGHT 35 - Bakery Product - ALFRED NICKLES BAKERY, INC.; *pg.* 836, *pg.* 1466

LIGHT AND DRY - Safety Product - WISCONSIN PHARMACAL COMPANY, LLC; *pg.* 1610, *pg.* 1861

LIGHT & MEDIUM TRUCK - Business Magazine - TRANSPORT TOPICS PUBLISHING GROUP; *pg.* 1696, *pg.* 1772

LIGHT & REFRESHING - Juice - SUN-RYPE PRODUCTS LTD.; *pg.* 899, *pg.* 1908

LIGHT CRAN POMEGRANATE - Juice Drink - OCEAN SPRAY CRANBERRIES, INC.; *pg.* 887, *pg.* 827

LIGHT CRANGRAPE - Juice Drink - OCEAN SPRAY CRANBERRIES, INC.; *pg.* 887, *pg.* 827

LIGHT CRAWLER - Flashlight - ENERGIZER HOLDINGS, INC.; *pg.* 637, *pg.* 996

LIGHT MAGNUM - Enhanced Velocity Ammunition - HORNADY MANUFACTURING COMPANY; *pg.* 1836, *pg.* 1010

LIGHT MOVER - Fiber Optics - LOCKHEED MARTIN CORPORATION; *pg.* 229, *pg.* 762

LIGHT 'N DELIGHTFUL - Entrees - EAT'N PARK HOSPITALITY GROUP; *pg.* 1728, *pg.* 1539

LIGHT 'N EASY - Aluminum Beach Chairs - TELESCOPE CASUAL FURNITURE INC.; *pg.* 944, *pg.* 1162

LIGHT 'N FIT - Lowfat Yogurt - THE DANNON COMPANY, INC.; *pg.* 851, *pg.* 1351

LIGHT 'N FLUFFY - Noodles - NEW WORLD PASTA COMPANY; *pg.* 885, *pg.* 1537

LIGHT OAK - Furniture - BUSH INDUSTRIES INC.; *pg.* 919, *pg.* 1170

LIGHT-PULSE - Filter Cartridge - W.L. GORE & ASSOCIATES, INC.; *pg.* 122, *pg.* 388

LIGHT RUBY - Juice - OCEAN SPRAY CRANBERRIES, INC.; *pg.* 887, *pg.* 827

LIGHT SHAPING DIFFUSERS - Filter & Attenuator - NEWPORT CORPORATION; *pg.* 1424, *pg.* 114

LIGHT STICKS - Fiber Optic Fixtures - REVOLUTION LIGHTING TECHNOLOGIES, INC.; *pg.* 1304, *pg.* 377

LIGHT TONIGHT - Microwaveable Fish Fillets - HIGH LINER FOODS INCORPORATED; *pg.* 862, *pg.* 1917

LIGHT-TOUCH - Internal Blinds - ODL INCORPORATED; *pg.* 101, *pg.* 914

LIGHT WAND - Illuminating Stylet - VITAL SIGNS, INC.; *pg.* 1607, *pg.* 1126

LIGHT WAVE SUNGLASSES - Sun Lens - COSTA DEL MAR SUNGLASSES, INC.; *pg.* 1407, *pg.* 419

LIGHT WITHOUT LIMITS - Slogan - PHILIPS SOLID-STATE LIGHTING SOLUTIONS; *pg.* 1303, *pg.* 806

LIGHTBAND - Electronic Components - MOLEX INCORPORATED; *pg.* 655, *pg.* 628

LIGHTBLOCKER - Vinyl Blinds - SPRINGS WINDOW FASHIONS LLC; *pg.* 943, *pg.* 1872

LIGHTBOX - Computer Application - FACEBOOK, INC.; *pg.* 1245, *pg.* 143

LIGHTBRIDGE - Telescope - MEADE INSTRUMENTS CORPORATION; *pg.* 1422, *pg.* 113

LIGHTDEALER - Electronic Components - MOLEX INCORPORATED; *pg.* 655, *pg.* 628

LIGHTEN UP - Beauty Product - AVON PRODUCTS, INC.; *pg.* 500, *pg.* 1198

LIGHTEN UP! - Low Fat Salad Dressings - NEWMAN'S OWN, INC.; *pg.* 886, *pg.* 384

LIGHTER - Resin - THE DOW CHEMICAL COMPANY; *pg.* 1157, *pg.* 898

LIGHTER AQUAFONTIS - Polyethylene Resins - THE DOW CHEMICAL COMPANY; *pg.* 1157, *pg.* 898

LIGHTER BAKE - Food Product - SUNSWEET GROWERS, INC.; *pg.* 900, *pg.* 309

LIGHTER BY CHOICE - Culinary Service - LACKMANN CULINARY SERVICES; *pg.* 1026, *pg.* 1356

THE LIGHTER SIDE - Mail Order Catalog - JOHNSON SMITH COMPANY; *pg.* 1774, *pg.* 414

LIGHTFAST - Thermal Laminating Film - TRANSILWRAP COMPANY, INC.; *pg.* 1470, *pg.* 613

LIGHTGATE - Digital & Data Service - AT&T SOUTHEAST; *pg.* 1868, *pg.* 489

LIGHTGUARD - Emergency Lighting - PHILIPS LIGHTING; *pg.* 1303, *pg.* 806

LIGHTHOUSE - Bookmark - HERITAGE LACE INC.; *pg.* 694, *pg.* 711

LIGHTHOUSE - Pool Filter Sand - U.S. SILICA COMPANY; *pg.* 1185, *pg.* 1849

LIGHTHOUSE LOOT - Game - WMS INDUSTRIES INC.; *pg.* 593, *pg.* 666

LIGHTHOUSE SELECTIONS - Select Seafood - RED LOBSTER; *pg.* 1747, *pg.* 455

LIGHTING FIXTURES - Commercial Lighting - SWIVELIER CO., INC.; *pg.* 1307, *pg.* 1142

LIGHTING FROM HOLLYWOOD - Slogan - MOLE-RICHARDSON CO.; *pg.* 1302, *pg.* 103

LIGHTLIFE - Food Product - CONAGRA FOODS, INC.; *pg.* 826, *pg.* 1014

LIGHTLINES - Aluminium Horizontal Blinds with Maximum Light Control - HUNTER DOUGLAS, INC.; *pg.* 928, *pg.* 1320

LIGHTLINK - Optical Waveguide - DOW CHEMICAL; *pg.* 1156, *pg.* 1563

LIGHTLY EXPRESSED - Fiber Optic Lighting System - ENERGY FOCUS, INC.; *pg.* 1411, *pg.* 1472

LIGHTNIN - Mixers & Aerators - SPX PROCESS EQUIPMENT; *pg.* 1378, *pg.* 1337

LIGHTNING - Dock Connector Trademark - APPLE INC.; *pg.* 350, *pg.* 73

LIGHTNING - Motorcycles - HARLEY-DAVIDSON, INC.; *pg.* 178, *pg.* 1874

LIGHTNING - Software - SS&C TECHNOLOGIES HOLDINGS, INC.; *pg.* 473, *pg.* 386

LIGHTNING - Electric Instrument - UNIVERSAL INSTRUMENTS CORPORATION; *pg.* 683, *pg.* 1154

LIGHTNING AUDIO - Car Audio System - ROCKFORD CORPORATION; *pg.* 667, *pg.* 26

LIGHTNING BUG - Video Game - INTERNATIONAL GAME TECHNOLOGY; *pg.* 957, *pg.* 1024

LIGHTNING HTA - Cutlery - BUCK KNIVES, INC.; *pg.* 1828, *pg.* 550

LIGHTNING POWDER - Finger Print Powder - BAE SYSTEMS PRODUCTS GROUP; *pg.* 359, *pg.* 432

LIGHTNING RICHES - Video Game - INTERNATIONAL GAME TECHNOLOGY; *pg.* 957, *pg.* 1024

LIGHTNING SPAR - Varnish - PETTIT PAINT COMPANY; *pg.* 1444, *pg.* 1116

LIGHTNING STRIKE - Game - WMS INDUSTRIES INC.; *pg.* 593, *pg.* 666

LIGHTNING TRADEDESK - Software - SS&C TECHNOLOGIES HOLDINGS, INC.; *pg.* 473, *pg.* 386

LIGHTNOTE BLEND - Coffee - STARBUCKS CORPORATION; *pg.* 897, *pg.* 1840

LIGHTOLIER - Lighting Fixture & Control - PHILIPS LIGHTING; *pg.* 1303, *pg.* 806

LIGHTOLIER CONTROLS - Lighting Controls - PHILIPS LIGHTING; *pg.* 1303, *pg.* 806

LIGHTORB - Lighting System - PHILIPS SOLID-STATE LIGHTING SOLUTIONS; *pg.* 1303, *pg.* 806

LIGHTPLAST - Medical & Aesthetic Product - DYNATRONICS CORPORATION; *pg.* 1526, *pg.* 1757

LIGHTPULSE - Host Bus Adapter - EMULEX CORPORATION; *pg.* 392, *pg.* 70

LIGHTS MANAGER - Software - VULCAN, INC.; *pg.* 687, *pg.* 5

LIGHTS OUT - Game - HASBRO, INC.; *pg.* 954, *pg.* 1603

LIGHTSAFE - Specialty Paper - APPVION INC.; *pg.* 1451, *pg.* 1852

LIGHTSAUCER - Lighting System - PHILIPS SOLID-STATE LIGHTING SOLUTIONS; *pg.* 1303, *pg.* 806

LIGHTSCAPER - Lighting Fixture - HUBBELL INCORPORATED; *pg.* 1299, *pg.* 370

LIGHTSHAPES - Lights - CYALUME TECHNOLOGIES HOLDINGS, INC.; *pg.* 1295, *pg.* 856

LIGHTSHEILD - Technology - WILD FLAVORS, INC.; *pg.* 910, *pg.* 728

LIGHTSOURCE.COM - Online Christian Ministries - SALEM MEDIA GROUP, INC.; *pg.* 307, *pg.* 57

LIGHTSPEED - Animal Clipper - ANDIS COMPANY; *pg.* 498, *pg.* 1895

LIGHTSPEED RT - Medical Device - GE HEALTHCARE TECHNOLOGIES; *pg.* 1533, *pg.* 1897

LIGHTSPRITE - Lighting System - PHILIPS SOLID-STATE LIGHTING SOLUTIONS; *pg.* 1303, *pg.* 806

LIGHTSTATION - Lights - CYALUME TECHNOLOGIES HOLDINGS, INC.; *pg.* 1295, *pg.* 856

LIGHTSTREAM - Switches - CISCO SYSTEMS, INC.; *pg.* 372, *pg.* 240

LIGHTTRO - Lighting System - PHILIPS SOLID-STATE LIGHTING SOLUTIONS; *pg.* 1303, *pg.* 806

LIGHTWAND - Lighting System - PHILIPS SOLID-STATE LIGHTING SOLUTIONS; *pg.* 1303, *pg.* 806

LIGHTWASH - Component Kit - COMMERCIAL VEHICLE GROUP, INC.; *pg.* 203, *pg.* 1467

LIGHTWASHER - Lighting System - PHILIPS SOLID-STATE LIGHTING SOLUTIONS; *pg.* 1303, *pg.* 806

LIGHTWATT - Lighting Product - HUBBELL INCORPORATED; *pg.* 1299, *pg.* 370

LIGHTWAVE - Electronic Device - LANTRONIX, INC.; *pg.* 426, *pg.* 112
LIGHTWEIGHT CARDINAL - Cutting System - EASTMAN MACHINE COMPANY; *pg.* 1331, *pg.* 1148
LIGHTWEIGHT TRAVELER - Whisky, Vodka, Gin, Rum & Schnapps - JIM BEAM BRANDS CO.; *pg.* 1965, *pg.* 601
LIGHTWORKS - Optical Networking System - CIENA CORPORATION; *pg.* 628, *pg.* 771
LIGHTWORKS EOS - Optical Networking System - CIENA CORPORATION; *pg.* 628, *pg.* 771
LIGHTWORKS IOS - Software - CIENA CORPORATION; *pg.* 628, *pg.* 771
LIGHTWORKS ON-CENTER - Software - CIENA CORPORATION; *pg.* 628, *pg.* 771
LIGHTWORKS OS - Optical Signaling & Routing Protocol - CIENA CORPORATION; *pg.* 628, *pg.* 771
LIGHTWORKS TOOLKIT - Software - CIENA CORPORATION; *pg.* 628, *pg.* 771
LIGHTWORX - Bowling Equipment - BRUNSWICK BOWLING & BILLIARDS CORP.; *pg.* 1828, *pg.* 622
LIGHTWORX - Automatic Conveyor System - PARAGON TECHNOLOGIES, INC.; *pg.* 1367, *pg.* 1528
LIGHTWRITER - Yag Marking Systems - GSI GROUP INC.; *pg.* 1415, *pg.* 784
LIGNOSOL - Chemical Product - WESTROCK COMPANY; *pg.* 1472, *pg.* 1805
LIHIT - Paper Punch - YASUTOMO & CO.; *pg.* 497, *pg.* 280
LIK-M-AID - Food & Beverage Product - NESTLE USA, INC.; *pg.* 883, *pg.* 96
LIL ANGELZ - Angel Dolls & Pets - MGA ENTERTAINMENT, INC.; *pg.* 964, *pg.* 300
LIL' BOWL BLU - Eucalyptus Mint - METHOD PRODUCTS INC.; *pg.* 332, *pg.* 223
LIL' BUCKAROO - Footwear - PHOENIX FOOTWEAR GROUP, INC.; *pg.* 1815, *pg.* 60
LIL' CHAMP - Convenience Stores - THE PANTRY, INC.; *pg.* 1029, *pg.* 1360
L'IL FISHER - Power Fishing System - GREENLEE TEXTRON INC.; *pg.* 1048, *pg.* 655
LIL' HELPERS - Children's Organization Products - HOME PRODUCTS INTERNATIONAL, INC.; *pg.* 1125, *pg.* 577
LIL' LADY - Video Game - INTERNATIONAL GAME TECHNOLOGY; *pg.* 957, *pg.* 1024
LI'L MISS DRESS UP - Doll - MATTEL, INC.; *pg.* 962, *pg.* 81
LI'L MISS MAKEUP - Doll - MATTEL, INC.; *pg.* 962, *pg.* 81
LIL' PAW - Leather Dog Collar - PETSMART, INC.; *pg.* 1481, *pg.* 18
LI'L ROUGHNECK - Children's Product Line - RUBBERMAID HOME PRODUCTS; *pg.* 1138, *pg.* 1453
L'IL SAFARI FRIENDS - Children's Toothbrushes - SUNSTAR AMERICAS INC.; *pg.* 1599, *pg.* 591
LIL SHAVER - Sno-Kone Machine - GOLD MEDAL PRODUCTS CO.; *pg.* 55, *pg.* 1414
LILA - Laser Imager for Lab Animals - IMAGING DIAGNOSTIC SYSTEMS, INC.; *pg.* 1544, *pg.* 425
LILA - Women's Clothing & Accessories - WOODEN SHIPS OF HOBOKEN; *pg.* 35, *pg.* 1315
LILABETH'S RIBBON - Fabric - SCALAMANDRE, INC.; *pg.* 941, *pg.* 1058
LILHCO - Lottery System - INTERNATIONAL GAME TECHNOLOGY; *pg.* 420, *pg.* 1606
LILJEHOLMENS - Home Fragrance Product - BLYTH, INC.; *pg.* 502, *pg.* 349
LILLIAN - Clothing - ABERCROMBIE & FITCH CO.; *pg.* 37, *pg.* 1466
LILLIAN - Fabric - NEMSCHOFF, INC.; *pg.* 936, *pg.* 1890
LILLIAN VERNON - Mail Order Catalog - LILLIAN VERNON CORPORATION; *pg.* 1776, *pg.* 315
LILLY - Furniture - AMISCO INDUSTRIES LTD.; *pg.* 913, *pg.* 1958
LILLY 2040 - Coating Products - RUSSEL METALS INC.; *pg.* 1180, *pg.* 1928
LILLY MILLER - Garden Seeds - FERRY-MORSE SEED COMPANY; *pg.* 1795, *pg.* 728
LILLY PULITZER - Apparel - SUGARTOWN WORLDWIDE INC.; *pg.* 33, *pg.* 1544
LILLY'S KIDS - Mail Order Catalog - LILLIAN VERNON CORPORATION; *pg.* 1776, *pg.* 315
LILT - Beverages - THE COCA-COLA COMPANY; *pg.* 240, *pg.* 493
LILT ZERO - Beverages - THE COCA-COLA COMPANY; *pg.* 240, *pg.* 493
LILY - Pillow - ETHAN ALLEN INTERIORS INC.; *pg.* 924, *pg.* 343
LILY - Seafood - TRIDENT SEAFOODS CORPORATION; *pg.* 902, *pg.* 1842
LILY FIELDS - Ceiling Fan - WESTINGHOUSE LIGHTING CORPORATION; *pg.* 687, *pg.* 1571
LILY OF FRANCE - Intimate Apparel - V.F. CORPORATION; *pg.* 34, *pg.* 1376
LILY OF THE VALLEY - Video Game - INTERNATIONAL GAME TECHNOLOGY; *pg.* 957, *pg.* 1024
LILYETTE - Intimate Apparel - HANESBRANDS INC.; *pg.* 26, *pg.* 1394
LILYPONS KOI CUISINE - Fish Food - LILYPONS WATER GARDENS INC.; *pg.* 1797, *pg.* 766
LILYTABS - Aquatic Plant Fertilizer - LILYPONS WATER GARDENS INC.; *pg.* 1797, *pg.* 766
LIMA - Food Product - THE HAIN CELESTIAL GROUP, INC.; *pg.* 860, *pg.* 1172
THE LIMA NEWS - Ohio Newspaper - FREEDOM COMMUNICATIONS, INC.; *pg.* 1643, *pg.* 110
LIMB-LOPPER - Hydraulic Pruners, Chain Saws - GREENLEE TEXTRON INC.; *pg.* 1048, *pg.* 655
LIMB-O - Ventilator Circuit - VITAL SIGNS, INC.; *pg.* 1607, *pg.* 1126
LIMBO - Fabric - NEMSCHOFF, INC.; *pg.* 936, *pg.* 1890
LIMBOARD - Arm Boards - CAS MEDICAL SYSTEMS, INC.; *pg.* 1513, *pg.* 339
LIMCA - Soft Drink - THE COCA-COLA COMPANY; *pg.* 240, *pg.* 493
LIME - Bicycle - TREK BICYCLE CORPORATION; *pg.* 1847, *pg.* 1896
LIME-A-WAY - Calcium & Rust Remover - RECKITT BENCKISER INC.; *pg.* 1136, *pg.* 1105
LIMELIGHT - Laser Product - CUTERA, INC.; *pg.* 1521, *pg.* 49
LIMELIGHTDELIVER - Internet Services - LIMELIGHT NETWORKS, INC.; *pg.* 1262, *pg.* 26
LIMELIGHTHD - Internet Services - LIMELIGHT NETWORKS, INC.; *pg.* 1262, *pg.* 26
LIMELIGHTPS - Internet Services - LIMELIGHT NETWORKS, INC.; *pg.* 1262, *pg.* 26
LIMELIGHTSITE - Internet Services - LIMELIGHT NETWORKS, INC.; *pg.* 1262, *pg.* 26
LIMELIGHTSTREAM - Internet Services - LIMELIGHT NETWORKS, INC.; *pg.* 1262, *pg.* 26
LIMELIGHTSUPPORT - Internet Services - LIMELIGHT NETWORKS, INC.; *pg.* 1262, *pg.* 26
LIMELITE - Beverages - THE COCA-COLA COMPANY; *pg.* 240, *pg.* 493
LIMELITE - Non-slip Boning Knives - DEXTER-RUSSELL INC.; *pg.* 1123, *pg.* 844
LIMEMOUND - Container Grown Plant - MONROVIA GROWERS; *pg.* 1797, *pg.* 44
LIMERICK - Chairs - HERMAN MILLER, INC.; *pg.* 926, *pg.* 913
LIMESTONE - Ceramic, Glass, Stone Tiles & Slabs - WALKER & ZANGER, INC.; *pg.* 119, *pg.* 281
LIMESTONE MOLDINGS - Ceramic, Glass, Stone Tiles & Slabs - WALKER & ZANGER, INC.; *pg.* 119, *pg.* 281
LIMIELIGHTEXCHANGE - Internet Services - LIMELIGHT NETWORKS, INC.; *pg.* 1262, *pg.* 26
LIMIT - Liquid Desiccant - FMC CORPORATION; *pg.* 1163, *pg.* 1564
LIMITED - Guitar - PEAVEY ELECTRONICS CORPORATION; *pg.* 662, *pg.* 970
LIMITORQUE - Valve - FLOWSERVE CORPORATION; *pg.* 82, *pg.* 1719
LIMON Y SAL - Apparel - KMART CORPORATION; *pg.* 1775, *pg.* 617
LIMONADE - Beverages - THE COCA-COLA COMPANY; *pg.* 240, *pg.* 493
LIMOUSINE - Fragrance - PARLUX FRAGRANCES, INC.; *pg.* 519, *pg.* 426
LIMOUSINE AND CHAUFFEURED TRANSPORTATION - Magazine - BOBIT BUSINESS MEDIA; *pg.* 1622, *pg.* 293
LIMPIDO - Bleach - THE CLOROX COMPANY; *pg.* 327, *pg.* 169
LIMU LEMON - Beverage - BAI BRANDS; *pg.* 238, *pg.* 1073
LINAGRAPH - Photo Papers, Film & Chemicals - EASTMAN KODAK COMPANY; *pg.* 1408, *pg.* 1333
LINAIRE GEL - Fragrant Gel - STEAMATIC INC.; *pg.* 60, *pg.* 1696
LINATRON-M - Linear Accelerator - VARIAN MEDICAL SYSTEMS, INC.; *pg.* 1434, *pg.* 178
LINBICMOS - Integrated Circuits - TEXAS INSTRUMENTS INCORPORATED; *pg.* 679, *pg.* 1688
LINC PUMPS - Fluid Control Product - MILTON ROY COMPANY; *pg.* 1361, *pg.* 1542
LINCMOS - Integrated Circuits & Operational Amplifiers - TEXAS INSTRUMENTS INCORPORATED; *pg.* 679, *pg.* 1688
LINCO-SPECTIN - Pharmaceutical Product - PFIZER INC.; *pg.* 1581, *pg.* 1278
LINCOCIN - Medicine - PFIZER INC.; *pg.* 1581, *pg.* 1278
LINCOCITY - Systems Integration & Aeronautics - LOCKHEED MARTIN CORPORATION; *pg.* 229, *pg.* 762
LINCOLN - Furniture - AMERICAN LEATHER LP; *pg.* 912, *pg.* 1673
LINCOLN - Furniture - JASPER GROUP; *pg.* 930, *pg.* 691
LINCOLN - Fruit Juice - KNOUSE FOODS COOPERATIVE INC.; *pg.* 869, *pg.* 1558
LINCOLN - Lubrication Equipment - LINCOLN INDUSTRIAL CORP.; *pg.* 1355, *pg.* 999
LINCOLN - Office Furniture - STEELCASE INC.; *pg.* 475, *pg.* 889
LINCOLN BENEFIT LIFE - Annuities & Savings - THE ALLSTATE CORPORATION; *pg.* 1189, *pg.* 639
LINCOLN CENTER - Performing Arts Center - LINCOLN CENTER FOR THE PERFORMING ARTS, INC.; *pg.* 557, *pg.* 1251
LINCOLN FINANCIAL GROUP - Financial Services - LINCOLN NATIONAL CORPORATION; *pg.* 776, *pg.* 1567
LINCOLN LIFE - Various Insurance & Financial Planning Services - LINCOLN NATIONAL CORPORATION; *pg.* 776, *pg.* 1567
LINCOLN LIFE DIRECTOR - Pension Product - LINCOLN NATIONAL CORPORATION; *pg.* 776, *pg.* 1567
LINCOLN NATIONAL - Various Insurance & Financial Planning Services - LINCOLN NATIONAL CORPORATION; *pg.* 776, *pg.* 1567
LINCOLN PARK - Furniture - STANLEY FURNITURE CO., INC.; *pg.* 943, *pg.* 1379
LINCOLN PARK AFTER DARK - Nail Care Product - OPI PRODUCTS INC.; *pg.* 518, *pg.* 167
LINCOLN ROAD - Furniture - ASHLEY FURNITURE INDUSTRIES, INC.; *pg.* 914, *pg.* 1852
LINCOLN SILHOUETTE DESIGN - Various Insurance & Financial Planning Services - LINCOLN NATIONAL CORPORATION; *pg.* 776, *pg.* 1567
LINCOLNWELD - Electrode - LINCOLN ELECTRIC HOLDINGS, INC.; *pg.* 1355, *pg.* 1432
LINCOMIX - Pharmaceutical Product - PFIZER INC.; *pg.* 1581, *pg.* 1278
LINCORE - Electrode - LINCOLN ELECTRIC HOLDINGS, INC.; *pg.* 1355, *pg.* 1432
LINCXPRESS SYSTEM - Telephony System - BLONDER TONGUE LABORATORIES, INC.; *pg.* 625, *pg.* 1100
LINDA MCCARTNEY - Food Product - THE HAIN CELESTIAL GROUP, INC.; *pg.* 860, *pg.* 1172
LINDAL - Doors - LINDAL CEDAR HOMES, INC.; *pg.* 94, *pg.* 1837
LINDE LSC VALVE - Four-way, Pilot-operated, Pressure Compensated & 420 Bar-rated Valve - LINDE HYDRAULICS CORPORATION; *pg.* 1356, *pg.* 1407
LINDEN FALLS - Furniture - ASHLEY FURNITURE INDUSTRIES, INC.; *pg.* 914, *pg.* 1852
LINDEN PONDS - Retirement Community - ERICKSON LIVING; *pg.* 1090, *pg.* 766
LINDENOL - Fragrance Ingredient - INTERNATIONAL FLAVORS & FRAGRANCES INC.; *pg.* 512, *pg.* 1244
LINDSEY - Dolls - AMERICAN GIRL LLC; *pg.* 949, *pg.* 1871
LINDSEY - Footwear - COBIAN CORP.; *pg.* 1806, *pg.* 253
LINDSEY BERGMAN - Doll And Toy - AMERICAN GIRL LLC; *pg.* 949, *pg.* 1871
LINDSEY PLAID - Pillow and Throw - HERITAGE LACE INC.; *pg.* 694, *pg.* 711
LINDSTROM - Hand Tools - SNAP-ON INCORPORATED; *pg.* 1062, *pg.* 1862
LINDT - Fine Chocolate - LINDT & SPRUNGLI (USA) INC.; *pg.* 1857, *pg.* 1039
LINDURE - Ferritic Nitrocarburizing Process - BODYCOTE THERMAL PROCESSING; *pg.* 71, *pg.* 632
LINE 'EM UP - Lottery Game - D.C. LOTTERY & CHARITABLE GAMES CONTROL BOARD; *pg.* 991, *pg.* 398
LINE 'EM UP - Lottery Game - KENTUCKY LOTTERY CORPORATION; *pg.* 996, *pg.* 735
LINE EM UP - Lotto Game - SOUTH DAKOTA LOTTERY; *pg.* 1006, *pg.* 1624
LINE GUARD - Maintenance Services - SPRINT CORPORATION; *pg.* 1874, *pg.* 719
LINE LEVEL - Software - TRIMBLE NAVIGATION LIMITED; *pg.* 1384, *pg.* 288

First page reference indicates Business Class Edition
Second page reference indicates Geographic Edition

LINE-O-GRAPH - Industrial Newsletter - EASTMAN KODAK COMPANY; *pg.* 1408, *pg.* 1333
LINE-OF-SIGHT ANTITANK - Mobile Guided Missile Systems - LOCKHEED MARTIN CORPORATION; *pg.* 229, *pg.* 762
LINE PHENIX - Bookcase - F.E. HALE MANUFACTURING COMPANY; *pg.* 925, *pg.* 1160
LINE POST - High Voltage Porcelain Insulators - LAPP INSULATOR COMPANY, LLC; *pg.* 1946, *pg.* 1173
LINE PRINTER PLUS - Printer - PRINTRONIX, INC.; *pg.* 456, *pg.* 115
LINE-R - Power Protection Product - SCHNEIDER ELECTRIC; *pg.* 467, *pg.* 1609
LINE-RUPTER - Circuit-Breaking Interrupter - S&C ELECTRIC COMPANY; *pg.* 1305, *pg.* 589
LINE STAR - Turf Maintenance Machinery - SMITHCO, INC.; *pg.* 1377, *pg.* 1592
LINE STAR JR. - Turf Maintenance Machinery - SMITHCO, INC.; *pg.* 1377, *pg.* 1592
LINE UP - Carpet - INTERFACE, INC.; *pg.* 695, *pg.* 512
LINEA - Needle - THE DMC CORPORATION; *pg.* 692, *pg.* 1076
LINEA - Print Cartridge - LEXMARK INTERNATIONAL, INC.; *pg.* 427, *pg.* 730
LINEA - Fabric - NEMSCHOFF, INC.; *pg.* 936, *pg.* 1890
LINEAR - Stair Treads - BURKE INDUSTRIES, INC.; *pg.* 919, *pg.* 239
LINEAR - Orthopedic Product - DJO SURGICAL; *pg.* 1525, *pg.* 1661
LINEAR - Medical Apparatus - MAQUET; *pg.* 1558, *pg.* 1082
LINEAR - Burner - NAO, INC.; *pg.* 1074, *pg.* 1567
LINEAR - Apparel - OAKLEY, INC.; *pg.* 1840, *pg.* 86
LINEAR - Lighting - SWIVELIER CO., INC.; *pg.* 1307, *pg.* 1142
LINEAR HIP SYSTEM - Hip Implant - DJO SURGICAL; *pg.* 1525, *pg.* 1661
LINEARFLOW - Molecular Probe Product - THERMO FISHER SCIENTIFIC INC.; *pg.* 1602, *pg.* 61
LINEARITY WEB - Software - BIO-RAD LABORATORIES, INC.; *pg.* 1504, *pg.* 101
LINEARPAK - Can - SONOCO PRODUCTS COMPANY; *pg.* 1469, *pg.* 1619
LINEBACKER - Water Service Line Repair Program - CONNECTICUT WATER SERVICE, INC.; *pg.* 1938, *pg.* 342
LINEBACKER - Antenna Product - PCTEL, INC.; *pg.* 452, *pg.* 557
LINEDRIVER - Line Striping - GRACO, INC.; *pg.* 1342, *pg.* 935
LINEGUARD - Control Equipment - HENKEL CORPORATION; *pg.* 1166, *pg.* 897
LINEIR - Radiant Heater for Heating Small Geometrics - PRECISION CONTROL SYSTEMS, INC./ RESEARCH INC.; *pg.* 1427, *pg.* 923
LINELAZER - Line Stripers - GRACO, INC.; *pg.* 1342, *pg.* 935
LINEMASTER - Customer Training Program - T.D. WILLIAMSON, INC.; *pg.* 1380, *pg.* 1490
LINEMELT - Line Frequency Channel Furnace Induction Melting Systems - INDUCTOTHERM CORP.; *pg.* 1348, *pg.* 1114
LINEN HOLLY - Table Textile - HERITAGE LACE INC.; *pg.* 694, *pg.* 711
LINEN-SET - Offset Printable Book Cloth - HOLLISTON LLC; *pg.* 1460, *pg.* 1630
LINENEASE - Outerwear - HABAND COMPANY, INC.; *pg.* 1772, *pg.* 1099
LINESIM - Software System - MENTOR GRAPHICS CORPORATION; *pg.* 432, *pg.* 1510
LINESPEC - Spectroscopy Instrument - NEWPORT CORPORATION; *pg.* 1424, *pg.* 114
LINETEC - Architectural Paint & Anodizing Finishers - APOGEE ENTERPRISES, INC.; *pg.* 67, *pg.* 930
LINETTE QUALITY CHOCOLATES - Chocolate Confections - CONAGRA FOODS; *pg.* 826, *pg.* 994
LINEUP - Service Program - ADVANCED ENERGY INDUSTRIES, INC.; *pg.* 613, *pg.* 328
LINEWORKS - Eyeliners - MAYBELLINE LLC; *pg.* 516, *pg.* 1257
LINEX - Herbicide - E.I. DU PONT DE NEMOURS & COMPANY; *pg.* 1159, *pg.* 390
LINGERIE - Furniture - HOOKER FURNITURE CORPORATION; *pg.* 928, *pg.* 1788
LINGUANOTTO - Food Product - MARS, INCORPORATED; *pg.* 1858, *pg.* 1792
LINIA - Bath Product - KOHLER CO.; *pg.* 91, *pg.* 1862
LINK MAPPER - Printed Circuit Boards - AVAGO TECHNOLOGIES; *pg.* 358, *pg.* 238
LINK-N-DOG - Food Product - ADVANCEPIERRE FOODS, INC.; *pg.* 1714, *pg.* 1409
LINKED BINGO GAMES - Game - FORTUNET, INC.; *pg.* 953, *pg.* 1024
LINKING PEOPLE, IDEAS, AND BUSINESS - Tag Line - CROIX CONNECT; *pg.* 1237, *pg.* 1809
LINKITE - Motorsports Entertainment - SPEEDWAY MOTORSPORTS, INC.; *pg.* 584, *pg.* 1370
LINKMATE - Image Acquisition Module - ST. JUDE MEDICAL, INC.; *pg.* 1596, *pg.* 963
LINKNET - Conveying System - MOTAN, INC.; *pg.* 1886, *pg.* 903
LINKOSITY - Electrical Connectors - LOCKHEED MARTIN CORPORATION; *pg.* 229, *pg.* 762
LINKS - Trademark & Golf Cart Tires - CARLISLE TIRE & WHEEL COMPANY; *pg.* 1880, *pg.* 1612
LINKSTAR - Network System - VIASAT, INC.; *pg.* 489, *pg.* 62
LINKSWITCH - Switch - POWER INTEGRATIONS, INC.; *pg.* 1369, *pg.* 249
LINKTENN - Computer Software Interface - SPX THERMAL PRODUCT SOLUTIONS; *pg.* 1378, *pg.* 1555
LINKWARE - Software - NEONODE, INC.; *pg.* 659, *pg.* 268
LINKWAY - Network System - VIASAT, INC.; *pg.* 489, *pg.* 62
LINKXPRESS - Computer Hardware - AVAGO TECHNOLOGIES; *pg.* 358, *pg.* 238
LINNEA - Watches - BAUME & MERCIER, INC.; *pg.* 1, *pg.* 1201
LINN'S STAMP NEWS - Publication - AMOS PRESS, INC.; *pg.* 1616, *pg.* 1472
LINNUSE - Beverages - THE COCA-COLA COMPANY; *pg.* 240, *pg.* 493
LINOFLAME - Burner - MAXON CORPORATION; *pg.* 1359, *pg.* 695
LINPACK - Benchmarks for Measurement - INTEL CORPORATION; *pg.* 645, *pg.* 266
LINQ - Hearing Aid - BELTONE ELECTRONICS LLC; *pg.* 1503, *pg.* 614
LINQ - Fabric - NEMSCHOFF, INC.; *pg.* 936, *pg.* 1890
LINT PIC-UP - Adhesive Tape Lint Remover - THE EVERCARE COMPANY; *pg.* 1124, *pg.* 483
LINTEK - Radar Cross Section Measurement - AEROFLEX INCORPORATED; *pg.* 614, *pg.* 1321
LINTPLUS - Polymer Product - CHEMTURA CORPORATION; *pg.* 1152, *pg.* 355
LINTRA - Rodless Actuators - NORGREN, INC.; *pg.* 231, *pg.* 333
LINTRAV - Engineered Product And System - SULZER METCO (WESTBURY) INC.; *pg.* 1064, *pg.* 1350
LINUX - Software - LYNX SOFTWARE TECHNOLOGIES; *pg.* 429, *pg.* 247
LINUX SDK - Network Testing System - IXIA; *pg.* 422, *pg.* 56
LINUXWORLD - Technology Magazine - INTERNATIONAL DATA GROUP; *pg.* 1653, *pg.* 796
LINX - Software - DIEBOLD, INCORPORATED; *pg.* 387, *pg.* 1407
LINXVIEW - Software - EMCORE CORPORATION; *pg.* 636, *pg.* 39
LIOFOL - Laminating Adhesives - HENKEL CORPORATION; *pg.* 1165, *pg.* 1535
LION - Footwear - COBIAN CORP.; *pg.* 1806, *pg.* 253
LION - Beverages - THE COCA-COLA COMPANY; *pg.* 240, *pg.* 493
LION - Coffee - HAWAII COFFEE COMPANY; *pg.* 861, *pg.* 543
LION BREWERY - Beer - THE LION BREWERY, INC.; *pg.* 254, *pg.* 1594
LION BREWERY ROOT BEER - Soft Drink - THE LION BREWERY, INC.; *pg.* 254, *pg.* 1594
LION DANCE - Video Game - INTERNATIONAL GAME TECHNOLOGY; *pg.* 957, *pg.* 1024
LION FISH - Video Slots - INTERNATIONAL GAME TECHNOLOGY; *pg.* 957, *pg.* 1024
THE LION KING - Cartoon Character - THE WALT DISNEY COMPANY; *pg.* 317, *pg.* 52
LIONACCESS - Software - LIONBRIDGE TECHNOLOGIES INC.; *pg.* 428, *pg.* 851
LIONEL KIDDIE CITY - Toy Train - LIONEL LLC; *pg.* 961, *pg.* 875
LIONEL LINES - Toy Train - LIONEL LLC; *pg.* 961, *pg.* 875
LIONEL PLAYWORLD - Toy Train - LIONEL LLC; *pg.* 961, *pg.* 875
LIONEL ZW - Volt Meter - LIONEL LLC; *pg.* 961, *pg.* 875
LIONELVILLE - Toy Train - LIONEL LLC; *pg.* 961, *pg.* 875
LIONGATE ENTERTAINMENT - Motion Pictures - LIONS GATE ENTERTAINMENT CORP.; *pg.* 296, *pg.* 274
LIONGATE HOME ENTERTAINMENT - Motion Pictures - LIONS GATE ENTERTAINMENT CORP.; *pg.* 296, *pg.* 274
LIONGATE TELEVISION - Motion Pictures - LIONS GATE ENTERTAINMENT CORP.; *pg.* 296, *pg.* 274
LIONITE - Wall Panel - BLUELINX HOLDINGS, INC.; *pg.* 70, *pg.* 491
LIONITE/LIONBLAST - Aluminum Oxide - IMERYS FUSED MINERALS; *pg.* 1348, *pg.* 1317
LIONLINGUIST - Software - LIONBRIDGE TECHNOLOGIES INC.; *pg.* 428, *pg.* 851
LIONMASTER - Toy Train - LIONEL LLC; *pg.* 961, *pg.* 875
LIONS HEAD - Insulated & Traditional Beverage Urns & Soup & Sauce Servers - CARLISLE FOODSERVICE PRODUCTS INCORPORATED; *pg.* 1455, *pg.* 1485
THE LIONS HEAD COLLECTION - Premium Chafers - CARLISLE FOODSERVICE PRODUCTS INCORPORATED; *pg.* 1455, *pg.* 1485
LIONSHEAD - Deluxe Pilsner Beer - THE LION BREWERY, INC.; *pg.* 254, *pg.* 1594
LIONSTREAM - Software - LIONBRIDGE TECHNOLOGIES INC.; *pg.* 428, *pg.* 851
LIP D'VOTION - Lip Color - THE BONNE BELL COMPANY; *pg.* 502, *pg.* 1480
LIP D'VOTION SHIMMERS - Lip Color - THE BONNE BELL COMPANY; *pg.* 502, *pg.* 1480
LIP EXPRESS - Lip Color - MAYBELLINE LLC; *pg.* 516, *pg.* 1257
LIP GLAM - Lip Color - THE BONNE BELL COMPANY; *pg.* 502, *pg.* 1480
LIP LITES - Cream Pop - THE BONNE BELL COMPANY; *pg.* 502, *pg.* 1480
LIP MEDEX - Cooling Relief - BLISTEX, INC.; *pg.* 502, *pg.* 644
LIP REVITALIZER - Alpha Hydroxy - BLISTEX, INC.; *pg.* 502, *pg.* 644
LIP SHAKE - Lip Color - THE BONNE BELL COMPANY; *pg.* 502, *pg.* 1480
LIP SMACKER - Cosmetics - THE BONNE BELL COMPANY; *pg.* 502, *pg.* 1480
LIP THERAPY - Personal Care Product - RBC LIFE SCIENCES, INC.; *pg.* 1588, *pg.* 1723
LIP TONE - Lip Care Product - BLISTEX, INC.; *pg.* 502, *pg.* 644
LIP TONOC - Compact Mirror - BROWN & BIGELOW, INC.; *pg.* 1624, *pg.* 959
LIPA - Amplifier - SKYWORKS SOLUTIONS, INC.; *pg.* 674, *pg.* 862
LIPAMIDE - Chemical Ingredient - LIPO CHEMICALS INC.; *pg.* 1171, *pg.* 1107
LIPBURST - Lip Gloss - THE BONNE BELL COMPANY; *pg.* 502, *pg.* 1480
LIPEX CELLECT - Phytosterol Canola Glyceride - JARCHEM INDUSTRIES, INC.; *pg.* 1169, *pg.* 1096
LIPIDOL - Nutritional Supplement - NU SKIN ENTERPRISES, INC.; *pg.* 518, *pg.* 1755
LIPIGUARD - Filter - PALL CORPORATION; *pg.* 232, *pg.* 1323
LIPIPOR - Filter Set - PALL CORPORATION; *pg.* 232, *pg.* 1323
LIPISORB - Enteral Nutritional for Patients with Fat Malabsorption - MEAD JOHNSON NUTRITION COMPANY; *pg.* 1561, *pg.* 615
LIPITOR - Cholesterol Reduction Medication - PFIZER INC.; *pg.* 1581, *pg.* 1278
LIPLITES - Lip Color - THE BONNE BELL COMPANY; *pg.* 502, *pg.* 1480
THE LIPMAN REPORT - Newsletter - GUARDSMARK, LLC; *pg.* 401, *pg.* 1237
LIPO CD - Chemical Ingredient - LIPO CHEMICALS INC.; *pg.* 1171, *pg.* 1107
LIPO POLYGLYCOL - Chemical Ingredient - LIPO CHEMICALS INC.; *pg.* 1171, *pg.* 1107
LIPO-TEARS - Lubricating Eye Drops - THE COOPER COMPANIES, INC.; *pg.* 1518, *pg.* 183
LIPOBEAD - Chemical Ingredient - LIPO CHEMICALS INC.; *pg.* 1171, *pg.* 1107
LIPOBRITE - Chemical Ingredient - LIPO CHEMICALS INC.; *pg.* 1171, *pg.* 1107
LIPOBRONZE - Chemical Ingredient - LIPO CHEMICALS INC.; *pg.* 1171, *pg.* 1107
LIPOCAPSULE - Chemical Ingredient - LIPO CHEMICALS INC.; *pg.* 1171, *pg.* 1107

LIPOCARE - Chemical Ingredient - LIPO CHEMICALS INC.; *pg.* 1171, *pg.* 1107
LIPOCLEAR - Diagnostic Urinalysis System - IRIS INTERNATIONAL, INC.; *pg.* 1547, *pg.* 64
LIPOCOL - Chemical Ingredient - LIPO CHEMICALS INC.; *pg.* 1171, *pg.* 1107
LIPODERMA - Chemical Ingredient - LIPO CHEMICALS INC.; *pg.* 1171, *pg.* 1107
LIPOFECTAMINE - Molecular Biology Product - THERMO FISHER SCIENTIFIC INC.; *pg.* 1602, *pg.* 61
LIPOFECTIN - Molecular Biology Product - THERMO FISHER SCIENTIFIC INC.; *pg.* 1602, *pg.* 61
LIPOLAN - Chemical Ingredient - LIPO CHEMICALS INC.; *pg.* 1171, *pg.* 1107
LIPOLIGHT - Chemical Ingredient - LIPO CHEMICALS INC.; *pg.* 1171, *pg.* 1107
LIPOMIC - Chemical Ingredient - LIPO CHEMICALS INC.; *pg.* 1171, *pg.* 1107
LIPOMULSE - Chemical Ingredient - LIPO CHEMICALS INC.; *pg.* 1171, *pg.* 1107
LIPONATE - Chemical Ingredient - LIPO CHEMICALS INC.; *pg.* 1171, *pg.* 1107
LIPONIC - Chemical Ingredient - LIPO CHEMICALS INC.; *pg.* 1171, *pg.* 1107
LIPONYL - Chemical Ingredient - LIPO CHEMICALS INC.; *pg.* 1171, *pg.* 1107
LIPOPEARL - Chemical Ingredient - LIPO CHEMICALS INC.; *pg.* 1171, *pg.* 1107
LIPOPEG - Chemical Ingredient - LIPO CHEMICALS INC.; *pg.* 1171, *pg.* 1107
LIPOQUAT - Chemical Ingredient - LIPO CHEMICALS INC.; *pg.* 1171, *pg.* 1107
LIPOSATIN - Chemical Ingredient - LIPO CHEMICALS INC.; *pg.* 1171, *pg.* 1107
LIPOSCRUB - Chemical Ingredient - LIPO CHEMICALS INC.; *pg.* 1171, *pg.* 1107
LIPOSERVE - Chemical Ingredient - LIPO CHEMICALS INC.; *pg.* 1171, *pg.* 1107
LIPOSIC - Dry Eye Product - BAUSCH & LOMB INCORPORATED; *pg.* 1401, *pg.* 1045
LIPOSILT - Chemical Ingredient - LIPO CHEMICALS INC.; *pg.* 1171, *pg.* 1107
LIPOSORB - Chemical Ingredient - LIPO CHEMICALS INC.; *pg.* 1171, *pg.* 1107
LIPOSPHERE - Chemical Ingredient - LIPO CHEMICALS INC.; *pg.* 1171, *pg.* 1107
LIPOTHIX - Chemical Ingredient - LIPO CHEMICALS INC.; *pg.* 1171, *pg.* 1107
LIPOVOL - Chemical Ingredient - LIPO CHEMICALS INC.; *pg.* 1171, *pg.* 1107
LIPOWAX - Chemical Ingredient - LIPO CHEMICALS INC.; *pg.* 1171, *pg.* 1107
LIPP - Phonetic Transcribing Program - INTELLIGENT HEARING SYSTEMS CORP.; *pg.* 1546, *pg.* 443
LIPPINCOTT MERCER - Corporate Identity & Image Management Consultants - MARSH & MCLENNAN COMPANIES INC.; *pg.* 1207, *pg.* 1256
LIPPKE - Leak Detection System - MOCON, INC.; *pg.* 1363, *pg.* 940
LIPSHAKE - Lip Color - THE BONNE BELL COMPANY; *pg.* 502, *pg.* 1480
LIPTON - Soup - UNILEVER UNITED STATES, INC.; *pg.* 904, *pg.* 1061
LIPTON BRISK - Teas - PEPSICO, INC.; *pg.* 259, *pg.* 1327
LIPTON'S ICED TEA - Teas - PEPSICO, INC.; *pg.* 259, *pg.* 1327
LIQ-GLASS - Robotic Product - HAMILTON CO., INC.; *pg.* 1415, *pg.* 1031
LIQ-PLAST - Robotic Product - HAMILTON CO., INC.; *pg.* 1415, *pg.* 1031
LIQ. SMOKEHOUSE CLEANER - Chemical Product - BIRKO CORPORATION; *pg.* 1149, *pg.* 332
LIQI-SEAL - Beauty Product Sampling System - ARCADE MARKETING, INC.; *pg.* 352, *pg.* 1196
LIQUAFEED - Gardens - THE SCOTTS MIRACLE-GRO COMPANY; *pg.* 1799, *pg.* 1459
LIQUAMYCIN - Antibiotic Veterinary Preparation - PFIZER INC.; *pg.* 1581, *pg.* 1278
LIQUAZINC - Polymer Product - CHEMTURA CORPORATION; *pg.* 1152, *pg.* 355
LIQUETTE - Pharmaceutical Product - LUMARA HEALTH INC.; *pg.* 1557, *pg.* 973
LIQUI-BOX - Liquid Packaging - E.I. DU PONT DE NEMOURS & COMPANY; *pg.* 1159, *pg.* 390
LIQUI-BOX - Molded Containers - LIQUI-BOX CORPORATION; *pg.* 1464, *pg.* 1802
LIQUI/DRY - Dual Chamber Prefill Syringe - BECTON, DICKINSON & COMPANY; *pg.* 1501, *pg.* 1068
LIQUI-FIRE - Ice Melter - MORGRO, INC.; *pg.* 1798, *pg.* 1759
LIQUI-MOVER - Condensate Handling Systems (Positive Displacement Pumps) - KADANT JOHNSON INC.; *pg.* 1073, *pg.* 909
LIQUI PASTE - Foundry Facing Compounds - ASHLAND INC.; *pg.* 972, *pg.* 726
LIQUICHEK - Clinical Diagnostic Product - BIO-RAD LABORATORIES, INC.; *pg.* 1504, *pg.* 101
LIQUID - Risk Management - STANDARD & POOR'S RATINGS SERVICES; *pg.* 805, *pg.* 1296
LIQUID ANT BAITS - Ant Control Products - SENORET CHEMICAL COMPANY; *pg.* 335, *pg.* 1548
LIQUID BONE POWER - Nutritional Supplement - NATURAL ORGANICS, INC.; *pg.* 1571, *pg.* 1181
LIQUID CONTROL - Fluid Handling System - GRACO, INC.; *pg.* 1342, *pg.* 935
LIQUID CONTROL & DESIGN - Fluid Handling System - GRACO, INC.; *pg.* 1342, *pg.* 935
LIQUID CONTROL CORPORATION - Fluid Handling System - GRACO, INC.; *pg.* 1342, *pg.* 935
LIQUID EYES - Eye Cosmetics - MAYBELLINE LLC; *pg.* 516, *pg.* 1257
LIQUID GARDEN GUARD - Agricultural Chemical - PBI/GORDON CORPORATION; *pg.* 1176, *pg.* 985
LIQUID GUM-GO - Cleaning Product - HILLYARD, INC.; *pg.* 331, *pg.* 990
LIQUID INK - Crystal Clear Ink - SERIGRAPH, INC.; *pg.* 1686, *pg.* 1899
LIQUID MAKEUP SPF 16 - Foundation - MERLE NORMAN COSMETICS, INC.; *pg.* 517, *pg.* 136
LIQUID MATE - Liquid Soap Dispenser - BOBRICK WASHROOM EQUIPMENT, INC.; *pg.* 1043, *pg.* 166
LIQUID NAILS - Adhesives - AKZONOBEL DECORATIVE PAINTS U.S.; *pg.* 1439, *pg.* 1474
LIQUID-PLUMR - Drain Opener; Regular & Professional Septic Buildup Remover - THE CLOROX COMPANY; *pg.* 327, *pg.* 169
LIQUID-PLUMR FOAMING PIPE SNAKE - Drain Opener - THE CLOROX COMPANY; *pg.* 327, *pg.* 169
LIQUID SPARKLE - Hair & Skin Product - AUBREY ORGANICS INC.; *pg.* 499, *pg.* 470
LIQUID SWABBY - Cleaning Product - HILLYARD, INC.; *pg.* 331, *pg.* 990
LIQUID TRAP SHOOTER - Cleaning Product - HILLYARD, INC.; *pg.* 331, *pg.* 990
LIQUID WIRELESS - Mobile Marketing Services - PUBLISHERS CLEARING HOUSE; *pg.* 1782, *pg.* 1324
LIQUID WONDER - Automotive Reconditioning Product - MOC PRODUCTS COMPANY, INC.; *pg.* 332, *pg.* 174
LIQUID WRENCH - Lubricant & Penetrant - RADIATOR SPECIALTY COMPANY; *pg.* 215, *pg.* 1380
LIQUIDATOR - Foam Eliminator - VON SCHRADER COMPANY; *pg.* 62, *pg.* 1890
LIQUIDCREDIT - Web-Based Instant Credit Decisioning Solution Services - FAIR ISAAC CORPORATION; *pg.* 1247, *pg.* 955
LIQUIDEMON - Steam Cleaning Solvent - CLAYTON INDUSTRIES CO.; *pg.* 1323, *pg.* 66
LIQUIDFRUIT - Beverage - MONSTER BEVERAGE CORPORATION; *pg.* 257, *pg.* 69
LIQUIDGOLD - Animal Feed - ARCHER-DANIELS-MIDLAND COMPANY; *pg.* 825, *pg.* 565
LIQUIDITYBRIDGE - Online Trading Services - MARKETAXESS HOLDINGS INC.; *pg.* 778, *pg.* 1256
LIQUIDOFFICE - Software - AUTONOMY, INC.; *pg.* 358, *pg.* 212
LIQUIDOFFICE - Software - SCANTRON CORPORATION; *pg.* 467, *pg.* 922
LIQUIDOW - Liquid Calcium Chloride - THE DOW CHEMICAL COMPANY; *pg.* 1157, *pg.* 898
LIQUIDPOWER - Flow Improver - CONOCOPHILLIPS; *pg.* 975, *pg.* 1703
LIQUIK - Cleaner - BIRKO CORPORATION; *pg.* 1149, *pg.* 332
LIQUIK 250 - Chemical Product - BIRKO CORPORATION; *pg.* 1149, *pg.* 332
LIQUILOC - Adhesive - H.B. FULLER COMPANY; *pg.* 1165, *pg.* 961
LIQUILON - Laundry Product - BIRKO CORPORATION; *pg.* 1149, *pg.* 332
LIQUINOX - Liquid Detergent - ALCONOX, INC.; *pg.* 325, *pg.* 1351
LIQUINOX - Chemical Product - SPECTRUM CHEMICALS & LABORATORY PRODUCTS, INC.; *pg.* 1181, *pg.* 94
LIQUIPAC - Plastics Product - AEP INDUSTRIES INC.; *pg.* 1878, *pg.* 1085
LIQUIPAK - Fibre Drum - GREIF INC.; *pg.* 1459, *pg.* 1447
LIQUISIZE - Ingredient System - PENFORD CORPORATION; *pg.* 1177, *pg.* 314
LIQUITAINER - Plastics Product - AEP INDUSTRIES INC.; *pg.* 1878, *pg.* 1085
LIQUITOUCH - Beauty Product Sampling System - ARCADE MARKETING, INC.; *pg.* 352, *pg.* 1196
LIQUOX - Chemical Product - CARUS CORPORATION; *pg.* 1152, *pg.* 652
LIQUOZON - Ozone Generator System - MKS INSTRUMENTS, INC.; *pg.* 1362, *pg.* 781
LISA - Sterilizer - A-DEC, INC.; *pg.* 1483, *pg.* 1500
LISA - Footwear - PHOENIX FOOTWEAR GROUP, INC.; *pg.* 1815, *pg.* 60
LISABETH - Furniture - HOOKER FURNITURE CORPORATION; *pg.* 928, *pg.* 1788
LISBEN - Furniture - AMERICAN LEATHER LP; *pg.* 912, *pg.* 1673
LISBEN WEDGE - Furniture - AMERICAN LEATHER LP; *pg.* 912, *pg.* 1673
LISBON - Guest Chairs - BERNHARDT DESIGN; *pg.* 918, *pg.* 1381
LISBON - Cookies - PEPPERIDGE FARM, INC.; *pg.* 888, *pg.* 363
LISETTE - Furniture - J. ROBERT SCOTT INC.; *pg.* 930, *pg.* 105
LISMORE - Fabric - NEMSCHOFF, INC.; *pg.* 936, *pg.* 1890
LISSAMINE - Molecular Probe Product - THERMO FISHER SCIENTIFIC INC.; *pg.* 1602, *pg.* 61
LISSOME - Furniture - HERMAN MILLER, INC.; *pg.* 926, *pg.* 913
LISTANALYST - Software - PITNEY BOWES INC.; *pg.* 454, *pg.* 376
LISTBAZAAR.COM - Online Lists - INFOGROUP INC.; *pg.* 1652, *pg.* 1016
LISTCLEANUP.COM - Online Direct Marketing Application - CONCLUSIVE ANALYTICS; *pg.* 1236, *pg.* 1380
LISTEN. THINK. DELIVER. - Tagline - CDM SMITH; *pg.* 74, *pg.* 807
LISTENHEAR - Preserving Hearing Health - STARKEY LABORATORIES, INC.; *pg.* 1597, *pg.* 923
LISTENING. LEARNING. LEADING - Slogan - EDUCATIONAL TESTING SERVICE INC.; *pg.* 1394, *pg.* 1111
LISTERINE - Mouthwash - JOHNSON & JOHNSON; *pg.* 1549, *pg.* 1091
LISTERINE - Mouthwash - MCNEIL-PPC, INC.; *pg.* 1560, *pg.* 1533
LISTERMINT - Mouthwash - MCNEIL-PPC, INC.; *pg.* 1560, *pg.* 1533
LISTMANAGER - Email Marketing Software - LYRIS, INC.; *pg.* 429, *pg.* 84
LISTNINGLOCK - Discrete Lock - NATIONAL ASSOCIATION OF REALTORS; *pg.* 1666, *pg.* 584
LISTO - Plastic Product - MYERS INDUSTRIES, INC.; *pg.* 1887, *pg.* 1402
LITE - Ankle Brace - MUELLER SPORTS MEDICINE, INC.; *pg.* 1570, *pg.* 1887
LITE-A-SITE - Electronic Components - MOLEX INCORPORATED; *pg.* 655, *pg.* 628
LITE ACCENTS - Salad Dressing - KEN'S FOODS, INC.; *pg.* 867, *pg.* 832
LITE & FREE - Food Product - SUBCO FOODS, INC.; *pg.* 899, *pg.* 668
LITE ANKLE BRACE - Hinged Brace for Protection & Flexibility - MUELLER SPORTS MEDICINE, INC.; *pg.* 1570, *pg.* 1887
LITE ASH STRATOCASTER - Electric Guitar - FENDER MUSICAL INSTRUMENTS CORPORATION; *pg.* 547, *pg.* 21
LITE ASH TELECASTER - Electric Guitar - FENDER MUSICAL INSTRUMENTS CORPORATION; *pg.* 547, *pg.* 21
LITE-BRITE - Toy & Game - HASBRO, INC.; *pg.* 954, *pg.* 1603
LITE-BRITE CUBE - Toy & Game - HASBRO, INC.; *pg.* 954, *pg.* 1603
LITE DETANGLER - Hair Care Product - JOHN PAUL MITCHELL SYSTEMS; *pg.* 512, *pg.* 133
LITE-DRI - Absorbent - SAFETY-KLEEN HOLDCO, INC.; *pg.*

First page reference indicates Business Class Edition
Second page reference indicates Geographic Edition

1180, *pg.* 1734
LITE-ENERGY - Lighting Fixture & Control - PHILIPS LIGHTING; *pg.* 1303, *pg.* 806
LITE-FLEX - Commercial Lighting - SWIVELIER CO., INC.; *pg.* 1307, *pg.* 1142
LITE KOTE - Paper Products - BOISE CASCADE HOLDINGS, L.L.C.; *pg.* 1453, *pg.* 546
LITE-LOC - Meat, Fish & Poultry Absorbent Pad - SEALED AIR CORPORATION; *pg.* 1468, *pg.* 1058
LITE LOFT - Security System - 3M COMPANY; *pg.* 1142, *pg.* 956
LITE-MART - Lighting - LSI INDUSTRIES INC.; *pg.* 58, *pg.* 1416
LITE MITE - Circular Flourescent Illuminator - PROPHOTONIX LIMITED; *pg.* 1427, *pg.* 1039
LITE-N-AIRE - Airmover/Heatvalve - SWARTWOUT DIVISION; *pg.* 114, *pg.* 978
LITE RAIL - Vanity Lights - CRAFTMADE INTERNATIONAL, INC.; *pg.* 1295, *pg.* 1670
LITE RIDER - Cart Bag - DATREK GOLF; *pg.* 1832, *pg.* 1801
LITE-SAVER - Commercial Lighting - SWIVELIER CO., INC.; *pg.* 1307, *pg.* 1142
LITE STREAMER - Temporary Lighting System - COLEMAN CABLE, INC.; *pg.* 1324, *pg.* 665
LITE-TOUCH ZOOM 140 - Photo Equipment - NIKON INC.; *pg.* 1424, *pg.* 1181
LITE WAY - Top Soil, Potting Soil, Organic Peat & Manure - PREMIER TECH HORTICULTURE LTD.; *pg.* 1799, *pg.* 1958
LITE WEIGHT - Clog-Free Lightweight Body Filler - ITW - EVERCOAT; *pg.* 1443, *pg.* 1415
LITEBLUE - 50% Less Calorie Drink - LEADING BRANDS, INC.; *pg.* 1026, *pg.* 1911
LITEBOX - Flashlight - STREAMLIGHT INC.; *pg.* 1306, *pg.* 1527
LITECAL - Graphic Film - FLEXCON CORPORATION; *pg.* 1457, *pg.* 844
LITECOTE - Kaolin Pigment - BASF CATALYSTS LLC; *pg.* 1148, *pg.* 1074
LITEFEIL - Light Weight Embankment - THE DOW CHEMICAL COMPANY; *pg.* 1157, *pg.* 898
LITEFLEX - Springs - MERITOR, INC.; *pg.* 212, *pg.* 911
LITELINK - PC Monitoring System - GEA REFRIGERATION NORTH AMERICA, INC.; *pg.* 1072, *pg.* 1597
LITEPEDAL - Clutch - MERITOR, INC.; *pg.* 212, *pg.* 911
LITEPORT - Playback System - INFOCUS CORPORATION; *pg.* 644, *pg.* 1503
LITEPRO - Apparatus - INFOCUS CORPORATION; *pg.* 644, *pg.* 1503
LITERARY CAVALCADE - Educational Materials - SCHOLASTIC INC.; *pg.* 1683, *pg.* 1288
LITERATURE TO THINK ABOUT - Educational Materials - SCHOLASTIC INC.; *pg.* 1683, *pg.* 1288
LITES - Safety & Protective Equipment - ENCON SAFETY PRODUCTS; *pg.* 1334, *pg.* 1705
LITES - Shoe - ETONIC WORLDWIDE LLC; *pg.* 1808, *pg.* 857
LITESHOW II - Mobile Projector - INFOCUS CORPORATION; *pg.* 644, *pg.* 1503
LITESPAN - Digital Telephone Equipment - ALCATEL-LUCENT USA, INC.; *pg.* 615, *pg.* 1728
LITESPEED - Software - DELL SOFTWARE; *pg.* 385, *pg.* 40
LITESPEED - Lighting System - LITECONTROL CORPORATION; *pg.* 1301, *pg.* 841
LITESPEED FOR SQL SERVER - Software - DELL SOFTWARE; *pg.* 385, *pg.* 40
LITESTRIP - Commercial Lighting - SWIVELIER CO., INC.; *pg.* 1307, *pg.* 1142
LITH-EASE - Lithium Lubricant - AMERICAN GREASE STICK CO.; *pg.* 971, *pg.* 902
LITHIC - Lamp - J. ROBERT SCOTT INC.; *pg.* 930, *pg.* 105
LITHION - Lithium Ion Cells/Batteries - YARDNEY TECHNICAL PRODUCTS, INC.; *pg.* 690, *pg.* 1601
LITHIUM COMMUNITIES - Platform for Brand-focused Conversations - LITHIUM TECHNOLOGIES; *pg.* 1263, *pg.* 221
LITHIUM ION - Battery - ULTRALIFE CORPORATION; *pg.* 1385, *pg.* 1317
LITHIUM MOBILE - Social Customer Experience App - LITHIUM TECHNOLOGIES; *pg.* 1263, *pg.* 221
LITHIUM POWER - Lithium Battery - ULTRALIFE CORPORATION; *pg.* 1385, *pg.* 1317
LITHIUM SOCIAL WEB - Web Experience Management Service - LITHIUM TECHNOLOGIES; *pg.* 1263, *pg.* 221
LITHO - Toolkit - SCHLUMBERGER LIMITED; *pg.* 801, *pg.* 1714
LITHO-FLUTE - Packaging Product - GRAPHIC PACKAGING HOLDING COMPANY; *pg.* 1459, *pg.* 509
LITHO MASTER - Offset Printing Blanket - ROTADYNE; *pg.* 1681, *pg.* 529
LITHOBID - Estradiol Transdermal System - NOVEN PHARMACEUTICALS, INC.; *pg.* 1576, *pg.* 445
LITHOCHROME - Concrete System - L.M. SCOFIELD COMPANY; *pg.* 94, *pg.* 134
LITHOCRUISER - Lithography Optimization System - BRION TECHNOLOGIES INC.; *pg.* 1319, *pg.* 265
LITHODIAMOND - Lithotripsy System - HEALTHTRONICS, INC.; *pg.* 1540, *pg.* 1663
LITHOGUARD - Filtration System - DONALDSON COMPANY, INC.; *pg.* 1329, *pg.* 917
LITHOJET - Digital Imaging Processes - THE DOW CHEMICAL COMPANY; *pg.* 1157, *pg.* 898
LITHOMAN - Press - MANROLAND INC.; *pg.* 430, *pg.* 669
LITHONIA LIGHTING - Lighting Fixture Product - ACUITY BRANDS, INC.; *pg.* 1294, *pg.* 487
LITHOPATTERNS - Lighting Product - HIGH END SYSTEMS, INC.; *pg.* 1299, *pg.* 1663
LITHOS - Simulation Technology - CAE INC.; *pg.* 226, *pg.* 1959
LITHOSEAL - Concrete System - L.M. SCOFIELD COMPANY; *pg.* 94, *pg.* 134
LITHOSTAT - Pharmaceutical Product - MISSION PHARMACAL COMPANY INC.; *pg.* 1568, *pg.* 1742
LITHOTEX - DUV Lithography - COHERENT, INC.; *pg.* 1406, *pg.* 265
LITHOTEX - Concrete System - L.M. SCOFIELD COMPANY; *pg.* 94, *pg.* 134
LITHOWARE - Inspection System - KLA-TENCOR CORPORATION; *pg.* 1353, *pg.* 146
LITMAS - Remote Plasma Source - ADVANCED ENERGY INDUSTRIES, INC.; *pg.* 613, *pg.* 328
LITRE LOG - Loyalty Program - PARKLAND FUEL CORPORATION; *pg.* 983, *pg.* 1906
LITTER GENIE - Pet Care - EDGEWELL PERSONAL CARE; *pg.* 1526, *pg.* 995
LITTER HAWK - Vacuums - TENNANT COMPANY; *pg.* 1381, *pg.* 944
LITTERLESS - Lunch Kit Eliminates Foil - RUBBERMAID HOME PRODUCTS; *pg.* 1138, *pg.* 1453
LITTLE AMERICA - Hotel Chain - SINCLAIR OIL CORPORATION; *pg.* 984, *pg.* 1760
LITTLE APPLE - Educational Materials - SCHOLASTIC INC.; *pg.* 1683, *pg.* 1288
LITTLE A'S - Ticket Program - OAKLAND ATHLETICS LIMITED PARTNERSHIP; *pg.* 571, *pg.* 172
LITTLE BEAR ORGANIC FOODS - Organic Food Products - THE HAIN CELESTIAL GROUP, INC.; *pg.* 860, *pg.* 1172
LITTLE BIG DOGS - Apparel & Accessories for Infants & Children - THE WALKING COMPANY HOLDINGS, INC.; *pg.* 50, *pg.* 263
LITTLE BIG MOUTH - Bicycle Accessories - SPECIALIZED BICYCLE COMPONENTS, INC.; *pg.* 1711, *pg.* 152
LITTLE BLACK DRESS - Fragrance - AVON PRODUCTS, INC.; *pg.* 500, *pg.* 1198
LITTLE BLACK DRESS - Wine - BROWN-FORMAN CORPORATION; *pg.* 1958, *pg.* 732
LITTLE BLESSINGS - Christian Literature for Children - TYNDALE HOUSE PUBLISHERS, INC.; *pg.* 1697, *pg.* 561
LITTLE BOOMEY - Beverage - TRINCHERO FAMILY ESTATES; *pg.* 1971, *pg.* 197
LITTLE BROWN - Book Publisher - TIME WARNER INC.; *pg.* 312, *pg.* 1302
LITTLE BUCKET - Parfaits - KFC CORPORATION; *pg.* 1733, *pg.* 735
LITTLE CAESAR'S - Carry-Out Pizza Restaurants - LITTLE CAESARS ENTERPRISES, INC.; *pg.* 1736, *pg.* 883
LITTLE CHAMP - Flush Cutter - CHANNELLOCK, INC.; *pg.* 1044, *pg.* 1551
LITTLE DEBBIE - Snack Cakes - MCKEE FOODS CORPORATION; *pg.* 1860, *pg.* 1630
LITTLE-DEMON - Resistor Product - OHMITE MANUFACTURING COMPANY; *pg.* 660, *pg.* 553
LITTLE-DEVIL - Resistor Product - OHMITE MANUFACTURING COMPANY; *pg.* 660, *pg.* 553
LITTLE ED - Flashlight - PELICAN PRODUCTS, INC.; *pg.* 1842, *pg.* 295
LITTLE EINSTEINS - Toy & Game - HASBRO, INC.; *pg.* 954, *pg.* 1603
LITTLE GIANT - Cutting System - EASTMAN MACHINE COMPANY; *pg.* 1331, *pg.* 1148
LITTLE GIANT - Water Gardening Kit - LILYPONS WATER GARDENS INC.; *pg.* 1797, *pg.* 766
LITTLE GIANT - Pumps - LITTLE GIANT PUMP COMPANY; *pg.* 1356, *pg.* 1486
LITTLE GREEN - Floor Care Product - BISSELL HOMECARE, INC.; *pg.* 52, *pg.* 887
LITTLE GREEN MEN - Video Slots - INTERNATIONAL GAME TECHNOLOGY; *pg.* 957, *pg.* 1024
LITTLE GREEN MEN FAMILY REUNION - Video Slots - INTERNATIONAL GAME TECHNOLOGY; *pg.* 957, *pg.* 1024
LITTLE KICKER - Bender - GREENLEE TEXTRON INC.; *pg.* 1048, *pg.* 655
LITTLE LEAP - Educational Toys - LEAPFROG ENTERPRISES, INC.; *pg.* 961, *pg.* 84
LITTLE LILY - Apparel - SUGARTOWN WORLDWIDE INC.; *pg.* 33, *pg.* 1544
LITTLE LOGIC - Integrated Circuits - TEXAS INSTRUMENTS INCORPORATED; *pg.* 679, *pg.* 1688
LITTLE LOTTO - Lottery Game - ILLINOIS STATE LOTTERY; *pg.* 995, *pg.* 578
LITTLE LUNCHMATE - Ice Chest - IGLOO PRODUCTS CORPORATION; *pg.* 1126, *pg.* 1724
LITTLE LUX - Hand Held Vacuum - AERUS LLC; *pg.* 51, *pg.* 1673
LITTLE MAN & GUN - Fluid Handling System - GRACO, INC.; *pg.* 1342, *pg.* 935
LITTLE MERMAID - Toy & Game - HASBRO, INC.; *pg.* 954, *pg.* 1603
LITTLE MOMMY - Toy - MATTEL, INC.; *pg.* 962, *pg.* 81
LITTLE MULE - Hoist - COLUMBUS MCKINNON CORPORATION; *pg.* 1325, *pg.* 1138
LITTLE OLLIE - Container Grown Plant - MONROVIA GROWERS; *pg.* 1797, *pg.* 44
LITTLE ONE - Container Grown Plant - MONROVIA GROWERS; *pg.* 1797, *pg.* 44
LITTLE PEOPLE - Pre-school Toys - FISHER-PRICE, INC.; *pg.* 953, *pg.* 1156
LITTLE PEOPLE, BIG BOOKS - Juvenile Book Series - DIRECT HOLDINGS AMERICAS INC.; *pg.* 1636, *pg.* 1780
LITTLE PLAYMATE - Ice Chest - IGLOO PRODUCTS CORPORATION; *pg.* 1126, *pg.* 1724
LITTLE PRETTY - Doll - MATTEL, INC.; *pg.* 962, *pg.* 81
LITTLE PRO - Small Floor Polisher - AERUS LLC; *pg.* 51, *pg.* 1673
LITTLE PRO - Food Processor - CUISINART INC.; *pg.* 1123, *pg.* 373
LITTLE PRO - Tools - VAUGHAN & BUSHNELL MANUFACTURING COMPANY, INC.; *pg.* 1066, *pg.* 616
LITTLE PURGE - Fluid Handling System - GRACO, INC.; *pg.* 1342, *pg.* 935
LITTLE RASCAL - Container Grown Plant - MONROVIA GROWERS; *pg.* 1797, *pg.* 44
LITTLE REBEL - Resistor Product - OHMITE MANUFACTURING COMPANY; *pg.* 660, *pg.* 553
LITTLE RED ROASTER - Ride-ons - RADIO FLYER INC.; *pg.* 966, *pg.* 588
LITTLE RED SCOOTER - Scooter - RADIO FLYER INC.; *pg.* 966, *pg.* 588
LITTLE RED TOOL BOX - Educational Materials - SCHOLASTIC INC.; *pg.* 1683, *pg.* 1288
LITTLE RHINE BEAR LIEBFRAUMILCH - German Wine - LAIRD & COMPANY, INC.; *pg.* 1966, *pg.* 1119
LITTLE SIMON - Children's Books - SIMON & SCHUSTER, INC.; *pg.* 1687, *pg.* 1292
LITTLE SIZZLERS - Pork Sausages - HORMEL FOODS CORPORATION; *pg.* 863, *pg.* 915
LITTLE SMOKIES - Smoked Sausage - JOHNSONVILLE SAUSAGE, LLC; *pg.* 867, *pg.* 1894
LITTLE SWIMMERS - Swim Diapers - KIMBERLY-CLARK CORPORATION; *pg.* 1461, *pg.* 1720
LITTLE SWITZERLAND - Specialty Retail Products - TIFFANY & CO.; *pg.* 13, *pg.* 1299
LITTLE THINGS - BIG DIFFERENCES - Cleaning Product - THE EVERCARE COMPANY; *pg.* 1124, *pg.* 483
LITTLE TIKES - Line of Toys - MGA ENTERTAINMENT, INC.; *pg.* 964, *pg.* 300
LITTLE TIKES - Bed Linen - SPRINGS GLOBAL, INC.; *pg.* 698, *pg.* 1616
LITTLE VISITS - Book - CONCORDIA PUBLISHING HOUSE; *pg.* 1629, *pg.* 995
LITTLE WHITE DRESS - Bridal Wear - ALFRED ANGELO, INC.; *pg.* 17, *pg.* 1532
LITTLEBUG - Bicycle - TREK BICYCLE CORPORATION; *pg.* 1847, *pg.* 1896

LITTLEFORD - Batch Mixer - LITTLEFORD DAY INC.; *pg.* 1356, *pg.* 728
LITTLEST PET SHOP - Toys - FUNRISE TOY CORP.; *pg.* 549, *pg.* 300
LITTLEST PET SHOP - Toy & Game - HASBRO, INC.; *pg.* 954, *pg.* 1603
LITTLETON - Coin Collections - LITTLETON COIN CO., INC.; *pg.* 1776, *pg.* 1035
LITTLETON'S CUSTOM COIN FOLDERS - Folder - LITTLETON COIN CO., INC.; *pg.* 1776, *pg.* 1035
LITTLETOUCH - Educational Toys - LEAPFROG ENTERPRISES, INC.; *pg.* 961, *pg.* 84
LITTMAN JEWELERS - Jewelry Store - THE KROGER CO.; *pg.* 1025, *pg.* 1416
LITTMANN - Stethoscopes - 3M COMPANY; *pg.* 1142, *pg.* 956
LIV CRAYOLA - School Supplies for Teen Girls - CRAYOLA LLC; *pg.* 951, *pg.* 1528
LIV/GIANT - Bicycle - GIANT BICYCLE INC.; *pg.* 1707, *pg.* 164
LIVALO - Cholesterol Reducing Drug - ELI LILLY AND COMPANY; *pg.* 1527, *pg.* 684
LIVE - Tile - ARTISTIC TILE INC.; *pg.* 914, *pg.* 1119
LIVE BETTER - Tagline - CHATTEM, INC.; *pg.* 1515, *pg.* 1628
LIVE COMFORTABLY - Slogan - HOLLANDER SLEEP PRODUCTS; *pg.* 927, *pg.* 411
LIVE/DEAD - Molecular Probe Product - THERMO FISHER SCIENTIFIC INC.; *pg.* 1602, *pg.* 61
LIVE FROM LINCOLN CENTER - Performing Arts Program - LINCOLN CENTER FOR THE PERFORMING ARTS, INC.; *pg.* 557, *pg.* 1251
LIVE FROM THE HEART - Cardiovascular Education Program - MUSEUM OF SCIENCE AND INDUSTRY; *pg.* 565, *pg.* 583
LIVE-ID - Software - 3M; *pg.* 339, *pg.* 179
LIVE IT UP - Carpet - BEAULIEU GROUP, LLC; *pg.* 917, *pg.* 529
LIVE LARGE. THINK BIG - Slogan - DALLAS CONVENTION & VISITORS BUREAU; *pg.* 991, *pg.* 1678
LIVE LIFE WELL - Pharmaceutical Benefit Management - EXPRESS SCRIPTS; *pg.* 1530, *pg.* 1070
LIVE LIFE.EVEN BETTER - Slogan - CALATLANTIC GROUP, INC.; *pg.* 1084, *pg.* 108
LIVE LOBSTERS DANCE PARTY - Game - WMS INDUSTRIES INC.; *pg.* 593, *pg.* 666
LIVE LOBSTERS DANCING NIGHTLY - Game - WMS INDUSTRIES INC.; *pg.* 593, *pg.* 666
LIVE LONGER & SAVE MONEY - Slogan - VITACOST.COM, INC.; *pg.* 1607, *pg.* 414
LIVE MAS - Slogan - TACO BELL CORP.; *pg.* 1752, *pg.* 117
LIVE OUT LOUD - Tagline - OXYGEN MEDIA LLC; *pg.* 303, *pg.* 1275
LIVE SOLID. BANK SOLID - Tagline - SUNTRUST BANKS, INC.; *pg.* 807, *pg.* 520
LIVE STRONGER. LIVE LONGER. - Tagline - JOHANNA FOODS INC.; *pg.* 866, *pg.* 1066
LIVE THE EXPERIENCE. ADMIRE THE VIEW. - Slogan - WCI COMMUNITIES, INC.; *pg.* 1118, *pg.* 414
LIVE UNINTERRUPTED - Slogan - DEXCOM INC; *pg.* 1524, *pg.* 202
LIVE WELL - Pillow and Throw - HERITAGE LACE INC.; *pg.* 694, *pg.* 711
LIVE YOUR LIFE - Slogan - AMERICAN EAGLE OUTFITTERS, INC.; *pg.* 37, *pg.* 1572
LIVE365.COM - Website - LIVE365, INC.; *pg.* 1264, *pg.* 89
LIVEALERTS - Software - PASSUR AEROSPACE, INC.; *pg.* 233, *pg.* 376
LIVEASSIST - Software - SUPPORT.COM, INC.; *pg.* 1283, *pg.* 192
LIVEBACK - Seating - STEELCASE INC.; *pg.* 475, *pg.* 889
LIVEBAR - Social Networking - LIVEWORLD, INC.; *pg.* 1264, *pg.* 246
LIVECAPTURE - Software - INTELLICORP, INC.; *pg.* 417, *pg.* 268
LIVECOMPARE - Software - INTELLICORP, INC.; *pg.* 417, *pg.* 268
LIVECYCLE - Software - ADOBE SYSTEMS INCORPORATED; *pg.* 342, *pg.* 235
LIVEDAILY - Entertainment News Website - IAC/INTERACTIVECORP; *pg.* 292, *pg.* 1242
LIVEINTERFACE - Software - INTELLICORP, INC.; *pg.* 417, *pg.* 268
LIVELED - Lighting Systems - REVOLUTION LIGHTING TECHNOLOGIES, INC.; *pg.* 1304, *pg.* 377
LIVELED 100 - Lighting Systems - REVOLUTION LIGHTING TECHNOLOGIES, INC.; *pg.* 1304, *pg.* 377
LIVELED 12 - Lighting Systems - REVOLUTION LIGHTING TECHNOLOGIES, INC.; *pg.* 1304, *pg.* 377
LIVELED 35 - Lighting Systems - REVOLUTION LIGHTING TECHNOLOGIES, INC.; *pg.* 1304, *pg.* 377
LIVELED BEAM BLASTER - Lighting Systems - REVOLUTION LIGHTING TECHNOLOGIES, INC.; *pg.* 1304, *pg.* 377
LIVELINK - Simulation Tool - RAYTHEON COMPANY; *pg.* 233, *pg.* 854
LIVELINK HLA - Simulation Tool - RAYTHEON COMPANY; *pg.* 233, *pg.* 854
LIVEMODEL - Software - INTELLICORP, INC.; *pg.* 417, *pg.* 268
LIVEMONITOR - Software - INTELLICORP, INC.; *pg.* 417, *pg.* 268
LIVEPAUSE - Digital Media System - REALNETWORKS, INC.; *pg.* 460, *pg.* 1839
LIVER GUARD - Vitamin & Herbal Supplement - SOURCE NATURALS; *pg.* 1595, *pg.* 278
LIVESCAN - Software - 3M; *pg.* 339, *pg.* 179
LIVESECURITY - Software - WATCHGUARD TECHNOLOGIES, INC.; *pg.* 491, *pg.* 1842
LIVESTATE - Software - SYMANTEC CORPORATION; *pg.* 478, *pg.* 161
LIVESTATE - Storage System - SYMANTEC CORPORATION; *pg.* 479, *pg.* 1753
LIVETYPE - Application Program - APPLE INC.; *pg.* 350, *pg.* 73
LIVEUPDATE - Software - SYMANTEC CORPORATION; *pg.* 478, *pg.* 161
LIVEWIRE - Catheters - ST. JUDE MEDICAL, INC.; *pg.* 1596, *pg.* 963
LIVEWIRE MOBILE - Wireless Technology - ONMOBILE LIVE, INC.; *pg.* 449, *pg.* 829
LIVEWIRE TC - Catheters - ST. JUDE MEDICAL, INC.; *pg.* 1596, *pg.* 963
LIVEWIRE911 - Emergency Services Provider - TELECOMMUNICATION SYSTEMS INC.; *pg.* 483, *pg.* 754
LIVIAL - Medicine - MERCK & CO., INC.; *pg.* 1566, *pg.* 1077
LIVIAN - Medical Device - BOSTON SCIENTIFIC CORPORATION; *pg.* 1508, *pg.* 831
LIVING - Dog Toy - THE HARTZ MOUNTAIN CORP.; *pg.* 1476, *pg.* 1120
THE LIVING BALANCE SHEET - Insurance Service - THE GUARDIAN LIFE INSURANCE COMPANY OF AMERICA; *pg.* 1202, *pg.* 1237
LIVING BOOKS - Christian Literature - TYNDALE HOUSE PUBLISHERS, INC.; *pg.* 1697, *pg.* 561
LIVING BRINGS IT IN. WE TAKE IT OUT. - Slogan - STANLEY STEEMER INTERNATIONAL, INC.; *pg.* 944, *pg.* 1450
LIVING CALCIUM - Health Supplement - GARDEN OF LIFE, INC.; *pg.* 1532, *pg.* 478
LIVING FLOWER - Scent Extraction Technology - INTERNATIONAL FLAVORS & FRAGRANCES INC.; *pg.* 512, *pg.* 1244
LIVING FOODS - Staple Food - GARDEN OF LIFE, INC.; *pg.* 1532, *pg.* 478
LIVING FRUIT - Scent Extraction Technology - INTERNATIONAL FLAVORS & FRAGRANCES INC.; *pg.* 512, *pg.* 1244
LIVING LANGUAGE - Publishing Imprint - PENGUIN RANDOM HOUSE; *pg.* 1675, *pg.* 1276
LIVING MEMORIAL - Tree Planting Program - BATESVILLE CASKET COMPANY, INC.; *pg.* 1393, *pg.* 673
LIVING MULTI - Health Supplement - GARDEN OF LIFE, INC.; *pg.* 1532, *pg.* 478
LIVING PROOF - Tagline - THE QUAKER OATS COMPANY; *pg.* 834, *pg.* 588
LIVING PUPPETS - Puppets - GUND, INC.; *pg.* 954, *pg.* 1056
LIVING SMARTER - Health Plan & Publication - MEDICA, INC.; *pg.* 1208, *pg.* 949
LIVING THE LIFE LOVING MY COURISTAN - Slogan - COURISTAN INC.; *pg.* 921, *pg.* 1067
LIVING VITAMIN C - Health Supplement - GARDEN OF LIFE, INC.; *pg.* 1532, *pg.* 478
LIVING WEDGE - Tools - VAUGHAN & BUSHNELL MANUFACTURING COMPANY, INC.; *pg.* 1066, *pg.* 616
LIVING WONDERS - Biological Product - CAROLINA BIOLOGICAL SUPPLY COMPANY; *pg.* 1513, *pg.* 1359
LIVING WORLD - Pet Product - PETSMART, INC.; *pg.* 1481, *pg.* 18
LIVINGSOCIAL - Social Buying, Instant Deals Smartphone Application - LIVINGSOCIAL, INC.; *pg.* 1264, *pg.* 401
LIVINGSTON - Guest Chairs - BERNHARDT DESIGN; *pg.* 918, *pg.* 1381
LIVINGSTON CELLARS - Wine - E&J GALLO WINERY; *pg.* 1962, *pg.* 149
LIVINGSTONE - Essentials Kit - LEVENGER COMPANY; *pg.* 1776, *pg.* 421
LIVINGSTYLE - Furniture - LEXINGTON HOME BRANDS; *pg.* 933, *pg.* 1391
LIVINGXL - Online & Print Catalog - DESTINATION XL GROUP, INC.; *pg.* 40, *pg.* 810
LIVOSTIN - Healthcare Product - JOHNSON & JOHNSON; *pg.* 1549, *pg.* 1091
LIX REAGENTS - Solvent Extraction Reagents - HENKEL CORPORATION; *pg.* 1165, *pg.* 1535
LIXOTINIC - Liquid Vitamin & Iron Supplement for Animals - PFIZER INC.; *pg.* 1581, *pg.* 1278
LIZ - Footwear - PHOENIX FOOTWEAR GROUP, INC.; *pg.* 1815, *pg.* 60
LIZ & ME - Apparel - ASCENA RETAIL GROUP, INC.; *pg.* 18, *pg.* 1081
LIZ CLAIBORNE - Women's Apparel - J.C. PENNEY COMPANY, INC.; *pg.* 1774, *pg.* 1732
LIZ CLAIBORNE - Sunglasses & Readers - SAFILO USA INC.; *pg.* 11, *pg.* 1106
LIZ CLAIBORNE COLLECTION - Optical Quality Sunglasses - SAFILO USA INC.; *pg.* 11, *pg.* 1106
LIZARD LIGHT - Flashlight - ENERGIZER HOLDINGS, INC.; *pg.* 637, *pg.* 996
LIZARD LUSTER - Body Lotion - ORANGE PEEL ENTERPRISES, INC.; *pg.* 1028, *pg.* 477
LJUNGSTROM - Rotary Air Preheaters - ABB INC.; *pg.* 1309, *pg.* 1359
LK - Chemical Products - AIR PRODUCTS AND CHEMICALS, INC.; *pg.* 1145, *pg.* 1513
LK BEAUTY IS IN THE CUTTING - Diamond Jewelry - LAZARE KAPLAN INTERNATIONAL, INC.; *pg.* 8, *pg.* 1250
LLANO - Furniture - AMERICAN LEATHER LP; *pg.* 912, *pg.* 1673
LLAZA - Retractable Awnings - ANCHOR INDUSTRIES, INC.; *pg.* 1825, *pg.* 678
LLCWDM - Fiber Optic Component - OPLINK COMMUNICATIONS, INC.; *pg.* 660, *pg.* 91
LLD EZ - Lead Locking Devices - THE SPECTRANETICS CORPORATION; *pg.* 1595, *pg.* 315
LLF - LED - CREE INC.; *pg.* 631, *pg.* 1371
LLOYD - Mattress - THERAPEDIC ASSOCIATES, INC.; *pg.* 945, *pg.* 1112
LLOYD AND PENFIELD - Mattress - THERAPEDIC ASSOCIATES, INC.; *pg.* 945, *pg.* 1112
LLOYD'S - Barbecue Products - HORMEL FOODS CORPORATION; *pg.* 863, *pg.* 915
LLS - LED - CREE INC.; *pg.* 631, *pg.* 1371
LLYNXINSURE++ - Analysis & Visualization Tools for LynxOS Applications - LYNX SOFTWARE TECHNOLOGIES; *pg.* 429, *pg.* 247
LM-EXPRESS - Messages & Other Digital Information Storage & Transmitting Applications - LOCKHEED MARTIN CORPORATION; *pg.* 229, *pg.* 762
LM PEOPLE - Computer Software Consultation - LOCKHEED MARTIN CORPORATION; *pg.* 229, *pg.* 762
LM SERIES - Line Matrix Printers - RICOH PRINTING SYSTEMS AMERICA, INC.; *pg.* 462, *pg.* 279
LM-STAR - Computer Controlled Test Equipment - LOCKHEED MARTIN CORPORATION; *pg.* 229, *pg.* 762
LMAX - Microplate Reader System - MOLECULAR DEVICES CORPORATION; *pg.* 1568, *pg.* 287
LMC - Systems Integration & Aeronautics - LOCKHEED MARTIN CORPORATION; *pg.* 229, *pg.* 762
LMCO - Systems Integration & Aeronautics - LOCKHEED MARTIN CORPORATION; *pg.* 229, *pg.* 762
LMS - Loan Management Software - SS&C TECHNOLOGIES HOLDINGS, INC.; *pg.* 473, *pg.* 386
LMS IPRO4 - Inspection System - KLA-TENCOR CORPORATION; *pg.* 1353, *pg.* 146
LMS LOAN SUITE - Software - SS&C TECHNOLOGIES HOLDINGS, INC.; *pg.* 473, *pg.* 386
LMS ORIGINATOR - Software - SS&C TECHNOLOGIES HOLDINGS, INC.; *pg.* 473, *pg.* 386
LMS SERVICER - Software - SS&C TECHNOLOGIES HOLDINGS, INC.; *pg.* 473, *pg.* 386
LMX - Soil Extraction System - VON SCHRADER COMPANY;

pg. 62, *pg.* 1890
LNC - Lincoln National Corporation - LINCOLN NATIONAL CORPORATION; *pg.* 776, *pg.* 1567
LNC CARTON - Egg Substitute - MICHAEL FOODS, INC.; *pg.* 877, *pg.* 949
LNCS - Invivo Sensors - MASIMO CORPORATION; *pg.* 1558, *pg.* 113
LNL - Software System - MENTOR GRAPHICS CORPORATION; *pg.* 432, *pg.* 1510
LNOP - Blue Sensors - MASIMO CORPORATION; *pg.* 1558, *pg.* 113
LNP DATA SERVER - Software - EVOLVING SYSTEMS, INC.; *pg.* 395, *pg.* 326
LNRM - Lincoln National Risk Management - LINCOLN NATIONAL CORPORATION; *pg.* 776, *pg.* 1567
LNS - Software - ECHELON CORPORATION; *pg.* 389, *pg.* 245
LO-CAL - Beverage - SPRECHER BREWING COMPANY; *pg.* 265, *pg.* 1858
LO-CAP - Foil Shield - GENERAL CABLE CORPORATION; *pg.* 83, *pg.* 729
LO-CARB CONEY BOWL - Low-carbohydrate Chili - SKYLINE CHILI, INC.; *pg.* 1033, *pg.* 1452
LO-COG - Brush Motor - PENN ENGINEERING & MANUFACTURING CORP.; *pg.* 1059, *pg.* 1525
LO-CONTOUR - Tracheal Tube - MEDTRONIC; *pg.* 1563, *pg.* 183
LO-DOWN BLUES - Fertilizer - SIMPLOT PARTNERS INC.; *pg.* 1800, *pg.* 548
LO-ERODE - Pressed & Monolithic Refractory - RESCO PRODUCTS, INC.; *pg.* 107, *pg.* 1581
LO-FLO - Regulators - ELSTER AMERICAN METER COMPANY; *pg.* 1411, *pg.* 1387
LO-HAT - Tripods & Supports - ALAN GORDON ENTERPRISES, INC.; *pg.* 1399, *pg.* 125
LO-KUT - Socks - WIGWAM MILLS, INC.; *pg.* 15, *pg.* 1894
LO LO - Ball - SCHOOL-TECH, INC.; *pg.* 1844, *pg.* 866
LO-NOX - Burner - MAXON CORPORATION; *pg.* 1359, *pg.* 695
LO-PRO - Tracheal Tube - MEDTRONIC; *pg.* 1563, *pg.* 183
LO-PRO - Adhesive - R.C.A. RUBBER COMPANY; *pg.* 1888, *pg.* 1402
LO-ROOT - Screws - ROBERTSON INC.; *pg.* 1372, *pg.* 1924
LO-SET - Pressed & Monolithic Refractory - RESCO PRODUCTS, INC.; *pg.* 107, *pg.* 1581
LO-SIL - Pressed & Monolithic Refractory - RESCO PRODUCTS, INC.; *pg.* 107, *pg.* 1581
LO-TOW - In-Floor Towline - PARAGON TECHNOLOGIES, INC.; *pg.* 1367, *pg.* 1528
LO-VEL - Flatting Agents for Industrial Arts Applications - PPG INDUSTRIES, INC.; *pg.* 1445, *pg.* 1579
LOA - Photonic Instrument - NEWPORT CORPORATION; *pg.* 1424, *pg.* 114
LOAD CONTROLLER II - On Board Air System - AIR LIFT COMPANY; *pg.* 198, *pg.* 895
LOAD CUSHION - Accumulator - CASCADE CORPORATION; *pg.* 1321, *pg.* 1497
LOAD KING - Axle Trailer - TEREX CORPORATION; *pg.* 1381, *pg.* 384
LOAD PROBE - Test - MAXIM INTEGRATED PRODUCTS, INC.; *pg.* 653, *pg.* 247
LOAD RUNNERS - Idler Rollers - OSBORN INTERNATIONAL; *pg.* 1367, *pg.* 1406
LOAD-SPAN - Truck Product - OSHKOSH CORPORATION; *pg.* 187, *pg.* 1885
LOAD TRAQ - Sterilizer Load Tracking System - AESCULAP, INC.; *pg.* 1487, *pg.* 1521
LOADALERT - Temperature Control - AERCO INTERNATIONAL INC.; *pg.* 1068, *pg.* 1142
LOADBUSTER - Tool - S&C ELECTRIC COMPANY; *pg.* 1305, *pg.* 589
LOADBUSTER DISCONNECT - Disconnect Switch - S&C ELECTRIC COMPANY; *pg.* 1305, *pg.* 589
LOADBUSTER DISCONNECTS - Loadbreak Tool - S&C ELECTRIC COMPANY; *pg.* 1305, *pg.* 589
LOADDXF - Software - TRIMBLE NAVIGATION LIMITED; *pg.* 1384, *pg.* 288
LOADERXPRESS - Enterprise Tape Library - OVERLAND STORAGE, INC.; *pg.* 451, *pg.* 205
LOADHOG - Battery - ENERSYS INC.; *pg.* 1334, *pg.* 1584
LOADMASTER - Pallet Wrap - AEP INDUSTRIES INC.; *pg.* 1878, *pg.* 1085
LOADMASTER - Lip System - ESCO CORPORATION; *pg.* 1335, *pg.* 1502
LOADMATCH - Cooling System - TACO INCORPORATED; *pg.* 1077, *pg.* 1601
LOADPLUS - IMS Database Utility - BMC SOFTWARE, INC.; *pg.* 362, *pg.* 1701
LOADRIGHT - Bulk Bag Carrier System - SONOCO PRODUCTS COMPANY; *pg.* 1469, *pg.* 1619
LOADSTAR - Container Crane Wire Rope - WIRECO WORLDGROUP; *pg.* 1389, *pg.* 987
LOADTRAC - Thermal Processing Equipment - SURFACE COMBUSTION, INC.; *pg.* 1077, *pg.* 1462
LOADUMPER - Handling Product - C.R. DANIELS, INC.; *pg.* 1456, *pg.* 769
LOANET - Software - SUNGARD DATA SYSTEMS INC.; *pg.* 477, *pg.* 1592
LOASTOFLEX - Coupling - LORD CORPORATION; *pg.* 1357, *pg.* 1360
LOBASE - Polymer Product - CHEMTURA CORPORATION; *pg.* 1152, *pg.* 355
LOBBYGUARD - Tracking System - PITNEY BOWES INC.; *pg.* 454, *pg.* 376
LOBE-AIRE - Positive Displacement Blower - THE SPENCER TURBINE CO.; *pg.* 1378, *pg.* 386
LOBE BLAST - Hygienic Product - GEA FARM TECHNOLOGIES; *pg.* 704, *pg.* 636
LOBLAW - Food Distribution - GEORGE WESTON LIMITED; *pg.* 858, *pg.* 1938
LOBO - Character - DC COMICS, INC.; *pg.* 1633, *pg.* 1221
LOBOY - Truck Seating - SEATS INCORPORATED; *pg.* 217, *pg.* 1890
LOBSTER KING - Specialty cutters - LINCOLN FOODSERVICE PRODUCTS, LLC; *pg.* 1127, *pg.* 1432
L.O.C. - Liquid Organic Cleaner - AMWAY CORPORATION; *pg.* 326, *pg.* 864
LOC - Pipe Thread Sealant - LA-CO INDUSTRIES MARKAL CO., INC.; *pg.* 1170, *pg.* 610
LOC DOT - Fluid Handling System - GRACO, INC.; *pg.* 1342, *pg.* 935
LOC-LEGS - Kitchen Organizer - HOME PRODUCTS INTERNATIONAL, INC.; *pg.* 1125, *pg.* 577
LOCAAS - Systems Integration & Aeronautics - LOCKHEED MARTIN CORPORATION; *pg.* 229, *pg.* 762
LOCAL COPY PLUS - Software - BMC SOFTWARE, INC.; *pg.* 362, *pg.* 1701
LOCAL PEOPLE SERVING LOCAL NEEDS - Tag Line - PLUMAS BANCORP; *pg.* 794, *pg.* 186
LOCAL.COM - Software - LOCAL.COM CORPORATION; *pg.* 1264, *pg.* 113
LOCALE - Fabric - NEMSCHOFF, INC.; *pg.* 936, *pg.* 1890
LOCALMOTION - Database - NIELSEN AUDIO; *pg.* 446, *pg.* 768
LOCALTALK - Computer Cable System & Network - APPLE INC.; *pg.* 350, *pg.* 73
LOCARNO - Footwear - K-SWISS; *pg.* 1837, *pg.* 306
LOCATE A POST OFFICE - Postal Services - UNITED STATES POSTAL SERVICE; *pg.* 1009, *pg.* 406
LOCATOR - Dental Implant System - LIFECORE BIOMEDICAL, LLC; *pg.* 1556, *pg.* 920
LOCATOR - Implant Tool - ST. JUDE MEDICAL, INC.; *pg.* 1596, *pg.* 963
LOCHMOR S - Fly Reels - DAIWA CORPORATION; *pg.* 1832, *pg.* 75
LOCK & LOAD - Metal Security Locks - MASTER LOCK COMPANY LLC; *pg.* 1055, *pg.* 1884
LOCK & RIDE - Cargo System - POLARIS INDUSTRIES INC.; *pg.* 1709, *pg.* 928
LOCK-EASE - Lock Fluid - AMERICAN GREASE STICK CO.; *pg.* 971, *pg.* 902
LOCK JAWS - Clip - BROWN & BIGELOW, INC.; *pg.* 1624, *pg.* 959
LOCK-N-LIFT - Universal Air Spring Spacer - AIR LIFT COMPANY; *pg.* 198, *pg.* 895
LOCK-O-RING - Valve - T.D. WILLIAMSON, INC.; *pg.* 1380, *pg.* 1490
LOCK-RIVET - Metal Building System - BUTLER MANUFACTURING COMPANY; *pg.* 72, *pg.* 981
LOCK-TEMP - Storage Tank - LOCHINVAR CORPORATION; *pg.* 1073, *pg.* 1640
LOCK TITE - Manual Shut-off Valve - ECLIPSE INC.; *pg.* 1332, *pg.* 655
LOCK-TITE - Anchored Flooring - ROBBINS, INC.; *pg.* 108, *pg.* 1425
LOCKBOX - Online Financial Services - ACI WORLDWIDE; *pg.* 710, *pg.* 1777
LOCKDOWN EDITION - Software - WEBSENSE, INC.; *pg.* 491, *pg.* 210
LOCKER SLIDE - Men's Footwear - UNDER ARMOUR, INC.; *pg.* 49, *pg.* 759
LOCKERS.COM - Online Shopping Website - SALSBURY INDUSTRIES; *pg.* 464, *pg.* 139
LOCKERTAG - Sport Apparel - UNDER ARMOUR, INC.; *pg.* 49, *pg.* 759
LOCKETS - Candy - WM. WRIGLEY JR. COMPANY; *pg.* 1863, *pg.* 596
LOCKHEED - Systems Integration & Aeronautics - LOCKHEED MARTIN CORPORATION; *pg.* 229, *pg.* 762
LOCKING COMPRESSION PLATE - Medical Device - DEPUY SYNTHES; *pg.* 1523, *pg.* 1593
LOCKLINK - Locking System - OSHKOSH CORPORATION; *pg.* 187, *pg.* 1885
LOCKNETICS - Electronic Access Control - INGERSOLL-RAND COMPANY; *pg.* 1349, *pg.* 1370
LOCKON - Toy Train - LIONEL LLC; *pg.* 961, *pg.* 875
LOCKON - Computer Software - NOVELL INC.; *pg.* 446, *pg.* 852
LOCKSLEY DAMASK - Fabric - SCALAMANDRE, INC.; *pg.* 941, *pg.* 1058
LOCKVAULT - Software - NETAPP, INC.; *pg.* 444, *pg.* 287
LOCO BLUE - Junior Women's Apparel - A&E STORES, INC.; *pg.* 17, *pg.* 1124
LOCOLOC - Oval and Stop Sleeves - LOOS & COMPANY, INC.; *pg.* 1356, *pg.* 368
LOCOMOTION - Cable - THE HEARST CORPORATION; *pg.* 1649, *pg.* 1239
LOCTITE - Consumer Adhesives - HENKEL CONSUMER ADHESIVES, INC.; *pg.* 403, *pg.* 1480
LOCTITE - Adhesive - HENKEL CORPORATION; *pg.* 1165, *pg.* 1535
LODELOK - Metal Hooks - COLUMBUS MCKINNON CORPORATION; *pg.* 1325, *pg.* 1138
LODEN - Fabric - NEMSCHOFF, INC.; *pg.* 936, *pg.* 1890
LODESTAR - Hoist - COLUMBUS MCKINNON CORPORATION; *pg.* 1325, *pg.* 1138
LODESTAR - Systems Integration & Aeronautics - LOCKHEED MARTIN CORPORATION; *pg.* 229, *pg.* 762
LODESTAR - Children's Hardcover Books - PENGUIN RANDOM HOUSE; *pg.* 1675, *pg.* 1276
LODGEMASTER - Debit Card - MASTERCARD INCORPORATED; *pg.* 779, *pg.* 1325
LOEW-CORNELL - Consumer Product - JARDEN CORPORATION; *pg.* 1885, *pg.* 412
LOEWENSTEIN - Furniture - BROWN JORDAN INTERNATIONAL COMPANY; *pg.* 919, *pg.* 740
LOEWS - Hotels & Resorts - LOEWS HOTELS HOLDING CORPORATION; *pg.* 1101, *pg.* 1252
LOFENALAC - Infant Formula - MEAD JOHNSON NUTRITION COMPANY; *pg.* 1561, *pg.* 615
LOFERO - Refractory Product - RESCO PRODUCTS, INC.; *pg.* 107, *pg.* 1581
LOFERO HM - Pressed & Monolithic Refractory - RESCO PRODUCTS, INC.; *pg.* 107, *pg.* 1581
L'OFFICE - Home Office Construction - KB HOME; *pg.* 90, *pg.* 134
LOFIBRA - Pharmaceutical Product - IMPAX LABORATORIES, INC.; *pg.* 1544, *pg.* 101
LOFT - Software - XEROX CORPORATION; *pg.* 494, *pg.* 365
LOFT POLO - Apparels - UNDER ARMOUR, INC.; *pg.* 49, *pg.* 759
LOFTEEZ - Activewear - FRUIT OF THE LOOM, INC.; *pg.* 41, *pg.* 725
LOG 911 - Newsletter - EASTMAN KODAK COMPANY; *pg.* 1408, *pg.* 1333
LOG CABIN - Fan - CRAFTMADE INTERNATIONAL, INC.; *pg.* 1295, *pg.* 1670
LOG CABIN - Syrup & Pancake Mix - PINNACLE FOODS GROUP LLC; *pg.* 889, *pg.* 1104
LOGAN - Dolls - AMERICAN GIRL LLC; *pg.* 949, *pg.* 1871
LOGAN - Leather Product - COACH, INC.; *pg.* 3, *pg.* 1214
LOGAN - Furniture - HOOKER FURNITURE CORPORATION; *pg.* 928, *pg.* 1788
LOGAN - Furniture - JASPER GROUP; *pg.* 930, *pg.* 691
LOGAN - Lighting Product - QUOIZEL INC.; *pg.* 1304, *pg.* 1616
LOGIC - Software Product - APPLE INC.; *pg.* 350, *pg.* 73
LOGIC - Printing Product - ELECTRONICS FOR IMAGING, INC.; *pg.* 390, *pg.* 88
LOGIC - Family Sampler Kit - THE HILSINGER CO.; *pg.* 1416, *pg.* 841
LOGIC - Apparel - OAKLEY, INC.; *pg.* 1840, *pg.* 86
LOGIC - Surgical Instrument - OSTEOMED CORPORATION; *pg.* 1425, *pg.* 1658
LOGIC - Fire Ant Bait - UNIVERSAL COOPERATIVES, INC.;

pg. 1482, *pg.* 922
LOGIC 7 - Software - HARMAN INTERNATIONAL INDUSTRIES, INCORPORATED; *pg.* 641, *pg.* 374
LOGIC BUILDER - Software System - MENTOR GRAPHICS CORPORATION; *pg.* 432, *pg.* 1510
LOGIC CELL ARRAYS - Xilinx Devices - XILINX, INC.; *pg.* 496, *pg.* 252
LOGIC DOUBLING - Programmable Logic - ATMEL CORPORATION; *pg.* 621, *pg.* 238
LOGIC HR. - Surgical Instrument - OSTEOMED CORPORATION; *pg.* 1425, *pg.* 1658
LOGIC PRO X - Application - APPLE INC.; *pg.* 350, *pg.* 73
LOGIC STUDIO - Software Product - APPLE INC.; *pg.* 350, *pg.* 73
LOGICAL CABLE - Software System - MENTOR GRAPHICS CORPORATION; *pg.* 432, *pg.* 1510
THE LOGICAL CHOICE - Slogan - BRENNAN INDUSTRIES INC.; *pg.* 1319, *pg.* 1429
LOGICBIST - Software System - MENTOR GRAPHICS CORPORATION; *pg.* 432, *pg.* 1510
LOGICLIB - Software System - MENTOR GRAPHICS CORPORATION; *pg.* 432, *pg.* 1510
LOGICLOCK - Software - ALTERA CORPORATION; *pg.* 348, *pg.* 237
LOGICOMM - Pattern Control & Verification System - NORDSON CORPORATION; *pg.* 1365, *pg.* 1480
LOGICORE - Predefined Cores of Logic Developed byXilinx - XILINX, INC.; *pg.* 496, *pg.* 252
LOGICPRO - Software - WATLOW ELECTRIC MANUFACTURING COMPANY; *pg.* 1078, *pg.* 1004
LOGICSOURCE - Computer Software - NOVELL INC.; *pg.* 446, *pg.* 852
LOGILITY VOYAGER COLLABORATE - Supply Chain Management Software - LOGILITY, INC.; *pg.* 428, *pg.* 513
LOGILITY VOYAGER SOLUTIONS - Supply Chain Management Software - LOGILITY, INC.; *pg.* 428, *pg.* 513
LOGINDATA - Telephone Service - IDT CORPORATION; *pg.* 643, *pg.* 1096
LOGIO - Software System - MENTOR GRAPHICS CORPORATION; *pg.* 432, *pg.* 1510
LOGIQ 3 - Medical Device - GE HEALTHCARE TECHNOLOGIES; *pg.* 1533, *pg.* 1897
LOGIQ 5 - Medical Device - GE HEALTHCARE TECHNOLOGIES; *pg.* 1533, *pg.* 1897
LOGIQ 7 - Medical Device - GE HEALTHCARE TECHNOLOGIES; *pg.* 1533, *pg.* 1897
LOGIQ 9 - Medical Device - GE HEALTHCARE TECHNOLOGIES; *pg.* 1533, *pg.* 1897
LOGIQ BOOK - Medical Device - GE HEALTHCARE TECHNOLOGIES; *pg.* 1533, *pg.* 1897
LOGITENN - Test Equipment - SPX THERMAL PRODUCT SOLUTIONS; *pg.* 1378, *pg.* 1555
LOGIX - Valve - FLOWSERVE CORPORATION; *pg.* 82, *pg.* 1719
LOGIX CONTROLLERS - Controllers for Autotrol Softener & Media Filter Valves - GE WATER & PROCESS TECHNOLOGIES; *pg.* 1339, *pg.* 1588
LOGMASTER - Software - BMC SOFTWARE, INC.; *pg.* 362, *pg.* 1701
LOGMEIN - Remote Computer Connectivity Product - LOGMEIN, INC.; *pg.* 428, *pg.* 861
LOGMEIN BACKUP - Remote Computer Connectivity Product - LOGMEIN, INC.; *pg.* 428, *pg.* 861
LOGMEIN CENTRAL - Remote Computer Connectivity Product - LOGMEIN, INC.; *pg.* 428, *pg.* 861
LOGMEIN FREE - Remote Computer Connectivity Product - LOGMEIN, INC.; *pg.* 428, *pg.* 861
LOGMEIN GRAVITY - Remote Computer Connectivity Product - LOGMEIN, INC.; *pg.* 428, *pg.* 861
LOGMEIN HAMACHI - Remote Computer Connectivity Product - LOGMEIN, INC.; *pg.* 428, *pg.* 861
LOGMEIN IGNITION - Remote Computer Connectivity Product - LOGMEIN, INC.; *pg.* 428, *pg.* 861
LOGMEIN IT REACH - Remote Computer Connectivity Product - LOGMEIN, INC.; *pg.* 428, *pg.* 861
LOGMEIN PRO - Remote Computer Connectivity Product - LOGMEIN, INC.; *pg.* 428, *pg.* 861
LOGMEIN RESCUE - Remote Computer Connectivity Product - LOGMEIN, INC.; *pg.* 428, *pg.* 861
LOGO EXPRESS - Headwear - MINE SAFETY APPLIANCES COMPANY; *pg.* 1361, *pg.* 1525
LOGOPORT - Software - LIONBRIDGE TECHNOLOGIES INC.; *pg.* 428, *pg.* 851
LOIS - Jewelry - UNCAS MANUFACTURING COMPANY; *pg.* 15, *pg.* 1608
LOIS LANE - Character - DC COMICS, INC.; *pg.* 1633, *pg.* 1221
LOJACK VEHICLE RECOVERY SYSTEM - Vehicle Tracking - LOJACK CORPORATION; *pg.* 210, *pg.* 811
LOK-ALL - Locker - AMERICAN LOCKER GROUP INCORPORATED; *pg.* 1041, *pg.* 1674
LOK-ALL - Locker - AMERICAN LOCKER SECURITY SYSTEMS, INC.; *pg.* 1042, *pg.* 1674
LOK-BOLT - Sleeve Anchor - POWERS FASTENERS INC.; *pg.* 1059, *pg.* 1143
LOK-DOWEL - Dowel Pin - DRIV-LOK, INC.; *pg.* 1046, *pg.* 662
LOK-FAST, SEMIFLEX, WEBLOK - Boxspring Components - LEGGETT & PLATT, INCORPORATED; *pg.* 933, *pg.* 974
LOK-GARD - Cleaning Product - HILLYARD, INC.; *pg.* 331, *pg.* 990
LOK-RIM - Fibre Drum - GREIF INC.; *pg.* 1459, *pg.* 1447
LOK-SUR - Tamper-Evident Closure - SEALED AIR CORPORATION; *pg.* 1468, *pg.* 1058
LOK-TOR - Power Tool - MILWAUKEE ELECTRIC TOOL CORP.; *pg.* 1056, *pg.* 1855
LOKATOP - Personal Care Product - WESTROCK COMPANY; *pg.* 1472, *pg.* 1805
LOLA - Clipper - ANDIS COMPANY; *pg.* 498, *pg.* 1895
LOLA - Fabric - NEMSCHOFF, INC.; *pg.* 936, *pg.* 1890
LOLLIPALOOZA - Dolls - THE GOLDBERGER COMPANY, LLC; *pg.* 954, *pg.* 1235
LOLO - Furniture - AMISCO INDUSTRIES LTD.; *pg.* 913, *pg.* 1958
LOLO - Molecular Probe Product - THERMO FISHER SCIENTIFIC INC.; *pg.* 1602, *pg.* 61
LOLO TINT - Cuprous Oxide - AMERICAN CHEMET CORPORATION; *pg.* 1147, *pg.* 599
LOLON - Hardware - LOOS & COMPANY, INC.; *pg.* 1356, *pg.* 368
LOMA LINDA - Meat Alternatives - KELLOGG COMPANY; *pg.* 831, *pg.* 870
LOMBARD - Lighting Product - QUOIZEL INC.; *pg.* 1304, *pg.* 1616
LOMBARDO - Wine - SHAW ROSS INTERNATIONAL IMPORTERS; *pg.* 1970, *pg.* 449
LOMOTIL - Medicine - PFIZER INC.; *pg.* 1581, *pg.* 1278
LON - Internet Servers - ECHELON CORPORATION; *pg.* 389, *pg.* 245
LON CHLOR - Chemical Product - BIRKO CORPORATION; *pg.* 1149, *pg.* 332
LONBUILDER - Software - ECHELON CORPORATION; *pg.* 389, *pg.* 245
LONDON - Furniture - AMERICAN LEATHER LP; *pg.* 912, *pg.* 1673
LONDON - Textiles - BERNHARDT DESIGN; *pg.* 918, *pg.* 1381
LONDON CLASSIC - Carpet - BEAULIEU GROUP, LLC; *pg.* 917, *pg.* 529
LONDON FOG - Apparel - ICONIX BRAND GROUP, INC.; *pg.* 26, *pg.* 1243
LONE STAR - Video Game - BALLY TECHNOLOGIES, INC.; *pg.* 531, *pg.* 1022
LONE STAR - Footwear - COBIAN CORP.; *pg.* 1806, *pg.* 253
LONE STAR - Beer - PABST BREWING COMPANY; *pg.* 258, *pg.* 137
LONE STAR - Designer Fragrance - PARFUMS DE COEUR LTD.; *pg.* 519, *pg.* 376
LONE STAR LIGHT - Light Beer - PABST BREWING COMPANY; *pg.* 258, *pg.* 137
LONESTAR - Uniforms - BLAUER MANUFACTURING COMPANY, INC.; *pg.* 20, *pg.* 789
LONESTAR - Footwear - STEVEN MADDEN, LTD.; *pg.* 1819, *pg.* 1176
LONEWS - Software - ECHELON CORPORATION; *pg.* 389, *pg.* 245
LONG CUT COUGAR - Moist Tobacco - AMERICAN SNUFF COMPANY; *pg.* 1893, *pg.* 1641
LONG DISTANCE TO GO - Communication Product - CENTURYLINK, INC; *pg.* 1870, *pg.* 317
LONG HAMMER IPA - Beverage - CRAFT BREWERS ALLIANCE, INC; *pg.* 247, *pg.* 1502
THE LONG ISLAND RAIL ROAD - Commuter Rail Service - LONG ISLAND RAIL ROAD; *pg.* 1914, *pg.* 1170
LONG JACK POWER MAX 200 - Nutritional Product - NUTRACEUTICAL INTERNATIONAL CORPORATION; *pg.* 1576, *pg.* 1753
LONG JOHN SILVERS - Fast Food - YUM! BRANDS, INC.; *pg.* 1756, *pg.* 738
LONG KEY - Carpet - BEAULIEU GROUP, LLC; *pg.* 917, *pg.* 529
LONG LEASE - Premium Roll Covers - VAIL RUBBER WORKS, INC.; *pg.* 1891, *pg.* 906
LONG LEASE III - Premium Roll Covers - VAIL RUBBER WORKS, INC.; *pg.* 1891, *pg.* 906
LONG-LIFE - Air Gun - BOLT TECHNOLOGY CORPORATION; *pg.* 1318, *pg.* 360
LONG-LIFE - Microchannel Plate - PHOTONIS USA PENNSYLVANIA; *pg.* 663, *pg.* 1547
LONG-LOK - Self-Locking Fasteners - LONG-LOK FASTENERS CORP.; *pg.* 1053, *pg.* 1416
LONG 'N LUSH - Mascara - COVER GIRL COSMETICS; *pg.* 506, *pg.* 772
LONG NECK - Wine - SHAW ROSS INTERNATIONAL IMPORTERS; *pg.* 1970, *pg.* 449
LONG RANGE ACOUSTIC DEVICE - Electronic Product - LRAD CORPORATION; *pg.* 652, *pg.* 204
LONG SHOT - Aluminum Beach Chaise - TELESCOPE CASUAL FURNITURE INC.; *pg.* 944, *pg.* 1162
LONG TRAIL II - Glove - KOMBI, LTD.; *pg.* 1838, *pg.* 1766
LONGABERGER TO GO - Basket - THE LONGABERGER COMPANY; *pg.* 1127, *pg.* 1467
LONGBOW - Systems Integration & Aeronautics - LOCKHEED MARTIN CORPORATION; *pg.* 229, *pg.* 762
LONGBOW HELLFIRE - Systems Integration & Aeronautics - LOCKHEED MARTIN CORPORATION; *pg.* 229, *pg.* 762
LONGCHAMP - Fabric - NEMSCHOFF, INC.; *pg.* 936, *pg.* 1890
LONGHORN STEAKHOUSE - Restaurant Chain - DARDEN RESTAURANTS, INC.; *pg.* 1724, *pg.* 453
LONGING - Women's Fragrance - COTY, INC.; *pg.* 506, *pg.* 1219
LONGITUDE - Swimwear - A.H. SCHREIBER CO., INC.; *pg.* 17, *pg.* 1188
LONGMONT - Turkey Products - BUTTERBALL, LLC; *pg.* 843, *pg.* 1385
LONGMONT - Food Product - CONAGRA FOODS, INC.; *pg.* 826, *pg.* 1014
LONGSHOT - Munition Range Extension System - LOCKHEED MARTIN CORPORATION; *pg.* 229, *pg.* 762
LONGSMOCK - Dress - STEVEN MADDEN, LTD.; *pg.* 1819, *pg.* 1176
LONGSTAFFE - Furniture - HOOKER FURNITURE CORPORATION; *pg.* 928, *pg.* 1788
LONGSTROKE - Cylinder - FABCO-AIR, INC.; *pg.* 1336, *pg.* 429
LONGTERM CARE REHAB CONTRACTS - ATS - HEALTHSOUTH CORPORATION; *pg.* 1540, *pg.* 3
LONGWEEKENDS - Best Places for Weekend Stays - GREAT LAKES PUBLISHING COMPANY; *pg.* 1646, *pg.* 1431
LONGWORTH - Furniture - ASHLEY FURNITURE INDUSTRIES, INC.; *pg.* 914, *pg.* 1852
LONLINK - Software - ECHELON CORPORATION; *pg.* 389, *pg.* 245
LONMAKER - Integration Tool - ECHELON CORPORATION; *pg.* 389, *pg.* 245
LONMAKER INTEGRATION TOOL - Software - ECHELON CORPORATION; *pg.* 389, *pg.* 245
LONMANAGER - Software - ECHELON CORPORATION; *pg.* 389, *pg.* 245
LONMARK - Integration Tool - ECHELON CORPORATION; *pg.* 389, *pg.* 245
LONOX - Volatile Organic Chemical Compliant Cleaning Agents - KYZEN CORPORATION; *pg.* 331, *pg.* 1652
LONPOINT - Router - ECHELON CORPORATION; *pg.* 389, *pg.* 245
LONRESPONSE - Software - ECHELON CORPORATION; *pg.* 389, *pg.* 245
LONSCANNER - Software - ECHELON CORPORATION; *pg.* 389, *pg.* 245
LONSUPPORT - Software - ECHELON CORPORATION; *pg.* 389, *pg.* 245
LONTALK - Control Communication Product - CYPRESS SEMICONDUCTOR CORPORATION; *pg.* 1326, *pg.* 243
LONTALK - Protocol - ECHELON CORPORATION; *pg.* 389, *pg.* 245
LONTREL - Herbicide - DOW AGROSCIENCES LLC; *pg.* 1156, *pg.* 684
LONUSERS - Software - ECHELON CORPORATION; *pg.* 389, *pg.* 245
LONWORKS - Networking Technology - ECHELON CORPORATION; *pg.* 389, *pg.* 245
LONWORLD - Event - ECHELON CORPORATION; *pg.* 389, *pg.* 245
LONZABAC-12 - Biocide for Germicidal Application - LONZA

INC.; pg. 1171, pg. 1041
LONZABAC-4 - Biocide for Germicidal Application - LONZA INC.; pg. 1171, pg. 1041
LONZACURE - Polyurethane Product - AIR PRODUCTS AND CHEMICALS, INC.; pg. 1145, pg. 1513
LONZACURE - M-Bis-Anilines - LONZA INC.; pg. 1171, pg. 1041
LONZAMONE - Monomer - LONZA INC.; pg. 1171, pg. 1041
LONZEST143-S - Skin Emollient - LONZA INC.; pg. 1171, pg. 1041
LOOK - Chocolate - ANNABELLE CANDY COMPANY, INC.; pg. 1850, pg. 100
LOOK! - Sideview Mirror Glass - DORMAN PRODUCTS, INC.; pg. 204, pg. 1522
LOOK - Furniture - HAWORTH, INC.; pg. 402, pg. 891
LOOK-AT-ME-BUTTON - Video Conferencing Product - POLYCOM, INC.; pg. 664, pg. 249
LOOK LIKE AN ATHELETE PERFORM LIKE AN ATHELETE - Tagline - FGX INTERNATIONAL, INC.; pg. 5, pg. 1608
LOOK 'N' FINE - Health & Beauty Product - BLUE CROSS LABORATORIES; pg. 326, pg. 277
THE LOOK OF A PROFESSIONAL - Slogan - LANDAU UNIFORMS INCORPORATED; pg. 28, pg. 971
LOOK OF NATURE - Setting Gel - THE GILLETTE COMPANY; pg. 509, pg. 795
LOOK TO THE PAST-LEARN FOR THE FUTURE - Doll And Toy - AMERICAN GIRL LLC; pg. 949, pg. 1871
LOOK UP A ZIP CODE - Postal Services - UNITED STATES POSTAL SERVICE; pg. 1009, pg. 406
LOOKING FIT - Publication - INFORMA EXHIBITIONS LLC; pg. 1653, pg. 17
LOOKOUT MOUNTAIN - Clothing - ABERCROMBIE & FITCH CO.; pg. 37, pg. 1466
LOONEY TUNES - Toy - MATTEL, INC.; pg. 962, pg. 81
LOOP DE LOOP - Carpet - INTERFACE, INC.; pg. 695, pg. 512
LOOP FLAGZ - Belt - SCHOOL-TECH, INC.; pg. 1844, pg. 866
LOOP-LOC - Swimming Pool Covers - LOOP-LOC LTD.; pg. 1838, pg. 1165
LOOP SCOUT - Software System - HONEYWELL INTERNATIONAL INC.; pg. 407, pg. 1088
LOOPER - Commercial Lighting - SWIVELIER CO., INC.; pg. 1307, pg. 1142
LOOS ENDS - Hardware - LOOS & COMPANY, INC.; pg. 1356, pg. 368
LOOSE CHANGE - Instant Lottery Game - NEW YORK STATE LOTTERY; pg. 1001, pg. 1340
LOOSE DIAMONDS - Game - WMS INDUSTRIES INC.; pg. 593, pg. 666
LOOSE KNIT - Women's Clothing & Accessories - WOODEN SHIPS OF HOBOKEN; pg. 35, pg. 1315
LOOSE POWDER PLUS REPLENISH - Beauty Product - AVEDA CORPORATION; pg. 499, pg. 917
LOOSEGEAR - Sport Apparel - UNDER ARMOUR, INC.; pg. 49, pg. 759
LOOSLAY - Plastic Impregnated Cables - LOOS & COMPANY, INC.; pg. 1356, pg. 368
LOOT PURSUIT - Lottery Game - IOWA LOTTERY; pg. 996, pg. 705
LOOZA - Juice & Nectar - TROPICANA PRODUCTS, INC.; pg. 902, pg. 592
LOPAC - Power Supply System - VICOR CORPORATION; pg. 1435, pg. 783
LOPID - Pharmaceutical Product - IMPAX LABORATORIES, INC.; pg. 1544, pg. 101
LOPID - Medicine - PFIZER INC.; pg. 1581, pg. 1278
LOPRO - Vacuum Valve - MKS INSTRUMENTS, INC.; pg. 1362, pg. 781
LOPRODYNE - Nylon Membrane - PALL CORPORATION; pg. 232, pg. 1323
L'OR J'ADORE - Women's Fragrance - PARFUMS CHRISTIAN DIOR, INC; pg. 519, pg. 1276
LOR ME IN - Sandals - AEROGROUP INTERNATIONAL, INC.; pg. 1803, pg. 1055
LORABID - Pharmaceutical Product - KING PHARMACEUTICALS, INC.; pg. 1553, pg. 1627
LORAD - Medical Test System - HOLOGIC, INC.; pg. 1416, pg. 784
LORAD DSM - Medical Product - HOLOGIC, INC.; pg. 1416, pg. 784
LORAD ELITE - Medical Product - HOLOGIC, INC.; pg. 1416, pg. 784
LORAIN - Rough Terrain & Truck Mobile Cranes - TEREX CORPORATION; pg. 1381, pg. 384
L'ORBETTE - Male Grooming Product - AMERICAN INTERNATIONAL INDUSTRIES COMPANY; pg. 498, pg. 126
LORD ACCELERATOR - Cyanoacrylate - LORD CORPORATION; pg. 1357, pg. 1360
LORD & MAYFAIR - Mouthwash - MARIETTA HOSPITALITY; pg. 1464, pg. 1155
LORD CALVERT - Whiskey - JIM BEAM BRANDS CO.; pg. 1965, pg. 601
LORD PAISLEY - Fabric - NEMSCHOFF, INC.; pg. 936, pg. 1890
LORD-PAK - Dispensing System - LORD CORPORATION; pg. 1357, pg. 1360
L'OREAL CLASSIC SALON PRODUCTS - Hair Care Products - L'OREAL USA; pg. 514, pg. 1252
L'OREAL PROFESSIONAL - Hair Care Products - L'OREAL USA; pg. 514, pg. 1252
L'OREAL TECHNIQUE - Hair Care Products - L'OREAL USA; pg. 514, pg. 1252
LOREN - Furniture - ETHAN ALLEN INTERIORS INC.; pg. 924, pg. 343
LOREN - Footwear - PHOENIX FOOTWEAR GROUP, INC.; pg. 1815, pg. 60
LORENTZ - Water Pump - CONERGY, INC.; pg. 1325, pg. 318
LORENZO - Fabric - NEMSCHOFF, INC.; pg. 936, pg. 1890
LORIA - Waiting Seating - STEELCASE INC.; pg. 475, pg. 889
LORIEN - Fabric - NEMSCHOFF, INC.; pg. 936, pg. 1890
LORNA - Women's Clothing & Accessories - WOODEN SHIPS OF HOBOKEN; pg. 35, pg. 1315
LORO JOSAM - Drainage System - JOSAM COMPANY; pg. 89, pg. 695
LOROX - Herbicide - E.I. DU PONT DE NEMOURS & COMPANY; pg. 1159, pg. 390
LORSBAN - Insecticide - DOW AGROSCIENCES LLC; pg. 1156, pg. 684
LOS ANGELES ANGELS - Baseball Team - ANGELS BASEBALL, L.P.; pg. 529, pg. 42
LOS ANGELES DODGERS - Baseball Team - LOS ANGELES DODGERS INC.; pg. 559, pg. 135
LOS ANGELES LAKERS - Basketball Team - CALIFORNIA SPORTS, INC.; pg. 536, pg. 78
LOS ANGELES SPARKS - Basketball Team - CALIFORNIA SPORTS, INC.; pg. 536, pg. 78
LOS ANGELES TIMES - Newspaper - LOS ANGELES TIMES COMMUNICATIONS, LLC; pg. 1660, pg. 135
LOS AZTECAS - Game - WMS INDUSTRIES INC.; pg. 593, pg. 666
LOS CONEJOS - Bleaches - THE CLOROX COMPANY; pg. 327, pg. 169
LOSALT - Corrosion Inhibitors - GE WATER & PROCESS TECHNOLOGIES; pg. 1339, pg. 1588
LOSAT - Mobile Guide Missile System - LOCKHEED MARTIN CORPORATION; pg. 229, pg. 762
LOSETA - Fabric - NEMSCHOFF, INC.; pg. 936, pg. 1890
LOSLIP - Catalyst - BASF CATALYSTS LLC; pg. 1148, pg. 1074
LOSONE - Ventilators - BROAN-NUTONE LLC; pg. 1069, pg. 1860
LOSONE - Fans - NORTEK, INC.; pg. 100, pg. 1607
LOSSSTATS - Credit Loss Information - STANDARD & POOR'S RATINGS SERVICES; pg. 805, pg. 1296
LOSSSTATS MODEL - Loss Analysis Tool - STANDARD & POOR'S RATINGS SERVICES; pg. 805, pg. 1296
LOST - Energy Drink - MONSTER BEVERAGE CORPORATION; pg. 257, pg. 69
THE LOST EXPEDITION - Game - ACTIVISION BLIZZARD, INC.; pg. 948, pg. 271
LOST KEY - Community Name - WCI COMMUNITIES, INC.; pg. 1118, pg. 414
LOST PACKET RECOVERY - QoS Technology - POLYCOM, INC.; pg. 664, pg. 249
LOST RIVER - Outerwear - KELLWOOD COMPANY; pg. 28, pg. 975
LOST TREASURE ADVENTURE - Game - MISSOURI LOTTERY; pg. 999, pg. 979
LOT #40 - Whisky - MCCORMICK DISTILLING CO., INC.; pg. 1966, pg. 1007
LOTCA - Cognitive Battery - ALIMED, INC.; pg. 1490, pg. 816
LOTEM - Platesetters - EASTMAN KODAK COMPANY; pg. 1408, pg. 1333
LOTEMAX - Pharmaceutical Product - BAUSCH & LOMB INCORPORATED; pg. 1401, pg. 1045
LOTEMP - Temperature Recorder - MESA LABORATORIES, INC.; pg. 1567, pg. 333
LOTREX - Medical Product - HOLOGIC, INC.; pg. 1416, pg. 784
LOTRIMIN - Antifungal Skin Preparation - MERCK & CO., INC.; pg. 1566, pg. 1077
LOTRISONE - Medicine - MERCK & CO., INC.; pg. 1566, pg. 1077
LOTS OF LUCK - Game - MISSOURI LOTTERY; pg. 999, pg. 979
LOTS OF WORK!!! PROVEN YIELD!!! - Tagline - TERRAL SEED, INC.; pg. 1801, pg. 748
LOTS TO FEEL GOOD ABOUT! - Tag Line - GARDEN FRESH RESTAURANT CORP.; pg. 1729, pg. 203
LOTSA LOVE - Flower Arrangement - 1-800-FLOWERS.COM, INC.; pg. 1758, pg. 1151
LOTTA LUCK - Instant Lottery Game - NEW YORK STATE LOTTERY; pg. 1001, pg. 1340
LOTTO - Lottery Game - ILLINOIS STATE LOTTERY; pg. 995, pg. 578
LOTTO - Lottery Game - LOUISIANA LOTTERY CORPORATION; pg. 997, pg. 742
LOTTO - Lottery Game - MISSOURI LOTTERY; pg. 999, pg. 979
LOTTO SOUL - Lottery Game - D.C. LOTTERY & CHARITABLE GAMES CONTROL BOARD; pg. 991, pg. 398
LOTTO TEXAS - Lottery - TEXAS LOTTERY COMMISSION; pg. 1007, pg. 1666
LOTUS - Footwear - EASTLAND SHOE CORPORATION; pg. 1808, pg. 750
LOTUS 103 - Rice - RICELAND FOODS, INC.; pg. 892, pg. 36
LOTUS DESIGNS - Paddling Gear - LOST ARROW CORPORATION; pg. 44, pg. 301
LOTUS POOL - Bath Product - KOHLER CO.; pg. 91, pg. 1862
LOTZEE - Weekly Computerized Numbers Game With Twenty-One Ways of Winning - NEW JERSEY STATE LOTTERY; pg. 1000, pg. 1126
LOU - Intimate Apparel - V.F. CORPORATION; pg. 34, pg. 1376
LOU ANA - Salad Oils - VENTURA FOODS, LLC; pg. 908, pg. 49
LOUD - Apparel - OAKLEY, INC.; pg. 1840, pg. 86
LOUIE LOOP - Roofing Fastener - POWERS FASTENERS INC.; pg. 1059, pg. 1143
LOUIS M. MARTINI - Wine - E&J GALLO WINERY; pg. 1962, pg. 149
LOUIS TRAUTH - Dairy Product - DEAN FOODS COMPANY; pg. 852, pg. 1679
LOUISA - Clothing - ABERCROMBIE & FITCH CO.; pg. 37, pg. 1466
LOUISIANA - Flatware - ONEIDA LTD; pg. 1129, pg. 1318
LOUISIANA DOWNS - Racetrack & Casino - CAESARS ENTERTAINMENT CORPORATION; pg. 1083, pg. 1023
LOUISIANA DOWNS - Race Track - HARRAH'S LOUISIANA DOWNS CASINO & RACETRACK; pg. 551, pg. 743
LOUISIANA GOLD - Hot Sauce - BRUCE FOODS CORPORATION; pg. 842, pg. 743
LOUISIANA LOUIE - Slots - INTERNATIONAL GAME TECHNOLOGY; pg. 957, pg. 1024
LOUISVILLE SLUGGER - Portable Pitching Machine - SCHOOL-TECH, INC.; pg. 1844, pg. 866
LOUISVILLE SLUGGER - Baseball Bats - WILSON SPORTING GOODS CO.; pg. 1848, pg. 596
LOUNGER - Seating - IRWIN SEATING COMPANY INC.; pg. 929, pg. 887
LOV-IT - Butter Blends - SCHREIBER FOODS, INC.; pg. 894, pg. 1859
LOVCAT - Network Product - VITESSE SEMICONDUCTOR CORPORATION; pg. 686, pg. 57
LOVE - Temperature Control - DWYER INSTRUMENTS INC.; pg. 1330, pg. 694
LOVE - Bookmark - HERITAGE LACE INC.; pg. 694, pg. 711
LOVE - Women's Fragrance - RALPH LAUREN CORPORATION; pg. 46, pg. 1284
LOVE AFFAIR - Carpet - BEAULIEU GROUP, LLC; pg. 917, pg. 529
LOVE BODY - Beverages - THE COCA-COLA COMPANY; pg. 240, pg. 493
LOVE BUFFS - Nutritional Supplement - NATURAL ORGANICS, INC.; pg. 1571, pg. 1181
LOVE EWE - Lace Curtain - HERITAGE LACE INC.; pg. 694, pg. 711

LOVE IN BLOOM - Pant Set - HABAND COMPANY, INC.; *pg.* 1772, *pg.* 1099
LOVE KNOTS - Flower Arrangement - 1-800-FLOWERS.COM, INC.; *pg.* 1758, *pg.* 1151
LOVE LETTER - Bedding - CROSCILL, INC.; *pg.* 1122, *pg.* 1220
LOVE-MY-LOOFAH - Soap - GRANDPA BRANDS COMPANY; *pg.* 1538, *pg.* 727
LOVE STORIES - Cable Television Channel - STARZ ENTERTAINMENT, LLC; *pg.* 310, *pg.* 327
LOVE TO WIN - Game - WMS INDUSTRIES INC.; *pg.* 593, *pg.* 666
LOVELADIES - Pointelle Sweater - HABAND COMPANY, INC.; *pg.* 1772, *pg.* 1099
LOVELINK - Logging Software - DWYER INSTRUMENTS INC.; *pg.* 1330, *pg.* 694
LOVENOX - Enoxaparin Sodium Injection - SANOFI US; *pg.* 1592, *pg.* 1046
LOVE'S FIRST BLOOM - Flower Arrangement - 1-800-FLOWERS.COM, INC.; *pg.* 1758, *pg.* 1151
LOVING CARE - Hair Coloring - P&G-CLAIROL, INC.; *pg.* 519, *pg.* 1418
LOVING FAMILY - Dollhouses and Accessories - FISHER-PRICE, INC.; *pg.* 953, *pg.* 1156
LOVITES - Nutritional Supplement - NATURAL ORGANICS, INC.; *pg.* 1571, *pg.* 1181
LOVOLT - Electronic Components - MOLEX INCORPORATED; *pg.* 655, *pg.* 628
LOW AIR LEAF - Chassis Suspension - PETERBILT MOTORS CO.; *pg.* 188, *pg.* 1691
LOW FARES, WAY BETTER - Slogan - AER LINGUS; *pg.* 1896, *pg.* 1171
LOW-LINE - Ventilators - SWARTWOUT DIVISION; *pg.* 114, *pg.* 978
LOW OGESTREL - Pharmaceutical Product - ALLERGAN; *pg.* 1490, *pg.* 1101
LOW PH/S - Veterinary Food - IAMS COMPANY; *pg.* 1477, *pg.* 1633
LOW PROFILE - Bathroom Fan - HUNTER FAN COMPANY; *pg.* 57, *pg.* 1631
LOW PROFILE - Seat Cushion - THE ROHO GROUP; *pg.* 1591, *pg.* 556
LOW PROFILE - Conveyor - SHUTTLEWORTH, INC.; *pg.* 1375, *pg.* 682
LOW-PROFILE - Floor - STEELCASE INC.; *pg.* 475, *pg.* 889
LOW PROFILE - Skylighting System - WASCO PRODUCTS, INC.; *pg.* 120, *pg.* 752
LOW PROFILE SIDE ENTRY - Fiber Optic Lighting System - ENERGY FOCUS, INC.; *pg.* 1411, *pg.* 1472
LOW-RESIDUE - Veterinary Food - IAMS COMPANY; *pg.* 1477, *pg.* 1633
LOW RIDER - Motorcycle - HARLEY-DAVIDSON, INC.; *pg.* 178, *pg.* 1874
LOW-T GRAY - Float Glass - AGC GLASS NORTH AMERICA, INC.; *pg.* 65, *pg.* 482
LOW-TEMP - Low Temperature, Extreme Pressure Grease for Industrial & Construction Use - LUBRIPLATE LUBRICANTS; *pg.* 980, *pg.* 1097
LOWARA - Fluid Technology - ITT CORPORATION; *pg.* 1351, *pg.* 1354
LOWDROP-CC - Switch - POWER INTEGRATIONS, INC.; *pg.* 1369, *pg.* 249
LOWELL - Carpet - INTERFACE, INC.; *pg.* 695, *pg.* 512
LOWELL WRENCH - Tool - LOWELL CORPORATION; *pg.* 1053, *pg.* 856
LOWER RISER & EMERGENCY DISCONNECT PACKAGES - Subsea Equipment - DRIL-QUIP, INC.; *pg.* 1330, *pg.* 1704
LOWER THE COST OF OWNERSHIP - Slogan - TENNANT COMPANY; *pg.* 1381, *pg.* 944
LOWERATOR - Oven - APW WYOTT FOOD SERVICE EQUIPMENT, INC.; *pg.* 1314, *pg.* 1658
LOWE'S DELIVERS - Tagline - LOWE'S COMPANIES, INC.; *pg.* 1053, *pg.* 1383
LOWILITE - Stabilizers - CHEMTURA CORPORATION; *pg.* 1152, *pg.* 355
LOWINOX - Polymer Product - CHEMTURA CORPORATION; *pg.* 1152, *pg.* 355
LOWOHM - Coating - VIAVI SOLUTIONS INC.; *pg.* 1435, *pg.* 148
LOWRY - Computer Products - LOWRY COMPUTER PRODUCTS, INC.; *pg.* 428, *pg.* 874
LOWY - Furniture - AMERICAN LEATHER LP; *pg.* 912, *pg.* 1673
LOXARMOR - Electrical Wire & Cable - THE OKONITE COMPANY; *pg.* 1302, *pg.* 1113
LOXITANE - Pharmaceutical Product - ALLERGAN; *pg.* 1490, *pg.* 1101
LOXON - Primer - THE SHERWIN-WILLIAMS COMPANY; *pg.* 1447, *pg.* 1435
LOYAL - Food Product - MARS, INCORPORATED; *pg.* 1858, *pg.* 1792
LOYAL TO THE SPORT - Slogan - SAUCONY, INC.; *pg.* 1818, *pg.* 828
LOYALL - Feeds - CARGILL, INC.; *pg.* 845, *pg.* 965
LOYALTY DRIVER - E-Newsletter - IMAKENEWS, INC.; *pg.* 413, *pg.* 851
LOYALTY. PROGRESS. ARTISTRY - Tagline - AMERICAN SOCIETY OF CINEMATOGRAPHERS; *pg.* 1616, *pg.* 103
LOYALTY THROUGH EXPERIENCE - Customer Solution - DELUXE CORPORATION; *pg.* 1634, *pg.* 964
LOZAN - Footwear - K-SWISS; *pg.* 1837, *pg.* 306
LOZANO - Publisher - IMPREMEDIA LLC; *pg.* 1652, *pg.* 133
LOZIER IMAX - Theater - OMAHA ZOOLOGICAL SOCIETY; *pg.* 572, *pg.* 1017
LP - Projector - INFOCUS CORPORATION; *pg.* 644, *pg.* 1503
LP - Musical Instrument - KAMAN CORPORATION; *pg.* 229, *pg.* 338
LP - Lumber Products - LOUISIANA-PACIFIC CORPORATION; *pg.* 94, *pg.* 1652
LP 2844 - Printers - AVERY WEIGH-TRONIX, INC.; *pg.* 1315, *pg.* 925
LP DATA VIEW - Software - BIO-RAD LABORATORIES, INC.; *pg.* 1504, *pg.* 101
LP OXO - Process Technology - THE DOW CHEMICAL COMPANY; *pg.* 1157, *pg.* 898
LP SERIES - Baseball Glove - HILLERICH & BRADSBY CO., INC.; *pg.* 1836, *pg.* 576
LP SOLUTIONS - Software - LOUISIANA-PACIFIC CORPORATION; *pg.* 94, *pg.* 1652
LP3000 - Narrow Web Press - MARK ANDY, INC.; *pg.* 1359, *pg.* 975
LPPS - Engineered Product And System - SULZER METCO (WESTBURY) INC.; *pg.* 1064, *pg.* 1350
LPR - QoS Technology - POLYCOM, INC.; *pg.* 664, *pg.* 249
LPS - Optical Product - LEUPOLD & STEVENS, INC.; *pg.* 1420, *pg.* 1492
LPT - Latchup Protection Technology - MAXWELL TECHNOLOGIES, INC.; *pg.* 653, *pg.* 204
LPTC - Coupler - OPLINK COMMUNICATIONS, INC.; *pg.* 660, *pg.* 91
LPV II - Medical Device - INTEGRA LIFESCIENCES HOLDINGS CORPORATION; *pg.* 1545, *pg.* 1109
LPX - Musical Instrument - GIBSON GUITAR CORP.; *pg.* 550, *pg.* 1650
LPXPRO - Medium Power Excimer Laser - COHERENT, INC.; *pg.* 1406, *pg.* 265
LPZ - Adjustable Angle Conveyor - DORNER MANUFACTURING CORP.; *pg.* 1329, *pg.* 1861
LQ-1070+ - Dot Matrix Printer - EPSON AMERICA INC.; *pg.* 394, *pg.* 122
LQ-1170 - Dot Matrix Printer - EPSON AMERICA INC.; *pg.* 394, *pg.* 122
LQ-2550 - Dot Matrix Printer - EPSON AMERICA INC.; *pg.* 394, *pg.* 122
LQ-570+ - Dot Matrix Printer - EPSON AMERICA INC.; *pg.* 394, *pg.* 122
LQ-870 - Dot Matrix Printer - EPSON AMERICA INC.; *pg.* 394, *pg.* 122
LR - Long Run Steel - A. FINKL & SONS CO.; *pg.* 1309, *pg.* 563
LR CLONASE - Biomolecule Product - THERMO FISHER SCIENTIFIC INC.; *pg.* 1602, *pg.* 61
LRAD - Hailing & Warning Device - LRAD CORPORATION; *pg.* 652, *pg.* 204
LRC - Folder - THOMAS & BETTS CORPORATION; *pg.* 680, *pg.* 1646
LRM TOSA - Electronic Component - EMCORE CORPORATION; *pg.* 636, *pg.* 39
LS - Particle Size Analyzer - BECKMAN COULTER, INC.; *pg.* 1402, *pg.* 48
LS-15 LINER HANGER SYSTEM - Liner Hanger Systems - DRIL-QUIP, INC.; *pg.* 1330, *pg.* 1704
LS ORTHO - Footwear - P.W. MINOR & SON, INC.; *pg.* 1816, *pg.* 1140
LS SENATOR - Footwear - P.W. MINOR & SON, INC.; *pg.* 1816, *pg.* 1140
LS SERIES - Baseball Glove - HILLERICH & BRADSBY CO., INC.; *pg.* 1836, *pg.* 576
LS SUPER X - Footwear - P.W. MINOR & SON, INC.; *pg.* 1816, *pg.* 1140
LS135 - Examination Light - WELCH ALLYN INC.; *pg.* 1436, *pg.* 1342
LS150 - Examination Light - WELCH ALLYN INC.; *pg.* 1436, *pg.* 1342
LS200 - Procedure Lighting - WELCH ALLYN INC.; *pg.* 1436, *pg.* 1342
LS3000 - Printer - RICOH AMERICAS CORPORATION; *pg.* 461, *pg.* 1131
LSA - Fluid Handling System - GRACO, INC.; *pg.* 1342, *pg.* 935
LSA PUMPS - Slurry Pump - GIW INDUSTRIES, INC.; *pg.* 1340, *pg.* 533
LSAMS - Software System - FAIR ISAAC CORPORATION; *pg.* 1247, *pg.* 955
LSC - Integrated Circuits - LATTICE SEMICONDUCTOR CORPORATION; *pg.* 651, *pg.* 1498
LSIM - Software System - MENTOR GRAPHICS CORPORATION; *pg.* 432, *pg.* 1510
LSIM DSM - Software System - MENTOR GRAPHICS CORPORATION; *pg.* 432, *pg.* 1510
LSIM GATE - Software System - MENTOR GRAPHICS CORPORATION; *pg.* 432, *pg.* 1510
LSIM POWER ANALYST - Software System - MENTOR GRAPHICS CORPORATION; *pg.* 432, *pg.* 1510
LSIM REVIEW - Software System - MENTOR GRAPHICS CORPORATION; *pg.* 432, *pg.* 1510
LSIM SWITCH - Software System - MENTOR GRAPHICS CORPORATION; *pg.* 432, *pg.* 1510
LSIM XL - Software System - MENTOR GRAPHICS CORPORATION; *pg.* 432, *pg.* 1510
LSIMNET - Software System - MENTOR GRAPHICS CORPORATION; *pg.* 432, *pg.* 1510
LSM - Accelerometer - JEWELL INSTRUMENTS, LLC; *pg.* 1418, *pg.* 1036
LSMSXPRESS - Software - EVOLVING SYSTEMS, INC.; *pg.* 395, *pg.* 326
LSO50 - Garage Door Operator - NORTEK SECURITY & CONTROL LLC; *pg.* 659, *pg.* 59
LSP ADVANTAGE - Emergency Portable Suction Unit - ALLIED HEALTHCARE PRODUCTS, INC.; *pg.* 1491, *pg.* 990
LSP HDX BACKBOARD - Trauma Product - ALLIED HEALTHCARE PRODUCTS, INC.; *pg.* 1491, *pg.* 990
LSP XTRA - Trauma Product - ALLIED HEALTHCARE PRODUCTS, INC.; *pg.* 1491, *pg.* 990
LSR - Fluid Handling System - GRACO, INC.; *pg.* 1342, *pg.* 935
LSS LIGHTWEIGHT SHOCK STOPPER - Medical Equipment - INVACARE CORPORATION; *pg.* 1546, *pg.* 1451
LST - Lightweight Pocket Knives - GERBER LEGENDARY BLADES; *pg.* 1834, *pg.* 1503
LST - Emission Testing System - MISTRAS GROUP, INC.; *pg.* 1362, *pg.* 1113
LT-CAGE - Lumbar Tapered Fusion Device - MEDTRONIC, INC.; *pg.* 1564, *pg.* 939
LT COLOURS - Color - FERRO CORPORATION; *pg.* 1162, *pg.* 1462
LTA - Transparent Glass & Plastic Laminate for Vehicle Window Applications - PPG INDUSTRIES, INC.; *pg.* 1445, *pg.* 1579
LTA/SECURITECT - Glass & Plastic Vehicle Window Laminate - PPG INDUSTRIES, INC.; *pg.* 1445, *pg.* 1579
LTC 1261/22DN - Camera - BOSCH SECURITY SYSTEMS, INC.; *pg.* 626, *pg.* 1158
LTC 1271 - Camera - BOSCH SECURITY SYSTEMS, INC.; *pg.* 626, *pg.* 1158
LTC 4600 - Data Processing Unit - BOSCH SECURITY SYSTEMS, INC.; *pg.* 626, *pg.* 1158
LTC 4700 - Data Processing Unit - BOSCH SECURITY SYSTEMS, INC.; *pg.* 626, *pg.* 1158
LTC 5231/90 - Amplifier - BOSCH SECURITY SYSTEMS, INC.; *pg.* 626, *pg.* 1158
LTC 5234/90 - Amplifier - BOSCH SECURITY SYSTEMS, INC.; *pg.* 626, *pg.* 1158
LTC-MAP - Monitoring Instrument - GE ENERGY; *pg.* 1338, *pg.* 506
LTC SOLUTION - Long Term Care Insurance - PENN TREATY AMERICAN CORPORATION; *pg.* 793, *pg.* 1514
LTC WORKS! - Insurance Administration - PENN TREATY AMERICAN CORPORATION; *pg.* 793, *pg.* 1514
LTD GRAPHITE - Fly Reel - CORTLAND LINE COMPANY; *pg.* 1831, *pg.* 1155
LTE - Mobile Solutions - SONUS NETWORKS INC.; *pg.* 1281,

pg. 858
LTI - Fluid Handling System - GRACO, INC.; *pg.* 1342, *pg.* 935
LTO - Drive - QUANTUM CORPORATION; *pg.* 458, *pg.* 250
LTO ULTRIUM - Barcode Labels - BACKUPWORKS.COM INC.; *pg.* 359, *pg.* 120
LTV - Seat Cushion - THE ROHO GROUP; *pg.* 1591, *pg.* 556
LTX - Liquids Recovery - CAMERON INTERNATIONAL; *pg.* 1151, *pg.* 1702
LU - Biscuits - MONDELEZ INTERNATIONAL, INC.; *pg.* 878, *pg.* 601
LUAU LOOT - Game - WMS INDUSTRIES INC.; *pg.* 593, *pg.* 666
LUBA - Furniture - AMISCO INDUSTRIES LTD.; *pg.* 913, *pg.* 1958
LUBE EZE - Lubricant - AERVOE INDUSTRIES INCORPORATED; *pg.* 1439, *pg.* 1021
LUBE MASTER - Fluid Handling System - GRACO, INC.; *pg.* 1342, *pg.* 935
THE LUBE-RARY - Online Dictionary - BEL-RAY COMPANY, INC.; *pg.* 972, *pg.* 1128
LUBEMASTER - Fluid Handling System - GRACO, INC.; *pg.* 1342, *pg.* 935
LUBOLID - Powered Chemical Substances - DOW CORNING CORPORATION; *pg.* 1159, *pg.* 900
LUBRAZINC - Polymer Product - CHEMTURA CORPORATION; *pg.* 1152, *pg.* 355
LUBRI-JOINT - Lubricant - LA-CO INDUSTRIES MARKAL CO., INC.; *pg.* 1170, *pg.* 610
LUBRI-SHINE - Automotive Surface Cleaner - ITW - EVERCOAT; *pg.* 1443, *pg.* 1415
LUBRI-TECH - Engineered Compound & Composite - POLYONE CORPORATION; *pg.* 1177, *pg.* 1404
THE LUBRICATION PROFESSIONALS (SM) - SERVICE MARK - Fluid Handling System - GRACO, INC.; *pg.* 1342, *pg.* 935
LUBRIDERM - Body Lotion - JOHNSON & JOHNSON; *pg.* 1549, *pg.* 1091
LUBRIGUIDE - Medical Device - BOSTON SCIENTIFIC CORPORATION; *pg.* 1508, *pg.* 831
LUBRILON - Plastic Compound & Resin - A. SCHULMAN, INC.; *pg.* 1144, *pg.* 1452
LUBRIMATE - Special Grade of Carbon/Graphite Seal Material for Severe Service - KADANT JOHNSON INC.; *pg.* 1073, *pg.* 909
LUBRIMATIC - Lubrication Equipment Accessories & Specialty Greases & Oils - PLEWS/EDELMANN; *pg.* 215, *pg.* 607
LUBRIONE - Wear Resistant Compounds - POLYONE CORPORATION; *pg.* 1177, *pg.* 1404
LUBRIPLATE - Lubricants - FISKE BROTHERS REFINING COMPANY; *pg.* 978, *pg.* 1096
LUBRIPLATE - Lubricants - LUBRIPLATE LUBRICANTS; *pg.* 980, *pg.* 1097
LUBRIQUIP - Fluid Handling System - GRACO, INC.; *pg.* 1342, *pg.* 935
LUBRIQUIP - Lubrication Equipment - IDEX CORPORATION; *pg.* 1347, *pg.* 623
LUBRIQUIP LUBRICATING & DISPENSING SOLUTIONS - Fluid Handling System - GRACO, INC.; *pg.* 1342, *pg.* 935
LUBRISIL OS - Silicone Lube & Heavy Duty Degreaser - PENETONE CORPORATION; *pg.* 333, *pg.* 1050
LUBRISYSTEM - Fluid Handling System - GRACO, INC.; *pg.* 1342, *pg.* 935
LUBRITAB - Natural Lubricant - PENFORD CORPORATION; *pg.* 1177, *pg.* 314
LUBRITAN - Acrylic Syntan - DOW CHEMICAL; *pg.* 1156, *pg.* 1563
LUBY'S - Cafeteria-Style Restaurants - LUBY'S, INC.; *pg.* 1736, *pg.* 1710
LUCAS - Furniture - AMISCO INDUSTRIES LTD.; *pg.* 913, *pg.* 1958
LUCAS - Ice Cream Bar - WELLS ENTERPRISES, INC.; *pg.* 909, *pg.* 709
LUCAS - Candy - WM. WRIGLEY JR. COMPANY; *pg.* 1863, *pg.* 596
LUCAS VALLEY - Bike - MARIN BIKES; *pg.* 1708, *pg.* 168
LUCENT - Software System - ALCATEL-LUCENT; *pg.* 615, *pg.* 1094
LUCENT BOOKS - Publisher - GALE CENGAGE LEARNING; *pg.* 1643, *pg.* 885
LUCENT SLC - Multiplexing System - CIENA CORPORATION; *pg.* 628, *pg.* 771
LUCENTIS - Anti-VEGF Antibody Fragment - GENENTECH, INC.; *pg.* 1533, *pg.* 279
LUCENTIS - Therapeutic Product - XOMA CORPORATION; *pg.* 1611, *pg.* 46
LUCERNE - Sedan - GENERAL MOTORS COMPANY; *pg.* 175, *pg.* 881
LUCERNE - Jewelry - HABAND COMPANY, INC.; *pg.* 1772, *pg.* 1099
LUCERNE - Wholesome Dairy Products & Eggs - SAFEWAY INC.; *pg.* 1032, *pg.* 184
LUCETTA - Bathroom Accessories - SYMMONS INDUSTRIES, INC.; *pg.* 114, *pg.* 803
LUCI-SOF - Dental Product - DENTSPLY INTERNATIONAL INC.; *pg.* 1522, *pg.* 1596
LUCIA - Footwear - COBIAN CORP.; *pg.* 1806, *pg.* 253
LUCIA - Footwear - PHOENIX FOOTWEAR GROUP, INC.; *pg.* 1815, *pg.* 60
LUCIAN - Furniture - ETHAN ALLEN INTERIORS INC.; *pg.* 924, *pg.* 343
LUCIANDO - Fabric - NEMSCHOFF, INC.; *pg.* 936, *pg.* 1890
LUCID - Computer Equipment - VIEWSONIC CORPORATION; *pg.* 489, *pg.* 303
LUCIDA - Jewelry Collection - TIFFANY & CO.; *pg.* 13, *pg.* 1299
LUCIDENE - Polymer - DOW CHEMICAL; *pg.* 1156, *pg.* 1563
LUCIEN DESCHAUX - Wines - LEONARD KREUSCH, INC.; *pg.* 254, *pg.* 1099
LUCITE - Paint Product - PPG INDUSTRIES, INC.; *pg.* 1445, *pg.* 1579
LUCITE SUPERTUF - Acrylic Polymer - LUCITE INTERNATIONAL, INC.; *pg.* 94, *pg.* 1631
LUCITE TUFCOAT - Acrylic Polymer - LUCITE INTERNATIONAL, INC.; *pg.* 94, *pg.* 1631
LUCIWAX - Additive - DOW CHEMICAL; *pg.* 1156, *pg.* 1563
LUCK HAPPENS HERE - Games - PENN NATIONAL GAMING, INC.; *pg.* 574, *pg.* 1595
LUCK OF THE IRISH - Lottery Game - OHIO LOTTERY COMMISSION; *pg.* 1002, *pg.* 1433
LUCK PLUS - Card Game - MATTEL GAMES/PUZZLES; *pg.* 962, *pg.* 80
LUCK'S - Food Product - CONAGRA FOODS, INC.; *pg.* 826, *pg.* 1014
LUCKY - Apparel & Accessories - KATE SPADE & COMPANY; *pg.* 27, *pg.* 1248
LUCKY - Food Product - MARS, INCORPORATED; *pg.* 1858, *pg.* 1792
LUCKY - Magazine - SCHOLASTIC INC.; *pg.* 1683, *pg.* 1288
LUCKY - Store - SUPERVALU, INC.; *pg.* 1035, *pg.* 924
LUCKY 5 - Numbers Game - THE STATE LOTTERY COMMISSION OF INDIANA; *pg.* 1006, *pg.* 690
LUCKY 7S - Game - MISSOURI LOTTERY; *pg.* 999, *pg.* 979
LUCKY 7'S - Lottery Game - NEW YORK STATE LOTTERY; *pg.* 1001, *pg.* 1340
LUCKY 7S BINGO - Game - MISSOURI LOTTERY; *pg.* 999, *pg.* 979
LUCKY BABY - Infant Clothing & Accessories - LUCKY BRAND DUNGAREES, INC.; *pg.* 29, *pg.* 301
LUCKY BARS - Video Game - INTERNATIONAL GAME TECHNOLOGY; *pg.* 957, *pg.* 1024
LUCKY BRAND - Apparel & Accessories - LUCKY BRAND DUNGAREES, INC.; *pg.* 29, *pg.* 301
LUCKY BUCKS - Game - MISSOURI LOTTERY; *pg.* 999, *pg.* 979
LUCKY BUG - Lottery Game - CALIFORNIA LOTTERY; *pg.* 990, *pg.* 196
LUCKY CATCH - Game - GAMEWRIGHT; *pg.* 953, *pg.* 836
LUCKY CHARM BINGO - Lottery Game - OHIO LOTTERY COMMISSION; *pg.* 1002, *pg.* 1433
LUCKY CHARMS - Cereal - GENERAL MILLS, INC.; *pg.* 828, *pg.* 933
LUCKY COIN - Video Game - INTERNATIONAL GAME TECHNOLOGY; *pg.* 957, *pg.* 1024
LUCKY CRICKETS - Video Game - INTERNATIONAL GAME TECHNOLOGY; *pg.* 957, *pg.* 1024
LUCKY DOG - Lottery Card - MISSOURI LOTTERY; *pg.* 999, *pg.* 979
LUCKY DOG DOUBLER - Lottery Game - OHIO LOTTERY COMMISSION; *pg.* 1002, *pg.* 1433
LUCKY DOUGH - Lottery Game - MISSOURI LOTTERY; *pg.* 999, *pg.* 979
LUCKY DRAGONFLY - Video Game - INTERNATIONAL GAME TECHNOLOGY; *pg.* 957, *pg.* 1024
LUCKY DREAMS - Underwear & Nightwear - LUCKY BRAND DUNGAREES, INC.; *pg.* 29, *pg.* 301
LUCKY FOR YOU - Games - PENN NATIONAL GAMING, INC.; *pg.* 574, *pg.* 1595
LUCKY FOUR LEAF CLOVER - Slots - INTERNATIONAL GAME TECHNOLOGY; *pg.* 957, *pg.* 1024
LUCKY FOX - Video Game - INTERNATIONAL GAME TECHNOLOGY; *pg.* 957, *pg.* 1024
LUCKY GIRLS - Children's Apparel - LUCKY BRAND DUNGAREES, INC.; *pg.* 29, *pg.* 301
LUCKY GOLD - Game - MISSOURI LOTTERY; *pg.* 999, *pg.* 979
LUCKY HEARTS - Video Game - INTERNATIONAL GAME TECHNOLOGY; *pg.* 957, *pg.* 1024
LUCKY HEARTS - Game - MISSOURI LOTTERY; *pg.* 999, *pg.* 979
LUCKY HEARTS - Lottery Game - NEW JERSEY STATE LOTTERY; *pg.* 1000, *pg.* 1126
LUCKY HORSESHOE - Toys - 1-800-FLOWERS.COM, INC.; *pg.* 1758, *pg.* 1151
LUCKY JOKERS - Video Game - INTERNATIONAL GAME TECHNOLOGY; *pg.* 957, *pg.* 1024
LUCKY LAGER - Beer - PABST BREWING COMPANY; *pg.* 258, *pg.* 137
LUCKY LARRY'S LOBSTERMANIA - Slots - INTERNATIONAL GAME TECHNOLOGY; *pg.* 957, *pg.* 1024
LUCKY LEAF - Pie Filling & Apple Products - KNOUSE FOODS COOPERATIVE INC.; *pg.* 869, *pg.* 1558
LUCKY LEMMINGS - Game - WMS INDUSTRIES INC.; *pg.* 593, *pg.* 666
LUCKY LINES - Lottery Game - MINNESOTA STATE LOTTERY; *pg.* 999, *pg.* 956
LUCKY LIZARD - Game - WMS INDUSTRIES INC.; *pg.* 593, *pg.* 666
LUCKY MEERKATS - Game - WMS INDUSTRIES INC.; *pg.* 593, *pg.* 666
LUCKY MONEY STACKS - Game - WMS INDUSTRIES INC.; *pg.* 593, *pg.* 666
LUCKY NUMBERS - Lottery Game - D.C. LOTTERY & CHARITABLE GAMES CONTROL BOARD; *pg.* 991, *pg.* 398
LUCKY NUMBERS - Lottery Game - KENTUCKY LOTTERY CORPORATION; *pg.* 996, *pg.* 735
LUCKY PENNY - Women's Accessories - URBAN OUTFITTERS, INC.; *pg.* 1789, *pg.* 1571
LUCKY SEALS - Game - WMS INDUSTRIES INC.; *pg.* 593, *pg.* 666
LUCKY SEVEN - Food Service - ARK RESTAURANTS CORP.; *pg.* 1715, *pg.* 1196
LUCKY STAR - Educational Materials - SCHOLASTIC INC.; *pg.* 1683, *pg.* 1288
LUCKY STARS - Textiles - BERNHARDT DESIGN; *pg.* 918, *pg.* 1381
LUCKY STREAK - Bus Transportation Service - GREYHOUND LINES, INC.; *pg.* 1910, *pg.* 1681
LUCKY STRIKE - Cigarette - REYNOLDS AMERICAN INC.; *pg.* 1894, *pg.* 1395
LUCKY TIMES TEN JR. - Lottery Game - OHIO LOTTERY COMMISSION; *pg.* 1002, *pg.* 1433
LUCKY YOU - Apparel & Accessories - LUCKY BRAND DUNGAREES, INC.; *pg.* 29, *pg.* 301
LUCKYSHOPS.COM - Online Shopping Site - THE LUCKY GROUP, INC.; *pg.* 1660, *pg.* 275
LUCY - Women's Activewear - V.F. CORPORATION; *pg.* 34, *pg.* 1376
LUCY MOSES SCHOOL - Performance Art Service - THE KAUFMAN CENTER; *pg.* 556, *pg.* 1248
LUDEN'S - Cough Drops - MCNEIL-PPC, INC.; *pg.* 1560, *pg.* 1533
LUER LOK - Needles & Syringes - CROSSTEX INTERNATIONAL INC.; *pg.* 1520, *pg.* 1164
LUERTIGHT - Pumps - IDEX CORPORATION; *pg.* 1347, *pg.* 623
LUFKIN - Oil Field & Industrial Equipment - LUFKIN INDUSTRIES, INC.; *pg.* 1357, *pg.* 1726
LUG NUT - Motorsports Entertainment - SPEEDWAY MOTORSPORTS, INC.; *pg.* 584, *pg.* 1370
LUGANO - Shoes - ALLEN-EDMONDS SHOE CORP.; *pg.* 1804, *pg.* 1887
LUGANO - Cheese - SAPUTO, INC.; *pg.* 893, *pg.* 1956
LUGZ - Casual Shoes - JACK SCHWARTZ SHOES, INC.; *pg.* 1810, *pg.* 1245
LUIGI'S - Italian Flavored Ice Beverages - J&J SNACK FOODS CORPORATION; *pg.* 865, *pg.* 1107
LUIGI'S SWIRL - Real Fruit Flavored & Dairy Free Smooth-Textured Ices - J&J SNACK FOODS CORPORATION; *pg.* 865, *pg.* 1107
LUIS - Furniture - AMISCO INDUSTRIES LTD.; *pg.* 913, *pg.* 1958

LUKAS - Hydraulic Equipment - IDEX CORPORATION; *pg.* 1347, *pg.* 623
LUKE - Lion Puppet - GUND, INC.; *pg.* 954, *pg.* 1056
LUKEY - Emission System - TENNECO, INC.; *pg.* 985, *pg.* 625
LULL - Telehandler - JLG INDUSTRIES, INC.; *pg.* 1351, *pg.* 1551
LULL - Light Construction Equipment - TEXTRON INC.; *pg.* 235, *pg.* 1607
LULLABY - Footwear - STEVEN MADDEN, LTD.; *pg.* 1819, *pg.* 1176
LUMA-CATH - Medical Device - BOSTON SCIENTIFIC CORPORATION; *pg.* 1508, *pg.* 831
LUMA-CATH - Diagnostic Catheter - ST. JUDE MEDICAL, INC.; *pg.* 1596, *pg.* 963
LUMA-SITE - Trouble Light - COLEMAN CABLE, INC.; *pg.* 1324, *pg.* 665
LUMA VI - Lighting Controls - PASS & SEYMOUR/LEGRAND; *pg.* 1303, *pg.* 1344
LUMABRITE HD - Cleaner - PENETONE CORPORATION; *pg.* 333, *pg.* 1050
LUMACELL - Emergency Lighting - THOMAS & BETTS CORPORATION; *pg.* 680, *pg.* 1646
LUMACORE - Electronic Components - MOLEX INCORPORATED; *pg.* 655, *pg.* 628
LUMAPRO - Lighting Products - W.W. GRAINGER, INC.; *pg.* 1390, *pg.* 625
LUMAR - Skin Treatment - LUZIER PERSONALIZED COSMETICS, INC.; *pg.* 515, *pg.* 978
LUMASPEC - Dimmers & Fan Speed Controls - PASS & SEYMOUR/LEGRAND; *pg.* 1303, *pg.* 1344
LUMAVIDIN - Microspheres - LUMINEX CORPORATION; *pg.* 1421, *pg.* 1664
LUMAX - Catheter - COOK GROUP, INC.; *pg.* 1518, *pg.* 674
LUMBAR TRACK - Medical Device - INTEGRA LIFESCIENCES HOLDINGS CORPORATION; *pg.* 1545, *pg.* 1109
LUMBARCUSHION - Cushion - TEMPUR SEALY INTERNATIONAL, INC.; *pg.* 944, *pg.* 731
LUMBROSACRAL - Orthopedic Product - DJO INCORPORATED; *pg.* 1524, *pg.* 302
LUMEC - Lighting Fixture & Control - PHILIPS LIGHTING; *pg.* 1303, *pg.* 806
LUMEC-SCHREDER - Lighting Fixture & Control - PHILIPS LIGHTING; *pg.* 1303, *pg.* 806
LUMEON360 - Lighting Systems - REVOLUTION LIGHTING TECHNOLOGIES, INC.; *pg.* 1304, *pg.* 377
LUMESSENCE - Hair & Skin Product - AUBREY ORGANICS INC.; *pg.* 499, *pg.* 470
LUMEX - Healthcare Product - GF HEALTH PRODUCTS, INC.; *pg.* 1535, *pg.* 508
LUMEXAIR - Healthcare Product - GF HEALTH PRODUCTS, INC.; *pg.* 1535, *pg.* 508
LUMI - Software - BIO-RAD LABORATORIES, INC.; *pg.* 1504, *pg.* 101
LUMICON - Video Game Controller - MAD CATZ INTERACTIVE INC.; *pg.* 429, *pg.* 204
LUMICYTE - Medical Product - PROPPER MANUFACTURING COMPANY, INC.; *pg.* 1586, *pg.* 1175
LUMIDOC - Software - BIO-RAD LABORATORIES, INC.; *pg.* 1504, *pg.* 101
LUMIERE PLACE - Casino & Hotel - PINNACLE ENTERTAINMENT, INC.; *pg.* 576, *pg.* 1029
LUMIFICIENT - Lighting Systems - REVOLUTION LIGHTING TECHNOLOGIES, INC.; *pg.* 1304, *pg.* 377
LUMIGAN - Eye Care Product - ALLERGAN, INC.; *pg.* 1491, *pg.* 106
LUMIJET - Microplate Counter - PERKINELMER, INC.; *pg.* 1426, *pg.* 853
LUMILUX - Pigment - HONEYWELL INTERNATIONAL INC.; *pg.* 407, *pg.* 1088
LUMIMARK - Software - BIO-RAD LABORATORIES, INC.; *pg.* 1504, *pg.* 101
LUMIMARK PLUS - Software - BIO-RAD LABORATORIES, INC.; *pg.* 1504, *pg.* 101
LUMIN - Uterine Manipulation Tool - UTAH MEDICAL PRODUCTS, INC.; *pg.* 1605, *pg.* 1752
LUMINA - Pigment - BASF CATALYSTS LLC; *pg.* 1148, *pg.* 1074
LUMINATOR - Flashlights - DORCY INTERNATIONAL INC.; *pg.* 1046, *pg.* 1439
LUMINATOR - Laser System - GSI GROUP INC.; *pg.* 1415, *pg.* 784
LUMINESSE - Lipstick - COVER GIRL COSMETICS; *pg.* 506, *pg.* 772
LUMINESSE SATIN FINISH - Eye pencils - COVER GIRL COSMETICS; *pg.* 506, *pg.* 772
LUMINETTE - Soft Vertical Fabric Vanes Between Sheer Fabric Facings - HUNTER DOUGLAS, INC.; *pg.* 928, *pg.* 1320
LUMINEX 100 - Software - LUMINEX CORPORATION; *pg.* 1421, *pg.* 1664
LUMINEX 100 IS - Analytical Device - LUMINEX CORPORATION; *pg.* 1421, *pg.* 1664
LUMINEX 200 - Testing Technology - LUMINEX CORPORATION; *pg.* 1421, *pg.* 1664
LUMINEX HTS - Testing Technology - LUMINEX CORPORATION; *pg.* 1421, *pg.* 1664
LUMINEX IS - Software - LUMINEX CORPORATION; *pg.* 1421, *pg.* 1664
LUMINEX SD - Delivery System - LUMINEX CORPORATION; *pg.* 1421, *pg.* 1664
LUMINEX XYP - Analytical Device - LUMINEX CORPORATION; *pg.* 1421, *pg.* 1664
LUMINO - Plumbing Product - SLOAN VALVE COMPANY; *pg.* 1062, *pg.* 613
LUMINOSA - Candles - THE CLOROX COMPANY; *pg.* 327, *pg.* 169
LUMINOSA - Bath & Plumbing Product - JACUZZI BRANDS CORPORATION; *pg.* 554, *pg.* 65
LUMINOX - Cleaning Detergent - ALCONOX, INC.; *pg.* 325, *pg.* 1351
LUMIO - Molecular Biology Product - THERMO FISHER SCIENTIFIC INC.; *pg.* 1602, *pg.* 61
LUMITECH - Organ Technical System - ALLEN ORGAN COMPANY; *pg.* 527, *pg.* 1549
LUMIVENT - Automatic Fire Vent - THE BILCO COMPANY; *pg.* 70, *pg.* 383
LUMIX - Digital Cameras - PANASONIC CORPORATION OF NORTH AMERICA; *pg.* 661, *pg.* 1120
LUMIZYME - Lysosomal Storage Disorder - GENZYME CORPORATION; *pg.* 1534, *pg.* 808
LUMONICS - Lasers - GSI GROUP INC.; *pg.* 1415, *pg.* 784
LUNA - Bath & Plumbing Product - JACUZZI BRANDS CORPORATION; *pg.* 554, *pg.* 65
LUNA - Personal Care Product - WESTROCK COMPANY; *pg.* 1472, *pg.* 1805
LUNA BAR - Food Product - CLIF BAR INC.; *pg.* 848, *pg.* 83
LUNA PIER - Apparel - BRODER BROS., CO.; *pg.* 1828, *pg.* 1588
LUNADA - Furniture - VIRCO MANUFACTURING CORPORATION; *pg.* 946, *pg.* 297
LUNAR - Lighted Visor - LUND INTERNATIONAL, INC.; *pg.* 211, *pg.* 526
LUNAR - Predecorated Ceiling Board - USG CORPORATION; *pg.* 118, *pg.* 594
LUNAR PENGUIN - Defense System - RAYTHEON COMPANY; *pg.* 233, *pg.* 854
LUNAR PLANETARY IMAGER - Imagers - MEADE INSTRUMENTS CORPORATION; *pg.* 1422, *pg.* 113
LUNAR PROSPECTOR - Spacecraft Vehicles - LOCKHEED MARTIN CORPORATION; *pg.* 229, *pg.* 762
LUNARTRAINER - Footwear - NIKE, INC.; *pg.* 1812, *pg.* 1492
LUNARTRAINER+ID - Footwear - NIKE, INC.; *pg.* 1812, *pg.* 1492
LUNCH EXPRESS - Insulated Lunch Bag - IGLOO PRODUCTS CORPORATION; *pg.* 1126, *pg.* 1724
LUNCHABLES - Juices - THE KRAFT HEINZ COMPANY; *pg.* 870, *pg.* 1577
LUNCHLUGGER - Portable Insulated Coolers - THERMOS L.L.C.; *pg.* 61, *pg.* 660
LUNCHMAKERS - Food Product - CONAGRA FOODS, INC.; *pg.* 826, *pg.* 1014
LUNCHMAKERS - Meat Products - JOHN MORRELL FOOD GROUP; *pg.* 866, *pg.* 628
LUNCHMATE - Insulated Lunch Bag - IGLOO PRODUCTS CORPORATION; *pg.* 1126, *pg.* 1724
LUNCHTIME TRIVIA - General Knowledge 15 Minute Trivia Game - NTN BUZZTIME, INC.; *pg.* 659, *pg.* 60
LUND - Boats - BRUNSWICK CORPORATION; *pg.* 1828, *pg.* 623
LUND SUNVISOR - Truck & Van Windshield Sunvisor - LUND INTERNATIONAL, INC.; *pg.* 211, *pg.* 526
LUNDAHL NT - Footwear - K-SWISS; *pg.* 1837, *pg.* 306
LUNESTA - Pharmaceutical Product - SUNOVION PHARMACEUTICALS INC.; *pg.* 1599, *pg.* 832
LUNKER - Aluminum Boat - ALUMACRAFT BOAT COMPANY; *pg.* 1705, *pg.* 964
LUNNAR - Footwear - STEVEN MADDEN, LTD.; *pg.* 1819, *pg.* 1176
LUPRON - Synthetic Hormone - ABBOTT LABORATORIES; *pg.* 1484, *pg.* 551
LUPRON DEPOT - Drug - ABBOTT LABORATORIES; *pg.* 1484, *pg.* 551
LURAMIST - Pharmaceutical Preparations - VIVUS, INC.; *pg.* 1608, *pg.* 163
LURAWAVE - Software - ACD SYSTEMS INTERNATIONAL INC.; *pg.* 340, *pg.* 1913
LURCH 1.0 - Bicycles - G. JOANNOU CYCLE CO. INC.; *pg.* 1707, *pg.* 1098
LURCH 2.0 - Bicycles - G. JOANNOU CYCLE CO. INC.; *pg.* 1707, *pg.* 1098
LURE-EYES - Sunglasses & Accessories - ALLIANCE SPORTS GROUP, L.P.; *pg.* 1825, *pg.* 1698
LUS - Life Underwriting System - LINCOLN NATIONAL CORPORATION; *pg.* 776, *pg.* 1567
LUSH - Chewing Gum Flavor - WM. WRIGLEY JR. COMPANY; *pg.* 1863, *pg.* 596
LUSH LEAF - Carpet - INTERFACE, INC.; *pg.* 695, *pg.* 512
LUSKEY'S/RYON'S - Apparel Company - LUSKEY'S WESTERN STORES, INC.; *pg.* 44, *pg.* 1657
LUSOIL - Additive - BASF CATALYSTS LLC; *pg.* 1148, *pg.* 1074
LUSSANNE - Furniture - ASHLEY FURNITURE INDUSTRIES, INC.; *pg.* 914, *pg.* 1852
LUSSO - Carpet - INTERFACE, INC.; *pg.* 695, *pg.* 512
LUSTER-FLOC - Inorganic Coagulents - LUSTER-ON PRODUCTS, INC.; *pg.* 1171, *pg.* 845
LUSTER-FOS - Rust Preventative Oil - LUSTER-ON PRODUCTS, INC.; *pg.* 1171, *pg.* 845
LUSTER LITE - Burnishing Pad - AMERICO MANUFACTURING CO., INC.; *pg.* 325, *pg.* 482
LUSTER-ON - Metal Precipitants - LUSTER-ON PRODUCTS, INC.; *pg.* 1171, *pg.* 845
LUSTERCLEAN - Aqueous Cleaner - HUBBARD-HALL, INC.; *pg.* 1167, *pg.* 382
LUSTERTONE - Sink - ELKAY MANUFACTURING COMPANY; *pg.* 80, *pg.* 645
LUSTRA - Bath Product - KOHLER CO.; *pg.* 91, *pg.* 1862
LUSTRA-CAD - Metal Finishing Product - HEATBATH CORPORATION; *pg.* 1165, *pg.* 826
LUSTRA COLORS - Hair Coloring Preparations - THE GILLETTE COMPANY; *pg.* 509, *pg.* 795
LUSTRA-TIN - Plating Brightener - HEATBATH CORPORATION; *pg.* 1165, *pg.* 826
LUSTRA-TIN SN - Metal Finishing Product - HEATBATH CORPORATION; *pg.* 1165, *pg.* 826
LUSTRA-ZINC - Metal Finishing Product - HEATBATH CORPORATION; *pg.* 1165, *pg.* 826
LUSTRALITE - Paper Product - WESTROCK COMPANY; *pg.* 1472, *pg.* 1805
LUSTRASILK - Hair Care Products - INSPIRED BEAUTY BRANDS; *pg.* 512, *pg.* 1244
LUSTRE - Software - AUTODESK INC.; *pg.* 356, *pg.* 257
LUSTRE - Fabric - NEMSCHOFF, INC.; *pg.* 936, *pg.* 1890
LUSTRE - Vitamin & Herbal Supplement - SOURCE NATURALS; *pg.* 1595, *pg.* 278
LUSTRE-MIST - Furniture Cleaner & Polish - HILLYARD, INC.; *pg.* 331, *pg.* 990
LUSTRECLEAR - Pharmaceutical Ingredient - FMC CORPORATION; *pg.* 1163, *pg.* 1564
LUSTRILLO - Cleaning Utensils - THE CLOROX COMPANY; *pg.* 327, *pg.* 169
LUTALYSE - Pharmaceutical Product - PFIZER INC.; *pg.* 1581, *pg.* 1278
LUTECE - Four-Star French Restaurant Recently Trademarked for Potential Licensing - ARK RESTAURANTS CORP.; *pg.* 1715, *pg.* 1196
LUTEIN - Nutritional Supplement - NATURAL ORGANICS, INC.; *pg.* 1571, *pg.* 1181
LUTERA - Pharmaceutical Product - ALLERGAN; *pg.* 1490, *pg.* 1101
LUTHERAN BROTHERHOOD - Insurance - THRIVENT FINANCIAL FOR LUTHERANS; *pg.* 1219, *pg.* 944
THE LUTHERAN HOUR - Outreach Radio Programming - INTERNATIONAL LUTHERAN LAYMEN'S LEAGUE; *pg.* 293, *pg.* 998
LUV-A-PET - Collectible Plush Toys - PETSMART, INC.; *pg.* 1481, *pg.* 18
LUV BIRD - Shoe - AEROGROUP INTERNATIONAL, INC.; *pg.* 1803, *pg.* 1055
LUV CUBS - Toy & Game - HASBRO, INC.; *pg.* 954, *pg.* 1603
LUVS - Baby Care Product - THE PROCTER & GAMBLE

First page reference indicates Business Class Edition
Second page reference indicates Geographic Edition

COMPANY; *pg.* 1129, *pg.* 1418
LUX - Vacuum Cleaner - AERUS LLC; *pg.* 51, *pg.* 1673
LUX - Molecular Biology Product - THERMO FISHER SCIENTIFIC INC.; *pg.* 1602, *pg.* 61
LUX - Apparel - VANS, INC.; *pg.* 1821, *pg.* 76
LUX 7000 SERIES - Cannister Vacuum - AERUS LLC; *pg.* 51, *pg.* 1673
LUXE - Fabric - NEMSCHOFF, INC.; *pg.* 936, *pg.* 1890
LUXE - Footwear - PHOENIX FOOTWEAR GROUP, INC.; *pg.* 1815, *pg.* 60
LUXE CLASSIC - Footwear - K-SWISS; *pg.* 1837, *pg.* 306
LUXE PREMIUM CLASSIC - Footwear - K-SWISS; *pg.* 1837, *pg.* 306
LUXEL - Dosimetry Product - LANDAUER, INC.; *pg.* 1554, *pg.* 615
LUXIL - Cosmetic Microspheres - PQ CORPORATION; *pg.* 1178, *pg.* 1515
LUXIVA - Skincare Product - MERLE NORMAN COSMETICS, INC.; *pg.* 517, *pg.* 136
LUXLAYER - Mattress Pad - SELECT COMFORT CORPORATION; *pg.* 942, *pg.* 942
LUXLOFT - Pillow - SELECT COMFORT CORPORATION; *pg.* 942, *pg.* 942
LUXOL - Chemical Product - SPECTRUM CHEMICALS & LABORATORY PRODUCTS, INC.; *pg.* 1181, *pg.* 94
LUXOR - Audio Visual Material Storage Cabinets - LUXOR CORP.; *pg.* 428, *pg.* 666
LUXOR - Toilet Partition - METPAR CORP.; *pg.* 97, *pg.* 1350
LUXOR - Resort & Casino - MGM RESORTS INTERNATIONAL; *pg.* 1105, *pg.* 1028
LUXOR - Eye Protection Product - MINE SAFETY APPLIANCES COMPANY; *pg.* 1361, *pg.* 1525
LUXOR - Dry Air Generator - MOTAN, INC.; *pg.* 1886, *pg.* 903
LUXOR - Fabric - NEMSCHOFF, INC.; *pg.* 936, *pg.* 1890
LUXORBIN - Conveying System - MOTAN, INC.; *pg.* 1886, *pg.* 903
LUXORNET - Conveying System - MOTAN, INC.; *pg.* 1886, *pg.* 903
LUXOVAL - Undermount Lavatory - GERBER PLUMBING FIXTURES CORPORATION; *pg.* 84, *pg.* 672
LUXPRINT - Printing Ink - E.I. DU PONT DE NEMOURS & COMPANY; *pg.* 1159, *pg.* 390
LUXSICO - Paint Product - AKZO NOBEL; *pg.* 1439, *pg.* 1952
LUXSIL - Cosmetic Microspheres - POTTERS INDUSTRIES, INC.; *pg.* 105, *pg.* 1515
LUXURA - Bath & Plumbing Product - JACUZZI BRANDS CORPORATION; *pg.* 554, *pg.* 65
LUXURIA - Rug - COURISTAN INC.; *pg.* 921, *pg.* 1067
LUXURY - Pasta - AMERICAN ITALIAN PASTA COMPANY; *pg.* 837, *pg.* 980
LUXURY - Blousecoats - ELBECO INCORPORATED; *pg.* 40, *pg.* 1584
THE LUXURY COLLECTION - Carpet - BEAULIEU GROUP, LLC; *pg.* 917, *pg.* 529
THE LUXURY COLLECTION - Hotels - STARWOOD HOTELS & RESORTS WORLDWIDE, INC.; *pg.* 1114, *pg.* 378
LUXURY ESCAPES - Mattress - KING KOIL LICENSING COMPANY INC.; *pg.* 932, *pg.* 671
LUXURY INCLUDED - Vacation Program - SANDALS RESORTS INTERNATIONAL; *pg.* 1111, *pg.* 446
LUXURY PLUS - Trousers - ELBECO INCORPORATED; *pg.* 40, *pg.* 1584
LUXURYBAC - Fiber - BEAULIEU GROUP, LLC; *pg.* 917, *pg.* 529
LUXWORKS - Telecommunication Industry Software - AVAGO TECHNOLOGIES; *pg.* 358, *pg.* 238
LUZIER - Skincare Cream - LUZIER PERSONALIZED COSMETICS, INC.; *pg.* 515, *pg.* 978
LV100 OEM BOARD - Wireless Product - HEMISPHERE GPS INC.; *pg.* 642, *pg.* 1903
LVND - Video Displays - ITUS CORPORATION; *pg.* 422, *pg.* 1180
LVPLUS III - Universal Life Insurance Product - GENWORTH LIFE AND ANNUITY INSURANCE COMPANY; *pg.* 1201, *pg.* 1802
LVPS - Engineered Product And System - SULZER METCO (WESTBURY) INC.; *pg.* 1064, *pg.* 1350
LVS - Liquid Vehicle System Data Sheet - ANSUL, INCORPORATED; *pg.* 1147, *pg.* 1869
LVT - Light Valves - EASTMAN KODAK COMPANY; *pg.* 1408, *pg.* 1333
LVY - Bath Accessory - CROSCILL, INC.; *pg.* 1122, *pg.* 1220
LWI - Plastic Refractory - PLIBRICO CO. LLC; *pg.* 104, *pg.* 587
LWM9045 - Inspection System - KLA-TENCOR CORPORATION; *pg.* 1353, *pg.* 146
LX - Clinical Chemistry Analyzer & Reagents - BECKMAN COULTER, INC.; *pg.* 1402, *pg.* 48
LX - Information Therapy - HEALTHWISE, INCORPORATED; *pg.* 143, *pg.* 546
LX-1 - Wireless Product - HEMISPHERE GPS INC.; *pg.* 642, *pg.* 1903
LX-1035 - Resins - NEVILLE CHEMICAL COMPANY; *pg.* 1174, *pg.* 1578
LX-105 - Resins - NEVILLE CHEMICAL COMPANY; *pg.* 1174, *pg.* 1578
LX-1082 - Resins - NEVILLE CHEMICAL COMPANY; *pg.* 1174, *pg.* 1578
LX-1122 - Resins - NEVILLE CHEMICAL COMPANY; *pg.* 1174, *pg.* 1578
LX-1127 - Resins - NEVILLE CHEMICAL COMPANY; *pg.* 1174, *pg.* 1578
LX-1144 - Resins - NEVILLE CHEMICAL COMPANY; *pg.* 1174, *pg.* 1578
LX-1200 - Resins - NEVILLE CHEMICAL COMPANY; *pg.* 1174, *pg.* 1578
LX-125 - Resins - NEVILLE CHEMICAL COMPANY; *pg.* 1174, *pg.* 1578
LX-130 - Resins - NEVILLE CHEMICAL COMPANY; *pg.* 1174, *pg.* 1578
LX-1314 - Resins - NEVILLE CHEMICAL COMPANY; *pg.* 1174, *pg.* 1578
LX-135 - Resins - NEVILLE CHEMICAL COMPANY; *pg.* 1174, *pg.* 1578
LX-2000 - Resins - NEVILLE CHEMICAL COMPANY; *pg.* 1174, *pg.* 1578
LX-2600 - Resins - NEVILLE CHEMICAL COMPANY; *pg.* 1174, *pg.* 1578
LX-270 - Resins - NEVILLE CHEMICAL COMPANY; *pg.* 1174, *pg.* 1578
LX-280 - Resins - NEVILLE CHEMICAL COMPANY; *pg.* 1174, *pg.* 1578
LX-300 - Dot Matrix Printer - EPSON AMERICA INC.; *pg.* 394, *pg.* 122
LX-685 - Resins - NEVILLE CHEMICAL COMPANY; *pg.* 1174, *pg.* 1578
LX-782 - Resins - NEVILLE CHEMICAL COMPANY; *pg.* 1174, *pg.* 1578
LX-830 - Chemical Product - NEVILLE CHEMICAL COMPANY; *pg.* 1174, *pg.* 1578
LX-961 - Chemical Product - NEVILLE CHEMICAL COMPANY; *pg.* 1174, *pg.* 1578
LX SERIES - Wireless Microphones - SHURE INCORPORATED; *pg.* 672, *pg.* 638
LX200 - Telescope - MEADE INSTRUMENTS CORPORATION; *pg.* 1422, *pg.* 113
LX90 - Telescopes - MEADE INSTRUMENTS CORPORATION; *pg.* 1422, *pg.* 113
LXD55 - Optical Telescopes - MEADE INSTRUMENTS CORPORATION; *pg.* 1422, *pg.* 113
LXD75 - Telescope - MEADE INSTRUMENTS CORPORATION; *pg.* 1422, *pg.* 113
LXT - Pipe - DETREX CORPORATION; *pg.* 1156, *pg.* 906
LYBREL - Oral Contraceptive - PFIZER INC.; *pg.* 1581, *pg.* 1278
LYCRA - Stretch Fabrics - INVISTA B.V.; *pg.* 1168, *pg.* 723
LYCRA - Shampoo - MCNETT CORPORATION; *pg.* 1839, *pg.* 1817
LYDAIR - Separation Product - LYDALL, INC.; *pg.* 1357, *pg.* 354
LYDIA - Decorative Accessory - ETHAN ALLEN INTERIORS INC.; *pg.* 924, *pg.* 343
LYDIA - Dinnerware - THE HOMER LAUGHLIN CHINA COMPANY; *pg.* 1125, *pg.* 1850
LYFLEX - Separation Product - LYDALL, INC.; *pg.* 1357, *pg.* 354
LYKES - Food Products - SMITHFIELD FOODS, INC.; *pg.* 896, *pg.* 1806
LYLE - Furniture - LA-Z-BOY INCORPORATED; *pg.* 932, *pg.* 901
LYMAN - Reloading Press - LYMAN PRODUCTS CORPORATION; *pg.* 1839, *pg.* 356
LYMEVAX - Canine Lyme Disease Prevention Vaccine - PFIZER INC.; *pg.* 1581, *pg.* 1278
LYMPHOCIDE - Non Hodgkin's Lymphoma Therapy - IMMUNOMEDICS, INC.; *pg.* 1544, *pg.* 1087
LYMPHOSCAN - In-Vivo Non Hodgkin's Lymphoma Therapy - IMMUNOMEDICS, INC.; *pg.* 1544, *pg.* 1087
LYMPHOSTAT-B - Biopharmaceutical Product - GLAXOSMITHKLINE; *pg.* 1537, *pg.* 776
LYN LARSEN - Organ - ALLEN ORGAN COMPANY; *pg.* 527, *pg.* 1549
LYNN WILSON MEXICAN FOODS - Food Product - RESER'S FINE FOODS INC.; *pg.* 1032, *pg.* 1496
LYNWOOD - Kitchen Cabinets - KITCHEN KOMPACT, INC.; *pg.* 91, *pg.* 692
LYNX - Wafer Processing System - AIXTRON INC.; *pg.* 1310, *pg.* 283
LYNX - Computer Hardware & Software - AVAGO TECHNOLOGIES; *pg.* 358, *pg.* 238
LYNX - Catalyst - BASF CATALYSTS LLC; *pg.* 1148, *pg.* 1074
LYNX - Snowmobiles, Snowgrooming Equipment & Multi-Purpose Tracked Vehicles - BOMBARDIER RECREATIONAL PRODUCTS, INC.; *pg.* 201, *pg.* 1960
LYNX - Medical Device - BOSTON SCIENTIFIC CORPORATION; *pg.* 1508, *pg.* 831
LYNX - Paper - DOMTAR CORPORATION; *pg.* 1456, *pg.* 1954
LYNX - Golf Equipment - GOLFSMITH INTERNATIONAL HOLDINGS, INC.; *pg.* 1835, *pg.* 1662
LYNX - Control Panel - HONEYWELL INTERNATIONAL INC.; *pg.* 407, *pg.* 1088
LYNX - Medical Equipment - INVACARE CORPORATION; *pg.* 1546, *pg.* 1451
LYNX - Wireless Video Game Controller - MAD CATZ INTERACTIVE INC.; *pg.* 429, *pg.* 204
LYNX - Rescue Equipment - MINE SAFETY APPLIANCES COMPANY; *pg.* 1361, *pg.* 1525
LYNX - Amplifiers - SKYWORKS SOLUTIONS, INC.; *pg.* 674, *pg.* 862
LYNX - Spotting Scope - SWIFT OPTICAL INSTRUMENTS, INC.; *pg.* 1430, *pg.* 1744
LYNX - Paper Product - WEYERHAEUSER COMPANY; *pg.* 121, *pg.* 1820
LYNX 1000 - Polypropylene Catalyst - BASF CATALYSTS LLC; *pg.* 1148, *pg.* 1074
LYNX SX-3 - Three-wheel PMV - INVACARE CORPORATION; *pg.* 1546, *pg.* 1451
LYNX2 - CVD & ALD Single Wafer Process (200 mm) - AIXTRON INC.; *pg.* 1310, *pg.* 283
LYNX3 - CVD & ALD 300 mm - AIXTRON INC.; *pg.* 1310, *pg.* 283
LYNXARRAY II - Storage System - DOT HILL SYSTEMS CORP.; *pg.* 388, *pg.* 333
LYNXINSURE - Software - LYNX SOFTWARE TECHNOLOGIES; *pg.* 429, *pg.* 247
LYNXOS - Software - LYNX SOFTWARE TECHNOLOGIES; *pg.* 429, *pg.* 247
LYNXSOFT - Computer Programs - TEXAS INSTRUMENTS INCORPORATED; *pg.* 679, *pg.* 1688
LYNXSTACK - Storage System - DOT HILL SYSTEMS CORP.; *pg.* 388, *pg.* 333
LYOCELL - Pillow - SELECT COMFORT CORPORATION; *pg.* 942, *pg.* 942
LYOCELL DOWN - Mattress Pad - SELECT COMFORT CORPORATION; *pg.* 942, *pg.* 942
LYOGUARD - Tray - W.L. GORE & ASSOCIATES, INC.; *pg.* 122, *pg.* 388
LYONS - Speedometer Seals - PECO, INC.; *pg.* 1368, *pg.* 1505
THE LYONS PRESS - Publisher of Fly Fishing & Outdoor Books - THE GLOBE PEQUOT PRESS, INC.; *pg.* 1645, *pg.* 350
LYOPRINT - Auxiliaries & Thickeners - HUNTSMAN CORPORATION; *pg.* 1167, *pg.* 1758
LYOSCAN - High-Speed Inspection System - ATS AUTOMATION TOOLING SYSTEMS INC.; *pg.* 355, *pg.* 1919
LYOTEC - Stoppers - WEST PHARMACEUTICAL SERVICES, INC.; *pg.* 1472, *pg.* 1532
LYOVAC - Freeze Dryer - STERIS CORPORATION; *pg.* 1597, *pg.* 1464
LYPHLINE - Software - BIO-RAD LABORATORIES, INC.; *pg.* 1504, *pg.* 101
LYPHOCHEK - Clinical Diagnostic Product - BIO-RAD LABORATORIES, INC.; *pg.* 1504, *pg.* 101
LYPORE - Separation Product - LYDALL, INC.; *pg.* 1357, *pg.* 354
LYPTUS - Wood & Building Material - WEYERHAEUSER COMPANY; *pg.* 121, *pg.* 1820
LYRA - Laser System - AMERICAN MEDICAL SYSTEMS,

INC.; *pg.* 1399, *pg.* 238
LYRA - Lighting - STEELCASE INC.; *pg.* 475, *pg.* 889
LYRA-I - Surgical Laser System - AMERICAN MEDICAL SYSTEMS, INC.; *pg.* 1399, *pg.* 238
LYRA-I - Medical Laser System - IRIDEX CORPORATION; *pg.* 648, *pg.* 160
LYRAL - Fragrance Ingredient - INTERNATIONAL FLAVORS & FRAGRANCES INC.; *pg.* 512, *pg.* 1244
LYRIC - Software - CHYRONHEGO; *pg.* 371, *pg.* 1179
LYRIC - Kitchen Product - KOHLER CO.; *pg.* 91, *pg.* 1862
LYRIC - Bird Food - LEBANON SEABOARD CORPORATION; *pg.* 1797, *pg.* 1547
LYRIC - Fabric - NEMSCHOFF, INC.; *pg.* 936, *pg.* 1890
LYRIC - Office Furniture - STEELCASE INC.; *pg.* 475, *pg.* 889
LYRIC STREET RECORDS - Record Label - THE WALT DISNEY COMPANY; *pg.* 317, *pg.* 52
LYRIC SUPREME - Bird Food - LEBANON SEABOARD CORPORATION; *pg.* 1797, *pg.* 1547
LYRICA - Dinnerware - THE HOMER LAUGHLIN CHINA COMPANY; *pg.* 1125, *pg.* 1850
LYRICA - Nerve Pain & Epileptic Seizure Medication - PFIZER INC.; *pg.* 1581, *pg.* 1278
LYRIS - Furniture - HERMAN MILLER, INC.; *pg.* 926, *pg.* 913
LYRIS - Email Marketing Software - LYRIS, INC.; *pg.* 429, *pg.* 84
LYRIS HQ - Internet Making Tools - LYRIS, INC.; *pg.* 429, *pg.* 84
LYRIS HQ AGENCY EDITION - Email Marketing Software - LYRIS, INC.; *pg.* 429, *pg.* 84
LYSODREN - Health Care Product - BRISTOL-MYERS SQUIBB COMPANY; *pg.* 1509, *pg.* 1206
LYSOL - Filtration Product - FLANDERS CORPORATION; *pg.* 1336, *pg.* 1392
LYSOL - Cleaning Products & Disinfectant Spray - RECKITT BENCKISER INC.; *pg.* 1136, *pg.* 1105
LYSONIX - Medical Device - MENTOR CORPORATION; *pg.* 1565, *pg.* 263
LYSONIX - Medical Device - MISONIX INC.; *pg.* 1568, *pg.* 1159
LYSORB 218 - Absorbents - ARCHER-DANIELS-MIDLAND COMPANY; *pg.* 825, *pg.* 565
LYSORB 220 - Absorbents - ARCHER-DANIELS-MIDLAND COMPANY; *pg.* 825, *pg.* 565
LYSOSENSOR - Molecular Probe Product - THERMO FISHER SCIENTIFIC INC.; *pg.* 1602, *pg.* 61
LYSOTRACKER - Molecular Probe Product - THERMO FISHER SCIENTIFIC INC.; *pg.* 1602, *pg.* 61
LYTECASTER - Recessed Lighting - LIGHTOLIER; *pg.* 1301, *pg.* 819
LYTELAUNCH 150 - Illuminator - REVOLUTION LIGHTING TECHNOLOGIES, INC.; *pg.* 1304, *pg.* 377
LYTEPRO - HID Wallprisms - CRESCENT/STONCO SUPPLY DIVISION; *pg.* 1295, *pg.* 1121
LYTESPAN - Track Lighting - LIGHTOLIER; *pg.* 1301, *pg.* 819
LYTETRAK - Fiber Optic Fixtures - REVOLUTION LIGHTING TECHNOLOGIES, INC.; *pg.* 1304, *pg.* 377
LYTHERM - Hard Pack Battery System - LYDALL, INC.; *pg.* 1357, *pg.* 354
LYTICBLAZER - Molecular Probe Product - THERMO FISHER SCIENTIFIC INC.; *pg.* 1602, *pg.* 61
LYTOR - Tall Oil Rosin - GEORGIA-PACIFIC LLC; *pg.* 1458, *pg.* 507
LZR 1200 SERIES - Laser Printers - RICOH PRINTING SYSTEMS AMERICA, INC.; *pg.* 462, *pg.* 279
LZR 2600 SERIES - Laser Printers - RICOH PRINTING SYSTEMS AMERICA, INC.; *pg.* 462, *pg.* 279

M

M - Men's Fashion Magazine - CONDE NAST PUBLICATIONS, INC.; *pg.* 1629, *pg.* 1217
M 3 POWER - Blade & Razor - THE GILLETTE COMPANY; *pg.* 509, *pg.* 795
M-61 - Cosmetics & Skincare - BLUEMERCURY, INC.; *pg.* 502, *pg.* 396
M-A-C - Color Cosmetics, Makeup Tools, Skin Care, Foundations & Fragrances - THE ESTEE LAUDER COMPANIES INC.; *pg.* 508, *pg.* 1229
M/A-COM - Wireless Products - TE CONNECTIVITY LTD.; *pg.* 677, *pg.* 1515
M&M'S - Candy - MARS, INCORPORATED; *pg.* 1858, *pg.* 1792
M & P - Pistol - SMITH & WESSON HOLDING CORPORATION; *pg.* 1845, *pg.* 846
M&P45C - Pistol - SMITH & WESSON HOLDING CORPORATION; *pg.* 1845, *pg.* 846
M&P9 - Pistol - SMITH & WESSON HOLDING CORPORATION; *pg.* 1845, *pg.* 846
M&W - Mowers - ALAMO GROUP INC.; *pg.* 1311, *pg.* 1745
M. BUTTERFLY - Tile - ARTISTIC TILE INC.; *pg.* 914, *pg.* 1119
M-CAT - Glass & Ceramic Material - CORNING INCORPORATED; *pg.* 1122, *pg.* 1154
M-CLASS - Bar Code System - DATAMAX CORPORATION; *pg.* 1633, *pg.* 453
M-CORE - Communications Product - MOTOROLA SOLUTIONS, INC.; *pg.* 657, *pg.* 659
M-FIAM - Filter - VICOR CORPORATION; *pg.* 1435, *pg.* 783
M FRAME - Eyewear - OAKLEY, INC.; *pg.* 1840, *pg.* 86
M-GATOR - Military Utility Vehicle - DEERE & COMPANY; *pg.* 703, *pg.* 632
M-IV - Medical Product - HOLOGIC, INC.; *pg.* 1416, *pg.* 784
M-IV PLATINUM - Medical Product - HOLOGIC, INC.; *pg.* 1416, *pg.* 784
M-LINE - Steel Office Desk - INVINCIBLE OFFICE FURNITURE; *pg.* 420, *pg.* 1868
M-LINK - Graphics Card - ADVANCED MICRO DEVICES, INC.; *pg.* 613, *pg.* 282
M-LOC - Navigation Aid - TRIMBLE NAVIGATION LIMITED; *pg.* 1384, *pg.* 288
M ONE - Fly Reels - DAIWA CORPORATION; *pg.* 1832, *pg.* 75
M-PACK - Asphalt Equipment - ASTEC INDUSTRIES, INC.; *pg.* 69, *pg.* 1628
M-PAKT ULTRA LOW NOX - Burner - MAXON CORPORATION; *pg.* 1359, *pg.* 695
M-SERIES - Meter - BADGER METER, INC.; *pg.* 1401, *pg.* 1873
M SERIES - Serial Dot - RICOH PRINTING SYSTEMS AMERICA, INC.; *pg.* 462, *pg.* 279
M SERIES - Switch Operator - S&C ELECTRIC COMPANY; *pg.* 1305, *pg.* 589
M SERIES - CCT Defibrillator - ZOLL MEDICAL CORPORATION; *pg.* 1612, *pg.* 814
M SERVICE MAGIC - Home Improvement - IAC/INTERACTIVECORP; *pg.* 292, *pg.* 1242
M-STAR - Glass & Ceramic Material - CORNING INCORPORATED; *pg.* 1122, *pg.* 1154
M-STOPP - Pipeline Pigging Product - T.D. WILLIAMSON, INC.; *pg.* 1380, *pg.* 1490
M-TAPE - All Cotton Sports Tape - MUELLER SPORTS MEDICINE, INC.; *pg.* 1570, *pg.* 1887
M-TURBO - Ultrasound System - SONOSITE, INC.; *pg.* 1429, *pg.* 1818
M-VENTOR - Education & Entertainment Services - MOTOROLA SOLUTIONS, INC.; *pg.* 657, *pg.* 659
M-WRAP - Foam Underwrap - MUELLER SPORTS MEDICINE, INC.; *pg.* 1570, *pg.* 1887
M+PAC - Swine Pneumonia Vaccine - MERCK & CO., INC.; *pg.* 1566, *pg.* 1077
M1 MANUAL SILENCER - Animal Chute - BEHLEN MFG. CO.; *pg.* 701, *pg.* 1010
M1 MEDIABOLIC - Digital Directory - ROVI CORPORATION; *pg.* 463, *pg.* 269
M100 FIREGARD SYSTEM - Rolling Fire Door - CORNELL IRON WORKS, INC.; *pg.* 77, *pg.* 1554
M15 - Printer - XEROX CORPORATION; *pg.* 494, *pg.* 365
M2 - Case Tumbler - HORNADY MANUFACTURING COMPANY; *pg.* 1836, *pg.* 1010
M2 - Bicycle - SPECIALIZED BICYCLE COMPONENTS, INC.; *pg.* 1711, *pg.* 152
M20 - Printer - XEROX CORPORATION; *pg.* 494, *pg.* 365
M2300 - Fluid Handling System - GRACO, INC.; *pg.* 1342, *pg.* 935
M2A-38 ACETABULAR - Hip Product - ZIMMER BIOMET HOLDINGS, INC.; *pg.* 1611, *pg.* 699
M2A ACETABULAR - Hip Product - ZIMMER BIOMET HOLDINGS, INC.; *pg.* 1611, *pg.* 699
M2A-TAPER ACETABULAR - Hip Product - ZIMMER BIOMET HOLDINGS, INC.; *pg.* 1611, *pg.* 699
M2Z - Accident & Injury Prevention - WASTE MANAGEMENT, INC.; *pg.* 1954, *pg.* 1716
M3-X - Surgical Screws - OSTEOMED CORPORATION; *pg.* 1425, *pg.* 1658
M300 - Cosmetics - WESTROCK COMPANY; *pg.* 1472, *pg.* 1805
M35 - Printer - XEROX CORPORATION; *pg.* 494, *pg.* 365
M3O - Software - VITRIA TECHNOLOGY, INC.; *pg.* 490, *pg.* 289
M4 - Communication Product - J2 GLOBAL COMMUNICATIONS, INC.; *pg.* 1260, *pg.* 133
M4 - Controller - REVOLUTION LIGHTING TECHNOLOGIES, INC.; *pg.* 1304, *pg.* 377
M4 RIGID FIXATION SYSTEM - Surgical Instruments - OSTEOMED CORPORATION; *pg.* 1425, *pg.* 1658
M430 - Laser System - GSI GROUP INC.; *pg.* 1415, *pg.* 784
M45 - Printer - XEROX CORPORATION; *pg.* 494, *pg.* 365
M4K - Microprocessor Core - IMAGINATION TECHNOLOGIES; *pg.* 412, *pg.* 285
M50 - Medical Equipment - INVACARE CORPORATION; *pg.* 1546, *pg.* 1451
M51 - Medical Equipment - INVACARE CORPORATION; *pg.* 1546, *pg.* 1451
M55 - Printer - XEROX CORPORATION; *pg.* 494, *pg.* 365
M61 - Medical Equipment - INVACARE CORPORATION; *pg.* 1546, *pg.* 1451
M71 - Medical Equipment - INVACARE CORPORATION; *pg.* 1546, *pg.* 1451
M77 - Bolt-Action Rifles - STURM, RUGER & COMPANY, INC.; *pg.* 1846, *pg.* 371
M8 - Semiconductor Solution - CYPRESS SEMICONDUCTOR CORPORATION; *pg.* 1326, *pg.* 243
M9000 - Digital Cutting System - EASTMAN MACHINE COMPANY; *pg.* 1331, *pg.* 1148
M91 - Medical Equipment - INVACARE CORPORATION; *pg.* 1546, *pg.* 1451
M94 - Medical Equipment - INVACARE CORPORATION; *pg.* 1546, *pg.* 1451
MA-25S - Thermal Insulation & Ablative Material - LOCKHEED MARTIN CORPORATION; *pg.* 229, *pg.* 762
MAAX PEARL - Bathware - MAAX INC.-MINNEAPOLIS; *pg.* 1885, *pg.* 938
MAAZA - Soft Drink - THE COCA-COLA COMPANY; *pg.* 240, *pg.* 493
MAB PAINTS - Paints - THE SHERWIN-WILLIAMS COMPANY; *pg.* 1447, *pg.* 1435
MABBELL - Footwear - STEVEN MADDEN, LTD.; *pg.* 1819, *pg.* 1176
MABCAMPATH - Oncology - GENZYME CORPORATION; *pg.* 1534, *pg.* 808
MABEL - Fabric - NEMSCHOFF, INC.; *pg.* 936, *pg.* 1890
MABEL - Software System - SS&C TECHNOLOGIES HOLDINGS, INC.; *pg.* 473, *pg.* 386
MAC - Desktop and Portable Personal Computers - APPLE INC.; *pg.* 350, *pg.* 73
MAC - Mobile Air Conditioning - BACHARACH INC.; *pg.* 1400, *pg.* 1556
MAC - Deinking Flotation Unit - KADANT BLACK CLAWSON INC.; *pg.* 1352, *pg.* 1460
MAC - Tools - STANLEY BLACK & DECKER, INC.; *pg.* 1063, *pg.* 358
MAC - Joint Compound - USG CORPORATION; *pg.* 118, *pg.* 594
MAC APP - Application Program - APPLE INC.; *pg.* 350, *pg.* 73
MAC APP STORE - Online Store for Mac Apps - APPLE INC.; *pg.* 350, *pg.* 73
MAC AUDIO - Mobile & Consumer Electronics - VOXX INTERNATIONAL; *pg.* 686, *pg.* 1166
MAC II TEST - Educational Test - QUESTAR ASSESSMENT, INC.; *pg.* 1679, *pg.* 1143
MAC-LAC - Percutaneous - COOK GROUP, INC.; *pg.* 1518, *pg.* 674
MAC OS X SERVER ESSENTIALS - Training Course - APPLE INC.; *pg.* 350, *pg.* 73
MAC OS X SUPPORT ESSENTIALS - Training Course - APPLE INC.; *pg.* 350, *pg.* 73
MAC PRO - Desktop Computer - APPLE INC.; *pg.* 350, *pg.* 73
MAC SERIES - Eddy Current Testers - MAGNETIC ANALYSIS CORPORATION; *pg.* 1421, *pg.* 1158
MAC2000 - Professional Automotive Air Conditioning Service System - BACHARACH INC.; *pg.* 1400, *pg.* 1556
MACATAWA CONNECT - Online Non-downloadable Software - MACATAWA BANK CORPORATION; *pg.* 778, *pg.* 892
MACBETH - Glass & Ceramic Material - CORNING INCORPORATED; *pg.* 1122, *pg.* 1154
MACBETH - Cigar And Tobacco - SWISHER INTERNATIONAL, INC.; *pg.* 1895, *pg.* 345
MACBOOK - Computer - APPLE INC.; *pg.* 350, *pg.* 73
MACBOOK AIR - Portable Computer - APPLE INC.; *pg.* 350, *pg.* 73

First page reference indicates Business Class Edition
Second page reference indicates Geographic Edition

MACBOOK PRO - Portable Computer - APPLE INC.; *pg.* 350, *pg.* 73
MACCAFERRI GAWACWIN - Design Software - MACCAFERRI, INC.; *pg.* 95, *pg.* 780
MACCAFERRI GREEN TERRAMESH - Slope & Wall Reinforcement - MACCAFERRI, INC.; *pg.* 95, *pg.* 780
MACCAFERRI TERRAWALL - Slope & Wall Reinforcement - MACCAFERRI, INC.; *pg.* 95, *pg.* 780
MACCO - Adhesives, Caulks, Sealants - AKZONOBEL DECORATIVE PAINTS U.S.; *pg.* 1439, *pg.* 1474
MACDNS - Application Program - APPLE INC.; *pg.* 350, *pg.* 73
MACE - Aerosol Sprays - BAE SYSTEMS PRODUCTS GROUP; *pg.* 359, *pg.* 432
MACE - Security & Law Enforcement Products - MACE SECURITY INTERNATIONAL, INC.; *pg.* 1172, *pg.* 1541
MACE - Apparel - OAKLEY, INC.; *pg.* 1840, *pg.* 86
MACESS - Software - SUNGARD DATA SYSTEMS INC.; *pg.* 477, *pg.* 1592
MACFEET - Laptop Riser - LAPWORKS, INC.; *pg.* 426, *pg.* 187
MACGREGOR - Golf Equipment - GOLFSMITH INTERNATIONAL HOLDINGS, INC.; *pg.* 1835, *pg.* 1662
MACGRID EB SERIES - Slope & Wall Reinforcement - MACCAFERRI, INC.; *pg.* 95, *pg.* 780
MACGRID KG SERIES - Slope & Wall Reinforcement - MACCAFERRI, INC.; *pg.* 95, *pg.* 780
MACGRID WG SERIES - Slope & Wall Reinforcement - MACCAFERRI, INC.; *pg.* 95, *pg.* 780
MACH - Button - PRECISION VALVE CORPORATION; *pg.* 1060, *pg.* 1357
MACH - Sport Surface - ROBBINS, INC.; *pg.* 108, *pg.* 1425
MACH - Voice Link - VISTEON CORPORATION; *pg.* 221, *pg.* 912
MACH 1 - Medical Device - BOSTON SCIENTIFIC CORPORATION; *pg.* 1508, *pg.* 831
MACH 12 - Low Moisture, High Speed Carpet Extraction System - VON SCHRADER COMPANY; *pg.* 62, *pg.* 1890
MACH 3 TURBO - Blade & Razor - THE GILLETTE COMPANY; *pg.* 509, *pg.* 795
MACH ONE - Controller - ADVANCED ENERGY INDUSTRIES, INC.; *pg.* 613, *pg.* 328
MACH PA - Software System - MENTOR GRAPHICS CORPORATION; *pg.* 432, *pg.* 1510
MACH TA - Software System - MENTOR GRAPHICS CORPORATION; *pg.* 432, *pg.* 1510
MACH1 - Biomolecule Product - THERMO FISHER SCIENTIFIC INC.; *pg.* 1602, *pg.* 61
MACH3 - Blade And Razor - THE GILLETTE COMPANY; *pg.* 509, *pg.* 795
MACH4 - Storage System - HGST; *pg.* 406, *pg.* 260
MACH4 CF - Storage System - HGST; *pg.* 406, *pg.* 260
MACH4 SSD - Storage System - HGST; *pg.* 406, *pg.* 260
MACH8 - Storage System - HGST; *pg.* 406, *pg.* 260
MACH8 SSD - Storage System - HGST; *pg.* 406, *pg.* 260
MACH8IOPS SSD - Storage System - HGST; *pg.* 406, *pg.* 260
MACH8MLC SSD - Storage System - HGST; *pg.* 406, *pg.* 260
MACHINE MATED - Business Forms - THE STANDARD REGISTER COMPANY; *pg.* 473, *pg.* 1446
MACHINECLAD - Stains for Machine Application - AKZONOBEL DECORATIVE PAINTS U.S.; *pg.* 1439, *pg.* 1474
MACHINEFINDER - Online Search - DEERE & COMPANY; *pg.* 703, *pg.* 632
MACHINERY COOLANT - Fluid Sealing Product - A.W. CHESTERTON COMPANY; *pg.* 1315, *pg.* 861
MACHINES TRUST US - Slogan - NUMEREX CORP.; *pg.* 660, *pg.* 517
MACHO - After Shave Lotion - BLUE CROSS LABORATORIES; *pg.* 326, *pg.* 277
MACI - Cell Implantation - GENZYME CORPORATION; *pg.* 1534, *pg.* 808
MACIEIRA - Brandy - DIAGEO CANADA, INC.; *pg.* 1961, *pg.* 1937
MACINTOSH - Computer - APPLE INC.; *pg.* 350, *pg.* 73
MACINTOSH PRODUCTS GUIDE - Online Catalog - APPLE INC.; *pg.* 350, *pg.* 73
MACK - Trucks - MACK TRUCKS, INC.; *pg.* 183, *pg.* 1375
MACK VISION - Toys - TRACTOR SUPPLY COMPANY; *pg.* 708, *pg.* 1627
MACKENZIE - Footwear - PHOENIX FOOTWEAR GROUP, INC.; *pg.* 1815, *pg.* 60
MACKIE - Recording Equipment - LOUD TECHNOLOGIES INC.; *pg.* 652, *pg.* 1847
MACK'S - Earplugs - MCKEON PRODUCTS, INC.; *pg.* 1559, *pg.* 912
MACLAB - Laboratory Tools - STOELTING CO.; *pg.* 1430, *pg.* 671
MACLADIN - Pharmaceutical Product - ABBOTT LABORATORIES; *pg.* 1484, *pg.* 551
MACLAR - Pharmaceutical Product - ABBOTT LABORATORIES; *pg.* 1484, *pg.* 551
MACLINKPLUS - Software - DATAVIZ, INC.; *pg.* 383, *pg.* 356
MACLOCK - Fasteners - MACLEAN-FOGG COMPANY INC.; *pg.* 1358, *pg.* 635
MACMAT - Rockfall Protection - MACCAFERRI, INC.; *pg.* 95, *pg.* 780
MACMELT - Software - BIO-RAD LABORATORIES, INC.; *pg.* 1504, *pg.* 101
MACMILLAN REFERENCE USA - Reference Books - GALE CENGAGE LEARNING; *pg.* 1643, *pg.* 885
MACMURRAY RANCH - Wine - E&J GALLO WINERY; *pg.* 1962, *pg.* 149
MACNEIL - Shoes - ALLEN-EDMONDS SHOE CORP.; *pg.* 1804, *pg.* 1887
MACNEIL - Motor Vehicle Parts - MACNEIL AUTOMOTIVE PRODUCTS, LTD.; *pg.* 211, *pg.* 559
MACOPENER - Software - DATAVIZ, INC.; *pg.* 383, *pg.* 356
MACOR - Machinable Glassware - CORNING INCORPORATED; *pg.* 1122, *pg.* 1154
MACPOET - Software - WIND RIVER SYSTEMS, INC.; *pg.* 493, *pg.* 38
MACRAME - Window Treatment - CROSCILL, INC.; *pg.* 1122, *pg.* 1220
MACRAME - Window Treatment - HERITAGE LACE INC.; *pg.* 694, *pg.* 711
MACRO 5 SLR - Complete Compact Camera for Instant Close-up Photography - POLAROID CORPORATION; *pg.* 1426, *pg.* 815
MACRO-CON - Diagnostic Test Product - MERIDIAN BIOSCIENCE INC.; *pg.* 1422, *pg.* 1417
MACRO-LOCK - Electronic Components - MOLEX INCORPORATED; *pg.* 655, *pg.* 628
MACRO-PREP - Software - BIO-RAD LABORATORIES, INC.; *pg.* 1504, *pg.* 101
MACRO-SORB - BathRug - HABAND COMPANY, INC.; *pg.* 1772, *pg.* 1099
MACRO-SYMMAR - Lenses - SCHNEIDER OPTICS INC.; *pg.* 1428, *pg.* 1165
MACROBAT - Sandals - AEROGROUP INTERNATIONAL, INC.; *pg.* 1803, *pg.* 1055
MACROBEAD - Minerals - MINERALS TECHNOLOGIES INC.; *pg.* 1173, *pg.* 617
MACROBOLIC - Nutritional Supplement - MAXIMUM HUMAN PERFORMANCE, INC.; *pg.* 1559, *pg.* 1065
MACROBORE - Liquid Chromatograph Equipment - PPG INDUSTRIES, INC.; *pg.* 1445, *pg.* 1579
MACROFLEX - Coating Product - PPG INDUSTRIES, INC.; *pg.* 1445, *pg.* 1579
MACROMAX - Wireless Network Product - AIRSPAN NETWORKS INC.; *pg.* 346, *pg.* 410
MACROMAX - Pharmaceutical Product - VALEANT PHARMACEUTICALS INTERNATIONAL; *pg.* 1605, *pg.* 1047
MACROMAXE - Wireless Network Product - AIRSPAN NETWORKS INC.; *pg.* 346, *pg.* 410
MACROMEDIA - Software - ADOBE SYSTEMS INCORPORATED; *pg.* 342, *pg.* 235
MACROMELT - Hot Melt Adhesives - HENKEL CORPORATION; *pg.* 1165, *pg.* 1535
MACROMET - Rockwell-Type Hardness Tester - BUEHLER, LTD.; *pg.* 1403, *pg.* 622
MACROPLAST - Polyurethane Adhesives - HENKEL CORPORATION; *pg.* 1165, *pg.* 1535
MACROPLASTIQUE - Urological Tissue Bulking Products - COGENTIX MEDICAL, INC.; *pg.* 1516, *pg.* 948
MACROSEP - Centrifugal Device - PALL CORPORATION; *pg.* 232, *pg.* 1323
MACROVICKERS - Macroindentation Hardness Testers - BUEHLER, LTD.; *pg.* 1403, *pg.* 622
MACROVISION - Software - FLEXERA SOFTWARE INC.; *pg.* 398, *pg.* 658
MACROVISION - Anti-Piracy Rights Management - ROVI CORPORATION; *pg.* 463, *pg.* 269
MACRYNAL - Solventborne - CYTEC INDUSTRIES, INC.; *pg.* 1155, *pg.* 1131
MACSTAN - Immersion - MACDERMID, INC.; *pg.* 1172, *pg.* 321
MACSTARS 2000 - Soil Reinforcement Design Software - MACCAFERRI, INC.; *pg.* 95, *pg.* 780
MACSYM - Measurement & Control System - ANALOG DEVICES, INC.; *pg.* 617, *pg.* 839
MACTAC - Pressure Sensitive Adhesives - BEMIS COMPANY, INC.; *pg.* 1453, *pg.* 1882
MACTCP - Application Program - APPLE INC.; *pg.* 350, *pg.* 73
MACTEX - Slope & Wall Reinforcement - MACCAFERRI, INC.; *pg.* 95, *pg.* 780
MACUGEN - Biopharmaceutical Product - GILEAD SCIENCES, INC.; *pg.* 1535, *pg.* 88
MACUSPEC - Electroplate - MACDERMID, INC.; *pg.* 1172, *pg.* 321
MACUVERSE - Ophthalmological Preparations - PFIZER INC.; *pg.* 1581, *pg.* 1278
MACWHYTE - Wire Rope - WIRECO WORLDGROUP; *pg.* 1389, *pg.* 987
MACWORLD - Technology Magazine - INTERNATIONAL DATA GROUP; *pg.* 1653, *pg.* 796
MACY'S - Department Store - MACY'S, INC.; *pg.* 1778, *pg.* 1417
MACY'S CREDIT CARD - Credit Card - CITIGROUP INC.; *pg.* 735, *pg.* 1212
MAD ABOUT MOVIES - Magazine - MIDNIGHT MARQUEE PRESS, INC.; *pg.* 1665, *pg.* 758
MAD LIBS - Game - PENGUIN RANDOM HOUSE CHILDREN'S BOOKS; *pg.* 1676, *pg.* 1277
MAD MIXOLOGY - Beverages - RED ROBIN GOURMET BURGERS, INC.; *pg.* 1747, *pg.* 331
MAD RIVER - Beverages - THE COCA-COLA COMPANY; *pg.* 240, *pg.* 493
MAD RIVER - Canoes - CONFLUENCE WATERSPORTS CO. INC.; *pg.* 1706, *pg.* 1617
MADAGASCAR - Game - ACTIVISION BLIZZARD, INC.; *pg.* 948, *pg.* 271
MADAGASCAR - Video Game - INTERNATIONAL GAME TECHNOLOGY; *pg.* 957, *pg.* 1024
MADAGASCAR 2 - Children Product - TUPPERWARE BRANDS CORPORATION; *pg.* 1139, *pg.* 456
MADAME ALEXANDER - Collectible Dolls - ALEXANDER DOLL COMPANY, INC.; *pg.* 949, *pg.* 1545
MADAME POMPADOUR - Fabric - SCALAMANDRE, INC.; *pg.* 941, *pg.* 1058
MADAME X - Game - WMS INDUSTRIES INC.; *pg.* 593, *pg.* 666
MADD DASH - Racing Event - MOTHERS AGAINST DRUNK DRIVING (MADD); *pg.* 147, *pg.* 1723
MADDOX - Furniture - JOFCO INC.; *pg.* 931, *pg.* 691
MADDVOCATE - Publication - MOTHERS AGAINST DRUNK DRIVING (MADD); *pg.* 147, *pg.* 1723
MADDY - Elephant Puppet - GUND, INC.; *pg.* 954, *pg.* 1056
MADE FOR EACH OTHER - Manual - XEROX CORPORATION; *pg.* 494, *pg.* 365
MADE FOR HER - Nutritional Supplement - PHARMAVITE LLC; *pg.* 1584, *pg.* 167
MADE FOR ME - Toy & Game - HASBRO, INC.; *pg.* 954, *pg.* 1603
MADE FOR YOU - Slogan - MARVIN WINDOWS & DOORS; *pg.* 934, *pg.* 965
MADE IN AMERICA WITH LOVE - Tagline - ALEX AND ANI; *pg.* 1, *pg.* 1600
MADE TO ORDER. BUILT TO LAST - Computer Printers - TRANSACT TECHNOLOGIES INCORPORATED; *pg.* 484, *pg.* 351
MADE TO WORK - Footwear & Clothing - THE TIMBERLAND COMPANY; *pg.* 1821, *pg.* 1039
MADEIRA - Carpet - BEAULIEU GROUP, LLC; *pg.* 917, *pg.* 529
MADELEINE - Lounge Chairs - BERNHARDT DESIGN; *pg.* 918, *pg.* 1381
MADELINE - Footwear - PHOENIX FOOTWEAR GROUP, INC.; *pg.* 1815, *pg.* 60
MADELINE - Lighting Product - QUOIZEL INC.; *pg.* 1304, *pg.* 1616
MADELINE MONO - Beauty Product - COSMETIQUE, INC.; *pg.* 1765, *pg.* 664
MADELINE PLAID - Pillow and Throw - HERITAGE LACE INC.; *pg.* 694, *pg.* 711
MADEMAN.COM - Website - DEFYMEDIA; *pg.* 1237, *pg.* 1222
MADEWELL - Casual Clothing - J. CREW GROUP, INC.; *pg.* 1773, *pg.* 1245
MADHATTER II - Glove - KOMBI, LTD.; *pg.* 1838, *pg.* 1766

MADISON - Furniture - AMISCO INDUSTRIES LTD.; *pg.* 913, *pg.* 1958
MADISON - Lounge Chairs - BERNHARDT DESIGN; *pg.* 918, *pg.* 1381
MADISON - Table - BLATT BOWLING & BILLIARD CORP.; *pg.* 1827, *pg.* 1203
MADISON - Leather Product - COACH, INC.; *pg.* 3, *pg.* 1214
MADISON - Vanity Lights - CRAFTMADE INTERNATIONAL, INC.; *pg.* 1295, *pg.* 1670
MADISON - Furniture - ETHAN ALLEN INTERIORS INC.; *pg.* 924, *pg.* 343
MADISON - Portable Playpen - EVENFLO COMPANY, INC.; *pg.* 924, *pg.* 1470
MADISON - Watch - GEVRIL USA; *pg.* 6, *pg.* 1348
MADISON - Furniture - JASPER GROUP; *pg.* 930, *pg.* 691
MADISON - Women's Trousers - LANE BRYANT; *pg.* 1776, *pg.* 1441
MADISON - Face Driver - SPEEDGRIP CHUCK, INC.; *pg.* 1377, *pg.* 677
MADISON AVE - Carpet - BEAULIEU GROUP, LLC; *pg.* 917, *pg.* 529
MADISON CABLE - Jewelry - YURMAN DESIGN, INC.; *pg.* 15, *pg.* 1316
MADISON FLARE - Clothing - ABERCROMBIE & FITCH CO.; *pg.* 37, *pg.* 1466
MADONE - Bicycle - TREK BICYCLE CORPORATION; *pg.* 1847, *pg.* 1896
MADRAS - Furniture - ASHLEY FURNITURE INDUSTRIES, INC.; *pg.* 914, *pg.* 1852
MADRID - Furniture - AMERICAN LEATHER LP; *pg.* 912, *pg.* 1673
MADRID - Furniture - AMISCO INDUSTRIES LTD.; *pg.* 913, *pg.* 1958
MADRONA MARKET - Food Service - FOOD SERVICES OF AMERICA, INC.; *pg.* 856, *pg.* 21
MADRONE TRAIL - Bike - MARIN BIKES; *pg.* 1708, *pg.* 168
MADURO BLEND - Coffee - PEET'S COFFEE & TEA, INC.; *pg.* 1029, *pg.* 85
MAE - Furniture - AMISCO INDUSTRIES LTD.; *pg.* 913, *pg.* 1958
MAELSTROM IPA - Beverage - COASTAL EXTREME BREWING COMPANY; *pg.* 240, *pg.* 1602
MAESTRO - Upscale Baked Goods - AWREY BAKERIES, INC.; *pg.* 1015, *pg.* 896
MAESTRO - Software - CANDID COLOR SYSTEMS, INC.; *pg.* 1404, *pg.* 1485
MAESTRO - Candle Holder, Bud Vases, & Number Stands - CARLISLE FOODSERVICE PRODUCTS INCORPORATED; *pg.* 1455, *pg.* 1485
MAESTRO - Insulation - THE DOW CHEMICAL COMPANY; *pg.* 1157, *pg.* 898
MAESTRO - Musical Instrument - GIBSON GUITAR CORP.; *pg.* 550, *pg.* 1650
MAESTRO - Branding & Master Control System - GRASS VALLEY, INC.; *pg.* 641, *pg.* 164
MAESTRO - Bath Product - KOHLER CO.; *pg.* 91, *pg.* 1862
MAESTRO - Credit Card - MASTERCARD INCORPORATED; *pg.* 779, *pg.* 1325
MAESTRO - Office Furniture - STEELCASE INC.; *pg.* 475, *pg.* 889
MAESTRO - Fragrance - WESTROCK COMPANY; *pg.* 1472, *pg.* 1805
MAESTRO 3000 - Medical Device - BOSTON SCIENTIFIC CORPORATION; *pg.* 1508, *pg.* 831
MAESTRO COLORS - Paint & Colors for Paint - PPG INDUSTRIES, INC.; *pg.* 1445, *pg.* 1579
MAESTRO E-COMMERCE - Credit Card - MASTERCARD INCORPORATED; *pg.* 779, *pg.* 1325
MAESTROLINK - DVD Player - CSR; *pg.* 280, *pg.* 284
MAFIA WARS - Online Game - ZYNGA INC.; *pg.* 1292, *pg.* 235
MAG - Eyewear - MINE SAFETY APPLIANCES COMPANY; *pg.* 1361, *pg.* 1525
MAG-1 - Extreme Pressure Lubricant for Industrial & Construction Use - LUBRIPLATE LUBRICANTS; *pg.* 980, *pg.* 1097
MAG 7 - Slots - INTERNATIONAL GAME TECHNOLOGY; *pg.* 957, *pg.* 1024
MAG-FLUX - Refractory Product - RESCO PRODUCTS, INC.; *pg.* 107, *pg.* 1581
MAG-GATE - Software - 3M; *pg.* 339, *pg.* 179
MAG JACK - Connector Modules - BEL FUSE INC.; *pg.* 624, *pg.* 1075
MAG-PRO - Payment System - COIN ACCEPTORS, INC.; *pg.* 1324, *pg.* 994
MAG TOUCH - Fishing Equipment - CABELA'S INCORPORATED; *pg.* 535, *pg.* 1019
MAGA AO - Nutritional Supplement - USANA HEALTH SCIENCES, INC.; *pg.* 1605, *pg.* 1761
MAGAZINE - Leather Product - COACH, INC.; *pg.* 3, *pg.* 1214
MAGAZINE & BOOKSELLER - Magazine - NORTH AMERICAN PUBLISHING COMPANY; *pg.* 1671, *pg.* 1567
THE MAGAZINE ANTIQUES - Magazine - BRANT PUBLICATIONS, INC.; *pg.* 1623, *pg.* 1206
MAGCELLECT - Biological Product - TECHNE CORPORATION; *pg.* 1601, *pg.* 944
MAGELLAN - Electron Microscope - FEI COMPANY; *pg.* 1413, *pg.* 1498
MAGELLAN - Medical Device - RESMED INC.; *pg.* 1589, *pg.* 207
MAGELLAN - Software - SYNOPSYS, INC.; *pg.* 480, *pg.* 162
MAGELLAN - Electric Instrument - UNIVERSAL INSTRUMENTS CORPORATION; *pg.* 683, *pg.* 1154
MAGELLAN I - Computer Controller for Starfinder Telescope - MEADE INSTRUMENTS CORPORATION; *pg.* 1422, *pg.* 113
MAGELLAN II - Computer Controller for Starfinder Telescope - MEADE INSTRUMENTS CORPORATION; *pg.* 1422, *pg.* 113
MAGFORCE - Reels - DAIWA CORPORATION; *pg.* 1832, *pg.* 75
MAGGI - Bouillon Cubes, Soup Mixes, Seasonings - NESTLE USA, INC.; *pg.* 883, *pg.* 96
MAGGIANO'S LITTLE ITALY - Italian Restaurant - BRINKER INTERNATIONAL, INC.; *pg.* 1718, *pg.* 1676
MAGGIANO'S LITTLE ITALY - Italian Restaurant - LETTUCE ENTERTAIN YOU ENTERPRISES, INC.; *pg.* 1735, *pg.* 580
MAGGIE - Furniture - AMISCO INDUSTRIES LTD.; *pg.* 913, *pg.* 1958
MAGGIE - Footwear - PHOENIX FOOTWEAR GROUP, INC.; *pg.* 1815, *pg.* 60
MAGGIE - Fabric - SCALAMANDRE, INC.; *pg.* 941, *pg.* 1058
MAGGIE & THE MARTIANS - Video Game - INTERNATIONAL GAME TECHNOLOGY; *pg.* 957, *pg.* 1024
MAGI-MELT - Ice Melting Compound - TEXAS REFINERY CORP.; *pg.* 986, *pg.* 1696
MAGI MIRROR - Travel Mirror - ELECTRO-OPTIX, INC.; *pg.* 1046, *pg.* 459
MAGI-PATCH - Floor Product - TEXAS REFINERY CORP.; *pg.* 986, *pg.* 1696
MAGI-TUNE FM - Radio - CLARION CORPORATION OF AMERICA; *pg.* 629, *pg.* 75
MAGIA - Fabric - NEMSCHOFF, INC.; *pg.* 936, *pg.* 1890
MAGIC - Software - BMC SOFTWARE, INC.; *pg.* 362, *pg.* 1701
MAGIC - Ironing & Cleaning Product - FAULTLESS STARCH/BON AMI COMPANY; *pg.* 330, *pg.* 982
MAGIC - Binding Posts - FELLOWES, INC.; *pg.* 397, *pg.* 620
MAGIC - Household Cleaning Products - HOMAX PRODUCTS INC.; *pg.* 1442, *pg.* 1817
MAGIC - Women's Fragrance - MARILYN MIGLIN, L.P.; *pg.* 516, *pg.* 581
MAGIC 8 BALL - Game - INTERNATIONAL GAME TECHNOLOGY; *pg.* 957, *pg.* 1024
MAGIC 8 BALL - Toy - MATTEL, INC.; *pg.* 962, *pg.* 81
MAGIC 8 BALL - Lottery Game - OHIO LOTTERY COMMISSION; *pg.* 1002, *pg.* 1433
MAGIC BULLET - Blender - CAPITAL BRANDS, LLC; *pg.* 53, *pg.* 127
MAGIC BUTTERFLY - Video Game - INTERNATIONAL GAME TECHNOLOGY; *pg.* 957, *pg.* 1024
MAGIC CABIN - Toys - 1-800-FLOWERS.COM, INC.; *pg.* 1758, *pg.* 1151
MAGIC CABIN DOLLS - Retail Store Services - 1-800-FLOWERS.COM, INC.; *pg.* 1758, *pg.* 1151
MAGIC CABIN FAIRIES - Toys - 1-800-FLOWERS.COM, INC.; *pg.* 1758, *pg.* 1151
MAGIC CARPET RIDE - Video Game - INTERNATIONAL GAME TECHNOLOGY; *pg.* 957, *pg.* 1024
MAGIC CHEF - Home Appliance - WHIRLPOOL CORPORATION; *pg.* 62, *pg.* 872
MAGIC CHOPPER - Chopper - HABAND COMPANY, INC.; *pg.* 1772, *pg.* 1099
MAGIC CLASPS - Jewelry - HABAND COMPANY, INC.; *pg.* 1772, *pg.* 1099
MAGIC COIN - Video Game - INTERNATIONAL GAME TECHNOLOGY; *pg.* 957, *pg.* 1024
MAGIC COLOR - Plastic & Rubber - TEKNOR APEX COMPANY; *pg.* 1889, *pg.* 1605
MAGIC CRYSTAL - Game - WMS INDUSTRIES INC.; *pg.* 593, *pg.* 666
MAGIC DECOR - Carpet - BEAULIEU GROUP, LLC; *pg.* 917, *pg.* 529
MAGIC DSP - Integrated Circuit - ATMEL CORPORATION; *pg.* 621, *pg.* 238
MAGIC KINGDOM - Amusement Park - THE WALT DISNEY COMPANY; *pg.* 317, *pg.* 52
MAGIC LAMP - Game - WMS INDUSTRIES INC.; *pg.* 593, *pg.* 666
MAGIC MALT - Ice Cream - UNITED DAIRY FARMERS, INC.; *pg.* 906, *pg.* 1426
MAGIC MOMENTS - Educational Toys - LEAPFROG ENTERPRISES, INC.; *pg.* 961, *pg.* 84
MAGIC MONEY - Lottery Game - MASSACHUSETTS STATE LOTTERY; *pg.* 998, *pg.* 802
MAGIC MONEY - Games - PENN NATIONAL GAMING, INC.; *pg.* 574, *pg.* 1595
MAGIC MOONS - Game - INTERNATIONAL GAME TECHNOLOGY; *pg.* 420, *pg.* 1606
MAGIC NURSERY - Dolls - MATTEL, INC.; *pg.* 962, *pg.* 81
MAGIC PACKET - Technical Documentation - ADVANCED MICRO DEVICES, INC.; *pg.* 613, *pg.* 282
MAGIC-PAK - Heating & Cooling Product - LENNOX INTERNATIONAL INC.; *pg.* 1073, *pg.* 1736
MAGIC PAN CREPE STAND - Food Stand - LETTUCE ENTERTAIN YOU ENTERPRISES, INC.; *pg.* 1735, *pg.* 580
MAGIC PREMIUM STARCH - Starch Product - FAULTLESS STARCH/BON AMI COMPANY; *pg.* 330, *pg.* 982
MAGIC RADIO - Radio Station - ORLANDO MAGIC; *pg.* 572, *pg.* 455
THE MAGIC SCHOOL BUS - Educational Materials - SCHOLASTIC INC.; *pg.* 1683, *pg.* 1288
MAGIC SCREEN LEARNING PAL - Toy & Game - HASBRO, INC.; *pg.* 954, *pg.* 1603
MAGIC SHELL - Ice Cream Toppings - THE J.M. SMUCKER COMPANY; *pg.* 865, *pg.* 1468
MAGIC SIZING - Starch Product - FAULTLESS STARCH/BON AMI COMPANY; *pg.* 330, *pg.* 982
MAGIC SPIN - Video Game - INTERNATIONAL GAME TECHNOLOGY; *pg.* 957, *pg.* 1024
MAGIC SPOON - Educational Materials - SCHOLASTIC INC.; *pg.* 1683, *pg.* 1288
MAGIC START - Spray - THE WOODSTREAM CORPORATION; *pg.* 1801, *pg.* 1549
MAGIC STRIPES - Yarn - LION BRAND YARN COMPANY; *pg.* 696, *pg.* 1050
MAGIC TALKIN' KITCHEN - Toy & Game - HASBRO, INC.; *pg.* 954, *pg.* 1603
MAGIC: THE GATHERING - Toy & Game - HASBRO, INC.; *pg.* 954, *pg.* 1603
MAGIC TIME - Game - WMS INDUSTRIES INC.; *pg.* 593, *pg.* 666
MAGIC TORQUE - Medical Device - BOSTON SCIENTIFIC CORPORATION; *pg.* 1508, *pg.* 831
MAGIC UNIVERSITY - Educational Materials - SCHOLASTIC INC.; *pg.* 1683, *pg.* 1288
MAGIC WINDOW - Shipment Service - FEDEX CORPORATION; *pg.* 1907, *pg.* 1642
MAGIC WISH - Video Game - INTERNATIONAL GAME TECHNOLOGY; *pg.* 957, *pg.* 1024
MAGICAL - Container Grown Plant - MONROVIA GROWERS; *pg.* 1797, *pg.* 44
MAGICAL - Nutritional Product - RBC LIFE SCIENCES, INC.; *pg.* 1588, *pg.* 1723
MAGICAL MOONLIGHT - Flower Arrangement - 1-800-FLOWERS.COM, INC.; *pg.* 1758, *pg.* 1151
MAGICALLY WILD - Video Game - INTERNATIONAL GAME TECHNOLOGY; *pg.* 957, *pg.* 1024
MAGICCYLINDER - Powder Coating System - GEMA USA INC.; *pg.* 1339, *pg.* 686
MAGICLEAN - Liquid Cleaner - KAO BRANDS CO. INC.; *pg.* 513, *pg.* 1415
MAGICLIFT - Bra & Shapewear - GLAMORISE FOUNDATIONS, INC.; *pg.* 25, *pg.* 1235
MAGICLIP - Wind & Rain Deflectors - MACNEIL AUTOMOTIVE PRODUCTS, LTD.; *pg.* 211, *pg.* 559
MAGICMARK - Molecular Biology Product - THERMO FISHER SCIENTIFIC INC.; *pg.* 1602, *pg.* 61
MAGICO - Chocolate Powder - PEPSICO, INC.; *pg.* 259, *pg.* 1327
MAGICO - Chocolate Powder - THE QUAKER OATS

COMPANY; *pg.* 834, *pg.* 588
MAGICSLIM - Jeans - HABAND COMPANY, INC.; *pg.* 1772, *pg.* 1099
MAGICSTOMP - Effects Pedal - YAMAHA CORPORATION OF AMERICA; *pg.* 595, *pg.* 51
MAGICUTS - Hair Service Center - REGIS CORPORATION; *pg.* 521, *pg.* 941
MAGIK BRUSH - Lint Brush - THE EVERCARE COMPANY; *pg.* 1124, *pg.* 483
MAGIKITCH'N - Cooking & Warming Equipment - THE MIDDLEBY CORPORATION; *pg.* 1361, *pg.* 610
MAGKRIMP - Connector - MOLEX INCORPORATED; *pg.* 655, *pg.* 628
MAGLIFT - Magnetic Lifter - BUNTING MAGNETICS CO.; *pg.* 1320, *pg.* 717
MAGLINER - Hand Trucks - MAGLINE, INC.; *pg.* 1358, *pg.* 908
MAGMA - Mobile Electronic Device - IGO, INC.; *pg.* 644, *pg.* 22
MAGNA-BAR - Peg Display System - CANNON EQUIPMENT COMPANY; *pg.* 1321, *pg.* 920
MAGNA BRIGHT - Automotive Reconditioning Product - MOC PRODUCTS COMPANY, INC.; *pg.* 332, *pg.* 174
MAGNA BUFF - Wax - MOC PRODUCTS COMPANY, INC.; *pg.* 332, *pg.* 174
MAGNA-BULB - Bolts & Nuts - ALCOA INC.; *pg.* 65, *pg.* 1188
MAGNA CRYSTAL - Automotive Reconditioning Product - MOC PRODUCTS COMPANY, INC.; *pg.* 332, *pg.* 174
MAGNA GLAZE - Automotive Reconditioning Product - MOC PRODUCTS COMPANY, INC.; *pg.* 332, *pg.* 174
MAGNA-GRIP - Bolts & Nuts - ALCOA INC.; *pg.* 65, *pg.* 1188
MAGNA KLEEN - Board Cleaner - MAGNA VISUAL, INC.; *pg.* 429, *pg.* 999
MAGNA-LOK - Bolts & Nuts - ALCOA INC.; *pg.* 65, *pg.* 1188
MAGNA PLATINUM - Card Printer - DATACARD CORPORATION; *pg.* 382, *pg.* 948
MAGNA SEAL - Wax - MOC PRODUCTS COMPANY, INC.; *pg.* 332, *pg.* 174
MAGNA-SEP - Molecular Biology Product - THERMO FISHER SCIENTIFIC INC.; *pg.* 1602, *pg.* 61
MAGNA TEC - Gaming Product - GLD PRODUCTS, INC.; *pg.* 1835, *pg.* 1882
MAGNABRITE - Bentonite Clay - MINERALS TECHNOLOGIES INC.; *pg.* 1173, *pg.* 617
MAGNABRITE - Magnesium Sulfate - PQ CORPORATION; *pg.* 1178, *pg.* 1515
MAGNACOOL - Coating Product - PPG INDUSTRIES, INC.; *pg.* 1445, *pg.* 1579
MAGNACORE - Toy & Game - HASBRO, INC.; *pg.* 954, *pg.* 1603
MAGNADIZE - Coating - GENERAL MAGNAPLATE CORPORATION; *pg.* 1164, *pg.* 1079
MAGNAFLUX - Magnetic Particle Inspection Product - ITW MAGNAFLUX; *pg.* 1418, *pg.* 615
MAGNAFLUX SPOTCHECK - Penetrant Crack Detection Kit - FLEXBAR MACHINE CORP.; *pg.* 1337, *pg.* 1169
MAGNAFRAME - Window & Door - JELD-WEN, INC.; *pg.* 1051, *pg.* 1499
MAGNAGLO - Fluorescent Magnetic Particle Testing - ITW MAGNAFLUX; *pg.* 1418, *pg.* 615
MAGNAGOLD - Coating - GENERAL MAGNAPLATE CORPORATION; *pg.* 1164, *pg.* 1079
MAGNAGROW - Magnesium Sulfate - PQ CORPORATION; *pg.* 1178, *pg.* 1515
MAGNAHELIC - Filtration Product - FLANDERS CORPORATION; *pg.* 1336, *pg.* 1392
MAGNALERT - Magnetic Drive Pump - FLOWSERVE CORPORATION; *pg.* 82, *pg.* 1719
MAGNALITE - Kitchen Houseware Product - WORLD KITCHEN LLC; *pg.* 1141, *pg.* 657
MAGNALUBE - Cylinder - BIMBA MANUFACTURING COMPANY; *pg.* 1317, *pg.* 633
MAGNAMITE - Carbon Fiber - HEXCEL CORPORATION; *pg.* 1884, *pg.* 375
MAGNANIMALS - Magnet & Clip - ADAMS MFG. CO.; *pg.* 51, *pg.* 1427
MAGNAPAK - Motion Control Product - GRAHAM MOTORS AND CONTROLS; *pg.* 177, *pg.* 1692
MAGNAPLATE HCR - Coating - GENERAL MAGNAPLATE CORPORATION; *pg.* 1164, *pg.* 1079
MAGNAPLATE HMF - Coating - GENERAL MAGNAPLATE CORPORATION; *pg.* 1164, *pg.* 1079
MAGNAPLATE HTR - Coating - GENERAL MAGNAPLATE CORPORATION; *pg.* 1164, *pg.* 1079
MAGNAPLATE TNS - Coating - GENERAL MAGNAPLATE CORPORATION; *pg.* 1164, *pg.* 1079
MAGNAPOP - Advertising & Promotional Brochure Design - STRUCTURAL GRAPHICS, LLC; *pg.* 1689, *pg.* 346
MAGNAPURE - Wastewater Treatment System - ITW MAGNAFLUX; *pg.* 1418, *pg.* 615
MAGNARACK - Molecular Biology Product - THERMO FISHER SCIENTIFIC INC.; *pg.* 1602, *pg.* 61
MAGNASIV - Cracking Catalyst - BASF CATALYSTS LLC; *pg.* 1148, *pg.* 1074
MAGNASPERSE - Minerals - MINERALS TECHNOLOGIES INC.; *pg.* 1173, *pg.* 617
MAGNASWEET - Sweetener - MAFCO WORLDWIDE CORPORATION; *pg.* 1858, *pg.* 1049
MAGNATE - Mobile & Consumer Electronics - VOXX INTERNATIONAL; *pg.* 686, *pg.* 1166
MAGNATHIN - Firearms - REMINGTON ARMS COMPANY, LLC; *pg.* 1844, *pg.* 1382
MAGNATRAN - Vacuum Process Tool - BROOKS AUTOMATION, INC.; *pg.* 1320, *pg.* 813
MAGNAVALVE - Ventilator - SWARTWOUT DIVISION; *pg.* 114, *pg.* 978
MAGNE-TRACTION - Toy Train - LIONEL LLC; *pg.* 961, *pg.* 875
MAGNEDUR - Alloy - CARPENTER TECHNOLOGY CORPORATION; *pg.* 73, *pg.* 1584
MAGNEHELIC - Differential Pressure Gauge - GE ENERGY; *pg.* 1338, *pg.* 506
MAGNEMAX - Nutritional Product - NUTRITION 21, INC.; *pg.* 1577, *pg.* 1327
MAGNEQUICK - Kitchen Appliance - VIKING RANGE CORPORATION; *pg.* 61, *pg.* 968
MAGNERIDE - Magneto-Rheological - LORD CORPORATION; *pg.* 1357, *pg.* 1360
MAGNESIL - Testing Instrument System - BECKMAN COULTER, INC.; *pg.* 1402, *pg.* 48
MAGNESITE - Pressed & Monolithic Refractory - RESCO PRODUCTS, INC.; *pg.* 107, *pg.* 1581
MAGNESIUM - Molecular Probe Product - THERMO FISHER SCIENTIFIC INC.; *pg.* 1602, *pg.* 61
MAGNET - Apparel - OAKLEY, INC.; *pg.* 1840, *pg.* 86
MAGNET MAN - Magnet & Clip - ADAMS MFG. CO.; *pg.* 51, *pg.* 1427
MAGNET-MASTER - Bail Assemblies - GRC ENTERPRISES, INC.; *pg.* 1344, *pg.* 677
MAGNET SPRAY - Air-Assisted Electrostatic Sprayer - PULLMAN-HOLT CORPORATION; *pg.* 333, *pg.* 475
MAGNETEC - Interposer Solenoids - JEWELL INSTRUMENTS, LLC; *pg.* 1418, *pg.* 1036
MAGNETEK - Power Control Product - MAGNETEK, INC.; *pg.* 1301, *pg.* 1870
MAGNETIC 7'S - Game - WMS INDUSTRIES INC.; *pg.* 593, *pg.* 666
MAGNETIC E3 CERAMICSTEEL - Porcelain Boards - MAGNA VISUAL, INC.; *pg.* 429, *pg.* 999
MAGNETIC KIDBOARDS - Educational Product - BARKER CREEK PUBLISHING INC.; *pg.* 1619, *pg.* 1818
MAGNETOFLOW - Meter - BADGER METER, INC.; *pg.* 1401, *pg.* 1873
MAGNI-FOCUSER - Magnifier-Headband - EDROY PRODUCTS CO., INC.; *pg.* 1411, *pg.* 1318
MAGNI-FOCUSER BIFOCAL - Magnifier-Headband with Bifocal Lense - EDROY PRODUCTS CO., INC.; *pg.* 1411, *pg.* 1318
MAGNI-FOCUSER WITH LIGHT - Magnifier - EDROY PRODUCTS CO., INC.; *pg.* 1411, *pg.* 1318
MAGNI-GUIDE - Healthcare Product - MEDICOOL, INC.; *pg.* 1562, *pg.* 294
MAGNI-SPECS - Hands-Free Magnifier - EDROY PRODUCTS CO., INC.; *pg.* 1411, *pg.* 1318
MAGNIFIER-FLEX - Flexible Illuminated Magnifier - DAZOR MANUFACTURING CORP.; *pg.* 1296, *pg.* 995
MAGNIFIN - Chemical Product - ALBEMARLE CORPORATION; *pg.* 1146, *pg.* 741
MAGNIFIQUE - Topcoats - ORLY INTERNATIONAL, INC.; *pg.* 518, *pg.* 137
MAGNIFOODS - Food Product - HORMEL FOODS CORPORATION; *pg.* 863, *pg.* 915
MAGNIVIEW 800 - Data Projector - DUKANE CORPORATION; *pg.* 634, *pg.* 658
MAGNIVIEW 807 - Data Projector; International Model - DUKANE CORPORATION; *pg.* 634, *pg.* 658
MAGNIVIEW 822 - Data Projector - DUKANE CORPORATION; *pg.* 634, *pg.* 658
MAGNIVIEW 840 - True Color Computer Data Projector - DUKANE CORPORATION; *pg.* 634, *pg.* 658
MAGNIVIEW 860 - Data Projector - DUKANE CORPORATION; *pg.* 634, *pg.* 658
MAGNIVIEW SERIES - LCD Computer Data Projection Panels - DUKANE CORPORATION; *pg.* 634, *pg.* 658
MAGNIVISION - Sunglasses - FGX INTERNATIONAL, INC.; *pg.* 5, *pg.* 1608
MAGNIVISION - Toy Train - LIONEL LLC; *pg.* 961, *pg.* 875
MAGNOLIA - Soft Drink - THE COCA-COLA COMPANY; *pg.* 240, *pg.* 493
MAGNOLIA - Video Game - INTERNATIONAL GAME TECHNOLOGY; *pg.* 957, *pg.* 1024
MAGNOLIA - Fragrance - NATURAL DECORATIONS, INC.; *pg.* 936, *pg.* 5
MAGNU-SPRAY - Coating Product - PPG INDUSTRIES, INC.; *pg.* 1445, *pg.* 1579
MAGNUDRAW - Coating Product - PPG INDUSTRIES, INC.; *pg.* 1445, *pg.* 1579
MAGNULITER - Lighting Product - HUBBELL INCORPORATED; *pg.* 1299, *pg.* 370
MAGNUM - Automotive Lifts - AMERICAN TIRE DISTRIBUTORS HOLDINGS, INC.; *pg.* 199, *pg.* 1379
MAGNUM - Fire Truck - ANSUL, INCORPORATED; *pg.* 1147, *pg.* 1869
MAGNUM - Water Heater - BRADFORD-WHITE CORPORATION; *pg.* 1069, *pg.* 1514
MAGNUM - Motor - CARTER MOTOR COMPANY; *pg.* 1321, *pg.* 665
MAGNUM - Reusable Biopsy System - C.R. BARD, INC.; *pg.* 1519, *pg.* 1094
MAGNUM - Resin - THE DOW CHEMICAL COMPANY; *pg.* 1157, *pg.* 898
MAGNUM - Transducer - DUKANE CORPORATION; *pg.* 634, *pg.* 658
MAGNUM - Electrical Product - EATON CORPORATION; *pg.* 1331, *pg.* 1429
MAGNUM - Airless Paint Sprayers - GRACO, INC.; *pg.* 1342, *pg.* 935
MAGNUM - Pump Product - IDEX CORPORATION; *pg.* 1347, *pg.* 623
MAGNUM - Gun & Cable - LINCOLN ELECTRIC HOLDINGS, INC.; *pg.* 1355, *pg.* 1432
MAGNUM - Hood Shield - LUND INTERNATIONAL, INC.; *pg.* 211, *pg.* 526
MAGNUM - Padlocks - MASTER LOCK COMPANY LLC; *pg.* 1055, *pg.* 1884
MAGNUM - Drill - MILWAUKEE ELECTRIC TOOL CORP.; *pg.* 1056, *pg.* 1855
MAGNUM - Electron Multiplier Detector - PHOTONIS USA PENNSYLVANIA; *pg.* 663, *pg.* 1547
MAGNUM - Power System - SCHNEIDER ELECTRIC; *pg.* 467, *pg.* 1609
MAGNUM - Revolver - SMITH & WESSON HOLDING CORPORATION; *pg.* 1845, *pg.* 846
MAGNUM - Ice Cream - UNILEVER UNITED STATES, INC.; *pg.* 904, *pg.* 1061
MAGNUM - Implant Product - ZIMMER BIOMET HOLDINGS, INC.; *pg.* 1611, *pg.* 699
MAGNUM ALERT - Control Panels - NAPCO SECURITY SYSTEMS, INC.; *pg.* 658, *pg.* 1138
MAGNUM DX - Paint Sprayers - GRACO, INC.; *pg.* 1342, *pg.* 935
MAGNUM FIRE ALERT - Fire Alarm Panels - NAPCO SECURITY SYSTEMS, INC.; *pg.* 658, *pg.* 1138
MAGNUM II - Memory-Test Product - TERADYNE INC.; *pg.* 679, *pg.* 838
MAGNUM MACE - Security & Law Enforcement Products - MACE SECURITY INTERNATIONAL, INC.; *pg.* 1172, *pg.* 1541
MAGNUM MALT LIQUOR - Malt Liquor - MILLERCOORS; *pg.* 254, *pg.* 1877
MAGNUM RS PRO - Fluid Handling System - GRACO, INC.; *pg.* 1342, *pg.* 935
MAGNUM SERIES - Seating for Office & Highway Equipment - SEATS INCORPORATED; *pg.* 217, *pg.* 1890
MAGNUM TEXFINISH - Fluid Handling System - GRACO, INC.; *pg.* 1342, *pg.* 935
MAGNUM-Z-CATH - Electrosurgical Devices - ANGIODYNAMICS, INC.; *pg.* 1495, *pg.* 1173
MAGNUS - Platesetters - EASTMAN KODAK COMPANY; *pg.* 1408, *pg.* 1333
MAGNUS - Transformer - GE ENERGY; *pg.* 1338, *pg.* 506
MAGNUS - Pumps - IDEX CORPORATION; *pg.* 1347, *pg.* 623
MAGNUSQUARE - Lighting Fixture - HUBBELL

INCORPORATED; *pg.* 1299, *pg.* 370
MAGNUSSON - Office Desks - KNOLL, INC.; *pg.* 425, *pg.* 1527
MAGNUTS - Toys - 1-800-FLOWERS.COM, INC.; *pg.* 1758, *pg.* 1151
MAGPIE - Pipeline - T.D. WILLIAMSON, INC.; *pg.* 1380, *pg.* 1490
MAGPLEX - Microspheres - LUMINEX CORPORATION; *pg.* 1421, *pg.* 1664
MAGPLEX C - Analytical Component - LUMINEX CORPORATION; *pg.* 1421, *pg.* 1664
MAGPRO - Bill Acceptor - COIN ACCEPTORS, INC.; *pg.* 1324, *pg.* 994
MAGSAFE - Power Adapters - APPLE INC.; *pg.* 350, *pg.* 73
MAGSLIDE - Conveyor - BUNTING MAGNETICS CO.; *pg.* 1320, *pg.* 717
MAGTRATE - Pharmaceutical Product - MISSION PHARMACAL COMPANY INC.; *pg.* 1568, *pg.* 1742
MAH - Enclosure - CHANNELL COMMERCIAL CORP.; *pg.* 1870, *pg.* 291
MAH JONG LIGHTNING - Game - WMS INDUSTRIES INC.; *pg.* 593, *pg.* 666
MAHA CHOCO - Confectionery - THE HERSHEY CO.; *pg.* 1855, *pg.* 1538
MAHA COFFEE ECLAIRS - Confectionery - THE HERSHEY CO.; *pg.* 1855, *pg.* 1538
MAHA LACTO - Confectionery - THE HERSHEY CO.; *pg.* 1855, *pg.* 1538
MAHAL - Rug - ETHAN ALLEN INTERIORS INC.; *pg.* 924, *pg.* 343
MAHARAJA - Video Game - INTERNATIONAL GAME TECHNOLOGY; *pg.* 957, *pg.* 1024
MAHATMA - Rice - RIVIANA FOODS INC.; *pg.* 892, *pg.* 1713
MAHI - Eyewear - MAUI JIM, INC.; *pg.* 9, *pg.* 651
MAHOGANY - Furniture - BUSH INDUSTRIES INC.; *pg.* 919, *pg.* 1170
MAHOGANY COLLECTION - Fiberglass Door System - THERMA-TRU CORP.; *pg.* 115, *pg.* 1462
MAHOGANY PRINCESS - Home & Garden Product - ENESCO, LLC; *pg.* 1124, *pg.* 620
MAHR - Measuring Instrument Company - MAHR FEDERAL, INC.; *pg.* 1358, *pg.* 1606
MAI BOCK - Beverage - SPRECHER BREWING COMPANY; *pg.* 265, *pg.* 1858
MAIA - Furniture - JOFCO INC.; *pg.* 931, *pg.* 691
MAIA LOUNGE - Office Furniture - JOFCO INC.; *pg.* 931, *pg.* 691
MAID OF MONEY - Video Game - INTERNATIONAL GAME TECHNOLOGY; *pg.* 957, *pg.* 1024
MAID RIGHT - Cleaning Services - PREMIUM FRANCHISE BRANDS LLC; *pg.* 333, *pg.* 485
MAIDEN - Bath Product - KOHLER CO.; *pg.* 91, *pg.* 1862
MAIDENFORM - Slippers - HABAND COMPANY, INC.; *pg.* 1772, *pg.* 1099
MAIDENFORM - Intimate Apparel - HANESBRANDS INC.; *pg.* 26, *pg.* 1394
MAIFAIR PLACE - Furniture - ASHLEY FURNITURE INDUSTRIES, INC.; *pg.* 914, *pg.* 1852
MAIL BOXES ETC - Communication Services - UNITED PARCEL SERVICE, INC.; *pg.* 1928, *pg.* 522
MAIL EXPRESS - Software - GLOBALSCAPE INC.; *pg.* 401, *pg.* 1740
MAIL-GEAR - Software - SYMANTEC CORPORATION; *pg.* 478, *pg.* 161
MAIL LITE - Air Cellular Lined Mailers - SEALED AIR CORPORATION; *pg.* 1468, *pg.* 1058
MAIL POUCH - Chewing Tobacco - SWISHER INTERNATIONAL, INC.; *pg.* 1895, *pg.* 345
MAIL-WELL - Mailing Envelopes - CENVEO INC.; *pg.* 1626, *pg.* 372
MAILBOX MONEY - Video Game - INTERNATIONAL GAME TECHNOLOGY; *pg.* 957, *pg.* 1024
MAILBOXES.COM - Online Shopping Website - SALSBURY INDUSTRIES; *pg.* 464, *pg.* 139
MAILCHIMP - E-Mail Marketing Service - THE ROCKET SCIENCE GROUP, LLC; *pg.* 1278, *pg.* 519
MAILERS - Software - MELISSA DATA CORP.; *pg.* 432, *pg.* 188
MAILER'S CHOICE - Software - PITNEY BOWES INC.; *pg.* 454, *pg.* 376
MAILLEFER - Dental Product - DENTSPLY INTERNATIONAL INC.; *pg.* 1522, *pg.* 1596
MAILMARK - Advertising Publication - DOMINION ENTERPRISES; *pg.* 1636, *pg.* 1796
MAILMASTER - Inserter - STANDARD DUPLICATING MACHINES CORPORATION; *pg.* 473, *pg.* 783
MAILMASTER - Plastic Product - THE STEP2 COMPANY LLC; *pg.* 1889, *pg.* 1474
MAILMAX - Mail Application - TRUSTWAVE HOLDINGS, INC.; *pg.* 1285, *pg.* 593
MAILSCAPE - Software - EASTMAN KODAK COMPANY; *pg.* 1408, *pg.* 1333
MAILSMART - Software - ARI NETWORK SERVICES, INC.; *pg.* 353, *pg.* 1873
MAILSMITH - Software - BARE BONES SOFTWARE, INC.; *pg.* 360, *pg.* 838
MAILSTATION - Postage Meter - PITNEY BOWES INC.; *pg.* 454, *pg.* 376
MAILTUFF - Mailers - SEALED AIR CORPORATION; *pg.* 1468, *pg.* 1058
MAILWRAP - Polywrapper - STANDARD DUPLICATING MACHINES CORPORATION; *pg.* 473, *pg.* 783
MAIN ST. BISTRO - Food Product - RESER'S FINE FOODS INC.; *pg.* 1032, *pg.* 1496
MAIN STREET - Area Lighting - JUNO LIGHTING, INC.; *pg.* 1300, *pg.* 606
MAIN STREET BOOKS - Publishing Imprint - THE KNOPF DOUBLEDAY GROUP; *pg.* 1657, *pg.* 1249
MAIN STREET STATION HOTEL, CASINO & BREWERY - Hotel, Casino & Brewery - BOYD GAMING CORPORATION; *pg.* 1082, *pg.* 1022
MAIN STREET, U.S.A. - Amusement Park - THE WALT DISNEY COMPANY; *pg.* 317, *pg.* 52
MAINE - Golf Apparel - BONOBOS; *pg.* 39, *pg.* 1205
MAINE GUIDE - Wool Vest - L.L. BEAN, INC.; *pg.* 1777, *pg.* 750
MAINE-IAC MAUVE - Nail Care Product - OPI PRODUCTS INC.; *pg.* 518, *pg.* 167
MAINFRAME - Software - BIO-RAD LABORATORIES, INC.; *pg.* 1504, *pg.* 101
MAINGATE - Embedded Site Server - COMVERGE, INC.; *pg.* 1325, *pg.* 536
MAINLINER - Hose - HBD INDUSTRIES, INC.; *pg.* 207, *pg.* 1449
MAINSTAGE - Application Program - APPLE INC.; *pg.* 350, *pg.* 73
MAINSTAY - The MacKay-Shields MainStay Family of Funds - NEW YORK LIFE INSURANCE COMPANY; *pg.* 1211, *pg.* 1268
MAINSTAY - Suture Anchor - STRYKER CORPORATION; *pg.* 1598, *pg.* 894
MAINSTAY ELITE - Nonionic Surfactant - KALO, INC.; *pg.* 1796, *pg.* 719
MAINSTAY SUITES - Extended Stay Hotels - CHOICE HOTELS INTERNATIONAL, INC.; *pg.* 1086, *pg.* 775
MAINSTAYS - Compressed Pillows - WAL-MART STORES, INC.; *pg.* 1790, *pg.* 29
MAINSTREET - Cigarettes - ROCK CREEK PHARMACEUTICALS, INC.; *pg.* 1895, *pg.* 466
MAINSTREETXPRESS - Insurance Underwriting Services - WESTERN NATIONAL MUTUAL INSURANCE CO.; *pg.* 1223, *pg.* 946
MAINTAINER - Floor Cleaner - SWISHER HYGIENE INC.; *pg.* 336, *pg.* 1507
MAINTENANCE USA - Maintenance, Repair & Operations Products - INTERLINE BRANDS, INC.; *pg.* 1051, *pg.* 433
MAINVIEW - Software - BMC SOFTWARE, INC.; *pg.* 362, *pg.* 1701
MAISON - Furniture - ASHLEY FURNITURE INDUSTRIES, INC.; *pg.* 914, *pg.* 1852
MAISON FRANCAISE - Terra Cotta - WALKER & ZANGER, INC.; *pg.* 119, *pg.* 281
MAITLAND-SMITH - Furniture - HERITAGE HOME GROUP; *pg.* 926, *pg.* 1379
MAIZETOS - Tortilla Chips - GOLDEN FLAKE SNACK FOODS, INC.; *pg.* 1854, *pg.* 3
MAJESTIC - Classic Chafers - CARLISLE FOODSERVICE PRODUCTS INCORPORATED; *pg.* 1455, *pg.* 1485
MAJESTIC - Vinyl Tile - CONGOLEUM CORPORATION; *pg.* 921, *pg.* 1084
MAJESTIC - Donut Mixes - DAWN FOOD PRODUCTS, INC.; *pg.* 1018, *pg.* 893
MAJESTIC - Vacuum Cleaner - HMI INDUSTRIES INC.; *pg.* 56, *pg.* 1475
MAJESTIC - Seating Product - IRWIN SEATING COMPANY INC.; *pg.* 929, *pg.* 887
MAJESTIC - Door Glass - ODL INCORPORATED; *pg.* 101, *pg.* 914
MAJESTIC - Intimate Apparel - V.F. CORPORATION; *pg.* 34, *pg.* 1376
MAJESTIC BEAUTY - Container Grown Plant - MONROVIA GROWERS; *pg.* 1797, *pg.* 44
MAJESTIC II - Vacuum Cleaner - HMI INDUSTRIES INC.; *pg.* 56, *pg.* 1475
MAJESTIC ORCHID - Container Grown Plant - MONROVIA GROWERS; *pg.* 1797, *pg.* 44
MAJESTIC WOLF - Game - WMS INDUSTRIES INC.; *pg.* 593, *pg.* 666
MAJESTICWARE - Tableware - ONEIDA LTD; *pg.* 1129, *pg.* 1318
MAJESTIK COLOR SERIES - Printer - XEROX CORPORATION; *pg.* 494, *pg.* 365
MAJESTIK COLOR SERIES DESIGN - Copier - XEROX CORPORATION; *pg.* 494, *pg.* 365
MAJESTIQUE - Biscuit - WORLD'S FINEST CHOCOLATE, INC.; *pg.* 1864, *pg.* 597
MAJESTY OF THE SEAS - Cruise Ship - ROYAL CARIBBEAN CRUISES LTD; *pg.* 1921, *pg.* 446
MAJESTYY - Footwear - STEVEN MADDEN, LTD.; *pg.* 1819, *pg.* 1176
MAJIC - Software System - MENTOR GRAPHICS CORPORATION; *pg.* 432, *pg.* 1510
MAJIC - Paints - YENKIN-MAJESTIC PAINT CORPORATION; *pg.* 1450, *pg.* 1445
MAJOR - Knife - COAST CUTLERY COMPANY; *pg.* 1121, *pg.* 1501
MAJOR - Fabric - NEMSCHOFF, INC.; *pg.* 936, *pg.* 1890
THE MAJOR ALTERNATIVE - Slogan - E1 ENTERTAINMENT U.S. LP; *pg.* 284, *pg.* 1323
MAJOR BRITE - Cleaner - BLUE CROSS LABORATORIES; *pg.* 326, *pg.* 277
MAJOR BUCKS AUSSIE ADVENTURE - Video Game - INTERNATIONAL GAME TECHNOLOGY; *pg.* 957, *pg.* 1024
MAJOR DICKASON'S BLEND - Coffee - PEET'S COFFEE & TEA, INC.; *pg.* 1029, *pg.* 85
MAJOR JACKPOTS - Video Game - INTERNATIONAL GAME TECHNOLOGY; *pg.* 957, *pg.* 1024
MAJORA - Bath & Plumbing Product - JACUZZI BRANDS CORPORATION; *pg.* 554, *pg.* 65
MAJORBUCKS - Video Game - INTERNATIONAL GAME TECHNOLOGY; *pg.* 957, *pg.* 1024
MAJORCA - Broadloom - COURISTAN INC.; *pg.* 921, *pg.* 1067
MAJORITY OF PLUMSETS - Medical Device - HOSPIRA, INC.; *pg.* 1542, *pg.* 623
MAKA - Eyewear - MAUI JIM, INC.; *pg.* 9, *pg.* 651
MAKAHA - Eyewear - MAUI JIM, INC.; *pg.* 9, *pg.* 651
MAKE-A-CASHWORD - Lottery Game - NEW YORK STATE LOTTERY; *pg.* 1001, *pg.* 1340
MAKE A FRIEND FOR LIFE - Teddy Bear Company - THE VERMONT TEDDY BEAR COMPANY; *pg.* 969, *pg.* 1767
MAKE A MARK - Non-Profit Humanitarian Organization - TRAVEL GUARD GROUP, INC.; *pg.* 1925, *pg.* 1895
MAKE A.COM NAME WITH US! - Slogan - GO DADDY INC.; *pg.* 1249, *pg.* 21
MAKE DINNER. BETTER. - Tagline - BARBER FOODS, INC.; *pg.* 839, *pg.* 751
MAKE EVERY MOMENT COUNT - Slogan - NETJETS INC.; *pg.* 1917, *pg.* 1442
MAKE HERR'S YOURS - Slogan - HERR FOODS INC.; *pg.* 861, *pg.* 1557
MAKE IT BETTER - Slogan - THE TIMBERLAND COMPANY; *pg.* 1821, *pg.* 1039
MAKE IT COOL - Craft Kit - JANLYNN CORPORATION; *pg.* 696, *pg.* 815
MAKE IT HAPPEN - Slogan - GATE CITY BANK; *pg.* 761, *pg.* 1397
MAKE IT REAL - Slogan - STRATASYS, INC.; *pg.* 476, *pg.* 923
MAKE IT UP! - Game - GAMEWRIGHT; *pg.* 953, *pg.* 836
MAKE KILLER FLASH - Effects For Website - COFFEECUP SOFTWARE INC.; *pg.* 1236, *pg.* 501
MAKE LEMONADE - Flower Arrangement - 1-800-FLOWERS.COM, INC.; *pg.* 1758, *pg.* 1151
MAKE LIFE MORE BEAUTIFUL - Slogan - MENTOR CORPORATION; *pg.* 1565, *pg.* 263
MAKE MANAGE MOVE - Tagline - AVID TECHNOLOGY, INC.; *pg.* 622, *pg.* 804
MAKE OUR NUMBERS - Tagline - INFOACCESS.NET LLC; *pg.* 1258, *pg.* 1456
MAKE SOMETHING GREAT - Slogan - STANLEY BLACK & DECKER, INC.; *pg.* 1063, *pg.* 358
MAKE THE WORLD A BETTER PLACE. - Tagline -

First page reference indicates Business Class Edition
Second page reference indicates Geographic Edition

BLACKBAUD, INC.; *pg.* 361, *pg.* 1613
MAKEAMENDS - Hair Care Product - NU SKIN ENTERPRISES, INC.; *pg.* 518, *pg.* 1755
MAKEOVER FUN 101 - Educational Materials - SCHOLASTIC INC.; *pg.* 1683, *pg.* 1288
MAKERART/COLOR 'N SEEK - Puzzle - B. DAZZLE, INC.; *pg.* 949, *pg.* 188
THE MAKER'S DIET - Health & Wellness Product - GARDEN OF LIFE, INC.; *pg.* 1532, *pg.* 478
MAKER'S MARK - Bourbon - JIM BEAM BRANDS CO.; *pg.* 1965, *pg.* 601
MAKEUPMATE - Cosmetic Products - COVER GIRL COSMETICS; *pg.* 506, *pg.* 772
MAKING A DIFFERENCE IN HEALTHCARE - Slogan - GE HEALTHCARE; *pg.* 399, *pg.* 1765
MAKING A DIFFERENCE WITH NOVEL THERAPIES - Tagline - DEPOMED, INC.; *pg.* 1523, *pg.* 143
MAKING DATA USEFUL - Tagline - TIGERLOGIC CORPORATION; *pg.* 484, *pg.* 117
MAKING FILMS FUNCTION AROUND THE GLOBE AND BEYOND - Slogan - DUNMORE CORPORATION; *pg.* 1456, *pg.* 1518
MAKING GREAT HEALTH CARE A LITTLE EASIER - Tag Line - HARVARD PILGRIM HEALTH CARE, INC.; *pg.* 1539, *pg.* 856
MAKING HEALTHCARE WORK - Slogan - HORIZON BLUE CROSS BLUE SHIELD OF NEW JERSEY; *pg.* 1203, *pg.* 1096
MAKING HOME AFFORDABLE - Home Modification Program - FEDERAL HOME LOAN MORTGAGE CORPORATION; *pg.* 751, *pg.* 1790
MAKING IT HOME - Slogan - HAVERTY FURNITURE COMPANIES, INC.; *pg.* 926, *pg.* 509
MAKING IT SIMPLE - Tagline - BCE INC.; *pg.* 1936, *pg.* 1960
MAKING IT WORK AS ONE - Slogan - NOVELL INC.; *pg.* 446, *pg.* 852
MAKING LEADERS SUCCESSFUL EVERY DAY - Tagline - FORRESTER RESEARCH, INC.; *pg.* 1642, *pg.* 807
MAKING LIVES EASIER, HEALTHIER, HAPPIER - Tagline - HY-VEE, INC.; *pg.* 1023, *pg.* 713
MAKING MEALS EASY - Tagline - HANOVER FOODS CORPORATION; *pg.* 861, *pg.* 1535
MAKING NETWORKS AND APPLICATIONS PERFORM - Slogan - RIVERBED PERFORMANCE MANAGEMENT; *pg.* 462, *pg.* 765
MAKING NEXT-GENERATION NETWORKS A REALITY. - Tagline - VITESSE SEMICONDUCTOR CORPORATION; *pg.* 686, *pg.* 57
MAKING PAPER WORK - Slogan - NUANCE DOCUMENT IMAGING SOLUTIONS; *pg.* 1271, *pg.* 1037
MAKING PLEASURABLE DINING AFFORDABLE - Tag Line - GOLDEN CORRAL CORPORATION; *pg.* 1730, *pg.* 1387
MAKING SCENTS - Catalog Order Services - 1-800-FLOWERS.COM, INC.; *pg.* 1758, *pg.* 1151
MAKING SEAFOOD A BIGGER PART OF LIFE - Slogan - PHILLIPS FOODS INC.; *pg.* 1030, *pg.* 758
MAKING SENSE OF INVESTING - Tagline - EDWARD D. JONES & CO., LP; *pg.* 746, *pg.* 995
MAKING SENSE OUT OF LIFE - Slogan - ILLUMINA, INC.; *pg.* 412, *pg.* 203
MAKING STRIDES - Breast Cancer Awareness Programs - AMERICAN CANCER SOCIETY, INC.; *pg.* 126, *pg.* 487
MAKING TECHNOLOGY WORK FOR YOU - Tag Line - BEST BUY CO., INC.; *pg.* 1761, *pg.* 954
MAKING WAVES IN POWER - Slogan - OCEAN POWER TECHNOLOGIES, INC.; *pg.* 1948, *pg.* 1107
MAKING WIRELESS M2M EASY - Tagline - DIGI INTERNATIONAL INC.; *pg.* 387, *pg.* 948
MAKING YOU LOOK GOOD IS WHAT WE DO BEST - Tag Line - HAIR CLUB FOR MEN, LTD., INC.; *pg.* 511, *pg.* 411
MAKO - Commercial Printing System - ECRM IMAGING SYSTEMS, INC.; *pg.* 1410, *pg.* 848
MAKO 2 CTP - Commercial Printing System - ECRM IMAGING SYSTEMS, INC.; *pg.* 1410, *pg.* 848
MAKO IMAGESETTER - Commercial Printing System - ECRM IMAGING SYSTEMS, INC.; *pg.* 1410, *pg.* 848
MAKON - Chemical Product - STEPAN COMPANY; *pg.* 1182, *pg.* 643
MAKROFOL - Plastic Film - TEKRA CORPORATION; *pg.* 1184, *pg.* 1884
MALAFENE - Pharmaceutical Product - ABBOTT LABORATORIES; *pg.* 1484, *pg.* 551
MALAGA WINE - Nail Care Product - OPI PRODUCTS INC.; *pg.* 518, *pg.* 167
MALATHION - Home & Farm Product - PBI/GORDON CORPORATION; *pg.* 1176, *pg.* 985
MALATHION - Insecticide - SOUTHERN AGRICULTURAL INSECTICIDES, INC.; *pg.* 1181, *pg.* 458
MALAWI MANGO - Beverage - BAI BRANDS; *pg.* 238, *pg.* 1073
MALAYSIA.COM - Travel Website - LIVE CURRENT MEDIA INC.; *pg.* 1263, *pg.* 1911
MALAYSIAN MIST - Nail Care Product - OPI PRODUCTS INC.; *pg.* 518, *pg.* 167
MALC - Medical Product - HOLOGIC, INC.; *pg.* 1416, *pg.* 784
MALCO - Nusoft Fabric Softener - MALCO PRODUCTS, INC.; *pg.* 1172, *pg.* 1404
MALD - Defense System - RAYTHEON COMPANY; *pg.* 233, *pg.* 854
MALDEN POWER STRETCH - Glove Liner - KOMBI, LTD.; *pg.* 1838, *pg.* 1766
MALDI - Mass Spectrometer - WATERS CORPORATION; *pg.* 1436, *pg.* 834
MALDI MATRICES - Analytical Component - BRUKER CORPORATION; *pg.* 1511, *pg.* 788
MALDIMICRO - Mass Spectrometer - WATERS CORPORATION; *pg.* 1436, *pg.* 834
MALE FACTOR 1000 - Herbal Formula with Swiss Oats - HERBALIFE INTERNATIONAL OF AMERICA, INC.; *pg.* 1541, *pg.* 132
MALE RESPONSE - Vitamin & Herbal Supplement - SOURCE NATURALS; *pg.* 1595, *pg.* 278
MALIA - Eyewear - MAUI JIM, INC.; *pg.* 9, *pg.* 651
MALIBU - Flavored Rum - PERNOD RICARD USA, INC.; *pg.* 1968, *pg.* 1332
MALIBU - Medical Device - RESMED INC.; *pg.* 1589, *pg.* 207
MALIBU - Office Furniture - STEELCASE INC.; *pg.* 475, *pg.* 889
MALIBU MUSK - Designer Fragrance - PARFUMS DE COEUR LTD.; *pg.* 519, *pg.* 376
MALIBU TOO - Waiting Seating - STEELCASE INC.; *pg.* 475, *pg.* 889
MALL MADNESS - Game - HASBRO, INC.; *pg.* 954, *pg.* 1603
MALL WITHOUT WALLS - Brokerage System - MARKET AMERICA WORLDWIDE, INC.; *pg.* 1265, *pg.* 1375
MALLO CUP - Confectionery - BOYER CANDY COMPANY INC.; *pg.* 1851, *pg.* 1514
MALLORY-HEAD - Implant Product - ZIMMER BIOMET HOLDINGS, INC.; *pg.* 1611, *pg.* 699
MALLORY HEAD HIP SYSTEM - Hip Stem - ZIMMER BIOMET HOLDINGS, INC.; *pg.* 1611, *pg.* 699
MALLORY SQUARE - Carpet - BEAULIEU GROUP, LLC; *pg.* 917, *pg.* 529
MALPENSA - Carpet - INTERFACE, INC.; *pg.* 695, *pg.* 512
MALPOTANE - Vitamin - HEALTH PRODUCTS CORPORATION; *pg.* 1540, *pg.* 1356
MALT - Snack Food - SNYDER'S-LANCE, INC.; *pg.* 896, *pg.* 1368
MALTA - Software Development Board - IMAGINATION TECHNOLOGIES; *pg.* 412, *pg.* 285
MALTED MICRO SHAKE - Frozen Milkshake - UNITED DAIRY FARMERS, INC.; *pg.* 906, *pg.* 1426
MALTESE FORTUNE - Video Game - INTERNATIONAL GAME TECHNOLOGY; *pg.* 957, *pg.* 1024
MALTESERS - Chocolate - MARS, INCORPORATED; *pg.* 1858, *pg.* 1792
MALTEVOL 12 - Multivitamin - CHURCH & DWIGHT CANADA CORP.; *pg.* 503, *pg.* 1925
MALTIDEX - Starch Derivative - CARGILL, INC.; *pg.* 845, *pg.* 965
MALTRIN - Corn Syrup Solids - GRAIN PROCESSING CORPORATION; *pg.* 859, *pg.* 709
MALTRIN QD - Pharmaceutical Ingredient - GRAIN PROCESSING CORPORATION; *pg.* 859, *pg.* 709
MALUBE - Industrial Synthetic Lubricant Additive - PPG INDUSTRIES, INC.; *pg.* 1445, *pg.* 1579
MALVERN - Beverages - THE COCA-COLA COMPANY; *pg.* 240, *pg.* 493
MAMA - Magazine for Expecting Parents - MARCH OF DIMES BIRTH DEFECTS FOUNDATION; *pg.* 146, *pg.* 1354
MAMA BURGER - Fast Food - A&W FOOD SERVICES OF CANADA INC.; *pg.* 1714, *pg.* 1908
MAMA MOORE'S BAKESHOP - Birthday Basket - 1-800-FLOWERS.COM, INC.; *pg.* 1758, *pg.* 1151
MAMA SBARRO'S - Pizzeria Restaurant - SBARRO, INC.; *pg.* 1749, *pg.* 1182
MAMA SPANX - Clothing - SPANX INC.; *pg.* 32, *pg.* 520
MAMBA - Amusement & Water Park - CEDAR FAIR, L.P.; *pg.* 537, *pg.* 1471
MAMMA BELLA - Frozen Breads - LANCASTER COLONY CORPORATION; *pg.* 873, *pg.* 1441
MAMMA BELLA - Food Product - T. MARZETTI COMPANY; *pg.* 900, *pg.* 1444
MAMMA.COM - Internet Search Engine - COPERNIC INC.; *pg.* 1237, *pg.* 1958
MAMMOMAT - Mammography Imaging System - SIEMENS CORPORATION; *pg.* 803, *pg.* 1291
MAMMOPAD - Medical Product - HOLOGIC, INC.; *pg.* 1416, *pg.* 784
MAMMOSITE - Radiation Therapy System - HOLOGIC, INC.; *pg.* 1416, *pg.* 784
MAMMOTH - Tobacco Product - AMERICAN SNUFF COMPANY; *pg.* 1893, *pg.* 1641
MAMMOTH - Air Conditioners - NORTEK, INC.; *pg.* 100, *pg.* 1607
MAMMOTH BASKETBALL EQUIPMENT - Basketball Backboards - LIFETIME PRODUCTS INC.; *pg.* 933, *pg.* 1751
MAMMOTH CAVE - Twist Tobacco - AMERICAN SNUFF COMPANY; *pg.* 1893, *pg.* 1641
MAMMOTH RECORDS - Record Label - THE WALT DISNEY COMPANY; *pg.* 317, *pg.* 52
MAMMOTOME - Healthcare Product - JOHNSON & JOHNSON; *pg.* 1549, *pg.* 1091
MAMONDE - skin Care Products - AMOREPACIFIC US, INC.; *pg.* 498, *pg.* 1195
MAMORAY - Mamography Films & Screens - AGFA CORPORATION; *pg.* 1398, *pg.* 1114
MAN - Fragrance - HERBALIFE INTERNATIONAL OF AMERICA, INC.; *pg.* 1541, *pg.* 132
MAN-ALOE CLASSIC - Healthcare Product - MANNATECH, INCORPORATED; *pg.* 1558, *pg.* 1671
MAN & GUN - Fluid Handling System - GRACO, INC.; *pg.* 1342, *pg.* 935
MAN ROLANDS - Printing Press - MANROLAND INC.; *pg.* 430, *pg.* 669
MANAGE - Software - EPICOR SOFTWARE CORPORATION; *pg.* 393, *pg.* 110
MANAGE YOUR CONNECTION - Service - ELEMICA, INC.; *pg.* 1242, *pg.* 1591
MANAGED EQUIPMENT PROGRAM - Centralized Supply Contracts & Inventory Accounting & Maintenance Services - GRACO, INC.; *pg.* 1342, *pg.* 935
MANAGED PKI - Online Transaction Security Product - VERISIGN, INC.; *pg.* 488, *pg.* 1799
MANAGED SERVICES - Global Services - SONUS NETWORKS INC.; *pg.* 1281, *pg.* 858
MANAGED SERVICES MANAGED BETTER - Slogan - ARAMARK; *pg.* 1013, *pg.* 1558
MANAGEFUSION - Software - SYMANTEC CORPORATION; *pg.* 478, *pg.* 161
MANAGEMENT ACCOUNTING QUARTERLY - Quarterly, Refereed Online Journal Devoted to Accounting & Finance - INSTITUTE OF MANAGEMENT ACCOUNTANTS, INC.; *pg.* 144, *pg.* 1086
MANAGEMENT CONSOLE - Software - DELL SOFTWARE; *pg.* 385, *pg.* 40
MANAGEMENT PACK FOR AS400 - Software - DELL SOFTWARE; *pg.* 385, *pg.* 40
MANAGEMENT PACK FOR .NET - Software - DELL SOFTWARE; *pg.* 385, *pg.* 40
MANAGEMENT REPORTER - Tool - NIELSEN AUDIO; *pg.* 446, *pg.* 768
MANAGEMENT SERVER - Web Tool - OPENCONNECT SYSTEMS, INC.; *pg.* 449, *pg.* 1685
MANAGEMENT SUITE - Software - DELL SOFTWARE; *pg.* 385, *pg.* 40
MANAGEMENT TEAM - Trade Magazine - THE NIELSEN COMPANY B.V.; *pg.* 1671, *pg.* 1272
MANAGEMENT XTENSIONS - CONFIGURATION MANAGER 2007 - Software - DELL SOFTWARE; *pg.* 385, *pg.* 40
MANAGEMENT XTENSIONS FOR SMS - Software - DELL SOFTWARE; *pg.* 385, *pg.* 40
MANAGEMENT XTENSIONS - OPERATIONS MANAGER 2007 - Software - DELL SOFTWARE; *pg.* 385, *pg.* 40
MANAGERSUITE - Software - SKILLSOFT PLC; *pg.* 470, *pg.* 1037
MANAGERVIEW - Software - OPENTEXT; *pg.* 450, *pg.* 1665
MANAGING GOAL ACHIEVEMENT - Software - INTEGRITY SOLUTIONS; *pg.* 145, *pg.* 22
MANAGING THE DOCUMENTS YOU CAN'T LIVE WITHOUT

- Slogan - THE STANDARD REGISTER COMPANY; *pg.* 473, *pg.* 1446
MANANTIAL - Beverages - THE COCA-COLA COMPANY; *pg.* 240, *pg.* 493
MANCHESTER - Furniture - ASHLEY FURNITURE INDUSTRIES, INC.; *pg.* 914, *pg.* 1852
MANDALAY BAY - Resort & Casino - MGM RESORTS INTERNATIONAL; *pg.* 1105, *pg.* 1028
MANDARIN MAGIC - Hair & Skin Product - AUBREY ORGANICS INC.; *pg.* 499, *pg.* 470
MANDARIN MAGIC - Mandarin Orange Juice Drink - OCEAN SPRAY CRANBERRIES, INC.; *pg.* 887, *pg.* 827
MANDARIN TOFU - Organic Tofu - SUNRISE SOYA FOODS; *pg.* 900, *pg.* 1912
MANDATE - Fabric - NEMSCHOFF, INC.; *pg.* 936, *pg.* 1890
MANDELAY - Male Genital Desensitizer - MAJESTIC DRUG COMPANY, INC.; *pg.* 516, *pg.* 1343
MANDIBULAR FRACTURE SYSTEM - Surgical Instruments - OSTEOMED CORPORATION; *pg.* 1425, *pg.* 1658
MANDOLINS - Musical Instrument - GIBSON GUITAR CORP.; *pg.* 550, *pg.* 1650
MANDREL SLEEVES & SEGMENTS - Roll Covering - VAIL RUBBER WORKS, INC.; *pg.* 1891, *pg.* 906
MANDRILL - E-Mail Infrastructure Service - THE ROCKET SCIENCE GROUP, LLC; *pg.* 1278, *pg.* 519
MANDYY - Footwear - STEVEN MADDEN, LTD.; *pg.* 1819, *pg.* 1176
MANE 'N TAIL - Personal Care Product - STRAIGHT ARROW PRODUCTS, INC.; *pg.* 523, *pg.* 1517
MANEX - Fungicide - E.I. DU PONT DE NEMOURS & COMPANY; *pg.* 1159, *pg.* 390
MANFACT - Software - EPICOR SOFTWARE CORPORATION; *pg.* 393, *pg.* 110
MANGABRAZE - Steel Product - RUSSEL METALS INC.; *pg.* 1180, *pg.* 1928
MANGE MEDICINE - Pet Supplies - HAPPY JACK INC.; *pg.* 1476, *pg.* 1390
MANGO - Fabric - NEMSCHOFF, INC.; *pg.* 936, *pg.* 1890
MANGO-A-GO-GO - Fruit Drink - JAMBA, INC.; *pg.* 1024, *pg.* 84
MANGO KIWI BLOSSOM - Fruit Arrangements - EDIBLE ARRANGEMENTS INTERNATIONAL, INC.; *pg.* 1768, *pg.* 382
MANGO KIWI FESTIVAL - Fruit Arrangements - EDIBLE ARRANGEMENTS INTERNATIONAL, INC.; *pg.* 1768, *pg.* 382
MANGO MANTRA - Low Calorie Fruit Drink - JAMBA, INC., *pg.* 1024, *pg.* 84
MANGO MELON - Decorative Fragrance - AROMATIQUE INC.; *pg.* 499, *pg.* 32
MANGO PEACH TOPPER - Fruit Smoothie With Granola - JAMBA, INC.; *pg.* 1024, *pg.* 84
MANHASSET - Lounge Chairs - BERNHARDT DESIGN; *pg.* 918, *pg.* 1381
MANHATTAN - Watch - A. T. CROSS COMPANY; *pg.* 339, *pg.* 1602
MANHATTAN - Furniture - ASHLEY FURNITURE INDUSTRIES, INC.; *pg.* 914, *pg.* 1852
MANHATTAN - Footwear - CAPEZIO BALLET MAKERS INC.; *pg.* 1805, *pg.* 1125
MANHATTAN - Quality Chafers - CARLISLE FOODSERVICE PRODUCTS INCORPORATED; *pg.* 1455, *pg.* 1485
MANHATTAN - Video Game - INTERNATIONAL GAME TECHNOLOGY; *pg.* 957, *pg.* 1024
MANHATTAN - Furniture - JASPER GROUP; *pg.* 930, *pg.* 691
MANHATTAN - Fabric - NEMSCHOFF, INC.; *pg.* 936, *pg.* 1890
MANHATTAN - Dress & Casual Clothing - PERRY ELLIS INTERNATIONAL, INC.; *pg.* 45, *pg.* 445
MANHATTAN BAGEL - Food Store - EINSTEIN NOAH RESTAURANT GROUP, INC.; *pg.* 1019, *pg.* 332
MANHATTAN CLASSICS - Rug - COURISTAN INC.; *pg.* 921, *pg.* 1067
THE MANHATTAN COLLECTION - Honeycomb Shades Featuring Sleek New Headrail & Woven Fabrics - HUNTER DOUGLAS, INC.; *pg.* 928, *pg.* 1320
MANHATTAN FAST TRACK - Educational Servicees - MANHATTAN ASSOCIATES, INC.; *pg.* 430, *pg.* 513
MANHATTAN SCOPE - Software - MANHATTAN ASSOCIATES, INC.; *pg.* 430, *pg.* 513
MANHATTEN MINI STORAGE - Storage - EDISON PROPERTIES, LLC; *pg.* 1906, *pg.* 1096
MANHOLE COVER/SAFETY POOL - Prevents Outside Sparks & Gases from Entering Sewer Lines - STANDARD SAFETY EQUIPMENT CO.; *pg.* 1379, *pg.* 632
MANICURE PEDICURE STATION - Nailcare Product - MEDICOOL, INC.; *pg.* 1562, *pg.* 294
MANINI - Eyewear - MAUI JIM, INC.; *pg.* 9, *pg.* 651
MANISCHEWITZ - Food Products - MANISCHEWITZ COMPANY; *pg.* 875, *pg.* 1097
MANITOWOC - Cranes & Boom Trucks - THE MANITOWOC COMPANY, INC.; *pg.* 1358, *pg.* 1868
MANITOWOC CRANE CARE - Crane Services - THE MANITOWOC COMPANY, INC.; *pg.* 1358, *pg.* 1868
MANKOCIDE - Fungicide - E.I. DU PONT DE NEMOURS & COMPANY; *pg.* 1159, *pg.* 390
MANNA - Bread - NATURE'S PATH FOODS INC.; *pg.* 833, *pg.* 1908
MANNA-BEARS - Nutritional Product - MANNATECH, INCORPORATED; *pg.* 1558, *pg.* 1671
MANNA-C - Nutritional Product - MANNATECH, INCORPORATED; *pg.* 1558, *pg.* 1671
MANNA E - Concentrated Microbial Supplements for Animal Feeds - MANNA PRO CORPORATION; *pg.* 1478, *pg.* 975
MANNA MATE - Calf & Lamb Feed - MANNA PRO CORPORATION; *pg.* 1478, *pg.* 975
MANNA SENIOR - Horse Feed - MANNA PRO CORPORATION; *pg.* 1478, *pg.* 975
MANNACLEANSE - Nutritional Product - MANNATECH, INCORPORATED; *pg.* 1558, *pg.* 1671
MANNATECH OPTIMAL SKIN CARE SYSTEM - Healthcare Product - MANNATECH, INCORPORATED; *pg.* 1558, *pg.* 1671
MANNAZ - Footwear - VANS, INC.; *pg.* 1821, *pg.* 76
MANNERLY - Faucets - MOEN INCORPORATED; *pg.* 1056, *pg.* 1468
MANNI - Bear - GUND, INC.; *pg.* 954, *pg.* 1056
MANNIDEX - Food Additives - CARGILL, INC.; *pg.* 845, *pg.* 965
MANNIGLAS - Thermal Control Unit - LYDALL, INC.; *pg.* 1357, *pg.* 354
MANNING - Industrial Paper Products - LYDALL, INC.; *pg.* 1357, *pg.* 354
MANNY'S - Tortilla Products - HORMEL FOODS CORPORATION; *pg.* 863, *pg.* 915
MANOR HALL - Coating Product - PPG INDUSTRIES, INC.; *pg.* 1445, *pg.* 1579
MANOR HALL TIMELESS - Coating Product - PPG INDUSTRIES, INC.; *pg.* 1445, *pg.* 1579
MANORCARE HEALTH SERVICES - Long Term Care Centers - HCR MANORCARE, INC.; *pg.* 1539, *pg.* 1476
MAN'S LAV - Bath Product - KOHLER CO.; *pg.* 91, *pg.* 1862
MANSAFE - Fall Protection Equipment - MINE SAFETY APPLIANCES COMPANY; *pg.* 1361, *pg.* 1525
MANSFIELD - Table - BLATT BOWLING & BILLIARD CORP.; *pg.* 1827, *pg.* 1203
MANSFIELD - Furniture - J. ROBERT SCOTT INC.; *pg.* 930, *pg.* 105
MANSFIELD - Office Furniture - STEELCASE INC.; *pg.* 475, *pg.* 889
MANTA - Laser Sorter - KEY TECHNOLOGY, INC.; *pg.* 868, *pg.* 1847
MANTA - Floor Cleaning Product - NSS ENTERPRISES, INC.; *pg.* 59, *pg.* 1476
MANTECA - Footwear - PHOENIX FOOTWEAR GROUP, INC.; *pg.* 1815, *pg.* 60
MANTIS - Knife - BUCK KNIVES, INC.; *pg.* 1828, *pg.* 550
MANTIS - Amusement & Water Park - CEDAR FAIR, L.P.; *pg.* 537, *pg.* 1471
MANTIS - Software - CINCOM SYSTEMS, INC.; *pg.* 372, *pg.* 1411
MANTIS - Oscillator - COHERENT, INC.; *pg.* 1406, *pg.* 265
MANTIS - Stereo Magnifier System - EDMUND INDUSTRIAL OPTICS INC.; *pg.* 1411, *pg.* 1041
MANTIS - Tiller - SCHILLER-PFEIFFER, INC.; *pg.* 1061, *pg.* 1587
MANTLE - Fabric - NEMSCHOFF, INC.; *pg.* 936, *pg.* 1890
MANTRA - Carpet - INTERFACE, INC.; *pg.* 695, *pg.* 512
MANTRA - Lighting System - LITECONTROL CORPORATION; *pg.* 1301, *pg.* 841
MANTRA - Ceramic, Glass, Stone Tiles & Slabs - WALKER & ZANGER, INC.; *pg.* 119, *pg.* 281
MANU-KLENZ - Detergent - STERIS CORPORATION; *pg.* 1597, *pg.* 1464
MANUAL PME - Pad-Mounted Gear - S&C ELECTRIC COMPANY; *pg.* 1305, *pg.* 589
MANUAL PMH - Pad-Mounted Gear - S&C ELECTRIC COMPANY; *pg.* 1305, *pg.* 589
MANUAL VRA - Visual Reinforcement Audiometry - INTELLIGENT HEARING SYSTEMS CORP.; *pg.* 1546, *pg.* 443
MANUFACTURERS PROTECTOR PLAN - Insurance Package Program - BROWN & BROWN, INC.; *pg.* 1196, *pg.* 419
MANUFACTUREVIEW - Software System - MENTOR GRAPHICS CORPORATION; *pg.* 432, *pg.* 1510
MANUFACTURING ADVISOR - Software System - MENTOR GRAPHICS CORPORATION; *pg.* 432, *pg.* 1510
MANUFACTURING CABLE - Software System - MENTOR GRAPHICS CORPORATION; *pg.* 432, *pg.* 1510
MANUFACTURING ENGINEERING - SME's Monthly Flagship Periodical - SOCIETY OF MANUFACTURING ENGINEERS; *pg.* 157, *pg.* 878
MANUFACTURING.NET - Trade Website - ADVANTAGE BUSINESS MEDIA; *pg.* 1613, *pg.* 1116
MANULIFE - Financial Services - MANULIFE FINANCIAL CORPORATION; *pg.* 778, *pg.* 1939
MANVER - Chemical Reagent - HACH COMPANY; *pg.* 1415, *pg.* 334
MANWICH - Food Product - CONAGRA FOODS, INC.; *pg.* 826, *pg.* 1014
MANY VOICES - Magazine - SCHOLASTIC INC.; *pg.* 1683, *pg.* 1288
MANZANA MIA - Soft Drink - THE COCA-COLA COMPANY; *pg.* 240, *pg.* 493
MANZANITA SOL - Beverage - PEPSICO, INC.; *pg.* 259, *pg.* 1327
MANZATE - Fungicide - E.I. DU PONT DE NEMOURS & COMPANY; *pg.* 1159, *pg.* 390
MANZEL - Fluid Handling System - GRACO, INC.; *pg.* 1342, *pg.* 935
MANZEL - Lubrication Equipment - IDEX CORPORATION; *pg.* 1347, *pg.* 623
MAORI RICHES - Game - WMS INDUSTRIES INC.; *pg.* 593, *pg.* 666
M.A.P - Screw Feeder - METALFAB, INC.; *pg.* 1360, *pg.* 1127
MAP - Medical Device - RESMED INC.; *pg.* 1589, *pg.* 207
MAP-IN - Software - SYNOPSYS, INC.; *pg.* 480, *pg.* 162
MAP-O-GRAM - Medical Equipment - INVACARE CORPORATION; *pg.* 1546, *pg.* 1451
MAP-PAK - Pocket Portfolio Folder For Maps - AMERICAN AUTOMOBILE ASSOCIATION; *pg.* 1190, *pg.* 429
MAP PRODUCTION SYSTEM - Software - ENVIRONMENTAL SYSTEMS RESEARCH INSTITUTE INC.; *pg.* 393, *pg.* 188
MAP-SHIELD - AF Barrier Film - HONEYWELL INTERNATIONAL INC.; *pg.* 407, *pg.* 1088
MAP XTEND - Location-Based Wireless Handheld Tool - PITNEY BOWES SOFTWARE INC.; *pg.* 455, *pg.* 1346
MAPAC - Plastic Film - AEP INDUSTRIES INC.; *pg.* 1878, *pg.* 1085
MAPBASIC - Software - PITNEY BOWES SOFTWARE INC.; *pg.* 455, *pg.* 1346
MAPBEANS - Software - ENVIRONMENTAL SYSTEMS RESEARCH INSTITUTE INC.; *pg.* 393, *pg.* 188
MAPCAFE - Software - ENVIRONMENTAL SYSTEMS RESEARCH INSTITUTE INC.; *pg.* 393, *pg.* 188
MAPCO EXPRESS - Retail Fuel & Convenience Stores - DELEK US HOLDINGS, INC.; *pg.* 975, *pg.* 1627
MAPCO MART - Retail Fuel & Convenience Stores - DELEK US HOLDINGS, INC.; *pg.* 975, *pg.* 1627
MAPDATA - Software - ENVIRONMENTAL SYSTEMS RESEARCH INSTITUTE INC.; *pg.* 393, *pg.* 188
MAPINFO MAP X - Mapping Software - PITNEY BOWES SOFTWARE INC.; *pg.* 455, *pg.* 1346
MAPINFO MAPXTREME - Mapping Application Software - PITNEY BOWES SOFTWARE INC.; *pg.* 455, *pg.* 1346
MAPINFO PROFESSIONAL - Mapping & Geographic Analysis Software - PITNEY BOWES SOFTWARE INC.; *pg.* 455, *pg.* 1346
MAPINFO PROVIEWER - Tool for Viewing Maps & Tables - PITNEY BOWES SOFTWARE INC.; *pg.* 455, *pg.* 1346
MAPINFO SPATIALWARE - Tool for Storage, Management & Manipulation of Location-Based Data - PITNEY BOWES SOFTWARE INC.; *pg.* 455, *pg.* 1346
MAPLE - Flooring - LUMBER LIQUIDATORS HOLDINGS, INC.; *pg.* 94, *pg.* 1808
MAPLE CINN - Frozen Waffles - NATURE'S PATH FOODS INC.; *pg.* 833, *pg.* 1908
MAPLE CREEK - Cabinetry - MASTERBRAND CABINETS, INC.; *pg.* 96, *pg.* 692
MAPLE GLAZED HONEY COAT - Food Product - BOAR'S HEAD PROVISIONS CO., INC.; *pg.* 841, *pg.* 465

First page reference indicates Business Class Edition
Second page reference indicates Geographic Edition

MAPLE GROVE - Ceiling Fan - WESTINGHOUSE LIGHTING CORPORATION; *pg.* 687, *pg.* 1571
MAPLE GROVE FARMS OF VERMONT - Pure Maple Syrup & Salad Dressings - B&G FOODS, INC.; *pg.* 838, *pg.* 1102
MAPLE LEAF MEDALLION NATURALLY - Pork - MAPLE LEAF FOODS INC.; *pg.* 875, *pg.* 1927
MAPLE LEAF NATURES GOURMET - Frozen Dinners - MAPLE LEAF FOODS INC.; *pg.* 875, *pg.* 1927
MAPLE LEAF PRIME NATURALLY - Chicken - MAPLE LEAF FOODS INC.; *pg.* 875, *pg.* 1927
MAPLE LEAF SIMPLY FRESH - Food Product - MAPLE LEAF FOODS INC.; *pg.* 875, *pg.* 1927
MAPLE RIDGE - Shirts - ABERCROMBIE & FITCH CO.; *pg.* 37, *pg.* 1466
MAPLEHURST - Milk Product - DEAN FOODS COMPANY; *pg.* 852, *pg.* 1679
MAPLESTORY - Toy & Game - HASBRO, INC.; *pg.* 954, *pg.* 1603
MAPLETON - Shoes - ALLEN-EDMONDS SHOE CORP.; *pg.* 1804, *pg.* 1887
MAPLEWOOD - Carpet - BEAULIEU GROUP, LLC; *pg.* 917, *pg.* 529
MAPLEX - Software - ENVIRONMENTAL SYSTEMS RESEARCH INSTITUTE INC.; *pg.* 393, *pg.* 188
MAPLOX - Program - MULTISORB TECHNOLOGIES, INC.; *pg.* 1570, *pg.* 1150
MAPMAAKER DIRECT - Software - NIELSEN AUDIO; *pg.* 446, *pg.* 768
MAPMAKER DIRECT - Presentations - NIELSEN AUDIO; *pg.* 446, *pg.* 768
MAPMAKER'S TOOLKIT - Educational Materials - SCHOLASTIC INC.; *pg.* 1683, *pg.* 1288
MAPMAN - Educational Materials - SCHOLASTIC INC.; *pg.* 1683, *pg.* 1288
MAPMARKER - Software - PITNEY BOWES SOFTWARE INC.; *pg.* 455, *pg.* 1346
MAPOBJECTS - Software - ENVIRONMENTAL SYSTEMS RESEARCH INSTITUTE INC.; *pg.* 393, *pg.* 188
MAPP GAS - Fuel Gas - LINDE GAS LLC; *pg.* 1356, *pg.* 1095
MAPPAIRS - Molecular Biology Product - THERMO FISHER SCIENTIFIC INC.; *pg.* 1602, *pg.* 61
MAPRI - Fastening Systems - TEXTRON INC.; *pg.* 235, *pg.* 1607
MAPROSY - Chemical Product - STEPAN COMPANY; *pg.* 1182, *pg.* 643
MAPS - Software - BIO-RAD LABORATORIES, INC.; *pg.* 1504, *pg.* 101
MAPS - Ingredient System - PENFORD CORPORATION; *pg.* 1177, *pg.* 314
MAPS - Sourcing & Hiring Technology - SELECTREMEDY; *pg.* 468, *pg.* 263
MAPS BRAND CHARTING - Copier - XEROX CORPORATION; *pg.* 494, *pg.* 365
MAPSHOP - Software - PITNEY BOWES SOFTWARE INC.; *pg.* 455, *pg.* 1346
MAPSTAR - Software - HEMISPHERE GPS INC.; *pg.* 642, *pg.* 1903
MAPSTAR II - Measurement Tool - LASER TECHNOLOGY, INC.; *pg.* 1419, *pg.* 314
MAPSTUDIO - Software - ENVIRONMENTAL SYSTEMS RESEARCH INSTITUTE INC.; *pg.* 393, *pg.* 188
MAPTRAK EXPRESS - Wafer Sorter - BROOKS AUTOMATION, INC.; *pg.* 1320, *pg.* 813
MAPX - Software - PITNEY BOWES SOFTWARE INC.; *pg.* 455, *pg.* 1346
MAPXTEND - Software - PITNEY BOWES SOFTWARE INC.; *pg.* 455, *pg.* 1346
MAPXTREME - Software - PITNEY BOWES SOFTWARE INC.; *pg.* 455, *pg.* 1346
MAQUINA LATINA - Video Game - INTERNATIONAL GAME TECHNOLOGY; *pg.* 957, *pg.* 1024
MAR-TEMP - Heat Treating Product - HOUGHTON INTERNATIONAL INC.; *pg.* 1167, *pg.* 1589
MAR-X - Mold Steel - A. FINKL & SONS CO.; *pg.* 1309, *pg.* 563
MARA - Fabric - NEMSCHOFF, INC.; *pg.* 936, *pg.* 1890
MARABOND - Motor Vehicle Product - JASON INDUSTRIES, INC.; *pg.* 208, *pg.* 1875
MARABOU - Chocolate - MONDELEZ INTERNATIONAL, INC.; *pg.* 878, *pg.* 601
MARACAS - Fabric - NEMSCHOFF, INC.; *pg.* 936, *pg.* 1890
MARACAY HOMES - Wood & Building Material - WEYERHAEUSER COMPANY; *pg.* 121, *pg.* 1820
MARAIS - Women's Clothing & Accessories - WOODEN SHIPS OF HOBOKEN; *pg.* 35, *pg.* 1315
MARATEA - Bath Product - KOHLER CO.; *pg.* 91, *pg.* 1862
MARATEX - Motor Vehicle Product - JASON INDUSTRIES, INC.; *pg.* 208, *pg.* 1875
MARATEX PLUS - Motor Vehicle Product - JASON INDUSTRIES, INC.; *pg.* 208, *pg.* 1875
MARATHON - Food Product - BUNGE LIMITED; *pg.* 842, *pg.* 1351
MARATHON - Single Control - THE CHICAGO FAUCET COMPANY; *pg.* 1044, *pg.* 606
MARATHON - Posterior Composite Resin Restorative - DEN-MAT CORPORATION; *pg.* 1522, *pg.* 271
MARATHON - Battery - EXIDE TECHNOLOGIES; *pg.* 204, *pg.* 483
MARATHON - Tire - THE GOODYEAR TIRE & RUBBER COMPANY; *pg.* 1883, *pg.* 1401
MARATHON - Pump Product - IDEX CORPORATION; *pg.* 1347, *pg.* 623
MARATHON - Vibratory Conveyor - KEY TECHNOLOGY, INC.; *pg.* 868, *pg.* 1847
MARATHON - Energy Bar - MARS, INCORPORATED; *pg.* 1858, *pg.* 1792
MARATHON - Saw Blades - NEWELL RUBBERMAID INC.; *pg.* 1128, *pg.* 515
MARATHON - Architectural & Marine Paints & Wood Stains - PPG INDUSTRIES, INC.; *pg.* 1445, *pg.* 1579
MARATHON - Fuse Holders, Terminal Blocks & Power Blocks - REGAL BELOIT CORPORATION; *pg.* 106, *pg.* 1854
MARATHON - Water Heater - RHEEM MANUFACTURING COMPANY; *pg.* 1075, *pg.* 519
MARATHON - Carpet Extractor - TORNADO INDUSTRIES, INC.; *pg.* 1383, *pg.* 591
MARATHON 2 - Vacuum Process Tool - BROOKS AUTOMATION, INC.; *pg.* 1320, *pg.* 813
MARATHON ELECTRIC - Electric Motors and Generators - REGAL BELOIT CORPORATION; *pg.* 106, *pg.* 1854
MARATHON EXPRESS - Vacuum Process Tool - BROOKS AUTOMATION, INC.; *pg.* 1320, *pg.* 813
MARATHON MILKER - Milking Machine - FLEXFAB HORIZONS INTERNATIONAL, LLC; *pg.* 1072, *pg.* 891
MARAUDER - Rodenticide Pellets & Blocks - KENT NUTRITION GROUP; *pg.* 1477, *pg.* 710
MARAX - Medicine - PFIZER INC.; *pg.* 1581, *pg.* 1278
MARAX-DF - Pharmaceutical Product - PFIZER INC.; *pg.* 1581, *pg.* 1278
MARBIG - Office Products - ACCO BRANDS CORPORATION; *pg.* 340, *pg.* 626
MARBLE - Ceramic, Glass, Stone Tiles & Slabs - WALKER & ZANGER, INC.; *pg.* 119, *pg.* 281
MARBLE ODYSSEY - Doll - MGA ENTERTAINMENT, INC.; *pg.* 964, *pg.* 300
MARBLESTONE - Fabric - UNIROYAL ENGINEERED PRODUCTS; *pg.* 699, *pg.* 467
MARBLEWOOD - Faux Marble Finishes for Mantels - WHITE RIVER HARDWOODS-WOODWORKS, INC.; *pg.* 121, *pg.* 31
MARBS - Sports & Leisure Product - JAKKS PACIFIC, INC.; *pg.* 960, *pg.* 142
MARC - Software - MSC SOFTWARE CORPORATION; *pg.* 441, *pg.* 262
MARCAD - Diversity Wireless Microphone Receiver - SHURE INCORPORATED; *pg.* 672, *pg.* 638
MARCATO - Kitchen Product - KOHLER CO.; *pg.* 91, *pg.* 1862
MARCELINA - Wine - E&J GALLO WINERY; *pg.* 1962, *pg.* 149
MARCELLA - Footwear - PHOENIX FOOTWEAR GROUP, INC.; *pg.* 1815, *pg.* 60
MARCELLE - Furniture - ETHAN ALLEN INTERIORS INC.; *pg.* 924, *pg.* 343
MARCH - Pumps - MARCH MANUFACTURING INC.; *pg.* 1359, *pg.* 615
MARCHEX ADHERE - Computer Services - MARCHEX, INC.; *pg.* 1395, *pg.* 1837
MARCHEX CONNECT - Online Advertising - MARCHEX, INC.; *pg.* 1395, *pg.* 1837
MARCHON - Aqueous Dispersants - HUNTSMAN CORPORATION; *pg.* 1167, *pg.* 1758
MARCHON - Company Name - MARCHON EYEWEAR, INC.; *pg.* 1421, *pg.* 1180
MARCIA - Furniture - AMISCO INDUSTRIES LTD.; *pg.* 913, *pg.* 1958
MARCO - Furniture - NEMSCHOFF, INC.; *pg.* 936, *pg.* 1890
MARCO GRANDE - Furniture - NEMSCHOFF, INC.; *pg.* 936, *pg.* 1890
MARCO ISLAND - Rug - COURISTAN INC.; *pg.* 921, *pg.* 1067
MARCO POLO - Video Game - INTERNATIONAL GAME TECHNOLOGY; *pg.* 957, *pg.* 1024
MARCO POLO CLUB - Travel Membership Group - ABERCROMBIE & KENT USA, LLC; *pg.* 1896, *pg.* 607
MARCOS-ESTATES - Furniture - ASHLEY FURNITURE INDUSTRIES, INC.; *pg.* 914, *pg.* 1852
MARCSTAR - Remote Control Transmitter & Receiver - TEXAS INSTRUMENTS INCORPORATED; *pg.* 679, *pg.* 1688
MARCUS - Cookware - REGAL WARE, INC.; *pg.* 1137, *pg.* 1862
THE MARCUS CORPORATION - Lodging & Entertainment - THE MARCUS CORPORATION; *pg.* 1102, *pg.* 1877
MARCUS THEATERS - Theatre - THE MARCUS CORPORATION; *pg.* 1102, *pg.* 1877
MARDI GRAS - Plastic Laminates - GEORGIA-PACIFIC LLC; *pg.* 1458, *pg.* 507
MARDI GRAS MADNESS - Game - WMS INDUSTRIES INC.; *pg.* 593, *pg.* 666
MARE ROSSO - Soft Drink - THE COCA-COLA COMPANY; *pg.* 240, *pg.* 493
MAREGA - Italian Wine - LAIRD & COMPANY, INC.; *pg.* 1966, *pg.* 1119
MARESSA - Furniture - ASHLEY FURNITURE INDUSTRIES, INC.; *pg.* 914, *pg.* 1852
MARFAID - Valve - HAYS FLUID CONTROLS; *pg.* 1049, *pg.* 1370
MARGARITAVILLE - Shoes - THE MEN'S WEARHOUSE, INC.; *pg.* 44, *pg.* 1711
THE MARGATE - Home Floor Plan - JACOBSEN MANUFACTURING, INC.; *pg.* 1098, *pg.* 460
MARGEAUX - Women's Clothing & Accessories - WOODEN SHIPS OF HOBOKEN; *pg.* 35, *pg.* 1315
MARGHERITA - Meat Product - JOHN MORRELL FOOD GROUP; *pg.* 866, *pg.* 628
MARGHERITA - Food Products - SMITHFIELD FOODS, INC.; *pg.* 896, *pg.* 1806
MARGI - Multimedia Products for Mobile Systems - HARMAN INTERNATIONAL INDUSTRIES, INCORPORATED; *pg.* 641, *pg.* 374
MARGILLES - Furniture - ASHLEY FURNITURE INDUSTRIES, INC.; *pg.* 914, *pg.* 1852
MARGINMAN - Software - SS&C TECHNOLOGIES HOLDINGS, INC.; *pg.* 473, *pg.* 386
MARGO - Women's Clothing - ANN INC.; *pg.* 18, *pg.* 1195
MARGOT - Footwear - PHOENIX FOOTWEAR GROUP, INC.; *pg.* 1815, *pg.* 60
MARIA - Clothing - ABERCROMBIE & FITCH CO.; *pg.* 37, *pg.* 1466
MARIA - Furniture - HAWORTH, INC.; *pg.* 402, *pg.* 891
MARIACHI - Pizza - DONATOS PIZZERIA CORPORATION; *pg.* 1727, *pg.* 1439
MARIACHI BEEF - Pizza - DONATOS PIZZERIA CORPORATION; *pg.* 1727, *pg.* 1439
MARIACHI CHICKEN - Pizza - DONATOS PIZZERIA CORPORATION; *pg.* 1727, *pg.* 1439
MARIAH - California Wines - BROWN-FORMAN CORPORATION; *pg.* 1958, *pg.* 732
MARIAH - Food Product - PEER FOODS INC.; *pg.* 888, *pg.* 587
MARIAH CAREY - Fragrance - ELIZABETH ARDEN, INC.; *pg.* 507, *pg.* 448
MARIANA - Fabric - NEMSCHOFF, INC.; *pg.* 936, *pg.* 1890
MARIANGELA - Footwear - PHOENIX FOOTWEAR GROUP, INC.; *pg.* 1815, *pg.* 60
MARIANI - Faucet - MASCO CORPORATION; *pg.* 96, *pg.* 909
MARIANNA - Footwear - VANS, INC.; *pg.* 1821, *pg.* 76
MARIE CALLENDER'S - Food Product - CONAGRA FOODS, INC.; *pg.* 826, *pg.* 1014
MARIE CALLENDER'S - Restaurants - PERKINS & MARIE CALLENDER'S INC.; *pg.* 1744, *pg.* 1645
MARIE CLAIRE - Magazine - THE HEARST CORPORATION; *pg.* 1649, *pg.* 1239
MARIE OSMOND - Doll - CHARISMA BRANDS, LLC; *pg.* 2, *pg.* 120
MARIE OSMOND COLLECTION - Porcelain Dolls - CHARISMA BRANDS, LLC; *pg.* 2, *pg.* 120
MARIETTA - Furniture - FLEXSTEEL INDUSTRIES, INC.; *pg.* 925, *pg.* 707
MARILLA - Footwear - STEVEN MADDEN, LTD.; *pg.* 1819, *pg.* 1176
MARILYN MIGLIN - Perfume - MARILYN MIGLIN, L.P.; *pg.*

516, *pg.* 581
MARILYN MONROE - Sleepwear - HABAND COMPANY, INC.; *pg.* 1772, *pg.* 1099
MARIMBA - Software - BMC SOFTWARE, INC.; *pg.* 362, *pg.* 1701
MARIMBA - Furniture - HERMAN MILLER, INC.; *pg.* 926, *pg.* 913
MARIMBA RUM - Distilled Spirits - HOOD RIVER DISTILLERS INC.; *pg.* 1964, *pg.* 1498
MARINA BLUE - Molecular Probe Product - THERMO FISHER SCIENTIFIC INC.; *pg.* 1602, *pg.* 61
MARINA POWER - Lighting Product - EATON CORPORATION; *pg.* 1331, *pg.* 1429
MARINCO - Salt - DOW CHEMICAL; *pg.* 1156, *pg.* 1563
MARINE - Binocular - BUSHNELL OUTDOOR PRODUCTS, INC.; *pg.* 1403, *pg.* 718
MARINE CONCIERGE - Magazine - TRAVELHOST, INC.; *pg.* 1696, *pg.* 1689
MARINE DECK - Plywood Designed for Rigorous Marine Use - PLUM CREEK TIMBER COMPANY, INC.; *pg.* 105, *pg.* 1838
MARINE DRILLING RISER CONNECTORS - Riser Systems - DRIL-QUIP, INC.; *pg.* 1330, *pg.* 1704
MARINE DRILLING RISER SYSTEMS - Riser Systems - DRIL-QUIP, INC.; *pg.* 1330, *pg.* 1704
MARINE ENDURANCE - Unmanned Surveillance Aircraft - LOCKHEED MARTIN CORPORATION; *pg.* 229, *pg.* 762
MARINE LOG - Monthly Magazine - SIMMONS-BOARDMAN PUBLISHING CORP.; *pg.* 1686, *pg.* 1292
MARINE MAGNUM - Firearms - REMINGTON ARMS COMPANY, LLC; *pg.* 1844, *pg.* 1382
MARINE ROLLER - Ice Chest on Wheels - IGLOO PRODUCTS CORPORATION; *pg.* 1126, *pg.* 1724
MARINEOMEGA - Nutritional Supplement - NU SKIN ENTERPRISES, INC.; *pg.* 518, *pg.* 1755
MARINER - Electrosurgical Devices - ANGIODYNAMICS, INC.; *pg.* 1495, *pg.* 1173
MARINER - Boats - BRUNSWICK CORPORATION; *pg.* 1828, *pg.* 623
MARINER - Cleaning Product - HILLYARD, INC.; *pg.* 331, *pg.* 990
MARINER - Medical Equipment - INVACARE CORPORATION; *pg.* 1546, *pg.* 1451
MARINER - French Fries - J.R. SIMPLOT COMPANY; *pg.* 867, *pg.* 547
MARINER - Marine Forklift - MARINE TRAVELIFT, INC.; *pg.* 1359, *pg.* 1895
MARINER - Marine Lighting - SWIVELIER CO., INC.; *pg.* 1307, *pg.* 1142
MARINER - Molecular Biology Product - THERMO FISHER SCIENTIFIC INC.; *pg.* 1602, *pg.* 61
MARINER OF THE SEAS - Cruise Ship - ROYAL CARIBBEAN CRUISES LTD; *pg.* 1921, *pg.* 446
MARINER'S - Skin Lotion - THE GILLETTE COMPANY; *pg.* 509, *pg.* 795
MARINO - Furniture - ETHAN ALLEN INTERIORS INC.; *pg.* 924, *pg.* 343
MARINR - Catheter - MEDTRONIC, INC.; *pg.* 1564, *pg.* 939
MARIPOSA - Footwear - COBIAN CORP.; *pg.* 1806, *pg.* 253
MARIPOSA - Fabric - NEMSCHOFF, INC.; *pg.* 936, *pg.* 1890
MARIPOSA - Magazine - SCHOLASTIC INC.; *pg.* 1683, *pg.* 1288
MARIPOSA SCHOLASTIC EN ESPANOL - Magazine - SCHOLASTIC INC.; *pg.* 1683, *pg.* 1288
MARIS GROVE - Retirement Community - ERICKSON LIVING; *pg.* 1090, *pg.* 766
MARISAIL - Chemical Product - SACHEM INC.; *pg.* 1180, *pg.* 1665
MARISTAR - Power Boat - MASTERCRAFT BOAT COMPANY LLC; *pg.* 1709, *pg.* 1656
MARK. - Beauty Brand for Young Women - AVON PRODUCTS, INC.; *pg.* 500, *pg.* 1198
MARK - Polymer Product - CHEMTURA CORPORATION; *pg.* 1152, *pg.* 355
MARK - Electrical Test & Measurement - HD ELECTRIC COMPANY; *pg.* 1299, *pg.* 666
MARK - Optical Product - LEUPOLD & STEVENS, INC.; *pg.* 1420, *pg.* 1492
MARK - Rifle - STURM, RUGER & COMPANY, INC.; *pg.* 1846, *pg.* 371
MARK 4 - Tactical Optic Scope - LEUPOLD & STEVENS, INC.; *pg.* 1420, *pg.* 1492
MARK II - Wind Speed Indicator - DWYER INSTRUMENTS INC.; *pg.* 1330, *pg.* 694
MARK II STANDARD - Rimfire Pistol - STURM, RUGER & COMPANY, INC.; *pg.* 1846, *pg.* 371
MARK II TARGET - Rimfire Pistol - STURM, RUGER & COMPANY, INC.; *pg.* 1846, *pg.* 371
MARK III - Pistol - STURM, RUGER & COMPANY, INC.; *pg.* 1846, *pg.* 371
MARK III SERIES AIR FEED - Automatic Tension Control & Tension Indicators - P/A INDUSTRIES, INC.; *pg.* 1367, *pg.* 339
MARK-IT - Sneaker - STEVEN MADDEN, LTD.; *pg.* 1819, *pg.* 1176
MARK IV - Door - JAMISON DOOR COMPANY; *pg.* 89, *pg.* 771
MARK KNOPFLER STRATOCASTER - Electric Guitar - FENDER MUSICAL INSTRUMENTS CORPORATION; *pg.* 547, *pg.* 21
MARK LEVINSON - Electronic Components - HARMAN INTERNATIONAL INDUSTRIES, INCORPORATED; *pg.* 641, *pg.* 374
MARK LL - Healthcare - WESTROCK COMPANY; *pg.* 1472, *pg.* 1805
MARK OBS - Liquid Stabilizer - CHEMTURA CORPORATION; *pg.* 1152, *pg.* 355
MARK OF A PRO - Athletic Equipment & Sporting Goods - RAWLINGS SPORTING GOODS CO., INC.; *pg.* 1843, *pg.* 1002
MARK OF QUALITY IN BEVERAGE EQUIPMENT WORLDWIDE - Slogan - BUNN-O-MATIC CORPORATION; *pg.* 53, *pg.* 661
MARK RIGHT - Paint - KELLY-MOORE PAINT COMPANY, INC.; *pg.* 1443, *pg.* 198
MARK TIME - Timers & Timing Devices - MARKTIME; *pg.* 1421, *pg.* 371
MARK V - Extruder - DAVIS-STANDARD LLC; *pg.* 1328, *pg.* 368
MARK V - Texture Sprayer - GRACO, INC.; *pg.* 1342, *pg.* 935
MARK V - Rifle - WEATHERBY, INC.; *pg.* 1848, *pg.* 181
MARK V PROVIS - Injection System - MEDRAD, INC.; *pg.* 1563, *pg.* 1591
MARK V SYNTHETIC - Rifle Bolt Action - WEATHERBY, INC.; *pg.* 1848, *pg.* 181
MARK VB - Camera Accessories - ALAN GORDON ENTERPRISES, INC.; *pg.* 1399, *pg.* 125
MARK VI - Extruder - DAVIS-STANDARD LLC; *pg.* 1328, *pg.* 368
MARK VL - Personal Care Product - WESTROCK COMPANY; *pg.* 1472, *pg.* 1805
MARK VLL - Healthcare - WESTROCK COMPANY; *pg.* 1472, *pg.* 1805
MARK XXII - Rifle - WEATHERBY, INC.; *pg.* 1848, *pg.* 181
MARK12 - Molecular Biology Product - THERMO FISHER SCIENTIFIC INC.; *pg.* 1602, *pg.* 61
MARKATHON - Permanent & Whiteboard Markers - PENTEL OF AMERICA, LTD.; *pg.* 453, *pg.* 295
MARKER - Apparel - OAKLEY, INC.; *pg.* 1840, *pg.* 86
MARKER CHANNEL - Telemetry - MEDTRONIC, INC.; *pg.* 1564, *pg.* 939
MARKER MATE - Electronic Marker - GREENLEE TEXTRON INC.; *pg.* 1048, *pg.* 655
MARKET-BASED MANAGEMENT - Business Approach - KOCH INDUSTRIES, INC.; *pg.* 1463, *pg.* 724
MARKET CLUB - Trading Service - INO.COM; *pg.* 1259, *pg.* 777
MARKET DISTRICT - Groceries - GIANT EAGLE, INC.; *pg.* 1020, *pg.* 1575
MARKET DYNAMICS - Software System - IMS HEALTH, INC.; *pg.* 1544, *pg.* 344
MARKET EXPANSION LINE - Communication Product - CENTURYLINK, INC; *pg.* 1870, *pg.* 317
MARKET LABORATORY - Financial Products - DOW JONES & COMPANY, INC.; *pg.* 1637, *pg.* 1225
MARKET MANAGER - Software - JDA SOFTWARE GROUP, INC.; *pg.* 423, *pg.* 22
MARKET MOSAIC - Software - MONEY.NET, INC.; *pg.* 1268, *pg.* 1261
MARKET MOSAIC PRO - Software - MONEY.NET, INC.; *pg.* 1268, *pg.* 1261
MARKET PANTRY - Grocery Products - TARGET CORPORATION; *pg.* 1786, *pg.* 942
MARKET PROGNOSIS - Software System - IMS HEALTH, INC.; *pg.* 1544, *pg.* 344
MARKET PROS - Market Survey - CARGILL LIMITED; *pg.* 1475, *pg.* 1914
MARKET SIZZLE - Software - CAMO SOFTWARE, INC.; *pg.* 368, *pg.* 1133
MARKET UMBRELLAS - Wood & Aluminum Outdoor Furniture - TELESCOPE CASUAL FURNITURE INC.; *pg.* 944, *pg.* 1162
MARKET WATCH - Financial Products - DOW JONES & COMPANY, INC.; *pg.* 1637, *pg.* 1225
MARKET WEEK - Financial Products - DOW JONES & COMPANY, INC.; *pg.* 1637, *pg.* 1225
MARKETEXPERT XR - Promotional Software - VALASSIS COMMUNICATIONS, INC.; *pg.* 1287, *pg.* 897
MARKETHEAT - Software - MONEY.NET, INC.; *pg.* 1268, *pg.* 1261
MARKETING COMPUTERS - Advertisers & Agencies Magazine - NIELSEN BUSINESS MEDIA; *pg.* 1671, *pg.* 1272
MARKETING MAGAZINE - Magazine - MARKETING MAGAZINE; *pg.* 1661, *pg.* 1940
MARKETING RESOURCES PLUS - Software - NIELSEN AUDIO; *pg.* 446, *pg.* 768
MARKETLOOK - Software - SS&C TECHNOLOGIES HOLDINGS, INC.; *pg.* 473, *pg.* 386
MARKETMATH - Market Analysis & Segmentation System for Canada - PITNEY BOWES SOFTWARE INC.; *pg.* 455, *pg.* 1346
MARKETMETER - Software - MONEY.NET, INC.; *pg.* 1268, *pg.* 1261
MARKETMOVER - Business Consulting - EASTMAN KODAK COMPANY; *pg.* 1408, *pg.* 1333
MARKETOTE - Grocery Bags - PACTIV CORPORATION; *pg.* 1466, *pg.* 624
MARKETPLACE - Online Shopping Site - INSPERITY, INC.; *pg.* 416, *pg.* 1725
MARKETPLACE REPLENISH - Software - JDA SOFTWARE GROUP, INC.; *pg.* 423, *pg.* 22
MARKETRACK - Real-Time Quote Processing & Analytical System for Investment Professionals - TRACK DATA CORPORATION; *pg.* 1284, *pg.* 1147
MARKETRACK MX-NT - Direct Communications of Exchange-Traded Instrument & News - TRACK DATA CORPORATION; *pg.* 1284, *pg.* 1147
MARKETSCOPE - Market Analysis - STANDARD & POOR'S RATINGS SERVICES; *pg.* 805, *pg.* 1296
MARKETSCREEN - Financial Analytic Engine - MONEY.NET, INC.; *pg.* 1268, *pg.* 1261
MARKETSMART DECISION SYSTEM - Software System - FAIR ISAAC CORPORATION; *pg.* 1247, *pg.* 955
MARKETTRACK - Consumer Information - ACNIELSEN CORPORATION; *pg.* 341, *pg.* 1187
MARKINGS - Stepping Stones - C.R. GIBSON, LLC; *pg.* 1631, *pg.* 1650
MARKINGS - Gift Products - THOMAS NELSON INC.; *pg.* 1692, *pg.* 1654
MARKINGS MANAGER - Software - VULCAN, INC.; *pg.* 687, *pg.* 5
MARKK - Electronic Components - MOLEX INCORPORATED; *pg.* 655, *pg.* 628
MARKLEAR - Polymer Product - CHEMTURA CORPORATION; *pg.* 1152, *pg.* 355
MARKLIFT - Capital Equipment - TEREX CORPORATION; *pg.* 1381, *pg.* 384
MARKLUBE - Polymer Product - CHEMTURA CORPORATION; *pg.* 1152, *pg.* 355
MARKNET - Print Server - LEXMARK INTERNATIONAL, INC.; *pg.* 427, *pg.* 730
MARKON - Fresh Food Service - GORDON FOOD SERVICE INC.; *pg.* 1021, *pg.* 913
MARKS-A-LOT - Marking Pen - AVERY DENNISON CORPORATION; *pg.* 1452, *pg.* 95
MARKS & MORGAN - Jewelers - STERLING JEWELERS INC.; *pg.* 13, *pg.* 1402
MARKSCREEN - Polymer Product - CHEMTURA CORPORATION; *pg.* 1152, *pg.* 355
MARKSMAN - Laser Device - LASER TECHNOLOGY, INC.; *pg.* 1419, *pg.* 314
MARKSMAN - Filter Housing - PALL CORPORATION; *pg.* 232, *pg.* 1323
MARKSMAN - Surface Maintenance Machine - TENNANT COMPANY; *pg.* 1381, *pg.* 944
MARKSTAT - Polymer Product - CHEMTURA CORPORATION; *pg.* 1152, *pg.* 355
MARKTRACK - Printer Software - LEXMARK INTERNATIONAL, INC.; *pg.* 427, *pg.* 730
MARKVISION - Printing Device - LEXMARK INTERNATIONAL, INC.; *pg.* 427, *pg.* 730
MARLBORO - Cigarettes - PHILIP MORRIS USA INC.; *pg.* 1894, *pg.* 1803

First page reference indicates Business Class Edition
Second page reference indicates Geographic Edition

MARLBORO FILTER CIGARETTES LONG - Cigarettes - PHILIP MORRIS USA INC.; *pg.* 1894, *pg.* 1803
MARLBORO MENTHOL - Menthol Cigarette - PHILIP MORRIS USA INC.; *pg.* 1894, *pg.* 1803
MARLBORO MENTHOL NO. 2 - Menthol Cigarette - PHILIP MORRIS USA INC.; *pg.* 1894, *pg.* 1803
MARLBORO SMOOTH - Menthol Cigarette - PHILIP MORRIS USA INC.; *pg.* 1894, *pg.* 1803
MARLBORO UNLIMITED - Cigarettes - PHILIP MORRIS USA INC.; *pg.* 1894, *pg.* 1803
MARLBROUGH - Dinnerware - THE HOMER LAUGHLIN CHINA COMPANY; *pg.* 1125, *pg.* 1850
MARLENE - Footwear - STEVEN MADDEN, LTD.; *pg.* 1819, *pg.* 1176
MARLETTE - Manufactured Homes - CLAYTON HOMES, INC.; *pg.* 1086, *pg.* 1640
MARLEY - Women's Clothing & Accessories - WOODEN SHIPS OF HOBOKEN; *pg.* 35, *pg.* 1315
MARLIN - Magazine - BONNIER CORPORATION; *pg.* 1622, *pg.* 480
MARLIN - Newspaper Publishing System - ECRM IMAGING SYSTEMS, INC.; *pg.* 1410, *pg.* 848
MARLIN - Fiberglass Boat Product - GRADY-WHITE BOATS, INC.; *pg.* 1707, *pg.* 1377
MARLITE - Commercial Wall Systems - MARLITE, INC.; *pg.* 95, *pg.* 1448
MARLITE FRP - Wall System - MARLITE, INC.; *pg.* 95, *pg.* 1448
MARLITE MODULES - Wall System - MARLITE, INC.; *pg.* 95, *pg.* 1448
MARLITE PLANK - Wall System - MARLITE, INC.; *pg.* 95, *pg.* 1448
MARLO - Furniture Retailer - MARLO FURNITURE CO., INC.; *pg.* 934, *pg.* 769
MARLOWE - Modern Occasional Tables - BERNHARDT DESIGN; *pg.* 918, *pg.* 1381
MARNOT - Hardcoated Plastic Film - TEKRA CORPORATION; *pg.* 1184, *pg.* 1884
MAROCHA - Soft Drink - THE COCA-COLA COMPANY; *pg.* 240, *pg.* 493
MAROONE - Car Dealerships - AUTONATION, INC.; *pg.* 165, *pg.* 423
MAROONED ON THE MAGNIFICENT MILE - Nail Care Product - OPI PRODUCTS INC.; *pg.* 518, *pg.* 167
MARQUEE - Furniture - ASHLEY FURNITURE INDUSTRIES, INC.; *pg.* 914, *pg.* 1852
MARQUEE - Seating Product - IRWIN SEATING COMPANY INC.; *pg.* 929, *pg.* 887
MARQUEE - Fabric - NEMSCHOFF, INC.; *pg.* 936, *pg.* 1890
MARQUENCH - Quenching Salt - HEATBATH CORPORATION; *pg.* 1165, *pg.* 826
MARQUES DE MURRIETA - Rioja Wine - WILLIAM GRANT & SONS, INC.; *pg.* 1972, *pg.* 1057
MARQUES DE RISCAL - Wine - SHAW ROSS INTERNATIONAL IMPORTERS; *pg.* 1970, *pg.* 449
MARQUESA - Actuator - PRECISION VALVE CORPORATION; *pg.* 1060, *pg.* 1357
MARQUETTE - Flatware - ONEIDA LTD; *pg.* 1129, *pg.* 1318
MARQUIS - Coating - ARCHER-DANIELS-MIDLAND COMPANY; *pg.* 825, *pg.* 565
MARQUIS - Furniture - ASHLEY FURNITURE INDUSTRIES, INC.; *pg.* 914, *pg.* 1852
MARQUIS - Vanity Lights - CRAFTMADE INTERNATIONAL, INC.; *pg.* 1295, *pg.* 1670
MARQUIS - Wallcovering - YORK WALLCOVERINGS INC.; *pg.* 947, *pg.* 1598
MARQUIS D'MAUVE - Nail Care Product - OPI PRODUCTS INC.; *pg.* 518, *pg.* 167
MARQUIS JET CARD - Jet Card - MARQUIS JET PARTNERS INC.; *pg.* 1915, *pg.* 1256
MARQUISE - Baked Goods - AWREY BAKERIES, INC.; *pg.* 1015, *pg.* 896
MARQUISE - Window Treatment - HERITAGE LACE INC.; *pg.* 694, *pg.* 711
MARRAKESH - Carpet - INTERFACE, INC.; *pg.* 695, *pg.* 512
MARRAKESH EXPRESS - Mediterranean Food Products - HORMEL FOODS CORPORATION; *pg.* 863, *pg.* 915
MARREKESH - Container Grown Plant - MONROVIA GROWERS; *pg.* 1797, *pg.* 44
MARRETTE - Wire Connector - THOMAS & BETTS CORPORATION; *pg.* 680, *pg.* 1646
MARRIAGE PARTNERSHIP - Magazine - CHRISTIANITY TODAY INTERNATIONAL; *pg.* 1627, *pg.* 561
MARRIETTA - Furniture - ASHLEY FURNITURE INDUSTRIES, INC.; *pg.* 914, *pg.* 1852
MARRIOT EXECUTIVE APARTMENTS - Extended Stay - MARRIOTT INTERNATIONAL, INC.; *pg.* 1102, *pg.* 764
MARRIOTT - Lodging - MARRIOTT INTERNATIONAL, INC.; *pg.* 1102, *pg.* 764
MARRIOTT REWARDS PROGRAM - Rewards Program - MARRIOTT INTERNATIONAL, INC.; *pg.* 1102, *pg.* 764
MARRIOTT VACATION CLUB - Hotels - MARRIOTT INTERNATIONAL, INC.; *pg.* 1102, *pg.* 764
MARRIS - Furniture - ETHAN ALLEN INTERIORS INC.; *pg.* 924, *pg.* 343
MARROWMAX - Cell Culture Product - THERMO FISHER SCIENTIFIC INC.; *pg.* 1602, *pg.* 61
MARRVEL - Footwear - STEVEN MADDEN, LTD.; *pg.* 1819, *pg.* 1176
MARS - Framers - AVAGO TECHNOLOGIES; *pg.* 358, *pg.* 238
MARS - Laboratory Microwave System - HACKER INSTRUMENTS & INDUSTRIES INC.; *pg.* 1415, *pg.* 1623
MARS - Snack Foods - MARS, INCORPORATED; *pg.* 1858, *pg.* 1792
MARS - Turbine Products - SOLAR TURBINES INCORPORATED; *pg.* 1377, *pg.* 209
MARS - Software - SYNOPSYS, INC.; *pg.* 480, *pg.* 162
MARS FLYING BOAT - Systems Integration & Aeronautics - LOCKHEED MARTIN CORPORATION; *pg.* 229, *pg.* 762
MARS-RAIL - Software - SYNOPSYS, INC.; *pg.* 480, *pg.* 162
MARS XPRESS - Analyzer - CEM CORPORATION; *pg.* 1405, *pg.* 1382
MARS-XTALK - Software - SYNOPSYS, INC.; *pg.* 480, *pg.* 162
MARSACK - Furniture - NEMSCHOFF, INC.; *pg.* 936, *pg.* 1890
MARSALA - Kitchen Product - KOHLER CO.; *pg.* 91, *pg.* 1862
MARSEILLES - Women's Clothing & Accessories - WOODEN SHIPS OF HOBOKEN; *pg.* 35, *pg.* 1315
MARSH - Footwear - LACROSSE FOOTWEAR, INC.; *pg.* 1811, *pg.* 1503
MARSH - Insurance Broking Services - MARSH & MCLENNAN COMPANIES INC.; *pg.* 1207, *pg.* 1256
MARSH - Printers - VIDEOJET TECHNOLOGIES INC.; *pg.* 489, *pg.* 671
MARSH ENCORE - Printers - VIDEOJET TECHNOLOGIES INC.; *pg.* 489, *pg.* 671
MARSH OVERTURE - Printers - VIDEOJET TECHNOLOGIES INC.; *pg.* 489, *pg.* 671
MARSH PATRIONPLUS - Printers - VIDEOJET TECHNOLOGIES INC.; *pg.* 489, *pg.* 671
MARSH THE WORLD'S #1 RISK SPECIALIST - Tag Line - MARSH & MCLENNAN COMPANIES INC.; *pg.* 1207, *pg.* 1256
MARSH UNICORN - Printers - VIDEOJET TECHNOLOGIES INC.; *pg.* 489, *pg.* 671
MARSHALL - Furniture - ETHAN ALLEN INTERIORS INC.; *pg.* 924, *pg.* 343
MARSHALL - Amplifiers - KORG USA, INC.; *pg.* 556, *pg.* 1180
MARSHALL - Pet Product - PETSMART, INC.; *pg.* 1481, *pg.* 18
MARSHALL - Food - WESTERN SIZZLIN CORPORATION; *pg.* 1755, *pg.* 1806
MARSHALL'S - Canned Seafood - ATALANTA CORPORATION; *pg.* 838, *pg.* 1057
MARSHFIELD - Furniture - FLEXSTEEL INDUSTRIES, INC.; *pg.* 925, *pg.* 707
MARSHMALLOW CIRCUS PEANUTS - Candy - SPANGLER CANDY COMPANY; *pg.* 1862, *pg.* 1407
MARSHMALLOW FROOT LOOPS - Cereal - KELLOGG COMPANY; *pg.* 831, *pg.* 870
MARSHMALLOW MATEYS - Cereal - POST CONSUMER BRANDS; *pg.* 833, *pg.* 927
MARSHMALLOW PEEPS - Candy - JUST BORN, INC.; *pg.* 1857, *pg.* 1516
MARSHMELLOW - Air Spring - FIRESTONE INDUSTRIAL PRODUCTS DIVISION; *pg.* 1882, *pg.* 686
MARSON - Paint Pails - THE SHERWIN-WILLIAMS COMPANY; *pg.* 1447, *pg.* 1435
MARSPAC - Split Face Marble - WALKER & ZANGER, INC.; *pg.* 119, *pg.* 281
THE MARSUPIAL - Healthcare Product - DERMA SCIENCES, INC.; *pg.* 1523, *pg.* 1111
MARTEL - Canned Seafood - ATALANTA CORPORATION; *pg.* 838, *pg.* 1057
MARTEST 21 - Plastic - VIRCO MANUFACTURING CORPORATION; *pg.* 946, *pg.* 297
MARTHA - Sunglasses - COACH, INC.; *pg.* 3, *pg.* 1214
MARTHA - Furniture - FLEXSTEEL INDUSTRIES, INC.; *pg.* 925, *pg.* 707
MARTHA GOOCH - Pasta - AMERICAN ITALIAN PASTA COMPANY; *pg.* 837, *pg.* 980
MARTHA STEWART COLLECTION - Housewares - MARTHA STEWART LIVING OMNIMEDIA, INC.; *pg.* 1661, *pg.* 1256
MARTHA STEWART EVERYDAY - Mass-Market Housewares - MARTHA STEWART LIVING OMNIMEDIA, INC.; *pg.* 1661, *pg.* 1256
MARTHA STEWART FLOWERS - Magazine - MARTHA STEWART LIVING OMNIMEDIA, INC.; *pg.* 1661, *pg.* 1256
MARTHA STEWART KIDS - Magazine - MARTHA STEWART LIVING OMNIMEDIA, INC.; *pg.* 1661, *pg.* 1256
MARTHA STEWART LIVING - Magazine - MARTHA STEWART LIVING OMNIMEDIA, INC.; *pg.* 1661, *pg.* 1256
MARTHA STEWART SHOW - Television Program - MARTHA STEWART LIVING OMNIMEDIA, INC.; *pg.* 1661, *pg.* 1256
MARTHA STEWART SIGNATURE - High-End Housewares - MARTHA STEWART LIVING OMNIMEDIA, INC.; *pg.* 1661, *pg.* 1256
MARTHA STEWART WEDDINGS - Magazine - MARTHA STEWART LIVING OMNIMEDIA, INC.; *pg.* 1661, *pg.* 1256
MARTHA WHITE - Baking Mix - THE J.M. SMUCKER COMPANY; *pg.* 865, *pg.* 1468
MARTHASTEWART.COM - Community Website - MARTHA STEWART LIVING OMNIMEDIA, INC.; *pg.* 1661, *pg.* 1256
MARTIAL ARTS MASTERS - Apparel - OTOMIX, INC.; *pg.* 30, *pg.* 105
THE MARTIAN MANHUNTER - Character - DC COMICS, INC.; *pg.* 1633, *pg.* 1221
MARTIAN MATTER - Toy & Game - HASBRO, INC.; *pg.* 954, *pg.* 1603
MARTIE - Footwear - PHOENIX FOOTWEAR GROUP, INC.; *pg.* 1815, *pg.* 60
MARTIFILL - Chemical Product - ALBEMARLE CORPORATION; *pg.* 1146, *pg.* 741
MARTIFIN - Chemical Product - ALBEMARLE CORPORATION; *pg.* 1146, *pg.* 741
MARTIGLOSS - Pigments & Fillers - ALBEMARLE CORPORATION; *pg.* 1146, *pg.* 741
MARTILE - Marble Tile - WALKER & ZANGER, INC.; *pg.* 119, *pg.* 281
MARTIN - Fishing Reels - ZEBCO; *pg.* 1848, *pg.* 1491
MARTIN DOORS - Door - MARTIN DOOR MANUFACTURING, INC.; *pg.* 96, *pg.* 1759
MARTIN ROBERTS - Doorset System - INGERSOLL-RAND COMPANY; *pg.* 1349, *pg.* 1370
MARTIN-SENOUR - Paints & Coatings - THE SHERWIN-WILLIAMS COMPANY; *pg.* 1447, *pg.* 1435
MARTINA - Educational Materials - SCHOLASTIC INC.; *pg.* 1683, *pg.* 1288
MARTINAL - Chemical Product - ALBEMARLE CORPORATION; *pg.* 1146, *pg.* 741
MARTINI - Modern Occasional Tables - BERNHARDT DESIGN; *pg.* 918, *pg.* 1381
MARTINI - Software - SUNGARD DATA SYSTEMS INC.; *pg.* 477, *pg.* 1592
MARTINIQUE - Bedding - CROSCILL, INC.; *pg.* 1122, *pg.* 1220
MARTINIQUE - Surface Material - STEELCASE INC.; *pg.* 475, *pg.* 889
MARTIN'S - Uniforms - SUPERIOR UNIFORM GROUP, INC.; *pg.* 33, *pg.* 468
MARTINSVILLE SPEEDWAY - Motorsports Facility - INTERNATIONAL SPEEDWAY CORPORATION; *pg.* 553, *pg.* 420
MARTIQUES - Dinnerware - THE HOMER LAUGHLIN CHINA COMPANY; *pg.* 1125, *pg.* 1850
MARTOXID - Chemical Product - ALBEMARLE CORPORATION; *pg.* 1146, *pg.* 741
MARTOXIN - Pigments & Fillers - ALBEMARLE CORPORATION; *pg.* 1146, *pg.* 741
MARVEL - Office Furniture - MASCO CORPORATION; *pg.* 96, *pg.* 909
MARVEL - Sturdilite Floodlight - PHOENIX PRODUCTS COMPANY; *pg.* 1304, *pg.* 1879
MARVEL MYSTERY OIL - Oil Additive - TURTLE WAX, INC.; *pg.* 220, *pg.* 671
MARVELL PXA3XX - Development Platform - BSQUARE CORPORATION; *pg.* 366, *pg.* 1813
MARVELON - Oral Contraceptive - MERCK & CO., INC.; *pg.* 1566, *pg.* 1077
MARVELOUS MIDDLE - Mattress - RESTONIC MATTRESS CORPORATION; *pg.* 941, *pg.* 553

MARVID - Footwear - K-SWISS; *pg.* 1837, *pg.* 306
MARVIN RICHARDS - Apparel - G-III APPAREL GROUP, LTD.; *pg.* 41, *pg.* 1233
MARWIN - Valve - RICHARDS INDUSTRIES VALVE GROUP; *pg.* 107, *pg.* 1425
MARWIN BALL VALVES - Ball Valve - RICHARDS INDUSTRIES VALVE GROUP; *pg.* 107, *pg.* 1425
MARY - Clothing - ABERCROMBIE & FITCH CO.; *pg.* 37, *pg.* 1466
MARY - Footwear - VANS, INC.; *pg.* 1821, *pg.* 76
MARY B'S - Frozen Biscuits - J&J SNACK FOODS CORPORATION; *pg.* 865, *pg.* 1107
MARY ELLEN - Preserves & Jellies - THE J.M. SMUCKER COMPANY; *pg.* 865, *pg.* 1468
MARY ENGELBREIT - Home & Garden Products - ENESCO, LLC; *pg.* 1124, *pg.* 620
MARY ENGELBREIT'S HOME COMPANION - Lifestyle Magazine - BELVOIR MEDIA GROUP, LLC; *pg.* 1620, *pg.* 360
MARY JANE - Footwear - CAPEZIO BALLET MAKERS INC.; *pg.* 1805, *pg.* 1125
MARY JANE - Taffy - NEW ENGLAND CONFECTIONERY COMPANY INC.; *pg.* 1860, *pg.* 842
MARY-KATE & ASHLEY - Toy - MATTEL, INC.; *pg.* 962, *pg.* 81
MARY MARY - Footwear - PHOENIX FOOTWEAR GROUP, INC.; *pg.* 1815, *pg.* 60
MARY MAXIM - Handcrafted Needlework Kits - MARY MAXIM, INC.; *pg.* 696, *pg.* 905
MARYANN - Bakery Products - ALPHA BAKING COMPANY; *pg.* 836, *pg.* 564
MARYJANESFARM - Organic Lifestyle Magazine - BELVOIR MEDIA GROUP, LLC; *pg.* 1620, *pg.* 360
MARYLAND GAZETTE - Newspaper - CAPITAL GAZETTE COMMUNICATIONS INC.; *pg.* 1625, *pg.* 754
MARYS MOO MOOS - Collectibles - ENESCO, LLC; *pg.* 1124, *pg.* 620
MARZETTI - Salad Dressings - LANCASTER COLONY CORPORATION; *pg.* 873, *pg.* 1441
MARZETTI - Salad Dressings, Condiments & Croutons - T. MARZETTI COMPANY; *pg.* 900, *pg.* 1444
MARZOCCHI - Forks & Struts - TENNECO, INC.; *pg.* 985, *pg.* 625
MAS - Surgical Platform - NUVASIVE, INC.; *pg.* 1577, *pg.* 205
MASAREPA BLANCA - Corn Flour - GOYA FOODS, INC.; *pg.* 859, *pg.* 1075
MASARICA - Corn mix - GOYA FOODS, INC.; *pg.* 859, *pg.* 1075
MASATHENTIC - Flavor Enhancer - CARGILL, INC.; *pg.* 845, *pg.* 965
MASCAGNI - Flatware - ONEIDA LTD; *pg.* 1129, *pg.* 1318
MASCARA PLUS ROSE - Mascara - AVEDA CORPORATION; *pg.* 499, *pg.* 917
MASCHERONI - Pillow - AMERICAN LEATHER LP; *pg.* 912, *pg.* 1673
MASCOLINO - Designer Fragrance - PARFUMS DE COEUR LTD.; *pg.* 519, *pg.* 376
MASDA - Biotechnology Product - GENZYME CORPORATION; *pg.* 1534, *pg.* 808
MASHIDA - LCD Touch Panel Phone - OVERSTOCK.COM, INC.; *pg.* 1273, *pg.* 1760
MASI - Wine - REMY COINTREAU USA INC.; *pg.* 1969, *pg.* 1285
MASIMO SET - Oximeter Sensors - MASIMO CORPORATION; *pg.* 1558, *pg.* 113
MASK-A-WAY - Waterproof Mask - DELTA FOREMOST CHEMICAL CORPORATION; *pg.* 1155, *pg.* 1642
MASK OFF - Cleansing Product - DELTA FOREMOST CHEMICAL CORPORATION; *pg.* 1155, *pg.* 1642
MASK-OR - Pre Press Film - PLASTIC SUPPLIERS, INC.; *pg.* 1888, *pg.* 1443
MASKCOMPOSE - Software - CADENCE DESIGN SYSTEMS, INC.; *pg.* 367, *pg.* 239
MASKCOMPOSE - Software System - MENTOR GRAPHICS CORPORATION; *pg.* 432, *pg.* 1510
MASLAND - Carpet - THE DIXIE GROUP, INC.; *pg.* 692, *pg.* 1629
MASO CANALI - Wine - E&J GALLO WINERY; *pg.* 1962, *pg.* 149
MASON - Furniture - AMISCO INDUSTRIES LTD.; *pg.* 913, *pg.* 1958
MASON - Candlelamps - STANDEX INTERNATIONAL CORPORATION; *pg.* 60, *pg.* 1039
MASON - Casegoods - STEELCASE INC.; *pg.* 475, *pg.* 889
MASON CROWS - Candy - TOOTSIE ROLL INDUSTRIES, INC.; *pg.* 1863, *pg.* 591
MASON DOTS - Candy - TOOTSIE ROLL INDUSTRIES, INC.; *pg.* 1863, *pg.* 591
MASON STREET FUNDS - Mutual Funds - THE NORTHWESTERN MUTUAL LIFE INSURANCE COMPANY; *pg.* 1212, *pg.* 1879
MASON'S - Soft Drink - THE MONARCH BEVERAGE COMPANY, INC.; *pg.* 257, *pg.* 514
THE MASQUE - Hair Care Product - JOHN PAUL MITCHELL SYSTEMS; *pg.* 512, *pg.* 133
MASQUE - Office Furniture - STEELCASE INC.; *pg.* 475, *pg.* 889
MASQUEPEN - Art Product - DANIEL SMITH INC.; *pg.* 1766, *pg.* 1835
MASQUERADE - Textiles - BERNHARDT DESIGN; *pg.* 918, *pg.* 1381
MASQUERADE - Fabric - NEMSCHOFF, INC.; *pg.* 936, *pg.* 1890
MASQUERADER - Sofa Sleepers - FLEXSTEEL INDUSTRIES, INC.; *pg.* 925, *pg.* 707
MASROLL - Vacuum Suction Rolls - VAIL RUBBER WORKS, INC.; *pg.* 1891, *pg.* 906
MASS CASH - Lottery Game - MASSACHUSETTS STATE LOTTERY; *pg.* 998, *pg.* 802
MASS-FLO - Gas-Flow Measurement & Control Instruments - MKS INSTRUMENTS, INC.; *pg.* 1362, *pg.* 781
MASS FRAGMENT - Software - WATERS CORPORATION; *pg.* 1436, *pg.* 834
MASS PROBAR - Flowmeter - EMERSON PROCESS MANAGEMENT ROSEMOUNT INC.; *pg.* 1334, *pg.* 920
MASS TRANSIT - Bicycle Accessories - SPECIALIZED BICYCLE COMPONENTS, INC.; *pg.* 1711, *pg.* 152
MASSACHUSETTS LAWYERS WEEKLY - Newspaper - MASSACHUSETTS LAWYERS WEEKLY, INC.; *pg.* 1662, *pg.* 798
MASSACHUSETTS MEDICAL LAW REPORT - Newspaper - MASSACHUSETTS LAWYERS WEEKLY, INC.; *pg.* 1662, *pg.* 798
MASSAGE MASTER - Two-Speed Massager - WAHL CLIPPER CORPORATION; *pg.* 524, *pg.* 662
MASSAGE SYSTEM - Massage Product - HUMAN TOUCH; *pg.* 928, *pg.* 123
MASSARRAY - Software - SEQUENOM, INC.; *pg.* 1593, *pg.* 209
MASSARRAY EPITYPER - Software - SEQUENOM, INC.; *pg.* 1593, *pg.* 209
MASSARRAY MALDI TOF MS - Diagnostic Tool - SEQUENOM, INC.; *pg.* 1593, *pg.* 209
MASSARRAY NANODISPENSER RS1000 - Diagnostic Device - SEQUENOM, INC.; *pg.* 1593, *pg.* 209
MASSARRAY OLIGOCHECK - Software - SEQUENOM, INC.; *pg.* 1593, *pg.* 209
MASSARRAY QGE - Diagnostic Tool - SEQUENOM, INC.; *pg.* 1593, *pg.* 209
MASSARRAY SNP DISCOVERY - Software - SEQUENOM, INC.; *pg.* 1593, *pg.* 209
MASSARRAY TYPER - Software - SEQUENOM, INC.; *pg.* 1593, *pg.* 209
MASSCLEAVE - Kit - SEQUENOM, INC.; *pg.* 1593, *pg.* 209
MASSENEZ - French Fruit Brandies & Liquers - DREYFUS ASHBY INC.; *pg.* 1962, *pg.* 1226
MASSIVELY MINI MEDIA - Toy & Game - HASBRO, INC.; *pg.* 954, *pg.* 1603
MASSLYNX - Software - WATERS CORPORATION; *pg.* 1436, *pg.* 834
MASSPREP - Peptide Standard Mixture - WATERS CORPORATION; *pg.* 1436, *pg.* 834
MASSSEQ - Automated Sequencing Algorithm - WATERS CORPORATION; *pg.* 1436, *pg.* 834
MASSWEIGH - En Masse Gravimetric Feeder - VIBRA SCREW INC.; *pg.* 1387, *pg.* 1126
MAST - Software - SYNOPSYS, INC.; *pg.* 480, *pg.* 162
MAST MICROWAVE - Microwave - KEVLIN CORPORATION; *pg.* 649, *pg.* 1034
MASTER - Clipper - ANDIS COMPANY; *pg.* 498, *pg.* 1895
MASTER - Tire Repair - CUSTOM ACCESSORIES INC.; *pg.* 203, *pg.* 653
MASTER - Bristle Dartboard - ESCALADE INC.; *pg.* 1833, *pg.* 678
MASTER - Food Products - THE KRAFT HEINZ COMPANY; *pg.* 870, *pg.* 1577
MASTER - Vehicle Security Products - MASTER LOCK COMPANY LLC; *pg.* 1055, *pg.* 1884
MASTER - Spindle & Slide - SETCO SALES COMPANY; *pg.* 1061, *pg.* 1426
MASTER AND VARITEMP - Gun - MASTER APPLIANCE CORP.; *pg.* 1055, *pg.* 1888
MASTER-BILT - Food Service Equipment - STANDEX INTERNATIONAL CORPORATION; *pg.* 60, *pg.* 1039
MASTER BLASTER - Software - BIO-RAD LABORATORIES, INC.; *pg.* 1504, *pg.* 101
MASTER BLOCK - Steering Wheel Lock - MASTER LOCK COMPANY LLC; *pg.* 1055, *pg.* 1884
MASTER BOND - Fencing - MASTER HALCO; *pg.* 96, *pg.* 474
MASTER BUILDER - Software - INTUIT INC.; *pg.* 769, *pg.* 158
MASTER CHEF - Oils & Shortenings - CARGILL, INC.; *pg.* 845, *pg.* 965
MASTER CHEF COLLECTION - Cooktops Designed Specifically for the American Home - MIELE INC.; *pg.* 59, *pg.* 1112
MASTER CHEF IN A BOX - Garden Kit - AEROGROW INTERNATIONAL, INC.; *pg.* 1393, *pg.* 310
MASTER CHILL - Beverages - THE COCA-COLA COMPANY; *pg.* 240, *pg.* 493
MASTER CHOICE - Food Products - THE GREAT ATLANTIC & PACIFIC TEA COMPANY, INC.; *pg.* 1021, *pg.* 1086
MASTER COLOR - Fencing - MASTER HALCO; *pg.* 96, *pg.* 474
MASTER CYLINDER - Commercial Lighting - SWIVELIER CO., INC.; *pg.* 1307, *pg.* 1142
MASTER EQUIPMENT - Pet Bathing System - PETEDGE; *pg.* 1481, *pg.* 787
MASTER-FIT - Commercial Water Heater - A.O. SMITH CORPORATION; *pg.* 1313, *pg.* 1872
MASTER FLASH - Roof Flashing - OATEY SUPPLY CHAIN SERVICES; *pg.* 30, *pg.* 1433
MASTER FLOW - Heat Blower - MASTER APPLIANCE CORP.; *pg.* 1055, *pg.* 1888
MASTER-GRIT - Blade - LENOX; *pg.* 1053, *pg.* 817
MASTER GROOMING TOOLS - Pet Grooming Products - PETEDGE; *pg.* 1481, *pg.* 787
MASTER GT - General Industrial Torch - MASTER APPLIANCE CORP.; *pg.* 1055, *pg.* 1888
MASTER-GUARD - Int./Ext. Acrylic Latex Paint - AKZONOBEL DECORATIVE PAINTS U.S.; *pg.* 1439, *pg.* 1474
MASTER GUIDE - Hunting Boots - CABELA'S INCORPORATED; *pg.* 535, *pg.* 1019
MASTER HEAT - Gun - MASTER APPLIANCE CORP.; *pg.* 1055, *pg.* 1888
MASTER HEAT GUN - Heat Gun - MASTER APPLIANCE CORP.; *pg.* 1055, *pg.* 1888
MASTER LOCK - Hardware - FORTUNE BRANDS HOME & SECURITY, INC.; *pg.* 55, *pg.* 600
MASTER LOCK - Locks & Security Products - MASTER LOCK COMPANY LLC; *pg.* 1055, *pg.* 1884
MASTER MATH - Application - AMERICAN TECHNICAL PUBLISHERS, INC.; *pg.* 1616, *pg.* 649
MASTER MICROPRO - Soldering Iron - MASTER APPLIANCE CORP.; *pg.* 1055, *pg.* 1888
MASTER-MITE - Heat Shrink System - MASTER APPLIANCE CORP.; *pg.* 1055, *pg.* 1888
MASTER-MITE ESD - Heat Shrink System - MASTER APPLIANCE CORP.; *pg.* 1055, *pg.* 1888
THE MASTER PALETTE - Color System - AKZONOBEL DECORATIVE PAINTS U.S.; *pg.* 1439, *pg.* 1474
MASTER POUR - Beverages - THE COCA-COLA COMPANY; *pg.* 240, *pg.* 493
MASTER PRO - Levels & Squares - THE L.S. STARRETT COMPANY; *pg.* 1421, *pg.* 783
MASTER PRO - Metal Padlocks - MASTER LOCK COMPANY LLC; *pg.* 1055, *pg.* 1884
MASTER PROSEAL - Connectors Bulk - MASTER APPLIANCE CORP.; *pg.* 1055, *pg.* 1888
MASTER-RAIL - Adapter - PHOTOGENIC PROFESSIONAL LIGHTING; *pg.* 1426, *pg.* 556
MASTER ROADASSIST - Credit Card - MASTERCARD INCORPORATED; *pg.* 779, *pg.* 1325
MASTER SERIES - Home Stereo Components - KRELL INDUSTRIES, INC.; *pg.* 650, *pg.* 367
MASTER TIRE REPAIR - Tire - CUSTOM ACCESSORIES INC.; *pg.* 203, *pg.* 653
MASTER WORKS - Composite Material - DOW CHEMICAL; *pg.* 1156, *pg.* 1563
MASTERBILT - Musical Instrument - GIBSON GUITAR CORP.; *pg.* 550, *pg.* 1650
MASTERBRAND CABINETS - Hardware - FORTUNE

BRANDS HOME & SECURITY, INC.; pg. 55, pg. 600
MASTERCARD - Cash Card - CITIGROUP INC.; pg. 735, pg. 1212
MASTERCARD - Software System - FAIR ISAAC CORPORATION; pg. 1247, pg. 955
MASTERCARD CORPORATE CARD - Credit Card - MASTERCARD INCORPORATED; pg. 779, pg. 1325
MASTERCARD CORPORATE EXECUTIVE CARD - Credit Card - MASTERCARD INCORPORATED; pg. 779, pg. 1325
MASTERCARD CORPORATE FLEET CARD - Credit Card - MASTERCARD INCORPORATED; pg. 779, pg. 1325
MASTERCARD CORPORATE MULTI CARD - Credit Card - MASTERCARD INCORPORATED; pg. 779, pg. 1325
MASTERCARD CORPORATE PURCHASING CARD - Credit Card - MASTERCARD INCORPORATED; pg. 779, pg. 1325
MASTERCARD EXECUTIVE BUSINESSCARD - Credit Card - MASTERCARD INCORPORATED; pg. 779, pg. 1325
MASTERCARD GOVERNMENT FLEET CARD - Credit Card - MASTERCARD INCORPORATED; pg. 779, pg. 1325
MASTERCARD GOVERNMENT INTEGRATED CARD - Credit Card - MASTERCARD INCORPORATED; pg. 779, pg. 1325
MASTERCARD GOVERNMENT PURCHASING CARD - Credit Card - MASTERCARD INCORPORATED; pg. 779, pg. 1325
MASTERCARD GOVERNMENT TRAVEL CARD - Credit Card - MASTERCARD INCORPORATED; pg. 779, pg. 1325
MASTERCARD INCENTIVE CARD - Credit Card - MASTERCARD INCORPORATED; pg. 779, pg. 1325
MASTERCARD INSTALLMENT CARD - Credit Card - MASTERCARD INCORPORATED; pg. 779, pg. 1325
MASTERCARD MARKET ADVISOR - Software - MASTERCARD INCORPORATED; pg. 779, pg. 1325
MASTERCARD MARKETACCESS - Software - MASTERCARD INCORPORATED; pg. 779, pg. 1325
MASTERCARD MASTERTAGGER - Software - MASTERCARD INCORPORATED; pg. 779, pg. 1325
MASTERCARD MATCH - Software - MASTERCARD INCORPORATED; pg. 779, pg. 1325
MASTERCARD MEETING CARD - Credit Card - MASTERCARD INCORPORATED; pg. 779, pg. 1325
MASTERCARD OPEN DATA STORAGE - Software - MASTERCARD INCORPORATED; pg. 779, pg. 1325
MASTERCARD PAYPASS - Prepaid Card - MASTERCARD INCORPORATED; pg. 779, pg. 1325
MASTERCARD PAYROLL CARD - Credit Card - MASTERCARD INCORPORATED; pg. 779, pg. 1325
MASTERCARD PROFESSIONAL CARD - Credit Card - MASTERCARD INCORPORATED; pg. 779, pg. 1325
MASTERCARD PROJECT CARD - Credit Card - MASTERCARD INCORPORATED; pg. 779, pg. 1325
MASTERCARD PUBLIC SECTOR FLEET CARD - Credit Card - MASTERCARD INCORPORATED; pg. 779, pg. 1325
MASTERCARD PUBLIC SECTOR MULTI CARD - Credit Card - MASTERCARD INCORPORATED; pg. 779, pg. 1325
MASTERCARD PUBLIC SECTOR PAYMENT SOLUTIONS - Payment Solution - MASTERCARD INCORPORATED; pg. 779, pg. 1325
MASTERCARD PUBLIC SECTOR PURCHASING CARD - Credit Card - MASTERCARD INCORPORATED; pg. 779, pg. 1325
MASTERCARD PUBLIC SECTOR TRAVEL CARD - Credit Card - MASTERCARD INCORPORATED; pg. 779, pg. 1325
MASTERCARD RELOCATION CARD - Credit Card - MASTERCARD INCORPORATED; pg. 779, pg. 1325
MASTERCARD REWARDS - Credit Card - MASTERCARD INCORPORATED; pg. 779, pg. 1325
MASTERCARD TRAVEL PER DIEM CARD - Credit Card - MASTERCARD INCORPORATED; pg. 779, pg. 1325
MASTERCARD TRAVELERS CHEQUE - Check - MASTERCARD INCORPORATED; pg. 779, pg. 1325
MASTERCELL - Batteries - DORCY INTERNATIONAL INC.; pg. 1046, pg. 1439
MASTERCELL EXCHANGE - Software - BMC SOFTWARE, INC.; pg. 362, pg. 1701
MASTERCLAD - Switchgear - SCHNEIDER ELECTRIC USA, INC.; pg. 1306, pg. 650
MASTERCLEAR - Egg Lid - PACTIV CORPORATION; pg. 1466, pg. 624
MASTERCOTE - Chemical - SENSIENT COLORS INC.; pg. 1180, pg. 1003
MASTERCRAFT - Furniture - BAKER KNAPP & TUBBS INC.; pg. 916, pg. 566
MASTERCRAFT - Tires - COOPER TIRE & RUBBER COMPANY; pg. 1881, pg. 1453
MASTERCUTS - Hair Salons - REGIS CORPORATION; pg. 521, pg. 941
MASTERDUO - Carton - PACTIV CORPORATION; pg. 1466, pg. 624
MASTERFEED - End-of-Day Pricing & Securities Data - STANDARD & POOR'S RATINGS SERVICES; pg. 805, pg. 1296
MASTERFEEDS - Grain - AG PROCESSING INC.; pg. 835, pg. 1013
MASTERFIT - Armature - HAMILTON CO., INC.; pg. 1415, pg. 1031
MASTERFLOW - Heat Blower - MASTER APPLIANCE CORP.; pg. 1055, pg. 1888
MASTERFOOD SERVICES - Food Services - MARS, INCORPORATED; pg. 1858, pg. 1792
MASTERFOODS - Food Products - MARS, INCORPORATED; pg. 1858, pg. 1792
MASTERGEAR - Manual Valve Actuators for Liquid & Gas Flow Control - REGAL BELOIT CORPORATION; pg. 106, pg. 1854
MASTERHAND - Tools - TRACTOR SUPPLY COMPANY; pg. 708, pg. 1627
MASTERLINE - Broad Band Amplifiers - BLONDER TONGUE LABORATORIES, INC.; pg. 625, pg. 1100
MASTERMARK - Doors - SIMPSON DOOR COMPANY; pg. 110, pg. 1823
MASTERMIND - Game - PRESSMAN TOY CORPORATION; pg. 965, pg. 1734
MASTERMONEY BUSINESSCARD - Credit Card - MASTERCARD INCORPORATED; pg. 779, pg. 1325
MASTERNAVIGATOR - Software - BMC SOFTWARE, INC.; pg. 362, pg. 1701
MASTERPACT - Circuit Breakers - SCHNEIDER ELECTRIC USA, INC.; pg. 1306, pg. 650
MASTERPIECE - Rug - COURISTAN INC.; pg. 921, pg. 1067
MASTERPURCHASE - Credit Card - MASTERCARD INCORPORATED; pg. 779, pg. 1325
MASTERS - Furniture - JASPER GROUP; pg. 930, pg. 691
MASTERS COLLECTION - Domestic Cigars - ALTADIS USA, INC.; pg. 1893, pg. 423
MASTER'S STUDIO FLARE - Basket - THE LONGABERGER COMPANY; pg. 1127, pg. 1467
MASTERSHOWER - Bath Product - KOHLER CO.; pg. 91, pg. 1862
MASTERSPEC - Glass Product - GUARDIAN INDUSTRIES CORP.; pg. 85, pg. 869
MASTERSUITE - Garage Organization - CLOSETMAID CORPORATION; pg. 920, pg. 452
MASTERSWITCH - Power Distribution Unit (PDU) - SCHNEIDER ELECTRIC; pg. 467, pg. 1609
MASTERTEX - Fabric - NEMSCHOFF, INC.; pg. 936, pg. 1890
MASTERTRAK - Services - CARDIAC SCIENCE CORPORATION; pg. 1512, pg. 1897
MASTERTRIP - Credit Card - MASTERCARD INCORPORATED; pg. 779, pg. 1325
MASTERVUE - Carton - PACTIV CORPORATION; pg. 1466, pg. 624
MASTRAL - Textiles - BERNHARDT DESIGN; pg. 918, pg. 1381
MAT - Furniture - AMISCO INDUSTRIES LTD.; pg. 913, pg. 1958
MAT - Multipath Assessment & Tool Software - NOVATEL INC.; pg. 1424, pg. 1904
MAT HOFFMAN'S PRO BMX - Game - ACTIVISION BLIZZARD, INC.; pg. 948, pg. 271
MATA HARI - Slots - INTERNATIONAL GAME TECHNOLOGY; pg. 957, pg. 1024
MATADOOR - Breakaway Curtain Bottom Section - CORNELL IRON WORKS, INC.; pg. 77, pg. 1554
MATCH-A-PAYMENT - Banking Service - THE BANK OF NOVA SCOTIA; pg. 721, pg. 1935
MATCH & WIN - Lottery Game - OHIO LOTTERY COMMISSION; pg. 1002, pg. 1433
MATCH-BLOMATIC - Foundry Mold Making Machine - PETTIBONE, LLC; pg. 1368, pg. 609
MATCH-UP - Labels - AMERICAN GREASE STICK CO.; pg. 971, pg. 902
MATCH UP - Games - LEAPFROG ENTERPRISES, INC.; pg. 961, pg. 84
MATCHA GREEN TEA BLAST - Fruit Drink - JAMBA, INC.; pg. 1024, pg. 84
MATCHA GREEN TEA SHOT - Fruit Drink - JAMBA, INC.; pg. 1024, pg. 84
MATCHBLOMATIC - Piper - SIMPSON TECHNOLOGIES CORPORATION; pg. 111, pg. 555
MATCHBOX - Fruit Flavored Snacks - KELLOGG COMPANY; pg. 831, pg. 870
MATCHBOX - Toy - MATTEL, INC.; pg. 962, pg. 81
MATCH.COM - Online Services - IAC/INTERACTIVECORP; pg. 292, pg. 1242
MATCH.COM - Website - MATCH.COM, LLC; pg. 1265, pg. 1683
MATCHED PERFORMANCE - Consumer Information - BALDOR ELECTRIC COMPANY; pg. 1316, pg. 32
MATCHED TECHNOLOGY SYSTEM - Software - GERBER SCIENTIFIC, INC.; pg. 1414, pg. 380
MATCHLESS - Carpet - BEAULIEU GROUP, LLC; pg. 917, pg. 529
MATCHLINK - Phone - ADVANCED TELECOM SERVICES; pg. 1865, pg. 1591
MATCHMAKER - Power Transmission Belting - THE GOODYEAR TIRE & RUBBER COMPANY; pg. 1883, pg. 1401
MATCHMOVER - Software - AUTODESK INC.; pg. 356, pg. 257
MATCHPORT - Electronic Device - LANTRONIX, INC.; pg. 426, pg. 112
MATCHPRINT - CHEMICALS - EASTMAN KODAK COMPANY; pg. 1408, pg. 1333
MATCHPRINT - Color Proofing Systems - IMATION CORP.; pg. 413, pg. 952
MATCHRITE IVUE - Spectrophotometer - X-RITE, INCORPORATED; pg. 1437, pg. 891
MATCHSTIK - Handheld Color Matching Tool - X-RITE, INCORPORATED; pg. 1437, pg. 891
MATCHWORK - Impedance Matching Network - MKS INSTRUMENTS, INC.; pg. 1362, pg. 781
MATCO TOOLS - Tool & Toolbox - DANAHER CORPORATION; pg. 1044, pg. 397
MAT.DB - Engineering Software - ASM INTERNATIONAL; pg. 132, pg. 1461
MATERIALS & PROCESSES FOR MEDICAL DEVICES - Trade Magazine - ASM INTERNATIONAL; pg. 132, pg. 1461
MATERNALINK - Pharmaceutical Product - ALERE INC.; pg. 1488, pg. 849
MATERNITYMALL.COM - Online Shopping - DESTINATION MATERNITY CORPORATION; pg. 23, pg. 1563
MATGRIP - Non-Metal Fasteners - MACNEIL AUTOMOTIVE PRODUCTS, LTD.; pg. 211, pg. 559
MATH 180 - Magazine - SCHOLASTIC INC.; pg. 1683, pg. 1288
MATH CIRCUS - Educational Kit - LEAPFROG ENTERPRISES, INC.; pg. 961, pg. 84
MATH MAN - Educational Materials - SCHOLASTIC INC.; pg. 1683, pg. 1288
MATH MANIA - Math Puzzle Books - HIGHLIGHTS FOR CHILDREN, INC.; pg. 1650, pg. 1440
MATH MOVES U - Program - RAYTHEON COMPANY; pg. 233, pg. 854
MATH MYSTERIES - Educational Materials - SCHOLASTIC INC.; pg. 1683, pg. 1288
MATH RENAISSANCE - Educational Materials - RENAISSANCE LEARNING, INC.; pg. 607, pg. 1899
MATH SAFARI - Electronic Learning Aid - EDUCATIONAL INSIGHTS, INC.; pg. 951, pg. 187
MATH SHOP - Educational Materials - SCHOLASTIC INC.; pg. 1683, pg. 1288
MATH TUTOR - Educational Materials - SCHOLASTIC INC.; pg. 1683, pg. 1288
MATHCAD - Software - PARAMETRIC TECHNOLOGY CORPORATION; pg. 452, pg. 835
MATHDOC - Document Delivery Service - AMERICAN MATHEMATICAL SOCIETY, INC.; pg. 129, pg. 1605
MATHEMATICAL WORLD - Publication - AMERICAN MATHEMATICAL SOCIETY, INC.; pg. 129, pg. 1605
MATHFACTS IN A FLASH - Educational Materials - RENAISSANCE LEARNING, INC.; pg. 607, pg. 1899
MATHLETICS - Workbook - OAKLAND ATHLETICS LIMITED PARTNERSHIP; pg. 571, pg. 172
MATHSCI - Database - AMERICAN MATHEMATICAL SOCIETY, INC.; pg. 129, pg. 1605
MATHSCINET - Online Database - AMERICAN

MATHEMATICAL SOCIETY, INC.; *pg.* 129, *pg.* 1605
MATHWORKS - Software Product - WOODWARD, INC.; *pg.* 122, *pg.* 329
MATINEE - Furniture - AMERICAN LEATHER LP; *pg.* 912, *pg.* 1673
MATINEE - Fabric - NEMSCHOFF, INC.; *pg.* 936, *pg.* 1890
MATISSE - Fabric - NEMSCHOFF, INC.; *pg.* 936, *pg.* 1890
MATOUCHE - Ceramic, Glass, Stone Tiles & Slabs - WALKER & ZANGER, INC.; *pg.* 119, *pg.* 281
MATRAVEL - Airline Service - MARKET AMERICA WORLDWIDE, INC.; *pg.* 1265, *pg.* 1375
MATRI-MONEY - Lottery Game - NEW JERSEY STATE LOTTERY; *pg.* 1000, *pg.* 1126
MATRIA - Pharmaceutical Product - ALERE INC.; *pg.* 1488, *pg.* 849
MATRIA HEALTHCARE - Pharmaceutical Product - ALERE INC.; *pg.* 1488, *pg.* 849
MATRIMID - Bismaleimide System - HUNTSMAN CORPORATION; *pg.* 1167, *pg.* 1758
MATRITECH - Pharmaceutical Product - ALERE INC.; *pg.* 1488, *pg.* 849
MATRIX - Furniture - ASHLEY FURNITURE INDUSTRIES, INC.; *pg.* 914, *pg.* 1852
MATRIX - Switch - BROCADE CORPORATION; *pg.* 365, *pg.* 312
MATRIX - Lasers - COHERENT, INC.; *pg.* 1406, *pg.* 265
MATRIX - Raised Access Floor Systems - DAW TECHNOLOGIES, INC.; *pg.* 78, *pg.* 1756
MATRIX - Bridge Product - THE D.S. BROWN COMPANY; *pg.* 79, *pg.* 1468
MATRIX - Herbicide - E.I. DU PONT DE NEMOURS & COMPANY; *pg.* 1159, *pg.* 390
MATRIX - Furniture - ETHAN ALLEN INTERIORS INC.; *pg.* 924, *pg.* 343
MATRIX - Fluid Dispensing System - GRACO, INC.; *pg.* 1342, *pg.* 935
MATRIX - Chairs - GROUPE DUTAILIER INC.; *pg.* 926, *pg.* 1960
MATRIX - Hair Care Products - L'OREAL USA; *pg.* 514, *pg.* 1252
MATRIX - Faceshield - MCR SAFETY; *pg.* 1422, *pg.* 1630
MATRIX - Fabric - NEMSCHOFF, INC.; *pg.* 936, *pg.* 1890
MATRIX - Apparel - OAKLEY, INC.; *pg.* 1840, *pg.* 86
MATRIX - Protective Eyewear - SELLSTROM MANUFACTURING CO.; *pg.* 1428, *pg.* 659
MATRIX - Fertilizer - SIMPLOT PARTNERS INC.; *pg.* 1800, *pg.* 548
MATRIX - Chopped Glass - SMOOTH-ON INC.; *pg.* 111, *pg.* 1528
MATRIX - Hand Tools - USG CORPORATION; *pg.* 118, *pg.* 594
MATRIX - Wood & Building Material - WEYERHAEUSER COMPANY; *pg.* 121, *pg.* 1820
MATRIX 44 - Closed-Circuit Television Equipment - VICON INDUSTRIES, INC.; *pg.* 685, *pg.* 1166
MATRIX 88 - Closed-Circuit Television Equipment - VICON INDUSTRIES, INC.; *pg.* 685, *pg.* 1166
MATRIX PLUS - Healthcare Product - GF HEALTH PRODUCTS, INC.; *pg.* 1535, *pg.* 508
MATRIX POKER - Video Poker - INTERNATIONAL GAME TECHNOLOGY; *pg.* 957, *pg.* 1024
MATRIX SERIES - Washroom Equipment - BOBRICK WASHROOM EQUIPMENT, INC.; *pg.* 1043, *pg.* 166
MATRIX-UPS - Uninterruptible Power Supplies - SCHNEIDER ELECTRIC; *pg.* 467, *pg.* 1609
MATRIXONE - Software - DASSAULT SYSTEMS ENOVIA; *pg.* 382, *pg.* 851
MATRIXONE DESIGNER CENTRAL - Design Software - DASSAULT SYSTEMS ENOVIA; *pg.* 382, *pg.* 851
MATRIXONE DOCUMENT CENTRAL - Software - DASSAULT SYSTEMS ENOVIA; *pg.* 382, *pg.* 851
MATRIXONE ENGINEERING CENTRAL - Software - DASSAULT SYSTEMS ENOVIA; *pg.* 382, *pg.* 851
MATRIXONE LIBRARY CENTRAL - Product Development Software - DASSAULT SYSTEMS ENOVIA; *pg.* 382, *pg.* 851
MATRIXONE MATERIALS COMPLIANCE CENTRAL - Software - DASSAULT SYSTEMS ENOVIA; *pg.* 382, *pg.* 851
MATRIXONE PROGRAM CENTRAL - Software - DASSAULT SYSTEMS ENOVIA; *pg.* 382, *pg.* 851
MATRIXONE SUPPLIER CENTRAL - Software - DASSAULT SYSTEMS ENOVIA; *pg.* 382, *pg.* 851
MATRIXONE TEAM CENTRAL - Software - DASSAULT SYSTEMS ENOVIA; *pg.* 382, *pg.* 851
MATRYOSHKA - Women's Clothing & Accessories - WOODEN SHIPS OF HOBOKEN; *pg.* 35, *pg.* 1315
MATS - Furniture - THE COMMERCIAL FURNITURE GROUP; *pg.* 920, *pg.* 994
MATSIDE - Scoreboard & Sports Product - DAKTRONICS, INC.; *pg.* 633, *pg.* 1624
MATSON - Ocean Transportation - ALEXANDER & BALDWIN, INC.; *pg.* 1079, *pg.* 543
MATSURI - Carpet - INTERFACE, INC.; *pg.* 695, *pg.* 512
MATSURI - Fabric - NEMSCHOFF, INC.; *pg.* 936, *pg.* 1890
MATT-KLEEN - Cleaner - SCHOOL-TECH, INC.; *pg.* 1844, *pg.* 866
MATT O'NEILL - Doll - TONNER DOLL COMPANY, INC.; *pg.* 968, *pg.* 1171
MATTA PELVIC - Surgical & Medical Product - STRYKER CORPORATION; *pg.* 1598, *pg.* 894
MATTE BLACK CINEFOIL - Film & Video Product - ROSCO LABORATORIES, INC.; *pg.* 1782, *pg.* 378
MATTE LEAO - Beverages - THE COCA-COLA COMPANY; *pg.* 240, *pg.* 493
MATTEFLEX - Plastic Product - PLASTIC SUPPLIERS, INC.; *pg.* 1888, *pg.* 1443
MATTEL CLASSIC GAMES - Toy - MATTEL, INC.; *pg.* 962, *pg.* 81
MATTEL GAMES - Games - MATTEL, INC.; *pg.* 962, *pg.* 81
MATTEO - Fabric - NEMSCHOFF, INC.; *pg.* 936, *pg.* 1890
MATTER OF FACT - Shoe - AEROGROUP INTERNATIONAL, INC.; *pg.* 1803, *pg.* 1055
MATTHEW - Vanity Lights - CRAFTMADE INTERNATIONAL, INC.; *pg.* 1295, *pg.* 1670
MATTISON GRINDERS - Machine Tool Product - BOURN & KOCH MACHINE TOOL COMPANY; *pg.* 1319, *pg.* 654
MATTISON WOODWORKING - Machine Tool Product - BOURN & KOCH MACHINE TOOL COMPANY; *pg.* 1319, *pg.* 654
THE MATTRESS PROFESSIONALS - Tagline - SLEEPY'S, INC.; *pg.* 943, *pg.* 1167
MATTRIX - Dual-Lead Neurostimulation Sys. - MEDTRONIC, INC.; *pg.* 1564, *pg.* 939
MATURE LIVING CHOICES - Real Estate Guide - NETWORK COMMUNICATIONS INC.; *pg.* 1271, *pg.* 534
MATUSALEM RUM - Spirits - PROXIMO SPIRITS, INC.; *pg.* 1969, *pg.* 1076
MATUSOV PRAMEN - Beverages - THE COCA-COLA COMPANY; *pg.* 240, *pg.* 493
MATUTANO - Food & Beverage - PEPSICO, INC.; *pg.* 259, *pg.* 1327
MATVAR 53 - Matte Finish Varnish - MARTIN/F. WEBER COMPANY; *pg.* 962, *pg.* 1567
MATZEL & MUMFORD - Homebuilder of Residential Communities - HOVNANIAN ENTERPRISES, INC.; *pg.* 1096, *pg.* 1114
MAUDITE - Beer - SLEEMAN UNIBROUE QUEBEC; *pg.* 265, *pg.* 1950
MAUI - Washed Raw Sugar - ALEXANDER & BALDWIN, INC.; *pg.* 1079, *pg.* 543
MAUI - Kayaks - HOBIE CAT COMPANY; *pg.* 1708, *pg.* 173
MAUI - Eyewear - MAUI JIM, INC.; *pg.* 9, *pg.* 651
MAUI JIM - Logo - MAUI JIM, INC.; *pg.* 9, *pg.* 651
MAUI MALL - Shopping Center Service - ALEXANDER & BALDWIN, INC.; *pg.* 1079, *pg.* 543
MAUI STYLE - Potato Crisps - FRITO-LAY NORTH AMERICA, INC.; *pg.* 1853, *pg.* 1730
MAULL'S BARBECUE SAUCE - Barbecue Sauce - LOUIS MAULL COMPANY; *pg.* 875, *pg.* 999
MAUNA LOA - Eyewear - MAUI JIM, INC.; *pg.* 9, *pg.* 651
MAURER - Bridge Product - THE D.S. BROWN COMPANY; *pg.* 79, *pg.* 1468
MAURICE - One-Piece Toilet - GERBER PLUMBING FIXTURES CORPORATION; *pg.* 84, *pg.* 672
MAURICE - Furniture - NEMSCHOFF, INC.; *pg.* 936, *pg.* 1890
MAUTZ - Paint - THE SHERWIN-WILLIAMS COMPANY; *pg.* 1447, *pg.* 1435
MAUVING TO MANITOBA - Nail Care Product - OPI PRODUCTS INC.; *pg.* 518, *pg.* 167
MAVERICK - Medical Device - BOSTON SCIENTIFIC CORPORATION; *pg.* 1508, *pg.* 831
MAVERICK - Furniture - LA-Z-BOY INCORPORATED; *pg.* 932, *pg.* 901
MAVERICK - Eye Protection Product - MINE SAFETY APPLIANCES COMPANY; *pg.* 1361, *pg.* 1525
MAVERICK - Selective Herbicide - MONSANTO COMPANY; *pg.* 1173, *pg.* 999
MAVERICK - Fabric - NEMSCHOFF, INC.; *pg.* 936, *pg.* 1890
MAVERICK - Automatic Test Equipment - NEXTEST SYSTEMS CORPORATION; *pg.* 445, *pg.* 248
MAVERICK - Floor Cleaning Product - NSS ENTERPRISES, INC.; *pg.* 59, *pg.* 1476
MAVERICK - Missile - RAYTHEON COMPANY; *pg.* 233, *pg.* 854
MAVERICK - Playing Cards - THE UNITED STATES PLAYING CARD COMPANY; *pg.* 969, *pg.* 727
MAVERICK - Jeanswear - V.F. CORPORATION; *pg.* 34, *pg.* 1376
MAVERICK - Record Label - WARNER MUSIC GROUP CORP.; *pg.* 590, *pg.* 1313
MAVERICK - Soil Disruption Guard - YETTER MANUFACTURING CO., INC.; *pg.* 708, *pg.* 598
MAVERICK GT - Automatic Test Equipment - NEXTEST SYSTEMS CORPORATION; *pg.* 445, *pg.* 248
MAVERICK HD - Automatic Test Equipment - NEXTEST SYSTEMS CORPORATION; *pg.* 445, *pg.* 248
MAVERICK TESTER - Automatic Test Equipment - NEXTEST SYSTEMS CORPORATION; *pg.* 445, *pg.* 248
MAVERICK VT - Automatic Test Equipment - NEXTEST SYSTEMS CORPORATION; *pg.* 445, *pg.* 248
MAVERIK FLEET CARD - Credit Card - MAVERIK COUNTRY STORES, INC.; *pg.* 1027, *pg.* 1752
MAVERIK GIFT CARD - Gift Card - MAVERIK COUNTRY STORES, INC.; *pg.* 1027, *pg.* 1752
MAVERIK MASTERCARD - Credit Card - MAVERIK COUNTRY STORES, INC.; *pg.* 1027, *pg.* 1752
MAVID - Pharmaceutical Product - ABBOTT LABORATORIES; *pg.* 1484, *pg.* 551
MAVIK - Tablet - ABBOTT LABORATORIES; *pg.* 1484, *pg.* 551
MAVIN - Fabric - NEMSCHOFF, INC.; *pg.* 936, *pg.* 1890
MAX - CLPD Device - ALTERA CORPORATION; *pg.* 348, *pg.* 237
MAX - Software - AMX CORPORATION; *pg.* 349, *pg.* 1735
MAX - Analyzer - ARIZONA INSTRUMENT LLC; *pg.* 1400, *pg.* 12
MAX - Software - CLEARONE COMMUNICATIONS, INC.; *pg.* 629, *pg.* 1756
THE MAX - Food Product - CONAGRA FOODS, INC.; *pg.* 826, *pg.* 1014
MAX - Character - CONSTELLATION; *pg.* 1938, *pg.* 373
THE MAX - Music Center - DETROIT SYMPHONY ORCHESTRA, INC.; *pg.* 544, *pg.* 880
MAX - Voice Processing Platform - ELECTRONIC TELE-COMMUNICATIONS, INC.; *pg.* 390, *pg.* 1897
MAX - Battery - ENERGIZER HOLDINGS, INC.; *pg.* 637, *pg.* 996
MAX - Software - HURCO COMPANIES, INC.; *pg.* 409, *pg.* 686
MAX - Tungsten Deposition System - LAM RESEARCH CORPORATION; *pg.* 1354, *pg.* 246
MAX - Mats - MACNEIL AUTOMOTIVE PRODUCTS, LTD.; *pg.* 211, *pg.* 559
MAX - Building Wrap - PACTIV CORPORATION; *pg.* 1466, *pg.* 624
MAX - Insect Killer For Lawns - THE SCOTTS MIRACLE-GRO COMPANY; *pg.* 1799, *pg.* 1459
MAX - Thermal Processing Equipment - SURFACE COMBUSTION, INC.; *pg.* 1077, *pg.* 1462
MAX - Control Cable - TUTHILL CORPORATION; *pg.* 1385, *pg.* 561
MAX - Wireless Control Product - UNIVERSAL ELECTRONICS, INC.; *pg.* 683, *pg.* 262
MAX - Slicer - UNIVEX CORPORATION; *pg.* 1386, *pg.* 1039
MAX 1000-MOISTURE ANALYZER - Analyzer - ARIZONA INSTRUMENT LLC; *pg.* 1400, *pg.* 12
MAX 2000-MOISTURE ANALYZER - Analyzer - ARIZONA INSTRUMENT LLC; *pg.* 1400, *pg.* 12
MAX 2000XL - Moisture Analyzer - ARIZONA INSTRUMENT LLC; *pg.* 1400, *pg.* 12
MAX 3000 - High-performance CPLD - ALTERA CORPORATION; *pg.* 348, *pg.* 237
MAX 3000 - Towel Dispensing System - GEORGIA-PACIFIC LLC; *pg.* 1458, *pg.* 507
MAX 3000A - High-Performance CPLD - ALTERA CORPORATION; *pg.* 348, *pg.* 237
MAX 5 - Whole House Electronic - TRION, INC.; *pg.* 682, *pg.* 1390
MAX-50 - Moisture Analyzer - ARIZONA INSTRUMENT LLC; *pg.* 1400, *pg.* 12
MAX 5000 - Mature Device - ALTERA CORPORATION; *pg.* 348, *pg.* 237
MAX 7000 - High-Performance CPLD - ALTERA

First page reference indicates Business Class Edition
Second page reference indicates Geographic Edition

CORPORATION; pg. 348, pg. 237
MAX 7000A - High-performance CPLD - ALTERA CORPORATION; pg. 348, pg. 237
MAX 7000B - High-performance CPLD - ALTERA CORPORATION; pg. 348, pg. 237
MAX 7000S - High-performance CPLD - ALTERA CORPORATION; pg. 348, pg. 237
MAX 9000 - Mature Device - ALTERA CORPORATION; pg. 348, pg. 237
MAX 9000A - Mature Device - ALTERA CORPORATION; pg. 348, pg. 237
MAX A MILLION - Lottery Game - MASSACHUSETTS STATE LOTTERY; pg. 998, pg. 802
MAX ALL PURPOSE - Cleaner - SWISHER HYGIENE INC.; pg. 336, pg. 1507
MAX-AMINE - Gas Treating Technology - GE WATER & PROCESS TECHNOLOGIES; pg. 1339, pg. 1588
MAX & ERMA'S - Restaurants - AMERICAN BLUE RIBBON HOLDINGS; pg. 1714, pg. 1648
MAX AZRIA - Clothing & Accessories for Women - BCBG MAX AZRIA GROUP LLC; pg. 19, pg. 301
M.A.X. BACKBONE - Bicycle Accessories - SPECIALIZED BICYCLE COMPONENTS, INC.; pg. 1711, pg. 152
MAX COAT II - Premium Roll Covers - VAIL RUBBER WORKS, INC.; pg. 1891, pg. 906
MAX DISINFECTANT - Cleaner - SWISHER HYGIENE INC.; pg. 336, pg. 1507
MAX-E-GLO - Animal Feed Supplement - MANNA PRO CORPORATION; pg. 1478, pg. 975
MAX EFFICIENCY - Molecular Biology Product - THERMO FISHER SCIENTIFIC INC.; pg. 1602, pg. 61
MAX-FAST - Medical Device - MALLINCKRODT PHARMACEUTICALS; pg. 1557, pg. 978
MAX FIT - Pipe - AP EXHAUST PRODUCTS, INC.; pg. 199, pg. 1373
MAX FLO - Fluid Handling System - GRACO, INC.; pg. 1342, pg. 935
MAX-FLO - Pump - HAYWARD POOL PRODUCTS; pg. 1049, pg. 1057
MAX FOAMING TUB & TILE - Cleaner - SWISHER HYGIENE INC.; pg. 336, pg. 1507
MAX HT - Sodalite Scale Inhibitor - CYTEC INDUSTRIES, INC.; pg. 1155, pg. 1131
MAX-I-PROBE - Dental Product - DENTSPLY INTERNATIONAL INC.; pg. 1522, pg. 1596
MAX II - High-Performance CPLD - ALTERA CORPORATION; pg. 348, pg. 237
MAX IV, 32 - Modular Application Executive Operating System - CSPI TECHNOLOGY SOLUTIONS; pg. 381, pg. 421
MAX LIFE - Automotive Oil Change Pans - ASHLAND INC.; pg. 972, pg. 726
MAX-LOC - Electronic Components - MOLEX INCORPORATED; pg. 655, pg. 628
MAX M. FISHER MUSIC CENTER - Music Center - DETROIT SYMPHONY ORCHESTRA, INC.; pg. 544, pg. 880
MAX MOUNT - Telescopes - MEADE INSTRUMENTS CORPORATION; pg. 1422, pg. 113
MAX-PHY - Digital Interface - MAXIM INTEGRATED PRODUCTS, INC.; pg. 653, pg. 247
MAX PLUS - Software - ALTERA CORPORATION; pg. 348, pg. 237
MAX PLUS II - Software - ALTERA CORPORATION; pg. 348, pg. 237
MAX PRIME - Coating Product - PPG INDUSTRIES, INC.; pg. 1445, pg. 1579
MAX RETRIEVER - Software - EMC CORPORATION; pg. 391, pg. 825
MAX-ROM HIP SYSTEM - Hip Product - ZIMMER BIOMET HOLDINGS, INC.; pg. 1611, pg. 699
MAX SPEARMINT - Cleaner - SWISHER HYGIENE INC.; pg. 336, pg. 1507
MAX SPEED - Ammo & Accessories - DAISY MANUFACTURING COMPANY; pg. 1831, pg. 35
MAX-STACKER - Chairs - STEELCASE INC.; pg. 475, pg. 889
MAX-SUPPORT - Medical Device - VASCULAR SOLUTIONS, INC.; pg. 1434, pg. 946
M.A.X. TAILBONE - Bicycle Accessories - SPECIALIZED BICYCLE COMPONENTS, INC.; pg. 1711, pg. 152
MAX TNT - Software System - ALCATEL-LUCENT; pg. 615, pg. 1094
MAX VANILLA - Cleaner - SWISHER HYGIENE INC.; pg. 336, pg. 1507
MAX-WALL - Interior Flat Paint - DUNN-EDWARDS CORPORATION; pg. 1442, pg. 129
MAX WAX - Lubricant & Protectant - MCNETT CORPORATION; pg. 1839, pg. 1817
MAX-WELD - Adhesive - H.B. FULLER COMPANY; pg. 1165, pg. 961
MAX WIRELESS PHONE - Wireless Conference Phone - CLEARONE COMMUNICATIONS, INC.; pg. 629, pg. 1756
MAX YOUR EDGE - Tagline - WMS INDUSTRIES INC.; pg. 593, pg. 666
MAXAIR ETS - Mattress - KINETIC CONCEPTS, INC.; pg. 1553, pg. 1741
MAXAM - Seating Product - HUSSEY SEATING CO.; pg. 929, pg. 751
MAXAMET - Alloy - CARPENTER TECHNOLOGY CORPORATION; pg. 73, pg. 1584
MAXATTACH - Software - CLEARONE COMMUNICATIONS, INC.; pg. 629, pg. 1756
MAXBAK - Epoxy Crusher - ESCO CORPORATION; pg. 1335, pg. 1502
MAXBOND - Refractory Product - RESCO PRODUCTS, INC.; pg. 107, pg. 1581
MAXCAST - Video Services - NU SKIN ENTERPRISES, INC.; pg. 518, pg. 1755
MAXCESS - Surgery System - NUVASIVE, INC.; pg. 1577, pg. 205
MAXCHANGER - Compact All-Welded Plate & Frame Heat Exchangers - TRANTER PHE, INC.; pg. 1383, pg. 1749
MAXCL - Insurance Service - MODERN WOODMEN OF AMERICA; pg. 1209, pg. 654
MAXCL PRO - Insurance Service - MODERN WOODMEN OF AMERICA; pg. 1209, pg. 654
MAXCOLD - Ice Chest - IGLOO PRODUCTS CORPORATION; pg. 1126, pg. 1724
MAXCORE - Fiber Optic Lighting System - ENERGY FOCUS, INC.; pg. 1411, pg. 1472
MAXDRP - Replacement Teeth - ESCO CORPORATION; pg. 1335, pg. 1502
MAXE2 SYSTEM - Eligibility Determination System for Medicaid - MAXIMUS, INC.; pg. 780, pg. 1799
MAXECON - Hose - HBD INDUSTRIES, INC.; pg. 207, pg. 1449
MAXECON 300 - Air or Water Hose for Where Moderate Oil Resistance is Required - HBD INDUSTRIES, INC.; pg. 207, pg. 1449
MAXECON PLUS - All Purpose Hose for Industrial Applications - HBD INDUSTRIES, INC.; pg. 207, pg. 1449
MAXECON WASHDOWN - Hose Designed for Low Pressure Steam & Hot Water Washdown Service - HBD INDUSTRIES, INC.; pg. 207, pg. 1449
MAXEMERGE - Planters - DEERE & COMPANY; pg. 703, pg. 632
MAXFIELD - Shoes - ALLEN-EDMONDS SHOE CORP.; pg. 1804, pg. 1887
MAXFIELD - Corner System - LINDSAY CORPORATION; pg. 1356, pg. 1016
MAXFILE ATTACHE - USB Micro Hard Drive - PNY TECHNOLOGIES, INC.; pg. 455, pg. 1105
MAXFLEET - Maintenance Program - MIKE ALBERT LEASING, INC.; pg. 185, pg. 1417
MAXFLO 3 - Valves - FLOWSERVE CORPORATION; pg. 82, pg. 1719
MAXFORCE - Professional Insecticides - THE CLOROX COMPANY; pg. 327, pg. 169
MAXGRIP - Pliers - STANLEY BLACK & DECKER, INC.; pg. 1063, pg. 358
MAXGUARD - Resins - ASHLAND INC.; pg. 972, pg. 726
MAXGUARD - Masking Product - KELLY-MOORE PAINT COMPANY, INC.; pg. 1443, pg. 198
MAXI - Controller - RAIN BIRD CORPORATION; pg. 707, pg. 44
MAXI-BUNDLE - Fiber Optic Cable - CORNING CABLE SYSTEMS LLC; pg. 1407, pg. 1378
MAXI-BUNDLE - Glass & Ceramic Material - CORNING INCORPORATED; pg. 1122, pg. 1154
MAXI-FLO - Fluid Handling System - GRACO, INC.; pg. 1342, pg. 935
MAXI FUSE - Large Automotive Fuse - LITTELFUSE, INC.; pg. 1301, pg. 580
MAXI-GRIP - Mop Handles - GEERPRES INC.; pg. 1339, pg. 901
MAXI MINDER - Clip - BROWN & BIGELOW, INC.; pg. 1624, pg. 959
MAXI-MONITOR - Fluid Handling System - GRACO, INC.; pg. 1342, pg. 935
MAXI-MOVERS - Storage Tank - CHEM-TAINER INDUSTRIES, INC.; pg. 1455, pg. 1349
MAXI-MOX - Resistor - OHMITE MANUFACTURING COMPANY; pg. 660, pg. 553
MAXI-PAC - Actuator - DUFF-NORTON; pg. 204, pg. 1365
MAXI-THERM - Medical Product - CINCINNATI SUB-ZERO PRODUCTS, INC.; pg. 1070, pg. 1411
MAXIBAN - Narasin & Nicarbazin - ELANCO ANIMAL HEALTH; pg. 1475, pg. 681
MAXICAP - Ionomer Cement Restorative - 3M COMPANY; pg. 1142, pg. 956
MAXICHECK - Test Kit - THE DOW CHEMICAL COMPANY; pg. 1157, pg. 898
MAXICOM2 - Central Control - RAIN BIRD CORPORATION; pg. 707, pg. 44
MAXIDONE - Pharmaceutical Product - ALLERGAN; pg. 1490, pg. 1101
MAXIGATOR - Irrigation Equipment Lateral Move - REINKE MANUFACTURING COMPANY, INC.; pg. 707, pg. 1010
MAXIKLEEN - Liquid CIP Cleaner - BOUMATIC LLC; pg. 701, pg. 1865
MAXILON - Cationic Dyes - HUNTSMAN CORPORATION; pg. 1167, pg. 1758
MAXIM - Furniture - AMISCO INDUSTRIES LTD.; pg. 913, pg. 1958
MAXIM - Hand Mixer - BROWN & BIGELOW, INC.; pg. 1624, pg. 959
MAXIM - Fluid Handling System - GRACO, INC.; pg. 1342, pg. 935
MAXIM - Pump Product - IDEX CORPORATION; pg. 1347, pg. 623
MAXIM - Repair Products - ITW - EVERCOAT; pg. 1443, pg. 1415
MAXIM - Semiconductor Chips - MAXIM INTEGRATED PRODUCTS, INC.; pg. 653, pg. 247
MAXIM - Fabric - NEMSCHOFF, INC.; pg. 936, pg. 1890
MAXIM REVISION KNEE SYSTEM - Knee Product - ZIMMER BIOMET HOLDINGS, INC.; pg. 1611, pg. 699
MAXIMA - Automobile - NISSAN NORTH AMERICA, INC.; pg. 186, pg. 1633
MAXIMA - MP&G Accelerator - SIGMA DESIGNS, INC.; pg. 469, pg. 148
MAXIMA PRO - MP&G Accelerator - SIGMA DESIGNS, INC.; pg. 469, pg. 148
MAXIMICE - Ice Slurry System - PAUL MUELLER COMPANY; pg. 706, pg. 1007
MAXIMILLIAN - Kitchenware - THE VOLLRATH COMPANY LLC; pg. 1139, pg. 1894
MAXIMISE. OPTIMIZE. NEVER COMPROMISE. - Tagline - TRICO MFG. CORP.; pg. 219, pg. 1886
MAXIMISER - Data Services - NIELSEN AUDIO; pg. 446, pg. 768
MAXIMISER PLUS - Software - NIELSEN AUDIO; pg. 446, pg. 768
MAXIMIZER - Conveyor System - AUTOMATED PACKAGING SYSTEMS INC.; pg. 1452, pg. 1474
MAXIMIZER - Food Bar - CARLISLE FOODSERVICE PRODUCTS INCORPORATED; pg. 1455, pg. 1485
MAXIMIZER - Insurance Service - MODERN WOODMEN OF AMERICA; pg. 1209, pg. 654
MAXIMIZER - Software - RADIO FREQUENCY SYSTEMS, INC.; pg. 666, pg. 354
MAXIMIZER - Bulk Seed Conveyor - YETTER MANUFACTURING CO., INC.; pg. 708, pg. 598
MAXIMMUNE - Blend of Ingredients - WILD FLAVORS, INC.; pg. 910, pg. 728
MAXIMO - Defibrillator - MEDTRONIC, INC.; pg. 1564, pg. 939
MAXIMO - Footwear - STEVEN MADDEN, LTD.; pg. 1819, pg. 1176
MAXIMUM - Vinyl Product - CRANE PLASTICS HOLDING COMPANY; pg. 1881, pg. 1439
MAXIMUM - Paint - PPG INDUSTRIES, INC.; pg. 1445, pg. 1579
MAXIMUM - Cardiology & Vascular Access Products - ST. JUDE MEDICAL, INC.; pg. 1596, pg. 963
MAXIMUM-CALORIE - Veterinary Food - IAMS COMPANY; pg. 1477, pg. 1633
MAXIMUM ENERGY - Battery Cables - COLEMAN CABLE, INC.; pg. 1324, pg. 665
MAXIMUM LOCKDOWN - Game - MULTIMEDIA GAMES INC.; pg. 442, pg. 1664
MAXIMUM PERFORMANCE DISTINCTION - Coating Product - PPG INDUSTRIES, INC.; pg. 1445, pg. 1579
MAXIMUM PLUS - Interior & Exterior Paints - PPG INDUSTRIES, INC.; pg. 1445, pg. 1579
MAXIMUM POLY - Orthopedic Product - DJO SURGICAL; pg.

1525, *pg.* 1661
MAXIMUM STRENGTH TYLENOL SINUS MEDICATION - Sinus Medication - MCNEIL-PPC, INC.; *pg.* 1560, *pg.* 1533
MAXIMUM VALUE PARTNERSHIP - Inventory Control Services - GUARDSMARK, LLC; *pg.* 401, *pg.* 1237
MAXINE - Footwear - PHOENIX FOOTWEAR GROUP, INC.; *pg.* 1815, *pg.* 60
MAXIPEDIC - Mattress - SIMMONS COMPANY; *pg.* 943, *pg.* 520
MAXIPLAN - Systems Integration & Aeronautics - LOCKHEED MARTIN CORPORATION; *pg.* 229, *pg.* 762
MAXIPOWER - Power Transmission Belt - HBD INDUSTRIES, INC.; *pg.* 207, *pg.* 1449
MAXIPRES - Machinery - NATIONAL MACHINERY LLC; *pg.* 1363, *pg.* 1475
MAXIPURGE - Systems Integration & Aeronautics - LOCKHEED MARTIN CORPORATION; *pg.* 229, *pg.* 762
MAXIS - Simulation & Strategy Games - ELECTRONIC ARTS INC.; *pg.* 951, *pg.* 189
MAXISHIP - Software - UNITED PARCEL SERVICE, INC.; *pg.* 1928, *pg.* 522
MAXISLEEVE - Animal Safety Product - NEOGEN CORPORATION; *pg.* 883, *pg.* 896
MAXISORT - Systems Integration & Aeronautics - LOCKHEED MARTIN CORPORATION; *pg.* 229, *pg.* 762
MAXISORT - Software - OPEX CORPORATION; *pg.* 450, *pg.* 1087
MAXISTAB - Stabilizer - THE DOW CHEMICAL COMPANY; *pg.* 1157, *pg.* 898
MAXISTAR - Systems Integration & Aeronautics - LOCKHEED MARTIN CORPORATION; *pg.* 229, *pg.* 762
MAXISTAR ONSCHEDULE - Systems Integration & Aeronautics - LOCKHEED MARTIN CORPORATION; *pg.* 229, *pg.* 762
MAXITORQ - Clutches & Brakes - THE CARLYLE JOHNSON MACHINE COMPANY, L.L.C.; *pg.* 1321, *pg.* 339
MAXITRAC - Software - UNITED PARCEL SERVICE, INC.; *pg.* 1928, *pg.* 522
MAXIVAC - Influenza Vaccines - MERCK & CO., INC.; *pg.* 1566, *pg.* 1077
MAXLIFE - Fluid Handling System - GRACO, INC.; *pg.* 1342, *pg.* 935
MAXLIFE - Insurance Service - MODERN WOODMEN OF AMERICA; *pg.* 1209, *pg.* 654
MAXLINE - Pressed & Monolithic Refractory - RESCO PRODUCTS, INC.; *pg.* 107, *pg.* 1581
MAXLINE - Bathroom Accessories - SYMMONS INDUSTRIES, INC.; *pg.* 114, *pg.* 803
MAXLINK - Optical Networking Product - HARMONIC, INC.; *pg.* 402, *pg.* 246
MAXM - Testing Instrument System - BECKMAN COULTER, INC.; *pg.* 1402, *pg.* 48
MAXM - Software - BMC SOFTWARE, INC.; *pg.* 362, *pg.* 1701
MAXM DATABASE ADVISOR - Software - BMC SOFTWARE, INC.; *pg.* 362, *pg.* 1701
MAXM REORG/EP - Software - BMC SOFTWARE, INC.; *pg.* 362, *pg.* 1701
MAXM REORG/EP EXPRESS - Software - BMC SOFTWARE, INC.; *pg.* 362, *pg.* 1701
MAXMATIC - Self-Feeding Riveter - ALLFAST FASTENING SYSTEMS, INC.; *pg.* 1041, *pg.* 66
MAXMC - Payment Software - LANDACORP, INC.; *pg.* 426, *pg.* 65
MAXNIBP - Vital Sign Monitor - CAS MEDICAL SYSTEMS, INC.; *pg.* 1513, *pg.* 339
MAXON - Office Furniture - HNI CORPORATION; *pg.* 927, *pg.* 709
MAXONLINE - Internet Advertising Sales Network - IAC SEARCH & MEDIA, INC.; *pg.* 1257, *pg.* 171
MAXORB - Medical Product - MEDLINE INDUSTRIES, INC.; *pg.* 1562, *pg.* 635
MAXP - Motion Controller - PRO-DEX, INC.; *pg.* 1586, *pg.* 115
MAXPAC - Power Controllers - CHROMALOX, INC.; *pg.* 1070, *pg.* 1574
MAXPRO - Healthcare Product - JOHNSON & JOHNSON; *pg.* 1549, *pg.* 1091
MAXPRO - Scrub Head - TENNANT COMPANY; *pg.* 1381, *pg.* 944
MAXQ - Microcontrollers - MAXIM INTEGRATED PRODUCTS, INC.; *pg.* 653, *pg.* 247
MAXQUALITATIVE - Software - NIELSEN AUDIO; *pg.* 446, *pg.* 768
MAXRAD - Antenna Products - PCTEL, INC.; *pg.* 452, *pg.* 557
MAXRATE - Lead Batteries - C&D TECHNOLOGIES, INC.; *pg.* 627, *pg.* 1517
MAXREG - Software Product - MAXIMUS, INC.; *pg.* 780, *pg.* 1799
MAXSIZE - Roller Cover - VAIL RUBBER WORKS, INC.; *pg.* 1891, *pg.* 906
MAXSTAR - Software Product - MAXIMUS, INC.; *pg.* 780, *pg.* 1799
MAXSTAR - Welding & Cutting Equip. - MILLER ELECTRIC MANUFACTURING CO.; *pg.* 1361, *pg.* 1852
MAXSTREAM - Electronic Devices - DIGI INTERNATIONAL INC.; *pg.* 387, *pg.* 948
MAXSTREAM - Fire Pumps - IDEX CORPORATION; *pg.* 1347, *pg.* 623
MAXSYS - Software - LANDACORP, INC.; *pg.* 426, *pg.* 65
MAXSYS II - Medical Management Software - LANDACORP, INC.; *pg.* 426, *pg.* 65
MAXTEMP - Steel Plate - ESCO CORPORATION; *pg.* 1335, *pg.* 1502
MAXTOUCH - Integrated Circuit - ATMEL CORPORATION; *pg.* 621, *pg.* 238
MAXTRACK - Software Product - MAXIMUS, INC.; *pg.* 780, *pg.* 1799
MAXTRAX - Orthopedic Product - DJO INCORPORATED; *pg.* 1524, *pg.* 302
MAXUM - Medical Device - COOK GROUP, INC.; *pg.* 1518, *pg.* 674
MAXUM - Vacuum Systems - H-P PRODUCTS, INC.; *pg.* 85, *pg.* 1458
MAXUMPLUS - Ball Bonder - KULICKE & SOFFA INDUSTRIES, INC.; *pg.* 650, *pg.* 1533
MAXUS - Avilamycin - ELANCO ANIMAL HEALTH; *pg.* 1475, *pg.* 681
MAXVAULT - Digital Content Storage - NU SKIN ENTERPRISES, INC.; *pg.* 518, *pg.* 1755
MAXVIEW - Protective Eyewear - SELLSTROM MANUFACTURING CO.; *pg.* 1428, *pg.* 659
MAXVUE - Image Generator - CAE INC.; *pg.* 226, *pg.* 1959
MAXWAX - Ring - OATEY SUPPLY CHAIN SERVICES; *pg.* 30, *pg.* 1433
MAXWELL - Close-Coupled Toilet - GERBER PLUMBING FIXTURES CORPORATION; *pg.* 84, *pg.* 672
MAXWELL - Navigation Aid - TRIMBLE NAVIGATION LIMITED; *pg.* 1384, *pg.* 288
MAXWELL HOUSE - Coffees - THE KRAFT HEINZ COMPANY; *pg.* 870, *pg.* 1577
MAXWORKFLOW - Scalable Digital Prepress Workflow System - ECRM IMAGING SYSTEMS, INC.; *pg.* 1410, *pg.* 848
MAXXAM - Hair Care Product - HAIR CLUB FOR MEN, LTD., INC.; *pg.* 511, *pg.* 411
MAXXAM - Polyolefin Compound - POLYONE CORPORATION; *pg.* 1177, *pg.* 1404
MAXXAM FR - Flame-Retardant Polypropylene Compounds - POLYONE CORPORATION; *pg.* 1177, *pg.* 1404
MAXXGRIP PRO - Putty Knives, Scrapers - HYDE TOOLS, INC.; *pg.* 1125, *pg.* 844
MAXXIM - Hose - THE GOODYEAR TIRE & RUBBER COMPANY; *pg.* 1883, *pg.* 1401
MAXXIS - Bed System - KINETIC CONCEPTS, INC.; *pg.* 1553, *pg.* 1741
MAXXMAIL - Promotional Service - T.J. MAXX; *pg.* 1788, *pg.* 822
MAY WEST - Bakery Product - SAPUTO, INC.; *pg.* 893, *pg.* 1956
MAY WEST - Bakery Product - VACHON BAKERY INC.; *pg.* 907, *pg.* 1959
MAYA - Software - AUTODESK INC.; *pg.* 356, *pg.* 257
MAYA - Fabric - NEMSCHOFF, INC.; *pg.* 936, *pg.* 1890
MAYA MADNESS - Game - GAMEWRIGHT; *pg.* 953, *pg.* 836
MAYAN SUN - Game - WMS INDUSTRIES INC.; *pg.* 593, *pg.* 666
MAYANA - Footwear - STEVEN MADDEN, LTD.; *pg.* 1819, *pg.* 1176
MAYER - Hosiery & Related Apparel - MAYER/BERKSHIRE CORPORATION; *pg.* 29, *pg.* 1129
MAYFAIR - Computer Bag - A. T. CROSS COMPANY; *pg.* 339, *pg.* 1602
MAYFAIR - Supermarkets - ARDEN GROUP, INC.; *pg.* 1014, *pg.* 68
MAYFAIR - Dinnerware - THE HOMER LAUGHLIN CHINA COMPANY; *pg.* 1125, *pg.* 1850
MAYFAIR - Fabric - NEMSCHOFF, INC.; *pg.* 936, *pg.* 1890
MAYFIELD - Furniture - ASHLEY FURNITURE INDUSTRIES, INC.; *pg.* 914, *pg.* 1852
MAYFIELD - Milk & Ice Cream - DEAN FOODS COMPANY; *pg.* 852, *pg.* 1679
MAYFIELD - Medical Device - INTEGRA LIFESCIENCES HOLDINGS CORPORATION; *pg.* 1545, *pg.* 1109
MAYFIELD - Kitchen Product - KOHLER CO.; *pg.* 91, *pg.* 1862
MAYFIELD DAIRY - Dairy Product - DEAN FOODS COMPANY; *pg.* 852, *pg.* 1679
MAYFLOWER - Bath Product - KOHLER CO.; *pg.* 91, *pg.* 1862
MAYFLOWER TRANSIT - Transportation System - UNIGROUP, INC.; *pg.* 1927, *pg.* 977
MAYO CLINIC PROCEEDINGS - Healthcare Publication - LEBHAR-FRIEDMAN INC.; *pg.* 1658, *pg.* 1250
MAYORS - Jewelry - BIRKS & MAYORS INC.; *pg.* 1, *pg.* 470
MAYORS - Jewelry - BIRKS & MAYORS INC.; *pg.* 1, *pg.* 1953
MAYROSE - Meat Product - JOHN MORRELL FOOD GROUP; *pg.* 866, *pg.* 628
MAYTAG - Home & Commercial Appliances - WHIRLPOOL CORPORATION; *pg.* 62, *pg.* 872
MAYURI - Bath Accessory - CROSCILL, INC.; *pg.* 1122, *pg.* 1220
MAZACA - Ingredient System - PENFORD CORPORATION; *pg.* 1177, *pg.* 314
MAZE - Specialty Nails - W.H. MAZE COMPANY; *pg.* 1389, *pg.* 652
MAZE PEN - Puzzle - BROWN & BIGELOW, INC.; *pg.* 1624, *pg.* 959
MAZEMADE - Specialty Nails - W.H. MAZE COMPANY; *pg.* 1389, *pg.* 652
MAZIN - Colloidal Silica Products - E.I. DU PONT DE NEMOURS & COMPANY; *pg.* 1159, *pg.* 390
MAZING SQUARES - Fabric - NEUTRAL POSTURE, INC.; *pg.* 939, *pg.* 1669
MAZOE - Beverages - THE COCA-COLA COMPANY; *pg.* 240, *pg.* 493
MAZURI - Pet Product - PETSMART, INC.; *pg.* 1481, *pg.* 18
MAZZETTI GRAPPA - Italian Grappa - LAIRD & COMPANY, INC.; *pg.* 1966, *pg.* 1119
MAZZIOS ITALIAN EATERY - Fast Food Restaurants - MAZZIO'S CORPORATION; *pg.* 1737, *pg.* 1490
MB - LED - CREE INC.; *pg.* 631, *pg.* 1371
MB-COLOR - Conveying System - MOTAN, INC.; *pg.* 1886, *pg.* 903
MB MAX - LED - CREE INC.; *pg.* 631, *pg.* 1371
MB PLUS - LED - CREE INC.; *pg.* 631, *pg.* 1371
MBA - Medical Device - INTEGRA LIFESCIENCES HOLDINGS CORPORATION; *pg.* 1545, *pg.* 1109
MBANKING 365 - Banking Product - SAP; *pg.* 465, *pg.* 78
MBB - Pumps - IDEX CORPORATION; *pg.* 1347, *pg.* 623
MBG - Metal Gas Burners - HAUCK MANUFACTURING COMPANY, INC.; *pg.* 1345, *pg.* 1522
MBIST - Software System - MENTOR GRAPHICS CORPORATION; *pg.* 432, *pg.* 1510
MBIST FLEX - Software System - MENTOR GRAPHICS CORPORATION; *pg.* 432, *pg.* 1510
MBIST FULL-SPEED - Software System - MENTOR GRAPHICS CORPORATION; *pg.* 432, *pg.* 1510
MBIST IN-PLACE - Software System - MENTOR GRAPHICS CORPORATION; *pg.* 432, *pg.* 1510
MBIST MANAGER - Software System - MENTOR GRAPHICS CORPORATION; *pg.* 432, *pg.* 1510
MBISTARCHITECT - Software System - MENTOR GRAPHICS CORPORATION; *pg.* 432, *pg.* 1510
MBOSS - Plastic & Rubber - TEKNOR APEX COMPANY; *pg.* 1889, *pg.* 1605
MBR - Doll - MGA ENTERTAINMENT, INC.; *pg.* 964, *pg.* 300
MBT - Appliance System - 3M COMPANY; *pg.* 1142, *pg.* 956
MBX-4 - Wireless Product - HEMISPHERE GPS INC.; *pg.* 642, *pg.* 1903
MC - Glass & Ceramic Material - CORNING INCORPORATED; *pg.* 1122, *pg.* 1154
MC-1 - Microphone Coupler - ALAN GORDON ENTERPRISES, INC.; *pg.* 1399, *pg.* 125
MC-100 - Multimedia Controller - ANDREA ELECTRONICS CORPORATION; *pg.* 617, *pg.* 1143
MC LADY - Golf Balls - BRIDGESTONE GOLF, INC.; *pg.* 1828, *pg.* 528
MC-LITE - Metal Clad Cable - AFC CABLE SYSTEMS, INC.; *pg.* 1294, *pg.* 835
MC/OF - Power & Fiber Optic Cable - AFC CABLE SYSTEMS,

INC.; pg. 1294, pg. 835
MC/OS - Operating System - MERCURY COMPUTER SYSTEMS, INC.; pg. 434, pg. 813
MC/OS CERTIFIED - Certifies Interoperability of Third Party SBCs in a Mercury System - MERCURY COMPUTER SYSTEMS, INC.; pg. 434, pg. 813
MC TUFF - Cable - AFC CABLE SYSTEMS, INC.; pg. 1294, pg. 835
MC-V - Meter Reading System - BADGER METER, INC.; pg. 1401, pg. 1873
MC1213 - Horizontal Machining Center - MAKINO INC.; pg. 1358, pg. 1461
MC1513 - Horizontal Machining Center - MAKINO INC.; pg. 1358, pg. 1461
MC1813 - Horizontal Machining Center - MAKINO INC.; pg. 1358, pg. 1461
MC2210 - Horizontal Machining Center - MAKINO INC.; pg. 1358, pg. 1461
MCARTHUR - Milk - DEAN FOODS COMPANY; pg. 852, pg. 1679
MCARTHUR DAIRY - Dairy Product - DEAN FOODS COMPANY; pg. 852, pg. 1679
MCBABY - Fast Food - MCDONALD'S CORPORATION; pg. 1737, pg. 645
MCBACON - Fast Food - MCDONALD'S CORPORATION; pg. 1737, pg. 645
MCBURGER - Fast Food - MCDONALD'S CORPORATION; pg. 1737, pg. 645
MCBUS - Fast Food - MCDONALD'S CORPORATION; pg. 1737, pg. 645
MCC - Missile Check-Out Console - BAE SYSTEMS-INFORMATION WARFARE; pg. 623, pg. 1036
MCC - Game Management - BALLY TECHNOLOGIES, INC.; pg. 531, pg. 1022
MCCABE STEEL - Steel Related Products & Wheelabrating - RUSSEL METALS INC.; pg. 1180, pg. 1928
MCCADAM - Cheese - AGRI-MARK, INC.; pg. 1012, pg. 833
MCCAFE - Specialty Coffees - MCDONALD'S CORPORATION; pg. 1737, pg. 645
MCCAIN - Food Product - MCCAIN FOODS LIMITED; pg. 876, pg. 1915
MCCALLS - Vodka - MONTEBELLO BRANDS INC.; pg. 1967, pg. 758
MCCALLS CANADIAN - Whiskey - MONTEBELLO BRANDS INC.; pg. 1967, pg. 758
MCCANNA - Valve - FLOWSERVE CORPORATION; pg. 82, pg. 1719
MCCANNA-MARPAC - Pump - FLOWSERVE CORPORATION; pg. 82, pg. 1719
MCCARTY - Guitar - PAUL REED SMITH GUITARS; pg. 574, pg. 779
MCCARTY HOLLOWBODY - Guitar - PAUL REED SMITH GUITARS; pg. 574, pg. 779
MCCARTY SOAPBAR - Guitar - PAUL REED SMITH GUITARS; pg. 574, pg. 779
MCCHICKEN - Chicken Sandwich - MCDONALD'S CORPORATION; pg. 1737, pg. 645
MCCONNELL - Tractor Attachment - ALAMO GROUP INC.; pg. 1311, pg. 1745
MCCORMICK & SCHMICK'S SEAFOOD RESTAURANT - Restaurant - MCCORMICK & SCHMICK'S SEAFOOD RESTAURANTS, INC.; pg. 1737, pg. 1711
MCCORMICK'S IRISH CREAM - Liqueur - MCCORMICK DISTILLING CO., INC.; pg. 1966, pg. 1007
MCCOY - High-Quality Coated Printing Paper - POTLATCH CORPORATION; pg. 1467, pg. 1844
MCCOY - Door Lock - SOUTHCO, INC.; pg. 1063, pg. 1522
MCCROMETER - Flowmeter - DANAHER CORPORATION; pg. 1044, pg. 397
MCCUBBIN - Hosiery - MCCUBBIN HOSIERY, INC.; pg. 9, pg. 1486
MCD - Apparel - PERRY ELLIS INTERNATIONAL, INC.; pg. 45, pg. 445
MCDIRECT SHARES - Financial Services - MCDONALD'S CORPORATION; pg. 1737, pg. 645
MCDONALDLAND - Playground - MCDONALD'S CORPORATION; pg. 1737, pg. 645
MCDONALD'S HAMBURGERS - Sandwich - MCDONALD'S CORPORATION; pg. 1737, pg. 645
MCDONELLS - Food Product - CAMPBELL SOUP COMPANY; pg. 844, pg. 1048
MCDONNELL & MILLER - Fluid Technology - ITT CORPORATION; pg. 1351, pg. 1354
MCDONNELL & MILLER - Boiler Controls & Flow Switches - XYLEM INC.; pg. 1078, pg. 1339
MCDOUBLE - Fast Food - MCDONALD'S CORPORATION; pg. 1737, pg. 645
MCDOUGAL LITTELL - Textbook Publishers - HOUGHTON MIFFLIN HARCOURT; pg. 1650, pg. 611
MCDRIVE - Fast Food - MCDONALD'S CORPORATION; pg. 1737, pg. 645
MCEXEC - API Kernel - MERCURY COMPUTER SYSTEMS, INC.; pg. 434, pg. 813
MCEXPRESS - Fast Food - MCDONALD'S CORPORATION; pg. 1737, pg. 645
MCFLURRY - Dessert - MCDONALD'S CORPORATION; pg. 1737, pg. 645
MCGILL - Electrical Products - EMERSON INDUSTRIAL AUTOMATION; pg. 1296, pg. 657
MCGOVERN - Canned Salmon - OCEAN BEAUTY SEAFOODS, INC.; pg. 1028, pg. 1838
MCGRAW-HILL - Publisher - THE MCGRAW-HILL COMPANIES INC.; pg. 1663, pg. 1257
MCGRIDDLES - Breakfast Sandwich - MCDONALD'S CORPORATION; pg. 1737, pg. 645
MCGRUFF THE CRIME DOG - Crime Prevention Campaign - THE ADVERTISING COUNCIL, INC.; pg. 125, pg. 1187
MCGUFFEY - Educational Books - JOHN WILEY & SONS, INC.; pg. 1655, pg. 1073
MCGUIRE - Furniture - KOHLER CO.; pg. 91, pg. 1862
MCGUIRE - Door Levelers/Seals/Shelters; Traffic Doors - OVERHEAD DOOR CORPORATION; pg. 102, pg. 1725
MCGUNN - Safe & Security Product - FIRE KING SECURITY GROUP; pg. 1336, pg. 696
MCH6 - Embedded Processors - MERCURY COMPUTER SYSTEMS, INC.; pg. 434, pg. 813
MCH9 - Embedded Processors - MERCURY COMPUTER SYSTEMS, INC.; pg. 434, pg. 813
MCHERO - Fast Food - MCDONALD'S CORPORATION; pg. 1737, pg. 645
MCIA - Electronic Components - MOLEX INCORPORATED; pg. 655, pg. 628
MCILHENNY FARMS - BBQ Sauces, Mustards, Pickles & Apparel - MCILHENNY COMPANY; pg. 876, pg. 741
MCILWAIN - Tissue Chopper - STOELTING CO.; pg. 1430, pg. 671
MCKAY - Hard Surfaceing Product - HOBART BROTHERS COMPANY; pg. 1346, pg. 1477
MCKENZIE - Wall Panel - BLUELINX HOLDINGS, INC.; pg. 70, pg. 491
MCKENZIE COUNTRY CLASSICS - Food Product - KAYEM FOODS, INC.; pg. 867, pg. 814
MCKENZIE MOUNTAIN - Clothing - ABERCROMBIE & FITCH CO.; pg. 37, pg. 1466
MCKENZIE'S - Frozen Vegetables & Foods - PINNACLE FOODS GROUP LLC; pg. 889, pg. 1104
MCKIDS - Children's Clothing - MCDONALD'S CORPORATION; pg. 1737, pg. 645
MCKINLEY EXPLORER - Train Set - BACHMANN INDUSTRIES, INC.; pg. 950, pg. 1559
MCKINZIE - Shoe - ALDO GROUP; pg. 1804, pg. 1959
MCKROKET - Fast Food - MCDONALD'S CORPORATION; pg. 1737, pg. 645
MCLAUGHLIN - Hip Product - ZIMMER BIOMET HOLDINGS, INC.; pg. 1611, pg. 699
MCLEAN DELUXE - 91% Fat Free Hamburger Sandwich - MCDONALD'S CORPORATION; pg. 1737, pg. 645
MCLURE'S - Honey & Maple Syrup - DUTCH GOLD HONEY INC.; pg. 854, pg. 1546
MCM DESIGNER - Software System - MENTOR GRAPHICS CORPORATION; pg. 432, pg. 1510
MCM STATION - Software System - MENTOR GRAPHICS CORPORATION; pg. 432, pg. 1510
MCMEMORIES - Fast Food - MCDONALD'S CORPORATION; pg. 1737, pg. 645
MCMENU - Restaurant Services - MCDONALD'S CORPORATION; pg. 1737, pg. 645
MCMS - Software - MICROWAY, INC.; pg. 1267, pg. 841
MCMUFFIN - Breakfast Sandwich - MCDONALD'S CORPORATION; pg. 1737, pg. 645
MCMUSIC - Fast Food - MCDONALD'S CORPORATION; pg. 1737, pg. 645
MCN2000 - Automatic Conveyor System - PARAGON TECHNOLOGIES, INC.; pg. 1367, pg. 1528
MCNALLY'S EXTRA - Ale - BIG ROCK BREWERY INCOME TRUST; pg. 239, pg. 1902
MCNE - Computer Software - NOVELL INC.; pg. 446, pg. 852
MCNEILUS - Truck Product - OSHKOSH CORPORATION; pg. 187, pg. 1885
MCNI - Computer Software - NOVELL INC.; pg. 446, pg. 852
MCNIFICA - Fast Food - MCDONALD'S CORPORATION; pg. 1737, pg. 645
MCNUGGETS - Entree - MCDONALD'S CORPORATION; pg. 1737, pg. 645
MCNUGGETS KIP - Fast Food - MCDONALD'S CORPORATION; pg. 1737, pg. 645
MCOE - Software - MERCURY COMPUTER SYSTEMS, INC.; pg. 434, pg. 813
MCOZ - Fast Food - MCDONALD'S CORPORATION; pg. 1737, pg. 645
MCP - Software - BIO-RAD LABORATORIES, INC.; pg. 1504, pg. 101
MCP SERIES - Pump Product - IDEX CORPORATION; pg. 1347, pg. 623
MCPHILBEN - Lighting Fixture & Control - PHILIPS LIGHTING; pg. 1303, pg. 806
MCPHILBEN OUTDOOR - Lighting Fixtures - PHILIPS LIGHTING; pg. 1303, pg. 806
MCPIEXP - Software System - MENTOR GRAPHICS CORPORATION; pg. 432, pg. 1510
MCPLANE - Fast Food - MCDONALD'S CORPORATION; pg. 1737, pg. 645
MCPOLLO - Fast Food - MCDONALD'S CORPORATION; pg. 1737, pg. 645
MCPREP - Fast Food - MCDONALD'S CORPORATION; pg. 1737, pg. 645
MCRIB - Sandwich - MCDONALD'S CORPORATION; pg. 1737, pg. 645
MCROYAL - Fast Food - MCDONALD'S CORPORATION; pg. 1737, pg. 645
MCS - Pourous Coated Total Hip System - EXACTECH, INC.; pg. 1529, pg. 428
MCS - Medical Device - HAEMONETICS CORPORATION; pg. 1538, pg. 802
MCS - Technical Fabric - INTERNATIONAL TEXTILE GROUP, INC.; pg. 696, pg. 1374
MCS - Model of Motorized SETCO Spindle - SETCO SALES COMPANY; pg. 1061, pg. 1426
MCSALAD SHAKER - Salad - MCDONALD'S CORPORATION; pg. 1737, pg. 645
MCSCHOLAR - Educational Services - MCDONALD'S CORPORATION; pg. 1737, pg. 645
MCSCHOLAR OF THE YEAR - Educational Services - MCDONALD'S CORPORATION; pg. 1737, pg. 645
MCSKILLET BURRITO - Breakfast Food - MCDONALD'S CORPORATION; pg. 1737, pg. 645
MCSWING - Fast Food - MCDONALD'S CORPORATION; pg. 1737, pg. 645
MCT OIL - Dietary Fat Supplement - MEAD JOHNSON NUTRITION COMPANY; pg. 1561, pg. 615
MCT SMARTMARK - Laser Marking and Vision Inspection System - MCT WORLDWIDE LLC; pg. 653, pg. 939
MCT TAPESTRY - Second Generation Strip Test - MCT WORLDWIDE LLC; pg. 653, pg. 939
MCTAVISH FISHERMAN - Footwear - PHOENIX FOOTWEAR GROUP, INC.; pg. 1815, pg. 60
MCTAVISH OXFORD - Footwear - PHOENIX FOOTWEAR GROUP, INC.; pg. 1815, pg. 60
MCTAVISH SLIP-ON - Footwear - PHOENIX FOOTWEAR GROUP, INC.; pg. 1815, pg. 60
MCV6 - Software - MERCURY COMPUTER SYSTEMS, INC.; pg. 434, pg. 813
MCV9 - Software - MERCURY COMPUTER SYSTEMS, INC.; pg. 434, pg. 813
MCWRAP - Fast Food - MCDONALD'S CORPORATION; pg. 1737, pg. 645
MD 20/20 - Wine - THE WINE GROUP, INC.; pg. 1972, pg. 234
M.D. FORTE - Skin Care Product - ALLERGAN, INC.; pg. 1491, pg. 106
MD-HC - Magnetic Pumps - LITTLE GIANT PUMP COMPANY; pg. 1356, pg. 1486
MD SERIES - Magnetic Pumps - LITTLE GIANT PUMP COMPANY; pg. 1356, pg. 1486
MD150 - Cosmetics - WESTROCK COMPANY; pg. 1472, pg. 1805
MD3200 - Personal Care Product - WESTROCK COMPANY; pg. 1472, pg. 1805
MD7-4502 - Silicone Adhesive - DOW CORNING CORPORATION; pg. 1159, pg. 900
MD7-4602 - Silicone Adhesive - DOW CORNING CORPORATION; pg. 1159, pg. 900
MDA-7000 - Electronic Component - EMCORE CORPORATION; pg. 636, pg. 39
MD.ADAMS - Software - MSC SOFTWARE CORPORATION;

pg. 441, *pg.* 262
MDISNEY - Mobile Publishing - THE WALT DISNEY COMPANY; *pg.* 317, *pg.* 52
MDKEYBANK - Software - AUTHENTIDATE HOLDING CORP.; *pg.* 356, *pg.* 1044
MDLINK - Software - CARDIAC SCIENCE CORPORATION; *pg.* 1512, *pg.* 1897
MDM-7000 - Electronic Component - EMCORE CORPORATION; *pg.* 636, *pg.* 39
MDMS - Software - BIO-RAD LABORATORIES, INC.; *pg.* 1504, *pg.* 101
MDMX - Processor - IMAGINATION TECHNOLOGIES; *pg.* 412, *pg.* 285
MD.NASTRAN - Software - MSC SOFTWARE CORPORATION; *pg.* 441, *pg.* 262
MDOC - Manual - XEROX CORPORATION; *pg.* 494, *pg.* 365
MDOT - Chemical Products - AIR PRODUCTS AND CHEMICALS, INC.; *pg.* 1145, *pg.* 1513
MDRAM - Memory Technology - MOSYS INC.; *pg.* 657, *pg.* 268
MDS2GO - Data Collection Instrument - OMNICARE, INC; *pg.* 1578, *pg.* 1418
MDV - Software System - MENTOR GRAPHICS CORPORATION; *pg.* 432, *pg.* 1510
MDX - Software - BIO-RAD LABORATORIES, INC.; *pg.* 1504, *pg.* 101
MDX - Thermal Processing Equipment - SURFACE COMBUSTION, INC.; *pg.* 1077, *pg.* 1462
ME-1000 - Edger - SANTINELLI INTERNATIONAL INC.; *pg.* 1395, *pg.* 1165
ME-2 - Hardness Tester - NEWAGE TESTING INSTRUMENTS, INC.; *pg.* 1058, *pg.* 1532
MEA - Software - SAS INSTITUTE INC.; *pg.* 466, *pg.* 1361
MEA-JOSAM - Polyconcrete Trench Drain Systems - JOSAM COMPANY; *pg.* 89, *pg.* 695
MEAD - Chemical Product - HURST CHEMICAL COMPANY; *pg.* 1168, *pg.* 174
MEAD - Writing Pad - WESTROCK COMPANY; *pg.* 1472, *pg.* 1805
MEADE DS-2114ATS-LNT - Telescope - MEADE INSTRUMENTS CORPORATION; *pg.* 1422, *pg.* 113
MEADOW - Carpet - INTERFACE, INC.; *pg.* 695, *pg.* 512
MEADOW - Surface Material - STEELCASE INC.; *pg.* 475, *pg.* 889
MEADOW BROOK - Dairy - DEAN FOODS COMPANY; *pg.* 852, *pg.* 1679
MEADOW GOLD - Dairy - DEAN FOODS COMPANY; *pg.* 852, *pg.* 1679
MEADOWARE - Plastic Cutlery - PACTIV CORPORATION; *pg.* 1466, *pg.* 624
MEADOWBROOK - Vinyl Siding - PLY GEM SIDING GROUP; *pg.* 105, *pg.* 986
MEADOWLAND - Kitchen Product - KOHLER CO.; *pg.* 91, *pg.* 1862
MEAL MAKER - Kitchen Appliance - HAMILTON BEACH BRANDS, INC.; *pg.* 56, *pg.* 1783
MEAL MAKER EXPRESS - Kitchen Appliance - HAMILTON BEACH BRANDS, INC.; *pg.* 56, *pg.* 1783
MEAL ON-THE-GO - Snack Bars - SLIM-FAST FOODS COMPANY; *pg.* 896, *pg.* 1061
MEAL-TIME - Feeding System or Feeder - CTB INTERNATIONAL CORP.; *pg.* 850, *pg.* 695
MEAL TIME STARTERS - Prepared Entrees - PERDUE FARMS INCORPORATED; *pg.* 889, *pg.* 777
MEALMASTER - Cookware - PACTIV CORPORATION; *pg.* 1466, *pg.* 624
MEALMASTER FEEDKAR - Cage Feeder - CTB INTERNATIONAL CORP.; *pg.* 850, *pg.* 695
MEALS AND HERB - Hair & Skin Product - AUBREY ORGANICS INC.; *pg.* 499, *pg.* 470
MEALS & MORE - E-Newsletter - PERDUE FARMS INCORPORATED; *pg.* 889, *pg.* 777
MEANDER - Fabric - NEMSCHOFF, INC.; *pg.* 936, *pg.* 1890
MEANDER - Surface Material - STEELCASE INC.; *pg.* 475, *pg.* 889
MEANER - Cleaner - PETTIT PAINT COMPANY; *pg.* 1444, *pg.* 1116
MEANINGFUL BEAUTY - Skincare System - GUTHY-RENKER LLC; *pg.* 289, *pg.* 273
MEARLIN - Pigment - BASF CATALYSTS LLC; *pg.* 1148, *pg.* 1074
MEARLITE - Pigment - BASF CATALYSTS LLC; *pg.* 1148, *pg.* 1074
MEASUR-MIST - Insecticide - DELTA FOREMOST CHEMICAL CORPORATION; *pg.* 1155, *pg.* 1642
THE MEASURABLE DIFFERENCE - Gages - SIEMENS PROCESS INDUSTRIES AND DRIVE; *pg.* 1376, *pg.* 1587
MEASURABLY IMPROVING LIVES - Slogan - ALERE INC.; *pg.* 1488, *pg.* 849
MEASURE-IT - Molecular Probe Product - THERMO FISHER SCIENTIFIC INC.; *pg.* 1602, *pg.* 61
MEASURE MISER - Portion Control Serving Spoons - CARLISLE FOODSERVICE PRODUCTS INCORPORATED; *pg.* 1455, *pg.* 1485
THE MEASURE OF EXCELLENCE - Slogan - HAMILTON CO., INC.; *pg.* 1415, *pg.* 1031
MEASURE RITE - Truck Meter - BADGER METER, INC.; *pg.* 1401, *pg.* 1873
MEASUREMENT XPRESS - Software - GIGA-TRONICS INCORPORATED; *pg.* 640, *pg.* 260
MEAT & SEAFOOD MERCHANDISING - Magazine - VANCE PUBLISHING CORPORATION; *pg.* 1699, *pg.* 627
MEAT-E-OR - Pizza - STRAW HAT COOPERATIVE CORPORATION; *pg.* 1751, *pg.* 260
MEAT PROCESSING - Magazine Covering North America - WATT PUBLISHING COMPANY; *pg.* 1701, *pg.* 655
MEATBIND - Agricultural Product - ARCHER-DANIELS-MIDLAND COMPANY; *pg.* 825, *pg.* 565
MEATKUTTER - Band Saw Blades - THE L.S. STARRETT COMPANY; *pg.* 1421, *pg.* 783
MEATNEWS.COM - Electronic Newsletter - WATT PUBLISHING COMPANY; *pg.* 1701, *pg.* 655
MEATSHURE - Nutrition & Food Product - BALCHEM CORPORATION; *pg.* 839, *pg.* 1183
MEATY BONE - Pet Food - BIG HEART PET BRANDS; *pg.* 1474, *pg.* 213
MEATY CHEESY BOYS - Fictional Singing Sensations - JACK IN THE BOX INC.; *pg.* 1732, *pg.* 204
MEC-O-MATIC - Pump Product - IDEX CORPORATION; *pg.* 1347, *pg.* 623
MECADOX - Animal Health Product - PHIBROCHEM; *pg.* 1177, *pg.* 1124
MECHANIC - Apparel - OAKLEY, INC.; *pg.* 1840, *pg.* 86
MECHANICA - Mechanical Pencils - PENTEL OF AMERICA, LTD.; *pg.* 453, *pg.* 295
MECHANICAL DESKTOP - Software - AUTODESK INC.; *pg.* 356, *pg.* 257
MECHANICAL INTERFACE - Software System - MENTOR GRAPHICS CORPORATION; *pg.* 432, *pg.* 1510
MECHANICAL-T - Hole Cutting Tool - VICTAULIC COMPANY; *pg.* 1066, *pg.* 1529
MECHANICAL TECHNOLOGY - Micro Fuel Cells Technology - MECHANICAL TECHNOLOGY, INCORPORATED; *pg.* 1422, *pg.* 1137
MECHDIRECT - Banking Service - MECHANICS BANK; *pg.* 781, *pg.* 193
MECOMEC - Turf Product - PBI/GORDON CORPORATION; *pg.* 1176, *pg.* 985
MECOREF - Robotic Product - HAMILTON CO., INC.; *pg.* 1415, *pg.* 1031
MECOTRODE - Robotic Product - HAMILTON CO., INC.; *pg.* 1415, *pg.* 1031
MECTHENE - Solvent - THE DOW CHEMICAL COMPANY; *pg.* 1157, *pg.* 898
MED - Debug Technology - IMAGINATION TECHNOLOGIES; *pg.* 412, *pg.* 285
MED-CHECK - Pillow - MEDLINE INDUSTRIES, INC.; *pg.* 1562, *pg.* 635
MED ONE - Recreation Vehicle - WINNEBAGO INDUSTRIES, INC.; *pg.* 1712, *pg.* 707
MED-STAPH - Pharmaceutical Product - ALERE INC.; *pg.* 1488, *pg.* 849
MED-STREP - Pharmaceutical Product - ALERE INC.; *pg.* 1488, *pg.* 849
MEDAL OF HONOR - Video Game - ELECTRONIC ARTS INC.; *pg.* 951, *pg.* 189
MEDAL OF HONOR HEROES - Video Game - ELECTRONIC ARTS INC.; *pg.* 951, *pg.* 189
MEDALIST - In-Circuit Test System - AGILENT TECHNOLOGIES, INC.; *pg.* 614, *pg.* 264
MEDALIST - Contact Lens - BAUSCH & LOMB INCORPORATED; *pg.* 1401, *pg.* 1045
MEDALIST - Table - BLATT BOWLING & BILLIARD CORP.; *pg.* 1827, *pg.* 1203
MEDALIST - Hot Air Balloon - CAMERON BALLOONS U.S.; *pg.* 1829, *pg.* 884
MEDALIST - Paper Folder - THE CHALLENGE MACHINERY COMPANY; *pg.* 1322, *pg.* 902
MEDALIST - Photographic Paper, Cameras & Projectors - EASTMAN KODAK COMPANY; *pg.* 1408, *pg.* 1333
MEDALIST - Tires - MICHELIN NORTH AMERICA INC.; *pg.* 1886, *pg.* 1618
MEDALIST SST - Wiring Devices - PASS & SEYMOUR/LEGRAND; *pg.* 1303, *pg.* 1344
MEDALLION - Visual System - CAE INC.; *pg.* 226, *pg.* 1959
MEDALLION - Frequent Flyer Program - DELTA AIR LINES, INC.; *pg.* 1905, *pg.* 503
MEDALLION - Seating Product - HUSSEY SEATING CO.; *pg.* 929, *pg.* 751
MEDALLION - Furniture - JASPER GROUP; *pg.* 930, *pg.* 691
MEDALLION - Food Product - MAPLE LEAF FOODS INC.; *pg.* 875, *pg.* 1927
MEDALLION - Antenna Product - PCTEL, INC.; *pg.* 452, *pg.* 557
MEDALLION FOODS, INC. - Food Products - CONAGRA FOODS; *pg.* 826, *pg.* 994
MEDALLION-S - Image Generator - CAE INC.; *pg.* 226, *pg.* 1959
MEDALLIONS - Fabric - NEMSCHOFF, INC.; *pg.* 936, *pg.* 1890
MEDALLIONS - Ceramic, Glass, Stone Tiles & Slabs - WALKER & ZANGER, INC.; *pg.* 119, *pg.* 281
MEDASSETS NET REVENUE SYSTEMS - Computer Software - MEDASSETS INC.; *pg.* 1561, *pg.* 484
MEDCAROUSEL - Automated Storage System - MCKESSON CORPORATION; *pg.* 1560, *pg.* 222
MEDCHECK - Bill Review & Reimbursement Provider - CORVEL CORPORATION; *pg.* 1198, *pg.* 109
MEDCHECK SELECT - Hospital, Line Item Bill Review - CORVEL CORPORATION; *pg.* 1198, *pg.* 109
MEDCO MEDICARE PRESCRIPTION PLAN - Prescription Plan - EXPRESS SCRIPTS; *pg.* 1530, *pg.* 1070
MEDCYT - Medical Product - HOLOGIC, INC.; *pg.* 1416, *pg.* 784
MEDEC DENTAL COMMUNICATIONS - Dental Publications - TRUVEN HEALTH ANALYTICS; *pg.* 1696, *pg.* 867
MEDECO - Key Lock - FIRE KING SECURITY GROUP; *pg.* 1336, *pg.* 696
MEDEX - Electronic Healthcare Document - BOTTOMLINE TECHNOLOGIES (DE), INC.; *pg.* 727, *pg.* 1038
MEDEX - Software - BOTTOMLINE TECHNOLOGIES INC.; *pg.* 363, *pg.* 483
MEDFIX - Medical Product - MEDLINE INDUSTRIES, INC.; *pg.* 1562, *pg.* 635
MEDFLEX - Medical Device - MENTOR CORPORATION; *pg.* 1565, *pg.* 263
MEDFORD - Furniture - ASHLEY FURNITURE INDUSTRIES, INC.; *pg.* 914, *pg.* 1852
MEDFORD - Footwear - EASTLAND SHOE CORPORATION; *pg.* 1808, *pg.* 750
MEDFORD'S - Meat Products - HATFIELD QUALITY MEATS, INC.; *pg.* 861, *pg.* 1537
MEDFORMATION - Healthcare Product - ALLINA HEALTH SYSTEM, INC.; *pg.* 1491, *pg.* 929
MEDFORMS - Electronic Healthcare Document - BOTTOMLINE TECHNOLOGIES (DE), INC.; *pg.* 727, *pg.* 1038
MEDFORMS - Software - BOTTOMLINE TECHNOLOGIES INC.; *pg.* 363, *pg.* 483
MEDGENMED.COM - Online Medical Journal - WEBMD HEALTH CORPORATION; *pg.* 1288, *pg.* 1313
MEDGLIDER - Medication Reminders - MEDPORT, LLC; *pg.* 1563, *pg.* 1607
MEDGUARD - Patient Safety System - OMNICELL INC.; *pg.* 1578, *pg.* 161
MEDI-COIL - Mattress - THERAPEDIC ASSOCIATES, INC.; *pg.* 945, *pg.* 1112
MEDI-FRIDGE - Healthcare Product - MEDICOOL, INC.; *pg.* 1562, *pg.* 294
MEDI-PRO/MP - X-Ray Film Processor - IMAGEWORKS; *pg.* 1544, *pg.* 1158
MEDI-STAT - Spray on Bandage that Stops Bleeding - MUELLER SPORTS MEDICINE, INC.; *pg.* 1570, *pg.* 1887
MEDI-STRIPS - Adhesive - ALIMED, INC.; *pg.* 1490, *pg.* 816
MEDI-WRAP - CSR Wrap - MEDLINE INDUSTRIES, INC.; *pg.* 1562, *pg.* 635
MEDIA ARRAY LP - Storage Sub System - AVID TECHNOLOGY, INC.; *pg.* 622, *pg.* 804
MEDIA ARRAY XT - Storage Sub System - AVID TECHNOLOGY, INC.; *pg.* 622, *pg.* 804
MEDIA CENTER - Personal Computer - HEWLETT-PACKARD COMPANY; *pg.* 404, *pg.* 175
MEDIA GATEWAY - Wireline Solutions - SONUS NETWORKS INC.; *pg.* 1281, *pg.* 858
MEDIA GENERAL - Corporate Brand - MEDIA GENERAL,

INC.; *pg.* 297, *pg.* 1803
MEDIA MAIL - Postal Services - UNITED STATES POSTAL SERVICE; *pg.* 1009, *pg.* 406
MEDIA MATE - Computer Products - ESSELTE BUSINESS CORP; *pg.* 395, *pg.* 1179
MEDIA MATRIX - Computerized Sound Systems - PEAVEY ELECTRONICS CORPORATION; *pg.* 662, *pg.* 970
MEDIA NET - Cellular Phone Internet Service - AT&T MOBILITY LLC; *pg.* 619, *pg.* 488
MEDIA PROFESSIONAL - Software - NIELSEN AUDIO; *pg.* 446, *pg.* 768
MEDIA PROFESSIONAL PLUS - Software - NIELSEN AUDIO; *pg.* 446, *pg.* 768
MEDIA TRANSCODING - Wireline Solutions - SONUS NETWORKS INC.; *pg.* 1281, *pg.* 858
MEDIA+ - Software - BSQUARE CORPORATION; *pg.* 366, *pg.* 1813
MEDIABISTRO.COM - Online Network - MEDIABISTRO, INC.; *pg.* 1266, *pg.* 1258
MEDIACARE - Outsourced Solution - IRON MOUNTAIN INCORPORATED; *pg.* 421, *pg.* 796
MEDIACIPHER - Telecommunication Signal - MOTOROLA SOLUTIONS, INC.; *pg.* 657, *pg.* 659
MEDIACLIENT - Digital Video System - SEACHANGE INTERNATIONAL, INC.; *pg.* 1279, *pg.* 781
MEDIACLOCK - Clock & Buffer Product - CYPRESS SEMICONDUCTOR CORPORATION; *pg.* 1326, *pg.* 243
MEDIACLUSTER - Digital Video System - SEACHANGE INTERNATIONAL, INC.; *pg.* 1279, *pg.* 781
MEDIADIRECT - Software - TELLABS, INC.; *pg.* 678, *pg.* 637
MEDIADOCK 2+ - Removable Drive Solution - AVID TECHNOLOGY, INC.; *pg.* 622, *pg.* 804
MEDIADRIVE RS 320/RVD - Fixed Drive - AVID TECHNOLOGY, INC.; *pg.* 622, *pg.* 804
MEDIADRIVE RS FIREWIRE - Fixed Drive - AVID TECHNOLOGY, INC.; *pg.* 622, *pg.* 804
MEDIADSP - Graphics Card - ADVANCED MICRO DEVICES, INC.; *pg.* 613, *pg.* 282
MEDIAHAWK - Server - CONCURRENT COMPUTER CORPORATION; *pg.* 379, *pg.* 531
MEDIAKAP - Filtration System - SPECTRUM LABORATORIES INC.; *pg.* 1595, *pg.* 69
MEDIALIBRARY - Digital Video System - SEACHANGE INTERNATIONAL, INC.; *pg.* 1279, *pg.* 781
MEDIAMANAGER - Software - CRESTRON ELECTRONICS INC.; *pg.* 631, *pg.* 1116
MEDIAMARKER - Software - CRESTRON ELECTRONICS INC.; *pg.* 631, *pg.* 1116
MEDIAMASTER - Reporting Tool - NIELSEN AUDIO; *pg.* 446, *pg.* 768
MEDIAMATE - Multimedia Speaker - BOSE CORPORATION; *pg.* 626, *pg.* 820
MEDIAMVP - Digital Video Product - HAUPPAUGE DIGITAL, INC.; *pg.* 402, *pg.* 1164
MEDIANODE - Digital Video Product - HARMONIC, INC.; *pg.* 402, *pg.* 246
MEDIAPIK - Software - PURAFIL, INC.; *pg.* 333, *pg.* 530
MEDIAPLAN - Content Management - WEGENER CORPORATION; *pg.* 687, *pg.* 533
MEDIAPRINTS - Cable Data Set - PITNEY BOWES SOFTWARE INC.; *pg.* 455, *pg.* 1346
MEDIAPUBLISHER - Digital Video System - SEACHANGE INTERNATIONAL, INC.; *pg.* 1279, *pg.* 781
MEDIARRAY II - Fibre Channel Array - AVID TECHNOLOGY, INC.; *pg.* 622, *pg.* 804
MEDIA:SCAPE - Office Furniture - STEELCASE INC.; *pg.* 475, *pg.* 889
MEDIASHIELD - Storage System - NVIDIA CORPORATION; *pg.* 447, *pg.* 268
MEDIASHIELD - Tape Drive - QUANTUM CORPORATION; *pg.* 458, *pg.* 250
MEDIASITE - Media Publishing System - SONIC FOUNDRY, INC.; *pg.* 472, *pg.* 1867
MEDIASQUEEZE - Software - NVIDIA CORPORATION; *pg.* 447, *pg.* 268
MEDIASTOR - Software - EMC CORPORATION; *pg.* 391, *pg.* 825
MEDIATION CENTRAL - Software - EVOLVING SYSTEMS, INC.; *pg.* 395, *pg.* 326
MEDIATLAS - Newspaper - PR NEWSWIRE ASSOCIATION LLC; *pg.* 1678, *pg.* 1283
MEDIATONE - Security Components - CISCO SYSTEMS, INC.; *pg.* 372, *pg.* 240
MEDIATONE - Software - WEBEX COMMUNICATIONS, INC.; *pg.* 491, *pg.* 270
MEDIATWIST - Wire & Cable Products - BELDEN, INC.; *pg.* 624, *pg.* 993
MEDIAVAULT - Lockable Data Storage Chest - FIRE KING SECURITY GROUP; *pg.* 1336, *pg.* 696
MEDIC-AIR - Medical & Aesthetic Product - DYNATRONICS CORPORATION; *pg.* 1526, *pg.* 1757
MEDIC-AIR CERVIICAL SLEEP PILLO - Cushion Pillow - DYNATRONICS CORPORATION; *pg.* 1526, *pg.* 1757
MEDIC-AIR INFLATABLE BACK PILLO - Cushion Pillow - DYNATRONICS CORPORATION; *pg.* 1526, *pg.* 1757
MEDIC-AIR INFLATABLE LUMBAR ROLL PILLO - Cushion Pillow - DYNATRONICS CORPORATION; *pg.* 1526, *pg.* 1757
MEDICA ACCESSABILITY SOLUTION - Health Plan & Publication - MEDICA, INC.; *pg.* 1208, *pg.* 949
MEDICA ADVANTAGE SOLUTION - Health Plan & Publication - MEDICA, INC.; *pg.* 1208, *pg.* 949
MEDICA BASICS - Health Plan & Publication - MEDICA, INC.; *pg.* 1208, *pg.* 949
MEDICA BEHAVIORAL HEALTH - Health Plan & Publication - MEDICA, INC.; *pg.* 1208, *pg.* 949
MEDICA CALL LINK - Health Plan & Publication - MEDICA, INC.; *pg.* 1208, *pg.* 949
MEDICA CHOICE - Health Plan & Publication - MEDICA, INC.; *pg.* 1208, *pg.* 949
MEDICA CHOICE CARE - Health Plan & Publication - MEDICA, INC.; *pg.* 1208, *pg.* 949
MEDICA COMPLETE SOLUTION - Health Plan & Publication - MEDICA, INC.; *pg.* 1208, *pg.* 949
MEDICA CONNECTIONS - Health Plan & Publication - MEDICA, INC.; *pg.* 1208, *pg.* 949
MEDICA DENTALCARE - Health Plan & Publication - MEDICA, INC.; *pg.* 1208, *pg.* 949
MEDICA DENTALCHOICE - Health Plan & Publication - MEDICA, INC.; *pg.* 1208, *pg.* 949
MEDICA DIRECT - Health Plan & Publication - MEDICA, INC.; *pg.* 1208, *pg.* 949
MEDICA DIRECT DENTAL - Health Plan & Publication - MEDICA, INC.; *pg.* 1208, *pg.* 949
MEDICA DIRECT FOR INDIVIDUALS - Health Plan & Publication - MEDICA, INC.; *pg.* 1208, *pg.* 949
MEDICA DIRECT HSA FOR INDIVIDUALS - Health Plan & Publication - MEDICA, INC.; *pg.* 1208, *pg.* 949
MEDICA DIRECT SHORT-TERM FOR INDIVIDUALS - Health Plan & Publication - MEDICA, INC.; *pg.* 1208, *pg.* 949
MEDICA DIRECT VALUE FOR INDIVIDUALS - Health Plan & Publication - MEDICA, INC.; *pg.* 1208, *pg.* 949
MEDICA DUAL SOLUTION - Health Plan & Publication - MEDICA, INC.; *pg.* 1208, *pg.* 949
MEDICA ELECT - Health Plan & Publication - MEDICA, INC.; *pg.* 1208, *pg.* 949
MEDICA ELITE SOLUTION - Health Plan & Publication - MEDICA, INC.; *pg.* 1208, *pg.* 949
MEDICA ENCORE - Health Plan & Publication - MEDICA, INC.; *pg.* 1208, *pg.* 949
MEDICA ESSENTIAL - Health Plan & Publication - MEDICA, INC.; *pg.* 1208, *pg.* 949
MEDICA FIT STEPS - Health Plan & Publication - MEDICA, INC.; *pg.* 1208, *pg.* 949
MEDICA FOCUS - Health Plan & Publication - MEDICA, INC.; *pg.* 1208, *pg.* 949
MEDICA GROUP ADVANTAGE SOLUTION - Health Plan & Publication - MEDICA, INC.; *pg.* 1208, *pg.* 949
MEDICA GROUP PRIME SOLUTION - Health Plan & Publication - MEDICA, INC.; *pg.* 1208, *pg.* 949
MEDICA GROUP SELECT SOLUTION - Health Plan & Publication - MEDICA, INC.; *pg.* 1208, *pg.* 949
MEDICA INDICATORS - Health Plan & Publication - MEDICA, INC.; *pg.* 1208, *pg.* 949
MEDICA LINK - Health Plan & Publication - MEDICA, INC.; *pg.* 1208, *pg.* 949
MEDICA MEDICARE SOLUTIONS - Health Plan & Publication - MEDICA, INC.; *pg.* 1208, *pg.* 949
MEDICA PRIME SOLUTION - Health Plan & Publication - MEDICA, INC.; *pg.* 1208, *pg.* 949
MEDICA SELECT SOLUTION - Health Plan & Publication - MEDICA, INC.; *pg.* 1208, *pg.* 949
MEDICA SELECTCARE - Health Plan & Publication - MEDICA, INC.; *pg.* 1208, *pg.* 949
MEDICA SENIORCARE - Health Plan & Publication - MEDICA, INC.; *pg.* 1208, *pg.* 949
MEDICA SENIORDENTAL - Health Plan & Publication - MEDICA, INC.; *pg.* 1208, *pg.* 949
MEDICA SOLO - Health Plan & Publication - MEDICA, INC.; *pg.* 1208, *pg.* 949
MEDICAINE - Topical Pain & Itch Relief - JAMES ALEXANDER CORPORATION; *pg.* 1461, *pg.* 1044
MEDICAL ASSURANCE - Liability Insurance for Physicians, Hospitals & Dentists - PROASSURANCE CORPORATION; *pg.* 1214, *pg.* 3
MEDICAL DECISION POINT - Healthcare Publication - LEBHAR-FRIEDMAN INC.; *pg.* 1658, *pg.* 1250
MEDICAL DESIGN TECHNOLOGY - Trade Magazine - ADVANTAGE BUSINESS MEDIA; *pg.* 1613, *pg.* 1116
MEDICAL DEVICES LAW & INDUSTRY REPORT - Publisher - BLOOMBERG BNA; *pg.* 1621, *pg.* 1772
MEDICAL ECONOMICS - Business Publication Magazine - TRUVEN HEALTH ANALYTICS; *pg.* 1696, *pg.* 867
MEDICAL ECONOMICS-OBGYN EDITION - Business Publication - TRUVEN HEALTH ANALYTICS; *pg.* 1696, *pg.* 867
MEDICAL ECONOMICS-PEDIATRICS EDITION - Business Publication - TRUVEN HEALTH ANALYTICS; *pg.* 1696, *pg.* 867
MEDICALDOCTOR - Staffing Services - CROSS COUNTRY HEALTHCARE, INC.; *pg.* 1520, *pg.* 411
MEDICATOR - Baby Care Product - MUNCHKIN, INC.; *pg.* 964, *pg.* 300
MEDICHOICE - Medical & Surgical Supplies - OWENS & MINOR, INC.; *pg.* 1579, *pg.* 1795
MEDICINE MAN - Beverage - MONSTER BEVERAGE CORPORATION; *pg.* 257, *pg.* 69
THE MEDICINE SHOPPE - Professional Pharmacies - MEDICINE SHOPPE INTERNATIONAL, INC.; *pg.* 1561, *pg.* 976
MEDICINENET.COM - Health Information Web Site - WEBMD HEALTH CORPORATION; *pg.* 1288, *pg.* 1313
MEDICLAIM - Software - AUTONOMY, INC.; *pg.* 358, *pg.* 212
MEDICOE - Software - MEDIWARE INFORMATION SYSTEMS, INC.; *pg.* 431, *pg.* 716
MEDICOETM - Software - MEDIWARE INFORMATION SYSTEMS, INC.; *pg.* 431, *pg.* 716
MEDICOOLER - Healthcare Product - MEDICOOL, INC.; *pg.* 1562, *pg.* 294
MEDICOPASTE - Healthcare Product - GF HEALTH PRODUCTS, INC.; *pg.* 1535, *pg.* 508
MEDIDATA CRO CONTRACTOR - Medical Software - MEDIDATA SOLUTIONS, INC.; *pg.* 431, *pg.* 1258
MEDIDATA DESIGNER - Medical Software - MEDIDATA SOLUTIONS, INC.; *pg.* 431, *pg.* 1258
MEDIDATA GRANTS MANAGER - Medical Software - MEDIDATA SOLUTIONS, INC.; *pg.* 431, *pg.* 1258
MEDIDATA RAVE - Medical Software - MEDIDATA SOLUTIONS, INC.; *pg.* 431, *pg.* 1258
MEDIEVAL TIMES - Theme Restaurants - MEDIEVAL TIMES INC.; *pg.* 561, *pg.* 51
MEDIFAST - Powder Diet Supplement & Bars - MEDIFAST, INC.; *pg.* 1562, *pg.* 774
MEDIHONEY - Wound Care Product - DERMA SCIENCES, INC.; *pg.* 1523, *pg.* 1111
MEDIMAR - Software - MEDIWARE INFORMATION SYSTEMS, INC.; *pg.* 431, *pg.* 716
MEDIMARTM - Software - MEDIWARE INFORMATION SYSTEMS, INC.; *pg.* 431, *pg.* 716
MEDINA - Fan - CRAFTMADE INTERNATIONAL, INC.; *pg.* 1295, *pg.* 1670
MEDINA - Actuator - PRECISION VALVE CORPORATION; *pg.* 1060, *pg.* 1357
MEDINTECH - Wood Flooring Product - ARMSTRONG WORLD INDUSTRIES, INC.; *pg.* 914, *pg.* 1545
MEDIPORE - Dressing Cover - 3M COMPANY; *pg.* 1142, *pg.* 956
MEDIPURE - Filter Cones & Cartridges - HMI INDUSTRIES INC.; *pg.* 56, *pg.* 1475
MEDISOFT - Fabric - POLYMER GROUP, INC.; *pg.* 698, *pg.* 1368
MEDISTYP - Styptic Powder - PETEDGE; *pg.* 1481, *pg.* 787
MEDITATIONS - Carpet - INTERFACE, INC.; *pg.* 695, *pg.* 512
MEDITECH - Software - MEDICAL INFORMATION TECHNOLOGY, INC.; *pg.* 431, *pg.* 859
MEDITERRANEAN - Fragrance - ELIZABETH ARDEN, INC.; *pg.* 507, *pg.* 448
MEDIUM - Fabric - NEMSCHOFF, INC.; *pg.* 936, *pg.* 1890
MEDIUM GRIPPER - Bath Organizer & Accessory - HOME PRODUCTS INTERNATIONAL, INC.; *pg.* 1125, *pg.* 577
MEDLEY - Cryogenic Product - CHART INDUSTRIES, INC.; *pg.* 1405, *pg.* 1454

MEDLEY - Fabric - NEMSCHOFF, INC.; *pg.* 936, *pg.* 1890
MEDLING - Handbag - ALDO GROUP; *pg.* 1804, *pg.* 1959
MEDLINK - Mobile Healthcare - POLYCOM, INC.; *pg.* 664, *pg.* 249
MEDLL - Multipath Estimation Delay Lockloop - NOVATEL INC.; *pg.* 1424, *pg.* 1904
MEDLOCKER - Storage System - MTS MEDICATION TECHNOLOGIES, INC.; *pg.* 442, *pg.* 463
MEDMINED - Infection Surveillance Service - CARDINAL HEALTH, INC.; *pg.* 1512, *pg.* 1448
MEDNET - Software - HOSPIRA, INC.; *pg.* 1542, *pg.* 623
MEDO - Air Fresheners - SHELL LUBRICANTS; *pg.* 217, *pg.* 1714
MEDO-GOLD - Flavour - CARGILL LIMITED; *pg.* 1475, *pg.* 1914
MEDONCOLOGY - Software - VARIAN MEDICAL SYSTEMS, INC.; *pg.* 1434, *pg.* 178
MEDORA - Faucets - MOEN INCORPORATED; *pg.* 1056, *pg.* 1468
MEDPAQ - Software - TRADEPAQ CORPORATION; *pg.* 1284, *pg.* 1304
MEDPOINT - Patient Safety System - AMERISOURCEBERGEN CORPORATION; *pg.* 1493, *pg.* 1522
MEDRAD VISTRON CT - Injection System - MEDRAD, INC.; *pg.* 1563, *pg.* 1591
MEDROL - Medicine - PFIZER INC.; *pg.* 1581, *pg.* 1278
MEDSCAPE.COM - Physicians & Other Healthcare Professionals Web Site - WEBMD HEALTH CORPORATION; *pg.* 1288, *pg.* 1313
MEDSTAFF - Staffing Services - CROSS COUNTRY HEALTHCARE, INC.; *pg.* 1520, *pg.* 411
MEDSTAR - Coupler - ALLIED HEALTHCARE PRODUCTS, INC.; *pg.* 1491, *pg.* 990
MEDSTAR - Felt Products - AMERICAN FELT & FILTER COMPANY; *pg.* 1312, *pg.* 1184
MEDSTAT - Healthcare Publications - THOMSON REUTERS CORPORATION; *pg.* 1693, *pg.* 1944
MEDSTORM - Medication Software - AMERISOURCEBERGEN CORPORATION; *pg.* 1493, *pg.* 1522
MEDTEC - Truck Product - OSHKOSH CORPORATION; *pg.* 187, *pg.* 1885
MEDTRACK - Treadmill - CARDIAC SCIENCE CORPORATION; *pg.* 1512, *pg.* 1897
MEDTRONIC CARDIOVASCULAR ALLIANCE - Marketing Program - MEDTRONIC, INC.; *pg.* 1564, *pg.* 939
MEDTRONIC FIRST ALLIANCE - Program - MEDTRONIC, INC.; *pg.* 1564, *pg.* 939
MEDTRONIC HALL - Prosthetic Heart Valve - MEDTRONIC, INC.; *pg.* 1564, *pg.* 939
MEDTRONIC KAPPA - Pacemaker - MEDTRONIC, INC.; *pg.* 1564, *pg.* 939
MEDTRONIC MOSAIC - Prosthetic Heart Valve - MEDTRONIC, INC.; *pg.* 1564, *pg.* 939
MEDTRONIC NEURO - Pulse Generators & Accessories - MEDTRONIC, INC.; *pg.* 1564, *pg.* 939
MEDTRONIC PREFERRED ALLIANCE - Program - MEDTRONIC, INC.; *pg.* 1564, *pg.* 939
MEDUSA BOB - Apparel - OAKLEY, INC.; *pg.* 1840, *pg.* 86
MEDWIRE - Medical Wire - SIGMUND COHN CORP.; *pg.* 1062, *pg.* 1183
MEE TU - Bottled Food Product - ALLIED OLD ENGLISH, INC.; *pg.* 836, *pg.* 1110
MEET FOR THE CURE - Event - UNITED STATES BOWLING CONGRESS; *pg.* 159, *pg.* 1660
MEET YOU AT THE TOSTITOS - Tag Line - FRITO-LAY NORTH AMERICA, INC.; *pg.* 1853, *pg.* 1730
MEETING ADVANTAGE - Workshop - FRANKLIN COVEY CO.; *pg.* 1642, *pg.* 1758
MEETING CENTER - Software - WEBEX COMMUNICATIONS, INC.; *pg.* 491, *pg.* 270
MEETING TRAVELER - Magazine - BONNIER CORPORATION; *pg.* 1622, *pg.* 480
MEETINGMANGER - Software - AMX CORPORATION; *pg.* 349, *pg.* 1735
MEETINGPLACE - Web Conferencing Server - CISCO SYSTEMS, INC.; *pg.* 372, *pg.* 240
MEETINGRIGHT - Manual - XEROX CORPORATION; *pg.* 494, *pg.* 365
MEG - Clothing - ABERCROMBIE & FITCH CO.; *pg.* 37, *pg.* 1466
MEG - Furniture - AMISCO INDUSTRIES LTD.; *pg.* 913, *pg.* 1958
MEG - Dispensing Gun - NORDSON CORPORATION; *pg.* 1365, *pg.* 1480
MEGA - Fluid Handling System - GRACO, INC.; *pg.* 1342, *pg.* 935
MEGA - Black Plate Chemistry - HURST CHEMICAL COMPANY; *pg.* 1168, *pg.* 174
MEGA - Fuse Battery - LITTELFUSE, INC.; *pg.* 1301, *pg.* 580
MEGA - Filter Housing - PALL CORPORATION; *pg.* 232, *pg.* 1323
MEGA 97.9 FM - Radio Station - SPANISH BROADCASTING SYSTEM INC.; *pg.* 310, *pg.* 446
MEGA BITE - Cookie - COOKIE TREE BAKERIES; *pg.* 1851, *pg.* 1756
MEGA BLUE - Automotive Reconditioning Product - MOC PRODUCTS COMPANY, INC.; *pg.* 332, *pg.* 174
MEGA CASH - Game - MULTIMEDIA GAMES INC.; *pg.* 442, *pg.* 1664
MEGA CASH II - Lottery Game - KENTUCKY LOTTERY CORPORATION; *pg.* 996, *pg.* 735
MEGA-CHEL - Health Care Product - NATURE'S SUNSHINE PRODUCTS, INC.; *pg.* 1571, *pg.* 1754
MEGA CLA - Nutritional Supplement - NATURAL ORGANICS, INC.; *pg.* 1571, *pg.* 1181
MEGA-CYL - Cryogenic Product - CHART INDUSTRIES, INC.; *pg.* 1405, *pg.* 1454
MEGA FLAX - Vitamins - DESIGNING HEALTH, INC.; *pg.* 1523, *pg.* 299
MEGA-FLO - Melt-Rate Plate - GRACO, INC.; *pg.* 1342, *pg.* 935
MEGA-FORCE - Nutritional Supplement - NATURAL ORGANICS, INC.; *pg.* 1571, *pg.* 1181
MEGA FORTUNE - Game - FORTUNET, INC.; *pg.* 953, *pg.* 1024
MEGA-G - Diet-Aid Product - CCA INDUSTRIES, INC.; *pg.* 503, *pg.* 1114
MEGA GREEN - Pipe - ADVANCED DRAINAGE SYSTEMS, INC.; *pg.* 1878, *pg.* 1455
MEGA GRIP - Gaming Product - GLD PRODUCTS, INC.; *pg.* 1835, *pg.* 1882
MEGA HOT - Personal Care Electrical Product - HELEN OF TROY L.P.; *pg.* 511, *pg.* 1692
MEGA MANGO - Fruit Drink - JAMBA, INC.; *pg.* 1024, *pg.* 84
MEGA MART - Game - INTERNATIONAL GAME TECHNOLOGY; *pg.* 420, *pg.* 1606
MEGA MATCH - Lottery Game - THE SOUTH CAROLINA EDUCATION LOTTERY; *pg.* 1005, *pg.* 1614
MEGA MELTDOWN - Game - MULTIMEDIA GAMES INC.; *pg.* 442, *pg.* 1664
MEGA MEN - Nutritional Supplement - GENERAL NUTRITION CENTERS, INC.; *pg.* 1534, *pg.* 1575
MEGA MEXICO - Telephone Service - IDT CORPORATION; *pg.* 643, *pg.* 1096
MEGA MILE - Precure Products Retread System - OLIVER RUBBER COMPANY; *pg.* 1887, *pg.* 1358
MEGA MILLIONS - Lottery Game - ILLINOIS STATE LOTTERY; *pg.* 995, *pg.* 578
MEGA MILLIONS - Lottery Game - MASSACHUSETTS STATE LOTTERY; *pg.* 998, *pg.* 802
MEGA MILLIONS - Game - MICHIGAN STATE LOTTERY BUREAU; *pg.* 999, *pg.* 895
MEGA MILLIONS - Lottery Game - NEW YORK STATE LOTTERY; *pg.* 1001, *pg.* 1340
MEGA MILLIONS - Lottery - TEXAS LOTTERY COMMISSION; *pg.* 1007, *pg.* 1666
MEGA MONEY - Lottery Game - THE FLORIDA LOTTERY; *pg.* 992, *pg.* 469
MEGA MONOPOLY - Lottery Game - MINNESOTA STATE LOTTERY; *pg.* 999, *pg.* 956
MEGA MONOPOLY - Lottery Card - MISSOURI LOTTERY; *pg.* 999, *pg.* 979
MEGA MOUTH CANDY SPRAY - Candy - THE TOPPS COMPANY, INC.; *pg.* 588, *pg.* 1302
MEGA MULTIPLIER - Game - WMS INDUSTRIES INC.; *pg.* 593, *pg.* 666
MEGA MULTIPLIER 125X - Game - WMS INDUSTRIES INC.; *pg.* 593, *pg.* 666
MEGA PRO - Blenders - WARING PRODUCTS, INC.; *pg.* 62, *pg.* 379
MEGA-RAD - Power Semiconductor Device - INTERNATIONAL RECTIFIER CORPORATION; *pg.* 647, *pg.* 80
MEGA SLAM - Primary Impactor - STEDMAN MACHINE COMPANY; *pg.* 1379, *pg.* 673
MEGA SMARTIES - Sweet & Sour Candy Rolls - SMARTIES CANDY COMPANY; *pg.* 1861, *pg.* 1127
MEGA SOURCE - Pharmaceutical Product - ALERE INC.; *pg.* 1488, *pg.* 849
MEGA STINGER - Flashlight - STREAMLIGHT INC.; *pg.* 1306, *pg.* 1527
MEGA STRESS CAPSULES & TABLETS - B-Complex with 500 mg. Vitamin C - SCHIFF NUTRITION INTERNATIONAL, INC.; *pg.* 1592, *pg.* 1760
MEGA-T - Diet-Aid Product - CCA INDUSTRIES, INC.; *pg.* 503, *pg.* 1114
MEGA-T PLUS - Diet Supplement - CCA INDUSTRIES, INC.; *pg.* 503, *pg.* 1114
MEGAAVR - Integrated Circuit - ATMEL CORPORATION; *pg.* 621, *pg.* 238
MEGABASE - Computer Equipment - VIEWSONIC CORPORATION; *pg.* 489, *pg.* 303
MEGABAUD - Data Rates - MAXIM INTEGRATED PRODUCTS, INC.; *pg.* 653, *pg.* 247
MEGABINGO - Electronic Bingo Game - MULTIMEDIA GAMES INC.; *pg.* 442, *pg.* 1664
MEGABINGO SESSIONS - Game - MULTIMEDIA GAMES INC.; *pg.* 442, *pg.* 1664
MEGABRIGHT - Led - CREE INC.; *pg.* 631, *pg.* 1371
MEGABRIGHT PLUS - Semiconductor Product - CREE INC.; *pg.* 631, *pg.* 1371
MEGABUCKS - Game - INTERNATIONAL GAME TECHNOLOGY; *pg.* 957, *pg.* 1024
MEGABUCKS - Lottery Game - MASSACHUSETTS STATE LOTTERY; *pg.* 998, *pg.* 802
MEGACASH - Game - MULTIMEDIA GAMES INC.; *pg.* 442, *pg.* 1664
MEGACE - Health Care Product - BRISTOL-MYERS SQUIBB COMPANY; *pg.* 1509, *pg.* 1206
MEGACODE - Radio Frequency Components - NORTEK SECURITY & CONTROL LLC; *pg.* 659, *pg.* 59
MEGACORE - Software - ALTERA CORPORATION; *pg.* 348, *pg.* 237
MEGACYCLE - Battery - EXIDE TECHNOLOGIES; *pg.* 204, *pg.* 483
MEGADATA - Terminals; Intelligent, Non-Intelligent, Color, Graphics, Word Processing - PASSUR AEROSPACE, INC.; *pg.* 233, *pg.* 376
MEGAFIRE - Burner - MAXON CORPORATION; *pg.* 1359, *pg.* 695
MEGAFLON - Coating & Finish - NOV AMERON; *pg.* 100, *pg.* 187
MEGAFLON - Coating Product - PPG INDUSTRIES, INC.; *pg.* 1445, *pg.* 1579
MEGAFORCE I - Bait Casting Reels - DAIWA CORPORATION; *pg.* 1832, *pg.* 75
MEGAFUNCTION - Software System - MENTOR GRAPHICS CORPORATION; *pg.* 432, *pg.* 1510
MEGAHUB - High Capacity Telecommunications Switching System - ALCATEL-LUCENT USA, INC.; *pg.* 615, *pg.* 1728
MEGAJACKPOTS - Slot Machine - INTERNATIONAL GAME TECHNOLOGY; *pg.* 957, *pg.* 1024
MEGALINK - Business Service - AT&T SOUTHEAST; *pg.* 1868, *pg.* 489
MEGALITH - Chemical Product - HURST CHEMICAL COMPANY; *pg.* 1168, *pg.* 174
MEGALLELE - Custom Reagent Kit - AFFYMETRIX, INC.; *pg.* 1487, *pg.* 263
MEGALLOY - Dental Product - DENTSPLY INTERNATIONAL INC.; *pg.* 1522, *pg.* 1596
MEGALUSTER - Cosmetic Product - MERLE NORMAN COSMETICS, INC.; *pg.* 517, *pg.* 136
MEGAMACRO - Software System - MENTOR GRAPHICS CORPORATION; *pg.* 432, *pg.* 1510
MEGAMANIA - Game - MULTIMEDIA GAMES INC.; *pg.* 442, *pg.* 1664
MEGAMILLIONS BINGO - Game - MULTIMEDIA GAMES INC.; *pg.* 442, *pg.* 1664
MEGAMIX - Blender - WARING PRODUCTS, INC.; *pg.* 62, *pg.* 379
MEGAMOD - Power Converter - VICOR CORPORATION; *pg.* 1435, *pg.* 783
MEGAMONITOR - Computer Equipment - VIEWSONIC CORPORATION; *pg.* 489, *pg.* 303
MEGAN - Footwear - PHOENIX FOOTWEAR GROUP, INC.; *pg.* 1815, *pg.* 60
MEGANANZA - Game - MULTIMEDIA GAMES INC.; *pg.* 442, *pg.* 1664
MEGAPAC - Power Supply System - VICOR CORPORATION; *pg.* 1435, *pg.* 783
MEGAPICK - Game - MULTIMEDIA GAMES INC.; *pg.* 442, *pg.* 1664

MEGAPIXELCAM - Webcam Software - EARTHCAM, INC.; *pg.* 1239, *pg.* 1072
MEGAPLAST - Filter Equipment - PALL CORPORATION; *pg.* 232, *pg.* 1323
MEGAPLUG - Electronic Product - ACTIONTEC ELECTRONICS, INC.; *pg.* 342, *pg.* 282
MEGAPLUS - Image Sensing Cameras - EASTMAN KODAK COMPANY; *pg.* 1408, *pg.* 1333
MEGAPORT - Broadband System Equipment - BLONDER TONGUE LABORATORIES, INC.; *pg.* 625, *pg.* 1100
MEGAPOWER - Liquid Cleaners - FINE ORGANICS CORPORATION; *pg.* 330, *pg.* 1052
MEGAPRINT - Impact Printer Ribbon - NER HOLDINGS INC.; *pg.* 444, *pg.* 1071
MEGARAD - Polycarbonate Resins - THE DOW CHEMICAL COMPANY; *pg.* 1157, *pg.* 898
MEGARAID - Hard Disk Controls Circuits & Software - AVAGO TECHNOLOGIES; *pg.* 358, *pg.* 238
MEGARAID MANAGEMENT SUITE - Hard Disk Controls Circuits & Software - AVAGO TECHNOLOGIES; *pg.* 358, *pg.* 238
MEGARAID STORAGE MANAGER - Hard Disk Controls Circuits & Software - AVAGO TECHNOLOGIES; *pg.* 358, *pg.* 238
MEGARED - Nutritional Supplements - RECKITT BENCKISER INC.; *pg.* 1136, *pg.* 1105
MEGAREELS - Game - MULTIMEDIA GAMES INC.; *pg.* 442, *pg.* 1664
MEGASEAL - Coating Product - PPG INDUSTRIES, INC.; *pg.* 1445, *pg.* 1579
MEGASHOT - Animal Safety Product - NEOGEN CORPORATION; *pg.* 883, *pg.* 896
MEGASIM - Memory Card - SANDISK CORPORATION; *pg.* 465, *pg.* 147
MEGASKILL - Game - MULTIMEDIA GAMES INC.; *pg.* 442, *pg.* 1664
MEGASOFT - Softeners - HUNTSMAN CORPORATION; *pg.* 1167, *pg.* 1758
MEGASOLV NOC - Cleaning Product - PETROFERM INC.; *pg.* 1177, *pg.* 616
MEGASOURCE - Viewer - EASTMAN KODAK COMPANY; *pg.* 1408, *pg.* 1333
MEGASTIR - Drilling Product - SMITH INTERNATIONAL, INC.; *pg.* 1377, *pg.* 1715
MEGASWEEPS - Game - MULTIMEDIA GAMES INC.; *pg* 442, *pg.* 1664
MEGASYS - Total Gas Management Systems for the Electronic Industry - AIR PRODUCTS AND CHEMICALS, INC.; *pg.* 1145, *pg.* 1513
MEGATEL - Telephone Service - IDT CORPORATION; *pg.* 643, *pg.* 1096
MEGATHANE - Urethane Adhesive - MCNETT CORPORATION; *pg.* 1839, *pg.* 1817
MEGATHEATER - Electronics - CAMBRIDGE SOUNDWORKS, INC.; *pg.* 1234, *pg.* 781
MEGATONE - Toner - NER HOLDINGS INC.; *pg.* 444, *pg.* 1071
MEGATRIM CLA - Diet-Aid Product - CCA INDUSTRIES, INC.; *pg.* 503, *pg.* 1114
MEGAVAC - Cleaning Product - HILLYARD, INC.; *pg.* 331, *pg.* 990
MEGAVIEW - Healthcare Product - GF HEALTH PRODUCTS, INC.; *pg.* 1535, *pg.* 508
MEGAVIEW - CAMERAS - UNIVERSAL INSTRUMENTS CORPORATION; *pg.* 683, *pg.* 1154
MEGAWHEELS - Game - MULTIMEDIA GAMES INC.; *pg.* 442, *pg.* 1664
MEGAWORKS - Electronics - CAMBRIDGE SOUNDWORKS, INC.; *pg.* 1234, *pg.* 781
MEGGER - Electrical Insulation Testers - MEGGER INC.; *pg.* 1422, *pg.* 1557
MEGNAPEARL - Pigment - BASF CATALYSTS LLC; *pg.* 1148, *pg.* 1074
MEGOLITE - Refractory Product - RESCO PRODUCTS, INC.; *pg.* 107, *pg.* 1581
MEGUM - Adhesive & Sealant - DOW CHEMICAL; *pg.* 1156, *pg.* 1563
MEIDILAND - Garden Roses - THE CONARD-PYLE COMPANY; *pg.* 1794, *pg.* 1594
MEIGS - Ethernet Product - VITESSE SEMICONDUCTOR CORPORATION; *pg.* 686, *pg.* 57
MEIGS-II - Semiconductor Solution - VITESSE SEMICONDUCTOR CORPORATION; *pg.* 686, *pg.* 57
MEIGS-IIE - Semiconductor Solution - VITESSE SEMICONDUCTOR CORPORATION; *pg.* 686, *pg.* 57
MEIJER - Bakery Products - ALPHA BAKING COMPANY; *pg.* 836, *pg.* 564
MEIJIFF - Fragrance Ingredient - INTERNATIONAL FLAVORS & FRAGRANCES INC.; *pg.* 512, *pg.* 1244
MEILINK - Safes & Security Product - FIRE KING SECURITY GROUP; *pg.* 1336, *pg.* 696
MEISTERCHEF - Meat Product - KAYEM FOODS, INC.; *pg.* 867, *pg.* 814
MEISTERHAND - Medical Instrument - INTEGRA MILTEX, INC.; *pg.* 1546, *pg.* 1597
MEITE - Pharmaceutical Product - PURETEK CORPORATION; *pg.* 1587, *pg.* 211
MEKOR - Dispersing Agent - ASHLAND INC.; *pg.* 972, *pg.* 726
MEL-FRY - Shortening & Cooking Oil - VENTURA FOODS, LLC; *pg.* 908, *pg.* 49
MELAFIND - Medical Device - MELA SCIENCES, INC.; *pg.* 1422, *pg.* 1168
MELANGE - Tile - ARTISTIC TILE INC.; *pg.* 914, *pg.* 1119
MELANGE - Ceramic, Glass, Stone Tiles & Slabs - WALKER & ZANGER, INC.; *pg.* 119, *pg.* 281
MELANIE - Furniture - LA-Z-BOY INCORPORATED; *pg.* 932, *pg.* 901
MELARREST - Personal Care Material - BASF CATALYSTS LLC; *pg.* 1148, *pg.* 1074
MELATONEX - Health & Beauty Product - CHATTEM, INC.; *pg.* 1515, *pg.* 1628
MELATONIN PLUS - Nutritional Product - RBC LIFE SCIENCES, INC.; *pg.* 1588, *pg.* 1723
MELBOURNE - Footwear - P.W. MINOR & SON, INC.; *pg.* 1816, *pg.* 1140
MELCO - Seam Tape - MCNETT CORPORATION; *pg.* 1839, *pg.* 1817
MELINEX - Film - E.I. DU PONT DE NEMOURS & COMPANY; *pg.* 1159, *pg.* 390
MELINEX - Plastic Film - TEKRA CORPORATION; *pg.* 1184, *pg.* 1884
MELISSA - Footwear - PHOENIX FOOTWEAR GROUP, INC.; *pg.* 1815, *pg.* 60
MELLES GRIOT - Optical Designs & Electronic Shutters - CVI MELLES GRIOT; *pg.* 1407, *pg.* 59
MELLO - Beverages - THE COCA-COLA COMPANY; *pg.* 240, *pg.* 493
MELLO GOLD - Vegetable Oil - MALLET & COMPANY, INC.; *pg.* 875, *pg.* 1521
MELLO YELLO - Soft Drink - THE COCA-COLA COMPANY; *pg.* 240, *pg.* 493
MELLOW SUPREME - Vegetable Oil - MALLET & COMPANY, INC.; *pg.* 875, *pg.* 1521
MELLOWOOD - Kitchen Cabinets - KITCHEN KOMPACT, INC.; *pg.* 91, *pg.* 692
MELODIE - Fabric - NEMSCHOFF, INC.; *pg.* 936, *pg.* 1890
MELODIE - Fragrance - WESTROCK COMPANY; *pg.* 1472, *pg.* 1805
MELODY - Hardware - EVANS & SUTHERLAND COMPUTER CORPORATION; *pg.* 638, *pg.* 1757
MELODY - Dinnerware - THE HOMER LAUGHLIN CHINA COMPANY; *pg.* 1125, *pg.* 1850
MELODY - Furniture - NEMSCHOFF, INC.; *pg.* 936, *pg.* 1890
MELODY FARMS - Dairy - DEAN FOODS COMPANY; *pg.* 852, *pg.* 1679
MELOGRANO - Fabric - SCALAMANDRE, INC.; *pg.* 941, *pg.* 1058
MELON DELIGHT - Fruit Arrangements - EDIBLE ARRANGEMENTS INTERNATIONAL, INC.; *pg.* 1768, *pg.* 382
MELON OF TROY - Nail Care Product - OPI PRODUCTS INC.; *pg.* 518, *pg.* 167
MELONI CANNONAU - Italian Wine - LAIRD & COMPANY, INC.; *pg.* 1966, *pg.* 1119
MELROSE - Brick & Tile Product - CHEROKEE BRICK & TILE COMPANY; *pg.* 75, *pg.* 535
MELROSE - Furniture - JASPER GROUP; *pg.* 930, *pg.* 691
MELROSE STUDIO - Women's Coordinates - KELLWOOD COMPANY; *pg.* 28, *pg.* 975
MELT DOWN - Game - MULTIMEDIA GAMES INC.; *pg.* 442, *pg.* 1664
MELTCATOR - Glue & Adhesive - GLUEFAST COMPANY, INC.; *pg.* 1459, *pg.* 1090
MELTDOWN - Game - MULTIMEDIA GAMES INC.; *pg.* 442, *pg.* 1664
MELTDOWN CORE REACTION - Game - MULTIMEDIA GAMES INC.; *pg.* 442, *pg.* 1664
MELTMINDER - Computer Control & Maintenance System - INDUCTOTHERM CORP.; *pg.* 1348, *pg.* 1114
MELURAC - Chemical Product - CYTEC INDUSTRIES, INC.; *pg.* 1155, *pg.* 1131
MEM - Electrical Products - EATON CORPORATION; *pg.* 1331, *pg.* 1429
MEMBER POLO - Apparels - UNDER ARMOUR, INC.; *pg.* 49, *pg.* 759
MEMBERCONNECT WEB - Provides Internet-Based Home Banking & Commercial Cash Management - JACK HENRY & ASSOCIATES, INC.; *pg.* 422, *pg.* 988
MEMBERSHIP REWARDS - Incentive Program - AMERICAN EXPRESS COMPANY; *pg.* 712, *pg.* 1190
MEMBRA-CEL - Tubing - VISKASE COMPANIES, INC.; *pg.* 1471, *pg.* 599
MEMBRALOX - Filter Equipment - PALL CORPORATION; *pg.* 232, *pg.* 1323
MEMBRANES - Dental Implant System - LIFECORE BIOMEDICAL, LLC; *pg.* 1556, *pg.* 920
MEMBRELLE - Microporous Membranes for Medical Laboratory Electrophoresis Applications - PPG INDUSTRIES, INC.; *pg.* 1445, *pg.* 1579
MEMENTO - Personal Database - AT&T SOUTHEAST; *pg.* 1868, *pg.* 489
MEMENTO - Funeral Chests - BATESVILLE CASKET COMPANY, INC.; *pg.* 1393, *pg.* 673
MEMENTO - Fabric - NEMSCHOFF, INC.; *pg.* 936, *pg.* 1890
MEMERASE - Wallcovering - OMNOVA SOLUTIONS INC; *pg.* 1176, *pg.* 1453
MEMERASE II - Wallcovering - OMNOVA SOLUTIONS INC; *pg.* 1176, *pg.* 1453
MEMOIR - Operating System Software - AVAGO TECHNOLOGIES; *pg.* 358, *pg.* 238
MEMOIR COLLECTION - Frame - BROWN & BIGELOW, INC.; *pg.* 1624, *pg.* 959
MEMOIRS - Bath Product - KOHLER CO.; *pg.* 91, *pg.* 1862
MEMOR-X - Health Care Product - HEALTH PRODUCTS CORPORATION; *pg.* 1540, *pg.* 1356
MEMORASE - Eprom Eraser - UVP, INC.; *pg.* 1434, *pg.* 298
MEMOREX IWAKE - Clock Radio - IMATION CORP.; *pg.* 413, *pg.* 952
MEMORIALCARE - Healthcare Service - MEMORIAL HEALTH SERVICES INC.; *pg.* 1565, *pg.* 90
MEMORY - Toy & Game - HASBRO, INC.; *pg.* 954, *pg.* 1603
MEMORY ADVISOR - Hardware - MICRON TECHNOLOGY, INC.; *pg.* 435, *pg.* 547
MEMORY ARC - Pattern Control - RAIN BIRD CORPORATION; *pg.* 707, *pg.* 44
MEMORY BANK - Wallets & Clutch Bags - EASTMAN KODAK COMPANY; *pg.* 1408, *pg.* 1333
MEMORY BUILDER - Software System - MENTOR GRAPHICS CORPORATION; *pg.* 432, *pg.* 1510
MEMORY BUILDER CONDUCTOR - Software System - MENTOR GRAPHICS CORPORATION; *pg.* 432, *pg.* 1510
MEMORY BUILDER MOZART - Software System - MENTOR GRAPHICS CORPORATION; *pg.* 432, *pg.* 1510
MEMORY DESIGNER - Software System - MENTOR GRAPHICS CORPORATION; *pg.* 432, *pg.* 1510
THE MEMORY EXPERTS - Memory Product - MICRON TECHNOLOGY, INC.; *pg.* 435, *pg.* 547
MEMORY FIT PRESSURE - Baby Gate - EVENFLO COMPANY, INC.; *pg.* 924, *pg.* 1470
MEMORY FOEM CLASSIC - Pillows - SELECT COMFORT CORPORATION; *pg.* 942, *pg.* 942
MEMORY GARDEN - Table Wreath - 1-800-FLOWERS.COM, INC.; *pg.* 1758, *pg.* 1151
MEMORY MASTER - Memory Card - PNY TECHNOLOGIES, INC.; *pg.* 455, *pg.* 1105
MEMORY MODEL BUILDER - Software System - MENTOR GRAPHICS CORPORATION; *pg.* 432, *pg.* 1510
MEMORY ON DEMAND - Nutritional Supplement - PHARMAVITE LLC; *pg.* 1584, *pg.* 167
MEMORY PLUS - Medical & Aesthetic Product - DYNATRONICS CORPORATION; *pg.* 1526, *pg.* 1757
MEMORY STICK - Memory Card - LEXAR MEDIA, INC.; *pg.* 1262, *pg.* 146
MEMORY STICK DUO - Memory Card Device - SANDISK CORPORATION; *pg.* 465, *pg.* 147
MEMORY STICK PRO - Memory Card - SANDISK CORPORATION; *pg.* 465, *pg.* 147
MEMORY STICK PRO DUO - Memory Card - SANDISK CORPORATION; *pg.* 465, *pg.* 147
MEMORYBIST - Software System - MENTOR GRAPHICS CORPORATION; *pg.* 432, *pg.* 1510
MEMORYCALL - Call Feature - AT&T SOUTHEAST; *pg.* 1868, *pg.* 489
MEMORYGEL - Breast Implant - MENTOR CORPORATION;

pg. 1565, *pg.* 263
MEMORYTOUCH - Mattress - THERAPEDIC ASSOCIATES, INC.; *pg.* 945, *pg.* 1112
MEMPHIS - Dinnerware - THE HOMER LAUGHLIN CHINA COMPANY; *pg.* 1125, *pg.* 1850
MEMPHIS - Furniture - LA-Z-BOY INCORPORATED; *pg.* 932, *pg.* 901
MEMPHIS - Fabric - NEMSCHOFF, INC.; *pg.* 936, *pg.* 1890
MEMPHIS MOTORSPORTS PARK - Motor Racetrack - DOVER MOTORSPORTS, INC.; *pg.* 545, *pg.* 387
MEMPHIS PEABODY - Hotel - PEABODY HOTEL GROUP, INC.; *pg.* 1107, *pg.* 1645
MEMSCAN - Closed-Circuit Television Equipment - VICON INDUSTRIES, INC.; *pg.* 685, *pg.* 1166
MEMTREX - Pleated Membrane Filters - GE WATER & PROCESS TECHNOLOGIES; *pg.* 1339, *pg.* 1588
MEN OF INTEGRITY - Magazine - CHRISTIANITY TODAY INTERNATIONAL; *pg.* 1627, *pg.* 561
MENA - Fabric - NEMSCHOFF, INC.; *pg.* 936, *pg.* 1890
MENACE - Game - ACTIVISION BLIZZARD, INC.; *pg.* 948, *pg.* 271
MENAGE A TROIS - Beverage - TRINCHERO FAMILY ESTATES; *pg.* 1971, *pg.* 197
MENAGERIE - Carpet - INTERFACE, INC.; *pg.* 695, *pg.* 512
MENDAM - Furniture - ASHLEY FURNITURE INDUSTRIES, INC.; *pg.* 914, *pg.* 1852
MENEST - Pharmaceutical Product - KING PHARMACEUTICALS, INC.; *pg.* 1553, *pg.* 1627
MENLO PARK - Furniture - AMERICAN LEATHER LP; *pg.* 912, *pg.* 1673
MENLO WORLDWIDE - Logistic Service - XPO LOGISTICS, INC.; *pg.* 1931, *pg.* 350
MENNEN - Oil Soap - COLGATE-PALMOLIVE COMPANY; *pg.* 504, *pg.* 1215
MENO-HERBS - Herbal Preparation - AT LAST NATURALS, INC.; *pg.* 499, *pg.* 1347
MENOMUNE - Meningococcal Vaccine - SANOFI PASTEUR, INC; *pg.* 1591, *pg.* 1588
MENOPAUSE MULTIPLE - Vitamin & Herbal Supplement - SOURCE NATURALS; *pg.* 1595, *pg.* 278
MENOREST - Estradiol Transdermal System - NOVEN PHARMACEUTICALS, INC.; *pg.* 1576, *pg.* 445
MEN'S BERTUCCI - Watch - WOOLRICH, INC.; *pg.* 699, *pg.* 1595
MEN'S CHOICE - Body Wash - BLUE CROSS LABORATORIES; *pg.* 326, *pg.* 277
MEN'S COLLEGE CUP - Trademark (Div. I Men's Soccer) - NATIONAL COLLEGIATE ATHLETIC ASSOCIATION; *pg.* 567, *pg.* 688
MEN'S ELITE EIGHT - Trademark - NATIONAL COLLEGIATE ATHLETIC ASSOCIATION; *pg.* 567, *pg.* 688
MEN'S FINAL 4 - Trademark (Div. I Men's Basketball) - NATIONAL COLLEGIATE ATHLETIC ASSOCIATION; *pg.* 567, *pg.* 688
MEN'S FINAL FOUR - Trademark (Div. I Men's Basketball) - NATIONAL COLLEGIATE ATHLETIC ASSOCIATION; *pg.* 567, *pg.* 688
MEN'S FITNESS - Magazine - AMERICAN MEDIA, INC.; *pg.* 1615, *pg.* 410
MEN'S FROZEN FOUR - Trademark (Div. I Men's Ice Hockey) - NATIONAL COLLEGIATE ATHLETIC ASSOCIATION; *pg.* 567, *pg.* 688
MEN'S HEALTH - Magazine - RODALE, INC.; *pg.* 1681, *pg.* 1530
MEN'S JOURNAL - Magazine - WENNER MEDIA LLC; *pg.* 1701, *pg.* 1314
MEN'S NETWORK - Online Resource - INTERNATIONAL LUTHERAN LAYMEN'S LEAGUE; *pg.* 293, *pg.* 998
MEN'S SPORTSWEAR - Men's Apparel - PENDLETON WOOLEN MILLS, INC.; *pg.* 697, *pg.* 1505
MEN'S STOCK - Shaving Cream - AUBREY ORGANICS INC.; *pg.* 499, *pg.* 470
MEN'S VOGUE - Magazine - CONDE NAST PUBLICATIONS, INC.; *pg.* 1629, *pg.* 1217
MENSHEALTH.COM - Website - RODALE, INC.; *pg.* 1681, *pg.* 1530
MEN.STYLE.COM - Fashion Site - CONDE NAST DIGITAL; *pg.* 1237, *pg.* 1217
MEN.STYLE.COM - Magazine - CONDE NAST PUBLICATIONS, INC.; *pg.* 1629, *pg.* 1217
MENTA-FX - Natural Health Product - AFEXA LIFE SCIENCES INC.; *pg.* 1487, *pg.* 1905
MENTADENT - Toothpaste - CHURCH & DWIGHT CO., INC.; *pg.* 1153, *pg.* 1063
MENTAL EDGE - Vitamin & Herbal Supplement - SOURCE NATURALS; *pg.* 1595, *pg.* 278
MENTAT - Software - MSC SOFTWARE CORPORATION; *pg.* 441, *pg.* 262
MENTHOL H & R - Aroma Chemical - SYMRISE, INC.; *pg.* 1183, *pg.* 1125
MENTHOLATUM - Deep Heating Rub & Ointment - THE MENTHOLATUM COMPANY; *pg.* 1565, *pg.* 1320
MENTHOLATUM ARTHRITIS PATCH - Pain reliever - THE MENTHOLATUM COMPANY; *pg.* 1565, *pg.* 1320
MENTHOLATUM CHERRY CHEST RUB FOR KIDS - Pain reliever for kids - THE MENTHOLATUM COMPANY; *pg.* 1565, *pg.* 1320
MENTHOLATUM OINTMENT - Pain reliever rub - THE MENTHOLATUM COMPANY; *pg.* 1565, *pg.* 1320
MENTHOLATUM PAIN PATCH BRAND - External Analgesic - THE MENTHOLATUM COMPANY; *pg.* 1565, *pg.* 1320
MENTOR - Software System - MENTOR GRAPHICS CORPORATION; *pg.* 432, *pg.* 1510
MENTOR - Fabric - NEMSCHOFF, INC.; *pg.* 936, *pg.* 1890
MENU - Cheese - SCHREIBER FOODS, INC.; *pg.* 894, *pg.* 1859
MENUWALL - Electronic Display System - TRANS-LUX CORPORATION; *pg.* 681, *pg.* 365
MEOW MIX - Cat Food - BIG HEART PET BRANDS; *pg.* 1474, *pg.* 213
MEOW TOWN - Cat Furniture - PETEDGE; *pg.* 1481, *pg.* 787
MEP - Centralized Supply Contracts & Inventory Accounting & Maintenance Services - GRACO, INC.; *pg.* 1342, *pg.* 935
MEPAL - Medical Device - RESMED INC.; *pg.* 1589, *pg.* 207
MER - Beverages - THE COCA-COLA COMPANY; *pg.* 240, *pg.* 493
MERAK - Petroleum Economics - SCHLUMBERGER LIMITED; *pg.* 801, *pg.* 1714
MERAK FLOMATIC - Software - SCHLUMBERGER LIMITED; *pg.* 801, *pg.* 1714
MERANO - Furniture - ASHLEY FURNITURE INDUSTRIES, INC.; *pg.* 914, *pg.* 1852
MERCEDES - Furniture - ETHAN ALLEN INTERIORS INC.; *pg.* 924, *pg.* 343
MERCER - Watch - COACH, INC.; *pg.* 3, *pg.* 1214
MERCER - Jewelry - YURMAN DESIGN, INC.; *pg.* 15, *pg.* 1316
MERCER DELTA - Corporate Organizational Design & Change Management - MARSH & MCLENNAN COMPANIES INC.; *pg.* 1207, *pg.* 1256
MERCER HUMAN RESOURCE CONSULTING - Employee Benefits Services - MARSH & MCLENNAN COMPANIES INC.; *pg.* 1207, *pg.* 1256
MERCHANDISER - Light Fixtures - JUNO LIGHTING, INC.; *pg.* 1300, *pg.* 606
MERCHANDISERGROU.COM - Website - SUMNER COMMUNICATIONS INC.; *pg.* 1690, *pg.* 338
MERCHANDISERS - Food Storage Product - HOME PRODUCTS INTERNATIONAL, INC.; *pg.* 1125, *pg.* 577
MERCHANT BANKING CENTER - Automates Commercial Banking - DIEBOLD, INCORPORATED; *pg.* 387, *pg.* 1407
MERCHANT'S TIRE & AUTO CENTERS - Tire Retail Centers - TBC CORPORATION; *pg.* 1889, *pg.* 457
MERCKENS - Chocolate Confections - ARCHER-DANIELS-MIDLAND COMPANY; *pg.* 825, *pg.* 565
MERCOID - Flanged Chamber - DWYER INSTRUMENTS INC.; *pg.* 1330, *pg.* 694
MERCURIAL TALARIA - Footwear - NIKE, INC.; *pg.* 1812, *pg.* 1492
MERCURIAL VAPOR - Footwear - NIKE, INC.; *pg.* 1812, *pg.* 1492
MERCURY - Monitor - AKRON BRASS COMPANY; *pg.* 1311, *pg.* 1482
MERCURY - FPGA Device - ALTERA CORPORATION; *pg.* 348, *pg.* 237
MERCURY - Boats - BRUNSWICK CORPORATION; *pg.* 1828, *pg.* 623
MERCURY - Window Treatment - CROSCILL, INC.; *pg.* 1122, *pg.* 1220
MERCURY - Reinforced Vinyl Banner Material - HOLLISTON LLC; *pg.* 1460, *pg.* 1630
MERCURY - Thermoplastic Application System - M-B COMPANIES, INC.; *pg.* 1357, *pg.* 1884
MERCURY - Fabric - NEMSCHOFF, INC.; *pg.* 936, *pg.* 1890
MERCURY - Cruise Ship - ROYAL CARIBBEAN CRUISES LTD; *pg.* 1921, *pg.* 446
MERCURY - Turbine Products - SOLAR TURBINES INCORPORATED; *pg.* 1377, *pg.* 209
MERCURY CENTER - Electronic Information - SAN JOSE MERCURY NEWS; *pg.* 1683, *pg.* 250
MERCURY COMPUTER SYSTEMS - Embedded Computing System - MERCURY COMPUTER SYSTEMS, INC.; *pg.* 434, *pg.* 813
MERCURY LUGGAGE - Luggage Line - MERCURY LUGGAGE/SEWARD TRUNK; *pg.* 9, *pg.* 434
MERCURY MERCRUISER - Outboard Motors - MERCURY MARINE; *pg.* 1709, *pg.* 1857
MERCURY OUTBOARDS - Outboard Motors - MERCURY MARINE; *pg.* 1709, *pg.* 1857
MERCURY PRECISION PARTS - Marine Parts & Accessories - MERCURY MARINE; *pg.* 1709, *pg.* 1857
MERCURY-SC - Filters - NEWPORT CORPORATION; *pg.* 1424, *pg.* 114
MERCURY SMARTCRAFT - Controls & Gauges - MERCURY MARINE; *pg.* 1709, *pg.* 1857
MERCURYNEWS.COM - Web Site - SAN JOSE MERCURY NEWS; *pg.* 1683, *pg.* 250
MERCUTIO - Flatware - ONEIDA LTD; *pg.* 1129, *pg.* 1318
MERCUVER - Chemical Reagent - HACH COMPANY; *pg.* 1415, *pg.* 334
MEREDITH - Clothing - ABERCROMBIE & FITCH CO.; *pg.* 37, *pg.* 1466
MEREDITH - Footwear - PHOENIX FOOTWEAR GROUP, INC.; *pg.* 1815, *pg.* 60
MERFLEX - Flooring System - THE VALSPAR CORPORATION; *pg.* 1449, *pg.* 945
MERGAL - Metalworking Fluid Additive - TROY CORPORATION; *pg.* 1184, *pg.* 1067
MERGE TECHNOLOGY - Computer Software - MEDASSETS INC.; *pg.* 1561, *pg.* 484
MERGENT ACTIVE - Computer Program - MERGENT, INC.; *pg.* 1664, *pg.* 1616
MERGENT ANNUAL REPORTS - Data Feed - MERGENT, INC.; *pg.* 1664, *pg.* 1616
MERGENT BONDVIEWER - Computer Program - MERGENT, INC.; *pg.* 1664, *pg.* 1616
MERGENT EVENTSDATA - News Service - MERGENT, INC.; *pg.* 1664, *pg.* 1616
MERGENT EX-DATE SERVICE - Data Feed - MERGENT, INC.; *pg.* 1664, *pg.* 1616
MERGENT FIXED INCOME DATA MANAGEMENT PLATFORM - Data Feed - MERGENT, INC.; *pg.* 1664, *pg.* 1616
MERGENT FIXED INVESTMENT SECURITIES DATABASE - Data Feed - MERGENT, INC.; *pg.* 1664, *pg.* 1616
MERGENT GLOBAL COMPANY DATA - Data Feed - MERGENT, INC.; *pg.* 1664, *pg.* 1616
MERGENT HISTORICAL SECURITIES EQUITIES DATA - Data Feed - MERGENT, INC.; *pg.* 1664, *pg.* 1616
MERGENT HORIZON - Computer Program - MERGENT, INC.; *pg.* 1664, *pg.* 1616
MERGENT INDICATED ANNUAL DIVIDEND DATA - Data Feed - MERGENT, INC.; *pg.* 1664, *pg.* 1616
MERGENT ONLINE - Computer Program Suite - MERGENT, INC.; *pg.* 1664, *pg.* 1616
MERGENT RETAIL NOTES - Data Feed - MERGENT, INC.; *pg.* 1664, *pg.* 1616
MERGENT SHORT INTEREST MONITOR DATA - Data Feed - MERGENT, INC.; *pg.* 1664, *pg.* 1616
MERGENT UNIT INVESTMENT TRUST DATA - Data Feed - MERGENT, INC.; *pg.* 1664, *pg.* 1616
MERGENT WEBREPORTS - Online News Database - MERGENT, INC.; *pg.* 1664, *pg.* 1616
MERGER - Fabric - NEMSCHOFF, INC.; *pg.* 936, *pg.* 1890
MERIDEN - Footwear - EASTLAND SHOE CORPORATION; *pg.* 1808, *pg.* 750
MERIDIA - Tablet - ABBOTT LABORATORIES; *pg.* 1484, *pg.* 551
MERIDIAN - Acrylic Intraocular Lenses - BAUSCH & LOMB INCORPORATED; *pg.* 1401, *pg.* 1045
MERIDIAN - Hemodialysis Machine - BAXTER INTERNATIONAL INC.; *pg.* 1499, *pg.* 599
MERIDIAN - CMP Pads - THE DOW CHEMICAL COMPANY; *pg.* 1157, *pg.* 898
MERIDIAN - Jackets - ELBECO INCORPORATED; *pg.* 40, *pg.* 1584
MERIDIAN - Filing & Storage Products - HERMAN MILLER, INC.; *pg.* 926, *pg.* 913
MERIDIAN - Aircraft - PIPER AIRCRAFT, INC.; *pg.* 233, *pg.* 477
MERIDIAN - Medical Device - RESMED INC.; *pg.* 1589, *pg.* 207
MERIDIAN - Hot Cup - SOLO CUP COMPANY; *pg.* 1469, *pg.* 625
MERIDIAN - Motor Homes - WINNEBAGO INDUSTRIES,

First page reference indicates Business Class Edition
Second page reference indicates Geographic Edition

INC.; pg. 1712, pg. 707
MERIFLUOR - Diagnostic Test Product - MERIDIAN BIOSCIENCE INC.; pg. 1422, pg. 1417
MERILLAT - Kitchen & Bath Cabinetry - MASCO CORPORATION; pg. 96, pg. 909
MERINGUE - Surface Material - STEELCASE INC.; pg. 475, pg. 889
MERINO - Furniture - ASHLEY FURNITURE INDUSTRIES, INC.; pg. 914, pg. 1852
MERINO LANOLIN - Healthcare Product - MEDICOOL, INC.; pg. 1562, pg. 294
MERINO SKIN CREME - Health & Beauty Product - MEDICOOL, INC.; pg. 1562, pg. 294
MERISEF - Veterinary Antibiotic for Cats & Dogs - PFIZER INC.; pg. 1581, pg. 1278
MERISTAR - Diagnostic Test Product - MERIDIAN BIOSCIENCE INC.; pg. 1422, pg. 1417
MERIT - Mufflers & Pipes - AP EXHAUST PRODUCTS, INC.; pg. 199, pg. 1373
MERIT - Tires - THE HERCULES TIRE & RUBBER COMPANY; pg. 1884, pg. 1454
MERIT - Cleaning Product - HILLYARD, INC.; pg. 331, pg. 990
MERIT - Shampoo - KAO BRANDS CO. INC.; pg. 513, pg. 1415
MERIT - Heating & Cooling Product - LENNOX INTERNATIONAL INC.; pg. 1073, pg. 1736
MERIT - Cigarettes - PHILIP MORRIS USA INC.; pg. 1894, pg. 1803
MERIT PLUS - Electric Fireplace - LENNOX HEARTH PRODUCTS; pg. 93, pg. 1652
MERITAGE - Software - SERENA SOFTWARE, INC.; pg. 468, pg. 192
MERITEC - Rapid Agglutination Tests for Infectious Disease - MERIDIAN BIOSCIENCE INC.; pg. 1422, pg. 1417
MERITOR - Universal Joint - MERITOR, INC.; pg. 212, pg. 911
MERITZ - Decontaminant - MEDLINE INDUSTRIES, INC.; pg. 1562, pg. 635
MERKUR - Air Operated Pumps - GRACO, INC.; pg. 1342, pg. 935
MERLE NORMAN SHIMMERSTICK - Cosmetic Product - MERLE NORMAN COSMETICS, INC.; pg. 517, pg. 136
MERLIN - Footwear - EASTLAND SHOE CORPORATION; pg. 1808, pg. 750
MERLIN - Thermal Imaging System - FLIR SYSTEMS, INC.; pg. 1413, pg. 1510
MERLIN - Game - HASBRO, INC.; pg. 954, pg. 1603
MERLIN - software - INSTRON CORPORATION; pg. 1349, pg. 839
MERLIN - Fabric - NEMSCHOFF, INC.; pg. 936, pg. 1890
MERLIN - Actuator - PRECISION VALVE CORPORATION; pg. 1060, pg. 1357
MERLIN - Proximity Sensor - THE ROHO GROUP; pg. 1591, pg. 556
MERLIN - Patient Care System - ST. JUDE MEDICAL, INC.; pg. 1596, pg. 963
MERLIN - Analyzer - TELEDYNE LECROY; pg. 1431, pg. 1153
MERLIN - Electronic Lettering System - VARITRONICS, LLC; pg. 487, pg. 954
MERLIN EXPRESS - Presentation Lettering System - VARITRONICS, LLC; pg. 487, pg. 954
MERLIN EXPRESS ELITE - Thermal Lettering System - VARITRONICS, LLC; pg. 487, pg. 954
MERLIN EXPRESS XT - Lettering System - VARITRONICS, LLC; pg. 487, pg. 954
MERLIN HOME - Transmitter - ST. JUDE MEDICAL, INC.; pg. 1596, pg. 963
MERLIN II - Analyzers - TELEDYNE LECROY; pg. 1431, pg. 1153
MERLIN II - Printing System - VARITRONICS, LLC; pg. 487, pg. 954
MERLIN MAGIX - Telecommunication Product - AVAYA INC.; pg. 621, pg. 264
MERLIN.NET - Patient Care Network - ST. JUDE MEDICAL, INC.; pg. 1596, pg. 963
MERMAID - Lighting - ETHAN ALLEN INTERIORS INC.; pg. 924, pg. 343
MERMAID'S GOLD - Game - WMS INDUSTRIES INC.; pg. 593, pg. 666
MERMAID'S WONDERS - Game - WMS INDUSTRIES INC.; pg. 593, pg. 666
MERONA - Clothing - TARGET CORPORATION; pg. 1786, pg. 942
MERPOL - Chemical Product - STEPAN COMPANY; pg. 1182, pg. 643
MERRELL - Footwear - WOLVERINE WORLD WIDE, INC.; pg. 1822, pg. 905
MERRIAM-WEBSTER - Reference Books - MERRIAM-WEBSTER, INC.; pg. 1664, pg. 846
MERRIEE - Footwear - STEVEN MADDEN, LTD.; pg. 1819, pg. 1176
MERRILL DISCOVERY NAVIGATOR - Web-based Information Management System - MERRILL CORPORATION; pg. 1664, pg. 962
MERRILL NET:PROSPECT - Web-based Sales Prospecting Software - MERRILL CORPORATION; pg. 1664, pg. 962
MERRILLCONNECT - Business Information Software - MERRILL CORPORATION; pg. 1664, pg. 962
MERRILLREPORTS - Automated Fund Annual & Semi-Annual Reports Creation & Assembly Solution - MERRILL CORPORATION; pg. 1664, pg. 962
MERRY CAROLERS BOUQUET - Floral Bouquet - FTD GROUP, INC.; pg. 1795, pg. 608
MERRY CHRISTMAS - Pillow and Throw - HERITAGE LACE INC.; pg. 694, pg. 711
MERRY MAIDS - Maid Service - THE SERVICEMASTER COMPANY, LLC; pg. 335, pg. 1646
MERRY MONEY - Game - MISSOURI LOTTERY; pg. 999, pg. 979
MERRY PALS - Packaging - PACTIV CORPORATION; pg. 1466, pg. 624
MERRY WOOFMAS - Lottery Game - KENTUCKY LOTTERY CORPORATION; pg. 996, pg. 735
MESA - Film Handling Equipment - EASTMAN KODAK COMPANY; pg. 1408, pg. 1333
MESA - Dinnerware - THE HOMER LAUGHLIN CHINA COMPANY; pg. 1125, pg. 1850
MESA - Software - ION GEOPHYSICAL CORPORATION; pg. 1350, pg. 1708
MESA - Nitrogen - LEBANON SEABOARD CORPORATION; pg. 1797, pg. 1547
MESA - Binocular - LEUPOLD & STEVENS, INC.; pg. 1420, pg. 1492
MESA PACK - Controls - DAVIS-STANDARD LLC; pg. 1328, pg. 368
MESA PACK PRO - Controls - DAVIS-STANDARD LLC; pg. 1328, pg. 368
MESA SUNRISE - Breakfast Cereals - NATURE'S PATH FOODS INC.; pg. 833, pg. 1908
MESABI - Scalping Screen - KPI-JCI; pg. 1354, pg. 1626
MESAFEM - Estradiol Transdermal System - NOVEN PHARMACEUTICALS, INC.; pg. 1576, pg. 445
MESAM - Medical Device - RESMED INC.; pg. 1589, pg. 207
MESDA, THE OLD SALEM TOY MUSEUM - Museum - OLD SALEM, INCORPORATED; pg. 572, pg. 1395
MESH - Fabric - NEMSCHOFF, INC.; pg. 936, pg. 1890
MESH - Filtration System - SPECTRUM LABORATORIES INC.; pg. 1595, pg. 69
MESH KNIT SHORT - Clothing - K-SWISS; pg. 1837, pg. 306
MESH LONG SLEEVE - Clothing - K-SWISS; pg. 1837, pg. 306
MESH RUN TOP - Clothing - K-SWISS; pg. 1837, pg. 306
MESH STRIP - Gaskets - PARKER CHOMERICS; pg. 662, pg. 862
MESMERIZE - Beauty Product - AVON PRODUCTS, INC.; pg. 500, pg. 1198
MESNEX - Tablet - BAXTER INTERNATIONAL INC.; pg. 1499, pg. 599
MESQUITE BBQ - Potato Chip Flavor - ZAPP'S POTATO CHIPS, INC.; pg. 1864, pg. 743
MESSAGE ADVISOR - Software - BMC SOFTWARE, INC.; pg. 362, pg. 1701
MESSAGEPAD - Handheld Computer - APPLE INC.; pg. 350, pg. 73
MESSAGEREACH - Telecom Product - PREMIERE GLOBAL SERVICES, INC.; pg. 1275, pg. 518
MESSAGESTATS - Software - DELL SOFTWARE; pg. 385, pg. 40
MESSAGIN INTERACTION CENTER - Software - INTERACTIVE INTELLIGENCE, INC.; pg. 417, pg. 687
MESSAGING LINK - Software System - ALCATEL-LUCENT; pg. 615, pg. 1094
MESSAGING MAESTRO - Computer Application - THE ELECTRIC MAIL COMPANY; pg. 1242, pg. 1907
MESSENGER - Announcement System - ELECTRONIC TELE-COMMUNICATIONS, INC.; pg. 390, pg. 1897
MESSENGER - Single-Strap Bag - JANSPORT; pg. 1837, pg. 38
MESSENGER - Message-Based Communication Protocol - LYNX SOFTWARE TECHNOLOGIES; pg. 429, pg. 247
MESSENGER - Musical Instrument - PEAVEY ELECTRONICS CORPORATION; pg. 662, pg. 970
MESSENGER LUNCH - Insulated Lunch Bag - IGLOO PRODUCTS CORPORATION; pg. 1126, pg. 1724
MESSENGER PLUS - Document Management Software - J2 GLOBAL COMMUNICATIONS, INC.; pg. 1260, pg. 133
MESSSAGE-A-ROUND - Balloon - CONTINENTAL AMERICAN CORP.; pg. 1880, pg. 723
MESTINON - Pharmaceutical Product - IMPAX LABORATORIES, INC.; pg. 1544, pg. 101
MESTINON - Pharmaceutical Product - VALEANT PHARMACEUTICALS INTERNATIONAL; pg. 1605, pg. 1047
MESURFLO - Controls - HAYS FLUID CONTROLS; pg. 1049, pg. 1370
MET - Multipath Elimination Technology - NOVATEL INC.; pg. 1424, pg. 1904
MET-FLO - Cold Forming Taps - REGAL BELOIT CORPORATION; pg. 106, pg. 1854
MET-L-CHEK - Cleaner Product - MCGEAN-ROHCO, INC.; pg. 1172, pg. 1432
MET-L-X - Dry Chemical Agent - ANSUL, INCORPORATED; pg. 1147, pg. 1869
MET-RX - Nutritional Supplements - NBTY, INC.; pg. 1572, pg. 1338
META MAX PA - Pozzolanic Additive - BASF CATALYSTS LLC; pg. 1148, pg. 1074
META-PLAST - Ceramic & Plastic Product - COORSTEK, INC.; pg. 77, pg. 330
META-TEC - Cleaner - BIRKO CORPORATION; pg. 1149, pg. 332
META TEC 2C - Chemical Product - BIRKO CORPORATION; pg. 1149, pg. 332
METABO PARTNER - Wellness Tea - CELESTIAL SEASONINGS, INC.; pg. 846, pg. 310
METABOFIRM - Vitamin & Dietary Supplement - NATROL, INC.; pg. 1570, pg. 64
METABOLIC PROFILER - Analytical System - BRUKER CORPORATION; pg. 1511, pg. 788
METABOMAX - Health Care Product - NATURE'S SUNSHINE PRODUCTS, INC.; pg. 1571, pg. 1754
METABOTRIM - Nutritional Supplement - NU SKIN ENTERPRISES, INC.; pg. 518, pg. 1755
METACRAWLER - Website - BLUCORA; pg. 1232, pg. 1813
METACURE - Metal-Based Catalysts - AIR PRODUCTS AND CHEMICALS, INC.; pg. 1145, pg. 1513
METADATA - Software - SAS INSTITUTE INC.; pg. 466, pg. 1361
METAFLUOR - Software - MOLECULAR DEVICES CORPORATION; pg. 1568, pg. 287
METAFRAM - Self Lubricating Bearings - FEDERAL-MOGUL HOLDINGS CORPORATION; pg. 205, pg. 907
METAFRAME - Software - CITRIX SYSTEMS, INC.; pg. 375, pg. 424
METAFRAME XP - Software - CITRIX SYSTEMS, INC.; pg. 375, pg. 424
METAFUZE - Media Converter - AVID TECHNOLOGY, INC.; pg. 622, pg. 804
METAG - Tape & Webbing - FLETCHER INDUSTRIES, INC.; pg. 1337, pg. 1390
METAGLISS - Industrial Bearings - FEDERAL-MOGUL HOLDINGS CORPORATION; pg. 205, pg. 907
METAL-2-METAL - Aluminum Filled Body Repair Filler - ITW - EVERCOAT; pg. 1443, pg. 1415
METAL ART - Mousepad - ALLSOP, INC.; pg. 347, pg. 1817
METAL BRITE - Automotive Reconditioning Product - MOC PRODUCTS COMPANY, INC.; pg. 332, pg. 174
METAL DEVIL - Resistor - OHMITE MANUFACTURING COMPANY; pg. 660, pg. 553
METAL GLAZE - Polyester Finishing & Glazing Putty - ITW - EVERCOAT; pg. 1443, pg. 1415
METAL-GUARD - Films - DAUBERT INDUSTRIES, INC.; pg. 1155, pg. 561
METAL GUARD - Corrosion Inhibitors & Rust Preventatives - HUBBARD-HALL, INC.; pg. 1167, pg. 382
METAL MINUTES - Publisher - SECO/WARWICK CORPORATION; pg. 1076, pg. 1552
METAL-MITE - Resistor - OHMITE MANUFACTURING COMPANY; pg. 660, pg. 553
METAL ORGANICS - Industrial Material - DOW CHEMICAL; pg. 1156, pg. 1563
METAL POLISH - Metal Cleaner - CONNOISSEURS PRODUCTS CORPORATION; pg. 329, pg. 861

METAL REMOVAL - Tools - KENNAMETAL INC.; *pg.* 1052, *pg.* 1547
METAL REMOVAL - Carbide Tools - KENNAMETAL IPG; *pg.* 1353, *pg.* 1615
METAL SIGNATURE - Water Analysis Services - THE DOW CHEMICAL COMPANY; *pg.* 1157, *pg.* 898
METAL STAMPING - Computer Enclosure Line - TRITON INDUSTRIES, INC.; *pg.* 1384, *pg.* 592
METAL-STOP - Metal Detector - GEHL COMPANY; *pg.* 1339, *pg.* 1899
METAL TECH - Ceramic, Glass, Stone Tiles & Slabs - WALKER & ZANGER, INC.; *pg.* 119, *pg.* 281
METAL WORKS - Repair Products - ITW - EVERCOAT; *pg.* 1443, *pg.* 1415
METAL45 - Conductor Etch System - LAM RESEARCH CORPORATION; *pg.* 1354, *pg.* 91
METALBESTOS - Venting Material - SELKIRK CORPORATION; *pg.* 1076, *pg.* 1736
METALCURE - Graphic Art UV System - NORDSON CORPORATION; *pg.* 1365, *pg.* 1480
METALDAM - Pressed & Monolithic Refractory - RESCO PRODUCTS, INC.; *pg.* 107, *pg.* 1581
METALEAF - Aluminum Paint - PPG INDUSTRIES, INC.; *pg.* 1445, *pg.* 1579
METALEX - Gaskets - PARKER CHOMERICS; *pg.* 662, *pg.* 862
METALHIDE - Liquid & Paste Paints - PPG INDUSTRIES, INC.; *pg.* 1445, *pg.* 1579
METALICO - Fabric - NEMSCHOFF, INC.; *pg.* 936, *pg.* 1890
METALINE - Thermal Processing Equipment - SURFACE COMBUSTION, INC.; *pg.* 1077, *pg.* 1462
METALINED - Series of Inside/Outside Design Furnaces - SURFACE COMBUSTION, INC.; *pg.* 1077, *pg.* 1462
METALIX - Material - ROSCO LABORATORIES, INC.; *pg.* 1782, *pg.* 378
METALIZED - Apparel - OAKLEY, INC.; *pg.* 1840, *pg.* 86
METALJACKET - Coating - LORD CORPORATION; *pg.* 1357, *pg.* 1360
METALLEX - Laminated Engravable Plastic - GRAVOGRAPH-NEW HERMES; *pg.* 1344, *pg.* 531
METALLIC COLORS - Colorful Metallic Markers - DRI MARK PRODUCTS, INC.; *pg.* 388, *pg.* 1323
METALLIC GEL ROLLER - Pens - PENTEL OF AMERICA, LTD.; *pg.* 453, *pg.* 295
METALLICS - Lighting - STEELCASE INC.; *pg.* 475, *pg.* 889
METALLISMO - Metal Tile - WALKER & ZANGER, INC.; *pg.* 119, *pg.* 281
METALLURGICAL & MATERIALS TRANSACTIONS - Journal - ASM INTERNATIONAL; *pg.* 132, *pg.* 1461
METALMASTER - High Pressure Gas Quench Vacuum Furnace - IPSEN INTERNATIONAL, INC.; *pg.* 1073, *pg.* 562
METALMATE - Thermosetting Powder Coatings - JONES-BLAIR COMPANY; *pg.* 1443, *pg.* 1682
METALNOX - Cleaning Chemical Product - KYZEN CORPORATION; *pg.* 331, *pg.* 1652
METALOPTICS - Lighting Fixtures - ACUITY BRANDS, INC.; *pg.* 1294, *pg.* 487
METALS ABSTRACTS - Publication - ASM INTERNATIONAL; *pg.* 132, *pg.* 1461
METALS HANDBOOK - Comprehensive Reference Series - ASM INTERNATIONAL; *pg.* 132, *pg.* 1461
METALSET - Epoxy Adhesive - SMOOTH-ON INC.; *pg.* 111, *pg.* 1528
METALTRACE - Test Kit - HACH COMPANY; *pg.* 1415, *pg.* 334
METALWOOD - Real-Metal Finishes for Mantels - WHITE RIVER HARDWOODS-WOODWORKS, INC.; *pg.* 121, *pg.* 31
METALWORKS - Ceilings & Walls - ARMSTRONG WORLD INDUSTRIES, INC.; *pg.* 914, *pg.* 1545
METALYN - Rosin Esters - EASTMAN CHEMICAL COMPANY; *pg.* 1159, *pg.* 1636
METAMAP - Web Application - EOLAS TECHNOLOGIES, INC.; *pg.* 1243, *pg.* 573
METAMARE - Polymers, Preservatives, Stabilizers, Accelerants & Catalysts - DOW CHEMICAL; *pg.* 1156, *pg.* 1563
METAMEX - Pigment - BASF CATALYSTS LLC; *pg.* 1148, *pg.* 1074
METAMORPH - Software - MOLECULAR DEVICES CORPORATION; *pg.* 1568, *pg.* 287
METAMORPHIC - Carpet - INTERFACE, INC.; *pg.* 695, *pg.* 512
METAMUCIL - Health Care Product - THE PROCTER & GAMBLE COMPANY; *pg.* 1129, *pg.* 1418
METAPLAS IONON - Engineered Product And System - SULZER METCO (WESTBURY) INC.; *pg.* 1064, *pg.* 1350
METAPRINT - Software - AMERICAN REPROGRAPHICS COMPANY; *pg.* 1616, *pg.* 303
METASERV - Grinder/Polishers - BUEHLER, LTD.; *pg.* 1403, *pg.* 622
METASYNC - Audio & Video Process - AVID TECHNOLOGY, INC.; *pg.* 622, *pg.* 804
METASYS - Mechanical & Electrical System - JOHNSON CONTROLS, INC.; *pg.* 209, *pg.* 1876
METATECH - Screw Feeder - METALFAB, INC.; *pg.* 1360, *pg.* 1127
METATRON 21 - Software - GEA FARM TECHNOLOGIES; *pg.* 704, *pg.* 636
METAVUE - Software - MOLECULAR DEVICES CORPORATION; *pg.* 1568, *pg.* 287
METAXPRESS - Software - MOLECULAR DEVICES CORPORATION; *pg.* 1568, *pg.* 287
METAZENE - Odorless Odor Counteractant Additive - SURCO PRODUCTS, INC.; *pg.* 336, *pg.* 1581
METCALF - Global Messaging Services - VERISIGN, INC.; *pg.* 488, *pg.* 1799
METCOLITE - Auxiliary Material - SULZER METCO (WESTBURY) INC.; *pg.* 1064, *pg.* 1350
METCON-2 - 2mm Hard Metric Connectors - WINCHESTER ELECTRONICS CORP.; *pg.* 688, *pg.* 382
METCUT - Tools - KENNAMETAL INC.; *pg.* 1052, *pg.* 1547
METCUT - Indexable Tooling - KENNAMETAL IPG; *pg.* 1353, *pg.* 1615
METED - Shampoo - DUSA PHARMACEUTICALS, INC.; *pg.* 1525, *pg.* 860
METEOR - Pigment & Dispersion - BASF CATALYSTS LLC; *pg.* 1148, *pg.* 1074
METEOR - Process Technology - THE DOW CHEMICAL COMPANY; *pg.* 1157, *pg.* 898
METEOR - Seating Product - IRWIN SEATING COMPANY INC.; *pg.* 929, *pg.* 887
METEOR - Multi-Purpose Bond Paper & Envelopes - LINDENMEYR MUNROE; *pg.* 1464, *pg.* 1325
METEOR - Hammer Mills - WILLIAMS PATENT CRUSHER & PULVERIZER CO., INC.; *pg.* 1389, *pg.* 1005
METEOR COPY - Reprographic Paper - LINDENMEYR MUNROE; *pg.* 1464, *pg.* 1325
METEOSTAR - Systems Integration & Aeronautics - LOCKHEED MARTIN CORPORATION; *pg.* 229, *pg.* 762
METER MIST - Fluid Handling System - GRACO, INC.; *pg.* 1342, *pg.* 935
METER READER - Surge Protector - WIREMOLD/LEGRAND; *pg.* 689, *pg.* 383
METER RELEASE - Pharmaceutical Product - LUMARA HEALTH INC.; *pg.* 1557, *pg.* 973
METER TRAX - Clinical Diagnostic Product - BIO-RAD LABORATORIES, INC.; *pg.* 1504, *pg.* 101
METERASSISTANT - Software - XEROX CORPORATION; *pg.* 494, *pg.* 365
METERFLO - Fluid Handling System - GRACO, INC.; *pg.* 1342, *pg.* 935
METFLO - Metal Tubing, Bends & Fittings - H-P PRODUCTS, INC.; *pg.* 85, *pg.* 1458
METGARD - Corrosion Inhibitors - THE DOW CHEMICAL COMPANY; *pg.* 1157, *pg.* 898
METGLAS - Amorphous Metal - HONEYWELL INTERNATIONAL INC.; *pg.* 407, *pg.* 1088
METHADOSE - Pharmaceutical Product - MALLINCKRODT PHARMACEUTICALS; *pg.* 1557, *pg.* 978
METHAZATE - Polymer Product - CHEMTURA CORPORATION; *pg.* 1152, *pg.* 355
METHCAT - Hazardous Materials Training for Law Enforcement Responders at Meth Labs - ECOLOGY AND ENVIRONMENT, INC.; *pg.* 1410, *pg.* 1173
METHELON - Photo Developing Agent - EASTMAN KODAK COMPANY; *pg.* 1408, *pg.* 1333
METHOCARBAMOL - Pharmaceutical Product - LANNETT COMPANY, INC.; *pg.* 1555, *pg.* 1566
METHOCEL - Cellulose Ethers - THE DOW CHEMICAL COMPANY; *pg.* 1157, *pg.* 898
METHODBABY - Cleaner - METHOD PRODUCTS INC.; *pg.* 332, *pg.* 223
METHODE - Electronic Components - METHODE ELECTRONICS, INC.; *pg.* 654, *pg.* 581
METHYLATED SOYBEAN OIL PLUS - Spray Adjuvant - UNIVERSAL COOPERATIVES, INC.; *pg.* 1482, *pg.* 922
METLBOND - Chemical Product - CYTEC INDUSTRIES, INC.; *pg.* 1155, *pg.* 1131
METLIFE AUTO & HOME - Insurance - METLIFE, INC.; *pg.* 1208, *pg.* 1258
METOXILITE - Semi-Conductor Devices - SEMTECH CORPORATION; *pg.* 671, *pg.* 57
METPAK - Backplane Connector - 3M COMPANY; *pg.* 1142, *pg.* 956
METPAR MULTICAM - Hinge - METPAR CORP.; *pg.* 97, *pg.* 1350
METRA - Furniture - THE COMMERCIAL FURNITURE GROUP; *pg.* 920, *pg.* 994
METRA - Diagnostic Test Product - QUIDEL CORPORATION; *pg.* 1588, *pg.* 207
METREC - Connector - MOLEX INCORPORATED; *pg.* 655, *pg.* 628
METRI-PACK - Vehicle Safety System - GROTE INDUSTRIES, INC.; *pg.* 206, *pg.* 693
METRIC - Fabric - NEMSCHOFF, INC.; *pg.* 936, *pg.* 1890
METRIFLEX - Power Transmission Belt - HBD INDUSTRIES, INC.; *pg.* 207, *pg.* 1449
METRIS - Gas Meters - SCHLUMBERGER LIMITED; *pg.* 801, *pg.* 1714
METRIX 100 - Inline Opaque Films Metrology System - KLA-TENCOR CORPORATION; *pg.* 1353, *pg.* 146
METRO - Magazine - BOBIT BUSINESS MEDIA; *pg.* 1622, *pg.* 293
METRO - Knife - BUCK KNIVES, INC.; *pg.* 1828, *pg.* 550
METRO - Fan - CRAFTMADE INTERNATIONAL, INC.; *pg.* 1295, *pg.* 1670
METRO - Bedding - CROSCILL, INC.; *pg.* 1122, *pg.* 1220
METRO - Healthcare Product - GF HEALTH PRODUCTS, INC.; *pg.* 1535, *pg.* 508
METRO - Daypack - JANSPORT; *pg.* 1837, *pg.* 38
METRO - Furniture - JASPER GROUP; *pg.* 930, *pg.* 691
METRO - Spools - METRO MACHINE & ENGINEERING CORP.; *pg.* 1360, *pg.* 923
METRO - Fire Helmet - MINE SAFETY APPLIANCES COMPANY; *pg.* 1361, *pg.* 1525
METRO - Fabric - NEMSCHOFF, INC.; *pg.* 936, *pg.* 1890
METRO - Hair Cutting Kit - WAHL CLIPPER CORPORATION; *pg.* 524, *pg.* 662
METRO LE - Medical Product - GF HEALTH PRODUCTS, INC.; *pg.* 1535, *pg.* 508
METRO ML - Central Conveying System - MOTAN, INC.; *pg.* 1886, *pg.* 903
METRO POWER - Medical Product - GF HEALTH PRODUCTS, INC.; *pg.* 1535, *pg.* 508
METRO-PUCK COMICS NETWORK - Sunday Comics National Advertising Sales - METRO-PUCK COMICS NETWORK; *pg.* 1665, *pg.* 1259
METRO SILVER DINER - Restaurant Services - SILVER DINER, INC.; *pg.* 1750, *pg.* 776
METRO SUEDE - Ear Warmer - 180S, LLC; *pg.* 1824, *pg.* 754
METRO TV BOOK NETWORK - 800 Plus Newspapers Published, TV & Books - METRO NEWSPAPER ADVERTISING SERVICES, INC.; *pg.* 1664, *pg.* 1259
METRO WIRE - Medical Device - COOK GROUP, INC.; *pg.* 1518, *pg.* 674
METROACCESS - Airport Service - WASHINGTON METROPOLITAN AREA TRANSIT AUTHORITY; *pg.* 1930, *pg.* 407
METROBUS - Airport Service - WASHINGTON METROPOLITAN AREA TRANSIT AUTHORITY; *pg.* 1930, *pg.* 407
METROCARD - Automated Fare Collection - METROPOLITAN TRANSPORTATION AUTHORITY; *pg.* 1915, *pg.* 1260
METROCLUSTER - Software - NETAPP, INC.; *pg.* 444, *pg.* 287
METROCOR - Optical Fiber - CORNING INCORPORATED; *pg.* 1122, *pg.* 1154
METRODIRECTOR K2 - Software - CIENA CORPORATION; *pg.* 628, *pg.* 771
METROGEL - Pharmaceutical Products - GALDERMA LABORATORIES, L.P.; *pg.* 1532, *pg.* 1695
METROGUARD - Nuclear, Biological & Chemical Detection System - LOCKHEED MARTIN CORPORATION; *pg.* 229, *pg.* 762
METROLINK - Framer & Mapper Product - CYPRESS SEMICONDUCTOR CORPORATION; *pg.* 1326, *pg.* 243
METROLINK - Optical Networking Product - HARMONIC, INC.; *pg.* 402, *pg.* 246
METROLINK - Conveying System - MOTAN, INC.; *pg.* 1886, *pg.* 903
METROLINK2T-2 - Asynchronous SRAMs - CYPRESS

First page reference indicates Business Class Edition
Second page reference indicates Geographic Edition

SEMICONDUCTOR CORPORATION; *pg.* 1326, *pg.* 243
METROLUX - Conveying System - MOTAN, INC.; *pg.* 1886, *pg.* 903
METROLUX - Lighting - PHILIPS LIGHTING; *pg.* 1303, *pg.* 806
METROMASTER - Vehicles - SPARTAN MOTORS, INC.; *pg.* 217, *pg.* 874
METROMIX - Conveying System - MOTAN, INC.; *pg.* 1886, *pg.* 903
METRONATURAL - Tagline - SEATTLE CONVENTION & VISITORS BUREAU; *pg.* 1005, *pg.* 1839
METRONET - Conveying System - MOTAN, INC.; *pg.* 1886, *pg.* 903
METRONIDAZOLE - Pharmaceutical Product - G&W LABORATORIES INC.; *pg.* 1532, *pg.* 1123
METROPLEX - Networking Service - GENERAL DATACOMM INDUSTRIES, INC.; *pg.* 400, *pg.* 357
THE METROPOLIS - Software System - ALCATEL-LUCENT; *pg.* 615, *pg.* 1094
METROPOLIS - Software - COSTAR GROUP, INC.; *pg.* 742, *pg.* 397
METROPOLIS - Rug - COURISTAN INC.; *pg.* 921, *pg.* 1067
METROPOLIS - Flatware - ONEIDA LTD; *pg.* 1129, *pg.* 1318
METROPOLITAN - Floor Tile - AMERICAN BILTRITE INC.; *pg.* 1878, *pg.* 856
METROPOLITAN - Furniture - ETHAN ALLEN INTERIORS INC.; *pg.* 924, *pg.* 343
METROPOLITAN - Hat - WOODEN SHIPS OF HOBOKEN; *pg.* 35, *pg.* 1315
THE METROPOLITAN CAFE - Restaurant - ARK RESTAURANTS CORP.; *pg.* 1715, *pg.* 1196
METROPOLITAN CANVAS - Hat - WOODEN SHIPS OF HOBOKEN; *pg.* 35, *pg.* 1315
METROPOLITAN STRIPE - Hat - WOODEN SHIPS OF HOBOKEN; *pg.* 35, *pg.* 1315
METROPOLITAN VIEW - Men's Clothing - BLOOMINGDALE'S, INC.; *pg.* 1763, *pg.* 1204
METROPOLOTAN - Furniture - AMERICAN LEATHER LP; *pg.* 912, *pg.* 1673
METRORAIL - Airport Service - WASHINGTON METROPOLITAN AREA TRANSIT AUTHORITY; *pg.* 1930, *pg.* 407
METROSEAL - Valve Resilient Seat - UNITED STATES PIPE & FOUNDRY COMPANY, INC.; *pg.* 117, *pg.* 5
METROSTAR - Amplified Omnidirectional TV Antenna - WINEGARD COMPANY; *pg.* 688, *pg.* 702
METSMANAGER - Navigation Aid - TRIMBLE NAVIGATION LIMITED; *pg.* 1384, *pg.* 288
METSO - Silicate Powder - PQ CORPORATION; *pg.* 1178, *pg.* 1515
METSO BEADS - Silicate Powder - PQ CORPORATION; *pg.* 1178, *pg.* 1515
METSO PENTABEAD - Silicate Powder - PQ CORPORATION; *pg.* 1178, *pg.* 1515
METTA - Fabric - NEMSCHOFF, INC.; *pg.* 936, *pg.* 1890
METZ - Pet Product - PETSMART, INC.; *pg.* 1481, *pg.* 18
MEVATRON - Radiation Therapy System - SIEMENS CORPORATION; *pg.* 803, *pg.* 1291
MEWSS PIP - Systems Integration & Aeronautics - LOCKHEED MARTIN CORPORATION; *pg.* 229, *pg.* 762
MEXENE CHILI - Chili Powder & Beans - BRUCE FOODS CORPORATION; *pg.* 842, *pg.* 743
MEXI ROLLS - Filled, Fried Burrito-Like Product - TACO JOHN'S INTERNATIONAL, INC.; *pg.* 1753, *pg.* 1901
MEXICALL - Telephone Service - IDT CORPORATION; *pg.* 643, *pg.* 1096
MEXICAN CHEDDAR ON BLACK BEAN DIPPERS - Flavored Tortilla Chips - HERR FOODS INC.; *pg.* 861, *pg.* 1557
MEXICAN ORIGINAL - Mexican Cuisine - TYSON FOODS, INC.; *pg.* 902, *pg.* 35
MEXIDEK - International Trade Forms - UNZ & COMPANY, INC.; *pg.* 1698, *pg.* 1084
MEXIDIPS & CHIPS - Mexican Food - TACO BUENO RESTAURANTS, L.P.; *pg.* 1753, *pg.* 1692
MEXIMUM - Sandals - AEROGROUP INTERNATIONAL, INC.; *pg.* 1803, *pg.* 1055
MEXSANA - Medicated Powder - MERCK & CO., INC.; *pg.* 1566, *pg.* 1077
MEXX - Apparel - KATE SPADE & COMPANY; *pg.* 27, *pg.* 1248
MEYER - Mattresses - SEALY CORPORATION; *pg.* 942, *pg.* 1391
MEYER - Steel Pole - THOMAS & BETTS CORPORATION; *pg.* 680, *pg.* 1646
MEZCLA - Fabric - NEMSCHOFF, INC.; *pg.* 936, *pg.* 1890
MEZZANINE MINK - Tile - ARTISTIC TILE INC.; *pg.* 914, *pg.* 1119
MEZZANO - Fabric - NEMSCHOFF, INC.; *pg.* 936, *pg.* 1890
MEZZO - Lounge Chairs - BERNHARDT DESIGN; *pg.* 918, *pg.* 1381
MEZZO - Beverages - THE COCA-COLA COMPANY; *pg.* 240, *pg.* 493
MEZZO MIX - Beverages - THE COCA-COLA COMPANY; *pg.* 240, *pg.* 493
MFB - Electronic Components - MOLEX INCORPORATED; *pg.* 655, *pg.* 628
MFI SOLARC - Headlight - WELCH ALLYN INC.; *pg.* 1436, *pg.* 1342
MFP - Glass & Ceramic Material - CORNING INCORPORATED; *pg.* 1122, *pg.* 1154
MG-0153/PA-0153 - Solvent Rubber Adhesive - DOW CORNING CORPORATION; *pg.* 1159, *pg.* 900
MG-0560/PA 0560 - Emulsion Acrylic Adhesive - DOW CORNING CORPORATION; *pg.* 1159, *pg.* 900
MG-0580/PA-0580 - Emulsion Acrylic Adhesive - DOW CORNING CORPORATION; *pg.* 1159, *pg.* 900
MG-0607/PA-0607 - Solvent Acrylic Adhesive - DOW CORNING CORPORATION; *pg.* 1159, *pg.* 900
MG-0610/PA-0610 - Solvent Acrylic Adhesive - DOW CORNING CORPORATION; *pg.* 1159, *pg.* 900
MG SONICGUIDE - Digital Directory - ROVI CORPORATION; *pg.* 463, *pg.* 269
M.G. WALDBAUM - Brine Packed Eggs, Diced Eggs & Dry Packed Eggs - MICHAEL FOODS, INC.; *pg.* 877, *pg.* 949
MGAME - Game - MULTIMEDIA GAMES INC.; *pg.* 442, *pg.* 1664
MGB - Interface - IMAGINATION TECHNOLOGIES; *pg.* 412, *pg.* 285
MGC - United Conferencing Bridge - POLYCOM, INC.; *pg.* 664, *pg.* 249
MGD 64 - Beer - MILLERCOORS; *pg.* 254, *pg.* 1877
MGLURS - Pharmaceutical - NPS PHARMACEUTICALS, INC.; *pg.* 1576, *pg.* 1043
MGM BRAKES - Heavy Duty Truck & Bus Spring Brake Actuators - INDIAN HEAD INDUSTRIES, INC.; *pg.* 208, *pg.* 1367
MGM GRAND - Resort & Casino - MGM RESORTS INTERNATIONAL; *pg.* 1105, *pg.* 1028
MGM GRAND CASINO - Food Service - ARK RESTAURANTS CORP.; *pg.* 1715, *pg.* 1196
MGM GRAND DETROIT - Resort & Casino - MGM RESORTS INTERNATIONAL; *pg.* 1105, *pg.* 1028
MGM GRAND SANYA - Resort & Casino - MGM RESORTS INTERNATIONAL; *pg.* 1105, *pg.* 1028
MGPI CHEWTEX - Pet Food - MGP INGREDIENTS, INC.; *pg.* 877, *pg.* 714
MGPI PET-TEX - Pet Food - MGP INGREDIENTS, INC.; *pg.* 877, *pg.* 714
MGX - Switches - CISCO SYSTEMS, INC.; *pg.* 372, *pg.* 240
MH-60R - Systems Integration & Aeronautics - LOCKHEED MARTIN CORPORATION; *pg.* 229, *pg.* 762
MHBC - Cleaner - SWISHER HYGIENE INC.; *pg.* 336, *pg.* 1507
M.H.M. - Women's Dresses - KELLWOOD COMPANY; *pg.* 28, *pg.* 975
MI-15 - Thermal Insulation & Ablative Material - LOCKHEED MARTIN CORPORATION; *pg.* 229, *pg.* 762
MI ACCESS - Financial Services - FEDERAL HOME LOAN MORTGAGE CORPORATION; *pg.* 751, *pg.* 1790
MI CASA - Food Product - FLOWERS FOODS, INC.; *pg.* 855, *pg.* 541
MI-CLEAN - Aqueous Cleaner - HUBBARD-HALL, INC.; *pg.* 1167, *pg.* 382
MI CROSDHC - Memory Card - SANDISK CORPORATION; *pg.* 465, *pg.* 147
MI II - Electronic Components - MOLEX INCORPORATED; *pg.* 655, *pg.* 628
MI-TIQUE - Antiquing Solutions - HUBBARD-HALL, INC.; *pg.* 1167, *pg.* 382
MIA - Fan - CRAFTMADE INTERNATIONAL, INC.; *pg.* 1295, *pg.* 1670
MIA & MAXX - Hair Studio - REGIS CORPORATION; *pg.* 521, *pg.* 941
MIA PIZZA BELLA - Food Product - ADVANCEPIERRE FOODS, INC.; *pg.* 1714, *pg.* 1409
MIAMI - Software - AEROFLEX INCORPORATED; *pg.* 614, *pg.* 1321
MIAMI - Beverages - THE COCA-COLA COMPANY; *pg.* 240, *pg.* 493
MIAMI - Door - MASONITE INTERNATIONAL CORPORATION; *pg.* 1054, *pg.* 1920
MIAMI GRILL - Restaurant - NATHAN'S FAMOUS INC.; *pg.* 1741, *pg.* 1171
MIAMI HEAT - Professional Basketball Team - MIAMI HEAT LIMITED PARTNERSHIP; *pg.* 562, *pg.* 444
MIAMI INTERNATIONAL UNIVERSITY OF ART & DESIGN - Art School - EDUCATION MANAGEMENT CORPORATION; *pg.* 601, *pg.* 1575
MIAMI JAI-ALAI - Jai-Alai Game Center - FLORIDA GAMING CORPORATION; *pg.* 548, *pg.* 442
MIAMI JR. - Orthopedic Product - DJO INCORPORATED; *pg.* 1524, *pg.* 302
MIAMI SUITES - Dom Cigars - ALTADIS USA, INC.; *pg.* 1893, *pg.* 423
MIAWARE - Location Service Tool - PITNEY BOWES SOFTWARE INC.; *pg.* 455, *pg.* 1346
MIC - Glass & Ceramic Material - CORNING INCORPORATED; *pg.* 1122, *pg.* 1154
MIC PLUS - Electronic Catalog - MIGHTY DISTRIBUTING SYSTEM OF AMERICA; *pg.* 213, *pg.* 538
MIC TECHNOLOGY - Microelectronic Interconnect Products - AEROFLEX INCORPORATED; *pg.* 614, *pg.* 1321
MICAD - Systems Integration & Aeronautics - LOCKHEED MARTIN CORPORATION; *pg.* 229, *pg.* 762
MICAH - Clothing - ABERCROMBIE & FITCH CO.; *pg.* 37, *pg.* 1466
MICALLPLAN - Customer-Service Tool - PITNEY BOWES SOFTWARE INC.; *pg.* 455, *pg.* 1346
MICATIN - Anti-Itch Cream - MCNEIL-PPC, INC.; *pg.* 1560, *pg.* 1533
MICH - Ranger Communication System - MINE SAFETY APPLIANCES COMPANY; *pg.* 1361, *pg.* 1525
MICHAEL BERMAN - Bath Product - ROHL LLC; *pg.* 1061, *pg.* 116
MICHAEL THERMICS - Beverage Flavoring - DAVID MICHAEL & CO. INC.; *pg.* 852, *pg.* 1563
MICHAELANGELO - Flatware - ONEIDA LTD; *pg.* 1129, *pg.* 1318
MICHAELITE - Reduced Fat Product - DAVID MICHAEL & CO. INC.; *pg.* 852, *pg.* 1563
MICHAELOK - Spray Dried Flavors - DAVID MICHAEL & CO. INC.; *pg.* 852, *pg.* 1563
MICHAEL'S - Arts & Crafts Stores - MICHAELS STORES, INC.; *pg.* 1127, *pg.* 1722
MICHEAL KORS - Beauty Product - THE ESTEE LAUDER COMPANIES INC.; *pg.* 508, *pg.* 1229
MICHEL PICARD - French Wines - BROWN-FORMAN CORPORATION; *pg.* 1958, *pg.* 732
MICHELANGELO - Dispensing Equipment - IDEX CORPORATION; *pg.* 1347, *pg.* 623
MICHELANGELO - Faux Finish Applicators - USG CORPORATION; *pg.* 118, *pg.* 594
MICHELANGELO COLLECTION - Decorative Lighting Fixtures for the Showroom Market - WESTINGHOUSE LIGHTING CORPORATION; *pg.* 687, *pg.* 1571
MICHELIN - Tires - MICHELIN NORTH AMERICA INC.; *pg.* 1886, *pg.* 1618
MICHELIN - Footwear - ROCKY BRANDS, INC.; *pg.* 1818, *pg.* 1466
MICHELIN MAN - Mascot - MICHELIN NORTH AMERICA INC.; *pg.* 1886, *pg.* 1618
MICHELINA'S - Frozen Food - BELLISIO FOODS, INC.; *pg.* 840, *pg.* 931
MICHELLE - Clothing - ABERCROMBIE & FITCH CO.; *pg.* 37, *pg.* 1466
MICHELOB - Beer - ANHEUSER-BUSCH COMPANIES, LLC; *pg.* 237, *pg.* 991
MICHELOB AMBERBOCK - Beer - ANHEUSER-BUSCH COMPANIES, LLC; *pg.* 237, *pg.* 991
MICHELOB GOLDEN DRAFT - Beer - ANHEUSER-BUSCH COMPANIES, LLC; *pg.* 237, *pg.* 991
MICHELOB GOLDEN DRAFT LIGHT - Beer - ANHEUSER-BUSCH COMPANIES, LLC; *pg.* 237, *pg.* 991
MICHELOB HONEY LAGER - Beer - ANHEUSER-BUSCH COMPANIES, LLC; *pg.* 237, *pg.* 991
MICHELOB LIGHT - Beer - ANHEUSER-BUSCH COMPANIES, LLC; *pg.* 237, *pg.* 991
MICHELOB PORTER - Beer - ANHEUSER-BUSCH COMPANIES, LLC; *pg.* 237, *pg.* 991
MICHELOB ULTRA - Beer - ANHEUSER-BUSCH COMPANIES, LLC; *pg.* 237, *pg.* 991
MICHELOB ULTRA AMBER - Beer - ANHEUSER-BUSCH COMPANIES, LLC; *pg.* 237, *pg.* 991
MICHELOB ULTRA FRUIT - Beer - ANHEUSER-BUSCH

COMPANIES, LLC; *pg.* 237, *pg.* 991
MICHICO - Diamonds - ICE.COM, INC.; *pg.* 1258, *pg.* 1955
MICHIGAN FORMULA - Personal Defense Sprays - MACE SECURITY INTERNATIONAL, INC.; *pg.* 1172, *pg.* 1541
MICHIGAN INTERNATIONAL SPEEDWAY - Motorsports Facility - INTERNATIONAL SPEEDWAY CORPORATION; *pg.* 553, *pg.* 420
MICHIGAN LAWYERS WEEKLY - Newspaper - MASSACHUSETTS LAWYERS WEEKLY, INC.; *pg.* 1662, *pg.* 798
MICHIGAN MATCH - Steel Propeller - MICHIGAN WHEEL CORPORATION; *pg.* 1709, *pg.* 888
MICHIGAN PROPELLERS - Boat Propellers - MICHIGAN WHEEL CORPORATION; *pg.* 1709, *pg.* 888
MICHIGAN'S ADVENTURE - Amusement Park - CEDAR FAIR, L.P.; *pg.* 537, *pg.* 1471
MICHOICE - Debit Card - MARKETING INNOVATORS INTERNATIONAL, INC.; *pg.* 430, *pg.* 657
MICHTEX - Stabilizer - DAVID MICHAEL & CO. INC.; *pg.* 852, *pg.* 1563
MICKEY - Police Officer Puppet - GUND, INC.; *pg.* 954, *pg.* 1056
MICKEY MOUSE - Toy & Game - HASBRO, INC.; *pg.* 954, *pg.* 1603
MICKEY MOUSE - Toy - MATTEL, INC.; *pg.* 962, *pg.* 81
MICKEY MOUSE - Cartoon Character - THE WALT DISNEY COMPANY; *pg.* 317, *pg.* 52
MICKEY'S ICE - Malt Liquor - MILLERCOORS; *pg.* 254, *pg.* 1877
MICKEY'S MALT LIQUOR - Malt Liquor - MILLERCOORS; *pg.* 254, *pg.* 1877
MICKEY'S TOONTOWN - Amusement Park - THE WALT DISNEY COMPANY; *pg.* 317, *pg.* 52
MICKEY'S WISH - Bath Product - KOHLER CO.; *pg.* 91, *pg.* 1862
MICOR - Physiological Recording & Reporting Systems - SIEMENS CORPORATION; *pg.* 803, *pg.* 1291
MICORE - Graphic Monitoring System - FIKE CORPORATION; *pg.* 1047, *pg.* 973
MICORE - Mineral Fiber Board - USG CORPORATION; *pg.* 118, *pg.* 594
MICORE MICRO BEAD - Corner Bead Mineral Fiber Board - USG CORPORATION; *pg.* 118, *pg.* 594
MICR-TOP - Gear Inspection System - GLEASON - M&M PRECISION SYSTEMS CORPORATION; *pg.* 1341, *pg.* 1479
MICRA - Sapphire Oscillators - COHERENT, INC.; *pg.* 1406, *pg.* 265
MICRA - Cutting Tool - LEATHERMAN TOOL GROUP, INC.; *pg.* 1053, *pg.* 1504
MICRED - Software System - MENTOR GRAPHICS CORPORATION; *pg.* 432, *pg.* 1510
MICREL MINI 8 - Integrated Circuits - MICREL, INC.; *pg.* 654, *pg.* 247
MICRELNET - Wireless IC System - MICREL, INC.; *pg.* 654, *pg.* 247
MICRO - Face Strip - FLEXIBLE STEEL LACING COMPANY; *pg.* 1337, *pg.* 608
MICRO - Electronic Device - LANTRONIX, INC.; *pg.* 426, *pg.* 112
MICRO - Liquid Handling System - MOLECULAR DEVICES CORPORATION; *pg.* 1568, *pg.* 287
MICRO - Chemical Product - SPECTRUM CHEMICALS & LABORATORY PRODUCTS, INC.; *pg.* 1181, *pg.* 94
MICRO ABG - Arterial Blood Gas Sampler - VITAL SIGNS, INC.; *pg.* 1607, *pg.* 1126
MICRO AIR VENTS - Nurser System Feature - EVENFLO COMPANY, INC.; *pg.* 924, *pg.* 1470
MICRO-AT - Source Transfer Control Switch - S&C ELECTRIC COMPANY; *pg.* 1305, *pg.* 589
MICRO BEAD - Paper Faced Metal Offset Outside Corner Tape-On Bead - USG CORPORATION; *pg.* 118, *pg.* 594
MICRO BIO-SPIN - Software - BIO-RAD LABORATORIES, INC.; *pg.* 1504, *pg.* 101
MICRO-BIRD - Spinner - RAIN BIRD CORPORATION; *pg.* 707, *pg.* 44
MICRO BRAID - Braided Monofilament - CORTLAND LINE COMPANY; *pg.* 1831, *pg.* 1155
MICRO-C - Junction Box - MOLEX INCORPORATED; *pg.* 655, *pg.* 628
MICRO-C POLYPORT - Electronic Components - MOLEX INCORPORATED; *pg.* 655, *pg.* 628
MICRO CABMATIC - Automatic Train Control System - ALSTOM SIGNALING, INC.; *pg.* 1312, *pg.* 1350
MICRO-CARBON - Filter Cartridge - PALL CORPORATION; *pg.* 232, *pg.* 1323
MICRO CASE - Case - PELICAN PRODUCTS, INC.; *pg.* 1842, *pg.* 295
MICRO-CENTERED - Antenna - TRIMBLE NAVIGATION LIMITED; *pg.* 1384, *pg.* 288
MICRO CHAMP - Flush Cutter - CHANNELLOCK, INC.; *pg.* 1044, *pg.* 1551
MICRO-CHANGE - Electronic Components - MOLEX INCORPORATED; *pg.* 655, *pg.* 628
MICRO-CHEK - Antimicrobial Agent for PVC - FERRO CORPORATION; *pg.* 1162, *pg.* 1462
MICRO-CORR - Corrugated Box - CALUMET CARTON COMPANY; *pg.* 1454, *pg.* 661
MICRO-CROWN - Commercial Lighting - SWIVELIER CO., INC.; *pg.* 1307, *pg.* 1142
MICRO-DIP - Switch - TRANSICO INCORPORATED; *pg.* 682, *pg.* 49
MICRO DISPODIALYZER - Lab Dialysis Product - SPECTRUM LABORATORIES INC.; *pg.* 1595, *pg.* 69
MICRO-DOSE - Security X-Ray Inspection Equipment - AMERICAN SCIENCE AND ENGINEERING, INC.; *pg.* 1399, *pg.* 787
MICRO-DROP - Lube Systems - TRICO MFG. CORP.; *pg.* 219, *pg.* 1886
MICRO-FASTTRACK - Molecular Biology Product - THERMO FISHER SCIENTIFIC INC.; *pg.* 1602, *pg.* 61
MICRO-FILE - Microfilm - EASTMAN KODAK COMPANY; *pg.* 1408, *pg.* 1333
MICRO FINISH - Automotive Reconditioning Product - MOC PRODUCTS COMPANY, INC.; *pg.* 332, *pg.* 174
MICRO-FIT - Junction Box - MOLEX INCORPORATED; *pg.* 655, *pg.* 628
MICRO-FIT - Plastic Tube - SWAGELOK COMPANY; *pg.* 1064, *pg.* 1473
MICRO-FIT 3.0 - Electronic Components - MOLEX INCORPORATED; *pg.* 655, *pg.* 628
MICRO-FIT 3.0 BMI - Electronic Components - MOLEX INCORPORATED; *pg.* 655, *pg.* 628
MICRO-FIT BMI CPI - Electronic Components - MOLEX INCORPORATED; *pg.* 655, *pg.* 628
MICRO-FIT CPI - Electronic Components - MOLEX INCORPORATED; *pg.* 655, *pg.* 628
MICRO FOG - Cutting Room Equipment - EASTMAN MACHINE COMPANY; *pg.* 1331, *pg.* 1148
MICRO FOOT - Analog Switch & Multiplexer - VISHAY INTERTECHNOLOGY, INC.; *pg.* 1435, *pg.* 1551
MICRO-GO-ROUND - Automatic Food Rotator for Microwave Ovens - NORTHLAND ALUMINUM PRODUCTS INC.; *pg.* 1129, *pg.* 941
MICRO-GUARD - Software - BIO-RAD LABORATORIES, INC.; *pg.* 1504, *pg.* 101
MICRO III - Control Panel Line - GEA REFRIGERATION NORTH AMERICA, INC.; *pg.* 1072, *pg.* 1597
MICRO-INTRODUCERS - Catheter - VASCULAR SOLUTIONS, INC.; *pg.* 1434, *pg.* 946
MICRO IRT/C - Sensor - EXERGEN CORPORATION; *pg.* 1412, *pg.* 855
MICRO JEWEL - Implantable Cardioverter Defibrillator - MEDTRONIC, INC.; *pg.* 1564, *pg.* 939
MICRO-LATCH - Electronic Components - MOLEX INCORPORATED; *pg.* 655, *pg.* 628
MICRO-LIGHT - Beverage - SPRECHER BREWING COMPANY; *pg.* 265, *pg.* 1858
MICRO-LOC - Dual Oven Deli Pad - SEALED AIR CORPORATION; *pg.* 1468, *pg.* 1058
MICRO-LOCK - Electronic Components - MOLEX INCORPORATED; *pg.* 655, *pg.* 628
MICRO-LUBRICANT - Motorsports Entertainment - SPEEDWAY MOTORSPORTS, INC.; *pg.* 584, *pg.* 1370
MICRO-MAGNETIC - Electronic Article Surveillance System - SENTRY TECHNOLOGY CORPORATION; *pg.* 672, *pg.* 1339
MICRO MALT - Frozen Juices - UNITED DAIRY FARMERS, INC.; *pg.* 906, *pg.* 1426
MICRO-MAX - Mixer & Blender - STEDMAN MACHINE COMPANY; *pg.* 1379, *pg.* 673
MICRO-MELT - Stainless Steel Product - CARPENTER TECHNOLOGY CORPORATION; *pg.* 73, *pg.* 1584
MICRO MESH - Mesh Nets - L.L. BEAN, INC.; *pg.* 1777, *pg.* 750
MICRO-MINI - Commercial Lighting - SWIVELIER CO., INC.; *pg.* 1307, *pg.* 1142
MICRO-MOUNTS - Isolator - LORD CORPORATION; *pg.* 1357, *pg.* 1360
MICRO ONE - Cleaner - SWISHER HYGIENE INC.; *pg.* 336, *pg.* 1507
MICRO-PHASE - Liquid Detergent for Industrial Cleaning Applications - PPG INDUSTRIES, INC.; *pg.* 1445, *pg.* 1579
MICRO-PLATE - Diagnostic & Medical Product - ORASURE TECHNOLOGIES INC; *pg.* 1578, *pg.* 1516
MICRO-PRODICON - Filtration System - SPECTRUM LABORATORIES INC.; *pg.* 1595, *pg.* 69
MICRO-PUSH - Electronic Components - MOLEX INCORPORATED; *pg.* 655, *pg.* 628
MICRO-RATIO - Valve - MAXON CORPORATION; *pg.* 1359, *pg.* 695
MICRO-READY - Sandwiches - BRIDGFORD FOODS CORPORATION; *pg.* 842, *pg.* 42
MICRO RELEASE - Controlled Micro Release Technology - LUMARA HEALTH INC.; *pg.* 1557, *pg.* 973
MICRO-SAMOS - Emission Testing System - MISTRAS GROUP, INC.; *pg.* 1362, *pg.* 1113
MICRO-SCOPE - Diagnostic Software - MICRO 2000, INC.; *pg.* 434, *pg.* 96
MICRO-SCOPE SUITE - Hardware System - MICRO 2000, INC.; *pg.* 434, *pg.* 96
MICRO-SHIELD - Sport Product - FRANKLIN SPORTS, INC.; *pg.* 1834, *pg.* 847
MICRO-SPOT - Commercial Lighting - SWIVELIER CO., INC.; *pg.* 1307, *pg.* 1142
MICRO SPRING - Air Core - COILCRAFT, INC.; *pg.* 1324, *pg.* 562
MICRO STAG - Knife - COAST CUTLERY COMPANY; *pg.* 1121, *pg.* 1501
MICRO-STEP - Chemical Product - STEPAN COMPANY; *pg.* 1182, *pg.* 643
MICRO-STEP - Commercial Lighting - SWIVELIER CO., INC.; *pg.* 1307, *pg.* 1142
MICRO-STRIKE - Miniature Mallet Set - NUPLA CORPORATION; *pg.* 101, *pg.* 281
MICRO TECH - Micro Tools - SK HAND TOOL CORPORATION; *pg.* 1062, *pg.* 663
MICRO-TEMP - Medical Product - CINCINNATI SUB-ZERO PRODUCTS, INC.; *pg.* 1070, *pg.* 1411
MICRO-TENNA - Cable & Antenna System - RADIO FREQUENCY SYSTEMS, INC.; *pg.* 666, *pg.* 354
MICRO TERRAIN TITANS - Toy - SPIN MASTER LTD.; *pg.* 967, *pg.* 1943
MICRO TIP - Toothbrush - SUNSTAR AMERICAS INC.; *pg.* 1599, *pg.* 591
MICRO TIP CARTRIDGE - Intraocular Lenses - STAAR SURGICAL COMPANY; *pg.* 1597, *pg.* 151
MICRO-TOP - Metrology Product - GLEASON CORPORATION; *pg.* 1340, *pg.* 1335
MICRO TURBO - Small Turbo Hair Dryer - ANDIS COMPANY; *pg.* 498, *pg.* 1895
MICRO-TWIN - Bath Tissue Dispenser - GEORGIA-PACIFIC LLC; *pg.* 1458, *pg.* 507
MICROAIR - Mattress - INVACARE CORPORATION; *pg.* 1546, *pg.* 1451
MICROAIRE - Company Name - MICROAIRE SURGICAL INSTRUMENTS INC.; *pg.* 1423, *pg.* 1778
MICROALBUMIN - Reagents - BECKMAN COULTER, INC.; *pg.* 1402, *pg.* 48
MICROAMPLIFIER - Amplifiers - TEXAS INSTRUMENTS INCORPORATED; *pg.* 679, *pg.* 1688
MICROBAN - Disinfectant Spray - STEAMATIC INC.; *pg.* 60, *pg.* 1696
MICROBEAM - Micromanipulators Used in Laser Procedures - AMERICAN MEDICAL SYSTEMS, INC.; *pg.* 1399, *pg.* 238
MICROBEMAX - Bioremediation Products - ZEP INC.; *pg.* 338, *pg.* 524
MICROBETA - Liquid Scintillation Analyzer - PERKINELMER, INC.; *pg.* 1426, *pg.* 853
MICROBILT - Computers & Related Accessories - MICROBILT CORPORATION; *pg.* 782, *pg.* 534
MICROBLADE - Cable Assembly - MOLEX INCORPORATED; *pg.* 655, *pg.* 628
MICROBLAST RACERS - Toys - MGA ENTERTAINMENT, INC.; *pg.* 964, *pg.* 300
MICROBLAZE - Soft Processor Core - XILINX, INC.; *pg.* 496, *pg.* 252
MICROBORE - Liquid Chromatography System - BECKMAN COULTER, INC.; *pg.* 1402, *pg.* 48
MICROBOX - Chassis - CYBERRESEARCH INC.; *pg.* 381, *pg.* 339
MICROBREATHE - Coveralls - ALPHA PRO TECH, LTD.; *pg.* 1492, *pg.* 1922
MICROBRITE - Nutritional Product - RBC LIFE SCIENCES,

First page reference indicates Business Class Edition
Second page reference indicates Geographic Edition

INC.; *pg.* 1588, *pg.* 1723
MICROBUDDY - IC Device - SEMTECH CORPORATION; *pg.* 671, *pg.* 57
MICROCAB - Carborne Control System - ANSALDO STS; *pg.* 618, *pg.* 1573
MICROCAM SLR - Instant Camera Prints of Microscopic Specimens in Color & Black & White - POLAROID CORPORATION; *pg.* 1426, *pg.* 815
MICROCAP - ATC Parallel Plate (Single Layer) Ceramic Capacitors for DC to 50 GHz - AMERICAN TECHNICAL CERAMICS CORP.; *pg.* 616, *pg.* 1168
MICROCAT-HX - Computer Consultation Services & Software - LOCKHEED MARTIN CORPORATION; *pg.* 229, *pg.* 762
MICROCELL - Computer Software - ASTRO-MED, INC.; *pg.* 619, *pg.* 1609
MICROCHAMBER - Wafer Probing System - CASCADE MICROTECH, INC.; *pg.* 1405, *pg.* 1492
MICROCHECK - Filter Funnel - PALL CORPORATION; *pg.* 232, *pg.* 1323
MICROCHRON II - Microprocessor Timer - ALSTOM SIGNALING, INC.; *pg.* 1312, *pg.* 1350
MICROCLASP - Cable Assembly - MOLEX INCORPORATED; *pg.* 655, *pg.* 628
MICROCLAVE - Medical Device - HOSPIRA, INC.; *pg.* 1542, *pg.* 623
MICROCLEAR - Balloon - CONTINENTAL AMERICAN CORP.; *pg.* 1880, *pg.* 723
MICROCLIMATE - Medical Product - CINCINNATI SUB-ZERO PRODUCTS, INC.; *pg.* 1070, *pg.* 1411
MICROCLYPS - Clips - CHYRONHEGO; *pg.* 371, *pg.* 1179
MICROCOIL - Sensor - WATLOW ELECTRIC MANUFACTURING COMPANY; *pg.* 1078, *pg.* 1004
MICROCOILS - Medical Device - COOK GROUP, INC.; *pg.* 1518, *pg.* 674
MICROCON - Video Game Controller - MAD CATZ INTERACTIVE INC.; *pg.* 429, *pg.* 204
MICROCONTROL - Mustard - FUCHS NORTH AMERICA.; *pg.* 857, *pg.* 774
MICROCONVERTER - Analog Microcontroller - ANALOG DEVICES, INC.; *pg.* 617, *pg.* 839
MICROCOOLER - Thermal Imaging System - FLIR SYSTEMS, INC.; *pg.* 1413, *pg.* 1510
MICROCORR - Custom E-Flute Folding Cartons - CALUMET CARTON COMPANY; *pg.* 1454, *pg.* 661
MICROCROSS - Electronic Components - MOLEX INCORPORATED; *pg.* 655, *pg.* 628
MICROCYCLE - Packaging Product - CASCADES, INC.; *pg.* 73, *pg.* 1950
MICROCYTEPLUS - Medical & Diagnostic Testing - LABORATORY CORPORATION OF AMERICA HOLDINGS; *pg.* 1554, *pg.* 1359
MICRODIN - Electrical Controller - WATLOW ELECTRIC MANUFACTURING COMPANY; *pg.* 1078, *pg.* 1004
MICRODISP - Emission Testing System - MISTRAS GROUP, INC.; *pg.* 1362, *pg.* 1113
MICRODOL-X - Photo Developer & Replenisher - EASTMAN KODAK COMPANY; *pg.* 1408, *pg.* 1333
MICRODOT - Fragrance Sample - ARCADE MARKETING, INC.; *pg.* 352, *pg.* 1196
MICRODOWN - Apparel - CABELA'S INCORPORATED; *pg.* 535, *pg.* 1019
MICRODYNE - Chemical Product - ROCHESTER MIDLAND CORPORATION; *pg.* 334, *pg.* 1337
MICROE SYSTEMS - Precision Motion System - GSI GROUP INC.; *pg.* 1415, *pg.* 784
MICROEDGE - Photographic Films & Processing Chemicals - EASTMAN KODAK COMPANY; *pg.* 1408, *pg.* 1333
MICROFAST - Sprinkler - THE VIKING GROUP; *pg.* 119, *pg.* 891
MICROFAST HP - Fixed Temperature Release System - THE VIKING GROUP; *pg.* 119, *pg.* 891
MICROFERRET - Infusion Catheter - COOK GROUP, INC.; *pg.* 1518, *pg.* 674
MICROFIBRE - Mousepad - ALLSOP, INC.; *pg.* 347, *pg.* 1817
MICROFIL - Meltblown Systems - NORDSON CORPORATION; *pg.* 1365, *pg.* 1480
MICROFILL - Microvia Filling Technology - DOW CHEMICAL; *pg.* 1156, *pg.* 1563
MICROFINANCIAL - Leasing & Financing - MICROFINANCIAL INCORPORATED; *pg.* 782, *pg.* 805
MICROFINE - Polymer Product - CHEMTURA CORPORATION; *pg.* 1152, *pg.* 355
MICROFLAT - Ribbon Cable - W.L. GORE & ASSOCIATES, INC.; *pg.* 122, *pg.* 388
MICROFLEX - Servo Drive - BALDOR ELECTRIC COMPANY; *pg.* 1316, *pg.* 32
MICROFLEX - Miniature Condenser Microphones - SHURE INCORPORATED; *pg.* 672, *pg.* 638
MICROFLO - Basin - SPEAKMAN COMPANY; *pg.* 112, *pg.* 388
MICROFLO PROCESS - Paints - PPG INDUSTRIES, INC.; *pg.* 1445, *pg.* 1579
MICROFLOW - Abrasive Flow Machine - KENNAMETAL EXTRUDE HONE; *pg.* 1352, *pg.* 1542
MICROFLUIDICS - Fluid Service - MICROFLUIDICS INTERNATIONAL CORPORATION; *pg.* 58, *pg.* 836
MICROFLUIDICS REACTION TECHNOLOGY - Microreactor System - MICROFLUIDICS INTERNATIONAL CORPORATION; *pg.* 58, *pg.* 836
MICROFLUIDIZER - High and Low Pressure Processing Equip. for Emulsifying, Dispersing - MICROFLUIDICS INTERNATIONAL CORPORATION; *pg.* 58, *pg.* 836
MICROFLUIDIZER MIXER-REACTOR - Chemical Reactor - MICROFLUIDICS INTERNATIONAL CORPORATION; *pg.* 58, *pg.* 836
MICROFOAM - Foam Backing Stretchy Surgical Tape - 3M COMPANY; *pg.* 1142, *pg.* 956
MICROFOAM - Cookware - PACTIV CORPORATION; *pg.* 1466, *pg.* 624
MICROFOIL - Metallic Balloons - CONTINENTAL AMERICAN CORP.; *pg.* 1880, *pg.* 723
MICROFORCE - Wafer Test Product - FORMFACTOR, INC.; *pg.* 1882, *pg.* 122
MICROFRIDGE - Refrigerator/Freezer/ Microwave Oven Units - MAC-GRAY CORPORATION; *pg.* 58, *pg.* 852
MICROFUGE - Testing Instrument System - BECKMAN COULTER, INC.; *pg.* 1402, *pg.* 48
MICROFUNNEL - Filter Funnel - PALL CORPORATION; *pg.* 232, *pg.* 1323
MICROFUSE - Electronic Fuse - LITTELFUSE, INC.; *pg.* 1301, *pg.* 580
MICROFUSED - Sensor - MEASUREMENT SPECIALTIES INC.; *pg.* 1360, *pg.* 1783
MICROFUSION - Radiopaque Coating - IMPLANT SCIENCES CORPORATION; *pg.* 1348, *pg.* 860
MICROGARD - Glove - LAKELAND INDUSTRIES, INC.; *pg.* 1354, *pg.* 1338
MICROGON - Filtration System - SPECTRUM LABORATORIES INC.; *pg.* 1595, *pg.* 69
MICROGRIT - Optical Product - UNIVERSAL PHOTONICS, INC.; *pg.* 1433, *pg.* 1167
MICROHEDGE - Software - SUNGARD DATA SYSTEMS INC.; *pg.* 477, *pg.* 1592
MICROHYB - Molecular Biology Product - THERMO FISHER SCIENTIFIC INC.; *pg.* 1602, *pg.* 61
MICROHYDRIN - Nutritional Supplement - RBC LIFE SCIENCES, INC.; *pg.* 1588, *pg.* 1723
MICROJUST - Spacers for Nulok - NUPLA CORPORATION; *pg.* 101, *pg.* 281
MICROKA - Pharmaceutical Product - VALEANT PHARMACEUTICALS INTERNATIONAL; *pg.* 1605, *pg.* 1047
MICROKONTROL - MIDI Studio Controller - KORG USA, INC.; *pg.* 556, *pg.* 1180
MICROKORG - Synthesizer/Vocoder - KORG USA, INC.; *pg.* 556, *pg.* 1180
MICROKROS - Filtration System - SPECTRUM LABORATORIES INC.; *pg.* 1595, *pg.* 69
MICROKWIK CULTURE - Biological Product - CAROLINA BIOLOGICAL SUPPLY COMPANY; *pg.* 1513, *pg.* 1359
MICROLAB - Chart & Marking System - GRAPHIC CONTROLS LLC; *pg.* 401, *pg.* 1148
MICROLAB - Dispenser - HAMILTON CO., INC.; *pg.* 1415, *pg.* 1031
MICROLAN - Coupler - MAXIM INTEGRATED PRODUCTS, INC.; *pg.* 653, *pg.* 247
MICROLAP - Medical Equipment - CONMED CORPORATION; *pg.* 1517, *pg.* 1347
MICROLAS - Optical Subsystems - COHERENT, INC.; *pg.* 1406, *pg.* 265
MICROLASE - Marking System - GEORGE T. SCHMIDT, INC.; *pg.* 1340, *pg.* 637
MICROLEADFRAME - Packaging System - AMKOR TECHNOLOGY, INC.; *pg.* 67, *pg.* 25
MICROLECTRIC - Pole Line Hardware - THOMAS & BETTS CORPORATION; *pg.* 680, *pg.* 1646
MICROLEGEND - String - ASHAWAY LINE & TWINE MFG. CO.; *pg.* 1826, *pg.* 1600
MICROLIGHT - Software-Defined Radio - RAYTHEON COMPANY; *pg.* 233, *pg.* 854
MICROLIGHTWAND - Lighting System - PHILIPS SOLID-STATE LIGHTING SOLUTIONS; *pg.* 1303, *pg.* 806
MICROLITER - Fitted Stainless Steel Plunger Syringes - HAMILTON CO., INC.; *pg.* 1415, *pg.* 1031
MICROLITER - Lighting Product - HUBBELL INCORPORATED; *pg.* 1299, *pg.* 370
MICROLLAM - Wood & Building Material - WEYERHAEUSER COMPANY; *pg.* 121, *pg.* 1820
MICROLOGIC - Trip Units - SCHNEIDER ELECTRIC USA, INC.; *pg.* 1306, *pg.* 650
MICROLOGIX - Software - ROCKWELL AUTOMATION, INC.; *pg.* 668, *pg.* 1880
MICROLOK - Vital Interlocking Control System - ANSALDO STS; *pg.* 618, *pg.* 1573
MICROLOOP - Inline, Non-contact Electrical Defect Monitoring Solution - KLA-TENCOR CORPORATION; *pg.* 1353, *pg.* 146
MICROLOY - Rivetless Conveyor Chain - DAIFUKU WEBB; *pg.* 1327, *pg.* 885
MICROLUBE - Wax Emulsions - HERCULES INCORPORATED; *pg.* 1166, *pg.* 392
MICROLYZED - Jordan Filling - BOLTON-EMERSON AMERICAS, INC.; *pg.* 1318, *pg.* 827
MICROMASK - Pharmaceutical Product - LUMARA HEALTH INC.; *pg.* 1557, *pg.* 973
MICROMASS - Mass Spectrometer - WATERS CORPORATION; *pg.* 1436, *pg.* 834
MICROMAT - Clinical Diagnostic Product - BIO-RAD LABORATORIES, INC.; *pg.* 1504, *pg.* 101
MICROMATE - Microwave Shelves & Range Hoods - NORTEK, INC.; *pg.* 100, *pg.* 1607
MICROMATE - Flash Memory Card - SANDISK CORPORATION; *pg.* 465, *pg.* 147
MICROMATIC - Cleaning Product - HILLYARD, INC.; *pg.* 331, *pg.* 990
MICROMATIC - Sprinkler - THE VIKING GROUP; *pg.* 119, *pg.* 891
MICROMAX - Wireless Network Product - AIRSPAN NETWORKS INC.; *pg.* 346, *pg.* 410
MICROMAX - Clothing - LAKELAND INDUSTRIES, INC.; *pg.* 1354, *pg.* 1338
MICROMAX - Floor Care - NILFISK-ADVANCE, INC.; *pg.* 332, *pg.* 953
MICROMAXX - Ultrasound System - SONOSITE, INC.; *pg.* 1429, *pg.* 1818
MICROMD - Software - HENRY SCHEIN, INC.; *pg.* 1541, *pg.* 1180
MICROMEASURE - Software - SYMANTEC CORPORATION; *pg.* 478, *pg.* 161
MICROMEDEX - Software Tool And Application - TRUVEN HEALTH ANALYTICS; *pg.* 1696, *pg.* 867
MICROMELT 440-XH - Alloy - CARPENTER TECHNOLOGY CORPORATION; *pg.* 73, *pg.* 1584
MICROMETER - Drill - STOELTING CO.; *pg.* 1430, *pg.* 671
MICROMINUM - Cable - STANDARD WIRE & CABLE CO.; *pg.* 1306, *pg.* 187
MICROMIST - Fire Protection System - FIKE CORPORATION; *pg.* 1047, *pg.* 973
MICROMIST SYSTEM - Self-contained, Single-fluid, Pre-engineered Water Mist Suppression System - FIKE CORPORATION; *pg.* 1047, *pg.* 973
MICROMITE - Polymer Product - CHEMTURA CORPORATION; *pg.* 1152, *pg.* 355
MICROMITE - Medical Equipment - CONMED CORPORATION; *pg.* 1517, *pg.* 1347
MICROMIX - Compounding System - BAXTER INTERNATIONAL INC.; *pg.* 1499, *pg.* 599
MICROMONITOR - Electronic Devices - MAXIM INTEGRATED PRODUCTS, INC.; *pg.* 653, *pg.* 247
MICROMOTION - Control Panel - SERIGRAPH, INC.; *pg.* 1686, *pg.* 1899
MICROMOTOR - Stereotaxic Equipment - STOELTING CO.; *pg.* 1430, *pg.* 671
MICRON - Micrographic Reader - ANACOMP, INC.; *pg.* 350, *pg.* 1777
MICRON - Flying Backing - CORTLAND LINE COMPANY; *pg.* 1831, *pg.* 1155
MICRON - Gearhead - DANAHER CORPORATION; *pg.* 1044, *pg.* 397
MICRON AIR JET SIEVE - Processing System - HOSOKAWA MICRON POWDER SYSTEMS; *pg.* 1347, *pg.* 1124
MICRONAL - Polishing Agent for CR-39 Hard Resin Lenses - FERRO CORPORATION; *pg.* 1162, *pg.* 1462
MICRONASE - Medicine - PFIZER INC.; *pg.* 1581, *pg.* 1278

MICRONESTER - Embolization - COOK GROUP, INC.; *pg.* 1518, *pg.* 674
MICRONET - Microfiber Towel - MCNETT CORPORATION; *pg.* 1839, *pg.* 1817
MICRONET - Software Product - WOODWARD, INC.; *pg.* 122, *pg.* 329
MICRONET TMR - Turbine Control Unit Triple Modular Redundant - WOODWARD, INC.; *pg.* 122, *pg.* 329
MICRONIZER - Applicator - LENOX; *pg.* 1053, *pg.* 817
MICRONIZER - Fluid Energy Mill - STURTEVANT INC.; *pg.* 1379, *pg.* 824
MICRONODE - I/O Module - MKS INSTRUMENTS, INC.; *pg.* 1362, *pg.* 781
MICRONOVA - Vehicle Safety System - GROTE INDUSTRIES, INC.; *pg.* 206, *pg.* 693
MICRONOX - Cleaning Chemical Product - KYZEN CORPORATION; *pg.* 331, *pg.* 1652
MICRONSPOT - Laser Delivery Device - AMERICAN MEDICAL SYSTEMS, INC.; *pg.* 1399, *pg.* 238
MICRONY - Pacemakers - ST. JUDE MEDICAL, INC.; *pg.* 1596, *pg.* 963
MICROPAK - Filter Cartridge - PALL CORPORATION; *pg.* 232, *pg.* 1323
MICROPAQ - Wearable Monitor - WELCH ALLYN INC.; *pg.* 1436, *pg.* 1342
MICROPEL - Plastic Product - TROY CORPORATION; *pg.* 1184, *pg.* 1067
MICROPIRANI - Vacuum Gauge System - MKS INSTRUMENTS, INC.; *pg.* 1362, *pg.* 781
MICROPLAN - Software System - MENTOR GRAPHICS CORPORATION; *pg.* 432, *pg.* 1510
MICROPLASTY MINIMALLY INVASIVE PROGRAM - Knee Product - ZIMMER BIOMET HOLDINGS, INC.; *pg.* 1611, *pg.* 699
MICROPLATE MANAGER - Software - BIO-RAD LABORATORIES, INC.; *pg.* 1504, *pg.* 101
MICROPLEX - Analytical Device - LUMINEX CORPORATION; *pg.* 1421, *pg.* 1664
MICROPLUMB - Plumbing Product - SLOAN VALVE COMPANY; *pg.* 1062, *pg.* 613
MICROPOINT - Fluid Handling System - GRACO, INC.; *pg.* 1342, *pg.* 935
MICROPOWER - String - ASHAWAY LINE & TWINE MFG. CO.; *pg.* 1826, *pg.* 1600
MICROPOWER - Asynchronous SRAMs - CYPRESS SEMICONDUCTOR CORPORATION; *pg.* 1326, *pg.* 243
MICROPRESS - Printing Product - ELECTRONICS FOR IMAGING, INC.; *pg.* 390, *pg.* 88
MICROPRO - Pump Product - IDEX CORPORATION; *pg.* 1347, *pg.* 623
MICROPRO - Battery-Powered - MASTER APPLIANCE CORP.; *pg.* 1055, *pg.* 1888
MICROPRO BT-30 - Soldering Iron - MASTER APPLIANCE CORP.; *pg.* 1055, *pg.* 1888
MICROPULSE - Antenna Product - PCTEL, INC.; *pg.* 452, *pg.* 557
MICROPULSER - Software - BIO-RAD LABORATORIES, INC.; *pg.* 1504, *pg.* 101
MICROPUMP - Pumps - IDEX CORPORATION; *pg.* 1347, *pg.* 623
MICROPUNCTURE - Medical Device - COOK GROUP, INC.; *pg.* 1518, *pg.* 674
MICROQ - Software - QSOUND LABS, INC.; *pg.* 666, *pg.* 1904
MICRORAM - Ripple Attenuation Module - VICOR CORPORATION; *pg.* 1435, *pg.* 783
MICRORITE - Packaging Product - GRAPHIC PACKAGING HOLDING COMPANY; *pg.* 1459, *pg.* 509
MICROROTOFOR - Software - BIO-RAD LABORATORIES, INC.; *pg.* 1504, *pg.* 101
MICROROUTE - Software System - MENTOR GRAPHICS CORPORATION; *pg.* 432, *pg.* 1510
MICROROUTER - Router - RAYTHEON COMPANY; *pg.* 233, *pg.* 854
MICRORUPTOR - Medical Laser System - IRIDEX CORPORATION; *pg.* 648, *pg.* 160
MICROS 3700 - Software - MICROS SYSTEMS, INC.; *pg.* 435, *pg.* 768
MICROS 9700 - Software - MICROS SYSTEMS, INC.; *pg.* 435, *pg.* 768
MICROS E7 - Software - MICROS SYSTEMS, INC.; *pg.* 435, *pg.* 768
MICROSAFE - Security Product - FLEXCON CORPORATION; *pg.* 1457, *pg.* 844
MICROSCINT - Cocktail - PERKINELMER, INC.; *pg.* 1426, *pg.* 853
MICROSCRIBE - Digitizing System - IMMERSION CORPORATION; *pg.* 413, *pg.* 246
MICROSD - Flash Card - HGST; *pg.* 406, *pg.* 260
MICROSD - Memory Card - PNY TECHNOLOGIES, INC.; *pg.* 455, *pg.* 1105
MICROSD - Memory Card - SANDISK CORPORATION; *pg.* 465, *pg.* 147
MICROSEAL - Software - BIO-RAD LABORATORIES, INC.; *pg.* 1504, *pg.* 101
MICROSHIELD - Hose - TEKNOR APEX COMPANY; *pg.* 1889, *pg.* 1605
MICROSHORT - Sport Apparel - UNDER ARMOUR, INC.; *pg.* 49, *pg.* 759
MICROSIZED - Salt - CARGILL LIMITED; *pg.* 1475, *pg.* 1914
MICROSLICE - Wheel - URSCHEL LABORATORIES INCORPORATED; *pg.* 1386, *pg.* 698
MICROSLIP - Coverglass Cartridge - HACKER INSTRUMENTS & INDUSTRIES INC.; *pg.* 1415, *pg.* 1623
MICROSMART - Embroidery Machine - HIRSCH INTERNATIONAL CORP.; *pg.* 694, *pg.* 1164
MICROSOFT EDGE - Internet Browser - MICROSOFT CORPORATION; *pg.* 435, *pg.* 1824
MICROSOFT EXCHANGE - Computer Software - MICROSOFT CORPORATION; *pg.* 435, *pg.* 1824
MICROSOFT LYNC - Comuter Software - MICROSOFT CORPORATION; *pg.* 435, *pg.* 1824
MICROSOFT OFFICE WEB APPS - Software - MICROSOFT CORPORATION; *pg.* 435, *pg.* 1824
MICROSOFT PROJECT - Software - MICROSOFT CORPORATION; *pg.* 435, *pg.* 1824
MICROSOFT SHAREPOINT - Computer Software - MICROSOFT CORPORATION; *pg.* 435, *pg.* 1824
MICROSOFT VISIO - Software - MICROSOFT CORPORATION; *pg.* 435, *pg.* 1824
MICROSORB - Filtration Product - BASF CATALYSTS LLC; *pg.* 1148, *pg.* 1074
MICROSOURCE - Energy Management System - CARMANAH TECHNOLOGIES CORPORATION; *pg.* 628, *pg.* 1913
MICROSPRING - Interconnect Technology - FORMFACTOR, INC.; *pg.* 1882, *pg.* 122
MICROSTAAR - Injector - STAAR SURGICAL COMPANY; *pg.* 1597, *pg.* 151
MICROSTAR - Reader - LANDAUER, INC.; *pg.* 1554, *pg.* 615
MICROSTAR BGA - Integrated Circuit Packages - TEXAS INSTRUMENTS INCORPORATED; *pg.* 679, *pg.* 1688
MICROSTAR JUNIOR - Integrated Circuit Packages - TEXAS INSTRUMENTS INCORPORATED; *pg.* 679, *pg.* 1688
MICROSTAT - Handsets for Use with Laserscope Surgical Laser Systems - AMERICAN MEDICAL SYSTEMS, INC.; *pg.* 1399, *pg.* 238
MICROSTAT - Floor Care - NILFISK-ADVANCE, INC.; *pg.* 332, *pg.* 953
MICROSTATION - Software - BENTLEY SYSTEMS, INC.; *pg.* 361, *pg.* 1531
MICROSTATION - Software - EAGLE POINT SOFTWARE CORPORATION; *pg.* 389, *pg.* 707
MICROSTRATEGY 6 - Software - MICROSTRATEGY, INC.; *pg.* 1266, *pg.* 1809
MICROSTRATEGY 7 - Software - MICROSTRATEGY, INC.; *pg.* 1266, *pg.* 1809
MICROSTRATEGY 7I - Software - MICROSTRATEGY, INC.; *pg.* 1266, *pg.* 1809
MICROSTRATEGY 7I EVALUATION EDITION - Software - MICROSTRATEGY, INC.; *pg.* 1266, *pg.* 1809
MICROSTRATEGY 7I OLAP SERVICES - Software - MICROSTRATEGY, INC.; *pg.* 1266, *pg.* 1809
MICROSTRATEGY 8 - Software - MICROSTRATEGY, INC.; *pg.* 1266, *pg.* 1809
MICROSTRATEGY 9 - Software - MICROSTRATEGY, INC.; *pg.* 1266, *pg.* 1809
MICROSTRATEGY AGENT - Software - MICROSTRATEGY, INC.; *pg.* 1266, *pg.* 1809
MICROSTRATEGY ANALYST - Software - MICROSTRATEGY, INC.; *pg.* 1266, *pg.* 1809
MICROSTRATEGY BI AUTHOR - Software - MICROSTRATEGY, INC.; *pg.* 1266, *pg.* 1809
MICROSTRATEGY BI DEVELOPER KIT - Software - MICROSTRATEGY, INC.; *pg.* 1266, *pg.* 1809
MICROSTRATEGY BI MODELER - Software - MICROSTRATEGY, INC.; *pg.* 1266, *pg.* 1809
MICROSTRATEGY BROADCAST SERVER - Software - MICROSTRATEGY, INC.; *pg.* 1266, *pg.* 1809
MICROSTRATEGY BROADCASTER - Software - MICROSTRATEGY, INC.; *pg.* 1266, *pg.* 1809
MICROSTRATEGY BROADCASTER SERVER - Software - MICROSTRATEGY, INC.; *pg.* 1266, *pg.* 1809
MICROSTRATEGY BUSINESS INTELLIGENCE PLATFORM - Software - MICROSTRATEGY, INC.; *pg.* 1266, *pg.* 1809
MICROSTRATEGY COMMAND MANAGER - Software - MICROSTRATEGY, INC.; *pg.* 1266, *pg.* 1809
MICROSTRATEGY CONSULTING - Software - MICROSTRATEGY, INC.; *pg.* 1266, *pg.* 1809
MICROSTRATEGY CONSUMER - Software - MICROSTRATEGY, INC.; *pg.* 1266, *pg.* 1809
MICROSTRATEGY CUSTOMER ANALYZER - Software - MICROSTRATEGY, INC.; *pg.* 1266, *pg.* 1809
MICROSTRATEGY DESKTOP ANALYST - Software - MICROSTRATEGY, INC.; *pg.* 1266, *pg.* 1809
MICROSTRATEGY DISTRIBUTION SERVICES - Software - MICROSTRATEGY, INC.; *pg.* 1266, *pg.* 1809
MICROSTRATEGY ECRM 7 - Software - MICROSTRATEGY, INC.; *pg.* 1266, *pg.* 1809
MICROSTRATEGY EDUCATION - Software - MICROSTRATEGY, INC.; *pg.* 1266, *pg.* 1809
MICROSTRATEGY ETRAINER - Software - MICROSTRATEGY, INC.; *pg.* 1266, *pg.* 1809
MICROSTRATEGY EVALUATION EDITION - Software - MICROSTRATEGY, INC.; *pg.* 1266, *pg.* 1809
MICROSTRATEGY INFOCENTER - Software - MICROSTRATEGY, INC.; *pg.* 1266, *pg.* 1809
MICROSTRATEGY MDX ADAPTER - Software - MICROSTRATEGY, INC.; *pg.* 1266, *pg.* 1809
MICROSTRATEGY MULTISOURCE OPTION - Software - MICROSTRATEGY, INC.; *pg.* 1266, *pg.* 1809
MICROSTRATEGY OBJECT MANAGER - Software - MICROSTRATEGY, INC.; *pg.* 1266, *pg.* 1809
MICROSTRATEGY OBJECTS - Software - MICROSTRATEGY, INC.; *pg.* 1266, *pg.* 1809
MICROSTRATEGY OFFICE - Software - MICROSTRATEGY, INC.; *pg.* 1266, *pg.* 1809
MICROSTRATEGY OLAP PROVIDER - Software - MICROSTRATEGY, INC.; *pg.* 1266, *pg.* 1809
MICROSTRATEGY SDK - Software - MICROSTRATEGY, INC.; *pg.* 1266, *pg.* 1809
MICROSTRATEGY SUPPORT - Software - MICROSTRATEGY, INC.; *pg.* 1266, *pg.* 1809
MICROSTRATEGY TELECASTER - Software - MICROSTRATEGY, INC.; *pg.* 1266, *pg.* 1809
MICROSTRATEGY TRANSACTOR - Software - MICROSTRATEGY, INC.; *pg.* 1266, *pg.* 1809
MICROSTRATEGY WEB - Software - MICROSTRATEGY, INC.; *pg.* 1266, *pg.* 1809
MICROSTRATEGY WEB MMT - Software - MICROSTRATEGY, INC.; *pg.* 1266, *pg.* 1809
MICROSTRATEGY WEB SERVICES - Software - MICROSTRATEGY, INC.; *pg.* 1266, *pg.* 1809
MICROSTRATEGY WORLD - Software - MICROSTRATEGY, INC.; *pg.* 1266, *pg.* 1809
MICROSTREAM - Breath Sampling Products - MEDTRONIC; *pg.* 1563, *pg.* 183
MICROSTREAM - Flashlight - STREAMLIGHT INC.; *pg.* 1306, *pg.* 1527
MICROSUEDE - Fabric - NATIONAL SPINNING COMPANY, INC.; *pg.* 697, *pg.* 1265
MICROSURFACE - Cleaner - HOUGHTON INTERNATIONAL INC.; *pg.* 1167, *pg.* 1589
MICROSYN - Linear Encoder - CUSTOM SENSORS & TECHNOLOGIES; *pg.* 1407, *pg.* 152
MICROTALK - FRS Radio - COBRA ELECTRONICS CORPORATION; *pg.* 629, *pg.* 572
MICROTARGETING - Direct Mail System - VALASSIS; *pg.* 1698, *pg.* 386
MICROTEC - Software System - MENTOR GRAPHICS CORPORATION; *pg.* 432, *pg.* 1510
MICROTEC - Microalloy Steel - THE TIMKEN COMPANY; *pg.* 218, *pg.* 1408
MICROTECH - Software - BIO-RAD LABORATORIES, INC.; *pg.* 1504, *pg.* 101
MICROTECTOR - Portable Electronic Point Gage - DWYER INSTRUMENTS INC.; *pg.* 1330, *pg.* 694
MICROTEK - Duct-Free Range Hood Systems - NORTEK, INC.; *pg.* 100, *pg.* 1607
MICROTEL INNS & SUITES - Hotels - WYNDHAM WORLDWIDE CORPORATION; *pg.* 1119, *pg.* 1107
MICROTENN - Microprocessor Programmer - SPX THERMAL PRODUCT SOLUTIONS; *pg.* 1378, *pg.* 1555
MICROTERM - Alarm Lock System - NAPCO SECURITY

First page reference indicates Business Class Edition
Second page reference indicates Geographic Edition

SYSTEMS, INC.; *pg.* 658, *pg.* 1138
MICROTEST - Laboratory Product - BECTON, DICKINSON & COMPANY; *pg.* 1501, *pg.* 1068
MICROTEX - Toothbrush - RANIR LLC; *pg.* 520, *pg.* 888
MICROTHERM - Thermometer - COOPER-ATKINS CORPORATION; *pg.* 1407, *pg.* 355
MICROTIGHT - Pumps - IDEX CORPORATION; *pg.* 1347, *pg.* 623
MICROTORCH - Butane-Powered Microtorch - MASTER APPLIANCE CORP.; *pg.* 1055, *pg.* 1888
MICROTOUCH - Touch Screen - 3M COMPANY; *pg.* 1142, *pg.* 956
MICROTRAC - Disposable Razor - THE GILLETTE COMPANY; *pg.* 509, *pg.* 795
MICROTRAC - pump Product - IDEX CORPORATION; *pg.* 1347, *pg.* 623
MICROTRAC - Drives - MAGNETEK, INC.; *pg.* 1301, *pg.* 1870
MICROTRACE - Liquid Photoresist Technology - MACDERMID, INC.; *pg.* 1172, *pg.* 321
MICROTRACTRIX - Electronic Equipment - KLIPSCH GROUP, INC.; *pg.* 649, *pg.* 688
MICROTRAK - Sensor - MECHANICAL TECHNOLOGY, INCORPORATED; *pg.* 1422, *pg.* 1137
MICROTRAK 7000 - Laser Sensor - MTI INSTRUMENTS INC.; *pg.* 658, *pg.* 1137
MICROTRAK II - Laser Sensor - MTI INSTRUMENTS INC.; *pg.* 658, *pg.* 1137
MICROTRON - Advanced Performance Detector - PHOTONIS USA PENNSYLVANIA; *pg.* 663, *pg.* 1547
MICROTUBE - Adapter Kit - PRESSURE BIOSCIENCES, INC.; *pg.* 1586, *pg.* 844
MICROVEE - Loudspeakers - VELODYNE ACOUSTICS, INC.; *pg.* 685, *pg.* 152
MICROVISION - Pump Product - IDEX CORPORATION; *pg.* 1347, *pg.* 623
MICROVISION - Display Product - MICROVISION, INC.; *pg.* 654, *pg.* 1828
MICROVISION PLUS - Gas Analyzer - MKS INSTRUMENTS, INC.; *pg.* 1362, *pg.* 781
MICROVUE - Diagnostic Test Product - QUIDEL CORPORATION; *pg.* 1588, *pg.* 207
MICROWARE - Kitchenware - NORTHLAND ALUMINUM PRODUCTS INC.; *pg.* 1129, *pg.* 941
MICROWARE - Software - RADISYS CORPORATION; *pg.* 458, *pg.* 1498
MICROWAVE OFFICE - Computer Software - AWR CORPORATION; *pg.* 623, *pg.* 78
MICROWAVEABLE MALT - Frozen Juices - UNITED DAIRY FARMERS, INC.; *pg.* 906, *pg.* 1426
MICROWAVEABLE SHAKE - Frozen Milkshake - UNITED DAIRY FARMERS, INC.; *pg.* 906, *pg.* 1426
MICROWIRE - Bus Interface - MICREL, INC.; *pg.* 654, *pg.* 247
MICROWORKS - Electronics - CAMBRIDGE SOUNDWORKS, INC.; *pg.* 1234, *pg.* 781
MICROWRIST - Robotic Surgical System - INTUITIVE SURGICAL, INC.; *pg.* 1546, *pg.* 286
MICROX - Software Product - CHYRONHEGO; *pg.* 371, *pg.* 1179
MICROZORB - Cleaner - DELTA FOREMOST CHEMICAL CORPORATION; *pg.* 1155, *pg.* 1642
MICS - Multiplexer & Demultiplexer Module - ALLIANCE FIBER OPTIC PRODUCTS, INC.; *pg.* 1399, *pg.* 283
MID BRITE - Chemical Product - ROCHESTER MIDLAND CORPORATION; *pg.* 334, *pg.* 1337
MID CONTINENT CABINETRY - Builder/Remodeler/Dealer Market - NORCRAFT HOLDINGS, LP; *pg.* 100, *pg.* 921
MID-CORE - Cervical Pillow - DYNATRONICS CORPORATION; *pg.* 1526, *pg.* 1757
MID HIGH DUAL AIR - Waterproof Soft Toe - WEINBRENNER SHOE COMPANY, INC.; *pg.* 1822, *pg.* 1871
MID PROFILE - Cushion - THE ROHO GROUP; *pg.* 1591, *pg.* 556
MID RISE BOOT 553 - Jean - LEVI STRAUSS & CO.; *pg.* 43, *pg.* 220
MID RISE STRAIGHT 552 - Jean - LEVI STRAUSS & CO.; *pg.* 43, *pg.* 220
MID SUR - Golf Equipment - ACUSHNET COMPANY; *pg.* 1824, *pg.* 818
MID VALLEY TOWN CRIER - Texas Newspaper - FREEDOM COMMUNICATIONS, INC.; *pg.* 1643, *pg.* 110
MIDAS - Wireless Control Product - UNIVERSAL ELECTRONICS, INC.; *pg.* 683, *pg.* 262
MIDAS - Grinder - WELDON SOLUTIONS; *pg.* 1388, *pg.* 1598
MIDAS TOUCH - Maintenance Package - MIDAS, INC.; *pg.* 212, *pg.* 620
MIDAZOLAM HCL - Pharmaceutical Product - BAXTER INTERNATIONAL INC.; *pg.* 1499, *pg.* 599
MIDDLE SCHOOL MADNESS - Trademark (Div. I Men's & Women's Basketball) - NATIONAL COLLEGIATE ATHLETIC ASSOCIATION; *pg.* 567, *pg.* 688
MIDDLEBY MARSHALL - Conveyor Cooking Equipment - THE MIDDLEBY CORPORATION; *pg.* 1361, *pg.* 610
MIDDLETOWN - Lighting Product - WESTINGHOUSE LIGHTING CORPORATION; *pg.* 687, *pg.* 1571
MIDFILM - Ceramic & Plastic Product - COORSTEK, INC.; *pg.* 77, *pg.* 330
MIDGARD - Stereotaxic Equipment - STOELTING CO.; *pg.* 1430, *pg.* 671
MIDGEE - Container Grown Plant - MONROVIA GROWERS; *pg.* 1797, *pg.* 44
MIDGET SHADE - Commercial Lighting - SWIVELIER CO., INC.; *pg.* 1307, *pg.* 1142
MIDGUARD - Precision Current Source - STOELTING CO.; *pg.* 1430, *pg.* 671
MIDI - Bolt Down Version of the Maxi Fuse - LITTELFUSE, INC.; *pg.* 1301, *pg.* 580
MIDI ASSISTANT - MIDI Products - ALLEN ORGAN COMPANY; *pg.* 527, *pg.* 1549
MIDIKROS - Filtration System - SPECTRUM LABORATORIES INC.; *pg.* 1595, *pg.* 69
MIDKNIGHT BLUE - Container Grown Plant - MONROVIA GROWERS; *pg.* 1797, *pg.* 44
MIDLAND HARVEST - Milled Rice - ARCHER-DANIELS-MIDLAND COMPANY; *pg.* 825, *pg.* 565
MIDMARK - Bariatric Power Examination Table - ALIMED, INC.; *pg.* 1490, *pg.* 816
MIDNIGHT - Furniture - ASHLEY FURNITURE INDUSTRIES, INC.; *pg.* 914, *pg.* 1852
MIDNIGHT - Fabric - NEMSCHOFF, INC.; *pg.* 936, *pg.* 1890
MIDNIGHT - Stainless Steel Flatware - ONEIDA LTD; *pg.* 1129, *pg.* 1318
MIDNIGHT ECLIPSE - Video Game - INTERNATIONAL GAME TECHNOLOGY; *pg.* 957, *pg.* 1024
MIDNIGHT EXPRESS - Towing Unit - MILLER INDUSTRIES, INC.; *pg.* 185, *pg.* 1655
MIDNIGHT MADNESS - Trademark (Div. I Men's & Women's Basketball) - NATIONAL COLLEGIATE ATHLETIC ASSOCIATION; *pg.* 567, *pg.* 688
MIDNIGHT MARQUEE - Magazines - MIDNIGHT MARQUEE PRESS, INC.; *pg.* 1665, *pg.* 758
MIDNIGHT MATINEE - Video Game - INTERNATIONAL GAME TECHNOLOGY; *pg.* 957, *pg.* 1024
MIDNIGHT MIST - Furniture - BUSH INDUSTRIES INC.; *pg.* 919, *pg.* 1170
MIDNIGHT SUN EXPRESS ULTRA DOME - Rail Cars Tour - PRINCESS TOURS; *pg.* 1920, *pg.* 1838
MIDNIGHT TREASURES - Video Game - INTERNATIONAL GAME TECHNOLOGY; *pg.* 957, *pg.* 1024
MIDNITE BUFFET - Late Night Food Service - EAT'N PARK HOSPITALITY GROUP; *pg.* 1728, *pg.* 1539
MIDOL - Medicine - BAYER HEALTHCARE CONSUMER CARE DIVISION; *pg.* 1500, *pg.* 1087
MIDORO - Fan - CRAFTMADE INTERNATIONAL, INC.; *pg.* 1295, *pg.* 1670
MIDSOL - Food Product - MGP INGREDIENTS, INC.; *pg.* 877, *pg.* 714
MIDSUMMER NIGHT SWING - Performing Arts Program - LINCOLN CENTER FOR THE PERFORMING ARTS, INC.; *pg.* 557, *pg.* 1251
MIDSUMMERS NIGHT - Candle - THE YANKEE CANDLE COMPANY, INC.; *pg.* 1792, *pg.* 843
MIDTOWN - Fabric - NEMSCHOFF, INC.; *pg.* 936, *pg.* 1890
MIDTOWNE - Flatware - ONEIDA LTD; *pg.* 1129, *pg.* 1318
MIDWAY - Arcade Games - WMS INDUSTRIES INC.; *pg.* 593, *pg.* 666
MIDWAY'S FINEST - Caramel - GOLD MEDAL PRODUCTS CO.; *pg.* 55, *pg.* 1414
MIDWEIGHT - Joint Compound - USG CORPORATION; *pg.* 118, *pg.* 594
MIDWEST - Sight Flow Indicators - DWYER INSTRUMENTS INC.; *pg.* 1330, *pg.* 694
MIDWEST - Pet Product - PETSMART, INC.; *pg.* 1481, *pg.* 18
MIDWEST COUNTRY FARE - Food Product - HY-VEE, INC.; *pg.* 1023, *pg.* 713
MIDWEST GRAIN - Bakery Product - ALFRED NICKLES BAKERY, INC.; *pg.* 836, *pg.* 1466
MIDWEST IN-HOUSE - In-House Publication - MASSACHUSETTS LAWYERS WEEKLY, INC.; *pg.* 1662, *pg.* 798
MIDWEST LIVING - Magazine - MEREDITH CORPORATION; *pg.* 1663, *pg.* 705
MIDWEST MARKETER - Publication - IOWA FARMER TODAY; *pg.* 1653, *pg.* 702
MIDWEST MERCHANDISER - Magazine - SUMNER COMMUNICATIONS INC.; *pg.* 1690, *pg.* 338
MIDWEST STYLUS - Dental Product - DENTSPLY INTERNATIONAL INC.; *pg.* 1522, *pg.* 1596
MIDWEY - Glove - KOMBI, LTD.; *pg.* 1838, *pg.* 1766
MIELE - Home Appliance - MIELE INC.; *pg.* 59, *pg.* 1112
MIETHER - Bearing Products - MIETHER BEARING PRODUCTS, INC.; *pg.* 1361, *pg.* 1728
MIFI TECHNOLOGY - Recovery System - MILE MARKER INTERNATIONAL INC.; *pg.* 213, *pg.* 459
MIG - Electronic Components - MOLEX INCORPORATED; *pg.* 655, *pg.* 628
MIGERGOT - Pharmaceutical Product - G&W LABORATORIES INC.; *pg.* 1532, *pg.* 1123
MIGHTY ARROW - Beer - NEW BELGIUM BREWING COMPANY, INC.; *pg.* 258, *pg.* 328
MIGHTY FLOW! - Air Intake, Carburetor Preheater & Defroster Duct Hoses - DORMAN PRODUCTS, INC.; *pg.* 204, *pg.* 1522
MIGHTY GRIP - Jar Openers - LEWTAN INDUSTRIES CORP.; *pg.* 1658, *pg.* 352
MIGHTY GRIP - Baby Care Product - MUNCHKIN, INC.; *pg.* 964, *pg.* 300
MIGHTY KIDS MEAL - Child's Combination Meal - MCDONALD'S CORPORATION; *pg.* 1737, *pg.* 645
MIGHTY LEAN - Nutritional Supplement - NATURAL ORGANICS, INC.; *pg.* 1571, *pg.* 1181
MIGHTY M - Gaming Service - EMPIRE RESORTS, INC.; *pg.* 1090, *pg.* 1183
MIGHTY MALTS CHOCOLATE MALTED MILK BALLS - Food Product - PROMOTION IN MOTION, INC.; *pg.* 1861, *pg.* 1052
MIGHTY MINI - Vacuum - SHOP-VAC CORPORATION; *pg.* 1375, *pg.* 1595
MIGHTY MITE - Connector - COOPER INTERCONNECT; *pg.* 630, *pg.* 1118
MIGHTY MO - Extra Heavy Duty Hammer Tacker - ARROW FASTENER COMPANY, INC.; *pg.* 1042, *pg.* 1118
MIGHTY MOUSER - Fishing System - GREENLEE TEXTRON INC.; *pg.* 1048, *pg.* 655
MIGHTY MUGGS - Toy & Game - HASBRO, INC.; *pg.* 954, *pg.* 1603
MIGHTY SYSTEM XL - Brake Parts - MIGHTY DISTRIBUTING SYSTEM OF AMERICA; *pg.* 213, *pg.* 538
MIGHTY TECSELECT - Wiper Blades - MIGHTY DISTRIBUTING SYSTEM OF AMERICA; *pg.* 213, *pg.* 538
MIGHTY TINY - Cookies & Crackers - KELLOGG COMPANY; *pg.* 831, *pg.* 870
MIGHTY VS7 - Chemical - MIGHTY DISTRIBUTING SYSTEM OF AMERICA; *pg.* 213, *pg.* 538
MIGHTYMO - Digitized Speech Devices - DYNAVOX INC.; *pg.* 635, *pg.* 1574
MIGHTYMOLE - Drilling Tool - MCLAUGHLIN BORING SYSTEMS; *pg.* 1360, *pg.* 1617
MIGHTYMUX - Analog Switches & Cross Points - INTERSIL CORPORATION; *pg.* 647, *pg.* 146
MIGHTYPLATE - Roofing Products Line - TEXAS REFINERY CORP.; *pg.* 986, *pg.* 1696
MIGHTYPLY - Cold Applied Roofing Membrane - TEXAS REFINERY CORP.; *pg.* 986, *pg.* 1696
MIGHTYPRO - Cleaning Product - RUG DOCTOR, LP; *pg.* 1373, *pg.* 1734
MIGHTYVALVE - Pumps - IDEX CORPORATION; *pg.* 1347, *pg.* 623
MIGORO-NOMIGORO - Beverages - THE COCA-COLA COMPANY; *pg.* 240, *pg.* 493
MIGRAACTIN - Nutritional Supplement - NATURAL ORGANICS, INC.; *pg.* 1571, *pg.* 1181
MIGRAHEAL - Cable - COMMSCOPE, INC.; *pg.* 278, *pg.* 1378
MIGRAINE ICE - Cooling Pads - THE MENTHOLATUM COMPANY; *pg.* 1565, *pg.* 1320
MIGRATION MANAGER - Software - DELL SOFTWARE; *pg.* 385, *pg.* 40
MIGRATION MANAGER FOR EXCHANGE - Software - DELL SOFTWARE; *pg.* 385, *pg.* 40
MIGRATION MANAGER FOR SHAREPOINT - Software -

DELL SOFTWARE; *pg.* 385, *pg.* 40
MIGRATION SERVICES - Wireline Solutions - SONUS NETWORKS INC.; *pg.* 1281, *pg.* 858
MIGRATION SUITE - Software - DELL SOFTWARE; *pg.* 385, *pg.* 40
MIGRATION SUITE FOR ACTIVE DIRECTORY - Software - DELL SOFTWARE; *pg.* 385, *pg.* 40
MIGRATIONS - Office Furniture - STEELCASE INC.; *pg.* 475, *pg.* 889
MIGRATIONS ROUND - Office Furniture - STEELCASE INC.; *pg.* 475, *pg.* 889
MIGRATIONS TABLE - Tables - STEELCASE INC.; *pg.* 475, *pg.* 889
MIGRATOR FOR SAMETIME - Software - DELL SOFTWARE; *pg.* 385, *pg.* 40
MIGUEL - Footwear - COBIAN CORP.; *pg.* 1806, *pg.* 253
MIGUZI - Game & TV Show - THE CARTOON NETWORK; *pg.* 273, *pg.* 492
M.I.K.A - Orthopedic Implant Product - DJO SURGICAL; *pg.* 1525, *pg.* 1661
MIKADO - Dinnerware - THE HOMER LAUGHLIN CHINA COMPANY; *pg.* 1125, *pg.* 1850
MIKADO - Biscuit Sticks - MONDELEZ INTERNATIONAL, INC.; *pg.* 878, *pg.* 601
MIKADO - Fabric - NEMSCHOFF, INC.; *pg.* 936, *pg.* 1890
MIKASA - Dinnerware - LIFETIME BRANDS, INC.; *pg.* 1127, *pg.* 1161
MIKE - Cellular Phone - TELUS CORPORATION; *pg.* 1952, *pg.* 1912
MIKE AND IKE - Candy - JUST BORN, INC.; *pg.* 1857, *pg.* 1516
MIKE SHAD - Car Dealerships - AUTONATION, INC.; *pg.* 165, *pg.* 423
MIKE'S CLASSIC MARGARITA - Beverage - MIKE'S HARD LEMONADE CO.; *pg.* 1966, *pg.* 582
MIKE'S HARD LEMONADE - Beverage - MIKE'S HARD LEMONADE CO.; *pg.* 1966, *pg.* 582
MIKE'S HARD PUNCH - Beverage - MIKE'S HARD LEMONADE CO.; *pg.* 1966, *pg.* 582
MIKE'S HARDER LEMONADE - Beverage - MIKE'S HARD LEMONADE CO.; *pg.* 1966, *pg.* 582
MIKE'S HARDER PUNCH - Beverage - MIKE'S HARD LEMONADE CO.; *pg.* 1966, *pg.* 582
MIKE'S LITE HARD LEMONADE - Beverage - MIKE'S HARD LEMONADE CO.; *pg.* 1966, *pg.* 582
MIKEY STARS - Women's Clothing - MICHAEL STARS, INC.; *pg.* 29, *pg.* 100
MIKRO - Hammer & Screen Mill - HOSOKAWA MICRON POWDER SYSTEMS; *pg.* 1347, *pg.* 1124
MIKRO-ACM - Processing System - HOSOKAWA MICRON POWDER SYSTEMS; *pg.* 1347, *pg.* 1124
MIKRO-ACM CX - Processing System - HOSOKAWA MICRON POWDER SYSTEMS; *pg.* 1347, *pg.* 1124
MIKRO-AIRLOCK - Processing System - HOSOKAWA MICRON POWDER SYSTEMS; *pg.* 1347, *pg.* 1124
MIKRO-ATOMIZER - Processing System - HOSOKAWA MICRON POWDER SYSTEMS; *pg.* 1347, *pg.* 1124
MIKRO-BANTAM - Processing System - HOSOKAWA MICRON POWDER SYSTEMS; *pg.* 1347, *pg.* 1124
MIKRO-PULVERIZER - Processing System - HOSOKAWA MICRON POWDER SYSTEMS; *pg.* 1347, *pg.* 1124
MIKRO-SAMPLMILL - Processing System - HOSOKAWA MICRON POWDER SYSTEMS; *pg.* 1347, *pg.* 1124
MIKRO-SPRAY - Detergent/Sanitizer Dispenser - ECOLAB INC.; *pg.* 329, *pg.* 960
MIKRON - Commemorative Camera - NIKON INC.; *pg.* 1424, *pg.* 1181
MIL-ENE - Hook-Up Wire - W.L. GORE & ASSOCIATES, INC.; *pg.* 122, *pg.* 388
MIL/PAC - High Density Military Power Supplies - MARTEK POWER ABBOTT, INC.; *pg.* 652, *pg.* 294
MILAFIN - Furniture - HERMAN MILLER, INC.; *pg.* 926, *pg.* 913
MILAN - Watch - A. T. CROSS COMPANY; *pg.* 339, *pg.* 1602
MILAN - Textiles - BERNHARDT DESIGN; *pg.* 918, *pg.* 1381
MILAN - Decorative Accessory - ETHAN ALLEN INTERIORS INC.; *pg.* 924, *pg.* 343
MILAN - Furniture - LA-Z-BOY INCORPORATED; *pg.* 932, *pg.* 901
MILANO - Shoes - ALLEN-EDMONDS SHOE CORP.; *pg.* 1804, *pg.* 1887
MILANO - Furniture - BUSH INDUSTRIES INC.; *pg.* 919, *pg.* 1170
MILANO - Carpet - INTERFACE, INC.; *pg.* 695, *pg.* 512
MILANO - Bath & Plumbing Product - JACUZZI BRANDS CORPORATION; *pg.* 554, *pg.* 65
MILANO - Cookies - PEPPERIDGE FARM, INC.; *pg.* 888, *pg.* 363
MILANO - Surface Material - STEELCASE INC.; *pg.* 475, *pg.* 889
MILANO - Ceiling Fan - WESTINGHOUSE LIGHTING CORPORATION; *pg.* 687, *pg.* 1571
MILCAM - Thermal Imaging System - FLIR SYSTEMS, INC.; *pg.* 1413, *pg.* 1510
MILCAM RECON - Thermal Imaging System - FLIR SYSTEMS, INC.; *pg.* 1413, *pg.* 1510
MILCARE - Furniture - HERMAN MILLER, INC.; *pg.* 926, *pg.* 913
MILCLAW - Tooling System - KENNAMETAL INC.; *pg.* 1052, *pg.* 1547
MILD MEXICAN - Food Product - ANNIE'S INC.; *pg.* 1760, *pg.* 45
MILDEW CHECK - Mildewcidal/Algicidal House Wash - PPG INDUSTRIES, INC.; *pg.* 1445, *pg.* 1579
MILE MARKER - Off-Road Vehicle Accessories - MILE MARKER INTERNATIONAL INC.; *pg.* 213, *pg.* 459
MILEAGE PLUS - Travel Award Program - UNITED CONTINENTAL HOLDINGS, INC.; *pg.* 1927, *pg.* 593
MILEMAKER - Computerized Mileage System - RAND MCNALLY & COMPANY; *pg.* 1679, *pg.* 661
MILEMATE - Wheel Bearing - THE TIMKEN COMPANY; *pg.* 218, *pg.* 1408
MILEMAX - Mileage Improver - RADIATOR SPECIALTY COMPANY; *pg.* 215, *pg.* 1380
MILEPOST - Equine Products - TRACTOR SUPPLY COMPANY; *pg.* 708, *pg.* 1627
MILES - Gin - SAZERAC COMPANY, INC.; *pg.* 1969, *pg.* 745
MILES 2000 - Multiple Integrated Laser Engagement System - CUBIC CORPORATION; *pg.* 632, *pg.* 201
THE MILES CARD FROM DISCOVER CARD - Credit Cards - DISCOVER FINANCIAL SERVICES; *pg.* 744, *pg.* 653
MILES KIMBALL - Mail Order - SILVER STAR BRANDS; *pg.* 1785, *pg.* 1886
MILES THE MONSTER - Toy Action Figures - DOVER MOTORSPORTS, INC.; *pg.* 545, *pg.* 387
MILESTONE - Herbicide - DOW AGROSCIENCES LLC; *pg.* 1156, *pg.* 684
MILESTONE - Furniture - JASPER GROUP; *pg.* 930, *pg.* 691
MILESTONE - Fabric - NEMSCHOFF, INC.; *pg.* 936, *pg.* 1890
MILESTONE - Musical Instrument - PEAVEY ELECTRONICS CORPORATION; *pg.* 662, *pg.* 970
MILESTONE - Custom Mobile Serving Equipment - THE VOLLRATH COMPANY LLC; *pg.* 1139, *pg.* 1894
MILESTONE SCIENTIFIC - Medical & Dental Solutions - MILESTONE SCIENTIFIC, INC.; *pg.* 1568, *pg.* 1079
MILEX - Automotive Repair Service - MORAN INDUSTRIES, INC.; *pg.* 213, *pg.* 632
MILFLEX - Military Specification Packaging Foam - SEALED AIR CORPORATION; *pg.* 1468, *pg.* 1058
MILFORCE - Military Specification Packaging Foam - SEALED AIR CORPORATION; *pg.* 1468, *pg.* 1058
MILFORD - Furniture - ETHAN ALLEN INTERIORS INC.; *pg.* 924, *pg.* 343
MILFORD - Dinnerware - THE HOMER LAUGHLIN CHINA COMPANY; *pg.* 1125, *pg.* 1850
MILFORD PARK - Furniture - ASHLEY FURNITURE INDUSTRIES, INC.; *pg.* 914, *pg.* 1852
MILISTS - Online Marketing Service - PITNEY BOWES SOFTWARE INC.; *pg.* 455, *pg.* 1346
MILITARY - Battery - ULTRALIFE CORPORATION; *pg.* 1385, *pg.* 1317
MILITARY APPROVED FERRO-FILM - Films - DAUBERT INDUSTRIES, INC.; *pg.* 1155, *pg.* 561
MILITARY MERIT - Military Recognition Program - DRIVETIME AUTOMOTIVE GROUP, INC.; *pg.* 169, *pg.* 16
MILITARY MONEY - Magazine - INCHARGE INSTITUTE OF AMERICA, INC.; *pg.* 768, *pg.* 454
MILITARY.COM - Military Website - MILITARY ADVANTAGE, INC.; *pg.* 1267, *pg.* 223
MILK BONE - Dog Treats - BIG HEART PET BRANDS; *pg.* 1474, *pg.* 213
MILK CHOCOLATE PEANUT BUTTER CUP - Candy - BOYER CANDY COMPANY INC.; *pg.* 1851, *pg.* 1514
MILK DUDS - Chocolate Candy - THE HERSHEY CO.; *pg.* 1855, *pg.* 1538
MILK IT! - Lottery Game - IOWA LOTTERY; *pg.* 996, *pg.* 705
MILK MATE - Milk Replacer for Foals - MANNA PRO CORPORATION; *pg.* 1478, *pg.* 975
MILK MONEY - Game - WMS INDUSTRIES INC.; *pg.* 593, *pg.* 666
MILK 'N CEREAL BARS - Cereal Bars - GENERAL MILLS, INC.; *pg.* 828, *pg.* 933
MILKA - Chocolate - MONDELEZ INTERNATIONAL, INC.; *pg.* 878, *pg.* 601
MILKADE - Pet Supplies - HAPPY JACK INC.; *pg.* 1476, *pg.* 1390
MILKSHAKE - Cow Puppet - GUND, INC.; *pg.* 954, *pg.* 1056
MILKY GEL ROLLER - Pens - PENTEL OF AMERICA, LTD.; *pg.* 453, *pg.* 295
MILKY WAY - Candy Bar - MARS, INCORPORATED; *pg.* 1858, *pg.* 1792
MILKY WAY CRISPY ROLLS - Candy - MARS, INCORPORATED; *pg.* 1858, *pg.* 1792
MILKYWAY - Software - SYNOPSYS, INC.; *pg.* 480, *pg.* 162
MILL CITY - Carpet - INTERFACE, INC.; *pg.* 695, *pg.* 512
MILL CREEK - Vinyl Siding - PLY GEM SIDING GROUP; *pg.* 105, *pg.* 986
MILL DANCE BRAND - Packaged Foods - ATALANTA CORPORATION; *pg.* 838, *pg.* 1057
MILL-GARD - Fluid Handling System - GRACO, INC.; *pg.* 1342, *pg.* 935
MILL HOST - Sawmill Technology Software - CAE INC.; *pg.* 226, *pg.* 1959
MILL PACK - Fluid Sealing Product - A.W. CHESTERTON COMPANY; *pg.* 1315, *pg.* 861
MILL PACK 1730 - Fiber Packing - A.W. CHESTERTON COMPANY; *pg.* 1315, *pg.* 861
MILL VALLEY - Bike - MARIN BIKES; *pg.* 1708, *pg.* 168
MILL WHITE - Paint - KELLY-MOORE PAINT COMPANY, INC.; *pg.* 1443, *pg.* 198
MILLBRIDGE - Shoes - ALLEN-EDMONDS SHOE CORP.; *pg.* 1804, *pg.* 1887
MILLBRIDGE - Vinyl Siding - NORTEK, INC.; *pg.* 100, *pg.* 1607
MILLBROOK - Clothing - ABERCROMBIE & FITCH CO.; *pg.* 37, *pg.* 1466
MILLE BORNES - Game - WINNING MOVES GAMES, INC.; *pg.* 970, *pg.* 816
MILLENIA - Bagger - AUTOMATED PACKAGING SYSTEMS INC.; *pg.* 1452, *pg.* 1474
MILLENIA - Vertical Blinds - HUNTER DOUGLAS, INC.; *pg.* 928, *pg.* 1320
MILLENIA - Cooler - SEELEY INTERNATIONAL AMERICAS; *pg.* 1076, *pg.* 19
MILLENIUM - Medical Information Management Solution - CERNER CORPORATION; *pg.* 1514, *pg.* 981
MILLENIUM 4 - Remote Control - UNIVERSAL ELECTRONICS, INC.; *pg.* 683, *pg.* 262
MILLENIUM RO SYSTEMS - Reverse Osmosis for Medical Market - GE WATER & PROCESS TECHNOLOGIES; *pg.* 1339, *pg.* 1588
MILLENNIA - Home Appliance - DACOR; *pg.* 54, *pg.* 67
MILLENNIA - Furniture - TROPITONE FURNITURE CO., INC.; *pg.* 945, *pg.* 118
MILLENNIA - Ceiling Panel - USG CORPORATION; *pg.* 118, *pg.* 594
MILLENNIUM - Furniture - ASHLEY FURNITURE INDUSTRIES, INC.; *pg.* 914, *pg.* 1852
MILLENNIUM - Microsurgical Equipment - BAUSCH & LOMB INCORPORATED; *pg.* 1401, *pg.* 1045
MILLENNIUM - Table - BLATT BOWLING & BILLIARD CORP.; *pg.* 1827, *pg.* 1203
MILLENNIUM - Cosmetics - ELIZABETH ARDEN, INC.; *pg.* 507, *pg.* 448
MILLENNIUM - Bathroom Fan - HUNTER FAN COMPANY; *pg.* 57, *pg.* 1631
MILLENNIUM - Seating Product - IRWIN SEATING COMPANY INC.; *pg.* 929, *pg.* 887
MILLENNIUM - Gas Mask - MINE SAFETY APPLIANCES COMPANY; *pg.* 1361, *pg.* 1525
MILLENNIUM - Dual Frequency Receiver for Navigation Applications - NOVATEL INC.; *pg.* 1424, *pg.* 1904
MILLENNIUM - Musical Instrument - PEAVEY ELECTRONICS CORPORATION; *pg.* 662, *pg.* 970
MILLENNIUM - Cruise Ship - ROYAL CARIBBEAN CRUISES LTD; *pg.* 1921, *pg.* 446
MILLENNIUM - Infant/Pediatric Ventilators - SECHRIST INDUSTRIES, INC.; *pg.* 1593, *pg.* 43
MILLENNIUM - Film Core - SONOCO PRODUCTS COMPANY; *pg.* 1469, *pg.* 1619
MILLENNIUM - Software - WATERS CORPORATION; *pg.* 1436, *pg.* 834

MILLENNIUM DRIVER TRAINER SYSTEM - Training System - LOCKHEED MARTIN CORPORATION; *pg.* 229, *pg.* 762
MILLENNIUM FORCE - Amusement & Water Park - CEDAR FAIR, L.P.; *pg.* 537, *pg.* 1471
MILLENNIUM STAGE - Art Performance Service - JOHN F. KENNEDY CENTER FOR THE PERFORMING ARTS; *pg.* 555, *pg.* 401
MILLENNIUM ULTRA - Herbicide - NUFARM AMERICAS INC; *pg.* 1798, *pg.* 552
MILLER - Bag - DATREK GOLF; *pg.* 1832, *pg.* 1801
MILLER - Chemicals - MILLER CHEMICAL & FERTILIZER CORPORATION; *pg.* 706, *pg.* 1535
MILLER - Farm Machinery & Recycling Equipment - MILLER MANUFACTURING COMPANY; *pg.* 706, *pg.* 921
MILLER - Heating & Cooling Products - NORTEK GLOBAL HVAC; *pg.* 1075, *pg.* 989
MILLER - Air Conditioners & Furnaces - NORTEK, INC.; *pg.* 100, *pg.* 1607
MILLER - Skis & Snowboard Systems - REVOLUTION MFG.; *pg.* 1844, *pg.* 1753
MILLER - Cable - THE RIPLEY COMPANY; *pg.* 1305, *pg.* 342
MILLER CHILL - Lime & Salt Beer - MILLERCOORS; *pg.* 254, *pg.* 1877
MILLER DU-OP - Welding & Cutting Equipment - MILLER ELECTRIC MANUFACTURING CO.; *pg.* 1361, *pg.* 1852
MILLER GENUINE DRAFT - Beer - MILLERCOORS; *pg.* 254, *pg.* 1877
MILLER GENUINE DRAFT 64 - Beer - MILLERCOORS; *pg.* 254, *pg.* 1877
MILLER HIGH LIFE - Beer - MILLERCOORS; *pg.* 254, *pg.* 1877
MILLER HIGH LIFE LIGHT - Beer - MILLERCOORS; *pg.* 254, *pg.* 1877
MILLER HOT STRIPPER - Stripper - THE RIPLEY COMPANY; *pg.* 1305, *pg.* 342
MILLER LEGEND - Welding & Cutting Equip. - MILLER ELECTRIC MANUFACTURING CO.; *pg.* 1361, *pg.* 1852
MILLER LITE - Beer - MILLERCOORS; *pg.* 254, *pg.* 1877
MILLER MICROSTRIP - Strip - THE RIPLEY COMPANY; *pg.* 1305, *pg.* 342
MILLER SOFT - Ski Equip. - REVOLUTION MFG.; *pg.* 1844, *pg.* 1753
MILLERMATIC - Welding & Cutting Equipment - MILLER ELECTRIC MANUFACTURING CO.; *pg.* 1361, *pg.* 1852
MILLER'S CHOICE - Flour - NORTH DAKOTA MILL & ELEVATOR ASSOCIATION; *pg.* 833, *pg.* 1398
MILLERSTRIPE - Fabric - NEMSCHOFF, INC.; *pg.* 936, *pg.* 1890
MILLESTEAD - Furniture - ASHLEY FURNITURE INDUSTRIES, INC.; *pg.* 914, *pg.* 1852
MILLI-GRID - Cable Assembly - MOLEX INCORPORATED; *pg.* 655, *pg.* 628
MILLI-Z - Electronic Components - MOLEX INCORPORATED; *pg.* 655, *pg.* 628
MILLICENT - Fabric - NEMSCHOFF, INC.; *pg.* 936, *pg.* 1890
MILLIKEN - Carpet - MILLIKEN & COMPANY; *pg.* 696, *pg.* 1622
MILLIKEN-KEX - Dust Control Product - MILLIKEN & COMPANY; *pg.* 696, *pg.* 1622
MILLING ROAD - Furniture - BAKER KNAPP & TUBBS INC.; *pg.* 916, *pg.* 566
MILLION-AIR - Compressor - BADGER AIR BRUSH COMPANY; *pg.* 359, *pg.* 612
MILLION DOLLAR CHASE - Video Game - INTERNATIONAL GAME TECHNOLOGY; *pg.* 957, *pg.* 1024
MILLION DOLLAR JEWELS - Video Game - INTERNATIONAL GAME TECHNOLOGY; *pg.* 957, *pg.* 1024
MILLION DOLLAR MANIA & DESIGN - Games - PENN NATIONAL GAMING, INC.; *pg.* 574, *pg.* 1595
MILLION DOLLAR MYSTERY - Video Game - INTERNATIONAL GAME TECHNOLOGY; *pg.* 957, *pg.* 1024
MILLION DOLLAR VOICE - Video Game - INTERNATIONAL GAME TECHNOLOGY; *pg.* 957, *pg.* 1024
MILLIONAIRE - Baitcasting Reels - DAIWA CORPORATION; *pg.* 1832, *pg.* 75
MILLIONAIRE - Fabric - NEMSCHOFF, INC.; *pg.* 936, *pg.* 1890
MILLIONAIRE - Game - PRESSMAN TOY CORPORATION; *pg.* 965, *pg.* 1734
MILLIONAIRE CV-X - Bait Casting Reels - DAIWA CORPORATION; *pg.* 1832, *pg.* 75
MILLIONAIRE CV-Z - Bait Casting Reels - DAIWA CORPORATION; *pg.* 1832, *pg.* 75
MILLIONAIRE RAFFLE - Lottery Game - ILLINOIS STATE LOTTERY; *pg.* 995, *pg.* 578
MILLIONAIRE S - Bait Casting Reels - DAIWA CORPORATION; *pg.* 1832, *pg.* 75
MILLIONAIRE SEVENS - Video Game - BALLY TECHNOLOGIES, INC.; *pg.* 531, *pg.* 1022
MILLIONAIRES' CLUB - Audio Book - BOOKS-A-MILLION, INC.; *pg.* 1623, *pg.* 2
MILLITE - Dry Fog - AKZONOBEL DECORATIVE PAINTS U.S.; *pg.* 1439, *pg.* 1474
THE MILLS - Real Estate Platforms - SIMON PROPERTY GROUP, INC.; *pg.* 1112, *pg.* 690
MILL'S PRIDE - Cabinets - MASCO CORPORATION; *pg.* 96, *pg.* 909
MILLSPERSE - Antiscalants - ASHLAND INC.; *pg.* 972, *pg.* 726
MILLSTONE - Coffee - THE J.M. SMUCKER COMPANY; *pg.* 865, *pg.* 1468
MILNOR - Washers - PELLERIN MILNOR CORPORATION; *pg.* 1368, *pg.* 744
MILO - Food & Beverage Product - NESTLE USA, INC.; *pg.* 883, *pg.* 96
MILORI - Balloon - CONTINENTAL AMERICAN CORP.; *pg.* 1880, *pg.* 723
MILO'S KITCHEN - Pet Treats - BIG HEART PET BRANDS; *pg.* 1474, *pg.* 213
MILSCO - Motor Vehicle Product - JASON INDUSTRIES, INC.; *pg.* 208, *pg.* 1875
MILSTAR - Systems Integration & Aeronautics - LOCKHEED MARTIN CORPORATION; *pg.* 229, *pg.* 762
MILTECH - Military Specification Packaging Foam - SEALED AIR CORPORATION; *pg.* 1468, *pg.* 1058
MILTEX - Instrument Cleaning & Care Products - INTEGRA MILTEX, INC.; *pg.* 1546, *pg.* 1597
MILTON BRADLEY - Games - HASBRO, INC.; *pg.* 954, *pg.* 1603
MILTON ROY - Fluid Control Product - MILTON ROY COMPANY; *pg.* 1361, *pg.* 1542
MILWAUKEE - Tools - MILWAUKEE ELECTRIC TOOL CORP.; *pg.* 1056, *pg.* 1855
MILWAUKEE BRASS - Gaming Product - GLD PRODUCTS, INC.; *pg.* 1835, *pg.* 1882
MILWAUKEE HAND TRUCK - Hand Trucks, Dollies, Carts - GLEASON INDUSTRIAL PRODUCTS INC.; *pg.* 1341, *pg.* 1874
MILWAUKEE JOURNAL SENTINEL - Newspaper - JOURNAL SENTINEL, INC.; *pg.* 1655, *pg.* 1876
MILWAUKEE'S - Pickles, Peppers & Relish - PINNACLE FOODS GROUP LLC; *pg.* 889, *pg.* 1104
MILWAUKEE'S BEST - Beer - MILLERCOORS; *pg.* 254, *pg.* 1877
MILWAUKEE'S BEST ICE - Beverage - MILLERCOORS; *pg.* 254, *pg.* 1877
MILWAUKEE'S BEST LIGHT - Beverage - MILLERCOORS; *pg.* 254, *pg.* 1877
MIMAGIC - Application Processor - NEOMAGIC CORPORATION; *pg.* 1364, *pg.* 247
MIMAX - Wireless Network Product - AIRSPAN NETWORKS INC.; *pg.* 346, *pg.* 410
MIMI MATERNITY - Maternity Apparel - DESTINATION MATERNITY CORPORATION; *pg.* 23, *pg.* 1563
MIMIC - Fabric - NEMSCHOFF, INC.; *pg.* 936, *pg.* 1890
MIMIO - Recorder - NEWELL RUBBERMAID INC.; *pg.* 1128, *pg.* 515
MIMI'S CAFE - Restaurant - BOB EVANS FARMS, LLC; *pg.* 841, *pg.* 1467
MIMOSA - Ceiling Fan - WESTINGHOUSE LIGHTING CORPORATION; *pg.* 687, *pg.* 1571
MIMS - Information Management Solution - HOLOGIC, INC.; *pg.* 1416, *pg.* 784
MIMS - Vodka - SAZERAC COMPANY, INC.; *pg.* 1969, *pg.* 745
MIN-R - X-Ray Films & Screens - EASTMAN KODAK COMPANY; *pg.* 1408, *pg.* 1333
MIN-U-SIL - Hydrous Kaolin - U.S. SILICA COMPANY; *pg.* 1185, *pg.* 1849
MINA GEAR - Power Transmission Equipment - REGAL BELOIT CORPORATION; *pg.* 106, *pg.* 1854
MINAPURE - Dental Handpiece Lubricant - THE TIMKEN COMPANY; *pg.* 218, *pg.* 1408
MINAQUA - Beverages - THE COCA-COLA COMPANY; *pg.* 240, *pg.* 493
MINCRO - Dental Instrument - OSTEOMED CORPORATION; *pg.* 1425, *pg.* 1658
MIND BODY SPIRIT - Tag Line - HUGGER MUGGER YOGA PRODUCTS LLC; *pg.* 1836, *pg.* 1758
MIND MANIA - Educational Toys - LEAPFROG ENTERPRISES, INC.; *pg.* 961, *pg.* 84
MIND OF THE MARRIED MAN - Cable Television Show - HOME BOX OFFICE, INC.; *pg.* 290, *pg.* 1240
MIND STATION - Educational Toys - LEAPFROG ENTERPRISES, INC.; *pg.* 961, *pg.* 84
MIND TRAP - Toy - MATTEL, INC.; *pg.* 962, *pg.* 81
MIND WARS - Educational Toys - LEAPFROG ENTERPRISES, INC.; *pg.* 961, *pg.* 84
MINDJET - Software - VIEWSONIC CORPORATION; *pg.* 489, *pg.* 303
MINDPOWER FOR A CHANGING WORLD - Slogan - BUTLER AMERICA; *pg.* 366, *pg.* 370
MINDSPARK - Online Services - IAC/INTERACTIVECORP; *pg.* 292, *pg.* 1242
MINE - Safety & Health Equipment - MINE SAFETY APPLIANCES COMPANY; *pg.* 1361, *pg.* 1525
MINEIT - Software - BIO-RAD LABORATORIES, INC.; *pg.* 1504, *pg.* 101
MINELINE - Heavy-Duty Cartridge - FLEXIBLE STEEL LACING COMPANY; *pg.* 1337, *pg.* 608
MINELOADER - Fuel Cell System - AEROVIRONMENT, INC.; *pg.* 223, *pg.* 150
MINERAL - Bedcovering - ETHAN ALLEN INTERIORS INC.; *pg.* 924, *pg.* 343
MINERAL - Fabric - NEMSCHOFF, INC.; *pg.* 936, *pg.* 1890
MINERAL - Sleeper & Recliner Seating - STEELCASE INC.; *pg.* 475, *pg.* 889
MINERAL ICE - Animal Care Product - STRAIGHT ARROW PRODUCTS, INC.; *pg.* 523, *pg.* 1517
MINERAL POWER - Foundation - MAYBELLINE LLC; *pg.* 516, *pg.* 1257
MINERALIGHT - Short Wave Lamps - UVP, INC.; *pg.* 1434, *pg.* 298
MINERALOX - Stone & Mineral Polish - FERRO CORPORATION; *pg.* 1162, *pg.* 1462
MINESCOUT - Undersea Mines Detection - RAYTHEON APPLIED SIGNAL TECHNOLOGY, INC.; *pg.* 667, *pg.* 288
MINETECH - Specialty High Performance Lubricants - QUAKER CHEMICAL CORP.; *pg.* 1178, *pg.* 1524
MINGLE - Office Furniture - STEELCASE INC.; *pg.* 475, *pg.* 889
MINH - Food Product - ELLENBEE-LEGGETT COMPANY INC.; *pg.* 854, *pg.* 1452
MINH - Frozen Asian Cuisine - THE SCHWAN FOOD COMPANY; *pg.* 894, *pg.* 928
MINI - Ultralight Outfits - DAIWA CORPORATION; *pg.* 1832, *pg.* 75
MINI - Watch - GEVRIL USA; *pg.* 6, *pg.* 1348
MINI - Small Automotive Fuse - LITTELFUSE, INC.; *pg.* 1301, *pg.* 580
MINI - Lawn Fertilizer - THE SCOTTS MIRACLE-GRO COMPANY; *pg.* 1799, *pg.* 1459
MINI-14 - Semi-Automatic Rifles - STURM, RUGER & COMPANY, INC.; *pg.* 1846, *pg.* 371
MINI-ALERT - Horns & Strobes - SYSTEM SENSOR; *pg.* 676, *pg.* 658
MINI ALPHA HUNTER - Knife - BUCK KNIVES, INC.; *pg.* 1828, *pg.* 550
MINI ATTACHE - Flash Drive - PNY TECHNOLOGIES, INC.; *pg.* 455, *pg.* 1105
MINI-AXID - Electronic Components - MOLEX INCORPORATED; *pg.* 655, *pg.* 628
MINI B - In-Line Speaker - ACR ELECTRONICS, INC.; *pg.* 612, *pg.* 422
MINI BABYBEL - Natural Cheeses - BEL BRANDS USA; *pg.* 839, *pg.* 566
MINI BASEBALL ETCH A SKETCH - Toy - THE OHIO ART COMPANY, INC.; *pg.* 965, *pg.* 1406
MINI BASKETBALL ETCH A SKETCH - Toy - THE OHIO ART COMPANY, INC.; *pg.* 965, *pg.* 1406
MINI BEDFORD TIE-R - Air-operated, Manual or Automatically Fed Twist Tying Machine - BEDFORD INDUSTRIES, INC.; *pg.* 1453, *pg.* 967
MINI BIONIX II - Biomaterials Test System - MTS SYSTEMS CORPORATION; *pg.* 442, *pg.* 923
MINI BITES - Snack - FRITO-LAY NORTH AMERICA, INC.; *pg.* 1853, *pg.* 1730
MINI BRUSSELS - Mini Cookies - PEPPERIDGE FARM, INC.; *pg.* 888, *pg.* 363
MINI BUCK - Cutlery - BUCK KNIVES, INC.; *pg.* 1828, *pg.* 550
MINI-C - Connector - MOLEX INCORPORATED; *pg.* 655, *pg.*

628

MINI-C POLYPORT - Electronic Components - MOLEX INCORPORATED; *pg.* 655, *pg.* 628

MINI-CAM - Electronic Components - MOLEX INCORPORATED; *pg.* 655, *pg.* 628

MINI-CART - Smaller Automatic Guided Vehicles - DAIFUKU WEBB; *pg.* 1327, *pg.* 885

MINI-CARTRAC - Material Handling System - PARAGON TECHNOLOGIES, INC.; *pg.* 1367, *pg.* 1528

MINI-CAT - Air Hoists - HARRINGTON HOISTS, INC.; *pg.* 1345, *pg.* 1551

MINI-CATH - Winged Infusion Set - BECTON, DICKINSON & COMPANY; *pg.* 1501, *pg.* 1068

MINI-CHANGE - Electronic Components - MOLEX INCORPORATED; *pg.* 655, *pg.* 628

MINI-CHECK - Security Locker - AMERICAN LOCKER GROUP INCORPORATED; *pg.* 1041, *pg.* 1674

MINI CHESSMEN - Mini Cookies - PEPPERIDGE FARM, INC.; *pg.* 888, *pg.* 363

MINI-CLIP - Round Knife - THE WOLF MACHINE CO.; *pg.* 1389, *pg.* 1427

MINI-COM - Copper Product - PANDUIT CORP.; *pg.* 661, *pg.* 663

MINI CONE - Screw-In Light Converter - SWIVELIER CO., INC.; *pg.* 1307, *pg.* 1142

MINI COVERT - Knife - GERBER LEGENDARY BLADES; *pg.* 1834, *pg.* 1503

MINI CYCLE - Healthcare Product - MEDICOOL, INC.; *pg.* 1562, *pg.* 294

MINI DIAMOND - Jewelry - HELZBERG'S DIAMOND SHOPS, INC.; *pg.* 6, *pg.* 984

MINI-DIP - Miniature Printed Circuit Board Switch - TRANSICO INCORPORATED; *pg.* 682, *pg.* 49

MINI DROPIN - Bolt & Shield Anchor - POWERS FASTENERS INC.; *pg.* 1059, *pg.* 1143

MINI EGGS - Chocolates - THE HERSHEY CO.; *pg.* 1855, *pg.* 1538

MINI-FIN - Water Heater - LOCHINVAR CORPORATION; *pg.* 1073, *pg.* 1640

MINI-FIT - Connector - MOLEX INCORPORATED; *pg.* 655, *pg.* 628

MINI-FIT BMI - Electronic Components - MOLEX INCORPORATED; *pg.* 655, *pg.* 628

MINI-FIT BMI SLIDE-AND-LOCK - Electronic Components - MOLEX INCORPORATED; *pg.* 655, *pg.* 628

MINI-FIT CPI - Electronic Components - MOLEX INCORPORATED; *pg.* 655, *pg.* 628

MINI-FIT GW - Electronic Components - MOLEX INCORPORATED; *pg.* 655, *pg.* 628

MINI-FIT H20 - Electronic Components - MOLEX INCORPORATED; *pg.* 655, *pg.* 628

MINI-FIT HCS - Electronic Components - MOLEX INCORPORATED; *pg.* 655, *pg.* 628

MINI-FIT HCS BMI - Electronic Components - MOLEX INCORPORATED; *pg.* 655, *pg.* 628

MINI-FIT HIGH CYCLE - Electronic Components - MOLEX INCORPORATED; *pg.* 655, *pg.* 628

MINI-FIT IDT - Electronic Components - MOLEX INCORPORATED; *pg.* 655, *pg.* 628

MINI-FIT JR. - Electronic Components - MOLEX INCORPORATED; *pg.* 655, *pg.* 628

MINI-FIT PLUS - Electronic Components - MOLEX INCORPORATED; *pg.* 655, *pg.* 628

MINI-FIT PLUS HCS - Electronic Components - MOLEX INCORPORATED; *pg.* 655, *pg.* 628

MINI-FIT RTC - Electronic Components - MOLEX INCORPORATED; *pg.* 655, *pg.* 628

MINI-FIT SMC - Electronic Components - MOLEX INCORPORATED; *pg.* 655, *pg.* 628

MINI-FIT SR. - Electronic Components - MOLEX INCORPORATED; *pg.* 655, *pg.* 628

MINI-FIT TPA - Electronic Components - MOLEX INCORPORATED; *pg.* 655, *pg.* 628

MINI FLASHER - Flashlight - PELICAN PRODUCTS, INC.; *pg.* 1842, *pg.* 295

MINI FOOTBALL ETCH A SKETCH - Toy - THE OHIO ART COMPANY, INC.; *pg.* 965, *pg.* 1406

MINI-GEN - Signal Generator - WOODWARD, INC.; *pg.* 122, *pg.* 329

MINI HALOGEN - Screw-In Light Converter - SWIVELIER CO., INC.; *pg.* 1307, *pg.* 1142

MINI-HEEL - Coreless Holding Furnaces - INDUCTOTHERM CORP.; *pg.* 1348, *pg.* 1114

MINI HIGHLIGHTER - Writing Instrument - DRI MARK PRODUCTS, INC.; *pg.* 388, *pg.* 1323

MINI-HMC - Electronic Components - MOLEX INCORPORATED; *pg.* 655, *pg.* 628

MINI-JACK - Copper Product - PANDUIT CORP.; *pg.* 661, *pg.* 663

MINI-KEY - Network Processing Product - CYPRESS SEMICONDUCTOR CORPORATION; *pg.* 1326, *pg.* 243

MINI KISSES - Milk Chocolates - THE HERSHEY CO.; *pg.* 1855, *pg.* 1538

MINI KNOTS - Snack Food Product - INVENTURE FOODS, INC.; *pg.* 1023, *pg.* 17

MINI-LAB - Gas Analyzer - MKS INSTRUMENTS, INC.; *pg.* 1362, *pg.* 781

MINI-LATCH - Electronic Components - MOLEX INCORPORATED; *pg.* 655, *pg.* 628

MINI-LEVELSITE - Level Control - BARKSDALE, INC.; *pg.* 1317, *pg.* 126

MINI-LITE - Commercial Lighting - SWIVELIER CO., INC.; *pg.* 1307, *pg.* 1142

MINI-LOCK - Electronic Components - MOLEX INCORPORATED; *pg.* 655, *pg.* 628

MINI M-70 - Spray Nozzle - STRAHMAN VALVES, INC.; *pg.* 1379, *pg.* 1517

MINI-MAC - Electronic Components - MOLEX INCORPORATED; *pg.* 655, *pg.* 628

MINI MAG - Doll And Toy - AMERICAN GIRL LLC; *pg.* 949, *pg.* 1871

MINI MARGARITA BOUQUET - Bouquet - 1-800-FLOWERS.COM, INC.; *pg.* 1758, *pg.* 1151

MINI-MASTER - Flowmeter - DWYER INSTRUMENTS INC.; *pg.* 1330, *pg.* 694

MINI-MATE2 - Air Conditioning System - EMERSON NETWORK POWER LIEBERT; *pg.* 1071, *pg.* 1439

MINI-MATIC - Pump Product - IDEX CORPORATION; *pg.* 1347, *pg.* 623

MINI-MAX - Cushion - THE ROHO GROUP; *pg.* 1591, *pg.* 556

MINI-MEDICAL - X -Ray Film Processor - IMAGEWORKS; *pg.* 1544, *pg.* 1158

MINI MI II - Electronic Components - MOLEX INCORPORATED; *pg.* 655, *pg.* 628

MINI MILANO - Mini Cookies - PEPPERIDGE FARM, INC.; *pg.* 888, *pg.* 363

MINI MILL - Software - OPEX CORPORATION; *pg.* 450, *pg.* 1087

MINI MINDER - Clip - BROWN & BIGELOW, INC.; *pg.* 1624, *pg.* 959

MINI MINT MILANO - Mini Cookies - PEPPERIDGE FARM, INC.; *pg.* 888, *pg.* 363

MINI-MITE - Cordless Rotary Tools - DREMEL; *pg.* 1046, *pg.* 634

MINI MIX - Fluid Handling System - GRACO, INC.; *pg.* 1342, *pg.* 935

MINI-MIZER - Electronic/Pneumatic Interface - HUMPHREY PRODUCTS CORPORATION; *pg.* 1300, *pg.* 894

MINI-MOD - Adapter - PANDUIT CORP.; *pg.* 661, *pg.* 663

MINI-MONITOR - Musical Instrument - PEAVEY ELECTRONICS CORPORATION; *pg.* 662, *pg.* 970

MINI-MORNAP - Dispenser Napkin - GEORGIA-PACIFIC LLC; *pg.* 1458, *pg.* 507

MINI MUFFINS - Snack Cakes - HOSTESS BRANDS LLC; *pg.* 1856, *pg.* 984

MINI-MULE - Spare Tire Holders - SELAS HEAT TECHNOLOGY COMPANY LLC; *pg.* 1076, *pg.* 1553

MINI-MYTE - Electric Air Valves - HUMPHREY PRODUCTS CORPORATION; *pg.* 1300, *pg.* 894

MINI-NDT - Film Processor - IMAGEWORKS; *pg.* 1544, *pg.* 1158

MINI-PAC - Actuator - DUFF-NORTON; *pg.* 204, *pg.* 1365

MINI-PAL - Servo Accelerometer - HONEYWELL AEROSPACE ELECTRONIC SYSTEMS; *pg.* 228, *pg.* 17

MINI-PAW - Sprinklers - RAIN BIRD CORPORATION; *pg.* 707, *pg.* 44

MINI-PHOENIX - Sewage Odor Control - CALGON CARBON CORPORATION; *pg.* 1151, *pg.* 1574

MINI PROFILE - Capsule Filter - PALL CORPORATION; *pg.* 232, *pg.* 1323

MINI-PROTEAN - Software - BIO-RAD LABORATORIES, INC.; *pg.* 1504, *pg.* 101

MINI-PUSH - Electronic Components - MOLEX INCORPORATED; *pg.* 655, *pg.* 628

MINI-REVO - Medical Equipment - CONMED CORPORATION; *pg.* 1517, *pg.* 1347

MINI RIDGE - Knife - GERBER LEGENDARY BLADES; *pg.* 1834, *pg.* 1503

MINI-ROCKER - Mini-Rocker Blocks & Terminals - CHANNELL COMMERCIAL CORP.; *pg.* 1870, *pg.* 291

MINI SCONCE - Lighting System - REVOLUTION LIGHTING TECHNOLOGIES, INC.; *pg.* 1304, *pg.* 377

MINI SD - Memory Card - SANDISK CORPORATION; *pg.* 465, *pg.* 147

MINI-SHEETS - Ink Jet Label - AVERY DENNISON CORPORATION; *pg.* 1452, *pg.* 95

MINI-SHOT - Animal Safety Product - NEOGEN CORPORATION; *pg.* 883, *pg.* 896

MINI-SIP - Liquid Serving Pouches - E.I. DU PONT DE NEMOURS & COMPANY; *pg.* 1159, *pg.* 390

MINI SOCCER ETCH A SKETCH - Toy - THE OHIO ART COMPANY, INC.; *pg.* 965, *pg.* 1406

MINI-SPOX - Electronic Components - MOLEX INCORPORATED; *pg.* 655, *pg.* 628

MINI SQUIRT - Hot Melt Equipment - NORDSON CORPORATION; *pg.* 1365, *pg.* 1480

MINI-STACK - Car Wash Equipment - D&S CAR WASH EQUIPMENT CO.; *pg.* 1327, *pg.* 979

MINI-SUB - Software - BIO-RAD LABORATORIES, INC.; *pg.* 1504, *pg.* 101

MINI-SUN CHAISES - Aluminum Beach Chairs - TELESCOPE CASUAL FURNITURE INC.; *pg.* 944, *pg.* 1162

MINI SWDM59 - Splitter - OPLINK COMMUNICATIONS, INC.; *pg.* 660, *pg.* 91

MINI SWFC - Coupler - OPLINK COMMUNICATIONS, INC.; *pg.* 660, *pg.* 91

MINI-SWIRLZ - Food Product - KELLOGG COMPANY; *pg.* 831, *pg.* 870

MINI TAC - Torch - COAST CUTLERY COMPANY; *pg.* 1121, *pg.* 1501

MINI-TEMP - Hyperthermia Equipment - CINCINNATI SUB-ZERO PRODUCTS, INC.; *pg.* 1070, *pg.* 1411

MINI THIRTY - Rifle - STURM, RUGER & COMPANY, INC.; *pg.* 1846, *pg.* 371

MINI-TOOL - Cutting Tool - LEATHERMAN TOOL GROUP, INC.; *pg.* 1053, *pg.* 1504

MINI TRANS-BLOT - Software - BIO-RAD LABORATORIES, INC.; *pg.* 1504, *pg.* 101

MINI TRAPPER - Knife - BUCK KNIVES, INC.; *pg.* 1828, *pg.* 550

MINI-TRIGGER - Personal Care Product - WESTROCK COMPANY; *pg.* 1472, *pg.* 1805

MINI-WHEATS - Food Product - KELLOGG COMPANY; *pg.* 831, *pg.* 870

MINI WHINNIES - Toy Scale Model Animal - REEVES INTERNATIONAL, INC.; *pg.* 966, *pg.* 1108

MINI WINE CUBE - Wine - TARGET CORPORATION; *pg.* 1786, *pg.* 942

MINI-X250 - Electronic Components - MOLEX INCORPORATED; *pg.* 655, *pg.* 628

MINI Z - Recreational Vehicle - BOMBARDIER RECREATIONAL PRODUCTS, INC.; *pg.* 201, *pg.* 1960

MINI Z - Self-propelled Lawn Mower - EXCEL INDUSTRIES, INC.; *pg.* 1795, *pg.* 715

MINIARC - Medical Device - AMERICAN MEDICAL SYSTEMS HOLDINGS, INC.; *pg.* 1493, *pg.* 947

MINIATURE EDITIONS - Miniature Printings of Popular Books - RUNNING PRESS; *pg.* 1682, *pg.* 1570

MINIBLOCK - Parallel Synthesis - METTLER-TOLEDO INTERNATIONAL INC.; *pg.* 1423, *pg.* 1441

MINIBLUE - Hot Melt Dispensing Gun - NORDSON CORPORATION; *pg.* 1365, *pg.* 1480

MINIBON - Baked Goods - CINNABON, INC.; *pg.* 1723, *pg.* 493

MINIBREAK - Compact Height Switches - SCHNEIDER ELECTRIC USA, INC.; *pg.* 1306, *pg.* 650

MINIBUCKS - Video Game - INTERNATIONAL GAME TECHNOLOGY; *pg.* 957, *pg.* 1024

MINIBULK - Materials Containers - ATMI, INC.; *pg.* 1314, *pg.* 342

MINIBURR - Electrochemical Machine - KENNAMETAL EXTRUDE HONE; *pg.* 1352, *pg.* 1542

MINIBUS - Class "A" Motor Homes - REXHALL INDUSTRIES, INC.; *pg.* 1710, *pg.* 121

MINICAM - Camera - ALAN GORDON ENTERPRISES, INC.; *pg.* 1399, *pg.* 125

MINICARD - Photo Film, Chemicals Data Handling Equipment - EASTMAN KODAK COMPANY; *pg.* 1408, *pg.* 1333

MINICAST - Minisystem - DAIWA CORPORATION; *pg.* 1832, *pg.* 75

MINICHEF - Temperature Controllers & Timers - WATLOW ELECTRIC MANUFACTURING COMPANY; *pg.* 1078, *pg.* 1004

MINICHEF 2000 - Machine Function Controller - WATLOW

ELECTRIC MANUFACTURING COMPANY; *pg.* 1078, *pg.* 1004
MINICHIPS - Semi-Sweet Chocolates - THE HERSHEY CO.; *pg.* 1855, *pg.* 1538
MINICOLOR - Dosing & Blending Unit - MOTAN, INC.; *pg.* 1886, *pg.* 903
MINICURE - UV Conveyor System - NORDSON CORPORATION; *pg.* 1365, *pg.* 1480
MINICYCLER - Software - BIO-RAD LABORATORIES, INC.; *pg.* 1504, *pg.* 101
MINIDISC - Liquid Handling System - MOLECULAR DEVICES CORPORATION; *pg.* 1568, *pg.* 287
MINIGEL - Pharmaceutical Product - ALERE INC.; *pg.* 1488, *pg.* 849
MINIGRAPH - Recorders - DWYER INSTRUMENTS INC.; *pg.* 1330, *pg.* 694
MINIGROOVE - Ceramic & Plastic Product - COORSTEK, INC.; *pg.* 77, *pg.* 330
MINIKAP - Filtration System - SPECTRUM LABORATORIES INC.; *pg.* 1595, *pg.* 69
MINIKROS - Fluid Purification System - SPECTRUM LABORATORIES INC.; *pg.* 1595, *pg.* 69
MINILAN - Electronic Components - MOLEX INCORPORATED; *pg.* 655, *pg.* 628
MINILCD - Software - CRESTRON ELECTRONICS INC.; *pg.* 631, *pg.* 1116
MINILIBRARYXPRESS - Enterprise Tape Library - OVERLAND STORAGE, INC.; *pg.* 451, *pg.* 205
MINILIGHTWAND - Lighting System - PHILIPS SOLID-STATE LIGHTING SOLUTIONS; *pg.* 1303, *pg.* 806
MINILITER - Lighting Product - HUBBELL INCORPORATED; *pg.* 1299, *pg.* 370
MINILOONS - Foil Balloons - CTI INDUSTRIES CORPORATION; *pg.* 1881, *pg.* 555
MINIM - Capsule - PALL CORPORATION; *pg.* 232, *pg.* 1323
MINIMAC - Nondestructive Testing - MAGNETIC ANALYSIS CORPORATION; *pg.* 1421, *pg.* 1158
MINIMANIA - Video Game - INTERNATIONAL GAME TECHNOLOGY; *pg.* 957, *pg.* 1024
MINIMARATHON - Event - KENTUCKY DERBY FESTIVAL, INC.; *pg.* 556, *pg.* 735
MINIMASS - Glass & Ceramic Material - CORNING INCORPORATED; *pg.* 1122, *pg.* 1154
MINIMASTER - Flowmeter - DWYER INSTRUMENTS INC.; *pg.* 1330, *pg.* 694
MINIMATE - Ice Chest - IGLOO PRODUCTS CORPORATION; *pg.* 1126, *pg.* 1724
MINIMATE - Filter Equipment - PALL CORPORATION; *pg.* 232, *pg.* 1323
MINIMATE - Plastic Bags - SONOCO PRODUCTS COMPANY; *pg.* 1469, *pg.* 1619
MINIMAX - Power Pacs - CHROMALOX, INC.; *pg.* 1070, *pg.* 1574
MINIMAX - Wireless Product - HEMISPHERE GPS INC.; *pg.* 642, *pg.* 1903
MINIMAX PLUS - Oxygenator - MEDTRONIC, INC.; *pg.* 1564, *pg.* 939
MINIMED - Intravenous Infusion Device - SIEMENS CORPORATION; *pg.* 803, *pg.* 1291
MINIMET - Automatic Polisher/Grinder - BUEHLER, LTD.; *pg.* 1403, *pg.* 622
MINIMISER - Material & Alloy - ALLEGHENY TECHNOLOGIES INCORPORATED; *pg.* 66, *pg.* 1572
MINIMO - Digitized Speech Devices - DYNAVOX INC.; *pg.* 635, *pg.* 1574
MINIMS - Ophthalmic Drugs - BAUSCH & LOMB INCORPORATED; *pg.* 1401, *pg.* 1045
MINIMUFFS - Noise Attenuators - NATUS MEDICAL INCORPORATED; *pg.* 1572, *pg.* 199
MINION - Paint & Coating - DIAMOND VOGEL PAINT, INC.; *pg.* 1441, *pg.* 710
MINIOPTICON - Software - BIO-RAD LABORATORIES, INC.; *pg.* 1504, *pg.* 101
MINIOX - Oxygen Analyzer - MINE SAFETY APPLIANCES COMPANY; *pg.* 1361, *pg.* 1525
MINIPAX - Sorbent Packet - MULTISORB TECHNOLOGIES, INC.; *pg.* 1570, *pg.* 1150
MINIPRESS - Medicine - PFIZER INC.; *pg.* 1581, *pg.* 1278
MINIQUICK - Medicine - PFIZER INC.; *pg.* 1581, *pg.* 1278
MINISAX - Optical Scanner - GSI GROUP INC.; *pg.* 1415, *pg.* 784
MINISCAN - Bar Code Scanner - MOTOROLA ENTERPRISE MOBILITY; *pg.* 441, *pg.* 1167
MINISD - Flash Card - HGST; *pg.* 406, *pg.* 260
MINISD - Memory Card - LEXAR MEDIA, INC.; *pg.* 1262, *pg.* 146
MINISDHC - Memory Card - SANDISK CORPORATION; *pg.* 465, *pg.* 147
MINISHAPES - Foil Balloons - CTI INDUSTRIES CORPORATION; *pg.* 1881, *pg.* 555
MINISIGNATURE - Leather Product - COACH, INC.; *pg.* 3, *pg.* 1214
MINISPEC PLUS - Software - BRUKER CORPORATION; *pg.* 1511, *pg.* 788
MINISPEC PROFILER - Analytical Device - BRUKER CORPORATION; *pg.* 1511, *pg.* 788
MINISPIN - Minisystem - DAIWA CORPORATION; *pg.* 1832, *pg.* 75
MINISPO2T - Patient Monitoring System - CRITICARE SYSTEMS, INC.; *pg.* 1520, *pg.* 1897
MINISTRIES TODAY - Magazine - CHARISMA MEDIA; *pg.* 1627, *pg.* 436
MINISYSTEM - Chip Processing - PRAB, INC.; *pg.* 1369, *pg.* 894
MINITEMP - Sensor - WATLOW ELECTRIC MANUFACTURING COMPANY; *pg.* 1078, *pg.* 1004
MINITERM - Access Control System - NAPCO SECURITY SYSTEMS, INC.; *pg.* 658, *pg.* 1138
MINITOME - Medical Device - COOK GROUP, INC.; *pg.* 1518, *pg.* 674
MINITOUCH - Software - CRESTRON ELECTRONICS INC.; *pg.* 631, *pg.* 1116
MINITRACKER - Searchlights - BALLANTYNE STRONG, INC.; *pg.* 623, *pg.* 1013
MINITRAK - Robotic Liquid Handling System - PERKINELMER, INC.; *pg.* 1426, *pg.* 853
MINITRODE - Robotic Product - HAMILTON CO., INC.; *pg.* 1415, *pg.* 1031
MINIVEE - Audio Loudspeakers - VELODYNE ACOUSTICS, INC.; *pg.* 685, *pg.* 152
MINIVISION - Portable Recordable Endoscopy - PENTAX MEDICAL COMPANY; *pg.* 1580, *pg.* 1086
MINIWRAP - Plastics Product - AEP INDUSTRIES INC.; *pg.* 1878, *pg.* 1085
MINLON - Engineering Thermoplastic - E.I. DU PONT DE NEMOURS & COMPANY; *pg.* 1159, *pg.* 390
MINN KOTA - Electric Fishing Motors, Power Equipment & Accessories - JOHNSON OUTDOORS INC.; *pg.* 1837, *pg.* 1888
MINNAH - Footwear - STEVEN MADDEN, LTD.; *pg.* 1819, *pg.* 1176
MINNESOTA AUTOMATION - Packaging Product - GRAPHIC PACKAGING HOLDING COMPANY; *pg.* 1459, *pg.* 509
MINNESOTA LIFE - Insurance Company - THE MINNESOTA LIFE INSURANCE COMPANY; *pg.* 1209, *pg.* 962
MINNESOTA POWER - Electric Utility - ALLETE, INC.; *pg.* 1933, *pg.* 921
MINNESOTA RUBBER - Molded Rubber Parts - QUADION CORPORATION; *pg.* 1888, *pg.* 941
MINNESOTA TIMBERWOLVES - Basketball Team - MINNESOTA TIMBERWOLVES BASKETBALL LIMITED PARTNERSHIP; *pg.* 563, *pg.* 940
MINNESOTA TWINS - Lottery Game - MINNESOTA STATE LOTTERY; *pg.* 999, *pg.* 956
MINNESOTA TWINS - Baseball Team - MINNESOTA TWINS, LLC; *pg.* 563, *pg.* 940
MINNIE - Catheter - VASCULAR SOLUTIONS, INC.; *pg.* 1434, *pg.* 946
MINNIE - Motor Homes - WINNEBAGO INDUSTRIES, INC.; *pg.* 1712, *pg.* 707
MINNIE MOUSE - Cartoon Character - THE WALT DISNEY COMPANY; *pg.* 317, *pg.* 52
MINNIE WINNIE - Motor Homes - WINNEBAGO INDUSTRIES, INC.; *pg.* 1712, *pg.* 707
MINNOX - Burner - ECLIPSE INC.; *pg.* 1332, *pg.* 655
MINOCIN - Pharmaceutical Product - IMPAX LABORATORIES, INC.; *pg.* 1544, *pg.* 101
MINOR'S - Food & Beverage Product - NESTLE USA, INC.; *pg.* 883, *pg.* 96
MINOT - Lawn & Garden Tractors - TRACTOR SUPPLY COMPANY; *pg.* 708, *pg.* 1627
MINOTAUR - Vapor Phase Activated Carbons - CALGON CARBON CORPORATION; *pg.* 1151, *pg.* 1574
MINOTAUR - Rocket - ORBITAL ATK; *pg.* 1425, *pg.* 1779
MINOTAUR - Book - ST. MARTINS PRESS, INC.; *pg.* 1688, *pg.* 1295
MINT - Motion Control System - BALDOR ELECTRIC COMPANY; *pg.* 1316, *pg.* 32
MINT - Premium Class - JETBLUE AIRWAYS CORPORATION; *pg.* 1913, *pg.* 1174
MINT - Fabric - NEMSCHOFF, INC.; *pg.* 936, *pg.* 1890
MINT - Software - SUNGARD DATA SYSTEMS INC.; *pg.* 477, *pg.* 1592
MINT CONDITION - Car Care Products - AMWAY CORPORATION; *pg.* 326, *pg.* 864
MINT DREAM - Candy - RUSSELL STOVER CANDIES, INC.; *pg.* 1861, *pg.* 986
MINT JULEP - Container Grown Plant - MONROVIA GROWERS; *pg.* 1797, *pg.* 44
MINT MEDLEY - Herb Tea - R.C. BIGELOW, INC.; *pg.* 891, *pg.* 348
MINT MELTAWAYS - Chocolate Product - WORLD'S FINEST CHOCOLATE, INC.; *pg.* 1864, *pg.* 597
MINT STICKS - Candy - SWEET CANDY COMPANY; *pg.* 1862, *pg.* 1761
MINT.COM - Financial Planning Site - INTUIT INC.; *pg.* 769, *pg.* 158
MINTDRIVE - Servo Drive - BALDOR ELECTRIC COMPANY; *pg.* 1316, *pg.* 32
MINT'EES - Almonds - BLUE DIAMOND GROWERS; *pg.* 840, *pg.* 195
MINTREX - Health & Nutrition Product - NOVUS INTERNATIONAL, INC.; *pg.* 706, *pg.* 1001
MINTY GINGER - Nutritional Product - NUTRACEUTICAL INTERNATIONAL CORPORATION; *pg.* 1576, *pg.* 1753
MINUET - Case - ANTEC INCORPORATED; *pg.* 350, *pg.* 90
MINUET - Fabric - NEMSCHOFF, INC.; *pg.* 936, *pg.* 1890
MINUK - Doll And Toy - AMERICAN GIRL LLC; *pg.* 949, *pg.* 1871
MINUTE - Eyewear - OAKLEY, INC.; *pg.* 1840, *pg.* 86
MINUTE MAID - Regular & Diet Flavored Soda - THE COCA-COLA COMPANY; *pg.* 240, *pg.* 493
MINUTE MAID ACTIVE - Beverages - THE COCA-COLA COMPANY; *pg.* 240, *pg.* 493
MINUTE MAID ANTIOX - Beverages - THE COCA-COLA COMPANY; *pg.* 240, *pg.* 493
MINUTE MAID DELI - Beverages - THE COCA-COLA COMPANY; *pg.* 240, *pg.* 493
MINUTE MAID DUOFRUTAS - Beverages - THE COCA-COLA COMPANY; *pg.* 240, *pg.* 493
MINUTE MAID FRUIT PLUS - Beverages - THE COCA-COLA COMPANY; *pg.* 240, *pg.* 493
MINUTE MAID HEART WISE - Cholesterol-Cutting Orange Juice - THE COCA-COLA COMPANY; *pg.* 240, *pg.* 493
MINUTE MAID JUICES TO GO - Beverages - THE COCA-COLA COMPANY; *pg.* 240, *pg.* 493
MINUTE MAID JUST 10 - Beverages - THE COCA-COLA COMPANY; *pg.* 240, *pg.* 493
MINUTE MAID LIGHT - Beverages - THE COCA-COLA COMPANY; *pg.* 240, *pg.* 493
MINUTE MAID MAIS - Beverages - THE COCA-COLA COMPANY; *pg.* 240, *pg.* 493
MINUTE MAID MULTI-VITAMIN - Beverages - THE COCA-COLA COMPANY; *pg.* 240, *pg.* 493
MINUTE MAID NUTRI+ - Beverages - THE COCA-COLA COMPANY; *pg.* 240, *pg.* 493
MINUTE MAID PREMIUM - Beverages - THE COCA-COLA COMPANY; *pg.* 240, *pg.* 493
MINUTE MAID SOFT DRINK - Beverages - THE COCA-COLA COMPANY; *pg.* 240, *pg.* 493
MINUTE MAID SOJAPLUS - Beverages - THE COCA-COLA COMPANY; *pg.* 240, *pg.* 493
MINUTE MAID SPLASH - Beverages - THE COCA-COLA COMPANY; *pg.* 240, *pg.* 493
MINUTE MALT - Frozen Juices - UNITED DAIRY FARMERS, INC.; *pg.* 906, *pg.* 1426
MINUTE MANAGER - Wireless Communication System - AT&T SOUTHEAST; *pg.* 1868, *pg.* 489
MINUTE MEND - Epoxy Stick - CRC INDUSTRIES, INC.; *pg.* 329, *pg.* 1590
MINUTE RICE - Rice - RIVIANA FOODS INC.; *pg.* 892, *pg.* 1713
MINUTE SHAKE - Frozen Juices - UNITED DAIRY FARMERS, INC.; *pg.* 906, *pg.* 1426
MINUTEMAN - Investment Services - BAY STATE SAVINGS BANK; *pg.* 722, *pg.* 862
MINWAX - Wood Finishing Products - THE SHERWIN-WILLIAMS COMPANY; *pg.* 1447, *pg.* 1435
MINWAX - Wood Stain - SHERWIN-WILLIAMS DIVERSIFIED BRANDS DIVISION; *pg.* 1448, *pg.* 1435
MINWAX - Wood Finishing Products - SHERWIN-WILLIAMS WOOD CARE GROUP; *pg.* 1448, *pg.* 1127
MIO - Liquid Water Enhancer - THE KRAFT HEINZ COMPANY; *pg.* 870, *pg.* 1577
MIO - Instant Camera & Film for Wallet-Sized Photos -

POLAROID CORPORATION; *pg.* 1426, *pg.* 815
MIO PUP - Toy & Game - HASBRO, INC.; *pg.* 954, *pg.* 1603
MIOC3 - Circulator - OPLINK COMMUNICATIONS, INC.; *pg.* 660, *pg.* 91
MIOC4 - Circulator - OPLINK COMMUNICATIONS, INC.; *pg.* 660, *pg.* 91
MIONET - Hard Drive - WESTERN DIGITAL CORPORATION; *pg.* 492, *pg.* 118
MIONET DRIVEACCESS - Hard Drive - WESTERN DIGITAL CORPORATION; *pg.* 492, *pg.* 118
MIOS - Furniture - THE COMMERCIAL FURNITURE GROUP; *pg.* 920, *pg.* 994
MIPCO - Reefer Power Outlet - THOMAS & BETTS CORPORATION; *pg.* 680, *pg.* 1646
MIPS - Core - IMAGINATION TECHNOLOGIES; *pg.* 412, *pg.* 285
MIPS - RISC Processor - PMC-SIERRA, INC.; *pg.* 664, *pg.* 287
MIPS-3D - Processor - IMAGINATION TECHNOLOGIES; *pg.* 412, *pg.* 285
MIPS-BASED - Semiconductor - IMAGINATION TECHNOLOGIES; *pg.* 412, *pg.* 285
MIPS I - Processor - IMAGINATION TECHNOLOGIES; *pg.* 412, *pg.* 285
MIPS II - Processor - IMAGINATION TECHNOLOGIES; *pg.* 412, *pg.* 285
MIPS III - Processor - IMAGINATION TECHNOLOGIES; *pg.* 412, *pg.* 285
MIPS IV - Processor - IMAGINATION TECHNOLOGIES; *pg.* 412, *pg.* 285
MIPS V - Processor - IMAGINATION TECHNOLOGIES; *pg.* 412, *pg.* 285
MIPS-VERIFIED - Test Suite - IMAGINATION TECHNOLOGIES; *pg.* 412, *pg.* 285
MIPS16 - Processor - IMAGINATION TECHNOLOGIES; *pg.* 412, *pg.* 285
MIPS16E - Processor - IMAGINATION TECHNOLOGIES; *pg.* 412, *pg.* 285
MIPS32 - Computer Product - IMAGINATION TECHNOLOGIES; *pg.* 412, *pg.* 285
MIPS64 - Computer Product - IMAGINATION TECHNOLOGIES; *pg.* 412, *pg.* 285
MIPSPRO - Compiler - IMAGINATION TECHNOLOGIES; *pg.* 412, *pg.* 285
MIPSSIM - Simulator - IMAGINATION TECHNOLOGIES; *pg.* 412, *pg.* 285
MIQ - Mineral Insulated Heating Cables - THERMON AMERICAS INC.; *pg.* 1077, *pg.* 1744
MIR - Publication - R.R. BOWKER LLC; *pg.* 1682, *pg.* 1095
MIR-O-CRON - Coatings for Mirror Backing - PPG INDUSTRIES, INC.; *pg.* 1445, *pg.* 1579
MIR O SPRAY - Glass Cleaner - EDWARD DON & COMPANY; *pg.* 54, *pg.* 672
MIR O ZERO - Glass Cleaner - EDWARD DON & COMPANY; *pg.* 54, *pg.* 672
MIRA - Hearing Device - BELTONE ELECTRONICS LLC; *pg.* 1503, *pg.* 614
MIRA - Laser & Laser System - COHERENT, INC.; *pg.* 1406, *pg.* 265
MIRA - Claims Advisor for Reserving Payments - FAIR ISAAC CORPORATION; *pg.* 1247, *pg.* 955
MIRA - Publisher - HARLEQUIN ENTERPRISES LIMITED; *pg.* 1647, *pg.* 1938
MIRA-COIL - Continuous Coil Springs & Constructions - LEGGETT & PLATT, INCORPORATED; *pg.* 933, *pg.* 974
MIRA-FOAM - Polyurethane Foam Cushions & Pads - LEGGETT & PLATT, INCORPORATED; *pg.* 933, *pg.* 974
MIRABEAU SHEER - Window Treatment - CROSCILL, INC.; *pg.* 1122, *pg.* 1220
MIRABEL - Frozen Seafood - HIGH LINER FOODS INCORPORATED; *pg.* 862, *pg.* 1917
MIRACLE - Monofilament Fishing Line - CORTLAND LINE COMPANY; *pg.* 1831, *pg.* 1155
MIRACLE - Toy - IMPERIAL TOY CORPORATION; *pg.* 957, *pg.* 166
MIRACLE BABY - Toy - MATTEL, INC.; *pg.* 962, *pg.* 81
MIRACLE BOW - Bow Kit - E-Z BOWZ, LLC; *pg.* 692, *pg.* 1635
MIRACLE BUBBLEMAN - Game - IMPERIAL TOY CORPORATION; *pg.* 957, *pg.* 166
MIRACLE BUBBLES - Toys - IMPERIAL TOY CORPORATION; *pg.* 957, *pg.* 166
THE MIRACLE COLLECTION - Men's Clothing - JOS. A. BANK CLOTHIERS, INC.; *pg.* 42, *pg.* 771
MIRACLE-EAR - Hearing Aids - MIRACLE-EAR, INC.; *pg.* 1568, *pg.* 940
MIRACLE FINISH - Hair Care Product - ZOTOS INTERNATIONAL, INC.; *pg.* 524, *pg.* 345
MIRACLE GLAZE - Paint & Coating - DIAMOND VOGEL PAINT, INC.; *pg.* 1441, *pg.* 710
MIRACLE-GRO - Lawn & Garden Product - THE SCOTTS MIRACLE-GRO COMPANY; *pg.* 1799, *pg.* 1459
MIRACLE GROOM - Grooming Product - W.F. YOUNG, INC.; *pg.* 1610, *pg.* 817
MIRACLE HOME - Program - RE/MAX INTERNATIONAL, INC.; *pg.* 1109, *pg.* 322
THE MIRACLE OF PAINT - Slogan - DIAMOND VOGEL PAINT, INC.; *pg.* 1441, *pg.* 710
MIRACLE SEAL - Adhesive Tape Sealant - REVERE PRODUCTS; *pg.* 107, *pg.* 1435
MIRACLE STONE - Pumice Stone - LUZIER PERSONALIZED COSMETICS, INC.; *pg.* 515, *pg.* 978
MIRACLE THIGH - Health & Beauty Product - DIXIE HEALTH, INC.; *pg.* 1524, *pg.* 535
MIRACLE THIGH CREAM - Cellulite Control Cream - DIXIE HEALTH, INC.; *pg.* 1524, *pg.* 535
MIRACLE WHIP - Food Product - THE KRAFT HEINZ COMPANY; *pg.* 870, *pg.* 1577
THE MIRACLES OF SCIENCE - Slogan - E.I. DU PONT DE NEMOURS & COMPANY; *pg.* 1159, *pg.* 390
MIRACOL - Skincare Product - MERLE NORMAN COSMETICS, INC.; *pg.* 517, *pg.* 136
MIRACOLI - Pasta - MARS, INCORPORATED; *pg.* 1858, *pg.* 1792
MIRACRYL - Display Trays-Mirrored, Ice Pan Housing, Cubes, & Triple Tier Frames - CARLISLE FOODSERVICE PRODUCTS INCORPORATED; *pg.* 1455, *pg.* 1485
MIRADA - Carpet - BEAULIEU GROUP, LLC; *pg.* 917, *pg.* 529
MIRADA - Rug - COURISTAN INC.; *pg.* 921, *pg.* 1067
MIRADA - Eye Protection - MCR SAFETY; *pg.* 1422, *pg.* 1630
MIRAFILM - Pigment - BASF CATALYSTS LLC; *pg.* 1148, *pg.* 1074
MIRAFLEX - Glass Fiber Used in Insulation - OWENS CORNING; *pg.* 102, *pg.* 1476
MIRAGE - Architectural Roofing Shingles - BUILDING PRODUCTS OF CANADA CORP.; *pg.* 72, *pg.* 1951
MIRAGE - Rug - COURISTAN INC.; *pg.* 921, *pg.* 1067
MIRAGE - Cart Bag - DATREK GOLF; *pg.* 1832, *pg.* 1801
MIRAGE - Software - DIGIRAD CORPORATION; *pg.* 1524, *pg.* 185
MIRAGE - Toilet - GERBER PLUMBING FIXTURES CORPORATION; *pg.* 84, *pg.* 672
MIRAGE - Gaming Product - GLD PRODUCTS, INC.; *pg.* 1835, *pg.* 1882
MIRAGE - IR Scene Projector - HEICO CORPORATION; *pg.* 228, *pg.* 431
MIRAGE - Eyewear - MAUI JIM, INC.; *pg.* 9, *pg.* 651
THE MIRAGE - Resort & Casino - MGM RESORTS INTERNATIONAL; *pg.* 1105, *pg.* 1028
MIRAGE - Fabric - NEMSCHOFF, INC.; *pg.* 936, *pg.* 1890
MIRAGE - Aircraft - PIPER AIRCRAFT, INC.; *pg.* 233, *pg.* 477
MIRAGE - Headset - PLANTRONICS, INC.; *pg.* 663, *pg.* 270
MIRAGE - Nasal Mask - RESMED INC.; *pg.* 1589, *pg.* 207
MIRAGE - Light Imaging Laminate - SCHNELLER, INC.; *pg.* 234, *pg.* 1456
MIRAGE - Concealed Sprinkler - THE VIKING GROUP; *pg.* 119, *pg.* 891
MIRAGE ACTIVA - Nasal Mask - RESMED INC.; *pg.* 1589, *pg.* 207
MIRAGE CLASSIC - Pedaling Kayak - HOBIE CAT COMPANY; *pg.* 1708, *pg.* 173
MIRAGE MICRO - Nasal Mask - RESMED INC.; *pg.* 1589, *pg.* 207
MIRAGE MIRAGE LIBERTY - Medical Device - RESMED INC.; *pg.* 1589, *pg.* 207
MIRAGE OUTBACK - Pedaling Kayak - HOBIE CAT COMPANY; *pg.* 1708, *pg.* 173
MIRAGE OUTBACK FISHERMAN - Pedaling Kayak - HOBIE CAT COMPANY; *pg.* 1708, *pg.* 173
MIRAGE QUATTRO - Nasal Mask - RESMED INC.; *pg.* 1589, *pg.* 207
MIRAGE SPORT - Pedaling Kayak - HOBIE CAT COMPANY; *pg.* 1708, *pg.* 173
MIRAGE SWIFT - Diagnostic Product - RESMED INC.; *pg.* 1589, *pg.* 207
MIRAGE TANDEM - Pedaling Kayak - HOBIE CAT COMPANY; *pg.* 1708, *pg.* 173
MIRAGE VISTA - Nasal Mask - RESMED INC.; *pg.* 1589, *pg.* 207
MIRAGLOSS - Pigment - BASF CATALYSTS LLC; *pg.* 1148, *pg.* 1074
MIRAGLOSS - Adhesive & Sealant - DOW CHEMICAL; *pg.* 1156, *pg.* 1563
MIRAKLE - Footwear - STEVEN MADDEN, LTD.; *pg.* 1819, *pg.* 1176
MIRALAN - Dyeing Auxiliaries - HUNTSMAN CORPORATION; *pg.* 1167, *pg.* 1758
MIRALAX - Laxative - MERCK & CO., INC.; *pg.* 1566, *pg.* 1077
MIRAMAR - Kitchenware - THE VOLLRATH COMPANY LLC; *pg.* 1139, *pg.* 1894
MIRAMAX - Polishing Compound for Mirrors - FERRO CORPORATION; *pg.* 1162, *pg.* 1462
MIRANA - Pigment - BASF CATALYSTS LLC; *pg.* 1148, *pg.* 1074
MIRANDA - Furniture - ASHLEY FURNITURE INDUSTRIES, INC.; *pg.* 914, *pg.* 1852
MIRANDA - Fabric - NEMSCHOFF, INC.; *pg.* 936, *pg.* 1890
MIRASOL - Display Technology - QUALCOMM INCORPORATED; *pg.* 1873, *pg.* 207
MIRASSOU - Wine - E&J GALLO WINERY; *pg.* 1962, *pg.* 149
MIRATHEN - Compound - THE DOW CHEMICAL COMPANY; *pg.* 1157, *pg.* 898
MIRATI - Seating - THE HON COMPANY; *pg.* 928, *pg.* 709
MIRAVISTA - Shake Shingles - OWENS CORNING; *pg.* 102, *pg.* 1476
MIRAZYME - Cleaner & Rejuvenator - MCNETT CORPORATION; *pg.* 1839, *pg.* 1817
MIRCERA - Pharmaceutical Product - NEKTAR THERAPEUTICS; *pg.* 1572, *pg.* 224
MIREILLE - Beverages - THE COCA-COLA COMPANY; *pg.* 240, *pg.* 493
MIREL - Polymers - ARCHER-DANIELS-MIDLAND COMPANY; *pg.* 825, *pg.* 565
MIROIR - Door Panel - MASONITE INTERNATIONAL CORPORATION; *pg.* 1054, *pg.* 1920
MIROMET - Polishing Compound - BUEHLER, LTD.; *pg.* 1403, *pg.* 622
MIRRA - Furniture - HERMAN MILLER, INC.; *pg.* 926, *pg.* 913
MIRROLAC - All Purpose Enamel - AKZONOBEL DECORATIVE PAINTS U.S.; *pg.* 1439, *pg.* 1474
MIRROLAC WB - Waterborne Enamel - AKZONOBEL DECORATIVE PAINTS U.S.; *pg.* 1439, *pg.* 1474
MIRROR ACTIVATOR - Disaster Recovery - SAP; *pg.* 465, *pg.* 78
MIRROR-ACULOUS - Art Activities Kit - OOZ & OZ INC.; *pg.* 965, *pg.* 1838
MIRROR FINISH - Wall Base - BURKE INDUSTRIES, INC.; *pg.* 919, *pg.* 239
MIRROR POND - Brew - DESCHUTES BREWERY INC.; *pg.* 248, *pg.* 1496
MIRRORBIT - Flash Memory Product - ADVANCED MICRO DEVICES, INC.; *pg.* 613, *pg.* 282
MIRRORVIEW - Software - EMC CORPORATION; *pg.* 391, *pg.* 825
MIRV - Thermal Imaging System - FLIR SYSTEMS, INC.; *pg.* 1413, *pg.* 1510
MIRVADER - Medical Product - HOLOGIC, INC.; *pg.* 1416, *pg.* 784
MISCELLANEOUS DESIGN - Fluid Handling System - GRACO, INC.; *pg.* 1342, *pg.* 935
MISCELLANEOUS DROP DESIGN - Fluid Handling System - GRACO, INC.; *pg.* 1342, *pg.* 935
MISHLER - Medical Device - INTEGRA LIFESCIENCES HOLDINGS CORPORATION; *pg.* 1545, *pg.* 1109
MISO HAPPY WITH THIS COLOR - Nail Care Product - OPI PRODUCTS INC.; *pg.* 518, *pg.* 167
MISPACHA - Food Products - MANISCHEWITZ COMPANY; *pg.* 875, *pg.* 1097
MISQUINCEMAG.COM - Online Latina Teen Magazine - THE HEARST CORPORATION; *pg.* 1649, *pg.* 1239
MISS-A-PAYMENT - Banking Service - THE BANK OF NOVA SCOTIA; *pg.* 721, *pg.* 1935
MISS CHIQUITA - Fruit & Vegetable Product - CHIQUITA BRANDS INTERNATIONAL, INC.; *pg.* 847, *pg.* 1365
MISS CONTOUR - Footwear - P.W. MINOR & SON, INC.; *pg.* 1816, *pg.* 1140
MISS DAISY - Bicycle - G. JOANNOU CYCLE CO. INC.; *pg.* 1707, *pg.* 1098
MISS DORBY - Dresses & Career Apparel - KELLWOOD

COMPANY; *pg.* 28, *pg.* 975

MISS PIGGY - Muppet - THE WALT DISNEY COMPANY; *pg.* 317, *pg.* 52

MISS VICKIE'S - Potato Chips - FRITO-LAY NORTH AMERICA, INC.; *pg.* 1853, *pg.* 1730

MISSING LINK - Health Food Product - DESIGNING HEALTH, INC.; *pg.* 1523, *pg.* 299

THE MISSING PEACE - Jewelry - STULLER, INC.; *pg.* 13, *pg.* 745

MISSION - Table - BLATT BOWLING & BILLIARD CORP.; *pg.* 1827, *pg.* 1203

MISSION - Beverages - THE COCA-COLA COMPANY; *pg.* 240, *pg.* 493

MISSION - Mexican Food Products - GRUMA CORPORATION; *pg.* 860, *pg.* 951

MISSION BURRITO - Restaurant - MEXICAN RESTAURANTS, INC.; *pg.* 1741, *pg.* 1711

MISSION COMMAND TRAINER - Simulator System - EVANS & SUTHERLAND COMPUTER CORPORATION; *pg.* 638, *pg.* 1757

MISSION CONTROL - Organizing System - AVID TECHNOLOGY, INC.; *pg.* 622, *pg.* 804

MISSION. CRITICAL. CHEMISTRY - Tag Line - SACHEM INC.; *pg.* 1180, *pg.* 1665

MISSION ORCHARDS - Fruit & Snack Gifts - HICKORY FARMS, INC.; *pg.* 862, *pg.* 1462

MISSION: PAINTBALL - Game - HASBRO, INC.; *pg.* 954, *pg.* 1603

MISSION POINTE - Furniture - BUSH INDUSTRIES INC.; *pg.* 919, *pg.* 1170

MISSION SUCCESS - Technology Products - LOCKHEED MARTIN CORPORATION; *pg.* 229, *pg.* 762

MISSION ZERO - Carpet - INTERFACE, INC.; *pg.* 695, *pg.* 512

MISSIONCONTROL - Software - DELL SOFTWARE; *pg.* 385, *pg.* 40

MISSIONS - Game - ACTIVISION BLIZZARD, INC.; *pg.* 948, *pg.* 271

MISSISSIPPI BARBECUE SAUCE - Barbecue Sauce - THE FREMONT COMPANY; *pg.* 856, *pg.* 1454

MISSISSIPPI. FEELS LIKE COMING HOME - Slogan - MISSISSIPPI DEVELOPMENT AUTHORITY; *pg.* 999, *pg.* 969

MISSONI - Pillow - AMERICAN LEATHER LP; *pg.* 912, *pg.* 1673

MISSOURI LAWYERS WEEKLY - Newspaper - MASSACHUSETTS LAWYERS WEEKLY, INC.; *pg.* 1662, *pg.* 798

MISSY - Footwear - COBIAN CORP.; *pg.* 1806, *pg.* 253

MISSYY - Slipper - STEVEN MADDEN, LTD.; *pg.* 1819, *pg.* 1176

MIST - Cart Bag - DATREK GOLF; *pg.* 1832, *pg.* 1801

MIST COAT - Primer - JONES-BLAIR COMPANY; *pg.* 1443, *pg.* 1682

MIST-MASTER - Vane Mist Eliminator - ACS INDUSTRIES, INC.; *pg.* 1040, *pg.* 1602

MIST 'R K - Insecticide - KENT NUTRITION GROUP; *pg.* 1477, *pg.* 710

MISTAKE PROOF - Beauty Product - AVON PRODUCTS, INC.; *pg.* 500, *pg.* 1198

MISTERMESH - Mist Eliminator - ACS INDUSTRIES, INC.; *pg.* 1040, *pg.* 1602

MISTI-CIDE - Insecticide - DELTA FOREMOST CHEMICAL CORPORATION; *pg.* 1155, *pg.* 1642

MISTIC - Non-Carbonated Soft Drink - DR PEPPER SNAPPLE GROUP, INC.; *pg.* 250, *pg.* 1729

MISTIC - Office Furniture - STEELCASE INC.; *pg.* 475, *pg.* 889

MISTIQUE - Hot Cup - SOLO CUP COMPANY; *pg.* 1469, *pg.* 625

MISTLEDOUGH DOUBLER - Lottery Game - MASSACHUSETTS STATE LOTTERY; *pg.* 998, *pg.* 802

MISTLETOE - Candle - THE YANKEE CANDLE COMPANY, INC.; *pg.* 1792, *pg.* 843

MISTMATIC - Spray Coolant System - TRICO MFG. CORP.; *pg.* 219, *pg.* 1886

MISTOLIN - Cleaners - THE CLOROX COMPANY; *pg.* 327, *pg.* 169

MISTRALE - Sewage Treatment - HUNTSMAN CORPORATION; *pg.* 1167, *pg.* 1758

MISTTRAP - Filter - CAMERON INTERNATIONAL; *pg.* 1151, *pg.* 1702

MISTXPERT - Software - ACS INDUSTRIES, INC.; *pg.* 1040, *pg.* 1602

MISTY - Jewelry - ROMAN RESEARCH, INC.; *pg.* 11, *pg.* 824

MISTY - Cleaning Agents - ZEP INC.; *pg.* 338, *pg.* 524

MISTY MEADOW - Weather Jacket - HABAND COMPANY, INC.; *pg.* 1772, *pg.* 1099

MISTY-OX - Hydration Delivery Systems - VITAL SIGNS, INC.; *pg.* 1607, *pg.* 1126

MISTY OX MULTIFIT - Nebulizer Adapter - VITAL SIGNS, INC.; *pg.* 1607, *pg.* 1126

MISURA - Sweetener - MERISANT COMPANY; *pg.* 876, *pg.* 581

MITA-CLEAR - Veterinary Companion Animal Earmite Preparations - PFIZER INC.; *pg.* 1581, *pg.* 1278

MITABAN - Dog Ectoparasiticide - PFIZER INC.; *pg.* 1581, *pg.* 1278

MITCHELL - Furniture - ETHAN ALLEN INTERIORS INC.; *pg.* 924, *pg.* 343

MITCHELL REPAIR - Repair & Service Information & Shop Management Systems - SNAP-ON INCORPORATED; *pg.* 1062, *pg.* 1862

MITCHELL'S - Hair Salons - REGIS CORPORATION; *pg.* 521, *pg.* 941

MITCHELL'S HAIR STYLING - Hair Salons - REGIS CORPORATION; *pg.* 521, *pg.* 941

MITCHUM - Deodorant - REVLON, INC.; *pg.* 521, *pg.* 1286

MITE-Y-PIN - Connector - MOLEX INCORPORATED; *pg.* 655, *pg.* 628

MITEK 2000 - Truss Engineering Software - MITEK, INC.; *pg.* 1056, *pg.* 975

MITEL ENTERPRISE - Messaging System - MITEL NETWORKS CORPORATION; *pg.* 654, *pg.* 1921

MITEL TOTALSOLUTION - Service Program - MITEL NETWORKS CORPORATION; *pg.* 654, *pg.* 1921

MITEL UNIFIED COMMUNICATOR - Communicator Mobile - MITEL NETWORKS CORPORATION; *pg.* 654, *pg.* 1921

MITI-LITE - Lighting System - UNILUX, INC.; *pg.* 682, *pg.* 1118

MITIGATOR - Limited Use Chemical Resistant Fabric - STANDARD SAFETY EQUIPMENT CO.; *pg.* 1379, *pg.* 632

MITIN - Moth Proofing System - HUNTSMAN CORPORATION; *pg.* 1167, *pg.* 1758

MITO - Bath & Plumbing Product - JACUZZI BRANDS CORPORATION; *pg.* 554, *pg.* 65

MITO TRACKER - Biomolecule Product - THERMO FISHER SCIENTIFIC INC.; *pg.* 1602, *pg.* 61

MITOFLUOR - Molecular Probe Product - THERMO FISHER SCIENTIFIC INC.; *pg.* 1602, *pg.* 61

MITOMYCIN - Pharmaceutical Product - ASTEX PHARMACEUTICALS, INC; *pg.* 1497, *pg.* 77

MITOPROBE - Molecular Probe Product - THERMO FISHER SCIENTIFIC INC.; *pg.* 1602, *pg.* 61

MITOSOX - Molecular Probe Product - THERMO FISHER SCIENTIFIC INC.; *pg.* 1602, *pg.* 61

MITOTRACKER - Molecular Probe Product - THERMO FISHER SCIENTIFIC INC.; *pg.* 1602, *pg.* 61

MITRA - Waiting Seating - STEELCASE INC.; *pg.* 475, *pg.* 889

MITRA RECLINER - Patient Seating - STEELCASE INC.; *pg.* 475, *pg.* 889

MITSUBISHI FUSO - Trucks - MITSUBISHI FUSO TRUCK OF AMERICA, INC.; *pg.* 185, *pg.* 1045

MITTEN - Ornament - HERITAGE LACE INC.; *pg.* 694, *pg.* 711

MITTEN 4 SALE - Scarf - HERITAGE LACE INC.; *pg.* 694, *pg.* 711

MITUTOYO - Hardness Tester - NEWAGE TESTING INSTRUMENTS, INC.; *pg.* 1058, *pg.* 1532

MITY DELUXE - Stacking Chair - MITY ENTERPRISES, INC.; *pg.* 935, *pg.* 1753

MITY FLEX - Stacking Chair - MITY ENTERPRISES, INC.; *pg.* 935, *pg.* 1753

MITY HOST - Stacking Chair - MITY ENTERPRISES, INC.; *pg.* 935, *pg.* 1753

MITY-LITE - Furniture - MITY ENTERPRISES, INC.; *pg.* 935, *pg.* 1753

MITY NICE GRILL - Casual Dining Restaurant - LETTUCE ENTERTAIN YOU ENTERPRISES, INC.; *pg.* 1735, *pg.* 580

MITY STACK - Stacking Chair - MITY ENTERPRISES, INC.; *pg.* 935, *pg.* 1753

MITYLITE - Flashlight - PELICAN PRODUCTS, INC.; *pg.* 1842, *pg.* 295

MITZEL'S AMERICAN KITCHEN - Family Style Full Service Restaurant - ELMER'S RESTAURANTS, INC.; *pg.* 1728, *pg.* 1502

MIVACRON - Pharmaceutical Product - ABBOTT LABORATORIES; *pg.* 1484, *pg.* 551

MIVIDA - Sweetener - MERISANT COMPANY; *pg.* 876, *pg.* 581

MIX-ALL - Grinder Mixer - GEHL COMPANY; *pg.* 1339, *pg.* 1899

MIX & MATCH - Lottery Game - PENNSYLVANIA STATE LOTTERY; *pg.* 1003, *pg.* 1552

MIX & MATCH - Game - THE STATE LOTTERY COMMISSION OF INDIANA; *pg.* 1006, *pg.* 690

MIX-IT UP - Gift Box - BEER NUTS, INC.; *pg.* 1850, *pg.* 557

MIX-MILL - On-Farm Feed Processing Equipment - A.T. FERRELL COMPANY, INC.; *pg.* 701, *pg.* 674

MIX-MULLER - Batch Mixer - SIMPSON TECHNOLOGIES CORPORATION; *pg.* 111, *pg.* 555

MIX-N-FINE - Salt - CARGILL LIMITED; *pg.* 1475, *pg.* 1914

MIX 'N' FIX - Home Products - HABAND COMPANY, INC.; *pg.* 1772, *pg.* 1099

MIX-N-STOR - Kitchenware - TUPPERWARE BRANDS CORPORATION; *pg.* 1139, *pg.* 456

MIX-UPS - Candy - NESTLE USA, INC.; *pg.* 883, *pg.* 96

MIX2VIAL - Drug Administration System - WEST PHARMACEUTICAL SERVICES, INC.; *pg.* 1472, *pg.* 1532

MIXED QUATREFOIL - Jewelry - YURMAN DESIGN, INC.; *pg.* 15, *pg.* 1316

MIXED-SIGNAL PRO - Software System - MENTOR GRAPHICS CORPORATION; *pg.* 432, *pg.* 1510

MIXED VEGETABLES - Nutritional Supplement - NATURAL ORGANICS, INC.; *pg.* 1571, *pg.* 1181

MIXER TOO SALADSHOOTER - Electric Slicer, Shredder & Mixer - NATIONAL PRESTO INDUSTRIES, INC; *pg.* 1128, *pg.* 1857

MIXEVAC - Bone Cement System - STRYKER CORPORATION; *pg.* 1598, *pg.* 894

MIXEVAN - Vanilla - DAVID MICHAEL & CO. INC.; *pg.* 852, *pg.* 1563

MIXJECT - Drug Administration System - WEST PHARMACEUTICAL SERVICES, INC.; *pg.* 1472, *pg.* 1532

MIXMATE - Kitchen Appliance - HAMILTON BEACH BRANDS, INC.; *pg.* 56, *pg.* 1783

MIXOR - Home & Garden Product - WESTROCK COMPANY; *pg.* 1472, *pg.* 1805

MIXTRUDER - High-Torque Mixer - LITTLEFORD DAY INC.; *pg.* 1356, *pg.* 728

MIXTURE NO. 79 - Pipe Tobaccos - ALTADIS USA, INC.; *pg.* 1893, *pg.* 423

MIZANI - Hair Care Products - L'OREAL USA; *pg.* 514, *pg.* 1252

MIZERAK - Sporting Good Product - ESCALADE INC.; *pg.* 1833, *pg.* 678

MIZTIQUE - Nutritional Product - NUTRACEUTICAL INTERNATIONAL CORPORATION; *pg.* 1576, *pg.* 1753

MIZU - Ceramic Tile - WALKER & ZANGER, INC.; *pg.* 119, *pg.* 281

MIZUHIKI - Craft - YASUTOMO & CO.; *pg.* 497, *pg.* 280

MIZUNO - Footwear, Equipment & Apparel for Baseball/Softball, Running, Volleyball - MIZUNO USA, INC.; *pg.* 1839, *pg.* 538

MJ MINI - Thermal Cycler - BIO-RAD LABORATORIES, INC.; *pg.* 1504, *pg.* 101

MJ MODULE - Software - BIO-RAD LABORATORIES, INC.; *pg.* 1504, *pg.* 101

MJ RESEARCH & THE MJ RESEARCH LOGO - Software - BIO-RAD LABORATORIES, INC.; *pg.* 1504, *pg.* 101

MK - Healthcare - WESTROCK COMPANY; *pg.* 1472, *pg.* 1805

MK 5 - Medical Equipment - INVACARE CORPORATION; *pg.* 1546, *pg.* 1451

MK II - Miniature Chemical Agent Detector - MINE SAFETY APPLIANCES COMPANY; *pg.* 1361, *pg.* 1525

MK6I - Medical Equipment - INVACARE CORPORATION; *pg.* 1546, *pg.* 1451

MKIV - Medical Equipment - INVACARE CORPORATION; *pg.* 1546, *pg.* 1451

MKS INSTRUMENTS - Components & Subsystems - MKS INSTRUMENTS, INC.; *pg.* 1362, *pg.* 781

M.L. CAMPBELL - Wood Finishing Systems - THE SHERWIN-WILLIAMS COMPANY; *pg.* 1447, *pg.* 1435

ML910 - Rugged Notebook - MOTOROLA SOLUTIONS, INC.; *pg.* 657, *pg.* 659

MLA - Banking Software - JACK HENRY & ASSOCIATES, INC.; *pg.* 422, *pg.* 988

MLB SERIES - Baseball Bat - HILLERICH & BRADSBY CO., INC.; *pg.* 1836, *pg.* 576

MLRS - Mobile Projectile Launch Platforms - LOCKHEED

MARTIN CORPORATION; *pg.* 229, *pg.* 762

MLT - Microlaryngeal Tracheal Tube - MEDTRONIC; *pg.* 1563, *pg.* 183

MLX - Electronic Components - MOLEX INCORPORATED; *pg.* 655, *pg.* 628

MMA - Footwear - COBIAN CORP.; *pg.* 1806, *pg.* 253

MMC CAPITAL - Private Equity Firm - MARSH & MCLENNAN COMPANIES INC.; *pg.* 1207, *pg.* 1256

MMC ENTERPRISE RISK - Enterprise Risk Management - MARSH & MCLENNAN COMPANIES INC.; *pg.* 1207, *pg.* 1256

MMCMOBILE - Memory Card - SANDISK CORPORATION; *pg.* 465, *pg.* 147

MMCMODEM - Wireless Modems - MULTI-TECH SYSTEMS INC.; *pg.* 442, *pg.* 951

MMD ACCESS - Pension Fund Related List - STANDARD & POOR'S RATINGS SERVICES; *pg.* 805, *pg.* 1296

MMD MAILING LISTS - Pension Fund Related List - STANDARD & POOR'S RATINGS SERVICES; *pg.* 805, *pg.* 1296

MMFC 1X2 - Coupler - OPLINK COMMUNICATIONS, INC.; *pg.* 660, *pg.* 91

MMFC 2X2 - Coupler - OPLINK COMMUNICATIONS, INC.; *pg.* 660, *pg.* 91

MMMM...TOASTY! - Tag Line - THE QUIZNO'S MASTER LLC; *pg.* 1746, *pg.* 322

MMR XTREME - Air Mask - MINE SAFETY APPLIANCES COMPANY; *pg.* 1361, *pg.* 1525

MMS - Imaging Lens - EDMUND INDUSTRIAL OPTICS INC.; *pg.* 1411, *pg.* 1041

MMSR - Systems Integration & Aeronautics - LOCKHEED MARTIN CORPORATION; *pg.* 229, *pg.* 762

MMV - Fluid Handling System - GRACO, INC.; *pg.* 1342, *pg.* 935

MMV-110 MICRO - Electronic Component - EMCORE CORPORATION; *pg.* 636, *pg.* 39

MMV-110 MINI - Electronic Component - EMCORE CORPORATION; *pg.* 636, *pg.* 39

MMV-110 STANDARD - Electronic Component - EMCORE CORPORATION; *pg.* 636, *pg.* 39

MMV-120 A-C - Electronic Component - EMCORE CORPORATION; *pg.* 636, *pg.* 39

MMV-120A3C3 - Electronic Component - EMCORE CORPORATION; *pg.* 636, *pg.* 39

MN FOR MEN - Cosmetic Product - MERLE NORMAN COSMETICS, INC.; *pg.* 517, *pg.* 136

MNEMOTEST - Software System - MENTOR GRAPHICS CORPORATION; *pg.* 432, *pg.* 1510

MNI LEADS - Online Sales & Marketing Database - MANUFACTURERS' NEWS, INC.; *pg.* 1661, *pg.* 612

MNI-RUPTER - Switch - S&C ELECTRIC COMPANY; *pg.* 1305, *pg.* 589

MNSD - Desuperheaters - SPX PROCESS EQUIPMENT; *pg.* 1378, *pg.* 1551

MO' BABY - Musical Instrument - GIBSON GUITAR CORP.; *pg.* 550, *pg.* 1650

MOAB - Car Part Accessory - PRO-LINE, INC.; *pg.* 966, *pg.* 45

MOANA - Eyewear - MAUI JIM, INC.; *pg.* 9, *pg.* 651

MOBAN - Pharmaceutical Product - ENDO PHARMACEUTICALS HOLDINGS, INC.; *pg.* 1528, *pg.* 1549

MOBELLA - Door Lock - SOUTHCO, INC.; *pg.* 1063, *pg.* 1522

MOBI-MATE - IO System - MOLEX INCORPORATED; *pg.* 655, *pg.* 628

MOBIL - Petroleum Products - EXXON MOBIL CORPORATION; *pg.* 977, *pg.* 1718

MOBIL 1 - Synthetic Lubricants - EXXON MOBIL CORPORATION; *pg.* 977, *pg.* 1718

MOBIL-MIST - Medical Equipment - INVACARE CORPORATION; *pg.* 1546, *pg.* 1451

MOBILAID - Power Wheelchair - INVACARE CORPORATION; *pg.* 1546, *pg.* 1451

MOBILAIRE - Compressor - INVACARE CORPORATION; *pg.* 1546, *pg.* 1451

MOBILE ACUITY - Central Station - WELCH ALLYN INC.; *pg.* 1436, *pg.* 1342

MOBILE AMD ATHLON - Mobile Processor - ADVANCED MICRO DEVICES, INC.; *pg.* 613, *pg.* 282

MOBILE AMD SEMPRON - Mobile Processor - ADVANCED MICRO DEVICES, INC.; *pg.* 613, *pg.* 282

THE MOBILE & EMBEDDED SYSTEM EXPERTS - Tagline - BSQUARE CORPORATION; *pg.* 366, *pg.* 1813

THE MOBILE & INTERNET PERFORMANCE AUTHORITY - Slogan - KEYNOTE SYSTEMS INCORPORATED; *pg.* 425, *pg.* 255

MOBILE ANSWERS - Search Engine - ANSWERS CORPORATION; *pg.* 1229, *pg.* 1195

MOBILE CADDIE - Golf Product - CALLAWAY GOLF COMPANY; *pg.* 1829, *pg.* 58

MOBILE CUSTOMER SELF SERVICE - Customer Service - TELUS CORPORATION; *pg.* 1952, *pg.* 1912

MOBILE ELECTRONICS - Magazine - BOBIT BUSINESS MEDIA; *pg.* 1622, *pg.* 293

MOBILE ESSENTIALS - Software - RENTRAK CORPORATION; *pg.* 306, *pg.* 1506

MOBILE EXPRESS DRIVER - Software - XEROX CORPORATION; *pg.* 494, *pg.* 365

MOBILE MARKETING - Marketing Tool - PREMIERE GLOBAL SERVICES, INC.; *pg.* 1275, *pg.* 518

MOBILE MAXPURE - Portable Solar Powered Pumping & Purification System - ENTECH SOLAR, INC.; *pg.* 1335, *pg.* 1694

MOBILE ME - Online Services - APPLE INC.; *pg.* 350, *pg.* 73

MOBILE MEETING - Calling Applications - POLYCOM, INC.; *pg.* 664, *pg.* 249

MOBILE MERCHANDISING SYSTEMS - Merchandise Displays - MEG; *pg.* 97, *pg.* 675

MOBILE MODULAR - Relocatable Modular Offices - MCGRATH RENTCORP; *pg.* 1104, *pg.* 122

MOBILE ONDEMAND ESSENTIALS - Software - RENTRAK CORPORATION; *pg.* 306, *pg.* 1506

MOBILE REACH SPLITWARE - Software - BMC SOFTWARE, INC.; *pg.* 362, *pg.* 1701

MOBILE RESPONDER - Video Conferencing System - POLYCOM, INC.; *pg.* 664, *pg.* 249

MOBILE TOUR - Golf Product - CALLAWAY GOLF COMPANY; *pg.* 1829, *pg.* 58

MOBILE TV ESSENTIALS - Software - RENTRAK CORPORATION; *pg.* 306, *pg.* 1506

MOBILE XDR - Memory Architecture - RAMBUS INC.; *pg.* 459, *pg.* 288

MOBILECAST - Software - UNITED PARCEL SERVICE, INC.; *pg.* 1928, *pg.* 522

MOBILECME - Learning System - EPOCRATES, INC.; *pg.* 1529, *pg.* 254

MOBILEDGE 4000 - Access Node - SONUS NETWORKS INC.; *pg.* 1281, *pg.* 858

MOBILEDGE 9000 - Access Node - SONUS NETWORKS INC.; *pg.* 1281, *pg.* 858

MOBILEDOC - Manual - XEROX CORPORATION; *pg.* 494, *pg.* 365

MOBILEGT - Semiconductor Product - FREESCALE SEMICONDUCTOR, INC.; *pg.* 398, *pg.* 1662

MOBILEIQ - Intelligent Vehicle Protection - AIRIQ, INC.; *pg.* 346, *pg.* 1932

MOBILEMANAGER - PC Workstation - RUBBERMAID HOME PRODUCTS; *pg.* 1138, *pg.* 1453

MOBILEMARKETINFO - Personal Communication & Cellular Market Area Database - PITNEY BOWES SOFTWARE INC.; *pg.* 455, *pg.* 1346

MOBILEOUTCOMES - Educational Service - EPOCRATES, INC.; *pg.* 1529, *pg.* 254

MOBILE.PCMAG.COM - Web Site - PC MAGAZINE; *pg.* 1674, *pg.* 1276

MOBILESAFETY - Mobile Phone Security System - THE ADT CORPORATION; *pg.* 612, *pg.* 409

MOBILESEARCH - Mobile Security X-ray System - AMERICAN SCIENCE AND ENGINEERING, INC.; *pg.* 1399, *pg.* 787

MOBILEVIEW - Portable HMI Product - ROCKWELL AUTOMATION, INC.; *pg.* 668, *pg.* 1880

MOBILEWEAR - Caller ID Watch - FOSSIL GROUP, INC.; *pg.* 5, *pg.* 1735

MOBILITY - 3D Graphical Technology - ADVANCED MICRO DEVICES, INC.-MARKHAM; *pg.* 345, *pg.* 1922

MOBILITY FIREGL - Graphics Accelerator - ADVANCED MICRO DEVICES, INC.-MARKHAM; *pg.* 345, *pg.* 1922

MOBILITY FRIENDLY - Wireless LAN Card - SOCKET MOBILE, INC.; *pg.* 471, *pg.* 164

MOBILITY RADEON - Mobile Graphics Chip - ADVANCED MICRO DEVICES, INC.-MARKHAM; *pg.* 345, *pg.* 1922

MOBILITY TECHNOLOGIES - Wireless Digital Sensor Network - THE HEARST CORPORATION; *pg.* 1649, *pg.* 1239

MOBILITY1 - Medical Device - DERMA SCIENCES, INC.; *pg.* 1523, *pg.* 1111

MOBILITY,RESPONSE,PROTECTION - Tagline - IRT, INC.; *pg.* 1169, *pg.* 771

MOBILOX - Chemical Product - CARUS CORPORATION; *pg.* 1152, *pg.* 652

MOBIPLAYER - Game - FORTUNET, INC.; *pg.* 953, *pg.* 1024

MOBIPLAYER SR - Game - FORTUNET, INC.; *pg.* 953, *pg.* 1024

MOBIUS - Seating - THE HON COMPANY; *pg.* 928, *pg.* 709

MOBIUS - Medical Device - INTEGRA LIFESCIENCES HOLDINGS CORPORATION; *pg.* 1545, *pg.* 1109

MOBIUS SYSTEM - Recycle Technology - SACHEM INC.; *pg.* 1180, *pg.* 1665

MOBL - Semiconductor Architecture - CYPRESS SEMICONDUCTOR CORPORATION; *pg.* 1326, *pg.* 243

MOBL-USB - Semiconductor Architecture - CYPRESS SEMICONDUCTOR CORPORATION; *pg.* 1326, *pg.* 243

MOBL2 - Semiconductor Architecture - CYPRESS SEMICONDUCTOR CORPORATION; *pg.* 1326, *pg.* 243

MOBL3 - Semiconductor Architecture - CYPRESS SEMICONDUCTOR CORPORATION; *pg.* 1326, *pg.* 243

MOBL4 - Semiconductor Architecture - CYPRESS SEMICONDUCTOR CORPORATION; *pg.* 1326, *pg.* 243

MOBSIM - Software System - ALION SCIENCE AND TECHNOLOGY CORPORATION; *pg.* 615, *pg.* 1788

MOCHA - Pillow and Throw - HERITAGE LACE INC.; *pg.* 694, *pg.* 711

MOCHA - Dinnerware - THE HOMER LAUGHLIN CHINA COMPANY; *pg.* 1125, *pg.* 1850

MOCHA ALMOND CHILLER - Coffee Service - KEURIG GREEN MOUNTAIN, INC.; *pg.* 868, *pg.* 1768

MOCHA CHERRY - Furniture - BUSH INDUSTRIES INC.; *pg.* 919, *pg.* 1170

MOCHA MIX - Non-Dairy Creamer - TREEHOUSE FOODS, INC.; *pg.* 901, *pg.* 649

MOCHA OAK - Flooring - LUMBER LIQUIDATORS HOLDINGS, INC.; *pg.* 94, *pg.* 1808

MOCHASIPPI - Coffee Product - COMMUNITY COFFEE COMPANY LLC; *pg.* 849, *pg.* 741

MOCKTWISTAFE - Clothing - LAKELAND INDUSTRIES, INC.; *pg.* 1354, *pg.* 1338

MOCON AB PLUS - Automatic Balance System for Capsule or Tablet Weighing & Sorting System - MOCON, INC.; *pg.* 1363, *pg.* 940

MOD-22XA - Lighting System - LITECONTROL CORPORATION; *pg.* 1301, *pg.* 841

MOD-66 - Lighting System - LITECONTROL CORPORATION; *pg.* 1301, *pg.* 841

MOD EXPRESS - Generator - BALDOR ELECTRIC COMPANY; *pg.* 1316, *pg.* 32

MOD-PLUS - Fluid Handling System - GRACO, INC.; *pg.* 1342, *pg.* 935

MOD-SNAP - Electronic Components - MOLEX INCORPORATED; *pg.* 655, *pg.* 628

MOD2 - Lighting System - LITECONTROL CORPORATION; *pg.* 1301, *pg.* 841

MODA - Faucet - ELKAY MANUFACTURING COMPANY; *pg.* 80, *pg.* 645

MODA MOSAIC - Ceramic, Glass, Stone Tiles & Slabs - WALKER & ZANGER, INC.; *pg.* 119, *pg.* 281

MODAFLOW - Flow Modifiers - CYTEC INDUSTRIES, INC.; *pg.* 1155, *pg.* 1131

MODALGISTICS - Consulting Services - NORFOLK SOUTHERN CORPORATION; *pg.* 1917, *pg.* 1797

MODALVIEW - Consulting Services - NORFOLK SOUTHERN CORPORATION; *pg.* 1917, *pg.* 1797

MODAMP - Electronic Product - LRAD CORPORATION; *pg.* 652, *pg.* 204

MODAR - Acrylic Resins - ASHLAND INC.; *pg.* 972, *pg.* 726

MODBOX - Storage System - DOT HILL SYSTEMS CORP.; *pg.* 388, *pg.* 333

MODBUS - Protocol - EMERSON PROCESS MANAGEMENT ROSEMOUNT INC.; *pg.* 1334, *pg.* 920

MODE - Furniture - JOFCO INC.; *pg.* 931, *pg.* 691

MODEL 10 - Revolver - SMITH & WESSON HOLDING CORPORATION; *pg.* 1845, *pg.* 846

MODEL 101ZZ - Image Simulator Software - AMERICAN SCIENCE AND ENGINEERING, INC.; *pg.* 1399, *pg.* 787

MODEL 17 MASTERPIECE - Revolver - SMITH & WESSON HOLDING CORPORATION; *pg.* 1845, *pg.* 846

MODEL 18 MASTERPIECE - Revolver - SMITH & WESSON HOLDING CORPORATION; *pg.* 1845, *pg.* 846

MODEL 29 50TH ANNIVERSARY - Pistol - SMITH & WESSON HOLDING CORPORATION; *pg.* 1845, *pg.* 846

MODEL 3 SCHOFIELD - Pistol - SMITH & WESSON HOLDING CORPORATION; *pg.* 1845, *pg.* 846

MODEL 310 NIGHT GUARD - Revolver - SMITH & WESSON

First page reference indicates Business Class Edition
Second page reference indicates Geographic Edition

HOLDING CORPORATION; *pg.* 1845, *pg.* 846
MODEL 317 - Revolver - SMITH & WESSON HOLDING CORPORATION; *pg.* 1845, *pg.* 846
MODEL 327 TRR8 - Tactical Revolver - SMITH & WESSON HOLDING CORPORATION; *pg.* 1845, *pg.* 846
MODEL 340PD - Revolver - SMITH & WESSON HOLDING CORPORATION; *pg.* 1845, *pg.* 846
MODEL 357 NIGHT GUARD - Revolver - SMITH & WESSON HOLDING CORPORATION; *pg.* 1845, *pg.* 846
MODEL 360PD - Revolver - SMITH & WESSON HOLDING CORPORATION; *pg.* 1845, *pg.* 846
MODEL 3913TSW - Pistol - SMITH & WESSON HOLDING CORPORATION; *pg.* 1845, *pg.* 846
MODEL 40 CENTENNIAL - Pistol - SMITH & WESSON HOLDING CORPORATION; *pg.* 1845, *pg.* 846
MODEL 4003TSW - Pistol - SMITH & WESSON HOLDING CORPORATION; *pg.* 1845, *pg.* 846
MODEL 4006TSW - Pistol - SMITH & WESSON HOLDING CORPORATION; *pg.* 1845, *pg.* 846
MODEL 4013TSW - Pistol - SMITH & WESSON HOLDING CORPORATION; *pg.* 1845, *pg.* 846
MODEL 42 - Revolver - SMITH & WESSON HOLDING CORPORATION; *pg.* 1845, *pg.* 846
MODEL 442 - Revolver - SMITH & WESSON HOLDING CORPORATION; *pg.* 1845, *pg.* 846
MODEL 442 SAF - Revolver - SMITH & WESSON HOLDING CORPORATION; *pg.* 1845, *pg.* 846
MODEL 4513TSW - Pistol - SMITH & WESSON HOLDING CORPORATION; *pg.* 1845, *pg.* 846
MODEL 4563TSW - Pistol - SMITH & WESSON HOLDING CORPORATION; *pg.* 1845, *pg.* 846
MODEL 4566TSW - Pistol - SMITH & WESSON HOLDING CORPORATION; *pg.* 1845, *pg.* 846
MODEL 460XVR - Revolver System - SMITH & WESSON HOLDING CORPORATION; *pg.* 1845, *pg.* 846
MODEL 500 - Urine/Fluids Workstation - IRIS INTERNATIONAL, INC.; *pg.* 1547, *pg.* 64
MODEL 58 - Revolver - SMITH & WESSON HOLDING CORPORATION; *pg.* 1845, *pg.* 846
MODEL 5903TSW - Pistol - SMITH & WESSON HOLDING CORPORATION; *pg.* 1845, *pg.* 846
MODEL 5906TSW - Pistol - SMITH & WESSON HOLDING CORPORATION; *pg.* 1845, *pg.* 846
MODEL 60 - Revolver - SMITH & WESSON HOLDING CORPORATION; *pg.* 1845, *pg.* 846
MODEL 60LS - Revolver - SMITH & WESSON HOLDING CORPORATION; *pg.* 1845, *pg.* 846
MODEL 619 - Revolver - SMITH & WESSON HOLDING CORPORATION; *pg.* 1845, *pg.* 846
MODEL 620 - Revolver - SMITH & WESSON HOLDING CORPORATION; *pg.* 1845, *pg.* 846
MODEL 632 CARRY COMP PRO - Revolver - SMITH & WESSON HOLDING CORPORATION; *pg.* 1845, *pg.* 846
MODEL 637 - Revolver - SMITH & WESSON HOLDING CORPORATION; *pg.* 1845, *pg.* 846
MODEL 638 - Revolver - SMITH & WESSON HOLDING CORPORATION; *pg.* 1845, *pg.* 846
MODEL 64 - Revolver - SMITH & WESSON HOLDING CORPORATION; *pg.* 1845, *pg.* 846
MODEL 640 - Revolver - SMITH & WESSON HOLDING CORPORATION; *pg.* 1845, *pg.* 846
MODEL 642 - Revolver - SMITH & WESSON HOLDING CORPORATION; *pg.* 1845, *pg.* 846
MODEL 642LS - Revolver - SMITH & WESSON HOLDING CORPORATION; *pg.* 1845, *pg.* 846
MODEL 649 - Revolver - SMITH & WESSON HOLDING CORPORATION; *pg.* 1845, *pg.* 846
MODEL 67 - Revolver - SMITH & WESSON HOLDING CORPORATION; *pg.* 1845, *pg.* 846
MODEL 686 PLUS - Revolver - SMITH & WESSON HOLDING CORPORATION; *pg.* 1845, *pg.* 846
MODEL 88 BY HENRY KLOSS - Electronics - CAMBRIDGE SOUNDWORKS, INC.; *pg.* 1234, *pg.* 781
MODEL 88CD BY HENRY KLOSS - Electronics - CAMBRIDGE SOUNDWORKS, INC.; *pg.* 1234, *pg.* 781
MODEL 952 LONG SLIDE - Pistol - SMITH & WESSON HOLDING CORPORATION; *pg.* 1845, *pg.* 846
MODEL B - Screen - DA-LITE SCREEN COMPANY; *pg.* 632, *pg.* 698
MODEL C - Screen - DA-LITE SCREEN COMPANY; *pg.* 632, *pg.* 698
MODEL CS45 - Pistol - SMITH & WESSON HOLDING CORPORATION; *pg.* 1845, *pg.* 846
MODEL CS9 - Pistol - SMITH & WESSON HOLDING CORPORATION; *pg.* 1845, *pg.* 846
MODEL DAIRY - Dairy Product - DEAN FOODS COMPANY; *pg.* 852, *pg.* 1679
MODEL ELEVEN - Speaker - CAMBRIDGE SOUNDWORKS, INC.; *pg.* 1234, *pg.* 781
MODEL MASTER - Car Paints - THE TESTOR CORPORATION; *pg.* 968, *pg.* 655
MODEL MASTER FS - Paints - THE TESTOR CORPORATION; *pg.* 968, *pg.* 655
MODEL PAL - Assembly Equipment - BADGER AIR BRUSH COMPANY; *pg.* 359, *pg.* 612
MODEL RAILROADER - Magazine - KALMBACH PUBLISHING CO.; *pg.* 1656, *pg.* 1898
MODEL RETAILER - Magazine - KALMBACH PUBLISHING CO.; *pg.* 1656, *pg.* 1898
MODEL STAR - Valves - THE WM. POWELL COMPANY; *pg.* 1389, *pg.* 1427
MODEL SW1911 - Pistol - SMITH & WESSON HOLDING CORPORATION; *pg.* 1845, *pg.* 846
MODEL SW1911PD - Pistol - SMITH & WESSON HOLDING CORPORATION; *pg.* 1845, *pg.* 846
MODEL TECHNOLOGY - Software System - MENTOR GRAPHICS CORPORATION; *pg.* 432, *pg.* 1510
MODELBUILDER - Software - ENVIRONMENTAL SYSTEMS RESEARCH INSTITUTE INC.; *pg.* 393, *pg.* 188
MODELEDITOR - Software System - MENTOR GRAPHICS CORPORATION; *pg.* 432, *pg.* 1510
MODELER - Software Product & Module - RIVERBED PERFORMANCE MANAGEMENT; *pg.* 462, *pg.* 765
MODELFLEX - Paint - BADGER AIR BRUSH COMPANY; *pg.* 359, *pg.* 612
MODELITHICS - Track - COILCRAFT, INC.; *pg.* 1324, *pg.* 562
MODELL'S - Apparel - HENRY MODELL & COMPANY, INC.; *pg.* 1836, *pg.* 1240
MODELO - Beer - CROWN IMPORTS LLC; *pg.* 248, *pg.* 572
MODELSIM - Hardware Description Language Simulator Software - MENTOR GRAPHICS CORPORATION; *pg.* 432, *pg.* 1510
MODELSLIM - Software - ALTERA CORPORATION; *pg.* 348, *pg.* 237
MODELSOURCE - Software - SYNOPSYS, INC.; *pg.* 480, *pg.* 162
MODELSTATION - Software System - MENTOR GRAPHICS CORPORATION; *pg.* 432, *pg.* 1510
MODELTOOLS - Software - SYNOPSYS, INC.; *pg.* 480, *pg.* 162
MODELVIEWER - Software System - MENTOR GRAPHICS CORPORATION; *pg.* 432, *pg.* 1510
MODELVIEWERPLUS - Software System - MENTOR GRAPHICS CORPORATION; *pg.* 432, *pg.* 1510
MODEMASTER - Analyzer - COHERENT, INC.; *pg.* 1406, *pg.* 265
MODEMMODULE - Dial-up Modem - MULTI-TECH SYSTEMS INC.; *pg.* 442, *pg.* 951
MODENA - Furniture - ASHLEY FURNITURE INDUSTRIES, INC.; *pg.* 914, *pg.* 1852
MODERATE PH/O - Veterinary Food - IAMS COMPANY; *pg.* 1477, *pg.* 1633
MODERN - Pillow - AMERICAN LEATHER LP; *pg.* 912, *pg.* 1673
MODERN - Underground Storage Tank - MODERN WELDING COMPANY, INC.; *pg.* 1363, *pg.* 739
MODERN & IMAGE - Hair Product - THE STEPHAN COMPANY; *pg.* 1597, *pg.* 426
MODERN-ART - Circuits & Software For Mobile Phones - AVAGO TECHNOLOGIES; *pg.* 358, *pg.* 238
MODERN BRIDE - Magazine - CONDE NAST PUBLICATIONS, INC.; *pg.* 1629, *pg.* 1217
MODERN CAR CARE - Publication - INFORMA EXHIBITIONS LLC; *pg.* 1653, *pg.* 17
MODERN EAGLE - Guitar - PAUL REED SMITH GUITARS; *pg.* 574, *pg.* 779
MODERN ELIXIRS - Hair Care Product - JOHN PAUL MITCHELL SYSTEMS; *pg.* 512, *pg.* 133
MODERN HEALTHCARE - Newspaper - CRAIN COMMUNICATIONS, INC.; *pg.* 1631, *pg.* 879
MODERN MACHINE SHOP - Business to Business Magazine - GARDNER PUBLICATIONS, INC.; *pg.* 1644, *pg.* 1413
MODERN PHYSICIAN - Newspaper - CRAIN COMMUNICATIONS, INC.; *pg.* 1631, *pg.* 879
MODERN REFORMATION - Bi-Monthly Theological Magazine - ALLIANCE OF CONFESSING EVANGELICALS, INC.; *pg.* 126, *pg.* 1545
MODERN SALON - Magazine - VANCE PUBLISHING CORPORATION; *pg.* 1699, *pg.* 627
MODERN TIRE DEALER - Magazine - BOBIT BUSINESS MEDIA; *pg.* 1622, *pg.* 293
MODERN TRACK MACHINERY - Railroad Track Construction & Maintenance Equipment - MODERN TRACK MACHINERY; *pg.* 98, *pg.* 610
MODERN WOOD FINISH - Paint - KELLY-MOORE PAINT COMPANY, INC.; *pg.* 1443, *pg.* 198
MODERN WOODMEN - Insurance - MODERN WOODMEN OF AMERICA; *pg.* 1209, *pg.* 654
MODERNE - Musical Instrument - GIBSON GUITAR CORP.; *pg.* 550, *pg.* 1650
MODERNE - Silverware - ONEIDA LTD; *pg.* 1129, *pg.* 1318
MODERNISM - Carpet - INTERFACE, INC.; *pg.* 695, *pg.* 512
MODERNSCREEN - Fireplace Accessories - PORTLAND WILLAMETTE; *pg.* 1129, *pg.* 1505
MODESTO - Footwear - PHOENIX FOOTWEAR GROUP, INC.; *pg.* 1815, *pg.* 60
MODESTYY - Footwear - STEVEN MADDEN, LTD.; *pg.* 1819, *pg.* 1176
MODGEN - Software System - MENTOR GRAPHICS CORPORATION; *pg.* 432, *pg.* 1510
MODIFIED MICROFILTER - Robotic Product - HAMILTON CO., INC.; *pg.* 1415, *pg.* 1031
MODIFIED MICROLITER - Syringe - HAMILTON CO., INC.; *pg.* 1415, *pg.* 1031
MODIFIED WHOLE LIFE - Whole Life Insurance - CATHOLIC ORDER OF FORESTERS; *pg.* 1196, *pg.* 635
MODINE - Heat Transfer Products - MODINE MANUFACTURING COMPANY; *pg.* 1074, *pg.* 1888
MODIPUR - Polyurethane - HEXCEL CORPORATION; *pg.* 1884, *pg.* 375
MODIS - Software - SNAP-ON INCORPORATED; *pg.* 1062, *pg.* 1862
MODLINK - Electronic Components - MOLEX INCORPORATED; *pg.* 655, *pg.* 628
MODU-FLO - Fluid Handling System - GRACO, INC.; *pg.* 1342, *pg.* 935
MODUBAR - Foundations - RESTONIC MATTRESS CORPORATION; *pg.* 941, *pg.* 553
MODUCAL - Dietary Carbohydrate - MEAD JOHNSON NUTRITION COMPANY; *pg.* 1561, *pg.* 615
MODUCCI - Air Conditioners - NORTEK, INC.; *pg.* 100, *pg.* 1607
MODUCOIL - Spring Assemblies for Furniture - LEGGETT & PLATT, INCORPORATED; *pg.* 933, *pg.* 974
MODUL-R - Testing Method - TINIUS OLSEN, INC.; *pg.* 1432, *pg.* 1541
MODULAR FILTERPAC - Air Cleaner - TRION, INC.; *pg.* 682, *pg.* 1390
MODULAR LUBE - Centralized Lubrication Equipment for Industry - LINCOLN INDUSTRIAL CORP.; *pg.* 1355, *pg.* 999
MODULAR MATES - Kitchenware - TUPPERWARE BRANDS CORPORATION; *pg.* 1139, *pg.* 456
MODULARMATIC - Underground Construction Equipment - CHARLES MACHINE WORKS, INC.; *pg.* 1322, *pg.* 1488
MODULATION OPTICS - Company Name - SLANT/FIN CORPORATION; *pg.* 1076, *pg.* 1163
MODULE-AIRE - Ventilator - SWARTWOUT DIVISION; *pg.* 114, *pg.* 978
MODULE COMPILER - Software - SYNOPSYS, INC.; *pg.* 480, *pg.* 162
MODULE-MOUNT - Ceramic Fiber Furnace System - WATLOW ELECTRIC MANUFACTURING COMPANY; *pg.* 1078, *pg.* 1004
MODULEIR - Area Heater - PRECISION CONTROL SYSTEMS, INC./ RESEARCH INC.; *pg.* 1427, *pg.* 923
MODULEN - Food & Beverage Product - NESTLE USA, INC.; *pg.* 883, *pg.* 96
MODULEX - Boilers - AERCO INTERNATIONAL INC.; *pg.* 1068, *pg.* 1142
MODULINK - Mobile Microphone Cordset System - SHURE INCORPORATED; *pg.* 672, *pg.* 638
MODUPULSE - Closed-Circuit Television Equipment - VICON INDUSTRIES, INC.; *pg.* 685, *pg.* 1166
MOEN - Hardware - FORTUNE BRANDS HOME & SECURITY, INC.; *pg.* 55, *pg.* 600
MOEN - Plumbing Supplies - MOEN INCORPORATED; *pg.* 1056, *pg.* 1468
MOENSTONE - Sinks - MOEN INCORPORATED; *pg.* 1056, *pg.* 1468
MOET & CHANDON - Champagne - MOET HENNESSY; *pg.* 1966, *pg.* 1260
MOF - Armored Fiber Optical Cable - AFC CABLE SYSTEMS, INC.; *pg.* 1294, *pg.* 835

MOFLO - XDP Cell Sorter - BECKMAN COULTER, INC.; *pg.* 1402, *pg.* 48
MOGEN DAVID - Wine - THE WINE GROUP, INC.; *pg.* 1972, *pg.* 234
MOGUL - Carbon Black - CABOT CORPORATION; *pg.* 1151, *pg.* 792
MOGUL - Fabric - NEMSCHOFF, INC.; *pg.* 936, *pg.* 1890
MOHAWK - Farm Tools - AG-MEIER INDUSTRIES LLC; *pg.* 700, *pg.* 1668
MOHAWK - Furniture - F.E. HALE MANUFACTURING COMPANY; *pg.* 925, *pg.* 1160
MOHAWK - Window Shading - MOHAWK INDUSTRIES, INC.; *pg.* 935, *pg.* 527
MOHAWK 50/10 PLUS - Paper - MOHAWK FINE PAPERS, INC.; *pg.* 1464, *pg.* 1153
MOHAWK BRAND - Tires - YOKOHAMA TIRE CORPORATION; *pg.* 1892, *pg.* 94
MOHAWK COLOR COPY - Copy Paper - MOHAWK FINE PAPERS, INC.; *pg.* 1464, *pg.* 1153
MOHAWK DIGITAL IMAGING SURFACE - Copy Paper - MOHAWK FINE PAPERS, INC.; *pg.* 1464, *pg.* 1153
MOHAWK IRISH LINEN - Recycled & Virgin Premium Textured Uncoated Paper - MOHAWK FINE PAPERS, INC.; *pg.* 1464, *pg.* 1153
MOHAWK NAVAJO - Premium Non-Textured Uncoated Paper - MOHAWK FINE PAPERS, INC.; *pg.* 1464, *pg.* 1153
MOHAWK OPAQUE - Recycled Covered & Uncoated Paper - MOHAWK FINE PAPERS, INC.; *pg.* 1464, *pg.* 1153
MOHAWK OPTIONS - Paper - MOHAWK FINE PAPERS, INC.; *pg.* 1464, *pg.* 1153
MOHAWK SATIN - Recycled & Virgin Non-Textured Paper - MOHAWK FINE PAPERS, INC.; *pg.* 1464, *pg.* 1153
MOHAWK SUPERFINE - Premium Non-Textured Uncoated Paper - MOHAWK FINE PAPERS, INC.; *pg.* 1464, *pg.* 1153
MOHAWK TOMOHAWK - Recycled & Virgin Premium Textured Uncoated Paper - MOHAWK FINE PAPERS, INC.; *pg.* 1464, *pg.* 1153
MOHAWK ULTRAFELT - Premium Textured Uncoated Paper - MOHAWK FINE PAPERS, INC.; *pg.* 1464, *pg.* 1153
MOHAWK VELLUM - Recycled & Virgin Non-Textured Text & Cover Uncoated Paper - MOHAWK FINE PAPERS, INC.; *pg.* 1464, *pg.* 1153
MOHEGAN SUN - Casino - MOHEGAN TRIBAL GAMING AUTHORITY; *pg.* 564, *pg.* 381
MOHR - Footwear - K-SWISS; *pg.* 1837, *pg.* 306
MOI PROTO - Graphite Golf Shaft - ALDILA, INC.; *pg.* 1825, *pg.* 185
MOIRE - Fabric - NEMSCHOFF, INC.; *pg.* 936, *pg.* 1890
MOISSANITE - Jewelry - CHARLES & COLVARD LTD; *pg.* 3, *pg.* 1384
MOIST LIP COLOR - Lipcolor - MERLE NORMAN COSMETICS, INC.; *pg.* 517, *pg.* 136
MOISTOP E-Z SEAL - Flashing System - FORTIFIBER CORPORATION; *pg.* 83, *pg.* 1021
MOISTOP NEXT - Moisture Control Flashing System - FORTIFIBER CORPORATION; *pg.* 83, *pg.* 1021
MOISTURE BALANCE - Personal Care Product - RBC LIFE SCIENCES, INC.; *pg.* 1588, *pg.* 1723
MOISTURE BAN - Mattress - SIMMONS COMPANY; *pg.* 943, *pg.* 520
MOISTURE EYES - Eye Drop & Ointment - BAUSCH & LOMB INCORPORATED; *pg.* 1401, *pg.* 1045
MOISTURE-GONE - Chemical Product - SPECTRUM CHEMICALS & LABORATORY PRODUCTS, INC.; *pg.* 1181, *pg.* 94
MOISTURE MAX - Hair Care Products - INSPIRED BEAUTY BRANDS; *pg.* 512, *pg.* 1244
MOISTURE PLUS TINT - Beauty Product - AVEDA CORPORATION; *pg.* 499, *pg.* 917
MOISTURE RESTORE - Skin Care Product - NU SKIN ENTERPRISES, INC.; *pg.* 518, *pg.* 1755
MOISTURE SHIELD - Wax - MOC PRODUCTS COMPANY, INC.; *pg.* 332, *pg.* 174
MOISTURE SPLASH - Lip Care Product - BLISTEX, INC.; *pg.* 502, *pg.* 644
MOISTURE THERAPY - Beauty Product - AVON PRODUCTS, INC.; *pg.* 500, *pg.* 1198
MOISTURE WHIP - Makeup & Lipstick - MAYBELLINE LLC; *pg.* 516, *pg.* 1257
MOISTURESHIELD - Building Material - ADVANCED ENVIRONMENTAL RECYCLING TECHNOLOGIES, INC.; *pg.* 1310, *pg.* 35
MOISTURESHINE - Skin Care Product - NEUTROGENA CORPORATION; *pg.* 517, *pg.* 137
MOISTUREWEAR - Liquid, Cream, Powder, Blush & Concealer - COVER GIRL COSMETICS; *pg.* 506, *pg.* 772
MOISTURSHADE - Cosmetic Product - NU SKIN ENTERPRISES, INC.; *pg.* 518, *pg.* 1755
MOJAVE - Software - DESPATCH INDUSTRIES; *pg.* 1070, *pg.* 927
MOJAVE - Dinnerware - THE HOMER LAUGHLIN CHINA COMPANY; *pg.* 1125, *pg.* 1850
MOJAVE - All-Terrain Vehicle - KAWASAKI MOTORS CORP., U.S.A.; *pg.* 1708, *pg.* 111
MOJAVE HOT WINGS - Spicy Chicken Wings - STRAW HAT COOPERATIVE CORPORATION; *pg.* 1751, *pg.* 260
MOJAZZ - Records - UNIVERSAL MOTOWN RECORDS; *pg.* 315, *pg.* 1307
MOJO - Shoe - ALDO GROUP; *pg.* 1804, *pg.* 1959
MOJO BAR - Food Product - CLIF BAR INC.; *pg.* 848, *pg.* 83
MOLAR APLICAP - Glass Ionomer Restorative - 3M COMPANY; *pg.* 1142, *pg.* 956
MOLD CONTROL 500 - Skin Care Product - SCOTT'S LIQUID GOLD-INC.; *pg.* 335, *pg.* 323
MOLD-DIE - Steel Product - A. FINKL & SONS CO.; *pg.* 1309, *pg.* 563
MOLD MAX - Liquid Rubber - SMOOTH-ON INC.; *pg.* 111, *pg.* 1528
MOLD-TECH - Mold Engravings - STANDEX INTERNATIONAL CORPORATION; *pg.* 60, *pg.* 1039
MOLD TOUGH - Gypsum Panels - USG CORPORATION; *pg.* 118, *pg.* 594
MOLDCAST - Lighting Product - HUBBELL INCORPORATED; *pg.* 1299, *pg.* 370
MOLDFLOW - Simulation Software - AUTODESK INC.; *pg.* 356, *pg.* 257
MOLDFLOW PLASTICS INSIGHT - Software - AUTODESK INC.; *pg.* 356, *pg.* 257
MOLDMAX XL - Alloy - MATERION CORPORATION; *pg.* 1359, *pg.* 1463
MOLDPRO - Polymer Product - CHEMTURA CORPORATION; *pg.* 1152, *pg.* 355
MOLDSTAT - Disinfectants - THEOCHEM LABORATORIES, INC.; *pg.* 1184, *pg.* 476
MOLDWIZ - Plastic & Rubber Material - AXEL PLASTICS RESEARCH LABORATORIES, INC.; *pg.* 326, *pg.* 1356
MOLE - Software - ENVIRONMENTAL SYSTEMS RESEARCH INSTITUTE INC.; *pg.* 393, *pg.* 188
MOLE - Lighting Product - MOLE-RICHARDSON CO.; *pg.* 1302, *pg.* 103
MOLE-MED - Lawn Care Product - GARDENS ALIVE!, INC.; *pg.* 1796, *pg.* 693
MOLE-RELIEF - Mole Repellant - GARDENS ALIVE!, INC.; *pg.* 1796, *pg.* 693
MOLECULAR - Filtration System - SPECTRUM LABORATORIES INC.; *pg.* 1595, *pg.* 69
MOLECULAR ANALYST - Software - BIO-RAD LABORATORIES, INC.; *pg.* 1504, *pg.* 101
MOLECULAR GATE - Adsorption System - BASF CATALYSTS LLC; *pg.* 1148, *pg.* 1074
MOLECULAR IMAGER - Software - BIO-RAD LABORATORIES, INC.; *pg.* 1504, *pg.* 101
MOLECULAR IMAGER FX - Software - BIO-RAD LABORATORIES, INC.; *pg.* 1504, *pg.* 101
MOLECULAR/POR - Filtration System - SPECTRUM LABORATORIES INC.; *pg.* 1595, *pg.* 69
MOLECULAR PROBES - Biological Detection Products - THERMO FISHER SCIENTIFIC INC.; *pg.* 1602, *pg.* 61
MOLEMAX - Household Insect Control - BONIDE PRODUCTS, INC.; *pg.* 1794, *pg.* 1320
MOLETOWN - Lighting Product - MOLE-RICHARDSON CO.; *pg.* 1302, *pg.* 103
MOLETTO - Italian Wine - LAIRD & COMPANY, INC.; *pg.* 1966, *pg.* 1119
MOLEX - Separates Liquid Normal Paraffins from Branched & Cyclic Components - UOP LLC; *pg.* 1386, *pg.* 606
MOLEX-ETC - Electronic Components - MOLEX INCORPORATED; *pg.* 655, *pg.* 628
MOLEX PREMISE NETWORKS - Electronic Components - MOLEX INCORPORATED; *pg.* 655, *pg.* 628
MOLFINO - Cheese - SAPUTO, INC.; *pg.* 893, *pg.* 1956
MOLIC - Electronic Components - MOLEX INCORPORATED; *pg.* 655, *pg.* 628
MOLICARE - Medical Product - MEDLINE INDUSTRIES, INC.; *pg.* 1562, *pg.* 635
MOLINA OPTIONS PLUS - Medical Services - MOLINA HEALTHCARE, INC.; *pg.* 1569, *pg.* 123
MOLLELAST - Medical & Aesthetic Product - DYNATRONICS CORPORATION; *pg.* 1526, *pg.* 1757
MOLLIE - Footwear - PHOENIX FOOTWEAR GROUP, INC.; *pg.* 1815, *pg.* 60
MOLLRING CUTTER - Medical Device - LEMAITRE VASCULAR, INC.; *pg.* 1555, *pg.* 805
MOLLY - Doll And Toy - AMERICAN GIRL LLC; *pg.* 949, *pg.* 1871
MOLLY - Growth Control Software - VEECO INSTRUMENTS INC.; *pg.* 1434, *pg.* 1322
MOLLY BROWN - Floatation Cushions - POLYAIR INTER PACK INC.; *pg.* 1467, *pg.* 1941
MOLLY MALLOY - Women's Clothing - CHEROKEE GLOBAL BRANDS; *pg.* 21, *pg.* 278
MOLLY MCINTIRE - Doll And Toy - AMERICAN GIRL LLC; *pg.* 949, *pg.* 1871
MOLOKAI COCONUT - Beverage - BAI BRANDS; *pg.* 238, *pg.* 1073
MOLOTOF - Designing Integrated Circuit Software - AVAGO TECHNOLOGIES; *pg.* 358, *pg.* 238
MOLSON CANADIAN - Beer - MOLSON COORS BREWING COMPANY; *pg.* 256, *pg.* 321
MOLSON DRY - Beer - MOLSON COORS BREWING COMPANY; *pg.* 256, *pg.* 321
MOLSON DRY - Beer - MOLSON COORS CANADA INC.; *pg.* 256, *pg.* 1955
MOLSON EXPORT - Beer - MOLSON COORS BREWING COMPANY; *pg.* 256, *pg.* 321
MOLSON GOLDEN - Beer - MOLSON COORS BREWING COMPANY; *pg.* 256, *pg.* 321
MOLSON M - Microcarbonated Lager Beer - MOLSON COORS CANADA INC.; *pg.* 256, *pg.* 1955
MOLSON SMOOTH DRY - Beer - MOLSON COORS CANADA INC.; *pg.* 256, *pg.* 1955
MOLSON ULTRA - Low Carb Beer - MOLSON COORS CANADA INC.; *pg.* 256, *pg.* 1955
MOLY PRO-SPEC - Motor Oil - TEXAS REFINERY CORP.; *pg.* 986, *pg.* 1696
MOLY5 - Lubricant - D-A LUBRICANT COMPANY; *pg.* 975, *pg.* 693
MOLYKOTE - Specialty Lubricants - DOW CORNING CORPORATION; *pg.* 1159, *pg.* 900
MOLYVER - Chemical Reagent - HACH COMPANY; *pg.* 1415, *pg.* 334
MOM 'N' POPS - Food Product - ADVANCEPIERRE FOODS, INC.; *pg.* 1714, *pg.* 1409
MOM TO MOM - Baby Products Created by Moms for Moms - SAFEWAY INC.; *pg.* 1032, *pg.* 184
MOMA - Museum Art - THE MUSEUM OF MODERN ART; *pg.* 565, *pg.* 1263
THE MOMENT OF TRUTH - Toy & Game - HASBRO, INC.; *pg.* 954, *pg.* 1603
MOMENT TENSOR - Emission Testing System - MISTRAS GROUP, INC.; *pg.* 1362, *pg.* 1113
MOMENTS NOTICE - Sandals - AEROGROUP INTERNATIONAL, INC.; *pg.* 1803, *pg.* 1055
MOMENTUM - Shoe - AEROGROUP INTERNATIONAL, INC.; *pg.* 1803, *pg.* 1055
MOMENTUM - Enterprise Solution - CACI INTERNATIONAL INC.; *pg.* 367, *pg.* 1773
MOMENTUM - Single Board Computers - MERCURY COMPUTER SYSTEMS, INC.; *pg.* 434, *pg.* 813
MOMENTUM - Furniture - TELESCOPE CASUAL FURNITURE INC.; *pg.* 944, *pg.* 1162
MOMETAMAX - Dog Vaccine - MERCK & CO., INC.; *pg.* 1566, *pg.* 1077
MOMETASONE - Pharmaceutical Product - G&W LABORATORIES INC.; *pg.* 1532, *pg.* 1123
MOMMYISH.COM - Website - DEFYMEDIA; *pg.* 1237, *pg.* 1222
MOM'S FAVORITE - Flower Arrangement - 1-800-FLOWERS.COM, INC.; *pg.* 1758, *pg.* 1151
MOM'S GOOP - Cleaning Preparation - CRITZAS INDUSTRIES, INC.; *pg.* 329, *pg.* 995
MOM'S HOME STYLE FUDGE - Fudge Making Machine - GOLD MEDAL PRODUCTS CO.; *pg.* 55, *pg.* 1414
MON-A-THERM - Temperature Monitoring Systems - MALLINCKRODT PHARMACEUTICALS; *pg.* 1557, *pg.* 978
MON-A-THERM - Temperature Probes - MEDTRONIC; *pg.* 1563, *pg.* 183
MON AMI GABI - French Restaurant - LETTUCE ENTERTAIN YOU ENTERPRISES, INC.; *pg.* 1735, *pg.* 580
MON REALE - Architectural Mouldings - WHITE RIVER HARDWOODS-WOODWORKS, INC.; *pg.* 121, *pg.* 31
MONACO - Furniture - AMISCO INDUSTRIES LTD.; *pg.* 913,

First page reference indicates Business Class Edition
Second page reference indicates Geographic Edition

pg. 1958
MONACO - Computer Font - APPLE INC.; *pg.* 350, *pg.* 73
MONACO - Furniture - ASHLEY FURNITURE INDUSTRIES, INC.; *pg.* 914, *pg.* 1852
MONACO - Door & Wood Product - CONESTOGA WOOD SPECIALTIES CORP.; *pg.* 921, *pg.* 1527
MONACO - Software - ELEKTA; *pg.* 391, *pg.* 987
MONACO - Decorative Accessory - ETHAN ALLEN INTERIORS INC.; *pg.* 924, *pg.* 343
MONACO - Furniture - HAWORTH, INC.; *pg.* 402, *pg.* 891
MONACO - Fabric - NEMSCHOFF, INC.; *pg.* 936, *pg.* 1890
MONACOEXCOLOR - Software - X-RITE, INCORPORATED; *pg.* 1437, *pg.* 891
MONACOOPTIX - Software - X-RITE, INCORPORATED; *pg.* 1437, *pg.* 891
MONACOPROFILER - Software - X-RITE, INCORPORATED; *pg.* 1437, *pg.* 891
MONACOQCCOLOR - Software - X-RITE, INCORPORATED; *pg.* 1437, *pg.* 891
MONADNOCK - Security Product - BAE SYSTEMS PRODUCTS GROUP; *pg.* 359, *pg.* 432
MONARC - Medical Device - AMERICAN MEDICAL SYSTEMS HOLDINGS, INC.; *pg.* 1493, *pg.* 947
MONARC - Process Analytical Technology - METTLER-TOLEDO INTERNATIONAL INC.; *pg.* 1423, *pg.* 1441
MONARCH - Agricultural Product - ARCHER-DANIELS-MIDLAND COMPANY; *pg.* 825, *pg.* 565
MONARCH - Cable - ARRIS GROUP, INC.; *pg.* 353, *pg.* 541
MONARCH - Automatic Aluminum Can Crusher - A.T. FERRELL COMPANY, INC.; *pg.* 701, *pg.* 674
MONARCH - Table - BLATT BOWLING & BILLIARD CORP.; *pg.* 1827, *pg.* 1203
MONARCH - Carbon Black - CABOT CORPORATION; *pg.* 1151, *pg.* 792
MONARCH - Software - DATAWATCH CORPORATION; *pg.* 383, *pg.* 813
MONARCH - Tire And Rubber Product - THE GOODYEAR TIRE & RUBBER COMPANY; *pg.* 1883, *pg.* 1401
MONARCH - Distilled Spirits - HOOD RIVER DISTILLERS INC.; *pg.* 1964, *pg.* 1498
MONARCH - Door Hardware - INGERSOLL-RAND COMPANY; *pg.* 1349, *pg.* 1370
MONARCH BI SERVER - Software - DATAWATCH CORPORATION; *pg.* 383, *pg.* 813
MONARCH DATA PUMP - Business Intelligence Product - DATAWATCH CORPORATION; *pg.* 383, *pg.* 813
MONARCH DATA PUMP PRO - Business Intelligence Product - DATAWATCH CORPORATION; *pg.* 383, *pg.* 813
MONARCH DENTAL - Dental Services - SMILE BRANDS GROUP INC.; *pg.* 1594, *pg.* 116
MONARCH/ES - Software - DATAWATCH CORPORATION; *pg.* 383, *pg.* 813
MONARCH HOME VIDEO - Video Product Distributors - INGRAM ENTERTAINMENT INC.; *pg.* 292, *pg.* 1639
MONARCH LANDING - Retirement Community - ERICKSON LIVING; *pg.* 1090, *pg.* 766
MONARCH MOPAKO - Paint Product - PPG INDUSTRIES, INC.; *pg.* 1445, *pg.* 1579
MONARCH OF THE SEAS - Cruise Ship - ROYAL CARIBBEAN CRUISES LTD; *pg.* 1921, *pg.* 446
MONARCH PRO - Business Intelligence Product - DATAWATCH CORPORATION; *pg.* 383, *pg.* 813
MONARCH REPORT MINING SERVER - Business Intelligence Product - DATAWATCH CORPORATION; *pg.* 383, *pg.* 813
MONARCH RMS - Business Intelligence Product - DATAWATCH CORPORATION; *pg.* 383, *pg.* 813
MONARCH SQ - Door & Wood Product - CONESTOGA WOOD SPECIALTIES CORP.; *pg.* 921, *pg.* 1527
MONARCH-TACH - Digital Optical Tachometer, Hand Held with Pistol Grip Design - HYDRALIGN; *pg.* 1257, *pg.* 833
MONARCH VALLEY - Furniture - ASHLEY FURNITURE INDUSTRIES, INC.; *pg.* 914, *pg.* 1852
MONARK - Pumps - GRACO, INC.; *pg.* 1342, *pg.* 935
MONARK-SHROUD - Fluid Handling System - GRACO, INC.; *pg.* 1342, *pg.* 935
MONDO - Beauty Salon Furniture - BELVEDERE USA CORPORATION; *pg.* 917, *pg.* 556
MONDO - Food Product - MARS, INCORPORATED; *pg.* 1858, *pg.* 1792
MONDO DI MARCO - Dress Sportswear - PERRY ELLIS INTERNATIONAL, INC.; *pg.* 45, *pg.* 445
MONDO FRUIT SQUEEZERS - Food Product - THE JEL SERT COMPANY; *pg.* 865, *pg.* 668
MONDRIAN - Ceramic, Glass, Stone Tiles & Slabs - WALKER & ZANGER, INC.; *pg.* 119, *pg.* 281
MONDRIAN DESK - Furniture - J. ROBERT SCOTT INC.; *pg.* 930, *pg.* 105
MONE - Beverages - THE COCA-COLA COMPANY; *pg.* 240, *pg.* 493
MONEL - Knitted Mesh Product - ACS INDUSTRIES, INC.; *pg.* 1040, *pg.* 1602
MONEL - Alloy Product - SPECIAL METALS CORPORATION; *pg.* 1377, *pg.* 1850
MONET - Yarn - LION BRAND YARN COMPANY; *pg.* 696, *pg.* 1050
MONET - Software System - MENTOR GRAPHICS CORPORATION; *pg.* 432, *pg.* 1510
MONET - Fabric - NEMSCHOFF, INC.; *pg.* 936, *pg.* 1890
MONET'S GARDEN - Decorative Flower - NATURAL DECORATIONS, INC.; *pg.* 936, *pg.* 5
MONEY - Media Publication - TIME INC.; *pg.* 1693, *pg.* 1300
MONEY BAGS - Lottery Game - MASSACHUSETTS STATE LOTTERY; *pg.* 998, *pg.* 802
MONEY BELT - Game - WMS INDUSTRIES INC.; *pg.* 593, *pg.* 666
MONEY BURST - Game - WMS INDUSTRIES INC.; *pg.* 593, *pg.* 666
MONEY FEVER - Game - WMS INDUSTRIES INC.; *pg.* 593, *pg.* 666
MONEY FOR LIFE - Lottery Game - OHIO LOTTERY COMMISSION; *pg.* 1002, *pg.* 1433
THE MONEY GAME - Lottery Game - OHIO LOTTERY COMMISSION; *pg.* 1002, *pg.* 1433
MONEY GRAB - Game - WMS INDUSTRIES INC.; *pg.* 593, *pg.* 666
MONEY GROOVE - Game - WMS INDUSTRIES INC.; *pg.* 593, *pg.* 666
MONEY HIVE - Game - WMS INDUSTRIES INC.; *pg.* 593, *pg.* 666
MONEY HQ - Online Financial Service - ACI WORLDWIDE; *pg.* 710, *pg.* 1777
MONEY JACKPOT SOAP - Soap - LANMAN & KEMP-BARCLAY CO., INC.; *pg.* 514, *pg.* 1132
MONEY MAD MARTIANS - Slots - INTERNATIONAL GAME TECHNOLOGY; *pg.* 957, *pg.* 1024
MONEY MAID - Bar Change Trays - CARLISLE FOODSERVICE PRODUCTS INCORPORATED; *pg.* 1455, *pg.* 1485
MONEY MANIA - Lottery Game - RHODE ISLAND LOTTERY; *pg.* 1004, *pg.* 1600
MONEY MARKET MANAGER - Software - SS&C TECHNOLOGIES HOLDINGS, INC.; *pg.* 473, *pg.* 386
MONEY MASTER - Banking Service - THE BANK OF NOVA SCOTIA; *pg.* 721, *pg.* 1935
MONEY MAZE - Lottery Game - NEW YORK STATE LOTTERY; *pg.* 1001, *pg.* 1340
MONEY MINE - Lottery Game - MASSACHUSETTS STATE LOTTERY; *pg.* 998, *pg.* 802
MONEY MIXER - Video Game - INTERNATIONAL GAME TECHNOLOGY; *pg.* 957, *pg.* 1024
MONEY MONEY MONEY - Lottery Game - OHIO LOTTERY COMMISSION; *pg.* 1002, *pg.* 1433
MONEY MONEY MONEY - Game - WMS INDUSTRIES INC.; *pg.* 593, *pg.* 666
MONEY ON THE MOVE - Game - WMS INDUSTRIES INC.; *pg.* 593, *pg.* 666
MONEY ROLL - Lottery Game - OHIO LOTTERY COMMISSION; *pg.* 1002, *pg.* 1433
THE MONEY SHOW - Tradeshow - INVESTMENT SEMINARS, INC.; *pg.* 420, *pg.* 466
MONEY SHOW DIGEST - Publication - INVESTMENT SEMINARS, INC.; *pg.* 420, *pg.* 466
MONEY STACK - Lottery Card - MISSOURI LOTTERY; *pg.* 999, *pg.* 979
MONEY STORM - Video Game - INTERNATIONAL GAME TECHNOLOGY; *pg.* 957, *pg.* 1024
MONEY TO BURN - Game - WMS INDUSTRIES INC.; *pg.* 593, *pg.* 666
MONEY TREE - Lottery Game - NEW YORK STATE LOTTERY; *pg.* 1001, *pg.* 1340
MONEYGUARD - Financial Product - LINCOLN NATIONAL CORPORATION; *pg.* 776, *pg.* 1567
MONEYLINE - Game - WMS INDUSTRIES INC.; *pg.* 593, *pg.* 666
MONEYNEWS.COM - Financial Website - NEWSMAX MEDIA, INC.; *pg.* 1271, *pg.* 479
MONEYPRO - Banking Services - FIRST NIAGARA FINANCIAL GROUP, INC.; *pg.* 757, *pg.* 1148
MONEYSAVER - Air Conditioner - FRIEDRICH AIR CONDITIONING CO.; *pg.* 1072, *pg.* 1740
MONEYSTORM - Video Slots - INTERNATIONAL GAME TECHNOLOGY; *pg.* 957, *pg.* 1024
MONEYSTREAM - Software - WORDEN BROTHERS, INC.; *pg.* 823, *pg.* 1372
MONGOOSE - Shaker - M-I SWACO; *pg.* 980, *pg.* 1710
MONICA MERRILL - Doll - TONNER DOLL COMPANY, INC.; *pg.* 968, *pg.* 1171
MONIKA - Footwear - P.W. MINOR & SON, INC.; *pg.* 1816, *pg.* 1140
MONIKAA - Footwear - STEVEN MADDEN, LTD.; *pg.* 1819, *pg.* 1176
MONIS - Software - SUNGARD DATA SYSTEMS INC.; *pg.* 477, *pg.* 1592
MONISTAT - Healthcare Product - JOHNSON & JOHNSON; *pg.* 1549, *pg.* 1091
MONISTAT-DERM - Healthcare Product - JOHNSON & JOHNSON; *pg.* 1549, *pg.* 1091
MONITOR - Shower Valves - DELTA FAUCET COMPANY; *pg.* 78, *pg.* 684
THE MONITOR - Texas Newspaper - FREEDOM COMMUNICATIONS, INC.; *pg.* 1643, *pg.* 110
MONITOR - Plumbing Product - MASCO CORPORATION; *pg.* 96, *pg.* 909
THE MONITOR - Newspaper - THE MONITOR; *pg.* 1665, *pg.* 1726
MONITOR - Selective Herbicide - MONSANTO COMPANY; *pg.* 1173, *pg.* 999
MONITOR - Windows & Doors - NORTEK, INC.; *pg.* 100, *pg.* 1607
MONITOR - Magazine - PEAVEY ELECTRONICS CORPORATION; *pg.* 662, *pg.* 970
MONITOR - Germicidal Cabinet - SELLSTROM MANUFACTURING CO.; *pg.* 1428, *pg.* 659
MONITOR II - Shower Valves - DELTA FAUCET COMPANY; *pg.* 78, *pg.* 684
MONITORMARK - Product Exposure Indicators - 3M COMPANY; *pg.* 1142, *pg.* 956
MONITORPARTNER - Communication Product - CENTURYLINK, INC; *pg.* 1870, *pg.* 317
MONITRON - Electric Boiler - SLANT/FIN CORPORATION; *pg.* 1076, *pg.* 1163
MONK'S - Felt - AMERICAN FELT & FILTER COMPANY; *pg.* 1312, *pg.* 1184
MONKS FOOT QUALITY - Slogan - AMERICAN FELT & FILTER COMPANY; *pg.* 1312, *pg.* 1184
MONLAUN - Laundry Product - BIRKO CORPORATION; *pg.* 1149, *pg.* 332
MONLAUN #3 - Chemical Product - BIRKO CORPORATION; *pg.* 1149, *pg.* 332
MONO - Aluminum Foil - THE CLOROX COMPANY; *pg.* 327, *pg.* 169
MONO - Pressed & Monolithic Refractory - RESCO PRODUCTS, INC.; *pg.* 107, *pg.* 1581
MONO-COAT - Semipermanent Release Agent - CHEM-TREND LIMITED PARTNERSHIP; *pg.* 973, *pg.* 892
MONO-DIFF - Pharmaceutical Product - ALERE INC.; *pg.* 1488, *pg.* 849
MONO GUN - Pressed & Monolithic Refractory - RESCO PRODUCTS, INC.; *pg.* 107, *pg.* 1581
MONO-LATEX - Pharmaceutical Product - ALERE INC.; *pg.* 1488, *pg.* 849
MONO-LUBE - Tire Releasant - CHEM-TREND LIMITED PARTNERSHIP; *pg.* 973, *pg.* 892
MONO-PLUS - Pharmaceutical Product - ALERE INC.; *pg.* 1488, *pg.* 849
MONO-POLY - Software - BIO-RAD LABORATORIES, INC.; *pg.* 1504, *pg.* 101
MONO-TEST - Pharmaceutical Product - ALERE INC.; *pg.* 1488, *pg.* 849
MONOBOX - Electrical Cranes & Hoists - AMERICAN CRANE & EQUIPMENT CORPORATION; *pg.* 1312, *pg.* 1526
MONOBRYTE - Software - BIO-RAD LABORATORIES, INC.; *pg.* 1504, *pg.* 101
MONOCLATE-P - Pasteurized, Monoclonal Antibody Purified Antihemophilic Factor (Human) - CSL BEHRING LLC; *pg.* 1520, *pg.* 1543
MONOCOR - Pharmaceutical Product - VALEANT PHARMACEUTICALS INTERNATIONAL, INC.; *pg.* 1605, *pg.* 1957
MONOCRYL - Healthcare Product - JOHNSON & JOHNSON; *pg.* 1549, *pg.* 1091
MONOCURE - Graphic Art UV System - NORDSON CORPORATION; *pg.* 1365, *pg.* 1480
MONODOSE - Water Soluble Film - MONOSOL, LLC; *pg.* 59,

pg. 694
MONODOX - Pharmaceutical Product - ALLERGAN; *pg.* 1490, *pg.* 1101
MONOFILAMENT - Conveyor Belting - SHINGLE BELTING COMPANY; *pg.* 1375, *pg.* 1544
MONOFIRE - Racket String - ASHAWAY LINE & TWINE MFG. CO.; *pg.* 1826, *pg.* 1600
MONOFIRE XL - String - ASHAWAY LINE & TWINE MFG. CO.; *pg.* 1826, *pg.* 1600
MONOFLANGE - Butterfly Valve - HENRY PRATT COMPANY; *pg.* 1049, *pg.* 555
MONOFLUO - Clinical Diagnostic Product - BIO-RAD LABORATORIES, INC.; *pg.* 1504, *pg.* 101
MONOFLUOSCREEN - Software - BIO-RAD LABORATORIES, INC.; *pg.* 1504, *pg.* 101
MONOGRAM - Home Appliance - GENERAL ELECTRIC COMPANY; *pg.* 1297, *pg.* 347
MONOGRAM - Model Kits - REVELL; *pg.* 966, *pg.* 611
MONOGRAM BLEND - Gin - LAIRD & COMPANY, INC.; *pg.* 1966, *pg.* 1119
MONOGRAM CLASSICS - Plastic Model Kits - REVELL; *pg.* 966, *pg.* 611
MONOGRAMS - Budget Escorted Tours - GROUP VOYAGERS, INC.; *pg.* 1910, *pg.* 333
MONOGRAMS - Wall Decor - HERITAGE LACE INC.; *pg.* 694, *pg.* 711
MONOGUT - Racket Strings - ASHAWAY LINE & TWINE MFG. CO.; *pg.* 1826, *pg.* 1600
MONOKILL - Hybrid String - ASHAWAY LINE & TWINE MFG. CO.; *pg.* 1826, *pg.* 1600
MONOKORE - Cable - LOOS & COMPANY, INC.; *pg.* 1356, *pg.* 368
MONOKOTE - Coverings - HOBBICO, INC.; *pg.* 956, *pg.* 562
MONOLAR - Mastic & Coating - H.B. FULLER COMPANY; *pg.* 1165, *pg.* 961
MONOLERT - Rapid Test for Detecting Infectious Mononucleosis - MERIDIAN BIOSCIENCE INC.; *pg.* 1422, *pg.* 1417
MONOLISA - Software - BIO-RAD LABORATORIES, INC.; *pg.* 1504, *pg.* 101
MONOLITH - Chemical Coating - ENTHONE INC.; *pg.* 1161, *pg.* 381
MONONESSA - Pharmaceutical Product - ALLERGAN; *pg.* 1490, *pg.* 1101
MONONINE - Coagulation Factor IX (Human) Monoclonal Antibody Purified - CSL BEHRING LLC; *pg.* 1520, *pg.* 1543
MONOPAC - Performance Assessment Program - MONOSOL, LLC; *pg.* 59, *pg.* 694
MONOPANL - Metal Building System - BUTLER MANUFACTURING COMPANY; *pg.* 72, *pg.* 981
MONOPLACE - Hyperbaric Chambers - SECHRIST INDUSTRIES, INC.; *pg.* 1593, *pg.* 43
MONOPLANE - Fluid Handling System - GRACO, INC.; *pg.* 1342, *pg.* 935
MONOPOL - Water Soluble Resin - MONOSOL, LLC; *pg.* 59, *pg.* 694
MONOPOLY - Game - HASBRO, INC.; *pg.* 954, *pg.* 1603
MONOPOLY - Lottery Game - NEW YORK STATE LOTTERY; *pg.* 1001, *pg.* 1340
MONOPOLY - Game - WMS INDUSTRIES INC.; *pg.* 593, *pg.* 666
MONOPOLY THE CARD GAME - Game - WINNING MOVES GAMES, INC.; *pg.* 970, *pg.* 816
MONOPRIL - ACE Inhibitor for treatment of Hypertension - BRISTOL-MYERS SQUIBB U.S. PHARMACEUTICAL GROUP; *pg.* 1511, *pg.* 1110
MONOPTY - Liver Biopsy Instrument - CONMED CORPORATION; *pg.* 1517, *pg.* 1347
MONOPTY - Urological Instrument - C.R. BARD, INC.; *pg.* 1519, *pg.* 1094
MONOSEAL - Fluid Sealing Product - A.W. CHESTERTON COMPANY; *pg.* 1315, *pg.* 861
MONOSLAB - Carpet Cushion - DURA UNDERCUSHIONS LTD.; *pg.* 923, *pg.* 1954
MONOSPOT - Rapid Test for Detecting Infectious Mononucleosis - MERIDIAN BIOSCIENCE INC.; *pg.* 1422, *pg.* 1417
MONOTEST - Pharmaceutical Product - ALERE INC.; *pg.* 1488, *pg.* 849
MONOTHANE - Polyurethane Elastomer - THE DOW CHEMICAL COMPANY; *pg.* 1157, *pg.* 898
MONOTUBE TRIAX - Surgical & Medical Product - STRYKER CORPORATION; *pg.* 1598, *pg.* 894
MONOVER - Chemical Reagent - HACH COMPANY; *pg.* 1415, *pg.* 334
MONOXOR - Gas Analyzer - BACHARACH INC.; *pg.* 1400, *pg.* 1556
MONOXOR II - Carbon Monoxide Analyzer - BACHARACH INC.; *pg.* 1400, *pg.* 1556
MONOXOR III - Carbon Monoxide Analyzer - BACHARACH INC.; *pg.* 1400, *pg.* 1556
MONOZECLAR - Pharmaceutical Product - ABBOTT LABORATORIES; *pg.* 1484, *pg.* 551
MONPAC - Emission Testing System - MISTRAS GROUP, INC.; *pg.* 1362, *pg.* 1113
MONPAC-PLUS - Emission Testing System - MISTRAS GROUP, INC.; *pg.* 1362, *pg.* 1113
MONPRENE - Plastic & Rubber - TEKNOR APEX COMPANY; *pg.* 1889, *pg.* 1605
MONRO - Repair Services - MONRO MUFFLER BRAKE, INC.; *pg.* 213, *pg.* 1336
MONRO MUFFLER BRAKE & SERVICE - Auto Service - MONRO MUFFLER BRAKE, INC.; *pg.* 213, *pg.* 1336
MONROE - Furniture - BASSETT FURNITURE INDUSTRIES, INCORPORATED; *pg.* 916, *pg.* 1776
MONROE - Door & Wood Product - CONESTOGA WOOD SPECIALTIES CORP.; *pg.* 921, *pg.* 1527
MONROE - Upholstery - ETHAN ALLEN INTERIORS INC.; *pg.* 924, *pg.* 343
MONROE - Calculator Company - MONROE SYSTEMS FOR BUSINESS; *pg.* 441, *pg.* 1518
MONROE - Shock Absorber & Strut - TENNECO, INC.; *pg.* 985, *pg.* 625
MONROVIA ORGANICS - Plant Food - MONROVIA GROWERS; *pg.* 1797, *pg.* 44
MONSIEUR HENRI - Wines - SAZERAC COMPANY, INC.; *pg.* 1969, *pg.* 745
MONSOON - Footwear - EASTLAND SHOE CORPORATION; *pg.* 1808, *pg.* 750
MONSOON - Fabric - NEMSCHOFF, INC.; *pg.* 936, *pg.* 1890
MONSOY - Foundation Seed - MONSANTO COMPANY; *pg.* 1173, *pg.* 999
MONSTER - Bowling Equipment - BRUNSWICK BOWLING & BILLIARDS CORP.; *pg.* 1828, *pg.* 622
MONSTER - Apparel - OAKLEY, INC.; *pg.* 1840, *pg.* 86
MONSTER - Pet Product - PETSMART, INC.; *pg.* 1481, *pg.* 18
MONSTER ALE - Seasonal Beer - THE BROOKLYN BREWERY; *pg.* 239, *pg.* 1145
MONSTER AMINO - Protein Supplement - CYTOSPORT, INC.; *pg.* 1018, *pg.* 45
MONSTER BRIDGE - Automobile Races - DOVER MOTORSPORTS, INC.; *pg.* 545, *pg.* 387
MONSTER CABLE - Electronic Equipment - KLIPSCH GROUP, INC.; *pg.* 649, *pg.* 688
MONSTER CHOCOLATE - Chocolate - SONIC CORP.; *pg.* 1750, *pg.* 1487
MONSTER DOGGLE - Eyewear - OAKLEY, INC.; *pg.* 1840, *pg.* 86
MONSTER ENERGY - Energy Drink - MONSTER BEVERAGE CORPORATION; *pg.* 257, *pg.* 69
MONSTER KENO - Video Game - INTERNATIONAL GAME TECHNOLOGY; *pg.* 957, *pg.* 1024
MONSTER MAIZE - Protein Supplement - CYTOSPORT, INC.; *pg.* 1018, *pg.* 45
MONSTER MALTS - Food Product - PROMOTION IN MOTION, INC.; *pg.* 1861, *pg.* 1052
MONSTER MANSION - Slots - INTERNATIONAL GAME TECHNOLOGY; *pg.* 957, *pg.* 1024
MONSTER MASS - Protein Supplement - CYTOSPORT, INC.; *pg.* 1018, *pg.* 45
MONSTER MILE - Automobile Races - DOVER MOTORSPORTS, INC.; *pg.* 545, *pg.* 387
MONSTER MILK - Protein Supplement - CYTOSPORT, INC.; *pg.* 1018, *pg.* 45
MONSTER PUMP - Protein Supplement - CYTOSPORT, INC.; *pg.* 1018, *pg.* 45
MONSTER REHAB - Energy Drink - MONSTER BEVERAGE CORPORATION; *pg.* 257, *pg.* 69
MONSTER TACO - Tacos - JACK IN THE BOX INC.; *pg.* 1732, *pg.* 204
MONSTERTONES.COM - RingTone Service - ADVANCED TELECOM SERVICES; *pg.* 1865, *pg.* 1591
MONTABERT - Hydraulic Rock Breaker - INGERSOLL-RAND COMPANY; *pg.* 1349, *pg.* 1370
MONTAGE - Furniture - JOFCO INC.; *pg.* 931, *pg.* 691
MONTAGE - Office Furniture - STEELCASE INC.; *pg.* 475, *pg.* 889
MONTAGNA - Fabric - NEMSCHOFF, INC.; *pg.* 936, *pg.* 1890
MONTALCINO - Ceiling Fan - HUNTER FAN COMPANY; *pg.* 57, *pg.* 1631
MONTANA - Orthopedic Product - DJO INCORPORATED; *pg.* 1524, *pg.* 302
MONTANA - Lighting - ETHAN ALLEN INTERIORS INC.; *pg.* 924, *pg.* 343
MONTANA - Garage Door - MARTIN DOOR MANUFACTURING, INC.; *pg.* 96, *pg.* 1759
MONTANA - Binoculars - MEADE INSTRUMENTS CORPORATION; *pg.* 1422, *pg.* 113
MONTANA BIG SKY - Nutritional Product - NUTRACEUTICAL INTERNATIONAL CORPORATION; *pg.* 1576, *pg.* 1753
MONTANA BOOK - Paper Products - BOISE CASCADE HOLDINGS, L.L.C.; *pg.* 1453, *pg.* 546
MONTANA CASH - Lottery Game - MONTANA LOTTERY; *pg.* 1000, *pg.* 1008
MONTANA COVER - Paper & Nonwoven Material - FIBERMARK INC.; *pg.* 1457, *pg.* 1764
MONTANA GOLD - Distilled Spirits - HOOD RIVER DISTILLERS INC.; *pg.* 1964, *pg.* 1498
MONTANA MORN - Carpet - BEAULIEU GROUP, LLC; *pg.* 917, *pg.* 529
MONTANA SILVER - Distilled Spirits - HOOD RIVER DISTILLERS INC.; *pg.* 1964, *pg.* 1498
MONTANA'S - Western Lodge Themed Restaurants - CARA OPERATIONS LIMITED; *pg.* 1720, *pg.* 1947
MONTAVERDI - Fragrance Ingredient - INTERNATIONAL FLAVORS & FRAGRANCES INC.; *pg.* 512, *pg.* 1244
THE MONTCLAIR - Outerwear - HABAND COMPANY, INC.; *pg.* 1772, *pg.* 1099
MONTE CARLO - Dose Calculation - ACCURAY INCORPORATED; *pg.* 1486, *pg.* 282
MONTE CARLO - Bar Stool - BLATT BOWLING & BILLIARD CORP.; *pg.* 1827, *pg.* 1203
MONTE CARLO - Dinnerware - THE HOMER LAUGHLIN CHINA COMPANY; *pg.* 1125, *pg.* 1850
MONTE CARLO - Resort & Casino - MGM RESORTS INTERNATIONAL; *pg.* 1105, *pg.* 1028
MONTE CARLO - Lottery Card - MISSOURI LOTTERY; *pg.* 999, *pg.* 979
MONTEBAN - Narasin - ELANCO ANIMAL HEALTH; *pg.* 1475, *pg.* 681
MONTEBELLO - Table - BLATT BOWLING & BILLIARD CORP.; *pg.* 1827, *pg.* 1203
MONTEBELLO BLOODY MARIA - Bloody Mary Mix - MONTEBELLO BRANDS INC.; *pg.* 1967, *pg.* 758
MONTEBELLO ORIGINAL KIR - Cocktail - MONTEBELLO BRANDS INC.; *pg.* 1967, *pg.* 758
MONTEBELLO ORIGINAL LONG ISLAND ICED TEA - Cocktail - MONTEBELLO BRANDS INC.; *pg.* 1967, *pg.* 758
MONTECITO - Furniture - STANLEY FURNITURE CO., INC.; *pg.* 943, *pg.* 1379
MONTECRUZ - Cigars - ALTADIS USA, INC.; *pg.* 1893, *pg.* 423
MONTEFIORE - Beverages - THE COCA-COLA COMPANY; *pg.* 240, *pg.* 493
MONTEFRISCO - Spout - PRECISION VALVE CORPORATION; *pg.* 1060, *pg.* 1357
MONTEGO - Footwear - PHOENIX FOOTWEAR GROUP, INC.; *pg.* 1815, *pg.* 60
MONTEGO BAY - Rum - MCCORMICK DISTILLING CO., INC.; *pg.* 1966, *pg.* 1007
MONTEL 200 - Optics - BRUKER CORPORATION; *pg.* 1511, *pg.* 788
MONTENAPO - Carpet - INTERFACE, INC.; *pg.* 695, *pg.* 512
MONTEREY - Footwear - COBIAN CORP.; *pg.* 1806, *pg.* 253
MONTEREY - Rug - COURISTAN INC.; *pg.* 921, *pg.* 1067
MONTEREY - Dinnerware - THE HOMER LAUGHLIN CHINA COMPANY; *pg.* 1125, *pg.* 1850
MONTEREY - Tufted Area Rugs - MOHAWK HOME; *pg.* 935, *pg.* 541
MONTEREY BAY CLOTHING COMPANY - Apparel - ASCENA RETAIL GROUP, INC.; *pg.* 18, *pg.* 1081
MONTEREY PASTA - Pasta - MONTEREY GOURMET FOODS, INC.; *pg.* 881, *pg.* 94
MONTEREY'S LITTLE MEXICO - Restaurant - MEXICAN RESTAURANTS, INC.; *pg.* 1741, *pg.* 1711
MONTEREY'S TEX MEX CAFE - Restaurant - MEXICAN RESTAURANTS, INC.; *pg.* 1741, *pg.* 1711
MONTESSORI UNLIMITED - Preschools - LA PETITE ACADEMY, INC.; *pg.* 603, *pg.* 903
MONTEVINA - Beverage - TRINCHERO FAMILY ESTATES; *pg.* 1971, *pg.* 197

First page reference indicates Business Class Edition
Second page reference indicates Geographic Edition

MONTEZUMA - Fabric - NEMSCHOFF, INC.; *pg.* 936, *pg.* 1890
MONTEZUMA - Surface Material - STEELCASE INC.; *pg.* 475, *pg.* 889
MONTGOMERY - Furniture - BASSETT FURNITURE INDUSTRIES, INCORPORATED; *pg.* 916, *pg.* 1776
MONTGOMERY - Chair - LA-Z-BOY INCORPORATED; *pg.* 932, *pg.* 901
MONTHLY COMFORT - Vitamin & Herbal Supplement - SOURCE NATURALS; *pg.* 1595, *pg.* 278
MONTHS IN BLOOM - Blooming Plants - 1-800-FLOWERS.COM, INC.; *pg.* 1758, *pg.* 1151
MONTICELLO - Furniture - ASHLEY FURNITURE INDUSTRIES, INC.; *pg.* 914, *pg.* 1852
MONTICELLO - Kitchen & Bathroom Faucets - MOEN INCORPORATED; *pg.* 1056, *pg.* 1468
MONTICELLO - Spout - PRECISION VALVE CORPORATION; *pg.* 1060, *pg.* 1357
MONTOUR - Furniture - ASHLEY FURNITURE INDUSTRIES, INC.; *pg.* 914, *pg.* 1852
MONTRAIL - Outdoor Gear - MOUNTAIN HARDWEAR, INC.; *pg.* 1839, *pg.* 193
MONTREAL - Women's Clothing & Accessories - WOODEN SHIPS OF HOBOKEN; *pg.* 35, *pg.* 1315
MONTREAL CANADIENS - Professional Hockey Team - CLUB DE HOCKEY CANADIEN, INC.; *pg.* 541, *pg.* 1954
MONTREUX - Furniture - TROPITONE FURNITURE CO., INC.; *pg.* 945, *pg.* 118
MONTRIO - Guest Chairs - BERNHARDT DESIGN; *pg.* 918, *pg.* 1381
MONTROUGE - Ceramic, Glass, Stone Tiles & Slabs - WALKER & ZANGER, INC.; *pg.* 119, *pg.* 281
MONTY - Glove - KOMBI, LTD.; *pg.* 1838, *pg.* 1766
MONUMENTAL IRON WORKS - Fencing - MASTER HALCO; *pg.* 96, *pg.* 474
MOO-LA-MILLIONS - Lottery Game - NEW YORK STATE LOTTERY; *pg.* 1001, *pg.* 1340
MOO-LAH MONEY - Lottery Game - KENTUCKY LOTTERY CORPORATION; *pg.* 996, *pg.* 735
MOO SHOO - Apparel - VANS, INC.; *pg.* 1821, *pg.* 76
MOOD BALANCE - Vitamin & Herbal Supplement - SOURCE NATURALS; *pg.* 1595, *pg.* 278
MOOD MENDER - Herb Tea - CELESTIAL SEASONINGS, INC.; *pg.* 846, *pg.* 310
MOOD PLUS - Nutritional Supplement - PHARMAVITE LLC; *pg.* 1584, *pg.* 167
MOODLIFT - Herbal Formula - SHAKLEE CORPORATION; *pg.* 1593, *pg.* 184
MOODY - Bible Institute - MOODY BIBLE INSTITUTE; *pg.* 605, *pg.* 583
MOODY PRESS, THE NAME YOU CAN TRUST - Publishers of Books & Bibles - MOODY PUBLISHERS; *pg.* 1665, *pg.* 583
MOOG - Chassis Products - FEDERAL-MOGUL HOLDINGS CORPORATION; *pg.* 205, *pg.* 907
MOOLAH - Video Game - INTERNATIONAL GAME TECHNOLOGY; *pg.* 957, *pg.* 1024
MOOLAH ROUGE - Game - WMS INDUSTRIES INC.; *pg.* 593, *pg.* 666
MOOMBA - Power Boat - SKIER'S CHOICE INC.; *pg.* 1711, *pg.* 1640
MOON DELIGHT - Fruit Arrangements - EDIBLE ARRANGEMENTS INTERNATIONAL, INC.; *pg.* 1768, *pg.* 382
MOON RISING - Game - WMS INDUSTRIES INC.; *pg.* 593, *pg.* 666
MOON SAND - Toy - SPIN MASTER LTD.; *pg.* 967, *pg.* 1943
MOON WALKER - Video Game - INTERNATIONAL GAME TECHNOLOGY; *pg.* 957, *pg.* 1024
MOON WARRIORS - Video Game - INTERNATIONAL GAME TECHNOLOGY; *pg.* 957, *pg.* 1024
MOONBEAMS - Leather Moccasins - HABAND COMPANY, INC.; *pg.* 1772, *pg.* 1099
MOONDANCE - Audio Device - ALTEC LANSING LLC; *pg.* 348, *pg.* 1553
MOONDANCE - Furniture - STANLEY FURNITURE CO., INC.; *pg.* 943, *pg.* 1379
MOONGLOW - Vanity Lights - CRAFTMADE INTERNATIONAL, INC.; *pg.* 1295, *pg.* 1670
MOONLIGHT - Fabric - NEMSCHOFF, INC.; *pg.* 936, *pg.* 1890
MOONLIGHT - Computer Software - NOVELL INC.; *pg.* 446, *pg.* 852
MOONLIGHT PARFAIT - Container Grown Plant - MONROVIA GROWERS; *pg.* 1797, *pg.* 44
MOONPIE - Food Products - CHATTANOOGA BAKERY INC.; *pg.* 847, *pg.* 1628
MOONRISE - Space & Space Exploration Educational Materials - LOCKHEED MARTIN CORPORATION; *pg.* 229, *pg.* 762
MOONSHINE MONEY - Video Game - INTERNATIONAL GAME TECHNOLOGY; *pg.* 957, *pg.* 1024
MOONSTRUCK - Game - MULTIMEDIA GAMES INC.; *pg.* 442, *pg.* 1664
MOONVISOR - Lighted Visor - LUND INTERNATIONAL, INC.; *pg.* 211, *pg.* 526
MOOOLAH KIDS CLUB - Educational Program - MACATAWA BANK CORPORATION; *pg.* 778, *pg.* 892
MOOR-DENSE - Container Grown Plant - MONROVIA GROWERS; *pg.* 1797, *pg.* 44
MOOR 'N STOR - Boat Cover - TAYLOR MADE GROUP; *pg.* 1711, *pg.* 1162
MOORCRAFT - Professional Coatings - BENJAMIN MOORE & CO.; *pg.* 1440, *pg.* 1085
MOORCRAFT ROOF SPEC - Paint And Stain Product - BENJAMIN MOORE & CO.; *pg.* 1440, *pg.* 1085
MOORCRAFT SUPER CRAFT - Paint And Stain Product - BENJAMIN MOORE & CO.; *pg.* 1440, *pg.* 1085
MOORCRAFT SUPER HIDE - Paint And Stain Product - BENJAMIN MOORE & CO.; *pg.* 1440, *pg.* 1085
MOORCRAFT SUPER SPEC - Paint And Stain Product - BENJAMIN MOORE & CO.; *pg.* 1440, *pg.* 1085
MOORE - Fans - MOORE FANS LLC; *pg.* 1363, *pg.* 987
MOORE - Machine Tool & Measuring Machines - MOORE TOOL COMPANY, INC.; *pg.* 1057, *pg.* 339
MOORE TRAIL - Clothing - ABERCROMBIE & FITCH CO.; *pg.* 37, *pg.* 1466
MOORE WALLACE - Printing & Business Forms - R.R. DONNELLEY & SONS COMPANY; *pg.* 1682, *pg.* 589
MOORELAND - Natural Honey - DUTCH GOLD HONEY INC.; *pg.* 854, *pg.* 1546
MOORE'S - Tobacco Product - AMERICAN SNUFF COMPANY; *pg.* 1893, *pg.* 1641
MOORE'S - Paint And Stain Product - BENJAMIN MOORE & CO.; *pg.* 1440, *pg.* 1085
MOORE'S COATING COUNSELOR - Paint And Stain Product - BENJAMIN MOORE & CO.; *pg.* 1440, *pg.* 1085
MOORE'S COLORX AND DESIGN - Paint And Stain Product - BENJAMIN MOORE & CO.; *pg.* 1440, *pg.* 1085
MOORE'S RED LEAF - Twist Tobaccos - AMERICAN SNUFF COMPANY; *pg.* 1893, *pg.* 1641
MOORFIELD - Carpet - INTERFACE, INC.; *pg.* 695, *pg.* 512
MOORGARD - Latex House Paint - BENJAMIN MOORE & CO.; *pg.* 1440, *pg.* 1085
MOORGLO - Latex House Paint - BENJAMIN MOORE & CO.; *pg.* 1440, *pg.* 1085
MOORLASTIC - Paint And Stain Product - BENJAMIN MOORE & CO.; *pg.* 1440, *pg.* 1085
MOORLIFE - Paint And Stain Product - BENJAMIN MOORE & CO.; *pg.* 1440, *pg.* 1085
MOORMAN - Nutrition Products - ADM ALLIANCE NUTRITION, INC.; *pg.* 1474, *pg.* 653
MOORMATE - Recessed Boat Cleat - THE WORTH COMPANY; *pg.* 1848, *pg.* 1895
MOORMATE 19001 - Drainage Kit - THE WORTH COMPANY; *pg.* 1848, *pg.* 1895
MOORWHITE - Paint And Stain Product - BENJAMIN MOORE & CO.; *pg.* 1440, *pg.* 1085
MOORWOOD - Exterior Stains - BENJAMIN MOORE & CO.; *pg.* 1440, *pg.* 1085
MOOSE MUNCH - Popcorn Snacks - HARRY & DAVID HOLDINGS, INC.; *pg.* 1022, *pg.* 1499
MOOSE TRACKS - Ice Cream - TURKEY HILL DAIRY, INC.; *pg.* 902, *pg.* 1522
MOOSHKINS - Educational Materials - SCHOLASTIC INC.; *pg.* 1683, *pg.* 1288
MOOTOWN - Cheese Dip - SARGENTO FOODS INC.; *pg.* 894, *pg.* 1886
MOP & GLO - Multi-Surface Floor Cleaner - RECKITT BENCKISER INC.; *pg.* 1136, *pg.* 1105
MOP & SHINE - Floor Polish - BLUE CROSS LABORATORIES; *pg.* 326, *pg.* 277
MOPAR - Automobile Parts & Accessories - FCA US LLC; *pg.* 170, *pg.* 868
MOPAR ENTHUSIAST - Magazine - AMOS PRESS, INC.; *pg.* 1616, *pg.* 1472
MOPO - Laser - NEWPORT CORPORATION; *pg.* 1424, *pg.* 114
MOR-AD - Adhesive & Sealant - DOW CHEMICAL; *pg.* 1156, *pg.* 1563
MOR-ESTER - Adhesive & Sealant - DOW CHEMICAL; *pg.* 1156, *pg.* 1563
MOR-FLO - Specialty Chemicals - OMNOVA SOLUTIONS INC; *pg.* 1176, *pg.* 1453
MOR-FLOCK - Adhesive & Sealant - DOW CHEMICAL; *pg.* 1156, *pg.* 1563
MOR-FREE - Adhesive & Sealant - DOW CHEMICAL; *pg.* 1156, *pg.* 1563
MOR-FREE - Solventless Adhesives - THE DOW CHEMICAL COMPANY; *pg.* 1157, *pg.* 898
MOR-GLO - Chemical Product - OMNOVA SOLUTIONS INC; *pg.* 1176, *pg.* 1453
MOR GOLD PLUS - Butter Substitute - VENTURA FOODS, LLC; *pg.* 908, *pg.* 49
MOR-MELT - Adhesive & Sealant - DOW CHEMICAL; *pg.* 1156, *pg.* 1563
MOR-PRIME - Adhesive & Sealant - DOW CHEMICAL; *pg.* 1156, *pg.* 1563
MOR-QUIK - Adhesive & Sealant - DOW CHEMICAL; *pg.* 1156, *pg.* 1563
MOR-SHINE - Wallcovering - OMNOVA SOLUTIONS INC; *pg.* 1176, *pg.* 1453
MOR-TRIM - Adhesive & Sealant - DOW CHEMICAL; *pg.* 1156, *pg.* 1563
MORAINE - Plant Material - THE SIEBENTHALER CO.; *pg.* 1800, *pg.* 1446
MORBID MAKEUP - Makeup - HOT TOPIC, INC.; *pg.* 42, *pg.* 67
MORBID THREADS - Clothing - HOT TOPIC, INC.; *pg.* 42, *pg.* 67
MORCRYL - Resin - DOW CHEMICAL; *pg.* 1156, *pg.* 1563
MORE - Dish Detergent - KAO BRANDS CO. INC.; *pg.* 513, *pg.* 1415
MORE - Magazine - MEREDITH CORPORATION; *pg.* 1663, *pg.* 705
MORE BARS IN MORE PLACES - Slogan - AT&T MOBILITY LLC; *pg.* 619, *pg.* 488
MORE BATTERY LIFE - SRAM - CYPRESS SEMICONDUCTOR CORPORATION; *pg.* 1326, *pg.* 243
MORE BROKER FOR YOUR MONEY - Slogan - SCOTTRADE, INC.; *pg.* 802, *pg.* 1003
MORE CHOICES - Slogan - SIMON PROPERTY GROUP, INC.; *pg.* 1112, *pg.* 690
MORE CONTROL LESS RISK - Tagline - ST. JUDE MEDICAL, INC.; *pg.* 1596, *pg.* 963
MORE EQUIPMENT MORE INDUSTRIES - Tagline - ASTEC INDUSTRIES, INC.; *pg.* 69, *pg.* 1628
MORE INTIMATE - Sleepwear - KELLWOOD COMPANY; *pg.* 28, *pg.* 975
MORE IS LESS - Slogan - THE RATNER COMPANIES; *pg.* 520, *pg.* 1809
MORE MONSTERS UNDER THE BED - Carpet - INTERFACE, INC.; *pg.* 695, *pg.* 512
MORE POWER. MORE ENERGY. MORE IDEAS - Slogan - MAXWELL TECHNOLOGIES, INC.; *pg.* 653, *pg.* 204
MORE RIGHT THAN RAIN - Tagline - REINKE MANUFACTURING COMPANY, INC.; *pg.* 707, *pg.* 1010
MORE SAVING. MORE DOING - Slogan - THE HOME DEPOT, INC.; *pg.* 1050, *pg.* 510
MORE SHINE FOR TIRES - Car Care Product - STONER INC.; *pg.* 985, *pg.* 1583
MORE TASTE.MORE JOY - Slogan - DEL MONTE FOODS, INC.; *pg.* 852, *pg.* 304
MORE THAN A MACHINE - Slogan - DOUGLAS MACHINE, INC.; *pg.* 1456, *pg.* 915
MORE THAN CLEAN IT'S READYSPACE - Floor Maintenance Equipment - TENNANT COMPANY; *pg.* 1381, *pg.* 944
MORE THAN ENERGY - Slogan - GAINESVILLE REGIONAL UTILITIES INC.; *pg.* 1943, *pg.* 429
MORE THAN YOU THOUGHT - Tagline - THE SSI GROUP, INC.; *pg.* 473, *pg.* 7
MORE WAYS TO MAKE IT YOUR MARKET - Tagline - UNIFIED GROCERS, INC.; *pg.* 1036, *pg.* 66
THE MORE YOU USE IT, THE SMARTER YOU GET. - Tag Line - IMAKENEWS, INC.; *pg.* 413, *pg.* 851
MOREAU - Lounge Chairs - BERNHARDT DESIGN; *pg.* 918, *pg.* 1381
MOREHOUSE-COWLES - Electronic Equipment - MOREHOUSE-COWLES; *pg.* 1363, *pg.* 66
MOREMAX - Movie Channel - HOME BOX OFFICE, INC.; *pg.* 290, *pg.* 1240
MORET ULTRA - Gymwear & Casualwear - JACQUES MORET, INC.; *pg.* 27, *pg.* 1245
MOREZ - Resin - DOW CHEMICAL; *pg.* 1156, *pg.* 1563

MORGAGNI - Software Product - FEI COMPANY; *pg.* 1413, *pg.* 1498
MORGAN - Clothing - ABERCROMBIE & FITCH CO.; *pg.* 37, *pg.* 1466
MORGAN - Lighting - ETHAN ALLEN INTERIORS INC.; *pg.* 924, *pg.* 343
MORGANA - Paper Folder - THE CHALLENGE MACHINERY COMPANY; *pg.* 1322, *pg.* 902
MORGANA EZ FOLDER - Paper Folding Machine - THE CHALLENGE MACHINERY COMPANY; *pg.* 1322, *pg.* 902
MORGAN'S - Tobacco Product - AMERICAN SNUFF COMPANY; *pg.* 1893, *pg.* 1641
MORGRO - Fertilizer - MORGRO, INC.; *pg.* 1798, *pg.* 1759
MORI NO MIZUDAYORI - Beverages - THE COCA-COLA COMPANY; *pg.* 240, *pg.* 493
MORITZ BILEVEL - Medical Device - RESMED INC.; *pg.* 1589, *pg.* 207
MORLEX DEEA - Corrosion Inhibitor - THE DOW CHEMICAL COMPANY; *pg.* 1157, *pg.* 898
MORLEY - Footwear - K-SWISS; *pg.* 1837, *pg.* 306
MORLIFE - Additive - DOW CHEMICAL; *pg.* 1156, *pg.* 1563
MORLITE - Lighting - PHILIPS LIGHTING; *pg.* 1303, *pg.* 806
MORMATE - Ceramic Processing Additive - HUNTSMAN CORPORATION; *pg.* 1167, *pg.* 1758
MORNAP - Dispenser Napkin - GEORGIA-PACIFIC LLC; *pg.* 1458, *pg.* 507
MORNING COFFEE - Carpet - INTERFACE, INC.; *pg.* 695, *pg.* 512
MORNING DELI - Beverages - THE COCA-COLA COMPANY; *pg.* 240, *pg.* 493
MORNING DEW - Hand & Body Cream - ANNIE OAKLEY ENTERPRISES, INC.; *pg.* 499, *pg.* 693
MORNING GLORY - Dairy Products - FOREMOST FARMS USA COOPERATIVE; *pg.* 856, *pg.* 1854
MORNING MAC - Fast Food - MCDONALD'S CORPORATION; *pg.* 1737, *pg.* 645
MORNING SONG - Pet Product - PETSMART, INC.; *pg.* 1481, *pg.* 18
MORNING SONG - Wild Bird Food - THE SCOTTS MIRACLE-GRO COMPANY; *pg.* 1799, *pg.* 1459
MORNING TREAT - Coffee - FRESHBREW COFFEE, LLC; *pg.* 857, *pg.* 1706
MORNINGSTAR - Hardware Flooring - LUMBER LIQUIDATORS HOLDINGS, INC.; *pg.* 94, *pg.* 1808
MORNINGSTAR ADVISOR - Magazine - MORNINGSTAR, INC.; *pg.* 784, *pg.* 583
MORNINGSTAR ADVISOR WORKSTATION - Web-Based Investment Planning Tool for Financial Advisors - MORNINGSTAR, INC.; *pg.* 784, *pg.* 583
MORNINGSTAR DIRECT - Internet-Based Investment Research Platform - MORNINGSTAR, INC.; *pg.* 784, *pg.* 583
MORNINGSTAR FARMS - Food Product - KELLOGG COMPANY; *pg.* 831, *pg.* 870
MORNINGSTAR FUNDINVESTOR - Monthly Mutual Fund Newsletter - MORNINGSTAR, INC.; *pg.* 784, *pg.* 583
MORNINGSTAR FUNDS 500 - Mutual Fund Analysis Publication - MORNINGSTAR, INC.; *pg.* 784, *pg.* 583
MORNINGSTAR INDEXES - Equity Market Indexes - MORNINGSTAR, INC.; *pg.* 784, *pg.* 583
MORNINGSTAR INVESTMENT GUIDES - Investment Advice Publications - MORNINGSTAR, INC.; *pg.* 784, *pg.* 583
MORNINGSTAR INVESTMENT PROFILES - Single-Page Investment Reports - MORNINGSTAR, INC.; *pg.* 784, *pg.* 583
MORNINGSTAR MANAGED PORTFOLIOS - Mutual Fund Portfolio Management Program - MORNINGSTAR, INC.; *pg.* 784, *pg.* 583
MORNINGSTAR MUTUAL FUNDS - Twice-Monthly Mutual Fund Guide - MORNINGSTAR, INC.; *pg.* 784, *pg.* 583
MORNINGSTAR PRINCIPIA - Investment Planning Software for Financial Advisors - MORNINGSTAR, INC.; *pg.* 784, *pg.* 583
MORNINGSTAR STOCKINVESTOR - Monthly Investor Newsletter - MORNINGSTAR, INC.; *pg.* 784, *pg.* 583
MORNINGSTAR STOCKS 500 - Annual Stock Report - MORNINGSTAR, INC.; *pg.* 784, *pg.* 583
MORNINGSTARADVISOR.COM - Investor Advice Web Site - MORNINGSTAR, INC.; *pg.* 784, *pg.* 583
MORNINGSTAR.COM - Investor Advice Web Site - MORNINGSTAR, INC.; *pg.* 784, *pg.* 583
MOROCCO - Shoe - AEROGROUP INTERNATIONAL, INC.; *pg.* 1803, *pg.* 1055
MOROCCO - Container Grown Plant - MONROVIA GROWERS; *pg.* 1797, *pg.* 44
MOROCCO - Fabric - NEMSCHOFF, INC.; *pg.* 936, *pg.* 1890
MOROMEDEX - Healthcare Publications - THOMSON REUTERS CORPORATION; *pg.* 1693, *pg.* 1944
MORPH2 - Refill - A. T. CROSS COMPANY; *pg.* 339, *pg.* 1602
MORPHE - Fabric - NEMSCHOFF, INC.; *pg.* 936, *pg.* 1890
MORPHEUS - Electrosurgical Devices - ANGIODYNAMICS, INC.; *pg.* 1495, *pg.* 1173
MORPHOS - Metal Finishing Product - HEATBATH CORPORATION; *pg.* 1165, *pg.* 826
MORPHOSIS - Bath & Plumbing Product - JACUZZI BRANDS CORPORATION; *pg.* 554, *pg.* 65
MORR-CLEAR - Hose - MORRIS COUPLING COMPANY; *pg.* 1057, *pg.* 1530
MORR-LITE - Hose - MORRIS COUPLING COMPANY; *pg.* 1057, *pg.* 1530
MORR-THANE - Hose - MORRIS COUPLING COMPANY; *pg.* 1057, *pg.* 1530
MORR-TITE - Hose - MORRIS COUPLING COMPANY; *pg.* 1057, *pg.* 1530
MORR-TUFF - Hose - MORRIS COUPLING COMPANY; *pg.* 1057, *pg.* 1530
MORRIS HELI-GROOVE - Stainless Steel - MORRIS COUPLING COMPANY; *pg.* 1057, *pg.* 1530
MORRISON - Office Furniture - KNOLL, INC.; *pg.* 425, *pg.* 1527
MORRISON - Light Equipment - TEREX CORPORATION; *pg.* 1381, *pg.* 384
MORRITEX - Flooring System - THE VALSPAR CORPORATION; *pg.* 1449, *pg.* 945
MORSTIK - Adhesive & Sealant - DOW CHEMICAL; *pg.* 1156, *pg.* 1563
MORTAR PLAS - Chemical Product - WESTROCK COMPANY; *pg.* 1472, *pg.* 1805
MORTGAGE MATCH - Software - EQUIFAX INC.; *pg.* 748, *pg.* 504
MORTIMER - Cleaning Utensils - THE CLOROX COMPANY; *pg.* 327, *pg.* 169
MORTISE - Sunglass - 180S, LLC; *pg.* 1824, *pg.* 754
MORTITE - Consumer Products - THERMWELL PRODUCTS CO., INC.; *pg.* 1065, *pg.* 1082
MORTON - Furniture - ASHLEY FURNITURE INDUSTRIES, INC.; *pg.* 914, *pg.* 1852
MORTON - Salt - DOW CHEMICAL; *pg.* 1156, *pg.* 1563
MORTON'S THE STEAKHOUSE - Steakhouses - MORTON'S RESTAURANT GROUP, INC.; *pg.* 1741, *pg.* 583
MORTRACE - Marker - DOW CHEMICAL; *pg.* 1156, *pg.* 1563
MORTRACE - Marking Technologies - THE DOW CHEMICAL COMPANY; *pg.* 1157, *pg.* 898
MOS2WAP - Mobile Suite - CHYRONHEGO; *pg.* 371, *pg.* 1179
MOSAIC - Thermally Stable/PDC Bits - BAKER HUGHES INTEQ; *pg.* 1316, *pg.* 1700
MOSAIC - Architectural Roofing Shingles - BUILDING PRODUCTS OF CANADA CORP.; *pg.* 72, *pg.* 1951
MOSAIC - Ramekins - CARLISLE FOODSERVICE PRODUCTS INCORPORATED; *pg.* 1455, *pg.* 1485
MOSAIC - Coffees - GORDON FOOD SERVICE INC.; *pg.* 1021, *pg.* 913
MOSAIC - Fabric - NEMSCHOFF, INC.; *pg.* 936, *pg.* 1890
MOSAIC - Antenna Product - PCTEL, INC.; *pg.* 452, *pg.* 557
MOSAIC - Seat Cushion - THE ROHO GROUP; *pg.* 1591, *pg.* 556
MOSAIC - Tiles - SEARS HOLDINGS CORPORATION; *pg.* 1784, *pg.* 618
MOSAIC - Stone - WALKER & ZANGER, INC.; *pg.* 119, *pg.* 281
MOSAIC - Community Name - WCI COMMUNITIES, INC.; *pg.* 1118, *pg.* 414
MOSAIC MANIA - Mosaic Kits - E-Z BOWZ, LLC; *pg.* 692, *pg.* 1635
MOSAID CLASS-IC - Circuit Design Services - CONVERSANT INTELLECTUAL PROPERTY MANAGEMENT INC.; *pg.* 630, *pg.* 1931
MOSCATO - Bathroom Accessories - SYMMONS INDUSTRIES, INC.; *pg.* 114, *pg.* 803
MOSCATO D'ORO - Wine - ROBERT MONDAVI WINERY; *pg.* 1969, *pg.* 173
MOSCONI - Sporting Good Product - ESCALADE INC.; *pg.* 1833, *pg.* 678
MOSECURITY - Computer Software - TRUSTWAVE HOLDINGS, INC.; *pg.* 1285, *pg.* 593
MOSLEY - Baler - HARRIS WASTE MANAGEMENT GROUP, INC.; *pg.* 1345, *pg.* 526
MOSQUITO BEATER - Insect Chaser - BONIDE PRODUCTS, INC.; *pg.* 1794, *pg.* 1320
MOSS - Fabric - NEMSCHOFF, INC.; *pg.* 936, *pg.* 1890
MOSS-ASIDE - Moss Killer - GARDENS ALIVE!, INC.; *pg.* 1796, *pg.* 693
MOSS BLEND - Excelsior Fiber - AMERICAN EXCELSIOR COMPANY; *pg.* 1451, *pg.* 1659
MOSS GREEN COLOR - Container Grown Plant - MONROVIA GROWERS; *pg.* 1797, *pg.* 44
MOSS TWEED - Pillow and Throw - HERITAGE LACE INC.; *pg.* 694, *pg.* 711
MOSSBERG - Gun - O.F. MOSSBERG & SONS, INC.; *pg.* 1842, *pg.* 360
MOSSCARA - Eye Makeup - AVEDA CORPORATION; *pg.* 499, *pg.* 917
MOSSIMO - Sportswear - ICONIX BRAND GROUP, INC.; *pg.* 26, *pg.* 1243
MOSSIMO - Clothing - TARGET CORPORATION; *pg.* 1786, *pg.* 942
MOSSTOWN - Brick & Tile Product - CHEROKEE BRICK & TILE COMPANY; *pg.* 75, *pg.* 535
MOSSY OAK - Overall - KEY INDUSTRIES, INC.; *pg.* 43, *pg.* 714
MOSSY OAK - Powered Tool - MILWAUKEE ELECTRIC TOOL CORP.; *pg.* 1056, *pg.* 1855
MOSSY OAK - Apparel - RUSSELL BRANDS LLC; *pg.* 698, *pg.* 726
THE MOST EXCITING SEAT IN SPORTS! - Automobile Races - DOVER MOTORSPORTS, INC.; *pg.* 545, *pg.* 387
MOST HONORABLE RED - Nail Care Product - OPI PRODUCTS INC.; *pg.* 518, *pg.* 167
THE MOST TRUSTED - Educational Materials - SCHOLASTIC INC.; *pg.* 1683, *pg.* 1288
THE MOST TRUSTED NAME IN LEARNING - Educational Materials - SCHOLASTIC INC.; *pg.* 1683, *pg.* 1288
MOST VANGUARD - Engine Type - BRIGGS & STRATTON CORPORATION; *pg.* 201, *pg.* 1899
MOSTLY MOZART - Performing Arts Program - LINCOLN CENTER FOR THE PERFORMING ARTS, INC.; *pg.* 557, *pg.* 1251
MOTCH - Machine Tool Product - BOURN & KOCH MACHINE TOOL COMPANY; *pg.* 1319, *pg.* 654
MOTH-AWAY - Insect Pest Control Product - GARDENS ALIVE!, INC.; *pg.* 1796, *pg.* 693
MOTHER - Energy Drink - THE COCA-COLA COMPANY; *pg.* 240, *pg.* 493
MOTHER EARTH - Magazine Publishers - MOTHER EARTH NEWS; *pg.* 1666, *pg.* 722
MOTHER EARTH NEWS - Bi-Monthly Magazine - OGDEN PUBLICATIONS, INC.; *pg.* 1672, *pg.* 722
MOTHER NATURE'S CLEAN COAL - Slogan - READING ANTHRACITE COMPANY; *pg.* 1179, *pg.* 1583
THE MOTHER OF ALL SEARCH ENGINES - Slogan - COPERNIC INC.; *pg.* 1237, *pg.* 1958
MOTHER ROAD ROSE - Nail Care Product - OPI PRODUCTS INC.; *pg.* 518, *pg.* 167
MOTHER ROSE - Pillow and Throw - HERITAGE LACE INC.; *pg.* 694, *pg.* 711
MOTHERHOOD - Maternity Apparel - DESTINATION MATERNITY CORPORATION; *pg.* 23, *pg.* 1563
MOTHERHOOD MATERNITY - Maternity Clothing & Retail Stores - DESTINATION MATERNITY CORPORATION; *pg.* 23, *pg.* 1563
MOTHERHOOD MATTERS - Pregnancy Program - MOLINA HEALTHCARE, INC.; *pg.* 1569, *pg.* 123
MOTHERHOOD NURSINGWEAR - Nursing Apparel - DESTINATION MATERNITY CORPORATION; *pg.* 23, *pg.* 1563
MOTHER'S - Food Products - MANISCHEWITZ COMPANY; *pg.* 875, *pg.* 1097
MOTHER'S - Cereal - THE QUAKER OATS COMPANY; *pg.* 834, *pg.* 588
MOTHER'S CHOICE - Baby Product - HY-VEE, INC.; *pg.* 1023, *pg.* 713
MOTHER'S DAY - Lottery Game - OHIO LOTTERY COMMISSION; *pg.* 1002, *pg.* 1433
MOTHER'S DAY WISHES BOUQUET - Floral Bouquet - FTD GROUP, INC.; *pg.* 1795, *pg.* 608
MOTHER'S DEVOTION - Flower Arrangement - 1-800-FLOWERS.COM, INC.; *pg.* 1758, *pg.* 1151
MOTHER'S EMBRACE - Flower Arrangement - 1-800-FLOWERS.COM, INC.; *pg.* 1758, *pg.* 1151
MOTHER'S KITCHEN - Food Products - RICH PRODUCTS CORPORATION; *pg.* 892, *pg.* 1150
MOTHERSHIP WIT - Beer - NEW BELGIUM BREWING

First page reference indicates Business Class Edition
Second page reference indicates Geographic Edition

COMPANY, INC.; pg. 258, pg. 328

MOTIF - Digital Marketing Product - DOUBLECLICK, INC.; pg. 1239, pg. 1225

MOTIF - Furniture - JASPER GROUP; pg. 930, pg. 691

MOTIF - Footwear - STEVEN MADDEN, LTD.; pg. 1819, pg. 1176

MOTIFLEX - Servo Drive - BALDOR ELECTRIC COMPANY; pg. 1316, pg. 32

MOTILIUM - Healthcare Product - JOHNSON & JOHNSON; pg. 1549, pg. 1091

MOTION FIT SYSTEM - Sunglass - 180S, LLC; pg. 1824, pg. 754

MOTION MASTER - Ride Management System - LORD CORPORATION; pg. 1357, pg. 1360

MOTIONBUILDER - Software - AUTODESK INC.; pg. 356, pg. 257

MOTIONGRADE - Cable - AMPHENOL CORPORATION; pg. 616, pg. 381

MOTIONS - Hair Care Products - UNILEVER UNITED STATES, INC.; pg. 904, pg. 1061

MOTIVA - Women's Walking Shoe - SAUCONY, INC.; pg. 1818, pg. 828

MOTIVE - Fabric - NEMSCHOFF, INC.; pg. 936, pg. 1890

MOTO - Electronic Transmission - MOTOROLA SOLUTIONS, INC.; pg. 657, pg. 659

MOTO ALPHA - Software - BIO-RAD LABORATORIES, INC.; pg. 1504, pg. 101

MOTO FOUR - Mirror - COMMERCIAL VEHICLE GROUP, INC.; pg. 203, pg. 1467

MOTO GUZZI - Scooter - PIAGGIO USA, INC.; pg. 188, pg. 1282

MOTO-MASSAGE - Moving Hydrotherapy Jet - WATKINS MANUFACTURING CORPORATION; pg. 120, pg. 303

MOTO MIRROR - Mirror - COMMERCIAL VEHICLE GROUP, INC.; pg. 203, pg. 1467

MOTOCROSS - Magazine - BONNIER CORPORATION; pg. 1622, pg. 480

MOTOMASTER - Battery - CANADIAN TIRE CORPORATION LIMITED; pg. 202, pg. 1936

MOTOR BOATING - Magazine - BONNIER CORPORATION; pg. 1622, pg. 480

MOTOR BOATING - Magazine - YACHTING MAGAZINE; pg. 1703, pg. 1602

MOTOR-MEDIC - Oil Additive - RADIATOR SPECIALTY COMPANY; pg. 215, pg. 1380

MOTOR RACING NETWORK - Race-Related Programming Network - INTERNATIONAL SPEEDWAY CORPORATION; pg. 553, pg. 420

MOTORAZR - Electronic Transmission - MOTOROLA SOLUTIONS, INC.; pg. 657, pg. 659

MOTORAZR MAXX VE - Phone Handset - MOTOROLA SOLUTIONS, INC.; pg. 657, pg. 659

MOTORAZR2 - Electronic Transmission - MOTOROLA SOLUTIONS, INC.; pg. 657, pg. 659

MOTORBOATING - Magazine - BONNIER ACTIVE MEDIA, INC.; pg. 1622, pg. 1205

MOTORBOATING.COM - Web Site - BONNIER ACTIVE MEDIA, INC.; pg. 1622, pg. 1205

MOTORCLOTHES - Apparel - HARLEY-DAVIDSON, INC.; pg. 178, pg. 1874

MOTORCYCLE CONSUMER NEWS - Magazine - I-5 PUBLISHING LLC; pg. 1651, pg. 133

MOTORIZED SCENIC ROLLER - Screen - DA-LITE SCREEN COMPANY; pg. 632, pg. 698

MOTOROKR - Electronic Transmission - MOTOROLA SOLUTIONS, INC.; pg. 657, pg. 659

MOTOROLA - Communications Product - MOTOROLA SOLUTIONS, INC.; pg. 657, pg. 659

MOTORPACT - Motor Controllers - SCHNEIDER ELECTRIC USA, INC.; pg. 1306, pg. 650

MOTORSPORTS BY MAIL - Motorsports Entertainment - SPEEDWAY MOTORSPORTS, INC.; pg. 584, pg. 1370

MOTOSLVR - Cellular Telephone - MOTOROLA SOLUTIONS, INC.; pg. 657, pg. 659

MOTOTRBO - Communications Product - MOTOROLA SOLUTIONS, INC.; pg. 657, pg. 659

MOTOWI4 - Communications Product - MOTOROLA SOLUTIONS, INC.; pg. 657, pg. 659

MOTOWN - Records - UNIVERSAL MOTOWN RECORDS; pg. 315, pg. 1307

MOTOZINE - Electronic Transmission - MOTOROLA SOLUTIONS, INC.; pg. 657, pg. 659

MOTRIN - Healthcare Product - JOHNSON & JOHNSON; pg. 1549, pg. 1091

MOTRIN - Pain Reliever - MCNEIL-PPC, INC.; pg. 1560, pg. 1533

MOTTED - Apparel - VANS, INC.; pg. 1821, pg. 76

MOTTLED - Paper & Nonwoven Material - FIBERMARK INC.; pg. 1457, pg. 1764

MOTTO - Fabric - NEMSCHOFF, INC.; pg. 936, pg. 1890

MOTT'S - Non-Carbonated Soft Drink - DR PEPPER SNAPPLE GROUP, INC.; pg. 250, pg. 1729

MOUEIX - Bordeaux Wines - DREYFUS ASHBY INC.; pg. 1962, pg. 1226

MOULIN - Fabric - SCALAMANDRE, INC.; pg. 941, pg. 1058

MOUNT-A-SIGN - Laminating System - SOUTHWEST BINDING & LAMINATING; pg. 1377, pg. 988

MOUNT CARMEL DAILY REPUBLICAN REGISTER - Newspaper - DAILY REPUBLICAN REGISTER; pg. 1633, pg. 634

MOUNT-O-MATIC - Miscellaneous Plate Mounting - ANDERSON & VREELAND, INC.; pg. 1616, pg. 1064

MOUNT-O-MATIC PLUS - Miscellaneous Plate Mounting - ANDERSON & VREELAND, INC.; pg. 1616, pg. 1064

MOUNT VERNON - Wall Panel - BLUELINX HOLDINGS, INC.; pg. 70, pg. 491

MOUNT VERNON - Distilled Spirits - JIM BEAM BRANDS CO.; pg. 1965, pg. 601

MOUNT VISION - Bike - MARIN BIKES; pg. 1708, pg. 168

MOUNTAIN - Hardwood Floor - ANDERSON HARDWOOD FLOORS; pg. 67, pg. 1613

MOUNTAIN - Bar Chocolate - BROWN & HALEY; pg. 1851, pg. 1820

MOUNTAIN ATHLETICS - Footwear, Apparel & Accessories - THE TIMBERLAND COMPANY; pg. 1821, pg. 1039

MOUNTAIN BAR - Chocolate Coated Fondant Center - BROWN & HALEY; pg. 1851, pg. 1820

MOUNTAIN BELL - Communication Product - CENTURYLINK, INC; pg. 1870, pg. 317

MOUNTAIN BIKE - Magazine - RODALE, INC.; pg. 1681, pg. 1530

MOUNTAIN CAGE - Bicycle Accessories - SPECIALIZED BICYCLE COMPONENTS, INC.; pg. 1711, pg. 152

MOUNTAIN CHAI DECAF ORIGINAL - Teas - CELESTIAL SEASONINGS, INC.; pg. 846, pg. 310

MOUNTAIN CHAI ORIGINAL - Tea Product - CELESTIAL SEASONINGS, INC.; pg. 846, pg. 310

MOUNTAIN DEW - Soft Drink - PEPSICO, INC.; pg. 259, pg. 1327

MOUNTAIN DEW CODE RED - Soft Drink - PEPSICO, INC.; pg. 259, pg. 1327

MOUNTAIN DEW LIVEWIRE - Soft Drink - PEPSICO, INC.; pg. 259, pg. 1327

MOUNTAIN DEW MDX - Soft Drink - PEPSICO, INC.; pg. 259, pg. 1327

MOUNTAIN DEW VOLTAGE - Soft Drink - PEPSICO, INC.; pg. 259, pg. 1327

MOUNTAIN ENERGY PINE-SOL - All Purpose Cleaner - THE CLOROX COMPANY; pg. 327, pg. 169

MOUNTAIN HARDWEAR - Outdoor Gear - MOUNTAIN HARDWEAR, INC.; pg. 1839, pg. 193

MOUNTAIN HIGH - Dairy Product - DEAN FOODS COMPANY; pg. 852, pg. 1679

MOUNTAIN HIKERS - Hiking Boots - CABELA'S INCORPORATED; pg. 535, pg. 1019

MOUNTAIN HOUSE - Freeze Dried Food Prods. - OREGON FREEZE DRY, INC.; pg. 888, pg. 1492

MOUNTAIN KING - Game - WMS INDUSTRIES INC.; pg. 593, pg. 666

MOUNTAIN LIVING - Magazine - NETWORK COMMUNICATIONS INC.; pg. 1271, pg. 534

MOUNTAIN MAGIC - Learn to Ski & Snowboard Package - GUNSTOCK RECREATION AREA; pg. 1094, pg. 1034

MOUNTAIN MAGIC - Western Bark & Cedar - MOUNTAIN WEST, LLC; pg. 98, pg. 550

MOUNTAIN MAN - Bicycle Helmets - SPECIALIZED BICYCLE COMPONENTS, INC.; pg. 1711, pg. 152

MOUNTAIN MEADOW - Plant Growing Kit - AEROGROW INTERNATIONAL, INC.; pg. 1393, pg. 310

MOUNTAIN MELT - De-Icer - GRAIN PROCESSING CORPORATION; pg. 859, pg. 709

MOUNTAIN TOP - Frozen Unbaked Pies - LANCASTER COLONY CORPORATION; pg. 873, pg. 1441

MOUNTAIN TOP - Frozen Pies - T. MARZETTI COMPANY; pg. 900, pg. 1444

MOUNTAINEER CASINO RACETRACK & RESORT - Racetrack & Hotel-Casino - ELDORADO RESORTS, INC.; pg. 546, pg. 1031

MOUNTAINS - Fabric - NEMSCHOFF, INC.; pg. 936, pg. 1890

THE MOUNTED OFFICER - Motorcycle - HARLEY-DAVIDSON, INC.; pg. 178, pg. 1874

MOUSE EPIPANEL - Diagnostic Tool - SEQUENOM, INC.; pg. 1593, pg. 209

MOUSE TRAP - Toy & Game - HASBRO, INC.; pg. 954, pg. 1603

MOUSE TYPER - Software - BIO-RAD LABORATORIES, INC.; pg. 1504, pg. 101

MOUSE WORKS - Cartoon & Amusement Ride - THE WALT DISNEY COMPANY; pg. 317, pg. 52

MOUSE.COM - Advertising Website - LIVE CURRENT MEDIA INC.; pg. 1263, pg. 1911

MOUSETRAP - Game - HASBRO, INC.; pg. 954, pg. 1603

MOUTON-CADET WINES - Wine - DIAGEO NORTH AMERICA, INC.; pg. 1961, pg. 361

MOUZPAD - Snap-On, Rigid Plastic Mousing Surface for the Laptop Desk - LAPWORKS, INC.; pg. 426, pg. 187

MOVADO - Watch - MOVADO GROUP, INC.; pg. 10, pg. 1101

MOVE - Office Furniture - STEELCASE INC.; pg. 475, pg. 889

MOVE FREE - Dietary Supplements - RECKITT BENCKISER INC.; pg. 1136, pg. 1105

MOVE IN GET MORE - Tagline - MACK-CALI REALTY CORPORATION; pg. 1102, pg. 1056

MOVE-IT - Conveyor - BUNTING MAGNETICS CO.; pg. 1320, pg. 717

MOVE MAILBOX MANAGER - Software - DELL SOFTWARE; pg. 385, pg. 40

MOVE OVER BUTTER - Food Product - CONAGRA FOODS, INC.; pg. 826, pg. 1014

THE MOVE SCRATCH-ITS - Lottery Rules - OREGON STATE LOTTERY; pg. 1003, pg. 1508

MOVE UP - Tagline - M/I HOMES, INC.; pg. 95, pg. 1441

MOVE.COM - Website - MOVE, INC.; pg. 1268, pg. 247

MOVEMASTER - Patient Transfer - ALIMED, INC.; pg. 1490, pg. 816

MOVER - Power Transmission Belt - HBD INDUSTRIES, INC.; pg. 207, pg. 1449

MOVER - Split-type Expansion Joint - VICTAULIC COMPANY; pg. 1066, pg. 1529

MOVERS & SHAKERS - Game - WMS INDUSTRIES INC.; pg. 593, pg. 666

MOVERSANDSHAKERS - Toy - INFANTINO, LLC; pg. 957, pg. 203

MOVEXPRESS - Wireless Communication System - AT&T SOUTHEAST; pg. 1868, pg. 489

MOVIANCRYPT - Software - CERTICOM CORP.; pg. 371, pg. 1925

MOVIANDM - Software - CERTICOM CORP.; pg. 371, pg. 1925

MOVIANMAIL - Software - CERTICOM CORP.; pg. 371, pg. 1925

MOVIANVPN - Software - CERTICOM CORP.; pg. 371, pg. 1925

THE MOVIE CHANNEL - Cable Television - SHOWTIME NETWORKS INC.; pg. 308, pg. 1291

THE MOVIE CHANNEL ON DEMAND - On Demand Television - SHOWTIME NETWORKS INC.; pg. 308, pg. 1291

THE MOVIE COLLECTOR'S WEBSITE - Slogan - MOVIES UNLIMITED INC.; pg. 1779, pg. 1567

MOVIE MAGIC - Digital Photography System - NU SKIN ENTERPRISES, INC.; pg. 518, pg. 1755

MOVIEFONE - Movie Information - AOL INC.; pg. 1229, pg. 1195

MOVIELINE'S HOLLYWOOD LIFE - Magazine - LINE PUBLICATIONS, INC.; pg. 1659, pg. 134

MOVIEPLEX - Cable Television - STARZ ENTERTAINMENT, LLC; pg. 310, pg. 327

THE MOVIES - Game - ACTIVISION BLIZZARD, INC.; pg. 948, pg. 271

MOVIEWATCHER - Loyalty Program - AMC ENTERTAINMENT INC.; pg. 527, pg. 716

MOVIEWORKS - Speaker - CAMBRIDGE SOUNDWORKS, INC.; pg. 1234, pg. 781

MOVIMENTO - Software - AUTODESK INC.; pg. 356, pg. 257

MOVIN' VIEW - Digital Satellite Mobile Antenna - WINEGARD COMPANY; pg. 688, pg. 702

MOVING AT THE SPEED OF BUSINESS - Software - UNITED PARCEL SERVICE, INC.; pg. 1928, pg. 522

MOVING COMFORT - Women's Activewear - RUSSELL BRANDS LLC; pg. 698, pg. 726

MOVING IS QUICK WHEN YOU CLICK - Slogan - AT&T

First page reference indicates Business Class Edition
Second page reference indicates Geographic Edition

SOUTHEAST; *pg.* 1868, *pg.* 489
MOVING YOUR MEMORIES - Tagline - NATIONAL VAN LINES, INC.; *pg.* 1916, *pg.* 559
MOVIPREP - Pharmaceutical Product - SALIX PHARMACEUTICALS, INC.; *pg.* 1591, *pg.* 1388
MOW-N-GO - Turf Maintenance Machinery - SMITHCO, INC.; *pg.* 1377, *pg.* 1592
MOXIE - Furniture - HAWORTH, INC.; *pg.* 402, *pg.* 891
MOXIE - Bath Product - KOHLER CO.; *pg.* 91, *pg.* 1862
MOXIE - Beverage - THE MONARCH BEVERAGE COMPANY, INC.; *pg.* 257, *pg.* 514
MOXY - Software - ADVENT SOFTWARE, INC.; *pg.* 345, *pg.* 211
MOZAMBIQUE - Ceiling Fan - HUNTER FAN COMPANY; *pg.* 57, *pg.* 1631
MOZART MAGIC - Toy - MUNCHKIN, INC.; *pg.* 964, *pg.* 300
MOZART MAGIC CUBE - Toy - MUNCHKIN, INC.; *pg.* 964, *pg.* 300
MOZLEY SANDSPIN - Water Separation Product - CAMERON INTERNATIONAL; *pg.* 1151, *pg.* 1702
MOZLEY WELLSPIN - Desanding Hydrocyclones - CAMERON INTERNATIONAL; *pg.* 1151, *pg.* 1702
MOZOBIL - Plerixafor Injection - GENZYME CORPORATION; *pg.* 1534, *pg.* 808
MOZY - Software - EMC CORPORATION; *pg.* 391, *pg.* 825
MOZYENTERPRISE - Software - EMC CORPORATION; *pg.* 391, *pg.* 825
MOZYHOME - Software - EMC CORPORATION; *pg.* 391, *pg.* 825
MOZYPRO - Software - EMC CORPORATION; *pg.* 391, *pg.* 825
MOZZA BURGER - Fast Food - A&W FOOD SERVICES OF CANADA INC.; *pg.* 1714, *pg.* 1908
MOZZARELLA FRESCA - Cheese - LACTALIS AMERICAN GROUP; *pg.* 873, *pg.* 1149
MP-200 - Electronic Components - MOLEX INCORPORATED; *pg.* 655, *pg.* 628
MP-5 - Coating Technology - II-VI INCORPORATED; *pg.* 1417, *pg.* 1585
MP BRITES - Paper Product - BOISE CASCADE HOLDINGS, L.L.C.; *pg.* 1453, *pg.* 546
MP COLORS - Paper Product - BOISE CASCADE HOLDINGS, L.L.C.; *pg.* 1453, *pg.* 546
MP COVER - Paper Product - BOISE CASCADE HOLDINGS, L.L.C.; *pg.* 1453, *pg.* 546
MP GRANITES - Paper Products - BOISE CASCADE HOLDINGS, L.L.C.; *pg.* 1453, *pg.* 546
MP-LOCK - Electronic Components - MOLEX INCORPORATED; *pg.* 655, *pg.* 628
MP LOCKS - Manipulation-Proof Combination Locks - SARGENT & GREENLEAF, INC.; *pg.* 1061, *pg.* 739
MP35N - Alloys - CARPENTER TECHNOLOGY CORPORATION; *pg.* 73, *pg.* 1584
MP3.COM - Digital Music Website - CBS INTERACTIVE, INC.; *pg.* 369, *pg.* 215
MPB SERIES - Conveyor - DORNER MANUFACTURING CORP.; *pg.* 1329, *pg.* 1861
MPC - Cross-Sectioning System - BUEHLER, LTD.; *pg.* 1403, *pg.* 622
MPC - Glass & Ceramic Material - CORNING INCORPORATED; *pg.* 1122, *pg.* 1154
MPC - Pump Product - IDEX CORPORATION; *pg.* 1347, *pg.* 623
MPC 1000 - Fire Alarm System - FARADAY; *pg.* 638, *pg.* 1066
MPC 1500 - Fire Alarm System - FARADAY; *pg.* 638, *pg.* 1066
MPC 220 - Minerals - MINERALS TECHNOLOGIES INC.; *pg.* 1173, *pg.* 617
MPC-5000 - Cutting System - EASTMAN MACHINE COMPANY; *pg.* 1331, *pg.* 1148
MPCIEXP - Software System - MENTOR GRAPHICS CORPORATION; *pg.* 432, *pg.* 1510
MPDIOL - Chemical Product - LYONDELLBASELL INDUSTRIES; *pg.* 980, *pg.* 1710
MPE 7.5 - Multiple Purpose Extractor - OPEX CORPORATION; *pg.* 450, *pg.* 1087
MPE SOLUTIONS - Software - DELL SOFTWARE; *pg.* 385, *pg.* 40
MPEXTREMITY MRI - MRI Scanner - FONAR CORPORATION; *pg.* 1413, *pg.* 1179
MPI LINK-CHECKER - Software - MICROWAY, INC.; *pg.* 1267, *pg.* 841
MPIS - Electronic Components - MOLEX INCORPORATED; *pg.* 655, *pg.* 628
MPJ - Medical Equipment - INVACARE CORPORATION; *pg.* 1546, *pg.* 1451
MPM - Electronic Components - MOLEX INCORPORATED; *pg.* 655, *pg.* 628
MPM - Stencil & Screen Printing Equipment - SPEEDLINE TECHNOLOGIES, INC.; *pg.* 1378, *pg.* 823
MPORT - Disposable Delivery Device - BAUSCH & LOMB INCORPORATED; *pg.* 1401, *pg.* 1045
MPOWER TOOLS - Software - ACD SYSTEMS INTERNATIONAL INC.; *pg.* 340, *pg.* 1913
MPS 17 - Flats Sorter - OPEX CORPORATION; *pg.* 450, *pg.* 1087
MPS 40 - Multiple Purpose Sorter - OPEX CORPORATION; *pg.* 450, *pg.* 1087
MPS 7 - Multi-Purpose Sorter - OPEX CORPORATION; *pg.* 450, *pg.* 1087
MPSO - Software - SAND TECHNOLOGY, INC.; *pg.* 465, *pg.* 1961
MPX - Software - CITRIX SYSTEMS, INC.; *pg.* 375, *pg.* 424
MPX - Inspection System - KLA-TENCOR CORPORATION; *pg.* 1353, *pg.* 146
MPZ - Apparels - UNDER ARMOUR, INC.; *pg.* 49, *pg.* 759
MQFX - Wireless Audio Solution - QSOUND LABS, INC.; *pg.* 666, *pg.* 1904
MQH - Sprayers - AG-MEIER INDUSTRIES LLC; *pg.* 700, *pg.* 1668
MQSYNTH - Audio System - QSOUND LABS, INC.; *pg.* 666, *pg.* 1904
MR-24 - Roof System - BUTLER MANUFACTURING COMPANY; *pg.* 72, *pg.* 981
MR & MRS T - Non-Carbonated Soft Drink - DR PEPPER SNAPPLE GROUP, INC.; *pg.* 250, *pg.* 1729
MR. APPLIANCE - Appliance Repair Businesses - THE DWYER GROUP, INC.; *pg.* 79, *pg.* 1748
MR. ATLAS - Health & Fitness Product - CHARLES ATLAS, LTD.; *pg.* 538, *pg.* 1211
MR. CLEAN - House Care Product - THE PROCTER & GAMBLE COMPANY; *pg.* 1129, *pg.* 1418
MR. CLEAN AUTODRY - Carwash System - THE PROCTER & GAMBLE COMPANY; *pg.* 1129, *pg.* 1418
MR. COFFEE - Coffee Makers - JARDEN CONSUMER SOLUTIONS; *pg.* 57, *pg.* 412
MR. ELECTRIC - Electrical Repair & Service Businesses - THE DWYER GROUP, INC.; *pg.* 79, *pg.* 1748
MR. GATTI'S - Pizza Franchise - MR. GATTI'S, LP; *pg.* 1741, *pg.* 1664
MR. GOODBAR - Chocolate Candy - THE HERSHEY CO.; *pg.* 1855, *pg.* 1538
MR. JOHNS-ON - Men's & Boys Thermal Underwear - INDERA MILLS COMPANY; *pg.* 26, *pg.* 1396
MR. METAL - Metal Polish - NORTHERN LABS, INC.; *pg.* 517, *pg.* 1869
MR. MISTY - Slush-type Drink - INTERNATIONAL DAIRY QUEEN, INC.; *pg.* 1732, *pg.* 938
MR. MOUTH - Toy & Game - HASBRO, INC.; *pg.* 954, *pg.* 1603
MR. MUSCLE - Cleaning Product - S.C. JOHNSON & SON, INC.; *pg.* 334, *pg.* 1889
MR. MXYZPTLK - Character - DC COMICS, INC.; *pg.* 1633, *pg.* 1221
MR. OIL - Lubricant - AMERICAN GREASE STICK CO.; *pg.* 971, *pg.* 902
MR. OTTOMAN - Furniture - ETHAN ALLEN INTERIORS INC.; *pg.* 924, *pg.* 343
MR. PENETRANT - Lubricant - AMERICAN GREASE STICK CO.; *pg.* 971, *pg.* 902
MR. PIBB - Regular & Diet Sodas - THE COCA-COLA COMPANY; *pg.* 240, *pg.* 493
MR. POTATO HEAD - Game - HASBRO, INC.; *pg.* 954, *pg.* 1603
MR. PROPER - Personal & Household Product - THE PROCTER & GAMBLE COMPANY; *pg.* 1129, *pg.* 1418
MR. PURE - Juice & Juice Based Products - NATIONAL BEVERAGE CORP.; *pg.* 257, *pg.* 425
MR. ROADSTER - Automobile Parts - SPEEDWAY MOTORS INC.; *pg.* 218, *pg.* 1012
MR. SAD SAM - Stuffed Toy - 1-800-FLOWERS.COM, INC.; *pg.* 1758, *pg.* 1151
MR SOFTEE - Shoe - AEROGROUP INTERNATIONAL, INC.; *pg.* 1803, *pg.* 1055
MR. TIRE - Auto Service - MONRO MUFFLER BRAKE, INC.; *pg.* 213, *pg.* 1336
MR. TRANSMISSION - Transmission Repair & Service Centers - MORAN INDUSTRIES, INC.; *pg.* 213, *pg.* 632
MR. YOSHIDA'S - Marinade & Cooking Sauces - THE KRAFT HEINZ COMPANY; *pg.* 870, *pg.* 1577
MR. ZIP - Extra Fine Graphite - AMERICAN GREASE STICK CO.; *pg.* 971, *pg.* 902
MR. ZIP GRAPHITE - Graphite - AMERICAN GREASE STICK CO.; *pg.* 971, *pg.* 902
MR. ZIP KABLE-EASE - Lubricant - AMERICAN GREASE STICK CO.; *pg.* 971, *pg.* 902
MRA - Copper Connectivity - CHANNELL COMMERCIAL CORP.; *pg.* 1870, *pg.* 291
MRA - Staffing Services - CROSS COUNTRY HEALTHCARE, INC.; *pg.* 1520, *pg.* 411
MRA - Pumps - IDEX CORPORATION; *pg.* 1347, *pg.* 623
MRA SEARCH - Staffing Services - CROSS COUNTRY HEALTHCARE, INC.; *pg.* 1520, *pg.* 411
MRAD - Hailing & Warning Device - LRAD CORPORATION; *pg.* 652, *pg.* 204
MRB - Copper Connectivity - CHANNELL COMMERCIAL CORP.; *pg.* 1870, *pg.* 291
MRC - Bearing - SKF USA; *pg.* 217, *pg.* 1535
MRC MONSTER ROLL CAGE - Simulator - ENVIRONMENTAL TECTONICS CORPORATION; *pg.* 1411, *pg.* 1587
MRD 2 - Degreaser & Cleaner - HILLYARD, INC.; *pg.* 331, *pg.* 990
MRF - Copper Connectivity - CHANNELL COMMERCIAL CORP.; *pg.* 1870, *pg.* 291
MRINNERVU - System for Magnetic Resonance - MEDRAD, INC.; *pg.* 1563, *pg.* 1591
MRN RADIO - Sport Radio Network - INTERNATIONAL SPEEDWAY CORPORATION; *pg.* 553, *pg.* 420
MRNA CATCHER - Molecular Biology Product - THERMO FISHER SCIENTIFIC INC.; *pg.* 1602, *pg.* 61
MRNA DIRECT - Molecular Biology Product - THERMO FISHER SCIENTIFIC INC.; *pg.* 1602, *pg.* 61
MRO - Industrial Coatings & Chemicals - SEYMOUR OF SYCAMORE, INC.; *pg.* 1447, *pg.* 663
MRP - Software - NIELSEN AUDIO; *pg.* 446, *pg.* 768
MRS. ADLER'S - Food Products - MANISCHEWITZ COMPANY; *pg.* 875, *pg.* 1097
MRS. BAIRD'S - Bakery - MRS. BAIRD'S BAKERIES, INC.; *pg.* 1860, *pg.* 1695
MRS. BUTTERWORTHS - Pancake Syrup - PINNACLE FOODS GROUP LLC; *pg.* 889, *pg.* 1104
MRS. FILBERT'S - Mayonnaise - THE C.F. SAUER COMPANY; *pg.* 847, *pg.* 1801
MRS. FRESHLEY'S - Food Product - FLOWERS FOODS, INC.; *pg.* 855, *pg.* 541
MRS. GOODCOOKIE - Cookie Products - J&J SNACK FOODS CORPORATION; *pg.* 865, *pg.* 1107
MRS. GRASS - Noodles - AMERICAN ITALIAN PASTA COMPANY; *pg.* 837, *pg.* 980
MRS. KINSER'S - Pimento Cheese Spread - RESER'S FINE FOODS INC.; *pg.* 1032, *pg.* 1496
MRS. O'LEARY'S BBQ - Nail Care Product - OPI PRODUCTS INC.; *pg.* 518, *pg.* 167
MRS. PAUL'S - Frozen Seafood - PINNACLE FOODS GROUP LLC; *pg.* 889, *pg.* 1104
MRS. RICHARDSON'S - Food Product - BALDWIN RICHARDSON FOODS COMPANY; *pg.* 1850, *pg.* 612
MRS. SMITH'S - Frozen Desserts - THE SCHWAN FOOD COMPANY; *pg.* 894, *pg.* 928
MRS. WEAVERS - Food Product - RESER'S FINE FOODS INC.; *pg.* 1032, *pg.* 1496
MRS. WEISS - Food Product - NEW WORLD PASTA COMPANY; *pg.* 885, *pg.* 1537
MRSASELECT - Software - BIO-RAD LABORATORIES, INC.; *pg.* 1504, *pg.* 101
MRS. T'S PIEROGIES - Food Product - ATEECO, INC.; *pg.* 838, *pg.* 1586
MRT - Heat-Shrinkable Closures - CHANNELL COMMERCIAL CORP.; *pg.* 1870, *pg.* 291
MRX - Bicycle Component - SRAM CORPORATION; *pg.* 967, *pg.* 590
MRX - Endothermic Atmosphere Gas Generators - SURFACE COMBUSTION, INC.; *pg.* 1077, *pg.* 1462
MS-10 MUDLINE SUSPENSION SYSTEMS - Mudline Equipment - DRIL-QUIP, INC.; *pg.* 1330, *pg.* 1704
MS-10A - Paper Drill - THE CHALLENGE MACHINERY COMPANY; *pg.* 1322, *pg.* 902
MS-15 MUDLINE SUSPENSION SYSTEMS - Mudline Equipment - DRIL-QUIP, INC.; *pg.* 1330, *pg.* 1704
MS-2000 (M) - Military Standard Distress Marker Light - ACR ELECTRONICS, INC.; *pg.* 612, *pg.* 422
MS-5 - Paper Drill - THE CHALLENGE MACHINERY COMPANY; *pg.* 1322, *pg.* 902

MS ANALYZER - Software System - MENTOR GRAPHICS CORPORATION; *pg.* 432, *pg.* 1510
MS ARCHITECT - Software System - MENTOR GRAPHICS CORPORATION; *pg.* 432, *pg.* 1510
MS-CA - Pumps - IDEX CORPORATION; *pg.* 1347, *pg.* 623
MS CONTIN - Pharmaceutical Product - ENDO PHARMACEUTICALS HOLDINGS, INC.; *pg.* 1528, *pg.* 1549
MS CONTIN - Pharmaceutical Product - PURDUE PHARMA LP; *pg.* 1587, *pg.* 377
MS END-CAP - Test Cap - OATEY SUPPLY CHAIN SERVICES; *pg.* 30, *pg.* 1433
MS-EXPRESS - Software System - MENTOR GRAPHICS CORPORATION; *pg.* 432, *pg.* 1510
MS. LITTLE GREEN MEN - Slots - INTERNATIONAL GAME TECHNOLOGY; *pg.* 957, *pg.* 1024
MS. UNDERSTOOD - Wall Decor - HERITAGE LACE INC.; *pg.* 694, *pg.* 711
M.S. WALKER - Premium Scotch - M.S. WALKER, INC.; *pg.* 1967, *pg.* 843
MS2 - Telecommunication Protected Entrance Terminal - 3M COMPANY; *pg.* 1142, *pg.* 956
MS2000B - Analog Modeled Synthesizer - KORG USA, INC.; *pg.* 556, *pg.* 1180
MS2000BR - Analog Modeled Rack - KORG USA, INC.; *pg.* 556, *pg.* 1180
MS257 - Spectrograph - NEWPORT CORPORATION; *pg.* 1424, *pg.* 114
MS750 - Navigation Aid - TRIMBLE NAVIGATION LIMITED; *pg.* 1384, *pg.* 288
MS860 - Navigation Aid - TRIMBLE NAVIGATION LIMITED; *pg.* 1384, *pg.* 288
MSA - Safety & Health Equipment - MINE SAFETY APPLIANCES COMPANY; *pg.* 1361, *pg.* 1525
MSC - Software - MSC SOFTWARE CORPORATION; *pg.* 441, *pg.* 262
MSC.ACUMEN - Software - MSC SOFTWARE CORPORATION; *pg.* 441, *pg.* 262
MSC.ADAMS - Software - MSC SOFTWARE CORPORATION; *pg.* 441, *pg.* 262
MSC.AFEA - Software - MSC SOFTWARE CORPORATION; *pg.* 441, *pg.* 262
MSC.AKUSMOD - Software - MSC SOFTWARE CORPORATION; *pg.* 441, *pg.* 262
MSC.AMS FVA - Software - MSC SOFTWARE CORPORATION; *pg.* 441, *pg.* 262
MSC.ASTROS - Software - MSC SOFTWARE CORPORATION; *pg.* 441, *pg.* 262
MSC.CATCMM - Software - MSC SOFTWARE CORPORATION; *pg.* 441, *pg.* 262
MSC.CONSTRUCT - Software - MSC SOFTWARE CORPORATION; *pg.* 441, *pg.* 262
MSC.DROPTEST - Software - MSC SOFTWARE CORPORATION; *pg.* 441, *pg.* 262
MSC.DYNAMIC DESIGNER - Software - MSC SOFTWARE CORPORATION; *pg.* 441, *pg.* 262
MSC.DYTRAN - Software - MSC SOFTWARE CORPORATION; *pg.* 441, *pg.* 262
MSC.EASY5 - Software - MSC SOFTWARE CORPORATION; *pg.* 441, *pg.* 262
MSC.ENTERPRISE MVISION - Software - MSC SOFTWARE CORPORATION; *pg.* 441, *pg.* 262
MSC.EXPLORE - Software - MSC SOFTWARE CORPORATION; *pg.* 441, *pg.* 262
MSC.FATIGUE - Software - MSC SOFTWARE CORPORATION; *pg.* 441, *pg.* 262
MSC.FEA - Software - MSC SOFTWARE CORPORATION; *pg.* 441, *pg.* 262
MSC.FLIGHTLOADS - Software - MSC SOFTWARE CORPORATION; *pg.* 441, *pg.* 262
MSC.GS-MESHER - Detector - MSC SOFTWARE CORPORATION; *pg.* 441, *pg.* 262
MSC.MARC - Software - MSC SOFTWARE CORPORATION; *pg.* 441, *pg.* 262
MSC.MARC MENTAT - Software - MSC SOFTWARE CORPORATION; *pg.* 441, *pg.* 262
MSC.MASTERKEY - Software - MSC SOFTWARE CORPORATION; *pg.* 441, *pg.* 262
MSC.MVISION - Software - MSC SOFTWARE CORPORATION; *pg.* 441, *pg.* 262
MSC.NASTRAN - Software - MSC SOFTWARE CORPORATION; *pg.* 441, *pg.* 262
MSC.NVH MANAGER - Software - MSC SOFTWARE CORPORATION; *pg.* 441, *pg.* 262
MSC.PATRAN - Software - MSC SOFTWARE CORPORATION; *pg.* 441, *pg.* 262
MSC.PATRAN LAMINATE - Software - MSC SOFTWARE CORPORATION; *pg.* 441, *pg.* 262
MSC.ROBUST DESIGN - Software - MSC SOFTWARE CORPORATION; *pg.* 441, *pg.* 262
MSC.SIMMANAGER - Software - MSC SOFTWARE CORPORATION; *pg.* 441, *pg.* 262
MSC.SIMXPERT - Software - MSC SOFTWARE CORPORATION; *pg.* 441, *pg.* 262
MSC.SOFY - Software - MSC SOFTWARE CORPORATION; *pg.* 441, *pg.* 262
MSC.SUPERFORGE - Software - MSC SOFTWARE CORPORATION; *pg.* 441, *pg.* 262
MSC.SUPERFORM - Software - MSC SOFTWARE CORPORATION; *pg.* 441, *pg.* 262
MSC.SUPERMODEL - Software - MSC SOFTWARE CORPORATION; *pg.* 441, *pg.* 262
MSC.TFEA - Software - MSC SOFTWARE CORPORATION; *pg.* 441, *pg.* 262
MSC.THERMAL - Software - MSC SOFTWARE CORPORATION; *pg.* 441, *pg.* 262
MSC.ULTIMA - Software - MSC SOFTWARE CORPORATION; *pg.* 441, *pg.* 262
MSC.VISUALNASTRAN - Software - MSC SOFTWARE CORPORATION; *pg.* 441, *pg.* 262
MSC.VISUALNASTRAN 4D - Software - MSC SOFTWARE CORPORATION; *pg.* 441, *pg.* 262
MSD - Maintenance Support Device Based on the TSC-750 - MILTOPE GROUP, INC.; *pg.* 440, *pg.* 6
MSD ICE - Maintenance Support Device for Internal Combustion Engines - MILTOPE GROUP, INC.; *pg.* 440, *pg.* 6
MSDN MAGAZINE - Magazine - UNITED BUSINESS MEDIA LLC; *pg.* 1697, *pg.* 1177
MSDS - Medical Device - NATUS MEDICAL INCORPORATED; *pg.* 1572, *pg.* 199
MSE - Seal - GREENE, TWEED & CO.; *pg.* 1344, *pg.* 1544
MSENDUR - Switchgear - C&D TECHNOLOGIES, INC.; *pg.* 627, *pg.* 1517
MSHATF - Training Centre - CAE INC.; *pg.* 226, *pg.* 1959
MSI STUDIO FOR CONFIGURATION MANAGER - Software - DELL SOFTWARE; *pg.* 385, *pg.* 40
MSIMON - Software System - MENTOR GRAPHICS CORPORATION; *pg.* 432, *pg.* 1510
MSIR - Medical Product - PURDUE PHARMA LP; *pg.* 1587, *pg.* 377
MSL - Muffler - AP EXHAUST PRODUCTS, INC.; *pg.* 199, *pg.* 1373
MSLAB - Software System - MENTOR GRAPHICS CORPORATION; *pg.* 432, *pg.* 1510
MSM - Skin Care Soap & Cream - AT LAST NATURALS, INC.; *pg.* 499, *pg.* 1347
MSM WITH MICROHYDRIN - Nutritional Product - RBC LIFE SCIENCES, INC.; *pg.* 1588, *pg.* 1723
MSM6100 - Chipset - QUALCOMM INCORPORATED; *pg.* 1873, *pg.* 207
MSM6225 - Chipset - QUALCOMM INCORPORATED; *pg.* 1873, *pg.* 207
MSM6250 - Chipset - QUALCOMM INCORPORATED; *pg.* 1873, *pg.* 207
MSM6300 - Chipset - QUALCOMM INCORPORATED; *pg.* 1873, *pg.* 207
MSM6500 - Chipset - QUALCOMM INCORPORATED; *pg.* 1873, *pg.* 207
MSM7500 - Chipset - QUALCOMM INCORPORATED; *pg.* 1873, *pg.* 207
MSNBC - Cable News - NBC UNIVERSAL, INC.; *pg.* 300, *pg.* 1266
MSP - Opthalmic Knives - SURGICAL SPECIALTIES CORPORATION; *pg.* 1600, *pg.* 1912
MSPB - Single Pin Bus - MAXIM INTEGRATED PRODUCTS, INC.; *pg.* 653, *pg.* 247
MSR MULTI - Health System Product - LANELABS USA INC.; *pg.* 1554, *pg.* 1128
MSSLITE - Electronic Device - LANTRONIX, INC.; *pg.* 426, *pg.* 112
MSTA - Mumps Skin Test Antigen, USP - SANOFI PASTEUR, INC; *pg.* 1591, *pg.* 1588
MSTAR - Systems Integration & Aeronautics - LOCKHEED MARTIN CORPORATION; *pg.* 229, *pg.* 762
MSVIEW - Software System - MENTOR GRAPHICS CORPORATION; *pg.* 432, *pg.* 1510
MSX INTERNATIONAL - Technical Business Service - MSX INTERNATIONAL, INC.; *pg.* 98, *pg.* 912
MT-11 MICROTORCH - Soldering Iron & Heat Tool - MASTER APPLIANCE CORP.; *pg.* 1055, *pg.* 1888
MT-11K MICROTORCH - Soldering Iron & Heat Tool - MASTER APPLIANCE CORP.; *pg.* 1055, *pg.* 1888
MT-13 - Epoxy Adhesive - SMOOTH-ON INC.; *pg.* 111, *pg.* 1528
MT-95K2 - 8-32 Channel Recorder - ASTRO-MED, INC.; *pg.* 619, *pg.* 1609
MT. BALDY - Bicycle Accessories - SPECIALIZED BICYCLE COMPONENTS, INC.; *pg.* 1711, *pg.* 152
MT EXPRESS - Integrated Home Network System - NORTEK, INC.; *pg.* 100, *pg.* 1607
MT. MCKINLEY PRINCESS LODGE - Hotel - PRINCESS TOURS; *pg.* 1920, *pg.* 1838
MT. SHASTA - Spring & Carbonated Water Products - NATIONAL BEVERAGE CORP.; *pg.* 257, *pg.* 425
MT. TRACK - Bicycle - TREK BICYCLE CORPORATION; *pg.* 1847, *pg.* 1896
MT. TRAIN - Bicycle - TREK BICYCLE CORPORATION; *pg.* 1847, *pg.* 1896
MT050 - Rainwear - CABELA'S INCORPORATED; *pg.* 535, *pg.* 1019
MTA BRIDGES & TUNNELS - Tolled Bridges & Tunnels in New York City - METROPOLITAN TRANSPORTATION AUTHORITY; *pg.* 1915, *pg.* 1260
MTA LONG ISLAND BUS - Buses in Nassau, Western Suffolk & Eastern Queens Counties - METROPOLITAN TRANSPORTATION AUTHORITY; *pg.* 1915, *pg.* 1260
MTA LONG ISLAND RAILROAD - Rail Lines in Nassau, Suffolk Counties & New York City - METROPOLITAN TRANSPORTATION AUTHORITY; *pg.* 1915, *pg.* 1260
MTA METRO-NORTH RAILROAD - Rail Lines - METROPOLITAN TRANSPORTATION AUTHORITY; *pg.* 1915, *pg.* 1260
MTA NEW YORK CITY TRANSIT - Subways & Buses in New York City - METROPOLITAN TRANSPORTATION AUTHORITY; *pg.* 1915, *pg.* 1260
MTB - Tactical Bi-Pod - MCNETT CORPORATION; *pg.* 1839, *pg.* 1817
MTC - Electronic Components - MOLEX INCORPORATED; *pg.* 655, *pg.* 628
MTI-2000 - Measuring System - MTI INSTRUMENTS INC.; *pg.* 658, *pg.* 1137
MTN 2000 - Automatic Conveyor System - PARAGON TECHNOLOGIES, INC.; *pg.* 1367, *pg.* 1528
MTOC - Systems Integration & Aeronautics - LOCKHEED MARTIN CORPORATION; *pg.* 229, *pg.* 762
MTP - Glass & Ceramic Material - CORNING INCORPORATED; *pg.* 1122, *pg.* 1154
MTPI - Software System - MENTOR GRAPHICS CORPORATION; *pg.* 432, *pg.* 1510
MTS-350 - Packaging Device - MTS MEDICATION TECHNOLOGIES, INC.; *pg.* 442, *pg.* 463
MTS-400 - Packaging Device - MTS MEDICATION TECHNOLOGIES, INC.; *pg.* 442, *pg.* 463
MTS-500 - Packaging Device - MTS MEDICATION TECHNOLOGIES, INC.; *pg.* 442, *pg.* 463
MTS BIONIX - Orthopaedic Product - MTS SYSTEMS CORPORATION; *pg.* 442, *pg.* 923
MTS INSIGHT - Testing System - MTS SYSTEMS CORPORATION; *pg.* 442, *pg.* 923
MTS LANDMARK - Servohydraulic Test System - MTS SYSTEMS CORPORATION; *pg.* 442, *pg.* 923
MTS TEST SUITE - Software - MTS SYSTEMS CORPORATION; *pg.* 442, *pg.* 923
MTX: MOTOTRAX - Game - ACTIVISION BLIZZARD, INC.; *pg.* 948, *pg.* 271
MTX9509 / MRX9509 TX/RX - Electronic Component - EMCORE CORPORATION; *pg.* 636, *pg.* 39
MTX9516 / MRX9516 TX/RX - Electronic Component - EMCORE CORPORATION; *pg.* 636, *pg.* 39
MTX9552 / MRX9552 TX/RX - Electronic Component - EMCORE CORPORATION; *pg.* 636, *pg.* 39
MU AND GO - Wireless Remote Control System - CONTROL CHIEF HOLDINGS, INC.; *pg.* 630, *pg.* 1518
MUC-X - Medical Product - UTAH MEDICAL PRODUCTS, INC.; *pg.* 1605, *pg.* 1752
MUCHACO - Mexican Food - TACO BUENO RESTAURANTS, L.P.; *pg.* 1753, *pg.* 1692
MUCHMORE - Standard Grade Controlled Label Prods. - IGA, INC.; *pg.* 1023, *pg.* 578
MUCHO DINERO - Slots - INTERNATIONAL GAME TECHNOLOGY; *pg.* 957, *pg.* 1024
MUCINEX - Expectorant - RECKITT BENCKISER INC.; *pg.* 1136, *pg.* 1105
MUD CAT - Auger Dredge - ELLICOTT DREDGES, LLC; *pg.*

1333, *pg.* 757
MUD CHEK - Drilling Product - SMITH INTERNATIONAL, INC.; *pg.* 1377, *pg.* 1715
MUD HOG - Hydraulic Axle - TUTHILL CORPORATION; *pg.* 1385, *pg.* 561
MUDBOX - Software - AUTODESK INC.; *pg.* 356, *pg.* 257
MUDD - Health & Beauty Product - CHATTEM, INC.; *pg.* 1515, *pg.* 1628
MUDD - Jeans - ICONIX BRAND GROUP, INC.; *pg.* 26, *pg.* 1243
MUDDY PIGS - Baby Care Product - MUNCHKIN, INC.; *pg.* 964, *pg.* 300
MUDDY WATERS TELECASTER - Electric Guitar - FENDER MUSICAL INSTRUMENTS CORPORATION; *pg.* 547, *pg.* 21
MUDLINE CONVERSION SYSTEMS - Mudline Equipment - DRIL-QUIP, INC.; *pg.* 1330, *pg.* 1704
MUDRA - DVD - GAIAM, INC.; *pg.* 1532, *pg.* 334
MUELLER - Hinged Knee Brace - ALIMED, INC.; *pg.* 1490, *pg.* 816
MUELLER - Furniture - HAWORTH, INC.; *pg.* 402, *pg.* 891
MUELLER - Process Solutions Provider - PAUL MUELLER COMPANY; *pg.* 706, *pg.* 1007
MUELLER GUARD - Protective Dental Guard - MUELLER SPORTS MEDICINE, INC.; *pg.* 1570, *pg.* 1887
MUELLER MATIC - Automatic Washing System - PAUL MUELLER COMPANY; *pg.* 706, *pg.* 1007
MUELLERGESIC - Mild Analgesic Ointment - MUELLER SPORTS MEDICINE, INC.; *pg.* 1570, *pg.* 1887
MUELLERHINGE - Protective Knee Brace - MUELLER SPORTS MEDICINE, INC.; *pg.* 1570, *pg.* 1887
MUELLERKOLD - Instant Ice Pack - MUELLER SPORTS MEDICINE, INC.; *pg.* 1570, *pg.* 1887
MUELLER'S - Pasta - AMERICAN ITALIAN PASTA COMPANY; *pg.* 837, *pg.* 980
MUFFLE MODULE - Noise Enclosures - AUTOMATION DEVICES, INC.; *pg.* 1315, *pg.* 1532
MUG - Root Beer - PEPSICO, INC.; *pg.* 259, *pg.* 1327
MUGABLES - Flower Arrangement - 1-800-FLOWERS.COM, INC.; *pg.* 1758, *pg.* 1151
MUGS N MORE - Heat Transfer Paper - NEENAH PAPER, INC.; *pg.* 1465, *pg.* 484
MUGS SHOP TIL YOU DROP - Games - PENN NATIONAL GAMING, INC.; *pg.* 574, *pg.* 1595
MUGSHOTS - Software - 3M; *pg.* 339, *pg.* 179
MUIR - Fabric - NEMSCHOFF, INC.; *pg.* 936, *pg.* 1890
MUIR BEACH - Bike - MARIN BIKES; *pg.* 1708, *pg.* 168
MUIR GLEN - Organic Food Products - GENERAL MILLS, INC.; *pg.* 828, *pg.* 933
MUIRWOODS - Bike - MARIN BIKES; *pg.* 1708, *pg.* 168
MUKLUKS - Slipper Sox - RELIABLE OF MILWAUKEE; *pg.* 698, *pg.* 1879
MUL-TEX - Buckwheat Food Product - THE BIRKETT MILLS; *pg.* 826, *pg.* 1321
THE MULBERRY - Home Floor Plan - JACOBSEN MANUFACTURING, INC.; *pg.* 1098, *pg.* 460
MULBERRY - Fabrics, Furniture & Wallcoverings - LEE JOFA, INC.; *pg.* 933, *pg.* 1142
MULE - Utility Vehicle - KAWASAKI MOTORS CORP., U.S.A.; *pg.* 1708, *pg.* 111
MULE - Unmanned Military Vehicle - LOCKHEED MARTIN CORPORATION; *pg.* 229, *pg.* 762
MULLEN - Mold-Tech Testers - STANDEX INTERNATIONAL CORPORATION; *pg.* 60, *pg.* 1039
MULLER - Light Equipment - TEREX CORPORATION; *pg.* 1381, *pg.* 384
MULLINAX - Car Dealerships - AUTONATION, INC.; *pg.* 165, *pg.* 423
MULT-E-POXY - Paint & Coating - DIAMOND VOGEL PAINT, INC.; *pg.* 1441, *pg.* 710
MULT-O - Machinery & Complete Binding Systems - STANDEX INTERNATIONAL CORPORATION; *pg.* 60, *pg.* 1039
MULTEEJET - Spray Nozzle - SPRAYING SYSTEMS CO.; *pg.* 1063, *pg.* 670
MULTI-ACTIVE - Personal Care Product - RBC LIFE SCIENCES, INC.; *pg.* 1588, *pg.* 1723
MULTI-AD CREATOR - Ad-Layout Software - MULTI-AD, INC.; *pg.* 1666, *pg.* 652
MULTI-AD SEARCH - Image Indexing Software - MULTI-AD, INC.; *pg.* 1666, *pg.* 652
MULTI-ALERT - Horns & Strobes - SYSTEM SENSOR; *pg.* 676, *pg.* 658
MULTI-ANALYST - Software - BIO-RAD LABORATORIES, INC.; *pg.* 1504, *pg.* 101
MULTI-AXIAL SIMULATION TABLE - Software - MTS SYSTEMS CORPORATION; *pg.* 442, *pg.* 923
MULTI-AXIS - Piping - CRANE CHEMPHARMA & ENERGY; *pg.* 1044, *pg.* 1382
MULTI-BETIC - Diabetic Vitamins & Supplements - AKORN; *pg.* 1488, *pg.* 1138
MULTI-BOOST - Beauty Product - AVON PRODUCTS, INC.; *pg.* 500, *pg.* 1198
MULTI-CAM - Cabinet - METPAR CORP.; *pg.* 97, *pg.* 1350
MULTI-CARD - Card Reader - LEXAR MEDIA, INC.; *pg.* 1262, *pg.* 146
MULTI-CHEM - Hose - HBD INDUSTRIES, INC.; *pg.* 207, *pg.* 1449
MULTI-CLEAN - Engine Treatment - MOC PRODUCTS COMPANY, INC.; *pg.* 332, *pg.* 174
MULTI CODE - Radio Frequency Components - NORTEK, INC.; *pg.* 100, *pg.* 1607
MULTI-COOLER - Sand Cooler - SIMPSON TECHNOLOGIES CORPORATION; *pg.* 111, *pg.* 555
MULTI-DENOMINATION - Casino Gaming System - INTERNATIONAL GAME TECHNOLOGY; *pg.* 957, *pg.* 1024
MULTI-DISTANCE HEADBAND LOUPE - Magnifier - EDROY PRODUCTS CO., INC.; *pg.* 1411, *pg.* 1318
MULTI-DOMES - High Fillable Dome - SCHOOL-TECH, INC.; *pg.* 1844, *pg.* 866
MULTI-DOSE - Packaging System - MTS MEDICATION TECHNOLOGIES, INC.; *pg.* 442, *pg.* 463
MULTI-E-PROXY - Paint & Coating - DIAMOND VOGEL PAINT, INC.; *pg.* 1441, *pg.* 710
MULTI EXTERNAL COANDA - Vent Tip - NAO, INC.; *pg.* 1074, *pg.* 1567
MULTI-FLAME - Burner Monitoring System - ECLIPSE INC.; *pg.* 1332, *pg.* 655
MULTI-FLO - Adapter - BECTON, DICKINSON & COMPANY; *pg.* 1501, *pg.* 1068
MULTI FLO - Fluid Handling System - GRACO, INC.; *pg.* 1342, *pg.* 935
MULTI FLUTE CHAMFER-SINK - Solid Carbide Combination Chamfer Countersink - REGAL BELOIT CORPORATION; *pg.* 106, *pg.* 1854
MULTI-FOUNTS - Plumbing Fixtures - BRADLEY CORPORATION; *pg.* 71, *pg.* 1870
MULTI-FUND - Variable Annuity Product - LINCOLN NATIONAL CORPORATION; *pg.* 776, *pg.* 1567
MULTI GRAIN CHEERIOS - Cereal - GENERAL MILLS, INC.; *pg.* 828, *pg.* 933
MULTI-GRIP - Primer - JONES-BLAIR COMPANY; *pg.* 1443, *pg.* 1682
MULTI-GUIDE II - Micro Implant System - STRYKER CORPORATION; *pg.* 1598, *pg.* 894
MULTI-HAND BLACKJACK - Video Poker - INTERNATIONAL GAME TECHNOLOGY; *pg.* 957, *pg.* 1024
MULTI JET MIX - Vent Tip - NAO, INC.; *pg.* 1074, *pg.* 1567
MULTI-KILL - Rodent Control - THE WOODSTREAM CORPORATION; *pg.* 1801, *pg.* 1549
MULTI-KLEAN - Industrial Cleaner - TEXAS REFINERY CORP.; *pg.* 986, *pg.* 1696
MULTI-KLEEN - Metal Cleaner - HEATBATH CORPORATION; *pg.* 1165, *pg.* 826
MULTI-KUT - File Product - SIMONDS INTERNATIONAL CORPORATION; *pg.* 1376, *pg.* 819
MULTI-LENS - Material - ROSCO LABORATORIES, INC.; *pg.* 1782, *pg.* 378
MULTI-LINK FRONTIER - Coronary Bifurcation Stent System - ABBOTT LABORATORIES; *pg.* 1484, *pg.* 551
MULTI-LINK MINI VISION - Stent System - ABBOTT LABORATORIES; *pg.* 1484, *pg.* 551
MULTI-LINK PIXEL - Stent System - ABBOTT LABORATORIES; *pg.* 1484, *pg.* 551
MULTI-LINK ULTRA - Stent System - ABBOTT LABORATORIES; *pg.* 1484, *pg.* 551
MULTI-LINK VISION - Stent System - ABBOTT LABORATORIES; *pg.* 1484, *pg.* 551
MULTI-LINK ZETA - Stent System - ABBOTT LABORATORIES; *pg.* 1484, *pg.* 551
MULTI-LOK - Ladder Product - WERNER HOLDING CO.; *pg.* 121, *pg.* 1534
MULTI-LON - Fluid Sealing Product - A.W. CHESTERTON COMPANY; *pg.* 1315, *pg.* 861
MULTI MAGIC - Game - WMS INDUSTRIES INC.; *pg.* 593, *pg.* 666
MULTI MARKER INDEX - Pharmaceutical Product - ALERE INC.; *pg.* 1488, *pg.* 849
MULTI-MAT - Plastic & Rubber - TEKNOR APEX COMPANY; *pg.* 1889, *pg.* 1605
MULTI-MATRIX TECHNOLOGY - Ophthalmic Technology - SIGNET ARMORLITE, INC.; *pg.* 1429, *pg.* 60
MULTI-MAX - Nutritional Product - NUTRACEUTICAL INTERNATIONAL CORPORATION; *pg.* 1576, *pg.* 1753
MULTI-MEDIA COMMAND - Software - ATEX MEDIA COMMAND, INC.; *pg.* 355, *pg.* 848
MULTI-MILE - Tire - TBC CORPORATION; *pg.* 1889, *pg.* 457
MULTI-MIX - Software - BIO-RAD LABORATORIES, INC.; *pg.* 1504, *pg.* 101
MULTI OPS - Flashlight - STREAMLIGHT INC.; *pg.* 1306, *pg.* 1527
MULTI-PAK - Robotic Product - HAMILTON CO., INC.; *pg.* 1415, *pg.* 1031
MULTI/PAK - Hydronic Baseboard - SLANT/FIN CORPORATION; *pg.* 1076, *pg.* 1163
MULTI-PAY PLUS - Video Slot Machine - WMS INDUSTRIES INC.; *pg.* 593, *pg.* 666
MULTI-PAY PLUS POKER - Game - WMS INDUSTRIES INC.; *pg.* 593, *pg.* 666
MULTI-PAY POKER - Game - WMS INDUSTRIES INC.; *pg.* 593, *pg.* 666
MULTI-PLIER - Multi-function Tool - GERBER LEGENDARY BLADES; *pg.* 1834, *pg.* 1503
MULTI-PLY - String - ASHAWAY LINE & TWINE MFG. CO.; *pg.* 1826, *pg.* 1600
MULTI-POWER - Cylinder - FABCO-AIR, INC.; *pg.* 1336, *pg.* 429
MULTI-PURGE - Thermoplastic Colorant & Additive - POLYONE CORPORATION; *pg.* 1177, *pg.* 1404
MULTI-PURPOSE - Primer - JONES-BLAIR COMPANY; *pg.* 1443, *pg.* 1682
MULTI-RAM FT-RAMAN - Analytical Device - BRUKER CORPORATION; *pg.* 1511, *pg.* 788
MULTI-RANGE - Test Equipment - SPX THERMAL PRODUCT SOLUTIONS; *pg.* 1378, *pg.* 1555
MULTI-RATIO - Mixer - MAXON CORPORATION; *pg.* 1359, *pg.* 695
MULTI-SCREEN MEDIA MEASUREMENT - Tagline - RENTRAK CORPORATION; *pg.* 306, *pg.* 1506
MULTI-SENSE - Meter - UVP, INC.; *pg.* 1434, *pg.* 298
MULTI-STAGE - Regulator - THE HARRIS PRODUCTS GROUP; *pg.* 1345, *pg.* 533
MULTI-STRIKE POKER - Video Poker - INTERNATIONAL GAME TECHNOLOGY; *pg.* 957, *pg.* 1024
MULTI-TAP - Electronic Components - MOLEX INCORPORATED; *pg.* 655, *pg.* 628
MULTI-THREAD - Connector - DRIL-QUIP, INC.; *pg.* 1330, *pg.* 1704
MULTI-TOUCH - Touchscreen Interface - APPLE INC.; *pg.* 350, *pg.* 73
MULTI-TRAK - Multiple Output Induction Power Supply - INDUCTOTHERM CORP.; *pg.* 1348, *pg.* 1114
MULTI-TREATMENT - Cooling System - MOC PRODUCTS COMPANY, INC.; *pg.* 332, *pg.* 174
MULTI-V - Sports Drink - ENERGY BRANDS, INC.; *pg.* 854, *pg.* 1227
MULTI-VENT - Door - LARSON MANUFACTURING COMPANY; *pg.* 93, *pg.* 1624
MULTI-VEST - Dental Product - DENTSPLY INTERNATIONAL INC.; *pg.* 1522, *pg.* 1596
MULTI-X - Riflescope - BUSHNELL OUTDOOR PRODUCTS, INC.; *pg.* 1403, *pg.* 718
MULTIACCESS - Communication Product - MULTI-TECH SYSTEMS INC.; *pg.* 442, *pg.* 951
MULTIBAR - Thermal Processing Equipment - SURFACE COMBUSTION, INC.; *pg.* 1077, *pg.* 1462
MULTIBOND - Bonding System - MACDERMID, INC.; *pg.* 1172, *pg.* 321
MULTIBONNET - Designed to Allow Repair of Bonnet Stem Packings on Active Propane Systems - ENGINEERED CONTROLS INTERNATIONAL LLC; *pg.* 1334, *pg.* 1372
MULTICARE - Medical Product - HOLOGIC, INC.; *pg.* 1416, *pg.* 784
MULTICHECK - Drug Interaction Feature - EPOCRATES, INC.; *pg.* 1529, *pg.* 254
MULTICIDE - Pesticide - MCLAUGHLIN GORMLEY KING COMPANY; *pg.* 1797, *pg.* 939
MULTICOAT - Thermal Spray Equipment - SULZER METCO (WESTBURY) INC.; *pg.* 1064, *pg.* 1350
MULTICODE - Radio Frequency Components - NORTEK SECURITY & CONTROL LLC; *pg.* 659, *pg.* 59
MULTICOLOR - Paper & Nonwoven Material - FIBERMARK INC.; *pg.* 1457, *pg.* 1764

First page reference indicates Business Class Edition
Second page reference indicates Geographic Edition

MULTICONNECT - Slot Management System - BALLY TECHNOLOGIES, INC.; *pg.* 531, *pg.* 1022
MULTICONNECT - Communication Product - MULTI-TECH SYSTEMS INC.; *pg.* 442, *pg.* 951
MULTICOPY - Storage Management Software - AVAGO TECHNOLOGIES; *pg.* 358, *pg.* 238
MULTICORE DONE RIGHT - Integrated Circuitry - AVAGO TECHNOLOGIES; *pg.* 358, *pg.* 238
MULTICORE PLUS - Software Development Kit - MERCURY COMPUTER SYSTEMS, INC.; *pg.* 434, *pg.* 813
MULTIDOC-IT - Imaging System - UVP, INC.; *pg.* 1434, *pg.* 298
MULTIFIRE - Conductor Paste - FERRO CORPORATION; *pg.* 1162, *pg.* 1462
MULTIFIRE - Burner - MAXON CORPORATION; *pg.* 1359, *pg.* 695
MULTIFIT - Foam - THE DOW CHEMICAL COMPANY; *pg.* 1157, *pg.* 898
MULTIFIT CONTOUR - Toothbrush - RANIR LLC; *pg.* 520, *pg.* 888
MULTIFLECTION - Accessories - UNDER ARMOUR, INC.; *pg.* 49, *pg.* 759
MULTIFLEX - Medical Device - HOSPIRA, INC.; *pg.* 1542, *pg.* 623
MULTIFLEX SERIES - Service Fittings - WIREMOLD/LEGRAND; *pg.* 689, *pg.* 383
MULTIFLO - Feed Delivery System or Conveying System - CTB INTERNATIONAL CORP.; *pg.* 850, *pg.* 695
MULTIFLOW - Flow Modifiers - CYTEC INDUSTRIES, INC.; *pg.* 1155, *pg.* 1131
MULTIFLOW - Fluid Handling System - GRACO, INC.; *pg.* 1342, *pg.* 935
MULTIFLOW - Pumps - IDEX CORPORATION; *pg.* 1347, *pg.* 623
MULTIFLUOR - Halogenated Hydrocarbon Fluids - AIR PRODUCTS AND CHEMICALS, INC.; *pg.* 1145, *pg.* 1513
MULTIFORM - Tablet - MULTISORB TECHNOLOGIES, INC.; *pg.* 1570, *pg.* 1150
MULTIFORM CSF - Flip-Top Desiccant Vial - MULTISORB TECHNOLOGIES, INC.; *pg.* 1570, *pg.* 1150
MULTIFUSE - Resettable Fuses - BOURNS, INC.; *pg.* 627, *pg.* 193
MULTIGARD - Gas Monitor - MINE SAFETY APPLIANCES COMPANY; *pg.* 1361, *pg.* 1525
MULTIGAS - Gas Analyzer - MKS INSTRUMENTS, INC.; *pg.* 1362, *pg.* 781
MULTIGRAIN - Snacks - SNYDER'S OF HANOVER, INC.; *pg.* 1862, *pg.* 1536
MULTIGRAPHICS - Pre-Press, Press, Post Press Equipment & Supplies - PRESSTEK, INC.; *pg.* 456, *pg.* 606
MULTIGRIP - Fitness Accessories - ALLIANCE SPORTS GROUP, L.P.; *pg.* 1825, *pg.* 1698
MULTIHORN - Toy Train - LIONEL LLC; *pg.* 961, *pg.* 875
MULTIKEY - Software - PHOENIX TECHNOLOGIES LTD.; *pg.* 454, *pg.* 147
MULTIKUT - Paper & Nonwoven Material - FIBERMARK INC.; *pg.* 1457, *pg.* 1764
MULTILOAD II - Pumps - IDEX CORPORATION; *pg.* 1347, *pg.* 623
MULTILOOK - Laminated Flooring - UNIBOARD CANADA INC.; *pg.* 117, *pg.* 1952
MULTIMASTER - Semicontinuous Vacuum Furnace - IPSEN INTERNATIONAL, INC.; *pg.* 1073, *pg.* 562
MULTIMATE - Mating Software - HOLSTEIN ASSOCIATION USA, INC.; *pg.* 143, *pg.* 1764
MULTIMATIC - Commercial Lighting - SWIVELIER CO., INC.; *pg.* 1307, *pg.* 1142
MULTIMAX - Movie Channel - HOME BOX OFFICE, INC.; *pg.* 290, *pg.* 1240
MULTIMAX - Calorimeter - METTLER-TOLEDO INTERNATIONAL INC.; *pg.* 1423, *pg.* 1441
MULTIMAXIR - Reaction Analysis - METTLER-TOLEDO INTERNATIONAL INC.; *pg.* 1423, *pg.* 1441
MULTIMEDIA - Flash Media - PNY TECHNOLOGIES, INC.; *pg.* 455, *pg.* 1105
MULTIMEDIA APPLICATION DEVELOPMENT PLATFORM - Mobile Solutions - SONUS NETWORKS INC.; *pg.* 1281, *pg.* 858
MULTIMEDIA CENTER - Software - ADVANCED MICRO DEVICES, INC.-MARKHAM; *pg.* 345, *pg.* 1922
MULTIMEDIACARD - Flash Card - HGST; *pg.* 406, *pg.* 260
MULTIMEK - Pipettor - BECKMAN COULTER, INC.; *pg.* 1402, *pg.* 48
MULTIMIGRADE - Storage Resources Software - AVAGO TECHNOLOGIES; *pg.* 358, *pg.* 238
MULTIMIRROR - Storage Resources Software - AVAGO TECHNOLOGIES; *pg.* 358, *pg.* 238
MULTIMOBILE - Communication Product - MULTI-TECH SYSTEMS INC.; *pg.* 442, *pg.* 951
MULTIMODE - Atomic Force Microscope - VEECO INSTRUMENTS INC.; *pg.* 1434, *pg.* 1322
MULTIMODEM - Communication Product - MULTI-TECH SYSTEMS INC.; *pg.* 442, *pg.* 951
MULTIMODEMDID - Communication Product - MULTI-TECH SYSTEMS INC.; *pg.* 442, *pg.* 951
MULTIMODEMDSVD - Communication Product - MULTI-TECH SYSTEMS INC.; *pg.* 442, *pg.* 951
MULTINEX - Respiration Gas Monitor - MAQUET; *pg.* 1558, *pg.* 1082
MULTIPLAN - Treatment Planning System - ACCURAY INCORPORATED; *pg.* 1486, *pg.* 282
MULTIPLANE - Navigation Aid - TRIMBLE NAVIGATION LIMITED; *pg.* 1384, *pg.* 288
MULTIPLATE - Software - BIO-RAD LABORATORIES, INC.; *pg.* 1504, *pg.* 101
MULTIPLATE - Wiper And Cleaning Cloth - GEORGIA-PACIFIC LLC; *pg.* 1458, *pg.* 507
MULTIPLATE - Flat & Laminated Glass - PPG INDUSTRIES, INC.; *pg.* 1445, *pg.* 1579
MULTIPLE LAUNCH ROCKET SYSTEM - Mobile Projectile Launch Platforms - LOCKHEED MARTIN CORPORATION; *pg.* 229, *pg.* 762
MULTIPLES - Professional Apparel - BARCO UNIFORMS, INC.; *pg.* 19, *pg.* 94
MULTIPLETE - Pharmaceutical Product - ALERE INC.; *pg.* 1488, *pg.* 849
MULTIPLEXED PROTEOMICS - Molecular Biology Product - THERMO FISHER SCIENTIFIC INC.; *pg.* 1602, *pg.* 61
MULTIPLEXER VS8394 - Video Surveillance - BOSCH SECURITY SYSTEMS, INC.; *pg.* 626, *pg.* 1158
MULTIPLEXING - Pump Product - IDEX CORPORATION; *pg.* 1347, *pg.* 623
MULTIPLIER BOOST - Game - WMS INDUSTRIES INC.; *pg.* 593, *pg.* 666
MULTIPOINT - Software - SYNOPSYS, INC.; *pg.* 480, *pg.* 162
MULTIPOLE - Electronics - CAMBRIDGE SOUNDWORKS, INC.; *pg.* 1234, *pg.* 781
MULTIPORT - Pressure Relief Valve Manifold for Large Storage Containers - ENGINEERED CONTROLS INTERNATIONAL LLC; *pg.* 1334, *pg.* 1372
MULTIPORT - Mercury System - MERCURY COMPUTER SYSTEMS, INC.; *pg.* 434, *pg.* 813
MULTIPORT DBU MODULE - Network Termination - ADTRAN, INC.; *pg.* 344, *pg.* 6
MULTIPREP - Adhesion - MACDERMID, INC.; *pg.* 1172, *pg.* 321
MULTIPRIME - Paint Primers - PPG INDUSTRIES, INC.; *pg.* 1445, *pg.* 1579
MULTIPRO ROTARY TOOLS - Electric Tools - DREMEL; *pg.* 1046, *pg.* 634
MULTIPROBE - Automated Liquid Handling System - PERKINELMER, INC.; *pg.* 1426, *pg.* 853
MULTIPULL - Collision Correction-Automotive - BEE LINE COMPANY; *pg.* 200, *pg.* 701
MULTIPULSE - HVAC Equipment - MESTEK, INC.; *pg.* 1074, *pg.* 857
MULTIPUMP - Pump - IDEX CORPORATION; *pg.* 1347, *pg.* 623
MULTIPURPOSE - Software - MTS SYSTEMS CORPORATION; *pg.* 442, *pg.* 923
MULTIQUAL - Clinical Diagnostic Product - BIO-RAD LABORATORIES, INC.; *pg.* 1504, *pg.* 101
MULTIREACH - Cable - COMMSCOPE, INC.; *pg.* 278, *pg.* 1378
MULTIREADER PLUS - Microplate Reader - IMMUCOR, INC.; *pg.* 1544, *pg.* 537
MULTISAURUS - Nutritional Product - NUTRACEUTICAL INTERNATIONAL CORPORATION; *pg.* 1576, *pg.* 1753
MULTISAVER - Paper Towel Dispenser - GEORGIA-PACIFIC LLC; *pg.* 1458, *pg.* 507
MULTISCAN - Gear-Pump Melters - NORDSON CORPORATION; *pg.* 1365, *pg.* 1480
MULTISCAN - Laser Product - ROFIN-SINAR TECHNOLOGIES, INC.; *pg.* 668, *pg.* 904
MULTISCRIM - Furniture - HERMAN MILLER, INC.; *pg.* 926, *pg.* 913
MULTISCRIPTOR - Multi-Channel Cardiac & Circulation Recorder - PPG INDUSTRIES, INC.; *pg.* 1445, *pg.* 1579
MULTISEAL - Soldering Iron & Heat Tool - MASTER APPLIANCE CORP.; *pg.* 1055, *pg.* 1888
MULTISERVICE ACCESS PLATFORM - Network Management System - TELLABS, INC.; *pg.* 678, *pg.* 637
MULTISERVICEPLUS - Software - TELLABS, INC.; *pg.* 678, *pg.* 637
MULTISHOT - Molecular Biology Product - THERMO FISHER SCIENTIFIC INC.; *pg.* 1602, *pg.* 61
MULTISHOX - Footwear - WOLVERINE WORLD WIDE, INC.; *pg.* 1822, *pg.* 905
MULTISITE GATEWAY - Biomolecule Product - THERMO FISHER SCIENTIFIC INC.; *pg.* 1602, *pg.* 61
MULTISIZER - Testing Instrument System - BECKMAN COULTER, INC.; *pg.* 1402, *pg.* 48
MULTISPECK - Molecular Probe Product - THERMO FISHER SCIENTIFIC INC.; *pg.* 1602, *pg.* 61
MULTISPOT - Software - BIO-RAD LABORATORIES, INC.; *pg.* 1504, *pg.* 101
MULTISTATE TRANSMISSIONS - Transmission Repair & Service Centers - MORAN INDUSTRIES, INC.; *pg.* 213, *pg.* 632
MULTISTORE - Software - NETAPP, INC.; *pg.* 444, *pg.* 287
MULTISUITE - Financial Services - FEDERAL HOME LOAN MORTGAGE CORPORATION; *pg.* 751, *pg.* 1790
MULTITEMP - HVAC Equipment - MESTEK, INC.; *pg.* 1074, *pg.* 857
MULTITRAN - Industrial Dual Arm Robots - BROOKS AUTOMATION, INC.; *pg.* 1320, *pg.* 813
MULTITUBE/SPIRAL-FLOW - Tubular Heat Exchanger - PAUL MUELLER COMPANY; *pg.* 706, *pg.* 1007
MULTIVALVE - Gas Product - ENGINEERED CONTROLS INTERNATIONAL LLC; *pg.* 1334, *pg.* 1372
MULTIVANTAGE - Telecommunication Product - AVAYA INC.; *pg.* 621, *pg.* 264
MULTIVARIABLE - Transmitter - EMERSON PROCESS MANAGEMENT ROSEMOUNT INC.; *pg.* 1334, *pg.* 920
MULTIVERSE CHASSIS - Multi-Card Chassis - EMCORE CORPORATION; *pg.* 636, *pg.* 39
MULTIVERSE DTCR - Enclosure - EMCORE CORPORATION; *pg.* 636, *pg.* 39
MULTIVIEW - Storage Resources Software - AVAGO TECHNOLOGIES; *pg.* 358, *pg.* 238
MULTIVITA - Beverages - THE COCA-COLA COMPANY; *pg.* 240, *pg.* 493
MULTIVOIP - Communication Product - MULTI-TECH SYSTEMS INC.; *pg.* 442, *pg.* 951
MULTIVOLT - Interface - ALTERA CORPORATION; *pg.* 348, *pg.* 237
MULTIVU - Newspaper - PR NEWSWIRE ASSOCIATION LLC; *pg.* 1678, *pg.* 1283
MULTIWALL - High Pressure Layered Vessel - TEI STRUTHERS WELLS; *pg.* 1381, *pg.* 1590
MULTIWAVE - Optical Networking System - CIENA CORPORATION; *pg.* 628, *pg.* 771
MULTIWAVE METRO - Optical Networking System - CIENA CORPORATION; *pg.* 628, *pg.* 771
MULTIWAVE METRO ONE - Optical Networking System - CIENA CORPORATION; *pg.* 628, *pg.* 771
MULTIWAVE SENTRY - Optical Networking System - CIENA CORPORATION; *pg.* 628, *pg.* 771
MULTIWHISTLE - Toy Train - LIONEL LLC; *pg.* 961, *pg.* 875
MULTUM - Drug, Herbal & Nutraceutical Database - CERNER CORPORATION; *pg.* 1514, *pg.* 981
MULTVIEW - Graphics Card - ADVANCED MICRO DEVICES, INC.; *pg.* 613, *pg.* 282
MUMM VSOP COGNAC - Cognac - DIAGEO CANADA, INC.; *pg.* 1961, *pg.* 1937
MUMMY RUMMY - Game - GAMEWRIGHT; *pg.* 953, *pg.* 836
MUMZ - Software - BIO-RAD LABORATORIES, INC.; *pg.* 1504, *pg.* 101
MUNCHETTES - Containers with Easy-Lift Tabs - RUBBERMAID HOME PRODUCTS; *pg.* 1138, *pg.* 1453
MUNCHIE BASKETS - Baskets - CARLISLE FOODSERVICE PRODUCTS INCORPORATED; *pg.* 1455, *pg.* 1485
MUNCHKIN - Children's Dress Shoes - THE STRIDE RITE CORPORATION; *pg.* 1820, *pg.* 828
MUNCHOS - Potato Crisps - FRITO-LAY NORTH AMERICA, INC.; *pg.* 1853, *pg.* 1730
MUNCHOS - Potato Crisps - PEPSICO, INC.; *pg.* 259, *pg.* 1327
MUNCK - Electric Wire Rope Hoists & Cranes - AMERICAN CRANE & EQUIPMENT CORPORATION; *pg.* 1312, *pg.* 1526
MUNDIAL - Wireless Control Product - UNIVERSAL ELECTRONICS, INC.; *pg.* 683, *pg.* 262
MUNICH - Furniture - AMISCO INDUSTRIES LTD.; *pg.* 913,

pg. 1958
MUNISING LP - Paper - NEENAH PAPER, INC.; *pg.* 1465, *pg.* 484
MUNIVIEW - Interactive Data Tool - INTERACTIVE DATA PRICING & REFERENCE DATA, INC.; *pg.* 769, *pg.* 785
MUNSINGWEAR - Casual Clothing - PERRY ELLIS INTERNATIONAL, INC.; *pg.* 45, *pg.* 445
MUNSINGWEAR - Knit Golf Shirts - RIVER'S END TRADING COMPANY; *pg.* 47, *pg.* 1867
MUPPETS - Puppet Characters - THE WALT DISNEY COMPANY; *pg.* 317, *pg.* 52
MURAL - Fabric - NEMSCHOFF, INC.; *pg.* 936, *pg.* 1890
MURATEC - Digital Office Equipment - MURATEC AMERICA, INC.; *pg.* 443, *pg.* 1733
MURCO - Petroleum Products in the United Kingdom - MURPHY OIL CORPORATION; *pg.* 982, *pg.* 31
MURDER MYSTERY PARTY - Game - UNIVERSITY GAMES CORPORATION; *pg.* 969, *pg.* 230
MUREK - Wallcovering - OMNOVA SOLUTIONS INC; *pg.* 1176, *pg.* 1453
MURESCO - Paint And Stain Product - BENJAMIN MOORE & CO.; *pg.* 1440, *pg.* 1085
MURF - Audio Solution - VIQ SOLUTIONS INC.; *pg.* 490, *pg.* 1905
MURIEL - Clothing - ABERCROMBIE & FITCH CO.; *pg.* 37, *pg.* 1466
MURIEL - Domestic Cigars - ALTADIS USA, INC.; *pg.* 1893, *pg.* 423
MURIEL - Fabric - SCALAMANDRE, INC.; *pg.* 941, *pg.* 1058
MURINE - Healthcare Product - PRESTIGE BRANDS HOLDINGS, INC.; *pg.* 520, *pg.* 1345
MURO-128 - Pharmaceutical Product - BAUSCH & LOMB INCORPORATED; *pg.* 1401, *pg.* 1045
MURPHY - Household Care Product - COLGATE-PALMOLIVE COMPANY; *pg.* 504, *pg.* 1215
MURPHY - Character - CONSTELLATION; *pg.* 1938, *pg.* 373
MURPHY - Furniture - JASPER GROUP; *pg.* 930, *pg.* 691
MURPHY - Beds - MURPHY BED CO., INC.; *pg.* 935, *pg.* 1159
MURPHY AND MYRTLE - Educational Materials - SCHOLASTIC INC.; *pg.* 1683, *pg.* 1288
MURPHY USA - Gasoline in the United States - MURPHY OIL CORPORATION; *pg.* 982, *pg.* 31
MURRAY - Food Product - KELLOGG COMPANY; *pg.* 831, *pg.* 870
MURRAY - Electrical Distribution & Circuit Protection - SIEMENS PROCESS INDUSTRIES AND DRIVES; *pg.* 673, *pg.* 485
MURRAY AND TREGURTHA - Marine Propulsion & Steering System - HARBORMASTER MARINE, INC.; *pg.* 1707, *pg.* 896
MURRAY SUGAR FREE - Cookies - KELLOGG COMPANY; *pg.* 831, *pg.* 870
MURREY - Sporting Good Product - ESCALADE INC.; *pg.* 1833, *pg.* 678
MURRIETA'S WELL WINERY - Winery - WENTE VINEYARDS; *pg.* 1972, *pg.* 122
MUSART - Web Application - EOLAS TECHNOLOGIES, INC.; *pg.* 1243, *pg.* 573
MUSASHI - Sports Nutrition - POST HOLDINGS, INC.; *pg.* 833, *pg.* 1002
MUSCLE & FITNESS - Magazine - AMERICAN MEDIA, INC.; *pg.* 1615, *pg.* 410
MUSCLE MASS - Vitamin & Herbal Supplement - SOURCE NATURALS; *pg.* 1595, *pg.* 278
MUSCLE MILK - Protein Supplement - CYTOSPORT, INC.; *pg.* 1018, *pg.* 45
MUSCLE MILK LIGHT - Protein Supplement - CYTOSPORT, INC.; *pg.* 1018, *pg.* 45
MUSCLE MILK 'N OATS - Protein Supplement - CYTOSPORT, INC.; *pg.* 1018, *pg.* 45
MUSCLE MILK NATURALS - Protein Supplement - CYTOSPORT, INC.; *pg.* 1018, *pg.* 45
MUSCLE MILK REFUEL - Protein Supplement - CYTOSPORT, INC.; *pg.* 1018, *pg.* 45
MUSCLE MILK TETRA - Protein Supplement - CYTOSPORT, INC.; *pg.* 1018, *pg.* 45
MUSCLE TEE - Clothing - K-SWISS; *pg.* 1837, *pg.* 306
MUSCLECAR ENTHUSIAST - Magazine - AMOS PRESS, INC.; *pg.* 1616, *pg.* 1472
MUSE - Web Application - EOLAS TECHNOLOGIES, INC.; *pg.* 1243, *pg.* 573
MUSE - Fabric - NEMSCHOFF, INC.; *pg.* 936, *pg.* 1890
MUSE - Pharmaceutical Product - VIVUS, INC.; *pg.* 1608, *pg.* 163
MUSEE - Tile - ARTISTIC TILE INC.; *pg.* 914, *pg.* 1119
MUSEUM - Furniture - AMERICAN LEATHER LP; *pg.* 912, *pg.* 1673
MUSEUM - Paintbrushes - MARTIN/F. WEBER COMPANY; *pg.* 962, *pg.* 1567
MUSEUM OF EARLY SOUTHERN DECORATIVE ARTS - Museum - OLD SALEM, INCORPORATED; *pg.* 572, *pg.* 1395
MUSHROOMS - Leather Slides - HABAND COMPANY, INC.; *pg.* 1772, *pg.* 1099
MUSIC - Solderless Terminal - MOLEX INCORPORATED; *pg.* 655, *pg.* 628
MUSIC + INNOVATION - Tagline - MEGATRAX PRODUCTION MUSIC, INC.; *pg.* 297, *pg.* 167
MUSIC & MEDIA - Magazine in Amsterdam; Directories - NIELSEN BUSINESS MEDIA; *pg.* 1671, *pg.* 1272
MUSIC BOOKS & MORE - Online Retail Ordering Services - MUSICNOTES, INC.; *pg.* 1268, *pg.* 1866
MUSIC CIRCUS - Musical Theater Production - CALIFORNIA MUSICAL THEATRE CORPORATION; *pg.* 536, *pg.* 196
MUSIC GO ROUND - Musical Instrument Stores - WINMARK CORPORATION; *pg.* 1792, *pg.* 946
MUSIC IN THE KEY OF A2 - Slogan - ANN ARBOR SYMPHONY ORCHESTRA; *pg.* 529, *pg.* 865
MUSIC MAN - Guitar - ERNIE BALL INC.; *pg.* 1768, *pg.* 68
MUSIC MAP - Digital Directory - ROVI CORPORATION; *pg.* 463, *pg.* 269
MUSIC PATHWAYS - Music Publisher - CARL FISCHER, LLC; *pg.* 1625, *pg.* 1209
MUSIC PLUS - Satellite Delivered Services - MOOD MEDIA; *pg.* 298, *pg.* 1616
MUSIC VIDEO CONFERENCE AWARDS - Business Information Services - NIELSEN BUSINESS MEDIA; *pg.* 1671, *pg.* 1272
MUSICAL AMERICA INTERNATIONAL - Performing Arts Directory - JOC GROUP INC.; *pg.* 1654, *pg.* 1096
THE MUSICAL INSTRUMENT MEGASTORE - Slogan - SAM ASH MUSIC CORPORATION; *pg.* 669, *pg.* 1167
MUSICAL TOILETTE PLUS - Musical Toilet Trainer & Step Stool - DOREL JUVENILE GROUP, INC.; *pg.* 923, *pg.* 676
MUSICNOTES - Computer Software - MUSICNOTES, INC.; *pg.* 1268, *pg.* 1866
MUSICSHOP - Computer Programs - GIBSON GUITAR CORP.; *pg.* 550, *pg.* 1650
MUSICSOFT - Software for Use in the Yamaha Clavinova Digital Piano - YAMAHA CORPORATION OF AMERICA; *pg.* 595, *pg.* 51
MUSICTESTER - Software - NIELSEN AUDIO; *pg.* 446, *pg.* 768
MUSICWORKS - Speaker - CAMBRIDGE SOUNDWORKS, INC.; *pg.* 1234, *pg.* 781
MUSICYO GEAR - Musical Instrument - GIBSON GUITAR CORP.; *pg.* 550, *pg.* 1650
MUSICYO.COM - Online Musical Instrument Store - GIBSON GUITAR CORP.; *pg.* 550, *pg.* 1650
MUSK SPLASH - Hair & Skin Product - AUBREY ORGANICS INC.; *pg.* 499, *pg.* 470
THE MUSKEGON CHRONICLE - Newspaper - MLIVE MEDIA GROUP; *pg.* 1665, *pg.* 888
MUSKOKA - Flooring Product - TEMBEC INC.; *pg.* 114, *pg.* 1957
MUSKRAT - Knife - BUCK KNIVES, INC.; *pg.* 1828, *pg.* 550
MUSKY MASTER - Braided Fishing Line - CORTLAND LINE COMPANY; *pg.* 1831, *pg.* 1155
MUSSELMAN'S - Apple Products - KNOUSE FOODS COOPERATIVE INC.; *pg.* 869, *pg.* 1558
MUST. HAVE. WHEAT THINS. - Wheat Thins Slogan - MONDELEZ INTERNATIONAL, INC.; *pg.* 878, *pg.* 601
MUSTANG - Tractor Mowers - AG-MEIER INDUSTRIES LLC; *pg.* 700, *pg.* 1668
MUSTANG - Herbicide - DOW AGROSCIENCES LLC; *pg.* 1156, *pg.* 684
MUSTANG - Footwear - EASTLAND SHOE CORPORATION; *pg.* 1808, *pg.* 750
MUSTANG - Insecticide - FMC CORPORATION; *pg.* 1163, *pg.* 1564
MUSTANG - Skid Steer Loader - GEHL COMPANY; *pg.* 1339, *pg.* 1899
MUSTANG - Floor Cleaning Product - NSS ENTERPRISES, INC.; *pg.* 59, *pg.* 1476
MUSTANG - Capsule & Cartridge - PALL CORPORATION; *pg.* 232, *pg.* 1323
MUSTANG - Copolyester - PLASKOLITE, INC.; *pg.* 1888, *pg.* 1443
MUSTANG ENTHUSIAST - Magazine - AMOS PRESS, INC.; *pg.* 1616, *pg.* 1472
MUSTANG MAX - Insecticide - FMC CORPORATION; *pg.* 1163, *pg.* 1564
MUSTANG MAX EC - Insecticides & Miticides - FMC CORPORATION; *pg.* 1163, *pg.* 1564
MUSTANG MAX EW - Insecticides & Miticides - FMC CORPORATION; *pg.* 1163, *pg.* 1564
MUSTARD LOVERS - Mustard - PLOCHMAN, INC.; *pg.* 890, *pg.* 631
MUSTEE - Laundry Cabinet - E.L. MUSTEE & SONS, INC.; *pg.* 1124, *pg.* 1430
MUTA-GENE - Software - BIO-RAD LABORATORIES, INC.; *pg.* 1504, *pg.* 101
MUTANT FREAKS - Doll - MGA ENTERTAINMENT, INC.; *pg.* 964, *pg.* 300
MUTTSY - Bear - GUND, INC.; *pg.* 954, *pg.* 1056
MUTUAL SERIES - Mutual Funds - FRANKLIN RESOURCES, INC.; *pg.* 760, *pg.* 254
MUX/DUX - Fiber Optic Component - OPLINK COMMUNICATIONS, INC.; *pg.* 660, *pg.* 91
MUXIT - Interface Integrated Circuits - TEXAS INSTRUMENTS INCORPORATED; *pg.* 679, *pg.* 1688
MUXLINK - Electronic Components - MOLEX INCORPORATED; *pg.* 655, *pg.* 628
MUZAK - Satellite Delivered Instrumental Music - MOOD MEDIA; *pg.* 298, *pg.* 1616
MUZZLE - Security & Law Enforcement Products - MACE SECURITY INTERNATIONAL, INC.; *pg.* 1172, *pg.* 1541
MUZZLE CANINE - Personal Defense Sprays - MACE SECURITY INTERNATIONAL, INC.; *pg.* 1172, *pg.* 1541
MV-396 - Electronic Components - MOLEX INCORPORATED; *pg.* 655, *pg.* 628
MV-52 - Automatic Gear Burnishing System - GLEASON - M&M PRECISION SYSTEMS CORPORATION; *pg.* 1341, *pg.* 1479
MV AGUSTA - Motorcycle - HARLEY-DAVIDSON, INC.; *pg.* 178, *pg.* 1874
MVB - Stuffed Dog - GUND, INC.; *pg.* 954, *pg.* 1056
MVBASE - Multi Dimensional Database Solution - TIGERLOGIC CORPORATION; *pg.* 484, *pg.* 117
MVDESIGNER - Multi Dimensional Database Solution - TIGERLOGIC CORPORATION; *pg.* 484, *pg.* 117
MVENTERPRISE - Multi Dimensional Database Solution - TIGERLOGIC CORPORATION; *pg.* 484, *pg.* 117
MVISION DATABANKS - Software - MSC SOFTWARE CORPORATION; *pg.* 441, *pg.* 262
MVO - Relay Lens - EDMUND INDUSTRIAL OPTICS INC.; *pg.* 1411, *pg.* 1041
MVOA-R - Attenuator - OPLINK COMMUNICATIONS, INC.; *pg.* 660, *pg.* 91
MVOA-T3 - Attenuator - OPLINK COMMUNICATIONS, INC.; *pg.* 660, *pg.* 91
MVP - Self-Closing Faucets - THE CHICAGO FAUCET COMPANY; *pg.* 1044, *pg.* 606
MVP - Folding Wheelchair - INVACARE CORPORATION; *pg.* 1546, *pg.* 1451
MVP - Cam Locks - MEDECO HIGH SECURITY LOCKS, INC.; *pg.* 1055, *pg.* 1806
MVP GIS - Geographic Data Access Application - THOMSON REUTERS TAX & ACCOUNTING; *pg.* 484, *pg.* 905
MVP JR. - Folding Wheelchair - INVACARE CORPORATION; *pg.* 1546, *pg.* 1451
MVP TAX - Property Tax Assessment Software - THOMSON REUTERS TAX & ACCOUNTING; *pg.* 484, *pg.* 905
MVP.COM - Sport Media - CBS SPORTSLINE.COM, INC.; *pg.* 1234, *pg.* 423
MVS - Conveyor Belting - FENNER DRIVES; *pg.* 1336, *pg.* 1551
MVS-8000 - Machine Vision System - COGNEX CORPORATION; *pg.* 1406, *pg.* 834
MW - Watches - FOSSIL GROUP, INC.; *pg.* 5, *pg.* 1735
MW MICHELE - Watch - FOSSIL GROUP, INC.; *pg.* 5, *pg.* 1735
MWDMG1315 - Electronic Component - OPLINK COMMUNICATIONS, INC.; *pg.* 660, *pg.* 91
MWDMG1315/1513 - Fiber Optic Component - OPLINK COMMUNICATIONS, INC.; *pg.* 660, *pg.* 91
MWDMG13CS - Fiber Optic Component - OPLINK COMMUNICATIONS, INC.; *pg.* 660, *pg.* 91
MWDMG1415/1514 - Fiber Optic Component - OPLINK COMMUNICATIONS, INC.; *pg.* 660, *pg.* 91
MWDMG1514 - Electronic Component - OPLINK COMMUNICATIONS, INC.; *pg.* 660, *pg.* 91
MWDMG1598 - Fiber Optic Component - OPLINK COMMUNICATIONS, INC.; *pg.* 660, *pg.* 91

MWDMG6470/7064 - Fiber Optic Component - OPLINK COMMUNICATIONS, INC.; *pg.* 660, *pg.* 91
MWDMGCL - Electronic Component - OPLINK COMMUNICATIONS, INC.; *pg.* 660, *pg.* 91
MWDMGCR/CB - Fiber Optic Component - OPLINK COMMUNICATIONS, INC.; *pg.* 660, *pg.* 91
MWDMGCSU - Fiber Optic Component - OPLINK COMMUNICATIONS, INC.; *pg.* 660, *pg.* 91
MWDMGFTTX - Fiber Optic Component - OPLINK COMMUNICATIONS, INC.; *pg.* 660, *pg.* 91
MWDMGLR/LB - Fiber Optic Component - OPLINK COMMUNICATIONS, INC.; *pg.* 660, *pg.* 91
MWDMGLSU - Fiber Optic Component - OPLINK COMMUNICATIONS, INC.; *pg.* 660, *pg.* 91
MWT - Premium Wall Tubing - CHANNELL COMMERCIAL CORP.; *pg.* 1870, *pg.* 291
MX - Pump - IDEX CORPORATION; *pg.* 1347, *pg.* 623
MX - Software - INFORMATICA CORPORATION; *pg.* 414, *pg.* 190
MX - Electronic Components - MOLEX INCORPORATED; *pg.* 655, *pg.* 628
MX - Goggles - OAKLEY, INC.; *pg.* 1840, *pg.* 86
MX - Methanol Dissociators - SURFACE COMBUSTION, INC.; *pg.* 1077, *pg.* 1462
MX - Hardware - VERIFONE SYSTEMS, INC.; *pg.* 487, *pg.* 251
MX-250 - Electronic Components - MOLEX INCORPORATED; *pg.* 655, *pg.* 628
MX 2800 - Power Supply - ADTRAN, INC.; *pg.* 344, *pg.* 6
MX-4 - Manual Folding Wheelchair - INVACARE CORPORATION; *pg.* 1546, *pg.* 1451
MX CONNECT - Drilling Product - SMITH INTERNATIONAL, INC.; *pg.* 1377, *pg.* 1715
MX DIRECT - Drilling Product - SMITH INTERNATIONAL, INC.; *pg.* 1377, *pg.* 1715
MX LOCATE - Drilling Product - SMITH INTERNATIONAL, INC.; *pg.* 1377, *pg.* 1715
MX O FRAME - Goggles - OAKLEY, INC.; *pg.* 1840, *pg.* 86
MX-PLUS - Electronic Components - MOLEX INCORPORATED; *pg.* 655, *pg.* 628
MX-RPO - Patient Handling Equipment - STRYKER CORPORATION; *pg.* 1598, *pg.* 894
MX SELECT - Drilling Product - SMITH INTERNATIONAL, INC.; *pg.* 1377, *pg.* 1715
MX120 - Electronic Components - MOLEX INCORPORATED; *pg.* 655, *pg.* 628
MX150 - Electronic Components - MOLEX INCORPORATED; *pg.* 655, *pg.* 628
MX150L - Electronic Components - MOLEX INCORPORATED; *pg.* 655, *pg.* 628
MX2 - Software - INFORMATICA CORPORATION; *pg.* 414, *pg.* 190
MX250 - Smoke Detector - BOSCH SECURITY SYSTEMS, INC.; *pg.* 626, *pg.* 1158
MX280 - Smoke Detector - BOSCH SECURITY SYSTEMS, INC.; *pg.* 626, *pg.* 1158
MX2800 - M13/STS-1 Multiplexer - ADTRAN, INC.; *pg.* 344, *pg.* 6
MX64 - Electronic Components - MOLEX INCORPORATED; *pg.* 655, *pg.* 628
MXENERGY SAVERSGUIDE - Online Service - CONSTELLATION; *pg.* 1938, *pg.* 373
MXENERGY WIZARD - Energy Promotion - CONSTELLATION; *pg.* 1938, *pg.* 373
MXII - Electronic Components - MOLEX INCORPORATED; *pg.* 655, *pg.* 628
MXL - Drivelines - MERITOR, INC.; *pg.* 212, *pg.* 911
MXL-38999 - Electronic Components - MOLEX INCORPORATED; *pg.* 655, *pg.* 628
MXM - Printed Plastic Product - TRANSILWRAP COMPANY, INC.; *pg.* 1470, *pg.* 613
MXOS - Software System - ALCATEL-LUCENT; *pg.* 615, *pg.* 1094
MXRAIL - Software - BENTLEY SYSTEMS, INC.; *pg.* 361, *pg.* 1531
MXRENEW - Software - BENTLEY SYSTEMS, INC.; *pg.* 361, *pg.* 1531
MXROAD - Software - BENTLEY SYSTEMS, INC.; *pg.* 361, *pg.* 1531
MXSITE - Software - BENTLEY SYSTEMS, INC.; *pg.* 361, *pg.* 1531
MXT - Metal Detector - WHITE'S ELECTRONICS; *pg.* 688, *pg.* 1509
MXURBAN - Software - BENTLEY SYSTEMS, INC.; *pg.* 361, *pg.* 1531
MY 1 SCOOTER - Scooter - RADIO FLYER INC.; *pg.* 966, *pg.* 588
MY BEAUTIFUL NAILS - Nailcare Product - MEDICOOL, INC.; *pg.* 1562, *pg.* 294
MY BOOK - Hard Drive - WESTERN DIGITAL CORPORATION; *pg.* 492, *pg.* 118
MY BOOK ESSENTIAL EDITION - Hard Drive - WESTERN DIGITAL CORPORATION; *pg.* 492, *pg.* 118
MY BOOK HOME EDITION - Hard Drive - WESTERN DIGITAL CORPORATION; *pg.* 492, *pg.* 118
MY BOOK MIRROR EDITION - Hard Drive - WESTERN DIGITAL CORPORATION; *pg.* 492, *pg.* 118
MY BOOK OFFICE EDITION - Hard Drive - WESTERN DIGITAL CORPORATION; *pg.* 492, *pg.* 118
MY BOOK STUDIO EDITION - Hard Drive - WESTERN DIGITAL CORPORATION; *pg.* 492, *pg.* 118
MY BOOK WORLD EDITION - Hard Drive - WESTERN DIGITAL CORPORATION; *pg.* 492, *pg.* 118
MY CAFE - Electric Beverage Makers - BUNN-O-MATIC CORPORATION; *pg.* 53, *pg.* 661
MY-CATH - Touch-Free Self Catheter - MEDLINE INDUSTRIES, INC.; *pg.* 1562, *pg.* 635
MY CLIPPER.COM - Internet Coupons - CLIPPER MAGAZINE INC.; *pg.* 1628, *pg.* 1555
MY COMMUNITY MY BANK - Slogan - COMMUNITY WEST BANCSHARES; *pg.* 741, *pg.* 99
MY CREDENTIAL FOR ADOBE - Online Transaction Security Product - VERISIGN, INC.; *pg.* 488, *pg.* 1799
MY-D HAN-D - All Tillage & Seed Cleaner - MY-D HAN-D MFG. INC.; *pg.* 706, *pg.* 714
MY DAILY VEGGIES - Health System Product - LANELABS USA INC.; *pg.* 1554, *pg.* 1128
MY DAILY VISITOR - Newsletter - OUR SUNDAY VISITOR, INC.; *pg.* 1673, *pg.* 682
MY DAY - Golf Club - KARSTEN MANUFACTURING CORPORATION; *pg.* 1838, *pg.* 17
MY DEFENSE - Nutritional Product - NATROL, INC.; *pg.* 1570, *pg.* 64
MY DOG - Dog Food - MARS, INCORPORATED; *pg.* 1858, *pg.* 1792
MY DVR EXPANDER - Hard Drive - WESTERN DIGITAL CORPORATION; *pg.* 492, *pg.* 118
MY EBAY - Online Services - EBAY INC.; *pg.* 1240, *pg.* 243
MY FAVORITE MUFFIN - Restaurant - BAB, INC.; *pg.* 1715, *pg.* 599
MY FAVORITE MULTIPLE - Nutritional Product - NATROL, INC.; *pg.* 1570, *pg.* 64
MY FIRST - Baby Care Product - MUNCHKIN, INC.; *pg.* 964, *pg.* 300
MY FIRST CAMERA - Cameras - EASTMAN KODAK COMPANY; *pg.* 1408, *pg.* 1333
MY FIRST COLGATE - Children's Toothbrush - COLGATE-PALMOLIVE COMPANY; *pg.* 504, *pg.* 1215
MY FIRST HELLO READER! - Educational Materials - SCHOLASTIC INC.; *pg.* 1683, *pg.* 1288
MY FIRST LEAPPAD - Learning System - LEAPFROG ENTERPRISES, INC.; *pg.* 961, *pg.* 84
MY FIRST READ-ALONG - Children's Books - THE WALT DISNEY COMPANY; *pg.* 317, *pg.* 52
MY FIRST STEPS TO LEARNING - Educational Materials - SCHOLASTIC INC.; *pg.* 1683, *pg.* 1288
MY FIRST STEPS TO READING - Educational Materials - SCHOLASTIC INC.; *pg.* 1683, *pg.* 1288
MY FIRST UNO - Card Game - MATTEL, INC.; *pg.* 962, *pg.* 81
MY FUN CARDS - Online Services - IAC/INTERACTIVECORP; *pg.* 292, *pg.* 1242
MY GLOVEBOX - Vehicle History & Services Website - ASHLAND INC.; *pg.* 972, *pg.* 726
MY H-E-B TEXAS LIFE - Recipe - H-E-B; *pg.* 1022, *pg.* 1740
MY HEALTH MANAGER FROM MEDICA - Health Plan & Publication - MEDICA, INC.; *pg.* 1208, *pg.* 949
MY HEINZ - ketchup Bottles - THE KRAFT HEINZ COMPANY; *pg.* 870, *pg.* 1577
MY HOME MY EARTH - Homebuilding Services - KB HOME; *pg.* 90, *pg.* 134
MY INSURANCE CENTER - Software - MAJESCO; *pg.* 429, *pg.* 1089
MY ISLANDS - Women's Cologne - THE GILLETTE COMPANY; *pg.* 509, *pg.* 795
MY KIND OF BROWN - Nail Care Product - OPI PRODUCTS INC.; *pg.* 518, *pg.* 167
MY LAZARE DIAMOND - Diamonds - LAZARE KAPLAN INTERNATIONAL, INC.; *pg.* 8, *pg.* 1250
MY LIFE ACCORDING TO ME - Educational Materials - SCHOLASTIC INC.; *pg.* 1683, *pg.* 1288
MY LIFE.MY CANCER.MY TREATMENT - Tagline - CELL THERAPEUTICS, INC.; *pg.* 1514, *pg.* 1834
MY LITTLE KITCHEN FAIRIES - Home & Garden Products - ENESCO, LLC; *pg.* 1124, *pg.* 620
MY LITTLE PONY - Toys - FUNRISE TOY CORP.; *pg.* 549, *pg.* 300
MY LITTLE PONY - Game - HASBRO, INC.; *pg.* 954, *pg.* 1603
MY LOVELY FEET - Nailcare Product - MEDICOOL, INC.; *pg.* 1562, *pg.* 294
MY MEDICA - Health Plan & Publication - MEDICA, INC.; *pg.* 1208, *pg.* 949
MY MICHELLE - Junior Dresses & Sportswear - KELLWOOD COMPANY; *pg.* 28, *pg.* 975
MY NAME IS AMERICA - Educational Materials - SCHOLASTIC INC.; *pg.* 1683, *pg.* 1288
MY OWN LEARNING LEAP - Educational Toys - LEAPFROG ENTERPRISES, INC.; *pg.* 961, *pg.* 84
MY PASSPORT ELITE - Hard Drive - WESTERN DIGITAL CORPORATION; *pg.* 492, *pg.* 118
MY PASSPORT ESSENTIAL - Hard Drive - WESTERN DIGITAL CORPORATION; *pg.* 492, *pg.* 118
MY PASSPORT STUDIO - Hard Drive - WESTERN DIGITAL CORPORATION; *pg.* 492, *pg.* 118
MY RECIPES - Media Publication - TIME INC.; *pg.* 1693, *pg.* 1300
MY RED CARRYING CASE - Educational Product - BARKER CREEK PUBLISHING INC.; *pg.* 1619, *pg.* 1818
MY RED SORT 'N STORE CASE - Educational Product - BARKER CREEK PUBLISHING INC.; *pg.* 1619, *pg.* 1818
MY RICH UNCLE - Video Slots - INTERNATIONAL GAME TECHNOLOGY; *pg.* 957, *pg.* 1024
MY SCENE - Fashion Dolls & Accessories - MATTEL, INC.; *pg.* 962, *pg.* 81
MY SIZE - Towels - ORCHIDS PAPER PRODUCTS COMPANY; *pg.* 1465, *pg.* 1488
MY SONIC - Card - SONIC CORP.; *pg.* 1750, *pg.* 1487
MY SORT 'N STORE 5-PACK - Educational Product - BARKER CREEK PUBLISHING INC.; *pg.* 1619, *pg.* 1818
MY STEP - Stroller Entry Feature - EVENFLO COMPANY, INC.; *pg.* 924, *pg.* 1470
MY STYLE - Home Design Center - CALATLANTIC GROUP, INC.; *pg.* 1084, *pg.* 108
MY SWEET REVENGE - Health System Product - LANELABS USA INC.; *pg.* 1554, *pg.* 1128
MY-T-FINE - Food Product - THE JEL SERT COMPANY; *pg.* 865, *pg.* 668
MY-T-KLEEN - Pre-Treatment Cleaner - A BRITE COMPANY; *pg.* 1144, *pg.* 1697
MY TATTOO - Labeling Software - INTEGRATED SOFTWARE DESIGN, INC.; *pg.* 416, *pg.* 830
MY TIVO GETS ME - Tagline - TIVO INC.; *pg.* 313, *pg.* 251
MY TRAVELHOST - Social Networking Services - TRAVELHOST, INC.; *pg.* 1696, *pg.* 1689
MY TV GUIDE - Digital Directory - ROVI CORPORATION; *pg.* 463, *pg.* 269
MY WELLNESS REWARDS - Nutritional Supplement - PHARMAVITE LLC; *pg.* 1584, *pg.* 167
MY WHEY - Nutritional Product - NUTRACEUTICAL INTERNATIONAL CORPORATION; *pg.* 1576, *pg.* 1753
MY YAHOO! - Internet Services - YAHOO! INC.; *pg.* 1289, *pg.* 289
MYADEC - Vitamin & Mineral Supplement - MCNEIL-PPC, INC.; *pg.* 1560, *pg.* 1533
MYADVENT - Browser-Based Portal - ADVENT SOFTWARE, INC.; *pg.* 345, *pg.* 211
MYBEACHBODY - Online Premium Diet & Support Club - BEACHBODY, LLC; *pg.* 271, *pg.* 272
MYBIZ - Wireless Communication System - AT&T SOUTHEAST; *pg.* 1868, *pg.* 489
MYBUSINESSTRAVEL.COM - Business Travel Resource - SMARTER TRAVEL MEDIA LLC; *pg.* 1687, *pg.* 801
MYCALLER - Software - ONMOBILE LIVE, INC.; *pg.* 449, *pg.* 829
MYCAPTURE - Digital Video Product - HAUPPAUGE DIGITAL, INC.; *pg.* 402, *pg.* 1164
MYCAPTURE II - Video Product - HAUPPAUGE DIGITAL, INC.; *pg.* 402, *pg.* 1164
MYCASEPTIC - Animal Safety Product - NEOGEN CORPORATION; *pg.* 883, *pg.* 896
MYCELEX - Medicine - BAYER HEALTHCARE CONSUMER CARE DIVISION; *pg.* 1500, *pg.* 1087
MYCELX - Pipe - ADVANCED DRAINAGE SYSTEMS, INC.; *pg.* 1878, *pg.* 1455

MYCHOICE - Rewards Program - PINNACLE ENTERTAINMENT, INC.; pg. 576, pg. 1029
MYCMDB - Computer Software - NOVELL INC.; pg. 446, pg. 852
MYCOBOVIS - Bovine Respiratory Vaccine - PFIZER INC.; pg. 1581, pg. 1278
MYCOBUTIN - Medicine - PFIZER INC.; pg. 1581, pg. 1278
MYCOCURE - Pharmaceutical Product - ALVA/AMCO PHARMACAL COMPANIES, INC.; pg. 1492, pg. 637
MYCOFLUOR - Molecular Probe Product - THERMO FISHER SCIENTIFIC INC.; pg. 1602, pg. 61
MYCOGEN - Seeds - DOW AGROSCIENCES LLC; pg. 1156, pg. 684
MYCONOS - Rug - COURISTAN INC.; pg. 921, pg. 1067
MYCOOP - Software - TELECOMMUNICATION SYSTEMS INC.; pg. 483, pg. 754
MYCOPLASMA DUO - Software - BIO-RAD LABORATORIES, INC.; pg. 1504, pg. 101
MYCOPLUS - Bovine Respiratory Vaccine - PFIZER INC.; pg. 1581, pg. 1278
MYCOSTATIN - Antifungal Antibiotic used for Treatment of Vulvovaginal Candidiasis - BRISTOL-MYERS SQUIBB U.S. PHARMACEUTICAL GROUP; pg. 1511, pg. 1110
MYCOSURE - Bovine Respiratory Vaccine - PFIZER INC.; pg. 1581, pg. 1278
MYCRO - Distributed Control Systems - SIEMENS PROCESS INDUSTRIES AND DRIVE; pg. 1376, pg. 1587
MYCRO ADVANTAGE - Industrial Instrumentation - SIEMENS PROCESS INDUSTRIES AND DRIVE; pg. 1376, pg. 1587
MYCROMESH - Biomaterial - W.L. GORE & ASSOCIATES, INC.; pg. 122, pg. 388
MYCYCLER - Thermal Cycler - BIO-RAD LABORATORIES, INC.; pg. 1504, pg. 101
MYELO-NATE - Neonatal/Pediatric Luber Puncture Kit - UTAH MEDICAL PRODUCTS, INC.; pg. 1605, pg. 1752
MYELOMASCAN - Antibody - IMMUNOMEDICS, INC.; pg. 1544, pg. 1087
MYERS - Processed Frozen Entrees & Soups - HANOVER FOODS CORPORATION; pg. 861, pg. 1535
MYER'S GOLDEN RICH - Jamaican Rum - DIAGEO CANADA, INC.; pg. 1961, pg. 1937
MYER'S ORIGINAL DARK - Jamaican Rum - DIAGEO CANADA, INC.; pg. 1961, pg. 1937
MYER'S PLATINUM WHITE - Jamaican Rum - DIAGEO CANADA, INC.; pg. 1961, pg. 1937
MYERS TIRE SUPPLY - Tire Repair & Underbody Service Equipment, Tools & Supplies - MYERS INDUSTRIES, INC.; pg. 1887, pg. 1402
MYEXTRA! - Presentation Services - ATTACHMATE CORPORATION; pg. 356, pg. 1833
MYEXTRA! SMART CONNECTOR ENTERPRISE EDITION - Non-invasive, Programmatic Legacy Integration Solution - ATTACHMATE CORPORATION; pg. 356, pg. 1833
MYFI - Satellite Radio - DELPHI AUTOMOTIVE LLP; pg. 204, pg. 910
MYFICO - Credit Scoring Service - FAIR ISAAC CORPORATION; pg. 1247, pg. 955
MYGREENS - Magazine - DOLE FRESH VEGETABLES; pg. 854, pg. 198
MYHAVERTYS - Software - HAVERTY FURNITURE COMPANIES, INC.; pg. 926, pg. 509
MYIQ - Detection System - BIO-RAD LABORATORIES, INC.; pg. 1504, pg. 101
MYITFORUM.COM - Website - TECHTARGET, INC.; pg. 482, pg. 837
MYJOYS - Shoes - ACUSHNET COMPANY; pg. 1824, pg. 818
MYKEYNOTE - Computer Services - KEYNOTE SYSTEMS INCORPORATED; pg. 425, pg. 255
MYKON - Wallcovering - OMNOVA SOLUTIONS INC; pg. 1176, pg. 1453
MYKONOS - Footwear - STEVEN MADDEN, LTD.; pg. 1819, pg. 1176
MYKOSIL - Specialty Chemicals - OMNOVA SOLUTIONS INC; pg. 1176, pg. 1453
MYKOSOFT - Specialty Chemicals - OMNOVA SOLUTIONS INC; pg. 1176, pg. 1453
MYLAM - Online Support - LAM RESEARCH CORPORATION; pg. 1354, pg. 91
MYLANTA - Healthcare Product - JOHNSON & JOHNSON; pg. 1549, pg. 1091
MYLAR - Reinforced Tab and Hole - AMERICAN THERMOPLASTIC COMPANY; pg. 349, pg. 1573
MYLAR - Film - E.I. DU PONT DE NEMOURS & COMPANY; pg. 1159, pg. 390
MYLAR - Medical Device - OLIVER PRODUCTS COMPANY INC.; pg. 1367, pg. 888
MYLAR - Plastic Film - TEKRA CORPORATION; pg. 1184, pg. 1884
MYLAUNCH - Internet Services - YAHOO! INC.; pg. 1289, pg. 289
MYLICON - Healthcare Product - JOHNSON & JOHNSON; pg. 1549, pg. 1091
MYLOTARG - Cancer Treatment Pharmaceutical Preparation - PFIZER INC.; pg. 1581, pg. 1278
MYMEDICA - Health Plan & Publication - MEDICA, INC.; pg. 1208, pg. 949
MYMENTOR - Online Solution - MEDASSETS INC.; pg. 1561, pg. 484
MYOCHRYSINE - Pharmaceutical Product - AKORN, INC.; pg. 1488, pg. 622
MYOHIOWINE.COM - Wine Connoisseur Magazine - GREAT LAKES PUBLISHING COMPANY; pg. 1646, pg. 1431
MYOKO - Personal Care Prods. - THE GILLETTE COMPANY; pg. 500, pg. 795
MYORANGECOUNTY.COM - Website - FREEDOM COMMUNICATIONS, INC.; pg. 1643, pg. 110
MYOSSAGE - Lotion - ALIMED, INC.; pg. 1490, pg. 816
MYOSSAGE - Orthopedic Device - DJO SURGICAL; pg. 1525, pg. 1661
MYOVIEW - Medical Device - GE HEALTHCARE TECHNOLOGIES; pg. 1533, pg. 1897
MYOZYME - Lysosomal Storage Disorder - GENZYME CORPORATION; pg. 1534, pg. 808
MYPOINTS - Internet Service - UNITED ONLINE, INC.; pg. 1286, pg. 308
MYPULTE - Building Construction Services - PULTEGROUP, INC.; pg. 1109, pg. 873
MYRAH - Footwear - STEVEN MADDEN, LTD.; pg. 1819, pg. 1176
MYRI - Chemical Product - SPECTRUM CHEMICALS & LABORATORY PRODUCTS, INC.; pg. 1181, pg. 94
MYRIAD - Board-Level Product - MERCURY COMPUTER SYSTEMS, INC.; pg. 434, pg. 813
MYRIADE - Hose - THE GOODYEAR TIRE & RUBBER COMPANY; pg. 1883, pg. 1401
MYRIDE.COM - Online Car-Buying Site - AUTOBYTEL INC.; pg. 1230, pg. 107
MYRISK - Insurance - FACTORY MUTUAL INSURANCE COMPANY; pg. 1199, pg. 1601
MYRO - Home Improvement Products - HOMAX PRODUCTS INC.; pg. 1442, pg. 1817
MYROAM - Software - IRON MOUNTAIN INCORPORATED; pg. 421, pg. 796
MYRTLE - Furniture - HAWORTH, INC.; pg. 402, pg. 891
MYSEARCH - Search Website - IAC SEARCH & MEDIA, INC.; pg. 1257, pg. 171
MYSIMON - Consumer Products Comparison Shopping Website - CBS INTERACTIVE, INC.; pg. 369, pg. 215
MYSITE - Internet Service - UNITED ONLINE, INC.; pg. 1286, pg. 308
MYSKY PLUS - Multi-Media Tool - MEADE INSTRUMENTS CORPORATION; pg. 1422, pg. 113
MYSOLINE - Pharmaceutical Product - IMPAX LABORATORIES, INC.; pg. 1544, pg. 101
MYSOLINE - Pharmaceutical Product - LANNETT COMPANY, INC.; pg. 1555, pg. 1566
MYSOTROL - Wound Drainage Container Holder - DERMA SCIENCES, INC.; pg. 1523, pg. 1111
MYSTAIRE - Medical Device - MISONIX INC.; pg. 1568, pg. 1159
MYSTERE - Show And Ticket - CIRQUE DU SOLEIL INC.; pg. 540, pg. 1954
MYSTERIES OF THE UNKNOWN - Book Series - DIRECT HOLDINGS AMERICAS INC.; pg. 1636, pg. 1780
MYSTERIOUS PRESS - Books - HBG BOOKS, INC.; pg. 1648, pg. 1238
MYSTERY DATE - Toy & Game - HASBRO, INC.; pg. 954, pg. 1603
MYSTERY MIXINS - Yogurt Additives - THE DANNON COMPANY, INC.; pg. 851, pg. 1351
MYSTERY SENTENCES - Educational Materials - SCHOLASTIC INC.; pg. 1683, pg. 1288
MYSTIC - Women's Fragrance - MARILYN MIGLIN, L.P.; pg. 516, pg. 581
MYSTIC - Bicycle - TREK BICYCLE CORPORATION; pg. 1847, pg. 1896
MYSTIC - Potato Chips - UTZ QUALITY FOODS, INC.; pg. 907, pg. 1536
MYSTIC WHITE - Pool Sand - U.S. SILICA COMPANY; pg. 1185, pg. 1849
MYSTIC WOODS - Decorative Fragrance - AROMATIQUE INC.; pg. 499, pg. 32
MYSTICAL DRAGON - Game - WMS INDUSTRIES INC.; pg. 593, pg. 666
MYSTICAL FORTUNES - Game - WMS INDUSTRIES INC.; pg. 593, pg. 666
MYSTICAL LOTUS - Game - WMS INDUSTRIES INC.; pg. 593, pg. 666
MYSTICAL MERMAID PARTY - Video Game - INTERNATIONAL GAME TECHNOLOGY; pg. 957, pg. 1024
MYSTICAL MERMAIDS - Video Slots - INTERNATIONAL GAME TECHNOLOGY; pg. 957, pg. 1024
MYSTICAL PRINCESS - Video Game - INTERNATIONAL GAME TECHNOLOGY; pg. 957, pg. 1024
MYSTICAL ROSE - Video Game - INTERNATIONAL GAME TECHNOLOGY; pg. 957, pg. 1024
MYSTICAL SWORDS - Video Game - INTERNATIONAL GAME TECHNOLOGY; pg. 957, pg. 1024
MYSTICAL WIZARD - Video Game - INTERNATIONAL GAME TECHNOLOGY; pg. 957, pg. 1024
MYSTIK - Lubricants - CITGO PETROLEUM CORPORATION; pg. 974, pg. 1703
MYSTIQUE - Rug - COURISTAN INC.; pg. 921, pg. 1067
MYSTIQUE - Dental Product - DENTSPLY INTERNATIONAL INC.; pg. 1522, pg. 1596
MYSTIQUE - Lace Curtain - HERITAGE LACE INC.; pg. 694, pg. 711
MYSTIQUE - Dinnerware - THE HOMER LAUGHLIN CHINA COMPANY; pg. 1125, pg. 1850
MYSTIQUE - Sturdilite Floodlight - PHOENIX PRODUCTS COMPANY; pg. 1304, pg. 1879
MYSTO-GRIP - Felt - AMERICAN FELT & FILTER COMPANY; pg. 1312, pg. 1184
MYSTORAGE - Computer Software - AVAGO TECHNOLOGIES; pg. 358, pg. 238
MYSYMBOLCARE - Services - MOTOROLA ENTERPRISE MOBILITY; pg. 441, pg. 1167,
MYTH - Personal & Household Product - THE PROCTER & GAMBLE COMPANY; pg. 1129, pg. 1418
MYTHICAL BEASTS - Bath Product - KOHLER CO.; pg. 91, pg. 1862
MY.TI - Online Database - TEXAS INSTRUMENTS INCORPORATED; pg. 679, pg. 1688
MYTRACK - Online Trading & Real Time Quotes, News & Fundamental Data - TRACK DATA CORPORATION; pg. 1284, pg. 1147
MYTRACK PRO - Customizable Exchange Quotation System - TRACK DATA CORPORATION; pg. 1284, pg. 1147
MYTV - Digital Video Product - HAUPPAUGE DIGITAL, INC.; pg. 402, pg. 1164
MYTV/FM - Video Product - HAUPPAUGE DIGITAL, INC.; pg. 402, pg. 1164
MYTV2GO - Video Product - HAUPPAUGE DIGITAL, INC.; pg. 402, pg. 1164
MYTV.PVR - Digital Video Product - HAUPPAUGE DIGITAL, INC.; pg. 402, pg. 1164
MYVIDEO - Digital Video Product - HAUPPAUGE DIGITAL, INC.; pg. 402, pg. 1164
MYVIDEOSTORE.COM - Website - INGRAM ENTERTAINMENT INC.; pg. 292, pg. 1639
MYVIEW - Software - BROCADE COMMUNICATIONS SYSTEMS, INC.; pg. 365, pg. 239
MYWAY - Web Portal - IAC SEARCH & MEDIA, INC.; pg. 1257, pg. 171
MYWEBSEARCH - Search Website - IAC SEARCH & MEDIA, INC.; pg. 1257, pg. 171
MYWORKSTYLE - Computer Services - COMPUTER SCIENCES CORPORATION; pg. 378, pg. 1780
MYX FUSIONS - Fruit Juice Infused Alcoholic Beverage - MYX BEVERAGES LLC; pg. 257, pg. 1263
MZP - Electronic Components - MOLEX INCORPORATED; pg. 655, pg. 628

N

N-COMMAND - Networking Products - ADTRAN, INC.; pg. 344, pg. 6
N-DULGENT - Chair - NEUTRAL POSTURE, INC.; pg. 939, pg. 1669
N-DURE - Furniture - NEUTRAL POSTURE, INC.; pg. 939, pg. 1669
N-FLORAL - Scarves - STEVEN MADDEN, LTD.; pg. 1819,

First page reference indicates Business Class Edition
Second page reference indicates Geographic Edition

pg. 1176
N-FORM - Web-Based Network Management - ADTRAN, INC.; *pg.* 344, *pg.* 6
N. GARCIAPARRA SERIES - Batting Glove - HILLERICH & BRADSBY CO., INC.; *pg.* 1836, *pg.* 576
N-GENEOUS HDL - Diagnostic Product - GENZYME CORPORATION; *pg.* 1534, *pg.* 808
N-HANCE - Polymer - HERCULES INCORPORATED; *pg.* 1166, *pg.* 392
N-HANCEMENTS - Seating Accessories - NEUTRAL POSTURE, INC.; *pg.* 939, *pg.* 1669
N. K. HURST - Dried Bean Prods. - N.K. HURST CO., INC.; *pg.* 886, *pg.* 689
N-LITE - Lawn Care Product - GARDENS ALIVE!, INC.; *pg.* 1796, *pg.* 693
N-PEACE - Scarves - STEVEN MADDEN, LTD.; *pg.* 1819, *pg.* 1176
N-POINT - Chemical Product - SPECTRUM CHEMICALS & LABORATORY PRODUCTS, INC.; *pg.* 1181, *pg.* 94
N-R-G-FLOR - Infloor Wiring System - WIREMOLD/LEGRAND; *pg.* 689, *pg.* 383
'N RAGE - Hair Care Product - AMERICAN INTERNATIONAL INDUSTRIES COMPANY; *pg.* 498, *pg.* 126
N-SERVE - Nitrogen Stabilizer - THE DOW CHEMICAL COMPANY; *pg.* 1157, *pg.* 898
N-SHAPE - Networking Products - ADTRAN, INC.; *pg.* 344, *pg.* 6
N-SIDE - Chair - NEUTRAL POSTURE, INC.; *pg.* 939, *pg.* 1669
N-SPECT - Networking Products - ADTRAN, INC.; *pg.* 344, *pg.* 6
N-TIDIED - Scarves - STEVEN MADDEN, LTD.; *pg.* 1819, *pg.* 1176
N-TUNE - Seating System - NEUTRAL POSTURE, INC.; *pg.* 939, *pg.* 1669
N-TYPE - Hot Air Balloon - CAMERON BALLOONS U.S.; *pg.* 1829, *pg.* 884
N-WELL PIXEL - Image Sensor Product - CYPRESS SEMICONDUCTOR CORPORATION; *pg.* 1326, *pg.* 243
N ZIMES - Food Enzyme Product - NATIONAL ENZYME COMPANY; *pg.* 882, *pg.* 978
N2025 - Printer - XEROX CORPORATION; *pg.* 494, *pg.* 365
N2125 - Printer - XEROX CORPORATION; *pg.* 494, *pg.* 365
N2825 - Printer - XEROX CORPORATION; *pg.* 494, *pg.* 365
N32 - Printer - XEROX CORPORATION; *pg.* 494, *pg.* 365
N3225 - Printer - XEROX CORPORATION; *pg.* 494, *pg.* 365
N40 - Printer - XEROX CORPORATION; *pg.* 494, *pg.* 365
N4025 - Printer - XEROX CORPORATION; *pg.* 494, *pg.* 365
N5 - Sub-Micron Particle Size Analyzer - BECKMAN COULTER, INC.; *pg.* 1402, *pg.* 48
N65 SLR - Photo Equipment - NIKON INC.; *pg.* 1424, *pg.* 1181
N80 SLR - Photo Equipment - NIKON INC.; *pg.* 1424, *pg.* 1181
NA-LUBE - Chemical Product - KING INDUSTRIES, INC.; *pg.* 1443, *pg.* 363
NA-SUL - Chemical Product - KING INDUSTRIES, INC.; *pg.* 1443, *pg.* 363
NA72Z4W512M8M-A18JTG - Storage System - HGST; *pg.* 406, *pg.* 260
NABCO - Automatic Swinging & Sliding Doors - NABCO ENTRANCES, INC.; *pg.* 99, *pg.* 1882
NABISCO - Cereal Bars, Crackers & Confections - MONDELEZ INTERNATIONAL, INC.; *pg.* 878, *pg.* 601
NABISCO 100 CALORIE PACKS - Snack Packs - MONDELEZ INTERNATIONAL, INC.; *pg.* 878, *pg.* 601
NACCONOL - Chemical Product - STEPAN COMPANY; *pg.* 1182, *pg.* 643
NACEVAC - Software - COOPER WHEELOCK; *pg.* 630, *pg.* 1080
NACHEZ - Brick & Tile Product - CHEROKEE BRICK & TILE COMPANY; *pg.* 75, *pg.* 535
NACHITAS - Tortilla Chips - HERR FOODS INC.; *pg.* 861, *pg.* 1557
NACHOS NAVIDAD - Food Product - TACO JOHN'S INTERNATIONAL, INC.; *pg.* 1753, *pg.* 1901
NACIONAL 27 - Latin American Restaurant - LETTUCE ENTERTAIN YOU ENTERPRISES, INC.; *pg.* 1735, *pg.* 580
NACON - Chemical Product - KING INDUSTRIES, INC.; *pg.* 1443, *pg.* 363
NACORR - Corrosion Inhibitor - KING INDUSTRIES, INC.; *pg.* 1443, *pg.* 363
NACTOOL - Software - COOPER WHEELOCK; *pg.* 630, *pg.* 1080
NACURE - Chemical Product - KING INDUSTRIES, INC.; *pg.* 1443, *pg.* 363
NADA - Beverages - THE COCA-COLA COMPANY; *pg.* 240, *pg.* 493
NADIA - Clothing - ABERCROMBIE & FITCH CO.; *pg.* 37, *pg.* 1466
NADIA - Urinalysis Workstation - IRIS INTERNATIONAL, INC.; *pg.* 1547, *pg.* 64
NADIA - Footwear - PHOENIX FOOTWEAR GROUP, INC.; *pg.* 1815, *pg.* 60
NADIAH - Footwear - STEVEN MADDEN, LTD.; *pg.* 1819, *pg.* 1176
NADIC - Chemical Product - SPECTRUM CHEMICALS & LABORATORY PRODUCTS, INC.; *pg.* 1181, *pg.* 94
NADINOLA - Face Cream - J. STRICKLAND & COMPANY; *pg.* 512, *pg.* 970
NADRION - Pharmaceutical Preparation - PFIZER INC.; *pg.* 1581, *pg.* 1278
NAF - Pump - FLOWSERVE CORPORATION; *pg.* 82, *pg.* 1719
NAFE - National Association for Female Executives - THE NATIONAL ASSOCIATION FOR FEMALE EXECUTIVES; *pg.* 147, *pg.* 1263
NAFTA RAILWAY - Transportation Service - THE KANSAS CITY SOUTHERN RAILWAY COMPANY; *pg.* 1913, *pg.* 985
NAG BRACHYFLEX - Catheter Implant Set - COOK GROUP, INC.; *pg.* 1518, *pg.* 674
NAGOMI - Beverages - THE COCA-COLA COMPANY; *pg.* 240, *pg.* 493
NAIL ARMOR - Strengtheners - ORLY INTERNATIONAL, INC.; *pg.* 518, *pg.* 137
NAIL DEFENSE - Strengtheners - ORLY INTERNATIONAL, INC.; *pg.* 518, *pg.* 137
NAIL EATERS - BITS - GREENLEE TEXTRON INC.; *pg.* 1048, *pg.* 655
NAIL ENVY - Nail Care Product - OPI PRODUCTS INC.; *pg.* 518, *pg.* 167
NAIL EXPERTS - Beauty Product - AVON PRODUCTS, INC.; *pg.* 500, *pg.* 1198
NAIL FLAIR - Paint - BADGER AIR BRUSH COMPANY; *pg.* 359, *pg.* 612
NAIL MASTER - Electric Nailer - ARROW FASTENER COMPANY, INC.; *pg.* 1042, *pg.* 1118
NAIL RESCUE - Polish Removers & Repair - ORLY INTERNATIONAL, INC.; *pg.* 518, *pg.* 137
NAIL TRAIL - Bike - MARIN BIKES; *pg.* 1708, *pg.* 168
NAIL WHITENER - Nail Product - ORLY INTERNATIONAL, INC.; *pg.* 518, *pg.* 137
NAILAID - Manicuring Instruments - MILLERS FORGE INC.; *pg.* 1056, *pg.* 1733
NAILBOARD - Roof Insulation Board - JOHNS MANVILLE CORPORATION; *pg.* 89, *pg.* 320
NAILCLEAR - Nail Revitalizing Liquid - ALVA/AMCO PHARMACAL COMPANIES, INC.; *pg.* 1492, *pg.* 637
NAILGLIDE 2100 - Nailcare Product - MEDICOOL, INC.; *pg.* 1562, *pg.* 294
NAILPRO 2000 - Nailcare Product - MEDICOOL, INC.; *pg.* 1562, *pg.* 294
NAILS FOR MALES - Nail Product - ORLY INTERNATIONAL, INC.; *pg.* 518, *pg.* 137
NAILSAVER - No Scratch Sponge - 3M COMPANY; *pg.* 1142, *pg.* 956
NAILSLICKS - Polish - COVER GIRL COSMETICS; *pg.* 506, *pg.* 772
NAILWEAR - Beauty Product - AVON PRODUCTS, INC.; *pg.* 500, *pg.* 1198
NAIR - Personal Care Product - CHURCH & DWIGHT CO., INC.; *pg.* 1153, *pg.* 1063
NAIR FOR MEN - Personal Care Product - CHURCH & DWIGHT CO., INC.; *pg.* 1153, *pg.* 1063
NAIR PRETTY - Personal Care Product - CHURCH & DWIGHT CO., INC.; *pg.* 1153, *pg.* 1063
NAIR SENSITIVE FORMULA COLLECTION - Personal Care Product - CHURCH & DWIGHT CO., INC.; *pg.* 1153, *pg.* 1063
NAIVE - Candle Stand - ETHAN ALLEN INTERIORS INC.; *pg.* 924, *pg.* 343
NAKAO SPIDER-NET - Endoscopic Technologies - CONMED CORPORATION; *pg.* 1517, *pg.* 1347
NAKED - Fruit Juices - NAKED JUICE COMPANY, INC.; *pg.* 882, *pg.* 150
NAKS-PAK - Pouches of Popcorn - GOLD MEDAL PRODUCTS CO.; *pg.* 55, *pg.* 1414
NAKS POP - Bars of Coconut Oil - GOLD MEDAL PRODUCTS CO.; *pg.* 55, *pg.* 1414
NALA - Furniture - HERMAN MILLER, INC.; *pg.* 926, *pg.* 913
NALCO - Slurry - DOW CHEMICAL; *pg.* 1156, *pg.* 1563
NALKYLENE - Detergent Alkylate - SASOL NORTH AMERICA INC.; *pg.* 984, *pg.* 1713
NALLEY - Canned Meals - PINNACLE FOODS GROUP LLC; *pg.* 889, *pg.* 1104
NALLEY'S - Pickles - TREEHOUSE FOODS, INC.; *pg.* 901, *pg.* 649
NALTEX - Extruded Plastic Net - DELSTAR TECHNOLOGIES, INC.; *pg.* 1881, *pg.* 387
NALU - Soft Drink - THE COCA-COLA COMPANY; *pg.* 240, *pg.* 493
NALU - Eyewear - MAUI JIM, INC.; *pg.* 9, *pg.* 651
NAMCO JENNER - Safety Light Curtain - DANAHER CORPORATION; *pg.* 1044, *pg.* 397
NAME OBJECT - Software - MELISSA DATA CORP.; *pg.* 432, *pg.* 188
NAMEDROPPERS.COM - Internet Service - LOGIKA CORPORATION; *pg.* 1264, *pg.* 581
NAMEIT - Software - BIO-RAD LABORATORIES, INC.; *pg.* 1504, *pg.* 101
NAMTHIP - Beverages - THE COCA-COLA COMPANY; *pg.* 240, *pg.* 493
NAN A. TALESE - Publishing Imprint - THE KNOPF DOUBLEDAY GROUP; *pg.* 1657, *pg.* 1249
NANAIRO ACHA - Beverages - THE COCA-COLA COMPANY; *pg.* 240, *pg.* 493
NANCE'S - Food Product - BALDWIN RICHARDSON FOODS COMPANY; *pg.* 1850, *pg.* 612
NANCY - Furniture - NEMSCHOFF, INC.; *pg.* 936, *pg.* 1890
NANCY'S - Frozen Appetizers & Entrees - THE KRAFT HEINZ COMPANY; *pg.* 870, *pg.* 1577
NANDI - Personal Care Electrical Product - HELEN OF TROY L.P.; *pg.* 511, *pg.* 1692
NANI - Eyewear - MAUI JIM, INC.; *pg.* 9, *pg.* 651
NANIK - Furniture - SPRINGS GLOBAL, INC.; *pg.* 698, *pg.* 1616
NANIK - Window Blinds & Shades - SPRINGS WINDOW FASHIONS LLC; *pg.* 943, *pg.* 1872
NANO BANTAM - Knife - BUCK KNIVES, INC.; *pg.* 1828, *pg.* 550
NANO BIONIX - Biomaterials Test System - MTS SYSTEMS CORPORATION; *pg.* 442, *pg.* 923
NANO-CHANGE - Electronic Components - MOLEX INCORPORATED; *pg.* 655, *pg.* 628
NANO FLOW - Sprayer - WATERS CORPORATION; *pg.* 1436, *pg.* 834
NANO INDENTER - Silicon Wafer Property Mappers - MTS SYSTEMS CORPORATION; *pg.* 442, *pg.* 923
NANO LC - Column - WATERS CORPORATION; *pg.* 1436, *pg.* 834
NANO LIGHT - Flashlight - STREAMLIGHT INC.; *pg.* 1306, *pg.* 1527
NANO-POLISH - Automotive Waxes & Polishes - ASHLAND INC.; *pg.* 972, *pg.* 726
NANO-PROTECTANT - Automobile Interior Surface Cleaners - ASHLAND INC.; *pg.* 972, *pg.* 726
NANO TAC - Torch - COAST CUTLERY COMPANY; *pg.* 1121, *pg.* 1501
NANO2 SMF - Electronic Fuse - LITTELFUSE, INC.; *pg.* 1301, *pg.* 580
NANOARC - Nanoparticle Product - NANOPHASE TECHNOLOGIES CORPORATION; *pg.* 1174, *pg.* 656
NANOBLEND - Engineered Compound & Composite - POLYONE CORPORATION; *pg.* 1177, *pg.* 1404
NANOCD - Metrology Suite - NANOMETRICS INCORPORATED; *pg.* 1423, *pg.* 147
NANOCEUTICALS - Nutritional Supplement - RBC LIFE SCIENCES, INC.; *pg.* 1588, *pg.* 1723
NANOCHECK - Ceramic Nanomaterial Product - ALTAIR NANOTECHNOLOGIES INC.; *pg.* 1147, *pg.* 1031
NANOCLEAN - Motor Oils, Lubricants & Greases - ASHLAND INC.; *pg.* 972, *pg.* 726
NANODOT - Dosimeter - LANDAUER, INC.; *pg.* 1554, *pg.* 615
NANODRIVE - Controller - VEECO INSTRUMENTS INC.; *pg.* 1434, *pg.* 1322
NANODUR - Nanocrystalline Material - NANOPHASE TECHNOLOGIES CORPORATION; *pg.* 1174, *pg.* 656
NANOEASE - Column - WATERS CORPORATION; *pg.* 1436, *pg.* 834
NANOFILM - Balloon - CONTINENTAL AMERICAN CORP.; *pg.* 1880, *pg.* 723
NANOFILTER - Pumps - IDEX CORPORATION; *pg.* 1347,

pg. 623
NANOFOLD - Pumps - IDEX CORPORATION; *pg.* 1347, *pg.* 623
NANOFREE - Lead-Free Wafer Chip Scale Package - TEXAS INSTRUMENTS INCORPORATED; *pg.* 679, *pg.* 1688
NANOFUSE - Electronic Fuse - LITTELFUSE, INC.; *pg.* 1301, *pg.* 580
NANOGARD - Nanoparticle Product - NANOPHASE TECHNOLOGIES CORPORATION; *pg.* 1174, *pg.* 656
NANOGEL - Chemical Product - CABOT CORPORATION; *pg.* 1151, *pg.* 792
NANOGEL - Filled Polycarbonate - SUPER SKY PRODUCTS, INC.; *pg.* 113, *pg.* 1871
NANOGLASS - Electronic Material - HONEYWELL INTERNATIONAL INC.; *pg.* 407, *pg.* 1088
NANOGOLD - Molecular Probe Product - THERMO FISHER SCIENTIFIC INC.; *pg.* 1602, *pg.* 61
NANOKERNAL - Software System - MENTOR GRAPHICS CORPORATION; *pg.* 432, *pg.* 1510
NANOKNIFE - Surgical Instrument - ANGIODYNAMICS, INC., *pg.* 1495, *pg.* 1173
NANOKOTE - Ceramic Paint - THE MURALO COMPANY; *pg.* 1444, *pg.* 1042
NANOLIFT - Electron Microscope - FEI COMPANY; *pg.* 1413, *pg.* 1498
NANOLITH - Light Source - CYMER, INC.; *pg.* 1296, *pg.* 202
NANOMAX - Minerals - MINERALS TECHNOLOGIES INC.; *pg.* 1173, *pg.* 617
NANOMER - Minerals - MINERALS TECHNOLOGIES INC.; *pg.* 1173, *pg.* 617
NANOMETRICS ATLAS - Integrated Metrology System - NANOMETRICS INCORPORATED; *pg.* 1423, *pg.* 147
NANOMETRICS ATLAS-M - Metrology System - NANOMETRICS INCORPORATED; *pg.* 1423, *pg.* 147
NANOMETRICS ATLAS XP - Metrology System - NANOMETRICS INCORPORATED; *pg.* 1423, *pg.* 147
NANOMETRICS FLX - Metrology System - NANOMETRICS INCORPORATED; *pg.* 1423, *pg.* 147
NANOMETRICS LYNX - Metrology Platform - NANOMETRICS INCORPORATED; *pg.* 1423, *pg.* 147
NANOMIXER - Pumps - IDEX CORPORATION; *pg.* 1347, *pg.* 623
NANOOCD 9010M - Integrated Metrology System - NANOMETRICS INCORPORATED; *pg.* 1423, *pg.* 147
NANOORANGE - Molecular Probe Product - THERMO FISHER SCIENTIFIC INC.; *pg.* 1602, *pg.* 61
NANOPEAK - Pumps - IDEX CORPORATION; *pg.* 1347, *pg.* 623
NANOPICS - Atomic Force Profilometer - KLA-TENCOR CORPORATION; *pg.* 1353, *pg.* 146
NANOPORT - Pumps - IDEX CORPORATION; *pg.* 1347, *pg.* 623
NANOROUTE - Software - CADENCE DESIGN SYSTEMS, INC.; *pg.* 367, *pg.* 239
NANOSCOPE 3D - Controller - VEECO INSTRUMENTS INC.; *pg.* 1434, *pg.* 1322
NANOSCOPE V - Controller - VEECO INSTRUMENTS INC.; *pg.* 1434, *pg.* 1322
THE NANOSEMICONDUCTOR COMPANY - Slogan - KOPIN CORPORATION; *pg.* 425, *pg.* 847
NANOSEP - Centrifugal Device - PALL CORPORATION; *pg.* 232, *pg.* 1323
NANOSHIELD - Nanocrystalline Material - NANOPHASE TECHNOLOGIES CORPORATION; *pg.* 1174, *pg.* 656
NANOSIM - Software - SYNOPSYS, INC.; *pg.* 480, *pg.* 162
NANOSPEC - Metrology System - NANOMETRICS INCORPORATED; *pg.* 1423, *pg.* 147
NANOSPEC 3000 - Tabletop Metrology - NANOMETRICS INCORPORATED; *pg.* 1423, *pg.* 147
NANOSPEC 6100 - Tabletop Metrology - NANOMETRICS INCORPORATED; *pg.* 1423, *pg.* 147
NANOSPEC 9200 - Metrology System - NANOMETRICS INCORPORATED; *pg.* 1423, *pg.* 147
NANOSPOT - Glass & Ceramic Material - CORNING INCORPORATED; *pg.* 1122, *pg.* 1154
NANOSTAR - X-Ray System - BRUKER CORPORATION; *pg.* 1511, *pg.* 788
NANOSTAR - Chip Scale Packages - TEXAS INSTRUMENTS INCORPORATED; *pg.* 679, *pg.* 1688
NANOTECH - Stepper - ULTRATECH, INC.; *pg.* 1433, *pg.* 251
NANOTEK - Nanocrystalline Material - NANOPHASE TECHNOLOGIES CORPORATION; *pg.* 1174, *pg.* 656
NANOTIGHT - Pumps - IDEX CORPORATION; *pg.* 1347, *pg.* 623
NANOTURN - Ultra Precision CNC Lathe - PRECITECH, INC.; *pg.* 1427, *pg.* 1035
NANOUDI - Integrated Metrology System - NANOMETRICS INCORPORATED; *pg.* 1423, *pg.* 147
NANOUDI 9300 - Metrology System - NANOMETRICS INCORPORATED; *pg.* 1423, *pg.* 147
NANOVATIONS - Customer Newsletter - VEECO INSTRUMENTS INC.; *pg.* 1434, *pg.* 1322
NANOVETTE - Microliter Measurement Cell Spectrophotometer Accessory - BECKMAN COULTER, INC.; *pg.* 1402, *pg.* 48
NANOWAX - Automotive Waxes & Polishes - ASHLAND INC.; *pg.* 972, *pg.* 726
NANOWEB - Coating - W.L. GORE & ASSOCIATES, INC.; *pg.* 122, *pg.* 388
NANSA - Laundry Product - HUNTSMAN CORPORATION; *pg.* 1167, *pg.* 1758
NANTUCKET - Rug - COURISTAN INC.; *pg.* 921, *pg.* 1067
NANTUCKET - Window Shadings With 2-1/2" Vane Size - HUNTER DOUGLAS, INC.; *pg.* 928, *pg.* 1320
NANTUCKET - Bath Product - KOHLER CO.; *pg.* 91, *pg.* 1862
NANTUCKET - Cookies - PEPPERIDGE FARM, INC.; *pg.* 888, *pg.* 363
NANTUCKET BLEND - Coffee - KEURIG GREEN MOUNTAIN, INC.; *pg.* 868, *pg.* 1768
NANTUCKET MIST - Nail Care Product - OPI PRODUCTS INC.; *pg.* 518, *pg.* 167
NANTUCKET NECTARS - Non-Carbonated Soft Drink - DR PEPPER SNAPPLE GROUP, INC.; *pg.* 250, *pg.* 1729
NANTUCKET SOUND - Outerwear - HABAND COMPANY, INC.; *pg.* 1772, *pg.* 1099
NANTUCKET TODAY - Newspaper - THE INQUIRER & MIRROR; *pg.* 1653, *pg.* 834
NAOMI - Clothing - ABERCROMBIE & FITCH CO.; *pg.* 37, *pg.* 1466
NAOMI - Furniture - AMISCO INDUSTRIES LTD.; *pg.* 913, *pg.* 1958
NAOMI - Apparel - BEBE STORES, INC.; *pg.* 19, *pg.* 49
NAOMI - Footwear - PHOENIX FOOTWEAR GROUP, INC.; *pg.* 1815, *pg.* 60
NAP-GARD - Powder Coatings - E.I. DU PONT DE NEMOURS & COMPANY; *pg.* 1159, *pg.* 390
NAP GUARD - Diagnostic System - BECTON, DICKINSON & COMPANY; *pg.* 1501, *pg.* 1068
NAP OF THE AMERICAS - Software - VERIZON TERREMARK; *pg.* 685, *pg.* 447
NAPA - Distribution Centers - GENUINE PARTS COMPANY; *pg.* 206, *pg.* 506
NAPA - Automotive Parts - NATIONAL AUTOMOTIVE PARTS ASSOCIATION; *pg.* 213, *pg.* 515
NAPA - Wines - PERNOD RICARD USA, INC.; *pg.* 1968, *pg.* 1332
NAPA VALLEY - Wine - DREYFUS ASHBY INC.; *pg.* 1962, *pg.* 1226
NAPA VALLEY - Fan - WESTINGHOUSE LIGHTING CORPORATION; *pg.* 687, *pg.* 1571
NAPA VALLEY GRILLE - Restaurants - TAVISTOCK RESTAURANT GROUP; *pg.* 1753, *pg.* 803
NAPALM - Bicycle Accessories - SPECIALIZED BICYCLE COMPONENTS, INC.; *pg.* 1711, *pg.* 152
NAPAPIJRI - Apparel - V.F. CORPORATION; *pg.* 34, *pg.* 1376
NAPCO - Vinyl-Window Systems - NORTEK, INC.; *pg.* 100, *pg.* 1607
NAPCO PREMIUM - Windows & Doors - NORTEK, INC.; *pg.* 100, *pg.* 1607
NAPCO PRIME - Windows & Doors - NORTEK, INC.; *pg.* 100, *pg.* 1607
NAPHTHAMAX - Catalyst - BASF CATALYSTS LLC; *pg.* 1148, *pg.* 1074
NAPKIN DELI - Deli Displayware - CARLISLE FOODSERVICE PRODUCTS INCORPORATED; *pg.* 1455, *pg.* 1485
NAPLES - Furniture - ASHLEY FURNITURE INDUSTRIES, INC.; *pg.* 914, *pg.* 1852
NAPLES - Cookies - PEPPERIDGE FARM, INC.; *pg.* 888, *pg.* 363
NAPLES CHARITY REGISTER - Magazine - PALM BEACH MEDIA GROUP INC.; *pg.* 1674, *pg.* 457
NAPLES DAILY NEWS - Newspaper - THE E.W. SCRIPPS COMPANY; *pg.* 1639, *pg.* 1412
NAPLES DAILY NEWS - Publication - NAPLES DAILY NEWS; *pg.* 1666, *pg.* 451
NAPLES ILLUSTRATED - Magazine - PALM BEACH MEDIA GROUP INC.; *pg.* 1674, *pg.* 457
NAPLESNEWS.COM - News Website - NAPLES DAILY NEWS; *pg.* 1666, *pg.* 451
NAPOLI - Fabric - NEMSCHOFF, INC.; *pg.* 936, *pg.* 1890
NAPROSYN - Pharmaceutical Product - HOFFMANN-LA ROCHE INC.; *pg.* 1542, *pg.* 1099
NAR IS THE VOICE FOR REAL ESTATE - Slogan - NATIONAL ASSOCIATION OF REALTORS; *pg.* 1666, *pg.* 584
NARAGANSETT - Table - BLATT BOWLING & BILLIARD CORP.; *pg.* 1827, *pg.* 1203
NARAMUNE-2 - Canine Parainfluenza-Bordetella Bronchiseptica Vaccine - BOEHRINGER INGELHEIM VETMEDICA, INC.; *pg.* 1474, *pg.* 989
NARBLES - Candy - FERRARA CANDY CO.; *pg.* 1852, *pg.* 612
NARCAL - Refractory Product - RESCO PRODUCTS, INC.; *pg.* 107, *pg.* 1581
NARCAN - Pharmaceutical Product - ENDO PHARMACEUTICALS HOLDINGS, INC.; *pg.* 1528, *pg.* 1549
NARCSTATION - Software - MCKESSON CORPORATION; *pg.* 1560, *pg.* 222
NARDIL - Medicine - PFIZER INC.; *pg.* 1581, *pg.* 1278
NARRATIVE - Fabric - NEMSCHOFF, INC.; *pg.* 936, *pg.* 1890
NARROLINE - Window - ANDERSEN CORPORATION; *pg.* 67, *pg.* 916
NARROW CORRELATOR - Tracking Technology - NOVATEL INC.; *pg.* 1424, *pg.* 1904
NARROWCAST SERVER - Software - MICROSTRATEGY, INC.; *pg.* 1266, *pg.* 1809
NARROWCAST SERVICES GATEWAY - Digital Video Product - HARMONIC, INC.; *pg.* 402, *pg.* 246
NARTHEX - Furniture - IMPERIAL WOODWORKS, INC.; *pg.* 929, *pg.* 1749
NARU - Bathroom Accessories - SYMMONS INDUSTRIES, INC.; *pg.* 114, *pg.* 803
NAS - Software - NETAPP, INC.; *pg.* 444, *pg.* 287
NAS - High Performance Styrenics - NOVA CHEMICALS CORPORATION; *pg.* 1175, *pg.* 1904
NASAGUARD-B - Canine Vaccine - PFIZER INC.; *pg.* 1581, *pg.* 1278
NASAL RAE - Tracheal Tube - MEDTRONIC; *pg.* 1563, *pg.* 183
NASALCROM - Nasal Allergy Symptom Controller - MCNEIL-PPC, INC.; *pg.* 1560, *pg.* 1533
NASCAR - Gift - AVON PRODUCTS, INC.; *pg.* 500, *pg.* 1198
NASCAR - Tire - THE GOODYEAR TIRE & RUBBER COMPANY; *pg.* 1883, *pg.* 1401
NASCAR - Coolers & Bottle - THERMOS L.L.C.; *pg.* 61, *pg.* 660
NASCAR EXTREME - Battery - EXIDE TECHNOLOGIES; *pg.* 204, *pg.* 483
NASCAR SELECT - Battery - EXIDE TECHNOLOGIES; *pg.* 204, *pg.* 483
NASH - Liquid Ring Vacuum Pump - GARDNER DENVER, INC.; *pg.* 1338, *pg.* 1592
NASH - Pump - GARDNER DENVER NASH; *pg.* 1338, *pg.* 381
NASH-ELMO - Dry Vacuum Pump - GARDNER DENVER NASH; *pg.* 1338, *pg.* 381
NASH ENGINEERING - Vacuum Pumps & Compressors - GARDNER DENVER NASH; *pg.* 1338, *pg.* 381
NASHUA - Shoes - ALLEN-EDMONDS SHOE CORP.; *pg.* 1804, *pg.* 1887
NASHVILLE - Musical Instrument - PEAVEY ELECTRONICS CORPORATION; *pg.* 662, *pg.* 970
NASHVILLE - Fabric - SCALAMANDRE, INC.; *pg.* 941, *pg.* 1058
NASHVILLE B-BENDER TELE - Electric Guitar - FENDER MUSICAL INSTRUMENTS CORPORATION; *pg.* 547, *pg.* 21
NASHVILLE GAS - Energy - PIEDMONT NATURAL GAS COMPANY, INC.; *pg.* 1949, *pg.* 1368
NASHVILLE SUPERSPEEDWAY - Motor Racetrack - DOVER MOTORSPORTS, INC.; *pg.* 545, *pg.* 387
NASHVILLE TELE - Electric Guitar - FENDER MUSICAL INSTRUMENTS CORPORATION; *pg.* 547, *pg.* 21
NASON - Automotive Coatings - E.I. DU PONT DE NEMOURS & COMPANY; *pg.* 1159, *pg.* 390
NASONEX - Medicine - MERCK & CO., INC.; *pg.* 1566, *pg.* 1077
NASTAR - Flight Simulator - ENVIRONMENTAL TECTONICS CORPORATION; *pg.* 1411, *pg.* 1587

First page reference indicates Business Class Edition
Second page reference indicates Geographic Edition

NAT CHERRY - Furniture - BUSH INDUSTRIES INC.; *pg.* 919, *pg.* 1170
NATALIA - Fabric - NEMSCHOFF, INC.; *pg.* 936, *pg.* 1890
NATALIE - Clothing - ABERCROMBIE & FITCH CO.; *pg.* 37, *pg.* 1466
NATALIE - Footwear - EASTLAND SHOE CORPORATION; *pg.* 1808, *pg.* 750
NATALIE - Footwear - PHOENIX FOOTWEAR GROUP, INC.; *pg.* 1815, *pg.* 60
NATASHA - Furniture - AMISCO INDUSTRIES LTD.; *pg.* 913, *pg.* 1958
NATASHA - Software - GULF PUBLISHING COMPANY; *pg.* 1646, *pg.* 1707
NATCO-LESCER - Coalescing Media - CAMERON INTERNATIONAL; *pg.* 1151, *pg.* 1702
NATHAN'S - Sauce - GOLD PURE FOOD PRODUCTS CO., INC.; *pg.* 858, *pg.* 1166
NATHAN'S - Hot Dog Restaurants - NATHAN'S FAMOUS INC.; *pg.* 1741, *pg.* 1171
NATHAN'S MUSTARD - Food Product - GOLD PURE FOOD PRODUCTS CO., INC.; *pg.* 858, *pg.* 1166
NATIONAL - Bakery Products - ALPHA BAKING COMPANY; *pg.* 836, *pg.* 564
NATIONAL - Sealing Devices - FEDERAL-MOGUL HOLDINGS CORPORATION; *pg.* 205, *pg.* 907
NATIONAL - Office Furniture - KIMBALL INTERNATIONAL, INC.; *pg.* 931, *pg.* 692
NATIONAL - Outdoor Covering - METALS USA, INC.; *pg.* 97, *pg.* 425
NATIONAL - Cutting Systems - NATIONAL MACHINERY LLC; *pg.* 1363, *pg.* 1475
NATIONAL - Electronics - RICHARDSON ELECTRONICS, LTD.; *pg.* 667, *pg.* 622
NATIONAL ACME - Machine Tool Product - BOURN & KOCH MACHINE TOOL COMPANY; *pg.* 1319, *pg.* 654
NATIONAL ARTS EDUCATION INITIATIVE - Cancer Eradication Program - ENTERTAINMENT INDUSTRY FOUNDATION; *pg.* 140, *pg.* 130
NATIONAL ASSOCIATION OF PIZZA OPERATORS - Organization - MACFADDEN COMMUNICATIONS GROUP, LLC; *pg.* 1660, *pg.* 1254
NATIONAL AUDUBON SOCIETY - Pet Food - PETSMART, INC.; *pg.* 1481, *pg.* 18
NATIONAL BEEF - Beef Products - NATIONAL BEEF PACKING COMPANY, LLC; *pg.* 882, *pg.* 985
NATIONAL BOHEMIAN - Beer - PABST BREWING COMPANY; *pg.* 258, *pg.* 137
NATIONAL CAR RENTAL - Car Rental - NATIONAL CAR RENTAL; *pg.* 1916, *pg.* 1490
NATIONAL CARD REGISTRY - Credit Card Protection Services - AFFINION GROUP, INC.; *pg.* 1225, *pg.* 372
NATIONAL CARDIOVASCULAR RESEARCH INITIATIVE - Cancer Eradication Program - ENTERTAINMENT INDUSTRY FOUNDATION; *pg.* 140, *pg.* 130
NATIONAL CHAMPION OF CHAMPIONS - Trademark - NATIONAL COLLEGIATE ATHLETIC ASSOCIATION; *pg.* 567, *pg.* 688
NATIONAL CHEMICALS - Specialty Chemicals - ZEP INC.; *pg.* 338, *pg.* 524
NATIONAL COLLEGIATE ATHLETIC ASSOCIATION - Trademark - NATIONAL COLLEGIATE ATHLETIC ASSOCIATION; *pg.* 567, *pg.* 688
NATIONAL COLLEGIATE CHAMPIONSHIPS - Trademark - NATIONAL COLLEGIATE ATHLETIC ASSOCIATION; *pg.* 567, *pg.* 688
NATIONAL COLORECTAL CANCER RESEARCH ALLIANCE - Cancer Eradication Program - ENTERTAINMENT INDUSTRY FOUNDATION; *pg.* 140, *pg.* 130
NATIONAL DAIRY COUNCIL - Dairy Product - DAIRY MANAGEMENT, INC.; *pg.* 138, *pg.* 656
NATIONAL DATACAST - High-Speed Data Delivery Via Broadcast Signal's VBI - PUBLIC BROADCASTING SERVICE; *pg.* 305, *pg.* 1774
NATIONAL DISEASE AND THERAPEUTIC INDEX - Software System - IMS HEALTH, INC.; *pg.* 1544, *pg.* 344
NATIONAL DRAGSTER - Publisher - NATIONAL HOT ROD ASSOCIATION; *pg.* 149, *pg.* 99
NATIONAL ELECTRICAL CODE - Fire Prevention - NATIONAL FIRE PROTECTION ASSOCIATION; *pg.* 149, *pg.* 842
THE NATIONAL ENQUIRER - Magazine - AMERICAN MEDIA, INC.; *pg.* 1615, *pg.* 410
NATIONAL FIRE ALARM CODE - Fire Safety Book - NATIONAL FIRE PROTECTION ASSOCIATION; *pg.* 149, *pg.* 842
NATIONAL FIRE CODES - Fire Prevention - NATIONAL FIRE PROTECTION ASSOCIATION; *pg.* 149, *pg.* 842
NATIONAL FISHERMAN MAGAZINE - Magazine - DIVERSIFIED COMMUNICATIONS; *pg.* 284, *pg.* 751
NATIONAL GEOGRAPHIC - Magazine - NATIONAL GEOGRAPHIC SOCIETY; *pg.* 1667, *pg.* 402
NATIONAL GEOGRAPHIC ADVENTURE - Publication - NATIONAL GEOGRAPHIC SOCIETY; *pg.* 1667, *pg.* 402
NATIONAL GEOGRAPHIC KIDS MAGAZINE - Publication - NATIONAL GEOGRAPHIC SOCIETY; *pg.* 1667, *pg.* 402
NATIONAL GEOGRAPHIC TRAVELER - Publication - NATIONAL GEOGRAPHIC SOCIETY; *pg.* 1667, *pg.* 402
NATIONAL GOLD - Tin Surface Treatment - REGAL BELOIT CORPORATION; *pg.* 106, *pg.* 1854
NATIONAL INSPIRER - Educational Materials - SCHOLASTIC INC.; *pg.* 1683, *pg.* 1288
NATIONAL/INTERRENT - Car Rental Marketing Umbrellas - NATIONAL CAR RENTAL; *pg.* 1916, *pg.* 1490
NATIONAL JEWELER - Trade Magazine - THE NIELSEN COMPANY B.V.; *pg.* 1671, *pg.* 1272
THE NATIONAL LAW JOURNAL - Legal Publication - AMERICAN LAWYER MEDIA, INC.; *pg.* 1615, *pg.* 1193
NATIONAL PARKS - Knife - BUCK KNIVES, INC.; *pg.* 1828, *pg.* 550
NATIONAL PRESCRIPTION AUDIT - Software System - IMS HEALTH, INC.; *pg.* 1544, *pg.* 344
NATIONAL PRESS - Forging Product - SUPERIOR DIE SET CORP.; *pg.* 1379, *pg.* 1885
NATIONAL REHABILITATION HOSPITAL - Hospital - MEDSTAR HEALTH INC.; *pg.* 1563, *pg.* 767
NATIONAL RIVET - Machines - NATIONAL RIVET & MANUFACTURING COMPANY; *pg.* 1364, *pg.* 1898
NATIONAL RV TRADER - Advertising Publication - DOMINION ENTERPRISES; *pg.* 1636, *pg.* 1796
NATIONAL SALES PERSPECTIVES - Software System - IMS HEALTH, INC.; *pg.* 1544, *pg.* 344
NATIONAL TILDEN/INTERRENT - Car Rental Marketing Umbrellas - NATIONAL CAR RENTAL; *pg.* 1916, *pg.* 1490
NATIONAL TIRE & BATTERY - Retail Center - TBC CORPORATION; *pg.* 1889, *pg.* 457
NATIONAL VALUES - Coupon Books - ENTERTAINMENT PUBLICATIONS, INC.; *pg.* 1639, *pg.* 910
NATIONAL WINE WEEK - Promotional Wine Tasting Event - THE SMITH & WOLLENSKY RESTAURANT GROUP, INC.; *pg.* 1750, *pg.* 1293
NATIONAL WOMEN'S CANCER RESEARCH ALLIANCE - Cancer Eradication Program - ENTERTAINMENT INDUSTRY FOUNDATION; *pg.* 140, *pg.* 130
NATION'S RESTURANT NEWS - Industry Publication - LEBHAR-FRIEDMAN INC.; *pg.* 1658, *pg.* 1250
NATIONWIDE - Modular Homes - NATIONWIDE HOMES, INC.; *pg.* 99, *pg.* 1788
NATIONWIDE BLUE RIBBON - Auto Insurance Claim - NATIONWIDE MUTUAL INSURANCE COMPANY; *pg.* 1210, *pg.* 1442
NATIONWIDE EAGLE PLUS - Insurance Underwriting Service - NATIONWIDE MUTUAL INSURANCE COMPANY; *pg.* 1210, *pg.* 1442
NATIONWIDE IT SERVICES PROVIDER - Tag Line - BARRISTER GLOBAL SERVICES NETWORK, INC.; *pg.* 360, *pg.* 744
NATIONWIDE PLATINUM III - Insurance Service - NATIONWIDE MUTUAL INSURANCE COMPANY; *pg.* 1210, *pg.* 1442
NATIONWIDE PLATINUM V - Insurance Service - NATIONWIDE MUTUAL INSURANCE COMPANY; *pg.* 1210, *pg.* 1442
NATIONWIDE QUATRO SELECT ANNUITY - Insurance Service - NATIONWIDE MUTUAL INSURANCE COMPANY; *pg.* 1210, *pg.* 1442
NATIONWIDE TRIO SELECT+ - Insurance Service - NATIONWIDE MUTUAL INSURANCE COMPANY; *pg.* 1210, *pg.* 1442
NATIVE - Apparel - OAKLEY, INC.; *pg.* 1840, *pg.* 86
NATIVEMARK - Molecular Biology Product - THERMO FISHER SCIENTIFIC INC.; *pg.* 1602, *pg.* 61
NATIVEPAGE - Molecular Biology Product - THERMO FISHER SCIENTIFIC INC.; *pg.* 1602, *pg.* 61
NATIVEPURE - Molecular Biology Product - THERMO FISHER SCIENTIFIC INC.; *pg.* 1602, *pg.* 61
NATIVITY - Ornament - HERITAGE LACE INC.; *pg.* 694, *pg.* 711
NATRABIO - Nutritional Product - NUTRACEUTICAL INTERNATIONAL CORPORATION; *pg.* 1576, *pg.* 1753
NATRALOCK - Visual Packaging - WESTROCK COMPANY; *pg.* 1472, *pg.* 1805
NATRAPEL - Insect Repellent - TENDER CORPORATION; *pg.* 1601, *pg.* 1035
NATRASOL - Gloves - LAKELAND INDUSTRIES, INC.; *pg.* 1354, *pg.* 1338
NATRASORB - Bagged Sorbent - MULTISORB TECHNOLOGIES, INC.; *pg.* 1570, *pg.* 1150
NATRECOR - Healthcare Product - JOHNSON & JOHNSON; *pg.* 1549, *pg.* 1091
NATREL - Milk & Cheese Products - AGROPUR COOPERATIVE; *pg.* 836, *pg.* 1950
NATRELLE COLLECTION - Skin Care Product - ALLERGAN, INC.; *pg.* 1491, *pg.* 106
NATROL - Nutritional Product - NATROL, INC.; *pg.* 1570, *pg.* 64
NATROL COMPLETE BALANCE - Vitamins - NATROL, INC.; *pg.* 1570, *pg.* 64
NATROSOL - Polymer - HERCULES INCORPORATED; *pg.* 1166, *pg.* 392
NATSYN - Polyisoprene Rubber - THE GOODYEAR TIRE & RUBBER COMPANY; *pg.* 1883, *pg.* 1401
NATUGUARD - Health & Nutrition Product - NOVUS INTERNATIONAL, INC.; *pg.* 706, *pg.* 1001
NATUMI - Food Product - THE HAIN CELESTIAL GROUP, INC.; *pg.* 860, *pg.* 1172
NATURA - Ostomy Skin Barriers - ALIMED, INC.; *pg.* 1490, *pg.* 816
NATURA - Glazed Floor Tile - FLORIDA TILE INDUSTRIES, INC.; *pg.* 82, *pg.* 730
NATURAL - Canned Seafood - CROWN PRINCE, INC.; *pg.* 850, *pg.* 67
NATURAL - Pudding - KOZY SHACK INC.; *pg.* 869, *pg.* 1167
NATURAL - Footwear - P.W. MINOR & SON, INC.; *pg.* 1816, *pg.* 1140
NATURAL - Toothpaste - USANA HEALTH SCIENCES, INC.; *pg.* 1605, *pg.* 1761
NATURAL - Potato Chips - UTZ QUALITY FOODS, INC.; *pg.* 907, *pg.* 1536
NATURAL ADVANTAGE - Skin Care Product - GUTHY-RENKER LLC; *pg.* 289, *pg.* 273
NATURAL ANIMAL - Organic Pet Care Product - GARDENS ALIVE!, INC.; *pg.* 1796, *pg.* 693
NATURAL BABY - Hair Care Product - AUBREY ORGANICS INC.; *pg.* 499, *pg.* 470
NATURAL BALANCE - Pet Food - BIG HEART PET BRANDS; *pg.* 1474, *pg.* 213
NATURAL BALANCE - Nutritional Product - NUTRACEUTICAL INTERNATIONAL CORPORATION; *pg.* 1576, *pg.* 1753
NATURAL BEAUTY ESSENTIALS - Supplement & Food Product - NEW EARTH LIFE SCIENCES, INC.; *pg.* 1573, *pg.* 1499
NATURAL BEGINNINGS - Vegetable Gardening - GARDENS ALIVE!, INC.; *pg.* 1796, *pg.* 693
NATURAL BERRY FULL - Herbal Product - NOW HEALTH GROUP, INC.; *pg.* 1576, *pg.* 557
NATURAL BORDEAUX - Cherry - OREGON CHERRY GROWERS, INC.; *pg.* 1028, *pg.* 1508
NATURAL BREW - Food Product - THE J.M. SMUCKER COMPANY; *pg.* 865, *pg.* 1468
NATURAL CARE - Mattress - SIMMONS COMPANY; *pg.* 943, *pg.* 520
NATURAL CHANGES - Health Care Product - NATURE'S SUNSHINE PRODUCTS, INC.; *pg.* 1571, *pg.* 1754
NATURAL CHEETOS - Chips - PEPSICO, INC.; *pg.* 259, *pg.* 1327
NATURAL CHERRY - Furniture - BUSH INDUSTRIES INC.; *pg.* 919, *pg.* 1170
NATURAL CHOICE - Deli Lunch Meats - HORMEL FOODS CORPORATION; *pg.* 863, *pg.* 915
NATURAL CHOICE - Beverage - MONSTER BEVERAGE CORPORATION; *pg.* 257, *pg.* 69
NATURAL CHOICE - Petcare - TRACTOR SUPPLY COMPANY; *pg.* 708, *pg.* 1627
NATURAL CITRUS MOISTURE - Herbal Product - NOW HEALTH GROUP, INC.; *pg.* 1576, *pg.* 557
NATURAL COMFORT - Pacifier - EVENFLO COMPANY, INC.; *pg.* 924, *pg.* 1470
THE NATURAL CONFECTIONERY COMPANY - Candy Products - MONDELEZ INTERNATIONAL, INC.; *pg.* 878, *pg.* 601
NATURAL COUNTRY - Nectar - COUNTRY PURE FOODS, INC.; *pg.* 247, *pg.* 1400
NATURAL CREATIONS - Wood Flooring Product -

ARMSTRONG WORLD INDUSTRIES, INC.; *pg.* 914, *pg.* 1545
NATURAL DIMENSIONS - Hair Coloring - P&G-CLAIROL, INC.; *pg.* 519, *pg.* 1418
NATURAL ELEGANCE - Rug - COURISTAN INC.; *pg.* 921, *pg.* 1067
NATURAL EXPRESSIONS - Carpet - BEAULIEU GROUP, LLC; *pg.* 917, *pg.* 529
NATURAL FERN - Carpet - BEAULIEU GROUP, LLC; *pg.* 917, *pg.* 529
THE NATURAL GOODNESS OF MAINE - Slogan - OAKHURST DAIRY; *pg.* 887, *pg.* 752
NATURAL HARMONY - Skin Care - COMBE INCORPORATED; *pg.* 1516, *pg.* 1351
NATURAL HEALTH - Magazine - AMERICAN MEDIA, INC.; *pg.* 1615, *pg.* 410
NATURAL HERBAL - Hair & Skin Product - AUBREY ORGANICS INC.; *pg.* 499, *pg.* 470
NATURAL HERBAL REVIVAL - Herbal Product - NOW HEALTH GROUP, INC.; *pg.* 1576, *pg.* 557
NATURAL HOME - Publication - OGDEN PUBLICATIONS, INC.; *pg.* 1672, *pg.* 722
NATURAL ICE - Beer - ANHEUSER-BUSCH COMPANIES, LLC; *pg.* 237, *pg.* 991
NATURAL ICE - Lip Balm - THE MENTHOLATUM COMPANY; *pg.* 1565, *pg.* 1320
NATURAL ILLUSIONS - Rubber Tile - BURKE INDUSTRIES, INC.; *pg.* 919, *pg.* 239
NATURAL INSPIRATIONS - Ceilings & Walls - ARMSTRONG WORLD INDUSTRIES, INC.; *pg.* 914, *pg.* 1545
NATURAL INSTINCTS - Hair Coloring - P&G-CLAIROL, INC.; *pg.* 519, *pg.* 1418
NATURAL INSTINCTS FOR MEN - Hair Coloring - P&G-CLAIROL, INC.; *pg.* 519, *pg.* 1418
NATURAL ISSUE - Casual Clothing - PERRY ELLIS INTERNATIONAL, INC.; *pg.* 45, *pg.* 445
NATURAL LAYS - Potato Chips - FRITO-LAY NORTH AMERICA, INC.; *pg.* 1853, *pg.* 1730
NATURAL LAYS - Chips - PEPSICO, INC.; *pg.* 259, *pg.* 1327
NATURAL LIGHT - Beer - ANHEUSER-BUSCH COMPANIES, LLC; *pg.* 237, *pg.* 991
NATURAL LIGHT SUPPLEMENT - Lighting - OTTLITE; *pg.* 1303, *pg.* 475
NATURAL LIPS - Hair & Skin Product - AUBREY ORGANICS INC.; *pg.* 499, *pg.* 470
NATURAL MINT - Hair & Skin Product - AUBREY ORGANICS INC.; *pg.* 499, *pg.* 470
NATURAL MISSST - Hair & Skin Product - AUBREY ORGANICS INC.; *pg.* 499, *pg.* 470
NATURAL MULTI-VITAMIN JUICE SLAM - Beverage - MONSTER BEVERAGE CORPORATION; *pg.* 257, *pg.* 69
NATURAL PRODUCT INSIDER - Publication - INFORMA EXHIBITIONS LLC; *pg.* 1653, *pg.* 17
NATURAL RED - Cherry - OREGON CHERRY GROWERS, INC.; *pg.* 1028, *pg.* 1508
THE NATURAL RESOURCE - Natural Colors - SENSIENT COLORS INC.; *pg.* 1180, *pg.* 1003
NATURAL RUFFLES - Potato Chips - FRITO-LAY NORTH AMERICA, INC.; *pg.* 1853, *pg.* 1730
NATURAL RUFFLES - Chips - PEPSICO, INC.; *pg.* 259, *pg.* 1327
THE NATURAL SOURCE OF QUALITY - Tagline - DARIGOLD, INC.; *pg.* 852, *pg.* 1835
NATURAL SPA - Hair & Skin Product - AUBREY ORGANICS INC.; *pg.* 499, *pg.* 470
NATURAL SPORT - Nutritional Product - NUTRACEUTICAL INTERNATIONAL CORPORATION; *pg.* 1576, *pg.* 1753
THE NATURAL STATE - Tagline - ARKANSAS DEPARTMENT OF PARKS & TOURISM; *pg.* 988, *pg.* 33
NATURAL STONE GROUND - Mustard - PLOCHMAN, INC.; *pg.* 890, *pg.* 631
NATURAL TOSTITOS - Chips - FRITO-LAY NORTH AMERICA, INC.; *pg.* 1853, *pg.* 1730
NATURAL TOSTITOS - Chips - PEPSICO, INC.; *pg.* 259, *pg.* 1327
NATURAL TOUCH - Food Product - KELLOGG COMPANY; *pg.* 831, *pg.* 870
NATURAL TOUCH - Bio-Enzymatic Cleaning Formula - NILODOR, INC.; *pg.* 332, *pg.* 1406
NATURAL TOUCH KAFFREE ROMA - Roasted Grain Beverage - KELLOGG COMPANY; *pg.* 831, *pg.* 870
NATURAL TOUCH NINE BEAN LOAF - Beans & Organic Tofu Cheeses - KELLOGG COMPANY; *pg.* 831, *pg.* 870
NATURAL TOUCH VEGETARIAN TUNA - Tuna Substitute - KELLOGG COMPANY; *pg.* 831, *pg.* 870
NATURAL WOOL COLLECTION - Wool Tufted Rugs - MOHAWK HOME; *pg.* 935, *pg.* 541
NATURALAIRE - Filtration Product - FLANDERS CORPORATION; *pg.* 1336, *pg.* 1392
NATURALAMB - Condoms - CHURCH & DWIGHT CO., INC.; *pg.* 1153, *pg.* 1063
NATURALATCH - Flashlight - ENERGIZER HOLDINGS, INC.; *pg.* 637, *pg.* 996
NATURALCARE - Nutritional Product - NUTRACEUTICAL INTERNATIONAL CORPORATION; *pg.* 1576, *pg.* 1753
NATURALCRISP - French Fries - J.R. SIMPLOT COMPANY; *pg.* 867, *pg.* 547
NATURALE - Ladies' Wallets - BUXTON ACQUISITION CO., LLC; *pg.* 2, *pg.* 845
NATURALIGHT - Supplement & Food Product - NEW EARTH LIFE SCIENCES, INC.; *pg.* 1573, *pg.* 1499
NATURALINE - Play System - CREATIVE PLAYTHINGS LTD.; *pg.* 1831, *pg.* 820
NATURALITE - Architectural Product - BUTLER MANUFACTURING COMPANY; *pg.* 72, *pg.* 981
NATURALLY, A BETTER SOLUTION - Tag Line - HERCULES INCORPORATED; *pg.* 1166, *pg.* 392
NATURALLY ALOE - Healthful Nutritional Product - INTEGRATED BIOPHARMA, INC.; *pg.* 1546, *pg.* 1073
NATURALLY CAJUN - Cajun Seasoning - MODERN PRODUCTS, INC.; *pg.* 1568, *pg.* 1871
NATURALLY CREATIVE - Slogan - FIBERMARK INC.; *pg.* 1457, *pg.* 1764
NATURALLY, IT WORKS. - Slogan - TOM'S OF MAINE, INC.; *pg.* 523, *pg.* 750
NATURALLY MANGOSTEEN - Healthful Nutritional Product - INTEGRATED BIOPHARMA, INC.; *pg.* 1546, *pg.* 1073
NATURALLY NONI - Healthful Nutritional Product - INTEGRATED BIOPHARMA, INC.; *pg.* 1546, *pg.* 1073
NATURALLY PLAYFUL - Plastic Product - THE STEP2 COMPANY LLC; *pg.* 1889, *pg.* 1474
NATURALLY POMEGRANATE - Healthful Nutritional Product - INTEGRATED BIOPHARMA, INC.; *pg.* 1546, *pg.* 1073
NATURALLY PREFERRED - Natural & Organic Foods - THE KROGER CO.; *pg.* 1025, *pg.* 1416
NATURALLY SALT FREE - Line of Salt Free Seasonings - MODERN PRODUCTS, INC.; *pg.* 1568, *pg.* 1871
NATURALMAX - Nutritional Product - NUTRACEUTICAL INTERNATIONAL CORPORATION; *pg.* 1576, *pg.* 1753
NATURALS - Beauty Product - AVON PRODUCTS, INC.; *pg.* 500, *pg.* 1198
NATURALSOURCE - Visual Packaging - WESTROCK COMPANY; *pg.* 1472, *pg.* 1805
NATURALSPORT - Shoes - CALERES, INC.; *pg.* 1805, *pg.* 993
NATURALSTONE - Flooring Finish - WILSONART INTERNATIONAL, INC.; *pg.* 1450, *pg.* 1746
NATURALYTE - Bicarbonate Concentrate for Single Patient Systems - FRESENIUS MEDICAL CARE NORTH AMERICA; *pg.* 1531, *pg.* 851
NATURAQUA - Beverages - THE COCA-COLA COMPANY; *pg.* 240, *pg.* 493
NATURE CLEANSE - Nutritional Supplement - NATURAL ORGANICS, INC.; *pg.* 1571, *pg.* 1181
NATURE DE FRANCE - Soap & Detergent - GRANDPA BRANDS COMPANY; *pg.* 1538, *pg.* 727
NATURE MADE - Vitamins & Food Supplements - PHARMAVITE LLC; *pg.* 1584, *pg.* 167
NATURE MADE ADVANCE - Nutritional Supplement - PHARMAVITE LLC; *pg.* 1584, *pg.* 167
NATURE MADE DIET WISE - Nutritional Supplement - PHARMAVITE LLC; *pg.* 1584, *pg.* 167
NATURE MADE HEALTHSOLUTIONS - Nutritional Supplement - PHARMAVITE LLC; *pg.* 1584, *pg.* 167
THE NATURE OF HUMAN HEALTH - Tag Line - PROPHASE LABS, INC.; *pg.* 1586, *pg.* 1526
THE NATURE OF WHAT'S TO COME - Tagline - ARCHER-DANIELS-MIDLAND COMPANY; *pg.* 825, *pg.* 565
NATURE SAVER - Office Products - GENUINE PARTS COMPANY; *pg.* 206, *pg.* 506
NATURE SCAPES - Mulch & Decorative Groundcover - THE SCOTTS MIRACLE-GRO COMPANY; *pg.* 1799, *pg.* 1459
NATURE SCENT - Organic Fan Freshener - SURCO PRODUCTS, INC.; *pg.* 336, *pg.* 1581
NATURE. SCIENCE. SOLUTIONS. - Slogan - PENFORD CORPORATION; *pg.* 1177, *pg.* 314
NATURE SING - Pillow and Throw - HERITAGE LACE INC.; *pg.* 694, *pg.* 711
NATURE SOLE - Shoes - CALERES, INC.; *pg.* 1805, *pg.* 993
NATURE TRAILS - Carpet - INTERFACE, INC.; *pg.* 695, *pg.* 512
NATURE VALLEY - Food Product - GENERAL MILLS, INC.; *pg.* 828, *pg.* 933
NATURE WEAVE - Carpet - BEAULIEU GROUP, LLC; *pg.* 917, *pg.* 529
NATURE WORKS - Fibres - CARGILL LIMITED; *pg.* 1475, *pg.* 1914
NATURE ZONE - Pet Product - PETSMART, INC.; *pg.* 1481, *pg.* 18
NATURECARE - Beauty Product - TUPPERWARE BRANDS CORPORATION; *pg.* 1139, *pg.* 456
NATUREFORM - Flooring - MANNINGTON MILLS, INC.; *pg.* 934, *pg.* 1119
NATUREGUARD - Rosemary Extract - NEWLY WEDS FOODS, INC.; *pg.* 886, *pg.* 585
NATURELLA - Personal Care Product - THE PROCTER & GAMBLE COMPANY; *pg.* 1129, *pg.* 1418
NATURELLE - Personal Care Product - ROCHESTER MIDLAND CORPORATION; *pg.* 334, *pg.* 1337
NATURELLE - Perms, Shampoos, Conditioners & Styling Aids - ZOTOS INTERNATIONAL, INC.; *pg.* 524, *pg.* 345
NATURE'S BALANCE - Hair & Skin Product - AUBREY ORGANICS INC.; *pg.* 499, *pg.* 470
NATURE'S BASKET - Food Products - GIANT EAGLE, INC.; *pg.* 1020, *pg.* 1575
NATURE'S BEAUTY, OUR CRAFTSMANSHIP - Tagline - F.E. HALE MANUFACTURING COMPANY; *pg.* 925, *pg.* 1160
NATURE'S BEST - Health & Beauty Product - BLUE CROSS LABORATORIES; *pg.* 326, *pg.* 277
NATURE'S BOUNTY - Natural Vitamins & Cosmetics - NBTY, INC.; *pg.* 1572, *pg.* 1338
NATURE'S CHOICE - Odor Remover - THE FULLER BRUSH COMPANY; *pg.* 330, *pg.* 715
NATURE`S CRYSTAL - Hand Cream - MERLE NORMAN COSMETICS, INC.; *pg.* 517, *pg.* 136
NATURE'S GALLERY - Wood Flooring Product - ARMSTRONG WORLD INDUSTRIES, INC.; *pg.* 914, *pg.* 1545
NATURES GARDEN - Carpet - BEAULIEU GROUP, LLC; *pg.* 917, *pg.* 529
NATURE'S GOLD - Small Pet Products - THE HARTZ MOUNTAIN CORP.; *pg.* 1476, *pg.* 1120
NATURES LIFE - Nutritional Product - NUTRACEUTICAL INTERNATIONAL CORPORATION; *pg.* 1576, *pg.* 1753
NATURE'S LINING - Health System Product - LANELABS USA INC.; *pg.* 1554, *pg.* 1128
NATURE'S MIRROR - Multivitamin Skin Care Product - HERBALIFE INTERNATIONAL OF AMERICA, INC.; *pg.* 1541, *pg.* 132
NATURE'S OWN - Instant Mashed Potatoes & Hashbrowns - BASIC AMERICAN FOODS, INC.; *pg.* 839, *pg.* 303
NATURE'S OWN - Food Product - FLOWERS FOODS, INC.; *pg.* 855, *pg.* 541
NATURE'S PARTNER - Fruit & Vegetable Product - GIUMARRA VINEYARDS CORPORATION; *pg.* 1964, *pg.* 45
NATURE'S PATH - Organic Foods - NATURE'S PATH FOODS INC.; *pg.* 833, *pg.* 1908
NATURE'S PET - Pet Grooming Products - THE STEPHAN COMPANY; *pg.* 1597, *pg.* 426
NATURE'S PLUS - Nutritional Supplement - NATURAL ORGANICS, INC.; *pg.* 1571, *pg.* 1181
NATURE'S PROMISE - Groceries - GIANT FOOD STORES, LLC; *pg.* 1021, *pg.* 1520
NATURES PROMISE - Pet Product - PETSMART, INC.; *pg.* 1481, *pg.* 18
NATURE'S RECIPE - Pet Snacks - BIG HEART PET BRANDS; *pg.* 1474, *pg.* 213
NATURE'S SECRET - Healthcare Product - SWANSON HEALTH PRODUCTS INC.; *pg.* 1600, *pg.* 1397
NATURE'S SOLUTION FOR BETTER HEALTH - Slogan - PHARMAVITE LLC; *pg.* 1584, *pg.* 167
NATURE'S SOURCE - Natural Biodegradable Cleaning Products - S.C. JOHNSON & SON, INC.; *pg.* 334, *pg.* 1889
NATURE'S SUNSHINE - Health Products - NATURE'S SUNSHINE PRODUCTS, INC.; *pg.* 1571, *pg.* 1754
NATURE'S TOUCH - Dairy Products - KWIK TRIP INC.; *pg.* 1026, *pg.* 1864
NATURE'S WONDER - Pharmaceutical Product - ALERE INC.; *pg.* 1488, *pg.* 849
NATURESCAPE - Patio Room - PGT, INC.; *pg.* 104, *pg.* 452
NATURESOURCE - Angus Beef - NATIONAL BEEF

First page reference indicates Business Class Edition
Second page reference indicates Geographic Edition

PACKING COMPANY, LLC; *pg.* 882, *pg.* 985
NATURESQUE - Rug - COURISTAN INC.; *pg.* 921, *pg.* 1067
NATURESSENCE - Bodycare and Skincare - AMERICAN INTERNATIONAL INDUSTRIES COMPANY; *pg.* 498, *pg.* 126
NATUREVIEW - Binocular - BUSHNELL OUTDOOR PRODUCTS, INC.; *pg.* 1403, *pg.* 718
NATUREWELL - Beef Products - NATIONAL BEEF PACKING COMPANY, LLC; *pg.* 882, *pg.* 985
NATUREWOOD - Pine Play System - CREATIVE PLAYTHINGS LTD.; *pg.* 1831, *pg.* 820
NATURFRESH - Misc. Natural Food Items - MODERN PRODUCTS, INC.; *pg.* 1568, *pg.* 1871
NATURLOSE - Dietary Supplements - SPHERIX INC.; *pg.* 1596, *pg.* 1808
NATUROSE NATURAL ASTAXANTHIN - Coloring Agent - CYANOTECH CORPORATION; *pg.* 1154, *pg.* 545
NATVAR - Medical Tubing - TEKNI-PLEX, INC.; *pg.* 1470, *pg.* 1122
NAUGAHYDE - Medical & Aesthetic Product - DYNATRONICS CORPORATION; *pg.* 1526, *pg.* 1757
NAUGALEATHER - Fabric - UNIROYAL ENGINEERED PRODUCTS; *pg.* 699, *pg.* 467
NAUGALUBE - Polymer Product - CHEMTURA CORPORATION; *pg.* 1152, *pg.* 355
NAUGARD - Polymer Product - CHEMTURA CORPORATION; *pg.* 1152, *pg.* 355
NAUGASATIN - Fabric - UNIROYAL ENGINEERED PRODUCTS; *pg.* 699, *pg.* 467
NAUGASOFT - Fabric - NEMSCHOFF, INC.; *pg.* 936, *pg.* 1890
NAUGASOFT - Fabric - UNIROYAL ENGINEERED PRODUCTS; *pg.* 699, *pg.* 467
NAUGASYLK - Fabric - UNIROYAL ENGINEERED PRODUCTS; *pg.* 699, *pg.* 467
NAUGAWHITE - Polymer Product - CHEMTURA CORPORATION; *pg.* 1152, *pg.* 355
NAUGEX - Polymer Product - CHEMTURA CORPORATION; *pg.* 1152, *pg.* 355
NAUTA - Processing System - HOSOKAWA MICRON POWDER SYSTEMS; *pg.* 1347, *pg.* 1124
NAUTICA - Furniture - LEXINGTON HOME BRANDS; *pg.* 933, *pg.* 1391
NAUTICA - Apparel - V.F. CORPORATION; *pg.* 34, *pg.* 1376
NAUTICAL - Lighting Product - QUOIZEL INC.; *pg.* 1304, *pg.* 1616
NAUTILUS - Battery - EXIDE TECHNOLOGIES; *pg.* 204, *pg.* 483
NAUTILUS - Knife - GERBER LEGENDARY BLADES; *pg.* 1834, *pg.* 1503
NAUTILUS - Health & Fitness Product - NAUTILUS, INC.; *pg.* 1840, *pg.* 1846
NAUTILUS - Range Hoods - NORTEK, INC.; *pg.* 100, *pg.* 1607
NAUTIQUE NEWS - Magazine - CORRECT CRAFT, INC.; *pg.* 1706, *pg.* 452
NAUTIQUE SUPERSPORT - Power Boat - CORRECT CRAFT, INC.; *pg.* 1706, *pg.* 452
NAUTIQUES - Boats - CORRECT CRAFT, INC.; *pg.* 1706, *pg.* 452
NAUTOCONNING - Monitoring Display System - RAYTHEON COMPANY; *pg.* 233, *pg.* 854
NAUTOLEX - Upholstery - OMNOVA SOLUTIONS INC; *pg.* 1176, *pg.* 1453
NAUTOPILOT - Adaptive Digital Autopilot - RAYTHEON COMPANY; *pg.* 233, *pg.* 854
NAUZENE - Pharmaceutical Product - ALVA/AMCO PHARMACAL COMPANIES, INC.; *pg.* 1492, *pg.* 637
NAV ONE - Laser Detectors - COBRA ELECTRONICS CORPORATION; *pg.* 629, *pg.* 572
NAVAJO - Printing Paper - MOHAWK FINE PAPERS, INC.; *pg.* 1464, *pg.* 1153
NAVAL - Valve - FLOWSERVE CORPORATION; *pg.* 82, *pg.* 1719
NAVAL - Plumbing Product - SLOAN VALVE COMPANY; *pg.* 1062, *pg.* 613
NAVAL OPTIMA SMO - Flushometer - SLOAN VALVE COMPANY; *pg.* 1062, *pg.* 613
NAVAN - Beverage - MARNIER-LAPOSTOLLE INC.; *pg.* 1966, *pg.* 1256
NAVANE - Medicine - PFIZER INC.; *pg.* 1581, *pg.* 1278
NAVARRO - Carpet - BEAULIEU GROUP, LLC; *pg.* 917, *pg.* 529
NAVDISC - Screen Navigation - MOTOROLA SOLUTIONS, INC.; *pg.* 657, *pg.* 659
NAVE - Audio Encoder - WEGENER CORPORATION; *pg.* 687, *pg.* 533
NAVI-DRILL - Downhole Motor - BAKER HUGHES INTEQ; *pg.* 1316, *pg.* 1700
NAVI-STAR - Healthcare Product - JOHNSON & JOHNSON; *pg.* 1549, *pg.* 1091
NAVI-TRAC - Frame Tent System - ANCHOR INDUSTRIES, INC.; *pg.* 1825, *pg.* 678
NAVI-TRAC LITE - Convertible Clearspan Frame Tents - ANCHOR INDUSTRIES, INC.; *pg.* 1825, *pg.* 678
NAVI-TRAK - MWD - BAKER HUGHES INTEQ; *pg.* 1316, *pg.* 1700
NAVIGANT - Software - STEREOTAXIS, INC.; *pg.* 1597, *pg.* 1004
NAVIGATOR - Power Supply System - ADVANCED ENERGY INDUSTRIES, INC.; *pg.* 613, *pg.* 328
NAVIGATOR - Valve - AKRON BRASS COMPANY; *pg.* 1311, *pg.* 1482
NAVIGATOR - Aluminum Boat - ALUMACRAFT BOAT COMPANY; *pg.* 1705, *pg.* 964
NAVIGATOR - Software - BENTLEY SYSTEMS, INC.; *pg.* 361, *pg.* 1531
NAVIGATOR - Guidance Systems - BLUE OX; *pg.* 701, *pg.* 1019
NAVIGATOR - Medical Device - BOSTON SCIENTIFIC CORPORATION; *pg.* 1508, *pg.* 831
NAVIGATOR - Bath Accessory - CROSCILL, INC.; *pg.* 1122, *pg.* 1220
NAVIGATOR - Cart Bag - DATREK GOLF; *pg.* 1832, *pg.* 1801
NAVIGATOR - Pool Cleaner - HAYWARD POOL PRODUCTS; *pg.* 1049, *pg.* 1057
NAVIGATOR - Panels - HUFCOR INCORPORATED; *pg.* 87, *pg.* 1861
NAVIGATOR - EPM Treatment - IDEXX LABORATORIES, INC.; *pg.* 1543, *pg.* 753
NAVIGATOR - Camera Control System - INTUITIVE SURGICAL, INC.; *pg.* 1546, *pg.* 286
NAVIGATOR - Basketball Equipment - LIFETIME PRODUCTS INC.; *pg.* 933, *pg.* 1751
NAVIGATOR - Eyewear - MAUI JIM, INC.; *pg.* 9, *pg.* 651
NAVIGATOR - Q-Switched Laser - NEWPORT CORPORATION; *pg.* 1424, *pg.* 114
NAVIGATOR - Gps Controls - REINKE MANUFACTURING COMPANY, INC.; *pg.* 707, *pg.* 1010
NAVIGATOR - Precision Ophthalmic Lenses - SIGNET ARMORLITE, INC.; *pg.* 1429, *pg.* 60
NAVIGATOR - Software - TEXAS INSTRUMENTS INCORPORATED; *pg.* 679, *pg.* 1688
NAVIGATOR - Bicycle - TREK BICYCLE CORPORATION; *pg.* 1847, *pg.* 1896
NAVIGATOR - Remote Designed to Operate Up to Four Separate Electronic Devices - UNIVERSAL ELECTRONICS, INC.; *pg.* 683, *pg.* 262
NAVIGATOR - Construction Equipment - VERMEER MANUFACTURING COMPANY; *pg.* 708, *pg.* 711
NAVIGATOR-20 - Paint Gun - M-B COMPANIES, INC.; *pg.* 1357, *pg.* 1884
NAVIGATOR OF THE SEAS - Cruise Ship - ROYAL CARIBBEAN CRUISES LTD; *pg.* 1921, *pg.* 446
NAVIGATOR SHORT - Ophthalmic Lenses - SIGNET ARMORLITE, INC.; *pg.* 1429, *pg.* 60
NAVILINK - Semiconductors - TEXAS INSTRUMENTS INCORPORATED; *pg.* 679, *pg.* 1688
NAVION - Software - MICROWAY, INC.; *pg.* 1267, *pg.* 841
NAVION - Motor Homes - WINNEBAGO INDUSTRIES, INC.; *pg.* 1712, *pg.* 707
NAVION IQ - Motor Homes - WINNEBAGO INDUSTRIES, INC.; *pg.* 1712, *pg.* 707
NAVIS - Software System - ALCATEL-LUCENT; *pg.* 615, *pg.* 1094
NAVIS - Optical Management Solution - ALCATEL-LUCENT; *pg.* 615, *pg.* 38
NAVISACCESS - Software System - ALCATEL-LUCENT; *pg.* 615, *pg.* 1094
NAVISCORE - Software System - ALCATEL-LUCENT; *pg.* 615, *pg.* 1094
NAVISPHERE - Software - EMC CORPORATION; *pg.* 391, *pg.* 825
NAVISRADIUS - Software System - ALCATEL-LUCENT; *pg.* 615, *pg.* 1094
NAVISWORKS - Software - AUTODESK INC.; *pg.* 356, *pg.* 257
NAVISXTEND - Software System - ALCATEL-LUCENT; *pg.* 615, *pg.* 1094
NAVITRAC - Tire - TBC CORPORATION; *pg.* 1889, *pg.* 457
NAVMAG - Magnetic Mapping System - SCINTREX LTD.; *pg.* 1374, *pg.* 1920
NAVSTRIKE - Precision Guided Munition - ROCKWELL COLLINS, INC.; *pg.* 234, *pg.* 702
NAVSUITE - Medical Product - STRYKER CORPORATION; *pg.* 1598, *pg.* 894
NAVTEC - Construction Equipment - VERMEER MANUFACTURING COMPANY; *pg.* 708, *pg.* 711
NAVY - Pillow and Throw - HERITAGE LACE INC.; *pg.* 694, *pg.* 711
NAVY, ACCELERATE YOUR LIFE - Tag Line - UNITED STATES NAVY RECRUITING COMMAND; *pg.* 1009, *pg.* 1648
NAVY SWEET - Dry Snuff - SWISHER INTERNATIONAL, INC.; *pg.* 1895, *pg.* 345
NAXCEL - Pharmaceutical Product - PFIZER INC.; *pg.* 1581, *pg.* 1278
NAXY - Pharmaceutical Product - ABBOTT LABORATORIES; *pg.* 1484, *pg.* 551
NB & T - Stainless Steel - NATIONAL BAND & TAG CO.; *pg.* 1479, *pg.* 739
NB ZIP - Cushioning Technology - NEW BALANCE ATHLETIC SHOE, INC.; *pg.* 1811, *pg.* 798
NBA - National Basketball Association - NATIONAL BASKETBALL ASSOCIATION; *pg.* 566, *pg.* 1264
NBA - Automatic Conveyor System - PARAGON TECHNOLOGIES, INC.; *pg.* 1367, *pg.* 1528
NBA BASIC FLEECE - Ear Warmer - 180S, LLC; *pg.* 1824, *pg.* 754
NBA INSTANT GAME - Lottery Game - OHIO LOTTERY COMMISSION; *pg.* 1002, *pg.* 1433
NBACCELERATOR - Computer Program - COMPUTER SCIENCES CORPORATION; *pg.* 378, *pg.* 1780
NBC - Broadcast Stations - NBC UNIVERSAL, INC.; *pg.* 300, *pg.* 1266
NBC SPORTS - Television Network - NBC UNIVERSAL TELEVISION NETWORKS GROUP; *pg.* 302, *pg.* 1267
NBCNEWS.COM - News Site - NBC NEWS; *pg.* 300, *pg.* 1265
NBE - Container - NATIONAL BULK EQUIPMENT, INC.; *pg.* 1479, *pg.* 892
NBK NEWS - Educational Materials - SCHOLASTIC INC.; *pg.* 1683, *pg.* 1288
NBS - Belt Sorter - PARAGON TECHNOLOGIES, INC.; *pg.* 1367, *pg.* 1528
NBS 30 - Belt Sorter - PARAGON TECHNOLOGIES, INC.; *pg.* 1367, *pg.* 1528
NBS 90 - Belt Sorter - PARAGON TECHNOLOGIES, INC.; *pg.* 1367, *pg.* 1528
NBS 90-SP - Belt Sorter - PARAGON TECHNOLOGIES, INC.; *pg.* 1367, *pg.* 1528
NBS ADVANTAGE - Card Personalization - NBS TECHNOLOGIES INC.; *pg.* 786, *pg.* 1941
NBS HORIZON - Card Personalization - NBS TECHNOLOGIES INC.; *pg.* 786, *pg.* 1941
NBS HORIZON EVOLUTION - Card Personalization - NBS TECHNOLOGIES INC.; *pg.* 786, *pg.* 1941
NBS IMAGEMASTER IMX2 - Card Printer - NBS TECHNOLOGIES INC.; *pg.* 786, *pg.* 1941
NBS JAVELIN - Card Personalization - NBS TECHNOLOGIES INC.; *pg.* 786, *pg.* 1941
NBS WAFER PACKING SOLUTIONS - Packaging Software - NBS TECHNOLOGIES INC.; *pg.* 786, *pg.* 1941
NBT - Automatic Conveyor System - PARAGON TECHNOLOGIES, INC.; *pg.* 1367, *pg.* 1528
NBX - Performance Footwear - NEW BALANCE ATHLETIC SHOE, INC.; *pg.* 1811, *pg.* 798
NC-11 - Cellular Telephone Headset - ANDREA ELECTRONICS CORPORATION; *pg.* 617, *pg.* 1143
NC-300 - Digital Concert Piano - KORG USA, INC.; *pg.* 556, *pg.* 1180
NC-3000 - De-Icer - ARCHER-DANIELS-MIDLAND COMPANY; *pg.* 825, *pg.* 565
NC-500 - Digital Concert Piano - KORG USA, INC.; *pg.* 556, *pg.* 1180
NC-61 - Noise Cancellation - ANDREA ELECTRONICS CORPORATION; *pg.* 617, *pg.* 1143
NC-65 - Noise Cancellation - ANDREA ELECTRONICS CORPORATION; *pg.* 617, *pg.* 1143
NC-7100 - Noise Cancellation w/ USB - ANDREA ELECTRONICS CORPORATION; *pg.* 617, *pg.* 1143
NC-STAT - Neuropathy Diagnostic System - NEUROMETRIX, INC.; *pg.* 1572, *pg.* 852
NCAA - Trademark - NATIONAL COLLEGIATE ATHLETIC

ASSOCIATION; *pg.* 567, *pg.* 688
NCAA BASKETBALL - Trademark - NATIONAL COLLEGIATE ATHLETIC ASSOCIATION; *pg.* 567, *pg.* 688
NCAA CHAMIONSHIPS - Trademark - NATIONAL COLLEGIATE ATHLETIC ASSOCIATION; *pg.* 567, *pg.* 688
NCAA CHAMPIONSHIPS - Trademark - NATIONAL COLLEGIATE ATHLETIC ASSOCIATION; *pg.* 567, *pg.* 688
NCAA COLLEGE CUP - Trademark (Div. I Men's & Women's Soccer) - NATIONAL COLLEGIATE ATHLETIC ASSOCIATION; *pg.* 567, *pg.* 688
THE NCAA EXPERIENCE - Trademark - NATIONAL COLLEGIATE ATHLETIC ASSOCIATION; *pg.* 567, *pg.* 688
NCAA HALL OF CHAMPIONS - Trademark - NATIONAL COLLEGIATE ATHLETIC ASSOCIATION; *pg.* 567, *pg.* 688
NCAA INTERNATIONAL - Trademark - NATIONAL COLLEGIATE ATHLETIC ASSOCIATION; *pg.* 567, *pg.* 688
NCAA KIDS - Trademark - NATIONAL COLLEGIATE ATHLETIC ASSOCIATION; *pg.* 567, *pg.* 688
NCAA NEWS - Trademark - NATIONAL COLLEGIATE ATHLETIC ASSOCIATION; *pg.* 567, *pg.* 688
NCAA PHOTOS - Trademark - NATIONAL COLLEGIATE ATHLETIC ASSOCIATION; *pg.* 567, *pg.* 688
NCAA SWEET 16 - Trademark (Collegiate Basketball) - NATIONAL COLLEGIATE ATHLETIC ASSOCIATION; *pg.* 567, *pg.* 688
NCAASPORTS.COM - Sport Media - CBS SPORTSLINE.COM, INC.; *pg.* 1234, *pg.* 423
NCAPS - Sensors - CUSTOM SENSORS & TECHNOLOGIES; *pg.* 1407, *pg.* 152
NCE - Animation Motor - ALAN GORDON ENTERPRISES, INC.; *pg.* 1399, *pg.* 125
NCENDX - Chemical Product - ALBEMARLE CORPORATION; *pg.* 1146, *pg.* 741
N.C.F.R. - Building Product - HOMASOTE COMPANY; *pg.* 87, *pg.* 1126
NCI - Furniture - NEMSCHOFF, INC.; *pg.* 936, *pg.* 1890
NCJ - Bi-Monthly Magazine - AMERICAN RADIO RELAY LEAGUE, INC.; *pg.* 130, *pg.* 359
NCNG - Energy - PIEDMONT NATURAL GAS COMPANY, INC.; *pg.* 1949, *pg.* 1368
NCOA LINK - Software - MELISSA DATA CORP.; *pg.* 432, *pg.* 188
NCOALINK - List Cleaner - USADATA, INC.; *pg.* 1287, *pg.* 1308
NCOEPAYMENTS - Payment Service - EGS FINANCIAL CARE, INC.; *pg.* 746, *pg.* 1540
NCOMMAND - Pharmaceutical Preparation - PFIZER INC.; *pg.* 1581, *pg.* 1278
NCOMPASS - Software Product & Module - RIVERBED PERFORMANCE MANAGEMENT; *pg.* 462, *pg.* 765
NCONCERT - Financial Aid Delivery Management - NELNET, INC.; *pg.* 786, *pg.* 1012
NCORE - Software - CITRIX SYSTEMS, INC.; *pg.* 375, *pg.* 424
NCP - Computer Software - NOVELL INC.; *pg.* 446, *pg.* 852
NCR @ YOUR SERVICE - Brochure - NCR CORPORATION; *pg.* 443, *pg.* 531
NCR FASTLANE - Software - NCR CORPORATION; *pg.* 443, *pg.* 531
NCR PAPER - Carbonless Paper - APPVION INC.; *pg.* 1451, *pg.* 1852
NCR REALPOS - Point-of-Service Operator - NCR CORPORATION; *pg.* 443, *pg.* 531
NCR REALPRICE - Label System - NCR CORPORATION; *pg.* 443, *pg.* 531
NCR REALSCAN - Price Scanner - NCR CORPORATION; *pg.* 443, *pg.* 531
NCR REALSOLUTIONS - Software - NCR CORPORATION; *pg.* 443, *pg.* 531
NCR SELFSERV - Automatic Teller Machine - NCR CORPORATION; *pg.* 443, *pg.* 531
NCS DESIGNEXPERT - Educational Software - PEARSON ASSESSMENTS; *pg.* 1674, *pg.* 918
NCS DOCUSCAN PATIENT ENCOUNTER SYSTEM - Healthcare Software - PEARSON ASSESSMENTS; *pg.* 1674, *pg.* 918
NCT - Protective & Decorative Motor Vehicle Coatings - PPG INDUSTRIES, INC.; *pg.* 1445, *pg.* 1579
NCVO - Software - TRIZETTO CORPORATION; *pg.* 485, *pg.* 327
NDS MIGRATOR - Software - DELL SOFTWARE; *pg.* 385, *pg.* 40
NEAP - Computer Software - NOVELL INC.; *pg.* 446, *pg.* 852
NEAPCO - Constant Velocity Joints - NEAPCO, INC.; *pg.* 214, *pg.* 1582
NEAR EAST - Rice & Noodle Products - PEPSICO, INC.; *pg.* 259, *pg.* 1327
NEAR EAST - Side Dishes - THE QUAKER OATS COMPANY; *pg.* 834, *pg.* 588
NEARSTORE - Software - NETAPP, INC.; *pg.* 444, *pg.* 287
NEAT - Electromechanical Positioning System - DANAHER CORPORATION; *pg.* 1044, *pg.* 397
NEAT - Custom Travel Packages - TRAVELPORT LIMITED; *pg.* 1925, *pg.* 521
NEAT FEET - Hair & Skin Product - AUBREY ORGANICS INC.; *pg.* 499, *pg.* 470
NEAT FEET - Nail Care Product - THE W.E. BASSETT COMPANY; *pg.* 524, *pg.* 371
NEAT PLEAT - Pleated Shades - SPRINGS WINDOW FASHIONS LLC; *pg.* 943, *pg.* 1872
NEAT SHEET - Ground Cover - KIMBERLY-CLARK CORPORATION; *pg.* 1461, *pg.* 1720
NEAX - Internet Tool - NEC CORPORATION OF AMERICA, INC.; *pg.* 658, *pg.* 1723
NEBO - Sports Equipment - ALLIANCE SPORTS GROUP, L.P.; *pg.* 1825, *pg.* 1698
NEBRASKA 2 BY 2 - Online Lottery Game - NEBRASKA LOTTERY; *pg.* 1000, *pg.* 1012
NEBRASKA PICK 3 - Lottery Game - NEBRASKA LOTTERY; *pg.* 1000, *pg.* 1012
NEBRASKA PICK 5 - Online Lottery Game - NEBRASKA LOTTERY; *pg.* 1000, *pg.* 1012
NEBS - Business Forms - DELUXE CORPORATION; *pg.* 1634, *pg.* 964
NEBULA - Fabric - NEMSCHOFF, INC.; *pg.* 936, *pg.* 1890
NEBULITE - Healthcare Product - GF HEALTH PRODUCTS, INC.; *pg.* 1535, *pg.* 508
NEC - Fire Safety Book - NATIONAL FIRE PROTECTION ASSOCIATION; *pg.* 149, *pg.* 842
NEC - Semiconductor Company - RENESAS ELECTRONICS AMERICA INC.; *pg.* 667, *pg.* 269
NEC EXPERT - Fire Safety Book - NATIONAL FIRE PROTECTION ASSOCIATION; *pg.* 149, *pg.* 842
NECCO CANDY BUTTONS - Candy Buttons - NEW ENGLAND CONFECTIONERY COMPANY INC.; *pg.* 1860, *pg.* 842
NECCO CHOCOLATE WAFERS - Candy Buttons & Wafers - NEW ENGLAND CONFECTIONERY COMPANY INC.; *pg.* 1860, *pg.* 842
NECDIGEST - Fire Safety Book - NATIONAL FIRE PROTECTION ASSOCIATION; *pg.* 149, *pg.* 842
NECK DOCTOR - Medical & Aesthetic Product - DYNATRONICS CORPORATION; *pg.* 1526, *pg.* 1757
NECK NACK - Travel Pillow - MCNETT CORPORATION; *pg.* 1839, *pg.* 1817
NECK NACK MD - Inflatable Neck Pillow - MCNETT CORPORATION; *pg.* 1839, *pg.* 1817
NECK TYE - Footwear - OAKLEY, INC.; *pg.* 1840, *pg.* 86
NECKPILLOW - Pillow - TEMPUR SEALY INTERNATIONAL, INC.; *pg.* 944, *pg.* 731
NECKSUPPORT - Pillow - TEMPUR SEALY INTERNATIONAL, INC.; *pg.* 944, *pg.* 731
NECKY - Kayaks - JOHNSON OUTDOORS INC.; *pg.* 1837, *pg.* 1888
NECON - Pharmaceutical Product - ALLERGAN; *pg.* 1490, *pg.* 1101
NECPLUS - Fire Safety Book - NATIONAL FIRE PROTECTION ASSOCIATION; *pg.* 149, *pg.* 842
NECTAR - Food Product - CLIF BAR INC.; *pg.* 848, *pg.* 83
NECTAR - Apparels - UNDER ARMOUR, INC.; *pg.* 49, *pg.* 759
NECTARIN - Beverages - THE COCA-COLA COMPANY; *pg.* 240, *pg.* 493
NECTARINE WALDORF SALAD - Food Product - GAY LEA FOODS CO-OPERATIVE LIMITED; *pg.* 858, *pg.* 1926
NECTO - Friction Products - FEDERAL-MOGUL HOLDINGS CORPORATION; *pg.* 205, *pg.* 907
NEDA - Apparel - BEBE STORES, INC.; *pg.* 19, *pg.* 49
NEDA BY BEBE - Apparel - BEBE STORES, INC.; *pg.* 19, *pg.* 49
NEDERBURG - South African Wines - DREYFUS ASHBY INC.; *pg.* 1962, *pg.* 1226
NEDHC - Head Capper - NEW ENGLAND MACHINERY, INC.; *pg.* 1364, *pg.* 415
NEDOX - Coating - GENERAL MAGNAPLATE CORPORATION; *pg.* 1164, *pg.* 1079
NEDP - Gap Transfer Flyer - NEW ENGLAND MACHINERY, INC.; *pg.* 1364, *pg.* 415
NEED FOR SPEED - Video Game - ELECTRONIC ARTS INC.; *pg.* 951, *pg.* 189
NEEDAHOTEL.COM - Hotel Accommodations Website - ORBITZ WORLDWIDE, INC.; *pg.* 1918, *pg.* 586
NEEDLEEZE - Bleached Cotton - BARNHARDT MANUFACTURING COMPANY; *pg.* 1498, *pg.* 1364
NEEDLEGARD - Animal Safety Product - NEOGEN CORPORATION; *pg.* 883, *pg.* 896
NEEDLESCOPIC - Instrument System Used for Laparoscopic, General & Pediatric Procedures - AESCULAP, INC.; *pg.* 1487, *pg.* 1521
NEEDLEWORK - Carpet - INTERFACE, INC.; *pg.* 695, *pg.* 512
NEEDS MET - Tagline - MAJESTIC DRUG COMPANY, INC.; *pg.* 516, *pg.* 1343
NEELA - Dolls - AMERICAN GIRL LLC; *pg.* 949, *pg.* 1871
NEENAH - Construction & Industrial Castings - NEENAH FOUNDRY COMPANY; *pg.* 99, *pg.* 1883
NEENAH DIGITAL - Paper - NEENAH PAPER, INC.; *pg.* 1465, *pg.* 484
NEGOCIOS BLOOMBERG - Financial News & Data - BLOOMBERG L.P.; *pg.* 725, *pg.* 1204
NEHA - Adjustable Unscrambler - NEW ENGLAND MACHINERY, INC.; *pg.* 1364, *pg.* 415
NEHCP - Adjustable Unscrambler - NEW ENGLAND MACHINERY, INC.; *pg.* 1364, *pg.* 415
NEHHBT - Adjustable Unscrambler - NEW ENGLAND MACHINERY, INC.; *pg.* 1364, *pg.* 415
NEHHLP - Adjustable Unscrambler - NEW ENGLAND MACHINERY, INC.; *pg.* 1364, *pg.* 415
NEIGHBOR - Office Furniture - STEELCASE INC.; *pg.* 475, *pg.* 889
NEIGHBORHOOD MAPMACHINE - Educational Materials - SCHOLASTIC INC.; *pg.* 1683, *pg.* 1288
NEIMAN MARCUS - Retail Stores & Catalogs - NEIMAN MARCUS, INC.; *pg.* 30, *pg.* 1684
NEK-STENDER - Animal Cage Bars - BEHLEN MFG. CO.; *pg.* 701, *pg.* 1010
NEKOT - Snack Food - SNYDER'S-LANCE, INC.; *pg.* 896, *pg.* 1368
NELC - Lane Combiner Flyer - NEW ENGLAND MACHINERY, INC.; *pg.* 1364, *pg.* 415
NELLCOR - Medical Products - MEDTRONIC; *pg.* 1563, *pg.* 183
NELLIE MAE - Magazine - SLM CORPORATION; *pg.* 804, *pg.* 388
NELSON - Seafood - BON SECOUR FISHERIES INC.; *pg.* 841, *pg.* 5
NELSON - Filtration And Exhaust System - CUMMINS INC.; *pg.* 1326, *pg.* 676
NELSON - Furniture - HERMAN MILLER, INC.; *pg.* 926, *pg.* 913
NELSON - Furniture - JASPER GROUP; *pg.* 930, *pg.* 691
NELSON - Wall System - SMITH-MIDLAND CORPORATION; *pg.* 111, *pg.* 1795
NELSON - Books - THOMAS NELSON INC.; *pg.* 1692, *pg.* 1654
NELSON E & C - Electrical Products - EMERSON INDUSTRIAL AUTOMATION; *pg.* 1296, *pg.* 657
NELSON FIRESTOP - Electrical Products - EMERSON INDUSTRIAL AUTOMATION; *pg.* 1296, *pg.* 657
NELSON HEAT TRACE - Electrical Products - EMERSON INDUSTRIAL AUTOMATION; *pg.* 1296, *pg.* 657
NELSON-ZIMMER - Printed Circuit Board Preparation System - BUEHLER, LTD.; *pg.* 1403, *pg.* 622
NELSON'S - Oysters - BON SECOUR FISHERIES INC.; *pg.* 841, *pg.* 5
NEM - Electrosurgery Generator - BOVIE MEDICAL CORPORATION; *pg.* 1402, *pg.* 1178
NEM - Unscrambling Systems - NEW ENGLAND MACHINERY, INC.; *pg.* 1364, *pg.* 415
NEMA 4X - Industrial Control - PECO, INC.; *pg.* 1368, *pg.* 1505
NEMA-JECT - Insect Pest Control Product - GARDENS ALIVE!, INC.; *pg.* 1796, *pg.* 693
NEMEX - Veterinary Anthelmintic Preparations - PFIZER INC.; *pg.* 1581, *pg.* 1278
NEMO - Flashlight - PELICAN PRODUCTS, INC.; *pg.* 1842, *pg.* 295
NEMO PUMPS - Progressing Cavity Pumps - NETZSCH PUMPS NORTH AMERICA, LLC; *pg.* 1364, *pg.* 1532

First page reference indicates Business Class Edition
Second page reference indicates Geographic Edition

NEN - New England Nuclear - PERKINELMER, INC.; *pg.* 1426, *pg.* 853

NENNOS - Signal Management Software - GRASS VALLEY, INC.; *pg.* 641, *pg.* 164

NEO - Computer Peripheral Equipment - DIGI INTERNATIONAL INC.; *pg.* 387, *pg.* 948

NEO - Fluorescent Yo-Yo - DUNCAN TOYS COMPANY; *pg.* 951, *pg.* 1465

NEO - Bath & Plumbing Product - JACUZZI BRANDS CORPORATION; *pg.* 554, *pg.* 65

NEO - Tape Backup & Archive Appliances - OVERLAND STORAGE, INC.; *pg.* 451, *pg.* 205

NEO 2 - Educational Materials - RENAISSANCE LEARNING, INC.; *pg.* 607, *pg.* 1899

NEO 2000 - Data Backup & Recovery - OVERLAND STORAGE, INC.; *pg.* 451, *pg.* 205

NEO 4100 - Data Backup & Recovery - OVERLAND STORAGE, INC.; *pg.* 451, *pg.* 205

NEO 4200 - Data Backup & Recovery - OVERLAND STORAGE, INC.; *pg.* 451, *pg.* 205

NEO 8000 - Data Backup & Recovery - OVERLAND STORAGE, INC.; *pg.* 451, *pg.* 205

NEO-FIT - Gloves - FRANKLIN SPORTS, INC.; *pg.* 1834, *pg.* 847

NEO-FLEX - Flat Panel Mounting System - ERGOTRON, INC.; *pg.* 395, *pg.* 960

NEO-PREDEF - Veterinary Antibiotic & Steroid Preparation - PFIZER INC.; *pg.* 1581, *pg.* 1278

NEO/SCI - Educational Resources - SCHOOL SPECIALTY, INC.; *pg.* 467, *pg.* 1860

NEO-STACK - Stack Technology - ISC8; *pg.* 1350, *pg.* 71

NEO-SYNEPHRINE - Medicine - BAYER HEALTHCARE CONSUMER CARE DIVISION; *pg.* 1500, *pg.* 1087

NEO-TERRAMYCIN - Animal Health Product - PHIBROCHEM; *pg.* 1177, *pg.* 1124

NEO TEXT2SPEECH - Educational Materials - RENAISSANCE LEARNING, INC.; *pg.* 607, *pg.* 1899

NEOBEE - Chemical Product - STEPAN COMPANY; *pg.* 1182, *pg.* 643

NEOBLUE - Phototherapy System - NATUS MEDICAL INCORPORATED; *pg.* 1572, *pg.* 199

NEOBOR - Medicine And Agricultural Product - RIO TINTO BORAX; *pg.* 334, *pg.* 331

NEOCAR - Branched Vinyl Ester Latexes - THE DOW CHEMICAL COMPANY; *pg.* 1157, *pg.* 898

NEOCHEK - Software - BIO-RAD LABORATORIES, INC.; *pg.* 1504, *pg.* 101

NEOCHROME - Bath Organizer - HOME PRODUCTS INTERNATIONAL, INC.; *pg.* 1125, *pg.* 577

NEOCHROME - Fabric - NEMSCHOFF, INC.; *pg.* 936, *pg.* 1890

NEOCHROME - Fabric - UNIROYAL ENGINEERED PRODUCTS; *pg.* 699, *pg.* 467

NEOCLASSIC - Wallcovering - YORK WALLCOVERINGS INC.; *pg.* 947, *pg.* 1598

NEOCOLUMN - Food Safety Product - NEOGEN CORPORATION; *pg.* 883, *pg.* 896

NEODERM - Medical Equipment - CONMED CORPORATION; *pg.* 1517, *pg.* 1347

NEODYNE - Speaker - CAMBRIDGE SOUNDWORKS, INC.; *pg.* 1234, *pg.* 781

NEOFAB - Hose - FLEXFAB HORIZONS INTERNATIONAL, LLC; *pg.* 1072, *pg.* 891

NEOFAB-1 - Lightweight Hose - FLEXFAB HORIZONS INTERNATIONAL, LLC; *pg.* 1072, *pg.* 891

NEOFLEX - Hose - HBD INDUSTRIES, INC.; *pg.* 207, *pg.* 1449

NEOFORM - Magnetic Product - DEXTER MAGNETIC TECHNOLOGIES, INC.; *pg.* 634, *pg.* 610

NEOFORM - Breast Implant Product - MENTOR CORPORATION; *pg.* 1565, *pg.* 263

NEOGARD - Waterproofing Systems - JONES-BLAIR COMPANY; *pg.* 1443, *pg.* 1682

NEOGRAM - Software - PERKINELMER, INC.; *pg.* 1426, *pg.* 853

NEOGUARD - Neonatal Product - CAS MEDICAL SYSTEMS, INC.; *pg.* 1513, *pg.* 339

NEOHELIOPAN - Sunscreen - SYMRISE, INC.; *pg.* 1183, *pg.* 1125

NEOLAN - Metal Complex Dyes - HUNTSMAN CORPORATION; *pg.* 1167, *pg.* 1758

NEOLINK - Pharmaceutical Product - ALERE INC.; *pg.* 1488, *pg.* 849

NEOLITE - Shoe Prods. - THE GOODYEAR TIRE & RUBBER COMPANY; *pg.* 1883, *pg.* 1401

NEOLON - Medical Product - MEDLINE INDUSTRIES, INC.; *pg.* 1562, *pg.* 635

NEOLONE - Biocide - DOW CHEMICAL; *pg.* 1156, *pg.* 1563

NEOLYTICA - Analytical Testing - THE DOW CHEMICAL COMPANY; *pg.* 1157, *pg.* 898

NEOMEDIAM - Plumbing Fixtures - KOHLER CO.; *pg.* 91, *pg.* 1862

NEOMET - Metallograph - UNITRON INC.; *pg.* 1433, *pg.* 1153

NEOMETRICS - Medical Device - NATUS MEDICAL INCORPORATED; *pg.* 1572, *pg.* 199

NEOMIX - Medicinal Preparation for Animals - PFIZER INC.; *pg.* 1581, *pg.* 1278

NEON - Tabbing Film - AMERICAN THERMOPLASTIC COMPANY; *pg.* 349, *pg.* 1573

NEON - Paint - BADGER AIR BRUSH COMPANY; *pg.* 359, *pg.* 612

NEON - Furniture - HAWORTH, INC.; *pg.* 402, *pg.* 891

NEON - Kitchen Utensils - ROBINSON HOME PRODUCTS INC.; *pg.* 1060, *pg.* 1355

NEON 9'S - Lottery Game - LOUISIANA LOTTERY CORPORATION; *pg.* 997, *pg.* 742

NEON 9'S - Lottery Game - RHODE ISLAND LOTTERY; *pg.* 1004, *pg.* 1600

NEON CUSH - Footwear - COBIAN CORP.; *pg.* 1806, *pg.* 253

NEON FABRIC - Paint - BADGER AIR BRUSH COMPANY; *pg.* 359, *pg.* 612

NEON NIGHTS - Video Slots - INTERNATIONAL GAME TECHNOLOGY; *pg.* 957, *pg.* 1024

NEOPETS - Toy & Game - HASBRO, INC.; *pg.* 954, *pg.* 1603

NEOPLANAR - Film Magnetic Transducer - LRAD CORPORATION; *pg.* 652, *pg.* 204

NEOPOLITAN: REGISTRY RESORT & CLUB - Magazine - PALM BEACH MEDIA GROUP INC.; *pg.* 1674, *pg.* 457

NEOPOWER - Power Supply Product - ANTEC INCORPORATED; *pg.* 350, *pg.* 90

NEOPRENE - Insulation Product - ALPHA ASSOCIATES, INC.; *pg.* 691, *pg.* 1078

NEOPRENE - Sealants - CONAX TECHNOLOGIES LLC; *pg.* 1325, *pg.* 1148

NEOPRENE - Synthetic Fiber Material - E.I. DU PONT DE NEMOURS & COMPANY; *pg.* 1159, *pg.* 390

NEOPRENE - Mask - SELLSTROM MANUFACTURING CO.; *pg.* 1428, *pg.* 659

N.E.O.S. - Rubber - WEINBRENNER SHOE COMPANY, INC.; *pg.* 1822, *pg.* 1871

NEOSAT - Speaker - VIEWSONIC CORPORATION; *pg.* 489, *pg.* 303

NEOSOL - Gloves - LAKELAND INDUSTRIES, INC.; *pg.* 1354, *pg.* 1338

NEOSPORIN - Antibiotic Ointment - JOHNSON & JOHNSON; *pg.* 1549, *pg.* 1091

NEOSTAR - Elastomer - EASTMAN CHEMICAL COMPANY; *pg.* 1159, *pg.* 1636

NEOSURE - Infant Formula Designed for Premature & Low-birth-weight Babies - ABBOTT LABORATORIES; *pg.* 1484, *pg.* 551

NEOTERIC - Enzymes - BUCKMAN; *pg.* 1150, *pg.* 1641

NEOTERIC - Skin Care Products - SCOTT'S LIQUID GOLD-INC.; *pg.* 335, *pg.* 323

NEOTEX - Electronic Components - MOLEX INCORPORATED; *pg.* 655, *pg.* 628

NEOTRODE - Medical Equipment - CONMED CORPORATION; *pg.* 1517, *pg.* 1347

NEOVISUALS - Software - SAS INSTITUTE INC.; *pg.* 466, *pg.* 1361

NEOWASH 1575 - Software - BIO-RAD LABORATORIES, INC.; *pg.* 1504, *pg.* 101

NEOWAX - Dental Product - DENTSPLY INTERNATIONAL INC.; *pg.* 1522, *pg.* 1596

NEPAL - Carpet - BEAULIEU GROUP, LLC; *pg.* 917, *pg.* 529

NEPD - Nitrohydroxy Compound - THE DOW CHEMICAL COMPANY; *pg.* 1157, *pg.* 898

NEPHRO-CALCI - Pharmaceutical Product - ALLERGAN; *pg.* 1490, *pg.* 1101

NEPHRO-FER - Pharmaceutical Product - ALLERGAN; *pg.* 1490, *pg.* 1101

NEPHRO-VITE - Pharmaceutical Product - ALLERGAN; *pg.* 1490, *pg.* 1101

NEPHROMAX - Medical Device - BOSTON SCIENTIFIC CORPORATION; *pg.* 1508, *pg.* 831

NEPMT - Head Capper - NEW ENGLAND MACHINERY, INC.; *pg.* 1364, *pg.* 415

NEPRO - Specialized Nutritional Product - ABBOTT LABORATORIES; *pg.* 1484, *pg.* 551

NEPTUNE - Military Aircraft - LOCKHEED MARTIN CORPORATION; *pg.* 229, *pg.* 762

NEPTUNE - Ocean Clams - OCEAN BEAUTY SEAFOODS, INC.; *pg.* 1028, *pg.* 1838

NEPTUNE - Waste Management System - STRYKER CORPORATION; *pg.* 1598, *pg.* 894

NEPTUNE - Conveyor Chain - U.S. TSUBAKI, INC.; *pg.* 221, *pg.* 670

NEPTUNE'S KINGDOM - Game - WMS INDUSTRIES INC.; *pg.* 593, *pg.* 666

NERBU - Adjustable Unscrambler - NEW ENGLAND MACHINERY, INC.; *pg.* 1364, *pg.* 415

NERCA - Head Capper - NEW ENGLAND MACHINERY, INC.; *pg.* 1364, *pg.* 415

NERCC - Rotary Chuck Capper - NEW ENGLAND MACHINERY, INC.; *pg.* 1364, *pg.* 415

NERDS - Candy - NESTLE USA, INC.; *pg.* 883, *pg.* 96

NERF - Toy & Game - HASBRO, INC.; *pg.* 954, *pg.* 1603

NERO - Rotary Orienter - NEW ENGLAND MACHINERY, INC.; *pg.* 1364, *pg.* 415

NERPA - Head Capper - NEW ENGLAND MACHINERY, INC.; *pg.* 1364, *pg.* 415

NERSC - Rotary Servo Capper - NEW ENGLAND MACHINERY, INC.; *pg.* 1364, *pg.* 415

NERSI - Spout Inserter - NEW ENGLAND MACHINERY, INC.; *pg.* 1364, *pg.* 415

NERVI - Carpet - INTERFACE, INC.; *pg.* 695, *pg.* 512

NESA - Electrically Conductive Coated Glass - PPG INDUSTRIES, INC.; *pg.* 1445, *pg.* 1579

NESATRON - Electrically Conductive Glass - PPG INDUSTRIES, INC.; *pg.* 1445, *pg.* 1579

NESBITT - HVAC Equipment - MESTEK, INC.; *pg.* 1074, *pg.* 857

NESCAFE - Instant Coffee - NESTLE USA, INC.; *pg.* 883, *pg.* 96

NESCAFE ICED COFFEE - Food & Beverage Product - NESTLE USA, INC.; *pg.* 883, *pg.* 96

NESCAFE MOUNTAIN BLEND - Food & Beverage Product - NESTLE USA, INC.; *pg.* 883, *pg.* 96

NESCAFE SUNRISE - Food & Beverage Product - NESTLE USA, INC.; *pg.* 883, *pg.* 96

NESHC - Head Capper - NEW ENGLAND MACHINERY, INC.; *pg.* 1364, *pg.* 415

NESHC-S - Servo Capper - NEW ENGLAND MACHINERY, INC.; *pg.* 1364, *pg.* 415

NESOL - Lidder - NEW ENGLAND MACHINERY, INC.; *pg.* 1364, *pg.* 415

NESPRESSO - Instant Coffee - NESTLE USA, INC.; *pg.* 883, *pg.* 96

NESQUIK - Toy Train - LIONEL LLC; *pg.* 961, *pg.* 875

NESQUIK POWDER - Food & Beverage Product - NESTLE USA, INC.; *pg.* 883, *pg.* 96

NESQUIK READY TO DRINK - Food & Beverage Product - NESTLE USA, INC.; *pg.* 883, *pg.* 96

NESQUIK SYRUP - Food & Beverage Product - NESTLE USA, INC.; *pg.* 883, *pg.* 96

NESSEN - Lighting - PHILIPS LIGHTING; *pg.* 1303, *pg.* 806

NESSO - Floor - STEELCASE INC.; *pg.* 475, *pg.* 889

NESSTC - Head Capper - NEW ENGLAND MACHINERY, INC.; *pg.* 1364, *pg.* 415

NEST - Smart Home Products Incubator - ALPHABET INC.; *pg.* 347, *pg.* 153

NEST - Vena Cava Filter - COOK GROUP, INC.; *pg.* 1518, *pg.* 674

THE NEST - Online Home Design Resource - XO GROUP INC.; *pg.* 1289, *pg.* 1316

NESTEA - Tea - THE COCA-COLA COMPANY; *pg.* 240, *pg.* 493

NESTEA COOL - Soft Drink - THE COCA-COLA COMPANY; *pg.* 240, *pg.* 493

NESTEA HERITAGE - Food & Beverage Product - NESTLE USA, INC.; *pg.* 883, *pg.* 96

NESTEA ICE TEASERS - Food & Beverage Product - NESTLE USA, INC.; *pg.* 883, *pg.* 96

NESTEA NUEVO TEA - Food & Beverage Product - NESTLE USA, INC.; *pg.* 883, *pg.* 96

NESTEA SUNTEA - Food & Beverage Product - NESTLE USA, INC.; *pg.* 883, *pg.* 96

NESTER - Medical Device - COOK GROUP, INC.; *pg.* 1518, *pg.* 674

NESTER - Apparel - VANS, INC.; *pg.* 1821, *pg.* 76

NESTLE BUNCHA CRUNCH - Food & Beverage Product - NESTLE USA, INC.; *pg.* 883, *pg.* 96

NESTLE COFFEE-MATE - Coffee Creamer - NESTLE USA,

INC.; *pg.* 883, *pg.* 96

NESTLE CRUNCH - Candy - NESTLE USA, INC.; *pg.* 883, *pg.* 96

NESTLE CRUNCH GIRL SCOUT CANDY BARS - Candy Bars - NESTLE USA, INC.; *pg.* 883, *pg.* 96

NESTLE MILO - Chocolate Malt - NESTLE USA, INC.; *pg.* 883, *pg.* 96

NESTLE TIDY CATS - Cat Litter - NESTLE USA, INC.; *pg.* 883, *pg.* 96

NET - Software - DAKTRONICS, INC.; *pg.* 633, *pg.* 1624

NET ALERT - Electronic Components - MOLEX INCORPORATED; *pg.* 655, *pg.* 628

THE NET COLLECTION - Software - NETWORK SYSTEMS INTERNATIONAL, INC.; *pg.* 445, *pg.* 1375

NET ENGINE - Integrated Access Device - POLYCOM, INC.; *pg.* 664, *pg.* 249

NET EXEC - Software - NETWORK SYSTEMS INTERNATIONAL, INC.; *pg.* 445, *pg.* 1375

NET FLITE - Inflight Entertainment & Data Bus Cable - CARLISLE INTERCONNECT TECHNOLOGIES; *pg.* 1294, *pg.* 461

NET JET - Toy & Game - HASBRO, INC.; *pg.* 954, *pg.* 1603

NET POWER - Volume Buying Fuel Pricing Program - SIGNATURE FLIGHT SUPPORT CORP.; *pg.* 234, *pg.* 456

NET PROFIT - Fish Products - KENT NUTRITION GROUP; *pg.* 1477, *pg.* 710

NET SAAVER - Low Airline Fares - AMERICAN AIRLINES INC.; *pg.* 1898, *pg.* 1693

NET10 - Pre-Paid Phone Service - TRACFONE WIRELESS, INC.; *pg.* 681, *pg.* 447

NET2DINE.COM - Telephone Service - IDT CORPORATION; *pg.* 643, *pg.* 1096

NET2PHONE COMMCENTER - Communication Service - NET2PHONE, INC.; *pg.* 1269, *pg.* 1097

NET2PHONE DIRECT - Communication Service - NET2PHONE, INC.; *pg.* 1269, *pg.* 1097

NET2TORAH - Telephone Service - IDT CORPORATION; *pg.* 643, *pg.* 1096

NET4GUESTS - Restaurant Services - RED LION HOTELS CORP.; *pg.* 1110, *pg.* 1844

NETADVANTAGE - Investment Tool - STANDARD & POOR'S RATINGS SERVICES; *pg.* 805, *pg.* 1296

NETAFFX - Software - AFFYMETRIX, INC.; *pg.* 1487, *pg.* 263

NETALYTIX - Electronic Components - MOLEX INCORPORATED; *pg.* 655, *pg.* 628

NETAPP VTL - Software - NETAPP, INC.; *pg.* 444, *pg.* 287

NETBACKUP - Software - SYMANTEC CORPORATION; *pg.* 478, *pg.* 161

NETCARE - Janitorial Maintenance Products - NETWORK SERVICES COMPANY; *pg.* 1465, *pg.* 659

NETCELERA - Software - F5 NETWORKS, INC.; *pg.* 396, *pg.* 1835

NETCENTER - Hard Drive - WESTERN DIGITAL CORPORATION; *pg.* 492, *pg.* 118

NETCENTRAL - Facility Monitoring System - GRASS VALLEY, INC.; *pg.* 641, *pg.* 164

NETCHECK - Software System - MENTOR GRAPHICS CORPORATION; *pg.* 432, *pg.* 1510

NETCOMMERCE - Software - NETSUITE, INC.; *pg.* 1270, *pg.* 255

NETCON - Turbine Control System - WOODWARD, INC.; *pg.* 122, *pg.* 329

NETCRM - Web Tool - NETSUITE, INC.; *pg.* 1270, *pg.* 255

NETDEVICE - Computer Software - NOVELL INC.; *pg.* 446, *pg.* 852

NETDISCOVERY - Telecommunication Product - VERISIGN, INC.; *pg.* 488, *pg.* 1799

NETDISK - Hardware & Software - POLYWELL COMPUTERS, INC.; *pg.* 456, *pg.* 280

NETDISPATCH - Workstation Information - ACNIELSEN CORPORATION; *pg.* 341, *pg.* 1187

NET.DISTRO - Software - R.R. DONNELLEY & SONS COMPANY; *pg.* 1682, *pg.* 589

NETDOCTOR - Software Product Module - RIVERBED PERFORMANCE MANAGEMENT; *pg.* 462, *pg.* 765

NETED - Software System - MENTOR GRAPHICS CORPORATION; *pg.* 432, *pg.* 1510

NETENGINE - Software - ENVIRONMENTAL SYSTEMS RESEARCH INSTITUTE INC.; *pg.* 393, *pg.* 188

NETERP - Software - NETSUITE, INC.; *pg.* 1270, *pg.* 255

NET.FILTER - Software - R.R. DONNELLEY & SONS COMPANY; *pg.* 1682, *pg.* 589

NETFIRES - Systems Integration & Aeronautics - LOCKHEED MARTIN CORPORATION; *pg.* 229, *pg.* 762

NETFITS - Golf Accessories - CALLAWAY GOLF COMPANY; *pg.* 1829, *pg.* 58

NETFLEX - Software - NETSUITE, INC.; *pg.* 1270, *pg.* 255

NETFORCE - Network Storage System - CANDELIS, INC.; *pg.* 368, *pg.* 165

NETFORUMS - Banking Software - JACK HENRY & ASSOCIATES, INC.; *pg.* 422, *pg.* 988

NETFRAME - Rack & Cable - PANDUIT CORP.; *pg.* 661, *pg.* 663

NETG - Educational Publications - THOMSON REUTERS CORPORATION; *pg.* 1693, *pg.* 1944

NETI - Pot - HUGGER MUGGER YOGA PRODUCTS LLC; *pg.* 1836, *pg.* 1758

NETINFO - Computer Software - APPLE INC.; *pg.* 350, *pg.* 73

NETIQ - Computer Security Products - ATTACHMATE CORPORATION; *pg.* 356, *pg.* 1833

NETJETS - Fractional Ownership Program - NETJETS INC.; *pg.* 1917, *pg.* 1442

NETKEY - Module - PANDUIT CORP.; *pg.* 661, *pg.* 663

NETLINE - Clothesline & Utility Cord - MCNETT CORPORATION; *pg.* 1839, *pg.* 1817

NETLINK - Computer Products - BROADCOM CORPORATION; *pg.* 364, *pg.* 108

NETLINK - Alarm Reporting System - NAPCO SECURITY SYSTEMS, INC.; *pg.* 658, *pg.* 1138

NETMAIL - Computer Operations - NOVELL INC.; *pg.* 446, *pg.* 852

NETMANAGER - Cable Manager - PANDUIT CORP.; *pg.* 661, *pg.* 663

NETMAPPER - Software Product & Module - RIVERBED PERFORMANCE MANAGEMENT; *pg.* 462, *pg.* 765

NETMARK - Ultrasonic Locator - DUKANE CORPORATION; *pg.* 634, *pg.* 658

NETMARKET.COM - Secure Catalog Shopping Services - AFFINION GROUP, INC.; *pg.* 1225, *pg.* 372

NETMASTER - Laundry System - ALLIANCE LAUNDRY HOLDINGS LLC; *pg.* 51, *pg.* 1890

NETMETER - Electronic Components - MOLEX INCORPORATED; *pg.* 655, *pg.* 628

NETMINDER - Network Traffic Management Software - ALCATEL-LUCENT; *pg.* 615, *pg.* 1094

NETOPIA - Gateways & Routers - MOTOROLA SOLUTIONS, INC.; *pg.* 657, *pg.* 659

NETOWL - Software - SRA INTERNATIONAL, INC.; *pg.* 473, *pg.* 1780

NETOXYGEN - Software - WIPRO GALLAGHER SOLUTIONS; *pg.* 823, *pg.* 447

NETPHY - Connectivity Product - ADVANCED MICRO DEVICES, INC.; *pg.* 613, *pg.* 282

NETPROCESS - Software - INTELLICORP, INC.; *pg.* 417, *pg.* 268

NETPROFILER - Software - X-RITE, INCORPORATED; *pg.* 1437, *pg.* 891

NETPULSE - Software - DYNTEK, INC.; *pg.* 389, *pg.* 165

NETRACK - Rack & Cable - PANDUIT CORP.; *pg.* 661, *pg.* 663

NETRS - Navigation Aid - TRIMBLE NAVIGATION LIMITED; *pg.* 1384, *pg.* 288

NETSCALER - Software - CITRIX SYSTEMS, INC.; *pg.* 375, *pg.* 424

NETSCAPE - Entertainment Product - TIME WARNER INC.; *pg.* 312, *pg.* 1302

NETSCREEN - Hardware Security Product - JUNIPER NETWORKS, INC.; *pg.* 1260, *pg.* 286

NETSCRIBE - Audio Solution - VIQ SOLUTIONS INC.; *pg.* 490, *pg.* 1905

NETSERVER - Internet Services - IPASS, INC.; *pg.* 1259, *pg.* 193

NETSHELTER - Enclosure - SCHNEIDER ELECTRIC; *pg.* 467, *pg.* 1609

NETSIM - Software Product - WOODWARD, INC.; *pg.* 122, *pg.* 329

NETSOL FINANCIAL SUITE - Software - NETSOL TECHNOLOGIES, INC.; *pg.* 1270, *pg.* 56

NETSOLUTIONS - Software System - MITEL NETWORKS, INC.; *pg.* 1872, *pg.* 13

NETSPAN - Wireless Network Product - AIRSPAN NETWORKS INC.; *pg.* 346, *pg.* 410

NETSPOKE - Conferencing - PREMIERE GLOBAL SERVICES, INC.; *pg.* 1275, *pg.* 518

NETSPOKE & DESIGN - Telecom Product - PREMIERE GLOBAL SERVICES, INC.; *pg.* 1275, *pg.* 518

NETSTAMPS - Postage - STAMPS.COM INC.; *pg.* 1282, *pg.* 82

NETSTAR - Digital Jukeboxes - ROWE INTERNATIONAL CORP; *pg.* 669, *pg.* 889

NETSTREAM - PC Add-In Card - SIGMA DESIGNS, INC.; *pg.* 469, *pg.* 148

NETSUITE - Software - NETSUITE, INC.; *pg.* 1270, *pg.* 255

NETSUITE CENTRAL - Knowledge Center - NETSUITE, INC.; *pg.* 1270, *pg.* 255

NETSUITE CRM+ - Software - NETSUITE, INC.; *pg.* 1270, *pg.* 255

NETSUITE ONEWORLD - Software - NETSUITE, INC.; *pg.* 1270, *pg.* 255

NETSUITE SMALL BUSINESS - Software - NETSUITE, INC.; *pg.* 1270, *pg.* 255

NETSURE - Telecommunication Product - VERISIGN, INC.; *pg.* 488, *pg.* 1799

NETSWITCH - LAN Connections - VICON INDUSTRIES, INC.; *pg.* 685, *pg.* 1166

NETTELLER ONLINE BANKING - On-Line Banking Solution - JACK HENRY & ASSOCIATES, INC.; *pg.* 422, *pg.* 988

NETTER ANATOMY - Health Science Publications & Software - ELSEVIER HEALTH SCIENCES; *pg.* 1838, *pg.* 1564

NETTING - Apparel - OAKLEY, INC.; *pg.* 1840, *pg.* 86

NETTRANSACT - Software System - BOTTOMLINE TECHNOLOGIES (DE), INC.; *pg.* 727, *pg.* 1038

NETTREKKER - Search Engine - KNOVATION; *pg.* 1261, *pg.* 1415

NETTREKKER CLASSIC - Search Engine - KNOVATION; *pg.* 1261, *pg.* 1415

NETTREKKER D.I. - Search Tool - KNOVATION; *pg.* 1261, *pg.* 1415

NETVANTA - Computer Software - ADTRAN, INC.; *pg.* 344, *pg.* 6

NETVANTAGE - Software - EVOLVING SYSTEMS, INC.; *pg.* 395, *pg.* 326

NETVENTURE - Telephone Service - IDT CORPORATION; *pg.* 643, *pg.* 1096

NETVISION - Network Appliances & Telephony - MOTOROLA ENTERPRISE MOBILITY; *pg.* 441, *pg.* 1167

NETWARE - Network Operating System Software - NOVELL INC.; *pg.* 446, *pg.* 852

NETWATCH - Optical Networking Product - HARMONIC, INC.; *pg.* 402, *pg.* 246

NETWELL - Glass & Ceramic Material - CORNING INCORPORATED; *pg.* 1122, *pg.* 1154

NETWIN - Software - EMC CORPORATION; *pg.* 391, *pg.* 825

NETWISDOM - Monitor - FINISAR CORPORATION; *pg.* 639, *pg.* 285

NETWIZARD - Software - ATTACHMATE CORPORATION; *pg.* 356, *pg.* 1833

NETWORK - Lighting System - LITECONTROL CORPORATION; *pg.* 1301, *pg.* 841

NET.WORK - Software - R.R. DONNELLEY & SONS COMPANY; *pg.* 1682, *pg.* 589

NETWORK ACCESS LOCKDOWN - Software - WEBSENSE, INC.; *pg.* 491, *pg.* 210

NETWORK & END-TO-END PERFORMANCE STARTER PACK - Software - BMC SOFTWARE, INC.; *pg.* 362, *pg.* 1701

NETWORK ANYTHING. NETWORK EVERYTHING. - Slogan - LANTRONIX, INC.; *pg.* 426, *pg.* 112

NETWORK AUDIT SERVICES - Global Services - SONUS NETWORKS INC.; *pg.* 1281, *pg.* 858

NETWORK AVAILABILITY NUMBER - Telecommunication Services - VONAGE HOLDINGS CORP.; *pg.* 686, *pg.* 1074

NETWORK AWARE SCHEDULER - Scheduling Software - POLYCOM, INC.; *pg.* 664, *pg.* 249

NETWORK BORDER SWITCH - Network Product - SONUS NETWORKS INC.; *pg.* 1281, *pg.* 858

NETWORK COMMISSIONING - Global Services - SONUS NETWORKS INC.; *pg.* 1281, *pg.* 858

NETWORK COMPUTING - Publisher - UNITED BUSINESS MEDIA LLC; *pg.* 1697, *pg.* 1177

NETWORK DEPLOYMENT DESIGN - Global Services - SONUS NETWORKS INC.; *pg.* 1281, *pg.* 858

NETWORK FLOOR OF THE FUTURE - Slogan - BALLY TECHNOLOGIES, INC.; *pg.* 531, *pg.* 1022

NETWORK II.5 - Computer Architecture Simulator - CACI INTERNATIONAL INC.; *pg.* 367, *pg.* 1773

NETWORK INDIANA - Radio News Network - EMMIS COMMUNICATIONS CORPORATION; *pg.* 285, *pg.* 685

NETWORK MANAGEMENT - Wireline Solutions - SONUS NETWORKS INC.; *pg.* 1281, *pg.* 858

NETWORK MATTERS - Newsletter - HARVARD PILGRIM

HEALTH CARE, INC.; pg. 1539, pg. 856
NETWORK OPTIMIZATION - Software - JDA SOFTWARE GROUP, INC.; pg. 423, pg. 22
NETWORK REGISTRAR - Data Backup - CISCO SYSTEMS, INC.; pg. 372, pg. 240
THE NETWORK SPECIALIST - Tagline - CIENA CORPORATION; pg. 628, pg. 771
NETWORK VERIFICATION - Global Services - SONUS NETWORKS INC.; pg. 1281, pg. 858
NETWORK WORLD - Technology Magazine - INTERNATIONAL DATA GROUP; pg. 1653, pg. 796
NETWORKAIR - Cooling System - SCHNEIDER ELECTRIC; pg. 467, pg. 1609
NETWORKER - Software - EMC CORPORATION; pg. 391, pg. 825
NETWORKERS - Broadband Networks - CISCO SYSTEMS, INC.; pg. 372, pg. 240
NETWORKING ACADEMY - E-Learning Program - CISCO SYSTEMS, INC.; pg. 372, pg. 240
NETWORKING SOLUTION - Software - OPEX CORPORATION; pg. 450, pg. 1087
NETWORKING THE WORLD'S BUSINESS DATA - Slogan - BROCADE CORPORATION; pg. 365, pg. 312
NETWORKING TOGETHER - Slogan - WESTCON GROUP, INC.; pg. 492, pg. 1345
NETWORKLINK - Software - CITRIX SYSTEMS, INC.; pg. 375, pg. 424
NETWORKS - Carpet - BEAULIEU GROUP, LLC; pg. 917, pg. 529
NETWORX - Software - TRIZETTO CORPORATION; pg. 485, pg. 327
NETWORXMODELER - Software - TRIZETTO CORPORATION; pg. 485, pg. 327
NETXTREME - Computer Products - BROADCOM CORPORATION; pg. 364, pg. 108
NETZERO - Internet Service - UNITED ONLINE, INC.; pg. 1286, pg. 308
NEU-TRI - Solvent - THE DOW CHEMICAL COMPANY; pg. 1157, pg. 898
NEU-VISION - Advanced Neutron Imaging Detection System - RAYTHEON APPLIED SIGNAL TECHNOLOGY, INC.; pg. 667, pg. 288
NEUE CLASSIC - Binder Cover - XEROX CORPORATION; pg. 494, pg. 365
NEUE MODERN FAMILY - Manual - XEROX CORPORATION; pg. 494, pg. 365
NEULASTA - Medicine - AMGEN INC.; pg. 1493, pg. 291
NEULASTA - Pharmaceutical Product - NEKTAR THERAPEUTICS; pg. 1572, pg. 224
NEULEVEL - Internet Business Address Registry - NEUSTAR, INC.; pg. 1872, pg. 1807
NEUMEGA - Blood Platelet Stimulation Medicine - PFIZER INC.; pg. 1581, pg. 1278
NEUP - Bottle Uprighter System - NEW ENGLAND MACHINERY, INC.; pg. 1364, pg. 415
NEUPOGEN - Medicine - AMGEN INC.; pg. 1493, pg. 291
NEUPREX - Biopharmaceutical Product - XOMA CORPORATION; pg. 1611, pg. 46
NEURAGEN - Medical Device - INTEGRA LIFESCIENCES HOLDINGS CORPORATION; pg. 1545, pg. 1109
NEURALSTEP - Control Technology - ADVANCED ENERGY INDUSTRIES, INC.; pg. 613, pg. 328
NEURAWRAP - Medical Device - INTEGRA LIFESCIENCES HOLDINGS CORPORATION; pg. 1545, pg. 1109
NEURO-COOL - Medical Product - CINCINNATI SUB-ZERO PRODUCTS, INC.; pg. 1070, pg. 1411
NEURO-PULSE - Electrosurgery Generators & Accessories - BOVIE MEDICAL CORPORATION; pg. 1402, pg. 1178
NEUROBASAL - Biomolecule Product - THERMO FISHER SCIENTIFIC INC.; pg. 1602, pg. 61
NEUROCLIP - Micro Implant System - STRYKER CORPORATION; pg. 1598, pg. 894
NEURODEX - Therapeutic Product - AVANIR PHARMACEUTICALS; pg. 1498, pg. 40
NEUROFORM - Medical Device - BOSTON SCIENTIFIC CORPORATION; pg. 1508, pg. 831
NEUROFORM3 - Medical Device - BOSTON SCIENTIFIC CORPORATION; pg. 1508, pg. 831
NEUROGENIC - Nutritional Supplement - NATURAL ORGANICS, INC.; pg. 1571, pg. 1181
NEUROMINS - Nutritional Product - NATROL, INC.; pg. 1570, pg. 64
NEURON - Control Communication Product - CYPRESS SEMICONDUCTOR CORPORATION; pg. 1326, pg. 243
NEURON - Chip - ECHELON CORPORATION; pg. 389, pg. 245
NEURONTIN - Neuralgia Medication - PFIZER INC.; pg. 1581, pg. 1278
NEUROPEN - Flexible Neuroendoscope - MEDTRONIC, INC.; pg. 1564, pg. 939
NEUROTRACE - Molecular Probe Product - THERMO FISHER SCIENTIFIC INC.; pg. 1602, pg. 61
NEUROVIEW - Medical Device - INTEGRA LIFESCIENCES HOLDINGS CORPORATION; pg. 1545, pg. 1109
NEUROVISION - Surgery System - NUVASIVE, INC.; pg. 1577, pg. 205
NEUTONE - Cleaning Product - HILLYARD, INC.; pg. 331, pg. 990
NEUTRA - Dry Cleaning & Laundry Product - ADCO, INC.; pg. 325, pg. 482
NEUTRA-FOAM - Cleaner - BIRKO CORPORATION; pg. 1149, pg. 332
NEUTRA-SOL - Cleaner - BIRKO CORPORATION; pg. 1149, pg. 332
NEUTRAFILM - Inhibitor - GE WATER & PROCESS TECHNOLOGIES; pg. 1339, pg. 1588
NEUTRAL CLEANER - Cleaning Preparation - WALTER G. LEGGE COMPANY, INC.; pg. 337, pg. 1321
NEUTRAL POSTURE - Furniture - NEUTRAL POSTURE, INC.; pg. 939, pg. 1669
NEUTRALITE - Conditioning Agent - GE ENERGY; pg. 1338, pg. 506
NEUTRAMEEN - Neutralizing Amine - GE WATER & PROCESS TECHNOLOGIES; pg. 1339, pg. 1588
NEUTRAPLEX - Vial - COMAR INC.; pg. 1455, pg. 1047
NEUTRAVIDIN - Molecular Probe Product - THERMO FISHER SCIENTIFIC INC.; pg. 1602, pg. 61
NEUTROGENA - Skin Care Product - JOHNSON & JOHNSON; pg. 1549, pg. 1091
NEUTROGENA - Skin Care Product - NEUTROGENA CORPORATION; pg. 517, pg. 137
NEUTROGENA WAVE - Skin Care Product - JOHNSON & JOHNSON; pg. 1549, pg. 1091
NEUTRONYX - Chemical Product - STEPAN COMPANY; pg. 1182, pg. 643
NEUTROSORB PLUS - Stainless Steel Product - CARPENTER TECHNOLOGY CORPORATION; pg. 73, pg. 1584
NEVADA - Beverages - THE COCA-COLA COMPANY; pg. 240, pg. 493
NEVADA - Footwear - P.W. MINOR & SON, INC.; pg. 1816, pg. 1140
NEVADA BELL - Telecommunications Equipment - AT&T SOUTHEAST; pg. 1868, pg. 489
NEVADA NICKELS - Video Game - INTERNATIONAL GAME TECHNOLOGY; pg. 957, pg. 1024
NEVADA POWER - Electric Utility in South Nevada - NV ENERGY, INC.; pg. 1948, pg. 1028
NEVAILLAC - Hydroxy Modified Resin - NEVILLE CHEMICAL COMPANY; pg. 1174, pg. 1578
NEVAMAR - Decorative Laminate Product - PANOLAM INDUSTRIES INTERNATIONAL, INC.; pg. 103, pg. 370
NEVASTAIN - Hydroxy Modified Resin - NEVILLE CHEMICAL COMPANY; pg. 1174, pg. 1578
NEVCHEM - Petroleum Resin - NEVILLE CHEMICAL COMPANY; pg. 1174, pg. 1578
NEVER COMPROMISE - Slogan - PRATT & LAMBERT PAINTS; pg. 1446, pg. 1434
NEVER COMPROMISE - Golf Club - ROGER CLEVELAND GOLF COMPANY, INC.; pg. 1844, pg. 105
NEVER GET CAUGHT OFF GUARD - Tagline - HENKEL CONSUMER GOODS; pg. 511, pg. 22
NEVER IRON - Shirt - LEVI STRAUSS & CO.; pg. 43, pg. 220
NEVER RUST - Duty Soap Pad - 3M COMPANY; pg. 1142, pg. 956
NEVER-SEEZ - Lubricating Compounds - BOSTIK INC.; pg. 1150, pg. 833
NEVER STOP GETTING BETTER - Slogan - DJO INCORPORATED; pg. 1524, pg. 302
NEVER STOP IMPROVING - Tagline - LOWE'S COMPANIES, INC.; pg. 1053, pg. 1383
NEVER STOP LOOKING - Tagline - ICAD, INC.; pg. 643, pg. 1037
NEVERFAIL - Beverages - THE COCA-COLA COMPANY; pg. 240, pg. 493
NEVERFLAT - Balls - SPALDING; pg. 1845, pg. 846
NEVERGREEN - Bleaching Clay - BASF CATALYSTS LLC; pg. 1148, pg. 1074
NEVERKINK - Plastic & Rubber - TEKNOR APEX COMPANY; pg. 1889, pg. 1605
NEVEROUT - Dispensing System - GEORGIA-PACIFIC LLC; pg. 1458, pg. 507
NEVEROUT 3000 - Dispensing System - GEORGIA-PACIFIC LLC; pg. 1458, pg. 507
NEVERTOUCH - Electrosurgical Devices - ANGIODYNAMICS, INC.; pg. 1495, pg. 1173
NEVEX - Resins - NEVILLE CHEMICAL COMPANY; pg. 1174, pg. 1578
NEVILLAC - Resins - NEVILLE CHEMICAL COMPANY; pg. 1174, pg. 1578
NEVIS - Carpet - BEAULIEU GROUP, LLC; pg. 917, pg. 529
NEVO - Wireless Control Product - UNIVERSAL ELECTRONICS, INC.; pg. 683, pg. 262
NEVOXY - Hydroxy Modified Resin - NEVILLE CHEMICAL COMPANY; pg. 1174, pg. 1578
NEVPENE - Hydrocarbon Resin - NEVILLE CHEMICAL COMPANY; pg. 1174, pg. 1578
NEVROZ - Hydrocarbon Resin - NEVILLE CHEMICAL COMPANY; pg. 1174, pg. 1578
NEVTAC - Aliphatic Hydrocarbon Resin - NEVILLE CHEMICAL COMPANY; pg. 1174, pg. 1578
NEW AGE OF OPPORTUNITY - Tagline - POPEYES LOUISIANA KITCHEN, INC.; pg. 1745, pg. 517
NEW AMERICAN LIVING - Furniture - BASSETT FURNITURE INDUSTRIES, INCORPORATED; pg. 916, pg. 1776
NEW AMSTERDAM - Seating Product - IRWIN SEATING COMPANY INC.; pg. 929, pg. 887
NEW & EXCEPTIONAL - Container Grown Plant - MONROVIA GROWERS; pg. 1797, pg. 44
NEW ANGLES - Lighting - SWIVELIER CO., INC.; pg. 1307, pg. 1142
NEW BALANCE - Sneakers - HABAND COMPANY, INC.; pg. 1772, pg. 1099
NEW BALANCE - Athletic Shoes & Apparel - NEW BALANCE ATHLETIC SHOE, INC.; pg. 1811, pg. 798
NEW BEADS - Detergent - KAO BRANDS CO. INC.; pg. 513, pg. 1415
NEW BEARCAT - Revolver - STURM, RUGER & COMPANY, INC.; pg. 1846, pg. 371
THE NEW BOOK OF KNOWLEDGE - Educational Materials - SCHOLASTIC INC.; pg. 1683, pg. 1288
NEW BOWL - Toilet Cleaner - SWISHER HYGIENE INC.; pg. 336, pg. 1507
NEW BRITAIN - Machine Tool Product - BOURN & KOCH MACHINE TOOL COMPANY; pg. 1319, pg. 654
NEW BUSINESS ACCELERATOR - Computer Program - COMPUTER SCIENCES CORPORATION; pg. 378, pg. 1780
THE NEW BUSINESS OF PRINTING - Manual - XEROX CORPORATION; pg. 494, pg. 365
NEW BUSINESS OF PRINTING, THE - Printer - XEROX CORPORATION; pg. 494, pg. 365
NEW CENTURY - Tension Tent - ANCHOR INDUSTRIES, INC.; pg. 1825, pg. 678
NEW COMPLEXION - Foundations, Powders & Blushers - REVLON, INC.; pg. 521, pg. 1286
NEW COUNTRY - Furniture - ETHAN ALLEN INTERIORS INC.; pg. 924, pg. 343
NEW DECADE - Grip - EATON CORPORATION; pg. 1331, pg. 1429
NEW DIMENSION - Reloading Dies - HORNADY MANUFACTURING COMPANY; pg. 1836, pg. 1010
NEW DIMENSIONS - Carpet - BEAULIEU GROUP, LLC; pg. 917, pg. 529
NEW DIMENSIONS IN DIAGNOSIS - Pharmaceutical Product - ALERE INC.; pg. 1488, pg. 849
NEW DIMENSIONS IN DIAGNOSIS - Quantitative Test - ALERE SAN DIEGO; pg. 1489, pg. 199
NEW ELITE - Scissors - ACME UNITED CORPORATION; pg. 1040, pg. 346
NEW ENGLAND IN-HOUSE - In-House Publication - MASSACHUSETTS LAWYERS WEEKLY, INC.; pg. 1662, pg. 798
THE NEW ENGLAND INSTITUTE OF ART - Art School - EDUCATION MANAGEMENT CORPORATION; pg. 601, pg. 1575
THE NEW ENGLAND JOURNAL OF MEDICINE - General Medical Periodical - THE NEW ENGLAND JOURNAL OF MEDICINE; pg. 1667, pg. 799
NEW ENGLAND PASTURES - Milk - COOPERATIVE REGIONS OF ORGANIC PRODUCER POOLS; pg. 850, pg. 1864
NEW ENGLAND.COM - Travel Magazine Covering the New

England Region - YANKEE PUBLISHING INC.; *pg.* 1703, *pg.* 1033
NEW ERA FITS - Slogan - NEW ERA CAP COMPANY INC.; *pg.* 1840, *pg.* 1155
NEW EXPERIENCE IV - Mattresses - KINGSDOWN, INC.; *pg.* 932, *pg.* 1383
NEW EXPERIENCE VI - Mattresses - KINGSDOWN, INC.; *pg.* 932, *pg.* 1383
NEW FREEDOM - Feminine Pads & Pantyliners - KIMBERLY-CLARK CORPORATION; *pg.* 1461, *pg.* 1720
NEW GENERATION - Wire & Cable Products - BELDEN, INC.; *pg.* 624, *pg.* 993
NEW GUINEA - Coffee - PEET'S COFFEE & TEA, INC.; *pg.* 1029, *pg.* 85
NEW HAMPSHIRE MOTOR SPEEDWAY - Entertainment Venue - SPEEDWAY MOTORSPORTS, INC.; *pg.* 584, *pg.* 1370
NEW HANDS - Skin Care Product - NEUTROGENA CORPORATION; *pg.* 517, *pg.* 137
NEW HERRINGBONE - Laminated Parquet - ROBBINS, INC.; *pg.* 108, *pg.* 1425
NEW HOLLAND - Semi-Soft Cheese - BONGRAIN NORTH AMERICA; *pg.* 841, *pg.* 1556
NEW HOME FINDER - Real Estate Guide - NETWORK COMMUNICATIONS INC.; *pg.* 1271, *pg.* 534
NEW HOME GUIDE - Magazine - RENTPATH, INC.; *pg.* 1680, *pg.* 538
NEW HOMES & LIVING - Advertising Publication - DOMINION ENTERPRISES; *pg.* 1636, *pg.* 1796
NEW HORIZONS COMPUTER LEARNING CENTERS - IT Training Service - NEW HORIZONS WORLDWIDE, INC.; *pg.* 445, *pg.* 43
NEW IDEA - Manure Spreader - AGCO CORPORATION; *pg.* 700, *pg.* 530
NEW JAMESTOWN - Rugs - COURISTAN INC.; *pg.* 921, *pg.* 1067
NEW JEFFERSONIAN - Laminated Parquet - ROBBINS, INC.; *pg.* 108, *pg.* 1425
NEW JERSEY MONTHLY - Publication - NEW JERSEY MONTHLY; *pg.* 1667, *pg.* 1089
THE NEW JERUSALEM BIBLE - Publishing Imprint - THE KNOPF DOUBLEDAY GROUP; *pg.* 1657, *pg.* 1249
NEW KASHIMAR - Rug - COURISTAN INC.; *pg.* 921, *pg.* 1067
NEW LEADER - Truck-Mounted Agricultural Fertilizer & Lime Spreaders - HIGHWAY EQUIPMENT COMPANY; *pg.* 704, *pg.* 702
NEW LIBERTY - Digital RF System - CHECKPOINT SYSTEMS, INC.; *pg.* 628, *pg.* 1559
NEW LINE - Entertainment Product - TIME WARNER INC.; *pg.* 312, *pg.* 1302
NEW LITTLE FRIEND BOUQUET - Floral Bouquet - FTD GROUP, INC.; *pg.* 1795, *pg.* 608
NEW LIVING TRANSLATION - Complete Reference Bible - TYNDALE HOUSE PUBLISHERS, INC.; *pg.* 1697, *pg.* 561
THE NEW LOOK OF COMFORT - Advertising Campaign - LA-Z-BOY INCORPORATED; *pg.* 932, *pg.* 901
NEW MAN - Magazine - CHARISMA MEDIA; *pg.* 1627, *pg.* 436
NEW MEDIA SERVICES - Provides Custom Research and Start-up Services for New Syndicated Products - NIELSEN MEDIA RESEARCH, INC.; *pg.* 303, *pg.* 1272
NEW MEDICINE. NEW HOPE. - Tagline - PHARMACEUTICAL RESEARCH & MANUFACTURERS OF AMERICA; *pg.* 153, *pg.* 404
NEW MODEL BLACKHAWK - Single Action Revolvers - STURM, RUGER & COMPANY, INC.; *pg.* 1846, *pg.* 371
NEW MODEL SUPER BLACKHAWK - Single Action Revolvers - STURM, RUGER & COMPANY, INC.; *pg.* 1846, *pg.* 371
NEW MUSK - Perfume - PARFUMS DE COEUR LTD.; *pg.* 519, *pg.* 376
NEW MUSK FOR MEN - Fragrance - PARFUMS DE COEUR LTD.; *pg.* 519, *pg.* 376
NEW MUSK FOR WOMEN - Fragrance - PARFUMS DE COEUR LTD.; *pg.* 519, *pg.* 376
NEW ONAN - Replacement Controls - FLIGHT SYSTEMS, INC.; *pg.* 1337, *pg.* 1548
NEW ONE-ELEVEN - Degreaser - TEXAS REFINERY CORP.; *pg.* 986, *pg.* 1696
NEW ORIENTAL - Carpet - STARK CARPET CORPORATION; *pg.* 944, *pg.* 1296
NEW ORLEAN BLEND - Coffee - COMMUNITY COFFEE COMPANY LLC; *pg.* 849, *pg.* 741
NEW ORLEANS - Smoked Sausage - JOHNSONVILLE SAUSAGE, LLC; *pg.* 867, *pg.* 1894
NEW ORLEANS JAZZ AND HERITAGE FESTIVAL - Annual Jazz Festival - FAIR GROUNDS CORPORATION; *pg.* 547, *pg.* 747
NEW ORLEANS MARDI-GRAS - T-Shirt - ZAPP'S POTATO CHIPS, INC.; *pg.* 1864, *pg.* 743
NEW ORLEANS PUBLIC SERVICE - Utility Distributors - ENTERGY NEW ORLEANS, INC.; *pg.* 1942, *pg.* 746
NEW ORLEAN'S SQUARE - Amusement Park - THE WALT DISNEY COMPANY; *pg.* 317, *pg.* 52
NEW PERSPECTIVE - Fabric - NEUTRAL POSTURE, INC.; *pg.* 939, *pg.* 1669
NEW PHASE - Menopausal Supplement - CHATTEM, INC.; *pg.* 1515, *pg.* 1628
THE NEW POWER GENERATION - Lithium Battery - ULTRALIFE CORPORATION; *pg.* 1385, *pg.* 1317
NEW PRODUCT PLACEMENT PROGRAM - Delivery System - AMERISOURCEBERGEN CORPORATION; *pg.* 1493, *pg.* 1522
NEW PRODUCT SPECTRA - Software System - IMS HEALTH, INC.; *pg.* 1544, *pg.* 344
NEW PRODUCTS NEW SOLUTIONS NEW OPPORTUNITIES - Tagline - DORMAN PRODUCTS, INC.; *pg.* 204, *pg.* 1522
THE NEW REPUBLIC - Magazine - THE NEW REPUBLIC INC.; *pg.* 1667, *pg.* 403
NEW SEASONS - Supplement & Food Product - NEW EARTH LIFE SCIENCES, INC.; *pg.* 1573, *pg.* 1499
NEW SINCE 1918 - Marketing Launch - DORMAN PRODUCTS, INC.; *pg.* 204, *pg.* 1522
NEW STRATFORD - Carpet - INTERFACE, INC.; *pg.* 695, *pg.* 512
NEW STUDENT RECORD - Yearbooks - HERFF JONES, INC.; *pg.* 7, *pg.* 686
NEW TRADITIONS - Furniture - BASSETT FURNITURE INDUSTRIES, INCORPORATED; *pg.* 916, *pg.* 1776
NEW VACQERO - Single Action Revolvers - STURM, RUGER & COMPANY, INC.; *pg.* 1846, *pg.* 371
NEW VISE ACTION - Latch - SOUTHCO, INC.; *pg.* 1063, *pg.* 1522
THE NEW WAVE IN BANKING - Slogan - FLAGSTAR BANCORP, INC.; *pg.* 758, *pg.* 910
NEW WAYS. NEW ANSWERS. - Slogan - SEI INVESTMENTS COMPANY; *pg.* 802, *pg.* 1558
NEW WAYS TO KNOW - Tag Line - HOUGHTON MIFFLIN HARCOURT PUBLISHING COMPANY; *pg.* 1651, *pg.* 796
NEW WESTCOTT - Scissors - ACME UNITED CORPORATION; *pg.* 1040, *pg.* 346
NEW WOOD DEFENDER - Coating & Paint - AKZO NOBEL DECORATIVE PAINTS, USA; *pg.* 1439, *pg.* 1474
NEW WORLD COFFEE - Bakery Product - EINSTEIN NOAH RESTAURANT GROUP, INC.; *pg.* 1019, *pg.* 332
NEW WORLDS - Consumer Catalog - LLEWELLYN WORLDWIDE LIMITED; *pg.* 1660, *pg.* 967
NEW YORK - Computer Font - APPLE INC.; *pg.* 350, *pg.* 73
NEW YORK - Cameras - EASTMAN KODAK COMPANY; *pg.* 1408, *pg.* 1333
NEW YORK - Frozen Bread - T. MARZETTI COMPANY; *pg.* 900, *pg.* 1444
NEW YORK APPLE ASSOCIATION, INC. - Growers Association Representing Apple Growers in New York State - NEW YORK APPLE ASSOCIATION, INC.; *pg.* 152, *pg.* 1160
NEW YORK BAGEL - Bagels - MAPLE LEAF FOODS INC.; *pg.* 875, *pg.* 1927
NEW YORK BAGEL BOYS - Bagels - UNITED STATES BAKERY; *pg.* 907, *pg.* 1507
NEW YORK FROZEN FOODS - Partially Baked Frozen Bread - LANCASTER COLONY CORPORATION; *pg.* 873, *pg.* 1441
NEW YORK LAW JOURNAL - Legal Publication - AMERICAN LAWYER MEDIA, INC.; *pg.* 1615, *pg.* 1193
NEW YORK MAGAZINE SHOP - Magazine - RENTPATH, INC.; *pg.* 1680, *pg.* 538
NEW YORK-NEW YORK - Hotel & Casino - MGM RESORTS INTERNATIONAL; *pg.* 1105, *pg.* 1028
NEW YORK NIGHTS - Designer Fragrance - PARFUMS DE COEUR LTD.; *pg.* 519, *pg.* 376
NEW YORK PAN - Food Product - PIZZA INN, INC.; *pg.* 1745, *pg.* 1746
NEW YORK POST - Newspaper - THE NEW YORK POST; *pg.* 1668, *pg.* 1269
NEW YORK SPORTS CLUBS - Fitness Center - TOWN SPORTS INTERNATIONAL HOLDINGS, INC.; *pg.* 589, *pg.* 1303
NEW YORK STYLE - Food Products - NONNI'S FOOD COMPANY INC.; *pg.* 886, *pg.* 1490
THE NEW YORK TIMES - Newspaper - THE NEW YORK TIMES COMPANY; *pg.* 1668, *pg.* 1270
NEW YORK TIMES MAGAZINE - Magazine - THE NEW YORK TIMES COMPANY; *pg.* 1668, *pg.* 1270
THE NEW YORK TIMES STYLE MAGAZINE - Magazine - THE NEW YORK TIMES COMPANY; *pg.* 1668, *pg.* 1270
NEW YORK YANKEES - Professional Baseball Team - NEW YORK YANKEES; *pg.* 570, *pg.* 1144
NEW YORKER - Table - BLATT BOWLING & BILLIARD CORP.; *pg.* 1827, *pg.* 1203
NEW YORKER - Residential Boilers - BURNHAM HOLDINGS, INC.; *pg.* 1069, *pg.* 1546
THE NEW YORKER - Magazine - CONDE NAST PUBLICATIONS, INC.; *pg.* 1629, *pg.* 1217
NEW YORKER - Fire Helmet - MINE SAFETY APPLIANCES COMPANY; *pg.* 1361, *pg.* 1525
NEW YORK'S FAVORITE PIZZA - Slogan - FAMIGLIA - DEBARTOLO, LLC; *pg.* 1728, *pg.* 1352
NEW2USA.COM - Website - SYNTEL, INC.; *pg.* 480, *pg.* 911
NEWAIR I.B - Inflatable Cushioning System - SEALED AIR CORPORATION; *pg.* 1468, *pg.* 1058
NEWBERRY - Textiles - BERNHARDT DESIGN; *pg.* 918, *pg.* 1381
NEWBOATS.COM - Website - BONNIER CORPORATION; *pg.* 1622, *pg.* 480
NEWBRIDGE - Publisher - HAIGHTS CROSS COMMUNICATIONS, INC.; *pg.* 1646, *pg.* 1237
NEWBRIDGE BANCORP - Banking Service - NEWBRIDGE BANCORP; *pg.* 787, *pg.* 1375
NEWBURGH REGISTER - Newspaper - WARRICK PUBLISHING CO. INC.; *pg.* 1701, *pg.* 675
NEWBURY - Fabric - NEMSCHOFF, INC.; *pg.* 936, *pg.* 1890
THE NEWBURY COLLECTION - Dinnerware - MARYLAND PLASTICS, INC.; *pg.* 1885, *pg.* 769
NEWBURY NETWORKS - Software - IDEALAB, INC.; *pg.* 1258, *pg.* 180
NEWCASTLE - Beer - HEINEKEN USA INC.; *pg.* 252, *pg.* 1352
NEWCASTLE BROWN ALE - Beer - JIM BEAM BRANDS CO.; *pg.* 1965, *pg.* 601
NEWDAMP - Elastomers Tutorial - NEWPORT CORPORATION; *pg.* 1424, *pg.* 114
NEWDEAL - Medical Device - INTEGRA LIFESCIENCES HOLDINGS CORPORATION; *pg.* 1545, *pg.* 1109
NEWEGG - Online Store - NEWEGG INC.; *pg.* 1271, *pg.* 67
NEWEGG MALL - Online Store - NEWEGG INC.; *pg.* 1271, *pg.* 67
NEWFORM - Flexible Packaging System - ATMI, INC.; *pg.* 1314, *pg.* 342
NEWHOUSE - Furniture - ASHLEY FURNITURE INDUSTRIES, INC.; *pg.* 914, *pg.* 1852
NEWLEADSUSA - Online Lists - INFOGROUP INC.; *pg.* 1652, *pg.* 1016
NEWLEAF - Agricultural Product - MONSANTO COMPANY; *pg.* 1173, *pg.* 999
NEWLIFE - Plant Cleaner - NATURAL DECORATIONS, INC.; *pg.* 936, *pg.* 5
NEWLY WEDS ADHESION BATTERS - Breaded Coatings - NEWLY WEDS FOODS, INC.; *pg.* 886, *pg.* 585
NEWLY WEDS SPECIALTY BATTERS - Flavored Batters - NEWLY WEDS FOODS, INC.; *pg.* 886, *pg.* 585
NEWMAN - Watchclock - DETEX CORPORATION; *pg.* 633, *pg.* 1728
NEWMAN QUARTZ - Watchclock - DETEX CORPORATION; *pg.* 633, *pg.* 1728
NEWMAN'S OWN - Food Products - NEWMAN'S OWN, INC.; *pg.* 886, *pg.* 384
NEWMAN'S OWN ORGANICS - Organic Food - NEWMAN'S OWN, INC.; *pg.* 886, *pg.* 384
NEWMARK - Rug Line - MOHAWK INDUSTRIES, INC.; *pg.* 935, *pg.* 527
NEWMARKET - Grocery Stores - SUPERVALU, INC.; *pg.* 1035, *pg.* 924
NEWPORT - Golf Equipment - ACUSHNET COMPANY; *pg.* 1824, *pg.* 818
NEWPORT - Shoes - ALLEN-EDMONDS SHOE CORP.; *pg.* 1804, *pg.* 1887
NEWPORT - Rug - COURISTAN INC.; *pg.* 921, *pg.* 1067
NEWPORT - Play System - CREATIVE PLAYTHINGS LTD.; *pg.* 1831, *pg.* 820
THE NEWPORT - Natural Pine Swing Set - CREATIVE PLAYTHINGS LTD.; *pg.* 1831, *pg.* 820
NEWPORT - Footwear - EASTLAND SHOE CORPORATION;

pg. 1808, pg. 750
NEWPORT - Furniture - ETHAN ALLEN INTERIORS INC.; pg. 924, pg. 343
NEWPORT - Outerwear - HABAND COMPANY, INC.; pg. 1772, pg. 1099
NEWPORT - Dinnerware - THE HOMER LAUGHLIN CHINA COMPANY; pg. 1125, pg. 1850
NEWPORT - Furniture - JOFCO INC.; pg. 931, pg. 691
NEWPORT - Cigarette - REYNOLDS AMERICAN INC.; pg. 1894, pg. 1395
NEWPORT - Ceramic Tile - WALKER & ZANGER, INC.; pg. 119, pg. 281
NEWPORT BEACH - Golf Equipment - ACUSHNET COMPANY; pg. 1824, pg. 818
NEWPORT BRASS - Faucet - MASCO CORPORATION; pg. 96, pg. 909
NEWPORT COVE - Furniture - BUSH INDUSTRIES INC.; pg. 919, pg. 1170
NEWPORT DENTAL - Dental Services - SMILE BRANDS GROUP INC.; pg. 1594, pg. 116
NEWPORT GREEN - Molecular Probe Product - THERMO FISHER SCIENTIFIC INC.; pg. 1602, pg. 61
NEWPORT STORM - Beer - COASTAL EXTREME BREWING COMPANY; pg. 240, pg. 1602
NEWPORT TWO - Golf Equipment - ACUSHNET COMPANY; pg. 1824, pg. 818
THE NEWS CHIEF - Newspaper - NEWS CHIEF; pg. 1669, pg. 480
NEWS HERALD - Florida Newspaper - FREEDOM COMMUNICATIONS, INC.; pg. 1643, pg. 110
NEWS THAT MOVES - Flash Movies - DORNER MANUFACTURING CORP.; pg. 1329, pg. 1861
NEWS THAT MOVES MARKETS - Financial Broadcasting Services - BLOOMBERG L.P.; pg. 725, pg. 1204
NEWS TRANSCRIPT - Weekly Publication - GREATER MEDIA NEWSPAPERS, INC.; pg. 1646, pg. 1071
THE NEWS TRIBUNE - Newspaper - THE NEWS TRIBUNE; pg. 1670, pg. 1845
NEWS TRIBUNE - Newspaper - NEWS TRIBUNE CO.; pg. 1670, pg. 980
NEWSBROWSE - Web-Based Browser/Editor - GRASS VALLEY, INC.; pg. 641, pg. 164
NEWSCRAWL - Software - CHYRONHEGO; pg. 371, pg. 1179
NEWSEDIT - News Editing Equipment - GRASS VALLEY, INC.; pg. 641, pg. 164
NEWSMATIC - Newspaper Publishing System - ECRM IMAGING SYSTEMS, INC.; pg. 1410, pg. 848
NEWSMAX MAGAZINE - National Distributed Magazine - NEWSMAX MEDIA, INC.; pg. 1271, pg. 479
NEWSPAC - Newspaper - VALASSIS COMMUNICATIONS, INC.; pg. 1287, pg. 897
NEWSPOUCH - Newspaper - VALASSIS COMMUNICATIONS, INC.; pg. 1287, pg. 897
NEWSQ - News Playout System - GRASS VALLEY, INC.; pg. 641, pg. 164
NEWSSTREAM - Software - MONEY.NET, INC.; pg. 1268, pg. 1261
NEWSTEAD - Footwear - K-SWISS; pg. 1837, pg. 306
NEWSWATCH - PC Application for Market Data Retrieval - TRACK DATA CORPORATION; pg. 1284, pg. 1147
NEWSWATCH API - Software - TRACK DATA CORPORATION; pg. 1284, pg. 1147
NEWSWEEK - Magazine - GRAHAM HOLDINGS COMPANY; pg. 1645, pg. 1773
NEWSWEEK - Magazine - NEWSWEEK DAILY BEAST CO.; pg. 1670, pg. 1271
NEWSWORTHY - Printing Plates - EASTMAN KODAK COMPANY; pg. 1408, pg. 1333
NEWTEAM - Plumbing Product - MASCO CORPORATION; pg. 96, pg. 909
NEWTON - Furniture - AMISCO INDUSTRIES LTD.; pg. 913, pg. 1958
NEWTON - Dispensing Equipment - IDEX CORPORATION; pg. 1347, pg. 623
NEWTON - Wine - MOET HENNESSY; pg. 1966, pg. 1260
NEWTON SERIES - Electronics - CAMBRIDGE SOUNDWORKS, INC.; pg. 1234, pg. 781
NEWTONS - Cookies - MONDELEZ INTERNATIONAL, INC.; pg. 878, pg. 601
NEWTON'S LAW - Ceramic Mugs & Gift Bears - GUND, INC.; pg. 954, pg. 1056
NEWTOWN - Ceiling Fan - WESTINGHOUSE LIGHTING CORPORATION; pg. 687, pg. 1571
NEWVAC - Packaging Machinery - SEALED AIR CORPORATION; pg. 1468, pg. 1058
NEXA - Power Module - BALLARD POWER SYSTEMS, INC.; pg. 70, pg. 1907
NEXA-LOTTE - Lawn & Garden Products - THE SCOTTS MIRACLE-GRO COMPANY; pg. 1799, pg. 1459
NEXCARE - First Aid Cream - 3M COMPANY; pg. 1142, pg. 956
NEXCARE ACTIVE - Foam Bandage - 3M COMPANY; pg. 1142, pg. 956
NEXCOR - Single-Mode Fiber - CORNING INCORPORATED; pg. 1122, pg. 1154
NEXERA - Canola & Sunflower Seeds - DOW AGROSCIENCES LLC; pg. 1156, pg. 684
NEXGEN - Church Ministry Aid Books - DAVID C. COOK; pg. 1633, pg. 315
NEXGEN - LED Lighting System - GROTE INDUSTRIES, INC.; pg. 206, pg. 693
NEXGEN - Video Game - INTERNATIONAL GAME TECHNOLOGY; pg. 957, pg. 1024
NEXGEN - Electronic Vending Locks - MEDECO HIGH SECURITY LOCKS, INC.; pg. 1055, pg. 1806
NEXIS - Filter Cartridge - PALL CORPORATION; pg. 232, pg. 1323
NEXIV - Computerized NC Video Measuring Systems - NIKON INC.; pg. 1424, pg. 1181
NEXLEV - Connector - AMPHENOL CORPORATION; pg. 616, pg. 381
NEXLEV - Board Connector - TERADYNE INC.; pg. 679, pg. 838
NEXON - High Strength High Impact Packaging Materials - NEXUS PLASTICS, INC.; pg. 1465, pg. 1073
NEXRUTINE - Health Care Product - NATURE'S SUNSHINE PRODUCTS, INC.; pg. 1571, pg. 1754
NEXSAS - Electronic Devices - MAXIM INTEGRATED PRODUCTS, INC.; pg. 653, pg. 247
NEXSAS - Network Product - VITESSE SEMICONDUCTOR CORPORATION; pg. 686, pg. 57
NEXSTEP - Electronic Components - MOLEX INCORPORATED; pg. 655, pg. 628
NEXT - Beverages - THE COCA-COLA COMPANY; pg. 240, pg. 493
NEXT - Metallization System - LAM RESEARCH CORPORATION; pg. 1354, pg. 246
N.E.X.T. - Team - WILD FLAVORS, INC.; pg. 910, pg. 728
NEXT CENTURY - Publication - FRANKLIN ELECTRONIC PUBLISHERS, INC.; pg. 398, pg. 1048
NEXT DAY NEIGHBOR ISLAND SERVICE - Shipment Service - FEDEX CORPORATION; pg. 1907, pg. 1642
NEXT DIMENSION - Carburetor Cleaners - ZEP INC.; pg. 338, pg. 524
NEXT GEN - Cement Board - USG CORPORATION; pg. 118, pg. 594
NEXT GENERATION - Serving & Merchandising Systems - DUKE MANUFACTURING COMPANY, INC.; pg. 54, pg. 995
NEXT GENERATION - Digital Cable Assembly - W.L. GORE & ASSOCIATES, INC.; pg. 122, pg. 388
THE NEXT GENERATION DATA CENTER - Tagline - EXTREME NETWORKS INC; pg. 287, pg. 245
NEXT GENERATION ELECTRONIC MEASUREMENT - Slogan - NIELSEN AUDIO; pg. 446, pg. 768
NEXT GENERATION ELECTRONIC RATINGS - Slogan - NIELSEN AUDIO; pg. 446, pg. 768
THE NEXT GENERATION OF PROGRAMMABLE LOGIC - Tagline - SAJAN, INC.; pg. 1278, pg. 1890
NEXT IN LINE - Carpet - INTERFACE, INC.; pg. 695, pg. 512
NEXT STEP - Carseat - GRACO CHILDREN'S PRODUCTS INC.; pg. 954, pg. 1531
NEXT STEP - Elevator Product - OTIS ELEVATOR COMPANY; pg. 102, pg. 349
NEXT TO NOTHING - Boxer Brief - JOCKEY INTERNATIONAL, INC.; pg. 27, pg. 1861
NEXTEL - Fabric - 3M COMPANY; pg. 1142, pg. 956
NEXTEP - Furniture - NEUTRAL POSTURE, INC.; pg. 939, pg. 1669
NEXTGEN - Fiber Optic Cable - GENERAL CABLE CORPORATION; pg. 83, pg. 729
NEXTGEN EMR - Software - QUALITY SYSTEMS, INC.; pg. 1587, pg. 115
NEXTGEN EPM - Software - QUALITY SYSTEMS, INC.; pg. 1587, pg. 115
NEXTGEN FICO - Credit Scores - FAIR ISAAC CORPORATION; pg. 1247, pg. 955
NEXTGEN HEALTHCARE - Software - QUALITY SYSTEMS, INC.; pg. 1587, pg. 115
NEXT*IDEA - Product Used to Identify Effective Advertising at the Storyboard Stage - IPSOS-ASI, INC.; pg. 421, pg. 363
NEXT*KIDS - Research System Focused on Children-oriented Advertising - IPSOS-ASI, INC.; pg. 421, pg. 363
NEXTMAP - Countrywide Terrain Elevation Databases - INTERMAP TECHNOLOGIES CORPORATION; pg. 417, pg. 1903
NEXTMOVE - Motion Control System - BALDOR ELECTRIC COMPANY; pg. 1316, pg. 32
NEXTON - Polymer - HERCULES INCORPORATED; pg. 1166, pg. 392
NEXTPHASE - Wood & Building Material - WEYERHAEUSER COMPANY; pg. 121, pg. 1820
NEXT*PRINT - Worldwide Print Advertising Testing System - IPSOS-ASI, INC.; pg. 421, pg. 363
NEXTRAC - Retail System - LAVI INDUSTRIES INC.; pg. 93, pg. 299
NEXTSTITCH - Biotechnology Product - GENZYME CORPORATION; pg. 1534, pg. 808
NEXT*TV - Worldwide Copy Testing System for TV Commercials - IPSOS-ASI, INC.; pg. 421, pg. 363
NEXTVISION - Video Processor Turner - VIEWSONIC CORPORATION; pg. 489, pg. 303
NEXU-PAK - Formed Liners - NEXUS PLASTICS, INC.; pg. 1465, pg. 1073
NEXUS - Artwork System - ANDERSON & VREELAND, INC.; pg. 1616, pg. 1064
NEXUS - Software - DIEBOLD, INCORPORATED; pg. 387, pg. 1407
NEXUS - Car Seat - GRACO CHILDREN'S PRODUCTS INC.; pg. 954, pg. 1531
NEXUS - Furniture - JASPER GROUP; pg. 930, pg. 691
NEXUS - Workbench Accessory System - LISTA INTERNATIONAL CORPORATION; pg. 934, pg. 825
NEXUS - Lighting System - LITECONTROL CORPORATION; pg. 1301, pg. 841
NEXUS - Fabric - NEMSCHOFF, INC.; pg. 936, pg. 1890
NEXUS - Process Equipment - VEECO INSTRUMENTS INC.; pg. 1434, pg. 1322
NEXUS PIONEER - Compass - SCHOOL-TECH, INC.; pg. 1844, pg. 866
NEXUS SPIRIT - Seat Cushion - THE ROHO GROUP; pg. 1591, pg. 556
NEXXUS - Bonding Tool - KULICKE & SOFFA INDUSTRIES, INC.; pg. 650, pg. 1533
NEXXUS - Hair Care Products - UNILEVER UNITED STATES, INC.; pg. 904, pg. 1061
NEYTECH - Dental Product - DENTSPLY INTERNATIONAL INC.; pg. 1522, pg. 1596
NF-2 - Flashlight - STREAMLIGHT INC.; pg. 1306, pg. 1527
NFC - Fire Safety Book - NATIONAL FIRE PROTECTION ASSOCIATION; pg. 149, pg. 842
NFINITEFX - Engine - NVIDIA CORPORATION; pg. 447, pg. 268
NFL SPORT SHELL - Ear Warmer - 180S, LLC; pg. 1824, pg. 754
NFL SUNDAY TICKET - Channel Subscription Packs - VERIZON COMMUNICATIONS INC.; pg. 1875, pg. 1309
NFL.COM - Sport Media - CBS SPORTSLINE.COM, INC.; pg. 1234, pg. 423
NFORCE - Software - NVIDIA CORPORATION; pg. 447, pg. 268
NFPA - Cylinder - FABCO-AIR, INC.; pg. 1336, pg. 429
NFPA 101 - Fire Safety Book - NATIONAL FIRE PROTECTION ASSOCIATION; pg. 149, pg. 842
NFPA 1600 - Fire Safety Book - NATIONAL FIRE PROTECTION ASSOCIATION; pg. 149, pg. 842
NFPA 5000 - Fire Safety Book - NATIONAL FIRE PROTECTION ASSOCIATION; pg. 149, pg. 842
NFPA 70 - Fire Safety Book - NATIONAL FIRE PROTECTION ASSOCIATION; pg. 149, pg. 842
NFPA 70E - Fire Safety Book - NATIONAL FIRE PROTECTION ASSOCIATION; pg. 149, pg. 842
NFPA 72 - Fire Safety Book - NATIONAL FIRE PROTECTION ASSOCIATION; pg. 149, pg. 842
NFPA COMPLIANT TYCHEM - Garments - E.I. DU PONT DE NEMOURS & COMPANY; pg. 1159, pg. 390
NFPA JOURNAL - Magazine - NATIONAL FIRE PROTECTION ASSOCIATION; pg. 149, pg. 842
NFPA WORLD SAFETY CONFERENCE & EXPOSITION - Annual Event - NATIONAL FIRE PROTECTION ASSOCIATION; pg. 149, pg. 842
NFS - Software - NETAPP, INC.; pg. 444, pg. 287
NFUSE - Software - CITRIX SYSTEMS, INC.; pg. 375, pg. 424

NFZ - Animal Safety Product - NEOGEN CORPORATION; *pg.* 883, *pg.* 896
NG STRIP - Nasal Tube Fastener - DERMA SCIENCES, INC.; *pg.* 1523, *pg.* 1111
NGENIUS - Software - NELNET, INC.; *pg.* 786, *pg.* 1012
NGENIUS - Software - NETSCOUT SYSTEMS, INC.; *pg.* 1270, *pg.* 858
NGENIUS PERFORMANCE MANAGER - Software - NETSCOUT SYSTEMS, INC.; *pg.* 1270, *pg.* 858
NGENIUS PROBE - Software - NETSCOUT SYSTEMS, INC.; *pg.* 1270, *pg.* 858
NGM ROADWARRIOR - Fluid Handling System - GRACO, INC.; *pg.* 1342, *pg.* 935
NGN - Trade Publication - TECHNOLOGY MARKETING CORP.; *pg.* 1691, *pg.* 364
NGO - Natural Gas Odorants - OCCIDENTAL CHEMICAL CORPORATION; *pg.* 1175, *pg.* 1685
NHB - Cabinetry - MASTERBRAND CABINETS, INC.; *pg.* 96, *pg.* 692
NHI 1219 - Computerized Engraving - GRAVOGRAPH-NEW HERMES; *pg.* 1344, *pg.* 531
NHI 810 - Computerized Engraving - GRAVOGRAPH-NEW HERMES; *pg.* 1344, *pg.* 531
NHL CENTER ICE - Professional Hockey Television Programming Package - NATIONAL HOCKEY LEAGUE; *pg.* 568, *pg.* 1265
NHL GAMECENTER - Online Professional Hockey Game Tracker - NATIONAL HOCKEY LEAGUE; *pg.* 568, *pg.* 1265
NHL GAMECENTER LIVE - Live Online Professional Hockey Game Video Feed - NATIONAL HOCKEY LEAGUE; *pg.* 568, *pg.* 1265
NHL NETWORK - Professional Hockey Cable Television Network - NATIONAL HOCKEY LEAGUE; *pg.* 568, *pg.* 1265
NHL.COM - Website - NATIONAL HOCKEY LEAGUE; *pg.* 568, *pg.* 1265
NHRA LUCAS OIL - Drag Racing Series - NATIONAL HOT ROD ASSOCIATION; *pg.* 149, *pg.* 99
NHRA O.REILLY JR. - Drag Racing Series - NATIONAL HOT ROD ASSOCIATION; *pg.* 149, *pg.* 99
NHRA POWERADE - Drag Racing Series - NATIONAL HOT ROD ASSOCIATION; *pg.* 149, *pg.* 99
NHRA SUMMIT - Drag Racing Series - NATIONAL HOT ROD ASSOCIATION; *pg.* 149, *pg.* 99
NHRA'S YOUTH AND EDUCATION SERVICES - Educational Program - NATIONAL HOT ROD ASSOCIATION; *pg.* 149, *pg.* 99
NHT (NOW HEAR THIS) - Loudspeakers - NHT AUDIO, LLC; *pg.* 659, *pg.* 45
NI-CHEM II - Premium Roll Covers - VAIL RUBBER WORKS, INC.; *pg.* 1891, *pg.* 906
NI-SPAN-C - Alloy Product - SPECIAL METALS CORPORATION; *pg.* 1377, *pg.* 1850
NI TERNE XL - Steel Product - AK STEEL HOLDING CORPORATION; *pg.* 1311, *pg.* 1479
NIA 24 - Skin Care Product - MENTOR CORPORATION; *pg.* 1565, *pg.* 263
NIAC - Electronic Components - MOLEX INCORPORATED; *pg.* 655, *pg.* 628
NIACIN - Pharmaceutical Product - VALEANT PHARMACEUTICALS INTERNATIONAL; *pg.* 1605, *pg.* 1047
NIAGARA - Sponge Cloth Clean - 3M COMPANY; *pg.* 1142, *pg.* 956
NIAGARA - 3-Tab Roofing Shingles - BUILDING PRODUCTS OF CANADA CORP.; *pg.* 72, *pg.* 1951
NIAGARA FALLS - Nail Care Product - OPI PRODUCTS INC.; *pg.* 518, *pg.* 167
NIAGARA NATIONAL - Truck Wash Agents - ZEP INC.; *pg.* 338, *pg.* 524
NIAL - Alloy - CARPENTER TECHNOLOGY CORPORATION; *pg.* 73, *pg.* 1584
NIAPROOF - Surfactants - PVS CHEMICALS, INC.; *pg.* 1178, *pg.* 884
NIAS - Footwear - COBIAN CORP.; *pg.* 1806, *pg.* 253
NIASHURE - Animal Nutritional Product - BALCHEM CORPORATION; *pg.* 839, *pg.* 1183
NIASPAN - Tablets - ABBOTT LABORATORIES; *pg.* 1484, *pg.* 551
NIBBLE NOTES - Toy & Game - HASBRO, INC.; *pg.* 954, *pg.* 1603
NIBBLERS - Pretzel Snacks - SNYDER'S OF HANOVER, INC.; *pg.* 1862, *pg.* 1536
NIBLACK - Plating Process - A BRITE COMPANY; *pg.* 1144, *pg.* 1697
NIBRITE - Plating Process System - A BRITE COMPANY; *pg.* 1144, *pg.* 1697
NIBS - Candy - THE HERSHEY CO.; *pg.* 1855, *pg.* 1538
NIC - Network Information Computer - DIGITAL LIGHTWAVE, INC.; *pg.* 634, *pg.* 462
NICARB - Animal Health Product - PHIBROCHEM; *pg.* 1177, *pg.* 1124
NICASIO - Bike - MARIN BIKES; *pg.* 1708, *pg.* 168
NICE & FRESH - Air Freshener - SWISHER HYGIENE INC.; *pg.* 336, *pg.* 1507
NICE COLOR EH - Nail Care Product - OPI PRODUCTS INC.; *pg.* 518, *pg.* 167
NICE 'N CLEAN - Moist Towelettes - NICE-PAK PRODUCTS, INC.; *pg.* 1465, *pg.* 1319
NICE 'N EASY - Hair Coloring - P&G-CLAIROL, INC.; *pg.* 519, *pg.* 1418
NICHE - Fabric - NEMSCHOFF, INC.; *pg.* 936, *pg.* 1890
NICHE - Surface Material - STEELCASE INC.; *pg.* 475, *pg.* 889
NICHEM - Roller Cover - VAIL RUBBER WORKS, INC.; *pg.* 1891, *pg.* 906
NICHICON - Capacitor - AUDIO RESEARCH CORPORATION; *pg.* 621, *pg.* 953
NICHOLAS - Furniture - LA-Z-BOY INCORPORATED; *pg.* 932, *pg.* 901
NICHOLL FELLOWSHIPS - Awards - ACADEMY OF MOTION PICTURE ARTS & SCIENCES; *pg.* 526, *pg.* 46
NICHROLOY - Steel Product - RUSSEL METALS INC.; *pg.* 1180, *pg.* 1928
NICI - Encryption Modules - NOVELL INC.; *pg.* 446, *pg.* 852
NICKEL - Skin Care Product - INTER PARFUMS, INC.; *pg.* 512, *pg.* 1244
NICKEL PENTRATE - Metal Finishing Product - HEATBATH CORPORATION; *pg.* 1165, *pg.* 826
NICKEL TULIP - Lighting - ETHAN ALLEN INTERIORS INC.; *pg.* 924, *pg.* 343
NICKELODEON - Cable TV Network - VIACOM INC.; *pg.* 316, *pg.* 1310
NICKELS AND DIMES IN MASON JARS - Slogan - SBLI USA LIFE INSURANCE COMPANY, INC.; *pg.* 1216, *pg.* 1288
NICKLES - Bakery Products - ALFRED NICKLES BAKERY, INC.; *pg.* 836, *pg.* 1466
NICKY - Furniture - AMISCO INDUSTRIES LTD.; *pg.* 913, *pg.* 1958
NICO - Beverages - THE COCA-COLA COMPANY; *pg.* 240, *pg.* 493
NICOLETT - Footwear - STEVEN MADDEN, LTD.; *pg.* 1819, *pg.* 1176
NICOLETTE - Clothing - ABERCROMBIE & FITCH CO.; *pg.* 37, *pg.* 1466
NICOLETTE - Bedding - CROSCILL, INC.; *pg.* 1122, *pg.* 1220
NICOLINI - Footwear - CAPEZIO BALLET MAKERS INC.; *pg.* 1805, *pg.* 1125
NICOMIDE - Biopharmaceutical Products - DUSA PHARMACEUTICALS, INC.; *pg.* 1525, *pg.* 860
NICOMIDE-T - Biopharmaceutical Product - DUSA PHARMACEUTICALS, INC.; *pg.* 1525, *pg.* 860
NICOSEAL - Coatings - CARPENTER TECHNOLOGY CORPORATION; *pg.* 73, *pg.* 1584
NICOTROL - Medicine - PFIZER INC.; *pg.* 1581, *pg.* 1278
NICOTROL INHALER - Pharmaceutical Product - PFIZER INC.; *pg.* 1581, *pg.* 1278
NICOTROL NS - Pharmaceutical Product - PFIZER INC.; *pg.* 1581, *pg.* 1278
NICOYA - Footwear - COBIAN CORP.; *pg.* 1806, *pg.* 253
NICROBRAZ - Nickel Alloy - WALL COLMONOY CORPORATION; *pg.* 1185, *pg.* 898
NICROCRAFT - Aircraft Exhaust Systems - WALL COLMONOY CORPORATION; *pg.* 1185, *pg.* 898
NICROSPRAY - Coating System - WALL COLMONOY CORPORATION; *pg.* 1185, *pg.* 898
NICULOY - Electroless Nickel Product - DOW CHEMICAL; *pg.* 1156, *pg.* 1563
NIDEX - Plating Process - A BRITE COMPANY; *pg.* 1144, *pg.* 1697
NIDEX - Software Product - CLARY CORPORATION; *pg.* 226, *pg.* 150
NIDO - Footwear - K-SWISS; *pg.* 1837, *pg.* 306
NIEHOFF - Motor Product - STANDARD MOTOR PRODUCTS, INC.; *pg.* 218, *pg.* 1176
NIELSEN ADVERTISER SERVICES - Provides Advanced Information Solutions to Help National Advertisers - NIELSEN MEDIA RESEARCH, INC.; *pg.* 303, *pg.* 1272
NIELSEN HISPANIC TELEVISION SERVICES - Provides Comprehensive Measurement Services for Hispanic Television - NIELSEN MEDIA RESEARCH, INC.; *pg.* 303, *pg.* 1272
NIELSEN HOMEVIDEO INDEX - Provides a Measurement of Cable, Pay Cable, VCRs, DVD, Satellite Dish - NIELSEN MEDIA RESEARCH, INC.; *pg.* 303, *pg.* 1272
NIELSEN MONITOR PLUS - Links Television Ratings to Commercial Occurrence Data - NIELSEN MEDIA RESEARCH, INC.; *pg.* 303, *pg.* 1272
NIELSEN SPORTS MARKETING SERVICE - Marketing Unit - NIELSEN MEDIA RESEARCH, INC.; *pg.* 303, *pg.* 1272
NIELSEN STATION INDEX - Provides Continuous Metered-Market Overnight Measurement - NIELSEN MEDIA RESEARCH, INC.; *pg.* 303, *pg.* 1272
NIFTY - Vehicle Product - LUND INTERNATIONAL, INC.; *pg.* 211, *pg.* 526
NIFTY $50'S - Lottery Card - MISSOURI LOTTERY; *pg.* 999, *pg.* 979
NIGHT & DAY - Lenses - ALCON; *pg.* 1399, *pg.* 530
NIGHT COM - Flashlight - STREAMLIGHT INC.; *pg.* 1306, *pg.* 1527
NIGHT ENFORCER - Night Vision Products - ITT CORPORATION; *pg.* 1351, *pg.* 1354
NIGHT EYES - Residential Lighting - SWIVELIER CO., INC.; *pg.* 1307, *pg.* 1142
NIGHT LIFE - Shoes - CALERES, INC.; *pg.* 1805, *pg.* 993
NIGHT LIFE - Lighting Fixture - PHILIPS LIGHTING; *pg.* 1303, *pg.* 806
NIGHT OF THE FUTURE STARS - Entertainment Service - KENTUCKY DERBY FESTIVAL, INC.; *pg.* 556, *pg.* 735
NIGHT OWL - Women's Clothing & Accessories - WOODEN SHIPS OF HOBOKEN; *pg.* 35, *pg.* 1315
NIGHT ROLL - Cervical Pillow - DYNATRONICS CORPORATION; *pg.* 1526, *pg.* 1757
NIGHT SCAN - Combination Lighting - THE WILL-BURT CO., INC.; *pg.* 1437, *pg.* 1469
NIGHT SCAN CHIEF - Telescoping Mast for Emergency Lighting - THE WILL-BURT CO., INC.; *pg.* 1437, *pg.* 1469
NIGHT SCAN PROFILER - Remote Control Positioner - THE WILL-BURT CO., INC.; *pg.* 1437, *pg.* 1469
NIGHT SCAN VERTICAL - Remote Control Positioner - THE WILL-BURT CO., INC.; *pg.* 1437, *pg.* 1469
NIGHT SKY - Textiles - BERNHARDT DESIGN; *pg.* 918, *pg.* 1381
NIGHT SKY - Video Game - INTERNATIONAL GAME TECHNOLOGY; *pg.* 957, *pg.* 1024
NIGHT SUPPLY - Skin Care Product - NU SKIN ENTERPRISES, INC.; *pg.* 518, *pg.* 1755
NIGHT TRAIN - Motorcycle - HARLEY-DAVIDSON, INC.; *pg.* 178, *pg.* 1874
NIGHT VISION SAFETY - Automatic-Dimming Car Mirror - GENTEX CORPORATION; *pg.* 206, *pg.* 913
NIGHTCRAWLER - Bicycle Component - SRAM CORPORATION; *pg.* 967, *pg.* 590
NIGHTFIGHTER - Flashlight - STREAMLIGHT INC.; *pg.* 1306, *pg.* 1527
NIGHTFIGHTER-2 - Flashlight - STREAMLIGHT INC.; *pg.* 1306, *pg.* 1527
NIGHTHAWK - Musical Instrument - GIBSON GUITAR CORP.; *pg.* 550, *pg.* 1650
NIGHTHAWK - Military Jet-Powered Fighter - LOCKHEED MARTIN CORPORATION; *pg.* 229, *pg.* 762
NIGHTHAWK - Spotting Scope Series - SWIFT OPTICAL INSTRUMENTS, INC.; *pg.* 1430, *pg.* 1744
NIGHTHUNTER - Lightweight Illumination System - XENONICS HOLDINGS, INC.; *pg.* 1308, *pg.* 62
NIGHTIME FORMULA - Nutritional Product - NUTRACEUTICAL INTERNATIONAL CORPORATION; *pg.* 1576, *pg.* 1753
NIGHTLIFE - Apparel & Accessories - BROOKS SPORTS INC.; *pg.* 1805, *pg.* 1818
NIGHTLIGHT - Software - BSQUARE CORPORATION; *pg.* 366, *pg.* 1813
NIGHTMARES - Gaming Product - GLD PRODUCTS, INC.; *pg.* 1835, *pg.* 1882
NIGHTSTAR - Integrated Tool - CONCURRENT COMPUTER CORPORATION; *pg.* 379, *pg.* 531
NIGHTVIEW - Telescope - MEADE INSTRUMENTS CORPORATION; *pg.* 1422, *pg.* 113
NIGHTWATCH - CB Radio - COBRA ELECTRONICS CORPORATION; *pg.* 629, *pg.* 572
NIGHTWATCH - Metal Door Hardware - MASTER LOCK COMPANY LLC; *pg.* 1055, *pg.* 1884
NIGHTWING - Character - DC COMICS, INC.; *pg.* 1633, *pg.*

First page reference indicates Business Class Edition
Second page reference indicates Geographic Edition

1221
NIJI - Markers - YASUTOMO & CO.; *pg.* 497, *pg.* 280
NIK - Security Product - BAE SYSTEMS PRODUCTS GROUP; *pg.* 359, *pg.* 432
NIK-L-NIP - Candy - TOOTSIE ROLL INDUSTRIES, INC.; *pg.* 1863, *pg.* 591
NIKE - Shoes, Apparel & Bags - NIKE, INC.; *pg.* 1812, *pg.* 1492
NIKE 6.0 - Footwear - NIKE, INC.; *pg.* 1812, *pg.* 1492
NIKE AIR - Apparel - NIKE, INC.; *pg.* 1812, *pg.* 1492
NIKE PRO - Footwear - NIKE, INC.; *pg.* 1812, *pg.* 1492
NIKE SWIM - Apparel - PERRY ELLIS INTERNATIONAL, INC.; *pg.* 45, *pg.* 445
NIKEFREE - Footwear - NIKE, INC.; *pg.* 1812, *pg.* 1492
NIKEFREE DYNAMIC TRAINER - Footwear - NIKE, INC.; *pg.* 1812, *pg.* 1492
NIKKO - Carpet - INTERFACE, INC.; *pg.* 695, *pg.* 512
NIKKO - Fabric - NEMSCHOFF, INC.; *pg.* 936, *pg.* 1890
NIKKOR - Auto Focus Lenses - NIKON INC.; *pg.* 1424, *pg.* 1181
NIKNAK - Cheese Snacks - PEPSICO, INC.; *pg.* 259, *pg.* 1327
NIKNAKS - Cheese Snack - FRITO-LAY NORTH AMERICA, INC.; *pg.* 1853, *pg.* 1730
NIKOLAI - Vodka & Gin - SAZERAC COMPANY, INC.; *pg.* 1969, *pg.* 745
NIKON COOLPIX - Digital Camera - EDMUND INDUSTRIAL OPTICS INC.; *pg.* 1411, *pg.* 1041
NIKON LITE EFFORT - Ophthalmic Lenses - NIKON INC.; *pg.* 1424, *pg.* 1181
NIKON V-20B - Large-Scale Profile Projector - NIKON INC.; *pg.* 1424, *pg.* 1181
NIKONOS - Underwater Camera - NIKON INC.; *pg.* 1424, *pg.* 1181
NIKONOS RS - Underwater Camera - NIKON INC.; *pg.* 1424, *pg.* 1181
NIKOS SCULPTURE DELICATE FLEUR - Women's Fragrance - COTY, INC.; *pg.* 506, *pg.* 1219
NIL-O-FRESH - Powdered Rug/Room Deodorizer - NILODOR, INC.; *pg.* 332, *pg.* 1406
NIL-O-LITTER - Moisture Absorbent Deodorizing Granules for Cat Litter - NILODOR, INC.; *pg.* 332, *pg.* 1406
NILE CRUISES - Hotel & Resort - SONESTA INTERNATIONAL HOTELS CORPORATION; *pg.* 1113, *pg.* 836
NILE SPICE - Food Product - THE HAIN CELESTIAL GROUP, INC.; *pg.* 860, *pg.* 1172
NILFISK ACTION PLUS - Vacuum Cleaner - NILFISK-ADVANCE, INC.; *pg.* 332, *pg.* 953
NILFISK AERO - Vacuum Cleaner - NILFISK-ADVANCE, INC.; *pg.* 332, *pg.* 953
NILFISK BUDDY - Vacuum Cleaner - NILFISK-ADVANCE, INC.; *pg.* 332, *pg.* 953
NILFISK CENTIX - Vacuum Cleaner - NILFISK-ADVANCE, INC.; *pg.* 332, *pg.* 953
NILFISK COMBAT - Vacuum Cleaner - NILFISK-ADVANCE, INC.; *pg.* 332, *pg.* 953
NILFISK COMBAT ULTRA - Vacuum Cleaner - NILFISK-ADVANCE, INC.; *pg.* 332, *pg.* 953
NILFISK COMPACT - Vacuum Cleaner - NILFISK-ADVANCE, INC.; *pg.* 332, *pg.* 953
NILFISK COUPE - Vacuum Cleaner - NILFISK-ADVANCE, INC.; *pg.* 332, *pg.* 953
NILFISK EXTREME - Vacuum Cleaner - NILFISK-ADVANCE, INC.; *pg.* 332, *pg.* 953
NILFISK EXTREME ECO - Vacuum Cleaner - NILFISK-ADVANCE, INC.; *pg.* 332, *pg.* 953
NILFISK GM 80 - Vacuum Cleaner - NILFISK-ADVANCE, INC.; *pg.* 332, *pg.* 953
NILFISK POWER - Vacuum Cleaner - NILFISK-ADVANCE, INC.; *pg.* 332, *pg.* 953
NILFISK SOPRA - Vacuum Cleaner - NILFISK-ADVANCE, INC.; *pg.* 332, *pg.* 953
NILIUM - Water Soluble Surface Deodorizer - NILODOR, INC.; *pg.* 332, *pg.* 1406
NILLA - Cookies - MONDELEZ INTERNATIONAL, INC.; *pg.* 878, *pg.* 601
NILMA - Vegetable Wash - CHESHER EQUIPMENT LTD.; *pg.* 1323, *pg.* 1925
NILO - Alloy Product - SPECIAL METALS CORPORATION; *pg.* 1377, *pg.* 1850
NILODOR CONCENTRATE - Concentrated Deodorizer - NILODOR, INC.; *pg.* 332, *pg.* 1406
NILOMAG - Alloy - SPECIAL METALS CORPORATION; *pg.* 1377, *pg.* 1850
NILOSOL - Deodorizing Cleaner - NILODOR, INC.; *pg.* 332, *pg.* 1406
NILOTEX - Pet Spot & Stain Remover - NILODOR, INC.; *pg.* 332, *pg.* 1406
NILOTRON - Air Freshener - NILODOR, INC.; *pg.* 332, *pg.* 1406
NILUXA - Pharmaceutical Preparation - PFIZER INC.; *pg.* 1581, *pg.* 1278
NILYN - Food Ingredient - FMC CORPORATION; *pg.* 1163, *pg.* 1564
NIMARK - Alloy - CARPENTER TECHNOLOGY CORPORATION; *pg.* 73, *pg.* 1584
NIMBEX - Pharmaceutical Product - ABBOTT LABORATORIES; *pg.* 1484, *pg.* 551
NIMBLE - Wire Guide - COOK GROUP, INC.; *pg.* 1518, *pg.* 674
NIMBLE - Apparel - VANS, INC.; *pg.* 1821, *pg.* 76
NIMBLE-LITE - Wiring Devices - SWIVELIER CO., INC.; *pg.* 1307, *pg.* 1142
NIMBLEEXPRESS - Array - AFFYMETRIX, INC.; *pg.* 1487, *pg.* 263
NIMBUS - Footwear - CAPEZIO BALLET MAKERS INC.; *pg.* 1805, *pg.* 1125
NIMBUS - Bicycle Tire - SPECIALIZED BICYCLE COMPONENTS, INC.; *pg.* 1711, *pg.* 152
NIMEX - Color Concentrates - FERRO CORPORATION; *pg.* 1162, *pg.* 1462
NIMONIC - Alloy Product - SPECIAL METALS CORPORATION; *pg.* 1377, *pg.* 1850
NINA - Furniture - AMISCO INDUSTRIES LTD.; *pg.* 913, *pg.* 1958
NINA - Footwear - CAPEZIO BALLET MAKERS INC.; *pg.* 1805, *pg.* 1125
NINA - Footwear - PHOENIX FOOTWEAR GROUP, INC.; *pg.* 1815, *pg.* 60
NINA THE NAMING NEWT - Educational Materials - SCHOLASTIC INC.; *pg.* 1683, *pg.* 1288
NINATE - Chemical Product - STEPAN COMPANY; *pg.* 1182, *pg.* 643
NINE WEST - Apparel - G-III APPAREL GROUP, LTD.; *pg.* 41, *pg.* 1233
NINE WEST - Women's Shoes & Accessories - NINE WEST HOLDINGS, INC.; *pg.* 1815, *pg.* 1272
NINES - Cosmetics - REVLON, INC.; *pg.* 521, *pg.* 1286
NINES BY SOUTHWICK - Clothes for Men - SOUTHWICK CLOTHING LLC; *pg.* 48, *pg.* 824
NINETY NINE RESTAURANT & PUB - Restaurants - AMERICAN BLUE RIBBON HOLDINGS; *pg.* 1714, *pg.* 1648
NINEX - Chemical Product - STEPAN COMPANY; *pg.* 1182, *pg.* 643
NINFA - Fabric - NEMSCHOFF, INC.; *pg.* 936, *pg.* 1890
NING PO - Fabric - SCALAMANDRE, INC.; *pg.* 941, *pg.* 1058
NINJA - Motorcycles - KAWASAKI MOTORS CORP., U.S.A.; *pg.* 1708, *pg.* 111
NINJA - Designer Fragrance - PARFUMS DE COEUR LTD.; *pg.* 519, *pg.* 376
NINJA SPIRIT - Game - WMS INDUSTRIES INC.; *pg.* 593, *pg.* 666
NINOL - Chemical Product - STEPAN COMPANY; *pg.* 1182, *pg.* 643
NINTENDO 64 - Video Game System - NINTENDO OF AMERICA, INC.; *pg.* 965, *pg.* 1829
NINTENDO ENTERTAINMENT SYSTEM - Video Game System - NINTENDO OF AMERICA, INC.; *pg.* 965, *pg.* 1829
NINTENDO GAME CUBE - Video Game System - NINTENDO OF AMERICA, INC.; *pg.* 965, *pg.* 1829
NINTENDO POWER - Publication - NINTENDO OF AMERICA, INC.; *pg.* 965, *pg.* 1829
NIOBE - Software - STEREOTAXIS, INC.; *pg.* 1597, *pg.* 1004
NIOS - Software Tool - ALTERA CORPORATION; *pg.* 348, *pg.* 237
NIOS II - Software Tool - ALTERA CORPORATION; *pg.* 348, *pg.* 237
NIPAR - Nitroparaffin Solvents - THE DOW CHEMICAL COMPANY; *pg.* 1157, *pg.* 898
NIPCHEE - Snack Food - SNYDER'S-LANCE, INC.; *pg.* 896, *pg.* 1368
NIPENT - Pharmaceutical Product - ASTEX PHARMACEUTICALS, INC; *pg.* 1497, *pg.* 77
NIPLATE - Electroless Nickel Product - DOW CHEMICAL; *pg.* 1156, *pg.* 1563
NIPOL - Chemical Product - STEPAN COMPANY; *pg.* 1182, *pg.* 643
NIPOSIT - Electroless Nickel Product - DOW CHEMICAL; *pg.* 1156, *pg.* 1563
NIPPERT - Commutator - KIRKWOOD HOLDING, INC.; *pg.* 649, *pg.* 1469
NIPS - Candy - NESTLE USA, INC.; *pg.* 883, *pg.* 96
NIRON - Chemical Coating - ENTHONE INC.; *pg.* 1161, *pg.* 381
NIRVANA - Rotary Screw - INGERSOLL-RAND COMPANY; *pg.* 1349, *pg.* 1370
NISSAN - Cars & Trucks - NISSAN NORTH AMERICA, INC.; *pg.* 186, *pg.* 1633
NISTRIP - Metal Stripper - HEATBATH CORPORATION; *pg.* 1165, *pg.* 826
NIT-OFF - Coating - HEATBATH CORPORATION; *pg.* 1165, *pg.* 826
NIT-VU - High-Performance Micro Guidewire - ANGIODYNAMICS, INC.; *pg.* 1495, *pg.* 1173
NITA - Footwear - PHOENIX FOOTWEAR GROUP, INC.; *pg.* 1815, *pg.* 60
NITAMIN - Coated Sand - FAIRMOUNT SANTROL; *pg.* 1162, *pg.* 1409
NITE BURN - Weight Loss Supplement - BPI SPORTS, LLC; *pg.* 842, *pg.* 430
NITE-EYES - Road Lights - UNITY MANUFACTURING COMPANY; *pg.* 221, *pg.* 594
NITE-HAWK - Sweepers - ALAMO GROUP INC.; *pg.* 1311, *pg.* 1745
NITE-LITE - Awning Fabric - GLEN RAVEN, INC.; *pg.* 693, *pg.* 1373
NITE LITE - Hunting Apparel - NLC PRODUCTS INC.; *pg.* 99, *pg.* 34
NITE NITE - Pharmaceutical Product - ALERE INC.; *pg.* 1488, *pg.* 849
NITE TEC ACOUSTIC - Ear Warmer - 180S, LLC; *pg.* 1824, *pg.* 754
NITEBRITE - Colorant - POLYONE CORPORATION; *pg.* 1177, *pg.* 1404
NITEC - Metal Finishing Product - HEATBATH CORPORATION; *pg.* 1165, *pg.* 826
NITEGLO - Humidifier - HUNTER FAN COMPANY; *pg.* 57, *pg.* 1631
NITEHAWK - Footwear - K-SWISS; *pg.* 1837, *pg.* 306
NITELYTE - Parking Garage & Canopy Lighting - JUNO LIGHTING, INC.; *pg.* 1300, *pg.* 606
NITETORCH - Lighting Product - HUBBELL INCORPORATED; *pg.* 1299, *pg.* 370
NITEWORKS - Dietary Supplement - HERBALIFE INTERNATIONAL OF AMERICA, INC.; *pg.* 1541, *pg.* 132
NITEWRITER - Pen With Flashlight - ELECTRO-OPTIX, INC.; *pg.* 1046, *pg.* 459
NITOMAN - Pharmaceutical Product - VALEANT PHARMACEUTICALS INTERNATIONAL, INC.; *pg.* 1605, *pg.* 1957
NITRASEAL - Hygiene System - SIRONA DENTAL SYSTEMS, INC.; *pg.* 1429, *pg.* 1175
NITRAVER - Chemical Reagent - HACH COMPANY; *pg.* 1415, *pg.* 334
NITRENE - Fatty Diethanol Amides - HENKEL CORPORATION; *pg.* 1165, *pg.* 1535
NITRILE ALUMINIZED ROOF PRIMER - Nitrile Roof Primer - W.J. RUSCOE COMPANY; *pg.* 122, *pg.* 1403
NITRIVER - Chemical Reagent - HACH COMPANY; *pg.* 1415, *pg.* 334
NITRO - Energy Drink - LEADING BRANDS, INC.; *pg.* 1026, *pg.* 1911
NITRO - Bait And Scent Product - WRIGHT & MCGILL CO.; *pg.* 1848, *pg.* 324
NITRO 27 - Shotshell - REMINGTON ARMS COMPANY, LLC; *pg.* 1844, *pg.* 1382
NITRO-DUR - Medicine - MERCK & CO., INC.; *pg.* 1566, *pg.* 1077
NITRO MAG - Ammunition - REMINGTON ARMS COMPANY, LLC; *pg.* 1844, *pg.* 1382
NITRO XRC - Toy & Game - HASBRO, INC.; *pg.* 954, *pg.* 1603
NITROCARN - Nutritional Product - NUTRACEUTICAL INTERNATIONAL CORPORATION; *pg.* 1576, *pg.* 1753
NITRODE - Steel Product - A. FINKL & SONS CO.; *pg.* 1309, *pg.* 563
NITROFUEL - Racing Nitromethane - THE DOW CHEMICAL COMPANY; *pg.* 1157, *pg.* 898
NITROGEN ATMOSPHERE - Thermal Processing Equipment - SURFACE COMBUSTION, INC.; *pg.* 1077, *pg.* 1462
NITRONEAL - Gas Generators - BASF CATALYSTS LLC; *pg.* 1148, *pg.* 1074

NITRONIC - Steel Product - AK STEEL HOLDING CORPORATION; *pg.* 1311, *pg.* 1479
NITROPHYL - Material - ROGERS CORPORATION; *pg.* 1305, *pg.* 369
NITROSHURE - Animal Nutritional Product - BALCHEM CORPORATION; *pg.* 839, *pg.* 1183
NITROSOL - Gloves - LAKELAND INDUSTRIES, INC.; *pg.* 1354, *pg.* 1338
NITROSTAT - Medicine - PFIZER INC.; *pg.* 1581, *pg.* 1278
NITROSTEEL - Piston Rod - EDELBROCK CORPORATION; *pg.* 204, *pg.* 293
NITROWING - Cab Spoiler - LUND INTERNATIONAL, INC.; *pg.* 211, *pg.* 526
NITTY GRITTY - Cleaning Product - THE LIBMAN COMPANY; *pg.* 331, *pg.* 553
NITWIT - Beer - BJ'S RESTAURANTS, INC.; *pg.* 1716, *pg.* 104
NIV CHILDREN'S BIBLE - Illustrated Children's Bible - THE ZONDERVAN CORPORATION; *pg.* 1703, *pg.* 891
NIV PULPIT BIBLE - New International Version Pulpit Bible - THE ZONDERVAN CORPORATION; *pg.* 1703, *pg.* 891
NIV STUDY BIBLE - New International Version Study Bible - THE ZONDERVAN CORPORATION; *pg.* 1703, *pg.* 891
NIZORAL - Pharmaceutical - JANSSEN PHARMACEUTICA PRODUCTS, L.P.; *pg.* 1548, *pg.* 1125
NIZORAL - Healthcare Product - JOHNSON & JOHNSON; *pg.* 1549, *pg.* 1091
NJBIZ - Business Magazine - NJBIZ; *pg.* 1671, *pg.* 1122
NJBIZADVERTISING - Newspaper - NJBIZ; *pg.* 1671, *pg.* 1122
NJBIZ.COM - Newspaper - NJBIZ; *pg.* 1671, *pg.* 1122
NJBIZDAILY - Newspaper - NJBIZ; *pg.* 1671, *pg.* 1122
NJBIZDATA - Newspaper - NJBIZ; *pg.* 1671, *pg.* 1122
NJBIZEVENTS - Newspaper - NJBIZ; *pg.* 1671, *pg.* 1122
NK - Premium NK Garden Products - PLANTATION PRODUCTS INC; *pg.* 1799, *pg.* 839
NK - Corn & Soy Beans - SYNGENTA SEEDS, INC.; *pg.* 1801, *pg.* 950
NK MAGIC TOOL BOX - Equipment - CARGILL LIMITED; *pg.* 1475, *pg.* 1914
NK SERIES - Reeling & Coiling Machinery - REEL-O-MATIC, INC.; *pg.* 1371, *pg.* 1487
NKK - Electrical/electronic Switches - NKK SWITCHES; *pg.* 1302, *pg.* 23
NKL - Safes - FIRE KING SECURITY GROUP; *pg.* 1336, *pg.* 696
NKTR - Pharmaceutical Product - NEKTAR THERAPEUTICS; *pg.* 1572, *pg.* 224
NL - Regulator Bypass Switch - S&C ELECTRIC COMPANY; *pg.* 1305, *pg.* 589
NLAYERS - Software - EMC CORPORATION; *pg.* 391, *pg.* 825
NLIGHTEN - Web-Based Business Management Training - PIVOTAL RESOURCES, INC.; *pg.* 455, *pg.* 304
NLIGHTEN - Fiber Optic Module - W.L. GORE & ASSOCIATES, INC.; *pg.* 122, *pg.* 388
NLT - Christian Books - TYNDALE HOUSE PUBLISHERS, INC.; *pg.* 1697, *pg.* 561
NM CABLE T - Wire Stripper - IDEAL INDUSTRIES, INC.; *pg.* 1051, *pg.* 662
NM2000 PLUGMOLD - Nonmetallic Raceway - WIREMOLD/LEGRAND; *pg.* 689, *pg.* 383
NM2000 RACEWAY - Nonmetallic Raceway - WIREMOLD/LEGRAND; *pg.* 689, *pg.* 383
NMOA8100 - Amplifier - EMCORE CORPORATION; *pg.* 636, *pg.* 39
NMOA8200 - Amplifier - EMCORE CORPORATION; *pg.* 636, *pg.* 39
NMP179 - Pharmaceutical Product - ALERE INC.; *pg.* 1488, *pg.* 849
NMP22 - Pharmaceutical Product - ALERE INC.; *pg.* 1488, *pg.* 849
NMP22 BLADDERCHEK - Pharmaceutical Product - ALERE INC.; *pg.* 1488, *pg.* 849
NMP66 - Pharmaceutical Product - ALERE INC.; *pg.* 1488, *pg.* 849
NMS HEARSAY - Product - ONMOBILE LIVE, INC.; *pg.* 449, *pg.* 829
NMX DIGITAL SERVICE MANAGER - Digital Video Product - HARMONIC, INC.; *pg.* 402, *pg.* 246
NNR THERAPEUTICS - Pharmaceutical Preparations - TARGACEPT, INC.; *pg.* 1601, *pg.* 1395
NO. 1 - Single-Shot Rifle - STURM, RUGER & COMPANY, INC.; *pg.* 1846, *pg.* 371
NO. 1 JR - Alloys - CARPENTER TECHNOLOGY CORPORATION; *pg.* 73, *pg.* 1584
NO BALL GOES FARTHER - Tag Line - ACUSHNET COMPANY; *pg.* 1824, *pg.* 818
NO BARE WALLS - Tag Line - KIRKLAND'S INC.; *pg.* 1126, *pg.* 1652
NO BITE - Nail Product - ORLY INTERNATIONAL, INC.; *pg.* 518, *pg.* 137
NO BLADE - Skin Care Product - E.T. BROWNE DRUG COMPANY, INC.; *pg.* 509, *pg.* 1060
NO BOUNDARIES - Merchandise - WAL-MART STORES, INC.; *pg.* 1790, *pg.* 29
NO BUS LATENCY - Memory Product - CYPRESS SEMICONDUCTOR CORPORATION; *pg.* 1326, *pg.* 243
NO-CALK - Roof Flashing - OATEY SUPPLY CHAIN SERVICES; *pg.* 30, *pg.* 1433
NO-CARB - Coating - HEATBATH CORPORATION; *pg.* 1165, *pg.* 826
NO-CHOKE TIP CAP - Medical Device - COMAR INC.; *pg.* 1455, *pg.* 1047
NO CLEAN FLUX REMOVER - Aerosol Cleaner - TECH SPRAY, L.P.; *pg.* 1183, *pg.* 1659
NO DOUBT - Mission Assurance - RAYTHEON COMPANY; *pg.* 233, *pg.* 854
NO DOWN PAYMENT - Course - PROFESSIONAL EDUCATION INSTITUTE; *pg.* 457, *pg.* 561
NO DRAFT - Air Purifier - KAZ, INC.; *pg.* 58, *pg.* 844
NO-DRIFT - Force Stick Encoder - SEMTECH CORPORATION; *pg.* 671, *pg.* 57
NO GLARE STRIPS - Sun Glare Reducer - MUELLER SPORTS MEDICINE, INC.; *pg.* 1570, *pg.* 1887
NO-GO - Hydration Inhibitor - USG CORPORATION; *pg.* 118, *pg.* 594
NO HASSLE - Credit Card - CAPITAL ONE FINANCIAL CORPORATION; *pg.* 730, *pg.* 1789
NO-HOE - Garden Mulch - FLEX-O-GLASS, INC.; *pg.* 1457, *pg.* 574
NO-LEAK - Premium Stop Leak - GOLD EAGLE COMPANY; *pg.* 206, *pg.* 575
NO-LIFT BOOSTER - Patient Transfer Devices - ALIMED, INC.; *pg.* 1490, *pg.* 816
NO LINES ONLINE - Retail Store - COSTCO WHOLESALE CORPORATION; *pg.* 1765, *pg.* 1820
NO-LINT - Dry Cleaning & Laundry Product - ADCO, INC.; *pg.* 325, *pg.* 482
NO-MESS PEN - Household Product - WD-40 COMPANY; *pg.* 337, *pg.* 210
NO-MOIST - Bill Straps - GLORY GLOBAL SOLUTIONS; *pg.* 401, *pg.* 628
NO MORE DRY WIPES - Warmer - MUNCHKIN, INC.; *pg.* 964, *pg.* 300
NO NONSENSE - Legwear & Apparel - KAYSER-ROTH CORPORATION; *pg.* 28, *pg.* 1374
NO ONE DOES IT FOR LESS - Tag Line - IDT CORPORATION; *pg.* 643, *pg.* 1096
NO ONE ELSE EVEN COMES CLOSE - Slogan - PRECISION ROLL GRINDERS, INC.; *pg.* 1370, *pg.* 1514
NO ORDINARY ADVICE - Slogan - NORTHEAST BANCORP; *pg.* 787, *pg.* 751
NO ORDINARY BANK - Slogan - NORTHEAST BANCORP; *pg.* 787, *pg.* 751
NO-OX - Pumps - IDEX CORPORATION; *pg.* 1347, *pg.* 623
NO PALCE LIKE HOME - Pillow and Throw - HERITAGE LACE INC.; *pg.* 694, *pg.* 711
NO PANTY LINE PROMISE - Bikini - JOCKEY INTERNATIONAL, INC.; *pg.* 27, *pg.* 1861
NO PLACE LIKE HOME - Pharmaceutical Product - ALERE INC.; *pg.* 1488, *pg.* 849
THE NO PROBLEM PEOPLE - Slogan - AUTO-OWNERS INSURANCE GROUP; *pg.* 1194, *pg.* 895
NO-REACT - Medical Device - INTEGRA LIFESCIENCES HOLDINGS CORPORATION; *pg.* 1545, *pg.* 1109
NO RETURN - Pet Odor - ORECK CORPORATION; *pg.* 59, *pg.* 1653
NO-RUST - Rust Preventive & Inhibitor - SLIDE PRODUCTS, INC.; *pg.* 1181, *pg.* 670
NO-SAG - Automobile Seating Systems - LEGGETT & PLATT, INCORPORATED; *pg.* 933, *pg.* 974
NO SALT - Salt Alternative - RECKITT BENCKISER INC.; *pg.* 1136, *pg.* 1105
NO-SHA - Cleansing Conditioner for Hair - THE GILLETTE COMPANY; *pg.* 509, *pg.* 795
NO SMOKE - Engine Oil - BARDAHL MANUFACTURING CORPORATION; *pg.* 972, *pg.* 1833
NO-SOAK - Plastic Casing - VISKASE COMPANIES, INC.; *pg.* 1471, *pg.* 599
NO-SPILL - Slide Gate - BUNTING MAGNETICS CO.; *pg.* 1320, *pg.* 717
NO STRESS CHESS - Game - WINNING MOVES GAMES, INC.; *pg.* 970, *pg.* 816
NO SWEAT - Deodorant - REVLON, INC.; *pg.* 521, *pg.* 1286
NO SWEAT - Slogan - SUNBELT RENTALS; *pg.* 1786, *pg.* 1616
NO-TACK - Stencil Film - BADGER AIR BRUSH COMPANY; *pg.* 359, *pg.* 612
NO TORQUE RIGHT - Catheter - COOK GROUP, INC.; *pg.* 1518, *pg.* 674
NO-TOX - Lubricant - BEL-RAY COMPANY, INC.; *pg.* 972, *pg.* 1128
NO-TWEEZE - Body & brow wax - AMERICAN INTERNATIONAL INDUSTRIES COMPANY; *pg.* 498, *pg.* 126
NO TYE - Footwear - OAKLEY, INC.; *pg.* 1840, *pg.* 86
NO YOLKS - Noodles - NEW WORLD PASTA COMPANY; *pg.* 885, *pg.* 1537
NO610 - Alloy - CARPENTER TECHNOLOGY CORPORATION; *pg.* 73, *pg.* 1584
NO883 - Tool Steel - CARPENTER TECHNOLOGY CORPORATION; *pg.* 73, *pg.* 1584
NOAH'S ARK - Video Game - INTERNATIONAL GAME TECHNOLOGY; *pg.* 957, *pg.* 1024
NOAH'S NEW YORK BAGELS - Food Store - EINSTEIN NOAH RESTAURANT GROUP, INC.; *pg.* 1019, *pg.* 332
NOALOX - Anti-Oxidant Compound - IDEAL INDUSTRIES, INC.; *pg.* 1051, *pg.* 662
NOBHILL - Furniture - AMERICAN LEATHER LP; *pg.* 912, *pg.* 1673
NOBILITY - Authentic Chinese Dimsum - MITSUI FOODS, INC.; *pg.* 877, *pg.* 1099
NOBL - Semiconductor Architecture - CYPRESS SEMICONDUCTOR CORPORATION; *pg.* 1326, *pg.* 243
NOBLE - Composites - CRANE CO.; *pg.* 227, *pg.* 373
NOBLE ALLOY - Valve - FLOWSERVE CORPORATION; *pg.* 82, *pg.* 1719
NOBLE KNIGHTS - Video Game - INTERNATIONAL GAME TECHNOLOGY; *pg.* 957, *pg.* 1024
NOBLE ROMAN'S PIZZA - Pizza - NOBLE ROMAN'S, INC.; *pg.* 1741, *pg.* 689
NOBLEMAN - Knife - BUCK KNIVES, INC.; *pg.* 1828, *pg.* 550
NOBLES - Floor Maintenance Equipment - TENNANT COMPANY; *pg.* 1381, *pg.* 944
NOBLES CAPITAL - Floor Maintenance Equipment - TENNANT COMPANY; *pg.* 1381, *pg.* 944
NOBLES SPIN KLEEN - Parts Washing - NOBLES MANUFACTURING, INC.; *pg.* 59, *pg.* 1890
NOBLES TURBO - Centrifugal Dryer - NOBLES MANUFACTURING, INC.; *pg.* 59, *pg.* 1890
NOBLES TURBO DRYER - Parts Dryer - NOBLES MANUFACTURING, INC.; *pg.* 59, *pg.* 1890
NOBODY - Slogan - WCI COMMUNITIES, INC.; *pg.* 1118, *pg.* 414
NOBODY DOES IT BETTER - Slogan - WCI COMMUNITIES, INC.; *pg.* 1118, *pg.* 414
NOBODY KNOWS MORE ABOUT MOZZARELLA - Slogan - LEPRINO FOODS COMPANY; *pg.* 874, *pg.* 320
NOBODY LENDS YOU MORE SUPPORT - Slogan - SLM CORPORATION; *pg.* 804, *pg.* 388
NOC - Fragrance - WESTROCK COMPANY; *pg.* 1472, *pg.* 1805
NOCONA - Workboots - JUSTIN BRANDS, INC.; *pg.* 1810, *pg.* 1695
NOCTURN - Entertainment Lighting Product - BALLANTYNE STRONG, INC.; *pg.* 623, *pg.* 1013
NOCTURNE - Chocolate Product - GUITTARD CHOCOLATE COMPANY; *pg.* 1855, *pg.* 55
NODEBUILDER - Development Tool - ECHELON CORPORATION; *pg.* 389, *pg.* 245
NODEWATCH - Software - MICROWAY, INC.; *pg.* 1267, *pg.* 841
NOESIS - Emission Testing System - MISTRAS GROUP, INC.; *pg.* 1362, *pg.* 1113
NOGGIN NEST - Baby Product - THE BOPPY COMPANY, LLC; *pg.* 20, *pg.* 329
NOGUCHI - Table - HERMAN MILLER, INC.; *pg.* 926, *pg.* 913
NOHO - Fabric - NEMSCHOFF, INC.; *pg.* 936, *pg.* 1890
NOILLY PRAT - Vermouths - BROWN-FORMAN CORPORATION; *pg.* 1958, *pg.* 732
NOIR BRUT - Wine - BILTMORE ESTATE WINE COMPANY; *pg.* 1958, *pg.* 1358

First page reference indicates Business Class Edition
Second page reference indicates Geographic Edition

NOISEASSASSIN - Noise & Wind Canceling Technology - ALIPHCOM, INC.; *pg.* 616, *pg.* 212
NOISECOM - Telecommunications Test Equipment - WIRELESS TELECOM GROUP, INC.; *pg.* 689, *pg.* 1106
NOISEPRO - Noise Dosimeters - 3M DETECTION SOLUTIONS; *pg.* 1398, *pg.* 1885
NOJAX - Sausage Casing - VISKASE COMPANIES, INC.; *pg.* 1471, *pg.* 599
NOJO - Infant Bedding - CROWN CRAFTS INFANT PRODUCTS, INC.; *pg.* 922, *pg.* 68
NOKIA - Smart Phones - MICROSOFT CORPORATION; *pg.* 435, *pg.* 1824
NOL - Adjustable Unscrambler - NEW ENGLAND MACHINERY, INC.; *pg.* 1364, *pg.* 415
NOLAN - Furniture - AMERICAN LEATHER LP; *pg.* 912, *pg.* 1673
NOLEN - Footwear - VANS, INC.; *pg.* 1821, *pg.* 76
NOLITA - Fabric - NEMSCHOFF, INC.; *pg.* 936, *pg.* 1890
NOLITA - Surface Material - STEELCASE INC.; *pg.* 475, *pg.* 889
NOLVASAN - Veterinary Medicated Shampoos - PFIZER INC.; *pg.* 1581, *pg.* 1278
NOMAD - Scraper Matting - 3M COMPANY; *pg.* 1142, *pg.* 956
NOMAD - Display System - MICROVISION, INC.; *pg.* 654, *pg.* 1828
NOMAD - Fabric - NEMSCHOFF, INC.; *pg.* 936, *pg.* 1890
NOMAD - Towable Recreational Vehicle - SKYLINE CORPORATION; *pg.* 1711, *pg.* 677
NOMAD - Surface Material - STEELCASE INC.; *pg.* 475, *pg.* 889
NOMAD SERIES - Engine Powered Forklifts - NISSAN FORKLIFT CORPORATION, NORTH AMERICA; *pg.* 186, *pg.* 631
NOMAD'S DREAM - Nail Care Product - OPI PRODUCTS INC.; *pg.* 518, *pg.* 167
NOMAX - Electrical Test & Measurement - HD ELECTRIC COMPANY; *pg.* 1299, *pg.* 666
NOMAX 2000 - Capacitor Control - HD ELECTRIC COMPANY; *pg.* 1299, *pg.* 666
NOMEX - Fiber - DRAPER KNITTING CO., INC.; *pg.* 692, *pg.* 810
NOMEX - Fiber & Protective Apparel - E.I. DU PONT DE NEMOURS & COMPANY; *pg.* 1159, *pg.* 390
NOMEX - Heater Hose - FLEXFAB HORIZONS INTERNATIONAL, LLC; *pg.* 1072, *pg.* 891
NOMEX - Fabric - HBD INDUSTRIES, INC.; *pg.* 207, *pg.* 1449
NOMEX - Clothing - LAKELAND INDUSTRIES, INC.; *pg.* 1354, *pg.* 1338
NON-AMMONIATED FLOOR STRIPPER - Floor Cleaner - SWISHER HYGIENE INC.; *pg.* 336, *pg.* 1507
NON-FEDERAL SHARED SERVICE PROVIDER PKI - Internet Site Security Product - VERISIGN, INC.; *pg.* 488, *pg.* 1799
NON-FICTION CONNECTION - Nonfiction Readers' Advisory Tool - R.R. BOWKER LLC; *pg.* 1682, *pg.* 1095
NON-GLARE EXHIBITION (PATTERN 122) - Patterned Glass - AGC GLASS NORTH AMERICA, INC.; *pg.* 65, *pg.* 482
NON SCENTS - Hand Cleaner & Odor Eliminator - WISCONSIN PHARMACAL COMPANY, LLC; *pg.* 1610, *pg.* 1861
NON-SPARKING POWER DRIVE - Hammer - NUPLA CORPORATION; *pg.* 101, *pg.* 281
NON-SPARKING SPS - Hammer - NUPLA CORPORATION; *pg.* 101, *pg.* 281
NON-SPARKING STRIKE - Hammer - NUPLA CORPORATION; *pg.* 101, *pg.* 281
NON-STOP PRODUCTION - Tag Line - BUTLER AUTOMATIC, INC.; *pg.* 1320, *pg.* 833
NON-THERMALIZED - Skylight - WASCO PRODUCTS, INC.; *pg.* 120, *pg.* 752
NON-WET - Skin Packaging - FLEX-O-GLASS, INC.; *pg.* 1457, *pg.* 574
NONESUCH - Record Label - WARNER MUSIC GROUP CORP.; *pg.* 590, *pg.* 1313
NONI - Health Care Product - NATURE'S SUNSHINE PRODUCTS, INC.; *pg.* 1571, *pg.* 1754
NONIDET - Chemical Product - SPECTRUM CHEMICALS & LABORATORY PRODUCTS, INC.; *pg.* 1181, *pg.* 94
NONLEDEX - Conductor Insulation Material - ENCORE WIRE CORPORATION; *pg.* 637, *pg.* 1726
NONNI'S - Company Name - NONNI'S FOOD COMPANY INC.; *pg.* 886, *pg.* 1490
NONO - Furniture - NEMSCHOFF, INC.; *pg.* 936, *pg.* 1890
NONONSENSE - Writing Instruments - SHEAFFER PEN CORPORATION; *pg.* 469, *pg.* 371
NONOXOR - Gas Analyzer - BACHARACH INC.; *pg.* 1400, *pg.* 1556
NONSTOP - Networking Product - HEWLETT-PACKARD COMPANY; *pg.* 404, *pg.* 175
NONSTOP - Hosiery - KAYSER-ROTH CORPORATION; *pg.* 28, *pg.* 1374
NONYX - Home Products - HABAND COMPANY, INC.; *pg.* 1772, *pg.* 1099
NOODLEBORO - Toy & Game - HASBRO, INC.; *pg.* 954, *pg.* 1603
NOOGEN - Apparel - VANS, INC.; *pg.* 1821, *pg.* 76
NOOK - Electronic Reader - BARNES & NOBLE, INC.; *pg.* 1619, *pg.* 1201
NOR-LAKE - Food Service Equipment - STANDEX INTERNATIONAL CORPORATION; *pg.* 60, *pg.* 1039
NOR-QD - Pharmaceutical Product - ALLERGAN; *pg.* 1490, *pg.* 1101
NORA - Clothing - ABERCROMBIE & FITCH CO.; *pg.* 37, *pg.* 1466
NORA - Footwear - PHOENIX FOOTWEAR GROUP, INC.; *pg.* 1815, *pg.* 60
NORAMPAC - Packaging Product - CASCADES, INC.; *pg.* 73, *pg.* 1950
NORBA - Truck Product - OSHKOSH CORPORATION; *pg.* 187, *pg.* 1885
NORBOND - Adhesive - DEMCO INC.; *pg.* 386, *pg.* 1865
NORBRO - Valve - FLOWSERVE CORPORATION; *pg.* 82, *pg.* 1719
NORCALCIPHOS - Veterinary Vaccines - PFIZER INC.; *pg.* 1581, *pg.* 1278
NORCO - Pharmaceutical Product - ALLERGAN; *pg.* 1490, *pg.* 1101
NORCO - Window & Door - JELD-WEN, INC.; *pg.* 1051, *pg.* 1499
NORCRAFT CABINETRY - Designer Stock Framed Cabinetry - NORCRAFT HOLDINGS, LP; *pg.* 100, *pg.* 921
NORCURON - Muscle Relaxation - MERCK & CO., INC.; *pg.* 1566, *pg.* 1077
NORDBAK - Wearing Compounds - HENKEL CORPORATION; *pg.* 1049, *pg.* 369
NORDEL - Chemical Product - THE DOW CHEMICAL COMPANY; *pg.* 1157, *pg.* 898
NORDIC - Footwear - EASTLAND SHOE CORPORATION; *pg.* 1808, *pg.* 750
NORDIC MIST - Soft Drink - THE COCA-COLA COMPANY; *pg.* 240, *pg.* 493
NORDIC PRIDE - Packaged Foods - ATALANTA CORPORATION; *pg.* 838, *pg.* 1057
NORDICA - Cottage Cheese - GAY LEA FOODS CO-OPERATIVE LIMITED; *pg.* 858, *pg.* 1926
NORDICA SUMMER DRESSING - Food Product - GAY LEA FOODS CO-OPERATIVE LIMITED; *pg.* 858, *pg.* 1926
NORDICTRACK - Health & Fitness Product - ICON HEALTH & FITNESS, INC.; *pg.* 1837, *pg.* 1752
NORDSTORM - Valve - FLOWSERVE CORPORATION; *pg.* 82, *pg.* 1719
NORDSTROM 1901 - Apparels - NORDSTROM, INC.; *pg.* 1779, *pg.* 1837
NORDSTROM BABY - Apparels - NORDSTROM, INC.; *pg.* 1779, *pg.* 1837
NORDSTROM BUTTERFLY DESIGN - Apparels - NORDSTROM, INC.; *pg.* 1779, *pg.* 1837
NORDSTROM CRYSTAL COLLECTION - Apparels - NORDSTROM, INC.; *pg.* 1779, *pg.* 1837
NORDSTROM HORSE & CROWN DESIGN - Apparels - NORDSTROM, INC.; *pg.* 1779, *pg.* 1837
NORDSTROM LAYETTE - Apparels - NORDSTROM, INC.; *pg.* 1779, *pg.* 1837
NORDSTROM RACK - Apparels - NORDSTROM, INC.; *pg.* 1779, *pg.* 1837
NOR'EASTER - Magazine - DOMINION ENTERPRISES; *pg.* 1636, *pg.* 1796
NOREASTER - Glove - KOMBI, LTD.; *pg.* 1838, *pg.* 1766
NORELCO - Shavers - PHILIPS ELECTRONICS NORTH AMERICA; *pg.* 662, *pg.* 782
NORFLEX - Pharmaceutical Product - IMPAX LABORATORIES, INC.; *pg.* 1544, *pg.* 101
NORFOLK - Office Furniture - STEELCASE INC.; *pg.* 475, *pg.* 889
NORFORMS - Feminine Deodorant - FLEET LABORATORIES; *pg.* 1531, *pg.* 1787
NORINYL - Pharmaceutical Product - ALLERGAN; *pg.* 1490, *pg.* 1101
NORIT - Chemical Product - SPECTRUM CHEMICALS & LABORATORY PRODUCTS, INC.; *pg.* 1181, *pg.* 94
NORKOOL - Coolant - THE DOW CHEMICAL COMPANY; *pg.* 1157, *pg.* 898
NORM-O-TEMP - Medical Product - CINCINNATI SUB-ZERO PRODUCTS, INC.; *pg.* 1070, *pg.* 1411
NORM THOMPSON - Clothing & Accessories - NORM THOMPSON OUTFITTERS INC.; *pg.* 1780, *pg.* 1498
NORMAN ROCKWELL - Toy Train - LIONEL LLC; *pg.* 961, *pg.* 875
NORMANDIE - Door & Wood Product - CONESTOGA WOOD SPECIALTIES CORP.; *pg.* 921, *pg.* 1527
NORMBAU - Door System - INGERSOLL-RAND COMPANY; *pg.* 1349, *pg.* 1370
NORPACE - Medicine - PFIZER INC.; *pg.* 1581, *pg.* 1278
NORPACE CR - Pharmaceutical Product - PFIZER INC.; *pg.* 1581, *pg.* 1278
NORRGREVE SWISS - Cheese - A.V. OLSSON TRADING CO. INC.; *pg.* 838, *pg.* 372
NORSE DAIRY SYSTEMS - Cup Line - NORSE DAIRY SYSTEMS LLC; *pg.* 886, *pg.* 1442
NORTEX - Adhesive Removing - MCGEAN-ROHCO, INC.; *pg.* 1172, *pg.* 1432
NORTH AMERICAN - Relocation Services - SIRVA, INC.; *pg.* 1923, *pg.* 669
NORTH AMERICAN INTERNATIONAL - International Relocation & Management Services - SIRVA, INC.; *pg.* 1923, *pg.* 669
NORTH AMERICAN REASSURANCE - Life Reinsurance Company - SWISS REINSURANCE AMERICA CORPORATION; *pg.* 1218, *pg.* 1140
NORTH AMERICA'S RAILROAD - Tagline - CANADIAN NATIONAL RAILWAY COMPANY; *pg.* 1902, *pg.* 1953
NORTH BROOK - Furniture - ASHLEY FURNITURE INDUSTRIES, INC.; *pg.* 914, *pg.* 1852
NORTH CAROLINA LAWYERS WEEKLY - Newspaper - MASSACHUSETTS LAWYERS WEEKLY, INC.; *pg.* 1662, *pg.* 798
NORTH CAROLINA POWER - Electric Utility - DOMINION VIRGINIA POWER; *pg.* 1939, *pg.* 1802
THE NORTH FACE - Technically-Advanced Outerwear & Climbing Equipment - THE NORTH FACE, INC.; *pg.* 1840, *pg.* 252
THE NORTH FACE - Outdoor Gear & Apparel - V.F. CORPORATION; *pg.* 34, *pg.* 1376
NORTH LAKE - Sweaters - ABERCROMBIE & FITCH CO.; *pg.* 37, *pg.* 1466
NORTH PACIFIC BOAT AND SHORE - Salt - CARGILL LIMITED; *pg.* 1475, *pg.* 1914
NORTH SHORE - Eyewear - MAUI JIM, INC.; *pg.* 9, *pg.* 651
NORTH STAR - Encoder - DYNAPAR; *pg.* 1408, *pg.* 616
NORTH STAR - Cleaning Product - HILLYARD, INC.; *pg.* 331, *pg.* 990
NORTHAMPTON - Cast/Tubular Aluminum Outdoor Furniture - TELESCOPE CASUAL FURNITURE INC.; *pg.* 944, *pg.* 1162
NORTHBROOK LIFE - Life Insurance & Savings - THE ALLSTATE CORPORATION; *pg.* 1189, *pg.* 639
NORTHBROOK PROPERTY & CASUALTY - Commerce Insurance - THE ALLSTATE CORPORATION; *pg.* 1189, *pg.* 639
NORTHEAST PASTURES - Milk - COOPERATIVE REGIONS OF ORGANIC PRODUCER POOLS; *pg.* 850, *pg.* 1864
NORTHEAST PIZZA EXPO - Trade Show - MACFADDEN COMMUNICATIONS GROUP, LLC; *pg.* 1660, *pg.* 1254
NORTHEN NECK - Soft Drink - THE COCA-COLA COMPANY; *pg.* 240, *pg.* 493
NORTHERN - Bath Tissue - GEORGIA-PACIFIC LLC; *pg.* 1458, *pg.* 507
NORTHERN BRIGHTS - Business Paper - BPM INC.; *pg.* 1454, *pg.* 1886
NORTHERN HEALTH - Software - NIGHTINGALE; *pg.* 446, *pg.* 186
NORTHERN HEALTH ANESTHESIA - Software - NIGHTINGALE; *pg.* 446, *pg.* 186
NORTHERN HEIGHTS - Wood Blinds - SPRINGS WINDOW FASHIONS LLC; *pg.* 943, *pg.* 1872
NORTHERN ISLES - Men's & Women's Sweaters & Knit Tops - KELLWOOD COMPANY; *pg.* 28, *pg.* 975
NORTHERN LIGHT LAGER - Beer - GRANITE CITY FOOD & BREWERY LTD; *pg.* 1730, *pg.* 937
NORTHERN LIGHTS - Broadloom - COURISTAN INC.; *pg.* 921, *pg.* 1067
NORTHERN LIGHTS - Gaming Product - GLD PRODUCTS, INC.; *pg.* 1835, *pg.* 1882

NORTHERN LIGHTS - Video Game - INTERNATIONAL GAME TECHNOLOGY; *pg.* 957, *pg.* 1024
NORTHERN STAR - Food Service Product - MICHAEL FOODS, INC.; *pg.* 877, *pg.* 949
NORTHERN TRUST - Bank - NORTHERN TRUST CORPORATION; *pg.* 787, *pg.* 585
NORTHERN TURF - Lawn Care Product - GARDENS ALIVE!, INC.; *pg.* 1796, *pg.* 693
NORTHFIELD - Furniture - BUSH INDUSTRIES INC.; *pg.* 919, *pg.* 1170
NORTHFIELD PUBLISHING - Publishers of Books - MOODY PUBLISHERS; *pg.* 1665, *pg.* 583
NORTHFORK CRAFTSMAN - Furniture - ASHLEY FURNITURE INDUSTRIES, INC.; *pg.* 914, *pg.* 1852
NORTHLAND - Kitchen Product - KOHLER CO.; *pg.* 91, *pg.* 1862
NORTHPORT - Outerwear - HABAND COMPANY, INC.; *pg.* 1772, *pg.* 1099
NORTHRIDGE - Lighting Product - QUOIZEL INC.; *pg.* 1304, *pg.* 1616
NORTHSIDE TRAIL - Bike - MARIN BIKES; *pg.* 1708, *pg.* 168
NORTHSTAR - Telescope - BUSHNELL OUTDOOR PRODUCTS, INC.; *pg.* 1403, *pg.* 718
NORTHSTAR - Financial Forms - ENNIS, INC.; *pg.* 393, *pg.* 1727
NORTHSTAR - Pump - HAYWARD POOL PRODUCTS; *pg.* 1049, *pg.* 1057
NORTHSTAR - Generator - NORTHERN TOOL + EQUIPMENT; *pg.* 1366, *pg.* 919
NORTHSTAR CASH - Lottery - MINNESOTA STATE LOTTERY; *pg.* 999, *pg.* 956
NORTHSTAR LEARNING - Software - SRA INTERNATIONAL, INC.; *pg.* 473, *pg.* 1780
NORTHWEST FLORIDA DAILY NEWS - Florida Newspaper - FREEDOM COMMUNICATIONS, INC.; *pg.* 1643, *pg.* 110
NORTHWEST FLORIDA DAILY NEWS - Newspaper - NORTHWEST FLORIDA DAILY NEWS; *pg.* 1672, *pg.* 428
NORTHWEST FRESH! - Slogan - ELMER'S RESTAURANTS, INC.; *pg.* 1728, *pg.* 1502
NORTHWEST PASTURES - Milk - COOPERATIVE REGIONS OF ORGANIC PRODUCER POOLS; *pg.* 850, *pg.* 1864
NORTHWESTERN - Communication Product - CENTURYLINK, INC; *pg.* 1870, *pg.* 317
NORTHWESTERN MUTUAL - Life Insurance, Disability Income Insurance, Annuities, & Long Term Care - THE NORTHWESTERN MUTUAL LIFE INSURANCE COMPANY; *pg.* 1212, *pg.* 1879
NORTHWESTERN MUTUAL TRUST CO. - Trust & Asset Management Services - THE NORTHWESTERN MUTUAL LIFE INSURANCE COMPANY; *pg.* 1212, *pg.* 1879
NORTHWICH - Carpet - BEAULIEU GROUP, LLC; *pg.* 917, *pg.* 529
NORTHWOODS - Apparel - L.L. BEAN, INC.; *pg.* 1777, *pg.* 750
NORTON - Software - SYMANTEC CORPORATION; *pg.* 478, *pg.* 161
NORTON 360 - Software - SYMANTEC CORPORATION; *pg.* 478, *pg.* 161
NORTON ANTIVIRUS - Security Software - SYMANTEC CORPORATION; *pg.* 478, *pg.* 161
NORTON SYSTEMWORKS - Security Software - SYMANTEC CORPORATION; *pg.* 478, *pg.* 161
NORTON UTILITIES - Software - SYMANTEC CORPORATION; *pg.* 478, *pg.* 161
NORTON WINDOCTOR - Software - SYMANTEC CORPORATION; *pg.* 478, *pg.* 161
NORTRAK - Steerable Downhole Motor - BAKER HUGHES INTEQ; *pg.* 1316, *pg.* 1700
NORVAL - Paper & Nonwoven Material - FIBERMARK INC.; *pg.* 1457, *pg.* 1764
NORVASC - High Blood Pressure Medication - PFIZER INC.; *pg.* 1581, *pg.* 1278
NORVIR - Tablet - ABBOTT LABORATORIES; *pg.* 1484, *pg.* 551
NORWALK - Acetylene Compressor - NORWALK COMPRESSOR COMPANY, INC.; *pg.* 1366, *pg.* 380
NORWAY - Flat Head Elevator Bolts - SCREW CONVEYOR INDUSTRIES; *pg.* 1374, *pg.* 682
NORWEGIAN CROWN - Cruise Ship - NORWEGIAN CRUISE LINE; *pg.* 1917, *pg.* 444
NORWEGIAN CRUISE LINE - Cruise Line - NORWEGIAN CRUISE LINE; *pg.* 1917, *pg.* 444
NORWEGIAN DAWN - Cruise Ship - NORWEGIAN CRUISE LINE; *pg.* 1917, *pg.* 444
NORWEGIAN DREAM - Cruise Ship - NORWEGIAN CRUISE LINE; *pg.* 1917, *pg.* 444
NORWEGIAN DYNASTY - Cruise Ship - NORWEGIAN CRUISE LINE; *pg.* 1917, *pg.* 444
NORWEGIAN FORMULA - Skin Care Product - NEUTROGENA CORPORATION; *pg.* 517, *pg.* 137
NORWEGIAN MAJESTY - Cruise Ship - NORWEGIAN CRUISE LINE; *pg.* 1917, *pg.* 444
NORWEGIAN SEA - Cruise Ship - NORWEGIAN CRUISE LINE; *pg.* 1917, *pg.* 444
NORWEGIAN SKY - Cruise Ship - NORWEGIAN CRUISE LINE; *pg.* 1917, *pg.* 444
NORWEGIAN STAR - Norwegian Capricorn Line - NORWEGIAN CRUISE LINE; *pg.* 1917, *pg.* 444
NORWEGIAN WIND - Cruise Ship - NORWEGIAN CRUISE LINE; *pg.* 1917, *pg.* 444
NORWEST - Financial Services - WELLS FARGO FINANCIAL, INC.; *pg.* 821, *pg.* 707
NORYL - Engineered Plastics - GENERAL ELECTRIC COMPANY; *pg.* 1297, *pg.* 347
NORYL - Wiring Duct - PANDUIT CORP.; *pg.* 661, *pg.* 663
NORYL GTX - Engineered Plastics - GENERAL ELECTRIC COMPANY; *pg.* 1297, *pg.* 347
NORYLUX - Compression Molded Product - WESTLAKE PLASTICS COMPANY; *pg.* 1892, *pg.* 1548
NOS ENTENDEMOS - Beverages - THE COCA-COLA COMPANY; *pg.* 240, *pg.* 493
NOSE MAN - Magnet & Clip - ADAMS MFG. CO.; *pg.* 51, *pg.* 1427
NOSEL - Handbag - ALDO GROUP; *pg.* 1804, *pg.* 1959
NOSHOK - Valve - NOSHOK INC.; *pg.* 1366, *pg.* 1406
NOSTALGIA - Seed - PLANTATION PRODUCTS INC; *pg.* 1799, *pg.* 839
NOSTALGIC MOMENTS - Bath Salt Series - THE PAGE SEED CO.; *pg.* 1798, *pg.* 1163
NOSTER - Off-Highway Power Transmission Products - REGAL BELOIT CORPORATION; *pg.* 106, *pg.* 1854
NOSWEEP - Ball Bonder - KULICKE & SOFFA INDUSTRIES, INC.; *pg.* 650, *pg.* 1533
NOT ON TOBACCO - Smoking Cessation Program - AMERICAN LUNG ASSOCIATION; *pg.* 129, *pg.* 395
NOT SO BORA-BORA-ING PIN - Nail Care Product - OPI PRODUCTS INC.; *pg.* 518, *pg.* 167
NOT-SO-SLOPPY-JOE - Meat Sauce - HORMEL FOODS CORPORATION; *pg.* 863, *pg.* 915
NOT YOUR DAUGHTER'S JEANS - Slogan - NYDJ APPAREL, LLC; *pg.* 30, *pg.* 302
NOTEBIOS - Software - PHOENIX TECHNOLOGIES LTD.; *pg.* 454, *pg.* 147
NOTECAM - Webcam Software - EARTHCAM, INC.; *pg.* 1239, *pg.* 1072
NOTEDOCK - Software - PHOENIX TECHNOLOGIES LTD.; *pg.* 454, *pg.* 147
NOTES MIGRATOR - Software - DELL SOFTWARE; *pg.* 385, *pg.* 40
NOTES MIGRATOR FOR SHAREPOINT - Software - DELL SOFTWARE; *pg.* 385, *pg.* 40
NOTHING BREWS LIKE A BUNN - Slogan - BUNN-O-MATIC CORPORATION; *pg.* 53, *pg.* 661
NOTHING BUT HEAVY DUTY - Power Tool - MILWAUKEE ELECTRIC TOOL CORP.; *pg.* 1056, *pg.* 1855
NOTHING COMES CLOSE TO A COBRA - Slogan - COBRA ELECTRONICS CORPORATION; *pg.* 629, *pg.* 572
NOTHING RUNS LIKE A DEERE - Slogan - DEERE & COMPANY; *pg.* 703, *pg.* 632
NOTHING SATISFIES LIKE FRITOS - Tag Line - FRITO-LAY NORTH AMERICA, INC.; *pg.* 1853, *pg.* 1730
NOTHING SEWS LIKE A BERNINA. NOTHING - Slogan - BERNINA OF AMERICA INC.; *pg.* 51, *pg.* 554
NOTHING TASTES BETTER THAN HOMEMADE. - Slogan - UNITED DAIRY FARMERS, INC.; *pg.* 906, *pg.* 1426
NOTI-FIRE-NET - Email Tool - NOTIFIER CO.; *pg.* 659, *pg.* 360
NOTICE SYMBOL - Brandmark - UNITED PARCEL SERVICE, INC.; *pg.* 1928, *pg.* 522
NOTIFACT - HVAC Control Systems - HEAT-TIMER CORPORATION; *pg.* 1072, *pg.* 1065
NOTIFIER - Alarm System - HONEYWELL INTERNATIONAL INC.; *pg.* 407, *pg.* 1088
NOTIFIER - Alarms - NOTIFIER CO.; *pg.* 659, *pg.* 360
NOTIFYME - Software - HEALTHPORT, INC.; *pg.* 403, *pg.* 484
NOTION - Fabric - NEMSCHOFF, INC.; *pg.* 936, *pg.* 1890
NOTIONSTM - Little Card - LEANIN' TREE, INC.; *pg.* 1658, *pg.* 311
NOTOUCH - Ramp Load Technology - WESTERN DIGITAL CORPORATION; *pg.* 492, *pg.* 118
NOTP - Computer Software - NOVELL INC.; *pg.* 446, *pg.* 852
NOTTINGHAM - Shoes - ALLEN-EDMONDS SHOE CORP.; *pg.* 1804, *pg.* 1887
NOTTINGHAM - Carpet - BEAULIEU GROUP, LLC; *pg.* 917, *pg.* 529
NOTTINGHAM - Furniture - HAWORTH, INC.; *pg.* 402, *pg.* 891
NOURICHE - Smoothie - YOPLAIT USA, INC.; *pg.* 910, *pg.* 947
NOURISH - Meal & Dessert - NUTRISYSTEM, INC.; *pg.* 1577, *pg.* 1533
NOURISHING FAMILIES. ENRICHING LIVES. EVERY DAY. - Slogan - DEL MONTE FOODS, INC.; *pg.* 852, *pg.* 304
NOURISHING IDEAS, NOURISHING PEOPLE - Slogan - CARGILL, INC.; *pg.* 845, *pg.* 965
NOURISHING LIVES - Slogan - GENERAL MILLS, INC.; *pg.* 828, *pg.* 933
NOURISHING PEOPLE'S LIVES EVERYWHERE,EVERY DAY - Tagline - CAMPBELL SOUP COMPANY; *pg* 844, *pg.* 1048
NOURYBOND - Chemical Products - AIR PRODUCTS AND CHEMICALS, INC.; *pg.* 1145, *pg.* 1513
NOUVEAU - Tile - ARTISTIC TILE INC.; *pg.* 914, *pg.* 1119
NOUVEAU - Rug - COURISTAN INC.; *pg.* 921, *pg.* 1067
NOUVEAU - Furniture - FLEXSTEEL INDUSTRIES, INC.; *pg.* 925, *pg.* 707
NOUVEAU - Fabric - NEMSCHOFF, INC.; *pg.* 936, *pg.* 1890
NOUVEAU - Door Glass - ODL INCORPORATED; *pg.* 101, *pg.* 914
NOUVEAU GOURMET - Sink - ELKAY MANUFACTURING COMPANY; *pg.* 80, *pg.* 645
NOUVEAUX - Apparel - HAMPSHIRE GROUP LIMITED; *pg.* 25, *pg.* 1237
NOVA - Industrial Material - DOW CHEMICAL; *pg.* 1156, *pg.* 1563
NOVA - Ion & Electron Beam - FEI COMPANY; *pg.* 1413, *pg.* 1498
NOVA - Bicycle - G. JOANNOU CYCLE CO. INC.; *pg.* 1707, *pg.* 1098
NOVA - Airless Paint Sprayers - GRACO, INC.; *pg.* 1342, *pg.* , 935
NOVA - Serial Data Converter Modules - INDUSTRIAL ELECTRONIC ENGINEERS, INC.; *pg.* 644, *pg.* 300
NOVA - Bath & Plumbing Product - JACUZZI BRANDS CORPORATION; *pg.* 554, *pg.* 65
NOVA - Dicing Blade - KULICKE & SOFFA INDUSTRIES, INC.; *pg.* 650, *pg.* 1533
NOVA - Power Generator - MKS INSTRUMENTS, INC.; *pg.* 1362, *pg.* 781
NOVA - Flashlight - STREAMLIGHT INC.; *pg.* 1306, *pg.* 1527
NOVA - Remote Control Device - UNIVERSAL ELECTRONICS, INC.; *pg.* 683, *pg.* 262
NOVA - Central Processing Unit - VICON INDUSTRIES, INC.; *pg.* 685, *pg.* 1166
NOVA - Ceiling Fan - WESTINGHOUSE LIGHTING CORPORATION; *pg.* 687, *pg.* 1571
NOVA-BOND - Insulator Pads - LEGGETT & PLATT, INCORPORATED; *pg.* 933, *pg.* 974
NOVA CORK - Building Product - HOMASOTE COMPANY; *pg.* 87, *pg.* 1126
NOVA-LOF - Insulator Pads - LEGGETT & PLATT, INCORPORATED; *pg.* 933, *pg.* 974
NOVA-PAK - Analytical Column - WATERS CORPORATION; *pg.* 1436, *pg.* 834
NOVABLOT - Software - BIO-RAD LABORATORIES, INC.; *pg.* 1504, *pg.* 101
NOVABLOT II - Software - BIO-RAD LABORATORIES, INC.; *pg.* 1504, *pg.* 101
NOVABLOT VI - Software - BIO-RAD LABORATORIES, INC.; *pg.* 1504, *pg.* 101
NOVABOND - Surface Sizes - GEORGIA-PACIFIC LLC; *pg.* 1458, *pg.* 507
NOVABRIK - Splitter - BESSER COMPANY; *pg.* 1317, *pg.* 865
NOVACAT - Catalyst - NOVA CHEMICALS CORPORATION; *pg.* 1175, *pg.* 1904
NOVACHROME - Cast Aluminum Wheels - MAXION WHEELS; *pg.* 212, *pg.* 903
NOVACLEAN - Solvent & Roof Flashing - GENOVA PRODUCTS, INC.; *pg.* 83, *pg.* 875
NOVACOTE - Surface Sizes & Boxboard Coatings - GEORGIA-PACIFIC LLC; *pg.* 1458, *pg.* 507
NOVACRON - Reactive Dyes - HUNTSMAN CORPORATION;

First page reference indicates Business Class Edition
Second page reference indicates Geographic Edition

pg. 1167, *pg.* 1758
NOVACRON - Furniture Coating Composition - PPG INDUSTRIES, INC.; *pg.* 1445, *pg.* 1579
NOVACRYL - Chemical Product - OMNOVA SOLUTIONS INC; *pg.* 1176, *pg.* 1453
NOVAFLO - Liquid Size Agent Used in Papermaking - GEORGIA-PACIFIC LLC; *pg.* 1458, *pg.* 507
NOVAGEL - Silicone Gel Sheets - ALIMED, INC.; *pg.* 1490, *pg.* 816
NOVAGEL - Food Ingredient - FMC CORPORATION; *pg.* 1163, *pg.* 1564
NOVAGREEN - Carpet Chemicals - OMNOVA SOLUTIONS INC; *pg.* 1176, *pg.* 1453
NOVAL - Refractory Product - RESCO PRODUCTS, INC.; *pg.* 107, *pg.* 1581
NOVALINE - Lithography Excimer Laser - COHERENT, INC.; *pg.* 1406, *pg.* 265
NOVALIPID - Soybean Oil & Fats - ARCHER-DANIELS-MIDLAND COMPANY; *pg.* 825, *pg.* 565
NOVANE - Specialty Chemicals - OMNOVA SOLUTIONS INC; *pg.* 1176, *pg.* 1453
NOVAPATH - Software - BIO-RAD LABORATORIES, INC.; *pg.* 1504, *pg.* 101
NOVAPLUS - Rosin Sizes - GEORGIA-PACIFIC LLC; *pg.* 1458, *pg.* 507
NOVAPLUS - Fluid Handling System - GRACO, INC.; *pg.* 1342, *pg.* 935
NOVAPOL - Polyethylene - NOVA CHEMICALS CORPORATION; *pg.* 1175, *pg.* 1904
NOVAPOR - Health & Nutrition Product - NOVUS INTERNATIONAL, INC.; *pg.* 706, *pg.* 1001
NOVAPREP - Liquid Chromatography Apparatus - PPG INDUSTRIES, INC.; *pg.* 1445, *pg.* 1579
NOVAPRO - Staffing Services - CROSS COUNTRY HEALTHCARE, INC.; *pg.* 1520, *pg.* 411
NOVAPRO - Airless Paint Sprayer - GRACO, INC.; *pg.* 1342, *pg.* 935
NOVAPURE - Dry Chemical Scrubber - ATMI, INC.; *pg.* 1314, *pg.* 342
NOVAR - Security System - HONEYWELL INTERNATIONAL INC.; *pg.* 407, *pg.* 1088
NOVASAFE - Treatment System - ATMI, INC.; *pg.* 1314, *pg.* 342
NOVASET - Foundry Binder - ASHLAND INC.; *pg.* 972, *pg.* 726
NOVASIL - Medical Device - LEMAITRE VASCULAR, INC.; *pg.* 1555, *pg.* 805
NOVASIL - Flow Agent for Feeds - TROUW NUTRITION USA; *pg.* 1482, *pg.* 616
NOVASIL PLUS - Additive - BASF CATALYSTS LLC; *pg.* 1148, *pg.* 1074
NOVASILPLUS - Aluminosilicate - TROUW NUTRITION USA; *pg.* 1482, *pg.* 616
NOVASIP - Capsule Filter - PALL CORPORATION; *pg.* 232, *pg.* 1323
NOVASOL - Vat Dyes - HUNTSMAN CORPORATION; *pg.* 1167, *pg.* 1758
NOVASOY - Isoflavones Supplements - ARCHER-DANIELS-MIDLAND COMPANY; *pg.* 825, *pg.* 565
NOVASP - Fluid Handling System - GRACO, INC.; *pg.* 1342, *pg.* 935
NOVASPX - Airless Paint Sprayers - GRACO, INC.; *pg.* 1342, *pg.* 935
NOVASURE - Women's Health Product - HOLOGIC, INC.; *pg.* 1416, *pg.* 784
NOVATEL MERLIN - Software System - ALCATEL-LUCENT; *pg.* 615, *pg.* 1094
NOVATEX - Photomask Writing - COHERENT, INC.; *pg.* 1406, *pg.* 265
NOVATION - Hip System - EXACTECH, INC.; *pg.* 1529, *pg.* 428
NOVATO - Bike - MARIN BIKES; *pg.* 1708, *pg.* 168
NOVATOL - Feed Ingredient - ARCHER-DANIELS-MIDLAND COMPANY; *pg.* 825, *pg.* 565
NOVAVENT - Valve - GENOVA PRODUCTS, INC.; *pg.* 83, *pg.* 875
NOVAWELD - Solvent & Roof Flashing - GENOVA PRODUCTS, INC.; *pg.* 83, *pg.* 875
NOVAXAN - Xanthan Gum Ingredients - ARCHER-DANIELS-MIDLAND COMPANY; *pg.* 825, *pg.* 565
NOVAXAN XANTHAN GUM 200 MESH - Xanthan Gum - ARCHER-DANIELS-MIDLAND COMPANY; *pg.* 825, *pg.* 565
NOVAXAN XANTHAN GUM 40 MESH - Xanthan Gum - ARCHER-DANIELS-MIDLAND COMPANY; *pg.* 825, *pg.* 565
NOVAXAN XANTHAN GUM 80 MESH DUST FREE - Xanthan Gum - ARCHER-DANIELS-MIDLAND COMPANY; *pg.* 825, *pg.* 565
NOVAXAN XANTHAN GUM DISPERSIBLE - Xanthan Gum - ARCHER-DANIELS-MIDLAND COMPANY; *pg.* 825, *pg.* 565
NOVAXAN XANTHAN GUM PET FOOD - Xanthan Gum - ARCHER-DANIELS-MIDLAND COMPANY; *pg.* 825, *pg.* 565
NOVAZONE - Polymer Product - CHEMTURA CORPORATION; *pg.* 1152, *pg.* 355
NOVEC - Fire Protection Fluid - 3M COMPANY; *pg.* 1142, *pg.* 956
NOVEL - Grout Whitener - A.L. WILSON CHEMICAL CO.; *pg.* 325, *pg.* 1076
NOVEL - Fabric - NEMSCHOFF, INC.; *pg.* 936, *pg.* 1890
NOVEL - Biodegradable Nonionics - SASOL NORTH AMERICA INC.; *pg.* 984, *pg.* 1713
NOVELL - Software & Ecosystem - NOVELL INC.; *pg.* 446, *pg.* 852
NOVELLA - Razzle Dazzle Timepiece - HABAND COMPANY, INC.; *pg.* 1772, *pg.* 1099
NOVEN - Pharmaceutical Product - NOVEN PHARMACEUTICALS, INC.; *pg.* 1576, *pg.* 445
NOVEON - Consumer Specialties - THE LUBRIZOL CORPORATION; *pg.* 1171, *pg.* 1481
NOVEX - Molecular Biology Product - THERMO FISHER SCIENTIFIC INC.; *pg.* 1602, *pg.* 61
NOVI - Wireless Intercoms & Videophones - NORTEK, INC.; *pg.* 100, *pg.* 1607
NOVIBRA - Latch - SOUTHCO, INC.; *pg.* 1063, *pg.* 1522
NOVICA - Furniture - NOVICA UNITED, INC.; *pg.* 1271, *pg.* 137
NOVO - Fabric - NEMSCHOFF, INC.; *pg.* 936, *pg.* 1890
NOVOGYNE - Pharmaceutical Product - NOVEN PHARMACEUTICALS, INC.; *pg.* 1576, *pg.* 445
NOVOLAC - Chemical - MILLER-STEPHENSON CHEMICAL COMPANY, INC.; *pg.* 1172, *pg.* 344
NOVONIC - Conductive Fabric - AMPHENOL CORPORATION; *pg.* 616, *pg.* 381
NOVUS - Hydraulic Oils - CARGILL LIMITED; *pg.* 1475, *pg.* 1914
NOVUS - Polymers - GE WATER & PROCESS TECHNOLOGIES; *pg.* 1339, *pg.* 1588
NOVUS - Medical Device - INTEGRA LIFESCIENCES HOLDINGS CORPORATION; *pg.* 1545, *pg.* 1109
NOVUS - Pressed & Monolithic Refractory - RESCO PRODUCTS, INC.; *pg.* 107, *pg.* 1581
NOW - Dietary Supplements - NOW HEALTH GROUP, INC.; *pg.* 1576, *pg.* 557
NOW - Cigarette - REYNOLDS AMERICAN INC.; *pg.* 1894, *pg.* 1395
NOW - Spray Paint - SHERWIN-WILLIAMS DIVERSIFIED BRANDS DIVISION; *pg.* 1448, *pg.* 1435
NOW&LATER - Candy - FERRARA CANDY CO.; *pg.* 1852, *pg.* 612
NOW CARD - Games - PENN NATIONAL GAMING, INC.; *pg.* 574, *pg.* 1595
NOW CLUB - Games - PENN NATIONAL GAMING, INC.; *pg.* 574, *pg.* 1595
NOW I'M READING! - Toy And Game - INNOVATIVE USA, INC.; *pg.* 957, *pg.* 363
NOW ON DISPLAY - Computer Equipment - VIEWSONIC CORPORATION; *pg.* 489, *pg.* 303
NOW THAT'S BETTER - Tagline - THE WENDY'S COMPANY; *pg.* 1755, *pg.* 1450
NOW YOU KNOW - Software - INFORMATICA CORPORATION; *pg.* 414, *pg.* 190
NOW YOU'RE GOING SOMEWHERE - Slogan - SKYAUCTION.COM, INC.; *pg.* 1281, *pg.* 1293
NOW YOU'RE STYLIN - Styling Gel - BLUE CROSS LABORATORIES; *pg.* 326, *pg.* 277
NOWCAM - Coiled Tubing & Nitrogen Services - SCHLUMBERGER WELL COMPLETIONS; *pg.* 1373, *pg.* 1714
NOWPAK - Dispense Connection System - ATMI, INC.; *pg.* 1314, *pg.* 342
NOWPAK - Container - HONEYWELL INTERNATIONAL INC.; *pg.* 407, *pg.* 1088
NOWTRAK - Inventory Management System - ATMI, INC.; *pg.* 1314, *pg.* 342
NOX-RUST - Rust Proofing Protection - DAUBERT INDUSTRIES, INC.; *pg.* 1155, *pg.* 561
NOX-SPOTS - Dry Cleaning & Laundry Product - ADCO, INC.; *pg.* 325, *pg.* 482
NOXAFIL - Antifungal Preparation - MERCK & CO., INC.; *pg.* 1566, *pg.* 1077
NOXCAT - Catalyst - BASF CATALYSTS LLC; *pg.* 1148, *pg.* 1074
NOXGETTER - Catalyst Additive - JOHNSON MATTHEY PROCESS TECHNOLOGIES; *pg.* 1169, *pg.* 1083
NOXMATIC - Burner - S.T. JOHNSON CO.; *pg.* 1077, *pg.* 173
NOXON - Metal Polish - RECKITT BENCKISER INC.; *pg.* 1136, *pg.* 1105
NOXOUT - Crop Nutrition - CARGILL LIMITED; *pg.* 1475, *pg.* 1914
NOXYLANE - Health System Product - LANELABS USA INC.; *pg.* 1554, *pg.* 1128
NOXZEMA - Skin Care Products - UNILEVER UNITED STATES, INC.; *pg.* 904, *pg.* 1061
NOZ-L-MIX - Burner - SELAS HEAT TECHNOLOGY COMPANY LLC; *pg.* 1076, *pg.* 1553
NP-10 - Plasticizers - NEVILLE CHEMICAL COMPANY; *pg.* 1174, *pg.* 1578
NP-25 - Plasticizers - NEVILLE CHEMICAL COMPANY; *pg.* 1174, *pg.* 1578
NP-LE AIRFLO - Burner - MAXON CORPORATION; *pg.* 1359, *pg.* 695
NPD - Paint & Paint Sundries Retailers/Distributors - PRO GROUP, INC.; *pg.* 1782, *pg.* 331
NPH - Valve - INTEGRA LIFESCIENCES HOLDINGS CORPORATION; *pg.* 1545, *pg.* 1109
NPLATE - Peptibody Protein - AMGEN INC.; *pg.* 1493, *pg.* 291
NPS PHARMACEUTICALS - Pharmaceutical Product - NPS PHARMACEUTICALS, INC.; *pg.* 1576, *pg.* 1043
NRG - L.E.D. Curing Light - DENTSPLY INTERNATIONAL INC.; *pg.* 1522, *pg.* 1596
NRG PAINTBALL - Sport & Leisure Product - JAKKS PACIFIC, INC.; *pg.* 960, *pg.* 142
NRL - Hazardous Area Lighting Products - FEDERAL SIGNAL CORPORATION; *pg.* 638, *pg.* 645
NRS - Pharmaceutical Product - ALLERGAN; *pg.* 1490, *pg.* 1101
NS-BOS - Software - NETSUITE, INC.; *pg.* 1270, *pg.* 255
NSBEES - Plastic Bins - MYERS INDUSTRIES, INC.; *pg.* 1887, *pg.* 1402
NSERVICE - Software - NELNET, INC.; *pg.* 786, *pg.* 1012
NSG - Digital Video Product - HARMONIC, INC.; *pg.* 402, *pg.* 246
NSM - Software - JUNIPER NETWORKS, INC.; *pg.* 1260, *pg.* 286
NSMXPRESS - Software - JUNIPER NETWORKS, INC.; *pg.* 1260, *pg.* 286
NSO - Art Performance Service - NATIONAL SYMPHONY ORCHESTRA; *pg.* 568, *pg.* 403
NSPLUS - Software - XEROX CORPORATION; *pg.* 494, *pg.* 365
NST - Rotor - FARREL CORPORATION; *pg.* 1336, *pg.* 337
NSURE - Software - NOVELL INC.; *pg.* 446, *pg.* 852
NT - Bearing - THE TIMKEN COMPANY; *pg.* 218, *pg.* 1408
NT1 ACE - ISDN Network Termination - ADTRAN, INC.; *pg.* 344, *pg.* 6
NT1 ACE3 - Videoconferencing Application - ADTRAN, INC.; *pg.* 344, *pg.* 6
NT300D - Navigation Aid - TRIMBLE NAVIGATION LIMITED; *pg.* 1384, *pg.* 288
NTERACT - Software - NELNET, INC.; *pg.* 786, *pg.* 1012
NTERCHANGE - Software - NELNET, INC.; *pg.* 786, *pg.* 1012
NTERPRISE - Software - NOVELL INC.; *pg.* 446, *pg.* 852
NTRAK - Test Kit - HACH COMPANY; *pg.* 1415, *pg.* 334
NTRUST - Software - NELNET, INC.; *pg.* 786, *pg.* 1012
NTUNE - Software - NVIDIA CORPORATION; *pg.* 447, *pg.* 268
NU-CLING - Paint & Coating - DIAMOND VOGEL PAINT, INC.; *pg.* 1441, *pg.* 710
NU COLOUR - Cosmetic Product - NU SKIN ENTERPRISES, INC.; *pg.* 518, *pg.* 1755
NU CON SEAL - Concrete Coating - DELTA FOREMOST CHEMICAL CORPORATION; *pg.* 1155, *pg.* 1642
NU DAY - Shoe - AEROGROUP INTERNATIONAL, INC.; *pg.* 1803, *pg.* 1055
NU-FLOOR FLEX-JOINT - Epoxy Resin - TEXAS REFINERY CORP.; *pg.* 986, *pg.* 1696
NU GAUZE - Sponges - STOELTING CO.; *pg.* 1430, *pg.* 671
NU-GAUZE - Surgical Supplies - STOELTING CO.; *pg.* 1430, *pg.* 671

NU-GEL - Healthcare Product - JOHNSON & JOHNSON; *pg.* 1549, *pg.* 1091
NU HUE - Spray Enamel - SHERWIN-WILLIAMS DIVERSIFIED BRANDS DIVISION; *pg.* 1448, *pg.* 1435
NU-KLAD - Protective Surfacing - NOV AMERON; *pg.* 100, *pg.* 187
NU-POLE - Fire Tools - NUPLA CORPORATION; *pg.* 101, *pg.* 281
NU-POT - Reusable Planting Tray - SUMMIT PLASTIC CO.; *pg.* 1470, *pg.* 1403
NU-SAFE - Cleaner Product - AERVOE INDUSTRIES INCORPORATED; *pg.* 1439, *pg.* 1021
NU-SAL - Neutral Salt - HEATBATH CORPORATION; *pg.* 1165, *pg.* 826
NU-SALT - Salt Substitute - CUMBERLAND PACKING CORP.; *pg.* 851, *pg.* 1146
NU SCALD - Scalding Product - BIRKO CORPORATION; *pg.* 1149, *pg.* 332
NU SKIN 180 - Skin Therapy System - NU SKIN ENTERPRISES, INC.; *pg.* 518, *pg.* 1755
NU SKIN CLEAR ACTION - Skin Care Product - NU SKIN ENTERPRISES, INC.; *pg.* 518, *pg.* 1755
NU-SURFACE - Concrete Coating - DELTA FOREMOST CHEMICAL CORPORATION; *pg.* 1155, *pg.* 1642
NU-TEK - Ball Bonder - KULICKE & SOFFA INDUSTRIES, INC.; *pg.* 650, *pg.* 1533
NU-TRAYS - Reusable Planting Tray - SUMMIT PLASTIC CO.; *pg.* 1470, *pg.* 1403
NU-TRED - Flat Rib Vinyl Mat - THE BILTRITE CORPORATION; *pg.* 1879, *pg.* 850
NU-TRISH - Diary Product - OAKHURST DAIRY; *pg.* 887, *pg.* 752
NU-VU - Cooking & Warming Equipment - THE MIDDLEBY CORPORATION; *pg.* 1361, *pg.* 610
NU-WELD - Flange - SCREW CONVEYOR INDUSTRIES; *pg.* 1374, *pg.* 682
NUB SCOUT - Shoe - AEROGROUP INTERNATIONAL, INC.; *pg.* 1803, *pg.* 1055
NUBARK - Spray - THE WOODSTREAM CORPORATION; *pg.* 1801, *pg.* 1549
NUBASICS - Food & Beverage Product - NESTLE USA, INC.; *pg.* 883, *pg.* 96
NUBILL - Telephone Service - IDT CORPORATION; *pg.* 643, *pg.* 1096
NUBILL.COM - Telephone Service - IDT CORPORATION; *pg.* 643, *pg.* 1096
NUBRITE - Bleached Linerboard - GEORGIA-PACIFIC LLC; *pg.* 1458, *pg.* 507
NUCHAR - Chemical Product - WESTROCK COMPANY; *pg.* 1472, *pg.* 1805
NUCLAY - Kaolin for use in The Paper Industry - BASF CATALYSTS LLC; *pg.* 1148, *pg.* 1074
NUCLEAR - Imaging Service - DIGIRAD CORPORATION; *pg.* 1524, *pg.* 185
NUCLEAR SQWORMS GUMMI WORMS - Food Product - PROMOTION IN MOTION, INC.; *pg.* 1861, *pg.* 1052
NUCLEUS - Software - CASCADE MICROTECH, INC.; *pg.* 1405, *pg.* 1492
NUCLEUS - Software System - MENTOR GRAPHICS CORPORATION; *pg.* 432, *pg.* 1510
NUCLEUS EDGE - Software System - MENTOR GRAPHICS CORPORATION; *pg.* 432, *pg.* 1510
NUCON - Pressed & Monolithic Refractory - RESCO PRODUCTS, INC.; *pg.* 107, *pg.* 1581
NUCOR BEARING PRODUCTS - Precision Bearings & Other Steel Machined Products - NUCOR CORPORATION; *pg.* 101, *pg.* 1368
NUCOR BUILDING SYSTEMS - Pre-Engineered Steel Building Systems - NUCOR CORPORATION; *pg.* 101, *pg.* 1368
NUCOR COLD FINISHED BAR - Steel Cold Finished Bars - NUCOR CORPORATION; *pg.* 101, *pg.* 1368
NUCOR FASTENERS - Steel Industrial Fasteners - NUCOR CORPORATION; *pg.* 101, *pg.* 1368
NUCOR GRINDING BALLS - Steel Grinding Media - NUCOR CORPORATION; *pg.* 101, *pg.* 1368
NUCOR STEEL - Hot Rolled Steel Bar, Sheet, Structural Products - NUCOR CORPORATION; *pg.* 101, *pg.* 1368
NUCORE - Metal Framing Products - KAWNEER COMPANY, INC.; *pg.* 90, *pg.* 537
NUCREL - Acid Copolymer Resins - E.I. DU PONT DE NEMOURS & COMPANY; *pg.* 1159, *pg.* 390
NUCUISINE - Calorie Controlled Entrees - NUTRISYSTEM, INC.; *pg.* 1577, *pg.* 1533
NUESTRA GENTE - Spanish Language Consumer Goods Magazine - SEARS HOLDINGS CORPORATION; *pg.* 1784, *pg.* 618
NUESTRA VOZ - Telephone Service - IDT CORPORATION; *pg.* 643, *pg.* 1096
NUEVO GRILLE - Frozen Mexican Foods - CIRCLE FOODS, LLC; *pg.* 848, *pg.* 201
NUFAB - Protective Apparel - E.I. DU PONT DE NEMOURS & COMPANY; *pg.* 1159, *pg.* 390
NUFILMS - Residue Control Agent - MILLER CHEMICAL & FERTILIZER CORPORATION; *pg.* 706, *pg.* 1535
NUFLOR - Medicine - MERCK & CO., INC.; *pg.* 1566, *pg.* 1077
NUGENESIS - Software - WATERS CORPORATION; *pg.* 1436, *pg.* 834
NUGGET - Food Product - ELLENBEE-LEGGETT COMPANY INC.; *pg.* 854, *pg.* 1452
NUGGET - Shoe Polish - RECKITT BENCKISER INC.; *pg.* 1136, *pg.* 1105
NUISANCE - Dust Mask - SELLSTROM MANUFACTURING CO.; *pg.* 1428, *pg.* 659
NUKEPOET - Software - WIND RIVER SYSTEMS, INC.; *pg.* 493, *pg.* 38
NULINE - Pressed & Monolithic Refractory - RESCO PRODUCTS, INC.; *pg.* 107, *pg.* 1581
NULLFIRE - Intumescent Fireproofing - CARBOLINE CO.; *pg.* 1152, *pg.* 994
NULLMATIC - Industrial Instrumentation - SIEMENS PROCESS INDUSTRIES AND DRIVE; *pg.* 1376, *pg.* 1587
NULLO - Internal Deodorant - MONTICELLO DRUG CO.; *pg.* 1569, *pg.* 434
NULOJIX - Health Care Product - BRISTOL-MYERS SQUIBB COMPANY; *pg.* 1509, *pg.* 1206
NULOK - Handle to Head Attachment - NUPLA CORPORATION; *pg.* 101, *pg.* 281
NUMANTHIA - Wine - MOET HENNESSY; *pg.* 1966, *pg.* 1260
#1 BALL IN GOLF - Tag Line - ACUSHNET COMPANY; *pg.* 1824, *pg.* 818
THE #1 GOLF CAR IN THE WORLD - Slogan - E-Z-GO TEXTRON; *pg.* 1706, *pg.* 525
#497 AUTOSTAR - Computer Controlled Telescope Alignment Device - MEADE INSTRUMENTS CORPORATION; *pg.* 1422, *pg.* 113
NUMBER PORTABILITY - Wireline Solutions - SONUS NETWORKS INC.; *pg.* 1281, *pg.* 858
NUMBER1EXPERT.COM - Real Estate Website - DOMINION ENTERPRISES; *pg.* 1636, *pg.* 1796
NUMBER.COM - Advertising Website - LIVE CURRENT MEDIA INC.; *pg.* 1263, *pg.* 1911
NUMBERS - iWork App for Spreadsheets - APPLE INC.; *pg.* 350, *pg.* 73
NUMBERS - Lottery Game - NEW YORK STATE LOTTERY; *pg.* 1001, *pg.* 1340
NUMBERS NOW - Lottery Game - ILLINOIS STATE LOTTERY; *pg.* 995, *pg.* 578
NUMBERSMASHER - Software - MICROWAY, INC.; *pg.* 1267, *pg.* 841
NUMELOCK - Surgical & Medical Product - STRYKER CORPORATION; *pg.* 1598, *pg.* 894
NUMEREX DNA - Communication Technology - NUMEREX CORP.; *pg.* 660, *pg.* 517
NUMEREX FAST - Software Technology - NUMEREX CORP.; *pg.* 660, *pg.* 517
NUMERITRACK - Software - EVOLVING SYSTEMS, INC.; *pg.* 395, *pg.* 326
NUMERO UNO - Pizza - UNO RESTAURANT HOLDINGS CORPORATION; *pg.* 1754, *pg.* 856
NUMORPHAN - Pharmaceutical Product - ENDO PHARMACEUTICALS HOLDINGS, INC.; *pg.* 1528, *pg.* 1549
NUNN-BUSH - Shoes - WEYCO GROUP, INC.; *pg.* 1822, *pg.* 1858
NUNN BUSH NXXT - Shoes - WEYCO GROUP, INC.; *pg.* 1822, *pg.* 1858
NUPAGE - Telephone Service - IDT CORPORATION; *pg.* 643, *pg.* 1096
NUPAGE - Molecular Biology Product - THERMO FISHER SCIENTIFIC INC.; *pg.* 1602, *pg.* 61
NUPAL - Coating Product - PPG INDUSTRIES, INC.; *pg.* 1445, *pg.* 1579
NUPLABOND - Epoxy Material - NUPLA CORPORATION; *pg.* 101, *pg.* 281
NUPLAFLEX - Soft Face Tips - NUPLA CORPORATION; *pg.* 101, *pg.* 281
NUPLAGLAS - Fiberglass - NUPLA CORPORATION; *pg.* 101, *pg.* 281
NUPOINT UNIFIED MESSAGING - Communications Solution - MITEL NETWORKS CORPORATION; *pg.* 654, *pg.* 1921
NUPOLAR - Polarized Lens - YOUNGER OPTICS; *pg.* 1437, *pg.* 297
NUPRO - Dental Product - DENTSPLY INTERNATIONAL INC.; *pg.* 1522, *pg.* 1596
NUPRO - Plastic Tube - SWAGELOK COMPANY; *pg.* 1064, *pg.* 1473
NUR - Ink-Jet Printer - COOLEY GROUP, INC.; *pg.* 691, *pg.* 1603
NURAL - Piston Product - FEDERAL-MOGUL HOLDINGS CORPORATION; *pg.* 205, *pg.* 907
NURESCA - Pharmaceutical Preparation - PFIZER INC.; *pg.* 1581, *pg.* 1278
NURIT - Hardware - VERIFONE SYSTEMS, INC.; *pg.* 487, *pg.* 251
NURLED - Belt - COACH, INC.; *pg.* 3, *pg.* 1214
NUROLL - Towel Dispensing System - GEORGIA-PACIFIC LLC; *pg.* 1458, *pg.* 507
NURSE FOLLIES - Video Slots - INTERNATIONAL GAME TECHNOLOGY; *pg.* 957, *pg.* 1024
NURSEADVOCATE - Power System - STINGER MEDICAL LLC; *pg.* 476, *pg.* 1648
NURSEALL - Animal Nutrition Product - MANNA PRO CORPORATION; *pg.* 1478, *pg.* 975
NURSEMATE - Integrated Review & Charting Station - ST. JUDE MEDICAL, INC.; *pg.* 1596, *pg.* 963
NURSERY RHYME - Game - HASBRO, INC.; *pg.* 954, *pg.* 1603
NURSESENSOR - Proximity Reader - STINGER MEDICAL LLC; *pg.* 476, *pg.* 1648
NURSETTE - Disposable Glass Bottle Service for Hospital Feedings - MEAD JOHNSON NUTRITION COMPANY; *pg.* 1561, *pg.* 615
NURSING HOME QUALITY GUIDE - Healthcare Product - HEALTH GRADES, INC.; *pg.* 1256, *pg.* 319
NURSING HOME REPORT CARDS - Healthcare Product - HEALTH GRADES, INC.; *pg.* 1256, *pg.* 319
NURSING SPECTRUM - Magazine Article - GANNETT HEALTHCARE GROUP; *pg.* 1644, *pg.* 617
NURSINGJOBS.COM - Internet Portal - AMN HEALTHCARE SERVICES, INC.; *pg.* 1494, *pg.* 200
NURSINGMATTERS - Publication - MADISON NEWSPAPERS, INC.; *pg.* 1661, *pg.* 1866
NURTURA - Beauty Product - AVON PRODUCTS, INC.; *pg.* 500, *pg.* 1198
NURTURELITE - Lighting Product - WESTINGHOUSE LIGHTING CORPORATION; *pg.* 687, *pg.* 1571
NUSONICS - Electronic Measurement Instrument - MESA LABORATORIES, INC.; *pg.* 1567, *pg.* 333
NUSSERVE - Telephone Service - IDT CORPORATION; *pg.* 643, *pg.* 1096
NUSUN - Sunflower Oil - ARCHER-DANIELS-MIDLAND COMPANY; *pg.* 825, *pg.* 565
NUT & HONEY CRUNCH - Flakes of Corn Coated with Nuts & Real Honey - KELLOGG COMPANY; *pg.* 831, *pg.* 870
NUT-FREE APPLE & APRICOT SMOOTHEES - Candies - LIBERTY ORCHARDS CO., INC.; *pg.* 1857, *pg.* 1819
NUT-FREE FRUIT PARFAITS - Candies - LIBERTY ORCHARDS CO., INC.; *pg.* 1857, *pg.* 1819
NUT FREE MINT-SMOOTHEES - Candies - LIBERTY ORCHARDS CO., INC.; *pg.* 1857, *pg.* 1819
NUT-FREE SMOOTHEES - Candy - LIBERTY ORCHARDS CO., INC.; *pg.* 1857, *pg.* 1819
NUT 'N SWEETIE - Ice Cream - TURKEY HILL DAIRY, INC.; *pg.* 902, *pg.* 1522
NUT-NOTS - Nuts - CARGILL LIMITED; *pg.* 1475, *pg.* 1914
NUT THINS - Almond, Hazelnut & Pecan Crackers - BLUE DIAMOND GROWERS; *pg.* 840, *pg.* 195
NUTBUSTER - Groove Plier - CHANNELLOCK, INC.; *pg.* 1044, *pg.* 1551
NUTCRACKER - Crackers - CONAGRA FOODS; *pg.* 826, *pg.* 994
NUTEK - Boxes & Covers - THOMAS & BETTS CORPORATION; *pg.* 680, *pg.* 1646
NUTMASTER - Hand Tool - IDEAL INDUSTRIES, INC.; *pg.* 1051, *pg.* 662
NUTRA - Nutritional Product - NUTRACEUTICAL INTERNATIONAL CORPORATION; *pg.* 1576, *pg.* 1753
NUTRA-FRY - Food Product - BUNGE LIMITED; *pg.* 842, *pg.* 1351
NUTRA NAIL - Nail Care Product - CCA INDUSTRIES, INC.; *pg.* 503, *pg.* 1114
NUTRA-RINSE - Cleaning Product - HILLYARD, INC.; *pg.*

First page reference indicates Business Class Edition
Second page reference indicates Geographic Edition

331, *pg.* 990
NUTRAFIBER - Dietary Fiber Blends - INTERNATIONAL FIBER CORP.; *pg.* 865, *pg.* 1317
NUTRAFIN MAX - Pet Product - PETSMART, INC.; *pg.* 1481, *pg.* 18
NUTRAFIRM - Personal Care Product - RBC LIFE SCIENCES, INC.; *pg.* 1588, *pg.* 1723
NUTRAGEOUS - Chocolate Candy - THE HERSHEY CO.; *pg.* 1855, *pg.* 1538
NUTRAMENT - Nutritional Drink - MEAD JOHNSON NUTRITION COMPANY; *pg.* 1561, *pg.* 615
NUTRAMIGEN - Hypoallergenic Powdered Protein Formula - MEAD JOHNSON NUTRITION COMPANY; *pg.* 1561, *pg.* 615
NUTRAPON - Chemical Product - STEPAN COMPANY; *pg.* 1182, *pg.* 643
NUTRASWEET - Sweetener - THE NUTRASWEET COMPANY; *pg.* 1860, *pg.* 585
NUTRAVIA - Sweetening Ingredient - MERISANT COMPANY; *pg.* 876, *pg.* 581
NUTRENA - Feeds - CARGILL, INC.; *pg.* 845, *pg.* 965
NUTREON - Agricultural Product - ARCHER-DANIELS-MIDLAND COMPANY; *pg.* 825, *pg.* 565
NUTRI-BLENDER - Blender - A.T. FERRELL COMPANY, INC.; *pg.* 701, *pg.* 674
NUTRI-BRAN - Bread - ROMAN MEAL COMPANY; *pg.* 834, *pg.* 1845
NUTRI-BURN - Health Care Product - NATURE'S SUNSHINE PRODUCTS, INC.; *pg.* 1571, *pg.* 1754
NUTRI-CALM - Health Care Product - NATURE'S SUNSHINE PRODUCTS, INC.; *pg.* 1571, *pg.* 1754
NUTRI-CATH - Long-Term Silicone Feeding Tubes - UTAH MEDICAL PRODUCTS, INC.; *pg.* 1605, *pg.* 1752
NUTRI-GENIC - Nutritional Supplement - NATURAL ORGANICS, INC.; *pg.* 1571, *pg.* 1181
NUTRI-GRAIN - Food Product - KELLOGG COMPANY; *pg.* 831, *pg.* 870
NUTRI-GRAIN STRAWBERRY YOGURT - Snacks - KELLOGG COMPANY; *pg.* 831, *pg.* 870
NUTRI-GRAIN VANILLA YOGURT - Snacks - KELLOGG COMPANY; *pg.* 831, *pg.* 870
NUTRI-LOK - Enteral Feeding Set - UTAH MEDICAL PRODUCTS, INC.; *pg.* 1605, *pg.* 1752
NUTRI-PHYSICAL - Internet-Based Analysis Tool - MARKET AMERICA WORLDWIDE, INC.; *pg.* 1265, *pg.* 1375
NUTRI/SYSTEM - Weight Loss Program - NUTRISYSTEM, INC.; *pg.* 1577, *pg.* 1533
NUTRIBULLET - Superfood Nutrition Extractor - CAPITAL BRANDS, LLC; *pg.* 53, *pg.* 127
NUTRICENTIALS - Nutritional Supplement - NU SKIN ENTERPRISES, INC.; *pg.* 518, *pg.* 1755
NUTRICHLOR - Health & Nutrition Product - NOVUS INTERNATIONAL, INC.; *pg.* 706, *pg.* 1001
NUTRIENE - Tocotrienols - EASTMAN CHEMICAL COMPANY; *pg.* 1159, *pg.* 1636
NUTRIENTIA - Sweetening Ingredient - MERISANT COMPANY; *pg.* 876, *pg.* 581
NUTRIFI - Nutritional Supplement - NU SKIN ENTERPRISES, INC.; *pg.* 518, *pg.* 1755
NUTRIGLOW - Nutritional Supplement - NATURAL ORGANICS, INC.; *pg.* 1571, *pg.* 1181
NUTRIHANCE - Vitamin - NUTRISYSTEM, INC.; *pg.* 1577, *pg.* 1533
NUTRIHEP - Food & Beverage Product - NESTLE USA, INC.; *pg.* 883, *pg.* 96
NUTRILAIT - Dairy Products - SAPUTO, INC.; *pg.* 893, *pg.* 1956
NUTRILAYER - Phytolipids - EASTMAN CHEMICAL COMPANY; *pg.* 1159, *pg.* 1636
NUTRILEAF - Fertilizer - MILLER CHEMICAL & FERTILIZER CORPORATION; *pg.* 706, *pg.* 1535
NUTRILITE - Vitamin & Mineral Supplements - AMWAY CORPORATION; *pg.* 326, *pg.* 864
NUTRIMEAL - Nutritional Supplement - USANA HEALTH SCIENCES, INC.; *pg.* 1605, *pg.* 1761
NUTRIMETICS - Beauty Product - TUPPERWARE BRANDS CORPORATION; *pg.* 1139, *pg.* 456
NUTRIMIX - Food Ingredient - FOREMOST FARMS USA COOPERATIVE; *pg.* 856, *pg.* 1854
NUTRIMIX - Medical Device - HOSPIRA, INC.; *pg.* 1542, *pg.* 623
NUTRIMMUNE CHEWS - Nutritional Supplement - NU SKIN ENTERPRISES, INC.; *pg.* 518, *pg.* 1755
NUTRINE - Confectionery - THE HERSHEY CO.; *pg.* 1855, *pg.* 1538
NUTRINE GOLD - Confectionery - THE HERSHEY CO.; *pg.* 1855, *pg.* 1538
NUTRIOL - Hair Care Product - NU SKIN ENTERPRISES, INC.; *pg.* 518, *pg.* 1755
NUTRIPACK - Fertilizer - SIMPLOT PARTNERS INC.; *pg.* 1800, *pg.* 548
NUTRIPASS - Agricultural Product - ARCHER-DANIELS-MIDLAND COMPANY; *pg.* 825, *pg.* 565
NUTRIPHASE - Pet Product - PETSMART, INC.; *pg.* 1481, *pg.* 18
NUTRIRENAL - Food & Beverage Product - NESTLE USA, INC.; *pg.* 883, *pg.* 96
NUTRISH - A/B & Probiotic Culture - CHR. HANSEN; *pg.* 847, *pg.* 1873
NUTRISOURCE - Health Product - TRACTOR SUPPLY COMPANY; *pg.* 708, *pg.* 1627
NUTRISOY - Soy Protein Ingredients - ARCHER-DANIELS-MIDLAND COMPANY; *pg.* 825, *pg.* 565
NUTRISOY NEXT - Soy-Based Meat Substitutes - ARCHER-DANIELS-MIDLAND COMPANY; *pg.* 825, *pg.* 565
NUTRISPHERE-N - Agricultural Product - J.R. SIMPLOT COMPANY; *pg.* 867, *pg.* 547
NUTRISURE - Pharmaceutical Product - ABBOTT LABORATORIES; *pg.* 1484, *pg.* 551
NUTRISYSTEM NOURISH - Diet Program - NUTRISYSTEM, INC.; *pg.* 1577, *pg.* 1533
NUTRITEK - Food Ingredient - FOREMOST FARMS USA COOPERATIVE; *pg.* 856, *pg.* 1854
NUTRITION - Dog Toy - THE HARTZ MOUNTAIN CORP.; *pg.* 1476, *pg.* 1120
NUTRITION BAR - Nutritional Supplement - USANA HEALTH SCIENCES, INC.; *pg.* 1605, *pg.* 1761
NUTRITION HEADQUARTERS - Nutritional Product - NBTY, INC.; *pg.* 1572, *pg.* 1338
NUTRITION KNOWLEDGE BASE - Software - FIRST DATABANK, INC.; *pg.* 397, *pg.* 217
NUTRITION MADE SIMPLE LIFE MADE RICH - Tagline - RELIV INTERNATIONAL, INC.; *pg.* 1589, *pg.* 975
NUTRITIONDATA.COM - Health Related Website - CONDE NAST DIGITAL; *pg.* 1237, *pg.* 1217
NUTRITIONIST PRO - Software - FIRST DATABANK, INC.; *pg.* 397, *pg.* 217
NUTRITIONIST PRO FOOD LABELING - Software - FIRST DATABANK, INC.; *pg.* 397, *pg.* 217
NUTRIWHIP - Food Product - MAPLE LEAF FOODS INC.; *pg.* 875, *pg.* 1927
NUTRIZAC - Nutritional Supplement - NATURAL ORGANICS, INC.; *pg.* 1571, *pg.* 1181
NUTRO - Natural Pet Food - MARS, INCORPORATED; *pg.* 1858, *pg.* 1792
NUTRO - Pet Food - MARS PETCARE; *pg.* 1478, *pg.* 1633
NUTRON - Power Wheelchair - INVACARE CORPORATION; *pg.* 1546, *pg.* 1451
NUTROPIN - Human Growth Hormone - GENENTECH, INC.; *pg.* 1533, *pg.* 279
NUTROPIN AQ - Liquid Formulation Human Growth Hormone - GENENTECH, INC.; *pg.* 1533, *pg.* 279
NUTROPIN AQ PEN - Biotherapeutic - GENENTECH, INC.; *pg.* 1533, *pg.* 279
NUTROPIN DEPOT - Treatment for Growth Hormone Deficiency - GENENTECH, INC.; *pg.* 1533, *pg.* 279
NUTS FOR BERRIES - Strawberry Arrangements Dipped in Chocolate & Nuts - EDIBLE ARRANGEMENTS INTERNATIONAL, INC.; *pg.* 1768, *pg.* 382
NUTSIE - Mobile Phone Application - HEWLETT-PACKARD COMPANY; *pg.* 404, *pg.* 175
NUTTIN' BUT THE BEST - Peanut - BEER NUTS, INC.; *pg.* 1850, *pg.* 557
NUTTIN' TO IT - Video Game - INTERNATIONAL GAME TECHNOLOGY; *pg.* 957, *pg.* 1024
NUTTY BREWNETTE - Beer - BJ'S RESTAURANTS, INC.; *pg.* 1716, *pg.* 104
NUTTY CHOCOLATE MOOSE TRACKS - Ice Cream - TURKEY HILL DAIRY, INC.; *pg.* 902, *pg.* 1522
NUTTY ELEPHANT - Toy & Game - HASBRO, INC.; *pg.* 954, *pg.* 1603
NUVARING - Contraceptive Devices - MERCK & CO., INC.; *pg.* 1566, *pg.* 1077
NUVE - Footwear - COBIAN CORP.; *pg.* 1806, *pg.* 253
NUVERA - Printer - XEROX CORPORATION; *pg.* 494, *pg.* 365
NUVINCI - Transmission Technology - FALLBROOK TECHNOLOGIES INC.; *pg.* 1336, *pg.* 203
NUVION - Antibody - PDL BIOPHARMA INC.; *pg.* 1580, *pg.* 1022
NUVIS S 2000 - Compact Camera - NIKON INC.; *pg.* 1424, *pg.* 1181
NUVO - Personal Care Product - TUPPERWARE BRANDS CORPORATION; *pg.* 1139, *pg.* 456
NUVUE - Display System - EASTMAN KODAK COMPANY; *pg.* 1408, *pg.* 1333
NUWEAR - Fabric - NEMSCHOFF, INC.; *pg.* 936, *pg.* 1890
NUZZLE NEST - Pet Product - PETSMART, INC.; *pg.* 1481, *pg.* 18
NV - Golf Club Shafts - ALDILA, INC.; *pg.* 1825, *pg.* 185
NV PROTOPYPE - Golf Club Shafts - ALDILA, INC.; *pg.* 1825, *pg.* 185
NVE - Semiconductor - NVE CORPORATION; *pg.* 447, *pg.* 923
NVIDIA - Graphics Accelerator Card - PNY TECHNOLOGIES, INC.; *pg.* 455, *pg.* 1105
NVIDIA QUADRO - Graphic Accelerator Card - PNY TECHNOLOGIES, INC.; *pg.* 455, *pg.* 1105
NVIDIA QUADRO PLEX - System - PNY TECHNOLOGIES, INC.; *pg.* 455, *pg.* 1105
NVIEW - Software - NVIDIA CORPORATION; *pg.* 447, *pg.* 268
NVKEYSTONE - Software - NVIDIA CORPORATION; *pg.* 447, *pg.* 268
NVPP - National Vehicle Population Profile - IHS AUTOMOTIVE DRIVEN BY POLK; *pg.* 1652, *pg.* 907
NVROTATE - Software - NVIDIA CORPORATION; *pg.* 447, *pg.* 268
NVS - Golf Club Shafts - ALDILA, INC.; *pg.* 1825, *pg.* 185
NVX - Vibration Control Systems - LORD CORPORATION; *pg.* 1357, *pg.* 1360
NWAVE - Programmable Oscillators - CTS CORPORATION; *pg.* 631, *pg.* 677
NX - Medical Equipment - INVACARE CORPORATION; *pg.* 1546, *pg.* 1451
NX - Nitrogen Atmosphere Gas Generators - SURFACE COMBUSTION, INC.; *pg.* 1077, *pg.* 1462
NX-PRO - Fertilizers - LEBANON SEABOARD CORPORATION; *pg.* 1797, *pg.* 1547
NX56/64K V.35 MODULE - Networking Product - ADTRAN, INC.; *pg.* 344, *pg.* 6
NXG - Wireless Measurement Solutions - COMMSCOPE, INC.; *pg.* 278, *pg.* 1378
NXG - Floor Underlayment - USG CORPORATION; *pg.* 118, *pg.* 594
NXJ DEVELOPER - Software - DAEGIS INC; *pg.* 381, *pg.* 195
NXJ ENTERPRISE - Software - DAEGIS INC; *pg.* 381, *pg.* 195
NXSET - Personal Audio Communication - KOSS CORPORATION; *pg.* 649, *pg.* 1877
NXT - Golf Equipment - ACUSHNET COMPANY; *pg.* 1824, *pg.* 818
NXT - Fluid Handling System - GRACO, INC.; *pg.* 1342, *pg.* 935
NXTRAIN - Training System - LOCKHEED MARTIN CORPORATION; *pg.* 229, *pg.* 762
NY KNICKERBOCKERS - Basketball Team - NEW YORK KNICKERBOCKERS; *pg.* 570, *pg.* 1268
NY NY - Stainless Steel Roll Top Schaffer - THE VOLLRATH COMPANY LLC; *pg.* 1139, *pg.* 1894
NY-WHITE - Yarn Lubricants - HENKEL CORPORATION; *pg.* 1165, *pg.* 1535
NYAL - Pharmaceutical Product - VALEANT PHARMACEUTICALS INTERNATIONAL; *pg.* 1605, *pg.* 1047
NYBEX - Polyamide Compounds - FERRO CORPORATION; *pg.* 1162, *pg.* 1462
NYBRAD - Abrasive Monofilaments - HAHL INC.; *pg.* 1299, *pg.* 1620
NYCOR - Rubber Nylon Core - SHINGLE BELTING COMPANY; *pg.* 1375, *pg.* 1544
NYDAILYNEWS.COM - Website - DAILY NEWS, L.P.; *pg.* 1632, *pg.* 1221
NYDD - Video Game - INTERNATIONAL GAME TECHNOLOGY; *pg.* 957, *pg.* 1024
NYJER - Pet Food - PETSMART, INC.; *pg.* 1481, *pg.* 18
NYLAFLO - Membrane Disc Filter - PALL CORPORATION; *pg.* 232, *pg.* 1323
NYLAKRIMP - Electronic Components - MOLEX INCORPORATED; *pg.* 655, *pg.* 628
NYLAR - Pesticide - MCLAUGHLIN GORMLEY KING COMPANY; *pg.* 1797, *pg.* 939
NYLASORB - Membrane Disc Filter - PALL CORPORATION; *pg.* 232, *pg.* 1323

NYLATEX - Orthopedic Device - DJO SURGICAL; *pg.* 1525, *pg.* 1661
NYLATRAC - Cable & Hose System - DYNATECT MANUFACTURING INC.; *pg.* 1330, *pg.* 1883
NYLATUBE - Cable & Hose System - DYNATECT MANUFACTURING INC.; *pg.* 1330, *pg.* 1883
NYLIFE - Brand Name for Investment & Registered Products - NEW YORK LIFE INSURANCE COMPANY; *pg.* 1211, *pg.* 1268
NYLINER - Fluid Handling System - GRACO, INC.; *pg.* 1342, *pg.* 935
NYLO-BEARING - Equipped Conveyor - METZGAR CONVEYOR COMPANY; *pg.* 1360, *pg.* 875
NYLO-WHEEL - Equipped Conveyor - METZGAR CONVEYOR COMPANY; *pg.* 1360, *pg.* 875
NYLOCK - Conveyor Belting - HBD INDUSTRIES, INC.; *pg.* 207, *pg.* 1449
NYLOK - Surface Treatment Product - J.M. HUBER CORPORATION; *pg.* 1169, *pg.* 1056
NYLON-CORDURA - Pouch Carrier - KLEIN TOOLS INC.; *pg.* 1052, *pg.* 627
NYLON NAILIN - Pin Anchor - POWERS FASTENERS INC.; *pg.* 1059, *pg.* 1143
NYLOPAK - Plastic Film - THE DOW CHEMICAL COMPANY; *pg.* 1157, *pg.* 898
NYLOPLAST - Pipe - ADVANCED DRAINAGE SYSTEMS, INC.; *pg.* 1878, *pg.* 1455
NYLOSUEDE - Fabric - NEMSCHOFF, INC.; *pg.* 936, *pg.* 1890
NYMAG.COM - Website - NEW YORK MAGAZINE; *pg.* 1667, *pg.* 1269
NYMAX - Engineered Compound & Composite - POLYONE CORPORATION; *pg.* 1177, *pg.* 1404
NYPOST.COM - Magazine - THE NEW YORK POST; *pg.* 1668, *pg.* 1269
NYQUIL - Cold Remedy - THE PROCTER & GAMBLE COMPANY; *pg.* 1129, *pg.* 1418
NYQUIL PLUS VITAMIN C - Health Care Product - THE PROCTER & GAMBLE COMPANY; *pg.* 1129, *pg.* 1418
NYSILON - Seal & Thermoplastic Component - GREENE, TWEED & CO.; *pg.* 1344, *pg.* 1544
NYSOFACT - Catalyst - BASF CATALYSTS LLC; *pg.* 1148, *pg.* 1074
NYSOSEL - Catalyst - BASF CATALYSTS LLC; *pg.* 1148, *pg.* 1074
NYSTROM - Maps, Globes & Multimedia - HERFF JONES, INC.; *pg.* 7, *pg.* 686
NYTAL - Chemical Product - R.T. VANDERBILT COMPANY, INC.; *pg.* 1180, *pg.* 364
NZ GESTION - Nutritional Supplement - WHITEWING LABS, INC.; *pg.* 1610, *pg.* 99

O

O - Theatrical Production - CIRQUE DU SOLEIL INC.; *pg.* 540, *pg.* 1954
O-4 MINI - Lighting Product - GERBER LEGENDARY BLADES; *pg.* 1834, *pg.* 1503
O&K - Excavator - TEREX CORPORATION; *pg.* 1381, *pg.* 384
O BLADE - Golf Club - KARSTEN MANUFACTURING CORPORATION; *pg.* 1838, *pg.* 17
O-CEL-O - Cleaning Products - 3M COMPANY; *pg.* 1142, *pg.* 956
O-FLOW - Accessories - UNDER ARMOUR, INC.; *pg.* 49, *pg.* 759
O HOLY NIGHT - Scarf - HERITAGE LACE INC.; *pg.* 694, *pg.* 711
O-KE DOKE - Snack Food - SNYDER'S-LANCE, INC.; *pg.* 896, *pg.* 1368
O ORGANICS - Baby Products, Beverages, Breakfast & Bakery Items, Dairy Products & Eggs - SAFEWAY INC.; *pg.* 1032, *pg.* 184
O THE OPRAH MAGAZINE - Magazine - THE HEARST CORPORATION; *pg.* 1649, *pg.* 1239
O-TITE! - O-rings - DORMAN PRODUCTS, INC.; *pg.* 204, *pg.* 1522
O-TYPE - Hot Air Balloon - CAMERON BALLOONS U.S.; *pg.* 1829, *pg.* 884
O-Z/GEDNEY - Electrical Products - EMERSON INDUSTRIAL AUTOMATION; *pg.* 1296, *pg.* 657
O12 - Children's Clothing - BENETTON U.S.A. CORPORATION; *pg.* 19, *pg.* 1202
O2 - Frames - OAKLEY, INC.; *pg.* 1840, *pg.* 86
O3MEGA - Integrated Ozone Delivery System - MKS INSTRUMENTS, INC.; *pg.* 1362, *pg.* 781
O6 - Frames - OAKLEY, INC.; *pg.* 1840, *pg.* 86
O7 - Frames - OAKLEY, INC.; *pg.* 1840, *pg.* 86
OADJUSTER - Orthopedic Product - DJO INCORPORATED; *pg.* 1524, *pg.* 302
OADMG 100GHZ (1X2) - Fiber Optic Component - OPLINK COMMUNICATIONS, INC.; *pg.* 660, *pg.* 91
OADMG 100GHZ (2X2) - Fiber Optic Component - OPLINK COMMUNICATIONS, INC.; *pg.* 660, *pg.* 91
OADMG 200GHZ (1X2) - Fiber Optic Component - OPLINK COMMUNICATIONS, INC.; *pg.* 660, *pg.* 91
OADMG 200GHZ (2X2) - Fiber Optic Component - OPLINK COMMUNICATIONS, INC.; *pg.* 660, *pg.* 91
OAG EXECUTIVE FLIGHT GUIDE - Airline Service - OAG WORLDWIDE LIMITED; *pg.* 1672, *pg.* 609
OAGEXPRESS - Airline Service - OAG WORLDWIDE LIMITED; *pg.* 1672, *pg.* 609
OAHU - Carpet - BEAULIEU GROUP, LLC; *pg.* 917, *pg.* 529
OAK CREEK - Homes - AMERICAN HOMESTAR CORPORATION; *pg.* 67, *pg.* 1725
OAK CREST - Retirement Community - ERICKSON LIVING; *pg.* 1090, *pg.* 766
OAK FARMS - Dairy Product - DEAN FOODS COMPANY; *pg.* 852, *pg.* 1679
OAK HARBOR - Ceiling Fan - WESTINGHOUSE LIGHTING CORPORATION; *pg.* 687, *pg.* 1571
THE OAK HILL - Home Floor Plan - JACOBSEN MANUFACTURING, INC.; *pg.* 1098, *pg.* 460
OAK HILL FARMS - Salad Dressing & Beverages - VITA FOOD PRODUCTS, INC.; *pg.* 909, *pg.* 595
OAK LORE - Furniture - ASHLEY FURNITURE INDUSTRIES, INC.; *pg.* 914, *pg.* 1852
OAK MEADOW - Shoes - SHOE CARNIVAL, INC.; *pg.* 1819, *pg.* 679
THE OAK RIDGER - Newspaper - THE OAK RIDGER, LLC; *pg.* 1672, *pg.* 1655
OAKCRAFT - Door - MASONITE INTERNATIONAL CORPORATION; *pg.* 1054, *pg.* 1920
OAKLOK - Plybent Wood Chair - SAUDER MANUFACTURING COMPANY; *pg.* 941, *pg.* 1403
OAKPARK - Door Glass - ODL INCORPORATED; *pg.* 101, *pg.* 914
OAKRIDGE - Roofing Shingles with a Shadow Effect - OWENS CORNING; *pg.* 102, *pg.* 1476
OAKRIDGE PRO - Roofing System - OWENS CORNING; *pg.* 102, *pg.* 1476
OAKSTONE - Publisher - HAIGHTS CROSS COMMUNICATIONS, INC.; *pg.* 1646, *pg.* 1237
OAKTREE - Process Improvement Software - PIVOTAL RESOURCES, INC.; *pg.* 455, *pg.* 304
OAKWOOD - Manufactured Homes - CLAYTON HOMES, INC.; *pg.* 1086, *pg.* 1640
OAKWOOD - Fabric - NEMSCHOFF, INC.; *pg.* 936, *pg.* 1890
OAKWOOD - Fabric - UNIROYAL ENGINEERED PRODUCTS; *pg.* 699, *pg.* 467
OAKWOODD - Footwear - STEVEN MADDEN, LTD.; *pg.* 1819, *pg.* 1176
OASIS - Medical Device - COOK GROUP, INC.; *pg.* 1518, *pg.* 674
OASIS - Rug - COURISTAN INC.; *pg.* 921, *pg.* 1067
OASIS - Films - E.I. DU PONT DE NEMOURS & COMPANY; *pg.* 1159, *pg.* 390
OASIS - Wall Decor - ETHAN ALLEN INTERIORS INC.; *pg.* 924, *pg.* 343
OASIS - Dental Software - HENRY SCHEIN, INC.; *pg.* 1541, *pg.* 1180
OASIS - Dinnerware - THE HOMER LAUGHLIN CHINA COMPANY; *pg.* 1125, *pg.* 1850
OASIS - Isolator & Lens - LIGHTPATH TECHNOLOGIES INC; *pg.* 1420, *pg.* 454
OASIS - Fabric - NEMSCHOFF, INC.; *pg.* 936, *pg.* 1890
OASIS - Health & Nutrition Product - NOVUS INTERNATIONAL, INC.; *pg.* 706, *pg.* 1001
OASIS - Decking - PLY GEM SIDING GROUP; *pg.* 105, *pg.* 986
OASIS - Sample Extraction Product - WATERS CORPORATION; *pg.* 1436, *pg.* 834
OASIS 1750 - Protein Crystal Imaging System - VEECO INSTRUMENTS INC.; *pg.* 1434, *pg.* 1322
OASIS RESORT HOTEL & CASINO - Hotel & Casino - MESQUITE GAMING, LLC; *pg.* 1104, *pg.* 1030
OASYS - Orbit Analysis System - INTEGRAL SYSTEMS, INC.; *pg.* 416, *pg.* 767
OASYS - Overhead System - LEAR CORPORATION; *pg.* 229, *pg.* 907
OASYS - Spinal System - STRYKER CORPORATION; *pg.* 1598, *pg.* 894
OAT BRAN STICKS - Snacks - SNYDER'S OF HANOVER, INC.; *pg.* 1862, *pg.* 1536
OATEYWELD - Solvent - OATEY SUPPLY CHAIN SERVICES; *pg.* 30, *pg.* 1433
OATMEAL - Fabric - ETHAN ALLEN INTERIORS INC.; *pg.* 924, *pg.* 343
OATMEAL - Fabric - NEMSCHOFF, INC.; *pg.* 936, *pg.* 1890
OATMEAL CRISP - Cereal - GENERAL MILLS, INC.; *pg.* 828, *pg.* 933
OATMEAL TWEED - Pillow and Throw - HERITAGE LACE INC.; *pg.* 694, *pg.* 711
OATY BITES - Breakfast Cereals - NATURE'S PATH FOODS INC.; *pg.* 833, *pg.* 1908
OAXACA - Food Product - V&V SUPREMO FOODS, INC.; *pg.* 907, *pg.* 595
O.B. - Feminine Care - EDGEWELL PERSONAL CARE; *pg.* 1526, *pg.* 995
OB - Sanitary Tampons - JOHNSON & JOHNSON; *pg.* 1549, *pg.* 1091
OB-MX - Electronic Musical Sound Generating Module - GIBSON GUITAR CORP.; *pg.* 550, *pg.* 1650
OBAG-C RX - Skin Care Products - OBAGI MEDICAL PRODUCTS, INC.; *pg.* 1577, *pg.* 123
OBAGI - Skin Care Products - OBAGI MEDICAL PRODUCTS, INC.; *pg.* 1577, *pg.* 123
OBAM - Matrix Architecture - POLYCOM, INC.; *pg.* 664, *pg.* 249
OBC - Pharmaceutical Product - ALERE INC.; *pg.* 1488, *pg.* 849
OBD - Column Calculator - WATERS CORPORATION; *pg.* 1436, *pg.* 834
OBELISK - Paperweight - BROWN & BIGELOW, INC.; *pg.* 1624, *pg.* 959
OBELUS - Flatware - ONEIDA LTD; *pg.* 1129, *pg.* 1318
OBERDORFER - Pump - GARDNER DENVER, INC.; *pg.* 1338, *pg.* 1592
OBERHEIM - Synthesizers & Electronic Keyboards - GIBSON GUITAR CORP.; *pg.* 550, *pg.* 1650
OBERLIN - Guest Chairs - BERNHARDT DESIGN; *pg.* 918, *pg.* 1381
OBERTO - Meat Snack - FRITO-LAY NORTH AMERICA, INC.; *pg.* 1853, *pg.* 1730
OBERTO - Meat Snacks - PEPSICO, INC.; *pg.* 259, *pg.* 1327
OBG MANAGEMENT - Healthcare Publication - LEBHAR-FRIEDMAN INC.; *pg.* 1658, *pg.* 1250
OBJECT RESTORE - Software - DELL SOFTWARE; *pg.* 385, *pg.* 40
OBJECTARX - Software - AUTODESK INC.; *pg.* 356, *pg.* 257
OBJECTIVE-C - Computer Software - APPLE INC.; *pg.* 350, *pg.* 73
OBJECTSTORE - Software - PROGRESS SOFTWARE CORPORATION; *pg.* 457, *pg.* 786
OBJECTSTUDIO - Software - CINCOM SYSTEMS, INC.; *pg.* 372, *pg.* 1411
OBL - Electrical Pickups for Stringed Musical Instruments - GIBSON GUITAR CORP.; *pg.* 550, *pg.* 1650
OBSCURE WIRE GLASS - Patterned Glass - AGC GLASS NORTH AMERICA, INC.; *pg.* 65, *pg.* 482
OBSERVATIONS - Magazine - SAS INSTITUTE INC.; *pg.* 466, *pg.* 1361
THE OBSERVER - Newspaper - HOMETOWN COMMUNICATIONS NETWORK, INC.; *pg.* 1650, *pg.* 904
OBSERVER REPORTER - Newspaper - OBSERVER PUBLISHING COMPANY; *pg.* 1672, *pg.* 1591
OBSERVISION - Security & Law Enforcement Products - MACE SECURITY INTERNATIONAL, INC.; *pg.* 1172, *pg.* 1541
OBSESSION - Cap - BROWN & BIGELOW, INC.; *pg.* 1624, *pg.* 959
OBSESSION - Fragrance - CALVIN KLEIN, INC.; *pg.* 20, *pg.* 1209
OBSESSION - Lighting Control Console - ELECTRONIC THEATRE CONTROLS, INC.; *pg.* 1296, *pg.* 1872
OBSIDIAN - Brew - DESCHUTES BREWERY. INC.; *pg.* 248, *pg.* 1496
OBSTACLE DETECTION SYSTEM - Rear Motion Detection System - GROTE INDUSTRIES, INC.; *pg.* 206, *pg.* 693
OBSTACLEINFO - Physical Obstacles & AM Frequency Database - PITNEY BOWES SOFTWARE INC.; *pg.* 455, *pg.* 1346
OBTRYX - Medical Device - BOSTON SCIENTIFIC

First page reference indicates Business Class Edition
Second page reference indicates Geographic Edition

CORPORATION; *pg.* 1508, *pg.* 831
OCAL - Conduit - THOMAS & BETTS CORPORATION; *pg.* 680, *pg.* 1646
OCASSIONS - Year Round Gift Catalog - THE POPCORN FACTORY; *pg.* 1861, *pg.* 625
OCCASION GALLERIE - Cards - SPS STUDIOS, INC.; *pg.* 1688, *pg.* 311
OCCIGERM - Medical Waste Processors - MARINE ELECTRIC SYSTEMS, INC.; *pg.* 652, *pg.* 1123
OCCUCOAT - Viscoelastic - BAUSCH & LOMB INCORPORATED; *pg.* 1401, *pg.* 1045
OCCUSENSE - Seating System - LEAR CORPORATION; *pg.* 229, *pg.* 907
OCEAN - Clothing - DOLFIN INTERNATIONAL CORPORATION; *pg.* 23, *pg.* 1553
OCEAN - Fabric - NEMSCHOFF, INC.; *pg.* 936, *pg.* 1890
OCEAN - Personal Care Product - WESTROCK COMPANY; *pg.* 1472, *pg.* 1805
OCEAN 21 - Systems Integration & Aeronautics - LOCKHEED MARTIN CORPORATION; *pg.* 229, *pg.* 762
OCEAN BEAUTY - Salmon - OCEAN BEAUTY SEAFOODS, INC.; *pg.* 1028, *pg.* 1838
OCEAN BIKINI VILLAGE - Swimwear - GROUPE BIKINI VILLAGE INC.; *pg.* 25, *pg.* 1950
OCEAN BONITA - Seafood - OCEAN BEAUTY SEAFOODS, INC.; *pg.* 1028, *pg.* 1838
OCEAN BREEZE - Carpet - BEAULIEU GROUP, LLC; *pg.* 917, *pg.* 529
OCEAN COUNTY OBSERVER - Daily Newspaper - ASBURY PARK PRESS INC.; *pg.* 1617, *pg.* 1090
OCEAN KAYAK - Kayaks - JOHNSON OUTDOORS INC.; *pg.* 1837, *pg.* 1888
OCEAN PEARL - Video Game - INTERNATIONAL GAME TECHNOLOGY; *pg.* 957, *pg.* 1024
OCEAN PRINCE - Seafood - CROWN PRINCE, INC.; *pg.* 850, *pg.* 67
OCEAN TECHNOLOGY - Fabric - W.L. GORE & ASSOCIATES, INC.; *pg.* 122, *pg.* 388
OCEAN VILLAGE - Passenger Cruises & Tours - CARNIVAL CORPORATION; *pg.* 1902, *pg.* 441
OCEAN WATER - Drink - SONIC CORP.; *pg.* 1750, *pg.* 1487
OCEANITE - Pressed & Monolithic Refractory - RESCO PRODUCTS, INC.; *pg.* 107, *pg.* 1581
OCEANS 3 - Health Supplement - GARDEN OF LIFE, INC.; *pg.* 1532, *pg.* 478
OCEAN'S DEEP - Game - WMS INDUSTRIES INC.; *pg.* 593, *pg.* 666
OCEANS OF FUN - Waterpark - CEDAR FAIR, L.P.; *pg.* 537, *pg.* 1471
OCEANSIDE - Tile - ARTISTIC TILE INC.; *pg.* 914, *pg.* 1119
OCEANSIDE - Furniture - TELESCOPE CASUAL FURNITURE INC.; *pg.* 944, *pg.* 1162
OCEANVIEW - Bedding - CROSCILL, INC.; *pg.* 1122, *pg.* 1220
OCEANVIEW - Kitchen Product - KOHLER CO.; *pg.* 91, *pg.* 1862
OCELLUS - Bath Product - KOHLER CO.; *pg.* 91, *pg.* 1862
O'CHARLEY'S - Restaurant & Pub - AMERICAN BLUE RIBBON HOLDINGS; *pg.* 1714, *pg.* 1648
OCHI-LYNX - Integrated Circuits - TEXAS INSTRUMENTS INCORPORATED; *pg.* 679, *pg.* 1688
OCHO DIAS - Distilled Spirits - JIM BEAM BRANDS CO.; *pg.* 1965, *pg.* 601
OCI - Debug Logic - IMAGINATION TECHNOLOGIES; *pg.* 412, *pg.* 285
OCS - Software - BIO-RAD LABORATORIES, INC.; *pg.* 1504, *pg.* 101
OCTA-CAROTENE - Nutritional Supplement - NATURAL ORGANICS, INC.; *pg.* 1571, *pg.* 1181
OCTAFILM - Filming Amine - GE WATER & PROCESS TECHNOLOGIES; *pg.* 1339, *pg.* 1588
OCTAFINING - Aromatics Isomerization Process to Produce Paraxylene - BASF CATALYSTS LLC; *pg.* 1148, *pg.* 1074
OCTAGON - Clock - ETHAN ALLEN INTERIORS INC.; *pg.* 924, *pg.* 343
OCTAL - Software - DATA I/O CORPORATION; *pg.* 382, *pg.* 1824
OCTAL-PHY - Ethernet Transceiver - BROADCOM CORPORATION; *pg.* 364, *pg.* 108
OCTALMAC - Network Product - VITESSE SEMICONDUCTOR CORPORATION; *pg.* 686, *pg.* 57
OCTALPHY - Retimer Device - PMC-SIERRA, INC.; *pg.* 664, *pg.* 287
OCTAMAX - Catalyst Additive - JOHNSON MATTHEY PROCESS TECHNOLOGIES; *pg.* 1169, *pg.* 1083
OCTAMAX HP - Enhancement Additive - JOHNSON MATTHEY PROCESS TECHNOLOGIES; *pg.* 1169, *pg.* 1083
OCTAMINE - Polymer Product - CHEMTURA CORPORATION; *pg.* 1152, *pg.* 355
OCTANE8 - Software - SUNGARD DATA SYSTEMS INC.; *pg.* 477, *pg.* 1592
OCTAPETTE - Glass & Ceramic Material - CORNING INCORPORATED; *pg.* 1122, *pg.* 1154
OCTEK - Electromagnetic Ballasts - UNIVERSAL LIGHTING TECHNOLOGIES; *pg.* 1307, *pg.* 1655
OCTEL - Telecommunication Product - AVAYA INC.; *pg.* 621, *pg.* 264
OCTISIV - Cracking Catalyst - BASF CATALYSTS LLC; *pg.* 1148, *pg.* 1074
OCTOATE Z - Activators - R.T. VANDERBILT COMPANY, INC.; *pg.* 1180, *pg.* 364
OCTOBER - Furniture - HAWORTH, INC.; *pg.* 402, *pg.* 891
OCTOPUS - Cleaning Pad - AMERICO MANUFACTURING CO., INC.; *pg.* 325, *pg.* 482
OCTOPUS2 - Tissue Stabilization Sys. - MEDTRONIC, INC.; *pg.* 1564, *pg.* 939
OCTOPUSTRAVEL.COM - Hotel & Travel Services Website - ORBITZ WORLDWIDE, INC.; *pg.* 1918, *pg.* 586
OCTOSPLIT - Fiber Optic Splitter - COMMUNICATIONS SPECIALTIES, INC.; *pg.* 377, *pg.* 1338
OCTUPUS - Tissue Stabilization System - MEDTRONIC, INC.; *pg.* 1564, *pg.* 939
OCTYLENES - Mixture of Octene - NOVA CHEMICALS CORPORATION; *pg.* 1175, *pg.* 1904
OCU 45 - Optical Converter Unites - ADTRAN, INC.; *pg.* 344, *pg.* 6
OCU-CARE - Nutritional Supplement - NATURAL ORGANICS, INC.; *pg.* 1571, *pg.* 1181
OCU SUPPORT - Dietary Supplement - NOW HEALTH GROUP, INC.; *pg.* 1576, *pg.* 557
OCUACTIN - Nutritional Supplement - NATURAL ORGANICS, INC.; *pg.* 1571, *pg.* 1181
OCUFLOX - Eye Care Product - ALLERGAN, INC.; *pg.* 1491, *pg.* 106
OCULIGHT - Medical Laser System - IRIDEX CORPORATION; *pg.* 648, *pg.* 160
OCUSENSE - Vitamin & Dietary Supplement - NATROL, INC.; *pg.* 1570, *pg.* 64
OCUSHIELD - Pharmaceutical Product - AKORN, INC.; *pg.* 1488, *pg.* 622
OCUSITE - Liquid Microemulsion Delivery Intended for Topical Applications in the Eye - LUMARA HEALTH INC.; *pg.* 1557, *pg.* 973
OCUVITE - Vitamin & Mineral Supplement - BAUSCH & LOMB INCORPORATED; *pg.* 1401, *pg.* 1045
ODALISQUE - Fabric - NEMSCHOFF, INC.; *pg.* 936, *pg.* 1890
ODDBOUNDER - Ball - SCHOOL-TECH, INC.; *pg.* 1844, *pg.* 866
ODE - Hearing Aid - BELTONE ELECTRONICS LLC; *pg.* 1503, *pg.* 614
ODEN AT - Injection Test System - GE ENERGY; *pg.* 1338, *pg.* 506
ODESSA - Sunglasses - COACH, INC.; *pg.* 3, *pg.* 1214
ODESSA AMERICAN - Texas Newspaper - FREEDOM COMMUNICATIONS, INC.; *pg.* 1643, *pg.* 110
ODOMASTER - Odor Control System - SURCO PRODUCTS, INC.; *pg.* 336, *pg.* 1581
ODOR-BANE - Deodorizer - NILODOR, INC.; *pg.* 332, *pg.* 1406
ODOR-EATERS - Footcare Products - COMBE INCORPORATED; *pg.* 1516, *pg.* 1351
ODOR EXPLODER - Cleaning Product - VON SCHRADER COMPANY; *pg.* 62, *pg.* 1890
ODOR OUT - Odor Remover Spray - STANLEY STEEMER INTERNATIONAL, INC.; *pg.* 944, *pg.* 1450
ODOR-X - Interior Deodorizer - TURTLE WAX, INC.; *pg.* 220, *pg.* 671
ODORMATIC - Odor Control Product - STEAMATIC INC.; *pg.* 60, *pg.* 1696
O'DOULS - Non-Alcoholic Beer - ANHEUSER-BUSCH COMPANIES, LLC; *pg.* 237, *pg.* 991
ODRIK - Pharmaceutical Product - ABBOTT LABORATORIES; *pg.* 1484, *pg.* 551
ODV - Forensics Equipment - BAE SYSTEMS PRODUCTS GROUP; *pg.* 359, *pg.* 432
ODWALLA - Soft Drink - THE COCA-COLA COMPANY; *pg.* 240, *pg.* 493
ODYSSEY - Furniture - AMERICAN LEATHER LP; *pg.* 912, *pg.* 1673
ODYSSEY - Furniture - ASHLEY FURNITURE INDUSTRIES, INC.; *pg.* 914, *pg.* 1852
ODYSSEY - Cutlery - BUCK KNIVES, INC.; *pg.* 1828, *pg.* 550
ODYSSEY - Putters & Wedges with Stronomic & Lyconite Inserts - CALLAWAY GOLF COMPANY; *pg.* 1829, *pg.* 58
ODYSSEY - Microwave Synthesis Product - CEM CORPORATION; *pg.* 1405, *pg.* 1382
ODYSSEY - Educational Technology - COMPASSLEARNING, INC.; *pg.* 1628, *pg.* 1661
ODYSSEY - Car Wash Equipment - D&S CAR WASH EQUIPMENT CO.; *pg.* 1327, *pg.* 979
ODYSSEY - Battery - ENERSYS INC.; *pg.* 1334, *pg.* 1584
ODYSSEY - Cleaning Product - HILLYARD, INC.; *pg.* 331, *pg.* 990
ODYSSEY - Kayak - HOBIE CAT COMPANY; *pg.* 1708, *pg.* 173
ODYSSEY - Toy Train - LIONEL LLC; *pg.* 961, *pg.* 875
ODYSSEY - Fabric - NEMSCHOFF, INC.; *pg.* 936, *pg.* 1890
ODYSSEY - Sturdilite Floodlight - PHOENIX PRODUCTS COMPANY; *pg.* 1304, *pg.* 1879
ODYSSEY - Protective Goggle - SELLSTROM MANUFACTURING CO.; *pg.* 1428, *pg.* 659
ODYSSEY - Chafer - THE VOLLRATH COMPANY LLC; *pg.* 1139, *pg.* 1894
ODYSSEY - Ceiling Fan - WESTINGHOUSE LIGHTING CORPORATION; *pg.* 687, *pg.* 1571
ODYSSEY ACCESS CLIENT - Software - JUNIPER NETWORKS, INC.; *pg.* 1260, *pg.* 286
ODYSSEY ATLASPHERE - Polymer Coating - BATTELLE MEMORIAL INSTITUTE; *pg.* 1401, *pg.* 1437
OE SOLUTIONS - Radiator Fan Assemblies - DORMAN PRODUCTS, INC.; *pg.* 204, *pg.* 1522
OEC - Medical Device - GE HEALTHCARE TECHNOLOGIES; *pg.* 1533, *pg.* 1897
OEG - Electronic Component Product - TE CONNECTIVITY LTD.; *pg.* 677, *pg.* 1515
OELSCHLAGER - Fastening Systems - TEXTRON INC.; *pg.* 235, *pg.* 1607
OEM WIRE-NUT - Screw-On-Connector - IDEAL INDUSTRIES, INC.; *pg.* 1051, *pg.* 662
OENOCLEAR - Filter Cartridge - PALL CORPORATION; *pg.* 232, *pg.* 1323
OENOPURE - Filter Cartridge - PALL CORPORATION; *pg.* 232, *pg.* 1323
OFAC EVALUATOR - Computer Software - COMPUTER SCIENCES CORPORATION; *pg.* 378, *pg.* 1780
OFF! - Insect Repellent - S.C. JOHNSON & SON, INC.; *pg.* 334, *pg.* 1889
OFF 5TH - Discount Department Store - SAKS INCORPORATED; *pg.* 1783, *pg.* 1288
OFF BROADWAY - Paint - ROSCO LABORATORIES, INC.; *pg.* 1782, *pg.* 378
OFF-CENTERED STUFF FOR OFF-CENTERED PEOPLE - Tagline - DOGFISH HEAD CRAFT BREWERY, INC.; *pg.* 249, *pg.* 388
OFF DUTY - Personal Defense Sprays - MACE SECURITY INTERNATIONAL, INC.; *pg.* 1172, *pg.* 1541
OFF-HAND - Cleaning Towels - THE GILLETTE COMPANY; *pg.* 509, *pg.* 795
OFF LINE - Frames - OAKLEY, INC.; *pg.* 1840, *pg.* 86
OFF-SHOOT T - Polymer Product - CHEMTURA CORPORATION; *pg.* 1152, *pg.* 355
OFF THE CHARTS - Game - WMS INDUSTRIES INC.; *pg.* 593, *pg.* 666
OFFER ZONE - Card Member Rewards - AMERICAN EXPRESS COMPANY; *pg.* 712, *pg.* 1190
OFFERINGS IN THE OFFING - Financial Products - DOW JONES & COMPANY, INC.; *pg.* 1637, *pg.* 1225
OFFICE - Office Applications Software - MICROSOFT CORPORATION; *pg.* 435, *pg.* 1824
OFFICE BLOCK - Electronic Components - MOLEX INCORPORATED; *pg.* 655, *pg.* 628
OFFICE DATA - Computer Accessories - SMEAD MANUFACTURING COMPANY; *pg.* 470, *pg.* 926
THE OFFICE ENVIRONMENT COMPANY - Slogan - STEELCASE INC.; *pg.* 475, *pg.* 889
OFFICE-IN-A-BOX - Furniture - HERMAN MILLER, INC.; *pg.* 926, *pg.* 913
OFFICE-IN-A-MINUTE - Furniture - HERMAN MILLER, INC.; *pg.* 926, *pg.* 913
OFFICE INTELLIGENCE - Software - MICROSTRATEGY, INC.; *pg.* 1266, *pg.* 1809
OFFICE MATE - Freestanding Footrest - IAC INDUSTRIES,

INC.; *pg.* 929, *pg.* 48
OFFICE MEDIC - Software - CARDIAC SCIENCE CORPORATION; *pg.* 1512, *pg.* 1897
OFFICE MOBILE - Software - MICROSOFT CORPORATION; *pg.* 435, *pg.* 1824
OFFICE ONLINE - Software - MICROSOFT CORPORATION; *pg.* 435, *pg.* 1824
OFFICE REVOLUTION - Furniture - BUSH INDUSTRIES INC.; *pg.* 919, *pg.* 1170
OFFICE THEATER - Computer Equipment - VIEWSONIC CORPORATION; *pg.* 489, *pg.* 303
OFFICEBRIDGE - Facsimile Equipment - MURATEC AMERICA, INC.; *pg.* 443, *pg.* 1733
OFFICECARE - Orthopedic Product - DJO INCORPORATED; *pg.* 1524, *pg.* 302
OFFICEESSENTIALS - Software - SKILLSOFT PLC; *pg.* 470, *pg.* 1037
OFFICEGARDEN - Furniture - HAWORTH, INC.; *pg.* 402, *pg.* 891
OFFICEMATE - Mini C-Arm - HOLOGIC, INC.; *pg.* 1410, *pg.* 784
OFFICEMATE - Software - MARCHON EYEWEAR, INC.; *pg.* 1421, *pg.* 1180
OFFICEPACS - Software - STRYKER CORPORATION; *pg.* 1598, *pg.* 894
OFFICERIGHT - Folder - PITNEY BOWES INC.; *pg.* 454, *pg.* 376
OFFICETEAM - Specialized Temporary Administrative Support Staffing - ROBERT HALF INTERNATIONAL INC.; *pg.* 462, *pg.* 145
THE OFFICIAL JOANN - Online Store - JO-ANN STORES LLC; *pg.* 696, *pg.* 1455
OFFICIAL-KNOW-IT-ALL-GUIDE - Publisher - FREDERICK FELL PUBLISHERS, INC.; *pg.* 1643, *pg.* 431
OFFICIAL NHL - Sport Product - FRANKLIN SPORTS, INC.; *pg.* 1834, *pg.* 847
OFFICIAL OUTFITTERS OF THE WEST - Farm & Ranch Supplies Catalog - RUSH ENTERPRISES INC.; *pg.* 189, *pg.* 1728
OFFICIAL SCRABBLE PLAYERS' DICTIONARY - Publication - FRANKLIN ELECTRONIC PUBLISHERS, INC.; *pg.* 398, *pg.* 1048
OFFICIAL VISITORS GUIDE - Promotional Guide - SARASOTA CONVENTION & VISITORS BUREAU; *pg.* 1005, *pg.* 467
OFFLINE FOLDER WIZARD - Software - DELL SOFTWARE; *pg.* 385, *pg.* 40
OFFLINE RT - Software Feature - APPLE INC.; *pg.* 350, *pg.* 73
OFFSHORE - Eyewear - MAUI JIM, INC.; *pg.* 9, *pg.* 651
OFFSHORE - Door Lock - SOUTHCO, INC.; *pg.* 1063, *pg.* 1522
OFK - Fiber Optics - CHANNELL COMMERCIAL CORP.; *pg.* 1870, *pg.* 291
OFMS - Fiber Optic Component - OPLINK COMMUNICATIONS, INC.; *pg.* 660, *pg.* 91
OFMS 1X4 - Switch - OPLINK COMMUNICATIONS, INC.; *pg.* 660, *pg.* 91
OFMS 1X8 - Switch - OPLINK COMMUNICATIONS, INC.; *pg.* 660, *pg.* 91
OFMS CUSTOM - Switch - OPLINK COMMUNICATIONS, INC.; *pg.* 660, *pg.* 91
OFMS FULL 2X2 - Switch - OPLINK COMMUNICATIONS, INC.; *pg.* 660, *pg.* 91
OFMS MINI (1:8) - Switch - OPLINK COMMUNICATIONS, INC.; *pg.* 660, *pg.* 91
OFMS MINI 1X4 - Switch - OPLINK COMMUNICATIONS, INC.; *pg.* 660, *pg.* 91
OFMS MINI 1X8 - Switch - OPLINK COMMUNICATIONS, INC.; *pg.* 660, *pg.* 91
OFMS MULTI-MODE - Switch - OPLINK COMMUNICATIONS, INC.; *pg.* 660, *pg.* 91
OFMS NET-READY 1+1 - Switch - OPLINK COMMUNICATIONS, INC.; *pg.* 660, *pg.* 91
OFMS NET-READY (1:1) - Switch - OPLINK COMMUNICATIONS, INC.; *pg.* 660, *pg.* 91
OFMS SINGLE MODE - Fiber Optic Component - OPLINK COMMUNICATIONS, INC.; *pg.* 660, *pg.* 91
OFMS ULTRA-MINI - Switch - OPLINK COMMUNICATIONS, INC.; *pg.* 660, *pg.* 91
OG&E ELECTRIC SERVICES - Registered Tradename - OGE ENERGY CORP.; *pg.* 1948, *pg.* 1486
OGASTRO - Proton Pump Inhibitor Drug - ABBOTT LABORATORIES; *pg.* 1484, *pg.* 551
OGURA - Cutter - HOUGEN MANUFACTURING INC.; *pg.* 1347, *pg.* 908
OGV - Wrenching Machine - SK HAND TOOL CORPORATION; *pg.* 1062, *pg.* 663
OH BABY! BY MOTHERHOOD - Maternity Apparel - DESTINATION MATERNITY CORPORATION; *pg.* 23, *pg.* 1563
OH HENRY! - Chocolate Bar - THE HERSHEY CO.; *pg.* 1855, *pg.* 1538
OH HENRY - Candy Bar - NESTLE USA, INC.; *pg.* 883, *pg.* 96
OH2 - Lawn & Garden Product - THE SCOTTS MIRACLE-GRO COMPANY; *pg.* 1799, *pg.* 1459
OHANA - Soft Drink - NATIONAL BEVERAGE CORP.; *pg.* 257, *pg.* 425
O'HARE & NAILS LOOK GREAT - Nail Care Product - OPI PRODUCTS INC.; *pg.* 518, *pg.* 167
OHAUS - Lab Science Material - CAROLINA BIOLOGICAL SUPPLY COMPANY; *pg.* 1513, *pg.* 1359
OHAUS - Demonstration Spring Scale - SCHOOL-TECH, INC.; *pg.* 1844, *pg.* 866
OHIO - Brush - THE WOOSTER BRUSH COMPANY; *pg.* 1450, *pg.* 1482
OHIO BRASS - Power Systems - HUBBELL INCORPORATED; *pg.* 1299, *pg.* 370
OHIO BUSINESS MAGAZINE - Showcasing Ohio's Business Sectors - GREAT LAKES PUBLISHING COMPANY; *pg.* 1646, *pg.* 1431
OHIO ENTREPRENEUR - Great Startup Businesses in Ohio - GREAT LAKES PUBLISHING COMPANY; *pg.* 1646, *pg.* 1431
OHIO MAGAZINE - Magazine - GREAT LAKES PUBLISHING COMPANY; *pg.* 1646, *pg.* 1431
OHM-O-TONE - Audio Indicators - OHMITE MANUFACTURING COMPANY; *pg.* 660, *pg.* 553
OHM-RANGER - Portable Resistance Selector - OHMITE MANUFACTURING COMPANY; *pg.* 660, *pg.* 553
OHMALOY - Material & Alloy - ALLEGHENY TECHNOLOGIES INCORPORATED; *pg.* 66, *pg.* 1572
OHMEDA - Coupler - ALLIED HEALTHCARE PRODUCTS, INC.; *pg.* 1491, *pg.* 990
OHMEGA-PLY - Laser System - GSI GROUP INC.; *pg.* 1415, *pg.* 784
OHMICONE - Wirewound Resistor - OHMITE MANUFACTURING COMPANY; *pg.* 660, *pg.* 553
OH!PAQUE - Paper Products - BOISE CASCADE HOLDINGS, L.L.C.; *pg.* 1453, *pg.* 546
OIA - Pharmaceutical Product - ALERE INC.; *pg.* 1488, *pg.* 849
OIASYS - Pharmaceutical Product - ALERE INC.; *pg.* 1488, *pg.* 849
OIKOS - Yogurt - THE DANNON COMPANY, INC.; *pg.* 851, *pg.* 1351
OIL & GAS TECHNOLOGY - Trade Journal - GULF PUBLISHING COMPANY; *pg.* 1646, *pg.* 1707
OIL-AWAY - Insect Pest Control Product - GARDENS ALIVE!, INC.; *pg.* 1796, *pg.* 693
OIL BOOM - Specialty Products - COOLEY GROUP, INC.; *pg.* 691, *pg.* 1603
OIL-DRI - Floor Absorbent - OIL-DRI CORPORATION OF AMERICA; *pg.* 1480, *pg.* 586
OIL KING - Used Oil - GRACO, INC.; *pg.* 1342, *pg.* 935
OIL-N-WICK - Insecticide - KENT NUTRITION GROUP; *pg.* 1477, *pg.* 710
OIL OF LIFE - Body Wash - BLUE CROSS LABORATORIES; *pg.* 326, *pg.* 277
OIL-ONLY 4 IN 1 - Absorbent - SAFETY-KLEEN HOLDCO, INC.; *pg.* 1180, *pg.* 1734
OIL SAFE - Oil Dispensing Device - TRICO MFG. CORP.; *pg.* 219, *pg.* 1886
OIL TAINER - Storage Tank for Used Oil - CHEM-TAINER INDUSTRIES, INC.; *pg.* 1455, *pg.* 1349
OIL-TITE! - Oil Drain Plugs & Gaskets - DORMAN PRODUCTS, INC.; *pg.* 204, *pg.* 1522
OILACE - Used Oil - GRACO, INC.; *pg.* 1342, *pg.* 935
OILDRAULIC - Automotive Lifts - ROTARY LIFT; *pg.* 216, *pg.* 694
OILSPIN - Water Separation Product - CAMERON INTERNATIONAL; *pg.* 1151, *pg.* 1702
OIME - Drilling Mud Pumps & Equipment - PARKER DRILLING COMPANY; *pg.* 982, *pg.* 1712
OIXSG - Electronic Component - OPLINK COMMUNICATIONS, INC.; *pg.* 660, *pg.* 91
OJK - Fiber Optics - CHANNELL COMMERCIAL CORP.; *pg.* 1870, *pg.* 291
OJON - Skin Care Product - THE ESTEE LAUDER COMPANIES INC.; *pg.* 508, *pg.* 1229
OK! - News Source - AMERICAN MEDIA, INC.; *pg.* 1615, *pg.* 410
O.K. - Indicator Strip - PROPPER MANUFACTURING COMPANY, INC.; *pg.* 1586, *pg.* 1175
OK! MAGAZINE - Celebrity News Magazine - SPINMEDIA; *pg.* 1282, *pg.* 104
O.K. STRIPS - Sterilization Products - PROPPER MANUFACTURING COMPANY, INC.; *pg.* 1586, *pg.* 1175
OKA - Milk & Cheese Products - AGROPUR COOPERATIVE; *pg.* 836, *pg.* 1950
OKLAHOMA - Fabric - NEMSCHOFF, INC.; *pg.* 936, *pg.* 1890
OKLAHOMA TODAY MAGAZINE - Magazine - OKLAHOMA TOURISM & RECREATION DEPARTMENT; *pg.* 1003, *pg.* 1487
OKO - Industrial Oils - ARCHER-DANIELS-MIDLAND COMPANY; *pg.* 825, *pg.* 565
OKOBON - Electrical Wire & Cable - THE OKONITE COMPANY; *pg.* 1302, *pg.* 1113
OKOBUS - Electrical Wire & Cable - THE OKONITE COMPANY; *pg.* 1302, *pg.* 1113
OKOCLAD - Electrical Wire & Cable - THE OKONITE COMPANY; *pg.* 1302, *pg.* 1113
OKOCLEAR TP - Electrical Wire & Cable - THE OKONITE COMPANY; *pg.* 1302, *pg.* 1113
OKOCLEAR TS - Electrical Wire & Cable - THE OKONITE COMPANY; *pg.* 1302, *pg.* 1113
OKOCORD - Electrical Wire & Cable - THE OKONITE COMPANY; *pg.* 1302, *pg.* 1113
OKOGUARD - Electrical Wire & Cable - THE OKONITE COMPANY; *pg.* 1302, *pg.* 1113
OKOLENE - Electrical Wire & Cable - THE OKONITE COMPANY; *pg.* 1302, *pg.* 1113
OKOLENE-OKOSEAL - Electrical Wire & Cable - THE OKONITE COMPANY; *pg.* 1302, *pg.* 1113
OKOLON - Electrical Wire & Cable - THE OKONITE COMPANY; *pg.* 1302, *pg.* 1113
OKONITE - High Voltage Cable - THE OKONITE COMPANY; *pg.* 1302, *pg.* 1113
OKONITE FMR - Power & Control Cables - THE OKONITE COMPANY; *pg.* 1302, *pg.* 1113
OKONITE-OKOCLEAR - Electrical Wire & Cable - THE OKONITE COMPANY; *pg.* 1302, *pg.* 1113
OKONITE-OKOLON - Electrical Wire & Cable - THE OKONITE COMPANY; *pg.* 1302, *pg.* 1113
OKOPACT - Electrical Wire & Cable - THE OKONITE COMPANY; *pg.* 1302, *pg.* 1113
OKOPRENE - Electrical Wire & Cable - THE OKONITE COMPANY; *pg.* 1302, *pg.* 1113
OKOSEAL - Electrical Wire & Cable - THE OKONITE COMPANY; *pg.* 1302, *pg.* 1113
OKOSHEATH - Electrical Wire & Cable - THE OKONITE COMPANY; *pg.* 1302, *pg.* 1113
OKOSHEATH-CP - Electrical Wire & Cable - THE OKONITE COMPANY; *pg.* 1302, *pg.* 1113
OKOTHERM - Electrical Wire & Cable - THE OKONITE COMPANY; *pg.* 1302, *pg.* 1113
OKOZEL - Electrical Wire & Cable - THE OKONITE COMPANY; *pg.* 1302, *pg.* 1113
OKTOBERFEST - Seasonal Beer - THE BROOKLYN BREWERY; *pg.* 239, *pg.* 1145
OKTOBERFEST - Video Game - INTERNATIONAL GAME TECHNOLOGY; *pg.* 957, *pg.* 1024
OKTOBERFEST - Food Product - JOHNSONVILLE SAUSAGE, LLC; *pg.* 867, *pg.* 1894
OKTOBERFEST - Event - MAKE-A-WISH FOUNDATION OF GREATER LOS ANGELES; *pg.* 146, *pg.* 136
OKTOBERFEST - Food Product - MAPLE LEAF CONSUMER FOODS; *pg.* 875, *pg.* 1922
OKTOBERFEST - Beverage - SPRECHER BREWING COMPANY; *pg.* 265, *pg.* 1858
OL' MADRID 2 - Fan - CRAFTMADE INTERNATIONAL, INC.; *pg.* 1295, *pg.* 1670
OL' ROY - Dog Food - WAL-MART STORES, INC.; *pg.* 1790, *pg.* 29
OL1000 - Orthopedic Product - DJO INCORPORATED; *pg.* 1524, *pg.* 302
OLANA - Fabric - NEMSCHOFF, INC.; *pg.* 936, *pg.* 1890
OLAP - Software - ENVIRONMENTAL SYSTEMS RESEARCH INSTITUTE INC.; *pg.* 393, *pg.* 188
OLAP - Software - SAS INSTITUTE INC.; *pg.* 466, *pg.* 1361
OLAP SERVICES - Software - MICROSTRATEGY, INC.; *pg.* 1266, *pg.* 1809
OLAY - Personal & Beauty Product - THE PROCTER &

First page reference indicates Business Class Edition
Second page reference indicates Geographic Edition

GAMBLE COMPANY; *pg.* 1129, *pg.* 1418
OLAY DEFINITY - Anti-Aging Products - THE PROCTER & GAMBLE COMPANY; *pg.* 1129, *pg.* 1418
OLAY REGENERIST - Skincare - THE PROCTER & GAMBLE COMPANY; *pg.* 1129, *pg.* 1418
OLD AMERICAN DUNGAREES - Apparel & Accessories - LUCKY BRAND DUNGAREES, INC.; *pg.* 29, *pg.* 301
OLD ARMY - Cap & Ball Revolver - STURM, RUGER & COMPANY, INC.; *pg.* 1846, *pg.* 371
OLD AXE - Jeanswear - V.F. CORPORATION; *pg.* 34, *pg.* 1376
OLD BAY - Seasoning - MCCORMICK & COMPANY, INCORPORATED; *pg.* 1027, *pg.* 779
OLD BLUE - Laundry Starch - ADCO, INC.; *pg.* 325, *pg.* 482
OLD BROOKVILLE - Wine - BANFI VINTNERS; *pg.* 1957, *pg.* 1161
OLD CHARTER - Bourbon - SAZERAC COMPANY, INC.; *pg.* 1969, *pg.* 745
OLD CHICAGO - Pasta, Pizza & Beer - ROCK BOTTOM RESTAURANTS, INC.; *pg.* 1748, *pg.* 334
OLD COUNTRY BUFFET - Restaurants - OVATION BRANDS; *pg.* 1743, *pg.* 921
OLD CROW - Bourbon - JIM BEAM BRANDS CO.; *pg.* 1965, *pg.* 601
OLD DUTCH - Food Products - OLD DUTCH FOODS, INC.; *pg.* 888, *pg.* 956
OLD DUTCH COCOA - 22-24% Cocoa Butter Content Cocoa - GUITTARD CHOCOLATE COMPANY; *pg.* 1855, *pg.* 55
OLD EL PASO - Mexican Food Products - GENERAL MILLS, INC.; *pg.* 828, *pg.* 933
OLD ENGLISH - Furniture Polish - RECKITT BENCKISER INC.; *pg.* 1136, *pg.* 1105
OLD ENGLISH (PATTERN 124) - Patterned Glass - AGC GLASS NORTH AMERICA, INC.; *pg.* 65, *pg.* 482
THE OLD FARMER'S ALMANAC - Annual Almanac - YANKEE PUBLISHING INC.; *pg.* 1703, *pg.* 1033
OLD FASHIONED - Pudding - KOZY SHACK INC.; *pg.* 869, *pg.* 1167
OLD FASHIONED LEMONADE - Soft Drink - AUNTIE ANNE'S INC.; *pg.* 1715, *pg.* 1546
OLD-FASHIONED LOCOUM - Confection - LIBERTY ORCHARDS CO., INC.; *pg.* 1857, *pg.* 1819
OLD FASHIONED WAY - Potatoes - J.R. SIMPLOT COMPANY; *pg.* 867, *pg.* 547
OLD FITZGERALD - Bourbon - HEAVEN HILL DISTILLERIES, INC.; *pg.* 1964, *pg.* 725
OLD FORESTER - Bourbon Whiskey - BROWN-FORMAN CORPORATION; *pg.* 1958, *pg.* 732
OLD GRAND DAD - Bourbon - JIM BEAM BRANDS CO.; *pg.* 1965, *pg.* 601
OLD HAVANA - Video Game - INTERNATIONAL GAME TECHNOLOGY; *pg.* 957, *pg.* 1024
OLD LONDON - Food Products - NONNI'S FOOD COMPANY INC.; *pg.* 886, *pg.* 1490
OLD MASTERS Paint & Coating - DIAMOND VOGEL PAINT, INC.; *pg.* 1441, *pg.* 710
OLD MCCALL - Bourbon - MONTEBELLO BRANDS INC.; *pg.* 1967, *pg.* 758
OLD MCDONALD HAD A FARM - Toy & Game - HASBRO, INC.; *pg.* 954, *pg.* 1603
OLD MILL - Oats - SMUCKER FOODS OF CANADA CO.; *pg.* 896, *pg.* 1924
OLD MILWAUKEE - Beer - PABST BREWING COMPANY; *pg.* 258, *pg.* 137
OLD NATIONAL BANK - Banking Services - OLD NATIONAL BANCORP; *pg.* 789, *pg.* 679
OLD NATIONAL ONLINE - Internet Banking Service - OLD NATIONAL BANCORP; *pg.* 789, *pg.* 679
OLD NATIONAL REACH - Banking Services - OLD NATIONAL BANCORP; *pg.* 789, *pg.* 679
OLD NAVY - Retail Clothing Store - THE GAP, INC.; *pg.* 1770, *pg.* 218
OLD NO. 7 - Whiskey - JACK DANIEL'S DISTILLERY; *pg.* 1964, *pg.* 1640
OLD OVERHOLT - Bourbon - JIM BEAM BRANDS CO.; *pg.* 1965, *pg.* 601
OLD PALM GOLF CLUB - Residential Community Name - WCI COMMUNITIES, INC.; *pg.* 1118, *pg.* 414
OLD PUEBLO TRADERS - Online Apparel Site - ASCENA RETAIL GROUP, INC.; *pg.* 18, *pg.* 1081
OLD RED BARN - Botanical Salves & Sun Protection Products - WATKINS INCORPORATED; *pg.* 909, *pg.* 967
OLD SALEM - Museum - OLD SALEM, INCORPORATED; *pg.* 572, *pg.* 1395
THE OLD SALEM CHILDREN'S MUSEUM - Museum - OLD SALEM, INCORPORATED; *pg.* 572, *pg.* 1395
OLD SALT - Crab Cakes, Shrimp & Breaded Calamari - SEA WATCH INTERNATIONAL, LTD.; *pg.* 895, *pg.* 769
OLD SCHOOL - Turfgrass Seed Mixture - CROSMAN SEED CORPORATION; *pg.* 1794, *pg.* 1156
OLD SKOOL - Footwear - VANS, INC.; *pg.* 1821, *pg.* 76
OLD SKULL - Apparel - VANS, INC.; *pg.* 1821, *pg.* 76
OLD SMOKEHOUSE - Meat Products - HORMEL FOODS CORPORATION; *pg.* 863, *pg.* 915
OLD SPICE - Personal Care Products - THE PROCTER & GAMBLE COMPANY; *pg.* 1129, *pg.* 1418
OLD STYLE - Beer - PABST BREWING COMPANY; *pg.* 258, *pg.* 137
OLD TAYLOR - Twist Tobacco - AMERICAN SNUFF COMPANY; *pg.* 1893, *pg.* 1641
OLD TIME - Foods - ROUNDY'S SUPERMARKETS INC.; *pg.* 1032, *pg.* 1880
OLD TIME BODY & AGE - Flavoring - DAVID MICHAEL & CO. INC.; *pg.* 852, *pg.* 1563
OLD TOWN - Canoes & Kayaks - JOHNSON OUTDOORS INC.; *pg.* 1837, *pg.* 1888
OLD TYME - Bread - SCHMIDT BAKING CO., INC.; *pg.* 894, *pg.* 759
OLD WISCONSIN - Sausage & Cheese - CARL BUDDIG & COMPANY; *pg.* 846, *pg.* 619
OLD WORLD - Sauce - GOLD PURE FOOD PRODUCTS CO., INC.; *pg.* 858, *pg.* 1166
OLD WORLD PREMIUM - Processed Meats - BAR-S FOODS CO.; *pg.* 839, *pg.* 15
OLD WORLD TRADITION - Tagline - THE GREAT LAKES CHEESE CO., INC.; *pg.* 859, *pg.* 1455
OLDE BROOKLYN - Soda - WHITE ROCK PRODUCTS CORP.; *pg.* 266, *pg.* 1355
OLDE CAPE COD - Salad Dressings, Soups, Chowders, Jams, Jellies, Frozen Seafood Products - CAINS FOODS, L.P.; *pg.* 843, *pg.* 784
OLDE ENGLISH 800 MALT LIQUOR - Malt Liquor - MILLERCOORS; *pg.* 254, *pg.* 1877
OLDE ENGLISH HG800 - Malt Liquor - MILLERCOORS; *pg.* 254, *pg.* 1877
OLDE ENGLISH HG800 7.5 - Malt Liquor - MILLERCOORS; *pg.* 254, *pg.* 1877
OLDE PHILADELPHIA - Beer - THE LION BREWERY, INC.; *pg.* 254, *pg.* 1594
OLDE PHILADELPHIA BLACK CHERRY - Black Cherry Soda - THE LION BREWERY, INC.; *pg.* 254, *pg.* 1594
OLDE PHILADELPHIA CREAM - Cream Soda - THE LION BREWERY, INC.; *pg.* 254, *pg.* 1594
OLDE PHILADELPHIA DIET CREAM - Diet Cream Soda - THE LION BREWERY, INC.; *pg.* 254, *pg.* 1594
OLDE PHILADELPHIA GRAPE - Grape Soda - THE LION BREWERY, INC.; *pg.* 254, *pg.* 1594
OLDE PHILADELPHIA ORANGE CREAM - Cream Soda - THE LION BREWERY, INC.; *pg.* 254, *pg.* 1594
OLDE PROVIDENCE - Vinyl Siding - NORTEK, INC.; *pg.* 100, *pg.* 1607
OLDE TOWNE - Ceramic Tile - SUMMITVILLE TILES, INC.; *pg.* 113, *pg.* 1475
OLDE TYME - Pretzels - SNYDER'S OF HANOVER, INC.; *pg.* 1862, *pg.* 1536
OLDE TYME STICKS - Snacks - SNYDER'S OF HANOVER, INC.; *pg.* 1862, *pg.* 1536
OLDE WORLD - Health Supplement - GARDEN OF LIFE, INC.; *pg.* 1532, *pg.* 478
OLDHAM - Battery - ENERSYS INC.; *pg.* 1334, *pg.* 1584
OLE FOODS - Food Products - BROOKSHIRE GROCERY COMPANY; *pg.* 1016, *pg.* 1748
OLE SOUTH - Pork Sausage - WILLIAMS SAUSAGE CO., INC.; *pg.* 910, *pg.* 1656
OLE TEQUILA - Tequila - SAZERAC COMPANY, INC.; *pg.* 1969, *pg.* 745
OLEFLEX - Catalytic Dehydrogenation Technology for the Production of Light Olefins - UOP LLC; *pg.* 1386, *pg.* 606
OLEG CASSINI - Women's Clothing & Accessories - OLEG CASSINI, INC.; *pg.* 30, *pg.* 1274
OLEOGARD - Automotive Vent - W.L. GORE & ASSOCIATES, INC.; *pg.* 122, *pg.* 388
OLEVIA - Consumer Electronics - EMERSON RADIO CORP.; *pg.* 636, *pg.* 1087
OLFA - Kitchen Houseware Product - WORLD KITCHEN LLC; *pg.* 1141, *pg.* 657
OLICLINOMEL - Healthcare Product - BAXTER INTERNATIONAL INC.; *pg.* 1499, *pg.* 599
OLIGATOR - DNA Synthesis System - ILLUMINA, INC.; *pg.* 412, *pg.* 203
OLIGGO-FIBER - Inulin - CARGILL, INC.; *pg.* 845, *pg.* 965
OLIGGO-FIBER - Range of Natural Fibers - CARGILL LIMITED; *pg.* 1475, *pg.* 1914
OLIGOFECTAMINE - Molecular Biology Product - THERMO FISHER SCIENTIFIC INC.; *pg.* 1602, *pg.* 61
OLIGOPERFECT - Oligonucleotide Primer Designer - THERMO FISHER SCIENTIFIC INC.; *pg.* 1602, *pg.* 61
OLIGOPURE - Robotic Product - HAMILTON CO., INC.; *pg.* 1415, *pg.* 1031
OLIMPIJA - Beverages - THE COCA-COLA COMPANY; *pg.* 240, *pg.* 493
OLIN - Chemicals - OLIN CORPORATION; *pg.* 1176, *pg.* 976
OLINA - Cooking Oil - CARGILL LIMITED; *pg.* 1475, *pg.* 1914
OLIO - Carpet - INTERFACE, INC.; *pg.* 695, *pg.* 512
OLIVE GARDEN - Restaurant Chain - DARDEN RESTAURANTS, INC.; *pg.* 1724, *pg.* 453
OLIVER - Furniture - NEMSCHOFF, INC.; *pg.* 936, *pg.* 1890
OLIVER - Precure & Mold Cure Tread Rubber - OLIVER RUBBER COMPANY; *pg.* 1887, *pg.* 1358
OLIVEXTRA PLUS - Olive Oil - POMPEIAN, INC.; *pg.* 890, *pg.* 759
OLIVIA - Bedding - CROSCILL, INC.; *pg.* 1122, *pg.* 1220
OLIVIA - Furniture - ETHAN ALLEN INTERIORS INC.; *pg.* 924, *pg.* 343
OLIVIA - Furniture - NEMSCHOFF, INC.; *pg.* 936, *pg.* 1890
OLIVIER - Fan - CRAFTMADE INTERNATIONAL, INC.; *pg.* 1295, *pg.* 1670
OLIVIERI - Food Product - MAPLE LEAF FOODS INC.; *pg.* 875, *pg.* 1927
OLIVINIA - Food Product - PARMALAT CANADA INC.; *pg.* 888, *pg.* 1941
OLIVIO - Fabric - NEMSCHOFF, INC.; *pg.* 936, *pg.* 1890
OLNET - Supercomputing System - CRAY INC.; *pg.* 380, *pg.* 1834
OLYMPIA - Furniture - JASPER GROUP; *pg.* 930, *pg.* 691
OLYMPIA - Flatware - ONEIDA LTD; *pg.* 1129, *pg.* 1318
OLYMPIA - Beer - PABST BREWING COMPANY; *pg.* 258, *pg.* 137
OLYMPIA - Athletic Equip. - SCHOOL-TECH, INC.; *pg.* 1844, *pg.* 866
OLYMPIA BAY - Furniture - BASSETT FURNITURE INDUSTRIES, INCORPORATED; *pg.* 916, *pg.* 1776
OLYMPIA BBQ LIGHT - Light - BARBEQUES GALORE, INC.; *pg.* 51, *pg.* 173
OLYMPIAD - Seating Product - HUSSEY SEATING CO.; *pg.* 929, *pg.* 751
OLYMPIAN - Car Seat - DOREL JUVENILE GROUP, INC.; *pg.* 923, *pg.* 676
OLYMPIAN - Air Filters, Regulators & Lubricators - NORGREN, INC.; *pg.* 231, *pg.* 333
OLYMPIC - Organic Products - AGROPUR COOPERATIVE; *pg.* 836, *pg.* 1950
OLYMPIC - Binocular - LEUPOLD & STEVENS, INC.; *pg.* 1420, *pg.* 1492
OLYMPIC - Paint Product - PPG INDUSTRIES, INC.; *pg.* 1445, *pg.* 1579
OLYMPIC OVERCOAT - Wood Stains - PPG INDUSTRIES, INC.; *pg.* 1445, *pg.* 1579
OLYMPIC WEATHERSCREEN - Wood Stains & Paints - PPG INDUSTRIES, INC.; *pg.* 1445, *pg.* 1579
OLYMPUS - Laboratory Equipment - LECO CORPORATION; *pg.* 1355, *pg.* 906
OLYMPUS - Fabric - NEMSCHOFF, INC.; *pg.* 936, *pg.* 1890
OLYMPUS - Medical & Clinical Instruments, 35mm Cameras - OLYMPUS AMERICA INC.; *pg.* 1425, *pg.* 1521
OLYMPUS - Sorting System - PITNEY BOWES INC.; *pg.* 454, *pg.* 376
OLYMPUS II - Sorters - PITNEY BOWES INC.; *pg.* 454, *pg.* 376
OLYMPUS-SOC - Software System - MENTOR GRAPHICS CORPORATION; *pg.* 432, *pg.* 1510
OM - Necklace - HUGGER MUGGER YOGA PRODUCTS LLC; *pg.* 1836, *pg.* 1758
OM - Tea - STARBUCKS CORPORATION; *pg.* 897, *pg.* 1840
OM 5 - Fluid Handling System - GRACO, INC.; *pg.* 1342, *pg.* 935
OM 5000 - Fluid Handling System - GRACO, INC.; *pg.* 1342, *pg.* 935
OM SYSTEM - 35mm SLR Camera System - OLYMPUS AMERICA INC.; *pg.* 1425, *pg.* 1521
OMAC - Character - DC COMICS, INC.; *pg.* 1633, *pg.* 1221
OMAHA STEAKHOUSE - Restaurant - OMAHA STEAKS INTERNATIONAL, INC.; *pg.* 1780, *pg.* 1017
OMAHA STEAKS - Beef Products - OMAHA STEAKS

INTERNATIONAL, INC.; pg. 1780, pg. 1017

OMAHA STEAKS WINE CLUB - Wine Club - OMAHA STEAKS INTERNATIONAL, INC.; pg. 1780, pg. 1017

OMAHA XS - Baseball Bat - HILLERICH & BRADSBY CO., INC.; pg. 1836, pg. 576

OMAHA'S HENRY DOORLY ZOO - Zoo - OMAHA ZOOLOGICAL SOCIETY; pg. 572, pg. 1017

OMALON - Bedding Foam - CARPENTER CO.; pg. 920, pg. 1801

OMAP - Platform - TEXAS INSTRUMENTS INCORPORATED; pg. 679, pg. 1688

OMAP-VOX - Semiconductors - TEXAS INSTRUMENTS INCORPORATED; pg. 679, pg. 1688

OMAPI - Licensing Service - TEXAS INSTRUMENTS INCORPORATED; pg. 679, pg. 1688

OMASTEAK - Meat - OMAHA STEAKS INTERNATIONAL, INC.; pg. 1780, pg. 1017

OMBRE - Apparel - BEBE STORES, INC.; pg. 19, pg. 49

OMDIRECT - Online Order Management System - OWENS & MINOR, INC.; pg. 1579, pg. 1795

OMEGA - Little Cigars - ALTADIS USA, INC.; pg. 1893, pg. 423

OMEGA - Scoreboard & Sports Product - DAKTRONICS, INC.; pg. 633, pg. 1624

OMEGA - Chemical Product - FINE ORGANICS CORPORATION; pg. 330, pg. 1052

OMEGA - Software - GERBER SCIENTIFIC, INC.; pg. 1414, pg. 380

OMEGA - Joggers - HABAND COMPANY, INC.; pg. 1772, pg. 1099

OMEGA - Polyethylene Banner Material - HOLLISTON LLC; pg. 1460, pg. 1630

OMEGA - Cabinetry - MASTERBRAND CABINETS, INC.; pg. 96, pg. 692

OMEGA - Vitamin & Dietary Supplement - NATROL, INC.; pg. 1570, pg. 64

OMEGA - Membrane Disc Filter - PALL CORPORATION; pg. 232, pg. 1323

OMEGA - Lighting Fixture & Control - PHILIPS LIGHTING; pg. 1303, pg. 806

OMEGA - Surgical & Medical Product - STRYKER CORPORATION; pg. 1598, pg. 894

OMEGA - Remote Control Device - UNIVERSAL ELECTRONICS, INC.; pg. 683, pg. 262

OMEGA - Spincast - ZEBCO; pg. 1848, pg. 1491

OMEGA 3 BASIC - Health Food Product - DESIGNING HEALTH, INC.; pg. 1523, pg. 299

OMEGA BOOST ONE - Nutritional Product - RBC LIFE SCIENCES, INC.; pg. 1588, pg. 1723

OMEGA CABINETRY - Hardware - FORTUNE BRANDS HOME & SECURITY, INC.; pg. 55, pg. 600

OMEGA GOLD - Supplement & Food Product - NEW EARTH LIFE SCIENCES, INC.; pg. 1573, pg. 1499

OMEGA HMJ - Pharmaceutical Product - ALERE INC.; pg. 1488, pg. 849

OMEGA LASKA - Health Care Product - HEALTH PRODUCTS CORPORATION; pg. 1540, pg. 1356

OMEGA MULTI - Health System Product - LANELABS USA INC.; pg. 1554, pg. 1128

OMEGA ONE - Pet Product - PETSMART, INC.; pg. 1481, pg. 18

OMEGA PM - Herbal Cleanse - GARDEN OF LIFE, INC.; pg. 1532, pg. 478

OMEGA SEED - Nutritional Product - NUTRACEUTICAL INTERNATIONAL CORPORATION; pg. 1576, pg. 1753

OMEGA SUN - Supplement & Food Product - NEW EARTH LIFE SCIENCES, INC.; pg. 1573, pg. 1499

OMEGAFLEX - Gas Piping Systems - OMEGA FLEX, INC.; pg. 982, pg. 1532

OMEGATIN - Horse Feeds - KENT NUTRITION GROUP; pg. 1477, pg. 710

OMEGAXANTHIN - Health Supplement - GARDEN OF LIFE, INC.; pg. 1532, pg. 478

OMEGOLD - Antioxidant - LIFEPLUS INTERNATIONAL; pg. 1556, pg. 29

OMI - Dental Instrument - OSTEOMED CORPORATION; pg. 1425, pg. 1658

OMI FIDUCIAL FINDER - Machine Vision System - COGNEX CORPORATION; pg. 1406, pg. 834

OMISSION BEER - Craft Beer Brand - CRAFT BREWERS ALLIANCE, INC; pg. 247, pg. 1502

OMITE - Polymer Product - CHEMTURA CORPORATION; pg. 1152, pg. 355

OMMI - Remote Control Device - UNIVERSAL ELECTRONICS, INC.; pg. 683, pg. 262

OMNABLOC - Chemical Product - OMNOVA SOLUTIONS INC; pg. 1176, pg. 1453

OMNAGLIDE - Carpet Chemicals - OMNOVA SOLUTIONS INC; pg. 1176, pg. 1453

OMNAGLO - Specialty Chemicals - OMNOVA SOLUTIONS INC; pg. 1176, pg. 1453

OMNAPEL - Specialty Chemicals - OMNOVA SOLUTIONS INC; pg. 1176, pg. 1453

OMNARIS - Pharmaceutical Product - SUNOVION PHARMACEUTICALS INC.; pg. 1599, pg. 832

OMNATUF - Chemical Product - OMNOVA SOLUTIONS INC; pg. 1176, pg. 1453

OMNEPHASE - Industrial State Timers & Controls - INTERNATIONAL CONTROLS & MEASUREMENTS CORP.; pg. 1350, pg. 1317

OMNETIME - Industrial State Timers & Controls - INTERNATIONAL CONTROLS & MEASUREMENTS CORP.; pg. 1350, pg. 1317

OMNI - Electrosurgical Devices - ANGIODYNAMICS, INC.; pg. 1495, pg. 1173

OMNI - Furniture - ASHLEY FURNITURE INDUSTRIES, INC.; pg. 914, pg. 1852

OMNI - Airbrushes - BADGER AIR BRUSH COMPANY; pg. 359, pg. 612

OMNI - Furniture Collection - CENTURY FURNITURE INDUSTRIES; pg. 920, pg. 1377

OMNI - Fan - CRAFTMADE INTERNATIONAL, INC.; pg. 1295, pg. 1670

OMNI - Office Furniture - HNI CORPORATION; pg. 927, pg. 709

OMNI - Control Panel - HONEYWELL INTERNATIONAL INC.; pg. 407, pg. 1088

OMNI - Pump - IDEX CORPORATION; pg. 1347, pg. 623

OMNI - Health & Nutrition Product - NOVUS INTERNATIONAL, INC.; pg. 706, pg. 1001

OMNI - Hotel - OMNI HOTELS & RESORTS; pg. 1107, pg. 1685

OMNI - Door Lock - SOUTHCO, INC.; pg. 1063, pg. 1522

OMNI - Software - SUNGARD DATA SYSTEMS INC.; pg. 477, pg. 1592

OMNI - Laser Device - TRIMEDYNE, INC.; pg. 1432, pg. 121

OMNI-100 - Thermal Printer - GSI GROUP INC.; pg. 1415, pg. 784

OMNI 3750 - Hardware - VERIFONE SYSTEMS, INC.; pg. 487, pg. 251

OMNI-BLOK - Fuse Block - LITTELFUSE, INC.; pg. 1301, pg. 580

OMNI-DRY - Apparel - COLUMBIA SPORTSWEAR COMPANY; pg. 1830, pg. 1501

OMNI EXPRESS - Planning & Organization of Meetings for Businesses and Other Organizations - OMNI HOTELS & RESORTS; pg. 1107, pg. 1685

OMNI-FILL - Paint Filling System - SHERWIN-WILLIAMS DIVERSIFIED BRANDS DIVISION; pg. 1448, pg. 1435

OMNI-FLO - Eye & Face Wash - HAWS CORPORATION; pg. 56, pg. 1032

OMNI-FLOW - Medical Device - HOSPIRA, INC.; pg. 1542, pg. 623

OMNI-FLOW 4000 - Medical Device - HOSPIRA, INC.; pg. 1542, pg. 623

OMNI-GRIP - Footwear - COLUMBIA SPORTSWEAR COMPANY; pg. 1830, pg. 1501

OMNI HUNTER - Knife - BUCK KNIVES, INC.; pg. 1828, pg. 550

OMNI INTERNATIONAL - Rental of Commercial Space in a Planned Community - OMNI HOTELS & RESORTS; pg. 1107, pg. 1685

OMNI-KOTE - Paperboard Packaging System - GRAPHIC PACKAGING HOLDING COMPANY; pg. 1459, pg. 509

OMNI-LOK - Fastener - LONG-LOK FASTENERS CORP.; pg. 1053, pg. 1416

OMNI MANUFACTURING - Medical Product - GF HEALTH PRODUCTS, INC.; pg. 1535, pg. 508

OMNI MARKER - Electronic Marker - GREENLEE TEXTRON INC.; pg. 1048, pg. 655

OMNI-MATE - Stored-Energy Operator - S&C ELECTRIC COMPANY; pg. 1305, pg. 589

OMNI ONE - Staffing Firm - GENERAL EMPLOYMENT ENTERPRISES, INC.; pg. 400, pg. 636

OMNI-PAK - Paint Filling System - SHERWIN-WILLIAMS DIVERSIFIED BRANDS DIVISION; pg. 1448, pg. 1435

OMNI-PLUS - Voice & Data System - THOMAS & BETTS CORPORATION; pg. 680, pg. 1646

OMNI POCKET - Door Lock - SOUTHCO, INC.; pg. 1063, pg. 1522

OMNI-PURPOSE - Loudspeaker Mounting Bracket - ATLAS SOUND; pg. 621, pg. 1692

OMNI-RUPTER - Switching System - S&C ELECTRIC COMPANY; pg. 1305, pg. 589

OMNI-SHADE - Sun-Protective Apparel - COLUMBIA SPORTSWEAR COMPANY; pg. 1830, pg. 1501

OMNI-SMOOTH - Personal Care Product - MGP INGREDIENTS, INC.; pg. 877, pg. 714

OMNI SWEEP - Anchor & Plastic Block - CARLISLE FOODSERVICE PRODUCTS INCORPORATED; pg. 1455, pg. 1485

OMNI-TECH - Apparel - COLUMBIA SPORTSWEAR COMPANY; pg. 1830, pg. 1501

OMNI-VENT - Ventilator - ALLIED HEALTHCARE PRODUCTS, INC.; pg. 1491, pg. 990

OMNIAC - Musical Instrument - PEAVEY ELECTRONICS CORPORATION; pg. 662, pg. 970

OMNIBANK - Biopharmaceutical Product - LEXICON PHARMACEUTICALS, INC.; pg. 1555, pg. 1747

OMNIBER - Software - AGILENT TECHNOLOGIES, INC.; pg. 614, pg. 264

OMNIBOX - Plastic Houseware Product - STERILITE CORPORATION; pg. 1138, pg. 848

OMNIBOX - Floor Boxes - WIREMOLD/LEGRAND; pg. 689, pg. 383

OMNIBUYER - Software - OMNICELL INC.; pg. 1578, pg. 161

OMNICARE GERIATRIC PHARMACEUTICAL CARE GUIDELINES - Proprietary Drug Formulary Designed for the Elderly - OMNICARE, INC; pg. 1578, pg. 1418

OMNICEF - Tablet - ABBOTT LABORATORIES; pg. 1484, pg. 551

OMNICELL PHARMACYCENTRAL - Software - OMNICELL INC.; pg. 1578, pg. 161

OMNICENTER - Surgical Services Solutions - OMNICELL INC.; pg. 1578, pg. 161

OMNICLONAL - Pharmaceutical Product - ALERE INC.; pg. 1488, pg. 849

OMNIEXCEL - Reflow Soldering Systems - SPEEDLINE TECHNOLOGIES, INC.; pg. 1378, pg. 823

OMNIFAX - Fax Technology - XEROX CORPORATION; pg. 494, pg. 365

OMNIFIT - Anaerobic Adhesives - HENKEL CORPORATION; pg. 1165, pg. 1535

OMNIFLEX - Medical Product - HOLOGIC, INC.; pg. 1416, pg. 784

OMNIFLEX - Reflow Oven Systems - SPEEDLINE TECHNOLOGIES, INC.; pg. 1378, pg. 823

OMNIFOUNT - Electric-Heated Fountain - RITCHIE INDUSTRIES, INC.; pg. 707, pg. 703

OMNIGATE - Software - OMNICELL INC.; pg. 1578, pg. 161

OMNIGEST - Health & Beauty Product - CHATTEM, INC.; pg. 1515, pg. 1628

OMNIGRID - Packaging System - MOLEX INCORPORATED; pg. 655, pg. 628

OMNIGRID - Brand Rulers - PRYM CONSUMER USA; pg. 698, pg. 1622

OMNIGUARD - Software - SYMANTEC CORPORATION; pg. 478, pg. 161

OMNIISENSE - Medical Instrument - WALLACH SURGICAL DEVICES, INC.; pg. 1436, pg. 381

OMNILINK - Stent System - ABBOTT LABORATORIES; pg. 1484, pg. 551

OMNILINK - Computer Services - OMNI HOTELS & RESORTS; pg. 1107, pg. 1685

OMNILINK - Surface Raceway - THOMAS & BETTS CORPORATION; pg. 680, pg. 1646

OMNILINKRX - Software - OMNICELL INC.; pg. 1578, pg. 161

OMNILUX - Software - IDEALAB, INC.; pg. 1258, pg. 180

OMNIMAP - Inspection System - KLA-TENCOR CORPORATION; pg. 1353, pg. 146

OMNIMARKET - Software - SAS INSTITUTE INC.; pg. 466, pg. 1361

OMNIMAX - Motion Picture Projector - IMAX CORPORATION; pg. 1417, pg. 1926

OMNIMAX - Molecular Biology Product - THERMO FISHER SCIENTIFIC INC.; pg. 1602, pg. 61

OMNIMET - Image Analyzer - BUEHLER, LTD.; pg. 1403, pg. 622

OMNIMIX - Healthcare Testing Product - CEPHEID; pg. 1514, pg. 284

OMNINET - Software - AGILENT TECHNOLOGIES, INC.; pg. 614, pg. 264

OMNINET VERSION 6.0 - Software System - MENTOR

GRAPHICS CORPORATION; *pg.* 432, *pg.* 1510
OMNIPAGE PRO - Scanning & Imaging Software - NUANCE COMMUNICATIONS, INC.; *pg.* 447, *pg.* 806
OMNIPAQUE - Medical Device - GE HEALTHCARE TECHNOLOGIES; *pg.* 1533, *pg.* 1897
OMNIPLACE - Electric Instrument - UNIVERSAL INSTRUMENTS CORPORATION; *pg.* 683, *pg.* 1154
OMNIPRO - Health & Nutrition Product - NOVUS INTERNATIONAL, INC.; *pg.* 706, *pg.* 1001
OMNIPULSE - Air Gun - BOLT TECHNOLOGY CORPORATION; *pg.* 1318, *pg.* 360
OMNIPULSE - Laser Device - TRIMEDYNE, INC.; *pg.* 1432, *pg.* 121
OMNIPULSE JR. - Laser Device - TRIMEDYNE, INC.; *pg.* 1432, *pg.* 121
OMNIPULSE MAX - Laser Device - TRIMEDYNE, INC.; *pg.* 1432, *pg.* 121
OMNIPURE - Chemical Product - SPECTRUM CHEMICALS & LABORATORY PRODUCTS, INC.; *pg.* 1181, *pg.* 94
OMNIROLL - Furniture - AMERICAN LEATHER LP; *pg.* 912, *pg.* 1673
OMNIRX - Software - OMNICELL INC.; *pg.* 1578, *pg.* 161
OMNIS STUDIO - Rapid Application Development Tool - TIGERLOGIC CORPORATION; *pg.* 484, *pg.* 117
OMNISCAN - Medical Device - GE HEALTHCARE TECHNOLOGIES; *pg.* 1533, *pg.* 1897
OMNISENSE - Bradycardia Products - ST. JUDE MEDICAL, INC.; *pg.* 1596, *pg.* 963
OMNISHIELD - Polyurethane Coating - COLUMBIA SPORTSWEAR COMPANY; *pg.* 1830, *pg.* 1501
OMNISHIELD - Catalyst - DOW CHEMICAL; *pg.* 1156, *pg.* 1563
OMNISHUNT - Medical Device - INTEGRA LIFESCIENCES HOLDINGS CORPORATION; *pg.* 1545, *pg.* 1109
OMNISMART - Line Interactive UPS Systems - TRIPPE MANUFACTURING COMPANY; *pg.* 220, *pg.* 592
OMNISOLV - Chemical Product - SPECTRUM CHEMICALS & LABORATORY PRODUCTS, INC.; *pg.* 1181, *pg.* 94
OMNISPORT - Scoreboard & Sports Product - DAKTRONICS, INC.; *pg.* 633, *pg.* 1624
OMNISTAR - Systems Integration & Aeronautics - LOCKHEED MARTIN CORPORATION; *pg.* 229, *pg.* 762
OMNISTAR - Communications Product - MOTOROLA SOLUTIONS, INC.; *pg.* 657, *pg.* 659
OMNISTOR - Storage Array - SILICON GRAPHICS INTERNATIONAL CORP; *pg.* 470, *pg.* 148
OMNISUPPLIER - Software - OMNICELL INC.; *pg.* 1578, *pg.* 161
OMNITARG - HER Dimerization Inhibitor - GENENTECH, INC.; *pg.* 1533, *pg.* 279
OMNITIP - Laser Device - TRIMEDYNE, INC.; *pg.* 1432, *pg.* 121
OMNITRACS - Mobile Communication System - QUALCOMM INCORPORATED; *pg.* 1873, *pg.* 207
OMNITURE ONLINE MARKETING SUITE - Software - ADOBE SYSTEMS INCORPORATED; *pg.* 342, *pg.* 235
OMNIVIEW - Inspection System - AMERICAN SCIENCE AND ENGINEERING, INC.; *pg.* 1399, *pg.* 787
OMNIVIEW - Web Portal - OMNICARE, INC; *pg.* 1578, *pg.* 1418
OMNIVIEW - Laser Device - TRIMEDYNE, INC.; *pg.* 1432, *pg.* 121
OMNIVISION - Electronic Tracking - QUALCOMM INCORPORATED; *pg.* 1873, *pg.* 207
OMOP - Floor Care - METHOD PRODUCTS INC.; *pg.* 332, *pg.* 223
OMRI LISTED - Insecticidal Soap - THE WOODSTREAM CORPORATION; *pg.* 1801, *pg.* 1549
OMS - Software - CHYRONHEGO; *pg.* 371, *pg.* 1179
OMS-EZ - Motion Control Commands - PRO-DEX, INC.; *pg.* 1586, *pg.* 115
OMSOLUTIONS - Portfolio of Supply Chain Consulting, Implementation, Outsourcing Solutions - OWENS & MINOR, INC.; *pg.* 1579, *pg.* 1795
OMV - Pre Press Film - PLASTIC SUPPLIERS, INC.; *pg.* 1888, *pg.* 1443
ON A ROLL - Pulltab Game - IDAHO LOTTERY; *pg.* 995, *pg.* 547
ON-BOARD - Pump System - BROOKS AUTOMATION, INC.; *pg.* 1320, *pg.* 813
ON CALL - Engraving - STANDEX INTERNATIONAL CORPORATION; *pg.* 60, *pg.* 1039
ON CALL AIR PICKUP - Software - UNITED PARCEL SERVICE, INC.; *pg.* 1928, *pg.* 522
ON-CENTER - Ethernet Access Manager - CIENA CORPORATION; *pg.* 628, *pg.* 771
ON-DEMAND DESTINATION PRINTING - Slogan - VIATECH PUBLISHING SOLUTIONS; *pg.* 489, *pg.* 1141
ON DEMAND SOFTWARE FOR PUBLIC RELATIONS MANAGEMENT - Tagline - CISION, INC.; *pg.* 375, *pg.* 761
ON DUTY - Beauty Product - AVON PRODUCTS, INC.; *pg.* 500, *pg.* 1198
ON. EVERY DAY. - Tag Line - GREEN MOUNTAIN POWER CORPORATION; *pg.* 1944, *pg.* 1765
ON FIRE - Video Game - INTERNATIONAL GAME TECHNOLOGY; *pg.* 957, *pg.* 1024
ON-GLASS - Antenna Product - PCTEL, INC.; *pg.* 452, *pg.* 557
ON-LINE - Pump Product - IDEX CORPORATION; *pg.* 1347, *pg.* 623
ON-LINE KITCHEN - Gateway - WATLOW ELECTRIC MANUFACTURING COMPANY; *pg.* 1078, *pg.* 1004
ON-MACHINE - Mounting - ROCKWELL AUTOMATION, INC.; *pg.* 668, *pg.* 1880
ON POINT - Furniture - J. ROBERT SCOTT INC.; *pg.* 930, *pg.* 105
ON ROUTE - Tracking - PITNEY BOWES INC.; *pg.* 454, *pg.* 376
ON-SITE - Eyewash - BRADLEY CORPORATION; *pg.* 71, *pg.* 1870
ON-TAP - Bar Code Printing Software - INTEGRATED SOFTWARE DESIGN, INC.; *pg.* 416, *pg.* 830
ON-TAP PLUS - Labeling Software - INTEGRATED SOFTWARE DESIGN, INC.; *pg.* 416, *pg.* 830
ON TARGET TO DELIVER - Tagline - BALCHEM CORPORATION; *pg.* 839, *pg.* 1183
ON THE BORDER MEXICAN GRILL & CANTINA - Mexican Restaurant - BRINKER INTERNATIONAL, INC.; *pg.* 1718, *pg.* 1676
ON THE GO BISTRO - Food Service Concept - MORRISON MANAGEMENT SPECIALISTS, INC.; *pg.* 1028, *pg.* 515
ON THE GO LOUNGER - Soft Travel Product - INFANTINO, LLC; *pg.* 957, *pg.* 203
ON THE LEVEL. EVERY DAY. - Tag Line - EMERY-WATERHOUSE COMPANY; *pg.* 1047, *pg.* 751
ON THE MARK HOSPITALITY CONCIERGE PROGRAM - Community Program - WCI COMMUNITIES, INC.; *pg.* 1118, *pg.* 414
ON THE ROAD - Advertising Management Consultancy - DAKTRONICS, INC.; *pg.* 633, *pg.* 1624
ON THE RUN - Franchise System - EXXON MOBIL CORPORATION; *pg.* 977, *pg.* 1718
ON-THE-SPOT - Acne Medicine - NEUTROGENA CORPORATION; *pg.* 517, *pg.* 137
ON THE WAY - Convenience Stores - THE PANTRY, INC.; *pg.* 1029, *pg.* 1360
ON TOP - Non-Dairy Topping - RICH PRODUCTS CORPORATION; *pg.* 892, *pg.* 1150
ON-TRAC - Irrigation System - REINKE MANUFACTURING COMPANY, INC.; *pg.* 707, *pg.* 1010
ON TRACK - Publication - MOTHERS AGAINST DRUNK DRIVING (MADD); *pg.* 147, *pg.* 1723
ON YOUR SIDE - Slogan - NATIONWIDE MUTUAL INSURANCE COMPANY; *pg.* 1211, *pg.* 706
ONALERT - Software - EMC CORPORATION; *pg.* 391, *pg.* 825
ONAMER - Chemical Product - STEPAN COMPANY; *pg.* 1182, *pg.* 643
ONAN - Generator Sets - CUMMINS INC.; *pg.* 1326, *pg.* 676
ONCALL - Software - NEUROMETRIX, INC.; *pg.* 1572, *pg.* 852
ONCAP - Thermoplastic Colorant & Additive - POLYONE CORPORATION; *pg.* 1177, *pg.* 1404
ONCE-A-DAY - Sterilization Product - PROPPER MANUFACTURING COMPANY, INC.; *pg.* 1586, *pg.* 1175
ONCE-A-DAY - Twenty-Four Hour Odor Counteractant - SURCO PRODUCTS, INC.; *pg.* 336, *pg.* 1581
ONCE-A-MONTH - Flea & Tick Drops - THE HARTZ MOUNTAIN CORP.; *pg.* 1476, *pg.* 1120
ONCE AROUND - Game - WMS INDUSTRIES INC.; *pg.* 593, *pg.* 666
ONCE AROUND DELUXE - Game - WMS INDUSTRIES INC.; *pg.* 593, *pg.* 666
ONCE UPON A CHILD - Toy Stores - WINMARK CORPORATION; *pg.* 1792, *pg.* 946
ONCE YOU GO YOU GET IT - Tagline - STEIN MART, INC.; *pg.* 1786, *pg.* 435
ONCE YOU GO. YOU KNOW. - Tagline - JAMAICA TOURIST BOARD; *pg.* 996, *pg.* 443
ONCE YOU KNOW, YOU NEWEGG - Slogan - NEWEGG INC.; *pg.* 1271, *pg.* 67
ONCOLOR - Thermoplastic Colorant & Additive - POLYONE CORPORATION; *pg.* 1177, *pg.* 1404
ONCOLOR COMPETE - Colorants - POLYONE CORPORATION; *pg.* 1177, *pg.* 1404
ONCOR - Flame Retardants - CHEMTURA CORPORATION; *pg.* 1152, *pg.* 355
ONCORE - Cluster Tool - COLLABRX, INC.; *pg.* 1324, *pg.* 216
ONCORE - Global Positioning - MOTOROLA SOLUTIONS, INC.; *pg.* 657, *pg.* 659
ONCYTE - Molecular Biology Product - THERMO FISHER SCIENTIFIC INC.; *pg.* 1602, *pg.* 61
ONDACOM - Wireless Communication System - AT&T SOUTHEAST; *pg.* 1868, *pg.* 489
ONDEMAND - Software - EGAIN COMMUNICATIONS CORPORATION; *pg.* 1242, *pg.* 284
ONDEMAND ACCUFLEX - Packaging System - MTS MEDICATION TECHNOLOGIES, INC.; *pg.* 442, *pg.* 463
ONDEMAND ESSENTIALS - Software - RENTRAK CORPORATION; *pg.* 306, *pg.* 1506
ONDEMAND EXCELL - Packaging System - MTS MEDICATION TECHNOLOGIES, INC.; *pg.* 442, *pg.* 463
ONDEMAND EXPRESS - Dispenser - MTS MEDICATION TECHNOLOGIES, INC.; *pg.* 442, *pg.* 463
ONDEMAND EXPRESS II - Dispenser - MTS MEDICATION TECHNOLOGIES, INC.; *pg.* 442, *pg.* 463
ONDEMAND MULTI-MED - Packaging System - MTS MEDICATION TECHNOLOGIES, INC.; *pg.* 442, *pg.* 463
ONDINE - Freshwater Spinning Reels - DAIWA CORPORATION; *pg.* 1832, *pg.* 75
ONE - Wiper & Anti-Extrusion Ring - A W CHESTERTON COMPANY; *pg.* 1315, *pg.* 861
ONE! - Hearing Aid - BELTONE ELECTRONICS LLC; *pg.* 1503, *pg.* 614
ONE - Lounge Chairs - BERNHARDT DESIGN; *pg.* 918, *pg.* 1381
ONE - Computer Peripheral Equipment - DIGI INTERNATIONAL INC.; *pg.* 387, *pg.* 948
ONE - Urethane Adhesive - THE DOW CHEMICAL COMPANY; *pg.* 1157, *pg.* 898
ONE - Brand Alignment Consultation Services - MARITZ INC.; *pg.* 1914, *pg.* 977
THE ONE 800 NUMBER FOR FLOWERS - Slogan - 1-800-FLOWERS.COM, INC.; *pg.* 1758, *pg.* 1151
THE ONE 888 NUMBER FOR FLOWERS - Slogan - 1-800-FLOWERS.COM, INC.; *pg.* 1758, *pg.* 1151
ONE-A-DAY MULTIVITAMINS - Medicine - BAYER HEALTHCARE CONSUMER CARE DIVISION; *pg.* 1500, *pg.* 1087
ONE-A-DAY SPECIALIZED BLENDS - Medicine - BAYER HEALTHCARE CONSUMER CARE DIVISION; *pg.* 1500, *pg.* 1087
ONE-AP - Dry Adjuvant Blend - KALO, INC.; *pg.* 1796, *pg.* 719
ONE BAL HARBOUR - Community Name - WCI COMMUNITIES, INC.; *pg.* 1118, *pg.* 414
ONE BUC CLUB - Fan Club - BUCCANEERS LIMITED PARTNERSHIP; *pg.* 534, *pg.* 471
ONE-CANCELS-OTHER - Application Service Provider - OPTIONSXPRESS HOLDINGS, INC.; *pg.* 790, *pg.* 586
ONE CARD - Discount Savings Card - HOMELAND STORES, INC.; *pg.* 1023, *pg.* 1486
ONE COMPANY A WORLD OF INNOVATION - Tagline - MOLEX INCORPORATED; *pg.* 655, *pg.* 628
ONE COMPANY, ONE MISSION - Tag Line - HF GROUP INC.; *pg.* 1346, *pg.* 68
ONE-EYED JACK - Lottery Game - MASSACHUSETTS STATE LOTTERY; *pg.* 998, *pg.* 802
ONE FOR ALL - Wireless Control Product - UNIVERSAL ELECTRONICS, INC.; *pg.* 683, *pg.* 262
ONE FOR THE FANS - Game - WMS INDUSTRIES INC.; *pg.* 593, *pg.* 666
ONE-HANDED SPEED-FOCUS - Laser Technology - COAST CUTLERY COMPANY; *pg.* 1121, *pg.* 1501
ONE HANES PLACE - Apparel - HANESBRANDS INC.; *pg.* 26, *pg.* 1394
ONE HOUR MARTINIZING - Dry Cleaning Service - MARTIN FRANCHISES INC.; *pg.* 332, *pg.* 1458
ONE MAN JAM - Toys - MGA ENTERTAINMENT, INC.; *pg.* 964, *pg.* 300
ONE OF A KIND - Carpet - BEAULIEU GROUP, LLC; *pg.* 917, *pg.* 529
ONE PLACE. YOUR PLACE. - Tagline - WAKEFERN FOOD

CORPORATION; *pg.* 1037, *pg.* 1058
ONE PLUS - Cleaning Product - HILLYARD, INC.; *pg.* 331, *pg.* 990
ONE RATE USA - Software System - AT&T COMMUNICATIONS CORP.; *pg.* 1866, *pg.* 1043
ONE SHOT - Case Tumbler - HORNADY MANUFACTURING COMPANY; *pg.* 1836, *pg.* 1010
ONE SHOT - Pump - IDEX CORPORATION; *pg.* 1347, *pg.* 623
ONE SHOT - Cell Culture Product - THERMO FISHER SCIENTIFIC INC.; *pg.* 1602, *pg.* 61
ONE-SHOT KINETICS - Software - BIO-RAD LABORATORIES, INC.; *pg.* 1504, *pg.* 101
ONE SHOT ULTRA - Cattle Vaccine - PFIZER INC.; *pg.* 1581, *pg.* 1278
ONE SOLUTION - Phenolic Disinfectant - STERIS CORPORATION; *pg.* 1597, *pg.* 1464
ONE-SOLUTION - Software - WIND RIVER SYSTEMS, INC.; *pg.* 493, *pg.* 38
ONE SOURCE - Vitamins - WAL-MART STORES, INC., *pg.* 1790, *pg.* 29
ONE SOURCE. THE SOLUTION. - Tagline - AEP INDUSTRIES INC.; *pg.* 1878, *pg.* 1085
ONE STAR - Shoe - CONVERSE INC.; *pg.* 1831, *pg.* 793
ONE STEP - Wood Floor Care - BISSELL HOMECARE, INC.; *pg.* 52, *pg.* 887
ONE STEP - Sealing Compound - SMOOTH-ON INC.; *pg.* 111, *pg.* 1528
ONE SYSTEM. NO LIMITS. - Slogan - NETSUITE, INC.; *pg.* 1270, *pg.* 255
ONE TIME - Medical Product - HOLOGIC, INC.; *pg.* 1416, *pg.* 784
ONE-TIME PAY - Online Financial Services - ACI WORLDWIDE; *pg.* 710, *pg.* 1777
ONE TOOTH - Cutter - LENOX; *pg.* 1053, *pg.* 817
ONE TOUCH - Male Grooming Product - AMERICAN INTERNATIONAL INDUSTRIES COMPANY; *pg.* 498, *pg.* 126
ONE TOUCH - Invisible Tape & Dispenser - HENKEL CONSUMER ADHESIVES, INC.; *pg.* 403, *pg.* 1480
ONE TOUCH - Scented Oils - HENKEL CONSUMER GOODS; *pg.* 511, *pg.* 22
ONE TOUCH - Kitchenware - TUPPERWARE BRANDS CORPORATION; *pg.* 1139, *pg.* 456
ONE-TOUCH - Gas Grill - WEBER-STEPHEN PRODUCTS LLC; *pg.* 62, *pg.* 650
ONE TOUCH BUSINESS TRAVEL - Management Services - CONCUR TECHNOLOGIES, INC.; *pg.* 1236, *pg.* 1813
ONE-TOUCH INSPECTION DOOR - Power Transmission Product - U.S. TSUBAKI, INC.; *pg.* 221, *pg.* 670
ONE TOUCH SYSTEM - Packaging - INTERNATIONAL PAPER COMPANY; *pg.* 1460, *pg.* 1644
ONE-TRIGGERS-OTHER - Application Service Provider - OPTIONSXPRESS HOLDINGS, INC.; *pg.* 790, *pg.* 586
ONE TRIGGERS TWO - Application Service Provider - OPTIONSXPRESS HOLDINGS, INC.; *pg.* 790, *pg.* 586
ONE-UP - Pump Diaphragm - W.L. GORE & ASSOCIATES, INC.; *pg.* 122, *pg.* 388
THE ONE WITH REAL TASTE - Slogan - HOUSE OF RAEFORD FARMS, INC.; *pg.* 864, *pg.* 1386
ONE WORLD CAMPAIGN - Manual - XEROX CORPORATION; *pg.* 494, *pg.* 365
ONE WORLD. ONE SOURCE. - Slogan - AEP INDUSTRIES INC.; *pg.* 1878, *pg.* 1085
ONE WORLD. ONE VISION. ONE VOICE. - Tagline - FUSION TELECOMMUNICATIONS INTERNATIONAL, INC.; *pg.* 1248, *pg.* 1233
ONE600 CLASSIC - Instant Camera - POLAROID CORPORATION; *pg.* 1426, *pg.* 815
ONE600 JOBPRO - Rugged, Outdoors Instant Camera - POLAROID CORPORATION; *pg.* 1426, *pg.* 815
ONE600 PRO - Instant Camera - POLAROID CORPORATION; *pg.* 1426, *pg.* 815
ONE600 ULTRA - Instant Camera - POLAROID CORPORATION; *pg.* 1426, *pg.* 815
ONEBOX - Communication Product - J2 GLOBAL COMMUNICATIONS, INC.; *pg.* 1260, *pg.* 133
ONECALL - Truck Service Program - MACK TRUCKS, INC.; *pg.* 183, *pg.* 1375
ONECOLOR PLUS TWO - Make-up - AVEDA CORPORATION; *pg.* 499, *pg.* 917
ONECONNECT - Software - F5 NETWORKS, INC.; *pg.* 396, *pg.* 1835
ONECUP - Lid - PACTIV CORPORATION; *pg.* 1466, *pg.* 624
ONEDRIVE - File Storage & Sharing Service - MICROSOFT CORPORATION; *pg.* 435, *pg.* 1824
ONEDRIVER - Wireless Network - BROADCOM CORPORATION; *pg.* 364, *pg.* 108
ONEFAB - Hardware Product - BROOKS AUTOMATION, INC.; *pg.* 1320, *pg.* 813
ONEFAB AMHS - Factory Automation Software - BROOKS AUTOMATION, INC.; *pg.* 1320, *pg.* 813
ONEFLEX - Fiber-Optic Network System - CENTURYLINK, INC; *pg.* 1870, *pg.* 317
ONEIDA - Silverware - ONEIDA LTD; *pg.* 1129, *pg.* 1318
ONEIDAWARE - Stainless Steel Flatware - ONEIDA LTD; *pg.* 1129, *pg.* 1318
ONELINK - Software System - ALCATEL-LUCENT; *pg.* 615, *pg.* 1094
ONEPAGE DX - Medical Product - HOLOGIC, INC.; *pg.* 1416, *pg.* 784
ONEPAGE FX - Medical Product - HOLOGIC, INC.; *pg.* 1416, *pg.* 784
ONEPART - Medical Equipment - CONMED CORPORATION; *pg.* 1517, *pg.* 1347
ONEPIECE - Chain - THE LAITRAM LLC; *pg.* 1354, *pg.* 744
ONEPLACE.COM - Website - SALEM MEDIA GROUP, INC.; *pg.* 307, *pg.* 57
ONEPOINT - Software - THE SSI GROUP, INC.; *pg.* 473, *pg.* 7
ONEPRINT - Facsimile Equipment - MURATEC AMERICA, INC.; *pg.* 443, *pg.* 1733
ONEROW - Thermal Processing Equipment - SURFACE COMBUSTION, INC.; *pg.* 1077, *pg.* 1462
ONES - Dietary Food Products - THE KRAFT HEINZ COMPANY; *pg.* 870, *pg.* 1577
ONESCANNER - Computer Scanner - APPLE INC.; *pg.* 350, *pg.* 73
ONESEAL - Electric Airless Sprayer - GRACO, INC.; *pg.* 1342, *pg.* 935
ONESMART MASTERCARD - Credit Card - MASTERCARD INCORPORATED; *pg.* 779, *pg.* 1325
ONESOURCE - Pharmaceutical Product - CARDINAL HEALTH, INC.; *pg.* 1512, *pg.* 1448
ONESOURCE - No Transaction Fee Mutual Funds - CHARLES SCHWAB & COMPANY, INC.; *pg.* 734, *pg.* 215
ONESOURCE - Laboratory Service - PERKINELMER, INC.; *pg.* 1426, *pg.* 853
ONESOURCE EXPRESS - Transactional Web Site - AVENTION; *pg.* 1230, *pg.* 815
ONESTEP - Bagging Machine - AUTOMATED PACKAGING SYSTEMS INC.; *pg.* 1452, *pg.* 1474
ONETOONE - Service & Support Program - APPLE INC.; *pg.* 350, *pg.* 73
ONETOUCH - Software - ANIMAS CORPORATION; *pg.* 1495, *pg.* 1593
ONETOUCH - Health & Wellness Product - EXPRESS SCRIPTS; *pg.* 1530, *pg.* 1070
ONETOUCH - Wafer Probe Solution - FORMFACTOR, INC.; *pg.* 1882, *pg.* 122
ONETOUCH - Overhead Storage Unit - HAWORTH, INC.; *pg.* 402, *pg.* 891
ONETOUCH - Healthcare Product - JOHNSON & JOHNSON; *pg.* 1549, *pg.* 1091
ONETOUCH - Blood Glucose Monitoring Products - LIFESCAN INC; *pg.* 1556, *pg.* 146
ONETOUCH - Kitchen Faucet - MOEN INCORPORATED; *pg.* 1056, *pg.* 1468
ONETOUCH - Mirror Mount - OPTOSIGMA CORP.; *pg.* 1425, *pg.* 262
ONETOUCH BASIC - Blood Glucose Monitoring Products - LIFESCAN INC; *pg.* 1556, *pg.* 146
ONETOUCH FASTTAKE - Blood Glucose Monitoring Products - LIFESCAN INC; *pg.* 1556, *pg.* 146
ONETOUCH PROFILE - Blood Glucose Monitoring Products - LIFESCAN INC; *pg.* 1556, *pg.* 146
ONETOUCH SURE STEP - Blood Glucose Monitoring Products - LIFESCAN INC; *pg.* 1556, *pg.* 146
ONETOUCH TEST STRIPS - Blood Glucose Monitoring System - LIFESCAN INC; *pg.* 1556, *pg.* 146
ONETOUCH ULTRA - Blood Glucose Monitoring System - LIFESCAN INC; *pg.* 1556, *pg.* 146
ONETOUCH ULTRASMART - Blood Glucose Monitoring System - LIFESCAN INC; *pg.* 1556, *pg.* 146
ONEVIEW - Reprographic Product - AMERICAN REPROGRAPHICS COMPANY; *pg.* 1616, *pg.* 303
ONEWORLD UNITED STATES - Public Policy Initiative - BENTON FOUNDATION; *pg.* 134, *pg.* 396
ONEX-SEAL - Cleaning Product - HILLYARD, INC.; *pg.* 331, *pg.* 990
ONEZIP - Plastic Slider Bag - PACTIV CORPORATION; *pg.* 1466, *pg.* 624
ONFORCE LFT - Long Fiber Compounds - POLYONE CORPORATION; *pg.* 1177, *pg.* 1404
ONGARD - Flame Retardants - CHEMTURA CORPORATION; *pg.* 1152, *pg.* 355
ONGUARD - Technology - MERITOR, INC.; *pg.* 212, *pg.* 911
ONGUARD - Air Monitor - PURAFIL, INC.; *pg.* 333, *pg.* 530
ONICE MISTA - Tile - ARTISTIC TILE INC.; *pg.* 914, *pg.* 1119
ONION KING - Vegetable slicer - LINCOLN FOODSERVICE PRODUCTS, LLC; *pg.* 1127, *pg.* 1432
ONION MAGIC - Food Product - MODERN PRODUCTS, INC.; *pg.* 1568, *pg.* 1871
ONION PEEL - Food Product - ZAXBY'S FRANCHISING, INC.; *pg.* 1756, *pg.* 486
ONKO - Coffee - MONDELEZ INTERNATIONAL, INC.; *pg.* 878, *pg.* 601
ONLINE - Multiplexing System - CIENA CORPORATION; *pg.* 628, *pg.* 771
ONLINE - Broadband Services - MEDIACOM COMMUNICATIONS CORPORATION; *pg.* 653, *pg.* 1182
ONLINE DIRECT MARKETING MANAGER - Online Promotional Tool - VALASSIS COMMUNICATIONS, INC.; *pg.* 1287, *pg.* 897
ONLINE EXTRAS - Promoting Goods - AMERICAN EXPRESS COMPANY; *pg.* 712, *pg.* 1190
ONLINE INTRO - Broadband Services - MEDIACOM COMMUNICATIONS CORPORATION; *pg.* 653, *pg.* 1182
ONLINE KNOWLEDGE CENTER - Software System - MENTOR GRAPHICS CORPORATION; *pg.* 432, *pg.* 1510
ONLINE MAX - Broadband Services - MEDIACOM COMMUNICATIONS CORPORATION; *pg.* 653, *pg.* 1182
ONLINE METRO - Multiplexing System - CIENA CORPORATION; *pg.* 628, *pg.* 771
ONLINE PROMOTION LINK - Online Promotional Tool - VALASSIS COMMUNICATIONS, INC.; *pg.* 1287, *pg.* 897
THE ONLY FINANCING SOURCE YOU WILL EVER NEED - Slogan - MICROFINANCIAL INCORPORATED; *pg.* 782, *pg.* 805
ONLY NATURAL - Cosmetic Product - MERLE NORMAN COSMETICS, INC.; *pg.* 517, *pg.* 136
ONLY RESERVE - Handmade Cigar - ALTADIS USA, INC.; *pg.* 1893, *pg.* 423
ONLY THE BEST FOR YOUR FAMILY FROM OURS - Tagline - BIG Y FOODS, INC.; *pg.* 1015, *pg.* 845
ONLY WITH CHIHUAHUA - Slogan - V&V SUPREMO FOODS, INC.; *pg.* 907, *pg.* 595
ONLY YOU - Apparel - PLAYTEX APPAREL, INC.; *pg.* 31, *pg.* 1395
ONLY4VETS - Pharmaceutical Product - PFIZER INC.; *pg.* 1581, *pg.* 1278
ONLYSWEET - Stevia Extracts - WILD FLAVORS, INC.; *pg.* 910, *pg.* 728
ONO - Eyewear - MAUI JIM, INC.; *pg.* 9, *pg.* 651
ONOCARTA - Diagnostic Tool - SEQUENOM, INC.; *pg.* 1593, *pg.* 209
ONPOINT - Service Agreements - GENERAL ELECTRIC COMPANY; *pg.* 1297, *pg.* 347
ONPOINT - Microplates - PERKINELMER, INC.; *pg.* 1426, *pg.* 853
ONPULSE - LaserLife Program - CYMER, INC.; *pg.* 1296, *pg.* 202
ONSIDE - Beverages - THE COCA-COLA COMPANY; *pg.* 240, *pg.* 493
ONSITE - Surgical Instrument Service - CARDINAL HEALTH, INC.; *pg.* 1512, *pg.* 1448
ONSTAR - Vehicle - GENERAL MOTORS COMPANY; *pg.* 175, *pg.* 881
ONSTAR - Auto-Dimming Mirror - GENTEX CORPORATION; *pg.* 206, *pg.* 913
ONSTAR - Automotive Safety Technology - ONSTAR CORPORATION; *pg.* 214, *pg.* 884
ONSTEP - Bottle Eyewash - BRADLEY CORPORATION; *pg.* 71, *pg.* 1870
ONSTREAM MEDIA - Internet Broadcasting - ONSTREAM MEDIA CORPORATION; *pg.* 449, *pg.* 459
ONTAK - Pharmaceutical - EISAI INC.; *pg.* 1526, *pg.* 1133
ONTAP - Telecommunications Gateway - LEVEL 3 COMMUNICATIONS, INC.; *pg.* 1262, *pg.* 312
ONTRACK - Orthopedic Product - DJO INCORPORATED; *pg.* 1524, *pg.* 302
ONTRAK - Integrated Substance Dependence Solution - CATASYS, INC.; *pg.* 1514, *pg.* 127
ONTRAK - Software - RENTRAK CORPORATION; *pg.* 306,

First page reference indicates Business Class Edition
Second page reference indicates Geographic Edition

pg. 1506
ONVIEW - Computer Monitor - VIEWSONIC CORPORATION; *pg.* 489, *pg.* 303
ONWALL - Speaker - TRIAD SPEAKERS, INC.; *pg.* 682, *pg.* 1507
ONWAVE - Multiplexer Card - CIENA CORPORATION; *pg.* 628, *pg.* 771
ONYX - Tile - ARTISTIC TILE INC.; *pg.* 914, *pg.* 1119
ONYX - Micro Channel Cooled Package - COHERENT, INC.; *pg.* 1406, *pg.* 265
ONYX - Paint Brushes - DUNN-EDWARDS CORPORATION; *pg.* 1442, *pg.* 129
ONYX - Pest Control Product - FMC CORPORATION; *pg.* 1163, *pg.* 1564
ONYX - Flashing Cement - KOPPERS HOLDINGS INC.; *pg.* 1170, *pg.* 1577
ONYX - Energy-Absorbing Lanyard - MINE SAFETY APPLIANCES COMPANY; *pg.* 1361, *pg.* 1525
ONYX - Adult Mass Market Paperback Books - PENGUIN RANDOM HOUSE; *pg.* 1675, *pg.* 1276
ONYX SERIES - Security Control Panel - NOTIFIER CO.; *pg.* 659, *pg.* 360
ONYXIDE - Chemical Product - STEPAN COMPANY; *pg.* 1182, *pg.* 643
OO-LA-LA - Container Grown Plant - MONROVIA GROWERS; *pg.* 1797, *pg.* 44
OODLE - Fabric - NEMSCHOFF, INC.; *pg.* 936, *pg.* 1890
OOH LA LA! - Gown Set - HABAND COMPANY, INC.; *pg.* 1772, *pg.* 1099
OOMOO - Liquid Rubber - SMOOTH-ON INC.; *pg.* 111, *pg.* 1528
OOMPH! - Multipurpose Cleaner - THE CLOROX COMPANY; *pg.* 327, *pg.* 169
OP - Apparel - ICONIX BRAND GROUP, INC.; *pg.* 26, *pg.* 1243
OP-1 - Medical Product - STRYKER CORPORATION; *pg.* 1598, *pg.* 894
OP DROPS - Lens Cleaner - MCNETT CORPORATION; *pg.* 1839, *pg.* 1817
OPAA! - Food Product - GRECIAN DELIGHT FOODS INC.; *pg.* 859, *pg.* 610
OPAL - Orthopedic Product - DJO INCORPORATED; *pg.* 1524, *pg.* 302
OPAL - Footwear - EASTLAND SHOE CORPORATION; *pg.* 1808, *pg.* 750
OPAL EDGE - Balloon - CONTINENTAL AMERICAN CORP.; *pg.* 1880, *pg.* 723
OPAL RING - Game - WMS INDUSTRIES INC.; *pg.* 593, *pg.* 666
OPALIA - Bath & Plumbing Product - JACUZZI BRANDS CORPORATION; *pg.* 554, *pg.* 65
OPAMPPRO - Software - TEXAS INSTRUMENTS INCORPORATED; *pg.* 679, *pg.* 1688
OPANA - Pharmaceutical Product - ENDO PHARMACEUTICALS HOLDINGS, INC.; *pg.* 1528, *pg.* 1549
OPANA ER - Pharmaceutical Product - ENDO PHARMACEUTICALS HOLDINGS, INC.; *pg.* 1528, *pg.* 1549
OPANA ER - Pharmaceutical Product - IMPAX LABORATORIES, INC.; *pg.* 1544, *pg.* 101
OPAQUE - Printing Paper - MOHAWK FINE PAPERS, INC.; *pg.* 1464, *pg.* 1153
OPAXIO - Polyglutamate Paclitaxel Drug - CELL THERAPEUTICS, INC.; *pg.* 1514, *pg.* 1834
OPC PLUS - Nutritional Product - RBC LIFE SCIENCES, INC.; *pg.* 1588, *pg.* 1723
OPCENTER - Communication System - OMNITRACS, LLC; *pg.* 449, *pg.* 1685
OPCO - Fluid Handling System - GRACO, INC.; *pg.* 1342, *pg.* 935
OPCON-A - Eye Drop & Ointment - BAUSCH & LOMB INCORPORATED; *pg.* 1401, *pg.* 1045
OPCONET - Fluid Handling System - GRACO, INC.; *pg.* 1342, *pg.* 935
OPDITRACKER - Content Management Software - IMATION CORP.; *pg.* 413, *pg.* 952
OPEL - Vehicle - GENERAL MOTORS COMPANY; *pg.* 175, *pg.* 881
OPEN - Software - WIND RIVER SYSTEMS, INC.; *pg.* 493, *pg.* 38
OPEN ACCESS - Chip Boards - ONMOBILE LIVE, INC.; *pg.* 449, *pg.* 829
OPEN-ACCESS - Rack & Cable - PANDUIT CORP.; *pg.* 661, *pg.* 663
OPEN AIR - Firelog - DURAFLAME, INC.; *pg.* 1123, *pg.* 280
OPEN BLOOMBERG - Computer Software Program - BLOOMBERG L.P.; *pg.* 725, *pg.* 1204
OPEN CASINO MANAGER - Game Management - BALLY TECHNOLOGIES, INC.; *pg.* 531, *pg.* 1022
OPEN CHANNEL - Software - BIO-RAD LABORATORIES, INC.; *pg.* 1504, *pg.* 101
OPEN COURT - Basketball Backboards - LIFETIME PRODUCTS INC.; *pg.* 933, *pg.* 1751
OPEN FILE MANAGER - Software - EDGEWAVE INC; *pg.* 390, *pg.* 202
OPEN HOUSE - Integrated Home Network System - NORTEK, INC.; *pg.* 100, *pg.* 1607
OPEN JOIST - Open-Web Floor Truss - UNIVERSAL FOREST PRODUCTS, INC.; *pg.* 117, *pg.* 890
OPEN LDV - Software - ECHELON CORPORATION; *pg.* 389, *pg.* 245
OPEN ME FIRST - Camera, Film, Accessories - EASTMAN KODAK COMPANY; *pg.* 1408, *pg.* 1333
OPEN PLAN - Computer Applications - DELTEK, INC.; *pg.* 386, *pg.* 1784
OPEN PRAIRIE NATURAL ANGUS - Angus Beef - TYSON FOODS, INC.; *pg.* 902, *pg.* 35
OPEN SEVEN DAYS - Slogan - TCF FINANCIAL CORPORATION; *pg.* 808, *pg.* 966
OPEN SKY MRI - Magnetic Resonance Scan Room - FONAR CORPORATION; *pg.* 1413, *pg.* 1179
OPEN STANDARDS INTEGRATION - Software - NETAPP, INC.; *pg.* 444, *pg.* 287
OPEN SYSTEMS ALLIANCE - Software - ECHELON CORPORATION; *pg.* 389, *pg.* 245
OPEN SYSTEMS SNAPVAULT - Software - NETAPP, INC.; *pg.* 444, *pg.* 287
OPEN TEXT ECM - Software - OPENTEXT CORPORATION; *pg.* 450, *pg.* 1948
OPEN: THE SMALL BUSINESS NETWORK - Business Services - AMERICAN EXPRESS COMPANY; *pg.* 712, *pg.* 1190
OPEN THE VAULT - Game - WMS INDUSTRIES INC.; *pg.* 593, *pg.* 666
OPEN VIEW - Online Reviews - MARCHEX, INC.; *pg.* 1395, *pg.* 1837
OPEN YOUR EYES - Tagline - LENSCRAFTERS, INC.; *pg.* 1420, *pg.* 1460
OPENAIR.COM - Software - OPENAIR, INC.; *pg.* 1272, *pg.* 800
OPENBOOK - Online Documentation Library - CADENCE DESIGN SYSTEMS, INC.; *pg.* 367, *pg.* 239
OPENCAD DESIGN SYSTEM - Semiconductor Product - RENESAS ELECTRONICS AMERICA INC.; *pg.* 667, *pg.* 269
OPENCHOICE - Calibration Feature - DEXCOM INC; *pg.* 1524, *pg.* 202
OPENCL - Software Technology - APPLE INC.; *pg.* 350, *pg.* 73
OPENDOOR - Software System - MENTOR GRAPHICS CORPORATION; *pg.* 432, *pg.* 1510
OPENEASE - Kitchen Appliance - HAMILTON BEACH BRANDS, INC.; *pg.* 56, *pg.* 1783
OPENEDGE - Software - PROGRESS SOFTWARE CORPORATION; *pg.* 457, *pg.* 786
OPENFRAME - Rack-Mount Equipment - DELL INC.; *pg.* 383, *pg.* 1737
OPENGL - Graphic System - NVIDIA CORPORATION; *pg.* 447, *pg.* 268
OPENGL - Graphics Solution - QUALCOMM INCORPORATED; *pg.* 1873, *pg.* 207
OPENHOUSE - Structured Wiring Solutions - NORTEK SECURITY & CONTROL LLC; *pg.* 659, *pg.* 59
OPENLINE - Toll-Free Support - DELL INC.; *pg.* 383, *pg.* 1737
OPENLYNX - Software - WATERS CORPORATION; *pg.* 1436, *pg.* 834
OPENPAGES GRC - Risk & Compliance Platform - INTERNATIONAL BUSINESS MACHINES CORPORATION; *pg.* 418, *pg.* 1138
OPENPAGES IT GOVERNANCE - IT Operations Management Software - INTERNATIONAL BUSINESS MACHINES CORPORATION; *pg.* 418, *pg.* 1138
OPENPAGES PINANCIAL CONTROL MANAGEMENT - Financial Management Platform - INTERNATIONAL BUSINESS MACHINES CORPORATION; *pg.* 418, *pg.* 1138
OPENPLAY - Application Program - APPLE INC.; *pg.* 350, *pg.* 73
OPENSAIL - Catheter - ABBOTT LABORATORIES; *pg.* 1484, *pg.* 551
OPENSCALE - Software - EMC CORPORATION; *pg.* 391, *pg.* 825
OPENSPEECH - Speech Recognition Software - NUANCE COMMUNICATIONS, INC.; *pg.* 447, *pg.* 806
OPENSUSE - Computer Software - NOVELL INC.; *pg.* 446, *pg.* 852
OPENTABLE - Restaurant Software Products - OPENTABLE, INC.; *pg.* 450, *pg.* 224
OPENTABLE DINERS CHOICE - Dining Service - OPENTABLE, INC.; *pg.* 450, *pg.* 224
OPENTABLE.COM - Online Restaurant Reservations - THE PRICELINE GROUP INC.; *pg.* 1276, *pg.* 364
OPENTV - Television Service - NAGRA USA; *pg.* 443, *pg.* 223
OPENVERA - Software - SYNOPSYS, INC.; *pg.* 480, *pg.* 162
OPENVIEW - Software - HEWLETT-PACKARD COMPANY; *pg.* 404, *pg.* 175
OPENVPX - Industry Working Group - MERCURY COMPUTER SYSTEMS, INC.; *pg.* 434, *pg.* 813
OPERA - Hearing Aid - BELTONE ELECTRONICS LLC; *pg.* 1503, *pg.* 614
OPERA - Modern Occasional Tables - BERNHARDT DESIGN; *pg.* 918, *pg.* 1381
OPERA - Amplifier - COHERENT, INC.; *pg.* 1406, *pg.* 265
OPERA - Awning Fabric - GLEN RAVEN, INC.; *pg.* 693, *pg.* 1373
OPERA - Software - MICROS SYSTEMS, INC.; *pg.* 435, *pg.* 768
OPERA - Microplate Image Reader - PERKINELMER, INC.; *pg.* 1426, *pg.* 853
OPERA - Office Furniture - STEELCASE INC.; *pg.* 475, *pg.* 889
OPERA HOUSE - Carpet - BEAULIEU GROUP, LLC; *pg.* 917, *pg.* 529
THE OPERATING ROOM FOR THE 21ST CENTURY - Medical Equipment Leasing - AMERICAN SHARED HOSPITAL SERVICES; *pg.* 1493, *pg.* 212
OPERATING TRACK CONTROLLER - Remote Control - LIONEL LLC; *pg.* 961, *pg.* 875
OPERATION - Fruit Flavored Snacks - KELLOGG COMPANY; *pg.* 831, *pg.* 870
OPERATION ELIMINATE - Program - TOPFLIGHT CORPORATION; *pg.* 681, *pg.* 1534
OPERATION: FROG - Educational Materials - SCHOLASTIC INC.; *pg.* 1683, *pg.* 1288
OPERATIONS MANAGER - Software - NETAPP, INC.; *pg.* 444, *pg.* 287
OPERATIONWISE - Energy Control Program - XCEL ENERGY INC.; *pg.* 1955, *pg.* 946
OPERATOR - Security Product - BAE SYSTEMS PRODUCTS GROUP; *pg.* 359, *pg.* 432
OPERATOR OFFICE - Software - SIQURA; *pg.* 308, *pg* 771
OPERTUNE - DB2 Enhancement - BMC SOFTWARE, INC.; *pg.* 362, *pg.* 1701
OPEX - Polymer Product - CHEMTURA CORPORATION; *pg.* 1152, *pg.* 355
OPEX 80 - Polymer Product - CHEMTURA CORPORATION; *pg.* 1152, *pg.* 355
OPFORCE - Software - SYMANTEC CORPORATION; *pg.* 478, *pg.* 161
OPHELIA - Clothing - ABERCROMBIE & FITCH CO.; *pg.* 37, *pg.* 1466
OPHELIA - Fan - CRAFTMADE INTERNATIONAL, INC.; *pg.* 1295, *pg.* 1670
OPI - Beauty Products - OPI PRODUCTS INC.; *pg.* 518, *pg.* 167
OPI RED - Nail Care Product - OPI PRODUCTS INC.; *pg.* 518, *pg.* 167
OPI TOP COAT - Nail Treatment - OPI PRODUCTS INC.; *pg.* 518, *pg.* 167
OPINIONWORLD - Research Panel - SURVEY SAMPLING INTERNATIONAL LLC; *pg.* 1690, *pg.* 371
OPIS - Fiber Optic Product - ALLIANCE FIBER OPTIC PRODUCTS, INC.; *pg.* 1399, *pg.* 283
OPM - Multifunction Optical Power Meter - NEWPORT CORPORATION; *pg.* 1424, *pg.* 114
OPNET NCOMPASS - Software Product & Module - RIVERBED PERFORMANCE MANAGEMENT; *pg.* 462, *pg.* 765
OPORTO - Fabric - NEMSCHOFF, INC.; *pg.* 936, *pg.* 1890
OPPERMAN MASTERGEAR - Electrical Product - REGAL BELOIT CORPORATION; *pg.* 106, *pg.* 1854
OPPONENT POKER - Video Game - INTERNATIONAL

GAME TECHNOLOGY; *pg.* 957, *pg.* 1024
OPRAH WINFREY NETWORK - Television Network - DISCOVERY COMMUNICATIONS, INC.; *pg.* 282, *pg.* 777
OPRAH WINFREY NETWORK (OWN) - Cable Television Network - HARPO, INC.; *pg.* 290, *pg.* 576
OPRAH'S NEXT CHAPTER - Television Show - DISCOVERY COMMUNICATIONS, INC.; *pg.* 282, *pg.* 777
OPSCAN INSIGHT 70 - Scanning Software - PEARSON ASSESSMENTS; *pg.* 1674, *pg.* 918
OPSIM - Software System - MENTOR GRAPHICS CORPORATION; *pg.* 432, *pg.* 1510
OPSITE - Medical & Aesthetic Product - DYNATRONICS CORPORATION; *pg.* 1526, *pg.* 1757
OPSLOG - Web Based Tool - INTEGRAL SYSTEMS, INC.; *pg.* 416, *pg.* 767
OPSNET - Software - PASSUR AEROSPACE, INC.; *pg.* 233, *pg.* 376
OPTAFLEXX - Ractopamine Hydrochloride - ELANCO ANIMAL HEALTH; *pg.* 1475, *pg.* 681
OPTALOY - Dental Product - DENTSPLY INTERNATIONAL INC.; *pg.* 1522, *pg.* 1596
OPTAMINT - Flavors - SYMRISE, INC.; *pg.* 1183, *pg.* 1125
OPTAROME - Flavor - SYMRISE, INC.; *pg.* 1183, *pg.* 1125
OPTAS - Software - SUNGARD DATA SYSTEMS INC.; *pg.* 477, *pg.* 1592
OPTECH - Fiber-Optic Line - VICON INDUSTRIES, INC.; *pg.* 685, *pg.* 1166
OPTEFIL - Orthopaedic Implant Device - EXACTECH, INC.; *pg.* 1529, *pg.* 428
OPTEFORM - Orthopaedic Implant Device - EXACTECH, INC.; *pg.* 1529, *pg.* 428
OPTELICAM - IP Cameras - SIQURA; *pg.* 308, *pg.* 771
OPTELIDOME - IP Cameras - SIQURA; *pg.* 308, *pg.* 771
OPTEON CEMENTED HIP - Total Hip Implant System - EXACTECH, INC.; *pg.* 1529, *pg.* 428
OPTETRAK - Orthopaedic Implant Device - EXACTECH, INC.; *pg.* 1529, *pg.* 428
OPTEVA - Cash Dispenser - DIEBOLD, INCORPORATED; *pg.* 387, *pg.* 1407
OPTEVIEW - Remote Monitoring - DIEBOLD, INCORPORATED; *pg.* 387, *pg.* 1407
OPTI - Medical Device - IDEXX LABORATORIES, INC.; *pg.* 1543, *pg.* 753
OPTI - Packaging Product - SEALED AIR CORPORATION; *pg.* 1468, *pg.* 1058
OPTI-3 - OC-3 Multiplexer - ADTRAN, INC.; *pg.* 344, *pg.* 6
OPTI-4CN - Software - BIO-RAD LABORATORIES, INC.; *pg.* 1504, *pg.* 101
OPTI-6100 - Optical Network - ADTRAN, INC.; *pg.* 344, *pg.* 6
OPTI-CORE - Fiber Solution - PANDUIT CORP.; *pg.* 661, *pg.* 663
OPTI-CRIMP - Fiber Solution - PANDUIT CORP.; *pg.* 661, *pg.* 663
OPTI-FLEX - Reading Glasses - HABAND COMPANY, INC.; *pg.* 1772, *pg.* 1099
OPTI-GREEN - Computer Equipment - VIEWSONIC CORPORATION; *pg.* 489, *pg.* 303
OPTI-ICE - Orthopedic Device - DJO SURGICAL; *pg.* 1525, *pg.* 1661
OPTI-JACK - Connector - PANDUIT CORP.; *pg.* 661, *pg.* 663
OPTI-KAN - Vehicle Operators - I.D. SYSTEMS, INC.; *pg.* 643, *pg.* 1134
OPTI-MEM - Cell Culture Product - THERMO FISHER SCIENTIFIC INC.; *pg.* 1602, *pg.* 61
OPTI-MOUNT - Miscellaneous Plate Mounting - ANDERSON & VREELAND, INC.; *pg.* 1616, *pg.* 1064
OPTI-PAK - Packaging System - MTS MEDICATION TECHNOLOGIES, INC.; *pg.* 442, *pg.* 463
OPTI-PERM - Laboratory Services - MOCON, INC.; *pg.* 1363, *pg.* 940
OPTI-POUR - Plastic Closures & Caps - ALCOA INC.; *pg.* 65, *pg.* 1188
OPTI-PROBE - Inspection System - KLA-TENCOR CORPORATION; *pg.* 1353, *pg.* 146
OPTI-UPS - Computer Equipment - VIEWSONIC CORPORATION; *pg.* 489, *pg.* 303
OPTI-VIA - Engineering Structure - SANMINA-SCI CORPORATION; *pg.* 671, *pg.* 250
OPTI-VIEW - Operator Seat - ALTEC INDUSTRIES INC.; *pg.* 1312, *pg.* 1
OPTI-ZYME - Animal Feed - MANNA PRO CORPORATION; *pg.* 1478, *pg.* 975
OPTIBERRY - Nutritional Supplement - RELIV INTERNATIONAL, INC.; *pg.* 1589, *pg.* 975
OPTIBITE - Endoscopic Technologies - CONMED CORPORATION; *pg.* 1517, *pg.* 1347
OPTIBLIN - Lighting System - PHILIPS SOLID-STATE LIGHTING SOLUTIONS; *pg.* 1303, *pg.* 806
OPTIBOR - Boric Acid - RIO TINTO BORAX; *pg.* 334, *pg.* 331
OPTIBRONZE - Glass Product - PPG INDUSTRIES, INC.; *pg.* 1445, *pg.* 1579
OPTIC - Furniture - HERMAN MILLER, INC.; *pg.* 926, *pg.* 913
OPTIC - Software - WIND RIVER SYSTEMS, INC.; *pg.* 493, *pg.* 38
OPTIC RULE - Micro-Measuring System - SLANT/FIN CORPORATION; *pg.* 1076, *pg.* 1163
OPTIC SIGNATURE - Leather Product - COACH, INC.; *pg.* 3, *pg.* 1214
OPTICA - Bath & Plumbing Product - JACUZZI BRANDS CORPORATION; *pg.* 554, *pg.* 65
OPTICAID CLIP-ON - Clip-On Magnifier - EDROY PRODUCTS CO., INC.; *pg.* 1411, *pg.* 1318
OPTICAID SPRING-TOP - Ophthalmic Hard-Coated Lens - EDROY PRODUCTS CO., INC.; *pg.* 1411, *pg.* 1318
OPTICAL SERVICES PROTECTOR PLAN - Insurance Package Program - BROWN & BROWN, INC.; *pg.* 1196, *pg.* 419
OPTICAL SHUFFLE - Packaging System - MOLEX INCORPORATED; *pg.* 655, *pg.* 628
OPTICAL TABLES FEATURING IQ - Damping Technology - NEWPORT CORPORATION; *pg.* 1424, *pg.* 114
OPTICAL WAVELENGTH MANAGER - Network Monitoring Product - DIGITAL LIGHTWAVE, INC.; *pg.* 634, *pg.* 462
OPTICALC - Software - THE DOW CHEMICAL COMPANY; *pg.* 1157, *pg.* 898
OPTICAM - Fiber Solution - PANDUIT CORP.; *pg.* 661, *pg.* 663
OPTICARE ANIMAL HEALTH PRODUCTS - Animal Nutritional Supplement - HUBBARD FEEDS INC.; *pg.* 1477, *pg.* 928
OPTICATH - Medical Device - HOSPIRA, INC.; *pg.* 1542, *pg.* 623
OPTICHEM 132 - Fluorescent Dye for Water Leak Testing - PPG INDUSTRIES, INC.; *pg.* 1445, *pg.* 1579
OPTICITE - Chemical Product - THE DOW CHEMICAL COMPANY; *pg.* 1157, *pg.* 898
OPTICLEAN - Brush - CONAIR CORPORATION; *pg.* 505, *pg.* 1055
OPTICLEAR - Containers - OWENS-ILLINOIS, INC.; *pg.* 1466, *pg.* 1470
OPTICLONE - Testing Instrument System - BECKMAN COULTER, INC.; *pg.* 1402, *pg.* 48
OPTICLUDE - Orthoptic Eye Patch - 3M COMPANY; *pg.* 1142, *pg.* 956
OPTICOM - Tray And Drawer - PANDUIT CORP.; *pg.* 661, *pg.* 663
OPTICON - Software - BIO-RAD LABORATORIES, INC.; *pg.* 1504, *pg.* 101
OPTICON MONITOR - Software - BIO-RAD LABORATORIES, INC.; *pg.* 1504, *pg.* 101
OPTICORE - Software - AUTODESK INC.; *pg.* 356, *pg.* 257
OPTICORE - Fiber Optic Lighting System - ENERGY FOCUS, INC.; *pg.* 1411, *pg.* 1472
OPTICS - Fabric - NEMSCHOFF, INC.; *pg.* 936, *pg.* 1890
OPTICS GAS PURIFIER - Purifier - ENTEGRIS, INC.; *pg.* 1882, *pg.* 788
OPTICX - Software - ACXIOM CORPORATION; *pg.* 342, *pg.* 33
OPTIDURA - Scratch Resistant Coating - UVEX SAFETY; *pg.* 1433, *pg.* 1608
OPTIFECT - Molecular Biology Product - THERMO FISHER SCIENTIFIC INC.; *pg.* 1602, *pg.* 61
OPTIFILM - Enhancer - EASTMAN CHEMICAL COMPANY; *pg.* 1159, *pg.* 1636
OPTIFILTER - Respirator - MINE SAFETY APPLIANCES COMPANY; *pg.* 1361, *pg.* 1525
OPTIFIT - Fitting System - CALLAWAY GOLF COMPANY; *pg.* 1829, *pg.* 58
OPTIFIT - Glass & Ceramic Material - CORNING INCORPORATED; *pg.* 1122, *pg.* 1154
OPTIFIX - Chemical Product - SPECTRUM CHEMICALS & LABORATORY PRODUCTS, INC.; *pg.* 1181, *pg.* 94
OPTIFLAME - Electrical Heating Product - DIMPLEX NORTH AMERICA LIMITED; *pg.* 54, *pg.* 1920
OPTIFLEX - Forefoot Flexibility Channel - ACUSHNET COMPANY; *pg.* 1824, *pg.* 818
OPTIFLEX - Medical Device - BOSTON SCIENTIFIC CORPORATION; *pg.* 1508, *pg.* 831
OPTIFLEX - Orthopedic Device - DJO SURGICAL; *pg.* 1525, *pg.* 1661
OPTIFLEX - Video Inspection System - FLEXBAR MACHINE CORP.; *pg.* 1337, *pg.* 1169
OPTIFLEX - Packaging Product - FLEXCON CORPORATION; *pg.* 1457, *pg.* 844
OPTIFLEX - Retention & Drainage Aids - GE WATER & PROCESS TECHNOLOGIES; *pg.* 1339, *pg.* 1588
OPTIFLEX - Video Controller - HONEYWELL INTERNATIONAL INC.; *pg.* 407, *pg.* 1088
OPTIFLEX - Supply Management System - OMNICELL INC.; *pg.* 1578, *pg.* 161
OPTIFLEX - High Speed Programmable Surface Scanning - PERCEPTRON, INC.; *pg.* 215, *pg.* 904
OPTIFLEX CL - Software - OMNICELL INC.; *pg.* 1578, *pg.* 161
OPTIFLEX MS - Software - OMNICELL INC.; *pg.* 1578, *pg.* 161
OPTIFLEX SS - Software - OMNICELL INC.; *pg.* 1578, *pg.* 161
OPTIFLO - Medical Device - BOSTON SCIENTIFIC CORPORATION; *pg.* 1508, *pg.* 831
OPTIFLORA - Herbal Formula - SHAKLEE CORPORATION; *pg.* 1593, *pg.* 184
OPTIFOAM - Medical Product - MEDLINE INDUSTRIES, INC.; *pg.* 1562, *pg.* 635
OPTIFOCUS - Glass & Ceramic Material - CORNING INCORPORATED; *pg.* 1122, *pg.* 1154
OPTIFRESH - Nutritional Supplement - NATURAL ORGANICS, INC.; *pg.* 1571, *pg.* 1181
OPTIGARD - Waterblocking Agents - DOW CORNING CORPORATION; *pg.* 1159, *pg.* 900
OPTIGEN - Adjustable Speed Generator - BALDOR ELECTRIC COMPANY; *pg.* 1316, *pg.* 32
OPTIGRAY - Glass Product - PPG INDUSTRIES, INC.; *pg.* 1445, *pg.* 1579
OPTIGUARD - Quality Control Program - EASTMAN KODAK COMPANY; *pg.* 1408, *pg.* 1333
OPTILASE - Laser Device - TRIMEDYNE, INC.; *pg.* 1432, *pg.* 121
OPTILINX - Switch - EMCORE CORPORATION; *pg.* 636, *pg.* 39
OPTILINX OLX-1000 - Electronic Component - EMCORE CORPORATION; *pg.* 636, *pg.* 39
OPTILINX OLX-3000 - Electronic Component - EMCORE CORPORATION; *pg.* 636, *pg.* 39
OPTILINX X-6000 - Electronic Component - EMCORE CORPORATION; *pg.* 636, *pg.* 39
OPTILITE - Lenses - MCR SAFETY; *pg.* 1422, *pg.* 1630
OPTILOCK - Medical Device - LEMAITRE VASCULAR, INC.; *pg.* 1555, *pg.* 805
OPTILON - Filters & Reflectors - E.I. DU PONT DE NEMOURS & COMPANY; *pg.* 1159, *pg.* 390
OPTILYSE - Testing Instrument System - BECKMAN COULTER, INC.; *pg.* 1402, *pg.* 48
OPTIM - Glycerine - THE DOW CHEMICAL COMPANY; *pg.* 1157, *pg.* 898
OPTIM - Bradycardia Products - ST. JUDE MEDICAL, INC.; *pg.* 1596, *pg.* 963
OPTIMA - Credit Card Services - AMERICAN EXPRESS COMPANY; *pg.* 712, *pg.* 1190
OPTIMA - Ceilings & Walls - ARMSTRONG WORLD INDUSTRIES, INC.; *pg.* 914, *pg.* 1545
OPTIMA - Furniture - ASHLEY FURNITURE INDUSTRIES, INC.; *pg.* 914, *pg.* 1852
OPTIMA - Testing Instrument System - BECKMAN COULTER, INC.; *pg.* 1402, *pg.* 48
OPTIMA - Hearing Aid - BELTONE ELECTRONICS LLC; *pg.* 1503, *pg.* 614
OPTIMA - Thermoplastic Adhesive - H.B. FULLER COMPANY; *pg.* 1165, *pg.* 961
OPTIMA - Poly-Cotton Cover Material - HOLLISTON LLC; *pg.* 1460, *pg.* 1630
OPTIMA - Auto Batteries - JOHNSON CONTROLS, INC.; *pg.* 209, *pg.* 1876
OPTIMA - Power Generator - MKS INSTRUMENTS, INC.; *pg.* 1362, *pg.* 781
OPTIMA - ICP Spectrometer - PERKINELMER, INC.; *pg.* 1426, *pg.* 853
OPTIMA - Memory Card - PNY TECHNOLOGIES, INC.; *pg.* 455, *pg.* 1105
OPTIMA - Shakes, Meal Bars & Snack Bars - SLIM-FAST FOODS COMPANY; *pg.* 896, *pg.* 1061
OPTIMA - Plumbing Product - SLOAN VALVE COMPANY;

First page reference indicates Business Class Edition
Second page reference indicates Geographic Edition

pg. 1062, *pg.* 613
OPTIMA - Computer Modems - ZOOM TECHNOLOGIES, INC.; *pg.* 497, *pg.* 1317
OPTIMA COMPACTFLASH - Digital Camera - PNY TECHNOLOGIES, INC.; *pg.* 455, *pg.* 1105
OPTIMA HD - Semiconductor Processing Equipment - AXCELIS TECHNOLOGIES, INC.; *pg.* 1400, *pg.* 787
OPTIMA MD - Semiconductor Processing Equipment - AXCELIS TECHNOLOGIES, INC.; *pg.* 1400, *pg.* 787
OPTIMA PLUS - Electronic Faucet - SLOAN VALVE COMPANY; *pg.* 1062, *pg.* 613
OPTIMA ROYAL - Flushometer - SLOAN VALVE COMPANY; *pg.* 1062, *pg.* 613
OPTIMA ROYAL II - Flushometer - SLOAN VALVE COMPANY; *pg.* 1062, *pg.* 613
OPTIMA SECURE DIGITAL - Digital Camera - PNY TECHNOLOGIES, INC.; *pg.* 455, *pg.* 1105
OPTIMA XE - Ion Implanter - AXCELIS TECHNOLOGIES, INC.; *pg.* 1400, *pg.* 787
OPTIMAB - Biomolecule Product - THERMO FISHER SCIENTIFIC INC.; *pg.* 1602, *pg.* 61
OPTIMAIR - Air-Purifying Respirator - MINE SAFETY APPLIANCES COMPANY; *pg.* 1361, *pg.* 1525
OPTIMALFLOW - Software - COMPUWARE CORPORATION; *pg.* 379, *pg.* 879
OPTIMALJ - Software - COMPUWARE CORPORATION; *pg.* 379, *pg.* 879
OPTIMALVIEW - Software - COMPUWARE CORPORATION; *pg.* 379, *pg.* 879
OPTIMAT - Plastic & Rubber - TEKNOR APEX COMPANY; *pg.* 1889, *pg.* 1605
OPTIMAX - Healthcare Product - GF HEALTH PRODUCTS, INC.; *pg.* 1535, *pg.* 508
OPTIMELT - Low Temperature Application Hot Melt - H.B. FULLER COMPANY; *pg.* 1165, *pg.* 961
OPTIMENTAL - Pharmaceutical Product - ABBOTT LABORATORIES; *pg.* 1484, *pg.* 551
OPTIMICRO - Dissection Electrodes - UTAH MEDICAL PRODUCTS, INC.; *pg.* 1605, *pg.* 1752
OPTIMIL COMPLETE - Medicated Feed Supplement for Preventing or Treating Calf Scours - MANNA PRO CORPORATION; *pg.* 1478, *pg.* 975
OPTIMIN - Organic Trace Minerals - TROUW NUTRITION USA; *pg.* 1482, *pg.* 616
OPTIMISER - Spray Gun - GRACO, INC.; *pg.* 1342, *pg.* 935
OPTIMIZE - Nutritional Supplement - PHARMAVITE LLC; *pg.* 1584, *pg.* 167
OPTIMIZE ON DEMAND - Software - JDA SOFTWARE GROUP, INC.; *pg.* 423, *pg.* 22
OPTIMIZED FOR XEROX FREEFLOW - Software - XEROX CORPORATION; *pg.* 494, *pg.* 365
OPTIMIZEIT - Software - BIO-RAD LABORATORIES, INC.; *pg.* 1504, *pg.* 101
OPTIMIZER - Adjustable Dish Dolly - CARLISLE FOODSERVICE PRODUCTS INCORPORATED; *pg.* 1455, *pg.* 1485
OPTIMIZER - Filters & Manifolds - ENTEGRIS, INC.; *pg.* 1882, *pg.* 788
OPTIMIZER - Laptop Business Backpack - JANSPORT; *pg.* 1837, *pg.* 38
OPTIMIZER - Cable & Antenna System - RADIO FREQUENCY SYSTEMS, INC.; *pg.* 666, *pg.* 354
OPTIMIZING PERFORMANCE ... IN A CONVERGED WORLD - Tag Line - CARTESIAN; *pg.* 369, *pg.* 718
OPTIMIZING THE CUSTOMER EXPERIENCE - Tagline - PEGASYSTEMS INC.; *pg.* 453, *pg.* 74
OPTIML - Chemical Product - THE DOW CHEMICAL COMPANY; *pg.* 1157, *pg.* 898
OPTIMMUNE - Canine Ophthalmic Ointment - MERCK & CO., INC.; *pg.* 1566, *pg.* 1077
OPTIMO - Cigars - SWISHER INTERNATIONAL, INC.; *pg.* 1895, *pg.* 345
OPTIMODAL - Freight Transportation - SCHNEIDER; *pg.* 1922, *pg.* 1859
OPTIMOUNT - Helical Gear Drives - BOSTON GEAR; *pg.* 201, *pg.* 802
OPTIMUM - Technical Furniture - IAC INDUSTRIES, INC.; *pg.* 929, *pg.* 48
OPTIMUM - Metal Gondolas - MEG; *pg.* 97, *pg.* 675
OPTIMUM - Cold Cereal - NATURE'S PATH FOODS INC.; *pg.* 833, *pg.* 1908
OPTIMUM - Mattresses - TEMPUR SEALY INTERNATIONAL, INC.; *pg.* 944, *pg.* 731
OPTIMUM CHOICE - Motor Oils, Lubricants & Greases - ASHLAND INC.; *pg.* 972, *pg.* 726
OPTIMUM LIFE - Wellness Program - BROOKDALE SENIOR LIVING INC.; *pg.* 1511, *pg.* 1627
OPTIMUM POWER - Breakfast Cereals - NATURE'S PATH FOODS INC.; *pg.* 833, *pg.* 1908
OPTIMUM REBOUND - Cereals - NATURE'S PATH FOODS INC.; *pg.* 833, *pg.* 1908
OPTIMUM SERIES - Engine Powered Forklifts - NISSAN FORKLIFT CORPORATION, NORTH AMERICA; *pg.* 186, *pg.* 631
OPTIMUM SLIM - Waffles - NATURE'S PATH FOODS INC.; *pg.* 833, *pg.* 1908
OPTIMUM ZEN - Breakfast Cereals - NATURE'S PATH FOODS INC.; *pg.* 833, *pg.* 1908
OPTINDEX - Polymer - BREWER SCIENCE, INC.; *pg.* 1150, *pg.* 989
OPTIO DESIGNSTUDIO - Software - BOTTOMLINE TECHNOLOGIES INC.; *pg.* 363, *pg.* 483
OPTIO E.COMINTEGRATE - Software - BOTTOMLINE TECHNOLOGIES INC.; *pg.* 363, *pg.* 483
OPTIO E.COMPRESENT - Software - BOTTOMLINE TECHNOLOGIES INC.; *pg.* 363, *pg.* 483
OPTIO ENTERPRISE PROCESSPACKS - Software - BOTTOMLINE TECHNOLOGIES INC.; *pg.* 363, *pg.* 483
OPTIO HEALTHCARE PROCESSPACKS - Software - BOTTOMLINE TECHNOLOGIES INC.; *pg.* 363, *pg.* 483
OPTIO MEDEXFLEX - Software - BOTTOMLINE TECHNOLOGIES INC.; *pg.* 363, *pg.* 483
OPTIO MEDFORMS - Software - BOTTOMLINE TECHNOLOGIES INC.; *pg.* 363, *pg.* 483
OPTIODCS - Software - BOTTOMLINE TECHNOLOGIES INC.; *pg.* 363, *pg.* 483
OPTIOFAX - Software - BOTTOMLINE TECHNOLOGIES INC.; *pg.* 363, *pg.* 483
OPTIONAL RAPIDHEAT - Bath & Plumbing Product - JACUZZI BRANDS CORPORATION; *pg.* 554, *pg.* 65
OPTIONALL - Pipeline Pigging Product - T.D. WILLIAMSON, INC.; *pg.* 1380, *pg.* 1490
OPTIONS - Pigment & Dispersion - BASF CATALYSTS LLC; *pg.* 1148, *pg.* 1074
OPTIONS - Credit Card - CANADIAN TIRE CORPORATION LIMITED; *pg.* 202, *pg.* 1936
OPTIONS - Printing Paper - MOHAWK FINE PAPERS, INC.; *pg.* 1464, *pg.* 1153
OPTIONS - Publication - VALUE LINE, INC.; *pg.* 1699, *pg.* 1308
OPTIONSTATION - Investment Analysis Software - TRADESTATION GROUP, INC.; *pg.* 811, *pg.* 459
OPTIPATTERN - Chemical Products - AIR PRODUCTS AND CHEMICALS, INC.; *pg.* 1145, *pg.* 1513
OPTIPLATE - Microplates - PERKINELMER, INC.; *pg.* 1426, *pg.* 853
OPTIPLAY - Drive Technology - WESTERN DIGITAL CORPORATION; *pg.* 492, *pg.* 118
OPTIPLEX - Desktop Computers - DELL INC.; *pg.* 383, *pg.* 1737
OPTIPORE - Wound Care Product - CONVATEC LTD.; *pg.* 1518, *pg.* 1121
OPTIPRO - Biomolecule Product - THERMO FISHER SCIENTIFIC INC.; *pg.* 1602, *pg.* 61
OPTIQ - Medical Device - HOSPIRA, INC.; *pg.* 1542, *pg.* 623
OPTIQUANT - Software - PERKINELMER, INC.; *pg.* 1426, *pg.* 853
OPTIQUEL - Ophthalmic Preparation - ENZO BIOCHEM INC.; *pg.* 1529, *pg.* 1228
OPTIQUEST - Computer Monitor - VIEWSONIC CORPORATION; *pg.* 489, *pg.* 303
OPTIRHYTHM - Pulse Oximeters - IDEXX LABORATORIES, INC.; *pg.* 1543, *pg.* 753
OPTIRINSE - Chemical Products - AIR PRODUCTS AND CHEMICALS, INC.; *pg.* 1145, *pg.* 1513
OPTISENSE - Bradycardia Products - ST. JUDE MEDICAL, INC.; *pg.* 1596, *pg.* 963
OPTISHEATH - Glass & Ceramic Material - CORNING INCORPORATED; *pg.* 1122, *pg.* 1154
OPTISHIELD - Faucet Accessory - SLOAN VALVE COMPANY; *pg.* 1062, *pg.* 613
OPTISOL - Gas Treating Services - THE DOW CHEMICAL COMPANY; *pg.* 1157, *pg.* 898
OPTISOLV - Cleaning Chemical Product - KYZEN CORPORATION; *pg.* 331, *pg.* 1652
OPTISON - Medical Device - GE HEALTHCARE TECHNOLOGIES; *pg.* 1533, *pg.* 1897
OPTISOURCE - Pharmaceutical Product - NESTLE HEALTHCARE NUTRITION; *pg.* 1572, *pg.* 941
OPTISPEC - Electrosurgical Instruments - UTAH MEDICAL PRODUCTS, INC.; *pg.* 1605, *pg.* 1752
OPTISPERSE - Alkaline Cleaning Compounds - GE WATER & PROCESS TECHNOLOGIES; *pg.* 1339, *pg.* 1588
OPTISTAR - Microimage Terminals & Datawriters - EASTMAN KODAK COMPANY; *pg.* 1408, *pg.* 1333
OPTISTROKE - Needle Stroke Detection System - NORDSON CORPORATION; *pg.* 1365, *pg.* 1480
OPTISYNC - LCD Display - VIEWSONIC CORPORATION; *pg.* 489, *pg.* 303
OPTITEMP - Cooking Equipment Technology - AMWAY CORPORATION; *pg.* 326, *pg.* 864
OPTITINT - Lens Treatment Product - EMERGING VISION, INC.; *pg.* 1411, *pg.* 1227
OPTIUM XCEED - Pharmaceutical Product - ABBOTT LABORATORIES; *pg.* 1484, *pg.* 551
OPTIVA - Electronic Components - EMCORE CORPORATION; *pg.* 636, *pg.* 39
OPTIVA 1RU - Chassis - EMCORE CORPORATION; *pg.* 636, *pg.* 39
OPTIVA 3RU CHASSIS - Enclosure - EMCORE CORPORATION; *pg.* 636, *pg.* 39
OPTIVA AUDIO - Sound Transmission - EMCORE CORPORATION; *pg.* 636, *pg.* 39
OPTIVA RS232/422/485 - Electronic Component - EMCORE CORPORATION; *pg.* 636, *pg.* 39
OPTIVA S-VIDEO - Electronic Component - EMCORE CORPORATION; *pg.* 636, *pg.* 39
OPTIVA SDI - Electronic Component - EMCORE CORPORATION; *pg.* 636, *pg.* 39
OPTIVAC - Suction Equipment - ALLIED HEALTHCARE PRODUCTS, INC.; *pg.* 1491, *pg.* 990
OPTIVAVIEW - Software - EMCORE CORPORATION; *pg.* 636, *pg.* 39
OPTIVE - Eye Drop - ALLERGAN, INC.; *pg.* 1491, *pg.* 106
OPTIVIEW - Control Center - JOHNSON CONTROLS, INC.; *pg.* 209, *pg.* 1876
OPTIVISION - Software System - HONEYWELL INTERNATIONAL INC.; *pg.* 407, *pg.* 1088
OPTIWHITE - Calcined Kaolin - BURGESS PIGMENT COMPANY; *pg.* 1150, *pg.* 535
OPTIWHITE MX - Flash Calcined Kaolin - BURGESS PIGMENT COMPANY; *pg.* 1150, *pg.* 535
OPTIWHITE P - Calcined Kaolin - BURGESS PIGMENT COMPANY; *pg.* 1150, *pg.* 535
OPTIWRITER - Microfilm - EASTMAN KODAK COMPANY; *pg.* 1408, *pg.* 1333
OPTIX - Acrylic Flat Sheet - PLASKOLITE, INC.; *pg.* 1888, *pg.* 1443
OPTIXAN - High Quality Xanthan Gum for Industrial Applications - ARCHER-DANIELS-MIDLAND COMPANY; *pg.* 825, *pg.* 565
OPTIXAN T - Xantham Gum - ARCHER-DANIELS-MIDLAND COMPANY; *pg.* 825, *pg.* 565
OPTIXAN XANTHAN GUM 40 MESH - Xantham Gum - ARCHER-DANIELS-MIDLAND COMPANY; *pg.* 825, *pg.* 565
OPTIXAN XANTHAN GUM DISPERSIBLE - Xantham Gum - ARCHER-DANIELS-MIDLAND COMPANY; *pg.* 825, *pg.* 565
OPTIXAN XANTHAN GUM TRANSPARENT - Xantham Gum - ARCHER-DANIELS-MIDLAND COMPANY; *pg.* 825, *pg.* 565
OPTIXIA - Performance Analysis Platform - IXIA; *pg.* 422, *pg.* 56
OPTIYIELD - Chemical Products - AIR PRODUCTS AND CHEMICALS, INC.; *pg.* 1145, *pg.* 1513
OPTIZONE - Drive Technology - WESTERN DIGITAL CORPORATION; *pg.* 492, *pg.* 118
OPTO-MATIC - Constant Level Oiler - TRICO MFG. CORP.; *pg.* 219, *pg.* 1886
OPTOCERAMIC - Glass & Ceramic Material - CORNING INCORPORATED; *pg.* 1122, *pg.* 1154
OPTOCOMMERCE - Glass & Ceramic Material - CORNING INCORPORATED; *pg.* 1122, *pg.* 1154
OPTOCUBE - Fiber Optic Product - EMCORE CORPORATION; *pg.* 636, *pg.* 39
OPTOGRADE - Metalorganic Precursors - THE DOW CHEMICAL COMPANY; *pg.* 1157, *pg.* 898
OPTOMEGA - Nutritional Supplement - USANA HEALTH SCIENCES, INC.; *pg.* 1605, *pg.* 1761
THE OPTOMETRIC PROTECTOR PLAN - Insurance Package Program - BROWN & BROWN, INC.; *pg.* 1196, *pg.* 419
OPTOMETRISTS PROTECTOR PLAN - Insurance Package Program - BROWN & BROWN, INC.; *pg.* 1196, *pg.* 419

First page reference indicates Business Class Edition
Second page reference indicates Geographic Edition

OPTOMIKE - Motorized Positioner - OPTOSIGMA CORP.; pg. 1425, pg. 262
OPTOSHIELD - Laser Light Safety Scanner - OMRON SCIENTIFIC TECHNOLOGIES INCORPORATED; pg. 1425, pg. 91
OPTRA - Print Cartridge - LEXMARK INTERNATIONAL, INC.; pg. 427, pg. 730
OPTRACK - Option Strategy Search & Rank Tool - TRACK DATA CORPORATION; pg. 1284, pg. 1147
OPTUM - Thermoplastic Polymer Resin - FERRO CORPORATION; pg. 1162, pg. 1462
OPTUMHEALTH - Health & Well-Being Services - UNITEDHEALTH GROUP INCORPORATED; pg. 1221, pg. 950
OPTUS - Satellite - ORBITAL ATK; pg. 1425, pg. 1779
OPTX - Software - CIENA CORPORATION; pg. 628, pg. 771
OPTYON - Hardware Product - QUANTUM CORPORATION; pg. 458, pg. 250
OPTYX - Sorter - KEY TECHNOLOGY, INC.; pg. 868, pg. 1847
OPULENCE - Furniture - ASHLEY FURNITURE INDUSTRIES, INC.; pg. 914, pg. 1852
OPULENCE - Bedding - CROSCILL, INC.; pg. 1122, pg. 1220
OPULENCE - Ceiling Fan - WESTINGHOUSE LIGHTING CORPORATION; pg. 687, pg. 1571
OPULYN - Opacifiers - THE DOW CHEMICAL COMPANY; pg. 1157, pg. 898
OPUS - Metal Etch System - APPLIED MATERIALS, INC.; pg. 618, pg. 264
OPUS - Catheter/Stylet - MEDTRONIC, INC.; pg. 1564, pg. 939
OPUS - Pet Product - PETSMART, INC.; pg. 1481, pg. 18
OPUS - Tables - STEELCASE INC.; pg. 475, pg. 889
OPUS - Furniture - TROPITONE FURNITURE CO., INC.; pg. 945, pg. 118
OPUS - Lighting Product - WESTINGHOUSE LIGHTING CORPORATION; pg. 687, pg. 1571
OPUS ANTICATO - Stone Collections - WALKER & ZANGER, INC.; pg. 119, pg. 281
OPUS SERVICENET - Web Portal - OPUS CORPORATION; pg. 101, pg. 949
OPUSXPRESS - Electrophysiology System - MOLECULAR DEVICES CORPORATION; pg. 1568, pg. 287
OPX SERIES - Baseball Glove - HILLERICH & BRADSBY CO., INC.; pg. 1836, pg. 576
OQOQO - Sports Apparel - LULULEMON ATHLETICA INC.; pg. 44, pg. 1911
OR-360 - MRI Operating Room - FONAR CORPORATION; pg. 1413, pg. 1179
OR-E-O KRUMS 4 - Medicated Livestock Feed - KENT NUTRITION GROUP; pg. 1477, pg. 710
OR21 - Medical Equipment Leasing - AMERICAN SHARED HOSPITAL SERVICES; pg. 1493, pg. 212
ORA KEY - Nutritional Product - RBC LIFE SCIENCES, INC.; pg. 1588, pg. 1723
ORABASE - Lip Healer - COLGATE ORAL PHARMACEUTICAL; pg. 1516, pg. 1214
ORACID PLUS - Hygenic Product - GEA FARM TECHNOLOGIES; pg. 704, pg. 636
ORACLE - Microfilmers & Reader Printers - EASTMAN KODAK COMPANY; pg. 1408, pg. 1333
ORACLE - Software - ORACLE CORPORATION; pg. 450, pg. 191
ORACLE CLINICAL - Software - ENCORIUM GROUP, INC.; pg. 1528, pg. 1591
ORACLE TMS - Software - ENCORIUM GROUP, INC.; pg. 1528, pg. 1591
ORADISC - Adhesive Erodible Film Technology - ULURU INC.; pg. 1603, pg. 1658
ORAGARD-B - Dental Product - COLGATE-PALMOLIVE COMPANY; pg. 504, pg. 1215
ORAJEL - Oral Care - CHURCH & DWIGHT CO., INC.; pg. 1153, pg. 1063
ORAL-B - Oral Product - THE GILLETTE COMPANY; pg. 509, pg. 795
ORAL-B - Personal & Household Product - THE PROCTER & GAMBLE COMPANY; pg. 1129, pg. 1418
ORAL-B 3D EXCEL - Electric Toothbrush - GILLETTE; pg. 1536, pg. 795
ORAL-B ADVANTAGES FLOSS PICK - Oral Care Product - THE PROCTER & GAMBLE COMPANY; pg. 1129, pg. 1418
ORAL-B TRIUMPH SMARTGUIDE - Toothbrush - THE PROCTER & GAMBLE COMPANY; pg. 1129, pg. 1418
ORAL-LYN - Oral Insulin Spray - GENEREX BIOTECHNOLOGY CORPORATION; pg. 1534, pg. 1938
ORAL RAE - Tracheal Tube - MEDTRONIC; pg. 1563, pg. 183
ORALERT - Pharmaceutical Product - ALERE INC.; pg. 1488, pg. 849
ORALIUM - Dental Bands - BASF CATALYSTS LLC; pg. 1148, pg. 1074
ORALSTAT - Diagnostic Test Kit - AMERICAN BIO MEDICA CORPORATION; pg. 1493, pg. 1171
ORANGE-A-PEEL - Fruit Drink - JAMBA, INC.; pg. 1024, pg. 84
ORANGE ACTION - Wipes - S.C. JOHNSON & SON, INC.; pg. 334, pg. 1889
ORANGE BERRY BLITZ - Smoothie - JAMBA, INC.; pg. 1024, pg. 84
ORANGE BLOSSOM - Bouquet - EDIBLE ARRANGEMENTS INTERNATIONAL, INC.; pg. 1768, pg. 382
ORANGE BLOSSOM - Honey - MILLER'S HONEY COMPANY; pg. 1860, pg. 1759
THE ORANGE COUNTY REGISTER - California Newspaper - FREEDOM COMMUNICATIONS, INC.; pg. 1643, pg. 110
ORANGE COUNTY REGISTER - Newspaper - THE ORANGE COUNTY REGISTER; pg. 1673, pg. 262
ORANGE CREME DE LA CREME - Ice Cream - DIPPIN' DOTS LLC; pg. 853, pg. 739
ORANGE DEGREASER - Automotive Reconditioning Product - MOC PRODUCTS COMPANY, INC.; pg. 332, pg. 174
ORANGE DREAM - Beverage - SPRECHER BREWING COMPANY; pg. 265, pg. 1858
ORANGE DREAM - Ice Cream Bar - WELLS ENTERPRISES, INC.; pg. 909, pg. 709
ORANGE DREAM MACHINE - Fruit Drink - JAMBA, INC.; pg. 1024, pg. 84
ORANGE DREAM SODA - Soda - SPRECHER BREWING COMPANY; pg. 265, pg. 1858
ORANGE DRIVER - Cocktail Mix - MONTEBELLO BRANDS INC.; pg. 1967, pg. 758
ORANGE ENERGY PINE-SOL - All Purpose Cleaner - THE CLOROX COMPANY; pg. 327, pg. 169
ORANGE GLO - Household Cleaner - CHURCH & DWIGHT CO., INC.; pg. 1153, pg. 1063
ORANGE-GO - Urethane Belts - FENNER DRIVES; pg. 1336, pg. 1551
ORANGE GOOP - Hand Cleaner, Towels, Soaps & Hand Creme - CRITZAS INDUSTRIES, INC.; pg. 329, pg. 995
ORANGE JUICE JR - Nutritional Supplement - NATURAL ORGANICS, INC.; pg. 1571, pg. 1181
ORANGE LABEL SISALKRAFT - Vapor Retarder - FORTIFIBER CORPORATION; pg. 83, pg. 1021
ORANGE MAGIC - Premium Bullet Lube - LYMAN PRODUCTS CORPORATION; pg. 1839, pg. 356
ORANGE MANGO PASSION - Fruit Drink - JAMBA, INC.; pg. 1024, pg. 84
ORANGE MANGO TANGO - Fruit Juice Cocktail - NEWMAN'S OWN, INC.; pg. 886, pg. 384
ORANGE MEDICAL - Pharmaceutical Product - ALERE INC.; pg. 1488, pg. 849
ORANGE SQUEEZE - Roller Cover - VAIL RUBBER WORKS, INC.; pg. 1891, pg. 906
ORANGE STICKS - Candy - SWEET CANDY COMPANY; pg. 1862, pg. 1761
ORANGE (TIP COLOR) - Fluid Handling System - GRACO, INC.; pg. 1342, pg. 935
ORANGUTAN-O'S - Breakfast Cereals - NATURE'S PATH FOODS INC.; pg. 833, pg. 1908
ORAQIX - Dental Product - DENTSPLY INTERNATIONAL INC.; pg. 1522, pg. 1596
ORAQUICK - Medical Test Product - ABBOTT LABORATORIES; pg. 1484, pg. 551
ORAQUICK ADVANCE - Medical Test - ABBOTT LABORATORIES; pg. 1484, pg. 551
ORAQUICK ADVANCE - Antibody Test - ORASURE TECHNOLOGIES INC; pg. 1578, pg. 1516
ORASERT - Cough Tablet - LUMARA HEALTH INC.; pg. 1557, pg. 973
ORASITE - Orally Administered Controlled Release Mucoadhesive Delivery System - LUMARA HEALTH INC.; pg. 1557, pg. 973
ORASURE - Diagnostic Product - ORASURE TECHNOLOGIES INC; pg. 1578, pg. 1516
ORAVISUAL - Easels & Lecterns - DA-LITE SCREEN COMPANY; pg. 632, pg. 698
ORAXION - Software - IDEALAB, INC.; pg. 1258, pg. 180
ORBACUS - Software - PROGRESS SOFTWARE CORPORATION; pg. 457, pg. 786
ORBAX - Medicine - MERCK & CO., INC.; pg. 1566, pg. 1077
ORBESEAL - Pharmaceutical Product - PFIZER INC.; pg. 1581, pg. 1278
ORBISPHERE - Analytical Instrument - DANAHER CORPORATION; pg. 1044, pg. 397
ORBIT - Guest Chairs - BERNHARDT DESIGN; pg. 918, pg. 1381
ORBIT - Carpet - INTERFACE, INC.; pg. 695, pg. 512
ORBIT - Medical Equipment - INVACARE CORPORATION; pg. 1546, pg. 1451
ORBIT - Brushes - OSBORN INTERNATIONAL; pg. 1367, pg. 1406
ORBIT - Toothbrush - RANIR LLC; pg. 520, pg. 888
ORBIT - Gum - WM. WRIGLEY JR. COMPANY; pg. 1863, pg. 596
ORBIT-AIR - Air Seeder - GANDY COMPANY; pg. 703, pg. 952
ORBIT-FLOW - Fertilizer Applicator with Speed-Compensated Metering - GANDY COMPANY; pg. 703, pg. 952
ORBIT-SNARE - Endoscopic Technologies - CONMED CORPORATION; pg. 1517, pg. 1347
ORBITAL - Battery - EXIDE TECHNOLOGIES; pg. 204, pg. 483
ORBITAL - Apparel - OAKLEY, INC.; pg. 1840, pg. 86
ORBITER - Cleaning Product - ORECK CORPORATION; pg. 59, pg. 1653
ORBITER - Commercial Lighting - SWIVELIER CO., INC.; pg. 1307, pg. 1142
ORBITER 6000 - Rotary Filler - LIQUI-BOX CORPORATION; pg. 1464, pg. 1802
ORBITEX - Abrasive Flow Machine - KENNAMETAL EXTRUDE HONE; pg. 1352, pg. 1542
ORBITRAC 2 - Vinyl Record Cleaning System - ALLSOP, INC.; pg. 347, pg. 1817
ORBITZ - Online Travel Services - TRAVELPORT LIMITED; pg. 1925, pg. 521
ORBITZ FOR BUSINESS - Corporate Travel Services - TRAVELPORT LIMITED; pg. 1925, pg. 521
ORBITZ.COM - Travel Web Site - ORBITZ WORLDWIDE, INC.; pg. 1918, pg. 586
ORBIX STANDARD - Software - PROGRESS SOFTWARE CORPORATION; pg. 457, pg. 786
ORBOS - Blood Analysers - ABAXIS, INC.; pg. 1483, pg. 298
ORBS - Simulation - HASBRO, INC.; pg. 954, pg. 1603
ORBSCAN - Anterior Segment Analysis System - BAUSCH & LOMB INCORPORATED; pg. 1401, pg. 1045
ORBVIEW - Satellite - DIGITALGLOBE; pg. 227, pg. 1785
ORBVIEW - Satellite - ORBITAL ATK; pg. 1425, pg. 1779
ORCA - Testing Instrument System - BECKMAN COULTER, INC.; pg. 1402, pg. 48
ORCA - Liquid Cylinder - CHART INDUSTRIES, INC.; pg. 1405, pg. 1454
ORCA - Video Game - INTERNATIONAL GAME TECHNOLOGY; pg. 957, pg. 1024
ORCA - Control System - ION GEOPHYSICAL CORPORATION; pg. 1350, pg. 1708
ORCA - Packaging Product - PACTIV CORPORATION; pg. 1466, pg. 624
ORCAD - Software - CADENCE DESIGN SYSTEMS, INC.; pg. 367, pg. 239
ORCAS - Sport Knife - MCNETT CORPORATION; pg. 1839, pg. 1817
ORCAS - Integrated Financial & Clinical Software - OMNICARE, INC; pg. 1578, pg. 1418
ORCHARD BANK - Credit Card - CAPITAL ONE FINANCIAL CORPORATION; pg. 730, pg. 1789
ORCHARD BOOKS - Educational Materials - SCHOLASTIC INC.; pg. 1683, pg. 1288
ORCHARD BOY - Food Products - NATIONAL FRUIT PRODUCT COMPANY, INC.; pg. 882, pg. 1811
ORCHARD CHOICE - Fig - VALLEY FIG GROWERS, INC.; pg. 908, pg. 93
ORCHARD MIX - Food Product - SUNSWEET GROWERS, INC.; pg. 900, pg. 309
ORCHARD PARK - Food Product - SUBCO FOODS, INC.; pg. 899, pg. 668
ORCHARDMASTER - Agricultural Product - PBI/GORDON CORPORATION; pg. 1176, pg. 985
ORCHESTRA - Fragrance - WESTROCK COMPANY; pg. 1472, pg. 1805
ORCHID - Oil & Spray - AROMATIQUE INC.; pg. 499, pg. 32
ORCHID - Sleeper & Recliner Seating - STEELCASE INC.; pg. 475, pg. 889

First page reference indicates Business Class Edition
Second page reference indicates Geographic Edition

ORCHID EMBRACE - Flower Arrangement - 1-800-FLOWERS.COM, INC.; *pg.* 1758, *pg.* 1151
ORCHID MOSS - Potting Material - SUN BULB COMPANY, INC.; *pg.* 1800, *pg.* 409
ORCHID PLUS - Fertilizer - SUN BULB COMPANY, INC.; *pg.* 1800, *pg.* 409
ORCHIDS AND NARCISSUS - Bath Accessory - CROSCILL, INC.; *pg.* 1122, *pg.* 1220
ORCS AND ELVES - Video Game - ID SOFTWARE, INC.; *pg.* 956, *pg.* 1727
ORDER - Apparel - OAKLEY, INC.; *pg.* 1840, *pg.* 86
ORDER ACCELERATOR - Software - VITRIA TECHNOLOGY, INC.; *pg.* 490, *pg.* 289
ORDER ENTRY - Electronic Prescription Ordering Service - OMNICARE, INC; *pg.* 1578, *pg.* 1418
ORDER-MATIC - Printed Order Form - EASTMAN KODAK COMPANY; *pg.* 1408, *pg.* 1333
ORDER OPTIMIZATION - Software - JDA SOFTWARE GROUP, INC.; *pg.* 423, *pg.* 22
ORDEREXPRESS - Software - SCAN-OPTICS, LLC; *pg.* 467, *pg.* 354
ORDERKEYSTONE.COM - Online Store - LKQ CORP.; *pg.* 210, *pg.* 185
ORDERPATH - Software - EVOLVING SYSTEMS, INC.; *pg.* 395, *pg.* 326
ORDERQUIX - Software - XEROX CORPORATION; *pg.* 494, *pg.* 365
ORE - Apparel - OAKLEY, INC.; *pg.* 1840, *pg.* 86
ORE-IDA - Potato Based Food Products - THE KRAFT HEINZ COMPANY; *pg.* 870, *pg.* 1577
ORECK ALANITE - Cleaning Product - ORECK CORPORATION; *pg.* 59, *pg.* 1653
ORECK CAR VAC - Cleaning Product - ORECK CORPORATION; *pg.* 59, *pg.* 1653
ORECK DRY CARPET - Cleaning Product - ORECK CORPORATION; *pg.* 59, *pg.* 1653
ORECK FLOOR SWEEPER - Floor Sweeper - ORECK CORPORATION; *pg.* 59, *pg.* 1653
ORECK FRESH AIR - Cleaning Product - ORECK CORPORATION; *pg.* 59, *pg.* 1653
ORECK FULL RELEASE - Cleaning Product - ORECK CORPORATION; *pg.* 59, *pg.* 1653
ORECK HALO - Vacuum Cleaner Bag - ORECK CORPORATION; *pg.* 59, *pg.* 1653
ORECK HOUSEKEEPER - Cleaning Product - ORECK CORPORATION; *pg.* 59, *pg.* 1653
ORECK IRONMAN - Cleaning Product - ORECK CORPORATION; *pg.* 59, *pg.* 1653
ORECK LITTER EX - Cleaning Product - ORECK CORPORATION; *pg.* 59, *pg.* 1653
ORECK PREMIST - Cleaning Product - ORECK CORPORATION; *pg.* 59, *pg.* 1653
ORECK RESTAURATEUR - Cleaning Product - ORECK CORPORATION; *pg.* 59, *pg.* 1653
ORECK XL - Vacuum Cleaner - ORECK CORPORATION; *pg.* 59, *pg.* 1653
ORECKBRITE - Cleaning Product - ORECK CORPORATION; *pg.* 59, *pg.* 1653
OREF - Ice Machine - SCOTSMAN GROUP LLC; *pg.* 1374, *pg.* 665
OREFRESCO - Food Product - FROSTY ACRES BRANDS, INC.; *pg.* 1020, *pg.* 484
OREGON - Saw Chain, Bars & Sprockets - BLOUNT INTERNATIONAL, INC.; *pg.* 1043, *pg.* 1501
OREGON ALE AND BEER COMPANY - Beer & Ale - THE BOSTON BEER COMPANY, INC.; *pg.* 239, *pg.* 790
OREGON GOLD - Video Game - INTERNATIONAL GAME TECHNOLOGY; *pg.* 957, *pg.* 1024
OREGON GREEN - Biomolecule Product - THERMO FISHER SCIENTIFIC INC.; *pg.* 1602, *pg.* 61
OREGON LOTTERY - Lottery Game - OREGON STATE LOTTERY; *pg.* 1003, *pg.* 1508
OREGON SCIENTIFIC - Fitness Equipment - BALLY TOTAL FITNESS HOLDINGS CORPORATION; *pg.* 532, *pg.* 1200
OREGON. WE LOVE DREAMERS - Slogan - OREGON TOURISM COMMISSION; *pg.* 1003, *pg.* 1508
THE OREGONIAN - Daily & Sunday Paper - OREGONIAN PUBLISHING CO.; *pg.* 1673, *pg.* 1504
OREL - Tapered Polyester Paintbrush Filaments - E.I. DU PONT DE NEMOURS & COMPANY; *pg.* 1159, *pg.* 390
ORENCIA - Rheumatoid Arthritis Medication - BRISTOL-MYERS SQUIBB COMPANY; *pg.* 1509, *pg.* 1206
OREO - Cookies - MONDELEZ INTERNATIONAL, INC.; *pg.* 878, *pg.* 601
OREPREP - Chemical Product - CYTEC INDUSTRIES, INC.; *pg.* 1155, *pg.* 1131
ORFFGARAGE - Storage - WENGER CORPORATION; *pg.* 1307, *pg.* 952
ORFFMOBILE - Cart - WENGER CORPORATION; *pg.* 1307, *pg.* 952
ORFORD - Packaging Product - CASCADES, INC.; *pg.* 73, *pg.* 1950
ORG 14 - Bag - CALLAWAY GOLF COMPANY; *pg.* 1829, *pg.* 58
ORGANELLE LIGHTS - Molecular Probe Product - THERMO FISHER SCIENTIFIC INC.; *pg.* 1602, *pg.* 61
ORGANIC - Faucets - MOEN INCORPORATED; *pg.* 1056, *pg.* 1468
ORGANIC - Healthcare Product - SWANSON HEALTH PRODUCTS INC.; *pg.* 1600, *pg.* 1397
ORGANIC - Potato Chips - UTZ QUALITY FOODS, INC.; *pg.* 907, *pg.* 1536
ORGANIC BLACK PARROT BLEND - Coffee - KEURIG GREEN MOUNTAIN, INC.; *pg.* 868, *pg.* 1768
ORGANIC CHOICE - Fertilizers - THE SCOTTS MIRACLE-GRO COMPANY; *pg.* 1799, *pg.* 1459
ORGANIC GARDENING - Magazine - RODALE, INC.; *pg.* 1681, *pg.* 1530
ORGANIC HAZELNUT SELECT - Coffee - KEURIG GREEN MOUNTAIN, INC.; *pg.* 868, *pg.* 1768
ORGANIC HOUSE BLEND - Coffee - KEURIG GREEN MOUNTAIN, INC.; *pg.* 868, *pg.* 1768
ORGANIC MEXICAN SELECT - Coffee - KEURIG GREEN MOUNTAIN, INC.; *pg.* 868, *pg.* 1768
ORGANIC PEPPERMINT TEA - Tea Product - CELESTIAL SEASONINGS, INC.; *pg.* 846, *pg.* 310
ORGANIC PERUVIAN SELECT - Coffee - KEURIG GREEN MOUNTAIN, INC.; *pg.* 868, *pg.* 1768
ORGANIC PROMISE - Breakfast Cereal - KASHI COMPANY; *pg.* 830, *pg.* 119
ORGANIC PROMISE AUTUMN WHEAT - Cereal - KASHI COMPANY; *pg.* 830, *pg.* 119
ORGANIC PROMISE CRANBERRY SUNSHINE - Cereal - KASHI COMPANY; *pg.* 830, *pg.* 119
ORGANIC PROMISE STRAWBERRY FIELDS - Cereal - KASHI COMPANY; *pg.* 830, *pg.* 119
ORGANIC RAIN FOREST BLEND - Coffee - KEURIG GREEN MOUNTAIN, INC.; *pg.* 868, *pg.* 1768
ORGANIC SERENA BLEND - Coffee - STARBUCKS CORPORATION; *pg.* 897, *pg.* 1840
ORGANIC SUMATRAN RESERVE - Coffee - KEURIG GREEN MOUNTAIN, INC.; *pg.* 868, *pg.* 1768
ORGANIC SWEET MOOSE - Nutritional Product - NUTRACEUTICAL INTERNATIONAL CORPORATION; *pg.* 1576, *pg.* 1753
ORGANIC VALLEY - Organic Foods - COOPERATIVE REGIONS OF ORGANIC PRODUCER POOLS; *pg.* 850, *pg.* 1864
ORGANIC VIENNESE CINNAMON - Coffee - KEURIG GREEN MOUNTAIN, INC.; *pg.* 868, *pg.* 1768
ORGANICGARDENING.COM - Website - RODALE, INC.; *pg.* 1681, *pg.* 1530
ORGANIMALS - Hair & Skin Product - AUBREY ORGANICS INC.; *pg.* 499, *pg.* 470
ORGANIZEIT - Software - SOCKET MOBILE, INC.; *pg.* 471, *pg.* 164
ORGANIZER - Ladies' Wallet - BUXTON ACQUISITION CO., LLC; *pg.* 2, *pg.* 845
ORGANO-GRO - Minerals - MINERALS TECHNOLOGIES INC.; *pg.* 1173, *pg.* 617
ORGANOKROME - Protective Coatings for Metals - PPG INDUSTRIES, INC.; *pg.* 1445, *pg.* 1579
ORGARAN - Pharmaceutical Preparation - MERCK & CO., INC.; *pg.* 1566, *pg.* 1077
ORIANA - Office Furniture - STEELCASE INC.; *pg.* 475, *pg.* 889
ORIAS - Software - XEROX CORPORATION; *pg.* 494, *pg.* 365
ORICK - Footwear - K-SWISS; *pg.* 1837, *pg.* 306
ORIEL CORNERSTONE - Spectroscopy Instrument - NEWPORT CORPORATION; *pg.* 1424, *pg.* 114
ORIEL GOLDILUX - UV & Light Meters - NEWPORT CORPORATION; *pg.* 1424, *pg.* 114
ORIEL LINESPEC - CMOS & CCD Array Spectrometers - NEWPORT CORPORATION; *pg.* 1424, *pg.* 114
ORIEL MERLIN - Digital Lock-in Radiometry System - NEWPORT CORPORATION; *pg.* 1424, *pg.* 114
ORIEL MIR8025 - Modular IR Fourier Spectrometers - NEWPORT CORPORATION; *pg.* 1424, *pg.* 114
ORIELLE - Ceramic Tile - WALKER & ZANGER, INC.; *pg.* 119, *pg.* 281
ORIENT EXPRESS - Amusement & Water Park - CEDAR FAIR, L.P.; *pg.* 537, *pg.* 1471
ORIENT FLEXI-PAX TOURS - Tour Packages - ISRAM WHOLESALE TOURS & TRAVEL LTD.; *pg.* 1913, *pg.* 1244
ORIENT LINES LTD - Cruise Line - NORWEGIAN CRUISE LINE; *pg.* 1917, *pg.* 444
ORIENTAL - Seating Product - IRWIN SEATING COMPANY INC.; *pg.* 929, *pg.* 887
ORIENTAL - Stucco & Plaster - USG CORPORATION; *pg.* 118, *pg.* 594
ORIENTAL CHEF - Salad Dressings - Q&B FOODS, INC.; *pg.* 891, *pg.* 119
ORIENTAL HARVEST - Rice - RICELAND FOODS, INC.; *pg.* 892, *pg.* 36
ORIENTAL STYLE - Rice - RICELAND FOODS, INC.; *pg.* 892, *pg.* 36
ORIENTEAUX - Fabric - SCALAMANDRE, INC.; *pg.* 941, *pg.* 1058
ORIENTED LS - Steel Product - AK STEEL HOLDING CORPORATION; *pg.* 1311, *pg.* 1479
ORIENTER - Positioner - NEW ENGLAND MACHINERY, INC.; *pg.* 1364, *pg.* 415
ORIGIN - Footwear - K-SWISS; *pg.* 1837, *pg.* 306
ORIGIN - Electronic Components - MOLEX INCORPORATED; *pg.* 655, *pg.* 628
ORIGIN SELECT - Candy - RUSSELL STOVER CANDIES, INC.; *pg.* 1861, *pg.* 986
ORIGINAL - Art Product - DANIEL SMITH INC.; *pg.* 1766, *pg.* 1835
ORIGINAL - Pudding - KOZY SHACK INC.; *pg.* 869, *pg.* 1167
ORIGINAL - Woman's Apparel - PENDLETON WOOLEN MILLS, INC.; *pg.* 697, *pg.* 1505
ORIGINAL - Bakery Product - SAPUTO, INC.; *pg.* 893, *pg.* 1956
ORIGINAL 874 - Pant - WILLIAMSON-DICKIE MANUFACTURING COMPANY; *pg.* 50, *pg.* 1696
THE ORIGINAL AND STILL THE BEST - Tagline - SOLOFLEX, INC.; *pg.* 1845, *pg.* 1498
ORIGINAL BRATWURST - Food Product - JOHNSONVILLE SAUSAGE, LLC; *pg.* 867, *pg.* 1894
ORIGINAL CHILI - Bowl - WINDSOR QUALITY FOOD CO., LTD.; *pg.* 910, *pg.* 1717
ORIGINAL CHILI BOWL - Food Product - WINDSOR QUALITY FOOD CO., LTD.; *pg.* 910, *pg.* 1717
ORIGINAL ESSENTIALS - Supplement & Food Product - NEW EARTH LIFE SCIENCES, INC.; *pg.* 1573, *pg.* 1499
THE ORIGINAL FLAVORED CRUST PIZZA - Slogan - HUNGRY HOWIE'S PIZZA & SUBS INC.; *pg.* 1023, *pg.* 897
ORIGINAL FORMULA ENZYMES - Supplement & Food Product - NEW EARTH LIFE SCIENCES, INC.; *pg.* 1573, *pg.* 1499
ORIGINAL FRENCH MANICURE - Nail Product - ORLY INTERNATIONAL, INC.; *pg.* 518, *pg.* 137
ORIGINAL GRAND SLAM - Food Product - DENNY'S CORPORATION; *pg.* 1725, *pg.* 1622
THE ORIGINAL GUIDE TO LIVING WISELY - Slogan - MOTHER EARTH NEWS; *pg.* 1666, *pg.* 722
ORIGINAL HOUND DOG - Musical Instrument - GIBSON GUITAR CORP.; *pg.* 550, *pg.* 1650
ORIGINAL KINGSDOWN - Mattress & Box Spring Sets - KINGSDOWN, INC.; *pg.* 932, *pg.* 1383
THE ORIGINAL MANE'N TAIL - Slogan - STRAIGHT ARROW PRODUCTS, INC.; *pg.* 523, *pg.* 1517
ORIGINAL MEMORY GAME - Toy & Game - HASBRO, INC.; *pg.* 954, *pg.* 1603
THE ORIGINAL OUTDOOR CLOTHING COMPANY - Slogan - WOOLRICH, INC.; *pg.* 699, *pg.* 1595
ORIGINAL OUTFITTER - Tagline - FGX INTERNATIONAL, INC.; *pg.* 5, *pg.* 1608
ORIGINAL PANCAKE - Cylinder - FABCO-AIR, INC.; *pg.* 1336, *pg.* 429
ORIGINAL PENGUIN - Apparel - PERRY ELLIS INTERNATIONAL, INC.; *pg.* 45, *pg.* 445
ORIGINAL RECIPE - Fried Chicken - KFC CORPORATION; *pg.* 1733, *pg.* 735
THE ORIGINAL RING LEADER - Slogan - HASTINGS MANUFACTURING COMPANY, LLC; *pg.* 207, *pg.* 891
ORIGINAL ROBERTSON - Square Drive - ROBERTSON INC.; *pg.* 1372, *pg.* 1924
ORIGINAL RUMBLE - Snack Food - SNYDER'S-LANCE, INC.; *pg.* 896, *pg.* 1368

ORIGINAL SALADSHOOTER - Electrical Appliance & Housewares - NATIONAL PRESTO INDUSTRIES, INC; pg. 1128, pg. 1857
ORIGINAL SCENT - Perfume - MICHAEL STARS, INC.; pg. 29, pg. 100
THE ORIGINAL SEARCH ENGINE - Tagline - AT&T SOUTHEAST; pg. 1868, pg. 489
ORIGINAL TART - Frozen Yogurt - YOCREAM INTERNATIONAL INC.; pg. 1039, pg. 1508
THE ORIGINAL TEE - Apparel - MICHAEL STARS, INC.; pg. 29, pg. 100
ORIGINAL THIN - Food Product - PIZZA INN, INC.; pg. 1745, pg. 1746
ORIGINAL WOW! - Lawn Care Product - GARDENS ALIVE!, INC.; pg. 1796, pg. 693
ORIGINAL WRAPS - Food Product - TYSON FOODS, INC.; pg. 902, pg. 35
ORIGINALBED - Mattress System - TEMPUR SEALY INTERNATIONAL, INC.; pg. 944, pg. 731
ORIGINATORS OF THE TRUE FITTED - Slogan - NEW ERA CAP COMPANY INC.; pg. 1840, pg. 1155
ORIGINS - Beauty Products - THE ESTEE LAUDER COMPANIES INC.; pg. 508, pg. 1229
ORINASE DIAGNOSTIC - Medicine - PFIZER INC.; pg. 1581, pg. 1278
ORINOCO - Chocolate Product - GUITTARD CHOCOLATE COMPANY; pg. 1855, pg. 55
ORION - Mid-size Laser System for Outpatient Surgical Centers & Hospitals - AMERICAN MEDICAL SYSTEMS, INC.; pg. 1399, pg. 238
ORION - Furniture - AMISCO INDUSTRIES LTD.; pg. 913, pg. 1958
ORION - Automated Meter Reading System - BADGER METER, INC.; pg. 1401, pg. 1873
ORION - Furniture - BUSH INDUSTRIES INC.; pg. 919, pg. 1170
ORION - Mobile Audio Equipment - DEI HOLDINGS, INC.; pg. 633, pg. 302
ORION - Air Operated Pumps - GRACO, INC.; pg. 1342, pg. 935
ORION - Parking Garage & Canopy Lighting - JUNO LIGHTING, INC.; pg. 1300, pg. 606
ORION - Military Airplane - LOCKHEED MARTIN CORPORATION; pg. 229, pg. 762
ORION - Gas Detector - MINE SAFETY APPLIANCES COMPANY; pg. 1361, pg. 1525
ORION - Photonic Instrument - NEWPORT CORPORATION; pg. 1424, pg. 114
ORION - Elevator - SAVARIA CONCORD LIFTS INC.; pg. 1592, pg. 1919
ORION - Computer Software - SOLARWINDS, INC.; pg. 471, pg. 1666
ORION - Wireless Control Product - UNIVERSAL ELECTRONICS, INC.; pg. 683, pg. 262
ORION - Ceiling Panel - USG CORPORATION; pg. 118, pg. 594
ORION - Water Pitcher - THE VOLLRATH COMPANY LLC; pg. 1139, pg. 1894
ORION - O/U Shotgun - WEATHERBY, INC.; pg. 1848, pg. 181
ORION NETLEADS - Software - SRA INTERNATIONAL, INC.; pg. 473, pg. 1780
ORIONLEADS - Software - SRA INTERNATIONAL, INC.; pg. 473, pg. 1780
ORIONLINK - Software - SRA INTERNATIONAL, INC.; pg. 473, pg. 1780
ORIONMAGIC - Software - SRA INTERNATIONAL, INC.; pg. 473, pg. 1780
ORIONSEARCH - Software - SRA INTERNATIONAL, INC.; pg. 473, pg. 1780
ORIONVIA - Software - SRA INTERNATIONAL, INC.; pg. 473, pg. 1780
ORISSA - Rug - COURISTAN INC.; pg. 921, pg. 1067
ORISSA - Fabric - NEMSCHOFF, INC.; pg. 936, pg. 1890
ORJENE - Food Product - THE HAIN CELESTIAL GROUP, INC.; pg. 860, pg. 1172
ORKIN - Termite Control Services - ORKIN, INC.; pg. 1798, pg. 517
ORKIN - Pest Control - ROLLINS, INC.; pg. 1179, pg. 519
THE ORKIN MAN - Slogan - ORKIN, INC.; pg. 1798, pg. 517
ORKUT - Social Networking Site - GOOGLE INC.; pg. 1249, pg. 153
ORLANDO - Furniture - HAWORTH, INC.; pg. 402, pg. 891
ORLANDO MAGIC - Professional Basketball Team - ORLANDO MAGIC; pg. 572, pg. 455
ORLEAN - Shoes - ALLEN-EDMONDS SHOE CORP.; pg. 1804, pg. 1887
ORLEANS - Seafood Products - BUMBLE BEE FOODS LLC; pg. 842, pg. 201
ORLEANS - Window Treatment - CROSCILL, INC.; pg. 1122, pg. 1220
ORLEANS - Furniture - FLEXSTEEL INDUSTRIES, INC.; pg. 925, pg. 707
ORLEANS - Bathroom Fan - HUNTER FAN COMPANY; pg. 57, pg. 1631
ORLEANS - Cookies - PEPPERIDGE FARM, INC.; pg. 888, pg. 363
ORLEANS FORGE - Furniture - ASHLEY FURNITURE INDUSTRIES, INC.; pg. 914, pg. 1852
ORLY - Furniture - AMERICAN LEATHER LP; pg. 912, pg. 1673
ORLY PEDICURE SPA - Spa Products - ORLY INTERNATIONAL, INC.; pg. 518, pg. 137
ORNAMEC - Turf Product - PBI/GORDON CORPORATION; pg. 1170, pg. 985
ORNAMENT - Fabric - NEMSCHOFF, INC.; pg. 936, pg. 1890
ORNAMENTS - Window Accent - HERITAGE LACE INC.; pg. 694, pg. 711
OROCLAD - Chemicals for Electro Plating - TECHNIC INCORPORATED; pg. 1183, pg. 1601
OROMERSE - Chemicals For Electro Plating - TECHNIC INCORPORATED; pg. 1183, pg. 1601
ORONITE - Fuel & Lubricant Additives - CHEVRON CORPORATION; pg. 974, pg. 259
ORONITE ALKANE - Detergent Alkylate - CHEVRON CORPORATION; pg. 974, pg. 259
OROPON - Leather Chemical - DOW CHEMICAL; pg. 1156, pg. 1563
OROSENE - Chemicals for Electro Plating - TECHNIC INCORPORATED; pg. 1183, pg. 1601
OROTEMP - Chemicals for Electro Plating - TECHNIC INCORPORATED; pg. 1183, pg. 1601
OROTHERM - Chemicals for Electro Plating - TECHNIC INCORPORATED; pg. 1183, pg. 1601
ORPEUM - Seating Product - IRWIN SEATING COMPANY INC.; pg. 929, pg. 887
ORPHISM - Fabric - NEMSCHOFF, INC.; pg. 936, pg. 1890
ORSCO - Automated Lubrication Systems - LINCOLN INDUSTRIAL CORP.; pg. 1355, pg. 999
ORSON - Furniture - LA-Z-BOY INCORPORATED; pg. 932, pg. 901
ORTAC - Hose - THE GOODYEAR TIRE & RUBBER COMPANY; pg. 1883, pg. 1401
ORTEGA - Mexican Seasonings - B&G FOODS, INC.; pg. 838, pg. 1102
ORTEL - Fiber Optic Product - EMCORE CORPORATION; pg. 636, pg. 39
ORTHENE - Lawn & Garden Products - THE SCOTTS MIRACLE-GRO COMPANY; pg. 1799, pg. 1459
ORTHINOX - Surgical & Medical Product - STRYKER CORPORATION; pg. 1598, pg. 894
ORTHO - Healthcare Product - JOHNSON & JOHNSON; pg. 1549, pg. 1091
ORTHO - Garden Pest Control - THE SCOTTS MIRACLE-GRO COMPANY; pg. 1799, pg. 1459
ORTHO-BIOTIC - Medical Product - GF HEALTH PRODUCTS, INC.; pg. 1535, pg. 508
ORTHO-CEPT - Healthcare Product - JOHNSON & JOHNSON; pg. 1549, pg. 1091
ORTHO-CYCLEN - Healthcare Product - JOHNSON & JOHNSON; pg. 1549, pg. 1091
ORTHO-EASE - Medical Product - GF HEALTH PRODUCTS, INC.; pg. 1535, pg. 508
ORTHO EVRA - Healthcare Product - JOHNSON & JOHNSON; pg. 1549, pg. 1091
ORTHO MICRONOR - Healthcare Product - JOHNSON & JOHNSON; pg. 1549, pg. 1091
ORTHO TRI-CYCLEN - Healthcare Product - JOHNSON & JOHNSON; pg. 1549, pg. 1091
ORTHOCLONE OKT - Healthcare Product - JOHNSON & JOHNSON; pg. 1549, pg. 1091
ORTHOFORM - Orthodontic Wire - 3M UNITEK CORPORATION; pg. 1483, pg. 150
ORTHOGNATHIC SYSTEM - Surgical Instruments - OSTEOMED CORPORATION; pg. 1425, pg. 1658
ORTHOLOC - Orthopaedic Knee Implant - DOW CORNING CORPORATION; pg. 1159, pg. 900
ORTHOPAD - Software - STRYKER CORPORATION; pg. 1598, pg. 894
ORTHOPAT - Orthopedic Surgery System - HAEMONETICS CORPORATION; pg. 1538, pg. 802
ORTHOPHOS - Dental Equipment - SIRONA DENTAL SYSTEMS, INC.; pg. 1429, pg. 1175
ORTHOPILOT - CT-free Navigation System For Orthopedic Surgery - AESCULAP, INC.; pg. 1487, pg. 1521
ORTHOTRAC - Software - EASTMAN KODAK COMPANY; pg. 1408, pg. 1333
ORTHOVISION - Surgical Table - STERIS CORPORATION; pg. 1597, pg. 1464
ORTHOWARE - Software - EASTMAN KODAK COMPANY; pg. 1408, pg. 1333
ORTHOWASH - Sodium Fluoride Rinse - 3M COMPANY; pg. 1142, pg. 956
ORTHOWORKS - Dental Product - DENTSPLY INTERNATIONAL INC.; pg. 1522, pg. 1596
ORTHTEK - Seal & Thermoplastic Component - GREENE, TWEED & CO.; pg. 1344, pg. 1544
ORTLEY - Jacket - I. SPIEWAK & SONS, INC.; pg. 42, pg. 1242
ORV - Footwear - COBIAN CORP.; pg. 1806, pg. 253
ORVILLE - Guitars - GIBSON GUITAR CORP.; pg. 550, pg. 1650
ORVILLE & WILBUR'S - Chicken Wings - TYSON FOODS, INC.; pg. 902, pg. 35
ORVILLE REDENBACHER'S - Food Product - CONAGRA FOODS, INC.; pg. 826, pg. 1014
ORVIS DOG'S NEST - Dog Bed - THE ORVIS COMPANY, INC.; pg. 1781, pg. 1764
ORVIS MYLAR - Tinsel - THE ORVIS COMPANY, INC.; pg. 1781, pg. 1764
OS X - Mac Operating System - APPLE INC.; pg. 350, pg. 73
OSA SYSTEM - Surgical Instruments - OSTEOMED CORPORATION; pg. 1425, pg. 1658
OSB - Paper Product - GEORGIA-PACIFIC LLC; pg. 1458, pg. 507
OSB - Packaging Systems & Materials - SEALED AIR CORPORATION; pg. 1468, pg. 1058
OSBORN - Brush - JASON INDUSTRIES, INC.; pg. 208, pg. 1875
OSBORN - Industrial Brushes - OSBORN INTERNATIONAL; pg. 1367, pg. 1406
OSBORNE - Carpet - BEAULIEU GROUP, LLC; pg. 917, pg. 529
OSC - Plastics Product - AEP INDUSTRIES INC.; pg. 1878, pg. 1085
OSCAR MAYER - Food Products - THE KRAFT HEINZ COMPANY; pg. 870, pg. 1577
OSCAR NIGHT - Event - ACADEMY OF MOTION PICTURE ARTS & SCIENCES; pg. 526, pg. 46
OSCAR SCHMIDT - Musical Instrument - U.S. MUSIC CORPORATION; pg. 315, pg. 560
OSCARS - Movie Awards - ACADEMY OF MOTION PICTURE ARTS & SCIENCES; pg. 526, pg. 46
OSCILLAMET - Abrasive Cutter - BUEHLER, LTD.; pg. 1403, pg. 622
OSCILLATOR - Heater - KAZ, INC.; pg. 58, pg. 844
OSCILLOMATE - Medical Product - CAS MEDICAL SYSTEMS, INC.; pg. 1513, pg. 339
OSCODRUG - Drug Stores - ALBERTSON'S LLC; pg. 1013, pg. 546
OSEKWORKS, - Software - WIND RIVER SYSTEMS, INC.; pg. 493, pg. 38
OSEKWORKS - Software - WIND RIVER SYSTEMS, INC.; pg. 493, pg. 38
OSHKOSH - Trucks - OSHKOSH CORPORATION; pg. 187, pg. 1885
OSHKOSH BABY - Clothing - OSHKOSH B'GOSH, INC.; pg. 45, pg. 1885
OSHKOSH B'GOSH - Clothing - OSHKOSH B'GOSH, INC.; pg. 45, pg. 1885
OSHMAN'S SPORTING GOODS - Sporting Goods - THE SPORTS AUTHORITY, INC.; pg. 1846, pg. 326
OSIAO - Skin Care Product - THE ESTEE LAUDER COMPANIES INC.; pg. 508, pg. 1229
OSIRIS - Clinical Diagnostic Product - BIO-RAD LABORATORIES, INC.; pg. 1504, pg. 101
OSIRIS EVOLUTION - Software - BIO-RAD LABORATORIES, INC.; pg. 1504, pg. 101
OSK - Software - BIO-RAD LABORATORIES, INC.; pg. 1504, pg. 101
OSLO - Bedding - CROSCILL, INC.; pg. 1122, pg. 1220
OSLO - Furniture - FLEXSTEEL INDUSTRIES, INC.; pg. 925, pg. 707
OSM SERIES - Spectrometers - NEWPORT CORPORATION;

pg. 1424, *pg.* 114
OSMIUM - Semiconductor Device - MICRON TECHNOLOGY, INC.; *pg.* 435, *pg.* 547
OSMO BEV - RO Equipment & Membranes for Beverage Market - GE WATER & PROCESS TECHNOLOGIES; *pg.* 1339, *pg.* 1588
OSMO MUNI - RO Equipment & Membranes for Municipal Market - GE WATER & PROCESS TECHNOLOGIES; *pg.* 1339, *pg.* 1588
OSMO PHARMA - RO Equipment & Membranes for Pharmaceutical Market - GE WATER & PROCESS TECHNOLOGIES; *pg.* 1339, *pg.* 1588
OSMO PRO SERIES - RO Equipment for the Industrial & Power Markets - GE WATER & PROCESS TECHNOLOGIES; *pg.* 1339, *pg.* 1588
OSMOCOTE - Lawn & Garden Product - THE SCOTTS MIRACLE-GRO COMPANY; *pg.* 1799, *pg.* 1459
OSMOLITE - Isotonic Liquid Nutritional - ABBOTT LABORATORIES; *pg.* 1484, *pg.* 551
OSMONICS HOUSEHOLD FILTER - Residential Sediment & Cartridge Filters - GE WATER & PROCESS TECHNOLOGIES; *pg.* 1339, *pg.* 1588
OSMOPLASTIC - Wood Preservative - OSMOSE, INC.; *pg.* 102, *pg.* 1150
OSMOPREP - Colonoscopy Preparation - SALIX PHARMACEUTICALS, INC.; *pg.* 1591, *pg.* 1388
OSMOSE - Lumber & Supplies - OSMOSE, INC.; *pg.* 102, *pg.* 1150
OSMOSE K-33 - Wood Preservative - OSMOSE, INC.; *pg.* 102, *pg.* 1150
OSO - Aluminum Foil, Trash Bags, Food Bags & Plastic Wrap - THE CLOROX COMPANY; *pg.* 327, *pg.* 169
OSOLEAN - Healthcare Product - MANNATECH, INCORPORATED; *pg.* 1558, *pg.* 1671
OSOM - Diagnostic Product - GENZYME CORPORATION; *pg.* 1534, *pg.* 808
O'SOY - Organic Soy Yogurt - STONYFIELD FARM, INC.; *pg.* 899, *pg.* 1035
OSP-201 - Electronic Component - EMCORE CORPORATION; *pg.* 636, *pg.* 39
OSP-9500 - Programmable Spectral Source - NEWPORT CORPORATION; *pg.* 1424, *pg.* 114
OSPREY - Fishing Tackle - EPPINGER MANUFACTURING CO.; *pg.* 1833, *pg.* 876
OSPREY - Digital Media System - REALNETWORKS, INC.; *pg.* 460, *pg.* 1839
OSPREY - Drilling Software - SCHLUMBERGER LIMITED; *pg.* 801, *pg.* 1714
OSRP - Routing Protocol - CIENA CORPORATION; *pg.* 628, *pg.* 771
OSS INTEGRATION CONSULTING - Global Services - SONUS NETWORKS INC.; *pg.* 1281, *pg.* 858
OSSI - Software - SUNGARD DATA SYSTEMS INC.; *pg.* 477, *pg.* 1592
OSTASE - Testing Instrument System - BECKMAN COULTER, INC.; *pg.* 1402, *pg.* 48
OSTEO-BI-FLEX - Nutritional Supplements - NBTY, INC.; *pg.* 1572, *pg.* 1338
OSTEO-FORCE - Needle - COOK GROUP, INC.; *pg.* 1518, *pg.* 674
OSTEO OMEGA SOLUTIONS - Vitamin & Dietary Supplement - NATROL, INC.; *pg.* 1570, *pg.* 64
OSTEO-RX - Needle - COOK GROUP, INC.; *pg.* 1518, *pg.* 674
OSTEO SAFE - Nutritional Supplement - WHITEWING LABS, INC.; *pg.* 1610, *pg.* 99
OSTEO-SITE - Needle - COOK GROUP, INC.; *pg.* 1518, *pg.* 674
OSTEOCAP - Implant Product - ZIMMER BIOMET HOLDINGS, INC.; *pg.* 1611, *pg.* 699
OSTEOCAP RS HIP SYSTEM - Hip Product - ZIMMER BIOMET HOLDINGS, INC.; *pg.* 1611, *pg.* 699
OSTEOCARE - Medical Device - COMPUMED, INC.; *pg.* 378, *pg.* 128
OSTEOFARM MESH - Surgical Instrument - OSTEOMED CORPORATION; *pg.* 1425, *pg.* 1658
OSTEOFLAP - Surgical Instrument - OSTEOMED CORPORATION; *pg.* 1425, *pg.* 1658
OSTEOGRAF - Dental Product - DENTSPLY INTERNATIONAL INC.; *pg.* 1522, *pg.* 1596
OSTEOGRAFT - Grafting Instrument - OSTEOMED CORPORATION; *pg.* 1425, *pg.* 1658
OSTEOGRAM - Medical Device - COMPUMED, INC.; *pg.* 378, *pg.* 128
OSTEOGUIDES - Medical Device - INTEGRA LIFESCIENCES HOLDINGS CORPORATION; *pg.* 1545, *pg.* 1109
OSTEOHARVESTER - Grafting Instrument - OSTEOMED CORPORATION; *pg.* 1425, *pg.* 1658
OSTEOJECT - Medical Device - INTEGRA LIFESCIENCES HOLDINGS CORPORATION; *pg.* 1545, *pg.* 1109
OSTEOKINETIC - Herbal Formula - SHAKLEE CORPORATION; *pg.* 1593, *pg.* 184
OSTEOMARK - Pharmaceutical Product - ALERE INC.; *pg.* 1488, *pg.* 849
OSTEOMATCH - Implants - OSTEOMED CORPORATION; *pg.* 1425, *pg.* 1658
OSTEONICS - Medical Product - STRYKER CORPORATION; *pg.* 1598, *pg.* 894
OSTEOSAL - Software - BIO-RAD LABORATORIES, INC.; *pg.* 1504, *pg.* 101
OSTEOSUN - Supplement & Food Product - NEW EARTH LIFE SCIENCES, INC.; *pg.* 1573, *pg.* 1499
OSTEOVATION - Surgical Instrument - OSTEOMED CORPORATION; *pg.* 1425, *pg.* 1658
OSTEOVATIONEX - Surgical Instrument - OSTEOMED CORPORATION; *pg.* 1425, *pg.* 1658
OSTER - Kitchen Appliances - JARDEN CONSUMER SOLUTIONS; *pg.* 57, *pg.* 412
OSTERIA VIA STATO - Italian Restaurant - LETTUCE ENTERTAIN YOU ENTERPRISES, INC.; *pg.* 1735, *pg.* 580
OSTERMOOR - Bedding - THE STANDARD MATTRESS COMPANY; *pg.* 943, *pg.* 352
OSTIVONE - Nutritional Supplement - NATURAL ORGANICS, INC.; *pg.* 1571, *pg.* 1181
OSU 300 - Optical Service Units - ADTRAN, INC.; *pg.* 344, *pg.* 6
OSURANCE - Medical Device - OLIVER PRODUCTS COMPANY INC.; *pg.* 1367, *pg.* 888
OSV II - Valves - INTEGRA LIFESCIENCES HOLDINGS CORPORATION; *pg.* 1545, *pg.* 1109
OSV.COM - Website - OUR SUNDAY VISITOR, INC.; *pg.* 1673, *pg.* 682
OSWEGO - Cable Wire - COLEMAN CABLE, INC.; *pg.* 1324, *pg.* 665
OT-HD-TRLSC-IC - Electronic Component - EMCORE CORPORATION; *pg.* 636, *pg.* 39
OTC - Athletic Footwear - REEBOK INTERNATIONAL LTD.; *pg.* 1817, *pg.* 811
OTC - Healthcare Product - SWANSON HEALTH PRODUCTS INC.; *pg.* 1600, *pg.* 1397
OTHELLO - Radio - ANALOG DEVICES, INC.; *pg.* 617, *pg.* 839
OTHELLO - Toy - MATTEL, INC.; *pg.* 962, *pg.* 81
OTHELLO - Game - PRESSMAN TOY CORPORATION; *pg.* 965, *pg.* 1734
OTHER VOICES - Financial Products - DOW JONES & COMPANY, INC.; *pg.* 1637, *pg.* 1225
OTHERWORLDLY - Boots - AEROGROUP INTERNATIONAL, INC.; *pg.* 1803, *pg.* 1055
OTHINE - Skin Bleach - J. STRICKLAND & COMPANY; *pg.* 512, *pg.* 970
OTINUM - Pharmaceutical Product - VALEANT PHARMACEUTICALS INTERNATIONAL; *pg.* 1605, *pg.* 1047
OTIS - Elevator - OTIS ELEVATOR COMPANY; *pg.* 102, *pg.* 349
OTIS - Elevators - UNITED TECHNOLOGIES CORPORATION; *pg.* 235, *pg.* 353
OTIX - Ear Wax Removal Aid - MONTICELLO DRUG CO.; *pg.* 1569, *pg.* 434
OTOMAX - Medicine - MERCK & CO., INC.; *pg.* 1566, *pg.* 1077
OTOMIX - Sportswear - OTOMIX, INC.; *pg.* 30, *pg.* 105
OTOPROBE - Otolaryngology Product - IRIDEX CORPORATION; *pg.* 648, *pg.* 160
OTOSONIC - Hearing Aid - BELTONE ELECTRONICS LLC; *pg.* 1503, *pg.* 614
OTOTEMP - Thermometer System - EXERGEN CORPORATION; *pg.* 1412, *pg.* 855
OTP-1HD - Electronic Components - EMCORE CORPORATION; *pg.* 636, *pg.* 39
OTS - Optical Table System - NEWPORT CORPORATION; *pg.* 1424, *pg.* 114
OTS-128DTR - Electronic Component - EMCORE CORPORATION; *pg.* 636, *pg.* 39
OTS-16A - Electronic Component - EMCORE CORPORATION; *pg.* 636, *pg.* 39
OTS-16ATR - Electronic Component - EMCORE CORPORATION; *pg.* 636, *pg.* 39
OTS-16DA - Electronic Component - EMCORE CORPORATION; *pg.* 636, *pg.* 39
OTS-16DTR - Electronic Component - EMCORE CORPORATION; *pg.* 636, *pg.* 39
OTS-1DVI2A - Electronic Component - EMCORE CORPORATION; *pg.* 636, *pg.* 39
OTS-1DVI2A1D1KM - Electronic Component - EMCORE CORPORATION; *pg.* 636, *pg.* 39
OTS-1ETR - Electronic Component - EMCORE CORPORATION; *pg.* 636, *pg.* 39
OTS-1HD1ETR - Electronic Component - EMCORE CORPORATION; *pg.* 636, *pg.* 39
OTS-1HD2DA - Electronic Component - EMCORE CORPORATION; *pg.* 636, *pg.* 39
OTS-1HD2DTR - Electronic Component - EMCORE CORPORATION; *pg.* 636, *pg.* 39
OTS-1LT - Electronic Component - EMCORE CORPORATION; *pg.* 636, *pg.* 39
OTS-1REF - Electronic Component - EMCORE CORPORATION; *pg.* 636, *pg.* 39
OTS-1SD - Electronic Component - EMCORE CORPORATION; *pg.* 636, *pg.* 39
OTS-1SD1ETR - Electronic Component - EMCORE CORPORATION; *pg.* 636, *pg.* 39
OTS-1SD2A - Electronic Component - EMCORE CORPORATION; *pg.* 636, *pg.* 39
OTS-1SD2DA - Electronic Component - EMCORE CORPORATION; *pg.* 636, *pg.* 39
OTS-1SD2DTR - Electronic Component - EMCORE CORPORATION; *pg.* 636, *pg.* 39
OTS-1V - Electronic Component - EMCORE CORPORATION; *pg.* 636, *pg.* 39
OTS-1V1DTR - Electronic Component - EMCORE CORPORATION; *pg.* 636, *pg.* 39
OTS-1V1ETR - Electronic Component - EMCORE CORPORATION; *pg.* 636, *pg.* 39
OTS-1V2A - Electronic Component - EMCORE CORPORATION; *pg.* 636, *pg.* 39
OTS-1V2ATR1DTR - Electronic Component - EMCORE CORPORATION; *pg.* 636, *pg.* 39
OTS-1V2ATR1DTR1ETR - Electronic Component - EMCORE CORPORATION; *pg.* 636, *pg.* 39
OTS-1VTR2ATR - Electronic Component - EMCORE CORPORATION; *pg.* 636, *pg.* 39
OTS-1VTR2ATR4DTR - Electronic Component - EMCORE CORPORATION; *pg.* 636, *pg.* 39
OTS-1VTR2DTR - Electronic Component - EMCORE CORPORATION; *pg.* 636, *pg.* 39
OTS-2DA - Electronic Component - EMCORE CORPORATION; *pg.* 636, *pg.* 39
OTS-2DATR - Electronic Component - EMCORE CORPORATION; *pg.* 636, *pg.* 39
OTS-2V4A - Electronic Component - EMCORE CORPORATION; *pg.* 636, *pg.* 39
OTS-2V4ATR1ETR - Electronic Component - EMCORE CORPORATION; *pg.* 636, *pg.* 39
OTS-2V4DTR - Electronic Component - EMCORE CORPORATION; *pg.* 636, *pg.* 39
OTS-32DTR - Electronic Component - EMCORE CORPORATION; *pg.* 636, *pg.* 39
OTS-3SD - Electronic Component - EMCORE CORPORATION; *pg.* 636, *pg.* 39
OTS-3V - Electronic Component - EMCORE CORPORATION; *pg.* 636, *pg.* 39
OTS-4A - Electronic Component - EMCORE CORPORATION; *pg.* 636, *pg.* 39
OTS-4ATR - Electronic Component - EMCORE CORPORATION; *pg.* 636, *pg.* 39
OTS-4DA - Electronic Component - EMCORE CORPORATION; *pg.* 636, *pg.* 39
OTS-4DATR - Electronic Component - EMCORE CORPORATION; *pg.* 636, *pg.* 39
OTS-4V8A - Electronic Component - EMCORE CORPORATION; *pg.* 636, *pg.* 39
OTS-4VT - Electronic Component - EMCORE CORPORATION; *pg.* 636, *pg.* 39
OTS-6SD - Electronic Component - EMCORE CORPORATION; *pg.* 636, *pg.* 39
OTS-6V - Electronic Component - EMCORE CORPORATION; *pg.* 636, *pg.* 39
OTS-8A - Electronic Component - EMCORE CORPORATION; *pg.* 636, *pg.* 39
OTS-8ATR - Electronic Component - EMCORE CORPORATION; *pg.* 636, *pg.* 39
OTS-8DA - Electronic Component - EMCORE

First page reference indicates Business Class Edition
Second page reference indicates Geographic Edition

CORPORATION; *pg.* 636, *pg.* 39
OTS-8DTR - Electronic Component - EMCORE CORPORATION; *pg.* 636, *pg.* 39
OTS-8V - Electronic Component - EMCORE CORPORATION; *pg.* 636, *pg.* 39
OTTASEPT - Fungicides, Biocides for Cosmetics, Soaps - FERRO CORPORATION; *pg.* 1162, *pg.* 1462
OTTAWA SENATORS - Professional Hockey Team - OTTAWA SENATORS HOCKEY CLUB; *pg.* 573, *pg.* 1921
OTTER POPS - Food Product - THE JEL SERT COMPANY; *pg.* 865, *pg.* 668
OTTO VIENNA - Office Furniture - JOFCO INC.; *pg.* 931, *pg.* 691
OTTOVIENNA - Furniture - JOFCO INC.; *pg.* 931, *pg.* 691
OTTOWA - Footwear - STEVEN MADDEN, LTD.; *pg.* 1819, *pg.* 1176
OUIJA - Game - HASBRO, INC.; *pg.* 954, *pg.* 1603
OUISTITI - Fabric - SCALAMANDRE, INC.; *pg.* 941, *pg.* 1058
OULUSKA PASS - Clothing - ABERCROMBIE & FITCH CO.; *pg.* 37, *pg.* 1466
OUR BEST BURGERS EVER - Restaurant Services - JACK IN THE BOX INC.; *pg.* 1732, *pg.* 204
OUR BUSINESS BEGINS WITH PATIENTS - Slogan - ACCURAY INCORPORATED; *pg.* 1486, *pg.* 282
OUR CUSTOMERS POWER THE FUTURE - Tag Line - LAPP INSULATOR COMPANY, LLC; *pg.* 1946, *pg.* 1173
OUR EARTH, OUR TOMORROW - Digital Office Equipment - RICOH AMERICAS CORPORATION; *pg.* 461, *pg.* 1131
OUR ENERGY COMES THROUGH - Slogan - CHS INC.; *pg.* 702, *pg.* 926
OUR ENERGY IS WORKING FOR YOU. - Tagline - FIRSTENERGY CORP.; *pg.* 1942, *pg.* 1400
OUR FAMILY - Food Products - SPARTANNASH CO.; *pg.* 1034, *pg.* 925
OUR FAMILY PRIDE - Labels - SPARTANNASH CO.; *pg.* 1034, *pg.* 925
OUR FIRST PRIORITY IS YOU - Slogan - FIRST NIAGARA BANK; *pg.* 756, *pg.* 1174
OUR FOOD.YOUR PLACE - Slogan - RUBIO'S RESTAURANTS, INC.; *pg.* 1748, *pg.* 60
OUR GEAR. YOUR VISION. - Slogan - CINEQUIPT INC.; *pg.* 629, *pg.* 932
OUR GIRL BY HEALTHTEX - Children's Clothing - LT APPAREL GROUP; *pg.* 29, *pg.* 1254
OUR GOAL IS REACHING YOURS - Slogan - BARTLETT & CO.; *pg.* 722, *pg.* 1410
OUR GREEN DRINK - Supplement & Food Product - NEW EARTH LIFE SCIENCES, INC.; *pg.* 1573, *pg.* 1499
OUR INTEREST IS YOU - Slogan - TRUSTMARK CORPORATION; *pg.* 812, *pg.* 7
OUR JOB IS MAKING YOURS EASIER - Tagline - BALDOR ELECTRIC COMPANY; *pg.* 1316, *pg.* 32
OUR ONLY BUSINESS - Tagline - CONSUMERS KITCHENS & BATHS; *pg.* 77, *pg.* 1167
OUR PEOPLE. OUR WORK. OUR VALUES. - Channel Subscription Packs - VERIZON COMMUNICATIONS INC.; *pg.* 1875, *pg.* 1309
OUR POWER IS IN OUR PEOPLE - Slogan - BHI ENERGY; *pg.* 361, *pg.* 1489
OUR PRODUCTS ARE EVERYWHERE - Tagline - LEGGETT & PLATT, INCORPORATED; *pg.* 933, *pg.* 974
OUR PRODUCTS PROTECT YOUR PRODUCTS - Slogan - SEALED AIR CORPORATION; *pg.* 1468, *pg.* 1058
OUR PURSUIT. LIFE.S POTENTIAL. - Slogan - ALLERGAN, INC.; *pg.* 1491, *pg.* 106
OUR WORLD, OUR CHOICE - Slogan - NORFOLK SOUTHERN CORPORATION; *pg.* 1917, *pg.* 1797
OUST - Herbicide - E.I. DU PONT DE NEMOURS & COMPANY; *pg.* 1159, *pg.* 390
OUST - Air Sanitizer - S.C. JOHNSON & SON, INC.; *pg.* 334, *pg.* 1889
OUSTAR - Herbicide - E.I. DU PONT DE NEMOURS & COMPANY; *pg.* 1159, *pg.* 390
OUT IN FRONT - Slogan - RE/MAX INTERNATIONAL, INC.; *pg.* 1109, *pg.* 322
OUT O'SIGHT - Mole Trap - THE WOODSTREAM CORPORATION; *pg.* 1801, *pg.* 1549
OUT THINKING. OUT DOING. - Slogan - CONVERGYS CORPORATION; *pg.* 379, *pg.* 1412
OUT-U-SCUM - Bathroom Cleaner - BLUE CROSS LABORATORIES; *pg.* 326, *pg.* 277
OUT WEST - Domestic Cigars - ALTADIS USA, INC.; *pg.* 1893, *pg.* 423
OUTBACK - Australian Themed Restaurants - CARA OPERATIONS LIMITED; *pg.* 1720, *pg.* 1947
OUTBACK - Men's Boot - JACK SCHWARTZ SHOES, INC.; *pg.* 1810, *pg.* 1245
OUTBACK - Wall System - SMITH-MIDLAND CORPORATION; *pg.* 111, *pg.* 1795
OUTBACK - Biscuits - UNITED STATES BAKERY; *pg.* 907, *pg.* 1507
OUTBACK ODYSSEY - Video Game - INTERNATIONAL GAME TECHNOLOGY; *pg.* 957, *pg.* 1024
OUTBACK STEAKHOUSE - Australian-Themed Restaurant - BLOOMIN' BRANDS, INC.; *pg.* 1716, *pg.* 471
OUTBRUST - Toy - MATTEL, INC.; *pg.* 962, *pg.* 81
OUTBURST - Game - HASBRO, INC.; *pg.* 954, *pg.* 1603
OUTBURST JUNIOR - Toy & Game - HASBRO, INC.; *pg.* 954, *pg.* 1603
OUTCOMES RESEARCH - Pharmaceutical Product - PFIZER INC.; *pg.* 1581, *pg.* 1278
THE OUTDOOR - Speaker - CAMBRIDGE SOUNDWORKS, INC.; *pg.* 1234, *pg.* 781
THE OUTDOOR CHANNEL - Television Station - THE OUTDOOR CHANNEL; *pg.* 303, *pg.* 291
OUTDOOR LIFE - Magazine - BONNIER ACTIVE MEDIA, INC.; *pg.* 1622, *pg.* 1205
OUTDOOR LIFE - Magazine - BONNIER CORPORATION; *pg.* 1622, *pg.* 480
OUTDOOR MIA - Fan - CRAFTMADE INTERNATIONAL, INC.; *pg.* 1295, *pg.* 1670
OUTDOOR PATIO FAN - Fan - CRAFTMADE INTERNATIONAL, INC.; *pg.* 1295, *pg.* 1670
OUTDOOR RANGE - Kitchen Appliance - VIKING RANGE CORPORATION; *pg.* 61, *pg.* 968
OUTDOOR WORLD - Outdoor Sports Stores - BASS PRO SHOPS, INC.; *pg.* 1826, *pg.* 1006
OUTDOORLIFE.COM - Web Site - BONNIER ACTIVE MEDIA, INC.; *pg.* 1622, *pg.* 1205
OUTER BANK - Shirt - BROWN & BIGELOW, INC.; *pg.* 1624, *pg.* 959
OUTER BANKS - Sportswear - HANESBRANDS INC.; *pg.* 26, *pg.* 1394
OUTER NUTRITION - Nutritional Supplement - HERBALIFE INTERNATIONAL OF AMERICA, INC.; *pg.* 1541, *pg.* 132
OUTERMAX - Movie Channel - HOME BOX OFFICE, INC.; *pg.* 290, *pg.* 1240
OUTERSHIELD - Electrode - LINCOLN ELECTRIC HOLDINGS, INC.; *pg.* 1355, *pg.* 1432
OUTFIT - Apparel - OAKLEY, INC.; *pg.* 1840, *pg.* 86
OUTFITTER - Flashlight - ENERGIZER HOLDINGS, INC.; *pg.* 637, *pg.* 996
OUTLAW - Floor Cleaning Product - NSS ENTERPRISES, INC.; *pg.* 59, *pg.* 1476
THE OUTLAW - Gasoline Additives - SHELL LUBRICANTS; *pg.* 217, *pg.* 1714
OUTLETBUY.COM - Online Services - IAC/INTERACTIVECORP; *pg.* 292, *pg.* 1242
OUTLINE - Apparel - OAKLEY, INC.; *pg.* 1840, *pg.* 86
OUTLINER II - Hair Trimmer - ANDIS COMPANY; *pg.* 498, *pg.* 1895
OUTLOOK - Motor Homes - WINNEBAGO INDUSTRIES, INC.; *pg.* 1712, *pg.* 707
OUTLOOK EMPRESS - Waiting Seating - STEELCASE INC.; *pg.* 475, *pg.* 889
OUTLOOK HAWTHORNE - Waiting Seating - STEELCASE INC.; *pg.* 475, *pg.* 889
OUTLOOK JARRAH - Waiting Seating - STEELCASE INC.; *pg.* 475, *pg.* 889
OUTLOOK LINDEN - Waiting Seating - STEELCASE INC.; *pg.* 475, *pg.* 889
OUTLOOK NIKKO - Waiting Seating - STEELCASE INC.; *pg.* 475, *pg.* 889
OUTLOOK PLUGIN - Software - EGAIN COMMUNICATIONS CORPORATION; *pg.* 1242, *pg.* 284
OUTLOOK SEQUOIA - Waiting Seating - STEELCASE INC.; *pg.* 475, *pg.* 889
OUTLOOK.COM - Email Service - MICROSOFT CORPORATION; *pg.* 435, *pg.* 1824
OUTNET - Software System - MENTOR GRAPHICS CORPORATION; *pg.* 432, *pg.* 1510
OUTPAC - Box - PACTIV CORPORATION; *pg.* 1466, *pg.* 624
OUTPATIENT - Minor Surgery Light - MEDLINE INDUSTRIES, INC.; *pg.* 1562, *pg.* 635
OUTPOST - Software Product - CLARY CORPORATION; *pg.* 226, *pg.* 150
OUTPOST - Footwear - LACROSSE FOOTWEAR, INC.; *pg.* 1811, *pg.* 1503
OUTPOST BRAND - Beef Jerky - SNYDER'S-LANCE, INC.; *pg.* 896, *pg.* 1368
OUTPUT DESIGNER - Software - ADOBE SYSTEMS INCORPORATED; *pg.* 342, *pg.* 235
OUTPUT PAK FOR MYSAP.COM - Software - ADOBE SYSTEMS INCORPORATED; *pg.* 342, *pg.* 235
OUTPUT SOLUTIONS - Software - SUNGARD DATA SYSTEMS INC.; *pg.* 477, *pg.* 1592
OUTREACH - Cleaner - THE DOW CHEMICAL COMPANY; *pg.* 1157, *pg.* 898
OUTRIDER - Selective Herbicide - MONSANTO COMPANY; *pg.* 1173, *pg.* 999
OUTSHINE - Frozen Fruit Bars - NESTLE USA, INC.; *pg.* 883, *pg.* 96
THE OUTSIDERS - Character - DC COMICS, INC.; *pg.* 1633, *pg.* 1221
OUTSTANDING AGENTS. OUTSTANDING RESULTS. - Slogan - RE/MAX INTERNATIONAL, INC.; *pg.* 1109, *pg.* 322
OUZO 12 - Liquor - CAMPARI AMERICA; *pg.* 1960, *pg.* 214
OVAL - Self-Rimming Lavatory - GERBER PLUMBING FIXTURES CORPORATION; *pg.* 84, *pg.* 672
OVAL HOLLAND - Hat - WOODEN SHIPS OF HOBOKEN; *pg.* 35, *pg.* 1315
OVALITE - Enamel Undercoat Paint for Interiors - PPG INDUSTRIES, INC.; *pg.* 1445, *pg.* 1579
OVALTINE - Chocolate Drink Mix - NESTLE HEALTHCARE NUTRITION; *pg.* 1572, *pg.* 941
OVALTINE - Chocolate Malt - NESTLE USA, INC.; *pg.* 883, *pg.* 96
OVANTEX - Medical Device - OLIVER PRODUCTS COMPANY INC.; *pg.* 1367, *pg.* 888
OVATION - Software - ADOBE SYSTEMS INCORPORATED; *pg.* 342, *pg.* 235
OVATION - Power Supply System - ADVANCED ENERGY INDUSTRIES, INC.; *pg.* 613, *pg.* 328
OVATION - Tile - ARTISTIC TILE INC.; *pg.* 914, *pg.* 1119
OVATION - Carseat - GRACO CHILDREN'S PRODUCTS INC.; *pg.* 954, *pg.* 1531
OVATION - Service Provider - HONEYWELL INTERNATIONAL INC.; *pg.* 407, *pg.* 1088
OVATION - Furniture - JASPER GROUP; *pg.* 930, *pg.* 691
OVATION - Guitars - KAMAN CORPORATION; *pg.* 229, *pg.* 338
OVATION - Lighting - LSI INDUSTRIES INC.; *pg.* 58, *pg.* 1416
OVATION - Fabric - NEMSCHOFF, INC.; *pg.* 936, *pg.* 1890
OVATION - Semi-Transparent Latex & Alkyd for Faux Finishes & Decorative Techniques - PRATT & LAMBERT PAINTS; *pg.* 1446, *pg.* 1434
OVATION - Golf Product - TAYLORMADE-ADIDAS GOLF; *pg.* 1847, *pg.* 60
OVATIONONS - Laser Navigation Sensors - CYPRESS SEMICONDUCTOR CORPORATION; *pg.* 1326, *pg.* 243
OVATIONS - Health & Well-Being Services for Seniors - UNITEDHEALTH GROUP INCORPORATED; *pg.* 1221, *pg.* 950
OVATIONSLIM - Laser Navigation Sensors - CYPRESS SEMICONDUCTOR CORPORATION; *pg.* 1326, *pg.* 243
THE OVE GLOVE - Hot Surface Handler - JOSEPH ENTERPRISES, INC.; *pg.* 960, *pg.* 220
OVEN EASY - Fully Cooked Fried Chicken Drumsticks - TYSON FOODS, INC.; *pg.* 902, *pg.* 35
OVEN ESSENTIALS - Bakeware - NORTHLAND ALUMINUM PRODUCTS INC.; *pg.* 1129, *pg.* 941
OVEN GLO - Chemical Product - ROCHESTER MIDLAND CORPORATION; *pg.* 334, *pg.* 1337
OVEN KRISP - Lemon Pepper Fish & Barbeque & Spicy Chicken Batter Mixes - FRY KRISP COMPANY; *pg.* 857, *pg.* 893
OVEN STUFFER - Roaster - PERDUE FARMS INCORPORATED; *pg.* 889, *pg.* 777
OVENGOLD - Food Product - BOAR'S HEAD PROVISIONS CO., INC.; *pg.* 841, *pg.* 465
OVENPAK - Burner - MAXON CORPORATION; *pg.* 1359, *pg.* 695
OVENPAK-II - Gas Burner - MAXON CORPORATION; *pg.* 1359, *pg.* 695
OVER - Introducer - COOK GROUP, INC.; *pg.* 1518, *pg.* 674
OVER 30 - Nutritional Product - RBC LIFE SCIENCES, INC.; *pg.* 1588, *pg.* 1723
OVER A CENTURY OF CUTTING EXPERTISE - Tagline - EASTMAN MACHINE COMPANY; *pg.* 1331, *pg.* 1148
OVER-N-UNDER - Gravity-Flow, Overhead Transfer Conveyors - DAIFUKU WEBB; *pg.* 1327, *pg.* 885
OVER THE MOON - Dairy Product - DEAN FOODS

First page reference indicates Business Class Edition
Second page reference indicates Geographic Edition

COMPANY; *pg.* 852, *pg.* 1679
OVER THE TOP - Sunglasses - OAKLEY, INC.; *pg.* 1840, *pg.* 86
OVERC - Software - CINCOM SYSTEMS, INC.; *pg.* 372, *pg.* 1411
OVERCOAT - House Paint - PPG INDUSTRIES, INC.; *pg.* 1445, *pg.* 1579
OVERDRAFT ADVANTAGE - Banking Services - FIRST BUSEY CORPORATION; *pg.* 754, *pg.* 562
OVERDRIVE - Nutritional Supplement - NU SKIN ENTERPRISES, INC.; *pg.* 518, *pg.* 1755
OVERDRIVE - Footwear - OAKLEY, INC.; *pg.* 1840, *pg.* 86
OVERHEAD - Door Products - OVERHEAD DOOR CORPORATION; *pg.* 102, *pg.* 1725
OVERLAY - Concrete System - L.M. SCOFIELD COMPANY; *pg.* 94, *pg.* 134
OVERLAY - Fabric - NEMSCHOFF, INC.; *pg.* 936, *pg.* 1890
OVERLAY MANAGER - Software - SUNGARD DATA SYSTEMS INC.; *pg.* 477, *pg.* 1592
OVERLY - Metal Acoustical Door - OVERLY MANUFACTURING COMPANY; *pg.* 102, *pg.* 1534
OVERNIGHT SUCCESS - Skin Care Products - ELIZABETH ARDEN, INC.; *pg.* 507, *pg.* 448
OVERNIGHTER - Furniture - HSM SOLUTIONS; *pg.* 1884, *pg.* 1378
OVERNIGHTER - Boat - SEA RAY BOATS, INC.; *pg.* 1710, *pg.* 1638
OVERRULE - Footwear - K-SWISS; *pg.* 1837, *pg.* 306
OVERSEAS.COM - Advertising Website - LIVE CURRENT MEDIA INC.; *pg.* 1263, *pg.* 1911
OVERSPRAY AWAY - Liquid Product - DELTA FOREMOST CHEMICAL CORPORATION; *pg.* 1155, *pg.* 1642
OVERT - Furniture - HERMAN MILLER, INC.; *pg.* 926, *pg.* 913
OVERTIME SCHEDULER - Remote Button - TIVO INC.; *pg.* 313, *pg.* 251
OVERTON - Furniture - JASPER GROUP; *pg.* 930, *pg.* 691
OVERTURE - Case - ANTEC INCORPORATED; *pg.* 350, *pg.* 90
OVERTURE - Bath Product - KOHLER CO.; *pg.* 91, *pg.* 1862
OVERWRAP - Fingertips Without Seams - WELLS LAMONT CORPORATION; *pg.* 15, *pg.* 638
OVOL - Pharmaceutical Product - CHURCH & DWIGHT CANADA CORP.; *pg.* 503, *pg.* 1925
OVPD - Light Emitting Diode - UNIVFRSAL DISPLAY CORPORATION; *pg.* 683, *pg.* 1064
OVS - Refurbished Chambers - QUALMARK CORPORATION; *pg.* 1427, *pg.* 322
OWEN - Furniture - AMISCO INDUSTRIES LTD.; *pg.* 913, *pg.* 1958
OWEN - Bulk Material Handling - ANVIL ATTACHMENTS, LLC; *pg.* 1313, *pg.* 748
OWENS - Food Product - BOB EVANS FARMS, LLC; *pg.* 841, *pg.* 1467
OWEN'S - Supermarket - THE KROGER CO.; *pg.* 1025, *pg.* 1416
OWENS FAMILY RESTAURANTS - Family Restaurants - BOB EVANS FARMS, LLC; *pg.* 841, *pg.* 1467
OWENS FAMILY RESTAURANTS - Family Restaurants - BOB EVANS RESTAURANTS, INC.; *pg.* 1717, *pg.* 1438
OWENS FOODS - Food Products - BOB EVANS FARMS, LLC; *pg.* 841, *pg.* 1467
OWL CENTIPEDE - Molecular Biology Product - THERMO FISHER SCIENTIFIC INC.; *pg.* 1602, *pg.* 61
OWL LOGO - Software - SRA INTERNATIONAL, INC.; *pg.* 473, *pg.* 1780
OWLS NEST - Spreadable Cheese - BEL BRANDS USA; *pg.* 839, *pg.* 566
OWN IT ALL - Game - WMS INDUSTRIES INC.; *pg.* 593, *pg.* 666
OWNER'S CHOICE - Pet Foods - RITE AID CORPORATION; *pg.* 1590, *pg.* 1519
OX-TRAN - Permeation Instrument - MOCON, INC.; *pg.* 1363, *pg.* 940
OXABAN - Preservative - THE DOW CHEMICAL COMPANY; *pg.* 1157, *pg.* 898
OXAMIN - Amine Oxide - HUNTSMAN CORPORATION; *pg.* 1167, *pg.* 1758
OXBOARD - Strand Board - POTLATCH CORPORATION; *pg.* 1467, *pg.* 1844
OXBOW - Pet Product - PETSMART, INC.; *pg.* 1481, *pg.* 18
OXEN - Fabric - NEMSCHOFF, INC.; *pg.* 936, *pg.* 1890
OXEN - Fabric - UNIROYAL ENGINEERED PRODUCTS; *pg.* 699, *pg.* 467
OXEPA - Pharmaceutical Product - ABBOTT LABORATORIES; *pg.* 1484, *pg.* 551
OXEQUIP - Adapter - ALLIED HEALTHCARE PRODUCTS, INC.; *pg.* 1491, *pg.* 990
OXFORD - Computer Bag - A. T. CROSS COMPANY; *pg.* 339, *pg.* 1602
OXFORD - Furniture - ASHLEY FURNITURE INDUSTRIES, INC.; *pg.* 914, *pg.* 1852
OXFORD - Furniture - BASSETT FURNITURE INDUSTRIES, INCORPORATED; *pg.* 916, *pg.* 1776
OXFORD - Lounge Chairs - BERNHARDT DESIGN; *pg.* 918, *pg.* 1381
OXFORD - Table - BLATT BOWLING & BILLIARD CORP.; *pg.* 1827, *pg.* 1203
OXFORD - Pickles, Relishes (excluding Fruit Relishes), Peppers, Olives & Mayonnaise - CAINS FOODS, L.P.; *pg.* 843, *pg.* 784
OXFORD - Brick & Tile Product - CHEROKEE BRICK & TILE COMPANY; *pg.* 75, *pg.* 535
OXFORD - Filing Supplies, Binders, Report Covers, Desk Accessories - ESSELTE BUSINESS CORP; *pg.* 395, *pg.* 1179
THE OXFORD - Home Floor Plan - JACOBSEN MANUFACTURING, INC.; *pg.* 1098, *pg.* 460
OXFORD - Paper - NEENAH PAPER, INC.; *pg.* 1465, *pg.* 484
OXFORD - Fabric - NEMSCHOFF, INC.; *pg.* 936, *pg.* 1890
OXFORD - Bathroom Accessories - SYMMONS INDUSTRIES, INC.; *pg.* 114, *pg.* 803
OXFORD - Knee System - ZIMMER BIOMET HOLDINGS, INC.; *pg.* 1611, *pg.* 699
OXFORD APPAREL - Casual, Outerwear & Golf Apparel - OXFORD INDUSTRIES, INC.; *pg.* 30, *pg.* 517
OXFORD CUSTOM BLEND - Mayonnaise - CAINS FOODS, L.P.; *pg.* 843, *pg.* 784
OXI-CHEK - Antioxidants, High Purity Solid With Low Toxicity - FERRO CORPORATION; *pg.* 1162, *pg.* 1462
OXI MAGIC - Carpet & Upholstery Cleaner - THE CLOROX COMPANY; *pg.* 327, *pg.* 169
OXICLEAN - Pre-Wash Laundry Additive - CHURCH & DWIGHT CO., INC.; *pg.* 1153, *pg.* 1063
OXICLIQ - Medical Device - MALLINCKRODT PHARMACEUTICALS; *pg.* 1557, *pg.* 978
OXICLIQ - Sensor - MEDTRONIC; *pg.* 1563, *pg.* 183
OXICOAT - Metal Finishing Product - HEATBATH CORPORATION; *pg.* 1165, *pg.* 826
OXIDATION - Apparel - OAKLEY, INC.; *pg.* 1840, *pg.* 86
OXIFIRST - Medical Device - MALLINCKRODT PHARMACEUTICALS; *pg.* 1557, *pg.* 978
OXIFIRST - Fetal Pulse Oximetry System - MEDTRONIC; *pg.* 1563, *pg.* 183
OXILINE - Pressed & Monolithic Refractory - RESCO PRODUCTS, INC.; *pg.* 107, *pg.* 1581
OXILUBE - Lubricants - THE DOW CHEMICAL COMPANY; *pg.* 1157, *pg.* 898
OXIMAGIC - Carpet & Upholstery Cleaner - THE CLOROX COMPANY; *pg.* 327, *pg.* 169
OXIMAX - Pulse Oximetry System - MEDTRONIC; *pg.* 1563, *pg.* 183
OXINET - Pulse Oximetry Network - MEDTRONIC; *pg.* 1563, *pg.* 183
OXISENSOR - Medical Device - MALLINCKRODT PHARMACEUTICALS; *pg.* 1557, *pg.* 978
OXISENSOR - Adhesive Sensor - MEDTRONIC; *pg.* 1563, *pg.* 183
OXISENSOR II - Adhesive Sensor - MEDTRONIC; *pg.* 1563, *pg.* 183
OXLEY - Fabric - SCALAMANDRE, INC.; *pg.* 941, *pg.* 1058
OXO - Food Product - CAMPBELL SOUP COMPANY; *pg.* 844, *pg.* 1048
OXO - Personal Care Electrical Products - HELEN OF TROY L.P.; *pg.* 511, *pg.* 1692
OXO - Soup, Sauce and Seasoning - UNILEVER CANADA INC.; *pg.* 903, *pg.* 1946
OXONE - Oxidizing Compound - E.I. DU PONT DE NEMOURS & COMPANY; *pg.* 1159, *pg.* 390
OXOR - Gas Analyzer - BACHARACH INC.; *pg.* 1400, *pg.* 1556
OXPRO OR - Technology for Recycling Mixed Office Wastepaper - AIR PRODUCTS AND CHEMICALS, INC.; *pg.* 1145, *pg.* 1513
OXSOL - Non-Ozone Depleting Solvents - OCCIDENTAL CHEMICAL CORPORATION; *pg.* 1175, *pg.* 1685
OXSORALEN-ULTRA - Pharmaceutical Product - VALEANT PHARMACEUTICALS INTERNATIONAL; *pg.* 1605, *pg.* 1047
OXUS BLACK - Masterbatch Concentrates - FERRO CORPORATION; *pg.* 1162, *pg.* 1462
OXY-FORCE - Cleaner - NILODOR, INC.; *pg.* 332, *pg.* 1406
OXY-GARD - Hydrogen Peroxide-Based Teat Dip - ECOLAB INC.; *pg.* 329, *pg.* 960
OXY GEN2 - Floor Care Product - BISSELL HOMECARE, INC.; *pg.* 52, *pg.* 887
OXY-KIC - Stain Remover - BISSELL HOMECARE, INC.; *pg.* 52, *pg.* 887
OXY-NECTAR - Nutritional Supplement - NATURAL ORGANICS, INC.; *pg.* 1571, *pg.* 1181
OXY-PILOT - Burner - MAXON CORPORATION; *pg.* 1359, *pg.* 695
OXY POWER - Home Cleaner - S.C. JOHNSON & SON, INC.; *pg.* 334, *pg.* 1889
OXY POWER OUT - Carpet & Upholstery Cleaner - TURTLE WAX, INC.; *pg.* 220, *pg.* 671
OXY-SHIELD - Abrasion Resistant Epoxy Coating - QUAKER CHEMICAL CORP.; *pg.* 1178, *pg.* 1524
OXY-TET 8 PELLETS - Medicated Livestock Feed - KENT NUTRITION GROUP; *pg.* 1477, *pg.* 710
OXY-THERM - Burner - MAXON CORPORATION; *pg.* 1359, *pg.* 695
OXYBURST - Molecular Probe Product - THERMO FISHER SCIENTIFIC INC.; *pg.* 1602, *pg.* 61
OXYCHEM - Chemical Segment - OCCIDENTAL CHEMICAL CORPORATION; *pg.* 1175, *pg.* 1685
OXYCHLOR - Chlorine Dioxcide Generators - E.I. DU PONT DE NEMOURS & COMPANY; *pg.* 1159, *pg.* 390
OXYCLEAN - Additive - BASF CATALYSTS LLC; *pg.* 1148, *pg.* 1074
OXYCONTIN - Pharmaceutical Product - IMPAX LABORATORIES, INC.; *pg.* 1544, *pg.* 101
OXYCONTIN - Pharmaceutical Product - PURDUE PHARMA LP; *pg.* 1587, *pg.* 377
OXYFAST - Pharmaceutical Product - PURDUE PHARMA LP; *pg.* 1587, *pg.* 377
OXYFERM - Dissolved Oxygen Sensor - HAMILTON CO., INC.; *pg.* 1415, *pg.* 1031
OXYGARD - Special Application Filters - VITAL SIGNS, INC.; *pg.* 1607, *pg.* 1126
OXYGEN ALONE - Cable - OXYGEN MEDIA LLC; *pg.* 303, *pg.* 1275
OXYGEN BLEACH PLUS - Color Safe Bleach Product - BI-O-KLEEN INDUSTRIES, INC.; *pg.* 326, *pg.* 1845
OXYGEN MEDIA - Cable TV Network - OXYGEN MEDIA LLC; *pg.* 303, *pg.* 1275
OXYIR - Medical Product - PURDUE PHARMA LP; *pg.* 1587, *pg.* 377
OXYJET - Toothbrush - GILLETTE; *pg.* 1536, *pg.* 795
OXYKIC - Floor Care Product - BISSELL HOMECARE, INC.; *pg.* 52, *pg.* 887
OXYLITE - Robotic Product - HAMILTON CO., INC.; *pg.* 1415, *pg.* 1031
OXYLOCK - Medical Equipment - INVACARE CORPORATION; *pg.* 1546, *pg.* 1451
OXYPURGE - Compound - POLYONE CORPORATION; *pg.* 1177, *pg.* 1404
OXYRICH - Oxygen Generating Technology - AIR PRODUCTS AND CHEMICALS, INC.; *pg.* 1145, *pg.* 1513
OXYSEPT - Medical Device - ABBOTT MEDICAL OPTICS, INC.; *pg.* 1485, *pg.* 260
OXYSHIELD - Oxygen Barrier - HONEYWELL INTERNATIONAL INC.; *pg.* 407, *pg.* 1088
OXYSURE - Medical Grade Oxygen - OXYSURE SYSTEMS, INC.; *pg.* 1579, *pg.* 1697
OXYTITE - Thread Sealant - LA-CO INDUSTRIES MARKAL CO., INC.; *pg.* 1170, *pg.* 610
OXYTREX - Pain Medication - PAIN THERAPEUTICS, INC.; *pg.* 1579, *pg.* 1665
OXYTRODE - Robotic Product - HAMILTON CO., INC.; *pg.* 1415, *pg.* 1031
OXYTROL - Pharmaceutical Product - ALLERGAN; *pg.* 1490, *pg.* 1101
OXYVINYLS - Chemical Product - OCCIDENTAL PETROLEUM CORPORATION; *pg.* 1175, *pg.* 137
OYLTITE-STIK - Sealant - LA-CO INDUSTRIES MARKAL CO., INC.; *pg.* 1170, *pg.* 610
OYSTER - Suitcase - SAMSONITE CORPORATION; *pg.* 11, *pg.* 830
OYSTER COLLECTION - Watches - ROLEX WATCH U.S.A., INC.; *pg.* 11, *pg.* 1286
OYSTER KING - Oyster & clam opener - LINCOLN FOODSERVICE PRODUCTS, LLC; *pg.* 1127, *pg.* 1432
OZ - Cable Television Show - HOME BOX OFFICE, INC.; *pg.*

290, *pg.* 1240
OZ TEK - Test Socket - KULICKE & SOFFA INDUSTRIES, INC.; *pg.* 650, *pg.* 1533
OZARK - Footwear - EASTLAND SHOE CORPORATION; *pg.* 1808, *pg.* 750
OZARK TRAIL - Butane Lighters - WAL-MART STORES, INC.; *pg.* 1790, *pg.* 29
OZIO - Fabric - NEMSCHOFF, INC.; *pg.* 936, *pg.* 1890
OZONE - Dinnerware - THE HOMER LAUGHLIN CHINA COMPANY; *pg.* 1125, *pg.* 1850
OZONE - Fabric - NEMSCHOFF, INC.; *pg.* 936, *pg.* 1890
OZZIE - Monitor - AKRON BRASS COMPANY; *pg.* 1311, *pg.* 1482

P

P-10 - Preamplifier - KLIPSCH GROUP, INC.; *pg.* 649, *pg.* 688
P-100 - Power Adapter Plug - ANDREA ELECTRONICS CORPORATION; *pg.* 617, *pg.* 1143
P-24 DELTA TIE - Truss - DAYTON SUPERIOR CORPORATION; *pg.* 1328, *pg.* 1464
P-2V - Military Aircraft - LOCKHEED MARTIN CORPORATION; *pg.* 229, *pg.* 762
P-3 - Military Aircraft - LOCKHEED MARTIN CORPORATION; *pg.* 229, *pg.* 762
P-38 LIGHTNING - Systems Integration & Aeronautics - LOCKHEED MARTIN CORPORATION; *pg.* 229, *pg.* 762
P-38J LIGHTNING - Systems Integration & Aeronautics - LOCKHEED MARTIN CORPORATION; *pg.* 229, *pg.* 762
P-80 - Systems Integration & Aeronautics - LOCKHEED MARTIN CORPORATION; *pg.* 229, *pg.* 762
P/ACE - High Performance Capillary Electrophoresis System - BECKMAN COULTER, INC.; *pg.* 1402, *pg.* 48
P&H - Mining Equipment - JOY GLOBAL, INC.; *pg.* 1351, *pg.* 1876
P & L - Varnishes, Enamel, Etc. - PRATT & LAMBERT PAINTS; *pg.* 1446, *pg.* 1434
P&O CRUISES - Passenger Cruises & Tours - CARNIVAL CORPORATION; *pg.* 1902, *pg.* 441
P&O CRUISES AUSTRALIA - Passenger Cruises & Tours - CARNIVAL CORPORATION; *pg.* 1902, *pg.* 441
P&R - Pasta - NEW WORLD PASTA COMPANY; *pg.* 885, *pg.* 1537
P&RINTEGRATOR - Software System - MENTOR GRAPHICS CORPORATION; *pg.* 432, *pg.* 1510
P&S PLUGTAIL - Wiring Products - PASS & SEYMOUR/LEGRAND; *pg.* 1303, *pg.* 1344
P&S SIGNATURE - Wiring Products - PASS & SEYMOUR/LEGRAND; *pg.* 1303, *pg.* 1344
P&T PAD - Control Disc - VICON INDUSTRIES, INC.; *pg.* 685, *pg.* 1166
P-III - Cable Product - COMMSCOPE, INC.; *pg.* 278, *pg.* 1378
P/M UNI-DRAW - Thermal Processing Equipment - SURFACE COMBUSTION, INC.; *pg.* 1077, *pg.* 1462
P-NAP - Architecture - INTERNAP NETWORK SERVICES CORPORATION; *pg.* 417, *pg.* 513
P/S RADIANT II - Line Burner - MAXON CORPORATION; *pg.* 1359, *pg.* 695
P-SERIES - Centerfire Pistols - STURM, RUGER & COMPANY, INC.; *pg.* 1846, *pg.* 371
P-TEN - Computer-Related Vehicle Driver Training Applications - LOCKHEED MARTIN CORPORATION; *pg.* 229, *pg.* 762
P-TRAK - Switch - SOUTHWESTERN INDUSTRIES, INC.; *pg.* 1429, *pg.* 69
P-TRAK - Ultrafine Particle Counter - TSI INCORPORATED; *pg.* 1432, *pg.* 965
P-U-L-S-E - Water Cooling System Monitors - ASHLAND INC.; *pg.* 972, *pg.* 726
P1202 - Software - XEROX CORPORATION; *pg.* 494, *pg.* 365
P1210 - Software - XEROX CORPORATION; *pg.* 494, *pg.* 365
P175 - Punch Grinder - WELDON SOLUTIONS; *pg.* 1388, *pg.* 1598
P175 PUNCH GRINDER - High-Precision Grinder - WELDON SOLUTIONS; *pg.* 1388, *pg.* 1598
P2000 - Personal Care Product - WESTROCK COMPANY; *pg.* 1472, *pg.* 1805
P22 - Staples - ARROW FASTENER COMPANY, INC.; *pg.* 1042, *pg.* 1118
P2390 - Fluid Handling System - GRACO, INC.; *pg.* 1342, *pg.* 935
P2OLED - Light Emitting Diode - UNIVERSAL DISPLAY CORPORATION; *pg.* 683, *pg.* 1064
P3 - Cable - COMMSCOPE, INC.; *pg.* 278, *pg.* 1378
P3 - Metal Hose - PENFLEX, INC.; *pg.* 104, *pg.* 1534
P35 - Staples - ARROW FASTENER COMPANY, INC.; *pg.* 1042, *pg.* 1118
P4 - Automatic Conveyor System - PARAGON TECHNOLOGIES, INC.; *pg.* 1367, *pg.* 1528
P4 TECHNOLOGY - Semiconductor Device - APPLIED MATERIALS, INC; *pg.* 618, *pg.* 1009
P66 - Staples - ARROW FASTENER COMPANY, INC.; *pg.* 1042, *pg.* 1118
P7E - Medical Equipment - INVACARE CORPORATION; *pg.* 1546, *pg.* 1451
P900 - Bearings - THE TIMKEN COMPANY; *pg.* 218, *pg.* 1408
P9000 - Medical Equipment - INVACARE CORPORATION; *pg.* 1546, *pg.* 1451
P90X - Fitness Video & DVD - BEACHBODY, LLC; *pg.* 271, *pg.* 272
PA/5000 - Label Printer Applicator - DIAGRAPH; *pg.* 387, *pg.* 989
PA DUTCH - Sausages - HATFIELD QUALITY MEATS, INC.; *pg.* 861, *pg.* 1537
PA SERIES - Antenna Combiners - SHURE INCORPORATED; *pg.* 672, *pg.* 638
PA1X - Professional Arranger - KORG USA, INC.; *pg.* 556, *pg.* 1180
PA50 - Professional Arranger - KORG USA, INC.; *pg.* 556, *pg.* 1180
PA60 - Professional Arranger - KORG USA, INC.; *pg.* 556, *pg.* 1180
PA80 - Professional Arranger - KORG USA, INC.; *pg.* 556, *pg.* 1180
PAANI - Beverages - THE COCA-COLA COMPANY; *pg.* 240, *pg.* 493
PAASCHE - Airbrush - PAASCHE AIRBRUSH COMPANY; *pg.* 1444, *pg.* 587
PABLO - Furniture - AMISCO INDUSTRIES LTD.; *pg.* 913, *pg.* 1958
PABLO - Fabric - NEMSCHOFF, INC.; *pg.* 936, *pg.* 1890
PABST BLUE RIBBON - Beer - PABST BREWING COMPANY; *pg.* 258, *pg.* 137
PAC - Security Products - STANLEY BLACK & DECKER, INC.; *pg.* 1063, *pg.* 358
PAC-3 - Guided Missiles - LOCKHEED MARTIN CORPORATION; *pg.* 229, *pg.* 762
PAC CHECK - Package Analyzer - MOCON, INC.; *pg.* 1363, *pg.* 940
PAC GUARD - Package Leak Detection System - MOCON, INC.; *pg.* 1363, *pg.* 940
PAC-MAN - Lottery Game - NEW JERSEY STATE LOTTERY; *pg.* 1000, *pg.* 1126
PAC-SEAL - Seal - FLOWSERVE CORPORATION; *pg.* 82, *pg.* 1719
PAC-TOTE - Media Case - NER HOLDINGS INC.; *pg.* 444, *pg.* 1071
PACARO - Fabric - NEMSCHOFF, INC.; *pg.* 936, *pg.* 1890
PACE - Hardware - ACE HARDWARE CORPORATION; *pg.* 1040, *pg.* 644
PACE - Table - BLATT BOWLING & BILLIARD CORP.; *pg.* 1827, *pg.* 1203
PACE - Food Product - CAMPBELL COMPANY OF CANADA LTD; *pg.* 844, *pg.* 1935
PACE - Sauces - CAMPBELL SOUP COMPANY; *pg.* 844, *pg.* 1048
PACE - Suburban Transit System - PACE; *pg.* 1918, *pg.* 553
PACE - Clinical Trials - PAREXEL INTERNATIONAL CORPORATION; *pg.* 1580, *pg.* 853
PACE - Footwear - P.W. MINOR & SON, INC.; *pg.* 1816, *pg.* 1140
PACE/32 - Process Control Software - CSPI TECHNOLOGY SOLUTIONS; *pg.* 381, *pg.* 421
PACEL - Bipolar Pacing Catheters - ST. JUDE MEDICAL, INC.; *pg.* 1596, *pg.* 963
PACEMAKER - Spreader - EASTMAN MACHINE COMPANY; *pg.* 1331, *pg.* 1148
PACEMAKER - Sink - ELKAY MANUFACTURING COMPANY; *pg.* 80, *pg.* 645
PACEMAKER - Network Product - VITESSE SEMICONDUCTOR CORPORATION; *pg.* 686, *pg.* 57
PACER - Custom Wheels - AMERICAN TIRE DISTRIBUTORS HOLDINGS, INC.; *pg.* 199, *pg.* 1379
PACER - Track & Field Equipment - GILL ATHLETICS, INC.; *pg.* 1835, *pg.* 562
PACER - Floor Cleaning Product - NSS ENTERPRISES, INC.; *pg.* 59, *pg.* 1476
PACER - Pump for Agriculture, Marine, Irrigation, Petrochem - SERFILCO, LTD.; *pg.* 1375, *pg.* 641
PACER - Software - SS&C TECHNOLOGIES HOLDINGS, INC.; *pg.* 473, *pg.* 386
PACER - Glue - SUPER GLUE CORPORATION; *pg.* 1183, *pg.* 187
PACER - Cloth Cutter - THE WOLF MACHINE CO.; *pg.* 1389, *pg.* 1427
PACER JR. - Straight Knife - THE WOLF MACHINE CO.; *pg.* 1389, *pg.* 1427
PACER TECH INDUSTRIAL - Adhesive Product - SUPER GLUE CORPORATION; *pg.* 1183, *pg.* 187
PACESETTER - Bagging Machine - AUTOMATED PACKAGING SYSTEMS INC.; *pg.* 1452, *pg.* 1474
PACESETTER - Inverter Duty Motor - BODINE ELECTRIC COMPANY; *pg.* 1318, *pg.* 641
PACESETTER - Flooring Product - CONGOLEUM CORPORATION; *pg.* 921, *pg.* 1084
PACESETTER - Paperboard Packaging System - GRAPHIC PACKAGING HOLDING COMPANY; *pg.* 1459, *pg.* 509
PACESETTER PLUS - Computerized Chemical Feed & Monitoring System - GE WATER & PROCESS TECHNOLOGIES; *pg.* 1339, *pg.* 1588
PACESSETTER - Briquetter - PRAB, INC.; *pg.* 1369, *pg.* 894
PACHANGA - Boat - SEA RAY BOATS, INC.; *pg.* 1710, *pg.* 1638
PACHMAYR - Pistol Grips & Rifle Pads - LYMAN PRODUCTS CORPORATION; *pg.* 1839, *pg.* 356
PACIFIC - Footwear - EASTLAND SHOE CORPORATION; *pg.* 1808, *pg.* 750
PACIFIC - Furniture - FLEXSTEEL INDUSTRIES, INC.; *pg.* 925, *pg.* 707
PACIFIC - Milk Powder - SAPUTO, INC.; *pg.* 893, *pg.* 1956
PACIFIC BELL - Wireless Communication System - AT&T SOUTHEAST; *pg.* 1868, *pg.* 489
PACIFIC BELL - Telecommunications Products & Services - AT&T WEST; *pg.* 1869, *pg.* 212
PACIFIC BLUE - Molecular Probe Product - THERMO FISHER SCIENTIFIC INC.; *pg.* 1602, *pg.* 61
PACIFIC CENTURY BANK - Commercial Bank - BANK OF HAWAII CORPORATION; *pg.* 720, *pg.* 543
PACIFIC CENTURY LEASING - Leasing Subsidiary - BANK OF HAWAII CORPORATION; *pg.* 720, *pg.* 543
PACIFIC FINANCIAL PRODUCTS - Credit Risk & Default Protection - PACIFIC LIFE INSURANCE COMPANY; *pg.* 1213, *pg.* 166
PACIFIC GARDEN - Antibacterial Hand Soap - GEORGIA-PACIFIC LLC; *pg.* 1458, *pg.* 507
PACIFIC GOLD - Fruit & Vegetable Product - CHIQUITA BRANDS INTERNATIONAL, INC.; *pg.* 847, *pg.* 1365
PACIFIC LIFE & ANNUITY COMPANY - Financial Services & Group Employee Benefits - PACIFIC LIFE INSURANCE COMPANY; *pg.* 1213, *pg.* 166
PACIFIC LIFECORP - Stock Holding Company - PACIFIC LIFE INSURANCE COMPANY; *pg.* 1213, *pg.* 166
PACIFIC LIFE INSURANCE CO. - Financial Services - PACIFIC LIFE INSURANCE COMPANY; *pg.* 1213, *pg.* 166
PACIFIC NORTHWEST CANNED PEARS - Canned Pears - PACIFIC NORTHWEST CANNED PEAR SERVICE, INC.; *pg.* 153, *pg.* 1847
PACIFIC ORANGE - Molecular Probe Product - THERMO FISHER SCIENTIFIC INC.; *pg.* 1602, *pg.* 61
PACIFIC PARADISE - Ceiling Fan - WESTINGHOUSE LIGHTING CORPORATION; *pg.* 687, *pg.* 1571
PACIFIC POWER - ABN - PACIFICORP; *pg.* 1949, *pg.* 1504
PACIFIC RIDGE PALE ALE - Specialty Beer - ANHEUSER-BUSCH COMPANIES, LLC; *pg.* 237, *pg.* 991
PACIFIC SCIENTIFIC ATG - Motor & Drive - DANAHER CORPORATION; *pg.* 1044, *pg.* 397
PACIFIC SHIPPER - Shipping Publication - JOC GROUP INC.; *pg.* 1654, *pg.* 1096
PACIFIC SUNWEAR - Clothing - PACIFIC SUNWEAR OF CALIFORNIA, INC.; *pg.* 1781, *pg.* 43
PACIFIC SUNWEAR OF CALIFORNIA - Clothing - PACIFIC SUNWEAR OF CALIFORNIA, INC.; *pg.* 1781, *pg.* 43
PACIFIC WIETZ - Seal - FLOWSERVE CORPORATION; *pg.* 82, *pg.* 1719
PACIFICA - Tile - ARTISTIC TILE INC.; *pg.* 914, *pg.* 1119
PACIFICO - Beer - CROWN IMPORTS LLC; *pg.* 248, *pg.* 572
PACIFIER CLEAN 'N GO - Baby Care Product - MUNCHKIN, INC.; *pg.* 964, *pg.* 300

First page reference indicates Business Class Edition
Second page reference indicates Geographic Edition

PACIRA - Pharmaceutical Product - PACIRA PHARMACEUTICALS, INC.; pg. 1579, pg. 1104
PACK - Cleaning Towelette - MCKEON PRODUCTS, INC.; pg. 1559, pg. 912
PACK-CON - Vehicle Safety System - GROTE INDUSTRIES, INC.; pg. 206, pg. 693
PACK-IT - Cushion - THE ROHO GROUP; pg. 1591, pg. 556
PACK IT - Fishing Rods - WRIGHT & MCGILL CO.; pg. 1848, pg. 324
PACK-LITE - Footwear - LACROSSE FOOTWEAR, INC.; pg. 1811, pg. 1503
PACK MINI MICE - Pet Toy - THE HARTZ MOUNTAIN CORP.; pg. 1476, pg. 1120
PACK-O-FUN - Magazine - AMOS PRESS, INC.; pg. 1616, pg. 1472
PACKAGE - Software System - MENTOR GRAPHICS CORPORATION; pg. 432, pg. 1510
PACKARD - Vehicle Safety System - GROTE INDUSTRIES, INC.; pg. 206, pg. 693
PACKARD - Fabric - NEMSCHOFF, INC.; pg. 936, pg. 1890
PACKBOT - Robotic Equipment - IROBOT CORP.; pg. 1418, pg. 785
PACKER - Food Product - ELLENBEE-LEGGETT COMPANY INC.; pg. 854, pg. 1452
PACKER - Footwear - LACROSSE FOOTWEAR, INC.; pg. 1811, pg. 1503
THE PACKER - Magazine - VANCE PUBLISHING CORPORATION; pg. 1699, pg. 627
PACKET VELOCITY - Software - F5 NETWORKS, INC.; pg. 396, pg. 1835
PACKET8 - Telecommunications Technology for Internet Protocol - 8X8, INC.; pg. 1865, pg. 282
PACKET8 VIRTUAL OFFICE - Software - 8X8, INC.; pg. 1865, pg. 282
PACKETCABLE - Network Device Monitoring - ARRIS GROUP, INC.; pg. 353, pg. 541
PACKETCABLE 1.5 - Cable Solutions - SONUS NETWORKS INC.; pg. 1281, pg. 858
PACKETCABLE MIGRATION - Cable Solutions - SONUS NETWORKS INC.; pg. 1281, pg. 858
PACKETCABLE MULTIMEDIA (PCMM) - Cable Solutions - SONUS NETWORKS INC.; pg. 1281, pg. 858
PACKETCLOCK - Clock & Buffer Product - CYPRESS SEMICONDUCTOR CORPORATION; pg. 1326, pg. 243
PACKETIN - Software System - ALCATEL-LUCENT; pg. 615, pg. 1094
PACKETMAKER - Software - FINISAR CORPORATION; pg. 639, pg. 285
PACKETRAM - RAM - CYPRESS SEMICONDUCTOR CORPORATION; pg. 1326, pg. 243
PACKETSTAR - Software System - ALCATEL-LUCENT; pg. 615, pg. 1094
PACKETSYNC - Computer Products - BROADCOM CORPORATION; pg. 364, pg. 108
PACKFORUM - Food Marketing & Packaging Exhibition Center & Seminars - SEALED AIR CORPORATION; pg. 1468, pg. 1058
PACKING SEAL - Fluid Handling System - GRACO, INC.; pg. 1342, pg. 935
PACKMATE - Flashlight - STREAMLIGHT INC.; pg. 1306, pg. 1527
PACLITAXEL - Pharmaceutical Product - ASTEX PHARMACEUTICALS, INC; pg. 1497, pg. 77
PACLITE - Apparel - CABELA'S INCORPORATED; pg. 535, pg. 1019
PACLITE - Fabric - W.L. GORE & ASSOCIATES, INC.; pg. 122, pg. 388
PACLOG - Software - BMC SOFTWARE, INC.; pg. 362, pg. 1701
PACMED - Packager - MCKESSON CORPORATION; pg. 1560, pg. 222
PACNET - Software System - HONEYWELL INTERNATIONAL INC.; pg. 407, pg. 1088
PACO - Refractories - RESCO PRODUCTS GREENSBORO; pg. 107, pg. 1375
PACO - Pressed & Monolithic Refractory - RESCO PRODUCTS, INC.; pg. 107, pg. 1581
PACO MIX - Refractory Product - RESCO PRODUCTS, INC.; pg. 107, pg. 1581
PACOCAST - Pressed & Monolithic Refractory - RESCO PRODUCTS, INC.; pg. 107, pg. 1581
PACS - Software - IDEXX LABORATORIES, INC.; pg. 1543, pg. 753
PACS - Software - STRYKER CORPORATION; pg. 1598, pg. 894
PACSHARE - Emission Testing System - MISTRAS GROUP, INC.; pg. 1362, pg. 1113
PACTECON - Dust Filter - SLY, INC.; pg. 1376, pg. 1475
PACTIV - Food Service & Packaging - PACTIV CORPORATION; pg. 1466, pg. 624
PACTIV AIR - Table - PACTIV CORPORATION; pg. 1466, pg. 624
PACTRA - Paint - THE TESTOR CORPORATION; pg. 968, pg. 655
PACTRAC - Prepaid College Tuition Service - HDI SOLUTIONS, INC.; pg. 403, pg. 1
PACZOL - Polymer Product - CHEMTURA CORPORATION; pg. 1152, pg. 355
PAD/DOCK - Box - RUBBERMAID HOME PRODUCTS; pg. 1138, pg. 1453
PAD KOTE - Pet Supplies - HAPPY JACK INC.; pg. 1476, pg. 1390
PAD-LOC - Processor Pad - SEALED AIR CORPORATION; pg. 1468, pg. 1058
PADDOCK AND PASTURE - Animal Safety Product - NEOGEN CORPORATION; pg. 883, pg. 896
PADDOCK PALS - Toy Scale Model Animal - REEVES INTERNATIONAL, INC.; pg. 966, pg. 1108
PADDY WAGON - Padding Press - THE CHALLENGE MACHINERY COMPANY; pg. 1322, pg. 902
PADLOCK - Adhesive - H.B. FULLER COMPANY; pg. 1165, pg. 961
PADLOCK - Security Device - WINNER INTERNATIONAL, LLC; pg. 222, pg. 1586
PADPRO - Medical Equipment - CONMED CORPORATION; pg. 1517, pg. 1347
PADRON - Cigars - FINCK CIGAR CO.; pg. 1894, pg. 1740
PADS - Software System - MENTOR GRAPHICS CORPORATION; pg. 432, pg. 1510
PAEDIASURE - Nutritional Product - ABBOTT LABORATORIES; pg. 1484, pg. 551
PAELLA - Rice Mix - GOYA FOODS, INC.; pg. 859, pg. 1075
PAF - Power Assisted Fuse - G&W ELECTRIC COMPANY; pg. 1338, pg. 558
PAGE & TUTTLE - Knit Golf Shirts - RIVER'S END TRADING COMPANY; pg. 47, pg. 1867
PAGE PLUS PROGRAM - Manual - XEROX CORPORATION; pg. 494, pg. 365
PAGE SPEED SERVICE - Online Application - GOOGLE INC.; pg. 1249, pg. 153
PAGEANT - Motion Picture Projectors - EASTMAN KODAK COMPANY; pg. 1408, pg. 1333
PAGECAM - Manual - XEROX CORPORATION; pg. 494, pg. 365
PAGEFLOW - Software - R.R. DONNELLEY & SONS COMPANY; pg. 1682, pg. 589
PAGEKOM - Paging & Intercom System - ATLAS SOUND; pg. 621, pg. 1692
PAGEMAKER - Software - ADOBE SYSTEMS INCORPORATED; pg. 342, pg. 235
PAGEMARK - Publication - FRANKLIN ELECTRONIC PUBLISHERS, INC.; pg. 398, pg. 1048
PAGEMASTER - Computer Program - HERFF JONES, INC.; pg. 7, pg. 686
PAGENT - Fabric - NEMSCHOFF, INC.; pg. 936, pg. 1890
PAGEPLANNER - Planning Tools - R.R. DONNELLEY & SONS COMPANY; pg. 1682, pg. 589
PAGER - Mining Product - MINE SAFETY APPLIANCES COMPANY; pg. 1361, pg. 1525
PAGERANK - Internet Application - GOOGLE INC.; pg. 1249, pg. 153
PAGES - iWork App for Word Processing & Page Layout - APPLE INC.; pg. 350, pg. 73
PAGES - Software - SS&C TECHNOLOGIES HOLDINGS, INC.; pg. 473, pg. 386
PAGE'S PREMIUM - Packet Seeds - Vegetable, Flower & Herb, Wildflower & Perennial - THE PAGE SEED CO.; pg. 1798, pg. 1163
PAGETRAK - Manual - XEROX CORPORATION; pg. 494, pg. 365
PAGI-SET - Phototypesetting Film - EASTMAN KODAK COMPANY; pg. 1408, pg. 1333
PAGLIA - Fabric - NEMSCHOFF, INC.; pg. 936, pg. 1890
PAGODA - Rice - RICELAND FOODS, INC.; pg. 892, pg. 36
PAID SEARCH PLUS - Internet Search Service - LOCAL.COM CORPORATION; pg. 1264, pg. 113
PAIGE - Furniture - HOOKER FURNITURE CORPORATION; pg. 928, pg. 1788
PAIN & DISTRESS REPORT - Newsletter - THE HUMANE SOCIETY OF THE UNITED STATES; pg. 143, pg. 400
PAIN PAK - Medical Device - INTEGRA LIFESCIENCES HOLDINGS CORPORATION; pg. 1545, pg. 1109
PAIN THERAPEUTICS - Drug Development - PAIN THERAPEUTICS, INC.; pg. 1579, pg. 1665
PAINBLOCKER - Surgical Device - WALLACH SURGICAL DEVICES, INC.; pg. 1436, pg. 381
PAINLESS - Analgesia Instrument - STOELTING CO.; pg. 1430, pg. 671
PAINPAK - Medical Device - INTEGRA LIFESCIENCES HOLDINGS CORPORATION; pg. 1545, pg. 1109
PAINPUMP - Surgical Pain Instrument - STRYKER CORPORATION; pg. 1598, pg. 894
PAINT BOX - Carpet - INTERFACE, INC.; pg. 695, pg. 512
PAINT BUSTER - Cleaner - 3M COMPANY; pg. 1142, pg. 956
PAINT MISER - Painting Tool - HYDE TOOLS, INC.; pg. 1125, pg. 844
PAINT POD - Sample-Sized Containers - ACE HARDWARE CORPORATION; pg. 1040, pg. 644
PAINT POTTERY - Hobby Craft Kit - JANLYNN CORPORATION; pg. 696, pg. 815
PAINT SAVER - Electric Airless Paint Sprayer - GRACO, INC.; pg. 1342, pg. 935
PAINT SHOP - Software - COREL CORPORATION; pg. 380, pg. 1931
PAINT YOUR TORON-TOES ROSE - Nail Care Product - OPI PRODUCTS INC.; pg. 518, pg. 167
PAINTERS' HELPER - Surface Preps - W.M. BARR & COMPANY, INC.; pg. 338, pg. 1647
THE PAINTER'S PAINT STORE - Tagline - KELLY-MOORE PAINT COMPANY, INC.; pg. 1443, pg. 198
PAINTER'S PUTTY '53' - Putty - DAP PRODUCTS, INC.; pg. 1441, pg. 756
PAINTER'S PYRAMID - Painting Tool - HYDE TOOLS, INC.; pg. 1125, pg. 844
PAINTER'S TEAM - Fluid Handling System - GRACO, INC.; pg. 1342, pg. 935
PAINTGRIP - Steel Product - AK STEEL HOLDING CORPORATION; pg. 1311, pg. 1479
THE PAINTIN' PLACE - Paint Store Retail Services - ACE HARDWARE CORPORATION; pg. 1040, pg. 644
PAINTING - Magazine - AMOS PRESS, INC.; pg. 1616, pg. 1472
PAINTMASTER PRO - Pavement Striping Management Software - M-B COMPANIES, INC.; pg. 1357, pg. 1884
PAINTMATE PLUS - Power Roller - WAGNER SPRAY TECH CORPORATION; pg. 1449, pg. 954
PAINTNROLL PLUS - Power Roller - WAGNER SPRAY TECH CORPORATION; pg. 1449, pg. 954
PAINTSCAN - In-Line Inspection System that Maps Defects in Paint - PERCEPTRON, INC.; pg. 215, pg. 904
PAINTSTIK - Counter Display - LA-CO INDUSTRIES MARKAL CO., INC.; pg. 1170, pg. 610
PAIRSPAN - High Capacity Telecommunications Switching System - ALCATEL-LUCENT USA, INC.; pg. 615, pg. 1728
PAJAMA PARTY - Fragrance - PARFUMS DE COEUR LTD.; pg. 519, pg. 376
PAJAMAGRAM - Gift Product - THE VERMONT TEDDY BEAR COMPANY; pg. 969, pg. 1767
PAJCO - Paper & Nonwoven Material - FIBERMARK INC.; pg. 1457, pg. 1764
PAK-A-POTTI - Portable Toilets - THETFORD CORPORATION; pg. 337, pg. 867
PAK-ITS - Packing Strip - DERMA SCIENCES, INC.; pg. 1523, pg. 1111
PAK-LINE - Custom Industrial Packaging - HOMASOTE COMPANY; pg. 87, pg. 1126
PAK-RAK - Stock Truck - THE CHALLENGE MACHINERY COMPANY; pg. 1322, pg. 902
PAK SHACK - Ice Fishing Equipment - SWORDFISH FINANCIAL, INC.; pg. 1430, pg. 1737
PAKS - Icing And Filling - DAWN FOOD PRODUCTS, INC.; pg. 1018, pg. 893
PAKT - Burner - MAXON CORPORATION; pg. 1359, pg. 695
PAL - Office Product - HAWORTH, INC.; pg. 402, pg. 891
PAL - Computer Software - LOCKHEED MARTIN CORPORATION; pg. 229, pg. 762
PAL - Power Assisted Lipoplasty Device - MICROAIRE SURGICAL INSTRUMENTS INC.; pg. 1423, pg. 1778
PAL - Elevator - SAVARIA CONCORD LIFTS INC.; pg. 1592, pg. 1919
PAL - Patient Handling Equipment - STRYKER CORPORATION; pg. 1598, pg. 894
PAL - Control System - TECK RESOURCES LIMITED; pg.

1183, *pg.* 1912
PAL-KOR - Transit Protection Product - GREIF INC.; *pg.* 1459, *pg.* 1447
PAL PAK - Corrugated Container - GREIF INC.; *pg.* 1459, *pg.* 1447
PAL SYSTEM - Software - SUNGARD DATA SYSTEMS INC.; *pg.* 477, *pg.* 1592
PALA - Footwear - COBIAN CORP.; *pg.* 1806, *pg.* 253
PALA-NATE - Oral Protection Device - UTAH MEDICAL PRODUCTS, INC.; *pg.* 1605, *pg.* 1752
PALACE OF RICHES - Game - WMS INDUSTRIES INC.; *pg.* 593, *pg.* 666
PALACE STATION HOTEL AND CASINO - Hotel & Casino - STATION CASINOS, INC.; *pg.* 585, *pg.* 1030
PALACEE - Footwear - STEVEN MADDEN, LTD.; *pg.* 1819, *pg.* 1176
PALADIN - Laser & Laser System - COHERENT, INC.; *pg.* 1406, *pg.* 265
PALADIN - Flame Resistant Barrier - MILLIKEN & COMPANY; *pg.* 696, *pg.* 1622
PALADIN - Digital Correction Signal Processor - PMC-SIERRA, INC.; *pg.* 664, *pg.* 287
PALAIS - Door Glass - ODL INCORPORATED; *pg.* 101, *pg.* 914
PALAIS ROYAL - Department Stores - STAGE STORES, INC.; *pg.* 33, *pg.* 1715
PALATINE - Bathroom Fan - HUNTER FAN COMPANY; *pg.* 57, *pg.* 1631
PALATINO - Fabric - NEMSCHOFF, INC.; *pg.* 936, *pg.* 1890
PALAZZIO - Lighting Product - QUOIZEL INC.; *pg.* 1304, *pg.* 1616
PALAZZO - Tile - ARTISTIC TILE INC.; *pg.* 914, *pg.* 1119
PALAZZO - Furniture - JOFCO INC.; *pg.* 931, *pg.* 691
PALAZZO - Door - MASONITE INTERNATIONAL CORPORATION; *pg.* 1054, *pg.* 1920
PALE ALE - Ale - BIG ROCK BREWERY INCOME TRUST; *pg.* 239, *pg.* 1902
PALE LAGER - Beer - SPRECHER BREWING COMPANY; *pg.* 265, *pg.* 1858
PALE OIL - Dry Cleaning & Laundry Product - ADCO, INC.; *pg.* 325, *pg.* 482
PALERMO - Office Furniture - STEELCASE INC.; *pg.* 475, *pg.* 889
PALETTE - Color - FERRO CORPORATION; *pg.* 1162, *pg.* 1462
PALETTE - Fabric - NEMSCHOFF, INC.; *pg.* 936, *pg.* 1890
PALGARD - Epoxy Coating - PRATT & LAMBERT PAINTS; *pg.* 1446, *pg.* 1434
PALI - Eyewear - MAUI JIM, INC.; *pg.* 9, *pg.* 651
PALISADE - Receiver - TRIMBLE NAVIGATION LIMITED; *pg.* 1384, *pg.* 288
PALISADES TRAIL - Bike - MARIN BIKES; *pg.* 1708, *pg.* 168
PALL - Filters - PALL CORPORATION; *pg.* 232, *pg.* 1323
PALL ADVANTA - Filter Equipment - PALL CORPORATION; *pg.* 232, *pg.* 1323
PALL-AQUASAFE - Filter - PALL CORPORATION; *pg.* 232, *pg.* 1323
PALL-ARIA - Water Treatment System - PALL CORPORATION; *pg.* 232, *pg.* 1323
PALL DISC TUBE - Filter Technology - PALL CORPORATION; *pg.* 232, *pg.* 1323
PALL-FIT - Filter Element - PALL CORPORATION; *pg.* 232, *pg.* 1323
PALL MALL - Cigarette - REYNOLDS AMERICAN INC.; *pg.* 1894, *pg.* 1395
PALLABAR - Chemicals for Electro Plating - TECHNIC INCORPORATED; *pg.* 1183, *pg.* 1601
PALLADIA - Digital Cable & Satellite TV Network - MTV NETWORKS COMPANY; *pg.* 298, *pg.* 1262
PALLADIAN - Furniture - TROPITONE FURNITURE CO., INC.; *pg.* 945, *pg.* 118
PALLADIUM - Call Handling Solutions - INTRADO INC.; *pg.* 420, *pg.* 334
PALLADIUM - Amplifier - KLIPSCH GROUP, INC.; *pg.* 649, *pg.* 688
PALLADONE - Pharmaceutical Product - PURDUE PHARMA LP; *pg.* 1587, *pg.* 377
PALLAMERSE - Chemicals for Electro Plating - TECHNIC INCORPORATED; *pg.* 1183, *pg.* 1601
PALLASPEED - Chemicals for Electro Plating - TECHNIC INCORPORATED; *pg.* 1183, *pg.* 1601
PALLCELL - Filter Cartridge - PALL CORPORATION; *pg.* 232, *pg.* 1323
PALLCHEK - Rapid Microbiology System - PALL CORPORATION; *pg.* 232, *pg.* 1323
PALLETFAST - Plastics Product - AEP INDUSTRIES INC.; *pg.* 1878, *pg.* 1085
PALLETOTE - Plastic Box - HILLYARD, INC.; *pg.* 331, *pg.* 990
PALLETPRO - Battery - EXIDE TECHNOLOGIES; *pg.* 204, *pg.* 483
PALLETSEARCH - Security X-Ray System for Searching Pallets - AMERICAN SCIENCE AND ENGINEERING, INC.; *pg.* 1399, *pg.* 787
PALLINI - Lemon Liqueur - CASTLE BRANDS INC.; *pg.* 239, *pg.* 1209
PALLSEP - Crossflow System - PALL CORPORATION; *pg.* 232, *pg.* 1323
PALLTRONIC - Filter Equipment - PALL CORPORATION; *pg.* 232, *pg.* 1323
PALM BEACH - Carpet - BEAULIEU GROUP, LLC; *pg.* 917, *pg.* 529
PALM BEACH - Rug - COURISTAN INC.; *pg.* 921, *pg.* 1067
PALM BEACH - Furniture - HOOKER FURNITURE CORPORATION; *pg.* 928, *pg.* 1788
PALM BEACH - Custom Poly-Satin Vinyl Shutters - HUNTER DOUGLAS, INC.; *pg.* 928, *pg.* 1320
PALM BEACH CHARITY REGISTER - Magazine - PALM BEACH MEDIA GROUP INC.; *pg.* 1674, *pg.* 457
PALM BEACH ILLUSTRATED - Magazine - PALM BEACH MEDIA GROUP INC.; *pg.* 1674, *pg.* 457
PALM GROVE - Furniture - ETHAN ALLEN INTERIORS INC.; *pg.* 924, *pg.* 343
THE PALM HOUSE - Wall Decor - ETHAN ALLEN INTERIORS INC.; *pg.* 924, *pg.* 343
PALM SPRINGS - Carpet - BEAULIEU GROUP, LLC; *pg.* 917, *pg.* 529
PALM SPRINGS - Rug - COURISTAN INC.; *pg.* 921, *pg.* 1067
PALM SPRINGS LIFE - Magazine - DESERT PUBLICATIONS INC.; *pg.* 1635, *pg.* 174
PALMAZ-SCHATZ - Healthcare Product - JOHNSON & JOHNSON; *pg.* 1549, *pg.* 1091
PALMERA - Hand Tools - SNAP-ON INCORPORATED; *pg.* 1062, *pg.* 1862
PALMER'S - Skin Care Product - E.T. BROWNE DRUG COMPANY, INC.; *pg.* 509, *pg.* 1060
PALMER'S COCOA BUTTER FORMULA - Lotion - E.T. BROWNE DRUG COMPANY, INC.; *pg.* 509, *pg.* 1060
PALMER'S COCONUT OIL FORMULA - Lotion - E.T. BROWNE DRUG COMPANY, INC.; *pg.* 509, *pg.* 1060
PALMER'S HAIR CARE - Hair Care Products - E.T. BROWNE DRUG COMPANY, INC.; *pg.* 509, *pg.* 1060
PALMER'S HAIR SUCCESS - Hair Care Products - E.T. BROWNE DRUG COMPANY, INC.; *pg.* 509, *pg.* 1060
PALMER'S NO BLADE - Hair Care Products - E.T. BROWNE DRUG COMPANY, INC.; *pg.* 509, *pg.* 1060
PALMER'S SKIN SOFTENING CREAM - Creams - E.T. BROWNE DRUG COMPANY, INC.; *pg.* 509, *pg.* 1060
PALMER'S SKIN SUCCESS - Creams - E.T. BROWNE DRUG COMPANY, INC.; *pg.* 509, *pg.* 1060
PALMETTO - Food Product - A. DUDA & SONS INC.; *pg.* 835, *pg.* 457
PALMETTO PLUS - Nutritional Supplement - USANA HEALTH SCIENCES, INC.; *pg.* 1605, *pg.* 1761
PALMIA - Cooking Oil - CARGILL LIMITED; *pg.* 1475, *pg.* 1914
PALMIER - Fabric - SCALAMANDRE, INC.; *pg.* 941, *pg.* 1058
PALMOA - Fabric - NEMSCHOFF, INC.; *pg.* 936, *pg.* 1890
PALMOLIVE - Personal Care Product - COLGATE-PALMOLIVE COMPANY; *pg.* 504, *pg.* 1215
PALMOLIVE AROMA LIQUID HAND WASH - RELAX - Personal Care Product - COLGATE-PALMOLIVE COMPANY; *pg.* 504, *pg.* 1215
PALMOLIVE AROMA SHOWER GEL - RELAX - Personal Care Product - COLGATE-PALMOLIVE COMPANY; *pg.* 504, *pg.* 1215
PALMOLIVE AROMA SHOWER GEL - VITALITY - Personal Care Product - COLGATE-PALMOLIVE COMPANY; *pg.* 504, *pg.* 1215
PALMOLIVE CHARMIS CREAM - Personal Care Product - COLGATE-PALMOLIVE COMPANY; *pg.* 504, *pg.* 1215
PALMOLIVE NATURALS LIQUID HAND WASH - MILK & OLIVE - Personal Care Product - COLGATE-PALMOLIVE COMPANY; *pg.* 504, *pg.* 1215
PALMOLIVE NATURALS MOISTURIZING BODY WASH - Personal Care Product - COLGATE-PALMOLIVE COMPANY; *pg.* 504, *pg.* 1215
PALMOLIVE SHAVE CREAM - Personal Care Product - COLGATE-PALMOLIVE COMPANY; *pg.* 504, *pg.* 1215
PALMOLIVE THERMAL SPA - FIRMING & MASSAGE - Personal Care Product - COLGATE-PALMOLIVE COMPANY; *pg.* 504, *pg.* 1215
PALMS - Pillow - AMERICAN LEATHER LP; *pg.* 912, *pg.* 1673
PALMS - Pulltab Game - IDAHO LOTTERY; *pg.* 995, *pg.* 547
PALMS - Eyewear - MAUI JIM, INC.; *pg.* 9, *pg.* 651
PALMS - Software - SS&C TECHNOLOGIES HOLDINGS, INC.; *pg.* 473, *pg.* 386
PALMSTAT - Static Control Product - WALTER G. LEGGE COMPANY, INC.; *pg.* 337, *pg.* 1321
PALMVITEE - Health System Product - LANELABS USA INC.; *pg.* 1554, *pg.* 1128
PALMYRA - Rug - COURISTAN INC.; *pg.* 921, *pg.* 1067
PALODENT - Dental Product - DENTSPLY INTERNATIONAL INC.; *pg.* 1522, *pg.* 1596
PALOMA - Vanity Lights - CRAFTMADE INTERNATIONAL, INC.; *pg.* 1295, *pg.* 1670
PALOMA - Furniture - ETHAN ALLEN INTERIORS INC.; *pg.* 924, *pg.* 343
PALOMA - Footwear - PHOENIX FOOTWEAR GROUP, INC.; *pg.* 1815, *pg.* 60
PALOMAR - Area Rugs - COURISTAN INC.; *pg.* 921, *pg.* 1067
PALOMINO RESTAURANT ROTISSERIA BAR - Restaurant Chain - RESTAURANTS UNLIMITED, INC.; *pg.* 1748, *pg.* 1839
PALS - Tableware - PACTIV CORPORATION; *pg.* 1466, *pg.* 624
PAM - Food Product - CONAGRA FOODS, INC.; *pg.* 826, *pg.* 1014
PAM PROFESSIONAL - Cooking Oil - CONAGRA FOODS, INC.; *pg.* 826, *pg.* 1014
PAMELA - Clothing - ABERCROMBIE & FITCH CO.; *pg.* 37, *pg.* 1466
PAMELOR - Pharmaceutical Product - MALLINCKRODT PHARMACEUTICALS; *pg.* 1557, *pg.* 978
PAMOLYN - Fatty Acids - EASTMAN CHEMICAL COMPANY; *pg.* 1159, *pg.* 1636
PAMPA - Furniture - ASHLEY FURNITURE INDUSTRIES, INC.; *pg.* 914, *pg.* 1852
PAMPA - Beverages - THE COCA-COLA COMPANY; *pg.* 240, *pg.* 493
PAMPER KAT - Minerals - MINERALS TECHNOLOGIES INC.; *pg.* 1173, *pg.* 617
PAMPERS - Baby Care Product - THE PROCTER & GAMBLE COMPANY; *pg.* 1129, *pg.* 1418
PAMPERS KANDOO - Baby Care Product - THE PROCTER & GAMBLE COMPANY; *pg.* 1129, *pg.* 1418
PAMPERS SIMPLY DRY - Baby Care Product - THE PROCTER & GAMBLE COMPANY; *pg.* 1129, *pg.* 1418
PAMPERS UNDERJAMS - Personal & Household Product - THE PROCTER & GAMBLE COMPANY; *pg.* 1129, *pg.* 1418
PAMPHLET - Parish Resource - OUR SUNDAY VISITOR, INC.; *pg.* 1673, *pg.* 682
PAMPLEFLEUR - Fragrance Ingredient - INTERNATIONAL FLAVORS & FRAGRANCES INC.; *pg.* 512, *pg.* 1244
PAMPLONA - Video Game - INTERNATIONAL GAME TECHNOLOGY; *pg.* 957, *pg.* 1024
PAMPRIN - Health & Beauty Product - CHATTEM, INC.; *pg.* 1515, *pg.* 1628
PAMSELLO - Grated Cheese - MARS, INCORPORATED; *pg.* 1858, *pg.* 1792
PAN CASARI - Furniture - ASHLEY FURNITURE INDUSTRIES, INC.; *pg.* 914, *pg.* 1852
PAN-CLAMP - Wiring Accessory - PANDUIT CORP.; *pg.* 661, *pg.* 663
PAN CLEAN - Prewash Product - NORTHERN LABS, INC.; *pg.* 517, *pg.* 1869
PAN-CODE - Marker Card - PANDUIT CORP.; *pg.* 661, *pg.* 663
PAN-IN-PAN - Panel - RIGIDIZED METALS CORP.; *pg.* 108, *pg.* 1151
PAN-L-BOND - Construction Panel-Foam Adhesive - W.J. RUSCOE COMPANY; *pg.* 122, *pg.* 1403
PAN-LUG - Power and Grounding Connector - PANDUIT CORP.; *pg.* 661, *pg.* 663
PAN MANAGER - Software - EGENERA, INC.; *pg.* 390, *pg.* 802
PAN-MARK - Software - PANDUIT CORP.; *pg.* 661, *pg.* 663
PAN-NET - Network System - PANDUIT CORP.; *pg.* 661, *pg.* 663

PAN PAL - Vegetable Oil - BLUE CROSS LABORATORIES; *pg.* 326, *pg.* 277
PAN-PLUG - Copper Product - PANDUIT CORP.; *pg.* 661, *pg.* 663
PAN-POLE - Surface Raceway - PANDUIT CORP.; *pg.* 661, *pg.* 663
PAN-PUNCH - Copper Product - PANDUIT CORP.; *pg.* 661, *pg.* 663
PAN-QUIK - Labeling Product - PANDUIT CORP.; *pg.* 661, *pg.* 663
PAN-STEEL - Stainless Steel Product - PANDUIT CORP.; *pg.* 661, *pg.* 663
PAN-TERM - Terminal Loose Piece - PANDUIT CORP.; *pg.* 661, *pg.* 663
PAN-TY - Cable Tie - PANDUIT CORP.; *pg.* 661, *pg.* 663
PAN-WAY - Surface Raceway - PANDUIT CORP.; *pg.* 661, *pg.* 663
PAN-WRAP - Abrasion Product - PANDUIT CORP.; *pg.* 661, *pg.* 663
PAN-ZONE - Wall Mount Cabinet - PANDUIT CORP.; *pg.* 661, *pg.* 663
PANACEA - Labeling Product - PANDUIT CORP.; *pg.* 661, *pg.* 663
PANACEA - Kitchenware - THE VOLLRATH COMPANY LLC; *pg.* 1139, *pg.* 1894
PANACHE - Vanity Lights - CRAFTMADE INTERNATIONAL, INC.; *pg.* 1295, *pg.* 1670
PANACHE - Fabric - NEMSCHOFF, INC.; *pg.* 936, *pg.* 1890
PANACHE - Door Glass - ODL INCORPORATED; *pg.* 101, *pg.* 914
PANACHE - Pearl - STULLER, INC.; *pg.* 13, *pg.* 745
PANACHE SOFPRINT - Paper & Nonwoven Material - FIBERMARK INC.; *pg.* 1457, *pg.* 1764
PANACUR - Broad-Spectrum Antibiotic - MERCK & CO., INC.; *pg.* 1566, *pg.* 1077
PANAFLEX - Flexible on Premise Sign Faces - 3M COMPANY; *pg.* 1142, *pg.* 956
PANAGRAPHICS - Polyester - 3M COMPANY; *pg.* 1142, *pg.* 956
PANAID - Agricultural Product - ARCHER-DANIELS-MIDLAND COMPANY; *pg.* 825, *pg.* 565
PANAKARE - Animal Safety Product - NEOGEN CORPORATION; *pg.* 883, *pg.* 896
PANALITE - Agricultural Product - ARCHER-DANIELS-MIDLAND COMPANY; *pg.* 825, *pg.* 565
PANALURE - Photographic Paper - EASTMAN KODAK COMPANY; *pg.* 1408, *pg.* 1333
PANAMA CANAL RAILWAY COMPANY - Transportation Service - THE KANSAS CITY SOUTHERN RAILWAY COMPANY; *pg.* 1913, *pg.* 985
PANAMA JACK - Flooring - AMERICAN BILTRITE INC.; *pg.* 1878, *pg.* 856
PANAMA PEACH - Beverage - BAI BRANDS; *pg.* 238, *pg.* 1073
PANAMA PU2 - Impregnated Nylon Used in Ice Hockey Skates to Increase Lateral Stiffness - REEBOK-CCM HOCKEY, INC.; *pg.* 1844, *pg.* 1960
PANAMAX - Dome Cover - THE VOLLRATH COMPANY LLC; *pg.* 1139, *pg.* 1894
PANAMED - Medical Insurance - PAN-AMERICAN LIFE INSURANCE COMPANY; *pg.* 1213, *pg.* 747
PANAPRESS - One-Quarter Ton Arbor Presses - PANAVISE PRODUCTS, INC.; *pg.* 1058, *pg.* 1032
PANASONIC - Radios, Television, Appliances, Auto Products, VCR Products - PANASONIC CORPORATION OF NORTH AMERICA; *pg.* 661, *pg.* 1120
PANASONIC - Electric Products - PANASONIC ELECTRIC WORKS CORPORATION OF AMERICA; *pg.* 661, *pg.* 1095
PANATOMIC-X - Photo Film - EASTMAN KODAK COMPANY; *pg.* 1408, *pg.* 1333
PANAVIEW - Scoreboard & Sports Product - DAKTRONICS, INC.; *pg.* 633, *pg.* 1624
PANBIO - Pharmaceutical Product - ALERE INC.; *pg.* 1488, *pg.* 849
PANCAKE - Cylinder - FABCO-AIR, INC.; *pg.* 1336, *pg.* 429
PANCAKE II - Interchangeable Industrial Composite Body Air Cylinder - FABCO-AIR, INC.; *pg.* 1336, *pg.* 429
PANCAKE PODS - Food Products - J.R. SIMPLOT COMPANY; *pg.* 867, *pg.* 547
PANCREASE - Healthcare Product - JOHNSON & JOHNSON; *pg.* 1549, *pg.* 1091
PANDA - Pharmaceutical Product - ALERE INC.; *pg.* 1488, *pg.* 849
PANDA EXPRESS - Chinese Restaurants - PANDA RESTAURANT GROUP, INC.; *pg.* 1743, *pg.* 194
PANDA INN - Chinese Restaurants - PANDA RESTAURANT GROUP, INC.; *pg.* 1743, *pg.* 194
PANDA-MONEY-UM - Lottery Game - NEW YORK STATE LOTTERY; *pg.* 1001, *pg.* 1340
PANDA PARTY - Video Game - INTERNATIONAL GAME TECHNOLOGY; *pg.* 957, *pg.* 1024
PANDA PAWS - Ice Cream Product - PERRY'S ICE CREAM CO., INC.; *pg.* 1861, *pg.* 1137
PANDA PUFFS - Snack Mix & Breakfast Cereals - NATURE'S PATH FOODS INC.; *pg.* 833, *pg.* 1908
PANDA RICHES - Game - WMS INDUSTRIES INC.; *pg.* 593, *pg.* 666
PANDAC - Software - OWENS & MINOR, INC.; *pg.* 1579, *pg.* 1795
PANDAMONIUM - Game - GAMEWRIGHT; *pg.* 953, *pg.* 836
PANDA'S JADE - Game - WMS INDUSTRIES INC.; *pg.* 593, *pg.* 666
PANDEMIC - Video Game - ELECTRONIC ARTS INC.; *pg.* 951, *pg.* 189
PANDITA - Footwear - STEVEN MADDEN, LTD.; *pg.* 1819, *pg.* 1176
PANDORA - Software - EASTMAN KODAK COMPANY; *pg.* 1408, *pg.* 1333
PANDUCT - Heat Shrink Product - PANDUIT CORP.; *pg.* 661, *pg.* 663
PANEL ACCENTS - Sliding Panel - SPRINGS WINDOW FASHIONS LLC; *pg.* 943, *pg.* 1872
PANEL-LOK - Envelopes - TENSION ENVELOPE CORPORATION; *pg.* 483, *pg.* 986
PANEL MANAGER - Software - METRIXLAB; *pg.* 1266, *pg.* 223
PANEL-TRACK - Baseboard Heaters - EMBASSY INDUSTRIES, INC.; *pg.* 1071, *pg.* 1164
PANELBUILDER - Software - AMX CORPORATION; *pg.* 349, *pg.* 1735
PANELBUS - Signal Processing Circuits - TEXAS INSTRUMENTS INCORPORATED; *pg.* 679, *pg.* 1688
PANELETCH - Concrete System - L.M. SCOFIELD COMPANY; *pg.* 94, *pg.* 134
PANELINE - Photos & Posters - THE DOW CHEMICAL COMPANY; *pg.* 1157, *pg.* 898
PANELINE - Door Panic Exit Safety Bars - KAWNEER COMPANY, INC.; *pg.* 90, *pg.* 537
PANELLINE - Laser Engraving Solution - VIRTEK VISION INTERNATIONAL, INC.; *pg.* 1435, *pg.* 1948
PANELMATE - Polystrene Insulation - THE DOW CHEMICAL COMPANY; *pg.* 1157, *pg.* 898
PANELMATE - Electrical Product - EATON CORPORATION; *pg.* 1331, *pg.* 1429
PANELMATE - Connector - MOLEX INCORPORATED; *pg.* 655, *pg.* 628
PANELPREVIEW - Software - AMX CORPORATION; *pg.* 349, *pg.* 1735
PANELSAFE - Lockout System - 3M COMPANY; *pg.* 1142, *pg.* 956
PANELVIEW - Graphic Terminal - ROCKWELL AUTOMATION, INC.; *pg.* 668, *pg.* 1880
PANELVIEW LOGIX - Software - ROCKWELL AUTOMATION, INC.; *pg.* 668, *pg.* 1880
PANELVIEW PLUS - Operator Terminal - ROCKWELL AUTOMATION, INC.; *pg.* 668, *pg.* 1880
THE PANERA CARD - Complement Card - PANERA BREAD COMPANY; *pg.* 1029, *pg.* 1001
PANEX - Fiber - ZOLTEK COMPANIES, INC.; *pg.* 123, *pg.* 974
PANFIBRE - Medium Density Fiberboard - UNIBOARD CANADA INC.; *pg.* 117, *pg.* 1952
PANFLOR - Utility Floor Laminate - SCHNELLER, INC.; *pg.* 234, *pg.* 1456
PANFOIL - Decorative Paper Overlay - UNIBOARD CANADA INC.; *pg.* 117, *pg.* 1952
PANGBURNS - Chocolate Candy - RUSSELL STOVER CANDIES, INC.; *pg.* 1861, *pg.* 986
PANGBURNS MILLIONAIRES - Chocolate Candy - RUSSELL STOVER CANDIES, INC.; *pg.* 1861, *pg.* 986
PANGEN - Data Communication Product - GENERAL CABLE CORPORATION; *pg.* 83, *pg.* 729
PANIC GUARD - Panic Doors & Entrances - KAWNEER COMPANY, INC.; *pg.* 90, *pg.* 537
PANIPLEX - Dough Strengthener & Softener - ARCHER-DANIELS-MIDLAND COMPANY; *pg.* 825, *pg.* 565
PANISTAY - Agricultural Product - ARCHER-DANIELS-MIDLAND COMPANY; *pg.* 825, *pg.* 565
PANL-FRAME - Metal Building System - BUTLER MANUFACTURING COMPANY; *pg.* 72, *pg.* 981
PANL-LINE - Metal Building System - BUTLER MANUFACTURING COMPANY; *pg.* 72, *pg.* 981
PANLASTIC - Metal Building System - BUTLER MANUFACTURING COMPANY; *pg.* 72, *pg.* 981
PANLGARD - Prefinished Hardboard Paneling - CANFOR CORPORATION; *pg.* 1454, *pg.* 1910
PANNIDO - Sandwiches - JACK IN THE BOX INC.; *pg.* 1732, *pg.* 204
PANNIER - Commuter Bags - JANDD MOUNTAINEERING, INC.; *pg.* 1837, *pg.* 204
PANO-SITE - Lens - DANKER LABORATORIES INC.; *pg.* 1408, *pg.* 465
PANOGAUZE - Medical & Aesthetic Product - DYNATRONICS CORPORATION; *pg.* 1526, *pg.* 1757
PANOMER - Molecular Probe Product - THERMO FISHER SCIENTIFIC INC.; *pg.* 1602, *pg.* 61
PANOPOULOS - Hair Salons - REGIS CORPORATION; *pg.* 521, *pg.* 941
PANOPTIC - Otoscopes - WELCH ALLYN INC.; *pg.* 1436, *pg.* 1342
PANORAMA - Furniture - ASHLEY FURNITURE INDUSTRIES, INC.; *pg.* 914, *pg.* 1852
PANORAMA - Furniture - BASSETT FURNITURE INDUSTRIES, INCORPORATED; *pg.* 916, *pg.* 1776
PANORAMA - Carpet - INTERFACE, INC.; *pg.* 695, *pg.* 512
PANORAMA - Patient Monitoring Device - MAQUET; *pg.* 1558, *pg.* 1082
PANORAMA - Software Product & Module - RIVERBED PERFORMANCE MANAGEMENT; *pg.* 462, *pg.* 765
PANORAMA - Optical Networks System - TELLABS, INC.; *pg.* 678, *pg.* 637
PANORAMIO - Photo Sharing Community - GOOGLE INC.; *pg.* 1249, *pg.* 153
PANORAMIX - Software - ECHELON CORPORATION; *pg.* 389, *pg.* 245
PANOURA ULTRA - X-Ray System - IMAGEWORKS; *pg.* 1544, *pg.* 1158
PANOX - Fiber - DRAPER KNITTING CO., INC.; *pg.* 692, *pg.* 810
PANRETIN - Pharmaceutical - EISAI INC.; *pg.* 1526, *pg.* 1133
PANROAST - Gravy Mix - CUSTOM CULINARY, INC.; *pg.* 851, *pg.* 644
PANROAST - Food Product - GRIFFITH LABORATORIES, INC.; *pg.* 860, *pg.* 552
PANTA-PAK - Tray - PACTIV CORPORATION; *pg.* 1466, *pg.* 624
PANTALOON - Protective Liner - W.L. GORE & ASSOCIATES, INC.; *pg.* 122, *pg.* 388
PANTENDER - Stacking Robot - WELDON SOLUTIONS; *pg.* 1388, *pg.* 1598
PANTENE - Hair Care Products - THE PROCTER & GAMBLE COMPANY; *pg.* 1129, *pg.* 1418
PANTENE PRO-V - Hair Care Products - THE PROCTER & GAMBLE COMPANY; *pg.* 1129, *pg.* 1418
PANTERA - Snowmobile - ARCTIC CAT INC.; *pg.* 1705, *pg.* 953
PANTERA - Electro Optical Weapon Targeting Devices - LOCKHEED MARTIN CORPORATION; *pg.* 229, *pg.* 762
PANTERA - Picosecond UV Laser - NEWPORT CORPORATION; *pg.* 1424, *pg.* 114
PANTHEON - Distribution Automation System - ELSTER AMERICAN METER COMPANY; *pg.* 1411, *pg.* 1387
PANTHEON - Fabric - NEMSCHOFF, INC.; *pg.* 936, *pg.* 1890
PANTHEON BOOKS - Book Imprint - PENGUIN RANDOM HOUSE; *pg.* 1675, *pg.* 1276
PANTHER - Software - ALPHA CTP SYSTEM; *pg.* 347, *pg.* 848
PANTHER - Snowmobile - ARCTIC CAT INC.; *pg.* 1705, *pg.* 953
PANTHER - Pump - FLOWSERVE CORPORATION; *pg.* 82, *pg.* 1719
PANTHER - Hand-Held Racing Wheel - MAD CATZ INTERACTIVE INC.; *pg.* 429, *pg.* 204
PANTHER - Home & Small Business Communication Systems - MITEL NETWORKS CORPORATION; *pg.* 654, *pg.* 1921
PANTHER - Labeling Product - PANDUIT CORP.; *pg.* 661, *pg.* 663
PANTHER - Spotting Scopes - SWIFT OPTICAL INSTRUMENTS, INC.; *pg.* 1430, *pg.* 1744
PANTHER CREEK - Bentonite - MINERALS TECHNOLOGIES INC.; *pg.* 1173, *pg.* 617
PANTHER FASTRAK - Software - ALPHA CTP SYSTEM; *pg.*

347, *pg.* 848

PANTHER LX-4 - Four-Wheel PMV - INVACARE CORPORATION; *pg.* 1546, *pg.* 1451

PANTHER MARTIN - Lures - SEA EAGLE BOATS; *pg.* 1845, *pg.* 1322

PANTONE - Digital Color System - X-RITE, INCORPORATED; *pg.* 1437, *pg.* 891

THE PANTRY - Convenience Stores - THE PANTRY, INC.; *pg.* 1029, *pg.* 1360

PANVAL - Melamine - UNIBOARD CANADA INC.; *pg.* 117, *pg.* 1952

PANVERTER - Stacking Robot - WELDON SOLUTIONS; *pg.* 1388, *pg.* 1598

PANVIEW - Scanner - PANDUIT CORP.; *pg.* 661, *pg.* 663

PANZONE - Copper Product - PANDUIT CORP.; *pg.* 661, *pg.* 663

PAOLA - Footwear - PHOENIX FOOTWEAR GROUP, INC.; *pg.* 1815, *pg.* 60

PAOLI - Office Furniture - HNI CORPORATION; *pg.* 927, *pg.* 709

PAP - Air Package - ELLIOTT COMPANY; *pg.* 1333, *pg.* 1542

PAP PLUS - Air Package Centrifugal Compressors - ELLIOTT COMPANY; *pg.* 1333, *pg.* 1542

PAPA GINO'S - Pizza Restaurant Chain - PAPA GINOS-DEANGELO HOLDING CORPORATION, INC.; *pg.* 1743, *pg.* 817

PAPA VINO'S - Restaurant - QUALITY DINING, INC.; *pg.* 1746, *pg.* 695

PAPAGUS - Greek Restaurant - LETTUCE ENTERTAIN YOU ENTERPRISES, INC.; *pg.* 1735, *pg.* 580

PAPER - Art Paper - MONADNOCK PAPER MILLS, INC.; *pg.* 1464, *pg.* 1033

PAPER MATE - Pens & Pencils - NEWELL RUBBERMAID INC.; *pg.* 1128, *pg.* 515

PAPER, SCISSORS, ROCK - Educational Materials - SCHOLASTIC INC.; *pg.* 1683, *pg.* 1288

PAPER TAPER - Dispenser - 3M COMPANY; *pg.* 1142, *pg.* 956

PAPER THAT KNOWS WHERE IT IS GOING - Paper - XEROX CORPORATION; *pg.* 494, *pg.* 365

PAPER TYGER - Durable Paper - CHASE CORPORATION; *pg.* 1152, *pg.* 803

PAPER WARE - Software - XEROX CORPORATION; *pg.* 494, *pg.* 365

PAPERCREME - Fingertip Moistener - THE GILLETTE COMPANY; *pg.* 509, *pg.* 795

PAPERFLO - Document File Trays - STEELCASE INC.; *pg.* 475, *pg.* 889

PAPERMASTER - Communication Product - J2 GLOBAL COMMUNICATIONS, INC.; *pg.* 1260, *pg.* 133

PAPERMASTER PRO - Document Management Software - J2 GLOBAL COMMUNICATIONS, INC.; *pg.* 1260, *pg.* 133

PAPERMATCH - Plastic Compound & Resin - A. SCHULMAN, INC.; *pg.* 1144, *pg.* 1452

PAPERPORT - Document Management Software - NUANCE COMMUNICATIONS, INC.; *pg.* 447, *pg.* 806

PAPERSTONE - Knife - BUCK KNIVES, INC.; *pg.* 1828, *pg.* 550

PAPERTIGER - Sundry - KELLY-MOORE PAINT COMPANY, INC.; *pg.* 1443, *pg.* 198

PAPERWORKS - Magazine for Paper Crafters - ANNIE'S; *pg.* 1617, *pg.* 673

PAPERWORKS - Software - NUANCE DOCUMENT IMAGING SOLUTIONS; *pg.* 1271, *pg.* 1037

PAPETTE - Cervical Cell Sampler - WALLACH SURGICAL DEVICES, INC.; *pg.* 1436, *pg.* 381

PAPETTI'S - Food Service Product - MICHAEL FOODS, INC.; *pg.* 877, *pg.* 949

PAPI - Polymer - THE DOW CHEMICAL COMPANY; *pg.* 1157, *pg.* 898

PAPILLON - Nasal Mask - RESMED INC.; *pg.* 1589, *pg.* 207

PAPYRUS - Rug - COURISTAN INC.; *pg.* 921, *pg.* 1067

PAPYRUS - Fabric - NEMSCHOFF, INC.; *pg.* 936, *pg.* 1890

PAQUA - Paint And Stain Product - BENJAMIN MOORE & CO.; *pg.* 1440, *pg.* 1085

PAR - Air Gun - BOLT TECHNOLOGY CORPORATION; *pg.* 1318, *pg.* 360

PAR 5 - Hip Product - ZIMMER BIOMET HOLDINGS, INC.; *pg.* 1611, *pg.* 699

PAR-A-DICE HOTEL & CASINO - Hotel & Casino - BOYD GAMING CORPORATION; *pg.* 1082, *pg.* 1022

PAR-BEAM-LITE - Recessed Lighting - SWIVELIER CO., INC.; *pg.* 1307, *pg.* 1142

PAR FILTERS - Natural & Synthetic Fibers - BLOCKSOM & COMPANY; *pg.* 691, *pg.* 694

PARA-CARE - Orthopedic Device - DJO SURGICAL; *pg.* 1525, *pg.* 1661

PARA RENTAR - Advertising Publication - DOMINION ENTERPRISES; *pg.* 1636, *pg.* 1796

PARA SYSTEM - Nutritional Supplement - NATURAL ORGANICS, INC.; *pg.* 1571, *pg.* 1181

PARA TROOPER - Apparel - OAKLEY, INC.; *pg.* 1840, *pg.* 86

PARABIS - Resin Intermediates - THE DOW CHEMICAL COMPANY; *pg.* 1157, *pg.* 898

PARABODY - Fitness Equipment - BRUNSWICK CORPORATION; *pg.* 1828, *pg.* 623

PARABOLIC - Mining Teeth & Adapters - HENSLEY INDUSTRIES, INC.; *pg.* 1166, *pg.* 1682

PARACHEK - Invitro Diagnostic Kit for Animals - PFIZER INC.; *pg.* 1581, *pg.* 1278

PARACHUTE - Fluid Sealing Product - A.W. CHESTERTON COMPANY; *pg.* 1315, *pg.* 861

PARACIDE II SHAMPOO - Pet Supplies - HAPPY JACK INC.; *pg.* 1476, *pg.* 1390

PARACLEANSE - Nutritional Care Product - LIFEPLUS INTERNATIONAL; *pg.* 1556, *pg.* 29

PARACOL - Additive - HERCULES INCORPORATED; *pg.* 1166, *pg.* 392

PARACOX - Medicine - MERCK & CO., INC.; *pg.* 1566, *pg.* 1077

PARACUBE - Plastic Louvers - AMERICAN LOUVER COMPANY; *pg.* 1294, *pg.* 660

PARADE - Software System - MENTOR GRAPHICS CORPORATION; *pg.* 432, *pg.* 1510

PARADE - News Magazine - PARADE PUBLICATIONS INC.; *pg.* 1674, *pg.* 1276

PARADE - Office Furniture - STEELCASE INC.; *pg.* 475, *pg.* 889

PARADE.COM - Website - PARADE PUBLICATIONS INC.; *pg.* 1674, *pg.* 1276

PARADIFF - Flavor Ingredient - INTERNATIONAL FLAVORS & FRAGRANCES INC.; *pg.* 512, *pg.* 1244

PARADIGM - Block - 3M COMPANY; *pg.* 1142, *pg.* 956

PARADIGM - Pharmaceutical Product - ALERE INC.; *pg.* 1488, *pg.* 849

PARADIGM - Semiconductor Processing Equipment - AXCELIS TECHNOLOGIES, INC.; *pg.* 1400, *pg.* 787

PARADIGM - Detection Platform - BECKMAN COULTER, INC.; *pg.* 1402, *pg.* 48

PARADIGM - Chairs - STEELCASE INC.; *pg.* 475, *pg.* 889

PARADIGM - Ceramic, Glass, Stone Tiles & Slabs - WALKER & ZANGER, INC.; *pg.* 119, *pg.* 281

PARADIGMHEALTH - Pharmaceutical Product - ALERE INC.; *pg.* 1488, *pg.* 849

PARADISE - Rug - COURISTAN INC.; *pg.* 921, *pg.* 1067

PARADISE - Seating Product - IRWIN SEATING COMPANY INC.; *pg.* 929, *pg.* 887

PARADISE - Eyewear - MAUI JIM, INC.; *pg.* 9, *pg.* 651

PARADISE - Fabric - NEMSCHOFF, INC.; *pg.* 936, *pg.* 1890

PARADISE - Glace (Candied Fruit) - PARADISE, INC.; *pg.* 888, *pg.* 458

PARADISE GARDEN - Video Game - INTERNATIONAL GAME TECHNOLOGY; *pg.* 957, *pg.* 1024

PARADISE VALLEY - Furniture - STANLEY FURNITURE CO., INC.; *pg.* 943, *pg.* 1379

PARADISO - Coffee Blend - THE SECOND CUP LTD.; *pg.* 1749, *pg.* 1928

PARADOX - Carpet - BEAULIEU GROUP, LLC; *pg.* 917, *pg.* 529

PARADOX - Bath Product - KOHLER CO.; *pg.* 91, *pg.* 1862

PARADOX - Flatware - ONEIDA LTD; *pg.* 1129, *pg.* 1318

PARADOX PRESS - Book & Magazine Publishing Imprint - DC COMICS, INC.; *pg.* 1633, *pg.* 1221

PARADY - Footwear - STEVEN MADDEN, LTD.; *pg.* 1819, *pg.* 1176

PARADYNE - Fluid Handling System - GRACO, INC.; *pg.* 1342, *pg.* 935

PARADYNE - Critical Care Therapy System - KINETIC CONCEPTS, INC.; *pg.* 1553, *pg.* 1741

PARAFFIN BATH - Medical & Aesthetic Product - DYNATRONICS CORPORATION; *pg.* 1526, *pg.* 1757

PARAFILM - Laboratory Film - STOELTING CO.; *pg.* 1430, *pg.* 671

PARAFILM M - Surgical Supplies - STOELTING CO.; *pg.* 1430, *pg.* 671

PARAFLOOD - HID General Purpose Flood - CRESCENT/STONCO SUPPLY DIVISION; *pg.* 1295, *pg.* 1121

PARAFON FORTE - Healthcare Product - JOHNSON & JOHNSON; *pg.* 1549, *pg.* 1091

PARAGON - Electrophoresis System - BECKMAN COULTER, INC.; *pg.* 1402, *pg.* 48

PARAGON - Fan - CRAFTMADE INTERNATIONAL, INC.; *pg.* 1295, *pg.* 1670

PARAGON - Healthcare Information Technology System - MCKESSON CORPORATION; *pg.* 1560, *pg.* 222

PARAGON - Fabric - MOMENTUM TEXTILES INC.; *pg.* 697, *pg.* 114

PARAGON - Media Rack & Cabinet - NER HOLDINGS INC.; *pg.* 444, *pg.* 1071

PARAGON - Hearing Instrument - SEMTECH CORPORATION GENNUM PRODUCTS; *pg.* 671, *pg.* 1919

PARAGON - Molecular Probe Product - THERMO FISHER SCIENTIFIC INC.; *pg.* 1602, *pg.* 61

PARAGON 3000 - Grease - TEXAS REFINERY CORP.; *pg.* 986, *pg.* 1696

PARAGON CZE - Testing Instrument System - BECKMAN COULTER, INC.; *pg.* 1402, *pg.* 48

PARAGON PLUS - Shirts - ELBECO INCORPORATED; *pg.* 40, *pg.* 1584

PARALINE - Ceiling Panel - USG CORPORATION; *pg.* 118, *pg.* 594

PARALINK - Electronic Components - MOLEX INCORPORATED; *pg.* 655, *pg.* 628

PARALINK-P - Electronic Components - MOLEX INCORPORATED; *pg.* 655, *pg.* 628

PARALLAM - Wood & Building Material - WEYERHAEUSER COMPANY; *pg.* 121, *pg.* 1820

PARALLEL ACCELERATION SYSTEM - Software - MERCURY COMPUTER SYSTEMS, INC.; *pg.* 434, *pg.* 813

PARALLELE TRUETAG - Array - AFFYMETRIX, INC.; *pg.* 1487, *pg.* 263

PARALLEX - Broadloom - COURISTAN INC.; *pg.* 921, *pg.* 1067

PARALLEX - Slide System - VILTER MANUFACTURING LLC; *pg.* 1078, *pg.* 1856

PARALOID - Additive - DOW CHEMICAL; *pg.* 1156, *pg.* 1563

PARALUME - Commercial Retail Lighting - JUNO LIGHTING, INC.; *pg.* 1300, *pg.* 606

PARAMOUNT - RF Power Feeder - ADVANCED ENERGY INDUSTRIES, INC.; *pg.* 613, *pg.* 328

PARANET! - Internet Co-op Query System - ADVERTISING CHECKING BUREAU INCORPORATED; *pg.* 345, *pg.* 1187

PARAPAK - Collection, Preservation & Transport for Human Specimen - MERIDIAN BIOSCIENCE INC.; *pg.* 1422, *pg.* 1417

PARAPLATIN - Platinum Compound - BRISTOL-MYERS SQUIBB U.S. PHARMACEUTICAL GROUP; *pg.* 1511, *pg.* 1110

PARAPREMIUM - Steel - THE TIMKEN COMPANY; *pg.* 218, *pg.* 1408

PARASCOPE! - Competitive Ad Tracking Query System - ADVERTISING CHECKING BUREAU INCORPORATED; *pg.* 345, *pg.* 1187

PARASCRIPT - Software - OPEX CORPORATION; *pg.* 450, *pg.* 1087

PARASEAL - Roofing Material - TREMCO INCORPORATED; *pg.* 116, *pg.* 1405

PARASITE - Character - DC COMICS, INC.; *pg.* 1633, *pg.* 1221

PARASTAR - Resins - EASTMAN CHEMICAL COMPANY; *pg.* 1159, *pg.* 1636

PARATEX - Rubberized Fiber - BLOCKSOM & COMPANY; *pg.* 691, *pg.* 694

PARATHERAPY - Medical & Aesthetic Product - DYNATRONICS CORPORATION; *pg.* 1526, *pg.* 1757

PARATRON - Lighting - LSI INDUSTRIES INC.; *pg.* 58, *pg.* 1416

PARAWEDGE - Lighting Diffusers - AMERICAN LOUVER COMPANY; *pg.* 1294, *pg.* 660

PARBERT - Communication & Test System - AGILENT TECHNOLOGIES, INC.; *pg.* 614, *pg.* 264

PARC - Software - XEROX CORPORATION; *pg.* 494, *pg.* 365

PARC & DESIGN - Software - XEROX CORPORATION; *pg.* 494, *pg.* 365

PARC-CERTIFIED FIELDWORKER - Software - XEROX CORPORATION; *pg.* 494, *pg.* 365

PARCEL INSURANCE PLAN - Insurance Package Program - BROWN & BROWN, INC.; *pg.* 1196, *pg.* 419

PARCEL POST - Ground Shipping - UNITED STATES POSTAL SERVICE; *pg.* 1009, *pg.* 406
PARCEL SELECT - Ground Shipping - UNITED STATES POSTAL SERVICE; *pg.* 1009, *pg.* 406
PARCELSEARCH - Baggage Inspection System - AMERICAN SCIENCE AND ENGINEERING, INC.; *pg.* 1399, *pg.* 787
PARCHEESI - Toy & Game - HASBRO, INC.; *pg.* 954, *pg.* 1603
PARCO - Hydraulic Pumps, Rig Equipment - PARKER DRILLING COMPANY; *pg.* 982, *pg.* 1712
PARCURE - Rubber Cure Salt - HEATBATH CORPORATION; *pg.* 1165, *pg.* 826
PARDON THE INTERRUPTION - Sports Discussion Program - ESPN, INC.; *pg.* 285, *pg.* 340
PAREMYD - Ophthalmic Pharmaceutical Product - AKORN, INC.; *pg.* 1488, *pg.* 622
PARENT BAG BOOK - Educational Materials - SCHOLASTIC INC.; *pg.* 1683, *pg.* 1288
PARENTCENTER - Website - BABYCENTER, LLC; *pg.* 1231, *pg.* 212
PARENTCONNECTXP - Software - EDUPOINT EDUCATIONAL SYSTEMS, LLC; *pg.* 390, *pg.* 109
PARENTHOOD - Publication - DOMINION ENTERPRISES; *pg.* 1636, *pg.* 1796
PARENTING - Magazine - BONNIER CORPORATION; *pg.* 1622, *pg.* 480
PARENTS - Magazine - MEREDITH CORPORATION; *pg.* 1663, *pg.* 705
PARENT'S CHOICE - Organic Baby Formula - WAL-MART STORES, INC.; *pg.* 1790, *pg.* 29
PARENT'S FRIEND - Educational Materials - SCHOLASTIC INC.; *pg.* 1683, *pg.* 1288
PARENTS ON BOARD - Educational Program - ACTIVE PARENTING PUBLISHERS; *pg.* 1613, *pg.* 535
PARFUM DE VANILLE - Fragrances - CCA INDUSTRIES, INC.; *pg.* 503, *pg.* 1114
PARIET - Healthcare Product - JOHNSON & JOHNSON; *pg.* 1549, *pg.* 1091
PARIGI - Bath Product - KOHLER CO.; *pg.* 91, *pg.* 1862
PARIO CLEANERS - Metalworking Chemical - HENKEL CORPORATION; *pg.* 1166, *pg.* 897
PARIOLENE - Metalworking Chemical - HENKEL CORPORATION; *pg.* 1166, *pg.* 897
PARIS - Watch - A. T. CROSS COMPANY; *pg.* 339, *pg.* 1602
PARIS - Furniture - AMISCO INDUSTRIES LTD.; *pg.* 913, *pg.* 1958
PARIS - Textiles - BERNHARDT DESIGN; *pg.* 918, *pg.* 1381
PARIS - Casino - CAESARS ENTERTAINMENT CORPORATION; *pg.* 1083, *pg.* 1023
PARIS - Footwear - CAPEZIO BALLET MAKERS INC.; *pg.* 1805, *pg.* 1125
PARIS - Furniture - J. ROBERT SCOTT INC.; *pg.* 930, *pg.* 105
PARIS - Door Glass - ODL INCORPORATED; *pg.* 101, *pg.* 914
PARIS TONNEAU - Watch - A. T. CROSS COMPANY; *pg.* 339, *pg.* 1602
PARISIAN SKY - Video Game - INTERNATIONAL GAME TECHNOLOGY; *pg.* 957, *pg.* 1024
PARITY - Fabric - NEMSCHOFF, INC.; *pg.* 936, *pg.* 1890
PARK - Coater/Laminator Machine - BOLTON-EMERSON AMERICAS, INC.; *pg.* 1318, *pg.* 827
PARK - Polish And Compound - HEATBATH CORPORATION; *pg.* 1165, *pg.* 826
PARK AND PIPE - Glove - BURTON SNOWBOARD COMPANY; *pg.* 1829, *pg.* 1765
PARK AVE - Blazer - HABAND COMPANY, INC.; *pg.* 1772, *pg.* 1099
PARK AVENUE - Shoes - ALLEN-EDMONDS SHOE CORP.; *pg.* 1804, *pg.* 1887
PARK AVENUE - Wood Flooring Product - ARMSTRONG WORLD INDUSTRIES, INC.; *pg.* 914, *pg.* 1545
PARK AVENUE - Carpet - BEAULIEU GROUP, LLC; *pg.* 917, *pg.* 529
PARK AVENUE - Table - BLATT BOWLING & BILLIARD CORP.; *pg.* 1827, *pg.* 1203
PARK AVENUE - Bedding Product - HOLLANDER SLEEP PRODUCTS; *pg.* 927, *pg.* 411
PARK AVENUE - Lighting - LSI INDUSTRIES INC.; *pg.* 58, *pg.* 1416
PARK AVENUE - Formals, Stationary, Boxes - XPEDX; *pg.* 1473, *pg.* 1377
PARK FALLS - Kitchen Product - KOHLER CO.; *pg.* 91, *pg.* 1862
PARK INN - Hotels - CARLSON COMPANIES INC.; *pg.* 1084, *pg.* 947
PARK KASE - Carburizer - HEATBATH CORPORATION; *pg.* 1165, *pg.* 826
PARK PLAZA - Hotels & Resorts - CARLSON COMPANIES INC.; *pg.* 1084, *pg.* 947
PARK SHORE RESORT - Resort - SUNSTREAM, INC.; *pg.* 1116, *pg.* 428
PARK STREET - Executive Dress Shirts - UNIFIRST CORPORATION; *pg.* 50, *pg.* 860
PARK-ZONE - Parking Tool - MEASUREMENT SPECIALTIES INC.; *pg.* 1360, *pg.* 1783
PARKAY - Food Product - CONAGRA FOODS, INC.; *pg.* 826, *pg.* 1014
PARKER - Leather Products - COACH, INC.; *pg.* 3, *pg.* 1214
PARKER - Fabric - NEMSCHOFF, INC.; *pg.* 936, *pg.* 1890
PARKER - Pens - NEWELL RUBBERMAID INC.; *pg.* 1128, *pg.* 515
PARKER - Guitars - U.S. MUSIC CORPORATION; *pg.* 315, *pg.* 560
PARKER BROTHERS - Games - HASBRO, INC.; *pg.* 954, *pg.* 1603
PARKER HOUSE - Hotel - OMNI HOTELS & RESORTS; *pg.* 1107, *pg.* 1685
PARKERTON - Dinnerware - THE HOMER LAUGHLIN CHINA COMPANY; *pg.* 1125, *pg.* 1850
PARKHURST - Truck Trailers - PARKHURST MANUFACTURING CO., INC.; *pg.* 214, *pg.* 1005
PARKING DECK/LOT CABLE - PVC Jacketed Metal Clad Cable - AFC CABLE SYSTEMS, INC.; *pg.* 1294, *pg.* 835
PARKLAND GOLF & COUNTRY CLUB - Community Name - WCI COMMUNITIES, INC.; *pg.* 1118, *pg.* 414
PARKLUME - Area Lighting - JUNO LIGHTING, INC.; *pg.* 1300, *pg.* 606
PARKO - Chemical Product - HEATBATH CORPORATION; *pg.* 1165, *pg.* 826
PARKPILOT - Automotive Product - ROSTRA PRECISION CONTROLS, INC.; *pg.* 216, *pg.* 1381
PARKSIDE - Building Product - BLUELINX HOLDINGS, INC.; *pg.* 70, *pg.* 491
PARLAY - Fabric - NEMSCHOFF, INC.; *pg.* 936, *pg.* 1890
PARLE - Beverages - THE COCA-COLA COMPANY; *pg.* 240, *pg.* 493
PARLUX - Fragrance - PARLUX FRAGRANCES, INC.; *pg.* 519, *pg.* 426
PARMESAN CRUSTED SPLASH! - Seafood - CLEAR SPRINGS FOODS, INC.; *pg.* 848, *pg.* 548
PARNELLI JONES DIRT GRIPZ - Tires - THE HERCULES TIRE & RUBBER COMPANY; *pg.* 1884, *pg.* 1454
PARODI - Cigar - AVANTI CIGAR CORPORATION; *pg.* 1894, *pg.* 1527
PAROIL - Chemical Product - DOVER CHEMICAL CORPORATION; *pg.* 1156, *pg.* 1447
PARPHORM - Gaskets - PARKER CHOMERICS; *pg.* 662, *pg.* 862
PARQUENCH - Water-Base Quenchant - HEATBATH CORPORATION; *pg.* 1165, *pg.* 826
PARROT - Latch - SOUTHCO, INC.; *pg.* 1063, *pg.* 1522
PARROT-BEAK - Drum Handling Equipment - LIFTOMATIC MATERIAL HANDLING INC.; *pg.* 94, *pg.* 560
PARS - Bulb - WESTINGHOUSE LIGHTING CORPORATION; *pg.* 687, *pg.* 1571
PARSYSTEM - Software - SCANTRON CORPORATION; *pg.* 467, *pg.* 922
PART LIFECYCLE - System - IHS AUTOMOTIVE DRIVEN BY POLK; *pg.* 1652, *pg.* 907
PART-TIME FARM - Loan Services - FEDERAL AGRICULTURAL MORTGAGE CORPORATION; *pg.* 751, *pg.* 399
PARTBUILDER - Computer Services - AVNET, INC.; *pg.* 622, *pg.* 15
PARTECH - Hydraulic Pumps, Rig Equipment - PARKER DRILLING COMPANY; *pg.* 982, *pg.* 1712
PARTEX - Wire Marker System - THOMAS & BETTS CORPORATION; *pg.* 680, *pg.* 1646
PARTHERM - Heat Transfer Salt - HEATBATH CORPORATION; *pg.* 1165, *pg.* 826
PARTHUNTER - Alignment System Software - HUNTER ENGINEERING COMPANY; *pg.* 208, *pg.* 973
PARTIALLY HYDRO - Soybean Oil - ARCHER-DANIELS-MIDLAND COMPANY; *pg.* 825, *pg.* 565
PARTICLE DISPERSION SYSTEMS - Proprietary Drug Delivery Technology - IMPAX LABORATORIES, INC.; *pg.* 1544, *pg.* 101
PARTICLEAR - Flocculants - E.I. DU PONT DE NEMOURS & COMPANY; *pg.* 1159, *pg.* 390
PARTIDA ANEJO TEQUILA - Alcoholic Beverage - PARTIDA TEQUILA, LLC; *pg.* 1967, *pg.* 224
PARTIDA BLANCO TEQUILA - Alcoholic Beverage - PARTIDA TEQUILA, LLC; *pg.* 1967, *pg.* 224
PARTIDA ELEGANTE TEQUILA - Premium Tequila - PARTIDA TEQUILA, LLC; *pg.* 1967, *pg.* 224
PARTIDA REPOSADO TEQUILA - Aged Tequila - PARTIDA TEQUILA, LLC; *pg.* 1967, *pg.* 224
PARTILOK - Screening Vehicle - FERRO CORPORATION; *pg.* 1162, *pg.* 1462
PARTINI - Toy & Game - HASBRO, INC.; *pg.* 954, *pg.* 1603
PARTISAN - Pharmaceutical Product - ALERE INC.; *pg.* 1488, *pg.* 849
PARTITIONED ARCHITECTURE - ETC's Telephony Interface - ELECTRONIC TELE-COMMUNICATIONS, INC.; *pg.* 390, *pg.* 1897
PARTITIONMAGIC - Software - SYMANTEC CORPORATION; *pg.* 478, *pg.* 161
PARTITIONMAGIC - Storage System - SYMANTEC CORPORATION; *pg.* 479, *pg.* 1753
PARTIZAN - Pharmaceutical Product - ALERE INC.; *pg.* 1488, *pg.* 849
PARTLOW - Temperature Controller - DYNAPAR; *pg.* 1408, *pg.* 616
PARTLOW WEST - Circular Chart Recorder - DANAHER CORPORATION; *pg.* 1044, *pg.* 397
PARTNER - Telecommunication Product - AVAYA INC.; *pg.* 621, *pg.* 264
PARTNER - Software - INSTRON CORPORATION; *pg.* 1349, *pg.* 839
PARTNER PERFECT - Bed - KINGSDOWN, INC.; *pg.* 932, *pg.* 1383
PARTNER SOLUTIONS - Software - AVNET TECHNOLOGY SOLUTIONS; *pg.* 359, *pg.* 25
PARTNERFARM - Coffee - KEURIG GREEN MOUNTAIN, INC.; *pg.* 868, *pg.* 1768
PARTNERINGCARE - Senior Service - HEALTHPARTNERS, INC.; *pg.* 1203, *pg.* 918
PARTNERPAK - Computer Assisted Construction Planning Services - KAWNEER COMPANY, INC.; *pg.* 90, *pg.* 537
PARTNERPAK+ - Computer Assisted Construction Planning Services - KAWNEER COMPANY, INC.; *pg.* 90, *pg.* 537
PARTNERPOINT - Video Communication System - GLOWPOINT, INC.; *pg.* 401, *pg.* 1094
PARTNERS - Online Account Checking - ANDROSCOGGIN SAVINGS BANK; *pg.* 716, *pg.* 751
PARTNERS IN CASH - Game - WMS INDUSTRIES INC.; *pg.* 593, *pg.* 666
PARTNERS IN PROGRESS - Life Insurance - OLD AMERICAN INSURANCE COMPANY; *pg.* 1213, *pg.* 985
PARTNERS PLUS - Online Account Checking - ANDROSCOGGIN SAVINGS BANK; *pg.* 716, *pg.* 751
PARTNERS1 - Corporate Account Program - LIFTOMATIC MATERIAL HANDLING INC.; *pg.* 94, *pg.* 560
PARTNERSHIPS THAT WORK - Tagline - VISION FINANCIAL CORPORATION; *pg.* 1222, *pg.* 1035
PARTNERUP - Online Community - DELUXE CORPORATION; *pg.* 1634, *pg.* 964
PARTS WASH - Automotive Reconditioning Product - MOC PRODUCTS COMPANY, INC.; *pg.* 332, *pg.* 174
PARTSBANK - Shipment Service - FEDEX CORPORATION; *pg.* 1907, *pg.* 1642
PARTSDIRECT - Home Appliance Replacement Parts - SEARS HOLDINGS CORPORATION; *pg.* 1784, *pg.* 618
PARTSEARCH TECHNOLOGIES - Software - IDEALAB, INC.; *pg.* 1258, *pg.* 180
PARTSINMINUTES - Prototyping Materials - HUNTSMAN CORPORATION; *pg.* 1167, *pg.* 1758
PARTSMART - Software - ARI NETWORK SERVICES, INC.; *pg.* 353, *pg.* 1873
PARTSMART CART - Software - ARI NETWORK SERVICES, INC.; *pg.* 353, *pg.* 1873
PARTSMART CLASSIC - Software - ARI NETWORK SERVICES, INC.; *pg.* 353, *pg.* 1873
PARTSMART DATA MANAGER - Software - ARI NETWORK SERVICES, INC.; *pg.* 353, *pg.* 1873
PARTSMART DATA PUBLISHER - Software - ARI NETWORK SERVICES, INC.; *pg.* 353, *pg.* 1873
PARTSMART DIY - Software - ARI NETWORK SERVICES, INC.; *pg.* 353, *pg.* 1873
PARTSMART WEB - Software - ARI NETWORK SERVICES, INC.; *pg.* 353, *pg.* 1873
PARTSPEC - CAD Drawings on CD & the Internet - THOMAS REGISTER OF AMERICAN MANUFACTURERS; *pg.* 1692, *pg.* 1299

PARTY - Tents - ANCHOR INDUSTRIES, INC.; pg. 1825, pg. 678

PARTY - Fabric - NEMSCHOFF, INC.; pg. 936, pg. 1890

PARTY ANIMALS - Awareness Program - THE HUMANE SOCIETY OF THE UNITED STATES; pg. 143, pg. 400

PARTY ANIMALS - Video Game - INTERNATIONAL GAME TECHNOLOGY; pg. 957, pg. 1024

PARTY BULLET - Blender - CAPITAL BRANDS, LLC; pg. 53, pg. 127

PARTY COLORS - Packaging - PACTIV CORPORATION; pg. 1466, pg. 624

PARTY EXPRESS FROM HALLMARK - Greeting Card - HALLMARK CARDS, INC.; pg. 1646, pg. 983

PARTY FANTASTICO - Video Game - INTERNATIONAL GAME TECHNOLOGY; pg. 957, pg. 1024

PARTY LIKE A ROCKSTAR! - Slogan - ROCKSTAR, INC.; pg. 265, pg. 1029

THE PARTY PEOPLE - Slogan - AMSCAN HOLDINGS, INC.; pg. 1760, pg. 1158

PARTY PERFECT - Dresses & Sets - HABAND COMPANY, INC.; pg. 1772, pg. 1099

PARTY PICS - Software - CANDID COLOR SYSTEMS, INC.; pg. 1404, pg. 1485

PARTY PLATTER - Container Product - INLINE PLASTICS CORP.; pg. 1460, pg. 370

PARTY PULSE - E-Communication Platform - IMAKENEWS, INC.; pg. 413, pg. 851

PARTY TRAIN - Game - WMS INDUSTRIES INC.; pg. 593, pg. 666

PARTYLITE - Candle - BLYTH, INC.; pg. 502, pg. 349

PARTYMATE - Balloon - CONTINENTAL AMERICAN CORP.; pg. 1880, pg. 723

PARVOSOL - Animal Safety Product - NEOGEN CORPORATION; pg. 883, pg. 896

PAS - Parallel Acceleration System (SW) - MERCURY COMPUTER SYSTEMS, INC.; pg. 434, pg. 813

P.A.S. PORT - Drug Delivery Systems - SMITHS MEDICAL MD, INC.; pg. 1594, pg. 963

PASCAL - Furniture - ASHLEY FURNITURE INDUSTRIES, INC.; pg. 914, pg. 1852

PASER - Abrasive Jet Cutting System - FLOW INTERNATIONAL CORPORATION; pg. 1337, pg. 1821

PASIC380 - FPGA - CYPRESS SEMICONDUCTOR CORPORATION; pg. 1326, pg. 243

PASIO - Office Furniture - STEELCASE INC.; pg. 475, pg. 889

PASION - Footwear - STEVEN MADDEN, LTD.; pg. 1819, pg. 1176

PASLODE - Construction Equipment - PASLODE; pg. 1059, pg. 664

PASO DE LOS TOROS - Commercial - PEPSICO, INC.; pg. 259, pg. 1327

PASS - Cathodic Protection - CORRPRO COMPANIES, INC.; pg. 631, pg. 1464

PASS - Orthopedic Product - DJO SURGICAL; pg. 1525, pg. 1661

PASS - Portable Access Security System - LOWRY COMPUTER PRODUCTS, INC.; pg. 428, pg. 874

PASS/FAIL - Sterilization Integrator - PROPPER MANUFACTURING COMPANY, INC.; pg. 1586, pg. 1175

PASS IT ON - Outdoor Campaign - OUTDOOR ADVERTISING ASSOCIATION OF AMERICA; pg. 152, pg. 403

PASS KEY - Automotive Anti-Theft - DELPHI ELECTRONICS & SAFETY; pg. 633, pg. 692

PASS THE PIGS - Game - WINNING MOVES GAMES, INC.; pg. 970, pg. 816

PASSAGE - Textiles - BERNHARDT DESIGN; pg. 918, pg. 1381

PASSAGE - Sail Boats - MARLOW-HUNTER LLC; pg. 1709, pg. 409

PASSAGE MAKER - Magazine - DOMINION ENTERPRISES; pg. 1636, pg. 1796

PASSAGEWAY - Carpet - INTERFACE, INC.; pg. 695, pg. 512

PASSAIC - Medical Stool - BLICKMAN HEALTH INDUSTRIES, INC.; pg. 1506, pg. 1051

PASSERELLE - Office Furniture - STEELCASE INC.; pg. 475, pg. 889

PASSERELLE BENCH - Office Furniture - STEELCASE INC.; pg. 475, pg. 889

PASSION - Perfume - ELIZABETH ARDEN, INC.; pg. 507, pg. 448

PASSION - Tea - STARBUCKS CORPORATION; pg. 897, pg. 1840

PASSION - Healthcare Product - SWANSON HEALTH PRODUCTS INC.; pg. 1600, pg. 1397

PASSION FLAKIE - Bakery Product - SAPUTO, INC.; pg. 893, pg. 1956

PASSION FLAKIE - Bakery Product - VACHON BAKERY INC.; pg. 907, pg. 1959

PASSION FLOWERS - Video Game - INTERNATIONAL GAME TECHNOLOGY; pg. 957, pg. 1024

PASSION FOR PERFORMANCE - Flash Memory Card - SANDISK CORPORATION; pg. 465, pg. 147

PASSION FOR PRINTING IDEAS - Consultation Services - LEXMARK INTERNATIONAL, INC.; pg. 427, pg. 730

PASSION FOR PURPLE - Bouquet - 1-800-FLOWERS.COM, INC.; pg. 1758, pg. 1151

PASSION. PRIDE. PACERS - Tagline - PACERS BASKETBALL, LLC; pg. 573, pg. 689

PASSIONATE PLUMERIA - Fragrance - LUZIER PERSONALIZED COSMETICS, INC.; pg. 515, pg. 978

PASSIVE - Computer Support Worktools - STEELCASE INC.; pg. 475, pg. 889

PASSIVE-MATRIX - Light Emitting Device - UNIVERSAL DISPLAY CORPORATION; pg. 683, pg. 1064

PASSIVE PLUS - Passive-Fixation Leads - ST. JUDE MEDICAL, INC.; pg. 1596, pg. 963

PASSKEY-ENABLED - Software - PASSKEY INTERNATIONAL, INC.; pg. 1274, pg. 853

PASSOA LIQUEUR - Spirits - REMY COINTREAU USA INC.; pg. 1969, pg. 1285

PASSPORT - Medical Device - BOSTON SCIENTIFIC CORPORATION; pg. 1508, pg. 831

PASSPORT - Scotch - DIAGEO CANADA, INC.; pg. 1961, pg. 1937

PASSPORT - Radar And Laser Detector - ESCORT, INC.; pg. 1412, pg. 1479

PASSPORT - CSA Approved Aerosol Compressor - INVACARE CORPORATION; pg. 1546, pg. 1451

PASSPORT - Vital Signs Monitoring Device - MAQUET; pg. 1558, pg. 1082

PASSPORT - Electronic Components - MOLEX INCORPORATED; pg. 655, pg. 628

PASSPORT - Digital Directory - ROVI CORPORATION; pg. 463, pg. 269

PASSPORT - Hard Drive - WESTERN DIGITAL CORPORATION; pg. 492, pg. 118

PASSPORT 2 - Vital Signs Monitoring Device - MAQUET; pg. 1558, pg. 1082

PASSPORT DCT - Digital Directory - ROVI CORPORATION; pg. 463, pg. 269

PASSPORT ECHO - Digital Directory - ROVI CORPORATION; pg. 463, pg. 269

PASSPORT FROM MEDICA - Health Plan & Publication - MEDICA, INC.; pg. 1208, pg. 949

PASSPORT SERIES - Cabinets - KRAFTMAID CABINETRY, INC.; pg. 1053, pg. 1465

PASSPORT.ATM - National ATM Switching & Processing Services for Electronic Transactions - JACK HENRY & ASSOCIATES, INC.; pg. 422, pg. 988

PASSUR - Software - PASSUR AEROSPACE, INC.; pg. 233, pg. 376

PASSUR INSIGHT - Software - PASSUR AEROSPACE, INC.; pg. 233, pg. 376

PASSUR PULSE - Software - PASSUR AEROSPACE, INC.; pg. 233, pg. 376

PASSVAULT - Codeword Safe Deposit Box Access - DIEBOLD, INCORPORATED; pg. 387, pg. 1407

PASSWORD MANAGER - Software - DELL SOFTWARE; pg. 385, pg. 40

PASSWORD RESET MANAGER - Software - DELL SOFTWARE; pg. 385, pg. 40

PASSWORDS PLUS - Software - DATAVIZ, INC.; pg. 383, pg. 356

PAST - Carpet - INTERFACE, INC.; pg. 695, pg. 512

PASTA BRAVO - Pasta Food Preparations - YUM! BRANDS, INC.; pg. 1756, pg. 738

PASTA POWER - Food Product - MGP INGREDIENTS, INC.; pg. 877, pg. 714

PASTA RONI - Rice & Noodle Products - PEPSICO, INC.; pg. 259, pg. 1327

PASTA RONI - Side Dishes - THE QUAKER OATS COMPANY; pg. 834, pg. 588

PASTE WIZ - Plastic & Rubber Material - AXEL PLASTICS RESEARCH LABORATORIES, INC.; pg. 326, pg. 1356

PASTEL COATINGS - Colored Coating for Candy & Bakeries - GUITTARD CHOCOLATE COMPANY; pg. 1855, pg. 55

PASTEL PETS - Puzzles - HASBRO, INC.; pg. 954, pg. 1603

PASTELS - Pillow - AMERICAN LEATHER LP; pg. 912, pg. 1673

PASTILLE FRIEZE - Broadloom - COURISTAN INC.; pg. 921, pg. 1067

PASTOREX - Clinical Diagnostic Product - BIO-RAD LABORATORIES, INC.; pg. 1504, pg. 101

PASTURE PRO - Homeowner Product - PBI/GORDON CORPORATION; pg. 1176, pg. 985

PASTURE PROTECTION - Insecticide - W.F. YOUNG, INC.; pg. 1610, pg. 817

PASYS - Pacemakers & Associated Controller Apparatus - MEDTRONIC, INC.; pg. 1564, pg. 939

PATAGONIA - Outdoor Clothing - LOST ARROW CORPORATION; pg. 44, pg. 301

PATAGONIA FOOTWEAR - Footwear - WOLVERINE WORLD WIDE, INC.; pg. 1822, pg. 905

PATAK'S - Indian Food Product - HORMEL FOODS CORPORATION; pg. 863, pg. 915

PATCH MANAGEMENT - Software - DELL SOFTWARE; pg. 385, pg. 40

PATCH MANAGER - Software - BMC SOFTWARE, INC.; pg. 362, pg. 1701

PATCH MANAGER - Software - ECORA SOFTWARE CORPORATION; pg. 389, pg. 1662

PATCH RUBBER - Plastic Product - MYERS INDUSTRIES, INC.; pg. 1887, pg. 1402

PATCH STICK - Repair Product - DAP PRODUCTS, INC.; pg. 1441, pg. 756

PATCHLINK - Rack & Cable - PANDUIT CORP.; pg. 661, pg. 663

PATCHMASTER - Grass Seed - THE SCOTTS MIRACLE-GRO COMPANY; pg. 1799, pg. 1459

PATCHRUNNER - Rack & Cable - PANDUIT CORP.; pg. 661, pg. 663

PATCHWORK - Carpet - INTERFACE, INC.; pg. 695, pg. 512

PATCHXPRESS - Electrophysiology System - MOLECULAR DEVICES CORPORATION; pg. 1568, pg. 287

PATCOTE - Antifoam - BIRKO CORPORATION; pg. 1149, pg. 332

PATCRAFT - Commercial Carpets - SHAW INDUSTRIES GROUP, INC.; pg. 942, pg. 530

PATELLA DONUT - Orthopedic Product - DJO INCORPORATED; pg. 1524, pg. 302

PATELLOFEMORA - Orthopedic Product - DJO INCORPORATED; pg. 1524, pg. 302

PATENT - Leather Product - COACH, INC.; pg. 3, pg. 1214

PATENT - Fabric - NEMSCHOFF, INC.; pg. 936, pg. 1890

PATENT INDEX - Science & Healthcare Publications - THOMSON REUTERS CORPORATION; pg. 1693, pg. 1944

PATENTED STEADYGUIDE - Motion Tracking - AVID TECHNOLOGY, INC.; pg. 622, pg. 804

PATERSON - Gear Motors - REGAL BELOIT CORPORATION; pg. 106, pg. 1854

PATFLEX - Machine Vision System - COGNEX CORPORATION; pg. 1406, pg. 834

PATHBLAZER - Biomolecule Product - THERMO FISHER SCIENTIFIC INC.; pg. 1602, pg. 61

PATHCLEAR - Lawn & Garden Products - THE SCOTTS MIRACLE-GRO COMPANY; pg. 1799, pg. 1459

PATHCLONES - Molecular Biology Product - THERMO FISHER SCIENTIFIC INC.; pg. 1602, pg. 61

PATHFINDER - Clinical Diagnostic Product - BIO-RAD LABORATORIES, INC.; pg. 1504, pg. 101

PATHFINDER - Knife - BUCK KNIVES, INC.; pg. 1828, pg. 550

PATHFINDER - Steel-Framed Operable Partition - HUFCOR INCORPORATED; pg. 87, pg. 1861

PATHFINDER - Sport-Utility Vehicle - NISSAN NORTH AMERICA, INC.; pg. 186, pg. 1633

PATHFINDER - Footwear - P.W. MINOR & SON, INC.; pg. 1816, pg. 1140

PATHFINDER - Endoscopic Irrigation Device - UTAH MEDICAL PRODUCTS, INC.; pg. 1605, pg. 1752

PATHFINDER PLUS - Endoscopic Bulb Irrigators - UTAH MEDICAL PRODUCTS, INC.; pg. 1605, pg. 1752

PATHFINDER WAGON - Wagon - RADIO FLYER INC.; pg. 966, pg. 588

PATHLINK - Software System - MENTOR GRAPHICS CORPORATION; pg. 432, pg. 1510

PATHMAKER - Systems Integration & Aeronautics - LOCKHEED MARTIN CORPORATION; pg. 229, pg. 762

PATHMARK - Food Stores - THE GREAT ATLANTIC & PACIFIC TEA COMPANY, INC.; pg. 1021, pg. 1086

PATHMILL - Software - SYNOPSYS, INC.; pg. 480, pg. 162
PATHNAVIGATOR - Network Conferencing System - POLYCOM, INC.; pg. 664, pg. 249
PATHNET - Laboratory Information System - CERNER CORPORATION; pg. 1514, pg. 981
PATHPOINT - Auto-Dimming Mirror - GENTEX CORPORATION; pg. 206, pg. 913
PATHVIEW - 3D Well Path Visualization Tool - GULF PUBLISHING COMPANY; pg. 1646, pg. 1707
PATHVYSION - Testing Device - ABBOTT LABORATORIES; pg. 1484, pg. 551
PATHWAY - Network Switch - ELECTRO STANDARDS LABORATORIES INC.; pg. 390, pg. 1600
PATHWAY T - Apparels - UNDER ARMOUR, INC.; pg. 49, pg. 759
PATHWAYS - Office Furniture - STEELCASE INC.; pg. 475, pg. 889
PATIENCE - Footwear - EASTLAND SHOE CORPORATION; pg. 1808, pg. 750
PATIENCE - Footwear - PHOENIX FOOTWEAR GROUP, INC.; pg. 1815, pg. 60
PATIENT - Footwear - NIKE, INC.; pg. 1812, pg. 1492
PATIENT ACTIVATOR - Internal Marketing Program - FUTUREDONTICS, INC.; pg. 1532, pg. 131
PATIENT ADVISOR - Client Communication Program - IDEXX LABORATORIES, INC.; pg. 1543, pg. 753
PATIENT CARE - Medical Publication - TRUVEN HEALTH ANALYTICS; pg. 1696, pg. 867
PATIENT CARE FOR THE NURSE PRACTITIONER - Medical Publication - TRUVEN HEALTH ANALYTICS; pg. 1696, pg. 867
PATIENT CHOICE INSIGHTS - Health Plan & Publication - MEDICA, INC.; pg. 1208, pg. 949
PATIENT EMPOWERMENT MEDICINE - Medical Service - CANCER TREATMENT CENTERS OF AMERICA; pg. 1511, pg. 410
THE PATIENT FRIENDLY MRI - Slogan - FONAR CORPORATION; pg. 1413, pg. 1179
PATIENT SAFE - Syringes - RETRACTABLE TECHNOLOGIES INC.; pg. 1590, pg. 1725
PATIENT SELECT - Software - MICROS SYSTEMS, INC.; pg. 435, pg. 768
PATIENTNET - Control Station Monitoring Systems - MAQUET; pg. 1558, pg. 1082
PATIENTPLUS - Patient Care Initiative - AMERISOURCEBERGEN CORPORATION; pg. 1493, pg. 1522
PATINE - Metal Tile - WALKER & ZANGER, INC.; pg. 119, pg. 281
PATINSPECT - Machine Vision System - COGNEX CORPORATION; pg. 1406, pg. 834
PATIO - Food Product - CONAGRA FOODS, INC.; pg. 826, pg. 1014
PATIO - Dinnerware - THE HOMER LAUGHLIN CHINA COMPANY; pg. 1125, pg. 1850
PATIO - Fabric - NEMSCHOFF, INC.; pg. 936, pg. 1890
PATIO BISTRO - Grill - W.C. BRADLEY CO.; pg. 62, pg. 528
PATIO CADDIE - Grill - W.C. BRADLEY CO.; pg. 62, pg. 528
PATITAS - Toys - LEAPFROG ENTERPRISES, INC.; pg. 961, pg. 84
PATMAX - Machine Vision System - COGNEX CORPORATION; pg. 1406, pg. 834
PATRA - Rug - COURISTAN INC.; pg. 921, pg. 1067
PATRAN - Software - MSC SOFTWARE CORPORATION; pg. 441, pg. 262
PATRICIA - Clothing - ABERCROMBIE & FITCH CO.; pg. 37, pg. 1466
PATRICIA - Furniture - AMISCO INDUSTRIES LTD.; pg. 913, pg. 1958
PATRICIA - Healthcare Product - GF HEALTH PRODUCTS, INC.; pg. 1535, pg. 508
PATRICK CUDAHY - Bacon, Hams, Sausage - PATRICK CUDAHY INC.; pg. 888, pg. 1856
PATRICK CUDAHY - Food Products - SMITHFIELD FOODS, INC.; pg. 896, pg. 1806
PATRIOT - Cattle Ear Tag - BOEHRINGER INGELHEIM VETMEDICA, INC.; pg. 1474, pg. 989
PATRIOT - Wrapper - CAMPBELL WRAPPER CORPORATION; pg. 1454, pg. 1856
PATRIOT - Folding Wheelchair - INVACARE CORPORATION; pg. 1546, pg. 1451
PATRIOT - Seating Product - IRWIN SEATING COMPANY INC.; pg. 929, pg. 887
PATRIOT - Lighting - LSI INDUSTRIES INC.; pg. 58, pg. 1416
PATRIOT - Herbicide Product - NUFARM AMERICAS INC; pg. 1798, pg. 552
PATRIOT - Pressed & Monolithic Refractory - RESCO PRODUCTS, INC.; pg. 107, pg. 1581
PATRIOT 80 - Oil Furnace - HEAT CONTROLLER, INC.; pg. 1072, pg. 893
PATRIOT PLUS - Fabric - NEUTRAL POSTURE, INC.; pg. 939, pg. 1669
PATRIOT POLYESTER - Plastic & Rubber - TEKNOR APEX COMPANY; pg. 1889, pg. 1605
PATRIOT PROTECTOR - Computer Services - COMPUTER SCIENCES CORPORATION; pg. 378, pg. 1780
PATRIOTS - Professional Football Team - NEW ENGLAND PATRIOTS FOOTBALL CLUB, INC.; pg. 569, pg. 819
PATROL - Glove - 180S, LLC; pg. 1824, pg. 754
PATROL - Feeding Pump - ABBOTT LABORATORIES; pg. 1484, pg. 551
PATROL - Pump - BATTELLE MEMORIAL INSTITUTE; pg. 1401, pg. 1437
PATROL - Software - BMC SOFTWARE, INC.; pg. 362, pg. 1701
PATROL - Apparel - OAKLEY, INC.; pg. 1840, pg. 86
PATROL - Process Analyzer - WATERS CORPORATION; pg. 1436, pg. 834
PATROL CENTRAL ALERTS - WEB EDITION - Software - BMC SOFTWARE, INC.; pg. 362, pg. 1701
PATROL DASHBOARD - Software - BMC SOFTWARE, INC.; pg. 362, pg. 1701
PATROLE CAR - Boots - AEROGROUP INTERNATIONAL, INC.; pg. 1803, pg. 1055
PATRON - Beverage Company - THE PATRON SPIRITS COMPANY; pg. 1967, pg. 1029
PATRON ANEJO - Tequila - THE PATRON SPIRITS COMPANY; pg. 1967, pg. 1029
THE PATRON EDGE - Ticketing - BLACKBAUD, INC.; pg. 361, pg. 1613
THE PATRON EDGE ONLINE - Online Ticketing - BLACKBAUD, INC.; pg. 361, pg. 1613
PATRON REPOSADO - Tequila - THE PATRON SPIRITS COMPANY; pg. 1967, pg. 1029
PATRON SILVER - Tequila - THE PATRON SPIRITS COMPANY; pg. 1967, pg. 1029
PATRONBOOKSINPRINT.COM - Online Database - R.R. BOWKER LLC; pg. 1682, pg. 1095
PATTERN 62 - Patterned Glass - AGC GLASS NORTH AMERICA, INC.; pg. 65, pg. 482
PATTERN PLUS AUDITOR - Clinical Diagnostic Product - BIO-RAD LABORATORIES, INC.; pg. 1504, pg. 101
PATTERNCLAD - Glass - PPG INDUSTRIES, INC.; pg. 1445, pg. 1579
PATTERNLITE - Glass Panels - PPG INDUSTRIES, INC.; pg. 1445, pg. 1579
PATTERNPRO - Variable Pitch Dispensing Gun - NORDSON CORPORATION; pg. 1365, pg. 1480
PATTERNS PROFILER - Pharmaceutical & Medical/Surgical Solutions - MCKESSON CORPORATION; pg. 1560, pg. 222
PATTERSON, FLYNN & MARTIN - High-End Decorative Carpet Business - F. SCHUMACHER & CO.; pg. 925, pg. 1230
PATTI LABELLE - Fragrance - COLOR ME BEAUTIFUL, INC.; pg. 505, pg. 1787
PATTON - Fire Control System - ASTRONAUTICS CORPORATION OF AMERICA; pg. 224, pg. 1873
PATTON - Heaters, Air Conditioners, & Fans - JARDEN CONSUMER SOLUTIONS; pg. 57, pg. 412
PAUL - Furniture - AMISCO INDUSTRIES LTD.; pg. 913, pg. 1958
PAUL - Medical Cabinet - BLICKMAN HEALTH INDUSTRIES, INC.; pg. 1506, pg. 1051
PAUL MITCHELL LAB - Hair Care Products - JOHN PAUL MITCHELL SYSTEMS; pg. 512, pg. 133
PAUL REED SMITH - Guitar - PAUL REED SMITH GUITARS; pg. 574, pg. 779
PAUL REVERE - Flatware - ONEIDA LTD; pg. 1129, pg. 1318
PAUL STUART - Apparel - PAUL STUART, INC.; pg. 1781, pg. 1276
PAULA - Clothing - ABERCROMBIE & FITCH CO.; pg. 37, pg. 1466
PAULA YOUNG - Wig Supplier - SPECIALTY CATALOG CORPORATION; pg. 1786, pg. 856
PAULMAC'S PET FOOD - Pet Food Product - PET VALU CANADA, INC.; pg. 1480, pg. 1924
PAULUHN - Hazardous Area Lighting Products - FEDERAL SIGNAL CORPORATION; pg. 638, pg. 645
PAUSE - Lounge Chairs - BERNHARDT DESIGN; pg. 918, pg. 1381
PAVAROTTI PEARL - Tile - ARTISTIC TILE INC.; pg. 914, pg. 1119
PAVE - Additive - DOW CHEMICAL; pg. 1156, pg. 1563
PAVE BOND - Additive - DOW CHEMICAL; pg. 1156, pg. 1563
PAVECRAFTERS - Concrete System - L.M. SCOFIELD COMPANY; pg. 94, pg. 134
PAVECRYL - Emulsion - DOW CHEMICAL; pg. 1156, pg. 1563
PAVERLYTE FIXTURE - Fiber Optic Fixtures - REVOLUTION LIGHTING TECHNOLOGIES, INC.; pg. 1304, pg. 377
PAVERS - Fabric - NEMSCHOFF, INC.; pg. 936, pg. 1890
PAVESAVER - Bridge Product - THE D.S. BROWN COMPANY; pg. 79, pg. 1468
PAVEWAY - Defense System - RAYTHEON COMPANY; pg. 233, pg. 854
PAVIA ANTICO - Stone - WALKER & ZANGER, INC.; pg. 119, pg. 281
PAVIA ANTICO PINTURA - Ceramic, Glass, Stone Tiles & Slabs - WALKER & ZANGER, INC.; pg. 119, pg. 281
PAVILION - Fan - CRAFTMADE INTERNATIONAL, INC.; pg. 1295, pg. 1670
PAVILION - Computer - HEWLETT-PACKARD COMPANY; pg. 404, pg. 175
PAVILION - Furniture - JOFCO INC.; pg. 931, pg. 691
PAVILION PANTRY - Hotel Shops - HILTON WORLDWIDE, INC.; pg. 1094, pg. 1791
PAVILION WOOD - Office Furniture - JOFCO INC.; pg. 931, pg. 691
PAVLOWA - Footwear - CAPEZIO BALLET MAKERS INC.; pg. 1805, pg. 1125
PAVONE - Food Product - PATRICK CUDAHY INC.; pg. 888, pg. 1856
PAW PAW CELL-REG - Health Care Product - NATURE'S SUNSHINE PRODUCTS, INC.; pg. 1571, pg. 1754
PAWS - Pet Products - BASHAS' SUPERMARKETS; pg. 1015, pg. 12
PAWS - Food Product - HAGGEN, INC.; pg. 1022, pg. 1817
PAWS 'N CLAWS - Pet Food - TRACTOR SUPPLY COMPANY; pg. 708, pg. 1627
PAWS PREMIUM - Toys, Treat & Food - HY-VEE, INC.; pg. 1023, pg. 713
PAWTUCKET FALLS - Carpet - INTERFACE, INC.; pg. 695, pg. 512
PAXBAC - Medical Equipment - INVACARE CORPORATION; pg. 1546, pg. 1451
PAXSCAN - X-Ray Detector - VARIAN MEDICAL SYSTEMS, INC.; pg. 1434, pg. 178
PAXWAY - Internet Service Provider - ION MEDIA NETWORKS, INC.; pg. 293, pg. 479
PAY DAY - Game - WINNING MOVES GAMES, INC.; pg. 970, pg. 816
PAY LESS - Supermarket - THE KROGER CO.; pg. 1025, pg. 1416
PAY PER TRANSACTION - Software - RENTRAK CORPORATION; pg. 306, pg. 1506
PAY YOURSELF TOO PLAN - Banking Service - THE BANK OF NOVA SCOTIA; pg. 721, pg. 1935
PAYANYONE - Payment Service - ACI WORLDWIDE; pg. 710, pg. 1777
PAYBACK - Insurance Policy - SENTRY INSURANCE GROUP; pg. 1217, pg. 1895
PAYBACK - Fire Ant Bait - SOUTHERN AGRICULTURAL INSECTICIDES, INC.; pg. 1181, pg. 458
PAYBACK - Office Furniture - STEELCASE INC.; pg. 475, pg. 889
PAYBASE - Software System - BOTTOMLINE TECHNOLOGIES (DE), INC.; pg. 727, pg. 1038
PAYCHECK DIRECT - Employee Purchase Program - BLUESTEM BRANDS, INC.; pg. 1763, pg. 922
PAYCHEX ONLINE PAYROLL - Software - PAYCHEX, INC.; pg. 792, pg. 1336
PAYCHEX PREMIER - Human Resources Software - PAYCHEX, INC.; pg. 792, pg. 1336
PAYDAY - Game - HASBRO, INC.; pg. 954, pg. 1603
PAYDAY - Candy - THE HERSHEY CO.; pg. 1855, pg. 1538
PAYDAY POKER - Rewards Game - BALLY TECHNOLOGIES, INC.; pg. 531, pg. 1022
PAYDIRT - Software - TRIMBLE NAVIGATION LIMITED; pg. 1384, pg. 288
PAYEN - Gaskets - FEDERAL-MOGUL HOLDINGS CORPORATION; pg. 205, pg. 907

PAYERVIEW - Payment System - ATHENAHEALTH, INC.; *pg.* 1497, *pg.* 855
PAYETTE FARMS - French Fries - J.R. SIMPLOT COMPANY; *pg.* 867, *pg.* 547
PAYFAST - Pre-Paid Self-Service - EDISON PROPERTIES, LLC; *pg.* 1906, *pg.* 1096
PAYFIRST - Sports Marketing System - CANDID COLOR SYSTEMS, INC.; *pg.* 1404, *pg.* 1485
PAYGEL - Agricultural Product - ARCHER-DANIELS-MIDLAND COMPANY; *pg.* 825, *pg.* 565
PAYHAULER - Capital Equipment - TEREX CORPORATION; *pg.* 1381, *pg.* 384
PAYLEAN - Ractopamine - ELANCO ANIMAL HEALTH; *pg.* 1475, *pg.* 681
PAYLINK - Software - PAYCHEX, INC.; *pg.* 792, *pg.* 1336
PAYLOAD - Magazine - DOMINION ENTERPRISES; *pg.* 1636, *pg.* 1796
PAYLOAD PLUS - Network Processors - AVAGO TECHNOLOGIES; *pg.* 358, *pg.* 238
PAYMENT OPTIMIZER - Fraud Detection Systems - FAIR ISAAC CORPORATION; *pg.* 1247, *pg.* 955
PAYMENTECH - Electronic Payment System - CYBERSOURCE CORPORATION; *pg.* 381, *pg.* 216
PAYNE - Air Conditioning & Heating - CARRIER CORPORATION; *pg.* 1070, *pg.* 349
PAYOFFPAK - Fibre Drum - GREIF INC.; *pg.* 1459, *pg.* 1447
PAYROLL - Video Game - INTERNATIONAL GAME TECHNOLOGY; *pg.* 957, *pg.* 1024
PAYROLLMATION - Human Resources Software - API HEALTHCARE CORP.; *pg.* 350, *pg.* 1860
PAYSMART - Billing Service - XCEL ENERGY INC.; *pg.* 1955, *pg.* 946
PAYSTATION - Customer Service Terminal - DIEBOLD, INCORPORATED; *pg.* 387, *pg.* 1407
PAYTENN - Footwear - STEVEN MADDEN, LTD.; *pg.* 1819, *pg.* 1176
PAYTON - Furniture - AMISCO INDUSTRIES LTD.; *pg.* 913, *pg.* 1958
PAYWARE - Credit & Gift Card Readers - VERIFONE SYSTEMS, INC.; *pg.* 487, *pg.* 251
PAYWISE - Accounts Payable Solution - SCAN-OPTICS, LLC; *pg.* 467, *pg.* 354
PAZZAZZ - Cameras - EASTMAN KODAK COMPANY; *pg.* 1408, *pg.* 1333
PB 7000 - Mode-Locked Laser - EMCORE CORPORATION; *pg.* 636, *pg.* 39
PB 7100 - Spectrometer - EMCORE CORPORATION; *pg.* 636, *pg.* 39
PB&J ROLLUPS - Peanut Butter & Jelly Filled Tortillas - TYSON FOODS, INC.; *pg.* 902, *pg.* 35
PB BLASTER PENETRANT - Vehicle Maintenance - TRACTOR SUPPLY COMPANY; *pg.* 708, *pg.* 1627
PB FIRST - Software - PITNEY BOWES INC.; *pg.* 454, *pg.* 376
PB-MAX - Biomolecule Product - THERMO FISHER SCIENTIFIC INC.; *pg.* 1602, *pg.* 61
PB TEEN - Furniture - WILLIAMS-SONOMA, INC.; *pg.* 1140, *pg.* 234
PB TMS - Delivery Management & Tracking - PITNEY BOWES INC.; *pg.* 454, *pg.* 376
PBC - Console Copier - PITNEY BOWES INC.; *pg.* 454, *pg.* 376
PBCC - Electronic Components - TEXAS INSTRUMENTS INCORPORATED; *pg.* 679, *pg.* 1688
PBI - Fiber - DRAPER KNITTING CO., INC.; *pg.* 692, *pg.* 810
PBLU - Biological Product - CAROLINA BIOLOGICAL SUPPLY COMPANY; *pg.* 1513, *pg.* 1359
PBOC - Circulator - OPLINK COMMUNICATIONS, INC.; *pg.* 660, *pg.* 91
PBS - Bypass Equipment - MEDTRONIC, INC.; *pg.* 1564, *pg.* 939
PBS-4100 - Portable Balancing System - MTI INSTRUMENTS INC.; *pg.* 658, *pg.* 1137
PBS-4100R - Portable Balancing System - MTI INSTRUMENTS INC.; *pg.* 658, *pg.* 1137
PBS HOME VIDEO - Home Videocassette Label - PUBLIC BROADCASTING SERVICE; *pg.* 305, *pg.* 1774
PBS HOME VIDEO SUPPORT SERVICES - Fulfillment Service for PBS Home Video Program Orders - PUBLIC BROADCASTING SERVICE; *pg.* 305, *pg.* 1774
PBS VIDEO - Distribution of Videocassettes for Educational Use - PUBLIC BROADCASTING SERVICE; *pg.* 305, *pg.* 1774
PBX - Glass & Ceramic Material - CORNING INCORPORATED; *pg.* 1122, *pg.* 1154
PC-123 - Hair Culture Solution to Assist in Pressing & Curling Hair - THE GILLETTE COMPANY; *pg.* 509, *pg.* 795
PC-220 - Counting Scales - AVERY WEIGH-TRONIX, INC.; *pg.* 1315, *pg.* 925
PC-3 - Epoxy Adhesive - SMOOTH-ON INC.; *pg.* 111, *pg.* 1528
PC-802 - Counting Scales - AVERY WEIGH-TRONIX, INC.; *pg.* 1315, *pg.* 925
PC-805 - Counting Scales - AVERY WEIGH-TRONIX, INC.; *pg.* 1315, *pg.* 925
PC-820 - Counting Scales - AVERY WEIGH-TRONIX, INC.; *pg.* 1315, *pg.* 925
PC-821 - Counting Scales - AVERY WEIGH-TRONIX, INC.; *pg.* 1315, *pg.* 925
PC/AIM - Automatic Inventory Management Systems/PC's - DAIFUKU WEBB; *pg.* 1327, *pg.* 885
PC ANYWHERE - Software - SYMANTEC CORPORATION; *pg.* 478, *pg.* 161
PC CARE - Vitamin & Dietary Supplement - NATROL, INC.; *pg.* 1570, *pg.* 64
PC CONTINGENCY - Banking Software - JACK HENRY & ASSOCIATES, INC.; *pg.* 422, *pg.* 988
PC EXPO - Publisher - UNITED BUSINESS MEDIA LLC; *pg.* 1697, *pg.* 1177
PC EXPRESS - Software - USA TECHNOLOGIES, INC.; *pg.* 815, *pg.* 1550
PC HARDWARE MADE EASY - Hardware System - MICRO 2000, INC.; *pg.* 434, *pg.* 96
PC MAGNI-VIEWER - Magnifier - BAUSCH & LOMB INCORPORATED; *pg.* 1401, *pg.* 1045
PC POSTAGE - Postal Services - UNITED STATES POSTAL SERVICE; *pg.* 1009, *pg.* 406
PC PROFESSIONELL - Trade Magazine - THE NIELSEN COMPANY B.V.; *pg.* 1671, *pg.* 1272
PC WORLD - Technology Magazine - INTERNATIONAL DATA GROUP; *pg.* 1653, *pg.* 796
PCA - Opening Force & Bending Tester - THWING-ALBERT INSTRUMENT COMPANY; *pg.* 1432, *pg.* 1131
PCANYWHERE - Remote Control System - SYMANTEC CORPORATION; *pg.* 479, *pg.* 1753
PCB DESIGN CONFERENCE - Magazine - UNITED BUSINESS MEDIA LLC; *pg.* 1697, *pg.* 1177
PCB-GEN - Software System - MENTOR GRAPHICS CORPORATION; *pg.* 432, *pg.* 1510
PCC III - Digital Loop Controller - PREFERRED UTILITIES MANUFACTURING CORPORATION; *pg.* 1075, *pg.* 344
PCC WEB - Based Equipment Control System - PROCESS CONTROL CORPORATION; *pg.* 1370, *pg.* 518
PCCHARGE - Payment Software - VERIFONE SYSTEMS, INC.; *pg.* 487, *pg.* 251
PCCWEB - Software - PROCESS CONTROL CORPORATION; *pg.* 1370, *pg.* 518
PCDEFENSE - Software - LAPLINK SOFTWARE, INC.; *pg.* 426, *pg.* 1815
PCDNA - Molecular Biology Product - THERMO FISHER SCIENTIFIC INC.; *pg.* 1602, *pg.* 61
PCE - Erythromycin Particles in Tablets - ABBOTT LABORATORIES; *pg.* 1484, *pg.* 551
PCE EGG CURDS - Food Service Product - MICHAEL FOODS, INC.; *pg.* 877, *pg.* 949
PCE FILLED OMELETS - Food Service Product - MICHAEL FOODS, INC.; *pg.* 877, *pg.* 949
PCE LNC OMELETS - Food Service Product - MICHAEL FOODS, INC.; *pg.* 877, *pg.* 949
PCE PLAIN FRIED PATTIES - Food Service Product - MICHAEL FOODS, INC.; *pg.* 877, *pg.* 949
PCH CASH SLOTS - App - PUBLISHERS CLEARING HOUSE; *pg.* 1782, *pg.* 1324
PCH LOTTO BLAST - App - PUBLISHERS CLEARING HOUSE; *pg.* 1782, *pg.* 1324
PCH SWEEPS - App - PUBLISHERS CLEARING HOUSE; *pg.* 1782, *pg.* 1324
PCH VIP - App - PUBLISHERS CLEARING HOUSE; *pg.* 1782, *pg.* 1324
PCHBINGO.COM - Website - PUBLISHERS CLEARING HOUSE; *pg.* 1782, *pg.* 1324
PCHBLACKJACK.COM - Website - PUBLISHERS CLEARING HOUSE; *pg.* 1782, *pg.* 1324
PCH.COM - Website - PUBLISHERS CLEARING HOUSE; *pg.* 1782, *pg.* 1324
PCHFRONTPAGE.COM - Website - PUBLISHERS CLEARING HOUSE; *pg.* 1782, *pg.* 1324
PCHGAMES.COM - Website - PUBLISHERS CLEARING HOUSE; *pg.* 1782, *pg.* 1324
PCHLOTTO.COM - Website - PUBLISHERS CLEARING HOUSE; *pg.* 1782, *pg.* 1324
PCHSEARCHANDWIN.COM - Website - PUBLISHERS CLEARING HOUSE; *pg.* 1782, *pg.* 1324
PCHSLOTS.COM - Website - PUBLISHERS CLEARING HOUSE; *pg.* 1782, *pg.* 1324
PCI - Hardware Product - INTERPHASE CORPORATION; *pg.* 420, *pg.* 1732
PCI-DP - Dual-Port SRAM With PCI Controller - CYPRESS SEMICONDUCTOR CORPORATION; *pg.* 1326, *pg.* 243
PCI-DPPSI - Dual-Port SRAM With PCI Controller - CYPRESS SEMICONDUCTOR CORPORATION; *pg.* 1326, *pg.* 243
PCI EXPRESS - 3D Graphical Technology - ADVANCED MICRO DEVICES, INC.-MARKHAM; *pg.* 345, *pg.* 1922
PCI-EXPRESS - Ethernet Controller - BROADCOM CORPORATION; *pg.* 364, *pg.* 108
PCI EXPRESS - Graphics Card - CRUCIAL TECHNOLOGY DIV OF MICRON; *pg.* 1237, *pg.* 550
PCI EXPRESS - Hardware Product - INTERPHASE CORPORATION; *pg.* 420, *pg.* 1732
PCI EXPRESS - Interface System - NVIDIA CORPORATION; *pg.* 447, *pg.* 268
PCI EXPRESS - Turnkey Solution - SEMTECH CORPORATION GENNUM PRODUCTS; *pg.* 671, *pg.* 1919
PCIDAQ - Data Acquisition System - CYBERRESEARCH INC.; *pg.* 381, *pg.* 339
PCIEXPRESS - Chip Interface System - RAMBUS INC.; *pg.* 459, *pg.* 288
PCILYNX - Circuit Chips - TEXAS INSTRUMENTS INCORPORATED; *pg.* 679, *pg.* 1688
PCJ - Conditioning Shampoo - LUSTER PRODUCTS INC.; *pg.* 515, *pg.* 581
PCJ PRETTY-N-SILKY - Hair Relaxer - LUSTER PRODUCTS INC.; *pg.* 515, *pg.* 581
PCMAG.COM - Online Magazine - PC MAGAZINE; *pg.* 1674, *pg.* 1276
PCMAG.COM - Publication - ZIFF DAVIS, LLC; *pg.* 1703, *pg.* 1316
PCMOVER - Software - LAPLINK SOFTWARE, INC.; *pg.* 426, *pg.* 1815
PCMS - Laparoscopic Set Rental & Maintenance Program - AESCULAP, INC.; *pg.* 1487, *pg.* 1521
PCNET - Integrated Chipset - ADVANCED MICRO DEVICES, INC.; *pg.* 613, *pg.* 282
PCNET-FAST - Integrated Chipset - ADVANCED MICRO DEVICES, INC.; *pg.* 613, *pg.* 282
PCNET-PRO - Integrated Chipset - ADVANCED MICRO DEVICES, INC.; *pg.* 613, *pg.* 282
PCO2-14 - Oven - DESPATCH INDUSTRIES; *pg.* 1070, *pg.* 927
PCQUOTE.COM - Electronic Product - MONEY.NET, INC.; *pg.* 1268, *pg.* 1261
PCR KLEEN - Software - BIO-RAD LABORATORIES, INC.; *pg.* 1504, *pg.* 101
PCR OPTIMIZER - Molecular Biology Product - THERMO FISHER SCIENTIFIC INC.; *pg.* 1602, *pg.* 61
PCS - Plastic Injection Mold & Die Cast Tools - FEDERAL SIGNAL CORPORATION; *pg.* 638, *pg.* 645
PCS - Medical Device - HAEMONETICS CORPORATION; *pg.* 1538, *pg.* 802
PCS - Automation Software Platform - NEWPORT CORPORATION; *pg.* 1424, *pg.* 114
PCS CLEAR WIRELESS WORKPLACE - Software - SPRINT CORPORATION; *pg.* 1874, *pg.* 719
PCS VISION - Phone - SPRINT CORPORATION; *pg.* 1874, *pg.* 719
PCT - Casegoods - STEELCASE INC.; *pg.* 475, *pg.* 889
PCTI - Personal Computer Telephone Interface - ANDREA ELECTRONICS CORPORATION; *pg.* 617, *pg.* 1143
PCTI II - Personal Computer Telephone Interface - ANDREA ELECTRONICS CORPORATION; *pg.* 617, *pg.* 1143
PCWORKS - Electronics - CAMBRIDGE SOUNDWORKS, INC.; *pg.* 1234, *pg.* 781
PD 1200 - Defibrillator & Pacemaker - ZOLL MEDICAL CORPORATION; *pg.* 1612, *pg.* 814
PD 1400 - Defibrillator & Pacemaker - ZOLL MEDICAL CORPORATION; *pg.* 1612, *pg.* 814
PD 2000 - Defibrillator & Pacemaker - ZOLL MEDICAL CORPORATION; *pg.* 1612, *pg.* 814
PD ADVANTAGE - Software - NIELSEN AUDIO; *pg.* 446, *pg.* 768
PD-DIRECT - Biologic Safety Test - THERMO FISHER SCIENTIFIC INC.; *pg.* 1602, *pg.* 61
PD LINK - Peritoneal Dialyzer - BAXTER INTERNATIONAL INC.; *pg.* 1499, *pg.* 599

PD PLUS - Blower - TUTHILL CORPORATION; *pg.* 1385, *pg.* 561
PDA PLAYGROUND - Software - DATAVIZ, INC.; *pg.* 383, *pg.* 356
PDASYNC - Software - LAPLINK SOFTWARE, INC.; *pg.* 426, *pg.* 1815
PDASYNC 3.0 - Mobile Device Synchronization Software - LAPLINK SOFTWARE, INC.; *pg.* 426, *pg.* 1815
PDC - Digital Cameras - POLAROID CORPORATION; *pg.* 1426, *pg.* 815
PDEMS - Chemical Product - AIR PRODUCTS AND CHEMICALS, INC.; *pg.* 1145, *pg.* 1513
PDEST - Cell Culture Product - THERMO FISHER SCIENTIFIC INC.; *pg.* 1602, *pg.* 61
PDFPLUS - Diesel Fuel - MFA OIL COMPANY; *pg.* 981, *pg.* 976
PDHP - Adhesive Activator - VERTELLUS SPECIALTIES INC.; *pg.* 1185, *pg.* 690
PDI - Liquid Color & Dispersion Additives for Plastics - FERRO CORPORATION; *pg.* 1162, *pg.* 1462
PDI - Disposable Medical Products - NICE-PAK PRODUCTS, INC.; *pg.* 1465, *pg.* 1319
PDI ON DEMAND - Sales Service Solution - PDI, INC.; *pg.* 1580, *pg.* 1104
PDISPLAY - Molecular Biology Product - THERMO FISHER SCIENTIFIC INC.; *pg.* 1602, *pg.* 61
PDLSIM - Software System - MENTOR GRAPHICS CORPORATION; *pg.* 432, *pg.* 1510
PDMPAK - Delivery System - ATMI, INC.; *pg.* 1314, *pg.* 342
PDQ - Distribution & Logistics System - ADVANCE AUTO PARTS, INC.; *pg.* 197, *pg.* 1805
PDQ - Game - GAMEWRIGHT; *pg.* 953, *pg.* 836
PDQ LOGISTICS - Transport Services - UNITED STATES COLD STORAGE, INC.; *pg.* 61, *pg.* 1051
PDQ MEXICO - LTL Transportation for Refrigerated Foods to Mexico - UNITED STATES COLD STORAGE, INC.; *pg.* 61, *pg.* 1051
PDQUEST - Software - BIO-RAD LABORATORIES, INC.; *pg.* 1504, *pg.* 101
PDR - Science & Healthcare Publications - THOMSON REUTERS CORPORATION; *pg.* 1693, *pg.* 1944
PDR - Software Tool And Application - TRUVEN HEALTH ANALYTICS; *pg.* 1696, *pg.* 867
P.D.R.P. - Rust Preventive Lubricant - SHERWIN-WILLIAMS DIVERSIFIED BRANDS DIVISION; *pg.* 1448, *pg.* 1435
PDS-1000/HE - Software - BIO-RAD LABORATORIES, INC.; *pg.* 1504, *pg.* 101
PDT-440 - PC Programmable Two-Wire Transmitter - CONAX TECHNOLOGIES LLC; *pg.* 1325, *pg.* 1148
PDTRACE - Interface - IMAGINATION TECHNOLOGIES; *pg.* 412, *pg.* 285
PDX - Power Supply - ADVANCED ENERGY INDUSTRIES, INC.; *pg.* 613, *pg.* 328
PDX - Portland International Airport - PORT OF PORTLAND; *pg.* 1920, *pg.* 1505
PE - Medical Product - HOLOGIC, INC.; *pg.* 1416, *pg.* 784
PE PREP COURSE - Civil Engineering Exam Review - SMARTPROS LTD.; *pg.* 1281, *pg.* 1166
PE1000+ - Adhesive Anchors & Foam - POWERS FASTENERS INC.; *pg.* 1059, *pg.* 1143
PEABERRY - Coffee - PEET'S COFFEE & TEA, INC.; *pg.* 1029, *pg.* 85
PEABODY LITTLE ROCK - Hotel - PEABODY HOTEL GROUP, INC.; *pg.* 1107, *pg.* 1645
PEABODY ORLANDO - Hotel - PEABODY HOTEL GROUP, INC.; *pg.* 1107, *pg.* 1645
PEACE - Apparel - OAKLEY, INC.; *pg.* 1840, *pg.* 86
PEACE OF MIND - Life Insurance - OLD AMERICAN INSURANCE COMPANY; *pg.* 1213, *pg.* 985
PEACE TEA - Beverage - MONSTER BEVERAGE CORPORATION; *pg.* 257, *pg.* 69
PEACEFUL NITE - Nutritional Product - NUTRACEUTICAL INTERNATIONAL CORPORATION; *pg.* 1576, *pg.* 1753
PEACEFUL PET - Memorial Box - PETEDGE; *pg.* 1481, *pg.* 787
PEACEFUL PLANET - Nutritional Product - NUTRACEUTICAL INTERNATIONAL CORPORATION; *pg.* 1576, *pg.* 1753
PEACH - Tobacco Product - AMERICAN SNUFF COMPANY; *pg.* 1893, *pg.* 1641
PEACH APRICOT HONEYBUSH - Herb Tea - CELESTIAL SEASONINGS, INC.; *pg.* 846, *pg.* 310
PEACH DRIFT - Garden Roses - THE CONARD-PYLE COMPANY; *pg.* 1794, *pg.* 1594
PEACH PERFECTION - Fruit Drink - JAMBA, INC.; *pg.* 1024, *pg.* 84
PEACH PLEASURE - Fruit Drink - JAMBA, INC.; *pg.* 1024, *pg.* 84
PEACH SWEET - Snuff Tobacco - AMERICAN SNUFF COMPANY; *pg.* 1893, *pg.* 1641
PEACHEY - Tobacco Product - AMERICAN SNUFF COMPANY; *pg.* 1893, *pg.* 1641
PEACHSKIN - Eyebag - HUGGER MUGGER YOGA PRODUCTS LLC; *pg.* 1836, *pg.* 1758
PEACHTREE - Fabric - NEMSCHOFF, INC.; *pg.* 936, *pg.* 1890
PEACHTREE ACCOUNTING 2004 - Accounting Software Best Suited for Small Businesses - SAGE SOFTWARE, INC.; *pg.* 464, *pg.* 116
PEACHTREE COMPLETE ACCOUNTING 2004 - Accounting Software Best Suited for Small Businesses - SAGE SOFTWARE, INC.; *pg.* 464, *pg.* 116
PEACHTREE FIRST ACCOUNTING 2004 - Accounting Software Best Suited for Home Offices with One to Five Employees - SAGE SOFTWARE, INC.; *pg.* 464, *pg.* 116
PEACHY - Air Freshener - SWISHER HYGIENE INC.; *pg.* 336, *pg.* 1507
PEACOCK - Premium Art Paper - PACON CORPORATION; *pg.* 1466, *pg.* 1852
PEACOCK PAYS - Video Game - INTERNATIONAL GAME TECHNOLOGY; *pg.* 957, *pg.* 1024
PEAK - Anti-Freeze - OLD WORLD INDUSTRIES, INC.; *pg.* 1175, *pg.* 641
PEAK - Steam Turbine Control System - WOODWARD, INC.; *pg.* 122, *pg.* 329
PEAK DISTRICT - Carpet - INTERFACE, INC.; *pg.* 695, *pg.* 512
THE PEAK OF PERFECTION IN HANDMADE CHOCOLATES - Slogan - ROCKY MOUNTAIN CHOCOLATE FACTORY, INC.; *pg.* 1032, *pg.* 324
PEAKFLOW - Molecular Probe Product - THERMO FISHER SCIENTIFIC INC.; *pg.* 1602, *pg.* 61
PEAKS - Key Control Systems - KABA ILCO CORP.; *pg.* 1052, *pg.* 1390
PEAKSWITCH - Switcher IC - POWER INTEGRATIONS, INC.; *pg.* 1369, *pg.* 249
PEANUT BUTTER BUCKET - Chocolates - ROCKY MOUNTAIN CHOCOLATE FACTORY, INC.; *pg.* 1032, *pg.* 324
PEANUT BUTTER CHEERIOS - Cereal - GENERAL MILLS, INC.; *pg.* 828, *pg.* 933
PEANUT BUTTER MOO'D - Fruit Drink - JAMBA, INC.; *pg.* 1024, *pg.* 84
PEANUT BUTTER PAILS - Chocolate Candy - ROCKY MOUNTAIN CHOCOLATE FACTORY, INC.; *pg.* 1032, *pg.* 324
PEANUT BUTTER PANIC - Ice Cream - WELLS ENTERPRISES, INC.; *pg.* 909, *pg.* 709
PEANUT SELECT - Food Product - BUNGE LIMITED; *pg.* 842, *pg.* 1351
THE PEANUT SHOP OF WILLIAMSBURG - Food Products - SMITHFIELD FOODS, INC.; *pg.* 896, *pg.* 1806
PEAPOD - Online Grocery Shopping Service - PEAPOD, LLC; *pg.* 1029, *pg.* 661
PEAR BLOSSOM - Rice - AMERICAN RICE, INC.; *pg.* 837, *pg.* 1700
PEAR FANTASY - Fragrance - PARFUMS DE COEUR LTD.; *pg.* 519, *pg.* 376
PEARBEAR - Spokes Character Introducing Children to the Benefits of Eating Healthy - PEAR BUREAU NORTHWEST; *pg.* 153, *pg.* 1500
PEARCE - Fabric - NEMSCHOFF, INC.; *pg.* 936, *pg.* 1890
PEARL - Skin Treatment - CUTERA, INC.; *pg.* 1521, *pg.* 49
PEARL - Gaming Product - GLD PRODUCTS, INC.; *pg.* 1835, *pg.* 1882
PEARL - Soy Milk - KIKKOMAN INTERNATIONAL INC.; *pg.* 868, *pg.* 220
PEARL - Beer - PABST BREWING COMPANY; *pg.* 258, *pg.* 137
PEARL - Personal Care Product - WESTROCK COMPANY; *pg.* 1472, *pg.* 1805
PEARL - Wood & Building Material - WEYERHAEUSER COMPANY; *pg.* 121, *pg.* 1820
PEARL BAY - Video Game - INTERNATIONAL GAME TECHNOLOGY; *pg.* 957, *pg.* 1024
PEARL DROPS - Toothpaste - CHURCH & DWIGHT CO., INC.; *pg.* 1153, *pg.* 1063
PEARL FRACTIONAL - Skin Treatment - CUTERA, INC.; *pg.* 1521, *pg.* 49
PEARL HUNTER - Entertainment Services - YAHOO! INC.; *pg.* 1289, *pg.* 289
PEARL-KOTE - Paperboard Packaging System - GRAPHIC PACKAGING HOLDING COMPANY; *pg.* 1459, *pg.* 509
PEARLBRITE - Chemical Coating - ENTHONE INC.; *pg.* 1161, *pg.* 381
PEARLCORDER - Microcassette Recorders, Dictators & Transcribers - OLYMPUS AMERICA INC.; *pg.* 1425, *pg.* 1521
PEARLDRY - Printing Plate - PRESSTEK LLC; *pg.* 1678, *pg.* 1034
PEARLE VISION - Eyeglass & Contact Lens Retailer - LUXOTTICA RETAIL; *pg.* 8, *pg.* 1460
PEARLIZED - Paper - CANDID COLOR SYSTEMS, INC.; *pg.* 1404, *pg.* 1485
PEARLIZED ELEGANCE - Software - XEROX CORPORATION; *pg.* 494, *pg.* 365
PEARLS - Wall Decor - HERITAGE LACE INC.; *pg.* 694, *pg.* 711
PEARLS - Olives - MUSCO FAMILY OLIVE COMPANY; *pg.* 882, *pg.* 297
PEARONA - Beverages - THE COCA-COLA COMPANY; *pg.* 240, *pg.* 493
PEARSON PASERIES - Educational Software - PEARSON ASSESSMENTS; *pg.* 1674, *pg.* 918
PEARSON TEST ITEM BANKS - Educational Software - PEARSON ASSESSMENTS; *pg.* 1674, *pg.* 918
PEARSON'S NIPS - Food Product - NESTLE USA, INC.; *pg.* 883, *pg.* 96
PEAS IN A POD - Video Game - INTERNATIONAL GAME TECHNOLOGY; *pg.* 957, *pg.* 1024
PEATS RIDGE - Beverages - THE COCA-COLA COMPANY; *pg.* 240, *pg.* 493
PEAVEY MAX - Musical Instrument - PEAVEY ELECTRONICS CORPORATION; *pg.* 662, *pg.* 970
PEBBLE - Window Treatment - CROSCILL, INC.; *pg.* 1122, *pg.* 1220
PEBBLE BEACH - Fabric - NEMSCHOFF, INC.; *pg.* 936, *pg.* 1890
PEBBLE OPTIC - Tumbler & Pitchers - CARLISLE FOODSERVICE PRODUCTS INCORPORATED; *pg.* 1455, *pg.* 1485
PEBL - Telephones - MOTOROLA SOLUTIONS, INC.; *pg.* 657, *pg.* 659
PECAN CRUSTED SPLASH! - Seafood - CLEAR SPRINGS FOODS, INC.; *pg.* 848, *pg.* 548
PECO PAK - Memory Disc Pack - PECO, INC.; *pg.* 1368, *pg.* 1505
PECOBACK - Latex Compounds - THE DOW CHEMICAL COMPANY; *pg.* 1157, *pg.* 898
PECORA - Sealants & Adhesives - PECORA CORPORATION; *pg.* 1444, *pg.* 1536
PECOS - Resistor - OHMITE MANUFACTURING COMPANY; *pg.* 660, *pg.* 553
PECOS DIAMOND STEAKHOUSE - Restaurant - STAR BUFFET, INC.; *pg.* 1751, *pg.* 24
PEDAL - Shoe - AEROGROUP INTERNATIONAL, INC.; *pg.* 1803, *pg.* 1055
PEDAL-UP! - Replacement Parts - DORMAN PRODUCTS, INC.; *pg.* 204, *pg.* 1522
PEDASTOOL - Furniture - HERMAN MILLER, INC.; *pg.* 926, *pg.* 913
PEDBED - Footwear Product - DECKERS OUTDOOR CORPORATION; *pg.* 1807, *pg.* 100
PEDESTAL - Polymer Product - CHEMTURA CORPORATION; *pg.* 1152, *pg.* 355
PEDESTAL BREAKER - Stationary Mounted Breaker System - ALLIED CONSTRUCTION PRODUCTS, LLC; *pg.* 1311, *pg.* 1427
PEDESTRIAN-VU - Light Communication System - RITE-HITE HOLDING CORPORATION; *pg.* 1372, *pg.* 1880
PEDI BLUE II - Resuscitators - VITAL SIGNS, INC.; *pg.* 1607, *pg.* 1126
PEDI COMFY - Pediatric Orthotics - ALIMED, INC.; *pg.* 1490, *pg.* 816
PEDI PADZ - Electrode System - ZOLL MEDICAL CORPORATION; *pg.* 1612, *pg.* 814
PEDI-SOX - Pedicure Accessory - TWEEZERMAN INTERNATIONAL; *pg.* 524, *pg.* 1324
PEDIACARE - Children's Cough & Cold Medicine - MCNEIL-PPC, INC.; *pg.* 1560, *pg.* 1533
PEDIALYTE - Nutritional Supplement - ABBOTT LABORATORIES; *pg.* 1484, *pg.* 551
PEDIALYTE - Oral Electrolyte Solution - ABBOTT NUTRITION; *pg.* 1485, *pg.* 1437
PEDIASURE - Nutritional Supplement - ABBOTT

LABORATORIES; *pg.* 1484, *pg.* 551
PEDIASURE - Children's Nutritionals & Snacks - ABBOTT NUTRITION; *pg.* 1485, *pg.* 1437
PEDIATRIC - Peritoneal Dialyzer - BAXTER INTERNATIONAL INC.; *pg.* 1499, *pg.* 599
PEDIATRIC COMFY - Pediatric Orthotics - ALIMED, INC.; *pg.* 1490, *pg.* 816
PEDIATRIC SLIMLINE - Pediatric Orthotics - ALIMED, INC.; *pg.* 1490, *pg.* 816
PEDIDYNE - Critical Care Therapy System - KINETIC CONCEPTS, INC.; *pg.* 1553, *pg.* 1741
PEDIGREE - Petcare Product - MARS, INCORPORATED; *pg.* 1858, *pg.* 1792
PEDIGREE - Dog Food - MARS PETCARE; *pg.* 1478, *pg.* 1633
PEDIGREE DENTABONE - Dog Food - MARS, INCORPORATED; *pg.* 1858, *pg.* 1792
PEDIGREE MEATY BITES - Dog Food - MARS, INCORPORATED; *pg.* 1858, *pg.* 1792
PEDIGREE OPTIMUM - Dog Food - MARS, INCORPORATED; *pg.* 1858, *pg.* 1792
PEDIGREE PAL - Dog Food - MARS, INCORPORATED; *pg.* 1858, *pg.* 1792
PEDINI - Footwear - CAPEZIO BALLET MAKERS INC.; *pg.* 1805, *pg.* 1125
PEDINOVA III - Nailcare Product - MEDICOOL, INC.; *pg.* 1562, *pg.* 294
PEDIOTIC - Pharmaceutical Product - KING PHARMACEUTICALS, INC.; *pg.* 1553, *pg.* 1627
PEDISPHYG - Neonatal Product - CAS MEDICAL SYSTEMS, INC.; *pg.* 1513, *pg.* 339
PEDLAR - Light Workout Exerciser - BATTLE CREEK EQUIPMENT CO.; *pg.* 1499, *pg.* 870
PEDRERA - Fabric - NEMSCHOFF, INC.; *pg.* 936, *pg.* 1890
PEEBLES - Apparel Store - STAGE STORES, INC.; *pg.* 33, *pg.* 1715
PEEK - Office Furniture - STEELCASE INC.; *pg.* 475, *pg.* 889
PEEK BARSTOOL - Office Furniture - STEELCASE INC.; *pg.* 475, *pg.* 889
PEEL & STICK APPLY-R - Automatic Peel & Stick Closure Applicator - BEDFORD INDUSTRIES, INC.; *pg.* 1453, *pg.* 967
PEEL & SEAL - Plastics Product - AEP INDUSTRIES INC.; *pg.* 1878, *pg.* 1085
PEEL&SEAL - Silicone Foam - A.W. CHESTERTON COMPANY; *pg.* 1315, *pg.* 861
PEEL & STICK - Pressure Sensitive Closures - BEDFORD INDUSTRIES, INC.; *pg.* 1453, *pg.* 967
PEEL AND STICK - Wired Closure - BEDFORD INDUSTRIES, INC.; *pg.* 1453, *pg.* 967
PEEL-AWAY - Introducer Set - COOK GROUP, INC.; *pg.* 1518, *pg.* 674
PEEL IT - Home Products - HABAND COMPANY, INC.; *pg.* 1772, *pg.* 1099
PEEL N' SHIELD - Gasket - W.L. GORE & ASSOCIATES, INC.; *pg.* 122, *pg.* 388
PEEL N' STICK - Hook & Helper - HOME PRODUCTS INTERNATIONAL, INC.; *pg.* 1125, *pg.* 577
PEEL PAK - Packaging Product - GRAPHIC PACKAGING HOLDING COMPANY; *pg.* 1459, *pg.* 509
PEEL STOP - Sundry - KELLY-MOORE PAINT COMPANY, INC.; *pg.* 1443, *pg.* 198
PEELPRO - Electrosurgical Devices - ANGIODYNAMICS, INC.; *pg.* 1495, *pg.* 1173
PEEPS - Seasonal Marshmallow Candies - JUST BORN, INC.; *pg.* 1857, *pg.* 1516
PEERLESS - Lighting Fixture Product - ACUITY BRANDS, INC.; *pg.* 1294, *pg.* 487
PEERLESS - Faucets - MASCO CORPORATION; *pg.* 96, *pg.* 909
PEERVIEW - Medical Product - HOLOGIC, INC.; *pg.* 1416, *pg.* 784
PEET'S COFFEE GLOBAL JOURNEY - Coffee Club - PEET'S COFFEE & TEA, INC.; *pg.* 1029, *pg.* 85
PEET'S.COM - Coffee - PEET'S COFFEE & TEA, INC.; *pg.* 1029, *pg.* 85
PEFORMANCEPARTNER - Security Software - SYNCHRONOSS TECHNOLOGIES, INC.; *pg.* 479, *pg.* 1047
PEG-INTRON - Medicine - MERCK & CO., INC.; *pg.* 1566, *pg.* 1077
PEGA CUSTOMER PROCESS MANAGER - Software - PEGASYSTEMS INC.; *pg.* 453, *pg.* 809
PEGABANKING SMART ADJUST - Software - PEGASYSTEMS INC.; *pg.* 453, *pg.* 809
PEGABANKING SMART MONITOR - Software Product - PEGASYSTEMS INC.; *pg.* 453, *pg.* 809
PEGACARD - Software - PEGASYSTEMS INC.; *pg.* 453, *pg.* 809
PEGACSP - Software Product - PEGASYSTEMS INC.; *pg.* 453, *pg.* 809
PEGAHEALTH - Software - PEGASYSTEMS INC.; *pg.* 453, *pg.* 809
PEGAIMAGE MANAGER - Software - PEGASYSTEMS INC.; *pg.* 453, *pg.* 809
PEGAINDEX - Software Product - PEGASYSTEMS INC.; *pg.* 453, *pg.* 809
PEGAREACH - Software Product - PEGASYSTEMS INC.; *pg.* 453, *pg.* 809
PEGAREELAY - Software Product - PEGASYSTEMS INC.; *pg.* 453, *pg.* 809
PEGARESEARCH MANAGER - Software - PEGASYSTEMS INC.; *pg.* 453, *pg.* 809
PEGARULES - Software - PEGASYSTEMS INC.; *pg.* 453, *pg.* 800
PEGARULES PROCESS COMMANDER - Software Product - PEGASYSTEMS INC.; *pg.* 453, *pg.* 809
PEGASUS - Parade - KENTUCKY DERBY FESTIVAL, INC.; *pg.* 556, *pg.* 735
PEGASUS - Laboratory Equipment - LECO CORPORATION; *pg.* 1355, *pg.* 906
PEGASUS - Rocket - ORBITAL ATK; *pg.* 1425, *pg.* 1779
PEGASUS - Magazine - THE READER'S DIGEST ASSOCIATION, INC.; *pg.* 1679, *pg.* 1322
PEGASUS - Wireless System - SKYWORKS SOLUTIONS, INC.; *pg.* 674, *pg.* 862
PEGASUS - Game - WMS INDUSTRIES INC.; *pg.* 593, *pg.* 666
PEGASYS - Pharmaceutical Product - HOFFMANN-LA ROCHE INC.; *pg.* 1542, *pg.* 1099
PEGAVIEW - Software Product - PEGASYSTEMS INC.; *pg.* 453, *pg.* 809
PEGAWEB - Software Product - PEGASYSTEMS INC.; *pg.* 453, *pg.* 809
PEGAWORKBENCH - Software Product - PEGASYSTEMS INC.; *pg.* 453, *pg.* 809
PEGAWORKS - Software Product - PEGASYSTEMS INC.; *pg.* 453, *pg.* 809
PEGAWORLD - Software Product - PEGASYSTEMS INC.; *pg.* 453, *pg.* 809
PEGGI - Footwear - CAPEZIO BALLET MAKERS INC.; *pg.* 1805, *pg.* 1125
PEGGY HARCOURT - Doll - TONNER DOLL COMPANY, INC.; *pg.* 968, *pg.* 1171
PEGINTRON - Powder for Injection - MERCK & CO., INC.; *pg.* 1566, *pg.* 1077
PEGMATE - Commercial Lighting - SWIVELIER CO., INC.; *pg.* 1307, *pg.* 1142
PEGOSPERSE - Emulsifier - LONZA INC.; *pg.* 1171, *pg.* 1041
PEGSON - Crushing & Screening Equipment - TEREX CORPORATION; *pg.* 1381, *pg.* 384
PEI WEI - Restaurant - P.F. CHANG'S CHINA BISTRO, INC.; *pg.* 1030, *pg.* 24
PEI WEI ASIAN DINER - Restaurant - P.F. CHANG'S CHINA BISTRO, INC.; *pg.* 1030, *pg.* 24
PEINER - Crane - TEREX CORPORATION; *pg.* 1381, *pg.* 384
PEL/CIDS SE - High Resolution Large Character Ink Jet Printer - DIAGRAPH; *pg.* 387, *pg.* 989
PELADOW - Calcium Chloride - THE DOW CHEMICAL COMPANY; *pg.* 1157, *pg.* 898
PELASPAN - Expandable Polystyrene - THE DOW CHEMICAL COMPANY; *pg.* 1157, *pg.* 898
PELBEN - Minerals - MINERALS TECHNOLOGIES INC.; *pg.* 1173, *pg.* 617
PELHAM - Jacket - I. SPIEWAK & SONS, INC.; *pg.* 42, *pg.* 1242
PELICAN BAY - Rug - COURISTAN INC.; *pg.* 921, *pg.* 1067
PELICAN BAY NAPLES FLORIDA - Community Name - WCI COMMUNITIES, INC.; *pg.* 1118, *pg.* 414
PELICAN KINGLITE - Flashlight - PELICAN PRODUCTS, INC.; *pg.* 1842, *pg.* 295
PELICAN LANDING - Community Name - WCI COMMUNITIES, INC.; *pg.* 1118, *pg.* 414
PELICAN PAYS - Video Game - INTERNATIONAL GAME TECHNOLOGY; *pg.* 957, *pg.* 1024
PELICAN RINSER - Baby Care Product - MUNCHKIN, INC.; *pg.* 964, *pg.* 300
PELICAN SOUND - Community Name - WCI COMMUNITIES, INC.; *pg.* 1118, *pg.* 414
PELLA IMPERVIA - Duracast Fiberglass Composite Windows & Patio Doors - PELLA CORPORATION; *pg.* 104, *pg.* 711
PELLA ONE-TOUCH - Storm Door - PELLA CORPORATION; *pg.* 104, *pg.* 711
PELLAQ - Paper & Nonwoven Material - FIBERMARK INC.; *pg.* 1457, *pg.* 1764
PELLA'S PRECISION FIT - Window - PELLA CORPORATION; *pg.* 104, *pg.* 711
PELLER ESTATES - Wine - ANDREW PELLER LIMITED; *pg.* 1956, *pg.* 1920
PELLER ESTATES CANADA - Wines and Spirits - LEONARD KREUSCH, INC.; *pg.* 254, *pg.* 1099
PELLETHANE - Chemical Product - THE DOW CHEMICAL COMPANY; *pg.* 1157, *pg.* 898
PELLETHANE - Thermoplastic Polyurethanes - THE LUBRIZOL CORPORATION; *pg.* 1171, *pg.* 1481
PELOPONNESE - Mediterranean Food Product - HORMEL FOODS CORPORATION; *pg.* 863, *pg.* 915
PELOUZE - Scale - NEWELL RUBBERMAID INC.; *pg.* 1128, *pg.* 515
PELS - Chemical Product - PPG INDUSTRIES, INC.; *pg.* 1445, *pg.* 1579
PELUCAS - Ice Cream Bar - WELLS ENTERPRISES, INC.; *pg.* 909, *pg.* 709
PELVIC BLOCKS BY CORE - Cervical Pillow - DYNATRONICS CORPORATION; *pg.* 1526, *pg.* 1757
PEM - Controller - HINDS INSTRUMENTS, INC.; *pg.* 1416, *pg.* 1498
PEM - Fastener Product - PENN ENGINEERING & MANUFACTURING CORP.; *pg.* 1059, *pg.* 1525
PEM-90 - Photoelastic Modulator Systems - HINDS INSTRUMENTS, INC.; *pg.* 1416, *pg.* 1498
PEMCO - Casters & Wheels - STANDEX INTERNATIONAL CORPORATION; *pg.* 60, *pg.* 1039
PEMFLEX - Self-Locking Fastener - PENN ENGINEERING & MANUFACTURING CORP.; *pg.* 1059, *pg.* 1525
PEMHEX - Self-Locking Fastener - PENN ENGINEERING & MANUFACTURING CORP.; *pg.* 1059, *pg.* 1525
PEMKOHINGE - Threshold Product - RELIABLE AUTOMATIC SPRINKLER CO., INC.; *pg.* 1137, *pg.* 1158
PEMMICAN - Food Product - CONAGRA FOODS, INC.; *pg.* 826, *pg.* 1014
PEMSERT - Flush Fastener - PENN ENGINEERING & MANUFACTURING CORP.; *pg.* 1059, *pg.* 1525
PEMSERTER - Press - PENN ENGINEERING & MANUFACTURING CORP.; *pg.* 1059, *pg.* 1525
PEMSERTER 2000 - Automatic Press System - PENNENGINEERING FASTENING TECHNOLOGIES; *pg.* 1059, *pg.* 1526
PEMSERTER LT4 - Manual Press - PENNENGINEERING FASTENING TECHNOLOGIES; *pg.* 1059, *pg.* 1526
PEMSERTER MICROMATE - Micromate - PENNENGINEERING FASTENING TECHNOLOGIES; *pg.* 1059, *pg.* 1526
PEMSERTER PLUS - Self-Clinching Fastener Feeding System - PENNENGINEERING FASTENING TECHNOLOGIES; *pg.* 1059, *pg.* 1526
PEMSERTER SERIES 4 - Manual Press - PENNENGINEERING FASTENING TECHNOLOGIES; *pg.* 1059, *pg.* 1526
PEMSERTER SERIES B49 - Press System - PENNENGINEERING FASTENING TECHNOLOGIES; *pg.* 1059, *pg.* 1526
PEMSERTER SERIES P3 - Portable Hand Held Pressing Tool - PENNENGINEERING FASTENING TECHNOLOGIES; *pg.* 1059, *pg.* 1526
PEMSERTER TNT618 - Turret Nut Tool - PENNENGINEERING FASTENING TECHNOLOGIES; *pg.* 1059, *pg.* 1526
PEMSERTER TRU-MOTION - Automated Positioning Systems - PENNENGINEERING FASTENING TECHNOLOGIES; *pg.* 1059, *pg.* 1526
PEMULEN - Polymeric Emulsifiers - THE LUBRIZOL CORPORATION; *pg.* 1171, *pg.* 1481
PEN DIP - Metal Finishing Product - HEATBATH CORPORATION; *pg.* 1165, *pg.* 826
PEN KARB - Carburizing Product - HEATBATH CORPORATION; *pg.* 1165, *pg.* 826
PEN PRO - Flashlight - ENERGIZER HOLDINGS, INC.; *pg.* 637, *pg.* 996
PEN-RAY - Light Source - UVP, INC.; *pg.* 1434, *pg.* 298
PENAFIEL - Carbonated Soft Drink - DR PEPPER SNAPPLE GROUP, INC.; *pg.* 250, *pg.* 1729
PENAIR HD-1 RTU - Aircraft Cleaner - PENETONE

First page reference indicates Business Class Edition
Second page reference indicates Geographic Edition

CORPORATION; pg. 333, pg. 1050
PENAIR HD-4 RTU - Aircraft Spot Cleaner - PENETONE CORPORATION; pg. 333, pg. 1050
PENAIR M5572B RTU - Phosphate-Free Aircraft Cleaner - PENETONE CORPORATION; pg. 333, pg. 1050
PENBIND - Ingredient System - PENFORD CORPORATION; pg. 1177, pg. 314
PENBLAST 214M - Cleaner & Brightener - PENETONE CORPORATION; pg. 333, pg. 1050
PENBLAST 322L - Cleaner & Brightener - PENETONE CORPORATION; pg. 333, pg. 1050
PENBLAST 510M - Cleaner & Brightener - PENETONE CORPORATION; pg. 333, pg. 1050
PENCIL - Stand Bag - CALLAWAY GOLF COMPANY; pg. 1829, pg. 58
PENCLING - Ingredient System - PENFORD CORPORATION; pg. 1177, pg. 314
PENDAFLEX - Hanging File Folders - ESSELTE BUSINESS CORP; pg. 395, pg. 1179
PENDALINER - Truck Bedliner - PENDA CORPORATION; pg. 214, pg. 1887
PENDALYTE - Lighting - STEELCASE INC.; pg. 475, pg. 889
PENDENNIS - Table - BLATT BOWLING & BILLIARD CORP.; pg. 1827, pg. 1203
PENDLETON - Shirt - PENDLETON WOOLEN MILLS, INC.; pg. 697, pg. 1505
PENDLETON 10 YEAR CANADIAN WHISKY - Distilled Spirits - HOOD RIVER DISTILLERS INC.; pg. 1964, pg. 1498
PENE-LUBE - Penetrating Lubricant - DOW CORNING CORPORATION; pg. 1159, pg. 900
PENEFELD - Mattress - THERAPEDIC ASSOCIATES, INC.; pg. 945, pg. 1112
PENELOPE - Furniture - AMISCO INDUSTRIES LTD.; pg. 913, pg. 1958
PENELOPE - Leather Products - COACH, INC.; pg. 3, pg. 1214
PENELOPE - Fabric - SCALAMANDRE, INC.; pg. 941, pg. 1058
PENEPREP - Exterior Wood Prep - AKZO NOBEL DECORATIVE PAINTS, USA; pg. 1439, pg. 1474
PENETONE - Chemicals & Allied Products - PENETONE CORPORATION; pg. 333, pg. 1050
PENETONE AFW1 - Wire Cleaner - PENETONE CORPORATION; pg. 333, pg. 1050
PENETONE ET - Solvent Emulsion Cleaner - PENETONE CORPORATION; pg. 333, pg. 1050
PENETRANT PLUS - Rust Preventive - SLIDE PRODUCTS, INC.; pg. 1181, pg. 670
PENETRATOR - Cable & Antenna System - RADIO FREQUENCY SYSTEMS, INC.; pg. 666, pg. 354
PENETROL - Coating & Paint - AKZO NOBEL DECORATIVE PAINTS, USA; pg. 1439, pg. 1474
PENFLEX - Flexible Metal Hose - PENFLEX, INC.; pg. 104, pg. 1534
PENFLEX - Ingredient System - PENFORD CORPORATION; pg. 1177, pg. 314
PENFORD - Ingredient System - PENFORD CORPORATION; pg. 1177, pg. 314
PENGLOSS - Coating Binder - PENFORD CORPORATION; pg. 1177, pg. 314
PENGUIN - Food Product - BUNGE LIMITED; pg. 842, pg. 1351
THE PENGUIN - Character - DC COMICS, INC.; pg. 1633, pg. 1221
PENGUIN SPORT - Apparel - PERRY ELLIS INTERNATIONAL, INC.; pg. 45, pg. 445
PENICILLINN G PROCAINE - Injectable Suspension - KING PHARMACEUTICALS, INC.; pg. 1553, pg. 1627
PENINSULA - Furniture - HOOKER FURNITURE CORPORATION; pg. 928, pg. 1788
PENINSULA - Ceiling Fan - HUNTER FAN COMPANY; pg. 57, pg. 1631
PENINSULA - Fireplaces - LENNOX HEARTH PRODUCTS; pg. 93, pg. 1652
PENINSULA - Furniture - STANLEY FURNITURE CO., INC.; pg. 943, pg. 1379
PENN BOND - Embroidery - THE PENN COMPANIES; pg. 10, pg. 1568
PENN NATIONAL GAMING, INC. - Games - PENN NATIONAL GAMING, INC.; pg. 574, pg. 1595
PENN NATIONAL RACE COURSE - Racetrack - PENN NATIONAL GAMING, INC.; pg. 574, pg. 1595
PENN SEAL - Identification Products - THE PENN COMPANIES; pg. 10, pg. 1568
PENN STATE TEXTILES - Occupational Apparel - V.F. CORPORATION; pg. 34, pg. 1376
PENN TEXT - Fabric Print Emblem - THE PENN COMPANIES; pg. 10, pg. 1568
PENNANT - Glace (Candied Fruit) - PARADISE, INC.; pg. 888, pg. 458
PENNANTS - Pennant - BROWN & BIGELOW, INC.; pg. 1624, pg. 959
PENNEMBLEM - Emblem - THE PENN COMPANIES; pg. 10, pg. 1568
PENNIES PER CALL! - Communication Product - CENTURYLINK, INC; pg. 1870, pg. 317
PENNMULCH - Seed Accelerator - LEBANON SEABOARD CORPORATION; pg. 1797, pg. 1547
PENNSYLVANIA DUTCH - Noodles - AMERICAN ITALIAN PASTA COMPANY; pg. 837, pg. 980
PENNSYLVANIA SCALE - Scales - PENNSYLVANIA SCALE COMPANY; pg. 1059, pg. 1546
PENNTHANE - Hardwood Flooring - NYDREE FLOORING; pg. 939, pg. 1782
PENNTROWEL - Coatings - ARKEMA INC.; pg. 1147, pg. 1543
PENNY - Eyewear - OAKLEY, INC.; pg. 1840, pg. 86
PENNY BARN - Video Game - INTERNATIONAL GAME TECHNOLOGY; pg. 957, pg. 1024
PENNY BRITE - Porcelain Dolls - CHARISMA BRANDS, LLC; pg. 2, pg. 120
PENNY MEGABUCKS - Video Game - INTERNATIONAL GAME TECHNOLOGY; pg. 957, pg. 1024
PENNY RICHES - Video Game - INTERNATIONAL GAME TECHNOLOGY; pg. 957, pg. 1024
PENNY ROLL - Video Game - INTERNATIONAL GAME TECHNOLOGY; pg. 957, pg. 1024
PENNYSAVER - Newspaper - GAZETTE COMMUNICATIONS, INC.; pg. 1644, pg. 702
PENNYTALK - Communication Service - NET2PHONE, INC.; pg. 1269, pg. 1097
PENNZOIL - Motor Oil - SHELL LUBRICANTS; pg. 217, pg. 1714
PENPLUS - Potato Starch - PENFORD CORPORATION; pg. 1177, pg. 314
PENPLUS CASE - Healthcare Product - MEDICOOL, INC.; pg. 1562, pg. 294
PENROSE - Furniture - ASHLEY FURNITURE INDUSTRIES, INC.; pg. 914, pg. 1852
PENROSE - Food Product - CONAGRA FOODS, INC.; pg. 826, pg. 1014
PENSIONS & INVESTMENTS - Newspaper - CRAIN COMMUNICATIONS, INC.; pg. 1631, pg. 879
PENSIZE - Ingredient System - PENFORD CORPORATION; pg. 1177, pg. 314
PENSKE - Automotive Group - PENSKE AUTOMOTIVE GROUP, INC.; pg. 188, pg. 873
PENSOLV L805 - Cleaner - PENETONE CORPORATION; pg. 333, pg. 1050
PENSOLV L945 - Cleaner - PENETONE CORPORATION; pg. 333, pg. 1050
PENSOLV SAFE 100 - Cleaner - PENETONE CORPORATION; pg. 333, pg. 1050
PENSOLV SAFE 101 - Cleaner - PENETONE CORPORATION; pg. 333, pg. 1050
PENSOLV SAFE PB2000 - Cleaner - PENETONE CORPORATION; pg. 333, pg. 1050
PENSOLVE SAFE 150 - Cleaner - PENETONE CORPORATION; pg. 333, pg. 1050
PENTA - Heavy Body Impression Material - 3M COMPANY; pg. 1142, pg. 956
PENTA - Musical Instrument - PEAVEY ELECTRONICS CORPORATION; pg. 662, pg. 970
PENTA-CAT - Catalyst Additive - JOHNSON MATTHEY PROCESS TECHNOLOGIES; pg. 1169, pg. 1083
PENTA-CAT HP - Enhancement Additive - JOHNSON MATTHEY PROCESS TECHNOLOGIES; pg. 1169, pg. 1083
PENTA-CAT PLUS - Enhancement Additive - JOHNSON MATTHEY PROCESS TECHNOLOGIES; pg. 1169, pg. 1083
PENTA-CHANGE - Electronic Components - MOLEX INCORPORATED; pg. 655, pg. 628
PENTA-HIS - Molecular Probe Product - THERMO FISHER SCIENTIFIC INC.; pg. 1602, pg. 61
PENTA-LATCH - Tamper Resistant Door Latching Mechanism - S&C ELECTRIC COMPANY; pg. 1305, pg. 589
PENTABEAD - Sodium Metasilicate - PQ CORPORATION; pg. 1178, pg. 1515
PENTAC - Bevel Product - GLEASON CORPORATION; pg. 1340, pg. 1335
PENTAFLEX - Paint And Stain Product - BENJAMIN MOORE & CO.; pg. 1440, pg. 1085
PENTAGON - Paper Product - BOISE CASCADE HOLDINGS, L.L.C.; pg. 1453, pg. 546
PENTAGON PROTECTION - Power Inverters - COBRA ELECTRONICS CORPORATION; pg. 629, pg. 572
PENTALUMEN - Medical Device - HOSPIRA, INC.; pg. 1542, pg. 623
PENTALYN - Synthetic Resins - EASTMAN CHEMICAL COMPANY; pg. 1159, pg. 1636
PENTAMIX - Mixing Unit - 3M COMPANY; pg. 1142, pg. 956
PENTAPHAN - Adhesive & Sealant - DOW CHEMICAL; pg. 1156, pg. 1563
PENTASCOPE - Medical Instrument - WALLACH SURGICAL DEVICES, INC.; pg. 1436, pg. 381
PENTASTAR - Medical Instrument - WALLACH SURGICAL DEVICES, INC.; pg. 1436, pg. 381
PENTASTAR ONE - Plating Process - A BRITE COMPANY; pg. 1144, pg. 1697
PENTATONE - Musical Instrument - PEAVEY ELECTRONICS CORPORATION; pg. 662, pg. 970
PENTAX - Endoscopy Equipment - PENTAX MEDICAL COMPANY; pg. 1580, pg. 1086
PENTE - Game - WINNING MOVES GAMES, INC.; pg. 970, pg. 816
PENTECH - Writing Instrument - JAKKS PACIFIC, INC.; pg. 960, pg. 142
PENTEL R.S.V.P. - Ball Point Pen - PENTEL OF AMERICA, LTD.; pg. 453, pg. 295
PENTHOUSE - Magazine - FRIENDFINDER NETWORKS INC.; pg. 1643, pg. 411
THE PENTHOUSE COLLECTION - Community Name - WCI COMMUNITIES, INC.; pg. 1118, pg. 414
PENTHOUSE LETTERS - Magazine - FRIENDFINDER NETWORKS INC.; pg. 1643, pg. 411
PENTHOUSE SKI WEAR - Ski Wear - RELIABLE OF MILWAUKEE; pg. 698, pg. 1879
PENTR - Restriction Cloning - THERMO FISHER SCIENTIFIC INC.; pg. 1602, pg. 61
PENTRATE - Metal Finishing Product - HEATBATH CORPORATION; pg. 1165, pg. 826
PENTREX - Multi-Purpose Fertilizer - THE WOODSTREAM CORPORATION; pg. 1801, pg. 1549
PENZYM - Food Safety Product - NEOGEN CORPORATION; pg. 883, pg. 896
PENZYME - Food Safety Product - NEOGEN CORPORATION; pg. 883, pg. 896
PEONIES AND IVY - Bath Product - KOHLER CO.; pg. 91, pg. 1862
PEOPLE - Media Publication - TIME INC.; pg. 1693, pg. 1300
THE PEOPLE BEHIND EGOVERNMENT - Slogan - NIC INC.; pg. 445, pg. 718
THE PEOPLE BEHIND THE SCIENCE - Software - BIO-RAD LABORATORIES, INC.; pg. 1504, pg. 101
PEOPLE BUILDING BRANDS - Slogan - SHAW ROSS INTERNATIONAL IMPORTERS; pg. 1970, pg. 449
THE PEOPLE DEVELOPMENT PEOPLE - Slogan - CPP, INC.; pg. 1631, pg. 153
PEOPLE EN ESPANOL - Magazine - PEOPLE MAGAZINE; pg. 1676, pg. 1278
PEOPLE EN ESPANOL - Media Publication - TIME INC.; pg. 1693, pg. 1300
PEOPLE FINDING A BETTER WAY - Slogan - DANA HOLDING CORPORATION; pg. 203, pg. 1461
PEOPLE MAGAZINE - Magaziine - PEOPLE MAGAZINE; pg. 1676, pg. 1278
PEOPLE OF CHRIST WITH THE MESSAGE OF HOPE - Tag Line - INTERNATIONAL LUTHERAN LAYMEN'S LEAGUE; pg. 293, pg. 998
PEOPLE ON CONTENT - Collaboration Technology - POLYCOM, INC.; pg. 664, pg. 249
PEOPLE STYLEWATCH - Media Publication - TIME INC.; pg. 1693, pg. 1300
PEOPLEPLUS CONTENT - Video Conferencing Product - POLYCOM, INC.; pg. 664, pg. 249
PEOPLE'S CHOICE - Game - MULTIMEDIA GAMES INC.; pg. 442, pg. 1664
PEOPLESENSOR - Machine Vision System - COGNEX CORPORATION; pg. 1406, pg. 834
PEOPLESOFT ENTERPRISE - Software - ORACLE CORPORATION; pg. 450, pg. 191
PEP - Interactive Touch Display - INDUSTRIAL ELECTRONIC ENGINEERS, INC.; pg. 644, pg. 300

PEP - Educational Products - POLAROID CORPORATION; *pg.* 1426, *pg.* 815
PEP-BACK - Pharmaceutical Product - ALVA/AMCO PHARMACAL COMPANIES, INC.; *pg.* 1492, *pg.* 637
PEP IRIDIA - Automated Wafer Fabrication System - LAM RESEARCH CORPORATION; *pg.* 1354, *pg.* 246
PEP RALLY - Shoe - AEROGROUP INTERNATIONAL, INC.; *pg.* 1803, *pg.* 1055
PEP SET - Foundry Resin - ASHLAND INC.; *pg.* 972, *pg.* 726
PEPAC - Software - GULF PUBLISHING COMPANY; *pg.* 1646, *pg.* 1707
PEPCID - Healthcare Product - JOHNSON & JOHNSON; *pg.* 1549, *pg.* 1091
PEPCID - Pharmaceutical Product - SALIX PHARMACEUTICALS, INC.; *pg.* 1591, *pg.* 1388
PEPCID AC - Heartburn Relief - JOHNSON & JOHNSON - MERCK CONSUMER PHARMACEUTICALS CO.; *pg.* 1552, *pg.* 1533
PEPCID COMPLETE - Heartburn Relief - JOHNSON & JOHNSON - MERCK CONSUMER PHARMACEUTICALS CO.; *pg.* 1552, *pg.* 1533
PEPE LOPEZ - Tequilas - BROWN-FORMAN CORPORATION; *pg.* 1958, *pg.* 732
PEPE'S - Snack Food Product - RUDOLPH FOODS COMPANY; *pg.* 892, *pg.* 1458
PEPGEN - Dental Product - DENTSPLY INTERNATIONAL INC.; *pg.* 1522, *pg.* 1596
PEPGEN P-15 - Dental Product - DENTSPLY INTERNATIONAL INC.; *pg.* 1522, *pg.* 1596
PEPPADEW - Sweet Picante Fruit - STROHMEYER & ARPE COMPANY; *pg.* 899, *pg.* 1042
PEPPER - Personal Defense Sprays - MACE SECURITY INTERNATIONAL, INC.; *pg.* 1172, *pg.* 1541
PEPPER GEL - Security & Law Enforcement Products - MACE SECURITY INTERNATIONAL, INC.; *pg.* 1172, *pg.* 1541
PEPPER MACE - Security & Law Enforcement Products - MACE SECURITY INTERNATIONAL, INC.; *pg.* 1172, *pg.* 1541
PEPPER MILL - Dressings & Sauces - GORDON FOOD SERVICE INC.; *pg.* 1021, *pg.* 913
PEPPER SPRAY - Personal Defense Sprays - MACE SECURITY INTERNATIONAL, INC.; *pg.* 1172, *pg.* 1541
PEPPERCORN - Oil & Spray - AROMATIQUE INC.; *pg.* 499, *pg.* 32
PEPPERDINE - Footwear - EASTLAND SHOE CORPORATION; *pg.* 1808, *pg.* 750
PEPPERFEST - Service - MCILHENNY COMPANY; *pg.* 876, *pg.* 741
PEPPERGARD - Security & Law Enforcement Products - MACE SECURITY INTERNATIONAL, INC.; *pg.* 1172, *pg.* 1541
PEPPERIDGE FARM - Baked Goods - CAMPBELL SOUP COMPANY; *pg.* 844, *pg.* 1048
PEPPERIDGE FARM - Fresh & Frozen Bakery & Food Products - PEPPERIDGE FARM, INC.; *pg.* 888, *pg.* 363
PEPPERIDGE FARM CARB STYLE - Food Product - PEPPERIDGE FARM, INC.; *pg.* 888, *pg.* 363
PEPPERIDGE FARM CHOCOLATE HEAVEN - Food Product - PEPPERIDGE FARM, INC.; *pg.* 888, *pg.* 363
PEPPERIDGE FARM FARMHOUSE - Food Product - PEPPERIDGE FARM, INC.; *pg.* 888, *pg.* 363
PEPPERIDGE FARM GREAT BAKES - Bakery Goods - PEPPERIDGE FARM, INC.; *pg.* 888, *pg.* 363
PEPPERMINT-GINGER PLUS - Herbal Formula - SHAKLEE CORPORATION; *pg.* 1593, *pg.* 184
PEPPERMINT HERB TEA - Tea Product - CELESTIAL SEASONINGS, INC.; *pg.* 846, *pg.* 310
PEPPERMINT STICKS - Candy - SWEET CANDY COMPANY; *pg.* 1862, *pg.* 1761
PEPPERMINTSTICK - Molecular Probe Product - THERMO FISHER SCIENTIFIC INC.; *pg.* 1602, *pg.* 61
PEPPERONI MAGNIFICO - Food Product - MARCOS PIZZA INC.; *pg.* 1737, *pg.* 1476
PEPPERONI WRAPS - Italian Dough - PIZZA INN, INC.; *pg.* 1745, *pg.* 1746
PEPPERS & ROGERS GROUP - Marketing Service - CARLSON COMPANIES INC.; *pg.* 1084, *pg.* 947
PEPSEQ - Software - WATERS CORPORATION; *pg.* 1436, *pg.* 834
PEPSI - Soft Drink - PEPSICO, INC.; *pg.* 259, *pg.* 1327
PEPSI BLUE - Soft Drink - PEPSICO, INC.; *pg.* 259, *pg.* 1327
PEPSI-COLA - Food & Beverage - PEPSICO, INC.; *pg.* 259, *pg.* 1327
PEPSI LIGHT - Soft Drink - PEPSICO, INC.; *pg.* 259, *pg.* 1327
PEPSI LIME - Flavored Cola - PEPSICO, INC.; *pg.* 259, *pg.* 1327
PEPSI LIMON - Soft Drink - PEPSICO, INC.; *pg.* 259, *pg.* 1327
PEPSI MAX - Soft Drink - PEPSICO, INC.; *pg.* 259, *pg.* 1327
PEPSI ONE - Soft Drink - PEPSICO, INC.; *pg.* 259, *pg.* 1327
PEPSI TWIST - Soft Drink - PEPSICO, INC.; *pg.* 259, *pg.* 1327
PEPSI VANILLA - Soft Drink - PEPSICO, INC.; *pg.* 259, *pg.* 1327
PEPSIECOCHALLENGE.COM - Sustainability Program - PEPSICO, INC.; *pg.* 259, *pg.* 1327
PEPSIRECYCLING.COM - Sustainability Program - PEPSICO, INC.; *pg.* 259, *pg.* 1327
PEPSODENT - Toothpaste - CHURCH & DWIGHT CO., INC.; *pg.* 1153, *pg.* 1063
PEPTAMEN - Nutrition Supplement - NESTLE USA, INC.; *pg.* 883, *pg.* 96
PEPTIC DEFENSE - Nutritional Product - NUTRACEUTICAL INTERNATIONAL CORPORATION; *pg.* 1576, *pg.* 1753
PEPTIDESELECT - Molecular Biology Product - THERMO FISHER SCIENTIFIC INC.; *pg.* 1602, *pg.* 61
PEPTIS PLUS - Sweetening Ingredient - MERISANT COMPANY; *pg.* 876, *pg.* 581
PEPTO-BISMOL - Health Care Product - THE PROCTER & GAMBLE COMPANY; *pg.* 1129, *pg.* 1418
PER-LUX - Vehicle Safety System - GROTE INDUSTRIES, INC.; *pg.* 206, *pg.* 693
PERAIDA - Footwear - STEVEN MADDEN, LTD.; *pg.* 1819, *pg.* 1176
PERAL - Chemical Product - WESTROCK COMPANY; *pg.* 1472, *pg.* 1805
PERATEX - Pressed & Monolithic Refractory - RESCO PRODUCTS, INC.; *pg.* 107, *pg.* 1581
PERATIVE - Pharmaceutical Product - ABBOTT LABORATORIES; *pg.* 1484, *pg.* 551
PERC - Protective & Decorative Coatings - FERRO CORPORATION; *pg.* 1162, *pg.* 1462
PERCEIVE - Beauty Product - AVON PRODUCTS, INC.; *pg.* 500, *pg.* 1198
PERCEPTION - Fabric - NEMSCHOFF, INC.; *pg.* 936, *pg.* 1890
PERCEPTION - Educational Software - PEARSON ASSESSMENTS; *pg.* 1674, *pg.* 918
PERCEPTRON - Automotive - PERCEPTRON, INC.; *pg.* 215, *pg.* 904
PERCH - Furniture - HERMAN MILLER, INC.; *pg.* 926, *pg.* 913
PERCHIK BUTTON - Electrosurgical Devices - ANGIODYNAMICS, INC.; *pg.* 1495, *pg.* 1173
PERCIVAL - Fabric - NEMSCHOFF, INC.; *pg.* 936, *pg.* 1890
PERCLOSE - Pharmaceutical Product - ABBOTT LABORATORIES; *pg.* 1484, *pg.* 551
PERCLUDER - Aortic Balloon & Related Parts - MAQUET; *pg.* 1558, *pg.* 1082
PERCOCET - Pharmaceutical Product - ENDO PHARMACEUTICALS HOLDINGS, INC.; *pg.* 1528, *pg.* 1549
PERCODAN - Pharmaceutical Product - ENDO PHARMACEUTICALS HOLDINGS, INC.; *pg.* 1528, *pg.* 1549
PERCOR - Intra-Aortic Balloon & Related Parts - MAQUET; *pg.* 1558, *pg.* 1082
PERCOR STAT - Intra-Aortic Balloon & Related Parts - MAQUET; *pg.* 1558, *pg.* 1082
PERCOR STAT-DL - Intra-Aortic Balloon - MAQUET; *pg.* 1558, *pg.* 1082
PERCUFLEX - Medical Device - BOSTON SCIENTIFIC CORPORATION; *pg.* 1508, *pg.* 831
PERCUSURGE - Circulatory Product - MEDTRONIC, INC.; *pg.* 1564, *pg.* 939
PERDUE DONE IT! - Fully Cooked Poultry Food Line - PERDUE FARMS INCORPORATED; *pg.* 889, *pg.* 777
PERECON - Pressed & Monolithic Refractory - RESCO PRODUCTS, INC.; *pg.* 107, *pg.* 1581
PEREGRINE GOLDEN ALE - Ale - MENDOCINO BREWING COMPANY; *pg.* 254, *pg.* 298
PERENNIAL - Carpet - BEAULIEU GROUP, LLC; *pg.* 917, *pg.* 529
PERENNIAL - Books - HARPERCOLLINS PUBLISHERS INC.; *pg.* 1647, *pg.* 1237
PERENNIAL - Fabric - MOMENTUM TEXTILES INC.; *pg.* 697, *pg.* 114
PERENNIAL - Skin Care Product - NU SKIN ENTERPRISES, INC.; *pg.* 518, *pg.* 1755
PERFCARD SMARTLINE - Card - BROWN & BIGELOW, INC.; *pg.* 1624, *pg.* 959
PERFEC GRATE - Heavy Traffic Application - REESE ENTERPRISES, INC.; *pg.* 1888, *pg.* 955
PERFEC MAT - Aluminum Hinge - REESE ENTERPRISES, INC.; *pg.* 1888, *pg.* 955
PERFEC ROLL-UP - Rollup Grate - REESE ENTERPRISES, INC.; *pg.* 1888, *pg.* 955
PERFEC VIEW - Strip Door - REESE ENTERPRISES, INC.; *pg.* 1888, *pg.* 955
PERFECFLEX - Medical Films - BEMIS HEALTHCARE PACKAGING; *pg.* 1453, *pg.* 1885
PERFECFORMS - Trays - BEMIS HEALTHCARE PACKAGING; *pg.* 1453, *pg.* 1885
PERFECRAFT - Heat Seal Coated Paper - BEMIS HEALTHCARE PACKAGING; *pg.* 1453, *pg.* 1885
PERFECSEAL - Medical Packaging Products - BEMIS HEALTHCARE PACKAGING; *pg.* 1453, *pg.* 1885
PERFECT - Software - CLEARONE COMMUNICATIONS, INC.; *pg.* 629, *pg.* 1756
PERFECT - Chair - HUMAN TOUCH; *pg.* 928, *pg.* 123
PERFECT ABS - Fitness Program - GUTHY-RENKER LLC; *pg.* 289, *pg.* 273
PERFECT BALANCE - Plant Care Product - GARDENS ALIVE!, INC.; *pg.* 1796, *pg.* 693
PERFECT BALANCE - Treatment - MARILYN MIGLIN, L.P.; *pg.* 516, *pg.* 581
THE PERFECT BALANCE OF LEARNING & PLAY - Slogan - NOBEL LEARNING COMMUNITIES, INC.; *pg.* 605, *pg.* 1593
PERFECT CENTS - Video Game - INTERNATIONAL GAME TECHNOLOGY; *pg.* 957, *pg.* 1024
PERFECT CIRCLE - Piston Rings & Pins, Camshafts, Valve Seals & Chassis Parts - DANA HOLDING CORPORATION; *pg.* 203, *pg.* 1461
PERFECT CLEANSE - Nutritional Supplement - GARDEN OF LIFE, INC.; *pg.* 1532, *pg.* 478
PERFECT CONTOUR - Mattress - KING KOIL LICENSING COMPANY INC.; *pg.* 932, *pg.* 671
PERFECT CONTOUR EXTRAORDINAIRE - Mattresses - KING KOIL LICENSING COMPANY INC.; *pg.* 932, *pg.* 671
PERFECT FOOD - Health Supplement - GARDEN OF LIFE, INC.; *pg.* 1532, *pg.* 478
PERFECT FOR EVERY OCCASION - Tagline - CHARLES & COLVARD LTD; *pg.* 3, *pg.* 1384
PERFECT GAME - Game - WMS INDUSTRIES INC.; *pg.* 593, *pg.* 666
PERFECT-IT - Foam Glaze & Pads - 3M COMPANY; *pg.* 1142, *pg.* 956
PERFECT MATCH - Game - WMS INDUSTRIES INC.; *pg.* 593, *pg.* 666
PERFECT MEAL - Dietary Supplement - GARDEN OF LIFE, INC.; *pg.* 1532, *pg.* 478
PERFECT NIGHT - Mattress & Foundation - SERTA, INC.; *pg.* 942, *pg.* 619
THE PERFECT PAIRING OF PASTA AND POTATOES - Slogan - ATEECO, INC.; *pg.* 838, *pg.* 1586
PERFECT PASS - System - BISSELL HOMECARE, INC.; *pg.* 52, *pg.* 887
THE PERFECT PEACH - Coffee - KEURIG GREEN MOUNTAIN, INC.; *pg.* 868, *pg.* 1768
PERFECT PERFORMANCE - Slacks & Shorts - HABAND COMPANY, INC.; *pg.* 1772, *pg.* 1099
PERFECT PITA - Traditional Greek Recipe Pita Bread - KRONOS PRODUCTS, INC.; *pg.* 872, *pg.* 614
PERFECT PITCH - Customer Interactive Training Product - CX ACT, INC.; *pg.* 1394, *pg.* 1773
PERFECT PLANET - Cleaning Product - WEIMAN PRODUCTS, LLC; *pg.* 337, *pg.* 616
PERFECT PLAY - Digital Media System - REALNETWORKS, INC.; *pg.* 460, *pg.* 1839
PERFECT PORTIONS - Chicken Products - PERDUE FARMS INCORPORATED; *pg.* 889, *pg.* 777
PERFECT SAMPLE - Paints - THE VALSPAR CORPORATION; *pg.* 1449, *pg.* 945
PERFECT SLEEPER - Mattress & Foundation - SERTA, INC.; *pg.* 942, *pg.* 619
PERFECT SOLUTIONS - Mattress - KING KOIL LICENSING COMPANY INC.; *pg.* 932, *pg.* 671
PERFECT START - Soil Care Product - GARDENS ALIVE!, INC.; *pg.* 1796, *pg.* 693
PERFECT SWEEP - Floor Care Product - BISSELL HOMECARE, INC.; *pg.* 52, *pg.* 887

First page reference indicates Business Class Edition
Second page reference indicates Geographic Edition

PERFECT SWEEP TURBO - Rechargeable Sweeper - BISSELL HOMECARE, INC.; pg. 52, pg. 887
PERFECT TEETH - Dental Practice - BIRNER DENTAL MANAGEMENT SERVICES, INC.; pg. 1506, pg. 317
PERFECT VALVE - Ceramic Cartridge Valve - SPEAKMAN COMPANY; pg. 112, pg. 388
PERFECT WEAR - Beauty Product - AVON PRODUCTS, INC.; pg. 500, pg. 1198
PERFECT WEIGHT - Health Supplement - GARDEN OF LIFE, INC.; pg. 1532, pg. 478
PERFECTA GOLD - Paint Brushes - DUNN-EDWARDS CORPORATION; pg. 1442, pg. 129
PERFECTAIRE - Fresh Air Exchanger - RESEARCH PRODUCTS CORPORATION; pg. 1075, pg. 1867
PERFECTBOUND - Books - HARPERCOLLINS PUBLISHERS INC.; pg. 1647, pg. 1237
PERFECTCASH - Cash Handling System - FIRE KING SECURITY GROUP; pg. 1336, pg. 696
PERFECTDISK - Software Product - RAXCO SOFTWARE, INC.; pg. 459, pg. 770
PERFECTEMP - Zone Control System/Electric Thermostat - RESEARCH PRODUCTS CORPORATION; pg. 1075, pg. 1867
PERFECTFINISH - Print Cartridge - LEXMARK INTERNATIONAL, INC.; pg. 427, pg. 730
PERFECTFLAT - Computer Monitor - VIEWSONIC CORPORATION; pg. 489, pg. 303
PERFECTING THE HEALTHCARE PACKAGE - Slogan - BEMIS HEALTHCARE PACKAGING; pg. 1453, pg. 1885
PERFECTION - Toy & Game - HASBRO, INC.; pg. 954, pg. 1603
PERFECTION - Fabric - NEMSCHOFF, INC.; pg. 936, pg. 1890
PERFECTION - Rice - RICELAND FOODS, INC.; pg. 892, pg. 36
PERFECTION - Frozen Foods - SENECA FOODS CORPORATION; pg. 895, pg. 1177
PERFECTION 600 - Color Scanner - EPSON AMERICA INC.; pg. 394, pg. 122
PERFECTIONS - Jewelry - ROMAN RESEARCH, INC.; pg. 11, pg. 824
PERFECTLY SUITED - Dresses & Sets - HABAND COMPANY, INC.; pg. 1772, pg. 1099
PERFECTO PEANUT - Popcorn Oil - VENTURA FOODS, LLC; pg. 908, pg. 49
PERFECTOE - Trouser Socks - SPANX INC.; pg. 32, pg. 520
PERFECTPAK - Child-Resistant Vial & Cap System - BERRY PLASTICS LANCASTER; pg. 1453, pg. 1546
PERFECTPORTRAIT - Computer Equipment - VIEWSONIC CORPORATION; pg. 489, pg. 303
PERFECTREACH - Ethernet Network Equipment - VITESSE SEMICONDUCTOR CORPORATION; pg. 686, pg. 57
PERFECTSOUND - Computer Equipment - VIEWSONIC CORPORATION; pg. 489, pg. 303
PERFECTSPEED - Software Product - RAXCO SOFTWARE, INC.; pg. 459, pg. 770
PERFECTUM - Glass Syringe - STOELTING CO.; pg. 1430, pg. 671
PERFECTVIEW - Computer Equipment - VIEWSONIC CORPORATION; pg. 489, pg. 303
PERFEX - Disposable Tablecloths - THE CLOROX COMPANY; pg. 327, pg. 169
PERFIX - Surgical Product - C.R. BARD, INC.; pg. 1519, pg. 1094
PERFLYTE - Lighting - STEELCASE INC.; pg. 475, pg. 889
PERFO - Laser Product - ROFIN-SINAR TECHNOLOGIES, INC.; pg. 668, pg. 904
PERFOCUT - Plastics Product - AEP INDUSTRIES INC.; pg. 1878, pg. 1085
PERFORM - Tagline - CYPRESS SEMICONDUCTOR CORPORATION; pg. 1326, pg. 243
PERFORM - Retention, Drainage & Clarification Technology - HERCULES INCORPORATED; pg. 1166, pg. 392
PERFORM - Dance/Drill Team - PERFORM GROUP, LLC; pg. 31, pg. 1597
PERFORMA - Mount - CHECKPOINT SYSTEMS, INC.; pg. 628, pg. 1559
PERFORMA - Industrial Optical Mounts - NEWPORT CORPORATION; pg. 1424, pg. 114
PERFORMANCE - Hosiery & Related Apparel - MAYER/BERKSHIRE CORPORATION; pg. 29, pg. 1129
PERFORMANCE - Nutritional Product - NUTRACEUTICAL INTERNATIONAL CORPORATION; pg. 1576, pg. 1753
PERFORMANCE - Watch - OAKLEY, INC.; pg. 1840, pg. 86
PERFORMANCE 390 - Fluid Handling System - GRACO, INC.; pg. 1342, pg. 935
PERFORMANCE ACCELERATION MODULE - Software - NETAPP, INC.; pg. 444, pg. 287
PERFORMANCE ANALYSIS - Software - BMC SOFTWARE, INC.; pg. 362, pg. 1701
PERFORMANCE ASSURANCE SUITE - Software - BMC SOFTWARE, INC.; pg. 362, pg. 1701
PERFORMANCE BLEND RUST-SOLV - Lubricant - AERVOE INDUSTRIES INCORPORATED; pg. 1439, pg. 1021
PERFORMANCE BOOST - Boost - JAMBA, INC.; pg. 1024, pg. 84
PERFORMANCE DEFINED RESULTS DELIVERED - Slogan - SYNYGY, INC.; pg. 481, pg. 1521
PERFORMANCE DESIGN - Newsprint Cores - SONOCO PRODUCTS COMPANY; pg. 1469, pg. 1619
PERFORMANCE DRIVEN - Tagline - SPARTANNASH CO.; pg. 1034, pg. 925
PERFORMANCE GEAR - Microphone - SHURE INCORPORATED; pg. 672, pg. 638
PERFORMANCE GOLD - Oil Filter - K&N ENGINEERING INC.; pg. 210, pg. 194
PERFORMANCE II - Line of Computer Enclosures - ANTEC INCORPORATED; pg. 350, pg. 90
PERFORMANCE IP - Network-Based Optimization System - INTERNAP NETWORK SERVICES CORPORATION; pg. 417, pg. 513
PERFORMANCE MANAGEMENT SUITE - Software - DELL SOFTWARE; pg. 385, pg. 40
PERFORMANCE MANAGER PORTAL - Software - BMC SOFTWARE, INC.; pg. 362, pg. 1701
PERFORMANCE MAX 395 - Fluid Handling System - GRACO, INC.; pg. 1342, pg. 935
PERFORMANCE MAX 495 - Fluid Handling System - GRACO, INC.; pg. 1342, pg. 935
PERFORMANCE. NOT PROMISES. - Slogan - PROGRESS SOFTWARE CORPORATION; pg. 457, pg. 786
PERFORMANCE PERCEIVER - Software - BMC SOFTWARE, INC.; pg. 362, pg. 1701
PERFORMANCE PLUS - Plastics Product - AEP INDUSTRIES INC.; pg. 1878, pg. 1085
PERFORMANCE PLUS - Line of Computer Enclosures - ANTEC INCORPORATED; pg. 350, pg. 90
PERFORMANCE PLUS - Computer Program - COMPUTER SCIENCES CORPORATION; pg. 378, pg. 1780
PERFORMANCE PLUS - Reconditioned Timken AP Bearing - THE TIMKEN COMPANY; pg. 218, pg. 1408
PERFORMANCE PREDICTOR - Software - BMC SOFTWARE, INC.; pg. 362, pg. 1701
PERFORMANCE RACING NETWORK - Radio Network - SPEEDWAY MOTORSPORTS, INC.; pg. 584, pg. 1370
PERFORMANCE SERIES - Fluid Handling System - GRACO, INC.; pg. 1342, pg. 935
PERFORMANCE SERIES - Software - SCANTRON CORPORATION; pg. 467, pg. 922
PERFORMANCE SUITE - Software - DELL SOFTWARE; pg. 385, pg. 40
PERFORMANCE THAT'S BUILT TO LAST - Tagline - ATTWOOD CORPORATION; pg. 1705, pg. 897
PERFORMANCE THROUGH INNOVATION - Tagline - NOVUS INTERNATIONAL, INC.; pg. 706, pg. 1001
PERFORMANCE TRACKER - Software System - IMS HEALTH, INC.; pg. 1544, pg. 344
PERFORMANCE WELDING - Slogan - HOBART BROTHERS COMPANY; pg. 1346, pg. 1477
PERFORMANCESOFT ONPERFORMANCE - Software - ACTUATE CORPORATION; pg. 342, pg. 253
PERFORMANCESOFT ROOT CAUSE ANALYSIS - Software - ACTUATE CORPORATION; pg. 342, pg. 253
PERFORMANCESOFT TRACK - Software - ACTUATE CORPORATION; pg. 342, pg. 253
PERFORMANCESOFT VIEWS - Software - ACTUATE CORPORATION; pg. 342, pg. 253
PERFORMANCEXL - Horse Feed - MANNA PRO CORPORATION; pg. 1478, pg. 975
PERFORMASURE - Software - DELL SOFTWARE; pg. 385, pg. 40
PERFORMAX - Cooling Water Treatment - ASHLAND INC.; pg. 972, pg. 726
PERFORMAX - Oil Treater Product - CAMERON INTERNATIONAL; pg. 1151, pg. 1702
PERFORMAX - Strobe Light - PHOTOGENIC PROFESSIONAL LIGHTING; pg. 1426, pg. 556
PERFORMAX MILLENNIUM - Water Treatment - ASHLAND INC.; pg. 972, pg. 726
PERFORMER - Delivery System - A-DEC, INC.; pg. 1483, pg. 1500
PERFORMER - Introducer Set - COOK GROUP, INC.; pg. 1518, pg. 674
PERFORMER - Carb & Accessory - EDELBROCK CORPORATION; pg. 204, pg. 293
PERFORMER - Routing Switcher - GRASS VALLEY, INC.; pg. 641, pg. 164
PERFORMER - Vending Service Body - HACKNEY INTERNATIONAL; pg. 178, pg. 1392
THE PERFORMER - Windows - KAWNEER COMPANY, INC.; pg. 90, pg. 537
PERFORMER - Gas Grill - WEBER-STEPHEN PRODUCTS LLC; pg. 62, pg. 650
PERFORMER LINK - Timing Chains - EDELBROCK CORPORATION; pg. 204, pg. 293
PERFORMER-SV3 - Robot for Small Part Handling, Packaging & Welding Applications - INTELITEK, INC.; pg. 1349, pg. 1036
PERFORMICS - Digital Marketing Product - DOUBLECLICK, INC.; pg. 1239, pg. 1225
PERFORMIX - Agricultural Product - ARCHER-DANIELS-MIDLAND COMPANY; pg. 825, pg. 565
PERFORMIX - Wafer Handling System - NEWPORT CORPORATION; pg. 1424, pg. 114
PERFOROLL - Plastics Product - AEP INDUSTRIES INC.; pg. 1878, pg. 1085
PERFUME.COM - Advertising Website - LIVE CURRENT MEDIA INC.; pg. 1263, pg. 1911
PERGOPAK - Pigments & Fillers - ALBEMARLE CORPORATION; pg. 1146, pg. 741
PERHAPS - Fabric - NEMSCHOFF, INC.; pg. 936, pg. 1890
PERI-PRO - Automatic X-Ray Film Processor - AIR TECHNIQUES, INC.; pg. 1487, pg. 1178
PERICLASE - Refractory Product - RESCO PRODUCTS, INC.; pg. 107, pg. 1581
PERIDATA - Pharmaceutical Product - ALERE INC.; pg. 1488, pg. 849
PERIDIN-C - Dietary Supplement - BEUTLICH PHARMACEUTICALS LP; pg. 1503, pg. 665
PERIGEE - Medical Device - AMERICAN MEDICAL SYSTEMS HOLDINGS, INC.; pg. 1493, pg. 947
PERIMALUX - Lighting Product - HUBBELL INCORPORATED; pg. 1299, pg. 370
PERIMATE - Insulation - THE DOW CHEMICAL COMPANY; pg. 1157, pg. 898
PERIMETER - Conference Tables - BERNHARDT DESIGN; pg. 918, pg. 1381
PERIO PIC - Toothpick - SUNSTAR AMERICAS INC.; pg. 1599, pg. 591
PERIOD COLLECTION - Lighting Fixtures - AMERICAN PERIOD LIGHTING, INC.; pg. 1294, pg. 1545
PERIOGLAS - Operatory Products - SUNSTAR AMERICAS INC.; pg. 1599, pg. 591
PERIOPERATIVE SOLUTIONS - Operating Room Management System - MEDIWARE INFORMATION SYSTEMS, INC.; pg. 431, pg. 716
PERISCOPE - Medical Device - LEMAITRE VASCULAR, INC.; pg. 1555, pg. 805
PERIVAC - Medical Device - BOSTON SCIENTIFIC CORPORATION; pg. 1508, pg. 831
PERIVENT - Medical Device - STAAR SURGICAL COMPANY; pg. 1597, pg. 151
PERIWINKLE - Fabric - NEMSCHOFF, INC.; pg. 936, pg. 1890
PERK - Fertilizer - LEBANON SEABOARD CORPORATION; pg. 1797, pg. 1547
PERK SHEEN - Charge Soap - ADCO, INC.; pg. 325, pg. 482
PERK SHEEN 324 - Dry Cleaning & Laundry Product - ADCO, INC.; pg. 325, pg. 482
PERKARE - Dry Cleaning Solvent - PPG INDUSTRIES, INC.; pg. 1445, pg. 1579
PERKINS - Restaurants - PERKINS & MARIE CALLENDER'S INC.; pg. 1744, pg. 1645
PERKINS - Converting & Finishing Machinery & Systems - STANDEX INTERNATIONAL CORPORATION; pg. 60, pg. 1039
PERKS SAFETY WASHERS - Prevents Grinding Wheels from Fracturing or Exploding - STANDARD SAFETY EQUIPMENT CO.; pg. 1379, pg. 632
PERKUP - Coffee - FRESHBREW COFFEE, LLC; pg. 857, pg. 1706
PERKY PET - Pet Product - PETSMART, INC.; pg. 1481, pg. 18
PERLA - Personal & Household Product - THE PROCTER &

GAMBLE COMPANY; *pg.* 1129, *pg.* 1418
PERLINA - Bear - GUND, INC.; *pg.* 954, *pg.* 1056
PERLITE - Roof Insulation - KOPPERS HOLDINGS INC.; *pg.* 1170, *pg.* 1577
PERLS - Software - PRINCIPAL FINANCIAL GROUP, INC.; *pg.* 796, *pg.* 706
PERM-A-CLOR - Cleaning Solvents - DETREX CORPORATION; *pg.* 1156, *pg.* 906
PERM-NET - Software - MOCON, INC.; *pg.* 1363, *pg.* 940
PERM-WALL - Wall Screen - DA-LITE SCREEN COMPANY; *pg.* 632, *pg.* 698
PERMA-BRITE - Lens - DANKER LABORATORIES INC.; *pg.* 1408, *pg.* 465
PERMA-CRETE - Coating Product - PPG INDUSTRIES, INC.; *pg.* 1445, *pg.* 1579
PERMA-CYL - Cryogenic Product - CHART INDUSTRIES, INC.; *pg.* 1405, *pg.* 1454
PERMA-EZE - Furniture Seat & Back Springs - LEGGETT & PLATT, INCORPORATED; *pg.* 933, *pg.* 974
PERMA-FIT - Electronic Components - MOLEX INCORPORATED; *pg.* 655, *pg.* 628
PERMA-FLEX - Golf Equipment - ACUSHNET COMPANY; *pg.* 1824, *pg.* 818
PERMA FRAME - Filtration Product - FLANDERS CORPORATION; *pg.* 1336, *pg.* 1392
PERMA GRIP - Mattress - THERAPEDIC ASSOCIATES, INC.; *pg.* 945, *pg.* 1112
PERMA PASS - Chemical Coating - ENTHONE INC.; *pg.* 1161, *pg.* 381
PERMA-PATCH - Refractory Product - RESCO PRODUCTS, INC.; *pg.* 107, *pg.* 1581
PERMA POWER - Surge Protector - WIREMOLD/LEGRAND; *pg.* 689, *pg.* 383
PERMA-SEAL - Connector - MOLEX INCORPORATED; *pg.* 655, *pg.* 628
PERMA-SEAL - Corrosion & Resistant Coating - POWERS FASTENERS INC.; *pg.* 1059, *pg.* 1143
PERMA-SHIELD - Window - ANDERSEN CORPORATION; *pg.* 67, *pg.* 916
PERMA-SOFT - Golf Equipment - ACUSHNET COMPANY; *pg.* 1824, *pg.* 818
PERMA-STAR - Pressed & Monolithic Refractory - RESCO PRODUCTS, INC.; *pg.* 107, *pg.* 1581
PERMA-STRIPE - Striping Paint - TEXAS REFINERY CORP.; *pg.* 986, *pg.* 1696
PERMA-TECH - Golf Equipment - ACUSHNET COMPANY; *pg.* 1824, *pg.* 818
PERMA-TITE - Closure - ATLAS BOLT & SCREW COMPANY; *pg.* 1042, *pg.* 1403
PERMACAST - Pressed & Monolithic Refractory - RESCO PRODUCTS, INC.; *pg.* 107, *pg.* 1581
PERMACELL - Cathodic Protection - CORRPRO COMPANIES, INC.; *pg.* 631, *pg.* 1464
PERMACLIP - Medical Equipment - CONMED CORPORATION; *pg.* 1517, *pg.* 1347
PERMACOLOR - Paper & Nonwoven Material - FIBERMARK INC.; *pg.* 1457, *pg.* 1764
PERMACOLOR - Filter - ROSCO LABORATORIES, INC.; *pg.* 1782, *pg.* 378
PERMACON - Pressed & Monolithic Refractory - RESCO PRODUCTS, INC.; *pg.* 107, *pg.* 1581
PERMACOTE - Lens - DANKER LABORATORIES INC.; *pg.* 1408, *pg.* 465
PERMACOTE - Paper & Nonwoven Material - FIBERMARK INC.; *pg.* 1457, *pg.* 1764
PERMACRYL - Paint & Coating - DIAMOND VOGEL PAINT, INC.; *pg.* 1441, *pg.* 710
PERMADIZE - Hardcoat Finishes - KAWNEER COMPANY, INC.; *pg.* 90, *pg.* 537
PERMADYNE - Impression Material - 3M COMPANY; *pg.* 1142, *pg.* 956
PERMAFIBER - Paper & Nonwoven Material - FIBERMARK INC.; *pg.* 1457, *pg.* 1764
PERMAFLEX - Soft, Flexible-Wear Contact Lens - THE COOPER COMPANIES, INC.; *pg.* 1518, *pg.* 183
PERMAFLEX - Paint & Coating - DIAMOND VOGEL PAINT, INC.; *pg.* 1441, *pg.* 710
PERMAFLEX NATURALS - Soft, Flexible-Wear Contact Lens - THE COOPER COMPANIES, INC.; *pg.* 1518, *pg.* 183
PERMAFLEX THIN - Soft, Flexible-Wear Contact Lens - THE COOPER COMPANIES, INC.; *pg.* 1518, *pg.* 183
PERMAFLEX UV NATURALS - Soft, Flexible-Wear Contact Lens - THE COOPER COMPANIES, INC.; *pg.* 1518, *pg.* 183
PERMAFLO - Pump - NORDSON CORPORATION; *pg.* 1365, *pg.* 1480
PERMAFOCUS - Binocular - BUSHNELL OUTDOOR PRODUCTS, INC.; *pg.* 1403, *pg.* 718
PERMAFRESH - Wallcovering - OMNOVA SOLUTIONS INC; *pg.* 1176, *pg.* 1453
PERMAFUSE - Fittings - UNITED STATES PIPE & FOUNDRY COMPANY, INC.; *pg.* 117, *pg.* 5
PERMAFUSED - Fencing - MASTER HALCO; *pg.* 96, *pg.* 474
PERMAGLAS ULTRA COAT - Coating - A.O. SMITH CORPORATION; *pg.* 1313, *pg.* 1872
PERMAGLOSS - Interior & Exterior Acrylic Gloss Paint - DUNN-EDWARDS CORPORATION; *pg.* 1442, *pg.* 129
PERMAGRID - Medical Product - HOLOGIC, INC.; *pg.* 1416, *pg.* 784
PERMAGUN - Pressed & Monolithic Refractory - RESCO PRODUCTS, INC.; *pg.* 107, *pg.* 1581
PERMALBA - Art Materials - MARTIN/F. WEBER COMPANY; *pg.* 962, *pg.* 1567
PERMALENS - Soft, Flexible-Wear Contact Lens - THE COOPER COMPANIES, INC.; *pg.* 1518, *pg.* 183
PERMALENS APHAKIC - Soft, Specialty-Wear Contact Lens - THE COOPER COMPANIES, INC.; *pg.* 1518, *pg.* 183
PERMALENS THERAPEUTIC - Soft, Specialty-Wear Contact Lens - THE COOPER COMPANIES, INC.; *pg.* 1518, *pg.* 183
PERMALENS XL - Soft, Flexible-Wear Contact Lens - THE COOPER COMPANIES, INC.; *pg.* 1518, *pg.* 183
PERMALEX - Paper & Nonwoven Material - FIBERMARK INC.; *pg.* 1457, *pg.* 1764
PERMALIN - Paper & Nonwoven Material - FIBERMARK INC.; *pg.* 1457, *pg.* 1764
PERMALOCK - Fastener - CHANNELLOCK, INC.; *pg.* 1044, *pg.* 1551
PERMALYN - Resins - EASTMAN CHEMICAL COMPANY; *pg.* 1159, *pg.* 1636
PERMAMOP - Asphalt - OWENS CORNING; *pg.* 102, *pg.* 1476
PERMANENT METALLIC - Block Seal - CRC INDUSTRIES, INC.; *pg.* 329, *pg.* 1590
PERMANENT-SEALER - Sealer - W.J. RUSCOE COMPANY; *pg.* 122, *pg.* 1403
PERMANENTE - Pressed & Monolithic Refractory - RESCO PRODUCTS, INC.; *pg.* 107, *pg.* 1581
PERMANET - Server Driver - ADVANCED MICRO DEVICES, INC.; *pg.* 613, *pg.* 282
PERMANIZER - Coating Product - PPG INDUSTRIES, INC.; *pg.* 1445, *pg.* 1579
PERMANIZER PLUS - Wood-Treating Coating - PPG INDUSTRIES, INC.; *pg.* 1445, *pg.* 1579
PERMANODE - Cathodic Protection - CORRPRO COMPANIES, INC.; *pg.* 631, *pg.* 1464
PERMAPEN - Medicine - PFIZER INC.; *pg.* 1581, *pg.* 1278
PERMAPLEX - Lubricant - D-A LUBRICANT COMPANY; *pg.* 975, *pg.* 693
PERMAPOL - Specialty Polymers - PPG AEROSPACE; *pg.* 1178, *pg.* 290
PERMAPOL - Insulating Glass Sealant - PPG INDUSTRIES, INC.; *pg.* 1445, *pg.* 1579
PERMASHEEN - Interior & Exterior Acrylic Semi-Gloss Paint - DUNN-EDWARDS CORPORATION; *pg.* 1442, *pg.* 129
PERMASHELL - Interior & Exterior Acrylic Eggshell Paint - DUNN-EDWARDS CORPORATION; *pg.* 1442, *pg.* 129
PERMASHIELD - Carpet - BEAULIEU GROUP, LLC; *pg.* 917, *pg.* 529
PERMASOFT - Carpet - BEAULIEU GROUP, LLC; *pg.* 917, *pg.* 529
PERMASOIL - Underground Construction Equipment - CHARLES MACHINE WORKS, INC.; *pg.* 1322, *pg.* 1488
PERMASTAR - Air Cleaner - EDELBROCK CORPORATION; *pg.* 204, *pg.* 293
PERMATAC - Resin Dispersion - NEVILLE CHEMICAL COMPANY; *pg.* 1174, *pg.* 1578
PERMATEARS - Lens - DANKER LABORATORIES INC.; *pg.* 1408, *pg.* 465
PERMATHERM - Skylighting Product - WASCO PRODUCTS, INC.; *pg.* 120, *pg.* 752
PERMATRAN-C - Carbon Dioxide Permeation Instrument - MOCON, INC.; *pg.* 1363, *pg.* 940
PERMATRAN-W - Water Vapor Permeation Instrument - MOCON, INC.; *pg.* 1363, *pg.* 940
PERMATREAT - Conversion Coating for Metals - GE WATER & PROCESS TECHNOLOGIES; *pg.* 1339, *pg.* 1588
PERMAWEAR - Coating Product - PPG INDUSTRIES, INC.; *pg.* 1445, *pg.* 1579
PERMAXIM - Pharmaceutical Product - ALERE INC.; *pg.* 1488, *pg.* 849
PERMBLOK - Multilayer Fuel - TI AUTOMOTIVE LIMITED; *pg.* 191, *pg.* 869
PERMEABLE PRIVACY - Furniture - HERMAN MILLER, INC.; *pg.* 926, *pg.* 913
PERMECTRIN - Insecticide - BOEHRINGER INGELHEIM VETMEDICA, INC.; *pg.* 1474, *pg.* 989
PERMECTRIN II - Insecticide Spray - BOEHRINGER INGELHEIM VETMEDICA, INC.; *pg.* 1474, *pg.* 989
PERMENTRY - Basement Entrance - THE BILCO COMPANY; *pg.* 70, *pg.* 383
PERMEOX - Chemical - FMC CORPORATION; *pg.* 1163, *pg.* 1564
PERMEX - Synthetic Rubber - SLOAN VALVE COMPANY; *pg.* 1062, *pg.* 613
PERMIC - Cleaning And Conditioning Product - HEATBATH CORPORATION; *pg.* 1165, *pg.* 826
PERMION - Coating Product - PPG INDUSTRIES, INC.; *pg.* 1445, *pg.* 1579
PERMISO - Office Furniture - STEELCASE INC.; *pg.* 475, *pg.* 889
PERMISSION TO SPEAK FREELY - Slogan - METROPCS, INC.; *pg.* 1872, *pg.* 1683
PERMIT - Apparel - OAKLEY, INC.; *pg.* 1840, *pg.* 86
PERMX - Films - E.I. DU PONT DE NEMOURS & COMPANY; *pg.* 1159, *pg.* 390
PERMYL - Ultraviolet Absorber - FERRO CORPORATION; *pg.* 1162, *pg.* 1462
PERNESTA - Medical Product - HOLOGIC, INC.; *pg.* 1416, *pg.* 784
PERNOD - Liquor - PERNOD RICARD USA, INC.; *pg.* 1968, *pg.* 1332
PERONI NASTRO AZZURRO - Beer - MILLERCOORS; *pg.* 254, *pg.* 1877
PEROX-PURE - UV System - CALGON CARBON CORPORATION; *pg.* 1151, *pg.* 1574
PEROXYL - First Aid Rinse - COLGATE ORAL PHARMACEUTICAL; *pg.* 1516, *pg.* 1214
PERPETUA - Flatware - ONEIDA LTD; *pg.* 1129, *pg.* 1318
PERRIN & ROWE - Bath Product - ROHL LLC; *pg.* 1061, *pg.* 116
PERRY - Farm Implement - THE PERRY COMPANY; *pg.* 706, *pg.* 1749
PERRY ELLIS - Apparel - PERRY ELLIS INTERNATIONAL, INC.; *pg.* 45, *pg.* 445
PERRY ELLIS AMERICA - Jeanswear - PERRY ELLIS INTERNATIONAL, INC.; *pg.* 45, *pg.* 445
PERRY ELLIS PORTFOLIO - Apparel - PERRY ELLIS INTERNATIONAL, INC.; *pg.* 45, *pg.* 445
PERRY WHITE - Character - DC COMICS, INC.; *pg.* 1633, *pg.* 1221
PERSA-GEL - Healthcare Product - JOHNSON & JOHNSON; *pg.* 1549, *pg.* 1091
PERSANTINE - Pharmaceutical Product - IMPAX LABORATORIES, INC.; *pg.* 1544, *pg.* 101
PERSEA BUTTER - Chemical Ingredient - LIPO CHEMICALS INC.; *pg.* 1171, *pg.* 1107
PERSIAN PRINCESS - Video Game - INTERNATIONAL GAME TECHNOLOGY; *pg.* 957, *pg.* 1024
PERSIMMON - Pillow - ETHAN ALLEN INTERIORS INC.; *pg.* 924, *pg.* 343
PERSIMMON - Pillow and Throw - HERITAGE LACE INC.; *pg.* 694, *pg.* 711
PERSIS - Footwear - STEVEN MADDEN, LTD.; *pg.* 1819, *pg.* 1176
PERSISTENCE EDGEXTEND - Software - PROGRESS SOFTWARE CORPORATION; *pg.* 457, *pg.* 786
PERSISTENCE POWERTIER - Software - PROGRESS SOFTWARE CORPORATION; *pg.* 457, *pg.* 786
PERSONA - Fertility Monitoring Device - ALERE INC.; *pg.* 1488, *pg.* 849
PERSONA - Bath Product - KOHLER CO.; *pg.* 91, *pg.* 1862
PERSONAL - Table - LIFETIME PRODUCTS INC.; *pg.* 933, *pg.* 1751
PERSONAL - Safety Product - WISCONSIN PHARMACAL COMPANY, LLC; *pg.* 1610, *pg.* 1861
PERSONAL ATTENTION POWERFUL RESULTS - Manual - XEROX CORPORATION; *pg.* 494, *pg.* 365
PERSONAL BACK 10 - Chair - INVACARE CORPORATION; *pg.* 1546, *pg.* 1451
PERSONAL BACK 10 PLUS - Chair - INVACARE CORPORATION; *pg.* 1546, *pg.* 1451
PERSONAL BUILDER - Building Program - DAVID WEEKLEY HOMES, LP; *pg.* 78, *pg.* 1704

First page reference indicates Business Class Edition
Second page reference indicates Geographic Edition

PERSONAL CAREADVANCE - Software - TRIZETTO CORPORATION; *pg.* 485, *pg.* 327
PERSONAL CHOICE PROGRAM - Weight Loss Program - WEIGHT WATCHERS INTERNATIONAL, INC.; *pg.* 1609, *pg.* 1313
PERSONAL CINEMA - Graphic System - NVIDIA CORPORATION; *pg.* 447, *pg.* 268
PERSONAL EXPRESSIONS - Casket Personalization - AURORA CASKET COMPANY, INC.; *pg.* 1393, *pg.* 673
THE PERSONAL FREEDOM - Home HealthCare - PENN TREATY AMERICAN CORPORATION; *pg.* 793, *pg.* 1514
PERSONAL JWORKS - Software - WIND RIVER SYSTEMS, INC.; *pg.* 493, *pg.* 38
PERSONAL LUCKY COIN - Video Game - INTERNATIONAL GAME TECHNOLOGY; *pg.* 957, *pg.* 1024
PERSONAL MATCH - Beauty Product - AVON PRODUCTS, INC.; *pg.* 500, *pg.* 1198
PERSONAL MOLECULAR IMAGER - Software - BIO-RAD LABORATORIES, INC.; *pg.* 1504, *pg.* 101
PERSONAL MOLECULAR IMAGER FX - Software - BIO-RAD LABORATORIES, INC.; *pg.* 1504, *pg.* 101
PERSONAL NURSE - Health Care Guidance & Information Service - HUMANA, INC.; *pg.* 1204, *pg.* 734
PERSONAL PIERCER - Ear Piercing System - INVERNESS CORPORATION; *pg.* 512, *pg.* 783
PERSONAL POST - Postage Meter - PITNEY BOWES INC.; *pg.* 454, *pg.* 376
PERSONAL RESPONSE SYSTEM (PRS) - Emergency Response System - HEALTH WATCH INC.; *pg.* 1540, *pg.* 411
PERSONAL SEAT VF - Medical Equipment - INVACARE CORPORATION; *pg.* 1546, *pg.* 1451
PERSONAL TRAFFIC MASTER - Cost-effective, Computerized Automatic Train Dispatching System - ALSTOM SIGNALING, INC.; *pg.* 1312, *pg.* 1350
PERSONAL UNDERLINE - Lighting - STEELCASE INC.; *pg.* 475, *pg.* 889
PERSONALDESIGNER - Software - X-RITE, INCORPORATED; *pg.* 1437, *pg.* 891
PERSONALIZED GIFTS - Mail Order Catalog - LILLIAN VERNON CORPORATION; *pg.* 1776, *pg.* 315
PERSONALIZED PROFILE - Characteristics Assessment - NUTRISYSTEM, INC.; *pg.* 1577, *pg.* 1533
PERSONALS - Premium Light Ice Cream - WELLS ENTERPRISES, INC.; *pg.* 909, *pg.* 709
PERSONAS - Automatic Teller Machine - NCR CORPORATION; *pg.* 443, *pg.* 531
PERSONATOR 3 - Software - MELISSA DATA CORP.; *pg.* 432, *pg.* 188
PERSONICX - Data Product - ACXIOM CORPORATION; *pg.* 342, *pg.* 33
PERSONICX GEO - Geodemographic Segmentation System - ACXIOM CORPORATION; *pg.* 342, *pg.* 33
PERSONICX VISIONSCAPE - Visualization Application - ACXIOM CORPORATION; *pg.* 342, *pg.* 33
PERSONNA - Shaving Products - EDGEWELL PERSONAL CARE; *pg.* 1526, *pg.* 995
PERSONNEL MANAGEMENT SYSTEM - Temporary Staffing - INSPERITY, INC.; *pg.* 416, *pg.* 1725
PERSONNELLE - Health & Beauty Product - THE JEAN COUTU GROUP (PJC) INC.; *pg.* 1548, *pg.* 1952
PERSONNELLE SHREK - Training Pant - THE JEAN COUTU GROUP (PJC) INC.; *pg.* 1548, *pg.* 1952
PERSPECTIVE - Collaboration Tool Integrating Video Conferencing & Web Conferencing - APPLIED GLOBAL TECHNOLOGIES; *pg.* 352, *pg.* 460
PERSPECTIVE - Computer Services - KEYNOTE SYSTEMS INCORPORATED; *pg.* 425, *pg.* 255
PERSPECTIVE - Fabric - NEMSCHOFF, INC.; *pg.* 936, *pg.* 1890
PERSPEX - Acrylic Polymer - LUCITE INTERNATIONAL, INC.; *pg.* 94, *pg.* 1631
PERSUADER - Cable & Antenna System - RADIO FREQUENCY SYSTEMS, INC.; *pg.* 666, *pg.* 354
PERSUASION - Fabric - NEMSCHOFF, INC.; *pg.* 936, *pg.* 1890
PERSUEDE - Fabric - NEMSCHOFF, INC.; *pg.* 936, *pg.* 1890
PERT PLUS - Hair Care Products - HELEN OF TROY L.P.; *pg.* 511, *pg.* 1692
PERU - Fabric - NEMSCHOFF, INC.; *pg.* 936, *pg.* 1890
PERU-B-RUBY - Nail Care Product - OPI PRODUCTS INC.; *pg.* 518, *pg.* 167
PERUGINA - Chocolate - NESTLE USA, INC.; *pg.* 883, *pg.* 96
PERUGINA GIANDUIA - Food Product - NESTLE USA, INC.; *pg.* 883, *pg.* 96
PERUGINA ORE LIETE - Food Product - NESTLE USA, INC.; *pg.* 883, *pg.* 96
PERVASIVE SOFTWARE FOR A CONNECTED WORLD - Slogan - RECURSION SOFTWARE, INC.; *pg.* 460, *pg.* 1697
PESARO - Guest Chairs - BERNHARDT DESIGN; *pg.* 918, *pg.* 1381
PESCA LETRAS - Educational Kit - LEAPFROG ENTERPRISES, INC.; *pg.* 961, *pg.* 84
PESTCHASER - Pest Control - THE WOODSTREAM CORPORATION; *pg.* 1801, *pg.* 1549
PESTISOLV - Chemical Product - SPECTRUM CHEMICALS & LABORATORY PRODUCTS, INC.; *pg.* 1181, *pg.* 94
PESTO - Dinnerware - THE HOMER LAUGHLIN CHINA COMPANY; *pg.* 1125, *pg.* 1850
PESTO - Fabric - NEMSCHOFF, INC.; *pg.* 936, *pg.* 1890
PET - Evaporated Milk - THE J.M. SMUCKER COMPANY; *pg.* 865, *pg.* 1468
PET AISLE - Publication - MACFADDEN COMMUNICATIONS GROUP, LLC; *pg.* 1660, *pg.* 1254
PET BUSINESS MAGAZINE - Publication - MACFADDEN COMMUNICATIONS GROUP, LLC; *pg.* 1660, *pg.* 1254
PET-CAL - Veterinary Vitamin Supplement - PFIZER INC.; *pg.* 1581, *pg.* 1278
PET CLUB - Pet Products - TOPCO HOLDINGS INC.; *pg.* 901, *pg.* 661
PET DAIRY - Dairy Product - DEAN FOODS COMPANY; *pg.* 852, *pg.* 1679
PET DREAMS - Pet Product - PETSMART, INC.; *pg.* 1481, *pg.* 18
PET EFFECTS - Pet Shampoo - PETEDGE; *pg.* 1481, *pg.* 787
PET-F.A. - Liquid Fatty Acid Dietary Supplement for Dogs and Cats - PFIZER INC.; *pg.* 1581, *pg.* 1278
PET FIT - Weight Control Plan - HILL'S PET NUTRITION, INC.; *pg.* 1476, *pg.* 721
PET GOODS - Pet Product - PETSMART, INC.; *pg.* 1481, *pg.* 18
PET-I-CURE - Home Products - HABAND COMPANY, INC.; *pg.* 1772, *pg.* 1099
PET PREFERRED - Pet Care Product - GARDENS ALIVE!, INC.; *pg.* 1796, *pg.* 693
PET PRODUCT NEWS - Magazine - I-5 PUBLISHING LLC; *pg.* 1651, *pg.* 133
THE PET PRODUCT NEWS BUYING GUIDE DIRECTORY - Magazine - I-5 PUBLISHING LLC; *pg.* 1651, *pg.* 133
PET-RITZ - Food Product - GENERAL MILLS, INC.; *pg.* 828, *pg.* 933
PET SCREENER - Hearing Test Equipment - INTELLIGENT HEARING SYSTEMS CORP.; *pg.* 1546, *pg.* 443
PET SHOPPE - Pet Products - THE HARTZ MOUNTAIN CORP.; *pg.* 1476, *pg.* 1120
PET STAIN - Household Product - BLUE CROSS LABORATORIES; *pg.* 326, *pg.* 277
PET STUDIO - Pet Gifts - PETEDGE; *pg.* 1481, *pg.* 787
PET TINIC - Veterinary Vitamin & Mineral Supplement - PFIZER INC.; *pg.* 1581, *pg.* 1278
PETAL MIST - Plates, Bowls, Trays, Servingware & Buffetware - CARLISLE FOODSERVICE PRODUCTS INCORPORATED; *pg.* 1455, *pg.* 1485
PETALO - Lighting Product - QUOIZEL INC.; *pg.* 1304, *pg.* 1616
PETALS - Fabric - NEMSCHOFF, INC.; *pg.* 936, *pg.* 1890
PETBOOK - Travel Guide Book For Persons Traveling With Pets - AMERICAN AUTOMOBILE ASSOCIATION; *pg.* 1190, *pg.* 429
PETCAT - Flame Retardants - CHEMTURA CORPORATION; *pg.* 1152, *pg.* 355
PETCHEK - Diagnostic Product - IDEXX LABORATORIES, INC.; *pg.* 1543, *pg.* 753
PETCO.COM - Website - PETCO ANIMAL SUPPLIES, INC.; *pg.* 1480, *pg.* 206
PETER PAN - Food Product - CONAGRA FOODS, INC.; *pg.* 826, *pg.* 1014
PETER PAN - Canned Salmon - PETER PAN SEAFOODS, INC.; *pg.* 889, *pg.* 1838
PETER PAUL ALMOND JOY - Candy Bars - THE HERSHEY CO.; *pg.* 1855, *pg.* 1538
PETER PIPER - Pickles - TREEHOUSE FOODS, INC.; *pg.* 901, *pg.* 649
PETER VELLA - Wine - E&J GALLO WINERY; *pg.* 1962, *pg.* 149
PETERBILT - Trucks - PACCAR INC.; *pg.* 187, *pg.* 1816
PETERBILT - Toys - TRACTOR SUPPLY COMPANY; *pg.* 708, *pg.* 1627
PETER'S BROC - Food Product - NESTLE USA, INC.; *pg.* 883, *pg.* 96
PETER'S BROKEN ORINOCO - Food Product - NESTLE USA, INC.; *pg.* 883, *pg.* 96
PETER'S BURGUNDY - Food Product - NESTLE USA, INC.; *pg.* 883, *pg.* 96
PETER'S CHATHAM - Food Product - NESTLE USA, INC.; *pg.* 883, *pg.* 96
PETER'S COMMANDER - Food Product - NESTLE USA, INC.; *pg.* 883, *pg.* 96
PETER'S CREMA - Food Product - NESTLE USA, INC.; *pg.* 883, *pg.* 96
PETERS EXCEL - Lawn & Garden Product - THE SCOTTS MIRACLE-GRO COMPANY; *pg.* 1799, *pg.* 1459
PETER'S GIBRALTAR - Food Product - NESTLE USA, INC.; *pg.* 883, *pg.* 96
PETERS PROFESSIONAL - Lawn & Garden Product - THE SCOTTS MIRACLE-GRO COMPANY; *pg.* 1799, *pg.* 1459
PETERSON'S - Nuts - KANAN ENTERPRISES, INC.; *pg.* 1857, *pg.* 1473
PETE'S TOFU - Organic Tofu - SUNRISE SOYA FOODS; *pg.* 900, *pg.* 1912
PETFOOD FORUM - North American & European Seminars & Trade Shows - WATT PUBLISHING COMPANY; *pg.* 1701, *pg.* 655
PETFOOD INDUSTRY - Global Magazine For Petfood Manufacturing - WATT PUBLISHING COMPANY; *pg.* 1701, *pg.* 655
PETIT AMPERE - Electrochemistry Product - BIOANALYTICAL SYSTEMS, INC.; *pg.* 1402, *pg.* 700
PETIT POINT - Carpet - BEAULIEU GROUP, LLC; *pg.* 917, *pg.* 529
PETIT-POINT CLASSICS - Area Rugs - COURISTAN INC.; *pg.* 921, *pg.* 1067
PETITE - Hearing Aid - BELTONE ELECTRONICS LLC; *pg.* 1503, *pg.* 614
PETITE - Poultry Product - PILGRIM'S PRIDE CORPORATION; *pg.* 889, *pg.* 330
PETITE - Ceiling Fan - WESTINGHOUSE LIGHTING CORPORATION; *pg.* 687, *pg.* 1571
PETITE 7 - HVAC Equipment - MESTEK, INC.; *pg.* 1074, *pg.* 857
PETITE EMBERS - Container Grown Plant - MONROVIA GROWERS; *pg.* 1797, *pg.* 44
PETITE ENCHANTMENT - Flower Arrangement - 1-800-FLOWERS.COM, INC.; *pg.* 1758, *pg.* 1151
PETITE INDIGO - Container Grown Plant - MONROVIA GROWERS; *pg.* 1797, *pg.* 44
PETITE MISS - Toy - IMPERIAL TOY CORPORATION; *pg.* 957, *pg.* 166
PETITE ORCHID - Container Grown Plant - MONROVIA GROWERS; *pg.* 1797, *pg.* 44
PETITE PINKIE - Container Grown Plant - MONROVIA GROWERS; *pg.* 1797, *pg.* 44
PETITE PLUM - Container Grown Plant - MONROVIA GROWERS; *pg.* 1797, *pg.* 44
PETITE PLUS - Hearing Aid - BELTONE ELECTRONICS LLC; *pg.* 1503, *pg.* 614
PETITE RED IMP - Container Grown Plant - MONROVIA GROWERS; *pg.* 1797, *pg.* 44
PETITE SNOW - Container Grown Plant - MONROVIA GROWERS; *pg.* 1797, *pg.* 44
PETITE SOPHISTICATE OUTLET - Women's Apparel - ASCENA RETAIL GROUP, INC.; *pg.* 18, *pg.* 1081
PETITION - Apparel - OAKLEY, INC.; *pg.* 1840, *pg.* 86
PETKEEPING WITH MARC MORRONE - Television Program - MARTHA STEWART LIVING OMNIMEDIA, INC.; *pg.* 1661, *pg.* 1256
PETMATE - Pet Product - PETSMART, INC.; *pg.* 1481, *pg.* 18
PETOSEED - Fruit & Vegetable Seeds - MONSANTO COMPANY; *pg.* 1173, *pg.* 999
PETPERKS - Savings Card - PETSMART, INC.; *pg.* 1481, *pg.* 18
PETRAC - Wax & Lubricant - FERRO CORPORATION; *pg.* 1162, *pg.* 1462
PETRACER - Analyzer - TELEDYNE LECROY; *pg.* 1431, *pg.* 1153
PETRAINER - Analyzer - TELEDYNE LECROY; *pg.* 1431, *pg.* 1153
PETREL - Software - SCHLUMBERGER LIMITED; *pg.* 801, *pg.* 1714
PETRI - Cigar - AVANTI CIGAR CORPORATION; *pg.* 1894, *pg.* 1527

PETRIFILM - Microbiological Pour Plate - 3M COMPANY; *pg.* 1142, *pg.* 956
PETRO-ALERT - Instruments - MOCON, INC.; *pg.* 1363, *pg.* 940
PETRO-CARBO - Salve - WATKINS INCORPORATED; *pg.* 909, *pg.* 967
PETRO-CARD 24 - Unattended Fueling System - MFA OIL COMPANY; *pg.* 981, *pg.* 976
PETRO EXPRESS - Convenience Stores - THE PANTRY, INC.; *pg.* 1029, *pg.* 1360
PETRO-MIX - Plastic Refractory - PLIBRICO CO. LLC; *pg.* 104, *pg.* 587
PETRO-THIN - Petrographic Polishing & Grinding Device - BUEHLER, LTD.; *pg.* 1403, *pg.* 622
PETROCALC - Software - GULF PUBLISHING COMPANY; *pg.* 1646, *pg.* 1707
PETROCARB - Fuel Oil - NOVA CHEMICALS CORPORATION; *pg.* 1175, *pg.* 1904
PETROCARE - Reservoir Souring Inhibitor - BAKER PETROLITE CORPORATION; *pg.* 1148, *pg.* 1745
PETROCUT - Abrasive Cutter - BUEHLER, LTD.; *pg.* 1403, *pg.* 622
PETRODEX ENZYMATIC - Toothpaste for Cats - PETEDGE; *pg.* 1481, *pg.* 787
PETROFLO - Petroleum Process Additives - GE WATER & PROCESS TECHNOLOGIES; *pg.* 1339, *pg.* 1588
PETROMEEN - Product Inhibitor - GE WATER & PROCESS TECHNOLOGIES; *pg.* 1339, *pg.* 1588
PETRONATE - Polymer Product - CHEMTURA CORPORATION; *pg.* 1152, *pg.* 355
PETROPOL - Polishing System - BUEHLER, LTD.; *pg.* 1403, *pg.* 622
PETROSTEP - Chemical Product - STEPAN COMPANY; *pg.* 1182, *pg.* 643
PETS ALIVE! - Organic Pet Care Product - GARDENS ALIVE!, INC.; *pg.* 1796, *pg.* 693
PETS FOR LIFE - Awareness Program - THE HUMANE SOCIETY OF THE UNITED STATES; *pg.* 143, *pg.* 400
PETS FOR PEOPLE - Pet Care Product - NESTLE PURINA PETCARE COMPANY; *pg.* 1479, *pg.* 1000
PETSAFE - Pet Product - PETSMART, INC.; *pg.* 1481, *pg.* 18
PETSMART - Pet Store - PETSMART, INC.; *pg.* 1481, *pg.* 18
PETSMART CHARITIES - Mouse Pad - PETSMART, INC.; *pg.* 1481, *pg.* 18
PETSMART HOLIDAY VILLAGE - Pet Services - PETSMART, INC.; *pg.* 1481, *pg.* 18
PETSMART PETSHOTEL - Pet Boarding Services - PETSMART, INC.; *pg.* 1481, *pg.* 18
PETSMART.COM - Pet Supply Website - PETSMART, INC.; *pg.* 1481, *pg.* 18
PETSTEP - Car Accessories - MACNEIL AUTOMOTIVE PRODUCTS, LTD.; *pg.* 211, *pg.* 559
PETTERINO'S - Fine Dining Restaurant - LETTUCE ENTERTAIN YOU ENTERPRISES, INC.; *pg.* 1735, *pg.* 580
PETTIBONE KRANE - Hydraulic Cranes and Parts - PETTIBONE, LLC; *pg.* 1368, *pg.* 609
PETTIBONE MERCURY - Fork Lift & Tow Tractors & Parts - PETTIBONE, LLC; *pg.* 1368, *pg.* 609
PETTIBONE MICHIGAN - Extendable Forklifts - PETTIBONE, LLC; *pg.* 1368, *pg.* 609
PETTIT - Paints - PETTIT PAINT COMPANY; *pg.* 1444, *pg.* 1116
PETTITROL - Retarder - PETTIT PAINT COMPANY; *pg.* 1444, *pg.* 1116
PETUNIA - Furniture - AMISCO INDUSTRIES LTD.; *pg.* 913, *pg.* 1958
PETZAZZ - Water Dispenser - PETSMART, INC.; *pg.* 1481, *pg.* 18
PEWTER - Furniture - BUSH INDUSTRIES INC.; *pg.* 919, *pg.* 1170
PEXEVA - Estradiol Transdermal System - NOVEN PHARMACEUTICALS, INC.; *pg.* 1576, *pg.* 445
PEYCHAUD'S - Bitters - SAZERAC COMPANY, INC.; *pg.* 1969, *pg.* 745
PEYTON'S - Meat Products - JOHN MORRELL & CO.; *pg.* 866, *pg.* 1415
PF - Heat Transfer Products - MODINE MANUFACTURING COMPANY; *pg.* 1074, *pg.* 1888
P.F. CHANG'S - Frozen Meals - CONAGRA FOODS, INC.; *pg.* 826, *pg.* 1014
PF FLYERS - Action Shoes - NEW BALANCE ATHLETIC SHOE, INC.; *pg.* 1811, *pg.* 798
PFAELZER BROTHERS - Steaks; Gourmet Food - HICKORY FARMS, INC.; *pg.* 862, *pg.* 1462
PFAFF - Industrial Components - COLUMBUS MCKINNON CORPORATION; *pg.* 1325, *pg.* 1138
PFALTZGRAFF - Tableware - LIFETIME BRANDS, INC.; *pg.* 1127, *pg.* 1161
PFAUTER - Gear Cutting, Finishing & Hobbing Machines - GLEASON CORPORATION; *pg.* 1340, *pg.* 1335
PFAUTER-MAAG - Cutting Tools - GLEASON CORPORATION; *pg.* 1340, *pg.* 1335
PFC SIGMA TOTAL KNEE SYSTEM - Orthopedic Product - DEPUYSYNTHES; *pg.* 1523, *pg.* 699
PFEIFFER - Professional Development Books - JOHN WILEY & SONS, INC.; *pg.* 1655, *pg.* 1073
PFEIFFER - Salad Dressings - LANCASTER COLONY CORPORATION; *pg.* 873, *pg.* 1441
PFEIFFER - Salad Dressings - T. MARZETTI COMPANY; *pg.* 900, *pg.* 1444
PFG CUSTOM CUT MEATS - Custom Cut Meats - PERFORMANCE FOOD GROUP COMPANY, LLC; *pg.* 1030, *pg.* 1803
PFISTER - Table - BLATT BOWLING & BILLIARD CORP.; *pg.* 1827, *pg.* 1203
PFIZER FOR LIVING - Slogan - PFIZER INC.; *pg.* 1581, *pg.* 1278
PFIZER MEDNET - Pharmaceutical Product - PFIZER INC.; *pg.* 1581, *pg.* 1278
PFIZERPEN - Medicine - PFIZER INC.; *pg.* 1581, *pg.* 1278
PFKIDS - Health & Information - PRAIRIE FARMS DAIRY, INC.; *pg.* 890, *pg.* 561
PFL - Masks - ALPHA PRO TECH, LTD.; *pg.* 1492, *pg.* 1922
PFL - Dietary Fiber Compound - ARCHER-DANIELS-MIDLAND COMPANY; *pg.* 825, *pg.* 565
PFL ISOLATED - Soy Protein - ARCHER-DANIELS-MIDLAND COMPANY; *pg.* 825, *pg.* 565
PFRESHEST IDEAS IN PFAUCETS - Tag Line - PFISTER, INC.; *pg.* 1059, *pg.* 88
PFS - Snap-In Panel Fastener - PENNENGINEERING FASTENING TECHNOLOGIES; *pg.* 1059, *pg.* 1526
PFSWEB'S END2END ECOMMERCE - Ecommerce Service - PFSWEB, INC.; *pg.* 1275, *pg.* 1733
PFT - Panel Access Hardware - PENNENGINEERING FASTENING TECHNOLOGIES; *pg.* 1059, *pg.* 1526
PG 123 - Ribbon Window System - KAWNEER COMPANY, INC.; *pg.* 90, *pg.* 537
PG TIPS - Beverages - UNILEVER CANADA INC.; *pg.* 903, *pg.* 1946
PG-TXL - Polyglutamate Paclitaxel - CELL THERAPEUTICS, INC.; *pg.* 1514, *pg.* 1834
PGA TOUR - Apparel - PERRY ELLIS INTERNATIONAL, INC.; *pg.* 45, *pg.* 445
PGATOUR.COM - Sport Media - CBS SPORTSLINE.COM, INC.; *pg.* 1234, *pg.* 423
PGI & DESIGN - Telecom Software - PREMIERE GLOBAL SERVICES, INC.; *pg.* 1275, *pg.* 518
PGICONNECT - Telecommunication - PREMIERE GLOBAL SERVICES, INC.; *pg.* 1275, *pg.* 518
PGII - Glass & Ceramic Material - CORNING INCORPORATED; *pg.* 1122, *pg.* 1154
PGIMARKET - Software - PREMIERE GLOBAL SERVICES, INC.; *pg.* 1275, *pg.* 518
PGIMEET - Software - PREMIERE GLOBAL SERVICES, INC.; *pg.* 1275, *pg.* 518
PGINOTIFY - Software - PREMIERE GLOBAL SERVICES, INC.; *pg.* 1275, *pg.* 518
PGINOTIFY MEDS - Software - PREMIERE GLOBAL SERVICES, INC.; *pg.* 1275, *pg.* 518
PGISEND - Software - PREMIERE GLOBAL SERVICES, INC.; *pg.* 1275, *pg.* 518
PGITV - Promo Tool - PREMIERE GLOBAL SERVICES, INC.; *pg.* 1275, *pg.* 518
PGLO - Software - BIO-RAD LABORATORIES, INC.; *pg.* 1504, *pg.* 101
PGMM - Systems Integration & Aeronautics - LOCKHEED MARTIN CORPORATION; *pg.* 229, *pg.* 762
PGX - Glass & Ceramic Material - CORNING INCORPORATED; *pg.* 1122, *pg.* 1154
PH-1 POWERHOUSE - Power Supply - LIONEL LLC; *pg.* 961, *pg.* 875
PH 13-8 MO - Steel Product - AK STEEL HOLDING CORPORATION; *pg.* 1311, *pg.* 1479
PH 15-7 MO - Steel Product - AK STEEL HOLDING CORPORATION; *pg.* 1311, *pg.* 1479
PH BALANCE - Healthcare Product - SWANSON HEALTH PRODUCTS INC.; *pg.* 1600, *pg.* 1397
PHADE - Fading Gel - ALVA/AMCO PHARMACAL COMPANIES, INC.; *pg.* 1492, *pg.* 637
PHAGE CONTROL - Culture - CHR. HANSEN; *pg.* 847, *pg.* 1873
PHALANX - Vanity Lights - CRAFTMADE INTERNATIONAL, INC.; *pg.* 1295, *pg.* 1670
PHALANX - Gas Mask - MINE SAFETY APPLIANCES COMPANY; *pg.* 1361, *pg.* 1525
PHALANX - Radar-Controlled Gun System - RAYTHEON COMPANY; *pg.* 233, *pg.* 854
PHANTASY CAMP - Baseball Tournament - THE PHILLIES, L.P.; *pg.* 575, *pg.* 1569
PHANTOM - Power Supply Product - ANTEC INCORPORATED; *pg.* 350, *pg.* 90
PHANTOM - Tile - ARTISTIC TILE INC.; *pg.* 914, *pg.* 1119
PHANTOM - Footwear - CAPEZIO BALLET MAKERS INC.; *pg.* 1805, *pg.* 1125
PHANTOM - Pool Cleaner - HAYWARD POOL PRODUCTS; *pg.* 1049, *pg.* 1057
PHANTOM - Auto-Darkening Filter - SELLSTROM MANUFACTURING CO.; *pg.* 1428, *pg.* 659
PHANTOM ELECTRO - Welding Helmet - SELLSTROM MANUFACTURING CO.; *pg.* 1428, *pg.* 659
PHANTORN - Medical Device - GAMMEX RMI INC.; *pg.* 1532, *pg.* 1872
PHAR LAP - Software - INTERVALZERO INC.; *pg.* 420, *pg.* 851
PHAR LAP SOFTWARE - Software - INTERVALZERO INC.; *pg.* 420, *pg.* 851
PHARAOH'S PYRAMID - Game - WMS INDUSTRIES INC.; *pg.* 593, *pg.* 666
PHARMACEUTICAL LAW & INDUSTRY REPORT - Publisher - BLOOMBERG BNA; *pg.* 1621, *pg.* 1772
PHARMACEUTICAL PROCESSING - Trade Magazine - ADVANTAGE BUSINESS MEDIA; *pg.* 1613, *pg.* 1116
PHARMACEUTICAL STABILIZATION SYSTEM - Proprietary Drug Delivery Technology - IMPAX LABORATORIES, INC.; *pg.* 1544, *pg.* 101
PHARMACYCENTRAL - Software - OMNICELL INC.; *pg.* 1578, *pg.* 161
PHARMAFLEX - Pharmaceutical Product - PURETEK CORPORATION; *pg.* 1587, *pg.* 211
PHARMAKON - Pharmacy Information System - MEDIWARE INFORMATION SYSTEMS, INC.; *pg.* 431, *pg.* 716
PHARMAKON - Pharmaceutical Product - PDI, INC.; *pg.* 1580, *pg.* 1104
PHARMALYZIR - Software - BIO-RAD LABORATORIES, INC.; *pg.* 1504, *pg.* 101
PHARMANEX - Nutritional Supplement - NU SKIN ENTERPRISES, INC.; *pg.* 518, *pg.* 1755
PHARMAPRIX - Full-service Retail Drug Stores - SHOPPERS DRUG MART CORPORATION; *pg.* 1594, *pg.* 1943
PHARMAPURE - Pharmaceutical Product - PURETEK CORPORATION; *pg.* 1587, *pg.* 211
PHARMASHURE - Nutrition & Food Product - BALCHEM CORPORATION; *pg.* 839, *pg.* 1183
PHARMASORB - Activated Attapulgite for use in Medicines & Pharmaceuticals - BASF CATALYSTS LLC; *pg.* 1148, *pg.* 1074
PHARMASSURE - Pin - PALL CORPORATION; *pg.* 232, *pg.* 1323
PHARMAVITE - Nutritional Supplement - PHARMAVITE LLC; *pg.* 1584, *pg.* 167
PHARMFLASH - Newsletter - EPOCRATES, INC.; *pg.* 1529, *pg.* 254
PHARMFLO - Filtration System - SPECTRUM LABORATORIES INC.; *pg.* 1595, *pg.* 69
PHARMNET - Pharmacy Information System - CERNER CORPORATION; *pg.* 1514, *pg.* 981
PHARMOLIN - Pigment - BASF CATALYSTS LLC; *pg.* 1148, *pg.* 1074
PHAROAH'S GOLD - Lottery Game - MASSACHUSETTS STATE LOTTERY; *pg.* 998, *pg.* 802
PHAROS - Software - BIO-RAD LABORATORIES, INC.; *pg.* 1504, *pg.* 101
PHAROS - Actuators - FLOWSERVE CORPORATION; *pg.* 82, *pg.* 1719
PHAROS - Fabric - NEMSCHOFF, INC.; *pg.* 936, *pg.* 1890
PHAROSFX - Software - BIO-RAD LABORATORIES, INC.; *pg.* 1504, *pg.* 101
PHASCAST - Refractory Product - RESCO PRODUCTS, INC.; *pg.* 107, *pg.* 1581
PHASE - Specialty Product - JONES-HAMILTON CO.; *pg.* 1169, *pg.* 1478
PHASE - Software - SUNGARD DATA SYSTEMS INC.; *pg.* 477, *pg.* 1592

First page reference indicates Business Class Edition
Second page reference indicates Geographic Edition

PHASE - Liquid Butter Alternative - VENTURA FOODS, LLC; *pg.* 908, *pg.* 49
PHASE 2 STARCH NEUTRALIZER - Weight Control Product - NATROL, INC.; *pg.* 1570, *pg.* 64
PHASE 3 - Software - SUNGARD DATA SYSTEMS INC.; *pg.* 477, *pg.* 1592
PHASE ALPHA - Sheet Molding Compound Resins System - ASHLAND INC.; *pg.* 972, *pg.* 726
PHASE EIGHT - Closed-Circuit Television Equipment - VICON INDUSTRIES, INC.; *pg.* 685, *pg.* 1166
PHASE EPSILON - System for Molding Automotive Body Panels - ASHLAND INC.; *pg.* 972, *pg.* 726
PHASE IV - Software - DATATRAK INTERNATIONAL, INC.; *pg.* 383, *pg.* 1462
PHASEFLEX - Microwave Test Assembly - W.L. GORE & ASSOCIATES, INC.; *pg.* 122, *pg.* 388
PHASER - Bar Code Scanner - MOTOROLA ENTERPRISE MOBILITY; *pg.* 441, *pg.* 1167
PHASER - 3100 MFP/X Multifunction Printer - XEROX CORPORATION; *pg.* 494, *pg.* 365
PHASERCAL - Printer - XEROX CORPORATION; *pg.* 494, *pg.* 365
PHASERMATCH - Printer - XEROX CORPORATION; *pg.* 494, *pg.* 365
PHASERSHARE - Manual - XEROX CORPORATION; *pg.* 494, *pg.* 365
PHASERSMART - Printer - XEROX CORPORATION; *pg.* 494, *pg.* 365
PHASESEP - Coalescer System - PALL CORPORATION; *pg.* 232, *pg.* 1323
PHASGUN - Refractory Product - RESCO PRODUCTS, INC.; *pg.* 107, *pg.* 1581
PHASOR II - Membrane Contactor - ENTEGRIS, INC.; *pg.* 1882, *pg.* 788
PHASOR X - Heat Exchanger - ENTEGRIS, INC.; *pg.* 1882, *pg.* 788
PHAT MASTER CLIPPER - Clipper - ANDIS COMPANY; *pg.* 498, *pg.* 1895
PHAZE 1 - Car Audio Speakers - CLARION CORPORATION OF AMERICA; *pg.* 629, *pg.* 75
PHAZER - Actuator - FLOWSERVE CORPORATION; *pg.* 82, *pg.* 1719
PHD - Software - BIO-RAD LABORATORIES, INC.; *pg.* 1504, *pg.* 101
PH.D. - Chairs - VIRCO MANUFACTURING CORPORATION; *pg.* 946, *pg.* 297
PH.D.EXECUTIVE - Furniture - VIRCO MANUFACTURING CORPORATION; *pg.* 946, *pg.* 297
PHEASANT - Furniture - ASHLEY FURNITURE INDUSTRIES, INC.; *pg.* 914, *pg.* 1852
PHEASANT - Bath Product - KOHLER CO.; *pg.* 91, *pg.* 1862
PHEASANT RUN - Furniture - ASHLEY FURNITURE INDUSTRIES, INC.; *pg.* 914, *pg.* 1852
PHEASANTS FOREVER - Lotto Game - SOUTH DAKOTA LOTTERY; *pg.* 1006, *pg.* 1624
PHEDRA - Footwear - STEVEN MADDEN, LTD.; *pg.* 1819, *pg.* 1176
PHELPS MOUNTAIN - Clothing - ABERCROMBIE & FITCH CO.; *pg.* 37, *pg.* 1466
PHEMTS - Electronic Material - EMCORE CORPORATION; *pg.* 636, *pg.* 39
PHEN - Molecular Probe Product - THERMO FISHER SCIENTIFIC INC.; *pg.* 1602, *pg.* 61
PHENAFLEUR - Fragrance Ingredient - INTERNATIONAL FLAVORS & FRAGRANCES INC.; *pg.* 512, *pg.* 1244
PHENERGAN - Pharmaceutical Product - IMPAX LABORATORIES, INC.; *pg.* 1544, *pg.* 101
PHENEX - Nutritional Product - ABBOTT LABORATORIES; *pg.* 1484, *pg.* 551
PHENIX - Bookcase - F.E. HALE MANUFACTURING COMPANY; *pg.* 925, *pg.* 1160
PHENIX - Luxury Bus - FORETRAVEL INC.; *pg.* 1909, *pg.* 1728
PHENODUR - Solventborne - CYTEC INDUSTRIES, INC.; *pg.* 1155, *pg.* 1131
PHENOL - Resin - DOW CHEMICAL; *pg.* 1156, *pg.* 1563
PHENOLINE - Protective Coatings - CARBOLINE CO.; *pg.* 1152, *pg.* 994
PHENOM - Desktop SEM - FEI COMPANY; *pg.* 1413, *pg.* 1498
PHENOSCREEN - Clinical Drug Candidate Screening Product - MONOGRAM BIOSCIENCES, INC.; *pg.* 1569, *pg.* 280
PHENOSENSE - Healthcare Product - MONOGRAM BIOSCIENCES, INC.; *pg.* 1569, *pg.* 280
PHENOSENSE GT - Healthcare Product - MONOGRAM BIOSCIENCES, INC.; *pg.* 1569, *pg.* 280
PHENOXANOL - Fragrance Ingredient - INTERNATIONAL FLAVORS & FRAGRANCES INC.; *pg.* 512, *pg.* 1244
PHENTERMINE HCL - Pharmaceutical Product - LANNETT COMPANY, INC.; *pg.* 1555, *pg.* 1566
PHEOBE - Footwear - STEVEN MADDEN, LTD.; *pg.* 1819, *pg.* 1176
PHEONIX - Electronic Components - MOLEX INCORPORATED; *pg.* 655, *pg.* 628
PHEROMONE - Women's Fragance - MARILYN MIGLIN, L.P.; *pg.* 516, *pg.* 581
PHEROMONE FOR MEN - Men's Fragrance - MARILYN MIGLIN, L.P.; *pg.* 516, *pg.* 581
PHG - Hotel - PEABODY HOTEL GROUP, INC.; *pg.* 1107, *pg.* 1645
PHH ARVAL - Fleet Management Services - PHH CORPORATION; *pg.* 793, *pg.* 1090
PHH MORTGAGE - Direct Consumer Mortgages - PHH CORPORATION; *pg.* 793, *pg.* 1090
PHILADELPHIA - Orthopedic Product - DJO INCORPORATED; *pg.* 1524, *pg.* 302
PHILADELPHIA - Cream Cheeses - THE KRAFT HEINZ COMPANY; *pg.* 870, *pg.* 1577
PHILADELPHIA - Cream Cheese - MONDELEZ INTERNATIONAL, INC.; *pg.* 878, *pg.* 601
PHILADELPHIA - Carpets - SHAW INDUSTRIES GROUP, INC.; *pg.* 942, *pg.* 530
PHILADELPHIA SPORTS CLUBS - Fitness Center - TOWN SPORTS INTERNATIONAL HOLDINGS, INC.; *pg.* 589, *pg.* 1303
PHILCO - Air Conditioners & Furnaces - NORTEK GLOBAL HVAC; *pg.* 1075, *pg.* 989
PHILE+ - Software - WIND RIVER SYSTEMS, INC.; *pg.* 493, *pg.* 38
PHILIPP SPRING - Integrated Circuit - ATMEL CORPORATION; *pg.* 621, *pg.* 238
PHILIPPA - Furniture - HOOKER FURNITURE CORPORATION; *pg.* 928, *pg.* 1788
PHILIPS BODINE - LED Driver - PHILIPS EMERGENCY LIGHTING; *pg.* 1303, *pg.* 1631
PHILIPS COOLFLUX - Software - SYNOPSYS, INC.; *pg.* 480, *pg.* 162
PHILLIES - Little Cigars - ALTADIS USA, INC.; *pg.* 1893, *pg.* 423
PHILLIES BALLGIRLS - Baseball Tournament - THE PHILLIES, L.P.; *pg.* 575, *pg.* 1569
PHILLIES PHESTIVAL - Charity Service - THE PHILLIES, L.P.; *pg.* 575, *pg.* 1569
PHILLIES PHUNDAMENTALS - Educational Program - THE PHILLIES, L.P.; *pg.* 575, *pg.* 1569
PHILLIPS - Shield Icon - CONOCOPHILLIPS; *pg.* 975, *pg.* 1703
PHILLIPS - Processed Food - HANOVER FOODS CORPORATION; *pg.* 861, *pg.* 1535
PHILLIPS - Art Auctioneers - PHILLIPS DE PURY & COMPANY; *pg.* 576, *pg.* 1282
PHILLIPS 66 - Gasoline, Lubricants, Chemicals & Plastics - CONOCOPHILLIPS; *pg.* 975, *pg.* 1703
PHILLIPS 66-CONOCO-76 PERSONAL CARD - Credit Card - CITIGROUP INC.; *pg.* 735, *pg.* 1212
PHILLIPS AIRE - Heating & Ventilation Equipment - MESTEK, INC.; *pg.* 1074, *pg.* 857
PHILLIPS' HALEY'S M-O - Medicine - BAYER HEALTHCARE CONSUMER CARE DIVISION; *pg.* 1500, *pg.* 1087
PHILLIPS' MILK OF MAGNESIA - Medicine - BAYER HEALTHCARE CONSUMER CARE DIVISION; *pg.* 1500, *pg.* 1087
PHILLOCRAFT - Furniture - THE COMMERCIAL FURNITURE GROUP; *pg.* 920, *pg.* 994
PHILOS - Medical Device - DEPUY SYNTHES; *pg.* 1523, *pg.* 1593
PHILTERKOL - Anthracite - READING ANTHRACITE COMPANY; *pg.* 1179, *pg.* 1583
PHISODERM - Health & Beauty Product - CHATTEM, INC.; *pg.* 1515, *pg.* 1628
PHLASH - Software - PHOENIX TECHNOLOGIES LTD.; *pg.* 454, *pg.* 147
PHOBOL - Repellent Finishes - HUNTSMAN CORPORATION; *pg.* 1167, *pg.* 1758
PHOBOTEX - Repellent Finishes - HUNTSMAN CORPORATION; *pg.* 1167, *pg.* 1758
PHOBOTONE - Repellent Finishes - HUNTSMAN CORPORATION; *pg.* 1167, *pg.* 1758
PHOENICIAN - Rug - COURISTAN INC.; *pg.* 921, *pg.* 1067
THE PHOENICIAN - Hotels - STARWOOD HOTELS & RESORTS WORLDWIDE, INC.; *pg.* 1114, *pg.* 378
PHOENICIAN COLORS - Rug - COURISTAN INC.; *pg.* 921, *pg.* 1067
PHOENIX - Burners - ASTEC INDUSTRIES, INC.; *pg.* 69, *pg.* 1628
PHOENIX - Sewage Odor Control - CALGON CARBON CORPORATION; *pg.* 1151, *pg.* 1574
PHOENIX - Fan - CRAFTMADE INTERNATIONAL, INC.; *pg.* 1295, *pg.* 1670
PHOENIX - Thermal Imaging System - FLIR SYSTEMS, INC.; *pg.* 1413, *pg.* 1510
PHOENIX - Bevel Product - GLEASON CORPORATION; *pg.* 1340, *pg.* 1335
PHOENIX - Dinnerware - THE HOMER LAUGHLIN CHINA COMPANY; *pg.* 1125, *pg.* 1850
PHOENIX - Mobility Lift System - INVACARE CORPORATION; *pg.* 1546, *pg.* 1451
PHOENIX - Glove - KOMBI, LTD.; *pg.* 1838, *pg.* 1766
PHOENIX - Fabric - NEMSCHOFF, INC.; *pg.* 936, *pg.* 1890
PHOENIX - Sensor System - RAYTHEON COMPANY; *pg.* 233, *pg.* 854
PHOENIX - Fabric - UNIROYAL ENGINEERED PRODUCTS; *pg.* 699, *pg.* 467
PHOENIX - Grinder - WELDON SOLUTIONS; *pg.* 1388, *pg.* 1598
PHOENIX ALWAYS SDK - Software Tools - PHOENIX TECHNOLOGIES LTD.; *pg.* 454, *pg.* 147
PHOENIX ARENA SPORTS - Game - PHOENIX SUNS; *pg.* 576, *pg.* 19
PHOENIX AWARD - Software - PHOENIX TECHNOLOGIES LTD.; *pg.* 454, *pg.* 147
PHOENIX CB - Cutting Machine - GLEASON CORPORATION; *pg.* 1340, *pg.* 1335
PHOENIX EDGE - Eye Protection - MCR SAFETY; *pg.* 1422, *pg.* 1630
PHOENIX FAILSAFE - Theft-loss Protection Software - PHOENIX TECHNOLOGIES LTD.; *pg.* 454, *pg.* 147
PHOENIX FREEZE - Software - PHOENIX TECHNOLOGIES LTD.; *pg.* 454, *pg.* 147
PHOENIX I - Eye Protection - MCR SAFETY; *pg.* 1422, *pg.* 1630
PHOENIX ID GRINDER - Internal Dual Spindle Grinder - WELDON SOLUTIONS; *pg.* 1388, *pg.* 1598
PHOENIX II - Eye Protection - MCR SAFETY; *pg.* 1422, *pg.* 1630
PHOENIX INTERNATIONAL RACEWAY - Motorsports Facility - INTERNATIONAL SPEEDWAY CORPORATION; *pg.* 553, *pg.* 420
PHOENIX LINING SYSTEM - Corrosion Resistant System - ZCL COMPOSITES INC.; *pg.* 1892, *pg.* 1906
PHOENIX MERCURY - Game - PHOENIX SUNS; *pg.* 576, *pg.* 19
PHOENIX SECURECORE - Software - PHOENIX TECHNOLOGIES LTD.; *pg.* 454, *pg.* 147
PHOENIX SECURITY SDK - Software Tools - PHOENIX TECHNOLOGIES LTD.; *pg.* 454, *pg.* 147
PHOENIXBIOS - Software - PHOENIX TECHNOLOGIES LTD.; *pg.* 454, *pg.* 147
PHOENIXII - Grinding Machine - GLEASON CORPORATION; *pg.* 1340, *pg.* 1335
PHOLED - Organic Light Emitting Device - UNIVERSAL DISPLAY CORPORATION; *pg.* 683, *pg.* 1064
PHONATE - Medical Device - MALLINCKRODT PHARMACEUTICALS; *pg.* 1557, *pg.* 978
PHONE BACKER - Communication Product - CENTURYLINK, INC; *pg.* 1870, *pg.* 317
PHONE OBJECT - Software - MELISSA DATA CORP.; *pg.* 432, *pg.* 188
PHONE TAG - Video Slots - INTERNATIONAL GAME TECHNOLOGY; *pg.* 957, *pg.* 1024
PHONE+ - Publication - INFORMA EXHIBITIONS LLC; *pg.* 1653, *pg.* 17
PHONECAST TV - Data Tool - NEXAGE, INC.; *pg.* 1271, *pg.* 799
PHONEMAIL - Voice Processing System - SIEMENS CORPORATION; *pg.* 803, *pg.* 1291
PHONICS BUS - Educational Toys - LEAPFROG ENTERPRISES, INC.; *pg.* 961, *pg.* 84
PHONICS COMICS - Toy And Game - INNOVATIVE USA, INC.; *pg.* 957, *pg.* 363
PHONOCARD - Debit Card System - SIEMENS BUILDING TECHNOLOGIES, INC.; *pg.* 1376, *pg.* 560
PHOS DIP - Metal Finishing Product - HEATBATH CORPORATION; *pg.* 1165, *pg.* 826
PHOSBOOSTER - Chemical Product - DOVER CHEMICAL

CORPORATION; *pg.* 1156, *pg.* 1447
PHOSEAL - Metal Finishing Product - HEATBATH CORPORATION; *pg.* 1165, *pg.* 826
PHOSGARD - Metal Finishing Agents - GE WATER & PROCESS TECHNOLOGIES; *pg.* 1339, *pg.* 1588
PHOSHIELD - Phosphate System - A BRITE COMPANY; *pg.* 1144, *pg.* 1697
PHOSPHATIDYLSERINE - Nutritional Supplement - NATURAL ORGANICS, INC.; *pg.* 1571, *pg.* 1181
PHOSPHOR ANALYST - Software - BIO-RAD LABORATORIES, INC.; *pg.* 1504, *pg.* 101
PHOSVER - Chemical Reagent - HACH COMPANY; *pg.* 1415, *pg.* 334
PHOTAC - Light-Cured Glass Ionomer - 3M COMPANY; *pg.* 1142, *pg.* 956
PHOTO BOOTH - Application Program - APPLE INC.; *pg.* 350, *pg.* 73
PHOTO DISTRICT NEWS - Magazine Photography Market - NIELSEN BUSINESS MEDIA; *pg.* 1671, *pg.* 1272
PHOTO FINISH - Lottery Game - MASSACHUSETTS STATE LOTTERY; *pg.* 998, *pg.* 802
PHOTO-FLO - Photo Wetting Agent - EASTMAN KODAK COMPANY; *pg.* 1408, *pg.* 1333
PHOTO-FLOW - Software - R.R. DONNELLEY & SONS COMPANY; *pg.* 1682, *pg.* 589
PHOTO MARKER - Blueprint Paper - PINNACLE COATING & CONVERTING, INC.; *pg.* 1467, *pg.* 1622
PHOTO MECHANIC - Software - LEXAR MEDIA, INC.; *pg.* 1262, *pg.* 146
PHOTO MOUNT - Adhesives - 3M COMPANY; *pg.* 1142, *pg.* 956
THE PHOTO NETWORK - Website - CANDID COLOR SYSTEMS, INC.; *pg.* 1404, *pg.* 1485
PHOTO PC 550 - Digital Camera - EPSON AMERICA INC.; *pg.* 394, *pg.* 122
PHOTO PC 600 - Digital Camera - EPSON AMERICA INC.; *pg.* 394, *pg.* 122
PHOTO RITE - Management Services - RITE AID CORPORATION; *pg.* 1590, *pg.* 1519
PHOTO-TRANS - Heat Transfer Paper - NEENAH PAPER, INC.; *pg.* 1465, *pg.* 484
PHOTO WALLET ENVELOPES - Envelopes - TENSION ENVELOPE CORPORATION; *pg.* 483, *pg.* 986
PHOTOART - Jewelry - PUPPYPAWS, INC.; *pg.* 11, *pg.* 1463
PHOTOBROWN - Glass & Ceramic Material - CORNING INCORPORATED; *pg.* 1122, *pg.* 1154
PHOTOBROWN EXTRA - Glass & Ceramic Material - CORNING INCORPORATED; *pg.* 1122, *pg.* 1154
PHOTOCASTING - Digital Content Delivery Service - APPLE INC.; *pg.* 350, *pg.* 73
PHOTODOC-IT - Imaging System - UVP, INC.; *pg.* 1434, *pg.* 298
PHOTOFRAME - Electronic Picture Frame - PHILIPS ELECTRONICS NORTH AMERICA; *pg.* 662, *pg.* 782
PHOTOGLAZE - Coating - LORD CORPORATION; *pg.* 1357, *pg.* 1360
PHOTOGRAPHY FOR A LIFETIME - Slogan - LIFETOUCH, INC.; *pg.* 1420, *pg.* 922
PHOTOGRAY - Glass & Ceramic Material - CORNING INCORPORATED; *pg.* 1122, *pg.* 1154
PHOTOGRAY EXTRA - Glass & Ceramic Material - CORNING INCORPORATED; *pg.* 1122, *pg.* 1154
PHOTOHELIC - Differential Pressure Gauge - GE ENERGY; *pg.* 1338, *pg.* 506
PHOTOKLEEN - Filter Assembly - PALL CORPORATION; *pg.* 232, *pg.* 1323
PHOTOLIFE - Batteries - EASTMAN KODAK COMPANY; *pg.* 1408, *pg.* 1333
PHOTOLINK - Surface Modification Technology - SURMODICS, INC.; *pg.* 1600, *pg.* 924
PHOTOMAPPER - Software - DIGITALGLOBE, INC.; *pg.* 1408, *pg.* 333
PHOTOMAX - Digital Photography System - NU SKIN ENTERPRISES, INC.; *pg.* 518, *pg.* 1755
PHOTONICS DIRECTORY - Industry Reference for Photonics Technology - LAURIN PUBLISHING CO., INC.; *pg.* 1658, *pg.* 841
THE PHOTONICS PRODUCT & RESOURCE SHOWCASE - Photonics Product & Resource Guide - LAURIN PUBLISHING CO., INC.; *pg.* 1658, *pg.* 841
PHOTONICS SPECTRA - Photonics Industry & Science Magazine - LAURIN PUBLISHING CO., INC.; *pg.* 1658, *pg.* 841
PHOTONICS.COM - Web Site - LAURIN PUBLISHING CO., INC.; *pg.* 1658, *pg.* 841
PHOTONICSFIBER.COM - Photonics Industry News Web Site - LAURIN PUBLISHING CO., INC.; *pg.* 1658, *pg.* 841
PHOTONICSWEB DIRECTORY - Print Guide to the Photonics Web Sites - LAURIN PUBLISHING CO., INC.; *pg.* 1658, *pg.* 841
PHOTOPLAS - Ultra-Violet Curable Coating - RED SPOT PAINT & VARNISH CO., INC.; *pg.* 1446, *pg.* 679
PHOTOPOSIT - Resist Product - DOW CHEMICAL; *pg.* 1156, *pg.* 1563
PHOTOPRO - Software - ACD SYSTEMS INTERNATIONAL INC.; *pg.* 340, *pg.* 1913
PHOTOSCREEN - Assays & Reagents - PERKINELMER, INC.; *pg.* 1426, *pg.* 853
PHOTOSEE - Software - ACD SYSTEMS INTERNATIONAL INC.; *pg.* 340, *pg.* 1913
PHOTOSHOP - Software - ADOBE SYSTEMS INCORPORATED; *pg.* 342, *pg.* 235
PHOTOSILK - Skin Rejuvenation System - CYNOSURE, INC.; *pg.* 1521, *pg.* 858
PHOTOSMART - Digital Camera Products - HEWLETT-PACKARD COMPANY; *pg.* 404, *pg.* 175
PHOTOSOL - Optical Product - PPG INDUSTRIES, INC.; *pg.* 1445, *pg.* 1579
PHOTOSTAMPS - Postage - STAMPS.COM INC.; *pg.* 1282, *pg.* 82
PHOTOSWITCH - Photoelectric Controls & Sensors - ROCKWELL AUTOMATION, INC.; *pg.* 668, *pg.* 1880
PHRODO - Indicator - THERMO FISHER SCIENTIFIC INC.; *pg.* 1602, *pg.* 61
PHTHALIC ANHYDRIDE - Chemical Product - STEPAN COMPANY; *pg.* 1182, *pg.* 643
PHYCOTENE CREME - Personal Care Product - RBC LIFE SCIENCES, INC.; *pg.* 1588, *pg.* 1723
PHYNYLTROPE - Mydriotic Ophthalmic Solution - THE COOPER COMPANIES, INC.; *pg.* 1518, *pg.* 183
PHYSICAL ANALYST - Software - SYNOPSYS, INC.; *pg.* 480, *pg.* 162
PHYSICAL COMPILER - Software - SYNOPSYS, INC.; *pg.* 480, *pg.* 162
PHYSICIAN QUALITY GUIDE - Healthcare Product - HEALTH GRADES, INC.; *pg.* 1256, *pg.* 319
PHYSICIAN REPORT CARDS - Healthcare Product - HEALTH GRADES, INC.; *pg.* 1256, *pg.* 319
PHYSICIANS CARE - First Aid Kits - ACME UNITED CORPORATION; *pg.* 1040, *pg.* 346
PHYSICIANS' DESK REF. FOR NON-PRESCRIPTION DRUGS - Drug Publication - TRUVEN HEALTH ANALYTICS; *pg.* 1696, *pg.* 867
PHYSICIANS' DESK REFERENCE - Drug Publication - TRUVEN HEALTH ANALYTICS; *pg.* 1696, *pg.* 867
PHYSICIANS' DESK REFERENCE FOR HERBAL MEDICINES - Healthcare Publication - TRUVEN HEALTH ANALYTICS; *pg.* 1696, *pg.* 867
PHYSICIANS' DESK REFERENCE FOR OPTHALMOLOGY - Drug Publication - TRUVEN HEALTH ANALYTICS; *pg.* 1696, *pg.* 867
PHYSICIANS INTERACTIVE - Software - ALLSCRIPTS HEALTHCARE SOLUTIONS, INC.; *pg.* 1492, *pg.* 563
PHYSICIANS PROTECTOR PLAN - Insurance Package Program - BROWN & BROWN, INC.; *pg.* 1196, *pg.* 419
PHYSICIANS REPORT WRITER - Medical Product - HOLOGIC, INC.; *pg.* 1416, *pg.* 784
PHYSICIANS VIEWER - Medical Product - HOLOGIC, INC.; *pg.* 1416, *pg.* 784
PHYSICS - Software - ELEKTA; *pg.* 391, *pg.* 987
PHYSIOBALLS - Ball - SCHOOL-TECH, INC.; *pg.* 1844, *pg.* 866
PHYSIONEAL - Healthcare Product - BAXTER INTERNATIONAL INC.; *pg.* 1499, *pg.* 599
PHYT-ALOE - Medical Device - MANNATECH, INCORPORATED; *pg.* 1558, *pg.* 1671
PHYTO FEM - Herbal Formula - SHAKLEE CORPORATION; *pg.* 1593, *pg.* 184
PHYTO POWER - Nutritional Product - RBC LIFE SCIENCES, INC.; *pg.* 1588, *pg.* 1723
PHYTOCHROME - Healthcare Product - INTEGRATED BIOPHARMA, INC.; *pg.* 1546, *pg.* 1073
PHYTOESTRIN - Nutritional Supplement - USANA HEALTH SCIENCES, INC.; *pg.* 1605, *pg.* 1761
PHYTOGEN - Cottonseeds - DOW AGROSCIENCES LLC; *pg.* 1156, *pg.* 684
PHYTOMATRIX - Healthcare Product - MANNATECH, INCORPORATED; *pg.* 1558, *pg.* 1671
PHYTOSEL - Healthcare Product - INTEGRATED BIOPHARMA, INC.; *pg.* 1546, *pg.* 1073
PI-980 - Controller - ADVANCED ENERGY INDUSTRIES, INC.; *pg.* 613, *pg.* 328
PI CONVENTION - Pharmaceutical Sales Software - ALLSCRIPTS HEALTHCARE SOLUTIONS, INC.; *pg.* 1492, *pg.* 563
PI E-DETAILING - Pharmaceutical Promotional & Educational Program - ALLSCRIPTS HEALTHCARE SOLUTIONS, INC.; *pg.* 1492, *pg.* 563
PI EXPERT - Software - POWER INTEGRATIONS, INC.; *pg.* 1369, *pg.* 249
PI FACTS - Switch - POWER INTEGRATIONS, INC.; *pg.* 1369, *pg.* 249
PI SURVEY - Market Research Program - ALLSCRIPTS HEALTHCARE SOLUTIONS, INC.; *pg.* 1492, *pg.* 563
PIAA - Wiper Blades - MACNEIL AUTOMOTIVE PRODUCTS, LTD.; *pg.* 211, *pg.* 559
PIACENZA - Carpet - INTERFACE, INC.; *pg.* 695, *pg.* 512
PIANTA - Carpet - INTERFACE, INC.; *pg.* 695, *pg.* 512
PIAZZA'S - Food Product - ADVANCEPIERRE FOODS, INC.; *pg.* 1714, *pg.* 1409
PIBB XTRA - Soft Drink - THE COCA-COLA COMPANY; *pg.* 240, *pg.* 493
PIBB ZERO - Beverages - THE COCA-COLA COMPANY; *pg.* 240, *pg.* 493
PIBOX - Imagery Management Control Box - LOCKHEED MARTIN CORPORATION; *pg.* 229, *pg.* 762
PIC-200 - Programmable Infrared Remote Controller - RETZLAFF INCORPORATED; *pg.* 667, *pg.* 258
PIC 30 - Defibrillator - WELCH ALLYN INC.; *pg.* 1436, *pg.* 1342
PIC 40 - Defibrillator - WELCH ALLYN INC.; *pg.* 1436, *pg.* 1342
PIC 50 - Defibrillator - WELCH ALLYN INC.; *pg.* 1436, *pg.* 1342
PIC 77 - Icing Powders - MALLET & COMPANY, INC.; *pg.* 875, *pg.* 1521
PIC-PAK - Reusable Consumer Packaging - HINDLEY MANUFACTURING COMPANY, INC.; *pg.* 1049, *pg.* 1601
PIC-SURE-STAY - Picture Hanging Aid - MOORE PUSH PIN CO.; *pg.* 441, *pg.* 1595
PICADOR USA - Book - ST. MARTINS PRESS, INC.; *pg.* 1688, *pg.* 1295
PICASA - Internet Application - GOOGLE INC.; *pg.* 1249, *pg.* 153
PICAVIEW - Image Viewing & Manipulation Software - ACD SYSTEMS INTERNATIONAL INC.; *pg.* 340, *pg.* 1913
PICC-NATE - Neonatal Peripherally Inserted Central Catheters - UTAH MEDICAL PRODUCTS, INC.; *pg.* 1605, *pg.* 1752
PICCADILLY - Fabric - NEMSCHOFF, INC.; *pg.* 936, *pg.* 1890
PICCADILLY EXPRESS - Carry Out - PICCADILLY RESTAURANTS, LLC; *pg.* 1744, *pg.* 742
PICCIONE - Bridal Wear - ALFRED ANGELO, INC.; *pg.* 17, *pg.* 1532
PICCO - Hydrocarbon Resins - EASTMAN CHEMICAL COMPANY; *pg.* 1159, *pg.* 1636
PICCOLASTIC - Hydrocarbon Resins - EASTMAN CHEMICAL COMPANY; *pg.* 1159, *pg.* 1636
PICCOLO - Medical Instruments - ABAXIS, INC.; *pg.* 1483, *pg.* 298
PICCOLO - Fan - CRAFTMADE INTERNATIONAL, INC.; *pg.* 1295, *pg.* 1670
PICCOLO - Measuring Device - CROLL-REYNOLDS COMPANY, INC.; *pg.* 1326, *pg.* 1103
PICCOLO XPRESS - Diagnostic Instruments - ABAXIS, INC.; *pg.* 1483, *pg.* 298
PICCOTAC - Hydrocarbon Resins - EASTMAN CHEMICAL COMPANY; *pg.* 1159, *pg.* 1636
PICCOTEX - Hydrocarbon Resins - EASTMAN CHEMICAL COMPANY; *pg.* 1159, *pg.* 1636
THE PICK - Lottery Game - ARIZONA LOTTERY; *pg.* 988, *pg.* 14
PICK - Database Software product - TIGERLOGIC CORPORATION; *pg.* 484, *pg.* 117
PICK 10 - Lottery Game - NEW YORK STATE LOTTERY; *pg.* 1001, *pg.* 1340
PICK-2 DOUBLE-UP POKER - Game - INTERNATIONAL GAME TECHNOLOGY; *pg.* 420, *pg.* 1606
PICK 3 - Lottery Game - ARIZONA LOTTERY; *pg.* 988, *pg.* 14
PICK 3 - Lottery Game - ILLINOIS STATE LOTTERY; *pg.* 995, *pg.* 578
PICK 3 - Lottery Game - IOWA LOTTERY; *pg.* 996, *pg.* 705
PICK 3 - Lottery Game - LOUISIANA LOTTERY

CORPORATION; *pg.* 997, *pg.* 742
PICK 3 - Lottery Game - MISSOURI LOTTERY; *pg.* 999, *pg.* 979
PICK-3 - Three Digit Daily Numbers Game - NEW JERSEY STATE LOTTERY; *pg.* 1000, *pg.* 1126
PICK 3 - Lottery - TEXAS LOTTERY COMMISSION; *pg.* 1007, *pg.* 1666
PICK 3 NUMBERS - Lottery Game - OHIO LOTTERY COMMISSION; *pg.* 1002, *pg.* 1433
PICK 4 - Lottery Game - ILLINOIS STATE LOTTERY; *pg.* 995, *pg.* 578
PICK 4 - Lottery Game - LOUISIANA LOTTERY CORPORATION; *pg.* 997, *pg.* 742
PICK 4 - Lottery Game - MISSOURI LOTTERY; *pg.* 999, *pg.* 979
PICK-4 - Four Digit Daily Numbers Game - NEW JERSEY STATE LOTTERY; *pg.* 1000, *pg.* 1126
PICK 4 - Lottery Game - THE SOUTH CAROLINA EDUCATION LOTTERY; *pg.* 1005, *pg.* 1614
PICK 4 NUMBERS - Lottery Game - OHIO LOTTERY COMMISSION; *pg.* 1002, *pg.* 1433
PICK-6 LOTTO - Six Digit Lotto Game - NEW JERSEY STATE LOTTERY; *pg.* 1000, *pg.* 1126
PICK-A-POCKET - Educational Product - BARKER CREEK PUBLISHING INC.; *pg.* 1619, *pg.* 1818
PICK-ME-UP - Bouquet - FTD GROUP, INC.; *pg.* 1795, *pg.* 608
PICK 'N SAVE - Warehouse Food Stores - ROUNDY'S SUPERMARKETS INC.; *pg.* 1032, *pg.* 1880
PICK-N-SPIN - Game - WMS INDUSTRIES INC.; *pg.* 593, *pg.* 666
PICK OF THE PROFESSIONALS - Tagline - ANDIS COMPANY; *pg.* 498, *pg.* 1895
PICK UP STIX - Restaurants - CARLSON COMPANIES INC.; *pg.* 1084, *pg.* 947
PICK YOUR FORTUNE - Game - WMS INDUSTRIES INC.; *pg.* 593, *pg.* 666
PICKDBI - Database Product - TIGERLOGIC CORPORATION; *pg.* 484, *pg.* 117
PICKLEEN - Surface Activation Product - A BRITE COMPANY; *pg.* 1144, *pg.* 1697
PICKUP ON DEMAND - Postal Services - UNITED STATES POSTAL SERVICE; *pg.* 1009, *pg.* 406
PICKUP STICK - Hand Tool - GENERAL TOOLS & INSTRUMENTS LLC; *pg.* 1048, *pg.* 1234
PICNIC - Fabric - NEMSCHOFF, INC.; *pg.* 936, *pg.* 1890
PICNIC PLUS - Table - LIFETIME PRODUCTS INC.; *pg.* 933, *pg.* 1751
PICO - Fuse Product - LITTELFUSE, INC.; *pg.* 1301, *pg.* 580
PICO - Leak Detector - MKS INSTRUMENTS, INC.; *pg.* 1362, *pg.* 781
PICO - Software - ROCKWELL AUTOMATION, INC.; *pg.* 668, *pg.* 1880
PICO 50 - General-purpose Catheter Sampler - RADIOMETER AMERICA INC.; *pg.* 1588, *pg.* 1481
PICO-CHANGE - Electronic Components - MOLEX INCORPORATED; *pg.* 655, *pg.* 628
PICO-CLASP - Electronic Components - MOLEX INCORPORATED; *pg.* 655, *pg.* 628
PICO-EZMATE - Electronic Components - MOLEX INCORPORATED; *pg.* 655, *pg.* 628
PICO/FEMTOCELL CONVERGENCE - Cable Solutions - SONUS NETWORKS INC.; *pg.* 1281, *pg.* 858
PICO FUSE - Fast-Acting Subminiature Fuse with Axial Leads - LITTELFUSE, INC.; *pg.* 1301, *pg.* 580
PICO-GOLD - Electronic Components - MOLEX INCORPORATED; *pg.* 655, *pg.* 628
PICO-GRID - Electronic Components - MOLEX INCORPORATED; *pg.* 655, *pg.* 628
PICO-SPOX - Electronic Components - MOLEX INCORPORATED; *pg.* 655, *pg.* 628
PICO TAG - Acid Analysis Technique - WATERS CORPORATION; *pg.* 1436, *pg.* 834
PICOBLADE - Connector - MOLEX INCORPORATED; *pg.* 655, *pg.* 628
PICOBLAZE - Soft Processor Core - XILINX, INC.; *pg.* 496, *pg.* 252
PICOFLEX - Connector - MOLEX INCORPORATED; *pg.* 655, *pg.* 628
PICOGFX - Software - ROCKWELL AUTOMATION, INC.; *pg.* 668, *pg.* 1880
PICOLO - Footwear - STEVEN MADDEN, LTD.; *pg.* 1819, *pg.* 1176
PICOP - Display System - MICROVISION, INC.; *pg.* 654, *pg.* 1828
PICOPOWER - Microcontroller - ATMEL CORPORATION; *pg.* 621, *pg.* 238
PICOR - Input Filter - VICOR CORPORATION; *pg.* 1435, *pg.* 783
PICORAPTR - Electrochemistry Meters - BECKMAN COULTER, INC.; *pg.* 1402, *pg.* 48
PICS SIMULATION - Electronic Components - MOLEX INCORPORATED; *pg.* 655, *pg.* 628
PICTIONARY - Game - HASBRO, INC.; *pg.* 954, *pg.* 1603
PICTIONARY JUNIOR - Toy & Game - HASBRO, INC.; *pg.* 954, *pg.* 1603
PICTOGRAM - Fabric - NEMSCHOFF, INC.; *pg.* 936, *pg.* 1890
PICTOR-XT - Autoguider & Imagers - MEADE INSTRUMENTS CORPORATION; *pg.* 1422, *pg.* 113
PICTURE BOOK PARADE - Educational Materials - SCHOLASTIC INC.; *pg.* 1683, *pg.* 1288
PICTURE KING - Screen - DA-LITE SCREEN COMPANY; *pg.* 632, *pg.* 698
THE PICTURE PEOPLE - Greeting Card - HALLMARK CARDS, INC.; *pg.* 1646, *pg.* 983
PICTURE PERFECT - Mirror - CONAIR CORPORATION; *pg.* 505, *pg.* 1055
PICTURE PERFECT - Action Figures & Collectibles - HASBRO, INC.; *pg.* 954, *pg.* 1603
PICTURE PERFECT BINGO - Game - MISSOURI LOTTERY; *pg.* 999, *pg.* 979
PICTURE POPS - Flat Lollipops - SPANGLER CANDY COMPANY; *pg.* 1862, *pg.* 1407
PICTUREKA! - Toy & Game - HASBRO, INC.; *pg.* 954, *pg.* 1603
PICTUREWALL - Electronic Display System - TRANS-LUX CORPORATION; *pg.* 681, *pg.* 365
PICTURING LIFE - Diagnostic Imaging Product - HOLOGIC, INC.; *pg.* 1416, *pg.* 784
PID-TECH - Photoionization Sensor - MOCON, INC.; *pg.* 1363, *pg.* 940
PIE BABY - Desserts - FRISCH'S RESTAURANTS, INC.; *pg.* 1729, *pg.* 1413
PIELS LIGHT - Beer - PABST BREWING COMPANY; *pg.* 258, *pg.* 137
PIER 1 KIDS - Retail Outlet - PIER 1 IMPORTS, INC.; *pg.* 940, *pg.* 1695
PIERCE - Rust Remover - LA-CO INDUSTRIES MARKAL CO., INC.; *pg.* 1170, *pg.* 610
PIERCE - Fire & Emergency Trucks - OSHKOSH CORPORATION; *pg.* 187, *pg.* 1885
PIERCE - Fire & Emergency Apparatus - PIERCE MANUFACTURING, INC.; *pg.* 188, *pg.* 1852
PIERCE AIRROW - Underground Construction Equipment - CHARLES MACHINE WORKS, INC.; *pg.* 1322, *pg.* 1488
PIERPORT - Food Product - SHAMROCK FOODS COMPANY; *pg.* 895, *pg.* 20
PIERRE - Furniture - HOOKER FURNITURE CORPORATION; *pg.* 928, *pg.* 1788
PIERRE CLASSICS - Food Product - ADVANCEPIERRE FOODS, INC.; *pg.* 1714, *pg.* 1409
PIERRE CREATIONS - Food Product - ADVANCEPIERRE FOODS, INC.; *pg.* 1714, *pg.* 1409
PIERRE CUISINE - Food Product - ADVANCEPIERRE FOODS, INC.; *pg.* 1714, *pg.* 1409
PIERRE MAIN STREET DINER - Food Product - ADVANCEPIERRE FOODS, INC.; *pg.* 1714, *pg.* 1409
PIERRE SELECT - Food Product - ADVANCEPIERRE FOODS, INC.; *pg.* 1714, *pg.* 1409
PIERRE SIGNATURES - Food Product - ADVANCEPIERRE FOODS, INC.; *pg.* 1714, *pg.* 1409
PIETRA CAMPANIA - Ceramic, Glass, Stone Tiles & Slabs - WALKER & ZANGER, INC.; *pg.* 119, *pg.* 281
PIETRA DI FIANDRA - Ceramic, Glass, Stone Tiles & Slabs - WALKER & ZANGER, INC.; *pg.* 119, *pg.* 281
PIETRAFITTA - Italian Wine - LAIRD & COMPANY, INC.; *pg.* 1966, *pg.* 1119
PIEZOBALANCE - Electronic Monitor - TSI INCORPORATED; *pg.* 1432, *pg.* 965
PIEZOPOWER - Piezoelectric Ceramic Materials - CTS CORPORATION; *pg.* 631, *pg.* 677
PIG CHAMP - Software - FARMS.COM LTD.; *pg.* 1247, *pg.* 1922
PIG INT'L - Global Magazine for Pig Producers - WATT PUBLISHING COMPANY; *pg.* 1701, *pg.* 655
PIG NURSERY FORMULA - Animal Treatment - KENT NUTRITION GROUP; *pg.* 1477, *pg.* 710
PIG PROFILE - Record Keeping System - KENT NUTRITION GROUP; *pg.* 1477, *pg.* 710
PIG-SIG - Pipeline Pigging Product - T.D. WILLIAMSON, INC.; *pg.* 1380, *pg.* 1490
PIG-SIG IV - Scraper Passage Indicator - T.D. WILLIAMSON, INC.; *pg.* 1380, *pg.* 1490
PIG TAILS - Cables - EMCORE CORPORATION; *pg.* 636, *pg.* 39
PIGGSLY - Pig Puppet - GUND, INC.; *pg.* 954, *pg.* 1056
PIGGY BANKIN - Game - WMS INDUSTRIES INC.; *pg.* 593, *pg.* 666
PIGGYBACK - Labels - AVERY DENNISON CORPORATION; *pg.* 1452, *pg.* 95
PIGGYBACK - Stabilizer - BAKER HUGHES INTEQ; *pg.* 1316, *pg.* 1700
PIGGYBACK - Battery Charger - STREAMLIGHT INC.; *pg.* 1306, *pg.* 1527
PIGMENT - Fabric - NEMSCHOFF, INC.; *pg.* 936, *pg.* 1890
PIK-A-NUT - Hardware Product - DORMAN PRODUCTS, INC.; *pg.* 204, *pg.* 1522
PIKE CREEK - Whisky - MCCORMICK DISTILLING CO., INC.; *pg.* 1966, *pg.* 1007
PIKE PLACE ROAST - Coffee - STARBUCKS CORPORATION; *pg.* 897, *pg.* 1840
PIKEVILLE - Footwear - EASTLAND SHOE CORPORATION; *pg.* 1808, *pg.* 750
PIKO - Beverages - THE COCA-COLA COMPANY; *pg.* 240, *pg.* 493
PILATES ARC - Barrel - BALANCED BODY, INC.; *pg.* 1826, *pg.* 195
PILATES IQ - Reformer - BALANCED BODY, INC.; *pg.* 1826, *pg.* 195
PILE CHOPPER - Snowboarding Gloves - KOMBI, LTD.; *pg.* 1838, *pg.* 1766
PILEDRIVER - Piston Pumps - LINCOLN INDUSTRIAL CORP.; *pg.* 1355, *pg.* 999
PILGRIM'S PRIDE - Poultry Products - PILGRIM'S PRIDE CORPORATION; *pg.* 889, *pg.* 330
PILGRIM'S SIGNATURE - Poultry Products - PILGRIM'S PRIDE CORPORATION; *pg.* 889, *pg.* 330
PILKINGTON ACTIV - Self-Cleaning Glass - PILKINGTON NORTH AMERICA, INC.; *pg.* 215, *pg.* 1477
PILLAR - Software - SRA INTERNATIONAL, INC.; *pg.* 473, *pg.* 1780
PILLAR ROCK - Canned - OCEAN BEAUTY SEAFOODS, INC.; *pg.* 1028, *pg.* 1838
PILLMINDER - Carrying Case - MEDICOOL, INC.; *pg.* 1562, *pg.* 294
PILLOPOST - Carton - PACTIV CORPORATION; *pg.* 1466, *pg.* 624
PILLOW BUDDIES - Infant Toys - CROWN CRAFTS INFANT PRODUCTS, INC.; *pg.* 922, *pg.* 68
PILLOW SOFT - Moldable Silicone Earplugs - MCKEON PRODUCTS, INC.; *pg.* 1559, *pg.* 912
PILLOW TOPPER - Mattress Cover - JAMISON BEDDING, INC.; *pg.* 930, *pg.* 1651
PILLOWBACKS - Shoes - P.W. MINOR & SON, INC.; *pg.* 1816, *pg.* 1140
PILLOWFLEX - Foam - FXI; *pg.* 1163, *pg.* 1552
PILLSBURY - Food Products - GENERAL MILLS, INC.; *pg.* 828, *pg.* 933
PILLSBURY - Flour Products - THE J.M. SMUCKER COMPANY; *pg.* 865, *pg.* 1468
PILLSBURY PIZZA MINIS - Pizza Snacks - GENERAL MILLS, INC.; *pg.* 828, *pg.* 933
PILLSBURY PIZZA POPS - Pizza Snacks - GENERAL MILLS, INC.; *pg.* 828, *pg.* 933
PILOT - Automobile - AMERICAN HONDA MOTOR CO., INC.; *pg.* 163, *pg.* 292
PILOT - Knife - BUCK KNIVES, INC.; *pg.* 1828, *pg.* 550
PILOT - Knife - COAST CUTLERY COMPANY; *pg.* 1121, *pg.* 1501
PILOT - Eyewear - MAUI JIM, INC.; *pg.* 9, *pg.* 651
PILOT - Bicycle - TREK BICYCLE CORPORATION; *pg.* 1847, *pg.* 1896
PILOTEX - Ultra High Speed Deluge System - TYCO SIMPLEXGRINNELL LP; *pg.* 682, *pg.* 859
PILOTONLINE.COM - Online Newspaper - PILOT MEDIA; *pg.* 1677, *pg.* 1797
PILOTPAK - Burner - MAXON CORPORATION; *pg.* 1359, *pg.* 695
PILSKANIA - Beverages - THE COCA-COLA COMPANY; *pg.* 240, *pg.* 493
PILSNER - Beer - MOLSON COORS BREWING COMPANY; *pg.* 256, *pg.* 321
PILSNER - Beer - MOLSON COORS CANADA INC.; *pg.* 256, *pg.* 1955

PILSNER URQUELL - Beer - MILLERCOORS; *pg.* 254, *pg.* 1877
PILT - Wood Preservative Coating Composition - PPG INDUSTRIES, INC.; *pg.* 1445, *pg.* 1579
PIMA - Linens Fabrics - TEMPUR SEALY INTERNATIONAL, INC.; *pg.* 944, *pg.* 731
PIMIC - Metal Ion Control Services - THE DOW CHEMICAL COMPANY; *pg.* 1157, *pg.* 898
PIMSLEUR - Audio Publishing Imprint - SIMON & SCHUSTER, INC.; *pg.* 1687, *pg.* 1292
PIN BRINELL - Hardness Tester - NEWAGE TESTING INSTRUMENTS, INC.; *pg.* 1058, *pg.* 1532
PIN LATCH - Latch - SOUTHCO, INC.; *pg.* 1063, *pg.* 1522
PIN-TECH - Pressure Relief Vent - THE PROTECTOSEAL COMPANY; *pg.* 1370, *pg.* 556
PINACLE - Banking Services - THE PNC FINANCIAL SERVICES GROUP, INC.; *pg.* 795, *pg.* 1579
PINBALL WIZARD - Lottery Game - MASSACHUSETTS STATE LOTTERY; *pg.* 998, *pg.* 802
PINBALL WIZARD - Lottery Game - OHIO LOTTERY COMMISSION; *pg.* 1002, *pg.* 1433
PINCH-PROOF - Ladder Product - WERNER HOLDING CO.; *pg.* 121, *pg.* 1534
PINDOT - Custom Seating System - INVACARE CORPORATION; *pg.* 1546, *pg.* 1451
PINE FOREST - All Purpose Cleaner - BLUE CROSS LABORATORIES; *pg.* 326, *pg.* 277
PINE MOUNTAIN - Firelogs - JARDEN CORPORATION; *pg.* 1885, *pg.* 412
PINE MOUNTAIN - Bike - MARIN BIKES; *pg.* 1708, *pg.* 168
PINE-O-CIDE - Cleaning Product - HILLYARD, INC.; *pg.* 331, *pg.* 990
PINE POINT TRAIL - Clothing - ABERCROMBIE & FITCH CO.; *pg.* 37, *pg.* 1466
PINE RIDGE - Riflescopes - CABELA'S INCORPORATED; *pg.* 535, *pg.* 1019
PINE-SOL - Cleaning Product - THE CLOROX COMPANY; *pg.* 327, *pg.* 169
PINEALEN - Cleaning Product - ALEN AMERICAS INC.; *pg.* 325, *pg.* 1699
PINEAPPLE - Window Treatment - HERITAGE LACE INC.; *pg.* 694, *pg.* 711
PINECONE - Decorative Hook - HERITAGE LACE INC.; *pg.* 694, *pg.* 711
PINECONE HOLLY - Pillow and Throw - HERITAGE LACE INC.; *pg.* 694, *pg.* 711
PINEDALE - Furniture - ASHLEY FURNITURE INDUSTRIES, INC.; *pg.* 914, *pg.* 1852
PINEHURST - Fabric - NEMSCHOFF, INC.; *pg.* 936, *pg.* 1890
PINELLA - Furniture - ASHLEY FURNITURE INDUSTRIES, INC.; *pg.* 914, *pg.* 1852
PINES BROOK VINTNERS - Spirits - LEONARD KREUSCH, INC.; *pg.* 254, *pg.* 1099
PINEX - Cleaner - SWISHER HYGIENE INC.; *pg.* 336, *pg.* 1507
PINEXO - Cleaners - THE CLOROX COMPANY; *pg.* 327, *pg.* 169
PING - Shirt - BROWN & BIGELOW, INC.; *pg.* 1624, *pg.* 959
PING - Golf Equipment - KARSTEN MANUFACTURING CORPORATION; *pg.* 1838, *pg.* 17
PING - Golf Equipment - PING INC.; *pg.* 1842, *pg.* 19
PING PONG - Textiles - BERNHARDT DESIGN; *pg.* 918, *pg.* 1381
PING PONG - Sporting Good Product - ESCALADE INC.; *pg.* 1833, *pg.* 678
PINHOLEFREE - Mirror - NEWPORT CORPORATION; *pg.* 1424, *pg.* 114
PINION-PAC - Bearing - THE TIMKEN COMPANY; *pg.* 218, *pg.* 1408
PINK - Hair Lotion - LUSTER PRODUCTS INC.; *pg.* 515, *pg.* 581
PINK-A-BOO - Container Grown Plant - MONROVIA GROWERS; *pg.* 1797, *pg.* 44
PINK DIAMOND - Video Game - INTERNATIONAL GAME TECHNOLOGY; *pg.* 957, *pg.* 1024
PINK DISH - Liquid Detergent - EDWARD DON & COMPANY; *pg.* 54, *pg.* 672
PINK DOUBLE KNOCK OUT - Garden Roses - THE CONARD-PYLE COMPANY; *pg.* 1794, *pg.* 1594
PINK DRIFT - Garden Roses - THE CONARD-PYLE COMPANY; *pg.* 1794, *pg.* 1594
PINK ELEPHANTS - Belt - VANS, INC.; *pg.* 1821, *pg.* 76
PINK ELF - Container Grown Plant - MONROVIA GROWERS; *pg.* 1797, *pg.* 44
PINK FIBERGLAS - Insulation - OWENS CORNING; *pg.* 102, *pg.* 1476
PINK INCE RUE21 - Fragrance - RUE21, INC.; *pg.* 32, *pg.* 1591
PINK IS THE NEW BLOG - News & Gossip Blog - SPINMEDIA; *pg.* 1282, *pg.* 104
PINK KNOCK OUT - Garden Roses - THE CONARD-PYLE COMPANY; *pg.* 1794, *pg.* 1594
PINK LEMONADE LEMON - Rose - ARMSTRONG GARDEN CENTERS, INC.; *pg.* 1793, *pg.* 99
PINK 'N PRETTY - Container Grown Plant - MONROVIA GROWERS; *pg.* 1797, *pg.* 44
PINK NV - Golf Club Shafts - ALDILA, INC.; *pg.* 1825, *pg.* 185
PINK PANTHER - Lottery Game - ILLINOIS STATE LOTTERY; *pg.* 995, *pg.* 578
PINK PANTHER - Lottery Game - MINNESOTA STATE LOTTERY; *pg.* 999, *pg.* 956
PINK PARFAIT - Container Grown Plant - MONROVIA GROWERS; *pg.* 1797, *pg.* 44
PINK PEARL - Soap - SWISHER HYGIENE INC.; *pg.* 336, *pg.* 1507
PINK PERFECTION - Flower Arrangement - 1-800-FLOWERS.COM, INC.; *pg.* 1758, *pg.* 1151
PINK PONY - Apparel & Footwear - RALPH LAUREN CORPORATION; *pg.* 46, *pg.* 1284
THE PINK RIBBON - Bouquet - 1-800-FLOWERS.COM, INC.; *pg.* 1758, *pg.* 1151
PINK RIBBON - Cooler - THERMOS L.L.C.; *pg.* 61, *pg.* 660
PINK RIBBON BAGGEL - Bakery Product - PANERA BREAD COMPANY; *pg.* 1029, *pg.* 1001
PINK SHEETS - OTC Public Company Quotation Products - OTC MARKETS GROUP INC.; *pg.* 791, *pg.* 1275
PINK SUEDE - Beauty Product - AVON PRODUCTS, INC.; *pg.* 500, *pg.* 1198
PINK VIOLETS - Dinnerware - THE HOMER LAUGHLIN CHINA COMPANY; *pg.* 1125, *pg.* 1850
PINKCORE - Extruded Polystyrene Insulation & Connector Ties - OWENS CORNING; *pg.* 102, *pg.* 1476
PINKPLUS - Glass Fiber Residential Insulation - OWENS CORNING; *pg.* 102, *pg.* 1476
PINKSEAL - Polyurethane Foam Sealant - OWENS CORNING; *pg.* 102, *pg.* 1476
PINKWRAP - Insulating System - OWENS CORNING; *pg.* 102, *pg.* 1476
PINMATE - Commercial Lighting - SWIVELIER CO., INC.; *pg.* 1307, *pg.* 1142
PINNA - Cheese - CANADIAN FISH EXPORTERS, INC.; *pg.* 845, *pg.* 784
PINNACLE - Golf Balls - ACUSHNET COMPANY; *pg.* 1824, *pg.* 818
PINNACLE - Power Supply System - ADVANCED ENERGY INDUSTRIES, INC.; *pg.* 613, *pg.* 328
PINNACLE - Medical Device - BOSTON SCIENTIFIC CORPORATION; *pg.* 1508, *pg.* 831
PINNACLE - Case - BROWN & BIGELOW, INC.; *pg.* 1624, *pg.* 959
PINNACLE - Software - CHECKPOINT SYSTEMS, INC.; *pg.* 628, *pg.* 1559
PINNACLE - Paint & Coating - DIAMOND VOGEL PAINT, INC.; *pg.* 1441, *pg.* 710
PINNACLE - Tackboard Panels - HOMASOTE COMPANY; *pg.* 87, *pg.* 1126
PINNACLE - Publishing Imprint - KENSINGTON PUBLISHING CORP.; *pg.* 1656, *pg.* 1248
PINNACLE - Binocular - LEUPOLD & STEVENS, INC.; *pg.* 1420, *pg.* 1492
PINNACLE - Software System - MENTOR GRAPHICS CORPORATION; *pg.* 432, *pg.* 1510
PINNACLE - Equine Veterinary Vaccine - PFIZER INC.; *pg.* 1581, *pg.* 1278
PINNACLE - Finger-Jointed Construction Studs - POTLATCH CORPORATION; *pg.* 1467, *pg.* 1844
PINNACLE - Healthcare Product - SWANSON HEALTH PRODUCTS INC.; *pg.* 1600, *pg.* 1397
PINNACLE - Specialty Smoke Detector - SYSTEM SENSOR; *pg.* 676, *pg.* 658
PINNACLE - Skylighting Product - WASCO PRODUCTS, INC.; *pg.* 120, *pg.* 752
PINNACLE - Fiberglass Tank System - ZCL COMPOSITES INC.; *pg.* 1892, *pg.* 1906
THE PINNACLE AWAITS - Trademark (Div. I Women's Basketball) - NATIONAL COLLEGIATE ATHLETIC ASSOCIATION; *pg.* 567, *pg.* 688
PINNACLE FITNESS - Health Clubs - BALLY TOTAL FITNESS HOLDINGS CORPORATION; *pg.* 532, *pg.* 1200
PINNACLE GOLD - Golf Equipment - ACUSHNET COMPANY; *pg.* 1824, *pg.* 818
PINNACLE OF FITNESS - Trademark (Div. I Women's Basketball Only) - NATIONAL COLLEGIATE ATHLETIC ASSOCIATION; *pg.* 567, *pg.* 688
PINNACLE ORCHARDS - Fruit & Snack Gifts - HICKORY FARMS, INC.; *pg.* 862, *pg.* 1462
PINOIR - Bath Product - KOHLER CO.; *pg.* 91, *pg.* 1862
PINOLUZ - Cleaners - THE CLOROX COMPANY; *pg.* 327, *pg.* 169
PINOVA - Rosin & Terpene Derivatives - HERCULES INCORPORATED; *pg.* 1166, *pg.* 392
PINPAD - Debit Card Transaction System - VERIFONE SYSTEMS, INC.; *pg.* 487, *pg.* 251
PINPOINT - Medical Device - BOSTON SCIENTIFIC CORPORATION; *pg.* 1508, *pg.* 831
PINPOINT - Ad Platform for Place-Based Targeting - FOURSQUARE LABS, INC; *pg.* 1248, *pg.* 1232
PINPOINT REPORT RETRIEVAL - Storage & Retrieval of Computer-Generated Reports - JACK HENRY & ASSOCIATES, INC.; *pg.* 422, *pg.* 988
PINSEEKER - Laser Rangefinder - BUSHNELL OUTDOOR PRODUCTS, INC.; *pg.* 1403, *pg.* 718
PINSETTER - Electronic Components - MOLEX INCORPORATED; *pg.* 655, *pg.* 628
PINSTRIPE - Bath Product - KOHLER CO.; *pg.* 91, *pg.* 1862
PINSTRIPE - Fabric - NEMSCHOFF, INC.; *pg.* 936, *pg.* 1890
PINT SIZE TEMPTATIONS - Ice Cream - PERRY'S ICE CREAM CO., INC.; *pg.* 1861, *pg.* 1137
PINTERETTO - Ceramic Tile - WALKER & ZANGER, INC.; *pg.* 119, *pg.* 281
PINTO - Furniture - ASHLEY FURNITURE INDUSTRIES, INC.; *pg.* 914, *pg.* 1852
PINTO HAMBEENS - Dried Beans - N.K. HURST CO., INC.; *pg.* 886, *pg.* 689
PINTO POP - Popcorn Machine - GOLD MEDAL PRODUCTS CO.; *pg.* 55, *pg.* 1414
PINWHEEL - Fabric - NEMSCHOFF, INC.; *pg.* 936, *pg.* 1890
PINWHEEL - Antenna - NOVATEL INC.; *pg.* 1424, *pg.* 1904
PIONEER - Processing Equipment - ASTEC INDUSTRIES, INC.; *pg.* 69, *pg.* 1628
PIONEER - Wrapper - CAMPBELL WRAPPER CORPORATION; *pg.* 1454, *pg.* 1856
PIONEER - Agriculture, Ranching, Construction and Consumer Utility Vehicle - CLUB CAR, INC.; *pg.* 1830, *pg.* 532
PIONEER - Door & Wood Product - CONESTOGA WOOD SPECIALTIES CORP.; *pg.* 921, *pg.* 1527
PIONEER - Seed & Microbial Products - DUPONT PIONEER; *pg.* 1795, *pg.* 708
PIONEER - Hybrid Corn - E.I. DU PONT DE NEMOURS & COMPANY; *pg.* 1159, *pg.* 390
PIONEER - Pumps - GUSHER PUMPS, INC.; *pg.* 1344, *pg.* 727
PIONEER - Bottled Water & Dispensers - PRIMO WATER CORPORATION; *pg.* 1030, *pg.* 1395
PIONEER CREDIT RECOVERY - Magazine - SLM CORPORATION; *pg.* 804, *pg.* 388
PIONEER NODE - Reference Design - CYPRESS SEMICONDUCTOR CORPORATION; *pg.* 1326, *pg.* 243
PIONEER NUTRITI - Nutritional Product - NUTRACEUTICAL INTERNATIONAL CORPORATION; *pg.* 1576, *pg.* 1753
PIONEER PIPE - Steel Pipe Products - RUSSEL METALS INC.; *pg.* 1180, *pg.* 1928
PIONEER TRAIL - Bike - MARIN BIKES; *pg.* 1708, *pg.* 168
PIONEERING SCIENCE DELIVERS VITAL MEDICINES - Slogan - AMGEN INC.; *pg.* 1493, *pg.* 291
PIONERO - Premium Wine - THE DONUM ESTATE, INC; *pg.* 1962, *pg.* 279
PIONITE - Decorative Laminate Product - PANOLAM INDUSTRIES INTERNATIONAL, INC.; *pg.* 103, *pg.* 370
PIP - Molecular Probe Product - THERMO FISHER SCIENTIFIC INC.; *pg.* 1602, *pg.* 61
PIPA - Fabric - NEMSCHOFF, INC.; *pg.* 936, *pg.* 1890
PIPA - Power Monitor - OPLINK COMMUNICATIONS, INC.; *pg.* 660, *pg.* 91
PIPD - Power Monitor - OPLINK COMMUNICATIONS, INC.; *pg.* 660, *pg.* 91
PIPE - Organ - ALLEN ORGAN COMPANY; *pg.* 527, *pg.* 1549
PIPE - Software - ASPEN TECHNOLOGY, INC.; *pg.* 354, *pg.* 804
PIPECO - Piping System - VICTAULIC COMPANY; *pg.* 1066, *pg.* 1529

First page reference indicates Business Class Edition
Second page reference indicates Geographic Edition

PIPED KNIT SHORT - Clothing - K-SWISS; pg. 1837, pg. 306
PIPELINE - Software System - ALCATEL-LUCENT; pg. 615, pg. 1094
THE PIPELINE - Newsletter - IMAGINATION TECHNOLOGIES; pg. 412, pg. 285
PIPELINE - Software - R.R. DONNELLEY & SONS COMPANY; pg. 1682, pg. 589
PIPELINE - Bicycle Accessories - SPECIALIZED BICYCLE COMPONENTS, INC.; pg. 1711, pg. 152
PIPELINEONRAIL - Crude Oil Product - CANADIAN NATIONAL RAILWAY COMPANY; pg. 1902, pg. 1953
PIPEPRO 304 - Welding & Cutting Equipment - MILLER ELECTRIC MANUFACTURING CO.; pg. 1361, pg. 1852
PIPER - Personal, Training, Utility & Business Aircraft - PIPER AIRCRAFT, INC.; pg. 233, pg. 477
PIPER - Molecular Probe Product - THERMO FISHER SCIENTIFIC INC.; pg. 1602, pg. 61
PIPER SONOMA - Sparkling Wine - REMY COINTREAU USA INC.; pg. 1969, pg. 1285
PIPERLIME - Online Retail Shoes and Handbags - THE GAP, INC.; pg. 1770, pg. 218
PIPESIM - Gas Production System - SCHLUMBERGER LIMITED; pg. 801, pg. 1714
PIPETITE - Thread Sealant - LA-CO INDUSTRIES MARKAL CO., INC.; pg. 1170, pg. 610
PIPETITE-STIK - Thread Sealant - LA-CO INDUSTRIES MARKAL CO., INC.; pg. 1170, pg. 610
PIPETTE PUMP III - Laboratory Pump - BEL-ART PRODUCTS, INC.; pg. 1879, pg. 1129
PIPRACIL - Antibiotic - PFIZER INC.; pg. 1581, pg. 1278
PIQUE - Fabric - NEMSCHOFF, INC.; pg. 936, pg. 1890
PIRA - Software - LOCKHEED MARTIN CORPORATION; pg. 229, pg. 762
PIRANHA - Fire Suppression Systems - ANSUL, INCORPORATED; pg. 1147, pg. 1869
PIRANHA - Beer - BJ'S RESTAURANTS, INC.; pg. 1716, pg. 104
PIRANHA - Medical Device - BOSTON SCIENTIFIC CORPORATION; pg. 1508, pg. 831
PIRATE - Canned Fish - OCEAN BEAUTY SEAFOODS, INC.; pg. 1028, pg. 1838
PIRATE'S GETAWAY - Game - WMS INDUSTRIES INC.; pg. 593, pg. 666
PIRATES GOLD - Rewards Game - BALLY TECHNOLOGIES, INC.; pg. 531, pg. 1022
PIRATE'S GOLD - Lottery Game - KENTUCKY LOTTERY CORPORATION; pg. 996, pg. 735
PIRL - Coating - BREWER SCIENCE, INC.; pg. 1150, pg. 989
PIROETTA - Chair - THE WICKER WORKS; pg. 946, pg. 233
PIROR - Slimicide - THE DOW CHEMICAL COMPANY; pg. 1157, pg. 898
PIROUETTE - Footwear - CAPEZIO BALLET MAKERS INC.; pg. 1805, pg. 1125
PIROUETTE - Fabric - NEMSCHOFF, INC.; pg. 936, pg. 1890
PIROUETTE - Cookies - PEPPERIDGE FARM, INC.; pg. 888, pg. 363
PISA - Dinnerware - THE HOMER LAUGHLIN CHINA COMPANY; pg. 1125, pg. 1850
PISA - Footwear - PHOENIX FOOTWEAR GROUP, INC.; pg. 1815, pg. 60
PISA - Lighting - STEELCASE INC.; pg. 475, pg. 889
PISCES - Fabric - NEMSCHOFF, INC.; pg. 936, pg. 1890
PISCO CAPEL - Liqueurs - SHAW ROSS INTERNATIONAL IMPORTERS; pg. 1970, pg. 449
PISTACHIO - Fabric - NEMSCHOFF, INC.; pg. 936, pg. 1890
PISTOL PACKIN' PINK - Nail Care Product - OPI PRODUCTS INC.; pg. 518, pg. 167
PISTON FILLER - Liquid Filling - U.S. BOTTLERS MACHINERY COMPANY; pg. 1386, pg. 1369
PISTON PUMP - Pumps - GRACO, INC.; pg. 1342, pg. 935
PIT - Game - WINNING MOVES GAMES, INC.; pg. 970, pg. 816
PITA SNACKS - Sandwich - JACK IN THE BOX INC.; pg. 1732, pg. 204
PITA WRAP - Pita Bread - GRECIAN DELIGHT FOODS INC.; pg. 859, pg. 610
PITAPANE - Photos & Posters - THE DOW CHEMICAL COMPANY; pg. 1157, pg. 898
PITBOSS - Pipeline Pigging Product - T.D. WILLIAMSON, INC.; pg. 1380, pg. 1490
PITBULL - Gaming Product - GLD PRODUCTS, INC.; pg. 1835, pg. 1882
PITCH DUO - Power Adapter - IGO, INC.; pg. 644, pg. 22
PITCH SIX - Game - HASBRO, INC.; pg. 954, pg. 1603
PITCO FRIALATOR - Cooking & Warming Equipment - THE MIDDLEBY CORPORATION; pg. 1361, pg. 610
PITFALL - Game - ACTIVISION BLIZZARD, INC.; pg. 948, pg. 271
PITMAN - Utility Digger/Derrick - MARINE TRAVELIFT, INC.; pg. 1359, pg. 1895
PITNEY BOWES ENVIRONMENTAL LAB - Mailer - PITNEY BOWES INC.; pg. 454, pg. 376
PITOMETER - Underwater Log Systems - THE DEWEY ELECTRONICS CORPORATION; pg. 1328, pg. 1099
PITOMETER - Pump Product - IDEX CORPORATION; pg. 1347, pg. 623
PITT BULL - Spray Paints - PPG INDUSTRIES, INC.; pg. 1445, pg. 1579
PITT-CHAR - Fire-Retardant Building Material Coating - PPG INDUSTRIES, INC.; pg. 1445, pg. 1579
PITT-CRYL - Acrylic Paints - PPG INDUSTRIES, INC.; pg. 1445, pg. 1579
PITT-FLEX - Elastomeric Exterior Masonry Coating - PPG INDUSTRIES, INC.; pg. 1445, pg. 1579
PITT-GLAZE - Epoxy Coatings - PPG INDUSTRIES, INC.; pg. 1445, pg. 1579
PITT-GUARD - Heavy-Duty Maintenance Coating - PPG INDUSTRIES, INC.; pg. 1445, pg. 1579
PITT-THERM - Corrosion Protective Coating - PPG INDUSTRIES, INC.; pg. 1445, pg. 1579
PITTABS - Water Treatment Chemicals - PPG INDUSTRIES, INC.; pg. 1445, pg. 1579
PITTCHAR - Coating Product - PPG INDUSTRIES, INC.; pg. 1445, pg. 1579
PITTCHLOR - Hypochlorite - PPG INDUSTRIES, INC.; pg. 1445, pg. 1579
PITTEX - Abrasive-Containing Plastic Filaments - PPG INDUSTRIES, INC.; pg. 1445, pg. 1579
PITTGUARD - Coating Product - PPG INDUSTRIES, INC.; pg. 1445, pg. 1579
PITTHANE - Coating Product - PPG INDUSTRIES, INC.; pg. 1445, pg. 1579
PITTSBURGH - Paint Product - PPG INDUSTRIES, INC.; pg. 1445, pg. 1579
PITTSBURGH PENGUINS - Hockey Team - PITTSBURGH PENGUINS LLC; pg. 577, pg. 1578
PITTSBURGH PIRATES - Game - PITTSBURGH BASEBALL, INC.; pg. 576, pg. 1578
PITTSBURGH POST-GAZETTE - Newspaper - BLOCK COMMUNICATIONS, INC.; pg. 1621, pg. 1476
PITTSBURGH TUBE - Steel Tubing - PTC ALLIANCE CORP.; pg. 1370, pg. 1594
PIVOT - Office Furniture - JOFCO INC.; pg. 931, pg. 691
PIVOT BELT - Conveyor - PRAB, INC.; pg. 1369, pg. 894
PIVOT GUARD SYSTEM - Sunglass - 180S, LLC; pg. 1824, pg. 754
PIVOTAL - Medical Equipment - CONMED CORPORATION; pg. 1517, pg. 1347
PIX - Security Appliances - CISCO SYSTEMS, INC.; pg. 372, pg. 240
PIX - Magazine for the Photography Market - NIELSEN BUSINESS MEDIA; pg. 1671, pg. 1272
PIXANTRONE - Pharmaceutical Product - CELL THERAPEUTICS, INC.; pg. 1514, pg. 1834
PIXEL ENGINE - Software & Hardware - EVANS & SUTHERLAND COMPUTER CORPORATION; pg. 638, pg. 1757
PIXEL TAPESTRY - Graphics Card - ADVANCED MICRO DEVICES, INC.; pg. 613, pg. 282
PIXELINK - Display Products - RICHARDSON ELECTRONICS, LTD.; pg. 667, pg. 622
PIXELL - Footwear - STEVEN MADDEN, LTD.; pg. 1819, pg. 1176
PIXIE - Miniature Carnations - DENVER WHOLESALE FLORISTS COMPANY; pg. 1794, pg. 319
PIXIE DUST - Cartoon Character - THE WALT DISNEY COMPANY; pg. 317, pg. 52
PIXIPOINT - Pointing Device - SEMTECH CORPORATION; pg. 671, pg. 57
PIXL - Software - MERCURY COMPUTER SYSTEMS, INC.; pg. 434, pg. 813
PIXLET - Compression Application Program - APPLE INC.; pg. 350, pg. 73
PIXOGRAPHY - Manual - XEROX CORPORATION; pg. 494, pg. 365
PIXOS - Toy - SPIN MASTER LTD.; pg. 967, pg. 1943
PIXTOOLS - Software - EMC CORPORATION; pg. 391, pg. 825
PIXY STIX - Candy - NESTLE USA, INC.; pg. 883, pg. 96
PIZ BUIN - Healthcare Product - JOHNSON & JOHNSON; pg. 1549, pg. 1091
PIZOOKIE - Dessert - BJ'S RESTAURANTS, INC.; pg. 1716, pg. 104
PIZZA BEER - Beer - SPRECHER BREWING COMPANY; pg. 265, pg. 1858
PIZZA BY THE SLICE - Pizza - LITTLE CAESARS ENTERPRISES, INC.; pg. 1736, pg. 883
PIZZA DI CASA - Food Product - GIANT EAGLE, INC.; pg. 1020, pg. 1575
PIZZA HUT - Pizza Brand - PIZZA HUT, INC.; pg. 1744, pg. 1733
PIZZA HUT - Pizza Restaurants - YUM! BRANDS, INC.; pg. 1756, pg. 738
PIZZA PAPA JOHN'S - Restaurant Services - PAPA JOHN'S INTERNATIONAL, INC.; pg. 1743, pg. 737
PIZZA PARLOR - Food Product - ADVANCEPIERRE FOODS, INC.; pg. 1714, pg. 1409
PIZZA ROLLS - Pizza Snacks - GENERAL MILLS, INC.; pg. 828, pg. 933
PIZZA TODAY MAGAZINE - Publication - MACFADDEN COMMUNICATIONS GROUP, LLC; pg. 1660, pg. 1254
PIZZAZZ - Electrical Appliance & Housewares - NATIONAL PRESTO INDUSTRIES, INC; pg. 1128, pg. 1857
PIZZAZZ - Wallcovering - YORK WALLCOVERINGS INC.; pg. 947, pg. 1598
PIZZERIA REGINA - Restaurant - BOSTON RESTAURANT ASSOCIATES, INC.; pg. 1717, pg. 829
PIZZERIA UNO - Original Deep Dish Pizza - UNO RESTAURANT HOLDINGS CORPORATION; pg. 1754, pg. 856
PIZZERIA VIA STATO - Bar & Tavern Pizzeria - LETTUCE ENTERTAIN YOU ENTERPRISES, INC.; pg. 1735, pg. 580
PIZZERT - Dessert Pizza - PIZZA INN, INC.; pg. 1745, pg. 1746
PIZZO - Carpet - INTERFACE, INC.; pg. 695, pg. 512
PK - Gum - WM. WRIGLEY JR. COMPANY; pg. 1863, pg. 596
PK-100 - Fastener Kit for Sheetmetal - PENNENGINEERING FASTENING TECHNOLOGIES; pg. 1059, pg. 1526
PKMS - Inventory Management Software - MANHATTAN ASSOCIATES, INC.; pg. 430, pg. 513
PKWF - Solvent - THE DOW CHEMICAL COMPANY; pg. 1157, pg. 898
PL 998 - Cleaner - PENETONE CORPORATION; pg. 333, pg. 1050
PL SERIES - Roll Covering - VAIL RUBBER WORKS, INC.; pg. 1891, pg. 906
PL50 - Platelet Filter - PALL CORPORATION; pg. 232, pg. 1323
THE PLACE - Children's Clothing Stores - THE CHILDREN'S PLACE, INC.; pg. 22, pg. 1119
THE PLACE THAT LOVES YOU BACK - Slogan - PHILADELPHIA CONVENTION & VISITORS BUREAU; pg. 1004, pg. 1568
PLACE YOUR FAITH IN THE EXPERT - Tagline - GUIDEONE INSURANCE COMPANY; pg. 1202, pg. 713
PLACEMARK - Educational Materials - SCHOLASTIC INC.; pg. 1683, pg. 1288
PLACEMENTSPLUS - Account Placement & Management Systems - FAIR ISAAC CORPORATION; pg. 1247, pg. 955
PLACER - Navigation Aid - TRIMBLE NAVIGATION LIMITED; pg. 1384, pg. 288
PLACES - Wood & Metal Casegoods, Freestanding & Open Office Furniture - HAWORTH, INC.; pg. 402, pg. 891
PLACESETTER - Tableware - PACTIV CORPORATION; pg. 1466, pg. 624
PLACIDO - Premium Wines - BANFI VINTNERS; pg. 1957, pg. 1161
THE PLAIN DEALER - Newspaper - PLAIN DEALER PUBLISHING CO.; pg. 1677, pg. 1434
PLAIN LAZY - Toy & Game - HASBRO, INC.; pg. 954, pg. 1603
PLAIN TALK - Insurance Policy - SENTRY INSURANCE GROUP; pg. 1217, pg. 1895
PLAIN TALK - Retirement Plan - THE VANGUARD GROUP, INC.; pg. 816, pg. 1550
PLAIN WEAVE - Carpet - INTERFACE, INC.; pg. 695, pg. 512
PLAINCLOTHESMAN - Fabric - NEMSCHOFF, INC.; pg. 936, pg. 1890

PLAINLOCK - Pipe Couplings - VICTAULIC COMPANY; *pg.* 1066, *pg.* 1529
PLAINTALK - Application Program - APPLE INC.; *pg.* 350, *pg.* 73
PLAINVIEW - Footwear - EASTLAND SHOE CORPORATION; *pg.* 1808, *pg.* 750
PLAINVIEW - Fabric - NEMSCHOFF, INC.; *pg.* 936, *pg.* 1890
PLAN - Provides Educational Assessment & Guidance - ACT INC.; *pg.* 597, *pg.* 708
PLAN AHEAD - Service Program - GLOBALSCAPE INC.; *pg.* 401, *pg.* 1740
PLANACON - Photomultiplier - PHOTONIS USA PENNSYLVANIA; *pg.* 663, *pg.* 1547
PLANAR - Flat-Panel Display - PLANAR SYSTEMS, INC.; *pg.* 455, *pg.* 1495
PLANAR DLP - Projectors - PLANAR SYSTEMS, INC.; *pg.* 455, *pg.* 1495
PLANAR DRYING - Microwave System - THE LAITRAM LLC; *pg.* 1354, *pg.* 744
PLANARCAP - Filters - ENTEGRIS, INC.; *pg.* 1882, *pg.* 788
PLANARCHEM - Chemical Mechanical Polishing Slurry - ATMI, INC.; *pg.* 1314, *pg.* 342
PLANARCLEAN - Copper Integration - ATMI, INC.; *pg.* 1314, *pg.* 342
PLANARCORE - PVA Brushes - ENTEGRIS, INC.; *pg.* 1882, *pg.* 788
PLANARGARD - Filter - ENTEGRIS, INC.; *pg.* 1882, *pg.* 788
PLANASLO - Biological Product - CAROLINA BIOLOGICAL SUPPLY COMPANY; *pg.* 1513, *pg.* 1359
PLANET - Fabric - NEMSCHOFF, INC.; *pg.* 936, *pg.* 1890
PLANET - Apparel - OAKLEY, INC.; *pg.* 1840, *pg.* 86
PLANET - Software - SYNOPSYS, INC.; *pg.* 480, *pg.* 162
THE PLANET BEACH - Tanning Salon & Spa - PLANET BEACH FRANCHISING CORPORATION; *pg.* 520, *pg.* 745
PLANET BEACH CONTEMPO SPA - Spa - PLANET BEACH FRANCHISING CORPORATION; *pg.* 520, *pg.* 745
PLANET COLA - Colas in Assorted Flavors - THE MONARCH BEVERAGE COMPANY, INC.; *pg.* 257, *pg.* 514
PLANET FOOD - Animal & Plantcare Product - NEW EARTH LIFE SCIENCES, INC.; *pg.* 1573, *pg.* 1499
PLANET GREEN - Eco-Lifestyle Television Network - DISCOVERY COMMUNICATIONS, INC.; *pg.* 282, *pg.* 777
PLANET LOOT - Game - WMS INDUSTRIES INC.; *pg.* 593, *pg.* 666
PLANET-PAC - Bearings - THE TIMKEN COMPANY; *pg.* 218, *pg.* 1408
PLANET PDA - Online Publication - TECHNOLOGY MARKETING CORP.; *pg.* 1691, *pg.* 364
PLANET-PL - Software - SYNOPSYS, INC.; *pg.* 480, *pg.* 162
PLANET SPA - Beauty Product - AVON PRODUCTS, INC.; *pg.* 500, *pg.* 1198
PLANET ZOO - Educational Materials - SCHOLASTIC INC.; *pg.* 1683, *pg.* 1288
PLANETECHS - Aviation Staffing - TRUEBLUE, INC.; *pg.* 485, *pg.* 1845
PLANNET - Plan Sponsor Service - STANDARD INSURANCE COMPANY; *pg.* 1217, *pg.* 1506
PLANNING STATION - Software - SUNGARD DATA SYSTEMS INC.; *pg.* 477, *pg.* 1592
PLANO - Tackle & Tool Boxes & Cosmetic Organizers - PLANO MOLDING COMPANY; *pg.* 1887, *pg.* 652
PLANO OUTDOOR SYSTEMS - Storage Product - PLANO MOLDING COMPANY; *pg.* 1887, *pg.* 652
PLANOFORM - Ultra Precision Flycutting Machine - PRECITECH, INC.; *pg.* 1427, *pg.* 1035
PLANPLUS - Book - FRANKLIN COVEY CO.; *pg.* 1642, *pg.* 1758
PLANPROFESSOR - Newsletter - HUMANA, INC.; *pg.* 1204, *pg.* 734
PLANT GREEN - DVD - GAIAM, INC.; *pg.* 1532, *pg.* 334
PLANT HART'S SEEDS - Vegetable, Flower & Lawn Seeds - THE CHAS. C. HART SEED CO.; *pg.* 1794, *pg.* 384
PLANT PROTECTOR - Tagline - WILT-PRUF PRODUCTS, INC.; *pg.* 1801, *pg.* 346
PLANT SAVVY - Newsletter - MONROVIA GROWERS; *pg.* 1797, *pg.* 44
PLANTABBS - House Plant Foods - PLANTABBS PRODUCTS COMPANY; *pg.* 1799, *pg.* 758
PLANTAR - Test Apparatus - STOELTING CO.; *pg.* 1430, *pg.* 671
PLANTAR VON FREY - Lab Instrument - STOELTING CO.; *pg.* 1430, *pg.* 671
PLANTATION - Bottled Food Product - ALLIED OLD ENGLISH, INC.; *pg.* 836, *pg.* 1110
PLANTATION - Turkey Products - CARGILL LIMITED; *pg.* 1475, *pg.* 1914
PLANTATION - Rug - COURISTAN INC.; *pg.* 921, *pg.* 1067
PLANTATION - Food Product - KELLOGG COMPANY; *pg.* 831, *pg.* 870
PLANTATION KEY - Carpet - BEAULIEU GROUP, LLC; *pg.* 917, *pg.* 529
PLANTATION MINT - Tea - R.C. BIGELOW, INC.; *pg.* 891, *pg.* 348
PLANTERS - Peanuts - THE KRAFT HEINZ COMPANY; *pg.* 870, *pg.* 1577
PLANTEX - Microlithographic Polymer Films - E.I. DU PONT DE NEMOURS & COMPANY; *pg.* 1159, *pg.* 390
PLANTFLOW - Software - BENTLEY SYSTEMS, INC.; *pg.* 361, *pg.* 1531
PLANTLAND U. S. A. - Nursery Stock - FORREST KEELING NURSERY, INC.; *pg.* 1795, *pg.* 977
PLANTRAC - Software - DST SYSTEMS, INC.; *pg.* 388, *pg.* 982
PLANTRAK - Software System - IMS HEALTH, INC.; *pg.* 1544, *pg.* 344
PLANTSKYDD - Deer Repellant - GARDENS ALIVE!, INC.; *pg.* 1796, *pg.* 693
PLANTSPACE - Software - BENTLEY SYSTEMS, INC.; *pg.* 361, *pg.* 1531
PLANTSPEC - CAD Drawings on CD & the Internet - THOMAS REGISTER OF AMERICAN MANUFACTURERS; *pg.* 1692, *pg.* 1299
PLANTVAX - Polymer Product - CHEMTURA CORPORATION; *pg.* 1152, *pg.* 355
PLANWELL - Software - AMERICAN REPROGRAPHICS COMPANY; *pg.* 1616, *pg.* 303
PLANWELL BIDCASTER - Software - AMERICAN REPROGRAPHICS COMPANY; *pg.* 1616, *pg.* 303
PLANWELL ENTERPRISE - Reprographic Product - AMERICAN REPROGRAPHICS COMPANY; *pg.* 1616, *pg.* 303
PLANWELL EWO - Reprographic Product - AMERICAN REPROGRAPHICS COMPANY; *pg.* 1616, *pg.* 303
PLANWELL PDS - Reprographic Product - AMERICAN REPROGRAPHICS COMPANY; *pg.* 1616, *pg.* 303
PLANX - Truss Manufacturing Tool - MITEK, INC.; *pg.* 1056, *pg.* 975
PLAQUE REMOVER - Dental Tool - THE GILLETTE COMPANY; *pg.* 509, *pg.* 795
PLAS-CHEK - Plasticizers - FERRO CORPORATION; *pg.* 1162, *pg.* 1462
PLASADD - Chemical Product - CABOT CORPORATION; *pg.* 1151, *pg.* 792
PLASBLAK - Chemical Product - CABOT CORPORATION; *pg.* 1151, *pg.* 792
PLASGREY - Chemical Product - CABOT CORPORATION; *pg.* 1151, *pg.* 792
PLASMA-TECHNIK - Engineered Product And System - SULZER METCO (WESTBURY) INC.; *pg.* 1064, *pg.* 1350
PLASMACOAT - Rod - GRACO, INC.; *pg.* 1342, *pg.* 935
PLASMADIZE - Coating - GENERAL MAGNAPLATE CORPORATION; *pg.* 1164, *pg.* 1079
PLASMAPURE - Ceramic & Plastic Product - COORSTEK, INC.; *pg.* 77, *pg.* 330
PLASMAPURE-UC - Ceramic & Plastic Product - COORSTEK, INC.; *pg.* 77, *pg.* 330
PLASMARESIST - Ceramic & Plastic Product - COORSTEK, INC.; *pg.* 77, *pg.* 330
PLASMATEMP - Inspection System - KLA-TENCOR CORPORATION; *pg.* 1353, *pg.* 146
PLASMAVISION SLIMSCREEN - Plasma Screen - FUJITSU GENERAL AMERICA, INC.; *pg.* 55, *pg.* 1065
PLASMAVOLT - Inspection System - KLA-TENCOR CORPORATION; *pg.* 1353, *pg.* 146
PLASMED - Microbore Tubing - TEKNI-PLEX, INC.; *pg.* 1470, *pg.* 1122
PLASMID - Biomolecule Product - THERMO FISHER SCIENTIFIC INC.; *pg.* 1602, *pg.* 61
PLASMON - Food Products - THE KRAFT HEINZ COMPANY; *pg.* 870, *pg.* 1577
PLAST-O-MAT - Shelf Liner; Floor Runner - WARP BROTHERS; *pg.* 1471, *pg.* 595
PLAST-O-MERIC - Screen Printing Ink - POLYONE CORPORATION; *pg.* 1177, *pg.* 1404
PLASTAZOTE - Tubing - ALIMED, INC.; *pg.* 1490, *pg.* 816
PLASTI GLASS - Window Material - WARP BROTHERS; *pg.* 1471, *pg.* 595
PLASTI-NAMEL - Enamel - KELLY-MOORE PAINT COMPANY, INC.; *pg.* 1443, *pg.* 198
PLASTI-PANE - Window Material - WARP BROTHERS; *pg.* 1471, *pg.* 595
PLASTI-PASTE - Liquid Plastic - SMOOTH-ON INC.; *pg.* 111, *pg.* 1528
PLASTI-SHIELD - Containers - OWENS-ILLINOIS, INC.; *pg.* 1466, *pg.* 1470
PLASTI-TILE - Plastic & Rubber - TEKNOR APEX COMPANY; *pg.* 1889, *pg.* 1605
PLASTI-TUFF - Plastic & Rubber - TEKNOR APEX COMPANY; *pg.* 1889, *pg.* 1605
PLASTIC-DRUM - Shipping Containers of Molded Plastic Material - SONOCO PRODUCTS COMPANY; *pg.* 1469, *pg.* 1619
PLASTIC FOAMJET - Spray Product - SPRAYING SYSTEMS CO.; *pg.* 1063, *pg.* 670
PLASTIC MAN - Characters - DC COMICS, INC.; *pg.* 1633, *pg.* 1221
PLASTIC MASTER - Cutting Room Equipment - EASTMAN MACHINE COMPANY; *pg.* 1331, *pg.* 1148
PLASTIC WOOD - Repair Product - DAP PRODUCTS, INC.; *pg.* 1441, *pg.* 756
PLASTICHANGE - Packaging Product - CASCADES, INC.; *pg.* 73, *pg.* 1950
PLASTICIZER - Dry Cleaning & Laundry Product - ADCO, INC.; *pg.* 325, *pg.* 482
PLASTICIZER - Chemical Product - STEPAN COMPANY; *pg.* 1182, *pg.* 643
PLASTICS & RUBBER WEEKLY - Trade Magazine - CRAIN COMMUNICATIONS, INC.; *pg.* 1631, *pg.* 879
PLASTICS DATA SOURCE - Statistical Program - THE SOCIETY OF THE PLASTICS INDUSTRY, INC.; *pg.* 157, *pg.* 404
PLASTICS NEWS - Newspaper - CRAIN COMMUNICATIONS, INC.; *pg.* 1631, *pg.* 879
PLASTICVILLE - Plastic Buildings for Model Trains - BACHMANN INDUSTRIES, INC.; *pg.* 950, *pg.* 1559
PLASTIPAD - Medical Product - CINCINNATI SUB-ZERO PRODUCTS, INC.; *pg.* 1070, *pg.* 1411
PLASTIPAK - Hypodermic Syringes - BECTON, DICKINSON & COMPANY; *pg.* 1501, *pg.* 1068
PLASTIQUENCH - Water-Base Quenchant - HEATBATH CORPORATION; *pg.* 1165, *pg.* 826
PLASTISAND - General Purpose Resin-Coated Sand - HEXION; *pg.* 1166, *pg.* 1440
PLASTO-JOINT STIK - Pipe Thread Compound - LA-CO INDUSTRIES MARKAL CO., INC.; *pg.* 1170, *pg.* 610
PLASTOLYN - Hydrocarbon Resins - EASTMAN CHEMICAL COMPANY; *pg.* 1159, *pg.* 1636
PLASTONE - Thermoplastic Colorant & Additive - POLYONE CORPORATION; *pg.* 1177, *pg.* 1404
PLASTOP - Tamper-Evident Closure - OWENS-ILLINOIS, INC.; *pg.* 1466, *pg.* 1470
PLAST'R CRAFT - Modeling Material - PACON CORPORATION; *pg.* 1466, *pg.* 1852
PLASTRON PEARLS - Medical Tubing - TEKNI-PLEX, INC.; *pg.* 1470, *pg.* 1122
PLASTRONIC - Plastic Bag - ELKAY PLASTICS COMPANY, INC.; *pg.* 1882, *pg.* 68
PLASTUSA - Tape Backing Material - HOLLISTON LLC; *pg.* 1460, *pg.* 1630
PLASWITE - Chemical Product - CABOT CORPORATION; *pg.* 1151, *pg.* 792
PLAT CAT - Cure Accelerator - SMOOTH-ON INC.; *pg.* 111, *pg.* 1528
PLAT IT AGAIN SPORTS - Sporting Goods Stores - WINMARK CORPORATION; *pg.* 1792, *pg.* 946
PLAT SIDESTRIPE - Footwear - VANS, INC.; *pg.* 1821, *pg.* 76
PLATAMID - Textile Adhesives - ARKEMA INC.; *pg.* 1147, *pg.* 1543
PLATE-HIDING PORTION - Restaurant Service - SONNY'S FRANCHISE COMPANY INC.; *pg.* 1751, *pg.* 480
PLATE LIBRARIAN - Software - BIO-RAD LABORATORIES, INC.; *pg.* 1504, *pg.* 101
PLATE-PAK - Vane Mist Eliminator - ACS INDUSTRIES, INC.; *pg.* 1040, *pg.* 1602
PLATE-PERFECT - Mashed Potatoes - J.R. SIMPLOT COMPANY; *pg.* 867, *pg.* 547
PLATE SCAPERS - Fruit or Candy Based Decorative Dessert Toppings - THE J.M. SMUCKER COMPANY; *pg.* 865, *pg.* 1468
PLATEAU - Furniture - VIRCO MANUFACTURING CORPORATION; *pg.* 946, *pg.* 297
PLATEAU HS DOCK - Connector - MOLEX INCORPORATED; *pg.* 655, *pg.* 628

PLATEAU HS DOCK PG - Electronic Components - MOLEX INCORPORATED; *pg.* 655, *pg.* 628
PLATEAU HS MEZZ - Connector - MOLEX INCORPORATED; *pg.* 655, *pg.* 628
PLATEAU TECHNOLOGY - Electronic Components - MOLEX INCORPORATED; *pg.* 655, *pg.* 628
PLATECOIL - Prime Surface/Immersion Heat Exchangers - TRANTER PHE, INC.; *pg.* 1383, *pg.* 1749
PLATEFRAME - License Plate Frames - MACNEIL AUTOMOTIVE PRODUCTS, LTD.; *pg.* 211, *pg.* 559
PLATELIA - Clinical Diagnostic Product - BIO-RAD LABORATORIES, INC.; *pg.* 1504, *pg.* 101
PLATELIA PASTEUR - Software - BIO-RAD LABORATORIES, INC.; *pg.* 1504, *pg.* 101
PLATES BELLPULL - Wall Decor - HERITAGE LACE INC.; *pg.* 694, *pg.* 711
PLATESCOPE - Portable Plate Platereader - X-RITE, INCORPORATED; *pg.* 1437, *pg.* 891
PLATESPIN FORGE - Computer Software - NOVELL INC.; *pg.* 446, *pg.* 852
PLATESTAK - Liquid Handling Dispenser - PERKINELMER, INC.; *pg.* 1426, *pg.* 853
PLATETRAK - Integration - PERKINELMER, INC.; *pg.* 1426, *pg.* 853
PLATEWASH - Liquid Handling Dispenser - PERKINELMER, INC.; *pg.* 1426, *pg.* 853
PLATFORM - Platform Mattress - KINGSDOWN, INC.; *pg.* 932, *pg.* 1383
PLATFORM EXPRESS - Software System - MENTOR GRAPHICS CORPORATION; *pg.* 432, *pg.* 1510
THE PLATFORM FOR INTELLIGENT E-BUSINESS - Slogan - MICROSTRATEGY, INC.; *pg.* 1266, *pg.* 1809
PLATFORM PLUS - Special Platrform with Qualofil - KINGSDOWN, INC.; *pg.* 932, *pg.* 1383
PLATINUM - Homes - AMERICAN HOMESTAR CORPORATION; *pg.* 67, *pg.* 1725
PLATINUM - Optical Network Performance Systems - CORNING CABLE SYSTEMS LLC; *pg.* 1407, *pg.* 1378
PLATINUM - Customer Service - DAKTRONICS, INC.; *pg.* 633, *pg.* 1624
PLATINUM - Car Wash Systems - DAUBERT INDUSTRIES, INC.; *pg.* 1155, *pg.* 561
PLATINUM - Gaming Product - GLD PRODUCTS, INC.; *pg.* 1835, *pg.* 1882
PLATINUM - Medical Equipment - INVACARE CORPORATION; *pg.* 1546, *pg.* 1451
PLATINUM - Furniture - JASPER GROUP; *pg.* 930, *pg.* 691
PLATINUM - Apparel - LANDAU UNIFORMS INCORPORATED; *pg.* 28, *pg.* 971
PLATINUM - Molecular Biology Product - THERMO FISHER SCIENTIFIC INC.; *pg.* 1602, *pg.* 61
PLATINUM 2000 - Chocolate Coating - CARGILL LIMITED; *pg.* 1475, *pg.* 1914
PLATINUM CARD - Credit Card - AMERICAN EXPRESS COMPANY; *pg.* 712, *pg.* 1190
PLATINUM CIRCLE - Banking Services - COMERICA INCORPORATED; *pg.* 740, *pg.* 1677
PLATINUM ELITE - Customer Service - DAKTRONICS, INC.; *pg.* 633, *pg.* 1624
PLATINUM FOR WINDOWS - Comprehensive Financial Software Solution - SAGE SOFTWARE, INC.; *pg.* 464, *pg.* 116
PLATINUM FORCE - Floor Care Product - H-P PRODUCTS, INC.; *pg.* 85, *pg.* 1458
PLATINUM FUBU - Clothing - GTFM LLC; *pg.* 41, *pg.* 1236
PLATINUM LEAF - Bath Accessory - CROSCILL, INC.; *pg.* 1122, *pg.* 1220
PLATINUM MASTERCARD - Credit Card - MASTERCARD INCORPORATED; *pg.* 779, *pg.* 1325
PLATINUM MIST - Furniture - BUSH INDUSTRIES INC.; *pg.* 919, *pg.* 1170
PLATINUM PAYOUT - Lottery Game - MASSACHUSETTS STATE LOTTERY; *pg.* 998, *pg.* 802
PLATINUM PAYOUT - Lottery Game - OHIO LOTTERY COMMISSION; *pg.* 1002, *pg.* 1433
PLATINUM PLUME - Flatware - ONEIDA LTD; *pg.* 1129, *pg.* 1318
PLATINUM PLUS - Customer Service - DAKTRONICS, INC.; *pg.* 633, *pg.* 1624
PLATINUM PLUS - Cable - GENERAL CABLE CORPORATION; *pg.* 83, *pg.* 729
PLATINUM-PLUS - Blades - THE GILLETTE COMPANY; *pg.* 509, *pg.* 795
PLATINUM PLUS - Credit Card - HUNTINGTON BANCSHARES INCORPORATED; *pg.* 767, *pg.* 1440
PLATINUM PLUS - Generic Automobile Parts - LKQ CORP.; *pg.* 210, *pg.* 185
PLATINUM PLUS - Business Credit Card - SALEM FIVE CENTS SAVINGS BANK; *pg.* 800, *pg.* 843
PLATINUM REFINISH - Generic Automobile Parts - LKQ CORP.; *pg.* 210, *pg.* 185
PLATINUMPRO - Multimeter - IDEAL INDUSTRIES, INC.; *pg.* 1051, *pg.* 662
PLATO - Software - EDMENTUM, INC.; *pg.* 390, *pg.* 917
PLATO THE PUBLIXAURUS - Magazine - PUBLIX SUPER MARKETS, INC.; *pg.* 1031, *pg.* 437
PLATO VOCABULARY BUILDER - Software - EDMENTUM, INC.; *pg.* 390, *pg.* 917
PLATO'S CLOSET - Clothing Stores - WINMARK CORPORATION; *pg.* 1792, *pg.* 946
PLATTS - Publication - THE MCGRAW-HILL COMPANIES INC.; *pg.* 1663, *pg.* 1257
PLAVIX - Health Care Product - BRISTOL-MYERS SQUIBB COMPANY; *pg.* 1509, *pg.* 1206
PLAVIX - Clopidogrel Bisulfate - SANOFI US; *pg.* 1592, *pg.* 1046
PLAX - Dental Product - COLGATE-PALMOLIVE COMPANY; *pg.* 504, *pg.* 1215
PLAX - Mouthwash - MCNEIL-PPC, INC.; *pg.* 1560, *pg.* 1533
PLAY 4 - Lottery Game - THE FLORIDA LOTTERY; *pg.* 992, *pg.* 469
PLAY 60 - Volunteer Service - CLEVELAND BROWNS FOOTBALL COMPANY LLC; *pg.* 541, *pg.* 1406
PLAY ALONG - Leisure Product - JAKKS PACIFIC, INC.; *pg.* 960, *pg.* 142
PLAY BALL - Game - GAMEWRIGHT; *pg.* 953, *pg.* 836
PLAY BIG - Projector - INFOCUS CORPORATION; *pg.* 644, *pg.* 1503
PLAY DATE - Boots - AEROGROUP INTERNATIONAL, INC.; *pg.* 1803, *pg.* 1055
PLAY-DOH - Toy & Game - HASBRO, INC.; *pg.* 954, *pg.* 1603
PLAY-DOH DOH DOH ISLAND - Toy & Game - HASBRO, INC.; *pg.* 954, *pg.* 1603
PLAY DRY - Lightweight Clothing Line - REEBOK INTERNATIONAL LTD.; *pg.* 1817, *pg.* 811
PLAY ENGERY DRINK - Beverages - THE COCA-COLA COMPANY; *pg.* 240, *pg.* 493
PLAY FAVORITES - Slacks & Shorts - HABAND COMPANY, INC.; *pg.* 1772, *pg.* 1099
PLAY HARDER PLAY TOGETHER - Tagline - MAD CATZ INTERACTIVE INC.; *pg.* 429, *pg.* 204
PLAY 'N PAT WATER MAT - Toy - MUNCHKIN, INC.; *pg.* 964, *pg.* 300
PLAY ON WORDS - Game - WINNING MOVES GAMES, INC.; *pg.* 970, *pg.* 816
PLAY SAFE & LEARN - Toys, Educational Games - SCHOOL-TECH, INC.; *pg.* 1844, *pg.* 866
PLAY! SCHOLASTIC - Educational Materials - SCHOLASTIC INC.; *pg.* 1683, *pg.* 1288
PLAY TIME - Swimming Pool Paint - CALIFORNIA PRODUCTS CORPORATION; *pg.* 1441, *pg.* 781
PLAY WARM - Footwear - REEBOK INTERNATIONAL LTD.; *pg.* 1817, *pg.* 811
PLAYA - Footwear - COBIAN CORP.; *pg.* 1806, *pg.* 253
PLAYBACK - Hour-Long Music Trivia Game - NTN BUZZTIME, INC.; *pg.* 659, *pg.* 60
PLAYBOX ESSENTIALS - Toy & Game - HASBRO, INC.; *pg.* 954, *pg.* 1603
PLAYBOY - Men's Magazine - AMERICAN MEDIA, INC.; *pg.* 1615, *pg.* 410
PLAYBOY BY DON DIEGO - Premium Cigars - ALTADIS USA, INC.; *pg.* 1893, *pg.* 423
PLAYDOCK - Electronics - CAMBRIDGE SOUNDWORKS, INC.; *pg.* 1234, *pg.* 781
PLAYER - Office Furniture - STEELCASE INC.; *pg.* 475, *pg.* 889
PLAYER EXPRESS - Point of Sale Terminal - INTERNATIONAL GAME TECHNOLOGY; *pg.* 420, *pg.* 1606
PLAYERS - Golf Equipment - ACUSHNET COMPANY; *pg.* 1824, *pg.* 818
PLAYERS CHOICE - Games - PENN NATIONAL GAMING, INC.; *pg.* 574, *pg.* 1595
PLAYERS CLUB BY DON DIEGO - Handmade Cigar - ALTADIS USA, INC.; *pg.* 1893, *pg.* 423
PLAYER'S EDGE - Video Game - INTERNATIONAL GAME TECHNOLOGY; *pg.* 957, *pg.* 1024
PLAYER'S EDGE PLUS - Video Game - INTERNATIONAL GAME TECHNOLOGY; *pg.* 957, *pg.* 1024
PLAYER'S SUITE - Video Game - INTERNATIONAL GAME TECHNOLOGY; *pg.* 957, *pg.* 1024
PLAYFIL - Footwear - STEVEN MADDEN, LTD.; *pg.* 1819, *pg.* 1176
PLAYFILL - Shoe - AEROGROUP INTERNATIONAL, INC.; *pg.* 1803, *pg.* 1055
PLAYFULLY PLUSH - Fleece Set - HABAND COMPANY, INC.; *pg.* 1772, *pg.* 1099
PLAYITNOW - Game - HASBRO, INC.; *pg.* 954, *pg.* 1603
PLAYJAM - Interactive Television - NAGRA USA; *pg.* 443, *pg.* 223
PLAYMAKER - Orthopedic Product - DJO INCORPORATED; *pg.* 1524, *pg.* 302
PLAYMAKERS - Football Miniseries - ESPN, INC.; *pg.* 285, *pg.* 340
PLAYMATE - Commercial Lighting - SWIVELIER CO., INC.; *pg.* 1307, *pg.* 1142
PLAYMATE ELITE - Ice Chest - IGLOO PRODUCTS CORPORATION; *pg.* 1126, *pg.* 1724
PLAYMATE PLUS - Ice Chest - IGLOO PRODUCTS CORPORATION; *pg.* 1126, *pg.* 1724
PLAYS - Magazine - KALMBACH PUBLISHING CO.; *pg.* 1656, *pg.* 1898
PLAYSKOOL - Preschool & Infant Toys - HASBRO, INC.; *pg.* 954, *pg.* 1603
PLAYSTATION - Videogame Console - SONY COMPUTER ENTERTAINMENT AMERICA LLC; *pg.* 966, *pg.* 256
PLAYSTATION VUE - Cloud-Based Television Service - SONY COMPUTER ENTERTAINMENT AMERICA LLC; *pg.* 966, *pg.* 256
PLAYTEX - Feminine Care, Infant Care, Gloves - EDGEWELL PERSONAL CARE; *pg.* 1526, *pg.* 995
PLAYTEX - Intimate Apparel - HANESBRANDS INC.; *pg.* 26, *pg.* 1394
PLAYTEX BODY ZEN - Apparel - PLAYTEX APPAREL, INC.; *pg.* 31, *pg.* 1395
PLAYTEX SECRETS - Apparel - PLAYTEX APPAREL, INC.; *pg.* 31, *pg.* 1395
PLAYWRITE - DVD Recorder - MICROBOARDS TECHNOLOGY, LLC; *pg.* 434, *pg.* 920
PLAZA - Fabric - NEMSCHOFF, INC.; *pg.* 936, *pg.* 1890
PLAZA SOUTH - Misses' Dresses - KELLWOOD COMPANY; *pg.* 28, *pg.* 975
PLC - Programmable Logic Controllers - ROCKWELL AUTOMATION, INC.; *pg.* 668, *pg.* 1880
PLC-2 - Software - ROCKWELL AUTOMATION, INC.; *pg.* 668, *pg.* 1880
PLC-3 - Software - ROCKWELL AUTOMATION, INC.; *pg.* 668, *pg.* 1880
PLC-5 - Software - ROCKWELL AUTOMATION, INC.; *pg.* 668, *pg.* 1880
PLCS - Splitter - OPLINK COMMUNICATIONS, INC.; *pg.* 660, *pg.* 91
PLCS2 - Splitter - OPLINK COMMUNICATIONS, INC.; *pg.* 660, *pg.* 91
PLDTEST PLUS - Software - DATA I/O CORPORATION; *pg.* 382, *pg.* 1824
PLEASANT - Furniture - JASPER GROUP; *pg.* 930, *pg.* 691
PLEASANT COMPANY PUBLICATIONS - Doll And Toy - AMERICAN GIRL LLC; *pg.* 949, *pg.* 1871
PLEASANTLY PINK - Flower Arrangement - 1-800-FLOWERS.COM, INC.; *pg.* 1758, *pg.* 1151
PLEASURE - Footwear - P.W. MINOR & SON, INC.; *pg.* 1816, *pg.* 1140
PLEASURES - Designer Fragrance - PARFUMS DE COEUR LTD.; *pg.* 519, *pg.* 376
PLEAT+PLUS - Filter - MIDWESCO FILTER RESOURCES INC.; *pg.* 1464, *pg.* 1811
PLEATJET - Dust Filter - SLY, INC.; *pg.* 1376, *pg.* 1475
PLEATS N PLAIDS - Carpet - BEAULIEU GROUP, LLC; *pg.* 917, *pg.* 529
PLEDGE - Furniture Cleaning Product - S.C. JOHNSON & SON, INC.; *pg.* 334, *pg.* 1889
PLEDGE AEROSOL - Cleaner - S.C. JOHNSON & SON, INC.; *pg.* 334, *pg.* 1889
PLEDGE DUST - Cleaner - S.C. JOHNSON & SON, INC.; *pg.* 334, *pg.* 1889
PLEDGE EXTRA MOISTURIZING - Cleaner - S.C. JOHNSON & SON, INC.; *pg.* 334, *pg.* 1889
PLEDGE FLOOR CARE - Cleaner - S.C. JOHNSON & SON, INC.; *pg.* 334, *pg.* 1889
PLEDGE GRAB-IT - Home Cleaner - S.C. JOHNSON & SON, INC.; *pg.* 334, *pg.* 1889
PLEDGE LEMON TRIGGER - Cleaner - S.C. JOHNSON & SON, INC.; *pg.* 334, *pg.* 1889

PLEDGE ORANGE OIT - Cleaner - S.C. JOHNSON & SON, INC.; *pg.* 334, *pg.* 1889
PLEDGE WIPES - Home Cleaner - S.C. JOHNSON & SON, INC.; *pg.* 334, *pg.* 1889
PLENCOTE - Cable Handbook - COLEMAN CABLE, INC.; *pg.* 1324, *pg.* 665
PLENTIKOOL - Thermoelectric - IGLOO PRODUCTS CORPORATION; *pg.* 1126, *pg.* 1724
PLEUGER - Pump - FLOWSERVE CORPORATION; *pg.* 82, *pg.* 1719
PLEWS - Lubrication Equipment & Accessories - PLEWS/EDELMANN; *pg.* 215, *pg.* 607
PLEXIBOND-FIBERGLASS SYSTEM - Acrylic Resurface - CALIFORNIA PRODUCTS CORPORATION; *pg.* 1441, *pg.* 781
PLEXICHROME - Acrylic Coating - CALIFORNIA PRODUCTS CORPORATION; *pg.* 1441, *pg.* 781
PLEXICOURT - Polyvinyl Chloride - CALIFORNIA PRODUCTS CORPORATION; *pg.* 1441, *pg.* 781
PLEXICUSHION - Latex Cushion Subsurface - CALIFORNIA PRODUCTS CORPORATION; *pg.* 1441, *pg.* 781
PLEXICUSHION PATCH - Unit Latex Patching - CALIFORNIA PRODUCTS CORPORATION; *pg.* 1441, *pg.* 781
PLEXIFLOR - Acrylic Finish Coating - CALIFORNIA PRODUCTS CORPORATION; *pg.* 1441, *pg.* 781
PLEXIGLAS - Chemical - MILLER-STEPHENSON CHEMICAL COMPANY, INC.; *pg.* 1172, *pg.* 344
PLEXIGLAS - Glass Window - WAYNE-DALTON CORP.; *pg.* 120, *pg.* 1465
PLEXIPATCH - Acrylic Latex Patching - CALIFORNIA PRODUCTS CORPORATION; *pg.* 1441, *pg.* 781
PLEXIPAVE - Mixing Plexichrome - CALIFORNIA PRODUCTS CORPORATION; *pg.* 1441, *pg.* 781
PLEXIPAVE GRAND PRIX - Acrylic Textured Coating - CALIFORNIA PRODUCTS CORPORATION; *pg.* 1441, *pg.* 781
PLEXIPULSE - Compression Device - KINETIC CONCEPTS, INC.; *pg.* 1553, *pg.* 1741
PLEXITRAC - Pigment - CALIFORNIA PRODUCTS CORPORATION; *pg.* 1441, *pg.* 781
PLEXTOR - Computer System - ALIENWARE CORPORATION; *pg.* 346, *pg.* 439
PLI - Footwear - CAPEZIO BALLET MAKERS INC.; *pg.* 1805, *pg.* 1125
PLI-FLOW - Plastic Refractory - PLIBRICO CO. LLC; *pg.* 104, *pg.* 587
PLIA-CELL - Medical Equipment - CONMED CORPORATION; *pg.* 1517, *pg.* 1347
PLIABLE PULLS - Dog Toy - THE HARTZ MOUNTAIN CORP.; *pg.* 1476, *pg.* 1120
PLIBRICO - Plastic Refractory - PLIBRICO CO. LLC; *pg.* 104, *pg.* 587
PLICAST - Plastic Refractory - PLIBRICO CO. LLC; *pg.* 104, *pg.* 587
PLIGUN - Plastic Refractory - PLIBRICO CO. LLC; *pg.* 104, *pg.* 587
PLIO-TAC - Contact Adhesive - W.J. RUSCOE COMPANY; *pg.* 122, *pg.* 1403
PLIOBOND - Adhesives for Roofing - ASHLAND INC.; *pg.* 972, *pg.* 726
PLIOBOND - Adhesive-Cement - W.J. RUSCOE COMPANY; *pg.* 122, *pg.* 1403
PLIOCORD - Styrene Butadiene/Vinylpyridine Latices - THE GOODYEAR TIRE & RUBBER COMPANY; *pg.* 1883, *pg.* 1401
PLIODECK - Adhesives - ASHLAND INC.; *pg.* 972, *pg.* 726
PLIOFLEX - Styrene/Butadiene Rubber - THE GOODYEAR TIRE & RUBBER COMPANY; *pg.* 1883, *pg.* 1401
PLIOGRIP - Structural Adhesive - ASHLAND INC.; *pg.* 972, *pg.* 726
PLIOLITE - Latex & Resins - THE GOODYEAR TIRE & RUBBER COMPANY; *pg.* 1883, *pg.* 1401
PLION - Monofilament - CORTLAND LINE COMPANY; *pg.* 1831, *pg.* 1155
PLIOTEC LS - Tire And Rubber Product - THE GOODYEAR TIRE & RUBBER COMPANY; *pg.* 1883, *pg.* 1401
PLIOTONE - Resin - THE GOODYEAR TIRE & RUBBER COMPANY; *pg.* 1883, *pg.* 1401
PLIOVIC - Polyvinyl Chloride Resin - THE GOODYEAR TIRE & RUBBER COMPANY; *pg.* 1883, *pg.* 1401
PLIOWAY - Resin - THE GOODYEAR TIRE & RUBBER COMPANY; *pg.* 1883, *pg.* 1401
PLISSE CRINKLE - Wallcovering - YORK WALLCOVERINGS INC.; *pg.* 947, *pg.* 1598
PLISTIX - Plastic Refractory - PLIBRICO CO. LLC; *pg.* 104, *pg.* 587
PLISULATE - Plastic Refractory - PLIBRICO CO. LLC; *pg.* 104, *pg.* 587
PLIVIOPURE - Medical Device - DEPUY SYNTHES; *pg.* 1523, *pg.* 1593
PLIZ - Home Cleaner - S.C. JOHNSON & SON, INC.; *pg.* 334, *pg.* 1889
PLLTEST - Software System - MENTOR GRAPHICS CORPORATION; *pg.* 432, *pg.* 1510
PLOW & HEARTH - Catalog & Web Site - 1-800-FLOWERS.COM, INC.; *pg.* 1758, *pg.* 1151
PLOW BOY SYRUP - All Natural Syrup - WHITFIELD FOODS, INC.; *pg.* 910, *pg.* 8
PLR HIP SYSTEM - Hip Product - ZIMMER BIOMET HOLDINGS, INC.; *pg.* 1611, *pg.* 699
PLT - Poultry Litter Treatment - JONES-HAMILTON CO.; *pg.* 1169, *pg.* 1478
PLUG - Stereo Earbud - KOSS CORPORATION; *pg.* 649, *pg.* 1877
PLUG - Apparel - OAKLEY, INC.; *pg.* 1840, *pg.* 86
PLUG-A-LITE - Wiring Devices - SWIVELIER CO., INC.; *pg.* 1307, *pg.* 1142
PLUG-ALL - Automotive Equipment - THEXTON MANUFACTURING COMPANY, INC.; *pg.* 218, *pg.* 925
PLUG AND GO - Wireless Remote Control System - CONTROL CHIEF HOLDINGS, INC.; *pg.* 630, *pg.* 1518
PLUG & GROW - Gardening Appliance Systems - AEROGROW INTERNATIONAL, INC.; *pg.* 1393, *pg.* 310
PLUG&SIM - Software - WIND RIVER SYSTEMS, INC.; *pg.* 493, *pg.* 38
PLUG-IN OUTLET CENTER - Surge Protector - WIREMOLD/LEGRAND; *pg.* 689, *pg.* 383
PLUG-IT - Cords - GENERAL CABLE CORPORATION; *pg.* 83, *pg.* 729
PLUG IT IN & PLAY TV GAMES - Leisure Product - JAKKS PACIFIC, INC.; *pg.* 960, *pg.* 142
PLUG MOUNTS - Commercial Lighting - SWIVELIER CO., INC.; *pg.* 1307, *pg.* 1142
PLUG N GO - Wireless Remote Control System - CONTROL CHIEF HOLDINGS, INC.; *pg.* 630, *pg.* 1518
PLUG-N-PLAY - Game - FORTUNET, INC.; *pg.* 953, *pg.* 1024
PLUG-N-RUN - Profit-Building Systems - USA FINANCIAL; *pg.* 815, *pg.* 864
PLUG-RACK - Hospital Lighting - SWIVELIER CO., INC.; *pg.* 1307, *pg.* 1142
PLUGMATE - Commercial Lighting - SWIVELIER CO., INC.; *pg.* 1307, *pg.* 1142
PLUGMISER - Software - USA TECHNOLOGIES, INC.; *pg.* 815, *pg.* 1550
PLUGRA - Dairy Product - DAIRY FARMERS OF AMERICA, INC.; *pg.* 851, *pg.* 982
PLUM A - Infusion System - HOSPIRA, INC.; *pg.* 1542, *pg.* 623
PLUM A PLUS - Medical Device - HOSPIRA, INC.; *pg.* 1542, *pg.* 623
PLUM BLOSSOM - Bath Product - KOHLER CO.; *pg.* 91, *pg.* 1862
PLUM CRAZY - Flower Arrangement - 1-800-FLOWERS.COM, INC.; *pg.* 1758, *pg.* 1151
PLUM CRAZY - Container Grown Plant - MONROVIA GROWERS; *pg.* 1797, *pg.* 44
PLUM CREEK - Lumber, Plywood & Medium-Density Fiberboard - PLUM CREEK TIMBER COMPANY, INC.; *pg.* 105, *pg.* 1838
PLUM GROVE - Furniture - ASHLEY FURNITURE INDUSTRIES, INC.; *pg.* 914, *pg.* 1852
PLUM PASSION - Container Grown Plant - MONROVIA GROWERS; *pg.* 1797, *pg.* 44
PLUMAS BANK - Banking Services - PLUMAS BANCORP; *pg.* 794, *pg.* 186
PLUMB N' PLUG - Circulators - TACO INCORPORATED; *pg.* 1077, *pg.* 1601
PLUMB POINTER - Navigation Aid - TRIMBLE NAVIGATION LIMITED; *pg.* 1384, *pg.* 288
PLUMBSET - Pencil - LA-CO INDUSTRIES MARKAL CO., INC.; *pg.* 1170, *pg.* 610
PLUMBSHOP - Plumbing Product - MASCO CORPORATION; *pg.* 96, *pg.* 909
PLUME & MERIDIAN - Adult Paperback Books - PENGUIN RANDOM HOUSE; *pg.* 1675, *pg.* 1276
PLUMERIA FANTASY - Fragrance - PARFUMS DE COEUR LTD.; *pg.* 519, *pg.* 376
PLUMP PERFECT - Skin Care Product - ELIZABETH ARDEN, INC.; *pg.* 507, *pg.* 448
PLUMPKINS - Food Product - R.M. PALMER COMPANY; *pg.* 1861, *pg.* 1585
PLUMS - Fabric - NEMSCHOFF, INC.; *pg.* 936, *pg.* 1890
PLUMSMART - Beverage - SUNSWEET GROWERS, INC.; *pg.* 900, *pg.* 309
PLUMSMART LIGHT - Beverage - SUNSWEET GROWERS, INC.; *pg.* 900, *pg.* 309
PLUNGER LUBE - Lubricant - HILL & GRIFFITH COMPANY; *pg.* 1167, *pg.* 1414
PLURAFAC - Surfactants - PVS CHEMICALS, INC.; *pg.* 1178, *pg.* 884
PLURAL - Fabric - NEMSCHOFF, INC.; *pg.* 936, *pg.* 1890
PLURONIC - Surfactants - PVS CHEMICALS, INC.; *pg.* 1178, *pg.* 884
PLURONIC - Molecular Probe Product - THERMO FISHER SCIENTIFIC INC.; *pg.* 1602, *pg.* 61
PLUS - Nutritional Product - MANNATECH, INCORPORATED; *pg.* 1558, *pg.* 1671
PLUS - Molecular Biology Product - THERMO FISHER SCIENTIFIC INC.; *pg.* 1602, *pg.* 61
PLUS 1 - Mobile Electronic Product - DANFOSS POWER SOLUTIONS COMPANY; *pg.* 1328, *pg.* 701
PLUS 3 - Joint Compound - USG CORPORATION; *pg.* 118, *pg.* 594
PLUS APLICAP - Glass Ionomer Restorative - 3M COMPANY; *pg.* 1142, *pg.* 956
PLUS DVR - Wireless Communications Service - VERIZON COMMUNICATIONS INC.; *pg.* 1875, *pg.* 1309
PLUS-FIFTY - Dry Chemical Agent - ANSUL, INCORPORATED; *pg.* 1147, *pg.* 1869
PLUS HD DVR - Wireless Communications Service - VERIZON COMMUNICATIONS INC.; *pg.* 1875, *pg.* 1309
PLUS SIZE LIVING - Apparel - ALWAYS FOR ME INC.; *pg.* 17, *pg.* 1163
PLUS TYPAR - Roofing Ventilation Product - BENJAMIN OBDYKE, INC.; *pg.* 70, *pg.* 1540
PLUS WHITE - Oral Care Product - CCA INDUSTRIES, INC.; *pg.* 503, *pg.* 1114
PLUS-X - Photographic Film - EASTMAN KODAK COMPANY; *pg.* 1408, *pg.* 1333
PLUSCODE - Digital Directory - ROVI CORPORATION; *pg.* 463, *pg.* 269
PLUSH - Doll - MGA ENTERTAINMENT, INC.; *pg.* 964, *pg.* 300
PLUSH - Fabric - NEMSCHOFF, INC.; *pg.* 936, *pg.* 1890
PLUSH CROC - Carpet - INTERFACE, INC.; *pg.* 695, *pg.* 512
PLUSH SENSE - Bed - KINGSDOWN, INC.; *pg.* 932, *pg.* 1383
PLUSMARK - Gift Wrap - AMERICAN GREETINGS CORPORATION; *pg.* 1615, *pg.* 1428
PLUSPAK - Packaging System - MTS MEDICATION TECHNOLOGIES, INC.; *pg.* 442, *pg.* 463
PLUSWOOD - Decorative Laminate Product - PANOLAM INDUSTRIES INTERNATIONAL, INC.; *pg.* 103, *pg.* 370
PLY-BEAD - Wall Panel - BLUELINX HOLDINGS, INC.; *pg.* 70, *pg.* 491
PLY-BEAD - Building Product - GEORGIA-PACIFIC LLC; *pg.* 1458, *pg.* 507
PLY-CEL - Meat, Fish & Poultry Pad - SEALED AIR CORPORATION; *pg.* 1468, *pg.* 1058
PLYABLE - Adhesive - H.B. FULLER COMPANY; *pg.* 1165, *pg.* 961
PLYFOAM - Cold Storage Doors - JAMISON DOOR COMPANY; *pg.* 89, *pg.* 771
PLYFOAM II - Cold Storage Doors - JAMISON DOOR COMPANY; *pg.* 89, *pg.* 771
PLYFOLD - Plybent Wood Chair - SAUDER MANUFACTURING COMPANY; *pg.* 941, *pg.* 1403
PLYGLASS - Plywood With Reinforced Plastic - MOLDED FIBER GLASS COMPANIES; *pg.* 1886, *pg.* 1403
PLYLOC - Low-Slope Roofing Products - GAF MATERIALS CORP.; *pg.* 83, *pg.* 1681
PLYLOK - Chair Plybent Wood - SAUDER MANUFACTURING COMPANY; *pg.* 941, *pg.* 1403
PLYLON - Conveyor Belting - THE GOODYEAR TIRE & RUBBER COMPANY; *pg.* 1883, *pg.* 1401
PLYMOUTH COLONY - Desserts & Condiments - CAINS FOODS, L.P.; *pg.* 843, *pg.* 784
PLYMOUTH PROWLER - Automobile - FCA US LLC; *pg.* 170, *pg.* 868
PLYOBACK - Medical & Aesthetic Product - DYNATRONICS CORPORATION; *pg.* 1526, *pg.* 1757
PLYOROBICS - Fitness Regimen - STAGESTEP INC.; *pg.* 1688, *pg.* 1570

PLYOTRAMP - Exercise Product - DYNATRONICS CORPORATION; pg. 1526, pg. 1757
PLYTANIUM - Wall Panel - BLUELINX HOLDINGS, INC.; pg. 70, pg. 491
PLYTANIUM - Structural Panels - GEORGIA-PACIFIC LLC; pg. 1458, pg. 507
PM ERASER - Pavement Line Remover - M-B COMPANIES, INC.; pg. 1357, pg. 1884
PM SHINES - Hair Care Product - JOHN PAUL MITCHELL SYSTEMS; pg. 512, pg. 133
PM1D - Digital Mixing Desk - YAMAHA CORPORATION OF AMERICA; pg. 595, pg. 51
PMA - Software - 3M; pg. 339, pg. 179
PMC - Hardware Product - INTERPHASE CORPORATION; pg. 420, pg. 1732
PMC - Urethane Liquid Rubber - SMOOTH-ON INC.; pg. 111, pg. 1528
PMI - Software - BIO-RAD LABORATORIES, INC.; pg. 1504, pg. 101
PMI NUTRITION - Animal Feeds & Pet Foods - LAND O'LAKES, INC.; pg. 873, pg. 915
PML - Lights - CYALUME TECHNOLOGIES HOLDINGS, INC.; pg. 1295, pg. 856
PMMS - Financial Services - FEDERAL HOME LOAN MORTGAGE CORPORATION; pg. 751, pg. 1790
PMOC - Circulator - OPLINK COMMUNICATIONS, INC.; pg. 660, pg. 91
PMS CONTROL - Nutritional Product - NATROL, INC.; pg. 1570, pg. 64
PMS ESCAPE - Supplement - ENZYMATIC THERAPY INC.; pg. 1529, pg. 1859
PMS OMEGA SOLUTIONS - Vitamin & Dietary Supplement - NATROL, INC.; pg. 1570, pg. 64
PMT - Photographic Materials & Chemicals - EASTMAN KODAK COMPANY; pg. 1408, pg. 1333
PMT - Electronic Product - LRAD CORPORATION; pg. 652, pg. 204
PMTV - Thermal Viewer - ISC8; pg. 1350, pg. 71
PMV - Pump - FLOWSERVE CORPORATION; pg. 82, pg. 1719
PMX - Metal-Enclosed Switchgear - S&C ELECTRIC COMPANY; pg. 1305, pg. 589
PMXXX - Fluid Handling System - GRACO, INC.; pg. 1342, pg. 935
PNA+ - Software - WIND RIVER SYSTEMS, INC.; pg. 493, pg. 38
PNC MERCHANT SERVICES - Banking Services - THE PNC FINANCIAL SERVICES GROUP, INC.; pg. 795, pg. 1579
PNEU-MOMENT - Pneumatic Actuator - BIMBA MANUFACTURING COMPANY; pg. 1317, pg. 633
PNEU-TURN - Rotary Actuator - BIMBA MANUFACTURING COMPANY; pg. 1317, pg. 633
PNEUMACAPPER - Capping Machine - PNEUMATICSCALEANGELUS; pg. 1369, pg. 1445
PNEUMACLEANER - Air Cleaning - PNEUMATICSCALEANGELUS; pg. 1369, pg. 1445
PNEUMAFLOW - Liquid Filler - PNEUMATICSCALEANGELUS; pg. 1369, pg. 1445
PNEUMALL - Software - BIO-RAD LABORATORIES, INC.; pg. 1504, pg. 101
PNEUMANT - Tire And Rubber Product - THE GOODYEAR TIRE & RUBBER COMPANY; pg. 1883, pg. 1401
PNEUMAPLUGGERS - Pharmaceutical Product - PNEUMATICSCALEANGELUS; pg. 1369, pg. 1445
PNEUMATIC SUPERJET - System for Installing Fiber Optic Cable - SHERMAN & REILLY, INC.; pg. 1062, pg. 1629
PNEUMOMENT - Rotary Actuator - BIMBA MANUFACTURING COMPANY; pg. 1317, pg. 633
PNEUMOTROL - Software - BIO-RAD LABORATORIES, INC.; pg. 1504, pg. 101
PNL - Pulsed Nucleation Layer - LAM RESEARCH CORPORATION; pg. 1354, pg. 246
PO-FLIP - Software - ARIBA, INC.; pg. 353, pg. 283
PO-PRO - Molecular Probe Product - THERMO FISHER SCIENTIFIC INC.; pg. 1602, pg. 61
POCAHONTAS - Foodservice Products - PERFORMANCE FOOD GROUP COMPANY, LLC; pg. 1030, pg. 1803
POCKET BASS - Flashlight - ENERGIZER HOLDINGS, INC.; pg. 637, pg. 996
POCKET BOOKS - Paperback Publisher - SIMON & SCHUSTER, INC.; pg. 1687, pg. 1292
POCKET CPR - Personal CPR Coaching Device - ZOLL MEDICAL CORPORATION; pg. 1612, pg. 814
POCKET DOODLE SKETCH - Toy - THE OHIO ART COMPANY, INC.; pg. 965, pg. 1406
POCKET DR - Beverages - THE COCA-COLA COMPANY; pg. 240, pg. 493
POCKET DTS - Software - VIASAT, INC.; pg. 489, pg. 62
POCKET ETCH A SKETCH - Toy - THE OHIO ART COMPANY, INC.; pg. 965, pg. 1406
POCKET FOLDING MONEY - Lottery Game - KENTUCKY LOTTERY CORPORATION; pg. 996, pg. 735
POCKET HEAD - Fluid Handling System - GRACO, INC.; pg. 1342, pg. 935
POCKET HOLDER - Key Holder - BROWN & BIGELOW, INC.; pg. 1624, pg. 959
POCKET IETM - Portable Hand-held Technical Manual - TELEDYNE BROWN ENGINEERING, INC.; pg. 235, pg. 6
POCKET LED - Flashlight - ENERGIZER HOLDINGS, INC.; pg. 637, pg. 996
POCKET MINI - Camera Accessories - ALAN GORDON ENTERPRISES, INC.; pg. 1399, pg. 125
POCKET PREP - Publication - FRANKLIN ELECTRONIC PUBLISHERS, INC.; pg. 398, pg. 1048
POCKET RESPONDER - Portable Hand-held Emergency Response Information Device - TELEDYNE BROWN ENGINEERING, INC.; pg. 235, pg. 6
POCKET SABRELITE - Flashlight - PELICAN PRODUCTS, INC.; pg. 1842, pg. 295
POCKET SPOT - Flashlight - ENERGIZER HOLDINGS, INC.; pg. 637, pg. 996
POCKETED COIL - Mattress - SIMMONS COMPANY; pg. 943, pg. 520
POCKETMAX - Software - HEMISPHERE GPS INC.; pg. 642, pg. 1903
POCKETPRO - Wireless Print Server - TROY GROUP INC.; pg. 485, pg. 71
POCKETS - Children's Magazine - THE UPPER ROOM; pg. 1698, pg. 1655
POCKETSCOPE - Otoscopes - WELCH ALLYN INC.; pg. 1436, pg. 1342
POCKETSCRIPT - Software - ZIX CORPORATION; pg. 497, pg. 1691
POCKETVIEW - Software - CITRIX SYSTEMS, INC.; pg. 375, pg. 424
POCO - Brief - JOCKEY INTERNATIONAL, INC.; pg. 27, pg. 1861
POCONO - Buckwheat Food Product - THE BIRKETT MILLS; pg. 826, pg. 1321
POCONO - Beer - THE LION BREWERY, INC.; pg. 254, pg. 1594
POCONO - Fabric - NEMSCHOFF, INC.; pg. 936, pg. 1890
POCONO LAGER - Beer - THE LION BREWERY, INC.; pg. 254, pg. 1594
POCONO PALE ALE - Beer - THE LION BREWERY, INC.; pg. 254, pg. 1594
PODIACIN - Foot Care - COMBE INCORPORATED; pg. 1516, pg. 1351
PODLE - Personal Care Product - WESTROCK COMPANY; pg. 1472, pg. 1805
PODOUS - Orthopedic Product - DJO INCORPORATED; pg. 1524, pg. 302
PODULAR TECHNOLOGY - Apparel Technology - BROOKS SPORTS INC.; pg. 1805, pg. 1818
POET - Patient Monitoring Device - CRITICARE SYSTEMS, INC.; pg. 1520, pg. 1897
POET GATEWAY - Software - WIND RIVER SYSTEMS, INC.; pg. 493, pg. 38
POET PLUS 8100 - Healthcare System - CRITICARE SYSTEMS, INC.; pg. 1520, pg. 1897
POETT - Cleaners - THE CLOROX COMPANY; pg. 327, pg. 169
POGA - Footwear - VANS, INC.; pg. 1821, pg. 76
POGO - Dental Product - DENTSPLY INTERNATIONAL INC.; pg. 1522, pg. 1596
POGO - Game - ELECTRONIC ARTS INC.; pg. 951, pg. 189
POGO - Semiconductor Test Products - EVERETT CHARLES TECHNOLOGIES; pg. 638, pg. 185
POGO - Fabric - NEMSCHOFF, INC.; pg. 936, pg. 1890
POGOL - Polyethylene Glycol - HUNTSMAN CORPORATION; pg. 1167, pg. 1758
POGOSTIK - Vehicle System - MACLEAN-FOGG COMPANY INC.; pg. 1358, pg. 635
POIANA NEGRI - Beverages - THE COCA-COLA COMPANY; pg. 240, pg. 493
POINCIANA - Home Builders - AV HOMES INC.; pg. 1080, pg. 20
POINSETTIA GROVES - Citrus Fruit Gift Packages - POINSETTIA GROVES INC.; pg. 890, pg. 478
POINT - Educational Materials - SCHOLASTIC INC.; pg. 1683, pg. 1288
POINT 9 - Excimer Laser System - THE SPECTRANETICS CORPORATION; pg. 1595, pg. 315
POINT ELECTRIC - Residential Lighting - SWIVELIER CO., INC.; pg. 1307, pg. 1142
POINT-GUARD - Insecticide - KENT NUTRITION GROUP; pg. 1477, pg. 710
POINT I/O - Software - ROCKWELL AUTOMATION, INC.; pg. 668, pg. 1880
POINT IN - Computer Program - COMPUTER SCIENCES CORPORATION; pg. 378, pg. 1780
THE POINT OF VICTORY - Slogan - MATTHEWS INTERNATIONAL CORPORATION; pg. 1662, pg. 1578
POINT PLAY - Gaming Devices - INTERNATIONAL GAME TECHNOLOGY; pg. 957, pg. 1024
POINT REYES - Bike - MARIN BIKES; pg. 1708, pg. 168
POINT ROYALE - Carpet - BEAULIEU GROUP, LLC; pg. 917, pg. 529
POINT-TO-POINT MEDICATION SAFETY - Software - OMNICELL INC.; pg. 1578, pg. 161
POINTBUS - Software - ROCKWELL AUTOMATION, INC.; pg. 668, pg. 1880
POINTE ESTERO BEACH RESORT - Resort - SUNSTREAM, INC.; pg. 1116, pg. 428
POINTER - Unmanned Air Vehicle - AEROVIRONMENT, INC.; pg. 223, pg. 150
POINTER CHECKER PLUS - IMS Database Utility - BMC SOFTWARE, INC.; pg. 362, pg. 1701
POINTFORWARD - Software - COMPUWARE CORPORATION; pg. 379, pg. 879
POINTGUARD - Fall Protection Equipment - MINE SAFETY APPLIANCES COMPANY; pg. 1361, pg. 1525
POINTS - Weight Loss System - WEIGHT WATCHERS INTERNATIONAL, INC.; pg. 1609, pg. 1313
POINTS - Value - WELLS ENTERPRISES, INC.; pg. 909, pg. 709
POINTS.COM - Website - POINTS INTERNATIONAL LTD.; pg. 1275, pg. 1941
POINTTER - Footwear - STEVEN MADDEN, LTD.; pg. 1819, pg. 1176
POINTTS - Cryosurgical Product - ORASURE TECHNOLOGIES INC; pg. 1578, pg. 1516
POISE - Feminine Guards - KIMBERLY-CLARK CORPORATION; pg. 1461, pg. 1720
POISE - Kitchen Product - KOHLER CO.; pg. 91, pg. 1862
POISE - Fabric - NEMSCHOFF, INC.; pg. 936, pg. 1890
POISINDEX - Medical Information - TRUVEN HEALTH ANALYTICS; pg. 486, pg. 331
POISON - Apparel - OAKLEY, INC.; pg. 1840, pg. 86
POISON - Perfume - PARFUMS CHRISTIAN DIOR, INC; pg. 519, pg. 1276
POISON-FREE - Pest Control - THE WOODSTREAM CORPORATION; pg. 1801, pg. 1549
POKE HOME - Connector - COOPER INTERCONNECT; pg. 630, pg. 1118
POKER FACE - Lottery Game - OHIO LOTTERY COMMISSION; pg. 1002, pg. 1433
POKERPRO - Electronic Poker Table - MULTIMEDIA GAMES INC.; pg. 442, pg. 1664
POKERTEK - Electronic Poker Table - MULTIMEDIA GAMES INC.; pg. 442, pg. 1664
POKHARA - Rug - COURISTAN INC.; pg. 921, pg. 1067
POL - Office Paper - INTERNATIONAL PAPER COMPANY; pg. 1460, pg. 1644
POL-E-LOC - Tamper-Evident Closure - OWENS-ILLINOIS, INC.; pg. 1466, pg. 1470
POLA - Power Modules & Converters - TEXAS INSTRUMENTS INCORPORATED; pg. 679, pg. 1688
POLA-H - Gaskets - PARKER CHOMERICS; pg. 662, pg. 862
POLACOAT - Screen - DA-LITE SCREEN COMPANY; pg. 632, pg. 698
POLACOLOR - Print Film - POLAROID CORPORATION; pg. 1426, pg. 815
POLAFILM - Optical Film - MONOSOL, LLC; pg. 59, pg. 694
POLAND SPRING - Mineral Water - NESTLE WATERS NORTH AMERICA INC.; pg. 257, pg. 375
POLANER - Jams, Jellies & Spices - B&G FOODS, INC.; pg. 838, pg. 1102
POLAR - Medical & Aesthetic Product - DYNATRONICS CORPORATION; pg. 1526, pg. 1757
POLAR - Acid Dyes - HUNTSMAN CORPORATION; pg. 1167, pg. 1758
POLAR - Systems Integration & Aeronautics - LOCKHEED MARTIN CORPORATION; pg. 229, pg. 762

POLAR - Soft Drink - POLAR BEVERAGES; *pg.* 264, *pg.* 862
POLAR BARE - Nail Care Product - OPI PRODUCTS INC.; *pg.* 518, *pg.* 167
POLAR BEAR - Delivery Body or Trailer Styles - HACKNEY INTERNATIONAL; *pg.* 178, *pg.* 1392
POLAR BOOTS - Slipper Boots - RELIABLE OF MILWAUKEE; *pg.* 698, *pg.* 1879
POLAR BREW - Beverages - THE COCA-COLA COMPANY; *pg.* 240, *pg.* 493
POLAR EYES - Sunglasses - FGX INTERNATIONAL, INC.; *pg.* 5, *pg.* 1608
POLAR-FLEX - Bare Copper - COLEMAN CABLE, INC.; *pg.* 1324, *pg.* 665
POLAR-GLO - Booster Cables - COLEMAN CABLE, INC.; *pg.* 1324, *pg.* 665
POLAR ICE - Vodka - MCCORMICK DISTILLING CO., INC.; *pg.* 1966, *pg.* 1007
POLAR KERR - Inspection System - KLA-TENCOR CORPORATION; *pg.* 1353, *pg.* 146
POLAR KING - Shirt - KEY INDUSTRIES, INC.; *pg.* 43, *pg.* 714
POLAR KRAFT - Paper Product - CANFOR CORPORATION; *pg.* 1454, *pg.* 1910
POLAR LOOP - Transmit Architecture - SKYWORKS SOLUTIONS, INC.; *pg.* 674, *pg.* 862
POLAR-MAX - Steel Product - HAWKEYE STEEL PRODUCTS, INC.; *pg.* 704, *pg.* 708
POLAR PETE - Slush Machine - GOLD MEDAL PRODUCTS CO.; *pg.* 55, *pg.* 1414
POLAR-RIG 125 - Bare Copper - COLEMAN CABLE, INC.; *pg.* 1324, *pg.* 665
POLAR SOLAR - Extension Cords - COLEMAN CABLE, INC.; *pg.* 1324, *pg.* 665
POLAR-THERM - Activewear for Winter Weather - STANFIELD'S LIMITED; *pg.* 48, *pg.* 1917
POLARA - Home Appliance Products - WHIRLPOOL CORPORATION; *pg.* 62, *pg.* 872
POLARCATH - Medical Device - BOSTON SCIENTIFIC CORPORATION; *pg.* 1508, *pg.* 831
POLARCHIP - Electrochemical Material - W.L. GORE & ASSOCIATES, INC.; *pg.* 122, *pg.* 388
POLARFLEECE - Synthetic Fabric - POLARTEC LLC; *pg.* 697, *pg.* 827
POLARGEL - Bentonite Clay - MINERALS TECHNOLOGIES INC.; *pg.* 1173, *pg.* 617
POLARGUARD - Durable High-Performance Apparel & Sleeping Bag Insulation Products - INVISTA B.V.; *pg.* 1168, *pg.* 723
POLARIS - Resins - ASHLAND INC.; *pg.* 972, *pg.* 726
POLARIS - Medical Device - BOSTON SCIENTIFIC CORPORATION; *pg.* 1508, *pg.* 831
POLARIS - Medical Equipment - INVACARE CORPORATION; *pg.* 1546, *pg.* 1451
POLARIS - Toothbrush - RANIR LLC; *pg.* 520, *pg.* 888
POLARIS - Tranceiver - RF MICRO DEVICES, INC.; *pg.* 667, *pg.* 1376
POLARIS - Faucet - SLOAN VALVE COMPANY; *pg.* 1062, *pg.* 613
POLARIS - Software - SYNOPSYS, INC.; *pg.* 480, *pg.* 162
POLARIS - Remote Control Device - UNIVERSAL ELECTRONICS, INC.; *pg.* 683, *pg.* 262
POLARIS - Assembly Cell - UNIVERSAL INSTRUMENTS CORPORATION; *pg.* 683, *pg.* 1154
POLARIS - Medical System - VARIAN MEDICAL SYSTEMS, INC.; *pg.* 1434, *pg.* 178
POLARIS DX - Medical Device - BOSTON SCIENTIFIC CORPORATION; *pg.* 1508, *pg.* 831
POLARIS X - Medical Device - BOSTON SCIENTIFIC CORPORATION; *pg.* 1508, *pg.* 831
POLARIZED CLIC - Sportsman Goggles - CORTLAND LINE COMPANY; *pg.* 1831, *pg.* 1155
POLARIZING - Filter - ROSCO LABORATORIES, INC.; *pg.* 1782, *pg.* 378
POLARMATE - Cooler - IGLOO PRODUCTS CORPORATION; *pg.* 1126, *pg.* 1724
POLAROID - Instant Cameras, Film, Digital & Audio Products & Videocassettes - POLAROID CORPORATION; *pg.* 1426, *pg.* 815
POLARSHADES - Ophthalmic Lenses - SIGNET ARMORLITE, INC.; *pg.* 1429, *pg.* 60
POLARSNAP - Software - AUTODESK INC.; *pg.* 356, *pg.* 257
POLARSPUN - Yarn - LION BRAND YARN COMPANY; *pg.* 696, *pg.* 1050
POLARTEC - Synthetic Fabrics - POLARTEC LLC; *pg.* 697, *pg.* 827
POLARTEC - Fishing Gear Product - SIMMS FISHING PRODUCTS CORP.; *pg.* 1845, *pg.* 1008
POLARTEC CLASSIC - Synthetic Fabric - POLARTEC LLC; *pg.* 697, *pg.* 827
POLARTEC POWER DRY - Synthetic Fabric - POLARTEC LLC; *pg.* 697, *pg.* 827
POLARTEC POWER SHIELD - Synthetic Fabric - POLARTEC LLC; *pg.* 697, *pg.* 827
POLARTEC POWER STRETCH - Synthetic Fabric - POLARTEC LLC; *pg.* 697, *pg.* 827
POLARTEC THERMAL PRO - Synthetic Fabric - POLARTEC LLC; *pg.* 697, *pg.* 827
POLARTEC WINDBLOC - Synthetic Fabric - POLARTEC LLC; *pg.* 697, *pg.* 827
POLCARD - Debit & Credit Card - INTERNATIONAL GAME TECHNOLOGY; *pg.* 420, *pg.* 1606
POLCARI'S - Restaurant - BOSTON RESTAURANT ASSOCIATES, INC.; *pg.* 1717, *pg.* 829
POLE MEGGER - Earth Tester - IDEAL INDUSTRIES, INC.; *pg.* 1051, *pg.* 662
POLESTAR - Carpet - INTERFACE, INC.; *pg.* 695, *pg.* 512
POLESTAR - Neurosurgery Navigation Tool - MEDTRONIC, INC.; *pg.* 1564, *pg.* 939
POLICE - Magazine - BOBIT BUSINESS MEDIA; *pg.* 1622, *pg.* 293
POLICE BIKE - Bicycle - TREK BICYCLE CORPORATION; *pg.* 1847, *pg.* 1896
POLICOSANOL CHOLESTEROL COMPLEX - Vitamin & Herbal Supplement - SOURCE NATURALS; *pg.* 1595, *pg.* 278
POLICY AUTHORITY FOR UNIFIED COMMUNICATIONS - Software - DELL SOFTWARE; *pg.* 385, *pg.* 40
POLICY MANAGER - Software - AXEDA SYSTEMS INC.; *pg.* 359, *pg.* 819
POLILYTE - Robotic Product - HAMILTON CO., INC.; *pg.* 1415, *pg.* 1031
POLIPOM - Nutritional Product - NUTRACEUTICAL INTERNATIONAL CORPORATION; *pg.* 1576, *pg.* 1753
POLISHING PEEL - Skin Care Product - NU SKIN ENTERPRISES, INC.; *pg.* 518, *pg.* 1755
POLITEX PRIMA - Polishing Pad - DOW CHEMICAL; *pg.* 1156, *pg.* 1563
POLK AUDIO - Home & Mobile Audio Equipment - DEI HOLDINGS, INC.; *pg.* 633, *pg.* 302
POLK INSIGHT - Online Automotive Analysis System - IHS AUTOMOTIVE DRIVEN BY POLK; *pg.* 1652, *pg.* 907
POLK TOTAL MARKET PREDICTOR - Vehicle - IHS AUTOMOTIVE DRIVEN BY POLK; *pg.* 1652, *pg.* 907
POLKA - Fabric - NEMSCHOFF, INC.; *pg.* 936, *pg.* 1890
POLKA DOT - Hat - WOODEN SHIPS OF HOBOKEN; *pg.* 35, *pg.* 1315
POLLEN - On-Line Injector - BIOANALYTICAL SYSTEMS, INC.; *pg.* 1402, *pg.* 700
POLLEN POWER - Nutritional Product - NUTRACEUTICAL INTERNATIONAL CORPORATION; *pg.* 1576, *pg.* 1753
POLLENEX - Showerhead - CONAIR CORPORATION; *pg.* 505, *pg.* 1055
POLLINATOR PLUS - Inbred Seed Coatings - LANDEC CORPORATION; *pg.* 1419, *pg.* 145
POLLOCK FILLETS TRIDENT - Seafood - TRIDENT SEAFOODS CORPORATION; *pg.* 902, *pg.* 1842
POLLY - Cabinet - METPAR CORP.; *pg.* 97, *pg.* 1350
POLLY - Wall Anchor - POWERS FASTENERS INC.; *pg.* 1059, *pg.* 1143
POLLY PEP - Bread Emulsifiers - MALLET & COMPANY, INC.; *pg.* 875, *pg.* 1521
POLLY SEALE - Hobby Paint - THE TESTOR CORPORATION; *pg.* 968, *pg.* 655
POLLYPELLET - System For Reheating Plates - CARLISLE FOODSERVICE PRODUCTS INCORPORATED; *pg.* 1455, *pg.* 1485
POLO - Furniture - FLEXSTEEL INDUSTRIES, INC.; *pg.* 925, *pg.* 707
POLO - Fabric - NEMSCHOFF, INC.; *pg.* 936, *pg.* 1890
POLO - Apparel - OAKLEY, INC.; *pg.* 1840, *pg.* 86
POLO BLACK - Men's Fragrance - RALPH LAUREN CORPORATION; *pg.* 46, *pg.* 1284
POLO BLUE - Men's Fragrance - RALPH LAUREN CORPORATION; *pg.* 46, *pg.* 1284
POLO BY RALPH LAUREN - Accessories - RALPH LAUREN CORPORATION; *pg.* 46, *pg.* 1284
POLO GOLF - Men's Golf Apparel - RALPH LAUREN CORPORATION; *pg.* 46, *pg.* 1284
POLO GULF - Apparel - RALPH LAUREN CORPORATION; *pg.* 46, *pg.* 1284
POLO RALPH LAUREN - Men's Clothing - RALPH LAUREN CORPORATION; *pg.* 46, *pg.* 1284
POLO TENNIS - Apparel - RALPH LAUREN CORPORATION; *pg.* 46, *pg.* 1284
POLONAISE - Packaged Foods - ATALANTA CORPORATION; *pg.* 838, *pg.* 1057
POLSET - Converting & Specialty Papers - INTERNATIONAL PAPER COMPANY; *pg.* 1460, *pg.* 1644
POLY 2000 - Labeling - FLEXCON CORPORATION; *pg.* 1457, *pg.* 844
POLY-2000 - Sensitive Film & Adhesive - FLEXCON CORPORATION; *pg.* 1457, *pg.* 844
POLY BAG - Poly Bag Pop Corn - AMERICAN POP CORN COMPANY; *pg.* 825, *pg.* 712
POLY-BOND - Weatherstripping - SCHLEGEL SYSTEMS, INC.; *pg.* 109, *pg.* 1337
POLY C - Nutritional Supplement - USANA HEALTH SCIENCES, INC.; *pg.* 1605, *pg.* 1761
POLY-CAST PLUS - Premium Roll Covers - VAIL RUBBER WORKS, INC.; *pg.* 1891, *pg.* 906
POLY-CATH - Urethral Catheter - MEDLINE INDUSTRIES, INC.; *pg.* 1562, *pg.* 635
POLY CC - Roll Covers - VAIL RUBBER WORKS, INC.; *pg.* 1891, *pg.* 906
POLY-COVER - Plastic Sheeting - FLEX-O-GLASS, INC.; *pg.* 1457, *pg.* 574
POLY DNB - Conditioning Agents - LORD CORPORATION; *pg.* 1357, *pg.* 1360
POLY DRY - Elastomeric Roll Covering - VAIL RUBBER WORKS, INC.; *pg.* 1891, *pg.* 906
POLY-FINE - Filter Cartridge - PALL CORPORATION; *pg.* 232, *pg.* 1323
POLY-FLEX - Flexible Polyester Glazing Putty - ITW - EVERCOAT; *pg.* 1443, *pg.* 1415
POLY-FLO - Filter Media - AMERICO MANUFACTURING CO., INC.; *pg.* 325, *pg.* 482
POLY-FLOC - Coagulant Aid - GE WATER & PROCESS TECHNOLOGIES; *pg.* 1339, *pg.* 1588
POLY-LOK - Fastener - LONG-LOK FASTENERS CORP.; *pg.* 1053, *pg.* 1416
POLY LOK - Envelope - POLY PAK AMERICA, INC.; *pg.* 1467, *pg.* 138
POLY MAIL - Envelope - POLY PAK AMERICA, INC.; *pg.* 1467, *pg.* 138
POLY-MAT - Seal Cement - TEXAS REFINERY CORP.; *pg.* 986, *pg.* 1696
POLY MATE - Roller Cover - VAIL RUBBER WORKS, INC.; *pg.* 1891, *pg.* 906
POLY-MESAM - Diagnosis System - RESMED INC.; *pg.* 1589, *pg.* 207
POLY-N - Ammoniated Poly Phosphate Solution - POTASHCORP; *pg.* 1799, *pg.* 641
POLY-PAC - Promotional Kit for Papers - EASTMAN KODAK COMPANY; *pg.* 1408, *pg.* 1333
POLY-PALE - Resin - EASTMAN CHEMICAL COMPANY; *pg.* 1159, *pg.* 1636
POLY-PANE - Storm Window Kit - WARP BROTHERS; *pg.* 1471, *pg.* 595
POLY-PORE - Minerals - MINERALS TECHNOLOGIES INC.; *pg.* 1173, *pg.* 617
POLY-PREP - Software - BIO-RAD LABORATORIES, INC.; *pg.* 1504, *pg.* 101
POLY PRINTS - Binders - AMERICAN THERMOPLASTIC COMPANY; *pg.* 349, *pg.* 1573
POLY-RIB - Plastic Sheeting - FLEX-O-GLASS, INC.; *pg.* 1457, *pg.* 574
POLY-SD - Rupture Disc Product - FIKE CORPORATION; *pg.* 1047, *pg.* 973
POLY SEAL - Automotive Reconditioning Product - MOC PRODUCTS COMPANY, INC.; *pg.* 332, *pg.* 174
POLY-SHIELD - Plastic Packaging Product - POLY PAK AMERICA, INC.; *pg.* 1467, *pg.* 138
POLY-SOFT - X-Ray Film Packet - EASTMAN KODAK COMPANY; *pg.* 1408, *pg.* 1333
POLY-SOFT - Wheel - HAMILTON CASTER & MFG. CO.; *pg.* 206, *pg.* 1454
POLY-SPHERE - Minerals - MINERALS TECHNOLOGIES INC.; *pg.* 1173, *pg.* 617
POLY-STRAP - Ties for Fastening Large Bundles Including Cable, Hoses, Cords & Laundry - BEDFORD INDUSTRIES, INC.; *pg.* 1453, *pg.* 967
POLY TABLET - Hardware & Software - POLYWELL COMPUTERS, INC.; *pg.* 456, *pg.* 280
POLY-TECH - Wheel - HAMILTON CASTER & MFG. CO.; *pg.*

First page reference indicates Business Class Edition
Second page reference indicates Geographic Edition

206, *pg.* 1454
POLY-TOGGLE - Screw Anchor - POWERS FASTENERS INC.; *pg.* 1059, *pg.* 1143
POLY TUFF - Livestock Equipment - BEHLEN MFG. CO.; *pg.* 701, *pg.* 1010
POLY-TWIST - Twist Tie Closure - BEDFORD INDUSTRIES, INC.; *pg.* 1453, *pg.* 967
POLY-VI-FLOR WITH IRON - 11 Essential Vitamins Plus Fluoride & Iron - MEAD JOHNSON NUTRITION COMPANY; *pg.* 1561, *pg.* 615
POLY-VI-SOL - 10 Essential Vitamins for Infants & Children - MEAD JOHNSON NUTRITION COMPANY; *pg.* 1561, *pg.* 615
POLY-WRAP - Skin Packaging - FLEX-O-GLASS, INC.; *pg.* 1457, *pg.* 574
POLY-XL - Jacketed Composite Cable - ELECTRON BEAM TECHNOLOGIES, INC.; *pg.* 1046, *pg.* 621
POLYACTIVE - Drug Delivery System - SURMODICS, INC.; *pg.* 1600, *pg.* 924
POLYALDO - Emulsifier - LONZA INC.; *pg.* 1171, *pg.* 1041
POLYALPHA - Hardware & Software - POLYWELL COMPUTERS, INC.; *pg.* 456, *pg.* 280
POLYAXIS - Plastic Compound & Resin - A. SCHULMAN, INC.; *pg.* 1144, *pg.* 1452
POLYBACK - Towel - CROSSTEX INTERNATIONAL INC.; *pg.* 1520, *pg.* 1164
POLYBATCH - Plastic Compound & Resin - A. SCHULMAN, INC.; *pg.* 1144, *pg.* 1452
POLYBATCH COLOR - Plastic Compound & Resin - A. SCHULMAN, INC.; *pg.* 1144, *pg.* 1452
POLYBATCH FILM - Plastic Compound & Resin - A. SCHULMAN, INC.; *pg.* 1144, *pg.* 1452
POLYBLAK - Plastic Compound & Resin - A. SCHULMAN, INC.; *pg.* 1144, *pg.* 1452
POLYBOND - Polymer Product - CHEMTURA CORPORATION; *pg.* 1152, *pg.* 355
POLYBOR - Medicine And Agricultural Product - RIO TINTO BORAX; *pg.* 334, *pg.* 331
POLYCAP - Air Cellular Cushioning Materials - SEALED AIR CORPORATION; *pg.* 1468, *pg.* 1058
POLYCARBALLOY - Fluid Handling System - GRACO, INC.; *pg.* 1342, *pg.* 935
POLYCARBONATE - Lenses - YOUNGER OPTICS; *pg.* 1437, *pg.* 297
POLYCAST - Roller Cover - VAIL RUBBER WORKS, INC.; *pg.* 1891, *pg.* 906
POLYCAST PLUS - Roll Covering - VAIL RUBBER WORKS, INC.; *pg.* 1891, *pg.* 906
POLYCAT - Catalysts - AIR PRODUCTS AND CHEMICALS, INC.; *pg.* 1145, *pg.* 1513
POLYCELL - Paint - AKZONOBEL DECORATIVE PAINTS U.S.; *pg.* 1439, *pg.* 1474
POLYCENTER - Hardware & Software - POLYWELL COMPUTERS, INC.; *pg.* 456, *pg.* 280
POLYCERAGUARD - Spray Booth Grate Coatings - GE WATER & PROCESS TECHNOLOGIES; *pg.* 1339, *pg.* 1588
POLYCHEM - Pump - FLOWSERVE CORPORATION; *pg.* 82, *pg.* 1719
POLYCHROME - Chemical Product - HURST CHEMICAL COMPANY; *pg.* 1168, *pg.* 174
POLYCIN - Polyol Products - VERTELLUS SPECIALTIES INC.; *pg.* 1185, *pg.* 690
POLYCLAVE - Electrode - HAMILTON CO., INC.; *pg.* 1415, *pg.* 1031
POLYCLEAN - Bag & Pouch Material - AUTOMATED PACKAGING SYSTEMS INC.; *pg.* 1452, *pg.* 1474
POLYCLEAR - Polycarbonate Ophthalmic Lenses - SIGNET ARMORLITE, INC.; *pg.* 1429, *pg.* 60
POLYCLEAR - Optical Product - UNIVERSAL PHOTONICS, INC.; *pg.* 1433, *pg.* 1167
POLYCLUSTERING - Hardware & Software - POLYWELL COMPUTERS, INC.; *pg.* 456, *pg.* 280
POLYCLUTCH - Coatings, Paints, Enamels, Primers & Thinners - PPG INDUSTRIES, INC.; *pg.* 1445, *pg.* 1579
POLYCO - Copolymer Binder - DOW CHEMICAL; *pg.* 1156, *pg.* 1563
POLYCOLD - Refrigeration - BROOKS AUTOMATION, INC.; *pg.* 1320, *pg.* 813
POLYCOM COMMUNICATOR - Voice Conference System - POLYCOM, INC.; *pg.* 664, *pg.* 249
POLYCOM CONFERENCE SUITE - Software Package - POLYCOM, INC.; *pg.* 664, *pg.* 249
POLYCOM HD VOICE - Technology - POLYCOM, INC.; *pg.* 664, *pg.* 249
POLYCOM ONE DIAL - Intelligent Call Management - POLYCOM, INC.; *pg.* 664, *pg.* 249
POLYCOM PATH NAVIGATOR - Advanced Gatekeeper - POLYCOM, INC.; *pg.* 664, *pg.* 249
POLYCOM SNAP - Collaboration Solution - POLYCOM, INC.; *pg.* 664, *pg.* 249
POLYCOM TELEPRESENCE EXPERIENCE - Solution Suite - POLYCOM, INC.; *pg.* 664, *pg.* 249
POLYCOM ULTIMATE HD - Technology - POLYCOM, INC.; *pg.* 664, *pg.* 249
POLYCOM V500 - Video Conferencing Product - POLYCOM, INC.; *pg.* 664, *pg.* 249
POLYCOM VIDEO PLUS - Video Conferencing Product - POLYCOM, INC.; *pg.* 664, *pg.* 249
POLYCOM VOICE PLUS - Audio Conference - POLYCOM, INC.; *pg.* 664, *pg.* 249
POLYCONTRAST - Photo Paper & Filters - EASTMAN KODAK COMPANY; *pg.* 1408, *pg.* 1333
POLYCOSE - Nutritional Supplement - ABBOTT LABORATORIES; *pg.* 1484, *pg.* 551
POLYCRON - Coating Product - PPG INDUSTRIES, INC.; *pg.* 1445, *pg.* 1579
POLYCUP - Resins - HERCULES INCORPORATED; *pg.* 1166, *pg.* 392
POLYCUT - Coated Abrasive With Grinding Aid Additives - 3M COMPANY; *pg.* 1142, *pg.* 956
POLYDEK - Biotechnology Product - GENZYME CORPORATION; *pg.* 1534, *pg.* 808
POLYDOL - Photo Developer & Replenisher - EASTMAN KODAK COMPANY; *pg.* 1408, *pg.* 1333
POLYDUAL - Hardware & Software - POLYWELL COMPUTERS, INC.; *pg.* 456, *pg.* 280
POLYDUR - UHMW Plastic - THE SCHMIDT GROUP, INC.; *pg.* 1374, *pg.* 1618
POLYETHELENE - Plastic Compound & Resin - A. SCHULMAN, INC.; *pg.* 1144, *pg.* 1452
POLYETTE - PVC Gloves - STANDARD SAFETY EQUIPMENT CO.; *pg.* 1379, *pg.* 632
POLYFABS - Plastic Compound & Resin - A. SCHULMAN, INC.; *pg.* 1144, *pg.* 1452
POLYFAC - Chemical Product - WESTROCK COMPANY; *pg.* 1472, *pg.* 1805
POLYFERM - Robotic Product - HAMILTON CO., INC.; *pg.* 1415, *pg.* 1031
POLYFIBER - Photographic Paper - EASTMAN KODAK COMPANY; *pg.* 1408, *pg.* 1333
POLYFIL - Surface Treatment Product - J.M. HUBER CORPORATION; *pg.* 1169, *pg.* 1056
POLYFILM - Specialty Paper - APPVION INC.; *pg.* 1451, *pg.* 1852
POLYFLAM - Plastic Compound & Resin - A. SCHULMAN, INC.; *pg.* 1144, *pg.* 1452
POLYFLEX - Veterinary Sterile Injectable Ampicillin - BOEHRINGER INGELHEIM VETMEDICA, INC.; *pg.* 1474, *pg.* 989
POLYFLEX - Medical Device - BOSTON SCIENTIFIC CORPORATION; *pg.* 1508, *pg.* 831
POLYFLEX - House Paint - JONES-BLAIR COMPANY; *pg.* 1443, *pg.* 1682
POLYFLEX - Plastic Product - PLASTIC SUPPLIERS, INC.; *pg.* 1888, *pg.* 1443
POLYFLEX - Extruded Elastomeric Conveyor Belting - SHINGLE BELTING COMPANY; *pg.* 1375, *pg.* 1544
POLYFLOCK - Adhesive & Sealant - DOW CHEMICAL; *pg.* 1156, *pg.* 1563
POLYFON - Chemical Product - WESTROCK COMPANY; *pg.* 1472, *pg.* 1805
POLYFORM - Medical Device - BOSTON SCIENTIFIC CORPORATION; *pg.* 1508, *pg.* 831
POLYFORT - Plastic Compound & Resin - A. SCHULMAN, INC.; *pg.* 1144, *pg.* 1452
POLYFOX - Chemical Product - OMNOVA SOLUTIONS INC; *pg.* 1176, *pg.* 1453
POLYFROTH - Froth Flotation Reagents - HUNTSMAN CORPORATION; *pg.* 1167, *pg.* 1758
POLYFUSE - Hair Replacement - HAIR CLUB FOR MEN, LTD., INC.; *pg.* 511, *pg.* 411
POLYGARD - Polymer Product - CHEMTURA CORPORATION; *pg.* 1152, *pg.* 355
POLYGARD - Towel - CROSSTEX INTERNATIONAL INC.; *pg.* 1520, *pg.* 1164
POLYGLAS - Adhesive & Sealant - DOW CHEMICAL; *pg.* 1156, *pg.* 1563
POLYGLYDE - Ceramic & Plastic Product - COORSTEK, INC.; *pg.* 77, *pg.* 330
POLYGRIP - Adhesive & Sealant - DOW CHEMICAL; *pg.* 1156, *pg.* 1563
POLYGUN - Hot-Melt Adhesive Applicator Guns & Accessories - 3M COMPANY; *pg.* 1142, *pg.* 956
POLYGYR - Analog Electronic Controls - SIEMENS BUILDING TECHNOLOGIES, INC.; *pg.* 1376, *pg.* 560
POLYHAND - Animal Safety Product - NEOGEN CORPORATION; *pg.* 883, *pg.* 896
POLYIFF - Polymer Encapsulation Fragrance Delivery Platform - INTERNATIONAL FLAVORS & FRAGRANCES INC.; *pg.* 512, *pg.* 1244
POLYJEL NF - Dental Product - DENTSPLY INTERNATIONAL INC.; *pg.* 1522, *pg.* 1596
POLYLAST - Aluminum-Center Polyurethane Wheels - HAMILTON CASTER & MFG. CO.; *pg.* 206, *pg.* 1454
POLYLIFE - Coating - YENKIN-MAJESTIC PAINT CORPORATION; *pg.* 1450, *pg.* 1445
POLYLITE - Antioxidants - CHEMTURA CORPORATION; *pg.* 1152, *pg.* 355
POLYLITE - Motor Vehicle Product - JASON INDUSTRIES, INC.; *pg.* 208, *pg.* 1875
POLYLITE - Protective Packaging Material - PACTIV CORPORATION; *pg.* 1466, *pg.* 624
POLYLOCK - File - FELLOWES, INC.; *pg.* 397, *pg.* 620
POLYLOK - Plastic Packaging Product - POLY PAK AMERICA, INC.; *pg.* 1467, *pg.* 138
POLYLUBE - Adhesive & Sealant - DOW CHEMICAL; *pg.* 1156, *pg.* 1563
POLYLUX - Plastic Compound & Resin - A. SCHULMAN, INC.; *pg.* 1144, *pg.* 1452
POLYMAIR - Polyelectrolyte Processing System - ACRISON, INC.; *pg.* 1310, *pg.* 1087
POLYMAN - Plastic Compound & Resin - A. SCHULMAN, INC.; *pg.* 1144, *pg.* 1452
POLYMAR - Injection (Plastic) Molding Operation - SERFILCO, LTD.; *pg.* 1375, *pg.* 641
POLYMATIC - Presensitized Litho Plates, Processing Chemicals & Little Plate Processors - EASTMAN KODAK COMPANY; *pg.* 1408, *pg.* 1333
POLYMAX - Photographic Paper; Chemicals; Filters; Processing Apparatus - EASTMAN KODAK COMPANY; *pg.* 1408, *pg.* 1333
POLYMER - Battery - ULTRALIFE CORPORATION; *pg.* 1385, *pg.* 1317
POLYMETRON - Water Analyzer - DANAHER CORPORATION; *pg.* 1044, *pg.* 397
POLYMODAL - Emission Testing System - MISTRAS GROUP, INC.; *pg.* 1362, *pg.* 1113
POLYMOLD - Adhesive & Sealant - DOW CHEMICAL; *pg.* 1156, *pg.* 1563
POLYNESIAN - Bottled Food Product - ALLIED OLD ENGLISH, INC.; *pg.* 836, *pg.* 1110
POLYNESIAN PRINCESS - Game - WMS INDUSTRIES INC.; *pg.* 593, *pg.* 666
POLYNETRA - Hardware & Software - POLYWELL COMPUTERS, INC.; *pg.* 456, *pg.* 280
POLYNODIC - Inhibitor - GE WATER & PROCESS TECHNOLOGIES; *pg.* 1339, *pg.* 1588
POLYNOTE - Hardware & Software - POLYWELL COMPUTERS, INC.; *pg.* 456, *pg.* 280
POLYOX - Water-Soluble Resins - THE DOW CHEMICAL COMPANY; *pg.* 1157, *pg.* 898
POLYPAK - Reels - SONOCO PRODUCTS COMPANY; *pg.* 1469, *pg.* 1619
POLYPHASE - Metalworking Fluid Additive - TROY CORPORATION; *pg.* 1184, *pg.* 1067
POLYPHOBE - Rheology Modifiers - THE DOW CHEMICAL COMPANY; *pg.* 1157, *pg.* 898
POLYPLANK - Packaging Product - PACTIV CORPORATION; *pg.* 1466, *pg.* 624
POLYPORT - Junction Box - MOLEX INCORPORATED; *pg.* 655, *pg.* 628
POLYPOXY - Two-Part Epoxy Products - PETTIT PAINT COMPANY; *pg.* 1444, *pg.* 1116
POLYPREP - Consumer Products - AKZO NOBEL; *pg.* 1439, *pg.* 1952
POLYPRINT - Photographic Paper - EASTMAN KODAK COMPANY; *pg.* 1408, *pg.* 1333
POLYPRINT - Orthopedic Device - SYMMETRY MEDICAL INC.; *pg.* 1600, *pg.* 699
POLYPRO - Glove Liner - KOMBI, LTD.; *pg.* 1838, *pg.* 1766
POLYPROPYLENE - Plastic Compound & Resin - A. SCHULMAN, INC.; *pg.* 1144, *pg.* 1452
POLYPUR - Plastic Compound & Resin - A. SCHULMAN, INC.; *pg.* 1144, *pg.* 1452

POLYPURE - Capsule - PALL CORPORATION; *pg.* 232, *pg.* 1323
POLYQUENCH - Water-Base Quenchant - HEATBATH CORPORATION; *pg.* 1165, *pg.* 826
POLYRACK - Hardware & Software - POLYWELL COMPUTERS, INC.; *pg.* 456, *pg.* 280
POLYRAD - Insulated Electrical Wire & Cable - GENERAL CABLE CORPORATION; *pg.* 83, *pg.* 384
POLYRAD - Wire & Cable - GENERAL CABLE CORPORATION; *pg.* 83, *pg.* 729
POLYRAXX - Hardware & Software - POLYWELL COMPUTERS, INC.; *pg.* 456, *pg.* 280
POLYRESIST - Robotic Product - HAMILTON CO., INC.; *pg.* 1415, *pg.* 1031
POLYS - Medical & Aesthetic Product - DYNATRONICS CORPORATION; *pg.* 1526, *pg.* 1757
POLYSCREEN - Hybridization - PERKINELMER, INC.; *pg.* 1426, *pg.* 853
POLYSEAL - Plastic Film - HOLLISTON LLC; *pg.* 1460, *pg.* 1630
POLYSEC - Bentonite Clay - MINERALS TECHNOLOGIES INC.; *pg.* 1173, *pg.* 617
POLYSERVER - Hardware & Software - POLYWELL COMPUTERS, INC.; *pg.* 456, *pg.* 280
POLYSHIELD - Paint & Coating - AERVOE INDUSTRIES INCORPORATED; *pg.* 1439, *pg.* 1021
POLYSIL - Coagulant and Dispersant - HUNTSMAN CORPORATION; *pg.* 1167, *pg.* 1758
POLYSLEEVE - Animal Safety Product - NEOGEN CORPORATION; *pg.* 883, *pg.* 896
POLYSLIP - Solvent - THE DOW CHEMICAL COMPANY; *pg.* 1157, *pg.* 898
POLYSONIC - Ultrasonic Lotion - ALIMED, INC.; *pg.* 1490, *pg.* 816
POLYSORB - Medical & Aesthetic Product - DYNATRONICS CORPORATION; *pg.* 1526, *pg.* 1757
POLYSORB - Sorbent Components - MULTISORB TECHNOLOGIES, INC.; *pg.* 1570, *pg.* 1150
POLYSPEED - Laminate - HEXCEL CORPORATION; *pg.* 1884, *pg.* 375
POLYSTAT - Anti-Static Materials - A. SCHULMAN, INC.; *pg.* 1144, *pg.* 1452
POLYSTATION - Hardware & Software - POLYWELL COMPUTERS, INC.; *pg.* 456, *pg.* 280
POLYSTAY - Antioxidant - THE GOODYEAR TIRE & RUBBER COMPANY; *pg.* 1883, *pg.* 1401
POLYSTEP - Chemical Product - STEPAN COMPANY; *pg.* 1182, *pg.* 643
POLYSTINGER - Flashlight - STREAMLIGHT INC.; *pg.* 1306, *pg.* 1527
POLYSTINGER DS - Flashlight - STREAMLIGHT INC.; *pg.* 1306, *pg.* 1527
POLYSTRIP - Industrial Paint Stripper & Industrial Chemicals - PPG INDUSTRIES, INC.; *pg.* 1445, *pg.* 1579
POLYSTYLUS - Flashlight - STREAMLIGHT INC.; *pg.* 1306, *pg.* 1527
POLYSTYRENE - Plastic Compound & Resin - A. SCHULMAN, INC.; *pg.* 1144, *pg.* 1452
POLYSULFONE - Dialyzers - FRESENIUS MEDICAL CARE NORTH AMERICA; *pg.* 1531, *pg.* 851
POLYSURF - Polymer - HERCULES INCORPORATED; *pg.* 1166, *pg.* 392
POLYTAC - Flashlight - STREAMLIGHT INC.; *pg.* 1306, *pg.* 1527
POLYTEX - Motor Vehicle Product - JASON INDUSTRIES, INC.; *pg.* 208, *pg.* 1875
POLYTEX - Chemical Ingredient - LIPO CHEMICALS INC.; *pg.* 1171, *pg.* 1107
POLYTITE - Sealant - DAYTON SUPERIOR CORPORATION; *pg.* 1328, *pg.* 1464
POLYTRAP - Endoscopic Technologies - CONMED CORPORATION; *pg.* 1517, *pg.* 1347
POLYTRITICUM - Resin - MGP INGREDIENTS, INC.; *pg.* 877, *pg.* 714
POLYTRON - Vinyl Compound - POLYONE CORPORATION; *pg.* 1177, *pg.* 1404
POLYTROPE - Plastic Compound & Resin - A. SCHULMAN, INC.; *pg.* 1144, *pg.* 1452
POLYULTRA - Hardware & Software - POLYWELL COMPUTERS, INC.; *pg.* 456, *pg.* 280
POLYVALVE - Pump - FLOWSERVE CORPORATION; *pg.* 82, *pg.* 1719
POLYVAULT - Envelope - POLY PAK AMERICA, INC.; *pg.* 1467, *pg.* 138
POLYVIN - Plastic Compound & Resin - A. SCHULMAN, INC.; *pg.* 1144, *pg.* 1452
POLYWEB - Polymer - GEORGIA-PACIFIC LLC; *pg.* 1458, *pg.* 507
POLYWEB - Coating - W.L. GORE & ASSOCIATES, INC.; *pg.* 122, *pg.* 388
POLYWET - Polymer Product - CHEMTURA CORPORATION; *pg.* 1152, *pg.* 355
POM WONDERFUL - Juices & Teas Processed from Pomegranates - POM WONDERFUL, LLC; *pg.* 890, *pg.* 139
POMALUX - Compression Molded Product - WESTLAKE PLASTICS COMPANY; *pg.* 1892, *pg.* 1548
POMEGRAN PLUS - Granola - NATURE'S PATH FOODS INC.; *pg.* 833, *pg.* 1908
POMEGRANATE - Oil & Spray - AROMATIQUE INC.; *pg.* 499, *pg.* 32
POMEGRANATE HEART HAPPY - Fruit Drink - JAMBA, INC.; *pg.* 1024, *pg.* 84
POMEGRANATE PARADISE - Fruit Drink - JAMBA, INC.; *pg.* 1024, *pg.* 84
POMEGRANATE PICK-ME-UP - Fruit Drink - JAMBA, INC.; *pg.* 1024, *pg.* 84
POMERATROL - Nutritional Product - NOW HEALTH GROUP, INC.; *pg.* 1576, *pg.* 557
POMODORO - Fabric - NEMSCHOFF, INC.; *pg.* 936, *pg.* 1890
POMONA - Fabric - NEMSCHOFF, INC.; *pg.* 936, *pg.* 1890
POMPEII - Furniture - BROWN JORDAN INTERNATIONAL COMPANY; *pg.* 919, *pg.* 740
POMPEII - Dinnerware - THE HOMER LAUGHLIN CHINA COMPANY; *pg.* 1125, *pg.* 1850
POMPEII PURPLE - Nail Care Product - OPI PRODUCTS INC.; *pg.* 518, *pg.* 167
POMS - Beverages - THE COCA-COLA COMPANY; *pg.* 240, *pg.* 493
POMX ICED TEA - Beverage - POM WONDERFUL, LLC; *pg.* 890, *pg.* 139
PON - Transceiver - FINISAR CORPORATION; *pg.* 639, *pg.* 285
PONA 2100 - Amplifier - EMCORE CORPORATION; *pg.* 636, *pg.* 39
PONA 3000 - Amplifier - EMCORE CORPORATION; *pg.* 636, *pg.* 39
POND - Outdoor Pond Products - THE HARTZ MOUNTAIN CORP.; *pg.* 1476, *pg.* 1120
POND ALLCLEAR II - Algicide for Outdoor Fishpools - THE HARTZ MOUNTAIN CORP.; *pg.* 1476, *pg.* 1120
PONDMASTER - Turf Product - PBI/GORDON CORPORATION; *pg.* 1176, *pg.* 985
PONDPACK - Software - BENTLEY SYSTEMS, INC.; *pg.* 361, *pg.* 1531
POND'S - Skin Care Products - UNILEVER UNITED STATES, INC.; *pg.* 904, *pg.* 1061
PONDS MAGAZINE - Magazine - I-5 PUBLISHING LLC; *pg.* 1651, *pg.* 133
PONDS USA AND WATER GARDENS - Magazine - I-5 PUBLISHING LLC; *pg.* 1651, *pg.* 133
PONDTABBS - Aquatic Fertilizer - PLANTABBS PRODUCTS COMPANY; *pg.* 1799, *pg.* 758
PONG - Fabric - NEMSCHOFF, INC.; *pg.* 936, *pg.* 1890
PONKANA - Soft Drink - THE COCA-COLA COMPANY; *pg.* 240, *pg.* 493
PONM - Splitter - OPLINK COMMUNICATIONS, INC.; *pg.* 660, *pg.* 91
PONTIAC - Automobile - GENERAL MOTORS COMPANY; *pg.* 175, *pg.* 881
PONTIAC ENTHUSIAST - Magazine - AMOS PRESS, INC.; *pg.* 1616, *pg.* 1472
PONY - Floor Cleaning Product - NSS ENTERPRISES, INC.; *pg.* 59, *pg.* 1476
PONY GALS - Toy Scale Model Animal - REEVES INTERNATIONAL, INC.; *pg.* 966, *pg.* 1108
PONY OH'S - Hair Accessories - STA-RITE GINNIE LOU, INC.; *pg.* 523, *pg.* 660
PONY PALS - Educational Materials - SCHOLASTIC INC.; *pg.* 1683, *pg.* 1288
PONY PCU - Compact, Lightweight & Highly Integrated Portable Rugged Computer - MILTOPE GROUP, INC.; *pg.* 440, *pg.* 6
POOCH POPS - Food Product - THE JEL SERT COMPANY; *pg.* 865, *pg.* 668
POOKS - Beer - BJ'S RESTAURANTS, INC.; *pg.* 1716, *pg.* 104
POOL - Accessories - THE MEN'S WEARHOUSE, INC.; *pg.* 44, *pg.* 1711
POOL ADVISOR - Software - BMC SOFTWARE, INC.; *pg.* 362, *pg.* 1701
POOL BLOK - Pool & Spa Cleaner - U.S. PUMICE COMPANY; *pg.* 1185, *pg.* 65
POOL-COTE - Paint & Coating - DIAMOND VOGEL PAINT, INC.; *pg.* 1441, *pg.* 710
POOL VAC ULTRA - Pool Cleaner - HAYWARD POOL PRODUCTS; *pg.* 1049, *pg.* 1057
POOLPRUF - Swim Dress - JUNONIA LTD.; *pg.* 27, *pg.* 929
POORE BROTHERS - Salted Snack Food - INVENTURE FOODS, INC.; *pg.* 1023, *pg.* 17
POORE BROTHERS BBQ RANCH CHIPS - Snack Food - INVENTURE FOODS, INC.; *pg.* 1023, *pg.* 17
POORE BROTHERS JALAPENO CHIPS - Snack Food - INVENTURE FOODS, INC.; *pg.* 1023, *pg.* 17
POP - Beverages - THE COCA-COLA COMPANY; *pg.* 240, *pg.* 493
POP - Carpet - INTERFACE, INC.; *pg.* 695, *pg.* 512
POP - Cosmetics - MARKWINS INTERNATIONAL CORP.; *pg.* 516, *pg.* 67
POP 1-2-3 - Container Grown Plant - MONROVIA GROWERS; *pg.* 1797, *pg.* 44
POP-A-LOT - Popcorn Machine - GOLD MEDAL PRODUCTS CO.; *pg.* 55, *pg.* 1414
POP-A-WAY - Sprinklers - RAIN BIRD CORPORATION; *pg.* 707, *pg.* 44
POP-ALL - Vegetable Oil - VENTURA FOODS, LLC; *pg.* 908, *pg.* 49
POP BID - Magazine - RANDALL-REILLY PUBLISHING COMPANY LLC; *pg.* 1679, *pg.* 8
POP CULTURE - Music Compact Discs - THE SINGING MACHINE COMPANY, INC.; *pg.* 674, *pg.* 426
POP-FREE - Conductive Primers - RED SPOT PAINT & VARNISH CO., INC.; *pg.* 1446, *pg.* 679
POP GLOSS - Cosmetics - KOSS CORPORATION; *pg.* 649, *pg.* 1877
POP-ICE - Frozen Confection - THE JEL SERT COMPANY; *pg.* 865, *pg.* 668
POP-O-MATIC TONKA - Game - HASBRO, INC.; *pg.* 954, *pg.* 1603
POP-O-MATIC TROUBLE - Toy & Game - HASBRO, INC.; *pg.* 954, *pg.* 1603
POP SECRET - Microwave Popcorn - DIAMOND FOODS, INC.; *pg.* 1851, *pg.* 216
POP-TARTS - Food Product - KELLOGG COMPANY; *pg.* 831, *pg.* 870
POP-TARTS BROWN SUGAR CINNAMON - Snacks - KELLOGG COMPANY; *pg.* 831, *pg.* 870
POP-TARTS CHOCOLATE FUDGE - Snacks - KELLOGG COMPANY; *pg.* 831, *pg.* 870
POP-TARTS FROSTED HOT FUDGE SUNDAE - Snacks - KELLOGG COMPANY; *pg.* 831, *pg.* 870
POP-TARTS LOW FAT STRAWBERRY - Snacks - KELLOGG COMPANY; *pg.* 831, *pg.* 870
POP-TARTS RASPBERRY - Snacks - KELLOGG COMPANY; *pg.* 831, *pg.* 870
POP-TARTS STRAWBERRY - Snacks - KELLOGG COMPANY; *pg.* 831, *pg.* 870
POP-TARTS VANILLA CREME - Snacks - KELLOGG COMPANY; *pg.* 831, *pg.* 870
POP-TARTS WILD BERRY - Snacks - KELLOGG COMPANY; *pg.* 831, *pg.* 870
POP-TOGGLE - Wall Anchor - POWERS FASTENERS INC.; *pg.* 1059, *pg.* 1143
POP TOP - Buttery-Flavored Topping - VENTURA FOODS, LLC; *pg.* 908, *pg.* 49
POP-TOP LUNCH KIT - Insulated Lunch Bag - IGLOO PRODUCTS CORPORATION; *pg.* 1126, *pg.* 1724
POP TOPPERS - Toy & Game - HASBRO, INC.; *pg.* 954, *pg.* 1603
POP-UP WASHER - Software - WEBROOT SOFTWARE, INC.; *pg.* 1289, *pg.* 313
POP ZONE - Educational Materials - SCHOLASTIC INC.; *pg.* 1683, *pg.* 1288
POPCHIPS - Potato Snacks - POPCHIPS; *pg.* 890, *pg.* 182
POPCORN - Poultry Product - PILGRIM'S PRIDE CORPORATION; *pg.* 889, *pg.* 330
POPCORN - Women's Clothing & Accessories - WOODEN SHIPS OF HOBOKEN; *pg.* 35, *pg.* 1315
POPCORN CHICKEN - Tender Bites of Fried Chicken Breast - KFC CORPORATION; *pg.* 1733, *pg.* 735
THE POPCORN FACTORY - Popcorn - THE POPCORN FACTORY; *pg.* 1861, *pg.* 625
THE POPCORN FACTORY SMILEY - Cookies - 1-800-FLOWERS.COM, INC.; *pg.* 1758, *pg.* 1151

First page reference indicates Business Class Edition
Second page reference indicates Geographic Edition

POPCORNNOW - Electrical Appliance & Housewares - NATIONAL PRESTO INDUSTRIES, INC; *pg.* 1128, *pg.* 1857
POPE - Spindle & Slide - SETCO SALES COMPANY; *pg.* 1061, *pg.* 1426
POPEYE'S - Fast Food Restaurants - POPEYES LOUISIANA KITCHEN, INC.; *pg.* 1745, *pg.* 517
POPEYE'S CHICKEN & BISCUITS - Fast Food Restaurants - POPEYE'S CHICKEN & BISCUITS; *pg.* 1745, *pg.* 517
POPINFO - Long-Distance Telecom System - PITNEY BOWES SOFTWARE INC.; *pg.* 455, *pg.* 1346
POPLITE - Electrical Appliance & Housewares - NATIONAL PRESTO INDUSTRIES, INC; *pg.* 1128, *pg.* 1857
POPMATTERS - Cultural Criticism Magazine - SPINMEDIA; *pg.* 1282, *pg.* 104
POP'N LITE - Corn Oil - VENTURA FOODS, LLC; *pg.* 908, *pg.* 49
POPO - Molecular Probe Product - THERMO FISHER SCIENTIFIC INC.; *pg.* 1602, *pg.* 61
POPOUT PRISM - Software - XEROX CORPORATION; *pg.* 494, *pg.* 365
POPOV VODKA - Vodka - DIAGEO NORTH AMERICA, INC.; *pg.* 1961, *pg.* 361
POPPEOPLE - Educational Materials - SCHOLASTIC INC.; *pg.* 1683, *pg.* 1288
POPPERS - Bakery Product - J&J SNACK FOODS CORPORATION; *pg.* 865, *pg.* 1107
POPPERS - Frozen Snacks - THE KRAFT HEINZ COMPANY; *pg.* 870, *pg.* 1577
POPPET - Valve - VERNAY LABORATORIES, INC.; *pg.* 1891, *pg.* 1482
POPPIES - Restaurant - OMNI HOTELS & RESORTS; *pg.* 1107, *pg.* 1685
POPPIN' TOPPIN' - Popcorn Topping Oil - VENTURA FOODS, LLC; *pg.* 908, *pg.* 49
POPPY - Silverware - ONEIDA LTD; *pg.* 1129, *pg.* 1318
POPPYCOCK - Food Product - CONAGRA FOODS, INC.; *pg.* 826, *pg.* 1014
POPSCI.COM - Web Site - BONNIER ACTIVE MEDIA, INC.; *pg.* 1622, *pg.* 1205
POPSICLE - Ice Cream - UNILEVER UNITED STATES, INC.; *pg.* 904, *pg.* 1061
POPULAR DOGS SERIES - Magazine - I-5 PUBLISHING LLC; *pg.* 1651, *pg.* 133
POPULAR MECHANICS - Magazine - THE HEARST CORPORATION; *pg.* 1649, *pg.* 1239
POPULAR SCIENCE - Magazine - BONNIER ACTIVE MEDIA, INC.; *pg.* 1622, *pg.* 1205
POPULAR SCIENCE - Magazine - BONNIER CORPORATION; *pg.* 1622, *pg.* 480
POPULARSCREENSAVERS - Online Services - IAC/INTERACTIVECORP; *pg.* 292, *pg.* 1242
POPULATED AREA COMBUSTORS - Flare - NAO, INC.; *pg.* 1074, *pg.* 1567
POPULOUS - Video Game - ELECTRONIC ARTS INC.; *pg.* 951, *pg.* 189
POR EQUAL - Pre Permanent Conditioning for Extra Resistant Hair - THE GILLETTE COMPANY; *pg.* 509, *pg.* 795
PORAPAK - Chromatography Product - WATERS CORPORATION; *pg.* 1436, *pg.* 834
PORCH & FLOOR - Enamel - JONES-BLAIR COMPANY; *pg.* 1443, *pg.* 1682
PORCH & FLOOR - Paint - THE SHERWIN-WILLIAMS COMPANY; *pg.* 1447, *pg.* 1435
PORCH FAN - Fan - CRAFTMADE INTERNATIONAL, INC.; *pg.* 1295, *pg.* 1670
PORIDON - Animal Safety Product - NEOGEN CORPORATION; *pg.* 883, *pg.* 896
PORK - Magazine - VANCE PUBLISHING CORPORATION; *pg.* 1699, *pg.* 627
PORK FOCUS - Animal Nutrition - CARGILL LIMITED; *pg.* 1475, *pg.* 1914
PORK KING - Fountain - RITCHIE INDUSTRIES, INC.; *pg.* 707, *pg.* 703
PORK WORKS - Risk Management - CARGILL LIMITED; *pg.* 1475, *pg.* 1914
PORON - Urethane Product - ROGERS CORPORATION; *pg.* 1305, *pg.* 369
POROUS COAT - Slot Applicator - NORDSON CORPORATION; *pg.* 1365, *pg.* 1480
PORT - Patient Monitoring System - CRITICARE SYSTEMS, INC.; *pg.* 1520, *pg.* 1897
PORT - Ophthalmic Devices - LANDEC CORPORATION; *pg.* 1419, *pg.* 145
PORT-A-CATH - Catheter - SMITHS MEDICAL MD, INC.; *pg.* 1594, *pg.* 963
PORT-A-PIT - Gymnastic Exercise Mats - SPORT SUPPLY GROUP, INC.; *pg.* 1846, *pg.* 1687
PORT AND COMPANY - Cap - BROWN & BIGELOW, INC.; *pg.* 1624, *pg.* 959
PORT AUTHORITY OF NEW YORK & NEW JERSEY - Bi-State Transportation & Trade Agency - PORT AUTHORITY OF NEW YORK & NEW JERSEY; *pg.* 1919, *pg.* 1283
PORT CLYDE - Seafood - OCEAN BEAUTY SEAFOODS, INC.; *pg.* 1028, *pg.* 1838
PORT COLLECTION - Gift Box - BROWN & BIGELOW, INC.; *pg.* 1624, *pg.* 959
PORT-O-LET - Sanitation Services - WASTE MANAGEMENT, INC.; *pg.* 1954, *pg.* 1716
PORT OF CALL - Bath Accessory - CROSCILL, INC.; *pg.* 1122, *pg.* 1220
PORT OF SUBS - Logo - PORT OF SUBS INC.; *pg.* 1746, *pg.* 1032
PORT ROUGE - Furniture - ASHLEY FURNITURE INDUSTRIES, INC.; *pg.* 914, *pg.* 1852
PORT ROYAL - Furniture - FLEXSTEEL INDUSTRIES, INC.; *pg.* 925, *pg.* 707
PORT ROYALE - Video Game - INTERNATIONAL GAME TECHNOLOGY; *pg.* 957, *pg.* 1024
THE PORT ST. LUCIE NEWS - Newspaper - THE E.W. SCRIPPS COMPANY; *pg.* 1639, *pg.* 1412
PORTA-FLOW - Medical Equipment - THE COOPER COMPANIES, INC.; *pg.* 1518, *pg.* 183
PORTA-MATIC - Pump Product - IDEX CORPORATION; *pg.* 1347, *pg.* 623
PORTA POTTI - Portable Toilets - THETFORD CORPORATION; *pg.* 337, *pg.* 867
PORTA-RAMP - Portable Ramp for Intermittent Loading & Unloading - LIFTOMATIC MATERIAL HANDLING INC.; *pg.* 94, *pg.* 560
PORTA-TEST REVOLUTION - Cyclonic Inlet Device - CAMERON INTERNATIONAL; *pg.* 1151, *pg.* 1702
PORTA-TEST WHIRLYSCRUB - V Gas Scrubber - CAMERON INTERNATIONAL; *pg.* 1151, *pg.* 1702
PORTA-TEST WHIRLYSCRUB I - Inline Recycling Separator - CAMERON INTERNATIONAL; *pg.* 1151, *pg.* 1702
PORTA-TRUNK - Fume Exhauster - DONALDSON COMPANY, INC.; *pg.* 1329, *pg.* 917
PORTA VAC - Container - CHART INDUSTRIES, INC.; *pg.* 1405, *pg.* 1454
PORTABARRE - Flooring Product - ROSCO LABORATORIES, INC.; *pg.* 1782, *pg.* 378
PORTABELLO - Dinnerware - THE HOMER LAUGHLIN CHINA COMPANY; *pg.* 1125, *pg.* 1850
PORTABLE-AIRE - Air Conditioner - HEAT CONTROLLER, INC.; *pg.* 1072, *pg.* 893
PORTABOUT - Infant Car Seat - EVENFLO COMPANY, INC.; *pg.* 924, *pg.* 1470
PORTACOUNT - Fit Tester - TSI INCORPORATED; *pg.* 1432, *pg.* 965
PORTAGE DAILY REGISTER - Newspaper - MADISON NEWSPAPERS, INC.; *pg.* 1661, *pg.* 1866
PORTAGEN - Food Fat/Lactose Dietary Powder - MEAD JOHNSON NUTRITION COMPANY; *pg.* 1561, *pg.* 615
PORTAGRIP - Phone Holder - PANAVISE PRODUCTS, INC.; *pg.* 1058, *pg.* 1032
PORTAGRIP 2000 - Hand Held Electronics - PANAVISE PRODUCTS, INC.; *pg.* 1058, *pg.* 1032
PORTAL - Software - PASSUR AEROSPACE, INC.; *pg.* 233, *pg.* 376
PORTAL LADDER - Security Product - BAE SYSTEMS PRODUCTS GROUP; *pg.* 359, *pg.* 432
PORTAL TO THE FUTURE - Slogan - SEATTLE CONVENTION & VISITORS BUREAU; *pg.* 1005, *pg.* 1839
PORTALAB - Portable Turbidimeter - HACH COMPANY; *pg.* 1415, *pg.* 334
PORTALBUILDER - Computer Software - TIBCO SOFTWARE INC.; *pg.* 484, *pg.* 178
PORTALLOY - Steel Alloy - WEBSTER INDUSTRIES INC.; *pg.* 1388, *pg.* 1475
PORTAMEDIC - Healthcare Services & Health Information - HOOPER HOLMES, INC.; *pg.* 1542, *pg.* 718
PORTAPAC - Floor Maintenance Equipment - TENNANT COMPANY; *pg.* 1381, *pg.* 944
PORTAPRO - Stereo Headphone - KOSS CORPORATION; *pg.* 649, *pg.* 1877
PORTAPRO - Glue Gun - MASTER APPLIANCE CORP.; *pg.* 1055, *pg.* 1888
PORTAPUMP - Pump Product - IDEX CORPORATION; *pg.* 1347, *pg.* 623
PORTELLO - Beverages - THE COCA-COLA COMPANY; *pg.* 240, *pg.* 493
PORTER - Gaming Product - GLD PRODUCTS, INC.; *pg.* 1835, *pg.* 1882
PORTER - Floor Cleaning Product - NSS ENTERPRISES, INC.; *pg.* 59, *pg.* 1476
PORTER - Paint Product - PPG INDUSTRIES, INC.; *pg.* 1445, *pg.* 1579
PORTER-CABLE - Tools - STANLEY BLACK & DECKER, INC.; *pg.* 1063, *pg.* 358
PORTER DECK - Coating Product - PPG INDUSTRIES, INC.; *pg.* 1445, *pg.* 1579
PORTER GUARD - Coating Product - PPG INDUSTRIES, INC.; *pg.* 1445, *pg.* 1579
PORTER SEPT - Coating Product - PPG INDUSTRIES, INC.; *pg.* 1445, *pg.* 1579
PORTERVILLE RECORDER - California Newspaper - FREEDOM COMMUNICATIONS, INC.; *pg.* 1643, *pg.* 110
PORTERVILLE RECORDER - Newspaper - PORTERVILLE RECORDER; *pg.* 1677, *pg.* 185
PORTESCAP - Miniature Motor - DANAHER CORPORATION; *pg.* 1044, *pg.* 397
PORTESCAP - Mini Motors - DANAHER MOTION; *pg.* 1327, *pg.* 1593
PORTEXCHANGE - Software - EVOLVING SYSTEMS, INC.; *pg.* 395, *pg.* 326
PORTFOLIO - Business Magazine - CONDE NAST PUBLICATIONS, INC.; *pg.* 1629, *pg.* 1217
PORTFOLIO - Software - ENVIRONMENTAL SYSTEMS RESEARCH INSTITUTE INC.; *pg.* 393, *pg.* 188
PORTFOLIO - Software System - JDA SOFTWARE GROUP, INC.; *pg.* 423, *pg.* 22
PORTFOLIO CRM - Software - JDA SOFTWARE GROUP, INC.; *pg.* 423, *pg.* 22
PORTFOLIO DATA SYNCHRONIZATION - Software - JDA SOFTWARE GROUP, INC.; *pg.* 423, *pg.* 22
PORTFOLIO EXCHANGE - Business Management Solution - ADVENT SOFTWARE, INC.; *pg.* 345, *pg.* 211
PORTFOLIO MERCHANDISE MANAGEMENT - Software - JDA SOFTWARE GROUP, INC.; *pg.* 423, *pg.* 22
PORTFOLIO MOBILE ACCESS - Software - JDA SOFTWARE GROUP, INC.; *pg.* 423, *pg.* 22
PORTFOLIO POS - Software - JDA SOFTWARE GROUP, INC.; *pg.* 423, *pg.* 22
PORTFOLIO REGISTRY - Software - JDA SOFTWARE GROUP, INC.; *pg.* 423, *pg.* 22
PORTFOLIO SERIES - Artist Supplies - CRAYOLA LLC; *pg.* 951, *pg.* 1528
PORTFOLIO WORKFORCE MANAGEMENT - Software - JDA SOFTWARE GROUP, INC.; *pg.* 423, *pg.* 22
PORTFOLIOWALL - Software - AUTODESK INC.; *pg.* 356, *pg.* 257
PORTHOLE FLAP - Briefcase - SANTA FE LEATHER CORPORATION; *pg.* 12, *pg.* 1059
PORTIA - Software - THOMSON REUTERS CORPORATION; *pg.* 1693, *pg.* 1944
PORTICA - Furniture - ASHLEY FURNITURE INDUSTRIES, INC.; *pg.* 914, *pg.* 1852
PORTICO - Seafood - CLEAR SPRINGS FOODS, INC.; *pg.* 848, *pg.* 548
PORTICO - Furniture - TROPITONE FURNITURE CO., INC.; *pg.* 945, *pg.* 118
PORTICO - Lighting Product - WESTINGHOUSE LIGHTING CORPORATION; *pg.* 687, *pg.* 1571
PORTICO BOUNTY - Seafood - CLEAR SPRINGS FOODS, INC.; *pg.* 848, *pg.* 548
PORTICO MACRAME - Bath Accessory - CROSCILL, INC.; *pg.* 1122, *pg.* 1220
PORTICO SIMPLY - Seafood - CLEAR SPRINGS FOODS, INC.; *pg.* 848, *pg.* 548
PORTION PERFECT - Food Product - PATRICK CUDAHY INC.; *pg.* 888, *pg.* 1856
PORTION POUR - Portion Control Spout - CARLISLE FOODSERVICE PRODUCTS INCORPORATED; *pg.* 1455, *pg.* 1485
PORTLAND - Footwear - PHOENIX FOOTWEAR GROUP, INC.; *pg.* 1815, *pg.* 60
PORTLAND - Bicycle - TREK BICYCLE CORPORATION; *pg.* 1847, *pg.* 1896
PORTLAND GLASS FIRESCREEN - Glass Firescreen & Firescreen Enclosure - PORTLAND WILLAMETTE; *pg.* 1129, *pg.* 1505
PORTLAND TRAIL BLAZERS - Basketball Team - PORTLAND TRAIL BLAZERS; *pg.* 577, *pg.* 1505
PORTOBELLO YACHT CLUB - Restaurant - LEVY

RESTAURANTS, INC.; *pg.* 1736, *pg.* 580
PORTOFINA - Bike - MARIN BIKES; *pg.* 1708, *pg.* 168
PORTOFINO - Broadloom - COURISTAN INC.; *pg.* 921, *pg.* 1067
PORTOFINO - Bike - MARIN BIKES; *pg.* 1708, *pg.* 168
PORTOFINO - Furniture - STANLEY FURNITURE CO., INC.; *pg.* 943, *pg.* 1379
PORTOFINO - Furniture - TROPITONE FURNITURE CO., INC.; *pg.* 945, *pg.* 118
PORTPRO - Software - SS&C TECHNOLOGIES HOLDINGS, INC.; *pg.* 473, *pg.* 386
PORTPRO MALL - Software - SS&C TECHNOLOGIES HOLDINGS, INC.; *pg.* 473, *pg.* 386
PORTRA - Films - EASTMAN KODAK COMPANY; *pg.* 1408, *pg.* 1333
PORTRAIT - Lounge Chairs - BERNHARDT DESIGN; *pg.* 918, *pg.* 1381
PORTRAIT - Furniture - JOFCO INC.; *pg.* 931, *pg.* 691
PORTRAIT - Bath Product - KOHLER CO.; *pg.* 91, *pg.* 1862
PORTRAITS BY NORTHERN ISLES - Misses' & Petite Sportswear - KELLWOOD COMPANY; *pg.* 28, *pg.* 975
PORTRATI INNOVATIONS - Portrait Photography - PORTRAIT INNOVATIONS HOLDING COMPANY; *pg.* 1427, *pg.* 1368
PORTSERVER - Computer Peripheral Equipment - DIGI INTERNATIONAL INC.; *pg.* 387, *pg.* 948
PORTSIDE - Suitcase - SAMSONITE CORPORATION; *pg.* 11, *pg.* 830
PORTSS - Software - SLM CORPORATION; *pg.* 804, *pg.* 388
POS-E-KON - Connector - THOMAS & BETTS CORPORATION; *pg.* 680, *pg.* 1646
POS PLUS - Specialty Paper - APPVION INC.; *pg.* 1451, *pg.* 1852
POSEIDON - Medical Equipment - INVACARE CORPORATION; *pg.* 1546, *pg.* 1451
POSEIDON - Membrane - PALL CORPORATION; *pg.* 232, *pg.* 1323
POSEK - Software - WIND RIVER SYSTEMS, INC.; *pg.* 493, *pg.* 38
POSEY - Guard Rail Pads - ALIMED, INC.; *pg.* 1490, *pg.* 816
POSH - Furniture - ASHLEY FURNITURE INDUSTRIES, INC.; *pg.* 914, *pg.* 1852
POSH HAWAII - Upscale Deluxe Hawaii Holidays - PLEASANT HOLIDAYS LLC; *pg.* 1919, *pg.* 307
POSHMINA - Accessories - HABAND COMPANY, INC.; *pg.* 1772, *pg.* 1099
POSI-DRIVE - Linear Motion Component - DEL-TRON PRECISION, INC.; *pg.* 1328, *pg.* 337
POSI-LOCK - Truck Equipment - AMERICAN VAN EQUIPMENT INC.; *pg.* 199, *pg.* 1078
POSI-LOCK - Carriage Locking Mechanism - DEL-TRON PRECISION, INC.; *pg.* 1328, *pg.* 337
POSI-LOCK - Quick Connect System - ITT CORPORATION; *pg.* 1351, *pg.* 1354
POSI-LOK - Shaft Bushings - ZERO-MAX, INC.; *pg.* 222, *pg.* 954
POSI-MIX - Valve - SELAS HEAT TECHNOLOGY COMPANY LLC; *pg.* 1076, *pg.* 1553
POSI-PRESSURE - Steam Control System - ARMSTRONG INTERNATIONAL, INC.; *pg.* 1069, *pg.* 909
POSI-RATIO - Fluid Handling System - GRACO, INC.; *pg.* 1342, *pg.* 935
POSI-STEP - Ramp - MAGLINE, INC.; *pg.* 1358, *pg.* 908
POSI-STOP - Mini Arbor Press - PANAVISE PRODUCTS, INC.; *pg.* 1058, *pg.* 1032
POSI-STRUT - Truss System - MITEK, INC.; *pg.* 1056, *pg.* 975
POSI-TEMP - Valve - MOEN INCORPORATED; *pg.* 1056, *pg.* 1468
POSI-TORQUE - Locking Device - JOHANSON MANUFACTURING CORPORATION; *pg.* 648, *pg.* 1045
POSIBIN - Bin Activator With Bin - METALFAB, INC.; *pg.* 1360, *pg.* 1127
POSIBINS - Bin Activator - METALFAB, INC.; *pg.* 1360, *pg.* 1127
POSIC - Framer & Mapper Product - CYPRESS SEMICONDUCTOR CORPORATION; *pg.* 1326, *pg.* 243
POSIC10G - Framer & Mapper Product - CYPRESS SEMICONDUCTOR CORPORATION; *pg.* 1326, *pg.* 243
POSIC2G - Framer & Mapper Product - CYPRESS SEMICONDUCTOR CORPORATION; *pg.* 1326, *pg.* 243
POSIC2GVC - Framer & Mapper Product - CYPRESS SEMICONDUCTOR CORPORATION; *pg.* 1326, *pg.* 243
POSIC2GVCA - Framer & Mapper Product - CYPRESS SEMICONDUCTOR CORPORATION; *pg.* 1326, *pg.* 243
POSICAST - Medical Device - GAMMEX RMI INC.; *pg.* 1532, *pg.* 1872
POSICHARGE - Vehicle Product - AEROVIRONMENT, INC.; *pg.* 223, *pg.* 150
POSIDOT - Fluid Handling System - GRACO, INC.; *pg.* 1342, *pg.* 935
POSIDYNE - Filter Cartridge - PALL CORPORATION; *pg.* 232, *pg.* 1323
POSIFIX - Medical Device - GAMMEX RMI INC.; *pg.* 1532, *pg.* 1872
POSIFLO - Feed Flow Control - CTB INTERNATIONAL CORP.; *pg.* 850, *pg.* 695
POSIFRAME - Medical Device - GAMMEX RMI INC.; *pg.* 1532, *pg.* 1872
POSILAC - Bovine Somatotropin - ELANCO ANIMAL HEALTH; *pg.* 1475, *pg.* 681
POSILAC - Bovine Somatotropin - ELI LILLY AND COMPANY; *pg.* 1527, *pg.* 684
POSILOAD - Fluid Handling System - GRACO, INC.; *pg.* 1342, *pg.* 935
POSILOK - Tooth Equipment - ESCO CORPORATION; *pg.* 1335, *pg.* 1502
POSILOK PLUS - Tooth System - ESCO CORPORATION; *pg.* 1335, *pg.* 1502
POSIMETER - Fluid Handling System - GRACO, INC.; *pg.* 1342, *pg.* 935
POSIMIXER - Fluid Handling System - GRACO, INC.; *pg.* 1342, *pg.* 935
POSIPOWER - Fluid Handling System - GRACO, INC.; *pg.* 1342, *pg.* 935
POSIREST - Medical Device - GAMMEX RMI INC.; *pg.* 1532, *pg.* 1872
POSIT-BOND - Clad Metal - OLIN CORPORATION; *pg.* 1176, *pg.* 976
POSITAC - Servo Amplifier Positioning System - HENRY PRATT COMPANY; *pg.* 1049, *pg.* 555
POSITANO - Window Treatment - CROSCILL, INC.; *pg.* 1122, *pg.* 1220
POSITECT - Enclosed Distribution Cutout - S&C ELECTRIC COMPANY; *pg.* 1305, *pg.* 589
POSITILT - Medical Device - GAMMEX RMI INC.; *pg.* 1532, *pg.* 1872
POSITION & LOCK PLUS - Baby Gate - EVENFLO COMPANY, INC.; *pg.* 924, *pg.* 1470
POSITION BLOCK - Cushion Pillow - DYNATRONICS CORPORATION; *pg.* 1526, *pg.* 1757
POSITION IMAGING - MRI Scanner - FONAR CORPORATION; *pg.* 1413, *pg.* 1179
POSITIONAL PIXELING - Electronic Sign System - DAKTRONICS, INC.; *pg.* 633, *pg.* 1624
POSITIVE CHOICES - Marketing Program - AURORA CASKET COMPANY, INC.; *pg.* 1393, *pg.* 673
POSITIVE ELECTRO-IMAGING TRACING - Sensor - NAPCO SECURITY SYSTEMS, INC.; *pg.* 658, *pg.* 1138
POSITIVE PELLET - Animal Nutrition Product - MANNA PRO CORPORATION; *pg.* 1478, *pg.* 975
POSITIVE PLACEMENT - Fastening System for Metal Hardware Installation - PASLODE; *pg.* 1059, *pg.* 664
POSITIVE THOUGHTS - Vitamin & Herbal Supplement - SOURCE NATURALS; *pg.* 1595, *pg.* 278
POSITIVESTOP - Connector - COMMSCOPE; *pg.* 630, *pg.* 668
POSITOPE - Molecular Biology Product - THERMO FISHER SCIENTIFIC INC.; *pg.* 1602, *pg.* 61
POSITRACE - Medical Equipment - CONMED CORPORATION; *pg.* 1517, *pg.* 1347
POSITRIM - System For Weight Control - AMWAY CORPORATION; *pg.* 326, *pg.* 864
POSITROL - Fuse - S&C ELECTRIC COMPANY; *pg.* 1305, *pg.* 589
POSITRON - Motor Operator - HENRY PRATT COMPANY; *pg.* 1049, *pg.* 555
POSIX - Software - LYNX SOFTWARE TECHNOLOGIES; *pg.* 429, *pg.* 247
POSJET - Ink Jet Printers - TRANSACT TECHNOLOGIES INCORPORATED; *pg.* 484, *pg.* 351
POSSE - Apparel - VANS, INC.; *pg.* 1821, *pg.* 76
POSSIBILITIES - Textbook - ACADEMIC INNOVATIONS; *pg.* 1613, *pg.* 262
POSSIBILITIES...ENDLESS - Slogan - NEBRASKA DEPARTMENT OF ECONOMIC DEVELOPMENT; *pg.* 1000, *pg.* 1012
POSSIBILITY. IN EVERY DIRECTION. - Tag Line - PORT OF PORTLAND; *pg.* 1920, *pg.* 1505
POST - Residential Real Estate - POST PROPERTIES, INC.; *pg.* 1108, *pg.* 518
POST & BEAM - Office Furniture - STEELCASE INC.; *pg.* 475, *pg.* 889
POST-IT - Sticky Notes - 3M COMPANY; *pg.* 1142, *pg.* 956
POST-OP - Orthopedic Product - DJO INCORPORATED; *pg.* 1524, *pg.* 302
POST-PROBE - Hardware System - MICRO 2000, INC.; *pg.* 434, *pg.* 96
POST ROAD - Flatware - ONEIDA LTD; *pg.* 1129, *pg.* 1318
POST ROAD PUMPKIN ALE - Seasonal Beer - THE BROOKLYN BREWERY; *pg.* 239, *pg.* 1145
POST SELECTS BANANA NUT CRUNCH - Cereal - POST HOLDINGS, INC.; *pg.* 833, *pg.* 1002
POST SELECTS BLUEBERRY MORNING - Cereal - POST HOLDINGS, INC.; *pg.* 833, *pg.* 1002
POST SELECTS CRANBERRY ALMOND CRUNCH - Cereal - POST HOLDINGS, INC.; *pg.* 833, *pg.* 1002
POST SELECTS GREAT GRAINS - Cereal - POST HOLDINGS, INC.; *pg.* 833, *pg.* 1002
POST SELECTS MAPLE PECAN CRUNCH - Cereal - POST HOLDINGS, INC.; *pg.* 833, *pg.* 1002
POST STORY - Residential Real Estate - POST PROPERTIES, INC.; *pg.* 1108, *pg.* 518
POSTAGE BY PHONE - Software - PITNEY BOWES INC.; *pg.* 454, *pg.* 376
POSTAGE ON DEMAND - Slogan - STAMPS.COM INC.; *pg.* 1282, *pg.* 82
POSTAGE SAVER - CD Mail Pouches - CALUMET CARTON COMPANY; *pg.* 1454, *pg.* 661
POSTALONE - Postal Services - UNITED STATES POSTAL SERVICE; *pg.* 1009, *pg.* 406
POSTCODES - Software - PITNEY BOWES SOFTWARE INC.; *pg.* 455, *pg.* 1346
POSTECOACTIVE - Residential Real Estate - POST PROPERTIES, INC.; *pg.* 1108, *pg.* 518
POSTER PRINTER - Enlarges Originals to Poster Size - VARITRONICS, LLC; *pg.* 487, *pg.* 954
POSTHOPE - Residential Real Estate - POST PROPERTIES, INC.; *pg.* 1108, *pg.* 518
POSTINI - Email Security & Archiving Services - GOOGLE INC.; *pg.* 1249, *pg.* 153
POSTLINK - Hardware & Software for Determining & Printing Postage - HASLER, INC.; *pg.* 1459, *pg.* 356
POSTMAP - European Postal Code Maps - PITNEY BOWES SOFTWARE INC.; *pg.* 455, *pg.* 1346
POSTMARK - Paper - INTERNATIONAL PAPER COMPANY; *pg.* 1460, *pg.* 1644
POSTMASTER - Fencing - MASTER HALCO; *pg.* 96, *pg.* 474
POSTNET - Barcode Verifier - VIDEOJET TECHNOLOGIES INC.; *pg.* 489, *pg.* 671
POSTPERFECT - Postage Meter - PITNEY BOWES INC.; *pg.* 454, *pg.* 376
POSTPOINT - UK Geographic Postcode System - PITNEY BOWES SOFTWARE INC.; *pg.* 455, *pg.* 1346
POST*TESTING - In-Market Advertising Assessment Product - IPSOS-ASI, INC.; *pg.* 421, *pg.* 363
POSTURE-D - Calcium Supplement - ALERE INC.; *pg.* 1488, *pg.* 849
POTABLE AQUA - Safety Product - WISCONSIN PHARMACAL COMPANY, LLC; *pg.* 1610, *pg.* 1861
POTATO BUDS - Food Product - GENERAL MILLS, INC.; *pg.* 828, *pg.* 933
POTATO EXPRESS - Food Product - RESER'S FINE FOODS INC.; *pg.* 1032, *pg.* 1496
POTATO OLE'S - Potato Round, Seasoned - TACO JOHN'S INTERNATIONAL, INC.; *pg.* 1753, *pg.* 1901
POTATO PEARLS - Mashed Potatos - BASIC AMERICAN FOODS, INC.; *pg.* 839, *pg.* 303
POTATO PEARLS EXCEL - Instant Mashed Potatoes - BASIC AMERICAN FOODS, INC.; *pg.* 839, *pg.* 303
POTEN-ZYME - Health & Wellness Product - GARDEN OF LIFE, INC.; *pg.* 1532, *pg.* 478
POTENTIALS - Trade Publications - THE NIELSEN COMPANY B.V.; *pg.* 1671, *pg.* 1272
POTENZA - Passenger Tires - BRIDGESTONE AMERICAS, INC.; *pg.* 201, *pg.* 1649
POTENZA - Remote Control Device - UNIVERSAL ELECTRONICS, INC.; *pg.* 683, *pg.* 262
POTLATCH - Forest Practices - POTLATCH CORPORATION; *pg.* 1467, *pg.* 1844
POTLUCK - Fabric - NEMSCHOFF, INC.; *pg.* 936, *pg.* 1890
POTOCKY NEEDLE - Retractable Needle - THE COOPER COMPANIES, INC.; *pg.* 1518, *pg.* 183

POTTERY BARN KIDS - Furniture - WILLIAMS-SONOMA, INC.; *pg.* 1140, *pg.* 234
POTTSGROVE - Fabric - SCALAMANDRE, INC.; *pg.* 941, *pg.* 1058
POTTY FRESH - Portable Toilet Concentrate - SURCO PRODUCTS, INC.; *pg.* 336, *pg.* 1581
POTYI - Sweetening Ingredient - MERISANT COMPANY; *pg.* 876, *pg.* 581
POUCH - Boxer Brief - JOCKEY INTERNATIONAL, INC.; *pg.* 27, *pg.* 1861
POUCHO FOR INHALER - Healthcare Product - MEDICOOL, INC.; *pg.* 1562, *pg.* 294
POUCHO FOR INSULIN - Healthcare Product - MEDICOOL, INC.; *pg.* 1562, *pg.* 294
POUCHPAC - Plastics Product - AEP INDUSTRIES INC.; *pg.* 1878, *pg.* 1085
POULTICE - Sealers & Cleaners - PULLMAN-HOLT CORPORATION; *pg.* 333, *pg.* 475
POULTRY INT'L - Poultry Magazine - WATT PUBLISHING COMPANY; *pg.* 1701, *pg.* 655
POUNCE - Pet Food - BIG HEART PET BRANDS; *pg.* 1474, *pg.* 213
POUND OF LOVE - Yarn - LION BRAND YARN COMPANY; *pg.* 696, *pg.* 1050
POUND-X - Diet Aid - CCA INDUSTRIES, INC.; *pg.* 503, *pg.* 1114
POUR A NEW ENGINE INTO YOUR CAR - Slogan - SPEEDWAY MOTORSPORTS, INC.; *pg.* 584, *pg.* 1370
POUR FREE - Spout - CARLISLE FOODSERVICE PRODUCTS INCORPORATED; *pg.* 1455, *pg.* 1485
POUR-O-MATIC - Coffee Brewer - BUNN-O-MATIC CORPORATION; *pg.* 53, *pg.* 661
POUR YOUR HEART OUT - Flower Arrangement - 1-800-FLOWERS.COM, INC.; *pg.* 1758, *pg.* 1151
POURA-CLEAN - Pressurized Liquid Pourer Cleaning System - CARLISLE FOODSERVICE PRODUCTS INCORPORATED; *pg.* 1455, *pg.* 1485
POURABLE BEFORE DRYWALL - Underlayment - USG CORPORATION; *pg.* 118, *pg.* 594
POURCHEZ RETRO - Catheter - SPIRE CORPORATION; *pg.* 1378, *pg.* 786
POURCHEZ XPRESSO - Catheter - SPIRE CORPORATION; *pg.* 1378, *pg.* 786
POURQUIER - Test Kit - IDEXX LABORATORIES, INC.; *pg.* 1543, *pg.* 753
POURS - Consulting Services - AVNET, INC.; *pg.* 622, *pg.* 15
POURS REMOTE - Computer Workstation - AVNET, INC.; *pg.* 622, *pg.* 15
POURSTER - Circular Waste Refuse Container - MODERN WELDING COMPANY, INC.; *pg.* 1363, *pg.* 739
POW-R-BELT - Electronic Components - MOLEX INCORPORATED; *pg.* 655, *pg.* 628
POW-R-FUEL - Toy & Game - HASBRO, INC.; *pg.* 954, *pg.* 1603
POW-R-MATIC Electronic Components - MOLEX INCORPORATED; *pg.* 655, *pg.* 628
POW-R-MITE - Electronic Components - MOLEX INCORPORATED; *pg.* 655, *pg.* 628
POW-R-TAG - Electronic Components - MOLEX INCORPORATED; *pg.* 655, *pg.* 628
POWDASCENT - Olfactory Sampling System - ARCADE MARKETING, INC.; *pg.* 352, *pg.* 1196
POWDER - Booties - 180S, LLC; *pg.* 1824, *pg.* 754
POWDER BASE - Cosmetic Product - MERLE NORMAN COSMETICS, INC.; *pg.* 517, *pg.* 136
POWDER BRONZE - Face & Body Product - THE BONNE BELL COMPANY; *pg.* 502, *pg.* 1480
POWDER BURST - Personal Care Product - COLGATE-PALMOLIVE COMPANY; *pg.* 504, *pg.* 1215
POWDER FEEDER - Feeder - HYER INDUSTRIES INC.; *pg.* 1051, *pg.* 841
POWDER MATE - Soap Dispenser - BOBRICK WASHROOM EQUIPMENT, INC.; *pg.* 1043, *pg.* 166
POWDER MITT - Glove - 180S, LLC; *pg.* 1824, *pg.* 754
POWDER-PROOF - Zipper - ZIP-PAK; *pg.* 1473, *pg.* 631
POWDER PUFF - Container Grown Plant - MONROVIA GROWERS; *pg.* 1797, *pg.* 44
POWDER SOFT - Personal Care Product - COLGATE-PALMOLIVE COMPANY; *pg.* 504, *pg.* 1215
POWDERED DIRTEX - Cleaner - THE SAVOGRAN COMPANY; *pg.* 1447, *pg.* 840
POWDERFREE - Paint Product - AKZO NOBEL; *pg.* 1439, *pg.* 1952
POWDERIZER - Classifying Impact Mill - STURTEVANT INC.; *pg.* 1379, *pg.* 824
POWDERLINK - Chemical Product - CYTEC INDUSTRIES, INC.; *pg.* 1155, *pg.* 1131
POWDERMATE - Powder Coating - TROY CORPORATION; *pg.* 1184, *pg.* 1067
POWELL - Valves - THE WM. POWELL COMPANY; *pg.* 1389, *pg.* 1427
POWER - Vaporizers - ALGAS-SDI; *pg.* 1311, *pg.* 1831
POWER - Car Dealerships - AUTONATION, INC.; *pg.* 165, *pg.* 423
POWER - Toilet Bowl Cleaner - SWISHER HYGIENE INC.; *pg.* 336, *pg.* 1507
POWER 90 - Fitness Video & DVD - BEACHBODY, LLC; *pg.* 271, *pg.* 272
POWER 9000 - Medical Equipment - INVACARE CORPORATION; *pg.* 1546, *pg.* 1451
POWER-A-TACH - Attachment Mounting System - GEHL COMPANY; *pg.* 1339, *pg.* 1899
POWER-AIRE - Room Air Conditioners - HEAT CONTROLLER, INC.; *pg.* 1072, *pg.* 893
POWER ARCH - Furniture - TRENDWAY CORPORATION; *pg.* 945, *pg.* 892
THE POWER BASE - Wire Circuitry System - HAWORTH, INC.; *pg.* 402, *pg.* 891
POWER BEAM - Laminated Wood Products - ANTHONY FOREST PRODUCTS CO., INC.; *pg.* 67, *pg.* 31
THE POWER BEHIND EBUSINESS - Slogan - IPOWERWEB INC.; *pg.* 1259, *pg.* 274
THE POWER BEHIND PRODUCTION - Manual - XEROX CORPORATION; *pg.* 494, *pg.* 365
POWER BLADZ - Electronic Components - MOLEX INCORPORATED; *pg.* 655, *pg.* 628
POWER-BOLT - Anchor - POWERS FASTENERS INC.; *pg.* 1059, *pg.* 1143
POWER BONNET - Software - BIO-RAD LABORATORIES, INC.; *pg.* 1504, *pg.* 101
POWER BOX - Paver - GEHL COMPANY; *pg.* 1339, *pg.* 1899
POWER BREAKFAST - Waffles - NATURE'S PATH FOODS INC.; *pg.* 833, *pg.* 1908
POWER BUYING. BUYING POWER. - Tagline - LANDSTAR SYSTEM, INC.; *pg.* 1914, *pg.* 434
POWER-C - Sports Drink - ENERGY BRANDS, INC.; *pg.* 854, *pg.* 1227
POWER CHARGER - Battery System - ZOLL MEDICAL CORPORATION; *pg.* 1612, *pg.* 814
POWER CHIP - Resistor - OHMITE MANUFACTURING COMPANY; *pg.* 660, *pg.* 553
POWER CLEAN - Bath Product - KOHLER CO.; *pg.* 91, *pg.* 1862
POWER CLEANSE - Hand Cleaner - TEXAS REFINERY CORP.; *pg.* 986, *pg.* 1696
POWER COIL - Hose - TEKNOR APEX COMPANY; *pg.* 1889, *pg.* 1605
POWER COLUMN - Laminated Wood Product - ANTHONY FOREST PRODUCTS CO., INC.; *pg.* 67, *pg.* 31
POWER COMMANDER - Power Shift Transmissions & Electronic Control Systems - TWIN DISC, INCORPORATED; *pg.* 220, *pg.* 1889
POWER COMMANDER - Surge Protector - WIREMOLD/LEGRAND; *pg.* 689, *pg.* 383
POWER COMMANDER IQ - Sure Protector - WIREMOLD/LEGRAND; *pg.* 689, *pg.* 383
POWER COMMANDER PDU - Surge Protector - WIREMOLD/LEGRAND; *pg.* 689, *pg.* 383
POWER COMMANDER PLUS - Surge Protector - WIREMOLD/LEGRAND; *pg.* 689, *pg.* 383
POWER COMPILER - Software - SYNOPSYS, INC.; *pg.* 480, *pg.* 162
POWER COMPILING SOLUTIONS - Software - WIND RIVER SYSTEMS, INC.; *pg.* 493, *pg.* 38
POWER CONSOLE - Configure Raid System - AVAGO TECHNOLOGIES; *pg.* 358, *pg.* 238
POWER CONVECTION - Thermal Processing Equipment - SURFACE COMBUSTION, INC.; *pg.* 1077, *pg.* 1462
POWER CORE - Golf Equipment - ACUSHNET COMPANY; *pg.* 1824, *pg.* 818
POWER CRUISING - Magazine - BONNIER CORPORATION; *pg.* 1622, *pg.* 480
POWER-CUT - Cutting Fluid - THE DOALL COMPANY; *pg.* 1329, *pg.* 670
POWER CUTTING - Machines & Accessories - GLEASON CORPORATION; *pg.* 1340, *pg.* 1335
POWER-D - Oil - CONOCOPHILLIPS; *pg.* 975, *pg.* 1703
POWER DECK - Construction Equipment - JLG INDUSTRIES, INC.; *pg.* 1351, *pg.* 1551
POWER DELUXE - Kitchen Appliance - HAMILTON BEACH BRANDS, INC.; *pg.* 56, *pg.* 1783
POWER DOCK - Junction Box - MOLEX INCORPORATED; *pg.* 655, *pg.* 628
POWER DRIVE - Dead Blow Hammers - NUPLA CORPORATION; *pg.* 101, *pg.* 281
POWER DRY - Fishing Gear Product - SIMMS FISHING PRODUCTS CORP.; *pg.* 1845, *pg.* 1008
POWER DRY CUTTING - Machines & Accessories - GLEASON CORPORATION; *pg.* 1340, *pg.* 1335
POWER EAGLE - Surface Maintenance Machine - TENNANT COMPANY; *pg.* 1381, *pg.* 944
POWER EDGE - Work Tools & Engines - CATERPILLAR, INC.; *pg.* 1321, *pg.* 650
POWER EDGE - Connector - MOLEX INCORPORATED; *pg.* 655, *pg.* 628
POWER EDGERS - Power Equipment - ECHO INCORPORATED; *pg.* 1046, *pg.* 626
POWER-FAST - Injection Adhesive System - POWERS FASTENERS INC.; *pg.* 1059, *pg.* 1143
POWER-FIN - Water Heater - LOCHINVAR CORPORATION; *pg.* 1073, *pg.* 1640
POWER FLEX - Piston Rings - HASTINGS MANUFACTURING COMPANY, LLC; *pg.* 207, *pg.* 891
POWER-FLITE - Screw Conveyors - BLOOM MANUFACTURING, INC.; *pg.* 701, *pg.* 708
POWER FLO - Clutches - THE CARLSON COMPANY INC.; *pg.* 167, *pg.* 722
POWER-FLO - Applicator - HILLYARD, INC.; *pg.* 331, *pg.* 990
POWER-FLO II - Pump - HAYWARD POOL PRODUCTS; *pg.* 1049, *pg.* 1057
POWER-FLO LX - Pump Timer Control - HAYWARD POOL PRODUCTS; *pg.* 1049, *pg.* 1057
POWER FLUSH - Electric Airless Paint Sprayer - GRACO, INC.; *pg.* 1342, *pg.* 935
POWER FLUSH - Cleaning System - WYNN OIL COMPANY; *pg.* 987, *pg.* 173
POWER FLYER - Sport & Leisure Product - JAKKS PACIFIC, INC.; *pg.* 960, *pg.* 142
POWER FOR LIVING - Slogan - SCANA CORPORATION; *pg.* 1951, *pg.* 1612
POWER FORMULA - Beverage - MONSTER BEVERAGE CORPORATION; *pg.* 257, *pg.* 69
POWER/FULL SOLUTIONS - Slogan - ENERSYS INC.; *pg.* 1334, *pg.* 1584
POWER-GARD - Fuse Product - LITTELFUSE, INC.; *pg.* 1301, *pg.* 580
POWER GAUGE - Integrated Circuits - TEXAS INSTRUMENTS INCORPORATED; *pg.* 679, *pg.* 1688
POWER GLOSS - Car Wash Equipment - D&S CAR WASH EQUIPMENT CO.; *pg.* 1327, *pg.* 979
POWER GRATER - Size Reduction Machine - S. HOWES, INC.; *pg.* 1373, *pg.* 1342
POWER GROOM - Cattle Clipper - ANDIS COMPANY; *pg.* 498, *pg.* 1895
POWER HAWK - Computer System - CONCURRENT COMPUTER CORPORATION; *pg.* 379, *pg.* 531
POWER HEADER - Laminated Wood Product - ANTHONY FOREST PRODUCTS CO., INC.; *pg.* 67, *pg.* 31
POWER INFUSER - Fluid Resuscitation Pump - ZOLL MEDICAL CORPORATION; *pg.* 1612, *pg.* 814
POWER IT-PROTECT IT-CONNECT IT - Slogan - SEMTECH CORPORATION; *pg.* 671, *pg.* 57
POWER JOIST - Laminated Wood Product - ANTHONY FOREST PRODUCTS CO., INC.; *pg.* 67, *pg.* 31
POWER KENO - Video Game - INTERNATIONAL GAME TECHNOLOGY; *pg.* 957, *pg.* 1024
POWER KING - Tire - TBC CORPORATION; *pg.* 1889, *pg.* 457
POWER LESSONS - Educational Materials - RENAISSANCE LEARNING, INC.; *pg.* 607, *pg.* 1899
POWER LIFT - Electric Lifts - INVACARE CORPORATION; *pg.* 1546, *pg.* 1451
POWER LIFT - Basketball Equipment - LIFETIME PRODUCTS INC.; *pg.* 933, *pg.* 1751
POWER LINE - Laser Product - ROFIN-SINAR TECHNOLOGIES, INC.; *pg.* 668, *pg.* 904
POWER LOC - Track System - LIFOAM INDUSTRIES INC.; *pg.* 961, *pg.* 772
POWER-LOCK - Fluid Handling System - GRACO, INC.; *pg.* 1342, *pg.* 935
POWER-LOCK - Keyley Shaft-to-Hub Locking Device - U.S. TSUBAKI, INC.; *pg.* 221, *pg.* 670
POWER LOG - Home Building Log - ANTHONY FOREST

PRODUCTS CO., INC.; *pg.* 67, *pg.* 31
POWER-LUBE - Plunger Lubricant - CHEM-TREND LIMITED PARTNERSHIP; *pg.* 973, *pg.* 892
POWER LUBE - Tools & Coatings - GLEASON CORPORATION; *pg.* 1340, *pg.* 1335
POWER MAC - Computer - APPLE INC.; *pg.* 350, *pg.* 73
POWER MAMA - Clothing - SPANX INC.; *pg.* 32, *pg.* 520
POWER MASTER - 30 Degree Framing Nailer - PASLODE; *pg.* 1059, *pg.* 664
POWER MASTER - Amplifier - SHURE INCORPORATED; *pg.* 672, *pg.* 638
POWER MIND - Nutritional Supplement - WHITEWING LABS, INC.; *pg.* 1610, *pg.* 99
POWER MIZER - Cast Centrifugal Blower - THE SPENCER TURBINE CO.; *pg.* 1378, *pg.* 386
POWER MODULE - Electrochemistry Product - BIOANALYTICAL SYSTEMS, INC.; *pg.* 1402, *pg.* 700
POWER MONITOR - Electronic Components - MOLEX INCORPORATED; *pg.* 655, *pg.* 628
POWER MOS 7 - Power MOSFETs - MICROSEMI CORPORATION; *pg.* 435, *pg.* 41
POWER MOS 8 - Switch-mode Power Transistors - MICROSEMI CORPORATION; *pg.* 435, *pg.* 41
POWER MOS IV - Solid State Power Devices - MICROSEMI CORPORATION; *pg.* 435, *pg.* 41
POWER-MOX - Resistors - OHMITE MANUFACTURING COMPANY; *pg.* 660, *pg.* 553
THE POWER OF COLOR - Slogan - DE HAGO, INC.; *pg.* 4, *pg.* 1222
THE POWER OF DESIGN - Slogan - WESTERN DIGITAL CORPORATION; *pg.* 492, *pg.* 118
THE POWER OF EXPERIENCE - Slogan - ALTRA HOLDINGS, INC.; *pg.* 198, *pg.* 802
THE POWER OF HUMAN CONNECTIONS - Slogan - TOUCHSTONE ENERGY COOPERATIVES; *pg.* 1953, *pg.* 1775
THE POWER OF INTELLIGENT E-BUSINESS - Slogan - MICROSTRATEGY, INC.; *pg.* 1266, *pg.* 1809
THE POWER OF INTELLIGENT EBUSINESS - Slogan - MICROSTRATEGY, INC.; *pg.* 1266, *pg.* 1809
THE POWER OF MANAGEMENT - Tagline - CYBERSOURCE CORPORATION; *pg.* 381, *pg.* 216
POWER OF NATURE - Personal Care Product - COLGATE-PALMOLIVE COMPANY; *pg.* 504, *pg.* 1215
THE POWER OF NOW - Slogan - TIBCO SOFTWARE INC.; *pg.* 484, *pg.* 178
THE POWER OF ONE - Slogan - GENERAL CABLE CORPORATION; *pg.* 83, *pg.* 729
THE POWER OF PEOPLE - Slogan - ENTERGY CORPORATION; *pg.* 1941, *pg.* 746
THE POWER OF PINK - Hair Dryer - CONAIR CORPORATION; *pg.* 505, *pg.* 1055
THE POWER OF POSSIBILITY - Slogan - CANYON RANCH MANAGEMENT, LLC; *pg.* 1084, *pg.* 27
THE POWER OF PROOF - Slogan - SURETY, INC.; *pg.* 1283, *pg.* 1799
THE POWER OF TEACHING. THE WONDERS OF LEARNING - Slogan - SCHOOL SPECIALTY, INC.; *pg.* 467, *pg.* 1860
THE POWER OF THE DEALER NETWORK - Tag Line - HOLLYMATIC CORPORATION; *pg.* 1346, *pg.* 598
THE POWER OF THE INTERNET - Tagline - MOVE, INC.; *pg.* 1268, *pg.* 247
THE POWER OF TWO - Networking Software - DELL INC.; *pg.* 383, *pg.* 1737
THE POWER OF WE - Tagline - RADISYS CORPORATION; *pg.* 458, *pg.* 1498
POWER-OUT ALERT - Environmental Security Product - WINLAND ELECTRONICS, INC.; *pg.* 688, *pg.* 928
POWER PACKAGE - Power System - EDELBROCK CORPORATION; *pg.* 204, *pg.* 293
POWER-PAK - Cremation System - MATTHEWS INTERNATIONAL CORPORATION; *pg.* 1662, *pg.* 1578
POWER PANTIES - Body-Shaping Underwear - SPANX INC.; *pg.* 32, *pg.* 520
POWER PARTNER - Upright Vacuum Cleaner - BISSELL HOMECARE, INC.; *pg.* 52, *pg.* 887
POWER PINCHER - Energy Saving Kits - STEELCASE INC.; *pg.* 475, *pg.* 889
POWER PINNER - Machinery - GRIPNAIL CORPORATION; *pg.* 1048, *pg.* 1601
THE POWER-PISTON - Fluid Handling System - GRACO, INC.; *pg.* 1342, *pg.* 935
POWER PISTON - Shotshell - REMINGTON ARMS COMPANY, LLC; *pg.* 1844, *pg.* 1382
POWER PLANK - Laminated Wood Product - ANTHONY FOREST PRODUCTS CO., INC.; *pg.* 67, *pg.* 31
POWER PLAY - Lottery - MINNESOTA STATE LOTTERY; *pg.* 999, *pg.* 956
POWER PLUS - Connector - MOLEX INCORPORATED; *pg.* 655, *pg.* 628
POWER PLUS SR. - Electronic Components - MOLEX INCORPORATED; *pg.* 655, *pg.* 628
POWER POCKET - Printer Devices - TRANSACT TECHNOLOGIES INCORPORATED; *pg.* 484, *pg.* 351
POWER POINTS - Electrostatic Air Spray Gun - GRACO, INC.; *pg.* 1342, *pg.* 935
POWER PRESERVED COLUMN - Laminated Wood Product - ANTHONY FOREST PRODUCTS CO., INC.; *pg.* 67, *pg.* 31
POWER PRESERVED GLULAM - Laminated Wood Product - ANTHONY FOREST PRODUCTS CO., INC.; *pg.* 67, *pg.* 31
POWER-PRIME - Electrodeposition Coating - PPG INDUSTRIES, INC.; *pg.* 1445, *pg.* 1579
THE POWER PRINCIPLE: INFLUENCE WITH HONOR - Publication - FRANKLIN COVEY CO.; *pg.* 1642, *pg.* 1758
POWER PRO - Patient Handling Equipment - STRYKER CORPORATION; *pg.* 1598, *pg.* 894
POWER PRODUCTS - Wood Products - ANTHONY FOREST PRODUCTS CO., INC.; *pg.* 67, *pg.* 31
POWER PRUNER - Power Equipment - ECHO INCORPORATED; *pg.* 1046, *pg.* 626
POWER PYLON - Shovel - NUPLA CORPORATION; *pg.* 101, *pg.* 281
POWER RED DEGREASER - Automotive Reconditioning Product - MOC PRODUCTS COMPANY, INC.; *pg.* 332, *pg.* 174
POWER SCORE - Video Game - INTERNATIONAL GAME TECHNOLOGY; *pg.* 957, *pg.* 1024
POWER SEAT - Game - WMS INDUSTRIES INC.; *pg.* 593, *pg.* 666
POWER SEVENS - Game - WMS INDUSTRIES INC.; *pg.* 593, *pg.* 666
POWER SHADE - Reduces Solar Heat - ALCOA INC.; *pg.* 65, *pg.* 1188
POWER SHAVING - Cylindrical Product - GLEASON CORPORATION; *pg.* 1340, *pg.* 1335
POWER SHINE - Automotive Reconditioning Product - MOC PRODUCTS COMPANY, INC.; *pg.* 332, *pg.* 174
POWER SHOCK - Basketball Equipment - LIFETIME PRODUCTS INC.; *pg.* 933, *pg.* 1751
POWER-SHOK - Ammunition - FEDERAL PREMIUM AMMUNITION; *pg.* 1834, *pg.* 915
POWER SHOT - Residential Water Heater - A.O. SMITH CORPORATION; *pg.* 1313, *pg.* 1872
POWER-SHOT - Fluid Handling System - GRACO, INC.; *pg.* 1342, *pg.* 935
POWER SOLUTIONS WHEN THE STAKES ARE HIGH - Tagline - WARD LEONARD ELECTRIC COMPANY, INC.; *pg.* 687, *pg.* 380
POWER STAR - Fluid Handling System - GRACO, INC.; *pg.* 1342, *pg.* 935
POWER STATION - Unix-Based Proprietary System - ACXIOM CORPORATION; *pg.* 342, *pg.* 607
POWER STATION - Gaming Machine - INTERNATIONAL GAME TECHNOLOGY; *pg.* 420, *pg.* 1606
POWER STATION - A/V Stereo Component - SHURE INCORPORATED; *pg.* 672, *pg.* 638
POWER STEMMER - Blast Hole Stemming Device - ARNOLD MACHINERY COMPANY; *pg.* 1314, *pg.* 1755
POWER STOP - Excelsior Fiber - AMERICAN EXCELSIOR COMPANY; *pg.* 1451, *pg.* 1659
POWER STRETCH - Fabric - 180S, LLC; *pg.* 1824, *pg.* 754
POWER STRETCH - Fishing Gear Product - SIMMS FISHING PRODUCTS CORP.; *pg.* 1845, *pg.* 1008
POWER STRIP - Non-Ammoniated Stripper - HILLYARD, INC.; *pg.* 331, *pg.* 990
POWER-STUD - Anchor - POWERS FASTENERS INC.; *pg.* 1059, *pg.* 1143
POWER TAC - Torch - COAST CUTLERY COMPANY; *pg.* 1121, *pg.* 1501
POWER TIME - Vitamin & Dietary Supplement - NATROL, INC.; *pg.* 1570, *pg.* 64
THE POWER TO AMAZE YOURSELF - Weight Reduction Diet - CURVES INTERNATIONAL INC.; *pg.* 542, *pg.* 1748
POWER TO CHANGE - Tagline - MOTAN, INC.; *pg.* 1886, *pg.* 903
POWER TO CHANGE THE WORLD - Slogan - BALLARD POWER SYSTEMS, INC.; *pg.* 70, *pg.* 1907
THE POWER TO KNOW - Slogan - SAS INSTITUTE INC.; *pg.* 466, *pg.* 1361
THE POWER TO MAKE IT BETTER - Slogan - AARP; *pg.* 124, *pg.* 393
THE POWER TO PREDICT - Slogan - TIBCO SOFTWARE INC.; *pg.* 484, *pg.* 178
POWER TO THE PLAYERS - Slogan - GAMESTOP CORP.; *pg.* 399, *pg.* 1699
THE POWER TO TRANSFORM - Slogan - MENTOR CORPORATION; *pg.* 1565, *pg.* 263
POWER-TORQUE - Workshop Make-Up/Break-Out Machine - BAKER HUGHES INTEQ; *pg.* 1316, *pg.* 1700
POWER TOUR - Toy & Game - HASBRO, INC.; *pg.* 954, *pg.* 1603
POWER TRAK - Floor Care Product - BISSELL HOMECARE, INC.; *pg.* 52, *pg.* 887
POWER TRENDS - Electronic Components & Switching Power Supplies - TEXAS INSTRUMENTS INCORPORATED; *pg.* 679, *pg.* 1688
POWER TRIM - Clipper - ANDIS COMPANY; *pg.* 498, *pg.* 1895
POWER WAFER - Inductors - COILCRAFT, INC.; *pg.* 1324, *pg.* 562
POWER WALKER - Electric Treadmill - BATTLE CREEK EQUIPMENT CO.; *pg.* 1499, *pg.* 870
POWER WALL - Reduces Environmental Factor - ALCOA INC.; *pg.* 65, *pg.* 1188
POWER WALL - Screw Feeder - HYER INDUSTRIES INC.; *pg.* 1051, *pg.* 841
POWER WEB - Medical & Aesthetic Product - DYNATRONICS CORPORATION; *pg.* 1526, *pg.* 1757
POWER WEB - Office Product - HAWORTH, INC.; *pg.* 402, *pg.* 891
POWER WEB JR. - Rehabilitation Product - ALIMED, INC.; *pg.* 1490, *pg.* 816
POWER WHEELS - Toy Vehicles - FISHER-PRICE, INC.; *pg.* 953, *pg.* 1156
THE POWER WITHIN - Slogan - BRIGGS & STRATTON CORPORATION; *pg.* 201, *pg.* 1899
POWER XP - Electric LPG Vaporizer - ALGAS-SDI; *pg.* 1311, *pg.* 1831
POWER-ZONE 4 - Low Voltage Switchgear - SCHNEIDER ELECTRIC USA, INC.; *pg.* 1306, *pg.* 650
POWER2CLEAN - Degreasing Preparations - ASHLAND INC.; *pg.* 972, *pg.* 726
POWERADE - Sports Drink - THE COCA-COLA COMPANY; *pg.* 240, *pg.* 493
POWERADE ADVANCE - Beverages - THE COCA-COLA COMPANY; *pg.* 240, *pg.* 493
POWERADE ALIVE - Beverages - THE COCA-COLA COMPANY; *pg.* 240, *pg.* 493
POWERADE AQUA+ - Beverages - THE COCA-COLA COMPANY; *pg.* 240, *pg.* 493
POWERADE BALANCE - Beverages - THE COCA-COLA COMPANY; *pg.* 240, *pg.* 493
POWERADE LIGHT - Beverages - THE COCA-COLA COMPANY; *pg.* 240, *pg.* 493
POWERADE OPTION - Beverages - THE COCA-COLA COMPANY; *pg.* 240, *pg.* 493
POWERADE ZERO - Beverages - THE COCA-COLA COMPANY; *pg.* 240, *pg.* 493
POWERALERT - Universal UPS Management Software - TRIPPE MANUFACTURING COMPANY; *pg.* 220, *pg.* 592
POWERANALYZER INSIGHT - Software - INFORMATICA CORPORATION; *pg.* 414, *pg.* 190
POWERANALYZER MOBILE - Software - INFORMATICA CORPORATION; *pg.* 414, *pg.* 190
POWERARC - Lighting - STEELCASE INC.; *pg.* 475, *pg.* 889
POWERARMOR - Drive Technology - WESTERN DIGITAL CORPORATION; *pg.* 492, *pg.* 118
POWERBACK - Portable Rebounder - SCHOOL-TECH, INC.; *pg.* 1844, *pg.* 866
POWERBALL - Lottery Game - ARIZONA LOTTERY; *pg.* 988, *pg.* 14
POWERBALL - Lottery Game - D.C. LOTTERY & CHARITABLE GAMES CONTROL BOARD; *pg.* 991, *pg.* 398
POWERBALL - Lottery Game - THE FLORIDA LOTTERY; *pg.* 992, *pg.* 469
POWERBALL - Lottery Game - GEORGIA LOTTERY CORPORATION; *pg.* 993, *pg.* 506
POWERBALL - Lottery Game - LOUISIANA LOTTERY CORPORATION; *pg.* 997, *pg.* 742
POWERBALL - Lottery Game - MINNESOTA STATE LOTTERY; *pg.* 999, *pg.* 956

POWERBALL - Lottery Game - MISSOURI LOTTERY; *pg.* 999, *pg.* 979
POWERBALL - Lottery Game - MONTANA LOTTERY; *pg.* 1000, *pg.* 1008
POWERBALL - Online Lottery Game - NEBRASKA LOTTERY; *pg.* 1000, *pg.* 1012
POWERBALL - Jackpot Game - PENNSYLVANIA STATE LOTTERY; *pg.* 1003, *pg.* 1552
POWERBALL INSTANT MILLIONAIRE - Lottery Game - LOUISIANA LOTTERY CORPORATION; *pg.* 997, *pg.* 742
POWERBALL INSTANT MILLIONAIRE - Lottery Game - MINNESOTA STATE LOTTERY; *pg.* 999, *pg.* 956
POWERBAR - Nutrition Bar - POST HOLDINGS, INC.; *pg.* 833, *pg.* 1002
POWERBASE - Concentrator - NATIONAL PRESTO INDUSTRIES, INC; *pg.* 1128, *pg.* 1857
POWERBEAM - Furniture - HAWORTH, INC.; *pg.* 402, *pg.* 891
POWERBIKE - Electric Bicycle - ZAP; *pg.* 222, *pg.* 277
POWERBLADE - Cable Cutter - IDEAL INDUSTRIES, INC.; *pg.* 1051, *pg.* 662
POWERBLAST - Energy Drink - NATIONAL BEVERAGE CORP.; *pg.* 257, *pg.* 425
POWERBLOCK - Engineering Development Kit - MERCURY COMPUTER SYSTEMS, INC.; *pg.* 434, *pg.* 813
POWERBOOK - Hardware Product - APPLE INC.; *pg.* 350, *pg.* 73
POWERBOOK - Digital Video Product - HAUPPAUGE DIGITAL, INC.; *pg.* 402, *pg.* 1164
POWERBOOM - Pedestal Boom - ALLIED CONSTRUCTION PRODUCTS, LLC; *pg.* 1311, *pg.* 1427
POWERBOOST - Smoothie - JAMBA, INC.; *pg.* 1024, *pg.* 84
POWERBOOST - Software - SHAW COMMUNICATIONS INC.; *pg.* 307, *pg.* 1904
POWERBOSS - Cable - AMPHENOL CORPORATION; *pg.* 616, *pg.* 381
POWERBOSSLITE - Cable - AMPHENOL CORPORATION; *pg.* 616, *pg.* 381
POWERBRIDGE - Software - INFORMATICA CORPORATION; *pg.* 414, *pg.* 190
POWERBUILDER - Mining Product - MINE SAFETY APPLIANCES COMPANY; *pg.* 1361, *pg.* 1525
POWERBUILDER - Programming Environment - SAP; *pg.* 465, *pg.* 78
POWERBUOY - Utility Systems - OCEAN POWER TECHNOLOGIES, INC.; *pg.* 1948, *pg.* 1107
POWERCACHE - Power Backup System - MAXWELL TECHNOLOGIES, INC.; *pg.* 653, *pg.* 204
POWERCAM - Video Conferencing Product - POLYCOM, INC.; *pg.* 664, *pg.* 249
POWERCAPTURE - Software - INFORMATICA CORPORATION; *pg.* 414, *pg.* 190
POWERCARE ADVANTAGE - Rental Service for Power System Maintenance Equipment - CUMMINS POWER GENERATION; *pg.* 1326, *pg.* 932
POWERCASH - Cashless Wagering Solution - EVERI HOLDINGS INC.; *pg.* 749, *pg.* 1023
POWERCAT - Electronic Components - MOLEX INCORPORATED; *pg.* 655, *pg.* 628
POWERCAT 6 - Electronic Components - MOLEX INCORPORATED; *pg.* 655, *pg.* 628
POWERCELL - Control Unit - LITTELFUSE, INC.; *pg.* 1301, *pg.* 580
POWERCENTER - Pre-assembled Electrical Unit - HILL PHOENIX INC.; *pg.* 1072, *pg.* 528
POWERCENTER - Software - INFORMATICA CORPORATION; *pg.* 414, *pg.* 190
POWERCENTER CONNECT - Software - INFORMATICA CORPORATION; *pg.* 414, *pg.* 190
POWERCHAIN MANAGEMENT - Software - EATON CORPORATION; *pg.* 1331, *pg.* 1429
POWERCHANNEL - Software - INFORMATICA CORPORATION; *pg.* 414, *pg.* 190
POWERCHART - Electronic Medical Record System - CERNER CORPORATION; *pg.* 1514, *pg.* 981
POWERCHART OFFICE - Electronic Medical Record System - CERNER CORPORATION; *pg.* 1514, *pg.* 981
POWERCHECK - Guard Tour System - MORSE WATCHMANS INC.; *pg.* 656, *pg.* 368
POWERCHEQUING - Banking Service - THE BANK OF NOVA SCOTIA; *pg.* 721, *pg.* 1935
POWERCHUTE - Network Shutdown Software - SCHNEIDER ELECTRIC; *pg.* 467, *pg.* 1609
POWERCIVIL - Software - BENTLEY SYSTEMS, INC.; *pg.* 361, *pg.* 1531
POWERCLEAN - Filter - CAMERON INTERNATIONAL; *pg.* 1151, *pg.* 1702
POWERCLEARVIEW - Deep Cleaner - BISSELL HOMECARE, INC.; *pg.* 52, *pg.* 887
POWERCOAT - Antifouling Paint-High Speed Boats - PETTIT PAINT COMPANY; *pg.* 1444, *pg.* 1116
POWERCOM - Power Monitoring System - SPARTON CORPORATION; *pg.* 1377, *pg.* 660
POWERCOMMAND - Pre-integrated Power Systems - CUMMINS POWER GENERATION; *pg.* 1326, *pg.* 932
POWERCONNECT - Networking Products - DELL INC.; *pg.* 383, *pg.* 1737
POWERCONNECT - Software - INFORMATICA CORPORATION; *pg.* 414, *pg.* 190
POWERCONVERT - Computer Software - NOVELL INC.; *pg.* 446, *pg.* 852
POWERCORE - Air Filter - AMSOIL INC.; *pg.* 971, *pg.* 1896
POWERCORE - Air-Intake Filtration System - DONALDSON COMPANY, INC.; *pg.* 1329, *pg.* 917
POWERCORE - Spark Plugs - MIGHTY DISTRIBUTING SYSTEM OF AMERICA; *pg.* 213, *pg.* 538
POWERCRAFT - Power Steering Hoses & Repair Kits - PLEWS/EDELMANN; *pg.* 215, *pg.* 607
POWERCRETE - Coating Products - RUSSEL METALS INC.; *pg.* 1180, *pg.* 1928
POWERCRISP - Electrical Appliance & Housewares - NATIONAL PRESTO INDUSTRIES, INC; *pg.* 1128, *pg.* 1857
POWERCRON - Electrodeposition Coatings - PPG INDUSTRIES, INC.; *pg.* 1445, *pg.* 1579
POWERCUP - Concentrator - NATIONAL PRESTO INDUSTRIES, INC; *pg.* 1128, *pg.* 1857
POWERCURE - On-Site Monitoring - ALLIANT ENERGY CORPORATION; *pg.* 1933, *pg.* 1864
POWERCUTTING - Cylindrical Product - GLEASON CORPORATION; *pg.* 1340, *pg.* 1335
POWERDAS - Terminal Panel - CYBERRESEARCH INC.; *pg.* 381, *pg.* 339
POWERDATA - Software - SUNGARD DATA SYSTEMS INC.; *pg.* 477, *pg.* 1592
POWERDESIGNER - Data Modeling Tool - SAP; *pg.* 465, *pg.* 78
POWERDI - Semiconductors - DIODES INCORPORATED; *pg.* 634, *pg.* 1729
POWERDRIVE - Recreational Vehicle - CLUB CAR, INC.; *pg.* 1830, *pg.* 532
POWERDRYCUTTING - Cylindrical Product - GLEASON CORPORATION; *pg.* 1340, *pg.* 1335
POWEREASE - Molecular Biology Product - THERMO FISHER SCIENTIFIC INC.; *pg.* 1602, *pg.* 61
POWERED BY BALLARD - Fuel Cell Power - BALLARD POWER SYSTEMS, INC.; *pg.* 70, *pg.* 1907
POWERED BY E-QOE - Internet Video Quality Monitoring - AVAGO TECHNOLOGIES; *pg.* 358, *pg.* 238
POWERED BY INSIGHT - Slogan - AXCELIS TECHNOLOGIES, INC.; *pg.* 1400, *pg.* 787
POWERED BY PEOPLE-DRIVEN BY SOLUTIONS - Tagline - EMPLOYMENT ENTERPRISES INC.; *pg.* 392, *pg.* 1787
POWERED BY PREMIERE & DESIGN - Telecom Service - PREMIERE GLOBAL SERVICES, INC.; *pg.* 1275, *pg.* 518
POWERED BY PROGRESS - Software - PROGRESS SOFTWARE CORPORATION; *pg.* 457, *pg.* 786
POWERED BY TYSON - Tagline - TYSON FOODS, INC.; *pg.* 902, *pg.* 35
POWERED BY XEROX - Slogan - XEROX CORPORATION; *pg.* 494, *pg.* 365
POWEREDGE - Servers - DELL INC.; *pg.* 383, *pg.* 1737
POWEREXCHANGE - Software - INFORMATICA CORPORATION; *pg.* 414, *pg.* 190
POWEREXIT - Electro Magnetic Lock with Request-To-Exit Push Buttons - NAPCO SECURITY SYSTEMS, INC.; *pg.* 658, *pg.* 1138
POWERFILM - Software - EASTMAN KODAK COMPANY; *pg.* 1408, *pg.* 1333
POWERFIT - Battery - EXIDE TECHNOLOGIES; *pg.* 204, *pg.* 483
POWERFLEET - Vehicle Management System - I.D. SYSTEMS, INC.; *pg.* 643, *pg.* 1134
POWERFLEX - Fitness Product - BALLY TOTAL FITNESS HOLDINGS CORPORATION; *pg.* 532, *pg.* 1200
POWERFLEX - Industrial Drive - ROCKWELL AUTOMATION, INC.; *pg.* 668, *pg.* 1880
POWERFLO - Pneumatic Pump - GRACO, INC.; *pg.* 1342, *pg.* 935
POWERFLO MATRIX - Pump - HAYWARD POOL PRODUCTS; *pg.* 1049, *pg.* 1057
POWERFOAM - Foam - POWERS FASTENERS INC.; *pg.* 1059, *pg.* 1143
POWERFORCE - Floor Care Product - BISSELL HOMECARE, INC.; *pg.* 52, *pg.* 887
POWERFUL COMPACT - Water Heater - BRADFORD-WHITE CORPORATION; *pg.* 1069, *pg.* 1514
POWERGLIDE - Upright Vacuum Cleaner - BISSELL HOMECARE, INC.; *pg.* 52, *pg.* 887
POWERGLIDE - Bicycle Component - SRAM CORPORATION; *pg.* 967, *pg.* 590
POWERGLIDE 2 - Steam Iron - ROWENTA (USA), INC.; *pg.* 60, *pg.* 1084
POWERGRID - Cartridge Filter - NORDSON CORPORATION; *pg.* 1365, *pg.* 1480
POWERGROOM - Floor Care Product - BISSELL HOMECARE, INC.; *pg.* 52, *pg.* 887
POWERGUARD - Battery - ENERSYS INC.; *pg.* 1334, *pg.* 1584
POWERGUI - Software - DELL SOFTWARE; *pg.* 385, *pg.* 40
POWERGUT 65 & 66 - Badminton Strings - ASHAWAY LINE & TWINE MFG. CO.; *pg.* 1826, *pg.* 1600
POWERHEAD - Toothbrush - GILLETTE; *pg.* 1536, *pg.* 795
POWERHEART - Diagnostic Cardiology System - CARDIAC SCIENCE CORPORATION; *pg.* 1512, *pg.* 1897
POWERHOOK - Extruded Hook - YKK CORPORATION OF AMERICA; *pg.* 699, *pg.* 536
POWERHOUSE - Solar Shingle - THE DOW CHEMICAL COMPANY; *pg.* 1157, *pg.* 898
POWERHOUSE - Toy Train - LIONEL LLC; *pg.* 961, *pg.* 875
POWERHOUSE - Animal Nutrition Product - MANNA PRO CORPORATION; *pg.* 1478, *pg.* 975
POWERHOUSE STRAT - Electric Guitar - FENDER MUSICAL INSTRUMENTS CORPORATION; *pg.* 547, *pg.* 21
POWERIIWATCH - Panel - TIVO INC.; *pg.* 313, *pg.* 251
POWERIMAGE - Software - SUNGARD DATA SYSTEMS INC.; *pg.* 477, *pg.* 1592
POWERING A BETTER INTERNET - Tagline - AKAMAI TECHNOLOGIES, INC.; *pg.* 1226, *pg.* 807
POWERING BUSINESS WORLDWIDE - Tagline - EATON CORPORATION; *pg.* 1331, *pg.* 1429
POWERING CONNECTIVITY - Slogan - EXAR CORPORATION; *pg.* 395, *pg.* 91
POWERING EDUCATION. WORLDWIDE. - Slogan - FOLLETT CORPORATION; *pg.* 1641, *pg.* 669
POWERING NEW MEDIA - Tagline - MINDBLAZER, INC.; *pg.* 1267, *pg.* 1367
POWERING THE DIGITAL MEDIA GENERATION - Tagline - SIGMA DESIGNS, INC.; *pg.* 469, *pg.* 148
POWERING THE FUTURE - Tagline - MAXWELL TECHNOLOGIES, INC.; *pg.* 653, *pg.* 204
POWERIZED - Baseball Bat - HILLERICH & BRADSBY CO., INC.; *pg.* 1836, *pg.* 576
POWERJACK - Lighting Product - LEVITON MANUFACTURING COMPANY, INC.; *pg.* 1301, *pg.* 1180
POWERKILL - Racquetball - ASHAWAY LINE & TWINE MFG. CO.; *pg.* 1826, *pg.* 1600
POWERLAB - Laboratory Tools - STOELTING CO.; *pg.* 1430, *pg.* 671
POWERLEASE - Battery - ENERSYS INC.; *pg.* 1334, *pg.* 1584
POWERLEVER PROX 9000 - Self-Powered Electronic Lock - KABA ILCO CORP.; *pg.* 1052, *pg.* 1390
POWERLIFT - Coating & Paint - AKZO NOBEL DECORATIVE PAINTS, USA; *pg.* 1439, *pg.* 1474
POWERLIFT - Side Loaders - HEIL ENVIRONMENTAL INDUSTRIES, LTD.; *pg.* 207, *pg.* 1629
POWERLIFTER - Floor Care Product - BISSELL HOMECARE, INC.; *pg.* 52, *pg.* 887
POWERLIGHT - Monolight - PHOTOGENIC PROFESSIONAL LIGHTING; *pg.* 1426, *pg.* 556
POWERLINE - CIP Cleaner - BOUMATIC LLC; *pg.* 701, *pg.* 1865
POWERLINE - Adult Air Rifles, Pistols & Slingshots - DAISY MANUFACTURING COMPANY; *pg.* 1831, *pg.* 35
POWERLINE - Battery - ENERSYS INC.; *pg.* 1334, *pg.* 1584
POWERLINE - Plunger Pumps - HYPRO; *pg.* 705, *pg.* 951
POWERLINE - Pouch Carrier - KLEIN TOOLS INC.; *pg.* 1052, *pg.* 627
POWERLINE - Hockey Equipment - REEBOK-CCM HOCKEY, INC.; *pg.* 1844, *pg.* 1960
POWERLINE SERIES - Tool Pouches & Belts - KLEIN TOOLS INC.; *pg.* 1052, *pg.* 627
POWERLINER - Pavement Marking Equipment - M-B COMPANIES, INC.; *pg.* 1357, *pg.* 1884

POWERLINK - Power Transfer System - ANALOGIC CORPORATION; *pg.* 1399, *pg.* 840
POWERLINK - Network Management Product - ECESSA CORPORATION; *pg.* 635, *pg.* 953
POWERLINK - Software - EMC CORPORATION; *pg.* 391, *pg.* 825
POWERLINK - Medical Delivery System - ENDOLOGIX, INC.; *pg.* 1528, *pg.* 109
POWERLINK - Bicycle Component - SRAM CORPORATION; *pg.* 967, *pg.* 590
POWERLINK - Fastening System - TEXTRON INC.; *pg.* 235, *pg.* 1607
POWERLINK-IPLUS - Network Protection System - ECESSA CORPORATION; *pg.* 635, *pg.* 953
POWERLINK-IV - Network Protection System - ECESSA CORPORATION; *pg.* 635, *pg.* 953
POWERLINK-IVPLUS - Network Tool - ECESSA CORPORATION; *pg.* 635, *pg.* 953
POWERLITE - Roofing Fastener - POWERS FASTENERS INC.; *pg.* 1059, *pg.* 1143
POWERLITE 5000XB - Portable Projector - EPSON AMERICA INC.; *pg.* 394, *pg.* 122
POWERLITE 7000XB - Portable Projector - EPSON AMERICA INC.; *pg.* 394, *pg.* 122
POWERLITE 7300 - Portable Projection - EPSON AMERICA INC.; *pg.* 394, *pg.* 122
POWERLITE 822+ - Multimedia Projector - EPSON AMERICA INC.; *pg.* 394, *pg.* 122
POWERLITE 83+ - Multimedia Projector - EPSON AMERICA INC.; *pg.* 394, *pg.* 122
POWERLOADER - Storage System - OVERLAND STORAGE, INC.; *pg.* 451, *pg.* 205
POWERLOCK - Hand Tools - STANLEY BLACK & DECKER, INC.; *pg.* 1063, *pg.* 358
POWERLOGIC - Coffee - BUNN-O-MATIC CORPORATION; *pg.* 53, *pg.* 661
POWERLOGIC - Power Monitoring & Control Devices - SCHNEIDER ELECTRIC USA, INC.; *pg.* 1306, *pg.* 650
POWERLUBE - Multi-Purpose Lubricant with Teflon - CRC INDUSTRIES, INC.; *pg.* 329, *pg.* 1590
POWERLUBER - Battery-Powered Grease Gun - LINCOLN INDUSTRIAL CORP.; *pg.* 1355, *pg.* 999
POWERMAG - Electro Magnetic Locks - NAPCO SECURITY SYSTEMS, INC.; *pg.* 658, *pg.* 1138
POWERMANAGER - Software - GENERAC POWER SYSTEMS INC.; *pg.* 1340, *pg.* 1898
POWERMANAGER - Power Protection Product - SCHNEIDER ELECTRIC; *pg.* 467, *pg.* 1609
POWERMAP - Software - BENTLEY SYSTEMS, INC.; *pg.* 361, *pg.* 1531
POWERMART - Software - INFORMATICA CORPORATION; *pg.* 414, *pg.* 190
POWERMASTER - Piston Pumps - LINCOLN INDUSTRIAL CORP.; *pg.* 1355, *pg.* 999
POWERMASTER - Toy Train - LIONEL LLC; *pg.* 961, *pg.* 875
POWERMAX - Pedestal Boom - ALLIED CONSTRUCTION PRODUCTS, LLC; *pg.* 1311, *pg.* 1427
POWERMAX - Probe - COHERENT, INC.; *pg.* 1406, *pg.* 265
POWERMAX - Operating System - CONCURRENT COMPUTER CORPORATION; *pg.* 379, *pg.* 531
POWERMAX - Wireless Product - HEMISPHERE GPS INC.; *pg.* 642, *pg.* 1903
POWERMAX - Hoist & Drag Wire Ropes - WIRECO WORLDGROUP; *pg.* 1389, *pg.* 987
POWERMEASURE - Software - TELEDYNE LECROY; *pg.* 1431, *pg.* 1153
POWERMHS - Computer Program - COMPUTER SCIENCES CORPORATION; *pg.* 378, *pg.* 1780
POWERMIC - Video Conferencing Product - POLYCOM, INC.; *pg.* 664, *pg.* 249
POWERMIND - Electronic Devices - MAXIM INTEGRATED PRODUCTS, INC.; *pg.* 653, *pg.* 247
POWERMISER - Air Conditioners & Furnaces - NORTEK, INC.; *pg.* 100, *pg.* 1607
POWERMIZER - Software - NVIDIA CORPORATION; *pg.* 447, *pg.* 268
POWERNET - Golf Shoe - ACUSHNET COMPANY; *pg.* 1824, *pg.* 818
POWERNET - Software for Network Power Management - SCHNEIDER ELECTRIC; *pg.* 467, *pg.* 1609
POWERNICK - String - ASHAWAY LINE & TWINE MFG. CO.; *pg.* 1826, *pg.* 1600
POWEROHM - Resistor Paste - FERRO CORPORATION; *pg.* 1162, *pg.* 1462
POWEROLL - Pre-Printed Receipt Paper - TRANSACT TECHNOLOGIES INCORPORATED; *pg.* 484, *pg.* 351
POWERON - Software - GE ENERGY; *pg.* 1338, *pg.* 506
POWERONE - Floor Care - NILFISK-ADVANCE, INC.; *pg.* 332, *pg.* 953
POWERONE - Software - VIEWSONIC CORPORATION; *pg.* 489, *pg.* 303
POWERPAC - Software - BIO-RAD LABORATORIES, INC.; *pg.* 1504, *pg.* 101
POWERPAD - Semiconductor Chip Packages - TEXAS INSTRUMENTS INCORPORATED; *pg.* 679, *pg.* 1688
POWERPAK - Receiver - NOVATEL INC.; *pg.* 1424, *pg.* 1904
POWERPANELS - Protective Data Center - CISCO SYSTEMS, INC.; *pg.* 372, *pg.* 240
POWERPARTNER - Software - INFORMATICA CORPORATION; *pg.* 414, *pg.* 190
POWERPATH - Power Supply - COOPER WHEELOCK; *pg.* 630, *pg.* 1080
POWERPATH - Software - ELEKTA; *pg.* 391, *pg.* 284
POWERPATH - Software System - EMC CORPORATION; *pg.* 391, *pg.* 825
POWERPC - Semiconductor Product - FREESCALE SEMICONDUCTOR, INC.; *pg.* 398, *pg.* 1662
POWERPCB - Software System - MENTOR GRAPHICS CORPORATION; *pg.* 432, *pg.* 1510
POWERPHASE - Vehicle Propulsion System - UQM TECHNOLOGIES, INC.; *pg.* 684, *pg.* 334
POWERPICKUP - Shipment Service - FEDEX CORPORATION; *pg.* 1907, *pg.* 1642
POWERPIPE - Power-Generation Prototype - NORTHWEST PIPE COMPANY; *pg.* 100, *pg.* 1846
POWERPLAY - Graphics Card - ADVANCED MICRO DEVICES, INC.; *pg.* 613, *pg.* 282
POWERPLAY - Beverages - THE COCA-COLA COMPANY; *pg.* 240, *pg.* 493
POWERPLUG - Software - INFORMATICA CORPORATION; *pg.* 414, *pg.* 190
POWERPLUS - Pedestal Boom - ALLIED CONSTRUCTION PRODUCTS, LLC; *pg.* 1311, *pg.* 1427
POWERPLUS - Battery - ENERSYS INC.; *pg.* 1334, *pg.* 1584
POWERPLUS - Power Transmission Belt - HBD INDUSTRIES, INC.; *pg.* 207, *pg.* 1449
POWERPLUS - Integrated Electrical Distribution System - HILL PHOENIX INC.; *pg.* 1072, *pg.* 528
POWERPLUS - Billing Service - OGE ENERGY CORP.; *pg.* 1948, *pg.* 1486
POWERPOINT WELD PINS - Fastener - GRIPNAIL CORPORATION; *pg.* 1048, *pg.* 1601
POWERPOP - Electrical Appliance & Housewares - NATIONAL PRESTO INDUSTRIES, INC; *pg.* 1128, *pg.* 1857
POWERPORTAL - Tracker For Electricity Consumption - COMVERGE, INC.; *pg.* 1325, *pg.* 536
POWERPOST - Computer Hardware & Software for Modular Mailing Systems - HASLER, INC.; *pg.* 1459, *pg.* 356
POWERPRESS - Steam Iron - ROWENTA (USA), INC.; *pg.* 60, *pg.* 1084
POWERPRO - Fabric - BROOKS SPORTS INC.; *pg.* 1805, *pg.* 1818
POWERPRO - Grinder & Polisher - BUEHLER, LTD.; *pg.* 1403, *pg.* 622
POWERPRO - Medical Equipment - CONMED CORPORATION; *pg.* 1517, *pg.* 1347
POWERPRO - Bath & Plumbing Product - JACUZZI BRANDS CORPORATION; *pg.* 554, *pg.* 65
POWERPROMAX - Handpiece - CONMED CORPORATION; *pg.* 1517, *pg.* 1347
POWERPSOC - Programmable System-on-Chip - CYPRESS SEMICONDUCTOR CORPORATION; *pg.* 1326, *pg.* 243
POWERPUFF GIRLS - Animated Series - THE CARTOON NETWORK; *pg.* 273, *pg.* 492
POWERQUAD - Packaging System - AMKOR TECHNOLOGY, INC.; *pg.* 67, *pg.* 25
POWERQUEST - Monitoring & Control System for Power Transfer Switches - ASCO POWER TECHNOLOGIES, L.P.; *pg.* 1314, *pg.* 1066
POWERQUEST - Software - SYMANTEC CORPORATION; *pg.* 478, *pg.* 161
POWERQUICC - Semiconductor Product - FREESCALE SEMICONDUCTOR, INC.; *pg.* 398, *pg.* 1662
POWERRACK - Truck Equipment - AMERICAN VAN EQUIPMENT INC.; *pg.* 199, *pg.* 1078
POWERREBAR - Software - BENTLEY SYSTEMS, INC.; *pg.* 361, *pg.* 1531
POWERRUN - Electronic Components - MOLEX INCORPORATED; *pg.* 655, *pg.* 628
POWERSAFE - Reserve Power Batteries - ENERSYS INC.; *pg.* 1334, *pg.* 1584
POWERSAIL - Catheter - ABBOTT LABORATORIES; *pg.* 1484, *pg.* 551
POWERSAN - Software - INTERPHASE CORPORATION; *pg.* 420, *pg.* 1732
POWERSAVER - SDRAM Device - INTEGRATED SILICON SOLUTION, INC.; *pg.* 645, *pg.* 145
POWERSCREEN - Crushing & Screening Equipment - TEREX CORPORATION; *pg.* 1381, *pg.* 384
POWERSCRIBE - Medical Dictation Software - NUANCE COMMUNICATIONS, INC.; *pg.* 447, *pg.* 806
POWERSEARCH ADVANTAGE - Real Estate Lead Generation Tool - HOMES.COM, INC.; *pg.* 1256, *pg.* 203
POWERSERVER - Memory Semiconductor Product - INTEGRATED SILICON SOLUTION, INC.; *pg.* 645, *pg.* 145
POWERSEWER - Pump - LITTLE GIANT PUMP COMPANY; *pg.* 1356, *pg.* 1486
POWERSHADE - Curtain Walls - KAWNEER COMPANY, INC.; *pg.* 90, *pg.* 537
POWERSHIELD - Power System - SCHNEIDER ELECTRIC; *pg.* 467, *pg.* 1609
POWERSHIFT - Graphics Card - ADVANCED MICRO DEVICES, INC.; *pg.* 613, *pg.* 282
POWERSHIFT - Actuation System - MOOG INC.; *pg.* 231, *pg.* 1156
POWERSHIFT - Wireless Networking Product - NETGEAR, INC.; *pg.* 444, *pg.* 247
POWERSHOT - Staple Gun - ARROW FASTENER COMPANY, INC.; *pg.* 1042, *pg.* 1118
POWERSHOT - Injection System - MOOG INC.; *pg.* 231, *pg.* 1156
POWERSHRED - Office Shredders - FELLOWES, INC.; *pg.* 397, *pg.* 620
POWERSKI - Electric Scooter - ZAP; *pg.* 222, *pg.* 277
POWERSLOPE - Curtain Walls - KAWNEER COMPANY, INC.; *pg.* 90, *pg.* 537
POWERSMART - Home Appliance - B.C. HYDRO; *pg.* 1936, *pg.* 1909
POWERSNAP - Software - EMC CORPORATION; *pg.* 391, *pg.* 825
POWERSOP - Packaging System - AMKOR TECHNOLOGY, INC.; *pg.* 67, *pg.* 25
POWERSTACK - Box Spring - HSM SOLUTIONS; *pg.* 1884, *pg.* 1378
POWERSTAR - Power Boat - MASTERCRAFT BOAT COMPANY LLC; *pg.* 1709, *pg.* 1656
POWERSTAR - Power Amplifier - RF MICRO DEVICES, INC.; *pg.* 667, *pg.* 1376
POWERSTATION - Surge Protector - COLEMAN CABLE, INC.; *pg.* 1324, *pg.* 665
POWERSTATION-POWERHOUSE - Toy Train - LIONEL LLC; *pg.* 961, *pg.* 875
POWERSTEAMER - Floor Care Product - BISSELL HOMECARE, INC.; *pg.* 52, *pg.* 887
POWERSTEAMER PRO - Deep Cleaner - BISSELL HOMECARE, INC.; *pg.* 52, *pg.* 887
POWERSTEEL TECHNOLOGY - Wire Rope Manufacturing Process - WIRECO WORLDGROUP; *pg.* 1389, *pg.* 987
POWERSTEP - Recreational Vehicle Products - HSM SOLUTIONS; *pg.* 1884, *pg.* 1378
POWERSTEPP - Computer Program - COMPUTER SCIENCES CORPORATION; *pg.* 378, *pg.* 1780
POWERSTICK - Adhesive Anchor System - POWERS FASTENERS INC.; *pg.* 1059, *pg.* 1143
POWERSTORE - Software - DST SYSTEMS, INC.; *pg.* 388, *pg.* 982
POWERSTREAM - Board-Level Product - MERCURY COMPUTER SYSTEMS, INC.; *pg.* 434, *pg.* 813
POWERSTROKE - Air Filter - AMSOIL INC.; *pg.* 971, *pg.* 1896
POWERSTROKE - Fluid Handling System - GRACO, INC.; *pg.* 1342, *pg.* 935
POWERSTROKE - Car Part Accessory - PRO-LINE, INC.; *pg.* 966, *pg.* 45
POWERSUB - Circuit Breaker - SCHNEIDER ELECTRIC USA, INC.; *pg.* 1306, *pg.* 650
POWERSURVEY - Software - BENTLEY SYSTEMS, INC.; *pg.* 361, *pg.* 1531
POWERSWITCH - Mechanical Interlock - LEVITON MANUFACTURING COMPANY, INC.; *pg.* 1301, *pg.* 1180
POWERTECH PLUS - Engine - DEERE & COMPANY; *pg.*

First page reference indicates Business Class Edition
Second page reference indicates Geographic Edition

703, *pg.* 632
POWERTEK - Dynamometers - MTS SYSTEMS CORPORATION; *pg.* 442, *pg.* 923
POWERTHOLD - Powder And Cream - COMBE INCORPORATED; *pg.* 1516, *pg.* 1351
POWERTOUCH - Toy - MATTEL, INC.; *pg.* 962, *pg.* 81
POWERTRACK - Rear Loaders - HEIL ENVIRONMENTAL INDUSTRIES, LTD.; *pg.* 207, *pg.* 1629
POWERTWIST-V - Belts - FENNER DRIVES; *pg.* 1336, *pg.* 1551
POWERVAULT - Storage Products - DELL INC.; *pg.* 383, *pg.* 1737
POWERVERTER - Truck Equipment - AMERICAN VAN EQUIPMENT INC.; *pg.* 199, *pg.* 1078
POWERVERTER - Inverter - TRIPPE MANUFACTURING COMPANY; *pg.* 220, *pg.* 592
POWERVIEW - Software - ADVANCED ENERGY INDUSTRIES, INC.; *pg.* 613, *pg.* 328
POWERVIEW - Binocular - BUSHNELL OUTDOOR PRODUCTS, INC.; *pg.* 1403, *pg.* 718
POWERVIEW - Camera - TSI INCORPORATED; *pg.* 1432, *pg.* 965
POWERVIEW PLUS - Camera - TSI INCORPORATED; *pg.* 1432, *pg.* 965
POWERVISION - Application for Automating the Healthcare Management Process - CERNER CORPORATION; *pg.* 1514, *pg.* 981
POWERVPN - Software - SYMANTEC CORPORATION; *pg.* 478, *pg.* 161
POWERWALL - Electrical Distribution System for Use in Building Construction - HILL PHOENIX INC.; *pg.* 1072, *pg.* 528
POWERWALL - Metal Building Wall Framing & Metal Curtain Walls - KAWNEER COMPANY, INC.; *pg.* 90, *pg.* 537
POWERWAND - Small Vacuum - NILFISK-ADVANCE, INC.; *pg.* 332, *pg.* 953
POWERWARE - Electrical Products - EATON CORPORATION; *pg.* 1331, *pg.* 1429
POWERWATCH - Siamese Cable - COLEMAN CABLE, INC.; *pg.* 1324, *pg.* 665
POWERWAVE - Acoustic Cleaning Systems - GE ENERGY; *pg.* 1338, *pg.* 506
POWERWEB - Communication Product - CENTURYLINK, INC; *pg.* 1870, *pg.* 317
POWERWORKS - Healthcare Solutions - CERNER CORPORATION; *pg.* 1514, *pg.* 981
POWERZONE - Turf Product - PBI/GORDON CORPORATION; *pg.* 1176, *pg.* 985
POWIRTAB - Power Semiconductor Device - INTERNATIONAL RECTIFIER CORPORATION; *pg.* 647, *pg.* 80
POWIRTRAIN - Power Semiconductor Device - INTERNATIONAL RECTIFIER CORPORATION; *pg.* 647, *pg.* 80
POWR-CONNECT - Mechanical Lug - IDEAL INDUSTRIES, INC.; *pg.* 1051, *pg.* 662
POWR-CONNECTOR - Single Barrel Connector - IDEAL INDUSTRIES, INC.; *pg.* 1051, *pg.* 662
POWR FILM - Resistor Product - OHMITE MANUFACTURING COMPANY; *pg.* 660, *pg.* 553
POWR-FISH - Pulling Product - IDEAL INDUSTRIES, INC.; *pg.* 1051, *pg.* 662
POWR-FOLD - Door - RITE-HITE HOLDING CORPORATION; *pg.* 1372, *pg.* 1880
POW'R GARD - Generators - BALDOR ELECTRIC COMPANY; *pg.* 1316, *pg.* 32
POWR-GLO - Electrical Tester - IDEAL INDUSTRIES, INC.; *pg.* 1051, *pg.* 662
POW'R-GRIP - Hanger - HOME PRODUCTS INTERNATIONAL, INC.; *pg.* 1125, *pg.* 577
POWR-RIB - Resistor - OHMITE MANUFACTURING COMPANY; *pg.* 660, *pg.* 553
POWR-SLIDE - Door - RITE-HITE HOLDING CORPORATION; *pg.* 1372, *pg.* 1880
POWRFILM - Metal Alloy Film Resistor - OHMITE MANUFACTURING COMPANY; *pg.* 660, *pg.* 553
POWRIFSAFE - Power Semiconductor Device - INTERNATIONAL RECTIFIER CORPORATION; *pg.* 647, *pg.* 80
POWRLINER - Line Striping Equipment - TITAN TOOL, INC.; *pg.* 1383, *pg.* 1100
POWRMAX - Copper & Aluminum Cables - GENERAL CABLE CORPORATION; *pg.* 83, *pg.* 729
POWRNET - Cable - GENERAL CABLE CORPORATION; *pg.* 83, *pg.* 729
POWRPAK - Cable - GENERAL CABLE CORPORATION; *pg.* 83, *pg.* 729
POWRSERV - Copper & Aluminum Cable - GENERAL CABLE CORPORATION; *pg.* 83, *pg.* 729
POWRTWIN - Gasoline-powered Airless Paint Sprayers - TITAN TOOL, INC.; *pg.* 1383, *pg.* 1100
POWRWORKER - Transistor Control - CLARK MATERIAL HANDLING COMPANY; *pg.* 1323, *pg.* 729
POXYGRID - Vinyl, Nylon or Poxy Coated Racks - BEL-ART PRODUCTS, INC.; *pg.* 1879, *pg.* 1129
POYO PUTTY - Liquid Rubber - SMOOTH-ON INC.; *pg.* 111, *pg.* 1528
POZ-E-LOCK - Mold Base & Component - SUPERIOR DIE SET CORP.; *pg.* 1379, *pg.* 1885
POZ-LOC - Welded Steel Pipe - NORTHWEST PIPE COMPANY; *pg.* 100, *pg.* 1846
POZZI - Window & Door - JELD-WEN, INC.; *pg.* 1051, *pg.* 1499
PP46D - Compact Photographic Printer System - POLAROID CORPORATION; *pg.* 1426, *pg.* 815
PPA - Professional Putters Association - THE PROFESSIONAL PUTTERS ASSOCIATION; *pg.* 154, *pg.* 1735
PPFA - Awareness Program - PLANNED PARENTHOOD FEDERATION OF AMERICA, INC.; *pg.* 154, *pg.* 1282
PPG AUTOGLASS - Replacement Glass - APOGEE ENTERPRISES, INC.; *pg.* 67, *pg.* 930
PPLI - PurePlast - TEKNI-PLEX, INC.; *pg.* 1470, *pg.* 1122
PPM - Portable Television Rating System - NIELSEN AUDIO; *pg.* 446, *pg.* 768
PPM - Crane - TEREX CORPORATION; *pg.* 1381, *pg.* 384
PPM 100 - Fluid Handling System - GRACO, INC.; *pg.* 1342, *pg.* 935
PPM ANALYSIS TOOL - Reporting Tool - NIELSEN AUDIO; *pg.* 446, *pg.* 768
PPM WEEKLIES - Reporting Tool - NIELSEN AUDIO; *pg.* 446, *pg.* 768
PPMA - Software - HTC GLOBAL SERVICES INC.; *pg.* 409, *pg.* 911
PPOONE - Software System - FISERV, INC.; *pg.* 397, *pg.* 1855
PPROTINT - Colorant - POLYONE CORPORATION; *pg.* 1177, *pg.* 1404
PPT - Home Video - RENTRAK CORPORATION; *pg.* 306, *pg.* 1506
PR-24 - Side-Handle Control Batons - BAE SYSTEMS PRODUCTS GROUP; *pg.* 359, *pg.* 432
PR-80 - Riser Equipment - DRIL-QUIP, INC.; *pg.* 1330, *pg.* 1704
PR INDEX - Software - MKS INSTRUMENTS, INC.; *pg.* 1362, *pg.* 781
PR OPINIONLEADER - Pharmaceutical Products & Marketing Software - ALLSCRIPTS HEALTHCARE SOLUTIONS, INC.; *pg.* 1492, *pg.* 563
PRA E-TMF - Electronic Document Management System - PRAHEALTH SCIENCES; *pg.* 1585, *pg.* 1388
PRA TOOLKIT - Simulation Environment - RAYTHEON COMPANY; *pg.* 233, *pg.* 854
PRACTICAL PERIPHERALS - Computer Peripherals - ZOOM TECHNOLOGIES, INC.; *pg.* 497, *pg.* 1317
PRACTICAL TAX PROFESSIONAL - Software - CCH INC.; *pg.* 1626, *pg.* 653
PRACTICE DEVELOPER - Savings Program - IDEXX LABORATORIES, INC.; *pg.* 1543, *pg.* 753
PRACTICE EXPLORER - Software - IDEXX LABORATORIES, INC.; *pg.* 1543, *pg.* 753
PRACTICE PROFILE - Software - IDEXX LABORATORIES, INC.; *pg.* 1543, *pg.* 753
PRACTICEPLUS - Eyecare Services - SIGNET ARMORLITE, INC.; *pg.* 1429, *pg.* 60
PRADINES - Hand Tools - SNAP-ON INCORPORATED; *pg.* 1062, *pg.* 1862
PRADO - Fabric - NEMSCHOFF, INC.; *pg.* 936, *pg.* 1890
PRAESTOL - Chemical Product - ASHLAND INC.; *pg.* 972, *pg.* 726
PRAGUE - Lounge Chairs - BERNHARDT DESIGN; *pg.* 918, *pg.* 1381
PRAGUE POWDER - Curing Compound - GRIFFITH LABORATORIES, INC.; *pg.* 860, *pg.* 552
PRAINBERGER - Acoustic Pianos - YOUNG CHANG NORTH AMERICA; *pg.* 595, *pg.* 77
PRAIRIE - All-Terrain Vehicle - KAWASAKI MOTORS CORP., U.S.A.; *pg.* 1708, *pg.* 111
PRAIRIE - Fabric - NEMSCHOFF, INC.; *pg.* 936, *pg.* 1890
PRAIRIE CREEK - Food Product - SHAMROCK FOODS COMPANY; *pg.* 895, *pg.* 20
PRAIRIE FLOWERS - Bath Product - KOHLER CO.; *pg.* 91, *pg.* 1862
PRAIRIE MEADOWS - Carpet - BEAULIEU GROUP, LLC; *pg.* 917, *pg.* 529
PRAIRIE PARTY - Video Game - INTERNATIONAL GAME TECHNOLOGY; *pg.* 957, *pg.* 1024
PRAIRIE PILLAR - Container Grown Plant - MONROVIA GROWERS; *pg.* 1797, *pg.* 44
PRAIRIE VIEW - Furniture - ASHLEY FURNITURE INDUSTRIES, INC.; *pg.* 914, *pg.* 1852
PRAIRIEHOLLOW - Cutlery - PACTIV CORPORATION; *pg.* 1466, *pg.* 624
PRAIRIEWARE - Plastic Cutlery - PACTIV CORPORATION; *pg.* 1466, *pg.* 624
PRAISE - Pharmaceutical Product - ALERE INC.; *pg.* 1488, *pg.* 849
PRALINE - Liqueur - SAZERAC COMPANY, INC.; *pg.* 1969, *pg.* 745
PRAMITOL - Non-Selective Herbicide - UNIVERSAL COOPERATIVES, INC.; *pg.* 1482, *pg.* 922
PRANA - Fabric - NEMSCHOFF, INC.; *pg.* 936, *pg.* 1890
PRANAYAMA - Pillow - HUGGER MUGGER YOGA PRODUCTS LLC; *pg.* 1836, *pg.* 1758
PRANG - Art Materials, Watercolors & Crayons - DIXON TICONDEROGA COMPANY; *pg.* 388, *pg.* 430
PRASTOST - Cheese - A.V. OLSSON TRADING CO. INC.; *pg.* 838, *pg.* 372
PRATO - Cheese - SAPUTO, INC.; *pg.* 893, *pg.* 1956
PRATT - Furniture - ETHAN ALLEN INTERIORS INC.; *pg.* 924, *pg.* 343
PRATT - Footwear - K-SWISS; *pg.* 1837, *pg.* 306
PRATT & LAMBERT - Paints & Stains - THE SHERWIN-WILLIAMS COMPANY; *pg.* 1447, *pg.* 1435
PRATT & LAMBERT - Paints - SHERWIN-WILLIAMS DIVERSIFIED BRANDS DIVISION; *pg.* 1448, *pg.* 1435
PRATT & LARSON - Tile - ARTISTIC TILE INC.; *pg.* 914, *pg.* 1119
PRATT & WHITNEY - Aircraft Engines - UNITED TECHNOLOGIES CORPORATION; *pg.* 235, *pg.* 353
PRAXAIR - Industrial Gas - PRAXAIR, INC.; *pg.* 1178, *pg.* 344
PRAXAIR - Coating - PRECISION ROLL GRINDERS, INC.; *pg.* 1370, *pg.* 1514
PRAXIS SERIES - Educational Test - EDUCATIONAL TESTING SERVICE INC.; *pg.* 1394, *pg.* 1111
PRE/AFT - Shave Lotion - THE ELTRON COMPANY; *pg.* 507, *pg.* 103
PRE-ASSEMBLED PIXMOBILE - Screen - DA-LITE SCREEN COMPANY; *pg.* 632, *pg.* 698
PRE-BYPASS PLUS - Blood Filter - PALL CORPORATION; *pg.* 232, *pg.* 1323
PRE-CAT - Catalytic Converter - AP EXHAUST PRODUCTS, INC.; *pg.* 199, *pg.* 1373
PRE-COTE - In-Mold Coating - SMOOTH-ON INC.; *pg.* 111, *pg.* 1528
PRE-K TODAY - Educational Materials - SCHOLASTIC INC.; *pg.* 1683, *pg.* 1288
PRE-KLENZ - Instrument Transport Gel - STERIS CORPORATION; *pg.* 1597, *pg.* 1464
PRE PLEAT - Filter - FLANDERS CORPORATION; *pg.* 1336, *pg.* 1392
PRE-SAN - Turf Product - PBI/GORDON CORPORATION; *pg.* 1176, *pg.* 985
PREACHING TODAY - Audio Cassette - CHRISTIANITY TODAY INTERNATIONAL; *pg.* 1627, *pg.* 561
PREALBUMIN - Power Processor Core System - BECKMAN COULTER, INC.; *pg.* 1402, *pg.* 48
PREBENT - Pipe - AP EXHAUST PRODUCTS, INC.; *pg.* 199, *pg.* 1373
PRECAST - Carpet - INTERFACE, INC.; *pg.* 695, *pg.* 512
PRECEDENCE - Pharmaceutical Product - PFIZER INC.; *pg.* 1581, *pg.* 1278
PRECEDENT - Club Car - INGERSOLL-RAND COMPANY; *pg.* 1349, *pg.* 1370
PRECEDEX - Pharmaceutical Product - HOSPIRA, INC.; *pg.* 1542, *pg.* 623
PRECEDUS - Software - UNITED PARCEL SERVICE, INC.; *pg.* 1928, *pg.* 522
PRECEPT - Golf Clubs & Accessories - BRIDGESTONE GOLF, INC.; *pg.* 1828, *pg.* 528
PRECESS 24 - Software - BIO-RAD LABORATORIES, INC.; *pg.* 1504, *pg.* 101
PRECESS 48 - Software - BIO-RAD LABORATORIES, INC.; *pg.* 1504, *pg.* 101

PRECIOUS - Cheese - LACTALIS AMERICAN GROUP; *pg.* 873, *pg.* 1149
PRECIOUS CARGO - Fabric - SCALAMANDRE, INC.; *pg.* 941, *pg.* 1058
PRECIS - Sizing Agent - HERCULES INCORPORATED; *pg.* 1166, *pg.* 392
PRECISE - Bipolar Instrument - INTUITIVE SURGICAL, INC.; *pg.* 1546, *pg.* 286
PRECISE - Ophthalmic Lenses - SIGNET ARMORLITE, INC.; *pg.* 1429, *pg.* 60
PRECISE HCG - Pregnancy Test - BECTON, DICKINSON & COMPANY; *pg.* 1501, *pg.* 1068
PRECISEID - Software - WEBSENSE, INC.; *pg.* 491, *pg.* 210
PRECISERX - Medical Equipment - INVACARE CORPORATION; *pg.* 1546, *pg.* 1451
PRECISION - Medical Instrument - ABBOTT LABORATORIES; *pg.* 1484, *pg.* 551
PRECISION - Imprinter - AUTOMATED PACKAGING SYSTEMS INC.; *pg.* 1452, *pg.* 1474
PRECISION - Fluorocarbon Tapered Leader - CORTLAND LINE COMPANY; *pg.* 1831, *pg.* 1155
PRECISION - Linear Motion Component - DEL-TRON PRECISION, INC.; *pg.* 1328, *pg.* 337
PRECISION - U-Joints - FEDERAL-MOGUL HOLDINGS CORPORATION; *pg.* 205, *pg.* 907
PRECISION - Golf Club Shaft - TRUE TEMPER SPORTS, INC.; *pg.* 1847, *pg.* 1647
PRECISION - Jet - WATKINS MANUFACTURING CORPORATION; *pg.* 120, *pg.* 303
PRECISION-AIR - Pneumatic Isolator - FABREEKA INTERNATIONAL, INC.; *pg.* 1882, *pg.* 847
PRECISION AIR FEED - Air Feed - P/A INDUSTRIES, INC.; *pg.* 1367, *pg.* 339
PRECISION AIRE - Pneumatic Vibration Isolation Mount - FABREEKA INTERNATIONAL, INC.; *pg.* 1882, *pg.* 847
PRECISION-AIRE - Pneumatic - FABREEKA INTERNATIONAL, INC.; *pg.* 1882, *pg.* 847
PRECISION ANGLE - Broom - THE LIBMAN COMPANY; *pg.* 331, *pg.* 553
PRECISION AUTO WASH - Car Wash - PRECISION AUTO CARE, INC.; *pg.* 215, *pg.* 1787
PRECISION BALL LEVEL - Level - C.H. HANSON COMPANY; *pg.* 1322, *pg.* 636
PRECISION CASTPARTS - Forced & Fastener Product - PRECISION CASTPARTS CORP.; *pg.* 105, *pg.* 1506
PRECISION COMFORT - Bed - SELECT COMFORT CORPORATION; *pg.* 942, *pg.* 942
PRECISION COMMERCIAL GPS TECHNOLOGY - Tagline - HEMISPHERE GPS INC.; *pg.* 642, *pg.* 1903
PRECISION CONTAINER AERIAL DELIVERY SYSTEM - Packaging - INTERNATIONAL PAPER COMPANY; *pg.* 1460, *pg.* 1644
PRECISION CORE - Plywood - POTLATCH CORPORATION; *pg.* 1467, *pg.* 1844
PRECISION EDGE - Precision Frequency Synthesizer - MICREL, INC.; *pg.* 654, *pg.* 247
PRECISION I - Fly Rods & Leaders - CORTLAND LINE COMPANY; *pg.* 1831, *pg.* 1155
PRECISION INTERCONNECT - Electronic Component Product - TE CONNECTIVITY LTD.; *pg.* 677, *pg.* 1515
PRECISION IRRIGATION MADE EASY - Tag Line - VALMONT INDUSTRIES, INC.; *pg.* 1387, *pg.* 1019
PRECISION LINE - Photo Film, Plates - EASTMAN KODAK COMPANY; *pg.* 1408, *pg.* 1333
PRECISION-LITE - Photographic & Reprographic Films & Paper - EASTMAN KODAK COMPANY; *pg.* 1408, *pg.* 1333
PRECISION LUBE EXPRESS - Vehicle Oil Change & Lubrication Services - PRECISION AUTO CARE, INC.; *pg.* 215, *pg.* 1787
PRECISION MELT ANALYSIS - Software - BIO-RAD LABORATORIES, INC.; *pg.* 1504, *pg.* 101
PRECISION PAK - Filter - FLANDERS CORPORATION; *pg.* 1336, *pg.* 1392
PRECISION PLUS - Medical Device - BOSTON SCIENTIFIC CORPORATION; *pg.* 1508, *pg.* 831
PRECISION PLUS PROTEIN WESTERNC - Software - BIO-RAD LABORATORIES, INC.; *pg.* 1504, *pg.* 101
PRECISION POWER - Mobile Audio Equipment - DEI HOLDINGS, INC.; *pg.* 633, *pg.* 302
PRECISION PRO - Software - BIO-RAD LABORATORIES, INC.; *pg.* 1504, *pg.* 101
PRECISION PROTEIN - Software - BIO-RAD LABORATORIES, INC.; *pg.* 1504, *pg.* 101
PRECISION ROLLED STRIP - Metal Products - ALLEGHENY TECHNOLOGIES INCORPORATED; *pg.* 66, *pg.* 1572
PRECISION SPEED TAC - Medical Device - BOSTON SCIENTIFIC CORPORATION; *pg.* 1508, *pg.* 831
PRECISION TUNE - Vehicle Tune-Up Services - PRECISION AUTO CARE, INC.; *pg.* 215, *pg.* 1787
PRECISION TUNE AUTO CARE - Vehicle Repair, Maintenance & Lubrication Services - PRECISION AUTO CARE, INC.; *pg.* 215, *pg.* 1787
PRECISION TWIST - Medical Device - BOSTON SCIENTIFIC CORPORATION; *pg.* 1508, *pg.* 831
PRECISION VIEW - Process Monitoring System - GRACO, INC.; *pg.* 1342, *pg.* 935
PRECISIONBREW - Digital Decanters & Airpot Brewers - GRINDMASTER CORPORATION; *pg.* 56, *pg.* 734
PRECISIONCELL - Filtration Product - FLANDERS CORPORATION; *pg.* 1336, *pg.* 1392
PRECISIONCELL GT - Filtration Product - FLANDERS CORPORATION; *pg.* 1336, *pg.* 1392
PRECISIONCELL HT - Filtration Product - FLANDERS CORPORATION; *pg.* 1336, *pg.* 1392
PRECISIONCELL II - Filtration Product - FLANDERS CORPORATION; *pg.* 1336, *pg.* 1392
PRECISIONCELL M16 - Filtration Product - FLANDERS CORPORATION; *pg.* 1336, *pg.* 1392
PRECISIONCELL MSH - Filtration Product - FLANDERS CORPORATION; *pg.* 1336, *pg.* 1392
PRECISIONDOSE - Dispense System - GRACO, INC.; *pg.* 1342, *pg.* 935
PRECISIONFLO - Electronic Meters & Controls - GRACO, INC.; *pg.* 1342, *pg.* 935
PRECISIONFLO LT - Fluid Handling System - GRACO, INC.; *pg.* 1342, *pg.* 935
PRECISIONFLO PLUS - Electronic Meters - GRACO, INC.; *pg.* 1342, *pg.* 935
PRECISIONHEAT - Gas Grill - W.C. BRADLEY CO.; *pg.* 62, *pg.* 528
PRECISIONMIX - Plural Component Proportioners - GRACO, INC.; *pg.* 1342, *pg.* 935
PRECISIONPHOTO - Software - LEXMARK INTERNATIONAL, INC.; *pg.* 427, *pg.* 730
PRECISIONPRO - Electric Instrument - UNIVERSAL INSTRUMENTS CORPORATION; *pg.* 683, *pg.* 1154
PRECISIONSENSE - Repair Services - LEXMARK INTERNATIONAL, INC.; *pg.* 427, *pg.* 730
PRECISIONSWIRL - Spray Guns - GRACO, INC.; *pg.* 1342, *pg.* 935
PRECISIONWARE - Plastic Packaging Bottles - BEL-ART PRODUCTS, INC.; *pg.* 1879, *pg.* 1129
PRECISIONWEB - Web-Based System - ABBOTT LABORATORIES; *pg.* 1484, *pg.* 551
PRECISOR - Medical Equipment - CONMED CORPORATION; *pg.* 1517, *pg.* 1347
PRECISOR - Pneumatic Positioner - DWYER INSTRUMENTS INC.; *pg.* 1330, *pg.* 694
PRECLUDE - Head & Neck Product - W.L. GORE & ASSOCIATES, INC.; *pg.* 122, *pg.* 388
PRECLUDE MVP - Head & Neck Product - W.L. GORE & ASSOCIATES, INC.; *pg.* 122, *pg.* 388
PRECO - Music Wire - GIBBS WIRE & STEEL COMPANY, INC.; *pg.* 1048, *pg.* 371
PRECOR - Exercise Equip. - PRECOR, INC.; *pg.* 1843, *pg.* 1847
PRED FORTE - Topical Steroid - ALLERGAN, INC.; *pg.* 1491, *pg.* 106
PREDATOR - Systems Integration & Aeronautics - LOCKHEED MARTIN CORPORATION; *pg.* 229, *pg.* 762
PREDATOR - Floor Cleaning Product - NSS ENTERPRISES, INC.; *pg.* 59, *pg.* 1476
PREDATOR - Musical Instrument - PEAVEY ELECTRONICS CORPORATION; *pg.* 662, *pg.* 970
PREDATOR PLUS - Guitar - PEAVEY ELECTRONICS CORPORATION; *pg.* 662, *pg.* 970
PREDEF - Veterinary Antibiotic & Steroid Preparation - PFIZER INC.; *pg.* 1581, *pg.* 1278
PREDICTABLE SUCCESS - Tagline - SYNOPSYS, INC.; *pg.* 480, *pg.* 162
PREDICTEASE - Internal Drug Therapy - ENZYMATIC THERAPY INC.; *pg.* 1529, *pg.* 1859
PREDICTION - Digital Proofing System - ANDERSON & VREELAND, INC.; *pg.* 1616, *pg.* 1064
PREDICTIT - Software - BIO-RAD LABORATORIES, INC.; *pg.* 1504, *pg.* 101
PREDICTIVE BUSINESS - Enterprise Software - TIBCO SOFTWARE INC.; *pg.* 484, *pg.* 178
PREDICTIVE GATE DRIVE - Electronic Products - TEXAS INSTRUMENTS INCORPORATED; *pg.* 679, *pg.* 1688
PREDICTIVE METRICS FOR THE NANO WORLD - Tagline - NANOMETRICS INCORPORATED; *pg.* 1423, *pg.* 147
PREDICTOR - Medical Apparatus - ARRHYTHMIA RESEARCH TECHNOLOGY, INC.; *pg.* 1496, *pg.* 819
PREEMPT - Laminates - OMNOVA SOLUTIONS INC; *pg.* 1176, *pg.* 1453
PREEN - Garden & Lawn Products - LEBANON SEABOARD CORPORATION; *pg.* 1797, *pg.* 1547
PREEN 'N GREEN - Garden & Lawn Products - LEBANON SEABOARD CORPORATION; *pg.* 1797, *pg.* 1547
PREEN 'N GREEN FOR LAWNS - Lawn Products - LEBANON SEABOARD CORPORATION; *pg.* 1797, *pg.* 1547
PREET 33 - Automotive Paint Primers - PPG INDUSTRIES, INC.; *pg.* 1445, *pg.* 1579
PREFACE - Stand - WENGER CORPORATION; *pg.* 1307, *pg.* 952
PREFERENCE - Contact Lenses - THE COOPER COMPANIES, INC.; *pg.* 1518, *pg.* 183
PREFERENCE - Home Appliance - DACOR; *pg.* 54, *pg.* 67
PREFERENCE - Building Product - GEORGIA-PACIFIC LLC; *pg.* 1458, *pg.* 507
PREFERENCE - Software - SUMTOTAL SYSTEMS, INC.; *pg.* 477, *pg.* 429
PREFERENCE COLLECTION - Dental Furniture - A-DEC, INC.; *pg.* 1483, *pg.* 1500
PREFERENCE PLUS ACCOUNT - Variable Annuity Product - METLIFE, INC.; *pg.* 1208, *pg.* 1258
PREFERRED - Scissors - ACME UNITED CORPORATION; *pg.* 1040, *pg.* 346
PREFERRED - Tableware - PACTIV CORPORATION; *pg.* 1466, *pg.* 624
PREFERRED CARE - Healthcare Product - GF HEALTH PRODUCTS, INC.; *pg.* 1535, *pg.* 508
PREFERRED REWARDS - Debit Card - CHEMICAL FINANCIAL CORPORATION; *pg.* 734, *pg.* 898
PREFERRED STOCK - Men's Fragrance - COTY, INC.; *pg.* 506, *pg.* 1219
PREFIXX - Upholstery - OMNOVA SOLUTIONS INC; *pg.* 1176, *pg.* 1453
PREFLOW - Capsule Filter - PALL CORPORATION; *pg.* 232, *pg.* 1323
PREFYX PPS - Medical Device - BOSTON SCIENTIFIC CORPORATION; *pg.* 1508, *pg.* 831
PREGEL - Food Product - MGP INGREDIENTS, INC.; *pg.* 877, *pg.* 714
PREGEN-PLUS - Stool DNA Test - EXACT SCIENCES CORPORATION; *pg.* 1529, *pg.* 1865
PREGESTIMIL - Hypoallergenic Infant Formula - MEAD JOHNSON NUTRITION COMPANY; *pg.* 1561, *pg.* 615
PREGGUARD - Bovine Vaccine - PFIZER INC.; *pg.* 1581, *pg.* 1278
PREGNANCY & NEWBORN HEALTH EDUCATION CENTER - Health Site for Pregnant Women & Newborns - MARCH OF DIMES BIRTH DEFECTS FOUNDATION; *pg.* 146, *pg.* 1354
PREGNANCY MATTERS - Health Care - HEALTH NET, INC.; *pg.* 1540, *pg.* 308
PREGO - Pasta Sauce - CAMPBELL SOUP COMPANY; *pg.* 844, *pg.* 1048
PREKOTE - Filter - MIDWESCO FILTER RESOURCES INC.; *pg.* 1464, *pg.* 1811
PRELAM - Structural Laminating Adhesive - ASHLAND INC.; *pg.* 972, *pg.* 726
PRELATE - Seafood - TRIDENT SEAFOODS CORPORATION; *pg.* 902, *pg.* 1842
PRELIM - Cleaning Product - VON SCHRADER COMPANY; *pg.* 62, *pg.* 1890
PRELL - Shampoo - PRESTIGE BRANDS HOLDINGS, INC.; *pg.* 520, *pg.* 1345
PRELOX - Male Supplement - HERBALIFE INTERNATIONAL OF AMERICA, INC.; *pg.* 1541, *pg.* 132
PRELUDE - Modern Occasional Tables - BERNHARDT DESIGN; *pg.* 918, *pg.* 1381
PRELUDE - Flooring Product - CONGOLEUM CORPORATION; *pg.* 921, *pg.* 1084
PRELUDE - Embedded Control System - GRASS VALLEY, INC.; *pg.* 641, *pg.* 164
PRELUDE - Furniture - NEMSCHOFF, INC.; *pg.* 936, *pg.* 1890
PRELUDE - Writing Instrument - SHEAFFER PEN CORPORATION; *pg.* 469, *pg.* 371
PRELUDE - Furniture - TRENDWAY CORPORATION; *pg.* 945, *pg.* 892

PRELUDE - Cosmetics - WESTROCK COMPANY; *pg.* 1472, *pg.* 1805
PREMAIR - Catalyst - BASF CATALYSTS LLC; *pg.* 1148, *pg.* 1074
PREMAIR - Cylinder - INGERSOLL-RAND COMPANY; *pg.* 1349, *pg.* 1370
PREMAIRE - Air Respirator - MINE SAFETY APPLIANCES COMPANY; *pg.* 1361, *pg.* 1525
PREMARIN - Estrogen Hormone Medicine - PFIZER INC.; *pg.* 1581, *pg.* 1278
PREMASK - Paper - NEENAH PAPER, INC.; *pg.* 1465, *pg.* 484
PREMASOL - Injection - BAXTER INTERNATIONAL INC.; *pg.* 1499, *pg.* 599
PREMDOR - Interior Wood Door - MASONITE INTERNATIONAL CORPORATION; *pg.* 1054, *pg.* 1920
PREMERE - PFO Closure System - ST. JUDE MEDICAL, INC.; *pg.* 1596, *pg.* 963
PREMI-YUM - Cream Pie Shake - SONIC CORP.; *pg.* 1750, *pg.* 1487
PREMIAT - Wine - SAZERAC COMPANY, INC.; *pg.* 1969, *pg.* 745
PREMIE NESTIE - Neonatal Product - CAS MEDICAL SYSTEMS, INC.; *pg.* 1513, *pg.* 339
PREMIER - Software - ADOBE SYSTEMS INCORPORATED; *pg.* 342, *pg.* 235
PREMIER - Roofing System - BEHLEN MFG. CO.; *pg.* 701, *pg.* 1010
PREMIER - Salt - CARGILL LIMITED; *pg.* 1475, *pg.* 1914
PREMIER - Control Valve - CASHCO, INC.; *pg.* 1044, *pg.* 714
PREMIER - Industrial Sewing Machines - CONSEW; *pg.* 53, *pg.* 1049
PREMIER - Photo Paper & Printer Accessories - EASTMAN KODAK COMPANY; *pg.* 1408, *pg.* 1333
PREMIER - Meats - ELLENBEE-LEGGETT COMPANY INC.; *pg.* 854, *pg.* 1452
PREMIER - Cast Iron Free Weights - ESCALADE INC.; *pg.* 1833, *pg.* 678
PREMIER - Paper & Nonwoven Material - FIBERMARK INC.; *pg.* 1457, *pg.* 1764
PREMIER - Graphic Products - THE GOODYEAR TIRE & RUBBER COMPANY; *pg.* 1883, *pg.* 1401
PREMIER - Air-Operated Piston Pumps - GRACO, INC.; *pg.* 1342, *pg.* 935
PREMIER - Medical Product - HOLOGIC, INC.; *pg.* 1416, *pg.* 784
PREMIER - Stud Bumper Product - KULICKE & SOFFA INDUSTRIES, INC.; *pg.* 650, *pg.* 1533
PREMIER - Bed Cover - LUND INTERNATIONAL, INC.; *pg.* 211, *pg.* 526
PREMIER - Diagnostic Test Product - MERIDIAN BIOSCIENCE INC.; *pg.* 1422, *pg.* 1417
PREMIER - Manicuring Tools - MILLERS FORGE INC.; *pg.* 1056, *pg.* 1733
PREMIER - Nutritional Product - NUTRACEUTICAL INTERNATIONAL CORPORATION; *pg.* 1576, *pg.* 1753
PREMIER - Tableware - PACTIV CORPORATION; *pg.* 1466, *pg.* 624
PREMIER - Plastic Shielding - PARKER CHOMERICS; *pg.* 662, *pg.* 862
PREMIER - Toothbrush - RANIR LLC; *pg.* 520, *pg.* 888
PREMIER - Ammunition - REMINGTON ARMS COMPANY, LLC; *pg.* 1844, *pg.* 1382
PREMIER - Briefs - THE SALK COMPANY; *pg.* 1591, *pg.* 800
PREMIER - Educational Resources - SCHOOL SPECIALTY, INC.; *pg.* 467, *pg.* 1860
PREMIER - Rifle Scopes - SWIFT OPTICAL INSTRUMENTS, INC.; *pg.* 1430, *pg.* 1744
PREMIER - Molding Plaster - USG CORPORATION; *pg.* 118, *pg.* 594
PREMIER '66 C - Footwear - K-SWISS; *pg.* 1837, *pg.* 306
PREMIER ACCESS - Parts Shipments - DELL INC.; *pg.* 383, *pg.* 1737
THE PREMIER EMS COMPANY - Slogan - SANMINA-SCI CORPORATION; *pg.* 671, *pg.* 250
PREMIER ENCORE - Medical Product - HOLOGIC, INC.; *pg.* 1416, *pg.* 784
PREMIER MARKET PRESENCE - Service - RE/MAX INTERNATIONAL, INC.; *pg.* 1109, *pg.* 322
PREMIER NIGHT - Game - WMS INDUSTRIES INC.; *pg.* 593, *pg.* 666
PREMIER ONE - Nutritional Product - NUTRACEUTICAL INTERNATIONAL CORPORATION; *pg.* 1576, *pg.* 1753
PREMIER PAGES - Tracking Tool - DELL INC.; *pg.* 383, *pg.* 1737
PREMIER PAYROLL SERVICE - Software Services - NETSUITE, INC.; *pg.* 1270, *pg.* 255
PREMIER PLATINUM - Enzyme Immunoassays for Infectious Disease Diagnosis - MERIDIAN BIOSCIENCE INC.; *pg.* 1422, *pg.* 1417
PREMIER SELECTION - Food Product - HARRIS TEETER, INC.; *pg.* 1022, *pg.* 1383
PREMIER SERIES - Wood - PACIFIC COLUMNS, INC.; *pg.* 103, *pg.* 49
PREMIER TRAVEL TOOTHBRUSH - Toothbrush - RANIR LLC; *pg.* 520, *pg.* 888
PREMIERE - Microsurgical Equipment - BAUSCH & LOMB INCORPORATED; *pg.* 1401, *pg.* 1045
PREMIERE - Personal Care Electrical Product - HELEN OF TROY L.P.; *pg.* 511, *pg.* 1692
PREMIERE - Wood - PACIFIC COLUMNS, INC.; *pg.* 103, *pg.* 49
PREMIERE - Fertilizer - SIMPLOT PARTNERS INC.; *pg.* 1800, *pg.* 548
PREMIERE COLLECTION - Ballet Apparel - ATTITUDES IN DRESSING INC.; *pg.* 19, *pg.* 1057
PREMIERE GLOBAL SERVICES & DESIGN - Telecom Product - PREMIERE GLOBAL SERVICES, INC.; *pg.* 1275, *pg.* 518
PREMIERE SERIES DUMP BODIES - Dump Body - HIGHWAY EQUIPMENT COMPANY; *pg.* 704, *pg.* 702
PREMIERECALL AUDITORIUM - Conferencing - PREMIERE GLOBAL SERVICES, INC.; *pg.* 1275, *pg.* 518
PREMIERECALL CONNECT - Conferencing - PREMIERE GLOBAL SERVICES, INC.; *pg.* 1275, *pg.* 518
PREMIERECALL EVENT - Conferencing - PREMIERE GLOBAL SERVICES, INC.; *pg.* 1275, *pg.* 518
PREMIO - Tire And Rubber Product - THE GOODYEAR TIRE & RUBBER COMPANY; *pg.* 1883, *pg.* 1401
PREMIS - Clock & Buffer Product - CYPRESS SEMICONDUCTOR CORPORATION; *pg.* 1326, *pg.* 243
PREMISE - Office Furniture & Systems - HAWORTH, INC.; *pg.* 402, *pg.* 891
PREMISEPRO - Security Systems - THE ADT CORPORATION; *pg.* 612, *pg.* 409
PREMIUM - Ammunition - FEDERAL PREMIUM AMMUNITION; *pg.* 1834, *pg.* 915
PREMIUM - Wire Stripper - IDEAL INDUSTRIES, INC.; *pg.* 1051, *pg.* 662
PREMIUM - Floor Mats - KRACO ENTERPRISES, LLC; *pg.* 210, *pg.* 68
PREMIUM - Crackers - MONDELEZ INTERNATIONAL, INC.; *pg.* 878, *pg.* 601
PREMIUM - Healthcare Product - SWANSON HEALTH PRODUCTS INC.; *pg.* 1600, *pg.* 1397
PREMIUM ANGUS BEEF - Meat - GORDON FOOD SERVICE INC.; *pg.* 1021, *pg.* 913
PREMIUM ARCTIC EXPRESS - Diesel Additive - POWER SERVICE PRODUCTS, INC.; *pg.* 983, *pg.* 1749
PREMIUM CANADIAN - Brandy - LAIRD & COMPANY, INC.; *pg.* 1966, *pg.* 1119
PREMIUM CHOCOLATE MASTERPIECES COLLECTION - Boxed Chocolate - GHIRARDELLI CHOCOLATE COMPANY; *pg.* 1854, *pg.* 252
PREMIUM CHOICE - Bentonite Clay - MINERALS TECHNOLOGIES INC.; *pg.* 1173, *pg.* 617
PREMIUM DIJON - Mustard - PLOCHMAN, INC.; *pg.* 890, *pg.* 631
PREMIUM DOMAIN FOR TODAY'S BROADCASTING INDUSTRY! - Slogan - BRS MEDIA INC.; *pg.* 1233, *pg.* 214
PREMIUM EDITION - Hard Drive - WESTERN DIGITAL CORPORATION; *pg.* 492, *pg.* 118
PREMIUM ES EDITION - Hard Drive - WESTERN DIGITAL CORPORATION; *pg.* 492, *pg.* 118
PREMIUM FUEL GUARD - Wax - MOC PRODUCTS COMPANY, INC.; *pg.* 332, *pg.* 174
PREMIUM GROUPS - Software - WEBSENSE, INC.; *pg.* 491, *pg.* 210
PREMIUM HEARTLAND QUALITY - Steaks & Meats - OMAHA STEAKS INTERNATIONAL, INC.; *pg.* 1780, *pg.* 1017
PREMIUM HOMEMADE ICE CREAM - Ice Cream - UNITED DAIRY FARMERS, INC.; *pg.* 906, *pg.* 1426
PREMIUM INSIGHTS - Health Plan & Publication - MEDICA, INC.; *pg.* 1208, *pg.* 949
PREMIUM KILBURN - Clothing - ABERCROMBIE & FITCH CO.; *pg.* 37, *pg.* 1466
PREMIUM METAL-GUARD - Films - DAUBERT INDUSTRIES, INC.; *pg.* 1155, *pg.* 561
PREMIUM ONLY PLAN - Employee Benefits - PAYCHEX, INC.; *pg.* 792, *pg.* 1336
PREMIUM OUTLET CENTERS - Real Estate Platforms - SIMON PROPERTY GROUP, INC.; *pg.* 1112, *pg.* 690
PREMIUM PLAN - Banking Services - THE PNC FINANCIAL SERVICES GROUP, INC.; *pg.* 795, *pg.* 1579
PREMIUM POLARIZED SUNWEAR - Tagline - FGX INTERNATIONAL, INC.; *pg.* 5, *pg.* 1608
PREMIUM POOLS - In-Ground Vinyl Pools - POOL CORPORATION; *pg.* 1843, *pg.* 743
PREMIUM POSTCARD - Postal Services - UNITED STATES POSTAL SERVICE; *pg.* 1009, *pg.* 406
PREMIUM QUALITY CARDS FOR A LASTING IMPRESSION - Slogan - PRUDENT PUBLISHING COMPANY, INC.; *pg.* 1678, *pg.* 1115
PREMIUM SELECTIONS - Chocolate - BROWN & HALEY; *pg.* 1851, *pg.* 1820
PREMIUM TEAK - Gardening Hand Tools - SMITH & HAWKEN, LTD.; *pg.* 1786, *pg.* 168
PREMIUM XL - Brushes - THE SHERWIN-WILLIAMS COMPANY; *pg.* 1447, *pg.* 1435
PREMIUMGRADE - Electronic Components - MOLEX INCORPORATED; *pg.* 655, *pg.* 628
PREMIUMLISTENER - Audio Publication Membership Plan - AUDIBLE, INC.; *pg.* 1230, *pg.* 1095
PREMIX - Metal Casting Product - HILL & GRIFFITH COMPANY; *pg.* 1167, *pg.* 1414
PREMIX - Valve - MAXON CORPORATION; *pg.* 1359, *pg.* 695
PREMO-FLEX - Connector - MOLEX INCORPORATED; *pg.* 655, *pg.* 628
PREMOID - Paper & Nonwoven Material - FIBERMARK INC.; *pg.* 1457, *pg.* 1764
PREMONITION - Video Game - INTERNATIONAL GAME TECHNOLOGY; *pg.* 957, *pg.* 1024
PREMPHASE - Hormonal Replacement Therapy - PFIZER INC.; *pg.* 1581, *pg.* 1278
PREMPRO - Menopause Treatment Medicine - PFIZER INC.; *pg.* 1581, *pg.* 1278
PREMSYN - Health & Beauty Product - CHATTEM, INC.; *pg.* 1515, *pg.* 1628
PRENTICE - Log Loaders, Feller Buncher & Harvesters - BLOUNT INTERNATIONAL, INC.; *pg.* 1043, *pg.* 1501
PREOS - Pharmaceutical Product - NPS PHARMACEUTICALS, INC.; *pg.* 1576, *pg.* 1043
PREOTACT - Pharmaceutical Product - NPS PHARMACEUTICALS, INC.; *pg.* 1576, *pg.* 1043
PREP - Shave Lotion - THE ELTRON COMPANY; *pg.* 507, *pg.* 103
PREP - Liquid Chromatography Instrument - WATERS CORPORATION; *pg.* 1436, *pg.* 834
PREP-A-GENE - Software - BIO-RAD LABORATORIES, INC.; *pg.* 1504, *pg.* 101
PREP CHEF - Food Product - HORMEL FOODS CORPORATION; *pg.* 863, *pg.* 915
PREP CREW - Brush - THE WOOSTER BRUSH COMPANY; *pg.* 1450, *pg.* 1482
PREP-DISC - Software - BIO-RAD LABORATORIES, INC.; *pg.* 1504, *pg.* 101
PREP-O-MATIC - Chopper - HABAND COMPANY, INC.; *pg.* 1772, *pg.* 1099
PREP POWER - Automotive Cleaner - DELTA FOREMOST CHEMICAL CORPORATION; *pg.* 1155, *pg.* 1642
PREP SCHOOL - Shoe - AEROGROUP INTERNATIONAL, INC.; *pg.* 1803, *pg.* 1055
PREP-STEP - Dirt & Stain Cleaner - THE VALSPAR CORPORATION; *pg.* 1449, *pg.* 945
PREPAIR - Footwear - CROCS, INC.; *pg.* 1806, *pg.* 335
PREPAK - Reaction Systems - RELIABLE AUTOMATIC SPRINKLER CO., INC.; *pg.* 1137, *pg.* 1158
PREPARATION H - Hemorrhoidal Symptom Relief - PFIZER INC.; *pg.* 1581, *pg.* 1278
PREPARE TO LIVE - Tagline - THE HARTFORD FINANCIAL SERVICES GROUP, INC.; *pg.* 1202, *pg.* 352
PREPARED TO RESPOND - Crude Oil & Fuel Services - BAKER PETROLITE CORPORATION; *pg.* 1148, *pg.* 1745
PREPAYIN - Telecommunication Product - VERISIGN, INC.; *pg.* 488, *pg.* 1799
PREPC+ - Software - WIND RIVER SYSTEMS, INC.; *pg.* 493, *pg.* 38
PREPCLEAN - Buffing Compound Remover - L&R MANUFACTURING COMPANY; *pg.* 1419, *pg.* 1076
PREPCLEAN PLUS - Buffing Compound Remover - L&R

MANUFACTURING COMPANY; *pg.* 1419, *pg.* 1076
PREPIDIL - Medicine - PFIZER INC.; *pg.* 1581, *pg.* 1278
PREPLEAT - Filtration Product - FLANDERS CORPORATION; *pg.* 1336, *pg.* 1392
PREPLUS - Software - SCHLUMBERGER LIMITED; *pg.* 801, *pg.* 1714
PREPPLUS - Testing Instrument System - BECKMAN COULTER, INC.; *pg.* 1402, *pg.* 48
PREPRINTED INSERT - Targeted Inserts - VALASSIS COMMUNICATIONS, INC.; *pg.* 1287, *pg.* 897
PREPRITE - Primer - THE SHERWIN-WILLIAMS COMPANY; *pg.* 1447, *pg.* 1435
PREPSAVER - Slicer - UNIVEX CORPORATION; *pg.* 1386, *pg.* 1039
PREPSTAIN - Diagnostic Product - BD DIAGNOSTICS - TRIPATH; *pg.* 1402, *pg.* 1358
PREPSTAR - Kitchen Appliance - HAMILTON BEACH BRANDS, INC.; *pg.* 56, *pg.* 1783
PREPY - Apparel - VANS, INC.; *pg.* 1821, *pg.* 76
PREQUEL - Liquid Reactive Size - HERCULES INCORPORATED; *pg.* 1166, *pg.* 392
PRESCOLITE - Lighting Product - HUBBELL INCORPORATED; *pg.* 1299, *pg.* 370
PRESCOLITE - Lighting Fixtures - PRESCOLITE INC.; *pg.* 1304, *pg.* 1622
PRESCORE - Credit Scoring Service - FAIR ISAAC CORPORATION; *pg.* 1247, *pg.* 955
PRESCOTT - Furniture - HAWORTH, INC.; *pg.* 402, *pg.* 891
PRESCOTT - Footwear - STEVEN MADDEN, LTD.; *pg.* 1819, *pg.* 1176
PRESCRIPTION CARE - Health & Beauty Product - BLUE CROSS LABORATORIES; *pg.* 326, *pg.* 277
PRESCRIPTION DIET - Dietary Animal Food - HILL'S PET NUTRITION, INC.; *pg.* 1476, *pg.* 721
THE PRESCRIPTION FOR POSITIVE OUTCOMES - Slogan - OMNICARE, INC; *pg.* 1578, *pg.* 1418
PRESCRIPTION OPTICIANS OF AMERICA - Guild - OPTICIANS ASSOCIATION OF AMERICA; *pg.* 152, *pg.* 1639
PRESCRIPTION TREATMENT - Pest-Control Equipment - BASF; *pg.* 1793, *pg.* 992
PRESCRIPTIVES - Beauty Products - THE ESTEE LAUDER COMPANIES INC.; *pg.* 508, *pg.* 1229
PRESEASON - Clothing Collection - REEBOK INTERNATIONAL LTD.; *pg.* 1817, *pg.* 811
PRESEIS - Hydrophones - ION GEOPHYSICAL CORPORATION; *pg.* 1350, *pg.* 1708
PRESENT - Carpet - INTERFACE, INC.; *pg.* 695, *pg.* 512
PRESENTATION ADVANTAGE - Workshop - FRANKLIN COVEY CO.; *pg.* 1642, *pg.* 1758
PRESENTATION EXPRESS - Software - QVIDIAN; *pg.* 458, *pg.* 829
PRESENTER - Software - ADOBE SYSTEMS INCORPORATED; *pg.* 342, *pg.* 235
PRESENTERPRO - Digital Media System - REALNETWORKS, INC.; *pg.* 460, *pg.* 1839
PRESENTING A BETTER WAY - Tagline - BOXLIGHT CORPORATION; *pg.* 627, *pg.* 1813
PRESERVCYT - Medical Product - HOLOGIC, INC.; *pg.* 1416, *pg.* 784
PRESERVE - Furniture - HERMAN MILLER, INC.; *pg.* 926, *pg.* 913
PRESERVISION - Vitamin & Mineral Supplement - BAUSCH & LOMB INCORPORATED; *pg.* 1401, *pg.* 1045
PRESIDENT - Pumps - GRACO, INC.; *pg.* 1342, *pg.* 935
PRESIDENT - Cheese - LACTALIS AMERICAN GROUP; *pg.* 873, *pg.* 1149
PRESIDENT-SHROUD - Fluid Handling System - GRACO, INC.; *pg.* 1342, *pg.* 935
PRESIDENTIAL - Door & Wood Product - CONESTOGA WOOD SPECIALTIES CORP.; *pg.* 921, *pg.* 1527
PRESIDENTIAL LL - Fan - CRAFTMADE INTERNATIONAL, INC.; *pg.* 1295, *pg.* 1670
PRESIDENT'S CHOICE - Private Label Food Brand - PROVIGO INC.; *pg.* 1030, *pg.* 1959
PRESIDENTS PRIDE - Meat & Cheese Products - BAR-S FOODS CO.; *pg.* 839, *pg.* 15
PRESIDER - Control Unit - DIEBOLD, INCORPORATED; *pg.* 387, *pg.* 1407
PRESORB - Absorbent - BASF CATALYSTS LLC; *pg.* 1148, *pg.* 1074
PRESPONSE - Cattle Pneumonic Pasteurellosis Vaccine - BOEHRINGER INGELHEIM VETMEDICA, INC.; *pg.* 1474, *pg.* 989
PRESQUE ISLE DOWNS & CASINO - Racetrack & Casino - ELDORADO RESORTS, INC.; *pg.* 546, *pg.* 1031
PRESS - Apparel - OAKLEY, INC.; *pg.* 1840, *pg.* 86
PRESS CLUB BLEND - Whiskey - LAIRD & COMPANY, INC.; *pg.* 1966, *pg.* 1119
PRESS DIE - Steel Product - A. FINKL & SONS CO.; *pg.* 1309, *pg.* 563
PRESS FIT'S - Connector - BOMAR INTERCONNECT PRODUCTS, INC.; *pg.* 1318, *pg.* 1079
PRESS-LOCK - Cold Plate - LYTRON INCORPORATED; *pg.* 1074, *pg.* 861
PRESS MATE - Paper & Nonwoven Material - FIBERMARK INC.; *pg.* 1457, *pg.* 1764
PRESS-ON - Optical Lenses - 3M COMPANY; *pg.* 1142, *pg.* 956
PRESS PAK - Cleaning Preparation - WALTER G. LEGGE COMPANY, INC.; *pg.* 337, *pg.* 1321
PRESS-TO-SEAL - Molecular Probe Product - THERMO FISHER SCIENTIFIC INC.; *pg.* 1602, *pg.* 61
PRESSBELT - Process Belt - ALBANY INTERNATIONAL CORP.; *pg.* 691, *pg.* 1038
PRESSED POWDER PLUS ANTI-OXIDANTS - Beauty Product - AVEDA CORPORATION; *pg.* 499, *pg.* 917
PRESSFIT - Electrical Pressing Tool - VICTAULIC COMPANY; *pg.* 1066, *pg.* 1529
PRESSGUARD - Paper & Nonwoven Material - FIBERMARK INC.; *pg.* 1457, *pg.* 1764
PRESSLOCK I - Cold Plate - LYTRON INCORPORATED; *pg.* 1074, *pg.* 861
PRESSLOCK II - Cold Plate - LYTRON INCORPORATED; *pg.* 1074, *pg.* 861
PRESSMAN - Toys & Games - PRESSMAN TOY CORPORATION; *pg.* 965, *pg.* 1734
PRESS'N GO - Car Seat Handle Release - EVENFLO COMPANY, INC.; *pg.* 924, *pg.* 1470
PRESSPRO - Specialty Paper - APPVION INC.; *pg.* 1451, *pg.* 1852
PRESSPRO RT - Drilling Support Software - M-I SWACO; *pg.* 980, *pg.* 1710
PRESSRITE - Ironing Center - BROAN-NUTONE LLC; *pg.* 1069, *pg.* 1860
PRESSSION - Orthopedic Device - DJO SURGICAL; *pg.* 1525, *pg.* 1661
PRESSTAPE - Film Splicer - EASTMAN KODAK COMPANY; *pg.* 1408, *pg.* 1333
PRESSTEQ - Drilling Pressure Management Service - BAKER HUGHES INTEQ; *pg.* 1316, *pg.* 1700
PRESSURA - Pressure Controller - TSI INCORPORATED; *pg.* 1432, *pg.* 965
PRESSURE - Apparel - OAKLEY, INC.; *pg.* 1840, *pg.* 86
PRESSURE & SWING - Baby Gate - EVENFLO COMPANY, INC.; *pg.* 924, *pg.* 1470
PRESSURE CONTROL - Nutritional Supplement - WHITEWING LABS, INC.; *pg.* 1610, *pg.* 99
PRESSURE CORING - In-Situ Coring System - BAKER HUGHES INTEQ; *pg.* 1316, *pg.* 1700
PRESSURE-FX - Natural Health Product - AFEXA LIFE SCIENCES INC.; *pg.* 1487, *pg.* 1905
PRESSURE GRAVITY FILLER - Liquid Filling - U.S. BOTTLERS MACHINERY COMPANY; *pg.* 1386, *pg.* 1369
PRESSURE LITE - Bath Product - KOHLER CO.; *pg.* 91, *pg.* 1862
PRESSURE POINT - Utility Knives - THE L.S. STARRETT COMPANY; *pg.* 1421, *pg.* 783
PRESSURE-SEAL - Window - ANDERSEN CORPORATION; *pg.* 67, *pg.* 916
PRESSURE ULCER PREVENTION - Medical Product - MEDLINE INDUSTRIES, INC.; *pg.* 1562, *pg.* 635
PRESSUREGUARD - Polyurethane Foam - SPAN-AMERICA MEDICAL SYSTEMS, INC.; *pg.* 1595, *pg.* 1618
PRESSUREGUARD RENEW - Polyurethane Foam - SPAN-AMERICA MEDICAL SYSTEMS, INC.; *pg.* 1595, *pg.* 1618
PRESTA - Beverages - THE COCA-COLA COMPANY; *pg.* 240, *pg.* 493
PRESTA LIGHT - Beverages - THE COCA-COLA COMPANY; *pg.* 240, *pg.* 493
PRESTIGE - Endoscopic Instruments - AESCULAP, INC.; *pg.* 1487, *pg.* 1521
PRESTIGE - Software - ATEX MEDIA COMMAND, INC.; *pg.* 355, *pg.* 848
PRESTIGE - Fishing Equipment - CABELA'S INCORPORATED; *pg.* 535, *pg.* 1019
PRESTIGE - Door & Wood Product - CONESTOGA WOOD SPECIALTIES CORP.; *pg.* 921, *pg.* 1527
PRESTIGE - Rug - COURISTAN INC.; *pg.* 921, *pg.* 1067
PRESTIGE - Photographic Paper - EASTMAN KODAK COMPANY; *pg.* 1408, *pg.* 1333
PRESTIGE - Pocket Trousers - ELBECO INCORPORATED; *pg.* 40, *pg.* 1584
PRESTIGE - Gaming Product - GLD PRODUCTS, INC.; *pg.* 1835, *pg.* 1882
PRESTIGE - Ceiling Fan - HUNTER FAN COMPANY; *pg.* 57, *pg.* 1631
PRESTIGE - Fabric - NEMSCHOFF, INC.; *pg.* 936, *pg.* 1890
PRESTIGE - In-Ground Vinyl Pools - POOL CORPORATION; *pg.* 1843, *pg.* 743
PRESTIGE - Cooler - SEELEY INTERNATIONAL AMERICAS; *pg.* 1076, *pg.* 19
PRESTIGE - Wood Office Furniture - TAB PRODUCTS CO. LLC; *pg.* 481, *pg.* 1869
PRESTIGE - Auto Sound - VOXX INTERNATIONAL; *pg.* 686, *pg.* 1166
PRESTIGE ADVANCE - Shirts - ELBECO INCORPORATED; *pg.* 40, *pg.* 1584
PRESTIGE COLLECTION - Advertising Publication - DOMINION ENTERPRISES; *pg.* 1636, *pg.* 1796
PRESTIGE IQ - Monitor - NIPRO DIAGNOSTICS, INC.; *pg.* 1573, *pg.* 426
PRESTIGE LX - Blood Glucose Monitors - NIPRO DIAGNOSTICS, INC.; *pg.* 1573, *pg.* 426
PRESTIGE POPLIN - Professional Apparel - BARCO UNIFORMS, INC.; *pg.* 19, *pg.* 94
PRESTIGE-SEAL - Door - LARSON MANUFACTURING COMPANY; *pg.* 93, *pg.* 1624
PRESTIGE SERIES - Video Consoles - LUXOR CORP.; *pg.* 428, *pg.* 666
PRESTIGE SMART SYSTEM - Blood Glucose Testing System - NIPRO DIAGNOSTICS, INC.; *pg.* 1573, *pg.* 426
PRESTIGE VODKA - Spirits - LEONARD KREUSCH, INC.; *pg.* 254, *pg.* 1099
PRESTIGO - Wireless Remote Control - PHILIPS ELECTRONICS NORTH AMERICA; *pg.* 662, *pg.* 782
PRESTO - Dry Color Mill Coloring Leather - HENKEL CORPORATION; *pg.* 1165, *pg.* 1535
PRESTO - Pressure Cooker - NATIONAL PRESTO INDUSTRIES, INC; *pg.* 1128, *pg.* 1857
PRESTO - Watch - NIKE, INC.; *pg.* 1812, *pg.* 1492
PRESTO! - ATM - PUBLIX SUPER MARKETS, INC.; *pg.* 1031, *pg.* 437
PRESTO - Footwear - P.W. MINOR & SON, INC.; *pg.* 1816, *pg.* 1140
PRESTO - Storage Bags & Reusable Containers - REYNOLDS CONSUMER PRODUCTS; *pg.* 1138, *pg.* 625
PRESTO - Food Products - RICH PRODUCTS CORPORATION; *pg.* 892, *pg.* 1150
PRESTO ORVILLE REDENBACHER - Electric Hot Air Popcorn Popper - NATIONAL PRESTO INDUSTRIES, INC; *pg.* 1128, *pg.* 1857
PRESTO-PAK - Fluid Handling System - GRACO, INC.; *pg.* 1342, *pg.* 935
PRESTO PATCH - Repair Product - DAP PRODUCTS, INC.; *pg.* 1441, *pg.* 756
PRESTO PRIDE - Housemark - NATIONAL PRESTO INDUSTRIES, INC; *pg.* 1128, *pg.* 1857
PRESTO-TITE - Fascia - JOHNS MANVILLE CORPORATION; *pg.* 89, *pg.* 320
PRESTOBARBA/BLUE - Disposable Razors - THE PROCTER & GAMBLE COMPANY; *pg.* 1129, *pg.* 1418
PRESTOBURGER - Electrical Appliance & Housewares - NATIONAL PRESTO INDUSTRIES, INC; *pg.* 1128, *pg.* 1857
PRESTOLOCK - Combination Padlocks - THE EASTERN COMPANY; *pg.* 1331, *pg.* 357
PRESTON - Furniture - ETHAN ALLEN INTERIORS INC.; *pg.* 924, *pg.* 343
PRESTON - Furniture - JASPER GROUP; *pg.* 930, *pg.* 691
PRESTONE - Antifreeze & Car Care Products - HONEYWELL CONSUMER PRODUCTS GROUP; *pg.* 208, *pg.* 344
PRESTONE - Refrigerants - HONEYWELL INTERNATIONAL INC.; *pg.* 407, *pg.* 1088
PRESTONE 0 TO 60 - Booster - HONEYWELL CONSUMER PRODUCTS GROUP; *pg.* 208, *pg.* 344
PRESTONE BUG WASH - Windshield Product - HONEYWELL CONSUMER PRODUCTS GROUP; *pg.* 208, *pg.* 344
PRESTONE COLD START - Fuel System - HONEYWELL CONSUMER PRODUCTS GROUP; *pg.* 208, *pg.* 344
PRESTONE JUMP IT - Battery - HONEYWELL CONSUMER PRODUCTS GROUP; *pg.* 208, *pg.* 344
PRESTONE TIRE JACK - Inflator And Sealer - HONEYWELL CONSUMER PRODUCTS GROUP; *pg.* 208, *pg.* 344

First page reference indicates Business Class Edition
Second page reference indicates Geographic Edition

PRESTONE WINDSHIELD MELT - De-Icer Concentrated Additive - HONEYWELL CONSUMER PRODUCTS GROUP; *pg.* 208, *pg.* 344
PRETTY & PRACTICAL - Pocket Smocks - HABAND COMPANY, INC.; *pg.* 1772, *pg.* 1099
PRETTY BIRD - Pet Product - PETSMART, INC.; *pg.* 1481, *pg.* 18
PRETTY IN PURPLE - Lace - HERITAGE LACE INC.; *pg.* 694, *pg.* 711
PRETTY LAIDY - Shoe - AEROGROUP INTERNATIONAL, INC.; *pg.* 1803, *pg.* 1055
PRETTY PRETTY PRINCESS - Game - HASBRO, INC.; *pg.* 954, *pg.* 1603
PRETTY QUICK - Fast Heating Curling Irons/Brush - ANDIS COMPANY; *pg.* 498, *pg.* 1895
PRETZEL CRISPS - Snack Food - SNYDER'S-LANCE, INC.; *pg.* 896, *pg.* 1368
PRETZEL FILLERS - Stuffed Soft Pretzels - J&J SNACK FOODS CORPORATION; *pg.* 865, *pg.* 1107
PRETZEL PERFECT - Pretzel - AUNTIE ANNE'S INC.; *pg.* 1715, *pg.* 1546
PRETZELFILS - Stuffed Soft Pretzel Sticks - J&J SNACK FOODS CORPORATION; *pg.* 865, *pg.* 1107
PREVACID - Tablet - ABBOTT LABORATORIES; *pg.* 1484, *pg.* 551
PREVAGE - Skin Care Product - ALLERGAN, INC.; *pg.* 1491, *pg.* 106
PREVAGE - Anti-Aging Product - ELIZABETH ARDEN, INC.; *pg.* 507, *pg.* 448
PREVAGE MD - Skin Care Product - ALLERGAN, INC.; *pg.* 1491, *pg.* 106
PREVAIL - Resin - THE DOW CHEMICAL COMPANY; *pg.* 1157, *pg.* 898
PREVAIL - Pest Control Product - FMC CORPORATION; *pg.* 1163, *pg.* 1564
PREVAIL - Paper - NEENAH PAPER, INC.; *pg.* 1465, *pg.* 484
PREVAILL - Upholstery - OMNOVA SOLUTIONS INC; *pg.* 1176, *pg.* 1453
PREVENT - Dust Suppressant - FAIRMOUNT SANTROL; *pg.* 1162, *pg.* 1409
PREVENT ZERO - Bicycle Accessories - SPECIALIZED BICYCLE COMPONENTS, INC.; *pg.* 1711, *pg.* 152
PREVENTAGE - Skincare Product - MERLE NORMAN COSMETICS, INC.; *pg.* 517, *pg.* 136
PREVENTIC - Veterinary Product - VIRBAC CORPORATION; *pg.* 1606, *pg.* 1696
PREVENTION - Magazine - RODALE, INC.; *pg.* 1681, *pg.* 1530
PREVENTION AND A CURE IN OUR LIFETIME - Tag Line - BREAST CANCER RESEARCH FOUNDATION; *pg.* 134, *pg.* 1206
PREVENTION.COM - Website - RODALE, INC.; *pg.* 1681, *pg.* 1530
PREVENTIP - Anti-Tipping System - LISTA INTERNATIONAL CORPORATION; *pg.* 934, *pg.* 825
PREVENTIVE - Hot Melt Replacement Part - NORDSON CORPORATION; *pg.* 1365, *pg.* 1480
PREVENTIVE MAINTENANCE PROS - Tag Line - GREASE MONKEY INTERNATIONAL, INC.; *pg.* 84, *pg.* 331
PREVENTIVE NUTRITION - Nutritional Supplement - GENERAL NUTRITION CENTERS, INC.; *pg.* 1534, *pg.* 1575
PREVIEW - Carpet - BEAULIEU GROUP, LLC; *pg.* 917, *pg.* 529
PREVIEW - Software - PAYCHEX, INC.; *pg.* 792, *pg.* 1336
PREVIEW - Bicycle Accessories - SPECIALIZED BICYCLE COMPONENTS, INC.; *pg.* 1711, *pg.* 152
PREVIEW THE PLACE TO STOP BEFORE YOU SHOP - Tagline - PIER 1 IMPORTS, INC.; *pg.* 940, *pg.* 1695
PREVNAR - Vaccine - PFIZER INC.; *pg.* 1581, *pg.* 1278
PREVUE - Pharmaceutical Product - ALERE INC.; *pg.* 1488, *pg.* 849
PREZENT - Veterinary Vaccine Component - PFIZER INC.; *pg.* 1581, *pg.* 1278
PREZERVE - Storage Product - CALGON CARBON CORPORATION; *pg.* 1151, *pg.* 1574
PREZERVER - Fiberglass Tank System - ZCL COMPOSITES INC.; *pg.* 1892, *pg.* 1906
PREZERVER+PLUS+ - Interior Coating Of Storage Tank - ZCL COMPOSITES INC.; *pg.* 1892, *pg.* 1906
PRGORESS APAMA - Software - PROGRESS SOFTWARE CORPORATION; *pg.* 457, *pg.* 786
PRICE CHECK - Video Slots - INTERNATIONAL GAME TECHNOLOGY; *pg.* 957, *pg.* 1024
PRICE CHOPPER - Grocery Store - GOLUB CORPORATION; *pg.* 1021, *pg.* 1340
PRICE CLUB - Club Industry - COSTCO WHOLESALE CORPORATION; *pg.* 1765, *pg.* 1820
THE PRICE IS RIGHT - Lottery Game - D.C. LOTTERY & CHARITABLE GAMES CONTROL BOARD; *pg.* 991, *pg.* 398
THE PRICE IS RIGHT - Lottery Game - KENTUCKY LOTTERY CORPORATION; *pg.* 996, *pg.* 735
THE PRICE IS RIGHT - Lottery Game - OHIO LOTTERY COMMISSION; *pg.* 1002, *pg.* 1433
PRICE LESS FOODS - Food Markets - C&K MARKET, INC.; *pg.* 1016, *pg.* 1496
PRICE PFISTER - Kitchen & Bathroom Fixtures - STANLEY BLACK & DECKER, INC.; *pg.* 1063, *pg.* 358
PRICE PROBE - Software - FIRST DATABANK, INC.; *pg.* 397, *pg.* 217
PRICECUTTER FOOD WAREHOUSE - Food Club - HARPS FOOD STORES, INC.; *pg.* 1022, *pg.* 35
PRICELINE.COM - Online Accomodations - THE PRICELINE GROUP INC.; *pg.* 1276, *pg.* 364
PRICEMAN - Workstation Information - ACNIELSEN CORPORATION; *pg.* 341, *pg.* 1187
PRICEPLUS - Electronic Display Signs - DAKTRONICS, INC.; *pg.* 633, *pg.* 1624
PRICEPOINT RX - Software - FIRST DATABANK, INC.; *pg.* 397, *pg.* 217
PRICE'S - Milk - DEAN FOODS COMPANY; *pg.* 852, *pg.* 1679
PRICE'S CREAMERIES - Dairy Product - DEAN FOODS COMPANY; *pg.* 852, *pg.* 1679
PRIDE - Snowmobile - ARCTIC CAT INC.; *pg.* 1705, *pg.* 953
PRIDE - Food Service - FOOD SERVICES OF AMERICA, INC.; *pg.* 856, *pg.* 21
PRIDE GAUCHO GRILLS - Poultry Product - PILGRIM'S PRIDE CORPORATION; *pg.* 889, *pg.* 330
PRIDE MASTERCRAFT - Paint Sundries Products - PRO GROUP, INC.; *pg.* 1782, *pg.* 331
PRIDE OF ALASKA - Seafood Products - UNISEA FOODS, INC.; *pg.* 906, *pg.* 1829
PRIDE OF LIFE - Butter Alternative - VENTURA FOODS, LLC; *pg.* 908, *pg.* 49
PRIDE OF NEBRASKA - Meat Products - OMAHA STEAKS INTERNATIONAL, INC.; *pg.* 1780, *pg.* 1017
PRIDE OF THE FARM - Livestock Equipment - HAWKEYE STEEL PRODUCTS, INC.; *pg.* 704, *pg.* 708
PRIDE OF THE PORT - Tea - PEET'S COFFEE & TEA, INC.; *pg.* 1029, *pg.* 85
THE PRIEST - Online Magazine - OUR SUNDAY VISITOR, INC.; *pg.* 1673, *pg.* 682
PRILCO - Private Label Division - AKZO NOBEL; *pg.* 1439, *pg.* 1952
PRILOSEC - Pharmaceutical Product - IMPAX LABORATORIES, INC.; *pg.* 1544, *pg.* 101
PRILOSEC OTC - Health Care Product - THE PROCTER & GAMBLE COMPANY; *pg.* 1129, *pg.* 1418
PRIMA - Art Materials - MARTIN/F. WEBER COMPANY; *pg.* 962, *pg.* 1567
PRIMA CONNEX - Dental Implant System - LIFECORE BIOMEDICAL, LLC; *pg.* 1556, *pg.* 920
PRIMA-KARE - Skin Care Product - STERIS CORPORATION; *pg.* 1597, *pg.* 1464
PRIMA PORTA - Sausages - HATFIELD QUALITY MEATS, INC.; *pg.* 861, *pg.* 1537
PRIMA SOLO - Dental Implant System - LIFECORE BIOMEDICAL, LLC; *pg.* 1556, *pg.* 920
PRIMA SPORT - Socks - KAYSER-ROTH CORPORATION; *pg.* 28, *pg.* 1374
PRIMABED - Mattress System - TEMPUR SEALY INTERNATIONAL, INC.; *pg.* 944, *pg.* 731
PRIMACARE - Bandage - DERMA SCIENCES, INC.; *pg.* 1523, *pg.* 1111
PRIMACARE - Disposable Adult Diapers - THE SALK COMPANY; *pg.* 1591, *pg.* 800
PRIMACAST - Unpadded Splint - 3M COMPANY; *pg.* 1142, *pg.* 956
PRIMACOL - Wound Dressing - DERMA SCIENCES, INC.; *pg.* 1523, *pg.* 1111
PRIMACOR - Chemical Product - THE DOW CHEMICAL COMPANY; *pg.* 1157, *pg.* 898
PRIMADERM - Wound Cleanser - DERMA SCIENCES, INC.; *pg.* 1523, *pg.* 1111
PRIMAFLO - Polymer - HERCULES INCORPORATED; *pg.* 1166, *pg.* 392
PRIMAL - Emulsion - DOW CHEMICAL; *pg.* 1156, *pg.* 1563
PRIMAL - Acrylics - THE DOW CHEMICAL COMPANY; *pg.* 1157, *pg.* 898
PRIMAL DEFENSE - Health Supplement - GARDEN OF LIFE, INC.; *pg.* 1532, *pg.* 478
PRIMALOFT - Insulation - 180S, LLC; *pg.* 1824, *pg.* 754
PRIMALOFT - Synthetic Down Insulation - ALBANY INTERNATIONAL CORP.; *pg.* 691, *pg.* 1038
PRIMALOFT - Pillow - SELECT COMFORT CORPORATION; *pg.* 942, *pg.* 942
PRIMAPAD - Wound Dressing Pad - DERMA SCIENCES, INC.; *pg.* 1523, *pg.* 1111
PRIMAPAD - Disposable Underpad - THE SALK COMPANY; *pg.* 1591, *pg.* 800
PRIMAPLY 28 - Roof Membranes - JOHNS MANVILLE CORPORATION; *pg.* 89, *pg.* 320
PRIMAPORE - Medical & Aesthetic Product - DYNATRONICS CORPORATION; *pg.* 1526, *pg.* 1757
PRIMARC - UV Curing Lamps - NORDSON CORPORATION; *pg.* 1365, *pg.* 1480
PRIMARY - Bath Product - KOHLER CO.; *pg.* 91, *pg.* 1862
PRIMARY AIR - Suspension Systems - AIR LIFT COMPANY; *pg.* 198, *pg.* 895
PRIMARY IMAGE - Manual - XEROX CORPORATION; *pg.* 494, *pg.* 365
PRIMARY SOURCE MICROFILM - Publisher - GALE CENGAGE LEARNING; *pg.* 1643, *pg.* 885
PRIMASET - Cyanate Esters - LONZA INC.; *pg.* 1171, *pg.* 1041
PRIMATENE - Asthma Relief - PFIZER INC.; *pg.* 1581, *pg.* 1278
PRIMAX - Polyurethane Product - AIR PRODUCTS AND CHEMICALS, INC.; *pg.* 1145, *pg.* 1513
PRIMAX - Label Film - AVERY DENNISON CORPORATION; *pg.* 1452, *pg.* 95
PRIMAX - Replacement Window & Door - TRUE HOME VALUE, INC.; *pg.* 117, *pg.* 738
PRIME - Dinnerware - THE HOMER LAUGHLIN CHINA COMPANY; *pg.* 1125, *pg.* 1850
PRIME - Food Product - MAPLE LEAF FOODS INC.; *pg.* 875, *pg.* 1927
PRIME - Composite Material - MOLDED FIBER GLASS COMPANIES; *pg.* 1886, *pg.* 1403
PRIME AND BOND - Dental Product - DENTSPLY INTERNATIONAL INC.; *pg.* 1522, *pg.* 1596
PRIME ANGLE - Slotted Angle System - UNISTRUT CORPORATION; *pg.* 117, *pg.* 913
PRIME CATCH - Canned Tuna - STARKIST FOODS INC.; *pg.* 898, *pg.* 1581
PRIME FRY - Liquid Frying Fat - MALLET & COMPANY, INC.; *pg.* 875, *pg.* 1521
PRIME MINISTER - Footwear - P.W. MINOR & SON, INC.; *pg.* 1816, *pg.* 1140
PRIME MOVER - Power Transmission Belt - HBD INDUSTRIES, INC.; *pg.* 207, *pg.* 1449
PRIME-O-SEAL - Paint & Coating - DIAMOND VOGEL PAINT, INC.; *pg.* 1441, *pg.* 710
PRIME PARTS - Cut-up Poultry Parts - PERDUE FARMS INCORPORATED; *pg.* 889, *pg.* 777
PRIME PUBS - Pubs - PRIME RESTAURANTS INC.; *pg.* 1746, *pg.* 1947
PRIME SELECTIONS - Seafood - F.W. BRYCE, INC.; *pg.* 857, *pg.* 823
PRIME SIRLOIN BUFFET BAKERY STEAKS - Restaurants - ADVANCEPIERRE FOODS, INC.; *pg.* 1714, *pg.* 1409
PRIME SIRLOIN FAMILY STEAK HOUSE - Restaurants - ADVANCEPIERRE FOODS, INC.; *pg.* 1714, *pg.* 1409
PRIME TIME - Software - SYNOPSYS, INC.; *pg.* 480, *pg.* 162
PRIME TIME MATH - Educational Materials - SCHOLASTIC INC.; *pg.* 1683, *pg.* 1288
PRIME TURKEY - Food Product - MAPLE LEAF FOODS INC.; *pg.* 875, *pg.* 1927
PRIMEA - Fuel Cell Vehicle - W.L. GORE & ASSOCIATES, INC.; *pg.* 122, *pg.* 388
PRIMEBASE - Paper Product - WESTROCK COMPANY; *pg.* 1472, *pg.* 1805
PRIMECOAT - Alkyd Shop/Field Primer - AKZONOBEL DECORATIVE PAINTS U.S.; *pg.* 1439, *pg.* 1474
PRIMEFIRE - Burner System - ECLIPSE INC.; *pg.* 1332, *pg.* 655
PRIMEGLOS - Adhesive Coated Paper - SPINNAKER COATING, LLC; *pg.* 1470, *pg.* 1477
PRIMELINE - Labeler - AVERY DENNISON CORPORATION; *pg.* 1452, *pg.* 95
PRIMELINE - Hose - THE GOODYEAR TIRE & RUBBER

COMPANY; *pg.* 1883, *pg.* 1401
PRIMEMAX - Wireless Network Product - AIRSPAN NETWORKS INC.; *pg.* 346, *pg.* 410
PRIMENE - Amine - DOW CHEMICAL; *pg.* 1156, *pg.* 1563
PRIMER - Paint & Coating - AERVOE INDUSTRIES INCORPORATED; *pg.* 1439, *pg.* 1021
PRIMER - Bandages - DERMA SCIENCES, INC.; *pg.* 1523, *pg.* 1111
PRIMERA - Furniture - TELESCOPE CASUAL FURNITURE INC.; *pg.* 944, *pg.* 1162
PRIMERICA - Financial Services - CITIGROUP INC.; *pg.* 735, *pg.* 1212
PRIMESCAN - Adhesive Coated Paper - SPINNAKER COATING, LLC; *pg.* 1470, *pg.* 1477
PRIMESINGLES.NET - Online Dating Service - SPARK NETWORKS, INC.; *pg.* 472, *pg.* 140
PRIMESMART - Diabetes Treatment Products - ANIMAS CORPORATION; *pg.* 1495, *pg.* 1593
PRIMET - Modular Dispensing System Satellite - BUEHLER, LTD.; *pg.* 1403, *pg.* 622
PRIMETIME - Film - EASTMAN KODAK COMPANY; *pg.* 1408, *pg.* 1333
PRIMETIME - Software - SYNOPSYS, INC.; *pg.* 480, *pg.* 162
PRIMETRIM - Building Product - BLUELINX HOLDINGS, INC.; *pg.* 70, *pg.* 491
PRIMETRIM - Engineered Wood Trim - GEORGIA-PACIFIC LLC; *pg.* 1458, *pg.* 507
PRIMIDONE - Pharmaceutical Product - LANNETT COMPANY, INC.; *pg.* 1555, *pg.* 1566
PRIMITIVE - Fabric - NEMSCHOFF, INC.; *pg.* 936, *pg.* 1890
PRIMMMO - Footwear - STEVEN MADDEN, LTD.; *pg.* 1819, *pg.* 1176
PRIMO - Mag File - BADGER METER, INC.; *pg.* 1401, *pg.* 1873
PRIMO - Fabric - NEMSCHOFF, INC.; *pg.* 936, *pg.* 1890
PRIMO - Designer Fragrance - PARFUMS DE COEUR LTD.; *pg.* 519, *pg.* 376
PRIMO - Bottled Water & Dispensers - PRIMO WATER CORPORATION; *pg.* 1030, *pg.* 1395
PRIMO DEL REY - Premium Cigars - ALTADIS USA, INC.; *pg.* 1893, *pg.* 423
PRIMO GUSTO - Italian Food - GORDON FOOD SERVICE INC.; *pg.* 1021, *pg.* 913
PRIMO ISLAND - Beer - PABST BREWING COMPANY; *pg.* 258, *pg.* 137
PRIMO TAGLIO - Aged Cheeses & Hand-Trimmed Meats - SAFEWAY INC.; *pg.* 1032, *pg.* 184
PRIMOR - Medicine - PFIZER INC.; *pg.* 1581, *pg.* 1278
PRIMROSE - Window Treatment - CROSCILL, INC.; *pg.* 1122, *pg.* 1220
PRIMROSE - Window Treatment - HERITAGE LACE INC.; *pg.* 694, *pg.* 711
PRIMROSE AND LAVENDER - Hair & Skin Product - AUBREY ORGANICS INC.; *pg.* 499, *pg.* 470
PRIMROSE TANGLE-GO - Hair & Skin Product - AUBREY ORGANICS INC.; *pg.* 499, *pg.* 470
PRINCE - Knife - BUCK KNIVES, INC.; *pg.* 1828, *pg.* 550
PRINCE - Knife - COAST CUTLERY COMPANY; *pg.* 1121, *pg.* 1501
PRINCE - Fluid Handling System - GRACO, INC.; *pg.* 1342, *pg.* 935
PRINCE - Biscuits - MONDELEZ INTERNATIONAL, INC.; *pg.* 878, *pg.* 601
PRINCE - Food Product - NEW WORLD PASTA COMPANY; *pg.* 885, *pg.* 1537
PRINCE MATCHABELLI - Fragrance - PARFUMS DE COEUR LTD.; *pg.* 519, *pg.* 376
PRINCE STREET HOUSE & HOME - Fabric & Flooring - INTERFACE, INC.; *pg.* 695, *pg.* 512
PRINCESS - Bedding - CROSCILL, INC.; *pg.* 1122, *pg.* 1220
PRINCESS - Pillow and Throw - HERITAGE LACE INC.; *pg.* 694, *pg.* 711
PRINCESS - Vacuum Cleaner - HMI INDUSTRIES INC.; *pg.* 56, *pg.* 1475
PRINCESS - Ocean Cruises - PRINCESS CRUISE LINES LTD.; *pg.* 1920, *pg.* 270
PRINCESS - Theater Glasses - SWIFT OPTICAL INSTRUMENTS, INC.; *pg.* 1430, *pg.* 1744
PRINCESS - Fan - WESTINGHOUSE LIGHTING CORPORATION; *pg.* 687, *pg.* 1571
PRINCESS AMBIANCE - Ceiling Fan - WESTINGHOUSE LIGHTING CORPORATION; *pg.* 687, *pg.* 1571
PRINCESS & THE PEA - Game - WINNING MOVES GAMES, INC.; *pg.* 970, *pg.* 816
PRINCESS BELLA - Puppet - GUND, INC.; *pg.* 954, *pg.* 1056
PRINCESS CRUISE LINE - Passenger Cruises & Tours - CARNIVAL CORPORATION; *pg.* 1902, *pg.* 441
PRINCESS LIVIA - Beauty Product - COSMETIQUE, INC.; *pg.* 1765, *pg.* 664
PRINCESS RADIANCE - Ceiling Fan - WESTINGHOUSE LIGHTING CORPORATION; *pg.* 687, *pg.* 1571
PRINCESS TOURS - Air, Land & Cruise Tours - PRINCESS TOURS; *pg.* 1920, *pg.* 1838
PRINCETON - Guitar Amplifier - FENDER MUSICAL INSTRUMENTS CORPORATION; *pg.* 547, *pg.* 21
PRINCETON PLANK - Solid 3-4-5" Plank-Beveled - ROBBINS, INC.; *pg.* 108, *pg.* 1425
PRINCETON REVIEW - Publishing Imprint - PENGUIN RANDOM HOUSE; *pg.* 1675, *pg.* 1276
THE PRINCETON REVIEW - Test Preparation Services & Related Publications - TPR EDUCATION, LLC; *pg.* 1695, *pg.* 822
THE PRINCIPAL - Brokerage - PRINCIPAL FINANCIAL GROUP, INC.; *pg.* 796, *pg.* 706
PRINCIPAL ANNUITY LEGACY - Management Services - PRINCIPAL FINANCIAL GROUP, INC.; *pg.* 796, *pg.* 706
PRINCIPAL BANK - Online Banking - PRINCIPAL FINANCIAL GROUP, INC.; *pg.* 796, *pg.* 706
PRINCIPAL BANK VISA - Gift Card - PRINCIPAL FINANCIAL GROUP, INC.; *pg.* 796, *pg.* 706
PRINCIPAL E-DISTRIBUTION SERVICES - Software - PRINCIPAL FINANCIAL GROUP, INC.; *pg.* 796, *pg.* 706
THE PRINCIPAL FINANCIAL GROUP - Mutual Life Insurance - PRINCIPAL FINANCIAL GROUP, INC.; *pg.* 796, *pg.* 706
THE PRINCIPAL FINANCIAL WELL-BEING INDEX - Management Services - PRINCIPAL FINANCIAL GROUP, INC.; *pg.* 796, *pg.* 706
PRINCIPAL HEALTH NEWS - Management Services - PRINCIPAL FINANCIAL GROUP, INC.; *pg.* 796, *pg.* 706
PRINCIPAL IRA EXCHANGE - Management Services - PRINCIPAL FINANCIAL GROUP, INC.; *pg.* 796, *pg.* 706
PRINCIPAL PROVIDER SERVICE CENTER - Management Services - PRINCIPAL FINANCIAL GROUP, INC.; *pg.* 796, *pg.* 706
PRINCIPAL REIMBURSEMENT ARRANGEMENT - Management Services - PRINCIPAL FINANCIAL GROUP, INC.; *pg.* 796, *pg.* 706
PRINCIPAL RETURN-TO-WORK RESOURCES - Management Services - PRINCIPAL FINANCIAL GROUP, INC.; *pg.* 796, *pg.* 706
PRINCIPAL ROLLOVER CHOICE - Management Services - PRINCIPAL FINANCIAL GROUP, INC.; *pg.* 796, *pg.* 706
PRINCIPAL SECRET - Skin Care Product - GUTHY-RENKER LLC; *pg.* 289, *pg.* 273
PRINCIPAL TOTAL RETIREMENT SUITE - Retirement Plans - PRINCIPAL FINANCIAL GROUP, INC.; *pg.* 796, *pg.* 706
PRINCIPAL WORK SECURE - Management Services - PRINCIPAL FINANCIAL GROUP, INC.; *pg.* 796, *pg.* 706
PRINCIPESSA GAVI - Wine - BANFI VINTNERS; *pg.* 1957, *pg.* 1161
PRINCIPLE - Dental Product - DENTSPLY INTERNATIONAL INC.; *pg.* 1522, *pg.* 1596
PRINCIPLE-CENTERED LEADERSHIP - Book & Workshop - FRANKLIN COVEY CO.; *pg.* 1642, *pg.* 1758
PRINCIPLE-CENTERED LEADERSHIP WEEK - Workshop - FRANKLIN COVEY CO.; *pg.* 1642, *pg.* 1758
PRINERGY - Software - EASTMAN KODAK COMPANY; *pg.* 1408, *pg.* 1333
PRINGLES - Potato Chips - KELLOGG COMPANY; *pg.* 831, *pg.* 870
PRINORM - Pharmaceutical Product - VALEANT PHARMACEUTICALS INTERNATIONAL; *pg.* 1605, *pg.* 1047
PRINT ENGINE - Software - ADOBE SYSTEMS INCORPORATED; *pg.* 342, *pg.* 235
PRINT FOR SUCCESS - Manual - XEROX CORPORATION; *pg.* 494, *pg.* 365
PRINT MANAGEMENT - Print Tools - R.R. DONNELLEY & SONS COMPANY; *pg.* 1682, *pg.* 589
PRINT MANAGER - Software - BOTTOMLINE TECHNOLOGIES INC.; *pg.* 363, *pg.* 483
PRINT MASTER - Offset Printing Blanket - ROTADYNE; *pg.* 1681, *pg.* 529
PRINT-N-PLAY - Lottery Game - MINNESOTA STATE LOTTERY; *pg.* 999, *pg.* 956
PRINT-N-PLAY TEE IT UP - Lottery Game - MINNESOTA STATE LOTTERY; *pg.* 999, *pg.* 956
PRINT TO WIN - Tagline - ELECTRONICS FOR IMAGING, INC.; *pg.* 390, *pg.* 88
PRINT4 - Managed Print - NER HOLDINGS INC.; *pg.* 444, *pg.* 1071
PRINTCOM - Program - EASTMAN KODAK COMPANY; *pg.* 1408, *pg.* 1333
PRINTCRYPTON - Printed Circuit Boards - LEXMARK INTERNATIONAL, INC.; *pg.* 427, *pg.* 730
PRINTED CIRCUIT BOARDS - Switch - TRANSICO INCORPORATED; *pg.* 682, *pg.* 49
PRINTERACT - Software - XEROX CORPORATION; *pg.* 494, *pg.* 365
PRINTERMAP - Software - XEROX CORPORATION; *pg.* 494, *pg.* 365
PRINTERS - Cameras - KONICA MINOLTA BUSINESS SOLUTIONS USA, INC.; *pg.* 1419, *pg.* 1113
PRINTING IMPRESSIONS - Magazine - NORTH AMERICAN PUBLISHING COMPANY; *pg.* 1671, *pg.* 1567
PRINTING INNOVATION WITH XEROX IMAGING AWARDS - Software - XEROX CORPORATION; *pg.* 494, *pg.* 365
PRINTINGSCOUT - Software - XEROX CORPORATION; *pg.* 494, *pg.* 365
PRINTIQUES - Photo Seminars - EASTMAN KODAK COMPANY; *pg.* 1408, *pg.* 1333
PRINTKOTE - Paperboard Packaging Product - WESTROCK COMPANY; *pg.* 1472, *pg.* 1805
PRINTMANAGER 2000 - Data Management System - VIDEOJET TECHNOLOGIES INC.; *pg.* 489, *pg.* 671
PRINTME - Printing Products - ELECTRONICS FOR IMAGING, INC.; *pg.* 390, *pg.* 88
PRINTNET - Software - PRINTRONIX, INC.; *pg.* 456, *pg.* 115
PRINTOSOL - Solvent - THE DOW CHEMICAL COMPANY; *pg.* 1157, *pg.* 898
PRINTOVISC - Polyurethane Component - THE DOW CHEMICAL COMPANY; *pg.* 1157, *pg.* 898
PRINTPLUS - Software - NIELSEN AUDIO; *pg.* 446, *pg.* 768
PRINTPRO - Clock - BROWN & BIGELOW, INC.; *pg.* 1624, *pg.* 959
PRINTRIO - Desktop Multifunction Ink - LEXMARK INTERNATIONAL, INC.; *pg.* 427, *pg.* 730
PRINTSCAN - Software - NIELSEN AUDIO; *pg.* 446, *pg.* 768
PRINTSMITH - Printing Product - ELECTRONICS FOR IMAGING, INC.; *pg.* 390, *pg.* 88
PRINTWATCH - Network Printer - RICOH PRINTING SYSTEMS AMERICA, INC.; *pg.* 462, *pg.* 279
PRINTXCHANGE - Software - XEROX CORPORATION; *pg.* 494, *pg.* 365
PRINTZ - Furniture - ASHLEY FURNITURE INDUSTRIES, INC.; *pg.* 914, *pg.* 1852
PRINTZTON - Shoe - AEROGROUP INTERNATIONAL, INC.; *pg.* 1803, *pg.* 1055
PRIORITY LINE - Products - DESPATCH INDUSTRIES; *pg.* 1070, *pg.* 927
PRIORITY MAIL - 2 to 3 Day Shipping - UNITED STATES POSTAL SERVICE; *pg.* 1009, *pg.* 406
PRIORITY MAIL INTERNATIONAL - Postal Services - UNITED STATES POSTAL SERVICE; *pg.* 1009, *pg.* 406
PRIORITY ONE - Software - WEBSENSE, INC.; *pg.* 491, *pg.* 210
PRIORITY OVERNIGHT - Shipment Service - FEDEX CORPORATION; *pg.* 1907, *pg.* 1642
PRIORITY PACK - Automated Packaging System - SEALED AIR CORPORATION; *pg.* 1468, *pg.* 1058
PRIORITY PET CARE - Scientifically Formulated Nutritional Pet Foods & Products - SAFEWAY INC.; *pg.* 1032, *pg.* 184
PRISCILLA - Clothing - ABERCROMBIE & FITCH CO.; *pg.* 37, *pg.* 1466
PRISM - Pressure Swing Absorption & Membrane Systems - AIR PRODUCTS AND CHEMICALS, INC.; *pg.* 1145, *pg.* 1513
PRISM - Desktop Application Software - APPLIED GLOBAL TECHNOLOGIES; *pg.* 352, *pg.* 460
PRISM - Imprinter - AUTOMATED PACKAGING SYSTEMS INC.; *pg.* 1452, *pg.* 1474
PRISM - Table - BLATT BOWLING & BILLIARD CORP.; *pg.* 1827, *pg.* 1203
PRISM - Electronic Previewing System - EASTMAN KODAK COMPANY; *pg.* 1408, *pg.* 1333
PRISM - Sorter - KEY TECHNOLOGY, INC.; *pg.* 868, *pg.* 1847
PRISM - Motor Controls & Panelboards - KILLARK ELECTRIC; *pg.* 1300, *pg.* 998
PRISM - Fabric - NEMSCHOFF, INC.; *pg.* 936, *pg.* 1890
PRISM - Cleaning Product - VON SCHRADER COMPANY; *pg.* 62, *pg.* 1890
PRISM - Metal detectors - WHITE'S ELECTRONICS; *pg.* 688,

pg. 1509
PRISM 2 - Sorter - KEY TECHNOLOGY, INC.; *pg.* 868, *pg.* 1847
PRISM SONTARA - Cleaning Product - HILLYARD, INC.; *pg.* 331, *pg.* 990
PRISMA - Lasers - COHERENT, INC.; *pg.* 1406, *pg.* 265
PRISMA - Dental Product - DENTSPLY INTERNATIONAL INC.; *pg.* 1522, *pg.* 1596
PRISMA-GHI - Advanced Packaging - ULTRATECH, INC.; *pg.* 1433, *pg.* 251
PRISMA-LUX - Light Fixtures - JUNO LIGHTING, INC.; *pg.* 1300, *pg.* 606
PRISMAPAK - Contract Packaging Service - UNETTE CORPORATION; *pg.* 1184, *pg.* 1114
PRISMAPRO - Dispensing Equipment - IDEX CORPORATION; *pg.* 1347, *pg.* 623
PRISMATIC - Coating - LORD CORPORATION; *pg.* 1357, *pg.* 1360
PRISMATIC - Fabric - NEMSCHOFF, INC.; *pg.* 936, *pg.* 1890
PRISMATIC - Pattern - ROSCO LABORATORIES, INC.; *pg.* 1782, *pg.* 378
PRISMATICS - Battery - THE GILLETTE COMPANY; *pg.* 509, *pg.* 795
PRISMATICS - Gobo Rotator - ROSCO LABORATORIES, INC.; *pg.* 1782, *pg.* 378
PRISMCAL - Graphic Film - FLEXCON CORPORATION; *pg.* 1457, *pg.* 844
PRISON - Plumbing Product - SLOAN VALVE COMPANY; *pg.* 1062, *pg.* 613
PRIST - Fuel Additive, Cleaning Preparations & Polishing Compounds - PPG INDUSTRIES, INC.; *pg.* 1445, *pg.* 1579
PRISTINE - Paint And Stain Product - BENJAMIN MOORE & CO.; *pg.* 1440, *pg.* 1085
PRISTINE - Dinnerware - THE HOMER LAUGHLIN CHINA COMPANY; *pg.* 1125, *pg.* 1850
PRISTIQ - Anti-Depressant - PFIZER INC.; *pg.* 1581, *pg.* 1278
PRISTO - Furniture - NEMSCHOFF, INC.; *pg.* 936, *pg.* 1890
PRISTYNE - Filter Media - W.L. GORE & ASSOCIATES, INC.; *pg.* 122, *pg.* 388
PRITEC - Coating Products - RUSSEL METALS INC.; *pg.* 1180, *pg.* 1928
PRIUS - Hybrid Car - TOYOTA MOTOR NORTH AMERICA, INC.; *pg.* 192, *pg.* 1303
PRIUS C - Hybrid Car - TOYOTA MOTOR NORTH AMERICA, INC.; *pg.* 192, *pg.* 1303
PRIUS PLUG-IN - Hybrid Car - TOYOTA MOTOR NORTH AMERICA, INC.; *pg.* 192, *pg.* 1303
PRIUS V - Hybrid Car - TOYOTA MOTOR NORTH AMERICA, INC.; *pg.* 192, *pg.* 1303
PRIVACY DIRECTOR - Calling Feature - AT&T SOUTHEAST; *pg.* 1868, *pg.* 489
PRIVACY WITHOUT WALLS - Furniture - HERMAN MILLER, INC.; *pg.* 926, *pg.* 913
PRIVACYGUARD - Credit Card Protection Services - AFFINION GROUP, INC.; *pg.* 1225, *pg.* 372
PRIVACYTOUCH - Screen - 3M COMPANY; *pg.* 1142, *pg.* 956
PRIVATE COUNTRY CLUB GUEST POLICY DIRECTORY - Annual Publication - PAZDUR PUBLISHING CO.; *pg.* 1674, *pg.* 115
PRIVATE ESTATES - Mausoleums - COLD SPRING GRANITE COMPANY; *pg.* 76, *pg.* 920
PRIVATE EYES - Sunglasses - FGX INTERNATIONAL, INC.; *pg.* 5, *pg.* 1608
PRIVATE FILE - Software - SMITH MICRO SOFTWARE, INC.; *pg.* 471, *pg.* 41
PRIVATE GARDENS - Laundry & Cleaning Product - FAULTLESS STARCH/BON AMI COMPANY; *pg.* 330, *pg.* 982
PRIVATE LABEL - Ice Cream - FIELDBROOK FOODS INC.; *pg.* 1852, *pg.* 1156
PRIVATE LABEL - Label Designs - WEIBEL, INC.; *pg.* 1972, *pg.* 122
PRIVATE LABEL - Tires - YOKOHAMA TIRE CORPORATION; *pg.* 1892, *pg.* 94
PRIVATE-PAK - Beverage - GREEN SPOT, INC.; *pg.* 251, *pg.* 68
PRIVATE PAYMENTS - Financial Services - AMERICAN EXPRESS COMPANY; *pg.* 712, *pg.* 1190
PRIVATE PORTRAIT - Banking Website Portal - NATIONAL BANK OF INDIANAPOLIS CORPORATION; *pg.* 785, *pg.* 688
PRIVATE RESERVE - Coffee Product - COMMUNITY COFFEE COMPANY LLC; *pg.* 849, *pg.* 741
PRIVATE RESERVE - Steaks - OMAHA STEAKS INTERNATIONAL, INC.; *pg.* 1780, *pg.* 1017
PRIVATE SELECTION - Organic Foods - THE KROGER CO.; *pg.* 1025, *pg.* 1416
PRIVATE STOCK - Bourbon Whiskey - LAIRD & COMPANY, INC.; *pg.* 1966, *pg.* 1119
PVTI - Software - SCHLUMBERGER LIMITED; *pg.* 801, *pg.* 1714
PRIVE - Fabric - MOMENTUM TEXTILES INC.; *pg.* 697, *pg.* 114
PRIVILEGE MANAGER FOR UNIX - Software - DELL SOFTWARE; *pg.* 385, *pg.* 40
PRIVOT - Fabric - NEMSCHOFF, INC.; *pg.* 936, *pg.* 1890
PRIZE SPIN - Game - WMS INDUSTRIES INC.; *pg.* 593, *pg.* 666
PRIZEFECTA - Games - PENN NATIONAL GAMING, INC.; *pg.* 574, *pg.* 1595
PRIZM II - Metal Detector - WHITE'S ELECTRONICS; *pg.* 688, *pg.* 1509
PRIZM III - Metal Detector - WHITE'S ELECTRONICS; *pg.* 688, *pg.* 1509
PRIZM IV - Metal Detector - WHITE'S ELECTRONICS; *pg.* 688, *pg.* 1509
PRIZM V - Metal Detector - WHITE'S ELECTRONICS; *pg.* 688, *pg.* 1509
PRM-100 - Phase Rotation Meter - HD ELECTRIC COMPANY; *pg.* 1299, *pg.* 666
PRO - Tool Belts, Backpacks & Eyewear - THE TIMBERLAND COMPANY; *pg.* 1821, *pg.* 1039
PRO 10 - Health & Beauty Product - DIXIE HEALTH, INC.; *pg.* 1524, *pg.* 535
PRO 115 - Musical Instrument - PEAVEY ELECTRONICS CORPORATION; *pg.* 662, *pg.* 970
PRO 150 - Glove - 180S, LLC; *pg.* 1824, *pg.* 754
PRO-16 - Tools - VAUGHAN & BUSHNELL MANUFACTURING COMPANY, INC.; *pg.* 1066, *pg.* 616
PRO 210 - Musical Instrument - PEAVEY ELECTRONICS CORPORATION; *pg.* 662, *pg.* 970
PRO 350 - Glove - 180S, LLC; *pg.* 1824, *pg.* 754
PRO 360 - Glove - 180S, LLC; *pg.* 1824, *pg.* 754
PRO 410 - Musical Instrument - PEAVEY ELECTRONICS CORPORATION; *pg.* 662, *pg.* 970
PRO 48 - Refrigerator - SUB ZERO WOLF; *pg.* 60, *pg.* 1867
PRO 750 - Glove - 180S, LLC; *pg.* 1824, *pg.* 754
PRO 810 - Musical Instrument - PEAVEY ELECTRONICS CORPORATION; *pg.* 662, *pg.* 970
PRO-88 - Paper Products - BOISE CASCADE HOLDINGS, L.L.C.; *pg.* 1453, *pg.* 546
PRO-92 - Paper Products - BOISE CASCADE HOLDINGS, L.L.C.; *pg.* 1453, *pg.* 546
PRO ACTION ROD - Sport Product - FRANKLIN SPORTS, INC.; *pg.* 1834, *pg.* 847
PRO-ALIGN - Laser Alignment System - U.S. TSUBAKI, INC.; *pg.* 221, *pg.* 670
PRO AM - Pencil - PENTEL OF AMERICA, LTD.; *pg.* 453, *pg.* 295
PRO-AP - Sprayer - KALO, INC.; *pg.* 1796, *pg.* 719
PRO ATTACHMENT SERIES - Power Equipment - ECHO INCORPORATED; *pg.* 1046, *pg.* 626
PRO BATCH - Electronic Fluid Batch - GRACO, INC.; *pg.* 1342, *pg.* 935
PRO C - Footwear - K-SWISS; *pg.* 1837, *pg.* 306
PRO CAL - Plastic Product - MYERS INDUSTRIES, INC.; *pg.* 1887, *pg.* 1402
PRO CARD - Peritoneal Dialyzer - BAXTER INTERNATIONAL INC.; *pg.* 1499, *pg.* 599
PRO-CHEF - Work Table - JOHN BOOS & CO.; *pg.* 1126, *pg.* 609
PRO-CHIP - Wood Chipper - M-B COMPANIES, INC.; *pg.* 1357, *pg.* 1884
PRO CHIP 625 - Brush Chipper - M-B COMPANIES, INC.; *pg.* 1357, *pg.* 1884
PRO CITRUS - Cleaner - SWISHER HYGIENE INC.; *pg.* 336, *pg.* 1507
PRO-CLAIM - Space Equipment - SIMPSON TECHNOLOGIES CORPORATION; *pg.* 111, *pg.* 555
PRO COMM - Coating Product - PPG INDUSTRIES, INC.; *pg.* 1445, *pg.* 1579
PRO COMMANDER - Sport Product - FRANKLIN SPORTS, INC.; *pg.* 1834, *pg.* 847
PRO COOKCENTER - Kitchen Product - KOHLER CO.; *pg.* 91, *pg.* 1862
PRO COOKSINK - Kitchen Product - KOHLER CO.; *pg.* 91, *pg.* 1862
PRO-COTE - Soy Polymer - E.I. DU PONT DE NEMOURS & COMPANY; *pg.* 1159, *pg.* 390
PRO COURT - Portable Basketball Standards - LIFETIME PRODUCTS INC.; *pg.* 933, *pg.* 1751
PRO-CUT - Plasma Cutter - LINCOLN ELECTRIC HOLDINGS, INC.; *pg.* 1355, *pg.* 1432
PRO-CUTS - Hair Service Center - REGIS CORPORATION; *pg.* 521, *pg.* 941
PRO/DESKTOP - Software - PARAMETRIC TECHNOLOGY CORPORATION; *pg.* 452, *pg.* 835
PRO DEX 550 - Glove - 180S, LLC; *pg.* 1824, *pg.* 754
PRO DISPENSE - Electronic Batch Station - GRACO, INC.; *pg.* 1342, *pg.* 935
PRO DOWN - Sports Equipment - SPORT SUPPLY GROUP, INC.; *pg.* 1846, *pg.* 1687
PRO-DUCT - Wiring Duct - HELLERMANNTYTON; *pg.* 642, *pg.* 1875
PRO EDITION - Hard Drive - WESTERN DIGITAL CORPORATION; *pg.* 492, *pg.* 118
PRO ELITE - Gaming Product - GLD PRODUCTS, INC.; *pg.* 1835, *pg.* 1882
PRO-ENDORPHIN - Health & Beauty Product - DIXIE HEALTH, INC.; *pg.* 1524, *pg.* 535
PRO ENGINEER - Software - MSC SOFTWARE CORPORATION; *pg.* 441, *pg.* 262
PRO/ENGINEER - Software - PARAMETRIC TECHNOLOGY CORPORATION; *pg.* 452, *pg.* 835
PRO-EX - Plastics Product - AEP INDUSTRIES INC.; *pg.* 1878, *pg.* 1085
PRO-EX - Lumber Crayons - LA-CO INDUSTRIES MARKAL CO., INC.; *pg.* 1170, *pg.* 610
PRO-FAM - Soy Proteins for both Meat & Food Applications - ARCHER DANIELS MIDLAND COMPANY; *pg.* 825, *pg.* 565
PRO-FAM 646 - Soy Protein - ARCHER-DANIELS-MIDLAND COMPANY; *pg.* 825, *pg.* 565
PRO-FAM 648 - Soy Protein - ARCHER-DANIELS-MIDLAND COMPANY; *pg.* 825, *pg.* 565
PRO-FAM 780 - Soy Protein - ARCHER-DANIELS-MIDLAND COMPANY; *pg.* 825, *pg.* 565
PRO-FAM 781 - Soy Protein - ARCHER-DANIELS-MIDLAND COMPANY; *pg.* 825, *pg.* 565
PRO-FAM 825 - Soy Protein - ARCHER-DANIELS-MIDLAND COMPANY; *pg.* 825, *pg.* 565
PRO-FAM 875 - Soy Protein - ARCHER-DANIELS-MIDLAND COMPANY; *pg.* 825, *pg.* 565
PRO-FAM 891 - Soy Protein - ARCHER-DANIELS-MIDLAND COMPANY; *pg.* 825, *pg.* 565
PRO-FAM 892 - Soy Protein - ARCHER-DANIELS-MIDLAND COMPANY; *pg.* 825, *pg.* 565
PRO-FAM 922 - Soy Protein - ARCHER-DANIELS-MIDLAND COMPANY; *pg.* 825, *pg.* 565
PRO-FAM 931 - Soy Protein - ARCHER-DANIELS-MIDLAND COMPANY; *pg.* 825, *pg.* 565
PRO-FAM 932 - Soy Protein - ARCHER-DANIELS-MIDLAND COMPANY; *pg.* 825, *pg.* 565
PRO-FAM 955 - Soy Protein - ARCHER-DANIELS-MIDLAND COMPANY; *pg.* 825, *pg.* 565
PRO-FAM 974 - Soy Protein - ARCHER-DANIELS-MIDLAND COMPANY; *pg.* 825, *pg.* 565
PRO-FAM H200 - Soy Protein - ARCHER-DANIELS-MIDLAND COMPANY; *pg.* 825, *pg.* 565
PRO-FECTED - String - ASHAWAY LINE & TWINE MFG. CO.; *pg.* 1826, *pg.* 1600
PRO-FINISH - Spray Gun - TITAN TOOL, INC.; *pg.* 1383, *pg.* 1100
PRO-FIRE - Power Equipment - ECHO INCORPORATED; *pg.* 1046, *pg.* 626
PRO FITTER - Medical & Aesthetic Product - DYNATRONICS CORPORATION; *pg.* 1526, *pg.* 1757
PRO FLAT - Coating Product - PPG INDUSTRIES, INC.; *pg.* 1445, *pg.* 1579
PRO FLEX - Sport Product - FRANKLIN SPORTS, INC.; *pg.* 1834, *pg.* 847
PRO-FLO - Air Cleaner - EDELBROCK CORPORATION; *pg.* 204, *pg.* 293
PRO-FLO - Metered Unit for Bonding & Sealing Applications - NORDSON CORPORATION; *pg.* 1365, *pg.* 1480
PRO-FLOW - Software - THE PROTECTOSEAL COMPANY; *pg.* 1370, *pg.* 556
PRO-FORM - Health & Fitness Product - ICON HEALTH & FITNESS, INC.; *pg.* 1837, *pg.* 1752
PRO-FORMANCE - Food Product - BUNGE LIMITED; *pg.* 842, *pg.* 1351
PRO-G-YAM - Health Care Product - NATURE'S SUNSHINE

PRODUCTS, INC.; *pg.* 1571, *pg.* 1754
PRO GENERIX - Software - AMERISOURCEBERGEN CORPORATION; *pg.* 1493, *pg.* 1522
PRO-GENOLOGIX - Therapy System - PROMETHEUS LABORATORIES, INC.; *pg.* 1586, *pg.* 206
PRO-GH - Nutritional Product - NOW HEALTH GROUP, INC.; *pg.* 1576, *pg.* 557
PRO GLASS - Basketball Backboards - LIFETIME PRODUCTS INC.; *pg.* 933, *pg.* 1751
PRO-GRIP - Tools - VAUGHAN & BUSHNELL MANUFACTURING COMPANY, INC.; *pg.* 1066, *pg.* 616
PRO-GUIDE - Fishing Equipment - CABELA'S INCORPORATED; *pg.* 535, *pg.* 1019
PRO HARDWARE - Hardware, Building Supplies Distributors/Retailers - PRO GROUP, INC.; *pg.* 1782, *pg.* 331
PRO-HGH - Health & Beauty Product - DIXIE HEALTH, INC.; *pg.* 1524, *pg.* 535
PRO-HIDE - Paints - PRATT & LAMBERT PAINTS; *pg.* 1446, *pg.* 1434
PRO-HIDE PLUS - Paint - PRATT & LAMBERT PAINTS; *pg.* 1446, *pg.* 1434
PRO HUMMER - Sport Product - FRANKLIN SPORTS, INC.; *pg.* 1834, *pg.* 847
PRO IMAGER - Wall Screen - DA-LITE SCREEN COMPANY; *pg.* 632, *pg.* 698
PRO-JECT - Software System - SS&C TECHNOLOGIES HOLDINGS, INC.; *pg.* 473, *pg.* 386
PRO-KEDS - Men's, Boys' Footwear - THE STRIDE RITE CORPORATION; *pg.* 1820, *pg.* 828
PRO LAB - Sports Nutrition - NATROL, INC.; *pg.* 1570, *pg.* 64
PRO LANE - Bowling Equipment - BRUNSWICK BOWLING & BILLIARDS CORP.; *pg.* 1828, *pg.* 622
PRO-LINE - Bulk Material Handling - ANVIL ATTACHMENTS, LLC; *pg.* 1313, *pg.* 748
PRO-LINE - Liquid Paint Marker - LA-CO INDUSTRIES MARKAL CO., INC.; *pg.* 1170, *pg.* 610
PRO-LINE - Molded Replacement Carpet - LUND INTERNATIONAL, INC.; *pg.* 211, *pg.* 526
PRO LINE - Integrated Avionic System - ROCKWELL COLLINS, INC.; *pg.* 234, *pg.* 702
PRO LINE - Paints - SHERWIN WILLIAMS; *pg.* 1448, *pg.* 1436
PRO LINE 21 - Integrated Display System - ROCKWELL COLLINS, INC.; *pg.* 234, *pg.* 702
PRO LINE FUSION - Integrated Avionics System - ROCKWELL COLLINS, INC.; *pg.* 234, *pg.* 702
PRO LINE PREMIUM - Paints - SHERWIN WILLIAMS; *pg.* 1448, *pg.* 1436
PRO LINE SUPREME - Paints - SHERWIN WILLIAMS; *pg.* 1448, *pg.* 1436
PRO LOGIC - Semiconductor Product - FREESCALE SEMICONDUCTOR, INC.; *pg.* 398, *pg.* 1662
PRO-LOK - Glue - SUPER GLUE CORPORATION; *pg.* 1183, *pg.* 187
PRO-LONG - Bicycle Accessories - SPECIALIZED BICYCLE COMPONENTS, INC.; *pg.* 1711, *pg.* 152
PRO-LOUPE - Magnifier-Headband - EDROY PRODUCTS CO., INC.; *pg.* 1411, *pg.* 1318
PRO MASTER - Coating Product - PPG INDUSTRIES, INC.; *pg.* 1445, *pg.* 1579
PRO MASTER - Power Console & Speaker System - SHURE INCORPORATED; *pg.* 672, *pg.* 638
PRO MAX - Door - THE GENIE COMPANY; *pg.* 55, *pg.* 1403
PRO-MAX - Liquid Paint Marker - LA-CO INDUSTRIES MARKAL CO., INC.; *pg.* 1170, *pg.* 610
PRO-MAX - Storage Product - PLANO MOLDING COMPANY; *pg.* 1887, *pg.* 652
PRO/MECHANIC - Software - PARAMETRIC TECHNOLOGY CORPORATION; *pg.* 452, *pg.* 835
PRO-MET - Cable Tie - IDEAL INDUSTRIES, INC.; *pg.* 1051, *pg.* 662
PRO-METER - High-viscosity Adhesives Dispensing System - NORDSON CORPORATION; *pg.* 1365, *pg.* 1480
PRO-MIST - Filter & Lens - THE TIFFEN COMPANY LLC; *pg.* 1432, *pg.* 1165
PRO-MIX - Soilless Mixes - PREMIER TECH HORTICULTURE LTD.; *pg.* 1799, *pg.* 1958
PRO MIX - Peat Moss - PREMIER TECH LTD.; *pg.* 1799, *pg.* 1959
PRO-MOSS - Peat Moss - PREMIER TECH HORTICULTURE LTD.; *pg.* 1799, *pg.* 1958
PRO-MOTION - Video Conferencing Product - POLYCOM, INC.; *pg.* 664, *pg.* 249
PRO MOUND - Packing Clay - OIL-DRI CORPORATION OF AMERICA; *pg.* 1480, *pg.* 586
PRO-OX - Health Care Product - HEALTH PRODUCTS CORPORATION; *pg.* 1540, *pg.* 1356
PRO-PAD - Abrasive - 3M COMPANY; *pg.* 1142, *pg.* 956
PRO PADZ - Electrode System - ZOLL MEDICAL CORPORATION; *pg.* 1612, *pg.* 814
PRO PAINTER'S PLUS - Contractor Painting Products - HENKEL CONSUMER ADHESIVES, INC.; *pg.* 403, *pg.* 1480
PRO PASSPORT - Program - EASTMAN KODAK COMPANY; *pg.* 1408, *pg.* 1333
PRO PERFORMANCE - Nutritional Supplement - GENERAL NUTRITION CENTERS, INC.; *pg.* 1534, *pg.* 1575
PRO-PERM - Hair Care Product - CCA INDUSTRIES, INC.; *pg.* 503, *pg.* 1114
PRO-PHREE - Nutritional Product - ABBOTT LABORATORIES; *pg.* 1484, *pg.* 551
PRO-PISTOL - Animal Safety Product - NEOGEN CORPORATION; *pg.* 883, *pg.* 896
PRO PLAN - Premium Cat & Dog Foods - NESTLE PURINA PETCARE COMPANY; *pg.* 1479, *pg.* 1000
PRO PLAN - Petcare - TRACTOR SUPPLY COMPANY; *pg.* 708, *pg.* 1627
PRO PLATE - Paint & Coating - DIAMOND VOGEL PAINT, INC.; *pg.* 1441, *pg.* 710
P.R.O. (PLATFORM RESPONSIVE OUTSOLE) - Shoe And Glove - ACUSHNET COMPANY; *pg.* 1824, *pg.* 818
PRO PLAYER - Apparel - PERRY ELLIS INTERNATIONAL, INC.; *pg.* 45, *pg.* 445
PRO PLUS - Clinical Assesment - ALIMED, INC.; *pg.* 1490, *pg.* 816
PRO PLUS - Paint & Coating - DIAMOND VOGEL PAINT, INC.; *pg.* 1441, *pg.* 710
PRO-POINT - Tooling System - KENNAMETAL INC.; *pg.* 1052, *pg.* 1547
PRO POWER - Oxy Blast Laundry Detergent - BLUE CROSS LABORATORIES; *pg.* 326, *pg.* 277
PRO POWER 20K - Nailcare Product - MEDICOOL, INC.; *pg.* 1562, *pg.* 294
PRO POWER 30K - Podiatry Machine - MEDICOOL, INC.; *pg.* 1562, *pg.* 294
PRO POWER 35K - Healthcare Product - MEDICOOL, INC.; *pg.* 1562, *pg.* 294
PRO-PREDICTRX - Therapy System - PROMETHEUS LABORATORIES, INC.; *pg.* 1586, *pg.* 206
PRO-PRINT - Synthetic Paper - TRANSILWRAP COMPANY, INC.; *pg.* 1470, *pg.* 613
PRO-PULL - Pulling Product - IDEAL INDUSTRIES, INC.; *pg.* 1051, *pg.* 662
PRO PVS 100 INNERNET - Volleyball Net System - FRANKLIN SPORTS, INC.; *pg.* 1834, *pg.* 847
PRO-Q - Molecular Probe Product - THERMO FISHER SCIENTIFIC INC.; *pg.* 1602, *pg.* 61
PRO RELEASE - Golf Products - FEEL GOLF CO., INC.; *pg.* 1834, *pg.* 465
PRO-RELIEF - Food Supplement - ORANGE PEEL ENTERPRISES, INC.; *pg.* 1028, *pg.* 477
PRO-RELIEF+ - Vitamins - ORANGE PEEL ENTERPRISES, INC.; *pg.* 1028, *pg.* 477
PRO-ROCKER - Tools - VAUGHAN & BUSHNELL MANUFACTURING COMPANY, INC.; *pg.* 1066, *pg.* 616
PRO-SA - Medical Equipment - INVACARE CORPORATION; *pg.* 1546, *pg.* 1451
PRO-SEAL - Sealants - PPG AEROSPACE; *pg.* 1178, *pg.* 290
PRO-SEAL - Coating Product - PPG INDUSTRIES, INC.; *pg.* 1445, *pg.* 1579
PRO SEAL - Adhesive Product - SUPER GLUE CORPORATION; *pg.* 1183, *pg.* 187
PRO SERIES - Torch Handle - THE HARRIS PRODUCTS GROUP; *pg.* 1345, *pg.* 533
PRO SERIES - Baseball Glove - HILLERICH & BRADSBY CO., INC.; *pg.* 1836, *pg.* 576
PRO SERIES - Furniture - IAC INDUSTRIES, INC.; *pg.* 929, *pg.* 48
PRO SERIES - Pump Product - IDEX CORPORATION; *pg.* 1347, *pg.* 623
PRO SERIES - Printed Circuitboard - IMAGINATION TECHNOLOGIES; *pg.* 412, *pg.* 285
PRO SERIES - Padlocks - MASTER LOCK COMPANY LLC; *pg.* 1055, *pg.* 1884
PRO SERIES - Stock Framed Cabinetry - NORCRAFT HOLDINGS, LP; *pg.* 100, *pg.* 921
PRO-SERIES - Window - ODL INCORPORATED; *pg.* 101, *pg.* 914
PRO SERIES - Volleyball Net - SCHOOL-TECH, INC.; *pg.* 1844, *pg.* 866
PRO SERIES - Tools - TRACTOR SUPPLY COMPANY; *pg.* 708, *pg.* 1627
PRO SERVICES - Metal Pump - GOULDS PUMPS, INCORPORATED; *pg.* 1342, *pg.* 1341
PRO-SET - Software - ROCKWELL AUTOMATION, INC.; *pg.* 668, *pg.* 1880
PRO-SHARP - Pencil Sharpener - C.H. HANSON COMPANY; *pg.* 1322, *pg.* 636
PRO-SHOT - Animal Safety Product - NEOGEN CORPORATION; *pg.* 883, *pg.* 896
PRO SLUGGER - Baseball Bat - HILLERICH & BRADSBY CO., INC.; *pg.* 1836, *pg.* 576
PRO-SPEC - Single & Multi-Viscosity Oils - TEXAS REFINERY CORP.; *pg.* 986, *pg.* 1696
PRO SPORT - Bike Locks - MASTER LOCK COMPANY LLC; *pg.* 1055, *pg.* 1884
PRO STANDARD - 3-Tab Roofing Shingles - BUILDING PRODUCTS OF CANADA CORP.; *pg.* 72, *pg.* 1951
PRO-STAT - Medical Product - MEDLINE INDUSTRIES, INC.; *pg.* 1562, *pg.* 635
PRO STOCKLITE - Baseball Bat - HILLERICH & BRADSBY CO., INC.; *pg.* 1836, *pg.* 576
PRO STYLER - Hair Care Product - CONAIR CORPORATION; *pg.* 505, *pg.* 1055
PRO SUPREME - Coating Product - PPG INDUSTRIES, INC.; *pg.* 1445, *pg.* 1579
PRO: SYS - Central System Software Platform - INTERNATIONAL GAME TECHNOLOGY; *pg.* 420, *pg.* 1606
PRO-T - Medical Equipment - INVACARE CORPORATION; *pg.* 1546, *pg.* 1451
PRO TACKS - Ice Skates - REEBOK-CCM HOCKEY, INC.; *pg.* 1844, *pg.* 1960
PRO TALC - Lubricant - MCNETT CORPORATION; *pg.* 1839, *pg.* 1817
PRO-TALK - Publication - EASTMAN KODAK COMPANY; *pg.* 1408, *pg.* 1333
PRO TASKCENTER - Kitchen Product - KOHLER CO.; *pg.* 91, *pg.* 1862
PRO TASKSINK - Kitchen Product - KOHLER CO.; *pg.* 91, *pg.* 1862
PRO TEC - Engineered Buildings - SIOUX STEEL COMPANY; *pg.* 707, *pg.* 1625
PRO TEC - Helmets - VANS, INC.; *pg.* 1821, *pg.* 76
PRO-TECH - Floor Care Product - BISSELL HOMECARE, INC.; *pg.* 52, *pg.* 887
PRO-TECT - Animal Care Product - STRAIGHT ARROW PRODUCTS, INC.; *pg.* 523, *pg.* 1517
PRO-TECTIVE - Filter & Lens - THE TIFFEN COMPANY LLC; *pg.* 1432, *pg.* 1165
PRO-TEK - Film Preservation System - EASTMAN KODAK COMPANY; *pg.* 1408, *pg.* 1333
PRO TITANIUM - Golf Equipment - ACUSHNET COMPANY; *pg.* 1824, *pg.* 818
PRO-TO-GO - Lipstick - AVON PRODUCTS, INC.; *pg.* 500, *pg.* 1198
PRO-TRACKING - Software System - OMNICARE, INC; *pg.* 1578, *pg.* 1418
PRO TRAJECTORY - Golf Equipment - ACUSHNET COMPANY; *pg.* 1824, *pg.* 818
PRO-TUNER - Electronic Kit - EDELBROCK CORPORATION; *pg.* 204, *pg.* 293
PRO V1 - Golf Ball - ACUSHNET COMPANY; *pg.* 1824, *pg.* 818
PRO V1X - Golf Ball - ACUSHNET COMPANY; *pg.* 1824, *pg.* 818
PRO VANTAGE - Coating Product - PPG INDUSTRIES, INC.; *pg.* 1445, *pg.* 1579
PRO WASH - Gun Washers - GRACO, INC.; *pg.* 1342, *pg.* 935
PRO WELD - Glue - SUPER GLUE CORPORATION; *pg.* 1183, *pg.* 187
PRO WICK - Chemical Cleaner Product - TECH SPRAY, L.P.; *pg.* 1183, *pg.* 1659
PRO XS - Fluid Handling System - GRACO, INC.; *pg.* 1342, *pg.* 935
PRO-ZONE - Talking Sports Action Figures & Playsets - PLAYMATES TOYS INC.; *pg.* 965, *pg.* 82
PRO-ZORB - Packaging Product - CASCADES, INC.; *pg.* 73, *pg.* 1950
PRO2 - Pulse Oximetry - CONMED CORPORATION; *pg.* 1517, *pg.* 1347

PRO2GO - Nutritional Supplement - GARDEN OF LIFE, INC.; *pg.* 1532, *pg.* 478
PROACT - Industrial Enzymes - EASTMAN KODAK COMPANY; *pg.* 1408, *pg.* 1333
PROACT - Actuator - WOODWARD, INC.; *pg.* 122, *pg.* 329
PROACTAZYME - Health Care Product - NATURE'S SUNSHINE PRODUCTS, INC.; *pg.* 1571, *pg.* 1754
PROACTIV - Acne Skin Care System - GUTHY-RENKER LLC; *pg.* 289, *pg.* 273
PROACTIVE CONSUMABLES MANAGEME - Software - XEROX CORPORATION; *pg.* 494, *pg.* 365
PROACTIVE PHARMACY CARE - Health Management - CVS HEALTH CORPORATION; *pg.* 1765, *pg.* 1610
PROACTIVE SERVICE DESK PACKAGE - Software - BMC SOFTWARE, INC.; *pg.* 362, *pg.* 1701
PROAD - Video Product - DAKTRONICS, INC.; *pg.* 633, *pg.* 1624
PROADVANTAGE - Fastening System - TEXTRON INC.; *pg.* 235, *pg.* 1607
PROAMATINE - Pharmaceutical Product - IMPAX LABORATORIES, INC.; *pg.* 1544, *pg.* 101
PROANTHENOLS - Nutritional Care Product - LIFEPLUS INTERNATIONAL; *pg.* 1556, *pg.* 29
PROASSURANCE - Liability Insurance for Physicians, Hospitals & Dentists - PROASSURANCE CORPORATION; *pg.* 1214, *pg.* 3
PROAVATAR - Kitchen Product - KOHLER CO.; *pg.* 91, *pg.* 1862
PROBACK - Towel - CROSSTEX INTERNATIONAL INC.; *pg.* 1520, *pg.* 1164
PROBAK - Blades - THE GILLETTE COMPANY; *pg.* 509, *pg.* 795
PROBAK JR. - Blades - THE GILLETTE COMPANY; *pg.* 509, *pg.* 795
PROBALANCE - Nutrition Supplement - NESTLE USA, INC.; *pg.* 883, *pg.* 96
PROBAR - Flowmeter - EMERSON PROCESS MANAGEMENT ROSEMOUNT INC.; *pg.* 1334, *pg.* 920
PROBATCH - Batch Metering Dipense System - GRACO, INC.; *pg.* 1342, *pg.* 935
PROBE - Commercial Lighting - SWIVELIER CO., INC.; *pg.* 1307, *pg.* 1142
PROBE+ - Software - WIND RIVER SYSTEMS, INC.; *pg.* 493, *pg.* 38
PROBEACON - Receiver - TRIMBLE NAVIGATION LIMITED; *pg.* 1384, *pg.* 288
PROBEAM - Electron Beam - KLA-TENCOR CORPORATION; *pg.* 1353, *pg.* 146
PROBECARDMANAGER - Software - KEITHLEY INSTRUMENTS, INC.; *pg.* 1418, *pg.* 1473
PROBELIA - Software - BIO-RAD LABORATORIES, INC.; *pg.* 1504, *pg.* 101
PROBENCH - Bench Scales - AVERY WEIGH-TRONIX, INC.; *pg.* 1315, *pg.* 925
PROBENT - Minerals - MINERALS TECHNOLOGIES INC.; *pg.* 1173, *pg.* 617
PROBIO PCC - Nutritional Supplement - NU SKIN ENTERPRISES, INC.; *pg.* 518, *pg.* 1755
PROBIOTIC DEFENSE - Nutritional Product - NOW HEALTH GROUP, INC.; *pg.* 1576, *pg.* 557
PROBIOTIC ELEVEN - Health Care Product - NATURE'S SUNSHINE PRODUCTS, INC.; *pg.* 1571, *pg.* 1754
PROBIOTICS - Healthcare Product - SWANSON HEALTH PRODUCTS INC.; *pg.* 1600, *pg.* 1397
PROBLEM SOLVED - Tag Line - WILLIS HRH, INC.; *pg.* 1223, *pg.* 1314
PROBLEM SOLVERS - Garden Tools - 1-800-FLOWERS.COM, INC.; *pg.* 1758, *pg.* 1151
THE PROBLEM SOLVERS - Slogan - MAXONS RESTORATIONS; *pg.* 332, *pg.* 1257
PROBLEM SOLVERS - Bicycle Accessories - QUALITY BICYCLE PRODUCTS; *pg.* 1710, *pg.* 918
PROBLER P2 - Spray Gun - COHESANT, INC.; *pg.* 1154, *pg.* 1405
PROBLOCK - Primer - THE SHERWIN-WILLIAMS COMPANY; *pg.* 1447, *pg.* 1435
PROBLUE - Adhesive Melter - NORDSON CORPORATION; *pg.* 1365, *pg.* 1480
PROBOND - Dental Product - DENTSPLY INTERNATIONAL INC.; *pg.* 1522, *pg.* 1596
PROBOND - Glue - ELMER'S PRODUCTS, INC.; *pg.* 1442, *pg.* 1479
PROBOND - Minerals - MINERALS TECHNOLOGIES INC.; *pg.* 1173, *pg.* 617
PROBOND - Molecular Biology Product - THERMO FISHER SCIENTIFIC INC.; *pg.* 1602, *pg.* 61
PROBOX - Seed Handling System - E.I. DU PONT DE NEMOURS & COMPANY; *pg.* 1159, *pg.* 390
PROBUGS - Organic Whole Milk Product - LIFEWAY FOODS, INC.; *pg.* 874, *pg.* 634
PROC - Development Kit - CYPRESS SEMICONDUCTOR CORPORATION; *pg.* 1326, *pg.* 243
PROCALL - Home Care Information Management System - CERNER CORPORATION; *pg.* 1514, *pg.* 981
PROCANBID - Pharmaceutical Product - KING PHARMACEUTICALS, INC.; *pg.* 1553, *pg.* 1627
PROCARDIA - Medicine - PFIZER INC.; *pg.* 1581, *pg.* 1278
PROCARDIA XL - Pharmaceutical Product - PFIZER INC.; *pg.* 1581, *pg.* 1278
PROCARE - Service & Support Program - APPLE INC.; *pg.* 350, *pg.* 73
PROCARE - Orthopedic Product - DJO INCORPORATED; *pg.* 1524, *pg.* 302
PROCART - Turbine Sprayer - GRACO, INC.; *pg.* 1342, *pg.* 935
PROCAST - Electronic Display - DAKTRONICS, INC.; *pg.* 633, *pg.* 1624
PROCAST - Pressed & Monolithic Refractory - RESCO PRODUCTS, INC.; *pg.* 107, *pg.* 1581
PROCASTER - Bait Casting Reels - DAIWA CORPORATION; *pg.* 1832, *pg.* 75
PROCASTER ROJO - Bait Casting Reels - DAIWA CORPORATION; *pg.* 1832, *pg.* 75
PROCASTER TOURNAMENT SERIES - Bait Casting Reels - DAIWA CORPORATION; *pg.* 1832, *pg.* 75
PROCASTER Z - Bait Casting Reels - DAIWA CORPORATION; *pg.* 1832, *pg.* 75
PROCAT - Additive - BASF CATALYSTS LLC; *pg.* 1148, *pg.* 1074
PROCAT - Catalytic Heater - THE COLEMAN COMPANY, INC.; *pg.* 1830, *pg.* 723
PROCEED - Software - BIO-RAD LABORATORIES, INC.; *pg.* 1504, *pg.* 101
PROCEED TO HEALTH ASSESSMENTS - Management Services - PRINCIPAL FINANCIAL GROUP, INC.; *pg.* 796, *pg.* 706
PROCEL - Fabric - W.L. GORE & ASSOCIATES, INC.; *pg.* 122, *pg.* 388
PROCELERANT - Embedded Computer System - RADISYS CORPORATION; *pg.* 458, *pg.* 1498
PROCELL - Batteries & Emergency Lights - DURACELL; *pg.* 635, *pg.* 337
PROCESS - Magazine - VANCE PUBLISHING CORPORATION; *pg.* 1699, *pg.* 627
THE PROCESS ENGINEER - Trade Magazine - ADVANTAGE BUSINESS MEDIA; *pg.* 1613, *pg.* 1116
PROCESS EYE - Software - MKS INSTRUMENTS, INC.; *pg.* 1362, *pg.* 781
PROCESS INSIGHT - Software - CYBEROPTICS CORPORATION; *pg.* 1408, *pg.* 925
PROCESS KLENZ - Process & Research Cleaner - STERIS CORPORATION; *pg.* 1597, *pg.* 1464
PROCESS KNOWLEDGE SYSTEM - Automation System - HONEYWELL INTERNATIONAL INC.; *pg.* 407, *pg.* 1088
PROCESS SENSE - Gas Analyzer - MKS INSTRUMENTS, INC.; *pg.* 1362, *pg.* 781
PROCESS SENTRY - Diagnostics Controller - NORDSON CORPORATION; *pg.* 1365, *pg.* 1480
PROCESS VIEW - Software - SERENA SOFTWARE, INC.; *pg.* 468, *pg.* 192
PROCESS360 - Software - OPENTEXT; *pg.* 450, *pg.* 1665
PROCESSGARD - Filter - ENTEGRIS, INC.; *pg.* 1882, *pg.* 788
PROCESSING BLADE - Software Product - EGENERA, INC.; *pg.* 390, *pg.* 802
PROCESSING CENTER PKI - Online Transaction Security Product - VERISIGN, INC.; *pg.* 488, *pg.* 1799
PROCESSION - Software - BIO-RAD LABORATORIES, INC.; *pg.* 1504, *pg.* 101
PROCESSIT - Software - BIO-RAD LABORATORIES, INC.; *pg.* 1504, *pg.* 101
PROCESSTRAC - Thermal Processing Equipment - SURFACE COMBUSTION, INC.; *pg.* 1077, *pg.* 1462
PROCESSVIEW COMPOSER - Software - SERENA SOFTWARE, INC.; *pg.* 468, *pg.* 192
PROCHIEVE - Pharmaceutical Product - JUNIPER PHARMACEUTICALS; *pg.* 1552, *pg.* 797
PROCHIP DESIGNER - Electronic Design Automation - ATMEL CORPORATION; *pg.* 621, *pg.* 238
PROCHLORPERAZINE - Pharmaceutical Product - G&W LABORATORIES INC.; *pg.* 1532, *pg.* 1123
PROCIDIA - Process Controller - SIEMENS PROCESS INDUSTRIES AND DRIVE; *pg.* 1376, *pg.* 1587
PROCIPHER - Digital Video Product - HARMONIC, INC.; *pg.* 402, *pg.* 246
PROCITE - Film - THE DOW CHEMICAL COMPANY; *pg.* 1157, *pg.* 898
PROCLASSIC - Paint - THE SHERWIN-WILLIAMS COMPANY; *pg.* 1447, *pg.* 1435
PROCLEAN - Solid Imaging Material - 3D SYSTEMS CORPORATION; *pg.* 339, *pg.* 1621
PROCLEAN - Gasoline - CONOCOPHILLIPS; *pg.* 975, *pg.* 1703
PROCLEAN - Protective Apparel - E.I. DU PONT DE NEMOURS & COMPANY; *pg.* 1159, *pg.* 390
PROCLEAN - Cleaning Preparation - STAGESTEP INC.; *pg.* 1688, *pg.* 1570
PROCOAT - Appliance Connectors - BRASSCRAFT MANUFACTURING COMPANY; *pg.* 1043, *pg.* 902
PROCOLOR - Projection Screens - DA-LITE SCREEN COMPANY; *pg.* 632, *pg.* 698
PROCOLOR ACCENTS - Hair Care Product - CONAIR CORPORATION; *pg.* 505, *pg.* 1055
PROCOMM - Software - SYMANTEC CORPORATION; *pg.* 478, *pg.* 161
PROCOMM PLUS - Software - SYMANTEC CORPORATION; *pg.* 478, *pg.* 161
PROCOMP - Turbine Sprayer - GRACO, INC.; *pg.* 1342, *pg.* 935
PROCON - Carbonator Pumps - STANDEX INTERNATIONAL CORPORATION; *pg.* 60, *pg.* 1039
PROCONCRETE - Software - BENTLEY SYSTEMS, INC.; *pg.* 361, *pg.* 1531
PROCONNECT - Wood Flooring Product - ARMSTRONG WORLD INDUSTRIES, INC.; *pg.* 914, *pg.* 1545
PROCONNECT - 4-Port CPU Switch - CISCO SYSTEMS, INC.; *pg.* 372, *pg.* 240
PROCOSA - Nutritional Supplement - USANA HEALTH SCIENCES, INC.; *pg.* 1605, *pg.* 1761
PROCRIT - Healthcare Product - JOHNSON & JOHNSON; *pg.* 1549, *pg.* 1091
PROCROP - Fertilizer - CARGILL LIMITED; *pg.* 1475, *pg.* 1914
PROCTOCORT - Pharmaceutical Product - SALIX PHARMACEUTICALS, INC.; *pg.* 1591, *pg.* 1388
PROCTOR-SILEX - Small Appliances - HAMILTON BEACH BRANDS, INC.; *pg.* 56, *pg.* 1783
PROCURE - Solid Imaging Material - 3D SYSTEMS CORPORATION; *pg.* 339, *pg.* 1621
PROCURE - Supply Chain Information System - CERNER CORPORATION; *pg.* 1514, *pg.* 981
PROCURE - Polymer Product - CHEMTURA CORPORATION; *pg.* 1152, *pg.* 355
PROCUREMENT VISION - Software - SAS INSTITUTE INC.; *pg.* 466, *pg.* 1361
PROCURVE - Networking Product - HEWLETT-PACKARD COMPANY; *pg.* 404, *pg.* 175
PROCYON - Bait Casting Reels - DAIWA CORPORATION; *pg.* 1832, *pg.* 75
PRODASHER - Electronic Sign Display - DAKTRONICS, INC.; *pg.* 633, *pg.* 1624
PRODATA - Software - KLA-TENCOR CORPORATION; *pg.* 1353, *pg.* 146
PRODENTAL - Pet Care Product - PETEDGE; *pg.* 1481, *pg.* 787
PRODERM - Skin Analyzer - NU SKIN ENTERPRISES, INC.; *pg.* 518, *pg.* 1755
PRODETAILER - Automobile Cleaners - ASHLAND INC.; *pg.* 972, *pg.* 726
PRODIGY - Fishing Equipment - CABELA'S INCORPORATED; *pg.* 535, *pg.* 1019
PRODIGY - Furniture - JASPER GROUP; *pg.* 930, *pg.* 691
PRODIGY - Instant Color Selector - NORDSON CORPORATION; *pg.* 1365, *pg.* 1480
PRODIGY - Ice Machine - SCOTSMAN GROUP LLC; *pg.* 1374, *pg.* 665
PRODIGY BRAND - Tires - YOKOHAMA TIRE CORPORATION; *pg.* 1892, *pg.* 94
PRODIGY MATTRESS OVERLAY - Medical Mattress - THE ROHO GROUP; *pg.* 1591, *pg.* 556
PRODISPENSE - Electronic Metering System - GRACO, INC.; *pg.* 1342, *pg.* 935
PRODOS - Operating System Software - APPLE INC.; *pg.* 350, *pg.* 73
PRODRY - Shoes - ACUSHNET COMPANY; *pg.* 1824, *pg.*

818
PRODUCE CONCEPTS - Magazine - VANCE PUBLISHING CORPORATION; *pg.* 1699, *pg.* 627
PRODUCE MERCHANDISING - Magazine - VANCE PUBLISHING CORPORATION; *pg.* 1699, *pg.* 627
PRODUCE PARTNERS - Food Product - MCCORMICK & COMPANY, INCORPORATED; *pg.* 1027, *pg.* 779
PRODUCE SOLUTIONS - Fruit & Vegetable Product - CHIQUITA BRANDS INTERNATIONAL, INC.; *pg.* 847, *pg.* 1365
PRODUCER - Advanced Patterning Film - APPLIED MATERIALS, INC.; *pg.* 618, *pg.* 264
PRODUCER - Carpet - INTERFACE, INC.; *pg.* 695, *pg.* 512
PRODUCER GT - CVD Platform - APPLIED MATERIALS, INC.; *pg.* 618, *pg.* 264
THE PRODUCER ONLINE - Software - THE ROUGH NOTES COMPANY, INC.; *pg.* 1681, *pg.* 675
PRODUCER VIEW - Web Portal - THE HARTFORD FINANCIAL SERVICES GROUP, INC.; *pg.* 1202, *pg.* 352
PRODUCER WORLD - Online Service Center - AETNA INC.; *pg.* 1187, *pg.* 351
THE PRODUCER'S MASTERGUIDE - Directories - NIELSEN BUSINESS MEDIA; *pg.* 1671, *pg.* 1272
PRODUCERS PRIDE - Livestock Feed - TRACTOR SUPPLY COMPANY; *pg.* 708, *pg.* 1627
PRODUCT 19 - Flakes of Toasted Corn, Oats, Wheat & Rice Cereal with Iron & Zinc - KELLOGG COMPANY; *pg.* 831, *pg.* 870
PRODUCT ACCELERATOR - Computer Software - COMPUTER SCIENCES CORPORATION; *pg.* 378, *pg.* 1780
PRODUCT DESIGN & DEVELOPMENT - Trade Magazine - ADVANTAGE BUSINESS MEDIA; *pg.* 1613, *pg.* 1116
PRODUCTION - Aluminum Oxide-Coated Abrasives - 3M COMPANY; *pg.* 1142, *pg.* 956
PRODUCTION MASTER - Crusher Jaws - ESCO CORPORATION; *pg.* 1335, *pg.* 1502
PRODUCTION PAINTER - Brush - THE WOOSTER BRUSH COMPANY; *pg.* 1450, *pg.* 1482
PRODUCTION TECHNOLOGY NEWS - Trade Magazine - ADVANTAGE BUSINESS MEDIA; *pg.* 1613, *pg.* 1116
PRODUCTIVIT - Asset Management Software - DYNTEK, INC.; *pg.* 389, *pg.* 165
PRODUCTIVITY PG - Software - WEBSENSE, INC.; *pg.* 491, *pg.* 210
PRODUCTIVITY PLUS - Service Agreement - COHERENT, INC.; *pg.* 1406, *pg.* 265
PRODUCTIVITY+ - Software - BSQUARE CORPORATION; *pg.* 366, *pg.* 1813
PRODUCTO - Tooling Components - MOORE TOOL COMPANY, INC.; *pg.* 1057, *pg.* 339
PRODUCTS AND ANSWERS THAT WORK - Tag Line - HUBBARD FEEDS INC.; *pg.* 1477, *pg.* 928
PRODUCTS FINISHING - Business to Business Magazine - GARDNER PUBLICATIONS, INC.; *pg.* 1644, *pg.* 1413
PRODUCTS FOR INDUSTRY - Trade Magazine - ADVANTAGE BUSINESS MEDIA; *pg.* 1613, *pg.* 1116
PRODUCTS THAT MAKE LIFE EASIER - Tag Line - NORM THOMPSON OUTFITTERS INC.; *pg.* 1780, *pg.* 1498
PRODUCTS UNLIMITED - Electronic Component Product - TE CONNECTIVITY LTD.; *pg.* 677, *pg.* 1515
PRODUCTVIEW - Software - PARAMETRIC TECHNOLOGY CORPORATION; *pg.* 452, *pg.* 835
PRODYN - Software - INSTRON CORPORATION; *pg.* 1349, *pg.* 839
PROEAR - Ear Cleaner - PETEDGE; *pg.* 1481, *pg.* 787
PROENGINEER WILDFIRE - Software - PARAMETRIC TECHNOLOGY CORPORATION; *pg.* 452, *pg.* 835
PROEXTREME - Beauty Product - AVON PRODUCTS, INC.; *pg.* 500, *pg.* 1198
PROEYE - Tear Stain Remover - PETEDGE; *pg.* 1481, *pg.* 787
PROFENCE - Electronic Sign Display - DAKTRONICS, INC.; *pg.* 633, *pg.* 1624
PROFES - Software - ASPEN TECHNOLOGY, INC.; *pg.* 354, *pg.* 804
PROFESSIONAL - Workstation Accessory - ALLSOP, INC.; *pg.* 347, *pg.* 1817
PROFESSIONAL - Software - PITNEY BOWES SOFTWARE INC.; *pg.* 455, *pg.* 1346
PROFESSIONAL - Ratchets - SK HAND TOOL CORPORATION; *pg.* 1062, *pg.* 663
PROFESSIONAL & CONSULTING SERVICES - Software - TELLABS, INC.; *pg.* 678, *pg.* 637
PROFESSIONAL BAKEWARE FROM CALPHALON - Bakeware - CALPHALON CORPORATION; *pg.* 1121, *pg.* 1470
PROFESSIONAL COLLECTION - Photo Prints for Professionals - EASTMAN KODAK COMPANY; *pg.* 1408, *pg.* 1333
PROFESSIONAL DOOR DEALER - Publication - INFORMA EXHIBITIONS LLC; *pg.* 1653, *pg.* 17
PROFESSIONAL ELECTROL - Electric Screen - DA-LITE SCREEN COMPANY; *pg.* 632, *pg.* 698
PROFESSIONAL HORSEMAN'S SUPPLY - Equipment & Accessories - DOVER SADDLERY, INC.; *pg.* 1833, *pg.* 829
PROFESSIONAL INVESTOR INSIGHT - Online Buy-Side Research - STANDARD & POOR'S RATINGS SERVICES; *pg.* 805, *pg.* 1296
PROFESSIONAL LAPTOP - Briefcase - SANTA FE LEATHER CORPORATION; *pg.* 12, *pg.* 1059
PROFESSIONAL LUXE - Steam Iron - ROWENTA (USA), INC.; *pg.* 60, *pg.* 1084
PROFESSIONAL NONSTICK FROM CALPHALON - Cookware - CALPHALON CORPORATION; *pg.* 1121, *pg.* 1470
PROFESSIONAL PARTS PEOPLE - Tagline - O'REILLY AUTOMOTIVE, INC.; *pg.* 214, *pg.* 1006
PROFESSIONAL PLUS - Cleaning Product - RUBBERMAID HOME PRODUCTS; *pg.* 1138, *pg.* 1453
THE PROFESSIONAL PORTFOLIO - Business Management Solutions - ADVENT SOFTWARE, INC.; *pg.* 345, *pg.* 211
PROFESSIONAL PROTECTOR PLAN - Insurance Package Program - BROWN & BROWN, INC.; *pg.* 1196, *pg.* 419
THE PROFESSIONAL PROTECTOR PLAN - Insurance Package Program - BROWN & BROWN, INC.; *pg.* 1196, *pg.* 419
PROFESSIONAL SALADSHOOTER PLUS - Electric Slicer & Shredder - NATIONAL PRESTO INDUSTRIES, INC; *pg.* 1128, *pg.* 1857
PROFESSIONAL SERVICES PLANS - Insurance Package Program - BROWN & BROWN, INC.; *pg.* 1196, *pg.* 419
PROFESSIONAL SNO-THROS - Lawn Product - ARIENS COMPANY INC.; *pg.* 700, *pg.* 1855
PROFESSIONAL STAFFING - Tagline - KFORCE INC.; *pg.* 1261, *pg.* 473
PROFESSIONAL STAINLESS FROM CALPHALON - Cookware - CALPHALON CORPORATION; *pg.* 1121, *pg.* 1470
PROFESSIONAL STRENGTH LIQUID-PLUMR - Gel - THE CLOROX COMPANY; *pg.* 327, *pg.* 169
THE PROFESSIONALS. CHOICE. - Slogan - AEP INDUSTRIES INC.; *pg.* 1878, *pg.* 1085
PROFESSIONALS DEMAND LITTLE WONDER. SHOULDN'T YOU? - Slogan - SCHILLER-PFEIFFER, INC.; *pg.* 1061, *pg.* 1587
THE PROFESSIONALS' EDGE - Slogan - SIMONDS INTERNATIONAL CORPORATION; *pg.* 1376, *pg.* 819
PROFESSIONALS GROUP - Liability Insurance for Physicians, Hospitals & Dentists - PROASSURANCE CORPORATION; *pg.* 1214, *pg.* 3
PROFESSOR ZOOM - Character - DC COMICS, INC.; *pg.* 1633, *pg.* 1221
PROFIBUS - Sensor - EMERSON PROCESS MANAGEMENT ROSEMOUNT INC.; *pg.* 1334, *pg.* 920
PROFIBUS - Software - MKS INSTRUMENTS, INC.; *pg.* 1362, *pg.* 781
PROFICY - Automation & Production Software - GE INTELLIGENT PLATFORMS; *pg.* 1339, *pg.* 1777
PROFILATED - Screwdriver - KLEIN TOOLS INC.; *pg.* 1052, *pg.* 627
PROFILE - Hearing Aid - BELTONE ELECTRONICS LLC; *pg.* 1503, *pg.* 614
PROFILE - Endodonic Instrument - DENTSPLY INTERNATIONAL INC.; *pg.* 1522, *pg.* 1596
PROFILE - Software - FIDELITY NATIONAL INFORMATION SERVICES; *pg.* 397, *pg.* 1549
PROFILE - Carpet - INTERFACE, INC.; *pg.* 695, *pg.* 512
PROFILE - Furniture - JASPER GROUP; *pg.* 930, *pg.* 691
PROFILE - Bath Product - KOHLER CO.; *pg.* 91, *pg.* 1862
PROFILE - Furniture - LA-Z-BOY INCORPORATED; *pg.* 932, *pg.* 901
PROFILE - Diagnostic Product - MEDTOX SCIENTIFIC, INC.; *pg.* 1422, *pg.* 962
PROFILE - Filter Cartridge - PALL CORPORATION; *pg.* 232, *pg.* 1323
PROFILE ARCTICA - Refrigerators - GENERAL ELECTRIC COMPANY; *pg.* 1297, *pg.* 347
PROFILE FOR WINDOWS - Software - FIDELITY NATIONAL INFORMATION SERVICES; *pg.* 397, *pg.* 1549
PROFILE.21 - Logistics Software - ASPEN TECHNOLOGY, INC.; *pg.* 354, *pg.* 804
PROFILEIT - Software - BIO-RAD LABORATORIES, INC.; *pg.* 1504, *pg.* 101
PROFILEMAKER5 - Software - X-RITE, INCORPORATED; *pg.* 1437, *pg.* 891
PROFILER - Truck Equipment - AMERICAN VAN EQUIPMENT INC.; *pg.* 199, *pg.* 1078
PROFILER - Electrosurgical Devices - ANGIODYNAMICS, INC.; *pg.* 1495, *pg.* 1173
PROFILER - Software - AUTONOMY, INC.; *pg.* 358, *pg.* 212
PROFILER - Off-Line Film Gauging System - MOCON, INC.; *pg.* 1363, *pg.* 940
PROFILER TARGET IDENTIFICATION - Manual - XEROX CORPORATION; *pg.* 494, *pg.* 365
PROFILES - Paint And Stain Product - BENJAMIN MOORE & CO.; *pg.* 1440, *pg.* 1085
PROFILES - Personal Care Electrical Product - HELEN OF TROY L.P.; *pg.* 511, *pg.* 1692
PROFILINK - Software - ACRISON, INC.; *pg.* 1310, *pg.* 1087
PROFILL CORP. - Fluid Handling System - GRACO, INC.; *pg.* 1342, *pg.* 935
PROFINIA - Software - BIO-RAD LABORATORIES, INC.; *pg.* 1504, *pg.* 101
PROFINISH - Snap-Tite & Easy Glue Pre-Painted Model Kits - REVELL; *pg.* 966, *pg.* 611
PROFINISH - Laminating System - VARITRONICS, LLC; *pg.* 487, *pg.* 954
PROFINITY - Software - BIO-RAD LABORATORIES, INC.; *pg.* 1504, *pg.* 101
PROFINITY EXACT - Software - BIO-RAD LABORATORIES, INC.; *pg.* 1504, *pg.* 101
PROFIRE EXCEL - Imaging Technology for CTP & DI - PRESSTEK LLC; *pg.* 1678, *pg.* 1034
PROFIREF - Robotic Product - HAMILTON CO., INC.; *pg.* 1415, *pg.* 1031
PROFIT - Patient Accounting Solution for Healthcare Professionals - CERNER CORPORATION; *pg.* 1514, *pg.* 981
PROFIT - Software System - HONEYWELL INTERNATIONAL INC.; *pg.* 407, *pg.* 1088
PROFIT FROM OUR KNOWLEDGE - Slogan - GUIDELINE, INC.; *pg.* 402, *pg.* 1237
PROFIT STRIP - Packaging Configuration for Batteries - EASTMAN KODAK COMPANY; *pg.* 1408, *pg.* 1333
PROFITACCELERATOR - Software - XEROX CORPORATION; *pg.* 494, *pg.* 365
PROFIT$MAKER - Portable Hydraulic Punch Press - KAWNEER COMPANY, INC.; *pg.* 90, *pg.* 537
PROFITMAX - Software System - HONEYWELL INTERNATIONAL INC.; *pg.* 407, *pg.* 1088
PROFITQUICK - Software - XEROX CORPORATION; *pg.* 494, *pg.* 365
PROFITRODE - Robotic Product - HAMILTON CO., INC.; *pg.* 1415, *pg.* 1031
PROFITS IN EVERY DEPARTMENT - Program - DAUBERT INDUSTRIES, INC.; *pg.* 1155, *pg.* 561
PROFIX - Animal Safety Product - NEOGEN CORPORATION; *pg.* 883, *pg.* 896
PROFLAVANOL - Nutritional Supplement - USANA HEALTH SCIENCES, INC.; *pg.* 1605, *pg.* 1761
PROFLAVANOL-T - Health Care Product - USANA HEALTH SCIENCES, INC.; *pg.* 1605, *pg.* 1761
PROFLEX - Glove - ALIMED, INC.; *pg.* 1490, *pg.* 816
PROFLEX - Bath Product - KOHLER CO.; *pg.* 91, *pg.* 1862
PROFLEX - Animal Safety Product - NEOGEN CORPORATION; *pg.* 883, *pg.* 896
PROFLEX - Packaging Product - PACTIV CORPORATION; *pg.* 1466, *pg.* 624
PROFLOW - Poured Floor Underlayment - USG CORPORATION; *pg.* 118, *pg.* 594
PROFLOW - Kitchen Appliance - VIKING RANGE CORPORATION; *pg.* 61, *pg.* 968
PROFLOWERS - Perishable Product - PROVIDE COMMERCE, INC.; *pg.* 1276, *pg.* 206
PROFNET - Newspaper - PR NEWSWIRE ASSOCIATION LLC; *pg.* 1678, *pg.* 1283
PROFORCE - Motor Oil & Lubricants - J.D. STREETT & CO., INC.; *pg.* 980, *pg.* 988
PROFORE - 4-Layer Bandage System - ALIMED, INC.; *pg.* 1490, *pg.* 816
PROFORE - Medical & Aesthetic Product - DYNATRONICS CORPORATION; *pg.* 1526, *pg.* 1757
PROFORM - Apparel - OAKLEY, INC.; *pg.* 1840, *pg.* 86

First page reference indicates Business Class Edition
Second page reference indicates Geographic Edition

PROFORM CS - Bakery Product - MALLET & COMPANY, INC.; pg. 875, pg. 1521

PROFORMA - Medical Equipment - CONMED CORPORATION; pg. 1517, pg. 1347

PROFORMA - Semiconductor Product - MECHANICAL TECHNOLOGY, INCORPORATED; pg. 1422, pg. 1137

PROFORMA 300 - Wafer Thickness Gauge - MTI INSTRUMENTS INC.; pg. 658, pg. 1137

PROFORMANCE FILMS - Plastics Product - AEP INDUSTRIES INC.; pg. 1878, pg. 1085

PROFORMER - Apparel - OAKLEY, INC.; pg. 1840, pg. 86

PROFRY - Electrical Appliance & Housewares - NATIONAL PRESTO INDUSTRIES, INC; pg. 1128, pg. 1857

PROFUME - Gas Fumigant - DOW AGROSCIENCES LLC; pg. 1156, pg. 684

PROGAGE - Thickness Tester - THWING-ALBERT INSTRUMENT COMPANY; pg. 1432, pg. 1131

PROGAINE - Hair Care Products - MCNEIL-PPC, INC.; pg. 1560, pg. 1533

PROGATOR - Utility Vehicle - DEERE & COMPANY; pg. 703, pg. 632

PROGEL - Minerals - MINERALS TECHNOLOGIES INC.; pg. 1173, pg. 617

PROGENY - Office Furniture - STEELCASE INC.; pg. 475, pg. 889

PROGESTA-CARE - Nutritional Product - NUTRACEUTICAL INTERNATIONAL CORPORATION; pg. 1576, pg. 1753

PROGESTONE - Health & Beauty Product - DIXIE HEALTH, INC.; pg. 1524, pg. 535

PROGESTONE-900 - Progesterone Cream - DIXIE HEALTH, INC.; pg. 1524, pg. 535

PROGESTONE HP - Moisturizing Cream for Young Women Experiencing PMS Symptoms - DIXIE HEALTH, INC.; pg. 1524, pg. 535

PROGESTONE TEN - Moisturizing Cream for Stubborn PMS & Menopause Symptoms - DIXIE HEALTH, INC.; pg. 1524, pg. 535

PROGLAZE - Roofing Material - TREMCO INCORPORATED; pg. 116, pg. 1405

PROGLO - Shampoo - PETEDGE; pg. 1481, pg. 787

PROGLYDE - Glycol - THE DOW CHEMICAL COMPANY; pg. 1157, pg. 898

PROGRAM MANAGEMENT - Global Services - SONUS NETWORKS INC.; pg. 1281, pg. 858

PROGRAM PLUS - Financial Services - FEDERAL HOME LOAN MORTGAGE CORPORATION; pg. 751, pg. 1790

PROGRAM TABLETS - Pet Medication - PETMED EXPRESS, INC.; pg. 1781, pg. 460

PROGRAMFINDER - Software - CERC; pg. 990, pg. 369

PROGRAMMABLE MATCHING ACCELERATOR - Software - 3M; pg. 339, pg. 179

PROGRAMMABLE SERIAL INTERFACE - Software - CYPRESS SEMICONDUCTOR CORPORATION; pg. 1326, pg. 243

PROGRAMMER'S PARADISE - Software, Systems & Services Reseller - WAYSIDE TECHNOLOGY GROUP, INC.; pg. 491, pg. 1121

PROGRAMMING ON AIR & ONLINE! - Tag Line - BRS MEDIA INC.; pg. 1233, pg. 214

PROGRASP - Forceps - INTUITIVE SURGICAL, INC.; pg. 1546, pg. 286

PROGRESS ACTIONAL - Client Security Enforcement - PROGRESS SOFTWARE CORPORATION; pg. 457, pg. 786

PROGRESS ACTIONAL FLEX POINT FOR SONIC - Governance Integration Module - PROGRESS SOFTWARE CORPORATION; pg. 457, pg. 786

PROGRESS APAMA - Cameron Fix Adapter - PROGRESS SOFTWARE CORPORATION; pg. 457, pg. 786

PROGRESS APPSALIVE - Software - PROGRESS SOFTWARE CORPORATION; pg. 457, pg. 786

PROGRESS ASPEN - Software - PROGRESS SOFTWARE CORPORATION; pg. 457, pg. 786

PROGRESS BUSINESSEDGE - Software - PROGRESS SOFTWARE CORPORATION; pg. 457, pg. 786

PROGRESS DATAXTEND - Data Integration Tool - PROGRESS SOFTWARE CORPORATION; pg. 457, pg. 786

PROGRESS EMPOWERMENT CENTER - Software - PROGRESS SOFTWARE CORPORATION; pg. 457, pg. 786

PROGRESS INTELLISTREAM - Software - PROGRESS SOFTWARE CORPORATION; pg. 457, pg. 786

PROGRESS LIGHTING - Lighting - HUBBELL INCORPORATED; pg. 1299, pg. 370

PROGRESS OBJECTSTORE - Activex Tool Kit - PROGRESS SOFTWARE CORPORATION; pg. 457, pg. 786

PROGRESS OPENEDGE - Workgroup Rdbms - PROGRESS SOFTWARE CORPORATION; pg. 457, pg. 786

PROGRESS POSSE - Software - PROGRESS SOFTWARE CORPORATION; pg. 457, pg. 786

PROGRESS POSSENET - Software - PROGRESS SOFTWARE CORPORATION; pg. 457, pg. 786

PROGRESS PRO VISION - Software - PROGRESS SOFTWARE CORPORATION; pg. 457, pg. 786

PROGRESS PS SELECT - Software - PROGRESS SOFTWARE CORPORATION; pg. 457, pg. 786

PROGRESS RESULTS - Software - PROGRESS SOFTWARE CORPORATION; pg. 457, pg. 786

PROGRESS SOFTWARE BUSINESS MAKING PROGRESS - Software - PROGRESS SOFTWARE CORPORATION; pg. 457, pg. 786

PROGRESS SOFTWARE DEVELOPERS NETWORK - Software - PROGRESS SOFTWARE CORPORATION; pg. 457, pg. 786

PROGRESS SONICMQ CLIENT BRIDGE - Software - PROGRESS SOFTWARE CORPORATION; pg. 457, pg. 786

PROGRESS SONICMQ CLIENT PLUS - Software - PROGRESS SOFTWARE CORPORATION; pg. 457, pg. 786

PROGRESS SONICMQ .NET CLIENT - Software - PROGRESS SOFTWARE CORPORATION; pg. 457, pg. 786

PROGRESS SONICMQ RESOURCE ADAPTERS - Software - PROGRESS SOFTWARE CORPORATION; pg. 457, pg. 786

PROGRESS SPEEDSCRIPT - Software - PROGRESS SOFTWARE CORPORATION; pg. 457, pg. 786

PROGRESS STORMGLASS - Software - PROGRESS SOFTWARE CORPORATION; pg. 457, pg. 786

PROGRESS WEBSPEED - Transaction Server - PROGRESS SOFTWARE CORPORATION; pg. 457, pg. 786

PROGRESSION - Carpet - BEAULIEU GROUP, LLC; pg. 917, pg. 529

PROGRESSIONS - Rug - COURISTAN INC.; pg. 921, pg. 1067

PROGRESSIONS - Hair Salons - REGIS CORPORATION; pg. 521, pg. 941

PROGRESSIVE - Multi-Game Table - SCHOOL-TECH, INC.; pg. 1844, pg. 866

PROGRESSIVE - Ceramic, Glass, Stone Tiles & Slabs - WALKER & ZANGER, INC.; pg. 119, pg. 281

PROGRESSIVE - Implant Product - ZIMMER BIOMET HOLDINGS, INC.; pg. 1611, pg. 699

PROGRESSIVE BAKER - Flour - CARGILL LIMITED; pg. 1475, pg. 1914

PROGRESSIVE ELECTRONICS - Telecommunication Installation, Maintenance & Testing - TEXTRON INC.; pg. 235, pg. 1607

PROGRESSIVE HIP SYSTEM - Hip Product - ZIMMER BIOMET HOLDINGS, INC.; pg. 1611, pg. 699

PROGRESSIVE STREAK - Video Game - INTERNATIONAL GAME TECHNOLOGY; pg. 957, pg. 1024

PROGRESSO - Soup - GENERAL MILLS, INC.; pg. 828, pg. 933

PROGRIP2 - Masking Product - KELLY-MOORE PAINT COMPANY, INC.; pg. 1443, pg. 198

PROGUARD - Pest Elimination System - ECOLAB INC.; pg. 329, pg. 960

PROGUARD - Masking Product - KELLY-MOORE PAINT COMPANY, INC.; pg. 1443, pg. 198

PROGUARD - Vinyl Skirting - NORTEK, INC.; pg. 100, pg. 1607

PROGUIDE - Medical Apparatus - MAQUET; pg. 1558, pg. 1082

PROGUN - Pressed & Monolithic Refractory - RESCO PRODUCTS, INC.; pg. 107, pg. 1581

PROHEART - Canine Heatworm Prevention Preparation - PFIZER INC.; pg. 1581, pg. 1278

PROHEAT - Deep Cleaner - BISSELL HOMECARE, INC.; pg. 52, pg. 887

PROHEAT - Gun - MASTER APPLIANCE CORP.; pg. 1055, pg. 1888

PROHEAT PRO-TECH - Deep Cleaner - BISSELL HOMECARE, INC.; pg. 52, pg. 887

PROINERT - Fire Protection System - FIKE CORPORATION; pg. 1047, pg. 973

PROJAX - Toy & Game - HASBRO, INC.; pg. 954, pg. 1603

PROJECT 70+ - Alloys - CARPENTER TECHNOLOGY CORPORATION; pg. 73, pg. 1584

PROJECT A+ - Promotion - TYSON FOODS, INC.; pg. 902, pg. 35

PROJECT ASSURANCE - Therapeutic Product - PRAHEALTH SCIENCES; pg. 1585, pg. 1388

PROJECT LOGIC - Software - KEPNER-TREGOE, INC.; pg. 424, pg. 1112

PROJECT MANAGEMENT - AN APPROACH THAT REALLY WORKS - Workshop - FRANKLIN COVEY CO.; pg. 1642, pg. 1758

PROJECT-O-STAND - Multi-Purpose Projection Stands - DA-LITE SCREEN COMPANY; pg. 632, pg. 698

PROJECT TURNAROUND - Business Management Consultation - THE CASEY GROUP; pg. 369, pg. 1102

PROJECT YOU - Fitness Video & DVD - BEACHBODY, LLC; pg. 271, pg. 272

PROJECTA - Projection Screens & Support Furniture - DA-LITE SCREEN COMPANY; pg. 632, pg. 698

PROJECT:INSPIRATION - Craft Product - HOB-LOB LIMITED PARTNERSHIP; pg. 552, pg. 1486

PROJECTOR NET - Cutting Edge Projector - INFOCUS CORPORATION; pg. 644, pg. 1503

PROJECTPOINT - Software - AUTODESK INC.; pg. 356, pg. 257

PROJECTS BY DESIGN - Educational Resources - SCHOOL SPECIALTY, INC.; pg. 467, pg. 1860

PROJECTSTATION - Software - BUGOPOLIS, INC.; pg. 366, pg. 278

PROJECTWISE - Software - BENTLEY SYSTEMS, INC.; pg. 361, pg. 1531

PROJECTZONE - Dedicated Server Hosting - BUGOPOLIS, INC.; pg. 366, pg. 278

PROJET - 3-D Production System - 3D SYSTEMS CORPORATION; pg. 339, pg. 1621

PROJO.COM - Website - THE PROVIDENCE JOURNAL; pg. 1678, pg. 1607

PROKLENZ - Alkaline Cleaner - STERIS CORPORATION; pg. 1597, pg. 1464

PROLECTRIC - Thermal Processing Equipment - SURFACE COMBUSTION, INC.; pg. 1077, pg. 1462

PROLENE - Healthcare Product - JOHNSON & JOHNSON; pg. 1549, pg. 1091

PROLIA - Soy Flour - CARGILL, INC.; pg. 845, pg. 965

PROLIANT - Networking Product - HEWLETT-PACKARD COMPANY; pg. 404, pg. 175

PROLIEVE - Medical Device - BOSTON SCIENTIFIC CORPORATION; pg. 1508, pg. 831

PROLIEVE THERMODILATATION - Medical Device - BOSTON SCIENTIFIC CORPORATION; pg. 1508, pg. 831

PROLIFIC - Shoe - AEROGROUP INTERNATIONAL, INC.; pg. 1803, pg. 1055

PROLIFT SCL - Elevator - SAVARIA CONCORD LIFTS INC.; pg. 1592, pg. 1919

PROLIFT VOYAGER - Elevator - SAVARIA CONCORD LIFTS INC.; pg. 1592, pg. 1919

PROLINC - Real Life Beauty Solutions - AMERICAN INTERNATIONAL INDUSTRIES COMPANY; pg. 498, pg. 126

PROLINE - EnduraClad Wood Windows & Patio Doors - PELLA CORPORATION; pg. 104, pg. 711

PROLINE - Software - TRANS-LUX CORPORATION; pg. 681, pg. 365

PROLINE - Cartoning Machinery - TRIANGLE PACKAGE MACHINERY CO.; pg. 1383, pg. 592

PROLINE 900 - Skate - ROLLER DERBY SKATE CORP.; pg. 966, pg. 630

PROLINE-ROADRUNNER - Flash Memory Device - DATA I/O CORPORATION; pg. 382, pg. 1824

PROLINK - Melters - NORDSON CORPORATION; pg. 1365, pg. 1480

PROLITE - Agricultural Product - ARCHER-DANIELS-MIDLAND COMPANY; pg. 825, pg. 565

PROLITE - Upright Vacuum Cleaner - BISSELL HOMECARE, INC.; pg. 52, pg. 887

PROLITE - Cart Bag - DATREK GOLF; pg. 1832, pg. 1801

PROLITE - Power Equipment - ECHO INCORPORATED; pg. 1046, pg. 626

PROLITE - Plastic Packaging Product - POLY PAK AMERICA, INC.; pg. 1467, pg. 138

PROLITE - Ice Skate Blades - REEBOK-CCM HOCKEY, INC.; pg. 1844, pg. 1960

PROLITE 100 - Binder - ARCHER-DANIELS-MIDLAND COMPANY; pg. 825, pg. 565

PROLITE 200 - Isolates - ARCHER-DANIELS-MIDLAND

COMPANY; pg. 825, pg. 565
PROLITE 3 - Ice Skate Blades - REEBOK-CCM HOCKEY, INC.; pg. 1844, pg. 1960
PROLITE LOW FLAVOR - Wheat Gluten - ARCHER-DANIELS-MIDLAND COMPANY; pg. 825, pg. 565
PROLITE SHIPPER - Envelope - POLY PAK AMERICA, INC.; pg. 1467, pg. 138
PROLITH - Optimization Tool - KLA-TENCOR CORPORATION; pg. 1353, pg. 146
PROLMAGE - Printer - VARITRONICS, LLC; pg. 487, pg. 954
PROLOGUE - Microphones & Circuitry - SHURE INCORPORATED; pg. 672, pg. 638
PROLOGUE SUNDAYPLUS - Software - DUKANE CORPORATION; pg. 634, pg. 658
PROLONG - Christmas Tree Preservative - PLANTABBS PRODUCTS COMPANY; pg. 1799, pg. 758
PROLONG - Molecular Probe Product - THERMO FISHER SCIENTIFIC INC.; pg. 1602, pg. 61
PROLUMEN - Medical Device - MAQUET; pg. 1558, pg. 1082
PROLYSTICA - Cleaner - STERIS CORPORATION; pg. 1597, pg. 1464
PROM - Home Permanent, Hand Lotion & Shampoo - THE GILLETTE COMPANY; pg. 509, pg. 795
PROMAC - Nondestructive Testing - MAGNETIC ANALYSIS CORPORATION; pg. 1421, pg. 1158
PROMARK - Stamp - AMERICAN MARKING SYSTEMS, INC.; pg. 349, pg. 1051
PROMASTER - Kitchen Product - KOHLER CO.; pg. 91, pg. 1862
PROMATCH - Resin - THE DOW CHEMICAL COMPANY; pg. 1157, pg. 898
PROMAX - Residential Water Heater - A.O. SMITH CORPORATION; pg. 1313, pg. 1872
PROMAX - Spray Product - SPRAYING SYSTEMS CO.; pg. 1063, pg. 670
PROMEDIA - Electronic Equipment - KLIPSCH GROUP, INC.; pg. 649, pg. 688
PROMENTUM - Embedded Computer System - RADISYS CORPORATION; pg. 458, pg. 1498
PROMEON - Polymers, Hydrogels - MEDTRONIC, INC.; pg. 1564, pg. 939
PROMETA - Integrated Treatment Protocol - CATASYS, INC.; pg. 1514, pg. 127
PROMETA CENTER - Recovery Consulting - CATASYS, INC.; pg. 1514, pg. 127
PROMETHEGAN - Pharmaceutical Product - G&W LABORATORIES INC.; pg. 1532, pg. 1123
PROMETRIC - Educational Publications - THOMSON REUTERS CORPORATION; pg. 1693, pg. 1944
PROMETRIX - Metrology Product - KLA-TENCOR CORPORATION; pg. 1353, pg. 146
PROMETRIX - Line of Precision Belt Driven Block & Cartridge Spindles - SETCO SALES COMPANY; pg. 1061, pg. 1426
PROMIERE - Consulting Services - AVNET, INC.; pg. 622, pg. 15
PROMINENCE - Carpet - BEAULIEU GROUP, LLC; pg. 917, pg. 529
PROMINENCE - Roofing Shingles - OWENS CORNING; pg. 102, pg. 1476
PROMIS - Software - BROOKS AUTOMATION, INC.; pg. 1320, pg. 813
PROMISE - Pharmaceutical Product - ENDO PHARMACEUTICALS HOLDINGS, INC.; pg. 1528, pg. 1549
THE PROMISE - Furniture - HERMAN MILLER, INC.; pg. 926, pg. 913
PROMISE - Vegetable Oil Spread - UNILEVER UNITED STATES, INC.; pg. 904, pg. 1061
PROMISE OF VALUE - Fiber-Optic Network System - CENTURYLINK, INC; pg. 1870, pg. 317
PROMIX - Dental Product - DENTSPLY INTERNATIONAL INC.; pg. 1522, pg. 1596
PROMIX - Plural Component Proportioners - GRACO, INC.; pg. 1342, pg. 935
PROMIX AUTO - Fluid Handling System - GRACO, INC.; pg. 1342, pg. 935
PROMLINK - Software - DATA I/O CORPORATION; pg. 382, pg. 1824
PROMO - Briefcase - SANTA FE LEATHER CORPORATION; pg. 12, pg. 1059
THE PROMO COLLECTION - CD Package - MEGATRAX PRODUCTION MUSIC, INC.; pg. 297, pg. 167
PROMOBILE - Network Storage System - CANDELIS, INC.; pg. 368, pg. 165
PROMOCLIP - Clip - BROWN & BIGELOW, INC.; pg. 1624, pg. 959
PROMOD - Protein Supplement - ABBOTT LABORATORIES; pg. 1484, pg. 551
PROMODELER - Plastic Model Kits & Modeling Accessories - REVELL; pg. 966, pg. 611
PROMOTE - Nutritional Product - ABBOTT LABORATORIES; pg. 1484, pg. 551
PROMOTE - Feed Applications - CARGILL LIMITED; pg. 1475, pg. 1914
PROMOTE - CRT Therapy - ST. JUDE MEDICAL, INC.; pg. 1596, pg. 963
PROMOTE ACCEL - CRT System - ST. JUDE MEDICAL, INC.; pg. 1596, pg. 963
PROMOTION WATCH - Promotion Security & Accountability Services - VALASSIS COMMUNICATIONS, INC.; pg. 1287, pg. 897
PROMOTIONS IN PLASTIC - Tagline - PILGRIM PLASTIC PRODUCTS COMPANY; pg. 1887, pg. 803
PROMOTOR - Hair Dryer & Hair Clipper - ANDIS COMPANY; pg. 498, pg. 1895
PROMOUNT - TV & VCR Mounting Systems - LUXOR CORP.; pg. 428, pg. 666
PROMOWALL - Electronic Display System - TRANS-LUX CORPORATION; pg. 681, pg. 365
PROMPT L-POP - Dental Adhesive System - 3M COMPANY; pg. 1142, pg. 956
PRONATIONAL - Liability Insurance for Physicians, Hospitals & Dentists - PROASSURANCE CORPORATION; pg. 1214, pg. 3
PRONEA 6 I - Advanced Photo System SLR Camera - NIKON INC.; pg. 1424, pg. 1181
PRONGHORN - Footwear - LACROSSE FOOTWEAR, INC.; pg. 1811, pg. 1503
PRONOVA - Healthcare Product - JOHNSON & JOHNSON; pg. 1549, pg. 1091
PRONTO - Cleaner - BIRKO CORPORATION; pg. 1149, pg. 332
PRONTO - Metal Building System - BUTLER MANUFACTURING COMPANY; pg. 72, pg. 981
PRONTO - Wheelchair - INVACARE CORPORATION; pg. 1546, pg. 1451
PRONTO - Homeowner Product - PBI/GORDON CORPORATION; pg. 1176, pg. 985
PRONTO - Home Cleaner - S.C. JOHNSON & SON, INC.; pg. 334, pg. 1889
PRONTO - Medical Device - VASCULAR SOLUTIONS, INC.; pg. 1434, pg. 946
PRONTO BIG N' TUF - Farm & Ranch Product - PBI/GORDON CORPORATION; pg. 1176, pg. 985
PRONTO BIG N' TUF - Weed & Grass Killer - TRACTOR SUPPLY COMPANY; pg. 708, pg. 1627
PRONTO LP - Extraction Catheter - VASCULAR SOLUTIONS, INC.; pg. 1434, pg. 946
PRONTO PROGRAM - Office Furniture - JOFCO INC.; pg. 931, pg. 691
PRONTO PUP MIX - Coating Mix for Hot Dogs - GOLD MEDAL PRODUCTS CO.; pg. 55, pg. 1414
PRONTO-SHORT - Catheter - VASCULAR SOLUTIONS, INC.; pg. 1434, pg. 946
PRONTO UOMO - Apparels - THE MEN'S WEARHOUSE, INC.; pg. 44, pg. 1711
PRONTO.COM - Online Services - IAC/INTERACTIVECORP; pg. 292, pg. 1242
PRONTOW - Automatic Guided Vehicles, Towing - DAIFUKU WEBB; pg. 1327, pg. 885
PROO - Brush - THE WOOSTER BRUSH COMPANY; pg. 1450, pg. 1482
PROOF PERFECT - Pizza Dough - THE SCHWAN FOOD COMPANY; pg. 894, pg. 928
PROOFEXPRESS - Software - SCAN-OPTICS, LLC; pg. 467, pg. 354
PROOFREAD - Machine Vision System - COGNEX CORPORATION; pg. 1406, pg. 834
PROOFWRITER - Online Writing Tool - EDUCATIONAL TESTING SERVICE INC.; pg. 1394, pg. 1111
PROPACK DATA - Software - ROCKWELL AUTOMATION, INC.; pg. 668, pg. 1880
PROPADDLE - Power Equipment - ECHO INCORPORATED; pg. 1046, pg. 626
PROPAFOAM - Packaging Product - PACTIV CORPORATION; pg. 1466, pg. 624
PROPAK - Extrusion Die - DAVIS-STANDARD LLC; pg. 1328, pg. 368
PROPAK - Receiver - NOVATEL INC.; pg. 1424, pg. 1904
PROPAK - Food Product - SHAMROCK FOODS COMPANY; pg. 895, pg. 20
PROPANE - Software - BROADCOM CORPORATION; pg. 364, pg. 108
PROPANEL - Furniture - BUSH INDUSTRIES INC.; pg. 919, pg. 1170
PROPAQ - Patient Monitor - WELCH ALLYN INC.; pg. 1436, pg. 1342
PROPARTNER - Floor Care Product - BISSELL HOMECARE, INC.; pg. 52, pg. 887
PROPARTNER - Software - TELLABS, INC.; pg. 678, pg. 637
PROPATCH - Soft Tissue Repair Matrix - CRYOLIFE, INC.; pg. 1520, pg. 534
PROPATEN - Vascular Graft Coated - W.L. GORE & ASSOCIATES, INC.; pg. 122, pg. 388
PROPAUSE - Nutritional Supplement - WHITEWING LABS, INC.; pg. 1610, pg. 99
PROPE - Antifreeze - THE DOW CHEMICAL COMPANY; pg. 1157, pg. 898
PROPEL - Propellant & Regulator - BADGER AIR BRUSH COMPANY; pg. 359, pg. 612
PROPEL - Plastic Foam - THE DOW CHEMICAL COMPANY; pg. 1157, pg. 898
PROPEL - Adhesive - H.B. FULLER COMPANY; pg. 1165, pg. 961
PROPEL - Medical Equipment - INVACARE CORPORATION; pg. 1546, pg. 1451
PROPEL - Fortified Water - PEPSICO, INC.; pg. 259, pg. 1327
PROPELL - Chemical Product - SACHEM INC.; pg. 1180, pg. 1665
PROPELLER - Office Furniture - KNOLL, INC.; pg. 425, pg. 1527
PROPELLER - Fan - WESTINGHOUSE LIGHTING CORPORATION; pg. 687, pg. 1571
PROPER CHAIR - Furniture - HERMAN MILLER, INC.; pg. 926, pg. 913
PROPERTY PREDICTR - Scoring Solutions - FAIR ISAAC CORPORATION; pg. 1247, pg. 955
PROPET - Leather Walkers - HABAND COMPANY, INC.; pg. 1772, pg. 1099
PROPET - Shoes - MASON COMPANIES, INC.; pg. 1811, pg. 1856
PROPEX - Plastics Product - AEP INDUSTRIES INC.; pg. 1878, pg. 1085
PROPHECY - Software Used for Color Proofing Systems - EASTMAN KODAK COMPANY; pg. 1408, pg. 1333
PROPHECY - Misses' Sportswear - KELLWOOD COMPANY; pg. 28, pg. 975
PROPHETS - Flower Grower - ARIS HORTICULTURE, INC.; pg. 1793, pg. 1404
PROPILE - Thermal Pile - HELLY-HANSEN (US), INC.; pg. 26, pg. 1813
PROPIMEX-1 - Nutritional Product - ABBOTT LABORATORIES; pg. 1484, pg. 551
PROPINK - Insulating System - OWENS CORNING; pg. 102, pg. 1476
PROPIXEL - Electronic Sign Display - DAKTRONICS, INC.; pg. 633, pg. 1624
PROPLATE - Molecular Probe Product - THERMO FISHER SCIENTIFIC INC.; pg. 1602, pg. 61
PROPLEX - Lubricant - D-A LUBRICANT COMPANY; pg. 975, pg. 693
PROPLEX T - Biopharmaceutical Product - BAXTER INTERNATIONAL INC.; pg. 1499, pg. 599
PROPLUS - Sensor - WATLOW ELECTRIC MANUFACTURING COMPANY; pg. 1078, pg. 1004
PROPMAN - Defense Communication System - ROCKWELL COLLINS, INC.; pg. 234, pg. 702
PROPOFLO - Injectable Anesthetic for Dogs - ABBOTT LABORATORIES; pg. 1484, pg. 551
PROPOFOL - Anesthetic Injection - ABBOTT LABORATORIES; pg. 1484, pg. 551
PROPOFOL - Pharmaceutical Product - BAXTER INTERNATIONAL INC.; pg. 1499, pg. 599
PROPOLYMER - Flashlight - STREAMLIGHT INC.; pg. 1306, pg. 1527
PROPORTIONAL POINT SOURCE - Loudspeaker Technology - IMAX CORPORATION; pg. 1417, pg. 1926
PROPOSAL AUTOMATION SUITE - Software - QVIDIAN; pg. 458, pg. 829
PROPOSALEXPRESS - Software - QVIDIAN; pg. 458, pg. 829

First page reference indicates Business Class Edition
Second page reference indicates Geographic Edition

PROPPER - Surgical, Hospital & Laboratory Supplies - PROPPER MANUFACTURING COMPANY, INC.; *pg.* 1586, *pg.* 1175
PROPPER PLUS - Diagnostic Product - PROPPER MANUFACTURING COMPANY, INC.; *pg.* 1586, *pg.* 1175
PROPPER STAR - Diagnostic Product - PROPPER MANUFACTURING COMPANY, INC.; *pg.* 1586, *pg.* 1175
PROPRINTER - Computer Printers - LEXMARK INTERNATIONAL, INC.; *pg.* 427, *pg.* 730
PROPULSE - Hybrid-Electric Drive - OSHKOSH CORPORATION; *pg.* 187, *pg.* 1885
PROPULSID - Pharmaceutical - JANSSEN PHARMACEUTICA PRODUCTS, L.P.; *pg.* 1548, *pg.* 1125
PROPULSION - Apparel - OAKLEY, INC.; *pg.* 1840, *pg.* 86
PROPYFLEX - PVC-Free Bag - PACTIV CORPORATION; *pg.* 1466, *pg.* 624
PROPYL ZITHATE - Accelerators - R.T. VANDERBILT COMPANY, INC.; *pg.* 1180, *pg.* 364
PROPYLUX - Compression Molded Product - WESTLAKE PLASTICS COMPANY; *pg.* 1892, *pg.* 1548
PROQUATICS - Water Clarifier - PETSMART, INC.; *pg.* 1481, *pg.* 18
PROQUEST - Molecular Biology Product - THERMO FISHER SCIENTIFIC INC.; *pg.* 1602, *pg.* 61
PROQUIN - Pharmaceutical Product - DEPOMED, INC.; *pg.* 1523, *pg.* 143
PRORAIL - Software - DAKTRONICS, INC.; *pg.* 633, *pg.* 1624
PRORECO - Marine Rubber Caulk - PPG AEROSPACE; *pg.* 1178, *pg.* 290
PROROM - Orthopedic Product - DJO INCORPORATED; *pg.* 1524, *pg.* 302
PROS PICK - Water Softening Salt - CARGILL, INC.; *pg.* 845, *pg.* 965
PRO'S PICK - Salt - CARGILL LIMITED; *pg.* 1475, *pg.* 1914
PROSACEA - Pharmaceutical Product - ALVA/AMCO PHARMACAL COMPANIES, INC.; *pg.* 1492, *pg.* 637
PROSAFE - Wireless Networking Product - NETGEAR, INC.; *pg.* 444, *pg.* 247
PROSANTE - Soy Flour - CARGILL, INC.; *pg.* 845, *pg.* 965
PROSANTE PLUS - Soy Flour - CARGILL, INC.; *pg.* 845, *pg.* 965
PROSAS - Synthetic Aperture Sonar Processor - RAYTHEON APPLIED SIGNAL TECHNOLOGY, INC.; *pg.* 667, *pg.* 288
PROSCANARRAY - Microarray Scanner - PERKINELMER, INC.; *pg.* 1426, *pg.* 853
PROSE - Flatware - ONEIDA LTD; *pg.* 1129, *pg.* 1318
PROSEAL - Interior Pigmented Sealer - DUNN-EDWARDS CORPORATION; *pg.* 1442, *pg.* 129
PROSEAL - Wiring Harness Connectors - MASTER APPLIANCE CORP.; *pg.* 1055, *pg.* 1888
PROSECURE - Wireless Networking Product - NETGEAR, INC.; *pg.* 444, *pg.* 247
PROSELECT - Stainless Steel Dishes - PETEDGE; *pg.* 1481, *pg.* 787
PROSERIES - Digital Photo Center - GIANT EAGLE, INC.; *pg.* 1020, *pg.* 1575
PROSERIES - Tax Preparation Software - INTUIT INC.; *pg.* 769, *pg.* 158
PROSERIES - Tackle Box Line - RUBBERMAID HOME PRODUCTS; *pg.* 1138, *pg.* 1453
PROSERIES - Computer Monitor - VIEWSONIC CORPORATION; *pg.* 489, *pg.* 303
PROSHIELD - Protective Apparel - E.I. DU PONT DE NEMOURS & COMPANY; *pg.* 1159, *pg.* 390
PROSHIELD - Corrosion Control Agents - GE WATER & PROCESS TECHNOLOGIES; *pg.* 1339, *pg.* 1588
PROSHINE - Hair Straightener - CONAIR CORPORATION; *pg.* 505, *pg.* 1055
PROSHOT 1 - Brad Nail Gun - ARROW FASTENER COMPANY, INC.; *pg.* 1042, *pg.* 1118
PROSHOT 2 - Narrow Crown Stapler - ARROW FASTENER COMPANY, INC.; *pg.* 1042, *pg.* 1118
PROSHOTS - Studio Software - EASTMAN KODAK COMPANY; *pg.* 1408, *pg.* 1333
PROSITE - Measuring Product - THE L.S. STARRETT COMPANY; *pg.* 1421, *pg.* 783
PROSLIC - Integrated Circuit Product - SILICON LABORATORIES INC.; *pg.* 674, *pg.* 1666
PROSMART - Monitoring System - ITT CORPORATION; *pg.* 1351, *pg.* 1354
PROSOFT - Tissue Technology - HERCULES INCORPORATED; *pg.* 1166, *pg.* 392
PROSOM - Sleep Medication - ABBOTT LABORATORIES; *pg.* 1484, *pg.* 551
PROSOURCE - Protein Supplement Powder - MEDLINE INDUSTRIES, INC.; *pg.* 1562, *pg.* 635
PROSOURCE - Software - SCHLUMBERGER LIMITED; *pg.* 801, *pg.* 1714
PROSPARK - Spark Plug Wire Sets - GENERAL CABLE CORPORATION; *pg.* 83, *pg.* 729
PROSPEC - Marketing System - BALDOR ELECTRIC COMPANY; *pg.* 1316, *pg.* 32
PROSPEC - Museum Grade Track Lighting - LIGHTOLIER; *pg.* 1301, *pg.* 819
PROSPEC - Industrial Safety Eyewear - UVEX SAFETY; *pg.* 1433, *pg.* 1608
PROSPECT FARMS - Pre-Cooked Frozen Chicken - TYSON FOODS, INC.; *pg.* 902, *pg.* 35
PROSPECT RATING SYSTEM - Rating System - BLACKBAUD, INC.; *pg.* 361, *pg.* 1613
PROSPECTOR - Software - NIELSEN AUDIO; *pg.* 446, *pg.* 768
PROSPECTOR - Poppet Valves - NORGREN, INC.; *pg.* 231, *pg.* 333
PROSPECTS - Furniture - HERMAN MILLER, INC.; *pg.* 926, *pg.* 913
PROSPECTUS BUILDER - Software - R.R. DONNELLEY & SONS COMPANY; *pg.* 1682, *pg.* 589
PROSPER - Educational Software - PEARSON ASSESSMENTS; *pg.* 1674, *pg.* 918
PROSPER ASSESSMENT SYSTEM - Educational Software - PEARSON ASSESSMENTS; *pg.* 1674, *pg.* 918
PROSPERITY BANCSHARES - Banking Services - PROSPERITY BANCSHARES, INC.; *pg.* 796, *pg.* 1713
PROSPIN - Medical Equipment - INVACARE CORPORATION; *pg.* 1546, *pg.* 1451
PROSPORT - Beauty Product - AVON PRODUCTS, INC.; *pg.* 500, *pg.* 1198
PROST - Wireless Network Product - AIRSPAN NETWORKS INC.; *pg.* 346, *pg.* 410
PROST-ACTIN - Nutritional Supplement - NATURAL ORGANICS, INC.; *pg.* 1571, *pg.* 1181
PROST-WI-FI - Wireless Network Product - AIRSPAN NETWORKS INC.; *pg.* 346, *pg.* 410
PROSTA-RESPONSE - Vitamin & Herbal Supplement - SOURCE NATURALS; *pg.* 1595, *pg.* 278
PROSTAR - Suture-Mediated Closure - ABBOTT LABORATORIES; *pg.* 1484, *pg.* 551
PROSTAR - Data Sheet - AMERICAN FELT & FILTER COMPANY; *pg.* 1312, *pg.* 1184
PROSTAR - Video Product - DAKTRONICS, INC.; *pg.* 633, *pg.* 1624
PROSTAR - Photo Processing Apparatus & Chemicals - EASTMAN KODAK COMPANY; *pg.* 1408, *pg.* 1333
PROSTAR - Power Boat - MASTERCRAFT BOAT COMPANY LLC; *pg.* 1709, *pg.* 1656
PROSTAR - VHF/UHF FM Antennas - WINEGARD COMPANY; *pg.* 688, *pg.* 702
PROSTAR 1000 - UHF Antenna - WINEGARD COMPANY; *pg.* 688, *pg.* 702
PROSTAR BASKETBALL - Fan - CRAFTMADE INTERNATIONAL, INC.; *pg.* 1295, *pg.* 1670
PROSTARS - Glass Product - PPG INDUSTRIES, INC.; *pg.* 1445, *pg.* 1579
PROSTART - Animal Feed - ARCHER-DANIELS-MIDLAND COMPANY; *pg.* 825, *pg.* 565
PROSTART - Fluid Handling System - GRACO, INC.; *pg.* 1342, *pg.* 935
PROSTATEXCELL - Vitamin & Dietary Supplement - NATROL, INC.; *pg.* 1570, *pg.* 64
PROSTATRON - Medical Device - UROLOGIX, INC.; *pg.* 1604, *pg.* 945
PROSTEEL - Software - BENTLEY SYSTEMS, INC.; *pg.* 361, *pg.* 1531
PROSTIN - Medicine - PFIZER INC.; *pg.* 1581, *pg.* 1278
PROSTIN VR PEDIATRIC - Pharmaceutical Product - PFIZER INC.; *pg.* 1581, *pg.* 1278
PROSTREAM - Digital Video Product - HARMONIC, INC.; *pg.* 402, *pg.* 246
PROSTRETCH - Bathroom Safety Product - ALIMED, INC.; *pg.* 1490, *pg.* 816
PROSTRETCH - Medical & Aesthetic Product - DYNATRONICS CORPORATION; *pg.* 1526, *pg.* 1757
PROSTRIP - Nails - PASLODE; *pg.* 1059, *pg.* 664
PROSTSAFE - Nutritional Supplement - WHITEWING LABS, INC.; *pg.* 1610, *pg.* 99
PROSTSAFE PLUS - Nutritional Supplement - WHITEWING LABS, INC.; *pg.* 1610, *pg.* 99
PROSTYLE - Hair Dryer - ANDIS COMPANY; *pg.* 498, *pg.* 1895
PROSURA - Food Safety Program - G&K SERVICES INC.; *pg.* 693, *pg.* 949
PROSURE - Nutritional Product - ABBOTT LABORATORIES; *pg.* 1484, *pg.* 551
PROSVUE - Urinalysis Workstation - IRIS INTERNATIONAL, INC.; *pg.* 1547, *pg.* 64
PROSWEEP - Power Equipment - ECHO INCORPORATED; *pg.* 1046, *pg.* 626
PROSWEET - Flavor Additives - VIRGINIA DARE EXTRACT CO., INC.; *pg.* 908, *pg.* 1147
PROSYSTEM FX - Software - CCH INC.; *pg.* 1626, *pg.* 653
PROSYSTEM FX OFFICE - Integrated Software Tools Used to Increase Office Productivity - CCH INC.; *pg.* 1626, *pg.* 653
PROT/ELEC - Software - BIO-RAD LABORATORIES, INC.; *pg.* 1504, *pg.* 101
PROTABLE - Scoreboard & Sports Product - DAKTRONICS, INC.; *pg.* 633, *pg.* 1624
PROTACID - Pharmaceutical Ingredient - FMC CORPORATION; *pg.* 1163, *pg.* 1564
PROTAL - Engineered Product And System - SULZER METCO (WESTBURY) INC.; *pg.* 1064, *pg.* 1350
PROTALC - Lubricant & Protectant - MCNETT CORPORATION; *pg.* 1839, *pg.* 1817
PROTAMATE - Healthcare Product - GF HEALTH PRODUCTS, INC.; *pg.* 1535, *pg.* 508
PROTANDIM - Nutritional Supplement - LIFEVANTAGE CORPORATION; *pg.* 1556, *pg.* 1762
PROTAPER - Dental Product - DENTSPLY INTERNATIONAL INC.; *pg.* 1522, *pg.* 1596
PROTEAN - Software - BIO-RAD LABORATORIES, INC.; *pg.* 1504, *pg.* 101
PROTEAN - Remote Control Kit - CONDUCTIX INC., *pg.* 1295, *pg.* 1015
PROTEAR - Tearing Tester - THWING-ALBERT INSTRUMENT COMPANY; *pg.* 1432, *pg.* 1131
PROTEC - Overhead System - LEAR CORPORATION; *pg.* 229, *pg.* 907
PROTEC - Tamper-Evident Closure - SEALED AIR CORPORATION; *pg.* 1468, *pg.* 1058
PROTECDOR - Power Door - RITE-HITE HOLDING CORPORATION; *pg.* 1372, *pg.* 1880
PROTECDOR XL - Power Door - RITE-HITE HOLDING CORPORATION; *pg.* 1372, *pg.* 1880
PROTECH - Security Product - BAE SYSTEMS PRODUCTS GROUP; *pg.* 359, *pg.* 432
PROTECH - Flame Barrier - CARPENTER CO.; *pg.* 920, *pg.* 1801
PROTECH - Closed Circuit Television Equipment - VICON INDUSTRIES, INC.; *pg.* 685, *pg.* 1166
PROTECH - Overspeed Protection System - WOODWARD, INC.; *pg.* 122, *pg.* 329
PROTECRITE - Protective Films - AMERICAN BILTRITE INC.; *pg.* 1878, *pg.* 856
PROTECT - Containment System - CALGON CARBON CORPORATION; *pg.* 1151, *pg.* 1574
PROTECT - Coating - E.I. DU PONT DE NEMOURS & COMPANY; *pg.* 1159, *pg.* 390
PROTECT - Flame Resistant Garment - G&K SERVICES INC.; *pg.* 693, *pg.* 949
PROTECT - Toothbrush with Antibacterial Bristles & Replaceable Heads - SUNSTAR AMERICAS INC.; *pg.* 1599, *pg.* 591
PROTECT-A-BOARD - Strap Protection - CARAUSTAR INDUSTRIES, INC.; *pg.* 1455, *pg.* 525
PROTECT-A-COIL - Strap Protection - CARAUSTAR INDUSTRIES, INC.; *pg.* 1455, *pg.* 525
PROTECT-A-FLEX - Strap Protection - CARAUSTAR INDUSTRIES, INC.; *pg.* 1455, *pg.* 525
PROTECT-A-POOL - Above Ground Fencing - POLYAIR INTER PACK INC.; *pg.* 1467, *pg.* 1941
PROTECT-A-WRAP - Strap Protection - CARAUSTAR INDUSTRIES, INC.; *pg.* 1455, *pg.* 525
PROTECT-O-SHEET - Polyethylene Masking Film - FLEX-O-GLASS, INC.; *pg.* 1457, *pg.* 574
PROTECT THE CORE - Tagline - FGX INTERNATIONAL, INC.; *pg.* 5, *pg.* 1608
PROTECTA - Truck Bed Liners - LANCASTER COLONY CORPORATION; *pg.* 873, *pg.* 1441
PROTECTA-COAT - Pads - ALIMED, INC.; *pg.* 1490, *pg.* 816
PROTECTADRIVE - Drive Assembly System - GEHL COMPANY; *pg.* 1339, *pg.* 1899
PROTECTAIR - Portable Instrument - TSI INCORPORATED; *pg.* 1432, *pg.* 965
PROTECTALL - Healthcare Product - MEDICOOL, INC.; *pg.*

1562, *pg.* 294
PROTECTASSIST - Travel Insurance - TRAVEL GUARD GROUP, INC.; *pg.* 1925, *pg.* 1895
PROTECTING YOUR WORLD FROM THE ELEMENTS - Slogan - FORTIFIBER CORPORATION; *pg.* 83, *pg.* 1021
PROTECTION - Software - CONDUSIV TECHNOLOGIES; *pg.* 379, *pg.* 51
PROTECTION MANAGER - Software - NETAPP, INC.; *pg.* 444, *pg.* 287
PROTECTION PLUS - Medical Product - MEDLINE INDUSTRIES, INC.; *pg.* 1562, *pg.* 635
PROTECTIONPAC - Software - OVERLAND STORAGE, INC.; *pg.* 451, *pg.* 205
PROTECTITNOW! - Security & Law Enforcement Products - MACE SECURITY INTERNATIONAL, INC.; *pg.* 1172, *pg.* 1541
PROTECTIVE BENEFITS COMMUNICATIONS - Insurance Services - PROTECTIVE LIFE CORPORATION; *pg.* 1215, *pg.* 4
PROTECTIVE EQUITY SERVICES - Insurance Services - PROTECTIVE LIFE CORPORATION; *pg.* 1215, *pg.* 4
PROTECTIVE FINANCIAL CORPORATION - Insurance Company - PROTECTIVE LIFE CORPORATION; *pg.* 1215, *pg.* 4
PROTECTIVE LIFE CORPORATION - Insurance Company - PROTECTIVE LIFE CORPORATION; *pg.* 1215, *pg.* 4
PROTECTIVE LIFE INSURANCE COMPANY - Insurance Company - PROTECTIVE LIFE CORPORATION; *pg.* 1215, *pg.* 4
PROTECTIVE VEIL - Lotion - MERLE NORMAN COSMETICS, INC.; *pg.* 517, *pg.* 136
PROTECTME - Shopping Cart Liner - THE BOPPY COMPANY, LLC; *pg.* 20, *pg.* 329
PROTECTNET - Power Protection Product - SCHNEIDER ELECTRIC; *pg.* 467, *pg.* 1609
THE PROTECTOR - Rust Protection - DAUBERT INDUSTRIES, INC.; *pg.* 1155, *pg.* 561
PROTECTOR - Carpet Cushion - DURA UNDERCUSHIONS LTD.; *pg.* 923, *pg.* 1954
THE PROTECTOR - Insurance Policy - STANDARD INSURANCE COMPANY; *pg.* 1217, *pg.* 1506
PROTECTOR - Mobile Law Enforcement - WINNEBAGO INDUSTRIES, INC.; *pg.* 1712, *pg.* 707
PROTECTOR SERIES - Storage Product - PLANO MOLDING COMPANY; *pg.* 1887, *pg.* 652
PROTECTOSEAL PLUS - Safety Storage Cabinet - THE PROTECTOSEAL COMPANY; *pg.* 1370, *pg.* 556
PROTEGE - Organs - ALLEN ORGAN COMPANY; *pg.* 527, *pg.* 1549
PROTEGE - Furniture - ASHLEY FURNITURE INDUSTRIES, INC.; *pg.* 914, *pg.* 1852
PROTEGE - Knife - BUCK KNIVES, INC.; *pg.* 1828, *pg.* 550
PROTEGE - Office Furniture - STEELCASE INC.; *pg.* 475, *pg.* 889
PROTEGE - Ceiling Fan - WESTINGHOUSE LIGHTING CORPORATION; *pg.* 687, *pg.* 1571
PROTEGEL - Robotic Product - HAMILTON CO., INC.; *pg.* 1415, *pg.* 1031
PROTEGENT - Software - SUNGARD DATA SYSTEMS INC.; *pg.* 477, *pg.* 1592
PROTEGO - Purifiers - ENTEGRIS, INC.; *pg.* 1882, *pg.* 788
PROTEGRA - Antioxidant Vitamin & Mineral Supplement Product - ALERE INC.; *pg.* 1488, *pg.* 849
PROTEIN - Entree - IN-N-OUT BURGERS, INC.; *pg.* 1732, *pg.* 111
PROTEIN 29 - Hair Groom - THE STEPHAN COMPANY; *pg.* 1597, *pg.* 426
PROTEIN BERRY PIZZAZZ - Smoothie - JAMBA, INC.; *pg.* 1024, *pg.* 84
PROTEIN BERRY WORKOUT - Fruit Drink - JAMBA, INC.; *pg.* 1024, *pg.* 84
PROTEIN GREENS - Food Supplement - ORANGE PEEL ENTERPRISES, INC.; *pg.* 1028, *pg.* 477
PROTEIN GREENS+ - Vitamins - ORANGE PEEL ENTERPRISES, INC.; *pg.* 1028, *pg.* 477
PROTEINCHIP - Proteomics Research Technologies - BIO-RAD LABORATORIES, INC.; *pg.* 1504, *pg.* 101
PROTEINEER FC - Analytical Component - BRUKER CORPORATION; *pg.* 1511, *pg.* 788
PROTEINEX - Nutritional Product - VICTUS, INC.; *pg.* 1606, *pg.* 447
PROTEK - Coating - BREWER SCIENCE, INC.; *pg.* 1150, *pg.* 989
PROTEK - Plastic Film - TEKRA CORPORATION; *pg.* 1184, *pg.* 1884
PROTEK WRAP - Corrosion Inhibitor - DAUBERT INDUSTRIES, INC.; *pg.* 1155, *pg.* 561
PROTEKTAGARD - Underwear Providing Protection Against Fire & Electrical Hazards - STANFIELD'S LIMITED; *pg.* 48, *pg.* 1917
PROTEKTOR - Fiberglass Tank System - ZCL COMPOSITES INC.; *pg.* 1892, *pg.* 1906
PROTELYTE - Robotic Product - HAMILTON CO., INC.; *pg.* 1415, *pg.* 1031
PROTEMP - Temporization Material - 3M COMPANY; *pg.* 1142, *pg.* 956
PROTEO-C - Health Care Product - USANA HEALTH SCIENCES, INC.; *pg.* 1605, *pg.* 1761
PROTEOME BIOKNOWLEDGE - Library - INCYTE CORPORATION; *pg.* 1545, *pg.* 392
PROTEOME PROFILER - Biological Product - TECHNE CORPORATION; *pg.* 1601, *pg.* 944
PROTEOMELAB - Testing Instrument System - BECKMAN COULTER, INC.; *pg.* 1402, *pg.* 48
PROTEOMEWORKS - Software - BIO-RAD LABORATORIES, INC.; *pg.* 1504, *pg.* 101
PROTEOMINER - Software - BIO-RAD LABORATORIES, INC.; *pg.* 1504, *pg.* 101
PROTEOMWEAVER - Software - BIO-RAD LABORATORIES, INC.; *pg.* 1504, *pg.* 101
PROTEON - Software - BIO-RAD LABORATORIES, INC.; *pg.* 1504, *pg.* 101
PROTEON MANAGER - Software - BIO-RAD LABORATORIES, INC.; *pg.* 1504, *pg.* 101
PROTEOQWEST - Western Blotting Kit - SIGMA-ALDRICH CORPORATION; *pg.* 1181, *pg.* 1003
PROTEOSOLVE-SB - LRS Kit - PRESSURE BIOSCIENCES, INC.; *pg.* 1586, *pg.* 844
PROTERA - Fabric - E.I. DU PONT DE NEMOURS & COMPANY; *pg.* 1159, *pg.* 390
PROTERRA - Personal Care Product - MARIETTA HOSPITALITY; *pg.* 1464, *pg.* 1155
PROTEUMPLUS - Software - BRUKER CORPORATION; *pg.* 1511, *pg.* 788
PROTEUS - Software - CTI GROUP HOLDINGS INC.; *pg.* 381, *pg.* 684
PROTEX - Cobalt Alloy Stent System - SURMODICS, INC.; *pg.* 1600, *pg.* 924
PROTHATCH - Power Equipment - ECHO INCORPORATED; *pg.* 1046, *pg.* 626
PROTIMAX - Specialized Egg Protein - TROUW NUTRITION USA; *pg.* 1482, *pg.* 616
PROTIONE - For Baby Pig Diets - TROUW NUTRITION USA; *pg.* 1482, *pg.* 616
PROTIVITI - Consulting Services - ROBERT HALF INTERNATIONAL INC.; *pg.* 462, *pg.* 145
PROTIVITY - Nutritional Product - RBC LIFE SCIENCES, INC.; *pg.* 1588, *pg.* 1723
PROTO - Industrial Tools - STANLEY BLACK & DECKER, INC.; *pg.* 1063, *pg.* 358
PROTO 1000 - Model Trains - LIFOAM INDUSTRIES INC.; *pg.* 961, *pg.* 772
PROTO 2000 - Model Trains - LIFOAM INDUSTRIES INC.; *pg.* 961, *pg.* 772
PROTO-KUT - Electroluminescence BackLighting Panel - EDMUND INDUSTRIAL OPTICS INC.; *pg.* 1411, *pg.* 1041
PROTO SPEED - Men's Footwear - UNDER ARMOUR, INC.; *pg.* 49, *pg.* 759
PROTOARRAY - Molecular Biology Product - THERMO FISHER SCIENTIFIC INC.; *pg.* 1602, *pg.* 61
PROTOCOL - Refrigeration System - HUSSMANN INTERNATIONAL, INC.; *pg.* 1347, *pg.* 973
PROTOCOL MANAGER - Software - DESPATCH INDUSTRIES; *pg.* 1070, *pg.* 927
PROTOCOL PLUS - Oven - DESPATCH INDUSTRIES; *pg.* 1070, *pg.* 927
PROTOCOLCATCHER - Software - WEBSENSE, INC.; *pg.* 491, *pg.* 210
PROTOFORM - Car Part Accessory - PRO-LINE, INC.; *pg.* 966, *pg.* 45
PROTONIX - Proton Pump Inhibitor - PFIZER INC.; *pg.* 1581, *pg.* 1278
PROTOOL LUBE - Cutting Tool Fluid - LENOX; *pg.* 1053, *pg.* 817
PROTOSLO - Biological Supplies - CAROLINA BIOLOGICAL SUPPLY COMPANY; *pg.* 1513, *pg.* 1359
PROTOTE - Fluid Handling System - GRACO, INC.; *pg.* 1342, *pg.* 935
PROTOTRAK - Software - SOUTHWESTERN INDUSTRIES, INC.; *pg.* 1429, *pg.* 69
PROTOUCH 1000 - Nailcare Product - MEDICOOL, INC.; *pg.* 1562, *pg.* 294
PROTOUR - Video Product - DAKTRONICS, INC.; *pg.* 633, *pg.* 1624
PROTRACK - Internet-Based Trading & Market Data for Professional Retail Brokers - TRACK DATA CORPORATION; *pg.* 1284, *pg.* 1147
PROTRANS CREAM - Natural Progesterone Cream - WHITEWING LABS, INC.; *pg.* 1610, *pg.* 99
PROTROPIN - Human Growth Hormone - GENENTECH, INC.; *pg.* 1533, *pg.* 279
PROUD TO BE AN AMERICAN GIRL - Doll And Toy - AMERICAN GIRL LLC; *pg.* 949, *pg.* 1871
PROUDLY POWERING THE WORLD - Tag Line - TYSON FOODS, INC.; *pg.* 902, *pg.* 35
PROVAL - Brushes - THE SHERWIN-WILLIAMS COMPANY; *pg.* 1447, *pg.* 1435
PROVAL - Property Valuation Software - THOMSON REUTERS TAX & ACCOUNTING; *pg.* 484, *pg.* 905
PROVAL PLUS - Property Valuation Software - THOMSON REUTERS TAX & ACCOUNTING; *pg.* 484, *pg.* 905
PROVANT - Wound Closure System - PROGRESSIVE MEDICAL, INC.; *pg.* 1586, *pg.* 1480
PROVANTAGE - Nutritional Product - RELIV INTERNATIONAL, INC.; *pg.* 1589, *pg.* 975
PROVECTA - Intraoral X-Ray System - AIR TECHNIQUES, INC.; *pg.* 1487, *pg.* 1178
PROVEN BRANDS - Line of Quality Paint & Related Products - PRO GROUP, INC.; *pg.* 1782, *pg.* 331
PROVEN EVERYDAY // PROVEN EVERYWHERE - Slogan - LA-CO INDUSTRIES MARKAL CO., INC.; *pg.* 1170, *pg.* 610
PROVEN MARKETING GROUP - Cabinet Hardware Distributors/Retailers - PRO GROUP, INC.; *pg.* 1782, *pg.* 331
PROVEN PERFORMANCE FROM INNOVATIVE NUTRITION - Slogan - ADM ALLIANCE NUTRITION, INC.; *pg.* 1474, *pg.* 653
PROVEN QUALITY LEADING TECHNOLOGY - Tagline - GRACO, INC.; *pg.* 1342, *pg.* 935
PROVEN SOLUTIONS FOR A GROWING WORLD - Tagline - THE DAVEY TREE EXPERT COMPANY; *pg.* 1794, *pg.* 1456
PROVENAIR - Cylinder - INGERSOLL-RAND COMPANY; *pg.* 1349, *pg.* 1370
PROVENANCE - Furniture - THE COMMERCIAL FURNITURE GROUP; *pg.* 920, *pg.* 994
PROVENANCE - Custom Made Woven Wood Shades - HUNTER DOUGLAS, INC.; *pg.* 928, *pg.* 1320
PROVENCE - Door & Wood Product - CONESTOGA WOOD SPECIALTIES CORP.; *pg.* 921, *pg.* 1527
PROVENGE - Treatment Drug for Prostate Cancer - DENDREON CORPORATION; *pg.* 1522, *pg.* 1835
PROVENTIL - Medicine - MERCK & CO., INC.; *pg.* 1566, *pg.* 1077
PROVERA - Medicine - PFIZER INC.; *pg.* 1581, *pg.* 1278
PROVIDE-A-RIDE - Health Plan & Publication - MEDICA, INC.; *pg.* 1208, *pg.* 949
PROVIDENCE - Lounge Chairs & Textiles - BERNHARDT DESIGN; *pg.* 918, *pg.* 1381
PROVIDENCE - Brick & Tile Product - CHEROKEE BRICK & TILE COMPANY; *pg.* 75, *pg.* 535
PROVIDENCE - Footwear - EASTLAND SHOE CORPORATION; *pg.* 1808, *pg.* 750
PROVIDENCE - Bath Product - KOHLER CO.; *pg.* 91, *pg.* 1862
PROVIDENT BANK - Banking Services - PROVIDENT FINANCIAL HOLDINGS, INC.; *pg.* 796, *pg.* 194
PROVIDENT MUSIC - Christian Record Label - SONY MUSIC ENTERTAINMENT; *pg.* 309, *pg.* 1294
PROVIDING KNOWLEDGE DELIVERING SOLUTIONS - Tagline - VIST FINANCIAL CORP.; *pg.* 818, *pg.* 1596
PROVIDING PROTEIN AND MENU SOLUTIONS - Slogan - QUANTUM FOODS, INC.; *pg.* 891, *pg.* 559
PROVIEW - Digital Video Product - HARMONIC, INC.; *pg.* 402, *pg.* 246
PROVIEW - Bicycle Accessories - SPECIALIZED BICYCLE COMPONENTS, INC.; *pg.* 1711, *pg.* 152
PROVIEWER - Software - PITNEY BOWES SOFTWARE INC.; *pg.* 455, *pg.* 1346
PROVIM ESP - Agricultural Product - ARCHER-DANIELS-MIDLAND COMPANY; *pg.* 825, *pg.* 565
PROVIM ESP VITAL - Gluten - ARCHER-DANIELS-MIDLAND COMPANY; *pg.* 825, *pg.* 565
PROVINCIAL - Bath Product - KOHLER CO.; *pg.* 91, *pg.*

First page reference indicates Business Class Edition
Second page reference indicates Geographic Edition

1862
PROVINCIAL - Lighting Product - WESTINGHOUSE LIGHTING CORPORATION; *pg.* 687, *pg.* 1571
PROVISION - Image Management Solution for Use with Electronic Medical Records - CERNER CORPORATION; *pg.* 1514, *pg.* 981
PROVISION - Industrial Safety Eyewear - UVEX SAFETY; *pg.* 1433, *pg.* 1608
PROVISIONING SOFTWARE - Software - NETAPP, INC.; *pg.* 444, *pg.* 287
PROVISIONS - Office Furniture - HNI CORPORATION; *pg.* 927, *pg.* 709
PROVISTA - Copolymer - EASTMAN CHEMICAL COMPANY; *pg.* 1159, *pg.* 1636
PROVOCATIVE - Spray - ELIZABETH ARDEN, INC.; *pg.* 507, *pg.* 448
PROW - Home Design - LINDAL CEDAR HOMES, INC.; *pg.* 94, *pg.* 1837
PROWAVE 770 - Hair Removal Products - CUTERA, INC.; *pg.* 1521, *pg.* 49
PROWOOD - Wood Product - UNIVERSAL FOREST PRODUCTS, INC.; *pg.* 117, *pg.* 890
PROWRAP - Housewrap - JOHNS MANVILLE CORPORATION; *pg.* 89, *pg.* 320
PROXABRUSH - Toothbrush with Antibacterial Bristles - SUNSTAR AMERICAS INC.; *pg.* 1599, *pg.* 591
PROXACOL - Antiseptic - MCNEIL-PPC, INC.; *pg.* 1560, *pg.* 1533
PROXAPIC - Oral Hygiene Aids - SUNSTAR AMERICAS INC.; *pg.* 1599, *pg.* 591
PROXCISION - Proteomics Gel Cutting Robot - PERKINELMER, INC.; *pg.* 1426, *pg.* 853
PROXI - Chemical Product - ROCHESTER MIDLAND CORPORATION; *pg.* 334, *pg.* 1337
PROXIAS - Application Server - POLYCOM, INC.; *pg.* 664, *pg.* 249
PROXIMA - Digital Projector - INFOCUS CORPORATION; *pg.* 644, *pg.* 1503
PROXIMATE - Surgical Staplers - CARDINAL HEALTH, INC.; *pg.* 1512, *pg.* 1448
PROXIMATE - Healthcare Product - JOHNSON & JOHNSON; *pg.* 1549, *pg.* 1091
PROXIMITY - Wireless Network Product - AIRSPAN NETWORKS INC.; *pg.* 346, *pg.* 410
PROXIMITY - Level Control, Valve Position Indicator - DWYER INSTRUMENTS INC.; *pg.* 1330, *pg.* 694
PROXIMITY DETECTOR - Position Sensor - DWYER INSTRUMENTS INC.; *pg.* 1330, *pg.* 694
PROXIMITY MARK - Magnetic Coupling - DWYER INSTRUMENTS INC.; *pg.* 1330, *pg.* 694
PROXIMITY PLUS - Mount - CHECKPOINT SYSTEMS, INC.; *pg.* 628, *pg.* 1559
PROXIPLATE - Microplates - PERKINELMER, INC.; *pg.* 1426, *pg.* 853
PROXIS - Embolic Protection System - ST. JUDE MEDICAL, INC.; *pg.* 1596, *pg.* 963
PROXPRESS - Proteomic Imaging System - PERKINELMER, INC.; *pg.* 1426, *pg.* 853
PROXPRESSION - Manual Enrichment Kit - PERKINELMER, INC.; *pg.* 1426, *pg.* 853
PROXXXX - Fluid Handling System - GRACO, INC.; *pg.* 1342, *pg.* 935
PROXYAV - Software - BLUE COAT SYSTEMS, INC.; *pg.* 362, *pg.* 284
PROXYSG - Software - BLUE COAT SYSTEMS, INC.; *pg.* 362, *pg.* 284
PROZAC - Pharmaceutical Product - ELI LILLY AND COMPANY; *pg.* 1527, *pg.* 684
PROZAP - Animal Safety Product - NEOGEN CORPORATION; *pg.* 883, *pg.* 896
PROZONE - Environmentally Friendly Air Conditioners & Heat Pumps - RHEEM MANUFACTURING COMPANY; *pg.* 1075, *pg.* 519
PRPC+ - Software - WIND RIVER SYSTEMS, INC.; *pg.* 493, *pg.* 38
PRS - Guitar - PAUL REED SMITH GUITARS; *pg.* 574, *pg.* 779
PRUFCOAT - Industrial Coating - AKZONOBEL DECORATIVE PAINTS U.S.; *pg.* 1439, *pg.* 1474
PRUITT - Medical Device - LEMAITRE VASCULAR, INC.; *pg.* 1555, *pg.* 805
PRUITT-INAHARA - Medical Device - LEMAITRE VASCULAR, INC.; *pg.* 1555, *pg.* 805
PRUSTMAN - Mirror - COMMERCIAL VEHICLE GROUP, INC.; *pg.* 203, *pg.* 1467
PRUV - Lubricant - PENFORD CORPORATION; *pg.* 1177, *pg.* 314
PRYBABY - Bicycle Accessories - SPECIALIZED BICYCLE COMPONENTS, INC.; *pg.* 1711, *pg.* 152
PRYM - Buttons - PRYM CONSUMER USA; *pg.* 698, *pg.* 1622
PS - Corporate Business Forms - THE STANDARD REGISTER COMPANY; *pg.* 473, *pg.* 1446
PS-100 - Power Supply - EMCORE CORPORATION; *pg.* 636, *pg.* 39
PS-1205 - Power Supply - EMCORE CORPORATION; *pg.* 636, *pg.* 39
PS 22 - Closure Liner Sealings Materials - TEKNI-PLEX, INC.; *pg.* 1470, *pg.* 1122
PS 300 - Automated Device Programming System - DATA I/O CORPORATION; *pg.* 382, *pg.* 1824
PS-59 - Systems Integration & Aeronautics - LOCKHEED MARTIN CORPORATION; *pg.* 229, *pg.* 762
PS FINE COLOGNE FOR MEN - Fragrance - ELIZABETH ARDEN, INC.; *pg.* 507, *pg.* 448
PS-SERIES - Programmable Power System Controllers - POWER INTEGRATIONS, INC.; *pg.* 1369, *pg.* 249
PS-SPECK - Molecular Probe Product - THERMO FISHER SCIENTIFIC INC.; *pg.* 1602, *pg.* 61
PS155 MICR - Mid-Volume Digital Printing System - DELPHAX TECHNOLOGIES INC.; *pg.* 386, *pg.* 917
PS75 MICR - Mid-Volume Digital Printing System - DELPHAX TECHNOLOGIES INC.; *pg.* 386, *pg.* 917
PSA - Printer - PRINTRONIX, INC.; *pg.* 456, *pg.* 115
PSAP PRO - Public Safety Answering Point Database - PITNEY BOWES SOFTWARE INC.; *pg.* 455, *pg.* 1346
PSARRAY - Medical Device - HOSPIRA, INC.; *pg.* 1542, *pg.* 623
PSAT/NMSQT - Educational Test - EDUCATIONAL TESTING SERVICE INC.; *pg.* 1394, *pg.* 1111
PSB COMPANY - Manufacturing Company - WHITE CASTLE MANAGEMENT CO.; *pg.* 1756, *pg.* 1444
PSC - Optical Coating - BREWER SCIENCE, INC.; *pg.* 1150, *pg.* 989
PSC-200 - Navigation Aid - TRIMBLE NAVIGATION LIMITED; *pg.* 1384, *pg.* 288
PSE - Sporting Good Product - ESCALADE INC.; *pg.* 1833, *pg.* 678
PSET - Software - WIND RIVER SYSTEMS, INC.; *pg.* 493, *pg.* 38
P'SGHETTI LOOPS - Food Product - ANNIE'S INC.; *pg.* 1760, *pg.* 45
PSHOOTER - Molecular Biology Product - THERMO FISHER SCIENTIFIC INC.; *pg.* 1602, *pg.* 61
PSI - Printing Product - ELECTRONICS FOR IMAGING, INC.; *pg.* 390, *pg.* 88
PSK - Optical Coating - BREWER SCIENCE, INC.; *pg.* 1150, *pg.* 989
PSM - Personal Stereo Monitors - SHURE INCORPORATED; *pg.* 672, *pg.* 638
PSOC - Programmable System-on-Chip - CYPRESS SEMICONDUCTOR CORPORATION; *pg.* 1326, *pg.* 243
PSOC DESIGNER - Programmable System-on-Chip - CYPRESS SEMICONDUCTOR CORPORATION; *pg.* 1326, *pg.* 243
PSOC EXPRESS - Programmable System-on-Chip - CYPRESS SEMICONDUCTOR CORPORATION; *pg.* 1326, *pg.* 243
PSOC ONS - Programmable System-on-Chip - CYPRESS SEMICONDUCTOR CORPORATION; *pg.* 1326, *pg.* 243
PSOC PROS - Programmable System-on-Chip - CYPRESS SEMICONDUCTOR CORPORATION; *pg.* 1326, *pg.* 243
PSORIASIN - Pharmaceutical Product - ALVA/AMCO PHARMACAL COMPANIES, INC.; *pg.* 1492, *pg.* 637
PSORIATEC - Biopharmaceutical Products - DUSA PHARMACEUTICALS, INC.; *pg.* 1525, *pg.* 860
PSOS+ - Software - WIND RIVER SYSTEMS, INC.; *pg.* 493, *pg.* 38
PSOS+M - Software - WIND RIVER SYSTEMS, INC.; *pg.* 493, *pg.* 38
PSOSIM - Software - WIND RIVER SYSTEMS, INC.; *pg.* 493, *pg.* 38
PSOSYSTEM 3 - Software - WIND RIVER SYSTEMS, INC.; *pg.* 493, *pg.* 38
PSPICE - Software - CADENCE DESIGN SYSTEMS, INC.; *pg.* 367, *pg.* 239
PSRC9 SERIES - Service Fittings - WIREMOLD/LEGRAND; *pg.* 689, *pg.* 383
PST - Periodontal Disease Diagnostic Tool - INTERLEUKIN GENETICS, INC.; *pg.* 1546, *pg.* 851
PST - Cutting Tool - LEATHERMAN TOOL GROUP, INC.; *pg.* 1053, *pg.* 1504
PSTAR - Systems Integration & Aeronautics - LOCKHEED MARTIN CORPORATION; *pg.* 229, *pg.* 762
PSV-4000 - High Quality Medical Video Camera for Flexible Endoscopes - PENTAX MEDICAL COMPANY; *pg.* 1580, *pg.* 1086
PSX - Fiberglass Pipe Product - NOV AMERON; *pg.* 100, *pg.* 187
PSX CENTRALIZED ROUTE SERVER - Network Product - SONUS NETWORKS INC.; *pg.* 1281, *pg.* 858
PSYCHEDELIC - Carpet - INTERFACE, INC.; *pg.* 695, *pg.* 512
PSYCHO PAINT - Silicone Paint Base - SMOOTH-ON INC.; *pg.* 111, *pg.* 1528
PSYTE - Geodemographic Neighborhood Segmentation System - PITNEY BOWES SOFTWARE INC.; *pg.* 455, *pg.* 1346
PT - Pumps - AG-MEIER INDUSTRIES LLC; *pg.* 700, *pg.* 1668
PT - Filling Machinery - R.A. JONES & CO.; *pg.* 1371, *pg.* 704
PT 1000 - Rear Loaders - HEIL ENVIRONMENTAL INDUSTRIES, LTD.; *pg.* 207, *pg.* 1629
PT-103 - Chemical Product - BIRKO CORPORATION; *pg.* 1149, *pg.* 332
PT 385 - Resistance Wire - SIGMUND COHN CORP.; *pg.* 1062, *pg.* 1183
PT. KROMEKOTE - Adhesive Coated Paper - SPINNAKER COATING, LLC; *pg.* 1470, *pg.* 1477
PT SNAPPY - Footwear - P.W. MINOR & SON, INC.; *pg.* 1816, *pg.* 1140
PT6 - Aircraft Engine - PRATT & WHITNEY CANADA CORP.; *pg.* 1370, *pg.* 1952
PT9 - Protective Eyewear - SELLSTROM MANUFACTURING CO.; *pg.* 1428, *pg.* 659
PTC - Systems Integration & Aeronautics - LOCKHEED MARTIN CORPORATION; *pg.* 229, *pg.* 762
PTC-100 - Software - BIO-RAD LABORATORIES, INC.; *pg.* 1504, *pg.* 101
PTDCHECK - Medical Product - HOLOGIC, INC.; *pg.* 1416, *pg.* 784
PTI - Systems Integration & Aeronautics - LOCKHEED MARTIN CORPORATION; *pg.* 229, *pg.* 762
PTQ - Implants & Wound Care Products - COGENTIX MEDICAL, INC.; *pg.* 1516, *pg.* 948
PTS - Financial Modeling & Decision Support System for Life & Health Insurers - SS&C TECHNOLOGIES HOLDINGS, INC.; *pg.* 473, *pg.* 386
PTX - Catalytic Exhaust Gas Purifier - BASF CATALYSTS LLC; *pg.* 1148, *pg.* 1074
PTXXXX - Fluid Handling System - GRACO, INC.; *pg.* 1342, *pg.* 935
PTZCAM - Software - CLEARONE COMMUNICATIONS, INC.; *pg.* 629, *pg.* 1756
PUB - Mobile Game - BLUCORA; *pg.* 1232, *pg.* 1813
PUB ALE - Beverage - SPRECHER BREWING COMPANY; *pg.* 265, *pg.* 1858
PUB FIGHT - Cell Phone Game - BLUCORA; *pg.* 1232, *pg.* 1813
PUB FRUITY - Mobile Game - BLUCORA; *pg.* 1232, *pg.* 1813
PUB WEAR - T-Shirt - DESCHUTES BREWERY INC.; *pg.* 248, *pg.* 1496
PUBEASY - Global Publishing e-Marketplace - R.R. BOWKER LLC; *pg.* 1682, *pg.* 1095
PUBHOUSE - Seafood - TRIDENT SEAFOODS CORPORATION; *pg.* 902, *pg.* 1842
PUBLI-SAC - Newspaper - TRANSCONTINENTAL INC.; *pg.* 1695, *pg.* 1957
PUBLIC FOLDER MIGRATOR FOR SHAREPOINT - Software - DELL SOFTWARE; *pg.* 385, *pg.* 40
PUBLIC RISK UNDERWRITERS - Insurance Package Program - BROWN & BROWN, INC.; *pg.* 1196, *pg.* 419
PUBLISH & PRODUCTION EXECUTIVE - Publisher - NORTH AMERICAN PUBLISHING COMPANY; *pg.* 1671, *pg.* 1567
PUBLISHER - Software - AUTONOMY, INC.; *pg.* 358, *pg.* 212
PUBLISHER OF TABER'S - Tagline - F.A. DAVIS PUBLISHING COMPANY; *pg.* 1640, *pg.* 1564
PUBLISHERS CLEARING HOUSE - Magazine Subscriptions by Mail - PUBLISHERS CLEARING HOUSE; *pg.* 1782, *pg.* 1324
PUBLISHERS WEEKLY - Publication - R.R. BOWKER LLC; *pg.* 1682, *pg.* 1095

PUBLIX BABY CLUB - Club - PUBLIX SUPER MARKETS, INC.; *pg.* 1031, *pg.* 437
PUBLIX FAMILYSTYLE - Newsletter - PUBLIX SUPER MARKETS, INC.; *pg.* 1031, *pg.* 437
PUBLIX GRAPE - Magazine - PUBLIX SUPER MARKETS, INC.; *pg.* 1031, *pg.* 437
PUBLIX GREENWISE MARKET - Magazine - PUBLIX SUPER MARKETS, INC.; *pg.* 1031, *pg.* 437
PUBLIX PARTNERS - Food Product - PUBLIX SUPER MARKETS, INC.; *pg.* 1031, *pg.* 437
PUBLIX PIX - Store - PUBLIX SUPER MARKETS, INC.; *pg.* 1031, *pg.* 437
PUBLIX PRESCHOOL PALS - Kid's Club - PUBLIX SUPER MARKETS, INC.; *pg.* 1031, *pg.* 437
PUBLIX.COM - Food Product Website - PUBLIX SUPER MARKETS, INC.; *pg.* 1031, *pg.* 437
PUBNET - Electronic Commerce Services - R.R. BOWKER LLC; *pg.* 1682, *pg.* 1095
PUBSELECT - Software - R.R. DONNELLEY & SONS COMPANY; *pg.* 1682, *pg.* 589
PUBSPRING - Software - R.R. DONNELLEY & SONS COMPANY; *pg.* 1682, *pg.* 589
PUBTRACK - Accurate, Reliable & Actionable Data Solutions - R.R. BOWKER LLC; *pg.* 1682, *pg.* 1095
PUCCI - Pedi Hand Orthosis - ALIMED, INC.; *pg.* 1490, *pg.* 816
PUCCI - Fabric - NEMSCHOFF, INC.; *pg.* 936, *pg.* 1890
PUCCINI - Flatware - ONEIDA LTD; *pg.* 1129, *pg.* 1318
PUCKER - Fabric - NEMSCHOFF, INC.; *pg.* 936, *pg.* 1890
PUDENZ - Medical Device - INTEGRA LIFESCIENCES HOLDINGS CORPORATION; *pg.* 1545, *pg.* 1109
PUDLISZKI - Prepared Meals & Ketchups - THE KRAFT HEINZ COMPANY; *pg.* 870, *pg.* 1577
PUEBLA - Dinnerware - THE HOMER LAUGHLIN CHINA COMPANY; *pg.* 1125, *pg.* 1850
PUEBLO - Furniture - AMERICAN LEATHER LP; *pg.* 912, *pg.* 1673
PUFF - Air Freshener - SWISHER HYGIENE INC.; *pg.* 336, *pg.* 1507
PUFFED RICE - Bag Cereal - POST CONSUMER BRANDS; *pg.* 833, *pg.* 927
PUFFED WHEAT - Bag Cereal - POST CONSUMER BRANDS; *pg.* 833, *pg.* 927
PUFFNS - Lab Science Material - CAROLINA BIOLOGICAL SUPPLY COMPANY; *pg.* 1513, *pg.* 1359
PUFFS - Paper Product - THE PROCTER & GAMBLE COMPANY; *pg.* 1129, *pg.* 1418
PUFFS PLUS WITH THE SCENT OF VICKS - Facial Tissue - THE PROCTER & GAMBLE COMPANY; *pg.* 1129, *pg.* 1418
PUFFY - Apparel - OAKLEY, INC.; *pg.* 1840, *pg.* 86
PUFFY AMI YUMI - Game & TV Show - THE CARTOON NETWORK; *pg.* 273, *pg.* 492
PUFFY QUILT - Ear Warmer - 180S, LLC; *pg.* 1824, *pg.* 754
PUGLIELLI - Golf Product - TAYLORMADE-ADIDAS GOLF; *pg.* 1847, *pg.* 60
PULASKI - Furniture - HOME MERIDIAN INTERNATIONAL, INC.; *pg.* 928, *pg.* 1379
PULASTIC - Floor System - ROBBINS, INC.; *pg.* 108, *pg.* 1425
PULL BACK AUTOS - Toy - THE OHIO ART COMPANY, INC.; *pg.* 965, *pg.* 1406
PULL-ON PAC - Footwear - LACROSSE FOOTWEAR, INC.; *pg.* 1811, *pg.* 1503
PULL-OPE - Envelopes - TENSION ENVELOPE CORPORATION; *pg.* 483, *pg.* 986
PULL-TABS - Lottery Game - MISSOURI LOTTERY; *pg.* 999, *pg.* 979
PULL-TITE - Plastic Bag - ELKAY PLASTICS COMPANY, INC.; *pg.* 1882, *pg.* 68
PULL-UPS - Training Pant - KIMBERLY-CLARK CORPORATION; *pg.* 1461, *pg.* 1720
PULLABLES - Dog Toy - THE HARTZ MOUNTAIN CORP.; *pg.* 1476, *pg.* 1120
PULLMAN - Dress Shoes - JOHNSTON & MURPHY CO.; *pg.* 1810, *pg.* 1651
PULLMOR - Toy Train - LIONEL LLC; *pg.* 961, *pg.* 875
PULLOVER - Body Harness - MINE SAFETY APPLIANCES COMPANY; *pg.* 1361, *pg.* 1525
PULLTAP - Corkscrew - THE VOLLRATH COMPANY LLC; *pg.* 1139, *pg.* 1894
PULMO-GUARD - Bacterin-Toxoid for Vaccination of Cattle - BOEHRINGER INGELHEIM VETMEDICA, INC.; *pg.* 1474, *pg.* 989
PULMO-GUARD MPB - Mycoplasma Bovis Vaccine. - BOEHRINGER INGELHEIM VETMEDICA, INC.; *pg.* 1474, *pg.* 989
PULMOCARE - Liquid Nutritional - ABBOTT LABORATORIES; *pg.* 1484, *pg.* 551
PULMOSITE - Bioadhesive & Controlled Release Site Release Technology - LUMARA HEALTH INC.; *pg.* 1557, *pg.* 973
PULMOSOL - Pharmaceutical Product - NEKTAR THERAPEUTICS; *pg.* 1572, *pg.* 224
PULMOSPHERE - Pharmaceutical Product - NEKTAR THERAPEUTICS; *pg.* 1572, *pg.* 224
PULMOTIL - Tilmicosin - ELANCO ANIMAL HEALTH; *pg.* 1475, *pg.* 681
PULP ORANGE - Beverages - THE COCA-COLA COMPANY; *pg.* 240, *pg.* 493
PULPAID - Defoamer in Liquid Concentrate Form - DOW CORNING CORPORATION; *pg.* 1159, *pg.* 900
PULPEX - Tray - PACTIV CORPORATION; *pg.* 1466, *pg.* 624
PULSA SERIES - Pump Product - IDEX CORPORATION; *pg.* 1347, *pg.* 623
PULSAJET - Spray Product - SPRAYING SYSTEMS CO.; *pg.* 1063, *pg.* 670
PULSAR - Integrated Circuits - ANALOG DEVICES, INC.; *pg.* 617, *pg.* 839
PULSAR - Pump Product - IDEX CORPORATION; *pg.* 1347, *pg.* 623
PULSAR - Single Gas Detector - MINE SAFETY APPLIANCES COMPANY; *pg.* 1361, *pg.* 1525
PULSATROL - Pump Product - IDEX CORPORATION; *pg.* 1347, *pg.* 623
PULSATRON - Pump Product - IDEX CORPORATION; *pg.* 1347, *pg.* 623
PULSATRON PLUS - Pump Product - IDEX CORPORATION; *pg.* 1347, *pg.* 623
PULSE - Resin - THE DOW CHEMICAL COMPANY; *pg.* 1157, *pg.* 898
PULSE - Cutting Tool - LEATHERMAN TOOL GROUP, INC.; *pg.* 1053, *pg.* 1504
PULSE - Electronics Components - PULSE ELECTRONICS CORPORATION; *pg.* 666, *pg.* 206
PULSE - Slither Scooter - SEARS HOLDINGS CORPORATION; *pg.* 1784, *pg.* 618
PULSE - Bag - SOLO; *pg.* 12, *pg.* 1165
PULSE-BREW - Coffee And Beverage Equipment - BUNN-O-MATIC CORPORATION; *pg.* 53, *pg.* 661
PULSE JETTER - Drain Cleaner - GOODWAY TECHNOLOGIES CORPORATION; *pg.* 1341, *pg.* 374
PULSE-LOK - Connector - AMPHENOL CORPORATION; *pg.* 616, *pg.* 381
PULSE-NET - Ethernet - AMPHENOL CORPORATION; *pg.* 616, *pg.* 381
PULSE OF THE ECONOMY - Financial Products - DOW JONES & COMPANY, INC.; *pg.* 1637, *pg.* 1225
PULSE-ON-DEMAND - Electric Controller - GE ENERGY; *pg.* 1338, *pg.* 506
PULSE-PLUS - Thread - AMPHENOL CORPORATION; *pg.* 616, *pg.* 381
PULSE SPRAY - Electrosurgical Devices - ANGIODYNAMICS, INC.; *pg.* 1495, *pg.* 1173
PULSE STAR - Exerciser - BATTLE CREEK EQUIPMENT CO.; *pg.* 1499, *pg.* 870
PULSE-VU - Electrosurgical Devices - ANGIODYNAMICS, INC.; *pg.* 1495, *pg.* 1173
PULSE WAVE - Brew Routines - BUNN-O-MATIC CORPORATION; *pg.* 53, *pg.* 661
PULSEATERS - Resistor Product - OHMITE MANUFACTURING COMPANY; *pg.* 660, *pg.* 553
PULSECOM - Telecommunication Product - HUBBELL INCORPORATED; *pg.* 1299, *pg.* 370
PULSELIFE - Packaging Process - COHERENT, INC.; *pg.* 1406, *pg.* 265
PULSELINK - Wireless Communication System - AT&T SOUTHEAST; *pg.* 1868, *pg.* 489
PULSEMASTER - Laser System - GSI GROUP INC.; *pg.* 1415, *pg.* 784
PULSESELECT - Medical Device - MISONIX INC.; *pg.* 1568, *pg.* 1159
PULSETRAC - Software - BIO-RAD LABORATORIES, INC.; *pg.* 1504, *pg.* 101
PULSEWAVE - Software - BIO-RAD LABORATORIES, INC.; *pg.* 1504, *pg.* 101
PULTE HOMES - Home Builders - PULTEGROUP, INC.; *pg.* 1109, *pg.* 873
PULTE MASTER BUILDER - Home Builders - PULTEGROUP, INC.; *pg.* 1109, *pg.* 873
PULTE MORTGAGE - Administration Services - PULTEGROUP, INC.; *pg.* 1109, *pg.* 873
PULVERLAC - Industrial Material - DOW CHEMICAL; *pg.* 1156, *pg.* 1563
PULVERMILL - Vertical Air Swept Hammer Mill - STURTEVANT INC.; *pg.* 1379, *pg.* 824
PUMA - Unmanned Air Vehicle - AEROVIRONMENT, INC.; *pg.* 223, *pg.* 150
PUMA - Wafer Inspection System - KLA-TENCOR CORPORATION; *pg.* 1353, *pg.* 146
PUMA - Personal & Household Product - THE PROCTER & GAMBLE COMPANY; *pg.* 1129, *pg.* 1418
PUMA KOLA - Beverage - SPRECHER BREWING COMPANY; *pg.* 265, *pg.* 1858
PUMICIDE - Dental Product - DENTSPLY INTERNATIONAL INC.; *pg.* 1522, *pg.* 1596
PUMIE - Scouring Stick - U.S. PUMICE COMPANY; *pg.* 1185, *pg.* 65
PUMP - Beverages - THE COCA-COLA COMPANY; *pg.* 240, *pg.* 493
THE PUMP - Athletic Shoe Technology - REEBOK INTERNATIONAL LTD.; *pg.* 1817, *pg.* 811
P.U.M.P. - Footwear - REEBOK INTERNATIONAL LTD.; *pg.* 1817, *pg.* 811
PUMP ACTION 500 - Gun - O.F. MOSSBERG & SONS, INC.; *pg.* 1842, *pg.* 360
PUMP ACTION 835 - Gun - O.F. MOSSBERG & SONS, INC.; *pg.* 1842, *pg.* 360
PUMP ARMOR - Fluid Handling System - GRACO, INC.; *pg.* 1342, *pg.* 935
PUMP-COLORIMETER - On-Line Process Monitor - HACH COMPANY; *pg.* 1415, *pg.* 334
PUMP DEFENDER - Fluid Handling System - GRACO, INC.; *pg.* 1342, *pg.* 935
PUMP LIFE - Fluid Handling System - GRACO, INC.; *pg.* 1342, *pg.* 935
THE PUMP PEOPLE - Slogan - THE GORMAN-RUPP COMPANY; *pg.* 1341, *pg.* 1458
PUMP ROOM - Restaurant - OMNI HOTELS & RESORTS; *pg.* 1107, *pg.* 1685
PUMP SYSTEMALERT - Pump System Monitor - TEXAS INSTRUMENTS INCORPORATED; *pg.* 679, *pg.* 1688
PUMP WORKS - Fluid Handling System - GRACO, INC.; *pg.* 1342, *pg.* 935
PUMPED ENHANCED HYDRATION - Beverages - THE COCA-COLA COMPANY; *pg.* 240, *pg.* 493
PUMPER LOG - Software - ASPEN TECHNOLOGY, INC.; *pg.* 354, *pg.* 804
PUMPERPARTS - Pump Product - IDEX CORPORATION; *pg.* 1347, *pg.* 623
PUMPFLEX - Hose - HBD INDUSTRIES, INC.; *pg.* 207, *pg.* 1449
PUMPFLEX I - Gasoline Curb Pump Hose - HBD INDUSTRIES, INC.; *pg.* 207, *pg.* 1449
PUMPFLEX II - Gasoline Curb Pump Hose - HBD INDUSTRIES, INC.; *pg.* 207, *pg.* 1449
PUMPHREY'S BLEND - Tea - PEET'S COFFEE & TEA, INC.; *pg.* 1029, *pg.* 85
PUMPING PLASTIC - Educational Materials - SCHOLASTIC INC.; *pg.* 1683, *pg.* 1288
PUMPKIN FACE - Candy - SWEET CANDY COMPANY; *pg.* 1862, *pg.* 1761
PUMPKIN FLAX PLUS - Granola Bar - NATURE'S PATH FOODS INC.; *pg.* 833, *pg.* 1908
PUMPKINS ON PARADE - Popcorn - THE POPCORN FACTORY; *pg.* 1861, *pg.* 625
PUMPKLEEN - Filter Assembly - PALL CORPORATION; *pg.* 232, *pg.* 1323
PUMPMASTER - Software - BENTLEY SYSTEMS, INC.; *pg.* 361, *pg.* 1531
PUMPORTATION - Air Powered Pump Color - GRACO, INC.; *pg.* 1342, *pg.* 935
PUMPSMART - Process Control Systems - GOULDS PUMPS, INCORPORATED; *pg.* 1342, *pg.* 1341
PUMPSMART - Flow System - ITT CORPORATION; *pg.* 1351, *pg.* 1354
PUNCH - Fungicide - E.I. DU PONT DE NEMOURS & COMPANY; *pg.* 1159, *pg.* 390
PUNCH-PRO - Hydraulic Hole Punchers - HOUGEN MANUFACTURING INC.; *pg.* 1347, *pg.* 908
PUNCTUR-GUARD - Winged Set - HOSPIRA, INC.; *pg.* 1542, *pg.* 623
PUNCTURE SEAL - Seals & Inflates Tires - RADIATOR SPECIALTY COMPANY; *pg.* 215, *pg.* 1380
PUNK NEWS - Alternative Music News Outlet - SPINMEDIA;

First page reference indicates Business Class Edition
Second page reference indicates Geographic Edition

pg. 1282, pg. 104

PUNK SKULL - Apparel - OAKLEY, INC.; pg. 1840, pg. 86

PUNKIN ALE - Seasonal Beer - DOGFISH HEAD CRAFT BREWERY, INC.; pg. 249, pg. 388

PUP - Combustible Gas Leak Detector - BACHARACH INC.; pg. 1400, pg. 1556

PUP - Hand Held Power Shears - THE WOLF MACHINE CO.; pg. 1389, pg. 1427

PUP & AIR PUP - Round Knife - THE WOLF MACHINE CO.; pg. 1389, pg. 1427

PUP-PERONI - Pet Food - BIG HEART PET BRANDS; pg. 1474, pg. 213

PUPPIES USA - Magazine - I-5 PUBLISHING LLC; pg. 1651, pg. 133

PUPPY CHOW - Dog Food - NESTLE PURINA PETCARE COMPANY; pg. 1479, pg. 1000

PUPPY GOLD - Food for Developing Dogs - FROMM FAMILY PET FOODS, INC.; pg. 1476, pg. 1870

PUPPY PRIME - Puppy Food - KENT NUTRITION GROUP; pg. 1477, pg. 710

PUPPYPAWS - Dog Jewelry - PUPPYPAWS, INC.; pg. 11, pg. 1463

PUR - Water Filtration Device - HELEN OF TROY L.P.; pg. 511, pg. 1692

PUR - Water Filters - KAZ, INC.; pg. 58, pg. 844

PURA - Release Agent - CHEM-TREND LIMITED PARTNERSHIP; pg. 973, pg. 892

PURAFIL - Air Filters - KAYDON CORPORATION; pg. 1352, pg. 866

PURAFILTER - Air Filter - PURAFIL, INC.; pg. 333, pg. 530

PURDY - Brush And Roller - THE SHERWIN-WILLIAMS COMPANY; pg. 1447, pg. 1435

PURDY - Brushes - SHERWIN-WILLIAMS DIVERSIFIED BRANDS DIVISION; pg. 1448, pg. 1435

PURDY ECO PRO - Brushes - THE SHERWIN-WILLIAMS COMPANY; pg. 1447, pg. 1435

PURE - Musical Instrument - GIBSON GUITAR CORP.; pg. 550, pg. 1650

PURE - Bicycle - TREK BICYCLE CORPORATION; pg. 1847, pg. 1896

PURE AIR - Floor Care Product - BISSELL HOMECARE, INC.; pg. 52, pg. 887

PURE AIR - Bath & Plumbing Product - JACUZZI BRANDS CORPORATION; pg. 554, pg. 65

PURE & NATURAL - Bar Soap - HENKEL CONSUMER GOODS; pg. 511, pg. 22

PURE-BIND - Food Ingredient - GRAIN PROCESSING CORPORATION; pg. 859, pg. 709

PURE CONVECTION - Home Appliance - DACOR; pg. 54, pg. 67

PURE-COTE - Pharmaceutical Ingredient - GRAIN PROCESSING CORPORATION; pg. 859, pg. 709

PURE DARK - Candy - MARS, INCORPORATED; pg. 1858, pg. 1792

PURE DATA FOR A HEALTHY PLANET - Slogan - YSI INCORPORATED; pg. 1438, pg. 1483

PURE-DENT - Pharmaceutical Ingredient - GRAIN PROCESSING CORPORATION; pg. 859, pg. 709

PURE DIGITAL FIBERLINK - Fiber Optic - COMMUNICATIONS SPECIALTIES, INC.; pg. 377, pg. 1338

PURE ENERGY - Nutritional Product - NUTRACEUTICAL INTERNATIONAL CORPORATION; pg. 1576, pg. 1753

PURE ENVIRONMENT - Slogan - YOCREAM INTERNATIONAL INC.; pg. 1039, pg. 1508

PURE-FLO - Adsorbent Product - OIL-DRI CORPORATION OF AMERICA; pg. 1480, pg. 586

PURE-FLOW - Pharmaceutical & Bioprocessing Product - ITT CORPORATION; pg. 1351, pg. 1354

PURE FOOD - Slogan - YOCREAM INTERNATIONAL INC.; pg. 1039, pg. 1508

PURE-FUME - Perfume - AVEDA CORPORATION; pg. 499, pg. 917

PURE-GEL - Pharmaceutical Ingredient - GRAIN PROCESSING CORPORATION; pg. 859, pg. 709

PURE GOODNESS - Slogan For Cascadian Farm - GENERAL MILLS, INC.; pg. 828, pg. 933

PURE HONEST TO GOODNESS - Tag Line - FOSTER FARMS; pg. 856, pg. 122

PURE INGREDIENTS. PURE RESULTS - Tagline - NATUROPATHICA LTD.; pg. 517, pg. 1156

PURE PERFORMANCE - Oil - CONOCOPHILLIPS; pg. 975, pg. 1703

PURE PERFORMANCE - Coating Product - PPG INDUSTRIES, INC.; pg. 1445, pg. 1579

PURE PIXEL - Electronic Sign Display - DAKTRONICS, INC.; pg. 633, pg. 1624

PURE PLAST - Packaging Product - TEKNI-PLEX, INC.; pg. 1470, pg. 1122

PURE PLEASURE - Slots - INTERNATIONAL GAME TECHNOLOGY; pg. 957, pg. 1024

PURE PLEASURE - Slogan - YOCREAM INTERNATIONAL INC.; pg. 1039, pg. 1508

PURE PLEASURE BONUS WHEEL - Slots - INTERNATIONAL GAME TECHNOLOGY; pg. 957, pg. 1024

PURE POLARIS - Apparel - POLARIS INDUSTRIES INC.; pg. 1709, pg. 928

PURE PREMIUM - Grass Seed - THE SCOTTS MIRACLE-GRO COMPANY; pg. 1799, pg. 1459

PURE-SET - Food Ingredient - GRAIN PROCESSING CORPORATION; pg. 859, pg. 709

PURE SHINE - Hair Care Products - INSPIRED BEAUTY BRANDS; pg. 512, pg. 1244

PURE SPRING - Bath & Body Products - RITE AID CORPORATION; pg. 1590, pg. 1519

PURE STAY - Powder & Foundation - MAYBELLINE LLC; pg. 516, pg. 1257

PURE TAC - Tacky, Adhesive, Highly Water Resistant, USDA Authorized Class H-1 Grease - LUBRIPLATE LUBRICANTS; pg. 980, pg. 1097

PURE TIFFANY - Fragrance Products - TIFFANY & CO.; pg. 13, pg. 1299

PUREAIR BIO RESPONSE KIT - Respirator - IRT, INC.; pg. 1169, pg. 771

PUREAIR PAPR C8 - Air Respirator - IRT, INC.; pg. 1169, pg. 771

PUREAIR PAPR K7 - Respirator - IRT, INC.; pg. 1169, pg. 771

PUREAUDIO - Desktop System - ANDREA ELECTRONICS CORPORATION; pg. 617, pg. 1143

PUREBASS - Electronic Product - LRAD CORPORATION; pg. 652, pg. 204

PUREBLEND - Pump Product - IDEX CORPORATION; pg. 1347, pg. 623

PUREBLUE - Juice - LEADING BRANDS, INC.; pg. 1026, pg. 1911

PUREBOND - Fusible Piping Product - ENTEGRIS, INC.; pg. 1882, pg. 788

PURECELL - Filter - PALL CORPORATION; pg. 232, pg. 1323

PUREDISK - Software - SYMANTEC CORPORATION; pg. 478, pg. 161

PUREFIX - Orthopaedic Product - STRYKER CORPORATION; pg. 1598, pg. 894

PUREFLO - Filter - FLANDERS CORPORATION; pg. 1336, pg. 1392

PUREFORM - Filtration Product - FLANDERS CORPORATION; pg. 1336, pg. 1392

PURELAM - Laminating Adhesives - ASHLAND INC.; pg. 972, pg. 726

PURELIGHT - Laser & Laser System - COHERENT, INC.; pg. 1406, pg. 265

PURELINK - Molecular Biology Product - THERMO FISHER SCIENTIFIC INC.; pg. 1602, pg. 61

PURELL - Hand Sanitizer - JOHNSON & JOHNSON; pg. 1549, pg. 1091

PURELY MAGNESIUM - Nutritional Product - NUTRACEUTICAL INTERNATIONAL CORPORATION; pg. 1576, pg. 1753

PUREOLOGY - Color Treated Hair Care Products - L'OREAL USA; pg. 514, pg. 1252

PUREPATH DIGITAL - Computer Chips - TEXAS INSTRUMENTS INCORPORATED; pg. 679, pg. 1688

PUREPLAST - Pharmaceutical Packaging Film - TEKNI-PLEX, INC.; pg. 1470, pg. 1122

PUREPOLYMER - Polymer Service - ENTEGRIS, INC.; pg. 1882, pg. 788

PURESIC - Ceramic & Plastic Product - COORSTEK, INC.; pg. 77, pg. 330

PURESPEED - Receiver - LATTICE SEMICONDUCTOR CORPORATION; pg. 651, pg. 1498

PURESTEEM - Water Treatment System - UNIFIED BRANDS INC.; pg. 1385, pg. 970

PURETECH - Recycled Material - TEKNI-PLEX, INC.; pg. 1470, pg. 1122

PURETOUCH - Kitchen Faucet - MOEN INCORPORATED; pg. 1056, pg. 1468

PURETOUCH - Mattress - THERAPEDIC ASSOCIATES, INC.; pg. 945, pg. 1112

PURETOUCH AQUASUITE - Faucet - MOEN INCORPORATED; pg. 1056, pg. 1468

PURETOUCH CLASSIC - Faucet - MOEN INCORPORATED; pg. 1056, pg. 1468

PURETOUCH EURO - Faucet & Water Filter - MOEN INCORPORATED; pg. 1056, pg. 1468

PURETOUCH PROFESSIONAL - Faucet & Water Filter - MOEN INCORPORATED; pg. 1056, pg. 1468

PUREVIDEO - High Definition Video Technology - NVIDIA CORPORATION; pg. 447, pg. 268

PUREVISION - Soft Contact Lens - BAUSCH & LOMB INCORPORATED; pg. 1401, pg. 1045

PUREVISION - Optical Character Recognition Software - LOCKHEED MARTIN CORPORATION; pg. 229, pg. 762

PUREVISION - Software - OPEX CORPORATION; pg. 450, pg. 1087

PUREVOLUME - Social Listening Site - SPINMEDIA; pg. 1282, pg. 104

PUREWAVE - Source-Transfer System - S&C ELECTRIC COMPANY; pg. 1305, pg. 589

PUREWAVE AVC - Adaptive VAR Compensator - S&C ELECTRIC COMPANY; pg. 1305, pg. 589

PUREWAVE DSTATCOM - Distribution Static Compensator - S&C ELECTRIC COMPANY; pg. 1305, pg. 589

PUREWAVE DVR - Dynamic Voltage Restorer - S&C ELECTRIC COMPANY; pg. 1305, pg. 589

PUREWAVE UPS - System - S&C ELECTRIC COMPANY; pg. 1305, pg. 589

PUREX - Laundry Care Products - HENKEL CONSUMER GOODS; pg. 511, pg. 22

PUREX BABY - Hypoallergenic Laundry Detergent - HENKEL CONSUMER GOODS; pg. 511, pg. 22

PUREZOL - Software - BIO RAD LABORATORIES, INC.; pg. 1504, pg. 101

PURFICTPURGE - Purge Compounds - FERRO CORPORATION; pg. 1162, pg. 1462

PURI-CLEAR - Air Purifier - SLANT/FIN CORPORATION; pg. 1076, pg. 1163

PURIFIRE - Atmosphere Systems - AIR PRODUCTS AND CHEMICALS, INC.; pg. 1145, pg. 1513

PURIFYING - Nutritional Product - RBC LIFE SCIENCES, INC.; pg. 1588, pg. 1723

PURILEV - Canola Oil - CARGILL LIMITED; pg. 1475, pg. 1914

PURINA - Petcare - TRACTOR SUPPLY COMPANY; pg. 708, pg. 1627

PURINA ONE - Dog Food - NESTLE PURINA PETCARE COMPANY; pg. 1479, pg. 1000

PURIST - Bath Product - KOHLER CO.; pg. 91, pg. 1862

PURIST NATURALS - Natural Skin Care - AMERICAN INTERNATIONAL INDUSTRIES COMPANY; pg. 498, pg. 126

PURITAN - Buckwheat Food Product - THE BIRKETT MILLS; pg. 826, pg. 1321

PURITAN - Pottery Plaster - USG CORPORATION; pg. 118, pg. 594

PURITAN - Merchandise - WAL-MART STORES, INC.; pg. 1790, pg. 29

PURITAN'S PRIDE - Nutritional Supplements - NBTY, INC.; pg. 1572, pg. 1338

PURITY - Milk Product - DEAN FOODS COMPANY; pg. 852, pg. 1679

PURITY - Lighting - ETHAN ALLEN INTERIORS INC.; pg. 924, pg. 343

PURITY MILK - Milk - PURITY DAIRIES, LLC; pg. 891, pg. 1653

PURO - Dry Cleaning & Laundry Product - ADCO, INC.; pg. 325, pg. 482

PUROCAST - Pressed & Monolithic Refractory - RESCO PRODUCTS, INC.; pg. 107, pg. 1581

PUROCRETE - Pressed & Monolithic Refractory - RESCO PRODUCTS, INC.; pg. 107, pg. 1581

PUROLITE - Pressed & Monolithic Refractory - RESCO PRODUCTS, INC.; pg. 107, pg. 1581

PUROTAB - Pressed & Monolithic Refractory - RESCO PRODUCTS, INC.; pg. 107, pg. 1581

PURPLE COPP - Copper Powder - AMERICAN CHEMET CORPORATION; pg. 1147, pg. 599

PURPLE HAZE - Beer - ABITA BREWING COMPANY; pg. 237, pg. 741

PURPLE LABEL - Apparel - RALPH LAUREN CORPORATION; pg. 46, pg. 1284

PURPLE PASSION - Slots - INTERNATIONAL GAME TECHNOLOGY; pg. 957, pg. 1024

PURPLE QUEEN - Container Grown Plant - MONROVIA

GROWERS; *pg.* 1797, *pg.* 44
PURPLE RAIN - Container Grown Plant - MONROVIA GROWERS; *pg.* 1797, *pg.* 44
PURPLE STUFF - Automotive Reconditioning Product - MOC PRODUCTS COMPANY, INC.; *pg.* 332, *pg.* 174
PURPOSE - Furniture - JOFCO INC.; *pg.* 931, *pg.* 691
PURPOSE - Healthcare Product - JOHNSON & JOHNSON; *pg.* 1549, *pg.* 1091
PURPOSE MATADOR - Cleaning Product - HILLYARD, INC.; *pg.* 331, *pg.* 990
PURPOSE MONEY - Bank Card - ATLANTICUS CORPORATION; *pg.* 717, *pg.* 490
PURRFECTLY FRESH - Activated Carbon Product - CALGON CARBON CORPORATION; *pg.* 1151, *pg.* 1574
PURSUE - Disinfectant Products - AMWAY CORPORATION; *pg.* 326, *pg.* 864
PURSUIT - Angioplasty - COOK GROUP, INC.; *pg.* 1518, *pg.* 674
PURSUIT - Kayak - HOBIE CAT COMPANY; *pg.* 1708, *pg.* 173
PURSUIT - Security Products - VOXX INTERNATIONAL; *pg.* 686, *pg.* 1166
THE PURSUIT OF QUALITY - Tagline - PACCAR INC.; *pg.* 187, *pg.* 1816
PURUS - Pump Product - IDEX CORPORATION; *pg.* 1347, *pg.* 623
PURVEYORS OF THE PRACTICAL & HARD-TO-FIND - Tagline - VERMONT COUNTRY STORE, INC.; *pg.* 1789, *pg.* 1766
PURWIPE - Chemical Cleaner Product - TECH SPRAY, L.P.; *pg.* 1183, *pg.* 1659
PUSH BUTTON PICKUP BOX - Library Security System - AMERICAN LOCKER SECURITY SYSTEMS, INC.; *pg.* 1042, *pg.* 1674
PUSH CAP - Test Cap - OATEY SUPPLY CHAIN SERVICES; *pg.* 30, *pg.* 1433
PUSH-EZ - Connector - BOMAR INTERCONNECT PRODUCTS, INC.; *pg.* 1318, *pg.* 1079
PUSH-LOCK - Extension Cords - COLEMAN CABLE, INC.; *pg.* 1324, *pg.* 665
PUSH-PAC - Agricultural Push-only Conveyors - CHRISTIANSON SYSTEMS, INC.; *pg.* 1323, *pg.* 917
PUSH POP LOLLIPOPS - Candy - THE TOPPS COMPANY, INC.; *pg.* 588, *pg.* 1302
PUSH-UP PAYS - Video Game - INTERNATIONAL GAME TECHNOLOGY; *pg.* 957, *pg.* 1024
PUSH UPS - Fruity Sherbert Swirls - NESTLE USA, INC.; *pg.* 883, *pg.* 96
THE PUSHER - Medical Product - PROPPER MANUFACTURING COMPANY, INC.; *pg.* 1586, *pg.* 1175
PUSHLNSTALLER - Software - CONDUSIV TECHNOLOGIES; *pg.* 379, *pg.* 51
PUSH'N RIDE - Walker - RUBBERMAID HOME PRODUCTS; *pg.* 1138, *pg.* 1453
PUSSER'S ORIGINAL NAVY RUM - Pums - SHAW ROSS INTERNATIONAL IMPORTERS; *pg.* 1970, *pg.* 449
PUT YOUR DAY TO REST - Slogan - RESTONIC MATTRESS CORPORATION; *pg.* 941, *pg.* 553
PUT YOUR LIFE ON IT - Slogan - WESTERN DIGITAL CORPORATION; *pg.* 492, *pg.* 118
PUTNAM - End Mills - KENNAMETAL IPG; *pg.* 1353, *pg.* 1615
PUTREX - Depth Filters - GE WATER & PROCESS TECHNOLOGIES; *pg.* 1339, *pg.* 1588
PUTTING CHALLENGE - Golf Product - CALLAWAY GOLF COMPANY; *pg.* 1829, *pg.* 58
PUTTING GOVERNMENT AT YOUR FINGERTIPS - Slogan - NIC INC.; *pg.* 445, *pg.* 718
PUZZ 3D - Toy & Game - HASBRO, INC.; *pg.* 954, *pg.* 1603
PUZZLE - Furniture - HERMAN MILLER, INC.; *pg.* 926, *pg.* 913
PUZZLE - Fabric - NEMSCHOFF, INC.; *pg.* 936, *pg.* 1890
THE PUZZLE CLUB - Animated Program - INTERNATIONAL LUTHERAN LAYMEN'S LEAGUE; *pg.* 293, *pg.* 998
PUZZLE FUN BOUQUET - Floral Bouquet - FTD GROUP, INC.; *pg.* 1795, *pg.* 608
PUZZLE GLUE - Adhesive - HOBBICO, INC.; *pg.* 956, *pg.* 562
PUZZLE MANIA - Puzzle Books - HIGHLIGHTS FOR CHILDREN, INC.; *pg.* 1650, *pg.* 1440
PUZZLE SHOTS - Toy & Game - HASBRO, INC.; *pg.* 954, *pg.* 1603
PV ISOSTATION - Vibration Isolation Workstations - NEWPORT CORPORATION; *pg.* 1424, *pg.* 114
PV JR - Mini Vise Tool - PANAVISE PRODUCTS, INC.; *pg.* 1058, *pg.* 1032
PV SUN TIMES - E-Newsletter - ADVANCED ENERGY INDUSTRIES, INC.; *pg.* 613, *pg.* 328
PVAC - Container - CHART INDUSTRIES, INC.; *pg.* 1405, *pg.* 1454
PVAX - Molecular Probe Product - THERMO FISHER SCIENTIFIC INC.; *pg.* 1602, *pg.* 61
PVC AND NATVAR - Medical Tubing - TEKNI-PLEX, INC.; *pg.* 1470, *pg.* 1122
PVC DYNAMIC DUO - Trap Adapter - GENOVA PRODUCTS, INC.; *pg.* 83, *pg.* 875
PVI METHOD - People Vehicle Interface Technology - LEAR CORPORATION; *pg.* 229, *pg.* 907
PVM - Particle System - METTLER-TOLEDO INTERNATIONAL INC.; *pg.* 1423, *pg.* 1441
PVM - Musical Instrument - PEAVEY ELECTRONICS CORPORATION; *pg.* 662, *pg.* 970
PVX - Desktop Software - POLYCOM, INC.; *pg.* 664, *pg.* 249
PW100 - Aircraft Engine - PRATT & WHITNEY CANADA CORP.; *pg.* 1370, *pg.* 1952
PW200 - Aircraft Engine - PRATT & WHITNEY CANADA CORP.; *pg.* 1370, *pg.* 1952
PW300 - Aircraft Engine - PRATT & WHITNEY CANADA CORP.; *pg.* 1370, *pg.* 1952
PW500 - Aircraft Engine - PRATT & WHITNEY CANADA CORP.; *pg.* 1370, *pg.* 1952
PW901A - Aircraft Engine - PRATT & WHITNEY CANADA CORP.; *pg.* 1370, *pg.* 1952
PWCTRADERONLINE.COM - Advertising Website - DOMINION ENTERPRISES; *pg.* 1636, *pg.* 1796
PWM - Led Drivers - MICREL, INC.; *pg.* 654, *pg.* 247
PWQ - Inspection System - KLA-TENCOR CORPORATION; *pg.* 1353, *pg.* 146
PWRBLAZER - Optical Networking Product - HARMONIC, INC.; *pg.* 402, *pg.* 246
PWRLINK - Optical Networking Product - HARMONIC, INC.; *pg.* 402, *pg.* 246
PWT - Premium Wall Tubing - CHANNELL COMMERCIAL CORP.; *pg.* 1870, *pg.* 291
PWT - Poultry Water Treatment - JONES-HAMILTON CO.; *pg.* 1169, *pg.* 1478
PX - Black Oxide - HEATBATH CORPORATION; *pg.* 1165, *pg.* 826
PX-SERIES - Tape Libraries - QUANTUM CORPORATION; *pg.* 458, *pg.* 250
PX11+ - Software - WIND RIVER SYSTEMS, INC.; *pg.* 493, *pg.* 38
PXP - Color Toner - RICOH AMERICAS CORPORATION; *pg.* 461, *pg.* 1131
PY-O-MY - Coffee Cake Mixes - GILSTER-MARY LEE CORPORATION; *pg.* 858, *pg.* 563
PYCAL - Chemical Product - SPECTRUM CHEMICALS & LABORATORY PRODUCTS, INC.; *pg.* 1181, *pg.* 94
PYCNOGENOL - Vitamin & Dietary Supplement - NATROL, INC.; *pg.* 1570, *pg.* 64
PYGANIC - Pesticide - MCLAUGHLIN GORMLEY KING COMPANY; *pg.* 1797, *pg.* 939
PYLES - Pump Extruder - GRACO, INC.; *pg.* 1342, *pg.* 935
PYLORITROL - Software - BIO-RAD LABORATORIES, INC.; *pg.* 1504, *pg.* 101
PYOLA - Insect Pest Control Product - GARDENS ALIVE!, INC.; *pg.* 1796, *pg.* 693
PYRALUX - Film - E.I. DU PONT DE NEMOURS & COMPANY; *pg.* 1159, *pg.* 390
PYRAMAX - Thermal Processing System - BTU INTERNATIONAL, INC.; *pg.* 1320, *pg.* 838
PYRAMID - Textiles - BERNHARDT DESIGN; *pg.* 918, *pg.* 1381
PYRAMID - Bovine Vaccine - BOEHRINGER INGELHEIM VETMEDICA, INC.; *pg.* 1474, *pg.* 989
PYRAMID - Probe Card - CASCADE MICROTECH, INC.; *pg.* 1405, *pg.* 1492
PYRAMID - Cage Layer System or Cages - CTB INTERNATIONAL CORP.; *pg.* 850, *pg.* 695
PYRAMID - Dinnerware - THE HOMER LAUGHLIN CHINA COMPANY; *pg.* 1125, *pg.* 1850
PYRAMID - Game - INTERNATIONAL GAME TECHNOLOGY; *pg.* 957, *pg.* 1024
PYRAMID OF THE KINGS - Game - WMS INDUSTRIES INC.; *pg.* 593, *pg.* 666
PYRAMIS - Data Management System - CARDIAC SCIENCE CORPORATION; *pg.* 1512, *pg.* 1897
PYRAX - Mineral Fillers - R.T. VANDERBILT COMPANY, INC.; *pg.* 1180, *pg.* 364
PYRENA - Footwear - STEVEN MADDEN, LTD.; *pg.* 1819, *pg.* 1176
PYRENEES - Eyewear - MINE SAFETY APPLIANCES COMPANY; *pg.* 1361, *pg.* 1525
PYREX - Glassware - CORNING INCORPORATED; *pg.* 1122, *pg.* 1154
PYREX PORTABLES - Glass & Ceramic Material - CORNING INCORPORATED; *pg.* 1122, *pg.* 1154
PYREXPLUS - Glass & Ceramic Material - CORNING INCORPORATED; *pg.* 1122, *pg.* 1154
PYRIL-PAM - Animal Safety Product - NEOGEN CORPORATION; *pg.* 883, *pg.* 896
PYRO-CHEK - Chemical Product - ALBEMARLE CORPORATION; *pg.* 1146, *pg.* 741
PYRO-GUARD - Fire-Retardant Treated Wood - NORTEK, INC.; *pg.* 100, *pg.* 1607
PYROBATCH - Thermal Processing Equipment - SURFACE COMBUSTION, INC.; *pg.* 1077, *pg.* 1462
PYROBLOC - Flame Retardants - CHEMTURA CORPORATION; *pg.* 1152, *pg.* 355
PYROCAST - Pressed & Monolithic Refractory - RESCO PRODUCTS, INC.; *pg.* 107, *pg.* 1581
PYROCERAM - Glass & Ceramic Material - CORNING INCORPORATED; *pg.* 1122, *pg.* 1154
PYROCIDE - Pesticide - MCLAUGHLIN GORMLEY KING COMPANY; *pg.* 1797, *pg.* 939
PYROCRETE - Fireproofing - CARBOLINE CO.; *pg.* 1152, *pg.* 994
PYRODOME - Skylighting Product - WASCO PRODUCTS, INC.; *pg.* 120, *pg.* 752
PYROFILL - Plaster - USG CORPORATION; *pg.* 118, *pg.* 594
PYROFRAC - Pressed & Monolithic Refractory - RESCO PRODUCTS, INC.; *pg.* 107, *pg.* 1581
PYROFUZE - Fuse Wire - SIGMUND COHN CORP.; *pg.* 1062, *pg.* 1183
PYROIL - Automotive Additives - ASHLAND INC.; *pg.* 972, *pg.* 726
PYROJECTOR - Relief Unit - SWARTWOUT DIVISION; *pg.* 114, *pg.* 978
PYROLON - Clothing - LAKELAND INDUSTRIES, INC.; *pg.* 1354, *pg.* 1338
PYROLON PLUS 2 - Clothing - LAKELAND INDUSTRIES, INC.; *pg.* 1354, *pg.* 1338
PYROLON XT - Clothing - LAKELAND INDUSTRIES, INC.; *pg.* 1354, *pg.* 1338
PYROMET - Stainless Steel Product - CARPENTER TECHNOLOGY CORPORATION; *pg.* 73, *pg.* 1584
PYRON - Fiber - ZOLTEK COMPANIES, INC.; *pg.* 123, *pg.* 974
PYROPEL - Material - ALBANY INTERNATIONAL CORP.; *pg.* 691, *pg.* 1038
PYROPHYL - Pressed & Monolithic Refractory - RESCO PRODUCTS, INC.; *pg.* 107, *pg.* 1581
PYROPURE - Water Purification Systems - PAUL MUELLER COMPANY; *pg.* 706, *pg.* 1007
PYROSET - Chemical Product - CYTEC INDUSTRIES, INC.; *pg.* 1155, *pg.* 1131
PYROSET - Pressed & Monolithic Refractory - RESCO PRODUCTS, INC.; *pg.* 107, *pg.* 1581
PYROTHERM - Thermal Processing Equipment - SURFACE COMBUSTION, INC.; *pg.* 1077, *pg.* 1462
PYROTOOL - Alloy - CARPENTER TECHNOLOGY CORPORATION; *pg.* 73, *pg.* 1584
PYROTROL - Pressed & Monolithic Refractory - RESCO PRODUCTS, INC.; *pg.* 107, *pg.* 1581
PYROVATEX - Flame Retardant Finishes - HUNTSMAN CORPORATION; *pg.* 1167, *pg.* 1758
PYROVATIM - Flame Retardant Finishes - HUNTSMAN CORPORATION; *pg.* 1167, *pg.* 1758
PYROVENT - Skylighting Product - WASCO PRODUCTS, INC.; *pg.* 120, *pg.* 752
PYROWEAR - Stainless Steel Product - CARPENTER TECHNOLOGY CORPORATION; *pg.* 73, *pg.* 1584
PYTHON - Automobile Electronics - DEI HOLDINGS, INC.; *pg.* 633, *pg.* 302
PYTHON - Socket Interface - DIGI INTERNATIONAL INC.; *pg.* 387, *pg.* 948
PYTHON - Automated Collection Vehicle - HEIL ENVIRONMENTAL INDUSTRIES, LTD.; *pg.* 207, *pg.* 1629
PYTHON - Locks - MASTER LOCK COMPANY LLC; *pg.* 1055, *pg.* 1884
PYTHONS - Gaming Product - GLD PRODUCTS, INC.; *pg.* 1835, *pg.* 1882
PYXIS - Health Care Automation Technology - CARDINAL HEALTH, INC.; *pg.* 1512, *pg.* 1448

PYXIS 24 - Software - BIO-RAD LABORATORIES, INC.; *pg.* 1504, *pg.* 101
PZERO - Biomolecule Product - THERMO FISHER SCIENTIFIC INC.; *pg.* 1602, *pg.* 61
PZI VET - Pharmaceutical Product - IDEXX LABORATORIES, INC.; *pg.* 1543, *pg.* 753

Q

Q - Motor Oil - SHELL LUBRICANTS; *pg.* 217, *pg.* 1714
Q-CEL - Polymer - POTTERS INDUSTRIES, INC.; *pg.* 105, *pg.* 1515
Q-CEL - Hollow Spheres - PQ CORPORATION; *pg.* 1178, *pg.* 1515
Q CHECKER - Software - RAND A TECHNOLOGY CORPORATION; *pg.* 459, *pg.* 774
Q CLUBS - Fitness Centers - 24 HOUR FITNESS WORLDWIDE INC.; *pg.* 526, *pg.* 258
Q-EYE - Inspection Lighting System - UNILUX, INC.; *pg.* 682, *pg.* 1118
Q-FACTOR - Cushioning Insoles - ALIMED, INC.; *pg.* 1490, *pg.* 816
Q-FLASH - Flash Memory - MICRON TECHNOLOGY, INC.; *pg.* 435, *pg.* 547
Q-FLEX - Servo Accelerometer - HONEYWELL AEROSPACE ELECTRONIC SYSTEMS; *pg.* 228, *pg.* 17
Q-FLOOR - Metal Building Product - CENTRIA, INC.; *pg.* 74, *pg.* 1554
Q-LAB - Process Monitoring System - EASTMAN KODAK COMPANY; *pg.* 1408, *pg.* 1333
Q-LAC - Paint - KELLY-MOORE PAINT COMPANY, INC.; *pg.* 1443, *pg.* 198
Q-LINK - Software - QUALSTAR CORPORATION; *pg.* 458, *pg.* 279
Q-LON - Weather Seal - SCHLEGEL SYSTEMS, INC.; *pg.* 109, *pg.* 1337
Q-MARK - Closure - ACUSHNET COMPANY; *pg.* 1824, *pg.* 818
Q-PACK - Labels - ADVANCED MICRO DEVICES, INC.; *pg.* 613, *pg.* 282
Q-PADS - Self-Adhering Restoration Products - ITW - EVERCOAT; *pg.* 1443, *pg.* 1415
Q-PIPE - Air Preheaters - ABB INC.; *pg.* 1309, *pg.* 1359
Q-PREP - Testing Instrument System - BECKMAN COULTER, INC.; *pg.* 1402, *pg.* 48
Q-ROK - Silica - U.S. SILICA COMPANY; *pg.* 1185, *pg.* 1849
Q-ROK 1 - Underground Silica - U.S. SILICA COMPANY; *pg.* 1185, *pg.* 1849
Q-ROK 2 - Underground Silica - U.S. SILICA COMPANY; *pg.* 1185, *pg.* 1849
Q-ROK 3 - Underground Silica - U.S. SILICA COMPANY; *pg.* 1185, *pg.* 1849
Q-SET - Flooring Tool & Accessory - Q.E.P. CO., INC.; *pg.* 1371, *pg.* 413
Q-STRESS - Diagnostic Cardiology System - CARDIAC SCIENCE CORPORATION; *pg.* 1512, *pg.* 1897
Q SYSTEM - Furniture - HERMAN MILLER, INC.; *pg.* 926, *pg.* 913
Q-TEC - Air Conditioner - BARD MANUFACTURING COMPANY; *pg.* 1069, *pg.* 1406
Q-TECHNOLOGY - Monitor Reservoirs - SCHLUMBERGER LIMITED; *pg.* 801, *pg.* 1714
Q-TEL - Monitoring System - CARDIAC SCIENCE CORPORATION; *pg.* 1512, *pg.* 1897
Q-TIPS - Swabs - UNILEVER UNITED STATES, INC.; *pg.* 904, *pg.* 1061
Q-TOF - Mass Spectrometer - WATERS CORPORATION; *pg.* 1436, *pg.* 834
Q-TOF MICRO - Mass Spectrometer - WATERS CORPORATION; *pg.* 1436, *pg.* 834
Q-TRAK - Air Quality Monitor - TSI INCORPORATED; *pg.* 1432, *pg.* 965
Q1 - Audio System - QSOUND LABS, INC.; *pg.* 666, *pg.* 1904
Q123 - Auxiliary Process - QSOUND LABS, INC.; *pg.* 666, *pg.* 1904
Q2 - Audio System - QSOUND LABS, INC.; *pg.* 666, *pg.* 1904
Q240AT - Overlay Metrology Tool - NANOMETRICS INCORPORATED; *pg.* 1423, *pg.* 147
Q2X - Audio System - QSOUND LABS, INC.; *pg.* 666, *pg.* 1904
Q3 - Audio System - QSOUND LABS, INC.; *pg.* 666, *pg.* 1904
Q3D - Audio System - QSOUND LABS, INC.; *pg.* 666, *pg.* 1904
Q3DIMENSION - Software - QUALCOMM INCORPORATED; *pg.* 1873, *pg.* 207
Q3DINTERACTIVE - Audio System - QSOUND LABS, INC.; *pg.* 666, *pg.* 1904
Q4 - Turf & Ornamental - PBI/GORDON CORPORATION; *pg.* 1176, *pg.* 985
Q4 - Audio System - QSOUND LABS, INC.; *pg.* 666, *pg.* 1904
Q4 QUADENSITY - Footwear - COLUMBIA SPORTSWEAR COMPANY; *pg.* 1830, *pg.* 1501
Q45 - Engine Type - BRIGGS & STRATTON CORPORATION; *pg.* 201, *pg.* 1899
Q45 INFINITI - Luxury Sedan - NISSAN NORTH AMERICA, INC.; *pg.* 186, *pg.* 1633
Q5 - Telecommunications System - ARRIS GROUP, INC.; *pg.* 353, *pg.* 541
Q6 COLUMBUS - Analytical Device - BRUKER CORPORATION; *pg.* 1511, *pg.* 788
Q7 - SUV - AUDI OF AMERICA, INC.; *pg.* 164, *pg.* 1784
QA CONTROLS - Surface Maintenance Machine - TENNANT COMPANY; *pg.* 1381, *pg.* 944
QACENTER - Software - COMPUWARE CORPORATION; *pg.* 379, *pg.* 879
QADIRECTOR - Software - COMPUWARE CORPORATION; *pg.* 379, *pg.* 879
QAMLINK - Computer Products - BROADCOM CORPORATION; *pg.* 364, *pg.* 108
QANTAS - Airlines - QANTAS AIRWAYS - USA; *pg.* 1920, *pg.* 139
QAS - Pharmaceutical Product - ALERE INC.; *pg.* 1488, *pg.* 849
QB1 - Football Strategy Game Played in Conjunction with Live NFL Telecasts - NTN BUZZTIME, INC.; *pg.* 659, *pg.* 60
QBASS - Audio System - QSOUND LABS, INC.; *pg.* 666, *pg.* 1904
QBC VETAUTOREAD - Hematology Analyzer - IDEXX LABORATORIES, INC.; *pg.* 1543, *pg.* 753
QBIS - Chemical Product - THE DOW CHEMICAL COMPANY; *pg.* 1157, *pg.* 898
QBN - Resource Center - CONTINENTAL AMERICAN CORP.; *pg.* 1880, *pg.* 723
QC - Electronic Tensile Tester - THWING-ALBERT INSTRUMENT COMPANY; *pg.* 1432, *pg.* 1131
QC MANAGER - Data Management System - ABBOTT LABORATORIES; *pg.* 1484, *pg.* 551
QC ONCALL - Software - BIO-RAD LABORATORIES, INC.; *pg.* 1504, *pg.* 101
QC-SMA - Quick Connect Plug - WINCHESTER ELECTRONICS CORP.; *pg.* 688, *pg.* 382
QC VALIDATOR - Software - BIO-RAD LABORATORIES, INC.; *pg.* 1504, *pg.* 101
QC3265 L CAPACITY - Check Weighers - AVERY WEIGH-TRONIX, INC.; *pg.* 1315, *pg.* 925
QC3265 M CAPACITY - Check Weighers - AVERY WEIGH-TRONIX, INC.; *pg.* 1315, *pg.* 925
QC3275 L CAPACITY - Check Weighers - AVERY WEIGH-TRONIX, INC.; *pg.* 1315, *pg.* 925
QCAMCORDER - Software - QUALCOMM INCORPORATED; *pg.* 1873, *pg.* 207
QCAMERA - Camera - QUALCOMM INCORPORATED; *pg.* 1873, *pg.* 207
QCC - Conduit - ELECTRON BEAM TECHNOLOGIES, INC.; *pg.* 1046, *pg.* 621
QCETTE - Medical Product - HOLOGIC, INC.; *pg.* 1416, *pg.* 784
QCF - Photographic Film - EASTMAN KODAK COMPANY; *pg.* 1408, *pg.* 1333
QCF7 - Photographic Film - EASTMAN KODAK COMPANY; *pg.* 1408, *pg.* 1333
QCHAT - Software - QUALCOMM INCORPORATED; *pg.* 1873, *pg.* 207
QCNET - Software - BIO-RAD LABORATORIES, INC.; *pg.* 1504, *pg.* 101
QCOMMERCE - Software - QSOUND LABS, INC.; *pg.* 666, *pg.* 1904
QCP - Graphic Arts Paper - EASTMAN KODAK COMPANY; *pg.* 1408, *pg.* 1333
QCPC - Coupler - OPLINK COMMUNICATIONS, INC.; *pg.* 660, *pg.* 91
QCREATOR - Software - QSOUND LABS, INC.; *pg.* 666, *pg.* 1904
QCS - Software - BIO-RAD LABORATORIES, INC.; *pg.* 1504, *pg.* 101
QD - Sprockets - U.S. TSUBAKI, INC.; *pg.* 221, *pg.* 670
QD 30 PLUS DESIGN - Paint And Stain Product - BENJAMIN MOORE & CO.; *pg.* 1440, *pg.* 1085
QD2 - Safety & Protective Equipment - ENCON SAFETY PRODUCTS; *pg.* 1334, *pg.* 1705
QDESIGNER - Software - DELL SOFTWARE; *pg.* 385, *pg.* 40
QDF - Photographic Film - EASTMAN KODAK COMPANY; *pg.* 1408, *pg.* 1333
QDF7 - Photographic Film - EASTMAN KODAK COMPANY; *pg.* 1408, *pg.* 1333
QDO - Vulcanizing Agents - LORD CORPORATION; *pg.* 1357, *pg.* 1360
QDOBA MEXICAN GRILL - Restaurants - JACK IN THE BOX INC.; *pg.* 1732, *pg.* 204
QDOT - Diagnostic Services - THERMO FISHER SCIENTIFIC INC.; *pg.* 1602, *pg.* 61
QDR - Memory Product - CYPRESS SEMICONDUCTOR CORPORATION; *pg.* 1326, *pg.* 243
QDR - Medical Product - HOLOGIC, INC.; *pg.* 1416, *pg.* 784
QDR-1000 - Medical Product - HOLOGIC, INC.; *pg.* 1416, *pg.* 784
QDR-4500 - Medical Product - HOLOGIC, INC.; *pg.* 1416, *pg.* 784
QDT - Hardware - TRANSACT TECHNOLOGIES INCORPORATED; *pg.* 484, *pg.* 351
QDVD - Audio System - QSOUND LABS, INC.; *pg.* 666, *pg.* 1904
Q.E.D. - Saliva Alcohol Test - ORASURE TECHNOLOGIES INC; *pg.* 1578, *pg.* 1516
QED - Educational Materials - SCHOLASTIC INC.; *pg.* 1683, *pg.* 1288
QEM - Audio System - QSOUND LABS, INC.; *pg.* 666, *pg.* 1904
QEMS - Event Management Software - CANDID COLOR SYSTEMS, INC.; *pg.* 1404, *pg.* 1485
QEP - Flooring Tool & Accessories - Q.E.P. CO., INC.; *pg.* 1371, *pg.* 413
QF-50 - Electronic Components - MOLEX INCORPORATED; *pg.* 655, *pg.* 628
QFC - Supermarket - THE KROGER CO.; *pg.* 1025, *pg.* 1416
QFIELD - Integrated Circuit - ATMEL CORPORATION; *pg.* 621, *pg.* 238
QFLO - Fire Pumps - IDEX CORPORATION; *pg.* 1347, *pg.* 623
QHD - Sprayers - AG-MEIER INDUSTRIES LLC; *pg.* 700, *pg.* 1668
QHD - Software - QSOUND LABS, INC.; *pg.* 666, *pg.* 1904
QHL75 LITE - Dental Product - DENTSPLY INTERNATIONAL INC.; *pg.* 1522, *pg.* 1596
QICLINK - Software - TRIZETTO CORPORATION; *pg.* 485, *pg.* 327
QIGONG - DVD - GAIAM, INC.; *pg.* 1532, *pg.* 334
QIK-FLECS - Electronic Components - MOLEX INCORPORATED; *pg.* 655, *pg.* 628
QINNEX - Styrenic - NOVA CHEMICALS CORPORATION; *pg.* 1175, *pg.* 1904
QINVADER - Medical Product - HOLOGIC, INC.; *pg.* 1416, *pg.* 784
QIX - Quick Insert Exchange - PARKER HANNIFIN WATTS FLUID AIR; *pg.* 1368, *pg.* 750
QLC - Quality-Locked Cheese - LEPRINO FOODS COMPANY; *pg.* 874, *pg.* 320
QLIKVIEW - Computer Software - QLIK TECHNOLOGIES INC.; *pg.* 457, *pg.* 1583
QLIMITER - Wireless Audio Solution - QSOUND LABS, INC.; *pg.* 666, *pg.* 1904
QLINE - Innerspace - STANLEY BLACK & DECKER, INC.; *pg.* 1063, *pg.* 358
QM - Packaged Propane & Air Vaporizer & Mixer System - ALGAS-SDI; *pg.* 1311, *pg.* 1831
QMAC - Analytical System - AIR PRODUCTS AND CHEMICALS, INC.; *pg.* 1145, *pg.* 1513
QMARK - Heaters - MARLEY ENGINEERED PRODUCTS; *pg.* 1074, *pg.* 1612
QMAT - Software - TINIUS OLSEN, INC.; *pg.* 1432, *pg.* 1541
QMAX - Fire Pumps - IDEX CORPORATION; *pg.* 1347, *pg.* 623
QMAX - Software - QSOUND LABS, INC.; *pg.* 666, *pg.* 1904
QMAXII - Audio System - QSOUND LABS, INC.; *pg.* 666, *pg.* 1904
QMDX - Audio System - QSOUND LABS, INC.; *pg.* 666, *pg.* 1904
QMF - Riser Equipment - DRIL-QUIP, INC.; *pg.* 1330, *pg.* 1704

QMFC - Riser Connector - DRIL-QUIP, INC.; *pg.* 1330, *pg.* 1704
QMIXER - Audio System - QSOUND LABS, INC.; *pg.* 666, *pg.* 1904
QMP3D - Software - QSOUND LABS, INC.; *pg.* 666, *pg.* 1904
QMSS - Audio System - QSOUND LABS, INC.; *pg.* 666, *pg.* 1904
QNAV - Integrated Circuit - ATMEL CORPORATION; *pg.* 621, *pg.* 238
QNEXA - Pharmaceutical Preparations - VIVUS, INC.; *pg.* 1608, *pg.* 163
QNX - Neutrino Realtime Operating Systems - HARMAN INTERNATIONAL INDUSTRIES, INCORPORATED; *pg.* 641, *pg.* 374
QNX MOMENTICS - Software - QNX SOFTWARE SYSTEMS LTD; *pg.* 458, *pg.* 1932
QNX NEUTRINO - Software - QNX SOFTWARE SYSTEMS LTD; *pg.* 458, *pg.* 1932
QNX PHOTON MICROGUI - Software - QNX SOFTWARE SYSTEMS LTD; *pg.* 458, *pg.* 1932
QOLLE - Broadcasting Equipment - TAMURA CORPORATION OF AMERICA; *pg.* 1380, *pg.* 291
QOO - Beverages - THE COCA-COLA COMPANY; *pg.* 240, *pg.* 493
QPAK - Fire Pumps - IDEX CORPORATION; *pg.* 1347, *pg.* 623
QPOINT - Software - QUALCOMM INCORPORATED; *pg.* 1873, *pg.* 207
QPP - Communication Product - CENTURYLINK, INC; *pg.* 1870, *pg.* 317
QPROX - Integrated Circuit - ATMEL CORPORATION; *pg.* 621, *pg.* 238
QPV - Pump Vacuum - SHOP-VAC CORPORATION; *pg.* 1375, *pg.* 1595
QR - Cable - COMMSCOPE, INC.; *pg.* 278, *pg.* 1378
QRG - Integrated Circuit - ATMEL CORPORATION; *pg.* 621, *pg.* 238
QRUMBLE - Wireless Audio Solution - QSOUND LABS, INC.; *pg.* 666, *pg.* 1904
QRW - Optical Product - LEUPOLD & STEVENS, INC.; *pg.* 1420, *pg.* 1492
QS - Plastic Core - SONOCO PRODUCTS COMPANY; *pg.* 1469, *pg.* 1619
QS-FRS - Full Rod Oxygen Analyzer - NANOMETRICS INCORPORATED; *pg.* 1423, *pg.* 147
QS1200 - FTIR Metrology Tool - NANOMETRICS INCORPORATED; *pg.* 1423, *pg.* 147
QS2200 - FTIR Metrology Tool - NANOMETRICS INCORPORATED; *pg.* 1423, *pg.* 147
QS3300 - FTIR Metrology Tool - NANOMETRICS INCORPORATED; *pg.* 1423, *pg.* 147
QSAC ACETABULAR - Hip Product - ZIMMER BIOMET HOLDINGS, INC.; *pg.* 1611, *pg.* 699
QSEC - Phone - QUALCOMM INCORPORATED; *pg.* 1873, *pg.* 207
QSI DENTAL SYSTEM - Software - QUALITY SYSTEMS, INC.; *pg.* 1587, *pg.* 115
QSIZZLE - Wireless Audio Solution - QSOUND LABS, INC.; *pg.* 666, *pg.* 1904
QSLIDE - Integrated Circuit - ATMEL CORPORATION; *pg.* 621, *pg.* 238
QSNAP - Software - COMMVAULT SYSTEMS, INC.; *pg.* 377, *pg.* 1125
QSOFT3D - Audio System - QSOUND LABS, INC.; *pg.* 666, *pg.* 1904
QSOUND 3D INTERACTIVE - Audio System Software - QSOUND LABS, INC.; *pg.* 666, *pg.* 1904
QSP - School Fund Raising - THE READER'S DIGEST ASSOCIATION, INC.; *pg.* 1679, *pg.* 1322
QSP - Quiet Wet/Dry Vacuum - SHOP-VAC CORPORATION; *pg.* 1375, *pg.* 1595
QST - Magazine - AMERICAN RADIO RELAY LEAGUE, INC.; *pg.* 130, *pg.* 359
QSTED - Pharmaceutical Preparation - PFIZER INC.; *pg.* 1581, *pg.* 1278
QSURROUND - Audio Processing Software - QSOUND LABS, INC.; *pg.* 666, *pg.* 1904
QSX - Web Conference - POLYCOM, INC.; *pg.* 664, *pg.* 249
QSYS - Audio System - QSOUND LABS, INC.; *pg.* 666, *pg.* 1904
QSYS/TDM - Plug-In Device - QSOUND LABS, INC.; *pg.* 666, *pg.* 1904
QSYSTEM - Hardware Processor - QSOUND LABS, INC.; *pg.* 666, *pg.* 1904
Q.T. - Hospital Disinfectant - HILLYARD, INC.; *pg.* 331, *pg.* 990
QT - Compressor - QUINCY COMPRESSOR INC.; *pg.* 1371, *pg.* 653
QT-TB - Disinfectant - HILLYARD, INC.; *pg.* 331, *pg.* 990
QTELNET - Telecommunications Services - QSOUND LABS, INC.; *pg.* 666, *pg.* 1904
QTEST - Material Test Systems - MTS SYSTEMS CORPORATION; *pg.* 442, *pg.* 923
QTI - Residential Sewage Grinder Package System - LITTLE GIANT PUMP COMPANY; *pg.* 1356, *pg.* 1486
QTOOLS/AX - Software - QSOUND LABS, INC.; *pg.* 666, *pg.* 1904
QTOOLS/SF - Audio System - QSOUND LABS, INC.; *pg.* 666, *pg.* 1904
QTOUCH - Integrated Circuit - ATMEL CORPORATION; *pg.* 621, *pg.* 238
QTR3400 - Media Converter - EMCORE CORPORATION; *pg.* 636, *pg.* 39
QTR3432 - Media Converter - EMCORE CORPORATION; *pg.* 636, *pg.* 39
QTR3500 - Media Converter - EMCORE CORPORATION; *pg.* 636, *pg.* 39
QTR3600 - Electronic Component - EMCORE CORPORATION; *pg.* 636, *pg.* 39
QTWO - Integrated Circuit - ATMEL CORPORATION; *pg.* 621, *pg.* 238
QTWO - Pumps - IDEX CORPORATION; *pg.* 1347, *pg.* 623
QUACAST - Liquid Casting Lubricants - QUAKER CHEMICAL CORP.; *pg.* 1178, *pg.* 1524
QUACK SHOT - Slots - INTERNATIONAL GAME TECHNOLOGY; *pg.* 957, *pg.* 1024
QUACKERS - Game - WMS INDUSTRIES INC.; *pg.* 593, *pg.* 666
QUAD - Software - DATA I/O CORPORATION; *pg.* 382, *pg.* 1824
QUAD - MRI Scanner - FONAR CORPORATION; *pg.* 1413, *pg.* 1179
QUAD - Fabric - NEMSCHOFF, INC.; *pg.* 936, *pg.* 1890
QUAD COMFORT - Footwear - LACROSSE FOOTWEAR, INC.; *pg.* 1811, *pg.* 1503
QUAD DATA RATE - Memory Product - CYPRESS SEMICONDUCTOR CORPORATION; *pg.* 1326, *pg.* 243
QUAD-DIS PLUS - Disinfectant & Deodorizing Liquid - DELTA FOREMOST CHEMICAL CORPORATION; *pg.* 1155, *pg.* 1642
QUAD GAS - Safety Monitor - MINE SAFETY APPLIANCES COMPANY; *pg.* 1361, *pg.* 1525
QUAD-GRIP - Toothbrush - SUNSTAR AMERICAS INC.; *pg.* 1599, *pg.* 591
QUAD-LINK - Bike - MARIN BIKES; *pg.* 1708, *pg.* 168
QUAD OFF ROAD - Magazine - BONNIER CORPORATION; *pg.* 1622, *pg.* 480
QUAD-PHY - Ethernet Transceiver - BROADCOM CORPORATION; *pg.* 364, *pg.* 108
QUAD-QUAD - Hamburger Sandwiches - IN-N-OUT BURGERS, INC.; *pg.* 1732, *pg.* 111
QUAD-RAIL - Electronic Sound Pickups for Guitars - GIBSON GUITAR CORP.; *pg.* 550, *pg.* 1650
QUADCHEK - Safety Test Instruments - ASSOCIATED RESEARCH INC.; *pg.* 1400, *pg.* 622
QUADCURE - Graphic Art UV System - NORDSON CORPORATION; *pg.* 1365, *pg.* 1480
QUADLOG - Safety System - SIEMENS PROCESS INDUSTRIES AND DRIVE; *pg.* 1376, *pg.* 1587
QUADNECTOR - Four Way Power Block - COLEMAN CABLE, INC.; *pg.* 1324, *pg.* 665
QUADPHY - Retimer Device - PMC-SIERRA, INC.; *pg.* 664, *pg.* 287
QUADPORT - Memory Product - CYPRESS SEMICONDUCTOR CORPORATION; *pg.* 1326, *pg.* 243
QUADPUTER - Software - MICROWAY, INC.; *pg.* 1267, *pg.* 841
QUADRA - Ceiling Panel - USG CORPORATION; *pg.* 118, *pg.* 594
QUADRA-CHECK - Video Measurement System - THE L.S. STARRETT COMPANY; *pg.* 1421, *pg.* 783
QUADRA-KLEAN - Industrial Cleaner - TEXAS REFINERY CORP.; *pg.* 986, *pg.* 1696
QUADRA PRESS - Filters - FLOWSERVE CORPORATION; *pg.* 82, *pg.* 1719
QUADRA-QUAT - Sanitizer - BIRKO CORPORATION; *pg.* 1149, *pg.* 332
QUADRA-VAC - Suction Regulator - ALLIED HEALTHCARE PRODUCTS, INC.; *pg.* 1491, *pg.* 990
QUADRAFLEX - Footwear - CAPEZIO BALLET MAKERS INC.; *pg.* 1805, *pg.* 1125
QUADRALAM - Technology - SIMMS FISHING PRODUCTS CORP.; *pg.* 1845, *pg.* 1008
QUADRAMATIC - Chemical Centrifugal - WESTERN STATES MACHINE COMPANY; *pg.* 1388, *pg.* 1455
QUADRANT - Orthopedic Product - DJO INCORPORATED; *pg.* 1524, *pg.* 302
QUADRANT - Furniture - HERMAN MILLER, INC.; *pg.* 926, *pg.* 913
QUADRANT - Fabric - NEMSCHOFF, INC.; *pg.* 936, *pg.* 1890
QUADRATAINER - Plastic Drum - GREIF INC.; *pg.* 1459, *pg.* 1447
QUADRETTI - Fabric - NEMSCHOFF, INC.; *pg.* 936, *pg.* 1890
QUADRIGA - Diagnostic Product - SIEMENS HEALTHCARE DIAGNOSTICS; *pg.* 673, *pg.* 604
QUADRIGA - Precision Navigation Aid - TRIMBLE NAVIGATION LIMITED; *pg.* 1384, *pg.* 288
QUADRILOK - Tooth Equipment - ESCO CORPORATION; *pg.* 1335, *pg.* 1502
QUADRO - Pumps - IDEX CORPORATION; *pg.* 1347, *pg.* 623
QUADRO - Satellite Communication Product - KVH INDUSTRIES INC; *pg.* 650, *pg.* 1602
QUADRO - Graphic System - NVIDIA CORPORATION; *pg.* 447, *pg.* 268
QUADRO - Professional Graphics Board - PNY TECHNOLOGIES, INC.; *pg.* 455, *pg.* 1105
QUADRO COMIL - Pump Product - IDEX CORPORATION; *pg.* 1347, *pg.* 623
QUADRO VAC - Pump Product - IDEX CORPORATION; *pg.* 1347, *pg.* 623
QUADRO YTRON - Pump Product - IDEX CORPORATION; *pg.* 1347, *pg.* 623
QUADSAFE - Safety Light Curtain - OMRON SCIENTIFIC TECHNOLOGIES INCORPORATED; *pg.* 1425, *pg.* 91
QUADSQUAD - Computer Products - BROADCOM CORPORATION; *pg.* 364, *pg.* 108
QUADSWITCH - Fiber Optic Transmission System - COMMUNICATIONS SPECIALTIES, INC.; *pg.* 377, *pg.* 1338
QUADTRO - Valve - OATEY SUPPLY CHAIN SERVICES; *pg.* 30, *pg.* 1433
QUADTRO - Seat Cushion - THE ROHO GROUP; *pg.* 1591, *pg.* 556
QUADTRO SELECT - Cushion - THE ROHO GROUP; *pg.* 1591, *pg.* 556
QUAIL HOLLOW - Apparel Mfr - DELTA APPAREL, INC.; *pg.* 39, *pg.* 1617
QUAIL RUN - Video Game - INTERNATIONAL GAME TECHNOLOGY; *pg.* 957, *pg.* 1024
QUAIL SPRINGS - Brew - DESCHUTES BREWERY INC.; *pg.* 248, *pg.* 1496
QUAKE - Video Game - ID SOFTWARE, INC.; *pg.* 956, *pg.* 1727
QUAKE - Bike - MARIN BIKES; *pg.* 1708, *pg.* 168
QUAKE 4 - Video Game - ID SOFTWARE, INC.; *pg.* 956, *pg.* 1727
QUAKE II - Video Game - ID SOFTWARE, INC.; *pg.* 956, *pg.* 1727
QUAKE III ARENA - Video Game - ID SOFTWARE, INC.; *pg.* 956, *pg.* 1727
QUAKE III GOLD - Video Game - ID SOFTWARE, INC.; *pg.* 956, *pg.* 1727
QUAKE III REVOLUTION - Video Game - ID SOFTWARE, INC.; *pg.* 956, *pg.* 1727
QUAKE III TEAM ARENA - Video Game - ID SOFTWARE, INC.; *pg.* 956, *pg.* 1727
QUAKER - Food & Beverage - PEPSICO, INC.; *pg.* 259, *pg.* 1327
QUAKER - Cereals, Puffed Wheat, Puffed Rice, Oatmeal, Rice Cakes & Grits - THE QUAKER OATS COMPANY; *pg.* 834, *pg.* 588
QUAKER 100% NATURAL CEREAL - Cereal - THE QUAKER OATS COMPANY; *pg.* 834, *pg.* 588
QUAKER BAKERIES - Beverage - THE QUAKER OATS COMPANY; *pg.* 834, *pg.* 588
QUAKER CHEWY - Granola Bars - PEPSICO, INC.; *pg.* 259, *pg.* 1327
QUAKER CHEWY - Granola Bars - THE QUAKER OATS COMPANY; *pg.* 834, *pg.* 588
QUAKER DIPPS - Granola Bars - PEPSICO, INC.; *pg.* 259, *pg.* 1327

QUAKER DIPPS - Granola Bars - THE QUAKER OATS COMPANY; *pg.* 834, *pg.* 588
QUAKER DRYCOTE - Dryfilms - QUAKER CHEMICAL CORP.; *pg.* 1178, *pg.* 1524
QUAKER FABRIC - Upholstery Fabric Line - VICTOR INNOVATIVE TEXTILES; *pg.* 699, *pg.* 819
QUAKER FORMULA - Cleaner - QUAKER CHEMICAL CORP.; *pg.* 1178, *pg.* 1524
QUAKER FRUIT & OATMEAL - Bars - THE QUAKER OATS COMPANY; *pg.* 834, *pg.* 588
QUAKER FRUIT & OATMEAL BITES - Snack - THE QUAKER OATS COMPANY; *pg.* 834, *pg.* 588
QUAKER FRUIT & OATMEAL TOASTABLES - Breakfast Food - THE QUAKER OATS COMPANY; *pg.* 834, *pg.* 588
QUAKER FRUT - Beverage - THE QUAKER OATS COMPANY; *pg.* 834, *pg.* 588
QUAKER INSTANT OATMEAL - Instant Oatmeal - THE QUAKER OATS COMPANY; *pg.* 834, *pg.* 588
QUAKER MAGICA - Beverage - THE QUAKER OATS COMPANY; *pg.* 834, *pg.* 588
QUAKER MAGICA CON SOJA - Beverage - THE QUAKER OATS COMPANY; *pg.* 834, *pg.* 588
QUAKER MAIS SABOR - Cereal - THE QUAKER OATS COMPANY; *pg.* 834, *pg.* 588
QUAKER MEU MINGAU - Beverage - THE QUAKER OATS COMPANY; *pg.* 834, *pg.* 588
QUAKER OAT BRAN - Ready-to-Eat Cereal - THE QUAKER OATS COMPANY; *pg.* 834, *pg.* 588
QUAKER OATMEAL - Breakfast Square - PEPSICO, INC.; *pg.* 259, *pg.* 1327
QUAKER OATMEAL - Cereal - THE QUAKER OATS COMPANY; *pg.* 834, *pg.* 588
QUAKER OATMEAL BREAKFAST SQUARES - Oat Bar - THE QUAKER OATS COMPANY; *pg.* 834, *pg.* 588
QUAKER OATMEAL BROWN SUGAR BLISS - Oatmeal - THE QUAKER OATS COMPANY; *pg.* 834, *pg.* 588
QUAKER OATMEAL HONEY NUT HEAVEN - Oatmeal - THE QUAKER OATS COMPANY; *pg.* 834, *pg.* 588
QUAKER OATMEAL-TO-GO - Oatmeal - THE QUAKER OATS COMPANY; *pg.* 834, *pg.* 588
QUAKER OATS - Oats - THE QUAKER OATS COMPANY; *pg.* 834, *pg.* 588
QUAKER OATSO SIMPLE - Hot Cereal - THE QUAKER OATS COMPANY; *pg.* 834, *pg.* 588
QUAKER OH'S! - Cereal - THE QUAKER OATS COMPANY; *pg.* 834, *pg.* 588
QUAKER PLUSH - Special Finished Upholstery Fabrics - VICTOR INNOVATIVE TEXTILES; *pg.* 699, *pg.* 819
QUAKER QUAKEROL - Liquid Casting Lubricants - QUAKER CHEMICAL CORP.; *pg.* 1178, *pg.* 1524
QUAKER QUAKES - Granola Product - PEPSICO, INC.; *pg.* 259, *pg.* 1327
QUAKER SOY CRISPS - Soy Snack - THE QUAKER OATS COMPANY; *pg.* 834, *pg.* 588
QUAKER SQUARES - Cereal - PEPSICO, INC.; *pg.* 259, *pg.* 1327
QUAKER STATE - Motor Oil - SHELL LUBRICANTS; *pg.* 217, *pg.* 1714
QUAKER SUEDE - Special Finished Upholstery Fabrics - VICTOR INNOVATIVE TEXTILES; *pg.* 699, *pg.* 819
QUAKER VITALY - Cookies - THE QUAKER OATS COMPANY; *pg.* 834, *pg.* 588
QUAKERAL - Lubricant - QUAKER CHEMICAL CORP.; *pg.* 1178, *pg.* 1524
QUAKERCLEAN - Lubricant & Cleaner - QUAKER CHEMICAL CORP.; *pg.* 1178, *pg.* 1524
QUAKERCOOL - Coolant - QUAKER CHEMICAL CORP.; *pg.* 1178, *pg.* 1524
QUAKERCUT - Cutting Oil - QUAKER CHEMICAL CORP.; *pg.* 1178, *pg.* 1524
QUAKERDRAW - Lubricant - QUAKER CHEMICAL CORP.; *pg.* 1178, *pg.* 1524
QUAKES - Rice Snacks - THE QUAKER OATS COMPANY; *pg.* 834, *pg.* 588
QUAL-E-FLEX - Gas Piping Systems - OMEGA FLEX, INC.; *pg.* 982, *pg.* 1532
QUAL-O-RIMETER - BTU Monitor & Control - SELAS HEAT TECHNOLOGY COMPANY LLC; *pg.* 1076, *pg.* 1553
QUALATEX - Bedding Foam - CARPENTER CO.; *pg.* 920, *pg.* 1801
QUALATEX B-BOPS - Balloon - CONTINENTAL AMERICAN CORP.; *pg.* 1880, *pg.* 723
QUALATEX BALLOON NETWORK - Balloon - CONTINENTAL AMERICAN CORP.; *pg.* 1880, *pg.* 723
QUALATEX BALLOONRIBBON - Balloon - CONTINENTAL AMERICAN CORP.; *pg.* 1880, *pg.* 723
QUALATEX MAGICPIPE - Balloon - CONTINENTAL AMERICAN CORP.; *pg.* 1880, *pg.* 723
QUALATEX MASTERBOW - Balloon - CONTINENTAL AMERICAN CORP.; *pg.* 1880, *pg.* 723
QUALATEX PROSIZER - Balloon - CONTINENTAL AMERICAN CORP.; *pg.* 1880, *pg.* 723
QUALATEX SPARKLE - Balloon - CONTINENTAL AMERICAN CORP.; *pg.* 1880, *pg.* 723
QUALATEX SPINNER - Balloon - CONTINENTAL AMERICAN CORP.; *pg.* 1880, *pg.* 723
QUALATEX SUPRAFOIL - Balloon - CONTINENTAL AMERICAN CORP.; *pg.* 1880, *pg.* 723
QUALCARE - Wheelchair Accessories - ALIMED, INC.; *pg.* 1490, *pg.* 816
QUALCRAFT - Diagnostic Imaging Accessories - ALIMED, INC.; *pg.* 1490, *pg.* 816
QUALFLO - Fiber Product - INTERNATIONAL FIBER CORP.; *pg.* 865, *pg.* 1317
QUALI-TOP - Non-Dispensing Closure - OWENS-ILLINOIS, INC.; *pg.* 1466, *pg.* 1470
QUALIBEADS - Software - IDEXX LABORATORIES, INC.; *pg.* 1543, *pg.* 753
QUALICHECK + - Analyzer Compatible Blood Gas Control Solution - RADIOMETER AMERICA INC.; *pg.* 1588, *pg.* 1481
QUALITAIR - Air Conditioning - NORTEK, INC.; *pg.* 100, *pg.* 1607
QUALITAP - Software - NIELSEN AUDIO; *pg.* 446, *pg.* 768
QUALITATE - Flour - CARGILL LIMITED; *pg.* 1475, *pg.* 1914
QUALITI - Footwear - STEVEN MADDEN, LTD.; *pg.* 1819, *pg.* 1176
QUALITY - Hotels & Resorts - CHOICE HOTELS INTERNATIONAL, INC.; *pg.* 1086, *pg.* 775
QUALITY AFFORDABLE RETIREMENT LIVING - Slogan - CAPITAL SENIOR LIVING CORPORATION; *pg.* 1084, *pg.* 1677
QUALITY ASSURANCE ADVANTAGE - Training Program - ATC HEALTHCARE, INC.; *pg.* 1497, *pg.* 1184
QUALITY BEVERAGE EQUIPMENT WORLDWIDE - Slogan - BUNN-O-MATIC CORPORATION; *pg.* 53, *pg.* 661
QUALITY CARE - Household Spray Cleaners - SHERWIN-WILLIAMS DIVERSIFIED BRANDS DIVISION; *pg.* 1448, *pg.* 1435
QUALITY DRESSINGS FOR GENERATIONS - Tagline - KEN'S FOODS, INC.; *pg.* 867, *pg.* 832
QUALITY EDUCATION DATA - Educational Materials - SCHOLASTIC INC.; *pg.* 1683, *pg.* 1288
QUALITY IN MOTION - Electric Motor - BODINE ELECTRIC COMPANY; *pg.* 1318, *pg.* 641
QUALITY IS OUR LEGACY - Tagline - DUMORE CORPORATION; *pg.* 1330, *pg.* 1869
QUALITY LIGHTING - Slogan - PHILIPS LIGHTING; *pg.* 1303, *pg.* 806
QUALITY-LOCKED - Individually Quick-Frozen Cheese - LEPRINO FOODS COMPANY; *pg.* 874, *pg.* 320
QUALITY NEVER LOOKED SO GOOD - Slogan - GORDON INDUSTRIES LTD.; *pg.* 6, *pg.* 1184
QUALITY ON TIME - Pharma Services - NORDION INC.; *pg.* 1573, *pg.* 1932
QUALITY, OUR MOST IMPORTANT PRODUCT - Tagline - WEBSTER INDUSTRIES INC.; *pg.* 1388, *pg.* 1475
QUALITY POWER FOR A DIGITAL WORLD - Slogan - ACTIVE POWER, INC.; *pg.* 1310, *pg.* 1660
QUALITY PRECISION INNOVATION ... SINCE 1880 - Tagline - THE L.S. STARRETT COMPANY; *pg.* 1421, *pg.* 783
QUALITY PRODUCTS FOR NATURAL LIVING - Slogan - FRONTIER NATURAL PRODUCTS CO-OP; *pg.* 509, *pg.* 710
QUALITY RATINGS SUITE - Healthcare Product - HEALTH GRADES, INC.; *pg.* 1256, *pg.* 319
QUALITY, SERVICE AND RELIABILITY AROUND THE WORLD - Slogan - REEL-O-MATIC, INC.; *pg.* 1371, *pg.* 1487
QUALITY, SERVICE, & SUPPORT - Tagline - INTEGRATED SILICON SOLUTION, INC.; *pg.* 645, *pg.* 145
QUALITY SERVICE THROUGHOUT THE YEAR - Tagline - BRISTOL MARINE; *pg.* 1705, *pg.* 1600
THE QUALITY SHOWS IN EVERY MOVE WE MAKE - Tag Line - UNITED VAN LINES, LLC; *pg.* 1929, *pg.* 978
QUALITY STREET - Food & Beverage Product - NESTLE USA, INC.; *pg.* 883, *pg.* 96
QUALITY THROUGH INTEGRITY & TECHNOLOGY - Tagline - ENVIRONMENTAL TECTONICS CORPORATION; *pg.* 1411, *pg.* 1587
QUALITY YOU CAN TASTE. - Slogan - IN-N-OUT BURGERS, INC.; *pg.* 1732, *pg.* 111
QUALITY, YOU CAN TASTE - Tagline - PRAIRIE FARMS DAIRY, INC.; *pg.* 890, *pg.* 561
QUALIZIP - Computer Application Software - NIELSEN AUDIO; *pg.* 446, *pg.* 768
QUAM - Speakers - QUAM-NICHOLS COMPANY; *pg.* 666, *pg.* 588
QUANIX - Powder Coating - NORDSON CORPORATION; *pg.* 1365, *pg.* 1480
QUANLYNX - Software - WATERS CORPORATION; *pg.* 1436, *pg.* 834
QUANT C6 - Medical Tests - IDEXX LABORATORIES, INC.; *pg.* 1543, *pg.* 753
QUANT-IT - Molecular Probe Product - THERMO FISHER SCIENTIFIC INC.; *pg.* 1602, *pg.* 61
QUANTA - Cell Lab - BECKMAN COULTER, INC.; *pg.* 1402, *pg.* 48
QUANTA - Ion & Electron Beam - FEI COMPANY; *pg.* 1413, *pg.* 1498
QUANTA RAY - Laser - NEWPORT CORPORATION; *pg.* 1424, *pg.* 114
QUANTACON - Photomultiplier - PHOTONIS USA PENNSYLVANIA; *pg.* 663, *pg.* 1547
QUANTAFLUOR - Software - BIO-RAD LABORATORIES, INC.; *pg.* 1504, *pg.* 101
QUANTANIUM - Fluoropolymer Coating System - WHITFORD WORLDWIDE COMPANY; *pg.* 1185, *pg.* 1529
QUANTAPHASE - Clinical Diagnostic Product - BIO-RAD LABORATORIES, INC.; *pg.* 1504, *pg.* 101
QUANTAR - Radio Frequency Communication - MOTOROLA SOLUTIONS, INC.; *pg.* 657, *pg.* 659
QUANTASE - Software - BIO-RAD LABORATORIES, INC.; *pg.* 1504, *pg.* 101
QUANTASURE - Scientific Research - LABORATORY CORPORATION OF AMERICA HOLDINGS; *pg.* 1554, *pg.* 1359
QUANTAX 400 STEEL - Analytical System - BRUKER CORPORATION; *pg.* 1511, *pg.* 788
QUANTEC - Software - THOMSON REUTERS CORPORATION; *pg.* 1693, *pg.* 1944
QUANTICUT - Dicer - URSCHEL LABORATORIES INCORPORATED; *pg.* 1386, *pg.* 698
QUANTIFY - Clinical Diagnostic Product - BIO-RAD LABORATORIES, INC.; *pg.* 1504, *pg.* 101
QUANTIKINE - Biological Product - TECHNE CORPORATION; *pg.* 1601, *pg.* 944
QUANTIM - Precision Flow Control - BROOKS INSTRUMENT, LLC; *pg.* 1403, *pg.* 1537
QUANTIMUNE - Software - BIO-RAD LABORATORIES, INC.; *pg.* 1504, *pg.* 101
QUANTISPEED - Computer Hardware - ADVANCED MICRO DEVICES, INC.; *pg.* 613, *pg.* 282
QUANTITY ONE - Software - BIO-RAD LABORATORIES, INC.; *pg.* 1504, *pg.* 101
QUANTOX - Electronic Instrument - KEITHLEY INSTRUMENTS, INC.; *pg.* 1418, *pg.* 1473
QUANTOX - Monitoring System - KLA-TENCOR CORPORATION; *pg.* 1353, *pg.* 146
QUANTOX XP - Non-Contract Oxide-Monitoring System - KLA-TENCOR CORPORATION; *pg.* 1353, *pg.* 146
QUANTRA - Volumetric Assessment Software - HOLOGIC, INC.; *pg.* 1416, *pg.* 784
QUANTREX - Ultrasonic Cleaning System - L&R MANUFACTURING COMPANY; *pg.* 1419, *pg.* 1076
QUANTREX PC3 - Personal-Sized Ultrasonic Cleaning Machine - L&R MANUFACTURING COMPANY; *pg.* 1419, *pg.* 1076
QUANTUM - Organs - ALLEN ORGAN COMPANY; *pg.* 527, *pg.* 1549
QUANTUM - Medical Device - BOSTON SCIENTIFIC CORPORATION; *pg.* 1508, *pg.* 831
QUANTUM - Medical Device - COOK GROUP, INC.; *pg.* 1518, *pg.* 674
QUANTUM - Paint & Coating - DIAMOND VOGEL PAINT, INC.; *pg.* 1441, *pg.* 710
QUANTUM - Pump Product - IDEX CORPORATION; *pg.* 1347, *pg.* 623
QUANTUM - Electrical Enclosures - KILLARK ELECTRIC; *pg.* 1300, *pg.* 998
QUANTUM - Fabric - NEMSCHOFF, INC.; *pg.* 936, *pg.* 1890
QUANTUM - Flatware - ONEIDA LTD; *pg.* 1129, *pg.* 1318
QUANTUM - Assay System - PERKINELMER, INC.; *pg.* 1426, *pg.* 853
QUANTUM - Advanced Performance Detector - PHOTONIS

USA PENNSYLVANIA; *pg.* 663, *pg.* 1547
QUANTUM - Fire Chassis - PIERCE MANUFACTURING, INC.; *pg.* 188, *pg.* 1852
QUANTUM - Bag - SAMSONITE CORPORATION; *pg.* 11, *pg.* 830
QUANTUM - Medical Instrument - WALLACH SURGICAL DEVICES, INC.; *pg.* 1436, *pg.* 381
QUANTUM - Garage Door - WAYNE-DALTON CORP.; *pg.* 120, *pg.* 1465
QUANTUM - Coating System - WHITFORD WORLDWIDE COMPANY; *pg.* 1185, *pg.* 1529
QUANTUM - Fishing Tackle - ZEBCO; *pg.* 1848, *pg.* 1491
QUANTUM BILIARY DILATOR - Medical Device - COOK GROUP, INC.; *pg.* 1518, *pg.* 674
QUANTUM DRY - Apparel - 180S, LLC; *pg.* 1824, *pg.* 754
QUANTUM PD - Overnight Cycler - BAXTER INTERNATIONAL INC.; *pg.* 1499, *pg.* 599
QUANTUM PREP - Software - BIO-RAD LABORATORIES, INC.; *pg.* 1504, *pg.* 101
QUANTUM RESEARCH GROUP - Integrated Circuit - ATMEL CORPORATION; *pg.* 621, *pg.* 238
QUANTUM SNIFFER - Explosive Detector - IMPLANT SCIENCES CORPORATION; *pg.* 1348, *pg.* 860
QUANTUM STEAKHOUSE - Strip - QUANTUM FOODS, INC.; *pg.* 891, *pg.* 559
QUANTUM TSI - Customer-Programmable Microcomputer CPU Switching System - VICON INDUSTRIES, INC.; *pg.* 685, *pg.* 1166
QUANTUM VENT - Apparel - 180S, LLC; *pg.* 1824, *pg.* 754
QUANTUM VIEW - Computer Software - UNITED PARCEL SERVICE, INC.; *pg.* 1928, *pg.* 522
QUANTUM VISION - Software - QUANTUM CORPORATION; *pg.* 458, *pg.* 250
QUANTUM2 - Fluoropolymer Coating System - WHITFORD WORLDWIDE COMPANY; *pg.* 1185, *pg.* 1529
QUANTUM38K - Software - CYPRESS SEMICONDUCTOR CORPORATION; *pg.* 1326, *pg.* 243
QUANTUMFOCUS - Glass & Ceramic Material - CORNING INCORPORATED; *pg.* 1122, *pg.* 1154
QUANTUMM - Footwear - STEVEN MADDEN, LTD.; *pg.* 1819, *pg.* 1176
QUANTUMONE - Screen Printing Ink - POLYONE CORPORATION; *pg.* 1177, *pg.* 1404
QUANTUMPRO - Coin Changer - COIN ACCEPTORS, INC.; *pg.* 1324, *pg.* 994
QUARK - Book Projects - CENVEO INC.; *pg.* 1626, *pg.* 372
QUARK DIGITAL MEDIA SYSTEM - Software - QUARK, INC.; *pg.* 458, *pg.* 322
QUARK PUBLISHING SYSTEM - Software - QUARK, INC.; *pg.* 458, *pg.* 322
QUARKCOMMERCE - Software - QUARK, INC.; *pg.* 458, *pg.* 322
QUARKCOPYDESK - Software - QUARK, INC.; *pg.* 458, *pg.* 322
QUARKCOPYDESK PASSPORT - Software - QUARK, INC.; *pg.* 458, *pg.* 322
QUARKCOPYDESK SPECIAL EDITION - Software - QUARK, INC.; *pg.* 458, *pg.* 322
QUARKDISPATCH - Software - QUARK, INC.; *pg.* 458, *pg.* 322
QUARKDMS - Software - QUARK, INC.; *pg.* 458, *pg.* 322
QUARKXPRESS - Software - QUARK, INC.; *pg.* 458, *pg.* 322
QUARKXPRESS PASSPORT - Software - QUARK, INC.; *pg.* 458, *pg.* 322
QUARROW - Fishing Rods - ALLIANCE SPORTS GROUP, L.P.; *pg.* 1825, *pg.* 1698
QUARTER MILLION - Video Game - BALLY TECHNOLOGIES, INC.; *pg.* 531, *pg.* 1022
QUARTER POUNDER - Sandwich - MCDONALD'S CORPORATION; *pg.* 1737, *pg.* 645
QUARTERBACK - Software - CHYRONHEGO; *pg.* 371, *pg.* 1179
QUARTERMANIA - Game - INTERNATIONAL GAME TECHNOLOGY; *pg.* 957, *pg.* 1024
QUARTERMASTER - Garage Building - BEHLEN MFG. CO.; *pg.* 701, *pg.* 1010
QUARTERS DELUXE - Video Game - INTERNATIONAL GAME TECHNOLOGY; *pg.* 957, *pg.* 1024
QUARTERVAC - Cleaning Product - HILLYARD, INC.; *pg.* 331, *pg.* 990
QUARTET - Jet - WATKINS MANUFACTURING CORPORATION; *pg.* 120, *pg.* 303
QUARTUS - Software - ALTERA CORPORATION; *pg.* 348, *pg.* 237
QUARTUS II - Design Software - ALTERA CORPORATION; *pg.* 348, *pg.* 237
QUARTZ - Graphics & Display Technology - APPLE INC.; *pg.* 350, *pg.* 73
QUARTZ-LUX - Flood Lighting - JUNO LIGHTING, INC.; *pg.* 1300, *pg.* 606
QUARTZELL - Load Cell - AVERY WEIGH-TRONIX, INC.; *pg.* 1315, *pg.* 925
QUARTZITE - Flooring System - THE VALSPAR CORPORATION; *pg.* 1449, *pg.* 945
QUASAR - Plating Process - A BRITE COMPANY; *pg.* 1144, *pg.* 1697
QUASAR - Gaming Product - GLD PRODUCTS, INC.; *pg.* 1835, *pg.* 1882
QUASAR - Area Lighting - JUNO LIGHTING, INC.; *pg.* 1300, *pg.* 606
QUASAR - TV, VCR, Microwave Ovens, Camcorders, Fax Machines - PANASONIC CORPORATION OF NORTH AMERICA; *pg.* 661, *pg.* 1120
QUASH - Plastic Foam - THE DOW CHEMICAL COMPANY; *pg.* 1157, *pg.* 898
QUATREFOIL - Fabric - NEMSCHOFF, INC.; *pg.* 936, *pg.* 1890
QUATRENE - Quaternary Ammonium Derivative - HENKEL CORPORATION; *pg.* 1165, *pg.* 1535
QUATREX - Benzoxazine Resins - HUNTSMAN CORPORATION; *pg.* 1167, *pg.* 1758
QUATRISOFT - HEC Derivatives - THE DOW CHEMICAL COMPANY; *pg.* 1157, *pg.* 898
QUATRIX - Photolithographic Test Technology - KULICKE & SOFFA INDUSTRIES, INC.; *pg.* 650, *pg.* 1533
QUATRO - Soft Drink - THE COCA-COLA COMPANY; *pg.* 240, *pg.* 493
QUATRO - Embedded Controller System - CSR; *pg.* 280, *pg.* 284
QUATRO - Carbide Drill Bit - POWERS FASTENERS INC.; *pg.* 1059, *pg.* 1143
QUATRO LIGHT - Beverages - THE COCA-COLA COMPANY; *pg.* 240, *pg.* 493
QUATTRO - Furniture - AMERICAN LEATHER LP; *pg.* 912, *pg.* 1673
QUATTRO - Seating Product - HUSSEY SEATING CO.; *pg.* 929, *pg.* 751
QUATTRO - Vacuum Transducer - MKS INSTRUMENTS, INC.; *pg.* 1362, *pg.* 781
QUATTRO - Electrophysiology System - MOLECULAR DEVICES CORPORATION; *pg.* 1568, *pg.* 287
QUATTRO - Fabric - NEMSCHOFF, INC.; *pg.* 936, *pg.* 1890
QUATTRO - Mass Spectrometer - WATERS CORPORATION; *pg.* 1436, *pg.* 834
QUATTRO MICRO - Mass Spectrometer - WATERS CORPORATION; *pg.* 1436, *pg.* 834
QUATTRO PREMIER - Mass Spectrometer - WATERS CORPORATION; *pg.* 1436, *pg.* 834
QUATURN - Cartridge - THE CHICAGO FAUCET COMPANY; *pg.* 1044, *pg.* 606
QUAVERS - Potato Snack - FRITO-LAY NORTH AMERICA, INC.; *pg.* 1853, *pg.* 1730
QUAVERS - Potato Chips - PEPSICO, INC.; *pg.* 259, *pg.* 1327
QUAVERS SNACKS - Snack - FRITO-LAY NORTH AMERICA, INC.; *pg.* 1853, *pg.* 1730
QUAY COUNTY SUN - New Mexico Newspaper - FREEDOM COMMUNICATIONS, INC.; *pg.* 1643, *pg.* 110
QUBE - Enterprise-Wide Client Management System - ADVENT SOFTWARE, INC.; *pg.* 345, *pg.* 211
QUBE - Modular FRL's - PARKER HANNIFIN WATTS FLUID AIR; *pg.* 1368, *pg.* 750
QUBES - Classic Cards - LEANIN' TREE, INC.; *pg.* 1658, *pg.* 311
QUCIKMEDIA - Software - CRESTRON ELECTRONICS INC.; *pg.* 631, *pg.* 1116
QUE TAL? - Educational Materials - SCHOLASTIC INC.; *pg.* 1683, *pg.* 1288
QUEBON - Fluid Milk & Ice Cream - AGROPUR COOPERATIVE; *pg.* 836, *pg.* 1950
QUEBON - Ice Cream and Frozen Novelties - UNILEVER CANADA INC.; *pg.* 903, *pg.* 1946
QUEEN - Carpets - SHAW INDUSTRIES GROUP, INC.; *pg.* 942, *pg.* 530
QUEEN ANNE - Furniture - ASHLEY FURNITURE INDUSTRIES, INC.; *pg.* 914, *pg.* 1852
QUEEN ANNE - Insulated & Traditional Beverage Urns & Buffetware - CARLISLE FOODSERVICE PRODUCTS INCORPORATED; *pg.* 1455, *pg.* 1485
QUEEN ANNE - Door & Wood Product - CONESTOGA WOOD SPECIALTIES CORP.; *pg.* 921, *pg.* 1527
QUEEN ANNE - Scotch - DIAGEO CANADA, INC.; *pg.* 1961, *pg.* 1937
QUEEN ANNE - Flatware - THE VOLLRATH COMPANY LLC; *pg.* 1139, *pg.* 1894
QUEEN ANNE'S LACE - Apparel - SAN FRANCISCO MERCANTILE COMPANY, INC.; *pg.* 32, *pg.* 227
QUEEN BEATER - Apparel - OAKLEY, INC.; *pg.* 1840, *pg.* 86
QUEEN CITY ICE - Ice Cream - UNITED DAIRY FARMERS, INC.; *pg.* 906, *pg.* 1426
QUEEN ELANCE - Brief - JOCKEY INTERNATIONAL, INC.; *pg.* 27, *pg.* 1861
QUEEN GUINEVERE - Cake Flour - THE KING ARTHUR FLOUR COMPANY, INC.; *pg.* 833, *pg.* 1767
QUEEN HELENE - Cosmetics - THE HAIN CELESTIAL GROUP, INC.; *pg.* 860, *pg.* 1172
QUEEN ZIP - Apparel - OAKLEY, INC.; *pg.* 1840, *pg.* 86
QUEEN'S CHOICE - Hard Ice Cream - INTERNATIONAL DAIRY QUEEN, INC.; *pg.* 1732, *pg.* 938
QUEEN'S KNIGHT - Game - WMS INDUSTRIES INC.; *pg.* 593, *pg.* 666
QUEENSDOWN - Mattresses - KINGSDOWN, INC.; *pg.* 932, *pg.* 1383
QUEENSGATE - Lighting Product - QUOIZEL INC.; *pg.* 1304, *pg.* 1616
QUELQUE CHOSE - Beer - SLEEMAN UNIBROUE QUEBEC; *pg.* 265, *pg.* 1950
QUENCH - Soft Drink - THE MONARCH BEVERAGE COMPANY, INC.; *pg.* 257, *pg.* 514
QUENCH GUM - Sports Gum - MUELLER SPORTS MEDICINE, INC.; *pg.* 1570, *pg.* 1887
QUENCHCARE - Heat Treating Product - HOUGHTON INTERNATIONAL INC.; *pg.* 1167, *pg.* 1589
QUENCHER - Floor Care - NILFISK-ADVANCE, INC.; *pg.* 332, *pg.* 953
QUERC - Electrical Rules Checker - MAXIM INTEGRATED PRODUCTS, INC.; *pg.* 653, *pg.* 247
QUERO - Food Products - THE KRAFT HEINZ COMPANY; *pg.* 870, *pg.* 1577
QUESADILLAS - Mexican Food - RUIZ FOOD PRODUCTS, INC.; *pg.* 893, *pg.* 77
QUESAPIZZA - Pizza - MAZZIO'S CORPORATION; *pg.* 1737, *pg.* 1490
QUESO ANEJO ENCHILADO - Food Product - V&V SUPREMO FOODS, INC.; *pg.* 907, *pg.* 595
QUESO RANCHERITO - Food Product - V&V SUPREMO FOODS, INC.; *pg.* 907, *pg.* 595
QUESO SIERRA - Food Product - V&V SUPREMO FOODS, INC.; *pg.* 907, *pg.* 595
QUESPRI - Pharmaceutical Preparation - PFIZER INC.; *pg.* 1581, *pg.* 1278
QUEST - Laser Rangefinder Binocular - BUSHNELL OUTDOOR PRODUCTS, INC.; *pg.* 1403, *pg.* 718
QUEST - Cardiac Stress Product - CARDIAC SCIENCE CORPORATION; *pg.* 1512, *pg.* 1897
QUEST - Fan - CRAFTMADE INTERNATIONAL, INC.; *pg.* 1295, *pg.* 1670
QUEST - Bicycle - G. JOANNOU CYCLE CO. INC.; *pg.* 1707, *pg.* 1098
QUEST - Turning Machine - HARDINGE INC.; *pg.* 1344, *pg.* 1157
QUEST - Navigation System - HARLEY-DAVIDSON, INC.; *pg.* 178, *pg.* 1874
QUEST - Slots - INTERNATIONAL GAME TECHNOLOGY; *pg.* 957, *pg.* 1024
QUEST - Fabric - NEMSCHOFF, INC.; *pg.* 936, *pg.* 1890
QUEST - Van - NISSAN NORTH AMERICA, INC.; *pg.* 186, *pg.* 1633
QUEST - Horses & Livestock Anthelmintic - PFIZER INC.; *pg.* 1581, *pg.* 1278
QUEST - Exterior Home Siding - PLY GEM SIDING GROUP; *pg.* 105, *pg.* 986
QUEST CENTRAL - Software - DELL SOFTWARE; *pg.* 385, *pg.* 40
QUEST CENTRAL FOR DB2 - Software - DELL SOFTWARE; *pg.* 385, *pg.* 40
QUEST CENTRAL FOR ORACLE - Software - DELL SOFTWARE; *pg.* 385, *pg.* 40
QUEST COEXISTENCE MANAGER FOR NOTES - Software - DELL SOFTWARE; *pg.* 385, *pg.* 40
QUEST FOR THE LOST CITY - Video Game - INTERNATIONAL GAME TECHNOLOGY; *pg.* 957, *pg.* 1024
QUEST PERFORMANCE TUNING SUITE FOR SYBASE

ASE - Software - DELL SOFTWARE; pg. 385, pg. 40
QUEST SOFTWARE - Software - DELL SOFTWARE; pg. 385, pg. 40
QUEST SQL OPTIMIZER SUITE FOR SYBASE ASE - Software - DELL SOFTWARE; pg. 385, pg. 40
QUEST WEB PARTS FOR SHAREPOINT - Software - DELL SOFTWARE; pg. 385, pg. 40
QUEST3 - Vinyl Siding - PLY GEM SIDING GROUP; pg. 105, pg. 986
QUESTA - Functional Verification Software - MENTOR GRAPHICS CORPORATION; pg. 432, pg. 1510
QUESTEMP - Heat Stress & Thermal Environment Monitors - 3M DETECTION SOLUTIONS; pg. 1398, pg. 1885
QUESTRA - Crystaline Polymers - THE DOW CHEMICAL COMPANY; pg. 1157, pg. 898
QUESTSUITE - Monitoring System Software - 3M DETECTION SOLUTIONS; pg. 1398, pg. 1885
QUETICO - Canoes - ALUMACRAFT BOAT COMPANY; pg. 1705, pg. 964
QUETZALCOATL - Chocolate Product - GUITTARD CHOCOLATE COMPANY; pg. 1855, pg. 55
QUEVEDO - Chocolate Product - GUITTARD CHOCOLATE COMPANY; pg. 1855, pg. 55
QUEX - Software - SAS INSTITUTE INC.; pg. 466, pg. 1361
QUIBBLE-FREE GUARANTEE - Money Back Guarantee Exclusive to Miles Kimball - SILVER STAR BRANDS; pg. 1785, pg. 1886
QUIC NETWORK - Software - QUALITY SYSTEMS, INC.; pg. 1587, pg. 115
QUICK - Rust Preventive - SLIDE PRODUCTS, INC.; pg. 1181, pg. 670
QUICK 7S - Game - MISSOURI LOTTERY; pg. 999, pg. 979
QUICK-ACCESS - Robotic Product - HAMILTON CO., INC.; pg. 1415, pg. 1031
QUICK ADJUST - Basketball Equipment - LIFETIME PRODUCTS INC.; pg. 933, pg. 1751
QUICK & CLEAN - Aerosol-Quarts-Wipes Systems - HILLYARD, INC.; pg. 331, pg. 990
QUICK & COOL - Ice Chest - IGLOO PRODUCTS CORPORATION; pg. 1126, pg. 1724
QUICK & EASY - Marinades - KIKKOMAN INTERNATIONAL INC.; pg. 868, pg. 220
QUICK & HOT - Hot Water Dispensers - ANAHEIM MANUFACTURING COMPANY; pg. 51, pg. 48
QUICK & SIMPLE - Magazine - THE HEARST CORPORATION; pg. 1649, pg. 1239
QUICK-AS-A-WINK - Sewer & Draincleaning Businesses - THE DWYER GROUP, INC.; pg. 79, pg. 1748
QUICK-ATTACH - Helmet - E.D. BULLARD COMPANY; pg. 1332, pg. 727
QUICK BEANS - Dried Beans - N.K. HURST CO., INC.; pg. 886, pg. 689
QUICK BRAID - Hair Care Product - CONAIR CORPORATION; pg. 505, pg. 1055
QUICK-BRIX - Brix Meter - METTLER-TOLEDO INTERNATIONAL INC.; pg. 1423, pg. 1441
QUICK BUSINESS CREDIT - Online Banking System - CENTRAL VALLEY COMMUNITY BANCORP; pg. 733, pg. 93
QUICK-CAL - Soil Care Product - GARDENS ALIVE!, INC.; pg. 1796, pg. 693
QUICK CAL - Densitometer - X-RITE, INCORPORATED; pg. 1437, pg. 891
QUICK-CAP - Dental Implant System - LIFECORE BIOMEDICAL, LLC; pg. 1556, pg. 920
QUICK CASH - Money Services - THE WESTERN UNION COMPANY; pg. 822, pg. 327
QUICK CHALLENGE - Sterilization Product - PROPPER MANUFACTURING COMPANY, INC.; pg. 1586, pg. 1175
QUICK CHANGE - Modular Dressing Table/Storage Cubes - DOREL JUVENILE GROUP, INC.; pg. 923, pg. 676
QUICK-CHANGE - Electronic Components - MOLEX INCORPORATED; pg. 655, pg. 628
QUICK-CHANGE - Reflector - PHOTOGENIC PROFESSIONAL LIGHTING; pg. 1426, pg. 556
QUICK CHANGE ARBOR - Fastening System - TEXTRON INC.; pg. 235, pg. 1607
QUICK-CHECK - Electrical Test & Measurement - HD ELECTRIC COMPANY; pg. 1299, pg. 666
QUICK CHEF - Kitchenware - TUPPERWARE BRANDS CORPORATION; pg. 1139, pg. 456
QUICK-CLAW - Drum Handling Equipment - LIFTOMATIC MATERIAL HANDLING INC.; pg. 94, pg. 560
QUICK CLEAN - Surface Maintenance Machine - TENNANT COMPANY; pg. 1381, pg. 944
QUICK/CLICK - Plastic Boxes - PASS & SEYMOUR/LEGRAND; pg. 1303, pg. 1344
QUICK-CLOSE - Nozzle - GRACO, INC.; pg. 1342, pg. 935
QUICK COALS - Charcoal Lighter - DURAFLAME, INC.; pg. 1123, pg. 280
QUICK CODE - Medical Equipment - INVACARE CORPORATION; pg. 1546, pg. 1451
QUICK COLLECT - Money Services - THE WESTERN UNION COMPANY; pg. 822, pg. 327
QUICK-CORE - Needle - COOK GROUP, INC.; pg. 1518, pg. 674
QUICK COURT - Backboard - LIFETIME PRODUCTS INC.; pg. 933, pg. 1751
QUICK-CROSS - Excimer Laser System - THE SPECTRANETICS CORPORATION; pg. 1595, pg. 315
QUICK-CYCLE SWITCH SYSTEM - Laser Technology - COAST CUTLERY COMPANY; pg. 1121, pg. 1501
QUICK DIGEST - Nutritional Product - NUTRACEUTICAL INTERNATIONAL CORPORATION; pg. 1576, pg. 1753
QUICK DISCONNECT - Hardware Product - DORMAN PRODUCTS, INC.; pg. 204, pg. 1522
QUICK DISCONNECT - Pumps - IDEX CORPORATION; pg. 1347, pg. 623
QUICK DRAW - Punch Driver - GREENLEE TEXTRON INC.; pg. 1048, pg. 655
QUICK DRAW - Lottery Game - NEW YORK STATE LOTTERY; pg. 1001, pg. 1340
QUICK DRAW - Game - THE STATE LOTTERY COMMISSION OF INDIANA; pg. 1006, pg. 690
QUICK DRAW - Fastening System - TEXTRON INC.; pg. 235, pg. 1607
QUICK DRY - Undercoater - JONES-BLAIR COMPANY; pg. 1443, pg. 1682
QUICK/ENTRY - Process for Entering Cable Into Plastic Boxes - PASS & SEYMOUR/LEGRAND; pg. 1303, pg. 1344
QUICK FEET - Med Belt - SCHOOL-TECH, INC.; pg. 1844, pg. 866
QUICK-FINISH - Photographic Processing Chemicals - EASTMAN KODAK COMPANY; pg. 1408, pg. 1333
QUICK-FIT - Replacement Cartridge - PHOTONIS USA PENNSYLVANIA; pg. 663, pg. 1547
QUICK-FIX - Fluid Handling System - GRACO, INC.; pg. 1342, pg. 935
QUICK-FIX - Surgical Screws - OSTEOMED CORPORATION; pg. 1425, pg. 1658
QUICK FRESH - Cleaner & Rejuvenator - MCNETT CORPORATION; pg. 1839, pg. 1817
QUICK GRIP - Strap - MASON COMPANIES, INC.; pg. 1811, pg. 1856
QUICK-GRIP - Clamps - NEWELL RUBBERMAID INC.; pg. 1128, pg. 515
QUICK HEAT - Heater - KAZ, INC.; pg. 58, pg. 844
QUICK-HITCH - Plow Mounting System - HINIKER COMPANY; pg. 704, pg. 927
QUICK HITCH SYSTEM - Fastening System - TEXTRON INC.; pg. 235, pg. 1607
QUICK-LIFT - Hydraulic Fluid - AMERICAN GREASE STICK CO.; pg. 971, pg. 902
QUICK LIFT - Basketball Standards - LIFETIME PRODUCTS INC.; pg. 933, pg. 1751
QUICK LINK - Ceiling Mount - DA-LITE SCREEN COMPANY; pg. 632, pg. 698
QUICK LOCATE - Software - MELISSA DATA CORP.; pg. 432, pg. 188
QUICK LOCK - Mounting Assembly - IN-SINK-ERATOR; pg. 57, pg. 1888
QUICK-LOCK CYLINDER PIN - Lock Cylinder - GRACO, INC.; pg. 1342, pg. 935
QUICK MAP 3D - Software - LASER TECHNOLOGY, INC.; pg. 1419, pg. 314
QUICK MATE - Wall Washing Kits - GEERPRES INC.; pg. 1339, pg. 901
QUICK-MOUNT - Commercial Lighting - SWIVELIER CO., INC.; pg. 1307, pg. 1142
QUICK-N-EASY - Food Products - SMITHFIELD FOODS, INC.; pg. 896, pg. 1806
QUICK-N-EASY - Ceiling Panel - USG CORPORATION; pg. 118, pg. 594
QUICK 'N HEARTY - Microwaveable Oatmeal - THE QUAKER OATS COMPANY; pg. 834, pg. 588
QUICK-OPE - Envelopes - TENSION ENVELOPE CORPORATION; pg. 483, pg. 986
QUICK PAY - Games - PENN NATIONAL GAMING, INC.; pg. 574, pg. 1595
QUICK PEEL - Office Product - AVERY DENNISON CORPORATION; pg. 1452, pg. 95
QUICK PLUG - Hydraulic Cement - DAP PRODUCTS, INC.; pg. 1441, pg. 756
QUICK POUCH - Cushioned Packaging Material - SEALED AIR CORPORATION; pg. 1468, pg. 1058
QUICK-PWM - Controllers - MAXIM INTEGRATED PRODUCTS, INC.; pg. 653, pg. 247
QUICK QUADS POKER - Video Game - INTERNATIONAL GAME TECHNOLOGY; pg. 957, pg. 1024
QUICK QUIZZES - Quiz - AMERICAN TECHNICAL PUBLISHERS, INC.; pg. 1616, pg. 649
QUICK RECOVERY - Software - COMMVAULT SYSTEMS, INC.; pg. 377, pg. 1125
QUICK RELEASE - Pumps - IDEX CORPORATION; pg. 1347, pg. 623
QUICK-RELEASE - Bath Product - KOHLER CO.; pg. 91, pg. 1862
QUICK RESPONSE - Management Program - CARDIAC SCIENCE CORPORATION; pg. 1512, pg. 1897
QUICK SCAN - Recorders - DWYER INSTRUMENTS INC.; pg. 1330, pg. 694
QUICK-SEAL - Test Plugs - TUTHILL CORPORATION PUMP GROUP; pg. 1385, pg. 553
QUICK-SERT - Inserts - YARDLEY PRODUCTS CORPORATION; pg. 1391, pg. 1596
QUICK SET - Medical Equipment - INVACARE CORPORATION; pg. 1546, pg. 1451
QUICK SHIP - Expedited Shipment - BOBRICK WASHROOM EQUIPMENT, INC.; pg. 1043, pg. 166
QUICK SHOPPING CART - Software Product - GO DADDY INC.; pg. 1249, pg. 21
QUICK SHOT - On-board Compressor Control System - AIR LIFT COMPANY; pg. 198, pg. 895
QUICK SHOT - Tube Cleaner - GOODWAY TECHNOLOGIES CORPORATION; pg. 1341, pg. 374
QUICK-SHOT - Fluid Handling System - GRACO, INC.; pg. 1342, pg. 935
QUICK SIT - Video Viewing System - SWORDFISH FINANCIAL, INC.; pg. 1430, pg. 1737
QUICK SLIP - Hair Care Product - JOHN PAUL MITCHELL SYSTEMS; pg. 512, pg. 133
QUICK SNAP - Software - COMMVAULT SYSTEMS, INC.; pg. 377, pg. 1125
QUICK SNAP - Muffs - SELLSTROM MANUFACTURING CO.; pg. 1428, pg. 659
QUICK-SPRAY - Powdered Wall Texture - USG CORPORATION; pg. 118, pg. 594
QUICK-START - Chili Mix - BASIC AMERICAN FOODS, INC.; pg. 839, pg. 303
QUICK START - Software - BIO-RAD LABORATORIES, INC.; pg. 1504, pg. 101
QUICK START - Firestarter - DURAFLAME, INC.; pg. 1123, pg. 280
QUICK START - Sensor - MOCON, INC.; pg. 1363, pg. 940
QUICK STEAMER - Carpet Deep Cleaner - BISSELL HOMECARE, INC.; pg. 52, pg. 887
QUICK STICK - Laboratory Tool - STOELTING CO.; pg. 1430, pg. 671
QUICK STOP - Convenience Stores - THE PANTRY, INC.; pg. 1029, pg. 1360
QUICK STUFF - Convenience Stores - JACK IN THE BOX INC.; pg. 1732, pg. 204
QUICK TACK - Medical Product - GENZYME CORPORATION; pg. 1534, pg. 808
QUICK TAKES - Healthcare Service - PUBLIX SUPER MARKETS, INC.; pg. 1031, pg. 437
QUICK TEEJET - Spray Nozzle - SPRAYING SYSTEMS CO.; pg. 1063, pg. 670
QUICK TEST - Chemical Cleaner Product - TECH SPRAY, L.P.; pg. 1183, pg. 1659
QUICK-TIES - Velcro Tape - GARDENS ALIVE!, INC.; pg. 1796, pg. 693
QUICK-VIEW - Rotary Valve Position Indicator - DWYER INSTRUMENTS INC.; pg. 1330, pg. 694
QUICKBASE - Software - INTUIT INC.; pg. 769, pg. 158
QUICKBID - Automated Bid/Contracting System - CACI INTERNATIONAL INC.; pg. 367, pg. 1773
QUICKBOOKS - Payroll Software - INTUIT INC.; pg. 769, pg. 158
QUICKBOOKS ENTERPRISE SOLUTIONS - Software - INTUIT INC.; pg. 769, pg. 158
QUICKBOOKS ONLINE BASIC - Software - INTUIT INC.; pg. 769, pg. 158
QUICKBOOKS ONLINE PLUS - Software - INTUIT INC.; pg.

769, pg. 158
QUICKBOOKS PREMIER - Software - INTUIT INC.; pg. 769, pg. 158
QUICKBOOKS PREMIER ACCOUNTANT - Software - INTUIT INC.; pg. 769, pg. 158
QUICKBOOKS PRO - Accounting Software - INTUIT INC.; pg. 769, pg. 158
QUICKBOOKS SIMPLE START - Software - INTUIT INC.; pg. 769, pg. 158
QUICKBRIDGE - Video Communication System - GLOWPOINT, INC.; pg. 401, pg. 1094
QUICKCAPS - Electrical Outlet Cover - FOAMPRO MANUFACTURING, INC.; pg. 1442, pg. 110
QUICKCHANGE - Filters & Membranes - ENTEGRIS, INC.; pg. 1882, pg. 788
QUICKCHART - Software - BOTTOMLINE TECHNOLOGIES INC.; pg. 363, pg. 483
QUICKCHECK - Self-Check Station - SENTRY TECHNOLOGY CORPORATION; pg. 672, pg. 1339
QUICKCHILLER - Refrigeration System - ALTO-SHAAM INC.; pg. 836, pg. 1869
QUICKCLAMP - Software - ROCKWELL AUTOMATION, INC.; pg. 668, pg. 1880
QUICKCLIP - Wall Mounted Poster Frame - LAVI INDUSTRIES INC.; pg. 93, pg. 299
QUICKCOOK - Kitchen Appliance - VIKING RANGE CORPORATION; pg. 61, pg. 968
QUICKDELIVERY - Software - BOTTOMLINE TECHNOLOGIES INC.; pg. 363, pg. 483
QUICKDRAW - Application Program - APPLE INC.; pg. 350, pg. 73
QUICKEDGE - Bevel Product - GLEASON CORPORATION; pg. 1340, pg. 1335
QUICKEN - Software - INTUIT INC.; pg. 769, pg. 158
QUICKEN.COM - Accounting Software - INTUIT INC.; pg. 769, pg. 158
QUICKER CLICKER - Pencils - PENTEL OF AMERICA, LTD.; pg. 453, pg. 295
QUICKEXCHANGE - Service - L.L. BEAN, INC.; pg. 1777, pg. 750
QUICKFIL - Chalk Product - C.H. HANSON COMPANY; pg. 1322, pg. 636
QUICKFINDER - Computer Software - NOVELL INC.; pg. 446, pg. 852
QUICKFLEX - CRT Therapy - ST. JUDE MEDICAL, INC.; pg. 1596, pg. 963
QUICKFLO - Packless Outlet Plug - GRACO, INC.; pg. 1342, pg. 935
QUICKFX - Software - MITEK SYSTEMS, INC.; pg. 440, pg. 204
QUICKFX PRO - Software - MITEK SYSTEMS, INC.; pg. 440, pg. 204
QUICKIC - IC Layout Editor - MAXIM INTEGRATED PRODUCTS, INC.; pg. 653, pg. 247
QUICKIE CLIPPER - Balloon - CONTINENTAL AMERICAN CORP.; pg. 1880, pg. 723
QUICKIE CLIPS - Balloon - CONTINENTAL AMERICAN CORP.; pg. 1880, pg. 723
QUICKJACK - Transaction Processing System - EVERI HOLDINGS INC.; pg. 749, pg. 1023
QUICKJAW - Connector - IDEAL INDUSTRIES, INC.; pg. 1051, pg. 662
QUICKJET - Spray Product - SPRAYING SYSTEMS CO.; pg. 1063, pg. 670
QUICKLABEL - Labeling System - ASTRO-MED, INC.; pg. 619, pg. 1609
QUICKLATCH - Medical Equipment - CONMED CORPORATION; pg. 1517, pg. 1347
QUICKLAWN - Home Products - HABAND COMPANY, INC.; pg. 1772, pg. 1099
QUICKLE - Bath Cleaner - KAO BRANDS CO. INC.; pg. 513, pg. 1415
QUICKLE WIPER - Cleaning Tool - KAO BRANDS CO. INC.; pg. 513, pg. 1415
QUICKLINK - Bus Transportation Service - GREYHOUND LINES, INC.; pg. 1910, pg. 1681
QUICKLINK - Software - SMITH MICRO SOFTWARE, INC.; pg. 471, pg. 41
QUICKLOCK - Coupler - PANDUIT CORP.; pg. 661, pg. 663
QUICKLOG - Software - SYMANTEC CORPORATION; pg. 478, pg. 161
QUICKLUB - Industrial Lubrication Equipment - LINCOLN INDUSTRIAL CORP.; pg. 1355, pg. 999
QUICKMASH - Mashed Potatoes - J.R. SIMPLOT COMPANY; pg. 867, pg. 547
QUICKMIPS - Hardware - IMAGINATION TECHNOLOGIES; pg. 412, pg. 285
QUICKMIST - Air Atomizing Nozzle - SPRAYING SYSTEMS CO.; pg. 1063, pg. 670
QUICKMOP - Surface Maintenance Machine - TENNANT COMPANY; pg. 1381, pg. 944
QUICKMOUNT - Safety Barricade Solution - LAVI INDUSTRIES INC.; pg. 93, pg. 299
QUICKNET - Fiber Solution - PANDUIT CORP.; pg. 661, pg. 663
QUICKO - Pet Product - PETSMART, INC.; pg. 1481, pg. 18
QUICKON II - Couplers - MORRIS COUPLING COMPANY; pg. 1057, pg. 1530
QUICKON II COUPLER - Coupling - MORRIS COUPLING COMPANY; pg. 1057, pg. 1530
QUICKOPT - CRT Therapy - ST. JUDE MEDICAL, INC.; pg. 1596, pg. 963
QUICKPART BUILDER - Software System - MENTOR GRAPHICS CORPORATION; pg. 432, pg. 1510
QUICKPART TABLES - Software System - MENTOR GRAPHICS CORPORATION; pg. 432, pg. 1510
QUICKPATH - Splitter Module - ALLIANCE FIBER OPTIC PRODUCTS, INC.; pg. 1399, pg. 283
QUICKPEAK - Chargers - HOBBICO, INC.; pg. 956, pg. 562
QUICKPEEK - Proofing System - THWING-ALBERT INSTRUMENT COMPANY; pg. 1432, pg. 1131
QUICKPLAN - Software - TRIMBLE NAVIGATION LIMITED; pg. 1384, pg. 288
QUICKPLAY - Software - PHILIPS SOLID-STATE LIGHTING SOLUTIONS; pg. 1303, pg. 806
QUICKPOINT - Software - IGO, INC.; pg. 644, pg. 22
QUICKRECORD - Electronic Healthcare Document - BOTTOMLINE TECHNOLOGIES (DE), INC.; pg. 727, pg. 1038
QUICKRECORD - Software - BOTTOMLINE TECHNOLOGIES INC.; pg. 363, pg. 483
QUICKRECORD INTELLIGENT HUB - Software - BOTTOMLINE TECHNOLOGIES INC.; pg. 363, pg. 483
QUICKSCAN - Software - BOTTOMLINE TECHNOLOGIES INC.; pg. 363, pg. 483
QUICKSCAN - Software - EMC CORPORATION; pg. 391, pg. 825
QUICKSCOPE - Critical Loss Information - MAXONS RESTORATIONS; pg. 332, pg. 1257
QUICKSCORE II - Software - SCANTRON CORPORATION; pg. 467, pg. 922
QUICKSEAL - Storefront Framing Systems - KAWNEER COMPANY, INC.; pg. 90, pg. 537
QUICKSET - Grill - W.C. BRADLEY CO.; pg. 62, pg. 528
QUICKSET TRADITIONAL - Grill - W.C. BRADLEY CO.; pg. 62, pg. 528
QUICKSHIFT - Power Transmission Equipment - TWIN DISC, INCORPORATED; pg. 220, pg. 1889
QUICKSHIP 1 - Quick Delivery Service for Custom Loose-Leaf Products - AMERICAN THERMOPLASTIC COMPANY; pg. 349, pg. 1573
QUICKSHIP 6 - Quick Delivery Service for Custom Loose-Leaf Products - AMERICAN THERMOPLASTIC COMPANY; pg. 349, pg. 1573
QUICKSHIP PROGRAM - Office Furniture - JOFCO INC.; pg. 931, pg. 691
QUICKSIGN - Software - BOTTOMLINE TECHNOLOGIES INC.; pg. 363, pg. 483
QUICKSILVER - Software Solutions - ENCORIUM GROUP, INC.; pg. 1528, pg. 1591
QUICKSILVER - Pest Control Product - FMC CORPORATION; pg. 1163, pg. 1564
QUICKSILVER - Content Tools - SEACHANGE INTERNATIONAL, INC.; pg. 1279, pg. 781
QUICKSILVER - Cohesive-Coated Laminate Polyethylene Foam - SEALED AIR CORPORATION; pg. 1468, pg. 1058
QUICKSITE - Pacing Leads - ST. JUDE MEDICAL, INC.; pg. 1596, pg. 963
QUICKSKILL - Software - SKILLSOFT PLC; pg. 470, pg. 1037
QUICKSON MULTIFRESH - Ink - VAN SON HOLLAND INK CORPORATION OF AMERICA; pg. 487, pg. 1169
QUICKSON PLUS - Ink - VAN SON HOLLAND INK CORPORATION OF AMERICA; pg. 487, pg. 1169
QUICKSON PRO - Ink - VAN SON HOLLAND INK CORPORATION OF AMERICA; pg. 487, pg. 1169
QUICKSOURCE - Telephone Information Service - AT&T INC.; pg. 1867, pg. 1674
QUICKSTART - Manual - XEROX CORPORATION; pg. 494, pg. 365
QUICKSTEAMER - Floor Care Product - BISSELL HOMECARE, INC.; pg. 52, pg. 887
QUICKSTIC - Electrosurgical Devices - ANGIODYNAMICS, INC.; pg. 1495, pg. 1173
QUICKSTROKES - Software - MITEK SYSTEMS, INC.; pg. 440, pg. 204
QUICKSUITE - Medical Product - MEDLINE INDUSTRIES, INC.; pg. 1562, pg. 635
QUICKSWITCH - Fiber Optic Switch - ELECTRO STANDARDS LABORATORIES INC.; pg. 390, pg. 1600
QUICKTAX - Software - INTUIT INC.; pg. 769, pg. 158
QUICKTIME - Software Product - APPLE INC.; pg. 350, pg. 73
QUICKTIME BROADCASTER - Application Program - APPLE INC.; pg. 350, pg. 73
QUICKTIX - Games - PENN NATIONAL GAMING, INC.; pg. 574, pg. 1595
QUICKTOOLS - Simulation - MAXIM INTEGRATED PRODUCTS, INC.; pg. 653, pg. 247
QUICKTOUCH - Power Roller - WAGNER SPRAY TECH CORPORATION; pg. 1449, pg. 954
QUICKTOUCH PRO - Power Roller - WAGNER SPRAY TECH CORPORATION; pg. 1449, pg. 954
QUICKVALVE - Valve Insertion - ROMAC INDUSTRIES, INC.; pg. 1061, pg. 1818
QUICKVHDL - Software System - MENTOR GRAPHICS CORPORATION; pg. 432, pg. 1510
QUICKVIEW - Software - HEALTHPORT, INC.; pg. 403, pg. 484
QUICKVUE - Diagnostic Test Product - QUIDEL CORPORATION; pg. 1588, pg. 207
QUICKVUE ADVANCE - Diagnostic Test Product - QUIDEL CORPORATION; pg. 1588, pg. 207
QUICKVUE IN-LINE - Diagnostic Test Product - QUIDEL CORPORATION; pg. 1588, pg. 207
QUICKVUE+ - Diagnostic Test Product - QUIDEL CORPORATION; pg. 1588, pg. 207
QUICPICS - Software - CANDID COLOR SYSTEMS, INC.; pg. 1404, pg. 1485
QUICPOST - Software - CANDID COLOR SYSTEMS, INC.; pg. 1404, pg. 1485
QUIDAM - Show And Ticket - CIRQUE DU SOLEIL INC.; pg. 540, pg. 1954
QUIDDITY - Open Architecture, On-Line Relational Marketing Database - ACXIOM CORPORATION; pg. 342, pg. 607
QUIET 1 - Power Equipment - ECHO INCORPORATED; pg. 1046, pg. 626
QUIET BRAKES - Battery & Windshield Treatment - MOC PRODUCTS COMPANY, INC.; pg. 332, pg. 174
QUIET CART - Shelf Style - WELLMASTER CARTS; pg. 1388, pg. 1934
QUIET CHOICE - Packaging - PACTIV CORPORATION; pg. 1466, pg. 624
QUIET-CLOSE - Bath Product - KOHLER CO.; pg. 91, pg. 1862
QUIET COAT SOUNDSHIELD - Automotive Reconditioning Product - MOC PRODUCTS COMPANY, INC.; pg. 332, pg. 174
QUIET ELEGANCE - Door Glass - ODL INCORPORATED; pg. 101, pg. 914
QUIET-FLO - Electric Fuel Pump - EDELBROCK CORPORATION; pg. 204, pg. 293
QUIET PIPES - Shock Absorber - OATEY SUPPLY CHAIN SERVICES; pg. 30, pg. 1433
QUIET SPOT - Headset - SHURE INCORPORATED; pg. 672, pg. 638
QUIET WEAR - Apparel - RELIABLE OF MILWAUKEE; pg. 698, pg. 1879
QUIET ZONE 2000 - Noise Reduction Stereo Headphone - KOSS CORPORATION; pg. 649, pg. 1877
QUIETCARE - Air Purifier - KAZ, INC.; pg. 58, pg. 844
QUIETCLEAN - Air Purifier - HONEYWELL INTERNATIONAL INC.; pg. 407, pg. 1088
QUIETCOMFORT - Audio Product - BOSE CORPORATION; pg. 626, pg. 820
QUIETDRIVE - Lighting Equipment - ELECTRONIC THEATRE CONTROLS, INC.; pg. 1296, pg. 1872
QUIETFLEX - Flex Duct - GOODMAN GROUP, INC.; pg. 1072, pg. 1706
QUIETFLO - Air Purifier - HUNTER FAN COMPANY; pg. 57, pg. 1631
QUIETIR - Power Semiconductor Device - INTERNATIONAL RECTIFIER CORPORATION; pg. 647, pg. 80
QUIETKEY - Keyboard - DELL INC.; pg. 383, pg. 1737
QUIETMASTER - Air Conditioner - FRIEDRICH AIR

CONDITIONING CO.; *pg.* 1072, *pg.* 1740
QUIETMASTER DELUXE - Room Air Conditioner - FRIEDRICH AIR CONDITIONING CO.; *pg.* 1072, *pg.* 1740
QUIETMASTER HEAVY DUTY - Room Air Conditioner - FRIEDRICH AIR CONDITIONING CO.; *pg.* 1072, *pg.* 1740
QUIETR - Fiber Glass Duct Product - OWENS CORNING; *pg.* 102, *pg.* 1476
QUIETSTEP - Flooring Product - STAGESTEP INC.; *pg.* 1688, *pg.* 1570
QUIETSTEP & DANCESTEP - Floors - STAGESTEP INC.; *pg.* 1688, *pg.* 1570
QUIETZONE - Noise Control System - OWENS CORNING; *pg.* 102, *pg.* 1476
QUIETZONE - Connector - W.L. GORE & ASSOCIATES, INC.; *pg.* 122, *pg.* 388
QUIK - Valve - STRAHMAN VALVES, INC.; *pg.* 1379, *pg.* 1517
QUIK ABG - Arterial Blood Gas Sampler - VITAL SIGNS, INC.; *pg.* 1607, *pg.* 1126
QUIK-CALC - ATC Multilayer Capacitor Calculator Disk - AMERICAN TECHNICAL CERAMICS CORP.; *pg.* 616, *pg.* 1168
QUIK CHANGE - Towel Dispenser - GEORGIA-PACIFIC LLC; *pg.* 1458, *pg.* 507
QUIK-CLAMP CONNECTOR - Surface Equipment - DRIL-QUIP, INC.; *pg.* 1330, *pg.* 1704
QUIK-COMM - E-mail System - OPENTEXT GXS; *pg.* 1272, *pg.* 770
QUIK-DEPLOY - Foldable Safety Road Marker - EAGLE MANUFACTURING COMPANY; *pg.* 79, *pg.* 1851
QUIK-FIX - Denture Care Products - COMBE INCORPORATED; *pg.* 1516, *pg.* 1351
QUIK FLIP - Chewing Gum - BROWN & BIGELOW, INC.; *pg.* 1624, *pg.* 959
QUIK-FLO - Flow Control - BIMBA MANUFACTURING COMPANY; *pg.* 1317, *pg.* 633
QUIK-FOLD - Furniture - ADAMS MFG. CO.; *pg.* 51, *pg.* 1427
QUIK-FREEZE - Chemical Product - MILLER-STEPHENSON CHEMICAL COMPANY, INC.; *pg.* 1172, *pg.* 344
QUIK-GO - Urethane Belts - FENNER DRIVES; *pg.* 1336, *pg.* 1551
QUIK-JAY CONNECTORS - Specialty Connectors - DRIL-QUIP, INC.; *pg.* 1330, *pg.* 1704
QUIK-LOK CONNECTORS - Specialty Connectors - DRIL-QUIP, INC.; *pg.* 1330, *pg.* 1704
QUIK-LOK CORD - Power Tool - MILWAUKEE ELECTRIC TOOL CORP.; *pg.* 1056, *pg.* 1855
QUIK-OUT - Sleeved Cylinder - GRACO, INC.; *pg.* 1342, *pg.* 935
QUIK PARTS PLUS PROGRAM (SM) - SERVICE MARK - Fluid Handling System - GRACO, INC.; *pg.* 1342, *pg.* 935
QUIK PICK 48 HOUR SHIPMENT SYSTEM - 48 Hour Shipment of Selected ATC Products - AMERICAN TECHNICAL CERAMICS CORP.; *pg.* 616, *pg.* 1168
QUIK-PREP - Preparation System - CARDIAC SCIENCE CORPORATION; *pg.* 1512, *pg.* 1897
QUIK-PREP - Power Cables - GENERAL CABLE CORPORATION; *pg.* 83, *pg.* 729
QUIK PRINT - Quick Printing Services - ALLEGRA NETWORK LLC; *pg.* 1614, *pg.* 904
QUIK SAMPLING VALVE - Sampling Valve - STRAHMAN VALVES, INC.; *pg.* 1379, *pg.* 1517
QUIK-STAB - Connector - DRIL-QUIP, INC.; *pg.* 1330, *pg.* 1704
QUIK-STAB CONNECTORS - Specialty Connectors - DRIL-QUIP, INC.; *pg.* 1330, *pg.* 1704
QUIK START - Chairside Bleaching System - DEN-MAT CORPORATION; *pg.* 1522, *pg.* 271
QUIK-START - Paper & Composite Cores - SONOCO PRODUCTS COMPANY; *pg.* 1469, *pg.* 1619
QUIK STIK - Marker - LA-CO INDUSTRIES MARKAL CO., INC.; *pg.* 1170, *pg.* 610
QUIK-STIK - Tubes for Winding of Web Material - SONOCO PRODUCTS COMPANY; *pg.* 1469, *pg.* 1619
QUIK-THREAD - Connector - DRIL-QUIP, INC.; *pg.* 1330, *pg.* 1704
QUIK-THREAD/MULTI THREAD CONNECTORS - Specialty Connectors - DRIL-QUIP, INC.; *pg.* 1330, *pg.* 1704
QUIK-TOP - Floor Underlayment - USG CORPORATION; *pg.* 118, *pg.* 594
QUIK-TUBE - Building Form Product - QUIKRETE COMPANIES; *pg.* 106, *pg.* 519
QUIK-WALL - Interior Flat Paint - DUNN-EDWARDS CORPORATION; *pg.* 1442, *pg.* 129
QUIKACCESS - Valve - GRACO, INC.; *pg.* 1342, *pg.* 935
QUIKCASH - Transaction Processing System - EVERI HOLDINGS INC.; *pg.* 749, *pg.* 1023
QUIKCASH PLUS - Transaction Processing System - EVERI HOLDINGS INC.; *pg.* 749, *pg.* 1023
QUIKCHANGE - Pump - GRACO, INC.; *pg.* 1342, *pg.* 935
QUIKCHAR - Polymers - THE DOW CHEMICAL COMPANY; *pg.* 1157, *pg.* 898
QUIKCHEK - Fit Test Adapter - MINE SAFETY APPLIANCES COMPANY; *pg.* 1361, *pg.* 1525
QUIKCLIP - Balloon - CONTINENTAL AMERICAN CORP.; *pg.* 1880, *pg.* 723
QUIKCONNECT - Pick Cable - EMG, INC.; *pg.* 636, *pg.* 277
QUIKDECK - Platform - SAFWAY SERVICES, LLC; *pg.* 109, *pg.* 1898
QUIKFRAME - Balloon - CONTINENTAL AMERICAN CORP.; *pg.* 1880, *pg.* 723
QUIKLOCK - Fiber Cable Routing - PANDUIT CORP.; *pg.* 661, *pg.* 663
QUIKLOK - Fastening Device - TELSMITH, INC.; *pg.* 1381, *pg.* 1871
QUIKMARKETING - Transaction Processing System - EVERI HOLDINGS INC.; *pg.* 749, *pg.* 1023
QUIKMATE - Plastic Grocery Bags - SONOCO PRODUCTS COMPANY; *pg.* 1469, *pg.* 1619
QUIKMATE EZ - Plastic Grocery Bags - SONOCO PRODUCTS COMPANY; *pg.* 1469, *pg.* 1619
QUIKMESSAGING - Marketing Messaging - EVERI HOLDINGS INC.; *pg.* 749, *pg.* 1023
QUIKOIN - Coin Purse - BROWN & BIGELOW, INC.; *pg.* 1624, *pg.* 959
QUIKOTE - Raycron Reinforcement - PPG INDUSTRIES, INC.; *pg.* 1445, *pg.* 1579
QUIKPIN - Fluid Handling System - GRACO, INC.; *pg.* 1342, *pg.* 935
QUIKPRO - Herbicide - MONSANTO COMPANY; *pg.* 1173, *pg.* 999
QUIKREPORTS - Transaction Processing System - EVERI HOLDINGS INC.; *pg.* 749, *pg.* 1023
QUIKSELECT - Fluid Handling System - GRACO, INC.; *pg.* 1342, *pg.* 935
QUIKSHAPE - Swim Dress - JUNONIA LTD.; *pg.* 27, *pg.* 929
QUIKSILVER - Apparel - QUIKSILVER, INC.; *pg.* 31, *pg.* 104
QUIKSILVEREDITION - Men's Apparel - QUIKSILVER, INC.; *pg.* 31, *pg.* 104
QUIKSPEC - Specification Tool - QUAM-NICHOLS COMPANY; *pg.* 666, *pg.* 588
QUIKSPLIT - Splitter - BESSER COMPANY; *pg.* 1317, *pg.* 865
QUIKSTAR - Cores for Winding - SONOCO PRODUCTS COMPANY; *pg.* 1469, *pg.* 1619
QUIKSTEP - Ladders - BAE SYSTEMS PRODUCTS GROUP; *pg.* 359, *pg.* 432
QUIKTAB - Plastic Bags - SONOCO PRODUCTS COMPANY; *pg.* 1469, *pg.* 1619
QUIKTICKET - Cashless Transaction - EVERI HOLDINGS INC.; *pg.* 749, *pg.* 1023
QUIKTRIP - Convenience Stores - QUIKTRIP CORPORATION; *pg.* 1031, *pg.* 1490
QUIKTUBE - Building Form - QUIKRETE COMPANIES; *pg.* 106, *pg.* 519
QUIKTURN - Pressed & Monolithic Refractory - RESCO PRODUCTS, INC.; *pg.* 107, *pg.* 1581
QUIKVENT - Power Equipment - ECHO INCORPORATED; *pg.* 1046, *pg.* 626
QUIKWAGER - Transaction Processing System - EVERI HOLDINGS INC.; *pg.* 749, *pg.* 1023
QUIKWALL - Concrete Product - QUIKRETE COMPANIES; *pg.* 106, *pg.* 519
QUIKWIK - Womens Clothing - JUNONIA LTD.; *pg.* 27, *pg.* 929
QUILL - Books - HARPERCOLLINS PUBLISHERS INC.; *pg.* 1647, *pg.* 1237
QUILT PATCH - Lace Curtain - HERITAGE LACE INC.; *pg.* 694, *pg.* 711
QUILT SCRAPS - Wall Decor - HERITAGE LACE INC.; *pg.* 694, *pg.* 711
QUILT WAVE - Packaging Product - GRAPHIC PACKAGING HOLDING COMPANY; *pg.* 1459, *pg.* 509
QUILTED NORTHERN - Bath Tissue - GEORGIA-PACIFIC LLC; *pg.* 1458, *pg.* 507
QUILTERS WORLD - Crafts Publications - ANNIE'S; *pg.* 1617, *pg.* 673
QUILTFLEX - Foam - FXI; *pg.* 1163, *pg.* 1552
QUILTING - Magazine - MEREDITH CORPORATION; *pg.* 1663, *pg.* 705
QUINCY - Compressor - QUINCY COMPRESSOR INC.; *pg.* 1371, *pg.* 653
QUINCY - Furniture - TRENDWAY CORPORATION; *pg.* 945, *pg.* 892
QUINCY - Footwear - VANS, INC.; *pg.* 1821, *pg.* 76
QUINCY AIR MASTER - Compressor - QUINCY COMPRESSOR INC.; *pg.* 1371, *pg.* 653
QUINCY COMPRESSOR - Air Compressors - ENPRO INDUSTRIES, INC.; *pg.* 1334, *pg.* 1366
QUINCY COMPRESSOR - Compressor - QUINCY COMPRESSOR INC.; *pg.* 1371, *pg.* 653
QUINCY PLT - Compressor - QUINCY COMPRESSOR INC.; *pg.* 1371, *pg.* 653
QUINGUARD - Health & Nutrition Product - NOVUS INTERNATIONAL, INC.; *pg.* 706, *pg.* 1001
QUINN - Clothing - ABERCROMBIE & FITCH CO.; *pg.* 37, *pg.* 1466
QUINN - Chair - LA-Z-BOY INCORPORATED; *pg.* 932, *pg.* 901
QUINNE - Footwear - STEVEN MADDEN, LTD.; *pg.* 1819, *pg.* 1176
QUINSANA - Powder - THE STEPHAN COMPANY; *pg.* 1597, *pg.* 426
QUINTA DOS OLIVAIS - Olive Oil - CARGILL LIMITED; *pg.* 1475, *pg.* 1914
QUINTESSENCE - Rug - COURISTAN INC.; *pg.* 921, *pg.* 1067
QUINTESSENTIALS - Furniture - ASHLEY FURNITURE INDUSTRIES, INC.; *pg.* 914, *pg.* 1852
QUINTOLUBRIC - Hydraulic Fluid - QUAKER CHEMICAL CORP.; *pg.* 1178, *pg.* 1524
QUINTON - Cardiology Products - CARDIAC SCIENCE CORPORATION; *pg.* 1512, *pg.* 1897
QUINTSULATION - Motor - BODINE ELECTRIC COMPANY; *pg.* 1318, *pg.* 641
QUISP - Cereal - PEPSICO, INC.; *pg.* 259, *pg.* 1327
QUISP - Cereal - THE QUAKER OATS COMPANY; *pg.* 834, *pg.* 588
QUITASSIST - Cigarette - PHILIP MORRIS USA INC.; *pg.* 1894, *pg.* 1803
QUITE POSSIBLY, THE WORLD'S PERFECT FOOD - Tag Line - CHIQUITA BRANDS INTERNATIONAL, INC.; *pg.* 847, *pg.* 1365
QUITTING MATTERS - Educational Services - HEALTH NET, INC.; *pg.* 1540, *pg.* 308
QUIVER - Bag - DATREK GOLF; *pg.* 1832, *pg.* 1801
QUIVER - Gaming Product - GLD PRODUCTS, INC.; *pg.* 1835, *pg.* 1882
QUIXELL - Research Instruments - STOELTING CO.; *pg.* 1430, *pg.* 671
QUIXX - Dental Product - DENTSPLY INTERNATIONAL INC.; *pg.* 1522, *pg.* 1596
QUIZ KIDZ - Meals - THE QUIZNO'S MASTER LLC; *pg* 1746, *pg.* 322
QUIZNOS SUB - Fast-food Franchise - THE QUIZNO'S MASTER LLC; *pg.* 1746, *pg.* 322
QUMPASS - Neuropsychological Computerized Testing Tools - CERORA, INC.; *pg.* 1405, *pg.* 1516
QUOTESCOPE - Stock Trading Tool - TD AMERITRADE HOLDING CORPORATION; *pg.* 808, *pg.* 1018
QUOTEWIRE - Custom Solutions - ONVIA, INC.; *pg.* 1272, *pg.* 1838
QUOTIEN - Online Financial Services - ACI WORLDWIDE; *pg.* 710, *pg.* 1777
QUWAT JABAL - Beverages - THE COCA-COLA COMPANY; *pg.* 240, *pg.* 493
QVERB - Audio System - QSOUND LABS, INC.; *pg.* 666, *pg.* 1904
QVIDEOPHONE - Mobile Video System - QUALCOMM INCORPORATED; *pg.* 1873, *pg.* 207
QVOICE - Wireless Audio Solution - QSOUND LABS, INC.; *pg.* 666, *pg.* 1904
QVPN BUILDER - Software System - ALCATEL-LUCENT; *pg.* 615, *pg.* 1094
QWERL - Fluid - QUAKER CHEMICAL CORP.; *pg.* 1178, *pg.* 1524
QWEST - Camping Trailer - JAYCO INC.; *pg.* 1708, *pg.* 695
QWEST ADVANTAGE - Communication Product - CENTURYLINK, INC; *pg.* 1870, *pg.* 317
QWEST BAJA - Camping Trailer - JAYCO INC.; *pg.* 1708, *pg.* 695
QWEST CHOICE - Communication Product - CENTURYLINK, INC; *pg.* 1870, *pg.* 317
QWEST CONNECT - Telecommunication Services -

CENTURYLINK, INC; *pg.* 1870, *pg.* 317
QWEST CONTROL - Communication Product - CENTURYLINK, INC; *pg.* 1870, *pg.* 317
QWEST DSL - Communication Product - CENTURYLINK, INC; *pg.* 1870, *pg.* 317
QWEST ENTERPRISE - Communication Product - CENTURYLINK, INC; *pg.* 1870, *pg.* 317
QWEST HIGH-SPEED INTERNET - Internet Services - CENTURYLINK, INC; *pg.* 1870, *pg.* 317
QWEST IQ - Integrated Access - CENTURYLINK, INC; *pg.* 1870, *pg.* 317
QWEST IQ NETWORKING - Communication Product - CENTURYLINK, INC; *pg.* 1870, *pg.* 317
QWEST PLATFORM PLUS - Communication Product - CENTURYLINK, INC; *pg.* 1870, *pg.* 317
QWEST TOTAL ADVANTAGE - Communication Product - CENTURYLINK, INC; *pg.* 1870, *pg.* 317
QWEST VOICE ADVANTAGE - Communication Product - CENTURYLINK, INC; *pg.* 1870, *pg.* 317
QWEST WIRELESS - Communication Product - CENTURYLINK, INC; *pg.* 1870, *pg.* 317
QWEST.NET - Communication Product - CENTURYLINK, INC; *pg.* 1870, *pg.* 317
QWHEEL - Integrated Circuit - ATMEL CORPORATION; *pg.* 621, *pg.* 238
QWIK CONNECT PLUS - Medical Product - UTAH MEDICAL PRODUCTS, INC.; *pg.* 1605, *pg.* 1752
QWIK FIT SYRINGE - Disposables - MEDRAD, INC.; *pg.* 1563, *pg.* 1591
QWIK-OFF - High Efficiency Cleaner - HILLYARD, INC.; *pg.* 331, *pg.* 990
QWIKGO - Stain Remover - A.L. WILSON CHEMICAL CO.; *pg.* 325, *pg.* 1076
QWIKRADIO - Receiver & Transmitter - MICREL, INC.; *pg.* 654, *pg.* 247
QWIP - Thermal Imaging System - FLIR SYSTEMS, INC.; *pg.* 1413, *pg.* 1510
QX - Stereo Enhancer - QSOUND LABS, INC.; *pg.* 666, *pg.* 1904
QX - Hardware - VERIFONE SYSTEMS, INC.; *pg.* 487, *pg.* 251
QX/TDM - Audio System - QSOUND LABS, INC.; *pg.* 666, *pg.* 1904
QX4 INFINITI - Sports Utility Vehicle - NISSAN NORTH AMERICA, INC.; *pg.* 186, *pg.* 1633
QXPANDER - Electronic Audio Device - QSOUND LABS, INC.; *pg.* 666, *pg.* 1904
QXSDII - Audio System - QSOUND LABS, INC.; *pg.* 666, *pg.* 1904
QXT PRO - Metal Detector - WHITE'S ELECTRONICS; *pg.* 688, *pg.* 1509

R

R-102 - Restaurant Fire Suppression Systems - ANSUL, INCORPORATED; *pg.* 1147, *pg.* 1869
R-16 PERMAFOAM - Insulation - A.O. SMITH CORPORATION; *pg.* 1313, *pg.* 1872
R-50 - Laser Device - TRIMEDYNE, INC.; *pg.* 1432, *pg.* 121
R&B - Medical Device - INTEGRA LIFESCIENCES HOLDINGS CORPORATION; *pg.* 1545, *pg.* 1109
R&D - Trade Magazine - ADVANTAGE BUSINESS MEDIA; *pg.* 1613, *pg.* 1116
R&F - Pasta - AMERICAN ITALIAN PASTA COMPANY; *pg.* 837, *pg.* 980
R&R - Dental Product - DENTSPLY INTERNATIONAL INC.; *pg.* 1522, *pg.* 1596
R&R 551 - Lecithin - ARCHER-DANIELS-MIDLAND COMPANY; *pg.* 825, *pg.* 565
R/BAK - Cushion Mounting Material - ROGERS CORPORATION; *pg.* 1305, *pg.* 369
R-CONTROL - Building Product - LESTER BUILDING SYSTEMS, LLC; *pg.* 93, *pg.* 927
R DOCS - Investment System - WILLIAM BLAIR & COMPANY LLC; *pg.* 822, *pg.* 596
R/EVOLUTION - Storage System - DOT HILL SYSTEMS CORP.; *pg.* 388, *pg.* 333
R FACTORS - Footwear - RED WING SHOE COMPANY, INC.; *pg.* 1817, *pg.* 954
R/FLEX - Flexible Laminate Material - ROGERS CORPORATION; *pg.* 1305, *pg.* 369
R-GENE-10 - Medicine - PFIZER INC.; *pg.* 1581, *pg.* 1278
R-MAX - Pressed & Monolithic Refractory - RESCO PRODUCTS, INC.; *pg.* 107, *pg.* 1581
R/S - Rheometer - BROOKFIELD ENGINEERING LABORATORIES, INC.; *pg.* 1403, *pg.* 833
R SERIES - Defibrillator - ZOLL MEDICAL CORPORATION; *pg.* 1612, *pg.* 814
R-SHINE - Cement - OATEY SUPPLY CHAIN SERVICES; *pg.* 30, *pg.* 1433
R. T. JUNIOR - Twist Tobacco - AMERICAN SNUFF COMPANY; *pg.* 1893, *pg.* 1641
R-TRAC - Intra-Aortic Balloon Pump Monitor Software - MAQUET; *pg.* 1558, *pg.* 1082
R. W. KNUDSEN FAMILY - Organic Juices, Concentrates, Light, Bottled Spritzers, & Sports Drinks - THE J.M. SMUCKER COMPANY; *pg.* 865, *pg.* 1468
R+/CHANGE ACCUM - Software - BMC SOFTWARE, INC.; *pg.* 362, *pg.* 1701
R1 - Index Register - CYPRESS SEMICONDUCTOR CORPORATION; *pg.* 1326, *pg.* 243
R100 - Wireless Product - HEMISPHERE GPS INC.; *pg.* 642, *pg.* 1903
R10000 - Microprocessor - IMAGINATION TECHNOLOGIES; *pg.* 412, *pg.* 285
R120 - Orthopedic Implant Product - DJO SURGICAL; *pg.* 1525, *pg.* 1661
R12000 - Microprocessor - IMAGINATION TECHNOLOGIES; *pg.* 412, *pg.* 285
R12000A - Microprocessor - IMAGINATION TECHNOLOGIES; *pg.* 412, *pg.* 285
R14000 - Microprocessor - IMAGINATION TECHNOLOGIES; *pg.* 412, *pg.* 285
R14000A - Microprocessor - IMAGINATION TECHNOLOGIES; *pg.* 412, *pg.* 285
R16000 - Microprocessor - IMAGINATION TECHNOLOGIES; *pg.* 412, *pg.* 285
R197A - Receiver - EMCORE CORPORATION; *pg.* 636, *pg.* 39
R198A - Receiver - EMCORE CORPORATION; *pg.* 636, *pg.* 39
R198P - Receiver - EMCORE CORPORATION; *pg.* 636, *pg.* 39
R2 - Pharmaceutical Product - ALERE INC.; *pg.* 1488, *pg.* 849
R2 - Index Register - CYPRESS SEMICONDUCTOR CORPORATION; *pg.* 1326, *pg.* 243
R2 - Medical Product - HOLOGIC, INC.; *pg.* 1416, *pg.* 784
R2 - Medical Equipment - INVACARE CORPORATION; *pg.* 1546, *pg.* 1451
R2 - Waiting Seating - STEELCASE INC.; *pg.* 475, *pg.* 889
R2 IMAGE CHECKER - Medical Product - HOLOGIC, INC.; *pg.* 1416, *pg.* 784
R204 MICRO FINE SUPERBALL - Pens - PENTEL OF AMERICA, LTD.; *pg.* 453, *pg.* 295
R206 SUPERBALL - Pens - PENTEL OF AMERICA, LTD.; *pg.* 453, *pg.* 295
R3 - Index Register - CYPRESS SEMICONDUCTOR CORPORATION; *pg.* 1326, *pg.* 243
R3 TECHNOLOGY - Response & Switching Efficiency - INTERSIL CORPORATION; *pg.* 647, *pg.* 146
R3000 - Microprocessor - IMAGINATION TECHNOLOGIES; *pg.* 412, *pg.* 285
R32 - Medical Equipment - INVACARE CORPORATION; *pg.* 1546, *pg.* 1451
R4 - Index Register - CYPRESS SEMICONDUCTOR CORPORATION; *pg.* 1326, *pg.* 243
R4000 - Microprocessor - IMAGINATION TECHNOLOGIES; *pg.* 412, *pg.* 285
R5 - Index Register - CYPRESS SEMICONDUCTOR CORPORATION; *pg.* 1326, *pg.* 243
R50 - Medical Equipment - INVACARE CORPORATION; *pg.* 1546, *pg.* 1451
R5000 - Microprocessor - IMAGINATION TECHNOLOGIES; *pg.* 412, *pg.* 285
R51 - Medical Equipment - INVACARE CORPORATION; *pg.* 1546, *pg.* 1451
R6 - Index Register - CYPRESS SEMICONDUCTOR CORPORATION; *pg.* 1326, *pg.* 243
R7 - Index Register - CYPRESS SEMICONDUCTOR CORPORATION; *pg.* 1326, *pg.* 243
R8 - Index Register - CYPRESS SEMICONDUCTOR CORPORATION; *pg.* 1326, *pg.* 243
R9 - Index Register - CYPRESS SEMICONDUCTOR CORPORATION; *pg.* 1326, *pg.* 243
RA - Restaurant - BENIHANA INC.; *pg.* 1716, *pg.* 409
RA40 - Mold Steel - A. FINKL & SONS CO.; *pg.* 1309, *pg.* 563
RAACO - Plastic Product - MYERS INDUSTRIES, INC.; *pg.* 1887, *pg.* 1402
RABBIT EARS BOOK & AUDIO - Children's Books & Audio Products - SIMON & SCHUSTER, INC.; *pg.* 1687, *pg.* 1292
RABBIT SEMICONDUCTOR - Electronic Devices - DIGI INTERNATIONAL INC.; *pg.* 387, *pg.* 948
RABBIT SKINS - Clock - BROWN & BIGELOW, INC.; *pg.* 1624, *pg.* 959
RABBIT SKINS - Sportswear - L.A. T SPORTSWEAR, LLC; *pg.* 1838, *pg.* 526
RABBITS - Magazine - I-5 PUBLISHING LLC; *pg.* 1651, *pg.* 133
R.A.B.O.S. - Software - HARMAN INTERNATIONAL INDUSTRIES, INCORPORATED; *pg.* 641, *pg.* 374
RAC - Card Product - ABNOTE NORTH AMERICA; *pg.* 1878, *pg.* 789
RAC - Fluid Handling System - GRACO, INC.; *pg.* 1342, *pg.* 935
RAC X - Tips for Spray Guns - GRACO, INC.; *pg.* 1342, *pg.* 935
RACCER - Footwear - STEVEN MADDEN, LTD.; *pg.* 1819, *pg.* 1176
RACCOONS TO RICHES - Video Game - INTERNATIONAL GAME TECHNOLOGY; *pg.* 957, *pg.* 1024
RACE - Office Furniture System - HAWORTH, INC.; *pg.* 402, *pg.* 891
RACE - Product Name/Architecture - MERCURY COMPUTER SYSTEMS, INC.; *pg.* 434, *pg.* 813
RACE AROUND THE BASES - Baseball Program - OAKLAND ATHLETICS LIMITED PARTNERSHIP; *pg.* 571, *pg.* 172
RACE CERTIFIED - Validates Inoperability of Third Party Raceway Products - MERCURY COMPUTER SYSTEMS, INC.; *pg.* 434, *pg.* 813
RACE FOR MONEY - Video Game - INTERNATIONAL GAME TECHNOLOGY; *pg.* 957, *pg.* 1024
RACE FOR THE GOLD - Game - WMS INDUSTRIES INC.; *pg.* 593, *pg.* 666
RACE PHOTO NETWORK - Website - CANDID COLOR SYSTEMS, INC.; *pg.* 1404, *pg.* 1485
RACE SERIES - Computer Architecture - MERCURY COMPUTER SYSTEMS, INC.; *pg.* 434, *pg.* 813
RACE SERIES MULTIPORT - Multiport System - MERCURY COMPUTER SYSTEMS, INC.; *pg.* 434, *pg.* 813
RACE SERIES MYRIAD - Multiport System - MERCURY COMPUTER SYSTEMS, INC.; *pg.* 434, *pg.* 813
RACE++ - Product Name/Architecture - MERCURY COMPUTER SYSTEMS, INC.; *pg.* 434, *pg.* 813
RACEPAC - Bearing Product - THE TIMKEN COMPANY; *pg.* 218, *pg.* 1408
RACER - Oven - APW WYOTT FOOD SERVICE EQUIPMENT, INC.; *pg.* 1314, *pg.* 1658
RACERBACK - Cabfairing - LUND INTERNATIONAL, INC.; *pg.* 211, *pg.* 526
RACETICKETS.COM - Website - INTERNATIONAL SPEEDWAY CORPORATION; *pg.* 553, *pg.* 420
RACETRACK - Bath Bars - CRAFTMADE INTERNATIONAL, INC.; *pg.* 1295, *pg.* 1670
RACETRACK - Third-Party Program - MERCURY COMPUTER SYSTEMS, INC.; *pg.* 434, *pg.* 813
RACETRACK - Fabric - NEMSCHOFF, INC.; *pg.* 936, *pg.* 1890
RACEWARE - Software Program - MERCURY COMPUTER SYSTEMS, INC.; *pg.* 434, *pg.* 813
RACEWAY - Convenience Stores - RACETRAC PETROLEUM, INC.; *pg.* 983, *pg.* 519
RACEWAY READY - Third-Party Marketing Program - MERCURY COMPUTER SYSTEMS, INC.; *pg.* 434, *pg.* 813
RACHEL - Clothing - ABERCROMBIE & FITCH CO.; *pg.* 37, *pg.* 1466
RACHEL'S - Dairy Product - DEAN FOODS COMPANY; *pg.* 852, *pg.* 1679
RACHEL'S - Yogurt - THE WHITEWAVE FOODS COMPANY; *pg.* 1037, *pg.* 324
RACHEL'S ORGANIC - Dairy Product - DEAN FOODS COMPANY; *pg.* 852, *pg.* 1679
RACINE SECO - Radial Piston Pumps - BOSCH REXROTH CORPORATION; *pg.* 1319, *pg.* 1516
RACING JACKET - Eyewear - OAKLEY, INC.; *pg.* 1840, *pg.* 86
RACING SAUSAGE - Fund Rising Program - MILWAUKEE BREWERS BASEBALL CLUB, INC.; *pg.* 562, *pg.* 1878
RACING TO BRING YOU THE BEST - Tag Line - PRO-LINE, INC.; *pg.* 966, *pg.* 45

RACK-ALL - Rack - FANCORT INDUSTRIES, INC.; pg. 1336, pg. 1131

RACK EXPRESS - Publication - MADISON NEWSPAPERS, INC.; pg. 1661, pg. 1866

RACK MOUNT - Surge Protector - WIREMOLD/LEGRAND; pg. 689, pg. 383

RACK MOUNT VAC - Attenuator Enclosure - JOHANSON MANUFACTURING CORPORATION; pg. 648, pg. 1045

RACK MOUNT VAC-PAK - Variable Attenuator Enclosure - JOHANSON MANUFACTURING CORPORATION; pg. 648, pg. 1045

RACK-N-ROLL - Mobile Racks - CRES-COR; pg. 1326, pg. 1464

RACK TOOLS - Tutorial - MIDDLE ATLANTIC PRODUCTS INC.; pg. 1360, pg. 1065

RACKET SPECS - Safety Goggle - SCHOOL-TECH, INC.; pg. 1844, pg. 866

RACKGUARD - Power Supply System - VICOR CORPORATION; pg. 1435, pg. 783

RACKMOUNT - Tape Drives - QUANTUM CORPORATION; pg. 458, pg. 250

RACKO - Game - HASBRO, INC.; pg. 954, pg. 1603

RACKS - Enclosure - MILLER ELECTRIC MANUFACTURING CO.; pg. 1361, pg. 1852

RACKSACK - Cargo Rack Expansion System - MACNEIL AUTOMOTIVE PRODUCTS, LTD.; pg. 211, pg. 559

RACO - Electrical Product - HUBBELL INCORPORATED; pg. 1299, pg. 370

RACPAK - Fluid Handling System - GRACO, INC.; pg. 1342, pg. 935

RACQUEL - Clothing - ABERCROMBIE & FITCH CO.; pg. 37, pg. 1466

RAD-CHECK - Medical Device - GAMMEX RMI INC.; pg. 1532, pg. 1872

RAD-COAT - Radiation Shielding Technology - MAXWELL TECHNOLOGIES, INC.; pg. 653, pg. 204

RAD-PAK - Radiation Shielding Technology - MAXWELL TECHNOLOGIES, INC.; pg. 653, pg. 204

RAD-STACK - Radiation Shielding Technology - MAXWELL TECHNOLOGIES, INC.; pg. 653, pg. 204

RADA - Water Temperature Control - ARMSTRONG INTERNATIONAL, INC.; pg. 1069, pg. 909

RADAR - Apparel - BURTON SNOWBOARD COMPANY; pg. 1829, pg. 1765

RADAR ONLINE - Gossip Site - AMERICAN MEDIA, INC.; pg. 1615, pg. 410

RADAR ONLINE - Entertainment News Site - SPINMEDIA; pg. 1282, pg. 104

RADARVISION - Safety Product - BAE SYSTEMS PRODUCTS GROUP; pg. 359, pg. 432

RADCLIFFE - Furniture - HOOKER FURNITURE CORPORATION; pg. 928, pg. 1788

RADCLIFFE - Misses', Women's & Petite Sportswear - KELLWOOD COMPANY; pg. 28, pg. 975

RADCUBE - Software - NUANCE COMMUNICATIONS, INC.; pg. 447, pg. 806

RADEC - Lumber - POTLATCH CORPORATION; pg. 1467, pg. 1844

RADEL - Resin - WESTLAKE PLASTICS COMPANY; pg. 1892, pg. 1548

RADEON - 3D Graphical Technology - ADVANCED MICRO DEVICES, INC.-MARKHAM; pg. 345, pg. 1922

RADEON - Graphics Card - CRUCIAL TECHNOLOGY DIV OF MICRON; pg. 1237, pg. 550

RADER FARMS - Snack Food - INVENTURE FOODS, INC.; pg. 1023, pg. 17

RADEX - General Radiographic System - HOLOGIC, INC.; pg. 1416, pg. 784

RADI-X - Lighting System - LITECONTROL CORPORATION; pg. 1301, pg. 841

RADIAFLEX - Cable & Antenna System - RADIO FREQUENCY SYSTEMS, INC.; pg. 666, pg. 354

RADIAL AIRE - Hose - HBD INDUSTRIES, INC.; pg. 207, pg. 1449

RADIAL BOLT CONNECTOR - Surface Equipment - DRIL-QUIP, INC.; pg. 1330, pg. 1704

RADIAL EDGE - Medical Device - BOSTON SCIENTIFIC CORPORATION; pg. 1508, pg. 831

RADIAL FIN - Electronic Components - MOLEX INCORPORATED; pg. 655, pg. 628

RADIAL FLEX - Hose - HBD INDUSTRIES, INC.; pg. 207, pg. 1449

RADIAL-PAK - Analytical Column - WATERS CORPORATION; pg. 1436, pg. 834

RADIAL TAPER PIPE TAP - Type of Taper Pipe Tap for Cast Iron - REGAL BELOIT CORPORATION; pg. 106, pg. 1854

RADIALSEAL - Filtration System - DONALDSON COMPANY, INC.; pg. 1329, pg. 917

RADIANCE - Glass - AGC GLASS NORTH AMERICA, INC.; pg. 65, pg. 482

RADIANCE - Photographic Color Paper - EASTMAN KODAK COMPANY; pg. 1408, pg. 1333

RADIANCE - Laminate - OMNOVA SOLUTIONS INC; pg. 1176, pg. 1453

RADIANCE - Fully Integrated STAT-testing Information Management System - RADIOMETER AMERICA INC.; pg. 1588, pg. 1481

RADIANCE - Furniture - TROPITONE FURNITURE CO., INC.; pg. 945, pg. 118

RADIANCE OF THE SEAS - Cruise Ship - ROYAL CARIBBEAN CRUISES LTD; pg. 1921, pg. 446

RADIANCE TI - Glass - AGC GLASS NORTH AMERICA, INC.; pg. 65, pg. 482

RADIANT - Software - BIO-RAD LABORATORIES, INC.; pg. 1504, pg. 101

RADIANT - Bath Product - KOHLER CO.; pg. 91, pg. 1862

RADIANT - Fabric - NEMSCHOFF, INC.; pg. 936, pg. 1890

RADIANT C - Face Quencher - HERBALIFE INTERNATIONAL OF AMERICA, INC.; pg. 1541, pg. 132

RADIANT ELEMENT - Laminate - OMNOVA SOLUTIONS INC; pg. 1176, pg. 1453

RADIANT HUES - Door Glass - ODL INCORPORATED; pg. 101, pg. 914

RADIANT MERCURY - Security Computer Software - LOCKHEED MARTIN CORPORATION; pg. 229, pg. 762

RADIANT STAR - Jewelry - HELZBERG'S DIAMOND SHOPS, INC.; pg. 6, pg. 984

RADIANT TRUST - Security Computer Software - LOCKHEED MARTIN CORPORATION; pg. 229, pg. 762

RADIANTLINE - Paper Product - WESTROCK COMPANY; pg. 1472, pg. 1805

RADIANTSTRIP - Semiconductor Processing Equipment - AXCELIS TECHNOLOGIES, INC.; pg. 1400, pg. 787

RADIAS - Software - BIO-RAD LABORATORIES, INC.; pg. 1504, pg. 101

RADIATA - Door - MASONITE INTERNATIONAL CORPORATION; pg. 1054, pg. 1920

RADIATORE - Food Product - ANNIE'S INC.; pg. 1760, pg. 45

RADIAX - Cable - COMMSCOPE; pg. 630, pg. 668

RADICAL - Men's Boot - JACK SCHWARTZ SHOES, INC.; pg. 1810, pg. 1245

RADICAL - Pulse Oximeter - MAQUET; pg. 1558, pg. 1082

RADICAL - Patient Monitors & Sensors - MASIMO CORPORATION; pg. 1558, pg. 113

RADICAL FRUIT - Beverage - PEPSICO, INC.; pg. 259, pg. 1327

RADICAL FRUITS - Health Supplement - GARDEN OF LIFE, INC.; pg. 1532, pg. 478

RADICALLY SIMPLE - Slogan - E-LOAN, INC.; pg. 745, pg. 657

RADICATOR - Thermal Processing Equipment - SURFACE COMBUSTION, INC.; pg. 1077, pg. 1462

RADID-EIGHTHS - Measuring Product - THE L.S. STARRETT COMPANY; pg. 1421, pg. 783

RADIESSE - Dermal Filler - MERZ AESTHETICS; pg. 1567, pg. 255

RADIO - Footwear - STEVEN MADDEN, LTD.; pg. 1819, pg. 1176

RADIO COUNTY COVERAGE - Reporting Tool - NIELSEN AUDIO; pg. 446, pg. 768

RADIO FIJI - Swimwear - QUIKSILVER, INC.; pg. 31, pg. 104

RADIO HEARD HERE - Slogan - INNER CITY BROADCASTING CORPORATION; pg. 292, pg. 1243

RADIO KING - Musical Instrument - GIBSON GUITAR CORP.; pg. 550, pg. 1650

RADIO LETRAS - Toys - LEAPFROG ENTERPRISES, INC.; pg. 961, pg. 84

RADIOACTIVE THREAT DETECTION - Detection Technology - AMERICAN SCIENCE AND ENGINEERING, INC.; pg. 1399, pg. 787

RADIO.AM - Radio & Multimedia Service - BRS MEDIA INC.; pg. 1233, pg. 214

RADIO.FM - Radio & Multimedia Service - BRS MEDIA INC.; pg. 1233, pg. 214

RADIOMATIC - Scintillation Analysers - PERKINELMER, INC.; pg. 1426, pg. 853

RADIOMETER - Blood Gas Analyzer - DANAHER CORPORATION; pg. 1044, pg. 397

RADIOMETER ANALYTICAL - Electrochemical And Titration System - DANAHER CORPORATION; pg. 1044, pg. 397

RADION-X - Medical Product - MEDLINE INDUSTRIES, INC.; pg. 1562, pg. 635

RADIOPASS - Digital Media System - REALNETWORKS, INC.; pg. 460, pg. 1839

RADIOTROL - Electrical Variable Speed Product - BOSTON GEAR; pg. 201, pg. 802

RADIOWIRE - Receiver & Transmitter - MICREL, INC.; pg. 654, pg. 247

RADISSON - Hotels & Resorts - CARLSON COMPANIES INC.; pg. 1084, pg. 947

RADIUS - Delivery System - A-DEC, INC.; pg. 1483, pg. 1500

RADIUS - Furniture - ETHAN ALLEN INTERIORS INC.; pg. 924, pg. 343

RADIUS - Transmitters - MOTOROLA SOLUTIONS, INC.; pg. 657, pg. 659

RADIUS - Stainless Steel Flatware - ONEIDA LTD; pg. 1129, pg. 1318

RADIX - Bonding Wire - KULICKE & SOFFA INDUSTRIES, INC.; pg. 650, pg. 1533

RADMAX - Burner - MAXON CORPORATION; pg. 1359, pg. 695

RADNET - Radiology Information System - CERNER CORPORATION; pg. 1514, pg. 981

RADNOR - Safety Glasses - AIRGAS, INC.; pg. 1146, pg. 1583

RADNOR - Casual Shoes - JOHNSTON & MURPHY CO.; pg. 1810, pg. 1651

RADORVISION - Security Product - BAE SYSTEMS PRODUCTS GROUP; pg. 359, pg. 432

RADOVAN - Medical Device - MENTOR CORPORATION; pg. 1565, pg. 263

RADPORT - Software - NUANCE COMMUNICATIONS, INC.; pg. 447, pg. 806

RADPRO - Dosimetry Data Management Software - LANDAUER, INC.; pg. 1554, pg. 615

RADSOK - Cable - AMPHENOL CORPORATION; pg. 616, pg. 381

RADSTEP - Running Boards - LUND INTERNATIONAL, INC.; pg. 211, pg. 526

RADTRAK - Radon Detection System - LANDAUER, INC.; pg. 1554, pg. 615

RADUCTIL - Pharmaceutical Product - ABBOTT LABORATORIES; pg. 1484, pg. 551

RAE LYNN - Apparel - VANS, INC.; pg. 1821, pg. 76

RAEFORD - Uniform Fabrics - INTERNATIONAL TEXTILE GROUP, INC.; pg. 696, pg. 1374

RAF SYSTEM - Modular Seating - STEELCASE INC.; pg. 475, pg. 889

RAFF - Drive Technology - WESTERN DIGITAL CORPORATION; pg. 492, pg. 118

RAFFIA - Decorative Accessory - ETHAN ALLEN INTERIORS INC.; pg. 924, pg. 343

RAFFINATO - Italian Food Service Items - PERFORMANCE FOOD GROUP COMPANY, LLC; pg. 1030, pg. 1803

RAFFLE - Lottery Game - OREGON STATE LOTTERY; pg. 1003, pg. 1508

RAFFLES - Fabric - NEMSCHOFF, INC.; pg. 936, pg. 1890

RAFFLES HOTELS & RESORTS - Hotels & Resorts - FAIRMONT HOTELS & RESORTS INC.; pg. 1091, pg. 1938

RAFOS - Oceanographic Product - TELEDYNE BENTHOS, INC.; pg. 1431, pg. 838

RAFT-R-MATE - Insulating System - OWENS CORNING; pg. 102, pg. 1476

RAFTMAN - Beer - SLEEMAN UNIBROUE QUEBEC; pg. 265, pg. 1950

RAGE - 3D Graphical Technology - ADVANCED MICRO DEVICES, INC.-MARKHAM; pg. 345, pg. 1922

RAGE - Herbicides - FMC CORPORATION; pg. 1163, pg. 1564

RAGE - Body Filler - ITW - EVERCOAT; pg. 1443, pg. 1415

RAGE - Apparel - OAKLEY, INC.; pg. 1840, pg. 86

RAGE - Musical Instrument - PEAVEY ELECTRONICS CORPORATION; pg. 662, pg. 970

RAGE D-TECH - Herbicides - FMC CORPORATION; pg. 1163, pg. 1564

RAGING 7S - Video Game - INTERNATIONAL GAME TECHNOLOGY; pg. 957, pg. 1024

RAGSDALE - Concord Cylinder - BUNTING MAGNETICS CO.; pg. 1320, pg. 717

RAGTIME - Fabric - NEMSCHOFF, INC.; pg. 936, pg. 1890

RAGU - Pasta Sauce - MIZKAN AMERICAS, INC.; pg. 877,

pg. 634
RAHAM - Microwave Product - KRATOS LANCASTER; pg. 1419, pg. 1546
RAID - Insect Spray - S.C. JOHNSON & SON, INC.; pg. 334, pg. 1889
RAID-DP - Software - NETAPP, INC.; pg. 444, pg. 287
RAIDAR - Wireless Networking Product - NETGEAR, INC.; pg. 444, pg. 247
RAIDCORE - Computer Products - BROADCOM CORPORATION; pg. 364, pg. 108
RAIDCORE - Internal Server Storage Software - DOT HILL SYSTEMS CORP.; pg. 388, pg. 333
RAIDER - Semiconductor Device - APPLIED MATERIALS, INC; pg. 618, pg. 1009
RAIDIATOR - Wireless Networking Product - NETGEAR, INC.; pg. 444, pg. 247
RAILCLAMP - Array - SEMTECH CORPORATION; pg. 671, pg. 57
RAILFOCUS - Software Product - MAXIMUS, INC.; pg. 780, pg. 1799
RAILPORT - Mechanical & Electrical System - JOHNSON CONTROLS, INC.; pg. 209, pg. 1876
RAILRIDER - Rescue Equipment - MINE SAFETY APPLIANCES COMPANY; pg. 1361, pg. 1525
RAILROAD MILLS - Dry Snuff - SWISHER INTERNATIONAL, INC.; pg. 1895, pg. 345
RAILROAD PROTECTOR PLAN - Insurance Package Program - BROWN & BROWN, INC.; pg. 1196, pg. 419
RAILSOUNDS - Toy Train - LIONEL LLC; pg. 961, pg. 875
RAILWAY AGE - Monthly Magazine - SIMMONS-BOARDMAN PUBLISHING CORP.; pg. 1686, pg. 1292
RAIMSA - Bearing - FEDERAL-MOGUL HOLDINGS CORPORATION; pg. 205, pg. 907
RAIN - Patterned Glass - AGC GLASS NORTH AMERICA, INC.; pg. 65, pg. 482
RAIN - Sports Drink - THE GATORADE COMPANY; pg. 251, pg. 574
RAIN - Organic Vodka - SAZERAC COMPANY, INC.; pg. 1969, pg. 745
RAIN - Chewing Gum Flavor - WM. WRIGLEY JR. COMPANY; pg. 1863, pg. 596
RAIN-BLO - Candy - FERRARA CANDY CO.; pg. 1852, pg. 612
RAIN CURTAIN - Nozzles - RAIN BIRD CORPORATION; pg. 707, pg. 44
RAIN DANCE - Waxes & Washes - THE CLOROX COMPANY; pg. 327, pg. 169
RAIN FOREST - Carpet - INTERFACE, INC.; pg. 695, pg. 512
RAIN FOREST - Candle - NATURAL DECORATIONS, INC.; pg. 936, pg. 5
RAIN FOREST NUT - Coffee - KEURIG GREEN MOUNTAIN, INC.; pg. 868, pg. 1768
RAIN GUARD - Header Seal - RITE-HITE HOLDING CORPORATION; pg. 1372, pg. 1880
RAIN GUN - Sprinklers - RAIN BIRD CORPORATION; pg. 707, pg. 44
RAIN OR SHINE - Reversible Hats - HABAND COMPANY, INC.; pg. 1772, pg. 1099
RAIN-X - Windshield Wiper Blades - SHELL LUBRICANTS; pg. 217, pg. 1714
RAINALERT II - Pump Product - IDEX CORPORATION; pg. 1347, pg. 623
RAINBOW - Chemical Product - CABOT CORPORATION; pg. 1151, pg. 792
RAINBOW - Digital Color Proofing System - IMATION CORP.; pg. 413, pg. 952
RAINBOW - Silicon Etch System - LAM RESEARCH CORPORATION; pg. 1354, pg. 91
RAINBOW - Systems Integration & Aeronautics - LOCKHEED MARTIN CORPORATION; pg. 229, pg. 762
RAINBOW - Art Paper - PACON CORPORATION; pg. 1466, pg. 1852
RAINBOW ADVENTURE - DVD Game - MATTEL, INC.; pg. 962, pg. 81
RAINBOW BEGINNER - Velcro Hand Grip - SCHOOL-TECH, INC.; pg. 1844, pg. 866
RAINBOW INTERNATIONAL - Carpet Care & Restoration Service - THE DWYER GROUP, INC.; pg. 79, pg. 1748
RAINBOW KNOCK OUT - Garden Roses - THE CONARD-PYLE COMPANY; pg. 1794, pg. 1594
RAINBOW OF BERRIES - Black Tea - CELESTIAL SEASONINGS, INC.; pg. 846, pg. 310
RAINBOW RICHES - Video Game - INTERNATIONAL GAME TECHNOLOGY; pg. 957, pg. 1024
RAINBOW SET - Oximeters - MASIMO CORPORATION; pg. 1558, pg. 113
RAINBOW SWEET - Snuff Tobacco - AMERICAN SNUFF COMPANY; pg. 1893, pg. 1641
RAINBOWWALL - Electronic Display System - TRANS-LUX CORPORATION; pg. 681, pg. 365
RAINBOX PAK - Plastic & Rubber - TEKNOR APEX COMPANY; pg. 1889, pg. 1605
RAINDANCE - Fabric - NEMSCHOFF, INC.; pg. 936, pg. 1890
RAINDROP - Mousepad - ALLSOP, INC.; pg. 347, pg. 1817
RAINDROP - Medical Device - MALLINCKRODT PHARMACEUTICALS; pg. 1557, pg. 978
RAINDROP - Nebulizers & Nebulizer Masks - MEDTRONIC; pg. 1563, pg. 183
RAINDROP - Packaging - PACTIV CORPORATION; pg. 1466, pg. 624
RAINFAIR - Rainwear & Protective Clothing - LACROSSE FOOTWEAR, INC.; pg. 1811, pg. 1503
RAINFINITY - Software - FMC CORPORATION; pg. 391, pg. 825
RAINFOREST - Fabric - NEMSCHOFF, INC.; pg. 936, pg. 1890
RAINFOREST CAFE - Restaurant Chain - LANDRY'S, INC.; pg. 1735, pg. 1709
RAINFOREST DESIGNER - Educational Materials - SCHOLASTIC INC.; pg. 1683, pg. 1288
RAINFOREST RESEARCHERS - Educational Materials - SCHOLASTIC INC.; pg. 1683, pg. 1288
RAINGO - Vinyl Rainwater System - GENOVA PRODUCTS, INC.; pg. 83, pg. 875
RAINGO & REPLAK - Gutter & Down Spouts - GENOVA PRODUCTS, INC.; pg. 83, pg. 875
RAINGRIP - Glove - ACUSHNET COMPANY; pg. 1824, pg. 818
RAINGUARD - Riflescope - BUSHNELL OUTDOOR PRODUCTS, INC.; pg. 1403, pg. 718
RAINGUARD - Construction Technology - SONOCO PRODUCTS COMPANY; pg. 1469, pg. 1619
RAINIER - Bedding - CROSCILL, INC.; pg. 1122, pg. 1220
RAINIER - Ceiling Fan - HUNTER FAN COMPANY; pg. 57, pg. 1631
RAINIER - Beer - PABST BREWING COMPANY; pg. 258, pg. 137
RAINMAKER - Software - ASA INTERNATIONAL LTD.; pg. 353, pg. 1036
RAINMAKER SYSTEM - Outsource Provider - RAINMAKER SYSTEMS INC.; pg. 458, pg. 58
RAINSPORT - Golf Accessories - CALLAWAY GOLF COMPANY; pg. 1829, pg. 58
RAINTREE - Dental Product - DENTSPLY INTERNATIONAL INC.; pg. 1522, pg. 1596
RAINTREE PUZZLES AND GAMES - Game - UNIVERSITY GAMES CORPORATION; pg. 969, pg. 230
RAINX - Vehicle Care - ZEP INC.; pg. 338, pg. 524
RAINY DAY CHANGE - Lottery Game - ILLINOIS STATE LOTTERY; pg. 995, pg. 578
RAINY RIVER - Apparel - CABELA'S INCORPORATED; pg. 535, pg. 1019
RAISE - Software - BIO-RAD LABORATORIES, INC.; pg. 1504, pg. 101
RAISE - Rug Shampoo - SWISHER HYGIENE INC.; pg. 336, pg. 1507
RAISE A READER - Community Foundation Program - EDMONTON OILERS HOCKEY CLUB; pg. 546, pg. 1906
RAISE YOUR SHOPPING I.Q. - Tag Line - BIZRATE.COM; pg. 1231, pg. 126
RAISED - Donut Mixes - DAWN FOOD PRODUCTS, INC.; pg. 1018, pg. 893
THE RAISER'S EDGE - Fundraising Software - BLACKBAUD, INC.; pg. 361, pg. 1613
THE RAISER'S EDGE ENTERPRISE - Constituent Relationship Management Software - BLACKBAUD, INC.; pg. 361, pg. 1613
RAISIN BLEND - Pet Product - PETSMART, INC.; pg. 1481, pg. 18
RAISIN BRAN - Crunchy Flakes - KELLOGG COMPANY; pg. 831, pg. 870
RAISIN BRAN - Cereal - POST HOLDINGS, INC.; pg. 833, pg. 1002
RAISIN NUT BRAN - Cereal - GENERAL MILLS, INC.; pg. 828, pg. 933
RAISINETS - Candy - NESTLE USA, INC.; pg. 883, pg. 96
RAISING BILLIONS TO EDUCATE MILLIONS! - Tagline - NEW YORK STATE LOTTERY; pg. 1001, pg. 1340
RAISING THE BAR - Slogan - AT&T MOBILITY LLC; pg. 619, pg. 488
RAISING THE STANDARD SINCE DAY ONE - Slogan - LKQ CORP.; pg. 210, pg. 185
RAISINMATE - Raisin Juice Concentrate Replacement - DAVID MICHAEL & CO. INC.; pg. 852, pg. 1563
RAISINS - Swimwear - QUIKSILVER, INC.; pg. 31, pg. 104
RAKIN' IT IN - Game - WMS INDUSTRIES INC.; pg. 593, pg. 666
RAKOLL - Adhesives - H.B. FULLER COMPANY; pg. 1165, pg. 961
RAKUTEN SUPER POINTS - Rewards Program - RAKUTEN.COM SHOPPING; pg. 1277, pg. 41
RALEIGH - Furniture - LA-Z-BOY INCORPORATED; pg. 932, pg. 901
RALEIGH COURT - Corporate Furniture - BERNHARDT DESIGN; pg. 918, pg. 1381
RALGRO - Medicine - MERCK & CO., INC.; pg. 1566, pg. 1077
RALIEGH - Table - BLATT BOWLING & BILLIARD CORP.; pg. 1827, pg. 1203
RALIVIA - Pharmaceutical Product - VALEANT PHARMACEUTICALS INTERNATIONAL, INC.; pg. 1605, pg. 1957
RALLY - Sport - AMERICAN KENNEL CLUB, INC.; pg. 129, pg. 1193
RALLY - String - ASHAWAY LINE & TWINE MFG. CO.; pg. 1826, pg. 1600
RALLY - Chrome Cleaner - GEERPRES INC.; pg. 1339, pg. 901
RALLY - Balloon, Hot Air Sport - RAVEN INDUSTRIES, INC.; pg. 1888, pg. 1625
RALLY - No Buff Wax - S.C. JOHNSON & SON, INC.; pg. 334, pg. 1889
RALLY - Office Furniture - STEELCASE INC.; pg. 475, pg. 889
RALLY'S - Restaurants - CHECKERS DRIVE-IN RESTAURANTS, INC.; pg. 1017, pg. 472
RALPH - Women's Fragrance - RALPH LAUREN CORPORATION; pg. 46, pg. 1284
RALPH BY RALPH LAUREN - Men's Apparel - RALPH LAUREN CORPORATION; pg. 46, pg. 1284
RALPH HOT - Women's Fragrance - RALPH LAUREN CORPORATION; pg. 46, pg. 1284
RALPH LAUREN BLACK LABEL - Men & Women's Apparel - RALPH LAUREN CORPORATION; pg. 46, pg. 1284
RALPH LAUREN BLUE - Women's Fragrance - RALPH LAUREN CORPORATION; pg. 46, pg. 1284
RALPH LAUREN BLUE LABEL - Women's Apparel - RALPH LAUREN CORPORATION; pg. 46, pg. 1284
RALPH LAUREN CHILDRENSWEAR - Children's Apparel - RALPH LAUREN CORPORATION; pg. 46, pg. 1284
RALPH LAUREN GOLF - Women's Golf Apparel - RALPH LAUREN CORPORATION; pg. 46, pg. 1284
RALPH LAUREN HOME - Bedding, Bath & Home Accessories - RALPH LAUREN CORPORATION; pg. 46, pg. 1284
RALPH LAUREN PAINT - Paint - RALPH LAUREN CORPORATION; pg. 46, pg. 1284
RALPH LAUREN PURPLE LABEL - Men's Clothing - RALPH LAUREN CORPORATION; pg. 46, pg. 1284
RALPH ROCKS - Fragrance - RALPH LAUREN CORPORATION; pg. 46, pg. 1284
RALPHS - Supermarket - THE KROGER CO.; pg. 1025, pg. 1416
RAM - Golf Product - HUFFY CORPORATION; pg. 1836, pg. 1409
RAM GOLF - Golf Company - HUFFY CORPORATION; pg. 1836, pg. 1409
RAM-RITE - Impact Doors - RITE-HITE HOLDING CORPORATION; pg. 1372, pg. 1880
RAM-STACK - Next Generation Technology - SANMINA-SCI CORPORATION; pg. 671, pg. 250
RAM1 - Memory - CYPRESS SEMICONDUCTOR CORPORATION; pg. 1326, pg. 243
RAM2 - Memory - CYPRESS SEMICONDUCTOR CORPORATION; pg. 1326, pg. 243
RAM3 - Memory - CYPRESS SEMICONDUCTOR CORPORATION; pg. 1326, pg. 243
RAM4 - Memory - CYPRESS SEMICONDUCTOR CORPORATION; pg. 1326, pg. 243
RAM5 - Memory - CYPRESS SEMICONDUCTOR CORPORATION; pg. 1326, pg. 243
RAM6 - Memory - CYPRESS SEMICONDUCTOR CORPORATION; pg. 1326, pg. 243
RAM7 - Memory - CYPRESS SEMICONDUCTOR

CORPORATION; pg. 1326, pg. 243
RAM8 - Memory - CYPRESS SEMICONDUCTOR CORPORATION; pg. 1326, pg. 243
RAM9 - Memory - CYPRESS SEMICONDUCTOR CORPORATION; pg. 1326, pg. 243
RAMADA - Hotels - MARRIOTT INTERNATIONAL, INC.; pg. 1102, pg. 764
RAMADA - Hotels - WYNDHAM WORLDWIDE CORPORATION; pg. 1119, pg. 1107
RAMAR - Meter Reading System - BADGER METER, INC.; pg. 1401, pg. 1873
RAMBLE - Software - SRA INTERNATIONAL, INC.; pg. 473, pg. 1780
RAMBLER - Knife - COAST CUTLERY COMPANY; pg. 1121, pg. 1501
RAMBLER'S - Leather Product - COACH, INC.; pg. 3, pg. 1214
RAMBLIN' - Beverages - THE COCA-COLA COMPANY; pg. 240, pg. 493
RAMBOLT - Bolts & Nuts - ALCOA INC.; pg. 65, pg. 1188
RAMCORDER - Electrical Test & Measurement - HD ELECTRIC COMPANY; pg. 1299, pg. 666
RAMCORDER OH1600 - System Measurement - HD ELECTRIC COMPANY; pg. 1299, pg. 666
RAMCORDER RCMB - Meter Base Recorder - HD ELECTRIC COMPANY; pg. 1299, pg. 666
RAMFIRE - Burner - MAXON CORPORATION; pg. 1359, pg. 695
RAMIK - Animal Safety Product - NEOGEN CORPORATION; pg. 883, pg. 896
RAMITEC - Impression Material - 3M COMPANY; pg. 1142, pg. 956
RAMLI - Footwear - K-SWISS; pg. 1837, pg. 306
RAMM - Remote Access Memory Modules - MAXXESS SYSTEMS, INC.; pg. 431, pg. 43
RAMONA - Furniture - ASHLEY FURNITURE INDUSTRIES, INC.; pg. 914, pg. 1852
RAMPAGE - Sportswear, Denim & Dresses - ICONIX BRAND GROUP, INC.; pg. 26, pg. 1243
RAMPAGE - Yacht - KCS INTERNATIONAL, INC.; pg. 556, pg. 1885
RAMPAGE - Auto Sound Systems - VOXX INTERNATIONAL; pg. 686, pg. 1166
RAMPANT REWARDS - Video Game - INTERNATIONAL GAME TECHNOLOGY; pg. 957, pg. 1024
RAMPART - 3-Tab Roofing Shingles - BUILDING PRODUCTS OF CANADA CORP.; pg. 72, pg. 1951
RAMRIGHT - Software Solution - DELL INC.; pg. 383, pg. 1737
RAMROD - Cigar - AVANTI CIGAR CORPORATION; pg. 1894, pg. 1527
RAMUC - Pool Paints - PETTIT PAINT COMPANY; pg. 1444, pg. 1116
RANAWAT-BURSTEIN HIP SYSTEM - Hip Product - ZIMMER BIOMET HOLDINGS, INC.; pg. 1611, pg. 699
RANCH - Garage Door - MARTIN DOOR MANUFACTURING, INC.; pg. 96, pg. 1759
RANCH - Gas Grill - WEBER-STEPHEN PRODUCTS LLC; pg. 62, pg. 650
RANCH HAND - Hand & Garden Tools - TRACTOR SUPPLY COMPANY; pg. 708, pg. 1627
RANCH STYLE - Food Product - CONAGRA FOODS, INC.; pg. 826, pg. 1014
RANCHER II - Glove - KOMBI, LTD.; pg. 1838, pg. 1766
RANCHERO - Wood Stain - JONES-BLAIR COMPANY; pg. 1443, pg. 1682
RANCHER'S RESERVE - Premium Quality Meats - SAFEWAY INC.; pg. 1032, pg. 184
RANCHERS STOCK - Salt - CARGILL LIMITED; pg. 1475, pg. 1914
RANCHMASTER - Livestock Equipment - BEHLEN MFG. CO.; pg. 701, pg. 1010
RANCHO - Furniture - ASHLEY FURNITURE INDUSTRIES, INC.; pg. 914, pg. 1852
RANCHO - Alkyd Gloss Enamel - DUNN-EDWARDS CORPORATION; pg. 1442, pg. 129
RANCHO - Shock & Suspension System - TENNECO, INC.; pg. 985, pg. 625
RANCHO ZABACO - Wine - E&J GALLO WINERY; pg. 1962, pg. 149
RAND MCNALLY FOR KIDS - Children's Publishing - RAND MCNALLY & COMPANY; pg. 1679, pg. 661
RANDALL - Furniture - AMERICAN LEATHER LP; pg. 912, pg. 1673
RANDALL - Amplifiers - U.S. MUSIC CORPORATION; pg. 315, pg. 560
RANDELL - Foodservice - UNIFIED BRANDS INC.; pg. 1385, pg. 970
RANDERS - Furniture - HOOKER FURNITURE CORPORATION; pg. 928, pg. 1788
RANDI - Handle And Fitting - INGERSOLL-RAND COMPANY; pg. 1349, pg. 1370
RANDOLPH - Shoes - ALLEN-EDMONDS SHOE CORP.; pg. 1804, pg. 1887
RANDOM HOUSE - Children's Books - PENGUIN RANDOM HOUSE CHILDREN'S BOOKS; pg. 1676, pg. 1277
RANDOM HOUSE PUZZLES & GAMES - Publishing Imprint - PENGUIN RANDOM HOUSE; pg. 1675, pg. 1276
RANDOM HOUSE REFERENCE - Publishing Imprint - PENGUIN RANDOM HOUSE; pg. 1675, pg. 1276
RANDOM PULSE - Phacoemulsification System - STAAR SURGICAL COMPANY; pg. 1597, pg. 151
RANDY OUZTS - Home & Garden Products - ENESCO, LLC; pg. 1124, pg. 620
RANGE - Apparel - OAKLEY, INC.; pg. 1840, pg. 86
RANGE ROVER - Sport Utility Vehicle - JAGUAR LAND ROVER NORTH AMERICA LLC; pg. 180, pg. 1081
RANGEFINDER - Sensor - HUNTER ENGINEERING COMPANY; pg. 208, pg. 973
RANGEMASTER - Range Hoods - BROAN-NUTONE LLC; pg. 1069, pg. 1860
RANGEMAX - Wireless Networking Product - NETGEAR, INC.; pg. 444, pg. 247
RANGER - Furniture - AMERICAN LEATHER LP; pg. 912, pg. 1673
RANGER - Cutlery - BUCK KNIVES, INC.; pg. 1828, pg. 550
RANGER - Material Handling Equipment - C&D TECHNOLOGIES, INC.; pg. 627, pg. 1517
RANGER - Thermal Imaging System - FLIR SYSTEMS, INC.; pg. 1413, pg. 1510
RANGER - Truck - FORD MOTOR COMPANY OF CANADA, LIMITED; pg. 174, pg. 1930
RANGER - Gaming Product - GLD PRODUCTS, INC.; pg. 1835, pg. 1882
RANGER - Wood Stain - JONES-BLAIR COMPANY; pg. 1443, pg. 1682
RANGER - Footwear - P.W. MINOR & SON, INC.; pg. 1816, pg. 1140
RANGER - Navigation Aid - TRIMBLE NAVIGATION LIMITED; pg. 1384, pg. 288
RANGER - Food - WESTERN SIZZLIN CORPORATION; pg. 1755, pg. 1806
RANGER AMERICAN - Security Monitoring System - THE ADT CORPORATION; pg. 612, pg. 409
RANGER II - Medical Equipment - INVACARE CORPORATION; pg. 1546, pg. 1451
RANGER QCT - Rotary Control Valve - CASHCO, INC.; pg. 1044, pg. 714
RANGER SX - Bicycles - G. JOANNOU CYCLE CO. INC.; pg. 1707, pg. 1098
RANGER X - Medical Equipment - INVACARE CORPORATION; pg. 1546, pg. 1451
RANGER XR - Bicycle - G. JOANNOU CYCLE CO. INC.; pg. 1707, pg. 1098
R'ANGLE - Right Angle Clinch Fastener - PENN ENGINEERING & MANUFACTURING CORP.; pg. 1059, pg. 1525
RANGOON - Furniture - ASHLEY FURNITURE INDUSTRIES, INC.; pg. 914, pg. 1852
RANGOON - Fabric - SCALAMANDRE, INC.; pg. 941, pg. 1058
RANIR - Dental Product - RANIR LLC; pg. 520, pg. 888
RANSCO - Products - DESPATCH INDUSTRIES; pg. 1070, pg. 927
RANSOMES - Golf, Turf & Specialty Products - TEXTRON INC.; pg. 235, pg. 1607
RAP - Latex - THE DOW CHEMICAL COMPANY; pg. 1157, pg. 898
RAP - Trading Edition - SAP; pg. 465, pg. 78
RAPAFLO - Pharmaceutical Product - ALLERGAN; pg. 1490, pg. 1101
RAPALA - Fishing Lures - RAPALA VMC CORPORATION; pg. 1843, pg. 949
RAPAMUNE - Autoimmune Disorder Treatment Pharmaceutical Preparation - PFIZER INC.; pg. 1581, pg. 1278
RAPHAEL - Software - SYNOPSYS, INC.; pg. 480, pg. 162
RAPHAEL - Lighting Product - WESTINGHOUSE LIGHTING CORPORATION; pg. 687, pg. 1571
RAPI-DRIV - Screwdriver With Rotating Blade - KLEIN TOOLS INC.; pg. 1052, pg. 627
RAPIBARRITAS - Frozen Seafood - HIGH LINER FOODS INCORPORATED; pg. 862, pg. 1917
RAPICOCINADOS - Frozen Seafood - HIGH LINER FOODS INCORPORATED; pg. 862, pg. 1917
RAPID ACCESS - Health Care Services - HEALTH NET, INC.; pg. 1540, pg. 308
RAPID ADVANCE - Wiper Control System - MAXIM INTEGRATED PRODUCTS, INC.; pg. 653, pg. 247
RAPID ARMOUR - Removable Protective Coatings - QUAKER CHEMICAL CORP.; pg. 1178, pg. 1524
RAPID/BONDER - Bonder - WSF INDUSTRIES, INC.; pg. 1390, pg. 1346
RAPID-CAM - Height-Adjustable Basketball Standards - LIFETIME PRODUCTS INC.; pg. 933, pg. 1751
RAPID/CANNER - Canner - WSF INDUSTRIES, INC.; pg. 1390, pg. 1346
RAPID/CAPPER - Tire Capper - WSF INDUSTRIES, INC.; pg. 1390, pg. 1346
RAPID CAPTURE - Molecular Diagnostic Test - QIAGEN GAITHERSBURG INC.; pg. 1587, pg. 771
RAPID-CLEAR - Eye Wash & Shower - SELLSTROM MANUFACTURING CO.; pg. 1428, pg. 659
RAPID/COOKER - Cooker - WSF INDUSTRIES, INC.; pg. 1390, pg. 1346
RAPID/COUPLER - Coupler - WSF INDUSTRIES, INC.; pg. 1390, pg. 1346
RAPID/CURE - Cable - WSF INDUSTRIES, INC.; pg. 1390, pg. 1346
RAPID DOCUMENT DESIGN - Software - BOTTOMLINE TECHNOLOGIES INC.; pg. 363, pg. 483
RAPID DOUBLE JACKPOT - Slot Machine - BALLY TECHNOLOGIES, INC.; pg. 531, pg. 1022
RAPID DRUG SCREEN - Diagnostic Test Kit - AMERICAN BIO MEDICA CORPORATION; pg. 1493, pg. 1171
RAPID DRY - Drying Agent - OIL-DRI CORPORATION OF AMERICA; pg. 1480, pg. 586
RAPID FILL - Air-Filled Packaging - SEALED AIR CORPORATION; pg. 1468, pg. 1058
RAPID FIT - Cable & Antenna System - RADIO FREQUENCY SYSTEMS, INC.; pg. 666, pg. 354
RAPID FLEX - Animal Feed Supplement - MANNA PRO CORPORATION; pg. 1478, pg. 975
RAPID GLOBALIZATION METHODOLOGY - Software - LIONBRIDGE TECHNOLOGIES INC.; pg. 428, pg. 851
RAPID JACKPOT - Slots - INTERNATIONAL GAME TECHNOLOGY; pg. 957, pg. 1024
RAPID LOAD - Commercial Washers - PELLERIN MILNOR CORPORATION; pg. 1368, pg. 744
RAPID/LOADER - Loader - WSF INDUSTRIES, INC.; pg. 1390, pg. 1346
RAPID LOGIC - Software - WIND RIVER SYSTEMS, INC.; pg. 493, pg. 38
RAPID ONE - Diagnostic Test Kit - AMERICAN BIO MEDICA CORPORATION; pg. 1493, pg. 1171
RAPID-PAK - Tape - IDEAL INDUSTRIES, INC.; pg. 1051, pg. 662
RAPID PLAY - Game - WMS INDUSTRIES INC.; pg. 593, pg. 666
RAPID PULSE - Dissolved Oxygen System - YSI INCORPORATED; pg. 1438, pg. 1483
RAPID RACK - Removable Rack Option - PELICAN PRODUCTS; pg. 1467, pg. 843
RAPID-RAIL - Side Loaders - HEIL ENVIRONMENTAL INDUSTRIES, LTD.; pg. 207, pg. 1629
RAPID READER - Diagnostic Test Kit - AMERICAN BIO MEDICA CORPORATION; pg. 1493, pg. 1171
RAPID RELOAD - Video Game - INTERNATIONAL GAME TECHNOLOGY; pg. 957, pg. 1024
RAPID RESPONSE - Expedited Shipment - BOBRICK WASHROOM EQUIPMENT, INC.; pg. 1043, pg. 166
RAPID RESPONSE - Support Services - DELL INC.; pg. 383, pg. 1737
RAPID RESPONSE - Heater - WATLOW ELECTRIC MANUFACTURING COMPANY; pg. 1078, pg. 1004
RAPID RESULTS - Fitness Product - BALLY TOTAL FITNESS HOLDINGS CORPORATION; pg. 532, pg. 1200
RAPID RETAIL - Retail Product - CIBER, INC.; pg. 372, pg. 330
RAPID REWARDS - Frequent Flyer Program - SOUTHWEST AIRLINES CO.; pg. 1923, pg. 1687
RAPID RIDGE - Roofing Ventilation Product - BENJAMIN OBDYKE, INC.; pg. 70, pg. 1540
RAPID-ROLL - Overhead Doors - ALBANY INTERNATIONAL CORP.; pg. 691, pg. 1038

RAPID RUSS - Food Product - ELLENBEE-LEGGETT COMPANY INC.; *pg.* 854, *pg.* 1452
RAPID SCAN - Software - HONEYWELL AEROSPACE ELECTRONIC SYSTEMS; *pg.* 228, *pg.* 17
RAPID TEC - Diagnostic Test Kit - AMERICAN BIO MEDICA CORPORATION; *pg.* 1493, *pg.* 1171
RAPID TOX - Diagnostic Test Kit - AMERICAN BIO MEDICA CORPORATION; *pg.* 1493, *pg.* 1171
RAPID/VAC - Vacuum - WSF INDUSTRIES, INC.; *pg.* 1390, *pg.* 1346
RAPID WRAP - Compression Bandage - SPECTRUM LABORATORIES INC.; *pg.* 1595, *pg.* 69
RAPIDARRAY - Supercomputing System - CRAY INC.; *pg.* 380, *pg.* 1834
RAPIDCIRC - Library Automation System - CHECKPOINT SYSTEMS, INC.; *pg.* 628, *pg.* 1559
RAPIDCONTROL - Software - WIND RIVER SYSTEMS, INC.; *pg.* 493, *pg.* 38
RAPIDCURE - Semiconductor Processing Equipment - AXCELIS TECHNOLOGIES, INC.; *pg.* 1400, *pg.* 787
RAPIDDITCH - Express Bag - ACR ELECTRONICS, INC.; *pg.* 612, *pg.* 422
RAPIDDITCH EXPRESS BAG - Survival Gear Bag - ACR ELECTRONICS, INC.; *pg.* 612, *pg.* 422
RAPID'E.COLI 2 - Software - BIO-RAD LABORATORIES, INC.; *pg.* 1504, *pg.* 101
RAPIDEX - Reactive Hot Melt Adhesive - H.B. FULLER COMPANY; *pg.* 1165, *pg.* 961
RAPIDFIND - Online Purchasing Database - TRICORBRAUN; *pg.* 1471, *pg.* 1004
RAPIDFIRE - Heating System for Aluminum, Non-Ferrous Metals - AIR PRODUCTS AND CHEMICALS, INC.; *pg.* 1145, *pg.* 1513
RAPIDFIRE - Medical Equipment - CONMED CORPORATION; *pg.* 1517, *pg.* 1347
RAPIDFIRE LIGHT - Automatic Vest Light/Strobe Light - ACR ELECTRONICS, INC.; *pg.* 612, *pg.* 422
RAPIDFIX 406 - 406-MHz EPIRB - ACR ELECTRONICS, INC.; *pg.* 612, *pg.* 422
RAPIDGX - Software - SANDISK CORPORATION; *pg.* 465, *pg.* 147
RAPID'L.MONO - Software - BIO-RAD LABORATORIES, INC.; *pg.* 1504, *pg.* 101
RAPIDMIST - Drug Delivery System - GENEREX BIOTECHNOLOGY CORPORATION; *pg.* 1534, *pg.* 1938
RAPIDOOR - Autoclaves Door - WSF INDUSTRIES, INC.; *pg.* 1390, *pg.* 1346
RAPIDPORT - Computer Peripheral Equipment - DIGI INTERNATIONAL INC.; *pg.* 387, *pg.* 948
RAPIDPORT/4 - Computer Peripheral Equipment - DIGI INTERNATIONAL INC.; *pg.* 387, *pg.* 948
RAPIDRELAY - Pharmaceutical Product - ALERE INC.; *pg.* 1488, *pg.* 849
RAPIDRESPONSE - Software - PASSUR AEROSPACE, INC.; *pg.* 233, *pg.* 376
RAPIDRY - Oil Paint Medium - MARTIN/F. WEBER COMPANY; *pg.* 962, *pg.* 1567
RAPIDRY - Nail Care Product - OPI PRODUCTS INC.; *pg.* 518, *pg.* 167
RAPIDS - Memory Product - ATMEL CORPORATION; *pg.* 621, *pg.* 238
RAPIDSCENE - Hardware & Software - EVANS & SUTHERLAND COMPUTER CORPORATION; *pg.* 638, *pg.* 1757
RAPIDSHIELD - Floor Coating System - QUAKER CHEMICAL CORP.; *pg.* 1178, *pg.* 1524
RAPIDSIGNAL - Pharmaceutical Product - ALERE INC.; *pg.* 1488, *pg.* 849
RAPIDSTART - Motor Start - INTERNATIONAL CONTROLS & MEASUREMENTS CORP.; *pg.* 1350, *pg.* 1317
RAPIDSTRIP - Semiconductor Processing Equipment - AXCELIS TECHNOLOGIES, INC.; *pg.* 1400, *pg.* 787
RAPIDVUE - Testing Instrument System - BECKMAN COULTER, INC.; *pg.* 1402, *pg.* 48
RAPIDWN - Diagnostic Test Product - SPECTRAL DIAGNOSTICS INC.; *pg.* 1430, *pg.* 1943
RAPIGEST - Reagant - WATERS CORPORATION; *pg.* 1436, *pg.* 834
RAPINA - Textiles - BERNHARDT DESIGN; *pg.* 918, *pg.* 1381
RAPINYL - Pharmaceutical Product - ENDO PHARMACEUTICALS HOLDINGS, INC.; *pg.* 1528, *pg.* 1549
RAPPORT - Bath Product - KOHLER CO.; *pg.* 91, *pg.* 1862
RAPPORT - Seating - STEELCASE INC.; *pg.* 475, *pg.* 889
RAPTIVA - Anti-CD11a Antibody for Psoriasis Treatments - GENENTECH, INC.; *pg.* 1533, *pg.* 279
RAPTOR - Amusement & Water Park - CEDAR FAIR, L.P.; *pg.* 537, *pg.* 1471
RAPTOR - Systems Integration & Aeronautics - LOCKHEED MARTIN CORPORATION; *pg.* 229, *pg.* 762
RAPTOR - Musical Instrument - PEAVEY ELECTRONICS CORPORATION; *pg.* 662, *pg.* 970
RAPTOR - Software - SYMANTEC CORPORATION; *pg.* 478, *pg.* 161
RAPTOR - Hard Drive - WESTERN DIGITAL CORPORATION; *pg.* 492, *pg.* 118
RAPTOR PLUS - Raptor Plus Guitar - PEAVEY ELECTRONICS CORPORATION; *pg.* 662, *pg.* 970
RAPTORS NBA TV - Television Channel - MAPLE LEAF SPORTS & ENTERTAINMENT LTD.; *pg.* 560, *pg.* 1940
RAPTURE - Stainless Steel Propeller - MICHIGAN WHEEL CORPORATION; *pg.* 1709, *pg.* 888
RAPUNZEL - Furniture - HERMAN MILLER, INC.; *pg.* 926, *pg.* 913
RAR - Photo Film - EASTMAN KODAK COMPANY; *pg.* 1408, *pg.* 1333
THE RARE AND THE EXTRAORDINARY - Slogan - DAVID BIRNBAUM/RARE 1 CORPORATION; *pg.* 4, *pg.* 1221
RARE EARTHS - Ethnobotanical Product - NU SKIN ENTERPRISES, INC.; *pg.* 518, *pg.* 1755
RARE GOLD - Beauty Product - AVON PRODUCTS, INC.; *pg.* 500, *pg.* 1198
RARE PEARLS - Beauty Product - AVON PRODUCTS, INC.; *pg.* 500, *pg.* 1198
RARE TREASURE - Carpet - BEAULIEU GROUP, LLC; *pg.* 917, *pg.* 529
RARIS - Food Product - MARS, INCORPORATED; *pg.* 1858, *pg.* 1792
RAS - Application Server - POLYCOM, INC.; *pg.* 664, *pg.* 249
RAS - Accessible Storage Products - REV-A-SHELF; *pg.* 1060, *pg.* 738
RA'S AL GHUL - Character - DC COMICS, INC.; *pg.* 1633, *pg.* 1221
RAS HOME OFFICE - Home Office Storage Products - REV-A-SHELF; *pg.* 1060, *pg.* 738
RA'S RICHES - Game - WMS INDUSTRIES INC.; *pg.* 593, *pg.* 666
RASCAL HOUSE - Food Product - JERRY'S FAMOUS DELI, INC.; *pg.* 1733, *pg.* 281
RASFINDER - Communication Product - MULTI-TECH SYSTEMS INC.; *pg.* 442, *pg.* 951
RASKAS - Cream Cheese - SCHREIBER FOODS, INC.; *pg.* 894, *pg.* 1859
RASPBERRY - Shoe - AEROGROUP INTERNATIONAL, INC.; *pg.* 1803, *pg.* 1055
RASPBERRY FANTASY - Fragrance - PARFUMS DE COEUR LTD.; *pg.* 519, *pg.* 376
RASPBERRY HEARTS - Candy - R.M. PALMER COMPANY; *pg.* 1861, *pg.* 1585
RASPBERRY LEMONADE BLAST - Lip Care Product - BLISTEX, INC.; *pg.* 502, *pg.* 644
RASPBERRY ROYALE - Tea - R.C. BIGELOW, INC.; *pg.* 891, *pg.* 348
RASPBERRY STICKS - Candy - SWEET CANDY COMPANY; *pg.* 1862, *pg.* 1761
RASPBERRY ZINGER - Herb Tea - CELESTIAL SEASONINGS, INC.; *pg.* 846, *pg.* 310
RASTER MATE - Sonar for Submarine Tracking - LOCKHEED MARTIN CORPORATION; *pg.* 229, *pg.* 762
RASTEX - Thread - W.L. GORE & ASSOCIATES, INC.; *pg.* 122, *pg.* 388
RAT-A-TAT CAT - Game - GAMEWRIGHT; *pg.* 953, *pg.* 836
RAT RODS - Die Cast Replicas - REVELL; *pg.* 966, *pg.* 611
RATA - Footwear - VANS, INC.; *pg.* 1821, *pg.* 76
RATALOC - Cutter - HOUGEN MANUFACTURING INC.; *pg.* 1347, *pg.* 908
RATATOUILLE - Shoe - AEROGROUP INTERNATIONAL, INC.; *pg.* 1803, *pg.* 1055
RATE - Systems Integration & Aeronautics - LOCKHEED MARTIN CORPORATION; *pg.* 229, *pg.* 762
RATE FINDER - Software - EQUIFAX INC.; *pg.* 748, *pg.* 504
RATE-MASTER - Plastic Flowmeter - DWYER INSTRUMENTS INC.; *pg.* 1330, *pg.* 694
RATEADVANTAGE - Interest Saver - DRIVETIME AUTOMOTIVE GROUP, INC.; *pg.* 169, *pg.* 16
RATECENTERINFO - Geographic Rate Center Boundary Tool - PITNEY BOWES SOFTWARE INC.; *pg.* 455, *pg.* 1346
RATESTOGO.COM - Accommodation Booking Website - ORBITZ WORLDWIDE, INC.; *pg.* 1918, *pg.* 586
RATH BLACK HAWK - Meat Products - JOHN MORRELL & CO.; *pg.* 866, *pg.* 1415
RATINGS IQUERY - Web-Based Reporting Tool - STANDARD & POOR'S RATINGS SERVICES; *pg.* 805, *pg.* 1296
RATINGSDIRECT - Web-Based Analysis - STANDARD & POOR'S RATINGS SERVICES; *pg.* 805, *pg.* 1296
RATINGSDIRECT ASIA - Online Analysis Tool - STANDARD & POOR'S RATINGS SERVICES; *pg.* 805, *pg.* 1296
RATINGSDIRECT CANADA - Online Analysis Tool - STANDARD & POOR'S RATINGS SERVICES; *pg.* 805, *pg.* 1296
RATINGSDIRECT CORPORATIONS & UTILITIES - Online Risk Analysis Tool - STANDARD & POOR'S RATINGS SERVICES; *pg.* 805, *pg.* 1296
RATINGSDIRECT FINANCIAL INSTITUTIONS - Online Risk Analysis Tool - STANDARD & POOR'S RATINGS SERVICES; *pg.* 805, *pg.* 1296
RATINGSDIRECT GLOBAL ISSUERS - Online Risk Analysis Tool - STANDARD & POOR'S RATINGS SERVICES; *pg.* 805, *pg.* 1296
RATINGSDIRECT INSURANCE - Online Risk Analysis Tool - STANDARD & POOR'S RATINGS SERVICES; *pg.* 805, *pg.* 1296
RATINGSDIRECT LATIN AMERICA - Online Risk Analysis Tool - STANDARD & POOR'S RATINGS SERVICES; *pg.* 805, *pg.* 1296
RATINGSDIRECT PACIFIC - Online Risk Analysis Tool - STANDARD & POOR'S RATINGS SERVICES; *pg.* 805, *pg.* 1296
RATINGSDIRECT PUBLIC FINANCE - Online Risk Analysis Tool - STANDARD & POOR'S RATINGS SERVICES; *pg.* 805, *pg.* 1296
RATINGSDIRECT SOVEREIGNS - Online Risk Analysis Tool - STANDARD & POOR'S RATINGS SERVICES; *pg.* 805, *pg.* 1296
RATINGSDIRECT STRUCTURED FINANCE - Online Risk Analysis Tool - STANDARD & POOR'S RATINGS SERVICES; *pg.* 805, *pg.* 1296
RATINGSXPRESS-CREDIT RATINGS - Online Risk Analysis Tool - STANDARD & POOR'S RATINGS SERVICES; *pg.* 805, *pg.* 1296
RATINGSXPRESS-CREDIT RESEARCH - Online Risk Analysis Tool - STANDARD & POOR'S RATINGS SERVICES; *pg.* 805, *pg.* 1296
RATIO - Turbidimeter-Laboratory & On-Line - HACH COMPANY; *pg.* 1415, *pg.* 334
RATIOMATIC - Burner - ECLIPSE INC.; *pg.* 1332, *pg.* 655
RATIOMETRIC - Digital Weight Resolver - ACRISON, INC.; *pg.* 1310, *pg.* 1087
RATIONALIQ - Health & Wellness Product - EXPRESS SCRIPTS; *pg.* 1530, *pg.* 1070
RATTAN - Fabric - NEMSCHOFF, INC.; *pg.* 936, *pg.* 1890
RATTANWEAVE - Coated Paper - BOISE CASCADE HOLDINGS, L.L.C.; *pg.* 1453, *pg.* 546
RATTLE 'N ROLL - Toy - MUNCHKIN, INC.; *pg.* 964, *pg.* 300
RATTLESNAKE - Firearms - REMINGTON ARMS COMPANY, LLC; *pg.* 1844, *pg.* 1382
RAUCH - Christmas Ornaments & Novelties - RAUCH INDUSTRIES, INC.; *pg.* 940, *pg.* 1373
RAULAND - Speaker And Horn - RAULAND-BORG CORPORATION; *pg.* 666, *pg.* 634
RAV-WARE - Software - CLEARONE COMMUNICATIONS, INC.; *pg.* 629, *pg.* 1756
RAV4 - Sports Utility Vehicle - TOYOTA MOTOR NORTH AMERICA, INC.; *pg.* 192, *pg.* 1303
RAV4 EV - Hybrid SUV - TOYOTA MOTOR NORTH AMERICA, INC.; *pg.* 192, *pg.* 1303
RAVE - Visualization Software - CAE INC.; *pg.* 226, *pg.* 1959
RAVE - Fabric - NEMSCHOFF, INC.; *pg.* 936, *pg.* 1890
RAVE - Flooring Product - STAGESTEP INC.; *pg.* 1688, *pg.* 1570
RAVE - Waiting Seating - STEELCASE INC.; *pg.* 475, *pg.* 889
RAVE TANDEM - Office Furniture - STEELCASE INC.; *pg.* 475, *pg.* 889
RAVE911 - Real Time Address Validation Engine - TELECOMMUNICATION SYSTEMS INC.; *pg.* 483, *pg.* 754
RAVEN - Unmanned Air Vehicle - AEROVIRONMENT, INC.; *pg.* 223, *pg.* 150
RAVEN - Footwear - CAPEZIO BALLET MAKERS INC.; *pg.* 1805, *pg.* 1125
RAVEN - Coating & Lining System - COHESANT, INC.; *pg.* 1154, *pg.* 1405

RAVEN - Furniture - JASPER GROUP; *pg.* 930, *pg.* 691
RAVEN - Helicopter - ROBINSON HELICOPTER COMPANY; *pg.* 234, *pg.* 295
RAVEN - Valve Trim - SPX PROCESS EQUIPMENT; *pg.* 1378, *pg.* 1551
RAVEN HILL FORGE - Metal Tile - WALKER & ZANGER, INC.; *pg.* 119, *pg.* 281
RAVIN - Footwear - STEVEN MADDEN, LTD.; *pg.* 1819, *pg.* 1176
RAVIN' RAISINS - Chocolate Product - WORLD'S FINEST CHOCOLATE, INC.; *pg.* 1864, *pg.* 597
RAVIN' RED - Beverage - SPRECHER BREWING COMPANY; *pg.* 265, *pg.* 1858
RAVIN' RED SODA - Soda - SPRECHER BREWING COMPANY; *pg.* 265, *pg.* 1858
RAVINA - Carpet - BEAULIEU GROUP, LLC; *pg.* 917, *pg.* 529
RAVING BEAUTY - Carpet - BEAULIEU GROUP, LLC; *pg.* 917, *pg.* 529
RAVINIA - Kitchen Product - KOHLER CO.; *pg.* 91, *pg.* 1862
RAVO - Sweeper Vehicles - FEDERAL SIGNAL CORPORATION; *pg.* 638, *pg.* 645
RAW - Hair Color - AMERICAN INTERNATIONAL INDUSTRIES COMPANY; *pg.* 498, *pg.* 126
RAW EARTH - Foot Care & Beauty Products - CREATIVE NAIL DESIGN, INC.; *pg.* 506, *pg.* 302
RAW ENERGY - Nutritional Product - NUTRACEUTICAL INTERNATIONAL CORPORATION; *pg.* 1576, *pg.* 1753
RAWL-BOLT - Expansion Anchor - POWERS FASTENERS INC.; *pg.* 1059, *pg.* 1143
RAWL-STUD - Wedge Anchor - POWERS FASTENERS INC.; *pg.* 1059, *pg.* 1143
RAWLDRILL - Masonry Drills - POWERS FASTENERS INC.; *pg.* 1059, *pg.* 1143
RAWLINGS - Athletic Equipment & Sporting Goods - RAWLINGS SPORTING GOODS CO., INC.; *pg.* 1843, *pg.* 1002
RAWLITE - Roofing Fastener - POWERS FASTENERS INC.; *pg.* 1059, *pg.* 1143
RAWLPLUG - Fiber Screw Anchors - POWERS FASTENERS INC.; *pg.* 1059, *pg.* 1143
RAWLY - Hollow Wall Anchor - POWERS FASTENERS INC.; *pg.* 1059, *pg.* 1143
RAY - Furniture - AMISCO INDUSTRIES LTD.; *pg.* 913, *pg.* 1958
RAY-JET - Fabric Filter Dust Collector - ABB INC.; *pg.* 1309, *pg.* 1359
RAY RAY - Footwear - VANS, INC.; *pg.* 1821, *pg.* 76
RAY-TECH - Boat - SEA RAY BOATS, INC.; *pg.* 1710, *pg.* 1638
RAY TEL - Boat - SEA RAY BOATS, INC.; *pg.* 1710, *pg.* 1638
RAY THREADED FUSION CAGE - Spinal System - STRYKER CORPORATION; *pg.* 1598, *pg.* 894
RAYA - Beverage Bottle & Coolers - THERMOS L.L.C.; *pg.* 61, *pg.* 660
RAYAH - Footwear - STEVEN MADDEN, LTD.; *pg.* 1819, *pg.* 1176
RAYAL MANOR - Flatware - ONEIDA LTD; *pg.* 1129, *pg.* 1318
RAYCRON - Coating Product - PPG INDUSTRIES, INC.; *pg.* 1445, *pg.* 1579
RAYITE - Machinable Media - USG CORPORATION; *pg.* 118, *pg.* 594
RAYLOC - Automotive Products - GENUINE PARTS COMPANY; *pg.* 206, *pg.* 506
RAYLOK - UV-Curable Resins - CYTEC INDUSTRIES, INC.; *pg.* 1155, *pg.* 1131
RAYLUX - Custom Lighting - SWIVELIER CO., INC.; *pg.* 1307, *pg.* 1142
RAYMAX - Heater - WATLOW ELECTRIC MANUFACTURING COMPANY; *pg.* 1078, *pg.* 1004
RAYMOND - Rotary Hazardous Material Incinerators - ABB INC.; *pg.* 1309, *pg.* 1359
RAYMOND - Mold Base & Component - SUPERIOR DIE SET CORP.; *pg.* 1379, *pg.* 1885
RAYMOTE - Wireless Remote Control System - CONTROL CHIEF HOLDINGS, INC.; *pg.* 630, *pg.* 1518
RAYNET - Boat - SEA RAY BOATS, INC.; *pg.* 1710, *pg.* 1638
RAYNOR - Overhead Doors & Door Operators - RAYNOR GARAGE DOORS; *pg.* 106, *pg.* 607
RAYO - Books - HARPERCOLLINS PUBLISHERS INC.; *pg.* 1647, *pg.* 1237
RAYOSCOPE - Radiographic Films - EASTMAN KODAK COMPANY; *pg.* 1408, *pg.* 1333
RAYOX - Oxidation System - CALGON CARBON CORPORATION; *pg.* 1151, *pg.* 1574
RAYPAK - Pool & Spa Heaters - RHEEM MANUFACTURING COMPANY; *pg.* 1075, *pg.* 519
RAY'S - Dairy Products - C&K MARKET, INC.; *pg.* 1016, *pg.* 1496
RAY'S FOOD PLACE - Food Markets - C&K MARKET, INC.; *pg.* 1016, *pg.* 1496
RAYTEK - Temperature Measurement Instrument - DANAHER CORPORATION; *pg.* 1044, *pg.* 397
RAYTHEON - Semiconductors & Electronic Equipment - RAYTHEON COMPANY; *pg.* 233, *pg.* 854
RAYTHEON SIX SIGMA - Training - RAYTHEON COMPANY; *pg.* 233, *pg.* 854
RAYTREX - Liquid Dispersion - EASTMAN KODAK COMPANY; *pg.* 1408, *pg.* 1333
RAZ - Eye Protection - MCR SAFETY; *pg.* 1422, *pg.* 1630
RAZADYNE - Healthcare Product - JOHNSON & JOHNSON; *pg.* 1549, *pg.* 1091
RAZE - Haircuts for Men - REGIS CORPORATION; *pg.* 521, *pg.* 941
RAZERTHIN - Led - CREE INC.; *pg.* 631, *pg.* 1371
RAZOR - Atmospheric Transfer Robot - BROOKS AUTOMATION, INC.; *pg.* 1320, *pg.* 813
RAZOR - Fluid Handling System - GRACO, INC.; *pg.* 1342, *pg.* 935
RAZOR - Floor Care - NILFISK-ADVANCE, INC.; *pg.* 332, *pg.* 953
RAZOR - Herbicide Product - NUFARM AMERICAS INC; *pg.* 1798, *pg.* 552
RAZOR - Apparel - OAKLEY, INC.; *pg.* 1840, *pg.* 86
RAZORBACK - Gaming Product - GLD PRODUCTS, INC.; *pg.* 1835, *pg.* 1882
RAZR - Cellular Telephone - MOTOROLA SOLUTIONS, INC.; *pg.* 657, *pg.* 659
RAZZ-MA-TAZZ RASPBERRY - Fruit Juice Cocktail - NEWMAN'S OWN, INC.; *pg.* 886, *pg.* 384
RAZZLEBERRI - Container Grown Plant - MONROVIA GROWERS; *pg.* 1797, *pg.* 44
RAZZLES - Candy - TOOTSIE ROLL INDUSTRIES, INC.; *pg.* 1863, *pg.* 591
RAZZMATAZZ - Fruit Drink - JAMBA, INC.; *pg.* 1024, *pg.* 84
RBK - Apparel - REEBOK INTERNATIONAL LTD.; *pg.* 1817, *pg.* 811
RBMWARE - Analysis Software for Vibration Monitors - EMERSON PROCESS MANAGEMENT; *pg.* 1334, *pg.* 1636
RC - Carbonated Soft Drink - DR PEPPER SNAPPLE GROUP, INC.; *pg.* 250, *pg.* 1729
RC DC - Software - BIO-RAD LABORATORIES, INC.; *pg.* 1504, *pg.* 101
RC1E - Calorimeter - METTLER-TOLEDO INTERNATIONAL INC.; *pg.* 1423, *pg.* 1441
RC3 POKE-THRU - Wiring Products - WIREMOLD/LEGRAND; *pg.* 689, *pg.* 383
RC4 POKE-THRU - Wiring Products - WIREMOLD/LEGRAND; *pg.* 689, *pg.* 383
RC7 POKE-THRU - Wiring Products - WIREMOLD/LEGRAND; *pg.* 689, *pg.* 383
RC91GHBTC POKE-THRU - Wiring Products - WIREMOLD/LEGRAND; *pg.* 689, *pg.* 383
RC92GHBTC POKE-THRU - Wiring Products - WIREMOLD/LEGRAND; *pg.* 689, *pg.* 383
RC9AFFTC POKE-THRU - Wiring Products - WIREMOLD/LEGRAND; *pg.* 689, *pg.* 383
RC9AM2TC POKE-THRU - Wiring Products - WIREMOLD/LEGRAND; *pg.* 689, *pg.* 383
RC9AMD POKE-THRU - Wiring Products - WIREMOLD/LEGRAND; *pg.* 689, *pg.* 383
RCA RECORDS - Pop Music Label - SONY MUSIC ENTERTAINMENT; *pg.* 309, *pg.* 1294
RCA VICTOR - Compact Disc - SONY MUSIC ENTERTAINMENT; *pg.* 309, *pg.* 1294
RCAL - Software - FLIR SYSTEMS, INC.; *pg.* 1413, *pg.* 1510
RCD - Fall Protection Product - MINE SAFETY APPLIANCES COMPANY; *pg.* 1361, *pg.* 1525
RCLWEB - Resources for College Libraries Publications - R.R. BOWKER LLC; *pg.* 1682, *pg.* 1095
RCM - Business & Technology Solutions - RCM TECHNOLOGIES, INC.; *pg.* 459, *pg.* 1108
RCN ESSENTIALS - Internet Service - RCN TELECOM SERVICES, LLC.; *pg.* 306, *pg.* 1785
RCR - Retroactive Claim Reprocessing - HEALTH MANAGEMENT SYSTEMS, INC.; *pg.* 1540, *pg.* 1238
RCR - Crystal - ONEIDA LTD; *pg.* 1129, *pg.* 1318
RCRD LBL - MP3 Downloads - SPINMEDIA; *pg.* 1282, *pg.* 104
RCS-6689 - RFID Conveyor Section - GLOBE COMPOSITE SOLUTIONS, LTD.; *pg.* 1883, *pg.* 842
RCU II - Pump - IDEX CORPORATION; *pg.* 1347, *pg.* 623
RCU WI-125 - Indicators - AVERY WEIGH-TRONIX, INC.; *pg.* 1315, *pg.* 925
RCX400 - Telescope - MEADE INSTRUMENTS CORPORATION; *pg.* 1422, *pg.* 113
RD-125 - Remote Displays - AVERY WEIGH-TRONIX, INC.; *pg.* 1315, *pg.* 925
RD-4100/6100 - Remote Displays - AVERY WEIGH-TRONIX, INC.; *pg.* 1315, *pg.* 925
RD-SERIES - Valve - HENRY PRATT COMPANY; *pg.* 1049, *pg.* 555
RDAC - Software - FLIR SYSTEMS, INC.; *pg.* 1413, *pg.* 1510
RDE-2 - Rotating Disk Electrode - BIOANALYTICAL SYSTEMS, INC.; *pg.* 1402, *pg.* 700
RDL - Test & Measurement Equipment - AEROFLEX INCORPORATED; *pg.* 614, *pg.* 1321
RDL - Lining System - GREIF INC.; *pg.* 1459, *pg.* 1447
RDRAM - Chip Interface System - RAMBUS INC.; *pg.* 459, *pg.* 288
RDS - Diagnostic Test Kit - AMERICAN BIO MEDICA CORPORATION; *pg.* 1493, *pg.* 1171
RDS INCUP - Drug Test Kit - AMERICAN BIO MEDICA CORPORATION; *pg.* 1493, *pg.* 1171
RE - Electric Motors - REULAND ELECTRIC COMPANY; *pg.* 1304, *pg.* 68
RE-1N - Residential Telephone Entry System - NORTEK SECURITY & CONTROL LLC; *pg.* 659, *pg.* 59
RE-BOOST - Wireless Systems - BOOST MOBILE; *pg.* 1869, *pg.* 107
RE-COIL - Flexible Air Hose - BADGER AIR BRUSH COMPANY; *pg.* 359, *pg.* 612
RE-ENTRY - Cleaning Product - PETROFERM INC.; *pg.* 1177, *pg.* 616
RE-IMAGINATION - Doll - TONNER DOLL COMPANY, INC.; *pg.* 968, *pg.* 1171
RE-ISSUE - Athletic Shoes - CONVERSE INC.; *pg.* 1831, *pg.* 793
RE-JUV-NAL - Cleaning Product - HILLYARD, INC.; *pg.* 331, *pg.* 990
RE-NEW-COAT - Masonry Coating - AKZONOBEL DECORATIVE PAINTS U.S.; *pg.* 1439, *pg.* 1474
RE-NU - Chemical - MILLER-STEPHENSON CHEMICAL COMPANY, INC.; *pg.* 1172, *pg.* 344
RE-SPIN & RE-PAY - Video Game - INTERNATIONAL GAME TECHNOLOGY; *pg.* 957, *pg.* 1024
RE-TECH - Capital Equipment - TEREX CORPORATION; *pg.* 1381, *pg.* 384
RE-UNION - Menswear - SEATTLE PACIFIC INDUSTRIES, INC.; *pg.* 48, *pg.* 1822
RE-USE-IT - Flooring Product - STAGESTEP INC.; *pg.* 1688, *pg.* 1570
RE-WORKS - Hair Care Product - JOHN PAUL MITCHELL SYSTEMS; *pg.* 512, *pg.* 133
REACH - Dental Care Products - JOHNSON & JOHNSON; *pg.* 1549, *pg.* 1091
REACH - Implant Product - ZIMMER BIOMET HOLDINGS, INC.; *pg.* 1611, *pg.* 699
REACH HIP SYSTEM - Hip Product - ZIMMER BIOMET HOLDINGS, INC.; *pg.* 1611, *pg.* 699
REACHING OUT - Educational Materials - SCHOLASTIC INC.; *pg.* 1683, *pg.* 1288
REACHING OUT ... THROUGH IT - Slogan - HTC GLOBAL SERVICES INC.; *pg.* 409, *pg.* 911
REACHLOCAL - Internet Advertising Services - REACHLOCAL, INC.; *pg.* 1277, *pg.* 308
REACHNXT - Ethernet Port - EXTREME NETWORKS INC; *pg.* 287, *pg.* 245
REACKTOR - Writing Instrument - SHEAFFER PEN CORPORATION; *pg.* 469, *pg.* 371
REACT - Electronic Temperature Control - THE CHICAGO FAUCET COMPANY; *pg.* 1044, *pg.* 606
REACT - Foot Apparel - CONVERSE INC.; *pg.* 1831, *pg.* 793
REACT - Naval Operations Workstation - RAYTHEON APPLIED SIGNAL TECHNOLOGY, INC.; *pg.* 667, *pg.* 288
REACT - Molecular Biology Product - THERMO FISHER SCIENTIFIC INC.; *pg.* 1602, *pg.* 61
REACTA-C - Nutritional Product - NUTRACEUTICAL INTERNATIONAL CORPORATION; *pg.* 1576, *pg.* 1753
REACTION - Furniture - HERMAN MILLER, INC.; *pg.* 926, *pg.* 913

REACTION CYCLING - Fitness Product - BALLY TOTAL FITNESS HOLDINGS CORPORATION; *pg.* 532, *pg.* 1200
REACTIR - Reaction Analysis - METTLER-TOLEDO INTERNATIONAL INC.; *pg.* 1423, *pg.* 1441
REACTIVAR - Harmonic Filtering Equipment - SCHNEIDER ELECTRIC USA, INC.; *pg.* 1306, *pg.* 650
REACTOPAQUE - Carpet Chemicals - OMNOVA SOLUTIONS INC; *pg.* 1176, *pg.* 1453
REACTOR - Software - AUTODESK INC.; *pg.* 356, *pg.* 257
REACTOR - Lighting Product - GERBER LEGENDARY BLADES; *pg.* 1834, *pg.* 1503
REACTOR - Electronic Proportioners - GRACO, INC.; *pg.* 1342, *pg.* 935
REACTOR - Apparel - OAKLEY, INC.; *pg.* 1840, *pg.* 86
REACTOR REBOUND - Basketball Equipment - LIFETIME PRODUCTS INC.; *pg.* 933, *pg.* 1751
READ - Canned Foods - SENECA FOODS CORPORATION; *pg.* 895, *pg.* 1177
READ 180 - Educational Materials - SCHOLASTIC INC.; *pg.* 1683, *pg.* 1288
READ ABOUT - Educational Materials - SCHOLASTIC INC.; *pg.* 1683, *pg.* 1288
READ AND RISE - Educational Materials - SCHOLASTIC INC.; *pg.* 1683, *pg.* 1288
READ AND SING - Educational Toys - LEAPFROG ENTERPRISES, INC.; *pg.* 961, *pg.* 84
READ-IT-ALL - Book Series for Struggling Readers - LEAPFROG ENTERPRISES, INC.; *pg.* 961, *pg.* 84
READ NOW POWER UP! - Educational Materials - RENAISSANCE LEARNING, INC.; *pg.* 607, *pg.* 1899
READ-O-MATIC - Remote Meter Reading System - BADGER METER, INC.; *pg.* 1401, *pg.* 1873
READ STREET BOOK FAIRS - Educational Materials - SCHOLASTIC INC.; *pg.* 1683, *pg.* 1288
READALL - Meter Reading System - BADGER METER, INC.; *pg.* 1401, *pg.* 1873
READCENTER - Reading Management Software - BADGER METER, INC.; *pg.* 1401, *pg.* 1873
READER - Software - ADOBE SYSTEMS INCORPORATED; *pg.* 342, *pg.* 235
READER - Newspaper - CHICAGO READER, INC.; *pg.* 1627, *pg.* 570
READER'S ADVANTAGE - Membership Program - BARNES & NOBLE, INC.; *pg.* 1619, *pg.* 1201
READER'S DIGEST - Magazine - THE READER'S DIGEST ASSOCIATION, INC.; *pg.* 1679, *pg.* 1322
READI-ACCESS - Competitive Print Ad Tracking - ADVERTISING CHECKING BUREAU INCORPORATED; *pg.* 345, *pg.* 1187
READI-BAKE - Cookie Product - J&J SNACK FOODS CORPORATION; *pg.* 865, *pg.* 1107
READI-STAIN - Biological Supplies - CAROLINA BIOLOGICAL SUPPLY COMPANY; *pg.* 1513, *pg.* 1359
READICONVENE - Network Conferencing System - POLYCOM, INC.; *pg.* 664, *pg.* 249
READIGEL - Agricultural Product - ARCHER-DANIELS-MIDLAND COMPANY; *pg.* 825, *pg.* 565
READIMANAGER - Network Conferencing System - POLYCOM, INC.; *pg.* 664, *pg.* 249
READING - Densitometers - EASTMAN KODAK COMPANY; *pg.* 1408, *pg.* 1333
READING ANTHRACITE - Anthracite Coal - READING ANTHRACITE COMPANY; *pg.* 1179, *pg.* 1583
READING ASSISTANT - Software - SCIENTIFIC LEARNING CORPORATION; *pg.* 607, *pg.* 172
READING CHANGES EVERYTHING - Slogan - SCHOLASTIC INC.; *pg.* 1683, *pg.* 1288
READING DISCOVERY - Educational Materials - SCHOLASTIC INC.; *pg.* 1683, *pg.* 1288
READING EDGE - Software - SCIENTIFIC LEARNING CORPORATION; *pg.* 607, *pg.* 172
READING FOR MEANING - Educational Materials - SCHOLASTIC INC.; *pg.* 1683, *pg.* 1288
READING INTERVENTION - Educational Materials - RENAISSANCE LEARNING, INC.; *pg.* 607, *pg.* 1899
READING IS BIG - Educational Materials - SCHOLASTIC INC.; *pg.* 1683, *pg.* 1288
READING MAGIC - Educational Materials - SCHOLASTIC INC.; *pg.* 1683, *pg.* 1288
READING POWER ESSENTIALS - Assessment Test - QUESTAR ASSESSMENT, INC.; *pg.* 1679, *pg.* 1143
READING ROVER - Software - SCIENTIFIC LEARNING CORPORATION; *pg.* 607, *pg.* 172
READING STARTS WITH US - Educational Materials - SCHOLASTIC INC.; *pg.* 1683, *pg.* 1288
READIRECORDER - Network Conferencing System - POLYCOM, INC.; *pg.* 664, *pg.* 249
READISERIES - Conferencing System - POLYCOM, INC.; *pg.* 664, *pg.* 249
READIVOICE - Audio Conferencing - POLYCOM, INC.; *pg.* 664, *pg.* 249
READY CRISP - Bacon - MAPLE LEAF FOODS INC.; *pg.* 875, *pg.* 1927
READY CRUST - Pie Crust - KELLOGG COMPANY; *pg.* 831, *pg.* 870
READY-CUT - Cheese - SCHREIBER FOODS, INC.; *pg.* 894, *pg.* 1859
READY-DOUGH - Frozen Bread - BRIDGFORD FOODS CORPORATION; *pg.* 842, *pg.* 42
READY FOR THE ROAD AHEAD - Tagline - GRACO CHILDREN'S PRODUCTS INC.; *pg.* 954, *pg.* 1531
READY GEL - Software - BIO-RAD LABORATORIES, INC.; *pg.* 1504, *pg.* 101
READY-LOAD - Molecular Biology Product - THERMO FISHER SCIENTIFIC INC.; *pg.* 1602, *pg.* 61
READY-MOUNT - Transparency Mounts - EASTMAN KODAK COMPANY; *pg.* 1408, *pg.* 1333
READY-PACK II - Radiographic Film Pack - EASTMAN KODAK COMPANY; *pg.* 1408, *pg.* 1333
THE READY PACK SYSTEM - Sterile Container Closure System - WEST PHARMACEUTICAL SERVICES, INC.; *pg.* 1472, *pg.* 1532
READY REMOTE - Mobile Electronics Equipment - DEI HOLDINGS, INC.; *pg.* 633, *pg.* 302
READY, SET, GROW - Program - FEDERAL AGRICULTURAL MORTGAGE CORPORATION; *pg.* 751, *pg.* 399
READY, SET, LEAP! - Research-based, Comprehensive & Multisensory Prekindergarten Curriculum - LEAPFROG ENTERPRISES, INC.; *pg.* 961, *pg.* 84
READY, SET, SCHOOL - Toy - VTECH ELECTRONICS NORTH AMERICA, LLC; *pg.* 969, *pg.* 554
READY SLEEVE - Paperboard Packaging Product - WESTROCK COMPANY; *pg.* 1472, *pg.* 1805
READY SPACE - Surface Maintenance Machine - TENNANT COMPANY; *pg.* 1381, *pg.* 944
READY-SPRAY - Insect Killer - THE SCOTTS MIRACLE-GRO COMPANY; *pg.* 1799, *pg.* 1459
READY-TEX - Ceiling System - CGC INC.; *pg.* 75, *pg.* 1925
READY TO GO SERVERS - Server - SOFTLAYER TECHNOLOGIES INC; *pg.* 471, *pg.* 1686
READY TO PLAY - Sport Product - FRANKLIN SPORTS, INC.; *pg.* 1834, *pg.* 847
READY-TO-ROLL - Air Cellular Cushioning Materials - SEALED AIR CORPORATION; *pg.* 1468, *pg.* 1058
READY TO WRITE - Educational Materials - SCHOLASTIC INC.; *pg.* 1683, *pg.* 1288
READY WALL - Steel Wall Panel - CLESTRA HAUSERMAN, INC.; *pg.* 76, *pg.* 1526
READY WRAP - Paperboard Packaging Product - WESTROCK COMPANY; *pg.* 1472, *pg.* 1805
READYAGAROSE - Software - BIO-RAD LABORATORIES, INC.; *pg.* 1504, *pg.* 101
READYBATH - Bathing Systems - MEDLINE INDUSTRIES, INC.; *pg.* 1562, *pg.* 635
READYCARE - Software - DYNTEK, INC.; *pg.* 389, *pg.* 165
READYCAST - Conferencing - PREMIERE GLOBAL SERVICES, INC.; *pg.* 1275, *pg.* 518
READYCONFERENCE - Telecom Product - PREMIERE GLOBAL SERVICES, INC.; *pg.* 1275, *pg.* 518
READYCONFERENCE PLUS - Marketing Tool - PREMIERE GLOBAL SERVICES, INC.; *pg.* 1275, *pg.* 518
READYDEPOSIT - Check Deposit Service - FIRSTRUST SAVINGS BANK; *pg.* 758, *pg.* 1523
READYFILL - Packaging - INTERNATIONAL PAPER COMPANY; *pg.* 1460, *pg.* 1644
READYFLEX - Microwave Cable Assembly - W.L. GORE & ASSOCIATES, INC.; *pg.* 122, *pg.* 388
READYLOAD - Photographic Film Packaging Configurations - EASTMAN KODAK COMPANY; *pg.* 1408, *pg.* 1333
READYMADE - Magazine - MEREDITH CORPORATION; *pg.* 1663, *pg.* 705
READYMATIC - Chemical - EASTMAN KODAK COMPANY; *pg.* 1408, *pg.* 1333
READYMOP - Cleaning System - THE CLOROX COMPANY; *pg.* 327, *pg.* 169
READYNAS - Wireless Networking Product - NETGEAR, INC.; *pg.* 444, *pg.* 247
READYON - Software - INTERVALZERO INC.; *pg.* 420, *pg.* 851
READYPREP - Software - BIO-RAD LABORATORIES, INC.; *pg.* 1504, *pg.* 101
READYPRESS - Cover & Pad - HOME PRODUCTS INTERNATIONAL, INC.; *pg.* 1125, *pg.* 577
READYPRO - Chemical - EASTMAN KODAK COMPANY; *pg.* 1408, *pg.* 1333
READYROCK - Liquid Gypsum - USG CORPORATION; *pg.* 118, *pg.* 594
READYSTRIP - Software - BIO-RAD LABORATORIES, INC.; *pg.* 1504, *pg.* 101
READYSUB-CELL - Software - BIO-RAD LABORATORIES, INC.; *pg.* 1504, *pg.* 101
READYWARE - Software Applications - DELL INC.; *pg.* 383, *pg.* 1737
REAG - Real Estate Advisory Group - AMERICAN APPRAISAL ASSOCIATES, INC.; *pg.* 349, *pg.* 1872
REAKTOR - Fruity, Carbonated Sweet Energy Drink - THE MONARCH BEVERAGE COMPANY, INC.; *pg.* 257, *pg.* 514
REAL - Bath & Plumbing Product - JACUZZI BRANDS CORPORATION; *pg.* 554, *pg.* 65
REAL - Pudding - KOZY SHACK INC.; *pg.* 869, *pg.* 1167
THE REAL BEAUTY IS IN THE TASTE - Tagline - THE CATFISH INSTITUTE; *pg.* 136, *pg.* 969
REAL BUBBLE - Digital Media System - REALNETWORKS, INC.; *pg.* 460, *pg.* 1839
REAL CALIFORNIA - Cheese - CALIFORNIA MILK ADVISORY BOARD; *pg.* 843, *pg.* 149
REAL CALIFORNIA CHEESE - Cheese - CALIFORNIA MILK ADVISORY BOARD; *pg.* 843, *pg.* 149
REAL CHARMER - Jewelry - AEROGROUP INTERNATIONAL, INC.; *pg.* 1803, *pg.* 1055
REAL CPR HELP - Management Services - ZOLL MEDICAL CORPORATION; *pg.* 1612, *pg.* 814
REAL CREAM - Non-Dairy Aerosol Whipped Topping - BROUGHTON FOODS COMPANY; *pg.* 842, *pg.* 1458
THE REAL CURL - Promotional Material for Hair Care Products - THE GILLETTE COMPANY; *pg.* 509, *pg.* 795
THE REAL DEAL - Beverage - MONSTER BEVERAGE CORPORATION; *pg.* 257, *pg.* 69
THE REAL DEAL - Machinery/Accessories - REEL-O-MATIC, INC.; *pg.* 1371, *pg.* 1487
THE REAL ESTATE BOOK - Magazine - NETWORK COMMUNICATIONS INC.; *pg.* 1271, *pg.* 534
REAL ESTATE FORUM - Real Estate Publication - AMERICAN LAWYER MEDIA, INC.; *pg.* 1615, *pg.* 1193
THE REAL ESTATE LEADERS - Slogan - RE/MAX INTERNATIONAL, INC.; *pg.* 1109, *pg.* 322
THE REAL ESTATE SUPERSTARS - Slogan - RE/MAX INTERNATIONAL, INC.; *pg.* 1109, *pg.* 322
REAL FOOD MADE EASY! - Slogan - MCCORMICK & COMPANY, INCORPORATED; *pg.* 1027, *pg.* 779
REAL FRESH - Canned Puddings & Cheese Sauces - ADVANCED FOOD PRODUCTS LLC; *pg.* 835, *pg.* 1555
REAL FRUIT FROM REAL PEOPLE - Slogan - TREE TOP, INC.; *pg.* 901, *pg.* 1843
REAL FRUIT GOODNESS - Tagline - SUN-RYPE PRODUCTS LTD.; *pg.* 899, *pg.* 1908
REAL GOLD - Soft Drink - THE COCA-COLA COMPANY; *pg.* 240, *pg.* 493
REAL GUIDE - Digital Media System - REALNETWORKS, INC.; *pg.* 460, *pg.* 1839
REAL/IX - Real-Time UNIX O/S - CSPI TECHNOLOGY SOLUTIONS; *pg.* 381, *pg.* 421
REAL LIFE - Educational Materials - SCHOLASTIC INC.; *pg.* 1683, *pg.* 1288
REAL MILK PAINT - Casein Paint - THE REAL MILK PAINT CO.; *pg.* 1446, *pg.* 1583
REAL MONITOR - Software Upgrade - 3D SYSTEMS CORPORATION; *pg.* 339, *pg.* 1621
THE REAL MOTHER GOOSE - Educational Materials - SCHOLASTIC INC.; *pg.* 1683, *pg.* 1288
REAL PAGES - Telephone Services - AT&T SOUTHEAST; *pg.* 1868, *pg.* 489
REAL PARTS - Thermoplastic - STRATASYS, INC.; *pg.* 476, *pg.* 923
REAL PEOPLE. REAL ADVICE. - Tagline - EHARMONY.COM, INC.; *pg.* 1242, *pg.* 180
REAL PEOPLE REAL SOLUTIONS - Slogan - SYKES ENTERPRISES, INCORPORATED; *pg.* 478, *pg.* 475
REAL PEPOPLE. REAL SOLUTIONS - Slogan - OPUS BANK; *pg.* 790, *pg.* 1819
REAL PLAY - Baseball - SCHOOL-TECH, INC.; *pg.* 1844, *pg.* 866
REAL PROFIT$ - Helpline - PROFESSIONAL EDUCATION

First page reference indicates Business Class Edition
Second page reference indicates Geographic Edition

INSTITUTE; *pg.* 457, *pg.* 561
REAL SANGRIA - Wine - SHAW ROSS INTERNATIONAL IMPORTERS; *pg.* 1970, *pg.* 449
REAL SIMPLE - Media Publication - TIME INC.; *pg.* 1693, *pg.* 1300
REAL SNP - Online Services - SEQUENOM, INC.; *pg.* 1593, *pg.* 209
REAL SOLUTIONS FOR REAL LIFE - Kitchen, Closet & Bath Storage Products - KNAPE & VOGT MANUFACTURING COMPANY; *pg.* 1052, *pg.* 913
REAL TALKING ADS - Wireless Communication System - AT&T SOUTHEAST; *pg.* 1868, *pg.* 489
REAL TIME - Banking Software - JACK HENRY & ASSOCIATES, INC.; *pg.* 422, *pg.* 988
REAL-TIME ANALYZER - Software - WEBSENSE, INC.; *pg.* 491, *pg.* 210
REAL-TIME DIGITAL SCANLINE - Online Service - ACI WORLDWIDE; *pg.* 710, *pg.* 1777
REAL TIME QA - Software - BIO-RAD LABORATORIES, INC.; *pg.* 1504, *pg.* 101
REAL TIME QC - Software - BIO-RAD LABORATORIES, INC.; *pg.* 1504, *pg.* 101
REAL-TIME ROTO - Software - AUTODESK INC.; *pg.* 356, *pg.* 257
REAL-TIME SECURITY UPDATES - Software - WEBSENSE, INC.; *pg.* 491, *pg.* 210
REAL TIME SERVICE MANAGEMENT - Software - SUPPORT.COM, INC.; *pg.* 1283, *pg.* 192
THE REAL WHITE PAGES - Telephone Directories - AT&T SOUTHEAST; *pg.* 1868, *pg.* 489
REAL WORLD SIGNAL PROCESSING - Semiconductors, Software & Integrated Circuits - TEXAS INSTRUMENTS INCORPORATED; *pg.* 679, *pg.* 1688
REAL WORLD TRAFFIC - Network Testing Solution - IXIA, *pg.* 422, *pg.* 56
REALARCADE - Digital Media System - REALNETWORKS, INC.; *pg.* 460, *pg.* 1839
REALAUDIO - Media Audio Files - REALNETWORKS, INC.; *pg.* 460, *pg.* 1839
REALEAN - Food Product - PATRICK CUDAHY INC.; *pg.* 888, *pg.* 1856
REALEASE - Enamel Coatings - FERRO CORPORATION; *pg.* 1162, *pg.* 1462
REALEAT - Food Product - THE HAIN CELESTIAL GROUP, INC.; *pg* 860, *pg.* 1172
REALEMON - Non-Carbonated Soft Drink - DR PEPPER SNAPPLE GROUP, INC.; *pg.* 250, *pg.* 1729
REALIMAGE - Bait - CABELA'S INCORPORATED; *pg.* 535, *pg.* 1019
REALITE - Lighting Product - WESTINGHOUSE LIGHTING CORPORATION; *pg.* 687, *pg.* 1571
REALITIES - Apparel - KATE SPADE & COMPANY; *pg.* 27, *pg.* 1248
REALITY - Fabric - NEMSCHOFF, INC.; *pg.* 936, *pg.* 1890
REALITY - Supplement & Food Product - NEW EARTH LIFE SCIENCES, INC.; *pg.* 1573, *pg.* 1499
REALITY CHECK - Banking Service - THE BANK OF NOVA SCOTIA; *pg.* 721, *pg.* 1935
REALITY RESEARCH - Software - UNITED BUSINESS MEDIA LLC; *pg.* 1697, *pg.* 1177
REALITYEXPANSION - Image Processing Product - SEMTECH CORPORATION GENNUM PRODUCTS; *pg.* 671, *pg.* 1919
REALIZE - Apparel - OAKLEY, INC.; *pg.* 1840, *pg.* 86
REALJUKEBOX - Digital Media System - REALNETWORKS, INC.; *pg.* 460, *pg.* 1839
REALLY RIPPED ABS - Fragrance - PARFUMS DE COEUR LTD.; *pg.* 519, *pg.* 376
REALMAGIC - PC Add-In Card - SIGMA DESIGNS, INC.; *pg.* 469, *pg.* 148
REALMEDIA - Media Player - REALNETWORKS, INC.; *pg.* 460, *pg.* 1839
REALMONEY.COM - Online News - THE STREET, INC.; *pg.* 1283, *pg.* 1296
REALMS - Book - CHARISMA MEDIA; *pg.* 1627, *pg.* 436
REALNETWORKS - Digital Media Service - REALNETWORKS, INC.; *pg.* 460, *pg.* 1839
REALONE - Software - NTI CORPORATION; *pg.* 446, *pg.* 114
REALONE - Digital Media Service - REALNETWORKS, INC.; *pg.* 460, *pg.* 1839
REALONE PLAYER - Digital Media System - REALNETWORKS, INC.; *pg.* 460, *pg.* 1839
REALONE SUPERPASS - Digital Media System - REALNETWORKS, INC.; *pg.* 460, *pg.* 1839
REALOPTIMIZER - Software - ACD SYSTEMS INTERNATIONAL INC.; *pg.* 340, *pg.* 1913
REALPAGES.COM - Wireless Communication System - AT&T SOUTHEAST; *pg.* 1868, *pg.* 489
REALPIX - Data Type - REALNETWORKS, INC.; *pg.* 460, *pg.* 1839
REALPLAYER - Digital Media System - REALNETWORKS, INC.; *pg.* 460, *pg.* 1839
REALPLAYER PLUS - Media Player - REALNETWORKS, INC.; *pg.* 460, *pg.* 1839
REALPORT - Computer Peripheral Equipment - DIGI INTERNATIONAL INC.; *pg.* 387, *pg.* 948
REALPRESENCE - Telepresence Conference - POLYCOM, INC.; *pg.* 664, *pg.* 249
REALPRESENTER - Media Presentation Software - REALNETWORKS, INC.; *pg.* 460, *pg.* 1839
REALPRODUCER - Digital Media System - REALNETWORKS, INC.; *pg.* 460, *pg.* 1839
REALRHAPSODY - Digital Media System - REALNETWORKS, INC.; *pg.* 460, *pg.* 1839
REALSEAL - Pipeline Pigging Product - T.D. WILLIAMSON, INC.; *pg.* 1380, *pg.* 1490
REALSLIDESHOW - Media Creator - REALNETWORKS, INC.; *pg.* 460, *pg.* 1839
REALSNP.COM - Website - SEQUENOM, INC.; *pg.* 1593, *pg.* 209
REALSPEAK - Text to Voice Converter - NUANCE COMMUNICATIONS, INC.; *pg.* 447, *pg.* 806
REALSSD - Hardware - MICRON TECHNOLOGY, INC.; *pg.* 435, *pg.* 547
REALTIME - Polymerase Chain Reaction Assay - ABBOTT LABORATORIES; *pg.* 1484, *pg.* 551
REALTIME - Active Balancing Technology - LORD CORPORATION; *pg.* 1357, *pg.* 1360
REALTIME - Electronic Components - MOLEX INCORPORATED; *pg.* 655, *pg.* 628
REALTOR - Personalized Account - M/I HOMES, INC.; *pg.* 95, *pg.* 1441
REALTOR - Magazine - NATIONAL ASSOCIATION OF REALTORS; *pg.* 1666, *pg.* 584
REALTOR BENEFITS - Service program - NATIONAL ASSOCIATION OF REALTORS; *pg.* 1666, *pg.* 584
REALTOR.COM - Website - MOVE, INC.; *pg.* 1268, *pg.* 247
REALTOR.COM - Online Resource - NATIONAL ASSOCIATION OF REALTORS; *pg.* 1666, *pg.* 584
REALTREE - Fabric - UNIROYAL ENGINEERED PRODUCTS; *pg.* 699, *pg.* 467
REALTYGENERATOR.COM - Website - MARKET LEADER, INC.; *pg.* 1102, *pg.* 1822
REALVIDEO - Video Media Files - REALNETWORKS, INC.; *pg.* 460, *pg.* 1839
REALVIZ - Software - AUTODESK INC.; *pg.* 356, *pg.* 257
REAM-A-MATIC - Tube Cleaner - GOODWAY TECHNOLOGIES CORPORATION; *pg.* 1341, *pg.* 374
REAM-EZE - Solid Carbide Reamer - REGAL BELOIT CORPORATION; *pg.* 106, *pg.* 1854
REAMASTER - Underreamer Tool - SMITH INTERNATIONAL, INC.; *pg.* 1377, *pg.* 1715
REAMES - Frozen Specialty Noodles, Pastas, & Breaded Specialty Items - LANCASTER COLONY CORPORATION; *pg.* 873, *pg.* 1441
REAMES - Egg Noodles & Soup Kits - T. MARZETTI COMPANY; *pg.* 900, *pg.* 1444
REAP - Fraternal Benefits - CATHOLIC ORDER OF FORESTERS; *pg.* 1196, *pg.* 635
REAR BLADES - Farm Tools - AG-MEIER INDUSTRIES LLC; *pg.* 700, *pg.* 1668
REARSENTRY - Vehicle - ROSTRA PRECISION CONTROLS, INC.; *pg.* 216, *pg.* 1381
REARSIGHT - Automotive Product - ROSTRA PRECISION CONTROLS, INC.; *pg.* 216, *pg.* 1381
REASHURE - Animal Nutritional Product - BALCHEM CORPORATION; *pg.* 839, *pg.* 1183
REAX - Chemical Product - WESTROCK COMPANY; *pg.* 1472, *pg.* 1805
REBA - Bicycle Component - SRAM CORPORATION; *pg.* 967, *pg.* 590
REBECA - Footwear - PHOENIX FOOTWEAR GROUP, INC.; *pg.* 1815, *pg.* 60
REBECCA - Clothing - ABERCROMBIE & FITCH CO.; *pg.* 37, *pg.* 1466
REBEE - Software - XEROX CORPORATION; *pg.* 494, *pg.* 365
REBEL 777 - Game - WMS INDUSTRIES INC.; *pg.* 593, *pg.* 666
REBETOL - Medicine - MERCK & CO., INC.; *pg.* 1566, *pg.* 1077
REBETRON - Hepatitis Treatment - MERCK & CO., INC.; *pg.* 1566, *pg.* 1077
REBOUND - Lamb Product - KENT NUTRITION GROUP; *pg.* 1477, *pg.* 710
REBOUND - Toy - MATTEL, INC.; *pg.* 962, *pg.* 81
REBOUND - Fabric - NEMSCHOFF, INC.; *pg.* 936, *pg.* 1890
REBOUND - Apparel - OAKLEY, INC.; *pg.* 1840, *pg.* 86
REBOUND - Silicone Rubber - SMOOTH-ON INC.; *pg.* 111, *pg.* 1528
REC OIL - Products for Separating Soluble Oils From Wastewaters - GE WATER & PROCESS TECHNOLOGIES; *pg.* 1339, *pg.* 1588
REC-TECH - Tennis Court Color Surfacing - MAINTENANCE, INC.; *pg.* 95, *pg.* 1482
RECALL CHECK - Information Retrieval Services - CARFAX INC.; *pg.* 202, *pg.* 1777
RECAP - Implant Product - ZIMMER BIOMET HOLDINGS, INC.; *pg.* 1611, *pg.* 699
RECAPIT - Cap & Crown Cement - MAJESTIC DRUG COMPANY, INC.; *pg.* 516, *pg.* 1343
RECARO - Seats - RECARO NORTH AMERICA, INC.; *pg.* 216, *pg.* 869
RECATH - Bypass Graft - COOK GROUP, INC.; *pg.* 1518, *pg.* 674
RECEPTAL - Fertility Management - MERCK & CO., INC.; *pg.* 1566, *pg.* 1077
RECESS - Fabric - NEMSCHOFF, INC.; *pg.* 936, *pg.* 1890
RECESS IS CALLING - Slogan - DAVE & BUSTER'S ENTERTAINMENT, INC.; *pg.* 1724, *pg.* 1679
RECESSED WALL - Lighting System - LITECONTROL CORPORATION; *pg.* 1301, *pg* 841
RECHARGE - Electrolyte Added Beverage - THE J.M. SMUCKER COMPANY; *pg.* 865, *pg.* 1468
RECHARGE COMPRESSION - Apparels - UNDER ARMOUR, INC.; *pg.* 49, *pg.* 759
RECHARGEABLE - Battery - ENERGIZER HOLDINGS, INC.; *pg.* 637, *pg.* 996
RECIFE - Rug - COURISTAN INC.; *pg.* 921, *pg.* 1067
RECIPROGRATE - Municipal & Industrial Stoker - DETROIT STOKER CO.; *pg.* 1070, *pg.* 900
RECITAL - Footwear - CAPEZIO BALLET MAKERS INC.; *pg.* 1805, *pg.* 1125
RECLAIM - Men's Jeans - THE BUCKLE, INC.; *pg.* 1764, *pg.* 1011
RECLINE SELECTOR - Furniture - HERMAN MILLER, INC.; *pg.* 926, *pg.* 913
RECOIL - Auto-plier - GERBER LEGENDARY BLADES; *pg.* 1834, *pg.* 1503
RECOIL - Flashlight - PELICAN PRODUCTS, INC.; *pg.* 1842, *pg.* 295
RECOMBINATE - Biopharmaceutical Product - BAXTER INTERNATIONAL INC.; *pg.* 1499, *pg.* 599
RECON - Software - SS&C TECHNOLOGIES HOLDINGS, INC.; *pg.* 473, *pg.* 386
RECON - Navigation Aid - TRIMBLE NAVIGATION LIMITED; *pg.* 1384, *pg.* 288
RECONIX - Medical Device - C.R. BARD, INC.; *pg.* 1519, *pg.* 1094
RECONSTRUCTOR - Personal Care Product - STRAIGHT ARROW PRODUCTS, INC.; *pg.* 523, *pg.* 1517
RECORD - Newspaper - NORTH JERSEY MEDIA GROUP INC.; *pg.* 1672, *pg.* 1072
RECORD CHECK - Information Retrieval Services - CARFAX INC.; *pg.* 202, *pg.* 1777
RECORD JACKPOTS - Game - WMS INDUSTRIES INC.; *pg.* 593, *pg.* 666
RECORD JOURNAL - Daily Newspaper - THE RECORD-JOURNAL PUBLISHING COMPANY; *pg.* 1680, *pg.* 354
THE RECORD PROGRAMS - Yearbooks - HERFF JONES, INC.; *pg.* 7, *pg.* 686
RECORD SEARCHLIGHT - Newspaper - THE E.W. SCRIPPS COMPANY; *pg.* 1639, *pg.* 1412
RECORDABLE - Audio System - VIQ SOLUTIONS INC.; *pg.* 490, *pg.* 1905
RECORDALL - Meter - BADGER METER, INC.; *pg.* 1401, *pg.* 1873
RECORDED BOOKS - Publisher - HAIGHTS CROSS COMMUNICATIONS, INC.; *pg.* 1646, *pg.* 1237
RECORDIAB - Software - VIQ SOLUTIONS INC.; *pg.* 490, *pg.* 1905
RECORDS COLLECTOR - Software - IRON MOUNTAIN INCORPORATED; *pg.* 421, *pg.* 796
RECORDVIEW - Software Product - MAXIMUS, INC.; *pg.*

780, *pg.* 1799
RECORE - Wallcovering - OMNOVA SOLUTIONS INC; *pg.* 1176, *pg.* 1453
RECOUP - Fabric - NEMSCHOFF, INC.; *pg.* 936, *pg.* 1890
RECOURSE TECHNOLOGIES - Software - SYMANTEC CORPORATION; *pg.* 478, *pg.* 161
RECOVER - Interior & Exterior Recycled Paint - DUNN-EDWARDS CORPORATION; *pg.* 1442, *pg.* 129
RECOVER PLUS - Software - BMC SOFTWARE, INC.; *pg.* 362, *pg.* 1701
RECOVERY DIRECTOR - Software - COMMVAULT SYSTEMS, INC.; *pg.* 377, *pg.* 1125
RECOVERY MANAGEMENT - Software - BMC SOFTWARE, INC.; *pg.* 362, *pg.* 1701
RECOVERY MANAGEMENT - Software - CA TECHNOLOGIES; *pg.* 366, *pg.* 1168
RECOVERY MANAGEMENT SYSTEM - Existing Collection Augmenting Solutions - FAIR ISAAC CORPORATION; *pg.* 1247, *pg.* 955
RECOVERY MANAGER - Software - BMC SOFTWARE, INC.; *pg.* 362, *pg.* 1701
RECOVERY MANAGER - Software - DELL SOFTWARE; *pg.* 385, *pg.* 40
RECOVERY MANAGER FOR EXCHANGE - Software - DELL SOFTWARE; *pg.* 385, *pg.* 40
RECOVERY MANAGER FOR SHAREPOINT - Software - DELL SOFTWARE; *pg.* 385, *pg.* 40
RECOVERY PLUS - Disaster Response Service - DIEBOLD, INCORPORATED; *pg.* 387, *pg.* 1407
RECOVERY PROTRUSIO CAGE - Hip Product - ZIMMER BIOMET HOLDINGS, INC.; *pg.* 1611, *pg.* 699
RECOVERY UTILITY - Software - BMC SOFTWARE, INC.; *pg.* 362, *pg.* 1701
RECRAFTING - Restoration Process for Shoes - ALLEN-EDMONDS SHOE CORP.; *pg.* 1804, *pg.* 1887
RECTAL THERMAL SENSING UNIT - Medical Device - UROLOGIX, INC.; *pg.* 1604, *pg.* 945
RECYCLEX - Erosion Control Product - AMERICAN EXCELSIOR COMPANY; *pg.* 1451, *pg.* 1659
RED - Restaurant - ARK RESTAURANTS CORP.; *pg.* 1715, *pg.* 1196
R.E.D - Protective Gear - BURTON SNOWBOARD COMPANY; *pg.* 1829, *pg.* 1765
RED ALERT - Fire Emergency Service - KIDDE FIRE FIGHTING; *pg.* 1170, *pg.* 1531
RED ALERT - Cable - SOUTHWIRE COMPANY; *pg.* 1063, *pg.* 527
RED ARROW - Software - UNITED PARCEL SERVICE, INC.; *pg.* 1928, *pg.* 522
RED ARROW MESSENGER - Software - UNITED PARCEL SERVICE, INC.; *pg.* 1928, *pg.* 522
RED BAG - Coffee Product - COMMUNITY COFFEE COMPANY LLC; *pg.* 849, *pg.* 741
RED BALL - Footwear - LACROSSE FOOTWEAR, INC.; *pg.* 1811, *pg.* 1503
RED BALL JETS - Footwear - LACROSSE FOOTWEAR, INC.; *pg.* 1811, *pg.* 1503
RED BARON - Frozen Pizza Products - THE SCHWAN FOOD COMPANY; *pg.* 894, *pg.* 928
RED BICYCLETTE - Wine - E&J GALLO WINERY; *pg.* 1962, *pg.* 149
RED BOOK PLUS - Sire Selection Software - HOLSTEIN ASSOCIATION USA, INC.; *pg.* 143, *pg.* 1764
RED BRAND - Fabricated Wire - KEYSTONE CONSOLIDATED INDUSTRIES, INC.; *pg.* 90, *pg.* 1683
RED BRAND - Agricultural Fencing Products - KEYSTONE STEEL & WIRE CO.; *pg.* 91, *pg.* 651
RED BURRITO - Quick Service Restaurant - CKE RESTAURANTS INC.; *pg.* 1723, *pg.* 63
RED CARPET - Computer Software - NOVELL INC.; *pg.* 446, *pg.* 852
RED CARPET CLUB - Conference Room - UNITED CONTINENTAL HOLDINGS, INC.; *pg.* 1927, *pg.* 593
RED CLAW LAGER - Seafood Product - RED LOBSTER; *pg.* 1747, *pg.* 455
RED COOPER - Air Distribution Products - STANDEX INTERNATIONAL CORPORATION; *pg.* 60, *pg.* 1039
RED-COTE - Oral Hygiene Aids - SUNSTAR AMERICAS INC.; *pg.* 1599, *pg.* 591
RED CROSS - Salt - CARGILL, INC.; *pg.* 845, *pg.* 965
RED CROSS - Table Salt - CARGILL SALT; *pg.* 846, *pg.* 926
RED CROSS - Toothache Drops & Canker Sore Medication - THE MENTHOLATUM COMPANY; *pg.* 1565, *pg.* 1320
RED CROSS SHOES - Leather Loafers - HABAND COMPANY, INC.; *pg.* 1772, *pg.* 1099
RED DEVIL - Hot Sauce - B&G FOODS, INC.; *pg.* 838, *pg.* 1102
RED DEVIL - Acrylic Latex Enamel - THE SHERWIN-WILLIAMS COMPANY; *pg.* 1447, *pg.* 1435
RED DEVIL - Floor Care Products - TTI FLOOR CARE NORTH AMERICA; *pg.* 61, *pg.* 1473
RED DIAMOND BLUE - Pulltab Game - IDAHO LOTTERY; *pg.* 995, *pg.* 547
RED DOG - Beer - MILLERCOORS; *pg.* 254, *pg.* 1877
RED DOOR REVEALED - Fragrance - ELIZABETH ARDEN, INC.; *pg.* 507, *pg.* 448
RED DOOR VELVET - Fragrance - ELIZABETH ARDEN, INC.; *pg.* 507, *pg.* 448
RED DOT - Box & Cover - THOMAS & BETTS CORPORATION; *pg.* 680, *pg.* 1646
RED DOT TANDEM ALIGNER - Truck & Trailer Tandem Aligner - BEE LINE COMPANY; *pg.* 200, *pg.* 701
RED DRAGON - Container Grown Plant - MONROVIA GROWERS; *pg.* 1797, *pg.* 44
RED DRIFT - Garden Roses - THE CONARD-PYLE COMPANY; *pg.* 1794, *pg.* 1594
RED ELF - Container Grown Plant - MONROVIA GROWERS; *pg.* 1797, *pg.* 44
RED ERASE - Red Stain Eliminator - EVERGREEN LABS, INC.; *pg.* 330, *pg.* 1847
RED FLASH - Beverages - THE COCA-COLA COMPANY; *pg.* 240, *pg.* 493
RED-FOUR - Chemical Product - SPECTRUM CHEMICALS & LABORATORY PRODUCTS, INC.; *pg.* 1181, *pg.* 94
RED FOX - Cocoa Butter - MAJESTIC DRUG COMPANY, INC.; *pg.* 516, *pg.* 1343
RED-GO 85 CXF - Reinforced Urethane Belts - FENNER DRIVES; *pg.* 1336, *pg.* 1551
RED GOAT - Waste Disposers - STANDEX INTERNATIONAL CORPORATION; *pg.* 60, *pg.* 1039
RED GOES GREEN - Environmental Program - THE PHILLIES, L.P.; *pg.* 575, *pg.* 1569
RED GOLD - Logo - RED GOLD, INC.; *pg.* 891, *pg.* 677
RED GOOSE - Shoes - CALERES, INC.; *pg.* 1805, *pg.* 993
RED HAT - Solenoid Valves - ASCO VALVE CANADA; *pg.* 619, *pg.* 1919
RED HAT II - Solenoid Valves - ASCO VALVE CANADA; *pg.* 619, *pg.* 1919
RED HEART - Yarn Hand Knitting - MAKE IT COATS; *pg.* 696, *pg.* 1367
RED HOT - Thermal - E.D. BULLARD COMPANY; *pg.* 1332, *pg.* 727
RED HOT - Video Game - INTERNATIONAL GAME TECHNOLOGY; *pg.* 957, *pg.* 1024
RED HOT CASH - Scratch-off - MISSOURI LOTTERY; *pg.* 999, *pg.* 979
RED HOT CHERRIES - Lottery Card - MISSOURI LOTTERY; *pg.* 999, *pg.* 979
RED HOT CHERRY - Video Game - INTERNATIONAL GAME TECHNOLOGY; *pg.* 957, *pg.* 1024
RED HOT DOUBLE WILD - Video Game - INTERNATIONAL GAME TECHNOLOGY; *pg.* 957, *pg.* 1024
RED HOT FUSION - Video Game - INTERNATIONAL GAME TECHNOLOGY; *pg.* 957, *pg.* 1024
RED HOT ICE - Video Game - INTERNATIONAL GAME TECHNOLOGY; *pg.* 957, *pg.* 1024
RED HOUSE - Educational Materials - SCHOLASTIC INC.; *pg.* 1683, *pg.* 1288
RED-I - Wood Joist - REDBUILT LLC; *pg.* 106, *pg.* 548
RED JACKET - Petroleum Pump - DANAHER CORPORATION; *pg.* 1044, *pg.* 397
RED JACKET - Water Product - ITT CORPORATION; *pg.* 1351, *pg.* 1354
RED KAP - Apparel - V.F. CORPORATION; *pg.* 34, *pg.* 1376
RED LABEL - Over-and-Under Shotgun - STURM, RUGER & COMPANY, INC.; *pg.* 1846, *pg.* 371
RED LINE - Hand Portable & Wheeled Fire Extinguishers - ANSUL, INCORPORATED; *pg.* 1147, *pg.* 1869
RED LOBSTER TO GO - Take-Out Food - RED LOBSTER; *pg.* 1747, *pg.* 455
RED MANSIONS - Video Game - INTERNATIONAL GAME TECHNOLOGY; *pg.* 957, *pg.* 1024
RED MAX - Degreaser - TEXAS REFINERY CORP.; *pg.* 986, *pg.* 1696
RED 'N PRETTY - Container Grown Plant - MONROVIA GROWERS; *pg.* 1797, *pg.* 44
RED OMEGA - Dietary Supplement - NOW HEALTH GROUP, INC.; *pg.* 1576, *pg.* 557
RED-OUT - Salt - CARGILL LIMITED; *pg.* 1475, *pg.* 1914
RED PACK - Tomato & Vegetable Juice - RED GOLD, INC.; *pg.* 891, *pg.* 677
RED PREMIUM - Cuprous Oxide - AMERICAN CHEMET CORPORATION; *pg.* 1147, *pg.* 599
RED RAGE - Alkaline Product - DELTA FOREMOST CHEMICAL CORPORATION; *pg.* 1155, *pg.* 1642
RED RASPBERRY - Herb Tea - R.C. BIGELOW, INC.; *pg.* 891, *pg.* 348
RED RED RHINE - Nail Care Product - OPI PRODUCTS INC.; *pg.* 518, *pg.* 167
RED REVERSIBLE - Pillow and Throw - HERITAGE LACE INC.; *pg.* 694, *pg.* 711
RED RHAPSODY - Container Grown Plant - MONROVIA GROWERS; *pg.* 1797, *pg.* 44
RED RIDER - Turf Maintenance Machinery - SMITHCO, INC.; *pg.* 1377, *pg.* 1592
RED-RITER - Metal Marker - LA-CO INDUSTRIES MARKAL CO., INC.; *pg.* 1170, *pg.* 610
RED RIVER - Cereals - THE J.M. SMUCKER COMPANY; *pg.* 865, *pg.* 1468
RED RIVER - Pet Product - PETSMART, INC.; *pg.* 1481, *pg.* 18
RED RIVER - Hose - TEKNOR APEX COMPANY; *pg.* 1889, *pg.* 1605
RED ROCK - Snacks - PEPSICO, INC.; *pg.* 259, *pg.* 1327
RED ROCK WINERY - Wine - E&J GALLO WINERY; *pg.* 1962, *pg.* 149
RED ROCKER - Beverage - MONSTER BEVERAGE CORPORATION; *pg.* 257, *pg.* 69
RED ROCKERS - Aluminum Roller Rocker Arms - EDELBROCK CORPORATION; *pg.* 204, *pg.* 293
RED ROOSTER - Video Game - INTERNATIONAL GAME TECHNOLOGY; *pg.* 957, *pg.* 1024
RED ROSE - Tea - REDCO FOODS, INC.; *pg.* 891, *pg.* 1174
RED ROSE - Beverages - UNILEVER CANADA INC.; *pg.* 903, *pg.* 1946
RED SAND - Apparel - PERRY ELLIS INTERNATIONAL, INC.; *pg.* 45, *pg.* 445
RED SEAL - Trolleys - DAIFUKU WEBB; *pg.* 1327, *pg.* 885
RED SEAL - Interior & Exterior Paints & Removers - PRATT & LAMBERT PAINTS; *pg.* 1446, *pg.* 1434
RED SEAL - Tobacco Product - U.S. SMOKELESS TOBACCO COMPANY; *pg.* 1895, *pg.* 1804
RED SEAL GUARD - Anti-Contaminant Seals - DAIFUKU WEBB; *pg.* 1327, *pg.* 885
RED SEAL SPECTRABLEND CLEAR - Chemical - SENSIENT COLORS INC.; *pg.* 1180, *pg.* 1003
RED SEAL SPECTRACOAT - Dispersions - SENSIENT COLORS INC.; *pg.* 1180, *pg.* 1003
RED SEAL SPECTRASPRAY - Chemical - SENSIENT COLORS INC.; *pg.* 1180, *pg.* 1003
RED SHED - Gifts & Collectibles - TRACTOR SUPPLY COMPANY; *pg.* 708, *pg.* 1627
RED SIREN 7S - Video Game - INTERNATIONAL GAME TECHNOLOGY; *pg.* 957, *pg.* 1024
RED SOX - Album - BOSTON SYMPHONY ORCHESTRA INC.; *pg.* 534, *pg.* 791
RED SQUARE - Video Game - INTERNATIONAL GAME TECHNOLOGY; *pg.* 957, *pg.* 1024
RED STREAK - Saw Blade - SIMONDS INTERNATIONAL CORPORATION; *pg.* 1376, *pg.* 819
RED TAB - Jean - LEVI STRAUSS & CO.; *pg.* 43, *pg.* 220
RED TAG - Media Packaging - WESTROCK COMPANY; *pg.* 1472, *pg.* 1805
RED TAIL ALE - Ale - MENDOCINO BREWING COMPANY; *pg.* 254, *pg.* 298
RED TAIL LAGER - Lager - MENDOCINO BREWING COMPANY; *pg.* 254, *pg.* 298
RED TOP - Fence Posts - KEYSTONE STEEL & WIRE CO.; *pg.* 91, *pg.* 651
RED TOP - Calcined Gypsum Wall Plasters, Hydrated Lime Soil Conditioners & Quicklime - USG CORPORATION; *pg.* 118, *pg.* 594
RED VALUFLEX - General Service Hose - HBD INDUSTRIES, INC.; *pg.* 207, *pg.* 1449
RED VINES - Candy Product - AMERICAN LICORICE CO. INC.; *pg.* 1850, *pg.* 692
RED WHITE & BLUE - Slots - INTERNATIONAL GAME TECHNOLOGY; *pg.* 957, *pg.* 1024
RED WHITE & BLUE DELUXE - Slots - INTERNATIONAL GAME TECHNOLOGY; *pg.* 957, *pg.* 1024
RED WING INTERNATIONAL - Footwear - RED WING SHOE COMPANY, INC.; *pg.* 1817, *pg.* 954
RED WOLF - Alcoholic Beverage - ANHEUSER-BUSCH COMPANIES, LLC; *pg.* 237, *pg.* 991
RED X - Golf Equipment - ACUSHNET COMPANY; *pg.* 1824,

pg. 818
REDA - Electric Submersible Pumping Systems - SCHLUMBERGER WELL COMPLETIONS; *pg.* 1373, *pg.* 1714
REDBOOK - Magazine - THE HEARST CORPORATION; *pg.* 1649, *pg.* 1239
REDBRICK CELLARS - Beverage - PHOENIX VINTNERS, LLC; *pg.* 1968, *pg.* 182
REDCO - Food Slicer - LINCOLN FOODSERVICE PRODUCTS, LLC; *pg.* 1127, *pg.* 1432
REDDI-SPONGE - Bakery Ingredient - FOREMOST FARMS USA COOPERATIVE; *pg.* 856, *pg.* 1854
REDDI-WIP - Food Product - CONAGRA FOODS, INC.; *pg.* 826, *pg.* 1014
REDDICK - Medical Device - LEMAITRE VASCULAR, INC.; *pg.* 1555, *pg.* 805
REDDIEGG - Food Product - NULAID FOODS INC.; *pg.* 887, *pg.* 193
REDDING RECORD SEARCHLIGHT - Newspaper - THE E.W. SCRIPPS COMPANY; *pg.* 1639, *pg.* 1412
REDDIT - Social News Website - ADVANCE PUBLICATIONS, INC.; *pg.* 1613, *pg.* 1343
REDD'S APPLE ALE - Apple Flavored Golden Ale - MILLERCOORS; *pg.* 254, *pg.* 1877
REDEFINING EXCELLENCE - Tag Line - INTEGRA MILTEX, INC.; *pg.* 1546, *pg.* 1597
REDEFINING THE BUILDING EXPERIENCE - Tag Line - WAUSAU HOMES, INC.; *pg.* 120, *pg.* 1890
REDEFINING VIDEO LIBRARY - Tagline - HARMONIC, INC.; *pg.* 402, *pg.* 246
REDEMPTION - Game - ACTIVISION BLIZZARD, INC.; *pg.* 948, *pg.* 271
REDEX - Car Care Product - HONEYWELL CONSUMER PRODUCTS GROUP; *pg.* 208, *pg.* 344
REDEX - Turbocharger - HONEYWELL INTERNATIONAL INC.; *pg.* 407, *pg.* 1088
REDEYE - RPM Service - STRATASYS, INC.; *pg.* 476, *pg.* 923
REDEYE RPM - Prototype & Part-Building Service - STRATASYS, INC.; *pg.* 476, *pg.* 923
REDFIELD - Clothing - ABERCROMBIE & FITCH CO.; *pg.* 37, *pg.* 1466
REDGRAVE - Furniture - ETHAN ALLEN INTERIORS INC.; *pg.* 924, *pg.* 343
REDGRAVE - Fabric - SCALAMANDRE, INC.; *pg.* 941, *pg.* 1058
REDHAWK - Software - CONCURRENT COMPUTER CORPORATION; *pg.* 379, *pg.* 531
REDHAWK - Revolver - STURM, RUGER & COMPANY, INC.; *pg.* 1846, *pg.* 371
REDHOOK BLONDE ALE - Beverage - CRAFT BREWERS ALLIANCE, INC; *pg.* 247, *pg.* 1502
REDHOOK BREWERY - Craft Brewery - CRAFT BREWERS ALLIANCE, INC; *pg.* 247, *pg.* 1502
REDHOOK ESB - Beverage - CRAFT BREWERS ALLIANCE, INC; *pg.* 247, *pg.* 1502
REDHOOK NUT BROWN ALE - Beverage - CRAFT BREWERS ALLIANCE, INC; *pg.* 247, *pg.* 1502
REDHOTS - Candy - FERRARA CANDY CO.; *pg.* 1852, *pg.* 612
REDI DRILL - Drills - SEARS HOLDINGS CORPORATION; *pg.* 1784, *pg.* 618
REDI-LINK - Compound - THE DOW CHEMICAL COMPANY; *pg.* 1157, *pg.* 898
REDI-MEAL - Backyard Birding - GARDENS ALIVE!, INC.; *pg.* 1796, *pg.* 693
REDI-MEASURE - Light Brown Sugar - IMPERIAL SUGAR COMPANY; *pg.* 864, *pg.* 1746
REDI-PRIME - Door - SIMPSON DOOR COMPANY; *pg.* 110, *pg.* 1823
REDI-ROOF - Metal Roofing - PETERSEN ALUMINUM CORPORATION; *pg.* 104, *pg.* 611
REDI-SEALS - Custom Sealing Solutions - THE TIMKEN COMPANY; *pg.* 218, *pg.* 1408
REDI-SERVE - Thermoformed Microwavable Trays - REXAM BEVERAGE CAN NORTH AMERICA; *pg.* 1468, *pg.* 588
REDI-SHAPE - Plastic Refractory - PLIBRICO CO. LLC; *pg.* 104, *pg.* 587
REDI SHRED - Potato Cheese Bake - BASIC AMERICAN FOODS, INC.; *pg.* 839, *pg.* 303
REDI-SLEEVES - Steel Wear - THE TIMKEN COMPANY; *pg.* 218, *pg.* 1408
REDI-SPRAY - Fluid Handling System - GRACO, INC.; *pg.* 1342, *pg.* 935
REDICARD - Preferred Member Program - RED ROOF INNS, INC.; *pg.* 1110, *pg.* 1443
REDICEL - Food Product - A. DUDA & SONS INC.; *pg.* 835, *pg.* 457
REDIGLYPH - Software - XEROX CORPORATION; *pg.* 494, *pg.* 365
REDIMARK - Writing Instrument - DIXON TICONDEROGA COMPANY; *pg.* 388, *pg.* 430
REDION - Battery - ENERSYS INC.; *pg.* 1334, *pg.* 1584
REDIPLATE - Molecular Probe Product - THERMO FISHER SCIENTIFIC INC.; *pg.* 1602, *pg.* 61
REDIPUS-OEDIPUS - Nail Care Product - OPI PRODUCTS INC.; *pg.* 518, *pg.* 167
REDISCOVER - Shoe - AEROGROUP INTERNATIONAL, INC.; *pg.* 1803, *pg.* 1055
REDISHARP - Writing Instrument - DIXON TICONDEROGA COMPANY; *pg.* 388, *pg.* 430
REDIT - Software - FLIR SYSTEMS, INC.; *pg.* 1413, *pg.* 1510
REDITABS - Pharmaceutical Product - IMPAX LABORATORIES, INC.; *pg.* 1544, *pg.* 101
REDITEST - Pharmaceutical Product - ALERE INC.; *pg.* 1488, *pg.* 849
REDKEN - Hair Care Products - L'OREAL USA; *pg.* 514, *pg.* 1252
REDLAM - Laminated Veneer Lumber Products - REDBUILT LLC; *pg.* 106, *pg.* 548
REDLINE - Golf Product - TAYLORMADE-ADIDAS GOLF; *pg.* 1847, *pg.* 60
REDONDO - Rubber Stair Tread - R.C.A. RUBBER COMPANY; *pg.* 1888, *pg.* 1402
REDOXSENSOR - Molecular Probe Product - THERMO FISHER SCIENTIFIC INC.; *pg.* 1602, *pg.* 61
REDPLEX - Lubricant - D-A LUBRICANT COMPANY; *pg.* 975, *pg.* 693
REDPLUM.COM - Web Site - VALASSIS COMMUNICATIONS, INC.; *pg.* 1287, *pg.* 897
REDPOINT - Knife - BUCK KNIVES, INC.; *pg.* 1828, *pg.* 550
REDRESS - Postal Services - UNITED STATES POSTAL SERVICE; *pg.* 1009, *pg.* 406
REDUCED POWER SPINUP - Drive Technology - WESTERN DIGITAL CORPORATION; *pg.* 492, *pg.* 118
REDUCER - Vortex Flowmeter - EMERSON PROCESS MANAGEMENT ROSEMOUNT INC.; *pg.* 1334, *pg.* 920
REDUCTASE - Pharmaceutical Product - ABBOTT LABORATORIES; *pg.* 1484, *pg.* 551
REDUCTONE - Chlorine & Caustic Soda - OLIN CORPORATION; *pg.* 1176, *pg.* 976
REDUX - Adhesive - HEXCEL CORPORATION; *pg.* 1884, *pg.* 375
REDUXADE - Pharmaceutical Product - ABBOTT LABORATORIES; *pg.* 1484, *pg.* 551
REDWOOD - Bike - MARIN BIKES; *pg.* 1708, *pg.* 168
REDWOOD - Moist Snuff Smokeless Tobacco - SWISHER INTERNATIONAL, INC.; *pg.* 1895, *pg.* 345
REDWOOD CREEK - Wine - E&J GALLO WINERY; *pg.* 1962, *pg.* 149
REEBOK CLASSIC - Shoe Line - REEBOK INTERNATIONAL LTD.; *pg.* 1817, *pg.* 811
REEBOK STRENGTH CYCLE - Exercise Bike - REEBOK INTERNATIONAL LTD.; *pg.* 1817, *pg.* 811
REECH - Software - SUNGARD DATA SYSTEMS INC.; *pg.* 477, *pg.* 1592
REED - Rock Bits - SCHLUMBERGER WELL COMPLETIONS; *pg.* 1373, *pg.* 1714
REEDRILL - Surface Drilling Equipment - TEREX CORPORATION; *pg.* 1381, *pg.* 384
REEDSBURG TIMES PRESS - Newspaper - MADISON NEWSPAPERS, INC.; *pg.* 1661, *pg.* 1866
REEF - Surf-Inspired Footwear & Apparel - V.F. CORPORATION; *pg.* 34, *pg.* 1376
REEFER GALLER - Household Product - WILLERT HOME PRODUCTS, INC.; *pg.* 1140, *pg.* 1005
REEL ADVENTURE - Game - WMS INDUSTRIES INC.; *pg.* 593, *pg.* 666
REEL CLUB - Restaurant - LETTUCE ENTERTAIN YOU ENTERPRISES, INC.; *pg.* 1735, *pg.* 580
REEL 'EM IN BIG BASS BUCKS - Game - WMS INDUSTRIES INC.; *pg.* 593, *pg.* 666
REEL 'EM IN CAST FOR CASH - Game - WMS INDUSTRIES INC.; *pg.* 593, *pg.* 666
REEL 'EM IN CATCH THAT BIG ONE - Game - WMS INDUSTRIES INC.; *pg.* 593, *pg.* 666
REEL 'EM IN POKER - Game - WMS INDUSTRIES INC.; *pg.* 593, *pg.* 666
REEL ESTATE - Game - WMS INDUSTRIES INC.; *pg.* 593, *pg.* 666
REEL ESTATE TYCOON - Game - WMS INDUSTRIES INC.; *pg.* 593, *pg.* 666
REEL GOLD - Video Game - INTERNATIONAL GAME TECHNOLOGY; *pg.* 957, *pg.* 1024
REEL HEROES - Game - WMS INDUSTRIES INC.; *pg.* 593, *pg.* 666
REEL HOSE - Hose - TEKNOR APEX COMPANY; *pg.* 1889, *pg.* 1605
REEL HOT WINS - Game - WMS INDUSTRIES INC.; *pg.* 593, *pg.* 666
REEL IN THE MONEY - Lottery Game - IOWA LOTTERY; *pg.* 996, *pg.* 705
REEL JAZZ - Video Game - INTERNATIONAL GAME TECHNOLOGY; *pg.* 957, *pg.* 1024
THE REEL LEADER. - Tagline - HANNAY REELS INC.; *pg.* 1344, *pg.* 1351
REEL LEGENDS - Game - WMS INDUSTRIES INC.; *pg.* 593, *pg.* 666
THE REEL-MAGIC - Limited Lifetime Warranty - REEL-O-MATIC, INC.; *pg.* 1371, *pg.* 1487
REEL MONEY - Video Game - BALLY TECHNOLOGIES, INC.; *pg.* 531, *pg.* 1022
REEL PEOPLE - Publication - EASTMAN KODAK COMPANY; *pg.* 1408, *pg.* 1333
REEL PROFIT - Video Game - INTERNATIONAL GAME TECHNOLOGY; *pg.* 957, *pg.* 1024
REEL RICH DEVIL - Game - WMS INDUSTRIES INC.; *pg.* 593, *pg.* 666
REEL RICHES - Game - WMS INDUSTRIES INC.; *pg.* 593, *pg.* 666
REEL ROCK - Premium Roll Covers - VAIL RUBBER WORKS, INC.; *pg.* 1891, *pg.* 906
REEL-SMART - Terminal Reel Fed - PANDUIT CORP.; *pg.* 661, *pg.* 663
REEL TOUGH - Flanged Spools & Reels - SONOCO PRODUCTS COMPANY; *pg.* 1469, *pg.* 1619
REEL VALUE - Flanged Spools & Reels - SONOCO PRODUCTS COMPANY; *pg.* 1469, *pg.* 1619
REELED HORSE - Lawn & Garden Care - TRACTOR SUPPLY COMPANY; *pg.* 708, *pg.* 1627
REELI-KLEAN - Melt Treatment - MINERALS TECHNOLOGIES INC.; *pg.* 1173, *pg.* 617
REELIN' IN THE DOUGH - Pull-tab Lottery Game - IDAHO LOTTERY; *pg.* 995, *pg.* 547
REELKASE - Plastic Casing - VISKASE COMPANIES, INC.; *pg.* 1471, *pg.* 599
REELPRINT - Adhesive Coated Paper - SPINNAKER COATING, LLC; *pg.* 1470, *pg.* 1477
REELS O'DUBLIN - Game - WMS INDUSTRIES INC.; *pg.* 593, *pg.* 666
REESE - Brass Stencil - C.H. HANSON COMPANY; *pg.* 1322, *pg.* 636
REESE - Furniture - LA-Z-BOY INCORPORATED; *pg.* 932, *pg.* 901
REESE - Trailer Hitch Systems - TRIMAS CORPORATION; *pg.* 1383, *pg.* 874
REESE FARM & RANCH - Interlock Ball Mount - TRACTOR SUPPLY COMPANY; *pg.* 708, *pg.* 1627
REESE PERFEC - Grating Products - REESE ENTERPRISES, INC.; *pg.* 1888, *pg.* 955
REESE'S - Candy - THE HERSHEY CO.; *pg.* 1855, *pg.* 1538
REESE'S CRUNCHY PEANUT BUTTER CUPS - Candy - THE HERSHEY CO.; *pg.* 1855, *pg.* 1538
REESE'S FAST BREAK - Chocolate Candy - THE HERSHEY CO.; *pg.* 1855, *pg.* 1538
REESE'S MINIS - Peanut Butter Milk Chocolate - THE HERSHEY CO.; *pg.* 1855, *pg.* 1538
REESE'S NUTRAGEOUS - Candy Bar - THE HERSHEY CO.; *pg.* 1855, *pg.* 1538
REESE'S PEANUT BUTTER CHIPS - Candy Chips - THE HERSHEY CO.; *pg.* 1855, *pg.* 1538
REESE'S PEANUT BUTTER CUPS - Candy - THE HERSHEY CO.; *pg.* 1855, *pg.* 1538
REESES PEANUT BUTTER PUFFS - Cereal - GENERAL MILLS, INC.; *pg.* 828, *pg.* 933
REESE'S PIECES - Candy - THE HERSHEY CO.; *pg.* 1855, *pg.* 1538
REESESTICKS - Chocolate Candy - THE HERSHEY CO.; *pg.* 1855, *pg.* 1538
REFACTO - Hemophilia Treatment Pharmaceutical Preparation - PFIZER INC.; *pg.* 1581, *pg.* 1278
REFER A FRIEND - Management Services - JACKSON HEWITT TAX SERVICE INC.; *pg.* 771, *pg.* 1103
REFER-A-FRIEND - Telecommunication Services - VONAGE

HOLDINGS CORP.; *pg.* 686, *pg.* 1074
REFERENCE - Loudspeakers - KLIPSCH GROUP, INC.; *pg.* 649, *pg.* 688
REFERENCE BILLS - Financial Services - FEDERAL HOME LOAN MORTGAGE CORPORATION; *pg.* 751, *pg.* 1790
REFERENCE BONDS - Financial Services - FEDERAL HOME LOAN MORTGAGE CORPORATION; *pg.* 751, *pg.* 1790
REFERENCE NOTES - Financial Services - FEDERAL HOME LOAN MORTGAGE CORPORATION; *pg.* 751, *pg.* 1790
REFERENCE POINT - Financial Services - FEDERAL HOME LOAN MORTGAGE CORPORATION; *pg.* 751, *pg.* 1790
REFERENCE REMIC - Financial Services - FEDERAL HOME LOAN MORTGAGE CORPORATION; *pg.* 751, *pg.* 1790
REFERENCE.COM - Reference Services - IAC/INTERACTIVECORP; *pg.* 292, *pg.* 1242
REFERENCEPOINT - Software - SUNGARD DATA SYSTEMS INC.; *pg.* 477, *pg.* 1592
REFERENCEWARE - Software - SKILLSOFT PLC; *pg.* 470, *pg.* 1037
REFERRAL EXPRESS! - Customer Solution - DELUXE CORPORATION; *pg.* 1634, *pg.* 964
REFF - Office Furniture - KNOLL, INC.; *pg.* 425, *pg.* 1527
REFILIT - Dental Product - MAJESTIC DRUG COMPANY, INC.; *pg.* 516, *pg.* 1343
REFINEIT - Software - BIO-RAD LABORATORIES, INC.; *pg.* 1504, *pg.* 101
REFINING CONDITIONER - Hair Care Product - JOHN PAUL MITCHELL SYSTEMS; *pg.* 512, *pg.* 133
REFINING SHAMPOO - Hair Care Product - JOHN PAUL MITCHELL SYSTEMS; *pg.* 512, *pg.* 133
REFLECT - Safety Product - WISCONSIN PHARMACAL COMPANY, LLC; *pg.* 1610, *pg.* 1861
REFLECTION - Software - ATTACHMATE CORPORATION; *pg.* 356, *pg.* 1833
REFLECTION - Flooring Product - CONGOLEUM CORPORATION; *pg.* 921, *pg.* 1084
REFLECTION - Church Worship Bulletins - WARNER PRESS, INC.; *pg.* 1701, *pg.* 673
REFLECTION FREE - Anti Reflective Coating - ICARE INDUSTRIES, INC.; *pg.* 1417, *pg.* 463
REFLECTIONS - Furniture - BUSH INDUSTRIES INC.; *pg.* 919, *pg.* 1170
REFLECTIONS - Cameras - EASTMAN KODAK COMPANY; *pg.* 1408, *pg.* 1333
REFLECTIONS - Office Furniture - JOFCO INC.; *pg.* 931, *pg.* 691
REFLECTIONS - Electric Fireplace - LENNOX HEARTH PRODUCTS; *pg.* 93, *pg.* 1652
REFLECTIONS - Flatware - ONEIDA LTD; *pg.* 1129, *pg.* 1318
REFLECTIONS: LONGBOAT KEY CLUB - Magazine - PALM BEACH MEDIA GROUP INC.; *pg.* 1674, *pg.* 457
REFLECTIVE CREW - Clothing - K-SWISS; *pg.* 1837, *pg.* 306
REFLECTIVE JACKET - Clothing - K-SWISS; *pg.* 1837, *pg.* 306
REFLECTIVE SLEEVELSS - Clothing - K-SWISS; *pg.* 1837, *pg.* 306
REFLECTIVE TANK - Clothing - K-SWISS; *pg.* 1837, *pg.* 306
REFLECTIX - Insulation Materials - SEALED AIR CORPORATION; *pg.* 1468, *pg.* 1058
REFLEJOS - Spanish Bilingual Newspaper - PADDOCK PUBLICATIONS, INC.; *pg.* 1674, *pg.* 554
REFLEX - Medical Equipment - CONMED CORPORATION; *pg.* 1517, *pg.* 1347
REFLEX - Plastics - FXI; *pg.* 1163, *pg.* 1552
REFLEX - Binning & Attribute Analysis - ION GEOPHYSICAL CORPORATION; *pg.* 1350, *pg.* 1708
REFLEX - Banking Services - THE PNC FINANCIAL SERVICES GROUP, INC.; *pg.* 795, *pg.* 1579
REFLEX - High Barrier Food Packaging Bulk Pouches - SEALED AIR CORPORATION; *pg.* 1468, *pg.* 1058
REFLEX - Spinal System - STRYKER CORPORATION; *pg.* 1598, *pg.* 894
REFLEX-BAR - Ice Skate Performance Enhancing Technology - REEBOK-CCM HOCKEY, INC.; *pg.* 1844, *pg.* 1960
REFLEX BOUNCE - Foam - FXI; *pg.* 1163, *pg.* 1552
REFLEX CORE - Foam - FXI; *pg.* 1163, *pg.* 1552
REFLEX MEMORY - Foam - FXI; *pg.* 1163, *pg.* 1552
REFLEX MESH - Hose - TEKNOR APEX COMPANY; *pg.* 1889, *pg.* 1605
REFLEX PLUS - Foam - FXI; *pg.* 1163, *pg.* 1552
REFLEX WRAP - Foam - FXI; *pg.* 1163, *pg.* 1552
REFLEXION - CMP System - APPLIED MATERIALS, INC.; *pg.* 618, *pg.* 264
REFLEXION - Surgical Instrument - OSTEOMED CORPORATION; *pg.* 1425, *pg.* 1658
REFLEXION - Bedding - SEALY CORPORATION; *pg.* 942, *pg.* 1391
REFLEXION - Steerable Catheters - ST. JUDE MEDICAL, INC.; *pg.* 1596, *pg.* 963
REFLEXION SPIRAL - Radius Catheter - ST. JUDE MEDICAL, INC.; *pg.* 1596, *pg.* 963
REFLEXION SPIRAL X - Mapping Catheter - ST. JUDE MEDICAL, INC.; *pg.* 1596, *pg.* 963
REFLEXITE - Reflective Cable - LOOS & COMPANY, INC.; *pg.* 1356, *pg.* 368
REFORMATION21 - Daily Devotional Magazine - ALLIANCE OF CONFESSING EVANGELICALS, INC.; *pg.* 126, *pg.* 1545
REFRESH - Eye Care Product - ALLERGAN, INC.; *pg.* 1491, *pg.* 106
REFRESH - Skin Care - CHEROKEE GLOBAL BRANDS; *pg.* 21, *pg.* 278
REFRESH - Tea - STARBUCKS CORPORATION; *pg.* 897, *pg.* 1840
REFRESH - Air Freshener - SWISHER HYGIENE INC.; *pg.* 336, *pg.* 1507
REFRESH CONTACTS - Eye Care Product - ALLERGAN, INC.; *pg.* 1491, *pg.* 106
REFRESH DRY EYE THERAPY - Eye Care - ALLERGAN, INC.; *pg.* 1491, *pg.* 106
REFRESH ENDURA - Eye Care Product - ALLERGAN, INC.; *pg.* 1491, *pg.* 106
REFRESH LIQUIGEL - Eye Care Product - ALLERGAN, INC.; *pg.* 1491, *pg.* 106
REFRESH PLUS - Eye Care Product - ALLERGAN, INC.; *pg.* 1491, *pg.* 106
REFRESH P.M. - Eye Care Product - ALLERGAN, INC.; *pg.* 1491, *pg.* 106
REFRESH TEARS - Eye Care Product - ALLERGAN, INC.; *pg.* 1491, *pg.* 106
REFRESHER COURSE - Financial Products - DOW JONES & COMPANY, INC.; *pg.* 1637, *pg.* 1225
REFRESHERS - Juice Drinks - OCEAN SPRAY CRANBERRIES, INC.; *pg.* 887, *pg.* 827
REFRESHMINT - Muscle Care Product - W.F. YOUNG, INC.; *pg.* 1610, *pg.* 817
REFRESHMINTS - Candy & Mints - PROMOTION IN MOTION, INC.; *pg.* 1861, *pg.* 1052
REFRIG/ARRANGERS - Laboratory Product - SPECTRUM LABORATORIES INC.; *pg.* 1595, *pg.* 69
REFRIGERANTSIDE - Refrigerant Side Performance Optimization Service - HUDSON TECHNOLOGIES, INC.; *pg.* 1073, *pg.* 1320
REFUELERS - Pumps - IDEX CORPORATION; *pg.* 1347, *pg.* 623
REG-9000 - Biodiesel - RENEWABLE ENERGY GROUP, INC.; *pg.* 984, *pg.* 701
REG-9000 BIOHEAT - Renewable Oil - RENEWABLE ENERGY GROUP, INC.; *pg.* 984, *pg.* 701
REGA - Amplifier - COHERENT, INC.; *pg.* 1406, *pg.* 265
REGAL - Resin Bond Cloth Belt & Fiber Disc - 3M COMPANY; *pg.* 1142, *pg.* 956
REGAL - In-Line Equalizer - ARRIS GROUP, INC.; *pg.* 353, *pg.* 541
REGAL - Furniture - ASHLEY FURNITURE INDUSTRIES, INC.; *pg.* 914, *pg.* 1852
REGAL - Paint And Stain Product - BENJAMIN MOORE & CO.; *pg.* 1440, *pg.* 1085
REGAL - Carbon Black - CABOT CORPORATION; *pg.* 1151, *pg.* 792
REGAL - Coating, Fats & Confections - CARGILL LIMITED; *pg.* 1475, *pg.* 1914
REGAL - Reels - DAIWA CORPORATION; *pg.* 1832, *pg.* 75
REGAL - Roses - DENVER WHOLESALE FLORISTS COMPANY; *pg.* 1794, *pg.* 319
REGAL - Furniture - JASPER GROUP; *pg.* 930, *pg.* 691
REGAL - Pool Water Treatment Products - POOL CORPORATION; *pg.* 1843, *pg.* 743
REGAL - Cutting Tools - REGAL BELOIT CORPORATION; *pg.* 106, *pg.* 1854
REGAL - Plybent Wood Chair - SAUDER MANUFACTURING COMPANY; *pg.* 941, *pg.* 1403
REGAL - Plumbing Product - SLOAN VALVE COMPANY; *pg.* 1062, *pg.* 613
REGAL - Rug - SPRINGS GLOBAL, INC.; *pg.* 698, *pg.* 1616
REGAL - Joint Compound - USG CORPORATION; *pg.* 118, *pg.* 594
REGAL AQUA PEARL - Interior Latex Enamel - BENJAMIN MOORE & CO.; *pg.* 1440, *pg.* 1085
REGAL AQUA VELVET - Interior Latex Enamel - BENJAMIN MOORE & CO.; *pg.* 1440, *pg.* 1085
REGAL AQUAGLO - Interior Latex Enamel - BENJAMIN MOORE & CO.; *pg.* 1440, *pg.* 1085
REGAL BRI - Saltwater Spinning Reels - DAIWA CORPORATION; *pg.* 1832, *pg.* 75
REGAL CINEMEETINGS AND EVENTS - Meetings & Seminars - REGAL ENTERTAINMENT GROUP; *pg.* 579, *pg.* 1638
REGAL CROWN CLUB - Loyalty Program - REGAL ENTERTAINMENT GROUP; *pg.* 579, *pg.* 1638
REGAL CUTTING TOOLS - Tools - REGAL BELOIT CORPORATION; *pg.* 106, *pg.* 1854
REGAL EXPRESS - Ticket Terminals & Kiosks - REGAL ENTERTAINMENT GROUP; *pg.* 579, *pg.* 1638
REGAL FIRST COAT - Paint And Stain Product - BENJAMIN MOORE & CO.; *pg.* 1440, *pg.* 1085
REGAL GOLD - Titanium Nitride Coating - REGAL BELOIT CORPORATION; *pg.* 106, *pg.* 1854
REGAL-LINE - Off Highway Power Transmission Products - REGAL BELOIT CORPORATION; *pg.* 106, *pg.* 1854
REGAL OPTIMA SMO - Flushometer - SLOAN VALVE COMPANY; *pg.* 1062, *pg.* 613
REGAL PLANK - Flooring Product - CONGOLEUM CORPORATION; *pg.* 921, *pg.* 1084
REGAL PLUS BRI - Freshwater Spinning Reels - DAIWA CORPORATION; *pg.* 1832, *pg.* 75
REGAL PREMIUM - Precision Cutting Tools; Gage Product & Standard Taps - REGAL BELOIT CORPORATION; *pg.* 106, *pg.* 1854
REGAL PRO - Flushometer - SLOAN VALVE COMPANY; *pg.* 1062, *pg.* 613
REGAL PRO OPTIMA - Flushometer - SLOAN VALVE COMPANY; *pg.* 1062, *pg.* 613
REGAL PRO OPTIMA SMO - Flushometer - SLOAN VALVE COMPANY; *pg.* 1062, *pg.* 613
REGAL RAPID ROUTER - 5 & 10 Degree Routers - REGAL BELOIT CORPORATION; *pg.* 106, *pg.* 1854
REGAL WALL SATIN - Interior Latex Flat Finish - BENJAMIN MOORE & CO.; *pg.* 1440, *pg.* 1085
REGAL WARE - Cookware - REGAL WARE, INC.; *pg.* 1137, *pg.* 1862
REGAL XC - Freshwater Spinning Reels - DAIWA CORPORATION; *pg.* 1832, *pg.* 75
REGAL ZC - Freshwater Spinning Reels - DAIWA CORPORATION; *pg.* 1832, *pg.* 75
REGALIA - Online Store - ASCENA RETAIL GROUP, INC.; *pg.* 18, *pg.* 1081
REGALITE - Resin Bond Abrasive Cloth - 3M COMPANY; *pg.* 1142, *pg.* 956
REGALITE - Hydrocarbon Resins - EASTMAN CHEMICAL COMPANY; *pg.* 1159, *pg.* 1636
REGALLOY - Dental Product - DENTSPLY INTERNATIONAL INC.; *pg.* 1522, *pg.* 1596
REGALREZ - Hydrocarbon Resins - EASTMAN CHEMICAL COMPANY; *pg.* 1159, *pg.* 1636
REGANBOOKS - Books - HARPERCOLLINS PUBLISHERS INC.; *pg.* 1647, *pg.* 1237
REGATTA - After Shave Lotion - BLUE CROSS LABORATORIES; *pg.* 326, *pg.* 277
REGATTA - Surface Material - STEELCASE INC.; *pg.* 475, *pg.* 889
REGATTA POOLS - In-Ground Vinyl Pools - POOL CORPORATION; *pg.* 1843, *pg.* 743
REGENAIR - Pump Product - IDEX CORPORATION; *pg.* 1347, *pg.* 623
REGENASURE - Glucosamine - CARGILL, INC.; *pg.* 845, *pg.* 965
REGENCY - Wall & House Paint - AKZONOBEL DECORATIVE PAINTS U.S.; *pg.* 1439, *pg.* 1474
REGENCY - Office Chairs - BERNHARDT DESIGN; *pg.* 918, *pg.* 1381
REGENCY - Icing And Base - DAWN FOOD PRODUCTS, INC.; *pg.* 1018, *pg.* 893
REGENCY - Faucet - ELKAY MANUFACTURING COMPANY; *pg.* 80, *pg.* 645
REGENCY - Cosmetic Product - MERLE NORMAN COSMETICS, INC.; *pg.* 517, *pg.* 136
REGENCY - Windows & Doors - NORTEK, INC.; *pg.* 100, *pg.* 1607
REGENCY - Pacemakers - ST. JUDE MEDICAL, INC.; *pg.* 1596, *pg.* 963
REGENCY PROFESSIONAL - Sanitary Maintenance Supplies

First page reference indicates Business Class Edition
Second page reference indicates Geographic Edition

- XPEDX; pg. 1473, pg. 1377

REGENERATE - Automation Tool - CACI INTERNATIONAL INC.; pg. 367, pg. 1773

REGENERATION - Nutritional Supplement - NATURAL ORGANICS, INC.; pg. 1571, pg. 1181

REGENEVER - Chemical Reagent - HACH COMPANY; pg. 1415, pg. 334

REGENSCHAUER OKTOBERFEST - Beverage - COASTAL EXTREME BREWING COMPANY; pg. 240, pg. 1602

REGENSI - Surface Preparation - ATMI, INC.; pg. 1314, pg. 342

REGENT - Canned Puddings & Cheese Sauces - ADVANCED FOOD PRODUCTS LLC; pg. 835, pg. 1555

REGENT - Hotels & Resorts - CARLSON COMPANIES INC.; pg. 1084, pg. 947

REGENT - Motor - CARTER MOTOR COMPANY; pg. 1321, pg. 665

REGENT - Photocopy Apparatus - EASTMAN KODAK COMPANY; pg. 1408, pg. 1333

REGENT - Fabric - NEMSCHOFF, INC.; pg. 936, pg. 1890

REGENT - Lubricant and Process Oil - ROCK VALLEY OIL & CHEMICAL COMPANY; pg. 1179, pg. 631

REGENT TAPE - Tape - THERMWELL PRODUCTS CO., INC.; pg. 1065, pg. 1082

REGGAE - Fabric - NEMSCHOFF, INC.; pg. 936, pg. 1890

REGGAETON 94 - Radio Station - SPANISH BROADCASTING SYSTEM INC.; pg. 310, pg. 446

REGGIE THE RHYMING RHINO - Educational Materials - SCHOLASTIC INC.; pg. 1683, pg. 1288

REGINA - Tile - ARTISTIC TILE INC.; pg. 914, pg. 1119

REGINA - Wine Vinegar - B&G FOODS, INC.; pg. 838, pg. 1102

REGINA - Table - BLATT BOWLING & BILLIARD CORP.; pg. 1827, pg. 1203

REGIOMAN - Press - MANROLAND INC.; pg. 430, pg. 669

REGIONAL - Tire - THE GOODYEAR TIRE & RUBBER COMPANY; pg. 1883, pg. 1401

REGIONAL RECIPE - Potato Side Dishes - BASIC AMERICAN FOODS, INC.; pg. 839, pg. 303

REGIONSERV - Telecommunications Transmission Services - AT&T SOUTHEAST; pg. 1868, pg. 489

REGIS - Fabric - NEMSCHOFF, INC.; pg. 936, pg. 1890

REGIS' CASH CLUB - Game - INTERNATIONAL GAME TECHNOLOGY; pg. 957, pg. 1024

REGIS SALONS - Hair Salons - REGIS CORPORATION; pg. 521, pg. 941

REGISIL - Dental Product - DENTSPLY INTERNATIONAL INC.; pg. 1522, pg. 1596

REGISTAR - Laser-Imageable Technology - DOW CHEMICAL; pg. 1156, pg. 1563

REGISTERED MAIL - Postal Services - UNITED STATES POSTAL SERVICE; pg. 1009, pg. 406

REGISTRATOR - Platens - THE STANDARD REGISTER COMPANY; pg. 473, pg. 1446

REGISTRY WIZARD - PC Update Software - PHOENIX TECHNOLOGIES LTD.; pg. 454, pg. 147

REGLINK - Software - PASSKEY INTERNATIONAL, INC.; pg. 1274, pg. 853

REGLO - Pump - IDEX CORPORATION; pg. 1347, pg. 623

REGO - Gas Product - ENGINEERED CONTROLS INTERNATIONAL LLC; pg. 1334, pg. 1372

REGRANEX - Healthcare Product - JOHNSON & JOHNSON; pg. 1549, pg. 1091

REGUARD - Agricultural Product - WILBUR-ELLIS COMPANY; pg. 1185, pg. 234

REGUL - Tires - MICHELIN NORTH AMERICA INC.; pg. 1886, pg. 1618

REGULAID - Spreader Activator - KALO, INC.; pg. 1796, pg. 719

REGULAR - Potato Chips - UTZ QUALITY FOODS, INC.; pg. 907, pg. 1536

REGULATION - Shirts - ELBECO INCORPORATED; pg. 40, pg. 1584

REGULATION PLUS - Trousers - ELBECO INCORPORATED; pg. 40, pg. 1584

REGULATORY SOLUTIONS - Wireline Solutions - SONUS NETWORKS INC.; pg. 1281, pg. 858

REGULUS - Diaphragm Pump - GRACO, INC.; pg. 1342, pg. 935

REGWICK - Fabric - NEMSCHOFF, INC.; pg. 936, pg. 1890

REHAB - Beverages - THE COCA-COLA COMPANY; pg. 240, pg. 493

REHAB - Orthopedic Product - DJO INCORPORATED; pg. 1524, pg. 302

REHAB JUST GOT EASIER - Medical Equipment - INVACARE CORPORATION; pg. 1546, pg. 1451

REHAB ONE - Medical Equipment - INVACARE CORPORATION; pg. 1546, pg. 1451

REHAB WITHOUT WALLS - Healthcare Product - GENTIVA HEALTH SERVICES, INC.; pg. 1534, pg. 506

REHABILITY CENTERS - Outpatient Clinics - HEALTHSOUTH CORPORATION; pg. 1540, pg. 3

REHABILITY HEALTH SERVICE - RHS - HEALTHSOUTH CORPORATION; pg. 1540, pg. 3

REI ADVENTURES - Adventure Travel - RECREATIONAL EQUIPMENT, INC.; pg. 1843, pg. 1821

REI COOP - Outdoor Apparel & Equipment Stores - RECREATIONAL EQUIPMENT, INC.; pg. 1843, pg. 1821

REI-OUTLET.COM - Online Outlet Store - RECREATIONAL EQUIPMENT, INC.; pg. 1843, pg. 1821

REI.COM - Online Store - RECREATIONAL EQUIPMENT, INC.; pg. 1843, pg. 1821

REILLEX - Diethenylbenzene - VERTELLUS SPECIALTIES INC.; pg. 1185, pg. 690

REILY - Decorative Accessory - ETHAN ALLEN INTERIORS INC.; pg. 924, pg. 343

REIMAN PUBLICATIONS - Magazine - THE READER'S DIGEST ASSOCIATION, INC.; pg. 1679, pg. 1322

REIMBURSEMENT CONNECTION - Professional Service - AMGEN INC.; pg. 1493, pg. 291

REINA - Actuator - PRECISION VALVE CORPORATION; pg. 1060, pg. 1357

REINFORCED COVERALL - Polyethylene Film - FLEX-O-GLASS, INC.; pg. 1457, pg. 574

REINVENTING TECHNOLOGY SUPPORT - Tagline - SUPPORT.COM, INC.; pg. 1283, pg. 192

REINVENTING THE OUTDOOR EXPERIENCE - Tagline - SWORDFISH FINANCIAL, INC.; pg. 1430, pg. 1737

REISHIMAX - Nutritional Supplement - NU SKIN ENTERPRISES, INC.; pg. 518, pg. 1755

REITER - Milk & Ice Cream - DEAN FOODS COMPANY; pg. 852, pg. 1679

REITER DAIRY - Dairy Product - DEAN FOODS COMPANY; pg. 852, pg. 1679

REITI - Footwear - PHOENIX FOOTWEAR GROUP, INC.; pg. 1815, pg. 60

REJOICE - Shampoo & Conditioner - THE PROCTER & GAMBLE COMPANY; pg. 1129, pg. 1418

REJUV - Food Product - SHAMROCK FOODS COMPANY; pg. 895, pg. 20

REKINDLE - Shoe - AEROGROUP INTERNATIONAL, INC.; pg. 1803, pg. 1055

REKINDLE - Nutritional Supplement - PHARMAVITE LLC; pg. 1584, pg. 167

RELASTYL - Health & Beauty Product - DIXIE HEALTH, INC.; pg. 1524, pg. 535

THE RELATIONSHIP COMPANY - Slogan - WESTERN NATIONAL MUTUAL INSURANCE CO.; pg. 1223, pg. 946

RELAX NOW - Herbal Supplement - HERBALIFE INTERNATIONAL OF AMERICA, INC.; pg. 1541, pg. 132

RELAX-R-BATH - Hair & Skin Product - AUBREY ORGANICS INC.; pg. 499, pg. 470

RELAX. YOU.VE PLACED YOUR BEST CLIENTS WITH CHUBB. - Slogan - THE CHUBB CORPORATION; pg. 1196, pg. 1128

RELAXED - Fabric - NEMSCHOFF, INC.; pg. 936, pg. 1890

RELAXED STRAIGHT 559 - Jean - LEVI STRAUSS & CO.; pg. 43, pg. 220

THE RELAXER - Hair Care System - JOHN PAUL MITCHELL SYSTEMS; pg. 512, pg. 133

RELAXIN - Valerian Root & Ayurvedic Passion Flower - DIXIE HEALTH, INC.; pg. 1524, pg. 535

RELAY - Textiles - BERNHARDT DESIGN; pg. 918, pg. 1381

RELAY - Wheat Cropping System - LANDEC CORPORATION; pg. 1419, pg. 145

RELAY - Molecular Biology Product - THERMO FISHER SCIENTIFIC INC.; pg. 1602, pg. 61

RELAY FOR LIFE - Fund-Raiser - AMERICAN CANCER SOCIETY, INC.; pg. 126, pg. 487

RELAY GEL - Battery - EXIDE TECHNOLOGIES; pg. 204, pg. 483

RELEASE - Fiberglass Boat Product - GRADY-WHITE BOATS, INC.; pg. 1707, pg. 1377

RELEASE - Golf Shaft - TRUE TEMPER SPORTS, INC.; pg. 1847, pg. 1647

RELENTLESS - Beverages - THE COCA-COLA COMPANY; pg. 240, pg. 493

RELEVANCE-X - Online Advertising Network - ACXIOM CORPORATION; pg. 342, pg. 33

RELEVANT - Office Furniture - STEELCASE INC.; pg. 475, pg. 889

RELEVE - Nutritional Supplement - MAXIMUM HUMAN PERFORMANCE, INC.; pg. 1559, pg. 1065

RELI - Molecular Biology Product - THERMO FISHER SCIENTIFIC INC.; pg. 1602, pg. 61

RELIABILITY BUILT IN - Slogan - T&S BRASS & BRONZE WORKS, INC.; pg. 114, pg. 1623

RELIABILITY FOR REAL LIFE - Slogan - JELD-WEN, INC.; pg. 1051, pg. 1499

RELIABLE - Bag - RELIABLE OF MILWAUKEE; pg. 698, pg. 1879

RELIALAB - Test Equipment - SPX THERMAL PRODUCT SOLUTIONS; pg. 1378, pg. 1555

RELIANCE - Carpet - BEAULIEU GROUP, LLC; pg. 917, pg. 529

RELIANCE - Atmospheric Direct Drive Robots - BROOKS AUTOMATION, INC.; pg. 1320, pg. 813

RELIANCE - Paper & Nonwoven Material - FIBERMARK INC.; pg. 1457, pg. 1764

RELIANCE - Vinyl Siding - OWENS CORNING; pg. 102, pg. 1476

RELIANCE - Horse Feeds - SOUTHERN STATES COOPERATIVE, INC.; pg. 1482, pg. 1804

RELIANCE - Automated Transport System - STERIS CORPORATION; pg. 1597, pg. 1464

RELIANCE ATR - Atmospheric Tool - BROOKS AUTOMATION, INC.; pg. 1320, pg. 813

RELIANT - Lubricant - D-A LUBRICANT COMPANY; pg. 975, pg. 693

RELIANT - Microfilming Machine & Accessories - EASTMAN KODAK COMPANY; pg. 1408, pg. 1333

RELIANT - Lift - INVACARE CORPORATION; pg. 1546, pg. 1451

RELIANT - Software - VERINT SYSTEMS INC.; pg. 488, pg. 1182

RELIANT 600 - Heavy Duty Stand-up Lift - INVACARE CORPORATION; pg. 1546, pg. 1451

RELIANT PLUS - Heavy Duty Stand-Up Lift - INVACARE CORPORATION; pg. 1546, pg. 1451

RELIC - Watch - FOSSIL GROUP, INC.; pg. 5, pg. 1735

RELICORE - Software - SYMANTEC CORPORATION; pg. 478, pg. 161

RELIEF - Eye Care Product - ALLERGAN, INC.; pg. 1491, pg. 106

RELIEF - Skin Care Lotion - BLUE CROSS LABORATORIES; pg. 326, pg. 277

RELIEF REFINANCE MORTAGES - Home Modification Program - FEDERAL HOME LOAN MORTGAGE CORPORATION; pg. 751, pg. 1790

RELIGIOUS EDUCATION ASSISTANCE PROGRAM - Fraternal Benefits - CATHOLIC ORDER OF FORESTERS; pg. 1196, pg. 635

RELISTOR - Opiod Induced Constipation Treatment - PFIZER INC.; pg. 1581, pg. 1278

RELISTOR - Pharmaceutical Product - SALIX PHARMACEUTICALS, INC.; pg. 1591, pg. 1388

RELIUS - Software - SUNGARD DATA SYSTEMS INC.; pg. 477, pg. 1592

RELIV CLASSIC - Nutritional Product - RELIV INTERNATIONAL, INC.; pg. 1589, pg. 975

RELIV NOW - Nutritional Product - RELIV INTERNATIONAL, INC.; pg. 1589, pg. 975

RELOCATING IN LAS VEGAS - Magazine - NETWORK COMMUNICATIONS INC.; pg. 1271, pg. 534

RELOCATING IN ST. LOUIS - Magazine - NETWORK COMMUNICATIONS INC.; pg. 1271, pg. 534

RELOCATION REDEFINED - Local & International Relocation Management Services - SIRVA, INC.; pg. 1923, pg. 669

RELORA - Health Care Product - NATURE'S SUNSHINE PRODUCTS, INC.; pg. 1571, pg. 1754

RELPAX - Migraine Medication - PFIZER INC.; pg. 1581, pg. 1278

RELSKA VODKA - Vodka - DIAGEO NORTH AMERICA, INC.; pg. 1961, pg. 361

RELY ON - Caulk And Sealant - DAP PRODUCTS, INC.; pg. 1441, pg. 756

RELYON - Disinfectants - E.I. DU PONT DE NEMOURS & COMPANY; pg. 1159, pg. 390

RELYX - Cement - 3M COMPANY; pg. 1142, pg. 956

REM - Patient Handling Equipment - STRYKER CORPORATION; pg. 1598, pg. 894

REM-LITE - Shotshell - REMINGTON ARMS COMPANY, LLC; pg. 1844, pg. 1382

REMARK CLASSIC OMR - Educational Software - PEARSON ASSESSMENTS; pg. 1674, pg. 918

REMARKABLE FINISH - Cosmetic Product - MERLE NORMAN COSMETICS, INC.; *pg.* 517, *pg.* 136
REMBRANDT - Bleaching Gel - DEN-MAT CORPORATION; *pg.* 1522, *pg.* 271
REMBRANDT - Window Treatment - HERITAGE LACE INC.; *pg.* 694, *pg.* 711
REMBRANDT - Teeth Cleaning Products - JOHNSON & JOHNSON; *pg.* 1549, *pg.* 1091
REMBRANDT - Decorative Polymer Stains - QUAKER CHEMICAL CORP.; *pg.* 1178, *pg.* 1524
REMBRANDT - Molecular Biology Product - THERMO FISHER SCIENTIFIC INC.; *pg.* 1602, *pg.* 61
REMBRANDT ALLEGRO - Dental Curing Light - DEN-MAT CORPORATION; *pg.* 1522, *pg.* 271
REMBRANDT RICHES - Video Game - INTERNATIONAL GAME TECHNOLOGY; *pg.* 957, *pg.* 1024
REMBRANDT SAPPHIRE - Dental Bleach - DEN-MAT CORPORATION; *pg.* 1522, *pg.* 271
REMCO - Toy Vehicles - JAKKS PACIFIC, INC.; *pg.* 960, *pg.* 142
REMEDE - Beauty Products - BLISSWORLD LLC; *pg.* 501, *pg.* 1204
REMEDI HS - Clinical Diagnostic Product - BIO-RAD LABORATORIES, INC.; *pg.* 1504, *pg.* 101
REMEDIA - Filter - W.L. GORE & ASSOCIATES, INC.; *pg.* 122, *pg.* 388
REMEDY - Software - BMC SOFTWARE, INC.; *pg.* 362, *pg.* 1701
REMEDY - Furniture - KIMBALL INTERNATIONAL, INC.; *pg.* 931, *pg.* 692
REMEDY - Skin Cream - MEDLINE INDUSTRIES, INC.; *pg.* 1562, *pg.* 635
REMEDY - Bicycle - TREK BICYCLE CORPORATION; *pg.* 1847, *pg.* 1896
REMEDY - Protection - WESTAMERICA BANCORPORATION; *pg.* 821, *pg.* 258
REMEDY CHECK PROTECTION - Protection - WESTAMERICA BANCORPORATION; *pg.* 821, *pg.* 258
REMEMBER-FX - Natural Health Product - AFEXA LIFE SCIENCES INC.; *pg.* 1487, *pg.* 1905
REMEMBER ME - Educational Product - BARKER CREEK PUBLISHING INC.; *pg.* 1619, *pg.* 1818
REMEMBER WHEN - Herbal And Vitamin Supplement - BEE-ALIVE INC.; *pg.* 1503, *pg.* 1348
REMEMBRANCE - Roller Shades on a Clutch System - HUNTER DOUGLAS, INC.; *pg.* 928, *pg.* 1320
REMEMBRANCE ADVERTISING - Slogan - BROWN & BIGELOW, INC.; *pg.* 1624, *pg.* 959
REMERON - Medicine - MERCK & CO., INC.; *pg.* 1566, *pg.* 1077
REMFORM - Screw - SFS INTEC, INC.; *pg.* 1061, *pg.* 1596
REMGRIT - Saw Blades - KENNAMETAL IPG; *pg.* 1353, *pg.* 1615
REMI - Nutritional Supplement - MAXIMUM HUMAN PERFORMANCE, INC.; *pg.* 1559, *pg.* 1065
REMIC - Home Modification Program - FEDERAL HOME LOAN MORTGAGE CORPORATION; *pg.* 751, *pg.* 1790
REMICADE - Healthcare Product - JOHNSON & JOHNSON; *pg.* 1549, *pg.* 1091
REMIFEMIN - Supplement Therapy - ENZYMATIC THERAPY INC.; *pg.* 1529, *pg.* 1859
REMINGTON - Tire And Rubber Product - THE GOODYEAR TIRE & RUBBER COMPANY; *pg.* 1883, *pg.* 1401
REMINGTON - Firearms, Ammunition, Traps - REMINGTON ARMS COMPANY, LLC; *pg.* 1844, *pg.* 1382
REMINGTON LEADLESS - Firearms - REMINGTON ARMS COMPANY, LLC; *pg.* 1844, *pg.* 1382
REMINISCE - Fabric - NEMSCHOFF, INC.; *pg.* 936, *pg.* 1890
REMINYL - Healthcare Product - JOHNSON & JOHNSON; *pg.* 1549, *pg.* 1091
REMIPAUSE - Pharmaceutical Product - ALERE INC.; *pg.* 1488, *pg.* 849
REMISOL - Data Manager Software - BECKMAN COULTER, INC.; *pg.* 1402, *pg.* 48
REMITCO - Payment Collection Service - FIRST DATA CORPORATION; *pg.* 754, *pg.* 505
REMITSTREAM - Software System - FISERV, INC.; *pg.* 397, *pg.* 1855
REMODEL - Magazine - MEREDITH CORPORATION; *pg.* 1663, *pg.* 705
REMODELINE - Sectional Showers & Tub/Showers - AQUATIC; *pg.* 68, *pg.* 42
REMOL - Flame Retardants - CHEMTURA CORPORATION; *pg.* 1152, *pg.* 355
REMOTE ALPHA DOCK - Software - BIO-RAD LABORATORIES, INC.; *pg.* 1504, *pg.* 101
REMOTE PARAMETER CONTROL - Software - MTS SYSTEMS CORPORATION; *pg.* 442, *pg.* 923
REMOTE TILT - Cable & Antenna System - RADIO FREQUENCY SYSTEMS, INC.; *pg.* 666, *pg.* 354
REMOTE WONDER - Remote Control - ADVANCED MICRO DEVICES, INC.; *pg.* 613, *pg.* 282
REMOTE WONDER - 3D Graphical Technology - ADVANCED MICRO DEVICES, INC.-MARKHAM; *pg.* 345, *pg.* 1922
REMOTELYANYWHERE - Remote Computer Connectivity Product - LOGMEIN, INC.; *pg.* 428, *pg.* 861
REMOTESCOPE - Hardware System - MICRO 2000, INC.; *pg.* 434, *pg.* 96
REMOTETELLER - Transaction Product - DIEBOLD, INCORPORATED; *pg.* 387, *pg.* 1407
REMOTEWARE - Retail Polling - SAP; *pg.* 465, *pg.* 78
REMOVABLE MEDIA LOCKDOWN - Software - WEBSENSE, INC.; *pg.* 491, *pg.* 210
REMOX - Chemical Product - CARUS CORPORATION; *pg.* 1152, *pg.* 652
REMOXY - Pain Medication - PAIN THERAPEUTICS, INC.; *pg.* 1579, *pg.* 1665
REMSEN SELVEDGE SLIM STRAIGHT - Clothing - ABERCROMBIE & FITCH CO.; *pg.* 37, *pg.* 1466
REMSEN SLIM STRAIGHT - Clothing - ABERCROMBIE & FITCH CO.; *pg.* 37, *pg.* 1466
REMY - Fabric - NEMSCHOFF, INC.; *pg.* 936, *pg.* 1890
REMY MARTIN 1738 - Cognac - REMY COINTREAU USA INC.; *pg.* 1969, *pg.* 1285
REMY MARTIN EXTRA - Cognac - REMY COINTREAU USA INC.; *pg.* 1969, *pg.* 1285
REMY MARTIN GRAND CRU - Cognac - REMY COINTREAU USA INC.; *pg.* 1969, *pg.* 1285
REMY MARTIN LOUIS XIII - Cognac - REMY COINTREAU USA INC.; *pg.* 1969, *pg.* 1285
REMY MARTIN VSOP - Cognac - REMY COINTREAU USA INC.; *pg.* 1969, *pg.* 1285
REMY MARTIN XO - Cognac - REMY COINTREAU USA INC.; *pg.* 1969, *pg.* 1285
REMY RED - Spirits - REMY COINTREAU USA INC.; *pg.* 1969, *pg.* 1285
RENAISSANCE - Organ - ALLEN ORGAN COMPANY; *pg.* 527, *pg.* 1549
RENAISSANCE - Furniture - ASHLEY FURNITURE INDUSTRIES, INC.; *pg.* 914, *pg.* 1852
RENAISSANCE - Dinnerware - THE HOMER LAUGHLIN CHINA COMPANY; *pg.* 1125, *pg.* 1850
RENAISSANCE - Hotels & Resorts - MARRIOTT INTERNATIONAL, INC.; *pg.* 1102, *pg.* 764
RENAISSANCE - Fabric - NEMSCHOFF, INC.; *pg.* 936, *pg.* 1890
RENAISSANCE - Traditional Kitchen Cabinets & Designs - WM OHS INC.; *pg.* 947, *pg.* 324
RENAISSANCE CLASSIC - Organs - ALLEN ORGAN COMPANY; *pg.* 527, *pg.* 1549
RENAISSANCE CLASSROOM RESPONSE SYSTEM - Software - RENAISSANCE LEARNING, INC.; *pg.* 607, *pg.* 1899
RENAISSANCE PIPE - Pipe Organs - ALLEN ORGAN COMPANY; *pg.* 527, *pg.* 1549
RENAISSANCE PLACE - Educational Materials - RENAISSANCE LEARNING, INC.; *pg.* 607, *pg.* 1899
RENAISSANCE QUANTUM - Organs - ALLEN ORGAN COMPANY; *pg.* 527, *pg.* 1549
RENAISSANCE THEATRE - Organs - ALLEN ORGAN COMPANY; *pg.* 527, *pg.* 1549
RENAKARE - Animal Safety Product - NEOGEN CORPORATION; *pg.* 883, *pg.* 896
RENALCAL - Food & Beverage Product - NESTLE USA, INC.; *pg.* 883, *pg.* 96
RENALPURE - Liquid Acid Concentrate - ROCKWELL MEDICAL TECHNOLOGIES, INC.; *pg.* 1590, *pg.* 913
RENALSOFT - Software Module - BAXTER INTERNATIONAL INC.; *pg.* 1499, *pg.* 599
RENARD - Automotive Electronics - WAIGLOBAL; *pg.* 221, *pg.* 1585
RENATA - Furniture - NEMSCHOFF, INC.; *pg.* 936, *pg.* 1890
RENATA CELINI - Diamonds - ICE.COM, INC.; *pg.* 1258, *pg.* 1955
RENAZORB - Ceramic Nanomaterial Product - ALTAIR NANOTECHNOLOGIES INC.; *pg.* 1147, *pg.* 1031
RENCAST - Casting System - HUNTSMAN CORPORATION; *pg.* 1167, *pg.* 1758
RENDER BEAST - Image Generator - EVANS & SUTHERLAND COMPUTER CORPORATION; *pg.* 638, *pg.* 1757
RENDERMAN - Computer Graphics Software - PIXAR ANIMATION STUDIOS; *pg.* 304, *pg.* 85
RENDERMAN ARTIST TOOLS - Graphics Software Suite - PIXAR ANIMATION STUDIOS; *pg.* 304, *pg.* 85
RENDERMAN FOR MAYA - Computer Graphics Software - PIXAR ANIMATION STUDIOS; *pg.* 304, *pg.* 85
RENDERMAN PRO SERVER - Artist Desktop Software - PIXAR ANIMATION STUDIOS; *pg.* 304, *pg.* 85
RENDEZVOUS - Furniture - ASHLEY FURNITURE INDUSTRIES, INC.; *pg.* 914, *pg.* 1852
RENDEZVOUS - Fabric - NEMSCHOFF, INC.; *pg.* 936, *pg.* 1890
RENDEZVOUS - Computer Software - TIBCO SOFTWARE INC.; *pg.* 484, *pg.* 178
RENDITION - Circuit - MICRON TECHNOLOGY, INC.; *pg.* 435, *pg.* 547
RENDITION - Fabric - NEMSCHOFF, INC.; *pg.* 936, *pg.* 1890
RENDITIONS - Bath & Plumbing Product - JACUZZI BRANDS CORPORATION; *pg.* 554, *pg.* 65
RENDURA - Wallcovering - OMNOVA SOLUTIONS INC; *pg.* 1176, *pg.* 1453
RENE JUNOT - Wine - REMY COINTREAU USA INC.; *pg.* 1969, *pg.* 1285
RENEE BEAUTY - Hair Salons - REGIS CORPORATION; *pg.* 521, *pg.* 941
RENEGADE - Monitor - AKRON BRASS COMPANY; *pg.* 1311, *pg.* 1482
RENEGADE - Airbrushes - BADGER AIR BRUSH COMPANY; *pg.* 359, *pg.* 612
RENEGADE - Medical Device - BOSTON SCIENTIFIC CORPORATION; *pg.* 1508, *pg.* 831
RENEGADE - Battery - ENERSYS INC.; *pg.* 1334, *pg.* 1584
RENEGADE - Eye Protection - MCR SAFETY; *pg.* 1422, *pg.* 1630
RENEGADE - Grill Guards - THE PERRY COMPANY; *pg.* 706, *pg.* 1749
RENEGADE - Vibratory Plow - VERMEER MANUFACTURING COMPANY; *pg.* 708, *pg.* 711
RENEGADE - Agricultural Product - WILBUR-ELLIS COMPANY; *pg.* 1185, *pg.* 234
RENESE - Medicine - PFIZER INC.; *pg.* 1581, *pg.* 1278
RENESSEN - Seeds - CARGILL LIMITED; *pg.* 1475, *pg.* 1914
RENEW - Dry Cleaning & Laundry Product - ADCO, INC.; *pg.* 325, *pg.* 482
RENEW - Concrete Treatment - FMC CORPORATION; *pg.* 1163, *pg.* 1564
RENEW - Testing System - MTS SYSTEMS CORPORATION; *pg.* 442, *pg.* 923
RENEW & REFRESH - Skin Care - AVON PRODUCTS, INC.; *pg.* 500, *pg.* 1198
RENEWAL BY ANDERSEN - Window Replacement Line - ANDERSEN CORPORATION; *pg.* 67, *pg.* 916
RENEX - Chemical Product - SPECTRUM CHEMICALS & LABORATORY PRODUCTS, INC.; *pg.* 1181, *pg.* 94
RENGEM - Gelcoat System - HUNTSMAN CORPORATION; *pg.* 1167, *pg.* 1758
RENLAM - Laminating System - HUNTSMAN CORPORATION; *pg.* 1167, *pg.* 1758
RENNER AIR - Apparel - OAKLEY, INC.; *pg.* 1840, *pg.* 86
RENNIE - Fabric - NEMSCHOFF, INC.; *pg.* 936, *pg.* 1890
RENO - Furniture - FLEXSTEEL INDUSTRIES, INC.; *pg.* 925, *pg.* 707
RENO MATTRESSES - Erosion Control Devices - MACCAFERRI, INC.; *pg.* 95, *pg.* 780
RENOIR RICHES - Video Game - INTERNATIONAL GAME TECHNOLOGY; *pg.* 957, *pg.* 1024
RENOLD GEARBOXES - Custom Made Gear Reducers for Industry - RENOLD, INC.; *pg.* 1371, *pg.* 1351
RENOVA - Healthcare Product - JOHNSON & JOHNSON; *pg.* 1549, *pg.* 1091
RENOVA - Dental Implant System - LIFECORE BIOMEDICAL, LLC; *pg.* 1556, *pg.* 920
RENOVATE - Reengineering Methodology - CACI INTERNATIONAL INC.; *pg.* 367, *pg.* 1773
RENOVATION - Carpet - BEAULIEU GROUP, LLC; *pg.* 917, *pg.* 529
RENOVATION STYLE - Magazine - MEREDITH CORPORATION; *pg.* 1663, *pg.* 705
RENOVATOR - Cleaning Product - HILLYARD, INC.; *pg.* 331, *pg.* 990
RENOVISIONS - Furniture Lift System - INTERFACE, INC.; *pg.* 695, *pg.* 512
RENOWNED - Fabric - NEMSCHOFF, INC.; *pg.* 936, *pg.*

First page reference indicates Business Class Edition
Second page reference indicates Geographic Edition

1890

RENPASTE - Modelling & Tooling Pastes - HUNTSMAN CORPORATION; *pg.* 1167, *pg.* 1758

RENPIM - Prototyping Materials - HUNTSMAN CORPORATION; *pg.* 1167, *pg.* 1758

RENSHAPE - Synthetic Materials - HUNTSMAN CORPORATION; *pg.* 1167, *pg.* 1758

RENT-A-TECH - Software - ENVIRONMENTAL SYSTEMS RESEARCH INSTITUTE INC.; *pg.* 393, *pg.* 188

RENTAL BUSINESS TODAY - Publication - INFORMA EXHIBITIONS LLC; *pg.* 1653, *pg.* 17

RENTAL-ZIP - Fluid Handling System - GRACO, INC.; *pg.* 1342, *pg.* 935

RENTALCARS.COM - Car Rental Booking Platform - THE PRICELINE GROUP INC.; *pg.* 1276, *pg.* 364

RENTALMAN - Software - UNITED RENTALS, INC.; *pg.* 1386, *pg.* 350

RENTALPRO - Fluid Handling System - GRACO, INC.; *pg.* 1342, *pg.* 935

RENTALS.COM - Website - RENTPATH, INC.; *pg.* 1680, *pg.* 538

RENTJILLSHOUSE.COM - Advertising Website - DOMINION ENTERPRISES; *pg.* 1636, *pg.* 1796

RENTNET.COM - Website - MOVE, INC.; *pg.* 1268, *pg.* 247

RENTRAK - Software - RENTRAK CORPORATION; *pg.* 306, *pg.* 1506

RENU - Soft Contact Lens Care - BAUSCH & LOMB INCORPORATED; *pg.* 1401, *pg.* 1045

RENUAC - Pharmaceutical Preparation - PFIZER INC.; *pg.* 1581, *pg.* 1278

RENUCARES.COM - Website - BAUSCH & LOMB INCORPORATED; *pg.* 1401, *pg.* 1045

RENUVA - Resource Technology - THE DOW CHEMICAL COMPANY; *pg.* 1157, *pg.* 898

RENUZIT - Air Fresheners - HENKEL CONSUMER GOODS; *pg.* 511, *pg.* 22

RENVAC - Vacuum Loading System - HI-VAC CORPORATION; *pg.* 56, *pg.* 1458

RENZE - Seeds - DOW AGROSCIENCES LLC; *pg.* 1156, *pg.* 684

REO - Disc Backup & Recovery Appliances - OVERLAND STORAGE, INC.; *pg.* 451, *pg.* 205

REO 1550 - Data Backup & Recovery - OVERLAND STORAGE, INC.; *pg.* 451, *pg.* 205

REO 4500 - Data Backup & Recovery - OVERLAND STORAGE, INC.; *pg.* 451, *pg.* 205

REO 4500C - Data Backup & Recovery - OVERLAND STORAGE, INC.; *pg.* 451, *pg.* 205

REO 9100 - Data Backup & Recovery - OVERLAND STORAGE, INC.; *pg.* 451, *pg.* 205

REO 9100C - Data Backup & Recovery - OVERLAND STORAGE, INC.; *pg.* 451, *pg.* 205

REO 9500D - Data Backup & Recovery - OVERLAND STORAGE, INC.; *pg.* 451, *pg.* 205

REO MANAGER - Financial Services - FEDERAL HOME LOAN MORTGAGE CORPORATION; *pg.* 751, *pg.* 1790

REO MULTISITEPAC - Software - OVERLAND STORAGE, INC.; *pg.* 451, *pg.* 205

REO PROTECTION OS - Software - OVERLAND STORAGE, INC.; *pg.* 451, *pg.* 205

REOFLEX - Liquid Rubber - SMOOTH-ON INC.; *pg.* 111, *pg.* 1528

REOFOS - Flame Retardants - CHEMTURA CORPORATION; *pg.* 1152, *pg.* 355

REOGARD - Flame Retardants - CHEMTURA CORPORATION; *pg.* 1152, *pg.* 355

REOPRO - Abciximab, Centocor - ELI LILLY AND COMPANY; *pg.* 1527, *pg.* 684

REORG PLUS - Software - BMC SOFTWARE, INC.; *pg.* 362, *pg.* 1701

REP-CAL - Pet Product - PETSMART, INC.; *pg.* 1481, *pg.* 18

REPAIRDISK MANAGER - Software Product - RAXCO SOFTWARE, INC.; *pg.* 459, *pg.* 770

REPEAT - Apparel - OAKLEY, INC.; *pg.* 1840, *pg.* 86

REPEATER - Laboratory Product - EPPENDORF NORTH AMERICA; *pg.* 1412, *pg.* 1164

REPEL - Safety Product - WISCONSIN PHARMACAL COMPANY, LLC; *pg.* 1610, *pg.* 1861

REPELLO - Concrete System - L.M. SCOFIELD COMPANY; *pg.* 94, *pg.* 134

REPETE - Recycled Polyester Resin - THE GOODYEAR TIRE & RUBBER COMPANY; *pg.* 1883, *pg.* 1401

REPHRESH - Pharmaceutical Product - JUNIPER PHARMACEUTICALS; *pg.* 1552, *pg.* 797

REPICCI - Knee System - ZIMMER BIOMET HOLDINGS, INC.; *pg.* 1611, *pg.* 699

REPICCI II UNICONDYLAR KNEE SYSTEM - Knee Product - ZIMMER BIOMET HOLDINGS, INC.; *pg.* 1611, *pg.* 699

REPLACE-ME - Toothbrush - RANIR LLC; *pg.* 520, *pg.* 888

REPLACEMENT NEWAGE - Voltage Regulators - FLIGHT SYSTEMS, INC.; *pg.* 1337, *pg.* 1548

REPLAY - Reconditioned Parts - DAKTRONICS, INC.; *pg.* 633, *pg.* 1624

REPLETE - Food & Beverage Product - NESTLE USA, INC.; *pg.* 883, *pg.* 96

REPLICARE - Medical & Aesthetic Product - DYNATRONICS CORPORATION; *pg.* 1526, *pg.* 1757

REPLICARE - Software - EMC CORPORATION; *pg.* 391, *pg.* 825

REPLICATION - Server - SAP; *pg.* 465, *pg.* 78

REPLICATION CAPACITY - Healthcare Product - MONOGRAM BIOSCIENCES, INC.; *pg.* 1569, *pg.* 280

REPLICATION EXEC - Software - SYMANTEC CORPORATION; *pg.* 478, *pg.* 161

REPLICATION EXPRESS - Computer Software - AVAGO TECHNOLOGIES; *pg.* 358, *pg.* 238

REPLICOPY - Xerographic - XPEDX; *pg.* 1473, *pg.* 1377

REPLIFAX - Fax Paper - XPEDX; *pg.* 1473, *pg.* 1377

REPLIFORM - Medical Device - BOSTON SCIENTIFIC CORPORATION; *pg.* 1508, *pg.* 831

REPLIFORM - Computer Paper - XPEDX; *pg.* 1473, *pg.* 1377

REPLISTOR - Software System - EMC CORPORATION; *pg.* 391, *pg.* 825

REPLY - Office Furniture - STEELCASE INC.; *pg.* 475, *pg.* 889

REPORT - Apparel - OAKLEY, INC.; *pg.* 1840, *pg.* 86

REPORT BUILDER - Software - DAEGIS INC; *pg.* 381, *pg.* 195

REPORT DESIGNER - Reporting Tool - NIELSEN AUDIO; *pg.* 446, *pg.* 768

REPORT MANAGER - Software - VULCAN, INC.; *pg.* 687, *pg.* 5

REPORT PARTNER - Communication Product - CENTURYLINK, INC; *pg.* 1870, *pg.* 317

REPORT SERVER - Software Product & Module - RIVERBED PERFORMANCE MANAGEMENT; *pg.* 462, *pg.* 765

REPORT SERVICES - Software - MICROSTRATEGY, INC.; *pg.* 1266, *pg.* 1809

REPORTADMIN FOR ACS - Software - DELL SOFTWARE; *pg.* 385, *pg.* 40

REPORTBUILDER - Software - R.R. DONNELLEY & SONS COMPANY; *pg.* 1682, *pg.* 589

REPORTER - Software - DELL SOFTWARE; *pg.* 385, *pg.* 40

REPORTER - Pump Product - IDEX CORPORATION; *pg.* 1347, *pg.* 623

REPORTER EXPRESS - Software - DELL SOFTWARE; *pg.* 385, *pg.* 40

REPORTING MADE EASY - Tagline - PROCESS ACADEMY, INC.; *pg.* 456, *pg.* 1951

REPORTIT - Software - BIO-RAD LABORATORIES, INC.; *pg.* 1504, *pg.* 101

REPORTLINK - Software - PAYCHEX, INC.; *pg.* 792, *pg.* 1336

REPORTS IMPACT MANAGER - Software - BMC SOFTWARE, INC.; *pg.* 362, *pg.* 1701

REPOVAC - Medical Device - GAMMEX RMI INC.; *pg.* 1532, *pg.* 1872

REPOWER - Prepaid Card - MASTERCARD INCORPORATED; *pg.* 779, *pg.* 1325

REPOWERING AMERICA - Generation of Electric Power - CALPINE CORPORATION; *pg.* 1936, *pg.* 1702

REPREXAIN - Pharmaceutical Product - ALLERGAN; *pg.* 1490, *pg.* 1101

REPRISE - Paper & Nonwoven Material - FIBERMARK INC.; *pg.* 1457, *pg.* 1764

REPRISE - Record Label - WARNER MUSIC GROUP CORP.; *pg.* 590, *pg.* 1313

REPROGRAPH - Apparel - OAKLEY, INC.; *pg.* 1840, *pg.* 86

REPRORUBBER - Rubber Dimensional Transfer Material - FLEXBAR MACHINE CORP.; *pg.* 1337, *pg.* 1169

REPROSIL - Dental Product - DENTSPLY INTERNATIONAL INC.; *pg.* 1522, *pg.* 1596

REPROVEL - Chart & Marking System - GRAPHIC CONTROLS LLC; *pg.* 401, *pg.* 1148

REPTILES MAGAZINE - Magazine - I-5 PUBLISHING LLC; *pg.* 1651, *pg.* 133

REPUBLIC - Shoe - AEROGROUP INTERNATIONAL, INC.; *pg.* 1803, *pg.* 1055

REPUBLIC - Tire And Rubber Product - THE GOODYEAR TIRE & RUBBER COMPANY; *pg.* 1883, *pg.* 1401

REPUBLIC - Apparel - OAKLEY, INC.; *pg.* 1840, *pg.* 86

REPUBLICANS FOR CHOICE - Awareness Program - PLANNED PARENTHOOD FEDERATION OF AMERICA, INC.; *pg.* 154, *pg.* 1282

REPUTATION - Food Products - NATIONAL FRUIT PRODUCT COMPANY, INC.; *pg.* 882, *pg.* 1811

REQDIRECT - Software - XEROX CORPORATION; *pg.* 494, *pg.* 365

REQDIRECT PLUS AND DESIGN - Software - XEROX CORPORATION; *pg.* 494, *pg.* 365

REQUEST SWITCHING - Software - CITRIX SYSTEMS, INC.; *pg.* 375, *pg.* 424

REQUIRE - Herbicide - E.I. DU PONT DE NEMOURS & COMPANY; *pg.* 1159, *pg.* 390

REQUIREMENTS - Apparel - HAMPSHIRE GROUP LIMITED; *pg.* 25, *pg.* 1237

RES 4.0 - Software - MICROS SYSTEMS, INC.; *pg.* 435, *pg.* 768

RES-N-GEL - Oil Painting Medium - MARTIN/F. WEBER COMPANY; *pg.* 962, *pg.* 1567

RES-Q - On-Site Ion Exchange Resin Cleaning - GE WATER & PROCESS TECHNOLOGIES; *pg.* 1339, *pg.* 1588

RESALARM - Medical Device - RESMED INC.; *pg.* 1589, *pg.* 207

RESAMIN - Solventborne - CYTEC INDUSTRIES, INC.; *pg.* 1155, *pg.* 1131

RESCAL - Pressed & Monolithic Refractory - RESCO PRODUCTS, INC.; *pg.* 107, *pg.* 1581

RESCAP - Medical Device - RESMED INC.; *pg.* 1589, *pg.* 207

RESCH - Computer Programs - GLEASON CORPORATION; *pg.* 1340, *pg.* 1335

RESCOAT - Pressed & Monolithic Refractory - RESCO PRODUCTS, INC.; *pg.* 107, *pg.* 1581

RESCOBOND - Pressed & Monolithic Refractory - RESCO PRODUCTS, INC.; *pg.* 107, *pg.* 1581

RESCOCAST - Pressed & Monolithic Refractory - RESCO PRODUCTS, INC.; *pg.* 107, *pg.* 1581

RESCOGUN - Pressed & Monolithic Refractory - RESCO PRODUCTS, INC.; *pg.* 107, *pg.* 1581

RESCOMAG - Pressed & Monolithic Refractory - RESCO PRODUCTS, INC.; *pg.* 107, *pg.* 1581

RESCONTROL - Medical Device - RESMED INC.; *pg.* 1589, *pg.* 207

RESCONTROL II - Medical Device - RESMED INC.; *pg.* 1589, *pg.* 207

RESCORAM - Pressed & Monolithic Refractory - RESCO PRODUCTS, INC.; *pg.* 107, *pg.* 1581

RESCOSET - Pressed & Monolithic Refractory - RESCO PRODUCTS, INC.; *pg.* 107, *pg.* 1581

RESCRIPTOR - Medicine - PFIZER INC.; *pg.* 1581, *pg.* 1278

RESCUE - Sports Drink - ENERGY BRANDS, INC.; *pg.* 854, *pg.* 1227

RESCUE LINK - Medical Software - CARDIAC SCIENCE CORPORATION; *pg.* 1512, *pg.* 1897

RESCUE READY - Medical Apparatus - CARDIAC SCIENCE CORPORATION; *pg.* 1512, *pg.* 1897

RESCUE ROOTER - Plumbing & Drain System Services - THE SERVICEMASTER COMPANY, LLC; *pg.* 335, *pg.* 1646

RESCUE ROVER - Video Game - ID SOFTWARE, INC.; *pg.* 956, *pg.* 1727

RESCUENET - Data Management Product - ZOLL MEDICAL CORPORATION; *pg.* 1612, *pg.* 814

RESCUEPRO - Software - SANDISK CORPORATION; *pg.* 465, *pg.* 147

RESCUEREADY - Patient Monitoring System - CRITICARE SYSTEMS, INC.; *pg.* 1520, *pg.* 1897

RESEARCH - Control Valve - BADGER METER, INC.; *pg.* 1401, *pg.* 1873

RESEARCH CONTROL - Precision Control Valves - BADGER METER, INC.; *pg.* 1401, *pg.* 1873

THE RESEARCH GROUP - Research Services - TRUVEN HEALTH ANALYTICS; *pg.* 1696, *pg.* 867

RESEARCH INSIGHT - Reference Tool - STANDARD & POOR'S RATINGS SERVICES; *pg.* 805, *pg.* 1296

RESEARCH INSIGHT ON THE WEB - Reference Tool - STANDARD & POOR'S RATINGS SERVICES; *pg.* 805, *pg.* 1296

RESERVATION BLACKJACK - Games - PENN NATIONAL GAMING, INC.; *pg.* 574, *pg.* 1595

RESERVATION BLACKJACK&DESIGN - Games - PENN NATIONAL GAMING, INC.; *pg.* 574, *pg.* 1595

RESERVE ALEXANDRE - Wine - GEYSER PEAK WINERY; *pg.* 1964, *pg.* 101

RESERVE AMERICA - Retail Shopping Network - IAC/INTERACTIVECORP; *pg.* 292, *pg.* 1242
RESERVOIR DOGS - Motion Pictures - LIONS GATE ENTERTAINMENT CORP.; *pg.* 296, *pg.* 274
RESFLOR - Broad-Spectrum Antibiotic - MERCK & CO., INC.; *pg.* 1566, *pg.* 1077
RESGEN - Molecular Biology Product - THERMO FISHER SCIENTIFIC INC.; *pg.* 1602, *pg.* 61
RESI-BOND - Resin Used in the Manufacture of Paper & Paperboard - GEORGIA-PACIFIC LLC; *pg.* 1458, *pg.* 507
RESI-MIX - Plywood Adhesive - GEORGIA-PACIFIC LLC; *pg.* 1458, *pg.* 507
RESI-STRAN - Resins for Use in the Manufacture of Oriented Strand Board - GEORGIA-PACIFIC LLC; *pg.* 1458, *pg.* 507
RESIDENCE INN - Hotel Chain - MARRIOTT INTERNATIONAL, INC.; *pg.* 1102, *pg.* 764
RESIDENT ENGINEER FOR NOC - Global Services - SONUS NETWORKS INC.; *pg.* 1281, *pg.* 858
RESIDENTIAL BUILDING BASICS - Workbook - VALE NATIONAL TRAINING CENTER INC.; *pg.* 610, *pg.* 1660
RESIDENTIAL LIGHTING - Magazine - VANCE PUBLISHING CORPORATION; *pg.* 1699, *pg.* 627
RESIDERM - Skin Disorder Treatment Technology - ULURU INC.; *pg.* 1603, *pg.* 1658
RESILIENCE - Lifetime Finish (Polished Brass & Brushed Nickel) - GERBER PLUMBING FIXTURES CORPORATION; *pg.* 84, *pg.* 672
RESILIENCE - Cleaning Product - HILLYARD, INC.; *pg.* 331, *pg.* 990
RESILIENCE - Paint - THE SHERWIN-WILLIAMS COMPANY; *pg.* 1447, *pg.* 1435
RESILIENTFLEX - Electronic Components - MOLEX INCORPORATED; *pg.* 655, *pg.* 628
RESILINE - Dental Product - DENTSPLY INTERNATIONAL INC.; *pg.* 1522, *pg.* 1596
RESILITEX - Foam - FXI; *pg.* 1163, *pg.* 1552
RESINEX - Plastics Product - AEP INDUSTRIES INC.; *pg.* 1878, *pg.* 1085
RESINITE - Film - AEP INDUSTRIES INC.; *pg.* 1878, *pg.* 1085
RESINITE HI LO - Plastics Product - AEP INDUSTRIES INC.; *pg.* 1878, *pg.* 1085
RESIST-A-BALL - Fitness Product - BALLY TOTAL FITNESS HOLDINGS CORPORATION; *pg.* 532, *pg.* 1200
RESIST-TORR - Cluster Tool Profiler - MKS INSTRUMENTS, INC.; *pg.* 1362, *pg.* 781
RESISTANCE - Supplement & Food Product - NEW EARTH LIFE SCIENCES, INC.; *pg.* 1573, *pg.* 1499
RESISTE - Specialty Paper - APPVION INC.; *pg.* 1451, *pg.* 1852
RESISTOHM - Alloy Product - SPECIAL METALS CORPORATION; *pg.* 1377, *pg.* 1850
RESISTORUST - Metal Primer - PETTIT PAINT COMPANY; *pg.* 1444, *pg.* 1116
RESKU - Fabric - INTERFACE, INC.; *pg.* 695, *pg.* 512
RESLINK - Medical Device - RESMED INC.; *pg.* 1589, *pg.* 207
RESLINK - Flow Control Devices - SCHLUMBERGER LIMITED; *pg.* 801, *pg.* 1714
RESMED - Medical Device - RESMED INC.; *pg.* 1589, *pg.* 207
RESNARE - Medical Device - COOK GROUP, INC.; *pg.* 1518, *pg.* 674
RESOLUT - Oral Health Product - W.L. GORE & ASSOCIATES, INC.; *pg.* 122, *pg.* 388
RESOLUTE - Chromatography Product - PALL CORPORATION; *pg.* 232, *pg.* 1323
RESOLUTION - Medical Device - BOSTON SCIENTIFIC CORPORATION; *pg.* 1508, *pg.* 831
RESOLUTION - Navigation Aid - TRIMBLE NAVIGATION LIMITED; *pg.* 1384, *pg.* 288
RESOLUTION ACCELERATOR - Software - VITRIA TECHNOLOGY, INC.; *pg.* 490, *pg.* 289
THE RESOLUTION EXPERTS - Slogan - JAMS, THE RESOLUTION EXPERTS; *pg.* 423, *pg.* 111
RESOLVE - Herbicide - E.I. DU PONT DE NEMOURS & COMPANY; *pg.* 1159, *pg.* 390
RESOLVE - Furniture System - HERMAN MILLER, INC.; *pg.* 926, *pg.* 913
RESOLVE - Carpet Cleaning Product - RECKITT BENCKISER INC.; *pg.* 1136, *pg.* 1105
RESOLVE - Analytical Column - WATERS CORPORATION; *pg.* 1436, *pg.* 834
RESOLVER - Food Ingredient - WILD FLAVORS, INC.; *pg.* 910, *pg.* 728
RESON8 - Speaker - SDI TECHNOLOGIES, INC.; *pg.* 671, *pg.* 1113
RESORSABOND - Resin Adhesive - GEORGIA-PACIFIC LLC; *pg.* 1458, *pg.* 507
THE RESORT AT SINGER ISLAND - Community Name - WCI COMMUNITIES, INC.; *pg.* 1118, *pg.* 414
RESORT CRUISING - On-Shore Resort Facilities - COSTA CRUISE LINES N.V.; *pg.* 1904, *pg.* 431
RESORTS & GREAT HOTELS - Magazine - BONNIER CORPORATION; *pg.* 1622, *pg.* 480
RE:SOURCE - Fabric & Flooring - INTERFACE, INC.; *pg.* 695, *pg.* 512
RESOURCE - Medical Product - MEDLINE INDUSTRIES, INC.; *pg.* 1562, *pg.* 635
RESOURCE - Floor Boxes - WIREMOLD/LEGRAND; *pg.* 689, *pg.* 383
RESOURCEFUL BY NATURE - Slogan - ARCHER-DANIELS-MIDLAND COMPANY; *pg.* 825, *pg.* 565
RESOURCEPAK - Software - EMC CORPORATION; *pg.* 391, *pg.* 825
RESOURCES FOR COLLEGE LIBRARIES - Curriculum Development, Student Research, Reference & Bibliographic Data - R.R. BOWKER LLC; *pg.* 1682, *pg.* 1095
RESOURCES FOR ENRICHING LIVES - Tagline - CHS INC.; *pg.* 702, *pg.* 926
RESOURCESMART - Design Practices - MAXIM INTEGRATED PRODUCTS, INC.; *pg.* 653, *pg.* 247
RESPIGAM - Respiratory Syncytial Virus Immune Globulin Intravenous (Human) - MEDIMMUNE LLC; *pg.* 1562, *pg.* 770
RESPIN PLUNDER - Game - WMS INDUSTRIES INC.; *pg.* 593, *pg.* 666
RESPIR-ALL - Nutritional Product - NOW HEALTH GROUP, INC.; *pg.* 1576, *pg.* 557
RESPIRATORY HEALTHWAYS - Disease Management - HEALTHWAYS, INC.; *pg.* 1540, *pg.* 1632
RESPIRGARD II - Medication Nebulizer - VITAL SIGNS, INC.; *pg.* 1607, *pg.* 1126
RESPISURE - Pharmaceutical Product - PFIZER INC.; *pg.* 1581, *pg.* 1278
RESPISURE-ONE - Pharmaceutical Product - PFIZER INC.; *pg.* 1581, *pg.* 1278
RESPIVENT - Pharmaceutical Product - CHIESI USA, INC.; *pg.* 1515, *pg.* 1359
RESPONDENT PRESERVATION INITIATIVE - Industry-Wide Program - SURVEY SAMPLING INTERNATIONAL LLC; *pg.* 1690, *pg.* 371
RESPONDER - Radio Frequency Electronics - DEI HOLDINGS, INC.; *pg.* 633, *pg.* 302
RESPONDER - Shoes - MASON COMPANIES, INC.; *pg.* 1811, *pg.* 1856
RESPONDER - Air Purifying Respirator - MINE SAFETY APPLIANCES COMPANY; *pg.* 1361, *pg.* 1525
RESPONDER - Communication Product - RAULAND-BORG CORPORATION; *pg.* 666, *pg.* 634
RESPONDER 4000 - Health Care Communication System - RAULAND-BORG CORPORATION; *pg.* 666, *pg.* 634
RESPONDER IV - Health Care Communication System - RAULAND-BORG CORPORATION; *pg.* 666, *pg.* 634
RESPONDER NET - Health Care Communication System - RAULAND-BORG CORPORATION; *pg.* 666, *pg.* 634
RESPONSE - Software - AUTONOMY, INC.; *pg.* 358, *pg.* 212
RESPONSE - Baseball Bat - HILLERICH & BRADSBY CO., INC.; *pg.* 1836, *pg.* 576
RESPONSE - Veterinary Food - IAMS COMPANY; *pg.* 1477, *pg.* 1633
RESPONSE - Escape Hood - MINE SAFETY APPLIANCES COMPANY; *pg.* 1361, *pg.* 1525
RESPONSE - Apparel - OAKLEY, INC.; *pg.* 1840, *pg.* 86
RESPONSE - Electrophysiology Products - ST. JUDE MEDICAL, INC.; *pg.* 1596, *pg.* 963
RESPONSE DX COLON - Medical Testing - RESPONSE GENETICS, INC.; *pg.* 1590, *pg.* 139
RESPONSE DX LUNGS - Mutation Analysis - RESPONSE GENETICS, INC.; *pg.* 1590, *pg.* 139
RESPONSE IS EVERYTHING - Tag Line - SELECTIVE INSURANCE GROUP, INC.; *pg.* 1216, *pg.* 1045
RESPONSE LLC - Commercial Road Service - AMERICAN AUTOMOBILE ASSOCIATION; *pg.* 1190, *pg.* 429
RESPONSEDX - Diagnostic Test - RESPONSE GENETICS, INC.; *pg.* 1590, *pg.* 139
RESPONSEPAK - Fiber Drums from Fiber Board - SONOCO PRODUCTS COMPANY; *pg.* 1469, *pg.* 1619
RESPONSIBLE BY NATURE - Slogan - XCEL ENERGY INC.; *pg.* 1955, *pg.* 946
RESPONSIBLE CARE - Chemical Product - CARUS CORPORATION; *pg.* 1152, *pg.* 652
RESPONSIBLE CARE - Management System - CHEMTURA CORPORATION; *pg.* 1152, *pg.* 355
RESPONSIBLE CARE - Slogan - NOVA CHEMICALS CORPORATION; *pg.* 1175, *pg.* 1904
RESPONSIBLE CARE - Chemical System - SOCIETY OF CHEMICAL MNAUFACTURERS & AFFILIATES, INC.; *pg.* 156, *pg.* 404
RESPONSIBLE CHOICES - Awareness Program - PLANNED PARENTHOOD FEDERATION OF AMERICA, INC.; *pg.* 154, *pg.* 1282
RESPUESTAS BELLSOUTH - Slogan (Spanish) - AT&T SOUTHEAST; *pg.* 1868, *pg.* 489
RESQPOD - Circulation Product - ZOLL MEDICAL CORPORATION; *pg.* 1612, *pg.* 814
RESSCAN - Medical Device - RESMED INC.; *pg.* 1589, *pg.* 207
RESSUM - Software - SCHLUMBERGER LIMITED; *pg.* 801, *pg.* 1714
REST ASSURED - Personal Care Product - ROCHESTER MIDLAND CORPORATION; *pg.* 334, *pg.* 1337
RESTASIS - Eye Care Product - ALLERGAN, INC.; *pg.* 1491, *pg.* 106
RESTAURANT NEWS - Foodservice Publication - LEBHAR-FRIEDMAN INC.; *pg.* 1658, *pg.* 1250
RESTON - Foam Pads, Self Adhesive - 3M COMPANY; *pg.* 1142, *pg.* 956
RESTORA - Coating & Paint - AKZO NOBEL DECORATIVE PAINTS, USA; *pg.* 1439, *pg.* 1474
RESTORATION - Lighting Product - QUOIZEL INC.; *pg.* 1304, *pg.* 1616
RESTORATION PALE ALE - Beer - ABITA BREWING COMPANY; *pg.* 237, *pg.* 741
RESTORATIVE - Fabric - NEMSCHOFF, INC.; *pg.* 936, *pg.* 1890
RESTORE - Health Supplement - GARDEN OF LIFE, INC.; *pg.* 1532, *pg.* 478
RESTORE - Water Conditioning Agent & Aciifier - KALO, INC.; *pg.* 1796, *pg.* 719
RESTORE - Dental Implant System - LIFECORE BIOMEDICAL, LLC; *pg.* 1556, *pg.* 920
RESTORE-X - Healthcare Product - BAXTER INTERNATIONAL INC.; *pg.* 1499, *pg.* 599
RESTORER - Cleaner - HILLYARD, INC.; *pg.* 331, *pg.* 990
RESTORIL - Pharmaceutical Product - MALLINCKRODT PHARMACEUTICALS; *pg.* 1557, *pg.* 978
RESTPIRATION - Nutritional Supplement - WHITEWING LABS, INC.; *pg.* 1610, *pg.* 99
RESTRAXX - Medical Device - RESMED INC.; *pg.* 1589, *pg.* 207
RESTRICTED-CALORIE - Veterinary Food - IAMS COMPANY; *pg.* 1477, *pg.* 1633
RESTWELL - Furniture - HSM SOLUTIONS; *pg.* 1884, *pg.* 1378
RESULTANTE - Treatment Line - PARFUMS CHRISTIAN DIOR, INC; *pg.* 519, *pg.* 1276
RESULTS ARE JUST THE BEGINING - Slogan - VHA INC.; *pg.* 1606, *pg.* 1724
RESULTS-DRIVEN COMPUTING - Business Consulting Services - COMPUTER SCIENCES CORPORATION; *pg.* 378, *pg.* 1780
RESULTS PLUS - Patient Histories - IDEXX LABORATORIES, INC.; *pg.* 1543, *pg.* 753
RESULTS THROUGH THE POWER OF EXPERIENCE. - Tagline - THE JUDGE GROUP, INC.; *pg.* 424, *pg.* 1594
RESULTS TRAVEL - Leisure Travel - CARLSON COMPANIES INC.; *pg.* 1084, *pg.* 947
RESULTSONDEMAND-COMPENSATION - Software - SUMTOTAL SYSTEMS, INC.; *pg.* 477, *pg.* 429
RESULTSONDEMAND-LEARNING - Software - SUMTOTAL SYSTEMS, INC.; *pg.* 477, *pg.* 429
RESULTSONDEMAND-PERFORMANCE - Software - SUMTOTAL SYSTEMS, INC.; *pg.* 477, *pg.* 429
RESUMANIA - Consulting Services - ROBERT HALF INTERNATIONAL INC.; *pg.* 462, *pg.* 145
RESUSCITIMER - Breathing Monitor - ALLIED HEALTHCARE PRODUCTS, INC.; *pg.* 1491, *pg.* 990
RESVAC - Bovine Immunization Vaccine - PFIZER INC.; *pg.* 1581, *pg.* 1278
RESVIEW - Medical Device - RESMED INC.; *pg.* 1589, *pg.* 207
RESX - Booking Tool - CONCUR TECHNOLOGIES; *pg.*

1903, *pg.* 501
RESYDROL - Waterborne - CYTEC INDUSTRIES, INC.; *pg.* 1155, *pg.* 1131
RET - Electronic Transmitter - BADGER METER, INC.; *pg.* 1401, *pg.* 1873
RETAIL CONNECTION - Account Specific Promotion - VALASSIS COMMUNICATIONS, INC.; *pg.* 1287, *pg.* 897
RETAIL DIRECT - Software - NIELSEN AUDIO; *pg.* 446, *pg.* 768
RETAIL ESSENTIALS - Software - RENTRAK CORPORATION; *pg.* 306, *pg.* 1506
RETAIL METHOD OF PAYMENT - Software System - IMS HEALTH, INC.; *pg.* 1544, *pg.* 344
RETAIL METHOD OF PAYMENT REPORT - Software Solution - IMS HEALTH, INC.; *pg.* 1544, *pg.* 344
RETAIL-PRO - Cold Storage Doors - JAMISON DOOR COMPANY; *pg.* 89, *pg.* 771
RETAIL PROFILING SYSTEM - Reporting Tool - NIELSEN AUDIO; *pg.* 446, *pg.* 768
RETAIL SPENDING POWER - Reporting Tool - NIELSEN AUDIO; *pg.* 446, *pg.* 768
RETAILDIRECT - Tool - NIELSEN AUDIO; *pg.* 446, *pg.* 768
RETAILRIGHT - Process Developed by Emery - EMERY-WATERHOUSE COMPANY; *pg.* 1047, *pg.* 751
RETAIN - Plastic Resin - THE DOW CHEMICAL COMPANY; *pg.* 1157, *pg.* 898
RETAIN - Minerals - MINERALS TECHNOLOGIES INC.; *pg.* 1173, *pg.* 617
RETAN - Acrylic Syntan - DOW CHEMICAL; *pg.* 1156, *pg.* 1563
RETARDER - Polymer Product - CHEMTURA CORPORATION; *pg.* 1152, *pg.* 355
RETARDINE - Dye Assistant - HENKEL CORPORATION; *pg.* 1165, *pg.* 1535
RETARDO - Paint And Stain Product - BENJAMIN MOORE & CO.; *pg.* 1440, *pg.* 1085
RETHINKING STRESS - Workshop - FRANKLIN COVEY CO.; *pg.* 1642, *pg.* 1758
RETICONE - Testing Instrument System - BECKMAN COULTER, INC.; *pg.* 1402, *pg.* 48
RETIMER - Software - AUTODESK INC.; *pg.* 356, *pg.* 257
RETIN-A MICRO - Healthcare Product - JOHNSON & JOHNSON; *pg.* 1549, *pg.* 1091
RETINA - Display - APPLE INC.; *pg.* 350, *pg.* 73
RETINA - Camera & Accessories - EASTMAN KODAK COMPANY; *pg.* 1408, *pg.* 1333
RETINAJECT - Subretinal Cannula - SURMODICS, INC.; *pg.* 1600, *pg.* 924
RETINAR - Lens - EASTMAN KODAK COMPANY; *pg.* 1408, *pg.* 1333
RETINETTE - Camera - EASTMAN KODAK COMPANY; *pg.* 1408, *pg.* 1333
RETINOMAX - Cordless Hand Held Auto Refract-Keratometer Refraction Measuring Devices - NIKON INC.; *pg.* 1424, *pg.* 1181
RETINYL A - Health Care Product - HEALTH PRODUCTS CORPORATION; *pg.* 1540, *pg.* 1356
RETIREMAX FLEX I - Fixed Annuity - NATIONAL LIFE INSURANCE COMPANY; *pg.* 1210, *pg.* 1766
RETIREMAX FLEX II - Fixed Annuity - NATIONAL LIFE INSURANCE COMPANY; *pg.* 1210, *pg.* 1766
RETIREMAX PREMIER + 1 - Fixed Annuity - NATIONAL LIFE INSURANCE COMPANY; *pg.* 1210, *pg.* 1766
RETIREMENT DIRECTIONS - Banking Services - THE PNC FINANCIAL SERVICES GROUP, INC.; *pg.* 795, *pg.* 1579
RETIREMENT HELP FOR LIFE - Slogan - FINANCIAL ENGINES, INC.; *pg.* 753, *pg.* 285
RETIREMENT SERVICE CENTER - Retirement Plans - PRINCIPAL FINANCIAL GROUP, INC.; *pg.* 796, *pg.* 706
RETISERT - Drug Implant - BAUSCH & LOMB INCORPORATED; *pg.* 1401, *pg.* 1045
RETORQUER - Cap Tightener - NEW ENGLAND MACHINERY, INC.; *pg.* 1364, *pg.* 415
RETOUCH COVER CREME - Cream - MERLE NORMAN COSMETICS, INC.; *pg.* 517, *pg.* 136
RETRACT-O-MATIC - Conversion Kit - ALLFLEX USA, INC.; *pg.* 1878, *pg.* 1717
RETRACTOFIT - Armature - HAMILTON CO., INC.; *pg.* 1415, *pg.* 1031
RETRACTOMASTER - Armature - HAMILTON CO., INC.; *pg.* 1415, *pg.* 1031
RETRACTOMATIC - Armature - HAMILTON CO., INC.; *pg.* 1415, *pg.* 1031
RETREAT - Furniture - ETHAN ALLEN INTERIORS INC.; *pg.* 924, *pg.* 343
RETRIEVALWARE - Information Retrieval Software - VERTICAL SEARCH WORKS INC.; *pg.* 489, *pg.* 1809
RETRIEVER - Storage/Retrieval Machine - DAIFUKU WEBB; *pg.* 1327, *pg.* 885
RETRIEVER - Satellite - HEIL ENVIRONMENTAL INDUSTRIES, LTD.; *pg.* 207, *pg.* 1629
RETRIEVER - Pet Food - TRACTOR SUPPLY COMPANY; *pg.* 708, *pg.* 1627
RETRO - Leather Product - COACH, INC.; *pg.* 3, *pg.* 1214
RETRO - Lighting - ETHAN ALLEN INTERIORS INC.; *pg.* 924, *pg.* 343
RETRO - Apparel - OAKLEY, INC.; *pg.* 1840, *pg.* 86
RETRO - Medical Device - SPIRE CORPORATION; *pg.* 1378, *pg.* 786
RETRO-FIT - Utility Board - JOHNS MANVILLE CORPORATION; *pg.* 89, *pg.* 320
RETRO-LINX - Broadband System Equipment - BLONDER TONGUE LABORATORIES, INC.; *pg.* 625, *pg.* 1100
RETRO ROCKER - Ride-ons - RADIO FLYER INC.; *pg.* 966, *pg.* 588
RETRO-SPEC - Workhorse Inspection System - PRESSCO TECHNOLOGY INC.; *pg.* 1370, *pg.* 1434
RETROBACK - Back Support System - THE ROHO GROUP; *pg.* 1591, *pg.* 556
RETROEASE - Custom Engineering of Cryopumps - BROOKS AUTOMATION, INC.; *pg.* 1320, *pg.* 813
RETROFAST - Electrical & Electronic Controls - BROOKS AUTOMATION, INC.; *pg.* 1320, *pg.* 813
RETROFIT TO CROSSOVER - LED Lighting - LSI INDUSTRIES INC.; *pg.* 58, *pg.* 1416
RETROPLEX - Premium TV Network Featuring Older Motion Pictures - STARZ ENTERTAINMENT, LLC; *pg.* 310, *pg.* 327
RETROSPECT - Software System - EMC CORPORATION; *pg.* 391, *pg.* 825
RETTRO - Footwear - STEVEN MADDEN, LTD.; *pg.* 1819, *pg.* 1176
RETURN OF THE TITANS - Game - WMS INDUSTRIES INC.; *pg.* 593, *pg.* 666
RETURN ON ENERGY - LED Technology - CREE INC.; *pg.* 631, *pg.* 1371
RETURN-RITE - Mold Base & Component - SUPERIOR DIE SET CORP.; *pg.* 1379, *pg.* 1885
RETURN TO CASTLE WOLFENSTEIN - Video Game - ID SOFTWARE, INC.; *pg.* 956, *pg.* 1727
RETURN TO PLANET LOOT - Game - WMS INDUSTRIES INC.; *pg.* 593, *pg.* 666
RETURN TO SENDER - Mailing Service - UNITED STATES POSTAL SERVICE; *pg.* 1009, *pg.* 406
RETURNING VALUE TO OUR CREDIT DRIVEN ECONOMY - Slogan - ASSET ACCEPTANCE CAPITAL CORP.; *pg.* 716, *pg.* 912
RETURNPLAY - Video Game - INTERNATIONAL GAME TECHNOLOGY; *pg.* 957, *pg.* 1024
REUNION - Office Furniture - STEELCASE INC.; *pg.* 475, *pg.* 889
REUNION NOMAD - Tables - STEELCASE INC.; *pg.* 475, *pg.* 889
REUNION RECORD - Yearbooks - HERFF JONES, INC.; *pg.* 7, *pg.* 686
REUTER SOAP - Soap - LANMAN & KEMP-BARCLAY CO., INC.; *pg.* 514, *pg.* 1132
REVACYCLE - Bevel Product - GLEASON CORPORATION; *pg.* 1340, *pg.* 1335
REVATIO - Medicine - PFIZER INC.; *pg.* 1581, *pg.* 1278
REV.CANVAS FRINGED CLOCHE - Hat - WOODEN SHIPS OF HOBOKEN; *pg.* 35, *pg.* 1315
REVEAL - Measures Nutrients In Real-Time - CARGILL, INC.; *pg.* 845, *pg.* 965
REVEAL - Light Bulbs - GENERAL ELECTRIC COMPANY; *pg.* 1297, *pg.* 347
REVEAL - Software - LATTICE SEMICONDUCTOR CORPORATION; *pg.* 651, *pg.* 1498
REVEAL - Fabric - NEMSCHOFF, INC.; *pg.* 936, *pg.* 1890
REVEAL - Food Safety Product - NEOGEN CORPORATION; *pg.* 883, *pg.* 896
REVEAL - Leak Detection System - UVP, INC.; *pg.* 1434, *pg.* 298
REVEL - Audio & Video Product - HARMAN INTERNATIONAL INDUSTRIES, INCORPORATED; *pg.* 641, *pg.* 374
REVEL - Revenue Assurance Software - LAVASTORM ANALYTICS; *pg.* 427, *pg.* 797
REVELATION - Orthopedic Implant Product - DJO SURGICAL; *pg.* 1525, *pg.* 1661
REVELATION HIP SYSTEM - Hip Implant - DJO SURGICAL; *pg.* 1525, *pg.* 1661
REVELL - Model Kits & Die-Cast Vehicles - REVELL; *pg.* 966, *pg.* 611
REVELL METAL BODY - Easy Glue Die-Cast Model Kits - REVELL; *pg.* 966, *pg.* 611
REVELLO - Ice Cream and Frozen Novelties - UNILEVER CANADA INC.; *pg.* 903, *pg.* 1946
REVELRY - Cleaning Product - ORECK CORPORATION; *pg.* 59, *pg.* 1653
REVELS - Food Product - MARS, INCORPORATED; *pg.* 1858, *pg.* 1792
REVERIE - Fabric - NEMSCHOFF, INC.; *pg.* 936, *pg.* 1890
REVERSAGE - Nutritional Supplement - RELIV INTERNATIONAL, INC.; *pg.* 1589, *pg.* 975
REVERSE - Orthopedic Implant Product - DJO SURGICAL; *pg.* 1525, *pg.* 1661
REVERSE-A-CLEAN - Reversible Tips for Paint Spray Guns - GRACO, INC.; *pg.* 1342, *pg.* 935
REVERSE-A-MATIC SYSTEM - Vehicle Safety System - GROTE INDUSTRIES, INC.; *pg.* 206, *pg.* 693
REVERSE OSMOSIS - Service Instrument - BAXTER INTERNATIONAL INC.; *pg.* 1499, *pg.* 599
REVERSET - Drug - INCYTE CORPORATION; *pg.* 1545, *pg.* 392
REVERSIFIT - Cover & Pad - HOME PRODUCTS INTERNATIONAL, INC.; *pg.* 1125, *pg.* 577
REVERT - Skate - ROLLER DERBY SKATE CORP.; *pg.* 966, *pg.* 630
REVERT ECO - Fragrance - RUE21, INC.; *pg.* 32, *pg.* 1591
REVEST - Refurbished & Restored Office Furniture - STEELCASE INC.; *pg.* 475, *pg.* 889
REVEX - Spiral Cutter - GLEASON CORPORATION; *pg.* 1340, *pg.* 1335
REVIEW AND PREVIEW - Financial Products - DOW JONES & COMPANY, INC.; *pg.* 1637, *pg.* 1225
REVISOR - Monitoring Security System - DIEBOLD, INCORPORATED; *pg.* 387, *pg.* 1407
REVIT - Software - SLOAN VALVE COMPANY; *pg.* 1062, *pg.* 613
REVIVAL - Kitchen Product - KOHLER CO.; *pg.* 91, *pg.* 1862
REVIVAL - Lighting Product - WESTINGHOUSE LIGHTING CORPORATION; *pg.* 687, *pg.* 1571
REVIVE - Sports Drink - ENERGY BRANDS, INC.; *pg.* 854, *pg.* 1227
REVIVEX - Water Repellent - MCNETT CORPORATION; *pg.* 1839, *pg.* 1817
REVIVEX - Water And Stain Repellent - W.L. GORE & ASSOCIATES, INC.; *pg.* 122, *pg.* 388
REVLON - Cosmetics - REVLON, INC.; *pg.* 521, *pg.* 1286
REVO - Medical Equipment - CONMED CORPORATION; *pg.* 1517, *pg.* 1347
REVO - Footwear - PHOENIX FOOTWEAR GROUP, INC.; *pg.* 1815, *pg.* 60
REVO - Performance Eyewear - SEQUENTIAL BRANDS GROUP, INC.; *pg.* 1395, *pg.* 1290
REVO FOOTBAR - Reformer Footbar - BALANCED BODY, INC.; *pg.* 1826, *pg.* 195
REVOLIX - Surgical Laser - HEALTHTRONICS, INC.; *pg.* 1540, *pg.* 1663
REVOLUTION - Floor Care Product - BISSELL HOMECARE, INC.; *pg.* 52, *pg.* 887
REVOLUTION - Apparel - CABELA'S INCORPORATED; *pg.* 535, *pg.* 1019
REVOLUTION - Wrapper - CAMPBELL WRAPPER CORPORATION; *pg.* 1454, *pg.* 1856
REVOLUTION - Laser Speed Detectors - COBRA ELECTRONICS CORPORATION; *pg.* 629, *pg.* 572
REVOLUTION - Lighting Equipment - ELECTRONIC THEATRE CONTROLS, INC.; *pg.* 1296, *pg.* 1872
REVOLUTION - Solar Pool Heater - FAFCO INC.; *pg.* 1071, *pg.* 65
REVOLUTION - Medical Device - GE HEALTHCARE TECHNOLOGIES; *pg.* 1533, *pg.* 1897
REVOLUTION - Gaming Product - GLD PRODUCTS, INC.; *pg.* 1835, *pg.* 1882
REVOLUTION - Integrated Remote Plasma - MKS INSTRUMENTS, INC.; *pg.* 1362, *pg.* 781
REVOLUTION - Mixer Drum - OSHKOSH CORPORATION; *pg.* 187, *pg.* 1885
REVOLUTION - Pet Medication - PETMED EXPRESS, INC.; *pg.* 1781, *pg.* 460
REVOLUTION - Pharmaceutical Product - PFIZER INC.; *pg.* 1581, *pg.* 1278
REVOLUTION - Bone Cement System - STRYKER CORPORATION; *pg.* 1598, *pg.* 894

REVOLUTIONIZING ROBOTICS - Fluid Handling System - GRACO, INC.; *pg.* 1342, *pg.* 935
REVOLUTIONS - Flooring - MANNINGTON MILLS, INC.; *pg.* 934, *pg.* 1119
REVOLVER - Apparel - OAKLEY, INC.; *pg.* 1840, *pg.* 86
REVOLVER - Car Part Accessory - PRO-LINE, INC.; *pg.* 966, *pg.* 45
REVOLVER-Z - VOC Emissions Treatment System - CALGON CARBON CORPORATION; *pg.* 1151, *pg.* 1574
REVOLVOR - Footwear - STEVEN MADDEN, LTD.; *pg.* 1819, *pg.* 1176
REVPRO - Removable Storage Media - GRASS VALLEY, INC.; *pg.* 641, *pg.* 164
REVPRO - Locking System - HIGHFIELD MANUFACTURING CO.; *pg.* 1346, *pg.* 339
REVTEX - Oil Fuel - CHEVRON CORPORATION; *pg.* 974, *pg.* 259
REVUE - Fabric - NEMSCHOFF, INC.; *pg.* 936, *pg.* 1890
REWARD - Canned Dog Food - HEINZ NORTH AMERICA; *pg.* 861, *pg.* 1576
REWARD - House Paint - PPG INDUSTRIES, INC.; *pg.* 1445, *pg.* 1579
REWARD CREDITS - Rewards Program - CAESARS ENTERTAINMENT CORPORATION; *pg.* 1083, *pg.* 1023
REWARD ZONE - Program - BEST BUY CO., INC.; *pg.* 1761, *pg.* 954
REX - Software - ADVENT SOFTWARE, INC.; *pg.* 345, *pg.* 211
REX - House Wrap - ALPHA PRO TECH, LTD.; *pg.* 1492, *pg.* 1922
REX - Computer Software - AVAGO TECHNOLOGIES; *pg.* 358, *pg.* 238
REX - Meat & Cheese Products - BAR-S FOODS CO.; *pg.* 839, *pg.* 15
REX - String Trimmer - BATTELLE MEMORIAL INSTITUTE; *pg.* 1401, *pg.* 1437
REX - Furniture - LA-Z-BOY INCORPORATED; *pg.* 932, *pg.* 901
REXAIR - Motorhome - REXHALL INDUSTRIES, INC.; *pg.* 1710, *pg.* 121
REXALL - Nutritional Supplements - NBTY, INC.; *pg.* 1572, *pg.* 1338
REXHALL - Motor Homes - REXHALL INDUSTRIES, INC.; *pg.* 1710, *pg.* 121
REXTAC - Bitumen Roofing - HUNTSMAN CORPORATION; *pg.* 1167, *pg.* 1758
REY - Paper - INTERNATIONAL PAPER COMPANY; *pg.* 1460, *pg.* 1644
REYATAZ - HIV Medication - BRISTOL-MYERS SQUIBB COMPANY; *pg.* 1509, *pg.* 1206
REYCO - Transportation Equipment - TUTHILL CORPORATION; *pg.* 1385, *pg.* 561
REYNA - Footwear - PHOENIX FOOTWEAR GROUP, INC.; *pg.* 1815, *pg.* 60
REYNAC PINEAU DES CHARENTES - Beverage - SIDNEY FRANK IMPORTING CO., INC.; *pg.* 1970, *pg.* 1184
REYNOLDS - Baking Cups; Freezer Paper; Oven Bags; Parchment Paper; Plastic Wrap - REYNOLDS CONSUMER PRODUCTS; *pg.* 1138, *pg.* 625
REYNOLDS - Stencil Inks - SHERWIN-WILLIAMS DIVERSIFIED BRANDS DIVISION; *pg.* 1448, *pg.* 1435
REYNOLDS - Beverage - TRINCHERO FAMILY ESTATES; *pg.* 1971, *pg.* 197
REYNOLDS CENTER ON AGING - Geriatric Clinic & Research - UNIVERSITY OF ARKANSAS FOR MEDICAL SCIENCES; *pg.* 608, *pg.* 34
REYNOLDS CUT RITE WAX PAPER - Consumer Product - REYNOLDS CONSUMER PRODUCTS; *pg.* 1138, *pg.* 625
REYNOLDS GRILL BUDDIES - Consumer Product - REYNOLDS CONSUMER PRODUCTS; *pg.* 1138, *pg.* 625
REYNOLDS HOT BAGS - Extra Heavy Duty Foil Bags - REYNOLDS CONSUMER PRODUCTS; *pg.* 1138, *pg.* 625
REYNOLDS OVEN BAGS - Consumer Product - REYNOLDS CONSUMER PRODUCTS; *pg.* 1138, *pg.* 625
REYNOLDS POT LUX - Disposable Cookware - REYNOLDS CONSUMER PRODUCTS; *pg.* 1138, *pg.* 625
REYNOLDS VINEYARDS - Winery - TRINCHERO FAMILY ESTATES; *pg.* 1971, *pg.* 197
REYNOLDS WRAP RELEASE - Non-Stick Aluminum Foil - REYNOLDS CONSUMER PRODUCTS; *pg.* 1138, *pg.* 625
REYNOLDS WRAPPERS - Pop-Up Foil Sheets - REYNOLDS CONSUMER PRODUCTS; *pg.* 1138, *pg.* 625
REZ - Interior/Exterior Wood & Masonry Stains & Sealer - PPG INDUSTRIES, INC.; *pg.* 1445, *pg.* 1579
REZICURE - Resin - SI GROUP, INC.; *pg.* 1181, *pg.* 1341
REZILUBE - Polymer Additive - THE DOW CHEMICAL COMPANY; *pg.* 1157, *pg.* 898
REZKLAD - Epoxy Flooring & Coatings - ATLAS MINERALS & CHEMICALS, INC.; *pg.* 69, *pg.* 1552
REZNOR - Heating Product - THOMAS & BETTS CORPORATION; *pg.* 680, *pg.* 1646
REZOOM - Medical Device - ABBOTT MEDICAL OPTICS, INC.; *pg.* 1485, *pg.* 260
REZOSOL - Cationic Resin - HERCULES INCORPORATED; *pg.* 1166, *pg.* 392
RF 3000 - Medical Device - BOSTON SCIENTIFIC CORPORATION; *pg.* 1508, *pg.* 831
RF ANALYST - Software System - ALION SCIENCE AND TECHNOLOGY CORPORATION; *pg.* 615, *pg.* 1788
RF CONDUCTR - Electrophysiology Catheter - MEDTRONIC, INC.; *pg.* 1564, *pg.* 939
RF GAIN - Electronics - RICHARDSON ELECTRONICS, LTD.; *pg.* 667, *pg.* 622
RF MARINR - Electrophysiology Catheter - MEDTRONIC, INC.; *pg.* 1564, *pg.* 939
RF NEULINK - Spectrum Radio Transceiver - RF INDUSTRIES, LTD.; *pg.* 461, *pg.* 208
RF PERFORMR - Electrophysiology Catheter - MEDTRONIC, INC.; *pg.* 1564, *pg.* 939
RF POWER - Surface Mount Components - ANAREN, INC.; *pg.* 617, *pg.* 1157
RF PURE - Ceramic & Plastic Product - COORSTEK, INC.; *pg.* 77, *pg.* 330
RF TO BITS - Radio Receivers - MAXIM INTEGRATED PRODUCTS, INC.; *pg.* 653, *pg.* 247
RFB11 A/V - Floor Boxes - WIREMOLD/LEGRAND; *pg.* 689, *pg.* 383
RFB6 - Floor Boxes - WIREMOLD/LEGRAND; *pg.* 689, *pg.* 383
RFB6 SERIES - Floor Boxes - WIREMOLD/LEGRAND; *pg.* 689, *pg.* 383
RFB9 A/V - Floor Boxes - WIREMOLD/LEGRAND; *pg.* 689, *pg.* 383
RFD LATEX - Barn Paint - JONES-BLAIR COMPANY; *pg.* 1443, *pg.* 1682
RFE SERIES - Enclosures - WIREMOLD/LEGRAND; *pg.* 689, *pg.* 383
RFG MORTAR - Pressed & Monolithic Refractory - RESCO PRODUCTS, INC.; *pg.* 107, *pg.* 1581
RFI - Interference Filters - DGT HOLDINGS; *pg.* 634, *pg.* 1223
RFID EASY - Program - TOPFLIGHT CORPORATION; *pg.* 681, *pg.* 1534
RFID IN A BOX - Software - MANHATTAN ASSOCIATES, INC.; *pg.* 430, *pg.* 513
RFMPLUS - 60-Day Revolving Catalog Database with Hotline Names from Mail Order Houses - INFOGROUP; *pg.* 769, *pg.* 1038
RFP MACHINE - Software - QVIDIAN; *pg.* 458, *pg.* 829
RFP TRACKING SYSTEM - Software - QVIDIAN; *pg.* 458, *pg.* 829
RG - Insulators - LAPP INSULATOR COMPANY, LLC; *pg.* 1946, *pg.* 1173
RG AIRFLO - Burner - MAXON CORPORATION; *pg.* 1359, *pg.* 695
RGB-4004 A/B/C - Electronic Component - EMCORE CORPORATION; *pg.* 636, *pg.* 39
RGB-4006 A/B/C - Electronic Component - EMCORE CORPORATION; *pg.* 636, *pg.* 39
RGB TOOLS - Software - CHYRONHEGO; *pg.* 371, *pg.* 1179
RGC350 - Radar Graphics Computer - L-3 AVIONICS SYSTEMS, INC.; *pg.* 650, *pg.* 888
RGEN - Dispense System - ENTEGRIS, INC.; *pg.* 1882, *pg.* 788
THE RGP MULTIFOCAL SPECIALISTS - Slogan - DANKER LABORATORIES INC.; *pg.* 1408, *pg.* 465
RGTS - Communication Service - ROCKEFELLER GROUP, INC.; *pg.* 1110, *pg.* 1286
RGX - Body Spray - HENKEL CONSUMER GOODS; *pg.* 511, *pg.* 22
R.H. FORSCHNER - Commercial Cutlery - VICTORINOX SWISS ARMY INC.; *pg.* 1139, *pg.* 357
RHAPSODY - Beverage Service, Stainless Steel Pitchers & Gravy Boats - CARLISLE FOODSERVICE PRODUCTS INCORPORATED; *pg.* 1455, *pg.* 1485
RHAPSODY - Software - NTI CORPORATION; *pg.* 446, *pg.* 114
RHAPSODY - Lighting Product - QUOIZEL INC.; *pg.* 1304, *pg.* 1616
RHAPSODY - Online Music Subscription Service - REALNETWORKS, INC.; *pg.* 460, *pg.* 1839
RHAPSODY - Cosmetics - WESTROCK COMPANY; *pg.* 1472, *pg.* 1805
RHAPSODY OF THE SEAS - Cruise Ship - ROYAL CARIBBEAN CRUISES LTD; *pg.* 1921, *pg.* 446
RHAPSODYBED - Mattress System - TEMPUR SEALY INTERNATIONAL, INC.; *pg.* 944, *pg.* 731
RHAPSODYPILLOW - Pillow - TEMPUR SEALY INTERNATIONAL, INC.; *pg.* 944, *pg.* 731
RHCA - Roller Hockey Coaches Association - ROLLER SKATING ASSOCIATION INTERNATIONAL; *pg.* 155, *pg.* 689
RHEBUILD - Pump Product - IDEX CORPORATION; *pg.* 1347, *pg.* 623
RHEEM - Water Heaters, Air Conditioners & Furnaces - RHEEM MANUFACTURING COMPANY; *pg.* 1075, *pg.* 519
RHEFLEX - Pump Product - IDEX CORPORATION; *pg.* 1347, *pg.* 623
RHELIANT - Synthetic Drilling Fluid - M-I SWACO; *pg.* 980, *pg.* 1710
RHENINGHAUS - Slicers - CHESHER EQUIPMENT LTD.; *pg.* 1323, *pg.* 1925
RHEO-LOADER - Software - BROOKFIELD ENGINEERING LABORATORIES, INC.; *pg.* 1403, *pg.* 833
RHEO2000 - Software - BROOKFIELD ENGINEERING LABORATORIES, INC.; *pg.* 1403, *pg.* 833
RHEO3000 - Software - BROOKFIELD ENGINEERING LABORATORIES, INC.; *pg.* 1403, *pg.* 833
RHEOCALC - Software - BROOKFIELD ENGINEERING LABORATORIES, INC.; *pg.* 1403, *pg.* 833
RHEOCHEM - Lubricant - HONEYWELL INTERNATIONAL INC.; *pg.* 407, *pg.* 1088
RHEODYNE - Pump Product - IDEX CORPORATION; *pg.* 1347, *pg.* 623
RHEOGEL - Starch for Salad Dressing Products - CARGILL LIMITED; *pg.* 1475, *pg.* 1914
RHEONETIC - Magnetic Fluids & Systems - LORD CORPORATION; *pg.* 1357, *pg.* 1360
RHEORANGER - Food Hydrocolloids - THE LUBRIZOL CORPORATION; *pg.* 1171, *pg.* 1481
RHEOSPAN - Minerals - MINERALS TECHNOLOGIES INC.; *pg.* 1173, *pg.* 617
RHEOVISION - Software - BROOKFIELD ENGINEERING LABORATORIES, INC.; *pg.* 1403, *pg.* 833
RHEUMATEX - Pharmaceutical Product - ALERE INC.; *pg.* 1488, *pg.* 849
RHEUMATON - Pharmaceutical Product - ALERE INC.; *pg.* 1488, *pg.* 849
RHINEBECK - Rug - COURISTAN INC.; *pg.* 921, *pg.* 1067
RHINO - Mower - ALAMO GROUP INC.; *pg.* 1311, *pg.* 1745
RHINO - Oxygen Regulator - ALLIED HEALTHCARE PRODUCTS, INC.; *pg.* 1491, *pg.* 990
RHINO - Steel Stamp - C.H. HANSON COMPANY; *pg.* 1322, *pg.* 636
RHINO - Metal Fabricated Enclosures - CHANNELL COMMERCIAL CORP.; *pg.* 1870, *pg.* 291
RHINO - High-viscosity Adhesives & Sealant Materials Dispensing System - NORDSON CORPORATION; *pg.* 1365, *pg.* 1480
RHINO - Plastic Packaging Product - POLY PAK AMERICA, INC.; *pg.* 1467, *pg.* 138
RHINO - Valve - SMITH INTERNATIONAL, INC.; *pg.* 1377, *pg.* 1715
RHINO - Record Label - WARNER MUSIC GROUP CORP.; *pg.* 590, *pg.* 1313
RHINO FLEX FLAIL - Flail Mower - ALAMO GROUP INC.; *pg.* 1311, *pg.* 1745
RHINO PLAY - Game Tables - ESCALADE INC.; *pg.* 1833, *pg.* 678
RHINO RAMPAGE - Video Game - INTERNATIONAL GAME TECHNOLOGY; *pg.* 957, *pg.* 1024
RHINO RUBDOWN - Body Lotion - ORANGE PEEL ENTERPRISES, INC.; *pg.* 1028, *pg.* 477
RHINO SKIN - Coated Foam Disc - SCHOOL-TECH, INC.; *pg.* 1844, *pg.* 866
RHINOFLOOR - Wood Flooring Product - ARMSTRONG WORLD INDUSTRIES, INC.; *pg.* 914, *pg.* 1545
RHINOGUARD - Antimicrobial Technology - STINGER MEDICAL LLC; *pg.* 476, *pg.* 1648
RHINOHIDE - Molecular Probe Product - THERMO FISHER SCIENTIFIC INC.; *pg.* 1602, *pg.* 61
RHINOMUNE - Pharmaceutical Product - PFIZER INC.; *pg.* 1581, *pg.* 1278
RHINOTUFF - Hardwood Floor - ANDERSON HARDWOOD

First page reference indicates Business Class Edition
Second page reference indicates Geographic Edition

FLOORS; *pg.* 67, *pg.* 1613
RHO-COR - Composite Sandwich Material System - UTC AEROSPACE SYSTEMS; *pg.* 236, *pg.* 1369
RHODAMINE GREEN - Biomolecule Product - THERMO FISHER SCIENTIFIC INC.; *pg.* 1602, *pg.* 61
RHODAMINE RED - Molecular Probe Product - THERMO FISHER SCIENTIFIC INC.; *pg.* 1602, *pg.* 61
RHODE ISLAND LAWYERS WEEKLY - Newspaper - MASSACHUSETTS LAWYERS WEEKLY, INC.; *pg.* 1662, *pg.* 798
RHODITE - Optical Product - UNIVERSAL PHOTONICS, INC.; *pg.* 1433, *pg.* 1167
RHODOL - Optical Product - UNIVERSAL PHOTONICS, INC.; *pg.* 1433, *pg.* 1167
RHODOL GREEN - Molecular Probe Product - THERMO FISHER SCIENTIFIC INC.; *pg.* 1602, *pg.* 61
RHODOS - Rug - COURISTAN INC.; *pg.* 921, *pg.* 1067
RHODZIN - Molecular Probe Product - THERMO FISHER SCIENTIFIC INC.; *pg.* 1602, *pg.* 61
RHOGAM - Healthcare Product - JOHNSON & JOHNSON; *pg.* 1549, *pg.* 1091
RHOMBUS - Fabric - NEMSCHOFF, INC.; *pg.* 936, *pg.* 1890
RHONDA - Footwear - COBIAN CORP.; *pg.* 1806, *pg.* 253
RHOPLEX - Adhesive & Sealant - DOW CHEMICAL; *pg.* 1156, *pg.* 1563
RHOPLEX - Aqueous Acrylic Polymer Emulsions - THE DOW CHEMICAL COMPANY; *pg.* 1157, *pg.* 898
RHT - Burner - ECLIPSE INC.; *pg.* 1332, *pg.* 655
RHUMBA - Beer - ANHEUSER-BUSCH COMPANIES, LLC; *pg.* 237, *pg.* 991
RHYME TIME READERS - Educational Materials - SCHOLASTIC INC.; *pg.* 1683, *pg.* 1288
RHYTHM - Bath Product - KOHLER CO.; *pg.* 91, *pg.* 1862
RHYTHMX - Software - CRITICARE SYSTEMS, INC.; *pg.* 1520, *pg.* 1897
RIA - Legal Publications - THOMSON REUTERS CORPORATION; *pg.* 1693, *pg.* 1944
RIALTA - Recreation Vehicle - WINNEBAGO INDUSTRIES, INC.; *pg.* 1712, *pg.* 707
RIALTO - Seating Product - IRWIN SEATING COMPANY INC.; *pg.* 929, *pg.* 887
RIALTO - Bath Product - KOHLER CO.; *pg.* 91, *pg.* 1862
RIATA - Chandeliers - CRAFTMADE INTERNATIONAL, INC.; *pg.* 1295, *pg.* 1670
RIATA - ICD Leads - ST. JUDE MEDICAL, INC.; *pg.* 1596, *pg.* 963
RIATRAC - Lab Control Product for Diagnostic Testing - BECTON, DICKINSON & COMPANY; *pg.* 1501, *pg.* 1068
RIAZZI - Bathroom Fan - HUNTER FAN COMPANY; *pg.* 57, *pg.* 1631
RIB-B-Q - Food Product - ADVANCEPIERRE FOODS, INC.; *pg.* 1714, *pg.* 1409
RIB CAGE - Water Bottle Holder - SPECIALIZED BICYCLE COMPONENTS, INC.; *pg.* 1711, *pg.* 152
RIB NIBBLERS - Food Product - ADVANCEPIFRRE FOODS, INC.; *pg.* 1714, *pg.* 1409
RIBBED ELANCE - Bikini - JOCKEY INTERNATIONAL, INC.; *pg.* 27, *pg.* 1861
RIBBED TOP - Women's Clothing & Accessories - WOODEN SHIPS OF HOBOKEN; *pg.* 35, *pg.* 1315
RIBBON - Hat - WOODEN SHIPS OF HOBOKEN; *pg.* 35, *pg.* 1315
RIBBON-AX - Cable Assembly - W.L. GORE & ASSOCIATES, INC.; *pg.* 122, *pg.* 388
RIBBONS & ROSEBUDS - Sleepwear - HABAND COMPANY, INC.; *pg.* 1772, *pg.* 1099
RIBETAK - Resin - SI GROUP, INC.; *pg.* 1181, *pg.* 1341
RIBFLEX - Conveyor Belting - HBD INDUSTRIES, INC.; *pg.* 207, *pg.* 1449
RIBOLYSER - Software - BIO-RAD LABORATORIES, INC.; *pg.* 1504, *pg.* 101
RIBOPRINTER - Microbial Characterization System - E.I. DU PONT DE NEMOURS & COMPANY; *pg.* 1159, *pg.* 390
RIBOSE - Nutritional Supplement - NATURAL ORGANICS, INC.; *pg.* 1571, *pg.* 1181
RICE - Soy Free Food Products - GALAXY NUTRITIONAL FOODS, INC.; *pg.* 857, *pg.* 1603
RICE-A-RONI - Flavored Rice Products - PEPSICO, INC.; *pg.* 259, *pg.* 1327
RICE-A-RONI - Pasta Products - THE QUAKER OATS COMPANY; *pg.* 834, *pg.* 588
RICE. A WORLD OF GREAT IDEAS - Slogan - USA RICE FEDERATION; *pg.* 160, *pg.* 1775
RICE DREAM - Food Product - THE HAIN CELESTIAL GROUP, INC.; *pg.* 860, *pg.* 1172
RICE KRISPIES - Food Product - KELLOGG COMPANY; *pg.* 831, *pg.* 870
RICE KRISPIES TREATS - Cereal - KELLOGG COMPANY; *pg.* 831, *pg.* 870
RICE 'N EASY - Rice Mix - RICELAND FOODS, INC.; *pg.* 892, *pg.* 36
RICE PAPER - Window Treatment - CROSCILL, INC.; *pg.* 1122, *pg.* 1220
RICE VEGAN - Soy Nutritious Food Product - GALAXY NUTRITIONAL FOODS, INC.; *pg.* 857, *pg.* 1603
RICH - Beverages - THE COCA-COLA COMPANY; *pg.* 240, *pg.* 493
RICH & SASSY - BBQ Sauce - FAMOUS DAVE'S OF AMERICA, INC.; *pg.* 1728, *pg.* 926
RICH GIRL - Video Slots - INTERNATIONAL GAME TECHNOLOGY; *pg.* 957, *pg.* 1024
RICH LITTLE PIGGIES - Game - WMS INDUSTRIES INC.; *pg.* 593, *pg.* 666
RICH MEDIA MADE SIMPLE - Slogan - EVEO INC.; *pg.* 1244, *pg.* 217
RICH RENEWAL - Ultra-Hydrating Creme - ORLY INTERNATIONAL, INC.; *pg.* 518, *pg.* 137
RICH REWARDS - Banking Services - COMERICA INCORPORATED; *pg.* 740, *pg.* 1677
RICHES OF ROME - Game - WMS INDUSTRIES INC.; *pg.* 593, *pg.* 666
RICHES OF THE AMAZON - Game - WMS INDUSTRIES INC.; *pg.* 593, *pg.* 666
RICHES OF THE PHARAOH - Game - WMS INDUSTRIES INC.; *pg.* 593, *pg.* 666
RICHES OF THE UNIVERSE - Game - WMS INDUSTRIES INC.; *pg.* 593, *pg.* 666
RICHFOAM - Bedding Foam - CARPENTER CO.; *pg.* 920, *pg.* 1801
RICHLAND PINES - Furniture - ASHLEY FURNITURE INDUSTRIES, INC.; *pg.* 914, *pg.* 1852
RICHMOND - Guest Chairs - BERNHARDT DESIGN; *pg.* 918, *pg.* 1381
RICHMOND - Furniture - HAWORTH, INC.; *pg.* 402, *pg.* 891
RICHMOND - Lighting - LSI INDUSTRIES INC.; *pg.* 58, *pg.* 1416
RICHMOND - Casket - MATTHEWS INTERNATIONAL CORPORATION; *pg.* 1662, *pg.* 1578
RICHMOND - Water Heaters - RHEEM MANUFACTURING COMPANY; *pg.* 1075, *pg.* 519
RICHMOND DENTAL - Dental Product And Dispenser - BARNHARDT MANUFACTURING COMPANY; *pg.* 1498, *pg.* 1364
RICHMOND GEAR - Performance Automotive Ring & Pinions & Transmissions - REGAL BELOIT CORPORATION; *pg.* 106, *pg.* 1854
RICHMOND INTERNATIONAL RACEWAY - Motorsports Facility - INTERNATIONAL SPEEDWAY CORPORATION; *pg.* 553, *pg.* 420
RICHMOND TIMES-DISPATCH - Daily Newspaper - MEDIA GENERAL, INC.; *pg.* 297, *pg.* 1803
RICH'S WELCOMES YOU LIKE ONLY A FAMILY CAN - Slogan - RICH PRODUCTS CORPORATION; *pg.* 892, *pg.* 1150
RICHTER - Fluid Technology - ITT CORPORATION; *pg.* 1351, *pg.* 1354
RICHWOOD - Exterior Siding Components - NORTEK, INC.; *pg.* 100, *pg.* 1607
RICHWOOD LITE - Kitchen Cabinets - KITCHEN KOMPACT, INC.; *pg.* 91, *pg.* 692
RICHY - Beverages - THE COCA-COLA COMPANY; *pg.* 240, *pg.* 493
RICKARD'S - Beer - MOLSON COORS CANADA INC.; *pg.* 256, *pg.* 1955
RICKARD'S RED - Beer - MOLSON COORS BREWING COMPANY; *pg.* 256, *pg.* 321
RICKSHAW - Fabric - NEMSCHOFF, INC.; *pg.* 936, *pg.* 1890
RICOCHET - Roller Coaster - CAROWINDS; *pg.* 537, *pg.* 1364
RICOCHET - Bath Product - KOHLER CO.; *pg.* 91, *pg.* 1862
RICOH DEVELOPER SUPPORT PROGRAM - Software - RICOH AMERICAS CORPORATION; *pg.* 461, *pg.* 1131
RICREM - Cheese - SAPUTO, INC.; *pg.* 893, *pg.* 1956
RID - Medicine - BAYER HEALTHCARE CONSUMER CARE DIVISION; *pg.* 1500, *pg.* 1087
RID FLEA - Flea Control Products - THE HARTZ MOUNTAIN CORP.; *pg.* 1476, *pg.* 1120
RID-OX - Chemical Cleaner Product - TECH SPRAY, L.P.; *pg.* 1183, *pg.* 1659
RID-X - Septic Tank Additive - EASTMAN KODAK COMPANY; *pg.* 1408, *pg.* 1333
RID-X - Septic Treatment - RECKITT BENCKISER INC.; *pg.* 1136, *pg.* 1105
RIDAURA - Therapy System - PROMETHEUS LABORATORIES, INC.; *pg.* 1586, *pg.* 206
RIDDLE - Eyewear - OAKLEY, INC.; *pg.* 1840, *pg.* 86
RIDE BMX - Magazine - BONNIER ACTIVE MEDIA, INC.; *pg.* 1622, *pg.* 1205
RIDE LINE - Boots - AEROGROUP INTERNATIONAL, INC.; *pg.* 1803, *pg.* 1055
RIDE ON - Bicycle Cable - W.L. GORE & ASSOCIATES, INC.; *pg.* 122, *pg.* 388
RIDE-RITE - Air Spring Applications for Personal Vehicles - FIRESTONE INDUSTRIAL PRODUCTS DIVISION; *pg.* 1882, *pg.* 686
RIDE RITE - Packaging Product - INTERNATIONAL PAPER COMPANY; *pg.* 1460, *pg.* 1644
RIDE THE WAVE - Petunia Seeds - PANAMERICAN SEED CO.; *pg.* 1798, *pg.* 668
THE RIDE WORKS - Entertainment - ENVIRONMENTAL TECTONICS CORPORATION; *pg.* 1411, *pg.* 1587
RIDE2ROLL SCOOTER - Toy & Game - HASBRO, INC.; *pg.* 954, *pg.* 1603
RIDEBMX - Magazine - BONNIER CORPORATION; *pg.* 1622, *pg.* 480
RIDECONTROL - Air Adjustable Kit - AIR LIFT COMPANY; *pg.* 198, *pg.* 895
RIDER SWEET - Sweetening Ingredient - MERISANT COMPANY; *pg.* 876, *pg.* 581
RIDERS - Jeanswear - V.F. CORPORATION; *pg.* 34, *pg.* 1376
RIDERS EDGE - Rider Training Program - HARLEY-DAVIDSON, INC.; *pg.* 178, *pg.* 1874
RIDERWOOD - Retirement Community - ERICKSON LIVING; *pg.* 1090, *pg.* 766
RIDESENTRY - Trailer Air Suspension - MERITOR, INC.; *pg.* 212, *pg.* 911
RIDG-AC - Bevel Product - GLEASON CORPORATION; *pg.* 1340, *pg.* 1335
RIDGE-FORM MESH - Dental Instrument - OSTEOMED CORPORATION; *pg.* 1425, *pg.* 1658
RIDGE SCRAPER - Plastic & Rubber - TEKNOR APEX COMPANY; *pg.* 1889, *pg.* 1605
RIDGECREST - Hip & Ridge Shingles - GAF MATERIALS CORP.; *pg.* 83, *pg.* 1681
RIDGELINE - Food Product - SHAMROCK FOODS COMPANY; *pg.* 895, *pg.* 20
RIDGEMARK - Software - NIGHTINGALE; *pg.* 446, *pg.* 186
RIDGETOP - Footwear - LACROSSE FOOTWEAR, INC.; *pg.* 1811, *pg.* 1503
RIDGETTS - Ridged Potato Chips - C.J. VITNER CO.; *pg.* 848, *pg.* 571
RIDGEWAY - Tents, Sleeping Bags & Backpacks - KELLWOOD COMPANY; *pg.* 28, *pg.* 975
RIDGID - Electric Drive - ROMAC INDUSTRIES, INC.; *pg.* 1061, *pg.* 1818
RIDGID/KOLLMAN - Tools - RIDGE TOOL COMPANY; *pg.* 1372, *pg.* 1452
RIDGLASS - Specialty Roofing Shingles - BUILDING PRODUCTS OF CANADA CORP.; *pg.* 72, *pg.* 1951
RIDGLASS - Hip & Ridge Shingles - GAF MATERIALS CORP.; *pg.* 83, *pg.* 1681
RIDGWOOD - Textiles - BERNHARDT DESIGN; *pg.* 918, *pg.* 1381
RIDING SPORT - Vests & Tights - DOVER SADDLERY, INC.; *pg.* 1833, *pg.* 829
RIDOLINE - Metalworking Chemical - HENKEL CORPORATION; *pg.* 1166, *pg.* 897
RIEDEL-DE HAEN - Laboratory Chemicals & Reagents for Research & Analysis - SIGMA-ALDRICH CORPORATION; *pg.* 1181, *pg.* 1003
RIEKE - Packaging System - TRIMAS CORPORATION; *pg.* 1383, *pg.* 874
RIFFS - Footwear - VANS, INC.; *pg.* 1821, *pg.* 76
RIFLE - Golf Club Shaft - TRUE TEMPER SPORTS, INC.; *pg.* 1847, *pg.* 1647
RIFLEMAN - Binocular - LEUPOLD & STEVENS, INC.; *pg.* 1420, *pg.* 1492
RIFOCS - Telecommunication Installation, Maintenance & Testing - TEXTRON INC.; *pg.* 235, *pg.* 1607
RIFT ZONE - Bike - MARIN BIKES; *pg.* 1708, *pg.* 168
RIG WASH - Powdered Cleaning Compound - TEXAS REFINERY CORP.; *pg.* 986, *pg.* 1696
RIGESA - Paperboard Packaging Product - WESTROCK COMPANY; *pg.* 1472, *pg.* 1805

RIGHT - Ear Muffs - MINE SAFETY APPLIANCES COMPANY; *pg.* 1361, *pg.* 1525
THE RIGHT BALANCE OF BREATHABILITY. - Slogan - RAVEN INDUSTRIES, INC.; *pg.* 1888, *pg.* 1625
THE RIGHT BANK - Slogan - PACIFIC CONTINENTAL CORPORATION; *pg.* 791, *pg.* 1497
THE RIGHT CHOICE FOR YOUR MATERIAL HANDLING NEEDS - Tagline - METZGAR CONVEYOR COMPANY; *pg.* 1360, *pg.* 875
THE RIGHT CONNECTION - Slogan - DIXON VALVE & COUPLING COMPANY; *pg.* 1045, *pg.* 766
RIGHT DECISION. RIGHT NOW - Tag Line - TRUVEN HEALTH ANALYTICS; *pg.* 486, *pg.* 331
THE RIGHT EQUIPMENT RIGHT NOW! - Tag Line - UNITED RENTALS, INC.; *pg.* 1386, *pg.* 350
RIGHT FROM THE BEGINNING - Tag Line - GRACO CHILDREN'S PRODUCTS INC.; *pg.* 954, *pg.* 1531
RIGHT GUARD - Deodorants & Body Sprays - HENKEL CONSUMER GOODS; *pg.* 511, *pg.* 22
RIGHT IN ANY LIGHT - Tag Line - TRANSITIONS OPTICAL, INC.; *pg.* 1432, *pg.* 458
RIGHT INNOVATION RIGHT HERE RIGHT NOW - Tagline - UTC AEROSPACE SYSTEMS; *pg.* 236, *pg.* 1369
RIGHT KIND - Oral Hygiene Aids - SUNSTAR AMERICAS INC.; *pg.* 1599, *pg.* 591
RIGHT-ON - Hair Preparations - THE GILLETTE COMPANY; *pg.* 509, *pg.* 795
RIGHT-ON - Curl Activator Styling Aids - INSPIRED BEAUTY BRANDS; *pg.* 512, *pg.* 1244
RIGHT ON COLOR - Tagline - X-RITE, INCORPORATED; *pg.* 1437, *pg.* 891
RIGHT-ON CURL - Hair Moisturizer & Conditioner - THE GILLETTE COMPANY; *pg.* 509, *pg.* 795
RIGHT-ON RIGHT BACK - Curl Restorer - THE GILLETTE COMPANY; *pg.* 509, *pg.* 795
RIGHT PORTION, RIGHT PRICE - Slogan - T.G.I. FRIDAY'S INC.; *pg.* 1754, *pg.* 1669
THE RIGHT ROAST - Process - THE COFFEE BEANERY LTD.; *pg.* 849, *pg.* 886
RIGHT TRACK - Publication - MOTHERS AGAINST DRUNK DRIVING (MADD); *pg.* 147, *pg.* 1723
RIGHT WHERE YOU ARE - Tagline - BANCORPSOUTH, INC.; *pg.* 717, *pg.* 971
RIGHTFIELDER 3 - Software - MELISSA DATA CORP.; *pg.* 432, *pg.* 188
RIGHTFIT - Pigment & Dispersion - BASF CATALYSTS LLC; *pg.* 1148, *pg.* 1074
RIGHTMIX - Software - R.R. DONNELLEY & SONS COMPANY; *pg.* 1682, *pg.* 589
RIGHTON - Medical Product - HOLOGIC, INC.; *pg.* 1416, *pg.* 784
RIGHTSIZE - Medical Product - HOLOGIC, INC.; *pg.* 1416, *pg.* 784
RIGHTSOURCE - Mail Order Health Coverage - HUMANA, INC.; *pg.* 1204, *pg.* 734
RIGHTTOUCH - Wireless Communication System - AT&T SOUTHEAST; *pg.* 1868, *pg.* 489
RIGI-BUMP - Sheet Metal - RIGIDIZED METALS CORP.; *pg.* 108, *pg.* 1151
RIGI-GRIP - Handrail - RIGIDIZED METALS CORP.; *pg.* 108, *pg.* 1151
RIGI-TILE - Metal Tile - RIGIDIZED METALS CORP.; *pg.* 108, *pg.* 1151
RIGID-AIR - Filtration Product - FLANDERS CORPORATION; *pg.* 1336, *pg.* 1392
RIGIDENT - Toothpaste - CHURCH & DWIGHT CO., INC.; *pg.* 1153, *pg.* 1063
RIGIDTEX - Textured Metals - RIGIDIZED METALS CORP.; *pg.* 108, *pg.* 1151
RIGIMESH - Filter Cartridge - PALL CORPORATION; *pg.* 232, *pg.* 1323
RIGITEX - Audio & Video Product - HARMAN INTERNATIONAL INDUSTRIES, INCORPORATED; *pg.* 641, *pg.* 374
RIGOROUS - Carpet - BEAULIEU GROUP, LLC; *pg.* 917, *pg.* 529
RIGS - Rate-Integrating Gyroscopic Survey System - BAKER HUGHES INTEQ; *pg.* 1316, *pg.* 1700
RIGTUFF - Marine Shipboard Cable - GENERAL CABLE CORPORATION; *pg.* 83, *pg.* 729
RIGUR - Plastic Packaging Product - POLY PAK AMERICA, INC.; *pg.* 1467, *pg.* 138
RIK - Wound Care Surface - KINETIC CONCEPTS, INC.; *pg.* 1553, *pg.* 1741
RIKEN - Tires - MICHELIN NORTH AMERICA INC.; *pg.* 1886, *pg.* 1618
RILEE - Metal Heating - AIR PRODUCTS AND CHEMICALS, INC.; *pg.* 1145, *pg.* 1513
RILONACEPT - Pharmaceutical Product - REGENERON PHARMACEUTICALS, INC.; *pg.* 1588, *pg.* 1345
RILUTEK - Pharmaceutical Product - IMPAX LABORATORIES, INC.; *pg.* 1544, *pg.* 101
RIM - Apparel - OAKLEY, INC.; *pg.* 1840, *pg.* 86
RIM - De-Icer - REVERE PRODUCTS; *pg.* 107, *pg.* 1435
RIM 1802G - OEM Radio Modem - BLACKBERRY LIMITED; *pg.* 625, *pg.* 1947
RIM 1902G - OEM Radio Modem - BLACKBERRY LIMITED; *pg.* 625, *pg.* 1947
RIM 802D - Radio Modem - BLACKBERRY LIMITED; *pg.* 625, *pg.* 1947
RIM 850 - Wireless Handheld - BLACKBERRY LIMITED; *pg.* 625, *pg.* 1947
RIM 850 WIRELESS HANDHELD - Wireless Handheld - BLACKBERRY LIMITED; *pg.* 625, *pg.* 1947
RIM 857 - Wireless Handheld - BLACKBERRY LIMITED; *pg.* 625, *pg.* 1947
RIM 857 WIRELESS HANDHELD - Wireless Handheld - BLACKBERRY LIMITED; *pg.* 625, *pg.* 1947
RIM 902M - Radio Modem - BLACKBERRY LIMITED; *pg.* 625, *pg.* 1947
RIM 950 - Wireless Handheld - BLACKBERRY LIMITED; *pg.* 625, *pg.* 1947
RIM 950 WIRELESS HANDHELD - Wireless Handheld - BLACKBERRY LIMITED; *pg.* 625, *pg.* 1947
RIM 957 - Wireless Handheld - BLACKBERRY LIMITED; *pg.* 625, *pg.* 1947
RIM 957 WIRELESS HANDHELD - Wireless Handheld - BLACKBERRY LIMITED; *pg.* 625, *pg.* 1947
RIM CELL PRIME MIX - Fluid Handling System - GRACO, INC.; *pg.* 1342, *pg.* 935
RIM EXCEL - Fluid Handling System - GRACO, INC.; *pg.* 1342, *pg.* 935
RIM FUSION - Fluid Handling System - GRACO, INC.; *pg.* 1342, *pg.* 935
RIM-LOC - Blast Wheels - PANGBORN CORPORATION; *pg.* 1367, *pg.* 532
RIM-LOCK - Dental Product - DENTSPLY INTERNATIONAL INC.; *pg.* 1522, *pg.* 1596
RIM PLUS - Rimboard - BOISE CASCADE HOLDINGS, L.L.C.; *pg.* 1453, *pg.* 546
RIM POLYMER - Fluid Handling System - GRACO, INC.; *pg.* 1342, *pg.* 935
RIM ROCKA - Children's Apparel - LT APPAREL GROUP; *pg.* 29, *pg.* 1254
RIM SUPRAMIX - Fluid Handling System - GRACO, INC.; *pg.* 1342, *pg.* 935
RIM TECHNOLOGY - Technology To Design The Flywheel - BEACON POWER, LLC; *pg.* 1936, *pg.* 848
RIM WIRELESS HANDHELD - Mobile Communication Service - BLACKBERRY LIMITED; *pg.* 625, *pg.* 1947
RIMA - Architectural Fixtures - BALLANTYNE STRONG, INC.; *pg.* 623, *pg.* 1013
RIMADYL - Pharmaceutical Product - IMPAX LABORATORIES, INC.; *pg.* 1544, *pg.* 101
RIMADYL - Pet Medication - PETMED EXPRESS, INC.; *pg.* 1781, *pg.* 460
RIMADYL - Carprofen - PFIZER INC.; *pg.* 1581, *pg.* 1278
RIMAGE - Disc Publisher - MICROBOARDS TECHNOLOGY, LLC; *pg.* 434, *pg.* 920
RIMCELL - Fluid Handling System - GRACO, INC.; *pg.* 1342, *pg.* 935
RIMCELL ACE - Fluid Handling System - GRACO, INC.; *pg.* 1342, *pg.* 935
RIMCELL SELECT - Fluid Handling System - GRACO, INC.; *pg.* 1342, *pg.* 935
RIMFLY - Fly Reel - CORTLAND LINE COMPANY; *pg.* 1831, *pg.* 1155
RIMINI - Footwear - PHOENIX FOOTWEAR GROUP, INC.; *pg.* 1815, *pg.* 60
RIMON - Polymer Product - CHEMTURA CORPORATION; *pg.* 1152, *pg.* 355
RIMPAK - Fluid Handling System - GRACO, INC.; *pg.* 1342, *pg.* 935
RIMSPRAY - Fluid Handling System - GRACO, INC.; *pg.* 1342, *pg.* 935
RIMSTAR - Computer Programs - MARSH & MCLENNAN COMPANIES INC.; *pg.* 1207, *pg.* 1256
RIN-T - Input/Output Device - MERCURY COMPUTER SYSTEMS, INC.; *pg.* 434, *pg.* 813
RINBROS - Apparel - HANESBRANDS INC.; *pg.* 26, *pg.* 1394
RINCINOL - Dental Rinse - SUNSTAR AMERICAS INC.; *pg.* 1599, *pg.* 591
RINDEX - Personal & Household Product - THE PROCTER & GAMBLE COMPANY; *pg.* 1129, *pg.* 1418
RING - Components - MOORE TOOL COMPANY, INC.; *pg.* 1057, *pg.* 339
RING-EEZE - Motor Oil - BARDAHL MANUFACTURING CORPORATION; *pg.* 972, *pg.* 1833
RING-FLEX - Furniture Edgings - LEGGETT & PLATT, INCORPORATED; *pg.* 933, *pg.* 974
RING IN THE HOLIDAYS - Game - MISSOURI LOTTERY; *pg.* 999, *pg.* 979
RING LEADER - O-Ring Sealed Joint Chains - DIAMOND CHAIN COMPANY; *pg.* 1328, *pg.* 684
RING-OF-AIR - Foot Drop Stop - SPAN-AMERICA MEDICAL SYSTEMS, INC.; *pg.* 1595, *pg.* 1618
RING OF FIRE - Game - WMS INDUSTRIES INC.; *pg.* 593, *pg.* 666
RING POP LOLLIPOPS - Candy - THE TOPPS COMPANY, INC.; *pg.* 588, *pg.* 1302
RING PULL MIRASTRIP - Containers - SONOCO PRODUCTS COMPANY; *pg.* 1469, *pg.* 1619
RING QUEST - Game - WMS INDUSTRIES INC.; *pg.* 593, *pg.* 666
RING SCREW - Fastening Systems - TEXTRON INC.; *pg.* 235, *pg.* 1607
RING TOSS - Textiles - BERNHARDT DESIGN; *pg.* 918, *pg.* 1381
RING TUFF - Paper - XEROX CORPORATION; *pg.* 494, *pg.* 365
RINGER - Pest Control - THE WOODSTREAM CORPORATION; *pg.* 1801, *pg.* 1549
RINGINGPHONE.COM - RingTone Service - ADVANCED TELECOM SERVICES; *pg.* 1865, *pg.* 1591
RINGLING BROS. & BARNUM & BAILEY - Circuses & Retail Toys - FELD ENTERTAINMENT, INC.; *pg.* 547, *pg.* 458
RINGLOC ACETABULAR - Hip Product - ZIMMER BIOMET HOLDINGS, INC.; *pg.* 1611, *pg.* 699
RINGMASTER - Wireless Communication System - AT&T SOUTHEAST; *pg.* 1868, *pg.* 489
RINGMASTER RICHES - Video Game - INTERNATIONAL GAME TECHNOLOGY; *pg.* 957, *pg.* 1024
RINGOS - Breaded Fish Rings - HIGH LINER FOODS INCORPORATED; *pg.* 862, *pg.* 1917
RINGS AND ROSES - Flower Arrangement - 1-800-FLOWERS.COM, INC.; *pg.* 1758, *pg.* 1151
RINI-REGO MARKETPLACE - Retail Grocery Stores - GIANT EAGLE AMERICAN SEAWAY FOODS; *pg.* 1020, *pg.* 1405
RINI-REGO STOP-N-SHOP - Retail Grocery Stores - GIANT EAGLE AMERICAN SEAWAY FOODS; *pg.* 1020, *pg.* 1405
RINN - Dental Product - DENTSPLY INTERNATIONAL INC.; *pg.* 1522, *pg.* 1596
THE RINSE - Hair Care Product - JOHN PAUL MITCHELL SYSTEMS; *pg.* 512, *pg.* 133
RINSE - Cleaning Chemical Product - KYZEN CORPORATION; *pg.* 331, *pg.* 1652
RINSE-A-MATIC STEEMER - Cleaning Product - ORECK CORPORATION; *pg.* 59, *pg.* 1653
RINSE-A-MATIC STEEMER ULTRA - Cleaning Product - ORECK CORPORATION; *pg.* 59, *pg.* 1653
RINSE KLEEN - Blackening Neutralizer - HEATBATH CORPORATION; *pg.* 1165, *pg.* 826
RINSEAID - Cleaning Enhancer - QUAKER CHEMICAL CORP.; *pg.* 1178, *pg.* 1524
RINSEGARD - Filters - ENTEGRIS, INC.; *pg.* 1882, *pg.* 788
RINSER - Liquid Cleaning - U.S. BOTTLERS MACHINERY COMPANY; *pg.* 1386, *pg.* 1369
RINZLER - Footwear - K-SWISS; *pg.* 1837, *pg.* 306
RIO - Casino - CAESARS ENTERTAINMENT CORPORATION; *pg.* 1083, *pg.* 1023
RIO - Broadloom - COURISTAN INC.; *pg.* 921, *pg.* 1067
RIO - Internal Server Storage Systems - DOT HILL SYSTEMS CORP.; *pg.* 388, *pg.* 333
RIO - Furniture - NEUTRAL POSTURE, INC.; *pg.* 939, *pg.* 1669
RIO GLANDE - Bottled Food Product - ALLIED OLD ENGLISH, INC.; *pg.* 836, *pg.* 1110
RIO GRANDE - Eggs - CAL-MAINE FOODS, INC.; *pg.* 843, *pg.* 969
RIO MAR - Furniture - ASHLEY FURNITURE INDUSTRIES, INC.; *pg.* 914, *pg.* 1852
RIO VIEJO - Food Service - FOOD SERVICES OF AMERICA,

INC.; pg. 856, pg. 21
RIO VISTA - Fruit & Vegetable Product - GIUMARRA VINEYARDS CORPORATION; pg. 1964, pg. 45
RIO XTREME - Storage Servers - DOT HILL SYSTEMS CORP.; pg. 388, pg. 333
RIP-A-PAK - Shank Kit - ESCO CORPORATION; pg. 1335, pg. 1502
RIP IT - Soft Drink - NATIONAL BEVERAGE CORP.; pg. 257, pg. 425
RIP-OPE - Envelopes - TENSION ENVELOPE CORPORATION; pg. 483, pg. 986
RIP TIDE - Thrill Ride - KNOTT'S BERRY FARM; pg. 556, pg. 50
RIPCORD - Split Release - BENJAMIN OBDYKE, INC.; pg. 70, pg. 1540
RIPCORD - Fabric - NEMSCHOFF, INC.; pg. 936, pg. 1890
RIPGUARD - Anti-Piracy Software - ROVI CORPORATION; pg. 463, pg. 269
RIPLEY MILLER - Cable Tool - THE RIPLEY COMPANY; pg. 1305, pg. 342
RIPLEY'S "BELIEVE IT OR NOT!" - Large & Unusual Vegetable & Flower Packet Seeds - THE PAGE SEED CO.; pg. 1798, pg. 1163
RIPPED GORE II - Glove - KOMBI, LTD.; pg. 1838, pg. 1766
RIPPLE - Snacks - SNYDER'S OF HANOVER, INC.; pg. 1862, pg. 1536
RIPPLE - Office Furniture - STEELCASE INC.; pg. 475, pg. 889
RIPPLES - Minerals - MINERALS TECHNOLOGIES INC.; pg. 1173, pg. 617
RIPPN - Electronic Components - MOLEX INCORPORATED; pg. 655, pg. 628
RIQUENT - Pharmaceutical Product - LA JOLLA PHARMACEUTICAL COMPANY; pg. 1554, pg. 204
RIRI - Fishing Gear Product - SIMMS FISHING PRODUCTS CORP.; pg. 1845, pg. 1008
RISE OF THE IMPERFECTS - Video Game - ELECTRONIC ARTS INC.; pg. 951, pg. 189
RISER - Computer Support Worktools - STEELCASE INC.; pg. 475, pg. 889
RISING FORTUNES - Game - WMS INDUSTRIES INC.; pg. 593, pg. 666
RISK - Game - HASBRO, INC.; pg. 954, pg. 1603
RISK 2210 AD - Toy & Game - HASBRO, INC.; pg. 954, pg. 1603
RISK-ADJUSTED SUPPLY CHAIN MANAGEMENT - Risk Management Services - MARSH & MCLENNAN COMPANIES INC.; pg. 1207, pg. 1256
RISK ASSESSMENT MANAGER - Credit Analysis Software - THE DUN & BRADSTREET CORP.; pg. 1637, pg. 1120
RISK GRADIENT - Security Risk Management Services - COMPUTER SCIENCES CORPORATION; pg. 378, pg. 1780
RISK MANAGEMENT HIERARCHY - Risk Management Consulting Services - MARSH & MCLENNAN COMPANIES INC.; pg. 1207, pg. 1256
RISKDATAINFO - Weather Peril & Natural Disaster Database - PITNEY BOWES SOFTWARE INC.; pg. 455, pg. 1346
RISKMARK - Risk Analysis Services - FACTORY MUTUAL INSURANCE COMPANY; pg. 1199, pg. 1601
RISKSPOTTER - Software - XEROX CORPORATION; pg. 494, pg. 365
RISKWATCH - Firesafety Education - NATIONAL FIRE PROTECTION ASSOCIATION; pg. 149, pg. 842
RISOTTERIA - Restaurants - IL FORNAIO (AMERICA) CORPORATION; pg. 1731, pg. 70
RISOTTO - Boots - AEROGROUP INTERNATIONAL, INC.; pg. 1803, pg. 1055
RISPERDAL - Antipsychotic Pharmaceutical - JANSSEN PHARMACEUTICA PRODUCTS, L.P.; pg. 1548, pg. 1125
RISPERDAL CONSTA - Pharmaceutical - JANSSEN PHARMACEUTICA PRODUCTS, L.P.; pg. 1548, pg. 1125
RISQUE BUSINESS - Video Slots - INTERNATIONAL GAME TECHNOLOGY; pg. 957, pg. 1024
RISTON - Dry Film Photoresist - E.I. DU PONT DE NEMOURS & COMPANY; pg. 1159, pg. 390
RITA MILLER'S - Honey - MILLER'S HONEY COMPANY; pg. 1860, pg. 1759
RITA SERVER - Electronic Transaction Product - VERIFONE SYSTEMS, INC.; pg. 487, pg. 251
RITAZZA - Food Service Concept - MORRISON MANAGEMENT SPECIALISTS, INC.; pg. 1028, pg. 515
RITE - Seafood - OCEAN BEAUTY SEAFOODS, INC.; pg. 1028, pg. 1838
RITE LITE - Hard Hat Light - HD ELECTRIC COMPANY; pg. 1299, pg. 666
RITE-LITE - Lighting Product - HD ELECTRIC COMPANY; pg. 1299, pg. 666
RITE-SIZE - Corrugated Box Machinery - THE ENTWISTLE CO.; pg. 637, pg. 826
RITE TEMP - Beverage Dispenser - ALADDIN TEMP-RITE, LLC; pg. 1013, pg. 1635
RITE-TEMP - Bath Product - KOHLER CO.; pg. 91, pg. 1862
RITE-VU - Light Communication System - RITE-HITE HOLDING CORPORATION; pg. 1372, pg. 1880
RITEBITE - Medical Equipment - CONMED CORPORATION; pg. 1517, pg. 1347
RITEGO - Laundry Spray Spotter - A.L. WILSON CHEMICAL CO.; pg. 325, pg. 1076
RITEHEIGHT - Mattress - SIMMONS COMPANY; pg. 943, pg. 520
RITEX - Pressed & Monolithic Refractory - RESCO PRODUCTS, INC.; pg. 107, pg. 1581
RITMO - Apparel - HANESBRANDS INC.; pg. 26, pg. 1394
RITWELL - Fabric - SCALAMANDRE, INC.; pg. 941, pg. 1058
RITZ - Shoes - ALLEN-EDMONDS SHOE CORP.; pg. 1804, pg. 1887
RITZ - Chair - LA-Z-BOY INCORPORATED; pg. 932, pg. 901
RITZ - Crackers - MONDELEZ INTERNATIONAL, INC.; pg. 878, pg. 601
RITZ - Soft Drink - NATIONAL BEVERAGE CORP.; pg. 257, pg. 425
RITZ-CARLTON - Hotels - MARRIOTT INTERNATIONAL, INC.; pg. 1102, pg. 764
THE RITZ-CARLTON DESINATION CLUB - Vacation Club - MARRIOTT INTERNATIONAL, INC.; pg. 1102, pg. 764
RIUNITE - Wine - BANFI VINTNERS; pg. 1957, pg. 1161
RIV-DEXTEEL - Bridge Deck Grating - ALABAMA METAL INDUSTRIES CORPORATION; pg. 65, pg. 1
RIVA - Storage - DOT HILL SYSTEMS CORP.; pg. 388, pg. 333
RIVA - Bath & Plumbing Product - JACUZZI BRANDS CORPORATION; pg. 554, pg. 65
RIVA - Furniture - NEMSCHOFF, INC.; pg. 936, pg. 1890
RIVA FC - High Bandwidth Storage Solutions - DOT HILL SYSTEMS CORP.; pg. 388, pg. 333
RIVAL - Cooking Appliances - JARDEN CONSUMER SOLUTIONS; pg. 57, pg. 412
RIVARD - Truck Equipment - ALAMO GROUP INC.; pg. 1311, pg. 1745
RIVARD - Furniture - ASHLEY FURNITURE INDUSTRIES, INC.; pg. 914, pg. 1852
RIVARD - Animal Safety Product - NEOGEN CORPORATION; pg. 883, pg. 896
RIVER - Rice - RIVIANA FOODS INC.; pg. 892, pg. 1713
RIVER BELLE 21 - Game - WMS INDUSTRIES INC.; pg. 593, pg. 666
RIVER CITY CHICKEN - Food Product - GIANT EAGLE, INC.; pg. 1020, pg. 1575
RIVER DOWNS - Carpet - BEAULIEU GROUP, LLC; pg. 917, pg. 529
RIVER FALLS - Kitchen Product - KOHLER CO.; pg. 91, pg. 1862
RIVER GUIDE - Tackle Storage - CABELA'S INCORPORATED; pg. 535, pg. 1019
RIVER MARSH - Dinnerware - THE HOMER LAUGHLIN CHINA COMPANY; pg. 1125, pg. 1850
RIVER OAK - Fiction Books - DAVID C. COOK; pg. 1633, pg. 315
RIVER QUEEN - Nut Products - THE LEAVITT CORPORATION; pg. 874, pg. 818
RIVER VALLEY BANCORP - Financial Services - RIVER VALLEY BANCORP; pg. 799, pg. 694
RIVERBATH - Bath Product - KOHLER CO.; pg. 91, pg. 1862
RIVERBEND - Glove - KOMBI, LTD.; pg. 1838, pg. 1766
RIVERBEND - Lighting Product - QUOIZEL INC.; pg. 1304, pg. 1616
RIVERS END - Denim Shirt - BROWN & BIGELOW, INC.; pg. 1624, pg. 959
RIVERSHED - Fishing Gear Product - SIMMS FISHING PRODUCTS CORP.; pg. 1845, pg. 1008
RIVERSIDE - Turkey & Turkey Parts - CARGILL LIMITED; pg. 1475, pg. 1914
RIVERSTONE - Tile - ARTISTIC TILE INC.; pg. 914, pg. 1119
RIVERTEK - Fishing Gear Product - SIMMS FISHING PRODUCTS CORP.; pg. 1845, pg. 1008
RIVERWASHED - Apparel - BARCO UNIFORMS, INC.; pg. 19, pg. 94
RIVET - Fabric - NEMSCHOFF, INC.; pg. 936, pg. 1890
RIVIERA - Watches - BAUME & MERCIER, INC.; pg. 1, pg. 1201
RIVIERA - Salad Dressing - CAINS FOODS, L.P.; pg. 843, pg. 784
RIVIERA - Cart Bag - DATREK GOLF; pg. 1832, pg. 1801
RIVIERA - Door Panel - MASONITE INTERNATIONAL CORPORATION; pg. 1054, pg. 1920
RIVOLI - Footwear - PHOENIX FOOTWEAR GROUP, INC.; pg. 1815, pg. 60
RIWA - Beverages - THE COCA-COLA COMPANY; pg. 240, pg. 493
RIXIE - PaperBoard - SONOCO PRODUCTS COMPANY; pg. 1469, pg. 1619
RIZZI ARC - Office Furniture - STEELCASE INC.; pg. 475, pg. 889
R.J. GRUNTS - Casual Dining Restaurant - LETTUCE ENTERTAIN YOU ENTERPRISES, INC.; pg. 1735, pg. 580
RJ-LNXX - Electronic Components - MOLEX INCORPORATED; pg. 655, pg. 628
RJ7 - Reject Processor - OPEX CORPORATION; pg. 450, pg. 1087
RJHRESORTS.COM - Advertising Website - DOMINION ENTERPRISES; pg. 1636, pg. 1796
RJMODEM - Communication Product - MULTI-TECH SYSTEMS INC.; pg. 442, pg. 951
RKE - Precision Eyepiece - EDMUND INDUSTRIAL OPTICS INC.; pg. 1411, pg. 1041
RKG - Electronic Components - MOLEX INCORPORATED; pg. 655, pg. 628
RKO CENTURY WARNER THEATRES - Motion Picture Theaters - CINEPLEX ENTERTAINMENT LP; pg. 275, pg. 1936
RLG NASHVILLE - Compact Disc - SONY MUSIC ENTERTAINMENT; pg. 309, pg. 1294
RLM - Paper, Paper Cones & Paper Tubes - SONOCO PRODUCTS COMPANY; pg. 1469, pg. 1619
RLX - Fan - CTB INTERNATIONAL CORP.; pg. 850, pg. 695
RLX - Athletic Apparel - RALPH LAUREN CORPORATION; pg. 46, pg. 1284
RLX PLUS - Scratch Resistant Ophthalmic Lenses - SIGNET ARMORLITE, INC.; pg. 1429, pg. 60
RLXPLUS - Scratch Resistant Lenses - SIGNET ARMORLITE, INC.; pg. 1429, pg. 60
RM-10 - Health Supplement - GARDEN OF LIFE, INC.; pg. 1532, pg. 478
RMC QUICK DRY - Chemical Product - ROCHESTER MIDLAND CORPORATION; pg. 334, pg. 1337
RMCC - Charitable Fundraising Services - MCDONALD'S CORPORATION; pg. 1737, pg. 645
RMF-61HY - Plastics Product - AEP INDUSTRIES INC.; pg. 1878, pg. 1085
RMHC - Charitable Fundraising Services - MCDONALD'S CORPORATION; pg. 1737, pg. 645
RN CAREER SEARCH - Recruitment Publication - TRUVEN HEALTH ANALYTICS; pg. 1696, pg. 867
RN MAGAZINE - Medical Publication - TRUVEN HEALTH ANALYTICS; pg. 1696, pg. 867
RNAAQUEOUS - Molecular Biology Product - THERMO FISHER SCIENTIFIC INC.; pg. 1602, pg. 61
RNAI - Biopharmaceutical Product - CYTRX CORPORATION; pg. 1521, pg. 129
RNAI TOPO - Biomolecule Product - THERMO FISHER SCIENTIFIC INC.; pg. 1602, pg. 61
RNASE - Biomolecule Product - THERMO FISHER SCIENTIFIC INC.; pg. 1602, pg. 61
RNASE AWAY - Molecular Biology Product - THERMO FISHER SCIENTIFIC INC.; pg. 1602, pg. 61
RNASELECT - Molecular Probe Product - THERMO FISHER SCIENTIFIC INC.; pg. 1602, pg. 61
RNASEOUT - Molecular Biology Product - THERMO FISHER SCIENTIFIC INC.; pg. 1602, pg. 61
RNASEZAP - Molecular Biology Product - THERMO FISHER SCIENTIFIC INC.; pg. 1602, pg. 61
RN.COM - Internet Portal - AMN HEALTHCARE SERVICES, INC.; pg. 1494, pg. 200
RO-CON - Fibre Drum - GREIF INC.; pg. 1459, pg. 1447
RO-LINX - Thermal Busbars - ROGERS CORPORATION; pg. 1305, pg. 369
RO PURE - Ceramic & Plastic Product - COORSTEK, INC.; pg. 77, pg. 330
RO TEL - Food Product - CONAGRA FOODS, INC.; pg. 826, pg. 1014
ROACH PRUFE - Insecticides - COPPER-BRITE, INC.; pg.

329, *pg.* 263
THE ROAD AHEAD IS INTELLIGENT - Tagline - AIRIQ, INC.; *pg.* 346, *pg.* 1932
ROAD & TRACK - Magazine - THE HEARST CORPORATION; *pg.* 1649, *pg.* 1239
ROAD CHAMPS - Toy & Collectible Vehicles - JAKKS PACIFIC, INC.; *pg.* 960, *pg.* 142
THE ROAD ENDS HERE - Trademark - NATIONAL COLLEGIATE ATHLETIC ASSOCIATION; *pg.* 567, *pg.* 688
ROAD GLIDE - Motorcycles - HARLEY-DAVIDSON, INC.; *pg.* 178, *pg.* 1874
ROAD I - Wine - WEIBEL, INC.; *pg.* 1972, *pg.* 122
ROAD KING - Motorcycle - HARLEY-DAVIDSON, INC.; *pg.* 178, *pg.* 1874
ROAD-KING - Screening - TELSMITH, INC.; *pg.* 1381, *pg.* 1871
ROAD MESH - Pavement Reinforcement - MACCAFERRI, INC.; *pg.* 95, *pg.* 780
ROAD MINER - Paving Equipment - ASTEC INDUSTRIES, INC.; *pg.* 69, *pg.* 1628
ROAD POWER - Booster Cables - COLEMAN CABLE, INC.; *pg.* 1324, *pg.* 665
ROAD RASH - Video Game - ELECTRONIC ARTS INC.; *pg.* 951, *pg.* 189
ROAD RESCUE - Vehicle - SPARTAN MOTORS, INC.; *pg.* 217, *pg.* 874
ROAD SERVICE ONLINE - Road Service - AMERICAN AUTOMOBILE ASSOCIATION; *pg.* 1190, *pg.* 429
ROAD SERVICE ONLINE - Online Road Service - AUTOMOBILE CLUB OF SOUTHERN CALIFORNIA; *pg.* 134, *pg.* 126
ROAD STAR - Motorcycle - YAMAHA MOTOR CORPORATION USA; *pg.* 1713, *pg.* 76
ROAD STAR MIDNIGHT - Motorcycle - YAMAHA MOTOR CORPORATION USA; *pg.* 1713, *pg.* 76
ROAD STAR SILVERADO - Motorcycle - YAMAHA MOTOR CORPORATION USA; *pg.* 1713, *pg.* 76
ROAD STAR WARRIOR - Motorcycle - YAMAHA MOTOR CORPORATION USA; *pg.* 1713, *pg.* 76
ROAD TECH - Navigation System - HARLEY-DAVIDSON, INC.; *pg.* 178, *pg.* 1874
THE ROAD TO ATLANTA - Trademark - NATIONAL COLLEGIATE ATHLETIC ASSOCIATION; *pg.* 567, *pg.* 688
THE ROAD TO CARY - Trademark - NATIONAL COLLEGIATE ATHLETIC ASSOCIATION; *pg.* 567, *pg.* 688
THE ROAD TO CLEVELAND - Trademark - NATIONAL COLLEGIATE ATHLETIC ASSOCIATION; *pg.* 567, *pg.* 688
THE ROAD TO DETROIT - Trademark - NATIONAL COLLEGIATE ATHLETIC ASSOCIATION; *pg.* 567, *pg.* 688
THE ROAD TO INDIANAPOLIS - Trademark - NATIONAL COLLEGIATE ATHLETIC ASSOCIATION; *pg.* 567, *pg.* 688
THE ROAD TO MINNEAPOLIS - Trademark - NATIONAL COLLEGIATE ATHLETIC ASSOCIATION; *pg.* 567, *pg.* 688
THE ROAD TO NEW ORLEANS - Trademark - NATIONAL COLLEGIATE ATHLETIC ASSOCIATION; *pg.* 567, *pg.* 688
THE ROAD TO OMAHA - Trademark - NATIONAL COLLEGIATE ATHLETIC ASSOCIATION; *pg.* 567, *pg.* 688
ROAD TO RICHES - Game - WMS INDUSTRIES INC.; *pg.* 593, *pg.* 666
THE ROAD TO SAN ANTONIO - Trademark - NATIONAL COLLEGIATE ATHLETIC ASSOCIATION; *pg.* 567, *pg.* 688
THE ROAD TO SAN DIEGO - Trademark - NATIONAL COLLEGIATE ATHLETIC ASSOCIATION; *pg.* 567, *pg.* 688
THE ROAD TO ST. LOUIS - Trademark - NATIONAL COLLEGIATE ATHLETIC ASSOCIATION; *pg.* 567, *pg.* 688
THE ROAD TO SUCCESS - Tagline - LANDSTAR SYSTEM, INC.; *pg.* 1914, *pg.* 434
ROAD TO THE FINAL FOUR - Trademark - NATIONAL COLLEGIATE ATHLETIC ASSOCIATION; *pg.* 567, *pg.* 688
THE ROAD TO THE FINAL FOUR - Trademark - NATIONAL COLLEGIATE ATHLETIC ASSOCIATION; *pg.* 567, *pg.* 688
ROADCALC - Software - EAGLE POINT SOFTWARE CORPORATION; *pg.* 389, *pg.* 707
ROADFORCE - Battery - EXIDE TECHNOLOGIES; *pg.* 204, *pg.* 483
ROADGUARD - Automotive Paints & Lacquers - PPG INDUSTRIES, INC.; *pg.* 1445, *pg.* 1579
ROADHOUSE - Fabric - NEMSCHOFF, INC.; *pg.* 936, *pg.* 1890
ROADHOUSE GOLD - Food Services - TEXAS ROADHOUSE, INC.; *pg.* 1753, *pg.* 738
ROADLAZER - Line Stripers - GRACO, INC.; *pg.* 1342, *pg.* 935
ROADLINK - Software - TRIMBLE NAVIGATION LIMITED; *pg.* 1384, *pg.* 288
ROADM - Wavelength Selective Switch - FINISAR CORPORATION; *pg.* 639, *pg.* 285
ROADMASTER - Tires - COOPER TIRE & RUBBER COMPANY; *pg.* 1881, *pg.* 1453
ROADNET - Software - UNITED PARCEL SERVICE, INC.; *pg.* 1928, *pg.* 522
ROADNET 5000 - Software - UNITED PARCEL SERVICE, INC.; *pg.* 1928, *pg.* 522
ROADNET ANYWHERE - Shipping Services - UNITED PARCEL SERVICE, INC.; *pg.* 1928, *pg.* 522
ROADRAMP - Multi-Lane Axle Sensor - INTERNATIONAL ROAD DYNAMICS INC.; *pg.* 1912, *pg.* 1962
ROADRANGER - Truck Components - EATON CORPORATION; *pg.* 1331, *pg.* 1429
ROADREADY - Laser Detectors - COBRA ELECTRONICS CORPORATION; *pg.* 629, *pg.* 572
ROADRUNNER - Erosion Control Product - AMERICAN EXCELSIOR COMPANY; *pg.* 1451, *pg.* 1659
ROADRUNNER - Medical Device - COOK GROUP, INC.; *pg.* 1518, *pg.* 674
ROADRUNNER - Record Label - WARNER MUSIC GROUP CORP.; *pg.* 590, *pg.* 1313
ROADRUNNER FOOTBAGS - Sand Filled Synthetic Leather Covers for Play - DUNCAN TOYS COMPANY; *pg.* 951, *pg.* 1465
ROADSIDE MANAGER - Software - VULCAN, INC.; *pg.* 687, *pg.* 5
ROADSTAR - Omnidirectional Antenna - WINEGARD COMPANY; *pg.* 688, *pg.* 702
ROADSTER - Children's Bed - RUBBERMAID HOME PRODUCTS; *pg.* 1138, *pg.* 1453
ROADSYNC - Software - DATAVIZ, INC.; *pg.* 383, *pg.* 356
ROADTEC - Paving Equipment - ASTEC INDUSTRIES, INC.; *pg.* 69, *pg.* 1628
ROADTRAX - Sensor System - MEASUREMENT SPECIALTIES INC.; *pg.* 1360, *pg.* 1783
ROADTRIP - Grill - THE COLEMAN COMPANY, INC.; *pg.* 1830, *pg.* 723
ROADTUFF - Turbocharger - HONEYWELL INTERNATIONAL INC.; *pg.* 407, *pg.* 1088
ROADWATCH 3 - Component Kit - COMMERCIAL VEHICLE GROUP, INC.; *pg.* 203, *pg.* 1467
ROADWATCH SS - Component Kit - COMMERCIAL VEHICLE GROUP, INC.; *pg.* 203, *pg.* 1467
ROADWHEEL - Tire Durability Testing System - MTS SYSTEMS CORPORATION; *pg.* 442, *pg.* 923
ROADY - Satellite Radio Receiver - DELPHI AUTOMOTIVE LLP; *pg.* 204, *pg.* 910
ROAMAN'S - Apparel - FULLBEAUTY BRANDS; *pg.* 1770, *pg.* 1233
ROAMER - Racing Boat - CHRIS-CRAFT CORPORATION; *pg.* 1706, *pg.* 465
ROAMEX - Software System - FAIR ISAAC CORPORATION; *pg.* 1247, *pg.* 955
ROAMIN RHINOS - Video Slots - INTERNATIONAL GAME TECHNOLOGY; *pg.* 957, *pg.* 1024
ROAMSERVER - Internet Services - IPASS, INC.; *pg.* 1259, *pg.* 193
ROANOKE TIMES NESWPAPER - Newspaper - THE ROANOKE TIMES; *pg.* 1680, *pg.* 1806
ROANOKE.COM - Online Newspaper - THE ROANOKE TIMES; *pg.* 1680, *pg.* 1806
ROARING 20S - Slot Machine - BALLY TECHNOLOGIES, INC.; *pg.* 531, *pg.* 1022
ROARING BROOK CREW - Clothing - ABERCROMBIE & FITCH CO.; *pg.* 37, *pg.* 1466
ROARING BROOK V-NECK - Clothing - ABERCROMBIE & FITCH CO.; *pg.* 37, *pg.* 1466
ROARR - Footwear - STEVEN MADDEN, LTD.; *pg.* 1819, *pg.* 1176
ROAST ALMOND - Chocolates - THE HERSHEY CO.; *pg.* 1855, *pg.* 1538
ROAST BEEF AND HORSERADISH GRILLED CHESSE - Food Product - GAY LEA FOODS CO-OPERATIVE LIMITED; *pg.* 858, *pg.* 1926
ROAST-N-HOLD - Under Counter Professional Ovens - CRES-COR; *pg.* 1326, *pg.* 1464
ROASTERS EXCHANGE - Coffee - PERFORMANCE FOOD GROUP COMPANY, LLC; *pg.* 1030, *pg.* 1803
ROASTWORKS - Food Products - J.R. SIMPLOT COMPANY; *pg.* 867, *pg.* 547
ROBAXIN - Pharmaceutical Product - LANNETT COMPANY, INC.; *pg.* 1555, *pg.* 1566
ROBBINS - Wood Flooring Products - ARMSTRONG WORLD INDUSTRIES, INC.; *pg.* 914, *pg.* 1545
ROBERT - Furniture - AMISCO INDUSTRIES LTD.; *pg.* 913, *pg.* 1958
ROBERT CRAY STRATOCASTER - Electric Guitar - FENDER MUSICAL INSTRUMENTS CORPORATION; *pg.* 547, *pg.* 21
ROBERT HALF - Professional Staffing Services - ROBERT HALF INTERNATIONAL INC.; *pg.* 462, *pg.* 145
ROBERT MONDAVI - Wine - CONSTELLATION BRANDS, INC.; *pg.* 1960, *pg.* 1348
ROBERT MONDAVI PRIVATE SELECTION - Wine - ROBERT MONDAVI WINERY; *pg.* 1969, *pg.* 173
ROBERT MONDAVI WINERY - Wine Company - ROBERT MONDAVI WINERY; *pg.* 1969, *pg.* 173
ROBERT STEMMLER - Premium Wine - THE DONUM ESTATE, INC; *pg.* 1962, *pg.* 279
ROBERTA - Furniture - ASHLEY FURNITURE INDUSTRIES, INC.; *pg.* 914, *pg.* 1852
ROBERTET - Essential Oils - ROBERTET, INC.; *pg.* 522, *pg.* 1100
ROBERTS - Sugar Centrifugal - WESTERN STATES MACHINE COMPANY; *pg.* 1388, *pg.* 1455
ROBERTSON - Furniture - AMISCO INDUSTRIES LTD.; *pg.* 913, *pg.* 1958
ROBERTSON - Company Name - ROBERTSON INC.; *pg.* 1372, *pg.* 1924
ROBIE HOUSE - Carpet - INTERFACE, INC.; *pg.* 695, *pg.* 512
ROBIN - Character - DC COMICS, INC.; *pg.* 1633, *pg.* 1221
ROBIN EGG QUADRANT - Pillow and Throw - HERITAGE LACE INC.; *pg.* 694, *pg.* 711
ROBIN ELECTRONICS - Testing Technology - DANAHER CORPORATION; *pg.* 1044, *pg.* 397
ROBIN HOOD - Baking Mix - THE J.M. SMUCKER COMPANY; *pg.* 865, *pg.* 1468
ROBIN HOOD - Flour & Mixes - SMUCKER FOODS OF CANADA CO.; *pg.* 896, *pg.* 1924
ROBIN HOOD'S SHERWOOD TREASURE - Game - WMS INDUSTRIES INC.; *pg.* 593, *pg.* 666
ROBINSON - Dairy Products - DEAN FOODS COMPANY; *pg.* 852, *pg.* 1679
ROBINSON R22 - 2-Seat Helicopter - ROBINSON HELICOPTER COMPANY; *pg.* 234, *pg.* 295
ROBINSON R44 - 4-Seat Helicopter - ROBINSON HELICOPTER COMPANY; *pg.* 234, *pg.* 295
ROBINWOOD PLAID - Pillow and Throw - HERITAGE LACE INC.; *pg.* 694, *pg.* 711
ROBITUSSIN - Cough Suppressant - PFIZER INC.; *pg.* 1581, *pg.* 1278
ROBO-HS - Ethernet Switches - BROADCOM CORPORATION; *pg.* 364, *pg.* 108
ROBO-MET.3D - Serial Sectioning System - UES, INC.; *pg.* 1449, *pg.* 1447
ROBOCLOCK - Clock & Buffer Product - CYPRESS SEMICONDUCTOR CORPORATION; *pg.* 1326, *pg.* 243
ROBOCLOCK II - Clock & Buffer Product - CYPRESS SEMICONDUCTOR CORPORATION; *pg.* 1326, *pg.* 243
ROBOCLOCK JR. - Clock & Buffer Product - CYPRESS SEMICONDUCTOR CORPORATION; *pg.* 1326, *pg.* 243
ROBOCONFIG - Clock & Buffer Product - CYPRESS SEMICONDUCTOR CORPORATION; *pg.* 1326, *pg.* 243
ROBOCOUCH - Patient Positioning System - ACCURAY INCORPORATED; *pg.* 1486, *pg.* 282
ROBODRIVE - Automatic Conveyor System - PARAGON TECHNOLOGIES, INC.; *pg.* 1367, *pg.* 1528
ROBOENHANCER - Software - ACD SYSTEMS INTERNATIONAL INC.; *pg.* 340, *pg.* 1913
ROBOFLASK - Glass & Ceramic Material - CORNING INCORPORATED; *pg.* 1122, *pg.* 1154
ROBOINFO - Software - ADOBE SYSTEMS INCORPORATED; *pg.* 342, *pg.* 235
ROBOLITE - Automatic Conveyor System - PARAGON

First page reference indicates Business Class Edition
Second page reference indicates Geographic Edition

TECHNOLOGIES, INC.; *pg.* 1367, *pg.* 1528
ROBOND - Adhesive & Sealant - DOW CHEMICAL; *pg.* 1156, *pg.* 1563
ROBOND - Acrylic Adhesives - THE DOW CHEMICAL COMPANY; *pg.* 1157, *pg.* 898
ROBORAIL - Automatic Conveyor System - PARAGON TECHNOLOGIES, INC.; *pg.* 1367, *pg.* 1528
ROBOSWITCH - Semiconductors - BROADCOM CORPORATION; *pg.* 364, *pg.* 108
ROBOSWITCH HS - Ethernet Switches - BROADCOM CORPORATION; *pg.* 364, *pg.* 108
ROBOT - Software - AUTODESK INC.; *pg.* 356, *pg.* 257
ROBOT-RX - Robotic Pharmacy Dispensing & Tracking System - MCKESSON CORPORATION; *pg.* 1560, *pg.* 222
ROBOT SERIES - Mirrorobot Compact Mirror - BROWN & BIGELOW, INC.; *pg.* 1624, *pg.* 959
ROBOTAG - Software - AT&T SOUTHEAST; *pg.* 1868, *pg.* 489
ROBOTIC MASSAGE - Massage Product - HUMAN TOUCH; *pg.* 928, *pg.* 123
ROBOTS THAT MAKE A DIFFERENCE - Tagline - IROBOT CORP.; *pg.* 1418, *pg.* 785
ROBOX - Robotic Compatible Storage Box - ENTEGRIS, INC.; *pg.* 1882, *pg.* 788
ROBUST - Food Flavorings - GRIFFITH LABORATORIES, INC.; *pg.* 860, *pg.* 552
ROBUSTONE - Flavor Ingredient - INTERNATIONAL FLAVORS & FRAGRANCES INC.; *pg.* 512, *pg.* 1244
ROC - Health Care Products - JOHNSON & JOHNSON; *pg.* 1549, *pg.* 1091
ROC - Adult Mass Market Paperback Books - PENGUIN RANDOM HOUSE; *pg.* 1675, *pg.* 1276
ROC-R - Pump Product - IDEX CORPORATION; *pg.* 1347, *pg.* 623
ROCA - Buttercrunch - BROWN & HALEY; *pg.* 1851, *pg.* 1820
ROCA BITS - Buttercrunch - BROWN & HALEY; *pg.* 1851, *pg.* 1820
ROCA LOCA - Footwear - VANS, INC.; *pg.* 1821, *pg.* 76
ROCALTROL - Pharmaceutical Product - HOFFMANN-LA ROCHE INC.; *pg.* 1542, *pg.* 1099
ROCAR - Wine - SHAW ROSS INTERNATIONAL IMPORTERS; *pg.* 1970, *pg.* 449
ROCATEC - Junior Bonding System - 3M COMPANY; *pg.* 1142, *pg.* 956
ROCAWEAR - Apparel - ICONIX BRAND GROUP, INC.; *pg.* 26, *pg.* 1243
ROCC - Coating Product - PPG INDUSTRIES, INC.; *pg.* 1445, *pg.* 1579
ROCCAL - Antiseptic & Disinfectant - PFIZER INC.; *pg.* 1581, *pg.* 1278
ROCCHE CASTAGMAGNA - Italian Wine - LAIRD & COMPANY, INC.; *pg.* 1966, *pg.* 1119
ROCCO - Office Furniture - STEELCASE INC.; *pg.* 475, *pg.* 889
ROCEPHIN - Pharmaceutical Product - CUBIST PHARMACEUTICALS, INC.; *pg.* 1521, *pg.* 828
ROCHESTER BIG & TALL CLOTHING - Men's Clothing - DESTINATION XL GROUP, INC.; *pg.* 40, *pg.* 810
ROCHESTER ROPES - Wire Rope - WIRECO WORLDGROUP; *pg.* 1389, *pg.* 987
THE ROCK - Beverage Bottle - THERMOS L.L.C.; *pg.* 61, *pg.* 660
ROCK A BYE BOUQUET - Fruit Arrangements - EDIBLE ARRANGEMENTS INTERNATIONAL, INC.; *pg.* 1768, *pg.* 382
ROCK BOTTOM RESTAURANT & BREWERY - Brew Pub - ROCK BOTTOM RESTAURANTS, INC.; *pg.* 1748, *pg.* 334
ROCK CREEK CIDER - Cider - BIG ROCK BREWERY INCOME TRUST; *pg.* 239, *pg.* 1902
ROCK FACE - Ceiling Panel - USG CORPORATION; *pg.* 118, *pg.* 594
ROCK FALLS - Furniture - ASHLEY FURNITURE INDUSTRIES, INC.; *pg.* 914, *pg.* 1852
ROCK FITNESS - Weight Benches - ALLIANCE SPORTS GROUP, L.P.; *pg.* 1825, *pg.* 1698
ROCK HARD - Fragrance - PARFUMS DE COEUR LTD.; *pg.* 519, *pg.* 376
ROCK HIS WORLD - Musical Instrument - GIBSON GUITAR CORP.; *pg.* 550, *pg.* 1650
ROCK IN COMFORT - Baby Product - THE BOPPY COMPANY, LLC; *pg.* 20, *pg.* 329
ROCK N' ROLL - Music Series - DIRECT HOLDINGS AMERICAS INC.; *pg.* 1636, *pg.* 1780
ROCK 'N SERVE - Kitchenware - TUPPERWARE BRANDS CORPORATION; *pg.* 1139, *pg.* 456
ROCK SPRINGS - Bike - MARIN BIKES; *pg.* 1708, *pg.* 168
ROCKAWAY - Jacket - I. SPIEWAK & SONS, INC.; *pg.* 42, *pg.* 1242
ROCKCUT - Metalworking Fluid - ROCK VALLEY OIL & CHEMICAL COMPANY; *pg.* 1179, *pg.* 631
ROCKEDGE - Metal Grave Markers - MATTHEWS INTERNATIONAL CORPORATION; *pg.* 1662, *pg.* 1578
ROCK'EM SOCK'EM ROBOTS - Toy - MATTEL, INC.; *pg.* 962, *pg.* 81
ROCKER GARD - Coating - 3M COMPANY; *pg.* 1142, *pg.* 956
ROCKET - Glove - 180S, LLC; *pg.* 1824, *pg.* 754
ROCKET - Educational Materials - SCHOLASTIC INC.; *pg.* 1683, *pg.* 1288
ROCKET - Bicycle Component - SRAM CORPORATION; *pg.* 967, *pg.* 590
ROCKET - Wiring Devices - SWIVELIER CO., INC.; *pg.* 1307, *pg.* 1142
ROCKET - Hammer Mills - WILLIAMS PATENT CRUSHER & PULVERIZER CO., INC.; *pg.* 1389, *pg.* 1005
ROCKET POWER - Toy - MATTEL, INC.; *pg.* 962, *pg.* 81
ROCKET RICHES - Game - WMS INDUSTRIES INC.; *pg.* 593, *pg.* 666
ROCKET TAP - Cold Forming Tap - REGAL BELOIT CORPORATION; *pg.* 106, *pg.* 1854
ROCKETFISH - Multimedia Bluetooth Keyboard - BEST BUY CO., INC.; *pg.* 1761, *pg.* 954
ROCKETSOC - Orthopedic Product - DJO INCORPORATED; *pg.* 1524, *pg.* 302
ROCKFIRE - Construction Equipment - VERMEER MANUFACTURING COMPANY; *pg.* 708, *pg.* 711
ROCKFORD ACOUSTIC DESIGN - Car Audio System - ROCKFORD CORPORATION; *pg.* 667, *pg.* 26
ROCKFORD FOSGATE - Car Audio System - ROCKFORD CORPORATION; *pg.* 667, *pg.* 26
ROCKFORD MACHINE TOOLS - Machine Tool Product - BOURN & KOCH MACHINE TOOL COMPANY; *pg.* 1319, *pg.* 654
ROCKFORD PUNCH PRESS - Machine Tool Product - BOURN & KOCH MACHINE TOOL COMPANY; *pg.* 1319, *pg.* 654
ROCKFORM - Metalworking Fluid - ROCK VALLEY OIL & CHEMICAL COMPANY; *pg.* 1179, *pg.* 631
ROCKHOPPER - Bicycle - SPECIALIZED BICYCLE COMPONENTS, INC.; *pg.* 1711, *pg.* 152
ROCKII - Sneaker - STEVEN MADDEN, LTD.; *pg.* 1819, *pg.* 1176
ROCKIN' HORSE GAME ROOM - Operator of Video Gaming Devices - FAIR GROUNDS CORPORATION; *pg.* 547, *pg.* 747
ROCKIN' RHYTHM BAND BOARD BOOKS - Educational Materials - SCHOLASTIC INC.; *pg.* 1683, *pg.* 1288
ROCKIN ROLL-UPS - Earplug - MCKEON PRODUCTS, INC.; *pg.* 1559, *pg.* 912
ROCKLAND - Shoes - ALLEN-EDMONDS SHOE CORP.; *pg.* 1804, *pg.* 1887
ROCKLATH - Plaster Base - USG CORPORATION; *pg.* 118, *pg.* 594
ROCKLINE - Belt Cleaner - FLEXIBLE STEEL LACING COMPANY; *pg.* 1337, *pg.* 608
ROCKMAN - Hardness Tester - NEWAGE TESTING INSTRUMENTS, INC.; *pg.* 1058, *pg.* 1532
ROCKMATE - Hardness Tester - NEWAGE TESTING INSTRUMENTS, INC.; *pg.* 1058, *pg.* 1532
ROCKPORT - Footwear - THE ROCKPORT GROUP; *pg.* 1818, *pg.* 812
ROCKPORT KIDS - Footwear - THE ROCKPORT GROUP; *pg.* 1818, *pg.* 812
ROCKPORT RESERVE - Footwear - THE ROCKPORT GROUP; *pg.* 1818, *pg.* 812
ROCKPORT XCS - Footwear - THE ROCKPORT GROUP; *pg.* 1818, *pg.* 812
ROCKQUENCH - Metalworking Fluid - ROCK VALLEY OIL & CHEMICAL COMPANY; *pg.* 1179, *pg.* 631
ROCKRESORTS - Resort - VAIL RESORTS, INC.; *pg.* 1117, *pg.* 313
ROCKSPIN - Lubricant and Process Oil - ROCK VALLEY OIL & CHEMICAL COMPANY; *pg.* 1179, *pg.* 631
ROCKSTAR - Energy Drink - ROCKSTAR, INC.; *pg.* 265, *pg.* 1029
ROCKSTAR JUICED - Energy Drink - ROCKSTAR, INC.; *pg.* 265, *pg.* 1029
ROCKSTAR PERFECTBERRY - Energy Drink - ROCKSTAR, INC.; *pg.* 265, *pg.* 1029
ROCKSTAR PUNCHED - Energy Drink - ROCKSTAR, INC.; *pg.* 265, *pg.* 1029
ROCKSTAR PUNCHED BLUE RASPBERRY - Energy Drink - ROCKSTAR, INC.; *pg.* 265, *pg.* 1029
ROCKSTAR PUNCHED GUAVA - Energy Drink - ROCKSTAR, INC.; *pg.* 265, *pg.* 1029
ROCKSTAR PURE ZERO BLUE ICE - Energy Drink - ROCKSTAR, INC.; *pg.* 265, *pg.* 1029
ROCKSTAR PURE ZERO MANGO ORANGE PASSIONFRUIT - Energy Drink - ROCKSTAR, INC.; *pg.* 265, *pg.* 1029
ROCKSTAR PURE ZERO PUNCHED - Energy Drink - ROCKSTAR, INC.; *pg.* 265, *pg.* 1029
ROCKSTAR PURE ZERO SILVER ICE - Energy Drink - ROCKSTAR, INC.; *pg.* 265, *pg.* 1029
ROCKSTAR RECOVERY LEMONADE - Energy Drink - ROCKSTAR, INC.; *pg.* 265, *pg.* 1029
ROCKSTAR RECOVERY ORANGE - Energy Drink - ROCKSTAR, INC.; *pg.* 265, *pg.* 1029
ROCKSTAR ROASED MOCHA - Energy Drink - ROCKSTAR, INC.; *pg.* 265, *pg.* 1029
ROCKSTAR ROASTED CARAMEL - Energy Drink - ROCKSTAR, INC.; *pg.* 265, *pg.* 1029
ROCKSTAR ROASTED LIGHT VANILLA - Energy Drink - ROCKSTAR, INC.; *pg.* 265, *pg.* 1029
ROCKSTAR SPARKLING CHERRY CITRUS - Energy Drink - ROCKSTAR, INC.; *pg.* 265, *pg.* 1029
ROCKSTAR SPARKLING PEACH - Energy Drink - ROCKSTAR, INC.; *pg.* 265, *pg.* 1029
ROCKSTAR SUGAR FREE - Energy Drink - ROCKSTAR, INC.; *pg.* 265, *pg.* 1029
ROCKSTAR SUPERSOURS BUBBLEBERRY - Energy Drink - ROCKSTAR, INC.; *pg.* 265, *pg.* 1029
ROCKSTAR SUPERSOURS GREEN APPLE - Energy Drink - ROCKSTAR, INC.; *pg.* 265, *pg.* 1029
ROCKSTAR XDURANCE - Energy Drink - ROCKSTAR, INC.; *pg.* 265, *pg.* 1029
ROCKSTAR ZERO CARB - Energy Drink - ROCKSTAR, INC.; *pg.* 265, *pg.* 1029
ROCKSUGAR PAN ASIAN KITCHEN - Food Product - CHEESECAKE FACTORY INCORPORATED; *pg.* 1017, *pg.* 56
ROCKVAC - Pneumatic Debris Removal Equipment - CHRISTIANSON SYSTEMS, INC.; *pg.* 1323, *pg.* 917
ROCKWAY - Lubricant and Process Oil - ROCK VALLEY OIL & CHEMICAL COMPANY; *pg.* 1179, *pg.* 631
ROCKWELL - Software - ROCKWELL AUTOMATION, INC.; *pg.* 668, *pg.* 1880
ROCKWELL COLLINS - Logo - ROCKWELL COLLINS, INC.; *pg.* 234, *pg.* 702
ROCKWELL SOFTWARE - Software - ROCKWELL AUTOMATION, INC.; *pg.* 668, *pg.* 1880
ROCKY - Furniture - AMISCO INDUSTRIES LTD.; *pg.* 913, *pg.* 1958
ROCKY - Office Furniture - STEELCASE INC.; *pg.* 475, *pg.* 889
ROCKY MOUNTAIN - Hardware Product - ROCKY MOUNTAIN HARDWARE INC.; *pg.* 1061, *pg.* 549
ROCKY MOUNTAIN - Log Homes - ROCKY MOUNTAIN LOG HOMES; *pg.* 108, *pg.* 1008
ROCKY MOUNTAIN MEDLEY - Candy Assortment - ROCKY MOUNTAIN CHOCOLATE FACTORY, INC.; *pg.* 1032, *pg.* 324
ROCKY MOUNTAIN MINTS - Mint-Flavored Chocolates - ROCKY MOUNTAIN CHOCOLATE FACTORY, INC.; *pg.* 1032, *pg.* 324
ROCKY MOUNTAIN NEWS - Newspaper - THE DENVER NEWSPAPER AGENCY; *pg.* 1634, *pg.* 318
ROCKY MOUNTAIN NEWS - Newspaper - THE E.W. SCRIPPS COMPANY; *pg.* 1639, *pg.* 1412
ROCKY MOUNTAIN PASTURES - Milk - COOPERATIVE REGIONS OF ORGANIC PRODUCER POOLS; *pg.* 850, *pg.* 1864
ROCKY MOUNTAIN SPLENDOR - Candy Assortment - ROCKY MOUNTAIN CHOCOLATE FACTORY, INC.; *pg.* 1032, *pg.* 324
ROCKY PEAK RIDGE - Clothing - ABERCROMBIE & FITCH CO.; *pg.* 37, *pg.* 1466
ROCKY POP - Candy Coated Popcorn - ROCKY MOUNTAIN CHOCOLATE FACTORY, INC.; *pg.* 1032, *pg.* 324
ROCKY RIDGE - Bike - MARIN BIKES; *pg.* 1708, *pg.* 168
ROCKY ROAD - Candy - ANNABELLE CANDY COMPANY, INC.; *pg.* 1850, *pg.* 100
ROCKY ROAD DARK - Candy Bar - ANNABELLE CANDY

COMPANY, INC.; pg. 1850, pg. 100
ROCKY ROAD DARK CHOCOLATE - Candy - ANNABELLE CANDY COMPANY, INC.; pg. 1850, pg. 100
ROCKY ROAD MINT - Candy - ANNABELLE CANDY COMPANY, INC.; pg. 1850, pg. 100
ROCKYROAD - Chocolate - ANNABELLE CANDY COMPANY, INC.; pg. 1850, pg. 100
ROCOCO - Rug - COURISTAN INC.; pg. 921, pg. 1067
ROCOL - Micro-Lubricant System - ITW FLUIDS NORTH AMERICA; pg. 980, pg. 614
ROCRYL - Alkyl Ester - DOW CHEMICAL; pg. 1156, pg. 1563
RODAR - Ultrasonic Pest Repellers - MICRON CORPORATION; pg. 654, pg. 840
RODDENBERRY'S NORTHWOODS - Sauces & Syrups - TREEHOUSE FOODS, INC.; pg. 901, pg. 649
RODEL - Industrial Material - DOW CHEMICAL; pg. 1156, pg. 1563
RODENT WORKSTATION - Scientific Instrument - BIOANALYTICAL SYSTEMS, INC.; pg. 1402, pg. 700
RODEO - Meat Products - JOHN MORRELL & CO.; pg. 866, pg. 1415
RODEO.COM - Advertising Website - LIVE CURRENT MEDIA INC.; pg. 1263, pg. 1911
RODERM - Chemicals & Adhesives - DOW CHEMICAL; pg. 1156, pg. 1563
RODEWAY INN - Hotels - CHOICE HOTELS INTERNATIONAL, INC.; pg. 1086, pg. 775
RODEX - Animal Safety Product - NEOGEN CORPORATION; pg. 883, pg. 896
RODINE - Metalworking Chemical - HENKEL CORPORATION; pg. 1166, pg. 897
RODON - Fly Rod Components - CORTLAND LINE COMPANY; pg. 1831, pg. 1155
RODOX - Chemical Product - ROCHESTER MIDLAND CORPORATION; pg. 334, pg. 1337
RODRIGUEZ - Classical Guitars - FENDER MUSICAL INSTRUMENTS CORPORATION; pg. 547, pg. 21
RODURFLEX - Insulator - LAPP INSULATOR COMPANY, LLC; pg. 1946, pg. 1173
ROEHLEN - Embossing Rolls & Plates - STANDEX INTERNATIONAL CORPORATION; pg. 60, pg. 1039
ROGAINE - Hair Regrowth Treatment - MCNEIL-PPC, INC.; pg. 1560, pg. 1533
ROGATOR - Sprayer And Spreader - AGCO CORPORATION; pg. 700, pg. 530
ROGERS - Silverware - ONEIDA LTD; pg. 1129, pg. 1318
ROGUE - Crossover SUV - NISSAN NORTH AMERICA, INC.; pg. 186, pg. 1633
ROGUE - Fabric - UNIROYAL ENGINEERED PRODUCTS; pg. 699, pg. 467
ROGUE RIVER - Shirt - SIMMS FISHING PRODUCTS CORP.; pg. 1845, pg. 1008
ROGUE WAVE SOURCEPRO C ++ - Software - ROGUE WAVE SOFTWARE, INC.; pg. 462, pg. 311
ROGUE WAVE STINGRAY STUDIO - Software - ROGUE WAVE SOFTWARE, INC.; pg. 462, pg. 311
ROH'LIX - Linear Actuators - ZERO-MAX, INC.; pg. 222, pg. 954
ROHM-CHROME - Paints & Coatings for Decorative & Protective Purposes - DOW CHEMICAL; pg. 1156, pg. 1563
ROHMIN - Mining Additive - DOW CHEMICAL; pg. 1156, pg. 1563
ROHNER COMFORT SOCKS - Healthcare Product - MEDICOOL, INC.; pg. 1562, pg. 294
ROHO - Heal Pads - ALIMED, INC.; pg. 1490, pg. 816
ROHO BARISELECT - Mattress - ALIMED, INC.; pg. 1490, pg. 816
ROHO MOJO - Designer Cover - THE ROHO GROUP; pg. 1591, pg. 556
ROHO SELECTAIR - Low Air Loss Mattress System - ALIMED, INC.; pg. 1490, pg. 816
ROHS COMPLIANT - Ceramic Chip - COILCRAFT, INC.; pg. 1324, pg. 562
ROHTO V - Lubricate for eyes - THE MENTHOLATUM COMPANY; pg. 1565, pg. 1320
ROHTO ZI - Eye Moisturizer - THE MENTHOLATUM COMPANY; pg. 1565, pg. 1320
ROI-TAN - Domestic Cigars - ALTADIS USA, INC.; pg. 1893, pg. 423
ROKEACH - Food Products - MANISCHEWITZ COMPANY; pg. 875, pg. 1097
ROKLITE - Armor Tile - THE DOW CHEMICAL COMPANY; pg. 1157, pg. 898
ROKU - Glass Tile - WALKER & ZANGER, INC.; pg. 119, pg. 281
ROL-A-DRAW - Foundry Mold Rollover Machine - PETTIBONE, LLC; pg. 1368, pg. 609
ROLAIDS - Antacid - CHATTEM, INC.; pg. 1515, pg. 1628
ROLARAM - Mechanical Actuator - DUFF-NORTON; pg. 204, pg. 1365
ROLATAPE - Electronic Measuring Tools - STANLEY BLACK & DECKER, INC.; pg. 1063, pg. 358
ROLD GOLD - Pretzels - FRITO-LAY NORTH AMERICA, INC.; pg. 1853, pg. 1730
ROLD GOLD - Pretzels - PEPSICO, INC.; pg. 259, pg. 1327
ROLEASE - Adhesive & Sealant - DOW CHEMICAL; pg. 1156, pg. 1563
ROLEPLAY - Software - SKILLSOFT PLC; pg. 470, pg. 1037
ROLETTE - Boots - AEROGROUP INTERNATIONAL, INC.; pg. 1803, pg. 1055
ROLL-A-CARD - File Cards For Rolodex Files - PILGRIM PLASTIC PRODUCTS COMPANY; pg. 1887, pg. 803
ROLL-A-DECK - Stage & Riser - WENGER CORPORATION; pg. 1307, pg. 952
ROLL-A-PUCK - Sport Product - FRANKLIN SPORTS, INC.; pg. 1834, pg. 847
ROLL-A-RAMA - Game Book - INNOVATIVE USA, INC.; pg. 957, pg. 363
ROLL & RHYME - Educational Toys - LEAPFROG ENTERPRISES, INC.; pg. 961, pg. 84
ROLL & WIN - Game - WMS INDUSTRIES INC.; pg. 593, pg. 666
ROLL ARMOR - Coating - PRECISION ROLL GRINDERS, INC.; pg. 1370, pg. 1514
ROLL CARRIER - Spreader - EASTMAN MACHINE COMPANY; pg. 1331, pg. 1148
ROLL CREDITS - Game - WMS INDUSTRIES INC.; pg. 593, pg. 666
ROLL-IN REFRIGERATOR RACKS - Racks for Roll-In or Pass-Thru Refrigerators, Freezers & Warming Cabinets - CRES-COR; pg. 1326, pg. 1464
ROLL N' GLUE - Art Materials - PENTEL OF AMERICA, LTD.; pg. 453, pg. 295
ROLL-O-WAX - Dental Product - DENTSPLY INTERNATIONAL INC.; pg. 1522, pg. 1596
ROLL-ON RELIEF - Rider Product - W.F. YOUNG, INC.; pg. 1610, pg. 817
ROLL OUT THE BARREL - Lottery Game - IOWA LOTTERY; pg. 996, pg. 705
ROLL RUNNER - Metal Building System - BUTLER MANUFACTURING COMPANY; pg. 72, pg. 981
ROLL STAND - Feed System - EASTMAN MACHINE COMPANY; pg. 1331, pg. 1148
ROLL STOCK - Durabubble Product - POLYAIR INTER PACK INC.; pg. 1467, pg. 1941
ROLL TO ROLL - Feeder - STANDARD DUPLICATING MACHINES CORPORATION; pg. 473, pg. 783
ROLL UP THE RIM TO WIN - Slogan - TIM HORTONS, INC.; pg. 1754, pg. 1930
ROLL VENT - Roofing Ventilation Product - BENJAMIN OBDYKE, INC.; pg. 70, pg. 1540
ROLLER ATTACKER - Toy & Game - HASBRO, INC.; pg. 954, pg. 1603
ROLLER BOWL - Game - WINNING MOVES GAMES, INC.; pg. 970, pg. 816
ROLLER COASTER TYCOON BOARD GAME - Board Game - HASBRO, INC.; pg. 954, pg. 1603
ROLLER COLOR - Eyeshadow - MAYBELLINE LLC; pg. 516, pg. 1257
ROLLER DERBY - Roller Skates - ROLLER DERBY SKATE CORP.; pg. 966, pg. 630
ROLLER PERM - Home Permanent - THE GILLETTE COMPANY; pg. 509, pg. 795
ROLLER SHIELD - Garage Door Child-Proofing Measure - MARTIN DOOR MANUFACTURING, INC.; pg. 96, pg. 1759
ROLLER STAR 350 - Skate - ROLLER DERBY SKATE CORP.; pg. 966, pg. 630
ROLLER STAR 550 - Skate - ROLLER DERBY SKATE CORP.; pg. 966, pg. 630
ROLLERRACK - Carton Flow Product - UNEX MANUFACTURING, INC.; pg. 1385, pg. 1075
ROLLING CASH 5 - Lottery Game - D.C. LOTTERY & CHARITABLE GAMES CONTROL BOARD; pg. 991, pg. 398
ROLLING CHASSIS - Chassis System - DANA HOLDING CORPORATION; pg. 203, pg. 1461
ROLLING ROCK - Lager - ANHEUSER-BUSCH COMPANIES, LLC; pg. 237, pg. 991
ROLLING ROCK LIGHT - Beer - ANHEUSER-BUSCH COMPANIES, LLC; pg. 237, pg. 991
ROLLING ROCK PREMIUM - Beer - ANHEUSER-BUSCH COMPANIES, LLC; pg. 237, pg. 991
ROLLING STONE - Magazine - WENNER MEDIA LLC; pg. 1701, pg. 1314
ROLLING WRITER - Pens - PENTEL OF AMERICA, LTD.; pg. 453, pg. 295
ROLLINS POND - Shirts - ABERCROMBIE & FITCH CO.; pg. 37, pg. 1466
ROLLITE - Rollator - INVACARE CORPORATION; pg. 1546, pg. 1451
ROLLMASTR - Bath Tissue - GEORGIA-PACIFIC LLC; pg. 1458, pg. 507
ROLLMATE - Plastic Bags - SONOCO PRODUCTS COMPANY; pg. 1469, pg. 1619
ROLLMATE II - Plastic Bags - SONOCO PRODUCTS COMPANY; pg. 1469, pg. 1619
ROLLMIX - Roller Mills - BLUE OX; pg. 701, pg. 1019
ROLLO - Furniture - AMERICAN LEATHER LP; pg. 912, pg. 1673
ROLLOVER - Cellular Phone Plan Feature - AT&T MOBILITY LLC; pg. 619, pg. 488
ROLLS - Wheelchair - INVACARE CORPORATION; pg. 1546, pg. 1451
ROLLS ROYCE - Automobile - BMW OF NORTH AMERICA, LLC; pg. 166, pg. 1133
ROLO - Chocolate Candy - THE HERSHEY CO.; pg. 1855, pg. 1538
ROLODEX - Publication - FRANKLIN ELECTRONIC PUBLISHERS, INC.; pg. 398, pg. 1048
ROLODEX - Filing System - NEWELL RUBBERMAID INC.; pg. 1128, pg. 515
ROLOX - Replacement Window & Door - TRUE HOME VALUE, INC.; pg. 117, pg. 738
ROLSCREEN - Retractable Screen - PELLA CORPORATION; pg. 104, pg. 711
ROM HIP - Orthopedic Product - DJO INCORPORATED; pg. 1524, pg. 302
ROMA - Shoes - ALLEN-EDMONDS SHOE CORP.; pg. 1804, pg. 1887
ROMA - Furniture - ETHAN ALLEN INTERIORS INC.; pg. 924, pg. 343
ROMA - Footwear - PHOENIX FOOTWEAR GROUP, INC.; pg. 1815, pg. 60
ROMAAN - Footwear - STEVEN MADDEN, LTD.; pg. 1819, pg. 1176
ROMAGRIP - Pipe Restraint Product - ROMAC INDUSTRIES, INC.; pg. 1061, pg. 1818
ROMAN - Dinnerware - THE HOMER LAUGHLIN CHINA COMPANY; pg. 1125, pg. 1850
ROMAN DYNASTY - Game - WMS INDUSTRIES INC.; pg. 593, pg. 666
ROMAN LIGHT - Bread - ROMAN MEAL COMPANY; pg. 834, pg. 1845
ROMAN MEAL - Bread; Waffles; Cereal; Refrigerated Products; Crackers - ROMAN MEAL COMPANY; pg. 834, pg. 1845
ROMAN MEAL - Breads - UNITED STATES BAKERY; pg. 907, pg. 1507
ROMAN MEAL CARB AWARE - Low-Carbohydrate Whole Wheat Bread - ROMAN MEAL COMPANY; pg. 834, pg. 1845
ROMAN MEAL COMPANY - Milling Company - ROMAN MEAL COMPANY; pg. 834, pg. 1845
ROMAN MEAL HIGH FIBER - High Fiber Bread - ROMAN MEAL COMPANY; pg. 834, pg. 1845
ROMAN MEAL HONEY COCONUT ALMOND GRANOLA - Whole Grain Granola Products - ROMAN MEAL COMPANY; pg. 834, pg. 1845
ROMAN MEAL HONEY NUT & OAT BRAN - Breads Made With Oats, Oat Bran, Almonds & Honey - ROMAN MEAL COMPANY; pg. 834, pg. 1845
ROMAN MEAL HONEY WHEATBERRY - Coarse Grained Breads with Soft Textures - ROMAN MEAL COMPANY; pg. 834, pg. 1845
ROMAN MEAL HONEYBRAN - Bread - ROMAN MEAL COMPANY; pg. 834, pg. 1845
ROMAN MEAL MULTIGRAIN PLUS - Multigrain Bread - ROMAN MEAL COMPANY; pg. 834, pg. 1845
ROMAN MEAL SEVEN GRAIN - Combination Grains Bread Products - ROMAN MEAL COMPANY; pg. 834, pg. 1845
ROMAN MEAL SUGAR FREE - Sugar Free Bread - ROMAN MEAL COMPANY; pg. 834, pg. 1845

ROMAN MEAL SUN GRAIN - Whole Grains Bread Products - ROMAN MEAL COMPANY; *pg.* 834, *pg.* 1845
ROMAN MEAL TWELVE GRAINS - Combination Grains Bread Products - ROMAN MEAL COMPANY; *pg.* 834, *pg.* 1845
ROMANBURGER - Burger - RESTAURANT DEVELOPERS CORP.; *pg.* 1747, *pg.* 1464
ROMANCE - Carpet - BEAULIEU GROUP, LLC; *pg.* 917, *pg.* 529
ROMANCE - Fragrance - RALPH LAUREN CORPORATION; *pg.* 46, *pg.* 1284
ROMANCE 106.7 FM - Radio Station - SPANISH BROADCASTING SYSTEM INC.; *pg.* 310, *pg.* 446
ROMANCE OF FLOWERS - Scent Extraction Technology - INTERNATIONAL FLAVORS & FRAGRANCES INC.; *pg.* 512, *pg.* 1244
ROMANCE SILVER - Fragrance - RALPH LAUREN CORPORATION; *pg.* 46, *pg.* 1284
ROMANESQUE - Wicker Furniture Collection - TELESCOPE CASUAL FURNITURE INC.; *pg.* 944, *pg.* 1162
ROMANOFF - Furniture - ASHLEY FURNITURE INDUSTRIES, INC.; *pg.* 914, *pg.* 1852
ROMANOFF - Caviar - LANCASTER COLONY CORPORATION; *pg.* 873, *pg.* 1441
ROMANOFF - Caviar - T. MARZETTI COMPANY; *pg.* 900, *pg.* 1444
ROMANO'S MACARONI GRILL - Italian Restaurant - BRINKER INTERNATIONAL, INC.; *pg.* 1718, *pg.* 1676
ROMANTIC TAJ - Rug - ETHAN ALLEN INTERIORS INC.; *pg.* 924, *pg.* 343
ROMANZA - Bath Accessory - CROSCILL, INC.; *pg.* 1122, *pg.* 1220
ROMATE - Wine - SHAW ROSS INTERNATIONAL IMPORTERS; *pg.* 1970, *pg.* 449
ROMAZICON - Pharmaceutical Product - HOFFMANN-LA ROCHE INC.; *pg.* 1542, *pg.* 1099
ROMBE - Dish - BROWN & BIGELOW, INC.; *pg.* 1624, *pg.* 959
ROMCHECK - Medical Product - HOLOGIC, INC.; *pg.* 1416, *pg.* 784
ROMCO - Industrial Sewing Light - CONSEW; *pg.* 53, *pg.* 1049
ROME - Furniture - AMISCO INDUSTRIES LTD.; *pg.* 913, *pg.* 1958
ROME & EGYPT - Game - WMS INDUSTRIES INC.; *pg.* 593, *pg.* 666
ROME IS BURNING - Sports Discussion Program - ESPN, INC.; *pg.* 285, *pg.* 340
ROMEO - Footwear - CAPEZIO BALLET MAKERS INC.; *pg.* 1805, *pg.* 1125
ROMEO - Eyewear - OAKLEY, INC.; *pg.* 1840, *pg.* 86
ROMEO AND JOLIET - Nail Care Product - OPI PRODUCTS INC.; *pg.* 518, *pg.* 167
ROMEO Y JULIETA RESERVA REAL - Cigars - FINCK CIGAR CO.; *pg.* 1894, *pg.* 1740
ROMERO - Bath Accessory - CROSCILL, INC.; *pg.* 1122, *pg.* 1220
ROMEX - Connector - MOLEX INCORPORATED; *pg.* 655, *pg.* 628
ROMEX - Residential & Commercial Electrical Wire - SOUTHWIRE COMPANY; *pg.* 1063, *pg.* 527
ROMS - Software Support Service - COMMVAULT SYSTEMS, INC.; *pg.* 377, *pg.* 1125
ROMY - Furniture - AMISCO INDUSTRIES LTD.; *pg.* 913, *pg.* 1958
RON LLAVE - Puerto Rican Rum - DIAGEO CANADA, INC.; *pg.* 1961, *pg.* 1937
RON LLAVE - Rum - HEAVEN HILL DISTILLERIES, INC.; *pg.* 1964, *pg.* 725
RON RIO - Rum - MCCORMICK DISTILLING CO., INC.; *pg.* 1966, *pg.* 1007
RON VIEJO DE CALDAS - Rums - SHAW ROSS INTERNATIONAL IMPORTERS; *pg.* 1970, *pg.* 449
RONA - Home Improvement Store - RONA, INC.; *pg.* 216, *pg.* 1950
RONACLEAN - Cleaner - DOW CHEMICAL; *pg.* 1156, *pg.* 1563
RONALD MCDONALD - Clown - MCDONALD'S CORPORATION; *pg.* 1737, *pg.* 645
RONALD MCDONALD CHILDREN'S CHARITIES - Charitable Organizations - MCDONALD'S CORPORATION; *pg.* 1737, *pg.* 645
RONALD MCDONALD HOUSE - Family Lodging for Medically Treated Children - MCDONALD'S CORPORATION; *pg.* 1737, *pg.* 645
RONALD MCDONALD HOUSE CHARITIES - Charitable Organizations - MCDONALD'S CORPORATION; *pg.* 1737, *pg.* 645
RONALD REDDING DESIGNS - Wallpaper - YORK WALLCOVERINGS INC.; *pg.* 947, *pg.* 1598
RONCO - Pasta - AMERICAN ITALIAN PASTA COMPANY; *pg.* 837, *pg.* 980
RONDO - Tables - HOWE FURNITURE CORPORATION; *pg.* 928, *pg.* 998
RONDO - Candy - WM. WRIGLEY JR. COMPANY; *pg.* 1863, *pg.* 596
RONIN - Apparel - BURTON SNOWBOARD COMPANY; *pg.* 1829, *pg.* 1765
RONINCAST - Software - WIRELESS RONIN TECHNOLOGIES INC.; *pg.* 689, *pg.* 951
RONNY - Furniture - AMISCO INDUSTRIES LTD.; *pg.* 913, *pg.* 1958
RONOCO CALCULATOR WHEELS - Software - THE ROUGH NOTES COMPANY, INC.; *pg.* 1681, *pg.* 675
RONRICO - Rum - JIM BEAM BRANDS CO.; *pg.* 1965, *pg.* 601
RONRON - Food Product - MARS, INCORPORATED; *pg.* 1858, *pg.* 1792
RONSEAL - Wood Finishing Products - THE SHERWIN-WILLIAMS COMPANY; *pg.* 1447, *pg.* 1435
RONZONI - Food Product - NEW WORLD PASTA COMPANY; *pg.* 885, *pg.* 1537
ROOF RIGS - Sprayers - GRACO, INC.; *pg.* 1342, *pg.* 935
ROOF RUNNER - Metal Building System - BUTLER MANUFACTURING COMPANY; *pg.* 72, *pg.* 981
ROOF SENTRY - Metal Building System - BUTLER MANUFACTURING COMPANY; *pg.* 72, *pg.* 981
ROOFER'S CHOICE - Corrosion Resistant Coil Nails - PASLODE; *pg.* 1059, *pg.* 664
ROOFGARD - Roofing Cap Sheet - GAF MATERIALS CORP.; *pg.* 83, *pg.* 1681
ROOFING SPIKE - Roofing Fastener - POWERS FASTENERS INC.; *pg.* 1059, *pg.* 1143
ROOFMASTER - Architectural Roofing Shingles - BUILDING PRODUCTS OF CANADA CORP.; *pg.* 72, *pg.* 1951
ROOFMATE - Insulation - THE DOW CHEMICAL COMPANY; *pg.* 1157, *pg.* 898
ROOFPAK - Spray System - THE DOW CHEMICAL COMPANY; *pg.* 1157, *pg.* 898
ROOFWALKS - Walkway Systems - UNISTRUT CORPORATION; *pg.* 117, *pg.* 913
ROOK - Game - HASBRO, INC.; *pg.* 954, *pg.* 1603
ROOKIE BIOGRAPHIES - Educational Materials - SCHOLASTIC INC.; *pg.* 1683, *pg.* 1288
ROOKIE CHOICES - Educational Materials - SCHOLASTIC INC.; *pg.* 1683, *pg.* 1288
ROOKIE LEAGUE - Baseball Season - THE PHILLIES, L.P.; *pg.* 575, *pg.* 1569
ROOKIE READ-ABOUT - Educational Materials - SCHOLASTIC INC.; *pg.* 1683, *pg.* 1288
ROOM ADAPTIVE BASS OPTIMIZATION SYSTEM - Software - HARMAN INTERNATIONAL INDUSTRIES, INCORPORATED; *pg.* 641, *pg.* 374
ROOM-ALERT - Sensor - NAPCO SECURITY SYSTEMS, INC.; *pg.* 658, *pg.* 1138
ROOM-FRIENDLY ACOUSTICAL DESIGN - Software - HARMAN INTERNATIONAL INDUSTRIES, INCORPORATED; *pg.* 641, *pg.* 374
ROOM MATE - Residential Lighting Decor Light - SWIVELIER CO., INC.; *pg.* 1307, *pg.* 1142
ROOM TECH - Toy & Game - HASBRO, INC.; *pg.* 954, *pg.* 1603
ROOMATE - Trash Cans - THE CLOROX COMPANY; *pg.* 327, *pg.* 169
ROOMBA - Robotic floor cleaner - IROBOT CORP.; *pg.* 1418, *pg.* 785
ROOMBA 500 SERIES - Robotic Floor Cleaner - IROBOT CORP.; *pg.* 1418, *pg.* 785
ROOMLAC - Translucent Plastic Foam - THE DOW CHEMICAL COMPANY; *pg.* 1157, *pg.* 898
ROOMMATE - Audio Product - BOSE CORPORATION; *pg.* 626, *pg.* 820
ROOMMATE - Mobile Partition - HUFCOR INCORPORATED; *pg.* 87, *pg.* 1861
ROOMS - Manual - XEROX CORPORATION; *pg.* 494, *pg.* 365
ROOMSAVER.COM - Travel Website - DOMINION ENTERPRISES; *pg.* 1636, *pg.* 1796
ROOMTUNE - Furniture - HERMAN MILLER, INC.; *pg.* 926, *pg.* 913
ROOMVIEW - Software - CRESTRON ELECTRONICS INC.; *pg.* 631, *pg.* 1116
ROOMWIZARD - Room Scheduling System - POLYVISION CORPORATION; *pg.* 665, *pg.* 531
ROOMWIZARD - Appliances - STEELCASE INC.; *pg.* 475, *pg.* 889
ROOSTER - Table Textile - HERITAGE LACE INC.; *pg.* 694, *pg.* 711
ROOT GUARDIAN - Soil Care Product - GARDENS ALIVE!, INC.; *pg.* 1796, *pg.* 693
ROOT PRODUCTION METHOD - Plant Growth Technology - FORREST KEELING NURSERY, INC.; *pg.* 1795, *pg.* 977
ROOT-RX - Treatment Program - THE F.A. BARTLETT TREE EXPERT COMPANY; *pg.* 1795, *pg.* 373
ROOT TUTOR - Reusable Planting Trays - SUMMIT PLASTIC CO.; *pg.* 1470, *pg.* 1403
ROOT ZX - Dental Product - DENTSPLY INTERNATIONAL INC.; *pg.* 1522, *pg.* 1596
ROOTSWEET - Plant Starter Kit - THE PAGE SEED CO.; *pg.* 1798, *pg.* 1163
ROP NETWORKS - Every United States Newspaper - METRO NEWSPAPER ADVERTISING SERVICES, INC.; *pg.* 1664, *pg.* 1259
ROPACO - Paper & Nonwoven Material - FIBERMARK INC.; *pg.* 1457, *pg.* 1764
ROPAQUE - Additive - DOW CHEMICAL; *pg.* 1156, *pg.* 1563
ROPAQUE - Opaque Polymers - THE DOW CHEMICAL COMPANY; *pg.* 1157, *pg.* 898
ROPE 'EM IN - Game - WMS INDUSTRIES INC.; *pg.* 593, *pg.* 666
ROPER - Home Appliance Product - WHIRLPOOL CORPORATION; *pg.* 62, *pg.* 872
ROPESPORT - Fitness Product - BALLY TOTAL FITNESS HOLDINGS CORPORATION; *pg.* 532, *pg.* 1200
ROS WALSH - Home & Garden Product - ENESCO, LLC; *pg.* 1124, *pg.* 620
ROSA - Office Furniture - STEELCASE INC.; *pg.* 475, *pg.* 889
ROSA MOSQUETA - Hair & Skin Product - AUBREY ORGANICS INC.; *pg.* 499, *pg.* 470
ROSACLEAR - Skin Care Products - OBAGI MEDICAL PRODUCTS, INC.; *pg.* 1577, *pg.* 123
ROSALIE - Footwear - EASTLAND SHOE CORPORATION; *pg.* 1808, *pg.* 750
ROSALITA - Fabric - NEMSCHOFF, INC.; *pg.* 936, *pg.* 1890
ROSALTA - Beverages - THE COCA-COLA COMPANY; *pg.* 240, *pg.* 493
ROSANIL - Topical Drug - GALDERMA LABORATORIES, L.P.; *pg.* 1532, *pg.* 1695
ROSARITA - Food Product - CONAGRA FOODS, INC.; *pg.* 826, *pg.* 1014
ROSAUER'S - Supermarkets - ROSAUERS SUPERMARKETS, INC.; *pg.* 1032, *pg.* 1844
ROSAUERS - Supermarkets - URM STORES, INC.; *pg.* 1036, *pg.* 1844
ROSAVE.Z - Depth Filter with Z.Plex Technology - GE WATER & PROCESS TECHNOLOGIES; *pg.* 1339, *pg.* 1588
ROSCO COOKIES - Film & Video Product - ROSCO LABORATORIES, INC.; *pg.* 1782, *pg.* 378
ROSCOFLAMEX - Coating - ROSCO LABORATORIES, INC.; *pg.* 1782, *pg.* 378
ROSCOGLO - Paint - ROSCO LABORATORIES, INC.; *pg.* 1782, *pg.* 378
ROSCOLENE - Filter - ROSCO LABORATORIES, INC.; *pg.* 1782, *pg.* 378
ROSCOLEUM - Flooring Product - ROSCO LABORATORIES, INC.; *pg.* 1782, *pg.* 378
ROSCOLUX - Filter - ROSCO LABORATORIES, INC.; *pg.* 1782, *pg.* 378
ROSCOTILES - Floor - ROSCO LABORATORIES, INC.; *pg.* 1782, *pg.* 378
ROSE - Furniture - AMISCO INDUSTRIES LTD.; *pg.* 913, *pg.* 1958
ROSE - Bookmark - HERITAGE LACE INC.; *pg.* 694, *pg.* 711
ROSE - Hat - WOODEN SHIPS OF HOBOKEN; *pg.* 35, *pg.* 1315
ROSE DOME - Cake Packaging - PACTIV CORPORATION; *pg.* 1466, *pg.* 624
ROSE ELEGANCE - Flower Arrangement - 1-800-FLOWERS.COM, INC.; *pg.* 1758, *pg.* 1151
ROSE GARDEN - Textiles - BERNHARDT DESIGN; *pg.* 918, *pg.* 1381
ROSE GARDEN - Bedding - CROSCILL, INC.; *pg.* 1122, *pg.* 1220

ROSE LOVER'S BOUQUET - Flower Arrangement - 1-800-FLOWERS.COM, INC.; *pg.* 1758, *pg.* 1151
ROSE MEDLEY - Rug - COURISTAN INC.; *pg.* 921, *pg.* 1067
ROSE OF CAIRO - Game - WMS INDUSTRIES INC.; *pg.* 593, *pg.* 666
ROSE PACKING - Smoked Meat Products - ROSE PACKING COMPANY; *pg.* 892, *pg.* 556
ROSE PETALS - Bear - GUND, INC.; *pg.* 954, *pg.* 1056
ROSE SYMBOL - Cleaning Services - DURACLEAN INTERNATIONAL, INC.; *pg.* 329, *pg.* 553
ROSE WITH TINY BUBBLES - Bath Set - 1-800-FLOWERS.COM, INC.; *pg.* 1758, *pg.* 1151
ROSEAIR - Motorhome - REXHALL INDUSTRIES, INC.; *pg.* 1710, *pg.* 121
ROSEAL - Industrial Material - DOW CHEMICAL; *pg.* 1156, *pg.* 1563
ROSEBUD - Table Textile - HERITAGE LACE INC.; *pg.* 694, *pg.* 711
ROSECORE - Fabric - F. SCHUMACHER & CO.; *pg.* 925, *pg.* 1230
ROSEDALE'S BEAUTY - Container Grown Plant - MONROVIA GROWERS; *pg.* 1797, *pg.* 44
ROSELYN STRIPE - Window Treatment - CROSCILL, INC.; *pg.* 1122, *pg.* 1220
ROSEMALING - Dinnerware - THE HOMER LAUGHLIN CHINA COMPANY; *pg.* 1125, *pg.* 1850
ROSEPRIDE - Lawn & Garden Products - THE SCOTTS MIRACLE-GRO COMPANY; *pg.* 1799, *pg.* 1459
ROSES - Beverages - THE COCA-COLA COMPANY; *pg.* 240, *pg.* 493
ROSES ALIVE! - Flower Gardening - GARDENS ALIVE!, INC.; *pg.* 1796, *pg.* 693
ROSETTA - Application Program - APPLE INC.; *pg.* 350, *pg.* 73
ROSETTA STONE LANGUAGE LEARNING SUCCESS - Language Learning Solutions - ROSETTA STONE INC.; *pg.* 462, *pg.* 1774
ROSETTA WORLD - Language Learning Solutions - ROSETTA STONE INC.; *pg.* 462, *pg.* 1774
ROSETTASTONE.COM - Language Learning Website - ROSETTA STONE INC.; *pg.* 462, *pg.* 1774
ROSETTAWORLD.COM - Language Learning Website - ROSETTA STONE INC.; *pg.* 462, *pg.* 1774
ROSETTO - Food Product - THE HAIN CELESTIAL GROUP, INC.; *pg.* 860, *pg.* 1172
ROSEWARE - Bowl - PACTIV CORPORATION; *pg.* 1466, *pg.* 624
ROSEWOOD - Furniture - ASHLEY FURNITURE INDUSTRIES, INC.; *pg.* 914, *pg.* 1852
ROSEWOOD - Guitar - PAUL REED SMITH GUITARS; *pg.* 574, *pg.* 779
ROSIDAL - Medical & Aesthetic Product - DYNATRONICS CORPORATION; *pg.* 1526, *pg.* 1757
ROSLIP - Adhesive & Sealant - DOW CHEMICAL; *pg.* 1156, *pg.* 1563
ROSPHALT - Asphalt Additive - CHASE CORPORATION; *pg.* 1152, *pg.* 803
ROSS - Glues - ELMER'S PRODUCTS, INC.; *pg.* 1442, *pg.* 1479
ROSS - Dinnerware - THE HOMER LAUGHLIN CHINA COMPANY; *pg.* 1125, *pg.* 1850
ROSS - THE KRAFT HEINZ COMPANY; *pg.* 870, *pg.* 1577
ROSS - Gift Cards - ROSS STORES, INC.; *pg.* 1783, *pg.* 78
ROSS - Automotive Product - ROSTRA PRECISION CONTROLS, INC.; *pg.* 216, *pg.* 1381
ROSS DRESS FOR LESS - Slogan - ROSS STORES, INC.; *pg.* 1783, *pg.* 78
ROSS REPORTS - Publication - NIELSEN BUSINESS MEDIA; *pg.* 1671, *pg.* 1272
ROSS STORES - Clothing, Shoes, Home Accents, Luggage & Cosmetics Retailing - ROSS STORES, INC.; *pg.* 1783, *pg.* 78
ROSSELLA - Food Product - CANADIAN FISH EXPORTERS, INC.; *pg.* 845, *pg.* 784
ROSSEY - Footwear - STEVEN MADDEN, LTD.; *pg.* 1819, *pg.* 1176
ROSSMORE - Apparel - VANS, INC.; *pg.* 1821, *pg.* 76
ROSTRA - Precision Control - ROSTRA PRECISION CONTROLS, INC.; *pg.* 216, *pg.* 1381
ROSWELL - Professional Digital Video Editing Systems - ALIENWARE CORPORATION; *pg.* 346, *pg.* 439
ROSWELL - Furniture - FLEXSTEEL INDUSTRIES, INC.; *pg.* 925, *pg.* 707
ROSYS - Blood Bank Automation System - IMMUCOR, INC.; *pg.* 1544, *pg.* 537
ROT-STOP - Disease Control Product - GARDENS ALIVE!, INC.; *pg.* 1796, *pg.* 693
ROTA - Trash Bags; Aluminum Foil - THE CLOROX COMPANY; *pg.* 327, *pg.* 169
ROTABLATOR - Medical Device - BOSTON SCIENTIFIC CORPORATION; *pg.* 1508, *pg.* 831
ROTABROACH - Cutter - HOUGEN MANUFACTURING INC.; *pg.* 1347, *pg.* 908
ROTACLEAN - Engineered Product And System - SULZER METCO (WESTBURY) INC.; *pg.* 1064, *pg.* 1350
ROTACLONE - Diagnostic Test Product - MERIDIAN BIOSCIENCE INC.; *pg.* 1422, *pg.* 1417
ROTACUT - Cutter - HOUGEN MANUFACTURING INC.; *pg.* 1347, *pg.* 908
ROTAFLO - Glass & Ceramic Material - CORNING INCORPORATED; *pg.* 1122, *pg.* 1154
ROTAJECTOR - Vacuum System - CROLL-REYNOLDS COMPANY, INC.; *pg.* 1326, *pg.* 1103
ROTAKOTE - Polyurethane Elastomer - THE DOW CHEMICAL COMPANY; *pg.* 1157, *pg.* 898
ROTALINK - Medical Device - BOSTON SCIENTIFIC CORPORATION; *pg.* 1508, *pg.* 831
ROTALIP - Seal & Thermoplastic Component - GREENE, TWEED & CO.; *pg.* 1344, *pg.* 1544
ROTALOC - Cutter - HOUGEN MANUFACTURING INC.; *pg.* 1347, *pg.* 908
ROTALOC PLUS - Annular Cutters - HOUGEN MANUFACTURING INC.; *pg.* 1347, *pg.* 908
ROTARY - Shoe - AEROGROUP INTERNATIONAL, INC.; *pg.* 1803, *pg.* 1055
ROTARY - Actuator - ECLIPSE INC.; *pg.* 1332, *pg.* 655
ROTARY-AIRE - Marine Air Conditioners - WESTERBEKE CORPORATION; *pg.* 1388, *pg.* 847
THE ROTARY UNION - Rotating Joint - DUFF-NORTON; *pg.* 204, *pg.* 1365
ROTASON - Ink - VAN SON HOLLAND INK CORPORATION OF AMERICA; *pg.* 487, *pg.* 1169
ROTATEQ - Medicine - MERCK & CO., INC.; *pg.* 1566, *pg.* 1077
ROTATEST - Pharmaceutical Product - ALERE INC.; *pg.* 1488, *pg.* 849
ROTATING WILD - Game - WMS INDUSTRIES INC.; *pg.* 593, *pg.* 666
ROTATION - Fabric - NEMSCHOFF, INC.; *pg.* 936, *pg.* 1890
ROTAWIRE - Medical Device - BOSTON SCIENTIFIC CORPORATION; *pg.* 1508, *pg.* 831
ROTAX - Engines - BOMBARDIER RECREATIONAL PRODUCTS, INC.; *pg.* 201, *pg.* 1960
ROTH IRA - Retirement Plans - PRINCIPAL FINANCIAL GROUP, INC.; *pg.* 796, *pg.* 706
ROTHBURY - Faucets - MOEN INCORPORATED; *pg.* 1056, *pg.* 1468
ROTILAND - Indian Flatbread - CIRCLE FOODS, LLC; *pg.* 848, *pg.* 201
ROTISSERIE - Chicken - PILGRIM'S PRIDE CORPORATION; *pg.* 889, *pg.* 330
ROTO-CUT - Asphalt Cutter - ALLIED CONSTRUCTION PRODUCTS, LLC; *pg.* 1311, *pg.* 1427
ROTO-RING - Tie Downs - GENERAL ENGINES COMPANY INC.; *pg.* 174, *pg.* 437
ROTO-ROOTER - Sewer Cleaning Machine - CHEMED CORPORATION; *pg.* 327, *pg.* 1410
ROTO-TECH - Machine Tool Product - BOURN & KOCH MACHINE TOOL COMPANY; *pg.* 1319, *pg.* 654
ROTO WITCH - Underground Construction Equipment - CHARLES MACHINE WORKS, INC.; *pg.* 1322, *pg.* 1488
ROTOBLAST - Fluid Handling System - GRACO, INC.; *pg.* 1342, *pg.* 935
ROTOBLAST - Cleaning System - PANGBORN CORPORATION; *pg.* 1367, *pg.* 532
ROTOCAGE - Lumpbreaker - WYSSMONT CO., INC.; *pg.* 1390, *pg.* 1068
ROTOCAST - Rotational Molding Machine - MCNEIL & NRM INC.; *pg.* 1360, *pg.* 1402
ROTOCLEAN - Spray Product - SPRAYING SYSTEMS CO.; *pg.* 1063, *pg.* 670
ROTOCOAT - Color Coated Alternative - FERRO CORPORATION; *pg.* 1162, *pg.* 1462
ROTOFLEX - Machining System - ATS AUTOMATION TOOLING SYSTEMS INC.; *pg.* 355, *pg.* 1919
ROTOFLEX - Fluid Handling System - GRACO, INC.; *pg.* 1342, *pg.* 935
ROTOFLUX - Nondestructive Testing - MAGNETIC ANALYSIS CORPORATION; *pg.* 1421, *pg.* 1158
ROTOFOR - Software - BIO-RAD LABORATORIES, INC.; *pg.* 1504, *pg.* 101
ROTOGRATE - Ash Discharge Stoker - DETROIT STOKER CO.; *pg.* 1070, *pg.* 900
ROTOLON - Seal & Thermoplastic Component - GREENE, TWEED & CO.; *pg.* 1344, *pg.* 1544
ROTOLYTE - Software - BIO-RAD LABORATORIES, INC.; *pg.* 1504, *pg.* 101
ROTOMAC - Nondestructive Testing - MAGNETIC ANALYSIS CORPORATION; *pg.* 1421, *pg.* 1158
ROTOMAN - Press - MANROLAND INC.; *pg.* 430, *pg.* 669
ROTOMIX - Capsule Mixer - 3M COMPANY; *pg.* 1142, *pg.* 956
ROTOPER - Machining System - ATS AUTOMATION TOOLING SYSTEMS INC.; *pg.* 355, *pg.* 1919
ROTOPRONE - Therapy System - KINETIC CONCEPTS, INC.; *pg.* 1553, *pg.* 1741
ROTOR - Blenders - CHESHER EQUIPMENT LTD.; *pg.* 1323, *pg.* 1925
ROTOR - Musical Instrument - PEAVEY ELECTRONICS CORPORATION; *pg.* 662, *pg.* 970
ROTOREST - Critical Care Therapy System - KINETIC CONCEPTS, INC.; *pg.* 1553, *pg.* 1741
ROTOROLLED - Steel Tubing - THE TIMKEN COMPANY; *pg.* 218, *pg.* 1408
ROTOSCOOP - Feeder - WYSSMONT CO., INC.; *pg.* 1390, *pg.* 1068
ROTOSTOKER VCG - Air Cooled Grate - DETROIT STOKER CO.; *pg.* 1070, *pg.* 900
ROTOVALVE - Core Valve - RODNEY HUNT COMPANY; *pg.* 1372, *pg.* 840
ROTTEN - Apparel - OAKLEY, INC.; *pg.* 1840, *pg.* 86
ROUDYBUSH - Pet Product - PETSMART, INC.; *pg.* 1481, *pg.* 18
ROUGH - Tobacco Product - AMERICAN SNUFF COMPANY; *pg.* 1893, *pg.* 1641
ROUGH AND READY - Surface Material - STEELCASE INC.; *pg.* 475, *pg.* 889
ROUGH COUNTRY - Twist Tobacco - AMERICAN SNUFF COMPANY; *pg.* 1893, *pg.* 1641
ROUGH NOTES - Magazine - THE ROUGH NOTES COMPANY, INC.; *pg.* 1681, *pg.* 675
ROUGH RIDER - Lawn Cart - RUBBERMAID HOME PRODUCTS; *pg.* 1138, *pg.* 1453
ROUGHAC - Spiral Cutter - GLEASON CORPORATION; *pg.* 1340, *pg.* 1335
ROUGHLYTE - Vaportight Fixtures - CRESCENT/STONCO SUPPLY DIVISION; *pg.* 1295, *pg.* 1121
ROUGHNECK - Storage Products - NEWELL RUBBERMAID INC.; *pg.* 1128, *pg.* 515
ROUGHNECK - Storage Box - SCHOOL-TECH, INC.; *pg.* 1844, *pg.* 866
ROUGHNECK - Impact Resistant Camera Domes - VICON INDUSTRIES, INC.; *pg.* 685, *pg.* 1166
ROUGHNECK - Stand - WENGER CORPORATION; *pg.* 1307, *pg.* 952
ROUGHRIDER - Foam Pig - T.D. WILLIAMSON, INC.; *pg.* 1380, *pg.* 1490
ROULEAU - Studded Rubber Floor Tile & Stairtreads - BURKE INDUSTRIES, INC.; *pg.* 919, *pg.* 239
ROULETTE - Fabric - NEMSCHOFF, INC.; *pg.* 936, *pg.* 1890
ROUND BACK - Lighting - SWIVELIER CO., INC.; *pg.* 1307, *pg.* 1142
ROUND HILL WHOLE - Poultry Product - PILGRIM'S PRIDE CORPORATION; *pg.* 889, *pg.* 330
ROUND SPECTRUM - Medical Device - MENTOR CORPORATION; *pg.* 1565, *pg.* 263
ROUND TABLE - Wheat Flour - THE KING ARTHUR FLOUR COMPANY, INC.; *pg.* 833, *pg.* 1767
ROUND TABLE PIZZA - Pizza - ROUND TABLE PIZZA; *pg.* 1748, *pg.* 69
ROUND-THE-CLOCK - Room Freshener - SURCO PRODUCTS, INC.; *pg.* 336, *pg.* 1581
ROUND TRIP - Hair Care Product - JOHN PAUL MITCHELL SYSTEMS; *pg.* 512, *pg.* 133
ROUND TRIP - Envelope - TENSION ENVELOPE CORPORATION; *pg.* 483, *pg.* 986
ROUND-UP - Gaming Product - GLD PRODUCTS, INC.; *pg.* 1835, *pg.* 1882
ROUND-UP - Horse Feed - MANNA PRO CORPORATION; *pg.* 1478, *pg.* 975
ROUNDRIVE - Headed Nails - PASLODE; *pg.* 1059, *pg.* 664
ROUNDUP - Steamers - CHESHER EQUIPMENT LTD.; *pg.* 1323, *pg.* 1925
ROUNDUP - Agricultural Product - MONSANTO COMPANY;

pg. 1173, pg. 999
ROUNDUP PRO - Herbicide - MONSANTO COMPANY; pg. 1173, pg. 999
ROUNDUP PRODRY - Herbicide - MONSANTO COMPANY; pg. 1173, pg. 999
ROUNDUP READY - Seed Corn - MOEWS SEED CO., INC.; pg. 1797, pg. 616
ROUNDUP READY - Cotton Seed Product - MONSANTO; pg. 1798, pg. 971
ROUNDUP READY - Herbicide Resistant Seeds - MONSANTO COMPANY; pg. 1173, pg. 999
ROUNDUP READY - Grain Seed Product - TERRAL SEED, INC.; pg. 1801, pg. 748
ROUNDUP READY - Soybean - UNIVERSAL COOPERATIVES, INC.; pg. 1482, pg. 922
ROUNDUP READY 2 YIELD - Insecticides - MONSANTO COMPANY; pg. 1173, pg. 999
ROUNDUP READY COTTON - Herbicide-Tolerant Seeds - MONSANTO; pg. 1798, pg. 971
ROUNDY'S - Food Wholesale Distribution - ROUNDY'S SUPERMARKETS INC.; pg. 1032, pg. 1880
ROUNTHANE - Extruded Thermoplastic Round Belting - SHINGLE BELTING COMPANY; pg. 1375, pg. 1544
ROUSSEAU - Tractor - ALAMO GROUP INC.; pg. 1311, pg. 1745
ROUST-A-BOUT - Pipe Couplings - VICTAULIC COMPANY; pg. 1066, pg. 1529
ROUT - Lawn & Garden Products - THE SCOTTS MIRACLE-GRO COMPANY; pg. 1799, pg. 1459
ROUT-T - Input/Output Device - MERCURY COMPUTER SYSTEMS, INC.; pg. 434, pg. 813
ROUTE 44 - Food Product - SONIC CORP.; pg. 1750, pg. 1487
ROUTE 44/BIG DRINK - Drink - SONIC CORP.; pg. 1750, pg. 1487
ROUTE 66 - Carpet - INTERFACE, INC.; pg. 695, pg. 512
ROUTE 66 RACEWAY - Motorsports Facility - INTERNATIONAL SPEEDWAY CORPORATION; pg. 553, pg. 420
ROUTEFINDER - Communication Product - MULTI-TECH SYSTEMS INC.; pg. 442, pg. 951
ROUTEMAP IMS - Software - ENVIRONMENTAL SYSTEMS RESEARCH INSTITUTE INC.; pg. 393, pg. 188
ROUTEMASTER - Paper Booklets Printed with Directional Information - AMERICAN AUTOMOBILE ASSOCIATION; pg. 1190, pg. 429
ROUTEMASTER - Ramps - MAGLINE, INC.; pg. 1358, pg. 908
ROUTENET - Software Services - UNITED PARCEL SERVICE, INC.; pg. 1928, pg. 522
ROUTER ENGINES - Software - WIND RIVER SYSTEMS, INC.; pg. 493, pg. 38
ROUTES TO VALUE - Software - BMC SOFTWARE, INC.; pg. 362, pg. 1701
ROV - Laser Bar Code Scanner - MICROVISION, INC.; pg. 654, pg. 1828
ROVER - Rust Remover - HACH COMPANY; pg. 1415, pg. 334
ROVER - Office Furniture - STEELCASE INC.; pg. 475, pg. 889
ROW ROW ROW YOUR BOAT - Game - HASBRO, INC.; pg. 954, pg. 1603
ROWBOAT - Shoe - AEROGROUP INTERNATIONAL, INC.; pg. 1803, pg. 1055
ROWE - HVAC Equipment - MESTEK, INC.; pg. 1074, pg. 857
ROWENTA - Small Household Appliances - ROWENTA (USA), INC.; pg. 60, pg. 1084
ROWOCO - Kitchen Gadget - WILTON PRODUCTS, INC.; pg. 1140, pg. 672
ROWTEC - Gauge Plastic Film - MULTI-PLASTICS, INC.; pg. 1886, pg. 1457
ROXANNE - Footwear - COBIAN CORP.; pg. 1806, pg. 253
ROXELL - Poultry System - CTB INTERNATIONAL CORP.; pg. 850, pg. 695
ROXIO BACKONTRACK SUITE - Media Protection Solution - COREL CORPORATION; pg. 380, pg. 1931
ROXIO CINEPLAYER - DVD Decoder - COREL CORPORATION; pg. 380, pg. 1931
ROXIO CREATOR - Software - COREL CORPORATION; pg. 380, pg. 1931
ROXIO EASY VHS TO DVD - VHS Conversion - COREL CORPORATION; pg. 380, pg. 1931
ROXIO GAME CAPTURE - Software & Hardware for Recording Console Gameplay - COREL CORPORATION; pg. 380, pg. 1931
ROXIO SECURE PRODUCTS - Encryption for Optical Media & USB Flash Drives - COREL CORPORATION; pg. 380, pg. 1931
ROXIO TOAST - Multimedia Toolkit for Mac - COREL CORPORATION; pg. 380, pg. 1931
ROXY - Thermogenic Softgels - BPI SPORTS, LLC; pg. 842, pg. 430
ROXY - Fabric - NEMSCHOFF, INC.; pg. 936, pg. 1890
ROXY - Casual Apparel - QUIKSILVER, INC.; pg. 31, pg. 104
ROXY - Lighting Product - QUOIZEL INC.; pg. 1304, pg. 1616
ROXY GIRL - Girls' Apparel - QUIKSILVER, INC.; pg. 31, pg. 104
ROYAL - Power Cable - COLEMAN CABLE, INC.; pg. 1324, pg. 665
ROYAL - Electrical Wire & Cable - ESSEX GROUP, INC.; pg. 638, pg. 680
ROYAL - Fruit & Vegetable Product - GIUMARRA VINEYARDS CORPORATION; pg. 1964, pg. 45
ROYAL - Food Product - THE JEL SERT COMPANY; pg. 865, pg. 668
ROYAL - Covering Products - METALS USA, INC.; pg. 97, pg. 425
ROYAL - Store Fixtures - PARISI INCORPORATED; pg. 103, pg. 1556
ROYAL - Plumbing Product - SLOAN VALVE COMPANY; pg. 1062, pg. 613
ROYAL - Commercial Lighting - SWIVELIER CO., INC.; pg. 1307, pg. 1142
ROYAL ALASKA - Seafood - OCEAN BEAUTY SEAFOODS, INC.; pg. 1028, pg. 1838
ROYAL BELL - Commercial Lighting - SWIVELIER CO., INC.; pg. 1307, pg. 1142
ROYAL BUSINESS FORMS - Financial Forms - ENNIS, INC.; pg. 393, pg. 1727
ROYAL CANIN - Pet Nutrition - MARS, INCORPORATED; pg. 1858, pg. 1792
ROYAL CANIN - Dog Food - MARS PETCARE; pg. 1478, pg. 1633
ROYAL CAPE - Container Grown Plant - MONROVIA GROWERS; pg. 1797, pg. 44
ROYAL CARIBBEAN INTERNATIONAL - Caribbean Cruises - ROYAL CARIBBEAN CRUISES LTD; pg. 1921, pg. 446
ROYAL COMPLEMENT - Paper Product - WASAU PAPER CORP.; pg. 1471, pg. 1882
ROYAL CORD - Rug - COURISTAN INC.; pg. 921, pg. 1067
ROYAL COTTON - Paper Product - WASAU PAPER CORP.; pg. 1471, pg. 1882
ROYAL CREST - Chafer - THE VOLLRATH COMPANY LLC; pg. 1139, pg. 1894
ROYAL CREST CHAFER - Food Chafer - THE VOLLRATH COMPANY LLC; pg. 1139, pg. 1894
ROYAL CROWN - Hair Conditioners - J. STRICKLAND & COMPANY; pg. 512, pg. 970
ROYAL DAMASK - Rug - COURISTAN INC.; pg. 921, pg. 1067
ROYAL DANSK - Men's Wallets - BUXTON ACQUISITION CO., LLC; pg. 2, pg. 845
ROYAL DANUBE - Packaged Foods - ATALANTA CORPORATION; pg. 838, pg. 1057
ROYAL DARK - Chocolates - THE HERSHEY CO.; pg. 1855, pg. 1538
ROYAL FAMILY - Game - WMS INDUSTRIES INC.; pg. 593, pg. 666
ROYAL FLUSH - Bowl Cleaner - BLUE CROSS LABORATORIES; pg. 326, pg. 277
ROYAL FLUSH BLUSH - Nail Care Product - OPI PRODUCTS INC.; pg. 518, pg. 167
ROYAL FRIEZE - Broadloom - COURISTAN INC.; pg. 921, pg. 1067
ROYAL G2 OPTIMA PLUS - Flushometer - SLOAN VALVE COMPANY; pg. 1062, pg. 613
ROYAL GUEST - Controlled Label Brand for Grocery Items - IGA, INC.; pg. 1023, pg. 578
ROYAL HYDRAULIC - Flushometer - SLOAN VALVE COMPANY; pg. 1062, pg. 613
ROYAL HYDRAULIC PRISON - Flushometer - SLOAN VALVE COMPANY; pg. 1062, pg. 613
ROYAL II - Flushometer - SLOAN VALVE COMPANY; pg. 1062, pg. 613
ROYAL IMPERIAL - Rug - COURISTAN INC.; pg. 921, pg. 1067
ROYAL JAMAICA - Cigars - ALTADIS USA, INC.; pg. 1893, pg. 423
ROYAL JELLY - Health & Beauty Product - DIXIE HEALTH, INC.; pg. 1524, pg. 535
ROYAL JELLY - Nutritional Product - NUTRACEUTICAL INTERNATIONAL CORPORATION; pg. 1576, pg. 1753
ROYAL JELLY BOOSTER - Physical, Mental, & Vitality Supplement Mix - DIXIE HEALTH, INC.; pg. 1524, pg. 535
ROYAL JELLY CAPSULES - Physical, Mental, & Vitality Enhancer Supplement - DIXIE HEALTH, INC.; pg. 1524, pg. 535
ROYAL KASHIMAR - Rug - COURISTAN INC.; pg. 921, pg. 1067
ROYAL KAUAI - Coffee - HAWAII COFFEE COMPANY; pg. 861, pg. 543
ROYAL KERRY - Wafers & Biscuits - ATALANTA CORPORATION; pg. 838, pg. 1057
ROYAL KICKER - Video Game - INTERNATIONAL GAME TECHNOLOGY; pg. 957, pg. 1024
ROYAL KINSDOWN - Mattress & Box Spring Sets - KINGSDOWN, INC.; pg. 932, pg. 1383
ROYAL KNIGHT - Table - BLATT BOWLING & BILLIARD CORP.; pg. 1827, pg. 1203
ROYAL KONA - Coffee - HAWAII COFFEE COMPANY; pg. 861, pg. 543
ROYAL LAID - Paper Product - WASAU PAPER CORP.; pg. 1471, pg. 1882
ROYAL LANCERS - Baseball Community - KANSAS CITY ROYALS BASEBALL CORPORATION; pg. 555, pg. 985
ROYAL LINEN - Paper Product - WASAU PAPER CORP.; pg. 1471, pg. 1882
ROYAL MAHOGANY - Door - MASONITE INTERNATIONAL CORPORATION; pg. 1054, pg. 1920
ROYAL MAHOUT - Packaged Foods - ATALANTA CORPORATION; pg. 838, pg. 1057
ROYAL MARBLE - Paper Product - WASAU PAPER CORP.; pg. 1471, pg. 1882
ROYAL MAUI - Coffee - HAWAII COFFEE COMPANY; pg. 861, pg. 543
ROYAL MELROSE - Monumental Products for the Memorial Industry - COLD SPRING GRANITE COMPANY; pg. 76, pg. 920
ROYAL MH - Polymer Product - CHEMTURA CORPORATION; pg. 1152, pg. 355
ROYAL OAK - Grinder - SENECA FALLS MACHINES; pg. 1374, pg. 1341
ROYAL OAK (R-O) - Form Relief Tool Grinders & CNC Cylindrical Grinders 8"x14" - SENECA FALLS MACHINES; pg. 1374, pg. 1341
ROYAL OPERA - Rug - COURISTAN INC.; pg. 921, pg. 1067
ROYAL OPTIMA - Flushometer - SLOAN VALVE COMPANY; pg. 1062, pg. 613
ROYAL OPTIMA SMO - Flushometer - SLOAN VALVE COMPANY; pg. 1062, pg. 613
THE ROYAL ORLEANS - Hotel - OMNI HOTELS & RESORTS; pg. 1107, pg. 1685
ROYAL PAISLEY - Bath Accessory - CROSCILL, INC.; pg. 1122, pg. 1220
ROYAL PAISLEY - Scotch - DIAGEO CANADA, INC.; pg. 1961, pg. 1937
ROYAL PLANTATION - Resort - SANDALS RESORTS INTERNATIONAL; pg. 1111, pg. 446
ROYAL PRISON - Flushometer - SLOAN VALVE COMPANY; pg. 1062, pg. 613
ROYAL PRISON REGAL - Flushometer - SLOAN VALVE COMPANY; pg. 1062, pg. 613
ROYAL RICHES - Video Game - INTERNATIONAL GAME TECHNOLOGY; pg. 957, pg. 1024
ROYAL RIVIERA - Fruit - HARRY & DAVID HOLDINGS, INC.; pg. 1022, pg. 1499
ROYAL SALUTE - Scotch - DIAGEO CANADA, INC.; pg. 1961, pg. 1937
ROYAL SEA - Frozen Seafood - HIGH LINER FOODS INCORPORATED; pg. 862, pg. 1917
ROYAL SILKPLUS - Paper Product - WASAU PAPER CORP.; pg. 1471, pg. 1882
ROYAL SLIMLINE HYDRAULIC - Bedpan Washer - SLOAN VALVE COMPANY; pg. 1062, pg. 613
ROYAL SLUIS - Fruit & Vegetable Seeds - MONSANTO COMPANY; pg. 1173, pg. 999
ROYAL STAR VENTURE - Motorcycle - YAMAHA MOTOR CORPORATION USA; pg. 1713, pg. 76
ROYAL STERLING - Silver Cream - WEIMAN PRODUCTS, LLC; pg. 337, pg. 616
ROYAL SUEDE II - Broadloom - COURISTAN INC.; pg. 921, pg. 1067

ROYAL TREASURES - Game - WMS INDUSTRIES INC.; pg. 593, pg. 666
ROYAL TREATMENT - Video Game - INTERNATIONAL GAME TECHNOLOGY; pg. 957, pg. 1024
ROYAL TRITON - Grease - CONOCOPHILLIPS; pg. 975, pg. 1703
ROYAL TRU - Beverages - THE COCA-COLA COMPANY; pg. 240, pg. 493
ROYAL TRU LIGHT - Beverages - THE COCA-COLA COMPANY; pg. 240, pg. 493
ROYAL UNICORN - Game - WMS INDUSTRIES INC.; pg. 593, pg. 666
ROYAL VELVET - Apparel - ICONIX BRAND GROUP, INC.; pg. 26, pg. 1243
ROYAL WAY KENO - Game - INTERNATIONAL GAME TECHNOLOGY; pg. 420, pg. 1606
ROYAL WILLAMETTE - Cherry - OREGON CHERRY GROWERS, INC.; pg. 1028, pg. 1508
ROYAL WING - Bird Feeding Supplies - TRACTOR SUPPLY COMPANY; pg. 708, pg. 1627
ROYAL-X - Photo Film - EASTMAN KODAK COMPANY; pg. 1408, pg. 1333
ROYALAC - Polymer Product - CHEMTURA CORPORATION; pg. 1152, pg. 355
ROYALAX - Rug - COURISTAN INC.; pg. 921, pg. 1067
ROYALE - Paint - AKZONOBEL DECORATIVE PAINTS U.S.; pg. 1439, pg. 1474
ROYALE - Specialty Paper - APPVION INC.; pg. 1451, pg. 1852
ROYALE - Dinnerware - THE HOMER LAUGHLIN CHINA COMPANY; pg. 1125, pg. 1850
ROYALE - Flooring Product - ROSCO LABORATORIES, INC.; pg. 1782, pg. 378
ROYALEDGE - Polymer Product - CHEMTURA CORPORATION; pg. 1152, pg. 355
ROYALENE - Polymer Product - CHEMTURA CORPORATION; pg. 1152, pg. 355
ROYALPRINT - Photo Processing Apparatus, Chemicals - EASTMAN KODAK COMPANY; pg. 1408, pg. 1333
ROYALTAC - Polymer Product - CHEMTURA CORPORATION; pg. 1152, pg. 355
ROYALTHERM - Polymer Product - CHEMTURA CORPORATION; pg. 1152, pg. 355
ROYALTUF - Polymer Product - CHEMTURA CORPORATION; pg. 1152, pg. 355
ROYALTY - Pineapple - CAMERICAN INTERNATIONAL; pg. 844, pg. 1101
ROYALTY - Fabric - NEMSCHOFF, INC.; pg. 936, pg. 1890
ROYALTY-GOLD - Furniture - ASHLEY FURNITURE INDUSTRIES, INC.; pg. 914, pg. 1852
ROYCO - Food Product - CAMPBELL SOUP COMPANY; pg. 844, pg. 1048
ROYCO - Food Product - MARS, INCORPORATED; pg. 1858, pg. 1792
ROYER - Capital Equipment - TEREX CORPORATION; pg. 1381, pg. 384
ROYLYN - Aircraft Parts - ROCKWELL COLLINS, INC.; pg. 234, pg. 702
ROY'S - Hawaiian Fusion Restaurant - BLOOMIN' BRANDS, INC.; pg. 1716, pg. 471
ROYSTON - Coating Product - CHASE CORPORATION; pg. 1152, pg. 803
ROYTYPE - Business Product - ROYAL CONSUMER INFORMATION PRODUCTS INC.; pg. 463, pg. 1122
RP - Aluminum Grease Filters - RESEARCH PRODUCTS CORPORATION; pg. 1075, pg. 1867
RPC PRO - Simulator Software for Vehicle Test Systems - MTS SYSTEMS CORPORATION; pg. 442, pg. 923
RPCS - Refined Printing Command Stream - RICOH AMERICAS CORPORATION; pg. 461, pg. 1131
RPEZ-KLEEN - Filter - RESEARCH PRODUCTS CORPORATION; pg. 1075, pg. 1867
RPL PERMALUBE - Universal Joint - MERITOR, INC.; pg. 212, pg. 911
RPM - Chemical Distribution System - ATMI, INC.; pg. 1314, pg. 342
RPM - Motor Oils - CHEVRON CORPORATION; pg. 974, pg. 259
RPM - Rotary Gas Meters - ELSTER AMERICAN METER COMPANY; pg. 1411, pg. 1387
RPM - Dragline Bucket - ESCO CORPORATION; pg. 1335, pg. 1502
RPM - Ergonomic Seating - KNOLL, INC.; pg. 425, pg. 1527
RPM - Software - RENTRAK CORPORATION; pg. 306, pg. 1506
RPM TREES - Root Production Method - FORREST KEELING NURSERY, INC.; pg. 1795, pg. 977
RPM2000 - PL Mapping Tool - NANOMETRICS INCORPORATED; pg. 1423, pg. 147
RPR RELIANCE - Optical Tables - NEWPORT CORPORATION; pg. 1424, pg. 114
RPRO - Software - FLIR SYSTEMS, INC.; pg. 1413, pg. 1510
RPROTEIN A - Protein - REPLIGEN CORPORATION; pg. 1589, pg. 854
RPS - Software - WATERS CORPORATION; pg. 1436, pg. 834
RPS VANTAGE - Paper Coating System - E.I. DU PONT DE NEMOURS & COMPANY; pg. 1159, pg. 390
RPT - Accessory - ADVANCED ENERGY INDUSTRIES, INC.; pg. 613, pg. 328
RPX - Fluid Handling System - GRACO, INC.; pg. 1342, pg. 935
RPX - Telepresence Solution - POLYCOM, INC.; pg. 664, pg. 249
RRL - Western Apparel - RALPH LAUREN CORPORATION; pg. 46, pg. 1284
RRPR - Systems Integration & Aeronautics - LOCKHEED MARTIN CORPORATION; pg. 229, pg. 762
RS-10 - Loudspeaker - KLIPSCH GROUP, INC.; pg. 649, pg. 688
RS-100 - Resistivity Measurement System - KLA-TENCOR CORPORATION; pg. 1353, pg. 146
RS-7 - Fluid Handling System - GRACO, INC.; pg. 1342, pg. 935
RS-MMC - Memory Card - SANDISK CORPORATION; pg. 465, pg. 147
RS4203 - Automated Sizing Clippers - TIPPER TIE, INC.; pg. 1382, pg. 1358
RSA - Computer Security Technologies - EMC CORPORATION; pg. 391, pg. 825
RSA ACCESS MANAGER - Web Security Software - RSA SECURITY INC.; pg. 463, pg. 786
RSA BSAFE - Computer Data Security Product - RSA SECURITY INC.; pg. 463, pg. 786
RSA ENVISION - Computer Security Product - RSA SECURITY INC.; pg. 463, pg. 786
RSA SEAL - Seal & Thermoplastic Component - GREENE, TWEED & CO.; pg. 1344, pg. 1544
RSA SECURID - Computer Security Authentication Product - RSA SECURITY INC.; pg. 463, pg. 786
RSAUTOMATION DESKTOP - Software - ROCKWELL AUTOMATION, INC.; pg. 668, pg. 1880
RSBATCH - Software - ROCKWELL AUTOMATION, INC.; pg. 668, pg. 1880
RSBIZWARE - Software - ROCKWELL AUTOMATION, INC.; pg. 668, pg. 1880
RSBIZWARE BATCH - Software - ROCKWELL AUTOMATION, INC.; pg. 668, pg. 1880
RSBIZWARE EPROCEDURE - Software - ROCKWELL AUTOMATION, INC.; pg. 668, pg. 1880
RSBIZWARE PLANTMETRICS - Software - ROCKWELL AUTOMATION, INC.; pg. 668, pg. 1880
RSCRIPT - Printer - RICOH AMERICAS CORPORATION; pg. 461, pg. 1131
RSEMULATE - Software - ROCKWELL AUTOMATION, INC.; pg. 668, pg. 1880
RSENERGYMETRIX - Software - ROCKWELL AUTOMATION, INC.; pg. 668, pg. 1880
RSFIELDBUS - Software - ROCKWELL AUTOMATION, INC.; pg. 668, pg. 1880
RSLADDER - Software - ROCKWELL AUTOMATION, INC.; pg. 668, pg. 1880
RSLINX - Software - ROCKWELL AUTOMATION, INC.; pg. 668, pg. 1880
RSLOGIX - Software - ROCKWELL AUTOMATION, INC.; pg. 668, pg. 1880
RSLOOP OPTIMIZER - Software - ROCKWELL AUTOMATION, INC.; pg. 668, pg. 1880
RSM - Roller Skating Manufacturers - ROLLER SKATING ASSOCIATION INTERNATIONAL; pg. 155, pg. 689
RSMACC - Software - ROCKWELL AUTOMATION, INC.; pg. 668, pg. 1880
RSNETWORX - Software - ROCKWELL AUTOMATION, INC.; pg. 668, pg. 1880
RSPOWER - Software - ROCKWELL AUTOMATION, INC.; pg. 668, pg. 1880
RSPRODUCTION - Software - ROCKWELL AUTOMATION, INC.; pg. 668, pg. 1880
RSR - CNC Cutter Sharpening Machine - GLEASON CORPORATION; pg. 1340, pg. 1335
RSR - Brake Seal - GREENE, TWEED & CO.; pg. 1344, pg. 1544
RSS - Elastomers Supply - GREENE, TWEED & CO.; pg. 1344, pg. 1544
RSS - Streaming Server - POLYCOM, INC.; pg. 664, pg. 249
RSSQL - Software - ROCKWELL AUTOMATION, INC.; pg. 668, pg. 1880
RSTESTSTAND - Software - ROCKWELL AUTOMATION, INC.; pg. 668, pg. 1880
RSTRAINER - Software - ROCKWELL AUTOMATION, INC.; pg. 668, pg. 1880
RSTUNE - Software - ROCKWELL AUTOMATION, INC.; pg. 668, pg. 1880
RSVIEW - Software - ROCKWELL AUTOMATION, INC.; pg. 668, pg. 1880
RSVIEW MACHINE EDITION - Software - ROCKWELL AUTOMATION, INC.; pg. 668, pg. 1880
RSVIEW SUPERVISORY EDITION - Software - ROCKWELL AUTOMATION, INC.; pg. 668, pg. 1880
RSVIEW32 - Software - ROCKWELL AUTOMATION, INC.; pg. 668, pg. 1880
RSVP - Raised Surface Variable Printing - THE STANDARD REGISTER COMPANY; pg. 473, pg. 1446
RT-2 - Kinematic System for Global Positioning Systems Applications - NOVATEL INC.; pg. 1424, pg. 1904
RT-20 - Kinematic System for Global Positioning Systems Applications - NOVATEL INC.; pg. 1424, pg. 1904
RT-200 - Rope Tester - HD ELECTRIC COMPANY; pg. 1299, pg. 666
R.T. JUNIOR - Tobacco Product - AMERICAN SNUFF COMPANY; pg. 1893, pg. 1641
R.T. JUNIOR (PRESSED) - Twist Tobacco - AMERICAN SNUFF COMPANY; pg. 1893, pg. 1641
RT-LAB RLX - Software - CONCURRENT COMPUTER CORPORATION; pg. 379, pg. 531
RT TCP/IP - Software - INTERVALZERO INC.; pg. 420, pg. 851
RTA - Regional Transit Authority - REGIONAL TRANSPORTATION AUTHORITY; pg. 1921, pg. 588
RTA SUITE - Software - WIND RIVER SYSTEMS, INC.; pg. 493, pg. 38
RTA TRAVEL INFORMATION - Telephone Information System for Transit Riders - REGIONAL TRANSPORTATION AUTHORITY; pg. 1921, pg. 588
RTC SOFT START - Soft Start Motor Control - REULAND ELECTRIC COMPANY; pg. 1304, pg. 68
RTCAL - Calorimeter - METTLER-TOLEDO INTERNATIONAL INC.; pg. 1423, pg. 1441
RTDX - Computer Software & Hardware - TEXAS INSTRUMENTS INCORPORATED; pg. 679, pg. 1688
RTEL - Software - LANTRONIX, INC.; pg. 426, pg. 112
RTF FLEXIPANEL - Vessel Heating Panel - THERMON AMERICAS INC.; pg. 1077, pg. 1744
RTI - Measurement & Control Module - ANALOG DEVICES, INC.; pg. 617, pg. 839
RTKNET - Software - TRIMBLE NAVIGATION LIMITED; pg. 1384, pg. 288
RTM - Software - SERENA SOFTWARE, INC.; pg. 468, pg. 192
RTMS - Radar - IMAGE SENSING SYSTEMS, INC.; pg. 412, pg. 961
RTP - Pumps - IDEX CORPORATION; pg. 1347, pg. 623
RTP FIELD MASTER - Gloves - FRANKLIN SPORTS, INC.; pg. 1834, pg. 847
RTQC DATA CONVERTER - Software - BIO-RAD LABORATORIES, INC.; pg. 1504, pg. 101
RTQC DATA MANAGER - Software - BIO-RAD LABORATORIES, INC.; pg. 1504, pg. 101
RTQC WEB - Software - BIO-RAD LABORATORIES, INC.; pg. 1504, pg. 101
RTR - Transmitter Register - BADGER METER, INC.; pg. 1401, pg. 1873
RTS 2000 - Software - BIO-RAD LABORATORIES, INC.; pg. 1504, pg. 101
RTS 400 - Skate - ROLLER DERBY SKATE CORP.; pg. 966, pg. 630
RTW - Tools - KENNAMETAL INC.; pg. 1052, pg. 1547
RTW - Metalworking Tools - KENNAMETAL IPG; pg. 1353, pg. 1615
RTX - Fluid Handling System - GRACO, INC.; pg. 1342, pg. 935
RTX - Software - INTERVALZERO INC.; pg. 420, pg. 851
RU - Sodium Silicate - PQ CORPORATION; pg. 1178, pg. 1515
RUB A535 - Analgesic - CHURCH & DWIGHT CANADA

CORP.; *pg.* 503, *pg.* 1925
RUB AND POUR-ON - Insecticide - KENT NUTRITION GROUP; *pg.* 1477, *pg.* 710
RUBALIT - Alumina Materials - CERAMTEC NORTH AMERICA ELECTRONIC APPLICATIONS, INC.; *pg.* 628, *pg.* 1620
RUBBER & PLASTICS NEWS - Trade Magazine - CRAIN COMMUNICATIONS, INC.; *pg.* 1631, *pg.* 879
RUBBER BASE PLUS - Ink - VAN SON HOLLAND INK CORPORATION OF AMERICA; *pg.* 487, *pg.* 1169
RUBBER CALK - Sealants - PPG AEROSPACE; *pg.* 1178, *pg.* 290
RUBBER GLASS - Glass Effects - SMOOTH-ON INC.; *pg.* 111, *pg.* 1528
RUBBER MATE - Rubber Injection Molding Machine - MCNEIL & NRM INC.; *pg.* 1360, *pg.* 1402
RUBBER SLEEVE - Rubber Core Inner Barrel - BAKER HUGHES INTEQ; *pg.* 1316, *pg.* 1700
RUBBERMAID - Home Products - NEWELL RUBBERMAID INC.; *pg.* 1128, *pg.* 515
RUBBERSET - Brushes & Rollers - THE SHERWIN-WILLIAMS COMPANY; *pg.* 1447, *pg.* 1435
RUBELLA-PLUS - Pharmaceutical Product - ALERE INC.; *pg.* 1488, *pg.* 849
RUBIA - Carpet - WOVEN LEGENDS INC.; *pg.* 947, *pg.* 1572
RUBIFLEX - Polyol - HUNTSMAN CORPORATION; *pg.* 1167, *pg.* 1758
RUBIG - Tools - KENNAMETAL INC.; *pg.* 1052, *pg.* 1547
RUBIGO - Beauty Product - COSMETIQUE, INC.; *pg.* 1765, *pg.* 664
RUBIK'S CUBE - Toy & Game - HASBRO, INC.; *pg.* 954, *pg.* 1603
RUBINATE - MDI Blends - HUNTSMAN CORPORATION; *pg.* 1167, *pg.* 1758
RUBINSTEIN'S - Seafood - TRIDENT SEAFOODS CORPORATION; *pg.* 902, *pg.* 1842
RUBIO'S A-GO-GO - Catering - RUBIO'S RESTAURANTS, INC.; *pg.* 1748, *pg.* 60
RUBY - Trimmer & Clipper - ANDIS COMPANY; *pg.* 498, *pg.* 1895
RUBY - Area Rugs - COURISTAN INC.; *pg.* 921, *pg.* 1067
RUBY - Flat Panel Display - EPSILON SYSTEMS SOLUTIONS; *pg.* 1412, *pg.* 202
RUBY - Juice - OCEAN SPRAY CRANBERRIES, INC.; *pg.* 887, *pg.* 827
RUBY LACE - Container Grown Plant - MONROVIA GROWERS; *pg.* 1797, *pg.* 44
RUBY RICHES - Lottery Game - KENTUCKY LOTTERY CORPORATION; *pg.* 996, *pg.* 735
RUBY RING - Game - WMS INDUSTRIES INC.; *pg.* 593, *pg.* 666
RUE BY RUE21 - Fragrance - RUE21, INC.; *pg.* 32, *pg.* 1591
RUE DE SEINE - Furniture - BASSETT FURNITURE INDUSTRIES, INCORPORATED; *pg.* 916, *pg.* 1776
RUE21 - Apparel - RUE21, INC.; *pg.* 32, *pg.* 1591
RUE21 ETC! - Apparel - RUE21, INC.; *pg.* 32, *pg.* 1591
RUEHL - Clothing - ABERCROMBIE & FITCH CO.; *pg.* 37, *pg.* 1466
RUFCO - Vapor Retarder - RAVEN INDUSTRIES, INC.; *pg.* 1888, *pg.* 1625
RUFF-LITE - Lightning - AMERICAN GREASE STICK CO.; *pg.* 971, *pg.* 902
RUFFINO - Fine Wine - CONSTELLATION BRANDS, INC.; *pg.* 1960, *pg.* 1348
RUFFLES - Potato Chips - FRITO-LAY NORTH AMERICA, INC.; *pg.* 1853, *pg.* 1730
RUFFLES - Potato Chips - PEPSICO, INC.; *pg.* 259, *pg.* 1327
RUFFLES FLAVOR RUSH - Potato Chips - FRITO-LAY NORTH AMERICA, INC.; *pg.* 1853, *pg.* 1730
RUFIO - Footwear - STEVEN MADDEN, LTD.; *pg.* 1819, *pg.* 1176
RUG AROMA - Carpet Freshener - SURCO PRODUCTS, INC.; *pg.* 336, *pg.* 1581
RUG RELIEF - Carpet Cleaner - BLUE CROSS LABORATORIES; *pg.* 326, *pg.* 277
RUGBY - Apparel - RALPH LAUREN CORPORATION; *pg.* 46, *pg.* 1284
RUGER - Pistol - STURM, RUGER & COMPANY, INC.; *pg.* 1846, *pg.* 371
RUGER MARK III - Pistols - STURM, RUGER & COMPANY, INC.; *pg.* 1846, *pg.* 371
RUGER MODEL 96 - Lever-Action Rifle - STURM, RUGER & COMPANY, INC.; *pg.* 1846, *pg.* 371
RUGER SR-556 - Rifle - STURM, RUGER & COMPANY, INC.; *pg.* 1846, *pg.* 371
RUGGED - Medical Product - STRYKER CORPORATION; *pg.* 1598, *pg.* 894
THE RUGGED CROSS - Ring - STULLER, INC.; *pg.* 13, *pg.* 745
RUGGED-RACK - Chassis - MICROWAY, INC.; *pg.* 1267, *pg.* 841
RUGGED TERRAIN - Carpet - INTERFACE, INC.; *pg.* 695, *pg.* 512
RUGGED ULTRA - Storage Box - STERILITE CORPORATION; *pg.* 1138, *pg.* 848
RUGGIE BEAR - Stuffed Toy - GRACO CHILDREN'S PRODUCTS INC.; *pg.* 954, *pg.* 1531
RUGGLES - Medical Device - INTEGRA LIFESCIENCES HOLDINGS CORPORATION; *pg.* 1545, *pg.* 1109
RUGLYDE - Rubber Lubricant - AMERICAN GREASE STICK CO.; *pg.* 971, *pg.* 902
RUGRATS - Toy - MATTEL, INC.; *pg.* 962, *pg.* 81
RUINART - Champagne - MOET HENNESSY; *pg.* 1966, *pg.* 1260
RULE 35 - Golf Accessories - CALLAWAY GOLF COMPANY; *pg.* 1829, *pg.* 58
RULE & PROFILE ADMINISTRATION - Software - WIPRO GALLAGHER SOLUTIONS; *pg.* 823, *pg.* 447
RULE BREAKER - Investing Service - THE MOTLEY FOOL, INC.; *pg.* 784, *pg.* 1771
RULE MAKER - Portfolio - THE MOTLEY FOOL, INC.; *pg.* 784, *pg.* 1771
RUMA-PASS - Agricultural Product - ARCHER-DANIELS-MIDLAND COMPANY; *pg.* 825, *pg.* 565
RUMATEL - Animal Health Product - PHIBROCHEM; *pg.* 1177, *pg.* 1124
RUMBA - Energy Drinks - MONSTER BEVERAGE CORPORATION; *pg.* 257, *pg.* 69
RUMBLE - Fabric - NEMSCHOFF, INC.; *pg.* 936, *pg.* 1890
RUMBLING RHINOS - Video Game - INTERNATIONAL GAME TECHNOLOGY; *pg.* 957, *pg.* 1024
RUMEN BUFF - Animal Feeds - KENT NUTRITION GROUP; *pg.* 1477, *pg.* 710
RUMESIN - Monensin Sodium - ELANCO ANIMAL HEALTH; *pg.* 1475, *pg.* 681
RUMMIKUB - Game - PRESSMAN TOY CORPORATION; *pg.* 965, *pg.* 1734
RUN A PRACTICE, NOT AN OBSTACLE COURSE. - Slogan - ATHENAHEALTH, INC.; *pg.* 1497, *pg.* 855
RUN-DRY - Fuel Impeller - GLOBE COMPOSITE SOLUTIONS, LTD.; *pg.* 1883, *pg.* 842
RUN FOR THE ROSE - Event - KENTUCKY DERBY FESTIVAL, INC.; *pg.* 556, *pg.* 735
RUN FOR YOUR MONEY - Slots - INTERNATIONAL GAME TECHNOLOGY; *pg.* 957, *pg.* 1024
RUN-OF-PRESS - Newspaper Promotion - VALASSIS COMMUNICATIONS, INC.; *pg.* 1287, *pg.* 897
RUN ONE MISOUL TECH - Footwear - K-SWISS; *pg.* 1837, *pg.* 306
RUN POWERPOINT - Software - ROSCO LABORATORIES, INC.; *pg.* 1782, *pg.* 378
RUN SHORT - Clothing - K-SWISS; *pg.* 1837, *pg.* 306
RUN THE TABLE - Instant Lottery Game - NEW YORK STATE LOTTERY; *pg.* 1001, *pg.* 1340
RUN WITH US - Tag Line - NAVISITE, INC.; *pg.* 1269, *pg.* 782
RUNABOUT - Eyewear - MAUI JIM, INC.; *pg.* 9, *pg.* 651
RUNCHEK - Electrical Leakage Tester - ASSOCIATED RESEARCH INC.; *pg.* 1400, *pg.* 622
RUNCO - Home Theater - PLANAR SYSTEMS, INC.; *pg.* 455, *pg.* 1495
RUNNER - Office Furniture - STEELCASE INC.; *pg.* 475, *pg.* 889
RUNNERS - Truck Step - LUND INTERNATIONAL, INC.; *pg.* 211, *pg.* 526
THE RUNNERS BODY - Book - RODALE, INC.; *pg.* 1681, *pg.* 1530
RUNNER'S WORLD - Magazine - RODALE, INC.; *pg.* 1681, *pg.* 1530
RUNNERSWORLD.COM - Website - RODALE, INC.; *pg.* 1681, *pg.* 1530
RUNNING JACKET - Clothing - K-SWISS; *pg.* 1837, *pg.* 306
RUNNING PANT - Clothing - K-SWISS; *pg.* 1837, *pg.* 306
RUNNING TIMES - Magazine - RODALE, INC.; *pg.* 1681, *pg.* 1530
RUNNINGTIMES.COM - Website - RODALE, INC.; *pg.* 1681, *pg.* 1530
RUNTS - Candy - NESTLE USA, INC.; *pg.* 883, *pg.* 96
RUNWAY - Medical Device - BOSTON SCIENTIFIC CORPORATION; *pg.* 1508, *pg.* 831
RUPS - Software Product - CLARY CORPORATION; *pg.* 226, *pg.* 150
RUSH - Knife - BUCK KNIVES, INC.; *pg.* 1828, *pg.* 550
RUSH - Women's Sport Watch Line - TIMEX CORPORATION; *pg.* 14, *pg.* 355
RUSH! ENERGY - Fruit-Flavored Carbonated Energy Drink - THE MONARCH BEVERAGE COMPANY, INC.; *pg.* 257, *pg.* 514
RUSH ENTERPRISES - Truck Dealerships - RUSH ENTERPRISES INC.; *pg.* 189, *pg.* 1728
RUSH EQUIPMENT CENTERS - Construction Machinery & Equipment Dealers - RUSH ENTERPRISES INC.; *pg.* 189, *pg.* 1728
RUSH ROX - Candy - SPANGLER CANDY COMPANY; *pg.* 1862, *pg.* 1407
RUSH TRUCK CENTERS - Truck Dealerships - RUSH ENTERPRISES INC.; *pg.* 189, *pg.* 1728
RUSHES - Photo Newsletter - EASTMAN KODAK COMPANY; *pg.* 1408, *pg.* 1333
RUSSEL DRILLING & INDUSTRIAL SUPPLY - Waterwell & Drilling Related Products - RUSSEL METALS INC.; *pg.* 1180, *pg.* 1928
RUSSEL METALS WILLIAMS BAHCALL - Metal Products - RUSSEL METALS INC.; *pg.* 1180, *pg.* 1928
RUSSELL - Hose - EDELBROCK CORPORATION; *pg.* 204, *pg.* 293
RUSSELL ARTWEAR - Apparel - RUSSELL BRANDS LLC; *pg.* 698, *pg.* 726
RUSSELL ATHLETIC - Knit Athletic Wear - RUSSELL BRANDS LLC; *pg.* 698, *pg.* 726
RUSSELL GREEN RIVER - Professional Knives - DEXTER-RUSSELL INC.; *pg.* 1123, *pg.* 844
RUSSELL INTERNATIONAL - Cutlery - DEXTER-RUSSELL INC.; *pg.* 1123, *pg.* 844
RUSSELL STOVER CANDIES - Candy - RUSSELL STOVER CANDIES, INC.; *pg.* 1861, *pg.* 986
RUSSELL STOVER COOKIE DOUGH - Cookies - RUSSELL STOVER CANDIES, INC.; *pg.* 1861, *pg.* 986
RUSSELLSTOLL - Interconnection System - THOMAS & BETTS CORPORATION; *pg.* 680, *pg.* 1646
RUSSER - Deli Products - TYSON FOODS, INC.; *pg.* 902, *pg.* 35
RUSSETT KETTLE COOKED POTATO CHIPS - Potato Snacks - HERR FOODS INC.; *pg.* 861, *pg.* 1557
RUSSIAN TEACUP - Bath Product - KOHLER CO.; *pg.* 91, *pg.* 1862
RUSSIAN TREASURE - Video Game - INTERNATIONAL GAME TECHNOLOGY; *pg.* 957, *pg.* 1024
RUST BLOK - Paint And Stain Product - BENJAMIN MOORE & CO.; *pg.* 1440, *pg.* 1085
RUST BREAKER - Penetrant - SHERWIN-WILLIAMS DIVERSIFIED BRANDS DIVISION; *pg.* 1448, *pg.* 1435
RUST BUSTER - Rust Remover - LA-CO INDUSTRIES MARKAL CO., INC.; *pg.* 1170, *pg.* 610
RUST FIX - Rust Convertor - SHERWIN-WILLIAMS DIVERSIFIED BRANDS DIVISION; *pg.* 1448, *pg.* 1435
RUST-NOT - Primer - JONES-BLAIR COMPANY; *pg.* 1443, *pg.* 1682
RUST RID - Rust Remover - JONES-BLAIR COMPANY; *pg.* 1443, *pg.* 1682
RUST TOUGH - Rust Preventive Enamel - SHERWIN-WILLIAMS DIVERSIFIED BRANDS DIVISION; *pg.* 1448, *pg.* 1435
RUST TRANSFORMER - Fluid Sealing Product - A.W. CHESTERTON COMPANY; *pg.* 1315, *pg.* 861
RUSTAMOR - Alkyd Enamel - PETTIT PAINT COMPANY; *pg.* 1444, *pg.* 1116
RUSTEC - Chemical Product - BIRKO CORPORATION; *pg.* 1149, *pg.* 332
RUSTGO - Stain Remover - A.L. WILSON CHEMICAL CO.; *pg.* 325, *pg.* 1076
RUSTIC - Aluminum Siding - PLY GEM SIDING GROUP; *pg.* 105, *pg.* 986
RUSTIC COLLECTION - Fiberglass Door System - THERMA-TRU CORP.; *pg.* 115, *pg.* 1462
RUSTLER - Jeanswear - V.F. CORPORATION; *pg.* 34, *pg.* 1376
RUSTLERS - Domestic Cigars - ALTADIS USA, INC.; *pg.* 1893, *pg.* 423
RUSTLER'S - Meat Snacks - FRITO-LAY NORTH AMERICA, INC.; *pg.* 1853, *pg.* 1730
RUSTLERS - Meat Snacks - PEPSICO, INC.; *pg.* 259, *pg.* 1327

RUSTLICK - Coolants & EDM Fluids - ITW FLUIDS NORTH AMERICA; *pg.* 980, *pg.* 614
RUSTLOK - Steel Primer - PETTIT PAINT COMPANY; *pg.* 1444, *pg.* 1116
RUSTMASTER - Paint - AKZONOBEL DECORATIVE PAINTS U.S.; *pg.* 1439, *pg.* 1474
RUSTMASTER METALLITE - Paint - AKZONOBEL DECORATIVE PAINTS U.S.; *pg.* 1439, *pg.* 1474
RUSTOP - Rust Remover - CARGILL LIMITED; *pg.* 1475, *pg.* 1914
RUSTPROOF - Paint & Coating - AERVOE INDUSTRIES INCORPORATED; *pg.* 1439, *pg.* 1021
RUSTSOLVO - Fluid Sealing Product - A.W. CHESTERTON COMPANY; *pg.* 1315, *pg.* 861
RUSTY WALLACE PRO - Eyewear - OAKLEY, INC.; *pg.* 1840, *pg.* 86
RUTHERFORD - Furniture - ASHLEY FURNITURE INDUSTRIES, INC.; *pg.* 914, *pg.* 1852
RUTHERFORD - Cylinder - BUNTING MAGNETICS CO.; *pg.* 1320, *pg.* 717
RUTHMAN PUMPS - Pumps - GUSHER PUMPS, INC.; *pg.* 1344, *pg.* 727
RUTH'S CHRIS - Dining & Restaurants - RUTH'S HOSPITALITY GROUP, INC.; *pg.* 1748, *pg.* 480
RUTLEDGE HILL PRESS - Books - THOMAS NELSON INC.; *pg.* 1692, *pg.* 1654
RUUD - Water Heaters, Air Conditioners & Furnaces - RHEEM MANUFACTURING COMPANY; *pg.* 1075, *pg.* 519
RUXXAC - Laundry & Cleaning Product - FAULTLESS STARCH/BON AMI COMPANY; *pg.* 330, *pg.* 982
RV/MARINE TOILET TISSUE - Economic 1-Ply Toilet Tissue - THETFORD CORPORATION; *pg.* 337, *pg.* 867
R.V. REAL VALUE - Loyalty Card - FJ MANAGEMENT, INC.; *pg.* 978, *pg.* 1758
RV TRADER - Magazine - DOMINION ENTERPRISES; *pg.* 1636, *pg.* 1796
RV14GD - Rivet Installation Tool - ALLFAST FASTENING SYSTEMS, INC.; *pg.* 1041, *pg.* 66
RV15GA - Rivet Installation Tool - ALLFAST FASTENING SYSTEMS, INC.; *pg.* 1041, *pg.* 66
RV2000 - Self-Feeding Pneumatic Riveter - ALLFAST FASTENING SYSTEMS, INC.; *pg.* 1041, *pg.* 66
RV3000 MAXMATIC - Self-Feeding Riveter - ALLFAST FASTENING SYSTEMS, INC.; *pg.* 1041, *pg.* 66
RV30GD - Rivet Installation Tool - ALLFAST FASTENING SYSTEMS, INC.; *pg.* 1041, *pg.* 66
RV50GB - Pneumatic Power Gun for Rivets - ALLFAST FASTENING SYSTEMS, INC.; *pg.* 1041, *pg.* 66
RV51GA - Pneumatic Power Gun for Rivets - ALLFAST FASTENING SYSTEMS, INC.; *pg.* 1041, *pg.* 66
RVT - Valve - HYDE TOOLS, INC.; *pg.* 1125, *pg.* 844
RX - Endothermic Atmosphere Gas Generators - SURFACE COMBUSTION, INC.; *pg.* 1077, *pg.* 1462
RX-90 HIP SYSTEM - Hip Product - ZIMMER BIOMET HOLDINGS, INC.; *pg.* 1611, *pg.* 699
RX CALCULATOR - Web Based Software - HUMANA, INC.; *pg.* 1204, *pg.* 734
RX-ERECT - Health & Beauty Product - DIXIE HEALTH, INC.; *pg.* 1524, *pg.* 535
RX M - Frames - OAKLEY, INC.; *pg.* 1840, *pg.* 86
RX SPECIAL - Footwear - P.W. MINOR & SON, INC.; *pg.* 1816, *pg.* 1140
RX WORKS - Newsletter - PHARMACEUTICAL RESEARCH & MANUFACTURERS OF AMERICA; *pg.* 153, *pg.* 404
RX-Z1 - Digital Home Theater Receiver - YAMAHA ELECTRONICS CORPORATION USA; *pg.* 689, *pg.* 51
RX-Z9 - Digital Home Theater Receiver - YAMAHA ELECTRONICS CORPORATION USA; *pg.* 689, *pg.* 51
RXERECT - Health & Beauty Product - DIXIE HEALTH, INC.; *pg.* 1524, *pg.* 535
RXFOCUS - Software - AMERISOURCEBERGEN CORPORATION; *pg.* 1493, *pg.* 1522
RXLIST.COM - Online Drug Directory - WEBMD HEALTH CORPORATION; *pg.* 1288, *pg.* 1313
RXLOY - EVA Containing Polymer for Medical - FERRO CORPORATION; *pg.* 1162, *pg.* 1462
RXMAP - Punch Cards - MTS MEDICATION TECHNOLOGIES, INC.; *pg.* 442, *pg.* 463
RXWEB - Software - FIRST DATABANK, INC.; *pg.* 397, *pg.* 217
RYAN - Vanity Lights - CRAFTMADE INTERNATIONAL, INC.; *pg.* 1295, *pg.* 1670
RYAN - Golf, Turf & Specialty Products - TEXTRON INC.; *pg.* 235, *pg.* 1607
RYAN'S - Restaurants - OVATION BRANDS; *pg.* 1743, *pg.* 921
RYDER FLEETCARE - Inventory Software - RYDER SYSTEM, INC.; *pg.* 1922, *pg.* 446
RYDERFLOW - Inventory Software - RYDER SYSTEM, INC.; *pg.* 1922, *pg.* 446
RYDERSHIP - Software - RYDER SYSTEM, INC.; *pg.* 1922, *pg.* 446
RYDERTRAC - Tracking Software - RYDER SYSTEM, INC.; *pg.* 1922, *pg.* 446
RYDESMART - GPS Tracking - RYDER SYSTEM, INC.; *pg.* 1922, *pg.* 446
RYE - Women's Clothing & Accessories - WOODEN SHIPS OF HOBOKEN; *pg.* 35, *pg.* 1315
RYKODISC - Record Label - WARNER MUSIC GROUP CORP.; *pg.* 590, *pg.* 1313
RYKRISP - Crackers - CONAGRA FOODS; *pg.* 826, *pg.* 994
RYLAND - Furniture - ASHLEY FURNITURE INDUSTRIES, INC.; *pg.* 914, *pg.* 1852
RYNEX - Dry Cleaning & Laundry Product - ADCO, INC.; *pg.* 325, *pg.* 482
RYNGLOK - Fitting - EATON CORPORATION; *pg.* 1331, *pg.* 1429
RYNITE - Thermoplastic Polyester - E.I. DU PONT DE NEMOURS & COMPANY; *pg.* 1159, *pg.* 390
RYNO-WELD - Adhesives - AMERICAN GREASE STICK CO.; *pg.* 971, *pg.* 902
RYOBI - Garden Equipment - MTD PRODUCTS, INC.; *pg.* 1057, *pg.* 1478
RYOLEX - Industrial Perlite - SILBRICO CORPORATION; *pg.* 110, *pg.* 617
RYON'S - Boots & Saddles - LUSKEY'S WESTERN STORES, INC.; *pg.* 44, *pg.* 1657
RYTEC - Software - RYERSON INC.; *pg.* 1373, *pg.* 589
RYTEX - Clothing - LAKELAND INDUSTRIES, INC.; *pg.* 1354, *pg.* 1338
RYTON - Energy Product - CONOCOPHILLIPS; *pg.* 975, *pg.* 1703
RYTZ - Footwear - STEVEN MADDEN, LTD.; *pg.* 1819, *pg.* 1176

S

S - Chemical Composition - DOW CORNING CORPORATION; *pg.* 1159, *pg.* 900
S - Symphony Orchestra - SEATTLE SYMPHONY ORCHESTRA; *pg.* 582, *pg.* 1840
S-100 - Signal Attenuator - ANDREA ELECTRONICS CORPORATION; *pg.* 617, *pg.* 1143
S-2 GLASS - Glass Yarns, Filaments, Strands & Rovings - OWENS CORNING; *pg.* 102, *pg.* 1476
S-2000 STABILIZER - Pneumatic Isolators - NEWPORT CORPORATION; *pg.* 1424, *pg.* 114
S-22 - Predispersed Coating Pigment - BASF CATALYSTS LLC; *pg.* 1148, *pg.* 1074
S-23 - Coating Pigment - BASF CATALYSTS LLC; *pg.* 1148, *pg.* 1074
S-3 - Systems Integration & Aeronautics - LOCKHEED MARTIN CORPORATION; *pg.* 229, *pg.* 762
S-3B - Systems Integration & Aeronautics - LOCKHEED MARTIN CORPORATION; *pg.* 229, *pg.* 762
S-4 PLUS - Carbide Drill Bit - POWERS FASTENERS INC.; *pg.* 1059, *pg.* 1143
S&G - Flower Seeds & Young Plants - SYNGENTA SEEDS, INC.; *pg.* 1801, *pg.* 630
S&K - Jets, Educators, Scrubbers - SCHUTTE & KOERTING INC.; *pg.* 1428, *pg.* 1589
S&P INDICES - Evaluation Tool - STANDARD & POOR'S RATINGS SERVICES; *pg.* 805, *pg.* 1296
S&S CAFETERIAS - Food Product - SMITH & SONS FOODS, INC.; *pg.* 1750, *pg.* 535
S AND W - Coffee Product - COFFEE HOLDING CO., INC.; *pg.* 849, *pg.* 1343
S&W - Canned Vegetables, Tomatoes & Fruit - DEL MONTE FOODS, INC.; *pg.* 852, *pg.* 304
S&W - Rice - RIVIANA FOODS INC.; *pg.* 892, *pg.* 1713
S-BLADE - Electric Shaver - THE ELTRON COMPANY; *pg.* 507, *pg.* 103
S BLADES - Silicon - DYNATEX INTERNATIONAL; *pg.* 635, *pg.* 277
S-CAP - Fire Escape Hood - MINE SAFETY APPLIANCES COMPANY; *pg.* 1361, *pg.* 1525
S-CARB - Chemical - FMC CORPORATION; *pg.* 1163, *pg.* 1564
S-CLASS - Bar Code System - DATAMAX CORPORATION; *pg.* 1633, *pg.* 453
S-CLASS - Fish Tape - IDEAL INDUSTRIES, INC.; *pg.* 1051, *pg.* 662
S-CON - Furniture - HAWORTH, INC.; *pg.* 402, *pg.* 891
S-CORE - Graphite Golf Shaft - ALDILA, INC.; *pg.* 1825, *pg.* 185
S-CURL - Hair Care Products - LUSTER PRODUCTS INC.; *pg.* 515, *pg.* 581
S-FTIGHT - Legwear - STEVEN MADDEN, LTD.; *pg.* 1819, *pg.* 1176
S H E AUDITOR - Software - GULF PUBLISHING COMPANY; *pg.* 1646, *pg.* 1707
S. HOWES - Processing Equipment - S. HOWES, INC.; *pg.* 1373, *pg.* 1342
S-K - Hand Tools - SK HAND TOOL CORPORATION; *pg.* 1062, *pg.* 663
S K SUPERSETS - Socket Set Packages - SK HAND TOOL CORPORATION; *pg.* 1062, *pg.* 663
S-LEGIN - Legwear - STEVEN MADDEN, LTD.; *pg.* 1819, *pg.* 1176
S-LINE - Steel Office Desk - INVINCIBLE OFFICE FURNITURE; *pg.* 420, *pg.* 1868
S-LINE - Insulated Tubing - O'BRIEN CORPORATION; *pg.* 1366, *pg.* 1001
S. ROSEN - Bakery Products - ALPHA BAKING COMPANY; *pg.* 836, *pg.* 564
S SERIES - Ultrasound Systems - SONOSITE, INC.; *pg.* 1429, *pg.* 1818
S SERIES - Hearing Instrument - STARKEY LABORATORIES, INC.; *pg.* 1597, *pg.* 923
S-SERIES - Roll Covering - VAIL RUBBER WORKS, INC.; *pg.* 1891, *pg.* 906
S-SERIES POSILOK - Tooth System - ESCO CORPORATION; *pg.* 1335, *pg.* 1502
S SONOCO - Plastic Cartridges - SONOCO PRODUCTS COMPANY; *pg.* 1469, *pg.* 1619
S-SPAN - Building Systems - BEHLEN MFG. CO.; *pg.* 701, *pg.* 1010
S WORKS - Bicycle - SPECIALIZED BICYCLE COMPONENTS, INC.; *pg.* 1711, *pg.* 152
S-XRS - Laser Detectors - COBRA ELECTRONICS CORPORATION; *pg.* 629, *pg.* 572
S1000 - Software - BIO-RAD LABORATORIES, INC.; *pg.* 1504, *pg.* 101
S2 RANGER - X-Ray System - BRUKER CORPORATION; *pg.* 1511, *pg.* 788
S2000 - Spinning Reel Platform - INTERNATIONAL GAME TECHNOLOGY; *pg.* 957, *pg.* 1024
S25 - Fertilizer - POTASHCORP; *pg.* 1799, *pg.* 641
S2H2 - Golf Accessories - CALLAWAY GOLF COMPANY; *pg.* 1829, *pg.* 58
S3 - Low Pressure, Sanitary Rupture Discs - FIKE CORPORATION; *pg.* 1047, *pg.* 973
S4 PIONEER - X-Ray System - BRUKER CORPORATION; *pg.* 1511, *pg.* 788
S4000 - Remote Control Device - UNIVERSAL ELECTRONICS, INC.; *pg.* 683, *pg.* 262
S563 - Footwear - STEVEN MADDEN, LTD.; *pg.* 1819, *pg.* 1176
S569 - Footwear - STEVEN MADDEN, LTD.; *pg.* 1819, *pg.* 1176
S7 ELITE - Flow Generator Product - RESMED INC.; *pg.* 1589, *pg.* 207
S7 LIGHTWEIGHT - Medical Device - RESMED INC.; *pg.* 1589, *pg.* 207
S8 AUTOSCORE - Ventilation Device - RESMED INC.; *pg.* 1589, *pg.* 207
S8 AUTOSET SPIRIT - Ventilation Device - RESMED INC.; *pg.* 1589, *pg.* 207
S8 AUTOSET VANTAGE - Ventilation Device - RESMED INC.; *pg.* 1589, *pg.* 207
S8 COMPACT - Mask - RESMED INC.; *pg.* 1589, *pg.* 207
S8 ELITE - Easy Breathe Technology - RESMED INC.; *pg.* 1589, *pg.* 207
S8 ESCAPE - Flow Generator Product - RESMED INC.; *pg.* 1589, *pg.* 207
S8 LIGHTWEIGHT - Easy Breathe Technology - RESMED INC.; *pg.* 1589, *pg.* 207
S8 PRIMA - Medical Device - RESMED INC.; *pg.* 1589, *pg.* 207
SA 3100 - Surface Area & Pore Size Analyzer - BECKMAN COULTER, INC.; *pg.* 1402, *pg.* 48
SA-50 - Insecticide - SOUTHERN AGRICULTURAL INSECTICIDES, INC.; *pg.* 1181, *pg.* 458
SA-SERIES - Check Valve - HENRY PRATT COMPANY; *pg.*

1049, *pg.* 555
SA-SON - Flavor Enhancer - B&G FOODS, INC.; *pg.* 838, *pg.* 1102
SA8 - Laundry Detergent - AMWAY CORPORATION; *pg.* 326, *pg.* 864
SAASPROTECT ESCROW SERVICE - Service Application - IRON MOUNTAIN INCORPORATED; *pg.* 421, *pg.* 796
SABA - Doll And Toy - AMERICAN GIRL LLC; *pg.* 949, *pg.* 1871
SABA ANALYTICS - Software - SABA SOFTWARE, INC.; *pg.* 464, *pg.* 192
SABA CERTIFICATION MANAGEMENT - Software - SABA SOFTWARE, INC.; *pg.* 464, *pg.* 192
SABA COLLABORATION - Software - SABA SOFTWARE, INC.; *pg.* 464, *pg.* 192
SABA CONTENT - Software - SABA SOFTWARE, INC.; *pg.* 464, *pg.* 192
SABA LEARNING - Software - SABA SOFTWARE, INC.; *pg.* 464, *pg.* 192
SABA LEARNING COMMERCE - Software - SABA SOFTWARE, INC.; *pg.* 464, *pg.* 192
SABA LEARNING NETWORK - Software - SABA SOFTWARE, INC.; *pg.* 464, *pg.* 192
SABA LEARNING PROVIDER NETWORK - Software - SABA SOFTWARE, INC.; *pg.* 464, *pg.* 192
SABA LN - Software - SABA SOFTWARE, INC.; *pg.* 464, *pg.* 192
SABA LPN - Software - SABA SOFTWARE, INC.; *pg.* 464, *pg.* 192
SABA PERFORMANCE - Software - SABA SOFTWARE, INC.; *pg.* 464, *pg.* 192
SABA PERFORMANCE REVIEWS - Software - SABA SOFTWARE, INC.; *pg.* 464, *pg.* 192
SABA PUBLISHER - Software - SABA SOFTWARE, INC.; *pg.* 464, *pg.* 192
SABA UNIVERSITY - Software - SABA SOFTWARE, INC.; *pg.* 464, *pg.* 192
SABA.THE PEOPLE MANAGEMENT SOLUTION. - Tagline - SABA SOFTWARE, INC.; *pg.* 464, *pg.* 192
SABATTUS - Footwear - EASTLAND SHOE CORPORATION; *pg.* 1808, *pg.* 750
SABEL - Shoes - P.W. MINOR & SON, INC.; *pg.* 1816, *pg.* 1140
SABEL OXFORD - Footwear - P.W. MINOR & SON, INC.; *pg.* 1816, *pg.* 1140
SABELLA - Bath & Plumbing Product - JACUZZI BRANDS CORPORATION; *pg.* 554, *pg.* 65
SABER - Gaming Product - GLD PRODUCTS, INC.; *pg.* 1835, *pg.* 1882
SABER - Apparel & Fabric - I. SPIEWAK & SONS, INC.; *pg.* 42, *pg.* 1242
SABER - Fire Chassis - PIERCE MANUFACTURING, INC.; *pg.* 188, *pg.* 1852
SABER SELECT - Feed System - EASTMAN MACHINE COMPANY; *pg.* 1331, *pg.* 1148
SABER-TOOTH - Self Drilling Anchors - POWERS FASTENERS INC.; *pg.* 1059, *pg.* 1143
SABERJET - Nozzle - AKRON BRASS COMPANY; *pg.* 1311, *pg.* 1482
SABERMASTER - Nozzle - AKRON BRASS COMPANY; *pg.* 1311, *pg.* 1482
SABERTOOTH - Game - WMS INDUSTRIES INC.; *pg.* 593, *pg.* 666
SABIAN - Musical Instrument - KAMAN CORPORATION; *pg.* 229, *pg.* 338
SABLE - Milk Chocolate - CARGILL LIMITED; *pg.* 1475, *pg.* 1914
SABLIME - Software System - ALCATEL-LUCENT; *pg.* 615, *pg.* 1094
SABOR LATINO - Yogurt & Drinks - JOHANNA FOODS INC.; *pg.* 866, *pg.* 1066
SABOR LATINO NECTARS - Nectar Drinks - JOHANNA FOODS INC.; *pg.* 866, *pg.* 1066
SABRA - Cleaning Utensils - THE CLOROX COMPANY; *pg.* 327, *pg.* 169
SABRA - Liqueur - DIAGEO CANADA, INC.; *pg.* 1961, *pg.* 1937
SABRE - Laser & Laser System - COHERENT, INC.; *pg.* 1406, *pg.* 265
SABRE - Medical Equipment - CONMED CORPORATION; *pg.* 1517, *pg.* 1347
SABRE - Glass & Ceramic Material - CORNING INCORPORATED; *pg.* 1122, *pg.* 1154
SABRE - Engineering Resins - THE DOW CHEMICAL COMPANY; *pg.* 1157, *pg.* 898
SABRE - Router - GERBER SCIENTIFIC, INC.; *pg.* 1414, *pg.* 380
SABRE - Agricultural Equipment - JOHN DEERE LTD.; *pg.* 705, *pg.* 1920
SABRE - Automated Wafer Fabrication System - LAM RESEARCH CORPORATION; *pg.* 1354, *pg.* 246
SABRE - Connector - MOLEX INCORPORATED; *pg.* 655, *pg.* 628
SABRE AIRLINE SOLUTIONS - Traveling Service - SABRE HOLDINGS CORPORATION; *pg.* 1922, *pg.* 1745
SABRE EXTREME - Copper Electrofill Product - LAM RESEARCH CORPORATION; *pg.* 1354, *pg.* 246
SABRE NEXT - Copper Electrofill Product - LAM RESEARCH CORPORATION; *pg.* 1354, *pg.* 246
SABRE SPIRIT - Boat - SABRE CORPORATION; *pg.* 1710, *pg.* 752
SABRE TRAVEL NETWORK - Traveling Service - SABRE HOLDINGS CORPORATION; *pg.* 1922, *pg.* 1745
SABRELINE - Motor Yachts - SABRE CORPORATION; *pg.* 1710, *pg.* 752
SABRELITE - Flashlight - PELICAN PRODUCTS, INC.; *pg.* 1842, *pg.* 295
SABRINA - Furniture - AMISCO INDUSTRIES LTD.; *pg.* 913, *pg.* 1958
SABRINA - Footwear - EASTLAND SHOE CORPORATION; *pg.* 1808, *pg.* 750
SABRINA - Furniture - HOOKER FURNITURE CORPORATION; *pg.* 928, *pg.* 1788
SABRITAS - Potato Chips - FRITO-LAY NORTH AMERICA, INC.; *pg.* 1853, *pg.* 1730
SABRITAS - Potato Chips - PEPSICO, INC.; *pg.* 259, *pg.* 1327
SABRITONES - Puffed Wheat Snacks - FRITO-LAY NORTH AMERICA, INC.; *pg.* 1853, *pg.* 1730
SABRO - Sweetening Ingredient - MERISANT COMPANY; *pg.* 876, *pg.* 581
SABROSO - Cigar And Tobacco - SWISHER INTERNATIONAL, INC.; *pg.* 1895, *pg.* 345
SACHS - Drop Line Hardware - THOMAS & BETTS CORPORATION; *pg.* 680, *pg.* 1646
SACHSTWINEXTEND - Clutch - MERITOR, INC.; *pg.* 212, *pg.* 911
SACONS - Automated Contracting System - CACI INTERNATIONAL INC.; *pg.* 367, *pg.* 1773
SACONS-FEDERAL - Automated Contracting System - CACI INTERNATIONAL INC.; *pg.* 367, *pg.* 1773
SACRAL DISH - Polyurethane Foam - SPAN-AMERICA MEDICAL SYSTEMS, INC.; *pg.* 1595, *pg.* 1618
SACRAMENTO - Lighting - LSI INDUSTRIES INC.; *pg.* 58, *pg.* 1416
SACRAMENTO - Tomato & Vegetable Juice - RED GOLD, INC.; *pg.* 891, *pg.* 677
SACRAMENTO BEE - Newspapers - MCCLATCHY NEWSPAPERS, INC.; *pg.* 1662, *pg.* 197
SACRAMENTO KINGS - Professional Basketball Team - SACRAMENTO KINGS; *pg.* 579, *pg.* 197
SADDLEBACK - Watch - OAKLEY, INC.; *pg.* 1840, *pg.* 86
SADDLEFORM - Desiccant Bag - MULTISORB TECHNOLOGIES, INC.; *pg.* 1570, *pg.* 1150
SADDLEPAK - Modular Support System - O'BRIEN CORPORATION; *pg.* 1366, *pg.* 1001
SADDLETRACE - Valve Heater - THERMON AMERICAS INC.; *pg.* 1077, *pg.* 1744
SADLIER - Religious Programs & Books - WILLIAM H. SADLIER, INC.; *pg.* 1702, *pg.* 1314
SADTLER - Software - BIO-RAD LABORATORIES, INC.; *pg.* 1504, *pg.* 101
SAE SYSTEM - Lighting System - LITECONTROL CORPORATION; *pg.* 1301, *pg.* 841
SAEGIS - Research Tool - THOMSON COMPUMARK; *pg.* 484, *pg.* 838
SAF-EAR-SHIELD - Ear Protection - MCR SAFETY; *pg.* 1422, *pg.* 1630
SAF-GEL - Wound Care Product - CONVATEC LTD.; *pg.* 1518, *pg.* 1121
SAF-I-CHEM - Eye Protection - MCR SAFETY; *pg.* 1422, *pg.* 1630
SAF-I-CHIPPER - Goggles - MCR SAFETY; *pg.* 1422, *pg.* 1630
SAF-I-FLEX - Eye Protection - MCR SAFETY; *pg.* 1422, *pg.* 1630
SAF-I-GARD - Lenses - MCR SAFETY; *pg.* 1422, *pg.* 1630
SAF-I-WELD - Welders Helmet & Goggles - MCR SAFETY; *pg.* 1422, *pg.* 1630
SAF SERIES - Floor Boxes - WIREMOLD/LEGRAND; *pg.* 689, *pg.* 383
SAF-STOR - Eyewear Tray - SELLSTROM MANUFACTURING CO.; *pg.* 1428, *pg.* 659
SAF STRESS & ANXIETY FORMULA - Stress & Mood Relief Product - NATROL, INC.; *pg.* 1570, *pg.* 64
SAF-T-BAR - Brace & Box - WESTINGHOUSE LIGHTING CORPORATION; *pg.* 687, *pg.* 1571
SAF-T-BLEND - Medical Product - MEDLINE INDUSTRIES, INC.; *pg.* 1562, *pg.* 635
SAF-T-BOX - Brace & Box - WESTINGHOUSE LIGHTING CORPORATION; *pg.* 687, *pg.* 1571
SAF-T-BRACE - Brace & Box - WESTINGHOUSE LIGHTING CORPORATION; *pg.* 687, *pg.* 1571
SAF-T-CATH - Intravenous Catheter Placement Unit - BECTON, DICKINSON & COMPANY; *pg.* 1501, *pg.* 1068
SAF-T-CUT - Scissors - ACME UNITED CORPORATION; *pg.* 1040, *pg.* 346
SAF-T-GAP - Height Contacts - PASS & SEYMOUR/LEGRAND; *pg.* 1303, *pg.* 1344
SAF-T-GARD - Closing Speed Governor - CORNELL IRON WORKS, INC.; *pg.* 77, *pg.* 1554
SAF-T-GRID - Brace & Box - WESTINGHOUSE LIGHTING CORPORATION; *pg.* 687, *pg.* 1571
SAF-T-LINK - Gas Hose Connector - T&S BRASS & BRONZE WORKS, INC.; *pg.* 114, *pg.* 1623
SAF-T-PAN - Brace & Box - WESTINGHOUSE LIGHTING CORPORATION; *pg.* 687, *pg.* 1571
SAF-T-POP - Lollipop - SPANGLER CANDY COMPANY; *pg.* 1862, *pg.* 1407
SAF-T-POPS - Candy - SPANGLER CANDY COMPANY; *pg.* 1862, *pg.* 1407
SAF-T-SHARP - Compact Sharpener with Tungsten Carbide Blades - GERBER LEGENDARY BLADES; *pg.* 1834, *pg.* 1503
SAF-TWIST - Respirator - MCR SAFETY; *pg.* 1422, *pg.* 1630
SAFARI - Web Browser - APPLE INC.; *pg.* 350, *pg.* 73
SAFARI - Rug - COURISTAN INC.; *pg.* 921, *pg.* 1067
SAFARI - Van - GENERAL MOTORS COMPANY; *pg.* 175, *pg.* 881
SAFARI - Magazine - O'REILLY MEDIA, INC.; *pg.* 1673, *pg.* 278
SAFARI - Fragrance - RALPH LAUREN CORPORATION; *pg.* 46, *pg.* 1284
SAFARI 7S - Video Game - INTERNATIONAL GAME TECHNOLOGY; *pg.* 957, *pg.* 1024
SAFARI-BURLAP - Furniture - ASHLEY FURNITURE INDUSTRIES, INC.; *pg.* 914, *pg.* 1852
SAFARI FLOWERS - Video Game - INTERNATIONAL GAME TECHNOLOGY; *pg.* 957, *pg.* 1024
SAFARILAND - Security Product - BAE SYSTEMS PRODUCTS GROUP; *pg.* 359, *pg.* 432
SAFE - Systems Integration & Aeronautics - LOCKHEED MARTIN CORPORATION; *pg.* 229, *pg.* 762
SAFE - Software - SERENA SOFTWARE, INC.; *pg.* 468, *pg.* 192
SAFE & SOPHISTICATED - Eyewear - MINE SAFETY APPLIANCES COMPANY; *pg.* 1361, *pg.* 1525
SAFE AND SOUND - Glass Product - PPG INDUSTRIES, INC.; *pg.* 1445, *pg.* 1579
SAFE-CO - Gasoline Generator - WESTERBEKE CORPORATION; *pg.* 1388, *pg.* 847
SAFE CRACKER - Lottery Game - KENTUCKY LOTTERY CORPORATION; *pg.* 996, *pg.* 735
SAFE-CUFF - Soft Fabric - CAS MEDICAL SYSTEMS, INC.; *pg.* 1513, *pg.* 339
SAFE ESCAPE - Respirator - MINE SAFETY APPLIANCES COMPANY; *pg.* 1361, *pg.* 1525
SAFE FLO - Solder - OATEY SUPPLY CHAIN SERVICES; *pg.* 30, *pg.* 1433
SAFE FOR THEM.SAFE FOR YOU - Tagline - MEDIWARE INFORMATION SYSTEMS, INC.; *pg.* 431, *pg.* 716
SAFE HARBOR - Retirement Plans - PRINCIPAL FINANCIAL GROUP, INC.; *pg.* 796, *pg.* 706
SAFE IMAGER - Molecular Probe Product - THERMO FISHER SCIENTIFIC INC.; *pg.* 1602, *pg.* 61
SAFE-LEC - Safety Equipment - CONDUCTIX INC.; *pg.* 1295, *pg.* 1015
SAFE-LOK - Screw - THE HILSINGER CO.; *pg.* 1416, *pg.* 841
SAFE' N SOUND - Door - MASONITE INTERNATIONAL CORPORATION; *pg.* 1054, *pg.* 1920
SAFE PERFORMANCE - Horse Feed - MANNA PRO CORPORATION; *pg.* 1478, *pg.* 975
SAFE-R - Employee Screening System - STOELTING CO.; *pg.* 1430, *pg.* 671

SAFE-RELEASE - Masking Tape - 3M COMPANY; *pg.* 1142, *pg.* 956
SAFE-RIM - Membrane End Closure - SONOCO PRODUCTS COMPANY; *pg.* 1469, *pg.* 1619
SAFE SAC - Laryngoscope Handle Covers - VITAL SIGNS, INC.; *pg.* 1607, *pg.* 1126
THE SAFE SCRUBBING ALTERNATIVE - Surface Maintenance Machine - TENNANT COMPANY; *pg.* 1381, *pg.* 944
SAFE SHUTDOWN - Software - WESTERN DIGITAL CORPORATION; *pg.* 492, *pg.* 118
SAFE-SOC - Security Platform - IMAGINATION TECHNOLOGIES; *pg.* 412, *pg.* 285
SAFE SOUND - Earplug - MCKEON PRODUCTS, INC.; *pg.* 1559, *pg.* 912
SAFE. SOUND. SECURE - Investment Strategy - AUTO-OWNERS INSURANCE GROUP; *pg.* 1194, *pg.* 895
SAFE STRIDES - Healthcare Product - GENTIVA HEALTH SERVICES, INC.; *pg.* 1534, *pg.* 506
SAFE-T-BEAM - Beam System - THE GENIE COMPANY; *pg.* 55, *pg.* 1403
SAFE-T-CHEK - Watchclock - DETEX CORPORATION; *pg.* 633, *pg.* 1728
SAFE-T-FRESH - Plastic Food Containers - INLINE PLASTICS CORP.; *pg.* 1460, *pg.* 370
SAFE-T-GARD - Fold Seatcover - GEORGIA-PACIFIC LLC; *pg.* 1458, *pg.* 507
SAFE-T-GARD - Tear Strip For Use In Plastic Food Containers To Ensure Freshness - INLINE PLASTICS CORP.; *pg.* 1460, *pg.* 370
SAFE-T-GAUGE - Tool for Precise Control in Loop Electrosurgery - UTAH MEDICAL PRODUCTS, INC.; *pg.* 1605, *pg.* 1752
SAFE-T-GRIP - Fuse Puller - IDEAL INDUSTRIES, INC.; *pg.* 1051, *pg.* 662
SAFE-T-HOLD - Hockey Hand Protector - SCHOOL-TECH, INC.; *pg.* 1844, *pg.* 866
SAFE-T-J - Wire Guide - COOK GROUP, INC.; *pg.* 1518, *pg.* 674
SAFE-T-LIGHT - Animal Trimmer - ANDIS COMPANY; *pg.* 498, *pg.* 1895
SAFE-T-LIP - Hydraulic Dock Leveler - RITE-HITE HOLDING CORPORATION; *pg.* 1372, *pg.* 1880
SAFE-T-NET - Frame Relay Network - ADTRAN, INC.; *pg.* 344, *pg.* 6
SAFE-T-OHM - Shoe Tester - DWYER INSTRUMENTS INC.; *pg.* 1330, *pg.* 694
SAFE-T-SPRINT - Power Door - RITE-HITE HOLDING CORPORATION; *pg.* 1372, *pg.* 1880
SAFE-T-STOP - Plier - CHANNELLOCK, INC.; *pg.* 1044, *pg.* 1551
SAFE-T-ZONE - Safety Showers - SPEAKMAN COMPANY; *pg.* 112, *pg.* 388
SAFE-TAINER - Containers - THE DOW CHEMICAL COMPANY; *pg.* 1157, *pg.* 898
SAFE-TIGUE - Vinyl Floor Matting - 3M COMPANY; *pg.* 1142, *pg.* 956
SAFE-TOP - Membrane End Closure; Can End - SONOCO PRODUCTS COMPANY; *pg.* 1469, *pg.* 1619
SAFECHEM - Analysis and Transport Services - THE DOW CHEMICAL COMPANY; *pg.* 1157, *pg.* 898
SAFECIRCUIT - Technology that Minimizes the Dangers of Overloaded Electrical Circuits - MAC-GRAY CORPORATION; *pg.* 58, *pg.* 852
SAFECLIP - Healthcare Product - MEDICOOL, INC.; *pg.* 1562, *pg.* 294
SAFECONNECT - Belt Bridge - MINE SAFETY APPLIANCES COMPANY; *pg.* 1361, *pg.* 1525
SAFEDESIGN INSIGHT - Visual Engineering & Validation Software - MTS SYSTEMS CORPORATION; *pg.* 442, *pg.* 923
SAFEFACE MR - Paperboard Products - CARAUSTAR INDUSTRIES, INC.; *pg.* 1455, *pg.* 525
SAFEGARD - Clothing - LAKELAND INDUSTRIES, INC.; *pg.* 1354, *pg.* 1338
SAFEGUARD - Service Program - ADVANCED ENERGY INDUSTRIES, INC.; *pg.* 613, *pg.* 328
SAFEGUARD - Medical Device - INTEGRA LIFESCIENCES HOLDINGS CORPORATION; *pg.* 1545, *pg.* 1109
SAFEGUARD - Triple-wall Construction Utilized in Kaz Steam Products - KAZ, INC.; *pg.* 58, *pg.* 844
SAFEGUARD - Post-Hemostatis Management Device - MAQUET; *pg.* 1558, *pg.* 1082
SAFEGUARD - Personal & Beauty Product - THE PROCTER & GAMBLE COMPANY; *pg.* 1129, *pg.* 1418
SAFEGUARD - Protective Eyewear - SELLSTROM MANUFACTURING CO.; *pg.* 1428, *pg.* 659
SAFEGUARDS - Protective Eyewear - SELLSTROM MANUFACTURING CO.; *pg.* 1428, *pg.* 659
SAFEHOLD - Permanent Lifting Magnet - ERIEZ MANUFACTURING CO. INC.; *pg.* 1335, *pg.* 1530
SAFEIR - Power Semiconductor Device - INTERNATIONAL RECTIFIER CORPORATION; *pg.* 647, *pg.* 80
SAFEKEEPERPLUS - Data Protection Service - IRON MOUNTAIN INCORPORATED; *pg.* 421, *pg.* 796
SAFEKEEPERPLUS.COM - Data Protection Service - IRON MOUNTAIN INCORPORATED; *pg.* 421, *pg.* 796
SAFELINC - Web-Based Access to Fire System Information - TYCO SIMPLEXGRINNELL LP; *pg.* 682, *pg.* 859
SAFELINE - Software - EMC CORPORATION; *pg.* 391, *pg.* 825
SAFELITE - Vehicle Glass Repair - SAFELITE SOLUTIONS LLC; *pg.* 109, *pg.* 1443
SAFELOCK - Safety Wiring Products - PASS & SEYMOUR/LEGRAND; *pg.* 1303, *pg.* 1344
SAFEMASTER - Security System - STANLEY BLACK & DECKER, INC.; *pg.* 1063, *pg.* 358
SAFENAV - On-Vehicle GPS-Based Navigation & Alert System - I.D. SYSTEMS, INC.; *pg.* 643, *pg.* 1134
SAFEPARK - Integrated Software Circuits - AVAGO TECHNOLOGIES; *pg.* 358, *pg.* 238
SAFEPASS 201 - Head-Impact Evaluation Software - MTS SYSTEMS CORPORATION; *pg.* 442, *pg.* 923
SAFEPATH - Audio Booster - COOPER WHEELOCK; *pg.* 630, *pg.* 1080
SAFER - Pest Control - THE WOODSTREAM CORPORATION; *pg.* 1801, *pg.* 1549
SAFER & SMARTER - Awareness Program - ALTEC INDUSTRIES INC.; *pg.* 1312, *pg.* 1
THE SAFER TANK - Fiberglass Tank System - ZCL COMPOSITES INC.; *pg.* 1892, *pg.* 1906
SAFESET - Medical Device - HOSPIRA, INC.; *pg.* 1542, *pg.* 623
SAFESHIELD - Motion Detector - THE ADT CORPORATION; *pg.* 612, *pg.* 409
SAFESHIELD - Healthcare Product - GF HEALTH PRODUCTS, INC.; *pg.* 1535, *pg.* 508
SAFESITE - Server Management Software - DELL INC.; *pg.* 383, *pg.* 1737
SAFESITE - Lens - EMERGING VISION, INC.; *pg.* 1411, *pg.* 1227
SAFESITE - Jobsite Safety Chests - JUSTRITE MANUFACTURING COMPANY, LLC; *pg.* 1394, *pg.* 606
SAFESITE - Gas Sensor - MINE SAFETY APPLIANCES COMPANY; *pg.* 1361, *pg.* 1525
SAFESMOKER - Cigarette Receptacle - EAGLE MANUFACTURING COMPANY; *pg.* 79, *pg.* 1851
SAFEST STRIPPER - Wood Refinishing Products - 3M COMPANY; *pg.* 1142, *pg.* 956
SAFESTART - Intravenous Start Kit with Gloves - BECTON, DICKINSON & COMPANY; *pg.* 1501, *pg.* 1068
SAFESTORE - Software - AVAGO TECHNOLOGIES; *pg.* 358, *pg.* 238
SAFETAP - Tapping Fluids - ITW FLUIDS NORTH AMERICA; *pg.* 980, *pg.* 614
SAFETE - Synthetic Film - SPINNAKER COATING, LLC; *pg.* 1470, *pg.* 1477
SAFETEMP - Pressure Balance Shower Valve - GERBER PLUMBING FIXTURES CORPORATION; *pg.* 84, *pg.* 672
SAFETFLEX - Animal Safety Product - NEOGEN CORPORATION; *pg.* 883, *pg.* 896
SAFETOX - Gas Monitor - MINE SAFETY APPLIANCES COMPANY; *pg.* 1361, *pg.* 1525
SAFETRAC - Medical Device - SPIRE CORPORATION; *pg.* 1378, *pg.* 786
SAFETRACE - Valve Heater - THERMON AMERICAS INC.; *pg.* 1077, *pg.* 1744
SAFETUBE - Storage Container - PHOENIX PRODUCTS COMPANY; *pg.* 1304, *pg.* 1879
SAFETY ALERT - Radar Detectors - COBRA ELECTRONICS CORPORATION; *pg.* 629, *pg.* 572
SAFETY & RELIABILITY REPORT - Information Retrieval Services - CARFAX INC.; *pg.* 202, *pg.* 1777
SAFETY AT HEIGHTS - Training - MINE SAFETY APPLIANCES COMPANY; *pg.* 1361, *pg.* 1525
THE SAFETY COMPANY - Tagline - MINE SAFETY APPLIANCES COMPANY; *pg.* 1361, *pg.* 1525
SAFETY EASE - Software - PANDUIT CORP.; *pg.* 661, *pg.* 663
SAFETY EDGE - Vinyl Diamond Plate Runner - THE BILTRITE CORPORATION; *pg.* 1879, *pg.* 850
SAFETY EDGE - Polyurethane Foam - SPAN-AMERICA MEDICAL SYSTEMS, INC.; *pg.* 1595, *pg.* 1618
SAFETY FIRST - Beverages - THE COCA-COLA COMPANY; *pg.* 240, *pg.* 493
SAFETY-FRESH - Coffee & Beverage Equipment - BUNN-O-MATIC CORPORATION; *pg.* 53, *pg.* 661
SAFETY HARBOR JOURNAL - Newspaper - TAMPA BAY NEWSPAPERS, INC.; *pg.* 1691, *pg.* 468
SAFETY IN COMMUNICATION - Tag Line - SAVOX COMMUNICATIONS LTD; *pg.* 671, *pg.* 1909
SAFETY LINK - Community Outreach Program - MIDAMERICAN ENERGY HOLDINGS COMPANY; *pg.* 1946, *pg.* 706
SAFETY-LUBE - Die Lubricant - CHEM-TREND LIMITED PARTNERSHIP; *pg.* 973, *pg.* 892
SAFETY-LUBE-SUPER - Die Lubricant - CHEM-TREND LIMITED PARTNERSHIP; *pg.* 973, *pg.* 892
SAFETY-MATE - Goggles - MCR SAFETY; *pg.* 1422, *pg.* 1630
SAFETY SCRAPE - Cleaning Product - HILLYARD, INC.; *pg.* 331, *pg.* 990
SAFETY, SECURITY, PROTECTION & SPORT - Tagline - SMITH & WESSON HOLDING CORPORATION; *pg.* 1845, *pg.* 846
SAFETY SOLVENT - Degreaser - TEXAS REFINERY CORP.; *pg.* 986, *pg.* 1696
SAFETY SPONGE - Medical Product - PATIENT SAFETY TECHNOLOGIES, INC.; *pg.* 1580, *pg.* 114
SAFETY STEP - Step-on-Can - WITT INDUSTRIES, INC.; *pg.* 1140, *pg.* 1461
SAFETY SUNBLOCK SHADE - Baby Care Product - MUNCHKIN, INC.; *pg.* 964, *pg.* 300
SAFETY THE ONLY CHOICE - Tagline - KLLM TRANSPORT SERVICES, INC.; *pg.* 1914, *pg.* 971
SAFETY TOUCH - Home Products - HABAND COMPANY, INC.; *pg.* 1772, *pg.* 1099
SAFETY TOWELS - Industrial Cleaner - SUNSHINE MAKERS, INC.; *pg.* 336, *pg.* 105
SAFETY TRAINING CUSTOMIZER - Training Program Design Software - J.J. KELLER & ASSOCIATES, INC.; *pg.* 1654, *pg.* 1883
SAFETY-TREAD - Safety Grating - ALABAMA METAL INDUSTRIES CORPORATION; *pg.* 65, *pg.* 1
SAFETY-WALK - Matting Product - 3M COMPANY; *pg.* 1142, *pg.* 956
SAFETY WITHOUT COMPROMISE - Tagline - THE PROTECTOSEAL COMPANY; *pg.* 1370, *pg.* 556
SAFETY+PLUS - Gas Valves - BRASSCRAFT MANUFACTURING COMPANY; *pg.* 1043, *pg.* 902
ENVIRO.BLR.COM - Website - BUSINESS & LEGAL REPORTS INC.; *pg.* 1624, *pg.* 367
SAFETYCADE - Barricade - UNITED RENTALS, INC.; *pg.* 1386, *pg.* 350
SAFETYCOR - Plastic Signs - UNITED RENTALS, INC.; *pg.* 1386, *pg.* 350
SAFETYDIRECT - Software - ITERIS, INC.; *pg.* 293, *pg.* 261
SAFETYFLEX - Hose - HBD INDUSTRIES, INC.; *pg.* 207, *pg.* 1449
SAFETYLIGHT 2100 - Vaporizer - KAZ, INC.; *pg.* 58, *pg.* 844
SAFETYLIGHT 2200 - Vaporizer - KAZ, INC.; *pg.* 58, *pg.* 844
SAFETYLOCK - Disposable Scalpel - CROSSTEX INTERNATIONAL INC.; *pg.* 1520, *pg.* 1164
SAFETYMED - Software - OMNICELL INC.; *pg.* 1578, *pg.* 161
SAFETYMED RN - Medicating Software - OMNICELL INC.; *pg.* 1578, *pg.* 161
SAFETYMIX - Pressure Balanced Safety Shower Systems - SYMMONS INDUSTRIES, INC.; *pg.* 114, *pg.* 803
SAFETYPAK - Software - OMNICELL INC.; *pg.* 1578, *pg.* 161
SAFETYSOLVE II - Degreaser - TEXAS REFINERY CORP.; *pg.* 986, *pg.* 1696
SAFETYSTATION - Ironing Board - HOME PRODUCTS INTERNATIONAL, INC.; *pg.* 1125, *pg.* 577
SAFETYSWEEP - Software - SYMANTEC CORPORATION; *pg.* 478, *pg.* 161
SAFETYVAP - Laboratory Product - EPPENDORF NORTH AMERICA; *pg.* 1412, *pg.* 1164
THE SAFETYWAND - Syringe - MILESTONE SCIENTIFIC, INC.; *pg.* 1568, *pg.* 1079
SAFEVOC - Gas Monitor - MINE SAFETY APPLIANCES COMPANY; *pg.* 1361, *pg.* 1525
SAFEWATCH - Home Security System - THE ADT CORPORATION; *pg.* 612, *pg.* 409

SAFEWAY - Electronic Components - MOLEX INCORPORATED; *pg.* 655, *pg.* 628
SAFEWAY SELECT - Premium Private Label Brand - SAFEWAY INC.; *pg.* 1032, *pg.* 184
SAFEWAY+ - Electronic Components - MOLEX INCORPORATED; *pg.* 655, *pg.* 628
SAFEWORK - Firesafety Education - NATIONAL FIRE PROTECTION ASSOCIATION; *pg.* 149, *pg.* 842
SAFEYE - Gas Detection System - MINE SAFETY APPLIANCES COMPANY; *pg.* 1361, *pg.* 1525
SAFFOLA - Margarine, Salad Oil & Mayonnaise - VENTURA FOODS, LLC; *pg.* 908, *pg.* 49
SAFFRAN - Fabric - NEMSCHOFF, INC.; *pg.* 936, *pg.* 1890
SAFIA - Beverages - THE COCA-COLA COMPANY; *pg.* 240, *pg.* 493
SAFIRE - Bi-directional Ablation Catheter - ST. JUDE MEDICAL, INC.; *pg.* 1596, *pg.* 963
SAFLIFT - Nuclear Cranes - AMERICAN CRANE & EQUIPMENT CORPORATION; *pg.* 1312, *pg.* 1526
SAFLOAD - Shoring System - SAFWAY SERVICES, LLC; *pg.* 109, *pg.* 1898
SAFMAX - Frame System - SAFWAY SERVICES, LLC; *pg.* 109, *pg.* 1898
SAFTEY-GRIP - Safety Grating - ALABAMA METAL INDUSTRIES CORPORATION; *pg.* 65, *pg.* 1
SAFTI-GRIP - Bathmat - HILLYARD, INC.; *pg.* 331, *pg.* 990
SAFWATCH - Nuclear Cranes - AMERICAN CRANE & EQUIPMENT CORPORATION; *pg.* 1312, *pg.* 1526
SAG HARBOR - Women's Sportswear & Dresses - KELLWOOD COMPANY; *pg.* 28, *pg.* 975
THE SAGA SYSTEM - Web Application - EOLAS TECHNOLOGIES, INC.; *pg.* 1243, *pg.* 573
SAGE - Gas Source - ATMI, INC.; *pg.* 1314, *pg.* 342
SAGE - Biotechnology Product - GENZYME CORPORATION; *pg.* 1534, *pg.* 808
SAGE - Pillow and Throw - HERITAGE LACE INC.; *pg.* 694, *pg.* 711
SAGE BLOSSOM - Honey - MILLER'S HONEY COMPANY; *pg.* 1860, *pg.* 1759
SAGE BORDER STRIPE - Pillow and Throw - HERITAGE LACE INC.; *pg.* 694, *pg.* 711
SAGE BRUSH - Natural Spray - ANNIE OAKLEY ENTERPRISES, INC.; *pg.* 499, *pg.* 693
SAGE SYSTEMS - High Pressure Spray Cleaners - T&S BRASS & BRONZE WORKS, INC.; *pg.* 114, *pg.* 1623
SAGEON - Power Plants - C&D TECHNOLOGIES, INC.; *pg.* 627, *pg.* 1517
SAGIAN - Testing Instrument System - BECKMAN COULTER, INC.; *pg.* 1402, *pg.* 48
THE SAGINAW NEWS - Newspaper - MLIVE MEDIA GROUP; *pg.* 1665, *pg.* 888
SAGRADA - Fabric - NEMSCHOFF, INC.; *pg.* 936, *pg.* 1890
SAGUARO - Video Game - INTERNATIONAL GAME TECHNOLOGY; *pg.* 957, *pg.* 1024
SAHALIE - Outdoor Clothing & Gear - NORM THOMPSON OUTFITTERS INC.; *pg.* 1780, *pg.* 1498
SAHARA - Ceilings & Walls - ARMSTRONG WORLD INDUSTRIES, INC.; *pg.* 914, *pg.* 1545
SAHARA - Footwear - COBIAN CORP.; *pg.* 1806, *pg.* 253
SAHARA - Bedding - CROSCILL, INC.; *pg.* 1122, *pg.* 1220
SAHARA - Masonry Coating - DAVIS PAINT COMPANY; *pg.* 1441, *pg.* 982
SAHARA - Biotechnology Product - GENZYME CORPORATION; *pg.* 1534, *pg.* 808
SAHARA - Medical Product - HOLOGIC, INC.; *pg.* 1416, *pg.* 784
SAHARA - Dinnerware - THE HOMER LAUGHLIN CHINA COMPANY; *pg.* 1125, *pg.* 1850
SAHARA - Furniture - NEUTRAL POSTURE, INC.; *pg.* 939, *pg.* 1669
SAHARA - Outdoor Lighting - SWIVELIER CO., INC.; *pg.* 1307, *pg.* 1142
SAHARA OASIS - Pool Paint - DAVIS PAINT COMPANY; *pg.* 1441, *pg.* 982
SAHARA SERIES - Drainage Pumps - LITTLE GIANT PUMP COMPANY; *pg.* 1356, *pg.* 1486
SAHASRA - Network Processing Product - CYPRESS SEMICONDUCTOR CORPORATION; *pg.* 1326, *pg.* 243
SAHORA - Suitcase - SAMSONITE CORPORATION; *pg.* 11, *pg.* 830
SAHTAIN - Beverages - THE COCA-COLA COMPANY; *pg.* 240, *pg.* 493
SAIA - Trucks Transportation - SAIA, INC.; *pg.* 1922, *pg.* 533
SAIA CUSTOMER SERVICE INDICATORS - Transport By Railway - SAIA, INC.; *pg.* 1922, *pg.* 533
SAIA GUARANTEED SELECT - Trucks - SAIA, INC.; *pg.* 1922, *pg.* 533
SAIA XTREME GUARANTEE - Freight Transportation - SAIA, INC.; *pg.* 1922, *pg.* 533
SAILCOAT - Antifouling Paint-Racing Sailboats - PETTIT PAINT COMPANY; *pg.* 1444, *pg.* 1116
SAILCOMP - Satellite Communication Product - KVH INDUSTRIES INC; *pg.* 650, *pg.* 1602
SAILFISH - Fiberglass Boat Product - GRADY-WHITE BOATS, INC.; *pg.* 1707, *pg.* 1377
SAILING WORLD - Magazine - BONNIER CORPORATION; *pg.* 1622, *pg.* 480
SAILOR JERRY - Rum - WILLIAM GRANT & SONS, INC.; *pg.* 1972, *pg.* 1057
THE SAILORS' CHOICE - Tagline - CATALINA YACHTS, INC.; *pg.* 1706, *pg.* 307
SAINT ALGUE - Hair Salons - REGIS CORPORATION; *pg.* 521, *pg.* 941
SAINT ANDREA - Silverware - ONEIDA LTD; *pg.* 1129, *pg.* 1318
SAINT CHARLES - Fan - WESTINGHOUSE LIGHTING CORPORATION; *pg.* 687, *pg.* 1571
SAINT IVES - Carpet - BEAULIEU GROUP, LLC; *pg.* 917, *pg.* 529
SAINT LOUIS BLUES - Professional Hockey Team - ST. LOUIS BLUES HOCKEY CLUB, LLC; *pg.* 585, *pg.* 1003
SAINT LUIS REY - Handmade Cigar - ALTADIS USA, INC.; *pg.* 1893, *pg.* 423
SAINT TROPEZ - Fan - WESTINGHOUSE LIGHTING CORPORATION; *pg.* 687, *pg.* 1571
SAINT TROPEZ WEST - Women's Active Wear - CHEROKEE GLOBAL BRANDS; *pg.* 21, *pg.* 278
SAIVI - Molecular Biology Product - THERMO FISHER SCIENTIFIC INC.; *pg.* 1602, *pg.* 61
SAKONITE - Pressed & Monolithic Refractory - RESCO PRODUCTS, INC.; *pg.* 107, *pg.* 1581
SAKRETE - Concrete Mixes - SAKRETE OF NORTH AMERICA, LLC; *pg.* 109, *pg.* 1425
SAKS FIFTH AVENUE - Department Stores - SAKS INCORPORATED; *pg.* 1783, *pg.* 1288
SAKURA - Dinnerware - ONEIDA LTD; *pg.* 1129, *pg.* 1318
SALAD BISTRO - Salad Products & Services - VENTURA FOODS, LLC; *pg.* 908, *pg.* 49
SALAD BOWLS - Container Product - INLINE PLASTICS CORP.; *pg.* 1460, *pg.* 370
SALAD LITE - Salad Dressing - CAINS FOODS, L.P.; *pg.* 843, *pg.* 784
SALAD SUPREME - Seasoning - MCCORMICK & COMPANY, INCORPORATED; *pg.* 1027, *pg.* 779
SALAD TOPPINS - Food Product - MCCORMICK & COMPANY, INCORPORATED; *pg.* 1027, *pg.* 779
SALADA - Tea - REDCO FOODS, INC.; *pg.* 891, *pg.* 1174
SALADA - Beverages - UNILEVER CANADA INC.; *pg.* 903, *pg.* 1946
SALADENA - Crumble Cheese - BONGRAIN NORTH AMERICA; *pg.* 841, *pg.* 1556
SALADMASTER - Cookware - SALADMASTER; *pg.* 60, *pg.* 1659
SALAGEN - Pharmaceutical - EISAI INC.; *pg.* 1526, *pg.* 1133
SALAGEN - Pharmaceutical Product - IMPAX LABORATORIES, INC.; *pg.* 1544, *pg.* 101
SALAMANDER - Restorative - MARTIN/F. WEBER COMPANY; *pg.* 962, *pg.* 1567
SALAMANDER - Lighting Product - QUOIZEL INC.; *pg.* 1304, *pg.* 1616
SALAMANDER SOOTHER - Body Lotion - ORANGE PEEL ENTERPRISES, INC.; *pg.* 1028, *pg.* 477
SALE OF THE CENTURY - Game - INTERNATIONAL GAME TECHNOLOGY; *pg.* 957, *pg.* 1024
SALEM - Chipset - ANALOG DEVICES, INC.; *pg.* 617, *pg.* 839
SALEM - Cash Settlement System - GLORY GLOBAL SOLUTIONS; *pg.* 401, *pg.* 628
SALEM FIVE ACCESSLINE - Banking Service - SALEM FIVE CENTS SAVINGS BANK; *pg.* 800, *pg.* 843
SALEM FIVE WORLDACCESS - Debit Card - SALEM FIVE CENTS SAVINGS BANK; *pg.* 800, *pg.* 843
SALEM MUSIC NETWORK - Radio Broadcasting Product - SALEM MEDIA GROUP, INC.; *pg.* 307, *pg.* 57
SALEM NEWS NETWORK - Radio Broadcasting Product - SALEM MEDIA GROUP, INC.; *pg.* 307, *pg.* 57
SALEM PUBLISHING - Christian-Themed Magazines - SALEM MEDIA GROUP, INC.; *pg.* 307, *pg.* 57
SALEM RADIO NETWORK - Radio Broadcasting Product - SALEM MEDIA GROUP, INC.; *pg.* 307, *pg.* 57
SALEM RADIO REPRESENTATIVES - Radio Broadcasting Product - SALEM MEDIA GROUP, INC.; *pg.* 307, *pg.* 57
SALEM WEB NETWORK - Online Christian Network - SALEM MEDIA GROUP, INC.; *pg.* 307, *pg.* 57
SALERNO - Fan - CRAFTMADE INTERNATIONAL, INC.; *pg.* 1295, *pg.* 1670
SALERNO - Dinnerware - THE HOMER LAUGHLIN CHINA COMPANY; *pg.* 1125, *pg.* 1850
SALES GENERATOR - Marketing Tool - PREMIERE GLOBAL SERVICES, INC.; *pg.* 1275, *pg.* 518
SALES LEADS. ON DEMAND - Slogan - USADATA, INC.; *pg.* 1287, *pg.* 1308
SALES MANAGER - Automated Sales System - VENDIO, INC.; *pg.* 1287, *pg.* 256
SALESGENIE.COM - Sales Lead Lists - INFOGROUP INC.; *pg.* 1652, *pg.* 1016
SALESLOGIX - CRM Solution - SAGE SOFTWARE, INC.; *pg.* 464, *pg.* 116
SALEST - Medical Product - HOLOGIC, INC.; *pg.* 1416, *pg.* 784
SALESTRACKER - Software - SILVON SOFTWARE INC.; *pg.* 470, *pg.* 669
SALINA - Furniture - AMERICAN LEATHER LP; *pg.* 912, *pg.* 1673
SALINGER - Furniture - ETHAN ALLEN INTERIORS INC.; *pg.* 924, *pg.* 343
SALISBURY PINK - Granite - ROCK OF AGES CORPORATION; *pg.* 108, *pg.* 1766
SALLIE MAE EDUCATION LOAN - Loan Service - SLM CORPORATION; *pg.* 804, *pg.* 388
THE SALLIE MAE FUND - Charitable Organization - SLM CORPORATION; *pg.* 804, *pg.* 388
SALLIE MAE MBA LOANS - Full Funding for Graduate Business Education - SLM CORPORATION; *pg.* 804, *pg.* 388
SALLLY - Footwear - STEVEN MADDEN, LTD.; *pg.* 1819, *pg.* 1176
SALLY - Furniture - AMISCO INDUSTRIES LTD.; *pg.* 913, *pg.* 1958
SALLY - Hat - WOODEN SHIPS OF HOBOKEN; *pg.* 35, *pg.* 1315
SALLY FLUTTER - Hat - WOODEN SHIPS OF HOBOKEN; *pg.* 35, *pg.* 1315
SALLY FOSTER - Giftwrap & Accessories - ENTERTAINMENT PUBLICATIONS, INC.; *pg.* 1639, *pg.* 910
SALLY SHELL - Hat - WOODEN SHIPS OF HOBOKEN; *pg.* 35, *pg.* 1315
SALLY STRIPED - Hat - WOODEN SHIPS OF HOBOKEN; *pg.* 35, *pg.* 1315
SALLY TIP - Hat - WOODEN SHIPS OF HOBOKEN; *pg.* 35, *pg.* 1315
SALMON ESSENTIALS - Biological Products - MERA PHARMACEUTICALS, INC.; *pg.* 1566, *pg.* 545
SALON - Fabric - NEMSCHOFF, INC.; *pg.* 936, *pg.* 1890
THE SALON - UK Salon Brand - REGIS CORPORATION; *pg.* 521, *pg.* 941
SALON CIELO & SPA - Hair Care Salon & Spa Services - THE RATNER COMPANIES; *pg.* 520, *pg.* 1809
SALON DESIGNS - Styling Mousse - BLUE CROSS LABORATORIES; *pg.* 326, *pg.* 277
SALON EDITION - Beauty Care Product - HELEN OF TROY L.P.; *pg.* 511, *pg.* 1692
SALON FORMULA - Cosmetic Product - MERLE NORMAN COSMETICS, INC.; *pg.* 517, *pg.* 136
SALON PLAZA - Hair Care Salon - THE RATNER COMPANIES; *pg.* 520, *pg.* 1809
SALON SILHOUETTES - Wig & Hairpiece Supplier to Salons - SPECIALTY CATALOG CORPORATION; *pg.* 1786, *pg.* 856
SALON STUDIO - Pinstriped Pant Set - HABAND COMPANY, INC.; *pg.* 1772, *pg.* 1099
SALON TODAY - Magazine - VANCE PUBLISHING CORPORATION; *pg.* 1699, *pg.* 627
SALOON BAR & GRILL - Restaurant - ARK RESTAURANTS CORP.; *pg.* 1715, *pg.* 1196
SALORA - Kitchen Faucet - MOEN INCORPORATED; *pg.* 1056, *pg.* 1468
SALSA - Tile - ARTISTIC TILE INC.; *pg.* 914, *pg.* 1119
SALSA - Fabric - NEMSCHOFF, INC.; *pg.* 936, *pg.* 1890
SALSA - Bicycle Components - QUALITY BICYCLE PRODUCTS; *pg.* 1710, *pg.* 918
SALSA EXPRESS - Salsa Food Products - STANDEX INTERNATIONAL CORPORATION; *pg.* 60, *pg.* 1039
SALSALITO - Food Product - BOAR'S HEAD PROVISIONS

CO., INC.; *pg.* 841, *pg.* 465
SALSALITTA - Chicken Product - MAPLE LODGE FARMS LTD.; *pg.* 876, *pg.* 1918
SALSBURY - Mail Box - SALSBURY INDUSTRIES; *pg.* 464, *pg.* 139
SALSERA - Footwear - STEVEN MADDEN, LTD.; *pg.* 1819, *pg.* 1176
SALT N PEPPER - Carpet - BEAULIEU GROUP, LLC; *pg.* 917, *pg.* 529
SALT SENSE - Plain & Iodized Salt - CARGILL LIMITED; *pg.* 1475, *pg.* 1914
SALT SENSE - Table Salt - CARGILL SALT; *pg.* 846, *pg.* 926
SALT STRIKER - Fishing Equipment - CABELA'S INCORPORATED; *pg.* 535, *pg.* 1019
SALT WATER SPORTSMAN - Magazine - BONNIER ACTIVE MEDIA, INC.; *pg.* 1622, *pg.* 1205
SALT WATER SPORTSMAN - Magazine - BONNIER CORPORATION; *pg.* 1622, *pg.* 480
SALT WATER TAFFY - Candy - SWEET CANDY COMPANY; *pg.* 1862, *pg.* 1761
SALTAIRE - Menswear - SEATTLE PACIFIC INDUSTRIES, INC.; *pg.* 48, *pg.* 1822
SALTIGA - Saltwater Spinning Reels - DAIWA CORPORATION; *pg.* 1832, *pg.* 75
SALTIMBANCO - Show And Ticket - CIRQUE DU SOLEIL INC.; *pg.* 540, *pg.* 1954
SALTTRIM - Flavor Technology - WILD FLAVORS, INC.; *pg.* 910, *pg.* 728
SALTWATERSPORTSMAN.COM - Web Site - BONNIER ACTIVE MEDIA, INC.; *pg.* 1622, *pg.* 1205
SALTWISE - Food Additives - CARGILL, INC.; *pg.* 845, *pg.* 965
SALUTE - Bath Product - KOHLER CO.; *pg.* 91, *pg.* 1862
SALVADOR - Footwear - COBIAN CORP.; *pg.* 1806, *pg.* 253
SALVATION - Cleaning Product - HILLYARD, INC.; *pg.* 331, *pg.* 990
SALVO - Personal & Household Product - THE PROCTER & GAMBLE COMPANY; *pg.* 1129, *pg.* 1418
SAM - Furniture - AMISCO INDUSTRIES LTD.; *pg.* 913, *pg.* 1958
SAM - Software - HEALTHPORT, INC.; *pg.* 403, *pg.* 484
S.A.M. - Software - NER HOLDINGS INC.; *pg.* 444, *pg.* 1071
SAM-BA - Integrated Circuit - ATMEL CORPORATION; *pg.* 621, *pg.* 238
SAM-E - Nutritional Supplement - PHARMAVITE LLC; *pg.* 1584, *pg.* 167
SAM-ICE - Integrated Circuit - ATMEL CORPORATION; *pg.* 621, *pg.* 238
SAM-PROG - Integrated Circuit - ATMEL CORPORATION; *pg.* 621, *pg.* 238
SAMANTHA - Beverages - THE COCA-COLA COMPANY; *pg.* 240, *pg.* 493
SAMANTHA PARKINGTON - Doll And Toy - AMERICAN GIRL LLC; *pg.* 949, *pg.* 1871
SAMANTHA'S BIRTHDAY TEA - Doll And Toy - AMERICAN GIRL LLC; *pg.* 949, *pg.* 1871
SAMBA - Bath Product - KOHLER CO.; *pg.* 91, *pg.* 1862
SAMBA - Fabric - NEMSCHOFF, INC.; *pg.* 936, *pg.* 1890
SAMBAPLUS - Color - FERRO CORPORATION; *pg.* 1162, *pg.* 1462
SAMBUKA - Footwear - STEVEN MADDEN, LTD.; *pg.* 1819, *pg.* 1176
SAMCURE - Photoinitiators for UV-Cured Coatings - KING INDUSTRIES, INC.; *pg.* 1443, *pg.* 363
SAME - Nutritional Supplement - NATURAL ORGANICS, INC.; *pg.* 1571, *pg.* 1181
SAME DAY SERVICE - Expedited Flight-Out Service - DHL HOLDINGS (USA), INC.; *pg.* 1906, *pg.* 459
SAMI - Testing Instrument System - BECKMAN COULTER, INC.; *pg.* 1402, *pg.* 48
SAMISH - Sport Knife - MCNETT CORPORATION; *pg.* 1839, *pg.* 1817
SAMOA - Outdoor Lighting - SWIVELIER CO., INC.; *pg.* 1307, *pg.* 1142
SAMONE - Footwear - VANS, INC.; *pg.* 1821, *pg.* 76
SAMOS - Rug - COURISTAN INC.; *pg.* 921, *pg.* 1067
SAMPI - Pump Product - IDEX CORPORATION; *pg.* 1347, *pg.* 623
SAMPLE CENTRIC - Software - WATERS CORPORATION; *pg.* 1436, *pg.* 834
SAMPLELOCK - Syringe - HAMILTON CO., INC.; *pg.* 1415, *pg.* 1031
SAMPLMET 2 - Abrasive Cutter - BUEHLER, LTD.; *pg.* 1403, *pg.* 622
SAMPSON - Footwear - P.W. MINOR & SON, INC.; *pg.* 1816, *pg.* 1140
SAM'S AMERICAN CHOICE - Grocery Items - WAL-MART STORES, INC.; *pg.* 1790, *pg.* 29
SAMS TOWN TUNICA HOTEL & GAMBLING HALL - Hotel & Casino - BOYD GAMING CORPORATION; *pg.* 1082, *pg.* 1022
SAMSON - Furniture - AMISCO INDUSTRIES LTD.; *pg.* 913, *pg.* 1958
SAMSON - Microphones, Amplifiers & Mixers - SAM ASH MUSIC CORPORATION; *pg.* 669, *pg.* 1167
SAMSON - Braided Rope - SAMSON ROPE TECHNOLOGIES; *pg.* 1468, *pg.* 1820
SAMSONITE BLACK LABEL - Suitcase - SAMSONITE CORPORATION; *pg.* 11, *pg.* 830
SAMSON'S - Tobacco Product - AMERICAN SNUFF COMPANY; *pg.* 1893, *pg.* 1641
SAMSON'S BIG 4 - Twist Tobacco - AMERICAN SNUFF COMPANY; *pg.* 1893, *pg.* 1641
SAMSUNG - Electronics Company - SAMSUNG TELECOMMUNICATIONS AMERICA, LLC; *pg.* 670, *pg.* 1736
SAMTRAK - Software - SS&C TECHNOLOGIES HOLDINGS, INC.; *pg.* 473, *pg.* 386
SAMUEL ADAMS - Brewer - THE BOSTON BEER COMPANY, INC.; *pg.* 239, *pg.* 790
SAMUEL ADAMS BOSTON LAGER - Beverage - THE BOSTON BEER COMPANY, INC.; *pg.* 239, *pg.* 790
SAMUEL ADAMS UTOPIAS - Beverage - THE BOSTON BEER COMPANY, INC.; *pg.* 239, *pg.* 790
SAMUEL ADAMS UTOPIAS MMII - Beverage - THE BOSTON BEER COMPANY, INC.; *pg.* 239, *pg.* 790
SAMUEL/LAWRENCE - Wood Bedroom Furniture - SEALY CORPORATION; *pg.* 942, *pg.* 1391
SAMUI - Footwear - STEVEN MADDEN, LTD.; *pg.* 1819, *pg.* 1176
SAMURAI - Restaurant - BENIHANA INC.; *pg.* 1716, *pg.* 409
SAMURAI - Soft Drink - THE COCA-COLA COMPANY; *pg.* 240, *pg.* 493
SAMURAI - Carpet - INTERFACE, INC.; *pg.* 695, *pg.* 512
SAMURAI - Circuit - MICRON TECHNOLOGY, INC.; *pg.* 435, *pg.* 547
SAMURAI JACK - Game & TV Show - THE CARTOON NETWORK; *pg.* 273, *pg.* 492
SAMURAI MASTER - Game - WMS INDUSTRIES INC.; *pg.* 593, *pg.* 666
SAMY - Medical Device - INTEGRA LIFESCIENCES HOLDINGS CORPORATION; *pg.* 1545, *pg.* 1109
SAN ADVISOR - Software - EMC CORPORATION; *pg.* 391, *pg.* 825
SAN AGUSTIN - Estate Coffee - THE SECOND CUP LTD.; *pg.* 1749, *pg.* 1928
SAN ANGELO - Hunting Goods - RIO BRANDS, INC.; *pg.* 941, *pg.* 1570
SAN ANGELO STANDARD-TIMES - Newspaper - THE E.W. SCRIPPS COMPANY; *pg.* 1639, *pg.* 1412
SAN ANSELMO - Bike - MARIN BIKES; *pg.* 1708, *pg.* 168
SAN ANTONIO FARMS - Sauces & Syrups - TREEHOUSE FOODS, INC.; *pg.* 901, *pg.* 649
SAN ANTONIO SPURS - Professional Basketball Team - SAN ANTONIO SPURS LLC; *pg.* 580, *pg.* 1742
SAN COPY - Software - EMC CORPORATION; *pg.* 391, *pg.* 825
SAN DIEGO PADRES - Baseball Team - PADRES L.P.; *pg.* 573, *pg.* 206
THE SAN DIEGO UNION-TRIBUNE - Newspaper - THE SAN DIEGO UNION-TRIBUNE, LLC; *pg.* 1682, *pg.* 208
SAN DIEGO ZOO - Zoo - ZOOLOGICAL SOCIETY OF SAN DIEGO; *pg.* 595, *pg.* 211
SAN-EZE - Plastic & Rubber - TEKNOR APEX COMPANY; *pg.* 1889, *pg.* 1605
SAN FRANCISCO CHRONICLE - Newspaper - THE HEARST CORPORATION; *pg.* 1649, *pg.* 1239
SAN FRANCISCO GIANTS - Major League Baseball - SAN FRANCISCO GIANTS BASEBALL CLUB; *pg.* 581, *pg.* 226
SAN GIORGIO - Food Product - NEW WORLD PASTA COMPANY; *pg.* 885, *pg.* 1537
SAN HEALTH - Health Diagnostics Capture - BROCADE COMMUNICATIONS SYSTEMS, INC.; *pg.* 365, *pg.* 239
SAN-J - Soy Sauce - SAN-J INTERNATIONAL, INC.; *pg.* 893, *pg.* 1803
SAN JUAN - Ceiling Fan - WESTINGHOUSE LIGHTING CORPORATION; *pg.* 687, *pg.* 1571
SAN LORENZ - Fan - CRAFTMADE INTERNATIONAL, INC.; *pg.* 1295, *pg.* 1670
SAN LUIS - Beverages - THE COCA-COLA COMPANY; *pg.* 240, *pg.* 493
SAN MANAGER - Software - EMC CORPORATION; *pg.* 391, *pg.* 825
SAN MARINO - Bike - MARIN BIKES; *pg.* 1708, *pg.* 168
SAN MATEO - Footwear - PHOENIX FOOTWEAR GROUP, INC.; *pg.* 1815, *pg.* 60
SAN MIGUEL - Fan - CRAFTMADE INTERNATIONAL, INC.; *pg.* 1295, *pg.* 1670
SAN MORITZ - Lighting Product - WESTINGHOUSE LIGHTING CORPORATION; *pg.* 687, *pg.* 1571
SAN PABLO - Food Product - SHAMROCK FOODS COMPANY; *pg.* 895, *pg.* 20
SAN RAFAEL - Bike - MARIN BIKES; *pg.* 1708, *pg.* 168
SAN RAPHAEL - Bath Product - KOHLER CO.; *pg.* 91, *pg.* 1862
SAN REMO - Dinnerware - THE HOMER LAUGHLIN CHINA COMPANY; *pg.* 1125, *pg.* 1850
SAN ROCCO - Italian Wine - LAIRD & COMPANY, INC.; *pg.* 1966, *pg.* 1119
SAN SEBASTIAN - Lighting Product - WESTINGHOUSE LIGHTING CORPORATION; *pg.* 687, *pg.* 1571
SAN-SIL - Synthetic Precipitated Silica for Papermaking Applications - PPG INDUSTRIES, INC.; *pg.* 1445, *pg.* 1579
SAN TROPEZ - Bath Product - KOHLER CO.; *pg.* 91, *pg.* 1862
SAN XING - Video Game - INTERNATIONAL GAME TECHNOLOGY; *pg.* 957, *pg.* 1024
SANA LA RANA - Pharmaceutical Product - PFIZER INC.; *pg.* 1581, *pg.* 1278
SANAMAT - Juice Extractors - CHESHER EQUIPMENT LTD.; *pg.* 1323, *pg.* 1925
SANARRAY - Computer Hardware - AVAGO TECHNOLOGIES; *pg.* 358, *pg.* 238
SANAVIGATOR - Software - BROCADE CORPORATION; *pg.* 365, *pg.* 312
SANCHEZ E-PROFILE - Software - FIDELITY NATIONAL INFORMATION SERVICES; *pg.* 397, *pg.* 1549
SANCHEZ FMS - Software - FIDELITY NATIONAL INFORMATION SERVICES; *pg.* 397, *pg.* 1549
SANCHEZ PROFILE - Software - FIDELITY NATIONAL INFORMATION SERVICES; *pg.* 397, *pg.* 1549
SANCHEZ WEALTHWARE - Software - FIDELITY NATIONAL INFORMATION SERVICES; *pg.* 397, *pg.* 1549
SANCHEZ WEBCLIENT - Software - FIDELITY NATIONAL INFORMATION SERVICES; *pg.* 397, *pg.* 1549
SANCHEZ WEBCSR - Software - FIDELITY NATIONAL INFORMATION SERVICES; *pg.* 397, *pg.* 1549
SANCHEZ XPRESS - Software - FIDELITY NATIONAL INFORMATION SERVICES; *pg.* 397, *pg.* 1549
SANCTUARY - Wines - BROWN-FORMAN CORPORATION; *pg.* 1958, *pg.* 732
SAND - Computer Program - SAND TECHNOLOGY, INC.; *pg.* 465, *pg.* 1961
SAND ANALYTIC SERVER - Software - SAND TECHNOLOGY, INC.; *pg.* 465, *pg.* 1961
SAND & SABLE - Cologne - COTY, INC.; *pg.* 506, *pg.* 1219
SAND/DNA - Software - SAND TECHNOLOGY, INC.; *pg.* 465, *pg.* 1961
SAND/DNA ACCESS - Software - SAND TECHNOLOGY, INC.; *pg.* 465, *pg.* 1961
SAND/DNA ACRM - Software - SAND TECHNOLOGY, INC.; *pg.* 465, *pg.* 1961
SAND/DNA ADVISE - Software - SAND TECHNOLOGY, INC.; *pg.* 465, *pg.* 1961
SAND/DNA ANALYTICS - Software - SAND TECHNOLOGY, INC.; *pg.* 465, *pg.* 1961
SAND DOLLAR - Bathroom Fan - HUNTER FAN COMPANY; *pg.* 57, *pg.* 1631
SAND DUNE - Flatware - ONEIDA LTD; *pg.* 1129, *pg.* 1318
SAND EXTENSIBLE WAREHOUSE - Analytic Application - SAND TECHNOLOGY, INC.; *pg.* 465, *pg.* 1961
SAND SEARCHABLE ARCHIVE - Software - SAND TECHNOLOGY, INC.; *pg.* 465, *pg.* 1961
SANDBAGER - Apparel - OAKLEY, INC.; *pg.* 1840, *pg.* 86
SANDBAR - Eyewear - MAUI JIM, INC.; *pg.* 9, *pg.* 651
SANDBLASTER - Abrasive - 3M COMPANY; *pg.* 1142, *pg.* 956
SANDBLASTER - Masking Product - KELLY-MOORE PAINT COMPANY, INC.; *pg.* 1443, *pg.* 198
SANDBOX - Fabric - NEMSCHOFF, INC.; *pg.* 936, *pg.* 1890
SANDFLEX - Hand Tools - SNAP-ON INCORPORATED; *pg.* 1062, *pg.* 1862
SANDI - Footwear - COBIAN CORP.; *pg.* 1806, *pg.* 253

First page reference indicates Business Class Edition
Second page reference indicates Geographic Edition

SANDIES - Cookies - KELLOGG COMPANY; *pg.* 831, *pg.* 870
SANDISK CRUZER - Flash Drive - SANDISK CORPORATION; *pg.* 465, *pg.* 147
SANDISK EXTREME - Memory Card - SANDISK CORPORATION; *pg.* 465, *pg.* 147
SANDISK FLASHBACK - Memory Card - SANDISK CORPORATION; *pg.* 465, *pg.* 147
SANDISK GRUVI - Music Card - SANDISK CORPORATION; *pg.* 465, *pg.* 147
SANDISK IMAGEMATE - Reader And Writer - SANDISK CORPORATION; *pg.* 465, *pg.* 147
SANDISK MOBILE ULTRA - Memory Card - SANDISK CORPORATION; *pg.* 465, *pg.* 147
SANDISK MOBILEMATE - Reader - SANDISK CORPORATION; *pg.* 465, *pg.* 147
SANDISK PSSD - Solid State Drive - SANDISK CORPORATION; *pg.* 465, *pg.* 147
SANDISK SANSA - MP3 Player - SANDISK CORPORATION; *pg.* 465, *pg.* 147
SANDISK SD - Memory Card - SANDISK CORPORATION; *pg.* 465, *pg.* 147
SANDISK ULTRA - Memory Card - SANDISK CORPORATION; *pg.* 465, *pg.* 147
SANDISK USSD - Solid State Drive - SANDISK CORPORATION; *pg.* 465, *pg.* 147
SANDISK VIDEO HD - Memory Card - SANDISK CORPORATION; *pg.* 465, *pg.* 147
SANDMAN - Character - DC COMICS, INC.; *pg.* 1633, *pg.* 1221
SANDMINER - Diesel Cutterhead Dredge - ELLICOTT DREDGES, LLC; *pg.* 1333, *pg.* 757
SANDPIPER - Pumps - IDEX CORPORATION; *pg.* 1347, *pg.* 623
SANDPIPER - Resort - TRADEWINDS ISLANDS RESORTS ON SAINT PETE BEACH; *pg.* 1116, *pg.* 461
SANDRA - Clothing - ABERCROMBIE & FITCH CO.; *pg.* 37, *pg.* 1466
SANDRA - Furniture - AMERICAN LEATHER LP; *pg.* 912, *pg.* 1673
SANDRIFT - Ceiling Panel - USG CORPORATION; *pg.* 118, *pg.* 594
SANDSCAPES - Faux Finishing Product - THE SHERWIN-WILLIAMS COMPANY; *pg.* 1447, *pg.* 1435
SANDSLINGER - Foundry Mold Ramming Machine - PETTIBONE, LLC; *pg.* 1368, *pg.* 609
SANDSTONE - Furniture - ASHLEY FURNITURE INDUSTRIES, INC.; *pg.* 914, *pg.* 1852
SANDSTONE - Bedding - CROSCILL, INC.; *pg.* 1122, *pg.* 1220
SANDSTONE PLAID - Pillow and Throw - HERITAGE LACE INC.; *pg.* 694, *pg.* 711
SANDSTORM - Medical Equipment - INVACARE CORPORATION; *pg.* 1546, *pg.* 1451
SANDWICH - Valve - T.D. WILLIAMSON, INC.; *pg.* 1380, *pg.* 1490
SANDWICH BUILDERS - Chicken - PERDUE FARMS INCORPORATED; *pg.* 889, *pg.* 777
SANDWICH SENSATIONS - Flavored Mayonnaise, Spreads, Pickles & Peppers - CAINS FOODS, L.P.; *pg.* 843, *pg.* 784
SANDY - Footwear - P.W. MINOR & SON, INC.; *pg.* 1816, *pg.* 1140
SANDY BEACH - Eyewear - MAUI JIM, INC.; *pg.* 9, *pg.* 651
SANDY SOIL - Turfgrass Seed Mixture - CROSMAN SEED CORPORATION; *pg.* 1794, *pg.* 1156
SANFORD - Markers & Writing Instruments - NEWELL RUBBERMAID INC.; *pg.* 1128, *pg.* 515
SANFORD - Footwear - VANS, INC.; *pg.* 1821, *pg.* 76
SANFRANN - Footwear - STEVEN MADDEN, LTD.; *pg.* 1819, *pg.* 1176
SANGAMO - Capacitor Control - HD ELECTRIC COMPANY; *pg.* 1299, *pg.* 666
SANGER - Furniture - ASHLEY FURNITURE INDUSTRIES, INC.; *pg.* 914, *pg.* 1852
SANGIOWESE - Wine - KENDALL-JACKSON WINE ESTATES, LTD.; *pg.* 1965, *pg.* 277
SANGO - Flash Memory Card - SANDISK CORPORATION; *pg.* 465, *pg.* 147
SANGO CORAL CALCIUM - Nutritional Product - RBC LIFE SCIENCES, INC.; *pg.* 1588, *pg.* 1723
SANI - Cleaners - THE CLOROX COMPANY; *pg.* 327, *pg.* 169
SANI-CLEAN - Chemical Product - BIRKO CORPORATION; *pg.* 1149, *pg.* 332
SANI-CLOTH - Wipe - CROSSTEX INTERNATIONAL INC.; *pg.* 1520, *pg.* 1164
SANI-CLOTH - Hard Surface Disinfectant Wipes - NICE-PAK PRODUCTS, INC.; *pg.* 1465, *pg.* 1319
SANI-DEX - Wipe - CROSSTEX INTERNATIONAL INC.; *pg.* 1520, *pg.* 1164
SANI-DEX - Hand Disinfectant Wipe - NICE-PAK PRODUCTS, INC.; *pg.* 1465, *pg.* 1319
SANI-DEX PLUS - Wipe - CROSSTEX INTERNATIONAL INC.; *pg.* 1520, *pg.* 1164
SANI-FLAKES - Pet Litter Deodorant Granules - SURCO PRODUCTS, INC.; *pg.* 336, *pg.* 1581
SANI-FLAT AND DESIGN - Paint And Stain Product - BENJAMIN MOORE & CO.; *pg.* 1440, *pg.* 1085
SANI-FOAM - Antibacterial Foam Soap - DELTA FOREMOST CHEMICAL CORPORATION; *pg.* 1155, *pg.* 1642
SANI-FOG - Disinfectant - DELTA FOREMOST CHEMICAL CORPORATION; *pg.* 1155, *pg.* 1642
SANI GUARD - Cleaner - SWISHER HYGIENE INC.; *pg.* 336, *pg.* 1507
SANI-HANDS - Hand Disinfectant Wipe - NICE-PAK PRODUCTS, INC.; *pg.* 1465, *pg.* 1319
SANI-KING - Conveyor Belting - HBD INDUSTRIES, INC.; *pg.* 207, *pg.* 1449
SANI-MATIC - Trash Room Odor Control System - SURCO PRODUCTS, INC.; *pg.* 336, *pg.* 1581
SANI-PADS - Pharmaceutical Product - G&W LABORATORIES INC.; *pg.* 1532, *pg.* 1123
SANI-PANT - Waterproof Diapers - THE SALK COMPANY; *pg.* 1591, *pg.* 800
SANI-PURE - Conveyor Belting - HBD INDUSTRIES, INC.; *pg.* 207, *pg.* 1449
SANI-ROLL - Packaging Accessory - CROSSTEX INTERNATIONAL INC.; *pg.* 1520, *pg.* 1164
SANI-SAFE - White Handled Cutlery - DEXTER-RUSSELL INC.; *pg.* 1123, *pg.* 844
SANI-SATIONS - Professional Quality Knives With Colorful Patterned Handles - DEXTER-RUSSELL INC.; *pg.* 1123, *pg.* 844
SANI-SCENT - Air Freshener - SURCO PRODUCTS, INC.; *pg.* 336, *pg.* 1581
SANI SUPP - Pharmaceutical Product - G&W LABORATORIES INC.; *pg.* 1532, *pg.* 1123
SANI-TAB - Towel - CROSSTEX INTERNATIONAL INC.; *pg.* 1520, *pg.* 1164
SANI-TIP - Dental Product - DENTSPLY INTERNATIONAL INC.; *pg.* 1522, *pg.* 1596
SANI-TUBE - Packaging Accessory - CROSSTEX INTERNATIONAL INC.; *pg.* 1520, *pg.* 1164
SANI-TUFF - Plastic & Rubber - TEKNOR APEX COMPANY; *pg.* 1889, *pg.* 1605
SANI-WHITE - Hose - HBD INDUSTRIES, INC.; *pg.* 207, *pg.* 1449
SANIBEL - Furniture - ASHLEY FURNITURE INDUSTRIES, INC.; *pg.* 914, *pg.* 1852
SANIBEL - Footwear - EASTLAND SHOE CORPORATION; *pg.* 1808, *pg.* 750
SANIBEL - Ceiling Fan - HUNTER FAN COMPANY; *pg.* 57, *pg.* 1631
SANIBROM - Chemical Product - ALBEMARLE CORPORATION; *pg.* 1146, *pg.* 741
SANICARE - Hand Care Product - CROSSTEX INTERNATIONAL INC.; *pg.* 1520, *pg.* 1164
SANICLEAN STRAINERS - Sanitary Strainer - NEWARK WIRE CLOTH CO.; *pg.* 99, *pg.* 1052
SANICLENZ - Hand Care Product - CROSSTEX INTERNATIONAL INC.; *pg.* 1520, *pg.* 1164
SANIGUARD - Bathroom Safety Product - ALIMED, INC.; *pg.* 1490, *pg.* 816
SANIJURA - Cabinetry - KOHLER CO.; *pg.* 91, *pg.* 1862
SANIPAD - Disposable Pad - THE SALK COMPANY; *pg.* 1591, *pg.* 800
SANISAC - Napkin Disposal Wall Unit - HILLYARD, INC.; *pg.* 331, *pg.* 990
SANISAC - Personal Care Product - ROCHESTER MIDLAND CORPORATION; *pg.* 334, *pg.* 1337
SANISEPT - Hand Care Product - CROSSTEX INTERNATIONAL INC.; *pg.* 1520, *pg.* 1164
SANISORB - Medical Liquid Absorber - MULTISORB TECHNOLOGIES, INC.; *pg.* 1570, *pg.* 1150
SANISORB X - Medical Liquid Solidifier - MULTISORB TECHNOLOGIES, INC.; *pg.* 1570, *pg.* 1150
SANISTAT - Medical & Aesthetic Product - DYNATRONICS CORPORATION; *pg.* 1526, *pg.* 1757
SANITAIR - Air Cleaner - U.S. BOTTLERS MACHINERY COMPANY; *pg.* 1386, *pg.* 1369
SANITAIRE - Fluid Technology - ITT CORPORATION; *pg.* 1351, *pg.* 1354
SANITARY RAM - Sampling Valve - STRAHMAN VALVES, INC.; *pg.* 1379, *pg.* 1517
SANITARY SHRINK - Wrapper - CAMPBELL WRAPPER CORPORATION; *pg.* 1454, *pg.* 1856
SANITEX PLUS - Spray - CROSSTEX INTERNATIONAL INC.; *pg.* 1520, *pg.* 1164
SANITITE - Pipe - ADVANCED DRAINAGE SYSTEMS, INC.; *pg.* 1878, *pg.* 1455
SANITIZING MACHINE - Cleaning Product - VON SCHRADER COMPANY; *pg.* 62, *pg.* 1890
SANITYZE - Hand Care Product - CROSSTEX INTERNATIONAL INC.; *pg.* 1520, *pg.* 1164
SANMAN - Storage System - DOT HILL SYSTEMS CORP.; *pg.* 388, *pg.* 333
SANMAPPING - Computer Hardware - AVAGO TECHNOLOGIES; *pg.* 358, *pg.* 238
SANNET - Storage System - DOT HILL SYSTEMS CORP.; *pg.* 388, *pg.* 333
SANNET II FC - Fibre Channel SAN Solution Controllers - DOT HILL SYSTEMS CORP.; *pg.* 388, *pg.* 333
SANOR - Chemical Product - ROCHESTER MIDLAND CORPORATION; *pg.* 334, *pg.* 1337
SANPATH - Storage Software Systems - DOT HILL SYSTEMS CORP.; *pg.* 388, *pg.* 333
SANPIPER - Flexible SAN Connectivity Solution - OVERLAND STORAGE, INC.; *pg.* 451, *pg.* 205
SANPOINT - Software - SYMANTEC CORPORATION; *pg.* 478, *pg.* 161
SANPOINT CONTROL - Software - SYMANTEC CORPORATION; *pg.* 478, *pg.* 161
SANSA - Mp3 Player - SANDISK CORPORATION; *pg.* 465, *pg.* 147
SANSA CONNECT - Mp3 Player - SANDISK CORPORATION; *pg.* 465, *pg.* 147
SANSA EXPRESS - Music Player - SANDISK CORPORATION; *pg.* 465, *pg.* 147
SANSA FUZE - Mp3 Player - SANDISK CORPORATION; *pg.* 465, *pg.* 147
SANSA SHAKER - Music Player - SANDISK CORPORATION; *pg.* 465, *pg.* 147
SANSCAPE - Storage Systems Software - DOT HILL SYSTEMS CORP.; *pg.* 388, *pg.* 333
SANSCREEN - Software - NETAPP, INC.; *pg.* 444, *pg.* 287
SANSHARE - Computer Software - AVAGO TECHNOLOGIES; *pg.* 358, *pg.* 238
SANSMART - Data Storage System - QUALSTAR CORPORATION; *pg.* 458, *pg.* 279
SANSURF - Personal Care Material - BASF CATALYSTS LLC; *pg.* 1148, *pg.* 1074
SANT' ANDREA - Serveware & Giftware - ONEIDA LTD; *pg.* 1129, *pg.* 1318
SANTA ANITA - Wine - LEONARD KREUSCH, INC.; *pg.* 254, *pg.* 1099
SANTA BARBARA - Furniture - ASHLEY FURNITURE INDUSTRIES, INC.; *pg.* 914, *pg.* 1852
SANTA BOWZ - Bows - E-Z BOWZ, LLC; *pg.* 692, *pg.* 1635
SANTA CLAUS - Pillow and Throw - HERITAGE LACE INC.; *pg.* 694, *pg.* 711
SANTA CLAWS - Pet Portrait Services - PETSMART, INC.; *pg.* 1481, *pg.* 18
SANTA CRUZ ORGANIC - Organic Fruit Juices, Fruit Spreads & Fruit Sauces - THE J.M. SMUCKER COMPANY; *pg.* 865, *pg.* 1468
SANTA DAMIANA - Premium Cigars - ALTADIS USA, INC.; *pg.* 1893, *pg.* 423
SANTA FE - Golf Equipment - ACUSHNET COMPANY; *pg.* 1824, *pg.* 818
SANTA FE - Rug - COURISTAN INC.; *pg.* 921, *pg.* 1067
SANTA FE - Dinnerware - THE HOMER LAUGHLIN CHINA COMPANY; *pg.* 1125, *pg.* 1850
SANTA FE - Footwear - P.W. MINOR & SON, INC.; *pg.* 1816, *pg.* 1140
SANTA FE - Cigars - SWISHER INTERNATIONAL, INC.; *pg.* 1895, *pg.* 345
SANTA FE - Charcoal Grill - W.C. BRADLEY CO.; *pg.* 62, *pg.* 528
SANTA FE - Coat Conditioner - W.F. YOUNG, INC.; *pg.* 1610, *pg.* 817
SANTA FE STATION HOTEL & CASINO - Hotel & Casino - STATION CASINOS, INC.; *pg.* 585, *pg.* 1030
SANTA ISABEL ARGENTINA - Wines and Spirits - LEONARD KREUSCH, INC.; *pg.* 254, *pg.* 1099
SANTA MARIA HARBOUR RESORT - Resort -

SUNSTREAM, INC.; *pg.* 1116, *pg.* 428

SANTA ROSA - Furniture - JASPER GROUP; *pg.* 930, *pg.* 691

SANTA ROSA - Bath Product - KOHLER CO.; *pg.* 91, *pg.* 1862

SANTA SOFIA - Italian Wine - LAIRD & COMPANY, INC.; *pg.* 1966, *pg.* 1119

SANTALIFF - Fragrance Ingredient - INTERNATIONAL FLAVORS & FRAGRANCES INC.; *pg.* 512, *pg.* 1244

SANTANA - Guitar - PAUL REED SMITH GUITARS; *pg.* 574, *pg.* 779

SANTAY - Food Products - MODERN PRODUCTS, INC.; *pg.* 1568, *pg.* 1871

SANTE FE - Furniture - FLEXSTEEL INDUSTRIES, INC.; *pg.* 925, *pg.* 707

SANTE-FE - Corner Bead - USG CORPORATION; *pg.* 118, *pg.* 594

SANTE FE - Lighting Product - WESTINGHOUSE LIGHTING CORPORATION; *pg.* 687, *pg.* 1571

SANTEGRITY - Software - BROCADE CORPORATION; *pg.* 365, *pg.* 312

SANTIAGO - Refried Beans - BASIC AMERICAN FOODS, INC.; *pg.* 839, *pg.* 303

SANTICIZER - Polymer Additives - FERRO CORPORATION; *pg.* 1162, *pg.* 1462

SANTITAS - Tortilla Chips - FRITO-LAY NORTH AMERICA, INC.; *pg.* 1853, *pg.* 1730

SANTOQUIN - Health & Nutrition Product - NOVUS INTERNATIONAL, INC.; *pg.* 706, *pg.* 1001

SANTORI - Furniture - ASHLEY FURNITURE INDUSTRIES, INC.; *pg.* 914, *pg.* 1852

SANTORINI - Rug - COURISTAN INC.; *pg.* 921, *pg.* 1067

SANTORNI - Footwear - STEVEN MADDEN, LTD.; *pg.* 1819, *pg.* 1176

SANTOSOL - Solvents - CYTEC INDUSTRIES, INC.; *pg.* 1155, *pg.* 1131

SANTRA GOLI - Confectionery - THE HERSHEY CO.; *pg.* 1855, *pg.* 1538

SANTRICITY - Computer Software - AVAGO TECHNOLOGIES; *pg.* 358, *pg.* 238

SANUK - Shoe/Sandal Hybrid, Vulcanized Footwear & Casual Canvas - DECKERS OUTDOOR CORPORATION; *pg.* 1807, *pg.* 100

SANVERGENCE - Software - BROCADE CORPORATION; *pg.* 365, *pg.* 312

SAO - Shoes - WEYCO GROUP, INC.; *pg.* 1822, *pg.* 1858

SAPACITABINE - Nucleoside Analog Prodrug - CYCLACEL PHARMACEUTICALS, INC.; *pg.* 1521, *pg.* 1044

SAPAMINE - Softeners - HUNTSMAN CORPORATION; *pg.* 1167, *pg.* 1758

SAPHARA - Organic Tea - CELESTIAL SEASONINGS, INC.; *pg.* 846, *pg.* 310

SAPHION - Lithium Ion Battery - VALENCE TECHNOLOGY, INC.; *pg.* 684, *pg.* 1667

SAPHLITE - Biotechnology Product - GENZYME CORPORATION; *pg.* 1534, *pg.* 808

SAPPER - Ergonomic Seating - KNOLL, INC.; *pg.* 425, *pg.* 1527

SAPPHIRE - Bridal Wear - ALFRED ANGELO, INC.; *pg.* 17, *pg.* 1532

SAPPHIRE - Clean-Agent Fire Extinguishers - ANSUL, INCORPORATED; *pg.* 1147, *pg.* 1869

SAPPHIRE - Laser & Laser System - COHERENT, INC.; *pg.* 1406, *pg.* 265

SAPPHIRE - Rug - COURISTAN INC.; *pg.* 921, *pg.* 1067

SAPPHIRE - Light - DEN-MAT CORPORATION; *pg.* 1522, *pg.* 271

SAPPHIRE - Roller & Conveyor Chain - DIAMOND CHAIN COMPANY; *pg.* 1328, *pg.* 684

SAPPHIRE - Flat Panel Display - EPSILON SYSTEMS SOLUTIONS; *pg.* 1412, *pg.* 202

SAPPHIRE - Fabric - NEMSCHOFF, INC.; *pg.* 936, *pg.* 1890

SAPPHIRE - Hardware - VERIFONE SYSTEMS, INC.; *pg.* 487, *pg.* 251

SAPPHIRE 7S - Lottery Game - OHIO LOTTERY COMMISSION; *pg.* 1002, *pg.* 1433

SAPPHIRE BLUE 5'S - Lottery Game - MINNESOTA STATE LOTTERY; *pg.* 999, *pg.* 956

SAPPHIRE BLUE 7S - Game - MISSOURI LOTTERY; *pg.* 999, *pg.* 979

SAPPHIRITE - Sharpening Wheels - NATIONAL PRESTO INDUSTRIES, INC; *pg.* 1128, *pg.* 1857

SAPPORO - Restaurants - TAVISTOCK RESTAURANT GROUP; *pg.* 1753, *pg.* 803

SARA - Dinnerware - THE HOMER LAUGHLIN CHINA COMPANY; *pg.* 1125, *pg.* 1850

SARA CLIP - Window Treatment - CROSCILL, INC.; *pg.* 1122, *pg.* 1220

SARA LEE - Deli Meats & Cheeses - TYSON FOODS, INC.; *pg.* 902, *pg.* 35

SARA LEE DESSERTS - Bakery Products - TYSON FOODS, INC.; *pg.* 902, *pg.* 35

SARA MORGAN - Dresses & Sets - HABAND COMPANY, INC.; *pg.* 1772, *pg.* 1099

SARA ST. JAMES - Beauty Product - COSMETIQUE, INC.; *pg.* 1765, *pg.* 664

SARAGASSO - Fabric - NEMSCHOFF, INC.; *pg.* 936, *pg.* 1890

SARAH - Furniture - HOOKER FURNITURE CORPORATION; *pg.* 928, *pg.* 1788

SARAH PLAID - Pillow and Throw - HERITAGE LACE INC.; *pg.* 694, *pg.* 711

SARAN - Resins and Films - THE DOW CHEMICAL COMPANY; *pg.* 1157, *pg.* 898

SARAN WRAP - Food Storage Wrap - S.C. JOHNSON & SON, INC.; *pg.* 334, *pg.* 1889

SARANAC - Furniture - F.E. HALE MANUFACTURING COMPANY; *pg.* 925, *pg.* 1160

SARANAC - Paper & Nonwoven Material - FIBERMARK INC.; *pg.* 1457, *pg.* 1764

SARANAC - Fabric - NEMSCHOFF, INC.; *pg.* 936, *pg.* 1890

SARANEX - Resin - THE DOW CHEMICAL COMPANY; *pg.* 1157, *pg.* 898

SARANO - Suitcase - SAMSONITE CORPORATION; *pg.* 11, *pg.* 830

SARASA - Laundry Product - THE PROCTER & GAMBLE COMPANY; *pg.* 1129, *pg.* 1418

SARASOTA - Furniture - LA-Z-BOY INCORPORATED; *pg.* 932, *pg.* 901

SARASOTA MAGAZINE - Magazine - OPEN SKY MEDIA; *pg.* 1673, *pg.* 451

SARASOTA/MANATEE BUSINESS - Magazine - OPEN SKY MEDIA; *pg.* 1673, *pg.* 451

SARATOGA - Medical & Aesthetic Product - DYNATRONICS CORPORATION; *pg.* 1526, *pg.* 1757

SARATOGA - Furniture - F.E. HALE MANUFACTURING COMPANY; *pg.* 925, *pg.* 1160

SARATOGA - Cigarettes - PHILIP MORRIS USA INC.; *pg.* 1894, *pg.* 1803

SARATOGA - Aircraft - PIPER AIRCRAFT, INC.; *pg.* 233, *pg.* 477

SARATOGA EXECUTIVE - Furniture - BUSH INDUSTRIES INC.; *pg.* 919, *pg.* 1170

SARATOGA REVERSIBLE - Hat - WOODEN SHIPS OF HOBOKEN; *pg.* 35, *pg.* 1315

SARDINIA - Rug - COURISTAN INC.; *pg.* 921, *pg.* 1067

SARDINIA - Dinnerware - THE HOMER LAUGHLIN CHINA COMPANY; *pg.* 1125, *pg.* 1850

SARDIS - Carpet - WOVEN LEGENDS INC.; *pg.* 947, *pg.* 1572

SAREE - Kitchen Product - KOHLER CO.; *pg.* 91, *pg.* 1862

SARGENT - Door Locks, Door Closers & Architectural Hardware - SARGENT MANUFACTURING COMPANY; *pg.* 1061, *pg.* 359

SARGENT AND GREENLEAF - Security System - STANLEY BLACK & DECKER, INC.; *pg.* 1063, *pg.* 358

SARGENTO - Food Product - PARMALAT CANADA INC.; *pg.* 888, *pg.* 1941

SARIS - Resistivity Technology - SCINTREX LTD.; *pg.* 1374, *pg.* 1920

SARKES TARZIAN - Radio & TV Broadcasting - SARKES TARZIAN INC.; *pg.* 307, *pg.* 674

SARM-X - Nutritional Supplement - MAXIMUM HUMAN PERFORMANCE, INC.; *pg.* 1559, *pg.* 1065

SAROUK - Rug - ETHAN ALLEN INTERIORS INC.; *pg.* 924, *pg.* 343

SARSI - Soft Drink - THE COCA-COLA COMPANY; *pg.* 240, *pg.* 493

SARTORI - Wine - BANFI VINTNERS; *pg.* 1957, *pg.* 1161

SARYUSAISAI - Beverages - THE COCA-COLA COMPANY; *pg.* 240, *pg.* 493

SAS - E-Intelligence Software & Services - SAS INSTITUTE INC.; *pg.* 466, *pg.* 1361

SAS/AF - Software - SAS INSTITUTE INC.; *pg.* 466, *pg.* 1361

SAS/ASSIST - Software - SAS INSTITUTE INC.; *pg.* 466, *pg.* 1361

SAS/CPE - Software - SAS INSTITUTE INC.; *pg.* 466, *pg.* 1361

SAS/DMI - Software - SAS INSTITUTE INC.; *pg.* 466, *pg.* 1361

SAS/ETS - Software - SAS INSTITUTE INC.; *pg.* 466, *pg.* 1361

SAS/GRAPH - Software - SAS INSTITUTE INC.; *pg.* 466, *pg.* 1361

SAS/IMS - Software - SAS INSTITUTE INC.; *pg.* 466, *pg.* 1361

SAS INFUSION - Analyzer - TELEDYNE LECROY; *pg.* 1431, *pg.* 1153

SAS INSCHOOL - Software - SAS INSTITUTE INC.; *pg.* 466, *pg.* 1361

SAS INSTITUTE - Software - SAS INSTITUTE INC.; *pg.* 466, *pg.* 1361

SAS ONLINE TUTOR - Online Classes - SAS INSTITUTE INC.; *pg.* 466, *pg.* 1361

SAS/QC - Software - SAS INSTITUTE INC.; *pg.* 466, *pg.* 1361

SAS/RTERM - Software - SAS INSTITUTE INC.; *pg.* 466, *pg.* 1361

SAS/SHARE - Software - SAS INSTITUTE INC.; *pg.* 466, *pg.* 1361

SAS/SPECTRAVIEW - Software - SAS INSTITUTE INC.; *pg.* 466, *pg.* 1361

SAS/STAT - Software - SAS INSTITUTE INC.; *pg.* 466, *pg.* 1361

SASALITO - Footwear - STEVEN MADDEN, LTD.; *pg.* 1819, *pg.* 1176

SASH LOCK - Window & Door Hardware - DECO PRODUCTS CO.; *pg.* 1045, *pg.* 704

SASHA - Clothing - ABERCROMBIE & FITCH CO.; *pg.* 37, *pg.* 1466

SASI - Software - EDUPOINT EDUCATIONAL SYSTEMS, LLC; *pg.* 390, *pg.* 109

SASIXP - Software - EDUPOINT EDUCATIONAL SYSTEMS, LLC; *pg.* 390, *pg.* 109

SASSAFRAZ - Vital Conditioner - LUSTER PRODUCTS INC.; *pg.* 515, *pg.* 581

SASSY - Child Product - SASSY, INC.; *pg.* 966, *pg.* 895

SASTRACER - Analyzer - TELEDYNE LECROY; *pg.* 1431, *pg.* 1153

SASWARE BALLOT - Software - SAS INSTITUTE INC.; *pg.* 466, *pg.* 1361

SAT - Scholastic Assessment Test - EDUCATIONAL TESTING SERVICE INC.; *pg.* 1394, *pg.* 1111

SAT-N-SHEEN - Wall & Trim Finish - KELLY-MOORE PAINT COMPANY, INC.; *pg.* 1443, *pg.* 198

SATA - Hand Tool - DANAHER CORPORATION; *pg.* 1044, *pg.* 397

SATCENTER - Systems Integration & Aeronautics - LOCKHEED MARTIN CORPORATION; *pg.* 229, *pg.* 762

SATCOM - Power Amplifier - KRATOS LANCASTER; *pg.* 1419, *pg.* 1546

SATCOM - Communication Product - ROCKWELL COLLINS, INC.; *pg.* 234, *pg.* 702

SATEC - Static Hydraulic Equipment - INSTRON CORPORATION; *pg.* 1349, *pg.* 839

SATELLITE - Watering System - CTB INTERNATIONAL CORP.; *pg.* 850, *pg.* 695

SATELLITE - Software - FINISAR CORPORATION; *pg.* 639, *pg.* 285

SATELLITE - Bicycles - G. JOANNOU CYCLE CO. INC.; *pg.* 1707, *pg.* 1098

SATELLITE CONTROL SYSTEM 21 - Satellite Command & Control Computer Software - LOCKHEED MARTIN CORPORATION; *pg.* 229, *pg.* 762

SATELLITE SERIES - Telephones - MOTOROLA SOLUTIONS, INC.; *pg.* 657, *pg.* 659

SATHERS - Candy - FERRARA CANDY CO.; *pg.* 1852, *pg.* 612

SATIETROL - Weight Loss Product - PACIFICHEALTH LABORATORIES, INC.; *pg.* 1579, *pg.* 1083

SATIETROL COMPLETE - Supplement - PACIFICHEALTH LABORATORIES, INC.; *pg.* 1579, *pg.* 1083

SATIN - Tape - 3M COMPANY; *pg.* 1142, *pg.* 956

SATIN - Printing Paper - MOHAWK FINE PAPERS, INC.; *pg.* 1464, *pg.* 1153

SATIN ACCENT - Flatware - ONEIDA LTD; *pg.* 1129, *pg.* 1318

SATIN CAMBER - Flatware - ONEIDA LTD; *pg.* 1129, *pg.* 1318

SATIN CANTATA - Flatware - ONEIDA LTD; *pg.* 1129, *pg.* 1318

SATIN CARE - Shave Gel - THE GILLETTE COMPANY; *pg.* 509, *pg.* 795

SATIN DONUT FRY - Frying Shortening - MALLET &

COMPANY, INC.; *pg.* 875, *pg.* 1521
SATIN DOVER - Flatware - ONEIDA LTD; *pg.* 1129, *pg.* 1318
SATIN DRIFTWOOD - Flatware - ONEIDA LTD; *pg.* 1129, *pg.* 1318
SATIN ETAGE - Flatware - ONEIDA LTD; *pg.* 1129, *pg.* 1318
SATIN FLOW - Enamel - THE MURALO COMPANY; *pg.* 1444, *pg.* 1042
SATIN FRY - Shortening - MALLET & COMPANY, INC.; *pg.* 875, *pg.* 1521
SATIN GLO - Shortening - MALLET & COMPANY, INC.; *pg.* 875, *pg.* 1521
SATIN IMPERVEX - Paint And Stain Product - BENJAMIN MOORE & CO.; *pg.* 1440, *pg.* 1085
SATIN IMPERVO - Paint And Stain Product - BENJAMIN MOORE & CO.; *pg.* 1440, *pg.* 1085
SATIN-L - Adhesive Coated Paper - SPINNAKER COATING, LLC; *pg.* 1470, *pg.* 1477
SATIN LINEA - Flatware - ONEIDA LTD; *pg.* 1129, *pg.* 1318
SATIN MOTIQUE - Adhesive Coated Paper - SPINNAKER COATING, LLC; *pg.* 1470, *pg.* 1477
SATIN PEAR - Personal Care Product - COLGATE-PALMOLIVE COMPANY; *pg.* 504, *pg.* 1215
SATIN PLUS - Emulsified Shortening - MALLET & COMPANY, INC.; *pg.* 875, *pg.* 1521
SATIN PRIME - Paint Primers & Sealers - PPG INDUSTRIES, INC.; *pg.* 1445, *pg.* 1579
SATIN ROSSINI - Flatware - ONEIDA LTD; *pg.* 1129, *pg.* 1318
SATIN SAXON - Flatware - ONEIDA LTD; *pg.* 1129, *pg.* 1318
SATIN SCOOP - Flatware - ONEIDA LTD; *pg.* 1129, *pg.* 1318
SATIN-SLIP - Medical Device - MALLINCKRODT PHARMACEUTICALS; *pg.* 1557, *pg.* 978
SATIN-SLIP - Intubating Stylet - MEDTRONIC; *pg.* 1563, *pg.* 183
SATIN SUZANA - Footwear - CAPEZIO BALLET MAKERS INC.; *pg.* 1805, *pg.* 1125
SATIN SWEET - Maltose Corn Syrup - CARGILL, INC.; *pg.* 845, *pg.* 965
SATIN TAHITA - Flatware - ONEIDA LTD; *pg.* 1129, *pg.* 1318
SATIN TRIBECA - Flatware - ONEIDA LTD; *pg.* 1129, *pg.* 1318
SATIN WOODCREST - Flatware - ONEIDA LTD; *pg.* 1129, *pg.* 1318
SATIN-X - Paint - JONES-BLAIR COMPANY; *pg.* 1443, *pg.* 1682
SATINAL - Polishing Agent for C-39 Hard Resin Lens - FERRO CORPORATION; *pg.* 1162, *pg.* 1462
SATINAMEL - Paint & Coating - DIAMOND VOGEL PAINT, INC.; *pg.* 1441, *pg.* 710
SATINFLOSS - Dental Floss - GILLETTE; *pg.* 1536, *pg.* 795
SATINGLO 30 - Kaolin Coating Pigment - BASF CATALYSTS LLC; *pg.* 1148, *pg.* 1074
SATINHIDE - Paint, Primers, Lacquers, Enamels & Varnishes - PPG INDUSTRIES, INC.; *pg.* 1445, *pg.* 1579
SATINIQUE - Plating Process - A BRITE COMPANY; *pg.* 1144, *pg.* 1697
SATINIQUE - Personal Care Products - AMWAY CORPORATION; *pg.* 326, *pg.* 864
SATINIQUE - Flatware - ONEIDA LTD; *pg.* 1129, *pg.* 1318
SATINTONE - Pigment - BASF CATALYSTS LLC; *pg.* 1148, *pg.* 1074
SATIS 2800 - Laser Displacement Sensor - VEECO INSTRUMENTS INC.; *pg.* 1434, *pg.* 1322
SATISFIT - Weight Care Technologies - THE DOW CHEMICAL COMPANY; *pg.* 1157, *pg.* 898
SATISFRIES - Reduced Calorie French Fries - BURGER KING CORPORATION; *pg.* 1719, *pg.* 440
SATLOC - Wireless Product - HEMISPHERE GPS INC.; *pg.* 642, *pg.* 1903
SATLOC M3 - Wireless Product - HEMISPHERE GPS INC.; *pg.* 642, *pg.* 1903
SATORI - Carpet - INTERFACE, INC.; *pg.* 695, *pg.* 512
SATRINE - Veterinary Preparation - PFIZER INC.; *pg.* 1581, *pg.* 1278
SATS - Systems Integration & Aeronautics - LOCKHEED MARTIN CORPORATION; *pg.* 229, *pg.* 762
SATURDAY MATINEE - Retail Video Stores - TRANS WORLD ENTERTAINMENT CORPORATION; *pg.* 313, *pg.* 1137
SATURDAY'S - Hair Service Center - REGIS CORPORATION; *pg.* 521, *pg.* 941
SATURN - Master Control System - GRASS VALLEY, INC.; *pg.* 641, *pg.* 164
SATURN - Polyester Outdoor Sign Material - HOLLISTON LLC; *pg.* 1460, *pg.* 1630
SATURN - Bathroom Fan - HUNTER FAN COMPANY; *pg.* 57, *pg.* 1631
SATURN - Seating Product - IRWIN SEATING COMPANY INC.; *pg.* 929, *pg.* 887
SATURN - Systems Integration & Aeronautics - LOCKHEED MARTIN CORPORATION; *pg.* 229, *pg.* 762
SATURN - Fabric - NEMSCHOFF, INC.; *pg.* 936, *pg.* 1890
SATURN - Filter Jackets - NORDSON CORPORATION; *pg.* 1365, *pg.* 1480
SATURN - Illuminated Magnifier - PROPHOTONIX LIMITED; *pg.* 1427, *pg.* 1039
SATURN - Turbine Products - SOLAR TURBINES INCORPORATED; *pg.* 1377, *pg.* 209
SATURN - Software - SYNOPSYS, INC.; *pg.* 480, *pg.* 162
SATURN WAFER STEPPER - Semiconductor Device - ULTRATECH, INC.; *pg.* 1433, *pg.* 251
SATURNA - Sport Knife - MCNETT CORPORATION; *pg.* 1839, *pg.* 1817
SAU-SEA - Seafood Products - SAU-SEA FOODS, INC.; *pg.* 894, *pg.* 1349
SAUCE - Lighting System - PHILIPS SOLID-STATE LIGHTING SOLUTIONS; *pg.* 1303, *pg.* 806
SAUCONY - Footwear - WOLVERINE WORLD WIDE, INC.; *pg.* 1822, *pg.* 905
SAUCY - Fabric - NEMSCHOFF, INC.; *pg.* 936, *pg.* 1890
SAUCY CHICKEN - Sauce - GOLD PURE FOOD PRODUCTS CO., INC.; *pg.* 858, *pg.* 1166
SAUCY RIB - Sauce - GOLD PURE FOOD PRODUCTS CO., INC.; *pg.* 858, *pg.* 1166
SAUCY SUSAN - Bottled Food Product - ALLIED OLD ENGLISH, INC.; *pg.* 836, *pg.* 1110
SAULSBURY - Fire & Rescue Vehicles - FEDERAL SIGNAL CORPORATION; *pg.* 638, *pg.* 645
SAUNDERS - Filter & Lens - THE TIFFEN COMPANY LLC; *pg.* 1432, *pg.* 1165
SAUS-A-RAGE - Food Product - ADVANCEPIERRE FOODS, INC.; *pg.* 1714, *pg.* 1409
SAUSAGE MCMUFFIN - Breakfast Sandwich - MCDONALD'S CORPORATION; *pg.* 1737, *pg.* 645
SAUSAGE N' EGGER - Fast Food - A&W FOOD SERVICES OF CANADA INC.; *pg.* 1714, *pg.* 1908
SAUSAGE PATTIES - Veggie Patties - KELLOGG COMPANY; *pg.* 831, *pg.* 870
SAUSAGE STYLE RECIPE CRUMBLES - Veggie Crumbles - KELLOGG COMPANY; *pg.* 831, *pg.* 870
SAUSALITO - Bike - MARIN BIKES; *pg.* 1708, *pg.* 168
SAUSALITO - Cookies - PEPPERIDGE FARM, INC.; *pg.* 888, *pg.* 363
SAUTEE EXPRESS - Cooking Squares - LAND O'LAKES, INC.; *pg.* 873, *pg.* 915
SAUTEJEAU - Muscadet - DREYFUS ASHBY INC.; *pg.* 1962, *pg.* 1226
SAUVAGE - Pen - A. T. CROSS COMPANY; *pg.* 339, *pg.* 1602
SAUZA - Tequila - JIM BEAM BRANDS CO.; *pg.* 1965, *pg.* 601
SAV-A-CENTER - Food Stores - THE GREAT ATLANTIC & PACIFIC TEA COMPANY, INC.; *pg.* 1021, *pg.* 1086
SAV-OIL - Crop Oil Concentrate - KALO, INC.; *pg.* 1796, *pg.* 719
SAVA - Tire And Rubber Product - THE GOODYEAR TIRE & RUBBER COMPANY; *pg.* 1883, *pg.* 1401
SAVAGE - Gaming Product - GLD PRODUCTS, INC.; *pg.* 1835, *pg.* 1882
SAVAGE - Magazine - PAISANO PUBLICATIONS, LLC; *pg.* 1674, *pg.* 38
SAVANA CARGO - Van - GENERAL MOTORS COMPANY; *pg.* 175, *pg.* 881
SAVANA PASSENGER - Van - GENERAL MOTORS COMPANY; *pg.* 175, *pg.* 881
SAVANAH - Furniture - ASHLEY FURNITURE INDUSTRIES, INC.; *pg.* 914, *pg.* 1852
SAVANE - Apparel - PERRY ELLIS INTERNATIONAL, INC.; *pg.* 45, *pg.* 445
SAVANNA - Sandals - AEROGROUP INTERNATIONAL, INC.; *pg.* 1803, *pg.* 1055
SAVANNA - Video Game - INTERNATIONAL GAME TECHNOLOGY; *pg.* 957, *pg.* 1024
SAVANNAH - Building Product - BLUELINX HOLDINGS, INC.; *pg.* 70, *pg.* 491
SAVANNAH - Brick & Tile Product - CHEROKEE BRICK & TILE COMPANY; *pg.* 75, *pg.* 535
SAVANNAH - Footwear - COBIAN CORP.; *pg.* 1806, *pg.* 253
SAVANNAH - Vanity Lights - CRAFTMADE INTERNATIONAL, INC.; *pg.* 1295, *pg.* 1670
SAVANNAH - Paper & Nonwoven Material - FIBERMARK INC.; *pg.* 1457, *pg.* 1764
SAVANNAH - Fabric - NEMSCHOFF, INC.; *pg.* 936, *pg.* 1890
SAVANNAH COLLECTION - Furniture - BUSH INDUSTRIES INC.; *pg.* 919, *pg.* 1170
SAVANNAH GOLD - Sugar & Sweetener Product - IMPERIAL SUGAR COMPANY; *pg.* 864, *pg.* 1746
SAVANT - Musical Instrument - GIBSON GUITAR CORP.; *pg.* 550, *pg.* 1650
SAVANYO - Kitchen Product - KOHLER CO.; *pg.* 91, *pg.* 1862
SAVE-A-LOT - Grocery Chain - SUPERVALU, INC.; *pg.* 1035, *pg.* 924
SAVE 'N PACK - Promotion - FOOD LION, LLC; *pg.* 1019, *pg.* 1390
SAVE THE EARTH SACRIFICE NOTHING - Slogan - GREEN EARTH TECHNOLOGIES, INC.; *pg.* 704, *pg.* 1352
SAVE THE WAVES - Cruise Ship - ROYAL CARIBBEAN CRUISES LTD; *pg.* 1921, *pg.* 446
SAVE THE WORLD - Game - WMS INDUSTRIES INC.; *pg.* 593, *pg.* 666
SAVE WRAPS FOR STUFF - Promotion - SPANGLER CANDY COMPANY; *pg.* 1862, *pg.* 1407
SAVEONCONFERENCES.COM - Telecom Product - PREMIERE GLOBAL SERVICES, INC.; *pg.* 1275, *pg.* 518
SAVEUR - Magazine - BONNIER CORPORATION; *pg.* 1622, *pg.* 480
SAVI - Lighting System - REVOLUTION LIGHTING TECHNOLOGIES, INC.; *pg.* 1304, *pg.* 377
SAVI - Infant/Pediatric Ventilators - SECHRIST INDUSTRIES, INC.; *pg.* 1593, *pg.* 43
SAVI 512 - Power Supply Components - REVOLUTION LIGHTING TECHNOLOGIES, INC.; *pg.* 1304, *pg.* 377
SAVI COVE RGB - Lighting Systems - REVOLUTION LIGHTING TECHNOLOGIES, INC.; *pg.* 1304, *pg.* 377
SAVI FLARE - Lighting Systems - REVOLUTION LIGHTING TECHNOLOGIES, INC.; *pg.* 1304, *pg.* 377
SAVI FLOOD - Lighting Systems - REVOLUTION LIGHTING TECHNOLOGIES, INC.; *pg.* 1304, *pg.* 377
SAVI FLOOD STRIP - Lighting Systems - REVOLUTION LIGHTING TECHNOLOGIES, INC.; *pg.* 1304, *pg.* 377
SAVI KEY PAD - Power Supply Components - REVOLUTION LIGHTING TECHNOLOGIES, INC.; *pg.* 1304, *pg.* 377
SAVI LINEAR - Lighting Systems - REVOLUTION LIGHTING TECHNOLOGIES, INC.; *pg.* 1304, *pg.* 377
SAVI MELODY - Lighting System - REVOLUTION LIGHTING TECHNOLOGIES, INC.; *pg.* 1304, *pg.* 377
SAVI MINI SCONCE - Lighting Systems - REVOLUTION LIGHTING TECHNOLOGIES, INC.; *pg.* 1304, *pg.* 377
SAVI NOTE - Lighting System - REVOLUTION LIGHTING TECHNOLOGIES, INC.; *pg.* 1304, *pg.* 377
SAVI POOL & SPA - Lighting Systems - REVOLUTION LIGHTING TECHNOLOGIES, INC.; *pg.* 1304, *pg.* 377
SAVI SHO WHITE - Lighting Systems - REVOLUTION LIGHTING TECHNOLOGIES, INC.; *pg.* 1304, *pg.* 377
SAVI SOURCE - Lighting Systems - REVOLUTION LIGHTING TECHNOLOGIES, INC.; *pg.* 1304, *pg.* 377
SAVING LIVES IS OUR GOAL - Slogan - ASTEX PHARMACEUTICALS, INC; *pg.* 1497, *pg.* 77
SAVING SPREE - Discount Coupon Book - ENTERTAINMENT PUBLICATIONS, INC.; *pg.* 1639, *pg.* 910
SAVINGS CLUB - Card - BIG Y FOODS, INC.; *pg.* 1015, *pg.* 845
SAVINGS. FOR EVERY STAGE OF YOUR LIFE - Insurance Product - SBLI USA LIFE INSURANCE COMPANY, INC.; *pg.* 1216, *pg.* 1288
SAVINGS PLUS - Discount Food & Household Products - THE GREAT ATLANTIC & PACIFIC TEA COMPANY, INC.; *pg.* 1021, *pg.* 1086
SAVOIR FAIRE - Bedding - CROSCILL, INC.; *pg.* 1122, *pg.* 1220
SAVON - Food Product And Drug - ALBERTSON'S LLC; *pg.* 1013, *pg.* 546
SAVON - Furniture Stores - KANE FURNITURE CORPORATION; *pg.* 931, *pg.* 458
SAVONA - Fan - WESTINGHOUSE LIGHTING CORPORATION; *pg.* 687, *pg.* 1571
SAVONA ES - Ceiling Fan - WESTINGHOUSE LIGHTING CORPORATION; *pg.* 687, *pg.* 1571
SAVONNIERE - Rug - ETHAN ALLEN INTERIORS INC.; *pg.* 924, *pg.* 343

First page reference indicates Business Class Edition
Second page reference indicates Geographic Edition

SAVOR - Cruise Ship - ROYAL CARIBBEAN CRUISES LTD; *pg.* 1921, *pg.* 446
SAVOR NOTES - Food Flavorings - GRIFFITH LABORATORIES, INC.; *pg.* 860, *pg.* 552
SAVOR THE GOOD LIFE - Slogan - CUISINART INC.; *pg.* 1123, *pg.* 373
SAVORCRAVE - Flavor Technology - WILD FLAVORS, INC.; *pg.* 910, *pg.* 728
SAVORY - Liquid Butter Alternative - VENTURA FOODS, LLC; *pg.* 908, *pg.* 49
SAVORY SERVINGS - Chicken - FOSTER FARMS; *pg.* 856, *pg.* 122
SAVORYSOY - Soybean Oil - CHS INC.; *pg.* 702, *pg.* 926
SAVOY - Furniture - AMERICAN LEATHER LP; *pg.* 912, *pg.* 1673
SAVOY - Furniture Collection - CENTURY FURNITURE INDUSTRIES; *pg.* 920, *pg.* 1377
SAVOY - Fabric - NEMSCHOFF, INC.; *pg.* 936, *pg.* 1890
SAVVY - Sandals - AEROGROUP INTERNATIONAL, INC.; *pg.* 1803, *pg.* 1055
SAVVY - Paper - INTERNATIONAL PAPER COMPANY; *pg.* 1460, *pg.* 1644
SAW - Apparel - OAKLEY, INC.; *pg.* 1840, *pg.* 86
SAW OFF - Apparel - OAKLEY, INC.; *pg.* 1840, *pg.* 86
SAW PALMETTO PLUS - Herbal Formula - SHAKLEE CORPORATION; *pg.* 1593, *pg.* 184
SAWGRASS - Fabric - NEMSCHOFF, INC.; *pg.* 936, *pg.* 1890
SAWTOOTH MOUNTAIN - Clothing - ABERCROMBIE & FITCH CO.; *pg.* 37, *pg.* 1466
SAWYER - Instrument Table - BLICKMAN HEALTH INDUSTRIES, INC.; *pg.* 1506, *pg.* 1051
SAWYER - Office Furniture - STEELCASE INC.; *pg.* 475, *pg.* 889
SAWZALL - Power Tools - MILWAUKEE ELECTRIC TOOL CORP.; *pg.* 1056, *pg.* 1855
SAWZALL PLUS - Power Tool - MILWAUKEE ELECTRIC TOOL CORP.; *pg.* 1056, *pg.* 1855
SAX ARTS & CRAFTS - Educational Resources - SCHOOL SPECIALTY, INC.; *pg.* 467, *pg.* 1860
SAX FAMILY & CONSUMER SCIENCES - Educational Resources - SCHOOL SPECIALTY, INC.; *pg.* 467, *pg.* 1860
SAXONY - Bath Accessory - CROSCILL, INC.; *pg.* 1122, *pg.* 1220
SAY YES TO BEANS - Nutritional Supplement - NATURAL ORGANICS, INC.; *pg.* 1571, *pg.* 1181
SAY YES TO DAIRY - Nutritional Supplement - NATURAL ORGANICS, INC.; *pg.* 1571, *pg.* 1181
SAYELLE - Commercial Knitting Yarn - NATIONAL SPINNING COMPANY, INC.; *pg.* 697, *pg.* 1265
SAYETT - Electronic Projection Equipment, Software - EASTMAN KODAK COMPANY; *pg.* 1408, *pg.* 1333
SAYTEX - Chemical Product - ALBEMARLE CORPORATION; *pg.* 1146, *pg.* 741
SAZON GOYA - Seasonings - GOYA FOODS, INC.; *pg.* 859, *pg.* 1075
SB - Video Game - INTERNATIONAL GAME TECHNOLOGY; *pg.* 957, *pg.* 1024
SB NEXGEN - Video Game - INTERNATIONAL GAME TECHNOLOGY; *pg.* 957, *pg.* 1024
SB-PLUGS - Subsea Equipment - DRIL-QUIP, INC.; *pg.* 1330, *pg.* 1704
SB POG - Oil and Grease Remover - ADCO, INC.; *pg.* 325, *pg.* 482
SBARRO THE ITALIAN EATERY - Slogan - SBARRO, INC.; *pg.* 1749, *pg.* 1182
SBECKLE - Shoe - AEROGROUP INTERNATIONAL, INC.; *pg.* 1803, *pg.* 1055
SBGANYTIME - Supplement And Food - NEW EARTH LIFE SCIENCES, INC.; *pg.* 1573, *pg.* 1499
SBLI USA EASY PAY - Insurance Product - SBLI USA LIFE INSURANCE COMPANY, INC.; *pg.* 1216, *pg.* 1288
SBLI USA FINANCIAL ENPOWERMENT COMPANY - Insurance Product - SBLI USA LIFE INSURANCE COMPANY, INC.; *pg.* 1216, *pg.* 1288
SBLI USA PAYCHECK PROTECTOR - Insurance Product - SBLI USA LIFE INSURANCE COMPANY, INC.; *pg.* 1216, *pg.* 1288
SBN - News - AMERICAN URBAN RADIO NETWORKS; *pg.* 269, *pg.* 1573
SBP - Insecticides - THE CLOROX COMPANY; *pg.* 327, *pg.* 169
SBR - Semiconductors - DIODES INCORPORATED; *pg.* 634, *pg.* 1729
SBR - Dust Filter - SLY, INC.; *pg.* 1376, *pg.* 1475
SBS - Polishing System - 3M COMPANY; *pg.* 1142, *pg.* 956
SBS - Chemical Product - SACHEM INC.; *pg.* 1180, *pg.* 1665
SBS - Automatic Balancing System - SCHMITT INDUSTRIES, INC.; *pg.* 1374, *pg.* 1506
SBX-4 - Wireless Product - HEMISPHERE GPS INC.; *pg.* 642, *pg.* 1903
SBX IP 320 - Telephone System - VERTICAL COMMUNICATIONS, INC.; *pg.* 488, *pg.* 270
SC-90 CONVENTIONAL WELLHEAD SYSTEMS - Surface Equipment - DRIL-QUIP, INC.; *pg.* 1330, *pg.* 1704
SC-DC - Glass & Ceramic Material - CORNING INCORPORATED; *pg.* 1122, *pg.* 1154
SC-GATE - Software - 3M; *pg.* 339, *pg.* 179
SC-QC - Glass & Ceramic Material - CORNING INCORPORATED; *pg.* 1122, *pg.* 1154
SC SERIES - Infrared Remote Controls - RETZLAFF INCORPORATED; *pg.* 667, *pg.* 258
SC SERIES - Wireless Microphones - SHURE INCORPORATED; *pg.* 672, *pg.* 638
SCA - Speed Coaches Association - ROLLER SKATING ASSOCIATION INTERNATIONAL; *pg.* 155, *pg.* 689
SCAASI - Perfume - REVLON, INC.; *pg.* 521, *pg.* 1286
SCADA - Data Aquisition System with Active Custom Graphics - PREFERRED UTILITIES MANUFACTURING CORPORATION; *pg.* 1075, *pg.* 344
SCADA-MATE - Switching System - S&C ELECTRIC COMPANY; *pg.* 1305, *pg.* 589
SCADA-MATE CX - Switching System - S&C ELECTRIC COMPANY; *pg.* 1305, *pg.* 589
SCADABASE - Scada Application Software Package - CSPI TECHNOLOGY SOLUTIONS; *pg.* 381, *pg.* 421
SCADACONNECT - Software - BENTLEY SYSTEMS, INC.; *pg.* 361, *pg.* 1531
SCAL - Software - SCHLUMBERGER LIMITED; *pg.* 801, *pg.* 1714
SCALA - Wood Flooring Product - ARMSTRONG WORLD INDUSTRIES, INC.; *pg.* 914, *pg.* 1545
SCALA - Rug - COURISTAN INC.; *pg.* 921, *pg.* 1067
SCALABLE NETWORK ACCELERATORS - Network Products - ALACRITECH, INC.; *pg.* 346, *pg.* 237
SCALAR - Tape Libraries - QUANTUM CORPORATION; *pg.* 458, *pg.* 250
SCALD GUARD - Shower Valves - DELTA FAUCET COMPANY; *pg.* 78, *pg.* 684
SCALE AUTO - Magazine - KALMBACH PUBLISHING CO.; *pg.* 1656, *pg.* 1898
SCALE KLEEN - Cleaning And Descaling Salt - HEATBATH CORPORATION; *pg.* 1165, *pg.* 826
SCALIBOR - Dog Collar - MERCK & CO., INC.; *pg.* 1566, *pg.* 1077
SCALINI - Tile - ARTISTIC TILE INC.; *pg.* 914, *pg.* 1119
SCALPICIN - Scalp Relief Medicine - COMBE INCORPORATED; *pg.* 1516, *pg.* 1351
SCALPICIN - Scalp Itch Medication - RECKITT BENCKISER INC.; *pg.* 1136, *pg.* 1105
SCAMPS - Furniture - HAWORTH, INC.; *pg.* 402, *pg.* 891
SCAN - Aluminia Nitrate - THE DOW CHEMICAL COMPANY; *pg.* 1157, *pg.* 898
SCAN - Carpet - INTERFACE, INC.; *pg.* 695, *pg.* 512
SCAN-A-DOSE PACKAGING - Medication Scanning Controls - AMERISOURCEBERGEN CORPORATION; *pg.* 1493, *pg.* 1522
SCAN-DE - Barcode Scanner - SENTRY TECHNOLOGY CORPORATION; *pg.* 672, *pg.* 1339
SCAN DIET - Nutritional Supplement - GENERAL NUTRITION CENTERS, INC.; *pg.* 1534, *pg.* 1575
SCAN DO - Scan Converter - COMMUNICATIONS SPECIALTIES, INC.; *pg.* 377, *pg.* 1338
SCAN-IT - Fluorescent Crayon - LA-CO INDUSTRIES MARKAL CO., INC.; *pg.* 1170, *pg.* 610
SCAN-IT PLUS - Fluorescent Crayon - LA-CO INDUSTRIES MARKAL CO., INC.; *pg.* 1170, *pg.* 610
SCAN-PRINT - Software - HURST CHEMICAL COMPANY; *pg.* 1168, *pg.* 174
SCAN-TECH - Volvo Product - DORMAN PRODUCTS, INC.; *pg.* 204, *pg.* 1522
SCAN TO PC DESKTOP - Software - XEROX CORPORATION; *pg.* 494, *pg.* 365
SCANBAY - Software - SNAP-ON INCORPORATED; *pg.* 1062, *pg.* 1862
SCANBOOK - Software - SCANTRON CORPORATION; *pg.* 467, *pg.* 922
SCANCOM - Data Processing & Retrieval Network - ALCATEL-LUCENT USA, INC.; *pg.* 615, *pg.* 1728
SCANDIA - Pillow and Throw - HERITAGE LACE INC.; *pg.* 694, *pg.* 711
SCANDIA - Footwear - P.W. MINOR & SON, INC.; *pg.* 1816, *pg.* 1140
SCANDIC FARMER - Cheese - A.V. OLSSON TRADING CO. INC.; *pg.* 838, *pg.* 372
SCANDIC GRAND FONTINA - Cheese - A.V. OLSSON TRADING CO. INC.; *pg.* 838, *pg.* 372
SCANDIC ORGANIC CHEDDAR - Cheese - A.V. OLSSON TRADING CO. INC.; *pg.* 838, *pg.* 372
SCANDINAVIAN DESIGN - Electrical Appliance & Housewares - NATIONAL PRESTO INDUSTRIES, INC; *pg.* 1128, *pg.* 1857
SCANDO-MINI - Elevator - ALIMAK HEK INC; *pg.* 66, *pg.* 1749
SCANEZE - Barcode Scanner - SENTRY TECHNOLOGY CORPORATION; *pg.* 672, *pg.* 1339
SCANGEL - Clinical Diagnostic Product - BIO-RAD LABORATORIES, INC.; *pg.* 1504, *pg.* 101
SCANGLOBE - Globe - REPLOGLE GLOBES, INC.; *pg.* 461, *pg.* 559
SCANGUARD - Card - ABNOTE NORTH AMERICA; *pg.* 1878, *pg.* 789
SCANLITE - Medical Laser System - IRIDEX CORPORATION; *pg.* 648, *pg.* 160
SCANMARK - Optical Mark Readers - SCANTRON CORPORATION; *pg.* 467, *pg.* 922
SCANMATEPRO - Laser & Laser System - COHERENT, INC.; *pg.* 1406, *pg.* 265
SCANNER-PACK - Microfilm Cartridge - EASTMAN KODAK COMPANY; *pg.* 1408, *pg.* 1333
SCANNING FOR LIFE - Slogan - IMAGING DIAGNOSTIC SYSTEMS, INC.; *pg.* 1544, *pg.* 425
SCANNING MOBILITY PARTICLE SIZER - Spectrometer - TSI INCORPORATED; *pg.* 1432, *pg.* 965
SCAN'O'VISION - Scoreboard & Sports Product - DAKTRONICS, INC.; *pg.* 633, *pg.* 1624
SCANPREP'S - Clinical Diagnostic Product - BIO-RAD LABORATORIES, INC.; *pg.* 1504, *pg.* 101
SCANPRO - Film Scanners - ANACOMP, INC.; *pg.* 350, *pg.* 1777
SCANSOURCE COMMUNICATIONS - Communication Solutions - SCANSOURCE, INC.; *pg.* 671, *pg.* 1618
SCANSOURCE POS & BARCODING - Software - SCANSOURCE, INC.; *pg.* 671, *pg.* 1618
SCANSOURCE SECURITY - Software - SCANSOURCE, INC.; *pg.* 671, *pg.* 1618
SCANTHERM - Adhesive Coated Paper - SPINNAKER COATING, LLC; *pg.* 1470, *pg.* 1477
SCANTHERM-POLY - Film - SPINNAKER COATING, LLC; *pg.* 1470, *pg.* 1477
SCANTOOLS PLUS - Scanning Software - PEARSON ASSESSMENTS; *pg.* 1674, *pg.* 918
SCANTOOLS PLUS SDK - Scanning Software - PEARSON ASSESSMENTS; *pg.* 1674, *pg.* 918
SCANTRACK - Consumer Information - ACNIELSEN CORPORATION; *pg.* 341, *pg.* 1187
SCANTRON - Designs, Develops, Products & Markets - SCANTRON CORPORATION; *pg.* 467, *pg.* 922
SCANVUE - Graphic Price Checker - INDUSTRIAL ELECTRONIC ENGINEERS, INC.; *pg.* 644, *pg.* 300
SCANWAVE - Collision Cell Technology - WATERS CORPORATION; *pg.* 1436, *pg.* 834
SCANWORKS - Software - PERCEPTRON, INC.; *pg.* 215, *pg.* 904
SCAP - Software System - MENTOR GRAPHICS CORPORATION; *pg.* 432, *pg.* 1510
SCARABEO - Scooter - PIAGGIO USA, INC.; *pg.* 188, *pg.* 1282
THE SCARECROW - Character - DC COMICS, INC.; *pg.* 1633, *pg.* 1221
SCARECROW - Character - DC COMICS, INC.; *pg.* 1633, *pg.* 1221
SCARLATTA - Wine - WILLIAM GRANT & SONS, INC.; *pg.* 1972, *pg.* 1057
SCARLATTI - Flatware - ONEIDA LTD; *pg.* 1129, *pg.* 1318
SCARLET - Semisweet Chocolate - CARGILL LIMITED; *pg.* 1475, *pg.* 1914
SCARLET MOON - Video Game - INTERNATIONAL GAME TECHNOLOGY; *pg.* 957, *pg.* 1024
SCARLETTE - Furniture - BASSETT FURNITURE INDUSTRIES, INCORPORATED; *pg.* 916, *pg.* 1776
SCAROWINDS - Halloween Attraction - CAROWINDS; *pg.* 537, *pg.* 1364
SCARY CASH - Lottery Card - MISSOURI LOTTERY; *pg.*

999, *pg.* 979
SCARY MONEY - Game - MISSOURI LOTTERY; *pg.* 999, *pg.* 979
SCARZONE - Skin Care Product - CCA INDUSTRIES, INC.; *pg.* 503, *pg.* 1114
SCATTER - Granular Deodorizers - SURCO PRODUCTS, INC.; *pg.* 336, *pg.* 1581
SCATTER BUCKS - Video Game - INTERNATIONAL GAME TECHNOLOGY; *pg.* 957, *pg.* 1024
SCATTER JOY - Pillow and Throw - HERITAGE LACE INC.; *pg.* 694, *pg.* 711
SCATTERBRAINED - Video Game - INTERNATIONAL GAME TECHNOLOGY; *pg.* 957, *pg.* 1024
SCATTERGORIES - Toy & Game - HASBRO, INC.; *pg.* 954, *pg.* 1603
SCATTERING BAR - Optical Proximity Correction Technology - BRION TECHNOLOGIES INC.; *pg.* 1319, *pg.* 265
SCATTERPILLAR - Video Game - INTERNATIONAL GAME TECHNOLOGY; *pg.* 957, *pg.* 1024
SCATTERTAINMENT - Game - WMS INDUSTRIES INC.; *pg.* 593, *pg.* 666
SCAVENGER - Manure Spreader System - GEHL COMPANY; *pg.* 1339, *pg.* 1899
SCAVENGER HUNT - Video Game - INTERNATIONAL GAME TECHNOLOGY; *pg.* 957, *pg.* 1024
SCBA - Ultrasonic Cleaning System - L&R MANUFACTURING COMPANY; *pg.* 1419, *pg.* 1076
SCC - Unit Modules - SCREW CONVEYOR INDUSTRIES; *pg.* 1374, *pg.* 682
THE SCENE - Music Library - MEGATRAX PRODUCTION MUSIC, INC.; *pg.* 297, *pg.* 167
SCENE IT - Toy - MATTEL, INC.; *pg.* 962, *pg.* 81
SCENE7 - Software - ADOBE SYSTEMS INCORPORATED; *pg.* 342, *pg.* 235
SCENES FROM RACEDAY - Photo Album - ATHLON SPORTS, INC.; *pg.* 1618, *pg.* 1648
SCENES FROM SATURDAY - Photo Album - ATHLON SPORTS, INC.; *pg.* 1618, *pg.* 1648
SCENES FROM SUNDAY - Photo Album - ATHLON SPORTS, INC.; *pg.* 1618, *pg.* 1648
SCENIC ROLLER - Screen - DA-LITE SCREEN COMPANY; *pg.* 632, *pg.* 698
SCENT FLO - Fan Air Freshener - SURCO PRODUCTS, INC.; *pg.* 336, *pg.* 1581
SCENT-LOK - Apparel - CABELA'S INCORPORATED; *pg.* 535, *pg.* 1019
SCENT OFF - Plant Chemicals - PLANTABBS PRODUCTS COMPANY; *pg.* 1799, *pg.* 758
SCENT-SATION - Fresher Unit - BLUE CROSS LABORATORIES; *pg.* 326, *pg.* 277
SCENT SEAL - Storage Bag - CABELA'S INCORPORATED; *pg.* 535, *pg.* 1019
SCENT SENSE - Potpourri - Advertising Specialty Custom Imprinted - THE PAGE SEED CO.; *pg.* 1798, *pg.* 1163
SCENT SKINZ - Apparel - CABELA'S INCORPORATED; *pg.* 535, *pg.* 1019
SCENT X-TERMINATOR - Kit - CABELA'S INCORPORATED; *pg.* 535, *pg.* 1019
SCENTED GARDEN - Scented Products - WILLERT HOME PRODUCTS, INC.; *pg.* 1140, *pg.* 1005
SCENTSATIONS - Hand & Body Lotions & Washes - CREATIVE NAIL DESIGN, INC.; *pg.* 506, *pg.* 302
SCENTSATIONS - Personal Care Product - ROCHESTER MIDLAND CORPORATION; *pg.* 334, *pg.* 1337
SCENTSCAPES - Air Fresheners - AMWAY CORPORATION; *pg.* 326, *pg.* 864
SCENTSEAL - Olfactory Sampling System - ARCADE MARKETING, INC.; *pg.* 352, *pg.* 1196
SCENTSTORIES BY FEBREZE - Scent Themed Cleaning Product - THE PROCTER & GAMBLE COMPANY; *pg.* 1129, *pg.* 1418
SCENTSTRIP - Olfactory Sampling System - ARCADE MARKETING, INC.; *pg.* 352, *pg.* 1196
SCEPTER - Semiconductor Device - APPLIED MATERIALS, INC; *pg.* 618, *pg.* 1009
SCF-19 - Alloy - CARPENTER TECHNOLOGY CORPORATION; *pg.* 73, *pg.* 1584
SCHAEFER - Beer - PABST BREWING COMPANY; *pg.* 258, *pg.* 137
SCHAEFER MARINE - Marine Hardware - SCHAEFER MARINE INC.; *pg.* 1373, *pg.* 835
SCHAEFF - Compact Equipment - TEREX CORPORATION; *pg.* 1381, *pg.* 384
SCHAEVITZ - Sensor System - MEASUREMENT SPECIALTIES INC.; *pg.* 1360, *pg.* 1783
SCHAUMBURG - Ethernet Product - VITESSE SEMICONDUCTOR CORPORATION; *pg.* 686, *pg.* 57
SCHEDULE-IT - Software - NIELSEN AUDIO; *pg.* 446, *pg.* 768
SCHEDULE TRACK - Navigation Aid - TRIMBLE NAVIGATION LIMITED; *pg.* 1384, *pg.* 288
SCHEDULEPOINT - Video Communication System - GLOWPOINT, INC.; *pg.* 401, *pg.* 1094
SCHEMA - Simulator Software - MTS SYSTEMS CORPORATION; *pg.* 442, *pg.* 923
SCHEMA MANAGER - Software - DELL SOFTWARE; *pg.* 385, *pg.* 40
SCHEMABSP - Development Tools - BSQUARE CORPORATION; *pg.* 366, *pg.* 1813
SCHEMAX - Computer Software - NOVELL INC.; *pg.* 446, *pg.* 852
SCHENKEL'S ALL STAR - Dairy Product - DEAN FOODS COMPANY; *pg.* 852, *pg.* 1679
SCHENLEY RESERVE - Whiskey Blend - CONSTELLATION BRANDS, INC.; *pg.* 1960, *pg.* 1348
SCHEPPS - Dairy Product - DEAN FOODS COMPANY; *pg.* 852, *pg.* 1679
SCHERR-TUMICO - Measuring Instruments - S-T INDUSTRIES, INC.; *pg.* 1428, *pg.* 956
SCHICK - Shaving Products - EDGEWELL PERSONAL CARE; *pg.* 1526, *pg.* 995
SCHILLING - Food Colorings - MCCORMICK & COMPANY, INCORPORATED; *pg.* 1027, *pg.* 779
SCHIRMER REFERENCES - College Textbooks & General Reference Books - GALE CENGAGE LEARNING; *pg.* 1643, *pg.* 885
SCHIZANDRA PLUS - Herbal Vitamin/Mineral Supplement - HERBALIFE INTERNATIONAL OF AMERICA, INC.; *pg.* 1541, *pg.* 132
SCHLAGE - Door Hardware - INGERSOLL-RAND COMPANY; *pg.* 1349, *pg.* 1370
SCHLEPP - Bear - GUND, INC.; *pg.* 954, *pg.* 1056
SCHLITZ - Beer - PABST BREWING COMPANY; *pg.* 258, *pg.* 137
SCHLOTZSKY'S - Deli - SCHLOTZSKY'S, LTD.; *pg.* 1749, *pg.* 1665
SCHLOTZSKY'S DELI - Food Product - SCHLOTZSKY'S, LTD.; *pg.* 1749, *pg.* 1665
SCHLUMBERGER - Oilfield Service Provider - SCHLUMBERGER LIMITED; *pg.* 801, *pg.* 1714
TIFFANY-SCHLUMBERGER - Jewelry & Watches - TIFFANY & CO.; *pg.* 13, *pg.* 1299
SCHMIDT - Couplings - ZERO-MAX, INC.; *pg.* 222, *pg.* 954
SCHMIDT ARMATUREN - Valve - FLOWSERVE CORPORATION; *pg.* 82, *pg.* 1719
SCHMIDT MICROLASE - Laser Marking - GEORGE T. SCHMIDT, INC.; *pg.* 1340, *pg.* 637
SCHMOOZE - Fabric - NEMSCHOFF, INC.; *pg.* 936, *pg.* 1890
SCHNEIDER FOODS - Meat Products - MAPLE LEAF FOODS INC.; *pg.* 875, *pg.* 1927
SCHNEIDER GUIDER - Medical Device - BOSTON SCIENTIFIC CORPORATION; *pg.* 1508, *pg.* 831
SCHNEIDER NATIONAL - Logo - SCHNEIDER; *pg.* 1922, *pg.* 1859
SCHOFIELD COBBLE - Clothing - ABERCROMBIE & FITCH CO.; *pg.* 37, *pg.* 1466
SCHOLAR - Knife - BUCK KNIVES, INC.; *pg.* 1828, *pg.* 550
SCHOLAR - Glass & Ceramic Material - CORNING INCORPORATED; *pg.* 1122, *pg.* 1154
SCHOLAR - Patient Monitoring System - CRITICARE SYSTEMS, INC.; *pg.* 1520, *pg.* 1897
SCHOLASTIC - Educational Materials - SCHOLASTIC INC.; *pg.* 1683, *pg.* 1288
SCHOLASTIC - THE MOST TRUSTED NAME IN LEARNING - Slogan - SCHOLASTIC INC.; *pg.* 1683, *pg.* 1288
SCHOLASTIC ACTION - Educational Materials - SCHOLASTIC INC.; *pg.* 1683, *pg.* 1288
SCHOLASTIC ADMINISTRATOR - Educational Materials - SCHOLASTIC INC.; *pg.* 1683, *pg.* 1288
SCHOLASTIC A.I. - Educational Materials - SCHOLASTIC INC.; *pg.* 1683, *pg.* 1288
SCHOLASTIC ART - Educational Materials - SCHOLASTIC INC.; *pg.* 1683, *pg.* 1288
SCHOLASTIC BANNERS - Educational Materials - SCHOLASTIC INC.; *pg.* 1683, *pg.* 1288
SCHOLASTIC BOOK FAIRS - Educational Materials - SCHOLASTIC INC.; *pg.* 1683, *pg.* 1288
SCHOLASTIC BOOKS ON TOUR - Educational Materials - SCHOLASTIC INC.; *pg.* 1683, *pg.* 1288
SCHOLASTIC CASSETTES - Educational Materials - SCHOLASTIC INC.; *pg.* 1683, *pg.* 1288
SCHOLASTIC CHOICES - Educational Materials - SCHOLASTIC INC.; *pg.* 1683, *pg.* 1288
SCHOLASTIC DECODABLE READERS - Educational Materials - SCHOLASTIC INC.; *pg.* 1683, *pg.* 1288
THE SCHOLASTIC EARLY CHILDHOOD WORKSHOP - Educational Materials - SCHOLASTIC INC.; *pg.* 1683, *pg.* 1288
SCHOLASTIC EXPLAINS - Educational Materials - SCHOLASTIC INC.; *pg.* 1683, *pg.* 1288
SCHOLASTIC EXPLORASTORY BOOK FAIR - Educational Materials - SCHOLASTIC INC.; *pg.* 1683, *pg.* 1288
SCHOLASTIC FAMILY BOOKSHELF - Educational Materials - SCHOLASTIC INC.; *pg.* 1683, *pg.* 1288
SCHOLASTIC HARDCOVER - Educational Materials - SCHOLASTIC INC.; *pg.* 1683, *pg.* 1288
SCHOLASTIC INTERACTIVE PHONICS READERS BOOSTER - Educational Materials - SCHOLASTIC INC.; *pg.* 1683, *pg.* 1288
SCHOLASTIC INTERNATIONAL - Educational Materials - SCHOLASTIC INC.; *pg.* 1683, *pg.* 1288
SCHOLASTIC LEARNING SIDE BY SIDE - Educational Materials - SCHOLASTIC INC.; *pg.* 1683, *pg.* 1288
SCHOLASTIC LITERACY FESTIVAL - Educational Materials - SCHOLASTIC INC.; *pg.* 1683, *pg.* 1288
SCHOLASTIC LITERACY PLACE - Educational Materials - SCHOLASTIC INC.; *pg.* 1683, *pg.* 1288
SCHOLASTIC MATH - Educational Materials - SCHOLASTIC INC.; *pg.* 1683, *pg.* 1288
SCHOLASTIC MATH PLACE - Educational Materials - SCHOLASTIC INC.; *pg.* 1683, *pg.* 1288
SCHOLASTIC MY FIRST LIBRARY - Educational Materials - SCHOLASTIC INC.; *pg.* 1683, *pg.* 1288
SCHOLASTIC NETWORK - Educational Materials - SCHOLASTIC INC.; *pg.* 1683, *pg.* 1288
SCHOLASTIC NEWS - Educational Materials - SCHOLASTIC INC.; *pg.* 1683, *pg.* 1288
SCHOLASTIC NEWS-EL PERIODICO - Educational Materials - SCHOLASTIC INC.; *pg.* 1683, *pg.* 1288
SCHOLASTIC PARENT & CHILD - Educational Materials - SCHOLASTIC INC.; *pg.* 1683, *pg.* 1288
SCHOLASTIC PHONICS CLUBHOUSE - Educational Materials - SCHOLASTIC INC.; *pg.* 1683, *pg.* 1288
SCHOLASTIC PHONICS READERS - Educational Materials - SCHOLASTIC INC.; *pg.* 1683, *pg.* 1288
SCHOLASTIC PRODUCTIONS - Educational Materials - SCHOLASTIC INC.; *pg.* 1683, *pg.* 1288
SCHOLASTIC READ XL - Educational Materials - SCHOLASTIC INC.; *pg.* 1683, *pg.* 1288
SCHOLASTIC READING COUNTS - Educational Materials - SCHOLASTIC INC.; *pg.* 1683, *pg.* 1288
SCHOLASTIC READING JAMBOREE - Educational Materials - SCHOLASTIC INC.; *pg.* 1683, *pg.* 1288
SCHOLASTIC READING LINE - Educational Materials - SCHOLASTIC INC.; *pg.* 1683, *pg.* 1288
SCHOLASTIC RECORDS - Educational Materials - SCHOLASTIC INC.; *pg.* 1683, *pg.* 1288
SCHOLASTIC RED - Educational Materials - SCHOLASTIC INC.; *pg.* 1683, *pg.* 1288
SCHOLASTIC REFERENCE - Educational Materials - SCHOLASTIC INC.; *pg.* 1683, *pg.* 1288
SCHOLASTIC SCIENCE PLACE - Educational Materials - SCHOLASTIC INC.; *pg.* 1683, *pg.* 1288
SCHOLASTIC SCOPE - Educational Materials - SCHOLASTIC INC.; *pg.* 1683, *pg.* 1288
SCHOLASTIC SHOWCASE - Educational Materials - SCHOLASTIC INC.; *pg.* 1683, *pg.* 1288
SCHOLASTIC SIDE BY SIDE - Educational Materials - SCHOLASTIC INC.; *pg.* 1683, *pg.* 1288
SCHOLASTIC SIDEKICKS - Educational Materials - SCHOLASTIC INC.; *pg.* 1683, *pg.* 1288
SCHOLASTIC SMART BOOKS - Educational Materials - SCHOLASTIC INC.; *pg.* 1683, *pg.* 1288
SCHOLASTIC SOLARES - Educational Materials - SCHOLASTIC INC.; *pg.* 1683, *pg.* 1288
SCHOLASTIC SOUND AND LETTER TIME - Educational Materials - SCHOLASTIC INC.; *pg.* 1683, *pg.* 1288
SCHOLASTIC SPELLING - Educational Materials - SCHOLASTIC INC.; *pg.* 1683, *pg.* 1288
SCHOLASTIC SPELLING STUDIO - Educational Materials - SCHOLASTIC INC.; *pg.* 1683, *pg.* 1288
SCHOLASTIC SPRINT READING - Educational Materials - SCHOLASTIC INC.; *pg.* 1683, *pg.* 1288
THE SCHOLASTIC STORE - Educational Materials -

SCHOLASTIC INC.; *pg.* 1683, *pg.* 1288
SCHOLASTIC STORYBOOK COLLECTIBLES - Educational Materials - SCHOLASTIC INC.; *pg.* 1683, *pg.* 1288
SCHOLASTIC SUPERPRINT! - Educational Materials - SCHOLASTIC INC.; *pg.* 1683, *pg.* 1288
SCHOLASTIC TEACHER - Educational Materials - SCHOLASTIC INC.; *pg.* 1683, *pg.* 1288
SCHOLASTIC TESTING - Educational Materials - SCHOLASTIC INC.; *pg.* 1683, *pg.* 1288
SCHOLASTIC TIME-TO-TIME DISCOVER READERS - Educational Materials - SCHOLASTIC INC.; *pg.* 1683, *pg.* 1288
SCHOLASTIC TRANSITION PROGRAM - Educational Materials - SCHOLASTIC INC.; *pg.* 1683, *pg.* 1288
SCHOLASTIC UPDATE - Educational Materials - SCHOLASTIC INC.; *pg.* 1683, *pg.* 1288
SCHOLASTIC VIDEO COLLECTION - Educational Materials - SCHOLASTIC INC.; *pg.* 1683, *pg.* 1288
SCHOLASTIC VOZ DEL LECTOR - Educational Materials - SCHOLASTIC INC.; *pg.* 1683, *pg.* 1288
SCHOLASTIC ZIP ZOOM - Educational Materials - SCHOLASTIC INC.; *pg.* 1683, *pg.* 1288
SCHON - Electrosurgical Devices - ANGIODYNAMICS, INC.; *pg.* 1495, *pg.* 1173
SCHON - Engineered Floors - LUMBER LIQUIDATORS HOLDINGS, INC.; *pg.* 94, *pg.* 1808
SCHON XL - Electrosurgical Devices - ANGIODYNAMICS, INC.; *pg.* 1495, *pg.* 1173
SCHONLAND'S - Frankfurters & Sausages - KAYEM FOODS, INC.; *pg.* 867, *pg.* 814
SCHOOL BUS FLEET - Magazine - BOBIT BUSINESS MEDIA; *pg.* 1622, *pg.* 293
SCHOOL CHOICE - Cheese - SCHREIBER FOODS, INC.; *pg.* 894, *pg.* 1859
SCHOOL CONSTRUCTION ALERT - Lead Generation Service - MARKET DATA RETRIEVAL; *pg.* 1661, *pg.* 370
SCHOOL DAYS - Apparel - ELDER MANUFACTURING COMPANY, INC.; *pg.* 40, *pg.* 996
SCHOOL OF HOMESTEAD LIVING - School Program - BOB EVANS FARMS, LLC; *pg.* 841, *pg.* 1467
SCHOOL RENAISSANCE - Educational Materials - RENAISSANCE LEARNING, INC.; *pg.* 607, *pg.* 1899
SCHOOL SAFE - Training Services - CARDIAC SCIENCE CORPORATION; *pg.* 1512, *pg.* 1897
SCHOOL SPECIALTY PUBLISHING - Educational Resources - SCHOOL SPECIALTY, INC.; *pg.* 467, *pg.* 1860
SCHOOL-TECH - Athletic Equipment - SCHOOL-TECH, INC.; *pg.* 1844, *pg.* 866
SCHOOLMAX - Software Product - MAXIMUS, INC.; *pg.* 780, *pg.* 1799
SCHOONER - Beer - LABATT BREWING COMPANY LIMITED; *pg.* 253, *pg.* 1939
SCHOTT - Glassware - ONEIDA LTD; *pg.* 1129, *pg.* 1318
SCHREIBER - Cheese - SCHREIBER FOODS, INC.; *pg.* 894, *pg.* 1859
SCHROCK - Hardware - FORTUNE BRANDS HOME & SECURITY, INC.; *pg.* 55, *pg.* 600
SCHROCK CABINETRY - Hardware - FORTUNE BRANDS HOME & SECURITY, INC.; *pg.* 55, *pg.* 600
SCHROEDER - Publishing Company - SCHROEDER PUBLISHING COMPANY; *pg.* 1685, *pg.* 739
SCHUCO - Nebulizer - ALLIED HEALTHCARE PRODUCTS, INC.; *pg.* 1491, *pg.* 990
SCHULABLEND - Plastic Compound & Resin - A. SCHULMAN, INC.; *pg.* 1144, *pg.* 1452
SCHULADUR - Plastic Compound & Resin - A. SCHULMAN, INC.; *pg.* 1144, *pg.* 1452
SCHULAFLEX - Plastic Compound & Resin - A. SCHULMAN, INC.; *pg.* 1144, *pg.* 1452
SCHULAFORM - Plastic Compound & Resin - A. SCHULMAN, INC.; *pg.* 1144, *pg.* 1452
SCHULAMID - Plastic Compound & Resin - A. SCHULMAN, INC.; *pg.* 1144, *pg.* 1452
SCHULATEC - Plastic Compound & Resin - A. SCHULMAN, INC.; *pg.* 1144, *pg.* 1452
SCHULINK - Plastic Compound & Resin - A. SCHULMAN, INC.; *pg.* 1144, *pg.* 1452
SCHULTE - Mower - ALAMO GROUP INC.; *pg.* 1311, *pg.* 1745
SCHULTE 5026 - Rotary Mower - ALAMO GROUP INC.; *pg.* 1311, *pg.* 1745
SCHUMACHER - Chemical Product - AIR PRODUCTS AND CHEMICALS, INC.; *pg.* 1145, *pg.* 1513
SCHUMACHER - Fabric - F. SCHUMACHER & CO.; *pg.* 925, *pg.* 1230
SCHUMACHER - Vehicle Maintenance - TRACTOR SUPPLY COMPANY; *pg.* 708, *pg.* 1627
SCHUSS - Educational Materials - SCHOLASTIC INC.; *pg.* 1683, *pg.* 1288
SCHWABFUNDS - Proprietary Mutual Funds - CHARLES SCHWAB & COMPANY, INC.; *pg.* 734, *pg.* 215
SCHWABPLAN - Retirement Plan Services - CHARLES SCHWAB & COMPANY, INC.; *pg.* 734, *pg.* 215
SCHWARTZ - Seasonings - MCCORMICK & COMPANY, INCORPORATED; *pg.* 1027, *pg.* 779
SCHWARTZ - Pickles - TREEHOUSE FOODS, INC.; *pg.* 901, *pg.* 649
SCHWARZ - Paper - SCHWARZ PAPER COMPANY; *pg.* 1468, *pg.* 634
SCHWARZE - Sweeper - ALAMO GROUP INC.; *pg.* 1311, *pg.* 1745
SCHWARZE M6000 - Street Sweeper - ALAMO GROUP INC.; *pg.* 1311, *pg.* 1745
SCHWEPPES - Carbonated Soft Drink - DR PEPPER SNAPPLE GROUP, INC.; *pg.* 250, *pg.* 1729
SCHWINN - Health & Fitness Product - NAUTILUS, INC.; *pg.* 1840, *pg.* 1846
SCHWINN A.C. - Health & Fitness Product - NAUTILUS, INC.; *pg.* 1840, *pg.* 1846
SCI FI CHANNEL UK - International Channel - NBC UNIVERSAL, INC.; *pg.* 300, *pg.* 1266
SCI-TECH AWARDS - Awards - ACADEMY OF MOTION PICTURE ARTS & SCIENCES; *pg.* 526, *pg.* 46
SCICLOPEDIA - Educational Materials - SCHOLASTIC INC.; *pg.* 1683, *pg.* 1288
SCIDYN - Communications Solution - LATTICE INC.; *pg.* 1872, *pg.* 1108
SCIENCE - Magazine - AMERICAN ASSOCIATION FOR THE ADVANCEMENT OF SCIENCE; *pg.* 126, *pg.* 394
SCIENCE ADVANCING HEALTH - Tagline - NORDION INC.; *pg.* 1573, *pg.* 1932
THE SCIENCE AND ART OF PEOPLE AND POTENTIAL - Slogan - MARITZ INC.; *pg.* 1914, *pg.* 977
SCIENCE AND TECHNOLOGY FOR CHILDREN - Integrated Hands On Science Program - CAROLINA BIOLOGICAL SUPPLY COMPANY; *pg.* 1513, *pg.* 1359
THE SCIENCE CHANNEL - Television Station - DISCOVERY COMMUNICATIONS, INC.; *pg.* 282, *pg.* 777
SCIENCE CHICAGO LIFE'S A LAB - Science Celebration Program - MUSEUM OF SCIENCE AND INDUSTRY; *pg.* 565, *pg.* 583
SCIENCE DARES YOU! - Educational Materials - SCHOLASTIC INC.; *pg.* 1683, *pg.* 1288
SCIENCE DESK - Tabletop - THORLABS INC.; *pg.* 1432, *pg.* 1098
SCIENCE DIET - Animal Food Products - HILL'S PET NUTRITION, INC.; *pg.* 1476, *pg.* 721
SCIENCE DIET - Pet Food - INTERMOUNTAIN FARMERS ASSOCIATION; *pg.* 705, *pg.* 1759
SCIENCE DIET ADVANCED PROTECTION - Pet Food - INTERMOUNTAIN FARMERS ASSOCIATION; *pg.* 705, *pg.* 1759
SCIENCE DUET - Petcare - TRACTOR SUPPLY COMPANY; *pg.* 708, *pg.* 1627
SCIENCE ILLUSTRATED - Magazine - BONNIER CORPORATION; *pg.* 1622, *pg.* 480
THE SCIENCE OF BEAUTIFUL EYES - Electrical & Scientific Apparatus - THE COOPER COMPANIES, INC.; *pg.* 1518, *pg.* 183
THE SCIENCE OF CELLULAR REJUVENATION - Slogan - FIBROCELL SCIENCE, INC.; *pg.* 1530, *pg.* 1531
THE SCIENCE OF COMFORT - Tag Line - ACUSHNET COMPANY; *pg.* 1824, *pg.* 818
THE SCIENCE OF RECOVERY - Tag Line - CATASYS, INC.; *pg.* 1514, *pg.* 127
THE SCIENCE OF WHAT.S POSSIBLE. - Slogan - WATERS CORPORATION; *pg.* 1436, *pg.* 834
SCIENCE PLACEMATS - Educational Materials - SCHOLASTIC INC.; *pg.* 1683, *pg.* 1288
SCIENCE SEEKERS - Educational Materials - SCHOLASTIC INC.; *pg.* 1683, *pg.* 1288
SCIENCE STORMS - Museum Exhibition Services - MUSEUM OF SCIENCE AND INDUSTRY; *pg.* 565, *pg.* 583
SCIENCE THINKMATS - Educational Materials - SCHOLASTIC INC.; *pg.* 1683, *pg.* 1288
SCIENCE WORLD - Educational Materials - SCHOLASTIC INC.; *pg.* 1683, *pg.* 1288
SCIENCEWARE - Scientific Supplies - BEL-ART PRODUCTS, INC.; *pg.* 1879, *pg.* 1129
SCIENCO - Pump - FLOWSERVE CORPORATION; *pg.* 82, *pg.* 1719
SCIENTIFIC AMERICAN - Magazine - SCIENTIFIC AMERICAN, INC.; *pg.* 1685, *pg.* 1290
SCIENTIFIC AMERICAN MIND - Magazine - SCIENTIFIC AMERICAN, INC.; *pg.* 1685, *pg.* 1290
SCIENTIFIC ANGLERS - Fly Fishing Products - 3M COMPANY; *pg.* 1142, *pg.* 956
SCIENTIFIC COMPUTING - Trade Magazine - ADVANTAGE BUSINESS MEDIA; *pg.* 1613, *pg.* 1116
SCIENTIST - Weather Instrument - SWIFT OPTICAL INSTRUMENTS, INC.; *pg.* 1430, *pg.* 1744
SCIFI.COM - Official Web Site - SYFY; *pg.* 311, *pg.* 1297
SCIFIT - Medical & Aesthetic Product - DYNATRONICS CORPORATION; *pg.* 1526, *pg.* 1757
SCIFLEX - Glove - ACUSHNET COMPANY; *pg.* 1824, *pg.* 818
SCINTIPLATES - Microplates - PERKINELMER, INC.; *pg.* 1426, *pg.* 853
SCION - Lighting System - LITECONTROL CORPORATION; *pg.* 1301, *pg.* 841
SCION - Wallcovering - OMNOVA SOLUTIONS INC; *pg.* 1176, *pg.* 1453
SCIOTO DOWNS RACINO - Racetrack & Casino - ELDORADO RESORTS, INC.; *pg.* 546, *pg.* 1031
SCIPION - Software - BIO-RAD LABORATORIES, INC.; *pg.* 1504, *pg.* 101
SCIQUEST - Computer Software - SCIQUEST, INC.; *pg.* 468, *pg.* 1361
SCIRAS - Sundstrand Coriolis Inertial Rate & Acceleration Sensor - HONEYWELL AEROSPACE ELECTRONIC SYSTEMS; *pg.* 228, *pg.* 17
SCIROCCO - Software - SYNOPSYS, INC.; *pg.* 480, *pg.* 162
SCIROCCO-I - Software - SYNOPSYS, INC.; *pg.* 480, *pg.* 162
SCITEX - Ink-Jet Printer - COOLEY GROUP, INC.; *pg.* 691, *pg.* 1603
SCL - Software - SRA INTERNATIONAL, INC.; *pg.* 473, *pg.* 1780
SCLAIR - Polyethylene - NOVA CHEMICALS CORPORATION; *pg.* 1175, *pg.* 1904
SCLAIRCOAT - Chemical Product - NOVA CHEMICALS CORPORATION; *pg.* 1175, *pg.* 1904
SCLAIRTECH - Advanced Technology - NOVA CHEMICALS CORPORATION; *pg.* 1175, *pg.* 1904
SCOFIELD FORMULA ONE - Liquid Dye - L.M. SCOFIELD COMPANY; *pg.* 94, *pg.* 134
SCONAPOR - Polystyrene Beads - THE DOW CHEMICAL COMPANY; *pg.* 1157, *pg.* 898
SCONCE - Lighting - ETHAN ALLEN INTERIORS INC.; *pg.* 924, *pg.* 343
SCOOBA - Robotic floor cleaner - IROBOT CORP.; *pg.* 1418, *pg.* 785
SCOOBY-DOO - Animated Series - THE CARTOON NETWORK; *pg.* 273, *pg.* 492
SCOOBY DOO BERRY BONES - Cereal - KELLOGG COMPANY; *pg.* 831, *pg.* 870
S'COOLMATE - Lunch Kit - IGLOO PRODUCTS CORPORATION; *pg.* 1126, *pg.* 1724
SCOOP AWAY - Clumping Litter - THE CLOROX COMPANY; *pg.* 327, *pg.* 169
SCOOP STOOL - Office Furniture - STEELCASE INC.; *pg.* 475, *pg.* 889
SCOOPS - Ice Cream - WELLS ENTERPRISES, INC.; *pg.* 909, *pg.* 709
SCOOT-ABOUT - Ride-ons - RADIO FLYER INC.; *pg.* 966, *pg.* 588
SCOOT-GARD - Medical & Aesthetic Product - DYNATRONICS CORPORATION; *pg.* 1526, *pg.* 1757
SCOOZI! - Italian Restaurant - LETTUCE ENTERTAIN YOU ENTERPRISES, INC.; *pg.* 1735, *pg.* 580
SCOPE - Software - BLUE COAT SYSTEMS, INC.; *pg.* 362, *pg.* 284
SCOPE - Apparel - OAKLEY, INC.; *pg.* 1840, *pg.* 86
SCOPE - Oral Care Product - THE PROCTER & GAMBLE COMPANY; *pg.* 1129, *pg.* 1418
SCOPE - Commercial Lighting - SWIVELIER CO., INC.; *pg.* 1307, *pg.* 1142
SCOPE - Software - SYNOPSYS, INC.; *pg.* 480, *pg.* 162
SCOPE SAVER - Medical Equipment - CONMED CORPORATION; *pg.* 1517, *pg.* 1347
SCOPE WHITE - Mouth Rinse - THE PROCTER & GAMBLE COMPANY; *pg.* 1129, *pg.* 1418
SCOPESMITH - Optical Product - LEUPOLD & STEVENS, INC.; *pg.* 1420, *pg.* 1492
SCORA-ER 14 - Robot Designed for Work in Industrial

First page reference indicates Business Class Edition
Second page reference indicates Geographic Edition

Training Facilities - INTELITEK, INC.; *pg.* 1349, *pg.* 1036
SCORBASE - Robotics Programming & Control Software for Use with SCORBOT Robots - INTELITEK, INC.; *pg.* 1349, *pg.* 1036
SCORBOT-ER 4U - Robot for Educational Use - INTELITEK, INC.; *pg.* 1349, *pg.* 1036
SCORBOT-ER 5PLUS - Robotic System Designed for Laboratory & Training Applications - INTELITEK, INC.; *pg.* 1349, *pg.* 1036
SCORBOT-ER 9 - Robot Designed for Work in Industrial Training Facilities - INTELITEK, INC.; *pg.* 1349, *pg.* 1036
SCORCHER - Men's Boot - JACK SCHWARTZ SHOES, INC.; *pg.* 1810, *pg.* 1245
SCORCHSHIELD - Cover & Pad - HOME PRODUCTS INTERNATIONAL, INC.; *pg.* 1125, *pg.* 577
SCORE - Stand Bag - DATREK GOLF; *pg.* 1832, *pg.* 1801
SCORE! - After-School Learning Centers - KAPLAN, INC.; *pg.* 603, *pg.* 425
SCORE - Analysis Software - MEDTRONIC; *pg.* 1563, *pg.* 183
SCORE CARD - Apparel - OAKLEY, INC.; *pg.* 1840, *pg.* 86
SCORE POWER - Software - EQUIFAX INC.; *pg.* 748, *pg.* 504
SCORE WATCH - Software - EQUIFAX INC.; *pg.* 748, *pg.* 504
SCOREGUARD - Pump - NORDSON CORPORATION; *pg.* 1365, *pg.* 1480
SCOREITNOW - Online Writing Practice - EDUCATIONAL TESTING SERVICE INC.; *pg.* 1394, *pg.* 1111
SCORENET - Database Network System - FAIR ISAAC CORPORATION; *pg.* 1247, *pg.* 955
SCORNED WOMAN - Hot Sauce-Based Products - VITA FOOD PRODUCTS, INC.; *pg.* 909, *pg.* 595
SCORPIO - Modern Chipset - AVAGO TECHNOLOGIES; *pg.* 358, *pg.* 238
SCORPIO - Orthopaedic Product - STRYKER CORPORATION; *pg.* 1598, *pg.* 894
SCORPIO - Hard Drive - WESTERN DIGITAL CORPORATION; *pg.* 492, *pg.* 118
SCORPION - Footwear - CAPEZIO BALLET MAKERS INC.; *pg.* 1805, *pg.* 1125
SCORPION - Land Recording System - ION GEOPHYSICAL CORPORATION; *pg.* 1350, *pg.* 1708
SCORPION - Flashlight - STREAMLIGHT INC.; *pg.* 1306, *pg.* 1527
SCOT - Slow-Closing Omni-Temperature Lavatory Faucet - SYMMONS INDUSTRIES, INC.; *pg.* 114, *pg.* 803
SCOTCH - Adhesive Tapes - 3M COMPANY; *pg.* 1142, *pg.* 956
SCOTCH - Cleaning Product - HILLYARD, INC.; *pg.* 331, *pg.* 990
SCOTCH-BRITE - Cleaning System - 3M COMPANY; *pg.* 1142, *pg.* 956
SCOTCH-MOUNT - Double Coated Foam Tapes - 3M COMPANY; *pg.* 1142, *pg.* 956
SCOTCH-SEAL - Sealants - 3M COMPANY; *pg.* 1142, *pg.* 956
SCOTCH-WELD - Structural Adhesives - 3M COMPANY; *pg.* 1142, *pg.* 956
SCOTCHAL - Graphic Film - 3M COMPANY; *pg.* 1142, *pg.* 956
SCOTCHBLOK - Masking Paper - 3M COMPANY; *pg.* 1142, *pg.* 956
SCOTCHBOND - Dental Adhesive - 3M COMPANY; *pg.* 1142, *pg.* 956
SCOTCHBRICK - Cleaning System - 3M COMPANY; *pg.* 1142, *pg.* 956
SCOTCHCAL - Film, Colored Film Vinyl, Drag Reduction Tape - 3M COMPANY; *pg.* 1142, *pg.* 956
SCOTCHCAST - Duct Sealing Foam - 3M COMPANY; *pg.* 1142, *pg.* 956
SCOTCHCODE - Wire Markers, Cable I.D. - 3M COMPANY; *pg.* 1142, *pg.* 956
SCOTCHFIL - Electrical Insulation Putty - 3M COMPANY; *pg.* 1142, *pg.* 956
SCOTCHGARD - Fabric Protector - 3M COMPANY; *pg.* 1142, *pg.* 956
SCOTCHH - Footwear - STEVEN MADDEN, LTD.; *pg.* 1819, *pg.* 1176
SCOTCHKOTE - Epoxy Protective Coatings - 3M COMPANY; *pg.* 1142, *pg.* 956
SCOTCHLITE - Personal Safety Product - 3M COMPANY; *pg.* 1142, *pg.* 956
SCOTCHLOK - Compression Connectors - 3M COMPANY; *pg.* 1142, *pg.* 956
SCOTCHMAN - Hydraulic Ironworkers, Punches & Shears - SCOTCHMAN INDUSTRIES, INC.; *pg.* 1374, *pg.* 1624
SCOTCHMARK - Label Stock, Marking Films, Printable Tapes, Marker System - 3M COMPANY; *pg.* 1142, *pg.* 956
SCOTCHMATE - Hook & Loop Fasteners - 3M COMPANY; *pg.* 1142, *pg.* 956
SCOTCHPAD - Label Protection Tapes in Pad Form - 3M COMPANY; *pg.* 1142, *pg.* 956
SCOTCHPRO - Film Backing for PSA Tapes - 3M COMPANY; *pg.* 1142, *pg.* 956
SCOTCHRAP - Corrosion Protection Tape; Veterinary Bandage - 3M COMPANY; *pg.* 1142, *pg.* 956
SCOTCHTINT - Films - 3M COMPANY; *pg.* 1142, *pg.* 956
SCOTIA - Banking Service - THE BANK OF NOVA SCOTIA; *pg.* 721, *pg.* 1935
SCOTIA 2020 - Mobile Terminal - THE BANK OF NOVA SCOTIA; *pg.* 721, *pg.* 1935
SCOTIA BANKING ADVANTAGE - Banking Plan - THE BANK OF NOVA SCOTIA; *pg.* 721, *pg.* 1935
SCOTIA BUSINESS LINK - Fund Transfer - THE BANK OF NOVA SCOTIA; *pg.* 721, *pg.* 1935
SCOTIA CANAM - Money Market Fund - THE BANK OF NOVA SCOTIA; *pg.* 721, *pg.* 1935
SCOTIA DIRECT - Electronic Fund - THE BANK OF NOVA SCOTIA; *pg.* 721, *pg.* 1935
SCOTIA GAIN PLAN - Investment Savings Account - THE BANK OF NOVA SCOTIA; *pg.* 721, *pg.* 1935
SCOTIA LEASING - Banking Service - THE BANK OF NOVA SCOTIA; *pg.* 721, *pg.* 1935
SCOTIA ONLINE - Online Banking - THE BANK OF NOVA SCOTIA; *pg.* 721, *pg.* 1935
SCOTIA PLAN - Banking Service - THE BANK OF NOVA SCOTIA; *pg.* 721, *pg.* 1935
SCOTIA PLUS - Banking Service - THE BANK OF NOVA SCOTIA; *pg.* 721, *pg.* 1935
SCOTIA POWERCHEQUING - Banking Service - THE BANK OF NOVA SCOTIA; *pg.* 721, *pg.* 1935
SCOTIA PROFESSIONAL - Student Plan - THE BANK OF NOVA SCOTIA; *pg.* 721, *pg.* 1935
SCOTIA REWARDS - Banking Service - THE BANK OF NOVA SCOTIA; *pg.* 721, *pg.* 1935
SCOTIA TOTAL EQUITY - Banking Service - THE BANK OF NOVA SCOTIA; *pg.* 721, *pg.* 1935
SCOTIA ULTIMATE - Banking Service - THE BANK OF NOVA SCOTIA; *pg.* 721, *pg.* 1935
SCOTIA VALUE - Banking Plan - THE BANK OF NOVA SCOTIA; *pg.* 721, *pg.* 1935
SCOTIABANK VALUE - Banking Service - THE BANK OF NOVA SCOTIA; *pg.* 721, *pg.* 1935
SCOTIABANK.CA - Banking Service - THE BANK OF NOVA SCOTIA; *pg.* 721, *pg.* 1935
SCOTIABANK.COM - Banking Service - THE BANK OF NOVA SCOTIA; *pg.* 721, *pg.* 1935
SCOTIABUSINESS - Electronic Banking - THE BANK OF NOVA SCOTIA; *pg.* 721, *pg.* 1935
SCOTIABUSINESS ELECTRONIC BANKING - Electronic Banking - THE BANK OF NOVA SCOTIA; *pg.* 721, *pg.* 1935
SCOTIACARD - Banking Service - THE BANK OF NOVA SCOTIA; *pg.* 721, *pg.* 1935
SCOTIACLUB - Business Plan - THE BANK OF NOVA SCOTIA; *pg.* 721, *pg.* 1935
SCOTIACONNECT - Electronic Banking - THE BANK OF NOVA SCOTIA; *pg.* 721, *pg.* 1935
SCOTIAFARM - Banking Service - THE BANK OF NOVA SCOTIA; *pg.* 721, *pg.* 1935
SCOTIAGOLD - Insurance Program - THE BANK OF NOVA SCOTIA; *pg.* 721, *pg.* 1935
SCOTIAGOLD PASSPORT - Business Cardholder - THE BANK OF NOVA SCOTIA; *pg.* 721, *pg.* 1935
SCOTIALINE - Banking Service - THE BANK OF NOVA SCOTIA; *pg.* 721, *pg.* 1935
SCOTIAPAY - Banking Service - THE BANK OF NOVA SCOTIA; *pg.* 721, *pg.* 1935
SCOTS LION - Scotch - LAIRD & COMPANY, INC.; *pg.* 1966, *pg.* 1119
SCOTT - Paper Products - KIMBERLY-CLARK CORPORATION; *pg.* 1461, *pg.* 1720
SCOTT - Oats - PEPSICO, INC.; *pg.* 259, *pg.* 1327
SCOTT NATURALS - Paper Products - KIMBERLY-CLARK CORPORATION; *pg.* 1461, *pg.* 1720
SCOTT STAMP MONTHLY - Publication - AMOS PRESS, INC.; *pg.* 1616, *pg.* 1472
SCOTTISH HIGHLANDS - Carpet - BEAULIEU GROUP, LLC; *pg.* 917, *pg.* 529
SCOTTKOTE - Lawn & Garden Products - THE SCOTTS MIRACLE-GRO COMPANY; *pg.* 1799, *pg.* 1459
SCOTTRADE ELITE - Trading Services - SCOTTRADE, INC.; *pg.* 802, *pg.* 1003
SCOTTRADE.COM - Brokerage Firm - SCOTTRADE, INC.; *pg.* 802, *pg.* 1003
SCOTTRADER - Trading Quotes & Charts - SCOTTRADE, INC.; *pg.* 802, *pg.* 1003
SCOTT'S LIQUID GOLD - Wood Cleaner & Preservative - SCOTT'S LIQUID GOLD-INC.; *pg.* 335, *pg.* 323
SCOTT'S PORAGE OATS - Rolled Oats - THE QUAKER OATS COMPANY; *pg.* 834, *pg.* 588
SCOTT'S SO EASY OATS - Rolled Oats - THE QUAKER OATS COMPANY; *pg.* 834, *pg.* 588
SCOTTSAVE.COM - Brokerage Firm - SCOTTRADE, INC.; *pg.* 802, *pg.* 1003
SCOTTSBLUFF - Furniture - ASHLEY FURNITURE INDUSTRIES, INC.; *pg.* 914, *pg.* 1852
SCOTTSDALE - Lighting - LSI INDUSTRIES INC.; *pg.* 58, *pg.* 1416
SCOTTWARREN - Automobile Refinishing Paints - THE SHERWIN-WILLIAMS COMPANY; *pg.* 1447, *pg.* 1435
SCOTTY CAMERON - Golf Clubs - ACUSHNET COMPANY; *pg.* 1824, *pg.* 818
SCOTTY CANNON - Eyewear - OAKLEY, INC.; *pg.* 1840, *pg.* 86
SCOUPE - Fabric - NEMSCHOFF, INC.; *pg.* 936, *pg.* 1890
SCOUR-EASE - Milk Replacer - MANNA PRO CORPORATION; *pg.* 1478, *pg.* 975
SCOUR-EASE PLUS - Animal Nutrition Product - MANNA PRO CORPORATION; *pg.* 1478, *pg.* 975
SCOUT - Connector & Adapter - ALLIANCE FIBER OPTIC PRODUCTS, INC.; *pg.* 1399, *pg.* 283
SCOUT - Laser Rangefinder - BUSHNELL OUTDOOR PRODUCTS, INC.; *pg.* 1403, *pg.* 718
SCOUT - Material Handling Equipment - C&D TECHNOLOGIES, INC.; *pg.* 627, *pg.* 1517
SCOUT - Knife - COAST CUTLERY COMPANY; *pg.* 1121, *pg.* 1501
SCOUT - Medical Equipment - INVACARE CORPORATION; *pg.* 1546, *pg.* 1451
SCOUT - Fabric - NEMSCHOFF, INC.; *pg.* 936, *pg.* 1890
SCOUT - Spotting Scope - SWIFT OPTICAL INSTRUMENTS, INC.; *pg.* 1430, *pg.* 1744
SCOUT - Inspection Lighting System - UNILUX, INC.; *pg.* 682, *pg.* 1118
SCOUT - Remote Control Device - UNIVERSAL ELECTRONICS, INC.; *pg.* 683, *pg.* 262
SCOUTING MAGAZINE - Magazine - BOYS' LIFE MAGAZINE; *pg.* 1623, *pg.* 1206
SCOUTMARC - Medical Product - HOLOGIC, INC.; *pg.* 1416, *pg.* 784
SCOVEL - Casual Shoes - JOHNSTON & MURPHY CO.; *pg.* 1810, *pg.* 1651
SCR-1 - Loudspeaker - KLIPSCH GROUP, INC.; *pg.* 649, *pg.* 688
SCR-2 - Loudspeaker - KLIPSCH GROUP, INC.; *pg.* 649, *pg.* 688
SCR-3 - Loudspeaker - KLIPSCH GROUP, INC.; *pg.* 649, *pg.* 688
SCRABBLE - Game - HASBRO, INC.; *pg.* 954, *pg.* 1603
SCRABBLE - Lottery Game - IDAHO LOTTERY; *pg.* 995, *pg.* 547
SCRAM - Odor Control - SWISHER HYGIENE INC.; *pg.* 336, *pg.* 1507
SCRAMBLE - Apparel - OAKLEY, INC.; *pg.* 1840, *pg.* 86
SCRAMBLE SQUARES - Puzzle - B. DAZZLE, INC.; *pg.* 949, *pg.* 188
THE SCRAMBLED STATES OF AMERICA - Game - GAMEWRIGHT; *pg.* 953, *pg.* 836
SCRANTON PRODUCTS - Building Products - CPG INTERNATIONAL, INC.; *pg.* 1881, *pg.* 1586
SCRAP MANAGER - Tilting Rotary Furnace System - SECO/WARWICK CORPORATION; *pg.* 1076, *pg.* 1552
SCRAPBOOK CARDS - Notelets - LEANIN' TREE, INC.; *pg.* 1658, *pg.* 311
SCRAPBOOK PARTY - Video Game - INTERNATIONAL GAME TECHNOLOGY; *pg.* 957, *pg.* 1024
SCRAPBOOKS ETC. - Magazine - MEREDITH CORPORATION; *pg.* 1663, *pg.* 705
SCRAPMASTER - Food Waste Disposer - THE SALVAJOR COMPANY; *pg.* 60, *pg.* 986
SCRAPPER - Recycle/Reclaim Extruder - DAVIS-STANDARD LLC; *pg.* 1328, *pg.* 368
SCRAPVEYOR - Conveyor - PRAB, INC.; *pg.* 1369, *pg.* 894

SCRATCH - Lottery Games - MONTANA LOTTERY; *pg.* 1000, *pg.* 1008
SCRATCH A WILD - Game - WMS INDUSTRIES INC.; *pg.* 593, *pg.* 666
SCRATCH-FIX - Liquid Auto Touch-Up Paint - SHERWIN-WILLIAMS DIVERSIFIED BRANDS DIVISION; *pg.* 1448, *pg.* 1435
SCRATCH GAMES - Lottery Game - IDAHO LOTTERY; *pg.* 995, *pg.* 547
SCRATCH GAMES - Lottery Games - MINNESOTA STATE LOTTERY; *pg.* 999, *pg.* 956
SCRATCH GAMES - Instant Win Scratch Tickets - NEBRASKA LOTTERY; *pg.* 1000, *pg.* 1012
SCRATCH N' MATCH - Jackpot Game - DAILY NEWS, L.P.; *pg.* 1632, *pg.* 1221
SCRATCHERS - Lottery Games - ARIZONA LOTTERY; *pg.* 988, *pg.* 14
SCRATCHERS - Lottery Tickets - CALIFORNIA LOTTERY; *pg.* 990, *pg.* 196
SCRATCHERS - Lottery Game - MISSOURI LOTTERY; *pg.* 999, *pg.* 979
SCREAMER - Software - MONEY.NET, INC.; *pg.* 1268, *pg.* 1261
SCREAMER - Hats - SCREAMER INC.; *pg.* 12, *pg.* 1839
SCREAMIN EAGLE - Motorcycle - HARLEY-DAVIDSON, INC.; *pg.* 178, *pg.* 1874
SCREAMING 3D AUDIO - Audio System - QSOUND LABS, INC.; *pg.* 666, *pg.* 1904
SCREECHER - Security & Law Enforcement Products - MACE SECURITY INTERNATIONAL, INC.; *pg.* 1172, *pg.* 1541
SCREEDPRO - Paving System - TRIMBLE NAVIGATION LIMITED; *pg.* 1384, *pg.* 288
SCREEN-GUARD - Software - BIO-RAD LABORATORIES, INC.; *pg.* 1504, *pg.* 101
SCREEN STARS - Apparel for Imprinting - FRUIT OF THE LOOM, INC.; *pg.* 41, *pg.* 725
SCREENARRAY - Cinema System - HARMAN INTERNATIONAL INDUSTRIES, INCORPORATED; *pg.* 641, *pg.* 374
SCREENCODER - Touch Screen Controller - SEMTECH CORPORATION; *pg.* 671, *pg.* 57
SCREENFRONT - Grille Insert - LUND INTERNATIONAL, INC.; *pg.* 211, *pg.* 526
SCREENGARD - Perforated Rolling Door - CORNELL IRON WORKS, INC.; *pg.* 77, *pg.* 1554
SCREENING ROOM - Video Content Management Software - VERTICAL SEARCH WORKS INC.; *pg.* 489, *pg.* 1809
SCREENJUNKIES.COM - Website - DEFYMEDIA; *pg.* 1237, *pg.* 1222
SCREENPLAY - Shoe - AEROGROUP INTERNATIONAL, INC.; *pg.* 1803, *pg.* 1055
SCREENPLAY - Mobile Projector - INFOCUS CORPORATION; *pg.* 644, *pg.* 1503
SCREENSTATION - Software - MOLECULAR DEVICES CORPORATION; *pg.* 1568, *pg.* 287
SCREW-DOWN - Specialty Nails - W.H. MAZE COMPANY; *pg.* 1389, *pg.* 652
SCREW-IN - Commercial Lighting - SWIVELIER CO., INC.; *pg.* 1307, *pg.* 1142
SCREW-LIFT - Conveyor - SCREW CONVEYOR INDUSTRIES; *pg.* 1374, *pg.* 682
SCREW-SHOOTERS - Power Tools - MILWAUKEE ELECTRIC TOOL CORP.; *pg.* 1056, *pg.* 1855
SCREWLOOSE - Super-Penetrant - CRC INDUSTRIES, INC.; *pg.* 329, *pg.* 1590
SCREWPULL - Corkscrew - INTERNATIONAL WINE ACCESSORIES, INC.; *pg.* 1964, *pg.* 71
SCREWS-ZINCLAD - Hot-Dipped - W.H. MAZE COMPANY; *pg.* 1389, *pg.* 652
SCREWY - Hooks & Fittings - ESCO CORPORATION; *pg.* 1335, *pg.* 1502
SCRIBBLE - Dinnerware - THE HOMER LAUGHLIN CHINA COMPANY; *pg.* 1125, *pg.* 1850
SCRIBBLE - Carpet - INTERFACE, INC.; *pg.* 695, *pg.* 512
SCRIBBLE & WRITE - Educational Product - LEAPFROG ENTERPRISES, INC.; *pg.* 961, *pg.* 84
SCRIBBLE STUDIO - Educational Materials - SCHOLASTIC INC.; *pg.* 1683, *pg.* 1288
SCRIBE-RITE - Floor Protection System - FORTIFIBER CORPORATION; *pg.* 83, *pg.* 1021
SCRIBELINER - Marking System - GEORGE T. SCHMIDT, INC.; *pg.* 1340, *pg.* 637
SCRIBESMART - Scan and Laser Control - GSI GROUP INC.; *pg.* 1415, *pg.* 784
SCRIBNER - Adult Publishing Imprint - SIMON & SCHUSTER, INC.; *pg.* 1687, *pg.* 1292
SCRIBNER'S - Book Stores - BARNES & NOBLE, INC.; *pg.* 1619, *pg.* 1201
SCRIPPS MEDIA CENTER - Newspaper - THE E.W. SCRIPPS COMPANY; *pg.* 1639, *pg.* 1412
SCRIPPS PRODUCTIONS - Producer of Cable Television Programming - THE E.W. SCRIPPS COMPANY; *pg.* 1639, *pg.* 1412
SCRIPSET - Resins - HERCULES INCORPORATED; *pg.* 1166, *pg.* 392
SCRIPTGEN - Network Testing System - IXIA; *pg.* 422, *pg.* 56
SCRIPTLINE - Pharmaceutical Product - CARDINAL HEALTH, INC.; *pg.* 1512, *pg.* 1448
SCRIPTS - Programming Language - AVAGO TECHNOLOGIES; *pg.* 358, *pg.* 238
SCROLL - Chandeliers - CRAFTMADE INTERNATIONAL, INC.; *pg.* 1295, *pg.* 1670
SCROLL TOP - Game - WMS INDUSTRIES INC.; *pg.* 593, *pg.* 666
SCROO-ZON - File Product - SIMONDS INTERNATIONAL CORPORATION; *pg.* 1376, *pg.* 819
SCROOP - Bleached Cotton - BARNHARDT MANUFACTURING COMPANY; *pg.* 1498, *pg.* 1364
SCRU-LEAD - Wall Anchor - POWERS FASTENERS INC.; *pg.* 1059, *pg.* 1143
SCRU-LOKT - Pump Product - IDEX CORPORATION; *pg.* 1347, *pg.* 623
SCRUB FREE - Cleaner - CHURCH & DWIGHT CO., INC.; *pg.* 1153, *pg.* 1063
SCRUB-IT - Scavenger & Odor Control - QUAKER CHEMICAL CORP.; *pg.* 1178, *pg.* 1524
SCRUB-VACTOR - Vacuum Pumps - CROLL-REYNOLDS COMPANY, INC.; *pg.* 1326, *pg.* 1103
SCRUBBA - Cleaning Pad - AMERICO MANUFACTURING CO., INC.; *pg.* 325, *pg.* 482
SCRUBBING BUBBLES - Cleaning Product - S.C. JOHNSON & SON, INC.; *pg.* 334, *pg.* 1889
SCRUBBING BUBBLES AEROSOL - Cleaner - S.C. JOHNSON & SON, INC.; *pg.* 334, *pg.* 1889
SCRUBBING BUBBLES FIZZ-ITS - Cleaner - S.C. JOHNSON & SON, INC.; *pg.* 334, *pg.* 1889
SCRUBBING BUBBLES FLUSHABLE - Cleaner - S.C. JOHNSON & SON, INC.; *pg.* 334, *pg.* 1889
SCRUBBING BUBBLES FRESH BRUSH - Cleaner - S.C. JOHNSON & SON, INC.; *pg.* 334, *pg.* 1889
SCRUBBING BUBBLES GEL BOWL - Cleaner - S.C. JOHNSON & SON, INC.; *pg.* 334, *pg.* 1889
SCRUBBING BUBBLES LEMON - Cleaner - S.C. JOHNSON & SON, INC.; *pg.* 334, *pg.* 1889
SCRUBBING BUBBLES MILDEW STAIN - Cleaner - S.C. JOHNSON & SON, INC.; *pg.* 334, *pg.* 1889
SCRUBBING BUBBLES SHOWER SHINE - Cleaner - S.C. JOHNSON & SON, INC.; *pg.* 334, *pg.* 1889
SCRUBBING BUBBLES SOAP SCUM - Cleaner - S.C. JOHNSON & SON, INC.; *pg.* 334, *pg.* 1889
SCRUBBLE - Household Product - ACS INDUSTRIES, INC.; *pg.* 1040, *pg.* 1602
SCRUBBY - Scrub Brush - BROWN & BIGELOW, INC.; *pg.* 1624, *pg.* 959
SCRUBMASTER - Cleaning Liquid - DELTA FOREMOST CHEMICAL CORPORATION; *pg.* 1155, *pg.* 1642
SCRUBMATE - Skin Care Product - STERIS CORPORATION; *pg.* 1597, *pg.* 1464
SCRUBOLT - Metal Building System - BUTLER MANUFACTURING COMPANY; *pg.* 72, *pg.* 981
SCRUBSTER - Cleaning Product - THE LIBMAN COMPANY; *pg.* 331, *pg.* 553
SCRUBZONE - Apparel - LANDAU UNIFORMS INCORPORATED; *pg.* 28, *pg.* 971
SCT (SPECTRUM CONTROL TECHNOLOGY) - Special Lens Technology - UVEX SAFETY; *pg.* 1433, *pg.* 1608
SCUBA - Electro-Hydraulic Activator - RODNEY HUNT COMPANY; *pg.* 1372, *pg.* 840
SCUBAPRO - Snorkeling & Underwater Diving Equipment - JOHNSON OUTDOORS INC.; *pg.* 1837, *pg.* 1888
SCUFF GUARD - Deck Stain - PPG INDUSTRIES, INC.; *pg.* 1445, *pg.* 1579
SCUFFIE FOOTLIGHTS - Slippers - RELIABLE OF MILWAUKEE; *pg.* 698, *pg.* 1879
SCUFFIES - Slippers - RELIABLE OF MILWAUKEE; *pg.* 698, *pg.* 1879
SCULPTING FOAM - Hair Care Product - JOHN PAUL MITCHELL SYSTEMS; *pg.* 512, *pg.* 133
SCULPTURE - Footwear - CAPEZIO BALLET MAKERS INC.; *pg.* 1805, *pg.* 1125
SCULPTURED ENDOSTATS - Disposable Instrument - AMERICAN MEDICAL SYSTEMS, INC.; *pg.* 1399, *pg.* 238
SCUNCI - Hair Accessory - CONAIR CORPORATION; *pg.* 505, *pg.* 1055
SCW-2 - Loudspeaker - KLIPSCH GROUP, INC.; *pg.* 649, *pg.* 688
SD - Memory Card Device - SANDISK CORPORATION; *pg.* 465, *pg.* 147
SD 100 - Personal Care Product - WESTROCK COMPANY; *pg.* 1472, *pg.* 1805
SD 1000 - Traction Drives - MAGNETEK, INC.; *pg.* 1301, *pg.* 1870
SD-1000 - Severe Duty Control Valves - SPX PROCESS EQUIPMENT; *pg.* 1378, *pg.* 1551
SD 200 - Personal Care Product - WESTROCK COMPANY; *pg.* 1472, *pg.* 1805
SD 20C - Personal Care Product - WESTROCK COMPANY; *pg.* 1472, *pg.* 1805
SD 300 E - Rotary Drilling Rig - THE GEORGE E. FAILING COMPANY; *pg.* 1340, *pg.* 1484
SD 400T - Personal Care Product - WESTROCK COMPANY; *pg.* 1472, *pg.* 1805
SD 500 - Traction Drives - MAGNETEK, INC.; *pg.* 1301, *pg.* 1870
SD 800T - Personal Care Product - WESTROCK COMPANY; *pg.* 1472, *pg.* 1805
SDA - Cleaning Product - THE AMERICAN CLEANING INSTITUTE; *pg.* 127, *pg.* 394
SDC - Financial Publications - THOMSON REUTERS CORPORATION; *pg.* 1693, *pg.* 1944
SDC CAMPGROUND - Entertainment Product - HERSCHEND FAMILY ENTERTAINMENT CORP.; *pg.* 552, *pg.* 973
SDC PLATINUM - Software - THOMSON REUTERS CORPORATION; *pg.* 1693, *pg.* 1944
SDF - Software System - MENTOR GRAPHICS CORPORATION; *pg.* 432, *pg.* 1510
SDHC - Memory Card - SANDISK CORPORATION; *pg.* 465, *pg.* 147
SDIO HX - Software - BSQUARE CORPORATION; *pg.* 366, *pg.* 1813
SDK - Software Development Kit for UMC - ATTACHMATE CORPORATION; *pg.* 356, *pg.* 1833
SDK - Printing Product - ELECTRONICS FOR IMAGING, INC.; *pg.* 390, *pg.* 88
SDM - Air Separator, High Efficiency - STURTEVANT INC.; *pg.* 1379, *pg.* 824
SDMO - Connector - MOLEX INCORPORATED; *pg.* 655, *pg.* 628
SDMS - Storage Management System - AVAGO TECHNOLOGIES; *pg.* 358, *pg.* 238
SDMS - Software - EMC CORPORATION; *pg.* 391, *pg.* 825
SDQ - Battery Monitor & Single Wire Serial Interface - TEXAS INSTRUMENTS INCORPORATED; *pg.* 679, *pg.* 1688
SDS - Gas Delivery System - ATMI, INC.; *pg.* 1314, *pg.* 342
SDS - Balloon - CONTINENTAL AMERICAN CORP.; *pg.* 1880, *pg.* 723
SDS - Student Detection System - ROSTRA PRECISION CONTROLS, INC.; *pg.* 216, *pg.* 1381
SDS - Paper Testing Machines - SONOCO PRODUCTS COMPANY; *pg.* 1469, *pg.* 1619
SDS - Home & Garden Product - WESTROCK COMPANY; *pg.* 1472, *pg.* 1805
SDS-MAX - Carbide Drill Bit - POWERS FASTENERS INC.; *pg.* 1059, *pg.* 1143
SDX - Lighting System - LITECONTROL CORPORATION; *pg.* 1301, *pg.* 841
SDX-300 - Service Deployment System - JUNIPER NETWORKS, INC.; *pg.* 1260, *pg.* 286
SE 300 ULTRA - Solder Paste Inspection - CYBEROPTICS CORPORATION; *pg.* 1408, *pg.* 925
SE-4 - Stimulator - MEDTRONIC, INC.; *pg.* 1564, *pg.* 939
SE-CURE - Encapsulant - KESTER, INC.; *pg.* 649, *pg.* 620
SE SOAPBAR - Guitar - PAUL REED SMITH GUITARS; *pg.* 574, *pg.* 779
SE500 - Solder Paste Inspection - CYBEROPTICS CORPORATION; *pg.* 1408, *pg.* 925
SEA ALASKA - Seafood - TRIDENT SEAFOODS CORPORATION; *pg.* 902, *pg.* 1842
SEA & LEARN - Baby Care Product - MUNCHKIN, INC.; *pg.* 964, *pg.* 300
SEA BAND - Dive Travel Product - MCNETT CORPORATION; *pg.* 1839, *pg.* 1817
SEA BEAM - Flashlight - ENERGIZER HOLDINGS, INC.; *pg.* 637, *pg.* 996

SEA-BOND - Denture Adhesive - COMBE INCORPORATED; *pg.* 1516, *pg.* 1351
SEA BREEZE - Personal Care Electrical Product - HELEN OF TROY L.P.; *pg.* 511, *pg.* 1692
SEA BUCKTHORN - Hair & Skin Product - AUBREY ORGANICS INC.; *pg.* 499, *pg.* 470
SEA BUFF - Anti-Fog Product - MCNETT CORPORATION; *pg.* 1839, *pg.* 1817
SEA CHOICE - Frozen Fillets - OCEAN BEAUTY SEAFOODS, INC.; *pg.* 1028, *pg.* 1838
SEA CLOUD - Watch - GEVRIL USA; *pg.* 6, *pg.* 1348
SEA COVE GALLERY - Deluxe Cards - LEANIN' TREE, INC.; *pg.* 1658, *pg.* 311
SEA CUISINE - Frozen Seafood - HIGH LINER FOODS INCORPORATED; *pg.* 862, *pg.* 1917
SEA-DOO - Recreational Vehicle - BOMBARDIER RECREATIONAL PRODUCTS, INC.; *pg.* 201, *pg.* 1960
SEA DROPS - Anti-Fog Product - MCNETT CORPORATION; *pg.* 1839, *pg.* 1817
SEA EAGLE - Inflatable Boats - SEA EAGLE BOATS; *pg.* 1845, *pg.* 1322
SEA FRIENDS - Children's Toothbrushes - SUNSTAR AMERICAS INC.; *pg.* 1599, *pg.* 591
SEA GOLD - Anti-Fog Product - MCNETT CORPORATION; *pg.* 1839, *pg.* 1817
SEA-GREEN - Household Insect Control - BONIDE PRODUCTS, INC.; *pg.* 1794, *pg.* 1320
SEA GUARD - Biocides for Use in Marine Anti-Foulant Applications - DOW CHEMICAL; *pg.* 1156, *pg.* 1563
SEA GUARD - Fishing Hook Finish - WRIGHT & MCGILL CO.; *pg.* 1848, *pg.* 324
SEA HAG IPA - Beer - NEW ENGLAND BREWING COMPANY; *pg.* 1967, *pg.* 386
SEA HAWK - Binoculars - SWIFT OPTICAL INSTRUMENTS, INC.; *pg.* 1430, *pg.* 1744
SEA ICE - Anti-Fog Product - MCNETT CORPORATION; *pg.* 1839, *pg.* 1817
SEA ISLAND - Residential Resort & Development - SEA ISLAND ACQUISITION LLC; *pg.* 1111, *pg.* 540
SEA KING - Binoculars - SWIFT OPTICAL INSTRUMENTS, INC.; *pg.* 1430, *pg.* 1744
SEA MONKEYS - Educational Toy - EDUCATIONAL INSIGHTS, INC.; *pg.* 951, *pg.* 187
SEA-NINE - Marine Antifouling Agent - DOW CHEMICAL; *pg.* 1156, *pg.* 1563
SEA OF GOLD - Container Grown Plant - MONROVIA GROWERS; *pg.* 1797, *pg.* 44
SEA OMEGA - Pharmaceutical Product - ALLERGAN; *pg.* 1490, *pg.* 1101
SEA PINES - Resort - SEA PINES RESORT, LLC; *pg.* 1112, *pg.* 1620
SEA QUICK - Anti-Fog Product - MCNETT CORPORATION; *pg.* 1839, *pg.* 1817
SEA RAM - Missile Defense System - RAYTHEON COMPANY; *pg.* 233, *pg.* 854
SEA RAY - Boats - BRUNSWICK CORPORATION; *pg.* 1828, *pg.* 623
SEA RAY - Boat - SEA RAY BOATS, INC.; *pg.* 1710, *pg.* 1638
SEA RAY LEGACY - Boat - SEA RAY BOATS, INC.; *pg.* 1710, *pg.* 1638
SEA RAY LIVING - Boat - SEA RAY BOATS, INC.; *pg.* 1710, *pg.* 1638
SEA RAY NAVIGATOR - Boat - SEA RAY BOATS, INC.; *pg.* 1710, *pg.* 1638
SEA RAY YACHT RENDEZVOUS - Boat - SEA RAY BOATS, INC.; *pg.* 1710, *pg.* 1638
SEA-RICH - Lawn Care Product - GARDENS ALIVE!, INC.; *pg.* 1796, *pg.* 693
SEA SALT - Kitchen Product - KOHLER CO.; *pg.* 91, *pg.* 1862
SEA SENTINEL - Undersea Surveillance System - LOCKHEED MARTIN CORPORATION; *pg.* 229, *pg.* 762
SEA SHELLS - Dinnerware - THE HOMER LAUGHLIN CHINA COMPANY; *pg.* 1125, *pg.* 1850
SEA SHELTER - Mounting Bracket - ACR ELECTRONICS, INC.; *pg.* 612, *pg.* 422
SEA SPA - Hair & Skin Product - AUBREY ORGANICS INC.; *pg.* 499, *pg.* 470
SEA-SPRAY - Fabric - NEMSCHOFF, INC.; *pg.* 936, *pg.* 1890
SEA STARSAFIRE - Thermal Imaging System - FLIR SYSTEMS, INC.; *pg.* 1413, *pg.* 1510
SEA TALON - Acoustic Sensor System - LOCKHEED MARTIN CORPORATION; *pg.* 229, *pg.* 762
SEA TREASURES - Slots - INTERNATIONAL GAME TECHNOLOGY; *pg.* 957, *pg.* 1024
SEA VUE - Surveillance Radar - RAYTHEON COMPANY; *pg.* 233, *pg.* 854
SEA WOLF - Binoculars - SWIFT OPTICAL INSTRUMENTS, INC.; *pg.* 1430, *pg.* 1744
SEA WONDERS - Natural Spa - AUBREY ORGANICS INC.; *pg.* 499, *pg.* 470
SEA WYNDE RUM - Rum - CASTLE BRANDS INC.; *pg.* 239, *pg.* 1209
SEABLENDS - Surimi Analogs - PETER PAN SEAFOODS, INC.; *pg.* 889, *pg.* 1838
SEABLUE - In-Ground Vinyl Pools - POOL CORPORATION; *pg.* 1843, *pg.* 743
SEABORG - Toy & Game - HASBRO, INC.; *pg.* 954, *pg.* 1603
SEABREEZE - Cooler - THERMOS L.L.C.; *pg.* 61, *pg.* 660
SEABROOK - Retirement Community - ERICKSON LIVING; *pg.* 1090, *pg.* 766
SEACEL - Magnesium Silver Chloride Batteries - YARDNEY TECHNICAL PRODUCTS, INC.; *pg.* 690, *pg.* 1601
SEACHEM - Pet Product - PETSMART, INC.; *pg.* 1481, *pg.* 18
SEACOM - Acoustical Device - DUKANE CORPORATION; *pg.* 634, *pg.* 658
SEAD - Development Board - IMAGINATION TECHNOLOGIES; *pg.* 412, *pg.* 285
SEAD-2 - Development Board - IMAGINATION TECHNOLOGIES; *pg.* 412, *pg.* 285
SEADREAM - Bath Product - KOHLER CO.; *pg.* 91, *pg.* 1862
SEAFARER - Fiberglass Boat Product - GRADY-WHITE BOATS, INC.; *pg.* 1707, *pg.* 1377
SEAFARER - Eyewear - MAUI JIM, INC.; *pg.* 9, *pg.* 651
SEAFARER'S - Salt - CARGILL LIMITED; *pg.* 1475, *pg.* 1914
SEAFAST - Stainless Steel Product - CARPENTER TECHNOLOGY CORPORATION; *pg.* 73, *pg.* 1584
SEAFLIR - Thermal Imaging System - FLIR SYSTEMS, INC.; *pg.* 1413, *pg.* 1510
SEAFOAM - Chocolate Candy - ROCKY MOUNTAIN CHOCOLATE FACTORY, INC.; *pg.* 1032, *pg.* 324
SEAFOOD BAR & GRILL - Slogan - FLANIGAN'S ENTERPRISES, INC.; *pg.* 1963, *pg.* 425
SEAFORTH - Bath Product - KOHLER CO.; *pg.* 91, *pg.* 1862
SEAFRESH - Seafood - HIGH LINER FOODS INCORPORATED; *pg.* 862, *pg.* 1917
SEAGATE - Carpet - BEAULIEU GROUP, LLC; *pg.* 917, *pg.* 529
SEAGRAMS - Soft Drink - THE COCA-COLA COMPANY; *pg.* 240, *pg.* 493
SEAGRAM'S - Gin - PERNOD RICARD USA, INC.; *pg.* 1968, *pg.* 1332
SEAGRASS - Table Tray - ETHAN ALLEN INTERIORS INC.; *pg.* 924, *pg.* 343
SEAGRASS - Fabric - NEMSCHOFF, INC.; *pg.* 936, *pg.* 1890
SEAGRAV - Gravity Meter - SCINTREX LTD.; *pg.* 1374, *pg.* 1920
SEAKEM - Food Ingredient - FMC CORPORATION; *pg.* 1163, *pg.* 1564
SEAL - Repair Clamp - ROMAC INDUSTRIES, INC.; *pg.* 1061, *pg.* 1818
SEAL 341 - Cleaning Product - HILLYARD, INC.; *pg.* 331, *pg.* 990
SEAL-A-RIDGE - Hip & Ridge Shingles - GAF MATERIALS CORP.; *pg.* 83, *pg.* 1681
SEAL& PROTECT - Dental Product - DENTSPLY INTERNATIONAL INC.; *pg.* 1522, *pg.* 1596
SEAL AND SHINE - Hair Care Product - JOHN PAUL MITCHELL SYSTEMS; *pg.* 512, *pg.* 133
SEAL & VIEW - Label Protectors - SMEAD MANUFACTURING COMPANY; *pg.* 470, *pg.* 926
SEAL CEMENT - Adhesive & Sealant - MCNETT CORPORATION; *pg.* 1839, *pg.* 1817
SEAL-CONNECT - Seal & Thermoplastic Component - GREENE, TWEED & CO.; *pg.* 1344, *pg.* 1544
SEAL-GRIP - Coating Product - PPG INDUSTRIES, INC.; *pg.* 1445, *pg.* 1579
SEAL KING - Low Profile Secondary Seal - HMT LLC; *pg.* 979, *pg.* 1747
SEAL-N-RIP - Plastic Bag - ELKAY PLASTICS COMPANY, INC.; *pg.* 1882, *pg.* 68
THE SEAL OF GOOD TASTE - Tagline - NEW ENGLAND APPLE ASSOCIATION; *pg.* 151, *pg.* 824
SEAL SAVER - Lubricant & Protectant - MCNETT CORPORATION; *pg.* 1839, *pg.* 1817
SEAL SENTRY - Control & Detection System - NORDSON CORPORATION; *pg.* 1365, *pg.* 1480
SEAL-TITE - Truck Storage Box - LUND INTERNATIONAL, INC.; *pg.* 211, *pg.* 526
SEAL-TRIM - Trimmer Capacitor - JOHANSON MANUFACTURING CORPORATION; *pg.* 648, *pg.* 1045
SEAL WRAP - Plastics Product - AEP INDUSTRIES INC.; *pg.* 1878, *pg.* 1085
SEAL-X - Control Stations - KILLARK ELECTRIC; *pg.* 1300, *pg.* 998
SEALAIR - Windows - KAWNEER COMPANY, INC.; *pg.* 90, *pg.* 537
SEALAMEAL - Home Vacuum Packaging Systems - JARDEN CONSUMER SOLUTIONS; *pg.* 57, *pg.* 412
SEALASTIN - Skin Care Product - NU SKIN ENTERPRISES, INC.; *pg.* 518, *pg.* 1755
SEALCLAMP - Muffler Clamp - DONALDSON COMPANY, INC.; *pg.* 1329, *pg.* 917
SEALED AIR - Packaging Materials - SEALED AIR CORPORATION; *pg.* 1468, *pg.* 1058
SEALED POWER - Engine Parts - FEDERAL-MOGUL HOLDINGS CORPORATION; *pg.* 205, *pg.* 907
SEALED-SAFE - Membrane End Closure - SONOCO PRODUCTS COMPANY; *pg.* 1469, *pg.* 1619
SEALED SHOT - Direct Vent Water Heater - A.O. SMITH CORPORATION; *pg.* 1313, *pg.* 1872
SEALEGS - Seafood - TRIDENT SEAFOODS CORPORATION; *pg.* 902, *pg.* 1842
SEALEZE - Brush - JASON INDUSTRIES, INC.; *pg.* 208, *pg.* 1875
SEALICIOUS - Seafood Products - GREAT NORTHERN PRODUCTS, LTD.; *pg.* 859, *pg.* 1609
SEALINE - Rods & Reels - DAIWA CORPORATION; *pg.* 1832, *pg.* 75
SEALINE BR - Saltwater Spinning Reels - DAIWA CORPORATION; *pg.* 1832, *pg.* 75
SEALINE H - Conventional Trolling Reels - DAIWA CORPORATION; *pg.* 1832, *pg.* 75
SEALINE LCA - Conventional Trolling Reels - DAIWA CORPORATION; *pg.* 1832, *pg.* 75
SEALINE LEVER DRAG - Conventional Trolling Reels - DAIWA CORPORATION; *pg.* 1832, *pg.* 75
SEALINE SGH - Conventional Trolling Reels - DAIWA CORPORATION; *pg.* 1832, *pg.* 75
SEALINE SL-D - Conventional Trolling Reels - DAIWA CORPORATION; *pg.* 1832, *pg.* 75
SEALINE SL-SH - Conventional Trolling Reels - DAIWA CORPORATION; *pg.* 1832, *pg.* 75
SEALINE SL-T - Conventional Trolling Reels - DAIWA CORPORATION; *pg.* 1832, *pg.* 75
SEALINE TOURNAMENT - Graphite Rods & Ocean Reels - DAIWA CORPORATION; *pg.* 1832, *pg.* 75
SEALINE X-HC - Conventional Trolling Reels - DAIWA CORPORATION; *pg.* 1832, *pg.* 75
SEALINE X-HV - Conventional Trolling Reels - DAIWA CORPORATION; *pg.* 1832, *pg.* 75
SEALING WITH CERTAINTY - Gasket - W.L. GORE & ASSOCIATES, INC.; *pg.* 122, *pg.* 388
SEALKLEEN - Filter Cartridge - PALL CORPORATION; *pg.* 232, *pg.* 1323
SEALMASTER - Corrugating & Bag - GRAIN PROCESSING CORPORATION; *pg.* 859, *pg.* 709
SEALMASTER - Plumbing Product - RADIATOR SPECIALTY COMPANY; *pg.* 215, *pg.* 1380
SEAL'N PEEL - Caulk And Sealant - DAP PRODUCTS, INC.; *pg.* 1441, *pg.* 756
SEAL'N RESEAL - Envelopes - TENSION ENVELOPE CORPORATION; *pg.* 483, *pg.* 986
SEALTEST - Dairy Products, Dips & Juices - AGROPUR COOPERATIVE; *pg.* 836, *pg.* 1950
SEALTIGHT - Pumps - IDEX CORPORATION; *pg.* 1347, *pg.* 623
SEALTITE - Sleeve & Leg Cuffs - STANDARD SAFETY EQUIPMENT CO.; *pg.* 1379, *pg.* 632
SEALY - Mattresses - ASHLEY FURNITURE INDUSTRIES, INC.; *pg.* 914, *pg.* 1852
SEALY - Mattresses - TEMPUR SEALY INTERNATIONAL, INC.; *pg.* 944, *pg.* 731
SEALY BACK SAVER - Mattresses - SEALY CORPORATION; *pg.* 942, *pg.* 1391
SEALY CORRECT COMFORT - Mattresses - SEALY CORPORATION; *pg.* 942, *pg.* 1391
SEALY KIDS - Mattresses - SEALY CORPORATION; *pg.* 942, *pg.* 1391
SEALY POSTURE PREMIER - Mattresses - SEALY

CORPORATION; *pg.* 942, *pg.* 1391
SEALY POSTUREMATIC - Mattresses - SEALY CORPORATION; *pg.* 942, *pg.* 1391
SEALY POSTUREPEDIC - Bedding - SEALY CORPORATION; *pg.* 942, *pg.* 1391
SEALY POSTUREPEDIC CROWN JEWEL - Mattresses - SEALY CORPORATION; *pg.* 942, *pg.* 1391
SEALY POSTURPEDIC - Mattresses - TEMPUR SEALY INTERNATIONAL, INC.; *pg.* 944, *pg.* 731
SEAM CLEANER - Cleaner & Rejuvenator - MCNETT CORPORATION; *pg.* 1839, *pg.* 1817
SEAM GRIP - Adhesive & Seam Sealer - MCNETT CORPORATION; *pg.* 1839, *pg.* 1817
SEAM SAVER - Box Cover - GARDNER DENVER NASH; *pg.* 1338, *pg.* 381
SEAM SURE - Adhesive & Seam Sealer - MCNETT CORPORATION; *pg.* 1839, *pg.* 1817
SEAMASTER CRUISES - Leisure Travel - CARLSON COMPANIES INC.; *pg.* 1084, *pg.* 947
SEAMFREE - Plastic Conveyor Belt - THE LAITRAM LLC; *pg.* 1354, *pg.* 744
SEAMGUARD - Cardiothoracic Product - W.L. GORE & ASSOCIATES, INC.; *pg.* 122, *pg.* 388
SEAMLESS MULLION - Thermal Window Framing Systems - KAWNEER COMPANY, INC.; *pg.* 90, *pg.* 537
SEAMLESS TUBE - Filter - MIDWESCO FILTER RESOURCES INC.; *pg.* 1464, *pg.* 1811
SEAMLESS WIDE SIGN - Seamless Flexible Back Lit Substrate Signs - COOLEY GROUP, INC.; *pg.* 691, *pg.* 1603
SEAMSTUFF - Seal - W.L. GORE & ASSOCIATES, INC.; *pg.* 122, *pg.* 388
SEAN JOHN - Sportswear - BAD BOY WORLDWIDE ENTERTAINMENT GROUP; *pg.* 270, *pg.* 1199
SEAN JOHN - Apparel - G-III APPAREL GROUP, LTD.; *pg.* 41, *pg.* 1233
SEAPAK - Insulated Tubing - O'BRIEN CORPORATION; *pg.* 1366, *pg.* 1001
SEAPAK - Seafood - RICH PRODUCTS CORPORATION; *pg.* 892, *pg.* 1150
SEARCH ALERT - Combination Locks - THE EASTERN COMPANY; *pg.* 1331, *pg.* 357
SEARCH-AND-LEARN - Software - SKILLSOFT PLC; *pg.* 470, *pg.* 1037
SEARCH FOR HEROES - Software - XEROX CORPORATION; *pg.* 494, *pg.* 365
SEARCH-GATE - Software - 3M; *pg.* 339, *pg.* 179
SEARCH THE SEARCH ENGINES! - Tag Line - BLUCORA; *pg.* 1232, *pg.* 1813
SEARCH390.COM - Website - TECHTARGET, INC.; *pg.* 482, *pg.* 837
SEARCH400.COM - Website - TECHTARGET, INC.; *pg.* 482, *pg.* 837
SEARCHCIO-MIDMARKET.COM - Website - TECHTARGET, INC.; *pg.* 482, *pg.* 837
SEARCHCIO.COM - Website - TECHTARGET, INC.; *pg.* 482, *pg.* 837
SEARCHCOMPLIANCE.COM - Website - TECHTARGET, INC.; *pg.* 482, *pg.* 837
SEARCHCRM.COM - Website - TECHTARGET, INC.; *pg.* 482, *pg.* 837
SEARCHDATABACKUP.COM - Website - TECHTARGET, INC.; *pg.* 482, *pg.* 837
SEARCHDATAMANAGEMENT.COM - Website - TECHTARGET, INC.; *pg.* 482, *pg.* 837
SEARCHDISASTERRECOVERY.COM - Website - TECHTARGET, INC.; *pg.* 482, *pg.* 837
SEARCHDOMINO.COM - Website - TECHTARGET, INC.; *pg.* 482, *pg.* 837
SEARCHENGINESMART - Software - ARI NETWORK SERVICES, INC.; *pg.* 353, *pg.* 1873
SEARCHENTERPRISEDESKTOP.COM - Website - TECHTARGET, INC.; *pg.* 482, *pg.* 837
SEARCHENTERPRISEWAN.COM - Website - TECHTARGET, INC.; *pg.* 482, *pg.* 837
SEARCHER - Spotting Scope - SWIFT OPTICAL INSTRUMENTS, INC.; *pg.* 1430, *pg.* 1744
SEARCHEXCHANGE.COM - Website - TECHTARGET, INC.; *pg.* 482, *pg.* 837
SEARCHFINANCIALSECURITY.COM - Website - TECHTARGET, INC.; *pg.* 482, *pg.* 837
SEARCHIT - Software - BIO-RAD LABORATORIES, INC.; *pg.* 1504, *pg.* 101
SEARCHLIGHT - Canned Salmon - OCEAN BEAUTY SEAFOODS, INC.; *pg.* 1028, *pg.* 1838
SEARCHLITE - Glass & Ceramic Material - CORNING INCORPORATED; *pg.* 1122, *pg.* 1154
SEARCHMANUFACTURINGERP.COM - Website - TECHTARGET, INC.; *pg.* 482, *pg.* 837
SEARCHMASTER - Software - BIO-RAD LABORATORIES, INC.; *pg.* 1504, *pg.* 101
SEARCHMIDMARKETSECURITY.COM - Website - TECHTARGET, INC.; *pg.* 482, *pg.* 837
SEARCHMOBILECOMPUTING.COM - Website - TECHTARGET, INC.; *pg.* 482, *pg.* 837
SEARCHNETWORKING.COM - Website - TECHTARGET, INC.; *pg.* 482, *pg.* 837
SEARCHORACLE.COM - Website - TECHTARGET, INC.; *pg.* 482, *pg.* 837
SEARCHSAP.COM - Website - TECHTARGET, INC.; *pg.* 482, *pg.* 837
SEARCHSECURITYCHANNEL.COM - Website - TECHTARGET, INC.; *pg.* 482, *pg.* 837
SEARCHSECURITY.COM - Website - TECHTARGET, INC.; *pg.* 482, *pg.* 837
SEARCHSECURITY.CO.UK - Website - TECHTARGET, INC.; *pg.* 482, *pg.* 837
SEARCHSMBSTORAGE.COM - Website - TECHTARGET, INC.; *pg.* 482, *pg.* 837
SEARCHSQLSERVER.COM - Website - TECHTARGET, INC.; *pg.* 482, *pg.* 837
SEARCHSTORAGE.COM - Website - TECHTARGET, INC.; *pg.* 482, *pg.* 837
SEARCHSTORAGE.CO.UK - Website - TECHTARGET, INC.; *pg.* 482, *pg.* 837
SEARCHTELECOM.COM - Website - TECHTARGET, INC.; *pg.* 482, *pg.* 837
SEARCHUNIFIEDCOMMUNICATIONS.COM - Website - TECHTARGET, INC.; *pg.* 482, *pg.* 837
SEARCHVB.COM - Website - TECHTARGET, INC.; *pg.* 482, *pg.* 837
SEARCHWEBSERVICES.COM - Website - TECHTARGET, INC.; *pg.* 482, *pg.* 837
SEARCHWIN2000.COM - Website - TECHTARGET, INC.; *pg.* 482, *pg.* 837
SEARCHWINDOWSSERVER.COM - Website - TECHTARGET, INC.; *pg.* 482, *pg.* 837
SEARCHWINIT.COM - Website - TECHTARGET, INC.; *pg.* 482, *pg.* 837
SEARCHWINSYSTEMS.COM - Website - TECHTARGET, INC.; *pg.* 482, *pg.* 837
SEARS - Carpet & Upholstery Care Program - SEARS CANADA INC.; *pg.* 1784, *pg.* 1943
SEARS - Retail Services - SEARS HOLDINGS CORPORATION; *pg.* 1784, *pg.* 618
SEARS AUTO CENTERS - Retail Automotive Services - SEARS HOLDINGS CORPORATION; *pg.* 1784, *pg.* 618
SEARS CANADA - Retail Services - SEARS HOLDINGS CORPORATION; *pg.* 1784, *pg.* 618
SEARS CANADA-CASUAL MALE - Clothing - DESTINATION XL GROUP, INC.; *pg.* 40, *pg.* 810
SEARS CARD - Cash Card - CITIGROUP INC.; *pg.* 735, *pg.* 1212
SEARS CARD - Credit Card Services - SEARS HOLDINGS CORPORATION; *pg.* 1784, *pg.* 618
SEARS FLOOR COVERINGS - Floor Coovering - SEARS CANADA INC.; *pg.* 1784, *pg.* 1943
SEARS HARDWARE - Retail Store Services - SEARS HOLDINGS CORPORATION; *pg.* 1784, *pg.* 618
SEARS HOME SERVICES - Home Improvement Services - SEARS HOLDINGS CORPORATION; *pg.* 1784, *pg.* 618
SEARS MEXICO - Retail Services - SEARS HOLDINGS CORPORATION; *pg.* 1784, *pg.* 618
SEARS POINT RACEWAY - Entertainment Venue - SPEEDWAY MOTORSPORTS, INC.; *pg.* 584, *pg.* 1370
SEARS PREMIER CARD - Credit Card Services - SEARS HOLDINGS CORPORATION; *pg.* 1784, *pg.* 618
SEARS.COM - Website - SEARS HOLDINGS CORPORATION; *pg.* 1784, *pg.* 618
SEASAFE - Fiberglass Grating - ALABAMA METAL INDUSTRIES CORPORATION; *pg.* 65, *pg.* 1
SEASCAPE - Table Textile - HERITAGE LACE INC.; *pg.* 694, *pg.* 711
SEASHELL - Womens Clothing - JUNONIA LTD.; *pg.* 27, *pg.* 929
SEASHELLS - Seafood - TRIDENT SEAFOODS CORPORATION; *pg.* 902, *pg.* 1842
SEASON - Seafood - MANISCHEWITZ COMPANY; *pg.* 875, *pg.* 1097
SEASON OF JOY BOUQUET - Floral Bouquet - FTD GROUP, INC.; *pg.* 1795, *pg.* 608
SEASON PASS - Digital Video Recorder - TIVO INC.; *pg.* 313, *pg.* 251
SEASONEDCRISP - French Fries - J.R. SIMPLOT COMPANY; *pg.* 867, *pg.* 547
SEASONITE - Wood Treatment - AKZO NOBEL DECORATIVE PAINTS, USA; *pg.* 1439, *pg.* 1474
SEASONS - Table - BLATT BOWLING & BILLIARD CORP.; *pg.* 1827, *pg.* 1203
SEASONS 52 - Restaurant Chain - DARDEN RESTAURANTS, INC.; *pg.* 1724, *pg.* 453
SEASTAR - Chip - CRAY INC.; *pg.* 380, *pg.* 1834
SEASTAR - FISHERIED INFORMATION SERVICE - DIGITALGLOBE; *pg.* 227, *pg.* 1785
SEASTAR - Frozen Seafood - HIGH LINER FOODS; *pg.* 862, *pg.* 1796
SEASTAR - Systems Integration & Aeronautics - LOCKHEED MARTIN CORPORATION; *pg.* 229, *pg.* 762
SEASYDE - Footwear - STEVEN MADDEN, LTD.; *pg.* 1819, *pg.* 1176
SEATCUSHION - Cushion - TEMPUR SEALY INTERNATIONAL, INC.; *pg.* 944, *pg.* 731
SEATMAKER - Seat Cushion - INVACARE CORPORATION; *pg.* 1546, *pg.* 1451
SEATTLE - Guest Chairs - BERNHARDT DESIGN; *pg.* 918, *pg.* 1381
SEATTLE CITY LIGHT - Municipal Electric Utility - SEATTLE CITY LIGHT; *pg.* 1951, *pg.* 1839
SEATTLE HOMES & LIFESTYLES - Magazine - NETWORK COMMUNICATIONS INC.; *pg.* 1271, *pg.* 534
SEATTLE INTERNATIONAL - Breads - UNITED STATES BAKERY; *pg.* 907, *pg.* 1507
SEATTLE MARINERS - Baseball Team - THE BASEBALL CLUB OF SEATTLE, L.P.; *pg.* 532, *pg.* 1833
SEATTLE MOUNTAIN - Bean & Ground Coffee - COSTCO WHOLESALE CORPORATION; *pg.* 1765, *pg.* 1820
SEATTLE P-I.COM - Web Site - SEATTLE POST-INTELLIGENCER; *pg.* 1685, *pg.* 1839
SEATTLE POPS - Music - SEATTLE SYMPHONY ORCHESTRA; *pg.* 582, *pg.* 1840
SEATTLE POST-INTELLIGENCER - Newspaper - SEATTLE POST-INTELLIGENCER; *pg.* 1685, *pg.* 1839
THE SEATTLE POST-INTELLIGENCER - Newspaper - SEATTLE TIMES COMPANY; *pg.* 1685, *pg.* 1840
SEATTLE SEAHAWKS - Football Team - SEATTLE SEAHAWKS; *pg.* 582, *pg.* 1830
SEATTLE SYMPHONY - Educational & Entertainment Services - SEATTLE SYMPHONY ORCHESTRA; *pg.* 582, *pg.* 1840
THE SEATTLE TIMES - Newspaper - SEATTLE TIMES COMPANY; *pg.* 1685, *pg.* 1840
SEATTLE'S BEST COFFEE - Coffee - SEATTLE COFFEE COMPANY; *pg.* 265, *pg.* 1839
SEATTLE'S BEST COFFEE - Coffee - STARBUCKS CORPORATION; *pg.* 897, *pg.* 1840
SEAVISION - Lenses - ICARE INDUSTRIES, INC.; *pg.* 1417, *pg.* 463
SEAVISION DIVE - Mask - ICARE INDUSTRIES, INC.; *pg.* 1417, *pg.* 463
SEAWALL - Bath Product - KOHLER CO.; *pg.* 91, *pg.* 1862
SEAWARE - Hair & Skin Product - AUBREY ORGANICS INC.; *pg.* 499, *pg.* 470
SEAWAY - Mop Wringers - GEERPRES INC.; *pg.* 1339, *pg.* 901
SEAWAY - Private Label for Food Products - GIANT EAGLE AMERICAN SEAWAY FOODS; *pg.* 1020, *pg.* 1405
SEBAGO - Furniture - ETHAN ALLEN INTERIORS INC.; *pg.* 924, *pg.* 343
SEBAGO - Footwear - WOLVERINE WORLD WIDE, INC.; *pg.* 1822, *pg.* 905
SEBASTIAN SUN - Newspaper - THE E.W. SCRIPPS COMPANY; *pg.* 1639, *pg.* 1412
SEBEKA - Wine - E&J GALLO WINERY; *pg.* 1962, *pg.* 149
SEBRING - Protective Eyewear - SELLSTROM MANUFACTURING CO.; *pg.* 1428, *pg.* 659
SEC N DRY - Quick Dry Nail Polish - ORLY INTERNATIONAL, INC.; *pg.* 518, *pg.* 137
SECADOR - Moisture Free Cabinets - BEL-ART PRODUCTS, INC.; *pg.* 1879, *pg.* 1129
SECANT - Office Furniture - STEELCASE INC.; *pg.* 475, *pg.* 889
SECCCO - Footwear - STEVEN MADDEN, LTD.; *pg.* 1819, *pg.* 1176
SECHE - Professional Nail Technic - AMERICAN INTERNATIONAL INDUSTRIES COMPANY; *pg.* 498, *pg.*

First page reference indicates Business Class Edition
Second page reference indicates Geographic Edition

126
SECLUSION 3D - Apparel - CABELA'S INCORPORATED; *pg.* 535, *pg.* 1019
SECLUSION 3D OUTFITTER - Apparel - CABELA'S INCORPORATED; *pg.* 535, *pg.* 1019
SECNET 11 - Secure Wireless Local Area Network - HARRIS CORPORATION; *pg.* 642, *pg.* 439
SECO - Adjustable Speed Drive - DANAHER CORPORATION; *pg.* 1044, *pg.* 397
SECOAT - Chemical Product - OMNOVA SOLUTIONS INC; *pg.* 1176, *pg.* 1453
SECOMIX - Chemical Product - STEPAN COMPANY; *pg.* 1182, *pg.* 643
SECOND CUP - Coffee Shop - CARA OPERATIONS LIMITED; *pg.* 1720, *pg.* 1947
SECOND LOOK - Ceilings & Walls - ARMSTRONG WORLD INDUSTRIES, INC.; *pg.* 914, *pg.* 1545
SECOND LOOK - Computer-Aided Detection Devices - ICAD, INC.; *pg.* 643, *pg.* 1037
SECOND NATURE - Distribution of Energy - ALLIANT ENERGY CORPORATION; *pg.* 1933, *pg.* 1864
SECOND NATURE - Wall System - SMITH-MIDLAND CORPORATION; *pg.* 111, *pg.* 1795
SECOND NATURE - Egg Substitute - TREEHOUSE FOODS, INC.; *pg.* 901, *pg.* 649
SECOND SKIN SATIN - Apparel - VICTORIA'S SECRET STORES, LLC; *pg.* 1789, *pg.* 1471
SECONDNATURE - Pet Care Product - NESTLE PURINA PETCARE COMPANY; *pg.* 1479, *pg.* 1000
SECORE - Molecular Biology Product - THERMO FISHER SCIENTIFIC INC.; *pg.* 1602, *pg.* 61
SECOSOL - Chemical Product - STEPAN COMPANY; *pg.* 1182, *pg.* 643
SECREFLO - Synthetic Secretin - REPLIGEN CORPORATION; *pg.* 1589, *pg.* 854
SECRET - Personal & Beauty Product - THE PROCTER & GAMBLE COMPANY; *pg.* 1129, *pg.* 1418
SECRET FIT BELLY - Maternity Apparel Technology - DESTINATION MATERNITY CORPORATION; *pg.* 23, *pg.* 1563
SECRET RINGS - Educational Materials - SCHOLASTIC INC.; *pg.* 1683, *pg.* 1288
SECRETAGOGUE-ONE - Nutritional Supplement - MAXIMUM HUMAN PERFORMANCE, INC.; *pg.* 1559, *pg.* 1065
SECRETS OF THE RAINFOREST - Software - BIO-RAD LABORATORIES, INC.; *pg.* 1504, *pg.* 101
SECRYL - Chemical Product - OMNOVA SOLUTIONS INC; *pg.* 1176, *pg.* 1453
SECSCONNECT - Computer Software - CIMETRIX INCORPORATED; *pg.* 372, *pg.* 1756
SECSTRACE - Trace Data Software - MKS INSTRUMENTS, INC.; *pg.* 1362, *pg.* 781
SECTION - Apparel - OAKLEY, INC.; *pg.* 1840, *pg.* 86
SECTOR - Banking Software - JACK HENRY & ASSOCIATES, INC.; *pg.* 422, *pg.* 988
SECTOR - Apparel - OAKLEY, INC.; *pg.* 1840, *pg.* 86
SECTORTRACKER - Software - MONEY.NET, INC.; *pg.* 1268, *pg.* 1261
SECUR-A-MATIC - Automatic Safety Cover - POLYAIR INTER PACK INC.; *pg.* 1467, *pg.* 1941
SECUR-A-POOL - Protective Pool Covering - POLYAIR INTER PACK INC.; *pg.* 1467, *pg.* 1941
SECUR-FIT - Medical Product - STRYKER CORPORATION; *pg.* 1598, *pg.* 894
SECUR-LUX - Security Lighting - JUNO LIGHTING, INC.; *pg.* 1300, *pg.* 606
SECUR-VENT - Garage Door - WAYNE-DALTON CORP.; *pg.* 120, *pg.* 1465
SECURA - Pacemakers - MEDTRONIC, INC.; *pg.* 1564, *pg.* 939
SECURA FENCE - Safety Fencing - ALABAMA METAL INDUSTRIES CORPORATION; *pg.* 65, *pg.* 1
SECURA INTEGRATED - Hardware - VERIFONE SYSTEMS, INC.; *pg.* 487, *pg.* 251
SECURA LATH - Heavy-Duty Security Lathing - ALABAMA METAL INDUSTRIES CORPORATION; *pg.* 65, *pg.* 1
SECURALL - Hospital Security System - API HEALTHCARE CORP.; *pg.* 350, *pg.* 1860
SECURCORE - Microcontroller - ATMEL CORPORATION; *pg.* 621, *pg.* 238
SECURE - Door Lock - SOUTHCO, INC.; *pg.* 1063, *pg.* 1522
SECURE - Patient Handling Equipment - STRYKER CORPORATION; *pg.* 1598, *pg.* 894
SECURE BACKUP - Software - WEBROOT SOFTWARE, INC.; *pg.* 1289, *pg.* 313
SECURE BY DESIGN - Break Resistant Glass - ODL INCORPORATED; *pg.* 101, *pg.* 914
SECURE CHECKFLOW ENTERPRISE - Software - TROY GROUP INC.; *pg.* 485, *pg.* 71
SECURE CLIENTCONNECT - Web Tool - OPENCONNECT SYSTEMS, INC.; *pg.* 449, *pg.* 1685
SECURE COM PORT REDIRECTOR - Software - LANTRONIX, INC.; *pg.* 426, *pg.* 112
SECURE COPY - Software - DELL SOFTWARE; *pg.* 385, *pg.* 40
SECURE CUP - Medical Product - UTAH MEDICAL PRODUCTS, INC.; *pg.* 1605, *pg.* 1752
SECURE DIGITAL - Digital Camera - PNY TECHNOLOGIES, INC.; *pg.* 455, *pg.* 1105
SECURE-FLOW - Nutritional Product - VICTUS, INC.; *pg.* 1606, *pg.* 447
SECURE I.V. - Catheter - SPAN-AMERICA MEDICAL SYSTEMS, INC.; *pg.* 1595, *pg.* 1618
SECURE-LOCK - Data Retention - MAXIM INTEGRATED PRODUCTS, INC.; *pg.* 653, *pg.* 247
SECURE LOGISTICS WORLDWIDE - Tagline - THE BRINK'S COMPANY; *pg.* 364, *pg.* 1800
SECURE 'N SAFE - Weed Control - GRAIN PROCESSING CORPORATION; *pg.* 859, *pg.* 709
SECURE PERF - Security Tape - AMERICAN CASTING & MANUFACTURING CORPORATION; *pg.* 1312, *pg.* 1321
SECURE PLUS SELECT - Equity Indexed Select - NATIONAL LIFE INSURANCE COMPANY; *pg.* 1210, *pg.* 1766
SECURE PLUS TSA - Equity Indexed Annuity - NATIONAL LIFE INSURANCE COMPANY; *pg.* 1210, *pg.* 1766
SECURE RINGS - Combat Label Switching - CHECKPOINT SYSTEMS, INC.; *pg.* 628, *pg.* 1559
SECURE-SEAL - Molecular Probe Product - THERMO FISHER SCIENTIFIC INC.; *pg.* 1602, *pg.* 61
SECURE SITE - Internet Site Security Product - VERISIGN, INC.; *pg.* 488, *pg.* 1799
SECURE SITE PRO - Internet Site Security Product - VERISIGN, INC.; *pg.* 488, *pg.* 1799
SECURE SITE PRO WITH EV - Internet Site Security Product - VERISIGN, INC.; *pg.* 488, *pg.* 1799
SECURE SITE WITH EV - Internet Site Security Product - VERISIGN, INC.; *pg.* 488, *pg.* 1799
SECURE SOCKETS LAYER - Software - CERTICOM CORP.; *pg.* 371, *pg.* 1925
SECURE SOLUTIONS SWING - Baby Gate - EVENFLO COMPANY, INC.; *pg.* 924, *pg.* 1470
SECURE TOUCH - Surface Wave Tempered Glass & Touch Screens - ELO TOUCH SOLUTIONS; *pg.* 635, *pg.* 145
SECURE T.R.A.C. - Self-Voiding Carton Sealing Tape - ALLIED SECURITY INNOVATIONS, INC.; *pg.* 1041, *pg.* 1066
SECURE VNC - Software - LAPLINK SOFTWARE, INC.; *pg.* 426, *pg.* 1815
SECUREAVR - Integrated Circuit - ATMEL CORPORATION; *pg.* 621, *pg.* 238
SECUREBASE - Software - IRON MOUNTAIN INCORPORATED; *pg.* 421, *pg.* 796
SECUREBOARD - Electronic Article Surveillance System - SENTRY TECHNOLOGY CORPORATION; *pg.* 672, *pg.* 1339
SECURECONNECT - Software - NIGHTINGALE; *pg.* 446, *pg.* 186
SECURECONNECT - Connector - WESTERN DIGITAL CORPORATION; *pg.* 492, *pg.* 118
THE SECURED RISK - Long Term Insurance Health - PENN TREATY AMERICAN CORPORATION; *pg.* 793, *pg.* 1514
SECUREDELETE - Software - CONDUSIV TECHNOLOGIES; *pg.* 379, *pg.* 51
SECUREDELETE - Software - SMITH MICRO SOFTWARE, INC.; *pg.* 471, *pg.* 41
SECUREDGE - Firewall Security Services - LOCKHEED MARTIN CORPORATION; *pg.* 229, *pg.* 762
SECUREDIGITAL - Flash Card - HGST; *pg.* 406, *pg.* 260
SECUREDX - Diagnostic Test - SEQUENOM, INC.; *pg.* 1593, *pg.* 209
SECUREEXCHANGE - Software - SYMANTEC CORPORATION; *pg.* 478, *pg.* 161
SECUREFORM - Thermoformed Desiccant Bags - MULTISORB TECHNOLOGIES, INC.; *pg.* 1570, *pg.* 1150
SECUREICA - Software - CITRIX SYSTEMS, INC.; *pg.* 375, *pg.* 424
SECUREIT - Chip Protector - RAYTHEON COMPANY; *pg.* 233, *pg.* 854
SECURELINE - Distribution Program for Life Product - LINCOLN NATIONAL CORPORATION; *pg.* 776, *pg.* 1567
SECURELINX - Electronic Device - LANTRONIX, INC.; *pg.* 426, *pg.* 112
SECURELINX SLK - PC Server Switch - LANTRONIX, INC.; *pg.* 426, *pg.* 112
SECURELINX SPIDER - Electronic Device - LANTRONIX, INC.; *pg.* 426, *pg.* 112
SECURELOK - Vehicle System - MACLEAN-FOGG COMPANY INC.; *pg.* 1358, *pg.* 635
SECUREPARK - Drive Technology - WESTERN DIGITAL CORPORATION; *pg.* 492, *pg.* 118
SECUREPLEX - Communication Product - RAULAND-BORG CORPORATION; *pg.* 666, *pg.* 634
SECURERIGHT - Car Seat Latch - EVENFLO COMPANY, INC.; *pg.* 924, *pg.* 1470
SECURESHIFT - Security Technology - VIAVI SOLUTIONS INC.; *pg.* 1435, *pg.* 148
SECURESTAT - Security Systems - DIEBOLD, INCORPORATED; *pg.* 387, *pg.* 1407
SECURESTOP - Brake Service - MIDAS, INC.; *pg.* 212, *pg.* 620
SECURESYNC - Software - IRON MOUNTAIN INCORPORATED; *pg.* 421, *pg.* 796
SECUREVAULT - Software - OMNICELL INC.; *pg.* 1578, *pg.* 161
SECURIAN FINANCIAL NETWORK - Insurance Product - THE MINNESOTA LIFE INSURANCE COMPANY; *pg.* 1209, *pg.* 962
SECURING DIGITAL IDENTITIES & INFORMATION - Tagline - ENTRUST, INC.; *pg.* 393, *pg.* 1680
SECURING PRODUCTIVITY - Slogan - WEBSENSE, INC.; *pg.* 491, *pg.* 210
SECURITECT - Coating - PPG INDUSTRIES, INC.; *pg.* 1445, *pg.* 1579
SECURITIES TRANSFER SYSTEMS - Software - DST SYSTEMS, INC.; *pg.* 388, *pg.* 982
SECURITY - Lighting Systems - HUBBELL INCORPORATED; *pg.* 1299, *pg.* 370
SECURITY BUILDER - Software - CERTICOM CORP.; *pg.* 371, *pg.* 1925
SECURITY BUILDER DRM - Software - CERTICOM CORP.; *pg.* 371, *pg.* 1925
SECURITY BUILDER ETS - Software - CERTICOM CORP.; *pg.* 371, *pg.* 1925
SECURITY BUILDER GSE - Software - CERTICOM CORP.; *pg.* 371, *pg.* 1925
SECURITY BUILDER PKI - Software - CERTICOM CORP.; *pg.* 371, *pg.* 1925
SECURITY BUILDER SSL - Software - CERTICOM CORP.; *pg.* 371, *pg.* 1925
SECURITY ENFORCER - Managed Internet Security Service - MAXIMUS, INC.; *pg.* 780, *pg.* 1799
SECURITY EXPLORER - Software - DELL SOFTWARE; *pg.* 385, *pg.* 40
SECURITY EXPLORER FOR EXCHANGE - Software - DELL SOFTWARE; *pg.* 385, *pg.* 40
SECURITY EXPLORER FOR FILE SERVERS - Software - DELL SOFTWARE; *pg.* 385, *pg.* 40
SECURITY EXPLORER FOR SQL SERVER - Software - DELL SOFTWARE; *pg.* 385, *pg.* 40
SECURITY EXPLORER FOR WORKSTATIONS - Software - DELL SOFTWARE; *pg.* 385, *pg.* 40
SECURITY FILTERING - Software - WEBSENSE, INC.; *pg.* 491, *pg.* 210
SECURITY LABS - Software - WEBSENSE, INC.; *pg.* 491, *pg.* 210
SECURITY MASTER PLAN - Periodic Economic Analysis - TRC COMPANIES, INC.; *pg.* 1383, *pg.* 386
SECURITY PG - Software - WEBSENSE, INC.; *pg.* 491, *pg.* 210
SECURITY PLUS - Life Insurance - OLD AMERICAN INSURANCE COMPANY; *pg.* 1213, *pg.* 985
SECURITY SALES & INTEGRATION - Magazine - BOBIT BUSINESS MEDIA; *pg.* 1622, *pg.* 293
SECURITY SERIES - Cables - WINNER INTERNATIONAL, LLC; *pg.* 222, *pg.* 1586
SECURITY THROUGH INNOVATION - Slogan - VERITEQ; *pg.* 488, *pg.* 422
SECURITYANDMORE - Security & Law Enforcement Products - MACE SECURITY INTERNATIONAL, INC.; *pg.* 1172, *pg.* 1541
SECURITYCAM - Webcam Software - EARTHCAM, INC.; *pg.* 1239, *pg.* 1072
SECURITY.HANDHELD. - Tagline - KASTLE SYSTEMS LLC; *pg.* 648, *pg.* 1773
SECURITYMANAGER - Software - DELL SOFTWARE; *pg.*

385, *pg.* 40
SECURITYPAQ - Software - TRADEPAQ CORPORATION; *pg.* 1284, *pg.* 1304
SECURITYSIGHT - Computer Programming & Integration Services - COMPUTER SCIENCES CORPORATION; *pg.* 378, *pg.* 1780
SECURITYWATCH.COM - Web Site - PC MAGAZINE; *pg.* 1674, *pg.* 1276
SECURMARK - Medical Product - HOLOGIC, INC.; *pg.* 1416, *pg.* 784
SECUROCK - Roof Board - USG CORPORATION; *pg.* 118, *pg.* 594
SECUROMATIC - Rotary Bank Depository - DIEBOLD, INCORPORATED; *pg.* 387, *pg.* 1407
SECURUS - Fiber - HONEYWELL INTERNATIONAL INC.; *pg.* 407, *pg.* 1088
SECURVIEW - Diagnostic Workstations - HOLOGIC, INC.; *pg.* 1416, *pg.* 784
SECURVIEW DX - Diagnostic Workstation - HOLOGIC, INC.; *pg.* 1416, *pg.* 784
THE SEDALIA DEMOCRAT - Missouri Newspaper - FREEDOM COMMUNICATIONS, INC.; *pg.* 1643, *pg.* 110
SEDALLIA - Furniture - ASHLEY FURNITURE INDUSTRIES, INC.; *pg.* 914, *pg.* 1852
SEDGEBROOK - Retirement Community - ERICKSON LIVING; *pg.* 1090, *pg.* 766
SEDIMENT LOG - Erosion Control Product - AMERICAN EXCELSIOR COMPANY; *pg.* 1451, *pg.* 1659
SEDONA - Guest Chairs - BERNHARDT DESIGN; *pg.* 918, *pg.* 1381
SEDONA - Paper & Nonwoven Material - FIBERMARK INC.; *pg.* 1457, *pg.* 1764
SEDONA - Bath & Plumbing Product - JACUZZI BRANDS CORPORATION; *pg.* 554, *pg.* 65
SEDONA - Eyewear - MINE SAFETY APPLIANCES COMPANY; *pg.* 1361, *pg.* 1525
SEDONA - Lighting Product - WESTINGHOUSE LIGHTING CORPORATION; *pg.* 687, *pg.* 1571
SEDUCTIVE - Carpet - BEAULIEU GROUP, LLC; *pg.* 917, *pg.* 529
S.E.E. - Lights - CYALUME TECHNOLOGIES HOLDINGS, INC.; *pg.* 1295, *pg.* 856
SEE & LEARN - Educational Toys - LEAPFROG ENTERPRISES, INC.; *pg.* 961, *pg.* 84
SEE & SPLICE - Electronic Components - MOLEX INCORPORATED; *pg.* 655, *pg.* 628
SEE-CLEAR - Eyeglass Wipes - CROSSTEX INTERNATIONAL INC.; *pg.* 1520, *pg.* 1164
SEE IT. BUY IT AND MORE @ BELLSOUTH.COM - Online Store - AT&T SOUTHEAST; *pg.* 1868, *pg.* 489
SEE IT LIKE THE PROS - Tagline - FGX INTERNATIONAL, INC.; *pg.* 5, *pg.* 1608
SEE ME, SHARE MY WORLD - Global Education Program - PLAN USA, INC.; *pg.* 154, *pg.* 1609
SEE SAW - Educational Materials - SCHOLASTIC INC.; *pg.* 1683, *pg.* 1288
SEE THE DIFFERENCE - Tagline - CANDELA CORPORATION; *pg.* 1404, *pg.* 855
SEE THE DIFFERENCE QUALITY MAKES - Software - XEROX CORPORATION; *pg.* 494, *pg.* 365
SEE THE LEARNING. - Slogan - LEAPFROG ENTERPRISES, INC.; *pg.* 961, *pg.* 84
SEE THE WORLD IN A NEW LIGHT - Slogan - OSRAM SYLVANIA, INC.; *pg.* 1302, *pg.* 816
SEE THERE WHEN YOU CAN'T BE THERE - Slogan - PANASONIC CORPORATION OF NORTH AMERICA; *pg.* 661, *pg.* 1120
SEE-THROUGH - Fireplaces - LENNOX HEARTH PRODUCTS; *pg.* 93, *pg.* 1652
SEE-THRU CPR - Filter - ZOLL MEDICAL CORPORATION; *pg.* 1612, *pg.* 814
SEE WHAT'S NEXT - Tagline - SMART SOFTWARE, INC.; *pg.* 470, *pg.* 787
SEEAMERICA - Annual Event - TRAVEL INDUSTRY ASSOCIATION OF AMERICA; *pg.* 158, *pg.* 405
SEEBLUE - Molecular Biology Product - THERMO FISHER SCIENTIFIC INC.; *pg.* 1602, *pg.* 61
SEED GERMINATION BLANKET - Seed Protection System - E.I. DU PONT DE NEMOURS & COMPANY; *pg.* 1159, *pg.* 390
SEED-LOK - Wheel - GREAT PLAINS MANUFACTURING, INCORPORATED; *pg.* 704, *pg.* 721
SEEDS - Food Product - CAMPBELL SOUP COMPANY; *pg.* 844, *pg.* 1048
SEEDS OF CHANGE - Food Product - MARS, INCORPORATED; *pg.* 1858, *pg.* 1792
SEEDS OF LIFE - Tree Kit - 1-800-FLOWERS.COM, INC.; *pg.* 1758, *pg.* 1151
SEEDVAC - Bulk Seed Conveyors - CHRISTIANSON SYSTEMS, INC.; *pg.* 1323, *pg.* 917
SEEGULL - Scanning Receivers & Receiver-Based Products - PCTEL, INC.; *pg.* 452, *pg.* 557
SEEING STARS - Game - WMS INDUSTRIES INC.; *pg.* 593, *pg.* 666
SEEKER - Rate-Gyro Surveying System - BAKER HUGHES INTEQ; *pg.* 1316, *pg.* 1700
SEEKURE - Floor Protection System - FORTIFIBER CORPORATION; *pg.* 83, *pg.* 1021
SEERI - Footwear - STEVEN MADDEN, LTD.; *pg.* 1819, *pg.* 1176
SEETHRU-SIGN - Graphic Film - FLEXCON CORPORATION; *pg.* 1457, *pg.* 844
SEFRONITE - Minerals - MINERALS TECHNOLOGIES INC.; *pg.* 1173, *pg.* 617
SEGAL - Dropbolts - MEDECO HIGH SECURITY LOCKS, INC.; *pg.* 1055, *pg.* 1806
SEGLDR - Supercomputing System - CRAY INC.; *pg.* 380, *pg.* 1834
SEGMENT - Fabric - NEMSCHOFF, INC.; *pg.* 936, *pg.* 1890
SEGMENTS - Furniture - BUSH INDUSTRIES INC.; *pg.* 919, *pg.* 1170
SEGMENTSAMPLER - Disposable Blood Handling Safety Device - IMMUCOR, INC.; *pg.* 1544, *pg.* 537
SEGUE - Fabric - NEMSCHOFF, INC.; *pg.* 936, *pg.* 1890
SEGURA - Actuator - PRECISION VALVE CORPORATION; *pg.* 1060, *pg.* 1357
SEGURA HEMISPHERE - Medical Device - BOSTON SCIENTIFIC CORPORATION; *pg.* 1508, *pg.* 831
SEISCLASS - Software - SCHLUMBERGER LIMITED; *pg.* 801, *pg.* 1714
SEKIDENKO - Emissometer - ADVANCED ENERGY INDUSTRIES, INC.; *pg.* 613, *pg.* 328
SEL-KLEEN - Safety Equipment Cleaning Packet - SELLSTROM MANUFACTURING CO.; *pg.* 1428, *pg.* 659
SELAH - Footwear - COBIAN CORP.; *pg.* 1806, *pg.* 253
SELAN - Polyurethane Foam - SPAN-AMERICA MEDICAL SYSTEMS, INC.; *pg.* 1595, *pg.* 1618
SELAR - Barrier Resins - E.I. DU PONT DE NEMOURS & COMPANY; *pg.* 1159, *pg.* 390
SELCO - Baler - HARRIS WASTE MANAGEMENT GROUP, INC.; *pg.* 1345, *pg.* 526
SELE-CONNECT - Connector System - GREENE, TWEED & CO.; *pg.* 1344, *pg.* 1544
SELECCIONES - Spanish-Language Magazine - THE READER'S DIGEST ASSOCIATION, INC.; *pg.* 1679, *pg.* 1322
SELECT - Software - BENTLEY SYSTEMS, INC.; *pg.* 361, *pg.* 1531
SELECT - Soup - CAMPBELL SOUP COMPANY; *pg.* 844, *pg.* 1048
SELECT - Labeling - FLEXCON CORPORATION; *pg.* 1457, *pg.* 844
SELECT - Beverage - GREEN SPOT, INC.; *pg.* 251, *pg.* 68
SELECT - Airborne - HONEYWELL INTERNATIONAL INC.; *pg.* 407, *pg.* 1088
SELECT - Committed Program - MEDASSETS INC.; *pg.* 1561, *pg.* 484
SELECT - Auto Delivery Program - NUTRISYSTEM, INC.; *pg.* 1577, *pg.* 1533
SELECT - Adsorbent Product - OIL-DRI CORPORATION OF AMERICA; *pg.* 1480, *pg.* 586
SELECT - Windows & Doors - PELLA CORPORATION; *pg.* 104, *pg.* 711
SELECT - Laboratory Product - PROPPER MANUFACTURING COMPANY, INC.; *pg.* 1586, *pg.* 1175
SELECT - Reduced-Salt Tuna Products - STARKIST FOODS INC.; *pg.* 898, *pg.* 1581
SELECT - Healthcare Product - SWANSON HEALTH PRODUCTS INC.; *pg.* 1600, *pg.* 1397
SELECT - Pretzels - UTZ QUALITY FOODS, INC.; *pg.* 907, *pg.* 1536
SELECT 55 - Light Beer - ANHEUSER-BUSCH COMPANIES, LLC; *pg.* 237, *pg.* 991
SELECT-A-BREW - Rubber & Plastic Carafe Stoppers - THERMOS L.L.C.; *pg.* 61, *pg.* 660
SELECT-A-NALYSIS - Bearing - THE TIMKEN COMPANY; *pg.* 218, *pg.* 1408
SELECT ACCESS - Electronic Key Storage Security Devices - MASTER LOCK COMPANY LLC; *pg.* 1055, *pg.* 1884
SELECT ACCESS - Pharmaceutical Product - PDI, INC.; *pg.* 1580, *pg.* 1104
SELECT BLEND - Coffee - QUIKTRIP CORPORATION; *pg.* 1031, *pg.* 1490
SELECT CHOCOLATE - Icing And Base - DAWN FOOD PRODUCTS, INC.; *pg.* 1018, *pg.* 893
SELECT CIRCLE - Speaker - CAMBRIDGE SOUNDWORKS, INC.; *pg.* 1234, *pg.* 781
SELECT COMFORT - Mattress - SELECT COMFORT CORPORATION; *pg.* 942, *pg.* 942
SELECT COMFORT CREATOR OF THE SLEEP NUMBER BED - Mattress - SELECT COMFORT CORPORATION; *pg.* 942, *pg.* 942
SELECT COMFORT GRIP - Air Swivel - GRACO, INC.; *pg.* 1342, *pg.* 935
SELECT COMFORT SLEEP NUMBER - Mattress - SELECT COMFORT CORPORATION; *pg.* 942, *pg.* 942
SELECT CURE - UV Conveyor System - NORDSON CORPORATION; *pg.* 1365, *pg.* 1480
SELECT CUT - Hair Clipper - ANDIS COMPANY; *pg.* 498, *pg.* 1895
SELECT DONUT - Icing And Filling - DAWN FOOD PRODUCTS, INC.; *pg.* 1018, *pg.* 893
SELECT EDITIONS - Magazine - THE READER'S DIGEST ASSOCIATION, INC.; *pg.* 1679, *pg.* 1322
SELECT LINE - Floor Care - NILFISK-ADVANCE, INC.; *pg.* 332, *pg.* 953
SELECT METALIZATION - Decorating Technology - SERIGRAPH, INC.; *pg.* 1686, *pg.* 1899
SELECT-RECIPE - French Fries - J.R. SIMPLOT COMPANY; *pg.* 867, *pg.* 547
SELECT SEAL - Packaging System - MTS MEDICATION TECHNOLOGIES, INC.; *pg.* 442, *pg.* 463
SELECT SERIES - Tractors - DEERE & COMPANY; *pg.* 703, *pg.* 632
SELECT SERIES - Gun & Hose - NORDSON CORPORATION; *pg.* 1365, *pg.* 1480
SELECT STEP - Repayment Plan - SLM CORPORATION; *pg.* 804, *pg.* 388
SELECT VAC - Livestock Health Management Program - PFIZER INC.; *pg.* 1581, *pg.* 1278
SELECT Z - Additive - BASF CATALYSTS LLC; *pg.* 1148, *pg.* 1074
SELECTACOM - Computer Weighers - TRIANGLE PACKAGE MACHINERY CO.; *pg.* 1383, *pg.* 592
SELECTAFIT - Instrument Fitting Software - BELTONE ELECTRONICS LLC; *pg.* 1503, *pg.* 614
SELECTAIR - Support Surface Product - THE ROHO GROUP; *pg.* 1591, *pg.* 556
SELECTAIRE - Hair Dryer - ANDIS COMPANY; *pg.* 498, *pg.* 1895
SELECTASHADE - Beauty Product Sampling System - ARCADE MARKETING, INC.; *pg.* 352, *pg.* 1196
SELECTCARE - Service & Support Program - DELL INC.; *pg.* 383, *pg.* 1737
SELECTCARE - Health Plan & Publication - MEDICA, INC.; *pg.* 1208, *pg.* 949
SELECTDL - Software - DELL SOFTWARE; *pg.* 385, *pg.* 40
SELECTEMP - HVAC Equipment - MESTEK, INC.; *pg.* 1074, *pg.* 857
SELECTEXT - Software - SAS INSTITUTE INC.; *pg.* 466, *pg.* 1361
SELECTFLUOR - Electrophilic Fluorinating Agent - AIR PRODUCTS AND CHEMICALS, INC.; *pg.* 1145, *pg.* 1513
SELECTFX - Molecular Probe Product - THERMO FISHER SCIENTIFIC INC.; *pg.* 1602, *pg.* 61
SELECTICA COMPOSER SUITE - Software - DETERMINE, INC.; *pg.* 386, *pg.* 254
SELECTICA CONFIGURATION PLATFORM - Software - DETERMINE, INC.; *pg.* 386, *pg.* 254
SELECTICA CONFIGURATOR - Software - DETERMINE, INC.; *pg.* 386, *pg.* 254
SELECTICA CONTRACT LIFECYCLE MANAGEMENT - Software - DETERMINE, INC.; *pg.* 386, *pg.* 254
SELECTICA CONTRACT PERFORMANCE MANAGEMENT - Software - DETERMINE, INC.; *pg.* 386, *pg.* 254
SELECTICA ENTERPRISE PRODUCTIVITY SUITE - Software - DETERMINE, INC.; *pg.* 386, *pg.* 254
SELECTICA KNOWLEDGEBASE DEVELOPMENT ENVIRONMENT - Software - DETERMINE, INC.; *pg.* 386, *pg.* 254
SELECTICA PRICER - Software - DETERMINE, INC.; *pg.* 386, *pg.* 254
SELECTICA QUOTER - Software - DETERMINE, INC.; *pg.* 386, *pg.* 254
SELECTICA REPOSITORY - Software - DETERMINE, INC.;

First page reference indicates Business Class Edition
Second page reference indicates Geographic Edition

pg. 386, pg. 254
SELECTICA SOLUTION ADVISOR - Software - DETERMINE, INC.; pg. 386, pg. 254
SELECTICA STUDIO - Software - DETERMINE, INC.; pg. 386, pg. 254
SELECTION AFM - Pacemaker - MEDTRONIC, INC.; pg. 1564, pg. 939
SELECTION SUNDAY - Trademark - NATIONAL COLLEGIATE ATHLETIC ASSOCIATION; pg. 567, pg. 688
SELECTIONS - Catalogues - TIFFANY & CO.; pg. 13, pg. 1299
SELECTION.SERVICE.SUPPORT - Tagline - ON SEMICONDUCTOR CORPORATION; pg. 101, pg. 18
SELECTIP - Pen - A. T. CROSS COMPANY; pg. 339, pg. 1602
SELECTO - Electro Lifting Magnet - ERIEZ MANUFACTURING CO. INC.; pg. 1335, pg. 1530
SELECTOL-SOFT - Photo Developer - EASTMAN KODAK COMPANY; pg. 1408, pg. 1333
SELECTOMAT - Photo Developer - EASTMAN KODAK COMPANY; pg. 1408, pg. 1333
SELECTOR - Medical Device - INTEGRA LIFESCIENCES HOLDINGS CORPORATION; pg. 1545, pg. 1109
SELECTPAY - Electronic Payment Service - SELECTIVE INSURANCE GROUP, INC.; pg. 1216, pg. 1045
SELECTPROTECT - Safety Enhancement System - THE ROHO GROUP; pg. 1591, pg. 556
SELECTQU - Advertising Publication - DOMINION ENTERPRISES; pg. 1636, pg. 1796
SELECTRA - Catalyst - BASF CATALYSTS LLC; pg. 1148, pg. 1074
SELECTRIC - Typewriter Ribbons - LEXMARK INTERNATIONAL, INC.; pg. 427, pg. 730
SELECTRONIC - Mixers & Mixer Controls - JARDEN CONSUMER SOLUTIONS; pg. 57, pg. 412
SELECTSCREEN - Molecular Biology Product - THERMO FISHER SCIENTIFIC INC.; pg. 1602, pg. 61
SELECTSECURA - Pacemakers - MEDTRONIC, INC.; pg. 1564, pg. 939
SELECTSOUND - Acoustic System - OWENS CORNING; pg. 102, pg. 1476
SELECTTECH - Dumbbells - NAUTILUS, INC.; pg. 1840, pg. 1846
SELECTVAC - Carpet Vacuum - HILLYARD, INC.; pg. 331, pg. 990
SELECTVAC - Floor Care - NILFISK-ADVANCE, INC.; pg. 332, pg. 953
SELENA - Clothing - ABERCROMBIE & FITCH CO.; pg. 37, pg. 1466
SELENA - Footwear - COBIAN CORP.; pg. 1806, pg. 253
SELENE E W/LECITHIN CAPSULES - Selenium/Lecithin Natural Anti-Oxidant Capsules - SCHIFF NUTRITION INTERNATIONAL, INC.; pg. 1592, pg. 1760
SELENIA - Mammography System - HOLOGIC, INC.; pg. 1416, pg. 784
SELENIUM NATURAL - Hair & Skin Product - AUBREY ORGANICS INC.; pg. 499, pg. 470
SELENOMAX - Selenium - NUTRITION 21, INC.; pg. 1577, pg. 1327
SELENOPURE - Yeast-Free Selenium - NUTRITION 21, INC.; pg. 1577, pg. 1327
SELEX - Depth Filters - GE WATER & PROCESS TECHNOLOGIES; pg. 1339, pg. 1588
SELEXOL - Solvent - THE DOW CHEMICAL COMPANY; pg. 1157, pg. 898
SELEXTRAC - Membrane Module - SPECTRUM LABORATORIES INC.; pg. 1595, pg. 69
SELF - Magazine - CONDE NAST PUBLICATIONS, INC.; pg. 1629, pg. 1217
SELF - Apparel - OAKLEY, INC.; pg. 1840, pg. 86
SELF-ALIGNING STATIONARY - Fluid Sealing Product - A.W. CHESTERTON COMPANY; pg. 1315, pg. 861
SELF-CENTERING LOCK RING - Seal - A.W. CHESTERTON COMPANY; pg. 1315, pg. 861
SELF-LOK - Clamping Systems - IDEX CORPORATION; pg. 1347, pg. 623
SELF-REGULATING - Cable - THERMON AMERICAS INC.; pg. 1077, pg. 1744
SELF-SEAL - Software - BIO-RAD LABORATORIES, INC.; pg. 1504, pg. 101
SELF-SEAL - Fastener - LONG-LOK FASTENERS CORP.; pg. 1053, pg. 1416
SELF-SERVE - Liquid Soap - ADCO, INC.; pg. 325, pg. 482
SELF-SERVICE SUITE - Software - SUPPORT.COM, INC.; pg. 1283, pg. 192
SELF-SERVICE WEB PORTAL - Software - DELL SOFTWARE; pg. 385, pg. 40
SELF WIPE - Toileting Hygiene Aids - ALIMED, INC.; pg. 1490, pg. 816
SELFIX - Houseware Products - HOME PRODUCTS INTERNATIONAL, INC.; pg. 1125, pg. 577
SELFPACE - Computer Program - MCKESSON CORPORATION; pg. 1560, pg. 222
SELFSERVICE - Software - EGAIN COMMUNICATIONS CORPORATION; pg. 1242, pg. 284
SELFSET - Medical Device - RESMED INC.; pg. 1589, pg. 207
SELFX - Stent System - ABBOTT LABORATORIES; pg. 1484, pg. 551
SELICICLIB - Biopharmaceutical Product - CYCLACEL PHARMACEUTICALS, INC.; pg. 1521, pg. 1044
SELIG - Chemical Product - ACUITY BRANDS, INC.; pg. 1294, pg. 487
SELIG - Specialty Chemicals - ZEP INC.; pg. 338, pg. 524
SELL MORE. LOSE LESS. - Slogan - CHECKPOINT SYSTEMS, INC.; pg. 628, pg. 1559
THE SELL OUT - Plastic Containers - PACTIV CORPORATION; pg. 1466, pg. 624
SELLO ROJO - Bleaches - THE CLOROX COMPANY; pg. 327, pg. 169
SELMER - Musical Instruments - CONN-SELMER, INC.; pg. 542, pg. 677
SELMER - Musical Instrument - STEINWAY MUSICAL INSTRUMENTS, INC.; pg. 586, pg. 854
SELSUN BLUE - Health & Beauty Product - CHATTEM, INC.; pg. 1515, pg. 1628
SELTON - Insecticides - THE CLOROX COMPANY; pg. 327, pg. 169
SELTZ - Beverages - THE COCA-COLA COMPANY; pg. 240, pg. 493
SELVA - Footwear - CAPEZIO BALLET MAKERS INC.; pg. 1805, pg. 1125
SELVAGE CUTTER - Round Knife - THE WOLF MACHINE CO.; pg. 1389, pg. 1427
SELZENTRY - Medicine - PFIZER INC.; pg. 1581, pg. 1278
SEMBLE - Sweetening Ingredient - MERISANT COMPANY; pg. 876, pg. 581
SEMCO - Coating Product - PPG INDUSTRIES, INC.; pg. 1445, pg. 1579
SEMCONN - Electronic Components - MOLEX INCORPORATED; pg. 655, pg. 628
SEMI-Q - Diagnostic Test Product - QUIDEL CORPORATION; pg. 1588, pg. 207
SEMI-SPERSE - Semiconductor Product - CABOT MICROELECTRONICS CORPORATION; pg. 1151, pg. 554
SEMI-WET - Dry Cleaning & Laundry Product - ADCO, INC.; pg. 325, pg. 482
SEMIFLEX - Cable - TIMES FIBER COMMUNICATIONS, INC.; pg. 681, pg. 382
SEMILLA'S FERRY'S - Garden Seeds - FERRY-MORSE SEED COMPANY; pg. 1795, pg. 728
SEMINIS - Fruit & Vegetable Seeds - MONSANTO COMPANY; pg. 1173, pg. 999
SEMINOLE - Aircraft - PIPER AIRCRAFT, INC.; pg. 233, pg. 477
SEMINOLE BEACON - Newspaper - TAMPA BAY NEWSPAPERS, INC.; pg. 1691, pg. 468
SEMKIT - Plastic Packaging - PPG AEROSPACE; pg. 1178, pg. 290
SEMOZON - Ozone Generator System - MKS INSTRUMENTS, INC.; pg. 1362, pg. 781
SEMPAK - Mixing & Dispensing Equipment - PPG AEROSPACE; pg. 1178, pg. 290
SENATOR - Gluing Machine - GLUEFAST COMPANY, INC.; pg. 1459, pg. 1090
SENATOR - Pumps - GRACO, INC.; pg. 1342, pg. 935
SENATOR - Seating Product - IRWIN SEATING COMPANY INC.; pg. 929, pg. 887
SENATORS CLUB - Whiskey - LAIRD & COMPANY, INC.; pg. 1966, pg. 1119
SEND-A-MESSAGE - Message Delivery Services - 1-800-FLOWERS.COM, INC.; pg. 1758, pg. 1151
SEND 'N RETURN - Envelopes - TENSION ENVELOPE CORPORATION; pg. 483, pg. 986
SEND.COM - Internet Property - SENDONLINE.COM, INC.; pg. 1280, pg. 1112
SENDD - Software - R.R. DONNELLEY & SONS COMPANY; pg. 1682, pg. 589
SENDERBASE - Real-Time Database - CISCO SYSTEMS, INC.; pg. 372, pg. 240
SENDFLORAL.COM - Internet Property - SENDONLINE.COM, INC.; pg. 1280, pg. 1112
SENDFOODS.COM - Internet Property - SENDONLINE.COM, INC.; pg. 1280, pg. 1112
SENDGIFTS.COM - Internet Property - SENDONLINE.COM, INC.; pg. 1280, pg. 1112
SENDING ALL THE RIGHT SIGNALS - Slogan - BELDEN, INC.; pg. 624, pg. 993
SENDLIQUOR.COM - Internet Property - SENDONLINE.COM, INC.; pg. 1280, pg. 1112
SENDONCE - Computer Software - IRON MOUNTAIN INCORPORATED; pg. 421, pg. 796
SENDORI - Online Services - IAC/INTERACTIVECORP; pg. 292, pg. 1242
SENDZIMIR - Mill - THE TIMKEN COMPANY; pg. 218, pg. 1408
SENECA - Shoes - ALLEN-EDMONDS SHOE CORP.; pg. 1804, pg. 1887
SENECA - Furniture - ASHLEY FURNITURE INDUSTRIES, INC.; pg. 914, pg. 1852
SENECA - Footwear - EASTLAND SHOE CORPORATION; pg. 1808, pg. 750
SENECA - Aircraft - PIPER AIRCRAFT, INC.; pg. 233, pg. 477
SENECA - Pressed & Monolithic Refractory - RESCO PRODUCTS, INC.; pg. 107, pg. 1581
SENECA - Endworking Equipment & Center Driven Lathes & CNC Production Lathes - SENECA FALLS MACHINES; pg. 1374, pg. 1341
SENECA - Apple Sauce - TREE TOP, INC.; pg. 901, pg. 1843
SENECA FALLS - Metal Cutting Machine - SENECA FALLS MACHINES; pg. 1374, pg. 1341
SENECAL - Surface Material - STEELCASE INC.; pg. 475, pg. 889
SENIOR - Screen - DA-LITE SCREEN COMPANY; pg. 632, pg. 698
SENIOR - Cable Instrument - PEAVEY ELECTRONICS CORPORATION; pg. 662, pg. 970
SENIOR DAYS - Ticket Program - OAKLAND ATHLETICS LIMITED PARTNERSHIP; pg. 571, pg. 172
SENIOR ELECTROL - Electric Screen - DA-LITE SCREEN COMPANY; pg. 632, pg. 698
SENIOR MARKET ADVISOR - Business-to-Business Magazine - WIESNER PUBLISHING, LLC; pg. 1702, pg. 328
SENIOR OUTLOOK - Advertising Publication - DOMINION ENTERPRISES; pg. 1636, pg. 1796
SENIOR PRIDE - Horse Feed - KENT NUTRITION GROUP; pg. 1477, pg. 710
SENIOR SCHOLASTIC - Educational Materials - SCHOLASTIC INC.; pg. 1683, pg. 1288
SENIOR TECHNOLOGIES - Monitoring & Tracking Devices - STANLEY BLACK & DECKER, INC.; pg. 1063, pg. 358
SENIORGLO - Pelleted Nutrition Product - ADM ALLIANCE NUTRITION, INC.; pg. 1474, pg. 653
SENIORS ESPECIALLY - Specialty Entrees for Seniors - EAT'N PARK HOSPITALITY GROUP; pg. 1728, pg. 1539
SENOR PICO - Powder Mix - TRADER VIC'S GOURMET PRODUCTS, INC.; pg. 901, pg. 69
SENORITA ROSE-ALITA - Nail Care Product - OPI PRODUCTS INC.; pg. 518, pg. 167
SENS-A-VIEW - Video Cameras - IMAGEWORKS; pg. 1544, pg. 1158
SENSA - Testing Instrument System - BECKMAN COULTER, INC.; pg. 1402, pg. 48
SENSABLES - Bakery Product - TASTY BAKING COMPANY; pg. 1862, pg. 1571
SENSAFLEX - Orthopedic Device - DJO SURGICAL; pg. 1525, pg. 1661
SENSAIRE - Fans - BROAN-NUTONE LLC; pg. 1069, pg. 1860
SENSAIRE - Spirometer - CARDIAC SCIENCE CORPORATION; pg. 1512, pg. 1897
SENSAIRE - Bathroom Exhaust Fans - NORTEK, INC.; pg. 100, pg. 1607
SENSALITE - Electronic Flash - EASTMAN KODAK COMPANY; pg. 1408, pg. 1333
SENSAR - Television Reception Product - WINEGARD COMPANY; pg. 688, pg. 702
SENSATION - Surface Cleaner - BLUE CROSS LABORATORIES; pg. 326, pg. 277
SENSATION - Medical Device - BOSTON SCIENTIFIC

CORPORATION; *pg.* 1508, *pg.* 831
SENSATION - Beverages - THE COCA-COLA COMPANY; *pg.* 240, *pg.* 493
SENSATION - Golf Products - FEEL GOLF CO., INC.; *pg.* 1834, *pg.* 465
SENSATION - Medical Apparatus - MAQUET; *pg.* 1558, *pg.* 1082
SENSATIONAL SIDES - Mashed Potatoes - RESER'S FINE FOODS INC.; *pg.* 1032, *pg.* 1496
SENSATIONS FROM ISOTONER - Slippers - TOTES ISOTONER CORPORATION; *pg.* 14, *pg.* 1426
SENSE - Fabric - NEMSCHOFF, INC.; *pg.* 936, *pg.* 1890
SENSE-A-MARK - Writing Instrument - DIXON TICONDEROGA COMPANY; *pg.* 388, *pg.* 430
SENSE OF SECURITY - Travel Insurance - TRAVEL GUARD GROUP, INC.; *pg.* 1925, *pg.* 1895
SENSELINK - Software - MKS INSTRUMENTS, INC.; *pg.* 1362, *pg.* 781
SENSEMATIC - Writing Instrument - DIXON TICONDEROGA COMPANY; *pg.* 388, *pg.* 430
SENSEO - Coffee Machine - PHILIPS ELECTRONICS NORTH AMERICA; *pg.* 662, *pg.* 782
SENSERT - Golf Accessories - CALLAWAY GOLF COMPANY; *pg.* 1829, *pg.* 58
SENSI-TEMP - Bath Water Thermometer - EVENFLO COMPANY, INC.; *pg.* 924, *pg.* 1470
SENSI-TRON - Detectors & Units - AUTOMATION DEVICES, INC.; *pg.* 1315, *pg.* 1532
SENSIA - Pacemakers - MEDTRONIC, INC.; *pg.* 1564, *pg.* 939
SENSIBLE SEATING - Office Seating - THE HON COMPANY; *pg.* 928, *pg.* 709
SENSICARE - Skin Care Product - CONVATEC LTD.; *pg.* 1518, *pg.* 1121
SENSICARE - Surgical Gloves - MEDLINE INDUSTRIES, INC.; *pg.* 1562, *pg.* 635
SENSICARE ADVANTIX - Polyurethane Exam Glove - MEDLINE INDUSTRIES, INC.; *pg.* 1562, *pg.* 635
SENSICHIP - Thermistor - YSI INCORPORATED; *pg.* 1438, *pg.* 1483
SENSICORE - Golf Shaft - TRUE TEMPER SPORTS, INC.; *pg.* 1847, *pg.* 1647
SENSIFLEX - Molecular Probe Product - THERMO FISHER SCIENTIFIC INC.; *pg.* 1602, *pg.* 61
SENSIFOOT - Medical & Aesthetic Product - DYNATRONICS CORPORATION; *pg.* 1526, *pg.* 1757
SENSIMAP - Formulating Concept - THE LUBRIZOL CORPORATION; *pg.* 1171, *pg.* 1481
SENSIPAR - Medicine - AMGEN INC.; *pg.* 1493, *pg.* 291
SENSITIVE - Beauty Product - THE STEPHAN COMPANY; *pg.* 1597, *pg.* 426
SENSITIVE EYES - Soft Contact Lens Care - BAUSCH & LOMB INCORPORATED; *pg.* 1401, *pg.* 1045
SENSO-MATIC - Detergent Dispenser - ECOLAB INC.; *pg.* 329, *pg.* 960
SENSOHM - Resistor Paste - FERRO CORPORATION; *pg.* 1162, *pg.* 1462
SENSONIC - In-Wall Power Subwoofer - BROAN-NUTONE LLC; *pg.* 1069, *pg.* 1860
SENSOR - Medical Device - BOSTON SCIENTIFIC CORPORATION; *pg.* 1508, *pg.* 831
SENSOR - Light Dimmer - ELECTRONIC THEATRE CONTROLS, INC.; *pg.* 1296, *pg.* 1872
SENSOR - Shaving System & Cartridges - THE GILLETTE COMPANY; *pg.* 509, *pg.* 795
SENSOR - Office Furniture - STEELCASE INC.; *pg.* 475, *pg.* 889
SENSOR EXCEL - Shaving System - THE GILLETTE COMPANY; *pg.* 509, *pg.* 795
SENSOR FOR WOMEN - Shaving System & Cartridges for Women - THE GILLETTE COMPANY; *pg.* 509, *pg.* 795
SENSOR GUARD - Rip Detection Device for Conveyor Belting - THE GOODYEAR TIRE & RUBBER COMPANY; *pg.* 1883, *pg.* 1401
SENSOR GUARD - Disposable Bandages for Pulse Oximetry Sensor - MAQUET; *pg.* 1558, *pg.* 1082
SENSOR LINE - Sensor System - MEASUREMENT SPECIALTIES INC.; *pg.* 1360, *pg.* 1783
SENSOR-PAC - Bearing - THE TIMKEN COMPANY; *pg.* 218, *pg.* 1408
SENSOR TEXTURE MAPS - Maps - RAYTHEON COMPANY; *pg.* 233, *pg.* 854
SENSOR3 - Blade And Razor - THE GILLETTE COMPANY; *pg.* 509, *pg.* 795
SENSORMATIC - Electronic Article Surveillance Systems - THE ADT CORPORATION; *pg.* 612, *pg.* 409
SENSORSELECT - Sensor System - MEASUREMENT SPECIALTIES INC.; *pg.* 1360, *pg.* 1783
SENSORTEXTURE - Sensor Simulation - EVANS & SUTHERLAND COMPUTER CORPORATION; *pg.* 638, *pg.* 1757
SENSUAL CURVES - Apparel - LANE BRYANT; *pg.* 1776, *pg.* 1441
SENSUALE - Designer Fragrance - PARFUMS DE COEUR LTD.; *pg.* 519, *pg.* 376
SENSUN GAZOZ - Beverages - THE COCA-COLA COMPANY; *pg.* 240, *pg.* 493
SENSUOUS - Carpet - BEAULIEU GROUP, LLC; *pg.* 917, *pg.* 529
SENSUS - Foam - FXI; *pg.* 1163, *pg.* 1552
SENSYNC - Software - DEXCOM INC; *pg.* 1524, *pg.* 202
SENTARA ECARE - Health Network - SENTARA HEALTHCARE; *pg.* 1593, *pg.* 1797
SENTER - Footwear - STEVEN MADDEN, LTD.; *pg.* 1819, *pg.* 1176
SENTEX - Gate Operators, Telephone Entry Systems & Radio Frequency Products - THE CHAMBERLAIN GROUP, INC.; *pg.* 75, *pg.* 611
SENTIA - Computer System - ALIENWARE CORPORATION; *pg.* 346, *pg.* 439
SENTIMENTAL - Carpet - BEAULIEU GROUP, LLC; *pg.* 917, *pg.* 529
SENTIMENTAL SURPRISE - Flower Arrangement - 1-800-FLOWERS.COM, INC.; *pg.* 1758, *pg.* 1151
SENTINEL - Mills Partitions - BRADLEY CORPORATION; *pg.* 71, *pg.* 1870
SENTINEL - Label Printer - BRADY CORPORATION; *pg.* 363, *pg.* 1873
SENTINEL - UV Disinfection System - CALGON CARBON CORPORATION; *pg.* 1151, *pg.* 1574
SENTINEL - Character - DC COMICS, INC.; *pg.* 1633, *pg.* 1221
SENTINEL - Headgear - E.D. BULLARD COMPANY; *pg.* 1332, *pg.* 727
SENTINEL - Gaming Product - GLD PRODUCTS, INC.; *pg.* 1835, *pg.* 1882
SENTINEL - Newspaper - GREATER MEDIA NEWSPAPERS, INC.; *pg.* 1646, *pg.* 1071
SENTINEL - Chair - HUSSEY SEATING CO.; *pg.* 929, *pg.* 751
SENTINEL - Computer Software - NOVELL INC.; *pg.* 446, *pg.* 852
SENTINEL - Pet Medication - PETMED EXPRESS, INC.; *pg.* 1781, *pg.* 460
SENTINEL - Writing Instrument - SHEAFFER PEN CORPORATION; *pg.* 469, *pg.* 371
SENTINEL - Cast Iron Gas Boiler - SLANT/FIN CORPORATION; *pg.* 1076, *pg.* 1163
SENTINEL - Surface Maintenance Machine - TENNANT COMPANY; *pg.* 1381, *pg.* 944
SENTINEL - Plastic Casing - VISKASE COMPANIES, INC.; *pg.* 1471, *pg.* 599
SENTINEL ADVANTAGE - Variable Annuity - NATIONAL LIFE INSURANCE COMPANY; *pg.* 1210, *pg.* 1766
SENTINEL CUSTOMER SATISFACTION - Manual - XEROX CORPORATION; *pg.* 494, *pg.* 365
SENTINEL FAMILY OF FUNDS - Mutual Funds Owned, Managed & Distributed By Sentinel Companies - NATIONAL LIFE INSURANCE COMPANY; *pg.* 1210, *pg.* 1766
SENTINEL MARK II - Shower Valve - SPEAKMAN COMPANY; *pg.* 112, *pg.* 388
SENTINEL NET EXPERIENCE SCORE - Services - XEROX CORPORATION; *pg.* 494, *pg.* 365
SENTINEL SATISFACTION ASSURANCE SYSTEM - Manual - XEROX CORPORATION; *pg.* 494, *pg.* 365
SENTINOL - Medical Device - BOSTON SCIENTIFIC CORPORATION; *pg.* 1508, *pg.* 831
SENTRA - Automobile - NISSAN NORTH AMERICA, INC.; *pg.* 186, *pg.* 1633
SENTREX - Surge Protector - WIREMOLD/LEGRAND; *pg.* 689, *pg.* 383
SENTRIANT - Security Appliance - EXTREME NETWORKS INC; *pg.* 287, *pg.* 245
SENTRIANT AG200 - Security Component - EXTREME NETWORKS INC; *pg.* 287, *pg.* 245
SENTRICON - Termite Colony Elimination System - DOW AGROSCIENCES LLC; *pg.* 1156, *pg.* 684
SENTRIX - Array - ILLUMINA, INC.; *pg.* 412, *pg.* 203
SENTRON - Circuit Protection - SIEMENS PROCESS INDUSTRIES AND DRIVES; *pg.* 673, *pg.* 485
SENTRY - Portable Fire Extinguisher - ANSUL, INCORPORATED; *pg.* 1147, *pg.* 1869
SENTRY - Hammermill - A.T. FERRELL COMPANY, INC.; *pg.* 701, *pg.* 674
SENTRY - Office Chairs - BERNHARDT DESIGN; *pg.* 918, *pg.* 1381
SENTRY - Medical Device - BOSTON SCIENTIFIC CORPORATION; *pg.* 1508, *pg.* 831
SENTRY - Wash Fountain - BRADLEY CORPORATION; *pg.* 71, *pg.* 1870
SENTRY - Spotting Scope - BUSHNELL OUTDOOR PRODUCTS, INC.; *pg.* 1403, *pg.* 718
SENTRY - Fan - CRAFTMADE INTERNATIONAL, INC.; *pg.* 1295, *pg.* 1670
SENTRY - Thermal Imaging System - FLIR SYSTEMS, INC.; *pg.* 1413, *pg.* 1510
SENTRY - Gaming Product - GLD PRODUCTS, INC.; *pg.* 1835, *pg.* 1882
SENTRY - Mattress Replacement System - MEDLINE INDUSTRIES, INC.; *pg.* 1562, *pg.* 635
SENTRY - Chemical Agent Detector - MINE SAFETY APPLIANCES COMPANY; *pg.* 1361, *pg.* 1525
SENTRY - Diary Farm Equipment - PAUL MUELLER COMPANY; *pg.* 706, *pg.* 1007
SENTRY - Command & Control System - RAYTHEON COMPANY; *pg.* 233, *pg.* 854
SENTRY - Filtration System - SERFILCO, LTD.; *pg.* 1375, *pg.* 641
SENTRY - Line of Precision Belt Driven Block & Cartridge Spindles - SETCO SALES COMPANY; *pg.* 1061, *pg.* 1426
SENTRY - Cast Iron Gas Boiler - SLANT/FIN CORPORATION; *pg.* 1076, *pg.* 1163
SENTRY - Inspection Lighting System - UNILUX, INC.; *pg.* 682, *pg.* 1118
SENTRY FIRE SAFE SECURITY CHEST - Fire Resistant Security Chest - SENTRY GROUP, INC.; *pg.* 468, *pg.* 1337
SENTRY GATE - Rolling Closure Products - CORNELL IRON WORKS, INC.; *pg.* 77, *pg.* 1554
SENTRY OWL - Military & Commercial Vehicles - LOCKHEED MARTIN CORPORATION; *pg.* 229, *pg.* 762
SENTRY SAFE - Security Product - SENTRY GROUP, INC.; *pg.* 468, *pg.* 1337
SENTRY VISION - Closed-Circuit Television - SENTRY TECHNOLOGY CORPORATION; *pg.* 672, *pg.* 1339
SENTRYGLAS - Intrusion Resistant Glass - E.I. DU PONT DE NEMOURS & COMPANY; *pg.* 1159, *pg.* 390
SENTRYS - Switch - BROADCOM CORPORATION; *pg.* 364, *pg.* 108
SENTRYWASH - Eye Wash Unit - SELLSTROM MANUFACTURING CO.; *pg.* 1428, *pg.* 659
SENZA - Bath Product - KOHLER CO.; *pg.* 91, *pg.* 1862
SENZAO - Soft Drink - THE COCA-COLA COMPANY; *pg.* 240, *pg.* 493
SENZO - Paper & Nonwoven Material - FIBERMARK INC.; *pg.* 1457, *pg.* 1764
SEOPRENE - Ultra Cold Weather - COLEMAN CABLE, INC.; *pg.* 1324, *pg.* 665
SEOPRENE - Cord - ENCORE WIRE CORPORATION; *pg.* 637, *pg.* 1726
SEP-PAK - Solid-Phase Extraction - WATERS CORPORATION; *pg.* 1436, *pg.* 834
SEP TECH - Liquid Chromatographs - PPG INDUSTRIES, INC.; *pg.* 1445, *pg.* 1579
SEPRA - Biotechnology Product - GENZYME CORPORATION; *pg.* 1534, *pg.* 808
SEPRACOR - Pharmaceuticals - SUNOVION PHARMACEUTICALS INC.; *pg.* 1599, *pg.* 832
SEPRAFILM - Adhesion Barrier - GENZYME CORPORATION; *pg.* 1534, *pg.* 808
SEPRASOL - Coalescer System - PALL CORPORATION; *pg.* 232, *pg.* 1323
SEPTA - Transportation System - SOUTHEASTERN PENNSYLVANIA TRANSPORTATION AUTHORITY; *pg.* 1923, *pg.* 1570
SEPTICARE - Antimicrobial Wound Cleanser - ALIMED, INC.; *pg.* 1490, *pg.* 816
SEPTIHOL - Alcohol Solution - STERIS CORPORATION; *pg.* 1597, *pg.* 1464
SEPTISOFT - Skin Care Product - CONVATEC LTD.; *pg.* 1518, *pg.* 1121
SEPTISOL - Skin Care Product - STERIS CORPORATION; *pg.* 1597, *pg.* 1464
SEPTOR - Flashlight - STREAMLIGHT INC.; *pg.* 1306, *pg.*

1527
SEPTRA - Pharmaceutical Product - KING PHARMACEUTICALS, INC.; *pg.* 1553, *pg.* 1627
SEQUABOND - Chemical Product - OMNOVA SOLUTIONS INC; *pg.* 1176, *pg.* 1453
SEQUAFLOW - Carpet Chemicals - OMNOVA SOLUTIONS INC; *pg.* 1176, *pg.* 1453
SEQUAPEL - Wallcovering - OMNOVA SOLUTIONS INC; *pg.* 1176, *pg.* 1453
SEQUAREZ - Chemical Product - OMNOVA SOLUTIONS INC; *pg.* 1176, *pg.* 1453
SEQUE/PRO - Software - BIO-RAD LABORATORIES, INC.; *pg.* 1504, *pg.* 101
SEQUEAKY KLEEN - Software - BIO-RAD LABORATORIES, INC.; *pg.* 1504, *pg.* 101
SEQUEL - Automated Wafer Fabrication System - LAM RESEARCH CORPORATION; *pg.* 1354, *pg.* 246
SEQUEL - Sealant - W.L. GORE & ASSOCIATES, INC.; *pg.* 122, *pg.* 388
SEQUEL EXPRESS - Plasma Enhanced Chemical Vapor Deposition System - LAM RESEARCH CORPORATION; *pg.* 1354, *pg.* 246
SEQUELINK - Software - PROGRESS DATADIRECT; *pg.* 457, *pg.* 1385
SEQUENCE - Fabric - NEMSCHOFF, INC.; *pg.* 936, *pg.* 1890
SEQUENCE - Apparel - OAKLEY, INC.; *pg.* 1840, *pg.* 86
SEQUENT - Health & Nutrition Product - NOVUS INTERNATIONAL, INC.; *pg.* 706, *pg.* 1001
SEQUENTIA - Composites - CRANE CO.; *pg.* 227, *pg.* 373
SEQUESTRA 1000 - Autotransfusion Sys. - MEDTRONIC, INC.; *pg.* 1564, *pg.* 939
SEQUI-BLOT - Software - BIO-RAD LABORATORIES, INC.; *pg.* 1504, *pg.* 101
SEQUI-GEN - Software - BIO-RAD LABORATORIES, INC.; *pg.* 1504, *pg.* 101
SEQUINE - Footwear - STEVEN MADDEN, LTD.; *pg.* 1819, *pg.* 1176
SEQUOIA - Restaurant - ARK RESTAURANTS CORP.; *pg.* 1715, *pg.* 1196
SEQUOIA - Footwear - EASTLAND SHOE CORPORATION; *pg.* 1808, *pg.* 750
SEQUOIA - Wine - GEYSER PEAK WINERY; *pg.* 1964, *pg.* 101
SEQUOIA - Spotting Scope - LEUPOLD & STEVENS, INC.; *pg.* 1420, *pg.* 1492
SEQUOIA - Fabric - NEMSCHOFF, INC.; *pg.* 936, *pg.* 1890
SEQUOIA - Bicycle - SPECIALIZED BICYCLE COMPONENTS, INC.; *pg.* 1711, *pg.* 152
SEQUOIA - Sports Utility Vehicle - TOYOTA MOTOR NORTH AMERICA, INC.; *pg.* 192, *pg.* 1303
SEQUOIA GROVE - Wines - KOBRAND CORPORATION; *pg.* 1965, *pg.* 1325
SER PADRES - Spanish-Language Parenting Magazine - MEREDITH CORPORATION; *pg.* 1663, *pg.* 705
SERA - Eyewear - NIKE, INC.; *pg.* 1812, *pg.* 1492
SERA-SHARP - Laboratory Product - PROPPER MANUFACTURING COMPANY, INC.; *pg.* 1586, *pg.* 1175
SERACULT - Laboratory Product - PROPPER MANUFACTURING COMPANY, INC.; *pg.* 1586, *pg.* 1175
SERAKET - Laboratory Product - PROPPER MANUFACTURING COMPANY, INC.; *pg.* 1586, *pg.* 1175
SERANADE - Footwear - STEVEN MADDEN, LTD.; *pg.* 1819, *pg.* 1176
SERANO - Community Name - WCI COMMUNITIES, INC.; *pg.* 1118, *pg.* 414
SERAPE - Fabric - NEMSCHOFF, INC.; *pg.* 936, *pg.* 1890
SERATURE - Medical & Surgical Product - PROPPER MANUFACTURING COMPANY, INC.; *pg.* 1586, *pg.* 1175
SERCOS - Metrology Product - GLEASON CORPORATION; *pg.* 1340, *pg.* 1335
SERDESTEST - Software System - MENTOR GRAPHICS CORPORATION; *pg.* 432, *pg.* 1510
SERDUCTOR - Pumps - SERFILCO, LTD.; *pg.* 1375, *pg.* 641
SEREFINA - Gas Stoves - LENNOX HEARTH PRODUCTS; *pg.* 93, *pg.* 1652
SERENA - Furniture - AMISCO INDUSTRIES LTD.; *pg.* 913, *pg.* 1958
SERENA CHANGEMAN - Software - SERENA SOFTWARE, INC.; *pg.* 468, *pg.* 192
SERENA COLLAGE - Software - SERENA SOFTWARE, INC.; *pg.* 468, *pg.* 192
SERENA DIMENSIONS - Software - SERENA SOFTWARE, INC.; *pg.* 468, *pg.* 192
SERENA PROFESSIONAL - Software - SERENA SOFTWARE, INC.; *pg.* 468, *pg.* 192
SERENA STARTOOL - Software - SERENA SOFTWARE, INC.; *pg.* 468, *pg.* 192
SERENA TEAMTRACK - Software - SERENA SOFTWARE, INC.; *pg.* 468, *pg.* 192
SERENADE - Modern Occasional Tables - BERNHARDT DESIGN; *pg.* 918, *pg.* 1381
SERENADE - Area Rugs - COURISTAN INC.; *pg.* 921, *pg.* 1067
SERENADE - Watch - GEVRIL USA; *pg.* 6, *pg.* 1348
SERENADE - Fabric - NEMSCHOFF, INC.; *pg.* 936, *pg.* 1890
SERENADE - Apparel - VANS, INC.; *pg.* 1821, *pg.* 76
SERENADE OF THE SEAS - Cruise Ship - ROYAL CARIBBEAN CRUISES LTD; *pg.* 1921, *pg.* 446
SERENDIPITY - Carpet - INTERFACE, INC.; *pg.* 695, *pg.* 512
SERENDIPITY - Fabric - NEMSCHOFF, INC.; *pg.* 936, *pg.* 1890
SERENE - Carpet - BEAULIEU GROUP, LLC; *pg.* 917, *pg.* 529
SERENE - Mattress - ETHAN ALLEN INTERIORS INC.; *pg.* 924, *pg.* 343
SERENE - Office Furniture - STEELCASE INC.; *pg.* 475, *pg.* 889
SERENE ELEMENTS - Shampoo - MARIETTA HOSPITALITY; *pg.* 1464, *pg.* 1155
SERENE GREEN - Bouquet - 1-800-FLOWERS.COM, INC.; *pg.* 1758, *pg.* 1151
SERENE HEAT - Gas Logs - LENNOX HEARTH PRODUCTS; *pg.* 93, *pg.* 1652
SERENGETI - Furniture - ASHLEY FURNITURE INDUSTRIES, INC.; *pg.* 914, *pg.* 1852
SERENGETI - Sport Optic Product - BUSHNELL OUTDOOR PRODUCTS, INC.; *pg.* 1403, *pg.* 718
SERENGETI - Rug - COURISTAN INC.; *pg.* 921, *pg.* 1067
SERENITI - Footwear - STEVEN MADDEN, LTD.; *pg.* 1819, *pg.* 1176
SERENITY - Fabric - NEMSCHOFF, INC.; *pg.* 936, *pg.* 1890
SERENITY - Furniture - STANLEY FURNITURE CO., INC.; *pg.* 943, *pg.* 1379
SERENO - Bathroom Accessories - SYMMONS INDUSTRIES, INC.; *pg.* 114, *pg.* 803
SERES - Wireless Product - HEMISPHERE GPS INC.; *pg.* 642, *pg.* 1903
SERFAS - Radio Frequency Ablation System - STRYKER CORPORATION; *pg.* 1598, *pg.* 894
SERFENE - Adhesive & Sealant - DOW CHEMICAL; *pg.* 1156, *pg.* 1563
SERFENE - Barrier Coatings - THE DOW CHEMICAL COMPANY; *pg.* 1157, *pg.* 898
SERGEANT WINBIG - Game - WMS INDUSTRIES INC.; *pg.* 593, *pg.* 666
SERGIO VALENTE - Jeans - SEATTLE PACIFIC INDUSTRIES, INC.; *pg.* 48, *pg.* 1822
SERIAL NUMBER SERVER - Software - DATA I/O CORPORATION; *pg.* 382, *pg.* 1824
SERIES 1600 - Nub Tops - INTRALOX LLC; *pg.* 1350, *pg.* 744
SERIES 1700 - Sprockets - INTRALOX LLC; *pg.* 1350, *pg.* 744
SERIES 2 - Conveyors - KPI-JCI; *pg.* 1354, *pg.* 1626
SERIES 2000 - Handle - MAGLINE, INC.; *pg.* 1358, *pg.* 908
SERIES 2000 - Healthcare Information Technology System - MCKESSON CORPORATION; *pg.* 1560, *pg.* 222
SERIES 2400 - Raised Rib Conveyor Belt - INTRALOX LLC; *pg.* 1350, *pg.* 744
SERIES 300 OXY-THERM - Burner - MAXON CORPORATION; *pg.* 1359, *pg.* 695
SERIES 4000 - Eyepieces & Photo-Visual Color Filters - MEADE INSTRUMENTS CORPORATION; *pg.* 1422, *pg.* 113
SERIES 5000 - Eyepieces & Photo-Visual Color Filters - MEADE INSTRUMENTS CORPORATION; *pg.* 1422, *pg.* 113
SERIES 511 - Alignment System - HUNTER ENGINEERING COMPANY; *pg.* 208, *pg.* 973
SERIES 66 AIRFLO - Burner - MAXON CORPORATION; *pg.* 1359, *pg.* 695
SERIES 811 - Alignment System - HUNTER ENGINEERING COMPANY; *pg.* 208, *pg.* 973
SERIES 900 - Rubber Flights - INTRALOX LLC; *pg.* 1350, *pg.* 744
SERIES 9000 - Office Components - STEELCASE INC.; *pg.* 475, *pg.* 889
SERIES FLO - Fluid Handling System - GRACO, INC.; *pg.* 1342, *pg.* 935
SERIES IX - Software - INSTRON CORPORATION; *pg.* 1349, *pg.* 839
SERIES K - Furniture - HAWORTH, INC.; *pg.* 402, *pg.* 891
SERIES LV AIRFLO - Burner - MAXON CORPORATION; *pg.* 1359, *pg.* 695
SERIES NP - Burner - MAXON CORPORATION; *pg.* 1359, *pg.* 695
SERIES SYSTEM 7 - Panel System - MITY ENTERPRISES, INC.; *pg.* 935, *pg.* 1753
SERIF - Bath Product - KOHLER CO.; *pg.* 91, *pg.* 1862
SERIGLAZE - Coating Technology - SERIGRAPH, INC.; *pg.* 1686, *pg.* 1899
SERILLUSION - Graphics Technology - SERIGRAPH, INC.; *pg.* 1686, *pg.* 1899
SERIOUS CHEESE - Pizza - DONATOS PIZZERIA CORPORATION; *pg.* 1727, *pg.* 1439
SERIOUS MEAT - Pizza - DONATOS PIZZERIA CORPORATION; *pg.* 1727, *pg.* 1439
SERIPHYL - Pressed & Monolithic Refractory - RESCO PRODUCTS, INC.; *pg.* 107, *pg.* 1581
SERK AUDCO - Valve - FLOWSERVE CORPORATION; *pg.* 82, *pg.* 1719
SERLING - Fabric - NEMSCHOFF, INC.; *pg.* 936, *pg.* 1890
SERMONSEARCH.COM - Online Spiritual Leaders Search - SALEM MEDIA GROUP, INC.; *pg.* 307, *pg.* 57
SEROCLUSTER - Glass & Ceramic Material - CORNING INCORPORATED; *pg.* 1122, *pg.* 1154
SEROJET - Injection System - BIOJECT MEDICAL TECHNOLOGIES INC.; *pg.* 1506, *pg.* 1509
SEROMAP - Analytical Device - LUMINEX CORPORATION; *pg.* 1421, *pg.* 1664
SEROTAIN - Nutritional Product - NATROL, INC.; *pg.* 1570, *pg.* 64
SEROTAIN - Nutritional Supplement - NATURAL ORGANICS, INC.; *pg.* 1571, *pg.* 1181
SERPANT - Footwear - STEVEN MADDEN, LTD.; *pg.* 1819, *pg.* 1176
SERPENTEE - Apparel - VANS, INC.; *pg.* 1821, *pg.* 76
SERPENTINE BRONZE - Bath Product - KOHLER CO.; *pg.* 91, *pg.* 1862
SERPICO - Footwear - STEVEN MADDEN, LTD.; *pg.* 1819, *pg.* 1176
SERRAZIMES - Food Enzyme Product - NATIONAL ENZYME COMPANY; *pg.* 882, *pg.* 978
SERTA - Mattresses - NATIONAL BEDDING CO.; *pg.* 935, *pg.* 618
SERTASERVIS - Tire And Rubber Product - THE GOODYEAR TIRE & RUBBER COMPANY; *pg.* 1883, *pg.* 1401
SERV-RITE - Cable - WATLOW ELECTRIC MANUFACTURING COMPANY; *pg.* 1078, *pg.* 1004
SERVALOT - Popcorn Warmers - GOLD MEDAL PRODUCTS CO.; *pg.* 55, *pg.* 1414
SERVE 'N STORE - Food Product - PACTIV CORPORATION; *pg.* 1466, *pg.* 624
SERVEND - Delivery Body Style - HACKNEY INTERNATIONAL; *pg.* 178, *pg.* 1392
SERVERBIOS - Software - PHOENIX TECHNOLOGIES LTD.; *pg.* 454, *pg.* 147
SERVERLOCK - Software - WATCHGUARD TECHNOLOGIES, INC.; *pg.* 491, *pg.* 1842
SERVERMAGIC - Software - SYMANTEC CORPORATION; *pg.* 478, *pg.* 161
SERVERPORT - Printer Technology - TRANSACT TECHNOLOGIES INCORPORATED; *pg.* 484, *pg.* 351
SERVER'S CHOICE - Processed Pork Products - AMERICAN FOODS GROUP, LLC; *pg.* 837, *pg.* 1859
SERVEWARE - Software - XEROX CORPORATION; *pg.* 494, *pg.* 365
SERVEWELL - Food Service Equipment - THE VOLLRATH COMPANY LLC; *pg.* 1139, *pg.* 1894
SERVICE - Software - AXEDA SYSTEMS INC.; *pg.* 359, *pg.* 819
SERVICE AUTOMATION SUITE - Software - SUPPORT.COM, INC.; *pg.* 1283, *pg.* 192
SERVICE BEYOND THE CLICK - Slogan - APPLE VACATIONS INC.; *pg.* 1899, *pg.* 1556
SERVICE DELIVERY PLATFORM - Wireline Solutions - SONUS NETWORKS INC.; *pg.* 1281, *pg.* 858
SERVICE DESK EXPRESS - Software - BMC SOFTWARE, INC.; *pg.* 362, *pg.* 1701
SERVICE EXPERTS - Heating & Cooling Service - LENNOX INTERNATIONAL INC.; *pg.* 1073, *pg.* 1736
SERVICE FEE - Online Financial Services - ACI

WORLDWIDE; *pg.* 710, *pg.* 1777

SERVICE LINK - Software - CARDIAC SCIENCE CORPORATION; *pg.* 1512, *pg.* 1897

THE SERVICE MACHINE - Solid Waste Landfill Services - WASTE MANAGEMENT, INC.; *pg.* 1954, *pg.* 1716

SERVICE MANAGEMENT SOLUTIONS - Global Services - SONUS NETWORKS INC.; *pg.* 1281, *pg.* 858

SERVICE MANAGER - Software - VULCAN, INC.; *pg.* 687, *pg.* 5

SERVICE MASTER HOME SERVICE CENTER - Online Home Services & Related Products - THE SERVICEMASTER COMPANY, LLC; *pg.* 335, *pg.* 1646

SERVICE PLUS - Insurance Program - FEDERATED MUTUAL INSURANCE COMPANY; *pg.* 1200, *pg.* 952

THE SERVICE PROFESSIONALS - Tagline - CINTAS CORPORATION; *pg.* 372, *pg.* 1411

SERVICE PROVISIONING - Wireline Solutions - SONUS NETWORKS INC.; *pg.* 1281, *pg.* 858

SERVICE SMART ENTERPRISE PROVEN - Tagline - ASTEA INTERNATIONAL INC.; *pg.* 355, *pg.* 1540

SERVICEGATEWAY - Software - SUPPORT.COM, INC.; *pg.* 1283, *pg.* 192

SERVICEGRADE - Electronic Components - MOLEX INCORPORATED; *pg.* 655, *pg.* 628

SERVICELINK - Software - EVOLVING SYSTEMS, INC.; *pg.* 395, *pg.* 326

SERVICELINK - Surface Maintenance Machine - TENNANT COMPANY; *pg.* 1381, *pg.* 944

SERVICEMAGIC - Online Services - IAC/INTERACTIVECORP; *pg.* 292, *pg.* 1242

SERVICEMASTER CLEAN - Cleaning Service - THE SERVICEMASTER COMPANY, LLC; *pg.* 335, *pg.* 1646

SERVICES & SOLUTIONS IMPLEMENTATION PROCESS - Software - XEROX CORPORATION; *pg.* 494, *pg.* 365

SERVICESMART - Software - ARI NETWORK SERVICES, INC.; *pg.* 353, *pg.* 1873

SERVICEVERIFY - Software - SUPPORT.COM, INC.; *pg.* 1283, *pg.* 192

SERVICEWATCH - Software - EXTREME NETWORKS INC; *pg.* 287, *pg.* 245

SERVICEXPRESS - Software - EVOLVING SYSTEMS, INC.; *pg.* 395, *pg.* 326

SERVIN' SAVER - Food Containers - RUBBERMAID HOME PRODUCTS; *pg.* 1138, *pg.* 1453

SERVING AMERICA`S TABLES TODAY AND TOMORROW - Slogan - FROSTY ACRES BRANDS, INC.; *pg.* 1020, *pg.* 484

SERVING THE NEEDS OF COMMERCIAL CUSTOMERS - Tagline - KATY INDUSTRIES, INC.; *pg.* 1126, *pg.* 973

SERVISIGNAL - Service Indicator - DONALDSON COMPANY, INC.; *pg.* 1329, *pg.* 917

SERVISTAR HARDWARE - Retail Stores - TRUE VALUE COMPANY; *pg.* 1065, *pg.* 592

SERVO - Chart & Marking System - GRAPHIC CONTROLS LLC; *pg.* 401, *pg.* 1148

SERVO CLASS - Couplings - ZERO-MAX, INC.; *pg.* 222, *pg.* 954

SERVO COMMAND - Apparatus Foam Proportioning - KIDDE FIRE FIGHTING; *pg.* 1170, *pg.* 1531

SERVO DRIVEN SHOT - Metering Unit - NORDSON CORPORATION; *pg.* 1365, *pg.* 1480

SERVOCHASSIS - Machining System - ATS AUTOMATION TOOLING SYSTEMS INC.; *pg.* 355, *pg.* 1919

SERVODRIVE - Wheel Balancer - HUNTER ENGINEERING COMPANY; *pg.* 208, *pg.* 973

SERVOJET - Control Valves - MOOG INC.; *pg.* 231, *pg.* 1156

SERVOMATIC - HVAC Equipment - MESTEK, INC.; *pg.* 1074, *pg.* 857

SERVOMAX - HVAC Equipment - MESTEK, INC.; *pg.* 1074, *pg.* 857

SERVOREADY - Actuators - CUSTOM SENSORS & TECHNOLOGIES; *pg.* 1407, *pg.* 152

SERVOSMART - Actuators - CUSTOM SENSORS & TECHNOLOGIES; *pg.* 1407, *pg.* 152

SERVOWELD - Spin Welder - DUKANE CORPORATION; *pg.* 634, *pg.* 658

SERVSAFE - Food Safety Service - GORDON FOOD SERVICE INC.; *pg.* 1021, *pg.* 913

SERVSAFE - Food Safety Program - INTERNATIONAL DAIRY-DELI-BAKERY-ASSOCIATION; *pg.* 145, *pg.* 1866

SESA - Software - SYMANTEC CORPORATION; *pg.* 478, *pg.* 161

SESAME STREET - Toy & Game - HASBRO, INC.; *pg.* 954, *pg.* 1603

SESAME STREET - Educational Children's Books - PENGUIN RANDOM HOUSE CHILDREN'S BOOKS; *pg.* 1676, *pg.* 1277

SESAMEE - Keyless Padlocks - THE EASTERN COMPANY; *pg.* 1331, *pg.* 357

SESQUI - Chemical - FMC CORPORATION; *pg.* 1163, *pg.* 1564

SESSION - Bicycle - TREK BICYCLE CORPORATION; *pg.* 1847, *pg.* 1896

SESSION BORDER CONTROL (ACCESS) - Wireline Solutions - SONUS NETWORKS INC.; *pg.* 1281, *pg.* 858

SESSION BORDER CONTROL/IP PEERING - Cable Solutions - SONUS NETWORKS INC.; *pg.* 1281, *pg.* 858

SESSION BORDER CONTROL (PEERING) - Wireline Solutions - SONUS NETWORKS INC.; *pg.* 1281, *pg.* 858

SESTINA - Flatware - ONEIDA LTD; *pg.* 1129, *pg.* 1318

SET AND SAVE - Thermostat - HUNTER FAN COMPANY; *pg.* 57, *pg.* 1631

SET-BOLT - Anchor - POWERS FASTENERS INC.; *pg.* 1059, *pg.* 1143

SET FOR LIFE - Lottery Game - MASSACHUSETTS STATE LOTTERY; *pg.* 998, *pg.* 802

SET FOR LIFE - Lottery Game - NEW YORK STATE LOTTERY; *pg.* 1001, *pg.* 1340

SET IT AND FORGET IT - Software - CONDUSIV TECHNOLOGIES; *pg.* 379, *pg.* 51

SET OF 4 TRAVEL BRIGHT - Home Products - HABAND COMPANY, INC.; *pg.* 1772, *pg.* 1099

SET-RIGHT - Bearing Product - THE TIMKEN COMPANY; *pg.* 218, *pg.* 1408

SET SAIL - Scarf - HERITAGE LACE INC.; *pg.* 694, *pg.* 711

SETCO - Stock & Custom Bottles - MCCORMICK & COMPANY, INCORPORATED; *pg.* 1027, *pg.* 779

SETCO - Lines of Precision Spindles, Accessories, & Machines - SETCO SALES COMPANY; *pg.* 1061, *pg.* 1426

SETRA - Transducer & Accelerometer - DANAHER CORPORATION; *pg.* 1044, *pg.* 397

SETRA CRAM - Sensor - SETRA SYSTEMS, INC.; *pg.* 1428, *pg.* 802

SETS - Severe Environment Tape System - HONEYWELL AEROSPACE ELECTRONIC SYSTEMS; *pg.* 228, *pg.* 17

SETSIT - Accelerators - R.T. VANDERBILT COMPANY, INC.; *pg.* 1180, *pg.* 364

SETSOURCE - Medical Device - HOSPIRA, INC.; *pg.* 1542, *pg.* 623

SETTING A GLOBAL STANDARD - Tagline - DRIL-QUIP, INC.; *pg.* 1330, *pg.* 1704

SETTING STANDARDS - Tagline - NILFISK-ADVANCE, INC.; *pg.* 332, *pg.* 953

SETTING THE PACE THROUGH INNOVATION - Tagline - GREAT PLAINS MANUFACTURING, INCORPORATED; *pg.* 704, *pg.* 721

SETTING THE STANDARD - Slogan - THE VOLLRATH COMPANY LLC; *pg.* 1139, *pg.* 1894

SETTING THE STANDARD FOR BRILLIANCE - Diamonds - LAZARE KAPLAN INTERNATIONAL, INC.; *pg.* 8, *pg.* 1250

SETTING THE STANDARDS - Tagline - SCINTREX LTD.; *pg.* 1374, *pg.* 1920

SETTLZ - Indigestion Medicine - WATKINS INCORPORATED; *pg.* 909, *pg.* 967

SETU - Furniture - HERMAN MILLER, INC.; *pg.* 926, *pg.* 913

SEVEN PLUS - Glucose Monitoring Device - DEXCOM INC; *pg.* 1524, *pg.* 202

SEVEN STAR - Blended Whiskey - LAIRD & COMPANY, INC.; *pg.* 1966, *pg.* 1119

SEVEN STARS - Rewards Program - CAESARS ENTERTAINMENT CORPORATION; *pg.* 1083, *pg.* 1023

SEVEN STREAK - Game - WMS INDUSTRIES INC.; *pg.* 593, *pg.* 666

SEVEN TIMES PAY - Game - INTERNATIONAL GAME TECHNOLOGY; *pg.* 957, *pg.* 1024

SEVEN UNDER SIX - Low-Fat Sandwich - SUBWAY RESTAURANTS; *pg.* 1751, *pg.* 356

SEVENSTAR - Tool Steel - CARPENTER TECHNOLOGY CORPORATION; *pg.* 73, *pg.* 1584

SEVENTEEN - Magazine - THE HEARST CORPORATION; *pg.* 1649, *pg.* 1239

SEVERE GEAR - Air Filter - AMSOIL INC.; *pg.* 971, *pg.* 1896

SEVERE SERVICE 500 - Hard Chrome Piston & Cylinder Assembly - TITAN TOOL, INC.; *pg.* 1383, *pg.* 1100

SEVERE WEATHER - Door Glass - ODL INCORPORATED; *pg.* 101, *pg.* 914

SEVEY'S CORNER - T-Shirts - ABERCROMBIE & FITCH CO.; *pg.* 37, *pg.* 1466

SEVIGNY'S - Ribbon Candy - F.B. WASHBURN CANDY CORP.; *pg.* 1852, *pg.* 803

SEVILLA - Footwear - COBIAN CORP.; *pg.* 1806, *pg.* 253

SEVILLE - Food Product - A. DUDA & SONS INC.; *pg.* 835, *pg.* 457

SEVILLE - Furniture - AMERICAN LEATHER LP; *pg.* 912, *pg.* 1673

SEVILLE - Area Rugs - COURISTAN INC.; *pg.* 921, *pg.* 1067

SEVILLE - Footwear - EASTLAND SHOE CORPORATION; *pg.* 1808, *pg.* 750

SEVILLE - Dinnerware - THE HOMER LAUGHLIN CHINA COMPANY; *pg.* 1125, *pg.* 1850

SEVILLE - Ceiling Fan - HUNTER FAN COMPANY; *pg.* 57, *pg.* 1631

SEVILLE - Commercial Lighting - SWIVELIER CO., INC.; *pg.* 1307, *pg.* 1142

SEVILLE - Envelopes - XPEDX; *pg.* 1473, *pg.* 1377

SEVOFLO - Inhalation Anesthetic - ABBOTT LABORATORIES; *pg.* 1484, *pg.* 551

SEVOFLUORANE - Pharmaceutical Product - BAXTER INTERNATIONAL INC.; *pg.* 1499, *pg.* 599

SEVORANE - Inhalation Anesthetic - ABBOTT LABORATORIES; *pg.* 1484, *pg.* 551

SEVURE COM PORT REDIRECTOR - Software - LANTRONIX, INC.; *pg.* 426, *pg.* 112

SEWARD RANGE - T-Shirts - ABERCROMBIE & FITCH CO.; *pg.* 37, *pg.* 1466

SEWERCAD - Software - BENTLEY SYSTEMS, INC.; *pg.* 361, *pg.* 1531

SEWERGEMS - Software - BENTLEY SYSTEMS, INC.; *pg.* 361, *pg.* 1531

SEWINGHELPER - Cover & Pad - HOME PRODUCTS INTERNATIONAL, INC.; *pg.* 1125, *pg.* 577

SEWN UP - Carpet - INTERFACE, INC.; *pg.* 695, *pg.* 512

SEX AND THE CITY - Cable Television Show - HOME BOX OFFICE, INC.; *pg.* 290, *pg.* 1240

SEXAUER - Specialty Plumbing & Facility Maintenance Products - INTERLINE BRANDS, INC.; *pg.* 1051, *pg.* 433

SEXHILARATE - Nutritional Supplement - WHITEWING LABS, INC.; *pg.* 1610, *pg.* 99

SEXY SOCCER - Mobile Game - BLUCORA; *pg.* 1232, *pg.* 1813

SEYMOUR - Primer - SEYMOUR OF SYCAMORE, INC.; *pg.* 1447, *pg.* 663

SFA - Film Adhesive - SPINNAKER COATING, LLC; *pg.* 1470, *pg.* 1477

SFD - Software - BIO-RAD LABORATORIES, INC.; *pg.* 1504, *pg.* 101

SFD HIV 1/2 PA - Software - BIO-RAD LABORATORIES, INC.; *pg.* 1504, *pg.* 101

SFF - Transceiver - FINISAR CORPORATION; *pg.* 639, *pg.* 285

SFGO ULTRA - Synthetic Lubricants - LUBRIPLATE LUBRICANTS; *pg.* 980, *pg.* 1097

SFP - Transceiver - FINISAR CORPORATION; *pg.* 639, *pg.* 285

SFP MODULES - Electronic Component - EMCORE CORPORATION; *pg.* 636, *pg.* 39

SFP PRO - Chipset - VITESSE SEMICONDUCTOR CORPORATION; *pg.* 686, *pg.* 57

SFP+ - Transceiver - FINISAR CORPORATION; *pg.* 639, *pg.* 285

SFPB-4800-IC - Electronic Component - EMCORE CORPORATION; *pg.* 636, *pg.* 39

SFPB-800-IC - Electronic Component - EMCORE CORPORATION; *pg.* 636, *pg.* 39

SFT - Electronic Product - LRAD CORPORATION; *pg.* 652, *pg.* 204

SFX - Filter - CAMERON INTERNATIONAL; *pg.* 1151, *pg.* 1702

SG1 - Fluid Handling System - GRACO, INC.; *pg.* 1342, *pg.* 935

SG1-EF - Fluid Handling System - GRACO, INC.; *pg.* 1342, *pg.* 935

SG2 - Fluid Handling System - GRACO, INC.; *pg.* 1342, *pg.* 935

SG3 - Fluid Handling System - GRACO, INC.; *pg.* 1342, *pg.* 935

SGIS - Agricultural Database - AGCO CORPORATION; *pg.* 700, *pg.* 530

SGL - Liquid Phase Carbon - CALGON CARBON CORPORATION; *pg.* 1151, *pg.* 1574

SGML VALIDATION STUDIO - Software - XEROX CORPORATION; *pg.* 494, *pg.* 365

SGS - Consumer Testing Service - SGS U.S. TESTING COMPANY INC.; *pg.* 1181, *pg.* 1065
SGT - Electronic Pressure Instrument - SOR, INC.; *pg.* 1306, *pg.* 716
SHA - Footwear - STEVEN MADDEN, LTD.; *pg.* 1819, *pg.* 1176
SHABUI - Stone - WALKER & ZANGER, INC.; *pg.* 119, *pg.* 281
SHAC - Catalysts - THE DOW CHEMICAL COMPANY; *pg.* 1157, *pg.* 898
SHACK FRIES - Side Order - FAMOUS DAVE'S OF AMERICA, INC.; *pg.* 1728, *pg.* 926
SHADE-X - Measurement Device - X-RITE, INCORPORATED; *pg.* 1437, *pg.* 891
SHADECASE - Enclosure - THERMON AMERICAS INC.; *pg.* 1077, *pg.* 1744
SHADEFACTORY - Internet Platform - HUNTSMAN CORPORATION; *pg.* 1167, *pg.* 1758
SHADES OF SILVER AND YELLOW - Flower Arrangement - 1-800-FLOWERS.COM, INC.; *pg.* 1758, *pg.* 1151
SHADES OF SILVER & YELOW - Plant - 1-800-FLOWERS.COM, INC.; *pg.* 1758, *pg.* 1151
SHADESEAL - Beauty Product Sampling System - ARCADE MARKETING, INC.; *pg.* 352, *pg.* 1196
SHADEVISION - Color Measurement System - X-RITE, INCORPORATED; *pg.* 1437, *pg.* 891
SHADMORE - Jacket - I. SPIEWAK & SONS, INC.; *pg.* 42, *pg.* 1242
SHADOW - Connector - BOMAR INTERCONNECT PRODUCTS, INC.; *pg.* 1318, *pg.* 1079
SHADOW - Musical Instrument - GIBSON GUITAR CORP.; *pg.* 550, *pg.* 1650
SHADOW - Cleaning Product - HILLYARD, INC.; *pg.* 331, *pg.* 990
SHADOW - Pump - IDEX CORPORATION; *pg.* 1347, *pg.* 623
SHADOW - Wiper Cowl - LUND INTERNATIONAL, INC.; *pg.* 211, *pg.* 526
SHADOW - Software - PROGRESS SOFTWARE CORPORATION; *pg.* 457, *pg.* 786
SHADOW 6000 - Men's & Women's Training Shoe - SAUCONY, INC.; *pg.* 1818, *pg.* 828
SHADOW PLANT - Software System - HONEYWELL INTERNATIONAL INC.; *pg.* 407, *pg.* 1088
SHADOW PLUS VITAMINS - Eyeshadow - AVEDA CORPORATION; *pg.* 499, *pg.* 917
SHADOWNET - Software - NETWOLVES CORPORATION; *pg.* 1271, *pg.* 474
SHADOWPLANT - Software System - HONEYWELL INTERNATIONAL INC.; *pg.* 407, *pg.* 1088
SHADOWRIB - Metal Building System - BUTLER MANUFACTURING COMPANY; *pg.* 72, *pg.* 981
SHADY - Fertilizer - SIMPLOT PARTNERS INC.; *pg.* 1800, *pg.* 548
SHADY SPOT - Turfgrass Seed Mixture - CROSMAN SEED CORPORATION; *pg.* 1794, *pg.* 1156
SHAFTFIT - Fitting System - TRUE TEMPER SPORTS, INC.; *pg.* 1847, *pg.* 1647
SHAFTKEEPER - Reconditioning Device - GLOBE COMPOSITE SOLUTIONS, LTD.; *pg.* 1883, *pg.* 842
SHAFTLAB - Fitting System - TRUE TEMPER SPORTS, INC.; *pg.* 1847, *pg.* 1647
SHAG-BAG - Sports Bag - FRANKLIN SPORTS, INC.; *pg.* 1834, *pg.* 847
SHAHEEN - Packaged Foods - ATALANTA CORPORATION; *pg.* 838, *pg.* 1057
SHAHISTAN - Rugs - COURISTAN INC.; *pg.* 921, *pg.* 1067
SHAKA - Eyewear - MAUI JIM, INC.; *pg.* 9, *pg.* 651
SHAKE - Software Product - APPLE INC.; *pg.* 350, *pg.* 73
SHAKE-FREE - Specialty Sand for Aluminum & Light Alloy Applications - HEXION; *pg.* 1166, *pg.* 1440
SHAKE-N-BAKE - Seasoned Coating Mixes - THE KRAFT HEINZ COMPANY; *pg.* 870, *pg.* 1577
SHAKE 'N FEED - Lawn & Garden Products - THE SCOTTS MIRACLE-GRO COMPANY; *pg.* 1799, *pg.* 1459
SHAKE RATTLE & DOUGH - Pulltab Game - IDAHO LOTTERY; *pg.* 995, *pg.* 547
SHAKEDOWN - Apparel - VANS, INC.; *pg.* 1821, *pg.* 76
SHAKEN PLANK - Solid 2 1/4-3 1/4" Plank-Beveled - ROBBINS, INC.; *pg.* 108, *pg.* 1425
SHAKER - Clock - ETHAN ALLEN INTERIORS INC.; *pg.* 924, *pg.* 343
SHAKER MAKER GIFT SET - Barware - GORDON INDUSTRIES LTD.; *pg.* 6, *pg.* 1184
SHAKESPEARE - Fishing Tackle - PURE FISHING, INC.; *pg.* 1843, *pg.* 1614
SHAKESPEARE COMPOSITE STRUCTURES - Lighting Fixture & Control - PHILIPS LIGHTING; *pg.* 1303, *pg.* 806
SHAKEY EGGS - Toy - MUNCHKIN, INC.; *pg.* 964, *pg.* 300
SHAKEY'S - Pizza Restaurants - SHAKEY'S USA, INC.; *pg.* 1749, *pg.* 40
SHAKIN' BACON - Game - WMS INDUSTRIES INC.; *pg.* 593, *pg.* 666
SHAKIRA - Toy - MATTEL, INC.; *pg.* 962, *pg.* 81
SHAKLEE - Vitamins, Food Supplements, Skin, Hair & Beauty Care Products - SHAKLEE CORPORATION; *pg.* 1593, *pg.* 184
SHAKLEE CLASSICS - PCP'S - SHAKLEE CORPORATION; *pg.* 1593, *pg.* 184
SHAKLEE CORENERGY - Herbal Formula - SHAKLEE CORPORATION; *pg.* 1593, *pg.* 184
SHAKLEE DR - Herbal Formula - SHAKLEE CORPORATION; *pg.* 1593, *pg.* 184
SHAKLEE PERFORMANCE - Sports Nutritional Products - SHAKLEE CORPORATION; *pg.* 1593, *pg.* 184
SHALLO-TOW - Low Profile, Chain-In-Floor Conveyors - DAIFUKU WEBB; *pg.* 1327, *pg.* 885
SHALLOW WATER ANGLER - Magazine - RENTPATH, INC.; *pg.* 1680, *pg.* 538
SHAMAL - Bearing - SMITH INTERNATIONAL, INC.; *pg.* 1377, *pg.* 1715
SHAMAN EARTHLY ORGANICS - Organic Food Products - THE HAIN CELESTIAL GROUP, INC.; *pg.* 860, *pg.* 1172
SHAMMY - Fabric - NEMSCHOFF, INC.; *pg.* 936, *pg.* 1890
SHAMPOO-AIDE - Bath Safety - ALIMED, INC.; *pg.* 1490, *pg.* 816
SHAMROCK - Institutional Food Service Products - SHAMROCK FOODS COMPANY; *pg.* 895, *pg.* 20
SHAMROCK - Conduit Product - THOMAS & BETTS CORPORATION; *pg.* 680, *pg.* 1646
SHAMROCK - Gasoline Retail Outlets - VALERO ENERGY CORPORATION; *pg.* 986, *pg.* 1743
SHAMROCK FARMS - Dairy Products & Ice Cream - SHAMROCK FOODS COMPANY; *pg.* 895, *pg.* 20
SHAMROCK SHUFFLE - Lottery Game - KENTUCKY LOTTERY CORPORATION; *pg.* 996, *pg.* 735
SHANA - Shoulder Bag - JANDD MOUNTAINEERING, INC.; *pg.* 1837, *pg.* 204
SHANE - Fabric - NEMSCHOFF, INC.; *pg.* 936, *pg.* 1890
SHANGHAI - Fabric - SCALAMANDRE, INC.; *pg.* 941, *pg.* 1058
SHANGHAI SHIMMER - Nail Care Product - OPI PRODUCTS INC.; *pg.* 518, *pg.* 167
SHANGRILA - Carpet - BEAULIEU GROUP, LLC; *pg.* 917, *pg.* 529
SHANKLIN - Packaging Machinery - SEALED AIR CORPORATION; *pg.* 1468, *pg.* 1058
SHANKLIN EDGE - Packaging Machinery - SEALED AIR CORPORATION; *pg.* 1468, *pg.* 1058
SHANKLIN HORIZON - Packaging Machinery - SEALED AIR CORPORATION; *pg.* 1468, *pg.* 1058
SHANNEN & SCOOCH - Toy - MATTEL, INC.; *pg.* 962, *pg.* 81
SHANNON - Candy Jar - BROWN & BIGELOW, INC.; *pg.* 1624, *pg.* 959
SHANTUNG - Fabric - NEMSCHOFF, INC.; *pg.* 936, *pg.* 1890
SHAPE - Fitness DVD - GAIAM, INC.; *pg.* 1532, *pg.* 334
SHAPE 1 - Toothbrush - SUNSTAR AMERICAS INC.; *pg.* 1599, *pg.* 591
SHAPE-A-LOONS - Foil Balloons - CTI INDUSTRIES CORPORATION; *pg.* 1881, *pg.* 555
SHAPE FITTING TECHNOLOGY - Slogan - THE ROHO GROUP; *pg.* 1591, *pg.* 556
SHAPE MAGAZINE - Magazine - AMERICAN MEDIA, INC.; *pg.* 1615, *pg.* 410
SHAPE 'N BLUSH - Face Make-Up - COVER GIRL COSMETICS; *pg.* 506, *pg.* 772
SHAPE-O - Toy - TUPPERWARE BRANDS CORPORATION; *pg.* 1139, *pg.* 456
SHAPE OF THE STAND MIXER - Slogan - WHIRLPOOL CORPORATION; *pg.* 62, *pg.* 872
SHAPE SORTER BOOK - Game Book - INNOVATIVE USA, INC.; *pg.* 957, *pg.* 363
SHAPE UPS - Food Product - J&J SNACK FOODS CORPORATION; *pg.* 865, *pg.* 1107
SHAPED ENERGY - Transmission Technology - AMERICAN SCIENCE AND ENGINEERING, INC.; *pg.* 1399, *pg.* 787
SHAPED PULSE - Electronic Control Device - TASER INTERNATIONAL, INC.; *pg.* 677, *pg.* 24
SHAPEMATE - Polystyrene Foam - THE DOW CHEMICAL COMPANY; *pg.* 1157, *pg.* 898
SHAPES OF THE CAPE - Crackers - CAPE COD POTATO CHIP COMPANY; *pg.* 845, *pg.* 826
THE SHAPES OF THINGS TO COME - Tagline - HINDLEY MANUFACTURING COMPANY, INC.; *pg.* 1049, *pg.* 1601
SHAPES WITH ELLA - Toys - LEAPFROG ENTERPRISES, INC.; *pg.* 961, *pg.* 84
SHAPESTERS - Cheese - LACTALIS AMERICAN GROUP; *pg.* 873, *pg.* 1149
SHAPEWORKS - Weight Loss Product - HERBALIFE INTERNATIONAL OF AMERICA, INC.; *pg.* 1541, *pg.* 132
SHAPING THE FUTURE OF SOUND - Slogan - LRAD CORPORATION; *pg.* 652, *pg.* 204
SHARC - Embedded Processor - ANALOG DEVICES, INC.; *pg.* 617, *pg.* 839
SHARE CARD - Pharmaceutical Product - PFIZER INC.; *pg.* 1581, *pg.* 1278
SHARE MOMENTS. SHARE LIFE. - Slogan - EASTMAN KODAK COMPANY; *pg.* 1408, *pg.* 1333
SHARE OUR PASSION. - Slogan - ARCTIC CAT INC.; *pg.* 1705, *pg.* 953
SHARED SERVICE PROVIDER PKI - Internet Site Security Product - VERISIGN, INC.; *pg.* 488, *pg.* 1799
SHAREDIRECT - Software - LAPLINK SOFTWARE, INC.; *pg.* 426, *pg.* 1815
SHAREPLEX - Software - DELL SOFTWARE; *pg.* 385, *pg.* 40
SHAREPOINT - Software - EGAIN COMMUNICATIONS CORPORATION; *pg.* 1242, *pg.* 284
SHARESCAN - Software - NUANCE DOCUMENT IMAGING SOLUTIONS; *pg.* 1271, *pg.* 1037
SHARESTREAM - Software - R.R. DONNELLEY & SONS COMPANY; *pg.* 1682, *pg.* 589
SHARING HOLIDAY MOMENTS FOR GENERATIONS - Tagline - COLONY BRANDS INC.; *pg.* 849, *pg.* 1881
SHARING KNOWLEDGE. BUILDING TRUST. - Slogan - OHIO FARMERS INSURANCE COMPANY; *pg.* 1213, *pg.* 1480
SHARK - Microprocessor Based Analog Addressable Fire Panel - FIKE CORPORATION; *pg.* 1047, *pg.* 973
SHARK - Herbicide - FMC CORPORATION; *pg.* 1163, *pg.* 1564
SHARK - Furniture - NEUTRAL POSTURE, INC.; *pg.* 939, *pg.* 1669
SHARK EW - Herbicides - FMC CORPORATION; *pg.* 1163, *pg.* 1564
SHARK H2O - Herbicides - FMC CORPORATION; *pg.* 1163, *pg.* 1564
SHARK TOOTH - Wheel - YETTER MANUFACTURING CO., INC.; *pg.* 708, *pg.* 598
SHARKY - Footwear - COBIAN CORP.; *pg.* 1806, *pg.* 253
SHARP - Watch - M.Z. BERGER & CO., INC.; *pg.* 10, *pg.* 1175
SHARP - Pencils - PENTEL OF AMERICA, LTD.; *pg.* 453, *pg.* 295
SHARP - Molecular Biology Product - THERMO FISHER SCIENTIFIC INC.; *pg.* 1602, *pg.* 61
SHARP CHEDDAR - Snack Food - SNYDER'S-LANCE, INC.; *pg.* 896, *pg.* 1368
SHARP-FIRE - Power Tool - MILWAUKEE ELECTRIC TOOL CORP.; *pg.* 1056, *pg.* 1855
SHARP-SERT - Fasteners - YARDLEY PRODUCTS CORPORATION; *pg.* 1391, *pg.* 1596
SHARPE - Fluid Handling System - GRACO, INC.; *pg.* 1342, *pg.* 935
SHARPE S - Fluid Handling System - GRACO, INC.; *pg.* 1342, *pg.* 935
SHARPIE - Markers - NEWELL RUBBERMAID INC.; *pg.* 1128, *pg.* 515
SHARPLET-2 - Pencil - PENTEL OF AMERICA, LTD.; *pg.* 453, *pg.* 295
SHARPOINT - Surgical Instruments - SURGICAL SPECIALTIES CORPORATION; *pg.* 1600, *pg.* 1912
SHARPRINT - Printing & Writing Paper - BPM INC.; *pg.* 1454, *pg.* 1886
SHARP'S - Non-Alcoholic Beer - MILLERCOORS; *pg.* 254, *pg.* 1877
SHARPSHOOTER - Cleaner - 3M COMPANY; *pg.* 1142, *pg.* 956
SHASTA - Food Product - BUNGE LIMITED; *pg.* 842, *pg.* 1351
SHASTA - Soft Drink - NATIONAL BEVERAGE CORP.; *pg.* 257, *pg.* 425
SHASTA - Brush - THE WOOSTER BRUSH COMPANY; *pg.* 1450, *pg.* 1482

SHAVATRON - Sno-Kone Machine - GOLD MEDAL PRODUCTS CO.; *pg.* 55, *pg.* 1414
SHAVE EASE - Aerosol Lubricant, Cleaner - THE ELTRON COMPANY; *pg.* 507, *pg.* 103
SHAVE STICK - Powder Stick - THE ELTRON COMPANY; *pg.* 507, *pg.* 103
SHAVED ICE - Bath Accessory - CROSCILL, INC.; *pg.* 1122, *pg.* 1220
SHAVE'R CORD - Shave Accessory - THE ELTRON COMPANY; *pg.* 507, *pg.* 103
SHAVEZONE - Hair Remover - CCA INDUSTRIES, INC.; *pg.* 503, *pg.* 1114
SHAW-BOX - Hoist - COLUMBUS MCKINNON CORPORATION; *pg.* 1325, *pg.* 1138
SHAW BUSINESS INTERNET - Internet Service - SHAW COMMUNICATIONS INC.; *pg.* 307, *pg.* 1904
SHAW MESSENGER - Software - SHAW COMMUNICATIONS INC.; *pg.* 307, *pg.* 1904
SHAW MUSIC - Online Music Source - SHAW COMMUNICATIONS INC.; *pg.* 307, *pg.* 1904
SHAW PHOTO SHARE - Software - SHAW COMMUNICATIONS INC.; *pg.* 307, *pg.* 1904
SHAW SECURE - Software - SHAW COMMUNICATIONS INC.; *pg.* 307, *pg.* 1904
SHAW SPAM FILTER - Email Management System - SHAW COMMUNICATIONS INC.; *pg.* 307, *pg.* 1904
SHAW WEBMAIL - Email Service - SHAW COMMUNICATIONS INC.; *pg.* 307, *pg.* 1904
SHAW WEBSPACE - Software - SHAW COMMUNICATIONS INC.; *pg.* 307, *pg.* 1904
SHAWE - Furniture - ETHAN ALLEN INTERIORS INC.; *pg.* 924, *pg.* 343
SHAWNEE NEWS STAR - Newspaper - SHAWNEE NEWS-STAR; *pg.* 1686, *pg.* 1488
SHAW'S CRAB HOUSE - Seafood Restaurant - LETTUCE ENTERTAIN YOU ENTERPRISES, INC.; *pg.* 1735, *pg.* 580
SHAZAM - Character - DC COMICS, INC.; *pg.* 1633, *pg.* 1221
SHE LOVES ME - Carpet - INTERFACE, INC.; *pg.* 695, *pg.* 512
SHEA BUTTER - Soap - GRANDPA BRANDS COMPANY; *pg.* 1538, *pg.* 727
SHEA BUTTER FORMULA - Skin Care Product - E.T. BROWNE DRUG COMPANY, INC.; *pg.* 509, *pg.* 1060
SHEA STICK 3000 - Shea Butter for Antiperspirant & Deodorant Stick Formulations - JARCHEM INDUSTRIES, INC.; *pg.* 1169, *pg.* 1096
SHEAF STOUT - Beer - MILLERCOORS; *pg.* 254, *pg.* 1877
SHEAFFER - Writing Instruments - SHEAFFER PEN CORPORATION; *pg.* 469, *pg.* 371
SHEAR-SEAL - Directional Control Valves - BARKSDALE, INC.; *pg.* 1317, *pg.* 126
SHEAR TECHNOLOGY - Personal Care Electrical Product - HELEN OF TROY L.P.; *pg.* 511, *pg.* 1692
SHEARMASTER - Sheep Shearing Machine - JARDEN CONSUMER SOLUTIONS; *pg.* 57, *pg.* 412
SHEARPROOF - Self Locking Pin - DRIV-LOK, INC.; *pg.* 1046, *pg.* 662
SHEBA - Petcare Product - MARS, INCORPORATED; *pg.* 1858, *pg.* 1792
SHEBOYGAN - Sausage & Other Processed Meat Products - AMERICAN FOODS GROUP, LLC; *pg.* 837, *pg.* 1859
SHEDD'S SPREAD COUNTRY CROCK - Margarine Spread - UNILEVER UNITED STATES, INC.; *pg.* 904, *pg.* 1061
SHEEN - Fabric - NEMSCHOFF, INC.; *pg.* 936, *pg.* 1890
SHEEPLOAD OF CASH - Game - WMS INDUSTRIES INC.; *pg.* 593, *pg.* 666
SHEER COVER - Beauty Product - GUTHY-RENKER LLC; *pg.* 289, *pg.* 273
SHEER DIVINE - Scarf - HERITAGE LACE INC.; *pg.* 694, *pg.* 711
SHEER ELEGANCE - Carpet - BEAULIEU GROUP, LLC; *pg.* 917, *pg.* 529
SHEER ENCHANTMENT - Vertical Solutions - SPRINGS WINDOW FASHIONS LLC; *pg.* 943, *pg.* 1872
SHEER ENDURANCE - Hosiery - KAYSER-ROTH CORPORATION; *pg.* 28, *pg.* 1374
SHEER ENERGY - Apparel - HANESBRANDS INC.; *pg.* 26, *pg.* 1394
SHEER FACE POWDER - Powder - MERLE NORMAN COSMETICS, INC.; *pg.* 517, *pg.* 136
SHEER HALSTON - Perfume - ELIZABETH ARDEN, INC.; *pg.* 507, *pg.* 448
SHEER MIST - Window Treatment - CROSCILL, INC.; *pg.* 1122, *pg.* 1220
SHEER ORGANICS - Apparel - BLUE CANOE BODYWEAR; *pg.* 20, *pg.* 94
SHEER RADIANCE - Hand & Body Lotion - ORLY INTERNATIONAL, INC.; *pg.* 518, *pg.* 137
SHEER ROSE - Beauty Product - AVON PRODUCTS, INC.; *pg.* 500, *pg.* 1198
SHEERWALL - Curtain Walls & Wall Panels - KAWNEER COMPANY, INC.; *pg.* 90, *pg.* 537
SHEERWARE - Apparel - LANE BRYANT; *pg.* 1776, *pg.* 1441
SHEETROCK - Gypsum Panel - USG CORPORATION; *pg.* 118, *pg.* 594
SHEETROCK B1 - Outside Bead - USG CORPORATION; *pg.* 118, *pg.* 594
SHEETROCK B2 - Offset Trim - USG CORPORATION; *pg.* 118, *pg.* 594
SHEETROCK B4 - No Bead L Trim - USG CORPORATION; *pg.* 118, *pg.* 594
SHEETROCK B9J - J Trim - USG CORPORATION; *pg.* 118, *pg.* 594
SHEETROCK SLIC OS - Offset Bead - USG CORPORATION; *pg.* 118, *pg.* 594
SHEETROCK SLOC - Bullnose Bead - USG CORPORATION; *pg.* 118, *pg.* 594
SHEETROCK TOTAL - Joint Compound - USG CORPORATION; *pg.* 118, *pg.* 594
SHEETROCK TOTAL LITE - Joint Compound - USG CORPORATION; *pg.* 118, *pg.* 594
SHEFFIELD - Furniture - LA-Z-BOY INCORPORATED; *pg.* 932, *pg.* 901
SHEFFIELD - Musical Instrument - PEAVEY ELECTRONICS CORPORATION; *pg.* 662, *pg.* 970
SHEFFIELD - Pharmaceutical Product - SHEFFIELD LABORATORIES; *pg.* 1375, *pg.* 359
SHEFFIELD CELLARS - Wine - E&J GALLO WINERY; *pg.* 1962, *pg.* 149
THE SHEILD - Car Safety Device - WINNER INTERNATIONAL, LLC; *pg.* 222, *pg.* 1586
SHELBY - Clothing - ABERCROMBIE & FITCH CO.; *pg.* 37, *pg.* 1466
SHELBY - Furniture - JOFCO INC.; *pg.* 931, *pg.* 691
SHELBY - Footwear - VANS, INC.; *pg.* 1821, *pg.* 76
SHELBY WILLIAMS - Furniture - THE COMMERCIAL FURNITURE GROUP; *pg.* 920, *pg.* 994
SHELCORE - Toys - FUNRISE TOY CORP.; *pg.* 549, *pg.* 300
SHELDON HARBOR - Furniture - ASHLEY FURNITURE INDUSTRIES, INC.; *pg.* 914, *pg.* 1852
SHELETS - Sox - RELIABLE OF MILWAUKEE; *pg.* 698, *pg.* 1879
SHELF CONVERTER - Drawer System for Shelving - LISTA INTERNATIONAL CORPORATION; *pg.* 934, *pg.* 825
SHELF LIFE - Shelving - SAUDER WOODWORKING CO.; *pg.* 941, *pg.* 1403
SHELF LIGHT-ADVANCED - Lighting - STEELCASE INC.; *pg.* 475, *pg.* 889
SHELF LIGHT-STANDARD - Lighting - STEELCASE INC.; *pg.* 475, *pg.* 889
SHELF LIGHT-UTILITY - Lighting - STEELCASE INC.; *pg.* 475, *pg.* 889
SHELF-MASTER - Two-Pli Tab - SMEAD MANUFACTURING COMPANY; *pg.* 470, *pg.* 926
SHELFMATE - Commercial Lighting - SWIVELIER CO., INC.; *pg.* 1307, *pg.* 1142
SHELFTRACK - Plastic Wheel Lane - UNEX MANUFACTURING, INC.; *pg.* 1385, *pg.* 1075
SHELL - Furniture - HERMAN MILLER, INC.; *pg.* 926, *pg.* 913
SHELL CARD - Cash Card - CITIGROUP INC.; *pg.* 735, *pg.* 1212
SHELL-LESS SELECT - Bird Seed - INTERMOUNTAIN FARMERS ASSOCIATION; *pg.* 705, *pg.* 1759
SHELL SHOCK - Liquid Plastic - SMOOTH-ON INC.; *pg.* 111, *pg.* 1528
SHELLBURST - Photo Film - EASTMAN KODAK COMPANY; *pg.* 1408, *pg.* 1333
SHELLDIE - Steel Product - A. FINKL & SONS CO.; *pg.* 1309, *pg.* 563
SHELLEX - Steel Product - A. FINKL & SONS CO.; *pg.* 1309, *pg.* 563
SHELLEY - Reading Glass - A. T. CROSS COMPANY; *pg.* 339, *pg.* 1602
SHELLPAK - Paperboard Packaging Product - WESTROCK COMPANY; *pg.* 1472, *pg.* 1805
SHELLS - Dinnerware - THE HOMER LAUGHLIN CHINA COMPANY; *pg.* 1125, *pg.* 1850
SHELTER LOGIC - Checkered Flag Canopy - TRACTOR SUPPLY COMPANY; *pg.* 708, *pg.* 1627
SHELTER-RITE - Vinyl-Coated Fabric - SHUR-CO, INC.; *pg.* 110, *pg.* 1626
SHELTON - Shoes - ALLEN-EDMONDS SHOE CORP.; *pg.* 1804, *pg.* 1887
SHEN MIN - Healthcare Product - SWANSON HEALTH PRODUCTS INC.; *pg.* 1600, *pg.* 1397
SHENANDOAH - Cabinet - AMERICAN WOODMARK CORPORATION; *pg.* 913, *pg.* 1811
SHENANDOAH - Poultry System - CTB INTERNATIONAL CORP.; *pg.* 850, *pg.* 695
SHENANDOAH - Food Products - NATIONAL FRUIT PRODUCT COMPANY, INC.; *pg.* 882, *pg.* 1811
SHENANDOAH CABINETRY - Cabinet - AMERICAN WOODMARK CORPORATION; *pg.* 913, *pg.* 1811
SHEPHERD BUSINESS INTELLIGENCE - Sales & Marketing Intelligence - TRAVELPORT LIMITED; *pg.* 1925, *pg.* 521
SHEPPARD & GREENE - Pet Product - PETSMART, INC.; *pg.* 1481, *pg.* 18
SHER-TIP - Brushes - THE SHERWIN-WILLIAMS COMPANY; *pg.* 1447, *pg.* 1435
SHERATON - Flatware - ONEIDA LTD; *pg.* 1129, *pg.* 1318
SHERATON - Hotel And Tower - STARWOOD HOTELS & RESORTS WORLDWIDE, INC.; *pg.* 1114, *pg.* 378
SHERBET - Ice Cream - BLUE BELL CREAMERIES, L.P.; *pg.* 1851, *pg.* 1668
SHERBROOKE - Furniture - HAWORTH, INC.; *pg.* 402, *pg.* 891
SHERGRIP - Brush - THE WOOSTER BRUSH COMPANY; *pg.* 1450, *pg.* 1482
SHERIDAN - Modern Occasional Tables & Textiles - BERNHARDT DESIGN; *pg.* 918, *pg.* 1381
SHERIDAN - Furniture - HOOKER FURNITURE CORPORATION; *pg.* 928, *pg.* 1788
SHERLOCK - Application Program - APPLE INC.; *pg.* 350, *pg.* 73
SHERLOCK - Scanning Equipment - ILLUMINA, INC.; *pg.* 412, *pg.* 203
SHERLOCK - Connector - MOLEX INCORPORATED; *pg.* 655, *pg.* 628
SHERLOCK - Brush - THE WOOSTER BRUSH COMPANY; *pg.* 1450, *pg.* 1482
SHERPA - Rug - COURISTAN INC.; *pg.* 921, *pg.* 1067
SHERTECH - Gear Pumps - HYPRO; *pg.* 705, *pg.* 951
SHERWOOD - Furniture - ASHLEY FURNITURE INDUSTRIES, INC.; *pg.* 914, *pg.* 1852
SHERWOOD - Footwear - EASTLAND SHOE CORPORATION; *pg.* 1808, *pg.* 750
SHERWOOD PARK - Carpet - BEAULIEU GROUP, LLC; *pg.* 917, *pg.* 529
SHE'S CHARMED & DANGEROUS - Game - GAMEWRIGHT; *pg.* 953, *pg.* 836
SHHIMER - Footwear - STEVEN MADDEN, LTD.; *pg.* 1819, *pg.* 1176
SHIATSU - Massage Chair - RELAX THE BACK CORPORATION; *pg.* 940, *pg.* 120
SHIDLER - Real Estate Investment - THE SHIDLER GROUP; *pg.* 1112, *pg.* 545
SHIELD - Systems Integration & Aeronautics - LOCKHEED MARTIN CORPORATION; *pg.* 229, *pg.* 762
SHIELD-ALL II - Disease Control Product - GARDENS ALIVE!, INC.; *pg.* 1796, *pg.* 693
SHIELD-ARC - Welder - LINCOLN ELECTRIC HOLDINGS, INC.; *pg.* 1355, *pg.* 1432
SHIELD BLASTER - Toy - MATTEL, INC.; *pg.* 962, *pg.* 81
SHIELD-KON - Connector - THOMAS & BETTS CORPORATION; *pg.* 680, *pg.* 1646
SHIELDED ZT-TAPE - Wire & Cable - THE ZIPPERTUBING COMPANY; *pg.* 1892, *pg.* 12
SHIELDGARD - Underlayment - GAF MATERIALS CORP.; *pg.* 83, *pg.* 1681
SHIELDMATE - Eyeshield Mask - ALPHA PRO TECH, LTD.; *pg.* 1492, *pg.* 1922
SHIFT - Corporate Furniture - BERNHARDT DESIGN; *pg.* 918, *pg.* 1381
SHIFTING SANDS - Carpet - BEAULIEU GROUP, LLC; *pg.* 917, *pg.* 529
SHIFTLOGIC - Software System - KRONOS INCORPORATED; *pg.* 425, *pg.* 813
SHIFTRONIC - Automatic Automobile Transmissions - HYUNDAI MOTOR AMERICA; *pg.* 179, *pg.* 89
SHIFTY - Glove - KOMBI, LTD.; *pg.* 1838, *pg.* 1766

First page reference indicates Business Class Edition
Second page reference indicates Geographic Edition

SHILEY - Tray - COOK GROUP, INC.; *pg.* 1518, *pg.* 674
SHILEY - Medical Device - MALLINCKRODT PHARMACEUTICALS; *pg.* 1557, *pg.* 978
SHILEY - Tracheostomy Tubes - MEDTRONIC; *pg.* 1563, *pg.* 183
SHIM-SELECT - Alignment System Software - HUNTER ENGINEERING COMPANY; *pg.* 208, *pg.* 973
SHIMADZU - Microhardness Tester - NEWAGE TESTING INSTRUMENTS, INC.; *pg.* 1058, *pg.* 1532
SHIMMER - Tile - ARTISTIC TILE INC.; *pg.* 914, *pg.* 1119
SHIMMER - Textiles - BERNHARDT DESIGN; *pg.* 918, *pg.* 1381
SHIMMER - Fabric - NEMSCHOFF, INC.; *pg.* 936, *pg.* 1890
SHIMMER - Game - WMS INDUSTRIES INC.; *pg.* 593, *pg.* 666
SHIMMER-E - Decorated Paper - HAZEN PAPER COMPANY; *pg.* 1459, *pg.* 825
SHIMMER SCRIM - Fabric - ROSCO LABORATORIES, INC.; *pg.* 1782, *pg.* 378
SHIMMERCAL - Graphic Film - FLEXCON CORPORATION; *pg.* 1457, *pg.* 844
SHIMMERS - Hosiery & Related Apparel - MAYER/BERKSHIRE CORPORATION; *pg.* 29, *pg.* 1129
SHIMMERSTICK - Eyeshadow Pencil - MERLE NORMAN COSMETICS, INC.; *pg.* 517, *pg.* 136
SHIMMY - Fabric - NEMSCHOFF, INC.; *pg.* 936, *pg.* 1890
SHIMMY - Surface Material - STEELCASE INC.; *pg.* 475, *pg.* 889
SHIN SPLINT - Orthopedic Product - DJO INCORPORATED; *pg.* 1524, *pg.* 302
THE SHINE - Hair Care Product - JOHN PAUL MITCHELL SYSTEMS; *pg.* 512, *pg.* 133
SHINE-A-LINE - Chemical Product - BIRKO CORPORATION; *pg.* 1149, *pg.* 332
SHINE EFFECTS - Hair Straightener - CONAIR CORPORATION; *pg.* 505, *pg.* 1055
SHINE FREE - Oil Control Makeup - MAYBELLINE LLC; *pg.* 516, *pg.* 1257
SHINE N' GUARD - Dressing - MOC PRODUCTS COMPANY, INC.; *pg.* 332, *pg.* 174
SHINE-ON - Animal Care Product - STRAIGHT ARROW PRODUCTS, INC.; *pg.* 523, *pg.* 1517
SHINES - Hair Care System - JOHN PAUL MITCHELL SYSTEMS; *pg.* 512, *pg.* 133
SHINEWHITE - Dental Product - ETS, LLC; *pg.* 54, *pg.* 685
SHINING STAR - Carpet - BEAULIEU GROUP, LLC; *pg.* 917, *pg.* 529
SHINING STARS - Toy - MATTEL, INC.; *pg.* 962, *pg.* 81
SHINNING EFFECTS - Cosmetic Product - NU SKIN ENTERPRISES, INC.; *pg.* 518, *pg.* 1755
SHINY STYLES - Hair Care Product - CONAIR CORPORATION; *pg.* 505, *pg.* 1055
SHIP AHOY - Frozen Seafood; Canned Seafood - ICICLE SEAFOODS, INC.; *pg.* 864, *pg.* 1836
SHIP 'N SHOP - Mobile Display Carts - CANNON EQUIPMENT COMPANY; *pg.* 1321, *pg.* 920
SHIPENDEC - Paint - PETTIT PAINT COMPANY; *pg.* 1444, *pg.* 1116
SHIPLAN - Military Cables - GENERAL CABLE CORPORATION; *pg.* 83, *pg.* 729
SHIPLEY - Industrial Material - DOW CHEMICAL; *pg.* 1156, *pg.* 1563
SHIPPING DIGEST - Shipping Publication - JOC GROUP INC.; *pg.* 1654, *pg.* 1096
SHIPPING-MATE - Packaging Aerosol Adhesives & Coatings - 3M COMPANY; *pg.* 1142, *pg.* 956
SHIPPING SAVVY - Shipment Service - FEDEX CORPORATION; *pg.* 1907, *pg.* 1642
SHIPREQUEST - Software - PITNEY BOWES INC.; *pg.* 454, *pg.* 376
SHIPSHAPE - Cruise Ship - ROYAL CARIBBEAN CRUISES LTD; *pg.* 1921, *pg.* 446
SHIPSTREAM - Mailing System - PITNEY BOWES INC.; *pg.* 454, *pg.* 376
SHIPSTREAM MANAGER - Mailer - PITNEY BOWES INC.; *pg.* 454, *pg.* 376
SHIPTRAK - Software System - IRON MOUNTAIN INCORPORATED; *pg.* 421, *pg.* 796
SHIRAZ - Rug - COURISTAN INC.; *pg.* 921, *pg.* 1067
SHIRMATIC - Plastic Casing - VISKASE COMPANIES, INC.; *pg.* 1471, *pg.* 599
SHISEIDO THE SKINCARE - Cosmetic Product - SHISEIDO COSMETICS AMERICA OF SAC; *pg.* 522, *pg.* 1291
SHIVERING TIMBERS - Amusement & Water Park - CEDAR FAIR, L.P.; *pg.* 537, *pg.* 1471
SHIZEN - Carpet - INTERFACE, INC.; *pg.* 695, *pg.* 512
SHO-FLEX - Animal Nutrition Product - MANNA PRO CORPORATION; *pg.* 1478, *pg.* 975
SHO-GLO - Animal Nutrition Product - MANNA PRO CORPORATION; *pg.* 1478, *pg.* 975
SHO-HOOF - Animal Nutrition Product - MANNA PRO CORPORATION; *pg.* 1478, *pg.* 975
SHO-RATE - Control Measurement - BROOKS INSTRUMENT, LLC; *pg.* 1403, *pg.* 1537
SHO RGB - Architectural Line Voltage - REVOLUTION LIGHTING TECHNOLOGIES, INC.; *pg.* 1304, *pg.* 377
SHOBBER - Hobbing And Shaping Machine - GLEASON CORPORATION; *pg.* 1340, *pg.* 1335
SHOCK - Beverages - THE COCA-COLA COMPANY; *pg.* 240, *pg.* 493
SHOCK ABSORBER - Sole Flex - HITCHCOCK SHOES, INC.; *pg.* 1810, *pg.* 824
SHOCK ABSORBING EXPANDER - Lanyard - SELLSTROM MANUFACTURING CO.; *pg.* 1428, *pg.* 659
SHOCK ABZZORBER - Box Spring - SEALY CORPORATION; *pg.* 942, *pg.* 1391
SHOCK-BLOK - Striking Tool - VAUGHAN & BUSHNELL MANUFACTURING COMPANY, INC.; *pg.* 1066, *pg.* 616
SHOCK-EZE - Shock Absorber - BAKER HUGHES INTEQ; *pg.* 1316, *pg.* 1700
SHOCK GUARD - Hard Drive - WESTERN DIGITAL CORPORATION; *pg.* 492, *pg.* 118
SHOCK-LESS - Cleaner - DELTA FOREMOST CHEMICAL CORPORATION; *pg.* 1155, *pg.* 1642
SHOCK SPRING - Cushioning System - K-SWISS; *pg.* 1837, *pg.* 306
SHOCK TOP BELGIAN WHITE - Beer - ANHEUSER-BUSCH COMPANIES, LLC; *pg.* 237, *pg.* 991
SHOCK TRAP - Extension Cord - SOUTHWIRE COMPANY; *pg.* 1063, *pg.* 527
SHOCKEN BOOKS - Book Imprint - PENGUIN RANDOM HOUSE; *pg.* 1675, *pg.* 1276
SHOCKERR - Footwear - STEVEN MADDEN, LTD.; *pg.* 1819, *pg.* 1176
SHOCKERS - Candy - NESTLE USA, INC.; *pg.* 883, *pg.* 96
SHOCKGUARD - Hose - HBD INDUSTRIES, INC.; *pg.* 207, *pg.* 1449
SHOCKGUARD 300 - Multipurpose Hose - HBD INDUSTRIES, INC.; *pg.* 207, *pg.* 1449
SHOCKPOD - Software - BIO-RAD LABORATORIES, INC.; *pg.* 1504, *pg.* 101
SHOCKROCK - Apparel - VANS, INC.; *pg.* 1821, *pg.* 76
SHOCKSHIELD - High-Density Foam Drop Protection for Laptops - JANSPORT; *pg.* 1837, *pg.* 38
SHOCKSHIELD - Drive Technology - WESTERN DIGITAL CORPORATION; *pg.* 492, *pg.* 118
SHOCKWAVE - Electronic Control Device - TASER INTERNATIONAL, INC.; *pg.* 677, *pg.* 24
SHOCKWAVE PLAYER - Software - ADOBE SYSTEMS INCORPORATED; *pg.* 342, *pg.* 235
SHOCKWAVE.COM - Gaming Website - DEFYMEDIA; *pg.* 1237, *pg.* 1222
SHODEX - Analytical Column - WATERS CORPORATION; *pg.* 1436, *pg.* 834
SHOEBOX LIBRARY - Educational Materials - SCHOLASTIC INC.; *pg.* 1683, *pg.* 1288
SHOEBUY.COM - Online Shoe Retailer - IAC/INTERACTIVECORP; *pg.* 292, *pg.* 1242
SHOEDAZZLE - Shoes - JUSTFAB, INC.; *pg.* 27, *pg.* 80
SHOES XL - Online & Print Catalog - DESTINATION XL GROUP, INC.; *pg.* 40, *pg.* 810
SHOGUN - Container Grown Plant - MONROVIA GROWERS; *pg.* 1797, *pg.* 44
SHOJI - Bath Accessory - CROSCILL, INC.; *pg.* 1122, *pg.* 1220
SHOK-SORB - Sport Product - FRANKLIN SPORTS, INC.; *pg.* 1834, *pg.* 847
SHOMY - Software - CRESTRON ELECTRONICS INC.; *pg.* 631, *pg.* 1116
SHONEY'S - Family Restaurants - SHONEY'S NORTH AMERICA, LLC; *pg.* 1749, *pg.* 1654
SHOOT - Trade Publication - THE NIELSEN COMPANY B.V.; *pg.* 1671, *pg.* 1272
SHOOT AND STORE - Memory Card - SANDISK CORPORATION; *pg.* 465, *pg.* 147
SHOOT CASE - Basketball Equipment - LIFETIME PRODUCTS INC.; *pg.* 933, *pg.* 1751
SHOOT CASE & DESIGN - Mini-Basketball Set - LIFETIME PRODUCTS INC.; *pg.* 933, *pg.* 1751
SHOOT 'N SCORE - Sport Product - FRANKLIN SPORTS, INC.; *pg.* 1834, *pg.* 847
SHOOT-N-SCORE - Basketball Equipment - LIFETIME PRODUCTS INC.; *pg.* 933, *pg.* 1751
SHOOTERR - Sneaker - STEVEN MADDEN, LTD.; *pg.* 1819, *pg.* 1176
SHOOTER'S PUTTY - Earplug - MCKEON PRODUCTS, INC.; *pg.* 1559, *pg.* 912
SHOOTING ARRAY - Eyewear - OAKLEY, INC.; *pg.* 1840, *pg.* 86
SHOOTING GALLERY - Slots - INTERNATIONAL GAME TECHNOLOGY; *pg.* 957, *pg.* 1024
SHOOTING STAR - Systems Integration & Aeronautics - LOCKHEED MARTIN CORPORATION; *pg.* 229, *pg.* 762
SHOOTING STAR - Lottery Game - MASSACHUSETTS STATE LOTTERY; *pg.* 998, *pg.* 802
SHOOTING TIMES - Magazine - RENTPATH, INC.; *pg.* 1680, *pg.* 538
SHOOTSAVER - Film Delivery Service - EASTMAN KODAK COMPANY; *pg.* 1408, *pg.* 1333
SHOP ABOUT - Furniture - ANTHRO CORPORATION; *pg.* 913, *pg.* 1509
SHOP AND DINE - Soft Travel Product - INFANTINO, LLC; *pg.* 957, *pg.* 203
SHOP CHANNEL - Retail Shopping Network - IAC/INTERACTIVECORP; *pg.* 292, *pg.* 1242
SHOP DIFFERENT - Slogan - APPLE INC.; *pg.* 350, *pg.* 73
SHOP MANAGER - Software - VULCAN, INC.; *pg.* 687, *pg.* 5
SHOP 'N SAVE - Retail Food & Drug Stores - HANNAFORD BROTHERS CO.; *pg.* 1022, *pg.* 752
SHOP 'N SAVE - Supermarkets & Pharmacies - SUPERVALU, INC.; *pg.* 1035, *pg.* 924
SHOP SMART - Food Markets - C&K MARKET, INC.; *pg.* 1016, *pg.* 1496
SHOP-SWEEP - Push Sweeper - SHOP-VAC CORPORATION; *pg.* 1375, *pg.* 1595
SHOP 'TIL YOU DROP - Lottery Game - NEW YORK STATE LOTTERY; *pg.* 1001, *pg.* 1340
SHOP WITH THE BIG DOGS - Tagline - THE WALKING COMPANY HOLDINGS, INC.; *pg.* 50, *pg.* 263
SHOPAMEX - Online Shopping - AMERICAN EXPRESS COMPANY; *pg.* 712, *pg.* 1190
SHOPANDPLAY - Shopping Cart Cover - INFANTINO, LLC; *pg.* 957, *pg.* 203
SHOPBLUE - Retail Store Services - JETBLUE AIRWAYS CORPORATION; *pg.* 1913, *pg.* 1174
SHOPKEY - Repair & Service Information & Shop Management Software - SNAP-ON INCORPORATED; *pg.* 1062, *pg.* 1862
SHOPMASTER - Wiper And Cleaning Cloth - GEORGIA-PACIFIC LLC; *pg.* 1458, *pg.* 507
SHOPNOVELL - Computer Software - NOVELL INC.; *pg.* 446, *pg.* 852
SHOPPER STOPPER - Publication - MADISON NEWSPAPERS, INC.; *pg.* 1661, *pg.* 1866
SHOPPERS - Store - SUPERVALU, INC.; *pg.* 1035, *pg.* 924
SHOPPERS ADVANTAGE - Discount Shopping Services - AFFINION GROUP, INC.; *pg.* 1225, *pg.* 372
SHOPPER'S FOOD WHAREHOUSE - Supermarket - SUPERVALU, INC.; *pg.* 1035, *pg.* 924
SHOPPERS HOME HEALTH CARE - Drug Stores - SHOPPERS DRUG MART CORPORATION; *pg.* 1594, *pg.* 1943
SHOPPERS OPTIMUM - Discount Card - SHOPPERS DRUG MART CORPORATION; *pg.* 1594, *pg.* 1943
SHOPPING SPREE - Golf Accessories - CALLAWAY GOLF COMPANY; *pg.* 1829, *pg.* 58
SHOPRANK - Shopping Search Algorithm - BIZRATE.COM; *pg.* 1231, *pg.* 126
SHOPRESULTS.NET - Online Alignment Service - HUNTER ENGINEERING COMPANY; *pg.* 208, *pg.* 973
SHOPRITE - Grocery Stores & Products - WAKEFERN FOOD CORPORATION; *pg.* 1037, *pg.* 1058
SHOPSMITH - Tools - SHOPSMITH, INC.; *pg.* 1375, *pg.* 1446
SHOPSY'S - Delicatessens & Meat Products - MAPLE LEAF FOODS INC.; *pg.* 875, *pg.* 1927
SHOPVOGUE.TV - Internet Channel - CONDE NAST PUBLICATIONS, INC.; *pg.* 1629, *pg.* 1217
SHOPVUE - Graphic Display - INDUSTRIAL ELECTRONIC ENGINEERS, INC.; *pg.* 644, *pg.* 300
SHOPWISE - Shared Advertising Mail Packets - VALASSIS; *pg.* 1698, *pg.* 386
SHORE - Durometer - INSTRON CORPORATION; *pg.* 1349, *pg.* 839
SHOREGUARD - Construction Material - CRANE PLASTICS

HOLDING COMPANY; *pg.* 1881, *pg.* 1439
SHOREHAM - Fabric - NEMSCHOFF, INC.; *pg.* 936, *pg.* 1890
THE SHOREHAM - Hotel - OMNI HOTELS & RESORTS; *pg.* 1107, *pg.* 1685
SHORELAND'R - Boat Trailers - MIDWEST INDUSTRIES, INC.; *pg.* 185, *pg.* 708
SHORELINE - Eyewear - MAUI JIM, INC.; *pg.* 9, *pg.* 651
SHORELINE - Furniture - TROPITONE FURNITURE CO., INC.; *pg.* 945, *pg.* 118
SHORESTATION - Boat Hoists & Docks - MIDWEST INDUSTRIES, INC.; *pg.* 185, *pg.* 708
SHORT CUTS - Fully Cooked Meats - PERDUE FARMS INCORPORATED; *pg.* 889, *pg.* 777
SHORT LOOKS - Texturizer Kit - LUSTER PRODUCTS INC.; *pg.* 515, *pg.* 581
SHORT NIGHTHAWK - Knife - BUCK KNIVES, INC.; *pg.* 1828, *pg.* 550
SHORT SLEEVE CREW NECK - Clothing - K-SWISS; *pg.* 1837, *pg.* 306
SHORT STOP - Wire Maintenance Solution - BULLSEYE TELECOM INC.; *pg.* 366, *pg.* 906
SHORT-STOP - Self-Retracting Lanyard - MINE SAFETY APPLIANCES COMPANY; *pg.* 1361, *pg.* 1525
SHORTCUT - Kitchen Appliance - HAMILTON BEACH BRANDS, INC.; *pg.* 56, *pg.* 1783
SHORTCUT - Brush - THE WOOSTER BRUSH COMPANY; *pg.* 1450, *pg.* 1482
SHORTCUTT - Plugging System - T.D. WILLIAMSON, INC.; *pg.* 1380, *pg.* 1490
SHORTI - Hoagie Sandwich - WAWA, INC.; *pg.* 1037, *pg.* 1552
SHORTIES - Glass & Ceramic Material - CORNING INCORPORATED; *pg.* 1122, *pg.* 1154
SHORTPLUG - Pipeline Pigging Product - T.D. WILLIAMSON, INC.; *pg.* 1380, *pg.* 1490
SHORTSLEEVE - Pipeline Pigging Product - T.D. WILLIAMSON, INC.; *pg.* 1380, *pg.* 1490
SHORTSTACK - Software - ECHELON CORPORATION; *pg.* 389, *pg.* 245
SHORTSTOPP - Plugging System - T.D. WILLIAMSON, INC.; *pg.* 1380, *pg.* 1490
SHORTSTOPP II - Device for Plugging Interior of Pipe - T.D. WILLIAMSON, INC.; *pg.* 1380, *pg.* 1490
SHORTY - Wire Guide - COOK GROUP, INC.; *pg.* 1518, *pg.* 674
SHOT - Fluid Handling System - GRACO, INC.; *pg.* 1342, *pg.* 935
SHOT BUSINESS - Magazine - BONNIER CORPORATION; *pg.* 1622, *pg.* 480
SHOT FOAM - Fluid Handling System - GRACO, INC.; *pg.* 1342, *pg.* 935
SHOT-FORM - Concrete Mesh - ALABAMA METAL INDUSTRIES CORPORATION; *pg.* 65, *pg.* 1
SHOT KING - Gaming Product - GLD PRODUCTS, INC.; *pg.* 1835, *pg.* 1882
SHOT-O - Nutritional Supplement - NATURAL ORGANICS, INC.; *pg.* 1571, *pg.* 1181
SHOT OF STEAM - Steam Irons - JARDEN CONSUMER SOLUTIONS; *pg.* 57, *pg.* 412
SHOT ZONE - Sport Product - FRANKLIN SPORTS, INC.; *pg.* 1834, *pg.* 847
SHOTGUN - Household Insect Control - BONIDE PRODUCTS, INC.; *pg.* 1794, *pg.* 1320
SHOUT - Cleaning Product - S.C. JOHNSON & SON, INC.; *pg.* 334, *pg.* 1889
SHOUT ABOUT MOVIES - Game - HASBRO, INC.; *pg.* 954, *pg.* 1603
SHOUT ACTION GEL - Cleaner - S.C. JOHNSON & SON, INC.; *pg.* 334, *pg.* 1889
SHOUT AEROSOL - Cleaner - S.C. JOHNSON & SON, INC.; *pg.* 334, *pg.* 1889
SHOUT COLOR CATCHER - Cleaner - S.C. JOHNSON & SON, INC.; *pg.* 334, *pg.* 1889
SHOUT GEL - Cleaner - S.C. JOHNSON & SON, INC.; *pg.* 334, *pg.* 1889
SHOUT OXYPOWER - Cleaner - S.C. JOHNSON & SON, INC.; *pg.* 334, *pg.* 1889
SHOUT TRIGGER & LIQUID - Cleaner - S.C. JOHNSON & SON, INC.; *pg.* 334, *pg.* 1889
SHOUT WIPE - Cleaner - S.C. JOHNSON & SON, INC.; *pg.* 334, *pg.* 1889
SHOUT WIPES - Portable Stain Treater Towelettes - S.C. JOHNSON & SON, INC.; *pg.* 334, *pg.* 1889
SHOVEL - Footwear - OAKLEY, INC.; *pg.* 1840, *pg.* 86
SHOW ME 5 PAYDOWN - Lottery Game - MISSOURI LOTTERY; *pg.* 999, *pg.* 979
SHOW ME CASH - Game - MISSOURI LOTTERY; *pg.* 999, *pg.* 979
SHOW-OFF - General Purpose Cleaner - DELTA FOREMOST CHEMICAL CORPORATION; *pg.* 1155, *pg.* 1642
THE SHOW OFF - Plastic Containers - PACTIV CORPORATION; *pg.* 1466, *pg.* 624
SHOW PONY - Apparel - OAKLEY, INC.; *pg.* 1840, *pg.* 86
SHOW PRO - Show Feeds - MANNA PRO CORPORATION; *pg.* 1478, *pg.* 975
SHOW YOUR LOVE BY WHAT YOU SERVE - Slogan - RHODES INTERNATIONAL, INC.; *pg.* 891, *pg.* 1760
SHOW YOUR TRUE COLORS - Photographic Film - EASTMAN KODAK COMPANY; *pg.* 1408, *pg.* 1333
SHOWBILL - Fabric - NEMSCHOFF, INC.; *pg.* 936, *pg.* 1890
SHOWBILL - Entertainment Magazine - PLAYBILL INCORPORATED; *pg.* 1677, *pg.* 1282
SHOWBOAT - Casino - CAESARS ENTERTAINMENT CORPORATION; *pg.* 1083, *pg.* 1023
SHOWBOAT BRANSON BELLE - Treasured Lake Adventure - HERSCHEND FAMILY ENTERTAINMENT CORP.; *pg.* 552, *pg.* 973
SHOWCAKE - Plastic Containers - PACTIV CORPORATION; *pg.* 1466, *pg.* 624
SHOWCASE - Software - AUTODESK INC.; *pg.* 356, *pg.* 257
SHOWCASE - Container - PACTIV CORPORATION; *pg.* 1466, *pg.* 624
SHOWCASE - Envelope - POLY PAK AMERICA, INC.; *pg.* 1467, *pg.* 138
SHOWCASE HOMES - Construction - M/I HOMES, INC.; *pg.* 95, *pg.* 1441
SHOWCLEAN - Grooming Product - W.F. YOUNG, INC.; *pg.* 1610, *pg.* 817
SHOWCLOTH - Fabric - ROSCO LABORATORIES, INC.; *pg.* 1782, *pg.* 378
SHOWDOWN - Advanced Trivia Challenge Covering All Topics - NTN BUZZTIME, INC.; *pg.* 659, *pg.* 60
SHOWDOWN - Video Viewing System - SWORDFISH FINANCIAL, INC.; *pg.* 1430, *pg.* 1737
SHOWDOWN SPORTS - Toy & Game - HASBRO, INC.; *pg.* 954, *pg.* 1603
SHOWER BRITE - Shower Cleaner - BLUE CROSS LABORATORIES; *pg.* 326, *pg.* 277
SHOWER FOAM - Cleaner - HILLYARD, INC.; *pg.* 331, *pg.* 990
SHOWER SHINE - Home Cleaner - S.C. JOHNSON & SON, INC.; *pg.* 334, *pg.* 1889
SHOWER THERAPY - Toiletries - THE HAIN CELESTIAL GROUP, INC.; *pg.* 860, *pg.* 1172
SHOWERGUARD - Glass Product - GUARDIAN INDUSTRIES CORP.; *pg.* 85, *pg.* 869
SHOWERGUARD - Personal Care Product - WESTROCK COMPANY; *pg.* 1472, *pg.* 1805
SHOWEROFF - Metering Shower Valve - SYMMONS INDUSTRIES, INC.; *pg.* 114, *pg.* 803
SHOWERS OF FLOWERS - Flower Arrangement - 1-800-FLOWERS.COM, INC.; *pg.* 1758, *pg.* 1151
SHOWHOUSE - Luxury Kitchen & Bath Products - MOEN INCORPORATED; *pg.* 1056, *pg.* 1468
SHOWMASTER - Electric Guitar - FENDER MUSICAL INSTRUMENTS CORPORATION; *pg.* 547, *pg.* 21
SHOWMASTER FAT HH - Electric Guitar - FENDER MUSICAL INSTRUMENTS CORPORATION; *pg.* 547, *pg.* 21
SHOWMASTER FAT SSS - Electric Guitar - FENDER MUSICAL INSTRUMENTS CORPORATION; *pg.* 547, *pg.* 21
SHOWMASTER QBT HH - Electric Guitar - FENDER MUSICAL INSTRUMENTS CORPORATION; *pg.* 547, *pg.* 21
SHOWMASTER QBT SSS - Electric Guitar - FENDER MUSICAL INSTRUMENTS CORPORATION; *pg.* 547, *pg.* 21
SHOWMOBILE - Riser - WENGER CORPORATION; *pg.* 1307, *pg.* 952
SHOWMOTION - Software - AUTODESK INC.; *pg.* 356, *pg.* 257
SHOWOFFS - Storage Box - STERILITE CORPORATION; *pg.* 1138, *pg.* 848
SHOWPIE - Container - PACTIV CORPORATION; *pg.* 1466, *pg.* 624
SHOWPLACE - Home Decorating Products - SEARS HOLDINGS CORPORATION; *pg.* 1784, *pg.* 618
SHOWSHEEN - Grooming Product - W.F. YOUNG, INC.; *pg.* 1610, *pg.* 817
SHOWTIME - Cable Television - SHOWTIME NETWORKS INC.; *pg.* 308, *pg.* 1291
SHOWTIME EN ESPANOL - Showtime In Spanish - SHOWTIME NETWORKS INC.; *pg.* 308, *pg.* 1291
SHOWTIME EVENT - Pay-Per-View Television - SHOWTIME NETWORKS INC.; *pg.* 308, *pg.* 1291
SHOWTIME HD - High Definition Television - SHOWTIME NETWORKS INC.; *pg.* 308, *pg.* 1291
SHOWTIME ON DEMAND - On Demand Television - SHOWTIME NETWORKS INC.; *pg.* 308, *pg.* 1291
SHOWVIEW - Video Recording Software - ROVI CORPORATION; *pg.* 463, *pg.* 269
SHOWWX - Projector - MICROVISION, INC.; *pg.* 654, *pg.* 1828
SHOX CLASSIC - Footwear - NIKE, INC.; *pg.* 1812, *pg.* 1492
SHOX EXPERIENCE - Footwear - NIKE, INC.; *pg.* 1812, *pg.* 1492
SHOX FIRST 2 - Footwear - NIKE, INC.; *pg.* 1812, *pg.* 1492
SHOX MVP - Footwear - NIKE, INC.; *pg.* 1812, *pg.* 1492
SHOX NAVINA - Footwear - NIKE, INC.; *pg.* 1812, *pg.* 1492
SHOX NZ - Footwear - NIKE, INC.; *pg.* 1812, *pg.* 1492
SHOX SLAM - Footwear - NIKE, INC.; *pg.* 1812, *pg.* 1492
SHOX TURBO - Footwear - NIKE, INC.; *pg.* 1812, *pg.* 1492
SHP-PRO - Fire Protection System - FIKE CORPORATION; *pg.* 1047, *pg.* 973
SHRED "N" VAC - Power Equipment - ECHO INCORPORATED; *pg.* 1046, *pg.* 626
SHREDDED HERITAGE BITES - Breakfast Cereals - NATURE'S PATH FOODS INC.; *pg.* 833, *pg.* 1908
SHREDDED WHEAT - Cereal - POST HOLDINGS, INC.; *pg.* 833, *pg.* 1002
SHREDDIES - Cheese - KRAFT CANADA INC.; *pg.* 869, *pg.* 1939
SHREK - Game - ACTIVISION BLIZZARD, INC.; *pg.* 948, *pg.* 271
SHRINK-IT - Window Sealer Kit - WARP BROTHERS; *pg.* 1471, *pg.* 595
SHRINK-KON - Insulation Product - THOMAS & BETTS CORPORATION; *pg.* 680, *pg.* 1646
SHRINK MATE - Plastics Product - AEP INDUSTRIES INC.; *pg.* 1878, *pg.* 1085
SHRINK-TO-FIT - Jean - LEVI STRAUSS & CO.; *pg.* 43, *pg.* 220
SHRINKVAC - Vacuum Shrink Packaging Films - SEALED AIR CORPORATION; *pg.* 1468, *pg.* 1058
SHRINKWRAP - Software - SMITH MICRO SOFTWARE, INC.; *pg.* 471, *pg.* 41
SHROCK - Cabinetry - MASTERBRAND CABINETS, INC.; *pg.* 96, *pg.* 692
SHRUBS-ALIVE - Fertilizer - GARDENS ALIVE!, INC.; *pg.* 1796, *pg.* 693
SHU-LOK - Ladder Product - WERNER HOLDING CO.; *pg.* 121, *pg.* 1534
SHULT - Manufactured Homes - CLAYTON HOMES, INC.; *pg.* 1086, *pg.* 1640
SHUNTZ - Apparel - VANS, INC.; *pg.* 1821, *pg.* 76
SHUR-CLENS - Wound Care Product - CONVATEC LTD.; *pg.* 1518, *pg.* 1121
SHUR-CONFORM - Bandage - DERMA SCIENCES, INC.; *pg.* 1523, *pg.* 1111
SHUR FINE - Food Product - WESTERN FAMILY HOLDING CO., INC.; *pg.* 1037, *pg.* 1509
SHUR-GAIN - Pet Foods & Livestock & Poultry Feeds - MAPLE LEAF FOODS INC.; *pg.* 875, *pg.* 1927
SHUR-LINE - Paint Brushes, Rollers & Accessories - NEWELL RUBBERMAID INC.; *pg.* 1128, *pg.* 515
SHUR-LOCK - Lid Opener - CTB INTERNATIONAL CORP.; *pg.* 850, *pg.* 695
SHUR-LOK - Roll Tarp System - SHUR-CO, INC.; *pg.* 110, *pg.* 1626
SHUR-MATIC - Tarp System & Component - SHUR-CO, INC.; *pg.* 110, *pg.* 1626
SHUR-MOUNT - Hospital Lighting - SWIVELIER CO., INC.; *pg.* 1307, *pg.* 1142
SHUR STRIP - Wound Closure Strip - DERMA SCIENCES, INC.; *pg.* 1523, *pg.* 1111
SHUR-TRAK - Tarp System & Component - SHUR-CO, INC.; *pg.* 110, *pg.* 1626
SHUR-WIPE - Wiper And Cleaning Cloth - GEORGIA-PACIFIC LLC; *pg.* 1458, *pg.* 507
SHURCO-LOK - Tarp System & Component - SHUR-CO, INC.; *pg.* 110, *pg.* 1626
SHUREFLEX - Connectors - THOMAS & BETTS CORPORATION; *pg.* 680, *pg.* 1646

First page reference indicates Business Class Edition
Second page reference indicates Geographic Edition

SHURESEAL - Conduits/Fittings - THOMAS & BETTS CORPORATION; *pg.* 680, *pg.* 1646
SHURFLO - Automatic Interlock Flow Switch - HAYS FLUID CONTROLS; *pg.* 1049, *pg.* 1370
SHURRITE - Glove - LAKELAND INDUSTRIES, INC.; *pg.* 1354, *pg.* 1338
SHURSTIK - Coating - HILL & GRIFFITH COMPANY; *pg.* 1167, *pg.* 1414
SHURTUFF - Durable Mailers - SEALED AIR CORPORATION; *pg.* 1468, *pg.* 1058
SHUSTER - Boot - ALDO GROUP; *pg.* 1804, *pg.* 1959
SHUT-EYE SERVICE - Travel Service - JETBLUE AIRWAYS CORPORATION; *pg.* 1913, *pg.* 1174
SHUT-EYE SHADE - Sleep Mask - MCKEON PRODUCTS, INC.; *pg.* 1559, *pg.* 912
SHUTT - Medical Equipment - CONMED CORPORATION; *pg.* 1517, *pg.* 1347
SHUTTERFLY - Photo Service - SHUTTERFLY, INC.; *pg.* 1280, *pg.* 192
SHUTTERFLY EXPRESS - Software - SHUTTERFLY, INC.; *pg.* 1280, *pg.* 192
SHUTTERFLY STUDIO - Software - SHUTTERFLY, INC.; *pg.* 1280, *pg.* 192
SHUTTLE - Introducer Set - COOK GROUP, INC.; *pg.* 1518, *pg.* 674
SHUTTLE - Personnel Carriers - E-Z-GO TEXTRON; *pg.* 1706, *pg.* 525
SHUTTLE - Footwear - STEVEN MADDEN, LTD.; *pg.* 1819, *pg.* 1176
SHUTTLE BUGGY - Mobile Self-Propelled Material Transfer Vehicle - ASTEC INDUSTRIES, INC.; *pg.* 69, *pg.* 1628
SHUTTLE PIP - Molecular Probe Product - THERMO FISHER SCIENTIFIC INC.; *pg.* 1602, *pg.* 61
SHUTTLE RELAY - Medical Equipment - CONMED CORPORATION; *pg.* 1517, *pg.* 1347
SHUTTLEKART - Agricultural Equipment - DEGELMAN INDUSTRIES LTD.; *pg.* 703, *pg.* 1962
SHUTTLELIFT - Industrial Mobile Gantry Crane - MARINE TRAVELIFT, INC.; *pg.* 1359, *pg.* 1895
SHUTTLETRAC - Thermal Processing Equipment - SURFACE COMBUSTION, INC.; *pg.* 1077, *pg.* 1462
SHV - Flare - CAMERON INTERNATIONAL; *pg.* 1151, *pg.* 1702
SHWEETZ - Bakery Items - SHEETZ, INC.; *pg.* 1033, *pg.* 1514
SI - Towline Vehicles - PARAGON TECHNOLOGIES, INC.; *pg.* 1367, *pg.* 1528
SI - Threaded Inserts - PENN ENGINEERING & MANUFACTURING CORP.; *pg.* 1059, *pg.* 1525
SI-18 BRISTEL - Footwear - K-SWISS; *pg.* 1837, *pg.* 306
SI-18 PREMIERE - Athletic Shoes - K-SWISS; *pg.* 1837, *pg.* 306
SI-CHROME - Saw Blade - SIMONDS INTERNATIONAL CORPORATION; *pg.* 1376, *pg.* 819
SI-LINK - Crosslinkable Polyethylene - THE DOW CHEMICAL COMPANY; *pg.* 1157, *pg.* 898
SI ORDERMATIC - Towline Vehicles - PARAGON TECHNOLOGIES, INC.; *pg.* 1367, *pg.* 1528
SI SERIES - Folding & Inserting Machines - NEOPOST CANADA LIMITED; *pg.* 1364, *pg.* 1924
SI SERIES - Solid Ink - RICOH PRINTING SYSTEMS AMERICA, INC.; *pg.* 462, *pg.* 279
SI2161/65 - Digital TV Demodulators - SILICON LABORATORIES INC.; *pg.* 674, *pg.* 1666
SI21XX - Satellite Receivers - SILICON LABORATORIES INC.; *pg.* 674, *pg.* 1666
SI4702/03 - FM Radio Receiver - SILICON LABORATORIES INC.; *pg.* 674, *pg.* 1666
SI4704/05 - FM Radio Receiver - SILICON LABORATORIES INC.; *pg.* 674, *pg.* 1666
SI4707 - Radio Receiver - SILICON LABORATORIES INC.; *pg.* 674, *pg.* 1666
SI4708/09 - FM Radio Receiver - SILICON LABORATORIES INC.; *pg.* 674, *pg.* 1666
SI4710/11 - FM Radio Transmitter - SILICON LABORATORIES INC.; *pg.* 674, *pg.* 1666
SI4712/13 - FM Radio Transmitter - SILICON LABORATORIES INC.; *pg.* 674, *pg.* 1666
SI472X - FM Radio Transceiver - SILICON LABORATORIES INC.; *pg.* 674, *pg.* 1666
SI4730/31 - Radio Receiver - SILICON LABORATORIES INC.; *pg.* 674, *pg.* 1666
SI4734/35 - Radio Receiver - SILICON LABORATORIES INC.; *pg.* 674, *pg.* 1666
SI4736/37 - Radio Receiver - SILICON LABORATORIES INC.; *pg.* 674, *pg.* 1666
SI4738/39 - Radio Receiver - SILICON LABORATORIES INC.; *pg.* 674, *pg.* 1666
SI474X - Radio Receiver - SILICON LABORATORIES INC.; *pg.* 674, *pg.* 1666
SIAM - Footwear - STEVEN MADDEN, LTD.; *pg.* 1819, *pg.* 1176
SIAP - Integrated Circuit - ATMEL CORPORATION; *pg.* 621, *pg.* 238
SIBLEY - Poultry System - CTB INTERNATIONAL CORP.; *pg.* 850, *pg.* 695
SIBOD - Thyristor - LITTELFUSE, INC.; *pg.* 1301, *pg.* 580
SIBUTRAL - Pharmaceutical Product - ABBOTT LABORATORIES; *pg.* 1484, *pg.* 551
SIBYTE - Semiconductors - BROADCOM CORPORATION; *pg.* 364, *pg.* 108
SICO - Consumer Products - AKZO NOBEL; *pg.* 1439, *pg.* 1952
SICOCERAM - Paint Product - AKZO NOBEL; *pg.* 1439, *pg.* 1952
SICOMET - Cyanoacrylate Adhesives - HENKEL CORPORATION; *pg.* 1165, *pg.* 1535
SICOPOXY - Paint Product - AKZO NOBEL; *pg.* 1439, *pg.* 1952
SICORAD - Industrial Product - AKZO NOBEL; *pg.* 1439, *pg.* 1952
SICS/NT - Computer Software & Manuals - COMPUTER SCIENCES CORPORATION; *pg.* 378, *pg.* 1780
SICURA - Laminator - HONEYWELL INTERNATIONAL INC.; *pg.* 407, *pg.* 1088
SIDARIS - Food Product - RESER'S FINE FOODS INC.; *pg.* 1032, *pg.* 1496
SIDE DRAFT - Air Classifier - STURTEVANT INC.; *pg.* 1379, *pg.* 824
SIDE ENTRY - Fiber Optic Lighting System - ENERGY FOCUS, INC.; *pg.* 1411, *pg.* 1472
SIDE I - Athletic Shoes - NIKE, INC.; *pg.* 1812, *pg.* 1492
SIDE KICK - Carts - GEERPRES INC.; *pg.* 1339, *pg.* 901
SIDE ROLL PROTECTION - Occupant Protection System - OSHKOSH CORPORATION; *pg.* 187, *pg.* 1885
SIDE-SNAP - Tee - CARTER'S, INC.; *pg.* 21, *pg.* 491
SIDE-TRAC - Mobile Shelf-Type Filing Cabinets - TAB PRODUCTS CO. LLC; *pg.* 481, *pg.* 1869
SIDE WINDER - Silicone Sealant - DAP PRODUCTS, INC.; *pg.* 1441, *pg.* 756
SIDEARM - Cutting Equipment - DEGELMAN INDUSTRIES LTD.; *pg.* 703, *pg.* 1962
SIDECLIP - Cutting Tool - LEATHERMAN TOOL GROUP, INC.; *pg.* 1053, *pg.* 1504
SIDEGLOW - Fiber Optic Cable - REVOLUTION LIGHTING TECHNOLOGIES, INC.; *pg.* 1304, *pg.* 377
SIDEKICK - Underground Construction Equipment - CHARLES MACHINE WORKS, INC.; *pg.* 1322, *pg.* 1488
SIDEKICK - Orthopedic Product - DJO INCORPORATED; *pg.* 1524, *pg.* 302
SIDEKICK - Diabetes Monitoring Product - NIPRO DIAGNOSTICS, INC.; *pg.* 1573, *pg.* 426
SIDEKICKERS - Food Product - THE WENDY'S COMPANY; *pg.* 1755, *pg.* 1450
SIDELINE SPIRIT - Sport Contest - ATHLON SPORTS, INC.; *pg.* 1618, *pg.* 1648
SIDEOUT - Apparel - CHEROKEE GLOBAL BRANDS; *pg.* 21, *pg.* 278
SIDEOUT SPORT - Sportswear - CHEROKEE GLOBAL BRANDS; *pg.* 21, *pg.* 278
SIDEPAK - Pump - TSI INCORPORATED; *pg.* 1432, *pg.* 965
SIDEPILLOW - Pillow - TEMPUR SEALY INTERNATIONAL, INC.; *pg.* 944, *pg.* 731
SIDEPOUCH - Bagging Machine - AUTOMATED PACKAGING SYSTEMS INC.; *pg.* 1452, *pg.* 1474
SIDEROLLER - Suitcase - SAMSONITE CORPORATION; *pg.* 11, *pg.* 830
SIDESTEP - Plate - UNIVERSAL FOREST PRODUCTS, INC.; *pg.* 117, *pg.* 890
SIDESTROY - Drive Technology - WESTERN DIGITAL CORPORATION; *pg.* 492, *pg.* 118
SIDETRACKER - Universal Running Boards - LUND INTERNATIONAL, INC.; *pg.* 211, *pg.* 526
SIDEWALK - Urban Infrastructure renewal Projects - ALPHABET INC.; *pg.* 347, *pg.* 153
SIDEWALK - Office Furniture - STEELCASE INC.; *pg.* 475, *pg.* 889
SIDEWALK MOBILE - Office Furniture - STEELCASE INC.; *pg.* 475, *pg.* 889
SIDEWALK OTTOMAN/BENCHES - Office Furniture - STEELCASE INC.; *pg.* 475, *pg.* 889
SIDEWALL CONCEALER - Industrial OREC HSW Concealed - RELIABLE AUTOMATIC SPRINKLER CO., INC.; *pg.* 1137, *pg.* 1158
SIDEWINDER - Pin System - ESCO CORPORATION; *pg.* 1335, *pg.* 1502
SIDEWINDER - Floor Cleaning Product - NSS ENTERPRISES, INC.; *pg.* 59, *pg.* 1476
SIDEWINDER - Flashlight - STREAMLIGHT INC.; *pg.* 1306, *pg.* 1527
SIDEWINDER HP - Flashlight - STREAMLIGHT INC.; *pg.* 1306, *pg.* 1527
SIDEXIS XG - Software - SIRONA DENTAL SYSTEMS, INC.; *pg.* 1429, *pg.* 1175
SIDNE - Voice Activation System - STRYKER CORPORATION; *pg.* 1598, *pg.* 894
SIDTEC - Condenser Tube Cleaners - GE WATER & PROCESS TECHNOLOGIES; *pg.* 1339, *pg.* 1588
SIEMPRE MUJER - Spanish-Language Magazine - MEREDITH CORPORATION; *pg.* 1663, *pg.* 705
SIENA - Shoes - ALLEN-EDMONDS SHOE CORP.; *pg.* 1804, *pg.* 1887
SIENA STUDIO - Apparel - G-III APPAREL GROUP, LTD.; *pg.* 41, *pg.* 1233
SIENNA - Furniture - ASHLEY FURNITURE INDUSTRIES, INC.; *pg.* 914, *pg.* 1852
SIENNA - Footwear - COBIAN CORP.; *pg.* 1806, *pg.* 253
SIENNA - Minivan - TOYOTA MOTOR NORTH AMERICA, INC.; *pg.* 192, *pg.* 1303
SIENNA - Ceiling Fan - WESTINGHOUSE LIGHTING CORPORATION; *pg.* 687, *pg.* 1571
SIENNA BAKERY - Baked Goods - GORDON FOOD SERVICE INC.; *pg.* 1021, *pg.* 913
SIENNA SUNRISE - Container Grown Plant - MONROVIA GROWERS; *pg.* 1797, *pg.* 44
SIENTO - Office Furniture - STEELCASE INC.; *pg.* 475, *pg.* 889
SIER-BATH - Pump - FLOWSERVE CORPORATION; *pg.* 82, *pg.* 1719
SIERASE - Drive Technology - WESTERN DIGITAL CORPORATION; *pg.* 492, *pg.* 118
SIERO INTENSIVO - Intensive Firming Serum for Skin - BORGHESE, INC.; *pg.* 502, *pg.* 1205
SIERRA - Toilet Partition - BOBRICK WASHROOM EQUIPMENT, INC.; *pg.* 1043, *pg.* 166
SIERRA - Footwear - EASTLAND SHOE CORPORATION; *pg.* 1808, *pg.* 750
SIERRA - Face Masks - E.I. DU PONT DE NEMOURS & COMPANY; *pg.* 1159, *pg.* 390
SIERRA - Pick-Up Truck - GENERAL MOTORS COMPANY; *pg.* 175, *pg.* 881
SIERRA - Valve - INGERSOLL-RAND COMPANY; *pg.* 1349, *pg.* 1370
SIERRA - Agricultural Fencing Products - KEYSTONE STEEL & WIRE CO.; *pg.* 91, *pg.* 651
SIERRA - Eyewear - MINE SAFETY APPLIANCES COMPANY; *pg.* 1361, *pg.* 1525
SIERRA - Antifreeze Solution - OLD WORLD INDUSTRIES, INC.; *pg.* 1175, *pg.* 641
SIERRA - Wall Plates - PASS & SEYMOUR/LEGRAND; *pg.* 1303, *pg.* 1344
SIERRA - Ethernet Services - TELLABS, INC.; *pg.* 678, *pg.* 637
SIERRA - Vinyl - TRANSILWRAP COMPANY, INC.; *pg.* 1470, *pg.* 613
SIERRA - Wireless Navigation Aid - TRIMBLE NAVIGATION LIMITED; *pg.* 1384, *pg.* 288
SIERRA - Food Product - V&V SUPREMO FOODS, INC.; *pg.* 907, *pg.* 595
SIERRA DESIGNS - Camping Accessories - EXXEL OUTDOORS LLC; *pg.* 1833, *pg.* 311
SIERRA DORADA - Coffee - PEET'S COFFEE & TEA, INC.; *pg.* 1029, *pg.* 85
SIERRA HSA - Banking & Financial Services - BANK OF THE SIERRA, INC.; *pg.* 721, *pg.* 185
SIERRA MADRE - Luggage - JANSPORT; *pg.* 1837, *pg.* 38
SIERRA MIST - Soft Drink - PEPSICO, INC.; *pg.* 259, *pg.* 1327
SIERRA MIST CRANBERRY SPLASH - Soft Drink - PEPSICO, INC.; *pg.* 259, *pg.* 1327
SIERRA MIST FREE CRANBERRY SPLASH - Soft Drink - PEPSICO, INC.; *pg.* 259, *pg.* 1327
SIERRA PACIFIC - Electric & Gas Utility in North Nevada - NV ENERGY, INC.; *pg.* 1948, *pg.* 1028
SIERRA PACIFIC COMMUNICATIONS - Telecommunications

Subsidiary - NV ENERGY, INC.; pg. 1948, pg. 1028
SIERRA PACIFIC POWER - Multi-State Electric Utility - NV ENERGY; pg. 1948, pg. 1032
SIERRA PACIFIC RESOURCES - Energy Services - NV ENERGY, INC.; pg. 1948, pg. 1028
SIERRA PERFORMANCE COATINGS - Industrial & Commercial Coating - RUST-OLEUM CORPORATION; pg. 1447, pg. 664
SIERRA WALL - Outdoor Concrete Sound & Sight Barrier - SMITH-MIDLAND CORPORATION; pg. 111, pg. 1795
SIERRA WIRELESS WATCHER - Connection Management Software - SIERRA WIRELESS INCORPORATED; pg. 673, pg. 1909
SIERRABLEN PLUS - Lawn & Garden Product - THE SCOTTS MIRACLE-GRO COMPANY; pg. 1799, pg. 1459
SIERRAPLEX - Wiring Devices - PASS & SEYMOUR/LEGRAND; pg. 1303, pg. 1344
SIESTA - Footwear - COBIAN CORP.; pg. 1806, pg. 253
SIESTA KEY - Carpet - BEAULIEU GROUP, LLC; pg. 917, pg. 529
THE SIESTA KEY - Home Floor Plan - JACOBSEN MANUFACTURING, INC.; pg. 1098, pg. 460
SIESTE - Office Furniture - STEELCASE INC.; pg. 475, pg. 889
SIEVE-GARD - Medical Equipment - INVACARE CORPORATION; pg. 1546, pg. 1451
SIFIR - Laser & Laser System - COHERENT, INC.; pg. 1406, pg. 265
SIGHT SAVERS - Magnifier - BAUSCH & LOMB INCORPORATED; pg. 1401, pg. 1045
SIGHT SAVERS - Silicone Treated Polishing Tissues - DOW CORNING CORPORATION; pg. 1159, pg. 900
SIGHTLINE - Protective Eyewear - SELLSTROM MANUFACTURING CO.; pg. 1428, pg. 659
SIGHTSEER - Motor Home - WINNEBAGO INDUSTRIES, INC.; pg. 1712, pg. 707
SIGLAN 350 - Cables - COLEMAN CABLE, INC.; pg. 1324, pg. 665
SIGLO 21 - Cigar And Tobacco - SWISHER INTERNATIONAL, INC.; pg. 1895, pg. 345
SIGMA - Laser System - GSI GROUP INC.; pg. 1415, pg. 784
SIGMA - Bonding Tool - KULICKE & SOFFA INDUSTRIES, INC.; pg. 650, pg. 1533
SIGMA - Bike Headlight - L.L. BEAN, INC.; pg. 1777, pg. 750
SIGMA - Wireless Antenna - PCTEL, INC.; pg. 452, pg. 557
SIGMA - Biochemicals & Reagents for Life Science Research - SIGMA-ALDRICH CORPORATION; pg. 1181, pg. 1003
SIGMA - Tire - TBC CORPORATION; pg. 1889, pg. 457
SIGMA 3 - Metrology Product - GLEASON CORPORATION; pg. 1340, pg. 1335
SIGMA 7 - Metrology Product - GLEASON CORPORATION; pg. 1340, pg. 1335
SIGMA DSP - Converters - ANALOG DEVICES, INC.; pg. 617, pg. 839
SIGMA HYBRI MAX - Biochemical Reagents - SIGMA-ALDRICH CORPORATION; pg. 1181, pg. 1003
SIGMA SAND - Resin-Coated Sand - HEXION; pg. 1166, pg. 1440
SIGMA STATION - Business Improvement Simulation Software - PIVOTAL RESOURCES, INC.; pg. 455, pg. 304
SIGMASTER - Banking Software - JACK HENRY & ASSOCIATES, INC.; pg. 422, pg. 988
SIGN & TRAVEL - Deferred Payment Service - AMERICAN EXPRESS COMPANY; pg. 712, pg. 1190
SIGN MANAGER - Software - VULCAN, INC.; pg. 687, pg. 5
SIGN ON SAN DIEGO - Local Newspaper Information Site - THE SAN DIEGO UNION-TRIBUNE, LLC; pg. 1682, pg. 208
SIGN PENS - Porous Point Pens - PENTEL OF AMERICA, LTD.; pg. 453, pg. 295
THE SIGN THAT BRINGS YOU HOME - Slogan - RE/MAX INTERNATIONAL, INC.; pg. 1109, pg. 322
SIGNA - Medical Device - GE HEALTHCARE TECHNOLOGIES; pg. 1533, pg. 1897
SIGNA - Bath & Plumbing Product - JACUZZI BRANDS CORPORATION; pg. 554, pg. 65
SIGNA-WAVE - Coaxial Cables - COLEMAN CABLE, INC.; pg. 1324, pg. 665
SIGNAL - Cable - COLEMAN CABLE, INC.; pg. 1324, pg. 665
SIGNAL - Apparel - OAKLEY, INC.; pg. 1840, pg. 86
SIGNAL EXTRACTION TECHNOLOGY - Medical Apparatus - MASIMO CORPORATION; pg. 1558, pg. 113
SIGNAL I.Q. - Medical Apparatus - MASIMO CORPORATION; pg. 1558, pg. 113
SIGNAL MANAGER - Software - VULCAN, INC.; pg. 687, pg. 5
SIGNAL PLUS - Receiver Coil - FONAR CORPORATION; pg. 1413, pg. 1179
SIGNAL POWER - Software Product - CLARY CORPORATION; pg. 226, pg. 150
SIGNAL SELECTIVE PROCESSING - Sensor - NAPCO SECURITY SYSTEMS, INC.; pg. 658, pg. 1138
SIGNAL VISION - Subscriber Drop Product - COMMSCOPE, INC.; pg. 278, pg. 1378
SIGNAL WAND - Flashlights - DORCY INTERNATIONAL INC.; pg. 1046, pg. 1439
SIGNAL WORKBENCH - Dynamic Analysis & Test System - CONCURRENT COMPUTER CORPORATION; pg. 379, pg. 531
SIGNALMAX - Wireless Product - PARKERVISION, INC.; pg. 1426, pg. 434
SIGNALPLUS - Interconnect Cables - COLEMAN CABLE, INC.; pg. 1324, pg. 665
SIGNALPROBE - Software - ALTERA CORPORATION; pg. 348, pg. 237
SIGNALSCREEN - Receptor Ligand Binding Assay - PERKINELMER, INC.; pg. 1426, pg. 853
SIGNALTRAP - Software - ALTERA CORPORATION; pg. 348, pg. 237
SIGNAMAX - Network Connectivity Product - AESP, INC.; pg. 345, pg. 439
SIGNATURE - Organ - ALLEN ORGAN COMPANY; pg. 527, pg. 1549
SIGNATURE - Frozen Food - BELLISIO FOODS, INC.; pg. 840, pg. 931
SIGNATURE - Electronic Games - CHECKPOINT SYSTEMS, INC.; pg. 628, pg. 1559
SIGNATURE - Leather Product - COACH, INC.; pg. 3, pg. 1214
SIGNATURE - Beverages - THE COCA-COLA COMPANY; pg. 240, pg. 493
SIGNATURE - Agricultural Equipment - DEGELMAN INDUSTRIES LTD.; pg. 703, pg. 1962
SIGNATURE - Color Proofing Materials, Equipment & Chemicals - EASTMAN KODAK COMPANY; pg. 1408, pg. 1333
SIGNATURE - Valve Cover - EDELBROCK CORPORATION; pg. 204, pg. 293
SIGNATURE - Bookcase - F.E. HALE MANUFACTURING COMPANY; pg. 925, pg. 1160
SIGNATURE - Sunglasses - FGX INTERNATIONAL, INC.; pg. 5, pg. 1608
SIGNATURE - Food Service - FOOD SERVICES OF AMERICA, INC.; pg. 856, pg. 21
SIGNATURE - Bleached Board And Kraft - GEORGIA-PACIFIC LLC; pg. 1458, pg. 507
SIGNATURE - Musical Instrument - GIBSON GUITAR CORP.; pg. 550, pg. 1650
SIGNATURE - Seating Product - IRWIN SEATING COMPANY INC.; pg. 929, pg. 887
SIGNATURE - Furniture - LA-Z-BOY INCORPORATED; pg. 932, pg. 901
SIGNATURE - Jewelry - LAGOS INC.; pg. 8, pg. 1566
SIGNATURE - Printer - MICROBOARDS TECHNOLOGY, LLC; pg. 434, pg. 920
SIGNATURE - Electronic Components - MOLEX INCORPORATED; pg. 655, pg. 628
SIGNATURE - All Natural Soda - MONSTER BEVERAGE CORPORATION; pg. 257, pg. 69
SIGNATURE - Guns - NORDSON CORPORATION; pg. 1365, pg. 1480
SIGNATURE - Steamtable Pan - PACTIV CORPORATION; pg. 1466, pg. 624
SIGNATURE - Suitcase - SAMSONITE CORPORATION; pg. 11, pg. 830
SIGNATURE - Clippers - TIPPER TIE, INC.; pg. 1382, pg. 1358
SIGNATURE - Ink - VAN SON HOLLAND INK CORPORATION OF AMERICA; pg. 487, pg. 1169
SIGNATURE - Stage & Riser - WENGER CORPORATION; pg. 1307, pg. 952
THE SIGNATURE AT MGM GRAND - Resort & Casino - MGM RESORTS INTERNATIONAL; pg. 1105, pg. 1028
SIGNATURE BY LEVI STRAUSS & CO. - Apparel - LEVI STRAUSS & CO.; pg. 43, pg. 220
SIGNATURE CAFE - Custom-Made Deli Sandwiches & Healthy Food Products - SAFEWAY INC.; pg. 1032, pg. 184
SIGNATURE CONFIRMATION - Postal Services - UNITED STATES POSTAL SERVICE; pg. 1009, pg. 406
SIGNATURE DRESS - Clothing - K-SWISS; pg. 1837, pg. 306
SIGNATURE EDUCATION LOAN - Fed & Private Loans - SLM CORPORATION; pg. 804, pg. 388
SIGNATURE II BY STAN HERMAN - Robes & Loungewear - KELLWOOD COMPANY; pg. 28, pg. 975
SIGNATURE LAQUERWARE - Bath Accessory - CROSCILL, INC.; pg. 1122, pg. 1220
SIGNATURE LINE - Chocolates - BLOMMER CHOCOLATE COMPANY; pg. 1851, pg. 566
SIGNATURE OF EXCELLENCE - Slogan - HOLLAND AMERICA LINE INC.; pg. 1911, pg. 1836
SIGNATURE POOLS - In-Ground Vinyl Pools - POOL CORPORATION; pg. 1843, pg. 743
SIGNATURE PRODUCTS - Alarm Systems - NAPCO SECURITY SYSTEMS, INC.; pg. 658, pg. 1138
SIGNATURE SELECT - Loan Program - SLM CORPORATION; pg. 804, pg. 388
SIGNATURE SERIES - Electric Coffee Grinders - BUNN-O-MATIC CORPORATION; pg. 53, pg. 661
SIGNATURE SERIES - Balloon - CONTINENTAL AMERICAN CORP.; pg. 1880, pg. 723
SIGNATURE SERIES - Chrome Accessories - EDELBROCK CORPORATION; pg. 204, pg. 293
SIGNATURE SERIES - Gaming Product - GLD PRODUCTS, INC.; pg. 1835, pg. 1882
SIGNATURE SERIES - DVD Player - HARMAN INTERNATIONAL INDUSTRIES, INCORPORATED; pg. 641, pg. 374
SIGNATURE SERIES - Wood - PACIFIC COLUMNS, INC.; pg. 103, pg. 49
SIGNATURE SERIES - Double Cutaway Guitar - PEAVEY ELECTRONICS CORPORATION; pg. 662, pg. 970
SIGNATURE SERVER - Entree Cart - THE VOLLRATH COMPANY LLC; pg. 1139, pg. 1894
SIGNATURE SERVICES CONCIERGE - Social Room - WCI COMMUNITIES, INC.; pg. 1118, pg. 414
SIGNATURE SOLUTIONS - Bleached Board And Kraft - GEORGIA-PACIFIC LLC; pg. 1458, pg. 507
SIGNATURE SOUND - Audio & Video Product - HARMAN INTERNATIONAL INDUSTRIES, INCORPORATED; pg. 641, pg. 374
SIGNED, SEALED, DELIVERED - Tag Line - HOUSTON ROCKETS; pg. 552, pg. 1707
SIGNET - Speaker Cable - COLEMAN CABLE, INC.; pg. 1324, pg. 665
SIGNET - Cameras - EASTMAN KODAK COMPANY; pg. 1408, pg. 1333
SIGNET - Tires - THE HERCULES TIRE & RUBBER COMPANY; pg. 1884, pg. 1454
SIGNET - Adult Mass Market Paperback Books - PENGUIN RANDOM HOUSE; pg. 1675, pg. 1276
SIGNI-PHY - Computer Products - BROADCOM CORPORATION; pg. 364, pg. 108
SIGNIFY - Rapid Membrane Test Products - ALERE INC.; pg. 1488, pg. 849
SIGNLUME - Specialty Lighting - JUNO LIGHTING, INC.; pg. 1300, pg. 606
SIGNMARK - Safety & Facility Identification Products - BRADY CORPORATION; pg. 363, pg. 1873
SIGNORA - Tile - ARTISTIC TILE INC.; pg. 914, pg. 1119
SIGNPOST - Fabric - NEMSCHOFF, INC.; pg. 936, pg. 1890
SIGNPOSTS EARLY LITERACY - Early Literacy Assessment System - QUESTAR ASSESSMENT, INC.; pg. 1679, pg. 1143
SIGNSYNC DESIGN - Software - XEROX CORPORATION; pg. 494, pg. 365
SIGN(WARE) - Document Frame - RUBBERMAID HOME PRODUCTS; pg. 1138, pg. 1453
SIGRID OLSEN - Apparel - KATE SPADE & COMPANY; pg. 27, pg. 1248
SII - Photographic Paper & Chemicals - EASTMAN KODAK COMPANY; pg. 1408, pg. 1333
SII - Industrial Tank - SNYDER INDUSTRIES, INC.; pg. 1377, pg. 1012
SIKEY - Drive Technology - WESTERN DIGITAL CORPORATION; pg. 492, pg. 118
SIKORSKY - Helicopters - UNITED TECHNOLOGIES CORPORATION; pg. 235, pg. 353
SIL-CELL - Plastics Filler - SILBRICO CORPORATION; pg. 110, pg. 617
SIL-CO-SIL - Ground Silica - U.S. SILICA COMPANY; pg. 1185, pg. 1849

SIL FIX - Silicon Repair Adhesive - MCNETT CORPORATION; *pg.* 1839, *pg.* 1817
SIL-GLYDE - Lubricating Compound - AMERICAN GREASE STICK CO.; *pg.* 971, *pg.* 902
SIL-KLEER - Filter Powder - SILBRICO CORPORATION; *pg.* 110, *pg.* 617
SIL-KORE - Cable - W.L. GORE & ASSOCIATES, INC.; *pg.* 122, *pg.* 388
SIL-MATRIX - Potassium Silicates - PQ CORPORATION; *pg.* 1178, *pg.* 1515
SIL NET - Silicone Seam Sealer - MCNETT CORPORATION; *pg.* 1839, *pg.* 1817
SIL-O-WET - Ink - SILBERLINE MANUFACTURING CO., INC.; *pg.* 110, *pg.* 1588
SIL-POXY - Silicone Adhesive - SMOOTH-ON INC.; *pg.* 111, *pg.* 1528
SILACOAT - Glass Product - GUARDIAN INDUSTRIES CORP.; *pg.* 85, *pg.* 869
SILACURE - Lead Coating - MEDTRONIC, INC.; *pg.* 1564, *pg.* 939
SILAGE SUPREME - Animal Treatment - KENT NUTRITION GROUP; *pg.* 1477, *pg.* 710
SILAPRENE - Adhesives & Sealants - ROYAL ADHESIVES & SEALANTS LLC; *pg.* 1179, *pg.* 697
SILAS - Pharmaceutical Product - ALERE INC.; *pg.* 1488, *pg.* 849
SILAS - Testing Instrument System - BECKMAN COULTER, INC.; *pg.* 1402, *pg.* 48
SILASTIC - Vulcanizable Elastomeric Caulking & Sealing Compounds - DOW CORNING CORPORATION; *pg.* 1159, *pg.* 900
SILBERCOTE - Coating - SILBERLINE MANUFACTURING CO., INC.; *pg.* 110, *pg.* 1588
SILC - Fabric - BROOKS SPORTS INC.; *pg.* 1805, *pg.* 1818
SILC PIG - Pigment - SMOOTH-ON INC.; *pg.* 111, *pg.* 1528
SILCON - Power Protection Product - SCHNEIDER ELECTRIC; *pg.* 467, *pg.* 1609
SILCROMA - Back Iron Flake - SILBERLINE MANUFACTURING CO., INC.; *pg.* 110, *pg.* 1588
SILEC - High Voltage Cables - GENERAL CABLE CORPORATION; *pg.* 83, *pg.* 729
SILENCE - Apparel - OAKLEY, INC.; *pg.* 1840, *pg.* 86
SILENCER - Saw Blade - THE DOALL COMPANY; *pg.* 1329, *pg.* 670
SILENCER - Brushless DC Motors - MOOG INC.; *pg.* 231, *pg.* 1156
SILENE - Alkaline Earth Metal & Synthetic Precipitated Silica for Industrial Arts - PPG INDUSTRIES, INC.; *pg.* 1445, *pg.* 1579
SILENT DRIVE - Electronic Components - MOLEX INCORPORATED; *pg.* 655, *pg.* 628
SILENT KEYER - Systems Integration & Aeronautics - LOCKHEED MARTIN CORPORATION; *pg.* 229, *pg.* 762
SILENT MAUVIE - Nail Care Product - OPI PRODUCTS INC.; *pg.* 518, *pg.* 167
SILENT PAPILLON - Medical Device - RESMED INC.; *pg.* 1589, *pg.* 207
SILENT PARTNER - Muffler - DONALDSON COMPANY, INC.; *pg.* 1329, *pg.* 917
SILENT SENTRY - Location Detection & Surveillance Air Tracking System - LOCKHEED MARTIN CORPORATION; *pg.* 229, *pg.* 762
SILENT SIGNAL - Hold-Up Emergency Reporting System - NORTEK, INC.; *pg.* 100, *pg.* 1607
SILENT STALK - Bow & Arrow Cases - CABELA'S INCORPORATED; *pg.* 535, *pg.* 1019
SILENT SUEDE - Guidewear - CABELA'S INCORPORATED; *pg.* 535, *pg.* 1019
SILENT SWIRL - Laboratory Product - SPECTRUM LABORATORIES INC.; *pg.* 1595, *pg.* 69
SILENT-TECH - Apparel - CABELA'S INCORPORATED; *pg.* 535, *pg.* 1019
SILENT TRAC - Automatic Transmission - TECUMSEH PRODUCTS COMPANY; *pg.* 1381, *pg.* 866
THE SILENT TURBINE - Pneumatic Vibrator - VIBCO INC.; *pg.* 1387, *pg.* 1611
SILENTCOMFORT - Air Purifier - KAZ, INC.; *pg.* 58, *pg.* 844
SILENTEX - Noise Control System - OWENS CORNING; *pg.* 102, *pg.* 1476
SILENTFECT - Software - BIO-RAD LABORATORIES, INC.; *pg.* 1504, *pg.* 101
SILENTFLO - Hydraulic Power Units - MTS SYSTEMS CORPORATION; *pg.* 442, *pg.* 923
SILENTGLIDE - Garage Door - WAYNE-DALTON CORP.; *pg.* 120, *pg.* 1465
SILENTMER - Software - BIO-RAD LABORATORIES, INC.; *pg.* 1504, *pg.* 101
SILFAB - Hose - FLEXFAB HORIZONS INTERNATIONAL, LLC; *pg.* 1072, *pg.* 891
SILFAB-1 - Lightweight Hose - FLEXFAB HORIZONS INTERNATIONAL, LLC; *pg.* 1072, *pg.* 891
SILFLEX - Ducting - HBD INDUSTRIES, INC.; *pg.* 207, *pg.* 1449
SILHOUET - Pacing Lead - MEDTRONIC, INC.; *pg.* 1564, *pg.* 939
SILHOUETTE - Pillow - AMERICAN LEATHER LP; *pg.* 912, *pg.* 1673
SILHOUETTE - Ultrafast Pulse Shaper - COHERENT, INC.; *pg.* 1406, *pg.* 265
SILHOUETTE - Glass & Ceramic Material - CORNING INCORPORATED; *pg.* 1122, *pg.* 1154
SILHOUETTE - Cart Bag - DATREK GOLF; *pg.* 1832, *pg.* 1801
SILHOUETTE - Guitar - ERNIE BALL INC.; *pg.* 1768, *pg.* 68
SILHOUETTE - Copyholders - FELLOWES, INC.; *pg.* 397, *pg.* 620
SILHOUETTE - Publisher - HARLEQUIN ENTERPRISES LIMITED; *pg.* 1647, *pg.* 1938
SILHOUETTE - Dinnerware - THE HOMER LAUGHLIN CHINA COMPANY; *pg.* 1125, *pg.* 1850
SILHOUETTE - Fabric Vanes Between Sheer Front & Back Fabric - HUNTER DOUGLAS, INC.; *pg.* 928, *pg.* 1320
SILHOUETTE - Fabric - NEMSCHOFF, INC.; *pg.* 936, *pg.* 1890
SILHOUETTE - Range Hoods - NORTEK, INC.; *pg.* 100, *pg.* 1607
SILHOUETTE - Suitcase - SAMSONITE CORPORATION; *pg.* 11, *pg.* 830
SILHOUETTE - Dispensing Systems - WAUSAU PAPER BAY WEST; *pg.* 1471, *pg.* 1465
SILHOUETTE BON SOIR - Room Darkening Shades - HUNTER DOUGLAS, INC.; *pg.* 928, *pg.* 1320
SILHOUETTE CLASSIC - Vinyl Siding - PLY GEM SIDING GROUP; *pg.* 105, *pg.* 986
SILHOUETTE DESIRE - Romance Paperbacks - HARLEQUIN MAGAZINES INC; *pg.* 1647, *pg.* 1237
SILHOUETTE III - Three-Inch Fabric Vanes Between Sheer Facings - HUNTER DOUGLAS, INC.; *pg.* 928, *pg.* 1320
SILHOUETTE INTIMATE MOMENTS - Romance Paperbacks - HARLEQUIN MAGAZINES INC; *pg.* 1647, *pg.* 1237
SILHOUETTE ROMANCE - Romance Paperbacks - HARLEQUIN MAGAZINES INC; *pg.* 1647, *pg.* 1237
SILHOUETTE SPECIAL EDITIONS - Romance Paperbacks - HARLEQUIN MAGAZINES INC; *pg.* 1647, *pg.* 1237
SILHOUETTES - Women's Larger Size Fashion Catalog-Career & Special Occasion - HANOVER DIRECT, INC.; *pg.* 1772, *pg.* 1130
SILHOUTTE - Wood Laboratory Cabinet - KEWAUNEE SCIENTIFIC CORPORATION; *pg.* 931, *pg.* 1391
SILICA-PAK - Cartridge - WATERS CORPORATION; *pg.* 1436, *pg.* 834
SILICA-SEAL - Dielectric Paste - FERRO CORPORATION; *pg.* 1162, *pg.* 1462
SILICON - Dicing Blade - KULICKE & SOFFA INDUSTRIES, INC.; *pg.* 650, *pg.* 1533
SILICON FOREST - Memory Storage Units - LATTICE SEMICONDUCTOR CORPORATION; *pg.* 651, *pg.* 1498
SILICON QOS - Semiconductor - AVAGO TECHNOLOGIES; *pg.* 358, *pg.* 238
SILICON STOR - Computer Hardware - AVAGO TECHNOLOGIES; *pg.* 358, *pg.* 238
SILICONBLADE - Drive Technology - WESTERN DIGITAL CORPORATION; *pg.* 492, *pg.* 118
SILICONCITY - Hardware Product - ATMEL CORPORATION; *pg.* 621, *pg.* 238
SILICONDRIVE - Drive Technology - WESTERN DIGITAL CORPORATION; *pg.* 492, *pg.* 118
SILICONDRIVE SECURE - Drive Technology - WESTERN DIGITAL CORPORATION; *pg.* 492, *pg.* 118
SILICONE - Mask - SELLSTROM MANUFACTURING CO.; *pg.* 1428, *pg.* 659
SILICONE - Intraocular Lenses - STAAR SURGICAL COMPANY; *pg.* 1597, *pg.* 151
SILICONE PUMP - Lubricant & Protectant - MCNETT CORPORATION; *pg.* 1839, *pg.* 1817
SILICONE THINNER - Chemical Preparation - SMOOTH-ON INC.; *pg.* 111, *pg.* 1528
SILICONINSIGHT - Software System - MENTOR GRAPHICS CORPORATION; *pg.* 432, *pg.* 1510
SILICORE - Duct Coextruded With a Super Slick Permanent Lining - DURA-LINE HOLDINGS; *pg.* 389, *pg.* 1636
SILICORE - Medical & Aesthetic Product - DYNATRONICS CORPORATION; *pg.* 1526, *pg.* 1757
SILIPON - Polymer - HERCULES INCORPORATED; *pg.* 1166, *pg.* 392
SILIPOS - Digital Care Kit - ALIMED, INC.; *pg.* 1490, *pg.* 816
SILIPOS - Medical & Aesthetic Product - DYNATRONICS CORPORATION; *pg.* 1526, *pg.* 1757
SILIPUR - Polymer - HERCULES INCORPORATED; *pg.* 1166, *pg.* 392
SILK - Semiconductor Dielectric Resins - THE DOW CHEMICAL COMPANY; *pg.* 1157, *pg.* 898
SILK - Soy Milk, Almond Milk & Coconut Milk - THE WHITEWAVE FOODS COMPANY; *pg.* 1037, *pg.* 324
SILK BLOSSOMS - Bedding - CROSCILL, INC.; *pg.* 1122, *pg.* 1220
SILK-EPIL - Hair Epilator - THE GILLETTE COMPANY; *pg.* 509, *pg.* 795
SILK KIMONO - Game - WMS INDUSTRIES INC.; *pg.* 593, *pg.* 666
SILK REFLECTIONS - Apparel - HANESBRANDS INC.; *pg.* 26, *pg.* 1394
SILK ROAD - Furniture Collection - CENTURY FURNITURE INDUSTRIES; *pg.* 920, *pg.* 1377
SILK ROUTE - Carpet - INTERFACE, INC.; *pg.* 695, *pg.* 512
SILKEDGE - Ceramic & Plastic Product - COORSTEK, INC.; *pg.* 77, *pg.* 330
SILKEN TOUCH - Coating Product - PPG INDUSTRIES, INC.; *pg.* 1445, *pg.* 1579
SILKEN TREASURES - Rug - COURISTAN INC.; *pg.* 921, *pg.* 1067
SILKIENCE - Shampoos, Conditioners & Hair Sprays - THE GILLETTE COMPANY; *pg.* 509, *pg.* 795
SILKOTE - Conditioner - PETEDGE; *pg.* 1481, *pg.* 787
SILKSTREAM - Drive Technology - WESTERN DIGITAL CORPORATION; *pg.* 492, *pg.* 118
SILKWEAVE - Bath Product - KOHLER CO.; *pg.* 91, *pg.* 1862
SILKWORM - Switch - BROCADE COMMUNICATIONS SYSTEMS, INC.; *pg.* 365, *pg.* 239
SILKY - Legwear - MAYER/BERKSHIRE CORPORATION; *pg.* 29, *pg.* 1129
SILKY & SLEEK - Blouses - HABAND COMPANY, INC.; *pg.* 1772, *pg.* 1099
SILKY FLO - Paint Brush - DUNN-EDWARDS CORPORATION; *pg.* 1442, *pg.* 129
SILLY CIRCUS WAGON - Flower Arrangement - 1-800-FLOWERS.COM, INC.; *pg.* 1758, *pg.* 1151
SILLY PUTTY - Toy - CRAYOLA LLC; *pg.* 951, *pg.* 1528
SILLY SOCCER - Toy & Game - HASBRO, INC.; *pg.* 954, *pg.* 1603
SILLY SPORTS - Game - HASBRO, INC.; *pg.* 954, *pg.* 1603
SILLY SYMPHONY - Sing-A-Long Toy - THE WALT DISNEY COMPANY; *pg.* 317, *pg.* 52
SILMAR - Resins & Clear Gel Coats - INTERPLASTIC CORPORATION; *pg.* 1168, *pg.* 961
SILNET - Adhesive & Seam Sealer - MCNETT CORPORATION; *pg.* 1839, *pg.* 1817
SILO - Fan - CRAFTMADE INTERNATIONAL, INC.; *pg.* 1295, *pg.* 1670
SILOAM - Book - CHARISMA MEDIA; *pg.* 1627, *pg.* 436
SILOPAD - Malleolar Gel Sleeve - ALIMED, INC.; *pg.* 1490, *pg.* 816
SILSOFT - Soft Contact Lens Care - BAUSCH & LOMB INCORPORATED; *pg.* 1401, *pg.* 1045
SILSOFT - Contact Lenses - DOW CORNING CORPORATION; *pg.* 1159, *pg.* 900
SILTEX - Medical Device - MENTOR CORPORATION; *pg.* 1565, *pg.* 263
SILTTRAP - Erosion Control Product - AMERICAN EXCELSIOR COMPANY; *pg.* 1451, *pg.* 1659
SILURIAN - Pool Filter Sand - U.S. SILICA COMPANY; *pg.* 1185, *pg.* 1849
SILV-EX - Foam Agent for Forest Fires - ANSUL, INCORPORATED; *pg.* 1147, *pg.* 1869
SILVA - Field Compasses - JOHNSON OUTDOORS INC.; *pg.* 1837, *pg.* 1888
SILVA-BRITE - Silver Plating Solution - BASF CATALYSTS LLC; *pg.* 1148, *pg.* 1074
SILVADENE - Pharmaceutical Product - KING PHARMACEUTICALS, INC.; *pg.* 1553, *pg.* 1627
SILVALOY - Brazing Alloys - BASF CATALYSTS LLC; *pg.* 1148, *pg.* 1074
SILVASORB - Medical Product - MEDLINE INDUSTRIES, INC.; *pg.* 1562, *pg.* 635

SILVASTAR - Wood Product - CANFOR CORPORATION; *pg.* 1454, *pg.* 1910
SILVATOL - Stain Removers - HUNTSMAN CORPORATION; *pg.* 1167, *pg.* 1758
SILVER - Office Furniture - JOFCO INC.; *pg.* 931, *pg.* 691
SILVER - Heat Transfer Papers - NEENAH PAPER, INC.; *pg.* 1465, *pg.* 484
SILVER - Nutritional Product - RBC LIFE SCIENCES, INC.; *pg.* 1588, *pg.* 1723
SILVER ANNIVERSARY - Carpet - BEAULIEU GROUP, LLC; *pg.* 917, *pg.* 529
SILVER BELLS - Lottery Game - MASSACHUSETTS STATE LOTTERY; *pg.* 998, *pg.* 802
SILVER BULLET - Pulltab Game - IDAHO LOTTERY; *pg.* 995, *pg.* 547
SILVER CAST PLUS - Spincast - DAIWA CORPORATION; *pg.* 1832, *pg.* 75
SILVER CLOUD - Electronic Article Surveillance System - SENTRY TECHNOLOGY CORPORATION; *pg.* 672, *pg* 1339
SILVER CREEK - Knife - BUCK KNIVES, INC.; *pg.* 1828, *pg.* 550
SILVER CURL - Home Permanent - THE GILLETTE COMPANY; *pg.* 509, *pg.* 795
SILVER FLOSS - Food Product - GLK FOODS, LLC; *pg.* 858, *pg.* 1852
SILVER-GUARD - Papers - DAUBERT INDUSTRIES, INC.; *pg.* 1155, *pg.* 561
SILVER ICE - Jewelry - YURMAN DESIGN, INC.; *pg.* 15, *pg.* 1316
SILVER KNIGHTS - Hunting Knives - GERBER LEGENDARY BLADES; *pg.* 1834, *pg.* 1503
SILVER KNIT - Healthcare Product - MEDICOOL, INC.; *pg.* 1562, *pg.* 294
SILVER LAKE - Furniture - ASHLEY FURNITURE INDUSTRIES, INC.; *pg.* 914, *pg.* 1852
SILVER LEGACY RESORT CASINO - Resort Casino - ELDORADO RESORTS, INC.; *pg.* 546, *pg.* 1031
SILVER MOON - Video Slots - INTERNATIONAL GAME TECHNOLOGY; *pg.* 957, *pg.* 1024
SILVER PIXEL PRESS - Filter & Lens - THE TIFFEN COMPANY LLC; *pg.* 1432, *pg.* 1165
SILVER PLUS - Spray Guns - GRACO, INC.; *pg.* 1342, *pg.* 935
SILVER POINSETTIA - Table Textile - HERITAGE LACE INC.; *pg.* 694, *pg.* 711
SILVER POLISH - Metal Cleaner - CONNOISSEURS PRODUCTS CORPORATION; *pg.* 329, *pg.* 861
SILVER PRINCESS - Container Grown Plant - MONROVIA GROWERS; *pg.* 1797, *pg.* 44
SILVER SATIN - Shirt System - FAULTLESS STARCH/BON AMI COMPANY; *pg.* 330, *pg.* 982
SILVER SAVER - Corrosion Inhibitor - DAUBERT INDUSTRIES, INC.; *pg.* 1155, *pg.* 561
SILVER SCREEN GAMING - Games - PENN NATIONAL GAMING, INC.; *pg.* 574, *pg.* 1595
SILVER SERIES - Dispenser - BUNN-O-MATIC CORPORATION; *pg.* 53, *pg.* 661
SILVER SERIES - Modular Homes - NATIONWIDE HOMES, INC.; *pg.* 99, *pg.* 1788
SILVER SERVICE - Company Motto - ARNOLD MACHINERY COMPANY; *pg.* 1314, *pg.* 1755
SILVER SET - Joint Compound - USG CORPORATION; *pg.* 118, *pg.* 594
SILVER SLUGGER - Baseball Bat - HILLERICH & BRADSBY CO., INC.; *pg.* 1836, *pg.* 576
SILVER SPREADER - Container Grown Plant - MONROVIA GROWERS; *pg.* 1797, *pg.* 44
SILVER STAIN PLUS - Software - BIO-RAD LABORATORIES, INC.; *pg.* 1504, *pg.* 101
SILVER STAR - Dry Fire Dummy Practice Rounds - LYMAN PRODUCTS CORPORATION; *pg.* 1839, *pg.* 356
SILVER-STREAK - Metal Marker - LA-CO INDUSTRIES MARKAL CO., INC.; *pg.* 1170, *pg.* 610
SILVER SWORD - Game - WMS INDUSTRIES INC.; *pg.* 593, *pg.* 666
SILVER THUNDER - Gaming Product - GLD PRODUCTS, INC.; *pg.* 1835, *pg.* 1882
SILVER THUNDER - Malt Liquor - PABST BREWING COMPANY; *pg.* 258, *pg.* 137
SILVER TRIDENT - Combat Knife - GERBER LEGENDARY BLADES; *pg.* 1834, *pg.* 1503
SILVER VEIN BUTTERFLY - Knife - BEAR & SON CUTLERY, INC.; *pg.* 1827, *pg.* 7
SILVER WHISPERS - Container Grown Plant - MONROVIA GROWERS; *pg.* 1797, *pg.* 44
SILVER WIPES - Metal Cleaner - CONNOISSEURS PRODUCTS CORPORATION; *pg.* 329, *pg.* 861
SILVERADO - Footwear - EASTLAND SHOE CORPORATION; *pg.* 1808, *pg.* 750
SILVERADO - Pick-Up Truck - GENERAL MOTORS COMPANY; *pg.* 175, *pg.* 881
SILVERADO - Fabric - NEMSCHOFF, INC.; *pg.* 936, *pg.* 1890
SILVERBACK - Sporting Good Product - ESCALADE INC.; *pg.* 1833, *pg.* 678
SILVERBACK - Game - WMS INDUSTRIES INC.; *pg.* 593, *pg.* 666
SILVERBROOK - Food Product - SHAMROCK FOODS COMPANY; *pg.* 895, *pg.* 20
SILVERCEL - Silver Zinc Batteries/Cells - YARDNEY TECHNICAL PRODUCTS, INC.; *pg.* 690, *pg.* 1601
SILVERCREEK - Moist Snuff Smokeless Tobacco - SWISHER INTERNATIONAL, INC.; *pg.* 1895, *pg.* 345
SILVERDALE ES - Ceiling Fan - WESTINGHOUSE LIGHTING CORPORATION; *pg.* 687, *pg.* 1571
SILVERLEAF - Clothing - LAKELAND INDUSTRIES, INC.; *pg.* 1354, *pg.* 1338
SILVERMASTER - Chemical Product - HURST CHEMICAL COMPANY; *pg.* 1168, *pg.* 174
SILVERQUEST - Molecular Biology Product - THERMO FISHER SCIENTIFIC INC.; *pg.* 1602, *pg.* 61
SILVERSEAL - Wound Dressing - DERMA SCIENCES, INC.; *pg.* 1523, *pg.* 1111
SILVERSHIELD - Fencing - MASTER HALCO; *pg.* 96, *pg.* 474
SILVERTON NORTHERN - Steam Locomotives - BACHMANN INDUSTRIES, INC.; *pg.* 950, *pg.* 1559
SILVERXPRESS - Molecular Biology Product - THERMO FISHER SCIENTIFIC INC.; *pg.* 1602, *pg.* 61
SILVET - Ink - SILBERLINE MANUFACTURING CO., INC.; *pg.* 110, *pg.* 1588
SILVEX - Ink - SILBERLINE MANUFACTURING CO., INC.; *pg.* 110, *pg.* 1588
SILVO - Seasonings - MCCORMICK & COMPANY, INCORPORATED; *pg.* 1027, *pg.* 779
SILVON - Medical Equipment - CONMED CORPORATION; *pg.* 1517, *pg.* 1347
SILX - Software - XEROX CORPORATION; *pg.* 494, *pg.* 365
SIM - Beverages - THE COCA-COLA COMPANY; *pg.* 240, *pg.* 493
SIM - Software - COMMVAULT SYSTEMS, INC.; *pg.* 377, *pg.* 1125
SIM-PULL - Envelope - TENSION ENVELOPE CORPORATION; *pg.* 483, *pg.* 986
SIM-PULL - Medical Product - W.L. GORE & ASSOCIATES, INC.; *pg.* 122, *pg.* 388
SIMAFLAME - Multifunctional Tester - ECLIPSE INC.; *pg.* 1332, *pg.* 655
SIMAG - Ice Machine - SCOTSMAN GROUP LLC; *pg.* 1374, *pg.* 665
SIMANIMALS - Video Game - ELECTRONIC ARTS INC.; *pg.* 951, *pg.* 189
SIMANT - Video Game - ELECTRONIC ARTS INC.; *pg.* 951, *pg.* 189
SIMATIC - Programmable Controllers - SIEMENS CORPORATION; *pg.* 803, *pg.* 1291
SIMBA - Beverages - THE COCA-COLA COMPANY; *pg.* 240, *pg.* 493
SIMBA - Food & Beverage - PEPSICO, INC.; *pg.* 259, *pg.* 1327
SIMBA - Publication - R.R. BOWKER LLC; *pg.* 1682, *pg.* 1095
SIMCITY 2000 - Video Game - ELECTRONIC ARTS INC.; *pg.* 951, *pg.* 189
SIMCOE - Commercial Retail Lighting - JUNO LIGHTING, INC.; *pg.* 1300, *pg.* 606
SIMCOR - Pharmaceutical Product - ABBOTT LABORATORIES; *pg.* 1484, *pg.* 551
SIMDESIGNER - Software - MSC SOFTWARE CORPORATION; *pg.* 441, *pg.* 262
SIMEARTH - Video Game - ELECTRONIC ARTS INC.; *pg.* 951, *pg.* 189
SIMET - Metal Cutting Saw Blade - SIMONDS INTERNATIONAL CORPORATION; *pg.* 1376, *pg.* 819
SIMFINITY - Simulation Technology - CAE INC.; *pg.* 226, *pg.* 1959
SIMFORCE - Force Reduction Simulation Software - CACI INTERNATIONAL INC.; *pg.* 367, *pg.* 1773
SIMFUSION - Software & Hardware - EVANS & SUTHERLAND COMPUTER CORPORATION; *pg.* 638, *pg.* 1757
SIMILAC - Nutritional Supplement - ABBOTT LABORATORIES; *pg.* 1484, *pg.* 551
SIMILAC - Infant Formula - ABBOTT NUTRITION; *pg.* 1485, *pg.* 1437
SIMILAC ADVANCE - Infant Nutritional Formulas - ABBOTT LABORATORIES; *pg.* 1484, *pg.* 551
SIMILAC ADVANCE - Infant Formula - ABBOTT NUTRITION; *pg.* 1485, *pg.* 1437
SIMILAC ALIMENTUM - Infant Nutritional Formulas - ABBOTT LABORATORIES; *pg.* 1484, *pg.* 551
SIMILAC GO & GROW - Infant Nutritional Formulas - ABBOTT LABORATORIES; *pg.* 1484, *pg.* 551
SIMILAC ISOMIL ADVANCE - Infant Nutritional Formulas - ABBOTT LABORATORIES; *pg.* 1484, *pg.* 551
SIMILAC NEOSURE - Prescription Infant Formula - ABBOTT LABORATORIES; *pg.* 1484, *pg.* 551
SIMILAC ORGANIC - Infant Nutritional Formulas - ABBOTT LABORATORIES; *pg.* 1484, *pg.* 551
SIMILAC SENSITIVE - Infant Nutritional Formulas - ABBOTT LABORATORIES; *pg.* 1484, *pg.* 551
SIMILKAMEEN - Wine - ANDREW PELLER LIMITED; *pg.* 1956, *pg.* 1920
SIMITRE - Bath Organizer & Accessory - HOME PRODUCTS INTERNATIONAL, INC.; *pg.* 1125, *pg.* 577
SIMLIPHY - Semiconductor Solution - VITESSE SEMICONDUCTOR CORPORATION; *pg.* 686, *pg.* 57
SIMLOCK - SIM/SAM Card Closed System - AMPHENOL CORPORATION; *pg.* 616, *pg.* 381
SIMMENTHAL - Canned Meat in Jelly - MONDELEZ INTERNATIONAL, INC.; *pg.* 878, *pg.* 601
SIMMER-SAFE - Electric Cooking Pots - JARDEN CONSUMER SOLUTIONS; *pg.* 57, *pg.* 412
SIMMONS - Matresses - ASHLEY FURNITURE INDUSTRIES, INC.; *pg.* 914, *pg.* 1852
SIMMONS - Healthcare Product - GF HEALTH PRODUCTS, INC.; *pg.* 1535, *pg.* 508
SIMMONS - Chicken Products - SIMMONS FOODS INC.; *pg.* 895, *pg.* 35
SIMMONS HEALTHCARE - Medical Product - GF HEALTH PRODUCTS, INC.; *pg.* 1535, *pg.* 508
SIMMS KEEN - Footwear - SIMMS FISHING PRODUCTS CORP.; *pg.* 1845, *pg.* 1008
SIMNOW - Simulator - ADVANCED MICRO DEVICES, INC.; *pg.* 613, *pg.* 282
SIMOFFICE - Software - MSC SOFTWARE CORPORATION; *pg.* 441, *pg.* 262
SIMOGRIT - Metal Cutting Saw Blade - SIMONDS INTERNATIONAL CORPORATION; *pg.* 1376, *pg.* 819
SIMON - Game - HASBRO, INC.; *pg.* 954, *pg.* 1603
SIMON - Real Estate Business - SIMON PROPERTY GROUP, INC.; *pg.* 1112, *pg.* 690
SIMON & SCHUSTER - Adult Publishing Imprint - SIMON & SCHUSTER, INC.; *pg.* 1687, *pg.* 1292
SIMON & SCHUSTER AUDIOWORKS - Audio Publishing Imprint - SIMON & SCHUSTER, INC.; *pg.* 1687, *pg.* 1292
SIMON & SCHUSTER BOOKS FOR YOUNG READERS - Children's Publishing Imprint - SIMON & SCHUSTER CHILDREN'S PUBLISHING; *pg.* 1686, *pg.* 1292
SIMON & SCHUSTER SOUND IDEAS - Audio Publishing Imprint - SIMON & SCHUSTER, INC.; *pg.* 1687, *pg.* 1292
SIMON FISCHER - Prune Butter & Apricot Butter - SOKOL & COMPANY; *pg.* 1862, *pg.* 598
SIMON GIFTACCOUNT - Electronic Payment Services - SIMON PROPERTY GROUP, INC.; *pg.* 1112, *pg.* 690
SIMON GIFTCARD - Giftcard - SIMON PROPERTY GROUP, INC.; *pg.* 1112, *pg.* 690
SIMON PULSE - Children's Publishing Imprint - SIMON & SCHUSTER CHILDREN'S PUBLISHING; *pg.* 1686, *pg.* 1292
SIMON SPOTLIGHT - Imprint that Publishes Tie-ins to Licensed Children's Media Properties - SIMON & SCHUSTER CHILDREN'S PUBLISHING; *pg.* 1686, *pg.* 1292
SIMONE - Clothing - ABERCROMBIE & FITCH CO.; *pg.* 37, *pg.* 1466
SIMONE - Decorative Accessory - ETHAN ALLEN INTERIORS INC.; *pg.* 924, *pg.* 343
SIMONIZ - Polish - HONEYWELL INTERNATIONAL INC.; *pg.* 407, *pg.* 1088
SIMONTON WINDOWS - Hardware - FORTUNE BRANDS HOME & SECURITY, INC.; *pg.* 55, *pg.* 600
SIMPACTOR - Impact Mill - STURTEVANT INC.; *pg.* 1379, *pg.* 824

First page reference indicates Business Class Edition
Second page reference indicates Geographic Edition

SIMPANA - Software Products - COMMVAULT SYSTEMS, INC.; *pg.* 377, *pg.* 1125
SIMPHONY - Software - MICROS SYSTEMS, INC.; *pg.* 435, *pg.* 768
SIMPL - Software - CRESTRON ELECTRONICS INC.; *pg.* 631, *pg.* 1116
SIMPLAIR - Software - INGERSOLL-RAND COMPANY; *pg.* 1349, *pg.* 1370
SIMPLE - Footwear Product - DECKERS OUTDOOR CORPORATION; *pg.* 1807, *pg.* 100
SIMPLE - Skin Care Products - UNILEVER UNITED STATES, INC.; *pg.* 904, *pg.* 1061
SIMPLE BLESSINGS - Pillow and Throw - HERITAGE LACE INC.; *pg.* 694, *pg.* 711
SIMPLE COMFORT - French Cut - JOCKEY INTERNATIONAL, INC.; *pg.* 27, *pg.* 1861
SIMPLE CUT - Haircutting Kit - CONAIR CORPORATION; *pg.* 505, *pg.* 1055
SIMPLE ELEGANCE - Pant Set - HABAND COMPANY, INC.; *pg.* 1772, *pg.* 1099
SIMPLE FRAMING SYSTEM - Building Products - BOISE CASCADE HOLDINGS, L.L.C.; *pg.* 1453, *pg.* 546
SIMPLE GREEN - Cleaning Product - SUNSHINE MAKERS, INC.; *pg.* 336, *pg.* 105
SIMPLE GREEN D PRO 3 - Germicidal Cleaner - SUNSHINE MAKERS, INC.; *pg.* 336, *pg.* 105
SIMPLE GREEN NATURALS - Dish Washing Liquid - SUNSHINE MAKERS, INC.; *pg.* 336, *pg.* 105
SIMPLE HARVEST - Breakfast Foods - THE QUAKER OATS COMPANY; *pg.* 834, *pg.* 588
SIMPLE PLEASURES - Lower Fat Chocolate Creme Candies - THE HERSHEY CO.; *pg.* 1855, *pg.* 1538
SIMPLE SEQUENCER - Semiconductors - ANALOG DEVICES, INC.; *pg.* 617, *pg.* 839
SIMPLE SHOES - Sport Sandals - DECKERS OUTDOOR CORPORATION; *pg.* 1807, *pg.* 100
SIMPLE SOLUTION FOR TODAY'S COMPLEX LIFESTYLES - Tagline - NEW EARTH LIFE SCIENCES, INC.; *pg.* 1573, *pg.* 1499
SIMPLE STEPS - Heat & Serve Food Packaging - SEALED AIR CORPORATION; *pg.* 1468, *pg.* 1058
SIMPLE SWAPPER - Hot Swap Switches - MAXIM INTEGRATED PRODUCTS, INC.; *pg.* 653, *pg.* 247
SIMPLE SWITCHER - Switching Regulator - COILCRAFT, INC.; *pg.* 1324, *pg.* 562
SIMPLECOMFORT - Thermostat - INTERNATIONAL CONTROLS & MEASUREMENTS CORP.; *pg.* 1350, *pg.* 1317
SIMPLEFI - Audio Receiver - MOTOROLA SOLUTIONS, INC.; *pg.* 657, *pg.* 659
SIMPLER IS BETTER - Software - CITRIX SYSTEMS, INC.; *pg.* 375, *pg.* 424
SIMPLESHARE - Storage System - HGST; *pg.* 406, *pg.* 260
SIMPLETRANSFER - Storage System - HGST; *pg.* 406, *pg.* 260
SIMPLEX - Flatwork Finishers - ALLIANCE LAUNDRY HOLDINGS LLC; *pg.* 51, *pg.* 1890
SIMPLEX - Movie Theater Equipment - BALLANTYNE STRONG, INC.; *pg.* 623, *pg.* 1013
SIMPLEX - Dental Product - DENTSPLY INTERNATIONAL INC.; *pg.* 1522, *pg.* 1596
SIMPLEX - Orthopaedic Product - STRYKER CORPORATION; *pg.* 1598, *pg.* 894
SIMPLEX - Fire Protection Products - TYCO SIMPLEXGRINNELL LP; *pg.* 682, *pg.* 859
SIMPLEX PACKAGES - Sewage Systems - LITTLE GIANT PUMP COMPANY; *pg.* 1356, *pg.* 1486
SIMPLGEL 30 - Pharmaceutical Product - HAWKINS, INC.; *pg.* 1165, *pg.* 937
SIMPLICITY - Computer Software - AVAGO TECHNOLOGIES; *pg.* 358, *pg.* 238
SIMPLICITY - Area Rugs - COURISTAN INC.; *pg.* 921, *pg.* 1067
SIMPLICITY - Herbicide - DOW AGROSCIENCES LLC; *pg.* 1156, *pg.* 684
SIMPLICITY - Solid Surfaces - E.I. DU PONT DE NEMOURS & COMPANY; *pg.* 1159, *pg.* 390
SIMPLICITY - High Chair - EVENFLO COMPANY, INC.; *pg.* 924, *pg.* 1470
SIMPLICITY - Door Glass - ODL INCORPORATED; *pg.* 101, *pg.* 914
SIMPLICITY - Light Bulbs - PHILIPS ELECTRONICS NORTH AMERICA; *pg.* 662, *pg.* 782
SIMPLICITY - Capital Equipment - TEREX CORPORATION; *pg.* 1381, *pg.* 384
SIMPLICITY ROSE - Dinnerware - THE HOMER LAUGHLIN CHINA COMPANY; *pg.* 1125, *pg.* 1850
SIMPLICITY THROUGH INNOVATION - Software - BIO-RAD LABORATORIES, INC.; *pg.* 1504, *pg.* 101
SIMPLICTY - Lace - HERITAGE LACE INC.; *pg.* 694, *pg.* 711
SIMPLIFICATION THROUGH INNOVATION - Slogan - CINCOM SYSTEMS, INC.; *pg.* 372, *pg.* 1411
SIMPLIFYING COMPLEXITY, DELIVERING POSSIBILITIES. - Tagline - SYNIVERSE HOLDINGS, INC.; *pg.* 479, *pg.* 475
SIMPLIFYING MOBILITY - Tagline - PCTEL, INC.; *pg.* 452, *pg.* 557
SIMPLIFYING THE VIEW OF BUSINESS - Tagline - SILVON SOFTWARE INC.; *pg.* 470, *pg.* 669
SIMPLIFYING YOUR INSURANCE DECISIONS - Slogan - INSWEB CORPORATION; *pg.* 1205, *pg.* 186
SIMPLIMET - Mounting Press - BUEHLER, LTD.; *pg.* 1403, *pg.* 622
SIMPLOT - Food Product - ELLENBEE-LEGGETT COMPANY INC.; *pg.* 854, *pg.* 1452
SIMPLOT CLASSIC - Food Products - J.R. SIMPLOT COMPANY; *pg.* 867, *pg.* 547
SIMPLOT PARTNERS - Fertilizer - SIMPLOT PARTNERS INC.; *pg.* 1800, *pg.* 548
SIMPLY APPLE - Beverages - THE COCA-COLA COMPANY; *pg.* 240, *pg.* 493
SIMPLY BEAUTIFUL - Carpet - BEAULIEU GROUP, LLC; *pg.* 917, *pg.* 529
SIMPLY BETTER RESULTS - Software - SYNOPSYS, INC.; *pg.* 480, *pg.* 162
SIMPLY BRILLIANT - Slogan - KWIAT INC.; *pg.* 8, *pg.* 1249
SIMPLY CINEMA - Audio & Video Product - HARMAN INTERNATIONAL INDUSTRIES, INCORPORATED; *pg.* 641, *pg.* 374
SIMPLY CLEAR - Pharmaceutical Product - ALERE INC.; *pg.* 1488, *pg.* 849
SIMPLY COUGH - Healthcare Product - JOHNSON & JOHNSON; *pg.* 1549, *pg.* 1091
SIMPLY DAISIES - Pineapple Fruit Arrangements - EDIBLE ARRANGEMENTS INTERNATIONAL, INC.; *pg.* 1768, *pg.* 382
SIMPLY DIVINE - Table Textile - HERITAGE LACE INC.; *pg.* 694, *pg.* 711
SIMPLY FRESH AMERICAN DINING - Tagline - RUBY TUESDAY, INC.; *pg.* 1748, *pg.* 1640
SIMPLY FRUIT - Fruit Juice-Sweetened Fruit Spreads - THE J.M. SMUCKER COMPANY; *pg.* 865, *pg.* 1468
SIMPLY GOURMET - Chicken Breast - QUANTUM FOODS, INC.; *pg.* 891, *pg.* 559
SIMPLY GRAPEFRUIT - Beverages - THE COCA-COLA COMPANY; *pg.* 240, *pg.* 493
SIMPLY IRRESISTIBLE - Carpet - BEAULIEU GROUP, LLC; *pg.* 917, *pg.* 529
SIMPLY LAZARE - Diamond Jewelry - LAZARE KAPLAN INTERNATIONAL, INC.; *pg.* 8, *pg.* 1250
SIMPLY LEMONADE - Beverages - THE COCA-COLA COMPANY; *pg.* 240, *pg.* 493
SIMPLY LIMEADE - Beverages - THE COCA-COLA COMPANY; *pg.* 240, *pg.* 493
SIMPLY ORANGE - Orange Juice - THE COCA-COLA COMPANY; *pg.* 240, *pg.* 493
SIMPLY ORGANIC - Food Product - ANNIE'S INC.; *pg.* 1760, *pg.* 45
SIMPLY ORGANIC - Organic Products - FRONTIER NATURAL PRODUCTS CO-OP; *pg.* 509, *pg.* 710
SIMPLY POTATOES - Refrigerated Potato Products - MICHAEL FOODS, INC.; *pg.* 877, *pg.* 949
SIMPLY SAVOUR - Meat Product - MAPLE LEAF FOODS INC.; *pg.* 875, *pg.* 1927
SIMPLY SBGA - Supplement & Food Product - NEW EARTH LIFE SCIENCES, INC.; *pg.* 1573, *pg.* 1499
SIMPLY SINGLES - Jewelry - ROMAN RESEARCH, INC.; *pg.* 11, *pg.* 824
SIMPLY SLEEP - Sleep Aid - MCNEIL-PPC, INC.; *pg.* 1560, *pg.* 1533
SIMPLY SMART DISPUTE - Software Product - PEGASYSTEMS INC.; *pg.* 453, *pg.* 809
SIMPLY SMARTER LIGHT - Optical Networking Solutions - CIENA CORPORATION; *pg.* 628, *pg.* 771
SIMPLY STAINLESS - Bathroom Design - DECOLAV, INC.; *pg.* 1123, *pg.* 411
SIMPLY STEAM - Vegetable Product - GENERAL MILLS, INC.; *pg.* 828, *pg.* 933
SIMPLY STUFFY - Healthcare Product - JOHNSON & JOHNSON; *pg.* 1549, *pg.* 1091
SIMPLY WHEY - Nutritional Supplement - MAXIMUM HUMAN PERFORMANCE, INC.; *pg.* 1559, *pg.* 1065
SIMPLY WHISPERS - Jewelry - ROMAN RESEARCH, INC.; *pg.* 11, *pg.* 824
SIMPLY YOURS - Furniture - BASSETT FURNITURE INDUSTRIES, INCORPORATED; *pg.* 916, *pg.* 1776
SIMPLYBLUE - Molecular Biology Product - THERMO FISHER SCIENTIFIC INC.; *pg.* 1602, *pg.* 61
SIMPLYBRILLIANT - Slogan - CIRCA LIGHTING, INC.; *pg.* 1295, *pg.* 539
SIMPLYDRI - Panties & Washable Pads - THE SALK COMPANY; *pg.* 1591, *pg.* 800
SIMPLYTHICK - Gel Thickeners - ALIMED, INC.; *pg.* 1490, *pg.* 816
SIMPROCESS - Object-Oriented Analytical Simulation Software - CACI INTERNATIONAL INC.; *pg.* 367, *pg.* 1773
SIMPSON - Doors - SIMPSON DOOR COMPANY; *pg.* 110, *pg.* 1823
SIMPSON MIX-MULLER - Industrial Mixer - SIMPSON TECHNOLOGIES CORPORATION; *pg.* 111, *pg.* 555
SIMPSON MULTI-MULL - Industrial Mixer - SIMPSON TECHNOLOGIES CORPORATION; *pg.* 111, *pg.* 555
THE SIMPSONS - Toy & Game - HASBRO, INC.; *pg.* 954, *pg.* 1603
SIMPULL - Communication Cable(Category Five) - SOUTHWIRE COMPANY; *pg.* 1063, *pg.* 527
SIMPULSE - Medical Device - C.R. BARD, INC.; *pg.* 1519, *pg.* 1094
THE SIMS - Video Game - ELECTRONIC ARTS INC.; *pg.* 951, *pg.* 189
THE SIMS CARNIVAL - Video Game - ELECTRONIC ARTS INC.; *pg.* 951, *pg.* 189
SIMSCRIPT - Object-Oriented Analytical Simulation Software - CACI INTERNATIONAL INC.; *pg.* 367, *pg.* 1773
SIMUL-RING - Telecommunication Services - VONAGE HOLDINGS CORP.; *pg.* 686, *pg.* 1074
SIMULATEIR - Space Thermal Simulation Module - PRECISION CONTROL SYSTEMS, INC./ RESEARCH INC.; *pg.* 1427, *pg.* 923
SIMULATING REALITY - Software - MSC SOFTWARE CORPORATION; *pg.* 441, *pg.* 262
SIMULATION CENTER - Software - MSC SOFTWARE CORPORATION; *pg.* 441, *pg.* 262
SIMULATION WORKBENCH - Real-Time Modeling Environment - CONCURRENT COMPUTER CORPORATION; *pg.* 379, *pg.* 531
SIMULCACHE - Storage System - DOT HILL SYSTEMS CORP.; *pg.* 388, *pg.* 333
SIMULCRYPT - Digital Video Product - HARMONIC, INC.; *pg.* 402, *pg.* 246
SIMUSOLV - Software - THE DOW CHEMICAL COMPANY; *pg.* 1157, *pg.* 898
SIMVIEWER - Visualization & Analysis Tool - ALION SCIENCE AND TECHNOLOGY CORPORATION; *pg.* 615, *pg.* 1788
SINALFA - Pharmaceutical Product - ABBOTT LABORATORIES; *pg.* 1484, *pg.* 551
SINBAR - Herbicide - E.I. DU PONT DE NEMOURS & COMPANY; *pg.* 1159, *pg.* 390
SINCERELY VISIONS - Frame - BROWN & BIGELOW, INC.; *pg.* 1624, *pg.* 959
SINCLAIR - Coating - AKZONOBEL DECORATIVE PAINTS U.S.; *pg.* 1439, *pg.* 1474
SINCLAIR - Furniture - AMERICAN LEATHER LP; *pg.* 912, *pg.* 1673
SINCLAIR - Lounge Chairs - BERNHARDT DESIGN; *pg.* 918, *pg.* 1381
SINE - Waiting Seating - STEELCASE INC.; *pg.* 475, *pg.* 889
SINE ON - Catalog & Information Services - TEXAS INSTRUMENTS INCORPORATED; *pg.* 679, *pg.* 1688
SINEMETCR - Pharmaceutical Product - IMPAX LABORATORIES, INC.; *pg.* 1544, *pg.* 101
SINEQUAN - Medicine - PFIZER INC.; *pg.* 1581, *pg.* 1278
SINFONIA - Cosmetics - WESTROCK COMPANY; *pg.* 1472, *pg.* 1805
SINFONY - Indirect Lab Composite - 3M COMPANY; *pg.* 1142, *pg.* 956
SING ALONG READ ALONG - Book Set - LEAPFROG ENTERPRISES, INC.; *pg.* 961, *pg.* 84
SING AND READ STORYBOOK - Educational Materials - SCHOLASTIC INC.; *pg.* 1683, *pg.* 1288
SING WITH ME MAGIC CUBE - Toy - MUNCHKIN, INC.; *pg.* 964, *pg.* 300
SINGAPORE - Furniture - AMISCO INDUSTRIES LTD.; *pg.*

913, *pg.* 1958
SINGAPORE AIRLINES - International Airlines - SINGAPORE AIRLINES; *pg.* 1923, *pg.* 82
SINGLE - Electric Coffee Maker - BUNN-O-MATIC CORPORATION; *pg.* 53, *pg.* 661
SINGLE - Bolt & Shield Anchor - POWERS FASTENERS INC.; *pg.* 1059, *pg.* 1143
SINGLE BARREL - Whiskey - JACK DANIEL'S DISTILLERY; *pg.* 1964, *pg.* 1640
SINGLE CYCLE - Cutting Method - GLEASON CORPORATION; *pg.* 1340, *pg.* 1335
SINGLE KIT - Eye Shadows - COVER GIRL COSMETICS; *pg.* 506, *pg.* 772
SINGLE MAILBOX RECOVERY - Software - NETAPP, INC.; *pg.* 444, *pg.* 287
SINGLE PACKET RADIO - Baseband Wireless Communications - SKYWORKS SOLUTIONS, INC.; *pg.* 674, *pg.* 862
SINGLE PATIENT USE VEST - Airway Clearance Product - ELECTROMED, INC.; *pg.* 1527, *pg.* 951
SINGLE PORE - Robotic Product - HAMILTON CO., INC.; *pg.* 1415, *pg.* 1031
SINGLE SIGN-ON FOR JAVA - Software - DELL SOFTWARE; *pg.* 385, *pg.* 40
SINGLE SIGN-ON FOR NETWEAVER - Software - DELL SOFTWARE; *pg.* 385, *pg.* 40
SINGLE SIX - Revolver - STURM, RUGER & COMPANY, INC.; *pg.* 1846, *pg.* 371
SINGLE SOFT HEAT - Beverage - BUNN-O-MATIC CORPORATION; *pg.* 53, *pg.* 661
SINGLE SOURCE - Pharmaceutical Product - ALERE INC.; *pg.* 1488, *pg.* 849
SINGLE-STAGE SNO-THROS - Lawn Product - ARIENS COMPANY INC.; *pg.* 700, *pg.* 1855
SINGLE STROKE - Honing Tool - SUNNEN PRODUCTS COMPANY; *pg.* 1379, *pg.* 1004
SINGLE STROKE HONING - Honing Tool - SUNNEN PRODUCTS COMPANY; *pg.* 1379, *pg.* 1004
SINGLE THERMOFRESH - Beverage - BUNN-O-MATIC CORPORATION; *pg.* 53, *pg.* 661
SINGLEBORE - Subsea Wellhead System - DRIL-QUIP, INC.; *pg.* 1330, *pg.* 1704
SINGLEBORE PRODUCTION SYSTEM - Subsea Equipment - DRIL-QUIP, INC.; *pg.* 1330, *pg.* 1704
SINGLECUT - Guitar - PAUL REED SMITH GUITARS; *pg.* 574, *pg.* 779
SINGLEPARENTSMINGLE.COM - Online Dating Service - SPARK NETWORKS, INC.; *pg.* 472, *pg.* 140
SINGLESCRUISE.COM - Leisure Travel - CARLSON COMPANIES INC.; *pg.* 1084, *pg.* 947
SINGLESTEP DEBUGGER - Software - WIND RIVER SYSTEMS, INC.; *pg.* 493, *pg.* 38
SINGLESTEP WITH VISION - Software - WIND RIVER SYSTEMS, INC.; *pg.* 493, *pg.* 38
SINGLET VCSELS - Electronic Component - EMCORE CORPORATION; *pg.* 636, *pg.* 39
SINGLWIPES - Windshield Towels - WAUSAU PAPER BAY WEST; *pg.* 1471, *pg.* 1465
SINGULAIR - Medicine - MERCK & CO., INC.; *pg.* 1566, *pg.* 1077
SINGULAR - Medical Equipment - CONMED CORPORATION; *pg.* 1517, *pg.* 1347
SINIGUAL - Mexican Restaurants - REAL MEX RESTAURANTS, INC.; *pg.* 1746, *pg.* 75
SINISTER CIRCUS - Doll - TONNER DOLL COMPANY, INC.; *pg.* 968, *pg.* 1171
SINNERR - Footwear - STEVEN MADDEN, LTD.; *pg.* 1819, *pg.* 1176
SINTERSCAN - Software - 3D SYSTEMS CORPORATION; *pg.* 339, *pg.* 1621
SINTERSTATION - Solid Imaging Material - 3D SYSTEMS CORPORATION; *pg.* 339, *pg.* 1621
SINTERSTATION HIQ - Solid Imaging Material - 3D SYSTEMS CORPORATION; *pg.* 339, *pg.* 1621
SINTHESIS - Computer Software - PARAGON TECHNOLOGIES, INC.; *pg.* 1367, *pg.* 1528
SINUS SUPPORT - Health Care Product - NATURE'S SUNSHINE PRODUCTS, INC.; *pg.* 1571, *pg.* 1754
SINUTAB - Sinus Medicine - MCNEIL-PPC, INC.; *pg.* 1560, *pg.* 1533
SIOUX - Furniture - ASHLEY FURNITURE INDUSTRIES, INC.; *pg.* 914, *pg.* 1852
SIOUX - Power Tools - SNAP-ON INCORPORATED; *pg.* 1062, *pg.* 1862
SIOUX CITY - Sarsaparilla Soft Drink - WHITE ROCK PRODUCTS CORP.; *pg.* 266, *pg.* 1355
SIP MAGAZINE - Trade Publication - TECHNOLOGY MARKETING CORP.; *pg.* 1691, *pg.* 364
SIP-N-CHEWS - Candy Product - AMERICAN LICORICE CO. INC.; *pg.* 1850, *pg.* 692
SIPHER - Photoluminescence Mapping System - NANOMETRICS INCORPORATED; *pg.* 1423, *pg.* 147
SIPHY - Integrated Circuit Product - SILICON LABORATORIES INC.; *pg.* 674, *pg.* 1666
SIPP - Natural Coffee Substitute - MODERN PRODUCTS, INC.; *pg.* 1568, *pg.* 1871
SIPPABLE SUNDAE - Milk Shakes - BIGLARI HOLDINGS INC.; *pg.* 1015, *pg.* 1739
SIPPIN SUE - Dolls - THE GOLDBERGER COMPANY, LLC; *pg.* 954, *pg.* 1235
SIPRITE - Spill-Proof Cup - EVENFLO COMPANY, INC.; *pg.* 924, *pg.* 1470
SIPROTECT - Drive Technology - WESTERN DIGITAL CORPORATION; *pg.* 492, *pg.* 118
SIPULEUCEL-T - Cancer Treatment - DENDREON CORPORATION; *pg.* 1522, *pg.* 1835
SIPURGE - Drive Technology - WESTERN DIGITAL CORPORATION; *pg.* 492, *pg.* 118
SIQURA - Hardware Components - SIQURA; *pg.* 308, *pg.* 771
SIR - Ground Fault Receptacles - PASS & SEYMOUR/LEGRAND; *pg.* 1303, *pg.* 1344
SIR CONTOUR - Footwear - P.W. MINOR & SON, INC.; *pg.* 1816, *pg.* 1140
SIR II - Academic Program - EDUCATIONAL TESTING SERVICE INC.; *pg.* 1394, *pg.* 1111
SIR MALCOLM - Scotch - SAZERAC COMPANY, INC.; *pg.* 1969, *pg.* 745
SIR SPEEDY - Printing Centers - SIR SPEEDY, INC.; *pg.* 1687, *pg.* 149
SIRBO - Educational Seminars - PFIZER INC.; *pg.* 1581, *pg.* 1278
SIRE - Record Label - WARNER MUSIC GROUP CORP.; *pg.* 590, *pg.* 1313
SIREN - Audio Technology - POLYCOM, INC.; *pg.* 664, *pg.* 249
SIRENLOCK - Alarm Systems - NAPCO SECURITY SYSTEMS, INC.; *pg.* 658, *pg.* 1138
SIRI - Voice Recognition Software - APPLE INC.; *pg.* 350, *pg.* 73
SIRIUS - Semiconductor Device - APPLIED MATERIALS, INC; *pg.* 618, *pg.* 1009
SIRIUS - Systems Integration & Aeronautics - LOCKHEED MARTIN CORPORATION; *pg.* 229, *pg.* 762
SIRIUS - Gas Detection System - MINE SAFETY APPLIANCES COMPANY; *pg.* 1361, *pg.* 1525
SIROCCO - Protein Precipitation Plate - WATERS CORPORATION; *pg.* 1436, *pg.* 834
SIROCCO - Ski Socks - WIGWAM MILLS, INC.; *pg.* 15, *pg.* 1894
SIRODEM - Hygiene System - SIRONA DENTAL SYSTEMS, INC.; *pg.* 1429, *pg.* 1175
SIROLASER - Dental Equipment - SIRONA DENTAL SYSTEMS, INC.; *pg.* 1429, *pg.* 1175
SIRONITI - Straight & Contra Angle Handpieces - SIRONA DENTAL SYSTEMS, INC.; *pg.* 1429, *pg.* 1175
SIROPURE - Straight & Contra Angle Handpieces - SIRONA DENTAL SYSTEMS, INC.; *pg.* 1429, *pg.* 1175
SIRRUS - Roll Towel - WAUSAU PAPER BAY WEST; *pg.* 1471, *pg.* 1465
SIRUS - Shoe - ALDO GROUP; *pg.* 1804, *pg.* 1959
SIRUS - Knife - BUCK KNIVES, INC.; *pg.* 1828, *pg.* 550
SIRVA MORTGAGE - Local & International Brokerage Services - SIRVA, INC.; *pg.* 1923, *pg.* 669
SIRVA RELOCATION - Relocation Services - SIRVA, INC.; *pg.* 1923, *pg.* 669
SIRVA SETTLEMENT - Management & Relocation Services - SIRVA, INC.; *pg.* 1923, *pg.* 669
SIRX - Integrated Circuit Product - SILICON LABORATORIES INC.; *pg.* 674, *pg.* 1666
SISAL - Tile - ARTISTIC TILE INC.; *pg.* 914, *pg.* 1119
SISAL TWIST - Carpet - INTERFACE, INC.; *pg.* 695, *pg.* 512
SISAL WEAVE - Carpet - BEAULIEU GROUP, LLC; *pg.* 917, *pg.* 529
SISAL WOOL - Rug - COURISTAN INC.; *pg.* 921, *pg.* 1067
SISCRUB - Drive Technology - WESTERN DIGITAL CORPORATION; *pg.* 492, *pg.* 118
SISECURE - Drive Technology - WESTERN DIGITAL CORPORATION; *pg.* 492, *pg.* 118
SISMART - Drive Technology - WESTERN DIGITAL CORPORATION; *pg.* 492, *pg.* 118
SISTER DREARY - Doll - TONNER DOLL COMPANY, INC.; *pg.* 968, *pg.* 1171
SISTER MOON - Womenswear - SEATTLE PACIFIC INDUSTRIES, INC.; *pg.* 48, *pg.* 1822
SISTER SCHUBERT'S - Yeast Rolls - LANCASTER COLONY CORPORATION; *pg.* 873, *pg.* 1441
SISTER SCHUBERT'S - Food Product - T. MARZETTI COMPANY; *pg.* 900, *pg.* 1444
SISTINA - Beauty Product - COSMETIQUE, INC.; *pg.* 1765, *pg.* 664
SISTOR - Drive Technology - WESTERN DIGITAL CORPORATION; *pg.* 492, *pg.* 118
SISU - Nutritional Supplements - NBTY, INC.; *pg.* 1572, *pg.* 1338
SISWEEP - Drive Technology - WESTERN DIGITAL CORPORATION; *pg.* 492, *pg.* 118
SIT 'N SPIN - Toy & Game - HASBRO, INC.; *pg.* 954, *pg.* 1603
SIT N STAND - Baby Carriages - BABY TREND, INC.; *pg.* 916, *pg.* 173
SITE ADMINISTRATOR FOR SHAREPOINT - Software - DELL SOFTWARE; *pg.* 385, *pg.* 40
SITE FOR SORE EYES - Eyewear - EMERGING VISION, INC.; *pg.* 1411, *pg.* 1227
SITE MASTER - Cable & Antenna Analyzer - ANRITSU COMPANY; *pg.* 618, *pg.* 152
SITE RELEASE - Pharmaceutical Product - LUMARA HEALTH INC.; *pg.* 1557, *pg.* 973
SITE RITE - Bender - GREENLEE TEXTRON INC.; *pg.* 1048, *pg.* 655
SITE SENTRY - Monitoring Security System - DIEBOLD, INCORPORATED; *pg.* 387, *pg.* 1407
SITE SURVEYOR - Navigation Aid - TRIMBLE NAVIGATION LIMITED; *pg.* 1384, *pg.* 288
SITEFINDER - Commercial Real Estate Database - CERC; *pg.* 990, *pg.* 369
SITEKEEPER - Software - CONDUSIV TECHNOLOGIES; *pg.* 379, *pg.* 51
SITEKEY - Key Control Device - MEDECO HIGH SECURITY LOCKS, INC.; *pg.* 1055, *pg.* 1806
SITELINE - Single Door Controller - MEDECO HIGH SECURITY LOCKS, INC.; *pg.* 1055, *pg.* 1806
SITEMAX - Asset Management Solutions - BECKMAN COULTER, INC.; *pg.* 1402, *pg.* 48
SITENET - Navigation Aid - TRIMBLE NAVIGATION LIMITED; *pg.* 1384, *pg.* 288
SITEPRO - Graphic Monitoring System - FIKE CORPORATION; *pg.* 1047, *pg.* 973
SITEREPORTER - Software - ENVIRONMENTAL SYSTEMS RESEARCH INSTITUTE INC.; *pg.* 393, *pg.* 188
SITESCAPE - Computer Software - NOVELL INC.; *pg.* 446, *pg.* 852
SITESEER - Guidewire - MEDTRONIC, INC.; *pg.* 1564, *pg.* 939
SITESPAN - Wireless Network Product - AIRSPAN NETWORKS INC.; *pg.* 346, *pg.* 410
SITESTAR - Construction Equipment - VERMEER MANUFACTURING COMPANY; *pg.* 708, *pg.* 711
SITESTOR - Software - SYMANTEC CORPORATION; *pg.* 478, *pg.* 161
SITEVISION - Navigation Aid - TRIMBLE NAVIGATION LIMITED; *pg.* 1384, *pg.* 288
SITEWATCHER - Software - WEBSENSE, INC.; *pg.* 491, *pg.* 210
SITEWEB - Communication System for the Monitoring & Control of Power Switches - ASCO POWER TECHNOLOGIES, L.P.; *pg.* 1314, *pg.* 1066
SITEWISE - Consultation Service - XCEL ENERGY INC.; *pg.* 1955, *pg.* 946
SIVL - Software - SYNOPSYS, INC.; *pg.* 480, *pg.* 162
SIX FEET UNDER - Cable Television Show - HOME BOX OFFICE, INC.; *pg.* 290, *pg.* 1240
SIX FLAGS - Theme Parks - SIX FLAGS ENTERTAINMENT CORPORATION; *pg.* 583, *pg.* 1698
SIX FLAGS AMERICA - Park - SIX FLAGS ENTERTAINMENT CORPORATION; *pg.* 583, *pg.* 1698
SIX FLAGS ASTROWORLD - Park - SIX FLAGS ENTERTAINMENT CORPORATION; *pg.* 583, *pg.* 1698
SIX FLAGS DARIEN LAKE - Park - SIX FLAGS ENTERTAINMENT CORPORATION; *pg.* 583, *pg.* 1698
SIX FLAGS DISCOVERY KINGDOM - Park - SIX FLAGS ENTERTAINMENT CORPORATION; *pg.* 583, *pg.* 1698
SIX FLAGS DUBAILAND - Park - SIX FLAGS ENTERTAINMENT CORPORATION; *pg.* 583, *pg.* 1698

SIX FLAGS ELITCH GARDENS - Park - SIX FLAGS ENTERTAINMENT CORPORATION; *pg.* 583, *pg.* 1698
SIX FLAGS FIESTA - Park Company - FIESTA TEXAS, INC.; *pg.* 548, *pg.* 1740
SIX FLAGS FIESTA TEXAS - Park - SIX FLAGS ENTERTAINMENT CORPORATION; *pg.* 583, *pg.* 1698
SIX FLAGS GREAT ADVENTURE - Park - SIX FLAGS ENTERTAINMENT CORPORATION; *pg.* 583, *pg.* 1698
SIX FLAGS GREAT AMERICA - Park - SIX FLAGS ENTERTAINMENT CORPORATION; *pg.* 583, *pg.* 1698
SIX FLAGS HURRICANE HARBOR - Park - SIX FLAGS ENTERTAINMENT CORPORATION; *pg.* 583, *pg.* 1698
SIX FLAGS KENTUCKY KINGDOM - Park - SIX FLAGS ENTERTAINMENT CORPORATION; *pg.* 583, *pg.* 1698
SIX FLAGS MAGIC MOUNTAIN - Park - SIX FLAGS ENTERTAINMENT CORPORATION; *pg.* 583, *pg.* 1698
SIX FLAGS MARINE WORLD - Park - SIX FLAGS ENTERTAINMENT CORPORATION; *pg.* 583, *pg.* 1698
SIX FLAGS NEW ENGLAND - Park - SIX FLAGS ENTERTAINMENT CORPORATION; *pg.* 583, *pg.* 1698
SIX FLAGS NEW ORLEANS - Park - SIX FLAGS ENTERTAINMENT CORPORATION; *pg.* 583, *pg.* 1698
SIX FLAGS OVER GEORGIA - Park - SIX FLAGS ENTERTAINMENT CORPORATION; *pg.* 583, *pg.* 1698
SIX FLAGS OVER TEXAS - Park - SIX FLAGS ENTERTAINMENT CORPORATION; *pg.* 583, *pg.* 1698
SIX FLAGS ST. LOUIS - Park - SIX FLAGS ENTERTAINMENT CORPORATION; *pg.* 583, *pg.* 1698
SIX FLAGS WHITE WATER - Park - SIX FLAGS ENTERTAINMENT CORPORATION; *pg.* 583, *pg.* 1698
SIX FLAGS WILD SAFARI - Park - SIX FLAGS ENTERTAINMENT CORPORATION; *pg.* 583, *pg.* 1698
SIX PACK - Portable, Self-Erecting Asphalt Equipment - ASTEC INDUSTRIES, INC.; *pg.* 69, *pg.* 1628
SIX PACK - Surface Material - STEELCASE INC.; *pg.* 475, *pg.* 889
SIX SHOOTER - Food - WESTERN SIZZLIN CORPORATION; *pg.* 1755, *pg.* 1806
SIX SIGMA - Communications Product - MOTOROLA SOLUTIONS, INC.; *pg.* 657, *pg.* 659
THE SIX SIGMA WAY - Business Management Textbook - PIVOTAL RESOURCES, INC.; *pg.* 455, *pg.* 304
THE SIX SIGMA WAY TEAM FIELDBOOK - Business Management Textbook - PIVOTAL RESOURCES, INC.; *pg.* 455, *pg.* 304
SIX STAR - Food Bar - CARLISLE FOODSERVICE PRODUCTS INCORPORATED; *pg.* 1455, *pg.* 1485
SIXTH DIMENSION - Software - COMVERGE, INC.; *pg.* 1325, *pg.* 536
SIXTH SENSE - Printer - XEROX CORPORATION; *pg.* 494, *pg.* 365
SIXTHMAN - Reward Program - PHOENIX SUNS; *pg.* 576, *pg.* 19
SIZE CONTROL - Gages - KENNAMETAL IPG; *pg.* 1353, *pg.* 1615
SIZESELECT - Molecular Biology Product - THERMO FISHER SCIENTIFIC INC.; *pg.* 1602, *pg.* 61
SIZEXCEL - Resin - GEORGIA-PACIFIC LLC; *pg.* 1458, *pg.* 507
SIZING UP SMALL CAPS - Financial Products - DOW JONES & COMPANY, INC.; *pg.* 1637, *pg.* 1225
SIZONE - Drive Technology - WESTERN DIGITAL CORPORATION; *pg.* 492, *pg.* 118
SIZZLI - Hot Breakfast Sandwich - WAWA, INC.; *pg.* 1037, *pg.* 1552
SIZZLIN - Restaurants & Food - WESTERN SIZZLIN CORPORATION; *pg.* 1755, *pg.* 1806
SIZZLIN' 7'S - Lottery Card - MISSOURI LOTTERY; *pg.* 999, *pg.* 979
SIZZLIN' SKILLET - Microwave Browner - NORTHLAND ALUMINUM PRODUCTS INC.; *pg.* 1129, *pg.* 941
SIZZLING 7 - Slots - INTERNATIONAL GAME TECHNOLOGY; *pg.* 957, *pg.* 1024
SIZZLING 7 TIMES PAY - Slots - INTERNATIONAL GAME TECHNOLOGY; *pg.* 957, *pg.* 1024
SJ - Musical Instrument - GIBSON GUITAR CORP.; *pg.* 550, *pg.* 1650
SJM - Annuloplasty Rings - ST. JUDE MEDICAL, INC.; *pg.* 1596, *pg.* 963
SJM BIOCOR - Tissue Heart Valves - ST. JUDE MEDICAL, INC.; *pg.* 1596, *pg.* 963
SJM CONFIRM - Cardiac Monitor - ST. JUDE MEDICAL, INC.; *pg.* 1596, *pg.* 963
SJM ENCAP - Medical Equipment - ST. JUDE MEDICAL, INC.; *pg.* 1596, *pg.* 963
SJM REGENT - Mechanical Heart Valves - ST. JUDE MEDICAL, INC.; *pg.* 1596, *pg.* 963
SJM TAILOR - Tissue Heart Valve - ST. JUDE MEDICAL, INC.; *pg.* 1596, *pg.* 963
SK-II - Skin Care Product - THE PROCTER & GAMBLE COMPANY; *pg.* 1129, *pg.* 1418
SKANDEX - Dispensing Equipment - IDEX CORPORATION; *pg.* 1347, *pg.* 623
SKANSEN - Herring - A.V. OLSSON TRADING CO. INC.; *pg.* 838, *pg.* 372
SKANSEN HERRING - Fish - A.V. OLSSON TRADING CO. INC.; *pg.* 838, *pg.* 372
SKANSTACKER - Liquid Handling System - MOLECULAR DEVICES CORPORATION; *pg.* 1568, *pg.* 287
SKANWASHER - Liquid Handling System - MOLECULAR DEVICES CORPORATION; *pg.* 1568, *pg.* 287
SKATE CHIC - Apparel - VANS, INC.; *pg.* 1821, *pg.* 76
SKATE CREW - Sock - OAKLEY, INC.; *pg.* 1840, *pg.* 86
SKATEBOARD SHANNEN - Toy - MATTEL, INC.; *pg.* 962, *pg.* 81
SKATEBOARDERS - Apparel - VANS, INC.; *pg.* 1821, *pg.* 76
SKATEBOARDING.COM - Web Site - BONNIER ACTIVE MEDIA, INC.; *pg.* 1622, *pg.* 1205
SKATES ON THE BAY - Restaurant - RESTAURANTS UNLIMITED, INC.; *pg.* 1748, *pg.* 1839
SKELAXIN - Pharmaceutical Product - KING PHARMACEUTICALS, INC.; *pg.* 1553, *pg.* 1627
SKELETAL ANCHORAE - Micro Implant System - STRYKER CORPORATION; *pg.* 1598, *pg.* 894
SKELETAL REPAIR SYSTEM - Medical Device - DEPUY SYNTHES; *pg.* 1523, *pg.* 1593
SKETCHBOOK - Software - AUTODESK INC.; *pg.* 356, *pg.* 257
SKETCHBOOK PRO - Software - VIEWSONIC CORPORATION; *pg.* 489, *pg.* 303
SKEW-SHEAR - Variable Rake Designed Tap - REGAL BELOIT CORPORATION; *pg.* 106, *pg.* 1854
SKEWMASTER - Wrap System - THE D.S. BROWN COMPANY; *pg.* 79, *pg.* 1468
SKF BEARINGS - Rolling Element Bearings for all Vehicles - SKF SEALING SOLUTIONS; *pg.* 217, *pg.* 610
SKI - Magazine - BONNIER ACTIVE MEDIA, INC.; *pg.* 1622, *pg.* 1205
SKI - Magazine - BONNIER CORPORATION; *pg.* 1622, *pg.* 480
SKI - Soft Drink - DOUBLE-COLA CO.-USA; *pg.* 249, *pg.* 1629
SKI-DOO - Snowmobiles, Snowgrooming Equipment & Multi-Purpose Tracked Vehicles - BOMBARDIER RECREATIONAL PRODUCTS, INC.; *pg.* 201, *pg.* 1960
SKI NAUTIQUE - Power Boat - CORRECT CRAFT, INC.; *pg.* 1706, *pg.* 452
SKI NAUTIQUE OPEN BOW - Power Boat - CORRECT CRAFT, INC.; *pg.* 1706, *pg.* 452
SKI ROUNDTOP - Ski And Snowboarding - SKI ROUNDTOP OPERATING CORP.; *pg.* 1113, *pg.* 1548
SKID-LOCK - Glue & Adhesive - GLUEFAST COMPANY, INC.; *pg.* 1459, *pg.* 1090
SKID-MATE - Cushion - PELICAN PRODUCTS; *pg.* 1467, *pg.* 843
SKID RESISTOR - Truck Bedliner - PENDA CORPORATION; *pg.* 214, *pg.* 1887
SKIDMASTER - Anti-Slip Shoe Accessories - STANDARD SAFETY EQUIPMENT CO.; *pg.* 1379, *pg.* 632
SKIING - Magazine - BONNIER ACTIVE MEDIA, INC.; *pg.* 1622, *pg.* 1205
SKIING - Magazine - BONNIER CORPORATION; *pg.* 1622, *pg.* 480
SKIINGMAG.COM - Web Site - BONNIER ACTIVE MEDIA, INC.; *pg.* 1622, *pg.* 1205
SKIL - Power Tools & Accessories - ROBERT BOSCH TOOL CORP; *pg.* 1060, *pg.* 634
SKIL-CARE - Vinyl Bed Rail Pads - ALIMED, INC.; *pg.* 1490, *pg.* 816
SKILL - Software - CADENCE DESIGN SYSTEMS, INC.; *pg.* 367, *pg.* 239
SKILLBAY - Software - SYNTEL, INC.; *pg.* 480, *pg.* 911
SKILLBUILDERS - Mat With Handles - ALIMED, INC.; *pg.* 1490, *pg.* 816
SKILLBUILDERS - Medical & Aesthetic Product - DYNATRONICS CORPORATION; *pg.* 1526, *pg.* 1757
SKILLCHOICE - Software - SKILLSOFT PLC; *pg.* 470, *pg.* 1037
SKILLPORT - Software - SKILLSOFT PLC; *pg.* 470, *pg.* 1037
SKILLS CONNECTION - Software - SCANTRON CORPORATION; *pg.* 467, *pg.* 922
SKILLSOFT DIALOGUE - Software - SKILLSOFT PLC; *pg.* 470, *pg.* 1037
SKILLSONE - Online Assessment - CPP, INC.; *pg.* 1631, *pg.* 153
SKILLVIEW - Software - SKILLSOFT PLC; *pg.* 470, *pg.* 1037
SKILLWARE - Training Software - MANPOWER INC.; *pg.* 430, *pg.* 1877
SKILSAW - Power Circular Saws - ROBERT BOSCH TOOL CORP; *pg.* 1060, *pg.* 634
SKIMAG.COM - Web Site - BONNIER ACTIVE MEDIA, INC.; *pg.* 1622, *pg.* 1205
SKIN ACTIVATOR - Skin Care Product - HERBALIFE INTERNATIONAL OF AMERICA, INC.; *pg.* 1541, *pg.* 132
SKIN BALM - Pet Supplies - HAPPY JACK INC.; *pg.* 1476, *pg.* 1390
SKIN BENEFICIAL - Cosmetic Product - NU SKIN ENTERPRISES, INC.; *pg.* 518, *pg.* 1755
SKIN BRACER - Personal Care Product - COLGATE-PALMOLIVE COMPANY; *pg.* 504, *pg.* 1215
SKIN ELATION CREAM - Nutritional Supplement - WHITEWING LABS, INC.; *pg.* 1610, *pg.* 99
SKIN ETERNAL PLUS - Vitamin & Herbal Supplement - SOURCE NATURALS; *pg.* 1595, *pg.* 278
SKIN MIRACLE - Personal Care Product - STRAIGHT ARROW PRODUCTS, INC.; *pg.* 523, *pg.* 1517
SKIN MUSK - Fragrance - PARFUMS DE COEUR LTD.; *pg.* 519, *pg.* 376
SKIN-SO-SOFT - Bath & Body Oil - AVON PRODUCTS, INC.; *pg.* 500, *pg.* 1198
SKIN THERAPY MIST - Personal Care Product - RBC LIFE SCIENCES, INC.; *pg.* 1588, *pg.* 1723
SKIN TITE - Prosthetic Adhesive - SMOOTH-ON INC.; *pg.* 111, *pg.* 1528
SKINCEUTICALS - Skin Care Products - L'OREAL USA; *pg.* 514, *pg.* 1252
SKINET.COM - Web Site - BONNIER ACTIVE MEDIA, INC.; *pg.* 1622, *pg.* 1205
SKINGUARD AQUA - Tissue - S.C. JOHNSON & SON, INC.; *pg.* 334, *pg.* 1889
SKINLIGHTS - Skin Lightening Lotions, Powders & Glide-on Sticks - REVLON, INC.; *pg.* 521, *pg.* 1286
SKINMILK - Personal Care Electrical Product - HELEN OF TROY L.P.; *pg.* 511, *pg.* 1692
SKINNER - Knife - BUCK KNIVES, INC.; *pg.* 1828, *pg.* 550
SKINNER - Knife - COAST CUTLERY COMPANY; *pg.* 1121, *pg.* 1501
SKINNER - Food Product - NEW WORLD PASTA COMPANY; *pg.* 885, *pg.* 1537
SKINNY 510 - Jean - LEVI STRAUSS & CO.; *pg.* 43, *pg.* 220
SKINNY 511 - Jean - LEVI STRAUSS & CO.; *pg.* 43, *pg.* 220
SKINNY COW - Ice Cream - NESTLE USA, INC.; *pg.* 883, *pg.* 96
SKINNY COW MILK - Dairy Product - DEAN FOODS COMPANY; *pg.* 852, *pg.* 1679
SKINNY DIP - Seasonal Beer - NEW BELGIUM BREWING COMPANY, INC.; *pg.* 258, *pg.* 328
SKINNY DIP'N LAKE MICHG'N - Nail Care Product - OPI PRODUCTS INC.; *pg.* 518, *pg.* 167
SKINNY FAST - Nutritional Product - NUTRACEUTICAL INTERNATIONAL CORPORATION; *pg.* 1576, *pg.* 1753
SKINNY MINI - Nutritional Supplement - NATURAL ORGANICS, INC.; *pg.* 1571, *pg.* 1181
SKINNY POP - Popcorn - SKINNYPOP POPCORN LLC; *pg.* 895, *pg.* 661
SKINNY SPIKES - Specialty Nails - W.H. MAZE COMPANY; *pg.* 1389, *pg.* 652
SKINNYGIRL COCKTAILS - Low Calorie Cocktails - JIM BEAM BRANDS CO.; *pg.* 1965, *pg.* 601
SKINSUCCESS - Skin Care Product - E.T. BROWNE DRUG COMPANY, INC.; *pg.* 509, *pg.* 1060
SKINTASTIC - Insect Repellent - S.C. JOHNSON & SON, INC.; *pg.* 334, *pg.* 1889
SKINTEGRITY - Medical Product - MEDLINE INDUSTRIES, INC.; *pg.* 1562, *pg.* 635
SKINTIMATE - Shaving Products - EDGEWELL PERSONAL CARE; *pg.* 1526, *pg.* 995
SKIP-BO - Card Game - MATTEL, INC.; *pg.* 962, *pg.* 81
SKIPID - Telephone Service - IDT CORPORATION; *pg.* 643, *pg.* 1096
SKIPPY - Peanut Butter - HORMEL FOODS CORPORATION; *pg.* 863, *pg.* 915
SKITTLES - Candy - WM. WRIGLEY JR. COMPANY; *pg.* 1863, *pg.* 596

SKIVERTEX - Paper & Nonwoven Material - FIBERMARK INC.; *pg.* 1457, *pg.* 1764
SKIVISION - Goggle - ICARE INDUSTRIES, INC.; *pg.* 1417, *pg.* 463
SKIWEAR FROM THE HEART OF MOUNTAINS - Tag Line - SPORT OBERMEYER LTD.; *pg.* 1846, *pg.* 310
SKLUTTERBY - Belt - VANS, INC.; *pg.* 1821, *pg.* 76
SKOAL - Tobacco Product - U.S. SMOKELESS TOBACCO COMPANY; *pg.* 1895, *pg.* 1804
SKOR - Chocolate Candy - THE HERSHEY CO.; *pg.* 1855, *pg.* 1538
SKORCH - Footwear - STEVEN MADDEN, LTD.; *pg.* 1819, *pg.* 1176
SKRIP - Writing Instrument - SHEAFFER PEN CORPORATION; *pg.* 469, *pg.* 371
SKROO-ZON - File Product - SIMONDS INTERNATIONAL CORPORATION; *pg.* 1376, *pg.* 819
SKUBE - Carton Flow Product - UNEX MANUFACTURING, INC.; *pg.* 1385, *pg.* 1075
SKULL - Lighter Light - CUSTOM ACCESSORIES INC.; *pg.* 203, *pg.* 653
SKULL - Apparel - VANS, INC.; *pg.* 1821, *pg.* 76
SKULLCANDY - Headphones - SKULLCANDY, INC.; *pg.* 674, *pg.* 1754
SKULLCAP - Cap - UNDER ARMOUR, INC.; *pg.* 49, *pg.* 759
SKULLGARD - Headwear - MINE SAFETY APPLIANCES COMPANY; *pg.* 1361, *pg.* 1525
SKWEEZE - Polystyrene Film - SPINNAKER COATING, LLC; *pg.* 1470, *pg.* 1477
SKY BAR - Candy Bar - NEW ENGLAND CONFECTIONERY COMPANY INC.; *pg.* 1860, *pg.* 842
SKY BLUE - Pillow and Throw - HERITAGE LACE INC.; *pg.* 694, *pg.* 711
SKY CABIN - Thrill Ride - KNOTT'S BERRY FARM; *pg.* 556, *pg.* 50
SKY DANCER - Textiles - BERNHARDT DESIGN; *pg.* 918, *pg.* 1381
SKY-HATCH - Metal Building System - BUTLER MANUFACTURING COMPANY; *pg.* 72, *pg.* 981
SKY HIGH CURVES - Mascara - MAYBELLINE LLC; *pg.* 516, *pg.* 1257
SKY HOMES - Community Name - WCI COMMUNITIES, INC.; *pg.* 1118, *pg.* 414
SKY LARK - Textiles - BERNHARDT DESIGN; *pg.* 918, *pg.* 1381
SKY MILES - Credit Cards - AMERICAN EXPRESS COMPANY; *pg.* 712, *pg.* 1190
SKY SPIRIT - Unmanned Aerial Vehicles - LOCKHEED MARTIN CORPORATION; *pg.* 229, *pg.* 762
SKY TEAM - Air Transportation Service - DELTA AIR LINES, INC.; *pg.* 1905, *pg.* 503
SKY TRAK - Light Construction Equipment - TEXTRON INC.; *pg.* 235, *pg.* 1607
SKY-WEB - Metal Building System - BUTLER MANUFACTURING COMPANY; *pg.* 72, *pg.* 981
SKYBONUS - Frequent Flyer Award Program - DELTA AIR LINES, INC.; *pg.* 1905, *pg.* 503
SKYBORNE - Communications Products - GLOBECOMM SYSTEMS INC.; *pg.* 640, *pg.* 1164
SKYCASH - Incentive Award Program - SKYAUCTION.COM, INC.; *pg.* 1281, *pg.* 1293
SKYCATCHER - Fastening System - TEXTRON INC.; *pg.* 235, *pg.* 1607
SKYDOME - Skylighting Product - WASCO PRODUCTS, INC.; *pg.* 120, *pg.* 752
SKYDOMES - Skylight - WASCO PRODUCTS, INC.; *pg.* 120, *pg.* 752
SKYFI - Satellite Radio Receiver - DELPHI AUTOMOTIVE LLP; *pg.* 204, *pg.* 910
SKYFLEX - Sealant - W.L. GORE & ASSOCIATES, INC.; *pg.* 122, *pg.* 388
SKYFRIES - Shoestring French Fries - SKYLINE CHILI, INC.; *pg.* 1033, *pg.* 1452
SKYGUIDE - Magazine - AMERICAN EXPRESS COMPANY; *pg.* 712, *pg.* 1190
SKYHAWK - Aircraft - CESSNA AIRCRAFT COMPANY; *pg.* 226, *pg.* 723
SKYHOOK - Commercial Lighting - SWIVELIER CO., INC.; *pg.* 1307, *pg.* 1142
SKYJACKER - Suspension Products - LONNIE MCCURRY'S FOUR WHEEL DRIVE CENTER, INC.; *pg.* 211, *pg.* 748
SKYLAND - Food Products - NATIONAL FRUIT PRODUCT COMPANY, INC.; *pg.* 882, *pg.* 1811
SKYLANE - Aircraft - CESSNA AIRCRAFT COMPANY; *pg.* 226, *pg.* 723
SKYLAR - Doll And Toy - AMERICAN GIRL LLC; *pg.* 949, *pg.* 1871
SKYLAR - Casegoods - STEELCASE INC.; *pg.* 475, *pg.* 889
SKYLARK - Publishing Imprint - PENGUIN RANDOM HOUSE CHILDREN'S BOOKS; *pg.* 1676, *pg.* 1277
SKYLER - Furniture - LA-Z-BOY INCORPORATED; *pg.* 932, *pg.* 901
SKYLIGHT - Laser & Laser System - COHERENT, INC.; *pg.* 1406, *pg.* 265
SKYLIGHT - Non-Yellowing Ceiling Paints - PRATT & LAMBERT PAINTS; *pg.* 1446, *pg.* 1434
SKYLINE - Flight Software & Hardware - LOCKHEED MARTIN CORPORATION; *pg.* 229, *pg.* 762
SKYLINE - Software - SS&C TECHNOLOGIES HOLDINGS, INC.; *pg.* 473, *pg.* 386
SKYLINE - Ceramic, Glass, Stone Tiles & Slabs - WALKER & ZANGER, INC.; *pg.* 119, *pg.* 281
SKYLINE CHILI - Cincinnati Style Chili - SKYLINE CHILI, INC.; *pg.* 1033, *pg.* 1452
SKYLINE PROPERTY MANAGEMENT - Software - SS&C TECHNOLOGIES HOLDINGS, INC.; *pg.* 473, *pg.* 386
SKYLINE II - Property Management, Accounting, & Reporting System for Realtors - SS&C TECHNOLOGIES HOLDINGS, INC.; *pg.* 473, *pg.* 386
SKYLINK - Fall Protection Equipment - MINE SAFETY APPLIANCES COMPANY; *pg.* 1361, *pg.* 1525
SKYLINX - Broadband Satellite Service - VIASAT, INC.; *pg.* 489, *pg.* 62
SKYLITE - Robotic Product - HAMILTON CO., INC.; *pg.* 1415, *pg.* 1031
SKYLITE PYROJECTOR - Projectors - SWARTWOUT DIVISION; *pg.* 114, *pg.* 978
SKYLOFTS AT MGM GRAND - Resort & Casino - MGM RESORTS INTERNATIONAL; *pg.* 1105, *pg.* 1028
SKYMILES - Frequent Flyer Membership - DELTA AIR LINES, INC.; *pg.* 1905, *pg.* 503
SKYPAK - Cooling Unit - JOHNSON CONTROLS, INC.; *pg.* 209, *pg.* 1876
SKYPE - Instant Messaging and File Sharing Service - MICROSOFT CORPORATION; *pg.* 435, *pg.* 1824
SKYPE FOR BUSINESS - Enterprise Communications Software Platform - MICROSOFT CORPORATION; *pg.* 435, *pg.* 1824
SKYPLUS - Color - FERRO CORPORATION; *pg.* 1162, *pg.* 1462
SKYSWEEP - Searchlights - BALLANTYNE STRONG, INC.; *pg.* 623, *pg.* 1013
SKYTHANE - Thermoplastic Polyurethanes - THE LUBRIZOL CORPORATION; *pg.* 1171, *pg.* 1481
SKYTRACK - Window System - SPRINGS WINDOW FASHIONS LLC; *pg.* 943, *pg.* 1872
SKYTRACKER - Entertainment Lighting Product - BALLANTYNE STRONG, INC.; *pg.* 623, *pg.* 1013
SKYTRACKER - Systems Integration & Aeronautics - LOCKHEED MARTIN CORPORATION; *pg.* 229, *pg.* 762
SKYTRAK - Telehandler - JLG INDUSTRIES, INC.; *pg.* 1351, *pg.* 1551
SKYWALL - Architectural Product - BUTLER MANUFACTURING COMPANY; *pg.* 72, *pg.* 981
SKYWATCH - Collision Avoidance Systems - L-3 AVIONICS SYSTEMS, INC.; *pg.* 650, *pg.* 888
SKYWAY - Elevator Product - OTIS ELEVATOR COMPANY; *pg.* 102, *pg.* 349
SKYWAY OTW - Catheter - VASCULAR SOLUTIONS, INC.; *pg.* 1434, *pg.* 946
SKYWAY RX - Catheter - VASCULAR SOLUTIONS, INC.; *pg.* 1434, *pg.* 946
SKYWEST AIRLINES - Airline Service - SKYWEST INC.; *pg.* 1923, *pg.* 1755
SKYWINDOW - Residential Skylights - WASCO PRODUCTS, INC.; *pg.* 120, *pg.* 752
SKYWINDOWS - Skylighting Product - WASCO PRODUCTS, INC.; *pg.* 120, *pg.* 752
SKYY - Alcoholic Beverages - CAMPARI AMERICA; *pg.* 1960, *pg.* 214
SKYY CITRUS - Beverage - CAMPARI AMERICA; *pg.* 1960, *pg.* 214
SKYY INFUSIONS - Beverage - CAMPARI AMERICA; *pg.* 1960, *pg.* 214
SL - Electronic Components - MOLEX INCORPORATED; *pg.* 655, *pg.* 628
SL-20X - Flashlight - STREAMLIGHT INC.; *pg.* 1306, *pg.* 1527
SL-20XP - Flashlight - STREAMLIGHT INC.; *pg.* 1306, *pg.* 1527
SL-35X - Flashlight - STREAMLIGHT INC.; *pg.* 1306, *pg.* 1527
SL FLEXOR - Introducer Set - COOK GROUP, INC.; *pg.* 1518, *pg.* 674
SL FRAME SYSTEM - Scaffolding System - SAFWAY SERVICES, LLC; *pg.* 109, *pg.* 1898
SL10 - Heat Sealer & Hot Tack Tester - THWING-ALBERT INSTRUMENT COMPANY; *pg.* 1432, *pg.* 1131
SL500 - Lighting Systems - REVOLUTION LIGHTING TECHNOLOGIES, INC.; *pg.* 1304, *pg.* 377
SL502 - Lighting Systems - REVOLUTION LIGHTING TECHNOLOGIES, INC.; *pg.* 1304, *pg.* 377
SL503 - Lighting Systems - REVOLUTION LIGHTING TECHNOLOGIES, INC.; *pg.* 1304, *pg.* 377
SL64F8W128M8L-A15LTG - Storage System - HGST; *pg.* 406, *pg.* 260
SL64F8W128M8L-A18JTG - Storage System - HGST; *pg.* 406, *pg.* 260
SL64F8W256M8L-A15LTG - Storage System - HGST; *pg.* 406, *pg.* 260
SL64Y8W128M8L-A15LTU - Storage System - HGST; *pg.* 406, *pg.* 260
SL64Y8W128M8L-A18JTU - Storage System - HGST; *pg.* 406, *pg.* 260
SL64Y8W256M8L-A15LTU - Storage System - HGST; *pg.* 406, *pg.* 260
SL64Y8W256M8L-A18JTU - Storage System - HGST; *pg.* 406, *pg.* 260
SL72Y8W128M8M-A15LTU - Storage System - HGST; *pg.* 406, *pg.* 260
SL72Y8W128M8M-A18JTU - Storage System - HGST; *pg.* 406, *pg.* 260
SL72Y8W256M8M-A15LTU - Storage System - HGST; *pg.* 406, *pg.* 260
SL72Y8W256M8M-A18JTU - Storage System - HGST; *pg.* 406, *pg.* 260
SL72Z4W256M8M-A15LTU - Storage System - HGST; *pg.* 406, *pg.* 260
SL72Z4W256M8M-A18JTU - Storage System - HGST; *pg.* 406, *pg.* 260
SL72Z4W512M8M-A15LTG - Storage System - HGST; *pg.* 406, *pg.* 260
SL72Z4W512M8M-A15LTU - Storage System - HGST; *pg.* 406, *pg.* 260
SL72Z4W512M8M-A18JTU - Storage System - HGST; *pg.* 406, *pg.* 260
SL72Z8W128M8M-A15LTU - Storage System - HGST; *pg.* 406, *pg.* 260
SL72Z8W128M8M-A18JTU - Storage System - HGST; *pg.* 406, *pg.* 260
SL72Z8W128M8M-B15LTU - Storage System - HGST; *pg.* 406, *pg.* 260
SL72Z8W128M8M-B18JTU - Storage System - HGST; *pg.* 406, *pg.* 260
SL72Z8W128M8M-B25GTU - Storage System - HGST; *pg.* 406, *pg.* 260
SL72Z8W256M8M-A15LTG - Storage System - HGST; *pg.* 406, *pg.* 260
SL72Z8W256M8M-A15LTU - Storage System - HGST; *pg.* 406, *pg.* 260
SL72Z8W256M8M-B25GTU - Storage System - HGST; *pg.* 406, *pg.* 260
SLA - Three Dimensional Imaging System - 3D SYSTEMS CORPORATION; *pg.* 339, *pg.* 1621
SLAB - Apparel - OAKLEY, INC.; *pg.* 1840, *pg.* 86
SLACK TUBE - U-Tube Manometer - DWYER INSTRUMENTS INC.; *pg.* 1330, *pg.* 694
SLACKER - Stuffed Dog - GUND, INC.; *pg.* 954, *pg.* 1056
SLACKER - Tactile Mutator - SMOOTH-ON INC.; *pg.* 111, *pg.* 1528
SLADDE - Footwear - STEVEN MADDEN, LTD.; *pg.* 1819, *pg.* 1176
SLAM - Magazine - RENTPATH, INC.; *pg.* 1680, *pg.* 538
SLAM AIR - Adjustable Air Spring - AIR LIFT COMPANY; *pg.* 198, *pg.* 895
SLAM CAM - 35 MM Camera - ALAN GORDON ENTERPRISES, INC.; *pg.* 1399, *pg.* 125
SLAM-IT - Basketball Rims - LIFETIME PRODUCTS INC.; *pg.* 933, *pg.* 1751
SLAM-IT-GOAL - Basketball Rim - LIFETIME PRODUCTS INC.; *pg.* 933, *pg.* 1751
SLAM-IT PRO - Basketball Rims - LIFETIME PRODUCTS INC.; *pg.* 933, *pg.* 1751
SLAM-PROOF - Retractable Screen - ODL INCORPORATED; *pg.* 101, *pg.* 914

First page reference indicates Business Class Edition
Second page reference indicates Geographic Edition

SLAMWICH - Game - GAMEWRIGHT; *pg.* 953, *pg.* 836
SLANT - Tweezer - TWEEZERMAN INTERNATIONAL; *pg.* 524, *pg.* 1324
SLANT ROCK - Clothing - ABERCROMBIE & FITCH CO.; *pg.* 37, *pg.* 1466
SLAP STIX - Caramep Sucker - NEW ENGLAND CONFECTIONERY COMPANY INC.; *pg.* 1860, *pg.* 842
SLAPPIES - Educational Materials - SCHOLASTIC INC.; *pg.* 1683, *pg.* 1288
SLASHDOT - Software - GEEKNET, INC.; *pg.* 1248, *pg.* 1780
SLASSSH - Footwear - STEVEN MADDEN, LTD.; *pg.* 1819, *pg.* 1176
SLAT MASTER - Fencing - MASTER HALCO; *pg.* 96, *pg.* 474
SLATA128MM1U(I) - Storage System - HGST; *pg.* 406, *pg.* 260
SLATA16GM1U(I) - Storage System - HGST; *pg.* 406, *pg.* 260
SLATA1GM1U(I) - Storage System - HGST; *pg.* 406, *pg.* 260
SLATA256MM1U(I) - Storage System - HGST; *pg.* 406, *pg.* 260
SLATA2GM1U(I) - Storage System - HGST; *pg.* 406, *pg.* 260
SLATA4GM1U(I) - Storage System - HGST; *pg.* 406, *pg.* 260
SLATA512MM1U(I) - Storage System - HGST; *pg.* 406, *pg.* 260
SLATA8GM1U(I) - Storage System - HGST; *pg.* 406, *pg.* 260
SLATE - Furniture - BUSH INDUSTRIES INC.; *pg.* 919, *pg.* 1170
SLATE - Ceramic, Glass, Stone Tiles & Slabs - WALKER & ZANGER, INC.; *pg.* 119, *pg.* 281
SLATER - Switch, Outlet, Ceiling Plastic Boxes - PASS & SEYMOUR/LEGRAND; *pg.* 1303, *pg.* 1344
SLATES - Men's Knit & Woven Tops, Sweaters, Dress Shirts & Outerwear - KELLWOOD COMPANY; *pg.* 28, *pg.* 975
SLATWALL/SLATRAIL - Computer Support Worktools - STEELCASE INC.; *pg.* 475, *pg.* 889
SLAUTTERBACK - Melters - NORDSON CORPORATION; *pg.* 1365, *pg.* 1480
SLC - Plastics Product - AEP INDUSTRIES INC.; *pg.* 1878, *pg.* 1085
SLC - Floor Underlayment - USG CORPORATION; *pg.* 118, *pg.* 594
SLC 500 - Software - ROCKWELL AUTOMATION, INC.; *pg.* 668, *pg.* 1880
SLCF128MM1U(I) - Storage System - HGST; *pg.* 406, *pg.* 260
SLCF16GM1T2U(I) - Storage System - HGST; *pg.* 406, *pg.* 260
SLCF16GM4U(I) - Storage System - HGST; *pg.* 406, *pg.* 260
SLCF1GM1U(I) - Storage System - HGST; *pg.* 406, *pg.* 260
SLCF256MM1U(I) - Storage System - HGST; *pg.* 406, *pg.* 260
SLCF2GM1U(I) - Storage System - HGST; *pg.* 406, *pg.* 260
SLCF4GM1U(I) - Storage System - HGST; *pg.* 406, *pg.* 260
SLCF512MM1U(I) - Storage System - HGST; *pg.* 406, *pg.* 260
SLCF8GM1U(I) - Storage System - HGST; *pg.* 406, *pg.* 260
SLCF8GM4U(I) - Storage System - HGST; *pg.* 406, *pg.* 260
SLCFAD(I)U - Storage System - HGST; *pg.* 406, *pg.* 260
SLCMATE - Thermal Processing Equipment - SURFACE COMBUSTION, INC.; *pg.* 1077, *pg.* 1462
SLE - Truck Seating - SEATS INCORPORATED; *pg.* 217, *pg.* 1890
SLEDGE HAMMER - Thrill Ride - CANADA'S WONDERLAND COMPANY; *pg.* 536, *pg.* 1947
SLEDGE HAMMER - Cleaner - DELTA FOREMOST CHEMICAL CORPORATION; *pg.* 1155, *pg.* 1642
SLEEK CANS - Metal Beverage Container - BALL CORPORATION; *pg.* 1452, *pg.* 311
SLEEKEND - Shoe - AEROGROUP INTERNATIONAL, INC.; *pg.* 1803, *pg.* 1055
SLEEMAN CREAM ALE - Beer - SLEEMAN BREWERIES, LTD.; *pg.* 265, *pg.* 1920
SLEEP 4A HEALTHY LIFE - Tagline - RESMED INC.; *pg.* 1589, *pg.* 207
SLEEP-ASSURE - Nutritional Supplement - NATURAL ORGANICS, INC.; *pg.* 1571, *pg.* 1181
SLEEP BETTER - Sleep Product - CARPENTER CO.; *pg.* 920, *pg.* 1801
SLEEP BETTER ON AIR - Mattress - SELECT COMFORT CORPORATION; *pg.* 942, *pg.* 942
THE SLEEP EASY - Baby Product - THE BOPPY COMPANY, LLC; *pg.* 20, *pg.* 329
SLEEP HAVEN - Sofa Sleeper - FLEXSTEEL INDUSTRIES, INC.; *pg.* 925, *pg.* 707
SLEEP-IN SOFA - Convertible Sleep Sofas - KINGSDOWN, INC.; *pg.* 932, *pg.* 1383
SLEEP INN - Hotels - CHOICE HOTELS INTERNATIONAL, INC.; *pg.* 1086, *pg.* 775
SLEEP-N-LOUNGE - Electric Bed - KINGSDOWN, INC.; *pg.* 932, *pg.* 1383
SLEEP 'N PLAY - Dress - CARTER'S, INC.; *pg.* 21, *pg.* 491
SLEEP N RESTORE - Vitamin & Dietary Supplement - NATROL, INC.; *pg.* 1570, *pg.* 64
SLEEP NOW - Dietary Supplement - HERBALIFE INTERNATIONAL OF AMERICA, INC.; *pg.* 1541, *pg.* 132
SLEEP NUMBER - Bed - SELECT COMFORT CORPORATION; *pg.* 942, *pg.* 942
THE SLEEP NUMBER BED BY SELECT COMFORT - Mattress - SELECT COMFORT CORPORATION; *pg.* 942, *pg.* 942
SLEEP SAFE - Nutritional Supplement - WHITEWING LABS, INC.; *pg.* 1610, *pg.* 99
THE SLEEP SHIRT - Healthcare Apparel - THE SALK COMPANY; *pg.* 1591, *pg.* 800
SLEEP TO LIVE - Slogan - KINGSDOWN, INC.; *pg.* 932, *pg.* 1383
SLEEP TO LIVE WAKE UP TO A BETTER LIFE - Slogan - KINGSDOWN, INC.; *pg.* 932, *pg.* 1383
SLEEPDRI - Budget Underpants - THE SALK COMPANY; *pg.* 1591, *pg.* 800
SLEEPING BEAR PRESS - Publisher - GALE CENGAGE LEARNING; *pg.* 1643, *pg.* 885
SLEEPING BEAUTY - Childrens Sleepwear - INDERA MILLS COMPANY; *pg.* 26, *pg.* 1396
SLEEPING BEAUTY - Mattresses - KINGSDOWN, INC.; *pg.* 932, *pg.* 1383
SLEEPING BEAUTY 2000 - Mattresses & Box Springs - KINGSDOWN, INC.; *pg.* 932, *pg.* 1383
SLEEPING BEAUTY ELOQUENCE - Mattress & Box Spring Sets - KINGSDOWN, INC.; *pg.* 932, *pg.* 1383
SLEEPING BEAUTY SOFTIE - Mattress & Box Spring - KINGSDOWN, INC.; *pg.* 932, *pg.* 1383
SLEEPING BEAUTY SYSTEM - Mattress Construction - KINGSDOWN, INC.; *pg.* 932, *pg.* 1383
SLEEPING BEAUTY TRADITION - Mattresses & Box Springs - KINGSDOWN, INC.; *pg.* 932, *pg.* 1383
SLEEPKIT SOLUTIONS - Medical Device - RESMED INC.; *pg.* 1589, *pg.* 207
SLEEPLIKELY - Gown - CARTER'S, INC.; *pg.* 21, *pg.* 491
SLEEPOVER - Furniture - NEMSCHOFF, INC.; *pg.* 936, *pg.* 1890
SLEEPSTRIP - Medical Product - MEDLINE INDUSTRIES, INC.; *pg.* 1562, *pg.* 635
SLEEPVANTAGE - Medical Device - RESMED INC.; *pg.* 1589, *pg.* 207
SLEEVELESS SPORT TOP - Clothing - K-SWISS; *pg.* 1837, *pg.* 306
SLEEVELINE - Valves - FLOWSERVE CORPORATION; *pg.* 82, *pg.* 1719
SLEEVIT - Pouch - PACTIV CORPORATION; *pg.* 1466, *pg.* 624
SLEIGH ME THE MONEY - Lottery Game - KENTUCKY LOTTERY CORPORATION; *pg.* 996, *pg.* 735
SLEIGH RIDE - Scratch Lottery Game - IDAHO LOTTERY; *pg.* 995, *pg.* 547
SLENDER PLUG - Cable - COLEMAN CABLE, INC.; *pg.* 1324, *pg.* 665
SLENDERWALL - Wall System - SMITH-MIDLAND CORPORATION; *pg.* 111, *pg.* 1795
SLENDYNE - Dynamic Microphone - SHURE INCORPORATED; *pg.* 672, *pg.* 638
SLENTROL - Canine Obesity Medication - PFIZER INC.; *pg.* 1581, *pg.* 1278
SLEUTH - Apparel - VANS, INC.; *pg.* 1821, *pg.* 76
SLFDM(40/44)H-8GM1U(I) - Storage System - HGST; *pg.* 406, *pg.* 260
SLFDM(40/44)(V/H)-128MM1U(I) - Storage System - HGST; *pg.* 406, *pg.* 260
SLFDM(40/44)(V/H)-1GM1U(I) - Storage System - HGST; *pg.* 406, *pg.* 260
SLFDM(40/44)(V/H)-256MM1U(I) - Storage System - HGST; *pg.* 406, *pg.* 260
SLFDM(40/44)(V/H)-2GM1U(I) - Storage System - HGST; *pg.* 406, *pg.* 260
SLFDM(40/44)(V/H)-4GM1U(I) - Storage System - HGST; *pg.* 406, *pg.* 260
SLFDM(40/44)(V/H)-512MM1U(I) - Storage System - HGST; *pg.* 406, *pg.* 260
SLFLD25-1 28MM 1 U(I) - Storage System - HGST; *pg.* 406, *pg.* 260
SLFLD25-1 6GM 1 U(I) - Storage System - HGST; *pg.* 406, *pg.* 260
SLFLD25-16GM1U(I) - Storage System - HGST; *pg.* 406, *pg.* 260
SLFLD25-1GM1U(L) - Storage System - HGST; *pg.* 406, *pg.* 260
SLFLD25-256MM1U(L) - Storage System - HGST; *pg.* 406, *pg.* 260
SLFLD25-2GM1U(I) - Storage System - HGST; *pg.* 406, *pg.* 260
SLFLD25-4GM1U(L) - Storage System - HGST; *pg.* 406, *pg.* 260
SLFLD25-512MM1U(L) - Storage System - HGST; *pg.* 406, *pg.* 260
SLFLD25-8GM 1 U(I) - Storage System - HGST; *pg.* 406, *pg.* 260
SLIC - Telecommunications Products - 3M COMPANY; *pg.* 1142, *pg.* 956
SLIC - Chemical Cleaner Product - TECH SPRAY, L.P.; *pg.* 1183, *pg.* 1659
SLIC-TITE - Counter Display - LA-CO INDUSTRIES MARKAL CO., INC.; *pg.* 1170, *pg.* 610
SLICCKK - Footwear - STEVEN MADDEN, LTD.; *pg.* 1819, *pg.* 1176
SLICE - Boats & Ships - LOCKHEED MARTIN CORPORATION; *pg.* 229, *pg.* 762
SLICE - Medicine - MERCK & CO., INC.; *pg.* 1566, *pg.* 1077
SLICE - Apparel - OAKLEY, INC.; *pg.* 1840, *pg.* 86
SLICE - Soft Drink - PEPSICO, INC.; *pg.* 259, *pg.* 1327
SLICE IN A BOX - Electronic Components - MOLEX INCORPORATED; *pg.* 655, *pg.* 628
SLICE OF LIFE - Flower Arrangement - 1-800-FLOWERS.COM, INC.; *pg.* 1758, *pg.* 1151
SLICEPAK - Packaging for Food Products - SEALED AIR CORPORATION; *pg.* 1468, *pg.* 1058
SLICING UP FRESHNESS - Tagline - ARBY'S RESTAURANT GROUP, INC.; *pg.* 1014, *pg.* 488
SLICK 50 - Engine Treatments - SHELL LUBRICANTS; *pg.* 217, *pg.* 1714
SLICK AIRCRAFT PRODUCTS - Aviation Ignition Equipment - UNISON INDUSTRIES, LLC; *pg.* 235, *pg.* 435
SLICK TINT - Beauty Product - AVON PRODUCTS, INC.; *pg.* 500, *pg.* 1198
SLICK WORKS - Hair Care Product - JOHN PAUL MITCHELL SYSTEMS; *pg.* 512, *pg.* 133
SLICKDIESEL - Diesel Additive - POWER SERVICE PRODUCTS, INC.; *pg.* 983, *pg.* 1749
SLICONNECT - Networking Software - OPENCONNECT SYSTEMS, INC.; *pg.* 449, *pg.* 1685
SLIDE - Industrial Aerosols - SLIDE PRODUCTS, INC.; *pg.* 1181, *pg.* 670
SLIDE-A-PACK - Conveyor Belting - HBD INDUSTRIES, INC.; *pg.* 207, *pg.* 1449
SLIDE-ACTION REAR SUSPENSION - Snowmobile - ARCTIC CAT INC.; *pg.* 1705, *pg.* 953
SLIDE CHAMBERS - Software - BIO-RAD LABORATORIES, INC.; *pg.* 1504, *pg.* 101
SLIDE GRIDDLE - Software - BIO-RAD LABORATORIES, INC.; *pg.* 1504, *pg.* 101
SLIDE-LAG - Rubber - VAN GORP CORPORATION; *pg.* 1387, *pg.* 711
SLIDE-LOC - Kitchen Organizer - HOME PRODUCTS INTERNATIONAL, INC.; *pg.* 1125, *pg.* 577
SLIDE LOCKS - Mold Base & Component - SUPERIOR DIE SET CORP.; *pg.* 1379, *pg.* 1885
SLIDE-ON - Vehicle Safety System - GROTE INDUSTRIES, INC.; *pg.* 206, *pg.* 693
SLIDE REEBOK - Video - REEBOK INTERNATIONAL LTD.; *pg.* 1817, *pg.* 811
SLIDE-RITE - Closure System - PACTIV CORPORATION; *pg.* 1466, *pg.* 624
SLIDE SHOP - Educational Materials - SCHOLASTIC INC.; *pg.* 1683, *pg.* 1288
SLIDER - Ramps - MAGLINE, INC.; *pg.* 1358, *pg.* 908
SLIDERFRAME - Gas Grill - WEBER-STEPHEN PRODUCTS LLC; *pg.* 62, *pg.* 650
SLIDERITE - Bags - BEMIS COMPANY, INC.; *pg.* 1453, *pg.* 1882
SLIDERZ - Connector - MOLEX INCORPORATED; *pg.* 655, *pg.* 628
SLIDETRACK - Chain Lubrication - BUNTING MAGNETICS CO.; *pg.* 1320, *pg.* 717
SLIDING BED - Thermal Processing Equipment - SURFACE

COMBUSTION, INC.; *pg.* 1077, *pg.* 1462
SLIK LEASE II - Premium Roll Covers - VAIL RUBBER WORKS, INC.; *pg.* 1891, *pg.* 906
SLIK LEASE III - Premium Roll Covers - VAIL RUBBER WORKS, INC.; *pg.* 1891, *pg.* 906
SLIKEASE - Metal Casting Product - HILL & GRIFFITH COMPANY; *pg.* 1167, *pg.* 1414
SLIM - Architecture - CYPRESS SEMICONDUCTOR CORPORATION; *pg.* 1326, *pg.* 243
SLIM - Rolling Writer Pens - PENTEL OF AMERICA, LTD.; *pg.* 453, *pg.* 295
SLIM - Footwear - VANS, INC.; *pg.* 1821, *pg.* 76
SLIM AND SLEEK - Beauty Product - AVON PRODUCTS, INC.; *pg.* 500, *pg.* 1198
SLIM BOOT 507 - Jean - LEVI STRAUSS & CO.; *pg.* 43, *pg.* 220
SLIM CHANCE - Beverage - CRAFT BREWERS ALLIANCE, INC; *pg.* 247, *pg.* 1502
SLIM-FAST - Weight Loss Product - SLIM-FAST FOODS COMPANY; *pg.* 896, *pg.* 1061
SLIM IN 6 - Fitness Video & DVD - BEACHBODY, LLC; *pg.* 271, *pg.* 272
SLIM JIM - Food Product - CONAGRA FOODS, INC.; *pg.* 826, *pg.* 1014
SLIM JIM - Round Knife - THE WOLF MACHINE CO.; *pg.* 1389, *pg.* 1427
SLIM-LINE - Panels - PROPHOTONIX LIMITED; *pg.* 1427, *pg.* 1039
SLIM-PAK - Unit-Dose Package - HOSPIRA, INC.; *pg.* 1542, *pg.* 623
SLIM SHAKE - Nutritional Product - RBC LIFE SCIENCES, INC.; *pg.* 1588, *pg.* 1723
SLIM STRAIGHT 514 - Jean - LEVI STRAUSS & CO.; *pg.* 43, *pg.* 220
SLIM STYLE - Cushion - DYNATRONICS CORPORATION; *pg.* 1526, *pg.* 1757
SLIM TOP HANDLE - Briefcase - SANTA FE LEATHER CORPORATION; *pg.* 12, *pg.* 1059
SLIM WEAR - Slacks & Shorts - HABAND COMPANY, INC.; *pg.* 1772, *pg.* 1099
SLIM6 - Dairy Food Product - LIFEWAY FOODS, INC.; *pg.* 874, *pg.* 634
SLIMCHIP - Semiconductor Suppliers - INTERDIGITAL, INC.; *pg.* 1872, *pg.* 1543
SLIMCORE - Integrated Circuits - POWER INTEGRATIONS, INC.; *pg.* 1369, *pg.* 249
SLIMDOWN - Beverage - MONSTER BEVERAGE CORPORATION; *pg.* 257, *pg.* 69
SLIME - Vehicle Maintenance - TRACTOR SUPPLY COMPANY; *pg.* 708, *pg.* 1627
SLIME-TROL - Biocides - GE WATER & PROCESS TECHNOLOGIES; *pg.* 1339, *pg.* 1588
SLIME-X - Diesel Fuel - POWER SERVICE PRODUCTS, INC.; *pg.* 983, *pg.* 1749
SLIMFIT - Glove Design - WELLS LAMONT CORPORATION; *pg.* 15, *pg.* 638
SLIMLINE - Trimmer - ANDIS COMPANY; *pg.* 498, *pg.* 1895
SLIMLINE - Workstation Table System - NEWPORT CORPORATION; *pg.* 1424, *pg.* 114
SLIMLINE - Compressor - NORWALK COMPRESSOR COMPANY, INC.; *pg.* 1366, *pg.* 380
SLIMLINE - Apparel - OAKLEY, INC.; *pg.* 1840, *pg.* 86
SLIMLINE - Pedestal Mount - PANAVISE PRODUCTS, INC.; *pg.* 1058, *pg.* 1032
SLIMLINE - Cable & Antenna System - RADIO FREQUENCY SYSTEMS, INC.; *pg.* 666, *pg.* 354
SLIMLINE - Plumbing Product - SLOAN VALVE COMPANY; *pg.* 1062, *pg.* 613
SLIMLINE - Computer Workstation Product - STINGER MEDICAL LLC; *pg.* 476, *pg.* 1648
SLIMLINE 2000 - Pedestal Mount - PANAVISE PRODUCTS, INC.; *pg.* 1058, *pg.* 1032
SLIMLINE ELECTROL - Screen - DA-LITE SCREEN COMPANY; *pg.* 632, *pg.* 698
SLIMLINE OPTIMA PLUS - Bedpan Washer - SLOAN VALVE COMPANY; *pg.* 1062, *pg.* 613
SLIMPAC - Semi-Conductor Devices - SEMTECH CORPORATION; *pg.* 671, *pg.* 57
SLIMPACK - Floppy Drive - CYBERRESEARCH INC.; *pg.* 381, *pg.* 339
SLIMPLICITY - Nutritional Supplement - RELIV INTERNATIONAL, INC.; *pg.* 1589, *pg.* 975
SLIMSTACK - Connector - MOLEX INCORPORATED; *pg.* 655, *pg.* 628
SLIMTRODE - Robotic Product - HAMILTON CO., INC.; *pg.* 1415, *pg.* 1031
SLIMWELL - Wellness Product - AVON PRODUCTS, INC.; *pg.* 500, *pg.* 1198
SLINGCHUTE - Educational Materials - SCHOLASTIC INC.; *pg.* 1683, *pg.* 1288
SLINGCHUTE - Toss and Catch Game - SCHOOL-TECH, INC.; *pg.* 1844, *pg.* 866
SLINGERLAND - Musical Instrument - GIBSON GUITAR CORP.; *pg.* 550, *pg.* 1650
SLINGO MAGIC - Scratch Lottery Game - IDAHO LOTTERY; *pg.* 995, *pg.* 547
SLINGO TRIO - Lottery Game - IDAHO LOTTERY; *pg.* 995, *pg.* 547
SLINGRIDER - Infant Carrier - INFANTINO, LLC; *pg.* 957, *pg.* 203
SLINKY - Guitar - ERNIE BALL INC.; *pg.* 1768, *pg.* 68
SLINKY - Footwear - STEVEN MADDEN, LTD.; *pg.* 1819, *pg.* 1176
SLINKY-FLEX - Conduit - SOUTHWIRE COMPANY; *pg.* 1063, *pg.* 527
SLIP - Self-Facing Display Shelving - CANNON EQUIPMENT COMPANY; *pg.* 1321, *pg.* 920
SLIP-CATH - Catheter - COOK GROUP, INC.; *pg.* 1518, *pg.* 674
SLIP/NOMOR - Floor & Flood Care Products - STAGESTEP INC.; *pg.* 1688, *pg.* 1570
SLIP NOMOR - Cleaning Preparation - STAGESTEP INC.; *pg.* 1688, *pg.* 1570
SLIP-ON - Cable Terminator - G&W ELECTRIC COMPANY; *pg.* 1338, *pg.* 558
SLIP-PIN - Lubricant - BIRKO CORPORATION; *pg.* 1149, *pg.* 332
SLIP-TORQUE - Conveyor - SHUTTLEWORTH, INC.; *pg.* 1375, *pg.* 682
SLIP-TRAK - Conveyor - SHUTTLEWORTH, INC.; *pg.* 1375, *pg.* 682
SLIP-X - Safety Product - VENTURI, INC.; *pg.* 1606, *pg.* 910
SLIPLOCK - Exercise Equipment - ALLIANCE SPORTS GROUP, L.P.; *pg.* 1825, *pg.* 1698
SLIPPER CHAIRS - Furniture - BASSETT FURNITURE INDUSTRIES, INCORPORATED; *pg.* 916, *pg.* 1776
SLIPPERY STUFF - Healthcare Product - MEDICOOL, INC.; *pg.* 1562, *pg.* 294
SLIPTOP - Conveyor Belting - HBD INDUSTRIES, INC.; *pg.* 207, *pg.* 1449
SLIQUE - Footwear - STEVEN MADDEN, LTD.; *pg.* 1819, *pg.* 1176
SLIQUID - Level Controls - DWYER INSTRUMENTS INC.; *pg.* 1330, *pg.* 694
SLITTER TOOLING - Tooling - ARTUS CORPORATION; *pg.* 1314, *pg.* 1059
SLIX - Lubricant - DELTA FOREMOST CHEMICAL CORPORATION; *pg.* 1155, *pg.* 1642
SLIX-IT - Lubricant - AERVOE INDUSTRIES INCORPORATED; *pg.* 1439, *pg.* 1021
SLM & AR SYSTEM & FLASHBOARDS - Software - BMC SOFTWARE, INC.; *pg.* 362, *pg.* 1701
SLM CORPORATION - Magazine - SLM CORPORATION; *pg.* 804, *pg.* 388
SLMPCI16GM4U-M - Storage System - HGST; *pg.* 406, *pg.* 260
SLMPCI32GM4U-M - Storage System - HGST; *pg.* 406, *pg.* 260
SLMPCI4GM4U-M - Storage System - HGST; *pg.* 406, *pg.* 260
SLMPCI8GM4U-M - Storage System - HGST; *pg.* 406, *pg.* 260
SLMSD128BS(I)U - Storage System - HGST; *pg.* 406, *pg.* 260
SLMSD1GBBS(I)U - Storage System - HGST; *pg.* 406, *pg.* 260
SLMSD256BS(I)U - Storage System - HGST; *pg.* 406, *pg.* 260
SLMSD2GBBS(I)U - Storage System - HGST; *pg.* 406, *pg.* 260
SLMSD512BS(I)U - Storage System - HGST; *pg.* 406, *pg.* 260
SLO BREWING CO. - Beer - UNITED STATES BEVERAGE LLC; *pg.* 266, *pg.* 379
SLO-JO - Platinum Silicone Cure Retarder - SMOOTH-ON INC.; *pg.* 111, *pg.* 1528
SLOAN - Table - BLATT BOWLING & BILLIARD CORP.; *pg.* 1827, *pg.* 1203
SLOAN OPTIMA - Electronic Faucet - SLOAN VALVE COMPANY; *pg.* 1062, *pg.* 613
SLOAN STONE - Lavatory System - SLOAN VALVE COMPANY; *pg.* 1062, *pg.* 613
SLOANE SQUARE - Furniture - STANLEY FURNITURE CO., INC.; *pg.* 943, *pg.* 1379
SLOANSTONE - Solid Surface Lavatory - SLOAN VALVE COMPANY; *pg.* 1062, *pg.* 613
SLOCHE - Cold Beverage - ALIMENTATION COUCHE-TARD INC.; *pg.* 1013, *pg.* 1951
SLOGGERS - Garden Footwear - PRINCIPLE PLASTICS, INC.; *pg.* 1816, *pg.* 94
SLOMIN'S - Heating & Cooling Services - SLOMIN'S INC.; *pg.* 1076, *pg.* 1167
THE SLOMIN'S SHIELD - Home Security System - SLOMIN'S INC.; *pg.* 1076, *pg.* 1167
SLOPER - Insulation - THE DOW CHEMICAL COMPANY; *pg.* 1157, *pg.* 898
SLOT ADDRESSABLE MANAGEMENT - Data Storage & System - NER HOLDINGS INC.; *pg.* 444, *pg.* 1071
SLOT-IT - Inventory Arrangement Software - MANHATTAN ASSOCIATES, INC.; *pg.* 430, *pg.* 513
SLOT MACHINE UNIVERSITY - Game - WMS INDUSTRIES INC.; *pg.* 593, *pg.* 666
SLOT MULTI-CARD - Card Reader - LEXAR MEDIA, INC.; *pg.* 1262, *pg.* 146
SLOT MUSIC - Musical Download - SANDISK CORPORATION; *pg.* 465, *pg.* 147
SLOT SPOT - Video Memory Card - SANDISK CORPORATION; *pg.* 465, *pg.* 147
SLOT SYSTEM - Lighting System - LITECONTROL CORPORATION; *pg.* 1301, *pg.* 841
SLOTOPTIMIZER - Hardware Product - INTERPHASE CORPORATION; *pg.* 420, *pg.* 1732
SLOTPLAY - Games - PENN NATIONAL GAMING, INC.; *pg.* 574, *pg.* 1595
SLOTS - Tailgate Covers - LUND INTERNATIONAL, INC.; *pg.* 211, *pg.* 526
SLOTS OF GOLD - Pulltab Game - IDAHO LOTTERY; *pg.* 995, *pg.* 547
SLOTS OF LUCK - Lottery Game - OHIO LOTTERY COMMISSION; *pg.* 1002, *pg.* 1433
SLOTSKY - Game - WMS INDUSTRIES INC.; *pg.* 593, *pg.* 666
SLOW CHURNED - Ice Cream - DREYER'S GRAND ICE CREAM HOLDINGS, INC.; *pg.* 1852, *pg.* 171
SLOWCOOK'NMORE - Electrical Appliance & Housewares - NATIONAL PRESTO INDUSTRIES, INC; *pg.* 1128, *pg.* 1857
SLOWFADE - Molecular Probe Product - THERMO FISHER SCIENTIFIC INC.; *pg.* 1602, *pg.* 61
SLS - Three Dimensional Imaging System - 3D SYSTEMS CORPORATION; *pg.* 339, *pg.* 1621
SLS - Burner - MAXON CORPORATION; *pg.* 1359, *pg.* 695
SLSD128BS(I)U - Storage System - HGST; *pg.* 406, *pg.* 260
SLSD1GBBS(I)U - Storage System - HGST; *pg.* 406, *pg.* 260
SLSD256BS(I)U - Storage System - HGST; *pg.* 406, *pg.* 260
SLSD2GBBS(I)U - Storage System - HGST; *pg.* 406, *pg.* 260
SLSD512BS(I)U - Storage System - HGST; *pg.* 406, *pg.* 260
SLT3S - Electronic Components - MOLEX INCORPORATED; *pg.* 655, *pg.* 628
SLUDGE DEVIL - Black Oxide Tank - HEATBATH CORPORATION; *pg.* 1165, *pg.* 826
SLUDGE GUARD - Engine Oil - BARDAHL MANUFACTURING CORPORATION; *pg.* 972, *pg.* 1833
SLUDGEMASTER - Pumps - IDEX CORPORATION; *pg.* 1347, *pg.* 623
SLUFD128MU1U(I)-Y - Storage System - HGST; *pg.* 406, *pg.* 260
SLUFD1GU1U(I)-Y - Storage System - HGST; *pg.* 406, *pg.* 260
SLUFD256MU1U(I)-Y - Storage System - HGST; *pg.* 406, *pg.* 260
SLUFD2GU1U(I)-Y - Storage System - HGST; *pg.* 406, *pg.* 260
SLUFD4GU1U(I)-Y - Storage System - HGST; *pg.* 406, *pg.* 260
SLUFD512MU1U(I)-Y - Storage System - HGST; *pg.* 406, *pg.* 260
SLUFDM128MU1U(I)-Y - Storage System - HGST; *pg.* 406, *pg.* 260
SLUFDM1GU1U(I)-Y - Storage System - HGST; *pg.* 406, *pg.* 260
SLUFDM256MU1U(I)-Y - Storage System - HGST; *pg.* 406, *pg.* 260
SLUFDM2GU1U(I)-Y - Storage System - HGST; *pg.* 406, *pg.* 260

SLUFDM4GU1U(I)-Y - Storage System - HGST; *pg.* 406, *pg.* 260
SLUFDM512MU1U(I)-Y - Storage System - HGST; *pg.* 406, *pg.* 260
SLUFDM8GU1U(I)-Y - Storage System - HGST; *pg.* 406, *pg.* 260
SLUG-BUSTER - Punch - GREENLEE TEXTRON INC.; *pg.* 1048, *pg.* 655
SLUG SPLITTER - Punch - GREENLEE TEXTRON INC.; *pg.* 1048, *pg.* 655
SLUGGER - Software - SCANTRON CORPORATION; *pg.* 467, *pg.* 922
SLUGGER CRUSHERS - Hammer Mills - WILLIAMS PATENT CRUSHER & PULVERIZER CO., INC.; *pg.* 1389, *pg.* 1005
SLUGGERRR - Mascot - KANSAS CITY ROYALS BASEBALL CORPORATION; *pg.* 555, *pg.* 985
SLUGGERS - Processed Poultry - TYSON FOODS, INC.; *pg.* 902, *pg.* 35
SLUMBER - Patient Seating - STEELCASE INC.; *pg.* 475, *pg.* 889
SLUMBER KING - Mattress - SIMMONS COMPANY; *pg.* 943, *pg.* 520
SLUMBER PET - Pet Beds - PETEDGE; *pg.* 1481, *pg.* 787
SLUMBER REST - Comforters & Mattress Pads - JARDEN CONSUMER SOLUTIONS; *pg.* 57, *pg.* 412
SLUMBER SOX - Bed Socks - RELIABLE OF MILWAUKEE; *pg.* 698, *pg.* 1879
SLUMBER TIME - Mattress - SIMMONS COMPANY; *pg.* 943, *pg.* 520
SLUMBERJACK - Sleeping Bag - EXXEL OUTDOORS LLC; *pg.* 1833, *pg.* 311
SLURP AND GULP - Frozen Beverage - 7-ELEVEN, INC.; *pg.* 1012, *pg.* 1672
SLURPEE - Frozen Carbonated Beverage - 7-ELEVEN, INC.; *pg.* 1012, *pg.* 1672
SLURPEE SPLITZ-O - Frozen Beverage - 7-ELEVEN, INC.; *pg.* 1012, *pg.* 1672
SLUSCD128MU1U(I)-Y - Storage System - HGST; *pg.* 406, *pg.* 260
SLUSCD1GU1U(I)-Y - Storage System - HGST; *pg.* 406, *pg.* 260
SLUSCD256MU1U(I)-Y - Storage System - HGST; *pg.* 406, *pg.* 260
SLUSCD2GU1U(I)-Y - Storage System - HGST; *pg.* 406, *pg.* 260
SLUSCD4GU1U(I)-Y - Storage System - HGST; *pg.* 406, *pg.* 260
SLUSCD512MU1U(I)-Y - Storage System - HGST; *pg.* 406, *pg.* 260
SLUSH POPS - Ice Cream Bar - WELLS ENTERPRISES, INC.; *pg.* 909, *pg.* 709
SLUSH PUPPIE - Fruit Flavored Ice Beverages - J&J SNACK FOODS CORPORATION; *pg.* 865, *pg.* 1107
SLUSH44.COM - E-Commerce Website - SONIC CORP.; *pg.* 1750, *pg.* 1487
SLX - Searchlights - BALLANTYNE STRONG, INC.; *pg.* 623, *pg.* 1013
SM - Power Fuse - S&C ELECTRIC COMPANY; *pg.* 1305, *pg.* 589
SM-4 - Power Fuse - S&C ELECTRIC COMPANY; *pg.* 1305, *pg.* 589
S.M.A - Boom Mounted Hedge - ALAMO GROUP INC.; *pg.* 1311, *pg.* 1745
SMACKER - Lip Product - THE BONNE BELL COMPANY; *pg.* 502, *pg.* 1480
SMALL BRA SAVER - Bra - BARE NECESSITIES, INC.; *pg.* 19, *pg.* 1056
SMALL BUSINESS SELECT - Wireless Communication System - AT&T SOUTHEAST; *pg.* 1868, *pg.* 489
SMALL CHIROPAK - Bag - SAMSONITE CORPORATION; *pg.* 11, *pg.* 830
SMALL OF SPRING - Decorative Fragrance - AROMATIQUE INC.; *pg.* 499, *pg.* 32
SMALL OVAL GATHERING - Basket - THE LONGABERGER COMPANY; *pg.* 1127, *pg.* 1467
SMALL TEAM DUFFEL - Footwear - NIKE, INC.; *pg.* 1812, *pg.* 1492
SMALL TWIN - Pumps - HYPRO; *pg.* 705, *pg.* 951
SMALL WORLD - Small Animal Feeds - MANNA PRO CORPORATION; *pg.* 1478, *pg.* 975
SMALLBIZSEARCH.COM - Search Engine - ENTREPRENEUR MEDIA, INC.; *pg.* 1639, *pg.* 110
SMALLCASE - Thermal Processing Equipment - SURFACE COMBUSTION, INC.; *pg.* 1077, *pg.* 1462
SMALLIR - Power Semiconductor Device - INTERNATIONAL RECTIFIER CORPORATION; *pg.* 647, *pg.* 80
SMALLTALK - Software - CINCOM SYSTEMS, INC.; *pg.* 372, *pg.* 1411
SMALSTRIP - Sterilization Product - PROPPER MANUFACTURING COMPANY, INC.; *pg.* 1586, *pg.* 1175
SMAP - Software - TELEDYNE LECROY; *pg.* 1431, *pg.* 1153
SMART - Software System - ALION SCIENCE AND TECHNOLOGY CORPORATION; *pg.* 615, *pg.* 1788
SMART - Beverages - THE COCA-COLA COMPANY; *pg.* 240, *pg.* 493
S.M.A.R.T - Stent Delivery System - CORDIS CORPORATION; *pg.* 1519, *pg.* 430
SMART-1 - Dataset - MITEL NETWORKS CORPORATION; *pg.* 654, *pg.* 1921
SMART 16/16E SHELVES - Central Site Rackmount - ADTRAN, INC.; *pg.* 344, *pg.* 6
SMART ADJUST - Software Product - PEGASYSTEMS INC.; *pg.* 453, *pg.* 809
SMART ADJUSTABILITY - Medical Equipment - INVACARE CORPORATION; *pg.* 1546, *pg.* 1451
SMART ALARM - Vehicle Safety System - GROTE INDUSTRIES, INC.; *pg.* 206, *pg.* 693
SMART & SNAPPY - Pocket Cobbler - HABAND COMPANY, INC.; *pg.* 1772, *pg.* 1099
SMART APEX - X-Ray System - BRUKER CORPORATION; *pg.* 1511, *pg.* 788
SMART APEX II - Analytical Device - BRUKER CORPORATION; *pg.* 1511, *pg.* 788
SMART AUDIOMETER - Hearing Test Equipment - INTELLIGENT HEARING SYSTEMS CORP.; *pg.* 1546, *pg.* 443
SMART BALANCE - Low-Fat Spreads - BOULDER BRANDS, INC.; *pg.* 1016, *pg.* 310
SMART BALL BLOWER - Game - FORTUNET, INC.; *pg.* 953, *pg.* 1024
SMART BALLS - Game - FORTUNET, INC.; *pg.* 953, *pg.* 1024
SMART BEARINGS - Railroad-Bearing - THE TIMKEN COMPANY; *pg.* 218, *pg.* 1408
SMART BENDER - Bender - GREENLEE TEXTRON INC.; *pg.* 1048, *pg.* 655
SMART BITES - Food Product - AUNTIE ANNE'S INC.; *pg.* 1715, *pg.* 1546
SMART BPM - Software - PEGASYSTEMS INC.; *pg.* 453, *pg.* 809
SMART BREAKER - Electrical Product - EATON CORPORATION; *pg.* 1331, *pg.* 1429
SMART BREEZE - X-Ray System - BRUKER CORPORATION; *pg.* 1511, *pg.* 788
SMART CAREER MOVE - Campaign - IOWA DEPARTMENT OF ECONOMIC DEVELOPMENT; *pg.* 995, *pg.* 705
SMART CHART - Paperless Recorder - DEVAR, INC.; *pg.* 633, *pg.* 339
SMART CHART II - Data Logger & Recorder - DEVAR, INC.; *pg.* 633, *pg.* 339
SMART CHECK - X-ray Screening System - AMERICAN SCIENCE AND ENGINEERING, INC.; *pg.* 1399, *pg.* 787
SMART CHECKS - Software Tool - OMNITRACS, LLC; *pg.* 449, *pg.* 1685
THE SMART CHOICE - Slogan - NIPRO DIAGNOSTICS, INC.; *pg.* 1573, *pg.* 426
THE SMART CHOICE - Slogan - SYMMONS INDUSTRIES, INC.; *pg.* 114, *pg.* 803
SMART CHOICES.MADE EASY. - Tagline - LOOKSMART, LTD.; *pg.* 1265, *pg.* 221
SMART CLAIMS - Software - VITRIA TECHNOLOGY, INC.; *pg.* 490, *pg.* 289
SMART CLIP - Orthodontic Appliances - 3M UNITEK CORPORATION; *pg.* 1483, *pg.* 150
SMART COIL - Technology - JAMISON BEDDING, INC.; *pg.* 930, *pg.* 1651
SMART COMFORT - Clothing - THE TIMBERLAND COMPANY; *pg.* 1821, *pg.* 1039
SMART CONNECTOR - Connector Services - ATTACHMATE CORPORATION; *pg.* 356, *pg.* 1833
SMART DATA - Medical Device - RESMED INC.; *pg.* 1589, *pg.* 207
SMART DESK - Game - FORTUNET, INC.; *pg.* 953, *pg.* 1024
SMART DIALOG - Software Product - PEGASYSTEMS INC.; *pg.* 453, *pg.* 809
SMART DISPLAY - Fluid Handling System - GRACO, INC.; *pg.* 1342, *pg.* 935
SMART DIVIDE - Kitchen Product - KOHLER CO.; *pg.* 91, *pg.* 1862
SMART DRIVE - Telescope - MEADE INSTRUMENTS CORPORATION; *pg.* 1422, *pg.* 113
SMART ENERGY MATRIX - Energy Storage System - BEACON POWER, LLC; *pg.* 1936, *pg.* 848
SMART EXPENSES - Financial Control - CONCUR TECHNOLOGIES, INC.; *pg.* 1236, *pg.* 1813
SMART FIT - Car seat - GRACO CHILDREN'S PRODUCTS INC.; *pg.* 954, *pg.* 1531
SMART FOLD - Baby Swing - EVENFLO COMPANY, INC.; *pg.* 924, *pg.* 1470
SMART FOOD - Pop Corn - PEPSICO, INC.; *pg.* 259, *pg.* 1327
SMART FUNNEL - Beverage - BUNN-O-MATIC CORPORATION; *pg.* 53, *pg.* 661
SMART-GATE - Software - 3M; *pg.* 339, *pg.* 179
SMART GATEWAY - Software - VITRIA TECHNOLOGY, INC.; *pg.* 490, *pg.* 289
SMART-GRIP - Plier - IDEAL INDUSTRIES, INC.; *pg.* 1051, *pg.* 662
SMART GUARD - Software - COMMAND SECURITY CORPORATION; *pg.* 377, *pg.* 1171
SMART HANDS - Telecommunication System - EQUINIX, INC.; *pg.* 394, *pg.* 190
SMART HOME: GREEN + WIRED - Museums Backyard - MUSEUM OF SCIENCE AND INDUSTRY; *pg.* 565, *pg.* 583
SMART HOPPER - Beverage - BUNN-O-MATIC CORPORATION; *pg.* 53, *pg.* 661
SMART INVESTIGATE - Software Product - PEGASYSTEMS INC.; *pg.* 453, *pg.* 809
SMART IRT/C - Sensor - EXERGEN CORPORATION; *pg.* 1412, *pg.* 855
SMART KENO - Game - FORTUNET, INC.; *pg.* 953, *pg.* 1024
SMART KIOSK - Game - FORTUNET, INC.; *pg.* 953, *pg.* 1024
SMART KIT - Software - XEROX CORPORATION; *pg.* 494, *pg.* 365
SMART LIDS - Lids for Food Pans - CARLISLE FOODSERVICE PRODUCTS INCORPORATED; *pg.* 1455, *pg.* 1485
SMART-LINK - Chipset - VITESSE SEMICONDUCTOR CORPORATION; *pg.* 686, *pg.* 57
SMART LOAN - Banking Services - SLM CORPORATION; *pg.* 804, *pg.* 388
SMART MONEY - Counterfeit Detector Pen - DRI MARK PRODUCTS, INC.; *pg.* 388, *pg.* 1323
SMART MOVE - Car Seat - GRACO CHILDREN'S PRODUCTS INC.; *pg.* 954, *pg.* 1531
SMART NUTRITION - Breads - UNITED STATES BAKERY; *pg.* 907, *pg.* 1507
SMART ONES - Low-Fat Frozen Food Entrees - WEIGHT WATCHERS INTERNATIONAL, INC.; *pg.* 1609, *pg.* 1313
SMART PACK - Game - FORTUNET, INC.; *pg.* 953, *pg.* 1024
SMART PADDLE - Medical Product - HOLOGIC, INC.; *pg.* 1416, *pg.* 784
SMART PARTS - Program - TOPFLIGHT CORPORATION; *pg.* 681, *pg.* 1534
SMART PETS - Toy - PETSMART, INC.; *pg.* 1481, *pg.* 18
SMART PLACE - Educational Materials - SCHOLASTIC INC.; *pg.* 1683, *pg.* 1288
SMART POCKET - Apparel - BARCO UNIFORMS, INC.; *pg.* 19, *pg.* 94
SMART POCKET - Suitcase - SAMSONITE CORPORATION; *pg.* 11, *pg.* 830
SMART PORT - Electrosurgical Devices - ANGIODYNAMICS, INC.; *pg.* 1495, *pg.* 1173
SMART POWER - Monitoring System - BEACON POWER, LLC; *pg.* 1936, *pg.* 848
SMART POWER SELECTOR - Circuitry - MAXIM INTEGRATED PRODUCTS, INC.; *pg.* 653, *pg.* 247
SMART RECORDER - Sequencer - ALLEN ORGAN COMPANY; *pg.* 527, *pg.* 1549
SMART SCAN - Game - FORTUNET, INC.; *pg.* 953, *pg.* 1024
SMART SCREENER - Hearing Screening Equipment - INTELLIGENT HEARING SYSTEMS CORP.; *pg.* 1546, *pg.* 443
SMART SENSIBLE LONG TERM CARE INSURANCE - Tagline - PENN TREATY AMERICAN CORPORATION; *pg.* 793, *pg.* 1514
SMART SET - Clock Radio - EMERSON RADIO CORP.; *pg.* 636, *pg.* 1087
SMART SHAKER - Vibratory Shakers - KEY TECHNOLOGY,

INC.; *pg.* 868, *pg.* 1847

SMART SHORE - IT Business Solution - RCM TECHNOLOGIES, INC.; *pg.* 459, *pg.* 1108

SMART SIGNS - Game - FORTUNET, INC.; *pg.* 953, *pg.* 1024

SMART SLEEVE - Suitcase - SAMSONITE CORPORATION; *pg.* 11, *pg.* 830

SMART SOLUTIONS - Compact Lighting Control Gear - ELECTRONIC THEATRE CONTROLS, INC.; *pg.* 1296, *pg.* 1872

SMART SOLUTIONS FOR A CONNECTED WORLD. - Tagline - ADTRAN, INC.; *pg.* 344, *pg.* 6

SMART SORT - Voice Activated Mail Sorter - HASLER, INC.; *pg.* 1459, *pg.* 356

SMART SOURCE - Food Product - SHAMROCK FOODS COMPANY; *pg.* 895, *pg.* 20

SMART SPEND - Business Consulting & Planning Services - COMPUTER SCIENCES CORPORATION; *pg.* 378, *pg.* 1780

SMART START - Food Product - KELLOGG COMPANY; *pg.* 831, *pg.* 870

SMART START - Power Tool - MILWAUKEE ELECTRIC TOOL CORP.; *pg.* 1056, *pg.* 1855

SMART START ANTIOXIDANTS - Cereal - KELLOGG COMPANY; *pg.* 831, *pg.* 870

SMART-STRAP - Retractable Shoulder Strap - SOLO; *pg.* 12, *pg.* 1165

SMART STRAW - Sprayer - WD-40 COMPANY; *pg.* 337, *pg.* 210

SMART SUBWOOFER, THE - Audio & Video Product - HARMAN INTERNATIONAL INDUSTRIES, INCORPORATED; *pg.* 641, *pg.* 374

SMART SYSTEM - Wireless Safety Monitoring System - HAWS CORPORATION; *pg.* 56, *pg.* 1032

SMART SYSTEM ADD-ON PANEL - Baby Gate - EVENFLO COMPANY, INC.; *pg.* 924, *pg.* 1470

SMART SYSTEM PRO - Eyewear - THE HILSINGER CO.; *pg.* 1416, *pg.* 841

SMART SYSTEMS - Electronic Control System - MERITOR, INC.; *pg.* 212, *pg.* 911

SMART T CAR - High Speed Automatic Transfer Vehicle - DAIFUKU WEBB; *pg.* 1327, *pg.* 885

SMART TAG - Computer Software - TRUSTWAVE HOLDINGS, INC.; *pg.* 1285, *pg.* 593

SMART TITLE SOLUTIONS - Property Data Services - CORELOGIC, INC.; *pg.* 1198, *pg.* 109

SMART TRAC - Microwave Fat & Moisture Analyzer - CEM CORPORATION; *pg.* 1405, *pg.* 1382

SMART TRACK - Integrated Processing System - HASLER, INC.; *pg.* 1459, *pg.* 356

SMART-UPS - Power Protection Product - SCHNEIDER ELECTRIC; *pg.* 467, *pg.* 1609

SMART VALVE - Medical Device - INTEGRA LIFESCIENCES HOLDINGS CORPORATION; *pg.* 1545, *pg.* 1109

SMART VIEWS - Software Product - PEGASYSTEMS INC.; *pg.* 453, *pg.* 809

SMART WHEEL - Software - COMMAND SECURITY CORPORATION; *pg.* 377, *pg.* 1171

SMART WIZARD - Software - NETGEAR, INC.; *pg.* 444, *pg.* 247

SMARTACCESS - Software - CITRIX SYSTEMS, INC.; *pg.* 375, *pg.* 424

SMARTACCESS - Software - SUPPORT.COM, INC.; *pg.* 1283, *pg.* 192

SMARTADVISOR - Software System - FAIR ISAAC CORPORATION; *pg.* 1247, *pg.* 955

SMARTAGENT - Software - ENVISION; *pg.* 393, *pg.* 1835

SMARTAGENT - Financial Systems Integration - ESM SOLUTIONS CORPORATION; *pg.* 1243, *pg.* 1591

SMARTAIR - Automatic Leveling System - AIR LIFT COMPANY; *pg.* 198, *pg.* 895

SMARTAMP - Amplifier - ADEPT TECHNOLOGY, INC.; *pg.* 1310, *pg.* 182

SMARTARC - Thermal Spray Equipment - SULZER METCO (WESTBURY) INC.; *pg.* 1064, *pg.* 1350

SMARTAXIS - Modular Building Block - ADEPT TECHNOLOGY, INC.; *pg.* 1310, *pg.* 182

SMARTBAR - Electronic Stabilizer System - AMERICAN AXLE & MANUFACTURING HOLDINGS, INC.; *pg.* 198, *pg.* 879

SMARTBATCH - Thermoplastic Colorant & Additive - POLYONE CORPORATION; *pg.* 1177, *pg.* 1404

SMARTBATTERY - Material Handling Equipment - C&D TECHNOLOGIES, INC.; *pg.* 627, *pg.* 1517

SMARTBEAM - Headlamp Control System - GENTEX CORPORATION; *pg.* 206, *pg.* 913

SMARTBEAM - Medical System - VARIAN MEDICAL SYSTEMS, INC.; *pg.* 1434, *pg.* 178

SMARTBILL - Software - CTI GROUP HOLDINGS INC.; *pg.* 381, *pg.* 684

SMARTBIND - Wheat Proteins - ARCHER-DANIELS-MIDLAND COMPANY; *pg.* 825, *pg.* 565

SMARTBLADE - Windshield Wiper Blades - OLD WORLD INDUSTRIES, INC.; *pg.* 1175, *pg.* 641

SMARTBLUE - Power Supply Product - ANTEC INCORPORATED; *pg.* 350, *pg.* 90

SMARTBLUE - Animal Nutritional Supplements - SMARTPAK EQUINE, LLC; *pg.* 1482, *pg.* 834

SMARTBPM - Software Product - PEGASYSTEMS INC.; *pg.* 453, *pg.* 809

SMARTBPO - Software Product - PEGASYSTEMS INC.; *pg.* 453, *pg.* 809

SMARTBRAN - Cereal - NATURE'S PATH FOODS INC.; *pg.* 833, *pg.* 1908

SMARTCALL - Software - SUNGARD DATA SYSTEMS INC.; *pg.* 477, *pg.* 1592

SMARTCARDS - Software Product - MAXIMUS, INC.; *pg.* 780, *pg.* 1799

SMARTCARE - Diagnostic Product - ALERE INC.; *pg.* 1488, *pg.* 849

SMARTCARE - Software - VITRIA TECHNOLOGY, INC.; *pg.* 490, *pg.* 289

SMARTCHARTS - Software - MONEY.NET, INC.; *pg.* 1268, *pg.* 1261

SMARTCHECK INR - Pharmaceutical Product - ALERE INC.; *pg.* 1488, *pg.* 849

SMARTCHOICE - Healthcare Product - HEALTH GRADES, INC.; *pg.* 1256, *pg.* 319

SMARTCHOICE - Security & Law Enforcement Products - MACE SECURITY INTERNATIONAL, INC.; *pg.* 1172, *pg.* 1541

SMARTCLAIMS - Software - VITRIA TECHNOLOGY, INC.; *pg.* 490, *pg.* 289

SMARTCLEAN - Cleaning System - ALTO-SHAAM INC.; *pg.* 836, *pg.* 1869

SMARTCLICK - Business Management Solutions - ADVENT SOFTWARE, INC.; *pg.* 345, *pg.* 211

SMARTCLIP - Self-Ligating Bracket System - 3M COMPANY; *pg.* 1142, *pg.* 956

SMARTCOLLABORATOR - Web Based Software - SMART SOFTWARE, INC.; *pg.* 470, *pg.* 787

SMARTCOM - Software - OMNITRACS, LLC; *pg.* 449, *pg.* 1685

SMARTCONTROL - Airless Paint Sprayers - GRACO, INC.; *pg.* 1342, *pg.* 935

SMARTCONTROLLER CS - Robot Controller - ADEPT TECHNOLOGY, INC.; *pg.* 1310, *pg.* 182

SMARTCONTROLLER CX - Robot Controller - ADEPT TECHNOLOGY, INC.; *pg.* 1310, *pg.* 182

SMARTCOOL - Power Supply Product - ANTEC INCORPORATED; *pg.* 350, *pg.* 90

SMARTCR - Compact Computed Radiology Image Processing System - FUJIFILM MEDICAL SYSTEMS USA, INC.; *pg.* 1531, *pg.* 374

SMARTCYCLER - Thermal Cycler - CEPHEID; *pg.* 1514, *pg.* 284

SMARTDBA - Software - BMC SOFTWARE, INC.; *pg.* 362, *pg.* 1701

SMARTDITCH - Water Liner - PENDA CORPORATION; *pg.* 214, *pg.* 1887

SMARTDM - Semiconductors - TEXAS INSTRUMENTS INCORPORATED; *pg.* 679, *pg.* 1688

SMARTDMA - Driver Software - ADVANCED MICRO DEVICES, INC.; *pg.* 613, *pg.* 282

SMARTDOCUMENT TRAVEL - Software - XEROX CORPORATION; *pg.* 494, *pg.* 365

SMARTDOGS - Slippers - TOTES ISOTONER CORPORATION; *pg.* 14, *pg.* 1426

SMARTDOT - Laser Levels - M-D BUILDING PRODUCTS, INC.; *pg.* 95, *pg.* 1486

SMARTDPOAE - Oto-Acoustic Emission Testing System - INTELLIGENT HEARING SYSTEMS CORP.; *pg.* 1546, *pg.* 443

SMARTE - Supercomputing System - CRAY INC.; *pg.* 380, *pg.* 1834

SMARTEC - Refrigerant Analyzer - BACHARACH INC.; *pg.* 1400, *pg.* 1556

SMARTEP - Hearing Diagnostic Equipment - INTELLIGENT HEARING SYSTEMS CORP.; *pg.* 1546, *pg.* 443

SMARTEP-ASSR - Auditory Testing System - INTELLIGENT HEARING SYSTEMS CORP.; *pg.* 1546, *pg.* 443

SMARTER BY THE YARD - Tag Line - ARIENS COMPANY INC.; *pg.* 700, *pg.* 1855

SMARTER DOCUMENT MANAGEMENT - Software - XEROX CORPORATION; *pg.* 494, *pg.* 365

SMARTER SYSTEM - Panel & Sensor - NAPCO SECURITY SYSTEMS, INC.; *pg.* 658, *pg.* 1138

THE SMARTER WAY TO DEFRAG - Tagline - RAXCO SOFTWARE, INC.; *pg.* 459, *pg.* 770

THE SMARTER WAY TO SEND MONEY - Tag Line - XOOM CORPORATION; *pg.* 1289, *pg.* 234

SMARTERM - Access Control System - NAPCO SECURITY SYSTEMS, INC.; *pg.* 658, *pg.* 1138

SMARTERSENSE - Detector - MAXIM INTEGRATED PRODUCTS, INC.; *pg.* 653, *pg.* 247

SMARTERTRAVEL.COM - Travel Resource - SMARTER TRAVEL MEDIA LLC; *pg.* 1687, *pg.* 801

SMARTFADE - Lighting Control Console - ELECTRONIC THEATRE CONTROLS, INC.; *pg.* 1296, *pg.* 1872

SMARTFEED - Multipacker Conveyor - SHUTTLEWORTH, INC.; *pg.* 1375, *pg.* 682

SMARTFILL - Automatic Tank Monitoring - FERRELLGAS PARTNERS, L.P.; *pg.* 977, *pg.* 718

SMARTFIRE - Burner - MAXON CORPORATION; *pg.* 1359, *pg.* 695

SMARTFIRE - Combustion Electronic Control - WOODWARD, INC.; *pg.* 122, *pg.* 329

SMARTFOLD - Seat Folding System - LEAR CORPORATION; *pg.* 229, *pg.* 907

SMARTFOOD - Popcorn - FRITO-LAY NORTH AMERICA, INC.; *pg.* 1853, *pg.* 1730

SMARTFORECASTS - Planning & Inventory Software - SMART SOFTWARE, INC.; *pg.* 470, *pg.* 787

SMARTFORECASTS ENTERPRISE - Software - SMART SOFTWARE, INC.; *pg.* 470, *pg.* 787

SMARTFRAME - Window Frame - ODL INCORPORATED; *pg.* 101, *pg.* 914

SMARTGART - Driver Software - ADVANCED MICRO DEVICES, INC.; *pg.* 613, *pg.* 282

SMARTGAUGE - Patient Monitoring System - CRITICARE SYSTEMS, INC.; *pg.* 1520, *pg.* 1897

SMARTGFI - Electrical Test Instruments - ASSOCIATED RESEARCH INC.; *pg.* 1400, *pg.* 622

SMARTGRIP - Toothbrush - RANIR LLC; *pg.* 520, *pg.* 888

SMARTHDHC - Memory Card - SANDISK CORPORATION; *pg.* 465, *pg.* 147

SMARTHEAT - Heating Pad - KAZ, INC.; *pg.* 58, *pg.* 844

SMARTHINKING - Online Tutoring Source - HOUGHTON MIFFLIN HARCOURT PUBLISHING COMPANY; *pg.* 1651, *pg.* 796

SMARTHOG - Battery - ENERSYS INC.; *pg.* 1334, *pg.* 1584

SMARTIES - Sweet & Sour Candy Rolls - SMARTIES CANDY COMPANY; *pg.* 1861, *pg.* 1127

SMARTIES LOLLIES - Sweet & Sour Lollipops - SMARTIES CANDY COMPANY; *pg.* 1861, *pg.* 1127

SMARTIES NECKLACES - Sweet & Sour Beaded Pieces - SMARTIES CANDY COMPANY; *pg.* 1861, *pg.* 1127

SMARTJUICE - Lighting System - PHILIPS SOLID-STATE LIGHTING SOLUTIONS; *pg.* 1303, *pg.* 806

SMARTKNIT - Socks - ALIMED, INC.; *pg.* 1490, *pg.* 816

SMARTLIFTS - Inground Lifts - ROTARY LIFT; *pg.* 216, *pg.* 694

SMARTLINE - Wireless Communication System - AT&T SOUTHEAST; *pg.* 1868, *pg.* 489

SMARTLINE - Card - BROWN & BIGELOW, INC.; *pg.* 1624, *pg.* 959

SMARTLINK - Software - AXEDA SYSTEMS INC.; *pg.* 359, *pg.* 819

SMARTLINK - Software - DYNISCO INSTRUMENTS LLC; *pg.* 1526, *pg.* 823

SMARTLINK - Fiber Optic Product - EMCORE CORPORATION; *pg.* 636, *pg.* 39

SMARTLINK - Software - HEALTHPORT, INC.; *pg.* 403, *pg.* 484

SMARTLINK - Valve - MAXON CORPORATION; *pg.* 1359, *pg.* 695

SMARTLIPO - Laser Body Sculpting Workstations - CYNOSURE, INC.; *pg.* 1521, *pg.* 858

SMARTLIST TO GO - Software - DATAVIZ, INC.; *pg.* 383, *pg.* 356

SMARTLITE - Dental Product - DENTSPLY INTERNATIONAL INC.; *pg.* 1522, *pg.* 1596

SMARTLITE - Soling Material - HUNTSMAN CORPORATION; *pg.* 1167, *pg.* 1758

SMARTLOAD - Micro Implant System - STRYKER

First page reference indicates Business Class Edition
Second page reference indicates Geographic Edition

CORPORATION; *pg.* 1598, *pg.* 894
SMARTLOCK - Quick Change Dumbbell System - ALLIANCE SPORTS GROUP, L.P.; *pg.* 1825, *pg.* 1698
SMARTLOCK - Container - PACTIV CORPORATION; *pg.* 1466, *pg.* 624
SMARTLOCK - Micro Implant System - STRYKER CORPORATION; *pg.* 1598, *pg.* 894
SMARTLOG - Correspondence Logging Software - HEALTHPORT, INC.; *pg.* 403, *pg.* 484
SMARTMAILER - Software - PITNEY BOWES INC.; *pg.* 454, *pg.* 376
SMARTMAILER 7 - Mail Management Software - PITNEY BOWES INC.; *pg.* 454, *pg.* 376
SMARTMARK - Automatic Test Equipment - MCT WORLDWIDE LLC; *pg.* 653, *pg.* 939
SMARTMATCH - Microwave Matching Unit - MKS INSTRUMENTS, INC.; *pg.* 1362, *pg.* 781
SMARTMEDIA - Memory Card - LEXAR MEDIA, INC.; *pg.* 1262, *pg.* 146
SMARTMEDIA - Card Reader - PNY TECHNOLOGIES, INC.; *pg.* 455, *pg.* 1105
SMARTMIPS - Card - IMAGINATION TECHNOLOGIES; *pg.* 412, *pg.* 285
SMARTMIX - Fluid Handling System - GRACO, INC.; *pg.* 1342, *pg.* 935
SMARTMODULES - Modular Building Block - ADEPT TECHNOLOGY, INC.; *pg.* 1310, *pg.* 182
SMARTMONEY - Magazine - THE HEARST CORPORATION; *pg.* 1649, *pg.* 1239
SMARTNET - Software - CISCO SYSTEMS, INC.; *pg.* 372, *pg.* 240
SMARTOCI - Search Engine - NETSOL TECHNOLOGIES, INC.; *pg.* 1270, *pg.* 56
SMARTOUCH - Software - CRESTRON ELECTRONICS INC.; *pg.* 631, *pg.* 1116
SMARTPACK - Lighting Equipment - ELECTRONIC THEATRE CONTROLS, INC.; *pg.* 1296, *pg.* 1872
SMARTPAK - Wrapping & Packaging Materials - SEALED AIR CORPORATION; *pg.* 1468, *pg.* 1058
SMARTPAPER - Manual - XEROX CORPORATION; *pg.* 494, *pg.* 365
SMARTPARTNER - Software - HEALTHPORT, INC.; *pg.* 403, *pg.* 484
SMARTPATH - Service - AT&T SOUTHEAST; *pg.* 1868, *pg.* 489
SMARTPATH - Computer Software - AVAGO TECHNOLOGIES; *pg.* 358, *pg.* 238
SMARTPAY - Telecommunication Product - VERISIGN, INC.; *pg.* 488, *pg.* 1799
SMARTPINK - Animal Nutritional Supplements - SMARTPAK EQUINE, LLC; *pg.* 1482, *pg.* 834
SMARTPLATE - Water Heaters - AERCO INTERNATIONAL INC.; *pg.* 1068, *pg.* 1142
SMARTPLATE - Software - HURST CHEMICAL COMPANY; *pg.* 1168, *pg.* 174
SMARTPLUS - Software - NIELSEN AUDIO; *pg.* 446, *pg.* 768
SMARTPOWER - Automatic Power-Off Mechanism - COBRA ELECTRONICS CORPORATION; *pg.* 629, *pg.* 572
SMARTPOWER - Microwave Power Generator - MKS INSTRUMENTS, INC.; *pg.* 1362, *pg.* 781
SMARTPOWER - Drive Management System - WESTERN DIGITAL CORPORATION; *pg.* 492, *pg.* 118
SMARTPRESENTER - Software - CRESTRON ELECTRONICS INC.; *pg.* 631, *pg.* 1116
SMARTPRESS - Printer - XEROX CORPORATION; *pg.* 494, *pg.* 365
SMARTPRESS PRODUCTION CONSULTA - Software - XEROX CORPORATION; *pg.* 494, *pg.* 365
SMARTPRESS SERVICES - Software - XEROX CORPORATION; *pg.* 494, *pg.* 365
SMARTPRESS TECHNOLOGY - Printer - XEROX CORPORATION; *pg.* 494, *pg.* 365
SMARTPRO - Intelligent Network UPS Systems - TRIPPE MANUFACTURING COMPANY; *pg.* 220, *pg.* 592
SMARTPROBE - High Purity Material Delivery Equipment - ATMI, INC.; *pg.* 1314, *pg.* 342
SMARTPROS ADVANTAGE - Training Service - SMARTPROS LTD.; *pg.* 1281, *pg.* 1166
SMARTPROS CONSULTING - Training Service - SMARTPROS LTD.; *pg.* 1281, *pg.* 1166
SMARTPROS ENGINEERING - Training Service - SMARTPROS LTD.; *pg.* 1281, *pg.* 1166
SMARTPROS FINANCIAL SERVICES - Training Service - SMARTPROS LTD.; *pg.* 1281, *pg.* 1166
SMARTPROS LEGAL - Training Service - SMARTPROS LTD.; *pg.* 1281, *pg.* 1166
SMARTRACK - Premium Enclosures & Accessories - TRIPPE MANUFACTURING COMPANY; *pg.* 220, *pg.* 592
SMARTRADIO - Computer Products - BROADCOM CORPORATION; *pg.* 364, *pg.* 108
SMARTRECORD - Software - CTI GROUP HOLDINGS INC.; *pg.* 381, *pg.* 684
SMARTRECTIFIER - Power Semiconductor Device - INTERNATIONAL RECTIFIER CORPORATION; *pg.* 647, *pg.* 80
SMARTREFLEX - Silicon, Circuit Design & Software - TEXAS INSTRUMENTS INCORPORATED; *pg.* 679, *pg.* 1688
SMARTREPORTS - Reporting Tool - NIELSEN AUDIO; *pg.* 446, *pg.* 768
SMARTRESPONSE - Software - VITRIA TECHNOLOGY, INC.; *pg.* 490, *pg.* 289
SMARTRIDER - Infant Carrier - INFANTINO, LLC; *pg.* 957, *pg.* 203
SMARTRIP - Rechargeable Farecard - WASHINGTON METROPOLITAN AREA TRANSIT AUTHORITY; *pg.* 1930, *pg.* 407
SMARTS - Software - EMC CORPORATION; *pg.* 391, *pg.* 825
SMARTSCAN - Laser Delivery Device - AMERICAN MEDICAL SYSTEMS, INC.; *pg.* 1399, *pg.* 238
SMARTSCHEDULE - Remote Schedule - ST. JUDE MEDICAL, INC.; *pg.* 1596, *pg.* 963
SMARTSECTOR - Software - SYMANTEC CORPORATION; *pg.* 478, *pg.* 161
SMARTSELECT - Health Coverage Plan - HUMANA, INC.; *pg.* 1204, *pg.* 734
SMARTSEND - Software - XEROX CORPORATION; *pg.* 494, *pg.* 365
SMARTSHADER - Graphics Card - ADVANCED MICRO DEVICES, INC.; *pg.* 613, *pg.* 282
SMARTSHIELD - Tape Autoloader - QUANTUM CORPORATION; *pg.* 458, *pg.* 250
SMARTSIDE - Siding - LOUISIANA-PACIFIC CORPORATION; *pg.* 94, *pg.* 1652
SMARTSIZE - Software - XEROX CORPORATION; *pg.* 494, *pg.* 365
SMARTSLIP - Needle Card - BECTON, DICKINSON & COMPANY; *pg.* 1501, *pg.* 1068
SMARTSOFT - Software - ELECTRONIC THEATRE CONTROLS, INC.; *pg.* 1296, *pg.* 1872
SMARTSOLUTIONS - CD-ROM-Based Product Catalog - KAWNEER COMPANY, INC.; *pg.* 90, *pg.* 537
SMARTSORT - Automatic Test Equipment - MCT WORLDWIDE LLC; *pg.* 653, *pg.* 939
SMARTSPAN - Software - CIENA CORPORATION; *pg.* 628, *pg.* 771
SMARTSPEC - Software - BIO-RAD LABORATORIES, INC.; *pg.* 1504, *pg.* 101
SMARTSPEND - Software System - CTI GROUP HOLDINGS INC.; *pg.* 381, *pg.* 684
SMARTSTART - Underwriting Life Insurance & Loan Service - AMERICAN AUTOMOBILE ASSOCIATION; *pg.* 1190, *pg.* 429
SMARTSTART - Medical Device - RESMED INC.; *pg.* 1589, *pg.* 207
SMARTSTEAM - Boilerless Steamer - UNIFIED BRANDS INC.; *pg.* 1385, *pg.* 970
SMARTSTEPS - Learning Toy - EVENFLO COMPANY, INC.; *pg.* 924, *pg.* 1470
SMARTSTREAM - Non-Contact Dispense Pumps - SPEEDLINE TECHNOLOGIES, INC.; *pg.* 1378, *pg.* 823
SMARTSTRIP - Labeling System - SMEAD MANUFACTURING COMPANY; *pg.* 470, *pg.* 926
SMARTSTYLE - Hair Salons - REGIS CORPORATION; *pg.* 521, *pg.* 941
SMARTSUCTION - Surgical Suction System - HAEMONETICS CORPORATION; *pg.* 1538, *pg.* 802
SMARTSUITE - Health Coverage Plan - HUMANA, INC.; *pg.* 1204, *pg.* 734
SMARTSUPPORT - Software - CIENA CORPORATION; *pg.* 628, *pg.* 771
SMARTSWITCH - Lighting Equipment - ELECTRONIC THEATRE CONTROLS, INC.; *pg.* 1296, *pg.* 1872
SMARTSYNC - Synchronized Ventilation Technology - SECHRIST INDUSTRIES, INC.; *pg.* 1593, *pg.* 43
SMARTTABLE - Optical Table System - NEWPORT CORPORATION; *pg.* 1424, *pg.* 114
SMARTTARGET - Collection Services Software - MICROBILT CORPORATION; *pg.* 782, *pg.* 534
SMARTTECH - Software - WEBEX COMMUNICATIONS, INC.; *pg.* 491, *pg.* 270
SMARTTEMP - Therapy System - KAZ, INC.; *pg.* 58, *pg.* 844
SMARTTOOL - Electronic Levels - M-D BUILDING PRODUCTS, INC.; *pg.* 95, *pg.* 1486
SMARTTOOLS - Optical Networking System - CIENA CORPORATION; *pg.* 628, *pg.* 771
SMARTTOTE - Box - PACTIV CORPORATION; *pg.* 1466, *pg.* 624
SMARTTOUCH - Camera Accessories - GRASS VALLEY, INC.; *pg.* 641, *pg.* 164
SMARTTOUCH - Nylon Hook & Loop - YKK CORPORATION OF AMERICA; *pg.* 699, *pg.* 536
SMARTTRAK - Automatic Test Equipment - MCT WORLDWIDE LLC; *pg.* 653, *pg.* 939
SMARTTRAK - Label - WEBER PACKAGING SOLUTIONS, INC.; *pg.* 491, *pg.* 554
SMARTTRAK IBIS - Equipment - MCT WORLDWIDE LLC; *pg.* 653, *pg.* 939
SMARTTRAK SOFTWARE SUITE - Software - MCT WORLDWIDE LLC; *pg.* 653, *pg.* 939
SMARTTROAE - Oto-acoustic Emissions Equipment - INTELLIGENT HEARING SYSTEMS CORP.; *pg.* 1546, *pg.* 443
SMARTUNE - Software - SYMANTEC CORPORATION; *pg.* 478, *pg.* 161
SMARTVANE - Pressure Compensated Pump With Electro-Hydraulic Controls - BOSCH REXROTH CORPORATION; *pg.* 1319, *pg.* 1516
SMARTVENT - Cookware - PACTIV CORPORATION; *pg.* 1466, *pg.* 624
SMARTVERIFY - Tape Drive - QUANTUM CORPORATION; *pg.* 458, *pg.* 250
SMARTVEST - Airway Clearance System - ELECTROMED, INC.; *pg.* 1527, *pg.* 951
SMARTVIEW - Machine Vision System - COGNEX CORPORATION; *pg.* 1406, *pg.* 834
SMARTVIEW - Internet Services - YAHOO! INC.; *pg.* 1289, *pg.* 289
SMARTVISION - Led Display - ANC SPORTS ENTERPRISES, LLC; *pg.* 1825, *pg.* 1325
SMARTVISION - Software - ATS AUTOMATION TOOLING SYSTEMS INC.; *pg.* 355, *pg.* 1919
SMARTVISION - Video Screens & Displays - LSI SACO TECHNOLOGIES, INC.; *pg.* 652, *pg.* 1955
SMARTWALL - Furniture - ETHAN ALLEN INTERIORS INC.; *pg.* 924, *pg.* 343
SMARTWARE - Software - IRIDEX CORPORATION; *pg.* 648, *pg.* 160
SMARTWATER - Distilled Bottled Water - ENERGY BRANDS, INC.; *pg.* 854, *pg.* 1227
SMARTWATER - Water Replacement Filters - GENERAL ELECTRIC COMPANY; *pg.* 1297, *pg.* 347
SMARTWAVE - Stand Alone AC/DC Power Source - AMETEK PROGRAMMABLE POWER, INC.; *pg.* 616, *pg.* 200
SMARTWAVE - Coffee Brewer - BUNN-O-MATIC CORPORATION; *pg.* 53, *pg.* 661
SMARTWEAR - Protective Apparel - ALPHA PRO TECH, LTD.; *pg.* 1492, *pg.* 1922
SMARTWINDOW - Medical Product - HOLOGIC, INC.; *pg.* 1416, *pg.* 784
SMARTWIPER - Control Circuitry - MAXIM INTEGRATED PRODUCTS, INC.; *pg.* 653, *pg.* 247
SMARTWIRE - Packaging Machinery - SEALED AIR CORPORATION; *pg.* 1468, *pg.* 1058
SMARTWORKPLACE - Management Consulting Services - COMPUTER SCIENCES CORPORATION; *pg.* 378, *pg.* 1780
SMARTWORKS - Software - HEALTHPORT, INC.; *pg.* 403, *pg.* 484
SMARTWORKS - Furniture - HOOKER FURNITURE CORPORATION; *pg.* 928, *pg.* 1788
SMARTXCHANGE - Software - LAPLINK SOFTWARE, INC.; *pg.* 426, *pg.* 1815
SMARTY DISH - Detergent - METHOD PRODUCTS INC.; *pg.* 332, *pg.* 223
SMARTYARD - Goods Transportation - CANADIAN NATIONAL RAILWAY COMPANY; *pg.* 1902, *pg.* 1953
SMARTZONE - Chocolate Candy - THE HERSHEY CO.; *pg.* 1855, *pg.* 1538
SMASH! PLASTIC - Liquid Plastic - SMOOTH-ON INC.; *pg.* 111, *pg.* 1528
'SMATH - Game - PRESSMAN TOY CORPORATION; *pg.* 965, *pg.* 1734
SMC-FLEX - Motor Controller - ROCKWELL AUTOMATION,

INC.; pg. 668, pg. 1880
SMD - Power Fuse - S&C ELECTRIC COMPANY; pg. 1305, pg. 589
SMD-20 - Power Fuse - S&C ELECTRIC COMPANY; pg. 1305, pg. 589
SMD-40 - Power Fuse - S&C ELECTRIC COMPANY; pg. 1305, pg. 589
SMEAD - Classification Folder - SMEAD MANUFACTURING COMPANY; pg. 470, pg. 926
SMF-28 - Glass & Ceramic Material - CORNING INCORPORATED; pg. 1122, pg. 1154
SMF-28E - Optical Fiber - CORNING CABLE SYSTEMS LLC; pg. 1407, pg. 1378
SMF-28E - Optical Fiber - CORNING INCORPORATED; pg. 1122, pg. 1154
SMF-28E+ - Glass & Ceramic Material - CORNING INCORPORATED; pg. 1122, pg. 1154
SMG II - Laser Marking Device - ROFIN-SINAR TECHNOLOGIES, INC.; pg. 668, pg. 904
SMI - Software - EAGLE POINT SOFTWARE CORPORATION; pg. 389, pg. 707
SMIDGEN - Knife - BUCK KNIVES, INC.; pg. 1828, pg. 550
SMILE BRANDS - Dental Services - SMILE BRANDS GROUP INC.; pg. 1594, pg. 116
SMILE SCRUB - Surgical Grade Aerosol Antibacterial Foam Soap - MUELLER SPORTS MEDICINE, INC.; pg. 1570, pg. 1887
SMILES FOR EVERYONE - Slogan - SMILE BRANDS GROUP INC.; pg. 1594, pg. 116
SMILESAVER - Safety Product - VENTURI, INC.; pg. 1606, pg. 910
SMILEWORKS - Dental Marketing Service - FUTUREDONTICS, INC.; pg. 1532, pg. 131
SMILEY - Cookies & Cookie Face - EAT'N PARK HOSPITALITY GROUP; pg. 1728, pg. 1539
SMILEY CENTRAL - Online Services - IAC/INTERACTIVECORP; pg. 292, pg. 1242
SMILING FACES. BEAUTIFUL PLACES - Slogan - SOUTH CAROLINA PARKS RECREATION & TOURISM; pg. 1005, pg. 1614
SMINT - Candy - SPANGLER CANDY COMPANY; pg. 1862, pg. 1407
SMIRNOFF - Vodka - DIAGEO NORTH AMERICA, INC.; pg. 1961, pg. 361
SMIRNOFF BLACK - Vodka - DIAGEO NORTH AMERICA, INC.; pg. 1961, pg. 361
SMIRNOFF CITRUS TWIST - Vodka - DIAGEO NORTH AMERICA, INC.; pg. 1961, pg. 361
SMITH & DAVIS - Medical Product - GF HEALTH PRODUCTS, INC.; pg. 1535, pg. 508
SMITH & FORGE - Hard Cider - MILLERCOORS; pg. 254, pg. 1877
SMITH & HAWKEN - Lawn Care Products - THE SCOTTS MIRACLE-GRO COMPANY; pg. 1799, pg. 1459
SMITH & WESSON - Firearms - SMITH & WESSON HOLDING CORPORATION; pg. 1845, pg. 846
SMITH+NOBLE - Online Gift Store - IAC/INTERACTIVECORP; pg. 292, pg. 1242
SMITHEREEN - Exterminators - SMITHEREEN PEST MANAGEMENT SERVICES; pg. 1800, pg. 638
SMITHFIELD - Meats - SMITHFIELD FOODS, INC.; pg. 896, pg. 1806
SMITHFIELD PREMIUM - Food Products - SMITHFIELD FOODS, INC.; pg. 896, pg. 1806
SMITHS - Potato Chips - FRITO-LAY NORTH AMERICA, INC.; pg. 1853, pg. 1730
SMITH'S - Supermarket - THE KROGER CO.; pg. 1025, pg. 1416
SMITHS - Food & Beverage - PEPSICO, INC.; pg. 259, pg. 1327
SMITHS SENSATIONS - Potato Snack - FRITO-LAY NORTH AMERICA, INC.; pg. 1853, pg. 1730
SMITHSONIAN - Monthly Magazine of Culture, History & Natural Science - SMITHSONIAN MAGAZINE; pg. 1687, pg. 404
SMITTIN - Footwear - STEVEN MADDEN, LTD.; pg. 1819, pg. 1176
SMJ BLOWER - Blower - ECLIPSE INC.; pg. 1332, pg. 655
SML-20 - Power Fuse - S&C ELECTRIC COMPANY; pg. 1305, pg. 589
SMM 106 - Wireless Microphone w/Microphone Receiver & Antenna - THE SINGING MACHINE COMPANY, INC.; pg. 674, pg. 426
SMM 107 - Wireless Microphone Pack - THE SINGING MACHINE COMPANY, INC.; pg. 674, pg. 426
SMM 111 - Headset Microphone - THE SINGING MACHINE COMPANY, INC.; pg. 674, pg. 426
SMM 112 - Wireless Microphone Headset - THE SINGING MACHINE COMPANY, INC.; pg. 674, pg. 426
SMM 117 - Karaoke Converter Accessory Pack - THE SINGING MACHINE COMPANY, INC.; pg. 674, pg. 426
SMM 205 - Dynamic Microphone - THE SINGING MACHINE COMPANY, INC.; pg. 674, pg. 426
SMOKE - On-Line Nonlinear Creative Editing & Finishing Solution - AUTODESK INC.; pg. 356, pg. 257
SMOKE - Footwear - OAKLEY, INC.; pg. 1840, pg. 86
SMOKE - Office Furniture - STEELCASE INC.; pg. 475, pg. 889
SMOKE CUTTER - Flashlight - STREAMLIGHT INC.; pg. 1306, pg. 1527
SMOKE ELIMINATOR - Air Conditioning System - TRION, INC.; pg. 682, pg. 1390
SMOKE MASTER - Plastic Casing - VISKASE COMPANIES, INC.; pg. 1471, pg. 599
SMOKE RING - Footwear - OAKLEY, INC.; pg. 1840, pg. 86
SMOKE SHARK - Electrosurgery Generators & Accessories - BOVIE MEDICAL CORPORATION; pg. 1402, pg. 1178
SMOKE STAR - Vaporizer - VAPOR CORP.; pg. 61, pg. 427
SMOKE TEST - Smoke Detector Tester - CRC INDUSTRIES, INC.; pg. 329, pg. 1590
SMOKEATER - Automotive Cleaner - DELTA FOREMOST CHEMICAL CORPORATION; pg. 1155, pg. 1642
SMOKEBLOC - Flame Retardants - CHEMTURA CORPORATION; pg. 1152, pg. 355
SMOKED YOUNG - Poultry Product - PILGRIM'S PRIDE CORPORATION; pg. 889, pg. 330
SMOKEHOUSE - Almonds - BLUE DIAMOND GROWERS; pg. 840, pg. 195
SMOKERS EXPRESS - Convenience Stores - THE PANTRY, INC.; pg. 1029, pg. 1360
SMOKERS' OUTPOST - Cigarette Waste Receptacle - THE PROTECTOSEAL COMPANY; pg. 1370, pg. 556
SMOKESHIELD - Smoke & Draft Control Doors - CORNELL IRON WORKS, INC.; pg. 77, pg. 1554
SMOKEVAC - Medical Device - C.R. BARD, INC.; pg. 1519, pg. 1094
SMOKEY BEAR - Forest Fire Campaign - THE ADVERTISING COUNCIL, INC.; pg. 125, pg. 1187
SMOKEY JOE - Gas Grill - WEBER-STEPHEN PRODUCTS LLC; pg. 62, pg. 650
SMOKEY MOUNTAIN COOKER - Gas Grill - WEBER-STEPHEN PRODUCTS LLC; pg. 62, pg. 650
SMOKIE GRILL - Food Product - ADVANCEPIERRE FOODS, INC.; pg. 1714, pg. 1409
SMOKIN' HOT 9'S - Lottery Game - IDAHO LOTTERY; pg. 995, pg. 547
SMOK'N IN HAVANA - Nail Care Product - OPI PRODUCTS INC.; pg. 518, pg. 167
SMOKREST - Processed Pork Products - AMERICAN FOODS GROUP, LLC; pg. 837, pg. 1859
SMOKY - Barbecue Sauce - LOUIS MAULL COMPANY; pg. 875, pg. 999
SMOKY CHIPOTLE CRISPY - Fried Chicken - KFC CORPORATION; pg. 1733, pg. 735
SMOOTH - Lip Color - THE BONNE BELL COMPANY; pg. 502, pg. 1480
SMOOTH - Flushometer - SLOAN VALVE COMPANY; pg. 1062, pg. 613
SMOOTH & TASTY - Slogan - YOCREAM INTERNATIONAL INC.; pg. 1039, pg. 1508
SMOOTH-CAST - Liquid Plastic - SMOOTH-ON INC.; pg. 111, pg. 1528
SMOOTH EDGE - Kitchen Appliance - HAMILTON BEACH BRANDS, INC.; pg. 56, pg. 1783
SMOOTH GLIDE - Swivel - GRACO, INC.; pg. 1342, pg. 935
SMOOTH-ON - Liquid Plastic - SMOOTH-ON INC.; pg. 111, pg. 1528
SMOOTH PERFORMANCE - Lingerie - LANE BRYANT; pg. 1776, pg. 1441
SMOOTH RESULT - Age Minimizing Pressed Powder - MAYBELLINE LLC; pg. 516, pg. 1257
SMOOTH-SIL - Liquid Rubber - SMOOTH-ON INC.; pg. 111, pg. 1528
SMOOTH-STAR - Fiberglass Exterior Doors - THERMA-TRU CORP.; pg. 115, pg. 1462
SMOOTH TRANSITION DOK SYSTEM - Back Pain Reliever - RITE-HITE HOLDING CORPORATION; pg. 1372, pg. 1880
SMOOTHBEAM - Diode Skin Treatment Laser - CANDELA CORPORATION; pg. 1404, pg. 855
SMOOTHCRETE - Concrete Mix - TRINITY INDUSTRIES, INC.; pg. 116, pg. 1690
SMOOTHEDGE - Ceramic & Plastic Product - COORSTEK, INC.; pg. 77, pg. 330
SMOOTHEE - Lighting Fixtures - SWIVELIER CO., INC.; pg. 1307, pg. 1142
SMOOTHGRIP - Scissors - ACME UNITED CORPORATION; pg. 1040, pg. 346
SMOOTHIE - Shoe - AEROGROUP INTERNATIONAL, INC.; pg. 1803, pg. 1055
SMOOTHIE - Candy - BOYER CANDY COMPANY INC.; pg. 1851, pg. 1514
SMOOTHIE O - Food Equipment - GOLD MEDAL PRODUCTS CO.; pg. 55, pg. 1414
SMOOTHIE PEANUT BUTTER CUP - Confectionery - BOYER CANDY COMPANY INC.; pg. 1851, pg. 1514
SMOOTHIES - Frozen Fruit - CHIQUITA BRANDS INTERNATIONAL, INC.; pg. 847, pg. 1365
SMOOTHLINE - Glass & Ceramic Material - CORNING INCORPORATED; pg. 1122, pg. 1154
SMOOTHPEEL - Laser - CANDELA CORPORATION; pg. 1404, pg. 855
SMOOTHROAMING - Software - CITRIX SYSTEMS, INC.; pg. 375, pg. 424
SMOOTHS - Material - ROSCO LABORATORIES, INC.; pg. 1782, pg. 378
SMOOTHTRAK - Mower Tractor - EXCEL INDUSTRIES, INC.; pg. 1795, pg. 715
SMOOTHVISION - Graphics Card - ADVANCED MICRO DEVICES, INC.; pg. 613, pg. 282
SMOQUE - Filter & Lens - THE TIFFEN COMPANY LLC; pg. 1432, pg. 1165
SMORZ - Cereal - KELLOGG COMPANY; pg. 831, pg. 870
SMOSH.COM - Website - DEFYMEDIA; pg. 1237, pg. 1222
SMP - Motor Product - STANDARD MOTOR PRODUCTS, INC.; pg. 218, pg. 1176
SMP II - Laser Marking Device - ROFIN-SINAR TECHNOLOGIES, INC.; pg. 668, pg. 904
SMRTSYSTEM - Network Product - NER HOLDINGS INC.; pg. 444, pg. 1071
SMS - Title & Escrow Systems - CORELOGIC, INC.; pg. 1198, pg. 109
SMS-1 - Subwoofer Management System - VELODYNE ACOUSTICS, INC.; pg. 685, pg. 152
SMS CASI - Micro Measurement Product - SCHMITT INDUSTRIES, INC.; pg. 1374, pg. 1506
SMS LOCAL - Software - LOCAL.COM CORPORATION; pg. 1264, pg. 113
SMSFINDER - Turnkey SMS Server - MULTI-TECH SYSTEMS INC.; pg. 442, pg. 951
SMSREACH - Telecom Product - PREMIERE GLOBAL SERVICES, INC.; pg. 1275, pg. 518
SMSXPRESS - Cellular Service - NUMEREX CORP.; pg. 660, pg. 517
SMT - Aerosol Cleaner - TECH SPRAY, L.P.; pg. 1183, pg. 1659
SMU-20 - Fuse Units - S&C ELECTRIC COMPANY; pg. 1305, pg. 589
SMU-40 - Fuse Units - S&C ELECTRIC COMPANY; pg. 1305, pg. 589
SMUCKER'S PUCKERS - Candy - THE J.M. SMUCKER COMPANY; pg. 865, pg. 1468
SMUDGE FIXER - Nail Product - ORLY INTERNATIONAL, INC.; pg. 518, pg. 137
SMVG 610 - Vertical Load CD/CD+G Karaoke System with Built-in Video Camera - THE SINGING MACHINE COMPANY, INC.; pg. 674, pg. 426
SNA ACCESS SERVER - Web Tool - OPENCONNECT SYSTEMS, INC.; pg. 449, pg. 1685
SNA PRINT SERVER - Web Tool - OPENCONNECT SYSTEMS, INC.; pg. 449, pg. 1685
SNACK A JACKS - Snack Food - PEPSICO, INC.; pg. 259, pg. 1327
SNACK BAR - Cheese Products - TILLAMOOK COUNTY CREAMERY ASSOCIATION; pg. 901, pg. 1509
SNACK 'N SERVE - Baby Care Product - MUNCHKIN, INC.; pg. 964, pg. 300
SNACK OF THE MONTH - Continuity Plan - THE POPCORN FACTORY; pg. 1861, pg. 625
SNACK PACK - Food Product - CONAGRA FOODS, INC.; pg. 826, pg. 1014
SNACK TO SCHOOL - Continuity Plan - THE POPCORN FACTORY; pg. 1861, pg. 625
SNACK WRAP - Chicken Wrap - MCDONALD'S CORPORATION; pg. 1737, pg. 645

SNACKARITOS - Food Product - TACO JOHN'S INTERNATIONAL, INC.; *pg.* 1753, *pg.* 1901
SNACKBARZ - Snack Product - THE HERSHEY CO.; *pg.* 1855, *pg.* 1538
SNACKEES - Frozen Product - DAWN FOOD PRODUCTS, INC.; *pg.* 1018, *pg.* 893
SNACKER - Sandwich - KFC CORPORATION; *pg.* 1733, *pg.* 735
SNACKIN' CAKE - Food Product - GENERAL MILLS, INC.; *pg.* 828, *pg.* 933
SNACKIN' FRUITS - Fruit Pastry Bars - SCHULZE & BURCH BISCUIT COMPANY; *pg.* 894, *pg.* 589
SNACKMISER - Software - USA TECHNOLOGIES, INC.; *pg.* 815, *pg.* 1550
SNACKSTERS - Snacks - THE HERSHEY CO.; *pg.* 1855, *pg.* 1538
SNACKWICHES - Meat Sandwiches - BOB EVANS FARMS, LLC; *pg.* 841, *pg.* 1467
SNAIL STACKER - Baby Care Product - MUNCHKIN, INC.; *pg.* 964, *pg.* 300
SNAK JAR - Insulated Food Container - THERMOS L.L.C.; *pg.* 61, *pg.* 660
SNAK N' FRESH - Bakery Goods - TASTY BAKING COMPANY; *pg.* 1862, *pg.* 1571
SNAKE - Mechanical Anchor & Fastener - POWERS FASTENERS INC.; *pg.* 1059, *pg.* 1143
SNAKE EYES - Golf Equipment - GOLFSMITH INTERNATIONAL HOLDINGS, INC.; *pg.* 1835, *pg.* 1662
SNAKE EYES - Reconnaissance & Surveillance Apparatus - LOCKHEED MARTIN CORPORATION; *pg.* 229, *pg.* 762
SNAKEEYE - Thermal Switch - EXERGEN CORPORATION; *pg.* 1412, *pg.* 855
SNAP - Game - GAMEWRIGHT; *pg.* 953, *pg.* 836
SNAP - Software - IDEALAB, INC.; *pg.* 1258, *pg.* 180
SNAP - Diagnostic Product - IDEXX LABORATORIES, INC.; *pg.* 1543, *pg.* 753
SNAP! - Cleaning Chemical - ROCHESTER MIDLAND CORPORATION; *pg.* 334, *pg.* 1337
SNAP - Gasoline Additives, Sealers, Cleaners, Degreasers, Dressings & Driers - SHELL LUBRICANTS; *pg.* 217, *pg.* 1714
S.N.A.P - Molecular Biology Product - THERMO FISHER SCIENTIFIC INC.; *pg.* 1602, *pg.* 61
SNAP 3DX - Test Kit - IDEXX LABORATORIES, INC.; *pg.* 1543, *pg.* 753
SNAP 4DX - Test Kit - IDEXX LABORATORIES, INC.; *pg.* 1543, *pg.* 753
SNAP-A-TAG - Twist Tie Closure - BEDFORD INDUSTRIES, INC.; *pg.* 1453, *pg.* 967
SNAP-BACK - Wing Pulley - VAN GORP CORPORATION; *pg.* 1387, *pg.* 711
SNAP-CAP - Film Magazines - EASTMAN KODAK COMPANY; *pg.* 1408, *pg.* 1333
SNAP-CLAD - Metal Roofing - PETERSEN ALUMINUM CORPORATION; *pg.* 104, *pg.* 611
SNAP! CRACKLE! POP! - Slogan - KELLOGG COMPANY; *pg.* 831, *pg.* 870
SNAP EDR EXPRESS - Software - OVERLAND STORAGE, INC.; *pg.* 451, *pg.* 205
SNAP EDR STANDARD - Software - OVERLAND STORAGE, INC.; *pg.* 451, *pg.* 205
SNAP ENTERPRISE DATA REPLICATOR - Data Replication & Protection Software - OVERLAND STORAGE, INC.; *pg.* 451, *pg.* 205
SNAP EXPANSION S50 - Data Storage - OVERLAND STORAGE, INC.; *pg.* 451, *pg.* 205
SNAP-EZE - Plastic Bag - ELKAY PLASTICS COMPANY, INC.; *pg.* 1882, *pg.* 68
SNAP-EZE - Hair Accessories - STA-RITE GINNIE LOU, INC.; *pg.* 523, *pg.* 660
SNAP-EZE T-SHIRT BAGS - T-Shirt Bags - ELKAY PLASTICS COMPANY, INC.; *pg.* 1882, *pg.* 68
SNAP-FIT - Solvent & Roof Flashing - GENOVA PRODUCTS, INC.; *pg.* 83, *pg.* 875
SNAP-FIT - Paddle Blade - INTUITIVE SURGICAL, INC.; *pg.* 1546, *pg.* 286
SNAP FITNESS 24/7 - Fitness Club Franchise - LIFT BRANDS; *pg.* 557, *pg.* 920
SNAP-GRIP - Wire & Cable - THE ZIPPERTUBING COMPANY; *pg.* 1892, *pg.* 12
SNAP-IT-UP - Favorite Fleece Jackets - HABAND COMPANY, INC.; *pg.* 1772, *pg.* 1099
SNAP-JOINT - Pipe Couplings - VICTAULIC COMPANY; *pg.* 1066, *pg.* 1529
SNAP-LET - Hole Cutting Tool - VICTAULIC COMPANY; *pg.* 1066, *pg.* 1529
SNAP-LINK - Software - SNAP-ON INCORPORATED; *pg.* 1062, *pg.* 1862
SNAP-LOCK - Electrosurgical Devices - ANGIODYNAMICS, INC.; *pg.* 1495, *pg.* 1173
SNAP LOCK - Food Storage Bags - THE CLOROX COMPANY; *pg.* 327, *pg.* 169
SNAP-N-GO - Infant Car Seat - BABY TREND, INC.; *pg.* 916, *pg.* 173
SNAP-N-SAVE - Sliding Transfer Ben - ALIMED, INC.; *pg.* 1490, *pg.* 816
SNAP-N-SEAL - Compression Drop Connector - THOMAS & BETTS CORPORATION; *pg.* 680, *pg.* 1646
SNAP-ON - Metal Roofing - PETERSEN ALUMINUM CORPORATION; *pg.* 104, *pg.* 611
SNAP-ON - Hand Tools, Power Tools, Tool Storage Units & Diagnostic Equipment - SNAP-ON INCORPORATED; *pg.* 1062, *pg.* 1862
SNAP PACK - Nutritional Supplement - PHARMAVITE LLC; *pg.* 1584, *pg.* 167
SNAP SERVER - Network & Desktop Storage Appliances - OVERLAND STORAGE, INC.; *pg.* 451, *pg.* 205
SNAP SERVER 110 - Data Storage - OVERLAND STORAGE, INC.; *pg.* 451, *pg.* 205
SNAP SERVER 210 - Data Storage - OVERLAND STORAGE, INC.; *pg.* 451, *pg.* 205
SNAP SERVER 410 - Data Storage - OVERLAND STORAGE, INC.; *pg.* 451, *pg.* 205
SNAP SERVER 520 - Data Storage - OVERLAND STORAGE, INC.; *pg.* 451, *pg.* 205
SNAP SERVER 620 - Data Storage - OVERLAND STORAGE, INC.; *pg.* 451, *pg.* 205
SNAP SERVER 650 - Data Storage - OVERLAND STORAGE, INC.; *pg.* 451, *pg.* 205
SNAP SERVER MANAGER - Software - OVERLAND STORAGE, INC.; *pg.* 451, *pg.* 205
SNAP TITE - Snap Together Hobby Kits - REVELL; *pg.* 966, *pg.* 611
SNAP-TOP - Standoffs for Metal Sheets & PCB - PENN ENGINEERING & MANUFACTURING CORP.; *pg.* 1059, *pg.* 1525
SNAP TRACE - Heat Transfer Compound - THERMON AMERICAS INC.; *pg.* 1077, *pg.* 1744
SNAPACTION - Fluid Handling System - GRACO, INC.; *pg.* 1342, *pg.* 935
SNAPBACK - Application Feature - APPLE INC.; *pg.* 350, *pg.* 73
SNAPBACK - Electrode - GRACO, INC.; *pg.* 1342, *pg.* 935
SNAPCOLOR - Manual - XEROX CORPORATION; *pg.* 494, *pg.* 365
SNAPDRAGON - Mobile Devices - QUALCOMM INCORPORATED; *pg.* 1873, *pg.* 207
SNAPDRIVE - Software - NETAPP, INC.; *pg.* 444, *pg.* 287
SNAPICOIL - Harness System - WIREMOLD/LEGRAND; *pg.* 689, *pg.* 383
SNAPIMAGE - Software - EMC CORPORATION; *pg.* 391, *pg.* 825
SNAPLIGHT - Lights - CYALUME TECHNOLOGIES HOLDINGS, INC.; *pg.* 1295, *pg.* 856
SNAPLIST - Software - DATAVIZ, INC.; *pg.* 383, *pg.* 356
SNAPLOCK - Storage Product - HOME PRODUCTS INTERNATIONAL, INC.; *pg.* 1125, *pg.* 577
SNAPLOCK - Software - NETAPP, INC.; *pg.* 444, *pg.* 287
SNAPMANAGER - Software - NETAPP, INC.; *pg.* 444, *pg.* 287
SNAPMATE - Electronic Components - MOLEX INCORPORATED; *pg.* 655, *pg.* 628
SNAPMIRROR - Software - NETAPP, INC.; *pg.* 444, *pg.* 287
SNAPMOVER - Software - NETAPP, INC.; *pg.* 444, *pg.* 287
SNAPPER - Electronic Components - MOLEX INCORPORATED; *pg.* 655, *pg.* 628
SNAPPER HOSE CLAMP - Hose Clamp - HELLERMANNTYTON; *pg.* 642, *pg.* 1875
SNAPPLE - Non-Carbonated Soft Drink - DR PEPPER SNAPPLE GROUP, INC.; *pg.* 250, *pg.* 1729
SNAPPY - Footwear - P.W. MINOR & SON, INC.; *pg.* 1816, *pg.* 1140
SNAPPY - Latch - SOUTHCO, INC.; *pg.* 1063, *pg.* 1522
SNAPPY - Air Distribution Product - STANDEX INTERNATIONAL CORPORATION; *pg.* 60, *pg.* 1039
SNAPPY FITTINGS - PVC Fittings - KILLARK ELECTRIC; *pg.* 1300, *pg.* 998
SNAPQUOTES - Software - MONEY.NET, INC.; *pg.* 1268, *pg.* 1261
SNAPRESTORE - Software - NETAPP, INC.; *pg.* 444, *pg.* 287
SNAPS - Candy Product - AMERICAN LICORICE CO. INC.; *pg.* 1850, *pg.* 692
SNAPS - Snacks - SNYDER'S OF HANOVER, INC.; *pg.* 1862, *pg.* 1536
SNAPSHOT - Computer With Attitude Verification - HONEYWELL AEROSPACE ELECTRONIC SYSTEMS; *pg.* 228, *pg.* 17
SNAPSHOT - Software - NETAPP, INC.; *pg.* 444, *pg.* 287
SNAPSHOT - Software - OVERLAND STORAGE, INC.; *pg.* 451, *pg.* 205
SNAPSHOT - EMI Shielding - W.L. GORE & ASSOCIATES, INC.; *pg.* 122, *pg.* 388
SNAPSHOT UPGRADE FEATURE - Software - BMC SOFTWARE, INC.; *pg.* 362, *pg.* 1701
SNAPSURE - Software - EMC CORPORATION; *pg.* 391, *pg.* 825
SNAPSWAB - Cleaning Materials for Magnetic Tapes - EASTMAN KODAK COMPANY; *pg.* 1408, *pg.* 1333
SNAPTICKET - Stock Trading Tool - TD AMERITRADE HOLDING CORPORATION; *pg.* 808, *pg.* 1018
SNAPTRACE - Medical Equipment - CONMED CORPORATION; *pg.* 1517, *pg.* 1347
SNAPVALIDATOR - Software - NETAPP, INC.; *pg.* 444, *pg.* 287
SNAPVAULT - Software - NETAPP, INC.; *pg.* 444, *pg.* 287
SNAPVIEW - Software - EMC CORPORATION; *pg.* 391, *pg.* 825
SNAPWRAP - Healthcare Apparel - THE SALK COMPANY; *pg.* 1591, *pg.* 800
SNARF - Molecular Probe Product - THERMO FISHER SCIENTIFIC INC.; *pg.* 1602, *pg.* 61
SNAUSAGES - Pet Treats - BIG HEART PET BRANDS; *pg.* 1474, *pg.* 213
SNAZZY - Carpet - BEAULIEU GROUP, LLC; *pg.* 917, *pg.* 529
SNAZZY - Fabric - NEMSCHOFF, INC.; *pg.* 936, *pg.* 1890
SNC - Graphite Machining Center - MAKINO INC.; *pg.* 1358, *pg.* 1461
SNEAK PREVIEW - Video Catalog System - FLEXSTEEL INDUSTRIES, INC.; *pg.* 925, *pg.* 707
SNELLING & SNELLING - Franchisors - SNELLING STAFFING SERVICES; *pg.* 471, *pg.* 1686
SNELLING PERSONNEL SERVICES - Staffing Service - SNELLING STAFFING SERVICES; *pg.* 471, *pg.* 1686
SNICKERS - Candy Bar - MARS, INCORPORATED; *pg.* 1858, *pg.* 1792
SNIFF+ - Software - WIND RIVER SYSTEMS, INC.; *pg.* 493, *pg.* 38
SNIFFER - Software - NETSCOUT SYSTEMS, INC.; *pg.* 1270, *pg.* 858
SNIFFERSTAR - Chemical Sensor for Detecting Chemical Warfare Agents - LOCKHEED MARTIN CORPORATION; *pg.* 229, *pg.* 762
SNIFIT - Gas Analyzer - BACHARACH INC.; *pg.* 1400, *pg.* 1556
SNIFIT 40 - Carbon Monoxide Analyzer - BACHARACH INC.; *pg.* 1400, *pg.* 1556
SNIFIT 50 - Carbon Monoxide Analyzer - BACHARACH INC.; *pg.* 1400, *pg.* 1556
SNIPER - Electro Optical Weapon Targeting Devices - LOCKHEED MARTIN CORPORATION; *pg.* 229, *pg.* 762
SNIPER XR - Systems Integration & Aeronautics - LOCKHEED MARTIN CORPORATION; *pg.* 229, *pg.* 762
SNIPP - Footwear - STEVEN MADDEN, LTD.; *pg.* 1819, *pg.* 1176
SNMP - Software - WIND RIVER SYSTEMS, INC.; *pg.* 493, *pg.* 38
SNO BALLS - Snack Cakes - HOSTESS BRANDS LLC; *pg.* 1856, *pg.* 984
SNO BOL - Cleaner - CHURCH & DWIGHT CO., INC.; *pg.* 1153, *pg.* 1063
SNO-CAPS - Candy - NESTLE USA, INC.; *pg.* 883, *pg.* 96
SNO KONE - Food Equipment - GOLD MEDAL PRODUCTS CO.; *pg.* 55, *pg.* 1414
SNO-KONER - Ice Ball Machine - GOLD MEDAL PRODUCTS CO.; *pg.* 55, *pg.* 1414
SNO-PLOW - Ice Melter - MORGRO, INC.; *pg.* 1798, *pg.* 1759
SNO PRO - Snowmobile - ARCTIC CAT INC.; *pg.* 1705, *pg.* 953
SNO-THRO - Walk Behind Snow Throwers, Tractors with Snow-Thro Attachments - ARIENS COMPANY INC.; *pg.* 700, *pg.* 1855
SNOBOY - Fresh Fruit & Vegetables - FOOD SERVICES OF

AMERICA, INC.; *pg.* 856, *pg.* 21
SNODGRASS - Office Furniture - STEELCASE INC.; *pg.* 475, *pg.* 889
SNOKONETTE - Sno-Kone Machine - GOLD MEDAL PRODUCTS CO.; *pg.* 55, *pg.* 1414
SNOLITE - Ready-Mixed White Liquid Paints & Enamel - PPG INDUSTRIES, INC.; *pg.* 1445, *pg.* 1579
SNOOP - Plastic Tube - SWAGELOK COMPANY; *pg.* 1064, *pg.* 1473
SNOOP LOOP - Loop Diagnostics - VITESSE SEMICONDUCTOR CORPORATION; *pg.* 686, *pg.* 57
SNOOPER - Card Counting System - DATACARD CORPORATION; *pg.* 382, *pg.* 948
SNOOTZ MATH TREK - Educational Materials - SCHOLASTIC INC.; *pg.* 1683, *pg.* 1288
SNOQUALMIE FALLS - Food Product - CONTINENTAL MILLS, INC.; *pg.* 827, *pg.* 1845
SNORE BLOCKERS - Earplug - MCKEON PRODUCTS, INC.; *pg.* 1559, *pg.* 912
SNORKEL - Light Construction Equipment - TEXTRON INC.; *pg.* 235, *pg.* 1607
SNORKELPRO - Masks, Snorkles, Fins & Vests - JOHNSON OUTDOORS INC.; *pg.* 1837, *pg.* 1888
SNOTRACE - Heat Exchanger - THERMON AMERICAS INC.; *pg.* 1077, *pg.* 1744
SNOW - Magazine - BONNIER CORPORATION; *pg.* 1622, *pg.* 480
SNOW - Goggles - OAKLEY, INC.; *pg.* 1840, *pg.* 86
SNOW BUCKET - Material Handling Equipment - DEGELMAN INDUSTRIES LTD.; *pg.* 703, *pg.* 1962
SNOW CROSS - Goggles - OAKLEY, INC.; *pg.* 1840, *pg.* 86
SNOW KISSES - Pillow and Throw - HERITAGE LACE INC.; *pg.* 694, *pg.* 711
SNOW LEOPARD - Tea - PEET'S COFFEE & TEA, INC.; *pg.* 1029, *pg.* 85
SNOW PHOTO - Table Textile - HERITAGE LACE INC.; *pg.* 694, *pg.* 711
SNOW TIME - Pillow and Throw - HERITAGE LACE INC.; *pg.* 694, *pg.* 711
SNOW WARNING SERVICE - Weather Information - ACCUWEATHER, INC.; *pg.* 268, *pg.* 1587
SNOW WHITE - Anhydrous Calcium Sulfate Filler - USG CORPORATION; *pg.* 118, *pg.* 594
SNOWBASIN - Ski Resort - SINCLAIR OIL CORPORATION; *pg.* 984, *pg.* 1760
SNOWBOARDER - Game - ACTIVISION BLIZZARD, INC.; *pg.* 948, *pg.* 271
SNOWBOARDER - Magazine - RENTPATH, INC.; *pg.* 1680, *pg.* 538
SNOWDEN PENCER - Surgical Instrumentation - CARDINAL HEALTH, INC.; *pg.* 1512, *pg.* 1448
SNOWFLAKE - Lace Flag - HERITAGE LACE INC.; *pg.* 694, *pg.* 711
SNOWFLAKES - Footwear - PHOENIX FOOTWEAR GROUP, INC.; *pg.* 1815, *pg.* 60
SNOWFLOSS - Sauerkraut Canned Products - THE FREMONT COMPANY; *pg.* 856, *pg.* 1454
SNOWJET - Spray Nozzle - SPRAYING SYSTEMS CO.; *pg.* 1063, *pg.* 670
SNOWMAN - Kitchen Appliance - HAMILTON BEACH BRANDS, INC.; *pg.* 56, *pg.* 1783
SNOWMEN - Lace - HERITAGE LACE INC.; *pg.* 694, *pg.* 711
SNOWMOBILETRADERONLINE.COM - Advertising Website - DOMINION ENTERPRISES; *pg.* 1636, *pg.* 1796
SNOWNMAN - Lace Flag - HERITAGE LACE INC.; *pg.* 694, *pg.* 711
SNOW*TEX - Calcined Clay - U.S. SILICA COMPANY; *pg.* 1185, *pg.* 1849
SNP CREDITS - Online Services - SEQUENOM, INC.; *pg.* 1593, *pg.* 209
SNP MANAGER - Software - BIO-RAD LABORATORIES, INC.; *pg.* 1504, *pg.* 101
SNPACTIVE - Cosmetics - GENELINK, INC.; *pg.* 1533, *pg.* 438
SNPSTREAM - Testing Instrument System - BECKMAN COULTER, INC.; *pg.* 1402, *pg.* 48
SNUB-IT - Hangers - MOORE PUSH PIN CO.; *pg.* 441, *pg.* 1595
SNUFFLES - Bear - GUND, INC.; *pg.* 954, *pg.* 1056
SNUG - Denture Cushions - THE MENTHOLATUM COMPANY; *pg.* 1565, *pg.* 1320
SNUG - Software - SYNOPSYS, INC.; *pg.* 480, *pg.* 162
SNUG PLUG - Safety Product - VENTURI, INC.; *pg.* 1606, *pg.* 910
SNUG TREDS - Slippers - R.G. BARRY CORPORATION; *pg.* 1818, *pg.* 1470
SNUGGIE - Fleece Blanket with Sleeves - ALLSTAR PRODUCTS GROUP LLC; *pg.* 17, *pg.* 1166
SNUGGLE - Fabric Softener - THE SUN PRODUCTS CORPORATION; *pg.* 336, *pg.* 385
SNUGGLE- ME - Sleeping Bag - CARTER'S, INC.; *pg.* 21, *pg.* 491
SNUGGLES - Carpet - BEAULIEU GROUP, LLC; *pg.* 917, *pg.* 529
SNUGGLEWEAR - Underwear - HABAND COMPANY, INC.; *pg.* 1772, *pg.* 1099
SNUGLI - Soft Infant Carriers - EVENFLO COMPANY, INC.; *pg.* 924, *pg.* 1470
SNYDER OF BERLIN - Potato Chips & Snack Foods - PINNACLE FOODS GROUP LLC; *pg.* 889, *pg.* 1104
SNYDER'S - Breads - UNITED STATES BAKERY; *pg.* 907, *pg.* 1507
SNYDER'S OF HANOVER - Snacks - SNYDER'S OF HANOVER, INC.; *pg.* 1862, *pg.* 1536
SO CAPTURE - Software - SCAN-OPTICS, LLC; *pg.* 467, *pg.* 354
SO DESIGNER - Software - SCAN-OPTICS, LLC; *pg.* 467, *pg.* 354
SO-DRI - Paper Towel - GEORGIA-PACIFIC LLC; *pg.* 1458, *pg.* 507
SO-FLEX - Flexibilizer - SMOOTH-ON INC.; *pg.* 111, *pg.* 1528
SO FRESH - Mattress Freshener - SURCO PRODUCTS, INC.; *pg.* 336, *pg.* 1581
SO/SAN - Biocidal Fabric Softeners - STEPAN COMPANY; *pg.* 1182, *pg.* 643
SO SERIES SCANNERS - Hardware Product - SCAN-OPTICS, LLC; *pg.* 467, *pg.* 354
SO SOFT - Shoe - AEROGROUP INTERNATIONAL, INC.; *pg.* 1803, *pg.* 1055
SO-STRONG - Color Tint - SMOOTH-ON INC.; *pg.* 111, *pg.* 1528
SO YOU THINK YOU CAN DANCE - Dance Television Program - DICK CLARK PRODUCTIONS, INC.; *pg.* 281, *pg.* 273
SOABAR - Label Machinery Tags - AVERY DENNISON CORPORATION; *pg.* 1452, *pg.* 95
SOAK CITY - Waterpark - CEDAR FAIR, L.P.; *pg.* 537, *pg.* 1471
SOAP OPERA DIGEST/SOAP OPERA WEEKLY - Magazine - AMERICAN MEDIA, INC.; *pg.* 1615, *pg.* 410
SOAP OPERA WEEKLY - Magazine - RENTPATH, INC.; *pg.* 1680, *pg.* 538
SOAP-SHIELD - Lawn Care Product - GARDENS ALIVE!, INC.; *pg.* 1796, *pg.* 693
SOAP STAYTION - Antibacterial Hand Soap - THETFORD CORPORATION; *pg.* 337, *pg.* 867
SOAP WEB - Online Trading Services - MARKETAXESS HOLDINGS INC.; *pg.* 778, *pg.* 1256
SOAP.COM - Household Goods - QUIDSI, INC.; *pg.* 1276, *pg.* 1076
SOAPER SHELF - Soap Dispenser & Shelf - BOBRICK WASHROOM EQUIPMENT, INC.; *pg.* 1043, *pg.* 166
SOAR - Spectra Outcome Analysis Report; Health Related Quality of Life Survey - FRESENIUS MEDICAL CARE NORTH AMERICA; *pg.* 1531, *pg.* 851
SOARING WINGS - Video Game - INTERNATIONAL GAME TECHNOLOGY; *pg.* 957, *pg.* 1024
SOBANCO - Financial Services - THE SOUTHERN BANC COMPANY, INC.; *pg.* 804, *pg.* 5
SOBE - Beverages - PEPSICO, INC.; *pg.* 259, *pg.* 1327
SOBO - Beverages - THE COCA-COLA COMPANY; *pg.* 240, *pg.* 493
SOBU - Ceramic, Glass, Stone Tiles & Slabs - WALKER & ZANGER, INC.; *pg.* 119, *pg.* 281
SOC-IT - Controller - IMAGINATION TECHNOLOGIES; *pg.* 412, *pg.* 285
SOCAPEX - Connectors - AMPHENOL CORPORATION; *pg.* 616, *pg.* 381
SOCCER - Sport Product - FRANKLIN SPORTS, INC.; *pg.* 1834, *pg.* 847
SOCCER - Apparels - UNDER ARMOUR, INC.; *pg.* 49, *pg.* 759
SOCCER - Ceiling Fan - WESTINGHOUSE LIGHTING CORPORATION; *pg.* 687, *pg.* 1571
SOCCER JR. - Educational Materials - SCHOLASTIC INC.; *pg.* 1683, *pg.* 1288
SOCFAT - All Purpose Shortening - CARGILL LIMITED; *pg.* 1475, *pg.* 1914
SOCIAL OCCASION - Mothers Wear - ALFRED ANGELO, INC.; *pg.* 17, *pg.* 1532
SOCIALITE - Fabric - NEMSCHOFF, INC.; *pg.* 936, *pg.* 1890
SOCIALITE LIFE - Entertainment News Site - SPINMEDIA; *pg.* 1282, *pg.* 104
SOCIETY - The Periodical of Record in Social Science & Public Policy - TRANSACTION PUBLISHERS, INC.; *pg.* 1695, *pg.* 1109
SOCK MONKEY - Flannel Sheet Set - VERMONT COUNTRY STORE, INC.; *pg.* 1789, *pg.* 1766
SOCKETETHERNET IP - Communication Product - MULTI-TECH SYSTEMS INC.; *pg.* 442, *pg.* 951
SOCKETMODEM - Dial-up Modem - MULTI-TECH SYSTEMS INC.; *pg.* 442, *pg.* 951
SOCKETSCAN - Software - SOCKET MOBILE, INC.; *pg.* 471, *pg.* 164
SOCKETSLIC - Communication Product - MULTI-TECH SYSTEMS INC.; *pg.* 442, *pg.* 951
SOCKETWIRELESS - Communication Product - MULTI-TECH SYSTEMS INC.; *pg.* 442, *pg.* 951
SOCKITTOME - Fabric - NEMSCHOFF, INC.; *pg.* 936, *pg.* 1890
SOCOLATE - Specialty Fats - CARGILL LIMITED; *pg.* 1475, *pg.* 1914
SOCON SYSTEM - Spinal Fixation Systems Designed for Pedicle Screw Fixation - AESCULAP, INC.; *pg.* 1487, *pg.* 1521
SOCRATES - Software - CINCOM SYSTEMS, INC.; *pg.* 372, *pg.* 1411
SOCRATES - Telecollaboration System - INTUITIVE SURGICAL, INC.; *pg.* 1546, *pg.* 286
SOCSCAN - Software System - MENTOR GRAPHICS CORPORATION; *pg.* 432, *pg.* 1510
SODNET - Turf Reinforcement Netting - RSI HOME PRODUCTS; *pg.* 108, *pg.* 1381
SOE INSTITUTE - Systems Integration & Aeronautics - LOCKHEED MARTIN CORPORATION; *pg.* 229, *pg.* 762
SOEHENDRA DILATOR - Medical Device - COOK GROUP, INC.; *pg.* 1518, *pg.* 674
SOEHENDRA LITHOTRIPTOR - Medical Device - COOK GROUP, INC.; *pg.* 1518, *pg.* 674
SOEHENDRA ROTARY DILATOR - Medical Device - COOK GROUP, INC.; *pg.* 1518, *pg.* 674
SOF-FOAM - Healthcare Product - JOHNSON & JOHNSON; *pg.* 1549, *pg.* 1091
SOF-LEX - Discs, Polishing, Dental - 3M COMPANY; *pg.* 1142, *pg.* 956
SOF 'N-SOIL - Lawn & Garden Gypsum - USG CORPORATION; *pg.* 118, *pg.* 594
SOF SPUN - Crepe Soles for Shoes - THE GOODYEAR TIRE & RUBBER COMPANY; *pg.* 1883, *pg.* 1401
S.O.F. SYSTEM - Mattress Unit - KINGSDOWN, INC.; *pg.* 932, *pg.* 1383
SOF-T - Salt - CARGILL LIMITED; *pg.* 1475, *pg.* 1914
SOF-T - Socks - WIGWAM MILLS, INC.; *pg.* 15, *pg.* 1894
SOF T-VISION - Mattress & Box Spring - KINGSDOWN, INC.; *pg.* 932, *pg.* 1383
SOF-TOUCH - Coin Purse - BROWN & BIGELOW, INC.; *pg.* 1624, *pg.* 959
SOF-WAIRE - Medical Equipment - INVACARE CORPORATION; *pg.* 1546, *pg.* 1451
SOFA PLUS - Sleeper Mechanisms - LEGGETT & PLATT, INCORPORATED; *pg.* 933, *pg.* 974
SOFEMATE - Ice Chest & Beverage Cooler - IGLOO PRODUCTS CORPORATION; *pg.* 1126, *pg.* 1724
SOFGRIP - Professional Cutlery With Cushioned Handles - DEXTER-RUSSELL INC.; *pg.* 1123, *pg.* 844
SOFIA - Furniture - AMISCO INDUSTRIES LTD.; *pg.* 913, *pg.* 1958
SOFIA - Footwear - CAPEZIO BALLET MAKERS INC.; *pg.* 1805, *pg.* 1125
SOFINA - Skin Care - KAO BRANDS CO. INC.; *pg.* 513, *pg.* 1415
SOFINA AUBE - Makeup - KAO BRANDS CO. INC.; *pg.* 513, *pg.* 1415
SOFISTICARTS - Carts Designed to be Used in the Kitchen or Dining Room - ECOLAB INC.; *pg.* 329, *pg.* 960
SOFJOY - Shoes - ACUSHNET COMPANY; *pg.* 1824, *pg.* 818
SOFKEY - Elastomer Key Panel - TRANSICO INCORPORATED; *pg.* 682, *pg.* 49
SOFLENS - Contact Lens - BAUSCH & LOMB INCORPORATED; *pg.* 1401, *pg.* 1045
SOFLEX SE - Contact Lens - BAUSCH & LOMB INCORPORATED; *pg.* 1401, *pg.* 1045
SOFPORT - Contact Lenses & Insertion Systems - BAUSCH &

First page reference indicates Business Class Edition
Second page reference indicates Geographic Edition

LOMB INCORPORATED; *pg.* 1401, *pg.* 1045
SOFPULL - Paper Towel - GEORGIA-PACIFIC LLC; *pg.* 1458, *pg.* 507
SOFSTRETCH - Paper - NEENAH PAPER, INC.; *pg.* 1465, *pg.* 484
SOFT - Filter - THE TIFFEN COMPANY LLC; *pg.* 1432, *pg.* 1165
SOFT-AIRE - Clutches & Brakes - P/A INDUSTRIES, INC.; *pg.* 1367, *pg.* 339
SOFT & DRI - Deodorant - HENKEL CONSUMER GOODS; *pg.* 511, *pg.* 22
SOFT & FIRM - Skin Care - AVON PRODUCTS, INC.; *pg.* 500, *pg.* 1198
SOFT & GLOW - Skin Care - AVON PRODUCTS, INC.; *pg.* 500, *pg.* 1198
SOFT ANIMAL STACKERS - Toy - MUNCHKIN, INC.; *pg.* 964, *pg.* 300
SOFT BATCH - Cookies - KELLOGG COMPANY; *pg.* 831, *pg.* 870
SOFT BLOOM - Towels & Tissues - XPEDX; *pg.* 1473, *pg.* 1377
SOFT CARE - Personal Care Product - DIVERSEY, INC.; *pg.* 1123, *pg.* 1896
SOFT-CELL - Tray - PACTIV CORPORATION; *pg.* 1466, *pg.* 624
SOFT CHORD - Carpet - INTERFACE, INC.; *pg.* 695, *pg.* 512
SOFT-EDGE - Safety System - RITE-HITE HOLDING CORPORATION; *pg.* 1372, *pg.* 1880
SOFT FEEL - Leather Like Coating - RED SPOT PAINT & VARNISH CO., INC.; *pg.* 1446, *pg.* 679
SOFT-FIT - Mattress Pad - MEDLINE INDUSTRIES, INC.; *pg.* 1562, *pg.* 635
SOFT-FLEX - Blanket - PROGRESSIVE DYNAMICS, INC.; *pg.* 665, *pg.* 898
SOFT-FLO - Aerator - THE CHICAGO FAUCET COMPANY; *pg.* 1044, *pg.* 606
SOFT-FLO - Anti-Surge Eye Wash Heads - HAWS CORPORATION; *pg.* 56, *pg.* 1032
SOFT/FX - Filter & Lens - THE TIFFEN COMPANY LLC; *pg.* 1432, *pg.* 1165
SOFT GRIPS - Bath Organizer & Accessory - HOME PRODUCTS INTERNATIONAL, INC.; *pg.* 1125, *pg.* 577
SOFT HEAT - Coffee & Beverage Equipment - BUNN-O-MATIC CORPORATION; *pg.* 53, *pg.* 661
SOFT KLEEN - Dry Cleaning & Laundry Product - ADCO, INC.; *pg.* 325, *pg.* 482
SOFT KLEEN XTRA - Charge Soap - ADCO, INC.; *pg.* 325, *pg.* 482
SOFT LOOK - Protective & Decorative Industrial & Automotive Coatings - PPG INDUSTRIES, INC.; *pg.* 1445, *pg.* 1579
SOFT-N-FRESH - Special Application Wipers - GEORGIA-PACIFIC LLC; *pg.* 1458, *pg.* 507
SOFT N INVITING - Carpet - BEAULIEU GROUP, LLC; *pg.* 917, *pg.* 529
SOFT 'N PERFECT - Foundation - LUZIER PERSONALIZED COSMETICS, INC.; *pg.* 515, *pg.* 978
SOFT N SAFE - Bare Floor Brush - BISSELL HOMECARE, INC.; *pg.* 52, *pg.* 887
SOFT N SURE - Skin Care Product - STERIS CORPORATION; *pg.* 1597, *pg.* 1464
SOFT NOTES - Casual Footwear - R.G. BARRY CORPORATION; *pg.* 1818, *pg.* 1470
SOFT SCOUR! - Household Scrubbing Sponge & Pad - 3M COMPANY; *pg.* 1142, *pg.* 956
SOFT SCRUB - Mild Abrasive Liquid Cleanser, Regular, with Bleach & Lemon Gel Formula - THE CLOROX COMPANY; *pg.* 327, *pg.* 169
SOFT SCRUB - Cleanser - HENKEL CONSUMER GOODS; *pg.* 511, *pg.* 22
SOFT SCULPTING SPRAY GEL - Hair Care Product - JOHN PAUL MITCHELL SYSTEMS; *pg.* 512, *pg.* 133
SOFT SENSE - Hand & Body Lotion - KAO BRANDS CO. INC.; *pg.* 513, *pg.* 1415
SOFT SET - Hair Setter - ANDIS COMPANY; *pg.* 498, *pg.* 1895
SOFT SHAPES - Toy And Game - INNOVATIVE USA, INC.; *pg.* 957, *pg.* 363
SOFT SHELL - Ear Warmer - 180S, LLC; *pg.* 1824, *pg.* 754
SOFT SHELL SATURDAY - Food Promotion - TACO JOHN'S INTERNATIONAL, INC.; *pg.* 1753, *pg.* 1901
SOFT-SHIELD - Low Closure Force EMI Gaskets - PARKER CHOMERICS; *pg.* 662, *pg.* 862
SOFT SHOULDERS - Bra & Shapewear - GLAMORISE FOUNDATIONS, INC.; *pg.* 25, *pg.* 1235
SOFT-SPAN - Knitted Sheet - MEDLINE INDUSTRIES, INC.; *pg.* 1562, *pg.* 635
SOFT SPOKES - Toss and Catch Game - SCHOOL-TECH, INC.; *pg.* 1844, *pg.* 866
SOFT SPORT - Sport Product - FRANKLIN SPORTS, INC.; *pg.* 1834, *pg.* 847
SOFT SPRAY - Hair Care Product - JOHN PAUL MITCHELL SYSTEMS; *pg.* 512, *pg.* 133
SOFT-START - Software - BIO-RAD LABORATORIES, INC.; *pg.* 1504, *pg.* 101
SOFT-STOP - Sensing System - RITE-HITE HOLDING CORPORATION; *pg.* 1372, *pg.* 1880
SOFT-STRIKE - Sport Product - FRANKLIN SPORTS, INC.; *pg.* 1834, *pg.* 847
SOFT SUPPLEX - Apparel - ATTITUDES IN DRESSING INC.; *pg.* 19, *pg.* 1057
SOFT-SURROUND - Fluid Handling System - GRACO, INC.; *pg.* 1342, *pg.* 935
SOFT TACO SUPREME - Beef Taco - TACO BELL CORP.; *pg.* 1752, *pg.* 117
SOFT TOP - Mousepad - ALLSOP, INC.; *pg.* 347, *pg.* 1817
SOFT TOP 2.0 - Frames - OAKLEY, INC.; *pg.* 1840, *pg.* 86
SOFT TOP 4.0 - Frames - OAKLEY, INC.; *pg.* 1840, *pg.* 86
SOFT TOUCH - Stuffed Animals - AMERICAN GREETINGS CORPORATION; *pg.* 1615, *pg.* 1428
SOFT-TOUCH - Rotary Hot Stamping System - ANDERSON & VREELAND, INC.; *pg.* 1616, *pg.* 1064
SOFT TOUCH - Agricultural Product - ARCHER-DANIELS-MIDLAND COMPANY; *pg.* 825, *pg.* 565
SOFT-TOUCH - Egg Collection System or Finger Collector - CTB INTERNATIONAL CORP.; *pg.* 850, *pg.* 695
SOFT TOUCH - Health & Beauty Product - DIXIE HEALTH, INC.; *pg.* 1524, *pg.* 535
SOFT TOUCH - Toiletries - THE GILLETTE COMPANY; *pg.* 509, *pg.* 795
SOFT TOUCH - Medical Product - UTAH MEDICAL PRODUCTS, INC.; *pg.* 1605, *pg.* 1752
SOFT-VU - Electrosurgical Devices - ANGIODYNAMICS, INC.; *pg.* 1495, *pg.* 1173
SOFT WASH - Healthcare Product - DERMA SCIENCES, INC.; *pg.* 1523, *pg.* 1111
SOFT YELLOW - Pillow and Throw - HERITAGE LACE INC.; *pg.* 694, *pg.* 711
SOFTAIDE - Robotic Product - HAMILTON CO., INC.; *pg.* 1415, *pg.* 1031
SOFTAIL - Motorcycle - HARLEY-DAVIDSON, INC.; *pg.* 178, *pg.* 1874
SOFTBACK - Sanding Sponge - 3M COMPANY; *pg.* 1142, *pg.* 956
SOFTCARE - Nonadhesive Sensors - MEDTRONIC; *pg.* 1563, *pg.* 183
SOFTCELL - Multicarrier Transceiver Chipset - ANALOG DEVICES, INC.; *pg.* 617, *pg.* 839
SOFTCHECK - Electrodes - CAS MEDICAL SYSTEMS, INC.; *pg.* 1513, *pg.* 339
SOFTCONNECT - Software - BIO-RAD LABORATORIES, INC.; *pg.* 1504, *pg.* 101
SOFTDENT - Software - EASTMAN KODAK COMPANY; *pg.* 1408, *pg.* 1333
SOFTEE - Medical Equipment - CONMED CORPORATION; *pg.* 1517, *pg.* 1347
SOFTENER CARE - Additive - CARGILL LIMITED; *pg.* 1475, *pg.* 1914
THE SOFTER SIDE OF SEARS - Tagline - SEARS HOLDINGS CORPORATION; *pg.* 1784, *pg.* 618
SOFTESSE - Protective Fabrics - E.I. DU PONT DE NEMOURS & COMPANY; *pg.* 1159, *pg.* 390
SOFTEX - Bath Mat - HENKEL CONSUMER ADHESIVES, INC.; *pg.* 403, *pg.* 1480
SOFTFEEL - Golf Ball - CALLAWAY GOLF COMPANY; *pg.* 1829, *pg.* 58
SOFTFONE - Chipset - ANALOG DEVICES, INC.; *pg.* 617, *pg.* 839
SOFTGRIP - Robotic Product - HAMILTON CO., INC.; *pg.* 1415, *pg.* 1031
SOFTIMAGE - 3D Animation Software - AUTODESK INC.; *pg.* 356, *pg.* 257
SOFTIMAGE XSI - Nonlinear Animation Solution - AVID TECHNOLOGY, INC.; *pg.* 622, *pg.* 804
SOFTINA - Dolls - THE GOLDBERGER COMPANY, LLC; *pg.* 954, *pg.* 1235
SOFTIP - Brush - THE WOOSTER BRUSH COMPANY; *pg.* 1450, *pg.* 1482
SOFTKINS - Sleepwear - HABAND COMPANY, INC.; *pg.* 1772, *pg.* 1099
SOFTLEAF - Tables - STEELCASE INC.; *pg.* 475, *pg.* 889
SOFTLINE - Eyeliner & Eyebrow Pencils - COVER GIRL COSMETICS; *pg.* 506, *pg.* 772
SOFTLINK - Software - PERKINELMER, INC.; *pg.* 1426, *pg.* 853
SOFTLIPS - Lip Protection - THE MENTHOLATUM COMPANY; *pg.* 1565, *pg.* 1320
SOFTLOGIX - Controller - ROCKWELL AUTOMATION, INC.; *pg.* 668, *pg.* 1880
SOFTMAX - Software - MOLECULAR DEVICES CORPORATION; *pg.* 1568, *pg.* 287
SOFTMOUSE - Hardware & Software - IMMERSION CORPORATION; *pg.* 413, *pg.* 246
SOFT'N FLUFFY - Bathroom Tissues & Towels - ORCHIDS PAPER PRODUCTS COMPANY; *pg.* 1465, *pg.* 1488
SOFT'N GENTLE - Bathroom Tissue - GEORGIA-PACIFIC LLC; *pg.* 1458, *pg.* 507
SOFTONE - Wrist & Ankle Weights - ALLIANCE SPORTS GROUP, L.P.; *pg.* 1825, *pg.* 1698
SOFTONES - Apparel - RELIABLE OF MILWAUKEE; *pg.* 698, *pg.* 1879
SOFTOP - Robotic Product - HAMILTON CO., INC.; *pg.* 1415, *pg.* 1031
SOFTOUCH - Wrist & Ankle Weights - ALLIANCE SPORTS GROUP, L.P.; *pg.* 1825, *pg.* 1698
SOFTOUCH - Furniture - NEUTRAL POSTURE, INC.; *pg.* 939, *pg.* 1669
SOFTPAY - Payment Software - VERIFONE SYSTEMS, INC.; *pg.* 487, *pg.* 251
SOFTPVR - Digital Video Product - HAUPPAUGE DIGITAL, INC.; *pg.* 402, *pg.* 1164
SOFTR - Fiber Glass Duct Product - OWENS CORNING; *pg.* 102, *pg.* 1476
SOFTSEAL-D - Disposable Respirator - MCR SAFETY; *pg.* 1422, *pg.* 1630
SOFTSEEK - Connector - WESTERN DIGITAL CORPORATION; *pg.* 492, *pg.* 118
SOFTSHEEN CARSON - Hair Care Products - L'OREAL USA; *pg.* 514, *pg.* 1252
SOFTSHOE - Internet Services - YAHOO! INC.; *pg.* 1289, *pg.* 289
SOFTSISAL - Carpet - INTERFACE, INC.; *pg.* 695, *pg.* 512
SOFTSOAP - Personal Care Product - COLGATE-PALMOLIVE COMPANY; *pg.* 504, *pg.* 1215
SOFTSPOON - Spoon - THE VOLLRATH COMPANY LLC; *pg.* 1139, *pg.* 1894
SOFTSTART - Robotic Product - HAMILTON CO., INC.; *pg.* 1415, *pg.* 1031
SOFTSTIX - Food Product - J&J SNACK FOODS CORPORATION; *pg.* 865, *pg.* 1107
SOFTSUEDE - Faux Finishing Product - THE SHERWIN-WILLIAMS COMPANY; *pg.* 1447, *pg.* 1435
SOFTSURV - Data Collection & Post Processing Software - NOVATEL INC.; *pg.* 1424, *pg.* 1904
SOFTSWEEP - Brush - ALLSOP, INC.; *pg.* 347, *pg.* 1817
SOFTTOUCH - Robotic Product - HAMILTON CO., INC.; *pg.* 1415, *pg.* 1031
SOFTTRACE - Medical Equipment - CONMED CORPORATION; *pg.* 1517, *pg.* 1347
SOFTUCK - Cones - SONOCO PRODUCTS COMPANY; *pg.* 1469, *pg.* 1619
SOFTVAC - Thermal Processing Equipment - SURFACE COMBUSTION, INC.; *pg.* 1077, *pg.* 1462
SOFTWALK - Women's Shoes - PHOENIX FOOTWEAR GROUP, INC.; *pg.* 1815, *pg.* 60
SOFTWARE - Software & Video - PUBLICATIONS & COMMUNICATIONS, INC.; *pg.* 1678, *pg.* 1665
SOFTWARE CAPITAL - Software - BMC SOFTWARE, INC.; *pg.* 362, *pg.* 1701
SOFTWARE DEVELOPMENT - Magazine - UNITED BUSINESS MEDIA LLC; *pg.* 1697, *pg.* 1177
SOFTWARE ETC. - Software Stores - BARNES & NOBLE, INC.; *pg.* 1619, *pg.* 1201
SOFTWARE MANAGEMENT - Software - AXEDA SYSTEMS INC.; *pg.* 359, *pg.* 819
SOFTWARE THAT NEVER WEARS OUT - Tagline - NETWORK SYSTEMS INTERNATIONAL, INC.; *pg.* 445, *pg.* 1375
SOFTWARE USAGE - Software - BMC SOFTWARE, INC.; *pg.* 362, *pg.* 1701
SOFTWEIGHER - Scales - PENNSYLVANIA SCALE COMPANY; *pg.* 1059, *pg.* 1546
SOFTWILL - Industrial Parts - UNIFIRST CORPORATION; *pg.* 50, *pg.* 860
SOFTWORKS - Personal Care Electrical Product - HELEN OF

TROY L.P.; *pg.* 511, *pg.* 1692
SOFTWORKS - Kitchen Tools - OXO; *pg.* 1058, *pg.* 1275
SOFTX - Medical Equipment - INVACARE CORPORATION; *pg.* 1546, *pg.* 1451
SOFTXHALE - Medical Equipment - INVACARE CORPORATION; *pg.* 1546, *pg.* 1451
SOFY - Software - MSC SOFTWARE CORPORATION; *pg.* 441, *pg.* 262
SOGAV - Valve - WOODWARD, INC.; *pg.* 122, *pg.* 329
SOGO - Chemical Detergent-Laundry - A.L. WILSON CHEMICAL CO.; *pg.* 325, *pg.* 1076
SOGO RECLAMATION SYSTEM - Laundry Stain Rewash - A.L. WILSON CHEMICAL CO.; *pg.* 325, *pg.* 1076
SOHO - Furniture - AMERICAN LEATHER LP; *pg.* 912, *pg.* 1673
SOHO - Rug - COURISTAN INC.; *pg.* 921, *pg.* 1067
SOHO - Furniture - ETHAN ALLEN INTERIORS INC.; *pg.* 924, *pg.* 343
SOHO - Ergonomic Seating - KNOLL, INC.; *pg.* 425, *pg.* 1527
SOHO - Chocolate - RUSSELL STOVER CANDIES, INC.; *pg.* 1861, *pg.* 986
SOHO - Coffee Blend - THE SECOND CUP LTD.; *pg.* 1749, *pg.* 1928
SOHO - Bicycle - TREK BICYCLE CORPORATION; *pg.* 1847, *pg.* 1896
SOHO - Ceramic Tile - WALKER & ZANGER, INC.; *pg.* 119, *pg.* 281
SOHO - Security Appliance - WATCHGUARD TECHNOLOGIES, INC.; *pg.* 491, *pg.* 1842
SOHO DELUXE - Watch - GEVRIL USA; *pg.* 6, *pg.* 1348
SOHO NICE TO MEET YOU - Nail Care Product - OPI PRODUCTS INC.; *pg.* 518, *pg.* 167
SOHO TWILL - Leather Product - COACH, INC.; *pg.* 3, *pg.* 1214
SOHOE - Footwear - STEVEN MADDEN, LTD.; *pg.* 1819, *pg.* 1176
SOIL & STAIN - Stain Remover - BLUE CROSS LABORATORIES; *pg.* 326, *pg.* 277
SOIL PEP - Mulch - MOUNTAIN WEST, LLC; *pg.* 98, *pg.* 550
SOIL RICH - Fertilizer Product - SYNAGRO TECHNOLOGIES, INC.; *pg.* 1800, *pg.* 759
SOIL-RX - Soil Analysis - THE F.A. BARTLETT TREE EXPERT COMPANY; *pg.* 1795, *pg.* 373
SOIL-STOP - Cleaning Product - HILLYARD, INC.; *pg.* 331, *pg.* 990
SOILAX - Laundry Soil-Out, Destainer, Neutralizer & Prep - ECOLAB INC.; *pg.* 329, *pg.* 960
SOILMASTER - Soil Conditioner - OIL-DRI CORPORATION OF AMERICA; *pg.* 1480, *pg.* 586
SOILMAX - Soil Stabilization Polymer - LINDSAY CORPORATION; *pg.* 1356, *pg.* 1016
SOILTEQ - Agricultural Equipment - AGCO CORPORATION; *pg.* 700, *pg.* 530
SOJOURN - Bath Product - KOHLER CO.; *pg.* 91, *pg.* 1862
SOK - Bath Product - KOHLER CO.; *pg.* 91, *pg.* 1862
SOKENBICHA - Soft Drink - THE COCA-COLA COMPANY; *pg.* 240, *pg.* 493
SOKREEM - Non-Dairy Sour Cream - BROUGHTON FOODS COMPANY; *pg.* 842, *pg.* 1458
SOL - Apparel - HANESBRANDS INC.; *pg.* 26, *pg.* 1394
SOL - Beverages - MOLSON COORS BREWING COMPANY; *pg.* 256, *pg.* 321
SOL Y ORO - Apparel - HANESBRANDS INC.; *pg.* 26, *pg.* 1394
SOLA - Ultra-Violet Thermal Processing System - LAM RESEARCH CORPORATION; *pg.* 1354, *pg.* 246
SOLA/HEVI-DUTY - Electrical Products - EMERSON INDUSTRIAL AUTOMATION; *pg.* 1296, *pg.* 657
SOLACE - Yoga Mat - HUGGER MUGGER YOGA PRODUCTS LLC; *pg.* 1836, *pg.* 1758
SOLACE - Medical Equipment - INVACARE CORPORATION; *pg.* 1546, *pg.* 1451
SOLACE - Bath Products - MOEN INCORPORATED; *pg.* 1056, *pg.* 1468
SOLAE - Soy Protein - E.I. DU PONT DE NEMOURS & COMPANY; *pg.* 1159, *pg.* 390
SOLAGE - Topical Solution - GALDERMA LABORATORIES, L.P.; *pg.* 1532, *pg.* 1695
SOLAMET - Conductor Composition - E.I. DU PONT DE NEMOURS & COMPANY; *pg.* 1159, *pg.* 390
SOLANA - Furniture - ASHLEY FURNITURE INDUSTRIES, INC.; *pg.* 914, *pg.* 1852
SOLANA - Footwear - COBIAN CORP.; *pg.* 1806, *pg.* 253
SOLANO - Gum - WM. WRIGLEY JR. COMPANY; *pg.* 1863, *pg.* 596
SOLAQUIN - Pharmaceutical Product - VALEANT PHARMACEUTICALS INTERNATIONAL; *pg.* 1605, *pg.* 1047
SOLAR - Reducing Apparel - ALLIANCE SPORTS GROUP, L.P.; *pg.* 1825, *pg.* 1698
SOLAR - Tool Steel - CARPENTER TECHNOLOGY CORPORATION; *pg.* 73, *pg.* 1584
SOLAR - Battery Charging Product - CLORE AUTOMOTIVE LLC; *pg.* 202, *pg.* 716
SOLAR - Visor - LUND INTERNATIONAL, INC.; *pg.* 211, *pg.* 526
SOLAR - Apparel - OAKLEY, INC.; *pg.* 1840, *pg.* 86
SOLAR - Turbine Products - SOLAR TURBINES INCORPORATED; *pg.* 1377, *pg.* 209
SOLAR - Orthopaedic Product - STRYKER CORPORATION; *pg.* 1598, *pg.* 894
SOLAR BLAST - Gaming Product - GLD PRODUCTS, INC.; *pg.* 1835, *pg.* 1882
SOLAR COMFORT - Heater - KAZ, INC.; *pg.* 58, *pg.* 844
SOLAR FLAIR - Tubular Sky Lights - ODL INCORPORATED; *pg.* 101, *pg.* 914
SOLAR FLARE - Paper - XEROX CORPORATION; *pg.* 494, *pg.* 365
SOLAR-FLO - Meter - BADGER METER, INC.; *pg.* 1401, *pg.* 1873
SOLAR FREEZE - Frozen Beverages - DIPPIN' DOTS LLC; *pg.* 853, *pg.* 739
SOLAR GREEN - Nutritional Supplement - NUTRACEUTICAL INTERNATIONAL CORPORATION; *pg.* 1576, *pg.* 1753
SOLAR LENS - Tubular Sky Lights - ODL INCORPORATED; *pg.* 101, *pg.* 914
SOLAR MAX - Clothing - MUSEUM OF SCIENCE AND INDUSTRY; *pg.* 565, *pg.* 583
SOLAR PLUS - Four Way Power Block - COLEMAN CABLE, INC.; *pg.* 1324, *pg.* 665
SOLAR SENSE - Skin Care Product - CCA INDUSTRIES, INC.; *pg.* 503, *pg.* 1114
SOLAR SHIELD - Sunglasses - FGX INTERNATIONAL, INC.; *pg.* 5, *pg.* 1608
SOLAR SUIT - Sauna Suit - ALLIANCE SPORTS GROUP, L.P.; *pg.* 1825, *pg.* 1698
SOLAR X-PUMP BLOCK - Solar Mixing System - TACO INCORPORATED; *pg.* 1077, *pg.* 1601
SOLARA - Wheelchair - INVACARE CORPORATION; *pg.* 1546, *pg.* 1451
SOLARA - Furniture - JOFCO INC.; *pg.* 931, *pg.* 691
SOLARA ION - Printer - GERBER SCIENTIFIC, INC.; *pg.* 1414, *pg.* 380
SOLARA LOUNGE - Office Furniture - JOFCO INC.; *pg.* 931, *pg.* 691
SOLARAM - Water Pump - CONERGY, INC.; *pg.* 1325, *pg.* 318
SOLARAY - Nutritional Product - NUTRACEUTICAL INTERNATIONAL CORPORATION; *pg.* 1576, *pg.* 1753
SOLARBAN - Glass Product - PPG INDUSTRIES, INC.; *pg.* 1445, *pg.* 1579
SOLARBRONZE - Glass Product - PPG INDUSTRIES, INC.; *pg.* 1445, *pg.* 1579
SOLARCAINE - Sun Care Products - MERCK & CO., INC.; *pg.* 1566, *pg.* 1077
SOLARCOOL - Glass Product - PPG INDUSTRIES, INC.; *pg.* 1445, *pg.* 1579
SOLARCURE - Adhesive - H.B. FULLER COMPANY; *pg.* 1165, *pg.* 961
SOLAREASE - Personal Care Material - BASF CATALYSTS LLC; *pg.* 1148, *pg.* 1074
SOLARFORCE - Water Pump - CONERGY, INC.; *pg.* 1325, *pg.* 318
SOLARGRAY - Glass Product - PPG INDUSTRIES, INC.; *pg.* 1445, *pg.* 1579
SOLARGREEN - Glass Product - PPG INDUSTRIES, INC.; *pg.* 1445, *pg.* 1579
SOLARIS - Manifold & Filters - ENTEGRIS, INC.; *pg.* 1882, *pg.* 788
SOLARIS - Police Lightbars - FEDERAL SIGNAL CORPORATION; *pg.* 638, *pg.* 645
SOLARIS - Multigas Detector - MINE SAFETY APPLIANCES COMPANY; *pg.* 1361, *pg.* 1525
SOLARMAX - Shirt - SIMMS FISHING PRODUCTS CORP.; *pg.* 1845, *pg.* 1008
SOLAROIL - Nail Care & Beauty Product - CREATIVE NAIL DESIGN, INC.; *pg.* 506, *pg.* 302
SOLARON - Inverter Support - ADVANCED ENERGY INDUSTRIES, INC.; *pg.* 613, *pg.* 328
SOLARSHIELD - Tinted Glass - AGC GLASS NORTH AMERICA, INC.; *pg.* 65, *pg.* 482
SOLASHIELD - Personal Care Product - TRI-K INDUSTRIES, INC.; *pg.* 523, *pg.* 1099
SOLATEX - Solar Glass - AGC GLASS NORTH AMERICA, INC.; *pg.* 65, *pg.* 482
SOLATRON - Electrical Products - EMERSON INDUSTRIAL AUTOMATION; *pg.* 1296, *pg.* 657
SOLD FOR THE CURE - Program - RE/MAX INTERNATIONAL, INC.; *pg.* 1109, *pg.* 322
SOLDER BRITE - Flux - LA-CO INDUSTRIES MARKAL CO., INC.; *pg.* 1170, *pg.* 610
SOLDER CHARGE - Electronic Components - MOLEX INCORPORATED; *pg.* 655, *pg.* 628
SOLDER CHARGE TECHNOLOGY - Electronic Components - MOLEX INCORPORATED; *pg.* 655, *pg.* 628
SOLDER SEAL - Auto Product - RADIATOR SPECIALTY COMPANY; *pg.* 215, *pg.* 1380
SOLDERFORMS - Pre Forms - KESTER, INC.; *pg.* 649, *pg.* 620
SOLDERMASK - Coating - DOW CHEMICAL; *pg.* 1156, *pg.* 1563
SOLDERSEAL - Wiring Harness Connector - MASTER APPLIANCE CORP.; *pg.* 1055, *pg.* 1888
SOLDIER OF FORTUNE - Game - ACTIVISION BLIZZARD, INC.; *pg.* 948, *pg.* 271
SOLE A - Shoe - AEROGROUP INTERNATIONAL, INC.; *pg.* 1803, *pg.* 1055
SOLE FLIP FLOPS - Footwear - HUGGER MUGGER YOGA PRODUCTS LLC; *pg.* 1836, *pg.* 1758
SOLE RIDE 100 - Bicycle - TREK BICYCLE CORPORATION; *pg.* 1847, *pg.* 1896
SOLE SOLUTION - Foot Treatment - NU SKIN ENTERPRISES, INC.; *pg.* 518, *pg.* 1755
SOLE ULTRA - Footwear - WELLCO ENTERPRISES, INC.; *pg.* 1822, *pg.* 1392
SOLEIL - Felt - AMERICAN FELT & FILTER COMPANY; *pg.* 1312, *pg.* 1184
SOLERA OPUS - Laser Product - CUTERA, INC.; *pg.* 1521, *pg.* 49
SOLERA TITAN - Laser Product - CUTERA, INC.; *pg.* 1521, *pg.* 49
SOLERIS - Food Safety Product - NEOGEN CORPORATION; *pg.* 883, *pg.* 896
SOLERRA - Paper & Nonwoven Material - FIBERMARK INC.; *pg.* 1457, *pg.* 1764
SOLESAVER - Footwear - CAPEZIO BALLET MAKERS INC.; *pg.* 1805, *pg.* 1125
SOLESTA - Pharmaceutical Product - SALIX PHARMACEUTICALS, INC.; *pg.* 1591, *pg.* 1388
SOLESTAT - Static Control Device for Shoes - WALTER G. LEGGE COMPANY, INC.; *pg.* 337, *pg.* 1321
SOLESUNITED - Donation Program - CROCS, INC.; *pg.* 1806, *pg.* 335
SOLEXIA - Glass Product - PPG INDUSTRIES, INC.; *pg.* 1445, *pg.* 1579
SOLEXTRA - Glass Product - PPG INDUSTRIES, INC.; *pg.* 1445, *pg.* 1579
SOLGAR - Nutritional Supplements - NBTY, INC.; *pg.* 1572, *pg.* 1338
SOLGAR - Healthcare Product - SWANSON HEALTH PRODUCTS INC.; *pg.* 1600, *pg.* 1397
SOLID - Bath Bars - CRAFTMADE INTERNATIONAL, INC.; *pg.* 1295, *pg.* 1670
SOLID - Molecular Biology Product - THERMO FISHER SCIENTIFIC INC.; *pg.* 1602, *pg.* 61
SOLID FOUNDATION - Carpet - INTERFACE, INC.; *pg.* 695, *pg.* 512
SOLID GROUND - Carpet - INTERFACE, INC.; *pg.* 695, *pg.* 512
SOLID HIDE - Rustic Stain - PRATT & LAMBERT PAINTS; *pg.* 1446, *pg.* 1434
SOLID START - Rim Board - LOUISIANA-PACIFIC CORPORATION; *pg.* 94, *pg.* 1652
SOLID SWING - Women's Clothing & Accessories - WOODEN SHIPS OF HOBOKEN; *pg.* 35, *pg.* 1315
SOLID WATER - Medical Device - GAMMEX RMI INC.; *pg.* 1532, *pg.* 1872
SOLIDBLUE - Hot Melt Pneumatic Gun - NORDSON CORPORATION; *pg.* 1365, *pg.* 1480
SOLIDCORE - Software - BSQUARE CORPORATION; *pg.* 366, *pg.* 1813
SOLIDIUM - Digital Gamma Camera - DIGIRAD CORPORATION; *pg.* 1524, *pg.* 185
SOLIDSTOR - Drive Technology - WESTERN DIGITAL

First page reference indicates Business Class Edition
Second page reference indicates Geographic Edition

CORPORATION; *pg.* 492, *pg.* 118
SOLILOQUY - Bath Product - KOHLER CO.; *pg.* 91, *pg.* 1862
SOLIMATE - Insulation - THE DOW CHEMICAL COMPANY; *pg.* 1157, *pg.* 898
SOLIRIS - Pharmaceutical - ALEXION PHARMACEUTICALS, INC.; *pg.* 1489, *pg.* 341
SOLIS - Laser System - AMERICAN MEDICAL SYSTEMS, INC.; *pg.* 1399, *pg.* 238
SOLIS - Plumbing Product - SLOAN VALVE COMPANY; *pg.* 1062, *pg.* 613
SOLITAIRE - Bouquet - 1-800-FLOWERS.COM, INC.; *pg.* 1758, *pg.* 1151
SOLITAIRE - Bath Fans & Fan Light - BROAN-NUTONE LLC; *pg.* 1069, *pg.* 1860
SOLITAIRE - Game - HASBRO, INC.; *pg.* 954, *pg.* 1603
SOLITAIRE - Bathroom Exhaust Fans - NORTEK, INC.; *pg.* 100, *pg.* 1607
SOLITAIRE TILES - Game - WINNING MOVES GAMES, INC.; *pg.* 970, *pg.* 816
SOLITAIRE ULTRA SILENT - Bathroom Exhaust Fans - NORTEK, INC.; *pg.* 100, *pg.* 1607
SOLITE - Solar Glass - AGC GLASS NORTH AMERICA, INC.; *pg.* 65, *pg.* 482
SOLITE - Stand Bag - DATREK GOLF; *pg.* 1832, *pg.* 1801
SOLITUDE - Apparel - OXFORD INDUSTRIES, INC.; *pg.* 30, *pg.* 517
SOLITUDE - Equine Fly Repellent - PFIZER INC.; *pg.* 1581, *pg.* 1278
SOLIVITA - Active Adult Community Development - AV HOMES INC.; *pg.* 1080, *pg.* 20
SOLKA-FLOC - Fiber Product - INTERNATIONAL FIBER CORP.; *pg.* 865, *pg.* 1317
SOLLEYS - Bakery - JERRY'S FAMOUS DELI, INC.; *pg.* 1733, *pg.* 281
SOLO - Knife - BUCK KNIVES, INC.; *pg.* 1828, *pg.* 550
SOLO - Beverages - THE COCA-COLA COMPANY; *pg.* 240, *pg.* 493
SOLO - Glass & Ceramic Material - CORNING INCORPORATED; *pg.* 1122, *pg.* 1154
SOLO - Fan - CRAFTMADE INTERNATIONAL, INC.; *pg.* 1295, *pg.* 1670
SOLO - Medium-duty Remanufactured Clutches - EATON CORPORATION; *pg.* 1331, *pg.* 1429
SOLO - Radar And Laser Detector - ESCORT, INC.; *pg.* 1412, *pg.* 1479
SOLO - Software - INTELLICORP, INC.; *pg.* 417, *pg.* 268
SOLO - Musical Instrument - PEAVEY ELECTRONICS CORPORATION; *pg.* 662, *pg.* 970
SOLO - Attaches & Portfolios - SOLO; *pg.* 12, *pg.* 1165
SOLO-CARE - Multipurpose Lens Care Solution - ALCON; *pg.* 1399, *pg.* 530
SOLO GLUE RITER - Glue & Adhesive - GLUEFAST COMPANY, INC.; *pg.* 1459, *pg.* 1090
SOLO LLANTAS - Tire And Rubber Product - THE GOODYEAR TIRE & RUBBER COMPANY; *pg.* 1883, *pg.* 1401
SOLO STEP - Heartworm Test System - HESKA CORPORATION; *pg.* 1542, *pg.* 335
SOLO SURGERY - Robotic-Assisted MIS - INTUITIVE SURGICAL, INC.; *pg.* 1546, *pg.* 286
SOLO2 - Graphics System Software - CHYRONHEGO; *pg.* 371, *pg.* 1179
SOLOCOAT - Metallizing Powder - WALL COLMONOY CORPORATION; *pg.* 1185, *pg.* 898
SOLODYN - Pharmaceutical Product - IMPAX LABORATORIES, INC.; *pg.* 1544, *pg.* 101
SOLOFLEX - Solution SBR - THE GOODYEAR TIRE & RUBBER COMPANY; *pg.* 1883, *pg.* 1401
SOLOIST - Medical Device - BOSTON SCIENTIFIC CORPORATION; *pg.* 1508, *pg.* 831
SOLOMIX - Healthcare Product - BAXTER INTERNATIONAL INC.; *pg.* 1499, *pg.* 599
SOLONOX - Turbine Products - SOLAR TURBINES INCORPORATED; *pg.* 1377, *pg.* 209
SOLOPHENYL - Direct Dyes - HUNTSMAN CORPORATION; *pg.* 1167, *pg.* 1758
SOLOXINE - Veterinary Product - VIRBAC CORPORATION; *pg.* 1606, *pg.* 1696
SOLSTICE - Shoe - AEROGROUP INTERNATIONAL, INC.; *pg.* 1803, *pg.* 1055
SOLSTICE - Knife - GERBER LEGENDARY BLADES; *pg.* 1834, *pg.* 1503
SOLSTICE - Chewing Gum Flavor - WM. WRIGLEY JR. COMPANY; *pg.* 1863, *pg.* 596
SOLSTICE SOLITAIRE - Ring - STULLER, INC.; *pg.* 13, *pg.* 745
SOLSTROM - Show And Ticket - CIRQUE DU SOLEIL INC.; *pg.* 540, *pg.* 1954
SOLTAB - Medicine - MERCK & CO., INC.; *pg.* 1566, *pg.* 1077
SOLTERRA - Ultraviolet Protection-Boosting Polymers - THE DOW CHEMICAL COMPANY; *pg.* 1157, *pg.* 898
SOLTES CP I - Ophthalmic Lenses - NIKON INC.; *pg.* 1424, *pg.* 1181
SOLTES CP II - Ophthalmic Lenses - NIKON INC.; *pg.* 1424, *pg.* 1181
SOLTEX - Waterproofing Polymer - THE DOW CHEMICAL COMPANY; *pg.* 1157, *pg.* 898
SOLTUF - Gauge Plastic Film - MULTI-PLASTICS, INC.; *pg.* 1886, *pg.* 1457
SOLU-CORTEF - Pharmaceutical Product - PFIZER INC.; *pg.* 1581, *pg.* 1278
SOLU-DELTA-CORTEF - Veterinary Medicinal Hormonal Preparation - PFIZER INC.; *pg.* 1581, *pg.* 1278
SOLU-MEDROL - Medicine - PFIZER INC.; *pg.* 1581, *pg.* 1278
SOLUCOR - Additives - AXIALL CORPORATION; *pg.* 69, *pg.* 491
SOLUCRYL - Solvent-based Acrylic Polymers - CYTEC INDUSTRIES, INC.; *pg.* 1155, *pg.* 1131
SOLUDEX - Tableting Agent for Pharmaceuticals - PENFORD CORPORATION; *pg.* 1177, *pg.* 314
SOLUJET - Cleaning Detergent - ALCONOX, INC.; *pg.* 325, *pg.* 1351
SOLULAC - Distillers Dried Grains with Solubles - GRAIN PROCESSING CORPORATION; *pg.* 859, *pg.* 709
SOLUMBRA - Apparel - SUN PRECAUTIONS, INC.; *pg.* 33, *pg.* 1820
SOLUPACK - Fertilizer - SIMPLOT PARTNERS INC.; *pg.* 1800, *pg.* 548
SOLUS - Performance Additive - EASTMAN CHEMICAL COMPANY; *pg.* 1159, *pg.* 1636
SOLUS - Diagnostic Tool - SNAP-ON INCORPORATED; *pg.* 1062, *pg.* 1862
SOLUS PRO - Diagnostic Tool - SNAP-ON INCORPORATED; *pg.* 1062, *pg.* 1862
SOLUSOL - Chemical Product - CYTEC INDUSTRIES, INC.; *pg.* 1155, *pg.* 1131
SOLUSTAPLE - Medical Device - INTEGRA LIFESCIENCES HOLDINGS CORPORATION; *pg.* 1545, *pg.* 1109
SOLUTION - Line of Mini-Tower PC Cases - ANTEC INCORPORATED; *pg.* 350, *pg.* 90
SOLUTION 21 - Systems Integration & Aeronautics - LOCKHEED MARTIN CORPORATION; *pg.* 229, *pg.* 762
SOLUTION ADVISOR - Wireless Communication System - AT&T SOUTHEAST; *pg.* 1868, *pg.* 489
SOLUTION ASSISTANT - Software System - AT&T COMMUNICATIONS CORP.; *pg.* 1866, *pg.* 1043
SOLUTION INTEGRATION - Global Services - SONUS NETWORKS INC.; *pg.* 1281, *pg.* 858
SOLUTION SELLING - Sales Techniques - SALES PERFORMANCE INTERNATIONAL, INC.; *pg.* 464, *pg.* 1368
SOLUTIONS - Software - BIO-RAD LABORATORIES, INC.; *pg.* 1504, *pg.* 101
SOLUTIONS - Household Products - NORM THOMPSON OUTFITTERS INC.; *pg.* 1780, *pg.* 1498
SOLUTIONS - Safety Product - VENTURI, INC.; *pg.* 1606, *pg.* 910
SOLUTIONS AT HAND - Slogan - DIMCO-GRAY COMPANY; *pg.* 1881, *pg.* 1409
SOLUTIONS@WORK - Publisher - SAS INSTITUTE INC.; *pg.* 466, *pg.* 1361
SOLUTIONS FOR A CLEANER WORLD - Slogan - THEOCHEM LABORATORIES, INC.; *pg.* 1184, *pg.* 476
SOLUTIONS FOR A NANOSCALE WORLD - Slogan - VEECO INSTRUMENTS INC.; *pg.* 1434, *pg.* 1322
SOLUTIONS FOR LIFE - Tagline - AMERICAN MEDICAL SYSTEMS HOLDINGS, INC.; *pg.* 1493, *pg.* 947
SOLUTIONS FROM HIRE TO RETIRE - Tagline - PAYCHEX, INC.; *pg.* 792, *pg.* 1336
SOLUTIONS IN MOTION - Tagline - LANDSTAR SYSTEM, INC.; *pg.* 1914, *pg.* 434
SOLUTIONS IN MOTION - Slogan - XTEK, INC.; *pg.* 1390, *pg.* 1427
SOLUTIONS IN STEEL - Business Strategy Services - ARCELORMITTAL DOFASCO INC.; *pg.* 68, *pg.* 1921
SOLUTIONS THAT WORK - Tag Line - U.S. TSUBAKI, INC.; *pg.* 221, *pg.* 670
SOLUTIONS WITH VISION - Slogan - DATALOGIC; *pg.* 382, *pg.* 1588
SOLUTIONS YOU NEED FROM A COMPANY YOU KNOW - Tag Line - INDIANA FARM BUREAU INSURANCE; *pg.* 1204, *pg.* 687
SOLVAC - Filter Holder - PALL CORPORATION; *pg.* 232, *pg.* 1323
SOLVE-A-SPOT - Cleaning Product - ORECK CORPORATION; *pg.* 59, *pg.* 1653
SOLVEX - Expanders - ANDERSON INTERNATIONAL CORP.; *pg.* 1313, *pg.* 1474
SOLVING FORWARD - Slogan - COMMVAULT SYSTEMS, INC.; *pg.* 377, *pg.* 1125
SOLVING HOLEMAKING PROBLEMS THROUGH INNOVATION - Tag Line - HOUGEN MANUFACTURING INC.; *pg.* 1347, *pg.* 908
SOLVING THE SYSTEM CARD PUZZLE - Communications Connecting Software - AVAGO TECHNOLOGIES; *pg.* 358, *pg.* 238
SOLVINGRIGHT - Manual - XEROX CORPORATION; *pg.* 494, *pg.* 365
SOLVNET - Software - SYNOPSYS, INC.; *pg.* 480, *pg.* 162
SOLVOL - Hand Cleaner - WD-40 COMPANY; *pg.* 337, *pg.* 210
SOLVSEAL - Closure Liner Sealings Materials - TEKNI-PLEX, INC.; *pg.* 1470, *pg.* 1122
SOLYX - Medical Device - BOSTON SCIENTIFIC CORPORATION; *pg.* 1508, *pg.* 831
SOMA - Stool - ALIMED, INC.; *pg.* 1490, *pg.* 816
SOMA - Lingerie - CHICO'S FAS, INC.; *pg.* 21, *pg.* 427
SOMA - Fabric - MOMENTUM TEXTILES INC.; *pg.* 697, *pg.* 114
SOMA FOAMA - Castable Foam - SMOOTH-ON INC.; *pg.* 111, *pg.* 1528
SOMAVERT - Medicine - PFIZER INC.; *pg.* 1581, *pg.* 1278
SOMERSAULTS - Footwear - DEER STAGS INC.; *pg.* 1807, *pg.* 1222
SOMERSET - Furniture - BUSH INDUSTRIES INC.; *pg.* 919, *pg.* 1170
SOMERSET - Fan - CRAFTMADE INTERNATIONAL, INC.; *pg.* 1295, *pg.* 1670
SOMERSET - Carpet - INTERFACE, INC.; *pg.* 695, *pg.* 512
SOMERSET - Furniture - TROPITONE FURNITURE CO., INC.; *pg.* 945, *pg.* 118
SOMETHIN NEW IS BREWIN - Coffee - FARMER BROTHERS COMPANY; *pg.* 855, *pg.* 293
SOMETHING FOR NOTHING - Game - WMS INDUSTRIES INC.; *pg.* 593, *pg.* 666
SOMETHING MORE - Tagline - AMC NETWORKS INC.; *pg.* 269, *pg.* 1189
SOMETHING SPECIAL - Scotch - DIAGEO CANADA, INC.; *pg.* 1961, *pg.* 1937
SOMETHING SPECIAL - Blouses - HABAND COMPANY, INC.; *pg.* 1772, *pg.* 1099
SOMETHING SPECIAL FROM WISCONSIN - Slogan - WISCONSIN DEPARTMENT OF AGRICULTURE, TRADE & CONSUMER PROTECTION; *pg.* 1011, *pg.* 1867
SOMETHING TO FEEL GOOD ABOUT. - Tagline - CROZER-KEYSTONE HEALTH SYSTEM INC.; *pg.* 1520, *pg.* 1587
SOMETHING UNEXPECTED - Slogan - GORDMANS STORES INC.; *pg.* 1771, *pg.* 1016
SOMETHING WILD HAS COME TO TOWN - Tagline - BUFFALO WILD WINGS, INC.; *pg.* 1718, *pg.* 931
SOMFY - Remote Control - SUNSETTER PRODUCTS, LP; *pg.* 113, *pg.* 830
SOMMER METALCRAFT - Metal Product - SOMMER METALCRAFT CORPORATION; *pg.* 112, *pg.* 676
SOMO - Handheld Computer - SOCKET MOBILE, INC.; *pg.* 471, *pg.* 164
SOMPOSURE - Pharmaceutical Preparation for Sleep Disorders - PFIZER INC.; *pg.* 1581, *pg.* 1278
SOMUBAC - Veterinary Pharmaceutical Preparation - PFIZER INC.; *pg.* 1581, *pg.* 1278
SONA - Bathroom Fan - HUNTER FAN COMPANY; *pg.* 57, *pg.* 1631
SONADRY - Ink - VAN SON HOLLAND INK CORPORATION OF AMERICA; *pg.* 487, *pg.* 1169
SONAGLOSS - Ink - VAN SON HOLLAND INK CORPORATION OF AMERICA; *pg.* 487, *pg.* 1169
SONAPRINT - Ink - VAN SON HOLLAND INK CORPORATION OF AMERICA; *pg.* 487, *pg.* 1169
SONAR - Software - SYMANTEC CORPORATION; *pg.* 478, *pg.* 161
SONATA - Case - ANTEC INCORPORATED; *pg.* 350, *pg.* 90
SONATA - Software - BIO-RAD LABORATORIES, INC.; *pg.*

First page reference indicates Business Class Edition
Second page reference indicates Geographic Edition

1504, *pg.* 101
SONATA - Pharmaceutical Product - KING PHARMACEUTICALS, INC.; *pg.* 1553, *pg.* 1627
SONATA - Bath Product - KOHLER CO.; *pg.* 91, *pg.* 1862
SONATA - Insomnia Treatment Pharmaceutical Preparation - PFIZER INC.; *pg.* 1581, *pg.* 1278
SONATA - Lighting Product - QUOIZEL INC.; *pg.* 1304, *pg.* 1616
SONATA - Office Furniture - STEELCASE INC.; *pg.* 475, *pg.* 889
SONATA - Cosmetics - WESTROCK COMPANY; *pg.* 1472, *pg.* 1805
SONATORQ - Tension Control - P/A INDUSTRIES, INC.; *pg.* 1367, *pg.* 339
SONDHI - Orthodontic Bonding Adhesive - 3M UNITEK CORPORATION; *pg.* 1483, *pg.* 150
SONERO - Coffee - PERFORMANCE FOOD GROUP COMPANY, LLC; *pg.* 1030, *pg.* 1803
SONESTA HOTELS & RESORTS - Hotel & Resort - SONESTA INTERNATIONAL HOTELS CORPORATION; *pg.* 1113, *pg.* 836
SONFIL - Beverages - THE COCA-COLA COMPANY; *pg.* 240, *pg.* 493
SONG AND BEAUTY - Bird Food - LEBANON SEABOARD CORPORATION; *pg.* 1797, *pg.* 1547
SONG BIRDS - Video Game - INTERNATIONAL GAME TECHNOLOGY; *pg.* 957, *pg.* 1024
SONGBIRD SELECTION - Bird Blend - THE SCOTTS MIRACLE-GRO COMPANY; *pg.* 1799, *pg.* 1459
SONHO DE VALSA - bonbon - MONDELEZ INTERNATIONAL, INC.; *pg.* 878, *pg.* 601
SONI-LOK - Packaging Product - GRAPHIC PACKAGING HOLDING COMPANY; *pg.* 1459, *pg.* 509
SONI-SEAL - Packaging Product - GRAPHIC PACKAGING HOLDING COMPANY; *pg.* 1459, *pg.* 509
SONIC - Lighting Product - GERBER LEGENDARY BLADES; *pg.* 1834, *pg.* 1503
SONIC - Software - PROGRESS SOFTWARE CORPORATION; *pg.* 457, *pg.* 786
SONIC BLAST - Drink - SONIC CORP.; *pg.* 1750, *pg.* 1487
SONIC BOOST - Cleaning Chemical Product - KYZEN CORPORATION; *pg.* 331, *pg.* 1652
SONIC CRUISERS - Fan Club - SONIC CORP.; *pg.* 1750, *pg.* 1487
SONIC DRIVE-IN - Restaurant Types - SONIC CORP.; *pg.* 1750, *pg.* 1487
SONIC-FRD - Power Semiconductor & Module - IXYS CORPORATION; *pg.* 422, *pg.* 146
SONIC PESTCHASER - Rodent Control - THE WOODSTREAM CORPORATION; *pg.* 1801, *pg.* 1549
SONIC PLUS - Mike Booms - ALAN GORDON ENTERPRISES, INC.; *pg.* 1399, *pg.* 125
SONIC-SIZE - Food Product - SONIC CORP.; *pg.* 1750, *pg.* 1487
SONIC SUNRISE - Drink - SONIC CORP.; *pg.* 1750, *pg.* 1487
SONIC WAVE - Purified Water - SONIC CORP.; *pg.* 1750, *pg.* 1487
SONIC WAVE - Medical System - STAAR SURGICAL COMPANY; *pg.* 1597, *pg.* 151
SONICAIDONE - Medical Instrument - WALLACH SURGICAL DEVICES, INC.; *pg.* 1436, *pg.* 381
SONICAIR - Software - UNITED PARCEL SERVICE, INC.; *pg.* 1928, *pg.* 522
SONICARE - Tooth Brushes - PHILIPS ELECTRONICS NORTH AMERICA; *pg.* 662, *pg.* 782
SONICARE ELITE - Fitness Equipment - BALLY TOTAL FITNESS HOLDINGS CORPORATION; *pg.* 532, *pg.* 1200
SONICATH - Medical Device - BOSTON SCIENTIFIC CORPORATION; *pg.* 1508, *pg.* 831
SONICATORS - Medical Device - MISONIX INC.; *pg.* 1568, *pg.* 1159
SONICFLO - Gas Fuel Control Valve - WOODWARD, INC.; *pg.* 122, *pg.* 329
SONIFI HEALTH SOLUTIONS - Healthcare Facilities - SONIFI SOLUTIONS; *pg.* 1281, *pg.* 1625
SONIFI SOLUTIONS - Hospitality Services - SONIFI SOLUTIONS; *pg.* 1281, *pg.* 1625
SONITE 16 - Hardener - SMOOTH-ON INC.; *pg.* 111, *pg.* 1528
SONIX - Protective Eyewear - SELLSTROM MANUFACTURING CO.; *pg.* 1428, *pg.* 659
SONNENSCHEIN - Battery - EXIDE TECHNOLOGIES; *pg.* 204, *pg.* 483
SONNET - Flatware - ONEIDA LTD; *pg.* 1129, *pg.* 1318
SONNET - Cosmetics - WESTROCK COMPANY; *pg.* 1472, *pg.* 1805
SONOBASE - Carriers - SONOCO PRODUCTS COMPANY; *pg.* 1469, *pg.* 1619
SONOBATTS - Glass Fiber Commercial Insulation - OWENS CORNING; *pg.* 102, *pg.* 1476
SONOBLASTER! - Work Zone Intrusion Alarm - INTERNATIONAL ROAD DYNAMICS INC.; *pg.* 1912, *pg.* 1962
SONOCALC - Ultrasound System - SONOSITE, INC.; *pg.* 1429, *pg.* 1818
SONOCO PACKAGING SYSTEM - Textiles, Film, Paper, Tape & Converting, Labels & Metals - SONOCO PRODUCTS COMPANY; *pg.* 1469, *pg.* 1619
SONOCO XCHB - Thermoformed Containers - SONOCO PRODUCTS COMPANY; *pg.* 1469, *pg.* 1619
SONOGLO - Colored Tip Cones - SONOCO PRODUCTS COMPANY; *pg.* 1469, *pg.* 1619
SONOHEART - Ultrasound System - SONOSITE, INC.; *pg.* 1429, *pg.* 1818
SONOLOC - Plastic Construction Forms - SONOCO PRODUCTS COMPANY; *pg.* 1469, *pg.* 1619
SONOMA - Furniture - AMERICAN LEATHER LP; *pg.* 912, *pg.* 1673
SONOMA - Furniture - ASHLEY FURNITURE INDUSTRIES, INC.; *pg.* 914, *pg.* 1852
SONOMA - Furniture - BUSH INDUSTRIES INC.; *pg.* 919, *pg.* 1170
SONOMA - Rug - COURISTAN INC.; *pg.* 921, *pg.* 1067
SONOMA - Cheese - MONTEREY GOURMET FOODS, INC.; *pg.* 881, *pg.* 94
SONOMA-CUTRER - Chardonnay Wines - BROWN-FORMAN CORPORATION; *pg.* 1958, *pg.* 732
SONOPOP - Display Systems - SONOCO PRODUCTS COMPANY; *pg.* 1469, *pg.* 1619
SONOPOST - Protective Corner Board - SONOCO PRODUCTS COMPANY; *pg.* 1469, *pg.* 1619
SONOPROCESS - Low Frequency Sonic Energy Technology - SONORO ENERGY LTD.; *pg.* 112, *pg.* 1905
SONORA - Carpet - BEAULIEU GROUP, LLC; *pg.* 917, *pg.* 529
SONORA - Paper Product - WEYERHAEUSER COMPANY; *pg.* 121, *pg.* 1820
SONORA SUNSET - Nail Care Product - OPI PRODUCTS INC.; *pg.* 518, *pg.* 167
SONORAN - Dinnerware - THE HOMER LAUGHLIN CHINA COMPANY; *pg.* 1125, *pg.* 1850
SONOSCORE - Confectionery Packaging - SONOCO PRODUCTS COMPANY; *pg.* 1469, *pg.* 1619
SONOTEC - Acoustic Product - LEAR CORPORATION; *pg.* 229, *pg.* 907
SONOTORT - Retort Pouches - SONOCO PRODUCTS COMPANY; *pg.* 1469, *pg.* 1619
SONOTRACK - Magnetic Sound-Track Striping - EASTMAN KODAK COMPANY; *pg.* 1408, *pg.* 1333
SONOTUBE - Fiber Forms for Concrete Columns - SONOCO PRODUCTS COMPANY; *pg.* 1469, *pg.* 1619
SONOTUBE FINISH FREE - Concrete Forms - SONOCO PRODUCTS COMPANY; *pg.* 1469, *pg.* 1619
SONOTUBE PLUS - Fiber Tubes for Concrete Column & Pier Construction - SONOCO PRODUCTS COMPANY; *pg.* 1469, *pg.* 1619
SONOVIEW - Packaging Systems - SONOCO PRODUCTS COMPANY; *pg.* 1469, *pg.* 1619
SONOVOID - Fiber Tubes for Voiding Concrete Slabs - SONOCO PRODUCTS COMPANY; *pg.* 1469, *pg.* 1619
SONOWARE - Molded Plastic Storage Trays - SONOCO PRODUCTS COMPANY; *pg.* 1469, *pg.* 1619
SONOWRAP - Adhesives & Sealants for Convolute Caulk Tube Labels - SONOCO PRODUCTS COMPANY; *pg.* 1469, *pg.* 1619
SONOXIDE - Ultrasonic Water Treatment Equipment - ASHLAND INC.; *pg.* 972, *pg.* 726
SONRIC - Snacks - PEPSICO, INC.; *pg.* 259, *pg.* 1327
SONRIC'S - Sweet Snack - FRITO-LAY NORTH AMERICA, INC.; *pg.* 1853, *pg.* 1730
SONTARA - Contamination Control Fabrics & Products - E.I. DU PONT DE NEMOURS & COMPANY; *pg.* 1159, *pg.* 390
SONTARA AC - Aircraft Wipes - E.I. DU PONT DE NEMOURS & COMPANY; *pg.* 1159, *pg.* 390
SONTARA FS - Food Service Wipes - E.I. DU PONT DE NEMOURS & COMPANY; *pg.* 1159, *pg.* 390
SONTARA PC - Printing Wipes - E.I. DU PONT DE NEMOURS & COMPANY; *pg.* 1159, *pg.* 390
SONUS NETWORKS HSX - Server - SONUS NETWORKS INC.; *pg.* 1281, *pg.* 858
SONUS NETWORKS PSX - Server - SONUS NETWORKS INC.; *pg.* 1281, *pg.* 858
SONUS NETWORKS SRX - Server - SONUS NETWORKS INC.; *pg.* 1281, *pg.* 858
SONY CLASSICAL - Compact Disc - SONY MUSIC ENTERTAINMENT; *pg.* 309, *pg.* 1294
SONY MUSIC INTERNATIONAL - Electronic Product - SONY MUSIC ENTERTAINMENT; *pg.* 309, *pg.* 1294
SONY MUSIC NASHVILLE - Electronic Product - SONY MUSIC ENTERTAINMENT; *pg.* 309, *pg.* 1294
SONY URBAN MUSIC - Electronic Product - SONY MUSIC ENTERTAINMENT; *pg.* 309, *pg.* 1294
SONY WONDER - Video - SONY MUSIC ENTERTAINMENT; *pg.* 309, *pg.* 1294
SOONSOO - Beverages - THE COCA-COLA COMPANY; *pg.* 240, *pg.* 493
SOOT-A-MATIC - Tube Cleaner - GOODWAY TECHNOLOGIES CORPORATION; *pg.* 1341, *pg.* 374
SOOT-VAC - Soot Vacuum - GOODWAY TECHNOLOGIES CORPORATION; *pg.* 1341, *pg.* 374
SOOTHE & COOL - Health Care Products for Medicinal or Therapeutic Use - MEDLINE INDUSTRIES, INC.; *pg.* 1562, *pg.* 635
SOOTHE-GUARD - Dental Product - DENTSPLY INTERNATIONAL INC.; *pg.* 1522, *pg.* 1596
SOOTHING LAVENDER - Doll - THE GOLDBERGER COMPANY, LLC; *pg.* 954, *pg.* 1235
SOOTHING SEVEN - Jet - WATKINS MANUFACTURING CORPORATION; *pg.* 120, *pg.* 303
SOOTHING SPLASH - Lip Care Product - BLISTEX, INC.; *pg.* 502, *pg.* 644
SOPC BUILDER - Design Tool - ALTERA CORPORATION; *pg.* 348, *pg.* 237
SOPHIA - Chair - LA-Z-BOY INCORPORATED; *pg.* 932, *pg.* 901
SOPHIA - Furniture - NEMSCHOFF, INC.; *pg.* 936, *pg.* 1890
SOPHIA - Furniture - STANLEY FURNITURE CO., INC.; *pg.* 943, *pg.* 1379
SOPHIE - Clothing - ABERCROMBIE & FITCH CO.; *pg.* 37, *pg.* 1466
SOPHIE - Women's Clothing & Accessories - WOODEN SHIPS OF HOBOKEN; *pg.* 35, *pg.* 1315
SOPHISTICATE - Faucets - MOEN INCORPORATED; *pg.* 1056, *pg.* 1468
SOPHY - Furniture - AMISCO INDUSTRIES LTD.; *pg.* 913, *pg.* 1958
THE SOPRANOS - Cable Television Show - HOME BOX OFFICE, INC.; *pg.* 290, *pg.* 1240
SOQUETE - Ready-Mixed Plaster - USG CORPORATION; *pg.* 118, *pg.* 594
SORA - Lighting - STEELCASE INC.; *pg.* 475, *pg.* 889
SORB-IT - Cleaning Product - HILLYARD, INC.; *pg.* 331, *pg.* 990
SORBACELL - Foam Dressing - DERMA SCIENCES, INC.; *pg.* 1523, *pg.* 1111
SORBAMINE - Liquid Process Purification Activated Carbons - CALGON CARBON CORPORATION; *pg.* 1151, *pg.* 1574
SORBAN - Bandage - DERMA SCIENCES, INC.; *pg.* 1523, *pg.* 1111
SORBARING - Desiccant Bag - MULTISORB TECHNOLOGIES, INC.; *pg.* 1570, *pg.* 1150
SORBEAD - Adsorbent - BASF CATALYSTS LLC; *pg.* 1148, *pg.* 1074
SORBEE - Sugar-Free Food Products - SORBEE INTERNATIONAL, LLC; *pg.* 1862, *pg.* 1570
SORBER - Survey - W.L. GORE & ASSOCIATES, INC.; *pg.* 122, *pg.* 388
SORBET - Shoe - AEROGROUP INTERNATIONAL, INC.; *pg.* 1803, *pg.* 1055
SORBET - Kitchen Product - KOHLER CO.; *pg.* 91, *pg.* 1862
SORBET - Seed - PANAMERICAN SEED CO.; *pg.* 1798, *pg.* 668
SORBET BOUQUET - Flower Arrangement - 1-800-FLOWERS.COM, INC.; *pg.* 1758, *pg.* 1151
SORBICAP - Desiccant Canister - MULTISORB TECHNOLOGIES, INC.; *pg.* 1570, *pg.* 1150
SORBIDEX - Starch Derivative - CARGILL, INC.; *pg.* 845, *pg.* 965
SORCE - Satellite - ORBITAL ATK; *pg.* 1425, *pg.* 1779
SOREL - Footwear - COLUMBIA SPORTSWEAR COMPANY; *pg.* 1830, *pg.* 1501
SORENTO - Furniture - ASHLEY FURNITURE INDUSTRIES, INC.; *pg.* 914, *pg.* 1852

First page reference indicates Business Class Edition
Second page reference indicates Geographic Edition

SORIATANE - Pharmaceutical Product - HOFFMANN-LA ROCHE INC.; *pg.* 1542, *pg.* 1099
SORONA - Polymer Fibers - E.I. DU PONT DE NEMOURS & COMPANY; *pg.* 1159, *pg.* 390
SORREL - Waiting Seating - STEELCASE INC.; *pg.* 475, *pg.* 889
SORRELL - Furniture - JASPER GROUP; *pg.* 930, *pg.* 691
SORRELL RIDGE - Bottled Food Product - ALLIED OLD ENGLISH, INC.; *pg.* 836, *pg.* 1110
SORRENTO - Table - BLATT BOWLING & BILLIARD CORP.; *pg.* 1827, *pg.* 1203
SORRENTO - Broadloom - COURISTAN INC.; *pg.* 921, *pg.* 1067
SORRENTO - Cheese - LACTALIS AMERICAN GROUP; *pg.* 873, *pg.* 1149
SORRENTO - Boat - SEA RAY BOATS, INC.; *pg.* 1710, *pg.* 1638
SORRENTO - Jewelry - UNCAS MANUFACTURING COMPANY; *pg.* 15, *pg.* 1608
SORRY! - Toy & Game - HASBRO, INC.; *pg.* 954, *pg.* 1603
SORTA CLEAR - Silicone Rubber - SMOOTH-ON INC.; *pg.* 111, *pg.* 1528
SORTA-CLEAR - Liquid Rubber - SMOOTH-ON INC.; *pg.* 111, *pg.* 1528
SORTHOEASE - Healthcare Product - GF HEALTH PRODUCTS, INC.; *pg.* 1535, *pg.* 508
S.O.S. - Steel Wool Soap Pads & Scrubber Sponges - THE CLOROX COMPANY; *pg.* 327, *pg.* 169
S.O.S - Lights - CYALUME TECHNOLOGIES HOLDINGS, INC.; *pg.* 1295, *pg.* 856
SOT-POT - Digital Potentiometers - MAXIM INTEGRATED PRODUCTS, INC.; *pg.* 653, *pg.* 247
SOTA WATER - Boots - AEROGROUP INTERNATIONAL, INC.; *pg.* 1803, *pg.* 1055
SOTAR - Air Brush - BADGER AIR BRUSH COMPANY; *pg.* 359, *pg.* 612
SOTHEBY'S - Art & Auction House - SOTHEBY'S INC.; *pg.* 472, *pg.* 1294
SOTHEBY'S INTERNATIONAL REALTY - Luxury Real Estate Brokerage - REALOGY CORPORATION; *pg.* 1109, *pg.* 1081
SOTRADECOL - Electrosurgical Devices - ANGIODYNAMICS, INC.; *pg.* 1495, *pg.* 1173
SOUL - Scent - HERBALIFE INTERNATIONAL OF AMERICA, INC.; *pg.* 1541, *pg.* 132
SOUL FUEL - Online Information - DARE 2 SHARE MINISTRIES INTERNATIONAL, INC.; *pg.* 138, *pg.* 310
SOUL MATE - Sandals - AEROGROUP INTERNATIONAL, INC.; *pg.* 1803, *pg.* 1055
SOUL SEARCH - Sandals - AEROGROUP INTERNATIONAL, INC.; *pg.* 1803, *pg.* 1055
SOUND - Musical Instrument - KAMAN CORPORATION; *pg.* 229, *pg.* 338
SOUND ASLEEP - Earplug - MCKEON PRODUCTS, INC.; *pg.* 1559, *pg.* 912
SOUND BEAUTY - Seafood - OCEAN BEAUTY SEAFOODS, INC.; *pg.* 1028, *pg.* 1838
SOUND DEFLECTION TECHNOLOGY - Muffler - EDELBROCK CORPORATION; *pg.* 204, *pg.* 293
SOUND GUARD SST - Marine Generator - WESTERBEKE CORPORATION; *pg.* 1388, *pg.* 847
SOUND HEALTH - Radio Show - ALLINA HEALTH SYSTEM, INC.; *pg.* 1491, *pg.* 929
SOUND INNOVATION - Slogan - PLANTRONICS, INC.; *pg.* 663, *pg.* 270
SOUND INVESTMENT. SOLID RETURN. - Tagline - SIOUX STEEL COMPANY; *pg.* 707, *pg.* 1625
SOUND VALUE - Promoting Products of Others To Auto Clubs - AMERICAN AUTOMOBILE ASSOCIATION; *pg.* 1190, *pg.* 429
SOUND X - Musical Instrument - THE SINGING MACHINE COMPANY, INC.; *pg.* 674, *pg.* 426
SOUNDBOOTH - Software - ADOBE SYSTEMS INCORPORATED; *pg.* 342, *pg.* 235
SOUNDBRIDGE - Music Education - SEATTLE SYMPHONY ORCHESTRA; *pg.* 582, *pg.* 1840
SOUNDCRAFT - Audio & Video Product - HARMAN INTERNATIONAL INDUSTRIES, INCORPORATED; *pg.* 641, *pg.* 374
SOUNDDIRECT - Electronic Product - LRAD CORPORATION; *pg.* 652, *pg.* 204
SOUNDDOCK - Audio Product - BOSE CORPORATION; *pg.* 626, *pg.* 820
SOUNDEFFECTS - Audio & Video Product - HARMAN INTERNATIONAL INDUSTRIES, INCORPORATED; *pg.* 641, *pg.* 374
SOUNDESIGN - Alarm Clock - SDI TECHNOLOGIES, INC.; *pg.* 671, *pg.* 1113
SOUNDGEAR - Audio & Video Product - HARMAN INTERNATIONAL INDUSTRIES, INCORPORATED; *pg.* 641, *pg.* 374
SOUNDINGS - Magazine - DOMINION ENTERPRISES; *pg.* 1636, *pg.* 1796
SOUNDINGS TRADE ONLY - Advertising Publication - DOMINION ENTERPRISES; *pg.* 1636, *pg.* 1796
SOUNDMASTER - Partitions - MODERNFOLD, INC.; *pg.* 98, *pg.* 681
SOUNDMATRIX TECHNOLOGY - Acoustic Technology for Use with Renaissance Organs - ALLEN ORGAN COMPANY; *pg.* 527, *pg.* 1549
SOUNDMAX - Microphone - ANDREA ELECTRONICS CORPORATION; *pg.* 617, *pg.* 1143
SOUNDOLIER - Integrated Home Electronics - ATLAS SOUND; *pg.* 621, *pg.* 1692
SOUNDPATH - Telecom Product - PREMIERE GLOBAL SERVICES, INC.; *pg.* 1275, *pg.* 518
SOUNDPLUS - Sampling Stereo Converter - TEXAS INSTRUMENTS INCORPORATED; *pg.* 679, *pg.* 1688
SOUNDPOINT - Audio & Video Product - HARMAN INTERNATIONAL INDUSTRIES, INCORPORATED; *pg.* 641, *pg.* 374
SOUNDPOINT - Voice Product - POLYCOM, INC.; *pg.* 664, *pg.* 249
SOUNDPORT - Hearing Instrument - STARKEY LABORATORIES, INC.; *pg.* 1597, *pg.* 923
SOUNDPRO - Sound Level Meters - 3M DETECTION SOLUTIONS; *pg.* 1398, *pg.* 1885
SOUNDS OF THE SEVENTIES - Music Series - DIRECT HOLDINGS AMERICAS INC.; *pg.* 1636, *pg.* 1780
SOUNDS SPECTACULAR - Music Publisher - CARL FISCHER, LLC; *pg.* 1625, *pg.* 1209
SOUNDSABER - Electronic Product - LRAD CORPORATION; *pg.* 652, *pg.* 204
SOUNDSATIONAL - Cable - COLEMAN CABLE, INC.; *pg.* 1324, *pg.* 665
SOUNDSCAPES - Ceilings & Walls - ARMSTRONG WORLD INDUSTRIES, INC.; *pg.* 914, *pg.* 1545
SOUNDSOAK - Acoustic System - OWENS CORNING; *pg.* 102, *pg.* 1476
SOUNDSTATION - Voice Product - POLYCOM, INC.; *pg.* 664, *pg.* 249
SOUNDSTATION PREMIER - Communication Product - POLYCOM, INC.; *pg.* 664, *pg.* 249
SOUNDSTATION PREMIER SATELLITE - Conference Phone - POLYCOM, INC.; *pg.* 664, *pg.* 249
SOUNDSTATION VTX 1000 - Conference Phone - POLYCOM, INC.; *pg.* 664, *pg.* 249
SOUNDSTATION2 - Conference Phone - POLYCOM, INC.; *pg.* 664, *pg.* 249
SOUNDSTATION2W - Conference Phone - POLYCOM, INC.; *pg.* 664, *pg.* 249
SOUNDSTICKS - Audio & Video Product - HARMAN INTERNATIONAL INDUSTRIES, INCORPORATED; *pg.* 641, *pg.* 374
SOUNDSTORM - Software - NVIDIA CORPORATION; *pg.* 447, *pg.* 268
SOUNDSTRUCTURE - Audio Solution - POLYCOM, INC.; *pg.* 664, *pg.* 249
SOUNDTECH - Musical Instrument - U.S. MUSIC CORPORATION; *pg.* 315, *pg.* 560
SOUNDTRACK - Application Program - APPLE INC.; *pg.* 350, *pg.* 73
SOUNDTRACKER - Communication Product - COBRA ELECTRONICS CORPORATION; *pg.* 629, *pg.* 572
SOUNDVECTOR - Electronic Product - LRAD CORPORATION; *pg.* 652, *pg.* 204
SOUNDWORKS - Speaker - CAMBRIDGE SOUNDWORKS, INC.; *pg.* 1234, *pg.* 781
SOUP AT HAND - Soup - CAMPBELL SOUP COMPANY; *pg.* 844, *pg.* 1048
SOUP2NUTS - Educational Materials - SCHOLASTIC INC.; *pg.* 1683, *pg.* 1288
SOUPLANTATION - Food Product - GARDEN FRESH RESTAURANT CORP.; *pg.* 1729, *pg.* 203
SOUR APPLE - Fabric - NEMSCHOFF, INC.; *pg.* 936, *pg.* 1890
SOUR BLOOPS - Candy & Mint - SNYDER'S-LANCE, INC.; *pg.* 896, *pg.* 1368
SOUR CREAM - Food Product - GAY LEA FOODS CO-OPERATIVE LIMITED; *pg.* 858, *pg.* 1926
SOUR JACKS - Candy - PROMOTION IN MOTION, INC.; *pg.* 1861, *pg.* 1052
SOUR JACKS SOUR CANDY - Food Product - PROMOTION IN MOTION, INC.; *pg.* 1861, *pg.* 1052
SOUR PUNCH - Candy Product - AMERICAN LICORICE CO. INC.; *pg.* 1850, *pg.* 692
SOURCE CAPTURE OPTIMIZATION - Payment Solution - FISERV, INC.; *pg.* 397, *pg.* 1855
SOURCE FOUR - Lighting Equipment - ELECTRONIC THEATRE CONTROLS, INC.; *pg.* 1296, *pg.* 1872
SOURCE FOUR REVOLUTION - Lighting Equipment for Theater - ELECTRONIC THEATRE CONTROLS, INC.; *pg.* 1296, *pg.* 1872
SOURCE I - Service Fittings - WIREMOLD/LEGRAND; *pg.* 689, *pg.* 383
SOURCE II - Service Fittings - WIREMOLD/LEGRAND; *pg.* 689, *pg.* 383
SOURCE OF LIFE - Nutritional Supplement - NATURAL ORGANICS, INC.; *pg.* 1571, *pg.* 1181
SOURCE OF NATURE - Garden Seeds - FERRY-MORSE SEED COMPANY; *pg.* 1795, *pg.* 728
THE SOURCE OF SMART SOLUTIONS - Slogan - RCM TECHNOLOGIES, INC.; *pg.* 459, *pg.* 1108
SOURCE RECORD PUNCH - Data Collection Devices - THE STANDARD REGISTER COMPANY; *pg.* 473, *pg.* 1446
SOURCEBOOK - Furniture - HAWORTH, INC.; *pg.* 402, *pg.* 891
SOURCEFORGE - Software - GEEKNET, INC.; *pg.* 1248, *pg.* 1780
SOURCEFORGE.NET - Software - GEEKNET, INC.; *pg.* 1248, *pg.* 1780
SOURCEMETER - Electronic Instrument - KEITHLEY INSTRUMENTS, INC.; *pg.* 1418, *pg.* 1473
SOURCESELECT - Software - BIO-RAD LABORATORIES, INC.; *pg.* 1504, *pg.* 101
SOURDOUGH JACK - Hamburger - JACK IN THE BOX INC.; *pg.* 1732, *pg.* 204
SOURZ - Liqueurs - JIM BEAM BRANDS CO.; *pg.* 1965, *pg.* 601
SOUTH BARSTOW - Furniture - ASHLEY FURNITURE INDUSTRIES, INC.; *pg.* 914, *pg.* 1852
SOUTH BEACH - Carpet - BEAULIEU GROUP, LLC; *pg.* 917, *pg.* 529
SOUTH BEACH - Rug - COURISTAN INC.; *pg.* 921, *pg.* 1067
SOUTH BEACH - Volleyball Complex - ONTARIO PLACE CORPORATION; *pg.* 572, *pg.* 1941
SOUTH CAROLINA LAWYERS WEEKLY - Newspaper - MASSACHUSETTS LAWYERS WEEKLY, INC.; *pg.* 1662, *pg.* 798
SOUTH CENTRAL BELL - Wireless Communication System - AT&T SOUTHEAST; *pg.* 1868, *pg.* 489
SOUTH DAKOTA LOTTERY - Lotto Game - SOUTH DAKOTA LOTTERY; *pg.* 1006, *pg.* 1624
SOUTH FORK - Footwear - SIMMS FISHING PRODUCTS CORP.; *pg.* 1845, *pg.* 1008
SOUTH HAMPTON - Carpet - BEAULIEU GROUP, LLC; *pg.* 917, *pg.* 529
SOUTH HAMPTON - Furniture - FLEXSTEEL INDUSTRIES, INC.; *pg.* 925, *pg.* 707
SOUTH MAID - Embroidery Thread - MAKE IT COATS; *pg.* 696, *pg.* 1367
SOUTH PACIFIC - Video Game - INTERNATIONAL GAME TECHNOLOGY; *pg.* 957, *pg.* 1024
SOUTH SEA - Tile - ARTISTIC TILE INC.; *pg.* 914, *pg.* 1119
SOUTH SHORE - Furniture - ASHLEY FURNITURE INDUSTRIES, INC.; *pg.* 914, *pg.* 1852
SOUTH SHORE - Eyewear - MAUI JIM, INC.; *pg.* 9, *pg.* 651
SOUTH UNIVERSITY - Universities - EDUCATION MANAGEMENT CORPORATION; *pg.* 601, *pg.* 1575
SOUTHAMPTON - Fabric - UNIROYAL ENGINEERED PRODUCTS; *pg.* 699, *pg.* 467
SOUTHBEND - Cooking & Warming Equipment - THE MIDDLEBY CORPORATION; *pg.* 1361, *pg.* 610
SOUTHERN 500 - Competitive Motorsport Event - INTERNATIONAL SPEEDWAY CORPORATION; *pg.* 553, *pg.* 420
SOUTHERN BELL - Wireless Communication System - AT&T SOUTHEAST; *pg.* 1868, *pg.* 489
SOUTHERN BELLE - Video Game - INTERNATIONAL GAME TECHNOLOGY; *pg.* 957, *pg.* 1024
SOUTHERN CALIFORNIA GAS - Public Utility Distributing Natural Gas - SOUTHERN CALIFORNIA GAS COMPANY; *pg.* 1952, *pg.* 140
SOUTHERN COMFORT - Liqueur - BROWN-FORMAN

CORPORATION; *pg.* 1958, *pg.* 732

SOUTHERN COMPANY - Regional Electric Utility - SOUTHERN COMPANY; *pg.* 1952, *pg.* 520

SOUTHERN ENGINEERING - Ventilators & UDS Conveyors - DUKE MANUFACTURING COMPANY, INC.; *pg.* 54, *pg.* 995

SOUTHERN EXPRESSIONS - Art Service - FRED'S INC.; *pg.* 1769, *pg.* 1644

SOUTHERN LIVING - Media Publication - TIME INC.; *pg.* 1693, *pg.* 1300

SOUTHERN PEARL - Food Product - SHAMROCK FOODS COMPANY; *pg.* 895, *pg.* 20

SOUTHERN PINE BY DESIGN - Pine Lumber - SOUTHERN FOREST PRODUCTS ASSOCIATION; *pg.* 157, *pg.* 744

SOUTHERN PINE COUNCIL - Council - SOUTHERN FOREST PRODUCTS ASSOCIATION; *pg.* 157, *pg.* 744

SOUTHERN PLAINS - Carpet - INTERFACE, INC.; *pg.* 695, *pg.* 512

SOUTHERN RECIPE - Snack Food Product - RUDOLPH FOODS COMPANY; *pg.* 892, *pg.* 1458

SOUTHERN SUN - Beverages - THE COCA-COLA COMPANY; *pg.* 240, *pg.* 493

SOUTHERN TURF ALIVE - Lawn Care Product - GARDENS ALIVE!, INC.; *pg.* 1796, *pg.* 693

SOUTHERNPINE.COM - Website - SOUTHERN FOREST PRODUCTS ASSOCIATION; *pg.* 157, *pg.* 744

SOUTHHAMPTON - Beer - PABST BREWING COMPANY; *pg.* 258, *pg.* 137

SOUTHPAW LIGHT - Beer - MILLERCOORS; *pg.* 254, *pg.* 1877

SOUTHPOINT - Furniture - ASHLEY FURNITURE INDUSTRIES, INC.; *pg.* 914, *pg.* 1852

SOUTHWESTERN - Educational Publications - THOMSON REUTERS CORPORATION; *pg.* 1693, *pg.* 1944

SOUTHWICK - Clothes for Men - SOUTHWICK CLOTHING LLC; *pg.* 48, *pg.* 824

SOUVLAKI - Food Product - KRONOS PRODUCTS, INC.; *pg.* 872, *pg.* 614

SOVEREIGN - Medical Device - ABBOTT MEDICAL OPTICS, INC.; *pg.* 1485, *pg.* 260

SOVEREIGN - Multifire Clip Applier - AESCULAP, INC.; *pg.* 1487, *pg.* 1521

SOVEREIGN - Carpet - BEAULIEU GROUP, LLC; *pg.* 917, *pg.* 529

SOVEREIGN - Power Cable - COLEMAN CABLE, INC.; *pg.* 1324, *pg.* 665

SOVEREIGN - Lighting - LSI INDUSTRIES INC.; *pg.* 58, *pg.* 1416

SOVEREIGN - Plastic Cutlery - MARYLAND PLASTICS, INC.; *pg.* 1885, *pg.* 769

SOVEREIGN - Furniture - NEMSCHOFF, INC.; *pg.* 936, *pg.* 1890

SOVEREIGN OF THE SEAS - Cruise Ship - ROYAL CARIBBEAN CRUISES LTD; *pg.* 1921, *pg.* 446

SOVONA - Dinnerware - THE HOMER LAUGHLIN CHINA COMPANY; *pg.* 1125, *pg.* 1850

SOX SPLIT RAFFLE - In Park Program - CHICAGO WHITE SOX LTD.; *pg.* 539, *pg.* 570

SOXCAT - Additive - BASF CATALYSTS LLC; *pg.* 1148, *pg.* 1074

SOXGETTER - Catalyst Additive - JOHNSON MATTHEY PROCESS TECHNOLOGIES; *pg.* 1169, *pg.* 1083

SOY A MELT - Soy Cheese - THE WHITEWAVE FOODS COMPANY; *pg.* 1037, *pg.* 324

SOY BALANCE - Nutritional Supplement - PHARMAVITE LLC; *pg.* 1584, *pg.* 167

SOY BLENDS - Cleaning Product - BI-O-KLEEN INDUSTRIES, INC.; *pg.* 326, *pg.* 1845

SOY DREAM - Food Product - THE HAIN CELESTIAL GROUP, INC.; *pg.* 860, *pg.* 1172

SOY GEL - Paint Stripper - THE REAL MILK PAINT CO.; *pg.* 1446, *pg.* 1583

SOY PLUS - Biodiesel Fuel - MFA OIL COMPANY; *pg.* 981, *pg.* 976

SOY PLUS - Breakfast Cereals & Waffles - NATURE'S PATH FOODS INC.; *pg.* 833, *pg.* 1908

SOY PROTEIN - Boost - JAMBA, INC.; *pg.* 1024, *pg.* 84

SOY TREAT - Dairy Food Product - LIFEWAY FOODS, INC.; *pg.* 874, *pg.* 634

SOY7 - Agricultural Product - ARCHER-DANIELS-MIDLAND COMPANY; *pg.* 825, *pg.* 565

SOYA - Footwear - STEVEN MADDEN, LTD.; *pg.* 1819, *pg.* 1176

SOYAMAX - Health Care Product - USANA HEALTH SCIENCES, INC.; *pg.* 1605, *pg.* 1761

SOYCARE - Soy Supplement for Menopause - ALERE INC.; *pg.* 1488, *pg.* 849

SOYCOMIL - Agricultural Product - ARCHER-DANIELS-MIDLAND COMPANY; *pg.* 825, *pg.* 565

SOYFOAM - Seating System - LEAR CORPORATION; *pg.* 229, *pg.* 907

SOYGOLD - Grain - AG PROCESSING INC.; *pg.* 835, *pg.* 1013

SOYL - Hand Cleaner - BATTELLE MEMORIAL INSTITUTE; *pg.* 1401, *pg.* 1437

SOYLEC - Agricultural Product - ARCHER-DANIELS-MIDLAND COMPANY; *pg.* 825, *pg.* 565

SOYLEC A-10 - Soy Flour - ARCHER-DANIELS-MIDLAND COMPANY; *pg.* 825, *pg.* 565

SOYLEC C-15 - Soy Flour - ARCHER-DANIELS-MIDLAND COMPANY; *pg.* 825, *pg.* 565

SOYMAX - Animal Feed Products - OWENSBORO GRAIN COMPANY, INC.; *pg.* 706, *pg.* 739

SOYNILLA - Weight Management System - WATKINS INCORPORATED; *pg.* 909, *pg.* 967

SOYSENSE - Nutritional Supplement - RELIV INTERNATIONAL, INC.; *pg.* 1589, *pg.* 975

SOYSENTIALS - Nutritional Product - RELIV INTERNATIONAL, INC.; *pg.* 1589, *pg.* 975

SOYTEIN - Nutritional Product - NUTRACEUTICAL INTERNATIONAL CORPORATION; *pg.* 1576, *pg.* 1753

SP - Room Air Conditioners - FRIEDRICH AIR CONDITIONING CO.; *pg.* 1072, *pg.* 1740

SP - Fluid Handling System - GRACO, INC.; *pg.* 1342, *pg.* 935

SP - Audio - INFOCUS CORPORATION; *pg.* 644, *pg.* 1503

SP - Glass Beverageware & Stemware - ONEIDA LTD; *pg.* 1129, *pg.* 1318

SP - Bearing - THE TIMKEN COMPANY; *pg.* 218, *pg.* 1408

SP-100 - Processor - AVERY WEIGH-TRONIX, INC.; *pg.* 1315, *pg.* 925

SP-200 - 88 Key Portable Digital Piano - KORG USA, INC.; *pg.* 556, *pg.* 1180

SP-300 - 88 Key Portable Digital Piano - KORG USA, INC.; *pg.* 556, *pg.* 1180

SP-500 - 88 Key Interactive Digital Piano - KORG USA, INC.; *pg.* 556, *pg.* 1180

SP GURU - Software Product & Module - RIVERBED PERFORMANCE MANAGEMENT; *pg.* 462, *pg.* 765

SP GURU NETWORK PLANNER - Software Product & Module - RIVERBED PERFORMANCE MANAGEMENT; *pg.* 462, *pg.* 765

SP GURU TRANSPORT PLANNER - Software Product & Module - RIVERBED PERFORMANCE MANAGEMENT; *pg.* 462, *pg.* 765

SP SENTINEL - Software Product & Module - RIVERBED PERFORMANCE MANAGEMENT; *pg.* 462, *pg.* 765

SP SERIES - Towing & Recovery Equipment - MILLER INDUSTRIES, INC.; *pg.* 185, *pg.* 1655

SP-VT - Heat Exchanger - ECLIPSE INC.; *pg.* 1332, *pg.* 655

SP101 - Double-Action Revolver - STURM, RUGER & COMPANY, INC.; *pg.* 1846, *pg.* 371

SPA - Computer Storage System Software - AVAGO TECHNOLOGIES; *pg.* 358, *pg.* 238

SPA - Magazine - BONNIER CORPORATION; *pg.* 1622, *pg.* 480

SPA AT THE BAY - Games - PENN NATIONAL GAMING, INC.; *pg.* 574, *pg.* 1595

SPA FANTASY - Perfumes & Facial Masks - JAKKS PACIFIC, INC.; *pg.* 960, *pg.* 142

SPA GLASS - Bath Accessory - CROSCILL, INC.; *pg.* 1122, *pg.* 1220

SPA GLASS - Tile - WALKER & ZANGER, INC.; *pg.* 119, *pg.* 281

SPA LEAF - Bedding - CROSCILL, INC.; *pg.* 1122, *pg.* 1220

SPA LOGIX - Personal Care Product - PURETEK CORPORATION; *pg.* 1587, *pg.* 211

SPA-N-DECK - Coating & Paint - AKZO NOBEL DECORATIVE PAINTS, USA; *pg.* 1439, *pg.* 1474

SPA SELECT - Bathroom Fan - HUNTER FAN COMPANY; *pg.* 57, *pg.* 1631

SP*ACE - Software - BIO-RAD LABORATORIES, INC.; *pg.* 1504, *pg.* 101

SPACE BAG - Vacuum Seal Space Saver Storage Bags - S.C. JOHNSON & SON, INC.; *pg.* 334, *pg.* 1889

SPACE CRAFT - Packaging - INTERNATIONAL PAPER COMPANY; *pg.* 1460, *pg.* 1644

SPACE EXPERT - Software - BMC SOFTWARE, INC.; *pg.* 362, *pg.* 1701

SPACE FOR RENT - Video Game - INTERNATIONAL GAME TECHNOLOGY; *pg.* 957, *pg.* 1024

SPACE-GARD - Air Cleaner - RESEARCH PRODUCTS CORPORATION; *pg.* 1075, *pg.* 1867

SPACE MANAGEMENT WITH LIVEREORG - Software - DELL SOFTWARE; *pg.* 385, *pg.* 40

SPACE-MATE - Commercial Lighting - SWIVELIER CO., INC.; *pg.* 1307, *pg.* 1142

SPACE MOUNTAIN - Amusement Park - THE WALT DISNEY COMPANY; *pg.* 317, *pg.* 52

SPACE PLANNING - Software - JDA SOFTWARE GROUP, INC.; *pg.* 423, *pg.* 22

SPACE RACE - Video Game - INTERNATIONAL GAME TECHNOLOGY; *pg.* 957, *pg.* 1024

SPACE-RAY - Gas Heating Product - GAS-FIRED PRODUCTS, INC.; *pg.* 1338, *pg.* 1367

SPACE SAVER - Health & Fitness Product - ICON HEALTH & FITNESS, INC.; *pg.* 1837, *pg.* 1752

SPACE-SAVER - Filtration System - SERFILCO, LTD.; *pg.* 1375, *pg.* 641

SPACE-SAVING FLAT-1 - Cylinder - BIMBA MANUFACTURING COMPANY; *pg.* 1317, *pg.* 633

SPACE SHIP - Educational Materials - SCHOLASTIC INC.; *pg.* 1683, *pg.* 1288

SPACED OUT - Carpet - INTERFACE, INC.; *pg.* 695, *pg.* 512

SPACEFINDER - Filing Cabinets - TAB PRODUCTS CO. LLC; *pg.* 481, *pg.* 1869

SPACEMAN - Consumer Information - ACNIELSEN CORPORATION; *pg.* 341, *pg.* 1187

SPACEMASTER - Spotting Scope - BUSHNELL OUTDOOR PRODUCTS, INC.; *pg.* 1403, *pg.* 718

SPACEMATE - Refrigerator - IGLOO PRODUCTS CORPORATION; *pg.* 1126, *pg.* 1724

SPACEPAK - HVAC Equipment - MESTEK, INC.; *pg.* 1074, *pg.* 857

SPACES - Operating System Feature - APPLE INC.; *pg.* 350, *pg.* 73

SPACESETTER - Partitions - MODERNFOLD, INC.; *pg.* 98, *pg.* 681

SPACESHIFT - Delay Management System - AVID TECHNOLOGY, INC.; *pg.* 622, *pg.* 804

SPACESTATION - Workstations - IAC INDUSTRIES, INC.; *pg.* 929, *pg.* 48

SPACETRAX - Innerspace - STANLEY BLACK & DECKER, INC.; *pg.* 1063, *pg.* 358

SPACEWORKS - Plastic Etagere - HOME PRODUCTS INTERNATIONAL, INC.; *pg.* 1125, *pg.* 577

SPACKLE - Patch & Repair - THE MURALO COMPANY; *pg.* 1444, *pg.* 1042

SPACKMAX - Airless Texture Sprayer - GRACO, INC.; *pg.* 1342, *pg.* 935

SPACLUB - Health Resort - CANYON RANCH MANAGEMENT, LLC; *pg.* 1084, *pg.* 27

SPACT - Audio Clock Recovery Architecture Systems - TEXAS INSTRUMENTS INCORPORATED; *pg.* 679, *pg.* 1688

SPAGHETTI TOP - Clothing - K-SWISS; *pg.* 1837, *pg.* 306

SPAGHETTI V-NECK TOP - Clothing - K-SWISS; *pg.* 1837, *pg.* 306

SPAGHETTIOS - Soup - CAMPBELL SOUP COMPANY; *pg.* 844, *pg.* 1048

SPAGO - Carpet - INTERFACE, INC.; *pg.* 695, *pg.* 512

SPALDING - Athletic Equipment - RUSSELL BRANDS LLC; *pg.* 698, *pg.* 726

SPALLSHIELD - Glass Laminate - E.I. DU PONT DE NEMOURS & COMPANY; *pg.* 1159, *pg.* 390

SPAM - Luncheon Meat Product - HORMEL FOODS CORPORATION; *pg.* 863, *pg.* 915

SPAM - Video Slots - INTERNATIONAL GAME TECHNOLOGY; *pg.* 957, *pg.* 1024

SPAMANICURE - Manicure Products - CREATIVE NAIL DESIGN, INC.; *pg.* 506, *pg.* 302

SPAMSMART - Spam Blocking Software - THE ELECTRIC MAIL COMPANY; *pg.* 1242, *pg.* 1907

SPAN - Data Library - ION GEOPHYSICAL CORPORATION; *pg.* 1350, *pg.* 1708

SPAN-RITE - Door - MASONITE INTERNATIONAL CORPORATION; *pg.* 1054, *pg.* 1920

SPAN-TECH - Steel Product - HAWKEYE STEEL PRODUCTS, INC.; *pg.* 704, *pg.* 708

SPAN-TRACK - Carton Flow Product - UNEX MANUFACTURING, INC.; *pg.* 1385, *pg.* 1075

SPAN+AIDS - Patient Positioners - SPAN-AMERICA MEDICAL SYSTEMS, INC.; *pg.* 1595, *pg.* 1618

SPANDRELITE - Coated Glass for Structural Applications - PPG INDUSTRIES, INC.; *pg.* 1445, *pg.* 1579

First page reference indicates Business Class Edition
Second page reference indicates Geographic Edition

SPANGLE - Neutral Floor Cleaner - 3M COMPANY; *pg.* 1142, *pg.* 956
SPANGLER CANDY CANES - Peppermint Cane - SPANGLER CANDY COMPANY; *pg.* 1862, *pg.* 1407
SPANGLER CHOCOLATES - Chocolates - SPANGLER CANDY COMPANY; *pg.* 1862, *pg.* 1407
SPANGLER GOLD LEAF - Chocolate - SPANGLER CANDY COMPANY; *pg.* 1862, *pg.* 1407
SPANISH AMERICAN BEAN SOUP - Dried Beans - N.K. HURST CO., INC.; *pg.* 886, *pg.* 689
SPANISH COTTO - Terra Cotta - WALKER & ZANGER, INC.; *pg.* 119, *pg.* 281
SPANISH MASTER - Language Dictionary - FRANKLIN ELECTRONIC PUBLISHERS, INC.; *pg.* 398, *pg.* 1048
SPANISH PARADISE - Game - WMS INDUSTRIES INC.; *pg.* 593, *pg.* 666
SPANISHBOOKSINPRINT.COM - Online Database - R.R. BOWKER LLC; *pg.* 1682, *pg.* 1095
SPANKY - Bicycle Accessories - SPECIALIZED BICYCLE COMPONENTS, INC.; *pg.* 1711, *pg.* 152
SPANLATCH - Locking Mechanism - ANCHOR INDUSTRIES, INC.; *pg.* 1825, *pg.* 678
SPANSION - Flash Memory Product - ADVANCED MICRO DEVICES, INC.; *pg.* 613, *pg.* 282
SPANX - Body-Shaping Hosiery - SPANX INC.; *pg.* 32, *pg.* 520
SPAPEDICURE - Pedicure Products - CREATIVE NAIL DESIGN, INC.; *pg.* 506, *pg.* 302
SPAR PRODUCTION & DRILLING RISER SYSTEMS - Riser Systems - DRIL-QUIP, INC.; *pg.* 1330, *pg.* 1704
SPAR PRODUCTION RISER CONNECTORS - Riser Systems - DRIL-QUIP, INC.; *pg.* 1330, *pg.* 1704
SPARC - Medical Device - AMERICAN MEDICAL SYSTEMS HOLDINGS, INC.; *pg.* 1493, *pg.* 947
SPARC - Bicycle Component - SRAM CORPORATION; *pg.* 967, *pg.* 590
SPARCO - Office Products - GENUINE PARTS COMPANY; *pg.* 206, *pg.* 506
SPARK - Automobile - GENERAL MOTORS COMPANY; *pg.* 175, *pg.* 881
SPARK - Suitcase - SAMSONITE CORPORATION; *pg.* 11, *pg.* 830
SPARK - Educational Resources - SCHOOL SPECIALTY, INC.; *pg.* 467, *pg.* 1860
SPARK-FAS - Adhesive - H.B. FULLER COMPANY; *pg.* 1165, *pg.* 961
SPARKLE - Soft Drink - THE COCA-COLA COMPANY; *pg.* 240, *pg.* 493
SPARKLE - Paper Towels & Napkins - GEORGIA-PACIFIC LLC; *pg.* 1458, *pg.* 507
SPARKLE - Imitation Butter Flavored Oil - MALLET & COMPANY, INC.; *pg.* 875, *pg.* 1521
SPARKLE RUE21 - Fragrance - RUE21, INC.; *pg.* 32, *pg.* 1591
SPARKLE SILVER - Automotive Coating - SILBERLINE MANUFACTURING CO., INC.; *pg.* 110, *pg.* 1588
SPARKLEEN - Pre-Treatment Cleaner - A BRITE COMPANY; *pg.* 1144, *pg.* 1697
SPARKLENE - Material - ROSCO LABORATORIES, INC.; *pg.* 1782, *pg.* 378
SPARKLER - Container Grown Plant - MONROVIA GROWERS; *pg.* 1797, *pg.* 44
SPARKLETTS - Soft Drink - THE COCA-COLA COMPANY; *pg.* 240, *pg.* 493
SPARKLEWRAP - Wrapping Material - SEALED AIR CORPORATION; *pg.* 1468, *pg.* 1058
SPARKLING ICE - Beverage - TALKINGRAIN BEVERAGE COMPANY; *pg.* 266, *pg.* 1823
SPARKLING ICE LEMONADE - Beverage - TALKINGRAIN BEVERAGE COMPANY; *pg.* 266, *pg.* 1823
SPARKLING ICE MOUNTAIN SPRING WATER - Beverage - TALKINGRAIN BEVERAGE COMPANY; *pg.* 266, *pg.* 1823
SPARKLING ICE TEA - Beverage - TALKINGRAIN BEVERAGE COMPANY; *pg.* 266, *pg.* 1823
SPARKLING-SEC - Wine - BILTMORE ESTATE WINE COMPANY; *pg.* 1958, *pg.* 1358
SPARKLING WAVE PINE-SOL - All Purpose Cleaner - THE CLOROX COMPANY; *pg.* 327, *pg.* 169
SPARKLIST - Hosted Email Marketing Solutions - LYRIS, INC.; *pg.* 429, *pg.* 84
SPARKLON - Adhesive & Sealant - DOW CHEMICAL; *pg.* 1156, *pg.* 1563
SPARKLY CLEAN - Dishwasher Soap - HY-VEE, INC.; *pg.* 1023, *pg.* 713
SPARKS - beer - MILLERCOORS; *pg.* 254, *pg.* 1877
SPARKS LIGHT - Beer - MILLERCOORS; *pg.* 254, *pg.* 1877
SPARKS PLUS 6% - Beer - MILLERCOORS; *pg.* 254, *pg.* 1877
SPARKS PLUS 7% - beer - MILLERCOORS; *pg.* 254, *pg.* 1877
SPARKS RESERVE HIGH GRAVITY - Beer - MILLERCOORS; *pg.* 254, *pg.* 1877
SPARKS RESERVE HIGH GRAVITY 6.0 - Beer - MILLERCOORS; *pg.* 254, *pg.* 1877
SPARKS RESERVE TRIPLE EXPORT 8.1% - Beer - MILLERCOORS; *pg.* 254, *pg.* 1877
SPARKY - Motorsports Entertainment - SPEEDWAY MOTORSPORTS, INC.; *pg.* 584, *pg.* 1370
SPARKY THE FIREDOG - Fire Safety Education - NATIONAL FIRE PROTECTION ASSOCIATION; *pg.* 149, *pg.* 842
SPARLETTA - Beverages - THE COCA-COLA COMPANY; *pg.* 240, *pg.* 493
SPARLETTA IRON BREW - Beverages - THE COCA-COLA COMPANY; *pg.* 240, *pg.* 493
SPARQ TR - Footwear - NIKE, INC.; *pg.* 1812, *pg.* 1492
SPARROW WEB - Software - XEROX CORPORATION; *pg.* 494, *pg.* 365
SPARTA - Foodservice Brushes, Cleaning Tools, Cutting Boards & Accessories - CARLISLE FOODSERVICE PRODUCTS INCORPORATED; *pg.* 1455, *pg.* 1485
SPARTA - Medical Device - INTEGRA LIFESCIENCES HOLDINGS CORPORATION; *pg.* 1545, *pg.* 1109
SPARTACUSA - Fabric - NEMSCHOFF, INC.; *pg.* 936, *pg.* 1890
SPARTAGLO - Interior & Exterior Semi-Gloss Paint - DUNN-EDWARDS CORPORATION; *pg.* 1442, *pg.* 129
SPARTAGLOSS - Interior & Exterior Gloss Paint - DUNN-EDWARDS CORPORATION; *pg.* 1442, *pg.* 129
SPARTAN - Paper Cutter - THE CHALLENGE MACHINERY COMPANY; *pg.* 1322, *pg.* 902
SPARTAN - Flexible Pipe - CRESLINE PLASTIC PIPE CO., INC.; *pg.* 1881, *pg.* 678
SPARTAN - Herbicide - FMC CORPORATION; *pg.* 1163, *pg.* 1564
SPARTAN - Medical Equipment - INVACARE CORPORATION; *pg.* 1546, *pg.* 1451
SPARTAN - Lubricant and Process Oil - ROCK VALLEY OIL & CHEMICAL COMPANY; *pg.* 1179, *pg.* 631
SPARTAN - Steel Products - RUSSEL METALS INC.; *pg.* 1180, *pg.* 1928
SPARTAN - Vehicles - SPARTAN MOTORS, INC.; *pg.* 217, *pg.* 874
SPARTAN - Food Products - SPARTANNASH CO; *pg.* 1034, *pg.* 889
SPARTAN - Commercial Lighting - SWIVELIER CO., INC.; *pg.* 1307, *pg.* 1142
SPARTAN ADVANCE - Herbicides - FMC CORPORATION; *pg.* 1163, *pg.* 1564
SPARTAN CHARGE - Herbicides - FMC CORPORATION; *pg.* 1163, *pg.* 1564
SPARTAN STAFFING - Warehouse & Manufacturing Staffing - TRUEBLUE, INC.; *pg.* 485, *pg.* 1845
SPARTAN Z - Skate - ROLLER DERBY SKATE CORP.; *pg.* 966, *pg.* 630
SPARTASHEEN - Interior & Exterior Low Sheen Paint - DUNN-EDWARDS CORPORATION; *pg.* 1442, *pg.* 129
SPARTASHELL - Interior & Exterior Eggshell Paint - DUNN-EDWARDS CORPORATION; *pg.* 1442, *pg.* 129
SPARTON MEDICAL SYSTEMS - Medical Services - SPARTON CORPORATION; *pg.* 1377, *pg.* 660
SPARVAR - Spray Paints - SHERWIN-WILLIAMS DIVERSIFIED BRANDS DIVISION; *pg.* 1448, *pg.* 1435
SPARX - Ethernet Network Equipment - VITESSE SEMICONDUCTOR CORPORATION; *pg.* 686, *pg.* 57
SPARY PREP - Water Conditioning Agent - KALO, INC.; *pg.* 1796, *pg.* 719
SPAS - Sonic Jewelry Cleaner - CONNOISSEURS PRODUCTS CORPORATION; *pg.* 329, *pg.* 861
SPATIAL DATABASE ENGINE - Software - ENVIRONMENTAL SYSTEMS RESEARCH INSTITUTE INC.; *pg.* 393, *pg.* 188
SPATIALWARE - Software - PITNEY BOWES SOFTWARE INC.; *pg.* 455, *pg.* 1346
SPATTER-GUARD FM - Blanket & Curtain - SELLSTROM MANUFACTURING CO.; *pg.* 1428, *pg.* 659
SPATTERWARE - Bath Accessory - CROSCILL, INC.; *pg.* 1122, *pg.* 1220
SPAULDING - Lighting Product - HUBBELL INCORPORATED; *pg.* 1299, *pg.* 370
S.P.D.E. 33 - Chemical Product - BIRKO CORPORATION; *pg.* 1149, *pg.* 332
SPEAK@EASE - PBX Switch - MITEL NETWORKS CORPORATION; *pg.* 654, *pg.* 1921
SPEAK OUT - Wireless Phone - 7-ELEVEN, INC.; *pg.* 1012, *pg.* 1672
SPEAKER'S - Scotch - LAIRD & COMPANY, INC.; *pg.* 1966, *pg.* 1119
SPEAKERS BUREAU - Event - CHICAGO WHITE SOX LTD.; *pg.* 539, *pg.* 570
SPEAKERSHOP - Audio & Video Product - HARMAN INTERNATIONAL INDUSTRIES, INCORPORATED; *pg.* 641, *pg.* 374
SPEAKING ACE - Speller - FRANKLIN ELECTRONIC PUBLISHERS, INC.; *pg.* 398, *pg.* 1048
SPEAKING WORDMASTER - Thesaurus - FRANKLIN ELECTRONIC PUBLISHERS, INC.; *pg.* 398, *pg.* 1048
SPEAR - Systems Integration & Aeronautics - LOCKHEED MARTIN CORPORATION; *pg.* 229, *pg.* 762
SPEAR OF DESTINY - Video Game - ID SOFTWARE, INC.; *pg.* 956, *pg.* 1727
SPEARHEAD - Boom Mowers - ALAMO GROUP INC.; *pg.* 1311, *pg.* 1745
SPEARMINT - Air Freshener - SWISHER HYGIENE INC.; *pg.* 336, *pg.* 1507
SPEC AID - Finished Fuel Additives - GE WATER & PROCESS TECHNOLOGIES; *pg.* 1339, *pg.* 1588
SPEC CLIPS - Mounting Tool - MIDDLE ATLANTIC PRODUCTS INC.; *pg.* 1360, *pg.* 1065
SPEC CPL - Medical Test - IDEXX LABORATORIES, INC.; *pg.* 1543, *pg.* 753
SPEC FPL - Medical Test - IDEXX LABORATORIES, INC.; *pg.* 1543, *pg.* 753
SPEC-KON - OEM Product And Tool - THOMAS & BETTS CORPORATION; *pg.* 680, *pg.* 1646
SPEC-TUSS - Animal Safety Product - NEOGEN CORPORATION; *pg.* 883, *pg.* 896
SPECBRIGHT - LED Module - PROPHOTONIX LIMITED; *pg.* 1427, *pg.* 1039
SPECDIRECT - Electronic Instrument - KEITHLEY INSTRUMENTS, INC.; *pg.* 1418, *pg.* 1473
SPECFIL - Polyurethane Component - THE DOW CHEMICAL COMPANY; *pg.* 1157, *pg.* 898
SPECFINDER - Software - BIO-RAD LABORATORIES, INC.; *pg.* 1504, *pg.* 101
SPECFLEX - Polyurethane Component - THE DOW CHEMICAL COMPANY; *pg.* 1157, *pg.* 898
SPECGRADE - Bag & Pouch Material - AUTOMATED PACKAGING SYSTEMS INC.; *pg.* 1452, *pg.* 1474
SPECI-CATCH - Specimen Collector - MEDLINE INDUSTRIES, INC.; *pg.* 1562, *pg.* 635
SPECI-CATH - Infant Urine Collector - MEDLINE INDUSTRIES, INC.; *pg.* 1562, *pg.* 635
SPECIAL - Knife - BUCK KNIVES, INC.; *pg.* 1828, *pg.* 550
SPECIAL - Car Washer - MOC PRODUCTS COMPANY, INC.; *pg.* 332, *pg.* 174
SPECIAL ALTERNATIVES - Insurance Claims Management Service - LINCOLN NATIONAL CORPORATION; *pg.* 776, *pg.* 1567
SPECIAL AMBER - Beverage - SPRECHER BREWING COMPANY; *pg.* 265, *pg.* 1858
SPECIAL APPLICATIONS CUTTINGS INJECTION SYSTEMS - Subsea Equipment - DRIL-QUIP, INC.; *pg.* 1330, *pg.* 1704
SPECIAL CARE - Skin Care Products - LUZIER PERSONALIZED COSMETICS, INC.; *pg.* 515, *pg.* 978
SPECIAL CRISP - Candy Bar - THE HERSHEY CO.; *pg.* 1855, *pg.* 1538
SPECIAL DARK - Semi-Sweet Chocolate Bar - THE HERSHEY CO.; *pg.* 1855, *pg.* 1538
SPECIAL DELIVERY B-12 PLUS - Jelly Product - BEE-ALIVE INC.; *pg.* 1503, *pg.* 1348
SPECIAL EFFECTS - Premium Vinyl Composition Floor Tile - CONGOLEUM CORPORATION; *pg.* 921, *pg.* 1084
SPECIAL EFFECTS - Optical Design Accessory - HIGH END SYSTEMS, INC.; *pg.* 1299, *pg.* 1663
SPECIAL EFFECTS - Stain Cleaner - THE VALSPAR CORPORATION; *pg.* 1449, *pg.* 945
SPECIAL EXPORT - Beer - PABST BREWING COMPANY; *pg.* 258, *pg.* 137
SPECIAL FAVORS - Customized Miniature Books - RUNNING PRESS; *pg.* 1682, *pg.* 1570
SPECIAL K - Food Product - KELLOGG COMPANY; *pg.* 831, *pg.* 870
SPECIAL K BAR STRAWBERRY - Snacks - KELLOGG

COMPANY; *pg.* 831, *pg.* 870
SPECIAL K BLISS BAR - Cereal Bar - KELLOGG COMPANY; *pg.* 831, *pg.* 870
SPECIAL K CRACKER CHIPS - Low Calorie Snack Foods - KELLOGG COMPANY; *pg.* 831, *pg.* 870
SPECIAL K PROTEIN SHAKE - Weight-Management Drink - KELLOGG COMPANY; *pg.* 831, *pg.* 870
SPECIAL MUSIC SCHOOL - Performance Art Service - THE KAUFMAN CENTER; *pg.* 556, *pg.* 1248
SPECIAL PINE - Outdoor Playsets - CREATIVE PLAYTHINGS LTD.; *pg.* 1831, *pg.* 820
SPECIAL PURPOSE 500 - Gun - O.F. MOSSBERG & SONS, INC.; *pg.* 1842, *pg.* 360
SPECIAL VALUE - Food Products - UNIFIED GROCERS, INC.; *pg.* 1036, *pg.* 66
SPECIAL WINDOWS - Envelope - TENSION ENVELOPE CORPORATION; *pg.* 483, *pg.* 986
SPECIALIZED PRINTED FORMS - Custom Printing - ENNIS, INC.; *pg.* 393, *pg.* 1727
SPECIALIZING IN NATIVE PLANTS - Tagline - FORREST KEELING NURSERY, INC.; *pg.* 1795, *pg.* 977
SPECIALRISE - Bicycle Accessories - SPECIALIZED BICYCLE COMPONENTS, INC.; *pg.* 1711, *pg.* 152
SPECIALTY - Door - MASONITE INTERNATIONAL CORPORATION; *pg.* 1054, *pg.* 1920
SPECIALTY COLLECTION - Sink - ELKAY MANUFACTURING COMPANY; *pg.* 80, *pg.* 645
SPECIALTY ENGINEERED PRODUCTS - Tagline - LYDALL, INC.; *pg.* 1357, *pg.* 354
SPECIALTY MATERIALS THAT MAKE OUR WORLD - Slogan - ALLEGHENY TECHNOLOGIES INCORPORATED; *pg.* 66, *pg.* 1572
SPECIALTY SLEEP - Mattress - SIMMONS COMPANY; *pg.* 943, *pg.* 520
SPECK FINDER - Electronic Video Microscope - DAZOR MANUFACTURING CORP.; *pg.* 1296, *pg.* 995
SPECKLE - Educational Materials - SCHOLASTIC INC.; *pg.* 1683, *pg.* 1288
SPECKLEMOUSE - Semiconductor Solution - CYPRESS SEMICONDUCTOR CORPORATION; *pg.* 1326, *pg.* 243
SPECMAKER - Screening - TELSMITH, INC.; *pg.* 1381, *pg.* 1871
SPECMASTER - Concrete Batching Equipment - BESSER COMPANY; *pg.* 1317, *pg.* 865
SPECMASTER II - Concrete Product Equipment - BESSER COMPANY; *pg.* 1317, *pg.* 865
SPECMATE LADDER - Wiring System - WIREMOLD/LEGRAND; *pg.* 689, *pg.* 383
SPECMATE SOLID BOTTOM - Wiring System - WIREMOLD/LEGRAND; *pg.* 689, *pg.* 383
SPECMATE TRAY - Wiring System - WIREMOLD/LEGRAND; *pg.* 689, *pg.* 383
SPECMATE TYPE I - Wiring System - WIREMOLD/LEGRAND; *pg.* 689, *pg.* 383
SPECMATE WALL - Wiring System - WIREMOLD/LEGRAND; *pg.* 689, *pg.* 383
SPEC'S - Retail Music Stores - TRANS WORLD ENTERTAINMENT CORPORATION; *pg.* 313, *pg.* 1137
SPECTA CLEAR - Lens Treatment Product - EMERGING VISION, INC.; *pg.* 1411, *pg.* 1227
SPECTAR - Copolyester - EASTMAN CHEMICAL COMPANY; *pg.* 1159, *pg.* 1636
SPECTATOR - Leather Product - COACH, INC.; *pg.* 3, *pg.* 1214
SPECTEK - Memory Chip - MICRON TECHNOLOGY, INC.; *pg.* 435, *pg.* 547
SPECTEK SELECT - Memory Chip - MICRON TECHNOLOGY, INC.; *pg.* 435, *pg.* 547
SPECTOR 2.2 - Software - SPECTORSOFT CORPORATION; *pg.* 1281, *pg.* 478
SPECTOR 3.0 - Software - SPECTORSOFT CORPORATION; *pg.* 1281, *pg.* 478
SPECTOR 360 - Software - SPECTORSOFT CORPORATION; *pg.* 1281, *pg.* 478
SPECTOR CNE - Software - SPECTORSOFT CORPORATION; *pg.* 1281, *pg.* 478
SPECTOR FOR WINDOWS - Software - SPECTORSOFT CORPORATION; *pg.* 1281, *pg.* 478
SPECTOR PRO 5.0 - Software - SPECTORSOFT CORPORATION; *pg.* 1281, *pg.* 478
SPECTOR PRO MAC - Software - SPECTORSOFT CORPORATION; *pg.* 1281, *pg.* 478
SPECTOUR - Digital Gamma Camera - DIGIRAD CORPORATION; *pg.* 1524, *pg.* 185
SPECTPAK PLUS - Medical Imaging Equipment - DIGIRAD CORPORATION; *pg.* 1524, *pg.* 185
SPECTRA - Furniture - ASHLEY FURNITURE INDUSTRIES, INC.; *pg.* 914, *pg.* 1852
SPECTRA - Fabric - HEXCEL CORPORATION; *pg.* 1884, *pg.* 375
SPECTRA - Fiber - HONEYWELL INTERNATIONAL INC.; *pg.* 407, *pg.* 1088
SPECTRA - Table System - HOWE FURNITURE CORPORATION; *pg.* 928, *pg.* 998
SPECTRA - Data Management System - ION GEOPHYSICAL CORPORATION; *pg.* 1350, *pg.* 1708
SPECTRA - Drift Retardant Solution - KALO, INC.; *pg.* 1796, *pg.* 719
SPECTRA - Metrology Product - KLA-TENCOR CORPORATION; *pg.* 1353, *pg.* 146
SPECTRA - Art Papers & Tissue - PACON CORPORATION; *pg.* 1466, *pg.* 1852
SPECTRA - Molecular Biology Product - THERMO FISHER SCIENTIFIC INC.; *pg.* 1602, *pg.* 61
SPECTRA AMS - Drift Retardant Solution - KALO, INC.; *pg.* 1796, *pg.* 719
SPECTRA/CHROM - Chromatography System - SPECTRUM LABORATORIES INC.; *pg.* 1595, *pg.* 69
SPECTRA/GEL - Absorbent - SPECTRUM LABORATORIES INC.; *pg.* 1595, *pg.* 69
SPECTRA LINK - Wireless Phone - POLYCOM, INC.; *pg.* 664, *pg.* 249
SPECTRA MAX TANK MIX - Drift Control Agent - KALO, INC.; *pg.* 1796, *pg.* 719
SPECTRA MAX TECH - Water Conditioner - KALO, INC.; *pg.* 1796, *pg.* 719
SPECTRA MESH - Filtration System - SPECTRUM LABORATORIES INC.; *pg.* 1595, *pg.* 69
SPECTRA POINT - Broadloom - COURISTAN INC.; *pg.* 921, *pg.* 1067
SPECTRA/POR - Biotech Cellulose Ester - SPECTRUM LABORATORIES INC.; *pg.* 1595, *pg.* 69
SPECTRA PRECISION - Navigation Aid - TRIMBLE NAVIGATION LIMITED; *pg.* 1384, *pg.* 288
SPECTRA SHIELD - Synthetic Fiber - HONEYWELL INTERNATIONAL INC.; *pg.* 407, *pg.* 1088
SPECTRA-STRIP - Connectors - AMPHENOL CORPORATION; *pg.* 616, *pg.* 381
SPECTRA SYSTEM - Instant Cameras, Films & Accessories - POLAROID CORPORATION; *pg.* 1426, *pg.* 815
SPECTRA-TEX - Paints - BADGER AIR BRUSH COMPANY; *pg.* 359, *pg.* 612
SPECTRABASE - Software - BIO-RAD LABORATORIES, INC.; *pg.* 1504, *pg.* 101
SPECTRABIOTIC - Supplement & Food Product - NEW EARTH LIFE SCIENCES, INC.; *pg.* 1573, *pg.* 1499
SPECTRACD - Inline Spectroscopic CD Metrology - KLA-TENCOR CORPORATION; *pg.* 1353, *pg.* 146
SPECTRACE - Marker - DOW CHEMICAL; *pg.* 1156, *pg.* 1563
SPECTRACEF - Pharmaceutical Product - CHIESI USA, INC.; *pg.* 1515, *pg.* 1359
SPECTRACLAD - Architectural Glass Panels - PPG INDUSTRIES, INC.; *pg.* 1445, *pg.* 1579
SPECTRACON - Coating Product - PPG INDUSTRIES, INC.; *pg.* 1445, *pg.* 1579
SPECTRAFLAIR - Pigment - VIAVI SOLUTIONS INC.; *pg.* 1435, *pg.* 148
SPECTRAFLEX - Lead Coating - MEDTRONIC, INC.; *pg.* 1564, *pg.* 939
SPECTRAFLO - Liquid Colorants - FERRO CORPORATION; *pg.* 1162, *pg.* 1462
SPECTRAFX 100 - Thin-film Metrology System - KLA-TENCOR CORPORATION; *pg.* 1353, *pg.* 146
SPECTRAGRAPH - Video Keying - AVID TECHNOLOGY, INC.; *pg.* 622, *pg.* 804
SPECTRAL - Pharmaceutical Product - ALERE INC.; *pg.* 1488, *pg.* 849
SPECTRAL SEARCHING MADE EASY - Software - BIO-RAD LABORATORIES, INC.; *pg.* 1504, *pg.* 101
SPECTRALENS - Molded Lens - TRANS-LUX CORPORATION; *pg.* 681, *pg.* 365
SPECTRALERT - Horns & Strobes - SYSTEM SENSOR; *pg.* 676, *pg.* 658
SPECTRALIFT - Vertical Wheelchair Lift - INCLINATOR COMPANY OF AMERICA; *pg.* 88, *pg.* 1536
SPECTRALIGHT - Light Booth - X-RITE, INCORPORATED; *pg.* 1437, *pg.* 891
SPECTRALINK - Wireless Phone System - RAULAND-BORG CORPORATION; *pg.* 666, *pg.* 634
SPECTRALINK NETLINK - Wireless Telephone - MITEL NETWORKS CORPORATION; *pg.* 654, *pg.* 1921
SPECTRALITE - Gauge Plastic Film - MULTI-PLASTICS, INC.; *pg.* 1886, *pg.* 1457
SPECTRALOOK - Image Processing - ICAD, INC.; *pg.* 643, *pg.* 1037
SPECTRAMATTE - Video Keying - AVID TECHNOLOGY, INC.; *pg.* 622, *pg.* 804
SPECTRAMAX - Connector & Adapter - ALLIANCE FIBER OPTIC PRODUCTS, INC.; *pg.* 1399, *pg.* 283
SPECTRAMAX - Software - MOLECULAR DEVICES CORPORATION; *pg.* 1568, *pg.* 287
SPECTRAMAX GEMINI - Spectrophotometer - MOLECULAR DEVICES CORPORATION; *pg.* 1568, *pg.* 287
SPECTRANETICS LASER SHEATH - Cardiac Lead Removal Device - THE SPECTRANETICS CORPORATION; *pg.* 1595, *pg.* 315
SPECTRAPLUS - Software - BRUKER CORPORATION; *pg.* 1511, *pg.* 788
SPECTRAQUARTZ Colored Play Sand - FAIRMOUNT SANTROL; *pg.* 1162, *pg.* 1409
SPECTRASHIELD - Powder Coat Finishes - CORNELL IRON WORKS, INC.; *pg.* 77, *pg.* 1554
SPECTRASOL - Animal Safety Product - NEOGEN CORPORATION; *pg.* 883, *pg.* 896
SPECTRASTREAM - Digital Video System - SIQURA; *pg.* 308, *pg.* 771
SPECTRATECH - Printing Papers - SAPPI FINE PAPER NORTH AMERICA; *pg.* 1468, *pg.* 801
SPECTRAX - Pacemaker - MEDTRONIC, INC.; *pg.* 1564, *pg.* 939
SPECTRAX SX - Pacemaker - MEDTRONIC, INC.; *pg.* 1564, *pg.* 939
SPECTRE - One-handed Opening Pocket/Belt Clip Knife - GERBER LEGENDARY BLADES; *pg.* 1834, *pg.* 1503
SPECTRE - Electronic Components - MOLEX INCORPORATED; *pg.* 655, *pg.* 628
SPECTRE ALERT - Laser Detectors - COBRA ELECTRONICS CORPORATION; *pg.* 629, *pg.* 572
SPECTREM - Roofing Material - TREMCO INCORPORATED; *pg.* 116, *pg.* 1405
SPECTRIM - Moldable Product - THE DOW CHEMICAL COMPANY; *pg.* 1157, *pg.* 898
SPECTRIS MR - Injection System - MEDRAD, INC.; *pg.* 1563, *pg.* 1591
SPECTRO - Nutritional Product - NUTRACEUTICAL INTERNATIONAL CORPORATION; *pg.* 1576, *pg.* 1753
SPECTRO CHIP - Clean Resin Chip - SEQUENOM, INC.; *pg.* 1593, *pg.* 209
SPECTROM - Color Light Mainline Signal - ALSTOM SIGNALING, INC.; *pg.* 1312, *pg.* 1350
SPECTROMAGIC - Game - THE WALT DISNEY COMPANY; *pg.* 317, *pg.* 52
SPECTRON - Braided Fishing Line - CORTLAND LINE COMPANY; *pg.* 1831, *pg.* 1155
SPECTRON - Lasers - GSI GROUP INC.; *pg.* 1415, *pg.* 784
SPECTRON - HMWPE Fiber Rope - SAMSON ROPE TECHNOLOGIES; *pg.* 1468, *pg.* 1820
SPECTRONIC - Graphic Art UV System - NORDSON CORPORATION; *pg.* 1365, *pg.* 1480
SPECTROPURE - Dental Mercury - BASF CATALYSTS LLC; *pg.* 1148, *pg.* 1074
SPECTROSOLV - Chemical Product - SPECTRUM CHEMICALS & LABORATORY PRODUCTS, INC.; *pg.* 1181, *pg.* 94
SPECTROVITE - Pharmaceutical Product - ALERE INC.; *pg.* 1488, *pg.* 849
SPECTRULITE - Screen-Printing Ink - FERRO CORPORATION; *pg.* 1162, *pg.* 1462
SPECTRUM - Semiconductor Device - APPLIED MATERIALS, INC; *pg.* 618, *pg.* 1009
SPECTRUM - Head & Neck Product - CARLISLE FOODSERVICE PRODUCTS INCORPORATED; *pg.* 1455, *pg.* 1485
SPECTRUM - Medical Equipment - CONMED CORPORATION; *pg.* 1517, *pg.* 1347
SPECTRUM - Dental Product - DENTSPLY INTERNATIONAL INC.; *pg.* 1522, *pg.* 1596
SPECTRUM - Mechanical Multipacker - DOUGLAS MACHINE, INC.; *pg.* 1456, *pg.* 915
SPECTRUM - Prefinished Interior Wall Paneling - GEORGIA-PACIFIC LLC; *pg.* 1458, *pg.* 507
SPECTRUM - Microbiological Control Technology - HERCULES INCORPORATED; *pg.* 1166, *pg.* 392
SPECTRUM - Steel-Framed Operable Partition - HUFCOR

First page reference indicates Business Class Edition
Second page reference indicates Geographic Edition

INCORPORATED; *pg.* 87, *pg.* 1861
SPECTRUM - Alternative Fuel Systems - IMPCO TECHNOLOGIES, INC.; *pg.* 208, *pg.* 261
SPECTRUM - Epilator - INSTANTRON CO., INC.; *pg.* 512, *pg.* 1608
SPECTRUM - Abrasive Flow Machine - KENNAMETAL EXTRUDE HONE; *pg.* 1352, *pg.* 1542
SPECTRUM - Grinder and Polisher - LECO CORPORATION; *pg.* 1355, *pg.* 906
SPECTRUM - Patient Monitoring Device - MAQUET; *pg.* 1558, *pg.* 1082
SPECTRUM - Medical Device - MENTOR CORPORATION; *pg.* 1565, *pg.* 263
SPECTRUM - Welding & Cutting Equip. - MILLER ELECTRIC MANUFACTURING CO.; *pg.* 1361, *pg.* 1852
SPECTRUM - Home & Small Business Communications Systems - MITEL NETWORKS CORPORATION; *pg.* 654, *pg.* 1921
SPECTRUM - Power Generator - MKS INSTRUMENTS, INC.; *pg.* 1362, *pg.* 781
SPECTRUM - Dispensing System - NORDSON CORPORATION; *pg.* 1365, *pg.* 1480
SPECTRUM - Surgical Instrument - OSTEOMED CORPORATION; *pg.* 1425, *pg.* 1658
SPECTRUM - Floor Finish - ROCHESTER MIDLAND CORPORATION; *pg.* 334, *pg.* 1337
SPECTRUM - Educational Resources - SCHOOL SPECIALTY, INC.; *pg.* 467, *pg.* 1860
SPECTRUM - Tablet Coating/Coutainment Machine - THOMAS ENGINEERING INC.; *pg.* 1382, *pg.* 619
SPECTRUM - Wireless Control Product - UNIVERSAL ELECTRONICS, INC.; *pg.* 683, *pg.* 262
SPECTRUM 24 - Wireless LAN - MOTOROLA ENTERPRISE MOBILITY; *pg.* 441, *pg.* 1167
SPECTRUM DP - Xerographic Paper - GEORGIA-PACIFIC LLC; *pg.* 1458, *pg.* 507
SPECTRUM ESSENTIALS - Nutritional Supplements - THE HAIN CELESTIAL GROUP, INC.; *pg.* 860, *pg.* 1172
SPECTRUM NATURALS - Food Product - THE HAIN CELESTIAL GROUP, INC.; *pg.* 860, *pg.* 1172
SPECTRUM OF CHOICE - Banking Services - COMERICA INCORPORATED; *pg.* 740, *pg.* 1677
SPECTRUM SPRAY BAR - Gun Technology - THOMAS ENGINEERING INC.; *pg.* 1382, *pg.* 619
SPECTRUMGOBOS - Gobo Rotator - ROSCO LABORATORIES, INC.; *pg.* 1782, *pg.* 378
SPEE-DEE - Dry Cleaning & Laundry Product - ADCO, INC.; *pg.* 325, *pg.* 482
SPEECH-WORLD - Trade Publication - TECHNOLOGY MARKETING CORP.; *pg.* 1691, *pg.* 364
SPEECHMAGIC - Software - NUANCE COMMUNICATIONS, INC.; *pg.* 447, *pg.* 806
SPEECHMINER - Software - ENVISION; *pg.* 393, *pg.* 1835
SPEECHSECURE - Voice Identification Software - NUANCE COMMUNICATIONS, INC.; *pg.* 447, *pg.* 806
SPEED - Automated Wafer Fabrication System - LAM RESEARCH CORPORATION; *pg.* 1354, *pg.* 246
SPEED 7'S - Pulltab Game - IDAHO LOTTERY; *pg.* 995, *pg.* 547
SPEED-BAND - Saw Blades - KENNAMETAL IPG; *pg.* 1353, *pg.* 1615
SPEED BEAD - Car Care Product - STONER INC.; *pg.* 985, *pg.* 1583
SPEED BENDER - Bender - GREENLEE TEXTRON INC.; *pg.* 1048, *pg.* 655
SPEED-CHUCK - Hand Tool - GENERAL TOOLS & INSTRUMENTS LLC; *pg.* 1048, *pg.* 1234
SPEED-COAT - Slot Applicator - NORDSON CORPORATION; *pg.* 1365, *pg.* 1480
SPEED-COMPOUNDER - Battery Paste Mixer - PETTIBONE, LLC; *pg.* 1368, *pg.* 609
SPEED-D - Switchboards & Motor Control Centers - SCHNEIDER ELECTRIC USA, INC.; *pg.* 1306, *pg.* 650
SPEED DISK - Software - SYMANTEC CORPORATION; *pg.* 478, *pg.* 161
SPEED-DRI - Graphic Arts Drying Systems - PRECISION CONTROL SYSTEMS, INC./ RESEARCH INC.; *pg.* 1427, *pg.* 923
SPEED DRY - Int./Ext. Primer & Enamels - AKZONOBEL DECORATIVE PAINTS U.S.; *pg.* 1439, *pg.* 1474
SPEED DRY - Beauty Product - AVON PRODUCTS, INC.; *pg.* 500, *pg.* 1198
SPEED-FEED - Reinsertion System - RITE-HITE HOLDING CORPORATION; *pg.* 1372, *pg.* 1880
SPEED FINISH PLUS - Coating Product - PPG INDUSTRIES, INC.; *pg.* 1445, *pg.* 1579
SPEED FRAME - 20 Degree Round Head Framing Nailer - PASLODE; *pg.* 1059, *pg.* 664
SPEED GATE - Automated Gate System - CANADIAN NATIONAL RAILWAY COMPANY; *pg.* 1902, *pg.* 1953
SPEED-GRIP - Mop Handles - GEERPRES INC.; *pg.* 1339, *pg.* 901
SPEED IRON - Iron Box - ORECK CORPORATION; *pg.* 59, *pg.* 1653
SPEED LINE - Lacquers - PPG INDUSTRIES, INC.; *pg.* 1445, *pg.* 1579
SPEED-MILL - Diamond Sidetracking/Window-Cutting Bit - BAKER HUGHES INTEQ; *pg.* 1316, *pg.* 1700
SPEED-PRO - Performance Products - FEDERAL-MOGUL HOLDINGS CORPORATION; *pg.* 205, *pg.* 907
SPEED QUEEN - Laundry Appliances & Equipment - ALLIANCE LAUNDRY HOLDINGS LLC; *pg.* 51, *pg.* 1890
SPEED-REX - Epoxy Ester Enamel - AKZONOBEL DECORATIVE PAINTS U.S.; *pg.* 1439, *pg.* 1474
SPEED SCRUB - Surface Maintenance Machine - TENNANT COMPANY; *pg.* 1381, *pg.* 944
SPEED SEAL - Primer - JONES-BLAIR COMPANY; *pg.* 1443, *pg.* 1682
SPEED SHIFT - Basketball Equipment - LIFETIME PRODUCTS INC.; *pg.* 933, *pg.* 1751
SPEED STAR - Rotary Drilling Rigs - THE GEORGE E. FAILING COMPANY; *pg.* 1340, *pg.* 1484
SPEED STICK - Personal Care Product - COLGATE-PALMOLIVE COMPANY; *pg.* 504, *pg.* 1215
SPEED STRIPS - Food Product - PROMOTION IN MOTION, INC.; *pg.* 1861, *pg.* 1052
SPEED TRANSFER - Tape Drive - QUANTUM CORPORATION; *pg.* 458, *pg.* 250
SPEED-WALL - Paint - AKZONOBEL DECORATIVE PAINTS U.S.; *pg.* 1439, *pg.* 1474
SPEED ZONE - Racing Shirt - BROWN & BIGELOW, INC.; *pg.* 1624, *pg.* 959
SPEED ZONE - Bicycle - SPECIALIZED BICYCLE COMPONENTS, INC.; *pg.* 1711, *pg.* 152
SPEEDAIRE - Air Compressor - W.W. GRAINGER, INC.; *pg.* 1390, *pg.* 625
SPEEDBAND SUPERVIEW SUPER7 - Medical Device - BOSTON SCIENTIFIC CORPORATION; *pg.* 1508, *pg.* 831
SPEEDBLADE - Material Handling Equipment - DEGELMAN INDUSTRIES LTD.; *pg.* 703, *pg.* 1962
SPEEDBOARD - Dielectric Material - W.L. GORE & ASSOCIATES, INC.; *pg.* 122, *pg.* 388
SPEEDBRIDGE - Software - CADENCE DESIGN SYSTEMS, INC.; *pg.* 367, *pg.* 239
SPEEDCOTE - Paint - AKZONOBEL DECORATIVE PAINTS U.S.; *pg.* 1439, *pg.* 1474
SPEEDCRAFT - Interior & Exterior Latex & Oil-Based Enamels - PPG INDUSTRIES, INC.; *pg.* 1445, *pg.* 1579
SPEEDECOLOR - Color Management System - POLYONE CORPORATION; *pg.* 1177, *pg.* 1404
SPEEDER - Household Product - BLUE CROSS LABORATORIES; *pg.* 326, *pg.* 277
SPEEDFEED - Security Product - BAE SYSTEMS PRODUCTS GROUP; *pg.* 359, *pg.* 432
SPEEDFLAME - Gas Burners - ADAMS MFG. CO.; *pg.* 51, *pg.* 1427
SPEEDFLOW - Process Continuous Mixer - PETTIBONE, LLC; *pg.* 1368, *pg.* 609
SPEEDGLAS - Auto-Darkening Welding Helmet - 3M COMPANY; *pg.* 1142, *pg.* 956
SPEEDHIDE - Coating Product - PPG INDUSTRIES, INC.; *pg.* 1445, *pg.* 1579
SPEEDI-BOOT! - Split Boots & Clamps - DORMAN PRODUCTS, INC.; *pg.* 204, *pg.* 1522
SPEEDI-DRI-OIL - Grease Absorbent - BASF CATALYSTS LLC; *pg.* 1148, *pg.* 1074
SPEEDI-NOTCH - Cutter - THE WOLF MACHINE CO.; *pg.* 1389, *pg.* 1427
SPEEDI PLUMB - Water Connectors - BRASSCRAFT MANUFACTURING COMPANY; *pg.* 1043, *pg.* 902
SPEEDI PLUMB PLUS - Water Connectors - BRASSCRAFT MANUFACTURING COMPANY; *pg.* 1043, *pg.* 902
SPEEDISET - Snap-Apart Sets - R.R. DONNELLEY & SONS COMPANY; *pg.* 1682, *pg.* 589
SPEEDKING - Powder Spray Booth - NORDSON CORPORATION; *pg.* 1365, *pg.* 1480
SPEEDLINE - Paint Brushes, Cleaning, Polishing, Smoothing & Dusting Brushes - PPG INDUSTRIES, INC.; *pg.* 1445, *pg.* 1579
SPEEDLINE - Golf Product - TAYLORMADE-ADIDAS GOLF; *pg.* 1847, *pg.* 60
SPEEDLINE DRAW - Golf Product - TAYLORMADE-ADIDAS GOLF; *pg.* 1847, *pg.* 60
SPEEDLINE TECH - Golf Product - TAYLORMADE-ADIDAS GOLF; *pg.* 1847, *pg.* 60
SPEEDLING FLATS - Growing Trays - SPEEDLING INCORPORATED; *pg.* 1800, *pg.* 468
SPEEDLOCK - Drum Handling Equipment - LIFTOMATIC MATERIAL HANDLING INC.; *pg.* 94, *pg.* 560
SPEEDLYSER - Electrosurgical Devices - ANGIODYNAMICS, INC.; *pg.* 1495, *pg.* 1173
SPEEDMASTER - Hair Clipper - ANDIS COMPANY; *pg.* 498, *pg.* 1895
SPEEDMULLOR - Foundry Sand Mullor - PETTIBONE, LLC; *pg.* 1368, *pg.* 609
SPEEDMULLOR - Cooler - SIMPSON TECHNOLOGIES CORPORATION; *pg.* 111, *pg.* 555
SPEEDNET - Radio - S&C ELECTRIC COMPANY; *pg.* 1305, *pg.* 589
SPEEDPAK - Knives - ACME UNITED CORPORATION; *pg.* 1040, *pg.* 346
SPEEDPASS - Paying System - EXXON MOBIL CORPORATION; *pg.* 977, *pg.* 1718
SPEEDPLUS - D/A Converter - TEXAS INSTRUMENTS INCORPORATED; *pg.* 679, *pg.* 1688
SPEEDPRO - Coating Product - PPG INDUSTRIES, INC.; *pg.* 1445, *pg.* 1579
SPEEDREACH - Integrated Circuits - AVAGO TECHNOLOGIES; *pg.* 358, *pg.* 238
SPEEDREAD - Meter Reading System - BADGER METER, INC.; *pg.* 1401, *pg.* 1873
SPEEDSCREEN - Software - CITRIX SYSTEMS, INC.; *pg.* 375, *pg.* 424
SPEEDSEND - Software - SYMANTEC CORPORATION; *pg.* 478, *pg.* 161
SPEEDSENTRY - Radar Display Sign - INTERNATIONAL ROAD DYNAMICS INC.; *pg.* 1912, *pg.* 1962
SPEEDSERT - Threaded Insert - GROOV-PIN CORPORATION; *pg.* 1049, *pg.* 1608
SPEEDSHINE - Surface Maintenance Machine - TENNANT COMPANY; *pg.* 1381, *pg.* 944
SPEEDSTAR - High Speed Steel - CARPENTER TECHNOLOGY CORPORATION; *pg.* 73, *pg.* 1584
SPEEDSTARS - Toy & Game - HASBRO, INC.; *pg.* 954, *pg.* 1603
SPEEDSTER - Recreational Vehicle - BOMBARDIER RECREATIONAL PRODUCTS, INC.; *pg.* 201, *pg.* 1960
SPEEDSTER - Speed Gun - BUSHNELL OUTDOOR PRODUCTS, INC.; *pg.* 1403, *pg.* 718
SPEEDSTER - Racing Boat - CHRIS-CRAFT CORPORATION; *pg.* 1706, *pg.* 465
SPEEDSUITE - Digital X-ray Room - FUJIFILM MEDICAL SYSTEMS USA, INC.; *pg.* 1531, *pg.* 374
SPEEDSUITE - Billing Services - VERISIGN, INC.; *pg.* 488, *pg.* 1799
SPEEDSYNC - Software - LAPLINK SOFTWARE, INC.; *pg.* 426, *pg.* 1815
SPEEDTALK - Push to Talk Service - UNITED STATES CELLULAR CORPORATION; *pg.* 1875, *pg.* 594
SPEEDTIP - Probe Card - KULICKE & SOFFA INDUSTRIES, INC.; *pg.* 650, *pg.* 1533
SPEEDWAY - Water Connectors - BRASSCRAFT MANUFACTURING COMPANY; *pg.* 1043, *pg.* 902
SPEEDWAY - Watch - FOSSIL GROUP, INC.; *pg.* 5, *pg.* 1735
SPEEDWAY - Fish Tapes - KLEIN TOOLS INC.; *pg.* 1052, *pg.* 627
SPEEDWAY - Plumbing Product - MASCO CORPORATION; *pg.* 96, *pg.* 909
SPEEDWAY - Gasoline Store - SPEEDWAY LLC; *pg.* 985, *pg.* 1452
THE SPEEDWAY CLUB - Motorsports Entertainment - SPEEDWAY MOTORSPORTS, INC.; *pg.* 584, *pg.* 1370
SPEEDWEEKS - Motorsports Event - INTERNATIONAL SPEEDWAY CORPORATION; *pg.* 553, *pg.* 420
SPEEDWELL - Cleanup Tools - M-I SWACO; *pg.* 980, *pg.* 1710
SPEEDWICK - Apparel - REEBOK INTERNATIONAL LTD.; *pg.* 1817, *pg.* 811
SPEEDY AUTOGLASS - Auto Glass Repair & Replacement - ZIEBART INTERNATIONAL CORPORATION; *pg.* 222, *pg.* 912
SPEEDY FACTS - Educational Materials - SCHOLASTIC INC.; *pg.* 1683, *pg.* 1288

SPEEDY PACKER INSIGHT - Packaging System - SEALED AIR CORPORATION; pg. 1468, pg. 1058
SPEEDY PASTA - Home Products - HABAND COMPANY, INC.; pg. 1772, pg. 1099
SPEEDY PRINTING - Quick Printing Services - ALLEGRA NETWORK LLC; pg. 1614, pg. 904
SPEEDYGREEN - Spreader - THE SCOTTS MIRACLE-GRO COMPANY; pg. 1799, pg. 1459
SPEEDYPACKER - Foam-in-Bag Packaging Film & Equipment - SEALED AIR CORPORATION; pg. 1468, pg. 1058
SPEEDZONE - Turf Product - PBI/GORDON CORPORATION; pg. 1176, pg. 985
SPELL BINDER - Video Game - INTERNATIONAL GAME TECHNOLOGY; pg. 957, pg. 1024
SPELLBOUND - Textiles - BERNHARDT DESIGN; pg. 918, pg. 1381
SPELLING ACE - Spell Corrector - FRANKLIN ELECTRONIC PUBLISHERS, INC.; pg. 398, pg. 1048
SPELLMASTER - Electronic Dictionary - FRANKLIN ELECTRONIC PUBLISHERS, INC.; pg. 398, pg. 1048
SPELLMASTER - Toy - MATTEL, INC.; pg. 962, pg. 81
SPENAX - Pneumatic Tools & Fasteners - STANLEY BLACK & DECKER, INC.; pg. 1063, pg. 358
SPENCER - Shoes - ALLEN-EDMONDS SHOE CORP.; pg. 1804, pg. 1887
SPENCER - Furniture - AMISCO INDUSTRIES LTD.; pg. 913, pg. 1958
SPENCER - Furniture - JASPER GROUP; pg. 930, pg. 691
SPENCER GIFTS - Retail Novelty Gift Shops - SPENCER GIFTS LLC; pg. 1786, pg. 1057
SPENCO - Medical & Aesthetic Product - DYNATRONICS CORPORATION; pg. 1526, pg. 1757
SPERRY - Marine Navigation - SPERRY MARINE INC.; pg. 1430, pg. 1778
SPERRY TOP-SIDER - Footwear - WOLVERINE WORLD WIDE, INC.; pg. 1822, pg. 905
SPERRY TOP-SIDERS - Men's, Women's & Children's Footwear - THE STRIDE RITE CORPORATION; pg. 1820, pg. 828
SPETZLER - Medical Device - INTEGRA LIFESCIENCES HOLDINGS CORPORATION; pg. 1545, pg. 1109
SPEX, THE BLOOMBERG - Trading Services - BLOOMBERG L.P.; pg. 725, pg. 1204
SPEXX - Bearing Product - THE TIMKEN COMPANY; pg. 218, pg. 1408
SPEYER - Footwear - K-SWISS; pg. 1837, pg. 306
SPEYSIDE 21-YEAR-OLD - Scotch - SAZERAC COMPANY, INC.; pg. 1969, pg. 745
SPF - Small Pupil Feature; Binocular Indirect Ophthalmoscope Capability - THE COOPER COMPANIES, INC.; pg. 1518, pg. 183
SPG - Hotels - STARWOOD HOTELS & RESORTS WORLDWIDE, INC.; pg. 1114, pg. 378
SPHERE - Biotechnology Product - GENZYME CORPORATION; pg. 1534, pg. 808
SPHERE - Athletic Shoe - JACK SCHWARTZ SHOES, INC.; pg. 1810, pg. 1245
SPHEREON - Switch - BROCADE CORPORATION; pg. 365, pg. 312
SPHERIC - Gear Honing Machines - GLEASON CORPORATION; pg. 1340, pg. 1335
SPHERICAL 3-WAY - Tee - T.D. WILLIAMSON, INC.; pg. 1380, pg. 1490
SPHERICEL - Hollow Glass Beads for Plastics - POTTERS INDUSTRIES, INC.; pg. 105, pg. 1515
SPHERICEL - Glass Spheres - PQ CORPORATION; pg. 1178, pg. 1515
SPHERIGLASS - Solid Glass Spheres for Plastics - POTTERS INDUSTRIES, INC.; pg. 105, pg. 1515
SPHERIGLASS - Glass Spheres - PQ CORPORATION; pg. 1178, pg. 1515
SPHERILOK - Lip Systems - ESCO CORPORATION; pg. 1335, pg. 1502
SPHERISORB - Preparative Column - WATERS CORPORATION; pg. 1436, pg. 834
SPHERO - Metal Security Locks - MASTER LOCK COMPANY LLC; pg. 1055, pg. 1884
SPHERODEX - Chromatography Product - PALL CORPORATION; pg. 232, pg. 1323
SPHERON - Carbon Black - CABOT CORPORATION; pg. 1151, pg. 792
SPHEROSIL - Chromatography Product - PALL CORPORATION; pg. 232, pg. 1323
SPHEROSYN - Linear Encoder - CUSTOM SENSORS & TECHNOLOGIES; pg. 1407, pg. 152
SPHINGOSTRIPS - Molecular Probe Product - THERMO FISHER SCIENTIFIC INC.; pg. 1602, pg. 61
SPHINX - Retouch Varnish - MARTIN/F. WEBER COMPANY; pg. 962, pg. 1567
SPHINX - Hanger Product - SMITH INTERNATIONAL, INC.; pg. 1377, pg. 1715
SPI-ARGENT - Infection Resistant Coating - SPIRE CORPORATION; pg. 1378, pg. 786
SPI-ARRAY TESTER - Photovoltaic Array Tester - SPIRE CORPORATION; pg. 1378, pg. 786
SPI-ASSEMBLER - Solar Cell Assembly - SPIRE CORPORATION; pg. 1378, pg. 786
SPI-CELL TEST - Photovoltaic Array Tester - SPIRE CORPORATION; pg. 1378, pg. 786
SPI-CERAMIC - Medical Device - SPIRE CORPORATION; pg. 1378, pg. 786
SPI-CONNECT 1000 - Cell Connector - SPIRE CORPORATION; pg. 1378, pg. 786
SPI-FRET - Mechanical Fretting Simulation System - SPIRE CORPORATION; pg. 1378, pg. 786
SPI IMPAX - Dead Blow Soft Face Hammers - NUPLA CORPORATION; pg. 101, pg. 281
SPI-ION 3Q00ME - Metal Ion Implantation Equipment - SPIRE CORPORATION; pg. 1378, pg. 786
SPI-LAMINATOR - Photovoltaic Module Laminator - SPIRE CORPORATION; pg. 1378, pg. 786
SPI-LASE50-50 - Watt Diode Laser 780-810nm - SPIRE CORPORATION; pg. 1378, pg. 786
SPI-LINE - Photovoltaic Array Tester - SPIRE CORPORATION; pg. 1378, pg. 786
SPI-MET - Medical Device - SPIRE CORPORATION; pg. 1378, pg. 786
SPI-POLYMER - Polymer - SPIRE CORPORATION; pg. 1378, pg. 786
SPI-SIGHT - Radiopaque Coatings for Medical Devices - SPIRE CORPORATION; pg. 1378, pg. 786
SPI-SPECTRUM - Metallic Component - SPIRE CORPORATION; pg. 1378, pg. 786
SPI-STRINGER - Solar Cell Assembly - SPIRE CORPORATION; pg. 1378, pg. 786
SPI-SUN SIMULATOR - Photovoltaic Module Tester - SPIRE CORPORATION; pg. 1378, pg. 786
SPI-TAB 1000 - Cell Tabber - SPIRE CORPORATION; pg. 1378, pg. 786
SPI-TAB 500 - Semi Automated Solar Cell Tabber - SPIRE CORPORATION; pg. 1378, pg. 786
SPI-TEXT - Material Treatment System - SPIRE CORPORATION; pg. 1378, pg. 786
SPI-TRIBOTESTER - Mechanical Wear Simulator & Friction Measurement Systems - SPIRE CORPORATION; pg. 1378, pg. 786
SPI-VAC PIK - Vacuum Transfer Machine - SPIRE CORPORATION; pg. 1378, pg. 786
SPIA-SINGLE PREMIUM IMMEDIATE ANNUITY - Immediate Annuities Providing Continuing Income Payments - NATIONAL LIFE INSURANCE COMPANY; pg. 1210, pg. 1766
SPIAGGIA - Private Dining & Conference Center - LEVY RESTAURANTS, INC.; pg. 1736, pg. 580
SPIC AND SPAN - Household Cleaning Product - PRESTIGE BRANDS HOLDINGS, INC.; pg. 520, pg. 1345
SPICE - Bedcovering - ETHAN ALLEN INTERIORS INC.; pg. 924, pg. 343
SPICE GARDEN - Brand of Spices and Herbs - MODERN PRODUCTS, INC.; pg. 1568, pg. 1871
SPICE HOT CASH - Pull-tab Lottery Game - IDAHO LOTTERY; pg. 995, pg. 547
SPICE HUNTER - Spices - THE C.F. SAUER COMPANY; pg. 847, pg. 1801
SPICE IT UP - Lottery Game - IOWA LOTTERY; pg. 996, pg. 705
SPICE OF LIFE - Food Service Concept - MORRISON MANAGEMENT SPECIALISTS, INC.; pg. 1028, pg. 515
SPICE PLAID - Pillow and Throw - HERITAGE LACE INC.; pg. 694, pg. 711
SPICER - Metal Stampings - DANA HOLDING CORPORATION; pg. 203, pg. 1461
SPICETEC - Food Product - CONAGRA FOODS, INC.; pg. 826, pg. 1014
SPICY 7'S - Lottery Game - MINNESOTA STATE LOTTERY; pg. 999, pg. 956
SPICY 7'S - Lottery Card - MISSOURI LOTTERY; pg. 999, pg. 979
SPICY CASH - Lottery Game - RHODE ISLAND LOTTERY; pg. 1004, pg. 1600
SPICY HONEY - Mustard - PLOCHMAN, INC.; pg. 890, pg. 631
SPICY HORSERADISH - Mustard - PLOCHMAN, INC.; pg. 890, pg. 631
SPICY PEPPA - Mustard - PLOCHMAN, INC.; pg. 890, pg. 631
SPIDER - Glove - ACUSHNET COMPANY; pg. 1824, pg. 818
SPIDER - Medical Device - INTEGRA LIFESCIENCES HOLDINGS CORPORATION; pg. 1545, pg. 1109
SPIDER - Insulation System - JOHNS MANVILLE CORPORATION; pg. 89, pg. 320
SPIDER - Herbicide Product - NUFARM AMERICAS INC; pg. 1798, pg. 552
SPIDER - Shelving Systems - ROUSSEAU METAL, INC.; pg. 463, pg. 1960
SPIDER FOOTBAGS - Sand Filled Synthetic Leather Covers for Perfect Play - DUNCAN TOYS COMPANY; pg. 951, pg. 1465
SPIDER LEG - Gaming Product - GLD PRODUCTS, INC.; pg. 1835, pg. 1882
SPIDER LIGHT - Commercial Lighting - SWIVELIER CO., INC.; pg. 1307, pg. 1142
SPIDER MAN - Toy & Game - HASBRO, INC.; pg. 954, pg. 1603
SPIDER-MEN - Game - ACTIVISION BLIZZARD, INC.; pg. 948, pg. 271
SPIDERGRIP - Glove - LAKELAND INDUSTRIES, INC.; pg. 1354, pg. 1338
SPIDERLABS - Computer Software - TRUSTWAVE HOLDINGS, INC.; pg. 1285, pg. 593
SPIDERMAN - Doll - MGA ENTERTAINMENT, INC.; pg. 964, pg. 300
SPIEGELAU - Glassware - WMF OF AMERICA, INC.; pg. 1140, pg. 1380
SPIELO - Lottery System - INTERNATIONAL GAME TECHNOLOGY; pg. 420, pg. 1606
SPIES HECKER - Automotive Coatings - E.I. DU PONT DE NEMOURS & COMPANY; pg. 1159, pg. 390
SPIEWAK - Apparel - I. SPIEWAK & SONS, INC.; pg. 42, pg. 1242
SPIFFNET! - Spiff & Site Draft Program Management - ADVERTISING CHECKING BUREAU INCORPORATED; pg. 345, pg. 1187
SPIIN - Footwear - STEVEN MADDEN, LTD.; pg. 1819, pg. 1176
SPIKE - Hardware - MIDDLE ATLANTIC PRODUCTS INC.; pg. 1360, pg. 1065
SPIKE - Brand of Spices & Herbs - MODERN PRODUCTS, INC.; pg. 1568, pg. 1871
SPIKE - Apparel - OAKLEY, INC.; pg. 1840, pg. 86
SPIKE - Impact Anchor - POWERS FASTENERS INC.; pg. 1059, pg. 1143
SPIKECUBE - Surge Suppressor - TRIPPE MANUFACTURING COMPANY; pg. 220, pg. 592
SPIKEFAST - Nail Hole Filler for Railroads - THE WILLAMETTE VALLEY COMPANY; pg. 1186, pg. 1497
SPIKESHIELD - Suppression Device - HUBBELL INCORPORATED; pg. 1299, pg. 370
SPIKESTIK - Surge Suppressor - TRIPPE MANUFACTURING COMPANY; pg. 220, pg. 592
SPILL - Apparel - OAKLEY, INC.; pg. 1840, pg. 86
SPILL-FREE - No Spill Funnel - LISLE CORPORATION; pg. 1356, pg. 703
SPILL-PROOF - Ladder Product - WERNER HOLDING CO.; pg. 121, pg. 1534
SPILL-X - Spill Control Products for Hazardous Spills - ANSUL, INCORPORATED; pg. 1147, pg. 1869
SPILLGUARD - Carpet Cushion - CARPENTER CO.; pg. 920, pg. 1801
SPIN - Curlers - THE GILLETTE COMPANY; pg. 509, pg. 795
SPIN - Medical Device - INTEGRA LIFESCIENCES HOLDINGS CORPORATION; pg. 1545, pg. 1109
SPIN - Fabric - NEMSCHOFF, INC.; pg. 936, pg. 1890
SPIN - Apparel - OAKLEY, INC.; pg. 1840, pg. 86
SPIN - Music Publication - SPINMEDIA; pg. 1282, pg. 104
SPIN & SING ALPHABET ZOO - Toys - LEAPFROG ENTERPRISES, INC.; pg. 961, pg. 84
SPIN CITY - Carpet - BEAULIEU GROUP, LLC; pg. 917, pg. 529
SPIN CYCLE - Video Game - INTERNATIONAL GAME TECHNOLOGY; pg. 957, pg. 1024
SPIN FOR CASH - Video Game - INTERNATIONAL GAME TECHNOLOGY; pg. 957, pg. 1024

SPIN-KLEEN - Washer - NOBLES MANUFACTURING, INC.; *pg.* 59, *pg.* 1890
SPIN MAGAZINE - Music Publication - SPINMEDIA; *pg.* 1282, *pg.* 104
SPIN MILLED - Golf Equipment - ACUSHNET COMPANY; *pg.* 1824, *pg.* 818
SPIN POKER - Video Poker - INTERNATIONAL GAME TECHNOLOGY; *pg.* 957, *pg.* 1024
SPIN POLO - Apparels - UNDER ARMOUR, INC.; *pg.* 49, *pg.* 759
SPIN POP - Toy & Game - HASBRO, INC.; *pg.* 954, *pg.* 1603
SPIN THE WHEEL - Video Game - INTERNATIONAL GAME TECHNOLOGY; *pg.* 957, *pg.* 1024
SPIN TO WIN - Rodeo Magazine - BELVOIR MEDIA GROUP, LLC; *pg.* 1620, *pg.* 360
SPIN-X - Glass & Ceramic Material - CORNING INCORPORATED; *pg.* 1122, *pg.* 1154
SPINAL AID - Mattresses - KINGSDOWN, INC.; *pg.* 932, *pg.* 1383
SPINALLOY - Magnetic & Video Heads - EASTMAN KODAK COMPANY; *pg.* 1408, *pg.* 1333
SPINALOGIC - Orthopedic Product - DJO INCORPORATED; *pg.* 1524, *pg.* 302
SPINBAR - Magneting Stirring Bars - BEL-ART PRODUCTS, INC.; *pg.* 1879, *pg.* 1129
SPINCHRON - Testing Instrument System - BECKMAN COULTER, INC.; *pg.* 1402, *pg.* 48
SPINCRAFT - Power Metal Spinning - STANDEX INTERNATIONAL CORPORATION; *pg.* 60, *pg.* 1039
SPINDLE - Footwear - OAKLEY, INC.; *pg.* 1840, *pg.* 86
SPINDLE-TITE! - Axle Spindle Nuts - DORMAN PRODUCTS, INC.; *pg.* 204, *pg.* 1522
SPINE SUPPORT - Mattress - KING KOIL LICENSING COMPANY INC.; *pg.* 932, *pg.* 671
SPINE SYSTEM EVOLUTION - Spinal Fixation Systems Designed for Pedicle Screw Fixation - AESCULAP, INC.; *pg.* 1487, *pg.* 1521
SPINE-TAG - Adhesive Strip - SENTRY TECHNOLOGY CORPORATION; *pg.* 672, *pg.* 1339
SPINECHILLERS - Publication - THOMAS NELSON INC.; *pg.* 1692, *pg.* 1654
SPINELLE - Flatware - ONEIDA LTD; *pg.* 1129, *pg.* 1318
SPINEPLEX - Radiopaque Bone Cement - STRYKER CORPORATION; *pg.* 1598, *pg.* 894
SPINESTAT - Handsets for Use with Laserscope Surgical Laser Systems - AMERICAN MEDICAL SYSTEMS, INC.; *pg.* 1399, *pg.* 238
SPINLACE - Wipe - POLYMER GROUP, INC.; *pg.* 698, *pg.* 1368
SPINMATIC ST - Freshwater Spinning Reels - DAIWA CORPORATION; *pg.* 1832, *pg.* 75
SPINMATIC XT - Freshwater Spinning Reels - DAIWA CORPORATION; *pg.* 1832, *pg.* 75
SPINMATIC ZT - Freshwater Spinning Reels - DAIWA CORPORATION; *pg.* 1832, *pg.* 75
SPINNAKER - Medical Device - BOSTON SCIENTIFIC CORPORATION; *pg.* 1508, *pg.* 831
SPINNAKER - Furniture - TROPITONE FURNITURE CO., INC.; *pg.* 945, *pg.* 118
SPINNER BOOKS - Game - UNIVERSITY GAMES CORPORATION; *pg.* 969, *pg.* 230
SPINNEYBECK - Leather Accessories - KNOLL, INC.; *pg.* 425, *pg.* 1527
SPINNING BEE - Gaming Product - GLD PRODUCTS, INC.; *pg.* 1835, *pg.* 1882
SPINNING STREAK - Game - WMS INDUSTRIES INC.; *pg.* 593, *pg.* 666
SPINOCCOLI - Pizza - UNO RESTAURANT HOLDINGS CORPORATION; *pg.* 1754, *pg.* 856
SPINSHOT - Footwear - K-SWISS; *pg.* 1837, *pg.* 306
SPINSTAR XC - Freshwater Spinning Reels - DAIWA CORPORATION; *pg.* 1832, *pg.* 75
SPINSTAR ZC - Freshwater Spinning Reels - DAIWA CORPORATION; *pg.* 1832, *pg.* 75
SPINSTER - Gaming Product - GLD PRODUCTS, INC.; *pg.* 1835, *pg.* 1882
SPINTRODE - Robotic Product - HAMILTON CO., INC.; *pg.* 1415, *pg.* 1031
SPINZ - Office Furniture - STEELCASE INC.; *pg.* 475, *pg.* 889
SPIRA-PAK - Cathodic Protection - CORRPRO COMPANIES, INC.; *pg.* 631, *pg.* 1464
SPIRACLE - Filtration System - DONALDSON COMPANY, INC.; *pg.* 1329, *pg.* 917
SPIRACON - Roller Screw - DUFF-NORTON; *pg.* 204, *pg.* 1365
SPIRAFLEX - Hose - THE GOODYEAR TIRE & RUBBER COMPANY; *pg.* 1883, *pg.* 1401
SPIRAHELIC - Pressure Indicating Transmitter - DWYER INSTRUMENTS INC.; *pg.* 1330, *pg.* 694
SPIRAL-LINK - Pumps - IDEX CORPORATION; *pg.* 1347, *pg.* 623
SPIRAL RADIUS - Spinal System - STRYKER CORPORATION; *pg.* 1598, *pg.* 894
SPIRALJET - Spray Product - SPRAYING SYSTEMS CO.; *pg.* 1063, *pg.* 670
SPIRALL - Footwear - STEVEN MADDEN, LTD.; *pg.* 1819, *pg.* 1176
SPIRALOK - Mattress - RESTONIC MATTRESS CORPORATION; *pg.* 941, *pg.* 553
SPIRALON - Steel Container - GREIF INC.; *pg.* 1459, *pg.* 1447
SPIRALOX - Plastic Conveyor Belt - THE LAITRAM LLC; *pg.* 1354, *pg.* 744
SPIRALTAINER - Steel Drums - GREIF INC.; *pg.* 1459, *pg.* 1447
SPIRALTRAC - Seal - A.W. CHESTERTON COMPANY; *pg.* 1315, *pg.* 861
SPIRALTRON - Electron Multiplier Detector - PHOTONIS USA PENNSYLVANIA; *pg.* 663, *pg.* 1547
SPIRAX SARCO - Steam System - SPIRAX SARCO, INC.; *pg.* 1076, *pg.* 1612
SPIRIT - Musical Instrument - GIBSON GUITAR CORP.; *pg.* 550, *pg.* 1650
SPIRIT - Audio Products - HARMAN INTERNATIONAL INDUSTRIES, INCORPORATED; *pg.* 641, *pg.* 374
SPIRIT - Steel Office Desk - INVINCIBLE OFFICE FURNITURE; *pg.* 420, *pg.* 1868
SPIRIT - Connector - MOLEX INCORPORATED; *pg.* 655, *pg.* 628
SPIRIT - Medical Device - RESMED INC.; *pg.* 1589, *pg.* 207
SPIRIT - Motor Homes - WINNEBAGO INDUSTRIES, INC.; *pg.* 1712, *pg.* 707
SPIRIT BEAR - Video Game - INTERNATIONAL GAME TECHNOLOGY; *pg.* 957, *pg.* 1024
SPIRIT BY CURTAIN CALL - Dance/Drill Team, Pep Squad & Competitive Apparel - PERFORM GROUP, LLC; *pg.* 31, *pg.* 1597
SPIRIT-FILLED LIFE - Bible Series - THOMAS NELSON INC.; *pg.* 1692, *pg.* 1654
SPIRIT HALLOWEEN SUPERSTORE - Retail Novelty Gift Shops - SPENCER GIFTS LLC; *pg.* 1786, *pg.* 1057
SPIRIT MILLENNIUM - Fabric - UNIROYAL ENGINEERED PRODUCTS; *pg.* 699, *pg.* 467
THE SPIRIT OF INNOVATION - Tagline - TEMBEC INC.; *pg.* 114, *pg.* 1957
SPIRIT OF SERVICE - Slogan - CENTURYLINK, INC; *pg.* 1870, *pg.* 317
SPIRIT RIDGE - Furniture - ASHLEY FURNITURE INDUSTRIES, INC.; *pg.* 914, *pg.* 1852
SPIRITLED WOMAN - Magazine - CHARISMA MEDIA; *pg.* 1627, *pg.* 436
SPIRITUAL SKY - Incenses & Oils - WILLERT HOME PRODUCTS, INC.; *pg.* 1140, *pg.* 1005
SPIRIVA HANDIHALER - Pharmaceutical Product - PFIZER INC.; *pg.* 1581, *pg.* 1278
SPIRO - Flatware - ONEIDA LTD; *pg.* 1129, *pg.* 1318
SPIRO-PAC - Paperboard Shipping Drums - SONOCO PRODUCTS COMPANY; *pg.* 1469, *pg.* 1619
SPIROCARD - Diagnostic Cardiology System - CARDIAC SCIENCE CORPORATION; *pg.* 1512, *pg.* 1897
SPIROFORM - Bevel Product - GLEASON CORPORATION; *pg.* 1340, *pg.* 1335
SPIROGARD - Special Application Filters - VITAL SIGNS, INC.; *pg.* 1607, *pg.* 1126
SPIROGRAPH - Toy & Game - HASBRO, INC.; *pg.* 954, *pg.* 1603
SPIROPET - Healthcare Product - GF HEALTH PRODUCTS, INC.; *pg.* 1535, *pg.* 508
SPIROVAC - Pharmaceutical Product - PFIZER INC.; *pg.* 1581, *pg.* 1278
SPIROXCARD - Spirometer & Pulse Oximeter - CARDIAC SCIENCE CORPORATION; *pg.* 1512, *pg.* 1897
SPIRU-TEIN - Nutritional Supplement - NATURAL ORGANICS, INC.; *pg.* 1571, *pg.* 1181
SPIRULINA - Nutritional Product - RBC LIFE SCIENCES, INC.; *pg.* 1588, *pg.* 1723
SPIRULINA PACIFICA - Nutrient-Rich Dietary Supplement - CYANOTECH CORPORATION; *pg.* 1154, *pg.* 545
SPIT NET - Officer Training Aids - BAE SYSTEMS PRODUCTS GROUP; *pg.* 359, *pg.* 432
SPITFIRE - Polymer Product - CHEMTURA CORPORATION; *pg.* 1152, *pg.* 355
SPITFIRE - Warning Lights - UNITY MANUFACTURING COMPANY; *pg.* 221, *pg.* 594
SPJ - Medical Equipment - INVACARE CORPORATION; *pg.* 1546, *pg.* 1451
SPL - Tachycardia Products - ST. JUDE MEDICAL, INC.; *pg.* 1596, *pg.* 963
SPL - Loudspeakers - VELODYNE ACOUSTICS, INC.; *pg.* 685, *pg.* 152
SPLASH - Beverages - THE COCA-COLA COMPANY; *pg.* 240, *pg.* 493
SPLASH - Rug - COURISTAN INC.; *pg.* 921, *pg.* 1067
SPLASH - Printing Products - ELECTRONICS FOR IMAGING, INC.; *pg.* 390, *pg.* 88
SPLASH OF COLOR - Plant Growing Kit - AEROGROW INTERNATIONAL, INC.; *pg.* 1393, *pg.* 310
SPLASH OF RAIN - Candle - THE YANKEE CANDLE COMPANY, INC.; *pg.* 1792, *pg.* 843
SPLASHFLASH - Umbrellas - TOTES ISOTONER CORPORATION; *pg.* 14, *pg.* 1426
SPLASHGARD - Beverage - BUNN-O-MATIC CORPORATION; *pg.* 53, *pg.* 661
SPLASHTOWN - HOUSTON - Park - SIX FLAGS ENTERTAINMENT CORPORATION; *pg.* 583, *pg.* 1698
SPLATTER - Apparel - OAKLEY, INC.; *pg.* 1840, *pg.* 86
SPLENDA - Sweetener - JOHNSON & JOHNSON; *pg.* 1549, *pg.* 1091
SPLENDID - Apparel - V.F. CORPORATION; *pg.* 34, *pg.* 1376
SPLENDID BEAUTY - Carpet - BEAULIEU GROUP, LLC; *pg.* 917, *pg.* 529
SPLENDOR - Decorative Fragrance - AROMATIQUE INC.; *pg.* 499, *pg.* 32
SPLENDOUR OF THE SEAS - Cruise Ship - ROYAL CARIBBEAN CRUISES LTD; *pg.* 1921, *pg.* 446
SPLICE - Beverages - THE COCA-COLA COMPANY; *pg.* 240, *pg.* 493
SPLICE - Eyewear - OAKLEY, INC.; *pg.* 1840, *pg.* 86
SPLICE KING - Tape - AMERICAN BILTRITE INC.; *pg.* 1878, *pg.* 856
SPLINE - Footwear - OAKLEY, INC.; *pg.* 1840, *pg.* 86
SPLINE GAUGES - Gauge & Master Gear - DANAHER CORPORATION; *pg.* 1044, *pg.* 397
SPLIT - Bath Bars - CRAFTMADE INTERNATIONAL, INC.; *pg.* 1295, *pg.* 1670
SPLIT - Leg Positioner - STERIS CORPORATION; *pg.* 1597, *pg.* 1464
SPLIT ATIVE - Air Conditioners - WHIRLPOOL CORPORATION; *pg.* 62, *pg.* 872
SPLIT CRATER - Footwear - OAKLEY, INC.; *pg.* 1840, *pg.* 86
SPLIT GRIP - Footwear - OAKLEY, INC.; *pg.* 1840, *pg.* 86
SPLIT-LESS - Nail & Screw - W.H. MAZE COMPANY; *pg.* 1389, *pg.* 652
SPLIT SCREEN - Digital Projector - INFOCUS CORPORATION; *pg.* 644, *pg.* 1503
SPLIT SMOKE - Footwear - OAKLEY, INC.; *pg.* 1840, *pg.* 86
SPLIT-SOLE - Footwear - CAPEZIO BALLET MAKERS INC.; *pg.* 1805, *pg.* 1125
SPLIT SYMBOLS - Video Game - INTERNATIONAL GAME TECHNOLOGY; *pg.* 957, *pg.* 1024
SPLIT TOP - Footwear - OAKLEY, INC.; *pg.* 1840, *pg.* 86
SPLITFIRE - Sparkplugs - OLD WORLD INDUSTRIES, INC.; *pg.* 1175, *pg.* 641
SPLITLEVEL - T.V.-Based Lottery Game - INTERNATIONAL GAME TECHNOLOGY; *pg.* 420, *pg.* 1606
SPLITTING HARES - Video Game - INTERNATIONAL GAME TECHNOLOGY; *pg.* 957, *pg.* 1024
SPLOX - Paper Product - BOISE CASCADE HOLDINGS, L.L.C.; *pg.* 1453, *pg.* 546
SPOKANE - Furniture - FLEXSTEEL INDUSTRIES, INC.; *pg.* 925, *pg.* 707
SPOKANE.NET - Online Service - THE SPOKESMAN-REVIEW; *pg.* 1687, *pg.* 1844
THE SPOKESMAN-REVIEW - Newspaper - THE SPOKESMAN-REVIEW; *pg.* 1687, *pg.* 1844
SPONGEBOB SQUAREPANTS - Toy & Game - HASBRO, INC.; *pg.* 954, *pg.* 1603
SPONGEBOB SQUAREPANTS - Toy - MATTEL, INC.; *pg.* 962, *pg.* 81
SPONGEBOB SQUAREPANTS 3D - 3D Motion Simulator Movie Ride - CANADA'S WONDERLAND COMPANY; *pg.* 536, *pg.* 1947

SPONSLER - Pump Product - IDEX CORPORATION; *pg.* 1347, *pg.* 623
SPOODLE - Kitchenware - THE VOLLRATH COMPANY LLC; *pg.* 1139, *pg.* 1894
SPOOKY - Video Game - INTERNATIONAL GAME TECHNOLOGY; *pg.* 957, *pg.* 1024
SPOOKY FRIENDS - Candy - JUST BORN, INC.; *pg.* 1857, *pg.* 1516
SPOOLMATE - Welding & Cutting Equip. - MILLER ELECTRIC MANUFACTURING CO.; *pg.* 1361, *pg.* 1852
SPOON - Watches - SEIKO CORPORATION OF AMERICA; *pg.* 12, *pg.* 1082
SPOONABLE BARREL CONTAINER - Mustard - PLOCHMAN, INC.; *pg.* 890, *pg.* 631
SPOR-KLENZ - Concentrate - STERIS CORPORATION; *pg.* 1597, *pg.* 1464
SPORANOX - Pharmaceutical - JANSSEN PHARMACEUTICA PRODUCTS, L.P.; *pg.* 1548, *pg.* 1125
SPORANOX - Healthcare Product - JOHNSON & JOHNSON; *pg.* 1549, *pg.* 1091
SPORDEX - Strip & Disc - STERIS CORPORATION; *pg.* 1597, *pg.* 1464
SPORDI - Strip & Disc - STERIS CORPORATION; *pg.* 1597, *pg.* 1464
SPORE - Video Game - ELECTRONIC ARTS INC.; *pg.* 951, *pg.* 189
SPORT - Laser Rangefinder - BUSHNELL OUTDOOR PRODUCTS, INC.; *pg.* 1403, *pg.* 718
SPORT - Beverages - THE COCA-COLA COMPANY; *pg.* 240, *pg.* 493
SPORT - Personal Care Product - COLGATE-PALMOLIVE COMPANY; *pg.* 504, *pg.* 1215
SPORT - Safety & Protective Equipment - ENCON SAFETY PRODUCTS; *pg.* 1334, *pg.* 1705
SPORT - Medical Device - MANNATECH, INCORPORATED; *pg.* 1558, *pg.* 1671
SPORT - Cigarettes - ROCK CREEK PHARMACEUTICALS, INC.; *pg.* 1895, *pg.* 466
SPORT BEANS - Candy - JELLY BELLY CANDY COMPANY; *pg.* 1857, *pg.* 86
SPORT BOWLING - Bowling Promotional Services - UNITED STATES BOWLING CONGRESS; *pg.* 159, *pg.* 1660
SPORT CARE - Trademark - MUELLER SPORTS MEDICINE, INC.; *pg.* 1570, *pg.* 1887
SPORT CROSS - Stand Bag - DATREK GOLF; *pg.* 1832, *pg.* 1801
SPORT DIVER - Magazine - BONNIER CORPORATION; *pg.* 1622, *pg.* 480
SPORT FISHING - Magazine - BONNIER CORPORATION; *pg.* 1622, *pg.* 480
SPORT GOBUG - Bicycle - TREK BICYCLE CORPORATION; *pg.* 1847, *pg.* 1896
SPORT HALEY - Golf Sportswear - SPORT HALEY, INC.; *pg.* 33, *pg.* 333
SPORT LIFTER - Floor Care Product - BISSELL HOMECARE, INC.; *pg.* 52, *pg.* 887
SPORT MATE 1200 - Blower/Dryer - JARDEN CONSUMER SOLUTIONS; *pg.* 57, *pg.* 412
SPORT NAUTIQUE - Power Boat - CORRECT CRAFT, INC.; *pg.* 1706, *pg.* 452
SPORT PAK - Safety Product - WISCONSIN PHARMACAL COMPANY, LLC; *pg.* 1610, *pg.* 1861
SPORT-RITE - Air Spring Applications for Personal Vehicles - FIRESTONE INDUSTRIAL PRODUCTS DIVISION; *pg.* 1882, *pg.* 686
SPORT SHAKE - Dairy Product - DAIRY FARMERS OF AMERICA, INC.; *pg.* 851, *pg.* 982
SPORT SHAKE MAX - Milk Shake - DAIRY FARMERS OF AMERICA, INC.; *pg.* 851, *pg.* 982
SPORT SUPPLY GROUP - Sporting Goods - SPORT SUPPLY GROUP, INC.; *pg.* 1846, *pg.* 1687
SPORT TABLE - Table - LIFETIME PRODUCTS INC.; *pg.* 933, *pg.* 1751
SPORT TEK - Clock - BROWN & BIGELOW, INC.; *pg.* 1624, *pg.* 959
SPORT-ZOOMS - Lawn Product - ARIENS COMPANY INC.; *pg.* 700, *pg.* 1855
SPORTAPRO - Stereo Headphone - KOSS CORPORATION; *pg.* 649, *pg.* 1877
SPORTBLOCKS - Medical & Aesthetic Product - DYNATRONICS CORPORATION; *pg.* 1526, *pg.* 1757
SPORTEASE - Clothing - SPANX INC.; *pg.* 32, *pg.* 520
SPORTEC - Knife - COAST CUTLERY COMPANY; *pg.* 1121, *pg.* 1501
SPORTER - Rifle - WEATHERBY, INC.; *pg.* 1848, *pg.* 181
SPORTIME - Educational Resources - SCHOOL SPECIALTY, INC.; *pg.* 467, *pg.* 1860
THE SPORTING NEWS - Magazine - THE SPORTING NEWS; *pg.* 1688, *pg.* 1295
SPORTMART - Sporting Goods - THE SPORTS AUTHORITY, INC.; *pg.* 1846, *pg.* 326
SPORTOCASINS - Shoes - G.H. BASS & CO.; *pg.* 1809, *pg.* 1234
SPORTOE - Semi Finished Product - STANBEE COMPANY, INC.; *pg.* 1819, *pg.* 1050
SPORTPLAY MX - Panel Floor System - ROBBINS, INC.; *pg.* 108, *pg.* 1425
SPORTRAILS - Curved Aluminum Side Rails - LUND INTERNATIONAL, INC.; *pg.* 211, *pg.* 526
SPORTREND - Running Boards - LUND INTERNATIONAL, INC.; *pg.* 211, *pg.* 526
SPORTRUNNER - Medical Equipment - INVACARE CORPORATION; *pg.* 1546, *pg.* 1451
SPORTS BLAST - Fruit Juices - CHIQUITA BRANDS INTERNATIONAL, INC.; *pg.* 847, *pg.* 1365
SPORTS ILLUSTRATED - Media Publication - TIME INC.; *pg.* 1693, *pg.* 1300
SPORTS ILLUSTRATED KIDS - Media Publication - TIME INC.; *pg.* 1693, *pg.* 1300
SPORTS INFORMATION DISPLAY - LED Text Displays - TRANS-LUX CORPORATION; *pg.* 681, *pg.* 365
SPORTS LADY - Golf Balls - BRIDGESTONE GOLF, INC.; *pg.* 1828, *pg.* 528
SPORTS PALS - Plate - PACTIV CORPORATION; *pg.* 1466, *pg.* 624
SPORTS TRIVIA CHALLENGE - Advanced Sports Trivia Covering Multiple Topics - NTN BUZZTIME, INC.; *pg.* 659, *pg.* 60
SPORTS WIRE - Software - DAKTRONICS, INC.; *pg.* 633, *pg.* 1624
SPORTSBALL - Balloon - CONTINENTAL AMERICAN CORP.; *pg.* 1880, *pg.* 723
SPORTSCENTER - Sports News Program - ESPN, INC.; *pg.* 285, *pg.* 340
SPORTSCREME - Health & Beauty Product - CHATTEM, INC.; *pg.* 1515, *pg.* 1628
SPORTSLITER - Lighting Product - HUBBELL INCORPORATED; *pg.* 1299, *pg.* 370
SPORTSMAN - Riflescope - BUSHNELL OUTDOOR PRODUCTS, INC.; *pg.* 1403, *pg.* 718
SPORTSMAN - Fiberglass Boat Product - GRADY-WHITE BOATS, INC.; *pg.* 1707, *pg.* 1377
THE SPORTSMAN'S GUIDE - Catalog & Internet Retailers - THE SPORTSMAN'S GUIDE, INC.; *pg.* 1846, *pg.* 965
SPORTSOUND - Scoreboard & Sports Product - DAKTRONICS, INC.; *pg.* 633, *pg.* 1624
SPORTSPIX - Software - XEROX CORPORATION; *pg.* 494, *pg.* 365
SPORTSTER - Recreational Vehicle - BOMBARDIER RECREATIONAL PRODUCTS, INC.; *pg.* 201, *pg.* 1960
SPORTSTER - Bag - DATREK GOLF; *pg.* 1832, *pg.* 1801
SPORTSTER - Motorcycle - HARLEY-DAVIDSON, INC.; *pg.* 178, *pg.* 1874
SPORTSTICKER - Electronic Display System - TRANS-LUX CORPORATION; *pg.* 681, *pg.* 365
SPORTTUBES - Side Rails - LUND INTERNATIONAL, INC.; *pg.* 211, *pg.* 526
SPORTVIEW - Spotting Scope - BUSHNELL OUTDOOR PRODUCTS, INC.; *pg.* 1403, *pg.* 718
SPORTWOOD - Sport Surface - ROBBINS, INC.; *pg.* 108, *pg.* 1425
SPORTWOOD PLUS - Glue-Down Flooring - ROBBINS, INC.; *pg.* 108, *pg.* 1425
SPORTWOOD PLUS ULTRA - Suspended/Anchored Sports Flooring - ROBBINS, INC.; *pg.* 108, *pg.* 1425
SPOT - Furniture - ASHLEY FURNITURE INDUSTRIES, INC.; *pg.* 914, *pg.* 1852
SPOT BALM - Pet Supplies - HAPPY JACK INC.; *pg.* 1476, *pg.* 1390
SPOT-BILT - Shoes for Coaches & Officials - SAUCONY, INC.; *pg.* 1818, *pg.* 828
SPOT GONE - Rug Cleaner - SWISHER HYGIENE INC.; *pg.* 336, *pg.* 1507
SPOT-LITE - Paste Putty - ITW - EVERCOAT; *pg.* 1443, *pg.* 1415
SPOT REMOVER - Automotive Reconditioning Product - MOC PRODUCTS COMPANY, INC.; *pg.* 332, *pg.* 174
SPOT VITAL SIGNS - Vital Signs Device - WELCH ALLYN INC.; *pg.* 1436, *pg.* 1342
SPOTARRAY - Microarray Printing System - PERKINELMER, INC.; *pg.* 1426, *pg.* 853
SPOTBOT - Floor Care Product - BISSELL HOMECARE, INC.; *pg.* 52, *pg.* 887
SPOTCHECK - Dye Penetrant - ITW MAGNAFLUX; *pg.* 1418, *pg.* 615
SPOTCOM - Shipment Service - FEDEX CORPORATION; *pg.* 1907, *pg.* 1642
SPOTCRAFT - Carpet Repair Services - DURACLEAN INTERNATIONAL, INC.; *pg.* 329, *pg.* 553
SPOTGLO - Seatbelt Light - HONEYWELL INTERNATIONAL INC.; *pg.* 407, *pg.* 1088
SPOTIR - Radiant Heater for Heating Small Objects - PRECISION CONTROL SYSTEMS, INC./ RESEARCH INC.; *pg.* 1427, *pg.* 923
SPOTLIFTER 2X - Floor Care Product - BISSELL HOMECARE, INC.; *pg.* 52, *pg.* 887
SPOTLIGHT - Textiles - BERNHARDT DESIGN; *pg.* 918, *pg.* 1381
SPOTLIGHT - Software - DELL SOFTWARE; *pg.* 385, *pg.* 40
SPOTLIGHT - Entertainment & Media-Based Trivia Game - NTN BUZZTIME, INC.; *pg.* 659, *pg.* 60
SPOTLIGHT - Presentation Boards - PACON CORPORATION; *pg.* 1466, *pg.* 1852
SPOTLIGHT ON DB2 LUW - Software - DELL SOFTWARE; *pg.* 385, *pg.* 40
SPOTLIGHT ON MESSAGING - Software - DELL SOFTWARE; *pg.* 385, *pg.* 40
SPOTLIGHT ON MYSQL - Software - DELL SOFTWARE; *pg.* 385, *pg.* 40
SPOTLIGHT ON ORACLE - Software - DELL SOFTWARE; *pg.* 385, *pg.* 40
SPOTLIGHT ON SQL SERVER ENTERPRISE - Software - DELL SOFTWARE; *pg.* 385, *pg.* 40
SPOTLIGHT ON SYBASE ASE - Software - DELL SOFTWARE; *pg.* 385, *pg.* 40
SPOTLIGHT ON UNIX/LINUX - Software - DELL SOFTWARE; *pg.* 385, *pg.* 40
SPOTLILFTER - Carpet Deep Cleaner - BISSELL HOMECARE, INC.; *pg.* 52, *pg.* 887
SPOTMAPPER - Software - BIO-RAD LABORATORIES, INC.; *pg.* 1504, *pg.* 101
SPOTSGO - Chemical Cleanser - A.L. WILSON CHEMICAL CO.; *pg.* 325, *pg.* 1076
SPOTSHOT - Carpet Stain - WD-40 COMPANY; *pg.* 337, *pg.* 210
SPOTTRAC - Audio Encoder - WEGENER CORPORATION; *pg.* 687, *pg.* 533
SPOTWHEEL - Fluid Handling System - GRACO, INC.; *pg.* 1342, *pg.* 935
SPOX - Connector - MOLEX INCORPORATED; *pg.* 655, *pg.* 628
SPOX BMI - Electronic Components - MOLEX INCORPORATED; *pg.* 655, *pg.* 628
SPR - Baseband Wireless Communications - SKYWORKS SOLUTIONS, INC.; *pg.* 674, *pg.* 862
SPRA-COUPE - Agricultural Sprayer - AGCO CORPORATION; *pg.* 700, *pg.* 530
SPRA-DRI - Dry Cleaning & Laundry Product - ADCO, INC.; *pg.* 325, *pg.* 482
SPRA-MAX - Texture Coatings - AKZONOBEL DECORATIVE PAINTS U.S.; *pg.* 1439, *pg.* 1474
SPRA-MAX 12 - Interior Coatings - AKZONOBEL DECORATIVE PAINTS U.S.; *pg.* 1439, *pg.* 1474
SPRA-MAX 40 - High Build Coatings - AKZONOBEL DECORATIVE PAINTS U.S.; *pg.* 1439, *pg.* 1474
SPRA-TOOL - Disposable Spray Gun - AERVOE INDUSTRIES INCORPORATED; *pg.* 1439, *pg.* 1021
SPRABRASS - Engineered Product And System - SULZER METCO (WESTBURY) INC.; *pg.* 1064, *pg.* 1350
SPRACO - Spray Nozzles - LECHLER, INC.; *pg.* 1444, *pg.* 658
SPRAFLEX - Fluid Sealing Product - A.W. CHESTERTON COMPANY; *pg.* 1315, *pg.* 861
SPRAGRIP - Fluid Sealing Product - A.W. CHESTERTON COMPANY; *pg.* 1315, *pg.* 861
SPRAGUE - Electronic Systems & Components - DGT HOLDINGS; *pg.* 634, *pg.* 1223
SPRASOLVO - Fluid Sealing Product - A.W. CHESTERTON COMPANY; *pg.* 1315, *pg.* 861
SPRATT'S KITCHEN & MARKET - Restaurant - LEVY RESTAURANTS, INC.; *pg.* 1736, *pg.* 580
SPRAY CENTER - Fluid Handling System - GRACO, INC.; *pg.* 1342, *pg.* 935
SPRAY-DAY-LITE - Paint - AKZONOBEL DECORATIVE PAINTS U.S.; *pg.* 1439, *pg.* 1474

SPRAY GUARD - Pump Product - IDEX CORPORATION; *pg.* 1347, *pg.* 623
SPRAY GUN (DESIGN) - Fluid Handling System - GRACO, INC.; *pg.* 1342, *pg.* 935
SPRAY MATE - Paint & Coating - AERVOE INDUSTRIES INCORPORATED; *pg.* 1439, *pg.* 1021
SPRAY MIST - Irons - JARDEN CONSUMER SOLUTIONS; *pg.* 57, *pg.* 412
SPRAY MIX - Pressed & Monolithic Refractory - RESCO PRODUCTS, INC.; *pg.* 107, *pg.* 1581
SPRAY-MOUNT - Adhesive Aerosol - 3M COMPANY; *pg.* 1142, *pg.* 956
SPRAY N' GLOSS - Automotive Reconditioning Product - MOC PRODUCTS COMPANY, INC.; *pg.* 332, *pg.* 174
SPRAY-N-GLUE - Adhesive - DAP PRODUCTS, INC.; *pg.* 1441, *pg.* 756
SPRAY 'N SPARKLE - Glass Cleaner - THE FULLER BRUSH COMPANY; *pg.* 330, *pg.* 715
SPRAY SATIN - Predispersed Coating Pigment - BASF CATALYSTS LLC; *pg.* 1148, *pg.* 1074
SPRAY SIZING - Dry Cleaning & Laundry Product - ADCO, INC.; *pg.* 325, *pg.* 482
SPRAY STAR - Turf Maintenance Machinery - SMITHCO, INC.; *pg.* 1377, *pg.* 1592
SPRAY START - Adjuvant - KALO, INC.; *pg.* 1796, *pg.* 719
SPRAY TECH - Paint Spraying Equipment - WAGNER SPRAY TECH CORPORATION; *pg.* 1449, *pg.* 954
SPRAY WAX - Hair Care Product - JOHN PAUL MITCHELL SYSTEMS; *pg.* 512, *pg.* 133
SPRAYCHECK - Spray Product - SPRAYING SYSTEMS CO.; *pg.* 1063, *pg.* 670
SPRAYCRON - Coating Product - PPG INDUSTRIES, INC.; *pg.* 1445, *pg.* 1579
SPRAYDRY - Spray Product - SPRAYING SYSTEMS CO.; *pg.* 1063, *pg.* 670
SPRAYETTE IV - Healthcare - WESTROCK COMPANY; *pg.* 1472, *pg.* 1805
SPRAYLOGIC - Software - SPRAYING SYSTEMS CO.; *pg.* 1063, *pg.* 670
SPRAYMASTER - Soil Releaser Applicator - DURACLEAN INTERNATIONAL, INC.; *pg.* 329, *pg.* 553
SPRAYMASTER - Spray Coolant System - TRICO MFG. CORP.; *pg.* 219, *pg.* 1886
SPRAYMASTER II - Spray Coolant System - TRICO MFG. CORP.; *pg.* 219, *pg.* 1886
SPRAYMATE - Actuator - PRECISION VALVE CORPORATION; *pg.* 1060, *pg.* 1357
SPRAYON - Chemicals & Lubricants - THE SHERWIN-WILLIAMS COMPANY; *pg.* 1447, *pg.* 1435
SPRAYON - Industrial Aerosol - SHERWIN-WILLIAMS DIVERSIFIED BRANDS DIVISION; *pg.* 1448, *pg.* 1435
SPRAYSENTRY - Engineered Product And System - SULZER METCO (WESTBURY) INC.; *pg.* 1064, *pg.* 1350
SPRAYWARE - Spray Product - SPRAYING SYSTEMS CO.; *pg.* 1063, *pg.* 670
SPRAYWELDER - Coating System - WALL COLMONOY CORPORATION; *pg.* 1185, *pg.* 898
SPRAYWIZARD - Engineered Product And System - SULZER METCO (WESTBURY) INC.; *pg.* 1064, *pg.* 1350
SPREAD AWARE - Clock & Buffer Product - CYPRESS SEMICONDUCTOR CORPORATION; *pg.* 1326, *pg.* 243
SPREADING SUNSHINE - Container Grown Plant - MONROVIA GROWERS; *pg.* 1797, *pg.* 44
SPRECHER + SCHUH - Software - ROCKWELL AUTOMATION, INC.; *pg.* 668, *pg.* 1880
SPRECKELS - Sugar & Sweetener Product - IMPERIAL SUGAR COMPANY; *pg.* 864, *pg.* 1746
SPRED - Paint - AKZONOBEL DECORATIVE PAINTS U.S.; *pg.* 1439, *pg.* 1474
SPRED 2000 - No-Voc Paint - AKZONOBEL DECORATIVE PAINTS U.S.; *pg.* 1439, *pg.* 1474
SPRED-DURA - Paint - AKZONOBEL DECORATIVE PAINTS U.S.; *pg.* 1439, *pg.* 1474
SPRED ENAMEL - Paint - AKZONOBEL DECORATIVE PAINTS U.S.; *pg.* 1439, *pg.* 1474
SPRED FLAT - Paint - AKZONOBEL DECORATIVE PAINTS U.S.; *pg.* 1439, *pg.* 1474
SPRED GLOSS - Paint - AKZONOBEL DECORATIVE PAINTS U.S.; *pg.* 1439, *pg.* 1474
SPRED HOUSE - Paint - AKZONOBEL DECORATIVE PAINTS U.S.; *pg.* 1439, *pg.* 1474
SPRED KITCHEN AND BATH - Paint - AKZONOBEL DECORATIVE PAINTS U.S.; *pg.* 1439, *pg.* 1474
SPRED LO-LUSTRE - Paint - AKZONOBEL DECORATIVE PAINTS U.S.; *pg.* 1439, *pg.* 1474
SPRED LUSTRE - Paint - AKZONOBEL DECORATIVE PAINTS U.S.; *pg.* 1439, *pg.* 1474
SPRED-RITE - Turf Product - PBI/GORDON CORPORATION; *pg.* 1176, *pg.* 985
SPRED SATIN - Paint - AKZONOBEL DECORATIVE PAINTS U.S.; *pg.* 1439, *pg.* 1474
SPRED SILK - Paint - AKZONOBEL DECORATIVE PAINTS U.S.; *pg.* 1439, *pg.* 1474
SPRED SOLO - Paint - AKZONOBEL DECORATIVE PAINTS U.S.; *pg.* 1439, *pg.* 1474
SPRED SUPREME - Paint - AKZONOBEL DECORATIVE PAINTS U.S.; *pg.* 1439, *pg.* 1474
SPREE - Candy - NESTLE USA, INC.; *pg.* 883, *pg.* 96
SPREE GT - Folding Wheelchair - INVACARE CORPORATION; *pg.* 1546, *pg.* 1451
SPREETA - Liquids & Gases Measuring Instruments - TEXAS INSTRUMENTS INCORPORATED; *pg.* 679, *pg.* 1688
SPRESS - Pharmaceutical Ingredient - GRAIN PROCESSING CORPORATION; *pg.* 859, *pg.* 709
SPRIG BREAK - Shoe - AEROGROUP INTERNATIONAL, INC.; *pg.* 1803, *pg.* 1055
SPRING - Glove - 180S, LLC; *pg.* 1824, *pg.* 754
SPRING! - Beverages - THE COCA-COLA COMPANY; *pg.* 240, *pg.* 493
SPRING - Basket - THE LONGABERGER COMPANY; *pg.* 1127, *pg.* 1467
SPRING - Apparel - OAKLEY, INC.; *pg.* 1840, *pg.* 86
SPRING AND MERCER - Apparel - HAMPSHIRE GROUP LIMITED; *pg.* 25, *pg.* 1237
SPRING AWAKENING - Art Performance - JOHN F. KENNEDY CENTER FOR THE PERFORMING ARTS; *pg.* 555, *pg.* 401
SPRING BLOSSOMS BOUQUET - Floral Bouquet - FTD GROUP, INC.; *pg.* 1795, *pg.* 608
SPRING CANISTER BOUQUET - Bouquet - 1-800-FLOWERS.COM, INC.; *pg.* 1758, *pg.* 1151
SPRING CREEK FARM BRAND - Smoked Meat Goods of Sausage - BOB EVANS FARMS, LLC; *pg.* 841, *pg.* 1467
SPRING DROPS - Nutritional Product - NUTRACEUTICAL INTERNATIONAL CORPORATION; *pg.* 1576, *pg.* 1753
SPRING FLING - Lottery Game - OHIO LOTTERY COMMISSION; *pg.* 1002, *pg.* 1433
SPRING GARDEN - Lettuce - DOLE FRESH VEGETABLES; *pg.* 854, *pg.* 198
SPRING GARDEN BOUQUET - Floral Bouquet - FTD GROUP, INC.; *pg.* 1795, *pg.* 608
SPRING GLEN - Snack Food Product - HANOVER FOODS CORPORATION; *pg.* 861, *pg.* 1535
SPRING GREEN - Furniture - ASHLEY FURNITURE INDUSTRIES, INC.; *pg.* 914, *pg.* 1852
SPRING HEARTH - Flour - CARGILL LIMITED; *pg.* 1475, *pg.* 1914
SPRING INSPIRATION - Flower Arrangement - 1-800-FLOWERS.COM, INC.; *pg.* 1758, *pg.* 1151
SPRING KING - Flour - CARGILL LIMITED; *pg.* 1475, *pg.* 1914
SPRING LAWNS ALIVE! - Lawn Care Product - GARDENS ALIVE!, INC.; *pg.* 1796, *pg.* 693
SPRING-LINE - Grounding Tabs - PARKER CHOMERICS; *pg.* 662, *pg.* 862
SPRING MEADOW - Flower Arrangement - 1-800-FLOWERS.COM, INC.; *pg.* 1758, *pg.* 1151
SPRING MOSAIC - Flower Arrangement - 1-800-FLOWERS.COM, INC.; *pg.* 1758, *pg.* 1151
SPRING PEARL - Doll And Toy - AMERICAN GIRL LLC; *pg.* 949, *pg.* 1871
SPRING RAPTURE - Container Grown Plant - MONROVIA GROWERS; *pg.* 1797, *pg.* 44
SPRING-TITE! - Multi-purpose Springs - DORMAN PRODUCTS, INC.; *pg.* 204, *pg.* 1522
SPRING VALLEY - Prenatal Vitamins - WAL-MART STORES, INC.; *pg.* 1790, *pg.* 29
SPRINGBOARD - Seasonal Beer - NEW BELGIUM BREWING COMPANY, INC.; *pg.* 258, *pg.* 328
SPRINGBOARD - Office Furniture - STEELCASE INC.; *pg.* 475, *pg.* 889
SPRINGBROO - Food Product - ELLENBEE-LEGGETT COMPANY INC.; *pg.* 854, *pg.* 1452
SPRINGER - Table - BLATT BOWLING & BILLIARD CORP.; *pg.* 1827, *pg.* 1203
SPRINGER - Motorcycle - HARLEY-DAVIDSON, INC.; *pg.* 178, *pg.* 1874
SPRINGFIELD - Machine Tool Product - BOURN & KOCH MACHINE TOOL COMPANY; *pg.* 1319, *pg.* 654
SPRINGFIELD - Furniture - FLEXSTEEL INDUSTRIES, INC.; *pg.* 925, *pg.* 707
SPRINGFIELD - Seating Product - IRWIN SEATING COMPANY INC.; *pg.* 929, *pg.* 887
SPRINGFIELD - Food Products & General Merchandise - UNIFIED GROCERS, INC.; *pg.* 1036, *pg.* 66
SPRINGHILL - Paper - INTERNATIONAL PAPER COMPANY; *pg.* 1460, *pg.* 1644
SPRINGHILL SUITES - Hotel Chain - MARRIOTT INTERNATIONAL, INC.; *pg.* 1102, *pg.* 764
SPRINGHOUSE - Study Aids for the Nursing Profession - LIPPINCOTT WILLIAMS & WILKINS, INC.; *pg.* 1659, *pg.* 1567
SPRINGLATCH - Deadbolt - MEDECO HIGH SECURITY LOCKS, INC.; *pg.* 1055, *pg.* 1806
SPRINGLINE - Window - ANDERSEN CORPORATION; *pg.* 67, *pg.* 916
SPRINGMAID - Window - SPRINGS GLOBAL, INC.; *pg.* 698, *pg.* 1616
SPRINGMESH - Gaskets - PARKER CHOMERICS; *pg.* 662, *pg.* 862
SPRINGSTEP - Flooring Product - STAGESTEP INC.; *pg.* 1688, *pg.* 1570
SPRINGTIME - Container Grown Plant - MONROVIA GROWERS; *pg.* 1797, *pg.* 44
SPRINGTIME II - Color - FERRO CORPORATION; *pg.* 1162, *pg.* 1462
SPRINKEL - Footwear - STEVEN MADDEN, LTD.; *pg.* 1819, *pg.* 1176
SPRINKLE - Granular Deodorizer - SURCO PRODUCTS, INC.; *pg.* 336, *pg.* 1581
SPRINKLER - Footwear - OAKLEY, INC.; *pg.* 1840, *pg.* 86
SPRINKLES - Fabric - NEMSCHOFF, INC.; *pg.* 936, *pg.* 1890
SPRINKL'INS - Lowfat Yogurt - THE DANNON COMPANY, INC.; *pg.* 851, *pg.* 1351
SPRINT - Bagging Machine - AUTOMATED PACKAGING SYSTEMS INC.; *pg.* 1452, *pg.* 1474
SPRINT - Engine Type - BRIGGS & STRATTON CORPORATION; *pg.* 201, *pg.* 1899
SPRINT - Delivery Body Style - HACKNEY INTERNATIONAL; *pg.* 178, *pg.* 1392
SPRINT - Medical Equipment - INVACARE CORPORATION; *pg.* 1546, *pg.* 1451
SPRINT - NAVIGATION PROCESSING - ION GEOPHYSICAL CORPORATION; *pg.* 1350, *pg.* 1708
SPRINT - Diagnostic Urinalysis System - IRIS INTERNATIONAL, INC.; *pg.* 1547, *pg.* 64
SPRINT - Convenience Stores - THE PANTRY, INC.; *pg.* 1029, *pg.* 1360
SPRINT - Footwear - P.W. MINOR & SON, INC.; *pg.* 1816, *pg.* 1140
SPRINT PCS - Wireless Network - SPRINT CORPORATION; *pg.* 1874, *pg.* 719
SPRINTER - Battery - EXIDE TECHNOLOGIES; *pg.* 204, *pg.* 483
SPRINTSCAN - High-Resolution Scanners - POLAROID CORPORATION; *pg.* 1426, *pg.* 815
SPIRALJET - Spray Product - SPRAYING SYSTEMS CO.; *pg.* 1063, *pg.* 670
SPRITE - Soft Drink - THE COCA-COLA COMPANY; *pg.* 240, *pg.* 493
SPRITE - Floor Care - NILFISK-ADVANCE, INC.; *pg.* 332, *pg.* 953
SPRITE 3G - Beverages - THE COCA-COLA COMPANY; *pg.* 240, *pg.* 493
SPRITE AIR SCOOP - Vacuum - HILLYARD, INC.; *pg.* 331, *pg.* 990
SPRITE DUO - Beverages - THE COCA-COLA COMPANY; *pg.* 240, *pg.* 493
SPRITE ICE - Beverages - THE COCA-COLA COMPANY; *pg.* 240, *pg.* 493
SPRITE LIGHT - Beverages - THE COCA-COLA COMPANY; *pg.* 240, *pg.* 493
SPRITE REMIX - Soft Drink - THE COCA-COLA COMPANY; *pg.* 240, *pg.* 493
SPRITE ZERO - Beverages - THE COCA-COLA COMPANY; *pg.* 240, *pg.* 493
SPRITZ DRY - Quick Dry Nail Polish - ORLY INTERNATIONAL, INC.; *pg.* 518, *pg.* 137
SPRO - Digital Imaging - 3D SYSTEMS CORPORATION; *pg.* 339, *pg.* 1621
SPROCKET - Apparel - OAKLEY, INC.; *pg.* 1840, *pg.* 86
SPRUCE - Lacquer - SEYMOUR OF SYCAMORE, INC.; *pg.* 1447, *pg.* 663
SPRUCE SPRAY - Coatings - SEYMOUR OF SYCAMORE,

INC.; *pg.* 1447, *pg.* 663

SPRYCEL - Leukemia Medication - BRISTOL-MYERS SQUIBB COMPANY; *pg.* 1509, *pg.* 1206

SPS - Sprayers - AG-MEIER INDUSTRIES LLC; *pg.* 700, *pg.* 1668

SPS - Soft Face Hammers - NUPLA CORPORATION; *pg.* 101, *pg.* 281

SPTIMES.COM - Website - TAMPA BAY TIMES; *pg.* 1691, *pg.* 464

SPUD JUMPERS - Potato Sack - SCHOOL-TECH, INC.; *pg.* 1844, *pg.* 866

SPUDDY BUDDY - Color Book - IDAHO POTATO COMMISSION; *pg.* 144, *pg.* 549

SPUDKA VODKA - Distilled Spirits - HOOD RIVER DISTILLERS INC.; *pg.* 1964, *pg.* 1498

SPUDSTERS - Potato Bites - J.R. SIMPLOT COMPANY; *pg.* 867, *pg.* 547

SPUDZ - Cereal - PEPSICO, INC.; *pg.* 259, *pg.* 1327

SPUDZ - Snack - THE QUAKER OATS COMPANY; *pg.* 834, *pg.* 588

SPUN GLASS - Bath Product - KOHLER CO.; *pg.* 91, *pg.* 1862

SPUNFLEX - Fabrics for RTW - GUILFORD PERFORMANCE TEXTILES; *pg.* 693, *pg.* 1393

SPUNKY - Stuffed Dog - GUND, INC.; *pg.* 954, *pg.* 1056

SPUR - Beverages - THE COCA-COLA COMPANY; *pg.* 240, *pg.* 493

SPUR - Petroleum Products in the United States & Canada - MURPHY OIL CORPORATION; *pg.* 982, *pg.* 31

SPURS FOUNDATION - Publisher - SAN ANTONIO SPURS LLC; *pg.* 580, *pg.* 1742

SPUTTER SPOTLIGHT - Newsletter - ADVANCED ENERGY INDUSTRIES, INC.; *pg.* 613, *pg.* 328

SPV - Minerals - MINERALS TECHNOLOGIES INC.; *pg.* 1173, *pg.* 617

SPX - Image Generator & Projector - EVANS & SUTHERLAND COMPUTER CORPORATION; *pg.* 638, *pg.* 1757

SPX - Fluid Handling System - GRACO, INC.; *pg.* 1342, *pg.* 935

SPY FIVE - Educational Materials - SCHOLASTIC INC.; *pg.* 1683, *pg.* 1288

SPY-PROOF - Combination Lock Dial - SARGENT & GREENLEAF, INC.; *pg.* 1061, *pg.* 739

SPY SWEEPER - Software - WEBROOT SOFTWARE, INC.; *pg.* 1289, *pg.* 313

SPY UNIVERSITY - Educational Materials - SCHOLASTIC INC.; *pg.* 1683, *pg.* 1288

SPY X - Educational Materials - SCHOLASTIC INC.; *pg.* 1683, *pg.* 1288

SPYDER - Flashlights - DORCY INTERNATIONAL INC.; *pg.* 1046, *pg.* 1439

SPYGLASS - Medical Device - BOSTON SCIENTIFIC CORPORATION; *pg.* 1508, *pg.* 831

SPYGLASS CARRIER MONITORING SYSTEM - Software - GLOBECOMM SYSTEMS INC.; *pg.* 640, *pg.* 1164

SPYKER - Software - LYNX SOFTWARE TECHNOLOGIES; *pg.* 429, *pg.* 247

SPYKER SPREADER - Lawn Spreaders - THE CYCLONE MFG. CO.; *pg.* 78, *pg.* 698

SPYKES - Malt Beverage - ANHEUSER-BUSCH COMPANIES, LLC; *pg.* 237, *pg.* 991

SPYLER - Educational Materials - SCHOLASTIC INC.; *pg.* 1683, *pg.* 1288

SPYWARE INTERCEPTOR - Software - BLUE COAT SYSTEMS, INC.; *pg.* 362, *pg.* 284

SQL ANYWHERE - Mobile & Embedded Database - SAP; *pg.* 465, *pg.* 78

SQL-BACKTRACK - Recovery Management - BMC SOFTWARE, INC.; *pg.* 362, *pg.* 1701

SQL EXPLORER - Software - BMC SOFTWARE, INC.; *pg.* 362, *pg.* 1701

SQL NAVIGATOR - Software - DELL SOFTWARE; *pg.* 385, *pg.* 40

SQL OPTIMIZER - Software - DELL SOFTWARE; *pg.* 385, *pg.* 40

SQL OPTIMIZER FOR ORACLE - Software - DELL SOFTWARE; *pg.* 385, *pg.* 40

SQL OPTIMIZER FOR SYBASE - Software - DELL SOFTWARE; *pg.* 385, *pg.* 40

SQL-PROGRAMMER - Software - BMC SOFTWARE, INC.; *pg.* 362, *pg.* 1701

SQL SERVER - Computer Software - MICROSOFT CORPORATION; *pg.* 435, *pg.* 1824

SQL TURBO - Software - DELL SOFTWARE; *pg.* 385, *pg.* 40

SQL WATCH - Software - DELL SOFTWARE; *pg.* 385, *pg.* 40

SQLBASE - Embedded Database - DAEGIS INC; *pg.* 381, *pg.* 195

SQLBASE TREASURY - Secure Database - DAEGIS INC; *pg.* 381, *pg.* 195

SQLCONNECT - Networking Software - OPENCONNECT SYSTEMS, INC.; *pg.* 449, *pg.* 1685

SQUARE - Cylinder - FABCO-AIR, INC.; *pg.* 1336, *pg.* 429

SQUARE 1 - Short Stroke Cylinder - FABCO-AIR, INC.; *pg.* 1336, *pg.* 429

SQUARE 1 - Software - SUREQUEST SYSTEMS, INC.; *pg.* 900, *pg.* 1669

SQUARE-A-WAY - Bag Sets - TUPPERWARE BRANDS CORPORATION; *pg.* 1139, *pg.* 456

SQUARE BARREL CONTAINER - Mustard - PLOCHMAN, INC.; *pg.* 890, *pg.* 631

SQUARE DANCER - Footwear - P.W. MINOR & SON, INC.; *pg.* 1816, *pg.* 1140

SQUARE-DUCT - Wireways - SCHNEIDER ELECTRIC USA, INC.; *pg.* 1306, *pg.* 650

SQUARE FLAT-1 - Cylinder - BIMBA MANUFACTURING COMPANY; *pg.* 1317, *pg.* 633

SQUARE O - Sports Eyewear - OAKLEY, INC.; *pg.* 1840, *pg.* 86

SQUARE PAIRS - Educational Materials - SCHOLASTIC INC.; *pg.* 1683, *pg.* 1288

SQUARE SHOOTER - Commercial Lighting - SWIVELIER CO., INC.; *pg.* 1307, *pg.* 1142

SQUARE SHOOTER - Capital Equipment - TEREX CORPORATION; *pg.* 1381, *pg.* 384

SQUARE SHOOTER - TV Antenna - WINEGARD COMPANY; *pg.* 688, *pg.* 702

SQUAREFOLD - Printer - XEROX CORPORATION; *pg.* 494, *pg.* 365

SQUARELOK - Tubing - PENFLEX, INC.; *pg.* 104, *pg.* 1534

SQUARESHOOT - Antenna System - WINEGARD COMPANY; *pg.* 688, *pg.* 702

SQUARESPOT - Thermal Imaging Heads - EASTMAN KODAK COMPANY; *pg.* 1408, *pg.* 1333

SQUAREWAY WOODS - Woods - CALLAWAY GOLF COMPANY; *pg.* 1829, *pg.* 58

SQUEAK - Bear - GUND, INC.; *pg.* 954, *pg.* 1056

SQUEAKY GREEN - Laundry Detergent - METHOD PRODUCTS INC.; *pg.* 332, *pg.* 223

SQUEAL MEDIC - Caliper Grease - RADIATOR SPECIALTY COMPANY; *pg.* 215, *pg.* 1380

SQUEEZ 'N GO - Food Product - CONAGRA FOODS, INC.; *pg.* 826, *pg.* 1014

SQUEEZABLE - Toothbrush Cover - RANIR LLC; *pg.* 520, *pg.* 888

SQUEEZE & SQUEAK - Doll - THE GOLDBERGER COMPANY, LLC; *pg.* 954, *pg.* 1235

SQUEEZE BAG - Blood Bag - DRAVON MEDICAL, INC.; *pg.* 1525, *pg.* 1497

SQUEEZE POP - Gum - WM. WRIGLEY JR. COMPANY; *pg.* 1863, *pg.* 596

SQUEEZEMATE - Commercial Lighting - SWIVELIER CO., INC.; *pg.* 1307, *pg.* 1142

SQUELLET - Ball - SCHOOL-TECH, INC.; *pg.* 1844, *pg.* 866

SQUIER - Guitar - FENDER MUSICAL INSTRUMENTS CORPORATION; *pg.* 547, *pg.* 21

SQUIRE - Knife - BUCK KNIVES, INC.; *pg.* 1828, *pg.* 550

SQUIRE - Classic Chafers - CARLISLE FOODSERVICE PRODUCTS INCORPORATED; *pg.* 1455, *pg.* 1485

SQUIRE - Animal Safety Product - NEOGEN CORPORATION; *pg.* 883, *pg.* 896

SQUIRES CHOICE - Candy, Nut & Confectionery Gifts - HICKORY FARMS, INC.; *pg.* 862, *pg.* 1462

SQUIRT - Footwear - COBIAN CORP.; *pg.* 1806, *pg.* 253

SQUIRT - Beverages - THE COCA-COLA COMPANY; *pg.* 240, *pg.* 493

SQUIRT - Carbonated Soft Drink - DR PEPPER SNAPPLE GROUP, INC.; *pg.* 250, *pg.* 1729

SQUIRT - Cutting Tool - LEATHERMAN TOOL GROUP, INC.; *pg.* 1053, *pg.* 1504

SQUIRT - Gas Bump Tester - MINE SAFETY APPLIANCES COMPANY; *pg.* 1361, *pg.* 1525

SQUISH N CHIPS - Shoe - AEROGROUP INTERNATIONAL, INC.; *pg.* 1803, *pg.* 1055

SQUISHING TRIP - Boots - AEROGROUP INTERNATIONAL, INC.; *pg.* 1803, *pg.* 1055

SQWEEZ - Massager - CONAIR CORPORATION; *pg.* 505, *pg.* 1055

SQWISH - Fruit Candy - PROMOTION IN MOTION, INC.; *pg.* 1861, *pg.* 1052

SR - Fluid Handling System - GRACO, INC.; *pg.* 1342, *pg.* 935

SR-71 - Systems Integration & Aeronautics - LOCKHEED MARTIN CORPORATION; *pg.* 229, *pg.* 762

SR9 - Centerfire Pistols - STURM, RUGER & COMPANY, INC.; *pg.* 1846, *pg.* 371

SRB - Sound Reduction Board - USG CORPORATION; *pg.* 118, *pg.* 594

SRC - Abrasion Resistant Coatings - RED SPOT PAINT & VARNISH CO., INC.; *pg.* 1446, *pg.* 679

SRDA OUT-OF-HOME ADVERTISING SOURCE - Media Directory - SRDS, INC.; *pg.* 1688, *pg.* 657

SRDF - Software - EMC CORPORATION; *pg.* 391, *pg.* 825

SRDS BUSINESS PUBLICATION ADVERTISING SOURCE - Media Directory - SRDS, INC.; *pg.* 1688, *pg.* 657

SRDS CIRCULATION - Media Directory - SRDS, INC.; *pg.* 1688, *pg.* 657

SRDS COMMUNITY PUBLICATION ADVERTISING SOURCE - Media Directory - SRDS, INC.; *pg.* 1688, *pg.* 657

SRDS CONSUMER MAGAZINE ADVERTISING SOURCE - Media Directory - SRDS, INC.; *pg.* 1688, *pg.* 657

SRDS DIRECT MARKETING LIST SOURCE - Media Directory - SRDS, INC.; *pg.* 1688, *pg.* 657

SRDS DIRECT NET - Media Directory - SRDS, INC.; *pg.* 1688, *pg.* 657

SRDS HISPANIC MEDIA & MARKET SOURCE - Media Directory - SRDS, INC.; *pg.* 1688, *pg.* 657

SRDS INTERACTIVE ADVERTISING SOURCE - Media Directory - SRDS, INC.; *pg.* 1688, *pg.* 657

SRDS MEDIA SOLUTIONS - Media Directory - SRDS, INC.; *pg.* 1688, *pg.* 657

SRDS NEWSPAPER ADVERTISING SOURCE - Media Directory - SRDS, INC.; *pg.* 1688, *pg.* 657

SRDS PRINT MEDIA PRODUCTION SOURCE - Media Directory - SRDS, INC.; *pg.* 1688, *pg.* 657

SRDS RADIO ADVERTISING SOURCE - Media Directory - SRDS, INC.; *pg.* 1688, *pg.* 657

SRDS TECHNOLOGY MEDIA SOURCE - Media Directory - SRDS, INC.; *pg.* 1688, *pg.* 657

SRDS TV & CABLE SOURCE - Media Directory - SRDS, INC.; *pg.* 1688, *pg.* 657

SRH - Welding Machine - MILLER ELECTRIC MANUFACTURING CO.; *pg.* 1361, *pg.* 1852

SRM - Colored Plastic Mulch Film - SONOCO PRODUCTS COMPANY; *pg.* 1469, *pg.* 1619

SRM-25 - Sound Reduction Mat - USG CORPORATION; *pg.* 118, *pg.* 594

SRM2 - Managed Network Security Service - NETWOLVES CORPORATION; *pg.* 1271, *pg.* 474

SROD - Software - LUFKIN INDUSTRIES, INC.; *pg.* 1357, *pg.* 1726

SRP PAYCENTERS - Utility Payment Centers - SALT RIVER PROJECT; *pg.* 707, *pg.* 26

SRP POWERWISE - Business Solutions - SALT RIVER PROJECT; *pg.* 707, *pg.* 26

SRS - Surface Maintenance Machine - TENNANT COMPANY; *pg.* 1381, *pg.* 944

SRSTA - Society of Roller Skating Teachers of America - ROLLER SKATING ASSOCIATION INTERNATIONAL; *pg.* 155, *pg.* 689

SRX - Sport Utility Vehicle - GENERAL MOTORS COMPANY; *pg.* 175, *pg.* 881

SRX - Thermal Processing Equipment - SURFACE COMBUSTION, INC.; *pg.* 1077, *pg.* 1462

SRX CALL SESSION SERVER - Network Product - SONUS NETWORKS INC.; *pg.* 1281, *pg.* 858

SS - Maintenance & Repair of Laboratory Equipment & Computers - DOW CORNING CORPORATION; *pg.* 1159, *pg.* 900

SS - Sodium Silicate - PQ CORPORATION; *pg.* 1178, *pg.* 1515

SS-10/SS-10C SUBSEA WELLHEAD SYSTEMS - Subsea Equipment - DRIL-QUIP, INC.; *pg.* 1330, *pg.* 1704

SS-15 BIGBORE SUBSEA WELLHEAD SYSTEMS - Subsea Equipment - DRIL-QUIP, INC.; *pg.* 1330, *pg.* 1704

SS-15 DEEPWATER SUBSEA WELLHEAD SYSTEMS - Subsea Equipment - DRIL-QUIP, INC.; *pg.* 1330, *pg.* 1704

SS-15 SUBSEA WELLHEAD SYSTEMS - Subsea Equipment - DRIL-QUIP, INC.; *pg.* 1330, *pg.* 1704

SS-15ES DEEPWATER SUBSEA WELLHEAD SYSTEMS - Subsea Equipment - DRIL-QUIP, INC.; *pg.* 1330, *pg.* 1704

SS-99 - Epilator - INSTANTRON CO., INC.; *pg.* 512, *pg.* 1608

SS TOURNAMENT - Freshwater Spinning Reels - DAIWA CORPORATION; *pg.* 1832, *pg.* 75
SS400 - Lighting Systems - REVOLUTION LIGHTING TECHNOLOGIES, INC.; *pg.* 1304, *pg.* 377
SS7/SIGTRAN MIGRATION - Wireline Solutions - SONUS NETWORKS INC.; *pg.* 1281, *pg.* 858
SSAL2000 - Stainless Steel & Aluminum Fry Pans & Cookware - CARLISLE FOODSERVICE PRODUCTS INCORPORATED; *pg.* 1455, *pg.* 1485
SSB - Servo Stepper Front End Brake - ELECTROID CO; *pg.* 1333, *pg.* 1123
SSD GUARD - Disk Control Computer Circuitry - AVAGO TECHNOLOGIES; *pg.* 358, *pg.* 238
SSI - Integrated Circuits - TEXAS INSTRUMENTS INCORPORATED; *pg.* 679, *pg.* 1688
SSI COMPASS - Newsletter - SURVEY SAMPLING INTERNATIONAL LLC; *pg.* 1690, *pg.* 371
SSI EQUIPMENT - Valve & Fluid Product - CIRCOR INTERNATIONAL, INC.; *pg.* 76, *pg.* 805
SSI-LITE - Targeted Samples - SURVEY SAMPLING INTERNATIONAL LLC; *pg.* 1690, *pg.* 371
SSI-ONE - Gun - O.F. MOSSBERG & SONS, INC.; *pg.* 1842, *pg.* 360
SSI-SNAP - On-Line Sampling Software - SURVEY SAMPLING INTERNATIONAL LLC; *pg.* 1690, *pg.* 371
SSI VERIFY - Technology-Based System - SURVEY SAMPLING INTERNATIONAL LLC; *pg.* 1690, *pg.* 371
SSIPS - Drink Boxes - JOHANNA FOODS INC.; *pg.* 866, *pg.* 1066
SSL FOR ENTERPRISE - Internet Site Security Product - VERISIGN, INC.; *pg.* 488, *pg.* 1799
SSOFAST - Software - BIO-RAD LABORATORIES, INC.; *pg.* 1504, *pg.* 101
SSR-100 - Blended Rope - SAMSON ROPE TECHNOLOGIES; *pg.* 1468, *pg.* 1820
SSR-101 - Blended Rope - SAMSON ROPE TECHNOLOGIES; *pg.* 1468, *pg.* 1820
SSR-1200 - Rope - SAMSON ROPE TECHNOLOGIES; *pg.* 1468, *pg.* 1820
SSR-301-R - Blended Rope - SAMSON ROPE TECHNOLOGIES; *pg.* 1468, *pg.* 1820
SSS - Cage Layer System or Cages - CTB INTERNATIONAL CORP.; *pg.* 850, *pg.* 695
SSSMART - Content Area Reading Program - QUESTAR ASSESSMENT, INC.; *pg.* 1679, *pg.* 1143
SST - Electronic Components - MOLEX INCORPORATED; *pg.* 655, *pg.* 628
SST CARBIDE - Blade - LENOX; *pg.* 1053, *pg.* 817
SSVG - Silicon Carbide Super Velocity Gas Burners - HAUCK MANUFACTURING COMPANY, INC.; *pg.* 1345, *pg.* 1522
SSW - Tempered Wire - SENECA WIRE & MANUFACTURING COMPANY; *pg.* 1061, *pg.* 1454
ST - Rotor - FARREL CORPORATION; *pg.* 1336, *pg.* 337
ST - Fluid Handling System - GRACO, INC.; *pg.* 1342, *pg.* 935
ST-246 - Anti-Viral Pharmaceutical - SIGA TECHNOLOGIES, INC.; *pg.* 1594, *pg.* 1292
ST-90 - Lens - DANKER LABORATORIES INC.; *pg.* 1408, *pg.* 465
ST-BIFOCAL - Lens - DANKER LABORATORIES INC.; *pg.* 1408, *pg.* 465
ST-BODIPY - Molecular Biology Product - THERMO FISHER SCIENTIFIC INC.; *pg.* 1602, *pg.* 61
ST. CHARLES - Lighting Product - WESTINGHOUSE LIGHTING CORPORATION; *pg.* 687, *pg.* 1571
ST. CLAIR - Office Furniture - STEELCASE INC.; *pg.* 475, *pg.* 889
ST-DRY - Connector System - GREENE, TWEED & CO.; *pg.* 1344, *pg.* 1544
ST. ELIENNE - Guest Chairs - BERNHARDT DESIGN; *pg.* 918, *pg.* 1381
ST. FRANCIS - Wines - KOBRAND CORPORATION; *pg.* 1965, *pg.* 1325
ST. GERMAIN - Bar stools - BERNHARDT DESIGN; *pg.* 918, *pg.* 1381
ST-HUBERT - Beer - SLEEMAN UNIBROUE QUEBEC; *pg.* 265, *pg.* 1950
ST. IDES - Malt Liquor - PABST BREWING COMPANY; *pg.* 258, *pg.* 137
ST. IVES - Body Wash - UNILEVER UNITED STATES, INC.; *pg.* 904, *pg.* 1061
ST. JAMES - Brick & Tile Product - CHEROKEE BRICK & TILE COMPANY; *pg.* 75, *pg.* 535
ST. JOHN - Women's Apparel - ST. JOHN KNITS INTERNATIONAL, INC.; *pg.* 33, *pg.* 116
ST. JOSEPH - Healthcare Product - JOHNSON & JOHNSON; *pg.* 1549, *pg.* 1091
ST. JOSEPH'S ASPIRIN - Pain Reliever - MCNEIL-PPC, INC.; *pg.* 1560, *pg.* 1533
ST. KITTS - Carpet - BEAULIEU GROUP, LLC; *pg.* 917, *pg.* 529
ST. LEONARD - Wines & Spirits - LEONARD KREUSCH, INC.; *pg.* 254, *pg.* 1099
ST. LOUIS HOMES & LIFESTYLES - Magazine - NETWORK COMMUNICATIONS INC.; *pg.* 1271, *pg.* 534
ST. LUCIA - Carpet - BEAULIEU GROUP, LLC; *pg.* 917, *pg.* 529
ST. MARTIN - Carpet - BEAULIEU GROUP, LLC; *pg.* 917, *pg.* 529
ST. MICHAEL - Guest Chairs - BERNHARDT DESIGN; *pg.* 918, *pg.* 1381
ST. MORITZ - Flatware - ONEIDA LTD; *pg.* 1129, *pg.* 1318
ST. NICK'S - Soft Drink - NATIONAL BEVERAGE CORP.; *pg.* 257, *pg.* 425
ST. PETERSBURG - Game - WMS INDUSTRIES INC.; *pg.* 593, *pg.* 666
ST. PETERSBURG TIMES - Daily Newspaper - THE TIMES PUBLISHING CO.; *pg.* 1695, *pg.* 464
ST PRO - Sensor - WATLOW ELECTRIC MANUFACTURING COMPANY; *pg.* 1078, *pg.* 1004
ST. REGIS - Hotels - STARWOOD HOTELS & RESORTS WORLDWIDE, INC.; *pg.* 1114, *pg.* 378
ST SERIES - Submersible Trash Pump - THE GORMAN-RUPP COMPANY; *pg.* 1341, *pg.* 1458
ST SLIM TWIN - Battery - ENERGIZER HOLDINGS, INC.; *pg.* 637, *pg.* 996
ST. TROPEZ - Dinnerware - THE HOMER LAUGHLIN CHINA COMPANY; *pg.* 1125, *pg.* 1850
ST. TROPEZ - Ceiling Fan - WESTINGHOUSE LIGHTING CORPORATION; *pg.* 687, *pg.* 1571
ST. VINCENT - Carpet - BEAULIEU GROUP, LLC; *pg.* 917, *pg.* 529
ST. VIVANT ARMAGNAC - Beverage - SIDNEY FRANK IMPORTING CO., INC.; *pg.* 1970, *pg.* 1184
ST3000 - Systems Integration & Aeronautics - LOCKHEED MARTIN CORPORATION; *pg.* 229, *pg.* 762
ST329 - Athletic Shoes - K-SWISS; *pg.* 1837, *pg.* 306
ST330 - Footwear - K-SWISS; *pg.* 1837, *pg.* 306
ST359 - Athletic Shoes - K-SWISS; *pg.* 1837, *pg.* 306
ST363 - Athletic Shoes - K-SWISS; *pg.* 1837, *pg.* 306
STA - Anesthesia System - MILESTONE SCIENTIFIC, INC.; *pg.* 1568, *pg.* 1079
STA-BIL - Fuel Stabilizer - GOLD EAGLE COMPANY; *pg.* 206, *pg.* 575
STA-CLEAR - Lens Cleaning Equipment - SELLSTROM MANUFACTURING CO.; *pg.* 1428, *pg.* 659
STA CRETE - Performance Coatings - QUAKER CHEMICAL CORP.; *pg.* 1178, *pg.* 1524
STA-DRY SYSTEM - Waterproof Shell - ACUSHNET COMPANY; *pg.* 1824, *pg.* 818
STA-FIL - All-Weather Chuckhole Repair - REVERE PRODUCTS; *pg.* 107, *pg.* 1435
STA-FLO - Liquid Starch - HENKEL CONSUMER GOODS; *pg.* 511, *pg.* 22
STA-FORM 60 - Urea Formaldehyde Reaction Product - GEORGIA-PACIFIC LLC; *pg.* 1458, *pg.* 507
STA-FRESH - Preservative - PLANTABBS PRODUCTS COMPANY; *pg.* 1799, *pg.* 758
STA-HARD - Neutral Salt - HEATBATH CORPORATION; *pg.* 1165, *pg.* 826
STA-HOME - Insect Pest Control Product - GARDENS ALIVE!, INC.; *pg.* 1796, *pg.* 693
STA-HOT - Non-Metal Sleeves - ASHLAND INC.; *pg.* 972, *pg.* 726
STA-KIL - Coating Product - PPG INDUSTRIES, INC.; *pg.* 1445, *pg.* 1579
STA-KLEEN - Wall Plates - PASS & SEYMOUR/LEGRAND; *pg.* 1303, *pg.* 1344
STA-KON - Terminal - THOMAS & BETTS CORPORATION; *pg.* 680, *pg.* 1646
STA-LUBE - Greases & Gear Oils - CRC INDUSTRIES, INC.; *pg.* 329, *pg.* 1590
STA-NATURAL - Water Repellant - QUAKER CHEMICAL CORP.; *pg.* 1178, *pg.* 1524
STA-PURE - Pump Tube - W.L. GORE & ASSOCIATES, INC.; *pg.* 122, *pg.* 388
STA-RITE - Hair Accessories - STA-RITE GINNIE LOU, INC.; *pg.* 523, *pg.* 660
STA-SOFT - Fabric - UNIROYAL ENGINEERED PRODUCTS; *pg.* 699, *pg.* 467
STA-STRAP - Cable Tie - PANDUIT CORP.; *pg.* 661, *pg.* 663
STA-TITE - Vehicle System - MACLEAN-FOGG COMPANY INC.; *pg.* 1358, *pg.* 635
STA-TRUE - Levels & Squares - THE L.S. STARRETT COMPANY; *pg.* 1421, *pg.* 783
STAAD - Software - BENTLEY SYSTEMS, INC.; *pg.* 361, *pg.* 1531
STAAR ELASTIC LENS - Lens - STAAR SURGICAL COMPANY; *pg.* 1597, *pg.* 151
STAAR ELASTIMIDE - Lens - STAAR SURGICAL COMPANY; *pg.* 1597, *pg.* 151
STAAR TORIC - Intraocular Lenses - STAAR SURGICAL COMPANY; *pg.* 1597, *pg.* 151
STAARVISC - Viscoelastic Gel - STAAR SURGICAL COMPANY; *pg.* 1597, *pg.* 151
STABIL-ION - Ionization Gauges - BROOKS AUTOMATION, INC.; *pg.* 1320, *pg.* 813
STABILAIRE - Liquid LPG Pumps - ALGAS-SDI; *pg.* 1311, *pg.* 1831
STABILCOAT - Stabilizer - SURMODICS, INC.; *pg.* 1600, *pg.* 924
STABILEYES - Medical Device - ABBOTT MEDICAL OPTICS, INC.; *pg.* 1485, *pg.* 260
STABILGUARD - Stabilizer - SURMODICS, INC.; *pg.* 1600, *pg.* 924
STABILIFE - Electrolyte Salts - AIR PRODUCTS AND CHEMICALS, INC.; *pg.* 1145, *pg.* 1513
STABILIFE - Optical Filter - NEWPORT CORPORATION; *pg.* 1424, *pg.* 114
STABILITE - Shoe - ETONIC WORLDWIDE LLC; *pg.* 1808, *pg.* 857
STABILITE - Systems Integration & Aeronautics - LOCKHEED MARTIN CORPORATION; *pg.* 229, *pg.* 762
STABILITY BRIDGE - Thermoplastic Urethane - ACUSHNET COMPANY; *pg.* 1824, *pg.* 818
STABILITY WEB - Midfoot Support - MASON COMPANIES, INC.; *pg.* 1811, *pg.* 1856
STABILIZER - Orthopedic Device - DJO SURGICAL; *pg.* 1525, *pg.* 1661
STABILIZER PRO - Glove - ETONIC WORLDWIDE LLC; *pg.* 1808, *pg.* 857
STABILIZING - Orthopedic Product - DJO INCORPORATED; *pg.* 1524, *pg.* 302
STABILON - Fiber Stabilizers - HUNTSMAN CORPORATION; *pg.* 1167, *pg.* 1758
STABILOR - Footwear - K-SWISS; *pg.* 1837, *pg.* 306
STABILOR MESH - Footwear - K-SWISS; *pg.* 1837, *pg.* 306
STABILOX - Sorbent Solution - MULTISORB TECHNOLOGIES, INC.; *pg.* 1570, *pg.* 1150
STABILZYME - Stabilizer - SURMODICS, INC.; *pg.* 1600, *pg.* 924
STABITEX - Starch - CARGILL, INC.; *pg.* 845, *pg.* 965
STABLE GOURMET - Animal Nutrition Product - MANNA PRO CORPORATION; *pg.* 1478, *pg.* 975
STABLE-RITE - Labeling Products - AVERY DENNISON CORPORATION; *pg.* 1452, *pg.* 95
STABLEC - Emulsifier - ARCHER-DANIELS-MIDLAND COMPANY; *pg.* 825, *pg.* 565
STABLEMATES - Toy Model Horse - REEVES INTERNATIONAL, INC.; *pg.* 966, *pg.* 1108
STABLETABLE - Cover & Pad - HOME PRODUCTS INTERNATIONAL, INC.; *pg.* 1125, *pg.* 577
STABLETRAC - Drive Technology - WESTERN DIGITAL CORPORATION; *pg.* 492, *pg.* 118
STABLEVIEW - Binocular - BUSHNELL OUTDOOR PRODUCTS, INC.; *pg.* 1403, *pg.* 718
STABROM - Chemical Product - ALBEMARLE CORPORATION; *pg.* 1146, *pg.* 741
STAC64 - Electronic Components - MOLEX INCORPORATED; *pg.* 655, *pg.* 628
STACCATO - Footwear - CAPEZIO BALLET MAKERS INC.; *pg.* 1805, *pg.* 1125
STACCATO - Computer Program - EASTMAN KODAK COMPANY; *pg.* 1408, *pg.* 1333
STACCATO - Kitchen Product - KOHLER CO.; *pg.* 91, *pg.* 1862
STACCATO - Fabric - NEUTRAL POSTURE, INC.; *pg.* 939, *pg.* 1669
STACK-A-SHELF - Closet Organization - CLOSETMAID CORPORATION; *pg.* 920, *pg.* 452
STACKABLE - Tumblers - CARLISLE FOODSERVICE PRODUCTS INCORPORATED; *pg.* 1455, *pg.* 1485
STACKABLE - Furniture - HERMAN MILLER, INC.; *pg.* 926, *pg.* 913

STACKED BUFFALO - Knife - BUCK KNIVES, INC.; *pg.* 1828, *pg.* 550
STACKED LEATHER - Knife - BUCK KNIVES, INC.; *pg.* 1828, *pg.* 550
STACKED WILDS - Video Game - INTERNATIONAL GAME TECHNOLOGY; *pg.* 957, *pg.* 1024
STACKER - Kitchen Organizer - HOME PRODUCTS INTERNATIONAL, INC.; *pg.* 1125, *pg.* 577
STACKER - Men's Boot - JACK SCHWARTZ SHOES, INC.; *pg.* 1810, *pg.* 1245
STACKFET - Switch - POWER INTEGRATIONS, INC.; *pg.* 1369, *pg.* 249
STACKING - Guest Chairs - BERNHARDT DESIGN; *pg.* 918, *pg.* 1381
STACKINS - Toys - FUNRISE TOY CORP.; *pg.* 549, *pg.* 300
STACKLINK - Cover Plate - QUANTUM CORPORATION; *pg.* 458, *pg.* 250
STACKPAK - Insulated Tubing - O'BRIEN CORPORATION; *pg.* 1366, *pg.* 1001
STACKS - Fabric - NEMSCHOFF, INC.; *pg.* 936, *pg.* 1890
STACKS OF CASH - Lottery Game - NEW YORK STATE LOTTERY; *pg.* 1001, *pg.* 1340
STACKS OF CASH - Lottery Game - OHIO LOTTERY COMMISSION; *pg.* 1002, *pg.* 1433
STACKVIEW - Software - PASSUR AEROSPACE, INC.; *pg.* 233, *pg.* 376
STACKWISE - EtherSwitch Service - CISCO SYSTEMS, INC.; *pg.* 372, *pg.* 240
STACO - Hog System - CTB INTERNATIONAL CORP.; *pg.* 850, *pg.* 695
STACOOLER - Shoes - ACUSHNET COMPANY; *pg.* 1824, *pg.* 818
STACOOLER SPORT - Shoes - ACUSHNET COMPANY; *pg.* 1824, *pg.* 818
STACY - Clothing - ABERCROMBIE & FITCH CO.; *pg.* 37, *pg.* 1466
STACY ADAMS - Footwear - WEYCO GROUP, INC.; *pg.* 1822, *pg.* 1858
STACY'S PITA CHIPS - Snack Food - STACY'S PITA CHIP COMPANY, INC.; *pg.* 1034, *pg.* 842
STACY'S SOY THIN CRISPS - Snack Food - STACY'S PITA CHIP COMPANY, INC.; *pg.* 1034, *pg.* 842
STADIA VIEW - Sliding Doors & Windows - KAWNEER COMPANY, INC.; *pg.* 90, *pg.* 537
STADIUM - Lounge Chairs - BERNHARDT DESIGN; *pg.* 918, *pg.* 1381
STADIUM BRATS - Bratwurst - JOHNSONVILLE SAUSAGE, LLC; *pg.* 867, *pg.* 1894
STADIUM CLUB SPORTS CARDS - Baseball, Football, Basketball & Hockey Cards - THE TOPPS COMPANY, INC.; *pg.* 588, *pg.* 1302
STADIUM SERIES - Outdoor Furnishings - WITT INDUSTRIES, INC.; *pg.* 1140, *pg.* 1461
STADOL IM/IV - Agonist-Antagonist Analgesic - BRISTOL-MYERS SQUIBB U.S. PHARMACEUTICAL GROUP; *pg.* 1511, *pg.* 1110
STAFAC - Animal Health Product - PHIBROCHEM; *pg.* 1177, *pg.* 1124
STAFF CARE - Staffing Services - AMN HEALTHCARE SERVICES, INC.; *pg.* 1494, *pg.* 200
STAFFING INDUSTRY ANALYSTS - Newspaper - CRAIN COMMUNICATIONS, INC.; *pg.* 1631, *pg.* 879
STAFFMETRICS - Human Resources Software - API HEALTHCARE CORP.; *pg.* 350, *pg.* 1860
STAFFORD - Lighting - ETHAN ALLEN INTERIORS INC.; *pg.* 924, *pg.* 343
STAFFORDSHIRE - Door & Wood Product - CONESTOGA WOOD SPECIALTIES CORP.; *pg.* 921, *pg.* 1527
STAFLEX - Apparel Interlining - HARODITE INDUSTRIES, INC.; *pg.* 693, *pg.* 847
STAG - Beer - PABST BREWING COMPANY; *pg.* 258, *pg.* 137
STAGE - Department Stores - STAGE STORES, INC.; *pg.* 33, *pg.* 1715
STAGE-1 - Dental Implant System - LIFECORE BIOMEDICAL, LLC; *pg.* 1556, *pg.* 920
STAGE 1000 - Guitar Amplifier - FENDER MUSICAL INSTRUMENTS CORPORATION; *pg.* 547, *pg.* 21
STAGE 1600 - Guitar Amplifier - FENDER MUSICAL INSTRUMENTS CORPORATION; *pg.* 547, *pg.* 21
THE STAGE IS SET FOR YOU - Tagline - TENNESSEE DEPARTMENT OF TOURIST DEVELOPMENT; *pg.* 1007, *pg.* 1654
STAGE IV - Mattress Replacement System - MEDLINE INDUSTRIES, INC.; *pg.* 1562, *pg.* 635
STAGE OF RICHES - Game - WMS INDUSTRIES INC.; *pg.* 593, *pg.* 666
STAGE PACK 3 - Electric Guitar Pack - PEAVEY ELECTRONICS CORPORATION; *pg.* 662, *pg.* 970
STAGE WORKS - Sound Equipment - SAM ASH MUSIC CORPORATION; *pg.* 669, *pg.* 1167
STAGEHAND - Stage & Riser - WENGER CORPORATION; *pg.* 1307, *pg.* 952
STAGEMOBILE - Riser - WENGER CORPORATION; *pg.* 1307, *pg.* 952
STAGES - Furniture - ASHLEY FURNITURE INDUSTRIES, INC.; *pg.* 914, *pg.* 1852
STAGES - Toothbrush - GILLETTE; *pg.* 1536, *pg.* 795
STAGG - Chili & Corned Beef Hash - HORMEL FOODS CORPORATION; *pg.* 863, *pg.* 915
STAGG BOWL - Trademark (Div. III Football) - NATIONAL COLLEGIATE ATHLETIC ASSOCIATION; *pg.* 567, *pg.* 688
STAIN ERASER - Cleaning Product - THE EVERCARE COMPANY; *pg.* 1124, *pg.* 483
STAIN LOCK - Paint - KELLY-MOORE PAINT COMPANY, INC.; *pg.* 1443, *pg.* 198
STAIN MATE - Floor Staining Tool - WAGNER SPRAY TECH CORPORATION; *pg.* 1449, *pg.* 954
STAIN SHIELD - Food Storage Containers - NEWELL RUBBERMAID INC.; *pg.* 1128, *pg.* 515
STAINEASE - Molecular Biology Product - THERMO FISHER SCIENTIFIC INC.; *pg.* 1602, *pg.* 61
STAINGUARD - Roofing Protectant - GAF MATERIALS CORP.; *pg.* 83, *pg.* 1681
STAINGUARD - Cover & Pad - HOME PRODUCTS INTERNATIONAL, INC.; *pg.* 1125, *pg.* 577
STAINLESS INTERCEPTOR - Wrap Bug Shield - LUND INTERNATIONAL, INC.; *pg.* 211, *pg.* 526
STAINLESS KING - Food Jar - THERMOS L.L.C.; *pg.* 61, *pg.* 660
STAINLESS MAX - Pump Product - IDEX CORPORATION; *pg.* 1347, *pg.* 623
STAINLESS STEEL FIXTURE - Fiber Optic Fixtures - REVOLUTION LIGHTING TECHNOLOGIES, INC.; *pg.* 1304, *pg.* 377
STAINLESS STEPSHIELD - Door Sill Protector - LUND INTERNATIONAL, INC.; *pg.* 211, *pg.* 526
STAINMASTER - Stain Resistant Fibers - INVISTA B.V.; *pg.* 1168, *pg.* 723
STAINSEAL - Interior Oil Stain - DUNN-EDWARDS CORPORATION; *pg.* 1442, *pg.* 129
STAINSHIELD - Latex Stains & Primers for Furniture, Lumber, Decking, Siding & Fences - PRATT & LAMBERT PAINTS; *pg.* 1446, *pg.* 1434
STAINSTRIP - Coating & Paint - AKZO NOBEL DECORATIVE PAINTS, USA; *pg.* 1439, *pg.* 1474
STAIR PRO - Patient Handling Equipment - STRYKER CORPORATION; *pg.* 1598, *pg.* 894
STAIRLIFT - Stair Rider - INCLINATOR COMPANY OF AMERICA; *pg.* 88, *pg.* 1536
STAIRMASTER - Health And Fitness Product - NAUTILUS, INC.; *pg.* 1840, *pg.* 1846
STAIRS - Software - COMMAND SECURITY CORPORATION; *pg.* 377, *pg.* 1171
STAIRS - Apparel - OAKLEY, INC.; *pg.* 1840, *pg.* 86
STAKLITE 500 - Light Fixture - LITECONTROL CORPORATION; *pg.* 1301, *pg.* 841
STALL FOUNT - Fountain - RITCHIE INDUSTRIES, INC.; *pg.* 707, *pg.* 703
STALL SAFE - Disinfectant - W.F. YOUNG, INC.; *pg.* 1610, *pg.* 817
STALLCUP'S - Fire Safety Book - NATIONAL FIRE PROTECTION ASSOCIATION; *pg.* 149, *pg.* 842
STALLION - Rigid Deck - AG-MEIER INDUSTRIES LLC; *pg.* 700, *pg.* 1668
STALLION - Floor Cleaning Product - NSS ENTERPRISES, INC.; *pg.* 59, *pg.* 1476
STAM-N-AID - Animal Safety Product - NEOGEN CORPORATION; *pg.* 883, *pg.* 896
STAMARK - Tape - 3M COMPANY; *pg.* 1142, *pg.* 956
STAMINA - Shoe - AEROGROUP INTERNATIONAL, INC.; *pg.* 1803, *pg.* 1055
STAMPED - Wallcovering - YORK WALLCOVERINGS INC.; *pg.* 947, *pg.* 1598
STAMPEDE! - Game - GAMEWRIGHT; *pg.* 953, *pg.* 836
STAMPEDE FOR MEN - Spray - ANNIE OAKLEY ENTERPRISES, INC.; *pg.* 499, *pg.* 693
STAMPS - Community - THE ZIEGLER COMPANIES, INC.; *pg.* 824, *pg.* 597
STAMPS HAPPEN - Rubber Stamp - JANLYNN CORPORATION; *pg.* 696, *pg.* 815
STAN HERMAN - Robes & Loungewear - KELLWOOD COMPANY; *pg.* 28, *pg.* 975
STAN-TONE - Colorant - POLYONE CORPORATION; *pg.* 1177, *pg.* 1404
STANAX - Durable Antistat - HENKEL CORPORATION; *pg.* 1165, *pg.* 1535
STANBEE - Shoe Components - STANBEE COMPANY, INC.; *pg.* 1819, *pg.* 1050
STANBOOK - Sales Books - THE STANDARD REGISTER COMPANY; *pg.* 473, *pg.* 1446
STANCADDY - Toothbrush Holder - SONOCO PRODUCTS COMPANY; *pg.* 1469, *pg.* 1619
STANCAPS - Glass Covers - SONOCO PRODUCTS COMPANY; *pg.* 1469, *pg.* 1619
STANCE - Floor Finish - 3M COMPANY; *pg.* 1142, *pg.* 956
STANCOTE - Wire Cable - STANDARD WIRE & CABLE CO.; *pg.* 1306, *pg.* 187
STANCUT - Continuous Tab Cards - THE STANDARD REGISTER COMPANY; *pg.* 473, *pg.* 1446
STAND-ALL - Saw Blade - SIMONDS INTERNATIONAL CORPORATION; *pg.* 1376, *pg.* 819
STAND 'N SWING - Swinging Accessory - CREATIVE PLAYTHINGS LTD.; *pg.* 1831, *pg.* 820
STANDAFIN - Fabric Hand Modifiers - HENKEL CORPORATION; *pg.* 1165, *pg.* 1535
STANDAPHOS - Phosphated Alcohols - HENKEL CORPORATION; *pg.* 1165, *pg.* 1535
STANDAPOL - Fiber Lubricants - HENKEL CORPORATION; *pg.* 1165, *pg.* 1535
STANDAPON - Detergents, Wetting Agents - HENKEL CORPORATION; *pg.* 1165, *pg.* 1535
STANDARD - Rainwear - BLAUER MANUFACTURING COMPANY, INC.; *pg.* 20, *pg.* 789
STANDARD - Lawn Fertilizer - THE SCOTTS MIRACLE-GRO COMPANY; *pg.* 1799, *pg.* 1459
STANDARD & POOR'S - Publication - THE MCGRAW-HILL COMPANIES INC.; *pg.* 1663, *pg.* 1257
STANDARD CARDINAL - Cutting System - EASTMAN MACHINE COMPANY; *pg.* 1331, *pg.* 1148
STANDARD-E - Industrial Electric Motors - BALDOR ELECTRIC COMPANY; *pg.* 1316, *pg.* 32
STANDARD ELECTRIC TIME - Clock Systems & Timers - FARADAY; *pg.* 638, *pg.* 1066
STANDARD EPIPANEL - Diagnostic Tool - SEQUENOM, INC.; *pg.* 1593, *pg.* 209
STANDARD EXAMINER - Daily Newspaper - OGDEN PUBLISHING CORPORATION; *pg.* 1672, *pg.* 1753
STANDARD FAST-FOLD - Portable Folding Screen - DA-LITE SCREEN COMPANY; *pg.* 632, *pg.* 698
STANDARD GRALITE - Lightweight Gray PVC Fabric - STANDARD SAFETY EQUIPMENT CO.; *pg.* 1379, *pg.* 632
STANDARD INSURANCE COMPANY - Insurance Company - STANDARD INSURANCE COMPANY; *pg.* 1217, *pg.* 1506
STANDARD MAIL - Postal Services - UNITED STATES POSTAL SERVICE; *pg.* 1009, *pg.* 406
STANDARD MELT - Underground Silica - U.S. SILICA COMPANY; *pg.* 1185, *pg.* 1849
THE STANDARD OF EXCELLENCE - Slogan - SEA RAY BOATS, INC.; *pg.* 1710, *pg.* 1638
STANDARD OVERNIGHT - Shipment Service - FEDEX CORPORATION; *pg.* 1907, *pg.* 1642
STANDARD PLUS - Ignition Wire - STANDARD MOTOR PRODUCTS, INC.; *pg.* 218, *pg.* 1176
STANDARD SIDERAIL - Adaptor - STERIS CORPORATION; *pg.* 1597, *pg.* 1464
STANDARD SUPER-SEALER - Wrap System - SOUTHWEST BINDING & LAMINATING; *pg.* 1377, *pg.* 988
STANDEX - Air Distribution Product - STANDEX INTERNATIONAL CORPORATION; *pg.* 60, *pg.* 1039
STANDING OVATIONS - Mugs - ENESCO, LLC; *pg.* 1124, *pg.* 620
STANDING WITH YOU. - Tagline - SENTRY TECHNOLOGY CORPORATION; *pg.* 672, *pg.* 1339
STANDOX - Automotive Coatings - E.I. DU PONT DE NEMOURS & COMPANY; *pg.* 1159, *pg.* 390
STANDS FOR SECURITY - Tag Line - WINNER INTERNATIONAL, LLC; *pg.* 222, *pg.* 1586
STANDUP - Furniture - NEUTRAL POSTURE, INC.; *pg.* 939, *pg.* 1669
STANFAST - Cut Sheet Printing - THE STANDARD REGISTER COMPANY; *pg.* 473, *pg.* 1446
STANFIX - Waterbased Adhesive - HENKEL CORPORATION;

First page reference indicates Business Class Edition
Second page reference indicates Geographic Edition

pg. 1165, pg. 1535
STANFLAKE - Flake Textile Softeners - HENKEL CORPORATION; pg. 1165, pg. 1535
STANFLEX - Construction Business Forms - THE STANDARD REGISTER COMPANY; pg. 473, pg. 1446
STANFLEX - Cable - STANDARD WIRE & CABLE CO.; pg. 1306, pg. 187
STANFORD - Shoes - ALLEN-EDMONDS SHOE CORP.; pg. 1804, pg. 1887
STANFORD - Table - BLATT BOWLING & BILLIARD CORP.; pg. 1827, pg. 1203
STANFORD - Furniture - BUSH INDUSTRIES INC.; pg. 919, pg. 1170
STANFORD - Footwear - EASTLAND SHOE CORPORATION; pg. 1808, pg. 750
STANFORD - Champagne - WEIBEL, INC.; pg. 1972, pg. 122
STANGUARD - Check Paper - THE STANDARD REGISTER COMPANY; pg. 473, pg. 1446
STANLEY - Electronic Systems & Components - DGT HOLDINGS; pg. 634, pg. 1223
STANLEY - Glove - KOMBI, LTD.; pg. 1838, pg. 1766
STANLEY - Hand Tools - STANLEY BLACK & DECKER, INC.; pg. 1063, pg. 358
STANLEY DOOR - Residential Entry Doors - MASONITE INTERNATIONAL CORPORATION; pg. 1054, pg. 1920
STANMORE - Implant Product - ZIMMER BIOMET HOLDINGS, INC.; pg. 1611, pg. 699
STANMORE HIP SYSTEM - Hip Product - ZIMMER BIOMET HOLDINGS, INC.; pg. 1611, pg. 699
STANNAVER - Chemical Reagent - HACH COMPANY; pg. 1415, pg. 334
STANPAC - Software - TINIUS OLSEN, INC.; pg. 1432, pg. 1541
STANPLAS - Semi Finished Product - STANBEE COMPANY, INC.; pg. 1819, pg. 1050
STANPRO - Sealing System - COOPER-STANDARD AUTOMOTIVE INC.; pg. 1880, pg. 903
STANSET - Construction Forms - THE STANDARD REGISTER COMPANY; pg. 473, pg. 1446
STANSOFT - Liquid Textile Softeners - HENKEL CORPORATION; pg. 1165, pg. 1535
STANSTEAD GRAY - Granite - ROCK OF AGES CORPORATION; pg. 108, pg. 1766
STANSTED - Ethernet Product - VITESSE SEMICONDUCTOR CORPORATION; pg. 686, pg. 57
STANTEK - Alloy Plating System - MACDERMID, INC.; pg. 1172, pg. 321
STANTEST - Enamel - JONES-BLAIR COMPANY; pg. 1443, pg. 1682
STANTEX - Textile Chemicals - HENKEL CORPORATION; pg. 1165, pg. 1535
STANVISION - Security Products - STANLEY BLACK & DECKER, INC.; pg. 1063, pg. 358
STANZOIL - Glove - MAPA PROFESSIONAL; pg. 1885, pg. 555
STAPH-GUARD - Commercial Washers - PELLERIN MILNOR CORPORATION; pg. 1368, pg. 744
STAPH-PLUS - Software - BIO-RAD LABORATORIES, INC.; pg. 1504, pg. 101
STAPHENE - Disinfectant - STERIS CORPORATION; pg. 1597, pg. 1464
STAPL-A-MATIC - Stapling Machines - THE STAPLEX COMPANY, INC.; pg. 474, pg. 1146
STAPLE - Herbicide - E.I. DU PONT DE NEMOURS & COMPANY; pg. 1159, pg. 390
STAPLEFORD - Men's Clothing - URBAN OUTFITTERS, INC.; pg. 1789, pg. 1571
STAPLEFORD - Ethernet Product - VITESSE SEMICONDUCTOR CORPORATION; pg. 686, pg. 57
STAPLES 365 SAVINGS - Card - STAPLES, INC.; pg. 474, pg. 821
STAPLES NATIONAL ADVANTAGE - Card - STAPLES, INC.; pg. 474, pg. 821
STAPLES REWARDS - Card - STAPLES, INC.; pg. 474, pg. 821
STAPLES TEACHER REWARDS - Card - STAPLES, INC.; pg. 474, pg. 821
STAPLES THE OFFICE SUPERSTORE - Tag Line - STAPLES, INC.; pg. 474, pg. 821
STAR - Doll And Toy - AMERICAN GIRL LLC; pg. 949, pg. 1871
STAR - Magazine - AMERICAN MEDIA, INC.; pg. 1615, pg. 410
STAR - Rose Plants - THE CONARD-PYLE COMPANY; pg. 1794, pg. 1594
STAR - Patient Monitoring System - CRITICARE SYSTEMS, INC.; pg. 1520, pg. 1897
STAR - Cameras - EASTMAN KODAK COMPANY; pg. 1408, pg. 1333
THE STAR - North Carolina Newspaper - FREEDOM COMMUNICATIONS, INC.; pg. 1643, pg. 110
STAR - Tire And Rubber Product - THE GOODYEAR TIRE & RUBBER COMPANY; pg. 1883, pg. 1401
STAR - Ornament - HERITAGE LACE INC.; pg. 694, pg. 711
STAR - Glove - KOMBI, LTD.; pg. 1838, pg. 1766
STAR - Silicon Etch - LAM RESEARCH CORPORATION; pg. 1354, pg. 91
STAR - Kitchen Equipment - THE MIDDLEBY CORPORATION; pg. 1361, pg. 610
STAR - Satellite - ORBITAL ATK; pg. 1425, pg. 1779
STAR - Sodium Silicate - PQ CORPORATION; pg. 1178, pg. 1515
STAR - Wearable Smart Tech Product - SENSEGIZ INC.; pg. 110, pg. 227
STAR - Olive Oil, Olives, Wine Vinegar, Capers, Pepperoni & Pickled Specialties - STAR FINE FOODS-BORGES USA; pg. 897, pg. 93
STAR - Biomolecule Product - THERMO FISHER SCIENTIFIC INC.; pg. 1602, pg. 61
STAR - Monitor - VIEWSONIC CORPORATION; pg. 489, pg. 303
STAR 2000 - Healthcare Information Technology System - MCKESSON CORPORATION; pg. 1560, pg. 222
STAR 2000 - Workbook - VALE NATIONAL TRAINING CENTER INC.; pg. 610, pg. 1660
STAR-3I - Digital Terrain Elevation Database - INTERMAP TECHNOLOGIES CORPORATION; pg. 417, pg. 1903
STAR ANTISTAT - Dry Cleaning & Laundry Product - ADCO, INC.; pg. 325, pg. 482
STAR BAG - Filtration Product - AEROFLEX INCORPORATED; pg. 614, pg. 1321
STAR BAR - Ice Cream Bar - WELLS ENTERPRISES, INC.; pg. 909, pg. 709
STAR BOOK CLUB - Educational Materials - SCHOLASTIC INC.; pg. 1683, pg. 1288
STAR BRITE - Marine Product - OCEAN BIO CHEM, INC.; pg. 1444, pg. 426
STAR CHECKING - Account - SALEM FIVE CENTS SAVINGS BANK; pg. 800, pg. 843
STAR CIRCUITS - Software - DAKTRONICS, INC.; pg. 633, pg. 1624
STAR COASTERS - Beverage Coasters - BOGDANCO CONSULTING; pg. 918, pg. 174
STAR COURIER - News Source Company - STAR COURIER; pg. 1689, pg. 621
STAR DISC - Laser Product - ROFIN-SINAR TECHNOLOGIES, INC.; pg. 668, pg. 904
STAR EARLY LITERACY - Educational Materials - RENAISSANCE LEARNING, INC.; pg. 607, pg. 1899
STAR FIRE - Gaming Product - GLD PRODUCTS, INC.; pg. 1835, pg. 1882
STAR-GATE - Software - VERINT SYSTEMS INC.; pg. 488, pg. 1182
STAR-KAP - Chimney Caps - FIELD CONTROLS LLC; pg. 1071, pg. 1380
STAR-KIST - Canned Tuna - STARKIST FOODS INC.; pg. 898, pg. 1581
STAR-KIST EATWELL - Sardines & Mackerel - STARKIST FOODS INC.; pg. 898, pg. 1581
STAR-LINE - Cable - AMPHENOL CORPORATION; pg. 616, pg. 381
STAR-LINE EX - Cable - AMPHENOL CORPORATION; pg. 616, pg. 381
STAR LINES - Telecommunications - AT&T SOUTHEAST; pg. 1868, pg. 489
STAR MART - Oil Fuel - CHEVRON CORPORATION; pg. 974, pg. 259
STAR MATH - Educational Materials - RENAISSANCE LEARNING, INC.; pg. 607, pg. 1899
STAR MAX - Tool Steel - CARPENTER TECHNOLOGY CORPORATION; pg. 73, pg. 1584
STAR OF INDEPENDENCE - Jewelry - HARRY WINSTON, INC.; pg. 6, pg. 1238
STAR OF INDIA - Game - WMS INDUSTRIES INC.; pg. 593, pg. 666
STAR OF SIERRA LEONE - Jewelry - HARRY WINSTON, INC.; pg. 6, pg. 1238
STAR OF WONDER - Pillow and Throw - HERITAGE LACE INC.; pg. 694, pg. 711
STAR PACK GIFT SET - Barware - GORDON INDUSTRIES LTD.; pg. 6, pg. 1184
STAR RANCH ANGUS - Beef Products - TYSON FOODS, INC.; pg. 902, pg. 35
STAR-RCXT - Software - SYNOPSYS, INC.; pg. 480, pg. 162
STAR READING - Educational Materials - RENAISSANCE LEARNING, INC.; pg. 607, pg. 1899
STAR S4 IR - Medical Device - ABBOTT MEDICAL OPTICS, INC.; pg. 1485, pg. 260
STAR SAFIRE - Thermal Imaging System - FLIR SYSTEMS, INC.; pg. 1413, pg. 1510
STAR SCRIBE - Laser Product - ROFIN-SINAR TECHNOLOGIES, INC.; pg. 668, pg. 904
STAR SHIELD BOOM - Turf Maintenance Machinery - SMITHCO, INC.; pg. 1377, pg. 1592
STAR SHOWERS - Container Grown Plant - MONROVIA GROWERS; pg. 1797, pg. 44
STAR-SIMXT - Software - SYNOPSYS, INC.; pg. 480, pg. 162
STAR SISTERZ - Game - HASBRO, INC.; pg. 954, pg. 1603
STAR TECK - Fittings - THOMAS & BETTS CORPORATION; pg. 680, pg. 1646
STAR-TELEGRAM - Newspaper - FORT WORTH STAR-TELEGRAM; pg. 1642, pg. 1694
STAR-TEX - Poster - MONADNOCK PAPER MILLS, INC.; pg. 1464, pg. 1033
STAR TRACK - Lighting Fixtures - SWIVELIER CO., INC.; pg. 1307, pg. 1142
STARACH - Software - TROY GROUP INC.; pg. 485, pg. 71
STARANE - Herbicide - DOW AGROSCIENCES LLC; pg. 1156, pg. 684
STARBEAM - Lighting - LSI INDUSTRIES INC.; pg. 58, pg. 1416
STARBLAST - Staurolite Sand - E.I. DU PONT DE NEMOURS & COMPANY; pg. 1159, pg. 390
STARBOND - Foam Product - POLYAIR INTER PACK INC.; pg. 1467, pg. 1941
STARBRITE - RV Care Product - OCEAN BIO CHEM, INC.; pg. 1444, pg. 426
STARBRITE - Automotive Coating - SILBERLINE MANUFACTURING CO., INC.; pg. 110, pg. 1588
STARBUCKS COFFEE - Coffee - STARBUCKS CORPORATION; pg. 897, pg. 1840
STARBUCKS DISCOVERIES - Ready to Drink Chilled Cup Coffee Beverage - STARBUCKS CORPORATION; pg. 897, pg. 1840
STARBUCKS HEAR MUSIC - Compact Discs - STARBUCKS CORPORATION; pg. 897, pg. 1840
STARBUCKS RESERVE - Coffee - STARBUCKS CORPORATION; pg. 897, pg. 1840
STARBUCKS VIA - Coffee - STARBUCKS CORPORATION; pg. 897, pg. 1840
STARBURST - Electrosurgical Devices - ANGIODYNAMICS, INC.; pg. 1405, pg. 1173
STARBURST - Incandescent Color Displays - DAKTRONICS, INC.; pg. 633, pg. 1624
STARBURST - Shower Floor - E.L. MUSTEE & SONS, INC.; pg. 1124, pg. 1430
STARBURST - Gaming Product - GLD PRODUCTS, INC.; pg. 1835, pg. 1882
STARBURST - Container Grown Plant - MONROVIA GROWERS; pg. 1797, pg. 44
STARBURST - Fabric - NEMSCHOFF, INC.; pg. 936, pg. 1890
STARBURST - Candy - WM. WRIGLEY JR. COMPANY; pg. 1863, pg. 596
STARCARD - Oil Fuel - CHEVRON CORPORATION; pg. 974, pg. 259
STARCENTER - Ice Skating Facility - DALLAS STARS L.P.; pg. 543, pg. 1697
STARCLEAR - Filter Cartridge - PALL CORPORATION; pg. 232, pg. 1323
STARCLOSE - Vascular Closure System - ABBOTT LABORATORIES; pg. 1484, pg. 551
STARCOLE - Packaging - INTERNATIONAL PAPER COMPANY; pg. 1460, pg. 1644
STARCORE - Communications Product - MOTOROLA SOLUTIONS, INC.; pg. 657, pg. 659
STARCREST - Mail Order House - STARCREST PRODUCTS OF CALIFORNIA; pg. 1786, pg. 181
STARCURED - Tobacco Product - ROCK CREEK PHARMACEUTICALS, INC.; pg. 1895, pg. 466
STARCUT - Laser Product - ROFIN-SINAR TECHNOLOGIES, INC.; pg. 668, pg. 904
STARDUST - Broadloom - COURISTAN INC.; pg. 921, pg.

1067
STARDUST - Fabric - NEMSCHOFF, INC.; *pg.* 936, *pg.* 1890
STARFIBER - Fiber Lasers - ROFIN-SINAR TECHNOLOGIES, INC.; *pg.* 668, *pg.* 904
STARFICHE - Microfiche Reader-Printers - EASTMAN KODAK COMPANY; *pg.* 1408, *pg.* 1333
STARFIELD TECHNOLOGIES - Software - GO DADDY INC.; *pg.* 1249, *pg.* 21
STARFILE - Microfilm Machine - EASTMAN KODAK COMPANY; *pg.* 1408, *pg.* 1333
STARFINDER - Equatorial & Dobsonian Telescope - MEADE INSTRUMENTS CORPORATION; *pg.* 1422, *pg.* 113
STARFIRE - Tires - COOPER TIRE & RUBBER COMPANY; *pg.* 1881, *pg.* 1453
STARFIRE - WAAS Receiver - DEERE & COMPANY; *pg.* 703, *pg.* 632
STARFIRE - Audio Visual Product - DUKANE CORPORATION; *pg.* 634, *pg.* 658
STARFIRE - Systems Integration & Aeronautics - LOCKHEED MARTIN CORPORATION; *pg.* 229, *pg.* 762
STARFIRE - Publishing Imprint - PENGUIN RANDOM HOUSE CHILDREN'S BOOKS; *pg.* 1676, *pg.* 1277
STARFISH - Tweeter Mounting System - HARMAN INTERNATIONAL INDUSTRIES, INCORPORATED; *pg.* 641, *pg.* 374
STARFISH - Glove - KOMBI, LTD.; *pg.* 1838, *pg.* 1766
STARFISH - Heart Positioner - MEDTRONIC, INC.; *pg.* 1564, *pg.* 939
STARFLASH - Camera - EASTMAN KODAK COMPANY; *pg.* 1408, *pg.* 1333
STARFLO - Valves - THE WM. POWELL COMPANY; *pg.* 1389, *pg.* 1427
STARFOAM - Foam Product - POLYAIR INTER PACK INC.; *pg.* 1467, *pg.* 1941
STARGLOSS - Metallized PET - DUNMORE CORPORATION; *pg.* 1456, *pg.* 1518
STARK - Fiberglass Filters - PENTAIR WATER POOL AND SPA, INC.; *pg.* 104, *pg.* 1171
STARKIST FLAVOR FRESH POUCH - Pouch Packaged Tuna - STARKIST FOODS INC.; *pg.* 898, *pg.* 1581
STARKIST TUNA CREATIONS - Marinated Tuna - STARKIST FOODS INC.; *pg.* 898, *pg.* 1581
STARKLEEN - Filter Capsule - PALL CORPORATION; *pg.* 232, *pg.* 1323
STARKRAFT - Foam Product - POLYAIR INTER PACK INC.; *pg.* 1467, *pg.* 1941
STARLIFTER - Systems Integration & Aeronautics - LOCKHEED MARTIN CORPORATION; *pg.* 229, *pg.* 762
STARLIGHT - Carpet - BEAULIEU GROUP, LLC; *pg.* 917, *pg.* 529
STARLIGHT - Inspection System - KLA-TENCOR CORPORATION; *pg.* 1353, *pg.* 146
STARLIGHT GLOBE - Globe - REPLOGLE GLOBES, INC.; *pg.* 461, *pg.* 559
STARLIGHTS - Paper Products - BOISE CASCADE HOLDINGS, L.L.C.; *pg.* 1453, *pg.* 546
STARLINE - Felt Products - AMERICAN FELT & FILTER COMPANY; *pg.* 1312, *pg.* 1184
STARLINE - Cable TV Distribution Equipment - MOTOROLA CANADA LIMITED; *pg.* 657, *pg.* 1924
STARLINE - Optical Node - MOTOROLA SOLUTIONS, INC.; *pg.* 657, *pg.* 659
STARLINK - Wall-mounted Internet-enabled Digital Jukeboxes - ROWE INTERNATIONAL CORP; *pg.* 669, *pg.* 889
STARLITE - Sink - ELKAY MANUFACTURING COMPANY; *pg.* 80, *pg.* 645
STARLITE - Bicycle - G. JOANNOU CYCLE CO. INC.; *pg.* 1707, *pg.* 1098
STARLITE - Doors - THERMA-TRU CORP.; *pg.* 115, *pg.* 1462
STARLITE MINTS - Candy - SORBEE INTERNATIONAL, LLC; *pg.* 1862, *pg.* 1570
STARLITY - Sink - ELKAY MANUFACTURING COMPANY; *pg.* 80, *pg.* 645
STARLOCK - Exercise Equipment - ALLIANCE SPORTS GROUP, L.P.; *pg.* 1825, *pg.* 1698
STARLOG - Magazine - STARLOG GROUP, INC.; *pg.* 1689, *pg.* 1296
STARMAN - Character - DC COMICS, INC.; *pg.* 1633, *pg.* 1221
STARMARK - Laser Product - ROFIN-SINAR TECHNOLOGIES, INC.; *pg.* 668, *pg.* 904
STARMARK CABINETRY - Semi-custom Cabinetry - NORCRAFT HOLDINGS, LP; *pg.* 100, *pg.* 921
STARMASK - Foam Product - POLYAIR INTER PACK INC.; *pg.* 1467, *pg.* 1941
STARMATE - Cameras, Microfilm Readers - EASTMAN KODAK COMPANY; *pg.* 1408, *pg.* 1333
STARMEDIA - Internet Media - THE HEARST CORPORATION; *pg.* 1649, *pg.* 1239
STARMILK - Animal Nutrition Product - VITUSA CORP.; *pg.* 1482, *pg.* 1063
STARMOVER - Foam Product - POLYAIR INTER PACK INC.; *pg.* 1467, *pg.* 1941
STARNAVIGATOR - Software - MEADE INSTRUMENTS CORPORATION; *pg.* 1422, *pg.* 113
STARNET - Foam Product - POLYAIR INTER PACK INC.; *pg.* 1467, *pg.* 1941
STARPAC - Valves - FLOWSERVE CORPORATION; *pg.* 82, *pg.* 1719
STARPHIRE - Glass Product - PPG INDUSTRIES, INC.; *pg.* 1445, *pg.* 1579
STARPOINTS - Hotels - STARWOOD HOTELS & RESORTS WORLDWIDE, INC.; *pg.* 1114, *pg.* 378
STARPOWER - Shirt System - FAULTLESS STARCH/BON AMI COMPANY; *pg.* 330, *pg.* 982
STARPRO - Integrated Circuits - AVAGO TECHNOLOGIES; *pg.* 358, *pg.* 238
STARPRO - Illuminator - REVOLUTION LIGHTING TECHNOLOGIES, INC.; *pg.* 1304, *pg.* 377
STARPULSE - Aura Feature Designed to Treat Benign Vascular & Pigmented Lesions - AMERICAN MEDICAL SYSTEMS, INC.; *pg.* 1399, *pg.* 238
STARPULSE - Pulsed Rod Lasers - ROFIN-SINAR TECHNOLOGIES, INC.; *pg.* 668, *pg.* 904
STARR - Semi-trailer Refuse Collection System - HEIL ENVIRONMENTAL INDUSTRIES, LTD.; *pg.* 207, *pg.* 1629
STARRSPACE 3000 - Partition Wall System - STARRCO COMPANY INC.; *pg.* 113, *pg.* 988
STARRSPACE 3500 - Partition Wall System - STARRCO COMPANY INC.; *pg.* 113, *pg.* 988
STARRY NIGHT - Carpet - WOVEN LEGENDS INC.; *pg.* 947, *pg.* 1572
STARS - Defense System - RAYTHEON COMPANY; *pg.* 233, *pg.* 854
STARS AND STRIPES - Game - MISSOURI LOTTERY; *pg.* 999, *pg.* 979
STARSET - Headset - PLANTRONICS, INC.; *pg.* 663, *pg.* 270
STARSHAPE - Laser Product - ROFIN-SINAR TECHNOLOGIES, INC.; *pg.* 668, *pg.* 904
STARSO - Sodium Silicate - PQ CORPORATION; *pg.* 1178, *pg.* 1515
STARSPAN - Digital Telephone Equipment & Telecommunications Equipment - ALCATEL-LUCENT USA, INC.; *pg.* 615, *pg.* 1728
STARSPOT - Lighting Fixtures - SWIVELIER CO., INC.; *pg.* 1307, *pg.* 1142
STARSYSTEM - Transmission Repair System - TRANSTAR INDUSTRIES, INC.; *pg.* 219, *pg.* 1478
START-TO-FINISH - Nail Care Product - OPI PRODUCTS INC.; *pg.* 518, *pg.* 167
STARTE PILOTE - Turbocharger - HONEYWELL INTERNATIONAL INC.; *pg.* 407, *pg.* 1088
STARTECH - Processor, Photographic Film - EASTMAN KODAK COMPANY; *pg.* 1408, *pg.* 1333
STARTER - Apparel - ICONIX BRAND GROUP, INC.; *pg.* 26, *pg.* 1243
STARTER - Lawn Fertilizer - THE SCOTTS MIRACLE-GRO COMPANY; *pg.* 1799, *pg.* 1459
STARTER STRIP - Specialty Roofing Shingles - BUILDING PRODUCTS OF CANADA CORP.; *pg.* 72, *pg.* 1951
STARTER-UP - Batteries - UNIVERSAL POWER GROUP, INC.; *pg.* 683, *pg.* 1671
STARTFEAR - Analgesia Instrument - STOELTING CO.; *pg.* 1430, *pg.* 671
STARTHANE - Automotive Coatings - PPG INDUSTRIES, INC.; *pg.* 1445, *pg.* 1579
STARTOOL - Software - SERENA SOFTWARE, INC.; *pg.* 468, *pg.* 192
STARTRON - Lighting Fixtures - SWIVELIER CO., INC.; *pg.* 1307, *pg.* 1142
STARVUE - Microfilm Readers & Reader-Printers - EASTMAN KODAK COMPANY; *pg.* 1408, *pg.* 1333
STARWAVE MOBILE - Mobile Publishing - THE WALT DISNEY COMPANY; *pg.* 317, *pg.* 52
STARWELD - Laser Product - ROFIN-SINAR TECHNOLOGIES, INC.; *pg.* 668, *pg.* 904
STARWHITE - Paper - NEENAH PAPER, INC.; *pg.* 1465, *pg.* 484
STARWIRE - Broadband Satellite Service - VIASAT, INC.; *pg.* 489, *pg.* 62
STARWNILLA - Chocolate - BIGLARI HOLDINGS INC.; *pg.* 1015, *pg.* 1739
STARWOOD PREFERRED GUEST - Customer Program - STARWOOD HOTELS & RESORTS WORLDWIDE, INC.; *pg.* 1114, *pg.* 378
STARZ! - Cable Television Channel - STARZ ENTERTAINMENT, LLC; *pg.* 310, *pg.* 327
STARZ! CINEMA - Cable Television Channel - STARZ ENTERTAINMENT, LLC; *pg.* 310, *pg.* 327
STARZ! FAMILY - Cable Television Channel - STARZ ENTERTAINMENT, LLC; *pg.* 310, *pg.* 327
STARZ! HD - Cable Television - STARZ ENTERTAINMENT, LLC; *pg.* 310, *pg.* 327
STARZ IN BLACK - Cable Television - STARZ ENTERTAINMENT, LLC; *pg.* 310, *pg.* 327
STARZ! KIDS - Cable Television - STARZ ENTERTAINMENT, LLC; *pg.* 310, *pg.* 327
STARZ ON DEMAND - Cable Channel - STARZ ENTERTAINMENT, LLC; *pg.* 310, *pg.* 327
STARZ SUPER PAK - Cable Television Programming Package - STARZ ENTERTAINMENT, LLC; *pg.* 310, *pg.* 327
STARZ! THEATER - Cable Television Channel - STARZ ENTERTAINMENT, LLC; *pg.* 310, *pg.* 327
STARZ TICKET - Broadband - STARZ ENTERTAINMENT, LLC; *pg.* 310, *pg.* 327
STARZ WAM - Cable Television Channel - STARZ ENTERTAINMENT, LLC; *pg.* 310, *pg.* 327
STASH TOP - Stopper - THERMOS L.L.C.; *pg.* 61, *pg.* 660
STASOF - Golf Glove - ACUSHNET COMPANY; *pg.* 1824, *pg.* 818
STASQUARE 32 - Paperboards - CARAUSTAR INDUSTRIES, INC.; *pg.* 1455, *pg.* 525
STAT - Medical Equipment - CONMED CORPORATION; *pg.* 1517, *pg.* 1347
STAT - Software - DELL SOFTWARE; *pg.* 385, *pg.* 40
STAT - Software - SAS INSTITUTE INC.; *pg.* 466, *pg.* 1361
STAT 2 - Medical Product - CONMED CORPORATION; *pg.* 1517, *pg.* 1347
STAT ACM - Software - DELL SOFTWARE; *pg.* 385, *pg.* 40
STAT ACM FOR PEOPLESOFT - Software - DELL SOFTWARE; *pg.* 385, *pg.* 40
STAT CREW - Software - DAKTRONICS, INC.; *pg.* 633, *pg.* 1624
STAT-CRIT - Pharmaceutical Product - ALERE INC.; *pg.* 1488, *pg.* 849
STAT FAX - Software - BIO-RAD LABORATORIES, INC.; *pg.* 1504, *pg.* 101
STAT-GARD - Electrical Tester - IDEAL INDUSTRIES, INC.; *pg.* 1051, *pg.* 662
STAT-LES - Static Dissipative Floor Finish - WALTER G. LEGGE COMPANY, INC.; *pg.* 337, *pg.* 1321
STAT ONE - Software - BIO-RAD LABORATORIES, INC.; *pg.* 1504, *pg.* 101
STAT PADZ - Electrode System - ZOLL MEDICAL CORPORATION; *pg.* 1612, *pg.* 814
STAT PRIME - Filter - PALL CORPORATION; *pg.* 232, *pg.* 1323
STAT-PRO - Material - ENTEGRIS, INC.; *pg.* 1882, *pg.* 788
STAT STAR - ESD Fabrics - GUILFORD PERFORMANCE TEXTILES; *pg.* 693, *pg.* 1393
STAT-TECH - Engineered Compound & Composite - POLYONE CORPORATION; *pg.* 1177, *pg.* 1404
STATE BRAND - Dairy Product - ASSOCIATED MILK PRODUCERS INC.; *pg.* 838, *pg.* 951
STATE FAIR - Video Slots - INTERNATIONAL GAME TECHNOLOGY; *pg.* 957, *pg.* 1024
STATE FAIR - Hot Dogs - TYSON FOODS, INC.; *pg.* 902, *pg.* 35
STATE FARM BANK - Bank - STATE FARM MUTUAL AUTOMOBILE INSURANCE CO.; *pg.* 1218, *pg.* 557
STATE JOURNAL REGISTER - Publisher - THE STATE JOURNAL-REGISTER; *pg.* 1689, *pg.* 662
STATE STREET - Fan - HUNTER FAN COMPANY; *pg.* 57, *pg.* 1631
STATEFARM.COM - Online Services - STATE FARM MUTUAL AUTOMOBILE INSURANCE CO.; *pg.* 1218, *pg.* 557
STATEMENT CREATION - Document Creation - PITNEY BOWES INC.; *pg.* 454, *pg.* 376
STATESMAN - Lockers - AMERICAN LOCKER GROUP INCORPORATED; *pg.* 1041, *pg.* 1674
STATESMAN - Power Equipment - SOUTHERN STATES

COOPERATIVE, INC.; pg. 1482, pg. 1804
STATESMAN JUNIOR - Locker - AMERICAN LOCKER GROUP INCORPORATED; pg. 1041, pg. 1674
STATHERZ - Pharmaceutical Preparation - PFIZER INC.; pg. 1581, pg. 1278
STATIBRUSH - Static Control System - DOYLE SYSTEMS; pg. 1330, pg. 1404
STATIC - After Shave - THE GILLETTE COMPANY; pg. 509, pg. 795
STATIC - Beanie - OAKLEY, INC.; pg. 1840, pg. 86
STATIC CONSUMER - Static Eliminator Tinsel - HYDRALIGN; pg. 1257, pg. 833
STATIC FACE - Seal & Thermoplastic Component - GREENE, TWEED & CO.; pg. 1344, pg. 1544
STATIC MIZER - Static Eliminating Ionizer Bars - HYDRALIGN; pg. 1257, pg. 833
STATIC O RING - Pressure Switches - SOR, INC.; pg. 1306, pg. 716
STATIC SENSITIVE BRUSHES - Aerosol Cleaner - TECH SPRAY, L.P.; pg. 1183, pg. 1659
STATIC SENSOR - Detects & Indicates Static Charge - HYDRALIGN; pg. 1257, pg. 833
STATICO - Anti-Static Spray - WALTER G. LEGGE COMPANY, INC.; pg. 337, pg. 1321
STATICSORB - Clothing - LAKELAND INDUSTRIES, INC.; pg. 1354, pg. 1338
STATIKIL - Static Control System - DOYLE SYSTEMS; pg. 1330, pg. 1404
STATION POST - High Voltage Porcelain Insulators - LAPP INSULATOR COMPANY, LLC; pg. 1946, pg. 1173
STATIONAIR - Aircraft - CESSNA AIRCRAFT COMPANY; pg. 226, pg. 723
STATIONARY - Game - FORTUNET, INC.; pg. 953, pg. 1024
STATIONMASTER - Bus Heat/Cool Units - CORNELIUS INC.; pg. 54, pg. 614
STATIONMASTER - Cable & Antenna System - RADIO FREQUENCY SYSTEMS, INC.; pg. 666, pg. 354
STATIONSOUNDS - Toy Train - LIONEL LLC; pg. 961, pg. 875
THE STATISTICAL DISCOVERY SOFTWARE - Slogan - SAS INSTITUTE INC.; pg. 466, pg. 1361
STATISTICAL POST PROCESSING - Integrated Circuits - AVAGO TECHNOLOGIES; pg. 358, pg. 238
STATITINSEL - Static Control System - DOYLE SYSTEMS; pg. 1330, pg. 1404
STATLOCK - Intra-Aortic Balloon Catheter Device - MAQUET; pg. 1558, pg. 1082
STATMEDIA - Irradiated Enrichment Media - E.I. DU PONT DE NEMOURS & COMPANY; pg. 1159, pg. 390
STATS ON-LINE - Computer Information Services - AVNET, INC.; pg. 622, pg. 15
STATSAFE - Ceramic & Plastic Product - COORSTEK, INC.; pg. 77, pg. 330
STATSAMPLER - Diagnostic Urinalysis System - IRIS INTERNATIONAL, INC.; pg. 1547, pg. 64
STATSHINE - Non Insulating Anti-Static Cleaner & Polish - WALTER G. LEGGE COMPANY, INC.; pg. 337, pg. 1321
STATSPIN - Diagnostic Urinalysis System - IRIS INTERNATIONAL, INC.; pg. 1547, pg. 64
STATTRACKER - Internet Services - YAHOO! INC.; pg. 1289, pg. 289
STATURE - Static Control Additives - THE DOW CHEMICAL COMPANY; pg. 1157, pg. 898
STATURE - Beverage - KENDALL-JACKSON WINE ESTATES, LTD.; pg. 1965, pg. 277
STATUSCHECK - Reliability Solutions - THE TIMKEN COMPANY; pg. 218, pg. 1408
STATVIEW - Software - SAS INSTITUTE INC.; pg. 466, pg. 1361
STATVISION - Software - DAKTRONICS, INC.; pg. 633, pg. 1624
STAUB COGNAC - Spirits - LEONARD KREUSCH, INC.; pg. 254, pg. 1099
STAVZOR - Estradiol Transdermal System - NOVEN PHARMACEUTICALS, INC.; pg. 1576, pg. 445
STAX - Stackable Pens - DRI MARK PRODUCTS, INC.; pg. 388, pg. 1323
STAX - Semiconductor Solution - VITESSE SEMICONDUCTOR CORPORATION; pg. 686, pg. 57
STAX-ON-STEEL - Filing System - FELLOWES, INC.; pg. 397, pg. 620
STAY BETWEEN THE LINES - Slogan - DEXCOM INC; pg. 1524, pg. 202
STAY-BRITE - Automotive Reconditioning Product - MOC PRODUCTS COMPANY, INC.; pg. 332, pg. 174
STAY COMFORTABLE - Restaurant Services - RED LION HOTELS CORP.; pg. 1110, pg. 1844
STAY-FORM - Leave-in-Place Concrete Form - ALABAMA METAL INDUSTRIES CORPORATION; pg. 65, pg. 1
STAY IN TOUCH BOUQUET - Floral Bouquet - FTD GROUP, INC.; pg. 1795, pg. 608
STAY OR GO - Kitchen Appliance - HAMILTON BEACH BRANDS, INC.; pg. 56, pg. 1783
STAY-PAK - Polyester Film - TRANSILWRAP COMPANY, INC.; pg. 1470, pg. 613
STAY-PUT - Baby Care Product - MUNCHKIN, INC.; pg. 964, pg. 300
STAY-PUT-STAKES - Hose - TEKNOR APEX COMPANY; pg. 1889, pg. 1605
STAY SMART - "But I Did Stay At a Holiday Inn Express Hotel Last Night" Tagline - INTERCONTINENTAL HOTELS CORPORATION; pg. 1097, pg. 511
STAYBELITE-E - Hydrogenated Rosins - EASTMAN CHEMICAL COMPANY; pg. 1159, pg. 1636
STAYBRED - Veterinary Vaccine - PFIZER INC.; pg. 1581, pg. 1278
STAYBRIDGE SUITES - All-Suites Hotel for Upscale Extended Stay Guests - INTERCONTINENTAL HOTELS CORPORATION; pg. 1097, pg. 511
STAYDARK - Jean - WILLIAMSON-DICKIE MANUFACTURING COMPANY; pg. 50, pg. 1696
STAYFLATS - Envelope - CALUMET CARTON COMPANY; pg. 1454, pg. 661
STAYFLATS PLUS - Envelope - CALUMET CARTON COMPANY; pg. 1454, pg. 661
STAYFREE - Feminine Care - EDGEWELL PERSONAL CARE; pg. 1526, pg. 995
STAYFREE - Healthcare Product - JOHNSON & JOHNSON; pg. 1549, pg. 1091
STAYFREE - Personal Care Product - ROCHESTER MIDLAND CORPORATION; pg. 334, pg. 1337
STAYFRESH - Antimicrobial Technology - 3M COMPANY; pg. 1142, pg. 956
STAYGARD - Fiber - HONEYWELL INTERNATIONAL INC.; pg. 407, pg. 1088
STAYPUT - Flex Mount - PANAVISE PRODUCTS, INC.; pg. 1058, pg. 1032
STAYS CLEAR - Paint And Stain Product - BENJAMIN MOORE & CO.; pg. 1440, pg. 1085
STAYSHARP - Ink Jet Label - AVERY DENNISON CORPORATION; pg. 1452, pg. 95
ST.BERNARD - Table - BLATT BOWLING & BILLIARD CORP.; pg. 1827, pg. 1203
STC - Lab Science Material - CAROLINA BIOLOGICAL SUPPLY COMPANY; pg. 1513, pg. 1359
STC/MS - Lab Science Material - CAROLINA BIOLOGICAL SUPPLY COMPANY; pg. 1513, pg. 1359
STD - Optical Product - LEUPOLD & STEVENS, INC.; pg. 1420, pg. 1492
STEAD-LITE - Circulars - PROPHOTONIX LIMITED; pg. 1427, pg. 1039
STEADFAST - Herbicide - E.I. DU PONT DE NEMOURS & COMPANY; pg. 1159, pg. 390
STEADICAM - Camera Stabilizing System - THE TIFFEN COMPANY LLC; pg. 1432, pg. 1165
STEADYLITE - Assays & Reagents - PERKINELMER, INC.; pg. 1426, pg. 853
THE STEAK LOVER'S COMPANION - Cook Book - OMAHA STEAKS INTERNATIONAL, INC.; pg. 1780, pg. 1017
STEAK N SHAKE FAMOUS FOR STEAKBURGERS - Restaurants - BIGLARI HOLDINGS INC.; pg. 1015, pg. 1739
STEAK N SHAKE ITS A MEAL - Tag Line - BIGLARI HOLDINGS INC.; pg. 1015, pg. 1739
STEAKBURGER - Food Product - BIGLARI HOLDINGS INC.; pg. 1015, pg. 1739
STEALTH - Cart Bag - DATREK GOLF; pg. 1832, pg. 1801
STEALTH - Pest Elimination System - ECOLAB INC.; pg. 329, pg. 960
STEALTH - Molecular Biology Product - THERMO FISHER SCIENTIFIC INC.; pg. 1602, pg. 61
STEALTH - Remote Control Device - UNIVERSAL ELECTRONICS, INC.; pg. 683, pg. 262
STEALTH - Safety Eyewear - UVEX SAFETY; pg. 1433, pg. 1608
STEALTH VECTOR - Diagnostic Product - ENZO BIOCHEM INC.; pg. 1529, pg. 1228
STEALTHLITE - Flashlight - PELICAN PRODUCTS, INC.; pg. 1842, pg. 295
STEALTHSTATION - Surgical Navigation System - MEDTRONIC, INC.; pg. 1564, pg. 939
STEALTHSTATION TREON TREATMENT GUIDANCE SYSTEM - Surgery System - MEDTRONIC, INC.; pg. 1564, pg. 939
STEAM-A-WARE - Software - ARMSTRONG INTERNATIONAL, INC.; pg. 1069, pg. 909
STEAM-DOT - Sterilization Product - PROPPER MANUFACTURING COMPANY, INC.; pg. 1586, pg. 1175
STEAM GUARD - Microwave Sterilizer - MUNCHKIN, INC.; pg. 964, pg. 300
STEAM-IT - Cleaning Product - ORECK CORPORATION; pg. 59, pg. 1653
STEAM JENNY - Steam Cleaner - JENNY PRODUCTS, INC.; pg. 331, pg. 1586
STEAM MOP - Floor Care Product - BISSELL HOMECARE, INC.; pg. 52, pg. 887
STEAM 'N CLEAN - Hand Held Steam Cleaner - BISSELL HOMECARE, INC.; pg. 52, pg. 887
STEAM 'N DRI - Curling Brush - JARDEN CONSUMER SOLUTIONS; pg. 57, pg. 412
STEAM PACK - Orthopedic Device - DJO SURGICAL; pg. 1525, pg. 1661
STEAM-SAFE 20 - Cleaning Products - CLAYTON INDUSTRIES CO.; pg. 1323, pg. 66
STEAM STORM - Kitchen Appliance - HAMILTON BEACH BRANDS, INC.; pg. 56, pg. 1783
STEAM TAPE - Indicator Tape - STERIS CORPORATION; pg. 1597, pg. 1464
STEAM TRACTION - Publication - OGDEN PUBLICATIONS, INC.; pg. 1672, pg. 722
STEAM VALET - Clothes Wrinkle Remover - JARDEN CONSUMER SOLUTIONS; pg. 57, pg. 412
STEAMATE - Corrosion Inhibitors - GE WATER & PROCESS TECHNOLOGIES; pg. 1339, pg. 1588
STEAMATIC THE TOTAL CLEANING SERVICE - Cleaning Services - STEAMATIC INC.; pg. 60, pg. 1696
STEAMATICARE - Regularly Scheduled Household Cleaning - STEAMATIC INC.; pg. 60, pg. 1696
STEAMER CREATIONS - Food Product - PHILLIPS FOODS INC.; pg. 1030, pg. 758
STEAMEYE - Remote Monitoring System - ARMSTRONG INTERNATIONAL, INC.; pg. 1069, pg. 909
STEAMFRESH - Microwavable Vegetables - PINNACLE FOODS GROUP LLC; pg. 889, pg. 1104
STEAMIN DEMON - Cleaning Products - CLAYTON INDUSTRIES CO.; pg. 1323, pg. 66
STEAMIX - Mixing Valve - ARMSTRONG INTERNATIONAL, INC.; pg. 1069, pg. 909
STEAMMOP - Bare Floor Steam Cleaner - BISSELL HOMECARE, INC.; pg. 52, pg. 887
STEAMPRESS - Ironing Board - HOME PRODUCTS INTERNATIONAL, INC.; pg. 1125, pg. 577
STEAMPRO - Bath & Plumbing Product - JACUZZI BRANDS CORPORATION; pg. 554, pg. 65
STEAMROLER - Boots - AEROGROUP INTERNATIONAL, INC.; pg. 1803, pg. 1055
STEAMSTAR - Software - ARMSTRONG INTERNATIONAL, INC.; pg. 1069, pg. 909
STEAMTEC - Vacuum Cleaner - NILFISK-ADVANCE, INC.; pg. 332, pg. 953
STEARNS & FOSTER - Mattresses & Box Springs - SEALY CORPORATION; pg. 942, pg. 1391
STEARNS & FOSTER - Mattresses - TEMPUR SEALY INTERNATIONAL, INC.; pg. 944, pg. 731
STEDESA - Pharmaceutical Product - SUNOVION PHARMACEUTICALS INC.; pg. 1599, pg. 832
STEDI-FLO - In-Line Water Conserving Apparatus - THE CHICAGO FAUCET COMPANY; pg. 1044, pg. 606
STEDMAN - Shirt - BROWN & BIGELOW, INC.; pg. 1624, pg. 959
STEDMAN BY HANES - Apparel - HANESBRANDS INC.; pg. 26, pg. 1394
STEDMAN FOR HER - Shirt - BROWN & BIGELOW, INC.; pg. 1624, pg. 959
STEDMAN'S MEDICAL DICTIONARIES - Medical Journal - LIPPINCOTT WILLIAMS & WILKINS, INC.; pg. 1659, pg. 1567
STEEL - Card - BROWN & BIGELOW, INC.; pg. 1624, pg. 959
STEEL - Kitchen Tools - OXO; pg. 1058, pg. 1275
STEEL-BEATER FIBERGLASS DOORS - Fiberglass Doors - THERMA-TRU CORP.; pg. 115, pg. 1462
THE STEEL BOXX - Container Box - MOORE PUSH PIN CO.; pg. 441, pg. 1595
STEEL BRIDGE - Pitless Trucking Scale - AVERY WEIGH-

TRONIX, INC.; *pg.* 1315, *pg.* 925
STEEL-BUILT - Apparel - REFRIGIWEAR, INC.; *pg.* 47, *pg.* 529
STEEL CITY - Spring Steel Fastener - THOMAS & BETTS CORPORATION; *pg.* 680, *pg.* 1646
STEEL DROPIN - Bolt & Shield Anchor - POWERS FASTENERS INC.; *pg.* 1059, *pg.* 1143
STEEL DYNAMICS, INC - Steel Product - STEEL DYNAMICS, INC.; *pg.* 113, *pg.* 681
STEEL EAGLE - Tools - VAUGHAN & BUSHNELL MANUFACTURING COMPANY, INC.; *pg.* 1066, *pg.* 616
STEEL FORCE - Amusement & Water Park - CEDAR FAIR, L.P.; *pg.* 537, *pg.* 1471
STEEL GLO - Ironing & Cleaning Product - FAULTLESS STARCH/BON AMI COMPANY; *pg.* 330, *pg.* 982
STEEL HAWG - Power Tools - MILWAUKEE ELECTRIC TOOL CORP.; *pg.* 1056, *pg.* 1855
STEEL-IT - Drum Handling Equipment - LIFTOMATIC MATERIAL HANDLING INC.; *pg.* 94, *pg.* 560
STEEL RENEW - Paint & Coating - AERVOE INDUSTRIES INCORPORATED; *pg.* 1439, *pg.* 1021
STEEL-RITE II - Sectional Dock Door - RITE-HITE HOLDING CORPORATION; *pg.* 1372, *pg.* 1880
STEEL SIX - Beer - MILLERCOORS; *pg.* 254, *pg.* 1877
STEEL TRAP - Fluid Sealing Product - A.W. CHESTERTON COMPANY; *pg.* 1315, *pg.* 861
STEEL WORK - Ceramic, Glass, Stone Tiles & Slabs - WALKER & ZANGER, INC.; *pg.* 119, *pg.* 281
STEELBOND - Coating & Finish - NOV AMERON; *pg.* 100, *pg.* 187
STEELCLAD - Cover - DYNATECT MANUFACTURING INC.; *pg.* 1330, *pg.* 1883
STEELCORE - Peripheral Guide Wire - ABBOTT LABORATORIES; *pg.* 1484, *pg.* 551
STEELCRAFT - Stainless Steel Door Frames - INGERSOLL-RAND COMPANY; *pg.* 1349, *pg.* 1370
STEELE FITNESS - Fitness Club Franchise - LIFT BRANDS; *pg.* 557, *pg.* 920
STEELFLEX - Bridge Product - THE D.S. BROWN COMPANY; *pg.* 79, *pg.* 1468
STEELFLEX - Roll Up Cover - DYNATECT MANUFACTURING INC.; *pg.* 1330, *pg.* 1883
STEELGUARD - Dropbolts - MEDECO HIGH SECURITY LOCKS, INC.; *pg.* 1055, *pg.* 1806
STEELGUARD - Coating & Finish - NOV AMERON; *pg.* 100, *pg.* 187
STEELHEAD - Sprinkler - RAIN BIRD CORPORATION; *pg.* 707, *pg.* 44
STEELHEAD X-16 - Golf Equipment - CALLAWAY GOLF COMPANY; *pg.* 1829, *pg.* 58
STEELMARK - Trade Association - AMERICAN IRON AND STEEL INSTITUTE; *pg.* 129, *pg.* 394
STEELMATE - Fencing - MASTER HALCO; *pg.* 96, *pg.* 474
STEELNET - Iron & Steel Service - CONSOLIDATED RAIL CORPORATION; *pg.* 1903, *pg.* 1562
STEELSAK - Bag - PACTIV CORPORATION; *pg.* 1466, *pg.* 624
STEELWORKS - Software - STEELCLOUD, INC.; *pg.* 476, *pg.* 1776
STEEMER ULTRA - Vacuum Cleaner - ORECK CORPORATION; *pg.* 59, *pg.* 1653
STEENS - Medical & Aesthetic Product - DYNATRONICS CORPORATION; *pg.* 1526, *pg.* 1757
STEEPING - Bath Product - KOHLER CO.; *pg.* 91, *pg.* 1862
STEER & STROLL - Trikes - RADIO FLYER INC.; *pg.* 966, *pg.* 588
STEER & STROLL COUPE - Ride-ons - RADIO FLYER INC.; *pg.* 966, *pg.* 588
STEER CRAZY - Game - WMS INDUSTRIES INC.; *pg.* 593, *pg.* 666
STEERINGWHEELS - Software - AUTODESK INC.; *pg.* 356, *pg.* 257
STEEROCATH-DX - Medical Device - BOSTON SCIENTIFIC CORPORATION; *pg.* 1508, *pg.* 831
STEEROCATH-T - Medical Device - BOSTON SCIENTIFIC CORPORATION; *pg.* 1508, *pg.* 831
STEERSEAL - Steering Fluid - RADIATOR SPECIALTY COMPANY; *pg.* 215, *pg.* 1380
STEEZ - Freshwater Fishing Rod - DAIWA CORPORATION; *pg.* 1832, *pg.* 75
STEIGMAIER - Beer - THE LION BREWERY, INC.; *pg.* 254, *pg.* 1594
STEIGMAIER PORTER - Beer - THE LION BREWERY, INC.; *pg.* 254, *pg.* 1594
STEIGMAIER SEASONALS - Beer - THE LION BREWERY, INC.; *pg.* 254, *pg.* 1594
STEIN OPTICAL - Eye Care Centers - VISIONWORKS OF AMERICA, INC.; *pg.* 1436, *pg.* 1744
THE STEINBECK REVIEW - Journal - SCARECROW PRESS, INC.; *pg.* 1683, *pg.* 773
STEINBERGER - Musical Instrument - GIBSON GUITAR CORP.; *pg.* 550, *pg.* 1650
STEINER - Golf, Turf & Specialty Products - TEXTRON INC.; *pg.* 235, *pg.* 1607
STEINFELD - Pickles - TREEHOUSE FOODS, INC.; *pg.* 901, *pg.* 649
STEINWAY - Musical Instrument - STEINWAY MUSICAL INSTRUMENTS, INC.; *pg.* 586, *pg.* 854
STEINWAY & SONS - Piano - STEINWAY & SONS; *pg.* 586, *pg.* 1176
STELLA ARTOIS - Beer - ANHEUSER-BUSCH COMPANIES, LLC; *pg.* 237, *pg.* 991
STELLA D'ORO - Snack Food - SNYDER'S-LANCE, INC.; *pg.* 896, *pg.* 1368
STELLAR - Floor Finish - 3M COMPANY; *pg.* 1142, *pg.* 956
STELLAR - Jin - BROWN-FORMAN CORPORATION; *pg.* 1958, *pg.* 732
STELLAR - Stereotaxic Instrument - STOELTING CO.; *pg.* 1430, *pg.* 671
STELTO - Pharmaceutical Preparation - PFIZER INC.; *pg.* 1581, *pg.* 1278
STELVIO - Bike - MARIN BIKES; *pg.* 1708, *pg.* 168
STEM-KIT - Reagents - BECKMAN COULTER, INC.; *pg.* 1402, *pg.* 48
STEM-TROL - Testing Instrument System - BECKMAN COULTER, INC.; *pg.* 1402, *pg.* 48
STEMCO - Truck Products - ENPRO INDUSTRIES, INC.; *pg.* 1334, *pg.* 1366
STEMPLEX - Supplement & Food Product - NEW EARTH LIFE SCIENCES, INC.; *pg.* 1573, *pg.* 1499
STENCIL FACTORY - Stencils - HIGHLIGHTS FOR CHILDREN, INC.; *pg.* 1650, *pg.* 1440
STEOL - Chemical Product - STEPAN COMPANY; *pg.* 1182, *pg.* 643
THE STEP - Aerobic Exercise System - ESCALADE INC.; *pg.* 1833, *pg.* 678
STEP - Spectra Traveling Education Program - FRESENIUS MEDICAL CARE NORTH AMERICA; *pg.* 1531, *pg.* 851
STEP - Software - SUNGARD DATA SYSTEMS INC.; *pg.* 477, *pg.* 1592
STEP BOND TAPE - Adhesive - BURKE INDUSTRIES, INC.; *pg.* 919, *pg.* 239
STEP CYLINDER - Lighting Fixtures - SWIVELIER CO., INC.; *pg.* 1307, *pg.* 1142
STEP-FLOW - Chemical Product - STEPAN COMPANY; *pg.* 1182, *pg.* 643
STEP HAPPY INSOLES - Healthcare Product - MEDICOOL, INC.; *pg.* 1562, *pg.* 294
STEP LIGHT - Plastic & Rubber - TEKNOR APEX COMPANY; *pg.* 1889, *pg.* 1605
STEP N UP - Footwear - PHOENIX FOOTWEAR GROUP, INC.; *pg.* 1815, *pg.* 60
STEP ONE - Insurance Service - MODERN WOODMEN OF AMERICA; *pg.* 1209, *pg.* 654
STEP REEBOK - Video - REEBOK INTERNATIONAL LTD.; *pg.* 1817, *pg.* 811
STEP SAVER - Floor Cleaner - S.C. JOHNSON & SON, INC.; *pg.* 334, *pg.* 1889
STEP SAVER WOOD STAIN & FINISH - Stain & Oil Finish - PPG AEROSPACE DEFT FACILITY; *pg.* 1445, *pg.* 115
STEP START WALK N' RIDE - Toy & Game - HASBRO, INC.; *pg.* 954, *pg.* 1603
STEPAN - Chemical Product - STEPAN COMPANY; *pg.* 1182, *pg.* 643
STEPAN-MILD - Chemical Product - STEPAN COMPANY; *pg.* 1182, *pg.* 643
STEPANATE - Chemical Product - STEPAN COMPANY; *pg.* 1182, *pg.* 643
STEPANFOAM - Chemical Product - STEPAN COMPANY; *pg.* 1182, *pg.* 643
STEPANFORM - Chemical Product - STEPAN COMPANY; *pg.* 1182, *pg.* 643
STEPANOL - Chemical Product - STEPAN COMPANY; *pg.* 1182, *pg.* 643
STEPANPOL - Chemical Product - STEPAN COMPANY; *pg.* 1182, *pg.* 643
STEPANQUAT - Chemical Product - STEPAN COMPANY; *pg.* 1182, *pg.* 643
STEPANTAN - Chemical Product - STEPAN COMPANY; *pg.* 1182, *pg.* 643
STEPANTEX - Chemical Product - STEPAN COMPANY; *pg.* 1182, *pg.* 643
STEPFAC - Chemical Product - STEPAN COMPANY; *pg.* 1182, *pg.* 643
STEPHAN'S - Shampoos & Hair Care Products - THE STEPHAN COMPANY; *pg.* 1597, *pg.* 426
STEPMAKER - Building Form - QUIKRETE COMPANIES; *pg.* 106, *pg.* 519
STEPMATES - Fiberglass Custom Truck Steps - LUND INTERNATIONAL, INC.; *pg.* 211, *pg.* 526
STEPOSOL - Chemical Product - STEPAN COMPANY; *pg.* 1182, *pg.* 643
STEPPING OUT - Dinnerware - THE HOMER LAUGHLIN CHINA COMPANY; *pg.* 1125, *pg.* 1850
STEPPING STONES - Books - C.R. GIBSON, LLC; *pg.* 1631, *pg.* 1650
STEPRAIL - Running Boards - LUND INTERNATIONAL, INC.; *pg.* 211, *pg.* 526
STEPSAVOR - Kitchen Appliance - HAMILTON BEACH BRANDS, INC.; *pg.* 56, *pg.* 1783
STEPSHIELD - Door Sill Protector - LUND INTERNATIONAL, INC.; *pg.* 211, *pg.* 526
STEPSPERSE - Chemical Product - STEPAN COMPANY; *pg.* 1182, *pg.* 643
STEPWET - Chemical Product - STEPAN COMPANY; *pg.* 1182, *pg.* 643
STERAFFIRM - Test Strips - STERIS CORPORATION; *pg.* 1597, *pg.* 1464
STEREO MIRROR - 3D Display - PLANAR SYSTEMS, INC.; *pg.* 455, *pg.* 1495
STEREO SURROUND - Home Theater Sound - SHURE INCORPORATED; *pg.* 672, *pg.* 638
STEREOGUM - Alternative & Independent Music Site - SPINMEDIA; *pg.* 1282, *pg.* 104
STEREOLOC - Diagnostic Imaging Product - HOLOGIC, INC.; *pg.* 1416, *pg.* 784
STEREOPTIC - Stand Magnifier - EDROY PRODUCTS CO., INC.; *pg.* 1411, *pg.* 1318
STEREOS.COM - Advertising Website - LIVE CURRENT MEDIA INC.; *pg.* 1263, *pg.* 1911
STEREOSURROUND - Video Conferencing Product - POLYCOM, INC.; *pg.* 664, *pg.* 249
STEREOTAXIS SYSTEM - Remote-Controlled Coronary Instrument Control & Navigation Platform - STEREOTAXIS, INC.; *pg.* 1597, *pg.* 1004
STERER - Wheel Steering System - EATON CORPORATION; *pg.* 1331, *pg.* 1429
STERI-DOT - Sterilization Product - PROPPER MANUFACTURING COMPANY, INC.; *pg.* 1586, *pg.* 1175
STERI-DRAPE - Surgical Drapes - 3M COMPANY; *pg.* 1142, *pg.* 956
STERI-GAS - Ethylene Oxide Cartridges - 3M COMPANY; *pg.* 1142, *pg.* 956
STERI-LOK - Sterilization Packaging - 3M COMPANY; *pg.* 1142, *pg.* 956
STERI-STRIP - Skin Closures - 3M COMPANY; *pg.* 1142, *pg.* 956
STERI-TAMP - Pharmaceutical Product - FRESENIUS KABI USA; *pg.* 1531, *pg.* 626
STERI-VAC - Aerator - 3M COMPANY; *pg.* 1142, *pg.* 956
STERI-WRAP - Sterilization Product - PROPPER MANUFACTURING COMPANY, INC.; *pg.* 1586, *pg.* 1175
STERIGAGE - Chemical Integrator Test - 3M COMPANY; *pg.* 1142, *pg.* 956
STERIGEL - Lab Science Material - CAROLINA BIOLOGICAL SUPPLY COMPANY; *pg.* 1513, *pg.* 1359
STERILCONTAINER - Sterile Processing Containers - AESCULAP, INC.; *pg.* 1487, *pg.* 1521
STERILEWARE - Sampling Supplies - BEL-ART PRODUCTS, INC.; *pg.* 1879, *pg.* 1129
STERILOBE - Pump Product - IDEX CORPORATION; *pg.* 1347, *pg.* 623
STERILYTE - Liquid Bicarbonate - ROCKWELL MEDICAL TECHNOLOGIES, INC.; *pg.* 1590, *pg.* 913
STERIPROBE - Medical Product - CINCINNATI SUB-ZERO PRODUCTS, INC.; *pg.* 1070, *pg.* 1411
STERISAFE - Sterilizer Treatment - GE WATER & PROCESS TECHNOLOGIES; *pg.* 1339, *pg.* 1588
STERIVENT - Filters - MEDTRONIC; *pg.* 1563, *pg.* 183
STERLING - Table - BLATT BOWLING & BILLIARD CORP.; *pg.* 1827, *pg.* 1203
STERLING - Medical Device - BOSTON SCIENTIFIC CORPORATION; *pg.* 1508, *pg.* 831
STERLING - Carbon Black - CABOT CORPORATION; *pg.* 1151, *pg.* 792

First page reference indicates Business Class Edition
Second page reference indicates Geographic Edition

STERLING - Table Salt - CARGILL SALT; *pg.* 846, *pg.* 926
STERLING - Guitar - ERNIE BALL INC.; *pg.* 1768, *pg.* 68
STERLING - Gaming Product - GLD PRODUCTS, INC.; *pg.* 1835, *pg.* 1882
STERLING - Furniture - JASPER GROUP; *pg.* 930, *pg.* 691
STERLING - Plumbing Fixtures - KOHLER CO.; *pg.* 91, *pg.* 1862
STERLING - Surface Finish - MACDERMID, INC.; *pg.* 1172, *pg.* 321
STERLING - Grinders - MCDONOUGH MANUFACTURING COMPANY; *pg.* 1360, *pg.* 1857
STERLING - HVAC Equipment - MESTEK, INC.; *pg.* 1074, *pg.* 857
STERLING - Drill - WAHL CLIPPER CORPORATION; *pg.* 524, *pg.* 662
STERLING - Paperboard Packaging Product - WESTROCK COMPANY; *pg.* 1472, *pg.* 1805
STERLING COLLECTION - Line of Polyester Fiber for Crafting - FEDERAL FOAM TECHNOLOGIES INC.; *pg.* 692, *pg.* 1884
THE STERLING EDITION - Mattress & Box Spring Sets - KINGSDOWN, INC.; *pg.* 932, *pg.* 1383
STERLING FILL - Automotive Body Filler - PPG INDUSTRIES, INC.; *pg.* 1445, *pg.* 1579
STERLING HOTELS & RESORTS - Hotels & Resorts - PREFERRED HOTEL GROUP; *pg.* 1108, *pg.* 587
STERLING LINE - Sleep Sofas - KINGSDOWN, INC.; *pg.* 932, *pg.* 1383
STERLING MONORAIL - Medical Device - BOSTON SCIENTIFIC CORPORATION; *pg.* 1508, *pg.* 831
STERLING OPTICAL - Eyewear - EMERGING VISION, INC.; *pg.* 1411, *pg.* 1227
STERLING POOLS - In-Ground Vinyl Pools - POOL CORPORATION; *pg.* 1843, *pg.* 743
STERLING RADIATOR - Heating & Ventilation Equipment - MESTEK, INC.; *pg.* 1074, *pg.* 857
STERLING SILVER - Jewelry Cleaner - AVON PRODUCTS, INC.; *pg.* 500, *pg.* 1198
STERLING SILVER - Meats - CARGILL, INC.; *pg.* 845, *pg.* 965
STERLING VINEYARDS - Wine - DIAGEO CANADA, INC.; *pg.* 1961, *pg.* 1937
STERLING VISIONCARE - Eyewear - EMERGING VISION, INC.; *pg.* 1411, *pg.* 1227
STERNER - Lighting Product - HUBBELL INCORPORATED; *pg.* 1299, *pg.* 370
STERNO - Portable Heating Fuel - BLYTH, INC.; *pg.* 502, *pg.* 349
STERRAD - Healthcare Product - JOHNSON & JOHNSON; *pg.* 1549, *pg.* 1091
STETSON - Fragrances - COTY, INC.; *pg.* 506, *pg.* 1219
STETSONN - Footwear - STEVEN MADDEN, LTD.; *pg.* 1819, *pg.* 1176
STEUBEN - Glassware - CORNING INCORPORATED; *pg.* 1122, *pg.* 1154
STEVA - Dry Cleaning & Laundry Product - ADCO, INC.; *pg.* 325, *pg.* 482
STEVE MADDEN MENS - Men's Shoes - STEVEN MADDEN, LTD.; *pg.* 1819, *pg.* 1176
STEVEN BY STEVE MADDEN - Belts - STEVEN MADDEN, LTD.; *pg.* 1819, *pg.* 1176
STEVEN GRAPHICS - Wireless Communication System - AT&T SOUTHEAST; *pg.* 1868, *pg.* 489
STEVENS - Centrifuge Components - WESTERN STATES MACHINE COMPANY; *pg.* 1388, *pg.* 1455
STEVIE AWARDS - Award - STEVIE AWARDS, INC.; *pg.* 157, *pg.* 1780
STEVIE RAY VAUGHAN STRATOCASTER - Electric Guitar - FENDER MUSICAL INSTRUMENTS CORPORATION; *pg.* 547, *pg.* 21
STEWARD - Insecticide - E.I. DU PONT DE NEMOURS & COMPANY; *pg.* 1159, *pg.* 390
STEWARDESS - Leather Product - COACH, INC.; *pg.* 3, *pg.* 1214
STEWARDSHIP - Coffee Service - KEURIG GREEN MOUNTAIN, INC.; *pg.* 868, *pg.* 1768
STEXCITE - Ignition System Driver - WOODWARD, INC.; *pg.* 122, *pg.* 329
STEYR - Agricultural Equipment - CNH AMERICA LLC; *pg.* 702, *pg.* 560
STICK-MATE - Printable Plastic Product - TRANSILWRAP COMPANY, INC.; *pg.* 1470, *pg.* 613
STICK-ONS - Game - UNIVERSITY GAMES CORPORATION; *pg.* 969, *pg.* 230
STICK-UMS - Toss and Catch Game - SCHOOL-TECH, INC.; *pg.* 1844, *pg.* 866
STICKER SCHOOLHOUSE - Educational Product - BARKER CREEK PUBLISHING INC.; *pg.* 1619, *pg.* 1818
STICKERUSA - Educational Product - BARKER CREEK PUBLISHING INC.; *pg.* 1619, *pg.* 1818
STICKNEY - Film Cleaning Equipment - EASTMAN KODAK COMPANY; *pg.* 1408, *pg.* 1333
STICKSCREW - Fastener Product - PENN ENGINEERING & MANUFACTURING CORP.; *pg.* 1059, *pg.* 1525
STICKSTERS - Cheese - LACTALIS AMERICAN GROUP; *pg.* 873, *pg.* 1149
STICKTITE - Burner - MAXON CORPORATION; *pg.* 1359, *pg.* 695
STIEGMANN-GOFF - Medical Equipment - CONMED CORPORATION; *pg.* 1517, *pg.* 1347
STIFF STUFF - Hair Product - THE STEPHAN COMPANY; *pg.* 1597, *pg.* 426
STIGA - Sporting Good Product - ESCALADE INC.; *pg.* 1833, *pg.* 678
STIGGLES - Stickers - HIGHLIGHTS FOR CHILDREN, INC.; *pg.* 1650, *pg.* 1440
STIKIT - Unlined Pressure-Sensitive Coated Abrasives - 3M COMPANY; *pg.* 1142, *pg.* 956
STILETTO - Office Furniture - STEELCASE INC.; *pg.* 475, *pg.* 889
STILETTO SLIM - Briefcase - SANTA FE LEATHER CORPORATION; *pg.* 12, *pg.* 1059
STILL THE FIRST - Tag Line - THE ADT CORPORATION; *pg.* 612, *pg.* 409
STILLHUNTER - Rainwear - CABELA'S INCORPORATED; *pg.* 535, *pg.* 1019
STILLNESS - Bath Product - KOHLER CO.; *pg.* 91, *pg.* 1862
STILLVER - Chemical Reagent - HACH COMPANY; *pg.* 1415, *pg.* 334
STILO - Tile - ARTISTIC TILE INC.; *pg.* 914, *pg.* 1119
STIMATE - Desmopressin Acetate - CSL BEHRING LLC; *pg.* 1520, *pg.* 1543
STIMOROL - Chewing Gum - MONDELEZ INTERNATIONAL, INC.; *pg.* 878, *pg.* 601
STIMPSON GS - Eyelet - THE STIMPSON COMPANY, INC.; *pg.* 1182, *pg.* 460
STIMUGEN - Vaccine Adjuvant - PFIZER INC.; *pg.* 1581, *pg.* 1278
STIMULAIRE - Aroma Therapy System - SURCO PRODUCTS, INC.; *pg.* 336, *pg.* 1581
STIMULATING - Carpet - BEAULIEU GROUP, LLC; *pg.* 917, *pg.* 529
STIMULUS PROGRESSION - Programming Format - MOOD MEDIA; *pg.* 298, *pg.* 1616
STINE - Bulk Seed Treatment - CARGILL LIMITED; *pg.* 1475, *pg.* 1914
STING - Card Game - MATTEL GAMES/PUZZLES; *pg.* 962, *pg.* 80
STING-EZE - Safety Product - WISCONSIN PHARMACAL COMPANY, LLC; *pg.* 1610, *pg.* 1861
STING FREE - Insect Bite Protector - GARDENS ALIVE!, INC.; *pg.* 1796, *pg.* 693
STINGER - Software System - ALCATEL-LUCENT; *pg.* 615, *pg.* 1094
STINGER - Computer Alignment Unit - BEE LINE COMPANY; *pg.* 200, *pg.* 701
STINGER - Inner Tubes - COOPER TIRE & RUBBER COMPANY; *pg.* 1881, *pg.* 1453
STINGER - Medical Device - C.R. BARD, INC.; *pg.* 1519, *pg.* 1094
STINGER - Portable Pin Marker - GEORGE T. SCHMIDT, INC.; *pg.* 1340, *pg.* 637
STINGER - Apparel - OAKLEY, INC.; *pg.* 1840, *pg.* 86
STINGER - Weapon System - RAYTHEON COMPANY; *pg.* 233, *pg.* 854
STINGER - Flashlight - STREAMLIGHT INC.; *pg.* 1306, *pg.* 1527
STINGER DS - Flashlight - STREAMLIGHT INC.; *pg.* 1306, *pg.* 1527
STINGER HP - Flashlight - STREAMLIGHT INC.; *pg.* 1306, *pg.* 1527
STINGER MODEL 2000 - AC & Refrigerant Recovery System - BACHARACH INC.; *pg.* 1400, *pg.* 1556
STINGER SPIKE - Tire Deflation Devices - FEDERAL SIGNAL CORPORATION; *pg.* 638, *pg.* 645
STINGER XT - Flashlight - STREAMLIGHT INC.; *pg.* 1306, *pg.* 1527
STINGER XT HP - Flashlight - STREAMLIGHT INC.; *pg.* 1306, *pg.* 1527
STINGERS - Food Product - TYSON FOODS, INC.; *pg.* 902, *pg.* 35
STINGRAY - Commercial Printing System - ECRM IMAGING SYSTEMS, INC.; *pg.* 1410, *pg.* 848
STINGRAY - Guitar - ERNIE BALL INC.; *pg.* 1768, *pg.* 68
STINGRAY - Skate - ROLLER DERBY SKATE CORP.; *pg.* 966, *pg.* 630
STINGRAY IMAGESETTER - Commercial Printing System - ECRM IMAGING SYSTEMS, INC.; *pg.* 1410, *pg.* 848
STINKIN' RICH - Lottery Game - NEW YORK STATE LOTTERY; *pg.* 1001, *pg.* 1340
STINNG - Footwear - STEVEN MADDEN, LTD.; *pg.* 1819, *pg.* 1176
STINSON - Bike - MARIN BIKES; *pg.* 1708, *pg.* 168
STIPPLE - Vinyl Matting - THE BILTRITE CORPORATION; *pg.* 1879, *pg.* 850
STIR-N-POUR - Paint & Coating - AERVOE INDUSTRIES INCORPORATED; *pg.* 1439, *pg.* 1021
STITCHER - Software - AUTODESK INC.; *pg.* 356, *pg.* 257
STITCHES - Footwear - COBIAN CORP.; *pg.* 1806, *pg.* 253
STITCHLINER - Bridge - STANDARD DUPLICATING MACHINES CORPORATION; *pg.* 473, *pg.* 783
STIVAL - Italian Wine - LAIRD & COMPANY, INC.; *pg.* 1966, *pg.* 1119
STIXSIL - Sodium Silicate - PQ CORPORATION; *pg.* 1178, *pg.* 1515
STIXSO - Sodium Silicate - PQ CORPORATION; *pg.* 1178, *pg.* 1515
STJ - Dust Filter - SLY, INC.; *pg.* 1376, *pg.* 1475
STK - Starter Kits - ATMEL CORPORATION; *pg.* 621, *pg.* 238
ST.LAURET - Furniture - ASHLEY FURNITURE INDUSTRIES, INC.; *pg.* 914, *pg.* 1852
ST.LUCIA - Shoes - ALLEN-EDMONDS SHOE CORP.; *pg.* 1804, *pg.* 1887
STOA - Furniture - HERMAN MILLER, INC.; *pg.* 926, *pg.* 913
STOCK-AID - Seasoning - MCCORMICK & COMPANY, INCORPORATED; *pg.* 1027, *pg.* 779
STOCK & CUSTOM PLASTIC AND POLY BAGS - Tagline - POLY PAK AMERICA, INC.; *pg.* 1467, *pg.* 138
STOCK LOCKS - Lock Mechanisms - COMPX INTERNATIONAL INC.; *pg.* 1044, *pg.* 1678
STOCKADE - Livestock Feeds & Feed Supplements - ALTAIR CORPORATION; *pg.* 1312, *pg.* 910
STOCKBRIDGE - Shoes - ALLEN-EDMONDS SHOE CORP.; *pg.* 1804, *pg.* 1887
STOCKMAN - Knife - BUCK KNIVES, INC.; *pg.* 1828, *pg.* 550
STOCKMAN ELK HOOF - Knife - BUCK KNIVES, INC.; *pg.* 1828, *pg.* 550
STOEGER - Firearm - BENELLI USA CORPORATION; *pg.* 1827, *pg.* 754
STOEGER BOOKS - Publication Book - BENELLI USA CORPORATION; *pg.* 1827, *pg.* 754
STOELTING - Stereotaxic Instrument - STOELTING CO.; *pg.* 1430, *pg.* 671
STOKED - Energy Drink - LEADING BRANDS, INC.; *pg.* 1026, *pg.* 1911
STOKLEY - Canned Foods - SENECA FOODS CORPORATION; *pg.* 895, *pg.* 1177
STOLICHNAYA - Premium Vodka - STOLI GROUP USA LLC; *pg.* 1970, *pg.* 1296
STOLZ - Injection Molded Plastic - TRIMAS CORPORATION; *pg.* 1383, *pg.* 874
STOMAHESIVE - Paste - ALIMED, INC.; *pg.* 1490, *pg.* 816
STOMASEAL - Adhesive Discs, Colostomy Dressings - 3M COMPANY; *pg.* 1142, *pg.* 956
STONCO - Outdoor Lighting & Access. - CRESCENT/STONCO SUPPLY DIVISION; *pg.* 1295, *pg.* 1121
STONCO - Lighting Fixture & Control - PHILIPS LIGHTING; *pg.* 1303, *pg.* 806
STONE - Software - AUTODESK INC.; *pg.* 356, *pg.* 257
STONE CLEAR TOP - Cleaning Product - ORECK CORPORATION; *pg.* 59, *pg.* 1653
STONE CONE - Medical Device - BOSTON SCIENTIFIC CORPORATION; *pg.* 1508, *pg.* 831
STONE MILL PALE ALE - Organic Beer - ANHEUSER-BUSCH COMPANIES, LLC; *pg.* 237, *pg.* 991
STONE SOUP - Game - GAMEWRIGHT; *pg.* 953, *pg.* 836
STONE TECH - Ceramic, Glass, Stone Tiles & Slabs - WALKER & ZANGER, INC.; *pg.* 119, *pg.* 281
STONEBRIDGE - Apparel - HAGGAR CORPORATION; *pg.* 41, *pg.* 1682
STONEBRIDGE - Ceiling Fan - HUNTER FAN COMPANY; *pg.* 57, *pg.* 1631

STONECOMP - Pharmaceutical Product - MISSION PHARMACAL COMPANY INC.; *pg.* 1568, *pg.* 1742
STONEHAVEN VINEYARDS - Wine - BANFI VINTNERS; *pg.* 1957, *pg.* 1161
STONEHURST - Carpet - BEAULIEU GROUP, LLC; *pg.* 917, *pg.* 529
STONEMILL KITCHENS - Premium Dips - RESER'S FINE FOODS INC.; *pg.* 1032, *pg.* 1496
STONERISK - Pharmaceutical Product - MISSION PHARMACAL COMPANY INC.; *pg.* 1568, *pg.* 1742
STONETECH - Stone Product Sealers, Cleaners & Refinishers - E.I. DU PONT DE NEMOURS & COMPANY; *pg.* 1159, *pg.* 390
STONETRACK - Pharmaceutical Product - MISSION PHARMACAL COMPANY INC.; *pg.* 1568, *pg.* 1742
STONEWALL - Moist & Dry Snuff - ROCK CREEK PHARMACEUTICALS, INC.; *pg.* 1895, *pg.* 466
STONEWALL HARD SNUFF - Tobacco Product - ROCK CREEK PHARMACEUTICALS, INC.; *pg.* 1895, *pg.* 466
STONEY GINGER BEER - Beverages - THE COCA-COLA COMPANY; *pg.* 240, *pg.* 493
STONINGTON - Furniture - BUSH INDUSTRIES INC.; *pg.* 919, *pg.* 1170
STONYFIELD FARM - Yogurt - STONYFIELD FARM, INC.; *pg.* 899, *pg.* 1035
STOOPER - Footwear - STEVEN MADDEN, LTD.; *pg.* 1819, *pg.* 1176
STOP - Safety Training Observation Program - E.I. DU PONT DE NEMOURS & COMPANY; *pg.* 1159, *pg.* 390
S.T.O.P. - Electrolyte - TROUW NUTRITION USA; *pg.* 1482, *pg.* 616
STOP-A-CLOG - Safety Product - VENTURI, INC.; *pg.* 1606, *pg.* 910
STOP & SHOP - Supermarkets - THE STOP & SHOP SUPERMARKET COMPANY LLC; *pg.* 1034, *pg.* 842
STOP LEAK - Engine Oil - BARDAHL MANUFACTURING CORPORATION; *pg.* 972, *pg.* 1833
STOP-N-FLOW - Light/Medium Duty Power-and-Free Conveyors - DAIFUKU WEBB; *pg.* 1327, *pg.* 885
STOP N GO - Gasoline Retail Outlets - VALERO ENERGY CORPORATION; *pg.* 986, *pg.* 1743
STOP OIL LEAKS - Oil Leak Treatment - AMERICAN GREASE STICK CO.; *pg.* 971, *pg.* 902
STOP SMOKIN - Engine Treatment - RADIATOR SPECIALTY COMPANY; *pg.* 215, *pg.* 1380
STOP SMOKING NOW!! - Health Care Product - HEALTH PRODUCTS CORPORATION; *pg.* 1540, *pg.* 1356
THE STOP THAT KEEPS YOU GOING. - Tagline - CUMBERLAND FARMS, INC.; *pg.* 1018, *pg.* 820
STOP THE WATCH - Educational Materials - SCHOLASTIC INC.; *pg.* 1683, *pg.* 1288
STOPLIGHT - Food Safety Product - CRC INDUSTRIES, INC.; *pg.* 329, *pg.* 1590
STOPPER - Outdoor Products - BLACK DIAMOND, INC.; *pg.* 1827, *pg.* 1756
STOPPER CYLINDER - Cylinder for Use in Conveyor Stopping Applications - FABCO-AIR, INC.; *pg.* 1336, *pg.* 429
STOPPLE - Plugging Machine - T.D. WILLIAMSON, INC.; *pg.* 1380, *pg.* 1490
STOR - Data Storage Product - CAMBEX CORPORATION; *pg.* 368, *pg.* 844
STOR-ALL - Storage & Utility Hooks - HINDLEY MANUFACTURING COMPANY, INC.; *pg.* 1049, *pg.* 1601
STOR/DRAWER - Filing System - FELLOWES, INC.; *pg.* 397, *pg.* 620
STOR-PAK - Reusable Consumer Packaging - HINDLEY MANUFACTURING COMPANY, INC.; *pg.* 1049, *pg.* 1601
STORABLE - Cup - SOLO CUP COMPANY; *pg.* 1469, *pg.* 625
STORAGE - Magazine - MEREDITH CORPORATION; *pg.* 1663, *pg.* 705
STORAGE ACCELERATION APPLIANCE - Software - NETAPP, INC.; *pg.* 444, *pg.* 287
THE STORAGE AND OFFICE SOLUTIONS SPECIALISTS - Tag Line - MOBILE MINI, INC.; *pg.* 1362, *pg.* 26
STORAGE ASSESSMENT TOOL - Software - DELL SOFTWARE; *pg.* 385, *pg.* 40
STORAGE CONSOLIDATOR - Software - DELL SOFTWARE; *pg.* 385, *pg.* 40
STORAGE EXEC - Software - SYMANTEC CORPORATION; *pg.* 478, *pg.* 161
STORAGE HORIZON - Software - DELL SOFTWARE; *pg.* 385, *pg.* 40
STORAGE MAGAZINE - Magazine - TECHTARGET, INC.; *pg.* 482, *pg.* 837
STORAGE PERFORMANCE ANALYSER - Computer Storage System Software - AVAGO TECHNOLOGIES; *pg.* 358, *pg.* 238
STORAGE SUITE - Software - DELL SOFTWARE; *pg.* 385, *pg.* 40
STORAGE SUITE FOR WINDOWS - Software - DELL SOFTWARE; *pg.* 385, *pg.* 40
STORAGE WALL - Drawer & Shelf Storage - LISTA INTERNATIONAL CORPORATION; *pg.* 934, *pg.* 825
STORAGECARE - ValueLoader - QUANTUM CORPORATION; *pg.* 458, *pg.* 250
STORAGECENTRAL - Software - SYMANTEC CORPORATION; *pg.* 478, *pg.* 161
STORAGELINK - Software - CITRIX SYSTEMS, INC.; *pg.* 375, *pg.* 424
STORAGESCOPE - Software - EMC CORPORATION; *pg.* 391, *pg.* 825
STORAGEX - Software - BROCADE COMMUNICATIONS SYSTEMS, INC.; *pg.* 365, *pg.* 239
STORARO - Filter - ROSCO LABORATORIES, INC.; *pg.* 1782, *pg.* 378
STORASSURE - Software - OVERLAND STORAGE, INC.; *pg.* 451, *pg.* 205
STORE 21 - Software - MICROS SYSTEMS, INC.; *pg.* 435, *pg.* 768
STORE & STREAM - Web Publishing Tool - ONSTREAM MEDIA CORPORATION; *pg.* 449, *pg.* 459
STORE-IT START-IT - Gas Stabilizer - AMERICAN GREASE STICK CO.; *pg.* 971, *pg.* 902
STORE YOUR WORLD IN OURS - Slogan - SANDISK CORPORATION; *pg.* 465, *pg.* 147
STOREAGE - Storage Resources Software - AVAGO TECHNOLOGIES; *pg.* 358, *pg.* 238
STORECOUNT - Visitors Counting System - CHECKPOINT SYSTEMS, INC.; *pg.* 628, *pg.* 1559
STOREFRONTDESIGN - Tagline - BIGLARI HOLDINGS INC.; *pg.* 1015, *pg.* 1739
STOREMORE - Outdoor Storage Sheds - FLOWTRON OUTDOOR PRODUCTS; *pg.* 639, *pg.* 830
STOREMORE - Slideout System - WINNEBAGO INDUSTRIES, INC.; *pg.* 1712, *pg.* 707
STORM - Ear Warmer - 180S, LLC; *pg.* 1824, *pg.* 754
STORM - Monitor - AKRON BRASS COMPANY; *pg.* 1311, *pg.* 1482
STORM - Semiconductor Device - APPLIED MATERIALS, INC; *pg.* 618, *pg.* 1009
STORM - Furniture - HOWE FURNITURE CORPORATION; *pg.* 928, *pg.* 998
STORM - Sport & Leisure Product - JAKKS PACIFIC, INC.; *pg.* 960, *pg.* 142
STORM - Precision Cleaning System - KENNAMETAL EXTRUDE HONE; *pg.* 1352, *pg.* 1542
STORM - Commercial CD Jukebox - ROWE INTERNATIONAL CORP; *pg.* 669, *pg.* 889
STORM - Fishing Gear Product - SIMMS FISHING PRODUCTS CORP.; *pg.* 1845, *pg.* 1008
THE STORM - Theme Park Ride - WET 'N WILD, INC.; *pg.* 592, *pg.* 457
STORM CASE - Transport Cases - PELICAN PRODUCTS; *pg.* 1467, *pg.* 843
STORM COAT - Exterior Stains & Clears - THE VALSPAR CORPORATION; *pg.* 1449, *pg.* 945
STORM-FIT - Apparel - NIKE, INC.; *pg.* 1812, *pg.* 1492
STORM GUARD - Wiper - MIGHTY DISTRIBUTING SYSTEM OF AMERICA; *pg.* 213, *pg.* 538
STORM HAWKS - Toy - SPIN MASTER LTD.; *pg.* 967, *pg.* 1943
STORM-PURE - Pipe - ADVANCED DRAINAGE SYSTEMS, INC.; *pg.* 1878, *pg.* 1455
STORM TRAK - Case - PELICAN PRODUCTS; *pg.* 1467, *pg.* 843
STORM WATCH - E-Newsletter - SEATTLE STORM; *pg.* 582, *pg.* 1839
STORM XTG - Glove - 180S, LLC; *pg.* 1824, *pg.* 754
STORM ZONE - Gloves - WELLS LAMONT CORPORATION; *pg.* 15, *pg.* 638
STORMCAD - Software - BENTLEY SYSTEMS, INC.; *pg.* 361, *pg.* 1531
STORMCORE - Golf Apparel - ROGER CLEVELAND GOLF COMPANY, INC.; *pg.* 1844, *pg.* 105
STORMGEMS - Software - BENTLEY SYSTEMS, INC.; *pg.* 361, *pg.* 1531
STORMGUARD - Nail & Screw - W.H. MAZE COMPANY; *pg.* 1389, *pg.* 652
STORMPAD - Software - WIND RIVER SYSTEMS, INC.; *pg.* 493, *pg.* 38
STORMROOM - Residential In-Home Storm Shelter - E.I. DU PONT DE NEMOURS & COMPANY; *pg.* 1159, *pg.* 390
STORMSCOPE - Weather Mapping Systems - L-3 AVIONICS SYSTEMS, INC.; *pg.* 650, *pg.* 888
STORMSTAIN - Exterior Wood Stain - CALIFORNIA PRODUCTS CORPORATION; *pg.* 1441, *pg.* 781
STORMTECH - Retention Chambers - ADVANCED DRAINAGE SYSTEMS, INC.; *pg.* 1878, *pg.* 1455
STORMWATCH - Window Protection - ANDERSEN CORPORATION; *pg.* 67, *pg.* 916
STORMY - Snack Food - SNYDER'S-LANCE, INC.; *pg.* 896, *pg.* 1368
STORNEXT - Software - QUANTUM CORPORATION; *pg.* 458, *pg.* 250
STORPLUS - Food Storage Boxes & Square Food Storage Containers - CARLISLE FOODSERVICE PRODUCTS INCORPORATED; *pg.* 1455, *pg.* 1485
STORVIEW - Software - SILICON GRAPHICS INTERNATIONAL CORP; *pg.* 470, *pg.* 148
STORY TREE - Educational Materials - SCHOLASTIC INC.; *pg.* 1683, *pg.* 1288
STORYBLOCK - Educational Toys - LEAPFROG ENTERPRISES, INC.; *pg.* 961, *pg.* 84
STORYBOOK HEIRLOOMS - Apparel - CELEBRATE EXPRESS, INC.; *pg.* 1764, *pg.* 1883
STORYBOOK.COM - Apparel - CELEBRATE EXPRESS, INC.; *pg.* 1764, *pg.* 1883
STORYTELLING CIRCLE - Educational Materials - SCHOLASTIC INC.; *pg.* 1683, *pg.* 1288
STORYWORKS - Magazine - SCHOLASTIC INC.; *pg.* 1683, *pg.* 1288
STORZ - Surgical Instruments - BAUSCH & LOMB INCORPORATED; *pg.* 1401, *pg.* 1045
STOUFFER'S - Food Product - ELLENBEE-LEGGETT COMPANY INC.; *pg.* 854, *pg.* 1452
STOUFFER'S - Frozen Entrees - NESTLE USA, INC.; *pg.* 883, *pg.* 96
STOUFFER'S ENTREES - Food & Beverage Product - NESTLE USA, INC.; *pg.* 883, *pg.* 96
STOUFFER'S FAMILY STYLE FAVORITES - Food & Beverage Product - NESTLE USA, INC.; *pg.* 883, *pg.* 96
STOUFFER'S FROZEN PIZZA - Food & Beverage Product - NESTLE USA, INC.; *pg.* 883, *pg.* 96
STOUFFER'S HEARTY PORTIONS - Food & Beverage Product - NESTLE USA, INC.; *pg.* 883, *pg.* 96
STOUFFER'S HOMESTYLE - Food & Beverage Product - NESTLE USA, INC.; *pg.* 883, *pg.* 96
STOUFFER'S LEAN CUISINE - Food & Beverage Product - NESTLE USA, INC.; *pg.* 883, *pg.* 96
STOUFFER'S LEAN CUISINE AMERICAN FAVORITES - Food & Beverage Product - NESTLE USA, INC.; *pg.* 883, *pg.* 96
STOUFFER'S LEAN CUISINE CAFE CLASSICS - Food & Beverage Product - NESTLE USA, INC.; *pg.* 883, *pg.* 96
STOUFFER'S LEAN CUISINE HEARTY PORTIONS - Food & Beverage Product - NESTLE USA, INC.; *pg.* 883, *pg.* 96
STOUFFER'S LEAN SKILLET SENSATIONS - Food & Beverage Product - NESTLE USA, INC.; *pg.* 883, *pg.* 96
STOUFFER'S OVEN SENSATIONS - Food & Beverage Product - NESTLE USA, INC.; *pg.* 883, *pg.* 96
STOUFFER'S SKILLET SENSATIONS - Food & Beverage Product - NESTLE USA, INC.; *pg.* 883, *pg.* 96
STOUT - Herbicide - E.I. DU PONT DE NEMOURS & COMPANY; *pg.* 1159, *pg.* 390
STOVE TOP - Stuffing Mixes - THE KRAFT HEINZ COMPANY; *pg.* 870, *pg.* 1577
STOW-A-WAY - Hose - TEKNOR APEX COMPANY; *pg.* 1889, *pg.* 1605
STOW AWAY - Basketball Standards - LIFETIME PRODUCTS INC.; *pg.* 933, *pg.* 1751
STOW DAVIS - Furniture - STEELCASE INC.; *pg.* 475, *pg.* 889
STOWAWAY - Battery - EXIDE TECHNOLOGIES; *pg.* 204, *pg.* 483
STOWAWAY RAINWEAR - Rainwear - L.L. BEAN, INC.; *pg.* 1777, *pg.* 750
STOWAWAYS - Food Storage Product - HOME PRODUCTS INTERNATIONAL, INC.; *pg.* 1125, *pg.* 577
STOWE - Shoes - ALLEN-EDMONDS SHOE CORP.; *pg.* 1804, *pg.* 1887
STOWE - Cookies - PEPPERIDGE FARM, INC.; *pg.* 888, *pg.* 363
STP - Automotive Aftermarket Appearance Products -

ARMORED AUTOGROUP INC.; *pg.* 199, *pg.* 342
STP - Automotive Additives - THE CLOROX COMPANY; *pg.* 327, *pg.* 169
STP MESSENGER - Online Trading Services - MARKETAXESS HOLDINGS INC.; *pg.* 778, *pg.* 1256
STP SON OF A GUN - Appearance Products - THE CLOROX COMPANY; *pg.* 327, *pg.* 169
STRADA - Shoes - CLARKS COMPANIES; *pg.* 1806, *pg.* 836
STRADA - Fabric - MOMENTUM TEXTILES INC.; *pg.* 697, *pg.* 114
STRADE - Guest Chairs - BERNHARDT DESIGN; *pg.* 918, *pg.* 1381
STRAIGHT - Tubing - AP EXHAUST PRODUCTS, INC.; *pg.* 199, *pg.* 1373
STRAIGHT APPLE B-I-B - Brandy - LAIRD & COMPANY, INC.; *pg.* 1966, *pg.* 1119
STRAIGHT CURVE - Instructional Supplements - EDMENTUM, INC.; *pg.* 390, *pg.* 917
STRAIGHT-IN - Medical Device - AMERICAN MEDICAL SYSTEMS HOLDINGS, INC.; *pg.* 1493, *pg.* 947
STRAIGHT JACKET - Eyewear - OAKLEY, INC.; *pg.* 1840, *pg.* 86
STRAIGHT-LINE SIGNAL PATH - Software - HARMAN INTERNATIONAL INDUSTRIES, INCORPORATED; *pg.* 641, *pg.* 374
STRAIGHT MICROSTATS - Surgical Instrument - AMERICAN MEDICAL SYSTEMS, INC.; *pg.* 1399, *pg.* 238
STRAIGHT 'N EASY - Wire Strengthener - ELECTRON BEAM TECHNOLOGIES, INC.; *pg.* 1046, *pg.* 621
STRAIGHT STYLES - Hair Care Product - CONAIR CORPORATION; *pg.* 505, *pg.* 1055
STRAIGHT TO THE MAXX - Personal Care Electrical Product - HELEN OF TROY L.P.; *pg.* 511, *pg.* 1692
STRAIGHT WORKS - Hair Care Product - JOHN PAUL MITCHELL SYSTEMS; *pg.* 512, *pg.* 133
STRAIGHTFIRE - Laser Device - TRIMEDYNE, INC.; *pg.* 1432, *pg.* 121
STRAIGHTFLASH - Flashing Tape - E.I. DU PONT DE NEMOURS & COMPANY; *pg.* 1159, *pg.* 390
STRAIGHTFX - Hair Care Products - LUSTER PRODUCTS INC.; *pg.* 515, *pg.* 581
STRAIGHTOP - Lens - DANKER LABORATORIES INC.; *pg.* 1408, *pg.* 465
STRAIT SHADES - Hair Care Products - LUSTER PRODUCTS INC.; *pg.* 515, *pg.* 581
STRANAHAN'S COLORADO WHISKEY - Spirits - PROXIMO SPIRITS, INC.; *pg.* 1969, *pg.* 1076
STRAND-BY-STRAND - Hair Replacement - HAIR CLUB FOR MEN, LTD., INC.; *pg.* 511, *pg.* 411
STRAND LIGHTING - Lighting - PHILIPS LIGHTING; *pg.* 1303, *pg.* 806
STRANDFOAM - Plastic Foam - THE DOW CHEMICAL COMPANY; *pg.* 1157, *pg.* 898
STRANDLINK - Automatic Connection Equipment - MACLEAN-FOGG COMPANY INC.; *pg.* 1358, *pg.* 635
STRANDVISE - Automatic Connection Equipment - MACLEAN-FOGG COMPANY INC.; *pg.* 1358, *pg.* 635
STRANTERM - Glass & Ceramic Material - CORNING INCORPORATED; *pg.* 1122, *pg.* 1154
STRAP-TOGGLE - Wall Anchor - POWERS FASTENERS INC.; *pg.* 1059, *pg.* 1143
STRAPACKER - Strapper - BESSER COMPANY; *pg.* 1317, *pg.* 865
STRAPOLOGY - Bag - CALLAWAY GOLF COMPANY; *pg.* 1829, *pg.* 58
STRAPPY TANKINI - Clothing - K-SWISS; *pg.* 1837, *pg.* 306
STRAT - Pickups & Accessories - EMG, INC.; *pg.* 636, *pg.* 277
STRAT HH - Electric Guitar - FENDER MUSICAL INSTRUMENTS CORPORATION; *pg.* 547, *pg.* 21
STRAT HSS - Electric Guitar - FENDER MUSICAL INSTRUMENTS CORPORATION; *pg.* 547, *pg.* 21
STRATA - Carpet - BEAULIEU GROUP, LLC; *pg.* 917, *pg.* 529
STRATA - Textiles - BERNHARDT DESIGN; *pg.* 918, *pg.* 1381
STRATA - Switch - BROADCOM CORPORATION; *pg.* 364, *pg.* 108
STRATA - Software - CGI TECHNOLOGIES & SOLUTIONS INC.; *pg.* 371, *pg.* 1779
STRATA - Bath Accessory - CROSCILL, INC.; *pg.* 1122, *pg.* 1220
STRATA - Air Cleaning System - DONALDSON COMPANY, INC.; *pg.* 1329, *pg.* 917
STRATA - Lamination Material - DOW CHEMICAL; *pg.* 1156, *pg.* 1563
STRATA - Ion & Electron Beam - FEI COMPANY; *pg.* 1413, *pg.* 1498
STRATA - Ceramic Tile - SUMMITVILLE TILES, INC.; *pg.* 113, *pg.* 1475
STRATA BY TOP-FLITE - Golf Balls - CALLAWAY GOLF BALL OPERATIONS, INC.; *pg.* 1829, *pg.* 814
STRATA STAR 15 - Rotary Drilling Rig - THE GEORGE E. FAILING COMPANY; *pg.* 1340, *pg.* 1484
STRATA STAR 25 - Rotary Drilling Rig - THE GEORGE E. FAILING COMPANY; *pg.* 1340, *pg.* 1484
STRATA STAR 5 - Rotary Drilling Rig - THE GEORGE E. FAILING COMPANY; *pg.* 1340, *pg.* 1484
STRATACRAWLER SERIES - Crawler Mounted Machines - TELSMITH, INC.; *pg.* 1381, *pg.* 1871
STRATAGEM - Atomic Layer Deposition System - AIXTRON INC.; *pg.* 1310, *pg.* 283
STRATAGUARD - Insulating System - OWENS CORNING; *pg.* 102, *pg.* 1476
STRATAMAX - Wood Flooring Product - ARMSTRONG WORLD INDUSTRIES, INC.; *pg.* 914, *pg.* 1545
STRATAMIX - Fluid Handling System - GRACO, INC.; *pg.* 1342, *pg.* 935
STRATASWITCH - Semiconductors - BROADCOM CORPORATION; *pg.* 364, *pg.* 108
STRATAXGS - Computer Products - BROADCOM CORPORATION; *pg.* 364, *pg.* 108
STRATCO - Clean Fuel Technologies - E.I. DU PONT DE NEMOURS & COMPANY; *pg.* 1159, *pg.* 390
STRATE-LINE - Sterilization Product - PROPPER MANUFACTURING COMPANY, INC.; *pg.* 1586, *pg.* 1175
STRATEGIC EMPLOYEE BENEFITS - Group Health & Disability Insurance - THE NORTHWESTERN MUTUAL LIFE INSURANCE COMPANY; *pg.* 1212, *pg.* 1879
STRATEGIC FINANCE - Monthly Magazine for Corporate Accounting & Finance Professionals - INSTITUTE OF MANAGEMENT ACCOUNTANTS, INC.; *pg.* 144, *pg.* 1086
STRATEGIC TECHNOTES - Twice-monthly Technology Newsletter - INSTITUTE OF MANAGEMENT ACCOUNTANTS, INC.; *pg.* 144, *pg.* 1086
STRATEGIES FOR SERIOUS MONEY - Slogan - CALAMOS ASSET MANAGEMENT INC; *pg.* 728, *pg.* 635
STRATEGIST - Software - TERADYNE INC.; *pg.* 679, *pg.* 838
STRATEGO - Game - HASBRO, INC.; *pg.* 954, *pg.* 1603
STRATEGO LEGENDS - Toy & Game - HASBRO, INC.; *pg.* 954, *pg.* 1603
STRATEGY MACHINE - Credit Scoring Solution - FAIR ISAAC CORPORATION; *pg.* 1247, *pg.* 955
STRATEGY SERIES - Loudspeaker Mounting System - ATLAS SOUND; *pg.* 621, *pg.* 1692
STRATEGY.COM - Website - MICROSTRATEGY, INC.; *pg.* 1266, *pg.* 1809
STRATEGYWARE - Software System - FAIR ISAAC CORPORATION; *pg.* 1247, *pg.* 955
STRATEX - Engineered Laminated Structures - DELSTAR TECHNOLOGIES, INC.; *pg.* 1881, *pg.* 387
STRATEX GX - High-Density Field-Programmable Gate Array - ALTERA CORPORATION; *pg.* 348, *pg.* 237
STRATFORD - Rug - COURISTAN INC.; *pg.* 921, *pg.* 1067
STRATFORD - Fabric - SCALAMANDRE, INC.; *pg.* 941, *pg.* 1058
STRATFORD - Fabric - UNIROYAL ENGINEERED PRODUCTS; *pg.* 699, *pg.* 467
STRATHMORE - Paper - INTERNATIONAL PAPER COMPANY; *pg.* 1460, *pg.* 1644
STRATHMORE - Paper - MOHAWK FINE PAPERS, INC.; *pg.* 1464, *pg.* 1153
STRATHMORE - Fabric - SCALAMANDRE, INC.; *pg.* 941, *pg.* 1058
STRATHMORE ARTIST - Paper - INTERNATIONAL PAPER COMPANY; *pg.* 1460, *pg.* 1644
STRATIFIED FIELD - Creative Engineered Solution - LRAD CORPORATION; *pg.* 652, *pg.* 204
STRATIX - FPGA Device - ALTERA CORPORATION; *pg.* 348, *pg.* 237
STRATIX II - High-Density Field-Programmable Gate Array - ALTERA CORPORATION; *pg.* 348, *pg.* 237
STRATIX III - Programmable Gate Array - ALTERA CORPORATION; *pg.* 348, *pg.* 237
STRATIX IV - Programmable Gate Array - ALTERA CORPORATION; *pg.* 348, *pg.* 237
STRATOCASTER - Electric Guitar - FENDER MUSICAL INSTRUMENTS CORPORATION; *pg.* 547, *pg.* 21
STRATOCASTER HARD TAIL - Electric Guitar - FENDER MUSICAL INSTRUMENTS CORPORATION; *pg.* 547, *pg.* 21
STRATOCASTER LEFT HAND - Electric Guitar - FENDER MUSICAL INSTRUMENTS CORPORATION; *pg.* 547, *pg.* 21
STRATOCELL - Packaging Product - SEALED AIR CORPORATION; *pg.* 1468, *pg.* 1058
STRATOGREY - Plastic Bag - ELKAY PLASTICS COMPANY, INC.; *pg.* 1882, *pg.* 68
STRATOS - Furniture - BUSH INDUSTRIES INC.; *pg.* 919, *pg.* 1170
STRATOS - Aerosol Compressor - INVACARE CORPORATION; *pg.* 1546, *pg.* 1451
STRATOSPHERE CASINO, HOTEL & TOWER - Hotel & Casino - STRATOSPHERE CORPORATION; *pg.* 1115, *pg.* 1030
STRATTERA - Pharmaceutical Product - ELI LILLY AND COMPANY; *pg.* 1527, *pg.* 684
STRATTON - Brick & Tile Product - CHEROKEE BRICK & TILE COMPANY; *pg.* 75, *pg.* 535
STRATUM - Lens Coating System - GERBER SCIENTIFIC, INC.; *pg.* 1414, *pg.* 380
STRATUM - Software - SILVON SOFTWARE INC.; *pg.* 470, *pg.* 669
STRATUS - Furniture - ASHLEY FURNITURE INDUSTRIES, INC.; *pg.* 914, *pg.* 1852
STRATUS - EPI Thickness Monitor - NANOMETRICS INCORPORATED; *pg.* 1423, *pg.* 147
STRATUS CS - Diagnostic Product - SIEMENS HEALTHCARE DIAGNOSTICS; *pg.* 673, *pg.* 604
STRAUSS - Flatware - ONEIDA LTD; *pg.* 1129, *pg.* 1318
STRAW - Fabric - NEMSCHOFF, INC.; *pg.* 936, *pg.* 1890
STRAWBERIFF - Fragrance Ingredient - INTERNATIONAL FLAVORS & FRAGRANCES INC.; *pg.* 512, *pg.* 1244
STRAWBERRIES ALIVE - Fertilizer - GARDENS ALIVE!, INC.; *pg.* 1796, *pg.* 693
STRAWBERRIES WILD - Fruit Drink - JAMBA, INC.; *pg.* 1024, *pg.* 84
STRAWBERRRY ENERGIZER - Fruit Drink - JAMBA, INC.; *pg.* 1024, *pg.* 84
STRAWBERRY FLORAL MARGARITA - Flower Arrangement - 1-800-FLOWERS.COM, INC.; *pg.* 1758, *pg.* 1151
STRAWBERRY KIWI - Herb Tea - CELESTIAL SEASONINGS, INC.; *pg.* 846, *pg.* 310
STRAWBERRY LEMONADE - Container Grown Plant - MONROVIA GROWERS; *pg.* 1797, *pg.* 44
STRAWBERRY NIRVANA - Low Calorie Fruit Drink - JAMBA, INC.; *pg.* 1024, *pg.* 84
STRAWBERRY SURF RIDER - Fruit Drink - JAMBA, INC.; *pg.* 1024, *pg.* 84
STRAWBERRY TSUNAMI - Smoothie - JAMBA, INC.; *pg.* 1024, *pg.* 84
STRAWBERRY WHIRL - Fruit Drink - JAMBA, INC.; *pg.* 1024, *pg.* 84
STRAWMASTER - Agricultural Equipment - DEGELMAN INDUSTRIES LTD.; *pg.* 703, *pg.* 1962
STREAKER - Pet Supplies - HAPPY JACK INC.; *pg.* 1476, *pg.* 1390
STREAM - Tape & Reel - ENTEGRIS, INC.; *pg.* 1882, *pg.* 788
STREAM - Memory Bandwidth Measurement - INTEL CORPORATION; *pg.* 645, *pg.* 266
STREAM - Apparel - OAKLEY, INC.; *pg.* 1840, *pg.* 86
STREAMER - Stand Bag - DATREK GOLF; *pg.* 1832, *pg.* 1801
STREAMING - Internet Tool - AKAMAI TECHNOLOGIES, INC.; *pg.* 1226, *pg.* 807
STREAMING MAD AT DIRT - Slogan - RUG DOCTOR, LP; *pg.* 1373, *pg.* 1734
STREAMING PUBLISHER - Web Publishing Solution - ONSTREAM MEDIA CORPORATION; *pg.* 449, *pg.* 459
STREAMIUM - Docking Cradle - PHILIPS ELECTRONICS NORTH AMERICA; *pg.* 662, *pg.* 782
STREAMJET - Spray Nozzle - SPRAYING SYSTEMS CO.; *pg.* 1063, *pg.* 670
STREAMLAB - Diagnostic Product - SIEMENS HEALTHCARE DIAGNOSTICS; *pg.* 673, *pg.* 604
STREAMLIGHT JR. - Flashlights - STREAMLIGHT INC.; *pg.* 1306, *pg.* 1527
STREAMLIGHT LITEBOX - Truck Equipment - AMERICAN VAN EQUIPMENT INC.; *pg.* 199, *pg.* 1078
STREAMLINE - Electronic Components - MOLEX INCORPORATED; *pg.* 655, *pg.* 628
STREAMLINE - Suitcase - SAMSONITE CORPORATION;

pg. 11, *pg.* 830
STREAMLINE - Software - WASTE MANAGEMENT, INC.; *pg.* 1954, *pg.* 1716
STREAMLINE - Carburetion Product - WOODWARD, INC.; *pg.* 122, *pg.* 329
STREAMLINE PLATFORM AUTOMATION - Fully-Automated Account Opening Solution - JACK HENRY & ASSOCIATES, INC.; *pg.* 422, *pg.* 988
STREAMLINER - Wireless Telecommunication Product - SYNIVERSE HOLDINGS, INC.; *pg.* 479, *pg.* 475
STREAMLINING ENTERPRISE INFORMATION SUPPLY CHAINS - Slogan - ACTUATE CANADA; *pg.* 1225, *pg.* 1933
STREAMMASTER - Monitor - AKRON BRASS COMPANY; *pg.* 1311, *pg.* 1482
STREAMPACK - Integrated Circuits - AVAGO TECHNOLOGIES; *pg.* 358, *pg.* 238
STREAMSEAL - Butterfly Valve - RODNEY HUNT COMPANY; *pg.* 1372, *pg.* 840
STREAMSHIELD - Vents - PARKER CHOMERICS; *pg.* 662, *pg.* 862
STREAMTREAD - Footwear - SIMMS FISHING PRODUCTS CORP.; *pg.* 1845, *pg.* 1008
STREAMVIEW - Software System - MENTOR GRAPHICS CORPORATION; *pg.* 432, *pg.* 1510
STREAMWEAVER - Software - PITNEY BOWES INC.; *pg.* 454, *pg.* 376
STREET COURT - Portable Basketball Standards - LIFETIME PRODUCTS INC.; *pg.* 933, *pg.* 1751
STREET CUFF - Metal Security Locks - MASTER LOCK COMPANY LLC; *pg.* 1055, *pg.* 1884
STREET CUSTOMS - Magazine - PAISANO PUBLICATIONS, LLC; *pg.* 1674, *pg.* 38
STREET LINKS - Metal Locks - MASTER LOCK COMPANY LLC; *pg.* 1055, *pg.* 1884
STREET MOUNTAIN - Clothing - ABERCROMBIE & FITCH CO.; *pg.* 37, *pg.* 1466
STREET SMART - Emergency Response Guide - E.I. DU PONT DE NEMOURS & COMPANY; *pg.* 1159, *pg.* 390
STREET SMART - Surface Maintenance Machine - TENNANT COMPANY; *pg.* 1381, *pg.* 944
STREET/SOCKET - Plumbing Fittings - GENOVA PRODUCTS, INC.; *pg.* 83, *pg.* 875
STREET TECH - Day Pack - JANSPORT; *pg.* 1837, *pg.* 38
STREET TUNNEL RAMS - Manifolds - EDELBROCK CORPORATION; *pg.* 204, *pg.* 293
STREETEDITOR - Software - ENVIRONMENTAL SYSTEMS RESEARCH INSTITUTE INC.; *pg.* 393, *pg.* 188
STREETFINDER - Software - COBRA ELECTRONICS CORPORATION; *pg.* 629, *pg.* 572
STREETFINDER - Street Map Book - RAND MCNALLY & COMPANY; *pg.* 1679, *pg.* 661
STREETGEAR - Shirt and Trouser - BLAUER MANUFACTURING COMPANY, INC.; *pg.* 20, *pg.* 789
STREETPRO - Software - PITNEY BOWES SOFTWARE INC.; *pg.* 455, *pg.* 1346
STREETPRO BASIC - Australian Mapping System - PITNEY BOWES SOFTWARE INC.; *pg.* 455, *pg.* 1346
STREETSMART - Drinking Fountain - HAWS CORPORATION; *pg.* 56, *pg.* 1032
STREETSTARS - Community-based Street Hockey Program - DALLAS STARS L.P.; *pg.* 543, *pg.* 1697
STREGA - Liquore - SHAW ROSS INTERNATIONAL IMPORTERS; *pg.* 1970, *pg.* 449
STRENGTH BENEATH THE SURFACE - Gypsum Board - USG CORPORATION; *pg.* 118, *pg.* 594
STRENGTH GROWTH VISION - Slogan - GUARANTY BANK; *pg.* 764, *pg.* 1006
STRENGTH IN THE FACE OF ALZHEIMER'S - Pharmaceutical Product - PFIZER INC.; *pg.* 1581, *pg.* 1278
STRENGTH, INTEGRITY & VALUE - Tag Line - REXHALL INDUSTRIES, INC.; *pg.* 1710, *pg.* 121
STRENGTH ON YOUR SIDE - Tag Line - GENERAL DYNAMICS CORPORATION; *pg.* 228, *pg.* 1781
STRENGTH . PROTECTION . VIGILANCE - Slogan - SENTRY INSURANCE GROUP; *pg.* 1217, *pg.* 1895
STRENGTHPACK - Flexible Packaging Structures - VALERON STRENGTH FILMS; *pg.* 1891, *pg.* 1716
STREP A OIA MAX - Pharmaceutical Product - ALERE INC.; *pg.* 1488, *pg.* 849
STREP A TWIST - Pharmaceutical Product - ALERE INC.; *pg.* 1488, *pg.* 849
STREPSILS - Sore Throat Lozenges - RECKITT BENCKISER INC.; *pg.* 1136, *pg.* 1105
STREPTASE - Streptokinase - CSL BEHRING LLC; *pg.* 1520, *pg.* 1543
STREPTONASE-B - Pharmaceutical Product - ALERE INC.; *pg.* 1488, *pg.* 849
STREPTOZYME - Pharmaceutical Product - ALERE INC.; *pg.* 1488, *pg.* 849
STRESS-B - Sports Drink - ENERGY BRANDS, INC.; *pg.* 854, *pg.* 1227
STRESS-DEX - Animal Safety Product - NEOGEN CORPORATION; *pg.* 883, *pg.* 896
STRESS EEZ - Nutritional Supplement - PHARMAVITE LLC; *pg.* 1584, *pg.* 167
STRESS GLOOP - Exerciser - BROWN & BIGELOW, INC.; *pg.* 1624, *pg.* 959
STRESS TESTING CARD - Card to Measure Stress Level - PILGRIM PLASTIC PRODUCTS COMPANY; *pg.* 1887, *pg.* 803
STRESSEDMETAL - Management Services - XEROX CORPORATION; *pg.* 494, *pg.* 365
STRESSFREE - Health Care Product - HEALTH PRODUCTS CORPORATION; *pg.* 1540, *pg.* 1356
STRESSTABS - B-Complex Vitamin Product - ALERE INC.; *pg.* 1488, *pg.* 849
STRETCH - Delivery Trailer Style - HACKNEY INTERNATIONAL; *pg.* 178, *pg.* 1392
STRETCH AND FIT - Cover & Pad - HOME PRODUCTS INTERNATIONAL, INC.; *pg.* 1125, *pg.* 577
STRETCH CROSS HATCH - Apparel - OAKLEY, INC.; *pg.* 1840, *pg.* 86
STRETCH DOWN - Glove - KOMBI, LTD.; *pg.* 1838, *pg.* 1766
STRETCH LACE - Bikini - JOCKEY INTERNATIONAL, INC.; *pg.* 27, *pg.* 1861
STRETCH MARK - Cream - THE STEPHAN COMPANY; *pg.* 1597, *pg.* 426
STRETCH PACK - Skin Packaging - FLEX-O-GLASS, INC.; *pg.* 1457, *pg.* 574
STRETCH PLAID - Apparel - OAKLEY, INC.; *pg.* 1840, *pg.* 86
STRETCH REPEAT - Apparel - OAKLEY, INC.; *pg.* 1840, *pg.* 86
STRETCH RIB - Boxer - JOCKEY INTERNATIONAL, INC.; *pg.* 27, *pg.* 1861
STRETCH TAB - Elastic Laminates - TREDEGAR CORPORATION; *pg.* 1890, *pg.* 1804
STRETCH TECH - Glove Liner - KOMBI, LTD.; *pg.* 1838, *pg.* 1766
STRETCH-TO-LENGTH - Gas Line Heating System - WATLOW ELECTRIC MANUFACTURING COMPANY; *pg.* 1078, *pg.* 1004
STRETCH VIEW - Magnifying Lamp - DAZOR MANUFACTURING CORP.; *pg.* 1296, *pg.* 995
STRETCH WRAP - Security Tape - AMERICAN CASTING & MANUFACTURING CORPORATION; *pg.* 1312, *pg.* 1321
STRETCH YOUR LIMITS - Tagline - EVERI HOLDINGS INC.; *pg.* 749, *pg.* 1023
STRETCHFIT - Cap - UNDER ARMOUR, INC.; *pg.* 49, *pg.* 759
STRI-DEX - Pimple Prevention - BLISTEX, INC.; *pg.* 502, *pg.* 644
STRIANT - Pharmaceutical Product - JUNIPER PHARMACEUTICALS; *pg.* 1552, *pg.* 797
STRICKLY MISSION - Furniture - ASHLEY FURNITURE INDUSTRIES, INC.; *pg.* 914, *pg.* 1852
STRIDE - Chewing Gum - MONDELEZ INTERNATIONAL, INC.; *pg.* 878, *pg.* 601
STRIDE - Footwear - P.W. MINOR & SON, INC.; *pg.* 1816, *pg.* 1140
STRIDE-RITE - Package Closures - REYNOLDS CONSUMER PRODUCTS; *pg.* 1138, *pg.* 625
STRIDE RITE - Children's Shoes - THE STRIDE RITE CORPORATION; *pg.* 1820, *pg.* 828
STRIDE RITE - Footwear - WOLVERINE WORLD WIDE, INC.; *pg.* 1822, *pg.* 905
STRIDER - Footwear - COBIAN CORP.; *pg.* 1806, *pg.* 253
STRIKE IT RICH - Lottery Game - MASSACHUSETTS STATE LOTTERY; *pg.* 998, *pg.* 802
STRIKE PRO - Dead Blow Hammers - NUPLA CORPORATION; *pg.* 101, *pg.* 281
STRIKE ZONE - Hard Drive Protection System - DELL INC.; *pg.* 383, *pg.* 1737
STRIKEFORCE - Bait Casting Reels - DAIWA CORPORATION; *pg.* 1832, *pg.* 75
STRIKEGUARD - Material - GERBER SCIENTIFIC, INC.; *pg.* 1414, *pg.* 380
STRIKER - Gaming Product - GLD PRODUCTS, INC.; *pg.* 1835, *pg.* 1882
STRIKER - Footwear - LACROSSE FOOTWEAR, INC.; *pg.* 1811, *pg.* 1503
STRIKER - Filter - SELLSTROM MANUFACTURING CO.; *pg.* 1428, *pg.* 659
STRIKERS - Door Accessory - SOUTHCO, INC.; *pg.* 1063, *pg.* 1522
THE STRIKING PRICE - Financial Products - DOW JONES & COMPANY, INC.; *pg.* 1637, *pg.* 1225
STRING ALONG - Craft Kit - JANLYNN CORPORATION; *pg.* 696, *pg.* 815
STRING AND BOOK - Design - SCHOLASTIC INC.; *pg.* 1683, *pg.* 1288
STRINGLES - Cheese - COOPERATIVE REGIONS OF ORGANIC PRODUCER POOLS; *pg.* 850, *pg.* 1864
STRINGLINGER - Masonry Line Reel - C.H. HANSON COMPANY; *pg.* 1322, *pg.* 636
STRINGSTERS - String Cheese - LACTALIS AMERICAN GROUP; *pg.* 873, *pg.* 1140
STRION - Flashlight - STREAMLIGHT INC.; *pg.* 1306, *pg.* 1527
STRIP-A-WAY - Detergent - DELTA FOREMOST CHEMICAL CORPORATION; *pg.* 1155, *pg.* 1642
STRIP-ALL - Stripper - HILLYARD, INC.; *pg.* 331, *pg.* 990
STRIP & SHINE - Cleaner - CHURCH & DWIGHT CO., INC.; *pg.* 1153, *pg.* 1063
STRIP-EAZE - Floor Stripper - SWISHER HYGIENE INC.; *pg.* 336, *pg.* 1507
STRIP-N-SEAL - Envelopes - TENSION ENVELOPE CORPORATION; *pg.* 483, *pg.* 986
STRIP-RITE - Adhesive Coated Paper - SPINNAKER COATING, LLC; *pg.* 1470, *pg.* 1477
STRIP-TAC - Pressure Sensitive Sheet & Roll Products - SPINNAKER COATING, LLC; *pg.* 1470, *pg.* 1477
STRIP-TAC PLUS - Pressure Sensitive Sheet - SPINNAKER COATING, LLC; *pg.* 1470, *pg.* 1477
STRIP TITE - Sport Surface - ROBBINS, INC.; *pg.* 108, *pg.* 1425
STRIPAID - Solvent - DYNATEX INTERNATIONAL; *pg.* 635, *pg.* 277
STRIPBURGERS AT CAFE BA-BA-REEBA! - Casual Dining Restaurant - LETTUCE ENTERTAIN YOU ENTERPRISES, INC.; *pg.* 1735, *pg.* 580
STRIPE - Marking Paint - SEYMOUR OF SYCAMORE, INC.; *pg.* 1447, *pg.* 663
STRIPED V - Women's Clothing & Accessories - WOODEN SHIPS OF HOBOKEN; *pg.* 35, *pg.* 1315
STRIPES - Extension Cords - COLEMAN CABLE, INC.; *pg.* 1324, *pg.* 665
STRIPES - Convenience Stores - SUSSER HOLDINGS CORPORATION; *pg.* 985, *pg.* 1671
STRIPETTE - Glass & Ceramic Material - CORNING INCORPORATED; *pg.* 1122, *pg.* 1154
STRIPIR - Infrared Heater - PRECISION CONTROL SYSTEMS, INC./ RESEARCH INC.; *pg.* 1427, *pg.* 923
STRIPMASTER - Wire Stripper - IDEAL INDUSTRIES, INC.; *pg.* 1051, *pg.* 662
STRIPPAX - Sorbent Packet - MULTISORB TECHNOLOGIES, INC.; *pg.* 1570, *pg.* 1150
STRIPPER - Chemical Coating - ENTHONE INC.; *pg.* 1161, *pg.* 381
STRIPPGARD - Strippable Coating for Substrate Protection - PPG INDUSTRIES, INC.; *pg.* 1445, *pg.* 1579
STRIPRITE - Stripper - A BRITE COMPANY; *pg.* 1144, *pg.* 1697
STRIPSWITCH - Switch - TRANSICO INCORPORATED; *pg.* 682, *pg.* 49
STRIVE - Software - CAE INC.; *pg.* 226, *pg.* 1959
STRIVE RIDER - Surface Maintenance Machine - TENNANT COMPANY; *pg.* 1381, *pg.* 944
STROBE - Software - COMPUWARE CORPORATION; *pg.* 379, *pg.* 879
STROBETOOL - Software - COOPER WHEELOCK; *pg.* 630, *pg.* 1080
STROBOFRAME - Filter & Lens - THE TIFFEN COMPANY LLC; *pg.* 1432, *pg.* 1165
STROH'S - Beer - PABST BREWING COMPANY; *pg.* 258, *pg.* 137
STROKE - Apparel - OAKLEY, INC.; *pg.* 1840, *pg.* 86
STROKE OF LUCK - Game - WMS INDUSTRIES INC.; *pg.* 593, *pg.* 666
STROKES SELECT - Pet Product - PETSMART, INC.; *pg.* 1481, *pg.* 18
STROL - Footwear - PHOENIX FOOTWEAR GROUP, INC.;

pg. 1815, *pg.* 60
STROLL - Stockinette - SPECTRUM LABORATORIES INC.; *pg.* 1595, *pg.* 69
STRONG - Entertainment Lighting Product - BALLANTYNE STRONG, INC.; *pg.* 623, *pg.* 1013
STRONG - Interest Inventory Assessments - CPP, INC.; *pg.* 1631, *pg.* 153
STRONG GUARD - Cleaning Product - HILLYARD, INC.; *pg.* 331, *pg.* 990
STRONG MAN - Heavy Duty Basketball Rims - LIFETIME PRODUCTS INC.; *pg.* 933, *pg.* 1751
STRONG. SOLID. UNCHANGING VALUES - Slogan - CENTRAL VALLEY COMMUNITY BANCORP; *pg.* 733, *pg.* 93
STRONG TIES. STRONG SOLUTONS. - Tagline - GERMAN AMERICAN BANCORP, INC.; *pg.* 762, *pg.* 691
STRONGARM - Bicycle Accessories - SPECIALIZED BICYCLE COMPONENTS, INC.; *pg.* 1711, *pg.* 152
STRONGBOX - Box Blade - DEGELMAN INDUSTRIES LTD.; *pg.* 703, *pg.* 1962
STRONGHOLD - Rivets & Bolts - ALCOA INC.; *pg.* 65, *pg.* 1188
STRONGHOLD - Medical Device - MALLINCKRODT PHARMACEUTICALS; *pg.* 1557, *pg.* 978
STRONGHOLD - Anti-Disconnect Devices - MEDTRONIC; *pg.* 1563, *pg.* 183
STRONGHOLD - Hair Care Product - NU SKIN ENTERPRISES, INC.; *pg.* 518, *pg.* 1755
STRONGHOLD - Agricultural Product - PBI/GORDON CORPORATION; *pg.* 1176, *pg.* 985
STRONGID - Pharmaceutical Product - PFIZER INC.; *pg.* 1581, *pg.* 1278
STRONGMOMS - Infant Nutritional Formulas - ABBOTT LABORATORIES; *pg.* 1484, *pg.* 551
STRONGSEAL - Roofing Underlayment - MINERALS TECHNOLOGIES INC.; *pg.* 1173, *pg.* 617
STRONG.SOLID.SECURE - Tagline - CATHOLIC ORDER OF FORESTERS; *pg.* 1196, *pg.* 635
STRONGWOMEN - DVD - GAIAM, INC.; *pg.* 1532, *pg.* 334
STROOPS - Medical & Aesthetic Product - DYNATRONICS CORPORATION; *pg.* 1526, *pg.* 1757
STRUCTO-BASE - Plaster - USG CORPORATION; *pg.* 118, *pg.* 594
STRUCTO-GAUGE - Plaster - USG CORPORATION; *pg.* 118, *pg.* 594
STRUCTOCORE - Security Wall - USG CORPORATION; *pg.* 118, *pg.* 594
STRUCTOLITE - Calcined Gypsum - USG CORPORATION; *pg.* 118, *pg.* 594
STRUCTURALL - Saw Blade - THE DOALL COMPANY; *pg.* 1329, *pg.* 670
STRUCTURE - Vinyl Siding - PLY GEM SIDING GROUP; *pg.* 105, *pg.* 986
STRUCTURE - Apparel - SEARS HOLDINGS CORPORATION; *pg.* 1784, *pg.* 618
STRUCTUREPAK - Wood & Building Material - WEYERHAEUSER COMPANY; *pg.* 121, *pg.* 1820
STRUCTURES - Carpet - BEAULIEU GROUP, LLC; *pg.* 917, *pg.* 529
STRUCTURES - Lighting Fixture - PHILIPS LIGHTING; *pg.* 1303, *pg.* 806
STRUCTVIEW - Software - SCHLUMBERGER LIMITED; *pg.* 801, *pg.* 1714
STRUGGLES FOR JUSTICE - Educational Materials - SCHOLASTIC INC.; *pg.* 1683, *pg.* 1288
STRUMMERTIME - Apparel - VANS, INC.; *pg.* 1821, *pg.* 76
STRUT - Automotive Parts & Clothing - STRUT, LLC; *pg.* 190, *pg.* 199
STRUT FEELING - Shoe - AEROGROUP INTERNATIONAL, INC.; *pg.* 1803, *pg.* 1055
STRUTT - Men's Shoe - JACK SCHWARTZ SHOES, INC.; *pg.* 1810, *pg.* 1245
STRUTT LO - Men's Shoe - JACK SCHWARTZ SHOES, INC.; *pg.* 1810, *pg.* 1245
STRUTT LO SE - Men's Shoe - JACK SCHWARTZ SHOES, INC.; *pg.* 1810, *pg.* 1245
STRUTWALL - Window - ANDERSEN CORPORATION; *pg.* 67, *pg.* 916
STRYKECAM - In-Light Camera - STRYKER CORPORATION; *pg.* 1598, *pg.* 894
STRYKER - Trademark & ATV Tires - CARLISLE TIRE & WHEEL COMPANY; *pg.* 1880, *pg.* 1612
STRYKEVAC - Smoke Evacuation System - STRYKER CORPORATION; *pg.* 1598, *pg.* 894
STRYPEEZE - Coating Remover - THE SAVOGRAN COMPANY; *pg.* 1447, *pg.* 840
STS - Dry Vacuum System - AIR TECHNIQUES, INC.; *pg.* 1487, *pg.* 1178
STS - Glucose Monitoring System - DEXCOM INC; *pg.* 1524, *pg.* 202
STS - Software - DST SYSTEMS, INC.; *pg.* 388, *pg.* 982
STS - Medical Device - DYNATRONICS CORPORATION; *pg.* 1526, *pg.* 1757
STS - Herbicide - E.I. DU PONT DE NEMOURS & COMPANY; *pg.* 1159, *pg.* 390
STS - Sedan - GENERAL MOTORS COMPANY; *pg.* 175, *pg.* 881
STS - Clay Targets - REMINGTON ARMS COMPANY, LLC; *pg.* 1844, *pg.* 1382
STS-V - Sedan - GENERAL MOTORS COMPANY; *pg.* 175, *pg.* 881
STT-100 - Viscometer - BROOKFIELD ENGINEERING LABORATORIES, INC.; *pg.* 1403, *pg.* 833
STUART - Shoes - ALLEN-EDMONDS SHOE CORP.; *pg.* 1804, *pg.* 1887
STUART - Furniture - FLEXSTEEL INDUSTRIES, INC.; *pg.* 925, *pg.* 707
STUART CLARK - Furniture - BROWN JORDAN INTERNATIONAL COMPANY; *pg.* 919, *pg.* 740
STUART LITTLE - Game - ACTIVISION BLIZZARD, INC.; *pg.* 948, *pg.* 271
THE STUART NEWS - Newspaper - THE E.W. SCRIPPS COMPANY; *pg.* 1639, *pg.* 1412
STUART PLAID - Pillow and Throw - HERITAGE LACE INC.; *pg.* 694, *pg.* 711
STUBBLE DEVICE - Shaver - WAHL CLIPPER CORPORATION; *pg.* 524, *pg.* 662
STUBHUB! - Online Ticket Marketplace - STUBHUB, INC.; *pg.* 586, *pg.* 228
STUCCO SEAL - Paint - KELLY-MOORE PAINT COMPANY, INC.; *pg.* 1443, *pg.* 198
STUCCOMATE - Insulation - THE DOW CHEMICAL COMPANY; *pg.* 1157, *pg.* 898
STUD-TO-STUD - Vehicle Safety System - GROTE INDUSTRIES, INC.; *pg.* 206, *pg.* 693
STUDENT ACADEMY AWARDS - Awards - ACADEMY OF MOTION PICTURE ARTS & SCIENCES; *pg.* 526, *pg.* 46
STUDENT LOAN FUNDING - Magazine - SLM CORPORATION; *pg.* 804, *pg.* 388
STUDENTCAM - Audio Conferencing System - CLEARONE COMMUNICATIONS, INC.; *pg.* 629, *pg.* 1756
STUDENTGUARD - Travel Insurance - TRAVEL GUARD GROUP, INC.; *pg.* 1925, *pg.* 1895
STUDENTPLUS - Software - SUNGARD DATA SYSTEMS INC.; *pg.* 477, *pg.* 1592
STUDER - Audio & Video Product - HARMAN INTERNATIONAL INDUSTRIES, INCORPORATED; *pg.* 641, *pg.* 374
STUDIO - Bar Stools & Guest Chairs - BERNHARDT DESIGN; *pg.* 918, *pg.* 1381
STUDIO 38 - Commercial Lighting - SWIVELIER CO., INC.; *pg.* 1307, *pg.* 1142
STUDIO B - Women's Clothing - BLOOMINGDALE'S, INC.; *pg.* 1763, *pg.* 1204
STUDIO BEAM - Lighting Product - HIGH END SYSTEMS, INC.; *pg.* 1299, *pg.* 1663
STUDIO COLOR - Lighting Product - HIGH END SYSTEMS, INC.; *pg.* 1299, *pg.* 1663
STUDIO COMMAND - Lighting Product - HIGH END SYSTEMS, INC.; *pg.* 1299, *pg.* 1663
STUDIO DEPOT - Lighting Product - MOLE-RICHARDSON CO.; *pg.* 1302, *pg.* 103
STUDIO EASE - Misses' Dresses - KELLWOOD COMPANY; *pg.* 28, *pg.* 975
STUDIO FINISHES - Paint And Stain Product - BENJAMIN MOORE & CO.; *pg.* 1440, *pg.* 1085
STUDIO JAX - Misses' & Women's Casual & Career Sportswear - KELLWOOD COMPANY; *pg.* 28, *pg.* 975
STUDIO KING - Drums - GIBSON GUITAR CORP.; *pg.* 550, *pg.* 1650
STUDIO MAX - Strobe Light - PHOTOGENIC PROFESSIONAL LIGHTING; *pg.* 1426, *pg.* 556
STUDIO ONE - Video Game - INTERNATIONAL GAME TECHNOLOGY; *pg.* 957, *pg.* 1024
STUDIO PRO - Musical Instrument - PEAVEY ELECTRONICS CORPORATION; *pg.* 662, *pg.* 970
STUDIO REFORMER - Reformer - BALANCED BODY, INC.; *pg.* 1826, *pg.* 195
STUDIO SERIES - Video Consoles - LUXOR CORP.; *pg.* 428, *pg.* 666
STUDIO SPOT - Lighting Product - HIGH END SYSTEMS, INC.; *pg.* 1299, *pg.* 1663
STUDIO VALUE COLLECTION - Oil Painting Equipment - MARTIN/F. WEBER COMPANY; *pg.* 962, *pg.* 1567
STUDIODEOT.COM - Lighting Product - MOLE-RICHARDSON CO.; *pg.* 1302, *pg.* 103
STUDIOPLUS DELUXE STUDIOS - Hotel - EXTENDED STAY HOTELS LLC; *pg.* 1091, *pg.* 1622
STUDIOSTREAM - Software - R.R. DONNELLEY & SONS COMPANY; *pg.* 1682, *pg.* 589
STUDS - Footwear - STEVEN MADDEN, LTD.; *pg.* 1819, *pg.* 1176
STUDYTRAK - Software - DATATRAK INTERNATIONAL, INC.; *pg.* 383, *pg.* 1462
THE STUFF YOU NEED OUT HERE - Tagline - TRACTOR SUPPLY COMPANY; *pg.* 708, *pg.* 1627
STUFFABLES - Kitchenware - TUPPERWARE BRANDS CORPORATION; *pg.* 1139, *pg.* 456
STUFFED CRUST - Food Product - PIZZA INN, INC.; *pg.* 1745, *pg.* 1746
STUFFIT DELUXE - Software - SMITH MICRO SOFTWARE, INC.; *pg.* 471, *pg.* 41
STUFFIT ENGINE - Software - SMITH MICRO SOFTWARE, INC.; *pg.* 471, *pg.* 41
STUFFIT EXPANDER - Software - SMITH MICRO SOFTWARE, INC.; *pg.* 471, *pg.* 41
STUFFIT EXPRESS - Software - SMITH MICRO SOFTWARE, INC.; *pg.* 471, *pg.* 41
STUFFIT LITE - Software - SMITH MICRO SOFTWARE, INC.; *pg.* 471, *pg.* 41
STULLER STUDIO - Custom Jewelry Resource - STULLER, INC.; *pg.* 13, *pg.* 745
STULSKI - Vodka - LAIRD & COMPANY, INC.; *pg.* 1966, *pg.* 1119
STUMP-OUT - Tree Stump Burner - BONIDE PRODUCTS, INC.; *pg.* 1794, *pg.* 1320
STUMPJUMPER - Bicycle Tire - SPECIALIZED BICYCLE COMPONENTS, INC.; *pg.* 1711, *pg.* 152
STURD-FLOOR - Building Product - BLUELINX HOLDINGS, INC.; *pg.* 70, *pg.* 491
STURD-I-FLOOR - Structural Panels - GEORGIA-PACIFIC LLC; *pg.* 1458, *pg.* 507
STURDIKWIK - Workstations & Computer Enclosures - KEWAUNEE SCIENTIFIC CORPORATION; *pg.* 931, *pg.* 1391
STURDILITE - Engineering Work Station - KEWAUNEE SCIENTIFIC CORPORATION; *pg.* 931, *pg.* 1391
STURDY SWEEP - Floor Care Product - BISSELL HOMECARE, INC.; *pg.* 52, *pg.* 887
STURM, RUGER - Pistols & Revolvers - STURM, RUGER & COMPANY, INC.; *pg.* 1846, *pg.* 371
STX - Fluid Handling System - GRACO, INC.; *pg.* 1342, *pg.* 935
STX1 - Searchlights - BALLANTYNE STRONG, INC.; *pg.* 623, *pg.* 1013
STYL-SAFE - Spectacle - MCR SAFETY; *pg.* 1422, *pg.* 1630
STYLE - Paperboard - WESTROCK COMPANY; *pg.* 1472, *pg.* 1805
STYLE-AIRE - Styler/Dryer - JARDEN CONSUMER SOLUTIONS; *pg.* 57, *pg.* 412
STYLE AMERICA - Hair Salons - REGIS CORPORATION; *pg.* 521, *pg.* 941
STYLE & CO. - Sportswear - MACY'S, INC.; *pg.* 1778, *pg.* 1417
STYLE-RIB - Metal Building Product - CENTRIA, INC.; *pg.* 74, *pg.* 1554
STYLE WEEKLY - Magazine - STYLE WEEKLY INC.; *pg.* 1690, *pg.* 1804
STYLECOAT - Chemical Product - OMNOVA SOLUTIONS INC; *pg.* 1176, *pg.* 1453
STYLE.COM - Fashion Site - CONDE NAST DIGITAL; *pg.* 1237, *pg.* 1217
STYLE.COM - Website - CONDE NAST PUBLICATIONS, INC.; *pg.* 1629, *pg.* 1217
STYLED FOR LIVING - Carpet - BEAULIEU GROUP, LLC; *pg.* 917, *pg.* 529
STYLELINE - Wall Panel - BLUELINX HOLDINGS, INC.; *pg.* 70, *pg.* 491
STYLELINE - Garage Door - WAYNE-DALTON CORP.; *pg.* 120, *pg.* 1465
STYLELITE - Camera - EASTMAN KODAK COMPANY; *pg.* 1408, *pg.* 1333
STYLEMATE - Bathtub Wall - E.L. MUSTEE & SONS, INC.; *pg.* 1124, *pg.* 1430
STYLER DRYER - Hair Care Product - CONAIR

CORPORATION; *pg.* 505, *pg.* 1055
STYLERS - Graphic Accents - LUND INTERNATIONAL, INC.; *pg.* 211, *pg.* 526
STYLEVIEW - Computer Cart - ERGOTRON, INC.; *pg.* 395, *pg.* 960
STYLEWRITER - Ink Jet Printer - APPLE INC.; *pg.* 350, *pg.* 73
STYLINER - Trimmer - ANDIS COMPANY; *pg.* 498, *pg.* 1895
STYLINER - Marking System - GEORGE T. SCHMIDT, INC.; *pg.* 1340, *pg.* 637
STYLINER MARK - Marking System - GEORGE T. SCHMIDT, INC.; *pg.* 1340, *pg.* 637
STYLINFOAM - Hair Care Product - NU SKIN ENTERPRISES, INC.; *pg.* 518, *pg.* 1755
STYLING CREME - Hair Care Product - JOHN PAUL MITCHELL SYSTEMS; *pg.* 512, *pg.* 133
STYLING SERUM - Hair Care Product - JOHN PAUL MITCHELL SYSTEMS; *pg.* 512, *pg.* 133
STYLINGEL - Hair Care Product - NU SKIN ENTERPRISES, INC.; *pg.* 518, *pg.* 1755
STYLIST - Pen - YASUTOMO & CO.; *pg.* 497, *pg.* 280
STYLIZED X DESIGN - Software - XEROX CORPORATION; *pg.* 494, *pg.* 365
STYLIZED X DESIGN, PIXELATED PORTION - Software - XEROX CORPORATION; *pg.* 494, *pg.* 365
STYLUS - Flashlight - STREAMLIGHT INC.; *pg.* 1306, *pg.* 1527
STYLUS COLOR 1520 - Ink Jet Prints - EPSON AMERICA INC.; *pg.* 394, *pg.* 122
STYLUS COLOR 3000 - Ink Jet Prints - EPSON AMERICA INC.; *pg.* 394, *pg.* 122
STYLUS COLOR 400 - Ink Jet Prints - EPSON AMERICA INC.; *pg.* 394, *pg.* 122
STYLUS COLOR 600 - Ink Jet Prints - EPSON AMERICA INC.; *pg.* 394, *pg.* 122
STYLUS COLOR 800 - Ink Jet Printer - EPSON AMERICA INC.; *pg.* 394, *pg.* 122
STYLUS PHOTO 700 EX - Ink Jet Prints - EPSON AMERICA INC.; *pg.* 394, *pg.* 122
STYLUS PRO - Flashlight - STREAMLIGHT INC.; *pg.* 1306, *pg.* 1527
STYLUS PRO 5000 - Digital Proofing System - EPSON AMERICA INC.; *pg.* 394, *pg.* 122
STYLUS REACH - Flashlight - STREAMLIGHT INC.; *pg.* 1306, *pg.* 1527
STYLUS STUDIO XML - Adapter Framework - PROGRESS SOFTWARE CORPORATION; *pg.* 457, *pg.* 786
STYREX - Petrochemical Processing Aids - GE WATER & PROCESS TECHNOLOGIES; *pg.* 1339, *pg.* 1588
STYROACE - Insulation - THE DOW CHEMICAL COMPANY; *pg.* 1157, *pg.* 898
STYROFOAM - Insulation Products - THE DOW CHEMICAL COMPANY; *pg.* 1157, *pg.* 898
STYROFOM - Building Product - BLUELINX HOLDINGS, INC.; *pg.* 70, *pg.* 491
STYRON - Resin - THE DOW CHEMICAL COMPANY; *pg.* 1157, *pg.* 898
STYRON A-TECH - Resin - THE DOW CHEMICAL COMPANY; *pg.* 1157, *pg.* 898
STYROSUN - Chemical Product - NOVA CHEMICALS CORPORATION; *pg.* 1175, *pg.* 1904
SU-90 - Wellhead System - DRIL-QUIP, INC.; *pg.* 1330, *pg.* 1704
SU-902 UNITIZED WELLHEAD SYSTEMS - Surface Equipment - DRIL-QUIP, INC.; *pg.* 1330, *pg.* 1704
SU VOCE - Beverages - THE COCA-COLA COMPANY; *pg.* 240, *pg.* 493
SUAV - Vehicle Product - AEROVIRONMENT, INC.; *pg.* 223, *pg.* 150
SUAVE - Footwear - COBIAN CORP.; *pg.* 1806, *pg.* 253
SUAVE - Hair Care Products - UNILEVER UNITED STATES, INC.; *pg.* 904, *pg.* 1061
SUAVE - Fluoropolymer Coating System - WHITFORD WORLDWIDE COMPANY; *pg.* 1185, *pg.* 1529
SUAVECITO - Fabric Softener - BLUE CROSS LABORATORIES; *pg.* 326, *pg.* 277
SUAVITEL - Fabric Care Product - COLGATE-PALMOLIVE COMPANY; *pg.* 504, *pg.* 1215
SUB-CELL - Software - BIO-RAD LABORATORIES, INC.; *pg.* 1504, *pg.* 101
SUB-G - Oral Hygiene Aids - SUNSTAR AMERICAS INC.; *pg.* 1599, *pg.* 591
SUB-HUB - Reprographic Product - AMERICAN REPROGRAPHICS COMPANY; *pg.* 1616, *pg.* 303
SUB-ZERO - Tools - VAUGHAN & BUSHNELL MANUFACTURING COMPANY, INC.; *pg.* 1066, *pg.* 616
SUB-ZERO FREEZER - Freezers & Built in Refrigerator Equipment - SUB ZERO WOLF; *pg.* 60, *pg.* 1867
SUBA - Polishing Pad - DOW CHEMICAL; *pg.* 1156, *pg.* 1563
SUBDOMAIN - Computer Software - NOVELL INC.; *pg.* 446, *pg.* 852
SUBJECT - Apparel - OAKLEY, INC.; *pg.* 1840, *pg.* 86
SUBLIMATED CREW - Clothing - K-SWISS; *pg.* 1837, *pg.* 306
SUBLIMATED POLO - Clothing - K-SWISS; *pg.* 1837, *pg.* 306
SUBLIMAZE - Pharmaceutical Product - AKORN, INC.; *pg.* 1488, *pg.* 622
SUBLIMINAL - Carpet - BEAULIEU GROUP, LLC; *pg.* 917, *pg.* 529
SUBONONE FILM - Partial Opioid Antagonist - RECKITT BENCKISER INC.; *pg.* 1136, *pg.* 1105
SUBOXONE - Pharmaceutical Preparation - MERCK & CO., INC.; *pg.* 1566, *pg.* 1077
SUBSCRIPTION MANAGER - Software - ERESEARCH TECHNOLOGY INC.; *pg.* 1243, *pg.* 1564
SUBSEA - Landing String - SCHLUMBERGER LIMITED; *pg.* 801, *pg.* 1714
SUBSEA TEMPLATE SYSTEMS - Subsea Equipment - DRIL-QUIP, INC.; *pg.* 1330, *pg.* 1704
SUBSEA TIE-BACK SYSTEM TO FIXED PLATFORM - Subsea Equipment - DRIL-QUIP, INC.; *pg.* 1330, *pg.* 1704
SUBSEA TIE-BACK SYSTEM TO TLP/SPAR - Subsea Equipment - DRIL-QUIP, INC.; *pg.* 1330, *pg.* 1704
SUBSITE - Underground Construction Equipment - CHARLES MACHINE WORKS, INC.; *pg.* 1322, *pg.* 1488
SUBSTANCE 257 - Apparel Technology - BROOKS SPORTS INC.; *pg.* 1805, *pg.* 1818
SUBSTRAL - Lawn & Garden Products - THE SCOTTS MIRACLE-GRO COMPANY; *pg.* 1799, *pg.* 1459
SUBTLE EFFECTS - Cosmetic Product - NU SKIN ENTERPRISES, INC.; *pg.* 518, *pg.* 1755
SUBURBAN - Extended Stay Hotels - CHOICE HOTELS INTERNATIONAL, INC.; *pg.* 1086, *pg.* 775
SUBURBAN - Sport Utility Vehicle - GENERAL MOTORS COMPANY; *pg.* 175, *pg.* 881
SUBURBAN - Weekly Publication - GREATER MEDIA NEWSPAPERS, INC.; *pg.* 1646, *pg.* 1071
SUBURBAN PROPANE - Gas Appliance Services - SUBURBAN PROPANE PARTNERS, L.P.; *pg.* 113, *pg.* 1132
SUBUTEX - Pharmaceutical Preparation - MERCK & CO., INC.; *pg.* 1566, *pg.* 1077
SUBWAY - Infloor Duct System - SCHNEIDER ELECTRIC USA, INC.; *pg.* 1306, *pg.* 650
SUBWAY - Deli-Style Restaurant Franchises - SUBWAY RESTAURANTS; *pg.* 1751, *pg.* 356
SUBWAY CLUB - Sliced Turkey Breast, Roast Beef & Ham Sandwich - SUBWAY RESTAURANTS; *pg.* 1751, *pg.* 356
SUBWAY FRESH FIT - Low-Fat Menu - SUBWAY RESTAURANTS; *pg.* 1751, *pg.* 356
SUBWAY MELT - Turkey, Ham, Melted Cheese & Bacon Sandwich - SUBWAY RESTAURANTS; *pg.* 1751, *pg.* 356
SUBWAY SELECTS - Sandwich Combination Meal - SUBWAY RESTAURANTS; *pg.* 1751, *pg.* 356
SUBZERO - Bicycle Accessories - SPECIALIZED BICYCLE COMPONENTS, INC.; *pg.* 1711, *pg.* 152
SUC - Natural Gas - SOUTHERN UNION COMPANY; *pg.* 1952, *pg.* 1715
SUCARYL - Sweetening Ingredient - MERISANT COMPANY; *pg.* 876, *pg.* 581
SUCCESS - Dental Product - DENTSPLY INTERNATIONAL INC.; *pg.* 1522, *pg.* 1596
SUCCESS - Horse Feeds - KENT NUTRITION GROUP; *pg.* 1477, *pg.* 710
SUCCESS - Instant Rice - RIVIANA FOODS INC.; *pg.* 892, *pg.* 1713
SUCCESS BY YOUR STANDARDS - Slogan - QUESTAR ASSESSMENT, INC.; *pg.* 1679, *pg.* 1143
SUCCESS ON DEMAND - Slogan - SALESFORCE.COM, INC.; *pg.* 1278, *pg.* 226
SUCCESS WITH TYPING - Educational Materials - SCHOLASTIC INC.; *pg.* 1683, *pg.* 1288
SUCCESS WITH WRITING - Educational Materials - SCHOLASTIC INC.; *pg.* 1683, *pg.* 1288
SUCCESSFOAL - Horse Products - KENT NUTRITION GROUP; *pg.* 1477, *pg.* 710
SUCCESSFUL FARMING - Magazine - MEREDITH CORPORATION; *pg.* 1663, *pg.* 705
SUCCESSFUL READER - Educational Materials - RENAISSANCE LEARNING, INC.; *pg.* 607, *pg.* 1899
SUCCESS.NOT SOFTWARE - Slogan - SALESFORCE.COM, INC.; *pg.* 1278, *pg.* 226
SUCHARD - Chocolate - MONDELEZ INTERNATIONAL, INC.; *pg.* 878, *pg.* 601
SUCKLE - Dairy Feed - MANNA PRO CORPORATION; *pg.* 1478, *pg.* 975
SUCOS MAIS - Beverages - THE COCA-COLA COMPANY; *pg.* 240, *pg.* 493
SUCTION-LOCK SHOWER ORGANIZERS - Shower Organizer - HOME PRODUCTS INTERNATIONAL, INC.; *pg.* 1125, *pg.* 577
SUCTIONLOCK - Shower Organizer - HOME PRODUCTS INTERNATIONAL, INC.; *pg.* 1125, *pg.* 577
SUDACARE - Cold Medicines - MCNEIL-PPC, INC.; *pg.* 1560, *pg.* 1533
SUDAFED - Cold, Flu & Sinus Medications - JOHNSON & JOHNSON; *pg.* 1549, *pg.* 1091
SUDAFED Cold, Sinus & Allergy Medicine - MCNEIL-PPC, INC.; *pg.* 1560, *pg.* 1533
SUDDEN CHANGE - Skin Care Product - CCA INDUSTRIES, INC.; *pg.* 503, *pg.* 1114
SUDDENLY SALAD - Dry Boxed Salad Mixes - GENERAL MILLS, INC.; *pg.* 828, *pg.* 933
SUDOKU - Lottery Game - IOWA LOTTERY; *pg.* 996, *pg.* 705
SUDOKU WORLD - Game - UNIVERSITY GAMES CORPORATION; *pg.* 969, *pg.* 230
SUDS-N-KLEEN - Automotive Cleaner - DELTA FOREMOST CHEMICAL CORPORATION; *pg.* 1155, *pg.* 1642
SUEDETEX - Paper & Nonwoven Material - FIBERMARK INC.; *pg.* 1457, *pg.* 1764
SUERORAL - Pharmaceutical Product - FLEET LABORATORIES; *pg.* 1531, *pg.* 1787
SUFENTA - Pharmaceutical Product - AKORN, INC.; *pg.* 1488, *pg.* 622
SUFFOLK - Lighting - ETHAN ALLEN INTERIORS INC.; *pg.* 924, *pg.* 343
SUFIO - Architectural Fixtures - BALLANTYNE STRONG, INC.; *pg.* 623, *pg.* 1013
SUG - Gloves - WELLS LAMONT CORPORATION; *pg.* 15, *pg.* 638
SUGA-LIK - Liquid Feed Product - UNITED STATES SUGAR CORPORATION; *pg.* 907, *pg.* 417
SUGAR & SPICE - Slots - INTERNATIONAL GAME TECHNOLOGY; *pg.* 957, *pg.* 1024
SUGAR BABIES - Caramel Candies - TOOTSIE ROLL INDUSTRIES, INC.; *pg.* 1863, *pg.* 591
SUGAR CONTROL - Nutritional Supplement - NATURAL ORGANICS, INC.; *pg.* 1571, *pg.* 1181
SUGAR CURE - Salt - DOW CHEMICAL; *pg.* 1156, *pg.* 1563
SUGAR DAD - Shoe - AEROGROUP INTERNATIONAL, INC.; *pg.* 1803, *pg.* 1055
SUGAR DADDY - Candy - TOOTSIE ROLL INDUSTRIES, INC.; *pg.* 1863, *pg.* 591
SUGAR FREE DELIGHT - Sugar-Free Candy Assortment - ROCKY MOUNTAIN CHOCOLATE FACTORY, INC.; *pg.* 1032, *pg.* 324
SUGAR-FREE DELIGHTS - Candy - LIBERTY ORCHARDS CO., INC.; *pg.* 1857, *pg.* 1819
SUGAR FREE ROCA - Net Carb - BROWN & HALEY; *pg.* 1851, *pg.* 1820
SUGAR N SPICE - Carpet - BEAULIEU GROUP, LLC; *pg.* 917, *pg.* 529
SUGAR-NO.11 - Agriculture Exchange - INTERCONTINENTALEXCHANGE, INC.; *pg.* 769, *pg.* 512
SUGAR-NO.16 - Agriculture Exchange - INTERCONTINENTALEXCHANGE, INC.; *pg.* 769, *pg.* 512
SUGAR PIE - Apparel - VANS, INC.; *pg.* 1821, *pg.* 76
SUGAR PLANET - Toys - MGA ENTERTAINMENT, INC.; *pg.* 964, *pg.* 300
SUGAR PLUM SPICE - Herb Tea - CELESTIAL SEASONINGS, INC.; *pg.* 846, *pg.* 310
SUGAR PUFFS - Cereal - THE QUAKER OATS COMPANY; *pg.* 834, *pg.* 588
SUGAR VANILLA - Fragrance - PARFUMS DE COEUR LTD.; *pg.* 519, *pg.* 376
SUGARDALE - Meats/Meat Products - FRESH MARK, INC.; *pg.* 856, *pg.* 1461
SUGARED PLUMS - Candle - THE YANKEE CANDLE COMPANY, INC.; *pg.* 1792, *pg.* 843
SUGARFIX - Spa Product - ORLY INTERNATIONAL, INC.; *pg.* 518, *pg.* 137
SUGARLOAF - Footwear - EASTLAND SHOE

CORPORATION; *pg.* 1808, *pg.* 750
SUGUS - Gum - WM. WRIGLEY JR. COMPANY; *pg.* 1863, *pg.* 596
SUI - Insurance - PAYCHEX, INC.; *pg.* 792, *pg.* 1336
SUICIDE SQUAD - Character - DC COMICS, INC.; *pg.* 1633, *pg.* 1221
SUISSE - Milk Chocolate - PROMOTION IN MOTION, INC.; *pg.* 1861, *pg.* 1052
SUITCASE - Wire Feeder - MILLER ELECTRIC MANUFACTURING CO.; *pg.* 1361, *pg.* 1852
SUITECONSULTING - Professional Services - NETSUITE, INC.; *pg.* 1270, *pg.* 255
SUITEFLEX - Software - NETSUITE, INC.; *pg.* 1270, *pg.* 255
SUITESCRIPT - Software - NETSUITE, INC.; *pg.* 1270, *pg.* 255
SUITESUCCESS - Professional Services - NETSUITE, INC.; *pg.* 1270, *pg.* 255
SUITESUPPORT - Professional Services - NETSUITE, INC.; *pg.* 1270, *pg.* 255
SUITETRAINING - Professional Services - NETSUITE, INC.; *pg.* 1270, *pg.* 255
SUL-RAY - Acne Treatment Products - AT LAST NATURALS, INC.; *pg.* 499, *pg.* 1347
SULAWESI-KALOSI - Coffee - PEET'S COFFEE & TEA, INC.; *pg.* 1029, *pg.* 85
SULFATREAT - Gas Conditioning Product - CAMERON INTERNATIONAL; *pg.* 1151, *pg.* 1702
SULFAVER - Chemical Reagent - HACH COMPANY; *pg.* 1415, *pg.* 334
SULFOBETAINE - Amphoteric Sulfobetaine - HENKEL CORPORATION; *pg.* 1165, *pg.* 1535
SULFONIC - Chemical Product - STEPAN COMPANY; *pg.* 1182, *pg.* 643
SULFONYLUREA-TOLERANT SOYBEAN - Soybean Seed Product - MONSANTO; *pg.* 1798, *pg.* 971
SULFOTEX - Sulphaten - HENKEL CORPORATION; *pg.* 1165, *pg.* 1535
SULFUR - Apparel - OAKLEY, INC.; *pg.* 1840, *pg.* 86
SULFUR-8 - Hair Products - J. STRICKLAND & COMPANY; *pg.* 512, *pg.* 970
SULFUR GUARD - Disease Control Product - GARDENS ALIVE!, INC.; *pg.* 1796, *pg.* 693
SULFUSORB - Activated Carbon Product - CALGON CARBON CORPORATION; *pg.* 1151, *pg.* 1574
SULLIVAN - Lighting - ETHAN ALLEN INTERIORS INC.; *pg.* 924, *pg.* 343
SULLIVAN - Comfort Bilevel Device - RESMED INC.; *pg.* 1589, *pg.* 207
SULLIVAN'S STEAKHOUSE - Steak Houses - LONE STAR STEAKHOUSE & SALOON, INC.; *pg.* 1736, *pg.* 1733
SULSIM - Software - ASPEN TECHNOLOGY, INC.; *pg.* 354, *pg.* 804
SULTAN - Rug - COURISTAN INC.; *pg.* 921, *pg.* 1067
SULTAN - Furniture - JASPER GROUP; *pg.* 930, *pg.* 691
SULTRIN - Healthcare Product - JOHNSON & JOHNSON; *pg.* 1549, *pg.* 1091
SULWHASOO - Skin Care Products - AMOREPACIFIC US, INC.; *pg.* 498, *pg.* 1195
SUMA - Machine Warewashing - DIVERSEY, INC.; *pg.* 1123, *pg.* 1896
SUMA - Hardware & Software - POLYWELL COMPUTERS, INC.; *pg.* 456, *pg.* 280
SUMAC RIDGE - Wine - CONSTELLATION BRANDS CANADA; *pg.* 1960, *pg.* 1925
SUMARE - Industrial Coatings - THE SHERWIN-WILLIAMS COMPANY; *pg.* 1447, *pg.* 1435
SUMARI - Ceramic Tile - WALKER & ZANGER, INC.; *pg.* 119, *pg.* 281
SUMATRA - Coffee - PEET'S COFFEE & TEA, INC.; *pg.* 1029, *pg.* 85
SUMATRA DRAGONFRUIT - Beverage - BAI BRANDS; *pg.* 238, *pg.* 1073
SUMAVEL DOSEPRO - Pharmaceutical Product - ZOGENIX, INC.; *pg.* 1612, *pg.* 211
SUMMA-SINO - Rugs - COURISTAN INC.; *pg.* 921, *pg.* 1067
SUMMER ALE - Seasonal Beer - THE BROOKLYN BREWERY; *pg.* 239, *pg.* 1145
SUMMER BERRY - Granola - KASHI COMPANY; *pg.* 830, *pg.* 119
SUMMER BLONDE - Hair Lightener - P&G-CLAIROL, INC.; *pg.* 519, *pg.* 1418
SUMMER CHILLS - Season Sponsor - ALLEY THEATRE; *pg.* 527, *pg.* 1699
SUMMER COOLERS - Cotton Capris - HABAND COMPANY, INC.; *pg.* 1772, *pg.* 1099
SUMMER FRESH - Candle - THE YANKEE CANDLE COMPANY, INC.; *pg.* 1792, *pg.* 843
SUMMER FRUIT - Fruit & Vegetable Product - GIUMARRA VINEYARDS CORPORATION; *pg.* 1964, *pg.* 45
SUMMER FUN - Above Ground Pools - POLYAIR INTER PACK INC.; *pg.* 1467, *pg.* 1941
SUMMER GARDEN - Embroidered Pant Set - HABAND COMPANY, INC.; *pg.* 1772, *pg.* 1099
SUMMER GLOW - Sunless Tanning Product - NEUTROGENA CORPORATION; *pg.* 517, *pg.* 137
SUMMER HOUSE - Iced Tea - PEET'S COFFEE & TEA, INC.; *pg.* 1029, *pg.* 85
SUMMER IS JUST AROUND THE CORNER - Slogan - TRUE VALUE COMPANY; *pg.* 1065, *pg.* 592
SUMMER OF LUCK - Games - PENN NATIONAL GAMING, INC.; *pg.* 574, *pg.* 1595
SUMMER RAIN - Bath & Plumbing Product - JACUZZI BRANDS CORPORATION; *pg.* 554, *pg.* 65
SUMMER SAFARI - Coffee - KEURIG GREEN MOUNTAIN, INC.; *pg.* 868, *pg.* 1768
SUMMER SNOW - Container Grown Plant - MONROVIA GROWERS; *pg.* 1797, *pg.* 44
SUMMER SOLSTICE - Game - WMS INDUSTRIES INC.; *pg.* 593, *pg.* 666
SUMMER SONG - Container Grown Plant - MONROVIA GROWERS; *pg.* 1797, *pg.* 44
SUMMER SORBET - Decorative Fragrance - AROMATIQUE INC.; *pg.* 499, *pg.* 32
SUMMER SPLASH - Insect Repellent - S.C. JOHNSON & SON, INC.; *pg.* 334, *pg.* 1889
SUMMER SUCCESS - Summer School Programs - HOUGHTON MIFFLIN HARCOURT PUBLISHING COMPANY; *pg.* 1651, *pg.* 796
SUMMER VACATION - Educational Activity Books - ENTERTAINMENT PUBLICATIONS, INC.; *pg.* 1639, *pg.* 910
SUMMERAIRE - Cleaning Products - CLAYTON INDUSTRIES CO.; *pg.* 1323, *pg.* 66
SUMMERIZER - Lawn Fertilizer - THE SCOTTS MIRACLE-GRO COMPANY; *pg.* 1799, *pg.* 1459
SUMMER'S EVE - Feminine Care - FLEET LABORATORIES; *pg.* 1531, *pg.* 1787
SUMMERSET - Table Textile - HERITAGE LACE INC.; *pg.* 694, *pg.* 711
SUMMERTIME PRO - Paint Brush - DUNN-EDWARDS CORPORATION; *pg.* 1442, *pg.* 129
SUMMIT - Power Supply System - ADVANCED ENERGY INDUSTRIES, INC.; *pg.* 613, *pg.* 328
SUMMIT - Furniture - ASHLEY FURNITURE INDUSTRIES, INC.; *pg.* 914, *pg.* 1852
SUMMIT - Semiconductor Processing Equipment - AXCELIS TECHNOLOGIES, INC.; *pg.* 1400, *pg.* 787
SUMMIT - Forms & Converting Paper - BOISE CASCADE HOLDINGS, L.L.C.; *pg.* 1453, *pg.* 546
SUMMIT - Recreational Vehicle - BOMBARDIER RECREATIONAL PRODUCTS, INC.; *pg.* 201, *pg.* 1960
SUMMIT - Food Service Distributors - CARA OPERATIONS LIMITED; *pg.* 1720, *pg.* 1947
SUMMIT - Wafer Probing System - CASCADE MICROTECH, INC.; *pg.* 1405, *pg.* 1492
SUMMIT - Wireless Control - CONTROL CHIEF HOLDINGS, INC.; *pg.* 630, *pg.* 1518
SUMMIT - Switch - EXTREME NETWORKS INC; *pg.* 287, *pg.* 245
SUMMIT - Software System - FISERV, INC.; *pg.* 397, *pg.* 1855
SUMMIT - Fixed Earth Stations - GLOBECOMM SYSTEMS INC.; *pg.* 640, *pg.* 1164
SUMMIT - Furniture - JASPER GROUP; *pg.* 930, *pg.* 691
SUMMIT - Window & Door - JELD-WEN, INC.; *pg.* 1051, *pg.* 1499
SUMMIT - Home Design - LINDAL CEDAR HOMES, INC.; *pg.* 94, *pg.* 1837
SUMMIT - Lamination Applicator - NORDSON CORPORATION; *pg.* 1365, *pg.* 1480
SUMMIT - Footwear - P.W. MINOR & SON, INC.; *pg.* 1816, *pg.* 1140
SUMMIT - Cruise Ship - ROYAL CARIBBEAN CRUISES LTD; *pg.* 1921, *pg.* 446
SUMMIT - Ceiling Panel - USG CORPORATION; *pg.* 118, *pg.* 594
SUMMIT - Grill - WEBER-STEPHEN PRODUCTS LLC; *pg.* 62, *pg.* 650
SUMMIT AVENUE - Furniture - ASHLEY FURNITURE INDUSTRIES, INC.; *pg.* 914, *pg.* 1852
SUMMIT DUTY - Jackets - ELBECO INCORPORATED; *pg.* 40, *pg.* 1584
SUMMIT HOTELS & RESORTS - Hotels & Resorts - PREFERRED HOTEL GROUP; *pg.* 1108, *pg.* 587
SUMMIT LECTERN - Mobile Lectern - MITY ENTERPRISES, INC.; *pg.* 935, *pg.* 1753
SUMMIT WM100 - Controller - EXTREME NETWORKS INC; *pg.* 287, *pg.* 245
SUMMIT WM20 - Controller - EXTREME NETWORKS INC; *pg.* 287, *pg.* 245
SUMMIT WM200 - Controller - EXTREME NETWORKS INC; *pg.* 287, *pg.* 245
SUMMIT WM2000 - Controller - EXTREME NETWORKS INC; *pg.* 287, *pg.* 245
SUMMIT X150 - Switch - EXTREME NETWORKS INC; *pg.* 287, *pg.* 245
SUMMIT X250E - Switch - EXTREME NETWORKS INC; *pg.* 287, *pg.* 245
SUMMIT X350 - Switch - EXTREME NETWORKS INC; *pg.* 287, *pg.* 245
SUMMIT X450A - Switch - EXTREME NETWORKS INC; *pg.* 287, *pg.* 245
SUMMIT X450E - Switch - EXTREME NETWORKS INC; *pg.* 287, *pg.* 245
SUMMIT X650 - Switch - EXTREME NETWORKS INC; *pg.* 287, *pg.* 245
SUMMIT48SI - Switch - EXTREME NETWORKS INC; *pg.* 287, *pg.* 245
SUMMON - Pest Control Product - FMC CORPORATION; *pg.* 1163, *pg.* 1564
SUMMUS - Protective Clothing - E.I. DU PONT DE NEMOURS & COMPANY; *pg.* 1159, *pg.* 390
SUMNERCOM.COM - Website - SUMNER COMMUNICATIONS INC.; *pg.* 1690, *pg.* 338
SUMNERHOST.COM - Website - SUMNER COMMUNICATIONS INC.; *pg.* 1690, *pg.* 338
SUMO - Surface Material - STEELCASE INC.; *pg.* 475, *pg.* 889
SUMO - Cells - VEECO INSTRUMENTS INC.; *pg.* 1434, *pg.* 1322
SUMP BUDDY - Time-Release Tablet - THE DOW CHEMICAL COMPANY; *pg.* 1157, *pg.* 898
SUMP-VAC - Cleanout Unit - THE SPENCER TURBINE CO.; *pg.* 1378, *pg.* 386
SUMTOTAL ENTERPRISE SUITE - Software - SUMTOTAL SYSTEMS, INC.; *pg.* 477, *pg.* 429
SUN - Beauty Product - AVON PRODUCTS, INC.; *pg.* 500, *pg.* 1198
THE SUN - Newspaper - THE BALTIMORE SUN COMPANY; *pg.* 1619, *pg.* 755
SUN 600 - Camera - POLAROID CORPORATION; *pg.* 1426, *pg.* 815
SUN AND SAND - Personal Care Product - MARIETTA HOSPITALITY; *pg.* 1464, *pg.* 1155
SUN & SAND CHAIRS - Aluminum Beach Chairs - TELESCOPE CASUAL FURNITURE INC.; *pg.* 944, *pg.* 1162
SUN & SHADE MIX - Grass Seed - THE SCOTTS MIRACLE-GRO COMPANY; *pg.* 1799, *pg.* 1459
SUN BURST - Sparkled Pigment - SEYMOUR OF SYCAMORE, INC.; *pg.* 1447, *pg.* 663
SUN CHIPS - Multigrain Snacks - FRITO-LAY NORTH AMERICA, INC.; *pg.* 1853, *pg.* 1730
SUN CHLORELLA - Healthcare Product - SWANSON HEALTH PRODUCTS INC.; *pg.* 1600, *pg.* 1397
SUN CITY CENTER - Community Name - WCI COMMUNITIES, INC.; *pg.* 1118, *pg.* 414
SUN CROP - French Fries - J.R. SIMPLOT COMPANY; *pg.* 867, *pg.* 547
SUN CURED - Plug Tobacco - AMERICAN SNUFF COMPANY; *pg.* 1893, *pg.* 1641
SUN DEVIL - UV Resistant Additive - SMOOTH-ON INC.; *pg.* 111, *pg.* 1528
SUN DOG AMBER WHEAT - Seasonal Beer - ANHEUSER-BUSCH COMPANIES, LLC; *pg.* 237, *pg.* 991
SUN DRY 44 - Cleaner - SWISHER HYGIENE INC.; *pg.* 336, *pg.* 1507
SUN GEMS - Salt - CARGILL LIMITED; *pg.* 1475, *pg.* 1914
SUN GEMS - Water Softener Salt - CARGILL SALT; *pg.* 846, *pg.* 926
SUN-GLEAM - Automotive Finishes - PPG INDUSTRIES, INC.; *pg.* 1445, *pg.* 1579
SUN-IN - Health & Beauty Product - CHATTEM, INC.; *pg.* 1515, *pg.* 1628
SUN JOURNAL - North Carolina Newspaper - FREEDOM

COMMUNICATIONS, INC.; *pg.* 1643, *pg.* 110
SUN LUCK - Chinese Food Products - ALLIED OLD ENGLISH, INC.; *pg.* 836, *pg.* 1110
SUN-MAID - Fig - VALLEY FIG GROWERS, INC.; *pg.* 908, *pg.* 93
SUN MAID MILK CHOCOLATE RAISINS - Food Product - PROMOTION IN MOTION, INC.; *pg.* 1861, *pg.* 1052
SUN MART - Retail Grocery Stores - SPARTANNASH CO.; *pg.* 1034, *pg.* 925
THE SUN NEWSPAPER - Publisher - THE SUN; *pg.* 1690, *pg.* 198
SUN PACER - Sun Care Products - AMWAY CORPORATION; *pg.* 326, *pg.* 864
SUN PRO - Horse & Dog Foods - INTERMOUNTAIN FARMERS ASSOCIATION; *pg.* 705, *pg.* 1759
SUN PRO FELINE - Pet Food - INTERMOUNTAIN FARMERS ASSOCIATION; *pg.* 705, *pg.* 1759
SUN PRO LITE - Pet Food - INTERMOUNTAIN FARMERS ASSOCIATION; *pg.* 705, *pg.* 1759
SUN PRO PREMIUM ADULT - Pet Food - INTERMOUNTAIN FARMERS ASSOCIATION; *pg.* 705, *pg.* 1759
SUN PRO SELECT - Pet Food - INTERMOUNTAIN FARMERS ASSOCIATION; *pg.* 705, *pg.* 1759
SUN PRO SELECT PUPPY - Pet Food - INTERMOUNTAIN FARMERS ASSOCIATION; *pg.* 705, *pg.* 1759
SUN-PROOF - Coating Product - PPG INDUSTRIES, INC.; *pg.* 1445, *pg.* 1579
SUN SEED - Pet Product - PETSMART, INC.; *pg.* 1481, *pg.* 18
SUN SHADE - Reduces Solar Heat - ALCOA INC.; *pg.* 65, *pg.* 1188
SUN SHADE - Hair & Skin Product - AUBREY ORGANICS INC.; *pg.* 499, *pg.* 470
SUN SHARP - Fabric - NATIONAL SPINNING COMPANY, INC.; *pg.* 697, *pg.* 1265
SUN SHELTER - Retractable Patio Awnings - DURASOL AWNINGS, INC.; *pg.* 79, *pg.* 1153
SUN SOY - Soy Milk - THE WHITEWAVE FOODS COMPANY; *pg.* 1037, *pg.* 324
SUN-SPORT - Boat - SEA RAY BOATS, INC.; *pg.* 1710, *pg.* 1638
SUN SPROUT - Food Product - HANOVER FOODS CORPORATION; *pg.* 861, *pg.* 1535
SUN STRIPE - Container Grown Plant - MONROVIA GROWERS; *pg.* 1797, *pg.* 44
SUN VALLEY - Furniture Collection - CENTURY FURNITURE INDUSTRIES; *pg.* 920, *pg.* 1377
SUN VALLEY - Ski Resort - SINCLAIR OIL CORPORATION; *pg.* 984, *pg.* 1760
SUNBANK - Interconnect Product - DANAHER CORPORATION; *pg.* 1044, *pg.* 397
SUNBEAM - Food Product - FLOWERS FOODS, INC.; *pg.* 855, *pg.* 541
SUNBEAM - Bread - SCHMIDT BAKING CO., INC.; *pg.* 894, *pg.* 759
SUNBEAM AUTOMATIC WARMING BLANKETS - Blanket - JARDEN CONSUMER SOLUTIONS; *pg.* 57, *pg.* 412
SUNBEAM CHILL-IT - Gel-Packs, Ice Bags, Cold Therapy Products - JARDEN CONSUMER SOLUTIONS; *pg.* 57, *pg.* 412
SUNBEAM DENTAL CARE - Dental Care Products - JARDEN CONSUMER SOLUTIONS; *pg.* 57, *pg.* 412
SUNBEAM HEAT TO GO - Portable Heating Pads - JARDEN CONSUMER SOLUTIONS; *pg.* 57, *pg.* 412
SUNBELT - Snacks & Cereals - MCKEE FOODS CORPORATION; *pg.* 1860, *pg.* 1630
SUNBELT - Steel Products - RUSSEL METALS INC.; *pg.* 1180, *pg.* 1928
SUNBELT BUSINESS ADVISORS - Business Broker - SUNBELT BUSINESS ADVISORS NETWORK, LLC; *pg.* 806, *pg.* 1456
SUNBLAZE - Pot Forcing Roses - THE CONARD-PYLE COMPANY; *pg.* 1794, *pg.* 1594
SUNBLOCK SHADE - Auto Accessory - MUNCHKIN, INC.; *pg.* 964, *pg.* 300
SUNBLUSH BRONZE - Face & Body Product - THE BONNE BELL COMPANY; *pg.* 502, *pg.* 1480
SUNBOND - Carpet Chemicals - OMNOVA SOLUTIONS INC; *pg.* 1176, *pg.* 1453
SUNBRELLA - Solution-dyed Acrylic Fabric for Awnings, Boat Covers & Outdoor Furniture - GLEN RAVEN, INC.; *pg.* 693, *pg.* 1373
SUNBRELLA - Fabric - NATIONAL SPINNING COMPANY, INC.; *pg.* 697, *pg.* 1265
SUNBRITE - Automotive Fabric - GLEN RAVEN, INC.; *pg.* 693, *pg.* 1373
SUNBRITE - Solder Brightener - HUBBARD-HALL, INC.; *pg.* 1167, *pg.* 382
SUNBURST - Books - FARRAR, STRAUS & GIROUX, INC.; *pg.* 1640, *pg.* 1231
SUNBURST - Container Grown Plant - MONROVIA GROWERS; *pg.* 1797, *pg.* 44
SUNBURST - Pan Coating - VENTURA FOODS, LLC; *pg.* 908, *pg.* 49
SUNBURST BOUQUET - Floral Bouquet - FTD GROUP, INC.; *pg.* 1795, *pg.* 608
SUNBURST C - Herb Tea - CELESTIAL SEASONINGS, INC.; *pg.* 846, *pg.* 310
SUNCATCHER - Retractable Window Awnings for Small to Medium Windows - DURASOL AWNINGS, INC.; *pg.* 79, *pg.* 1153
SUNCENTRIC - Water Pump - CONERGY, INC.; *pg.* 1325, *pg.* 318
SUNCLAVA - Fishing Gear Product - SIMMS FISHING PRODUCTS CORP.; *pg.* 1845, *pg.* 1008
SUNCLOUD - Sunglasses - SAFILO USA INC.; *pg.* 11, *pg.* 1106
SUNCOAST - Retail Music & Video Store - TRANS WORLD ENTERTAINMENT CORPORATION; *pg.* 313, *pg.* 1137
SUNCREST - Cola, Cherry, Blue Raspberry, Orange, Strawberry & Fruit Punch Drinks - THE MONARCH BEVERAGE COMPANY, INC.; *pg.* 257, *pg.* 514
SUNCRUISER - Motor Homes - WINNEBAGO INDUSTRIES, INC.; *pg.* 1712, *pg.* 707
SUNCRYL - Chemical Product - OMNOVA SOLUTIONS INC; *pg.* 1176, *pg.* 1453
SUNDAE CRUNCH - Ice Cream Bar - WELLS ENTERPRISES, INC.; *pg.* 909, *pg.* 709
SUNDANCE - Publisher - HAIGHTS CROSS COMMUNICATIONS, INC.; *pg.* 1646, *pg.* 1237
SUNDANCE - Herbicide - MONSANTO COMPANY; *pg.* 1173, *pg.* 999
SUNDANCE - Paper - NEENAH PAPER, INC.; *pg.* 1465, *pg.* 484
SUNDANCE - Footwear - PHOENIX FOOTWEAR GROUP, INC.; *pg.* 1815, *pg.* 60
SUNDANCE CAFE - Games - PENN NATIONAL GAMING, INC.; *pg.* 574, *pg.* 1595
SUNDANCER - Cart Bag - DATREK GOLF; *pg.* 1832, *pg.* 1801
SUNDANCER - Boat - SEA RAY BOATS, INC.; *pg.* 1710, *pg.* 1638
SUNDANCER - Motor Homes - WINNEBAGO INDUSTRIES, INC.; *pg.* 1712, *pg.* 707
SUNDANCETV - Cable & Satellite Television Network - AMC NETWORKS INC.; *pg.* 269, *pg.* 1189
SUNDAY MAGAZINE NETWORK - Twenty Two Newspaper Published Sunday Magazines - METRO NEWSPAPER ADVERTISING SERVICES, INC.; *pg.* 1664, *pg.* 1259
SUNDAY MORNING VALUES, SATURDAY MORNING FUN - Slogan - BIG IDEA, INC.; *pg.* 271, *pg.* 1632
SUNDAZE - Container Grown Plant - MONROVIA GROWERS; *pg.* 1797, *pg.* 44
SUNDECK - Boat - SEA RAY BOATS, INC.; *pg.* 1710, *pg.* 1638
SUNDECKER - Latch - SOUTHCO, INC.; *pg.* 1063, *pg.* 1522
SUNDIAL - Paint - JONES-BLAIR COMPANY; *pg.* 1443, *pg.* 1682
SUNDOG - Clamp-On Mattebox - ALAN GORDON ENTERPRISES, INC.; *pg.* 1399, *pg.* 125
SUNDOWN - Nutritional Supplements - NBTY, INC.; *pg.* 1572, *pg.* 1338
SUNDRESS CARDIGAN - Women's Clothing & Accessories - WOODEN SHIPS OF HOBOKEN; *pg.* 35, *pg.* 1315
SUNDT - Medical Device - INTEGRA LIFESCIENCES HOLDINGS CORPORATION; *pg.* 1545, *pg.* 1109
SUNDURA - Coatings for Woods - PPG INDUSTRIES, INC.; *pg.* 1445, *pg.* 1579
SUNFADER - Medicated Skin Care - OBAGI MEDICAL PRODUCTS, INC.; *pg.* 1577, *pg.* 123
SUNFILL - Soft Drink - THE COCA-COLA COMPANY; *pg.* 240, *pg.* 493
SUNFILM - Plastics Product - AEP INDUSTRIES INC.; *pg.* 1878, *pg.* 1085
SUNFIRE - Educational Materials - SCHOLASTIC INC.; *pg.* 1683, *pg.* 1288
SUNFIRE - Analytical Column - WATERS CORPORATION; *pg.* 1436, *pg.* 834
SUNFLECTOR - Rear Window Sun Deflector - LUND INTERNATIONAL, INC.; *pg.* 211, *pg.* 526
SUNFLOWER - Tillage System - AGCO CORPORATION; *pg.* 700, *pg.* 530
SUNFLOWER - Table Textile - HERITAGE LACE INC.; *pg.* 694, *pg.* 711
SUNFLOWERS - Fragrance - ELIZABETH ARDEN, INC.; *pg.* 507, *pg.* 448
SUNFRESH - Food Product - DEL MONTE FOODS, INC.; *pg.* 852, *pg.* 304
SUNFROST - Plastic Compound & Resin - A. SCHULMAN, INC.; *pg.* 1144, *pg.* 1452
SUNGARD - Software - SUNGARD DATA SYSTEMS INC.; *pg.* 477, *pg.* 1592
SUNGATE - Windshield - PPG INDUSTRIES, INC.; *pg.* 1445, *pg.* 1579
SUNGFIT - Cover & Pad - HOME PRODUCTS INTERNATIONAL, INC.; *pg.* 1125, *pg.* 577
SUNGLOW - Butter Alternative - VENTURA FOODS, LLC; *pg.* 908, *pg.* 49
SUNGUARD - Retractable Window Awnings - DURASOL AWNINGS, INC.; *pg.* 79, *pg.* 1153
SUNGUARD - Glass Product - GUARDIAN INDUSTRIES CORP.; *pg.* 85, *pg.* 869
SUNGUARD - Umbrellas - TOTES ISOTONER CORPORATION; *pg.* 14, *pg.* 1426
SUNJUNS - Shoes - G.H. BASS & CO.; *pg.* 1809, *pg.* 1234
SUNKEM - Carpet Chemicals - OMNOVA SOLUTIONS INC; *pg.* 1176, *pg.* 1453
SUNKIST - Citrus Fruits - SUNKIST GROWERS, INC.; *pg.* 899, *pg.* 299
SUNKOTE - Carpet Chemicals - OMNOVA SOLUTIONS INC; *pg.* 1176, *pg.* 1453
SUNLIGHT - Laundry Detergent - THE SUN PRODUCTS CORPORATION; *pg.* 336, *pg.* 385
SUNLINE SLIPPER - Felt - AMERICAN FELT & FILTER COMPANY; *pg.* 1312, *pg.* 1184
SUNLINK - Wireless Communication System - AT&T SOUTHEAST; *pg.* 1868, *pg.* 489
SUNLITE - Liquid Detergent - EDWARD DON & COMPANY; *pg.* 54, *pg.* 672
SUNLYTE - Battery - EXIDE TECHNOLOGIES; *pg.* 204, *pg.* 483
SUNNE - Temperature Controls - PECO, INC.; *pg.* 1368, *pg.* 1505
SUNNY - Fertilizer - SIMPLOT PARTNERS INC.; *pg.* 1800, *pg.* 548
SUNNY CASH UP - Lottery Game - RHODE ISLAND LOTTERY; *pg.* 1004, *pg.* 1600
SUNNY DAZE - Container Grown Plant - MONROVIA GROWERS; *pg.* 1797, *pg.* 44
SUNNY DELIGHT - Container Grown Plant - MONROVIA GROWERS; *pg.* 1797, *pg.* 44
SUNNY DELIGHT - Fruit Drinks - SUNNY DELIGHT BEVERAGES CO.; *pg.* 899, *pg.* 1426
SUNNY FRESH - Egg Products - CARGILL, INC.; *pg.* 845, *pg.* 965
SUNNY GOLD - Vegetable Corn Oil - MALLET & COMPANY, INC.; *pg.* 875, *pg.* 1521
SUNNY GREEN - Nutritional Product - NUTRACEUTICAL INTERNATIONAL CORPORATION; *pg.* 1576, *pg.* 1753
SUNNY ISLE - Processed Food - KAYEM FOODS, INC.; *pg.* 867, *pg.* 814
SUNNY KNOCK OUT - Garden Roses - THE CONARD-PYLE COMPANY; *pg.* 1794, *pg.* 1594
SUNNY MONEY - Lottery Game - D.C. LOTTERY & CHARITABLE GAMES CONTROL BOARD; *pg.* 991, *pg.* 398
SUNNYBROOK - Milk Chocolate - CARGILL LIMITED; *pg.* 1475, *pg.* 1914
SUNNYBROOK - Vinyl Siding - NORTEK, INC.; *pg.* 100, *pg.* 1607
SUNNYD - Fruit Juice - SUNNY DELIGHT BEVERAGES CO.; *pg.* 899, *pg.* 1426
SUNNYLAND - Food Products - SMITHFIELD FOODS, INC.; *pg.* 896, *pg.* 1806
SUNNYTIME - Children's Product - THE STEP2 COMPANY LLC; *pg.* 1889, *pg.* 1474
SUNOCO - Petroleum Products - SUNOCO INC.; *pg.* 985, *pg.* 1571
SUNOCO CARD - Credit Card - CITIGROUP INC.; *pg.* 735, *pg.* 1212
SUNOLITE - Polymer Product - CHEMTURA CORPORATION; *pg.* 1152, *pg.* 355
SUNOVA - Motor Home - WINNEBAGO INDUSTRIES, INC.; *pg.* 1712, *pg.* 707
SUNPORCH - Enclosed Patios - SUNPORCH STRUCTURES

INC.; pg. 113, pg. 384
SUNPORT - Soft Top - BESTOP, INC.; pg. 200, pg. 312
SUNPRENE - Plastic Compound & Resin - A. SCHULMAN, INC.; pg. 1144, pg. 1452
SUNPRO - Diagnostics & Service Equipment - SNAP-ON INCORPORATED; pg. 1062, pg. 1862
SUNPRO ADULT - Pet Food - INTERMOUNTAIN FARMERS ASSOCIATION; pg. 705, pg. 1759
SUNPROOF - Polymer Product - CHEMTURA CORPORATION; pg. 1152, pg. 355
SUNRAYCER - Solar Air Craft - AEROVIRONMENT, INC.; pg. 223, pg. 150
SUNREZ - Chemical Product - OMNOVA SOLUTIONS INC; pg. 1176, pg. 1453
SUNRIDER - Soft Top For Jeeps - BESTOP, INC.; pg. 200, pg. 312
SUNRIGHT - Skin Care Product - NU SKIN ENTERPRISES, INC.; pg. 518, pg. 1755
SUNRISE - Film Scanners - ANACOMP, INC.; pg. 350, pg. 1777
SUNRISE - Motor Homes - WINNEBAGO INDUSTRIES, INC.; pg. 1712, pg. 707
SUNRISE SPECIAL - Automotive Reconditioning Product - MOC PRODUCTS COMPANY, INC.; pg. 332, pg. 174
SUNRISE STRAWBERRY - Yogurt & Fruit Blend Drink - JAMBA, INC.; pg. 1024, pg. 84
SUNRISE TOFU - Tofu & Soy Beverages - SUNRISE SOYA FOODS; pg. 900, pg. 1912
SUNRON - Non-Stick Coatings - JARDEN CONSUMER SOLUTIONS; pg. 57, pg. 412
SUNRYE ALE - Beverage - CRAFT BREWERS ALLIANCE, INC; pg. 247, pg. 1502
SUNSASH - Architectural Lineal Components; Jambs, Heads, Sills, Sashes, ect. - PPG INDUSTRIES, INC.; pg. 1445, pg. 1579
SUNSATIA - Container Grown Plant - MONROVIA GROWERS; pg. 1797, pg. 44
SUNSATION - Container Grown Plant - MONROVIA GROWERS; pg. 1797, pg. 44
SUNSAVER - Solar Pool Heater - FAFCO INC.; pg. 1071, pg. 65
SUNSCREEN FOR NAILS - Topcoats - ORLY INTERNATIONAL, INC.; pg. 518, pg. 137
SUNSENSORS - Glass & Ceramic Material - CORNING INCORPORATED; pg. 1122, pg. 1154
SUNSET - Bath & Shower Gel - ANNIE OAKLEY ENTERPRISES, INC.; pg. 499, pg. 693
SUNSET - Eyewear - MAUI JIM, INC.; pg. 9, pg. 651
SUNSET - Fabric - NEMSCHOFF, INC.; pg. 936, pg. 1890
SUNSET - Paints, Enamels, Varnishes & Lacquers - PPG INDUSTRIES, INC.; pg. 1445, pg. 1579
SUNSET - Media Publication - TIME INC.; pg. 1693, pg. 1300
SUNSET HARVEST - Retail Variety Breads - BIMBO BAKERIES USA; pg. 840, pg. 151
SUNSET STATION HOTEL AND CASINO - Hotel & Casino - STATION CASINOS, INC.; pg. 585, pg. 1030
SUNSET STRIPS - Chicken Strip Food Service Option - TYSON FOODS, INC.; pg. 902, pg. 35
SUNSETTER OASIS - Awnings - SUNSETTER PRODUCTS, LP; pg. 113, pg. 830
SUNSHADE - Enclosure System - O'BRIEN CORPORATION; pg. 1366, pg. 1001
SUNSHADE - Tinted Automotive Glass - PPG INDUSTRIES, INC.; pg. 1445, pg. 1579
SUNSHINE - Footwear - COBIAN CORP.; pg. 1806, pg. 253
SUNSHINE - Color - FERRO CORPORATION; pg. 1162, pg. 1462
SUNSHINE - Snacks - KELLOGG COMPANY; pg. 831, pg. 870
SUNSHINE COUNTRY - Nuts - JOHN B. SANFILIPPO & SON, INC.; pg. 1024, pg. 610
SUNSHINE FRESH - Dry Cleaning & Laundry Product - ADCO, INC.; pg. 325, pg. 482
SUNSHINE JOE - Coffee - ALIMENTATION COUCHE-TARD INC.; pg. 1013, pg. 1951
SUNSHINE SMOOTHIE - Food Product - SONIC CORP.; pg. 1750, pg. 1487
SUNSHINE WHEAT - Beer - NEW BELGIUM BREWING COMPANY, INC.; pg. 258, pg. 328
SUNSMART - Hat - L.L. BEAN, INC.; pg. 1777, pg. 750
SUNSPLASH - Audio Visual Product - DUKANE CORPORATION; pg. 634, pg. 658
SUNSPOT - Scoreboard & Sports Product - DAKTRONICS, INC.; pg. 633, pg. 1624
SUNSPOT - Health System Product - LANELABS USA INC.; pg. 1554, pg. 1128
SUNSPOT - Lighting Fixtures - SWIVELIER CO., INC.; pg. 1307, pg. 1142
SUNSTAR - Gas Room Heaters - GAS-FIRED PRODUCTS, INC.; pg. 1338, pg. 1367
SUNSTAR - Lighting - INTERLINE BRANDS, INC.; pg. 1051, pg. 433
SUNSTAR - Software - SUNGARD DATA SYSTEMS INC.; pg. 477, pg. 1592
SUNSTAR - Motor Homes - WINNEBAGO INDUSTRIES, INC.; pg. 1712, pg. 707
SUNSTONE - Hotel - SUNSTONE HOTEL INVESTORS, INC.; pg. 1116, pg. 41
SUNSWEET FRESH - Quality Fresh Fruit & Vegetables - SUNSWEET GROWERS, INC.; pg. 900, pg. 309
SUNTRON - Automotive Refinish Coatings - PPG INDUSTRIES, INC.; pg. 1445, pg. 1579
SUNUPS - Eggs - CAL-MAINE FOODS, INC.; pg. 843, pg. 969
SUNVISOR - Visor - LUND INTERNATIONAL, INC.; pg. 211, pg. 526
SUNVISOR II - Visor - LUND INTERNATIONAL, INC.; pg. 211, pg. 526
SUNWARD - Bath Product - KOHLER CO.; pg. 91, pg. 1862
SUNWASH - Bike Cleaner - HARLEY-DAVIDSON, INC.; pg. 178, pg. 1874
SUNWASHED LINEN - Candle - THE YANKEE CANDLE COMPANY, INC.; pg. 1792, pg. 843
SUNWEST BANK ONLINE - Internet Cash Management Services - SUNWEST BANK; pg. 807, pg. 116
SUNWEST BANK RAPID REMID - Payment Processing - SUNWEST BANK; pg. 807, pg. 116
SUNWOOD - Wood Preservative - OSMOSE, INC.; pg. 102, pg. 1150
SUNWORKS - Construction Paper - PACON CORPORATION; pg. 1466, pg. 1852
SUONO - Theatrical Fixtures - BALLANTYNE STRONG, INC.; pg. 623, pg. 1013
SUP-R-CAULK - Expansion Screw Anchor - MKT FASTENING, LLC; pg. 1056, pg. 34
SUP-R-DROP - Masonry Anchor - MKT FASTENING, LLC; pg. 1056, pg. 34
SUP-R-LAG - Lag Shield - MKT FASTENING, LLC; pg. 1056, pg. 34
SUP-R-LEAD - Lead Anchor - MKT FASTENING, LLC; pg. 1056, pg. 34
SUP-R-SHORTY - Medium Duty Anchor - MKT FASTENING, LLC; pg. 1056, pg. 34
SUP-R-SLEEVE - Masonry Anchor - MKT FASTENING, LLC; pg. 1056, pg. 34
SUP-R-SPLIT - Light Duty Anchor - MKT FASTENING, LLC; pg. 1056, pg. 34
SUP-R-STUD - Masonry Anchor - MKT FASTENING, LLC; pg. 1056, pg. 34
SUP-R-TOGGLE - Toggle Bolt - MKT FASTENING, LLC; pg. 1056, pg. 34
SUPA-LOC - Meat, Fish & Poultry Absorbent Pad - SEALED AIR CORPORATION; pg. 1468, pg. 1058
SUPELCO - Chromatography Products for Analysis & Purification - SIGMA-ALDRICH CORPORATION; pg. 1181, pg. 1003
SUPER - Car Wash Equipment - D&S CAR WASH EQUIPMENT CO.; pg. 1327, pg. 979
SUPER - Pump - HAYWARD POOL PRODUCTS; pg. 1049, pg. 1057
SUPER - Footwear - VANS, INC.; pg. 1821, pg. 76
SUPER - Fishing Hooks - WRIGHT & MCGILL CO.; pg. 1848, pg. 324
SUPER 1 - Foods - URM STORES, INC.; pg. 1036, pg. 1844
SUPER-49 - Green & Clear Fertilizer - POTASH CORP.; pg. 1177, pg. 641
SUPER 5-HTP - Nutritional Product - NUTRACEUTICAL INTERNATIONAL CORPORATION; pg. 1576, pg. 1753
SUPER 5000 - Sizing, Brushless Automatic Carwash System - D&S CAR WASH EQUIPMENT CO.; pg. 1327, pg. 979
SUPER 6 - Environmental Control System - CTB INTERNATIONAL CORP.; pg. 850, pg. 695
SUPER 6 LOTTO - Jackpot Game - PENNSYLVANIA STATE LOTTERY; pg. 1003, pg. 1552
SUPER 60 - Socks - WIGWAM MILLS, INC.; pg. 15, pg. 1894
SUPER 60 JR. - Socks - WIGWAM MILLS, INC.; pg. 15, pg. 1894
SUPER 77 - Multipurpose Adhesive - 3M COMPANY; pg. 1142, pg. 956
SUPER 7'S - Lottery Card - MISSOURI LOTTERY; pg. 999, pg. 979
SUPER 8 - Hotels - WYNDHAM WORLDWIDE CORPORATION; pg. 1119, pg. 1107
SUPER ACRYLIC - Coating Product - PPG INDUSTRIES, INC.; pg. 1445, pg. 1579
SUPER ADAMANT - Refractory Product - RESCO PRODUCTS, INC.; pg. 107, pg. 1581
SUPER ARCOFLEX - Paper & Nonwoven Material - FIBERMARK INC.; pg. 1457, pg. 1764
SUPER AUTOCHOKE - Automatic Pressure Regulator - M-I SWACO; pg. 980, pg. 1710
SUPER B - Magnetic Trap - ERIEZ MANUFACTURING CO. INC.; pg. 1335, pg. 1530
SUPER BEARCAT - Single-Action Revolver - STURM, RUGER & COMPANY, INC.; pg. 1846, pg. 371
SUPER BEDFORD TIE-R - Air-operated, Manual or Automatically Fed Twist Tying Machine - BEDFORD INDUSTRIES, INC.; pg. 1453, pg. 967
SUPER BEE - Gaming Product - GLD PRODUCTS, INC.; pg. 1835, pg. 1882
SUPER BEE - Cleaner Product - MCGEAN-ROHCO, INC.; pg. 1172, pg. 1432
SUPER BETA PNP - Integrated Circuits - MICREL, INC.; pg. 654, pg. 247
SUPER BIG BURGER - Sandwich - 7-ELEVEN, INC.; pg. 1012, pg. 1672
SUPER BIG GULP - Fountain Soft Drink - 7-ELEVEN, INC.; pg. 1012, pg. 1672
SUPER BIG RED - Concentrated Cleaner - TEXAS REFINERY CORP.; pg. 986, pg. 1696
SUPER BLAZING 7S - Video Game - BALLY TECHNOLOGIES, INC.; pg. 531, pg. 1022
SUPER BLUE GREEN - Supplement And Food - NEW EARTH LIFE SCIENCES, INC.; pg. 1573, pg. 1499
SUPER BONUS - Lawn Fertilizer - THE SCOTTS MIRACLE-GRO COMPANY; pg. 1799, pg. 1459
SUPER BOOSTER - Aluminum Hose Reel - HANNAY REELS INC.; pg. 1344, pg. 1351
SUPER BRAVO B - Flooring Product - STAGESTEP INC.; pg. 1688, pg. 1570
SUPER BRAVO CLASSIC - Flooring Product - STAGESTEP INC.; pg. 1688, pg. 1570
SUPER BRIGHT - Car Washes - MACE SECURITY INTERNATIONAL, INC.; pg. 1172, pg. 1541
SUPER BRITE - Automotive Cleaner - DELTA FOREMOST CHEMICAL CORPORATION; pg. 1155, pg. 1642
SUPER BUBBLE - Gum - FERRARA CANDY CO.; pg. 1852, pg. 612
SUPER BUFFER - Clock & Buffer Product - CYPRESS SEMICONDUCTOR CORPORATION; pg. 1326, pg. 243
SUPER-BUILD - Paint & Coating - DIAMOND VOGEL PAINT, INC.; pg. 1441, pg. 710
SUPER CANT-LEG - Drive In Rack - SPEEDRACK PRODUCTS GROUP, LTD.; pg. 112, pg. 908
SUPER CASH - Game - MISSOURI LOTTERY; pg. 999, pg. 979
SUPER CE-RITE - High Speed Polish For Glass - FERRO CORPORATION; pg. 1162, pg. 1462
SUPER CHARGE - Flashlight - ENERGIZER HOLDINGS, INC.; pg. 637, pg. 996
SUPER-CHARGED MOISTURIZER - Hair Care Product - JOHN PAUL MITCHELL SYSTEMS; pg. 512, pg. 133
SUPER CHERRY - Video Slots - INTERNATIONAL GAME TECHNOLOGY; pg. 957, pg. 1024
SUPER CHUNKY COOKIE DOUGH - Ice Cream - WELLS ENTERPRISES, INC.; pg. 909, pg. 709
SUPER CINELUX - Cinema Lenses - SCHNEIDER OPTICS INC.; pg. 1428, pg. 1165
SUPER CLEAN - Hair Care System - JOHN PAUL MITCHELL SYSTEMS; pg. 512, pg. 133
SUPER CLEAN EXTRA - Hair Care Product - JOHN PAUL MITCHELL SYSTEMS; pg. 512, pg. 133
SUPER CLEAN LIGHT - Hair Care Product - JOHN PAUL MITCHELL SYSTEMS; pg. 512, pg. 133
SUPER CLEAN SCULPTING GEL - Hair Care Product - JOHN PAUL MITCHELL SYSTEMS; pg. 512, pg. 133
SUPER CLEAN SPRAY - Hair Care Product - JOHN PAUL MITCHELL SYSTEMS; pg. 512, pg. 133
SUPER CLIPS - Hair Care Product - CONAIR CORPORATION; pg. 505, pg. 1055
SUPER CONCENTRATE - Teknor Color - TEKNOR APEX COMPANY; pg. 1889, pg. 1605
SUPER CONCENTRATE - Freshner - AMERICAN GREASE STICK CO.; pg. 971, pg. 902
SUPER CONSTELLATION - Systems Integration &

Aeronautics - LOCKHEED MARTIN CORPORATION; *pg.* 229, *pg.* 762
SUPER CONTRYX XRAY GLASSES - X-Ray Shielding - HCS CORPORATION; *pg.* 86, *pg.* 1821
SUPER CRANK - Battery - EXIDE TECHNOLOGIES; *pg.* 204, *pg.* 483
SUPER CREDITS - Game - WMS INDUSTRIES INC.; *pg.* 593, *pg.* 666
SUPER CUSHION - Shoe And Glove - ACUSHNET COMPANY; *pg.* 1824, *pg.* 818
SUPER-CUSHION - Automotive & Industrial Air Springs - THE GOODYEAR TIRE & RUBBER COMPANY; *pg.* 1883, *pg.* 1401
SUPER CYLINDERS - Spring-Return Cylinders - MARSH BELLOFRAM CORPORATION; *pg.* 1885, *pg.* 1850
SUPER DEGREASER - Cleaner/Degreaser - CRC INDUSTRIES, INC.; *pg.* 329, *pg.* 1590
SUPER DEPTH - Footwear - P.W. MINOR & SON, INC.; *pg.* 1816, *pg.* 1140
SUPER DLTTAPE - 320 Gig Backup for Servers - IMATION CORP.; *pg.* 413, *pg.* 952
SUPER DOGEROO - Hot Dog Machine - GOLD MEDAL PRODUCTS CO.; *pg.* 55, *pg.* 1414
SUPER DOO-Z - Brush - THE WOOSTER BRUSH COMPANY; *pg.* 1450, *pg.* 1482
SUPER DOODLEBUG - Bike - TREK BICYCLE CORPORATION; *pg.* 1847, *pg.* 1896
SUPER DOUBLE DOUBLER - Lottery Game - OHIO LOTTERY COMMISSION; *pg.* 1002, *pg.* 1433
SUPER DRAGON - Dredges - ELLICOTT DREDGES, LLC; *pg.* 1333, *pg.* 757
SUPER-DUPER CROSSWORD - Lottery Game - LOUISIANA LOTTERY CORPORATION; *pg.* 997, *pg.* 742
SUPER DURA - Carpet Cushion - DURA UNDERCUSHIONS LTD.; *pg.* 923, *pg.* 1954
SUPER DURABRAKE II - Switchgear Enclosure Finish - S&C ELECTRIC COMPANY; *pg.* 1305, *pg.* 589
SUPER DUTY - Shovels - NUPLA CORPORATION; *pg.* 101, *pg.* 281
SUPER DUTY CARDINAL - Cutting System - EASTMAN MACHINE COMPANY; *pg.* 1331, *pg.* 1148
SUPER-E - Industrial Electric Motors - BALDOR ELECTRIC COMPANY; *pg.* 1316, *pg.* 32
SUPER E Z KLEEN - Aluminum Air Filters - RESEARCH PRODUCTS CORPORATION; *pg.* 1075, *pg.* 1867
SUPER EASY MONEY - Game - WMS INDUSTRIES INC.; *pg.* 593, *pg.* 666
SUPER EASY WASH - Front Loading Clothes Washer - WHIRLPOOL CORPORATION; *pg.* 62, *pg.* 872
SUPER EDGE - Mattress - RESTONIC MATTRESS CORPORATION; *pg.* 941, *pg.* 553
SUPER ELECTRONIC KER PLUNK - Toy - MATTEL, INC.; *pg.* 962, *pg.* 81
SUPER ENDURANCE - Casters - HAMILTON CASTER & MFG. CO.; *pg.* 206, *pg.* 1454
SUPER ET - Ophthalmic Product - CARL ZEISS OPTICAL, INC.; *pg.* 1405, *pg.* 1778
SUPER F - General Purpose Resin Coated Sand - HEXION; *pg.* 1166, *pg.* 1440
SUPER/FAB - Brush - THE WOOSTER BRUSH COMPANY; *pg.* 1450, *pg.* 1482
SUPER FEC - Semiconductor Solution - VITESSE SEMICONDUCTOR CORPORATION; *pg.* 686, *pg.* 57
SUPER FERRO-KLEEN - Detergent - DELTA FOREMOST CHEMICAL CORPORATION; *pg.* 1155, *pg.* 1642
SUPER FII - General Purpose Resin Coated Sand - HEXION; *pg.* 1166, *pg.* 1440
SUPER FINE PENTEL - Pens - PENTEL OF AMERICA, LTD.; *pg.* 453, *pg.* 295
SUPER FIT BURNERS - Nutritional Product - NUTRACEUTICAL INTERNATIONAL CORPORATION; *pg.* 1576, *pg.* 1753
SUPER FLANGELESS - Pumps - IDEX CORPORATION; *pg.* 1347, *pg.* 623
SUPER-FLEX - Fluid Handling System - GRACO, INC.; *pg.* 1342, *pg.* 935
SUPER-FLEX - Wheel - HAMILTON CASTER & MFG. CO.; *pg.* 206, *pg.* 1454
SUPER-FLO - Drag Conveyor - SCREW CONVEYOR INDUSTRIES; *pg.* 1374, *pg.* 682
SUPER FLOR - Carpet - INTERFACE, INC.; *pg.* 695, *pg.* 512
SUPER FLOSS - Dental Floss - GILLETTE; *pg.* 1536, *pg.* 795
SUPER FLOW - Filter - FLANDERS CORPORATION; *pg.* 1336, *pg.* 1392
SUPER FLOW-V - Filtration Product - FLANDERS CORPORATION; *pg.* 1336, *pg.* 1392
SUPER FOODMART - Drug & Food Product - THE GREAT ATLANTIC & PACIFIC TEA COMPANY, INC.; *pg.* 1021, *pg.* 1086
SUPER FRESH - Drug & Food Product - THE GREAT ATLANTIC & PACIFIC TEA COMPANY, INC.; *pg.* 1021, *pg.* 1086
SUPER FUDGE BROWNIE - Premium Light Ice Cream - WELLS ENTERPRISES, INC.; *pg.* 909, *pg.* 709
SUPER G - Grocery Stores - GIANT OF MARYLAND LLC; *pg.* 1021, *pg.* 773
SUPER G - Wireless Adapters - NETGEAR, INC.; *pg.* 444, *pg.* 247
SUPER GET INFO - Software - BARE BONES SOFTWARE, INC.; *pg.* 360, *pg.* 838
SUPER GLIDE - Motorcycle - HARLEY-DAVIDSON, INC.; *pg.* 178, *pg.* 1874
SUPER GLOBO - Bleach - THE CLOROX COMPANY; *pg.* 327, *pg.* 169
SUPER GLUE - Glue - SUPER GLUE CORPORATION; *pg.* 1183, *pg.* 187
SUPER GRAPHITE PACKING - Fluid Sealing Product - A.W. CHESTERTON COMPANY; *pg.* 1315, *pg.* 861
SUPER GREASE BUSTER - Cleaning Product - HILLYARD, INC.; *pg.* 331, *pg.* 990
SUPER GRIP - Camera Mount - ALAN GORDON ENTERPRISES, INC.; *pg.* 1399, *pg.* 125
SUPER-GRIP - Cable Tie - PANDUIT CORP.; *pg.* 661, *pg.* 663
SUPER GRIP 2000 - One Component Moisture Cured Urethane - BOSTIK INC.; *pg.* 1150, *pg.* 833
SUPER-GUARD - Automotive Cleaner - DELTA FOREMOST CHEMICAL CORPORATION; *pg.* 1155, *pg.* 1642
SUPER HAWG - High Torque Drill - MILWAUKEE ELECTRIC TOOL CORP.; *pg.* 1056, *pg.* 1855
SUPER HEAVY DUTY - Batteries - DORCY INTERNATIONAL INC.; *pg.* 1046, *pg.* 1439
SUPER HI-POLYMER - Leads - PENTEL OF AMERICA, LTD.; *pg.* 453, *pg.* 295
SUPER HIL-AIRE - Cleaning Product - HILLYARD, INC.; *pg.* 331, *pg.* 990
SUPER HIL-BRITE - Cleaning Product - HILLYARD, INC.; *pg.* 331, *pg.* 990
SUPER HIL-TONE - Cleaning Product - HILLYARD, INC.; *pg.* 331, *pg.* 990
SUPER HORSE - Animal Nutrition Product - MANNA PRO CORPORATION; *pg.* 1478, *pg.* 975
SUPER HUGE - Game - WMS INDUSTRIES INC.; *pg.* 593, *pg.* 666
SUPER HUGE 7S DESIGN - Game - WMS INDUSTRIES INC.; *pg.* 593, *pg.* 666
SUPER II - Counting Scale - SETRA SYSTEMS, INC.; *pg.* 1428, *pg.* 802
SUPER INDO-COLORS - Rug - COURISTAN INC.; *pg.* 921, *pg.* 1067
SUPER INDO-NATURAL - Rug - COURISTAN INC.; *pg.* 921, *pg.* 1067
SUPER INVAR - Breadboards - NEWPORT CORPORATION; *pg.* 1424, *pg.* 114
SUPER JACKPOT PARTY - Game - WMS INDUSTRIES INC.; *pg.* 593, *pg.* 666
SUPER KLEAN - Thinner - AKZONOBEL DECORATIVE PAINTS U.S.; *pg.* 1439, *pg.* 1474
SUPER KLEEN - Automotive Cleaner - DELTA FOREMOST CHEMICAL CORPORATION; *pg.* 1155, *pg.* 1642
SUPER KLEEN - Sewer & Draincleaning Businesses - THE DWYER GROUP, INC.; *pg.* 79, *pg.* 1748
SUPER KMART - Large Department Stores - KMART CORPORATION; *pg.* 1775, *pg.* 617
SUPER-KOTE - Paint - JONES-BLAIR COMPANY; *pg.* 1443, *pg.* 1682
SUPER KRIAL - Pressed & Monolithic Refractory - RESCO PRODUCTS, INC.; *pg.* 107, *pg.* 1581
SUPER-LOC - Waterborne Epoxy Masonry Primer - DUNN-EDWARDS CORPORATION; *pg.* 1442, *pg.* 129
SUPER-LON - Fluid Sealing Product - A.W. CHESTERTON COMPANY; *pg.* 1315, *pg.* 861
SUPER LOTTO PLUS - Lottery Tickets - CALIFORNIA LOTTERY; *pg.* 990, *pg.* 196
SUPER LOTTO PLUS - Lottery Game - OHIO LOTTERY COMMISSION; *pg.* 1002, *pg.* 1433
SUPER LUBE - Lubricants - CONSEW; *pg.* 53, *pg.* 1049
SUPER-LUBE - Skincare Product - MERLE NORMAN COSMETICS, INC.; *pg.* 517, *pg.* 136
SUPER LUCKY LINES - Lottery Game - IDAHO LOTTERY; *pg.* 995, *pg.* 547
SUPER LUSTROUS - Lipstick - REVLON, INC.; *pg.* 521, *pg.* 1286
SUPER MAG 7 - Slots - INTERNATIONAL GAME TECHNOLOGY; *pg.* 957, *pg.* 1024
SUPER MAX - Blind Rivet - ALLFAST FASTENING SYSTEMS, INC.; *pg.* 1041, *pg.* 66
SUPER MAXI - Dispensing System - COHESANT, INC.; *pg.* 1154, *pg.* 1405
SUPER MELATONIN PLUS - Nutritional Product - NUTRACEUTICAL INTERNATIONAL CORPORATION; *pg.* 1576, *pg.* 1753
SUPER MINI Z - Self-propelled Lawn Mower - EXCEL INDUSTRIES, INC.; *pg.* 1795, *pg.* 715
SUPER MOLY - Bullet Lube - LYMAN PRODUCTS CORPORATION; *pg.* 1839, *pg.* 356
SUPER MONOPOLY - Game - MISSOURI LOTTERY; *pg.* 999, *pg.* 979
SUPER MONOSEAL Fluid Sealing Product - A.W. CHESTERTON COMPANY; *pg.* 1315, *pg.* 861
SUPER MULTI-PAY - Game - WMS INDUSTRIES INC.; *pg.* 593, *pg.* 666
SUPER N - Deodorizer - NILODOR, INC.; *pg.* 332, *pg.* 1406
SUPER NATURAL - Rug - COURISTAN INC.; *pg.* 921, *pg.* 1067
SUPER NEUTRAL CABLE - Cable - AFC CABLE SYSTEMS, INC.; *pg.* 1294, *pg.* 835
SUPER NEVTAC - Aliphatic Hydrocarbon Resin - NEVILLE CHEMICAL COMPANY; *pg.* 1174, *pg.* 1578
SUPER NINTENDO ENTERTAINMENT SYSTEM - Video Game System - NINTENDO OF AMERICA, INC.; *pg.* 965, *pg.* 1829
SUPER NITELYTE - Fiber Optic Fixtures - REVOLUTION LIGHTING TECHNOLOGIES, INC.; *pg.* 1304, *pg.* 377
SUPER NOVA - Jewelry - LAGOS INC.; *pg.* 8, *pg.* 1566
SUPER NOVA - Halogen Exam Light - MEDLINE INDUSTRIES, INC.; *pg.* 1562, *pg.* 635
SUPER NOVA 700 - Electric Airless Paint Sprayer - GRACO, INC.; *pg.* 1342, *pg.* 935
SUPER ODOR NEUTRALIZER - Air Freshener Spray - HENKEL CONSUMER GOODS; *pg.* 511, *pg.* 22
SUPER OIL - Lubricant - RADIATOR SPECIALTY COMPANY; *pg.* 215, *pg.* 1380
SUPER OX SENSOR - Oxygen Sensing - ECLIPSE INC.; *pg.* 1332, *pg.* 655
SUPER P - Deicing Spreader - HIGHWAY EQUIPMENT COMPANY; *pg.* 704, *pg.* 702
SUPER-PAC - Actuator - DUFF-NORTON; *pg.* 204, *pg.* 1365
SUPER PAN - Table Pan - THE VOLLRATH COMPANY LLC; *pg.* 1139, *pg.* 1894
SUPER PAN 3 - Food Service Equipment - THE VOLLRATH COMPANY LLC; *pg.* 1139, *pg.* 1894
SUPER PAN II - Food Service Equipment - THE VOLLRATH COMPANY LLC; *pg.* 1139, *pg.* 1894
SUPER PAY ROYALS - Games - PENN NATIONAL GAMING, INC.; *pg.* 574, *pg.* 1595
SUPER PAYDAY - Lottery Game - NEW JERSEY STATE LOTTERY; *pg.* 1000, *pg.* 1126
SUPER PEA - Urinal Screen - AMERICO MANUFACTURING CO., INC.; *pg.* 325, *pg.* 482
SUPER PELILITE - Flashlight - PELICAN PRODUCTS, INC.; *pg.* 1842, *pg.* 295
SUPER POLAR PETE - Slush Machine - GOLD MEDAL PRODUCTS CO.; *pg.* 55, *pg.* 1414
SUPER POLY-SOFT - X-Ray Film Packet - EASTMAN KODAK COMPANY; *pg.* 1408, *pg.* 1333
SUPER-POR-SEAL - Water Repellent Sealer - AKZONOBEL DECORATIVE PAINTS U.S.; *pg.* 1439, *pg.* 1474
SUPER PORTABLE - Marine Portable Shipunloaders - CHRISTIANSON SYSTEMS, INC.; *pg.* 1323, *pg.* 917
SUPER POT - All-Purpose Electric Cooker - JARDEN CONSUMER SOLUTIONS; *pg.* 57, *pg.* 412
SUPER POWER-AIRE - Air Conditioner - HEAT CONTROLLER, INC.; *pg.* 1072, *pg.* 893
SUPER-PRECISION - Turning Machine - HARDINGE INC.; *pg.* 1344, *pg.* 1157
SUPER PRO - Paint & Coating - DIAMOND VOGEL PAINT, INC.; *pg.* 1441, *pg.* 710
SUPER/PRO - Brush - THE WOOSTER BRUSH COMPANY; *pg.* 1450, *pg.* 1482
SUPER PUMA - Model Helicopter - AIRBUS HELICOPTERS, INC.; *pg.* 223, *pg.* 1698
SUPER-PUNCH - Automotive Equipment - THEXTON MANUFACTURING COMPANY, INC.; *pg.* 218, *pg.* 925

SUPER Q10 - Supplement And Food - NEW EARTH LIFE SCIENCES, INC.; *pg.* 1573, *pg.* 1499
SUPER QUICK - Paint & Coating - DIAMOND VOGEL PAINT, INC.; *pg.* 1441, *pg.* 710
SUPER RAKE - Turf Maintenance Machinery - SMITHCO, INC.; *pg.* 1377, *pg.* 1592
SUPER RED - Container Grown Plant - MONROVIA GROWERS; *pg.* 1797, *pg.* 44
SUPER REDHAWK - Double Action Revolvers - STURM, RUGER & COMPANY, INC.; *pg.* 1846, *pg.* 371
SUPER-REFINED MDF2 - Medium Density Fiberboard - PLUM CREEK TIMBER COMPANY, INC.; *pg.* 105, *pg.* 1838
SUPER REVO - Medical Equipment - CONMED CORPORATION; *pg.* 1517, *pg.* 1347
SUPER-RIB - Metal Building Product - CENTRIA, INC.; *pg.* 74, *pg.* 1554
SUPER ROOM - Furniture - HERMAN MILLER, INC.; *pg.* 926, *pg.* 913
SUPER ROPES - Candy Product - AMERICAN LICORICE CO. INC.; *pg.* 1850, *pg.* 692
SUPER RUBY RED 7S - Game - MISSOURI LOTTERY; *pg.* 999, *pg.* 979
SUPER S - Water Soluble Air Freshener - SURCO PRODUCTS, INC.; *pg.* 336, *pg.* 1581
SUPER SABRELITE - Flashlight - PELICAN PRODUCTS, INC.; *pg.* 1842, *pg.* 295
SUPER SAFE SOLV - Safety Solvent - DELTA FOREMOST CHEMICAL CORPORATION; *pg.* 1155, *pg.* 1642
SUPER-SAFEWAY - Electronic Components - MOLEX INCORPORATED; *pg.* 655, *pg.* 628
SUPER SANI-CLOTH - Wipe - CROSSTEX INTERNATIONAL INC.; *pg.* 1520, *pg.* 1164
SUPER SAVER - Educational Toys - LEAPFROG ENTERPRISES, INC.; *pg.* 961, *pg.* 84
SUPER SAW PALMETTO PLUS - Nutritional Product - NUTRACEUTICAL INTERNATIONAL CORPORATION; *pg.* 1576, *pg.* 1753
SUPER SAWZALL - Power Tool - MILWAUKEE ELECTRIC TOOL CORP.; *pg.* 1056, *pg.* 1855
SUPER SCATTER - Game - WMS INDUSTRIES INC.; *pg.* 593, *pg.* 666
SUPER SCRABBLE - Game - WINNING MOVES GAMES, INC.; *pg.* 970, *pg.* 816
SUPER-SCRUBBER - Rotary Washer - TELSMITH, INC.; *pg.* 1381, *pg.* 1871
SUPER SCULPT - Hair Care Product - JOHN PAUL MITCHELL SYSTEMS; *pg.* 512, *pg.* 133
SUPER SEALS, EXCEPTIONAL SERVICE - Tagline - SEALING DEVICES INC.; *pg.* 1889, *pg.* 1173
SUPER SEED - Health Supplement - GARDEN OF LIFE, INC.; *pg.* 1532, *pg.* 478
SUPER SELECT - Clipper - ANDIS COMPANY; *pg.* 498, *pg.* 1895
SUPER SHARP - Power Tool - MILWAUKEE ELECTRIC TOOL CORP.; *pg.* 1056, *pg.* 1855
SUPER SHEATH - Medical Device - BOSTON SCIENTIFIC CORPORATION; *pg.* 1508, *pg.* 831
SUPER SHELF - Building Products - BOISE CASCADE HOLDINGS, L.L.C.; *pg.* 1453, *pg.* 546
SUPER SHINE-ALL - Cleaning Product - HILLYARD, INC.; *pg.* 331, *pg.* 990
SUPER SHOT SEVENS DESIGN - Game - WMS INDUSTRIES INC.; *pg.* 593, *pg.* 666
SUPER SKINNY - Hair Care Product - JOHN PAUL MITCHELL SYSTEMS; *pg.* 512, *pg.* 133
SUPER SLAM - Apparel - CABELA'S INCORPORATED; *pg.* 535, *pg.* 1019
SUPER SLIP - Floss - RANIR LLC; *pg.* 520, *pg.* 888
SUPER SLOTS - Lottery Game - OHIO LOTTERY COMMISSION; *pg.* 1002, *pg.* 1433
SUPER SOAKER - Toy & Game - HASBRO, INC.; *pg.* 954, *pg.* 1603
SUPER SOAKER MONSTER ROCKET - Toy & Game - HASBRO, INC.; *pg.* 954, *pg.* 1603
SUPER-SOLV - Solvent - DELTA FOREMOST CHEMICAL CORPORATION; *pg.* 1155, *pg.* 1642
SUPER SOXGETTER - Enhancement Additive - JOHNSON MATTHEY PROCESS TECHNOLOGIES; *pg.* 1169, *pg.* 1083
SUPER SPAR - Varnish - JONES-BLAIR COMPANY; *pg.* 1443, *pg.* 1682
SUPER SPEED - Aluminum Paint - JONES-BLAIR COMPANY; *pg.* 1443, *pg.* 1682
SUPER SPEED SOLUTIONS - Analytical System - BRUKER CORPORATION; *pg.* 1511, *pg.* 788
SUPER SPIKE - Tetherball - SCHOOL-TECH, INC.; *pg.* 1844, *pg.* 866
SUPER SPIN SIZZLING 7 - Slots - INTERNATIONAL GAME TECHNOLOGY; *pg.* 957, *pg.* 1024
SUPER SPORTS - Candy - R.M. PALMER COMPANY; *pg.* 1861, *pg.* 1585
SUPER SPOT - Screw-In Light Converter - SWIVELIER CO., INC.; *pg.* 1307, *pg.* 1142
SUPER SPRAY - Detergent - ADCO, INC.; *pg.* 325, *pg.* 482
SUPER SPROUTS AND ALGAE - Supplement & Food Product - NEW EARTH LIFE SCIENCES, INC.; *pg.* 1573, *pg.* 1499
SUPER STAR - Turf Maintenance Machinery - SMITHCO, INC.; *pg.* 1377, *pg.* 1592
SUPER STARS - Video Game - INTERNATIONAL GAME TECHNOLOGY; *pg.* 957, *pg.* 1024
SUPER STARS SPIN - Slots - INTERNATIONAL GAME TECHNOLOGY; *pg.* 957, *pg.* 1024
SUPER STEEL - Garage Door - MARTIN DOOR MANUFACTURING, INC.; *pg.* 96, *pg.* 1759
SUPER STEP - Building Products - BOISE CASCADE HOLDINGS, L.L.C.; *pg.* 1453, *pg.* 546
SUPER STEPPER BENCH SYSTEM - Aerobic Step & Weight Bench - ALLIANCE SPORTS GROUP, L.P.; *pg.* 1825, *pg.* 1698
SUPER STRATA SLURPEE - Frozen Beverage - 7-ELEVEN, INC.; *pg.* 1012, *pg.* 1672
SUPER STREAMMACHINE - Stock Trading Tool - TD AMERITRADE HOLDING CORPORATION; *pg.* 808, *pg.* 1018
SUPER STREET - Magazine - RENTPATH, INC.; *pg.* 1680, *pg.* 538
THE SUPER STRENGTHENER - Hair Care System - JOHN PAUL MITCHELL SYSTEMS; *pg.* 512, *pg.* 133
SUPER STRIP - Nonflammable Paint Remover - THE SAVOGRAN COMPANY; *pg.* 1447, *pg.* 840
SUPER STRONG - Hair Care Product - JOHN PAUL MITCHELL SYSTEMS; *pg.* 512, *pg.* 133
SUPER SUN SMOOTHIE - Supplement & Food Product - NEW EARTH LIFE SCIENCES, INC.; *pg.* 1573, *pg.* 1499
SUPER SUPREME - Vanilla - DAVID MICHAEL & CO. INC.; *pg.* 852, *pg.* 1563
SUPER T - Wire Stripper - IDEAL INDUSTRIES, INC.; *pg.* 1051, *pg.* 662
SUPER TAC - Flashlight - STREAMLIGHT INC.; *pg.* 1306, *pg.* 1527
SUPER TAK - Aerosol Adhesives - BOSTIK INC.; *pg.* 1150, *pg.* 833
SUPER TALL - Straight Knife - THE WOLF MACHINE CO.; *pg.* 1389, *pg.* 1427
SUPER-TAN - Dry Cleaning & Laundry Product - ADCO, INC.; *pg.* 325, *pg.* 482
SUPER TESTRON - Health & Beauty Product - DIXIE HEALTH, INC.; *pg.* 1524, *pg.* 535
SUPER TI POWDER - Powder - UNITED-GUARDIAN, INC.; *pg.* 1184, *pg.* 1165
SUPER TIMES JACKPOT - Video Game - INTERNATIONAL GAME TECHNOLOGY; *pg.* 957, *pg.* 1024
SUPER TIMES PAY - Video Poker - INTERNATIONAL GAME TECHNOLOGY; *pg.* 957, *pg.* 1024
SUPER TIMES STRIKE - Video Game - INTERNATIONAL GAME TECHNOLOGY; *pg.* 957, *pg.* 1024
SUPER TIP - Toothbrush - SUNSTAR AMERICAS INC.; *pg.* 1599, *pg.* 591
SUPER TOOL - Cutting Tool - LEATHERMAN TOOL GROUP, INC.; *pg.* 1053, *pg.* 1504
SUPER TOOL 200 - Knive - LEATHERMAN TOOL GROUP, INC.; *pg.* 1053, *pg.* 1504
SUPER TOP SPEED - Nail Polish - REVLON, INC.; *pg.* 521, *pg.* 1286
SUPER-TOUGH - Power Tool - MILWAUKEE ELECTRIC TOOL CORP.; *pg.* 1056, *pg.* 1855
SUPER TOUGHCOAT - Topcoats & Primers - SHERWIN WILLIAMS; *pg.* 1448, *pg.* 1436
SUPER TOWER - Pneumatic Shipunloader - CHRISTIANSON SYSTEMS, INC.; *pg.* 1323, *pg.* 917
SUPER TRACK - Phonograph Cartridge - SHURE INCORPORATED; *pg.* 672, *pg.* 638
SUPER-TRANSTAY - Overlay Films for Graphic Arts Anti-Static, Anti-HaloPoly. Layout Base - TRANSILWRAP COMPANY, INC.; *pg.* 1470, *pg.* 613
SUPER TREAT - Bentonite Clay - MINERALS TECHNOLOGIES INC.; *pg.* 1173, *pg.* 617
SUPER TRIMEC - Turf Product - PBI/GORDON CORPORATION; *pg.* 1176, *pg.* 985
SUPER TROUPE - Entertainment Lighting - BALLANTYNE STRONG, INC.; *pg.* 623, *pg.* 1013
THE SUPER TROUPER - Entertainment Lighting - BALLANTYNE STRONG, INC.; *pg.* 623, *pg.* 1013
SUPER TROWLEZE - Pressed & Monolithic Refractory - RESCO PRODUCTS, INC.; *pg.* 107, *pg.* 1581
SUPER TRUSS - Uprights for Selective & Drive-In Rack - SPEEDRACK PRODUCTS GROUP, LTD.; *pg.* 112, *pg.* 908
SUPER TUBE - Socks - WIGWAM MILLS, INC.; *pg.* 15, *pg.* 1894
SUPER TUF CUT END MILLS - Rex Seventy-Six End Mills - REGAL BELOIT CORPORATION; *pg.* 106, *pg.* 1854
SUPER-TUFF - Apparel - LACROSSE FOOTWEAR, INC.; *pg.* 1811, *pg.* 1503
SUPER TUFF - Welding Helmet - SELLSTROM MANUFACTURING CO.; *pg.* 1428, *pg.* 659
SUPER TUFF TAG - Custom Material - CHECKPOINT SYSTEMS, INC.; *pg.* 628, *pg.* 1559
SUPER TUGGER - Puller - GREENLEE TEXTRON INC.; *pg.* 1048, *pg.* 655
SUPER TURBO - Fan - KAZ, INC.; *pg.* 58, *pg.* 844
SUPER U-365 - Interior Alkyd Enamel Undercoater - DUNN-EDWARDS CORPORATION; *pg.* 1442, *pg.* 129
SUPER ULTRALAST - Wheel - HAMILTON CASTER & MFG. CO.; *pg.* 206, *pg.* 1454
SUPER V - Tooth Equipment - ESCO CORPORATION; *pg.* 1335, *pg.* 1502
SUPER-V - Drag Conveyors - SCREW CONVEYOR INDUSTRIES; *pg.* 1374, *pg.* 682
SUPER VALUE - Pipe Tobaccos, Cigarette Rolling Tobacco - ALTADIS USA, INC.; *pg.* 1893, *pg.* 423
SUPER VARMINTMASTER - Rifle - WEATHERBY, INC.; *pg.* 1848, *pg.* 181
SUPER VISION - Lighting Systems - REVOLUTION LIGHTING TECHNOLOGIES, INC.; *pg.* 1304, *pg.* 377
SUPER VU-TRON - Welding Cables - GENERAL CABLE CORPORATION; *pg.* 83, *pg.* 729
SUPER WALKBEHIND - Self-propelled Lawn Mower - EXCEL INDUSTRIES, INC.; *pg.* 1795, *pg.* 715
SUPER WHEEL POKER - Video Game - INTERNATIONAL GAME TECHNOLOGY; *pg.* 957, *pg.* 1024
SUPER WILD - Video Game - INTERNATIONAL GAME TECHNOLOGY; *pg.* 957, *pg.* 1024
SUPER WIPER - Fluid Sealing Product - A.W. CHESTERTON COMPANY; *pg.* 1315, *pg.* 861
SUPER WITCH - Underground Construction Equipment - CHARLES MACHINE WORKS, INC.; *pg.* 1322, *pg.* 1488
SUPER WITCH II - Underground Construction Equipment - CHARLES MACHINE WORKS, INC.; *pg.* 1322, *pg.* 1488
SUPER X - Sheet Packing - CHICAGO-WILCOX MFG. COMPANY, INC.; *pg.* 202, *pg.* 661
SUPER-X - Plastic Packaging Product - POLY PAK AMERICA, INC.; *pg.* 1467, *pg.* 138
SUPER X - Footwear - P.W. MINOR & SON, INC.; *pg.* 1816, *pg.* 1140
SUPER Z - Mower Tractor - EXCEL INDUSTRIES, INC.; *pg.* 1795, *pg.* 715
SUPER Z - Floor Polish - HILLYARD, INC.; *pg.* 331, *pg.* 990
SUPER Z - Catalyst Additive - JOHNSON MATTHEY PROCESS TECHNOLOGIES; *pg.* 1169, *pg.* 1083
SUPER Z DIESEL - Mower Tractor - EXCEL INDUSTRIES, INC.; *pg.* 1795, *pg.* 715
SUPER-ZIP - Fluid Handling System - GRACO, INC.; *pg.* 1342, *pg.* 935
SUPER1 FOOD - Food Store - URM STORES, INC.; *pg.* 1036, *pg.* 1844
SUPER1FOODS - Food Products - BROOKSHIRE GROCERY COMPANY; *pg.* 1016, *pg.* 1748
SUPERAGATE - Balloon - CONTINENTAL AMERICAN CORP.; *pg.* 1880, *pg.* 723
SUPERAMERICA - Gasoline Store - SPEEDWAY LLC; *pg.* 985, *pg.* 1452
SUPERB - Soybean Oil - ARCHER-DANIELS-MIDLAND COMPANY; *pg.* 825, *pg.* 565
SUPERB - Frame - BROWN & BIGELOW, INC.; *pg.* 1624, *pg.* 959
SUPERB SELECT - Sunflower Oil - ARCHER-DANIELS-MIDLAND COMPANY; *pg.* 825, *pg.* 565
SUPERB SELECT NU-SUN - Sunflower Oil - ARCHER-DANIELS-MIDLAND COMPANY; *pg.* 825, *pg.* 565
SUPERB SELECT POWER-SUN - Sunflower Oil - ARCHER-DANIELS-MIDLAND COMPANY; *pg.* 825, *pg.* 565
SUPERBA - Neckwear Producer Company - PVH

NECKWEAR GROUP; pg. 46, pg. 139
SUPERBAR - Nail Puller - VAUGHAN & BUSHNELL MANUFACTURING COMPANY, INC.; pg. 1066, pg. 616
SUPERBAY - Lighting Fixture - HUBBELL INCORPORATED; pg. 1299, pg. 370
SUPERBEAM - Software - ANDREA ELECTRONICS CORPORATION; pg. 617, pg. 1143
SUPERBGA - Packaging System - AMKOR TECHNOLOGY, INC.; pg. 67, pg. 25
SUPERBLUE - Led - CREE INC.; pg. 631, pg. 1371
SUPERBOND - Corrugating & Bag - GRAIN PROCESSING CORPORATION; pg. 859, pg. 709
SUPERBOT - Robot Server - ATS AUTOMATION TOOLING SYSTEMS INC.; pg. 355, pg. 1919
SUPERBOY - Character - DC COMICS, INC.; pg. 1633, pg. 1221
SUPERBRIGHT - Led - CREE INC.; pg. 631, pg. 1371
SUPERBRUSH - Agricultural Product - PBI/GORDON CORPORATION; pg. 1176, pg. 985
SUPERBUFF - Buffing Pad - 3M COMPANY; pg. 1142, pg. 956
SUPERBURGER - Burger Entree - EAT'N PARK HOSPITALITY GROUP; pg. 1728, pg. 1539
SUPERCASH - Lottery Game - OHIO LOTTERY COMMISSION; pg. 1002, pg. 1433
SUPERCAT - Data Communication Product - GENERAL CABLE CORPORATION; pg. 83, pg. 729
SUPERCAT - Plural Component Proportioners - GRACO, INC.; pg. 1342, pg. 935
SUPERCAVITY - Optical Spectrum Analyzer - NEWPORT CORPORATION; pg. 1424, pg. 114
SUPERCEM - Cement - LAFARGE CANADA INC.; pg. 92, pg. 1958
SUPERCENTER - Furniture - HSM SOLUTIONS; pg. 1884, pg. 1378
SUPERCERTIFICATE - Gift Card - GIFTCERTIFICATES.COM; pg. 1249, pg. 1015
SUPERCHANGER - Plate and Frame Heat Exchangers - TRANTER PHE, INC.; pg. 1383, pg. 1749
SUPERCHARGE - Ceramic & Plastic Product - COORSTEK, INC.; pg. 77, pg. 330
SUPERCHARTS - Investment Analysis Software - TRADESTATION GROUP, INC.; pg. 811, pg. 459
SUPERCHIPS - ATC 100 Series RF/Microwave Multilayer Porcelain Capacitors - AMERICAN TECHNICAL CERAMICS CORP.; pg. 616, pg. 1168
SUPERCHLOR - Alloy - FLOWSERVE CORPORATION; pg. 82, pg. 1719
SUPERCLEAR - Label - AVERY DENNISON CORPORATION; pg. 1452, pg. 95
SUPERCLEAR - Computer Monitor - VIEWSONIC CORPORATION; pg. 489, pg. 303
SUPERCLUSTER - Supercomputing System - CRAY INC.; pg. 380, pg. 1834
SUPERCOL - Polymer - HERCULES INCORPORATED; pg. 1166, pg. 392
SUPERCONNECT - Cable Modem Products - ALCATEL-LUCENT; pg. 615, pg. 1094
SUPERCONSOLE - Telephone Software - MITEL NETWORKS CORPORATION; pg. 654, pg. 1921
SUPERCONTRAST - Computer Equipment - VIEWSONIC CORPORATION; pg. 489, pg. 303
SUPERCOTE - Automotive Reconditioning Product - MOC PRODUCTS COMPANY, INC.; pg. 332, pg. 174
SUPERCUP - Fluid Sealing Product - A.W. CHESTERTON COMPANY; pg. 1315, pg. 861
SUPERCUTS - Hair Salons - REGIS CORPORATION; pg. 521, pg. 941
SUPERCYCLE - Packaging Product - CASCADES, INC.; pg. 73, pg. 1950
SUPERDISK - 120 Mb High Capacity Diskettes & Drives - IMATION CORP.; pg. 413, pg. 952
SUPERDRIVE - Computer Media Device - APPLE INC.; pg. 350, pg. 73
SUPERFABULOSO - Educational Materials - SCHOLASTIC INC.; pg. 1683, pg. 1288
SUPERFC - Packaging System - AMKOR TECHNOLOGY, INC.; pg. 67, pg. 25
SUPERFEET - Capsule - WELLCO ENTERPRISES, INC.; pg. 1822, pg. 1392
SUPERFICIAL - Apparel - OAKLEY, INC.; pg. 1840, pg. 86
THE SUPERFICIAL - Celebrity News Site - SPINMEDIA; pg. 1282, pg. 104
SUPERFINE - Food Product - HANOVER FOODS CORPORATION; pg. 861, pg. 1535
SUPERFINE - Printing Paper - MOHAWK FINE PAPERS, INC.; pg. 1464, pg. 1153
SUPERFINE - Air Classifier - STURTEVANT INC.; pg. 1379, pg. 824
SUPERFINE AIR SEPARATOR - Air Separators - STURTEVANT INC.; pg. 1379, pg. 824
SUPERFLEX - Lined Metal Hose/S.S. - FEDERAL HOSE MANUFACTURING INC.; pg. 1047, pg. 1469
SUPERFLEX - Seal & Thermoplastic Component - GREENE, TWEED & CO.; pg. 1344, pg. 1544
SUPERFLEX - Translating Mass Accelerometer - HONEYWELL AEROSPACE ELECTRONIC SYSTEMS; pg. 228, pg. 17
SUPERFLEX - Satellite Datacasting System - INTERNATIONAL DATACASTING CORPORATION; pg. 419, pg. 1921
SUPERFLEX - Filter - W.L. GORE & ASSOCIATES, INC.; pg. 122, pg. 388
SUPERFLO - Lab Dialysis Product - SPECTRUM LABORATORIES INC.; pg. 1595, pg. 69
SUPERFLOC - Chemical Product - CYTEC INDUSTRIES, INC.; pg. 1155, pg. 1131
SUPERFLOW - Refractory Product - RESCO PRODUCTS, INC.; pg. 107, pg. 1581
SUPERFLOW - Plastic & Rubber - TEKNOR APEX COMPANY; pg. 1889, pg. 1605
SUPERFOAM - Plastic & Rubber - TEKNOR APEX COMPANY; pg. 1889, pg. 1605
SUPERGARD - Motor Oil - CITGO PETROLEUM CORPORATION; pg. 974, pg. 1703
SUPERGARD ULTRALIFE - Motor Oil - CITGO PETROLEUM CORPORATION; pg. 974, pg. 1703
SUPERGEL - Filter - ROSCO LABORATORIES, INC.; pg. 1782, pg. 378
SUPERGIRL - Character - DC COMICS, INC.; pg. 1633, pg. 1221
SUPERGLUTEN - Agricultural Product - ARCHER-DANIELS-MIDLAND COMPANY; pg. 825, pg. 565
SUPERGOLD - Diesel Fuel - SOUTHERN STATES COOPERATIVE, INC.; pg. 1482, pg. 1804
SUPERGRIP - Cover & Pad - HOME PRODUCTS INTERNATIONAL, INC.; pg. 1125, pg. 577
SUPERHOG - Battery - ENERSYS INC.; pg. 1334, pg. 1584
SUPERHOT - Hot Water Boosters - CHESHER EQUIPMENT LTD.; pg. 1323, pg. 1925
SUPERIOR - Fire & Rescue Apparatus - FEDERAL SIGNAL CORPORATION; pg. 638, pg. 645
SUPERIOR - Healthcare Product - GF HEALTH PRODUCTS, INC.; pg. 1535, pg. 508
SUPERIOR - Fireplaces & Gas Logs - LENNOX HEARTH PRODUCTS; pg. 93, pg. 1652
SUPERIOR - Lubrication Equipment Accessories - PLEWS/EDELMANN; pg. 215, pg. 607
SUPERIOR - Dry Snuff - SWISHER INTERNATIONAL, INC.; pg. 1895, pg. 345
SUPERIOR DATA WRAPPED IN AN ENGAGING EXPERIENCE - Tag Line - SURVEY SAMPLING INTERNATIONAL LLC; pg. 1690, pg. 371
SUPERIOR ELECTRIC - Hardware & Software - DANAHER CORPORATION; pg. 1044, pg. 397
SUPERIOR HERBS - Healthcare Product - SWANSON HEALTH PRODUCTS INC.; pg. 1600, pg. 1397
SUPERIOR HONEY - Honey - MILLER'S HONEY COMPANY; pg. 1860, pg. 1759
SUPERIOR MISCIBLE - Refined Petroleum Distillate - UNIVERSAL COOPERATIVES, INC.; pg. 1482, pg. 922
SUPERIOR RELIABILITY & PERFORMANCE - Slogan - COHERENT, INC.; pg. 1406, pg. 265
SUPERIOR SOLUTIONS - Tagline - ZEP INC.; pg. 338, pg. 524
SUPERIOR SYSTEMS SOLUTIONS - Tagline - ELECTRO-SENSORS, INC.; pg. 1333, pg. 948
SUPERIORE - Mascara - BORGHESE, INC.; pg. 502, pg. 1205
SUPERIOR'S - Meat Product - FRESH MARK, INC.; pg. 856, pg. 1461
SUPERKILL - Tennis String - ASHAWAY LINE & TWINE MFG. CO.; pg. 1826, pg. 1600
SUPERKOTE - Plating Process - A BRITE COMPANY; pg. 1144, pg. 1697
SUPERKROME - High Polish Finish - SK HAND TOOL CORPORATION; pg. 1062, pg. 663
SUPERLA SIEVE - Test Sieve - NEWARK WIRE CLOTH CO.; pg. 99, pg. 1052
SUPERLAST - Wheel - HAMILTON CASTER & MFG. CO.; pg. 206, pg. 1454
SUPERLINE - Software System - ALCATEL-LUCENT; pg. 615, pg. 1094
SUPERLINEAR - Plastic Compound & Resin - A. SCHULMAN, INC.; pg. 1144, pg. 1452
SUPERLINK - Supercomputing System - CRAY INC.; pg. 380, pg. 1834
SUPERLITE - Hose - HBD INDUSTRIES, INC.; pg. 207, pg. 1449
SUPERLITE - Integrated Circuits - MICREL, INC.; pg. 654, pg. 247
SUPERLITE - Circulars - PROPHOTONIX LIMITED; pg. 1427, pg. 1039
SUPERLOAD - Software - BENTLEY SYSTEMS, INC.; pg. 361, pg. 1531
SUPERLOADER - Tape Autoloader - QUANTUM CORPORATION; pg. 458, pg. 250
SUPERLOONS - Foil Balloons - CTI INDUSTRIES CORPORATION; pg. 1881, pg. 555
SUPERLUME - Medical Product - PROPPER MANUFACTURING COMPANY, INC.; pg. 1586, pg. 1175
SUPERMAN - Character - DC COMICS, INC.; pg. 1633, pg. 1221
SUPERMAPPER - Integrated Circuits - AVAGO TECHNOLOGIES; pg. 358, pg. 238
SUPERMATIC - Home Appliance Product - WHIRLPOOL CORPORATION; pg. 62, pg. 872
SUPERMAX - Rivet - ALLFAST FASTENING SYSTEMS, INC.; pg. 1041, pg. 66
SUPERMAX - All-Welded Plate Heat Exchangers - TRANTER PHE, INC.; pg. 1383, pg. 1749
SUPERMELTS - Food Product - FRIENDLY ICE CREAM, LLC; pg. 1853, pg. 859
SUPERMERCADO DE WALMART - Hispanic Markets - WAL-MART STORES, INC.; pg. 1790, pg. 29
SUPERMET - High-Speed Abrasive Disc Grinder - BUEHLER, LTD.; pg. 1403, pg. 622
SUPERMICRO - Microperforated Films for Bread Packing - SEALED AIR CORPORATION; pg. 1468, pg. 1058
SUPERMIX - Fluid Handling System - GRACO, INC.; pg. 1342, pg. 935
SUPERMOIST - Cake Mixes - GENERAL MILLS, INC.; pg. 828, pg. 933
SUPERNAIL - Sculptured Nails - AMERICAN INTERNATIONAL INDUSTRIES COMPANY; pg. 498, pg. 126
SUPERNICK XL - String - ASHAWAY LINE & TWINE MFG. CO.; pg. 1826, pg. 1600
SUPERNICK XL MICRO - String - ASHAWAY LINE & TWINE MFG. CO.; pg. 1826, pg. 1600
SUPERNICK XL PRO - String - ASHAWAY LINE & TWINE MFG. CO.; pg. 1826, pg. 1600
SUPERNICK XL TITANIUM - String - ASHAWAY LINE & TWINE MFG. CO.; pg. 1826, pg. 1600
SUPERNOVA - Vehicle Safety System - GROTE INDUSTRIES, INC.; pg. 206, pg. 693
SUPERNOVA - Fabric - NEMSCHOFF, INC.; pg. 936, pg. 1890
SUPERNOVAPRO - Airless Paint Sprayer - GRACO, INC.; pg. 1342, pg. 935
SUPERNUMBER - Hotel & Motel Reservations Service - AMERICAN AUTOMOBILE ASSOCIATION; pg. 1190, pg. 429
SUPERPAC - Block Machine - BESSER COMPANY; pg. 1317, pg. 865
SUPERPAGES - Online Directory - DEX MEDIA INC; pg. 1635, pg. 1680
SUPERPAGES MOBILE - Online Directory - DEX MEDIA INC; pg. 1635, pg. 1680
SUPERPAGES.COM - Website - DEX MEDIA INC; pg. 1635, pg. 1680
SUPERPAINT - Paint - THE SHERWIN-WILLIAMS COMPANY; pg. 1447, pg. 1435
SUPERPANEL - Software - NIELSEN AUDIO; pg. 446, pg. 768
SUPERPANELIST - Software - NIELSEN AUDIO; pg. 446, pg. 768
SUPERPIPE - Software System - ALCATEL-LUCENT; pg. 615, pg. 1094
SUPERPLEX TC - Lubricant - D-A LUBRICANT COMPANY; pg. 975, pg. 693
SUPERPLEXUS - Game - HASBRO, INC.; pg. 954, pg. 1603
SUPERPOO - Grooming Product - W.F. YOUNG, INC.; pg. 1610, pg. 817
SUPERPRESS - Computer Equipment - VIEWSONIC

First page reference indicates Business Class Edition
Second page reference indicates Geographic Edition

CORPORATION; pg. 489, pg. 303
SUPERPRETZEL - Soft Pretzels - J&J SNACK FOODS CORPORATION; pg. 865, pg. 1107
SUPERSAFE - Battery - ENERSYS INC.; pg. 1334, pg. 1584
SUPERSAVER FOODS - Grocery Stores - ALBERTSON'S LLC; pg. 1013, pg. 546
SUPERSCIENCE - Educational Materials - SCHOLASTIC INC.; pg. 1683, pg. 1288
SUPERSCOOPER - Amphibious Aircraft - BOMBARDIER INC.; pg. 1318, pg. 1953
SUPERSCRIPT - Balloon - CONTINENTAL AMERICAN CORP.; pg. 1880, pg. 723
SUPERSCRIPT - Molecular Biology Product - THERMO FISHER SCIENTIFIC INC.; pg. 1602, pg. 61
SUPERSEAL - Custom Coated Products - ALLIED SECURITY INNOVATIONS, INC.; pg. 1041, pg. 1066
SUPERSEAL - Sealing Compound - SMOOTH-ON INC.; pg. 111, pg. 1528
SUPERSEED - Impatiens Seeds - PANAMERICAN SEED CO.; pg. 1798, pg. 668
SUPERSET 2 - Single Line Telephone - MITEL NETWORKS CORPORATION; pg. 654, pg. 1921
SUPERSET 3 - Advanced Business Telephones - MITEL NETWORKS CORPORATION; pg. 654, pg. 1921
SUPERSET 4 - Advanced Business Telephones - MITEL NETWORKS CORPORATION; pg. 654, pg. 1921
SUPERSET 7 - Attendant Console for SX-2000 - MITEL NETWORKS CORPORATION; pg. 654, pg. 1921
SUPERSETS - Socket Set Packages - SK HAND TOOL CORPORATION; pg. 1062, pg. 663
SUPERSHELL - Outerwear - BLAUER MANUFACTURING COMPANY, INC.; pg. 20, pg. 789
SUPERSHIELD - Gel Protective Coating - FERRO CORPORATION; pg. 1162, pg. 1462
SUPERSHIELD - Fly Control Product - W.F. YOUNG, INC.; pg. 1610, pg. 817
SUPERSHIELD GREEN - Horse Spray - W.F. YOUNG, INC.; pg. 1610, pg. 817
SUPERSHINE - Grooming Product - W.F. YOUNG, INC.; pg. 1610, pg. 817
SUPERSHOCK - Beauty Product - AVON PRODUCTS, INC.; pg. 500, pg. 1198
SUPERSHOT - Fluid Handling System - GRACO, INC.; pg. 1342, pg. 935
SUPERSIL - Precision Abrasive Product - SAINT-GOBAIN ABRASIVES, INC. - PHILADELPHIA; pg. 1180, pg. 1553
SUPERSLIMS - Cigarettes - PHILIP MORRIS USA INC.; pg. 1894, pg. 1803
SUPERSLIP - Coverglass Cartridge - HACKER INSTRUMENTS & INDUSTRIES INC.; pg. 1415, pg. 1623
SUPERSMITH - Software - GULF PUBLISHING COMPANY; pg. 1646, pg. 1707
SUPERSOCOLATE - Specialty Fats - CARGILL LIMITED; pg. 1475, pg. 1914
SUPERSOFT - Paper - INTERNATIONAL PAPER COMPANY; pg. 1460, pg. 1644
SUPERSOFT - Fabric - POLYMER GROUP, INC.; pg. 698, pg. 1368
SUPERSOFTMARK - Laser System - GSI GROUP INC.; pg. 1415, pg. 784
SUPERSOIL - Fertilizers - THE SCOTTS MIRACLE-GRO COMPANY; pg. 1799, pg. 1459
SUPERSOLE - Footwear - RED WING SHOE COMPANY, INC.; pg. 1817, pg. 954
SUPERSOLE 2.0 - Footwear - RED WING SHOE COMPANY, INC.; pg. 1817, pg. 954
SUPERSONIC - Cheeseburger - SONIC CORP.; pg. 1750, pg. 1487
SUPERSTAR CASH - Lottery Game - IOWA LOTTERY; pg. 996, pg. 705
SUPERSTAR COFFEE CREAM - Confectionery - THE HERSHEY CO.; pg. 1855, pg. 1538
SUPERSTAT - Thermostat - COMVERGE, INC.; pg. 1325, pg. 536
SUPERSTEEL - Hammer - VAUGHAN & BUSHNELL MANUFACTURING COMPANY, INC.; pg. 1066, pg. 616
SUPERSTEP - Universal Truck Steps - LUND INTERNATIONAL, INC.; pg. 211, pg. 526
SUPERSTRATE - Film Substrate - COORSTEK, INC.; pg. 77, pg. 330
SUPERSTRUT - Metal Framing - THOMAS & BETTS CORPORATION; pg. 680, pg. 1646
SUPERTARGET - Department Stores - TARGET CORPORATION; pg. 1786, pg. 942
SUPERTERM - Access Control System - NAPCO SECURITY SYSTEMS, INC.; pg. 658, pg. 1138
SUPERTEXTURE - Anisotropic Texture - EVANS & SUTHERLAND COMPUTER CORPORATION; pg. 638, pg. 1757
SUPERTONE - Nutritional Product - NUTRACEUTICAL INTERNATIONAL CORPORATION; pg. 1576, pg. 1753
SUPERTOP - Soft Top for Jeep - BESTOP, INC.; pg. 200, pg. 312
SUPERTRACKER - Shipment Service - FEDEX CORPORATION; pg. 1907, pg. 1642
SUPERTRAK - Conveyor & Linear Motor - ATS AUTOMATION TOOLING SYSTEMS INC.; pg. 355, pg. 1919
SUPERTRIM - Panel PC System - CYBERRESEARCH INC.; pg. 381, pg. 339
SUPERVALU - Food And Drug Product - SUPERVALU, INC.; pg. 1035, pg. 924
SUPERVAN - Vanillin Replacement - DAVID MICHAEL & CO. INC.; pg. 852, pg. 1563
SUPERVAULT - Aboveground Horizontal Storage Tank - MODERN WELDING COMPANY, INC.; pg. 1363, pg. 739
SUPERVIEW - Cable Television Services - AT&T SOUTHEAST; pg. 1868, pg. 489
SUPERVISION - Hand Held Night Vision Device - XENONICS HOLDINGS, INC.; pg. 1308, pg. 62
SUPERVISOR - Curtain - SELLSTROM MANUFACTURING CO.; pg. 1428, pg. 659
SUPERWHITE - Tent Fabric - ANCHOR INDUSTRIES, INC.; pg. 1825, pg. 678
SUPERWOMAN - Character - DC COMICS, INC.; pg. 1633, pg. 1221
SUPIMA - Linens Fabrics - TEMPUR SEALY INTERNATIONAL, INC.; pg. 944, pg. 731
SUPLENA - Nutritional Product - ABBOTT LABORATORIES; pg. 1484, pg. 551
SUPLEX - Tights - SCHOOL-TECH, INC.; pg. 1844, pg. 866
SUPOR - Filter Cartridge - PALL CORPORATION; pg. 232, pg. 1323
SUPPER BAKES - Soup - CAMPBELL SOUP COMPANY; pg. 844, pg. 1048
SUPPLE LEATHER STABILITY WALKER - Rubber Sole - MASON COMPANIES, INC.; pg. 1811, pg. 1856
SUPPLEMENTAL CASING HANGER SYSTEM - Subsea Equipment - DRIL-QUIP, INC.; pg. 1330, pg. 1704
SUPPLEMENTS SIMPLIFIED. - Tagline - SMARTPAK EQUINE, LLC; pg. 1482, pg. 834
SUPPLEX - Cotton-Soft Fabrics & Fibers - INVISTA B.V.; pg. 1168, pg. 723
SUPPLIES DEVELOPMENT CENTRE & DESIGN - Manual - XEROX CORPORATION; pg. 494, pg. 365
SUPPLIESASSISTANT - Software - XEROX CORPORATION; pg. 494, pg. 365
SUPPLY CHAIN ESSENTIALS - Software - RENTRAK CORPORATION; pg. 306, pg. 1506
SUPPLY CHAIN ITS ALL WE DO - Slogan - MANHATTAN ASSOCIATES, INC.; pg. 430, pg. 513
THE SUPPLY CHAIN PEOPLE - Slogan - MANHATTAN ASSOCIATES, INC.; pg. 430, pg. 513
SUPPLY LYNX - Management Service - VHA INC.; pg. 1606, pg. 1724
SUPPLYSCAN - Supply Management System - MCKESSON CORPORATION; pg. 1560, pg. 222
SUPPLYSIDE INSIDE COSMECEUTICALS - Publication - INFORMA EXHIBITIONS LLC; pg. 1653, pg. 17
SUPPLYWATCH - Software - ARIBA, INC.; pg. 353, pg. 283
SUPPORT IN STYLE - Maternity Band - THE BOPPY COMPANY, LLC; pg. 20, pg. 329
SUPPORT PLUS - Software Services - ELEKTA; pg. 391, pg. 284
SUPPORT SMARTER - Software - CITRIX SYSTEMS, INC.; pg. 375, pg. 424
SUPPORTIVE HOME - Promotional Services - TIAX LLC; pg. 115, pg. 829
SUPPORTMATE - Software - EMC CORPORATION; pg. 391, pg. 825
SUPPORTNET - Software System - MENTOR GRAPHICS CORPORATION; pg. 432, pg. 1510
SUPPORTNET - Desktop Application - MOTAN, INC.; pg. 1886, pg. 903
SUPPRESCENT - Fabric - W.L. GORE & ASSOCIATES, INC.; pg. 122, pg. 388
SUPRA - Software - CINCOM SYSTEMS, INC.; pg. 372, pg. 1411
SUPRA - Photographic Paper - EASTMAN KODAK COMPANY; pg. 1408, pg. 1333
SUPRA - Communication Headset Product - PLANTRONICS, INC.; pg. 663, pg. 270
SUPRA - Power Boat - SKIER'S CHOICE INC.; pg. 1711, pg. 1640
SUPRA CORE - Peripheral Guide Wire - ABBOTT LABORATORIES; pg. 1484, pg. 551
SUPRA GLUE - Adhesives - AMERICAN GREASE STICK CO.; pg. 971, pg. 902
SUPRACAP - Filter & Module - PALL CORPORATION; pg. 232, pg. 1323
SUPRACONDYLAR NAIL - Surgical & Medical Product - STRYKER CORPORATION; pg. 1598, pg. 894
SUPRADISC - Filter Cartridge - PALL CORPORATION; pg. 232, pg. 1323
SUPRALIFE - Alkaline Batteries - EASTMAN KODAK COMPANY; pg. 1408, pg. 1333
SUPRALINK - Digital Video Product - HARMONIC, INC.; pg. 402, pg. 246
SUPRAMESH - Membrane - PALL CORPORATION; pg. 232, pg. 1323
SUPRAMIX - Vertical Tub Mixer - ART'S-WAY MANUFACTURING CO., INC.; pg. 701, pg. 701
SUPRANE - Pharmaceutical Product - BAXTER INTERNATIONAL INC.; pg. 1499, pg. 599
SUPRAPLUS - Headset - PLANTRONICS, INC.; pg. 663, pg. 270
SUPRASEC - Diphenylmethane Diisocyanates - HUNTSMAN CORPORATION; pg. 1167, pg. 1758
SUPRASHIELD - Automotive Coating - E.I. DU PONT DE NEMOURS & COMPANY; pg. 1159, pg. 390
SUPRE SWEETS - Domestic Cigars - ALTADIS USA, INC.; pg. 1893, pg. 423
SUPREL - Non Woven Fabrics - E.I. DU PONT DE NEMOURS & COMPANY; pg. 1159, pg. 390
SUPREMA - Interior Low Sheen Wall Paint - DUNN-EDWARDS CORPORATION; pg. 1442, pg. 129
SUPREMA - Waterproof Camera - MCNETT CORPORATION; pg. 1839, pg. 1817
SUPREMA - Gas Monitor - MINE SAFETY APPLIANCES COMPANY; pg. 1361, pg. 1525
SUPREMA - Optical Mount - NEWPORT CORPORATION; pg. 1424, pg. 114
SUPREME - Fishing Lines - 3M COMPANY; pg. 1142, pg. 956
SUPREME - Crocks - CARLISLE FOODSERVICE PRODUCTS INCORPORATED; pg. 1455, pg. 1485
SUPREME - Vanilla - DAVID MICHAEL & CO. INC.; pg. 852, pg. 1563
SUPREME - Lawn Fertilizer - GARDENS ALIVE!, INC.; pg. 1796, pg. 693
SUPREME - Beverage - GREEN SPOT, INC.; pg. 251, pg. 68
SUPREME - Aluminum Paint - JONES-BLAIR COMPANY; pg. 1443, pg. 1682
SUPREME - Musical Instrument - PEAVEY ELECTRONICS CORPORATION; pg. 662, pg. 970
SUPREME - Pet Product - PETSMART, INC.; pg. 1481, pg. 18
SUPREME - Turf Maintenance Machinery - SMITHCO, INC.; pg. 1377, pg. 1592
SUPREME - Electrophysiology Products - ST. JUDE MEDICAL, INC.; pg. 1596, pg. 963
SUPREME 10HT - Epoxy Adhesive - MASTER BOND INC.; pg. 1172, pg. 1072
SUPREME 11F - Epoxy Adhesive - MASTER BOND INC.; pg. 1172, pg. 1072
SUPREME 3HTND-2GT - Glob Top Coating - MASTER BOND INC.; pg. 1172, pg. 1072
SUPREME AIR SERIES - Fume Hoods - KEWAUNEE SCIENTIFIC CORPORATION; pg. 931, pg. 1391
SUPREME COMFORT - Stationary & Sleep Sofas - LA-Z-BOY INCORPORATED; pg. 932, pg. 901
SUPREME ELEGANCE - Carpet - BEAULIEU GROUP, LLC; pg. 917, pg. 529
SUPREME LIVING - Carpet - BEAULIEU GROUP, LLC; pg. 917, pg. 529
SUPREME LUXURY - Carpet - BEAULIEU GROUP, LLC; pg. 917, pg. 529
SUPREME PRO - Ear Muffs - MINE SAFETY APPLIANCES COMPANY; pg. 1361, pg. 1525
SUPREME RUST SHIELD - Coating - AERVOE INDUSTRIES INCORPORATED; pg. 1439, pg. 1021
SUPREME STEAM - Kitchen Appliance - HAMILTON BEACH BRANDS, INC.; pg. 56, pg. 1783
SUPREME TENDER - Pork Products - TYSON FOODS, INC.; pg. 902, pg. 35

SUPREMES - Sweet - WELLS ENTERPRISES, INC.; *pg.* 909, *pg.* 709
SUPREMO - Food Product - V&V SUPREMO FOODS, INC.; *pg.* 907, *pg.* 595
SUPRIME - Acrylic Latex & Oil Primers - PRATT & LAMBERT PAINTS; *pg.* 1446, *pg.* 1434
SUPROX - Cleaning Product - HILLYARD, INC.; *pg.* 331, *pg.* 990
SUPRVISION - Magnifier - ULTRAOPTIX, INC.; *pg.* 1433, *pg.* 346
SUR DEL LAGO - Chocolate Product - GUITTARD CHOCOLATE COMPANY; *pg.* 1855, *pg.* 55
SUR-FIT - Ostomy Skin Barriers - ALIMED, INC.; *pg.* 1490, *pg.* 816
SUR-FIT AUTOLOCK - Ostomy Care Product - CONVATEC LTD.; *pg.* 1518, *pg.* 1121
SUR-FIT NATURA - Ostomy Care Product - CONVATEC LTD.; *pg.* 1518, *pg.* 1121
SUR-FLEX - Skin Packaging - FLEX-O-GLASS, INC.; *pg.* 1457, *pg.* 574
SUR LAST - Solution-Dyed Polyester Fabric - GLEN RAVEN, INC.; *pg.* 693, *pg.* 1373
SUR-WET - Aliphatic Amine - AIR PRODUCTS AND CHEMICALS, INC.; *pg.* 1145, *pg.* 1513
SURAN - Fertilizer - POTASHCORP; *pg.* 1799, *pg.* 641
SURCHEM - Polymer Product - CHEMTURA CORPORATION; *pg.* 1152, *pg.* 355
SURCOTECH - Odor Control Systems - SURCO PRODUCTS, INC.; *pg.* 336, *pg.* 1581
SURCOTTA - Solid Air Freshener - SURCO PRODUCTS, INC.; *pg.* 336, *pg.* 1581
SURE - Deodorant - HELEN OF TROY L.P.; *pg.* 511, *pg.* 1692
SURE - Protein - REPLIGEN CORPORATION; *pg.* 1589, *pg.* 854
SURE ACCESS - Personal Secured Loan Products - APPLE BANK FOR SAVINGS; *pg.* 716, *pg.* 1196
SURE AUDIT - Software - STEELCLOUD, INC.; *pg.* 476, *pg.* 1776
SURE-BLOCK - Paint & Coating - DIAMOND VOGEL PAINT, INC.; *pg.* 1441, *pg.* 710
SURE-CATCH - Insect Pest Control Product - GARDENS ALIVE!, INC.; *pg.* 1796, *pg.* 693
SURE CHECK - Packaging Accessory - CROSSTEX INTERNATIONAL INC.; *pg.* 1520, *pg.* 1164
SURE-CHECK - Shower Curtain - MEDLINE INDUSTRIES, INC.; *pg.* 1562, *pg.* 635
SURE-CHEK - Hospital Product - HERCULITE PRODUCTS, INC.; *pg.* 694, *pg.* 1529
SURE-CHEK - Leak Detector - LA-CO INDUSTRIES MARKAL CO., INC.; *pg.* 1170, *pg.* 610
SURE-CHEK COMFORT - Fabrics - HERCULITE PRODUCTS, INC.; *pg.* 694, *pg.* 1529
SURE-CHEK FUSION - Fabrics - HERCULITE PRODUCTS, INC.; *pg.* 694, *pg.* 1529
SURE CLEAN - Powder Spray System - NORDSON CORPORATION; *pg.* 1365, *pg.* 1480
SURE-CLIMB - Vertical Lifeline - MINE SAFETY APPLIANCES COMPANY; *pg.* 1361, *pg.* 1525
SURE CODE - Chart & Marking System - GRAPHIC CONTROLS LLC; *pg.* 401, *pg.* 1148
SURE CREDIT - Personal Secured Loan Products - APPLE BANK FOR SAVINGS; *pg.* 716, *pg.* 1196
SURE CURE - Flower Arrangement - 1-800-FLOWERS.COM, INC.; *pg.* 1758, *pg.* 1151
SURE-CURE - Light Source - UVP, INC.; *pg.* 1434, *pg.* 298
SURE-DNS - Software System - IRON MOUNTAIN INCORPORATED; *pg.* 421, *pg.* 796
SURE-FILL - Beverage System - CHART INDUSTRIES, INC.; *pg.* 1405, *pg.* 1454
SURE-FIT - Bottle Caps - BERRY PLASTICS LANCASTER; *pg.* 1453, *pg.* 1546
SURE-FIT - Universal Backing Ring - THE TIMKEN COMPANY; *pg.* 218, *pg.* 1408
SURE-GRAB - Fall Protection Product - MINE SAFETY APPLIANCES COMPANY; *pg.* 1361, *pg.* 1525
SURE GRIP - Shoe Cover - ALPHA PRO TECH, LTD.; *pg.* 1492, *pg.* 1922
SURE GRIP - Paint & Coating - DIAMOND VOGEL PAINT, INC.; *pg.* 1441, *pg.* 710
SURE GRIP - Gaming Product - GLD PRODUCTS, INC.; *pg.* 1835, *pg.* 1882
SURE-GRIP - Spindle Tooling - HARDINGE INC.; *pg.* 1344, *pg.* 1157
SURE-GUARD - Surge Protector - ELECTRO STANDARDS LABORATORIES INC.; *pg.* 390, *pg.* 1600
SURE-JELL - Jams, Jellies & Relishes - THE KRAFT HEINZ COMPANY; *pg.* 870, *pg.* 1577
SURE-LIFT - Medical Product - GF HEALTH PRODUCTS, INC.; *pg.* 1535, *pg.* 508
SURE LINE - Personal Secured Loan Products - APPLE BANK FOR SAVINGS; *pg.* 716, *pg.* 1196
SURE LOAN - Personal Secured Loan Products - APPLE BANK FOR SAVINGS; *pg.* 716, *pg.* 1196
SURE-LOCK - Ratchet Suspension System - E.D. BULLARD COMPANY; *pg.* 1332, *pg.* 727
SURE LOCK - Plastic Mesh Baby Gate - EVENFLO COMPANY, INC.; *pg.* 924, *pg.* 1470
SURE-LOCK - Fall Protection Equipment - MINE SAFETY APPLIANCES COMPANY; *pg.* 1361, *pg.* 1525
SURE-LOCK - Tools - VAUGHAN & BUSHNELL MANUFACTURING COMPANY, INC.; *pg.* 1066, *pg.* 616
SURE-LOK - Minus Head Kit - THE HILSINGER CO.; *pg.* 1416, *pg.* 841
SURE MARK - Chart & Marking System - GRAPHIC CONTROLS LLC; *pg.* 401, *pg.* 1148
SURE-MED - Medication Dispensing System - OMNICELL INC.; *pg.* 1578, *pg.* 161
SURE-OFF - Testers - RELIABLE AUTOMATIC SPRINKLER CO., INC.; *pg.* 1137, *pg.* 1158
SURE POP - Sprinkler - RAIN BIRD CORPORATION; *pg.* 707, *pg.* 44
SURE-SAFE - Medical Product - GF HEALTH PRODUCTS, INC.; *pg.* 1535, *pg.* 508
SURE-SAFE - Plastic Packaging Product - POLY PAK AMERICA, INC.; *pg.* 1467, *pg.* 138
SURE SCAN - Chart & Marking System - GRAPHIC CONTROLS LLC; *pg.* 401, *pg.* 1148
SURE-SCREEN - Drug Testing Device - MEDTOX SCIENTIFIC, INC.; *pg.* 1422, *pg.* 962
SURE SEAL - Sealer - JONES-BLAIR COMPANY; *pg.* 1443, *pg.* 1682
SURE-SEAL - Envelope - POLY PAK AMERICA, INC.; *pg.* 1467, *pg.* 138
SURE SEAT - Valve Springs - EDELBROCK CORPORATION; *pg.* 204, *pg.* 293
SURE-SET - Power Transmission Belt - HBD INDUSTRIES, INC.; *pg.* 207, *pg.* 1449
SURE SET - Medical Product - MEDLINE INDUSTRIES, INC.; *pg.* 1562, *pg.* 635
SURE SHOT - Residential Water Heater - A.O. SMITH CORPORATION; *pg.* 1313, *pg.* 1872
SURE SHOT - Medical Equipment - CONMED CORPORATION; *pg.* 1517, *pg.* 1347
SURE-SLIDE - Dimmer Switch - LEVITON MANUFACTURING COMPANY, INC.; *pg.* 1301, *pg.* 1180
SURE STEP - Coating Agent - DELTA FOREMOST CHEMICAL CORPORATION; *pg.* 1155, *pg.* 1642
SURE-STEP - Floor Product - TEXAS REFINERY CORP.; *pg.* 986, *pg.* 1696
SURE-STOP - Fall Protection Equipment - MINE SAFETY APPLIANCES COMPANY; *pg.* 1361, *pg.* 1525
SURE-STRONG - Rescue Equipment - MINE SAFETY APPLIANCES COMPANY; *pg.* 1361, *pg.* 1525
SURE TEST - Circuit Analyzer - IDEAL INDUSTRIES, INC.; *pg.* 1051, *pg.* 662
SURE-THANE - Healthcare Fabric - HERCULITE PRODUCTS, INC.; *pg.* 694, *pg.* 1529
SURE THING - Carpet - BEAULIEU GROUP, LLC; *pg.* 917, *pg.* 529
SURE TRAIL - Trademark; Camper & Trailer Tires - CARLISLE TIRE & WHEEL COMPANY; *pg.* 1880, *pg.* 1612
SURE TRAIL LT - Trademark & Trailer Tires - CARLISLE TIRE & WHEEL COMPANY; *pg.* 1880, *pg.* 1612
SURE-VENT - Valve - OATEY SUPPLY CHAIN SERVICES; *pg.* 30, *pg.* 1433
SURE WIN - Video Game - INTERNATIONAL GAME TECHNOLOGY; *pg.* 957, *pg.* 1024
SUREAIRE - Filtration Product - FLANDERS CORPORATION; *pg.* 1336, *pg.* 1392
SUREASSESS - Software - SUREQUEST SYSTEMS, INC.; *pg.* 900, *pg.* 1669
SUREBEAD - Hot Melt Pneumatic Gun - NORDSON CORPORATION; *pg.* 1365, *pg.* 1480
SURECARE - Eye Pads - DERMA SCIENCES, INC.; *pg.* 1523, *pg.* 1111
SURECHARGE - Medical Equipment - CONMED CORPORATION; *pg.* 1517, *pg.* 1347
SURECHIP - Power Semiconductor Device - INTERNATIONAL RECTIFIER CORPORATION; *pg.* 647, *pg.* 80
SURECONNECT - Cable Connector - WESTERN DIGITAL CORPORATION; *pg.* 492, *pg.* 118
SURECUT - Kitchen Appliance - HAMILTON BEACH BRANDS, INC.; *pg.* 56, *pg.* 1783
SUREFIL - Dental Product - DENTSPLY INTERNATIONAL INC.; *pg.* 1522, *pg.* 1596
SUREFIX - Pacing Lead - MEDTRONIC, INC.; *pg.* 1564, *pg.* 939
SUREFLO - Soap Dispenser - BOBRICK WASHROOM EQUIPMENT, INC.; *pg.* 1043, *pg.* 166
SUREFLO - Filter - FLANDERS CORPORATION; *pg.* 1336, *pg.* 1392
SUREFLOW - Pressed & Monolithic Refractory - RESCO PRODUCTS, INC.; *pg.* 107, *pg.* 1581
SUREFLOW - Adaptive Offset Controller - TSI INCORPORATED; *pg.* 1432, *pg.* 965
SUREFOOT - Ironing Board - HOME PRODUCTS INTERNATIONAL, INC.; *pg.* 1125, *pg.* 577
SUREGLIDE - Brake - INVACARE CORPORATION; *pg.* 1546, *pg.* 1451
SUREGRIP - Hanger - HOME PRODUCTS INTERNATIONAL, INC.; *pg.* 1125, *pg.* 577
SUREGRIP - Screw-On-Connector - IDEAL INDUSTRIES, INC.; *pg.* 1051, *pg.* 662
SUREGRIP - Ice & Water Guard - JOHNS MANVILLE CORPORATION; *pg.* 89, *pg.* 320
SUREGRIP - Slippers - THE SALK COMPANY; *pg.* 1591, *pg.* 800
SUREGRIP - Hex Design Wrenching Profile & Screwdrivers - SK HAND TOOL CORPORATION; *pg.* 1062, *pg.* 663
SURELIGHT - Protein Binding Essays - PERKINELMER, INC.; *pg.* 1426, *pg.* 853
SURELINE - Hose - THE GOODYEAR TIRE & RUBBER COMPANY; *pg.* 1883, *pg.* 1401
SURELINK - Integrated Circuits - AVAGO TECHNOLOGIES; *pg.* 358, *pg.* 238
SURELINK - Software - SUREQUEST SYSTEMS, INC.; *pg.* 900, *pg.* 1669
SURELOCK - Gasket Seal - FLANDERS CORPORATION; *pg.* 1336, *pg.* 1392
SURELOCK - Diagnostic Imaging Product - HOLOGIC, INC.; *pg.* 1416, *pg.* 784
SURELOCK - Cover & Pad - HOME PRODUCTS INTERNATIONAL, INC.; *pg.* 1125, *pg.* 577
SURELOCK - Plastic Food Containers - INLINE PLASTICS CORP.; *pg.* 1460, *pg.* 370
SUREMENU - Recipe Management - SUREQUEST SYSTEMS, INC.; *pg.* 900, *pg.* 1669
SUREMIX - Dispensing System - NORDSON CORPORATION; *pg.* 1365, *pg.* 1480
SUREPAK - Paperboard Packaging Product - WESTROCK COMPANY; *pg.* 1472, *pg.* 1805
SUREPATH - Diagnostic Product - BD DIAGNOSTICS - TRIPATH; *pg.* 1402, *pg.* 1358
SUREPAY - Software System - ALCATEL-LUCENT; *pg.* 615, *pg.* 1094
SUREPLAQUE - Software - VITAL IMAGES, INC.; *pg.* 1607, *pg.* 950
SUREPLEAT - Filtration Product - FLANDERS CORPORATION; *pg.* 1336, *pg.* 1392
SUREPOWER - Defibrillator Battery System - ZOLL MEDICAL CORPORATION; *pg.* 1612, *pg.* 814
SUREPRESS - Wound Care Product - CONVATEC LTD.; *pg.* 1518, *pg.* 1121
SURESEAL - Filtration Product - FLANDERS CORPORATION; *pg.* 1336, *pg.* 1392
SURESEAL - Sealer - MTS MEDICATION TECHNOLOGIES, INC.; *pg.* 442, *pg.* 463
SURESEAL - Electric Gun - NORDSON CORPORATION; *pg.* 1365, *pg.* 1480
SURESEAL - Ink Jet Cartridges - RICOH PRINTING SYSTEMS AMERICA, INC.; *pg.* 462, *pg.* 279
SURESEAL - Sealant - SOUTHWIRE COMPANY; *pg.* 1063, *pg.* 527
SURESEAL - Thermo Plastic Spacer System - VIRGINIA GLASS PRODUCTS CORPORATION; *pg.* 119, *pg.* 1788
SURESET - Scissors - ACME UNITED CORPORATION; *pg.* 1040, *pg.* 346
SURESET - Heater - KAZ, INC.; *pg.* 58, *pg.* 844
SURESIP - Drinking Cup Valve - EVENFLO COMPANY, INC.; *pg.* 924, *pg.* 1470
SURESTA - Chain Oil - TEXAS REFINERY CORP.; *pg.* 986, *pg.* 1696

First page reference indicates Business Class Edition
Second page reference indicates Geographic Edition

SURESTART - Low Voltage Disconnect Switch - COLE HERSEE COMPANY; *pg.* 202, *pg.* 792
SURESTEP - Rapid Membrane Test Products - ALERE INC.; *pg.* 1488, *pg.* 849
SURESTEP - Protective Disposable Shoe Covers - E.I. DU PONT DE NEMOURS & COMPANY; *pg.* 1159, *pg.* 390
SURESTEP - Wheelchair - INVACARE CORPORATION; *pg.* 1546, *pg.* 1451
SURESTREAM - Media System - REALNETWORKS, INC.; *pg.* 460, *pg.* 1839
SURESTRIP - Pharmaceutical Product - ALERE INC.; *pg.* 1488, *pg.* 849
SURETEMP - Electronic Thermometry - WELCH ALLYN INC.; *pg.* 1436, *pg.* 1342
SURETEST - Rolling Steel Fire Door - RAYNOR GARAGE DOORS; *pg.* 106, *pg.* 607
SURETRACE - Medical Equipment - CONMED CORPORATION; *pg.* 1517, *pg.* 1347
SURETRANS - Medical Device - C.R. BARD, INC.; *pg.* 1519, *pg.* 1094
SURETRAP - Filter - CAMERON INTERNATIONAL; *pg.* 1151, *pg.* 1702
SURETY LIFE - Annuities & Savings - THE ALLSTATE CORPORATION; *pg.* 1189, *pg.* 639
SURETYPE - Keyboard Technology - BLACKBERRY LIMITED; *pg.* 625, *pg.* 1947
SURETYPLUS - Commercial Insurance - THE CHUBB CORPORATION; *pg.* 1196, *pg.* 1128
SUREVIEW - Computer Program - COMPUTER SCIENCES CORPORATION; *pg.* 378, *pg.* 1780
SUREVUE - Daily-Wear Contact Lenses - JOHNSON & JOHNSON VISION CARE, INC.; *pg.* 1552, *pg.* 434
SUREWRAP - Hot Melt Adhesive Applicator - NORDSON CORPORATION; *pg.* 1365, *pg.* 1480
SURF - Toothbrush - RANIR LLC; *pg.* 520, *pg.* 888
SURF - Bag - SAMSONITE CORPORATION; *pg.* 11, *pg.* 830
SURF - Laundry Detergent - THE SUN PRODUCTS CORPORATION; *pg.* 336, *pg.* 385
SURF & COURT CANVAS - Footwear - K-SWISS; *pg.* 1837, *pg.* 306
SURF & COURT OG CNVS - Footwear - K-SWISS; *pg.* 1837, *pg.* 306
SURF CITY - Video Game - INTERNATIONAL GAME TECHNOLOGY; *pg.* 957, *pg.* 1024
SURF KING - Seafood - OCEAN BEAUTY SEAFOODS, INC.; *pg.* 1028, *pg.* 1838
SURF PI PRO - Metal Detector - WHITE'S ELECTRONICS; *pg.* 688, *pg.* 1509
SURF (X) - Wallcovering - OMNOVA SOLUTIONS INC; *pg.* 1176, *pg.* 1453
SURFACE - Tablet Computer - MICROSOFT CORPORATION; *pg.* 435, *pg.* 1824
SURFACE GUARD - Surface Protector - SWISHER HYGIENE INC.; *pg.* 336, *pg.* 1507
SURFACE PRO - Tablet Computer - MICROSOFT CORPORATION; *pg.* 435, *pg.* 1824
SURFACE PRODUCTION SYSTEMS - Surface Equipment - DRIL-QUIP, INC.; *pg.* 1330, *pg.* 1704
SURFACE SAFE - Pharmaceutical Product - ASTEX PHARMACEUTICALS, INC; *pg.* 1497, *pg.* 77
SURFACE SAVER - Lens Surfacing Systems - 3M COMPANY; *pg.* 1142, *pg.* 956
SURFACE SCATTER - Turbidimeter, On-Line - HACH COMPANY; *pg.* 1415, *pg.* 334
SURFACE SYSTEMS - Commercial Wall System - MARLITE, INC.; *pg.* 95, *pg.* 1448
SURFACE SYSTEMS RADIUS WALL - Wall System - MARLITE, INC.; *pg.* 95, *pg.* 1448
SURFACE WATER PRO - Agricultural Equipment - DEERE & COMPANY; *pg.* 703, *pg.* 632
SURFACEGUARD - Cleaner - ROCHESTER MIDLAND CORPORATION; *pg.* 334, *pg.* 1337
SURFACESTRIP - Photoresist Stripper - DOW CHEMICAL; *pg.* 1156, *pg.* 1563
SURFACO - Masonry Surface Conditioner - DUNN-EDWARDS CORPORATION; *pg.* 1442, *pg.* 129
SURFBEAM - Broadband Satellite Network - VIASAT, INC.; *pg.* 489, *pg.* 62
SURFBOARD - Cable Modem - MOTOROLA SOLUTIONS, INC.; *pg.* 657, *pg.* 659
SURFCHEM - Chemicals - ASHLAND INC.; *pg.* 972, *pg.* 726
SURFCOAT - Cleaning Product - HILLYARD, INC.; *pg.* 331, *pg.* 990
SURFER - Magazine - RENTPATH, INC.; *pg.* 1680, *pg.* 538
SURFER GIRL - Bicycle - TREK BICYCLE CORPORATION; *pg.* 1847, *pg.* 1896
SURFEX - Lampholders - PASS & SEYMOUR/LEGRAND; *pg.* 1303, *pg.* 1344
SURFMONITOR - Inspection System - KLA-TENCOR CORPORATION; *pg.* 1353, *pg.* 146
SURFOL - Linear Alcohol - HUNTSMAN CORPORATION; *pg.* 1167, *pg.* 1758
SURFONAMIDE - Alkanolamide - HUNTSMAN CORPORATION; *pg.* 1167, *pg.* 1758
SURFONAMINE - Surfactant Amines - HUNTSMAN CORPORATION; *pg.* 1167, *pg.* 1758
SURFONIC - Castor Oil - HUNTSMAN CORPORATION; *pg.* 1167, *pg.* 1758
SURFPACK - Fertilizer - SIMPLOT PARTNERS INC.; *pg.* 1800, *pg.* 548
SURFSCAN - Surface Inspection System - KLA-TENCOR CORPORATION; *pg.* 1353, *pg.* 146
SURFSIDE - Fabric - UNIROYAL ENGINEERED PRODUCTS; *pg.* 699, *pg.* 467
SURFTRAN - Thermal Energy Machine - KENNAMETAL EXTRUDE HONE; *pg.* 1352, *pg.* 1542
SURFYNOL - Surfactants - AIR PRODUCTS AND CHEMICALS, INC.; *pg.* 1145, *pg.* 1513
SURGATOL - Soap Scrub - SWISHER HYGIENE INC.; *pg.* 336, *pg.* 1507
SURGE - Soft Drink - THE COCA-COLA COMPANY; *pg.* 240, *pg.* 493
SURGE - Dairy Farm Equip. - GEA FARM TECHNOLOGIES; *pg.* 704, *pg.* 636
SURGE - Turf Product - PBI/GORDON CORPORATION; *pg.* 1176, *pg.* 985
SURGE DUFFLE - Accessories - UNDER ARMOUR, INC.; *pg.* 49, *pg.* 759
SURGE GRAPHIC HOODY - Apparels - UNDER ARMOUR, INC.; *pg.* 49, *pg.* 759
SURGE GUARD - Gas Guard Regulator - THE HARRIS PRODUCTS GROUP; *pg.* 1345, *pg.* 533
SURGEARREST - Power Protection Product - SCHNEIDER ELECTRIC; *pg.* 467, *pg.* 1609
SURGEX - Oxygen Therapy Equipment - ALLIED HEALTHCARE PRODUCTS, INC.; *pg.* 1491, *pg.* 990
SURGI-BAC - Hand Soap - ECOLAB INC.; *pg.* 329, *pg.* 960
SURGI-CARE - Male Grooming Product - AMERICAN INTERNATIONAL INDUSTRIES COMPANY; *pg.* 498, *pg.* 126
SURGI KLEEN - Cleaner - SWISHER HYGIENE INC.; *pg.* 336, *pg.* 1507
SURGICAL IMMERSION - Surgical System - INTUITIVE SURGICAL, INC.; *pg.* 1546, *pg.* 286
SURGICAL PRODUCTS - Trade Magazine - ADVANTAGE BUSINESS MEDIA; *pg.* 1613, *pg.* 1116
SURGICOUNTER - Medical Product - PATIENT SAFETY TECHNOLOGIES, INC.; *pg.* 1580, *pg.* 114
SURGICRYL - Animal Safety Product - NEOGEN CORPORATION; *pg.* 883, *pg.* 896
SURGIGRAPHIC - Surgical Table - STERIS CORPORATION; *pg.* 1597, *pg.* 1464
SURGIGRIP - Elastic Net Dressing - DERMA SCIENCES, INC.; *pg.* 1523, *pg.* 1111
SURGILAST - Elastic Net Dressing - DERMA SCIENCES, INC.; *pg.* 1523, *pg.* 1111
SURGILUBE - Surgical Lubricant - STOELTING CO.; *pg.* 1430, *pg.* 671
SURGINET - Surgery & Anesthesia Information System - CERNER CORPORATION; *pg.* 1514, *pg.* 981
SURGITRACK - Software - OWENS & MINOR, INC.; *pg.* 1579, *pg.* 1795
SURGITUBE - Elastic Net Dressing - DERMA SCIENCES, INC.; *pg.* 1523, *pg.* 1111
SURLY - Bikes & Frames - QUALITY BICYCLE PRODUCTS; *pg.* 1710, *pg.* 918
SURLYN - Ionomer Resin - E.I. DU PONT DE NEMOURS & COMPANY; *pg.* 1159, *pg.* 390
SURLYN REFLECTION SERIES - Super Gloss Molding Alloys - E.I. DU PONT DE NEMOURS & COMPANY; *pg.* 1159, *pg.* 390
SURMAX - Avilamycin - ELANCO ANIMAL HEALTH; *pg.* 1475, *pg.* 681
SUROFLEX - Motor Vehicle Product - JASON INDUSTRIES, INC.; *pg.* 208, *pg.* 1875
SURPASS - Polyethylene - NOVA CHEMICALS CORPORATION; *pg.* 1175, *pg.* 1904
SURPLUS WAREHOUSE - Building Materials - E.C. BARTON & COMPANY; *pg.* 80, *pg.* 33
SURPRISE! - Game - GAMEWRIGHT; *pg.* 953, *pg.* 836
SURPRISE - Office Furniture - STEELCASE INC.; *pg.* 475, *pg.* 889
SURPRISE BOUQUET - Container Grown Plant - MONROVIA GROWERS; *pg.* 1797, *pg.* 44
SURROUND - Crop Protectant - BASF CATALYSTS LLC; *pg.* 1148, *pg.* 1074
THE SURROUND - Electronics - CAMBRIDGE SOUNDWORKS, INC.; *pg.* 1234, *pg.* 781
SURROUND - Semiconductor Product - FREESCALE SEMICONDUCTOR, INC.; *pg.* 398, *pg.* 1662
SURROUND - Insect Pest Control Product - GARDENS ALIVE!, INC.; *pg.* 1796, *pg.* 693
SURROUNDS - Furniture - ASHLEY FURNITURE INDUSTRIES, INC.; *pg.* 914, *pg.* 1852
SURROUNDVIEW - Graphics Card - ADVANCED MICRO DEVICES, INC.; *pg.* 613, *pg.* 282
SURROUNDVIEW - Software - WIND RIVER SYSTEMS, INC.; *pg.* 493, *pg.* 38
SURSENSE - Sensor - HONEYWELL INTERNATIONAL INC.; *pg.* 407, *pg.* 1088
SURVAC - Thermal Processing Equipment - SURFACE COMBUSTION, INC.; *pg.* 1077, *pg.* 1462
SURVANTA - Healthcare System - ABBOTT LABORATORIES; *pg.* 1484, *pg.* 551
SURVEY - Paint & Coating - AERVOE INDUSTRIES INCORPORATED; *pg.* 1439, *pg.* 1021
SURVEY MANAGER - Software - TRIMBLE NAVIGATION LIMITED; *pg.* 1384, *pg.* 288
SURVEYOR - Software - FINISAR CORPORATION; *pg.* 639, *pg.* 285
SURVEYOR - Mini-Domed Closed-Circuit Television Equipment - VICON INDUSTRIES, INC.; *pg.* 685, *pg.* 1166
SURVEYSPOT - Panel - SURVEY SAMPLING INTERNATIONAL LLC; *pg.* 1690, *pg.* 371
SURVEYTRACKER - Educational Software - PEARSON ASSESSMENTS; *pg.* 1674, *pg.* 918
SURVEYTRACKER PLUS 5.0 - Educational Software - PEARSON ASSESSMENTS; *pg.* 1674, *pg.* 918
SURVEYTRACKER PLUS EMAIL WEB 5.0 - Educational Software - PEARSON ASSESSMENTS; *pg.* 1674, *pg.* 918
SURVIVAL KIT - Bicycle Accessories - SPECIALIZED BICYCLE COMPONENTS, INC.; *pg.* 1711, *pg.* 152
SURVIVALINK - Medical Apparatus - CARDIAC SCIENCE CORPORATION; *pg.* 1512, *pg.* 1897
SURVIVING FAMILY FUND - Insurance Product - SBLI USA LIFE INSURANCE COMPANY, INC.; *pg.* 1216, *pg.* 1288
SURVIVOR - Flashlight - STREAMLIGHT INC.; *pg.* 1306, *pg.* 1527
SURVIVOR - Multi-Species Oral Gel - TROUW NUTRITION USA; *pg.* 1482, *pg.* 616
SURVIVOR LIFE - Second to Die Product - GENWORTH LIFE AND ANNUITY INSURANCE COMPANY; *pg.* 1201, *pg.* 1802
SUS - Coated Unbleached Kraft Paperboard - GRAPHIC PACKAGING HOLDING COMPANY; *pg.* 1459, *pg.* 509
SUSAN SCHEEWE - Art Materials - MARTIN/F. WEBER COMPANY; *pg.* 962, *pg.* 1567
SUSANNE - Wall Decor - ETHAN ALLEN INTERIORS INC.; *pg.* 924, *pg.* 343
SUSE - Computer Operating System - NOVELL INC.; *pg.* 446, *pg.* 852
SUSIE - Clothing - ABERCROMBIE & FITCH CO.; *pg.* 37, *pg.* 1466
SUSSEX - Furniture - AMERICAN LEATHER LP; *pg.* 912, *pg.* 1673
SUSSEX - Furniture - ETHAN ALLEN INTERIORS INC.; *pg.* 924, *pg.* 343
SUSTACAL - Supplemental Food with High Protein & Low Fat - MEAD JOHNSON NUTRITION COMPANY; *pg.* 1561, *pg.* 615
SUSTAIN - Chemical Product - PPG INDUSTRIES, INC.; *pg.* 1445, *pg.* 1579
SUSTAINED PLATEAU BIASING - Digital Input & Output Bias Tracking Points Monitor Used in FPB Amplifiers - KRELL INDUSTRIES, INC.; *pg.* 650, *pg.* 367
SUSTANE SAIB - Resin - EASTMAN CHEMICAL COMPANY; *pg.* 1159, *pg.* 1636
SUSTIVA - HIV Medication - BRISTOL-MYERS SQUIBB COMPANY; *pg.* 1509, *pg.* 1206
SUTCLIFFE - Furniture - ASHLEY FURNITURE INDUSTRIES, INC.; *pg.* 914, *pg.* 1852
SUTENT - Renal & Gastrointestinal Cancer Medication - PFIZER INC.; *pg.* 1581, *pg.* 1278
SUTORBILT - Blower - GARDNER DENVER, INC.; *pg.* 1338,

pg. 1592
SUTTER HOME - Beverage - TRINCHERO FAMILY ESTATES; *pg.* 1971, *pg.* 197
SUTTON - Women's Clothing - BLOOMINGDALE'S, INC.; *pg.* 1763, *pg.* 1204
SUTTON - Fan - CRAFTMADE INTERNATIONAL, INC.; *pg.* 1295, *pg.* 1670
SUTTON - Furniture - JASPER GROUP; *pg.* 930, *pg.* 691
SUTTON - Carpets - SHAW INDUSTRIES GROUP, INC.; *pg.* 942, *pg.* 530
SUTTON - Commercial Lighting - SWIVELIER CO., INC.; *pg.* 1307, *pg.* 1142
SUTTON & DODGE - Meat Products - TARGET CORPORATION; *pg.* 1786, *pg.* 942
SUTTON PLACE - Table - BLATT BOWLING & BILLIARD CORP.; *pg.* 1827, *pg.* 1203
SUTURABLE DURAGEN - Medical Device - INTEGRA LIFESCIENCES HOLDINGS CORPORATION; *pg.* 1545, *pg.* 1109
SUTURE - Medical Product - ST. JUDE MEDICAL, INC.; *pg.* 1596, *pg.* 963
SUTURE STRIP - Wound Closure Strip - DERMA SCIENCES, INC.; *pg.* 1523, *pg.* 1111
SUTURE TRAM - Medical Equipment - CONMED CORPORATION; *pg.* 1517, *pg.* 1347
SUVA - Refrigerants - E.I. DU PONT DE NEMOURS & COMPANY; *pg.* 1159, *pg.* 390
SUVAXYN - Swine Disease Prevention Veterinary Preparation - PFIZER INC.; *pg.* 1581, *pg.* 1278
SUVAXYN RESPIFEND - Swine Disease Prevention Pharmaceutical Preparation - PFIZER INC.; *pg.* 1581, *pg.* 1278
SUZANA - Footwear - CAPEZIO BALLET MAKERS INC.; *pg.* 1805, *pg.* 1125
SUZI WAN - Oriental Food Products - MARS, INCORPORATED; *pg.* 1858, *pg.* 1792
SUZY-QS - Snack Cakes - HOSTESS BRANDS LLC; *pg.* 1856, *pg.* 984
SUZY SELL SUSHI BY THE SEASHORE - Nail Care Product - OPI PRODUCTS INC.; *pg.* 518, *pg.* 167
SV100EG - Lighting Systems - REVOLUTION LIGHTING TECHNOLOGIES, INC.; *pg.* 1304, *pg.* 377
SV126 - Lighting Systems - REVOLUTION LIGHTING TECHNOLOGIES, INC.; *pg.* 1304, *pg.* 377
SV12EG - Lighting Systems - REVOLUTION LIGHTING TECHNOLOGIES, INC.; *pg.* 1304, *pg.* 377
SV1500 - Illuminator - REVOLUTION LIGHTING TECHNOLOGIES, INC.; *pg.* 1304, *pg.* 377
SV150EG - Lighting Systems - REVOLUTION LIGHTING TECHNOLOGIES, INC.; *pg.* 1304, *pg.* 377
SV150EGW - Lighting Systems - REVOLUTION LIGHTING TECHNOLOGIES, INC.; *pg.* 1304, *pg.* 377
SV150T - Illuminator - REVOLUTION LIGHTING TECHNOLOGIES, INC.; *pg.* 1304, *pg.* 377
SV2 - Tooth System - ESCO CORPORATION; *pg.* 1335, *pg.* 1502
SV225EG - Lighting Systems - REVOLUTION LIGHTING TECHNOLOGIES, INC.; *pg.* 1304, *pg.* 377
SV225EGW - Lighting Systems - REVOLUTION LIGHTING TECHNOLOGIES, INC.; *pg.* 1304, *pg.* 377
SV25EG - Lighting Systems - REVOLUTION LIGHTING TECHNOLOGIES, INC.; *pg.* 1304, *pg.* 377
SV300C - Controller - REVOLUTION LIGHTING TECHNOLOGIES, INC.; *pg.* 1304, *pg.* 377
SV300EG - Lighting Systems - REVOLUTION LIGHTING TECHNOLOGIES, INC.; *pg.* 1304, *pg.* 377
SV300EGW - Lighting Systems - REVOLUTION LIGHTING TECHNOLOGIES, INC.; *pg.* 1304, *pg.* 377
SV32 - Lighting Systems - REVOLUTION LIGHTING TECHNOLOGIES, INC.; *pg.* 1304, *pg.* 377
SV42 - Lighting Systems - REVOLUTION LIGHTING TECHNOLOGIES, INC.; *pg.* 1304, *pg.* 377
SV42ULTRA - Lighting Systems - REVOLUTION LIGHTING TECHNOLOGIES, INC.; *pg.* 1304, *pg.* 377
SV4EG - Lighting Systems - REVOLUTION LIGHTING TECHNOLOGIES, INC.; *pg.* 1304, *pg.* 377
SV50EG - Lighting Systems - REVOLUTION LIGHTING TECHNOLOGIES, INC.; *pg.* 1304, *pg.* 377
SV6 - Van - GENERAL MOTORS COMPANY; *pg.* 175, *pg.* 881
SV600C - Controller - REVOLUTION LIGHTING TECHNOLOGIES, INC.; *pg.* 1304, *pg.* 377
SV750 - Illuminator - REVOLUTION LIGHTING TECHNOLOGIES, INC.; *pg.* 1304, *pg.* 377
SV75EG - Lighting Systems - REVOLUTION LIGHTING TECHNOLOGIES, INC.; *pg.* 1304, *pg.* 377
SV84 - Lighting Systems - REVOLUTION LIGHTING TECHNOLOGIES, INC.; *pg.* 1304, *pg.* 377
SV84ULTRA - Lighting Systems - REVOLUTION LIGHTING TECHNOLOGIES, INC.; *pg.* 1304, *pg.* 377
SV8EG - Lighting Systems - REVOLUTION LIGHTING TECHNOLOGIES, INC.; *pg.* 1304, *pg.* 377
SVA200 - Lighting Systems - REVOLUTION LIGHTING TECHNOLOGIES, INC.; *pg.* 1304, *pg.* 377
SVA205 - Lighting Systems - REVOLUTION LIGHTING TECHNOLOGIES, INC.; *pg.* 1304, *pg.* 377
SVALI - Beverages - THE COCA-COLA COMPANY; *pg.* 240, *pg.* 493
SVC30 - Cordless Hot Knife - REVOLUTION LIGHTING TECHNOLOGIES, INC.; *pg.* 1304, *pg.* 377
SVE30 - Electronic Hot Knife - REVOLUTION LIGHTING TECHNOLOGIES, INC.; *pg.* 1304, *pg.* 377
SVEE EIGHT PLUS GPS - Receiver - TRIMBLE NAVIGATION LIMITED; *pg.* 1384, *pg.* 288
SVENHARD'S - Pastries - UNITED STATES BAKERY; *pg.* 907, *pg.* 1507
SVF100 - Lighting Systems - REVOLUTION LIGHTING TECHNOLOGIES, INC.; *pg.* 1304, *pg.* 377
SVG - Super Velocity Gas Burners - HAUCK MANUFACTURING COMPANY, INC.; *pg.* 1345, *pg.* 1522
SVL - HID Vertical Lamp - CRESCENT/STONCO SUPPLY DIVISION; *pg.* 1295, *pg.* 1121
SVL300 - Lighting Systems - REVOLUTION LIGHTING TECHNOLOGIES, INC.; *pg.* 1304, *pg.* 377
SVM - Storage Resources Software - AVAGO TECHNOLOGIES; *pg.* 358, *pg.* 238
SVM APP-PACK - Computer Software - AVAGO TECHNOLOGIES; *pg.* 358, *pg.* 238
SVM REPORT GENERATOR - Computer Software - AVAGO TECHNOLOGIES; *pg.* 358, *pg.* 238
SVP CAFE - Software - SYNOPSYS, INC.; *pg.* 480, *pg.* 162
SVPAF60 - Lighting Systems - REVOLUTION LIGHTING TECHNOLOGIES, INC.; *pg.* 1304, *pg.* 377
SVPAVER4X4 - Lighting Systems - REVOLUTION LIGHTING TECHNOLOGIES, INC.; *pg.* 1304, *pg.* 377
SVPLUME - Image Rendering - RAYTHEON COMPANY; *pg.* 233, *pg.* 854
SVS - Spherical Video System - ALION SCIENCE AND TECHNOLOGY CORPORATION; *pg.* 615, *pg.* 1788
SVS - Laser System - GSI GROUP INC.; *pg.* 1415, *pg.* 784
SW PATRIOT RR - Canola Hybrids - MONSANTO; *pg.* 1798, *pg.* 1399
SW TITAN RRR - Canola Hybrids - MONSANTO; *pg.* 1798, *pg.* 1399
SW1911 .45ACP SUB COMPACT - Pistol - SMITH & WESSON HOLDING CORPORATION; *pg.* 1845, *pg.* 846
SW1911 COMPACT ES - Pistol - SMITH & WESSON HOLDING CORPORATION; *pg.* 1845, *pg.* 846
SW1911 PRO - Pistol - SMITH & WESSON HOLDING CORPORATION; *pg.* 1845, *pg.* 846
SWA - Airline Service - SOUTHWEST AIRLINES CO.; *pg.* 1923, *pg.* 1687
SWADCOTE - Detergent - ADCO, INC.; *pg.* 325, *pg.* 482
SWAE - AC Power Source for IEC Harmonic & Flicker Testing - AMETEK PROGRAMMABLE POWER, INC.; *pg.* 616, *pg.* 200
SWAGELOK.COM - Company Website - SWAGELOK COMPANY; *pg.* 1064, *pg.* 1473
SWAMP ASH - Guitar - PAUL REED SMITH GUITARS; *pg.* 574, *pg.* 779
SWAMP ASH SPECIAL - Guitar - PAUL REED SMITH GUITARS; *pg.* 574, *pg.* 779
SWAN - Garden Hose - TEKNI-PLEX, INC.; *pg.* 1470, *pg.* 1122
SWAN LAKE - Container Grown Plant - MONROVIA GROWERS; *pg.* 1797, *pg.* 44
SWANK - Blood Filters - CAS MEDICAL SYSTEMS, INC.; *pg.* 1513, *pg.* 339
SWANK - Gifts, Leather Accessories, Belts, Jewelry - SWANK, INC.; *pg.* 13, *pg.* 1297
SWANN MORTON - Medical Product - PROPPER MANUFACTURING COMPANY, INC.; *pg.* 1586, *pg.* 1175
SWANSON - Chicken & Broth - CAMPBELL SOUP COMPANY; *pg.* 844, *pg.* 1048
SWANSON - Frozen Dinner - PINNACLE FOODS GROUP LLC; *pg.* 889, *pg.* 1104
SWANSON HEALTH PRODUCTS - Healthcare Product - SWANSON HEALTH PRODUCTS INC.; *pg.* 1600, *pg.* 1397
SWAROVSKI BUTTERFLY - Flower Arrangement - 1-800-FLOWERS.COM, INC.; *pg.* 1758, *pg.* 1151
SWARTZ - Guiding Introducers - ST. JUDE MEDICAL, INC.; *pg.* 1596, *pg.* 963
SWASH - Cleanser - DERMA SCIENCES, INC.; *pg.* 1523, *pg.* 1111
SWASH BY TIDE - Laundry Product - THE PROCTER & GAMBLE COMPANY; *pg.* 1129, *pg.* 1418
S.W.A.T. - Awareness Program - ECOLAB INC.; *pg.* 329, *pg.* 960
SWAT 'N SWAY - Cat Toy - THE HARTZ MOUNTAIN CORP.; *pg.* 1476, *pg.* 1120
SWATH CONTROL PRO - Precision Agriculture - DEERE & COMPANY; *pg.* 703, *pg.* 632
SWATHMORE - Office Furniture - STEELCASE INC.; *pg.* 475, *pg.* 889
SWATHMORE GRAND MOBILE - Office Furniture - STEELCASE INC.; *pg.* 475, *pg.* 889
SWATHSTAR - Wireless Product - HEMISPHERE GPS INC.; *pg.* 642, *pg.* 1903
SWATHSTAR M3 - Wireless Product - HEMISPHERE GPS INC.; *pg.* 642, *pg.* 1903
SWAYED - Fabric - NEMSCHOFF, INC.; *pg.* 936, *pg.* 1890
SWAYYY - Footwear - STEVEN MADDEN, LTD.; *pg.* 1819, *pg.* 1176
SWDM 53 - Fiber Optic Component - OPLINK COMMUNICATIONS, INC.; *pg.* 660, *pg.* 91
SWDM 54 - Fiber Optic Component - OPLINK COMMUNICATIONS, INC.; *pg.* 660, *pg.* 91
SWDM 59 - Fiber Optic Component - OPLINK COMMUNICATIONS, INC.; *pg.* 660, *pg.* 91
SWDM53 - Splitters - OPLINK COMMUNICATIONS, INC.; *pg.* 660, *pg.* 91
SWDM54 - Splitters - OPLINK COMMUNICATIONS, INC.; *pg.* 660, *pg.* 91
SWDM59 - Splitters - OPLINK COMMUNICATIONS, INC.; *pg.* 660, *pg.* 91
SWEATIN' FLUX - Flux - LA-CO INDUSTRIES MARKAL CO., INC.; *pg.* 1170, *pg.* 610
SWEATME - Footwear - STEVEN MADDEN, LTD.; *pg.* 1819, *pg.* 1176
SWEDISH - Mirror - ETHAN ALLEN INTERIORS INC.; *pg.* 924, *pg.* 343
SWEDISH GLACE - Food Product - PERRY'S ICE CREAM CO., INC.; *pg.* 1861, *pg.* 1137
SWEDISH KITCHEN - Ginger Snap - A.V. OLSSON TRADING CO. INC.; *pg.* 838, *pg.* 372
SWEECHA - Beverages - THE COCA-COLA COMPANY; *pg.* 240, *pg.* 493
SWEEDEN - Footwear - COBIAN CORP.; *pg.* 1806, *pg.* 253
SWEEET N NEAT 65 GMF - Sweetener - ARCHER-DANIELS-MIDLAND COMPANY; *pg.* 825, *pg.* 565
SWEEP ARRAY - Eyewear - OAKLEY, INC.; *pg.* 1840, *pg.* 86
SWEEP MASTER - Turf Brush - GANDY COMPANY; *pg.* 703, *pg.* 952
SWEEP 'N CLEAN - Cleaning Product - THE EVERCARE COMPANY; *pg.* 1124, *pg.* 483
SWEEP STAR - Turf Maintenance Machinery - SMITHCO, INC.; *pg.* 1377, *pg.* 1592
SWEEP UP - Floor Care Product - BISSELL HOMECARE, INC.; *pg.* 52, *pg.* 887
SWEEPER - Office Furniture - STEELCASE INC.; *pg.* 475, *pg.* 889
SWEEPFIRE - Freshwater Spinning Reels - DAIWA CORPORATION; *pg.* 1832, *pg.* 75
SWEEPT - Footwear - STEVEN MADDEN, LTD.; *pg.* 1819, *pg.* 1176
SWEEPZONE - Ultrasonic Cleaning System - L&R MANUFACTURING COMPANY; *pg.* 1419, *pg.* 1076
SWEEPZONE AG - Ultrasonic Cleaning Systems - L&R MANUFACTURING COMPANY; *pg.* 1419, *pg.* 1076
SWEET 10 - Horse Feed - MANNA PRO CORPORATION; *pg.* 1478, *pg.* 975
SWEET ACIDOPHILUS - Milk - PURITY DAIRIES, LLC; *pg.* 891, *pg.* 1653
SWEET & MAXWELL - Legal Publications - THOMSON REUTERS CORPORATION; *pg.* 1693, *pg.* 1944
SWEET & ZESTY - BBQ Sauce - FAMOUS DAVE'S OF AMERICA, INC.; *pg.* 1728, *pg.* 926
SWEET APPLE WOOD SMOKE - Food Product - PATRICK CUDAHY INC.; *pg.* 888, *pg.* 1856
SWEET BABY BOY - Flower Arrangement - 1-800-FLOWERS.COM, INC.; *pg.* 1758, *pg.* 1151
SWEET BABY GIRL - Flower Arrangement - 1-800-FLOWERS.COM, INC.; *pg.* 1758, *pg.* 1151

SWEET BY NATURE - Slogan - THE SUGAR ASSOCIATION, INC.; *pg.* 157, *pg.* 405
SWEET CELEBRATION - Fruit Arrangements - EDIBLE ARRANGEMENTS INTERNATIONAL, INC.; *pg.* 1768, *pg.* 382
SWEET CHARITY - Video Game - INTERNATIONAL GAME TECHNOLOGY; *pg.* 957, *pg.* 1024
SWEET CORN ALIVE - Vegetable Gardening - GARDENS ALIVE!, INC.; *pg.* 1796, *pg.* 693
SWEET DEAL - Video Game - INTERNATIONAL GAME TECHNOLOGY; *pg.* 957, *pg.* 1024
SWEET DESIGN - Sweetener - CARGILL, INC.; *pg.* 845, *pg.* 965
SWEET DREAMS - Herb Tea - R.C. BIGELOW, INC.; *pg.* 891, *pg.* 348
SWEET DREAMS - Candy Assortment - ROCKY MOUNTAIN CHOCOLATE FACTORY, INC.; *pg.* 1032, *pg.* 324
SWEET DREAMS BOUQUET - Floral Bouquet - FTD GROUP, INC.; *pg.* 1795, *pg.* 608
SWEET DRIFT - Garden Roses - THE CONARD-PYLE COMPANY; *pg.* 1794, *pg.* 1594
SWEET EXPRESSIONS BOUQUET - Floral Bouquet - FTD GROUP, INC.; *pg.* 1795, *pg.* 608
SWEET FREEDOM - Sweet Cake & Sundae - WELLS ENTERPRISES, INC.; *pg.* 909, *pg.* 709
SWEET GOLD - Video Game - INTERNATIONAL GAME TECHNOLOGY; *pg.* 957, *pg.* 1024
SWEET HOME - Candle - THE YANKEE CANDLE COMPANY, INC.; *pg.* 1792, *pg.* 843
SWEET HONESTY - Beauty Product - AVON PRODUCTS, INC.; *pg.* 500, *pg.* 1198
SWEET INSPIRATION - Visor Clips - HABAND COMPANY, INC.; *pg.* 1772, *pg.* 1099
SWEET KISS - Dairy Food Product - LIFEWAY FOODS, INC.; *pg.* 874, *pg.* 634
SWEET MIST - Car Wash Equipment - D&S CAR WASH EQUIPMENT CO.; *pg.* 1327, *pg.* 979
SWEET 'N LOW - Saccharin-Based Sugar Substitute - CUMBERLAND PACKING CORP.; *pg.* 851, *pg.* 1146
SWEET N NEAT - Agricultural Product - ARCHER-DANIELS-MIDLAND COMPANY; *pg.* 825, *pg.* 565
SWEET N NEAT 2000 - Sweetener - ARCHER-DANIELS-MIDLAND COMPANY; *pg.* 825, *pg.* 565
SWEET N NEAT 3000 - Sweetener - ARCHER-DANIELS-MIDLAND COMPANY; *pg.* 825, *pg.* 565
SWEET N NEAT 4000 - Sweetener - ARCHER-DANIELS-MIDLAND COMPANY; *pg.* 825, *pg.* 565
SWEET N NEAT 50 - Sweetener - ARCHER-DANIELS-MIDLAND COMPANY; *pg.* 825, *pg.* 565
SWEET N NEAT 5000 - Sweetener - ARCHER-DANIELS-MIDLAND COMPANY; *pg.* 825, *pg.* 565
SWEET N NEAT TACK BLEND - Sweetener - ARCHER-DANIELS-MIDLAND COMPANY; *pg.* 825, *pg.* 565
SWEET N NEAT TACK BLEND S - Sweetener - ARCHER-DANIELS-MIDLAND COMPANY; *pg.* 825, *pg.* 565
SWEET N NEAT TACK BLEND T - Sweetener - ARCHER-DANIELS-MIDLAND COMPANY; *pg.* 825, *pg.* 565
SWEET N NEAT TS DRY - Sweetener - ARCHER-DANIELS-MIDLAND COMPANY; *pg.* 825, *pg.* 565
SWEET N NEAT TS OIL - Sweetener - ARCHER-DANIELS-MIDLAND COMPANY; *pg.* 825, *pg.* 565
SWEET PDZ - Horse Stall Refresher - MANNA PRO CORPORATION; *pg.* 1478, *pg.* 975
SWEET PEA - Flower Arrangement - 1-800-FLOWERS.COM, INC.; *pg.* 1758, *pg.* 1151
SWEET PEA - Dinnerware - THE HOMER LAUGHLIN CHINA COMPANY; *pg.* 1125, *pg.* 1850
SWEET PERKS TOO - Food Product - DOVER DOWNS GAMING & ENTERTAINMENT, INC.; *pg.* 545, *pg.* 387
SWEET RELY - Horse Feed - MANNA PRO CORPORATION; *pg.* 1478, *pg.* 975
SWEET RUBIES - Live Plants - AEROGROW INTERNATIONAL, INC.; *pg.* 1393, *pg.* 310
SWEET SENSATIONS - Carpet - BEAULIEU GROUP, LLC; *pg.* 917, *pg.* 529
SWEET SIMPLICITY - Sweetener - MERISANT COMPANY; *pg.* 876, *pg.* 581
SWEET SLEEPER - Bed - THE SHERATON CORPORATION; *pg.* 1112, *pg.* 378
SWEET SOUNDS - Baby Music Station - EVENFLO COMPANY, INC.; *pg.* 924, *pg.* 1470
SWEET SUE - Chicken Products - BUMBLE BEE FOODS LLC; *pg.* 842, *pg.* 201
SWEET SURPRISE BOUQUET - Floral Bouquet - FTD GROUP, INC.; *pg.* 1795, *pg.* 608
SWEET SWEATERS - Blouses - HABAND COMPANY, INC.; *pg.* 1772, *pg.* 1099
SWEET TALK - Mouthwash - BLUE CROSS LABORATORIES; *pg.* 326, *pg.* 277
SWEET TOMATOES - Food Product - GARDEN FRESH RESTAURANT CORP.; *pg.* 1729, *pg.* 203
SWEET TREATS BOUQUET - Floral Bouquet - FTD GROUP, INC.; *pg.* 1795, *pg.* 608
SWEET WATER PRESS - Book - BOOKS-A-MILLION, INC.; *pg.* 1623, *pg.* 2
SWEETARTS - Candy - NESTLE USA, INC.; *pg.* 883, *pg.* 96
SWEET'EES - Almonds - BLUE DIAMOND GROWERS; *pg.* 840, *pg.* 195
SWEETEST FLOWER - Pillow and Throw - HERITAGE LACE INC.; *pg.* 694, *pg.* 711
THE SWEETEST SITE ON THE WEB - Slogan - THE HERSHEY CO.; *pg.* 1855, *pg.* 1538
SWEETEX - Sweetening Ingredient - MERISANT COMPANY; *pg.* 876, *pg.* 581
SWEETGLO - Horse Products - KENT NUTRITION GROUP; *pg.* 1477, *pg.* 710
SWEETHEART - Carpet - BEAULIEU GROUP, LLC; *pg.* 917, *pg.* 529
SWEETHEART - Cup - SOLO CUP COMPANY; *pg.* 1469, *pg.* 625
SWEETHEART BOUQUET - Fruit Arrangements - EDIBLE ARRANGEMENTS INTERNATIONAL, INC.; *pg.* 1768, *pg.* 382
SWEETHEART CASH - Lottery Game - MASSACHUSETTS STATE LOTTERY; *pg.* 998, *pg.* 802
SWEETHEARTS - Conversation Hearts - NEW ENGLAND CONFECTIONERY COMPANY INC.; *pg.* 1860, *pg.* 842
SWEETIEZ - Footwear - STEVEN MADDEN, LTD.; *pg.* 1819, *pg.* 1176
SWEETMATE - Sweetener - MERISANT COMPANY; *pg.* 876, *pg.* 581
SWEETMEADOW FARMS - Honey & Maple Syrup - DUTCH GOLD HONEY INC.; *pg.* 854, *pg.* 1546
SWEET'S CINNAMON BEARS - Cinnamon Candy - SWEET CANDY COMPANY; *pg.* 1862, *pg.* 1761
SWEET'S ORANGE STICKS - Candy - SWEET CANDY COMPANY; *pg.* 1862, *pg.* 1761
SWEET'S SALTWATER TAFFY - Taffy - SWEET CANDY COMPANY; *pg.* 1862, *pg.* 1761
SWEETSTREET - Manhole Adsorber - CALGON CARBON CORPORATION; *pg.* 1151, *pg.* 1574
SWEETVENT - Vent Stack Adsorber - CALGON CARBON CORPORATION; *pg.* 1151, *pg.* 1574
SWEETWATER OAKS - Furniture - ASHLEY FURNITURE INDUSTRIES, INC.; *pg.* 914, *pg.* 1852
SWELL SPOTS - Medical & Aesthetic Product - DYNATRONICS CORPORATION; *pg.* 1526, *pg.* 1757
SWEPCO - Pipe & Tubing - SWEPCO TUBE CORPORATION; *pg.* 114, *pg.* 1052
SWERVE - Soft Drink - THE COCA-COLA COMPANY; *pg.* 240, *pg.* 493
SWERVE - Kitchen Product - KOHLER CO.; *pg.* 91, *pg.* 1862
SWFC 1X2 - Coupler - OPLINK COMMUNICATIONS, INC.; *pg.* 660, *pg.* 91
SWFC 1X3 - Coupler - OPLINK COMMUNICATIONS, INC.; *pg.* 660, *pg.* 91
SWFC1X4 - Coupler - OPLINK COMMUNICATIONS, INC.; *pg.* 660, *pg.* 91
SWIFFER - House Care Product - THE PROCTER & GAMBLE COMPANY; *pg.* 1129, *pg.* 1418
SWIFT - Simulator System - MTS SYSTEMS CORPORATION; *pg.* 442, *pg.* 923
SWIFT - Nasal Pillow - RESMED INC.; *pg.* 1589, *pg.* 207
SWIFT - Power Products & Voltage Regulators - TEXAS INSTRUMENTS INCORPORATED; *pg.* 679, *pg.* 1688
SWIFT - Gas Metering System - WOODWARD, INC.; *pg.* 122, *pg.* 329
SWIFT DENIM - Denim Producer - GALEY & LORD LLC; *pg.* 693, *pg.* 1621
SWIFT RIVER - Paper Products - BOISE CASCADE HOLDINGS, L.L.C.; *pg.* 1453, *pg.* 546
SWIFT RIVER - Apparel - L.L. BEAN, INC.; *pg.* 1777, *pg.* 750
SWIFT SWEEP - Floor Care Product - BISSELL HOMECARE, INC.; *pg.* 52, *pg.* 887
SWIFTCOMPLETE - Software - VITRIA TECHNOLOGY, INC.; *pg.* 490, *pg.* 289
SWIFTFLO - Bath Product - KOHLER CO.; *pg.* 91, *pg.* 1862
SWIFTLINK - Wireless Communication Product - TELECOMMUNICATION SYSTEMS INC.; *pg.* 483, *pg.* 754
SWIFTNET - Software - PEGASYSTEMS INC.; *pg.* 453, *pg.* 809
SWIFTPAY - Auto Debit Payment Option - SLM CORPORATION; *pg.* 804, *pg.* 388
SWIFTSET - Folding Chair - MITY ENTERPRISES, INC.; *pg.* 935, *pg.* 1753
SWIFTWRITER - PDF Converter Enables Electronic Integration with DMS/RMS Systems - OMTOOL, LTD.; *pg.* 449, *pg.* 782
SWIGER - Electric Motor Coils - WESTINGHOUSE AIR BRAKE TECHNOLOGIES CORPORATION; *pg.* 1388, *pg.* 1595
SWIMCLEAR - Cartridge Filter - HAYWARD POOL PRODUCTS; *pg.* 1049, *pg.* 1057
SWIMMER'S - Hair & Skin Product - AUBREY ORGANICS INC.; *pg.* 499, *pg.* 470
SWIMVISION - Goggle - ICARE INDUSTRIES, INC.; *pg.* 1417, *pg.* 463
SWIMVITATIONAL - Entertainment Services - MUTUAL OF OMAHA INSURANCE COMPANY; *pg.* 1210, *pg.* 1016
SWINDLEEV - Footwear - STEVEN MADDEN, LTD.; *pg.* 1819, *pg.* 1176
SWINE PRACTITIONER - Magazine - VANCE PUBLISHING CORPORATION; *pg.* 1699, *pg.* 627
SWINE SAFE-GUARD - Concentrated Nutrients for Internal Parasites - KENT NUTRITION GROUP; *pg.* 1477, *pg.* 710
SWING - Silverware - ONEIDA LTD; *pg.* 1129, *pg.* 1318
SWING - Footwear - P.W. MINOR & SON, INC.; *pg.* 1816, *pg.* 1140
SWING FAIR ISLE - Women's Clothing & Accessories - WOODEN SHIPS OF HOBOKEN; *pg.* 35, *pg.* 1315
SWING-OUT - Valves - AKRON BRASS COMPANY; *pg.* 1311, *pg.* 1482
SWING-TOP - Plastic Houseware Product - STERILITE CORPORATION; *pg.* 1138, *pg.* 848
SWINGER - Grooved & Swing Check Valve - VICTAULIC COMPANY; *pg.* 1066, *pg.* 1529
SWINGERS - Conveyor & Diverter - SHUTTLEWORTH, INC.; *pg.* 1375, *pg.* 682
SWINGIN' & SPINNIN' - Game - WMS INDUSTRIES INC.; *pg.* 593, *pg.* 666
SWINGIN' IN THE GREEN - Game - WMS INDUSTRIES INC.; *pg.* 593, *pg.* 666
SWINGLINE - Office Products - ACCO BRANDS CORPORATION; *pg.* 340, *pg.* 626
SWINGMASTER - Musical Instrument - GIBSON GUITAR CORP.; *pg.* 550, *pg.* 1650
SWIRL - Bread - PEPPERIDGE FARM, INC.; *pg.* 888, *pg.* 363
SWIRL - Footwear - VANS, INC.; *pg.* 1821, *pg.* 76
SWIRL - Ceiling Fan - WESTINGHOUSE LIGHTING CORPORATION; *pg.* 687, *pg.* 1571
SWIRL-OUT - Exhaust - SWARTWOUT DIVISION; *pg.* 114, *pg.* 978
SWIRL SERVE - Beverage Server - THE VOLLRATH COMPANY LLC; *pg.* 1139, *pg.* 1894
SWIRLS OF PEARLS - Jewelry - HABAND COMPANY, INC.; *pg.* 1772, *pg.* 1099
SWIRLY - Footwear - COBIAN CORP.; *pg.* 1806, *pg.* 253
SWISH - Cup Watering System or Waterer - CTB INTERNATIONAL CORP.; *pg.* 850, *pg.* 695
SWISHER SWEETS - Cigar - SWISHER INTERNATIONAL, INC.; *pg.* 1895, *pg.* 345
SWISS ARMY - Watches, Writing Instruments - VICTORINOX SWISS ARMY INC.; *pg.* 1139, *pg.* 357
SWISS CARBIDE - Healthcare Product - MEDICOOL, INC.; *pg.* 1562, *pg.* 294
SWISS CHALET - Chicken & Ribs Restaurants - CARA OPERATIONS LIMITED; *pg.* 1720, *pg.* 1947
SWISS COLONY - Gourmet Food Stores - COLONY BRANDS INC.; *pg.* 849, *pg.* 1881
SWISS DAIRY - Dairy Products - DEAN FOODS COMPANY; *pg.* 852, *pg.* 1679
SWISS FORMULA - Food Products - MODERN PRODUCTS, INC.; *pg.* 1568, *pg.* 1871
SWISS-KRISS - Laxative - MODERN PRODUCTS, INC.; *pg.* 1568, *pg.* 1871
SWISS LITHOCLAST - Medical Device - BOSTON SCIENTIFIC CORPORATION; *pg.* 1508, *pg.* 831
SWISS MADE - Athletic Shoes - K-SWISS; *pg.* 1837, *pg.* 306
SWISS MISS - Powdered Hot Beverage Products - CONAGRA FOODS, INC.; *pg.* 826, *pg.* 1014
SWISS WATER - Decaffeinate Coffee - SWISS WATER DECAFFEINATED COFFEE INCOME FUND; *pg.* 900, *pg.* 1907

First page reference indicates Business Class Edition
Second page reference indicates Geographic Edition

SWISSAIRE - Filtration Product - FLANDERS CORPORATION; *pg.* 1336, *pg.* 1392
SWISSGARDE - Personal Care Product - TUPPERWARE BRANDS CORPORATION; *pg.* 1139, *pg.* 456
SWITCH - Office Furniture - STEELCASE INC.; *pg.* 475, *pg.* 889
SWITCH BLADE - Software Product - EGENERA, INC.; *pg.* 390, *pg.* 802
SWITCH-BLADE - Pharmaceutical Product - GENZYME CORPORATION; *pg.* 1534, *pg.* 808
SWITCH-CART - Tow Chain Conveying Equipment - PARAGON TECHNOLOGIES, INC.; *pg.* 1367, *pg.* 1528
SWITCH EXECUTIVE - Office Furniture - STEELCASE INC.; *pg.* 475, *pg.* 889
SWITCH TIP - Tips for Spray Guns - GRACO, INC.; *pg.* 1342, *pg.* 935
SWITCH-TO-STARTER - Vehicle Safety System - GROTE INDUSTRIES, INC.; *pg.* 206, *pg.* 693
SWITCHCRAFT - Adapter - PEAVEY ELECTRONICS CORPORATION; *pg.* 662, *pg.* 970
SWITCHER VS7390 - Video Surveillance - BOSCH SECURITY SYSTEMS, INC.; *pg.* 626, *pg.* 1158
SWITCHMARK - Membrane Switch Component - FLEXCON CORPORATION; *pg.* 1457, *pg.* 844
SWITCHPLAN - Occupancy Sensing Controls - PASS & SEYMOUR/LEGRAND; *pg.* 1303, *pg.* 1344
SWITCHPLAY - Toy - SPIN MASTER LTD.; *pg.* 967, *pg.* 1943
SWITCHPOINT INFINITY - Touchpad - STRYKER CORPORATION; *pg.* 1598, *pg.* 894
SWIV-ALL - Swivel - LAPWORKS, INC.; *pg.* 426, *pg.* 187
SWIV-L-CUT - Windshield Removing Tools & Replacement Parts - PPG INDUSTRIES, INC.; *pg.* 1445, *pg.* 1579
SWIV-O-FLEX - Industrial Lighting - SWIVELIER CO., INC.; *pg.* 1307, *pg.* 1142
SWIVEL - Disposable Pivoting Head Razor - THE GILLETTE COMPANY; *pg.* 509, *pg.* 795
SWIVEL - Category Search - TIVO INC.; *pg.* 313, *pg.* 251
SWIVEL-BLADE - Cable Stripper - IDEAL INDUSTRIES, INC.; *pg.* 1051, *pg.* 662
SWIVEL-PRO - Adapter - STRAHMAN VALVES, INC.; *pg.* 1379, *pg.* 1517
SWIVELHOSE - Fluid Handling System - GRACO, INC.; *pg.* 1342, *pg.* 935
SWIVELIER - Light Converter And Extender - SWIVELIER CO., INC.; *pg.* 1307, *pg.* 1142
SWIVLPAD - Turntable Allowing for Full Rotation & Viewing of Notebook Computer Screens - LAPWORKS, INC.; *pg.* 426, *pg.* 187
SWIVOMATIC - Industrial & Hospital Lighting - SWIVELIER CO., INC.; *pg.* 1307, *pg.* 1142
SWIZZLE - Fabric - NEMSCHOFF, INC.; *pg.* 936, *pg.* 1890
SWOON - Fabric - NEMSCHOFF, INC.; *pg.* 936, *pg.* 1890
SWOOPS - Chocolate Candy - THE HERSHEY CO.; *pg.* 1855, *pg.* 1538
SWOOSH DESIGN - Apparel - NIKE, INC.; *pg.* 1812, *pg.* 1492
SWOPPERV - Vacuum Cutter - TIPPER TIE, INC.; *pg.* 1382, *pg.* 1358
SWORD - Thermal Plates - EASTMAN KODAK COMPANY; *pg.* 1408, *pg.* 1333
SWORD EXCEL - Thermal Plates - EASTMAN KODAK COMPANY; *pg.* 1408, *pg.* 1333
SWORD FLOSS - Dental Product - MAJESTIC DRUG COMPANY, INC.; *pg.* 516, *pg.* 1343
SWORD FLOSS PROXI-PLUS - Dental Product - MAJESTIC DRUG COMPANY, INC.; *pg.* 516, *pg.* 1343
SWORDS OF HONOR - Game - WMS INDUSTRIES INC.; *pg.* 593, *pg.* 666
SWR - Guitar - FENDER MUSICAL INSTRUMENTS CORPORATION; *pg.* 547, *pg.* 21
SWTC - Splitter - OPLINK COMMUNICATIONS, INC.; *pg.* 660, *pg.* 91
SWYPEOUT - Toy - SPIN MASTER LTD.; *pg.* 967, *pg.* 1943
SX - Self-Limiting Heating Cables - THERMON AMERICAS INC.; *pg.* 1077, *pg.* 1744
SX-200 - Analog PABX - MITEL NETWORKS CORPORATION; *pg.* 654, *pg.* 1921
SX-200 DIGITAL - Digital PABX - MITEL NETWORKS CORPORATION; *pg.* 654, *pg.* 1921
SX-200 EL - Digital PBX for Under 80 Lines - MITEL NETWORKS CORPORATION; *pg.* 654, *pg.* 1921
SX-200 LIGHT - Fiber Distributed PBX - MITEL NETWORKS CORPORATION; *pg.* 654, *pg.* 1921
SX-200 ML - Digital PBX for Under 150 Lines - MITEL NETWORKS CORPORATION; *pg.* 654, *pg.* 1921
SX-2000 - Digital Switching System - MITEL NETWORKS CORPORATION; *pg.* 654, *pg.* 1921
SX-2000 LIGHT - Fiber Distributed PBX - MITEL NETWORKS CORPORATION; *pg.* 654, *pg.* 1921
SX-2000 MICRO LIGHT - Fiber Distributed PBX - MITEL NETWORKS CORPORATION; *pg.* 654, *pg.* 1921
SX-50 - Digital PABX - MITEL NETWORKS CORPORATION; *pg.* 654, *pg.* 1921
SX COBRA - Sterndrive - VOLVO PENTA OF THE AMERICAS, INC.; *pg.* 1712, *pg.* 1778
SX DIESEL - Diesel Sterndrive - VOLVO PENTA OF THE AMERICAS, INC.; *pg.* 1712, *pg.* 1778
SX PRO INNERNET - Sport Product - FRANKLIN SPORTS, INC.; *pg.* 1834, *pg.* 847
SX3000 - Software - XEROX CORPORATION; *pg.* 494, *pg.* 365
SX3000T - Software - XEROX CORPORATION; *pg.* 494, *pg.* 365
SXR 61 - SX Receiver - NORTEK SECURITY & CONTROL LLC; *pg.* 659, *pg.* 59
SYBEL - Footwear - STEVEN MADDEN, LTD.; *pg.* 1819, *pg.* 1176
SYBEX - Training Books - JOHN WILEY & SONS, INC.; *pg.* 1655, *pg.* 1073
SYBR - Molecular Probe Product - THERMO FISHER SCIENTIFIC INC.; *pg.* 1602, *pg.* 61
SYBR SAFE - Molecular Biology Product - THERMO FISHER SCIENTIFIC INC.; *pg.* 1602, *pg.* 61
SYCAMORE LANE - Beverage - TRINCHERO FAMILY ESTATES; *pg.* 1971, *pg.* 197
SYCLONE - Flashlight - STREAMLIGHT INC.; *pg.* 1306, *pg.* 1527
SYDNEY - Furniture - ASHLEY FURNITURE INDUSTRIES, INC.; *pg.* 914, *pg.* 1852
SYDNEY CHASE - Doll - TONNER DOLL COMPANY, INC.; *pg.* 968, *pg.* 1171
SYGATE - Software - SYMANTEC CORPORATION; *pg.* 478, *pg.* 161
SYGENEX - Engineering Services - LOCKHEED MARTIN CORPORATION; *pg.* 229, *pg.* 762
SYKES PICAVENT - Facom Tools - STANLEY BLACK & DECKER, INC.; *pg.* 1063, *pg.* 358
SYL-OFF - Silicones & Silicone Compositions Used as Release Coatings - DOW CORNING CORPORATION; *pg.* 1159, *pg.* 900
SYLFAT - Tall Oil Products - ARIZONA CHEMICAL CO. LLC; *pg.* 1147, *pg.* 431
SYLGARD - Silicon-Based Adjuvant Compound - DOW CORNING CORPORATION; *pg.* 1159, *pg.* 900
SYLTHERM - Heat Transfer Fluid - THE DOW CHEMICAL COMPANY; *pg.* 1157, *pg.* 898
SYLVABLEND - Acid Tall Oil - ARIZONA CHEMICAL CO. LLC; *pg.* 1147, *pg.* 431
SYLVACLEAR - Gel - ARIZONA CHEMICAL CO. LLC; *pg.* 1147, *pg.* 431
SYLVACOTE - Polyamide Resin - ARIZONA CHEMICAL CO. LLC; *pg.* 1147, *pg.* 431
SYLVACYCLE - Packaging Product - CASCADES, INC.; *pg.* 73, *pg.* 1950
SYLVAGEL - Resin - ARIZONA CHEMICAL CO. LLC; *pg.* 1147, *pg.* 431
SYLVAGUM - Resin - ARIZONA CHEMICAL CO. LLC; *pg.* 1147, *pg.* 431
SYLVALITE - Resin - ARIZONA CHEMICAL CO. LLC; *pg.* 1147, *pg.* 431
SYLVAN - Dress Shoes - JOHNSTON & MURPHY CO.; *pg.* 1810, *pg.* 1651
SYLVAN - Software - SS&C TECHNOLOGIES HOLDINGS, INC.; *pg.* 473, *pg.* 386
SYLVAPINE - Alpha-Pinene - ARIZONA CHEMICAL CO. LLC; *pg.* 1147, *pg.* 431
SYLVAPRINT - Solid Fusion Resinate - ARIZONA CHEMICAL CO. LLC; *pg.* 1147, *pg.* 431
SYLVARES - Resin - ARIZONA CHEMICAL CO. LLC; *pg.* 1147, *pg.* 431
SYLVAROS - Tall Oil Resins - ARIZONA CHEMICAL CO. LLC; *pg.* 1147, *pg.* 431
SYLVATAC - Resin Esters - ARIZONA CHEMICAL CO. LLC; *pg.* 1147, *pg.* 431
SYLVATAL - Tall Oil Products - ARIZONA CHEMICAL CO. LLC; *pg.* 1147, *pg.* 431
SYLVATECH - Packaging Product - CASCADES, INC.; *pg.* 73, *pg.* 1950
SYMANTEC DEPLOYCENTER - Software - SYMANTEC CORPORATION; *pg.* 478, *pg.* 161
SYMANTEC ENTERPRISE SECURITY ARCHITECTURE - Software - SYMANTEC CORPORATION; *pg.* 478, *pg.* 161
SYMANTEC INFORM - Software - SYMANTEC CORPORATION; *pg.* 478, *pg.* 161
SYMANTEC INSIGHT - Software - SYMANTEC CORPORATION; *pg.* 478, *pg.* 161
SYMANTEC INTRUDER ALERT - Software - SYMANTEC CORPORATION; *pg.* 478, *pg.* 161
SYMANTEC MAIL-GEAR - Software - SYMANTEC CORPORATION; *pg.* 478, *pg.* 161
SYMANTEC MOBILE ESSENTIALS - Software - SYMANTEC CORPORATION; *pg.* 478, *pg.* 161
SYMANTEC ON COMMAND DISCOVERY - Software - SYMANTEC CORPORATION; *pg.* 478, *pg.* 161
SYMANTEC ON ICOMMAND - Software - SYMANTEC CORPORATION; *pg.* 478, *pg.* 161
SYMANTEC ON IPATCH - Software - SYMANTEC CORPORATION; *pg.* 478, *pg.* 161
SYMAPPS - Software - BIO-RAD LABORATORIES, INC.; *pg.* 1504, *pg.* 101
SYMBILL - Footwear - STEVEN MADDEN, LTD.; *pg.* 1819, *pg.* 1176
SYMBIO - Bath Product - KOHLER CO.; *pg.* 91, *pg.* 1862
SYMBIOS - Pacemaker - MEDTRONIC, INC.; *pg.* 1564, *pg.* 939
SYMBIOSIS - Carpet - INTERFACE, INC.; *pg.* 695, *pg.* 512
SYMBOL - Meter Reading System - BADGER METER, INC.; *pg.* 1401, *pg.* 1873
SYMBOL - Bath Product - KOHLER CO.; *pg.* 91, *pg.* 1862
SYMBOL - Fabric - NEMSCHOFF, INC.; *pg.* 936, *pg.* 1890
SYMBYAX - Pharmaceutical Product - ELI LILLY AND COMPANY; *pg.* 1527, *pg.* 684
SYMFUNNIES - Symphony - SPOKANE SYMPHONY ORCHESTRA; *pg.* 584, *pg.* 1844
SYMITAR - Banking Software - JACK HENRY & ASSOCIATES, INC.; *pg.* 422, *pg.* 988
SYMMAPI - Software - EMC CORPORATION; *pg.* 391, *pg.* 825
SYMMENABLER - Software - EMC CORPORATION; *pg.* 391, *pg.* 825
SYMMETRA - Power Protection Product - SCHNEIDER ELECTRIC; *pg.* 467, *pg.* 1609
SYMMETREL - Pharmaceutical Product - ENDO PHARMACEUTICALS HOLDINGS, INC.; *pg.* 1528, *pg.* 1549
SYMMETRIC - Patient Handling Equipment - STRYKER CORPORATION; *pg.* 1598, *pg.* 894
SYMMETRICAL FIELD GEOMETRY - Speaker Motor - HARMAN INTERNATIONAL INDUSTRIES, INCORPORATED; *pg.* 641, *pg.* 374
SYMMETRIX - Software - EMC CORPORATION; *pg.* 391, *pg.* 825
SYMMETRIX - Precision Kitchen & Lavatory Faucets - SYMMONS INDUSTRIES, INC.; *pg.* 114, *pg.* 803
SYMMETRIX DMX - Software - EMC CORPORATION; *pg.* 391, *pg.* 825
SYMMETRIX VMAX - Software - EMC CORPORATION; *pg.* 391, *pg.* 825
SYMMETRY - Medical Device - BOSTON SCIENTIFIC CORPORATION; *pg.* 1508, *pg.* 831
SYMMETRY - Fabric - NEMSCHOFF, INC.; *pg.* 936, *pg.* 1890
SYMMETRY - Analytical Column - WATERS CORPORATION; *pg.* 1436, *pg.* 834
SYMMIX - Neurological Lead - MEDTRONIC, INC.; *pg.* 1564, *pg.* 939
SYMMONS DESIGN STUDIO - Design Tool - SYMMONS INDUSTRIES, INC.; *pg.* 114, *pg.* 803
SYMPATEX - Blood Borne Pathogen Barrier - WEINBRENNER SHOE COMPANY, INC.; *pg.* 1822, *pg.* 1871
SYMPATHY SENTIMENTS - Bouquet - 1-800-FLOWERS.COM, INC.; *pg.* 1758, *pg.* 1151
SYMPHONY - Publication - AMERICAN SYMPHONY ORCHESTRA LEAGUE; *pg.* 528, *pg.* 1194
SYMPHONY - Editing & Audio Systems - AVID TECHNOLOGY, INC.; *pg.* 622, *pg.* 804
SYMPHONY - Furniture - THE COMMERCIAL FURNITURE GROUP; *pg.* 920, *pg.* 994
SYMPHONY - Electrical Heating Product - DIMPLEX NORTH AMERICA LIMITED; *pg.* 54, *pg.* 1920
SYMPHONY - Chocolate Candy - THE HERSHEY CO.; *pg.* 1855, *pg.* 1538
SYMPHONY - Medical Laser System - IRIDEX

First page reference indicates Business Class Edition
Second page reference indicates Geographic Edition

CORPORATION; *pg.* 648, *pg.* 160

SYMPHONY - Commercial CD Jukebox - ROWE INTERNATIONAL CORP; *pg.* 669, *pg.* 889

SYMPHONY - Wall Tissue Paper - THE SHERWIN-WILLIAMS COMPANY; *pg.* 1447, *pg.* 1435

SYMPHONY ON WHEELS - Music Education - SEATTLE SYMPHONY ORCHESTRA; *pg.* 582, *pg.* 1840

SYMPHONY SERIES - Swimming Pools - DELAIR GROUP, LLC; *pg.* 78, *pg.* 1053

SYMPHONY WITH A TWIST - Slogan - BALTIMORE SYMPHONY ORCHESTRA; *pg.* 532, *pg.* 755

SYMPHONYPILLOW - Pillow - TEMPUR SEALY INTERNATIONAL, INC.; *pg.* 944, *pg.* 731

SYMPT-X - Healthcare Product - BAXTER INTERNATIONAL INC.; *pg.* 1499, *pg.* 599

SYN CHECK - Software - F5 NETWORKS, INC.; *pg.* 396, *pg.* 1835

SYN-CHEK - Chlorinated Fatty Ester - FERRO CORPORATION; *pg.* 1162, *pg.* 1462

SYN-LUBE - Synthetic Lubricants for Rotary Screw & Rotary Vane Air Compressors - LUBRIPLATE LUBRICANTS; *pg.* 980, *pg.* 1097

SYN-LUSTRO - Alkyd Semi-Gloss & Gloss Enamel - DUNN-EDWARDS CORPORATION; *pg.* 1442, *pg.* 129

SYNAC - Synthetic Lubricants - LUBRIPLATE LUBRICANTS; *pg.* 980, *pg.* 1097

SYNAGIS - Medical Product - ABBOTT LABORATORIES; *pg.* 1484, *pg.* 551

SYNALOX - Lubricants - THE DOW CHEMICAL COMPANY; *pg.* 1157, *pg.* 898

SYNANTHIC - Veterinary Anthelmintic - PFIZER INC.; *pg.* 1581, *pg.* 1278

SYNAPPTEST - Software - SYNTEL, INC.; *pg.* 480, *pg.* 911

SYNAPPTOOL - Software - SYNTEL, INC.; *pg.* 480, *pg.* 911

SYNAPSE - Software - CRESTRON ELECTRONICS INC.; *pg.* 631, *pg.* 1116

SYNAPSE - Medical Image & Information Management System - FUJIFILM MEDICAL SYSTEMS USA, INC.; *pg.* 1531, *pg.* 374

SYNAPSE - Software - SUNGARD DATA SYSTEMS INC.; *pg.* 477, *pg.* 1592

SYNAPTA - Software - ATTACHMATE CORPORATION; *pg.* 356, *pg.* 1833

SYNAREL - Medicine - PFIZER INC.; *pg.* 1581, *pg.* 1278

SYNARO - Software - ISLAND PACIFIC; *pg.* 422, *pg.* 111

SYNBIOSYS - Drug Delivery System - SURMODICS, INC.; *pg.* 1600, *pg.* 924

SYNC - Voice-Activated In-Car Communications & Entertainment System - FORD MOTOR COMPANY; *pg.* 172, *pg.* 876

SYNC - Sales & Marketing Tool - R.R. DONNELLEY & SONS COMPANY; *pg.* 1682, *pg.* 589

SYNC - Modular Solutions - STEELCASE INC.; *pg.* 475, *pg.* 889

SYNCBURST - Hardware - MICRON TECHNOLOGY, INC.; *pg.* 435, *pg.* 547

SYNCHLOROZENE - Hide Processing Agent - BIRKO CORPORATION; *pg.* 1149, *pg.* 332

SYNCHRO - Valve - MAXON CORPORATION; *pg.* 1359, *pg.* 695

SYNCHRO2 - Medical Device - BOSTON SCIENTIFIC CORPORATION; *pg.* 1508, *pg.* 831

SYNCHROBELT - Power Transmission Belt - HBD INDUSTRIES, INC.; *pg.* 207, *pg.* 1449

SYNCHROFET - Drive Circuit - INTERSIL CORPORATION; *pg.* 647, *pg.* 146

SYNCHROMAX - Microplate Reader System - MOLECULAR DEVICES CORPORATION; *pg.* 1568, *pg.* 287

SYNCHROMED - Infusion System - MEDTRONIC, INC.; *pg.* 1564, *pg.* 939

SYNCHRON - Testing Instrument System - BECKMAN COULTER, INC.; *pg.* 1402, *pg.* 48

SYNCHRON - Spreading & Cutting System - GERBER SCIENTIFIC, INC.; *pg.* 1414, *pg.* 380

SYNCHRON CX - Clinical Analytical Instruments & Reagents - BECKMAN COULTER, INC.; *pg.* 1402, *pg.* 48

SYNCHRON LX - Clinical Chemistry Analyzers & Reagents - BECKMAN COULTER, INC.; *pg.* 1402, *pg.* 48

SYNCHRONET - Digital & Data Service - AT&T SOUTHEAST; *pg.* 1868, *pg.* 489

SYNCHRONETICS - Air & Ground Command Services - LOCKHEED MARTIN CORPORATION; *pg.* 229, *pg.* 762

SYNCHRONICITY - Carpet - INTERFACE, INC.; *pg.* 695, *pg.* 512

SYNCHRONICITY DEVELOPER SUITE - Software - DASSAULT SYSTEMS ENOVIA; *pg.* 382, *pg.* 851

SYNCHRONICITY DIGITAL DEVELOPER SUITE - Software - DASSAULT SYSTEMS ENOVIA; *pg.* 382, *pg.* 851

SYNCHRONICITY PHYSICAL DEVELOPER SUITE - Software - DASSAULT SYSTEMS ENOVIA; *pg.* 382, *pg.* 851

SYNCHRONICITY PUBLISHER AND CONSUMER SUITES - Software - DASSAULT SYSTEMS ENOVIA; *pg.* 382, *pg.* 851

SYNCHRONIZER - Lighting System - PHILIPS SOLID-STATE LIGHTING SOLUTIONS; *pg.* 1303, *pg.* 806

SYNCHRONY - Respiratory Tracking System - ACCURAY INCORPORATED; *pg.* 1486, *pg.* 282

SYNCHRONY - Software - CINCOM SYSTEMS, INC.; *pg.* 372, *pg.* 1411

SYNCHRONY - Herbicide - E.I. DU PONT DE NEMOURS & COMPANY; *pg.* 1159, *pg.* 390

SYNCHRONY - Bath Product - KOHLER CO.; *pg.* 91, *pg.* 1862

SYNCHROPOWER - Power Control Systems - ASCO POWER TECHNOLOGIES, L.P.; *pg.* 1314, *pg.* 1066

SYNCMIRROR - Software - NETAPP, INC.; *pg.* 444, *pg.* 287

SYNCOL - Synthetic Polymer - HUNTSMAN CORPORATION; *pg.* 1167, *pg.* 1758

SYNCOM - Stereo Test Equipment - BOSE CORPORATION; *pg.* 626, *pg.* 820

SYNCOOL - Synthetic Lubricants for Rotary Screw Air Compressors - LUBRIPLATE LUBRICANTS; *pg.* 980, *pg.* 1097

SYNCOPATION - Fabric - NEMSCHOFF, INC.; *pg.* 936, *pg.* 1890

SYNCRIA - Biological Product - GLAXOSMITHKLINE; *pg.* 1537, *pg.* 776

SYNCRO - Industrial Instrumentation - SIEMENS PROCESS INDUSTRIES AND DRIVE; *pg.* 1376, *pg.* 1587

SYNCRO SYSTEM - Shaving System - BRAUN NORTH AMERICA; *pg.* 52, *pg.* 792

SYNCROSIGN - Paper - XEROX CORPORATION; *pg.* 494, *pg.* 365

SYNCROWAVE - Welding & Cutting Equip. - MILLER ELECTRIC MANUFACTURING CO.; *pg.* 1361, *pg.* 1852

SYNCURE - Polyethylene Compound - POLYONE CORPORATION; *pg.* 1177, *pg.* 1404

SYNDECK - Adhesives & Sealers - QUAKER CHEMICAL CORP.; *pg.* 1178, *pg.* 1524

SYNDEO - Syringe Pump - BAXTER INTERNATIONAL INC.; *pg.* 1499, *pg.* 599

SYNDETIC SOLUTIONS - Publication - R.R. BOWKER LLC; *pg.* 1682, *pg.* 1095

SYNDETICS ICE - Indexed Content Enrichment Search Solutions - R.R. BOWKER LLC; *pg.* 1682, *pg.* 1095

SYNDICATED - Software - SYNOPSYS, INC.; *pg.* 480, *pg.* 162

SYNDION - 3-D IC Etch System - LAM RESEARCH CORPORATION; *pg.* 1354, *pg.* 91

SYNERCID - Injection - KING PHARMACEUTICALS, INC.; *pg.* 1553, *pg.* 1627

SYNERGIE - Medical Device - DYNATRONICS CORPORATION; *pg.* 1526, *pg.* 1757

SYNERGIE - Material Test Workstations - MTS SYSTEMS CORPORATION; *pg.* 442, *pg.* 923

SYNERGIE AESTHETIC MASSAGE SYSTEM - Massage System - DYNATRONICS CORPORATION; *pg.* 1526, *pg.* 1757

SYNERGIX - Printer - XEROX CORPORATION; *pg.* 494, *pg.* 365

SYNERGIZER GREEN - Capsule - WELLCO ENTERPRISES, INC.; *pg.* 1822, *pg.* 1392

SYNERGRAFT - Vascular Graft Replacement Product - CRYOLIFE, INC.; *pg.* 1520, *pg.* 534

SYNERGY - Pigment & Dispersion - BASF CATALYSTS LLC; *pg.* 1148, *pg.* 1074

SYNERGY - Bath Accessory - CROSCILL, INC.; *pg.* 1122, *pg.* 1220

SYNERGY - Plastic Foam - THE DOW CHEMICAL COMPANY; *pg.* 1157, *pg.* 898

SYNERGY - Neurostimulation System - MEDTRONIC, INC.; *pg.* 1564, *pg.* 939

SYNERGY - Air Respirator - MINE SAFETY APPLIANCES COMPANY; *pg.* 1361, *pg.* 1525

SYNERGY - Electronic Components - MOLEX INCORPORATED; *pg.* 655, *pg.* 628

SYNERGY - Grain Flake - NATURE'S PATH FOODS INC.; *pg.* 833, *pg.* 1908

SYNERGY - Coating Products - RUSSEL METALS INC.; *pg.* 1180, *pg.* 1928

SYNERGY - Washer - STERIS CORPORATION; *pg.* 1597, *pg.* 1464

SYNERGY INTEGRA - Wafer Cleaning System - LAM RESEARCH CORPORATION; *pg.* 1354, *pg.* 91

SYNERGY SERIES - Loudspeakers - KLIPSCH GROUP, INC.; *pg.* 649, *pg.* 688

SYNERGY SOLUTIONS - Business Tool - AVENTION; *pg.* 1230, *pg.* 815

SYNERGYCCS - Solvent Cleaning Agent - KYZEN CORPORATION; *pg.* 331, *pg.* 1652

SYNFIX-LR - Medical Device - DEPUY SYNTHES; *pg.* 1523, *pg.* 1593

SYNFLEX - Power Control Solutions - EATON CORPORATION; *pg.* 1331, *pg.* 1429

SYNIVERSE NEXT - Messaging Solution - SYNIVERSE HOLDINGS, INC.; *pg.* 479, *pg.* 475

SYNKAD - Lubricants - FERRO CORPORATION; *pg.* 1162, *pg.* 1462

SYNKO - Ceiling System - CGC INC.; *pg.* 75, *pg.* 1925

SYNOVEX - Veterinary Hormone - PFIZER INC.; *pg.* 1581, *pg.* 1278

SYNPAQUE - Chemical Product - WESTROCK COMPANY; *pg.* 1472, *pg.* 1805

SYNPLAST - Thermoplastic Colorant & Additive - POLYONE CORPORATION; *pg.* 1177, *pg.* 1404

SYNPLICITY - Software - SYNOPSYS, INC.; *pg.* 480, *pg.* 162

THE SYNPLICITY LOGO - Software - SYNOPSYS, INC.; *pg.* 480, *pg.* 162

SYNPLIFY - Software - SYNOPSYS, INC.; *pg.* 480, *pg.* 162

SYNPLIFY PRO - Software - SYNOPSYS, INC.; *pg.* 480, *pg.* 162

SYNPLUG - Medical Device - INTEGRA LIFESCIENCES HOLDINGS CORPORATION; *pg.* 1545, *pg.* 1109

SYNPOWER - Automotive Chemicals - ASHLAND INC.; *pg.* 972, *pg.* 726

SYNPRENE - Thermoplastic Elastomer Compound - POLYONE CORPORATION; *pg.* 1177, *pg.* 1404

SYNPRO - Polymer Additives - FERRO CORPORATION; *pg.* 1162, *pg.* 1462

SYNSURE - Lubricant - D-A LUBRICANT COMPANY; *pg.* 975, *pg.* 693

SYNTEGRA - Polyurethane Dispersion - THE DOW CHEMICAL COMPANY; *pg.* 1157, *pg.* 898

SYNTEQ - Air Filter - DONALDSON COMPANY, INC.; *pg.* 1329, *pg.* 917

SYNTHACRYL - Matting Agent - CYTEC INDUSTRIES, INC.; *pg.* 1155, *pg.* 1131

SYNTHESIS - Audio & Video Product - HARMAN INTERNATIONAL INDUSTRIES, INCORPORATED; *pg.* 641, *pg.* 374

SYNTHESIS - Fabric - NEMSCHOFF, INC.; *pg.* 936, *pg.* 1890

SYNTHESIS BOARDROOM - Audio & Video Product - HARMAN INTERNATIONAL INDUSTRIES, INCORPORATED; *pg.* 641, *pg.* 374

SYNTHESIS CONSTRAINTS OPTIMIZATION ENVIRONMENT - Software - SYNOPSYS, INC.; *pg.* 480, *pg.* 162

SYNTHROID - Tablet - ABBOTT LABORATORIES; *pg.* 1484, *pg.* 551

SYNTHROID - Pharmaceutical Product - LANNETT COMPANY, INC.; *pg.* 1555, *pg.* 1566

SYNTON - Polymer Product - CHEMTURA CORPORATION; *pg.* 1152, *pg.* 355

SYNVAR - Varnish - MARTIN/F. WEBER COMPANY; *pg.* 962, *pg.* 1567

SYNVISC - Pharmaceuticals & Syringes - GENZYME CORPORATION; *pg.* 1534, *pg.* 808

SYNVISC-ONE - Osteoarthritis Of Knee - GENZYME CORPORATION; *pg.* 1534, *pg.* 808

SYPHILAM - Clinical Diagnostic Product - BIO-RAD LABORATORIES, INC.; *pg.* 1504, *pg.* 101

SYPHILIA - Software - BIO-RAD LABORATORIES, INC.; *pg.* 1504, *pg.* 101

SYPRO - Molecular Biology Product - THERMO FISHER SCIENTIFIC INC.; *pg.* 1602, *pg.* 61

SYRACUSE - Footwear - EASTLAND SHOE CORPORATION; *pg.* 1808, *pg.* 750

SYRACUSE - Furniture - LA-Z-BOY INCORPORATED; *pg.* 932, *pg.* 901

SYRAH - Wine - BILTMORE ESTATE WINE COMPANY; *pg.* 1958, *pg.* 1358

SYRINGE AVITENE - Medical Device - C.R. BARD, INC.; *pg.*

1519, *pg.* 1094
SYS ADMIN - Software - UNITED BUSINESS MEDIA LLC; *pg.* 1697, *pg.* 1177
SYSCHANGE - Software - BMC SOFTWARE, INC.; *pg.* 362, *pg.* 1701
SYSCO - Food Products & Food-Related Products - SYSCO CORPORATION; *pg.* 1035, *pg.* 1716
SYSCO CLASSIC - Food Products - SYSCO CORPORATION; *pg.* 1035, *pg.* 1716
SYSCO IMPERIAL - Food Products - SYSCO CORPORATION; *pg.* 1035, *pg.* 1716
SYSCO NATURAL - Vegetables & Produce - SYSCO CORPORATION; *pg.* 1035, *pg.* 1716
SYSCO RELIANCE - Food Products - SYSCO CORPORATION; *pg.* 1035, *pg.* 1716
SYSCO SUPREME - Food Products - SYSCO CORPORATION; *pg.* 1035, *pg.* 1716
SYSMEX - Hemostasis Product - SIEMENS HEALTHCARE DIAGNOSTICS; *pg.* 673, *pg.* 604
SYSTEC - Pumps - IDEX CORPORATION; *pg.* 1347, *pg.* 623
THE SYSTEM - Medical Equipment - CONMED CORPORATION; *pg.* 1517, *pg.* 1347
SYSTEM 1 - Sterile Processing System - STERIS CORPORATION; *pg.* 1597, *pg.* 1464
SYSTEM 1 - Personal Care Product - WESTROCK COMPANY; *pg.* 1472, *pg.* 1805
SYSTEM 1-2-3 - Men's Electric Shaver - BRAUN NORTH AMERICA; *pg.* 52, *pg.* 792
SYSTEM 1000/TINA - Service Instrument - BAXTER INTERNATIONAL INC.; *pg.* 1499, *pg.* 599
SYSTEM 10K - Power Supply - EMCORE CORPORATION; *pg.* 636, *pg.* 39
SYSTEM 150 - High Speed Mail Extractor - OPEX CORPORATION; *pg.* 450, *pg.* 1087
SYSTEM 2000 - Grading System - ESCO CORPORATION; *pg.* 1335, *pg.* 1502
SYSTEM 2000 - Software - SAS INSTITUTE INC.; *pg.* 466, *pg.* 1361
SYSTEM 2450 - Medical Equipment - CONMED CORPORATION; *pg.* 1517, *pg.* 1347
THE SYSTEM 2500 - Medical Product - CONMED CORPORATION; *pg.* 1517, *pg.* 1347
SYSTEM 2500 - Fluid Handling System - GRACO, INC.; *pg.* 1342, *pg.* 935
SYSTEM 3 - Voice/Data Response System - ELECTRONIC TELE-COMMUNICATIONS, INC.; *pg.* 390, *pg.* 1897
SYSTEM 37 - Pharmaceutical Product - ALERE INC.; *pg.* 1488, *pg.* 849
SYSTEM 3800 - Fluid Handling System - GRACO, INC.; *pg.* 1342, *pg.* 935
SYSTEM 4 - Commercial Washers - PELLERIN MILNOR CORPORATION; *pg.* 1368, *pg.* 744
SYSTEM 48 - Recreational Vehicle - CLUB CAR, INC.; *pg.* 1830, *pg.* 532
SYSTEM 4900 - Fluid Handling System - GRACO, INC.; *pg.* 1342, *pg.* 935
THE SYSTEM 5000 - Medical Product - CONMED CORPORATION; *pg.* 1517, *pg.* 1347
SYSTEM 7 - Commercial Washers - PELLERIN MILNOR CORPORATION; *pg.* 1368, *pg.* 744
SYSTEM 7500 - Medical Product - CONMED CORPORATION; *pg.* 1517, *pg.* 1347
SYSTEM 7550 - Medical Equipment - CONMED CORPORATION; *pg.* 1517, *pg.* 1347
SYSTEM 98XT - Balloon Pump - MAQUET; *pg.* 1558, *pg.* 1082
SYSTEM ADVANTAGE - Warranty Services on Roofing Materials - OWENS CORNING; *pg.* 102, *pg.* 1476
SYSTEM CHANGE - Software - BMC SOFTWARE, INC.; *pg.* 362, *pg.* 1701
SYSTEM COMPILER - Software - SYNOPSYS, INC.; *pg.* 480, *pg.* 162
SYSTEM COREWARE - Printed Circuit Boards & Semiconductor Chips - AVAGO TECHNOLOGIES; *pg.* 358, *pg.* 238
SYSTEM DESIGNER - Software - SYNOPSYS, INC.; *pg.* 480, *pg.* 162
SYSTEM DIRECTOR - Operating System - MERU NETWORKS, INC.; *pg.* 434, *pg.* 286
SYSTEM EXPLORER - Software - BMC SOFTWARE, INC.; *pg.* 362, *pg.* 1701
SYSTEM FOUR - Seismic Acquisition System - ION GEOPHYSICAL CORPORATION; *pg.* 1350, *pg.* 1708
SYSTEM GOLD - Liquid Chromatograph Equipment - BECKMAN COULTER, INC.; *pg.* 1402, *pg.* 48
SYSTEM II - Piping System - VICTAULIC COMPANY; *pg.* 1066, *pg.* 1529
SYSTEM II MODULAR - Metal-Enclosed Switchgear - S&C ELECTRIC COMPANY; *pg.* 1305, *pg.* 589
SYSTEM III - Pest-Control Equipment - BASF; *pg.* 1793, *pg.* 992
SYSTEM III - Hot Water Dispensers - BUNN-O-MATIC CORPORATION; *pg.* 53, *pg.* 661
SYSTEM MANAGEMENT - Software - NETAPP, INC.; *pg.* 444, *pg.* 287
SYSTEM MANAGER - Software - VULCAN, INC.; *pg.* 687, *pg.* 5
SYSTEM #1 - Thermal Processing Equipment - SURFACE COMBUSTION, INC.; *pg.* 1077, *pg.* 1462
SYSTEM ONE - Truck Equipment - AMERICAN VAN EQUIPMENT INC.; *pg.* 199, *pg.* 1078
SYSTEM ONE - Seismic Acquisition System - ION GEOPHYSICAL CORPORATION; *pg.* 1350, *pg.* 1708
SYSTEM PERFORMANCE - Software - BMC SOFTWARE, INC.; *pg.* 362, *pg.* 1701
SYSTEM-PROCART - Fluid Handling System - GRACO, INC.; *pg.* 1342, *pg.* 935
SYSTEM-PROCOMP - Fluid Handling System - GRACO, INC.; *pg.* 1342, *pg.* 935
SYSTEM SMART - Amplifier - SKYWORKS SOLUTIONS, INC.; *pg.* 674, *pg.* 862
SYSTEM THINKING - Brand Promise - OWENS CORNING; *pg.* 102, *pg.* 1476
SYSTEM TWO - Seismic Acquisition System - ION GEOPHYSICAL CORPORATION; *pg.* 1350, *pg.* 1708
SYSTEM VI - Switchgear - S&C ELECTRIC COMPANY; *pg.* 1305, *pg.* 589
SYSTEM WATCH - Online Information - OGE ENERGY CORP.; *pg.* 1948, *pg.* 1486
SYSTEM6 - Light Commercial Baseboard Heaters - EMBASSY INDUSTRIES, INC.; *pg.* 1071, *pg.* 1164
SYSTEMATIC - Filing System - FELLOWES, INC.; *pg.* 397, *pg.* 620
SYSTEMAX - Label Product - SYSTEMAX, INC.; *pg.* 481, *pg.* 1324
SYSTEMS - Modular Scaffolds - SAFWAY SERVICES, LLC; *pg.* 109, *pg.* 1898
SYSTEMS - Healthcare Product - SWANSON HEALTH PRODUCTS INC.; *pg.* 1600, *pg.* 1397
SYSTEMS ADVANTAGE - Packaging System Program - AUTOMATED PACKAGING SYSTEMS INC.; *pg.* 1452, *pg.* 1474
SYSTEMS ENHANCEMENT - Software Product - CLARY CORPORATION; *pg.* 226, *pg.* 150
SYSTEMS ONE - Coulter - YETTER MANUFACTURING CO., INC.; *pg.* 708, *pg.* 598
SYSTEMSEATING - Furniture - HAWORTH, INC.; *pg.* 402, *pg.* 891
SYSTEMVIEW - Software - ITERIS, INC.; *pg.* 293, *pg.* 261
SYSTENET - Tube Gauze - DERMA SCIENCES, INC.; *pg.* 1523, *pg.* 1111
SYSTIMATIC - Saw Blade - SIMONDS INTERNATIONAL CORPORATION; *pg.* 1376, *pg.* 819
SYSTIMAX - Cable - COMMSCOPE, INC.; *pg.* 278, *pg.* 1378
SYTO - Molecular Probe Product - THERMO FISHER SCIENTIFIC INC.; *pg.* 1602, *pg.* 61
SYTON - Chemical Products - AIR PRODUCTS AND CHEMICALS, INC.; *pg.* 1145, *pg.* 1513
SYTON - Colloidal Silica - E.I. DU PONT DE NEMOURS & COMPANY; *pg.* 1159, *pg.* 390
SYTOX - Molecular Probe Product - THERMO FISHER SCIENTIFIC INC.; *pg.* 1602, *pg.* 61

T

T - Wire Striper - IDEAL INDUSTRIES, INC.; *pg.* 1051, *pg.* 662
T-100 - Adapter - ANDREA ELECTRONICS CORPORATION; *pg.* 617, *pg.* 1143
T-2 - Overhead Conductor - GENERAL CABLE CORPORATION; *pg.* 83, *pg.* 729
T-40 - Thinner - AKZONOBEL DECORATIVE PAINTS U.S.; *pg.* 1439, *pg.* 1474
T&B - Electrical Product Company - THOMAS & BETTS CORPORATION; *pg.* 680, *pg.* 1646
T&B EXPRESS TRAY - Tray - THOMAS & BETTS CORPORATION; *pg.* 680, *pg.* 1646
T. BAGGE: MERCHANT - Shop - OLD SALEM, INCORPORATED; *pg.* 572, *pg.* 1395
T-BEAR - Personal Care Product - ROCHESTER MIDLAND CORPORATION; *pg.* 334, *pg.* 1337
T-BOLT - Hose Clamp - DIXON VALVE & COUPLING COMPANY; *pg.* 1045, *pg.* 766
T-BOMB - Nutritional Supplement - MAXIMUM HUMAN PERFORMANCE, INC.; *pg.* 1559, *pg.* 1065
T-BOMB II - Nutritional Supplement - MAXIMUM HUMAN PERFORMANCE, INC.; *pg.* 1559, *pg.* 1065
T-BONE - Bag - SAMSONITE CORPORATION; *pg.* 11, *pg.* 830
T BONZ - Pet Care Product - NESTLE PURINA PETCARE COMPANY; *pg.* 1479, *pg.* 1000
T-CAM - Lifting System - THE BILCO COMPANY; *pg.* 70, *pg.* 383
T-CUBED - Telecommunications Service - NORFOLK SOUTHERN CORPORATION; *pg.* 1917, *pg.* 1797
T-D-I - Terminal Digital Indexing - SMEAD MANUFACTURING COMPANY; *pg.* 470, *pg.* 926
T-EDJER - Trimmer Razor - ANDIS COMPANY; *pg.* 498, *pg.* 1895
T-FOG - Satellite Communication Product - KVH INDUSTRIES INC; *pg.* 650, *pg.* 1602
T-GEL - Impact Mitt - ALIMED, INC.; *pg.* 1490, *pg.* 816
T/GEL - Therapeutic Shampoo & Conditioner - NEUTROGENA CORPORATION; *pg.* 517, *pg.* 137
T-GRAIN - Photographic Emulsions - EASTMAN KODAK COMPANY; *pg.* 1408, *pg.* 1333
T-HAB - Protective Lining Product - NOV AMERON; *pg.* 100, *pg.* 187
T-HYDRO - Chemical Product - LYONDELLBASELL INDUSTRIES; *pg.* 980, *pg.* 1710
T-JAK - Fastening Product - PEACE INDUSTRIES INC.; *pg.* 1368, *pg.* 656
T-LIGHT - Trimmer - ANDIS COMPANY; *pg.* 498, *pg.* 1895
T-LINE - Pumps; Valves - FLOWSERVE CORPORATION; *pg.* 82, *pg.* 1719
T-LOCK - Protective Lining Product - NOV AMERON; *pg.* 100, *pg.* 187
T-LOK - Vinyl Siding - PLY GEM SIDING GROUP; *pg.* 105, *pg.* 986
T-MAG II - Metallic Reloading Press - LYMAN PRODUCTS CORPORATION; *pg.* 1839, *pg.* 356
T. MARZETTI'S - Food Product - T. MARZETTI COMPANY; *pg.* 900, *pg.* 1444
T-MAT - Film - EASTMAN KODAK COMPANY; *pg.* 1408, *pg.* 1333
T-MAX - Photographic Film, Plates, Chemicals - EASTMAN KODAK COMPANY; *pg.* 1408, *pg.* 1333
T-MAX - Plastic Packaged MOSFET - MICROSEMI CORPORATION; *pg.* 435, *pg.* 41
T-MAX - Truck - WESTIN AUTOMOTIVE PRODUCTS, INC.; *pg.* 222, *pg.* 211
T-O-T - Thread Sealant - LA-CO INDUSTRIES MARKAL CO., INC.; *pg.* 1170, *pg.* 610
T-OUTLINER - Hair Trimmer - ANDIS COMPANY; *pg.* 498, *pg.* 1895
T-POLYM - Polyimide Material - BREWER SCIENCE, INC.; *pg.* 1150, *pg.* 989
"T" PORT - Adapter - BECTON, DICKINSON & COMPANY; *pg.* 1501, *pg.* 1068
T-PRENE - Booster Cables - COLEMAN CABLE, INC.; *pg.* 1324, *pg.* 665
T-REX - Pet Product - PETSMART, INC.; *pg.* 1481, *pg.* 18
T-REX - Molecular Biology Product - THERMO FISHER SCIENTIFIC INC.; *pg.* 1602, *pg.* 61
T-REX DOUBLE & WIDE - Motorhome - REXHALL INDUSTRIES, INC.; *pg.* 1710, *pg.* 121
T. REX SUE - On-Going Exhibit - THE FIELD MUSEUM; *pg.* 548, *pg.* 573
T. ROOSEVELT - Knife - BUCK KNIVES, INC.; *pg.* 1828, *pg.* 550
T/SAL - Shampoo - NEUTROGENA CORPORATION; *pg.* 517, *pg.* 137
T SERIES - Self Priming Centrifugal Trash Pump Solids Handling - THE GORMAN-RUPP COMPANY; *pg.* 1341, *pg.* 1458
T SERIES - Wireless Microphones - SHURE INCORPORATED; *pg.* 672, *pg.* 638
T-SERT - Fastener - LONG-LOK FASTENERS CORP.; *pg.* 1053, *pg.* 1416
T-STRAP - Footwear - CAPEZIO BALLET MAKERS INC.; *pg.* 1805, *pg.* 1125
T SYMBOL - Software - TELLABS, INC.; *pg.* 678, *pg.* 637
T-TECH - Battery Charging Product - CLORE AUTOMOTIVE LLC; *pg.* 202, *pg.* 716

T-TOP - Dispensing Closure - OWENS-ILLINOIS, INC.; *pg.* 1466, *pg.* 1470
T-WALL - Optimize Respiratory Mechanic - VITAL SIGNS, INC.; *pg.* 1607, *pg.* 1126
T-WATCH PRO - TSU & TDU Device Management - ADTRAN, INC.; *pg.* 344, *pg.* 6
T-WAVE - Collision Cell Technology - WATERS CORPORATION; *pg.* 1436, *pg.* 834
T-WING - Heat Spreaders - PARKER CHOMERICS; *pg.* 662, *pg.* 862
T-ZOID - Golf Equipment - MIZUNO USA, INC.; *pg.* 1839, *pg.* 538
T1 CSUS - Networking Products - ADTRAN, INC.; *pg.* 344, *pg.* 6
T1 ESF CSU - Networking Product - ADTRAN, INC.; *pg.* 344, *pg.* 6
T1 REVISION KNEE SYSTEM - Knee Product - ZIMMER BIOMET HOLDINGS, INC.; *pg.* 1611, *pg.* 699
T10 DROP CABLE - Cable - TIMES FIBER COMMUNICATIONS, INC.; *pg.* 681, *pg.* 382
T10 SEMIFLEX - Cable - TIMES FIBER COMMUNICATIONS, INC.; *pg.* 681, *pg.* 382
T10 TELEDROP - Cable - TIMES FIBER COMMUNICATIONS, INC.; *pg.* 681, *pg.* 382
T18 - Staples - ARROW FASTENER COMPANY, INC.; *pg.* 1042, *pg.* 1118
T1CSU ACE - Networking Product - ADTRAN, INC.; *pg.* 344, *pg.* 6
T2000 - Trucks - KENWORTH TRUCK CO.; *pg.* 181, *pg.* 1822
T2025 - Staples - ARROW FASTENER COMPANY, INC.; *pg.* 1042, *pg.* 1118
T203 - Tapping Machine - T.D. WILLIAMSON, INC.; *pg.* 1380, *pg.* 1490
T27 - Staples - ARROW FASTENER COMPANY, INC.; *pg.* 1042, *pg.* 1118
T3 - Tactical Targeting System - LOCKHEED MARTIN CORPORATION; *pg.* 229, *pg.* 762
T30 - Staples - ARROW FASTENER COMPANY, INC.; *pg.* 1042, *pg.* 1118
T300 - Trucks - KENWORTH TRUCK CO.; *pg.* 181, *pg.* 1822
T32 - Tacker Gun - ARROW FASTENER COMPANY, INC.; *pg.* 1042, *pg.* 1118
T37 - Staples - ARROW FASTENER COMPANY, INC.; *pg.* 1042, *pg.* 1118
T3LT - Thermal - E.D. BULLARD COMPANY; *pg.* 1332, *pg.* 727
T3MAX - Thermal - E.D. BULLARD COMPANY; *pg.* 1332, *pg.* 727
T3SU 300 - Networking Products - ADTRAN, INC.; *pg.* 344, *pg.* 6
T50 - Staple Gun - ARROW FASTENER COMPANY, INC.; *pg.* 1042, *pg.* 1118
T55 - Staples - ARROW FASTENER COMPANY, INC.; *pg.* 1042, *pg.* 1118
T59 - Staples - ARROW FASTENER COMPANY, INC.; *pg.* 1042, *pg.* 1118
T600 - Trucks - KENWORTH TRUCK CO.; *pg.* 181, *pg.* 1822
T660 - Snowmobile - ARCTIC CAT INC.; *pg.* 1705, *pg.* 953
T75 - Staples - ARROW FASTENER COMPANY, INC.; *pg.* 1042, *pg.* 1118
T800 - Trucks - KENWORTH TRUCK CO.; *pg.* 181, *pg.* 1822
TA CLONING - Molecular Biology Product - THERMO FISHER SCIENTIFIC INC.; *pg.* 1602, *pg.* 61
TA-NON-KA - Watermarked Paper - BPM INC.; *pg.* 1454, *pg.* 1886
TA2000 - Software - DST SYSTEMS, INC.; *pg.* 388, *pg.* 982
TA2000 DESKTOP - Software - DST SYSTEMS, INC.; *pg.* 388, *pg.* 982
TA2000/VOICE - Software - DST SYSTEMS, INC.; *pg.* 388, *pg.* 982
TAABOO - Footwear - STEVEN MADDEN, LTD.; *pg.* 1819, *pg.* 1176
TAAKA - Vodka & Gin - SAZERAC COMPANY, INC.; *pg.* 1969, *pg.* 745
TAARGET - Medical Device - LEMAITRE VASCULAR, INC.; *pg.* 1555, *pg.* 805
TAB - Regular & Diet Caffeine-Free Cola - THE COCA-COLA COMPANY; *pg.* 240, *pg.* 493
TAB - Books - SCHOLASTIC INC.; *pg.* 1683, *pg.* 1288
TAB-BLU - Bowl Cleaner - BLUE CROSS LABORATORIES; *pg.* 326, *pg.* 277
TAB BOOK CLUB - Educational Materials - SCHOLASTIC INC.; *pg.* 1683, *pg.* 1288
TAB ENERGY - Beverages - THE COCA-COLA COMPANY; *pg.* 240, *pg.* 493
TAB II - Child-Resistant Packaging - BERRY PLASTICS LANCASTER; *pg.* 1453, *pg.* 1546
TAB-SEAL - Caps - GREIF INC.; *pg.* 1459, *pg.* 1447
TAB-TRAC - Mobile Filing Equip. - TAB PRODUCTS CO. LLC; *pg.* 481, *pg.* 1869
TAB X-TRA - Beverages - THE COCA-COLA COMPANY; *pg.* 240, *pg.* 493
TABASCO - Slots - INTERNATIONAL GAME TECHNOLOGY; *pg.* 957, *pg.* 1024
TABASCO - Sauce - MCILHENNY COMPANY; *pg.* 876, *pg.* 741
TABASCO - Fabric - NEMSCHOFF, INC.; *pg.* 936, *pg.* 1890
TABLE TAILORS - Tables for Industry - JOHN BOOS & CO.; *pg.* 1126, *pg.* 609
TABLE TOUCH - Casino System - INTERNATIONAL GAME TECHNOLOGY; *pg.* 957, *pg.* 1024
TABLE VIEW - Table Management - BALLY TECHNOLOGIES, INC.; *pg.* 531, *pg.* 1022
TABLEAU - Bath Product - KOHLER CO.; *pg.* 91, *pg.* 1862
TABLERITE - Controlled Label for Fresh Meat & Processed Meat Prods. - IGA, INC.; *pg.* 1023, *pg.* 578
TABLES OF CONTENT - Buffet Accessories - EDWARD DON & COMPANY; *pg.* 54, *pg.* 672
TABLESOURCE - Power Portals - WIREMOLD/LEGRAND; *pg.* 689, *pg.* 383
TABLESTAR CUSTOM MEATS - Meat - OMAHA STEAKS INTERNATIONAL, INC.; *pg.* 1780, *pg.* 1017
TABOO - Game - HASBRO, INC.; *pg.* 954, *pg.* 1603
TABOO JUNIOR - Toy & Game - HASBRO, INC.; *pg.* 954, *pg.* 1603
TABORET - Kitchen Product - KOHLER CO.; *pg.* 91, *pg.* 1862
TABQUIK - Color-Coded Labels - TAB PRODUCTS CO. LLC; *pg.* 481, *pg.* 1869
TABSTER - Wafer Tab Applicators - THE STAPLEX COMPANY, INC.; *pg.* 474, *pg.* 1146
TABULA - Electrical Product - EATON CORPORATION; *pg.* 1331, *pg.* 1429
TAC - Air Valves - HUMPHREY PRODUCTS CORPORATION; *pg.* 1300, *pg.* 894
TAC 2 - Air Valves - HUMPHREY PRODUCTS CORPORATION; *pg.* 1300, *pg.* 894
TAC 3 - Electric Air Valves - HUMPHREY PRODUCTS CORPORATION; *pg.* 1300, *pg.* 894
TACC - Timed Access Cash Controllers-Electronic Cash Handling System - TIDEL ENGINEERING, L.P.; *pg.* 1382, *pg.* 1670
TACEE - Footwear - STEVEN MADDEN, LTD.; *pg.* 1819, *pg.* 1176
TACHISME - Fabric - NEMSCHOFF, INC.; *pg.* 936, *pg.* 1890
TACK-IT - Cleaning Product - HILLYARD, INC.; *pg.* 331, *pg.* 990
TACK-MATE - Horse Clipper - ANDIS COMPANY; *pg.* 498, *pg.* 1895
TACKBOLT - Rivet - ALLFAST FASTENING SYSTEMS, INC.; *pg.* 1041, *pg.* 66
TACKBOLT RIVET - Blind Rivet - ALLFAST FASTENING SYSTEMS, INC.; *pg.* 1041, *pg.* 66
TACKTILE - Adhesives - H.B. FULLER COMPANY; *pg.* 1165, *pg.* 961
TACKY COAT - Water-Based Protective Booth Coating - ITW - EVERCOAT; *pg.* 1443, *pg.* 1415
TACKY TAPE - Removable Transfer Tape - MOORE PUSH PIN CO.; *pg.* 441, *pg.* 1595
TACLINK - Tactical Modem Technology - RAYTHEON COMPANY; *pg.* 233, *pg.* 854
TACMS - Systems Integration & Aeronautics - LOCKHEED MARTIN CORPORATION; *pg.* 229, *pg.* 762
TACNAV - Satellite Communication Product - KVH INDUSTRIES INC; *pg.* 650, *pg.* 1602
TACNAV II - Military Navigation System - KVH INDUSTRIES INC; *pg.* 650, *pg.* 1602
TACNAV M100 GMENS - Military Navigation System - KVH INDUSTRIES INC; *pg.* 650, *pg.* 1602
TACNAV TLS - Military Navigation System - KVH INDUSTRIES INC; *pg.* 650, *pg.* 1602
TACO BELL - Fast Food Mexican Restaurants - YUM! BRANDS, INC.; *pg.* 1756, *pg.* 738
TACO BRAVO - Food Product - TACO JOHN'S INTERNATIONAL, INC.; *pg.* 1753, *pg.* 1901
TACO CABANA - Restaurant Company - TACO CABANA, INC.; *pg.* 1753, *pg.* 1743
TACO JOHN'S MEXPRESS - Alternative Distribution Unit - TACO JOHN'S INTERNATIONAL, INC.; *pg.* 1753, *pg.* 1901
TACO TECH - Training Program - TACO JOHN'S INTERNATIONAL, INC.; *pg.* 1753, *pg.* 1901
TACO TIME - Quick-Service Restaurant Chain - KAHALA FRANCHISING LLC; *pg.* 1025, *pg.* 23
TACO TUESDAY - Promotion - TACO JOHN'S INTERNATIONAL, INC.; *pg.* 1753, *pg.* 1901
TACOLYN - Resin Dispersions - EASTMAN CHEMICAL COMPANY; *pg.* 1159, *pg.* 1636
TACOMA - Furniture - ASHLEY FURNITURE INDUSTRIES, INC.; *pg.* 914, *pg.* 1852
TACOMA - Furniture - BUSH INDUSTRIES INC.; *pg.* 919, *pg.* 1170
TACOMA - Titling Equipment - EASTMAN KODAK COMPANY; *pg.* 1408, *pg.* 1333
TACOMA - Furniture - LA-Z-BOY INCORPORATED; *pg.* 932, *pg.* 901
TACOMA - Truck - TOYOTA MOTOR NORTH AMERICA, INC.; *pg.* 192, *pg.* 1303
TACOMA - Ceiling Fan - WESTINGHOUSE LIGHTING CORPORATION; *pg.* 687, *pg.* 1571
T.A.C.PIN - Medical Device - INTEGRA LIFESCIENCES HOLDINGS CORPORATION; *pg.* 1545, *pg.* 1109
TACPOLE - Fire Safety Product - E.D. BULLARD COMPANY; *pg.* 1332, *pg.* 727
TACPORT - Fire Safety Product - E.D. BULLARD COMPANY; *pg.* 1332, *pg.* 727
TACSCOPE - Fire Safety Product - E.D. BULLARD COMPANY; *pg.* 1332, *pg.* 727
TACSIGHT - Thermal - E.D. BULLARD COMPANY; *pg.* 1332, *pg.* 727
TACSTAR - Tactical Shotgun Accessories - LYMAN PRODUCTS CORPORATION; *pg.* 1839, *pg.* 356
TACTCAP - Flashlight - STREAMLIGHT INC.; *pg.* 1306, *pg.* 1527
TACTEL - Apparel - ATTITUDES IN DRESSING INC.; *pg.* 19, *pg.* 1057
TACTEL - Versatile, Lightweight Fabrics - INVISTA B.V.; *pg.* 1168, *pg.* 723
TACTESSE - Fiber - BEAULIEU GROUP, LLC; *pg.* 917, *pg.* 529
TACTICAL - Fall Protection Equipment - MINE SAFETY APPLIANCES COMPANY; *pg.* 1361, *pg.* 1525
TACTICAL - Apparel - OAKLEY, INC.; *pg.* 1840, *pg.* 86
TACTICAL - Apparels - UNDER ARMOUR, INC.; *pg.* 49, *pg.* 759
TACTICAL APPROACH - Apparels - UNDER ARMOUR, INC.; *pg.* 49, *pg.* 759
TACTICAL LIGHT - Flashlight - STREAMLIGHT INC.; *pg.* 1306, *pg.* 1527
TACTICS - Furniture - HAWORTH, INC.; *pg.* 402, *pg.* 891
TACTION - Fabric - NEMSCHOFF, INC.; *pg.* 936, *pg.* 1890
TACTIX - High Purity Epoxy Resins - HUNTSMAN CORPORATION; *pg.* 1167, *pg.* 1758
TADAS - Beverages - THE COCA-COLA COMPANY; *pg.* 240, *pg.* 493
TADS/PNVS - Systems Integration & Aeronautics - LOCKHEED MARTIN CORPORATION; *pg.* 229, *pg.* 762
TAE BO - Fitness DVD - GAIAM, INC.; *pg.* 1532, *pg.* 334
TAFFETA TRELLIS - Furniture - ASHLEY FURNITURE INDUSTRIES, INC.; *pg.* 914, *pg.* 1852
TAFFY - Fabric - NEMSCHOFF, INC.; *pg.* 936, *pg.* 1890
TAFT - Fabric - NEUTRAL POSTURE, INC.; *pg.* 939, *pg.* 1669
TAFT STREET - Wine - WILLIAM GRANT & SONS, INC.; *pg.* 1972, *pg.* 1057
TAG - Body Spray - THE GILLETTE COMPANY; *pg.* 509, *pg.* 795
TAG - Medical Equipment - INVACARE CORPORATION; *pg.* 1546, *pg.* 1451
TAG - Toys - LEAPFROG ENTERPRISES, INC.; *pg.* 961, *pg.* 84
TAG-200 - Electrical Test & Measurement - HD ELECTRIC COMPANY; *pg.* 1299, *pg.* 666
TAG-200MR - Electrical Test & Measurement - HD ELECTRIC COMPANY; *pg.* 1299, *pg.* 666
TAG-330 - Electrical Test & Measurement - HD ELECTRIC COMPANY; *pg.* 1299, *pg.* 666
TAG-5000 - Electrical Test & Measurement - HD ELECTRIC COMPANY; *pg.* 1299, *pg.* 666
TAG-IT - Radio Frequency Transponder Device - TEXAS INSTRUMENTS INCORPORATED; *pg.* 679, *pg.* 1688
TAG-ON-DEMAND - Molecular Biology Product - THERMO FISHER SCIENTIFIC INC.; *pg.* 1602, *pg.* 61
TAG PRINT PRO - Software - HELLERMANNTYTON; *pg.*

642, *pg.* 1875
TAG SERIES - Electrical Test & Measurement - HD ELECTRIC COMPANY; *pg.* 1299, *pg.* 666
TAG-X - Paper Products - BOISE CASCADE HOLDINGS, L.L.C.; *pg.* 1453, *pg.* 546
TAGGED - Social Networking Site - IF(WE); *pg.* 1258, *pg.* 219
TAGIT! - Identification Student Shears - ACME UNITED CORPORATION; *pg.* 1040, *pg.* 346
TAGLESS - Apparel - HANESBRANDS INC.; *pg.* 26, *pg.* 1394
T.A.G.S - Guide Service - CABELA'S INCORPORATED; *pg.* 535, *pg.* 1019
TAHITI - Carpet - BEAULIEU GROUP, LLC; *pg.* 917, *pg.* 529
TAHITI - Cookies - PEPPERIDGE FARM, INC.; *pg.* 888, *pg.* 363
TAHITI - Commercial Lighting - SWIVELIER CO., INC.; *pg.* 1307, *pg.* 1142
TAHITI SUNSET - Video Game - INTERNATIONAL GAME TECHNOLOGY; *pg.* 957, *pg.* 1024
TAHITIAN - Jewelry - YURMAN DESIGN, INC.; *pg.* 15, *pg.* 1316
TAHITIAN DAWN - Container Grown Plant - MONROVIA GROWERS; *pg.* 1797, *pg.* 44
TAHOE - Sport Utility Vehicle - GENERAL MOTORS COMPANY; *pg.* 175, *pg.* 881
TAHOE - Bath Product - KOHLER CO.; *pg.* 91, *pg.* 1862
TAHOE - Designer Fragrance - PARFUMS DE COEUR LTD.; *pg.* 519, *pg.* 376
TAHOE - Cookies - PEPPERIDGE FARM, INC.; *pg.* 888, *pg.* 363
TAHOE JOE'S - Restaurants - OVATION BRANDS; *pg.* 1743, *pg.* 921
TAI - Beverages - THE COCA-COLA COMPANY; *pg.* 240, *pg.* 493
TAI - Roof Systems & Building Prods - METALS USA, INC.; *pg.* 97, *pg.* 425
TAI AEROBICS - Aerobics System - ALLIANCE SPORTS GROUP, L.P.; *pg.* 1825, *pg.* 1698
TAI CHI - Video Game - INTERNATIONAL GAME TECHNOLOGY; *pg.* 957, *pg.* 1024
TAI LIGHT - Beverages - THE COCA-COLA COMPANY; *pg.* 240, *pg.* 493
TAI PAN - Video Game - INTERNATIONAL GAME TECHNOLOGY; *pg.* 957, *pg.* 1024
TAIL GATOR - Lottery Game - NEW JERSEY STATE LOTTERY; *pg.* 1000, *pg.* 1126
TAIL-LOADER - Cargo Carriers - LUND INTERNATIONAL, INC.; *pg.* 211, *pg.* 526
TAIL-LOADER II - Cargo Carriers - LUND INTERNATIONAL, INC.; *pg.* 211, *pg.* 526
TAIL-TAG - Adhesive Strip - SENTRY TECHNOLOGY CORPORATION; *pg.* 672, *pg.* 1339
TAILGATE - Magazine - PAISANO PUBLICATIONS, LLC; *pg.* 1674, *pg.* 38
TAILGATE PARTY - Video Slots - INTERNATIONAL GAME TECHNOLOGY; *pg.* 957, *pg.* 1024
TAILGATER - Blender - WARING PRODUCTS, INC.; *pg.* 62, *pg.* 379
TAILGATOR - Tailgate Protector - LUND INTERNATIONAL, INC.; *pg.* 211, *pg.* 526
TAILMATE - Rear Valance - LUND INTERNATIONAL, INC.; *pg.* 211, *pg.* 526
TAILORED PROTECTION - Insurance - AMERICAN REPUBLIC INSURANCE COMPANY; *pg.* 1191, *pg.* 704
TAILORED THERAPY - ICD Product - ST. JUDE MEDICAL, INC.; *pg.* 1596, *pg.* 963
TAILORED ULTRAFIT - Cover & Pad - HOME PRODUCTS INTERNATIONAL, INC.; *pg.* 1125, *pg.* 577
TAILSHADES - Blackout Taillight Covers - LUND INTERNATIONAL, INC.; *pg.* 211, *pg.* 526
TAILSHADES2 - Blackout Taillight Covers - LUND INTERNATIONAL, INC.; *pg.* 211, *pg.* 526
TAILVAC - Cleaning Product - HILLYARD, INC.; *pg.* 331, *pg.* 990
TAILWIND - Airborne TV System - ROCKWELL COLLINS, INC.; *pg.* 234, *pg.* 702
TAIPAN - Fabric - SCALAMANDRE, INC.; *pg.* 941, *pg.* 1058
TAJ MAHAL - Rug - COURISTAN INC.; *pg.* 921, *pg.* 1067
TAK-4 - Truck Product - OSHKOSH CORPORATION; *pg.* 187, *pg.* 1885
TAK-TAPE - Cable Tie - PANDUIT CORP.; *pg.* 661, *pg.* 663
TAK-TY - Cable Tie - PANDUIT CORP.; *pg.* 661, *pg.* 663
TAKAMINE - Guitars - KAMAN CORPORATION; *pg.* 229, *pg.* 338
TAKE 5 - Candy - THE HERSHEY CO.; *pg.* 1855, *pg.* 1538
TAKE A KID TO THE RACES - Automobile Races - DOVER MOTORSPORTS, INC.; *pg.* 545, *pg.* 387
TAKE A SHOT - Video Game - INTERNATIONAL GAME TECHNOLOGY; *pg.* 957, *pg.* 1024
TAKE BACK OUR PLATES - Tagline - WHOLE FOODS MARKET, INC.; *pg.* 1038, *pg.* 1667
TAKE CONTROL - LIVE UNINTERRUPTED - Slogan - DEXCOM INC; *pg.* 1524, *pg.* 202
TAKE CONTROL WITH DEPEND - Slogan - KIMBERLY-CLARK CORPORATION; *pg.* 1461, *pg.* 1720
TAKE DOWN - Cleaning Product - HILLYARD, INC.; *pg.* 331, *pg.* 990
TAKE 'EM - Apparel - VANS, INC.; *pg.* 1821, *pg.* 76
TAKE FIVE - Lottery Game - NEW YORK STATE LOTTERY; *pg.* 1001, *pg.* 1340
TAKE ME HOME - Bear Projects - BUILD-A-BEAR WORKSHOP, INC.; *pg.* 950, *pg.* 993
TAKE ME TO THE HILTON - Tag Line - HILTON WORLDWIDE, INC.; *pg.* 1094, *pg.* 1791
TAKE OFF! - Nutritional Supplement - MAXIMUM HUMAN PERFORMANCE, INC.; *pg.* 1559, *pg.* 1065
TAKE ONE - Vitamin & Dietary Supplement - NATROL, INC.; *pg.* 1570, *pg.* 64
TAKE OUT - Newsletter - OUR SUNDAY VISITOR, INC.; *pg.* 1673, *pg.* 682
TAKE PRIDE. ITS A DAISY - Tag Line - DAISY MANUFACTURING COMPANY; *pg.* 1831, *pg.* 35
TAKE THE FIELD WITH THE A'S - Baseball Program - OAKLAND ATHLETICS LIMITED PARTNERSHIP; *pg.* 571, *pg.* 172
TAKE THE LEAD - High School Assembly - MOTHERS AGAINST DRUNK DRIVING (MADD); *pg.* 147, *pg.* 1723
TAKE TV - Video Player - SANDISK CORPORATION; *pg.* 465, *pg.* 147
TAKE-TWO INTERACTIVE - Game - TAKE-TWO INTERACTIVE SOFTWARE, INC.; *pg.* 481, *pg.* 1297
TAKE WING - Bath Product - KOHLER CO.; *pg.* 91, *pg.* 1862
TAKE YOUR GAME FURTHER - Company Slogan - PRIMA GAMES; *pg.* 965, *pg.* 693
TAKE YOUR PICK - Video Game - INTERNATIONAL GAME TECHNOLOGY; *pg.* 957, *pg.* 1024
TAKEALONGS - Food Storage Containers - NEWELL RUBBERMAID INC.; *pg.* 1128, *pg.* 515
TAKEAWAY - Conveyor System - AUTOMATED PACKAGING SYSTEMS INC.; *pg.* 1452, *pg.* 1474
TAKEDOWN - Security & Law Enforcement Products - MACE SECURITY INTERNATIONAL, INC.; *pg.* 1172, *pg.* 1541
TAKEDOWN - Apparel - VANS, INC.; *pg.* 1821, *pg.* 76
TAKEFIVE - Software - WIND RIVER SYSTEMS, INC.; *pg.* 493, *pg.* 38
TAKENOTE - Software - AMX CORPORATION; *pg.* 349, *pg.* 1735
TAKHOMACARD - Giftcard - BIGLARI HOLDINGS INC.; *pg.* 1015, *pg.* 1739
TAKHOMACUP - CUP - BIGLARI HOLDINGS INC.; *pg.* 1015, *pg.* 1739
TAKING AIM AT CANCER - Tagline - ONCOTHYREON INC.; *pg.* 1578, *pg.* 1838
TAKING COMMAND OF YOUR SECURITY NEEDS - Tagline - COMMAND SECURITY CORPORATION; *pg.* 377, *pg.* 1171
TAKING ON THE WORLD.S TOUGHEST ENERGY CHALLENGES. - Slogan - EXXON MOBIL CORPORATION; *pg.* 977, *pg.* 1718
TAKING YOU FROM THE RED TO THE BLACK - Slogan - ASSET ACCEPTANCE CAPITAL CORP.; *pg.* 716, *pg.* 912
TAKU - Ventilation System - UNIFIED BRANDS INC.; *pg.* 1385, *pg.* 970
TAL - Tren/Alarm Log System - SURFACE COMBUSTION, INC.; *pg.* 1077, *pg.* 1462
TAL MICRODRAINAGE - Medical Device - BOSTON SCIENTIFIC CORPORATION; *pg.* 1508, *pg.* 831
TALALAY LATEX - Mattress - JAMISON BEDDING, INC.; *pg.* 930, *pg.* 1651
TALAR-FIT - Surgical Instrument - OSTEOMED CORPORATION; *pg.* 1425, *pg.* 1658
TALARIA - Systems Integration & Aeronautics - LOCKHEED MARTIN CORPORATION; *pg.* 229, *pg.* 762
TALBOTS - Clothing - THE TALBOTS, INC.; *pg.* 34, *pg.* 824
TALBOTS COLLECTION - Clothing - THE TALBOTS, INC.; *pg.* 34, *pg.* 824
TALBOTS MISSES - Clothing - THE TALBOTS, INC.; *pg.* 34, *pg.* 824
TALBOTS PETITES - Clothing - THE TALBOTS, INC.; *pg.* 34, *pg.* 824
TALBOTS WOMAN - Clothing - THE TALBOTS, INC.; *pg.* 34, *pg.* 824
TALBOTS WOMAN PETITES - Clothing - THE TALBOTS, INC.; *pg.* 34, *pg.* 824
TALE SPIN - Cartoon Character - THE WALT DISNEY COMPANY; *pg.* 317, *pg.* 52
TALENT - Musical Instrument - GIBSON GUITAR CORP.; *pg.* 550, *pg.* 1650
TALENT - Turning Machine - HARDINGE INC.; *pg.* 1344, *pg.* 1157
TALENT - Stent - MEDTRONIC, INC.; *pg.* 1564, *pg.* 939
TALENT MATCH - Professional Staffing Services - ROBERT HALF INTERNATIONAL INC.; *pg.* 462, *pg.* 145
TALENTI - Gelato & Sorbetto - UNILEVER UNITED STATES, INC.; *pg.* 904, *pg.* 1061
TALENTT - Footwear - STEVEN MADDEN, LTD.; *pg.* 1819, *pg.* 1176
TALES OF FANTASY - Educational Materials - SCHOLASTIC INC.; *pg.* 1683, *pg.* 1288
TALES OF HERCULES - Video Game - INTERNATIONAL GAME TECHNOLOGY; *pg.* 957, *pg.* 1024
TALES OF RICHES - Video Game - INTERNATIONAL GAME TECHNOLOGY; *pg.* 957, *pg.* 1024
TALIESIN - Carpet - INTERFACE, INC.; *pg.* 695, *pg.* 512
TALISKAR - Fiber Based Lasers - COHERENT, INC.; *pg.* 1406, *pg.* 265
TALISMAN - Carpet - BEAULIEU GROUP, LLC; *pg.* 917, *pg.* 529
TALK-A-PHONE - Intercom Systems - TALK-A-PHONE CO.; *pg.* 481, *pg.* 638
TALK ON WATER - Cellular Telephone Service - OCEAN POWER TECHNOLOGIES, INC.; *pg.* 1948, *pg.* 1107
TALKABOUT - Communications Product - MOTOROLA SOLUTIONS, INC.; *pg.* 657, *pg.* 659
TALKANYTIME - Communication Product - MULTI-TECH SYSTEMS INC.; *pg.* 442, *pg.* 951
TALKING CAR - Information Retrieval Services - CARFAX INC.; *pg.* 202, *pg.* 1777
TALKING RAIN FUSIONS - Beverage - TALKINGRAIN BEVERAGE COMPANY; *pg.* 266, *pg.* 1823
TALKING RAIN MOUNTAIN SPRING WATER - Beverage - TALKINGRAIN BEVERAGE COMPANY; *pg.* 266, *pg.* 1823
TALKING RAIN SPARKLING ESSENCE WATER - Beverage - TALKINGRAIN BEVERAGE COMPANY; *pg.* 266, *pg.* 1823
TALKING TEXT WRITER - Educational Materials - SCHOLASTIC INC.; *pg.* 1683, *pg.* 1288
TALKING WORDS FACTORY - Educational Toys - LEAPFROG ENTERPRISES, INC.; *pg.* 961, *pg.* 84
TALKTRACKER - Wireless Service - UNITED STATES CELLULAR CORPORATION; *pg.* 1875, *pg.* 594
TALKWORKS - Software - SYMANTEC CORPORATION; *pg.* 478, *pg.* 161
TALL TISSUE - Basket - THE LONGABERGER COMPANY; *pg.* 1127, *pg.* 1467
TALLADEGA SUPERSPEEDWAY - Motorsports Facility - INTERNATIONAL SPEEDWAY CORPORATION; *pg.* 553, *pg.* 420
TALLGRASS CREEK - Retirement Community - ERICKSON LIVING; *pg.* 1090, *pg.* 766
TALLY - Furniture - HAWORTH, INC.; *pg.* 402, *pg.* 891
TALMID - Convertible Briefcase - JANDD MOUNTAINEERING, INC.; *pg.* 1837, *pg.* 204
TALON - Integrated Processing System - BREWER SCIENCE, INC.; *pg.* 1150, *pg.* 989
TALON - Amusement & Water Park - CEDAR FAIR, L.P.; *pg.* 537, *pg.* 1471
TALON - Software - FLIR SYSTEMS, INC.; *pg.* 1413, *pg.* 1510
TALON - Handling Tools - S&C ELECTRIC COMPANY; *pg.* 1305, *pg.* 589
TALON - Door Lock - SOUTHCO, INC.; *pg.* 1063, *pg.* 1522
TALON - Apparels - UNDER ARMOUR, INC.; *pg.* 49, *pg.* 759
TALON TREAD - Rubber Stair Tread - R.C.A. RUBBER COMPANY; *pg.* 1888, *pg.* 1402
TALON ZX - Recreational Vehicles - JAYCO INC.; *pg.* 1708, *pg.* 695
TALSTAR - Insecticide - FMC CORPORATION; *pg.* 1163, *pg.* 1564
TALSTARONE - Pest Control Product - FMC CORPORATION; *pg.* 1163, *pg.* 1564
TALUHET - Cheese - SAPUTO, INC.; *pg.* 893, *pg.* 1956

First page reference indicates Business Class Edition
Second page reference indicates Geographic Edition

TAM O'SHANTER - Restaurant - LAWRY'S RESTAURANTS, INC.; *pg.* 1735, *pg.* 180
TAMA - Footwear - STEVEN MADDEN, LTD.; *pg.* 1819, *pg.* 1176
TAMALE RMS - Business Management Solution - ADVENT SOFTWARE, INC.; *pg.* 345, *pg.* 211
TAMALES - Mexican Food - RUIZ FOOD PRODUCTS, INC.; *pg.* 893, *pg.* 77
TAMARA - Furniture - AMISCO INDUSTRIES LTD.; *pg.* 913, *pg.* 1958
TAMAS ESTATES WINERY - Estate Winery - WENTE VINEYARDS; *pg.* 1972, *pg.* 122
TAMBORA - Video Game - INTERNATIONAL GAME TECHNOLOGY; *pg.* 957, *pg.* 1024
TAMBOUR - Wall Covering, Doors, Wall Panels & Furniture - OMEGA NATIONAL PRODUCTS; *pg.* 939, *pg.* 737
TAMERLANE - Area Rugs - COURISTAN INC.; *pg.* 921, *pg.* 1067
TAMIFLU - Biopharmaceutical Product - GILEAD SCIENCES, INC.; *pg.* 1535, *pg.* 88
TAMING SPRAY - Hair Care Product - JOHN PAUL MITCHELL SYSTEMS; *pg.* 512, *pg.* 133
TAMMY - Furniture - AMISCO INDUSTRIES LTD.; *pg.* 913, *pg.* 1958
TAMOL - Dispersant - DOW CHEMICAL; *pg.* 1156, *pg.* 1563
TAMOR - Houseware Products - HOME PRODUCTS INTERNATIONAL, INC.; *pg.* 1125, *pg.* 577
TAMPA BAY BUCCANEERS - Professional Football Team - BUCCANEERS LIMITED PARTNERSHIP; *pg.* 534, *pg.* 471
TAMPA BAY CHARITY REGISTER - Magazine - PALM BEACH MEDIA GROUP INC.; *pg.* 1674, *pg.* 457
TAMPA BAY DEVIL RAYS - Baseball Team - TAMPA BAY RAYS BASEBALL, LTD.; *pg.* 586, *pg.* 464
TAMPA BAY ILLUSTRATED - Magazine - PALM BEACH MEDIA GROUP INC.; *pg.* 1674, *pg.* 457
TAMPA BAY LIGHTNING - Hockey Team - LIGHTNING HOCKEY LP; *pg.* 557, *pg.* 474
TAMPA BAY MAGAZINE - Magazine - TAMPA BAY PUBLICATIONS, INC.; *pg.* 1691, *pg.* 416
TAMPA NUGGET - Domestic Cigars - ALTADIS USA, INC.; *pg.* 1893, *pg.* 423
TAMPA SWEET - Domestic Cigars - ALTADIS USA, INC.; *pg.* 1893, *pg.* 423
THE TAMPA TRIBUNE - Daily Newspaper - MEDIA GENERAL, INC.; *pg.* 297, *pg.* 1803
THE TAMPA TRIBUNE - Publication - THE TAMPA TRIBUNE; *pg.* 1691, *pg.* 476
TAMPABAY.COM - Website - TAMPA BAY TIMES; *pg.* 1691, *pg.* 464
TAMPAX - Personal Care Product - THE PROCTER & GAMBLE COMPANY; *pg.* 1129, *pg.* 1418
TAMPERPROOF - Livestock Tags - ALLFLEX USA, INC.; *pg.* 1878, *pg.* 1717
TAMROTOR - Marine Compressor - GARDNER DENVER, INC.; *pg.* 1338, *pg.* 1592
TAN - Pillow and Throw - HERITAGE LACE INC.; *pg.* 694, *pg.* 711
TAN HOUND'S TOOTH - Pillow and Throw - HERITAGE LACE INC.; *pg.* 694, *pg.* 711
TAN-TRU - Cutters - GLEASON CORPORATION; *pg.* 1340, *pg.* 1335
TANCHOI - Pillow - ETHAN ALLEN INTERIORS INC.; *pg.* 924, *pg.* 343
TANDA-TAC - Adhesive Coated Paper - SPINNAKER COATING, LLC; *pg.* 1470, *pg.* 1477
TANDEM - Burner - NAO, INC.; *pg.* 1074, *pg.* 1567
TANDEM - Valve Trim - SPX PROCESS EQUIPMENT; *pg.* 1378, *pg.* 1551
TANDEM - Bicycle - TREK BICYCLE CORPORATION; *pg.* 1847, *pg.* 1896
TANDEM-PINS - End-to-End Wire Contact Pins - BEAD INDUSTRIES INC.; *pg.* 200, *pg.* 356
TANDEM TONES - Construction Paper - PACON CORPORATION; *pg.* 1466, *pg.* 1852
TANDEM UNIPASS ACME TAP - Taps with a Roughing & Finishing Section - REGAL BELOIT CORPORATION; *pg.* 106, *pg.* 1854
TANE - Pillow and Throw - HERITAGE LACE INC.; *pg.* 694, *pg.* 711
TANEKO JAPANESE TAVERN - Tavern - P.F. CHANG'S CHINA BISTRO, INC.; *pg.* 1030, *pg.* 24
TANG - Powdered & Ready-to-Drink Soft Drink - MONDELEZ INTERNATIONAL, INC.; *pg.* 878, *pg.* 601
TANG KUEI - Herbal Tablets - HERBALIFE INTERNATIONAL OF AMERICA, INC.; *pg.* 1541, *pg.* 132
TANGENT - Fabric - NEMSCHOFF, INC.; *pg.* 936, *pg.* 1890
TANGENTPOS - Software - MICROS SYSTEMS, INC.; *pg.* 435, *pg.* 768
TANGERINE - Container Grown Plant - MONROVIA GROWERS; *pg.* 1797, *pg.* 44
TANGERINE ORANGE ZINGER WITH VITAMIN C - Herb Tea - CELESTIAL SEASONINGS, INC.; *pg.* 846, *pg.* 310
TANGERINE PRESS - Educational Materials - SCHOLASTIC INC.; *pg.* 1683, *pg.* 1288
TANGERINE TRIPLER - Lottery Game - ILLINOIS STATE LOTTERY; *pg.* 995, *pg.* 578
TANGIER - Bicycle - G. JOANNOU CYCLE CO. INC.; *pg.* 1707, *pg.* 1098
TANGIER - Container Grown Plant - MONROVIA GROWERS; *pg.* 1797, *pg.* 44
TANGIERS - Fabric - NEMSCHOFF, INC.; *pg.* 936, *pg.* 1890
TANGITA - Footwear - STEVEN MADDEN, LTD.; *pg.* 1819, *pg.* 1176
TANGLE RIDGE - Whiskey - JIM BEAM BRANDS CO.; *pg.* 1965, *pg.* 601
TANGLEWOOD - Music Venue - BOSTON SYMPHONY ORCHESTRA INC.; *pg.* 534, *pg.* 791
TANGO - Furniture - ETHAN ALLEN INTERIORS INC.; *pg.* 924, *pg.* 343
TANGO - Fabric - NEMSCHOFF, INC.; *pg.* 936, *pg.* 1890
TANGO - Mask Device - RESMED INC.; *pg.* 1589, *pg.* 207
TANGO - Paperboard Packaging Product - WESTROCK COMPANY; *pg.* 1472, *pg.* 1805
TANGO BINGO - Game - FORTUNET, INC.; *pg.* 953, *pg.* 1024
TANGO TWIRL - Container Grown Plant - MONROVIA GROWERS; *pg.* 1797, *pg.* 44
TANK BEATER - Apparel - OAKLEY, INC.; *pg.* 1840, *pg.* 86
TANK CLEANER - Cleaner - KALO, INC.; *pg.* 1796, *pg.* 719
TANK-IN-TANK - Floor Care Product - BISSELL HOMECARE, INC.; *pg.* 52, *pg.* 887
TANK MANAGEMENT - Software - ASPEN TECHNOLOGY, INC.; *pg.* 354, *pg.* 804
TANKHIDE - Liquid & Paste Paints, Primers, Enamels, Lacquers & Varnishes - PPG INDUSTRIES, INC.; *pg.* 1445, *pg.* 1579
TANKLITE - Protective Insulation - THE DOW CHEMICAL COMPANY; *pg.* 1157, *pg.* 808
TANKMASTER - Hose - HBD INDUSTRIES, INC.; *pg.* 207, *pg.* 1449
TANKPAC - Emission Testing System - MISTRAS GROUP, INC.; *pg.* 1362, *pg.* 1113
TANKSCOPE - Combustible Gas Indicator - MINE SAFETY APPLIANCES COMPANY; *pg.* 1361, *pg.* 1525
TANLINE - Bevel Product - GLEASON CORPORATION; *pg.* 1340, *pg.* 1335
TANNENBAUM - Medical Device - COOK GROUP, INC.; *pg.* 1518, *pg.* 674
TANNER - Misses Dresses - TANNER COMPANIES, LP; *pg.* 34, *pg.* 1390
TANNET - Storage System - DOT HILL SYSTEMS CORP.; *pg.* 388, *pg.* 333
TANNIVER - Chemical Reagent - HACH COMPANY; *pg.* 1415, *pg.* 334
TANOS - Fungicide - E.I. DU PONT DE NEMOURS & COMPANY; *pg.* 1159, *pg.* 390
TANQUERAY - Gin - DIAGEO NORTH AMERICA, INC.; *pg.* 1961, *pg.* 361
TANRUF - Gear Cutting Tools & Blades - GLEASON CORPORATION; *pg.* 1340, *pg.* 1335
TANS III - Customer Support - TRIMBLE NAVIGATION LIMITED; *pg.* 1384, *pg.* 288
TANS VECTOR - Sensor - TRIMBLE NAVIGATION LIMITED; *pg.* 1384, *pg.* 288
TANTLIZE - Footwear - STEVEN MADDEN, LTD.; *pg.* 1819, *pg.* 1176
TANTUNG - Proprietary Alloy - AGI-VR/WESSON INC; *pg.* 1041, *pg.* 415
TANZA - Building Product - BLUELINX HOLDINGS, INC.; *pg.* 70, *pg.* 491
TANZANIA LEMONADE TEA - Beverage - BAI BRANDS; *pg.* 238, *pg.* 1073
TAORMINA - Broadloom - COURISTAN INC.; *pg.* 921, *pg.* 1067
TAOS SKI & BOOT - Ski Soft & Hardgoods - TAOS SKI VALLEY, INC.; *pg.* 1116, *pg.* 1136
TAP - Fraternal Benefits - CATHOLIC ORDER OF FORESTERS; *pg.* 1196, *pg.* 635
TAP - Ammunition - HORNADY MANUFACTURING COMPANY; *pg.* 1836, *pg.* 1010
TAP-A-DROP - Deodorizer - NILODOR, INC.; *pg.* 332, *pg.* 1406
TAP-EASE - Lubricant - AMERICAN GREASE STICK CO.; *pg.* 971, *pg.* 902
TAP-IN - Software - SYNOPSYS, INC.; *pg.* 480, *pg.* 162
TAP JR. FOOTLIGHT - Footwear - CAPEZIO BALLET MAKERS INC.; *pg.* 1805, *pg.* 1125
TAP-LOK - Threaded Insert - GROOV-PIN CORPORATION; *pg.* 1049, *pg.* 1608
TAPAZOLE - Pharmaceutical Product - KING PHARMACEUTICALS, INC.; *pg.* 1553, *pg.* 1627
TAPCO - Recording Equipment - LOUD TECHNOLOGIES INC.; *pg.* 652, *pg.* 1847
TAPE CABLE - Multiple Wire Electrical Conductor - GENERAL CABLE CORPORATION; *pg.* 83, *pg.* 384
TAPE-ID - Labels for Tape Reels - TAB PRODUCTS CO. LLC; *pg.* 481, *pg.* 1869
TAPE-ON - Storm Window Kit - WARP BROTHERS; *pg.* 1471, *pg.* 595
TAPE-PAK - Fish Tape - IDEAL INDUSTRIES, INC.; *pg.* 1051, *pg.* 662
TAPE-SUPERBGA - Packaging System - AMKOR TECHNOLOGY, INC.; *pg.* 67, *pg.* 25
TAPEARRAY - Packaging System - AMKOR TECHNOLOGY, INC.; *pg.* 67, *pg.* 25
TAPECOAT - Coating Product - CHASE CORPORATION; *pg.* 1152, *pg.* 803
TAPER - Implant Product - ZIMMER BIOMET HOLDINGS, INC.; *pg.* 1611, *pg.* 699
TAPER BOLT - Masonry Anchor - MKT FASTENING, LLC; *pg.* 1056, *pg.* 34
TAPER-LOCK - Power Transmission Product - U.S. TSUBAKI, INC.; *pg.* 221, *pg.* 670
TAPERBEAM - Flow Cell Design - WATERS CORPORATION; *pg.* 1436, *pg.* 834
TAPERED ENRGY 3 - Roof Insulation Board - JOHNS MANVILLE CORPORATION; *pg.* 89, *pg.* 320
TAPERLOC - Implant Product - ZIMMER BIOMET HOLDINGS, INC.; *pg.* 1611, *pg.* 699
TAPERLOC HIP SYSTEM - Hip Stem - ZIMMER BIOMET HOLDINGS, INC.; *pg.* 1611, *pg.* 699
TAPERSLIT - Flow Cell Design - WATERS CORPORATION; *pg.* 1436, *pg.* 834
TAPERTIP - Laser Device - TRIMEDYNE, INC.; *pg.* 1432, *pg.* 121
TAPESHIELD - Tape Autoloader - QUANTUM CORPORATION; *pg.* 458, *pg.* 250
TAPESTRY - Automatic Test Equipment - MCT WORLDWIDE LLC; *pg.* 653, *pg.* 939
TAPESTRY - Fabric - NEMSCHOFF, INC.; *pg.* 936, *pg.* 1890
TAPESTRY - Music Management Software - ROVI CORPORATION; *pg.* 463, *pg.* 269
TAPESTRY - Women's Clothing & Accessories - WOODEN SHIPS OF HOBOKEN; *pg.* 35, *pg.* 1315
TAPESTRY BLEND DARK - Coffee - KEURIG GREEN MOUNTAIN, INC.; *pg.* 868, *pg.* 1768
TAPEWARE - Tape Drive - QUANTUM CORPORATION; *pg.* 458, *pg.* 250
TAPIOCA - Starch - CARGILL, INC.; *pg.* 845, *pg.* 965
TAPMATE - Drilling And Tapping Machine - ROMAC INDUSTRIES, INC.; *pg.* 1061, *pg.* 1818
TAPMEDIA - Software - NIELSEN AUDIO; *pg.* 446, *pg.* 768
TAP'N LOK - Sampler Kit - THE HILSINGER CO.; *pg.* 1416, *pg.* 841
TA'POT - Tester - HOWELL INSTRUMENTS INC.; *pg.* 1417, *pg.* 1695
TAPP - Controller Unit - ADTRAN, INC.; *pg.* 344, *pg.* 6
TAPPAN - Air Conditioners & Furnaces - NORTEK GLOBAL HVAC; *pg.* 1075, *pg.* 989
TAPPER - Screw Anchor - POWERS FASTENERS INC.; *pg.* 1059, *pg.* 1143
TAPPLE - Footwear - STEVEN MADDEN, LTD.; *pg.* 1819, *pg.* 1176
TAPROUTE - Metal Building Product - CENTRIA, INC.; *pg.* 74, *pg.* 1554
TAPTITE - Screw - SFS INTEC, INC.; *pg.* 1061, *pg.* 1596
TAPTONE - Oceanographic Product - TELEDYNE BENTHOS, INC.; *pg.* 1431, *pg.* 838
TAQUITOS - Frozen Mexican Food - RUIZ FOOD PRODUCTS, INC.; *pg.* 893, *pg.* 77
TAR GLAS - Reinforcing Felt - KOPPERS HOLDINGS INC.; *pg.* 1170, *pg.* 1577
TARA - Bath & Plumbing Product - JACUZZI BRANDS CORPORATION; *pg.* 554, *pg.* 65

TARA - Furniture - JASPER GROUP; *pg.* 930, *pg.* 691
TARA - Bike - MARIN BIKES; *pg.* 1708, *pg.* 168
TARA KEELY - Bridal Gowns - JLM COUTURE, INC.; *pg.* 27, *pg.* 1246
TARADIDDLE - Game - GAMEWRIGHT; *pg.* 953, *pg.* 836
TARAS - Information Management System - LOCKHEED MARTIN CORPORATION; *pg.* 229, *pg.* 762
TARASI - Software & Electronic Circuitry - AVAGO TECHNOLOGIES; *pg.* 358, *pg.* 238
TARCEVA - Therapeutic Product - IDERA PHARMACEUTICALS, INC.; *pg.* 1543, *pg.* 808
TARCEVA - Cancer Therapy - INCYTE CORPORATION; *pg.* 1545, *pg.* 392
TAREA BY RUE21 - Apparel - RUE21, INC.; *pg.* 32, *pg.* 1591
TARGA BY SHEAFFER - Writing Instruments - SHEAFFER PEN CORPORATION; *pg.* 469, *pg.* 371
TARGACEPT - Pharmaceutical Preparations - TARGACEPT, INC.; *pg.* 1601, *pg.* 1395
TARGACEUTICAL - Medical Device - LUITPOLD PHARMACEUTICALS, INC.; *pg.* 1557, *pg.* 1342
TARGARD - Safety Product - VENTURI, INC.; *pg.* 1606, *pg.* 910
TARGDOTS - Shooting Dot - LYMAN PRODUCTS CORPORATION; *pg.* 1839, *pg.* 356
TARGET - Adhesive - R.C.A. RUBBER COMPANY; *pg.* 1888, *pg.* 1402
TARGET - Department Stores - TARGET CORPORATION; *pg.* 1786, *pg.* 942
TARGET-7 - Vapor Suppression Foam System - ANSUL, INCORPORATED; *pg.* 1147, *pg.* 1869
TARGET ANALYTICS - Comprehensive Donor Management - BLACKBAUD, INC.; *pg.* 361, *pg.* 1613
TARGET CORPORATION - Shopping Destination - TARGET CORPORATION; *pg.* 1786, *pg.* 942
TARGET DESIGNER - Development Tools - BSQUARE CORPORATION; *pg.* 366, *pg.* 1813
TARGET GREY - Shotgun - STURM, RUGER & COMPANY, INC.; *pg.* 1846, *pg.* 371
TARGET KENO - Video Game - INTERNATIONAL GAME TECHNOLOGY; *pg.* 957, *pg.* 1024
TARGET LIFE - Universal Life Insurance - NEW YORK LIFE INSURANCE COMPANY; *pg.* 1211, *pg.* 1268
TARGET MARKETING - Magazine - NORTH AMERICAN PUBLISHING COMPANY; *pg.* 1671, *pg.* 1567
TARGET MARKETING MAINE - Advertising Publication - DOMINION ENTERPRISES; *pg.* 1636, *pg.* 1796
TARGET PRO - Demographic, Segmentation & Analysis System - PITNEY BOWES SOFTWARE INC.; *pg.* 455, *pg.* 1346
TARGET TECH - Warning Device - FEDERAL SIGNAL CORPORATION; *pg.* 638, *pg.* 645
TARGETED JOB FAIRS - Career Fairs - DHI GROUP, INC.; *pg.* 1238, *pg.* 1223
TARGETEXPERT XR - Promotional Software - VALASSIS COMMUNICATIONS, INC.; *pg.* 1287, *pg.* 897
TARGETING CANCER, TRANSFORMING LIVES - Slogan - DENDREON CORPORATION; *pg.* 1522, *pg.* 1835
TARGETMAN - Target Stand - LYMAN PRODUCTS CORPORATION; *pg.* 1839, *pg.* 356
TARGETMASTER - Firearms - REMINGTON ARMS COMPANY, LLC; *pg.* 1844, *pg.* 1382
TARGETONE - Software - NIELSEN AUDIO; *pg.* 446, *pg.* 768
TARGET:PILE - Software - TRIMBLE NAVIGATION LIMITED; *pg.* 1384, *pg.* 288
TARGET:STRUCTURES - Software - TRIMBLE NAVIGATION LIMITED; *pg.* 1384, *pg.* 288
TARGETVIEW - Software & Hardware - EVANS & SUTHERLAND COMPUTER CORPORATION; *pg.* 638, *pg.* 1757
TARGIS - Medical Device - UROLOGIX, INC.; *pg.* 1604, *pg.* 945
TARGO - Stain Remover - A.L. WILSON CHEMICAL CO.; *pg.* 325, *pg.* 1076
TARGRETIN - Pharmaceutical - EISAI INC.; *pg.* 1526, *pg.* 1133
TARGRETIN - Pharmaceutical Product - LIGAND PHARMACEUTICALS INC.; *pg.* 1556, *pg.* 119
TARKA - Tablet - ABBOTT LABORATORIES; *pg.* 1484, *pg.* 551
TARLETON - Furniture - LA-Z-BOY INCORPORATED; *pg.* 932, *pg.* 901
TARMINATOR - Car Care Product - STONER INC.; *pg.* 985, *pg.* 1583
TARN-X - Cleaner Deodorizer - JELMAR COMPANY; *pg.* 331, *pg.* 660
TARN-X COPPER GLAZE - Copper Polish - JELMAR COMPANY; *pg.* 331, *pg.* 660
TARN-X SILVER GLAZE - Silver Polish - JELMAR COMPANY; *pg.* 331, *pg.* 660
TARNEYY - Footwear - STEVEN MADDEN, LTD.; *pg.* 1819, *pg.* 1176
TARNI-SHIELD - Tarnish Preventing Metal Cleaner - 3M COMPANY; *pg.* 1142, *pg.* 956
TARNIBAN - Anti-tarnish for Silver - TECHNIC INCORPORATED; *pg.* 1183, *pg.* 1601
TARRAGON - Fabric - NEMSCHOFF, INC.; *pg.* 936, *pg.* 1890
TARREGA - Ceiling Fan - WESTINGHOUSE LIGHTING CORPORATION; *pg.* 687, *pg.* 1571
TARSO MEDIUS - Surgical Boots - MAURICE J. MARKELL SHOE CO., INC.; *pg.* 1811, *pg.* 1356
TARSO PRONATOR - Children's Corrective Shoes - MAURICE J. MARKELL SHOE CO., INC.; *pg.* 1811, *pg.* 1356
TARSO SUPINATOR - Children's Corrective Shoes - MAURICE J. MARKELL SHOE CO., INC.; *pg.* 1811, *pg.* 1356
TART - Candle - THE YANKEE CANDLE COMPANY, INC.; *pg.* 1792, *pg.* 843
TART 'N TANGY TOTALLY - Candy - SWEET CANDY COMPANY; *pg.* 1862, *pg.* 1761
TARTAN - Tape - 3M COMPANY; *pg.* 1142, *pg.* 956
TAS - Interoperability Software - AVAGO TECHNOLOGIES; *pg.* 358, *pg.* 238
TAS - Task Seating - HAWORTH, INC.; *pg.* 402, *pg.* 891
T.A.S.A.R - Ankle Support Against Rollover - WEINBRENNER SHOE COMPANY, INC.; *pg.* 1822, *pg.* 1871
TASC - Cathodic Protection - CORRPRO COMPANIES, INC.; *pg.* 631, *pg.* 1464
TASC-MECHANICAL - Software - ASPEN TECHNOLOGY, INC.; *pg.* 354, *pg.* 804
TASCAM - Rewritable Recorder - MICROBOARDS TECHNOLOGY, LLC; *pg.* 434, *pg.* 920
TASCAM - Professional Sound Equip. - TEAC AMERICA, INC.; *pg.* 678, *pg.* 151
TASCO - Sport Optic Product - BUSHNELL OUTDOOR PRODUCTS, INC.; *pg.* 1403, *pg.* 718
TASER C2 - Stun Gun - TASER INTERNATIONAL, INC.; *pg.* 677, *pg.* 24
TASER CAM - Electronic Control Device - TASER INTERNATIONAL, INC.; *pg.* 677, *pg.* 24
TASER MPH - Electronic Control Device - TASER INTERNATIONAL, INC.; *pg.* 677, *pg.* 24
TASER VDPM - Electronic Control Device - TASER INTERNATIONAL, INC.; *pg.* 677, *pg.* 24
TASER X12 - Electronic Control Device - TASER INTERNATIONAL, INC.; *pg.* 677, *pg.* 24
TASER X26 - Electronic Control Device - TASER INTERNATIONAL, INC.; *pg.* 677, *pg.* 24
TASER X26C - Electronic Control Device - TASER INTERNATIONAL, INC.; *pg.* 677, *pg.* 24
TASER XREP - Electronic Control Device - TASER INTERNATIONAL, INC.; *pg.* 677, *pg.* 24
TASHA - Sunglasses - COACH, INC.; *pg.* 3, *pg.* 1214
TASK - Polyurethane Elastomer - SMOOTH-ON INC.; *pg.* 111, *pg.* 1528
TASK INITIATOR - Software - INTEGRAL SYSTEMS, INC.; *pg.* 416, *pg.* 767
TASK-LIGHT - Flashlight - STREAMLIGHT INC.; *pg.* 1306, *pg.* 1527
TASK-LIGHTS - Flashlight - STREAMLIGHT INC.; *pg.* 1306, *pg.* 1527
TASK MASTER - Offset Printing Blanket - ROTADYNE; *pg.* 1681, *pg.* 529
TASK MASTER - Ladder Product - WERNER HOLDING CO.; *pg.* 121, *pg.* 1534
TASKFORCE - Software - SRA INTERNATIONAL, INC.; *pg.* 473, *pg.* 1780
TASKFORCE - Vacuum - TORNADO INDUSTRIES, INC.; *pg.* 1383, *pg.* 591
TASKI - Floor Care Machine - DIVERSEY, INC.; *pg.* 1123, *pg.* 1896
TASKIT - Medical Instrument Container - MEDLINE INDUSTRIES, INC.; *pg.* 1562, *pg.* 635
TASKLINK - Software - DATA I/O CORPORATION; *pg.* 382, *pg.* 1824
TASKMASTER - Warehouse Management System - UNITED STATES COLD STORAGE, INC.; *pg.* 61, *pg.* 1051
TASKMATE - Wiper And Cleaning Cloth - GEORGIA-PACIFIC LLC; *pg.* 1458, *pg.* 507
TASKMATE - Upper Structures for IAC Industries' Task Handling Systems - IAC INDUSTRIES, INC.; *pg.* 929, *pg.* 48
TASMAN - Receiver - TRIMBLE NAVIGATION LIMITED; *pg.* 1384, *pg.* 288
TASMAR - Pharmaceutical Product - HOFFMANN-LA ROCHE INC.; *pg.* 1542, *pg.* 1099
TASSIMO - Coffees - THE KRAFT HEINZ COMPANY; *pg.* 870, *pg.* 1577
TASSIMO - Coffee Maker/Hot Beverage System - MONDELEZ INTERNATIONAL, INC.; *pg.* 878, *pg.* 601
THE TASTE OF PARADISE - Slogan - FIJI WATER; *pg.* 251, *pg.* 130
TASTE OF TEA - Flower Arrangement - 1-800-FLOWERS.COM, INC.; *pg.* 1758, *pg.* 1151
TASTE PARADISE - Slogan - KING'S HAWAIIAN BAKERY WEST, INC.; *pg.* 869, *pg.* 293
TASTE PERFECTION - Slogan - PRIMO WATER CORPORATION; *pg.* 1030, *pg.* 1395
TASTE UPSTATE FRESHNESS - Slogan - UPSTATE NIAGARA COOPERATIVE, INC.; *pg.* 907, *pg.* 1151
TASTE WAVES - Nutritional Product - NUTRACEUTICAL INTERNATIONAL CORPORATION; *pg.* 1576, *pg.* 1753
TASTE YOU CAN BELIEVE IN - Tag Line for Cascadian Farm Products - GENERAL MILLS, INC.; *pg.* 828, *pg.* 933
TASTEE - Corn, Cane, Pancake & Waffle Syrups - WHITFIELD FOODS, INC.; *pg.* 910, *pg.* 8
TASTEE FREEZ - Fast Food Chain - GALARDI GROUP, INC.; *pg.* 1729, *pg.* 110
TASTER'S CHOICE - Coffee - NESTLE USA, INC.; *pg.* 883, *pg.* 96
TASTETATIONS - Candy - THE HERSHEY CO.; *pg.* 1855, *pg.* 1538
TASTY BITE - Processed Food - KAYEM FOODS, INC.; *pg.* 867, *pg.* 814
TASTY NUGGETS - Dog Food - KENT NUTRITION GROUP; *pg.* 1477, *pg.* 710
TASTY TATERS - Food Prods. - FROSTY ACRES BRANDS, INC.; *pg.* 1020, *pg.* 484
TASTYBIRD - Chicken Products - TYSON FOODS, INC.; *pg.* 902, *pg.* 35
THE TASTYGRAM COMPANY - Gift Product - THE VERMONT TEDDY BEAR COMPANY; *pg.* 969, *pg.* 1767
TASTYKAKE - Bakery Goods - TASTY BAKING COMPANY; *pg.* 1862, *pg.* 1571
TATAMI - Bath Collection - CROSCILL, INC.; *pg.* 1122, *pg.* 1220
TATAMI - Carpet - INTERFACE, INC.; *pg.* 695, *pg.* 512
TATAMI - Fabric - NEMSCHOFF, INC.; *pg.* 936, *pg.* 1890
TATCH-A-CLEAT - Conveyor Belt Cleats - FLEXIBLE STEEL LACING COMPANY; *pg.* 1337, *pg.* 608
TATER KING - Potato Peeler - LINCOLN FOODSERVICE PRODUCTS, LLC; *pg.* 1127, *pg.* 1432
TATER PALS - Food Products - J.R. SIMPLOT COMPANY; *pg.* 867, *pg.* 547
TATL - Software - MERCURY COMPUTER SYSTEMS, INC.; *pg.* 434, *pg.* 813
TATO SKINS - Snack Food Product - INVENTURE FOODS, INC.; *pg.* 1023, *pg.* 17
TATO SKINS CHEDDAR & BACON POTATO SKINS - Snack Food Product - INVENTURE FOODS, INC.; *pg.* 1023, *pg.* 17
TATO SKINS SOUR CREAM & ONION POTATO SKINS - Snack Food - INVENTURE FOODS, INC.; *pg.* 1023, *pg.* 17
TATONKA - Beer - BJ'S RESTAURANTS, INC.; *pg.* 1716, *pg.* 104
TATRA - Radio Test System - AEROFLEX INCORPORATED; *pg.* 614, *pg.* 1321
TATRA - Vehicle - TEREX CORPORATION; *pg.* 1381, *pg.* 384
TATTERSAIL - Carpet - BEAULIEU GROUP, LLC; *pg.* 917, *pg.* 529
TATTLE-TAPE - Detection System - 3M COMPANY; *pg.* 1142, *pg.* 956
TATTOO - Waterproof Bandage - 3M COMPANY; *pg.* 1142, *pg.* 956
TATTOO - Leather Product - COACH, INC.; *pg.* 3, *pg.* 1214
TATTOO - Magazine - PAISANO PUBLICATIONS, LLC; *pg.* 1674, *pg.* 38
TATTOO EXPRESS - Enables Faster Printing - INTEGRATED SOFTWARE DESIGN, INC.; *pg.* 416, *pg.* 830
TATTOO ID - Label, Design, Print & Barcode Platform -

First page reference indicates Business Class Edition
Second page reference indicates Geographic Edition

INTEGRATED SOFTWARE DESIGN, INC.; *pg.* 416, *pg.* 830

TATTOO ID BUSINESS - Labeling Software - INTEGRATED SOFTWARE DESIGN, INC.; *pg.* 416, *pg.* 830

TATTOO ID ENTERPRISE - Labeling Software - INTEGRATED SOFTWARE DESIGN, INC.; *pg.* 416, *pg.* 830

TATTOO LABEL - Software - INTEGRATED SOFTWARE DESIGN, INC.; *pg.* 416, *pg.* 830

TATTOO POSTSCRIPT - Barcode Printing Software - INTEGRATED SOFTWARE DESIGN, INC.; *pg.* 416, *pg.* 830

TATUM - Clothing - ABERCROMBIE & FITCH CO.; *pg.* 37, *pg.* 1466

TAUPE - Furniture - BUSH INDUSTRIES INC.; *pg.* 919, *pg.* 1170

TAURUS - Network Storage System - CANDELIS, INC.; *pg.* 368, *pg.* 165

TAURUS - Leather Cutting System - GERBER SCIENTIFIC, INC.; *pg.* 1414, *pg.* 380

TAURUS - Rocket - ORBITAL ATK; *pg.* 1425, *pg.* 1779

TAURUS - Turbine Products - SOLAR TURBINES INCORPORATED; *pg.* 1377, *pg.* 209

TAURUS - Software - SYNOPSYS, INC.; *pg.* 480, *pg.* 162

TAURUS - Remote Control Device - UNIVERSAL ELECTRONICS, INC.; *pg.* 683, *pg.* 262

TAUTLINER - Curtain Flatbed - UTILITY TRAILER MANUFACTURING COMPANY; *pg.* 1712, *pg.* 68

TAVERA - Automobile - GENERAL MOTORS COMPANY; *pg.* 175, *pg.* 881

TAVERN KING - Video Game - INTERNATIONAL GAME TECHNOLOGY; *pg.* 957, *pg.* 1024

TAVI - Footwear - COBIAN CORP.; *pg.* 1806, *pg.* 253

TAX ALERTS - Software - THOMSON REUTERS TAX & ACCOUNTING; *pg.* 1693, *pg.* 1299

TAX PAID 20 GRAND - Game - MISSOURI LOTTERY; *pg.* 999, *pg.* 979

TAX PREP PARTNER SERIES - Reference Material - CCH INC.; *pg.* 1626, *pg.* 653

TAX SERVICE - Tag Line - JACKSON HEWITT TAX SERVICE INC.; *pg.* 771, *pg.* 1103

TAXCORE - Publisher - BLOOMBERG BNA; *pg.* 1621, *pg.* 1772

TAXEXPRESS - Software - SCAN-OPTICS, LLC; *pg.* 467, *pg.* 354

TAXI - Bicycles - G. JOANNOU CYCLE CO. INC.; *pg.* 1707, *pg.* 1098

TAXI JAM - Miniature Roller Coaster - CAROWINDS; *pg.* 537, *pg.* 1364

TAXICAB CONFESSIONS - Cable Television Show - HOME BOX OFFICE, INC.; *pg.* 290, *pg.* 1240

TAXOL - Pharmaceutical Product - CELL THERAPEUTICS, INC.; *pg.* 1514, *pg.* 1834

TAXOPREXIN - Medical Device - LUITPOLD PHARMACEUTICALS, INC., *pg.* 1557, *pg.* 1342

TAXOTERE - Drug - ISIS PHARMACEUTICALS, INC.; *pg.* 1548, *pg.* 59

TAXOTERE - Docetaxel - SANOFI US; *pg.* 1592, *pg.* 1046

TAXPAY - Software - PAYCHEX, INC.; *pg.* 792, *pg.* 1336

TAXSCRIPTS TAXPRO - Software - CCH INC.; *pg.* 1626, *pg.* 653

TAXUS - Medical Device - BOSTON SCIENTIFIC CORPORATION; *pg.* 1508, *pg.* 831

TAXUS EXPRESS2 - Medical Device - BOSTON SCIENTIFIC CORPORATION; *pg.* 1508, *pg.* 831

TAXUS EXPRESS2 ATOM - Medical Device - BOSTON SCIENTIFIC CORPORATION; *pg.* 1508, *pg.* 831

TAXUS LIBERTE ATOM - Medical Device - BOSTON SCIENTIFIC CORPORATION; *pg.* 1508, *pg.* 831

TAYLA - Footwear - STEVEN MADDEN, LTD.; *pg.* 1819, *pg.* 1176

TAYLOR - Life Ring - TAYLOR MADE GROUP; *pg.* 1711, *pg.* 1162

TAYLOR - Wiring Duct - THOMAS & BETTS CORPORATION; *pg.* 680, *pg.* 1646

TAYLOR-BURTON DIAMOND - Jewelry - HARRY WINSTON, INC.; *pg.* 6, *pg.* 1238

TAYLOR HILL - Fan - WESTINGHOUSE LIGHTING CORPORATION; *pg.* 687, *pg.* 1571

TAYLOR RENTAL - Equipment Rental - TRUE VALUE COMPANY; *pg.* 1065, *pg.* 592

TAYLORBRITE - Interior Light - TAYLOR MADE GROUP; *pg.* 1711, *pg.* 1162

TAYLOR*MADE - Marine, Lawn & Garden, Luggage - TAYLOR MADE GROUP; *pg.* 1711, *pg.* 1162

TAYLOR'S PRIDE - Tobacco Product - AMERICAN SNUFF COMPANY; *pg.* 1893, *pg.* 1641

TAZO - Tea - STARBUCKS CORPORATION; *pg.* 897, *pg.* 1840

TAZORAC - Skin Care Product - ALLERGAN, INC.; *pg.* 1491, *pg.* 106

TBA - Helicopter Transportable Drilling rigs - PARKER DRILLING COMPANY; *pg.* 982, *pg.* 1712

TBG - Abuse Resistant Packaging Materials for Food Products - SEALED AIR CORPORATION; *pg.* 1468, *pg.* 1058

TBII - Glass & Ceramic Material - CORNING INCORPORATED; *pg.* 1122, *pg.* 1154

TBL - Diabetes Care Product - BECTON, DICKINSON & COMPANY; *pg.* 1501, *pg.* 1068

TBL - Footwear - THE TIMBERLAND COMPANY; *pg.* 1821, *pg.* 1039

TBMCS - Systems Integration & Aeronautics - LOCKHEED MARTIN CORPORATION; *pg.* 229, *pg.* 762

TBN WEEKLY ONLINE - Online Newspaper - TAMPA BAY NEWSPAPERS, INC.; *pg.* 1691, *pg.* 468

TBS - Steel - THE TIMKEN COMPANY; *pg.* 218, *pg.* 1408

TBS-600 - Steel - THE TIMKEN COMPANY; *pg.* 218, *pg.* 1408

TBS-9 - Steel - THE TIMKEN COMPANY; *pg.* 218, *pg.* 1408

TC-90 THINLINE - Electric Guitar - FENDER MUSICAL INSTRUMENTS CORPORATION; *pg.* 547, *pg.* 21

TC-FLASH - Molecular Biology Product - THERMO FISHER SCIENTIFIC INC.; *pg.* 1602, *pg.* 61

TC-REASH - Molecular Probe Product - THERMO FISHER SCIENTIFIC INC.; *pg.* 1602, *pg.* 61

TC4 - Tank Cleaner - ASHLAND INC.; *pg.* 972, *pg.* 726

TCA - Hardware Product - INTERPHASE CORPORATION; *pg.* 420, *pg.* 1732

TCA - Temporary Condyle Attachment - OSTEOMED CORPORATION; *pg.* 1425, *pg.* 1658

TCA PAINT - Animal Safety Product - NEOGEN CORPORATION; *pg.* 883, *pg.* 896

TCF - Photographic Film & Paper - EASTMAN KODAK COMPANY; *pg.* 1408, *pg.* 1333

TCF EXPRESS TELLERS - Automated Bank Teller Machines - TCF FINANCIAL CORPORATION; *pg.* 808, *pg.* 966

TCIHG - Electronic Component - OPLINK COMMUNICATIONS, INC.; *pg.* 660, *pg.* 91

TCIP - Test Cell Instrumentation Package - HOWELL INSTRUMENTS INC.; *pg.* 1417, *pg.* 1695

TCL API - Network Testing System - IXIA; *pg.* 422, *pg.* 56

TCLIBRARY - Software - KEITHLEY INSTRUMENTS, INC.; *pg.* 1418, *pg.* 1473

TCM4 - Continuous & Non-invasive Transcutaneous pO2 & pCO2 Information Monitor - RADIOMETER AMERICA INC.; *pg.* 1588, *pg.* 1481

TCM400 - Portable Instrument for Measuring Transcutaneous Oxygen Tension - RADIOMETER AMERICA INC.; *pg.* 1588, *pg.* 1481

TCMS - Total Charge Management System - PROGRESSIVE DYNAMICS, INC.; *pg.* 665, *pg.* 898

TCMS INTERFACE - Total Charge Management System - PROGRESSIVE DYNAMICS, INC.; *pg.* 665, *pg.* 898

TCP - Photographic Film & Paper - EASTMAN KODAK COMPANY; *pg.* 1408, *pg.* 1333

TCP - Silicon Etch System - LAM RESEARCH CORPORATION; *pg.* 1354, *pg.* 91

TCS - Apparel - CABELA'S INCORPORATED; *pg.* 535, *pg.* 1019

TCS SNAPTRACK - Wireless Communication Product - TELECOMMUNICATION SYSTEMS INC.; *pg.* 483, *pg.* 754

TCT GOLD LINE - Measure Spindle Accuracy - SETCO SALES COMPANY; *pg.* 1061, *pg.* 1426

TD - Tetanus and Diphtheria Toxoids Adsorbed For Adult - SANOFI PASTEUR, INC; *pg.* 1591, *pg.* 1588

TD-850 DRUMVERTER - Manual Drum Dumper - LIFTOMATIC MATERIAL HANDLING INC.; *pg.* 94, *pg.* 560

TD COLLECTION - Furniture - HERMAN MILLER, INC.; *pg.* 926, *pg.* 913

TDC1 - Data Collector - TRIMBLE NAVIGATION LIMITED; *pg.* 1384, *pg.* 288

TDC2 - Asset Surveyor - TRIMBLE NAVIGATION LIMITED; *pg.* 1384, *pg.* 288

TDF - Photographic Film & Paper - EASTMAN KODAK COMPANY; *pg.* 1408, *pg.* 1333

TDI - Batteries - TE CONNECTIVITY LTD.; *pg.* 677, *pg.* 1515

TDP - Electronic Components - MOLEX INCORPORATED; *pg.* 655, *pg.* 628

TDS - Pump Product - IDEX CORPORATION; *pg.* 1347, *pg.* 623

TDS-30 - Steel - THE TIMKEN COMPANY; *pg.* 218, *pg.* 1408

TDS-70 - Steel - THE TIMKEN COMPANY; *pg.* 218, *pg.* 1408

TDS-90 - Steel - THE TIMKEN COMPANY; *pg.* 218, *pg.* 1408

TDTNEWS.COM - Website - FRANK MAYBORN ENTERPRISES; *pg.* 1642, *pg.* 1746

TDX - Therapeutic Drug Monitoring System - ABBOTT LABORATORIES; *pg.* 1484, *pg.* 551

TE AMO - Premium Cigars - ALTADIS USA, INC.; *pg.* 1893, *pg.* 423

TEA AT ITS BEST - Slogan - BUNN-O-MATIC CORPORATION; *pg.* 53, *pg.* 661

TEA FOR AMERICA - Black Tea - CELESTIAL SEASONINGS, INC.; *pg.* 846, *pg.* 310

TEA-FOR-TWO - Bath Product - KOHLER CO.; *pg.* 91, *pg.* 1862

TEA FOR TWO BOUQUET - Floral Bouquet - FTD GROUP, INC.; *pg.* 1795, *pg.* 608

TEA ROSE - Scarf - HERITAGE LACE INC.; *pg.* 694, *pg.* 711

TEA TIME - Cotton Capris - HABAND COMPANY, INC.; *pg.* 1772, *pg.* 1099

TEA TREE - Salon Product - GREAT CLIPS, INC.; *pg.* 510, *pg.* 937

TEA TREE - Hair Care Product - JOHN PAUL MITCHELL SYSTEMS; *pg.* 512, *pg.* 133

TEA TREE SPECIAL - Hair Care System - JOHN PAUL MITCHELL SYSTEMS; *pg.* 512, *pg.* 133

TEA TRIO - Dietary Supplement - GARDEN OF LIFE, INC.; *pg.* 1532, *pg.* 478

TEA2GO - Food Product - 4C FOODS CORPORATION; *pg.* 835, *pg.* 1145

TEABAGS - Mix & RTD - COMMUNITY COFFEE COMPANY LLC; *pg.* 849, *pg.* 741

TEABERRY - Shoe - AEROGROUP INTERNATIONAL, INC.; *pg.* 1803, *pg.* 1055

TEAC - Electronic Products - TEAC AMERICA, INC.; *pg.* 678, *pg.* 151

TEACHCAM - Audio Conferencing System - CLEARONE COMMUNICATIONS, INC.; *pg.* 629, *pg.* 1756

TEACHER FREEBIES - Educational Materials - SCHOLASTIC INC.; *pg.* 1683, *pg.* 1288

TEACHER LIBRARIAN - Journal - SCARECROW PRESS, INC.; *pg.* 1598, *pg.* 773

THE TEACHER STORE - Educational Materials - SCHOLASTIC INC.; *pg.* 1683, *pg.* 1288

TEACHERS - Scotch Whiskey - JIM BEAM BRANDS CO.; *pg.* 1965, *pg.* 601

TEACHING - Magazine - HIGHLIGHTS FOR CHILDREN, INC.; *pg.* 1650, *pg.* 1440

TEACHING TOLERANCE - Magazine - THE SOUTHERN POVERTY LAW CENTER; *pg.* 157, *pg.* 7

TEACHWELL - Mobile Computer Workstation - ERGOTRON, INC.; *pg.* 395, *pg.* 960

TEAK COTE - Teak Wood Treatment - PETTIT PAINT COMPANY; *pg.* 1444, *pg.* 1116

TEAKWORKS - Coating & Paint - AKZO NOBEL DECORATIVE PAINTS, USA; *pg.* 1439, *pg.* 1474

TEAL - Fabric - NEMSCHOFF, INC.; *pg.* 936, *pg.* 1890

TEALTRAN - Isolation Transformer - SL INDUSTRIES, INC.; *pg.* 674, *pg.* 1090

TEALWATCH - Power Monitor - SL INDUSTRIES, INC.; *pg.* 674, *pg.* 1090

TEALWAVE - Filter - SL INDUSTRIES, INC.; *pg.* 674, *pg.* 1090

TEAM - Car Dealerships - AUTONATION, INC.; *pg.* 165, *pg.* 423

TEAM - Dairy Supplies & Animal Health Prods. - GEA FARM TECHNOLOGIES; *pg.* 704, *pg.* 636

TEAM - Network Elements - GENERAL DATACOMM INDUSTRIES, INC.; *pg.* 400, *pg.* 357

TEAM - Footwear - SAUCONY, INC.; *pg.* 1818, *pg.* 828

TEAM APPROACH - Fundraising Software - BLACKBAUD, INC.; *pg.* 361, *pg.* 1613

TEAM ARENA - Game - ACTIVISION BLIZZARD, INC.; *pg.* 948, *pg.* 271

TEAM CHEERIOS - Cereal - GENERAL MILLS, INC.; *pg.* 828, *pg.* 933

TEAM CONTROL - Bicycle Accessories - SPECIALIZED BICYCLE COMPONENTS, INC.; *pg.* 1711, *pg.* 152

TEAM DAIWA-ADVANTAGE - Freshwater Spinning Reels - DAIWA CORPORATION; *pg.* 1832, *pg.* 75

TEAM DAIWA FUEGO - Bait Casting Reels - DAIWA CORPORATION; *pg.* 1832, *pg.* 75

TEAM DAIWA LUNA - Bait Casting Reels - DAIWA

CORPORATION; *pg.* 1832, *pg.* 75
TEAM DAIWA SOL - Bait Casting Reels - DAIWA CORPORATION; *pg.* 1832, *pg.* 75
TEAM DAIWA VIENTO - Bait Casting Reels - DAIWA CORPORATION; *pg.* 1832, *pg.* 75
TEAM DAIWA X - Bait Casting Reels - DAIWA CORPORATION; *pg.* 1832, *pg.* 75
TEAM DAIWA-Z CU - Freshwater Spinning Reels - DAIWA CORPORATION; *pg.* 1832, *pg.* 75
TEAM DAIWA ZILLION - Saltwater Spinning Reels - DAIWA CORPORATION; *pg.* 1832, *pg.* 75
TEAM DEVELOPER - Software - DAEGIS INC; *pg.* 381, *pg.* 195
TEAM GRID - Apparel - OAKLEY, INC.; *pg.* 1840, *pg.* 86
TEAM MANAGER - Management Software - HIBBETT SPORTS, INC.; *pg.* 1836, *pg.* 3
TEAM MASTER - Bicycle Accessories - SPECIALIZED BICYCLE COMPONENTS, INC.; *pg.* 1711, *pg.* 152
TEAM TIME TRAIL - Bicycle - TREK BICYCLE CORPORATION; *pg.* 1847, *pg.* 1896
TEAM TRACK - Software - SERENA SOFTWARE, INC.; *pg.* 468, *pg.* 192
TEAM TURBO - Bicycle Accessories - SPECIALIZED BICYCLE COMPONENTS, INC.; *pg.* 1711, *pg.* 152
TEAM UP - Apparel - OAKLEY, INC.; *pg.* 1840, *pg.* 86
TEAM WIN-T - Systems Integration & Aeronautics - LOCKHEED MARTIN CORPORATION; *pg.* 229, *pg.* 762
TEAM - WORK - Claim Management - THE HARTFORD FINANCIAL SERVICES GROUP, INC.; *pg.* 1202, *pg.* 352
TEAMBOAT SPRINGS - Cartoon Character - THE WALT DISNEY COMPANY; *pg.* 317, *pg.* 52
TEAMBUILDER - Career Recruiting Website - CAREERBUILDER, LLC; *pg.* 1234, *pg.* 568
TEAMED WITH TEACHERS - Science & Math Products - CAROLINA BIOLOGICAL SUPPLY COMPANY; *pg.* 1513, *pg.* 1359
TEAMLEADER.COM - Website - MARKET LEADER, INC.; *pg.* 1102, *pg.* 1822
TEAMPCB - Software System - MENTOR GRAPHICS CORPORATION; *pg.* 432, *pg.* 1510
TEAMSOCK - Sock - UNDER ARMOUR, INC.; *pg.* 49, *pg.* 759
TEAMSOURCING - Employee Leasing Service - SYNTEL, INC.; *pg.* 480, *pg.* 911
TEAMTELEWORK - Wireless Communication System - AT&T SOUTHEAST; *pg.* 1868, *pg.* 489
TEAMTELEWORK CONNECTIONS - Wireless Communication System - AT&T SOUTHEAST; *pg.* 1868, *pg.* 489
TEAMTRACK - Software - SERENA SOFTWARE, INC.; *pg.* 468, *pg.* 192
TEAMWORK - Office Furniture - STEELCASE INC.; *pg.* 475, *pg.* 889
TEARDROP - Furniture - HERMAN MILLER, INC.; *pg.* 926, *pg.* 913
TEARDROP - Selective Rack - SPEEDRACK PRODUCTS GROUP, LTD.; *pg.* 112, *pg.* 908
TEARDROPS - Fabric - NEMSCHOFF, INC.; *pg.* 936, *pg.* 1890
TEARS RENEWED - Ophthalmic Ointment - AKORN, INC.; *pg.* 1488, *pg.* 622
TEARTESTER - Test Instrument - THWING-ALBERT INSTRUMENT COMPANY; *pg.* 1432, *pg.* 1131
TEASE - Fabric - NEMSCHOFF, INC.; *pg.* 936, *pg.* 1890
TEASPOON - Eyewear - OAKLEY, INC.; *pg.* 1840, *pg.* 86
TEAVANA - Teas & Teaware - STARBUCKS CORPORATION; *pg.* 897, *pg.* 1840
TEAZE - Leather Glove - KOMBI, LTD.; *pg.* 1838, *pg.* 1766
TEBO DECKER - Fastening Product - PEACE INDUSTRIES INC.; *pg.* 1368, *pg.* 656
TEBO FASTENER - Fastening Product - PEACE INDUSTRIES INC.; *pg.* 1368, *pg.* 656
TEBOL - Chemical Product - LYONDELLBASELL INDUSTRIES; *pg.* 980, *pg.* 1710
TEC 2000 - Construction Equipment - VERMEER MANUFACTURING COMPANY; *pg.* 708, *pg.* 711
TEC 2000.2 - Construction Equipment - VERMEER MANUFACTURING COMPANY; *pg.* 708, *pg.* 711
TEC BLUE - Toy - IMPERIAL TOY CORPORATION; *pg.* 957, *pg.* 166
TEC STRETCH - Glove - 180S, LLC; *pg.* 1824, *pg.* 754
TEC TOUCH - Glove - 180S, LLC; *pg.* 1824, *pg.* 754
TECATE - Beer - HEINEKEN USA INC.; *pg.* 252, *pg.* 1352
TECATE - All-Terrain Vehicle - KAWASAKI MOTORS CORP., U.S.A.; *pg.* 1708, *pg.* 111
TECENTER - Consulting Services - AVNET, INC.; *pg.* 622, *pg.* 15
TECFLOR - Office Product - HAWORTH, INC.; *pg.* 402, *pg.* 891
TECH - Sock - OAKLEY, INC.; *pg.* 1840, *pg.* 86
TECH - Magazine - SNAP-ON INCORPORATED; *pg.* 1062, *pg.* 1862
TECH - Bag - SOLO; *pg.* 12, *pg.* 1165
TECH 60/40 - Shirt - CORTLAND LINE COMPANY; *pg.* 1831, *pg.* 1155
TECH BITS - Technical Publication - EASTMAN KODAK COMPANY; *pg.* 1408, *pg.* 1333
TECH BRUSHES - Chemical Cleaner Product - TECH SPRAY, L.P.; *pg.* 1183, *pg.* 1659
TECH DECK - Toy - SPIN MASTER LTD.; *pg.* 967, *pg.* 1943
TECH-GUARD - Paints - PRATT & LAMBERT PAINTS; *pg.* 1446, *pg.* 1434
TECH HOLD - Chemical Cleaner Product - TECH SPRAY, L.P.; *pg.* 1183, *pg.* 1659
TECH-MET - Laboratory Furniture - BUEHLER, LTD.; *pg.* 1403, *pg.* 622
TECH PACK 2 - Photographic Film & Chemical Kit - EASTMAN KODAK COMPANY; *pg.* 1408, *pg.* 1333
TECH-POL - Optical Product - UNIVERSAL PHOTONICS, INC.; *pg.* 1433, *pg.* 1167
TECH-RAZOR - Razor & Blades - THE GILLETTE COMPANY; *pg.* 509, *pg.* 795
TECH-SELECT - Technical Product Catalog - AMERICAN TECHNICAL CERAMICS CORP.; *pg.* 616, *pg.* 1168
TECH SERIES - Gloves - CALLAWAY GOLF COMPANY; *pg.* 1829, *pg.* 58
TECH SPEC - Near Infrared Achromat - EDMUND INDUSTRIAL OPTICS INC.; *pg.* 1411, *pg.* 1041
TECH STEP - Molded Step Stool - DOREL JUVENILE GROUP, INC.; *pg.* 923, *pg.* 676
TECH TIPS - Medical Test System - HOLOGIC, INC.; *pg.* 1416, *pg.* 784
TECH TOE - Footwear - RED WING SHOE COMPANY, INC.; *pg.* 1817, *pg.* 954
TECH-TRAK - Conveyor - WES-TECH AUTOMATION SOLUTIONS; *pg.* 1388, *pg.* 560
TECH TWILL - Shirt - CORTLAND LINE COMPANY; *pg.* 1831, *pg.* 1155
TECH VENT - Shirt - CORTLAND LINE COMPANY; *pg.* 1831, *pg.* 1155
TECH3 - Pen - A. T. CROSS COMPANY; *pg.* 339, *pg.* 1602
TECHBRUSH - Cleaning Product - TECH SPRAY, L.P.; *pg.* 1183, *pg.* 1659
TECHCLEAN - Chemical Cleaner Product - TECH SPRAY, L.P.; *pg.* 1183, *pg.* 1659
TECHCONNECT - Software - ROCKWELL AUTOMATION, INC.; *pg.* 668, *pg.* 1880
TECHHEALTH CONNECTIONS - Integration Technology - TECHHEALTH, INC.; *pg.* 1283, *pg.* 476
TECHMATE - Resilient Moldable Beads - THE DOW CHEMICAL COMPANY; *pg.* 1157, *pg.* 898
TECHMATE - Workstations - HOLOGIC, INC.; *pg.* 1416, *pg.* 784
TECHNACURV - Full Body Harness - MINE SAFETY APPLIANCES COMPANY; *pg.* 1361, *pg.* 1525
TECHNI COPPER - Semiconductor - TECHNIC INCORPORATED; *pg.* 1183, *pg.* 1601
TECHNI FB BRIGHT ACID COPPER - Acid Copper - TECHNIC INCORPORATED; *pg.* 1183, *pg.* 1601
TECHNI-GOLDCLAD - Chemicals for Electro Plating - TECHNIC INCORPORATED; *pg.* 1183, *pg.* 1601
TECHNI NF COPPER - Matte Copper - TECHNIC INCORPORATED; *pg.* 1183, *pg.* 1601
TECHNI NICKEL JB - Nickel Sulfate Solution - TECHNIC INCORPORATED; *pg.* 1183, *pg.* 1601
TECHNI-PRINT - Heat Transfer Paper - NEENAH PAPER, INC.; *pg.* 1465, *pg.* 484
TECHNI-RHODIUM - Chemicals for Electro Plating - TECHNIC INCORPORATED; *pg.* 1183, *pg.* 1601
TECHNI-SILVER - Chemicals for Electro Plating - TECHNIC INCORPORATED; *pg.* 1183, *pg.* 1601
TECHNI-SOLDER - Chemicals for Electro Plating - TECHNIC INCORPORATED; *pg.* 1183, *pg.* 1601
TECHNI-TIN - Chemicals for Electro Plating - TECHNIC INCORPORATED; *pg.* 1183, *pg.* 1601
TECHNI X-CELL - Oxide Process - TECHNIC INCORPORATED; *pg.* 1183, *pg.* 1601
TECHNIC-COPPER - Semiconductor - TECHNIC INCORPORATED; *pg.* 1183, *pg.* 1601
TECHNIC-LAB - Equipment for Electro Plating - TECHNIC INCORPORATED; *pg.* 1183, *pg.* 1601
TECHNICA-X - Ball Point Pens & Auto Pencils - PENTEL OF AMERICA, LTD.; *pg.* 453, *pg.* 295
TECHNICAL COMMUNICATION SUITE - Software - ADOBE SYSTEMS INCORPORATED; *pg.* 342, *pg.* 235
TECHNICAL WRITING ADVANTAGE - Workshop - FRANKLIN COVEY CO.; *pg.* 1642, *pg.* 1758
TECHNICLICK - Ball Point Pens & Auto Pencils - PENTEL OF AMERICA, LTD.; *pg.* 453, *pg.* 295
TECHNICOLOR - Photographic Supplies & Services - TECHNICOLOR, INC.; *pg.* 311, *pg.* 57
TECHNICS - Audio & Professional Equipment - PANASONIC CORPORATION OF NORTH AMERICA; *pg.* 661, *pg.* 1120
TECHNIDOL - Photographic Developer - EASTMAN KODAK COMPANY; *pg.* 1408, *pg.* 1333
TECHNIGOLD - Chemicals for Electro Plating - TECHNIC INCORPORATED; *pg.* 1183, *pg.* 1601
TECHNIQUE - Office Furniture - STEELCASE INC.; *pg.* 475, *pg.* 889
TECHNIQUE - Toothbrush - SUNSTAR AMERICAS INC.; *pg.* 1599, *pg.* 591
TECHNO - Furniture - BUSH INDUSTRIES INC.; *pg.* 919, *pg.* 1170
TECHNOBEAM - Specialty Illumination Products - BALLANTYNE STRONG, INC.; *pg.* 623, *pg.* 1013
TECHNOBEAM - Lighting Product - HIGH END SYSTEMS, INC.; *pg.* 1299, *pg.* 1663
TECHNOCLIPPER - Manual Hand Clipper - TIPPER TIE, INC.; *pg.* 1382, *pg.* 1358
TECHNOCOLOR - Fabric - NEMSCHOFF, INC.; *pg.* 936, *pg.* 1890
TECHNOFLEX - Floor Mats - MACNEIL AUTOMOTIVE PRODUCTS, LTD.; *pg.* 211, *pg.* 559
TECHNOFLOW - Five-Layer Hose - TI AUTOMOTIVE LIMITED; *pg.* 191, *pg.* 869
TECHNOGRAPHICS - Technology Research Report - FORRESTER RESEARCH, INC.; *pg.* 1642, *pg.* 807
TECHNOLAB - Laboratory Equipment - FARREL CORPORATION; *pg.* 1336, *pg.* 337
TECHNOLAS 217 - Excimer Laser - BAUSCH & LOMB INCORPORATED; *pg.* 1401, *pg.* 1045
TECHNOLOGY AHEAD OF ITS TIME - Slogan - CYTEC INDUSTRIES, INC.; *pg.* 1155, *pg.* 1131
TECHNOLOGY & LEARNING - Magazine - UNITED BUSINESS MEDIA LLC; *pg.* 1697, *pg.* 1177
TECHNOLOGY & LEARNING SCHOOL TECH - Publisher - UNITED BUSINESS MEDIA LLC; *pg.* 1697, *pg.* 1177
TECHNOLOGY FOR INNOVATORS - Tag Line - TEXAS INSTRUMENTS INCORPORATED; *pg.* 679, *pg.* 1688
TECHNOLOGY FOR PRODUCTIVITY - Tagline - MKS INSTRUMENTS, INC.; *pg.* 1362, *pg.* 781
TECHNOLOGY FURNITURE - Slogan - ANTHRO CORPORATION; *pg.* 913, *pg.* 1509
TECHNOLOGY MEETS MEDICINE - Slogan - DATATRAK INTERNATIONAL, INC.; *pg.* 383, *pg.* 1462
TECHNOLOGY SMART - Tagline - KNOWLOGY CORPORATION; *pg.* 425, *pg.* 1809
TECHNOLOGY THAT FEEDS AMERICA! - Slogan - SUREQUEST SYSTEMS, INC.; *pg.* 900, *pg.* 1669
TECHNORA - Polyethylene Fiber - SAMSON ROPE TECHNOLOGIES; *pg.* 1468, *pg.* 1820
TECHNOSPHERE - Drug Delivery Platform - MANNKIND CORPORATION; *pg.* 1558, *pg.* 299
TECHNOSPORTS II - Protective Eyewear - SELLSTROM MANUFACTURING CO.; *pg.* 1428, *pg.* 659
TECHPACK - Fertilizer - SIMPLOT PARTNERS INC.; *pg.* 1800, *pg.* 548
TECHRANKINGS - Technology Research Report - FORRESTER RESEARCH, INC.; *pg.* 1642, *pg.* 807
TECHREPUBLIC - IT Website - CBS INTERACTIVE, INC.; *pg.* 369, *pg.* 215
TECHROLL - Chemical Cleaner Product - TECH SPRAY, L.P.; *pg.* 1183, *pg.* 1659
TECHRON - Fuel Additives - CHEVRON CORPORATION; *pg.* 974, *pg.* 259
TECHSWABS - Chemical Cleaner Product - TECH SPRAY, L.P.; *pg.* 1183, *pg.* 1659
TECHTRIM - Trim & Moulding Product - UNIVERSAL FOREST PRODUCTS, INC.; *pg.* 117, *pg.* 890
TECHWEB - Publisher - UNITED BUSINESS MEDIA LLC; *pg.* 1697, *pg.* 1177
TECHZONE - Ceilings & Walls - ARMSTRONG WORLD INDUSTRIES, INC.; *pg.* 914, *pg.* 1545
TECJET - Valve - WOODWARD, INC.; *pg.* 122, *pg.* 329

TECLAR - Blended Non-Woven Material - HOLLISTON LLC; *pg.* 1460, *pg.* 1630
TECNAI - Software - FEI COMPANY; *pg.* 1413, *pg.* 1498
TECNIS - Medical Device - ABBOTT MEDICAL OPTICS, INC.; *pg.* 1485, *pg.* 260
TECOFROST - Natural Gas Compressor - VILTER MANUFACTURING LLC; *pg.* 1078, *pg.* 1856
TECRETE - Office Furniture - HAWORTH, INC.; *pg.* 402, *pg.* 891
TECSOL - Solvents - EASTMAN CHEMICAL COMPANY; *pg.* 1159, *pg.* 1636
TECSTAR - Alkyd Enamel Primers & Topcoats - PPG INDUSTRIES, INC.; *pg.* 1445, *pg.* 1579
TECTILON - Acid Levelling Dyes - HUNTSMAN CORPORATION; *pg.* 1167, *pg.* 1758
TECTOR - Plastic Resins - THE DOW CHEMICAL COMPANY; *pg.* 1157, *pg.* 898
TECTYL - Corrosion Resistance - DAUBERT INDUSTRIES, INC.; *pg.* 1155, *pg.* 561
TEDDIE PEANUT BUTTER - Peanut Butter & Nut Products - THE LEAVITT CORPORATION; *pg.* 874, *pg.* 818
TEDDY BEAR - Fragrance - PARFUMS DE COEUR LTD.; *pg.* 519, *pg.* 376
TEDDY STOCKING - Ornament - HERITAGE LACE INC.; *pg.* 694, *pg.* 711
TEDECO - Aerospace Product - EATON CORPORATION; *pg.* 1331, *pg.* 1429
TEDLAR - Film - E.I. DU PONT DE NEMOURS & COMPANY; *pg.* 1159, *pg.* 390
TEDLAR - Wire & Cable - THE ZIPPERTUBING COMPANY; *pg.* 1892, *pg.* 12
TEDS-TAG - Sensor - ELECTRO STANDARDS LABORATORIES INC.; *pg.* 390, *pg.* 1600
TEDUGLUTIDE - Pharmaceutical - NPS PHARMACEUTICALS, INC.; *pg.* 1576, *pg.* 1043
TEE-BALL - Outdoor Lighting - SWIVELIER CO., INC.; *pg.* 1307, *pg.* 1142
TEE ONE UP - Lottery Game - IOWA LOTTERY; *pg.* 996, *pg.* 705
TEE TIME - Precision Blended Fertilizer - THE ANDERSONS INCORPORATED; *pg.* 1793, *pg.* 1461
TEE TIME - Pillow and Throw - HERITAGE LACE INC.; *pg.* 694, *pg.* 711
TEEJET - Nozzles - SPRAYING SYSTEMS CO.; *pg.* 1063, *pg.* 670
TEEN BUNGALOW - Furniture - STANLEY FURNITURE CO., INC.; *pg.* 943, *pg.* 1379
TEEN BURGER - Fast Food - A&W FOOD SERVICES OF CANADA INC.; *pg.* 1714, *pg.* 1908
TEEN PEOPLE - Magazine - PEOPLE MAGAZINE; *pg.* 1676, *pg.* 1278
TEEN SPIRIT - Personal Care Product - COLGATE-PALMOLIVE COMPANY; *pg.* 504, *pg.* 1215
TEEN TITANS - Game & TV Show - THE CARTOON NETWORK; *pg.* 273, *pg.* 492
TEEN TITANS - Character - DC COMICS, INC.; *pg.* 1633, *pg.* 1221
TEEN VOGUE - Magazine - CONDE NAST PUBLICATIONS, INC.; *pg.* 1629, *pg.* 1217
TEEN VOGUE - Magazine - VOGUE MAGAZINE; *pg.* 1700, *pg.* 1311
TEEN.COM - Teen & Tween Website - DEFYMEDIA; *pg.* 1237, *pg.* 1222
TEENEE BEENEE - Jelly Beans - JUST BORN, INC.; *pg.* 1857, *pg.* 1516
TEENFORM - Brassieres, Lingerie & Children's Nightwear - WACOAL AMERICA INC.; *pg.* 35, *pg.* 1312
TEENIE GENIE - Container Grown Plant - MONROVIA GROWERS; *pg.* 1797, *pg.* 44
TEENIE WAHINE - Girls' Apparel - QUIKSILVER, INC.; *pg.* 31, *pg.* 104
TEENWIRE.COM - Sexual Health Website - PLANNED PARENTHOOD FEDERATION OF AMERICA, INC.; *pg.* 154, *pg.* 1282
TEEPEA - Footwear - STEVEN MADDEN, LTD.; *pg.* 1819, *pg.* 1176
TEETER - Fabric - NEMSCHOFF, INC.; *pg.* 936, *pg.* 1890
TEETHER BABIES - Toy - MUNCHKIN, INC.; *pg.* 964, *pg.* 300
TEETHER BLANKER BUDDY - Toy - MUNCHKIN, INC.; *pg.* 964, *pg.* 300
TEETHING RING - Dog Toy - THE HARTZ MOUNTAIN CORP.; *pg.* 1476, *pg.* 1120
TEEVALVE - Control Valve - SPRAYING SYSTEMS CO.; *pg.* 1063, *pg.* 670
TEF-LUBE - Lubricant - AERVOE INDUSTRIES INCORPORATED; *pg.* 1439, *pg.* 1021
TEFGEN REGENERATIVE MEMBRANE - Non-Resorbable Membrane for Assisting the Regeneration of Bone Defects - LIFECORE BIOMEDICAL, LLC; *pg.* 1556, *pg.* 920
TEFLON - Gate Valves - DRIL-QUIP, INC.; *pg.* 1330, *pg.* 1704
TEFLON - Glass Flowmeter - DWYER INSTRUMENTS INC.; *pg.* 1330, *pg.* 694
TEFLON - Inner Liner - EDELBROCK CORPORATION; *pg.* 204, *pg.* 293
TEFLON - Cable - W.L. GORE & ASSOCIATES, INC.; *pg.* 122, *pg.* 388
TEFZEL - Film - E.I. DU PONT DE NEMOURS & COMPANY; *pg.* 1159, *pg.* 390
TEFZEL - Cable Tie - PANDUIT CORP.; *pg.* 661, *pg.* 663
TEG - Hemostasis Analyzer - HAEMONETICS CORPORATION; *pg.* 1538, *pg.* 802
TEGADERM - Medical Transparent Dressing - 3M COMPANY; *pg.* 1142, *pg.* 956
TEGAGEN - Alginate Dressing - 3M COMPANY; *pg.* 1142, *pg.* 956
TEGAPORE - Wound Contact Material - 3M COMPANY; *pg.* 1142, *pg.* 956
TEGASORB - Ulcer Dressing - 3M COMPANY; *pg.* 1142, *pg.* 956
TEGRA - Sorter - KEY TECHNOLOGY, INC.; *pg.* 868, *pg.* 1847
TEGREEN - Nutritional Supplement - NU SKIN ENTERPRISES, INC.; *pg.* 518, *pg.* 1755
TEGRIS - Thermoplastic Composite - MILLIKEN & COMPANY; *pg.* 696, *pg.* 1622
TEI - Technology Research Methodology - FORRESTER RESEARCH, INC.; *pg.* 1642, *pg.* 807
TEIJIN - Film - E.I. DU PONT DE NEMOURS & COMPANY; *pg.* 1159, *pg.* 390
TEIJIN - Plastic Film - TEKRA CORPORATION; *pg.* 1184, *pg.* 1884
TEIJIN TETORON - Polyester Film - E.I. DU PONT DE NEMOURS & COMPANY; *pg.* 1159, *pg.* 390
TEJAVA - Tea - CRYSTAL GEYSER WATER COMPANY; *pg.* 248, *pg.* 57
TEK - Series Resistance Heating Cables - THERMON AMERICAS INC.; *pg.* 1077, *pg.* 1744
TEK - Software - TRIMBLE NAVIGATION LIMITED; *pg.* 1384, *pg.* 288
TEK-CONNECT - Plastic & Rubber - TEKNOR APEX COMPANY; *pg.* 1889, *pg.* 1605
TEK-LOK - Fastener - LONG-LOK FASTENERS CORP.; *pg.* 1053, *pg.* 1416
TEK-SPHERES - Plastic & Rubber - TEKNOR APEX COMPANY; *pg.* 1889, *pg.* 1605
TEK-TOUGH - Plastic & Rubber - TEKNOR APEX COMPANY; *pg.* 1889, *pg.* 1605
TEK TWILL - Shirts - ELBECO INCORPORATED; *pg.* 40, *pg.* 1584
TEKALOID - Coating & Finish - NOV AMERON; *pg.* 100, *pg.* 187
TEKBOND - Plastic & Rubber - TEKNOR APEX COMPANY; *pg.* 1889, *pg.* 1605
TEKLAC - Food Ingredient - FOREMOST FARMS USA COOPERATIVE; *pg.* 856, *pg.* 1854
TEKNI-FILMS - Pharmaceutical Packaging Film - TEKNI-PLEX, INC.; *pg.* 1470, *pg.* 1122
TEKNI-PLEX - Pharmaceutical Packaging Film - TEKNI-PLEX, INC.; *pg.* 1470, *pg.* 1122
TEKNIFLEX - Film - TEKNI-PLEX, INC.; *pg.* 1470, *pg.* 1122
TEKNIK - Footwear - CAPEZIO BALLET MAKERS INC.; *pg.* 1805, *pg.* 1125
TEKNISEAL - Closure Liner Sealings Materials - TEKNI-PLEX, INC.; *pg.* 1470, *pg.* 1122
TEKNIT - Fabric & Flooring - INTERFACE, INC.; *pg.* 695, *pg.* 512
TEKNO - Fragrance - PARFUMS DE COEUR LTD.; *pg.* 519, *pg.* 376
TEKNO-LOW - Footwear - CAPEZIO BALLET MAKERS INC.; *pg.* 1805, *pg.* 1125
TEKPANEL - Thermoplastic Product - GARAGETEK INC.; *pg.* 1457, *pg.* 1179
TEKRAK - Vibration Resistant Measuring Equipment Support System - KEWAUNEE SCIENTIFIC CORPORATION; *pg.* 931, *pg.* 1391
TEKRON - Plastic & Rubber - TEKNOR APEX COMPANY; *pg.* 1889, *pg.* 1605
TEKSERVICE - Ceramic & Plastic Product - COORSTEK, INC.; *pg.* 77, *pg.* 330
TEKSOLUTIONS - Fabric & Flooring - INTERFACE, INC.; *pg.* 695, *pg.* 512
TEKTUFF - Plastic & Rubber - TEKNOR APEX COMPANY; *pg.* 1889, *pg.* 1605
TEKWARE - Sportswear - THE NORTH FACE, INC.; *pg.* 1840, *pg.* 252
TEKZONE - Wrist Brace - BECTON, DICKINSON & COMPANY; *pg.* 1501, *pg.* 1068
TEL-STIK - Equipment for Lifting & Lowering Materials - BLOUNT INTERNATIONAL, INC.; *pg.* 1043, *pg.* 1501
TELADAPTIVE - Software System - FAIR ISAAC CORPORATION; *pg.* 1247, *pg.* 955
TELAFLEX - Metal Telescopic Cover - DYNATECT MANUFACTURING INC.; *pg.* 1330, *pg.* 1883
TELALERT - Chemical Products - AIR PRODUCTS AND CHEMICALS, INC.; *pg.* 1145, *pg.* 1513
TELAR - Herbicide - E.I. DU PONT DE NEMOURS & COMPANY; *pg.* 1159, *pg.* 390
TELASSISTANCE - Computer Network - EASTMAN KODAK COMPANY; *pg.* 1408, *pg.* 1333
TELATUBES - Metal Telescopic Cover - DYNATECT MANUFACTURING INC.; *pg.* 1330, *pg.* 1883
TELAWEAVE - Furniture - TELESCOPE CASUAL FURNITURE INC.; *pg.* 944, *pg.* 1162
TELAWEAVE VINYL MESH - Indoor/Outdoor Aluminum Furniture - TELESCOPE CASUAL FURNITURE INC.; *pg.* 944, *pg.* 1162
TELAZOL - Veterinary Anesthetic - PFIZER INC.; *pg.* 1581, *pg.* 1278
TELCAR - Plastic & Rubber - TEKNOR APEX COMPANY; *pg.* 1889, *pg.* 1605
TELCOT - Electronic Marketing System - PLAINS COTTON COOPERATIVE ASSOCIATION; *pg.* 697, *pg.* 1726
TELE-CUSTOMER - Product Information Service - EASTMAN KODAK COMPANY; *pg.* 1408, *pg.* 1333
TELE-EKTRALITE - Cameras - EASTMAN KODAK COMPANY; *pg.* 1408, *pg.* 1333
TELE-STYLELITE - Cameras - EASTMAN KODAK COMPANY; *pg.* 1408, *pg.* 1333
TELE-THERMOMETER - Scientific Instruments - YSI INCORPORATED; *pg.* 1438, *pg.* 1483
TELE TONE - Footwear - CAPEZIO BALLET MAKERS INC.; *pg.* 1805, *pg.* 1125
TELEBELT - Telescopic-Truck Mounted Belt Conveyor - PUTZMEISTER AMERICA; *pg.* 1371, *pg.* 1896
TELEBET - Games - PENN NATIONAL GAMING, INC.; *pg.* 574, *pg.* 1595
TELEBROKER - Automated Telephone Trading System - CHARLES SCHWAB & COMPANY, INC.; *pg.* 734, *pg.* 215
TELECASTER - Electric Guitar - FENDER MUSICAL INSTRUMENTS CORPORATION; *pg.* 547, *pg.* 21
TELECASTER ASH - Electric Guitar - FENDER MUSICAL INSTRUMENTS CORPORATION; *pg.* 547, *pg.* 21
TELECASTER BLACKOUT - Electric Guitar - FENDER MUSICAL INSTRUMENTS CORPORATION; *pg.* 547, *pg.* 21
TELECASTER CUSTOM - Electric Guitar - FENDER MUSICAL INSTRUMENTS CORPORATION; *pg.* 547, *pg.* 21
TELECASTER DELUXE - Electric Guitar - FENDER MUSICAL INSTRUMENTS CORPORATION; *pg.* 547, *pg.* 21
TELECASTER LEFT HAND - Electric Guitar - FENDER MUSICAL INSTRUMENTS CORPORATION; *pg.* 547, *pg.* 21
TELECASTER THINLINE - Electric Guitar - FENDER MUSICAL INSTRUMENTS CORPORATION; *pg.* 547, *pg.* 21
TELECENTER - Communication Product - RAULAND-BORG CORPORATION; *pg.* 666, *pg.* 634
TELECHART - Computer Programs & Database - WORDEN BROTHERS, INC.; *pg.* 823, *pg.* 1372
TELECHIEF - Wireless Remote Control System - CONTROL CHIEF HOLDINGS, INC.; *pg.* 630, *pg.* 1518
TELE.COM - Publisher - UNITED BUSINESS MEDIA LLC; *pg.* 1697, *pg.* 1177
TELECOM GEAR - Magazine - DOMINION ENTERPRISES; *pg.* 1636, *pg.* 1796
TELECONNECT MAGAZINE - Magazine - UNITED BUSINESS MEDIA LLC; *pg.* 1697, *pg.* 1177
TELECONTINUITY SERVICE - Telecommunications Device - TELECOMMUNICATION SYSTEMS INC.; *pg.* 483, *pg.* 754
TELECOPIER - Printer - XEROX CORPORATION; *pg.* 494, *pg.* 365

TELEDESIGN - Radio Modem - RF INDUSTRIES, LTD.; *pg.* 461, *pg.* 208
TELEDROP - Cable - TIMES FIBER COMMUNICATIONS, INC.; *pg.* 681, *pg.* 382
TELEFLASH - Spectrophotometer - X-RITE, INCORPORATED; *pg.* 1437, *pg.* 891
TELEFLO - Pump Product - IDEX CORPORATION; *pg.* 1347, *pg.* 623
TELEFLORA - Flowers By Wire - TELEFLORA LLC; *pg.* 1801, *pg.* 140
TELEFORM - Software - AUTONOMY, INC.; *pg.* 358, *pg.* 212
TELEFORM - Software - SCANTRON CORPORATION; *pg.* 467, *pg.* 922
TELEFUSE - Telecom Fuses - BOURNS, INC.; *pg.* 627, *pg.* 193
THE TELEGRAPH - Illinois Newspaper - FREEDOM COMMUNICATIONS, INC.; *pg.* 1643, *pg.* 110
TELEGYR 8500 - EMS-Energy Management Systems - SIEMENS BUILDING TECHNOLOGIES, INC.; *pg.* 1376, *pg.* 560
TELELECT - Aerial Device - TEREX CORPORATION; *pg.* 1381, *pg.* 384
TELEMASTER - Spotting Scope/Telephoto Lens - SWIFT OPTICAL INSTRUMENTS, INC.; *pg.* 1430, *pg.* 1744
TELEMIX - Telephone interface - GATESAIR, INC.; *pg.* 640, *pg.* 1460
TELEMUNDO - Spanish-Language Television Station - NBC UNIVERSAL, INC.; *pg.* 300, *pg.* 1266
TELENABLE - Connector - MOLEX INCORPORATED; *pg.* 655, *pg.* 628
TELENAV - Navigation & Location Systems - TELENAV, INC.; *pg.* 678, *pg.* 288
TELENAV GPS NAVIGATOR - Navigation & Location Systems - TELENAV, INC.; *pg.* 678, *pg.* 288
TELENAV SHOTGUN - Navigation & Location Systems - TELENAV, INC.; *pg.* 678, *pg.* 288
TELENAV TRACK - Navigation & Location Systems - TELENAV, INC.; *pg.* 678, *pg.* 288
TELENAV VEHICLE MANAGER - Navigation & Location Systems - TELENAV, INC.; *pg.* 678, *pg.* 288
TELENAV VEHICLE TRACKER - Navigation & Location Systems - TELENAV, INC.; *pg.* 678, *pg.* 288
TELENOVEL - Educational Materials - SCHOLASTIC INC.; *pg.* 1683, *pg.* 1288
TELENURSE - Nurse Call Communications System - RAULAND-BORG CORPORATION; *pg.* 666, *pg.* 634
TELEPORT - VoIP Product - ZOOM TECHNOLOGIES, INC.; *pg.* 497, *pg.* 1317
TELESCOTIA - Banking Service - THE BANK OF NOVA SCOTIA; *pg.* 721, *pg.* 1935
TELESERVICES CALLMANAGER - Software System - ALCATEL-LUCENT; *pg.* 615, *pg.* 1094
TELESHIP - Software - UNITED PARCEL SERVICE, INC.; *pg.* 1928, *pg.* 522
TELESPAR - Telescoping Tubing - UNISTRUT CORPORATION; *pg.* 117, *pg.* 913
TELESTAR - Telescope - MEADE INSTRUMENTS CORPORATION; *pg.* 1422, *pg.* 113
TELESTREAM FLIPFACTORY - Software - EMC CORPORATION; *pg.* 391, *pg.* 825
TELESTRUT - Telescoping Strut - UNISTRUT CORPORATION; *pg.* 117, *pg.* 913
TELETAPE - Flat Undercarpet Telephone Cable - GENERAL CABLE CORPORATION; *pg.* 83, *pg.* 384
TELETILT - Antenna - COMMSCOPE; *pg.* 630, *pg.* 668
TELEVANTAGE - Computer Telephony System - VERTICAL COMMUNICATIONS, INC.; *pg.* 488, *pg.* 270
TELEVERSITY - Educational Services - 1-800-FLOWERS.COM, INC.; *pg.* 1758, *pg.* 1151
TELEVISION FOR WOMEN - Slogan - LIFETIME ENTERTAINMENT SERVICES LLC; *pg.* 296, *pg.* 1251
TELEVISION PROGRAMMING SOURCEBOOK - Programming Guide - NORTH AMERICAN PUBLISHING COMPANY; *pg.* 1671, *pg.* 1567
TELEVISIONWEEK - Newspaper - CRAIN COMMUNICATIONS, INC.; *pg.* 1631, *pg.* 879
TELEWIRE - Cable - ARRIS GROUP, INC.; *pg.* 353, *pg.* 541
TELEWIRE-DIGICON-S - Hand Tool - IDEAL INDUSTRIES, INC.; *pg.* 1051, *pg.* 662
TELEWIRE SUPPLY - Telecommunications System - ARRIS GROUP, INC.; *pg.* 353, *pg.* 541
TELEX - Communication Equipment - BOSCH COMMUNICATIONS INC.; *pg.* 626, *pg.* 919
TELEX LEGACY - Communication Equipment - BOSCH COMMUNICATIONS INC.; *pg.* 626, *pg.* 919
TELIGEN - Medical Device - BOSTON SCIENTIFIC CORPORATION; *pg.* 1508, *pg.* 831
TELINNOVATION - Echo Canceller Software - TEXAS INSTRUMENTS INCORPORATED; *pg.* 679, *pg.* 1688
TELKOM-2 - Satellite - ORBITAL ATK; *pg.* 1425, *pg.* 1779
TELL-I-VISION - Guides and Folders - SMEAD MANUFACTURING COMPANY; *pg.* 470, *pg.* 926
TELL YOUR STORY - Tagline - SHUTTERFLY, INC.; *pg.* 1280, *pg.* 192
TELLIANT - Software - TELLABS, INC.; *pg.* 678, *pg.* 637
TELLIEUR - Bath Product - KOHLER CO.; *pg.* 91, *pg.* 1862
TELOGY NETWORKS, INC. - Telecommunications Engineering Services - TEXAS INSTRUMENTS INCORPORATED; *pg.* 679, *pg.* 1688
TELONE - Soil Fumigant - DOW AGROSCIENCES LLC; *pg.* 1156, *pg.* 684
TELSMITH - Paving Equipment - ASTEC INDUSTRIES, INC.; *pg.* 69, *pg.* 1628
TELSMITH - Quarry Plants - TELSMITH, INC.; *pg.* 1381, *pg.* 1871
TELUS AGENTANYWHERE - Home Based Contact Centre - TELUS CORPORATION; *pg.* 1952, *pg.* 1912
TELUS ASSET TRACKER - Cellular Services - TELUS CORPORATION; *pg.* 1952, *pg.* 1912
TELUS BUSINESS ONE - Business Service - TELUS CORPORATION; *pg.* 1952, *pg.* 1912
TELUS FLEET TRACKER - Cellular Services - TELUS CORPORATION; *pg.* 1952, *pg.* 1912
TELUS MOBILITY - Cellular Services - TELUS CORPORATION; *pg.* 1952, *pg.* 1912
TELUS NAVIGATOR - Cellular Services - TELUS CORPORATION; *pg.* 1952, *pg.* 1912
TELUS RESOURCE TRACKER - Cellular Services - TELUS CORPORATION; *pg.* 1952, *pg.* 1912
TELUS SAFETYNET - Energy Solution - TELUS CORPORATION; *pg.* 1952, *pg.* 1912
TELUS XPRESS - Conferencing Service - TELUS CORPORATION; *pg.* 1952, *pg.* 1912
TELVISANT - Fleet Management System - TRIMBLE NAVIGATION LIMITED; *pg.* 1384, *pg.* 288
TELZIR - Pharmaceutical Product - VERTEX PHARMACEUTICALS INCORPORATED; *pg.* 1606, *pg.* 801
TEM - Telecom Expense Management - CALERO SOFTWARE, LLC; *pg.* 368, *pg.* 1333
TEM-COTE - Food Product - BUNGE LIMITED; *pg.* 842, *pg.* 1351
TEM-PLUS - Food Product - BUNGE LIMITED; *pg.* 842, *pg.* 1351
TEM-U-LAC - Screw Conveyor Coupling Bolts - SCREW CONVEYOR INDUSTRIES; *pg.* 1374, *pg.* 682
TEM-U-LOC - Casing Construction - SCREW CONVEYOR INDUSTRIES; *pg.* 1374, *pg.* 682
TEMARIL-P - Veterinary Antipruritic Antitussive - PFIZER INC.; *pg.* 1581, *pg.* 1278
TEMECULA - Furniture - FLEXSTEEL INDUSTRIES, INC.; *pg.* 925, *pg.* 707
TEMFLEX - Electrical Tape - 3M COMPANY; *pg.* 1142, *pg.* 956
TEMODAR - Medicine - MERCK & CO., INC.; *pg.* 1566, *pg.* 1077
TEMP-A-SURE - Indicator Strip - STERIS CORPORATION; *pg.* 1597, *pg.* 1464
TEMP & HUMIDITY ALERTS - Electronic Product - WINLAND ELECTRONICS, INC.; *pg.* 688, *pg.* 928
TEMP ASSURE - Nutritional Product - NUTRACEUTICAL INTERNATIONAL CORPORATION; *pg.* 1576, *pg.* 1753
TEMP-ASSURE AIR - Shipping Technology - FEDEX CORPORATION; *pg.* 1907, *pg.* 1642
TEMP-ASSURE VALIDATED AIR - Shipping Technology - FEDEX CORPORATION; *pg.* 1907, *pg.* 1642
TEMP-LITES - Utility Lighting - AFC CABLE SYSTEMS, INC.; *pg.* 1294, *pg.* 835
TEMP-PAD - Medical Product - CINCINNATI SUB-ZERO PRODUCTS, INC.; *pg.* 1070, *pg.* 1411
TEMP-PLATE - Heat Transfer System - PAUL MUELLER COMPANY; *pg.* 706, *pg.* 1007
TEMP PRO - Food Product - LEPRINO FOODS COMPANY; *pg.* 874, *pg.* 320
TEMP-RITE - Insulated Tray Systems - ALADDIN TEMP-RITE, LLC; *pg.* 1013, *pg.* 1635
TEMP-RITE II - Cook/Chill Meal Service Systems - ALADDIN TEMP-RITE, LLC; *pg.* 1013, *pg.* 1635
TEMP RITE II EXCEL - Cook/Chill Meal Service Systems - ALADDIN TEMP-RITE, LLC; *pg.* 1013, *pg.* 1635
TEMP ROCK - Premium Roll Covers - VAIL RUBBER WORKS, INC.; *pg.* 1891, *pg.* 906
TEMPA-DOT - Thermometer - 3M COMPANY; *pg.* 1142, *pg.* 956
TEMPALLOY - Plastic Compound & Resin - A. SCHULMAN, INC.; *pg.* 1144, *pg.* 1452
TEMPALUX - Static Control Product - WESTLAKE PLASTICS COMPANY; *pg.* 1892, *pg.* 1548
TEMPAR-GLAS - Custom-Tempered Glass - VIRGINIA GLASS PRODUCTS CORPORATION; *pg.* 119, *pg.* 1788
TEMPAR-GLAS ALL-GLASS ENTRANCES - Tempered Glass Entrance Doors & Sidelights - VIRGINIA GLASS PRODUCTS CORPORATION; *pg.* 119, *pg.* 1788
TEMPAR-GLAS SHOWER DOORS - Shower Doors - VIRGINIA GLASS PRODUCTS CORPORATION; *pg.* 119, *pg.* 1788
TEMPAR-GLAS SLIDING DOORS - Sliding Doors - VIRGINIA GLASS PRODUCTS CORPORATION; *pg.* 119, *pg.* 1788
TEMPAR-GLAS SPANDREL GLASS - Glass With Ceramic Enamel Coating - VIRGINIA GLASS PRODUCTS CORPORATION; *pg.* 119, *pg.* 1788
TEMPCAL - Tester - HOWELL INSTRUMENTS INC.; *pg.* 1417, *pg.* 1695
TEMPCAL TESTER - Thermal Sensor Tester - HOWELL INSTRUMENTS INC.; *pg.* 1417, *pg.* 1695
TEMPCONTROL - Thermostatic Water Controller - SYMMONS INDUSTRIES, INC.; *pg.* 114, *pg.* 803
TEMPEST - Knife - BUCK KNIVES, INC.; *pg.* 1828, *pg.* 550
TEMPEST - Tables - HOWE FURNITURE CORPORATION; *pg.* 928, *pg.* 998
TEMPESTT - Footwear - STEVEN MADDEN, LTD.; *pg.* 1819, *pg.* 1176
TEMPGARD - Paint And Stain Product - BENJAMIN MOORE & CO.; *pg.* 1440, *pg.* 1085
TEMPGARD - Test Equipment - SPX THERMAL PRODUCT SOLUTIONS; *pg.* 1378, *pg.* 1555
TEMPLATE - Office Furniture - STEELCASE INC.; *pg.* 475, *pg.* 889
TEMPLE OF GOLD - Video Game - INTERNATIONAL GAME TECHNOLOGY; *pg.* 957, *pg.* 1024
TEMPLE OF TREASURE - Video Game - INTERNATIONAL GAME TECHNOLOGY; *pg.* 957, *pg.* 1024
TEMPLETON - Mutual Funds - FRANKLIN RESOURCES, INC.; *pg.* 760, *pg.* 254
TEMPMASTER - Frame Warmer Machine - THE HILSINGER CO.; *pg.* 1416, *pg.* 841
TEMPMATE - Thermal Processing Equipment - SURFACE COMBUSTION, INC.; *pg.* 1077, *pg.* 1462
TEMPO - Furniture - ASHLEY FURNITURE INDUSTRIES, INC.; *pg.* 914, *pg.* 1852
TEMPO - Theatrical Fixtures - BALLANTYNE STRONG, INC.; *pg.* 623, *pg.* 1013
TEMPO - Textiles - BERNHARDT DESIGN; *pg.* 918, *pg.* 1381
TEMPO - Furniture - HAWORTH, INC.; *pg.* 402, *pg.* 891
TEMPO - Tequila - JIM BEAM BRANDS CO.; *pg.* 1965, *pg.* 601
TEMPO - Tissues - THE PROCTER & GAMBLE COMPANY; *pg.* 1129, *pg.* 1418
TEMPO - Auto Cleaning Product - S.C. JOHNSON & SON, INC.; *pg.* 334, *pg.* 1889
TEMPORALSCANNER - Thermometer System - EXERGEN CORPORATION; *pg.* 1412, *pg.* 855
TEMPOSONICS - Transducers - MTS SYSTEMS CORPORATION; *pg.* 442, *pg.* 923
TEMPRANO - Polymer Product - CHEMTURA CORPORATION; *pg.* 1152, *pg.* 355
TEMPRITE - Engineered Polymers - THE LUBRIZOL CORPORATION; *pg.* 1171, *pg.* 1481
TEMPRO - Flame Retardant Protective Garments - E.I. DU PONT DE NEMOURS & COMPANY; *pg.* 1159, *pg.* 390
TEMPROFJ - Lumber - TEMBEC INC.; *pg.* 114, *pg.* 1957
TEMPROOF - Fireplace Product - UNITED GILSONITE LABORATORIES; *pg.* 1449, *pg.* 1527
TEMPSCRIBE - Temperature Recorder - BACHARACH INC.; *pg.* 1400, *pg.* 1556
TEMPSHIELD - Thermostatic Pressure Valve - THE CHICAGO FAUCET COMPANY; *pg.* 1044, *pg.* 606
TEMPSHIELD - Reflective Foil Air Cellular Insulation - SEALED AIR CORPORATION; *pg.* 1468, *pg.* 1058
TEMPSHIELD-MFL - Reflective Air Cellular Insulation - SEALED AIR CORPORATION; *pg.* 1468, *pg.* 1058
TEMPTING - Carpet - BEAULIEU GROUP, LLC; *pg.* 917, *pg.* 529
TEMPTROL - Pressure Balanced Safety Shower Systems -

SYMMONS INDUSTRIES, INC.; *pg.* 114, *pg.* 803
TEMPTROL 2000 - Pressure-Balancing Tub - SYMMONS INDUSTRIES, INC.; *pg.* 114, *pg.* 803
TEMPTROL II - Pressure-Balancing Tub - SYMMONS INDUSTRIES, INC.; *pg.* 114, *pg.* 803
TEMPTUBE - Sterilization Product - PROPPER MANUFACTURING COMPANY, INC.; *pg.* 1586, *pg.* 1175
TEMPUR - Mattress - RELAX THE BACK CORPORATION; *pg.* 940, *pg.* 120
TEMPUR - Pressure Relieving Material - TEMPUR SEALY INTERNATIONAL, INC.; *pg.* 944, *pg.* 731
TEMPUR ADVANCED ERGO SYSTEM - Bed Base - TEMPUR SEALY INTERNATIONAL, INC.; *pg.* 944, *pg.* 731
TEMPUR-FIT - Linens - TEMPUR SEALY INTERNATIONAL, INC.; *pg.* 944, *pg.* 731
TEMPUR-FLEX - Mattress System - TEMPUR SEALY INTERNATIONAL, INC.; *pg.* 944, *pg.* 731
TEMPUR-HD - Mattress Material - TEMPUR SEALY INTERNATIONAL, INC.; *pg.* 944, *pg.* 731
TEMPUR PEDIC - Mattress - TEMPUR SEALY INTERNATIONAL, INC.; *pg.* 944, *pg.* 731
TEMPUR-PEDIC MATTRESS OVERLAY - Cushion - TEMPUR SEALY INTERNATIONAL, INC.; *pg.* 944, *pg.* 731
TEMTROL - Air Conditioners - NORTEK, INC.; *pg.* 100, *pg.* 1607
TEN MILE - Jacket - KEY INDUSTRIES, INC.; *pg.* 43, *pg.* 714
TEN-MILE - Socks - WOOLRICH, INC.; *pg.* 699, *pg.* 1595
TEN PLAY - Video Poker - INTERNATIONAL GAME TECHNOLOGY; *pg.* 957, *pg.* 1024
TEN REN - Beverages - THE COCA-COLA COMPANY; *pg.* 240, *pg.* 493
TEN-TEN - Medical Device - BOSTON SCIENTIFIC CORPORATION; *pg.* 1508, *pg.* 831
TEN TEN - Diagnostic Catheter - ST. JUDE MEDICAL, INC.; *pg.* 1596, *pg.* 963
TEN TERRIFIC NAILS - Applied Nails - COVER GIRL COSMETICS; *pg.* 506, *pg.* 772
TEN TIMES GOLD - Slots - INTERNATIONAL GAME TECHNOLOGY; *pg.* 957, *pg.* 1024
TEN TIMES PAY - Slots - INTERNATIONAL GAME TECHNOLOGY; *pg.* 957, *pg.* 1024
TEN TIMES PAY RED WHITE & BLUE - Slots - INTERNATIONAL GAME TECHNOLOGY; *pg.* 957, *pg.* 1024
TEN-TUF ENVELOPES - Envelopes - TENSION ENVELOPE CORPORATION; *pg.* 483, *pg.* 986
TENACIOUS - Adhesive Tape & Patch - MCNETT CORPORATION; *pg.* 1839, *pg.* 1817
TENACIOUS TAPE - Adhesive Backed Tape & Patching Material - MCNETT CORPORATION; *pg.* 1839, *pg.* 1817
TENARA - Fabric - W.L. GORE & ASSOCIATES, INC.; *pg.* 122, *pg.* 388
TENAX - Chemical Product - WESTROCK COMPANY; *pg.* 1472, *pg.* 1805
TENCHU - Game - ACTIVISION BLIZZARD, INC.; *pg.* 948, *pg.* 271
TENDER & TASTY - Chicken - PERDUE FARMS INCORPORATED; *pg.* 889, *pg.* 777
TENDER CHOICE - Meats - CARGILL, INC.; *pg.* 845, *pg.* 965
TENDER O'S - Breakfast Cereals - NATURE'S PATH FOODS INC.; *pg.* 833, *pg.* 1908
TENDER PLUS - Fresh Pork - HATFIELD QUALITY MEATS, INC.; *pg.* 861, *pg.* 1537
TENDER QUICK - Salt - DOW CHEMICAL; *pg.* 1156, *pg.* 1563
TENDER ROAST SANDWICH - Roasted Chicken - KFC CORPORATION; *pg.* 1733, *pg.* 735
TENDER TOUCH - Medical Product - UTAH MEDICAL PRODUCTS, INC.; *pg.* 1605, *pg.* 1752
TENDER VITTLES - Cat Food - NESTLE PURINA PETCARE COMPANY; *pg.* 1479, *pg.* 1000
TENDERCARE - Personal Care Product - THE HAIN CELESTIAL GROUP, INC.; *pg.* 860, *pg.* 1172
TENDERCLOUD - Healthcare Product - GF HEALTH PRODUCTS, INC.; *pg.* 1535, *pg.* 508
TENDERCRISP - Chicken Sandwich - BURGER KING CORPORATION; *pg.* 1719, *pg.* 440
TENDERFLAKE - Pastry - MAPLE LEAF FOODS INC.; *pg.* 875, *pg.* 1927
TENDERFLO - Medical Product - GF HEALTH PRODUCTS, INC.; *pg.* 1535, *pg.* 508
TENDERGRILL - Chicken Sandwich - BURGER KING CORPORATION; *pg.* 1719, *pg.* 440
TENDERLY - Bathroom Tissue - GEORGIA-PACIFIC LLC; *pg.* 1458, *pg.* 507
TENDERWET - Medical Product - MEDLINE INDUSTRIES, INC.; *pg.* 1562, *pg.* 635
TENDRE POISON - Women's Fragrance - PARFUMS CHRISTIAN DIOR, INC; *pg.* 519, *pg.* 1276
TENDRIL - Pacemaker Leads - ST. JUDE MEDICAL, INC.; *pg.* 1596, *pg.* 963
TENDU - Footwear - CAPEZIO BALLET MAKERS INC.; *pg.* 1805, *pg.* 1125
TENEO - Furniture - HERMAN MILLER, INC.; *pg.* 926, *pg.* 913
TENEO - Dental Equipment - SIRONA DENTAL SYSTEMS, INC.; *pg.* 1429, *pg.* 1175
TENETCARE - Diagnostic & Outpatient Care - TENET HEALTHCARE CORPORATION; *pg.* 1601, *pg.* 1688
TENITE - Cellulosics - EASTMAN CHEMICAL COMPANY; *pg.* 1159, *pg.* 1636
TENLEY - Furniture - ASHLEY FURNITURE INDUSTRIES, INC.; *pg.* 914, *pg.* 1852
TENLEY - Hat - WOODEN SHIPS OF HOBOKEN; *pg.* 35, *pg.* 1315
TENNANT CAPITAL - Surface Maintenance Machine - TENNANT COMPANY; *pg.* 1381, *pg.* 944
TENNANT FINANCIAL - Surface Maintenance Machine - TENNANT COMPANY; *pg.* 1381, *pg.* 944
TENNESSEE - Packaging Product - BUCKEYE CORRUGATED INC.; *pg.* 1454, *pg.* 1400
TENNESSEE PRIDE - Sausage - ODOM'S TENNESSEE PRIDE SAUSAGE, INC.; *pg.* 887, *pg.* 1640
TENNESSEE RIVER - Apparel - ENNIS, INC.; *pg.* 393, *pg.* 1727
TENNEY JR. - Test Equipment - SPX THERMAL PRODUCT SOLUTIONS; *pg.* 1378, *pg.* 1555
TENNEYMITE - Test Equipment - SPX THERMAL PRODUCT SOLUTIONS; *pg.* 1378, *pg.* 1555
TENNIS BALL TEE - Clothing - K-SWISS; *pg.* 1837, *pg.* 306
TENNTROL - Institute Control System - SPX THERMAL PRODUCT SOLUTIONS; *pg.* 1378, *pg.* 1555
TENOGLIDE - Medical Device - INTEGRA LIFESCIENCES HOLDINGS CORPORATION; *pg.* 1545, *pg.* 1109
TENOX - Food-Grade Antioxidants - EASTMAN CHEMICAL COMPANY; *pg.* 1159, *pg.* 1636
TENSETTE - Automatic Pipet - HACH COMPANY; *pg.* 1415, *pg.* 334
TENSIL BOLT - Wire Cloth - NEWARK WIRE CLOTH CO.; *pg.* 99, *pg.* 1052
TENSION GROOVED ENVELOPES - Envelopes - TENSION ENVELOPE CORPORATION; *pg.* 483, *pg.* 986
TENSIONED COSMOPOLITAN - Screen - DA-LITE SCREEN COMPANY; *pg.* 632, *pg.* 698
TENSIONERS - Tensioners - ELECTROID CO; *pg.* 1333, *pg.* 1123
TENSIONET - Packaging Net - RSI HOME PRODUCTS; *pg.* 108, *pg.* 1381
TENSOR - Home Care Product - BECTON, DICKINSON & COMPANY; *pg.* 1501, *pg.* 1068
TENSOR - Analytical Device - BRUKER CORPORATION; *pg.* 1511, *pg.* 788
TENT SURE - Water Repellent - MCNETT CORPORATION; *pg.* 1839, *pg.* 1817
TENTHSET - Adjustable Boring Bars - KENNAMETAL INC.; *pg.* 1052, *pg.* 1547
TENURE - Dental Bonding System - DEN-MAT CORPORATION; *pg.* 1522, *pg.* 271
TENURE QUIK - Bonding Adhesive - DEN-MAT CORPORATION; *pg.* 1522, *pg.* 271
TENURE UNIBOND - Dental Bonding System - DEN-MAT CORPORATION; *pg.* 1522, *pg.* 271
TEOMA - Internet Search Technology - IAC SEARCH & MEDIA, INC.; *pg.* 1257, *pg.* 171
TEONEX - Film - E.I. DU PONT DE NEMOURS & COMPANY; *pg.* 1159, *pg.* 390
TEONEX - Plastic Film - TEKRA CORPORATION; *pg.* 1184, *pg.* 1884
TEPEE - Socks & Knitted Headwear - WIGWAM MILLS, INC.; *pg.* 15, *pg.* 1894
TEPHRAM - Coating - PPG INDUSTRIES, INC.; *pg.* 1445, *pg.* 1579
TEQUILA CORAZON - Beverage - SIDNEY FRANK IMPORTING CO., INC.; *pg.* 1970, *pg.* 1184
TEQUILOCO - Beer - UNITED STATES BEVERAGE LLC; *pg.* 266, *pg.* 379
TEQUIZA - Malt Beverage - ANHEUSER-BUSCH COMPANIES, LLC; *pg.* 237, *pg.* 991
TERA - Seal - ENTEGRIS, INC.; *pg.* 1882, *pg.* 788
TERABYTE VOLUME ENGINE - Software - CONDUSIV TECHNOLOGIES; *pg.* 379, *pg.* 51
TERADATA - Data Warehousing Software - NCR CORPORATION; *pg.* 443, *pg.* 531
TERAFAB - Inspection System - KLA-TENCOR CORPORATION; *pg.* 1353, *pg.* 146
TERAHUB - High Capacity Broadband Telecommunications Switching Apparatus - ALCATEL-LUCENT USA, INC.; *pg.* 615, *pg.* 1728
TERALOADER - Data Storage System - QUALSTAR CORPORATION; *pg.* 458, *pg.* 279
TERASAM - Software - EMC CORPORATION; *pg.* 391, *pg.* 825
TERASCAN - Reticle Inspection System - KLA-TENCOR CORPORATION; *pg.* 1353, *pg.* 146
TERASCANHR - Inspection System - KLA-TENCOR CORPORATION; *pg.* 1353, *pg.* 146
TERASCANXR - Inspection System - KLA-TENCOR CORPORATION; *pg.* 1353, *pg.* 146
TERASIL - Disperse Dyes - HUNTSMAN CORPORATION; *pg.* 1167, *pg.* 1758
TERASTAR - Reticle Inspection System - KLA-TENCOR CORPORATION; *pg.* 1353, *pg.* 146
TERATHANE - Polyurethane Chemicals - INVISTA B.V.; *pg.* 1168, *pg.* 723
TERATHANE - Chemical Product - SPECTRUM CHEMICALS & LABORATORY PRODUCTS, INC.; *pg.* 1181, *pg.* 94
TERATOP - Disperse Dyes - HUNTSMAN CORPORATION; *pg.* 1167, *pg.* 1758
TERAYON - Digital Video Product - HARMONIC, INC.; *pg.* 402, *pg.* 246
TERAZOL - Healthcare Product - JOHNSON & JOHNSON; *pg.* 1549, *pg.* 1091
TERBUTALINE SULFATE - Pharmaceutical Product - LANNETT COMPANY, INC.; *pg.* 1555, *pg.* 1566
TERCET - Bath Product - KOHLER CO.; *pg.* 91, *pg.* 1862
TEREMEC - Turf Product - PBI/GORDON CORPORATION; *pg.* 1176, *pg.* 985
TEREX - Compact Equipment & Crane - TEREX CORPORATION; *pg.* 1381, *pg.* 384
TEREX AMERICAN - Crane - TEREX CORPORATION; *pg.* 1381, *pg.* 384
TEREXLIFT - Crane - TEREX CORPORATION; *pg.* 1381, *pg.* 384
TERG-A-ZYME - Cleaning Detergent - ALCONOX, INC.; *pg.* 325, *pg.* 1351
TERGAJET - Low-Foaming Phosphate-Free Powdered Detergent - ALCONOX, INC.; *pg.* 325, *pg.* 1351
TERGITOL - Surfactant - THE DOW CHEMICAL COMPANY; *pg.* 1157, *pg.* 898
TERGITOL - Chemical Product - SPECTRUM CHEMICALS & LABORATORY PRODUCTS, INC.; *pg.* 1181, *pg.* 94
TERIC - Alcohol Ethoxylate - HUNTSMAN CORPORATION; *pg.* 1167, *pg.* 1758
TERIYAKI - Chicken Product - MAPLE LODGE FARMS LTD.; *pg.* 876, *pg.* 1918
TERLIPRESSIN - Peptide - PDL BIOPHARMA INC.; *pg.* 1580, *pg.* 1022
TERM-A-NUT - Screw-On-Connector - IDEAL INDUSTRIES, INC.; *pg.* 1051, *pg.* 662
TERM LIFE - Insurance - PAN-AMERICAN LIFE INSURANCE COMPANY; *pg.* 1213, *pg.* 747
TERMINATOR - Mobile Firefighting Equipment - KIDDE FIRE FIGHTING; *pg.* 1170, *pg.* 1531
TERMINATOR - Connection System - THERMON AMERICAS INC.; *pg.* 1077, *pg.* 1744
THE TERMINATORS - Fastening System - TEXTRON INC.; *pg.* 235, *pg.* 1607
TERMINIX - Termite & Pest Control - THE SERVICEMASTER COMPANY, LLC; *pg.* 335, *pg.* 1646
TERMITE KILL III CONCENTRATE - Insect Controller - UNIVERSAL COOPERATIVES, INC.; *pg.* 1482, *pg.* 922
TERMITE PRUFE - Wood Destroying Insect - COPPER-BRITE, INC.; *pg.* 329, *pg.* 263
TERMOVIR - Plastics Product - AEP INDUSTRIES INC.; *pg.* 1878, *pg.* 1085
TERMUL - Emulsifiers - HUNTSMAN CORPORATION; *pg.* 1167, *pg.* 1758
TERRA - Chips - THE HAIN CELESTIAL GROUP, INC.; *pg.* 860, *pg.* 1172
TERRA - Yoga Kit - HUGGER MUGGER YOGA PRODUCTS LLC; *pg.* 1836, *pg.* 1758

TERRA - Carpet - INTERFACE, INC.; pg. 695, pg. 512
TERRA - Furniture - LA-Z-BOY INCORPORATED; pg. 932, pg. 901
TERRA - Fabric - NEUTRAL POSTURE, INC.; pg. 939, pg. 1669
TERRA - Floor Care - NILFISK-ADVANCE, INC.; pg. 332, pg. 953
TERRA CHIPS - Vegetable & Potato Snack Chips - THE HAIN CELESTIAL GROUP, INC.; pg. 860, pg. 1172
TERRA COPPER - Home & Garden Product - ENESCO, LLC; pg. 1124, pg. 620
TERRA CRAFT - Landscape Product - OWENS CORNING; pg. 102, pg. 1476
TERRA D ITALIA - Tile - ARTISTIC TILE INC.; pg. 914, pg. 1119
TERRA FORCE - Footwear - LACROSSE FOOTWEAR, INC.; pg. 1811, pg. 1503
TERRA-TIRE - High Flotation Tires - THE GOODYEAR TIRE & RUBBER COMPANY; pg. 1883, pg. 1401
TERRA-TITAN - Pump - FLOWSERVE CORPORATION; pg. 82, pg. 1719
TERRACE - Panel System - THE HON COMPANY; pg. 928, pg. 709
TERRACE - Furniture - JASPER GROUP; pg. 930, pg. 691
TERRACE CLUB - Assisted Living Services - SUNRISE SENIOR LIVING, INC.; pg. 1599, pg. 1795
TERRACE PLACE - Furniture - BASSETT FURNITURE INDUSTRIES, INCORPORATED; pg. 916, pg. 1776
TERRACINA - Bath Product - KOHLER CO.; pg. 91, pg. 1862
TERRACLOR - Polymer Product - CHEMTURA CORPORATION; pg. 1152, pg. 355
TERRACOTTA - Fabric - ETHAN ALLEN INTERIORS INC.; pg. 924, pg. 343
TERRADORO - Beverage - TRINCHERO FAMILY ESTATES; pg. 1971, pg. 197
TERRAFIRE - Construction Equipment - VERMEER MANUFACTURING COMPANY; pg. 708, pg. 711
TERRAGATOR - Agricultural Floater - AGCO CORPORATION; pg. 700, pg. 530
TERRAGUARD - Polymer Product - CHEMTURA CORPORATION; pg. 1152, pg. 355
TERRAIN - Apparel - URBAN OUTFITTERS, INC.; pg. 1789, pg. 1571
TERRALARGO - Home Builders - AV HOMES INC.; pg. 1080, pg. 20
TERRALOC - Dust Suppression Product - MONOSOL, LLC; pg. 59, pg. 694
TERRALOX - Lubricants - THE DOW CHEMICAL COMPANY; pg. 1157, pg. 898
TERRAM PARADRAIN - Slope & Wall Reinforcement - MACCAFERRI, INC.; pg. 95, pg. 780
TERRAM PARALINK - Slope & Wall Reinforcement - MACCAFERRI, INC.; pg. 95, pg. 780
TERRAMASTER - Polymer Product - CHEMTURA CORPORATION; pg. 1152, pg. 355
TERRAMESH - Slope & Wall Reinforcement - MACCAFERRI, INC.; pg. 95, pg. 780
TERRAMICA - Particleboard - POTLATCH CORPORATION; pg. 1467, pg. 1844
TERRAMM GRID - Slope & Wall Reinforcement - MACCAFERRI, INC.; pg. 95, pg. 780
TERRAMODAL - Navigation Aid - TRIMBLE NAVIGATION LIMITED; pg. 1384, pg. 288
TERRAMYCIN - Medicine - PFIZER INC.; pg. 1581, pg. 1278
TERRAMYCIN - Animal Health Product - PHIBROCHEM; pg. 1177, pg. 1124
TERRAPIN - Hardcoated Film - TEKRA CORPORATION; pg. 1184, pg. 1884
TERRAPIN RIDGES GOURMET LINE - Mustards & Sauces - FURST-MCNESS COMPANY; pg. 1476, pg. 613
TERRAQUENCH - Quenchants - THE DOW CHEMICAL COMPANY; pg. 1157, pg. 898
TERRASAIL - Chemical Product - SACHEM INC.; pg. 1180, pg. 1665
TERRASAT - Software - TRIMBLE NAVIGATION LIMITED; pg. 1384, pg. 288
TERRASOLES - Footwear - R.G. BARRY CORPORATION; pg. 1818, pg. 1470
TERRASURF - Surfactants - THE DOW CHEMICAL COMPANY; pg. 1157, pg. 898
TERRASYNC - Navigation Aid - TRIMBLE NAVIGATION LIMITED; pg. 1384, pg. 288
TERRATEK - Biodegradable Resins - MGP INGREDIENTS, INC.; pg. 877, pg. 714
TERRATEX - Fabric - INTERFACE, INC.; pg. 695, pg. 512
TERRATONE - Door - ANDERSEN CORPORATION; pg. 67, pg. 916
TERRAVISTA - Software - TRIMBLE NAVIGATION LIMITED; pg. 1384, pg. 288
TERRAWAVE - Wireless Networking Applications - TESSCO TECHNOLOGIES, INC.; pg. 679, pg. 773
TERRAZAS DE LOS ANDES - Wine - MOET HENNESSY; pg. 1966, pg. 1260
TERRAZOLE - Polymer Product - CHEMTURA CORPORATION; pg. 1152, pg. 355
TERRAZZINE - Sealant - HILLYARD, INC.; pg. 331, pg. 990
TERRAZZO - Fan - CRAFTMADE INTERNATIONAL, INC.; pg. 1295, pg. 1670
TERRAZZO - Office Furniture - STEELCASE INC.; pg. 475, pg. 889
TERREMARKS'S ENTERPRISE CLOUD - Server Platform - VERIZON TERREMARK; pg. 685, pg. 447
TERRENAP - Data Center - VERIZON TERREMARK; pg. 685, pg. 447
TERREON - Solid Surface Material - BRADLEY CORPORATION; pg. 71, pg. 1870
TERRESTRIAL TOTAL STATION - Navigation Aid - TRIMBLE NAVIGATION LIMITED; pg. 1384, pg. 288
TERRI - Clothing - ABERCROMBIE & FITCH CO.; pg. 37, pg. 1466
TERRIBLE - Beer - SLEEMAN UNIBROUE QUEBEC; pg. 265, pg. 1950
THE TERRITORY AHEAD - Online Clothing Store - IAC/INTERACTIVECORP; pg. 292, pg. 1242
TERRITORY PLANNER - Software - UNITED PARCEL SERVICE, INC.; pg. 1928, pg. 522
TERRO - Fly Ribbons - SENORET CHEMICAL COMPANY; pg. 335, pg. 1548
TERSPERSE - Dispersant - HUNTSMAN CORPORATION; pg. 1167, pg. 1758
TERTIO - Software - EVOLVING SYSTEMS, INC.; pg. 395, pg. 326
TERWET - Wetting Agents - HUNTSMAN CORPORATION; pg. 1167, pg. 1758
TESCOL - Textile Yarns - HUNTSMAN CORPORATION; pg. 1167, pg. 1758
TESCORP - Cables & Connectors - ION GEOPHYSICAL CORPORATION; pg. 1350, pg. 1708
TESEE - Software - BIO-RAD LABORATORIES, INC.; pg. 1504, pg. 101
TESEE PRECESS 24 - Software - BIO-RAD LABORATORIES, INC.; pg. 1504, pg. 101
TESEE PRECESS 48 - Software - BIO-RAD LABORATORIES, INC.; pg. 1504, pg. 101
TESLA - Software - NVIDIA CORPORATION; pg. 447, pg. 268
TESLIN - Synthetic Printing Sheet - PPG INDUSTRIES, INC.; pg. 1445, pg. 1579
TESLIN - Card Stock - TRANSILWRAP COMPANY, INC.; pg. 1470, pg. 613
TESMA - Automotive Parts - MAGNA INTERNATIONAL INC.; pg. 211, pg. 1918
TESORITOS - Food Product - FLOWERS FOODS, INC.; pg. 855, pg. 541
TESSA - Furniture - AMISCO INDUSTRIES LTD.; pg. 913, pg. 1958
TESSAA - Footwear - STEVEN MADDEN, LTD.; pg. 1819, pg. 1176
TESSCO.COM - Internet Based System - TESSCO TECHNOLOGIES, INC.; pg. 679, pg. 773
TESSELLATION EXPLORATION - Educational Materials - SCHOLASTIC INC.; pg. 1683, pg. 1288
TESSENT - Silicon Test & Yield Products - MENTOR GRAPHICS CORPORATION; pg. 432, pg. 1510
TESSERA - Glass Tile - WALKER & ZANGER, INC.; pg. 119, pg. 281
TESSUTO - Carpet - INTERFACE, INC.; pg. 695, pg. 512
TEST BOOKING CENTER - Quality Assurance Service - TRAVELZOO INC; pg. 1926, pg. 1304
TEST-GLO - Electrical Tester - IDEAL INDUSTRIES, INC.; pg. 1051, pg. 662
TEST LITE - Software - TINIUS OLSEN, INC.; pg. 1432, pg. 1541
TEST-M-LITE - Push Button Secondary Test - HD ELECTRIC COMPANY; pg. 1299, pg. 666
TEST MANAGER - Software - CRESTRON ELECTRONICS INC.; pg. 631, pg. 1116
TEST NAVIGATOR - Software - TINIUS OLSEN, INC.; pg. 1432, pg. 1541
TEST-PAK - Sterilization Product - PROPPER MANUFACTURING COMPANY, INC.; pg. 1586, pg. 1175
TEST-PRO - Multimeter - IDEAL INDUSTRIES, INC.; pg. 1051, pg. 662
TESTAMENT BOOKS - Publishing Imprint - PENGUIN RANDOM HOUSE; pg. 1675, pg. 1276
TESTCHECK - Educational Materials - RENAISSANCE LEARNING, INC.; pg. 607, pg. 1899
TESTCONNECT - Computer Software - CIMETRIX INCORPORATED; pg. 372, pg. 1756
TESTIR - Infrared Test Kit - PRECISION CONTROL SYSTEMS, INC./ RESEARCH INC.; pg. 1427, pg. 923
TESTKOMPRESS - Software System - MENTOR GRAPHICS CORPORATION; pg. 432, pg. 1510
TESTLINE - Testing Systems - MTS SYSTEMS CORPORATION; pg. 442, pg. 923
TESTMART - Online Search Tool - TECHNICAL COMMUNITIES, INC.; pg. 1283, pg. 198
TESTMASTER - Automation System - INSTRON CORPORATION; pg. 1349, pg. 839
TESTMASTER - Inspector's Test Module - VICTAULIC COMPANY; pg. 1066, pg. 1529
TESTNET - Circuit Tester - TERADYNE INC.; pg. 679, pg. 838
TESTOR - Brush-On Spray Enamel Paints, Model Kits - THE TESTOR CORPORATION; pg. 968, pg. 655
TESTORS - Models & Hobby Supplies - RPM INTERNATIONAL INC.; pg. 1447, pg. 1464
TESTOSTERONE MDTS - Treatment for Women with Low Sexual Desire - VIVUS, INC.; pg. 1608, pg. 163
TESTPACK - Testing Product - ABBOTT LABORATORIES; pg. 1484, pg. 551
TESTPACK PLUS - Testing Product - ABBOTT LABORATORIES; pg. 1484, pg. 551
TESTPOINT - Software - KEITHLEY INSTRUMENTS, INC.; pg. 1418, pg. 1473
TESTRAK - Drilling System - BAKER HUGHES INTEQ; pg. 1316, pg. 1700
TESTSTAR - Software - MTS SYSTEMS CORPORATION; pg. 442, pg. 923
TESTWARE - Software - MTS SYSTEMS CORPORATION; pg. 442, pg. 923
TESTWORKS - Software - MTS SYSTEMS CORPORATION; pg. 442, pg. 923
TETLEY - Tea Bags, Instant & Liquid Tea - TETLEY USA INC.; pg. 901, pg. 1095
TETLEY DRAWSTRING TEA BAGS - Tea - TETLEY USA INC.; pg. 901, pg. 1095
TETLEY ICED GOLD - Ready-to-Drink Iced Tea - TETLEY USA INC.; pg. 901, pg. 1095
TETLEY ICED TEA MIX - Iced Tea Mix - TETLEY USA INC.; pg. 901, pg. 1095
TETLEY MAKES IT BETTER - Tag Line - TETLEY USA INC.; pg. 901, pg. 1095
TETLEY ROUND TEA BAGS - Tea - TETLEY USA INC.; pg. 901, pg. 1095
TETORON - Plastic Film - TEKRA CORPORATION; pg. 1184, pg. 1884
TETRA - Advanced Reticle Etch System - APPLIED MATERIALS, INC.; pg. 618, pg. 264
TETRA - Pet Product - PETSMART, INC.; pg. 1481, pg. 18
TETRA-ETCH - Fluorocarbon Etchant - W.L. GORE & ASSOCIATES, INC.; pg. 122, pg. 388
TETRA PAK - Container - EDEN FOODS INC.; pg. 1019, pg. 875
TETRA-TEMP - Ceramic & Plastic Product - COORSTEK, INC.; pg. 77, pg. 330
TETRAD - Software - BIO-RAD LABORATORIES, INC.; pg. 1504, pg. 101
TETRAFLUOR - Ceramic & Plastic Product - COORSTEK, INC.; pg. 77, pg. 330
TETRAHUB - PCB Design Recommendation - CYPRESS SEMICONDUCTOR CORPORATION; pg. 1326, pg. 243
TETRAHYDRO MUGUOL - Fragrance Ingredient - INTERNATIONAL FLAVORS & FRAGRANCES INC.; pg. 512, pg. 1244
TETRALON - Ceramic & Plastic Product - COORSTEK, INC.; pg. 77, pg. 330
TETRAMAX - Software - SYNOPSYS, INC.; pg. 480, pg. 162
TETRAONE - Testing Instrument System - BECKMAN COULTER, INC.; pg. 1402, pg. 48
TETRASPECK - Molecular Probe Product - THERMO FISHER SCIENTIFIC INC.; pg. 1602, pg. 61
TETRASTAR - Food Safety Product - NEOGEN CORPORATION; pg. 883, pg. 896

First page reference indicates Business Class Edition
Second page reference indicates Geographic Edition

TETRATEX - Nanofiber Filter Media - DONALDSON COMPANY, INC.; *pg.* 1329, *pg.* 917
TETTEX - Electrical Utility Equipment - HUBBELL INCORPORATED; *pg.* 1299, *pg.* 370
TEVA - Footwear Product - DECKERS OUTDOOR CORPORATION; *pg.* 1807, *pg.* 100
TEVDEK - Biotechnology Product - GENZYME CORPORATION; *pg.* 1534, *pg.* 808
TEVETEN - Pharmaceutical Product - ABBOTT LABORATORIES; *pg.* 1484, *pg.* 551
TEVETEN - Pharmaceutical Product - VALEANT PHARMACEUTICALS INTERNATIONAL, INC.; *pg.* 1605, *pg.* 1957
TEX - Book Projects - CENVEO INC.; *pg.* 1626, *pg.* 372
TEX FINISH - Fluid Handling System - GRACO, INC.; *pg.* 1342, *pg.* 935
TEX MEX - Shoe - AEROGROUP INTERNATIONAL, INC.; *pg.* 1803, *pg.* 1055
TEX-TROP - Shirts - ELBECO INCORPORATED; *pg.* 40, *pg.* 1584
TEX TRU - Splitter - BESSER COMPANY; *pg.* 1317, *pg.* 865
TEXACO - Extended Life Coolant - CHEVRON CORPORATION; *pg.* 974, *pg.* 259
TEXACRAFT - Furniture - BROWN JORDAN INTERNATIONAL COMPANY; *pg.* 919, *pg.* 740
TEXANOL - Ester Alcohol - EASTMAN CHEMICAL COMPANY; *pg.* 1159, *pg.* 1636
TEXAS BEST - BBQ & Grilling Sauces - T. MARZETTI COMPANY; *pg.* 900, *pg.* 1444
TEXAS DAWN - Container Grown Plant - MONROVIA GROWERS; *pg.* 1797, *pg.* 44
TEXAS INSTRUMENTS - Calculators & Circuits - TEXAS INSTRUMENTS INCORPORATED; *pg.* 679, *pg.* 1688
TEXAS LAND & CATTLE COMPANY STEAK HOUSE - Steak Houses - LONE STAR STEAKHOUSE & SALOON, INC.; *pg.* 1736, *pg.* 1733
TEXAS MEXICAN RAILWAYS - Transportation Service - THE KANSAS CITY SOUTHERN RAILWAY COMPANY; *pg.* 1913, *pg.* 985
TEXAS MONTHLY - Magazine - TEXAS MONTHLY; *pg.* 1692, *pg.* 1666
TEXAS MOTOR SPEEDWAY - Entertainment Venue - SPEEDWAY MOTORSPORTS, INC.; *pg.* 584, *pg.* 1370
TEXAS PASTURES - Milk - COOPERATIVE REGIONS OF ORGANIC PRODUCER POOLS; *pg.* 850, *pg.* 1864
TEXAS PIT - BBQ Sauce - FAMOUS DAVE'S OF AMERICA, INC.; *pg.* 1728, *pg.* 926
TEXAS PRIDE - Food Product - JOHN B. SANFILIPPO & SON, INC.; *pg.* 1024, *pg.* 610
TEXAS RED - Molecular Probe Product - THERMO FISHER SCIENTIFIC INC.; *pg.* 1602, *pg.* 61
TEXAS STAR - Knife - BUCK KNIVES, INC.; *pg.* 1828, *pg.* 550
TEXAS STATION GAMBLING HALL AND HOTEL - Hotel & Casino - STATION CASINOS, INC.; *pg.* 585, *pg.* 1030
TEXAS STYLE - Salted Snack Food - INVENTURE FOODS, INC.; *pg.* 1023, *pg.* 17
TEXAS SWEETS - Cigars - FINCK CIGAR CO.; *pg.* 1894, *pg.* 1740
TEXAS TEA - Video Slots - INTERNATIONAL GAME TECHNOLOGY; *pg.* 957, *pg.* 1024
TEXAS TECH - Apparels - UNDER ARMOUR, INC.; *pg.* 49, *pg.* 759
TEXAS TWO STEP - Lottery - TEXAS LOTTERY COMMISSION; *pg.* 1007, *pg.* 1666
TEXAS WIDE OPEN FOR BUSINESS - Slogan - GOVERNOR'S OFFICE OF ECONOMIC DEVELOPMENT & TOURISM; *pg.* 993, *pg.* 1662
TEXINOL - Cleaning Preparation - WALTER G. LEGGE COMPANY, INC.; *pg.* 337, *pg.* 1321
TEXLMATE - Conductive Fabric - AMPHENOL CORPORATION; *pg.* 616, *pg.* 381
TEXMADE - Window - SPRINGS GLOBAL, INC.; *pg.* 698, *pg.* 1616
TEXO - Multi-strand Textured Fiber Glass Strand & Yarn - PPG INDUSTRIES, INC.; *pg.* 1445, *pg.* 1579
TEXOLITE - Texture - USG CORPORATION; *pg.* 118, *pg.* 594
TEXOPRINT - Durable Paper - NEENAH PAPER, INC.; *pg.* 1465, *pg.* 484
TEXSPAR - Heavy Duty Cleaner for Tile & Grout - WALTER G. LEGGE COMPANY, INC.; *pg.* 337, *pg.* 1321
TEXSPAR PLUS - Cleaning Preparation - WALTER G. LEGGE COMPANY, INC.; *pg.* 337, *pg.* 1321
TEXSPRAY - Sprayers - GRACO, INC.; *pg.* 1342, *pg.* 935
TEXSPRAY RTX 1000 - Fluid Handling System - GRACO, INC.; *pg.* 1342, *pg.* 935
TEXSPRAY RTX 750 - Fluid Handling System - GRACO, INC.; *pg.* 1342, *pg.* 935
TEXT & LEARN - Educational Product - LEAPFROG ENTERPRISES, INC.; *pg.* 961, *pg.* 84
TEXT-GUARD - Paper & Nonwoven Material - FIBERMARK INC.; *pg.* 1457, *pg.* 1764
TEXT MINER - Software - SAS INSTITUTE INC.; *pg.* 466, *pg.* 1361
TEXTAMER - Polymeric Acrylates - HENKEL CORPORATION; *pg.* 1165, *pg.* 1535
TEXTAMINE - Cationic Amines - HENKEL CORPORATION; *pg.* 1165, *pg.* 1535
TEXTAMINE OXIDE - Amine Oxides - HENKEL CORPORATION; *pg.* 1165, *pg.* 1535
TEXTBRIDGE PRO - Optical Character Recognition Software - NUANCE COMMUNICATIONS, INC.; *pg.* 447, *pg.* 806
TEXTERGE - Detergents - HENKEL CORPORATION; *pg.* 1165, *pg.* 1535
TEXTILE - Computer Font - APPLE INC.; *pg.* 350, *pg.* 73
TEXTOFOAM - Detergents - HENKEL CORPORATION; *pg.* 1165, *pg.* 1535
TEXTOOL - Flat Pack Socket - 3M COMPANY; *pg.* 1142, *pg.* 956
TEXTRANS - Transmission Fluid - TEXAS REFINERY CORP.; *pg.* 986, *pg.* 1696
TEXTRATEIN - Textured Soy Protein - CARGILL, INC.; *pg.* 845, *pg.* 965
TEXTRATEIN - Soy Flour - CARGILL LIMITED; *pg.* 1475, *pg.* 1914
TEXTSENSE - Summary Writing Program - QUESTAR ASSESSMENT, INC.; *pg.* 1679, *pg.* 1143
TEXTURA - Ceramic, Glass, Stone Tiles & Slabs - WALKER & ZANGER, INC.; *pg.* 119, *pg.* 281
TEXTURE CARE - Hair Care Product - ZOTOS INTERNATIONAL, INC.; *pg.* 524, *pg.* 345
TEXTURE-COTE - Metal Building System - BUTLER MANUFACTURING COMPANY; *pg.* 72, *pg.* 981
TEXTURE LIFE 2000 - Dry Cleaning & Laundry Product - ADCO, INC.; *pg.* 325, *pg.* 482
TEXTURED II POLO - Apparels - UNDER ARMOUR, INC.; *pg.* 49, *pg.* 759
TEXTURED MONEY - Leather Product - COACH, INC.; *pg.* 3, *pg.* 1214
TEXTURED PEWTER - Furniture - ASHLEY FURNITURE INDUSTRIES, INC.; *pg.* 914, *pg.* 1852
TEXTURES & TONES - Hair Coloring - P&G-CLAIROL, INC.; *pg.* 519, *pg.* 1418
TEXTURETOP - Concrete System - L.M. SCOFIELD COMPANY; *pg.* 94, *pg.* 134
TEXTURIZING BALM - Hair Care Product - JOHN PAUL MITCHELL SYSTEMS; *pg.* 512, *pg.* 133
TEXTWRANGLER - Software - BARE BONES SOFTWARE, INC.; *pg.* 360, *pg.* 838
TEZZATA - Food Product - HORMEL FOODS CORPORATION; *pg.* 863, *pg.* 915
TF - Fluid Handling System - GRACO, INC.; *pg.* 1342, *pg.* 935
TFB - Machinery - HARDINGE INC.; *pg.* 1344, *pg.* 1157
TFC HEADEND DROP CABLE - Cable - TIMES FIBER COMMUNICATIONS, INC.; *pg.* 681, *pg.* 382
T.F.E. - Lubricant - AERVOE INDUSTRIES INCORPORATED; *pg.* 1439, *pg.* 1021
TFM - Transportation Service - THE KANSAS CITY SOUTHERN RAILWAY COMPANY; *pg.* 1913, *pg.* 985
TFOCA-II - Connectors - AMPHENOL FIBER SYSTEMS INTERNATIONAL, INC.; *pg.* 617, *pg.* 1658
TFS - Surge Protectors - TII NETWORK TECHNOLOGIES, INC.; *pg.* 680, *pg.* 1157
TFX - Footwear - LACROSSE FOOTWEAR, INC.; *pg.* 1811, *pg.* 1503
TG GUARD - Security & Law Enforcement Products - MACE SECURITY INTERNATIONAL, INC.; *pg.* 1172, *pg.* 1541
T.G. LEE - Milk - DEAN FOODS COMPANY; *pg.* 852, *pg.* 1679
T.G. LEE DAIRY - Dairy Product - DEAN FOODS COMPANY; *pg.* 852, *pg.* 1679
TGF - Hair Salons - REGIS CORPORATION; *pg.* 521, *pg.* 941
TGFIII - Coating Products - RUSSEL METALS INC.; *pg.* 1180, *pg.* 1928
T.G.I. FRIDAY'S - Restaurants - CARLSON COMPANIES INC.; *pg.* 1084, *pg.* 947
TGI FRIDAYS - Food Products - THE KRAFT HEINZ COMPANY; *pg.* 870, *pg.* 1577
TGI FRIDAY'S CHEESE PIZZA CHIPS - Snack Food - INVENTURE FOODS, INC.; *pg.* 1023, *pg.* 17
T.G.I. FRIDAY'S FROZEN COCKTAILS - Frozen Cocktails - DIAGEO NORTH AMERICA, INC.; *pg.* 1961, *pg.* 361
TH - Weekly Entertainment Guide - TRAVELHOST, INC.; *pg.* 1696, *pg.* 1689
TH JR. - Test Equipment - SPX THERMAL PRODUCT SOLUTIONS; *pg.* 1378, *pg.* 1555
THAAD - Integrated Maintenance Management System - BAE SYSTEMS-INFORMATION WARFARE; *pg.* 623, *pg.* 1036
THAAD - Systems Integration & Aeronautics - LOCKHEED MARTIN CORPORATION; *pg.* 229, *pg.* 762
THAAD RADAR - Radar System - RAYTHEON COMPANY; *pg.* 233, *pg.* 854
THAI TREASURES - Game - WMS INDUSTRIES INC.; *pg.* 593, *pg.* 666
THALITONE - Pharmaceutical Product - KING PHARMACEUTICALS, INC.; *pg.* 1553, *pg.* 1627
THANK GOODNESS IT FITS - Apparel - PLAYTEX APPAREL, INC.; *pg.* 31, *pg.* 1395
THANK YOU GARDEN - Flower Arrangement - 1-800-FLOWERS.COM, INC.; *pg.* 1758, *pg.* 1151
THANKS A 1,000,000 - Lottery Game - OHIO LOTTERY COMMISSION; *pg.* 1002, *pg.* 1433
THANKS A BUNCH BOUQUET - Floral Bouquet - FTD GROUP, INC.; *pg.* 1795, *pg.* 608
THANKS-A-LATTE - Flower Arrangement - 1-800-FLOWERS.COM, INC.; *pg.* 1758, *pg.* 1151
THANKS A MILLION - Book - BOOKS-A-MILLION, INC.; *pg.* 1623, *pg.* 2
THANKS TO YOU BOUQUET - Floral Bouquet - FTD GROUP, INC.; *pg.* 1795, *pg.* 608
THANKSGIVING HARVEST BOUQUET - Flower Bouquet - FTD GROUP, INC.; *pg.* 1795, *pg.* 608
THAR - Dinnerware - THE HOMER LAUGHLIN CHINA COMPANY; *pg.* 1125, *pg.* 1850
THAT GIRL - Video Slots - INTERNATIONAL GAME TECHNOLOGY; *pg.* 957, *pg.* 1024
THAT THE FUTURE MAY LEARN FORM THE PAST - Tagline - COLONIAL WILLIAMSBURG FOUNDATION; *pg.* 541, *pg.* 1811
THAT WAS EASY - Slogan - STAPLES, INC.; *pg.* 474, *pg.* 821
THATCHMASTER - Gardening & Hardware Product - FAULTLESS STARCH/BON AMI COMPANY; *pg.* 330, *pg.* 982
THAT'S AN "EL" OF A COLOR - Nail Care Product - OPI PRODUCTS INC.; *pg.* 518, *pg.* 167
THAT'S MY GIRL - Cologne Spray - ENESCO, LLC; *pg.* 1124, *pg.* 620
THAT'S OUR PROMISE. THAT'S OUR WAY - Public Utility - EXELON CORPORATION; *pg.* 1942, *pg.* 573
THATS THE LOGIC OF LENNAR - Slogan - LENNAR CORPORATION; *pg.* 1100, *pg.* 443
THAT'S WHAT A HAMBURGER'S ALL ABOUT - Restaurant Services - IN-N-OUT BURGERS, INC.; *pg.* 1732, *pg.* 111
THAW-AND-SERVE - Cookie - COOKIE TREE BAKERIES; *pg.* 1851, *pg.* 1756
THAYER - Conveyor Belt - HYER INDUSTRIES INC.; *pg.* 1051, *pg.* 841
THAYER & CHANDLER - Airbrushes - BADGER AIR BRUSH COMPANY; *pg.* 359, *pg.* 612
THC - Sealant - TREMCO INCORPORATED; *pg.* 116, *pg.* 1405
THE INGLES ADVANTAGE - Slogan - INGLES MARKETS, INCORPORATED; *pg.* 1023, *pg.* 1358
THEA ARIZONA - Textiles - BERNHARDT DESIGN; *pg.* 918, *pg.* 1381
THEA DRESS - Women's Clothing & Accessories - WOODEN SHIPS OF HOBOKEN; *pg.* 35, *pg.* 1315
THEATER - 3D Graphical Technology - ADVANCED MICRO DEVICES, INC.-MARKHAM; *pg.* 345, *pg.* 1922
THEATRE DEPOT - Lighting Product - MOLE-RICHARDSON CO.; *pg.* 1302, *pg.* 103
THEATRE DESIGN PRO - Software for Designing Cinemas & Other Facilities Utilizing Projection - SCHNEIDER OPTICS INC.; *pg.* 1428, *pg.* 1165
THE THEATRE OF PRESIDENTS - Tag Line - THE NATIONAL THEATRE CORPORATION; *pg.* 569, *pg.* 403
THEATRE PROFILES - Online Information Service - THEATRE COMMUNICATIONS GROUP, INC.; *pg.* 587, *pg.* 1298
THEBESTCHOICE - Food Service - OMAHA STEAKS INTERNATIONAL, INC.; *pg.* 1780, *pg.* 1017

First page reference indicates Business Class Edition
Second page reference indicates Geographic Edition

THEDOMAINNAMEAFTERMARKET - Software - GO DADDY INC.; *pg.* 1249, *pg.* 21
THEFISH.COM - Christian Music - SALEM MEDIA GROUP, INC.; *pg.* 307, *pg.* 57
THEGLOSS.COM - Website - DEFYMEDIA; *pg.* 1237, *pg.* 1222
THEHEART.ORG - Cardiology Web Site - WEBMD HEALTH CORPORATION; *pg.* 1288, *pg.* 1313
THEHOTEL AT MANDALAY BAY - Resort & Casino - MGM RESORTS INTERNATIONAL; *pg.* 1105, *pg.* 1028
THEME PARK - Video Game - ELECTRONIC ARTS INC.; *pg.* 951, *pg.* 189
THEME STYLINGS - Multiple Style Kitchen Furniture Collections - WM OHS INC.; *pg.* 947, *pg.* 324
THEMED EVENTS - Target Specific Promotions - VALASSIS COMMUNICATIONS, INC.; *pg.* 1287, *pg.* 897
THEODORE - Furniture - AMISCO INDUSTRIES LTD.; *pg.* 913, *pg.* 1958
THEODORE PRESSER CO - Music Publishers & Importers - THEODORE PRESSER CO.; *pg.* 1692, *pg.* 1544
THEOREM - Office Furniture - STEELCASE INC.; *pg.* 475, *pg.* 889
THEORY - Fabric - NEMSCHOFF, INC.; *pg.* 936, *pg.* 1890
THERA - Pacemaker - MEDTRONIC, INC.; *pg.* 1564, *pg.* 939
THERA-BAND - Medical & Aesthetic Product - DYNATRONICS CORPORATION; *pg.* 1526, *pg.* 1757
THERA CANE - Massage Product - RELAX THE BACK CORPORATION; *pg.* 940, *pg.* 120
THERA-GESIC - Pharmaceutical Product - MISSION PHARMACAL COMPANY INC.; *pg.* 1568, *pg.* 1742
THERA-P - Medical & Aesthetic Product - DYNATRONICS CORPORATION; *pg.* 1526, *pg.* 1757
THERA-PUTTY - Healthcare Product - GF HEALTH PRODUCTS, INC.; *pg.* 1535, *pg.* 508
THERABATH - Cleanser - DERMA SCIENCES, INC.; *pg.* 1523, *pg.* 1111
THERABATH - Healthcare Product - GF HEALTH PRODUCTS, INC.; *pg.* 1535, *pg.* 508
THERABLOAT - Veterinary Pharmaceutical Preparation - PFIZER INC.; *pg.* 1581, *pg.* 1278
THERACYCLE - Exercise Equipment - EXERCYCLE CORPORATION; *pg.* 1833, *pg.* 823
THERACYS - Medication to Treat Bladder Cancer - SANOFI PASTEUR, INC; *pg.* 1591, *pg.* 1588
THERADENT - Pharmaceutical Product - ALVA/AMCO PHARMACAL COMPANIES, INC.; *pg.* 1492, *pg.* 637
THERAGRAN - Multivitamin Supplement - MEAD JOHNSON NUTRITION COMPANY; *pg.* 1561, *pg.* 615
THERALL - Healthcare Product - MEDICOOL, INC.; *pg.* 1562, *pg.* 294
THERAPIST HELPER - Software - NIGHTINGALE; *pg.* 446, *pg.* 186
THERAPRO - Bath & Plumbing Product - JACUZZI BRANDS CORPORATION; *pg.* 554, *pg.* 65
THERAPULSE - Wound Care Surface - KINETIC CONCEPTS, INC.; *pg.* 1553, *pg.* 1741
THERAPY - Ablation Catheter - ST. JUDE MEDICAL, INC.; *pg.* 1596, *pg.* 963
THERAPY FORECASTER - Software System - IMS HEALTH, INC.; *pg.* 1544, *pg.* 344
THERAREST - Mattress Replacement System - KINETIC CONCEPTS, INC.; *pg.* 1553, *pg.* 1741
THERASEED - Medical Device - THERAGENICS CORPORATION; *pg.* 1431, *pg.* 527
THERASIGHT - Brachytherapy System - THERAGENICS CORPORATION; *pg.* 1431, *pg.* 527
THERASOURCE - Brachytherapy System - THERAGENICS CORPORATION; *pg.* 1431, *pg.* 527
THERASURE - Scientific Research - LABORATORY CORPORATION OF AMERICA HOLDINGS; *pg.* 1554, *pg.* 1359
THERATEA - Mint & Lemongrass Tea - WATKINS INCORPORATED; *pg.* 909, *pg.* 967
THERATOGS - Full Body System - ALIMED, INC.; *pg.* 1490, *pg.* 816
THERATOPE - Vaccine - ONCOTHYREON INC.; *pg.* 1578, *pg.* 1838
THERATRIM - Weight Management System - WATKINS INCORPORATED; *pg.* 909, *pg.* 967
THERE IS A DIFFERENCE! - Tagline - WESTIN AUTOMOTIVE PRODUCTS, INC.; *pg.* 222, *pg.* 211
THERE IS ALWAYS AN AERVOE SOLUTION... - Tagline - AERVOE INDUSTRIES INCORPORATED; *pg.* 1439, *pg.* 1021
THERE WITH YOU - Tag Line - GREENLEE TEXTRON INC.; *pg.* 1048, *pg.* 655
THERE'S A NEW GAME IN TOWN - Slogan - PENN NATIONAL GAMING, INC.; *pg.* 574, *pg.* 1595
THERE'S A NEW WAY TO LOOK AT IT - Manual - XEROX CORPORATION; *pg.* 494, *pg.* 365
THERE'S AN APP FOR THAT - Tagline - APPLE INC.; *pg.* 350, *pg.* 73
THERE'S FAST FOOD..THEN THERE'S KFC! - Slogan - KFC CORPORATION; *pg.* 1733, *pg.* 735
THERE'S NOTHING SOFT ABOUT IT - Sprite Tagline - THE COCA-COLA COMPANY; *pg.* 240, *pg.* 493
THERE'S ONE LANGUAGE EVERYONE UNDERSTANDS - Tag Line - WORLD GOLD COUNCIL; *pg.* 162, *pg.* 1315
THERE'S SOMETHING GREATER AT WORK HERE - Slogan - UNITEDHEALTH GROUP INCORPORATED; *pg.* 1221, *pg.* 950
THERESA - Clothing - ABERCROMBIE & FITCH CO.; *pg.* 37, *pg.* 1466
THERM A FORM - Silicone Compounds - PARKER CHOMERICS; *pg.* 662, *pg.* 862
THERM-A-GAP - Thermally Conductive Gap Fillers - PARKER CHOMERICS; *pg.* 662, *pg.* 862
THERM-CHEK - Heat Stabilizers - FERRO CORPORATION; *pg.* 1162, *pg.* 1462
THERM-O-FLOW - Heated Ram Plates - GRACO, INC.; *pg.* 1342, *pg.* 935
THERM TRAC - Heat Tracing System - THERMON AMERICAS INC.; *pg.* 1077, *pg.* 1744
THERMA-FIT - Apparel - NIKE, INC.; *pg.* 1812, *pg.* 1492
THERMA-PROBE - Inspection System - KLA-TENCOR CORPORATION; *pg.* 1353, *pg.* 146
THERMA-STOR - Heat Recovery Unit - BOUMATIC LLC; *pg.* 701, *pg.* 1865
THERMA-TECH - Engineered Compound & Composite - POLYONE CORPORATION; *pg.* 1177, *pg.* 1404
THERMA-TEMP - Medical Product - CINCINNATI SUB-ZERO PRODUCTS, INC.; *pg.* 1070, *pg.* 1411
THERMA-TRU - Hardware - FORTUNE BRANDS HOME & SECURITY, INC.; *pg.* 55, *pg.* 600
THERMA TRU - Doors - THERMA-TRU CORP.; *pg.* 115, *pg.* 1462
THERMABLANKET - Metallized, Polyester Blanket - ACR ELECTRONICS, INC.; *pg.* 612, *pg.* 422
THERMACAM - Software - FLIR SYSTEMS, INC.; *pg.* 1413, *pg.* 1510
THERMACAM RESEARCHER - Software - FLIR SYSTEMS, INC.; *pg.* 1413, *pg.* 1510
THERMACARE - Heat Releasing Wraps - PFIZER INC.; *pg.* 1581, *pg.* 1278
THERMACELL - Hair Care Product - CONAIR CORPORATION; *pg.* 505, *pg.* 1055
THERMACHOICE - Healthcare Product - JOHNSON & JOHNSON; *pg.* 1549, *pg.* 1091
THERMACOL - Padding Auxiliaries - HUNTSMAN CORPORATION; *pg.* 1167, *pg.* 1758
THERMACOLOR - Video Print Paper, Cartridge, Kit - EASTMAN KODAK COMPANY; *pg.* 1408, *pg.* 1333
THERMADOR - Appliances - BSH HOME APPLIANCES CORPORATION; *pg.* 53, *pg.* 108
THERMADRAPE - Temperature Insulating Drape - VITAL SIGNS, INC.; *pg.* 1607, *pg.* 1126
THERMAFIL - Dental Product - DENTSPLY INTERNATIONAL INC.; *pg.* 1522, *pg.* 1596
THERMAFLEECE - Blouses - HABAND COMPANY, INC.; *pg.* 1772, *pg.* 1099
THERMAGARD - Insulation Product - ALPHA ASSOCIATES, INC.; *pg.* 691, *pg.* 1078
THERMAGOWN - Healthcare Apparel - THE SALK COMPANY; *pg.* 1591, *pg.* 800
THERMAGUARD - Protection - INTERSIL CORPORATION; *pg.* 647, *pg.* 146
THERMAGUARD - Wall System - SMITH-MIDLAND CORPORATION; *pg.* 111, *pg.* 1795
THERMAIR - Nozzle-mix Burner with a Packaged Combustion Air Blower - ECLIPSE INC.; *pg.* 1332, *pg.* 655
THERMAL AIR - Police Products - BAE SYSTEMS PRODUCTS GROUP; *pg.* 359, *pg.* 432
THERMAL BOB - Apparel - OAKLEY, INC.; *pg.* 1840, *pg.* 86
THERMAL-GARD - Windows & Patio Doors - NORTEK, INC.; *pg.* 100, *pg.* 1607
THERMAL GOLD - Digital Plate - EASTMAN KODAK COMPANY; *pg.* 1408, *pg.* 1333
THERMAL MATRIX - Radiant Energy Technology Used in SmartTemp Hot-cold Therapy Systems - KAZ, INC.; *pg.* 58, *pg.* 844
THERMAL MONOPANL - Metal Building System - BUTLER MANUFACTURING COMPANY; *pg.* 72, *pg.* 981
THERMAL PLATINUM - Digital Plate - EASTMAN KODAK COMPANY; *pg.* 1408, *pg.* 1333
THERMAL PRO - Finger Gloves - SIMMS FISHING PRODUCTS CORP.; *pg.* 1845, *pg.* 1008
THERMAL SOLUTIONS - Commercial & Industrial Boilers - BURNHAM HOLDINGS, INC.; *pg.* 1069, *pg.* 1546
THERMAL SOLUTIONS - Cooling System - LYTRON INCORPORATED; *pg.* 1074, *pg.* 861
THERMALACE - Molecular Biology Product - THERMO FISHER SCIENTIFIC INC.; *pg.* 1602, *pg.* 61
THERMALEEZE - Healthcare Product - GF HEALTH PRODUCTS, INC.; *pg.* 1535, *pg.* 508
THERMALGARD - Headwear - MINE SAFETY APPLIANCES COMPANY; *pg.* 1361, *pg.* 1525
THERMALGRAPH - Chemical Product - CYTEC INDUSTRIES, INC.; *pg.* 1155, *pg.* 1131
THERMALIZED - Skylighting Product - WASCO PRODUCTS, INC.; *pg.* 120, *pg.* 752
THERMALKYD - Paint Product - AKZO NOBEL; *pg.* 1439, *pg.* 1952
THERMALNEWS - Gold Digital Plus - EASTMAN KODAK COMPANY; *pg.* 1408, *pg.* 1333
THERMALOG - Chemical Integrator - 3M COMPANY; *pg.* 1142, *pg.* 956
THERMARITE - Absorbent & Refrigerant Pads - SEALED AIR CORPORATION; *pg.* 1468, *pg.* 1058
THERMARK - Wood Grain Foils - AVERY DENNISON CORPORATION; *pg.* 1452, *pg.* 95
THERMART - Thermal Paper - APPVION INC.; *pg.* 1451, *pg.* 1852
THERMASEAL - Seals & Gaskets - METAL TEXTILES CORPORATION; *pg.* 654, *pg.* 1057
THERMASEAM - Tank - THERMON AMERICAS INC.; *pg.* 1077, *pg.* 1744
THERMASOTE - Building Product - HOMASOTE COMPANY; *pg.* 87, *pg.* 1126
THERMASTAR BY PELLA - Energy-Efficient Vinyl Windows & Patio Doors - PELLA CORPORATION; *pg.* 104, *pg.* 711
THERMATEK - Fall Protection Equipment - MINE SAFETY APPLIANCES COMPANY; *pg.* 1361, *pg.* 1525
THERMATIC - Extruder - DAVIS-STANDARD LLC; *pg.* 1328, *pg.* 368
THERMATRX - Medical Device - AMERICAN MEDICAL SYSTEMS HOLDINGS, INC.; *pg.* 1493, *pg.* 947
THERMATTACH - Thermally Conductive Adhesive Tapes - PARKER CHOMERICS; *pg.* 662, *pg.* 862
THERMAX - Insulation - THE DOW CHEMICAL COMPANY; *pg.* 1157, *pg.* 898
THERMAX - Beverage Bottle - THERMOS L.L.C.; *pg.* 61, *pg.* 660
THERMAX SUPERGAP - Cryogenic Product - CHART INDUSTRIES, INC.; *pg.* 1405, *pg.* 1454
THERMBAR - Glove - LAKELAND INDUSTRIES, INC.; *pg.* 1354, *pg.* 1338
THERMEDICS - Polymer Products - THE LUBRIZOL CORPORATION; *pg.* 1171, *pg.* 1481
THERMEX - Plastic Compound & Resin - A. SCHULMAN, INC.; *pg.* 1144, *pg.* 1452
THERMFLOW - Phase Change Materials - PARKER CHOMERICS; *pg.* 662, *pg.* 862
THERMIC WELD - Machine Tool Covers - DYNATECT MANUFACTURING INC.; *pg.* 1330, *pg.* 1883
THERMISER - Insulated Rolling Door - CORNELL IRON WORKS, INC.; *pg.* 77, *pg.* 1554
THERMISTEMP - Industrial Instruments - YSI INCORPORATED; *pg.* 1438, *pg.* 1483
THERMIVOLT - Industrial Instruments - YSI INCORPORATED; *pg.* 1438, *pg.* 1483
THERMIXER - Thermostatic Water Controller - SYMMONS INDUSTRIES, INC.; *pg.* 114, *pg.* 803
THERMJET - Nozzle-mix Burner - ECLIPSE INC.; *pg.* 1332, *pg.* 655
THERMLFILM - Labeling - FLEXCON CORPORATION; *pg.* 1457, *pg.* 844
THERMLFILM SELECT - Sensitive Film & Adhesive - FLEXCON CORPORATION; *pg.* 1457, *pg.* 844
THERMO - Fabric - NEMSCHOFF, INC.; *pg.* 936, *pg.* 1890
THERMO BAN - Proximity Fire Clothing - STANDARD SAFETY EQUIPMENT CO.; *pg.* 1379, *pg.* 632
THERMO BURST - Nutritional Supplement - GENERAL NUTRITION CENTERS, INC.; *pg.* 1534, *pg.* 1575
THERMO CAFE - Automatic Drip Coffeemaker With Oster ThermoCarafe - JARDEN CONSUMER SOLUTIONS; *pg.*

First page reference indicates Business Class Edition
Second page reference indicates Geographic Edition

57, *pg.* 412
THERMO-DYNAMIC - Steam Traps - SPIRAX SARCO, INC.; *pg.* 1076, *pg.* 1612
THERMO-FOAM - Pillow - SELECT COMFORT CORPORATION; *pg.* 942, *pg.* 942
THERMO GLOSS - Thermoplastic Acrylic Floor - ROCHESTER MIDLAND CORPORATION; *pg.* 334, *pg.* 1337
THERMO GREENS - Food Supplement - ORANGE PEEL ENTERPRISES, INC.; *pg.* 1028, *pg.* 477
THERMO GREENS+ - Vitamins - ORANGE PEEL ENTERPRISES, INC.; *pg.* 1028, *pg.* 477
THERMO KING - Transport Temperature Control System - INGERSOLL-RAND COMPANY; *pg.* 1349, *pg.* 1370
THERMO KING - Refrigeration Systems - THERMO KING CORPORATION; *pg.* 1077, *pg.* 918
THERMO LIFE - Power Generator - VERITEQ; *pg.* 488, *pg.* 422
THERMO-LUBE - Sealer & Additive - QUIKRETE COMPANIES; *pg.* 106, *pg.* 519
THERMO-MIST - Humidifier - FIELD CONTROLS LLC; *pg.* 1071, *pg.* 1380
THERMO-PAK - Forced Draft Industrial #2-#6 Oil & Gas Burner - PREFERRED UTILITIES MANUFACTURING CORPORATION; *pg.* 1075, *pg.* 344
THERMO-PANEL - Sidewall - WINNEBAGO INDUSTRIES, INC.; *pg.* 1712, *pg.* 707
THERMO PRIDE - Residential Furnaces & Air Conditioners - BURNHAM HOLDINGS, INC.; *pg.* 1069, *pg.* 1546
THERMO-PRO - Spray Nozzle - STRAHMAN VALVES, INC.; *pg.* 1379, *pg.* 1517
THERMO-PRO 2000 - Spray Nozzle - STRAHMAN VALVES, INC.; *pg.* 1379, *pg.* 1517
THERMO-QUENCH - Quenching Salt - HEATBATH CORPORATION; *pg.* 1165, *pg.* 826
THERMO SCIENTIFIC - Laboratory Equipment & Chemicals - THERMO FISHER SCIENTIFIC INC.; *pg.* 1431, *pg.* 854
THERMO-SHRINK - Tubing - IDEAL INDUSTRIES, INC.; *pg.* 1051, *pg.* 662
THERMO-TEK - Industrial Filter - DONALDSON COMPANY, INC.; *pg.* 1329, *pg.* 917
THERMO TROPICS - Nutritional Supplement - NATURAL ORGANICS, INC.; *pg.* 1571, *pg.* 1181
THERMO-X - Molecular Biology Product - THERMO FISHER SCIENTIFIC INC.; *pg.* 1602, *pg.* 61
THERMOBOND - Document Heat Sealing Device - THE STANDARD REGISTER COMPANY; *pg.* 473, *pg.* 1446
THERMOBRITE - Diagnostic Urinalysis System - IRIS INTERNATIONAL, INC.; *pg.* 1547, *pg.* 64
THERMOBURR - Deburring And Finishing System - KENNAMETAL EXTRUDE HONE; *pg.* 1352, *pg.* 1542
THERMOCASE - Enclosure - THERMON AMERICAS INC.; *pg.* 1077, *pg.* 1744
THERMOCHRON - Hardware Protection - MAXIM INTEGRATED PRODUCTS, INC.; *pg.* 653, *pg.* 247
THERMOCOTE - Replacement Window & Door - TRUE HOME VALUE, INC.; *pg.* 117, *pg.* 738
THERMOCUBE - Cooling System - LYTRON INCORPORATED; *pg.* 1074, *pg.* 861
THERMOCUBE CHILLER - Cooling System - LYTRON INCORPORATED; *pg.* 1074, *pg.* 861
THERMODRY - Insulation Drainage Panel - THE DOW CHEMICAL COMPANY; *pg.* 1157, *pg.* 898
THERMOEXPRESS - Temperature Controlled Shipping Service - DHL HOLDINGS (USA), INC.; *pg.* 1906, *pg.* 459
THERMOFILL - Powdered Gypsum Products - USG CORPORATION; *pg.* 118, *pg.* 594
THERMOFLEX - Narrow Platesetter - EASTMAN KODAK COMPANY; *pg.* 1408, *pg.* 1333
THERMOFLOW - Flow Controls - XYLEM INC.; *pg.* 1078, *pg.* 1339
THERMOFORM - Resealable Packaging Solution - ZIP-PAK; *pg.* 1473, *pg.* 631
THERMOFRESH - Coffee & Beverage Equipment - BUNN-O-MATIC CORPORATION; *pg.* 53, *pg.* 661
THERMOGENICS - Fat Burning Products - PHYSICIANS WEIGHT LOSS CENTERS, INC.; *pg.* 1585, *pg.* 1402
THERMOGLAS - Fire & Rescue Product - E.D. BULLARD COMPANY; *pg.* 1332, *pg.* 727
THERMOGLAZE - Donut Glazing Equipment - BELSHAW ADAMATIC BAKERY GROUP; *pg.* 1317, *pg.* 1813
THERMOGRIP - Hot Metal Adhesives - BOSTIK INC.; *pg.* 1150, *pg.* 833
THERMOGUARD - Flame Retardants - CHEMTURA CORPORATION; *pg.* 1152, *pg.* 355
THERMOID - Hose - HBD INDUSTRIES, INC.; *pg.* 207, *pg.* 1449
THERMOINSULATOR - Insulated Divider for Food Carriers - CARLISLE FOODSERVICE PRODUCTS INCORPORATED; *pg.* 1455, *pg.* 1485
THERMOJET - Printer System - 3D SYSTEMS CORPORATION; *pg.* 339, *pg.* 1621
THERMOJETICS - Herbal Tablets - HERBALIFE INTERNATIONAL OF AMERICA, INC.; *pg.* 1541, *pg.* 132
THERMOKIT - Thermoplastic Applicator - M-B COMPANIES, INC.; *pg.* 1357, *pg.* 1884
THERMOLDS - Shoes - P.W. MINOR & SON, INC.; *pg.* 1816, *pg.* 1140
THERMOLEC - Nutritional Lecithin Products - ARCHER-DANIELS-MIDLAND COMPANY; *pg.* 825, *pg.* 565
THERMOLITE - Insulation - 180S, LLC; *pg.* 1824, *pg.* 754
THERMOLITE - Performance Fabrics & Insulations - INVISTA B.V.; *pg.* 1168, *pg.* 723
THERMOLITE - Fishing Gear Product - SIMMS FISHING PRODUCTS CORP.; *pg.* 1845, *pg.* 1008
THERMOLITE - Socks - WIGWAM MILLS, INC.; *pg.* 15, *pg.* 1894
THERMOLITE BASE - Glove Liner - KOMBI, LTD.; *pg.* 1838, *pg.* 1766
THERMOMAN - Garment Fire Test System - E.I. DU PONT DE NEMOURS & COMPANY; *pg.* 1159, *pg.* 390
THERMOMARK - Garage Doors - WAYNE-DALTON CORP.; *pg.* 120, *pg.* 1465
THERMOMAT - Insulating System - OWENS CORNING; *pg.* 102, *pg.* 1476
THERMOMAX - Software - MOLECULAR DEVICES CORPORATION; *pg.* 1568, *pg.* 287
THERMOMELT - Temperature Indicator - LA-CO INDUSTRIES MARKAL CO., INC.; *pg.* 1170, *pg.* 610
THERMOMOUNT - Enclosure - THERMON AMERICAS INC.; *pg.* 1077, *pg.* 1744
THERMON FIBREFORM - Enclosure - THERMON AMERICAS INC.; *pg.* 1077, *pg.* 1744
THERMOPHORE - Automatic Moist Heat Pack - BATTLE CREEK EQUIPMENT CO.; *pg.* 1499, *pg.* 870
THERMOPHORE - Medical & Aesthetic Product - DYNATRONICS CORPORATION; *pg.* 1526, *pg.* 1757
THERMOPIPE - Polyethylene Lining System - INSITUFORM TECHNOLOGIES INC; *pg.* 88, *pg.* 974
THERMOPOLYMER - Heater - WATLOW ELECTRIC MANUFACTURING COMPANY; *pg.* 1078, *pg.* 1004
THERMOPOWER - Bike Wear Material - W.L. GORE & ASSOCIATES, INC.; *pg.* 122, *pg.* 388
THERMOPROOF - Roof Insulation - THE DOW CHEMICAL COMPANY; *pg.* 1157, *pg.* 898
THERMOQUIET - Brakes - FEDERAL-MOGUL HOLDINGS CORPORATION; *pg.* 205, *pg.* 907
THERMORANGE - Insulating System - OWENS CORNING; *pg.* 102, *pg.* 1476
THERMOS NISSAN - Beverage Bottle - THERMOS L.L.C.; *pg.* 61, *pg.* 660
THERMOSCRIPT - Molecular Biology Product - THERMO FISHER SCIENTIFIC INC.; *pg.* 1602, *pg.* 61
THERMOSEL - Elevated Temperature Testing - BROOKFIELD ENGINEERING LABORATORIES, INC.; *pg.* 1403, *pg.* 833
THERMOSET - Medical Device - HOSPIRA, INC.; *pg.* 1542, *pg.* 623
THERMOSET - Epoxy - LORD CORPORATION; *pg.* 1357, *pg.* 1360
THERMOSIGHT - Thermal Imaging System - FLIR SYSTEMS, INC.; *pg.* 1413, *pg.* 1510
THERMOSPAN - Garage Door - WAYNE-DALTON CORP.; *pg.* 120, *pg.* 1465
THERMOSPEED - Film Splicer & Splicing Tape - EASTMAN KODAK COMPANY; *pg.* 1408, *pg.* 1333
THERMOSPRAY - Engineered Product And System - SULZER METCO (WESTBURY) INC.; *pg.* 1064, *pg.* 1350
THERMOSTAT - Building Product - BLUELINX HOLDINGS, INC.; *pg.* 70, *pg.* 491
THERMOSTAT - Structural Panels - GEORGIA-PACIFIC LLC; *pg.* 1458, *pg.* 507
THERMOTAINER - Food Holding Equipment - DUKE MANUFACTURING COMPANY, INC.; *pg.* 54, *pg.* 995
THERMOTRAP - Heat Loss Minimalizing System - A.O. SMITH CORPORATION; *pg.* 1313, *pg.* 1872
THERMOTUBE - Tubing - THERMON AMERICAS INC.; *pg.* 1077, *pg.* 1744
THERMOVIEW - Replacement Window & Door - TRUE HOME VALUE, INC.; *pg.* 117, *pg.* 738
THERMOVISION - Thermal Imaging System - FLIR SYSTEMS, INC.; *pg.* 1413, *pg.* 1510
THERMOVISION LABVIEW TOOLKIT - Software - FLIR SYSTEMS, INC.; *pg.* 1413, *pg.* 1510
THERMOVISION SDK - Software - FLIR SYSTEMS, INC.; *pg.* 1413, *pg.* 1510
THERMOWAYNE - Garage Door - WAYNE-DALTON CORP.; *pg.* 120, *pg.* 1465
THERMOWELL - Glass & Ceramic Material - CORNING INCORPORATED; *pg.* 1122, *pg.* 1154
THERMTHIEF - Flame Nozzle - ECLIPSE INC.; *pg.* 1332, *pg.* 655
THERMTILE - Ceramic & Plastic Product - COORSTEK, INC.; *pg.* 77, *pg.* 330
THERMTRAC - Cable - THERMON AMERICAS INC.; *pg.* 1077, *pg.* 1744
THERMX - Polyester Resin - E.I. DU PONT DE NEMOURS & COMPANY; *pg.* 1159, *pg.* 390
THEROSCA - Pharmaceutical Preparation for Bone Healing - PFIZER INC.; *pg.* 1581, *pg.* 1278
THESA - Software - FLIR SYSTEMS, INC.; *pg.* 1413, *pg.* 1510
THESAURUS.COM - Reference Service - IAC/INTERACTIVECORP; *pg.* 292, *pg.* 1242
THESTREET.COM - Online Investment Information - THE STREET, INC.; *pg.* 1283, *pg.* 1296
THESYS - Digital Video Product - HARMONIC, INC.; *pg.* 402, *pg.* 246
THETAFORM - Glass & Ceramic Material - CORNING INCORPORATED; *pg.* 1122, *pg.* 1154
THETFORD 735MSD - Marine Head - THETFORD CORPORATION; *pg.* 337, *pg.* 867
THETFORD 775MSD - Marine Head - THETFORD CORPORATION; *pg.* 337, *pg.* 867
THEXTONITE - Automotive Equipment - THEXTON MANUFACTURING COMPANY, INC.; *pg.* 218, *pg.* 925
THEXTONS - Beverages - THE COCA-COLA COMPANY; *pg.* 240, *pg.* 493
THEY ARE DELICIOUS - Tagline - MIKE-SELL'S POTATO CHIP COMPANY; *pg.* 1860, *pg.* 1446
THEY'RE OFF - Entertainment Service - KENTUCKY DERBY FESTIVAL, INC.; *pg.* 556, *pg.* 735
THEY'RE OFF - Game - WMS INDUSTRIES INC.; *pg.* 593, *pg.* 666
THI-VEX - Rubber - SMOOTH-ON INC.; *pg.* 111, *pg.* 1528
THICK & HEARTY BURGER - Food Product - WHATABURGER, INC.; *pg.* 1755, *pg.* 1744
THICK AND THIN - Carpet - INTERFACE, INC.; *pg.* 695, *pg.* 512
THICK CLASSIC MID - Footwear - K-SWISS; *pg.* 1837, *pg.* 306
THICK-IT - Dietary Product - ALIMED, INC.; *pg.* 1490, *pg.* 816
THICK-IT - Healthcare Food Thickener - MEDLINE INDUSTRIES, INC.; *pg.* 1562, *pg.* 635
THICK LASH 2 - Mascara - COVER GIRL COSMETICS; *pg.* 506, *pg.* 772
THICK 'N CRISPY - Frozen Poultry - TYSON FOODS, INC.; *pg.* 902, *pg.* 35
THICK 'N THIN - Eye Color Pencils - COVER GIRL COSMETICS; *pg.* 506, *pg.* 772
THICKBURGER - Hamburger Sandwich - HARDEES FOOD SYSTEMS, INC.; *pg.* 1731, *pg.* 998
THICKENUP - Pharmaceutical Product - NESTLE HEALTHCARE NUTRITION; *pg.* 1572, *pg.* 941
THICKET - Carpet - INTERFACE, INC.; *pg.* 695, *pg.* 512
THICKET - Fabric - NEMSCHOFF, INC.; *pg.* 936, *pg.* 1890
THIGH'M A BELIEVER - Clothing - SPANX INC.; *pg.* 32, *pg.* 520
THIN-BEZEL - Video Product - PLANAR SYSTEMS, INC.; *pg.* 455, *pg.* 1495
THIN CELL - Battery - ULTRALIFE CORPORATION; *pg.* 1385, *pg.* 1317
THIN ICE - Game - PRESSMAN TOY CORPORATION; *pg.* 965, *pg.* 1734
THIN PIN - Push-Pin - MOORE PUSH PIN CO.; *pg.* 441, *pg.* 1595
THIN SET - Tile Setting Product - QUIKRETE COMPANIES; *pg.* 106, *pg.* 519
THIN-TRIM - Capacitor - JOHANSON MANUFACTURING CORPORATION; *pg.* 648, *pg.* 1045
THINBAND - Heater - WATLOW ELECTRIC MANUFACTURING COMPANY; *pg.* 1078, *pg.* 1004
THINBAND BARREL HEATERS - Heater - WATLOW ELECTRIC MANUFACTURING COMPANY; *pg.* 1078, *pg.*

First page reference indicates Business Class Edition
Second page reference indicates Geographic Edition

1004
THINEDGE - LCD Display - VIEWSONIC CORPORATION; *pg.* 489, *pg.* 303
THINFLEX - Wood & Building Material - WEYERHAEUSER COMPANY; *pg.* 121, *pg.* 1820
THINFOLD - Men's Wallet - BUXTON ACQUISITION CO., LLC; *pg.* 2, *pg.* 845
THINGS YOU NEVER KNEW EXISTED - Mail Order Catalog - JOHNSON SMITH COMPANY; *pg.* 1774, *pg.* 414
THINK - Pharmaceutical Product - ENDO PHARMACEUTICALS HOLDINGS, INC.; *pg.* 1528, *pg.* 1549
THINK - Awareness Program - MOTHERS AGAINST DRUNK DRIVING (MADD); *pg.* 147, *pg.* 1723
THINK - Office Furniture - STEELCASE INC.; *pg.* 475, *pg.* 889
THINK ABOUT TOMORROW - Slogan - AMERICAN STUDENT ASSISTANCE; *pg.* 714, *pg.* 789
THINK BIG - Slogan - IMAX CORPORATION; *pg.* 1417, *pg.* 1926
THINK FORWARD - Slogan - BRUKER CORPORATION; *pg.* 1511, *pg.* 788
THINK GAMES - Solitaire Games - PRESSMAN TOY CORPORATION; *pg.* 965, *pg.* 1734
THINK GREEK - Website - GEEKNET, INC.; *pg.* 1248, *pg.* 1780
THINK GREEN - Slogan - WASTE MANAGEMENT, INC.; *pg.* 1954, *pg.* 1716
THINK INNODATA ISOGEN - Slogan - INNODATA ISOGEN, INC.; *pg.* 1259, *pg.* 1072
THINK IT. APPLY IT. - Slogan - APPLIED MATERIALS, INC.; *pg.* 618, *pg.* 264
THINK OF US AS FALVOR - Tagline - VIRGINIA DARE EXTRACT CO., INC.; *pg.* 908, *pg.* 1147
THINK QWEST FIRST - Communication Product - CENTURYLINK, INC; *pg.* 1870, *pg.* 317
THINK WESTERN - Banking Service - CANADIAN WESTERN BANK; *pg.* 729, *pg.* 1906
THINK WIDER - Manual - XEROX CORPORATION; *pg.* 494, *pg.* 365
THINKCURE - Charity Program - LOS ANGELES DODGERS INC.; *pg.* 559, *pg.* 135
THINKING AHEAD - Banking Service - THE BANK OF NOVA SCOTIA; *pg.* 721, *pg.* 1935
THINKING OUTSIDE THE BADGE - Slogan - LANDAUER, INC.; *pg.* 1554, *pg.* 615
THINKING READER - Educational Materials - SCHOLASTIC INC.; *pg.* 1683, *pg.* 1288
THINMAN - Truck Leveler - RITE-HITE HOLDING CORPORATION; *pg.* 1372, *pg.* 1880
THINNER - Scales - MEASUREMENT SPECIALTIES INC.; *pg.* 1360, *pg.* 1783
THINPREP - Pap Test - HOLOGIC, INC.; *pg.* 1416, *pg.* 784
THINSISTOR - Infrared Thermistor - MEASUREMENT SPECIALTIES/YSI TEMPERATURE; *pg.* 1074, *pg.* 1482
THINSULATE - Personal Safety Product - 3M COMPANY; *pg.* 1142, *pg.* 956
THINSULATE - Insulation - SELECT COMFORT CORPORATION; *pg.* 942, *pg.* 942
THINSULATOR - Insulator - T.D. WILLIAMSON, INC.; *pg.* 1380, *pg.* 1490
THINZ - Pharmaceutical Product - ALVA/AMCO PHARMACAL COMPANIES, INC.; *pg.* 1492, *pg.* 637
THINZ CARBOFAST - Weight Loss - ALVA/AMCO PHARMACAL COMPANIES, INC.; *pg.* 1492, *pg.* 637
THIODAN - Insecticide - UNIVERSAL COOPERATIVES, INC.; *pg.* 1482, *pg.* 922
THIOLA - Pharmaceutical Product - MISSION PHARMACAL COMPANY INC.; *pg.* 1568, *pg.* 1742
THE THIRD REICH - Book Series - DIRECT HOLDINGS AMERICAS INC.; *pg.* 1636, *pg.* 1780
THIRSTY GIANT - Decorated Paper Towels - HY-VEE, INC.; *pg.* 1023, *pg.* 713
THIRSTY PENGUIN - Recreational Hockey League - CANLAN ICE SPORTS CORPORATION; *pg.* 536, *pg.* 1907
THIS IS PINK - Umbrellas - TOTES ISOTONER CORPORATION; *pg.* 14, *pg.* 1426
THIS IS THE SPLIT-CHIP ADVANTAGE - Slogan - THE L.S. STARRETT COMPANY; *pg.* 1421, *pg.* 783
THIS OLD HOUSE - Magazine - BONNIER ACTIVE MEDIA, INC.; *pg.* 1622, *pg.* 1205
THIS OLD HOUSE - Media Publication - TIME INC.; *pg.* 1693, *pg.* 1300
THISNEXT - Social Shopping Site - SPINMEDIA; *pg.* 1282, *pg.* 104
THISOLDHOUSE.ORG - Web Site - BONNIER ACTIVE MEDIA, INC.; *pg.* 1622, *pg.* 1205
THIXMOLDING - Injection Molding Process for Semi-Solid Metal - BODYCOTE THERMAL PROCESSING; *pg.* 71, *pg.* 632
THIXOMAG - Alloy Granules - THE DOW CHEMICAL COMPANY; *pg.* 1157, *pg.* 898
THIXON - Adhesive & Sealant - DOW CHEMICAL; *pg.* 1156, *pg.* 1563
THOM-KATT - Trailer-Mounted Concrete Pump - PUTZMEISTER AMERICA; *pg.* 1371, *pg.* 1896
THOMAFLUID - Chemical Tubing - ACCURATE CHEMICAL & SCIENTIFIC CORPORATION; *pg.* 1145, *pg.* 1350
THOMAS - Furniture - ETHAN ALLEN INTERIORS INC.; *pg.* 924, *pg.* 343
THOMAS - Pressure Component - GARDNER DENVER, INC.; *pg.* 1338, *pg.* 1592
THOMAS - Replacement Window & Door - TRUE HOME VALUE, INC.; *pg.* 117, *pg.* 738
THOMAS & FRIENDS - Train Toys - FISHER-PRICE, INC.; *pg.* 953, *pg.* 1156
THOMAS CANADA - Lighting Fixture & Control - PHILIPS LIGHTING; *pg.* 1303, *pg.* 806
THOMAS ENGINEERING - Pharmaceutical Tablet Pressess & Coaters - THOMAS ENGINEERING INC.; *pg.* 1382, *pg.* 619
THE THOMAS GUIDE - Street Guide - RAND MCNALLY & COMPANY; *pg.* 1679, *pg.* 661
THOMAS LIGHTING RESIDENTIAL - Lighting Fixtures - PHILIPS LIGHTING; *pg.* 1303, *pg.* 806
THOMAS NELSON BIBLE - Publication - THOMAS NELSON INC.; *pg.* 1692, *pg.* 1654
THOMAS NELSON BOOKS - Books - THOMAS NELSON INC.; *pg.* 1692, *pg.* 1654
THOMAS REGISTER. COM - Product Information for Industry - THOMAS REGISTER OF AMERICAN MANUFACTURERS; *pg.* 1692, *pg.* 1299
THOMAS REGISTER ORDER ON LINE - E Commerce Service - THOMAS REGISTER OF AMERICAN MANUFACTURERS; *pg.* 1692, *pg.* 1299
THOMAS TABLET SENTINEL 5 (TTS 5) - Press Equipment Automation - THOMAS ENGINEERING INC.; *pg.* 1382, *pg.* 619
THOMAS THE TANK ENGINE - Model Trains - BACHMANN INDUSTRIES, INC.; *pg.* 950, *pg.* 1559
THOMASVILLE - Furniture - HERITAGE HOME GROUP; *pg.* 926, *pg.* 1379
THOMASVILLE - Furniture - THOMASVILLE FURNITURE INDUSTRIES, INC.; *pg.* 945, *pg.* 1391
THOMPSON - Cassettes - INTEGRA MILTEX, INC.; *pg.* 1546, *pg.* 1597
THOMPSON - Nutritional Product - NUTRACEUTICAL INTERNATIONAL CORPORATION; *pg.* 1576, *pg.* 1753
THOMPSON NUTRIT - Nutritional Product - NUTRACEUTICAL INTERNATIONAL CORPORATION; *pg.* 1576, *pg.* 1753
THOMPSON'S - Waterproofing Products - THE SHERWIN-WILLIAMS COMPANY; *pg.* 1447, *pg.* 1435
THOMPSON'S - Exterior Waterproofers; Wood Preservatives, Cleaners & Stains - SHERWIN-WILLIAMS WOOD CARE GROUP; *pg.* 1448, *pg.* 1127
THOMPSON'S WATER SEAL - Waterproofing Stains - SHERWIN-WILLIAMS DIVERSIFIED BRANDS DIVISION; *pg.* 1448, *pg.* 1435
THOMSON - Linear Motion System - DANAHER CORPORATION; *pg.* 1044, *pg.* 397
THOMSON - Mechanical Product - DANAHER MOTION; *pg.* 1327, *pg.* 1593
THOMSON ADVISOR - Software Tool And Application - THOMSON REUTERS MARKETS; *pg.* 810, *pg.* 1299
THOMSON ONE - Financial Publications - THOMSON REUTERS CORPORATION; *pg.* 1693, *pg.* 1944
THOMSON RESEARCH - Software - THOMSON REUTERS CORPORATION; *pg.* 1693, *pg.* 1944
THOMSON TECHNOLOGIES - Automatic Transfer Switches - REGAL BELOIT CORPORATION; *pg.* 106, *pg.* 1854
THOMSON TOLLO - Linear Motion System - DANAHER CORPORATION; *pg.* 1044, *pg.* 397
THONET - Furniture - THE COMMERCIAL FURNITURE GROUP; *pg.* 920, *pg.* 994
THOR - Powerline Protector - TII NETWORK TECHNOLOGIES, INC.; *pg.* 680, *pg.* 1157
THOR - Travel Marketing & Distribution Services - TRAVELPORT LIMITED; *pg.* 1925, *pg.* 521
THORA-CATH - Silicone Chest Drainage Catheter - UTAH MEDICAL PRODUCTS, INC.; *pg.* 1605, *pg.* 1752
THORA-KLEX - Biotechnology Product - GENZYME CORPORATION; *pg.* 1534, *pg.* 808
THORAWEDGE - Medical Device - GAMMEX RMI INC.; *pg.* 1532, *pg.* 1872
THORNDIKE PRESS - Large-Print Editions of Fiction & Non-Fiction Books - GALE CENGAGE LEARNING; *pg.* 1643, *pg.* 885
THORNEL - Chemical Product - CYTEC INDUSTRIES, INC.; *pg.* 1155, *pg.* 1131
THORNHILL - Flatware - THE VOLLRATH COMPANY LLC; *pg.* 1139, *pg.* 1894
THORNTON - Furniture - FLEXSTEEL INDUSTRIES, INC.; *pg.* 925, *pg.* 707
THORNTON - Multiparameter Analyzer - METTLER-TOLEDO INTERNATIONAL INC.; *pg.* 1423, *pg.* 1441
THOROBRED - Entertainment Service - KENTUCKY DERBY FESTIVAL, INC.; *pg.* 556, *pg.* 735
THOROGOOD - Uniform Work & Safety Shoes - WEINBRENNER SHOE COMPANY, INC.; *pg.* 1822, *pg.* 1871
THOROUGHBRED - Belly Tractor Mowers - AG-MEIER INDUSTRIES LLC; *pg.* 700, *pg.* 1668
THE THOROUGHBRED - Transportation - NORFOLK SOUTHERN CORPORATION; *pg.* 1917, *pg.* 1797
THOROUGHBRED - Floor Cleaning Product - NSS ENTERPRISES, INC.; *pg.* 59, *pg.* 1476
THOUGHT BUBBLE - Balloon - CONTINENTAL AMERICAN CORP.; *pg.* 1880, *pg.* 723
THOUGHTFUL LOUNGE - Office Furniture - STEELCASE INC.; *pg.* 475, *pg.* 889
THOUGHTS OF LIFE - Cards - SPS STUDIOS, INC.; *pg.* 1688, *pg.* 311
THREAD-EASY - Film Reels, Magazines - EASTMAN KODAK COMPANY; *pg.* 1408, *pg.* 1333
THREAD-MAGIC - Spark Plug Anti-Seize - AMERICAN GREASE STICK CO.; *pg.* 971, *pg.* 902
THREAD-O-RING - Pipeline Pigging Product - T.D. WILLIAMSON, INC.; *pg.* 1380, *pg.* 1490
THREAD-SEEKER - Locking Spring Hinge Screw - THE HILSINGER CO.; *pg.* 1416, *pg.* 841
THREADFORMER - Information Brochure - SUPERIOR DIE SET CORP.; *pg.* 1379, *pg.* 1885
THREADS - Gages - KENNAMETAL IPG; *pg.* 1353, *pg.* 1615
THREATSEEKER - Software - WEBSENSE, INC.; *pg.* 491, *pg.* 210
THREATSEEKER NETWORK - Software - WEBSENSE, INC.; *pg.* 491, *pg.* 210
THREATWATCHER - Software - WEBSENSE, INC.; *pg.* 491, *pg.* 210
THREE A - Auto Association Prints & Publications - AMERICAN AUTOMOBILE ASSOCIATION; *pg.* 1190, *pg.* 429
THREE BY THREE - Hamburger Sandwiches - IN-N-OUT BURGERS, INC.; *pg.* 1732, *pg.* 111
THREE CARD DRAW POKER - Video Poker - INTERNATIONAL GAME TECHNOLOGY; *pg.* 957, *pg.* 1024
THREE GALLON - Ice Cream - BRIDGEMAN'S RESTAURANTS INC.; *pg.* 1718, *pg.* 919
THREE GREAT BRANDS. ONE GREAT PLACE - Tagline - BAB, INC.; *pg.* 1715, *pg.* 599
THREE KIT - Eye Shadows - COVER GIRL COSMETICS; *pg.* 506, *pg.* 772
THREE MONKEYS - Wine - JIM BEAM BRANDS CO.; *pg.* 1965, *pg.* 601
THREE OLIVES VODKA - Spirits - PROXIMO SPIRITS, INC.; *pg.* 1969, *pg.* 1076
THREE PERFECT DAYS - Airline Service - UNITED CONTINENTAL HOLDINGS, INC.; *pg.* 1927, *pg.* 593
THREE-QUARTER SIZE STERISET - Container - MEDLINE INDUSTRIES, INC.; *pg.* 1562, *pg.* 635
THREE-STONE PENDANT - Diamond Product - BLUE NILE, INC.; *pg.* 2, *pg.* 1834
THREE-STONE RING - Diamond Product - BLUE NILE, INC.; *pg.* 2, *pg.* 1834
THE THREE STOOGES - Lottery Game - MICHIGAN STATE LOTTERY BUREAU; *pg.* 999, *pg.* 895
THREE THIEVES - Beverage - TRINCHERO FAMILY ESTATES; *pg.* 1971, *pg.* 197
THREE TIMES PAY - Game - INTERNATIONAL GAME TECHNOLOGY; *pg.* 957, *pg.* 1024
THREE TREES - Design - SCHOLASTIC INC.; *pg.* 1683, *pg.* 1288
THREESQUARES - Software - SUREQUEST SYSTEMS,

First page reference indicates Business Class Edition
Second page reference indicates Geographic Edition

INC.; *pg.* 900, *pg.* 1669
THRESHOLD - Screening System - MOLECULAR DEVICES CORPORATION; *pg.* 1568, *pg.* 287
THRESHOLDENTERPRISE - Software - CHECKPOINT SYSTEMS, INC.; *pg.* 628, *pg.* 1559
THRIF-T-LUBER - Fluid Handling System - GRACO, INC.; *pg.* 1342, *pg.* 935
THRIFT OVENS - Thermal Processing Equipment - SURFACE COMBUSTION, INC.; *pg.* 1077, *pg.* 1462
THRIFTEE - Depanning Compound - MALLET & COMPANY, INC.; *pg.* 875, *pg.* 1521
THRIFTEE GOLD - Vegetable Oils - MALLET & COMPANY, INC.; *pg.* 875, *pg.* 1521
THRIFTOOL - Clamping Systems - IDEX CORPORATION; *pg.* 1347, *pg.* 623
THRIFTWAY - Supermarkets (Ohio) - WINN DIXIE STORES, INC.; *pg.* 1038, *pg.* 435
THRIFTY KING - Fountain - RITCHIE INDUSTRIES, INC.; *pg.* 707, *pg.* 703
THE THRILL OF BRAZIL - Nail Care Product - OPI PRODUCTS INC.; *pg.* 518, *pg.* 167
THRILLERMAX - Movie Channel - HOME BOX OFFICE, INC.; *pg.* 290, *pg.* 1240
THRILLSEEKERS - Slogan - POPEYE'S CHICKEN & BISCUITS; *pg.* 1745, *pg.* 517
THRIVENT MAGAZINE - Financial Planning Magazine - THRIVENT FINANCIAL FOR LUTHERANS; *pg.* 1219, *pg.* 944
THROAT DISCS - Throat Lozenges - MONTICELLO DRUG CO.; *pg.* 1569, *pg.* 434
THROBOT - Bowling Equipment - BRUNSWICK BOWLING & BILLIARDS CORP.; *pg.* 1828, *pg.* 622
THROGRIP - Outsole - WEINBRENNER SHOE COMPANY, INC.; *pg.* 1822, *pg.* 1871
THROMBI-GEL - Foam Hemostat - KING PHARMACEUTICALS, INC.; *pg.* 1553, *pg.* 1627
THROMBI-PAD - Hemostatic Pad - KING PHARMACEUTICALS, INC.; *pg.* 1553, *pg.* 1627
THROMBIN-JMI - Pharmaceutical Product - KING PHARMACEUTICALS, INC.; *pg.* 1553, *pg.* 1627
THROMCAT - Excimer Laser System - THE SPECTRANETICS CORPORATION; *pg.* 1595, *pg.* 315
THROTTLE - Herbicide - E.I. DU PONT DE NEMOURS & COMPANY; *pg.* 1159, *pg.* 390
THROTTLE - Men's Shoe - JACK SCHWARTZ SHOES, INC.; *pg.* 1810, *pg.* 1245
THROUGH-THE-WALL - Water Heater - BRADFORD-WHITE CORPORATION; *pg.* 1069, *pg.* 1514
THROW ME A BONE - Toy & Game - HASBRO, INC.; *pg.* 954, *pg.* 1603
THRUSH - Exhaust Product - TENNECO, INC.; *pg.* 985, *pg.* 625
THRUSHCRUSHER - Animal Safety Product - NEOGEN CORPORATION; *pg.* 883, *pg.* 896
THRUST - Starting Fluid - RADIATOR SPECIALTY COMPANY; *pg.* 215, *pg.* 1380
THRUVIEW - Graphics Card - ADVANCED MICRO DEVICES, INC.; *pg.* 613, *pg.* 282
THRUWAY - Medical Device - BOSTON SCIENTIFIC CORPORATION; *pg.* 1508, *pg.* 831
THT - Sport Product - FRANKLIN SPORTS, INC.; *pg.* 1834, *pg.* 847
THUMB FUN LOLLIPOPS - Candy - THE TOPPS COMPANY, INC.; *pg.* 588, *pg.* 1302
THUMB-O-PRENE - Orthopedic Product - DJO INCORPORATED; *pg.* 1524, *pg.* 302
THUMB THING - Game - HASBRO, INC.; *pg.* 954, *pg.* 1603
THUMB THING - Hose - TEKNOR APEX COMPANY; *pg.* 1889, *pg.* 1605
THUMB WINDER - Tape - IDEAL INDUSTRIES, INC.; *pg.* 1051, *pg.* 662
THUMBELINA - Toy - MATTEL, INC.; *pg.* 962, *pg.* 81
THUMBPOT - Voltage Divider - TRANSICO INCORPORATED; *pg.* 682, *pg.* 49
THUMBS DOWN - Remote Button - TIVO INC.; *pg.* 313, *pg.* 251
THUMBS UP - Remote Button - TIVO INC.; *pg.* 313, *pg.* 251
THUMBWHEEL - Switch - TRANSICO INCORPORATED; *pg.* 682, *pg.* 49
THUMP - Eyewear - OAKLEY, INC.; *pg.* 1840, *pg.* 86
THUMPER - Massage Product - RELAX THE BACK CORPORATION; *pg.* 940, *pg.* 120
THUMS UP - Beverages - THE COCA-COLA COMPANY; *pg.* 240, *pg.* 493
THUNDER - Carb & Accessory - EDELBROCK CORPORATION; *pg.* 204, *pg.* 293
THUNDER - Salty Snacks - SNYDER'S-LANCE, INC.; *pg.* 896, *pg.* 1368
THUNDER - Appliances - STEELCASE INC.; *pg.* 475, *pg.* 889
THUNDER CREEK - Carpet - BEAULIEU GROUP, LLC; *pg.* 917, *pg.* 529
THUNDER DOWN - Water & Stain Repellent - MCNETT CORPORATION; *pg.* 1839, *pg.* 1817
THUNDER EXPRESS - Global Collaboration System - POLYVISION CORPORATION; *pg.* 665, *pg.* 531
THUNDER GRILL - Restaurant - ARK RESTAURANTS CORP.; *pg.* 1715, *pg.* 1196
THUNDER GUARD - Water & Stain Repellent - MCNETT CORPORATION; *pg.* 1839, *pg.* 1817
THUNDER PRO - Global Collaboration System - POLYVISION CORPORATION; *pg.* 665, *pg.* 531
THUNDER SHIELD - Water Repellent - MCNETT CORPORATION; *pg.* 1839, *pg.* 1817
THUNDER SQUADRON - Snap-Tite Model Kits - REVELL; *pg.* 966, *pg.* 611
THUNDERBIRD - Wine - E&J GALLO WINERY; *pg.* 1962, *pg.* 149
THUNDERBOLT - Welding & Cutting Equip. - MILLER ELECTRIC MANUFACTURING CO.; *pg.* 1361, *pg.* 1852
THUNDERBOLT - Power Tool - MILWAUKEE ELECTRIC TOOL CORP.; *pg.* 1056, *pg.* 1855
THUNDERBOLT - Navigation Clock - TRIMBLE NAVIGATION LIMITED; *pg.* 1384, *pg.* 288
THUNDERBOLT - High Watt Density Cartridge Heater - VULCAN ELECTRIC COMPANY; *pg.* 1078, *pg.* 751
THUNDERBOLT DISPLAY - Display - APPLE INC.; *pg.* 350, *pg.* 73
THUNDERBOLT IGBT - High Voltage Power IGBT - MICROSEMI CORPORATION; *pg.* 435, *pg.* 41
THUNDERHAWK - Amusement & Water Park - CEDAR FAIR, L.P.; *pg.* 537, *pg.* 1471
THUNDERHAWK - Game - WMS INDUSTRIES INC.; *pg.* 593, *pg.* 666
THUNDERHEAD IRISH RED - Beverage - COASTAL EXTREME BREWING COMPANY; *pg.* 240, *pg.* 1602
THUNDERMAX - Power Tool - MILWAUKEE ELECTRIC TOOL CORP.; *pg.* 1056, *pg.* 1855
THURAYA - Telecommunication Product - ITUS CORPORATION; *pg.* 422, *pg.* 1180
THURMADUKE - Streamtables - DUKE MANUFACTURING COMPANY, INC.; *pg.* 54, *pg.* 995
THUYA - Knife - COAST CUTLERY COMPANY; *pg.* 1121, *pg.* 1501
THV - Replacement Window & Door - TRUE HOME VALUE, INC.; *pg.* 117, *pg.* 738
THWACK - Computer Product - SOLARWINDS, INC.; *pg.* 471, *pg.* 1666
THX ULTRA - Electronic Equipment - KLIPSCH GROUP, INC.; *pg.* 649, *pg.* 688
THYBONY - Wall Coverings - THYBONY WALLCOVERINGS INC.; *pg.* 945, *pg.* 591
THYLOX - Soap - GRANDPA BRANDS COMPANY; *pg.* 1538, *pg.* 727
THYMOGLOBULIN - Transplant & Immune Disease - GENZYME CORPORATION; *pg.* 1534, *pg.* 808
THYRO-SLIM - Nutritional Supplement - MAXIMUM HUMAN PERFORMANCE, INC.; *pg.* 1559, *pg.* 1065
THYROGEN - Oncology - GENZYME CORPORATION; *pg.* 1534, *pg.* 808
THYROID ENERGY - Nutritional Supplement - NOW HEALTH GROUP, INC.; *pg.* 1576, *pg.* 557
THYROKARE - Animal Safety Product - NEOGEN CORPORATION; *pg.* 883, *pg.* 896
THYROMED - Chewable Tablet - HESKA CORPORATION; *pg.* 1542, *pg.* 335
THYROTEST - Thyroid Disease Test Product - ALERE INC.; *pg.* 1488, *pg.* 849
TI-83 PLUS - Calculators - TEXAS INSTRUMENTS INCORPORATED; *pg.* 679, *pg.* 1688
TI FLEX BOW - Scissors - ACME UNITED CORPORATION; *pg.* 1040, *pg.* 346
TI NAVIGATOR - Classroom Learning Network - TEXAS INSTRUMENTS INCORPORATED; *pg.* 679, *pg.* 1688
TI-NSPIRE - Hand-Held Electronic Instrument - TEXAS INSTRUMENTS INCORPORATED; *pg.* 679, *pg.* 1688
TI OMAP3 - Software Application - BSQUARE CORPORATION; *pg.* 366, *pg.* 1813
TI OMAP3 EVM - Development Platform - BSQUARE CORPORATION; *pg.* 366, *pg.* 1813
TI-OPC - Integrated Circuits - TEXAS INSTRUMENTS INCORPORATED; *pg.* 679, *pg.* 1688
TI-RFID - Radio Frequency Transceivers - TEXAS INSTRUMENTS INCORPORATED; *pg.* 679, *pg.* 1688
TI-SMARTVIEW - Software - TEXAS INSTRUMENTS INCORPORATED; *pg.* 679, *pg.* 1688
TI-TECH - Header - EDELBROCK CORPORATION; *pg.* 204, *pg.* 293
TI-TECH - Striking Tool - VAUGHAN & BUSHNELL MANUFACTURING COMPANY, INC.; *pg.* 1066, *pg.* 616
TIAMORA - Footwear - STEVEN MADDEN, LTD.; *pg.* 1819, *pg.* 1176
TIAN TEY - Soft Drink - THE COCA-COLA COMPANY; *pg.* 240, *pg.* 493
TIAN YU DI - Beverages - THE COCA-COLA COMPANY; *pg.* 240, *pg.* 493
TIARA - Yachts - S2 YACHTS, INC.; *pg.* 1710, *pg.* 892
TIAZAC - Pharmaceutical Product - VALEANT PHARMACEUTICALS INTERNATIONAL, INC.; *pg.* 1605, *pg.* 1957
TIBCO ACTIVEMATRIX BUSINESSWORKS - Productivity Software - TIBCO SOFTWARE INC.; *pg.* 484, *pg.* 178
TIBCO SILVER - Web Services - TIBCO SOFTWARE INC.; *pg.* 484, *pg.* 178
TIBERIAN SUN - Video Game - ELECTRONIC ARTS INC.; *pg.* 951, *pg.* 189
TIBERON - Ceramic Tile - WALKER & ZANGER, INC.; *pg.* 119, *pg.* 281
TIBET - Rug - COURISTAN INC.; *pg.* 921, *pg.* 1067
TIBET - Fabric - NEMSCHOFF, INC.; *pg.* 936, *pg.* 1890
TIBETAN FOREST - Carpet - INTERFACE, INC.; *pg.* 695, *pg.* 512
TIBIAL - Orthopedic Product - DJO INCORPORATED; *pg.* 1524, *pg.* 302
TIBURON - Rug - COURISTAN INC.; *pg.* 921, *pg.* 1067
TIBURON - Community Name - WCI COMMUNITIES, INC.; *pg.* 1118, *pg.* 414
TIBURON NAPLES - Community Name - WCI COMMUNITIES, INC.; *pg.* 1118, *pg.* 414
TIC TAC DOUGH - Game - MISSOURI LOTTERY; *pg.* 999, *pg.* 979
TIC TAC SNOW - Lottery Game - D.C. LOTTERY & CHARITABLE GAMES CONTROL BOARD; *pg.* 991, *pg.* 398
TIC TAC TURKEY - Scratch Lottery Game - IDAHO LOTTERY; *pg.* 995, *pg.* 547
TICINO - Bike - ELECTRA BICYCLE COMPANY; *pg.* 1706, *pg.* 303
TICKETBURST - Sensor - TRANSACT TECHNOLOGIES INCORPORATED; *pg.* 484, *pg.* 351
TICKLE - Web Applications - EOLAS TECHNOLOGIES, INC.; *pg.* 1243, *pg.* 573
TICKLED PINK - Instant Lottery Game - NEW YORK STATE LOTTERY; *pg.* 1001, *pg.* 1340
TICLID - Pharmaceutical Product - HOFFMANN-LA ROCHE INC.; *pg.* 1542, *pg.* 1099
TI.COM - Website - TEXAS INSTRUMENTS INCORPORATED; *pg.* 679, *pg.* 1688
TICON - Additive - FERRO CORPORATION; *pg.* 1162, *pg.* 1462
TICONDEROGA - Writing Instruments - DIXON TICONDEROGA COMPANY; *pg.* 388, *pg.* 430
TICONTROL - Medical Device - RESMED INC.; *pg.* 1589, *pg.* 207
TIDE - Fabric - NEMSCHOFF, INC.; *pg.* 936, *pg.* 1890
TIDE - Laundry Products - THE PROCTER & GAMBLE COMPANY; *pg.* 1129, *pg.* 1418
TIDE 2X ULTRA - Laundry Product - THE PROCTER & GAMBLE COMPANY; *pg.* 1129, *pg.* 1418
TIDE PODS - Laundry Product - THE PROCTER & GAMBLE COMPANY; *pg.* 1129, *pg.* 1418
TIDE SIMPLE PLEASURES - Laundry Detergent - THE PROCTER & GAMBLE COMPANY; *pg.* 1129, *pg.* 1418
TIDE TO GO PEN - Stain Remover - THE PROCTER & GAMBLE COMPANY; *pg.* 1129, *pg.* 1418
TIDEGUARD - Protective Cladding - NOV AMERON; *pg.* 100, *pg.* 187
TIDINGS - Kitchen Product - KOHLER CO.; *pg.* 91, *pg.* 1862
TIDY CATS - Pet Care Product - NESTLE PURINA PETCARE COMPANY; *pg.* 1479, *pg.* 1000
TIDY KIDS - Bath Organizer - HOME PRODUCTS INTERNATIONAL, INC.; *pg.* 1125, *pg.* 577
TIDY- VAC - Surface Maintenance Machine - TENNANT COMPANY; *pg.* 1381, *pg.* 944
TIDYNAP - Dispenser Napkin - GEORGIA-PACIFIC LLC; *pg.*

1458, *pg.* 507
TIE-DEX - Clamping Systems - IDEX CORPORATION; *pg.* 1347, *pg.* 623
TIE-DYE STRATOCASTER - Electric Guitar - FENDER MUSICAL INSTRUMENTS CORPORATION; *pg.* 547, *pg.* 21
TIE-LOK - Clamping Systems - IDEX CORPORATION; *pg.* 1347, *pg.* 623
TIE MASTERS - Railroad Tie - HARSCO RAIL; *pg.* 1345, *pg.* 1623
TIE ONE ON FOR SAFETY - Awareness Program - MOTHERS AGAINST DRUNK DRIVING (MADD); *pg.* 147, *pg.* 1723
TIEBACK - Healthcare Apparel - THE SALK COMPANY; *pg.* 1591, *pg.* 800
TIEBACK - Lanyard - SELLSTROM MANUFACTURING CO.; *pg.* 1428, *pg.* 659
TIELLE - Healthcare Product - JOHNSON & JOHNSON; *pg.* 1549, *pg.* 1091
TIEMPO - Radial Tires - THE GOODYEAR TIRE & RUBBER COMPANY; *pg.* 1883, *pg.* 1401
TIEMPO - Apparel - NIKE, INC.; *pg.* 1812, *pg.* 1492
TIEMPO - Weekly Newspaper - THE RECORD-JOURNAL PUBLISHING COMPANY; *pg.* 1680, *pg.* 354
TIENET - Software Product - MAXIMUS, INC.; *pg.* 780, *pg.* 1799
TIERRA - Furniture - JASPER GROUP; *pg.* 930, *pg.* 691
TIFFANY - Furniture - AMERICAN LEATHER LP; *pg.* 912, *pg.* 1673
TIFFANY - Door Panel - MASONITE INTERNATIONAL CORPORATION; *pg.* 1054, *pg.* 1920
TIFFANY - Fabric - NEMSCHOFF, INC.; *pg.* 936, *pg.* 1890
TIFFANY - Lighting Product - QUOIZEL INC.; *pg.* 1304, *pg.* 1616
TIFFANY & CO. - Jewelry, China, Crystal, Silver & Fragrance - TIFFANY & CO.; *pg.* 13, *pg.* 1299
TIFFANY ATLAS - Jewelry Collection - TIFFANY & CO.; *pg.* 13, *pg.* 1299
TIFFANY BLUE - Color - TIFFANY & CO.; *pg.* 13, *pg.* 1299
TIFFANY BLUE BOX - Box Packaging - TIFFANY & CO.; *pg.* 13, *pg.* 1299
TIFFANY CELEBRATION - Jewelry Collection - TIFFANY & CO.; *pg.* 13, *pg.* 1299
TIFFANY FOR MEN - Fragrance - TIFFANY & CO.; *pg.* 13, *pg.* 1299
TIFFANY MARK - Watch - TIFFANY & CO.; *pg.* 13, *pg.* 1299
TIFFANY NATURE - Jewelry Collection - TIFFANY & CO.; *pg.* 13, *pg.* 1299
TIFFANY SIGNATURE - Jewelry Collection - TIFFANY & CO.; *pg.* 13, *pg.* 1299
TIGER - Detergent - ADCO, INC.; *pg.* 325, *pg.* 482
TIGER - Mower - ALAMO GROUP INC.; *pg.* 1311, *pg.* 1745
TIGER - Sporting Goods - ASICS AMERICA CORPORATION; *pg.* 1826, *pg.* 106
TIGER - Biscuits - MONDELEZ INTERNATIONAL, INC.; *pg.* 878, *pg.* 601
TIGER - Label Product - SYSTEMAX, INC.; *pg.* 481, *pg.* 1324
TIGER BLUE - Wire Rope Process - BRIDON AMERICAN CORP.; *pg.* 1319, *pg.* 1594
TIGER BRAND - Structural Process Line/Mining - BRIDON AMERICAN CORP.; *pg.* 1319, *pg.* 1594
TIGER CLAW - Decking & Railing - TREX COMPANY, INC.; *pg.* 116, *pg.* 1812
TIGER COOL FUSION - Drinks - PEPSICO, INC.; *pg.* 259, *pg.* 1327
TIGER ELECTRONICS - Toy & Game - HASBRO, INC.; *pg.* 954, *pg.* 1603
TIGER GAMES - Toy & Game - HASBRO, INC.; *pg.* 954, *pg.* 1603
TIGER HAIR - Fiberglass Reinforced Filler - ITW - EVERCOAT; *pg.* 1443, *pg.* 1415
TIGER POWER - Food Product - KELLOGG COMPANY; *pg.* 831, *pg.* 870
TIGER QUITE STORM - Drinks - PEPSICO, INC.; *pg.* 259, *pg.* 1327
TIGER RED DRIVE - Drinks - PEPSICO, INC.; *pg.* 259, *pg.* 1327
TIGER RING - Flashlight - STREAMLIGHT INC.; *pg.* 1306, *pg.* 1527
TIGER RIVER SPAS - Spas - WATKINS MANUFACTURING CORPORATION; *pg.* 120, *pg.* 303
TIGER TRUCKAT - Truck-Mounted Boom Mower - ALAMO GROUP INC.; *pg.* 1311, *pg.* 1745
TIGER TUBE - Feeding Tube - COOK GROUP, INC.; *pg.* 1518, *pg.* 674
TIGERCAT PLATESETTER - Four Page Platesetter - ECRM IMAGING SYSTEMS, INC.; *pg.* 1410, *pg.* 848
TIGERLOGIC - Dashboard Product - TIGERLOGIC CORPORATION; *pg.* 484, *pg.* 117
TIGER'S MILK - Nutritional Bars - RECKITT BENCKISER INC.; *pg.* 1136, *pg.* 1105
TIGER'S REALM - Game - WMS INDUSTRIES INC.; *pg.* 593, *pg.* 666
TIGERSHARC - Baseband Processor - ANALOG DEVICES, INC.; *pg.* 617, *pg.* 839
TIGERSHARP - Scissors - ACME UNITED CORPORATION; *pg.* 1040, *pg.* 346
TIGERTOP - Soft Top - BESTOP, INC.; *pg.* 200, *pg.* 312
TIGERWIRE - Steerable Guidewire - ST. JUDE MEDICAL, INC.; *pg.* 1596, *pg.* 963
TIGHT CURL II - Curling Iron Brush Set - JARDEN CONSUMER SOLUTIONS; *pg.* 57, *pg.* 412
TIGHT LIES - Golf Product - TAYLORMADE-ADIDAS GOLF; *pg.* 1847, *pg.* 60
TIGI - Hair Care Products - UNILEVER UNITED STATES, INC.; *pg.* 904, *pg.* 1061
TIGLAZE - Copolyester - EASTMAN CHEMICAL COMPANY; *pg.* 1159, *pg.* 1636
TIGRIP - Hoist - COLUMBUS MCKINNON CORPORATION; *pg.* 1325, *pg.* 1138
TIGRIS - Fabric - NEMSCHOFF, INC.; *pg.* 936, *pg.* 1890
TIGRIS - Carpet - WOVEN LEGENDS INC.; *pg.* 947, *pg.* 1572
TIJUANA - Tequila - SAZERAC COMPANY, INC.; *pg.* 1969, *pg.* 745
TIK SERIES - Audio & Video Product - HARMAN INTERNATIONAL INDUSTRIES, INCORPORATED; *pg.* 641, *pg.* 374
TIKES PEAK - Road & Rail Set - RUBBERMAID HOME PRODUCTS; *pg.* 1138, *pg.* 1453
TIKI - Cone Metal Torch - W.C. BRADLEY CO.; *pg.* 62, *pg.* 528
TIKI BAY - Food Products - RICH PRODUCTS CORPORATION; *pg.* 892, *pg.* 1150
TIKI GOLD - Game - WMS INDUSTRIES INC.; *pg.* 593, *pg.* 666
TIKI TIME - Nail Color - ORLY INTERNATIONAL, INC.; *pg.* 518, *pg.* 137
TIKOSYN - Medicine - PFIZER INC.; *pg.* 1581, *pg.* 1278
TIKY - Soft Drink - THE COCA-COLA COMPANY; *pg.* 240, *pg.* 493
TILADE - Pharmaceutical Product - KING PHARMACEUTICALS, INC.; *pg.* 1553, *pg.* 1627
TILANX - Pharmaceutical Preparation - PFIZER INC.; *pg.* 1581, *pg.* 1278
TILE BOND - Roof Tile Adhesive - THE DOW CHEMICAL COMPANY; *pg.* 1157, *pg.* 898
TILE GROUT - Sealer - THE SAVOGRAN COMPANY; *pg.* 1447, *pg.* 840
TILE PERFECT - Adhesive - H.B. FULLER COMPANY; *pg.* 1165, *pg.* 961
TILE POWER - Stain Remover - BLUE CROSS LABORATORIES; *pg.* 326, *pg.* 277
TILES - Fabric - NEMSCHOFF, INC.; *pg.* 936, *pg.* 1890
TILEX - Daily Shower Cleaner - THE CLOROX COMPANY; *pg.* 327, *pg.* 169
TILEX MILDEW ROOT - Penetrator & Remover - THE CLOROX COMPANY; *pg.* 327, *pg.* 169
TILLAMOOK CHEESEBURGER - Cheese Products - TILLAMOOK COUNTY CREAMERY ASSOCIATION; *pg.* 901, *pg.* 1509
TILLEY - Leather Goods & Souvenirs - TILLEY OF CANADA LIMITED; *pg.* 14, *pg.* 1920
TILT-A-WHIRL - Fabric - NEMSCHOFF, INC.; *pg.* 936, *pg.* 1890
TILT & POUR - Beverage Server - THE VOLLRATH COMPANY LLC; *pg.* 1139, *pg.* 1894
TILT II - Electrical Test & Measurement - HD ELECTRIC COMPANY; *pg.* 1299, *pg.* 666
TILT-KOTE - Masonry Paint - DUNN-EDWARDS CORPORATION; *pg.* 1442, *pg.* 129
TILT-LOK - Power Tool - MILWAUKEE ELECTRIC TOOL CORP.; *pg.* 1056, *pg.* 1855
TILT N' TUMBLE - Game - PRESSMAN TOY CORPORATION; *pg.* 965, *pg.* 1734
TILT-PRIME - Masonry Primer - DUNN-EDWARDS CORPORATION; *pg.* 1442, *pg.* 129
TILT SWIVEL - Furniture - HOOKER FURNITURE CORPORATION; *pg.* 928, *pg.* 1788
TILT WALL WEDGE-BOLT - Screw Anchor - POWERS FASTENERS INC.; *pg.* 1059, *pg.* 1143
TILTBACK - Bucket Exchange System - GRACO, INC.; *pg.* 1342, *pg.* 935
TILTED STRAIGHT 523 - Jean - LEVI STRAUSS & CO.; *pg.* 43, *pg.* 220
TIM - Furniture - AMISCO INDUSTRIES LTD.; *pg.* 913, *pg.* 1958
TIM DRAKE - Character - DC COMICS, INC.; *pg.* 1633, *pg.* 1221
TIM HORTONS - Restaurant Chain - RESTAURANT BRANDS INTERNATIONAL INC.; *pg.* 1747, *pg.* 1930
TIMBER - Bear - GUND, INC.; *pg.* 954, *pg.* 1056
TIMBER CREEK BY WRANGLER - Casual Pants - V.F. CORPORATION; *pg.* 34, *pg.* 1376
TIMBER HD - Binocular - LEUPOLD & STEVENS, INC.; *pg.* 1420, *pg.* 1492
TIMBER RIDGE - Wall Panel - BLUELINX HOLDINGS, INC.; *pg.* 70, *pg.* 491
TIMBER WOLF - Amusement & Water Park - CEDAR FAIR, L.P.; *pg.* 537, *pg.* 1471
TIMBERGUARD - Construction Material - CRANE PLASTICS HOLDING COMPANY; *pg.* 1881, *pg.* 1439
TIMBERLAKE - Cabinet - AMERICAN WOODMARK CORPORATION; *pg.* 913, *pg.* 1811
TIMBERLAND - Wood Flooring Products - ARMSTRONG WORLD INDUSTRIES, INC.; *pg.* 914, *pg.* 1545
TIMBERLAND - Footwear, Apparel Accessories & Licensed Products - THE TIMBERLAND COMPANY; *pg.* 1821, *pg.* 1039
TIMBERLAND PRO - Work Boots - THE TIMBERLAND COMPANY; *pg.* 1821, *pg.* 1039
TIMBERLAST - Vinyl Siding - NORTEK, INC.; *pg.* 100, *pg.* 1607
TIMBERLINE - Furniture - ASHLEY FURNITURE INDUSTRIES, INC.; *pg.* 914, *pg.* 1852
TIMBERLINE BOND - Paper Product - BOISE CASCADE HOLDINGS, L.L.C.; *pg.* 1453, *pg.* 546
TIMBERMASTER - Footwear - LACROSSE FOOTWEAR, INC.; *pg.* 1811, *pg.* 1503
TIMBERSTRAND - Wood & Building Material - WEYERHAEUSER COMPANY; *pg.* 121, *pg.* 1820
TIMBERTECH - Building Product - CRANE PLASTICS HOLDING COMPANY; *pg.* 1881, *pg.* 1439
TIMBERWORK - Fastening System - SFS INTEC, INC.; *pg.* 1061, *pg.* 1596
TIMBERWORKS - Cleaning Product - ORECK CORPORATION; *pg.* 59, *pg.* 1653
TIMBITS - Bite Sized Donut - TIM HORTONS, INC.; *pg.* 1754, *pg.* 1930
TIME - Media Publication - TIME INC.; *pg.* 1693, *pg.* 1300
TIME-A-MATIC - Sprinklers - MELNOR, INC.; *pg.* 1055, *pg.* 1811
TIME ATTENDANT - Time Reporting System - AMANO CINCINNATI, INC.; *pg.* 348, *pg.* 1117
TIME-BASED SOLUTIONS FOR YOUR BUSINESS - Tagline - AMANO CINCINNATI, INC.; *pg.* 348, *pg.* 1117
TIME BOMB - Watch - OAKLEY, INC.; *pg.* 1840, *pg.* 86
TIME CAPSULE - Wireless Hard Drive - APPLE INC.; *pg.* 350, *pg.* 73
TIME FOR KIDS - Media Publication - TIME INC.; *pg.* 1693, *pg.* 1300
TIME FOR US GAMES - Toy & Game - HASBRO, INC.; *pg.* 954, *pg.* 1603
TIME GUARDIAN - Time Reporting System - AMANO CINCINNATI, INC.; *pg.* 348, *pg.* 1117
TIME IN A BOX - Time & Attendance System - PAYCHEX, INC.; *pg.* 792, *pg.* 1336
TIME INC. - Wireless Service Company - TIME WARNER INC.; *pg.* 312, *pg.* 1302
TIME IS LIFE - Slogan - BLACK DIAMOND, INC.; *pg.* 1827, *pg.* 1756
THE TIME IS RIGHT - Tag Line - HAIR CLUB FOR MEN, LTD., INC.; *pg.* 511, *pg.* 411
TIME-IT - Software System - MENTOR GRAPHICS CORPORATION; *pg.* 432, *pg.* 1510
TIME-LIFE VIDEO RECORDINGS - Videos - DIRECT HOLDINGS AMERICAS INC.; *pg.* 1636, *pg.* 1780
TIME MACHINE - Application Program - APPLE INC.; *pg.* 350, *pg.* 73
TIME MACHINE - Guitar - FENDER MUSICAL INSTRUMENTS CORPORATION; *pg.* 547, *pg.* 21
TIME MACHINE - Game - WMS INDUSTRIES INC.; *pg.* 593, *pg.* 666
TIME OPTIMAL PATH - Atmospheric Tool - BROOKS AUTOMATION, INC.; *pg.* 1320, *pg.* 813

First page reference indicates Business Class Edition
Second page reference indicates Geographic Edition

TIME TRAVEL - Software - SAND TECHNOLOGY, INC.; *pg.* 465, *pg.* 1961
TIME WARNER CABLE - Entertainment Product - TIME WARNER INC.; *pg.* 312, *pg.* 1302
TIME WARNER TRADE PUBLISHING - Entertainment Product - TIME WARNER INC.; *pg.* 312, *pg.* 1302
TIMEBINATION - Time-Delay Combination Lock - SARGENT & GREENLEAF, INC.; *pg.* 1061, *pg.* 739
TIMEBLOCK - Personal Care Electrical Product - HELEN OF TROY L.P.; *pg.* 511, *pg.* 1692
TIMEBUILDER - Application Specific Integrated Circuits - TEXAS INSTRUMENTS INCORPORATED; *pg.* 679, *pg.* 1688
TIMECARD - Medical Product - PROPPER MANUFACTURING COMPANY, INC.; *pg.* 1586, *pg.* 1175
TIMECELL - Application Specific Integrated Circuits - TEXAS INSTRUMENTS INCORPORATED; *pg.* 679, *pg.* 1688
TIMED MULTIPLE-ACTION DELIVERY SYSTEM - Proprietary Drug Delivery Technology - IMPAX LABORATORIES, INC.; *pg.* 1544, *pg.* 101
TIMEFINDER - Software - EMC CORPORATION; *pg.* 391, *pg.* 825
TIMEKEEPER CENTRAL - Software System - KRONOS INCORPORATED; *pg.* 425, *pg.* 813
TIMELESS - Hardwood Flooring - NYDREE FLOORING; *pg.* 939, *pg.* 1782
TIMELESS BEAUTY - Container Grown Plant - MONROVIA GROWERS; *pg.* 1797, *pg.* 44
TIMELESS RETREAT - Furniture - LEXINGTON HOME BRANDS; *pg.* 933, *pg.* 1391
TIMELESS SERIES - Flooring - NYDREE FLOORING; *pg.* 939, *pg.* 1782
TIMELESS SERIES 3 - Hardwood Flooring Product - NYDREE FLOORING; *pg.* 939, *pg.* 1782
TIMELESS TREASURES - Toy - MATTEL, INC.; *pg.* 962, *pg.* 81
TIMELESS TULIPS - Flower Arrangement - 1-800-FLOWERS.COM, INC.; *pg.* 1758, *pg.* 1151
TIMELESS TWIST - Carpet - BEAULIEU GROUP, LLC; *pg.* 917, *pg.* 529
TIMELINE - Process Technology - TEXAS INSTRUMENTS INCORPORATED; *pg.* 679, *pg.* 1688
TIMEMARK - Software - FALCONSTOR SOFTWARE, INC.; *pg.* 396, *pg.* 1179
TIMEMIST - Air Fragrancing & Sanitizing Products - ZEP INC.; *pg.* 338, *pg.* 524
TIMEPIECE - Kitchen Appliance - VIKING RANGE CORPORATION; *pg.* 61, *pg.* 968
TIMEPILOT - ASIC Design Tool - TEXAS INSTRUMENTS INCORPORATED; *pg.* 679, *pg.* 1688
TIMEPORT - Communications Product - MOTOROLA SOLUTIONS, INC.; *pg.* 657, *pg.* 659
TIMES COMMUNITY NEWS - Newspapers - LOS ANGELES TIMES COMMUNICATIONS, LLC; *pg.* 1660, *pg.* 135
TIMES FIBER - Fiber Optics - AMPHENOL CORPORATION; *pg.* 616, *pg.* 381
THE TIMES-NEWS - North Carolina Newspaper - FREEDOM COMMUNICATIONS, INC.; *pg.* 1643, *pg.* 110
THE TIMES-NEWS - Newspaper - THE TIMES-NEWS; *pg.* 1694, *pg.* 1359
THE TIMES-PICAYUNE - Daily Newspaper - NOLA MEDIA GROUP; *pg.* 1671, *pg.* 747
TIMES REMEMBERED - Deluxe Cards - LEANIN' TREE, INC.; *pg.* 1658, *pg.* 311
TIMESHARESAVER.COM - Advertising Website - DOMINION ENTERPRISES; *pg.* 1636, *pg.* 1796
TIMESHIFT - Communication Product - J2 GLOBAL COMMUNICATIONS, INC.; *pg.* 1260, *pg.* 133
TIMESLIPS - Time & Billing Solution for Service Professionals - SAGE SOFTWARE, INC.; *pg.* 464, *pg.* 116
TIMESOLV - Internet-Based Time Tracking & Invoicing Solution - THOMSON ELITE; *pg.* 484, *pg.* 72
TIMESPAN - Digital Telephone Equipment - ALCATEL-LUCENT USA, INC.; *pg.* 615, *pg.* 1728
TIMESTEP - Floors - STAGESTEP INC.; *pg.* 1688, *pg.* 1570
TIMESTEP T - Flooring Product - STAGESTEP INC.; *pg.* 1688, *pg.* 1570
TIMESTREAM - Semiconductor Solution - VITESSE SEMICONDUCTOR CORPORATION; *pg.* 686, *pg.* 57
TIMETER - Suction Regulator - ALLIED HEALTHCARE PRODUCTS, INC.; *pg.* 1491, *pg.* 990
TIMETRACK PAYROLL SYSTEM - Fully-Integrated Payroll & Human Resources Accounting & Management Tool - JACK HENRY & ASSOCIATES, INC.; *pg.* 422, *pg.* 988
TIMETRAX - Time & Expense Entry System - THOMSON ELITE; *pg.* 484, *pg.* 72
TIMEVIEW - Image Software - FALCONSTOR SOFTWARE, INC.; *pg.* 396, *pg.* 1179
TIMEXPO - Timekeeping Museum - TIMEX CORPORATION; *pg.* 14, *pg.* 355
TIMKEN - Bearing Product - THE TIMKEN COMPANY; *pg.* 218, *pg.* 1408
TIMONOX - Flame Retardants - CHEMTURA CORPORATION; *pg.* 1152, *pg.* 355
TIMPANI - Software - LIVEPERSON, INC.; *pg.* 1264, *pg.* 1252
TIMPANO - Restaurants - TAVISTOCK RESTAURANT GROUP; *pg.* 1753, *pg.* 803
TIM'S - Potato Chips & Snack Foods - PINNACLE FOODS GROUP LLC; *pg.* 889, *pg.* 1104
TIM'S OWN - Sandwiches - TIM HORTONS, INC.; *pg.* 1754, *pg.* 1930
TIN CAT - Trap - THE WOODSTREAM CORPORATION; *pg.* 1801, *pg.* 1549
TINA - Furniture - AMISCO INDUSTRIES LTD.; *pg.* 913, *pg.* 1958
TINA - Furniture - THE COMMERCIAL FURNITURE GROUP; *pg.* 920, *pg.* 994
TINACTIN - Antifungal Products - MERCK & CO., INC.; *pg.* 1566, *pg.* 1077
TINANO - Ceramic Nanomaterial Product - ALTAIR NANOTECHNOLOGIES INC.; *pg.* 1147, *pg.* 1031
TINDLE FEEDS - Animal Health Product - ADM ALLIANCE NUTRITION, INC.; *pg.* 1474, *pg.* 653
TINEGAL - Levelling Agents - HUNTSMAN CORPORATION; *pg.* 1167, *pg.* 1758
TINGSHA - Bell - HUGGER MUGGER YOGA PRODUCTS LLC; *pg.* 1836, *pg.* 1758
TINI - Microcontrollers - MAXIM INTEGRATED PRODUCTS, INC.; *pg.* 653, *pg.* 247
TINI PUPPINI - Toy - SPIN MASTER LTD.; *pg.* 967, *pg.* 1943
TINITE - Tin Coatings for Cutting Tools - GLEASON CORPORATION; *pg.* 1340, *pg.* 1335
TINKERTOYS - Construction Toys - HASBRO, INC.; *pg.* 954, *pg.* 1603
TINOS - Fabric - NEMSCHOFF, INC.; *pg.* 936, *pg.* 1890
TINTIA - Dispensing Equipment - IDEX CORPORATION; *pg.* 1347, *pg.* 623
TINTMASTER - Dispensing Equipment - IDEX CORPORATION; *pg.* 1347, *pg.* 623
TINTURA - Concrete System - L.M. SCOFIELD COMPANY; *pg.* 94, *pg.* 134
TINY CABLE - Women's Clothing & Accessories - WOODEN SHIPS OF HOBOKEN; *pg.* 35, *pg.* 1315
TINY FLOWER - Women's Clothing & Accessories - WOODEN SHIPS OF HOBOKEN; *pg.* 35, *pg.* 1315
TINY SHELL - Women's Clothing & Accessories - WOODEN SHIPS OF HOBOKEN; *pg.* 35, *pg.* 1315
TINY TIM - Connector - COOPER INTERCONNECT; *pg.* 630, *pg.* 1118
TINY TOWER - Container Grown Plant - MONROVIA GROWERS; *pg.* 1797, *pg.* 44
TINY TRAIL - Bike - MARIN BIKES; *pg.* 1708, *pg.* 168
TINY TWEEZ - Hair Accessories - STA-RITE GINNIE LOU, INC.; *pg.* 523, *pg.* 660
TINYAVR - Integrated Circuit - ATMEL CORPORATION; *pg.* 621, *pg.* 238
TINYFET - Integrated Circuits - MICREL, INC.; *pg.* 654, *pg.* 247
TINYLETTER - E-Mail Newsletter - THE ROCKET SCIENCE GROUP, LLC; *pg.* 1278, *pg.* 519
TINYPRINTS - Stationary & Print Invitations - SHUTTERFLY, INC.; *pg.* 1280, *pg.* 192
TINYSWITCH - Switch - POWER INTEGRATIONS, INC.; *pg.* 1369, *pg.* 249
TINYTIGHT - Pumps - IDEX CORPORATION; *pg.* 1347, *pg.* 623
TIO PEPE - Sherry - REMY COINTREAU USA INC.; *pg.* 1969, *pg.* 1285
TIO PEPE'S - Food Product - J&J SNACK FOODS CORPORATION; *pg.* 865, *pg.* 1107
TIO SOTO - Fortified Wine - LEONARD KREUSCH, INC.; *pg.* 254, *pg.* 1099
TIOPREM - Mineral Product - TOR MINERALS INTERNATIONAL INC.; *pg.* 1184, *pg.* 1672
TIOXIDE - Titanium Dioxide Pigments - HUNTSMAN CORPORATION; *pg.* 1167, *pg.* 1758
TIP - Access - IHS AUTOMOTIVE DRIVEN BY POLK; *pg.* 1652, *pg.* 907
TIP ACCESS - Vehicle - IHS AUTOMOTIVE DRIVEN BY POLK; *pg.* 1652, *pg.* 907
TIP-IT - Instrument Guards - INTEGRA MILTEX, INC.; *pg.* 1546, *pg.* 1597
TIP-IT - Toy - MATTEL, INC.; *pg.* 962, *pg.* 81
TIP NET - Vehicle - IHS AUTOMOTIVE DRIVEN BY POLK; *pg.* 1652, *pg.* 907
TIP-OFF - Cleaning Product - HILLYARD, INC.; *pg.* 331, *pg.* 990
TIP-ON - Process for Adhering Plastic to Paper - PLASTIC SUPPLIERS, INC.; *pg.* 1888, *pg.* 1443
TIP SEAL - Fluid Handling System - GRACO, INC.; *pg.* 1342, *pg.* 935
TIP TONI - Home Permanent - THE GILLETTE COMPANY; *pg.* 509, *pg.* 795
TIP TOP - Foods - SENECA FOODS CORPORATION; *pg.* 895, *pg.* 1177
TIP TORCON - Catheter - COOK GROUP, INC.; *pg.* 1518, *pg.* 674
TIP TORCON NB - Catheter - COOK GROUP, INC.; *pg.* 1518, *pg.* 674
TIPER - Office Furniture - JOFCO INC.; *pg.* 931, *pg.* 691
TIPPER CLIPPER - Manual Hand Clipper - TIPPER TIE, INC.; *pg.* 1382, *pg.* 1358
TIPPER TAGGER SYSTEM - Ultrasonic, Plastic Tag Closure System With the Ability to Print - TIPPER TIE, INC.; *pg.* 1382, *pg.* 1358
TIPPERARY - Fabric - SCALAMANDRE, INC.; *pg.* 941, *pg.* 1058
TIPSEEZ - Footwear - CAPEZIO BALLET MAKERS INC.; *pg.* 1805, *pg.* 1125
TIPTRODE - Robotic Product - HAMILTON CO., INC.; *pg.* 1415, *pg.* 1031
TIRE BUSINESS - Newspaper - CRAIN COMMUNICATIONS, INC.; *pg.* 1631, *pg.* 879
TIRE KINGDOM - Retail Center - TBC CORPORATION; *pg.* 1889, *pg.* 457
TIRE TECHNOLOGY FOR THE 21ST CENTURY - Slogan - AMERITYRE CORPORATION; *pg.* 1879, *pg.* 1021
TIREBUYER.COM - E-Commerce Website - AMERICAN TIRE DISTRIBUTORS HOLDINGS, INC.; *pg.* 199, *pg.* 1379
TIRECO - Tires - THE HERCULES TIRE & RUBBER COMPANY; *pg.* 1884, *pg.* 1454
TIREM - Software Product Module - RIVERBED PERFORMANCE MANAGEMENT; *pg.* 462, *pg.* 765
TIREP ROS - Franchise Systems - AMERICAN TIRE DISTRIBUTORS HOLDINGS, INC.; *pg.* 199, *pg.* 1379
TIRESEAL - Tire Sealant for Off Road - TEXAS REFINERY CORP.; *pg.* 986, *pg.* 1696
TIRIS - Radio Frequency Devices - TEXAS INSTRUMENTS INCORPORATED; *pg.* 679, *pg.* 1688
TIRON - Chemical Product - SPECTRUM CHEMICALS & LABORATORY PRODUCTS, INC.; *pg.* 1181, *pg.* 94
TISCOR - Mobile Software Solutions - BRADY CORPORATION; *pg.* 363, *pg.* 1873
TISEEL - Biopharmaceutical Product - BAXTER INTERNATIONAL INC.; *pg.* 1499, *pg.* 599
TISP - Thyristor Surge Protectors - BOURNS, INC.; *pg.* 627, *pg.* 193
TISSOMAT - Biopharmaceutical Product - BAXTER INTERNATIONAL INC.; *pg.* 1499, *pg.* 599
TISSUCOL - Healthcare Product - BAXTER INTERNATIONAL INC.; *pg.* 1499, *pg.* 599
TISSUE DIGESTER - Holding Tank Tissue Digester - THETFORD CORPORATION; *pg.* 337, *pg.* 867
TISSUEMEND - Orthopaedic Product - STRYKER CORPORATION; *pg.* 1598, *pg.* 894
TITAN - Single Brewer - BUNN-O-MATIC CORPORATION; *pg.* 53, *pg.* 661
TITAN - Adsorber - CALGON CARBON CORPORATION; *pg.* 1151, *pg.* 1574
TITAN - Motor - CARTER MOTOR COMPANY; *pg.* 1321, *pg.* 665
TITAN - Paper Cutter - THE CHALLENGE MACHINERY COMPANY; *pg.* 1322, *pg.* 902
TITAN - Software - CLEARONE COMMUNICATIONS, INC.; *pg.* 629, *pg.* 1756
TITAN - Light-Based Aesthetic System - CUTERA, INC.; *pg.* 1521, *pg.* 49
TITAN - Metal Vault Doors - DIEBOLD, INCORPORATED; *pg.* 387, *pg.* 1407
TITAN - Aircraft Engine Products - ENGINE COMPONENTS, INC.; *pg.* 227, *pg.* 1740
TITAN - Electron Microscope - FEI COMPANY; *pg.* 1413, *pg.* 1498
TITAN - Pump - FLOWSERVE CORPORATION; *pg.* 82, *pg.*

1719
TITAN - Prescription Lens Edgar - GERBER SCIENTIFIC, INC.; *pg.* 1414, *pg.* 380
TITAN - Popcorn Machine - GOLD MEDAL PRODUCTS CO.; *pg.* 55, *pg.* 1414
TITAN - Apparel & Fabric - I. SPIEWAK & SONS, INC.; *pg.* 42, *pg.* 1242
TITAN - Parking Garage & Canopy Lighting - JUNO LIGHTING, INC.; *pg.* 1300, *pg.* 606
TITAN - Space Vehicles - LOCKHEED MARTIN CORPORATION; *pg.* 229, *pg.* 762
TITAN - Vehicle - NISSAN NORTH AMERICA, INC.; *pg.* 186, *pg.* 1633
TITAN - Ice Hockey Equipment - REEBOK-CCM HOCKEY, INC.; *pg.* 1844, *pg.* 1960
TITAN - Lubricant and Process Oil - ROCK VALLEY OIL & CHEMICAL COMPANY; *pg.* 1179, *pg.* 631
TITAN - Protective Welding Helmet - SELLSTROM MANUFACTURING CO.; *pg.* 1428, *pg.* 659
TITAN - Turbine Products - SOLAR TURBINES INCORPORATED; *pg.* 1377, *pg.* 209
TITAN - Ultrasound System - SONOSITE, INC.; *pg.* 1429, *pg.* 1818
TITAN - Magnetic Coronary Guidewire - STEREOTAXIS, INC.; *pg.* 1597, *pg.* 1004
TITAN - Optical Networking System - TELLABS, INC.; *pg.* 678, *pg.* 637
TITAN - Fastening System - TEXTRON INC.; *pg.* 235, *pg.* 1607
TITAN - Footwear - THE TIMBERLAND COMPANY; *pg.* 1821, *pg.* 1039
TITAN - Paint Sprayers & Accessories - TITAN TOOL, INC.; *pg.* 1383, *pg.* 1100
TITAN - Remote Control Device - UNIVERSAL ELECTRONICS, INC.; *pg.* 683, *pg.* 262
TITAN - Paint Spraying Equipment - WAGNER SPRAY TECH CORPORATION; *pg.* 1449, *pg.* 954
TITAN - Garage Door - WAYNE-DALTON CORP.; *pg.* 120, *pg.* 1465
TITAN - Centrifuge - WESTERN STATES MACHINE COMPANY; *pg.* 1388, *pg.* 1455
TITAN - Fishing Equipment Hooks - WRIGHT & MCGILL CO.; *pg.* 1848, *pg.* 324
TITAN - Bulk Seed Handling - YETTER MANUFACTURING CO., INC.; *pg.* 708, *pg.* 598
TITAN 1000D - Thermoplastic Applicators - M-B COMPANIES, INC.; *pg.* 1357, *pg.* 1884
TITAN 90 - Filter-Permanent Media, Automatic Backwash - SERFILCO, LTD.; *pg.* 1375, *pg.* 641
TITAN FILTER - Permanent Media, Automatic Backwash Filter - SERFILCO, LTD.; *pg.* 1375, *pg.* 641
TITAN MOXI - Remote Control Device - UNIVERSAL ELECTRONICS, INC.; *pg.* 683, *pg.* 262
TITAN T-SERIES - Towing & Recovery Equipment - MILLER INDUSTRIES, INC.; *pg.* 185, *pg.* 1655
TITAN V - Light-Based Aesthetic System - CUTERA, INC.; *pg.* 1521, *pg.* 49
TITAN WAFER STEPPER - Semiconductor Device - ULTRATECH, INC.; *pg.* 1433, *pg.* 251
TITAN XL - Light-Based Aesthetic System - CUTERA, INC.; *pg.* 1521, *pg.* 49
TITANCL - Pump Product - IDEX CORPORATION; *pg.* 1347, *pg.* 623
TITANCOAT - Automotive Paints - UES, INC.; *pg.* 1449, *pg.* 1447
TITANEX - Pump Product - IDEX CORPORATION; *pg.* 1347, *pg.* 623
TITANFALL - Video Game - RESPAWN ENTERTAINMENT; *pg.* 579, *pg.* 278
TITANHP - Pump Product - IDEX CORPORATION; *pg.* 1347, *pg.* 623
TITANHT - Pump Product - IDEX CORPORATION; *pg.* 1347, *pg.* 623
TITANIA - Hair & Skin Product - AUBREY ORGANICS INC.; *pg.* 499, *pg.* 470
TITANIUM - Textiles - BERNHARDT DESIGN; *pg.* 918, *pg.* 1381
TITANIUM - Apparel - COLUMBIA SPORTSWEAR COMPANY; *pg.* 1830, *pg.* 1501
TITANIUM - Silicone Sealant - DAP PRODUCTS, INC.; *pg.* 1441, *pg.* 756
TITANIUM - Paper - DOMTAR CORPORATION; *pg.* 1456, *pg.* 1954
TITANIUM ALLOY - Apparel - COLUMBIA SPORTSWEAR COMPANY; *pg.* 1830, *pg.* 1501
TITANIUM BONDED - Scissors - ACME UNITED CORPORATION; *pg.* 1040, *pg.* 346
TITANIUM CHAIN - Frames - OAKLEY, INC.; *pg.* 1840, *pg.* 86
TITANIUM MASTERCARD - Credit Card - MASTERCARD INCORPORATED; *pg.* 779, *pg.* 1325
TITANIUM O3 - Frames - OAKLEY, INC.; *pg.* 1840, *pg.* 86
TITANIUM PLUS - Alkaline Batteries - VARTA MICROBATTERY, INC.; *pg.* 221, *pg.* 1339
TITANIUM-PRO - Paint Brush - DUNN-EDWARDS CORPORATION; *pg.* 1442, *pg.* 129
TITANIUM SERIES - Toy & Game - HASBRO, INC.; *pg.* 954, *pg.* 1603
TITANIUM TECHNOLOGY - Battery - ENERGIZER HOLDINGS, INC.; *pg.* 637, *pg.* 996
TITANIUM TI2 - Shelf Trays - ACME UNITED CORPORATION; *pg.* 1040, *pg.* 346
TITANIUM UL TRABAR - Medical Alloys - CARPENTER TECHNOLOGY CORPORATION; *pg.* 73, *pg.* 1584
TITANIUM WHY 3 - Frames - OAKLEY, INC.; *pg.* 1840, *pg.* 86
TITANPORT - Electrosurgical Devices - ANGIODYNAMICS, INC.; *pg.* 1495, *pg.* 1173
TITE LINER - Polyethylene Lining System - INSITUFORM TECHNOLOGIES INC; *pg.* 88, *pg.* 974
TITE-LOC - Metal Roofing - PETERSEN ALUMINUM CORPORATION; *pg.* 104, *pg.* 611
TITE-LOK - Interlocking Roofing Shingles - BUILDING PRODUCTS OF CANADA CORP.; *pg.* 72, *pg.* 1951
TITE-ON - Interlocking Roofing Shingles - BUILDING PRODUCTS OF CANADA CORP.; *pg.* 72, *pg.* 1951
TITERTUBE - Software - BIO-RAD LABORATORIES, INC.; *pg.* 1504, *pg.* 101
TITESEAL - Oil Treatment - RADIATOR SPECIALTY COMPANY; *pg.* 215, *pg.* 1380
TITLEIST - Golf Equipment - ACUSHNET COMPANY; *pg.* 1824, *pg.* 818
TITLEIST DT - Golf Ball - ACUSHNET COMPANY; *pg.* 1824, *pg.* 818
TITLEIST NXT - Golf Ball - ACUSHNET COMPANY; *pg.* 1824, *pg.* 818
TITLEIST SO-LO - Golf Ball - ACUSHNET COMPANY; *pg.* 1824, *pg.* 818
TITLEIST TITANIUM - Golf Equipment - ACUSHNET COMPANY; *pg.* 1824, *pg.* 818
TITLEPAC - Insurance Package Program - BROWN & BROWN, INC.; *pg.* 1196, *pg.* 419
TITO'S HANDMADE VODKA - Vodka - FIFTH GENERATION, INC.; *pg.* 1963, *pg.* 1662
TITRASTIR - Magnetic Stirrer - HACH COMPANY; *pg.* 1415, *pg.* 334
TITRIVER - Chemical Reagent - HACH COMPANY; *pg.* 1415, *pg.* 334
TIVO CENTRAL - Menu Screen - TIVO INC.; *pg.* 313, *pg.* 251
TIVO DVR - Digital Video Recorder - TIVO INC.; *pg.* 313, *pg.* 251
TIVOLI - Shoes - ALLEN-EDMONDS SHOE CORP.; *pg.* 1804, *pg.* 1887
TIVOLI - Packaged Foods - ATALANTA CORPORATION; *pg.* 838, *pg.* 1057
TIVOLUTION - Magazine - TIVO INC.; *pg.* 313, *pg.* 251
TIVOTOGO - Graphic System - NVIDIA CORPORATION; *pg.* 447, *pg.* 268
TIVOTOGO - Digital Video Recorder - TIVO INC.; *pg.* 313, *pg.* 251
TIX4DINNERS - Reservation and Booking Services - TIX CORPORATION; *pg.* 588, *pg.* 281
TIX4TONIGHT - Ticketing Services - TIX CORPORATION; *pg.* 588, *pg.* 281
TIZIANO - Pump Product - IDEX CORPORATION; *pg.* 1347, *pg.* 623
TIZOX - Silica Product - FERRO CORPORATION; *pg.* 1162, *pg.* 1462
TJ - Bicycle Accessories - SPECIALIZED BICYCLE COMPONENTS, INC.; *pg.* 1711, *pg.* 152
TJ BEARYTALES - Toy & Game - HASBRO, INC.; *pg.* 954, *pg.* 1603
T.J. CINNAMONS - Food Product - THE WENDY'S COMPANY; *pg.* 1755, *pg.* 1450
T.J. MAXX - Retail Stores - T.J. MAXX; *pg.* 1788, *pg.* 822
TJ-PRO - Wood & Building Material - WEYERHAEUSER COMPANY; *pg.* 121, *pg.* 1820
TJ-XPER - Wood & Building Material - WEYERHAEUSER COMPANY; *pg.* 121, *pg.* 1820
TJI - Wood & Building Material - WEYERHAEUSER COMPANY; *pg.* 121, *pg.* 1820
TK6 - Wireless Control - CONTROL CHIEF HOLDINGS, INC.; *pg.* 630, *pg.* 1518
TKL - Pump - FLOWSERVE CORPORATION; *pg.* 82, *pg.* 1719
TKO - Anti Reflux Device - HOSPIRA, INC.; *pg.* 1542, *pg.* 623
TL-2 - Flashlight - STREAMLIGHT INC.; *pg.* 1306, *pg.* 1527
TL-3 - Flashlight - STREAMLIGHT INC.; *pg.* 1306, *pg.* 1527
TLC - Medical Device - BOSTON SCIENTIFIC CORPORATION; *pg.* 1508, *pg.* 831
TLC - Television Station - DISCOVERY COMMUNICATIONS, INC.; *pg.* 282, *pg.* 777
TLC - Infant Car Seat/Carrier - DOREL JUVENILE GROUP, INC.; *pg.* 923, *pg.* 676
TLC COUNTRY CHEDDAR - Crackers - KASHI COMPANY; *pg.* 830, *pg.* 119
TLC CRACKERS - Crackers - KASHI COMPANY; *pg.* 830, *pg.* 119
TLC HONEY SESAME - Crackers - KASHI COMPANY; *pg.* 830, *pg.* 119
TLC NATURAL RANCH - Crackers - KASHI COMPANY; *pg.* 830, *pg.* 119
TLC ORIGINAL 7 GRAIN - Crackers - KASHI COMPANY; *pg.* 830, *pg.* 119
TLD MONITOR - Software System - IRON MOUNTAIN INCORPORATED; *pg.* 421, *pg.* 796
TLE SIDECAR - Motorcycle - HARLEY-DAVIDSON, INC.; *pg.* 178, *pg.* 1874
TLF - Leather Supplier - TANDY LEATHER FACTORY, INC.; *pg.* 48, *pg.* 1696
TLH - Audio & Video Product - HARMAN INTERNATIONAL INDUSTRIES, INCORPORATED; *pg.* 641, *pg.* 374
TLH II - Audio & Video Product - HARMAN INTERNATIONAL INDUSTRIES, INCORPORATED; *pg.* 641, *pg.* 374
TLH2 - Audio & Video Product - HARMAN INTERNATIONAL INDUSTRIES, INCORPORATED; *pg.* 641, *pg.* 374
TLI - Medical Product - HOLOGIC, INC.; *pg.* 1416, *pg.* 784
TLI IQ - Medical Product - HOLOGIC, INC.; *pg.* 1416, *pg.* 784
TLN - Treated Lumber Nails to Reduce Corrosion - PASLODE; *pg.* 1059, *pg.* 664
TLR-1 - Flashlight - STREAMLIGHT INC.; *pg.* 1306, *pg.* 1527
TLR-2 - Flashlight - STREAMLIGHT INC.; *pg.* 1306, *pg.* 1527
TLR-3 - Flashlight - STREAMLIGHT INC.; *pg.* 1306, *pg.* 1527
TLR-VIR - Flashlight - STREAMLIGHT INC.; *pg.* 1306, *pg.* 1527
TLS SERIES - Automatic Tank Gauging Systems - VEEDER-ROOT COMPANY; *pg.* 61, *pg.* 371
TM 2000 - Children's Orthopedic Sneakers - MAURICE J. MARKELL SHOE CO., INC.; *pg.* 1811, *pg.* 1356
TM-2000 - Electronic Components - MOLEX INCORPORATED; *pg.* 655, *pg.* 628
TM-234 IMPACT - Printers - AVERY WEIGH-TRONIX, INC.; *pg.* 1315, *pg.* 925
TM-3000 - Electronic Components - MOLEX INCORPORATED; *pg.* 655, *pg.* 628
TM-40 - Electronic Components - MOLEX INCORPORATED; *pg.* 655, *pg.* 628
TM-42 - Electronic Components - MOLEX INCORPORATED; *pg.* 655, *pg.* 628
TM APPLICATION RESPONSE TIME EXECUTION SERVER - Software - BMC SOFTWARE, INC.; *pg.* 362, *pg.* 1701
TM PLY - Thermoformable Laminate Sheets for Food Packaging - SEALED AIR CORPORATION; *pg.* 1468, *pg.* 1058
TM-U590 - Printers - AVERY WEIGH-TRONIX, INC.; *pg.* 1315, *pg.* 925
TMCC - Toy Train - LIONEL LLC; *pg.* 961, *pg.* 875
TMCNET.COM - Online Publication - TECHNOLOGY MARKETING CORP.; *pg.* 1691, *pg.* 364
TMI - Unsaturated Aliphatic Isocyanate - CYTEC INDUSTRIES, INC.; *pg.* 1155, *pg.* 1131
TML - Telecentric Lens - EDMUND INDUSTRIAL OPTICS INC.; *pg.* 1411, *pg.* 1041
TMMS - Computer Software & Facilities Maintenance - AVNET, INC.; *pg.* 622, *pg.* 15
TMNG QBC - Transaction Monitoring Business System - CARTESIAN; *pg.* 369, *pg.* 718
TMNG QSA - Methodology for IT Assessment - CARTESIAN; *pg.* 369, *pg.* 718
TMNS - Pharmaceutical Product - ALERE INC.; *pg.* 1488, *pg.* 849
TMOPS - Plastic Films Product - PLASTIC SUPPLIERS, INC.; *pg.* 1888, *pg.* 1443

First page reference indicates Business Class Edition
Second page reference indicates Geographic Edition

TMOS - Software - F5 NETWORKS, INC.; *pg.* 396, *pg.* 1835
TMOV - Thermally Protected Metal Oxide Varistors - LITTELFUSE, INC.; *pg.* 1301, *pg.* 580
TMPD - Glycol - EASTMAN CHEMICAL COMPANY; *pg.* 1159, *pg.* 1636
TMR - Roof System - BUTLER MANUFACTURING COMPANY; *pg.* 72, *pg.* 981
TMS - Table Tracking - BALLY TECHNOLOGIES, INC.; *pg.* 531, *pg.* 1022
TMS - Motorsports Entertainment - SPEEDWAY MOTORSPORTS, INC.; *pg.* 584, *pg.* 1370
TMS320 - Digital Signal Processors - TEXAS INSTRUMENTS INCORPORATED; *pg.* 679, *pg.* 1688
TMV - Technology - AMKOR TECHNOLOGY, INC.; *pg.* 67, *pg.* 25
TMV - Pricing System - EDMUNDS, INC.; *pg.* 1241, *pg.* 273
TMX - Teen Watches - TIMEX CORPORATION; *pg.* 14, *pg.* 355
TMXDI - Performance Chemicals - CYTEC INDUSTRIES, INC.; *pg.* 1155, *pg.* 1131
TMZ - Celebrity News & Gossip Channel - TIME WARNER INC.; *pg.* 312, *pg.* 1302
TMZ.COM - Celebrity News & Gossip Site - TIME WARNER INC.; *pg.* 312, *pg.* 1302
TMZF - Medical Product - STRYKER CORPORATION; *pg.* 1598, *pg.* 894
TNKASE - Treatment of Acute Myocardial Infarction - GENENTECH, INC.; *pg.* 1533, *pg.* 279
TNP TANK - Apparels - UNDER ARMOUR, INC.; *pg.* 49, *pg.* 759
TNT - Taslan Fabric Outerwear - BLAUER MANUFACTURING COMPANY, INC.; *pg.* 20, *pg.* 789
TNT DOS-EXTENDER - Software - INTERVALZERO INC.; *pg.* 420, *pg.* 851
TNT EMBEDDED TOOL SUITE - Software - INTERVALZERO INC.; *pg.* 420, *pg.* 851
TO EARN TRUST, EVERY DAY. - Slogan - MERCK & CO., INC.; *pg.* 1566, *pg.* 1077
TO EDUCATE, AMUSE & ENRICH - Slogan - THE MOTLEY FOOL, INC.; *pg.* 784, *pg.* 1771
TO EROS IS HUMAN - Nail Care Product - OPI PRODUCTS INC.; *pg.* 518, *pg.* 167
TO GUIDE AND PROVIDE - Tagline - HORTICA INSURANCE; *pg.* 1204, *pg.* 609
TO-PRO - Molecular Probe Product - THERMO FISHER SCIENTIFIC INC.; *pg.* 1602, *pg.* 61
TO THE CORE - Gypsum & Cement Board - USG CORPORATION; *pg.* 118, *pg.* 594
TO YOUR GOOD HEALTH - Tagline - BOB'S RED MILL NATURAL FOODS, INC.; *pg.* 841, *pg.* 1500
TOAD - Software - DELL SOFTWARE; *pg.* 385, *pg.* 40
TOAD DBA SUITE FOR IBM DB2 - Software - DELL SOFTWARE; *pg.* 385, *pg.* 40
TOAD DBA SUITE FOR ORACLE - Software - DELL SOFTWARE; *pg.* 385, *pg.* 40
TOAD DEVELOPMENT SUITE FOR ORACLE - Software - DELL SOFTWARE; *pg.* 385, *pg.* 40
TOAD FOR DATA ANALYSTS - Software - DELL SOFTWARE; *pg.* 385, *pg.* 40
TOAD FOR IBM DB2 LUW - Software - DELL SOFTWARE; *pg.* 385, *pg.* 40
TOAD FOR IBM DB2 Z/OS - Software - DELL SOFTWARE; *pg.* 385, *pg.* 40
TOAD FOR MYSQL - Software - DELL SOFTWARE; *pg.* 385, *pg.* 40
TOAD FOR ORACLE - Software - DELL SOFTWARE; *pg.* 385, *pg.* 40
TOAD FOR SQL SERVER - Software - DELL SOFTWARE; *pg.* 385, *pg.* 40
TOADSTOP - Tow Car Brake System - BLUE OX; *pg.* 701, *pg.* 1019
TOADSTOP II - Braking System - BLUE OX; *pg.* 701, *pg.* 1019
TOAST OF THE TOWN - Game - WMS INDUSTRIES INC.; *pg.* 593, *pg.* 666
TOASTCHEE - Food Product - SNYDER'S-LANCE, INC.; *pg.* 896, *pg.* 1368
TOASTED HEAD - Wine - CONSTELLATION BRANDS CANADA; *pg.* 1960, *pg.* 1925
TOASTEDS - Crackers - KELLOGG COMPANY; *pg.* 831, *pg.* 870
TOAST'EM POP-UPS - Toaster Pastries Products - SCHULZE & BURCH BISCUIT COMPANY; *pg.* 894, *pg.* 589
TOASTER - Food Product - SONIC CORP.; *pg.* 1750, *pg.* 1487
TOASTER SCRAMBLES - Food Product - GENERAL MILLS, INC.; *pg.* 828, *pg.* 933
TOASTER STRUDEL - Food Product - GENERAL MILLS, INC.; *pg.* 828, *pg.* 933
TOASTMASTER - Cooking & Warming Equipment - THE MIDDLEBY CORPORATION; *pg.* 1361, *pg.* 610
TOASTY - Food - THE QUIZNO'S MASTER LLC; *pg.* 1746, *pg.* 322
TOASTY - Snack Food - SNYDER'S-LANCE, INC.; *pg.* 896, *pg.* 1368
TOASTY BULLETS - Fast-food - THE QUIZNO'S MASTER LLC; *pg.* 1746, *pg.* 322
TOASTY O'S - Bag Cereal - POST CONSUMER BRANDS; *pg.* 833, *pg.* 927
TOASTY TORPEDO - Sandwich - THE QUIZNO'S MASTER LLC; *pg.* 1746, *pg.* 322
TOASTY TORPEDOES - Fast-food - THE QUIZNO'S MASTER LLC; *pg.* 1746, *pg.* 322
TOBACCO OUTLET PLUS - Tobacco Product Stores - KWIK TRIP INC.; *pg.* 1026, *pg.* 1864
TOBACCO SORTER 3 - Tobacco Sorting System - KEY TECHNOLOGY, INC.; *pg.* 868, *pg.* 1847
TOBACCO SORTER II - Tobacco Sorting System - KEY TECHNOLOGY, INC.; *pg.* 868, *pg.* 1847
TOBAGO - Fabric - NEMSCHOFF, INC.; *pg.* 936, *pg.* 1890
TOBIAS - Musical Instrument - GIBSON GUITAR CORP.; *pg.* 550, *pg.* 1650
TOBIAS - Fabric - SCALAMANDRE, INC.; *pg.* 941, *pg.* 1058
TOBIN'S FIRST PRIZE - Meat Products - JOHN MORRELL & CO.; *pg.* 866, *pg.* 1415
TOBIN'S MOTHER - Food Product - JOHN MORRELL & CO.; *pg.* 866, *pg.* 1415
TOBLERONE - Chocolates - MONDELEZ INTERNATIONAL, INC.; *pg.* 878, *pg.* 601
TOBOGGAN - Fabric - NEMSCHOFF, INC.; *pg.* 936, *pg.* 1890
TOCA - Drums - KAMAN CORPORATION; *pg.* 229, *pg.* 338
TOCARRA - Footwear - STEVEN MADDEN, LTD.; *pg.* 1819, *pg.* 1176
TOCCATA - Kitchen Product - KOHLER CO.; *pg.* 91, *pg.* 1862
TOCCATA - Stationery - THOMAS NELSON INC.; *pg.* 1692, *pg.* 1654
TOCOSOL - Pharmaceutical Product - ONCOGENEX PHARMACEUTICALS, INC.; *pg.* 1578, *pg.* 1818
TOCOTRIENOL - Nutritional Supplement - NATURAL ORGANICS, INC.; *pg.* 1571, *pg.* 1181
TODAY - Electric Irons - JARDEN CONSUMER SOLUTIONS; *pg.* 57, *pg.* 412
TODAY - Veterinary Antibiotic - PFIZER INC.; *pg.* 1581, *pg.* 1278
TODAY, TOMORROW, ALWAYS - Fragrance - AVON PRODUCTS, INC.; *pg.* 500, *pg.* 1198
TODAY.COM - Website Targeted to Women - NBC UNIVERSAL, INC.; *pg.* 300, *pg.* 1266
TODAY'S BEST NONFICTION - Magazine - THE READER'S DIGEST ASSOCIATION, INC.; *pg.* 1679, *pg.* 1322
TODAY'S BIG THING - Online Services - IAC/INTERACTIVECORP; *pg.* 292, *pg.* 1242
TODAY'S CARNIVAL - Cruise Line - CARNIVAL CRUISE LINES; *pg.* 1902, *pg.* 441
TODAY'S CHRISTIAN WOMAN - Magazine - CHRISTIANITY TODAY INTERNATIONAL; *pg.* 1627, *pg.* 561
TODAY'S HEALTHCARE - Health Care - AMERISOURCEBERGEN CORPORATION; *pg.* 1493, *pg.* 1522
TODAY'S MENU - Low-fat Food - OMAHA STEAKS INTERNATIONAL, INC.; *pg.* 1780, *pg.* 1017
TODAY'S RESEARCH. TOMORROW'S CURES - Tagline - PHARMACEUTICAL RESEARCH & MANUFACTURERS OF AMERICA; *pg.* 153, *pg.* 404
TODAY'S RESULTS...TOMORROW'S VISION - Slogan - SEMTECH CORPORATION; *pg.* 671, *pg.* 57
TODAY'S SURGICENTER - Publication - INFORMA EXHIBITIONS LLC; *pg.* 1653, *pg.* 17
TODAYSHOMEOWNER.COM - Web Site - BONNIER ACTIVE MEDIA, INC.; *pg.* 1622, *pg.* 1205
TODCO - Vehicular Door Products - OVERHEAD DOOR CORPORATION; *pg.* 102, *pg.* 1725
TODDLE TOTS - Building Block Toys - RUBBERMAID HOME PRODUCTS; *pg.* 1138, *pg.* 1453
TODDY - Chocolate Powder - THE QUAKER OATS COMPANY; *pg.* 834, *pg.* 588
TODDYNHO - Chocolate Drink - PEPSICO, INC.; *pg.* 259, *pg.* 1327
TODDYNHO - Chocolate Drink - THE QUAKER OATS COMPANY; *pg.* 834, *pg.* 588
TODO - Coupler - GARDNER DENVER, INC.; *pg.* 1338, *pg.* 1592
TODO - Office Furniture - HAWORTH, INC.; *pg.* 402, *pg.* 891
TODO-GAS - Couplers - GARDNER DENVER, INC.; *pg.* 1338, *pg.* 1592
TODO-MATIC - Couplers - GARDNER DENVER, INC.; *pg.* 1338, *pg.* 1592
TODOBEBE.COM - Multiplatform Media Brand - ENTRAVISION COMMUNICATIONS CORPORATION; *pg.* 285, *pg.* 273
TOE CLIPS - Protective Steel Toe Caps - STANDARD SAFETY EQUIPMENT CO.; *pg.* 1379, *pg.* 632
TOEFL - English Language Test - EDUCATIONAL TESTING SERVICE INC.; *pg.* 1394, *pg.* 1111
TOEIC - Speaking & Writing Test - EDUCATIONAL TESTING SERVICE INC.; *pg.* 1394, *pg.* 1111
TOEM5XX - OEM Connectivity Module - TROY GROUP INC.; *pg.* 485, *pg.* 71
TOFAX - Chemical Product - WESTROCK COMPANY; *pg.* 1472, *pg.* 1805
TOFPREP - Maldi Spotting System - PERKINELMER, INC.; *pg.* 1426, *pg.* 853
TOFRANIL - Pharmaceutical Product - MALLINCKRODT PHARMACEUTICALS; *pg.* 1557, *pg.* 978
TOFUTOWN - Tofu Product - THE HAIN CELESTIAL GROUP, INC.; *pg.* 860, *pg.* 1172
TOG-L-LOC - Metal Joining System - BTM CORPORATION; *pg.* 1320, *pg.* 898
TOG-L-LOK - One Hand Clamping Tool - CHANNELLOCK, INC.; *pg.* 1044, *pg.* 1551
TOGATHER - Shoe - AEROGROUP INTERNATIONAL, INC.; *pg.* 1803, *pg.* 1055
TOGETHER WE BREAK NEW GROUND EVERYDAY - Tagline - DDR CORP.; *pg.* 1089, *pg.* 1405
TOGETHER WE MAKE A GREAT TEAM - Tagline - AMERICAN SOCIETY OF HEALTH-SYSTEM PHARMACISTS; *pg.* 131, *pg.* 761
TOGETHER, WE'LL GET YOU THERE - Slogan - NORTHEAST BANCORP; *pg.* 787, *pg.* 751
TOGGI - Chocolate Wafer - PROMOTION IN MOTION, INC.; *pg.* 1861, *pg.* 1052
TOGGI CHOCOLATE COVERED WAFERS - Imported European Wafers - PROMOTION IN MOTION, INC.; *pg.* 1861, *pg.* 1052
TOGGLE - Women's Clothing & Accessories - WOODEN SHIPS OF HOBOKEN; *pg.* 35, *pg.* 1315
TOGGLETOUCH - Dimmer Switch - LEVITON MANUFACTURING COMPANY, INC.; *pg.* 1301, *pg.* 1180
TOGO'S - Sandwich Stores - DUNKIN' BRANDS GROUP, INC.; *pg.* 1727, *pg.* 810
TOILE - Furniture - ASHLEY FURNITURE INDUSTRIES, INC.; *pg.* 914, *pg.* 1852
TOILET BRITE - Cleaning Brush - BLUE CROSS LABORATORIES; *pg.* 326, *pg.* 277
TOILET DUCK - Cleaner - S.C. JOHNSON & SON, INC.; *pg.* 334, *pg.* 1889
TOILETTE - Child's Toilet - DOREL JUVENILE GROUP, INC.; *pg.* 923, *pg.* 676
TOILETTE PLUS - Toilet Trainer & Step Stool - DOREL JUVENILE GROUP, INC.; *pg.* 923, *pg.* 676
TOILETWAND - Cleaning System - THE CLOROX COMPANY; *pg.* 327, *pg.* 169
TOILEVATOR - Toilet Elevator - ALIMED, INC.; *pg.* 1490, *pg.* 816
TOKA - Beverages - THE COCA-COLA COMPANY; *pg.* 240, *pg.* 493
TOKEN - Fabric - NEMSCHOFF, INC.; *pg.* 936, *pg.* 1890
TOKI - Health System Product - LANELABS USA INC.; *pg.* 1554, *pg.* 1128
TOKI TOKI BOOM - Entertainment Services - YAHOO! INC.; *pg.* 1289, *pg.* 289
TOKUDEN - Roll Services - PRECISION ROLL GRINDERS, INC.; *pg.* 1370, *pg.* 1514
TOLA - Yoga Mat - HUGGER MUGGER YOGA PRODUCTS LLC; *pg.* 1836, *pg.* 1758
TOLAD - Corrosion Inhibitor - BAKER PETROLITE CORPORATION; *pg.* 1148, *pg.* 1745
TOLECTIN - Healthcare Product - JOHNSON & JOHNSON; *pg.* 1549, *pg.* 1091
TOLED - Organic Light Emitting Device - UNIVERSAL DISPLAY CORPORATION; *pg.* 683, *pg.* 1064
TOLEDO - Rugs - COURISTAN INC.; *pg.* 921, *pg.* 1067
TOLERAGENS - Pharmaceutical Product - LA JOLLA

PHARMACEUTICAL COMPANY; *pg.* 1554, *pg.* 204

TOLERANCE TECHNOLOGY - Proprietary Research & Development Platform - LA JOLLA PHARMACEUTICAL COMPANY; *pg.* 1554, *pg.* 204

TOLERANCE.ORG - Website - THE SOUTHERN POVERTY LAW CENTER; *pg.* 157, *pg.* 7

TOLINASE - Medicine - PFIZER INC.; *pg.* 1581, *pg.* 1278

TOLL BROTHERS - Homes - TOLL BROTHERS, INC.; *pg.* 115, *pg.* 1541

TOLL FREE PLUS - Telecommunication Services - VONAGE HOLDINGS CORP.; *pg.* 686, *pg.* 1074

TOLL HOUSE MORSELS - Food & Beverage Product - NESTLE USA, INC.; *pg.* 883, *pg.* 96

TOLL HOUSE REFRIGERATED COOKIE DOUGH - Food & Beverage Product - NESTLE USA, INC.; *pg.* 883, *pg.* 96

TOLNAFTATE - Pharmaceutical Product - G&W LABORATORIES INC.; *pg.* 1532, *pg.* 1123

TOM SAWYER - Boyswear - ELDER MANUFACTURING COMPANY, INC.; *pg.* 40, *pg.* 996

TOM SNYDER PRODUCTIONS - Educational Materials - SCHOLASTIC INC.; *pg.* 1683, *pg.* 1288

TOM WATSON - Golf Product - TAYLORMADE-ADIDAS GOLF; *pg.* 1847, *pg.* 60

TOMAHAWK - Heavy Duty Hammer Tacker - ARROW FASTENER COMPANY, INC.; *pg.* 1042, *pg.* 1118

TOMAHAWK - Cruise Missile - RAYTHEON COMPANY; *pg.* 233, *pg.* 854

TOMAHAWK - Fabric End Cutter - THE WOLF MACHINE CO.; *pg.* 1389, *pg.* 1427

TOMATO KING - Tomato Scooper - LINCOLN FOODSERVICE PRODUCTS, LLC; *pg.* 1127, *pg.* 1432

TOMATO PRO - Specialty cutters - LINCOLN FOODSERVICE PRODUCTS, LLC; *pg.* 1127, *pg.* 1432

TOMATOES ALIVE! - Vegetable Gardening - GARDENS ALIVE!, INC.; *pg.* 1796, *pg.* 693

TOMATOGARD - Tray - PACTIV CORPORATION; *pg.* 1466, *pg.* 624

TOMBSTONE - Pizza - NESTLE USA, INC.; *pg.* 883, *pg.* 96

TOMBSTONE BULLTUFF - Feeders - SIOUX STEEL COMPANY; *pg.* 707, *pg.* 1625

TOMIC - Fittings - PASS & SEYMOUR/LEGRAND; *pg.* 1303, *pg.* 1344

TOMLINSON/ERWIN-LAMBETH - Upholstered Furniture - TOMLINSON/ERWIN-LAMBETH, INC.; *pg.* 945, *pg.* 1391

TOMMY - Furniture - AMISCO INDUSTRIES LTD.; *pg.* 913, *pg.* 1958

TOMMY ARMOUR - Golf Product - HUFFY CORPORATION; *pg.* 1836, *pg.* 1409

TOMMY ARMOUR GOLF - Golf Company - HUFFY CORPORATION; *pg.* 1836, *pg.* 1409

TOMMY BAHAMA - Label Apparel - OXFORD INDUSTRIES, INC.; *pg.* 30, *pg.* 517

TOMMY BAHAMA - Beverage - SIDNEY FRANK IMPORTING CO., INC.; *pg.* 1970, *pg.* 1184

TOMMY BAHAMA - Sportswear - TOMMY BAHAMA; *pg.* 48, *pg.* 1842

TOMMY GUN - Plaster/Fireproofing Pump - PUTZMEISTER AMERICA; *pg.* 1371, *pg.* 1896

TOMMY HILFIGER - Fragrances & Toiletries - THE ESTEE LAUDER COMPANIES INC.; *pg.* 508, *pg.* 1229

TOMMY HILFIGER - Apparel - G-III APPAREL GROUP, LTD.; *pg.* 41, *pg.* 1233

TOMMY HILFIGER - Sportswear Product Company - TOMMY HILFIGER USA; *pg.* 48, *pg.* 1302

TOMMY NELSON - Children's Books - THOMAS NELSON INC.; *pg.* 1692, *pg.* 1654

TOMMYGEL - Pharmaceutical Product - HAWKINS, INC.; *pg.* 1165, *pg.* 937

TOMOHAWK - Printing Paper - MOHAWK FINE PAPERS, INC.; *pg.* 1464, *pg.* 1153

TOMORROW - Veterinary Antibiotic - PFIZER INC.; *pg.* 1581, *pg.* 1278

TOMORROWLAND - Amusement Park - THE WALT DISNEY COMPANY; *pg.* 317, *pg.* 52

TOM'S - Potato Chips, Fries, Tortilla Chips, Corn Chips & Pork Skins - SNYDER'S-LANCE, INC.; *pg.* 896, *pg.* 1368

TOMTEX - Non-Woven Protective Fabric - LAKELAND INDUSTRIES, INC.; *pg.* 1354, *pg.* 1338

TONA CERVEZA - Beer - UNITED STATES BEVERAGE LLC; *pg.* 266, *pg.* 379

TONAL - Carpet - INTERFACE, INC.; *pg.* 695, *pg.* 512

TONALIN - Vitamin & Dietary Supplement - NATROL, INC.; *pg.* 1570, *pg.* 64

TONDA - Chair - THE WICKER WORKS; *pg.* 946, *pg.* 233

TONE - Polymer - THE DOW CHEMICAL COMPANY; *pg.* 1157, *pg.* 898

TONE - Personal Cleansing Products - HENKEL CONSUMER GOODS; *pg.* 511, *pg.* 22

TONECRETE - Wall Coating - THE VALSPAR CORPORATION; *pg.* 1449, *pg.* 945

TONEDOWN - Hearing Protection - SELLSTROM MANUFACTURING CO.; *pg.* 1428, *pg.* 659

TONERGRIP - Paper Products - BOISE CASCADE HOLDINGS, L.L.C.; *pg.* 1453, *pg.* 546

TONES - Dinnerware - THE HOMER LAUGHLIN CHINA COMPANY; *pg.* 1125, *pg.* 1850

TONES - On Location Taped Music - MOOD MEDIA; *pg.* 298, *pg.* 1616

TONETIC - Fast Drying Wood Stains - PRATT & LAMBERT PAINTS; *pg.* 1446, *pg.* 1434

TONETTE - Children's Home Permanent - THE GILLETTE COMPANY; *pg.* 509, *pg.* 795

TONEWORKS - Special Effects - KORG USA, INC.; *pg.* 556, *pg.* 1180

TONGUE TORCH - Food Product - ZAXBY'S FRANCHISING, INC.; *pg.* 1756, *pg.* 486

TONI LIGHTWAVES - Home Permanent - THE GILLETTE COMPANY; *pg.* 509, *pg.* 795

TONI SILKWAVE - Home Permanent - THE GILLETTE COMPANY; *pg.* 509, *pg.* 795

TONKA - Preschool & Infant Toys - HASBRO, INC.; *pg.* 954, *pg.* 1603

TONKA TOUGH TRUCK ADVENTURES - Toy & Game - HASBRO, INC.; *pg.* 954, *pg.* 1603

TONKAFLO - High Pressure Pumps - GE WATER & PROCESS TECHNOLOGIES; *pg.* 1339, *pg.* 1588

TONNER CHARACTER FIGURES - Doll - TONNER DOLL COMPANY, INC.; *pg.* 968, *pg.* 1171

TONOX - Polymer Product - CHEMTURA CORPORATION; *pg.* 1152, *pg.* 355

TONY HAWK'S PRO SKATER - Game - ACTIVISION BLIZZARD, INC.; *pg.* 948, *pg.* 271

TONY HAWK'S UNDERGROUND - Game - ACTIVISION BLIZZARD, INC.; *pg.* 948, *pg.* 271

TONY LAMA - Cowboy Boots - JUSTIN BRANDS, INC.; *pg.* 1810, *pg.* 1695

TONY ROMA'S RED HOTS - Sauce - ROMACORP, INC.; *pg.* 1748, *pg.* 1734

TONY THE TIGER - Product Icon - KELLOGG COMPANY; *pg.* 831, *pg.* 870

TONY TRUJILLO - Footwear - VANS, INC.; *pg.* 1821, *pg.* 76

TONY'S - Pizza Products - THE SCHWAN FOOD COMPANY; *pg.* 894, *pg.* 928

TONY'S CINNAMON KRUNCHERS - Cereal - KELLOGG COMPANY; *pg.* 831, *pg.* 870

TOO TOUGH TO TAME - Motorsports Event - INTERNATIONAL SPEEDWAY CORPORATION; *pg.* 553, *pg.* 420

TOOL CRIB - Lube - SEYMOUR OF SYCAMORE, INC.; *pg.* 1447, *pg.* 663

TOOL/RITE - Chemical Product - CYTEC INDUSTRIES, INC.; *pg.* 1155, *pg.* 1131

TOOL TERRITORY - Retail Services - SEARS HOLDINGS CORPORATION; *pg.* 1784, *pg.* 618

TOOL TOTE - Fluid Handling System - GRACO, INC.; *pg.* 1342, *pg.* 935

TOOL TOWER - Tool Storage Products - WATERLOO INDUSTRIES, INC.; *pg.* 946, *pg.* 1885

TOOL-TRA-TOP - Ladder Product - WERNER HOLDING CO.; *pg.* 121, *pg.* 1534

TOOLBOOK - Software - SUMTOTAL SYSTEMS, INC.; *pg.* 477, *pg.* 429

TOOLBOSS - Software - KENNAMETAL INC.; *pg.* 1052, *pg.* 1547

TOOLBOX.COM - Network for IT Professionals - ZIFF DAVIS, LLC; *pg.* 1703, *pg.* 1316

TOOLLINK - Control System - MKS INSTRUMENTS, INC.; *pg.* 1362, *pg.* 781

TOOLS NOT TOYS - Flashlight - STREAMLIGHT INC.; *pg.* 1306, *pg.* 1527

TOOLTREATER - Vacuum Furnace - IPSEN INTERNATIONAL, INC.; *pg.* 1073, *pg.* 562

TOOLWEB - Software - MKS INSTRUMENTS, INC.; *pg.* 1362, *pg.* 781

TOONAMI - Action-Adventure Programming Block - THE CARTOON NETWORK; *pg.* 273, *pg.* 492

TOONTOWN - Cartoon - THE WALT DISNEY COMPANY; *pg.* 317, *pg.* 52

TOOSTRIPE - Fabric - NEMSCHOFF, INC.; *pg.* 936, *pg.* 1890

TOOTH TUNES - Toy & Game - HASBRO, INC.; *pg.* 954, *pg.* 1603

TOOTHPICK - Knife - BUCK KNIVES, INC.; *pg.* 1828, *pg.* 550

TOOTHY FROG - Bottle Opening Coaster - BOGDANCO CONSULTING; *pg.* 918, *pg.* 174

TOOTIE FRUITIES - Fruit-Flavored Cereal - POST CONSUMER BRANDS; *pg.* 833, *pg.* 927

TOOTSIE POPS - Candy - TOOTSIE ROLL INDUSTRIES, INC.; *pg.* 1863, *pg.* 591

TOP - Packaged Foods - ATALANTA CORPORATION; *pg.* 838, *pg.* 1057

TOP - Beverages - THE COCA-COLA COMPANY; *pg.* 240, *pg.* 493

TOP 2 BOTTOM - Basecoats - ORLY INTERNATIONAL, INC.; *pg.* 518, *pg.* 137

TOP 20 - Global Internet Media - TRAVELZOO INC; *pg.* 1926, *pg.* 1304

TOP AUTHORITY - Blousecoats - ELBECO INCORPORATED; *pg.* 40, *pg.* 1584

TOP AUTHORITY PLUS - Trousers - ELBECO INCORPORATED; *pg.* 40, *pg.* 1584

TOP BANANA - Game - WMS INDUSTRIES INC.; *pg.* 593, *pg.* 666

TOP BLEND - Coffee - PEET'S COFFEE & TEA, INC.; *pg.* 1029, *pg.* 85

TOP BRAND VITAMINS AT WHOLESALE COST - Slogan - VITACOST.COM, INC.; *pg.* 1607, *pg.* 414

TOP CARE - Health & Beauty Products - BASHAS' SUPERMARKETS; *pg.* 1015, *pg.* 12

TOP CARE - Food Product - HARRIS TEETER, INC.; *pg.* 1022, *pg.* 1383

TOP CARE - Health & Beauty Care Products - SPARTANNASH CO; *pg.* 1034, *pg.* 889

TOP CARE - HBC - TOPCO HOLDINGS INC.; *pg.* 901, *pg.* 661

TOP CAT - Dry Cleaning & Laundry Product - ADCO, INC.; *pg.* 325, *pg.* 482

TOP CAT - French Fries - J.R. SIMPLOT COMPANY; *pg.* 867, *pg.* 547

TOP CLEAN - Cleaning Product - HILLYARD, INC.; *pg.* 331, *pg.* 990

TOP COAT - Floor Finish - SWISHER HYGIENE INC.; *pg.* 336, *pg.* 1507

TOP COTE - Woodworking Machinery Lubricant - BOSTIK INC.; *pg.* 1150, *pg.* 833

TOP CREST - Non-Edible Products - BASHAS' SUPERMARKETS; *pg.* 1015, *pg.* 12

TOP CREST - General Merchandise - TOPCO HOLDINGS INC.; *pg.* 901, *pg.* 661

TOP DOGS - Hot Dogs - MAPLE LEAF FOODS INC.; *pg.* 875, *pg.* 1927

TOP DOLLAR - Game - INTERNATIONAL GAME TECHNOLOGY; *pg.* 957, *pg.* 1024

TOP DOLLAR DELUXE - Video Game - INTERNATIONAL GAME TECHNOLOGY; *pg.* 957, *pg.* 1024

TOP DOLLAR LUCKY ROLL - Video Game - INTERNATIONAL GAME TECHNOLOGY; *pg.* 957, *pg.* 1024

TOP DRUM - Separator - THE SPENCER TURBINE CO.; *pg.* 1378, *pg.* 386

TOP FIN - Pet Product - PETSMART, INC.; *pg.* 1481, *pg.* 18

TOP-FLITE - Golf Balls, Clubs, Accessories - CALLAWAY GOLF BALL OPERATIONS, INC.; *pg.* 1829, *pg.* 814

TOP-FLITE - Golf Products - DICK'S SPORTING GOODS, INC.; *pg.* 1832, *pg.* 1524

TOP FLITE - Models - HOBBICO, INC.; *pg.* 956, *pg.* 562

TOP FUEL - Bicycle - TREK BICYCLE CORPORATION; *pg.* 1847, *pg.* 1896

TOP GON - Railroad Cars - NORFOLK SOUTHERN CORPORATION; *pg.* 1917, *pg.* 1797

TOP GUN - Looping Jet Roller Coaster - CANADA'S WONDERLAND COMPANY; *pg.* 536, *pg.* 1947

TOP GUN - Caulks - PPG INDUSTRIES, INC.; *pg.* 1445, *pg.* 1579

TOP GUN - Bale Processor - VERMEER MANUFACTURING COMPANY; *pg.* 708, *pg.* 711

TOP GUN H10XPRO - Refrigerant Leak Detector - BACHARACH INC.; *pg.* 1400, *pg.* 1556

TOP GUN: THE JET COASTER - Roller Coaster - CAROWINDS; *pg.* 537, *pg.* 1364

TOP HANDLE - Briefcase - SANTA FE LEATHER CORPORATION; *pg.* 12, *pg.* 1059

TOP HAT PROGRESSIVES - Video Game - INTERNATIONAL GAME TECHNOLOGY; *pg.* 957, *pg.*

First page reference indicates Business Class Edition
Second page reference indicates Geographic Edition

1024
TOP LEASE - Premium Roll Covers - VAIL RUBBER WORKS, INC.; *pg.* 1891, *pg.* 906
TOP LEASE II - Premium Roll Covers - VAIL RUBBER WORKS, INC.; *pg.* 1891, *pg.* 906
TOP LEASE X - Premium Roll Covers - VAIL RUBBER WORKS, INC.; *pg.* 1891, *pg.* 906
TOP LINER - Turf Maintenance Machinery - SMITHCO, INC.; *pg.* 1377, *pg.* 1592
TOP NOTCH - Food Pans - CARLISLE FOODSERVICE PRODUCTS INCORPORATED; *pg.* 1455, *pg.* 1485
TOP NOTCH - Inserts For Metal Cutting Tools - KENNAMETAL INC.; *pg.* 1052, *pg.* 1547
TOP NOTCH - Tongue & Groove Flooring - LOUISIANA-PACIFIC CORPORATION; *pg.* 94, *pg.* 1652
TOP OF STAIR - Baby Gate - EVENFLO COMPANY, INC.; *pg.* 924, *pg.* 1470
TOP OF THE CLASS CELEBRATION - Fruit Arrangements - EDIBLE ARRANGEMENTS INTERNATIONAL, INC.; *pg.* 1768, *pg.* 382
TOP OF THE COP - Motorsports Entertainment - SPEEDWAY MOTORSPORTS, INC.; *pg.* 584, *pg.* 1370
TOP PAW - Pet Supplies - PETSMART, INC.; *pg.* 1481, *pg.* 18
TOP PERFORMANCE - Pet Care Product - PETEDGE; *pg.* 1481, *pg.* 787
TOP POST - Vehicle Safety System - GROTE INDUSTRIES, INC.; *pg.* 206, *pg.* 693
TOP PRO - Golf Product - FAIRMOUNT SANTROL; *pg.* 1162, *pg.* 1409
TOP PRODUCER FLAGSHIP 8I - Software - MOVE, INC.; *pg.* 1268, *pg.* 247
TOP SECRET ADVENTURES - Activity Kit Series - HIGHLIGHTS FOR CHILDREN, INC.; *pg.* 1650, *pg.* 1440
TOP SECRET SPINS - Video Game - INTERNATIONAL GAME TECHNOLOGY; *pg.* 957, *pg.* 1024
TOP SHAPE - Cleaning Product - HILLYARD, INC.; *pg.* 331, *pg.* 990
TOP SHOW - Rabbit Food - KENT NUTRITION GROUP; *pg.* 1477, *pg.* 710
TOP TEX - Premium Roll Covers - VAIL RUBBER WORKS, INC.; *pg.* 1891, *pg.* 906
TOP THRILL DRAGSTER - Amusement & Water Park - CEDAR FAIR, L.P.; *pg.* 537, *pg.* 1471
TOP TRUMPS - Game - HASBRO, INC.; *pg.* 954, *pg.* 1603
TOPAMAX - Healthcare Product - JOHNSON & JOHNSON; *pg.* 1549, *pg.* 1091
TOPANGA - Fabric - NEMSCHOFF, INC.; *pg.* 936, *pg.* 1890
TOPAS - Ultrafast Optical Parametric Amplifier - COHERENT, INC.; *pg.* 1406, *pg.* 265
TOPAS - Fabric - NEMSCHOFF, INC.; *pg.* 936, *pg.* 1890
TOPAS - Automated Ultrafast OPAOTS - NEWPORT CORPORATION; *pg.* 1424, *pg.* 114
TOPAZ - Rugs - COURISTAN INC.; *pg.* 921, *pg.* 1067
TOPAZ - Flat Panel Display - EPSILON SYSTEMS SOLUTIONS; *pg.* 1412, *pg.* 202
TOPAZ - Wheelchair - INVACARE CORPORATION; *pg.* 1546, *pg.* 1451
TOPAZ - Adult Mass Market Paperback Books - PENGUIN RANDOM HOUSE; *pg.* 1675, *pg.* 1276
TOPAZ - Office Furniture - STEELCASE INC.; *pg.* 475, *pg.* 889
TOPAZ XL - Hardware - VERIFONE SYSTEMS, INC.; *pg.* 487, *pg.* 251
TOPCARE - Food Product - HAGGEN, INC.; *pg.* 1022, *pg.* 1817
TOPCARE CYLINDERS - Engine Cylinder - CONTINENTAL MOTORS; *pg.* 227, *pg.* 7
TOPCAT - Ingredient System - PENFORD CORPORATION; *pg.* 1177, *pg.* 314
TOPCOUNT - Microplate - PERKINELMER, INC.; *pg.* 1426, *pg.* 853
TOPEIN - Petroleum Product - ALON USA ENERGY, INC.; *pg.* 971, *pg.* 1673
TOPGARD - Roof Coatings - JOHNS MANVILLE CORPORATION; *pg.* 89, *pg.* 320
TOPGARD - Headwear - MINE SAFETY APPLIANCES COMPANY; *pg.* 1361, *pg.* 1525
TOPGARD 4000 - Roof Coating - JOHNS MANVILLE CORPORATION; *pg.* 89, *pg.* 320
TOPGARD 5000 - Roof Coating - JOHNS MANVILLE CORPORATION; *pg.* 89, *pg.* 320
TOPHEL - Alloy - CARPENTER TECHNOLOGY CORPORATION; *pg.* 73, *pg.* 1584
TOPHET - Alloy - CARPENTER TECHNOLOGY CORPORATION; *pg.* 73, *pg.* 1584
TOPHOOF - Animal Safety Product - NEOGEN CORPORATION; *pg.* 883, *pg.* 896
TOPIARY - Fabric - NEMSCHOFF, INC.; *pg.* 936, *pg.* 1890
TOPIX - Theme-Driven Trivia Game Played Under Controlled Timing - NTN BUZZTIME, INC.; *pg.* 659, *pg.* 60
TOPLINE TOYS - Game - UNIVERSITY GAMES CORPORATION; *pg.* 969, *pg.* 230
TOPLITE - Recessed Lighting - SWIVELIER CO., INC.; *pg.* 1307, *pg.* 1142
TOPLOK - Shroud - ESCO CORPORATION; *pg.* 1335, *pg.* 1502
TOPMIKE - Mirror Mount - OPTOSIGMA CORP.; *pg.* 1425, *pg.* 262
TOPNOTES - Pet & Animal Food Additives - TYSON FOODS, INC.; *pg.* 902, *pg.* 35
TOPO - Office Furniture - STEELCASE INC.; *pg.* 475, *pg.* 889
TOPO - Molecular Biology Product - THERMO FISHER SCIENTIFIC INC.; *pg.* 1602, *pg.* 61
TOPO - Ceiling Tiles - USG CORPORATION; *pg.* 118, *pg.* 594
TOPO TA CLONING - Biomolecule Product - THERMO FISHER SCIENTIFIC INC.; *pg.* 1602, *pg.* 61
TOPOBASE - Software - AUTODESK INC.; *pg.* 356, *pg.* 257
TOPOGRAPHY - Fabric - NEMSCHOFF, INC.; *pg.* 936, *pg.* 1890
TOPOLOGY DISCOVERY - Software - BMC SOFTWARE, INC.; *pg.* 362, *pg.* 1701
TOPOLOGY EXTENSION - Software - BMC SOFTWARE, INC.; *pg.* 362, *pg.* 1701
TOPOLOGY MANAGER - Software - PITNEY BOWES SOFTWARE INC.; *pg.* 455, *pg.* 1346
TOPOMAP 250K - Mapping Overlay Tool - PITNEY BOWES SOFTWARE INC.; *pg.* 455, *pg.* 1346
TOPOSAR - Digital Terrain & Elevation Modeling Services - INTERMAP TECHNOLOGIES CORPORATION; *pg.* 417, *pg.* 1903
TOPOSAR - Medicine - PFIZER INC.; *pg.* 1581, *pg.* 1278
TOPPER - Fabric - SCALAMANDRE, INC.; *pg.* 941, *pg.* 1058
TOPPLE - Game - PRESSMAN TOY CORPORATION; *pg.* 965, *pg.* 1734
TOPPRINT - Balloon - CONTINENTAL AMERICAN CORP.; *pg.* 1880, *pg.* 723
TOPPS ARCHIVES - Sports Cards - THE TOPPS COMPANY, INC.; *pg.* 588, *pg.* 1302
TOPPS FINEST - Sports Cards - THE TOPPS COMPANY, INC.; *pg.* 588, *pg.* 1302
TOPPS GALLERY - Sports Cards - THE TOPPS COMPANY, INC.; *pg.* 588, *pg.* 1302
TOPPS SPORTS CARDS - Baseball, Football, Basketball & Hockey Cards - THE TOPPS COMPANY, INC.; *pg.* 588, *pg.* 1302
TOPPS VAULT - On-Line Auction for Trading Cards - THE TOPPS COMPANY, INC.; *pg.* 588, *pg.* 1302
TOPPUR - Water - THE COCA-COLA COMPANY; *pg.* 240, *pg.* 493
TOPREM - Gear Cutting Tools & Blades - GLEASON CORPORATION; *pg.* 1340, *pg.* 1335
TOP'S - Beverages - THE COCA-COLA COMPANY; *pg.* 240, *pg.* 493
TOPS MILD - Dry Snuff - SWISHER INTERNATIONAL, INC.; *pg.* 1895, *pg.* 345
TOPS SWEET - Dry Snuff - SWISHER INTERNATIONAL, INC.; *pg.* 1895, *pg.* 345
THE TOPSAIL ADVERTISER - North Carolina Newspaper - FREEDOM COMMUNICATIONS, INC.; *pg.* 1643, *pg.* 110
TOPSCENE - Computer Software - LOCKHEED MARTIN CORPORATION; *pg.* 229, *pg.* 762
TOPSIDER - Industrial Safety Eyewear - UVEX SAFETY; *pg.* 1433, *pg.* 1608
TOPSPOT - Flashlight - STREAMLIGHT INC.; *pg.* 1306, *pg.* 1527
TOPSTITCH POLO - Clothing - K-SWISS; *pg.* 1837, *pg.* 306
TOPSTYLE - Shirts & Sportswear - INDERA MILLS COMPANY; *pg.* 26, *pg.* 1396
TOPSWITCH - Switch - POWER INTEGRATIONS, INC.; *pg.* 1369, *pg.* 249
TOPSY TURVY TROLLS - Toys - 1-800-FLOWERS.COM, INC.; *pg.* 1758, *pg.* 1151
TOPSYNC - Communication Product - SEMTECH CORPORATION; *pg.* 671, *pg.* 57
TOPSYTAIL - Hair Styling Tool - CONAIR CORPORATION; *pg.* 505, *pg.* 1055
TOR BOOKS - Books - ST. MARTINS PRESS, INC.; *pg.* 1688, *pg.* 1295
TORADA - Margarita - SAZERAC COMPANY, INC.; *pg.* 1969, *pg.* 745
TORADOL - Pharmaceutical Product - HOFFMANN-LA ROCHE INC.; *pg.* 1542, *pg.* 1099
TORBUGESIC - Veterinary Analgesic Preparation - PFIZER INC.; *pg.* 1581, *pg.* 1278
TORBUTROL - Veterinary Antitussive - PFIZER INC.; *pg.* 1581, *pg.* 1278
THE TORCH - Power Tool - MILWAUKEE ELECTRIC TOOL CORP.; *pg.* 1056, *pg.* 1855
TORCON - Medical Device - COOK GROUP, INC.; *pg.* 1518, *pg.* 674
TORDERA - Vanity Lights - CRAFTMADE INTERNATIONAL, INC.; *pg.* 1295, *pg.* 1670
TORDON - Herbicide - DOW AGROSCIENCES LLC; *pg.* 1156, *pg.* 684
TORGENA - Pain Treatment Pharmaceutical Preparation - PFIZER INC.; *pg.* 1581, *pg.* 1278
TORI - Clothing - ABERCROMBIE & FITCH CO.; *pg.* 37, *pg.* 1466
TORI - Furniture - AMISCO INDUSTRIES LTD.; *pg.* 913, *pg.* 1958
TORIC - Intraocular Lenses - STAAR SURGICAL COMPANY; *pg.* 1597, *pg.* 151
TORIC ICL - Implantable Collamer Lens - STAAR SURGICAL COMPANY; *pg.* 1597, *pg.* 151
TORII - Furniture - NEMSCHOFF, INC.; *pg.* 936, *pg.* 1890
TORINO - Shoes - ALLEN-EDMONDS SHOE CORP.; *pg.* 1804, *pg.* 1887
TORINO - Window Treatment - CROSCILL, INC.; *pg.* 1122, *pg.* 1220
TORINO - Ceiling Fan - WESTINGHOUSE LIGHTING CORPORATION; *pg.* 687, *pg.* 1571
TORISEL - Cancer Treatment Pharmaceutical Preparation - PFIZER INC.; *pg.* 1581, *pg.* 1278
TORIT - Environmental Control Apparatus - DONALDSON COMPANY, INC.; *pg.* 1329, *pg.* 917
TORIT-BUILT - Air Filtration & Contaminant Collection System - DONALDSON COMPANY, INC.; *pg.* 1329, *pg.* 917
TORIT-TEX - Cartridge - DONALDSON COMPANY, INC.; *pg.* 1329, *pg.* 917
TORK MASTER - Sugar Centrifugal - WESTERN STATES MACHINE COMPANY; *pg.* 1388, *pg.* 1455
TORKER II - Manifolds - EDELBROCK CORPORATION; *pg.* 204, *pg.* 293
TORN RANCH - Flower Arrangement - 1-800-FLOWERS.COM, INC.; *pg.* 1758, *pg.* 1151
TORNADE - Malt-Based Lemonade - MOLSON COORS BREWING COMPANY; *pg.* 256, *pg.* 321
TORNADO - Pulper Machine - BOLTON-EMERSON AMERICAS, INC.; *pg.* 1318, *pg.* 827
TORNADO - Bowling Equipment - BRUNSWICK BOWLING & BILLIARDS CORP.; *pg.* 1828, *pg.* 622
TORNADO - Medical Device - COOK GROUP, INC.; *pg.* 1518, *pg.* 674
TORNADO - Cotton Candy Machine - GOLD MEDAL PRODUCTS CO.; *pg.* 55, *pg.* 1414
TORNADO - Cutter - HOUGEN MANUFACTURING INC.; *pg.* 1347, *pg.* 908
TORNADO - Cleaning Product - THE LIBMAN COMPANY; *pg.* 331, *pg.* 553
TORNADO - Cookware - TURBOCHEF TECHNOLOGIES, INC.; *pg.* 902, *pg.* 1670
TORNADO - Software - WIND RIVER SYSTEMS, INC.; *pg.* 493, *pg.* 38
TORNADO 2 - Oven - TURBOCHEF TECHNOLOGIES, INC.; *pg.* 902, *pg.* 1670
TORNADO AE - Software - WIND RIVER SYSTEMS, INC.; *pg.* 493, *pg.* 38
TORNADO BSP DEVELOPER'S KIT - Software - WIND RIVER SYSTEMS, INC.; *pg.* 493, *pg.* 38
TORNADOS - Mexican Food - RUIZ FOOD PRODUCTS, INC.; *pg.* 893, *pg.* 77
TORO PREMIUM CIGAR TASTER - Cigars - FINCK CIGAR CO.; *pg.* 1894, *pg.* 1740
TORO WHEEL HORSE - Riding Mower And Tractor - THE TORO COMPANY; *pg.* 1065, *pg.* 918
TORONADO - Electric Guitar - FENDER MUSICAL INSTRUMENTS CORPORATION; *pg.* 547, *pg.* 21
TORONTO - Fabric - NEMSCHOFF, INC.; *pg.* 936, *pg.* 1890
TORONTO BLUE JAYS - Baseball Team - TORONTO BLUE JAYS BASEBALL CLUB; *pg.* 588, *pg.* 1945
TORONTO MAPLE LEAFS - NHL Hockey Club - MAPLE LEAF SPORTS & ENTERTAINMENT LTD.; *pg.* 560, *pg.*

1940
TORONTO RAPTORS - NBA Basketball Club - MAPLE LEAF SPORTS & ENTERTAINMENT LTD.; *pg.* 560, *pg.* 1940
TORPEDO - Commercial Lighting - SWIVELIER CO., INC.; *pg.* 1307, *pg.* 1142
TORQ-FLEX - Wire Guide - COOK GROUP, INC.; *pg.* 1518, *pg.* 674
TORQR - Catheter - MEDTRONIC, INC.; *pg.* 1564, *pg.* 939
TORQUE - Wheelchair - INVACARE CORPORATION; *pg.* 1546, *pg.* 1451
TORQUE CONTROL - Shoe And Glove - ACUSHNET COMPANY; *pg.* 1824, *pg.* 818
TORQUE-ON-DEMAND - Automatic Transmission System - BORGWARNER INC.; *pg.* 167, *pg.* 867
TORQUE TEAM - Power Transmission Belting - THE GOODYEAR TIRE & RUBBER COMPANY; *pg.* 1883, *pg.* 1401
TORQUEMASTER - Garage Door - WAYNE-DALTON CORP.; *pg.* 120, *pg.* 1465
TORREFAZIONE ITALIA - Coffee - SEATTLE COFFEE COMPANY; *pg.* 265, *pg.* 1839
TORREFAZIONE ITALIA - Coffee - STARBUCKS CORPORATION; *pg.* 897, *pg.* 1840
TORRENT - Pumps - IDEX CORPORATION; *pg.* 1347, *pg.* 623
TORRENTO - Filters - ENTEGRIS, INC.; *pg.* 1882, *pg.* 788
TORRETTA - Bath & Plumbing Product - JACUZZI BRANDS CORPORATION; *pg.* 554, *pg.* 65
TORREXX - Electric LPG Vaporizer - ALGAS-SDI; *pg.* 1311, *pg.* 1831
TORRINGTON - Bearing Product - THE TIMKEN COMPANY; *pg.* 218, *pg.* 1408
TORSADA - Flatware - ONEIDA LTD; *pg.* 1129, *pg.* 1318
TORSADE - Stainless Steel Flatware - ONEIDA LTD; *pg.* 1129, *pg.* 1318
TORSION MOUNT - Vehicle Safety System - GROTE INDUSTRIES, INC.; *pg.* 206, *pg.* 693
TORSION MOUNT II - Shock-absorbing Bulb Cradle - GROTE INDUSTRIES, INC.; *pg.* 206, *pg.* 693
TORTILLALAND - Uncooked Tortillas - CIRCLE FOODS, LLC; *pg.* 848, *pg.* 201
TORTILLAS SAN ANTONIO - Food Product - RESER'S FINE FOODS INC.; *pg.* 1032, *pg.* 1496
TORX - Hand Tool - GENERAL TOOLS & INSTRUMENTS LLC; *pg.* 1048, *pg.* 1234
TORX - Screwdriver - KLEIN TOOLS INC.; *pg.* 1052, *pg.* 627
TORY BURCH - Women's Lifestyle Brand - TORY BURCH LLC; *pg.* 34, *pg.* 1302
TOSCANA - Furniture - AMERICAN LEATHER LP; *pg.* 912, *pg.* 1673
TOSCANA - Furniture - ASHLEY FURNITURE INDUSTRIES, INC.; *pg.* 914, *pg.* 1852
TOSCANA - Fan - CRAFTMADE INTERNATIONAL, INC.; *pg.* 1295, *pg.* 1670
TOSCANA - Bike - MARIN BIKES; *pg.* 1708, *pg.* 168
TOSCANA - Fabric - NEMSCHOFF, INC.; *pg.* 936, *pg.* 1890
TOSCANO - Cigar - AVANTI CIGAR CORPORATION; *pg.* 1894, *pg.* 1527
TOSS - Bioremediation Services - WASTE MANAGEMENT, INC.; *pg.* 1954, *pg.* 1716
TOSS ACROSS - Toy - MATTEL, INC.; *pg.* 962, *pg.* 81
TOSTADOS - White Corn Tortilla - GOLDEN FLAKE SNACK FOODS, INC.; *pg.* 1854, *pg.* 3
TOSTITOS - Tortilla Chips - FRITO-LAY NORTH AMERICA, INC.; *pg.* 1853, *pg.* 1730
TOSTITOS - Snack Food - PEPSICO, INC.; *pg.* 259, *pg.* 1327
TOT-LOK - Magnetic Cabinet Locking System - REV-A-SHELF; *pg.* 1060, *pg.* 738
TOTAL - Cereal - GENERAL MILLS, INC.; *pg.* 828, *pg.* 933
TOTAL ABSCESSION - Electrosurgical Devices - ANGIODYNAMICS, INC.; *pg.* 1495, *pg.* 1173
TOTAL ACCESS - Outside Plant Remote Access Terminal - ADTRAN, INC.; *pg.* 344, *pg.* 6
TOTAL ACCESS ELEMENT MANAGEMENT SYSTEM - Networking System - ADTRAN, INC.; *pg.* 344, *pg.* 6
TOTAL ACCESS OPTI-3 - Controller Module Installation - ADTRAN, INC.; *pg.* 344, *pg.* 6
TOTAL ANTIOXIDANT - Green Tea - CELESTIAL SEASONINGS, INC.; *pg.* 846, *pg.* 310
TOTAL CHARGING MANAGEMENT SYSTEM - Connector - PROGRESSIVE DYNAMICS, INC.; *pg.* 665, *pg.* 898
TOTAL CHOICE DINING - Cruise Line - CARNIVAL CRUISE LINES; *pg.* 1902, *pg.* 441
TOTAL CLEAN - Can Openers - JARDEN CONSUMER SOLUTIONS; *pg.* 57, *pg.* 412
TOTAL CLEAN - Floor Care - NILFISK-ADVANCE, INC.; *pg.* 332, *pg.* 953
TOTAL CONTAINMENT DEVICE - Sterile Connection Product - HAEMONETICS CORPORATION; *pg.* 1538, *pg.* 802
TOTAL CONTROL ACCOUNT - Life Insurance Settlement Option - METLIFE, INC.; *pg.* 1208, *pg.* 1258
TOTAL-E - DVD Solution Kit - CIRRUS LOGIC, INC.; *pg.* 629, *pg.* 1661
TOTAL ECLIPSE - Multi-function Tool - GERBER LEGENDARY BLADES; *pg.* 1834, *pg.* 1503
TOTAL ECONOMIC IMPACT - Technology Research Methodology - FORRESTER RESEARCH, INC.; *pg.* 1642, *pg.* 807
TOTAL ENVIRONMENTAL ACTIVITY MANAGEMENT - Specialized Customer Service - SAFETY-KLEEN HOLDCO, INC.; *pg.* 1180, *pg.* 1734
TOTAL FINISH - Cosmetic Product - MERLE NORMAN COSMETICS, INC.; *pg.* 517, *pg.* 136
TOTAL FITNESS - Fitness Product - BALLY TOTAL FITNESS HOLDINGS CORPORATION; *pg.* 532, *pg.* 1200
TOTAL FLUID MANAGEMENT SYSTEM - Fluid Handling System - GRACO, INC.; *pg.* 1342, *pg.* 935
TOTAL FOR AGILENT - Bioanalyzer - THERMO FISHER SCIENTIFIC INC.; *pg.* 1602, *pg.* 61
TOTAL GREEN - Nutritional Product - NUTRACEUTICAL INTERNATIONAL CORPORATION; *pg.* 1576, *pg.* 1753
TOTAL INSTRUMENT SOLUTION - Tagline - DWYER INSTRUMENTS INC.; *pg.* 1330, *pg.* 694
TOTAL LEAN - Nutritional Supplements - GENERAL NUTRITION CENTERS, INC.; *pg.* 1534, *pg.* 1575
TOTAL LEAN MRP - Nutritional Supplement - GENERAL NUTRITION CENTERS, INC.; *pg.* 1534, *pg.* 1575
TOTAL LIVING COVERAGE - Insurance Coverage - GENWORTH FINANCIAL, INC.; *pg.* 761, *pg.* 1802
TOTAL MATERNAL-NEWBORN SOLUTION - Pharmaceutical Product - ALERE INC.; *pg.* 1488, *pg.* 849
TOTAL PET HEALTH - Multi Vitamin Tablets - PETEDGE; *pg.* 1481, *pg.* 787
THE TOTAL POWER PACKAGE - Slogan - EDELBROCK CORPORATION; *pg.* 204, *pg.* 293
TOTAL PRO - Coating Product - PPG INDUSTRIES, INC.; *pg.* 1445, *pg.* 1579
TOTAL QUALITY KEEPS US ON TRACK! - Tag Line - HARSCO RAIL; *pg.* 1345, *pg.* 1623
TOTAL RADIO - Multi-Band Chipset - RF MICRO DEVICES, INC.; *pg.* 667, *pg.* 1376
TOTAL RAISIN BRAN - Cereal - GENERAL MILLS, INC.; *pg.* 828, *pg.* 933
TOTAL REACH - ISDN & DDS Extension - ADTRAN, INC.; *pg.* 344, *pg.* 6
TOTAL RECONCILIATION - Software System - SS&C TECHNOLOGIES HOLDINGS, INC.; *pg.* 473, *pg.* 386
TOTAL RESPONSE - Training Services - CARDIAC SCIENCE CORPORATION; *pg.* 1512, *pg.* 1897
TOTAL RETURN - Software - SS&C TECHNOLOGIES HOLDINGS, INC.; *pg.* 473, *pg.* 386
TOTAL REWARDS - Rewards Program - CAESARS ENTERTAINMENT CORPORATION; *pg.* 1083, *pg.* 1023
TOTAL SATISFACTION SERVICES - Manual - XEROX CORPORATION; *pg.* 494, *pg.* 365
TOTAL SCRIPTS - Multi-Purpose Prescription Labels - THE STANDARD REGISTER COMPANY; *pg.* 473, *pg.* 1446
TOTAL SOLUTIONS - Audio & Video Product - HARMAN INTERNATIONAL INDUSTRIES, INCORPORATED; *pg.* 641, *pg.* 374
TOTAL SOLUTIONS - Medical Testing & Services - SYMMETRY MEDICAL INC.; *pg.* 1600, *pg.* 699
TOTAL THERMAL SOLUTIONS - Slogan - LYTRON INCORPORATED; *pg.* 1074, *pg.* 861
TOTAL TURTLE - Professional Wax - TURTLE WAX, INC.; *pg.* 220, *pg.* 671
TOTAL UROLOGY. TOTAL CARE. - Tagline - HEALTHTRONICS, INC.; *pg.* 1540, *pg.* 1663
TOTAL WAR - Game - ACTIVISION BLIZZARD, INC.; *pg.* 948, *pg.* 271
TOTAL90 - Footwear - NIKE, INC.; *pg.* 1812, *pg.* 1492
TOTALACCESS - Software - SUMTOTAL SYSTEMS, INC.; *pg.* 477, *pg.* 429
TOTALCARE - Health Services - HEALTHTRONICS, INC.; *pg.* 1540, *pg.* 1663
TOTALCARE - Hospital Beds - HILL-ROM HOLDINGS, INC.; *pg.* 1542, *pg.* 673
TOTALCHROM - Chromatography Data System - PERKINELMER, INC.; *pg.* 1426, *pg.* 853
TOTALCOLLABORATION - Software - SUMTOTAL SYSTEMS, INC.; *pg.* 477, *pg.* 429
TOTALCOLLECT - Electronic Payment System - CYBERSOURCE CORPORATION; *pg.* 381, *pg.* 216
TOTALDASHBOARD - Software - SUMTOTAL SYSTEMS, INC.; *pg.* 477, *pg.* 429
TOTALFLEX - Pharmaceutical Product - ALERE INC.; *pg.* 1488, *pg.* 849
TOTALFOAM - Packaging System - POLYAIR INTER PACK INC.; *pg.* 1467, *pg.* 1941
TOTALINFORMATION - Software - SUMTOTAL SYSTEMS, INC.; *pg.* 477, *pg.* 429
TOTALLCMS - Software - SUMTOTAL SYSTEMS, INC.; *pg.* 477, *pg.* 429
TOTALLMS - Software - SUMTOTAL SYSTEMS, INC.; *pg.* 477, *pg.* 429
TOTALLOOK MAMMO ADVANTAGE - Converts Mammography Images - ICAD, INC.; *pg.* 643, *pg.* 1037
TOTALLY FERRET - Pet Product - PETSMART, INC.; *pg.* 1481, *pg.* 18
TOTALLY FREE - Checking Accounts - TCF FINANCIAL CORPORATION; *pg.* 808, *pg.* 966
TOTALLY GROSS - Game - UNIVERSITY GAMES CORPORATION; *pg.* 969, *pg.* 230
TOTALLY HAYWARD - Pool System - HAYWARD POOL PRODUCTS; *pg.* 1049, *pg.* 1057
TOTALLY KIDS CLUB - Savings Program for Children 12 & Under - COMMUNITY BANCORP; *pg.* 741, *pg.* 1766
TOTALLY LIGHT - Food Product - 4C FOODS CORPORATION; *pg.* 835, *pg.* 1145
TOTALLY OPEN - Data Protection Software - FALCONSTOR SOFTWARE, INC.; *pg.* 396, *pg.* 1179
TOTALLY PUZZLED - Video Game - INTERNATIONAL GAME TECHNOLOGY; *pg.* 957, *pg.* 1024
TOTALLY RICHIN - Video Game - INTERNATIONAL GAME TECHNOLOGY; *pg.* 957, *pg.* 1024
TOTALLY TAFFY - Tart & Tangy Taffy - SWEET CANDY COMPANY; *pg.* 1862, *pg.* 1761
TOTALLY TATTOO - Body Paints - BADGER AIR BRUSH COMPANY; *pg.* 359, *pg.* 612
TOTALLY TOGETHER - Eye Care Product - THE W.E. BASSETT COMPANY; *pg.* 524, *pg.* 371
TOTALPERFORMANCE - Software - SUMTOTAL SYSTEMS, INC.; *pg.* 477, *pg.* 429
TOTALPLANT - Software System - HONEYWELL INTERNATIONAL INC.; *pg.* 407, *pg.* 1088
TOTALRECALL - Software - SYNOPSYS, INC.; *pg.* 480, *pg.* 162
TOTALSOURCE - Service & Support - VIDEOJET TECHNOLOGIES INC.; *pg.* 489, *pg.* 671
TOTALSTRETCH - Convertible Tight - ATTITUDES IN DRESSING INC.; *pg.* 19, *pg.* 1057
TOTALVCS - Software - SUMTOTAL SYSTEMS, INC.; *pg.* 477, *pg.* 429
TOTALVIEW - Wireless Institute - LCC INTERNATIONAL, INC.; *pg.* 651, *pg.* 1792
TOTALVIEW - Embedded Debugger for LynxOS - LYNX SOFTWARE TECHNOLOGIES; *pg.* 429, *pg.* 247
TOTALVIEW - Software - MONEY.NET, INC.; *pg.* 1268, *pg.* 1261
TOTE-ALONG SOFT SHAPES - Game Book - INNOVATIVE USA, INC.; *pg.* 957, *pg.* 363
TOTE N STORE - Chafer Box - THE VOLLRATH COMPANY LLC; *pg.* 1139, *pg.* 1894
TOTEL FAILSAFE - Surge Protectors - TII NETWORK TECHNOLOGIES, INC.; *pg.* 680, *pg.* 1157
TOTELINE - Food Service & Bakery Display Trays, Boxes & Pans - MOLDED FIBER GLASS COMPANIES; *pg.* 1886, *pg.* 1403
TOTEM - Fabric - NEMSCHOFF, INC.; *pg.* 936, *pg.* 1890
TOTES - Leather Boots - HABAND COMPANY, INC.; *pg.* 1772, *pg.* 1099
TOTES - Waterproof Accessories - TOTES ISOTONER CORPORATION; *pg.* 14, *pg.* 1426
TOTEWHEELS - Luggage - RUBBERMAID HOME PRODUCTS; *pg.* 1138, *pg.* 1453
TOTINO'S - Food Product - GENERAL MILLS, INC.; *pg.* 828, *pg.* 933
TOTO - Molecular Probe Product - THERMO FISHER SCIENTIFIC INC.; *pg.* 1602, *pg.* 61
TOTS' CHOICE - Modular Playsystem - MIRACLE RECREATION EQUIPMENT COMPANY; *pg.* 1839, *pg.* 988
TOTT'S - Champagne - E&J GALLO WINERY; *pg.* 1962, *pg.* 149

TOUCAN - Footwear - EASTLAND SHOE CORPORATION; *pg.* 1808, *pg.* 750
TOUCAN - High Volume, Large Format Outdoor Industrial Printers - MUTOH AMERICA INC.; *pg.* 443, *pg.* 18
TOUCAN SAM - Product Icon - KELLOGG COMPANY; *pg.* 831, *pg.* 870
TOUCH - Softeners - KAO BRANDS CO. INC.; *pg.* 513, *pg.* 1415
TOUCH & TUG - Educational Toys - LEAPFROG ENTERPRISES, INC.; *pg.* 961, *pg.* 84
TOUCH 'N FOAM - One Component Expanding Polyurethane Foam - CLAYTON CORPORATION; *pg.* 1154, *pg.* 977
TOUCH N' GO CALIBRATION - Systems Integration & Aeronautics - LOCKHEED MARTIN CORPORATION; *pg.* 229, *pg.* 762
TOUCH 'N SEAL - One or Two Component Expanding or Reduced Expanding Polyurethane Foam - CLAYTON CORPORATION; *pg.* 1154, *pg.* 977
TOUCH 'N SEAL - Envelopes - TENSION ENVELOPE CORPORATION; *pg.* 483, *pg.* 986
TOUCH 'N STICK - Spray Adhesive for Household & Industrial Use - CLAYTON CORPORATION; *pg.* 1154, *pg.* 977
TOUCH 'N TONE - Massager - CONAIR CORPORATION; *pg.* 505, *pg.* 1055
TOUCH O' GOLD PEANUT OIL - Vegetable Oil - MALLET & COMPANY, INC.; *pg.* 875, *pg.* 1521
TOUCH OF LOVE - Perfume - LANMAN & KEMP-BARCLAY CO., INC.; *pg.* 514, *pg.* 1132
TOUCH OF ORANGE - Wax - MOC PRODUCTS COMPANY, INC.; *pg.* 332, *pg.* 174
TOUCH-OF-SCENT - Room Air Freshener - SCOTT'S LIQUID GOLD-INC.; *pg.* 335, *pg.* 323
TOUCH-OF-SCENT-TOO - Air Freshener - SCOTT'S LIQUID GOLD-INC.; *pg.* 335, *pg.* 323
TOUCH OF SUN - Hair Coloring - P&G-CLAIROL, INC.; *pg.* 519, *pg.* 1418
TOUCH TECHNOLOGY - Massage Product - HUMAN TOUCH; *pg.* 928, *pg.* 123
TOUCH TEST - Sensory Evaluator - STOELTING CO.; *pg.* 1430, *pg.* 671
TOUCH-THE-PC - Software - CRESTRON ELECTRONICS INC.; *pg.* 631, *pg.* 1116
TOUCH-TOP - Plastic Houseware Product - STERILITE CORPORATION; *pg.* 1138, *pg.* 848
TOUCH UP - Ironing & Cleaning Product - FAULTLESS STARCH/BON AMI COMPANY; *pg.* 330, *pg.* 982
THE TOUCHABLES - Mattress - THERAPEDIC ASSOCIATES, INC.; *pg.* 945, *pg.* 1112
TOUCHCHART - Software - ALLSCRIPTS HEALTHCARE SOLUTIONS, INC.; *pg.* 1492, *pg.* 563
TOUCHDOWN - Office Furniture - STEELCASE INC.; *pg.* 475, *pg.* 889
TOUCHE - Paper & Nonwoven Material - FIBERMARK INC.; *pg.* 1457, *pg.* 1764
TOUCHENGINE - Pharmaceutical Product - ALERE INC.; *pg.* 1488, *pg.* 849
TOUCHGARD - Station with Sensors - HUFCOR INCORPORATED; *pg.* 87, *pg.* 1861
TOUCHGUARD - Safety System - HUFCOR INCORPORATED; *pg.* 87, *pg.* 1861
TOUCHGUARD - Flash Drive - LEXAR MEDIA, INC.; *pg.* 1262, *pg.* 146
TOUCHING LIVES. SECURING FUTURES. - Slogan - MODERN WOODMEN OF AMERICA; *pg.* 1209, *pg.* 654
TOUCHPAD - Tablet Computer - HEWLETT-PACKARD COMPANY; *pg.* 404, *pg.* 175
TOUCHPEN - Screen - 3M COMPANY; *pg.* 1142, *pg.* 956
TOUCHSCRIPT - Software - ALLSCRIPTS HEALTHCARE SOLUTIONS, INC.; *pg.* 1492, *pg.* 563
TOUCHSENSE - Hardware & Software - IMMERSION CORPORATION; *pg.* 413, *pg.* 246
TOUCHSTAR - Wireless Communication System - AT&T SOUTHEAST; *pg.* 1868, *pg.* 489
TOUCHSTART - Switch - OMRON SCIENTIFIC TECHNOLOGIES INCORPORATED; *pg.* 1425, *pg.* 91
TOUCHSTONE - Cable - ARRIS GROUP, INC.; *pg.* 353, *pg.* 541
TOUCHSTONE - Motion Picture & Television Production Company - THE WALT DISNEY COMPANY; *pg.* 317, *pg.* 52
TOUCHSTONE - Software - WIND RIVER SYSTEMS, INC.; *pg.* 493, *pg.* 38
TOUCHTEC - Switch - LEAR CORPORATION; *pg.* 229, *pg.* 907
TOUCHWAKE - WirelessUSB - CYPRESS SEMICONDUCTOR CORPORATION; *pg.* 1326, *pg.* 243
TOUCHWARE - Hardware & Software - IMMERSION CORPORATION; *pg.* 413, *pg.* 246
TOUCHWORKS - Software - ALLSCRIPTS HEALTHCARE SOLUTIONS, INC.; *pg.* 1492, *pg.* 563
TOUGH - Thermal - E.D. BULLARD COMPANY; *pg.* 1332, *pg.* 727
TOUGH BIRD - Sprinkler - RAIN BIRD CORPORATION; *pg.* 707, *pg.* 44
TOUGH COOKIE - Strengtheners - ORLY INTERNATIONAL, INC.; *pg.* 518, *pg.* 137
TOUGH-FIBRE - Tools - VAUGHAN & BUSHNELL MANUFACTURING COMPANY, INC.; *pg.* 1066, *pg.* 616
TOUGH FURNITURE. TOTAL SERVICE. - Slogan - HAWORTH, INC.; *pg.* 402, *pg.* 891
TOUGH ON DIRT, GENTLE ON THE EARTH - Tagline - BI-O-KLEEN INDUSTRIES, INC.; *pg.* 326, *pg.* 1845
THE TOUGH ONES COME TO US - Tagline - VAIL RUBBER WORKS, INC.; *pg.* 1891, *pg.* 906
TOUGH PRIME - Coating - ROSCO LABORATORIES, INC.; *pg.* 1782, *pg.* 378
TOUGH TAPES - Measuring Product - THE L.S. STARRETT COMPANY; *pg.* 1421, *pg.* 783
TOUGH TEX - Ink - VAN SON HOLLAND INK CORPORATION OF AMERICA; *pg.* 487, *pg.* 1169
TOUGH TEX LR - Ink - VAN SON HOLLAND INK CORPORATION OF AMERICA; *pg.* 487, *pg.* 1169
TOUGH-TITE - Coupling - MORRIS COUPLING COMPANY; *pg.* 1057, *pg.* 1530
TOUGH TOOLS - Tools & Tool Kits - NEWELL RUBBERMAID INC.; *pg.* 1128, *pg.* 515
TOUGHCHEW - Dog's Nest - THE ORVIS COMPANY, INC.; *pg.* 1781, *pg.* 1764
TOUGHCOAT - Topcoats & Primers - SHERWIN WILLIAMS; *pg.* 1448, *pg.* 1436
TOUGHEST MIGHTY DUMP - Toy & Game - HASBRO, INC.; *pg.* 954, *pg.* 1603
TOUGHGUARD - Wood Flooring Product - ARMSTRONG WORLD INDUSTRIES, INC.; *pg.* 914, *pg.* 1545
TOUGHLITE - Warning Light - UNITED RENTALS, INC.; *pg.* 1386, *pg.* 350
TOUGHMET - Alloy - MATERION CORPORATION; *pg.* 1359, *pg.* 1463
TOUGHROCK - Gypsum Wallboard Product - G-P GYPSUM CORPORATION; *pg.* 978, *pg.* 505
TOUGHROCK - Building Product - GEORGIA-PACIFIC LLC; *pg.* 1458, *pg.* 507
TOUGHTOUCH - Screen - 3M COMPANY; *pg.* 1142, *pg.* 956
TOULON - Dinnerware - THE HOMER LAUGHLIN CHINA COMPANY; *pg.* 1125, *pg.* 1850
TOUR - Graphite Golf Shaft - ALDILA, INC.; *pg.* 1825, *pg.* 185
TOUR - Motor Homes - WINNEBAGO INDUSTRIES, INC.; *pg.* 1712, *pg.* 707
TOUR AUTHENTIC - Golf Accessories - CALLAWAY GOLF COMPANY; *pg.* 1829, *pg.* 58
TOUR BLEND - Golf Product - FAIRMOUNT SANTROL; *pg.* 1162, *pg.* 1409
TOUR GRADE - Golf Product - FAIRMOUNT SANTROL; *pg.* 1162, *pg.* 1409
TOUR I - Golf Ball - CALLAWAY GOLF COMPANY; *pg.* 1829, *pg.* 58
TOUR MAX - Trademark & Golf Vehicle Tires - CARLISLE TIRE & WHEEL COMPANY; *pg.* 1880, *pg.* 1612
TOUR OF STARS - Game - WMS INDUSTRIES INC.; *pg.* 593, *pg.* 666
TOUR-PAK - Bag & Pouch - HARLEY-DAVIDSON, INC.; *pg.* 178, *pg.* 1874
TOUR-PRO - Software - MORSE WATCHMANS INC.; *pg.* 656, *pg.* 368
TOUR VELVET - Grip - EATON CORPORATION; *pg.* 1331, *pg.* 1429
TOUREWARDS - Loyalty Card - FJ MANAGEMENT, INC.; *pg.* 978, *pg.* 1758
TOURISMCAM - Webcam Software - EARTHCAM, INC.; *pg.* 1239, *pg.* 1072
TOURMALINE CERAMIC - Hair Dryer - CONAIR CORPORATION; *pg.* 505, *pg.* 1055
TOURMASTER - Riser - WENGER CORPORATION; *pg.* 1307, *pg.* 952
TOURNAMENT - Aluminum Boat - ALUMACRAFT BOAT COMPANY; *pg.* 1705, *pg.* 964
TOURNAMENT - Fiberglass Boat Product - GRADY-WHITE BOATS, INC.; *pg.* 1707, *pg.* 1377
TOURNAMENT EDITION - Video Game - INTERNATIONAL GAME TECHNOLOGY; *pg.* 957, *pg.* 1024
TOURNAMENT KNOCKOUT - Video Game - INTERNATIONAL GAME TECHNOLOGY; *pg.* 957, *pg.* 1024
TOURNAMENT-READY - Soil Surfactant - KALO, INC.; *pg.* 1796, *pg.* 719
TOURNAMENT X-PRESS ROLLER - Turf Maintenance Machinery - SMITHCO, INC.; *pg.* 1377, *pg.* 1592
TOURNEAU - Watch - TOURNEAU INC.; *pg.* 14, *pg.* 1303
TOURNEY TRAIL - Fishing Equipment - CABELA'S INCORPORATED; *pg.* 535, *pg.* 1019
TOVOLO - Furniture - ASHLEY FURNITURE INDUSTRIES, INC.; *pg.* 914, *pg.* 1852
T.O.W. - Fertilizer Opener - YETTER MANUFACTURING CO., INC.; *pg.* 708, *pg.* 598
TOW-PRO - Construction Equipment - JLG INDUSTRIES, INC.; *pg.* 1351, *pg.* 1551
TOWARD MAN'S FULL LIFE - Service - MEDTRONIC, INC.; *pg.* 1564, *pg.* 939
TOWEL GRIP-ITS - Hook & Helper - HOME PRODUCTS INTERNATIONAL, INC.; *pg.* 1125, *pg.* 577
TOWER - Wallcovering - OMNOVA SOLUTIONS INC; *pg.* 1176, *pg.* 1453
TOWER BY HENRY KLOSS - Speaker - CAMBRIDGE SOUNDWORKS, INC.; *pg.* 1234, *pg.* 781
TOWER II BY HENRY KLOSS - Speaker - CAMBRIDGE SOUNDWORKS, INC.; *pg.* 1234, *pg.* 781
TOWER III BY HENRY KLOSS - Speaker - CAMBRIDGE SOUNDWORKS, INC.; *pg.* 1234, *pg.* 781
TOWER OF TREATS - Gifts - HARRY & DAVID HOLDINGS, INC.; *pg.* 1022, *pg.* 1499
TOWER POKER - Game - WMS INDUSTRIES INC.; *pg.* 593, *pg.* 666
TOWER TOO - Storage Product - STEELCASE INC.; *pg.* 475, *pg.* 889
TOWER TREET - Synergist - DELTA FOREMOST CHEMICAL CORPORATION; *pg.* 1155, *pg.* 1642
TOWERCOM - Toy Train - LIONEL LLC; *pg.* 961, *pg.* 875
TOWFLEX - Thermoplastic Material - HEXCEL CORPORATION; *pg.* 1884, *pg.* 375
TOWHAWK - Battery Powered UAV - ISC8; *pg.* 1350, *pg.* 71
TOWING & RECOVERY FOOTNOTES - Trade Publication - DOMINION ENTERPRISES; *pg.* 1636, *pg.* 1796
TOWING OPERATORS PROTECTOR PLAN - Insurance Package Program - BROWN & BROWN, INC.; *pg.* 1196, *pg.* 419
TOWLMASTR - Towel Dispensing System - GEORGIA-PACIFIC LLC; *pg.* 1458, *pg.* 507
TOWLSAVER - Towel Dispensing System - GEORGIA-PACIFIC LLC; *pg.* 1458, *pg.* 507
TOWN & COUNTRY - Furniture Collection - CENTURY FURNITURE INDUSTRIES; *pg.* 920, *pg.* 1377
TOWN & COUNTRY - Grass Seed Mixture - CROSMAN SEED CORPORATION; *pg.* 1794, *pg.* 1156
TOWN & COUNTRY - Minivan - FCA US LLC; *pg.* 170, *pg.* 868
TOWN & COUNTRY - Magazine - THE HEARST CORPORATION; *pg.* 1649, *pg.* 1239
TOWN AND COUNTRY - Building Product - LESTER BUILDING SYSTEMS, LLC; *pg.* 93, *pg.* 927
TOWN & COUNTRY TRAVEL - Magazine - THE HEARST CORPORATION; *pg.* 1649, *pg.* 1239
TOWN & COUNTRY WAGON - Wagon - RADIO FLYER INC.; *pg.* 966, *pg.* 588
TOWN HOUSE - Snacks - KELLOGG COMPANY; *pg.* 831, *pg.* 870
TOWNEPLACE SUITES - Hotels - MARRIOTT INTERNATIONAL, INC.; *pg.* 1102, *pg.* 764
TOWNHALL.COM - Online Interactive Community - SALEM MEDIA GROUP, INC.; *pg.* 307, *pg.* 57
TOWNHOUSE - Bedding - CROSCILL, INC.; *pg.* 1122, *pg.* 1220
TOWNHOUSE - Furniture - ETHAN ALLEN INTERIORS INC.; *pg.* 924, *pg.* 343
TOWNIE - Bike - ELECTRA BICYCLE COMPANY; *pg.* 1706, *pg.* 303
TOWNIE - Apparel - VANS, INC.; *pg.* 1821, *pg.* 76
TOWNSEND - Pens - A. T. CROSS COMPANY; *pg.* 339, *pg.* 1602
TOWNSEND - Fan - CRAFTMADE INTERNATIONAL, INC.; *pg.* 1295, *pg.* 1670
TOWNSEND - Furniture - ETHAN ALLEN INTERIORS INC.; *pg.* 924, *pg.* 343
TOWPRO - Boom Lift - JLG INDUSTRIES, INC.; *pg.* 1351, *pg.* 1551

TOWSEND - Footwear - EASTLAND SHOE CORPORATION; *pg.* 1808, *pg.* 750
TOWVEYOR - Conveyor Floor - DAIFUKU WEBB; *pg.* 1327, *pg.* 885
TOWWER - Footwear - STEVEN MADDEN, LTD.; *pg.* 1819, *pg.* 1176
TOX/SEE - Clinical Diagnostic Product - BIO-RAD LABORATORIES, INC.; *pg.* 1504, *pg.* 101
TOXBLAZER - Molecular Probe Product - THERMO FISHER SCIENTIFIC INC.; *pg.* 1602, *pg.* 61
TOXGARD - Safety Monitor - MINE SAFETY APPLIANCES COMPANY; *pg.* 1361, *pg.* 1525
TOXIBOND - Animal Nutrition Product - VITUSA CORP.; *pg.* 1482, *pg.* 1063
TOXIK - Software - AUTODESK INC.; *pg.* 356, *pg.* 257
TOXIMETER - Automatic Detector Tube Pump - MINE SAFETY APPLIANCES COMPANY; *pg.* 1361, *pg.* 1525
TOXIMUL - Chemical Product - STEPAN COMPANY; *pg.* 1182, *pg.* 643
TOY CREATOR - Game - UNIVERSITY GAMES CORPORATION; *pg.* 969, *pg.* 230
TOY POODLE - Carpet - INTERFACE, INC.; *pg.* 695, *pg.* 512
TOY STORY - Game - HASBRO, INC.; *pg.* 954, *pg.* 1603
TOYCON - Meeting & Conference - TOY INDUSTRY ASSOCIATION, INC.; *pg.* 158, *pg.* 1303
TOYMAKER 3000 - Educational Toys - MUSEUM OF SCIENCE AND INDUSTRY; *pg.* 565, *pg.* 583
TOYMAX - Toy & Leisure Product - JAKKS PACIFIC, INC.; *pg.* 960, *pg.* 142
TOYS YOU'LL FEEL GOOD ABOUT GIVING - Catalog Order Services - 1-800-FLOWERS.COM, INC.; *pg.* 1758, *pg.* 1151
TOYSRUS.COM - Online Toy Store - TOYS "R" US, INC.; *pg.* 968, *pg.* 1130
TP-4429 - Rugged Thermal Printer/Plotter Designed for Use in Commercial Aircraft - MILTOPE GROUP, INC.; *pg.* 440, *pg.* 6
TP-4840 - Rugged, Compact Thermal Printer for Use in Commercial Aircraft - MILTOPE GROUP, INC.; *pg.* 440, *pg.* 6
TPA - Electronic Components - MOLEX INCORPORATED; *pg.* 655, *pg.* 628
TPC 427 - Phosphate - CARUS CORPORATION; *pg.* 1152, *pg.* 652
TPC SOLVENT - Cleaner - PENETONE CORPORATION; *pg.* 333, *pg.* 1050
TPDOC - Software - KEITHLEY INSTRUMENTS, INC.; *pg.* 1418, *pg.* 1473
TPH - Dental Product - DENTSPLY INTERNATIONAL INC.; *pg.* 1522, *pg.* 1596
TPL - Third Party Liability Processing - HEALTH MANAGEMENT SYSTEMS, INC.; *pg.* 1540, *pg.* 1238
TPM-TEST - Pharmaceutical Product - ALERE INC.; *pg.* 1488, *pg.* 849
TPMA - Sprayers - AG-MEIER INDUSTRIES LLC; *pg.* 700, *pg.* 1668
TPS - Bearing - THE TIMKEN COMPANY; *pg.* 218, *pg.* 1408
TPS SERIES - Baseball Glove - HILLERICH & BRADSBY CO., INC.; *pg.* 1836, *pg.* 576
TPS40K - DC Controllers - TEXAS INSTRUMENTS INCORPORATED; *pg.* 679, *pg.* 1688
TPSD - Battery Charger/ Power Supply - LA MARCHE MANUFACTURING COMPANY; *pg.* 1300, *pg.* 606
TPX - Baseball Glove - HILLERICH & BRADSBY CO., INC.; *pg.* 1836, *pg.* 576
TPX - Telepresence Solution - POLYCOM, INC.; *pg.* 664, *pg.* 249
TQ-PREP - Testing Instrument System - BECKMAN COULTER, INC.; *pg.* 1402, *pg.* 48
TR FLEX - Ductile Iron Pipe & Fittings - UNITED STATES PIPE & FOUNDRY COMPANY, INC.; *pg.* 117, *pg.* 5
TR TELE FLEX - Extendable, Flexible, Restrained Joint Assembly - UNITED STATES PIPE & FOUNDRY COMPANY, INC.; *pg.* 117, *pg.* 5
TRA - Nutritional Supplement - NU SKIN ENTERPRISES, INC.; *pg.* 518, *pg.* 1755
TRA SERIES - Pump Product - IDEX CORPORATION; *pg.* 1347, *pg.* 623
TRABON - Fluid Handling System - GRACO, INC.; *pg.* 1342, *pg.* 935
TRABON - Lubrication Equipment - IDEX CORPORATION; *pg.* 1347, *pg.* 623
TRAC - Software - DST SYSTEMS, INC.; *pg.* 388, *pg.* 982
TRAC - Vascular Access Management Program - FRESENIUS MEDICAL CARE NORTH AMERICA; *pg.* 1531, *pg.* 851
TRAC - Nutritional Supplement - MAXIMUM HUMAN PERFORMANCE, INC.; *pg.* 1559, *pg.* 1065
TRAC AUTOVANTAGE - Retirement Solutions - DST SYSTEMS, INC.; *pg.* 388, *pg.* 982
TRAC-BALL - Toy - MATTEL, INC.; *pg.* 962, *pg.* 81
TRAC CHIEF - Trademark & Industrial Tire - CARLISLE TIRE & WHEEL COMPANY; *pg.* 1880, *pg.* 1612
TRAC EXTREME-NO - Nutritional Supplement - MAXIMUM HUMAN PERFORMANCE, INC.; *pg.* 1559, *pg.* 1065
TRAC II - Razors & Blades - THE GILLETTE COMPANY; *pg.* 509, *pg.* 795
TRAC STAR - Skate - ROLLER DERBY SKATE CORP.; *pg.* 966, *pg.* 630
TRAC WEB - Retirement Solutions - DST SYSTEMS, INC.; *pg.* 388, *pg.* 982
TRAC12 - Financial Management Information Service - EASTMAN KODAK COMPANY; *pg.* 1408, *pg.* 1333
TRACBALL - Toy - WHAM-O, INC.; *pg.* 969, *pg.* 308
TRACE - Meter Reading System - BADGER METER, INC.; *pg.* 1401, *pg.* 1873
TRACE - Automated Meter Reading System - ELSTER AMERICAN METER COMPANY; *pg.* 1411, *pg.* 1387
TRACE - Apparel - OAKLEY, INC.; *pg.* 1840, *pg.* 86
TRACE MINERALS - Healthcare Product - SWANSON HEALTH PRODUCTS INC.; *pg.* 1600, *pg.* 1397
TRACE TECHNOLOGIES - Aerosol Cleaner - TECH SPRAY, L.P.; *pg.* 1183, *pg.* 1659
TRACELESS - Computer Hardware - EASTMAN KODAK COMPANY; *pg.* 1408, *pg.* 1333
TRACEPAK - Tubing & Hose - O'BRIEN CORPORATION; *pg.* 1366, *pg.* 1001
TRACEPLUS - Nonmetallic Power Connection - THERMON AMERICAS INC.; *pg.* 1077, *pg.* 1744
TRACER - Wireless License-Free Digital Microwave Radios - ADTRAN, INC.; *pg.* 344, *pg.* 6
TRACER - Software - BIO-RAD LABORATORIES, INC.; *pg.* 1504, *pg.* 101
TRACER - Compact Forensic Laser System - COHERENT, INC.; *pg.* 1406, *pg.* 265
TRACER - Hunting Product - GERBER LEGENDARY BLADES; *pg.* 1834, *pg.* 1503
TRACER - Gaming Product - GLD PRODUCTS, INC.; *pg.* 1835, *pg.* 1882
TRACER - Wheelchair - INVACARE CORPORATION; *pg.* 1546, *pg.* 1451
TRACER - Skate - ROLLER DERBY SKATE CORP.; *pg.* 966, *pg.* 630
TRACER - Analyzer - TELEDYNE LECROY; *pg.* 1431, *pg.* 1153
TRACER NATURALYTE - Insect Control Products - DOW AGROSCIENCES LLC; *pg.* 1156, *pg.* 684
TRACERY - Wall Decor - HERITAGE LACE INC.; *pg.* 694, *pg.* 711
TRACERY - Fabric - NEMSCHOFF, INC.; *pg.* 936, *pg.* 1890
TRACEVIEW - Cable - THERMON AMERICAS INC.; *pg.* 1077, *pg.* 1744
TRACFONE - Wireless Telecommunication Instrument - TRACFONE WIRELESS, INC.; *pg.* 681, *pg.* 447
TRACGLIDE - Braking System - THE TIMKEN COMPANY; *pg.* 218, *pg.* 1408
TRACII - Footwear - STEVEN MADDEN, LTD.; *pg.* 1819, *pg.* 1176
TRACK - Bicycle - TREK BICYCLE CORPORATION; *pg.* 1847, *pg.* 1896
TRACK ECN - Electronic Communications Network - TRACK DATA CORPORATION; *pg.* 1284, *pg.* 1147
TRACK-IT - Electronic Components - MOLEX INCORPORATED; *pg.* 655, *pg.* 628
TRACK 'N TRAIL - Footwear - WOLVERINE WORLD WIDE, INC.; *pg.* 1822, *pg.* 905
TRACK POWER - Toy Train - LIONEL LLC; *pg.* 961, *pg.* 875
TRACK POWER CONTROLLER 300 - Remote Control - LIONEL LLC; *pg.* 961, *pg.* 875
TRACK POWER CONTROLLER 400 - Remote Control - LIONEL LLC; *pg.* 961, *pg.* 875
TRACKEASE - Diabetes Monitoring Product - NIPRO DIAGNOSTICS, INC.; *pg.* 1573, *pg.* 426
TRACKEASE SMART SYSTEM - Blood Glucose Testing System - NIPRO DIAGNOSTICS, INC.; *pg.* 1573, *pg.* 426
TRACKER - Medical Device - BOSTON SCIENTIFIC CORPORATION; *pg.* 1508, *pg.* 831
TRACKER - Food Product - MARS, INCORPORATED; *pg.* 1858, *pg.* 1792
TRACKER - Flashlight - PELICAN PRODUCTS, INC.; *pg.* 1842, *pg.* 295
TRACKER EXCEL - Medical Device - BOSTON SCIENTIFIC CORPORATION; *pg.* 1508, *pg.* 831
TRACKING SERVER - Software - ENVIRONMENTAL SYSTEMS RESEARCH INSTITUTE INC.; *pg.* 393, *pg.* 188
TRACKINGPORTAL.NET - Software - NETWORK SYSTEMS INTERNATIONAL, INC.; *pg.* 445, *pg.* 1375
TRACKIT - Molecular Biology Product - THERMO FISHER SCIENTIFIC INC.; *pg.* 1602, *pg.* 61
TRACKLIGHT - Navigation Aid - TRIMBLE NAVIGATION LIMITED; *pg.* 1384, *pg.* 288
TRACKMASTER - Hose - HBD INDUSTRIES, INC.; *pg.* 207, *pg.* 1449
TRACKMASTER - Wellbore Departure System - SMITH INTERNATIONAL, INC.; *pg.* 1377, *pg.* 1715
TRACKRECORD - Data Management Software - NIPRO DIAGNOSTICS, INC.; *pg.* 1573, *pg.* 426
TRACKTRADE - Trading Platform - TRACK DATA CORPORATION; *pg.* 1284, *pg.* 1147
TRACLINE - Gas Piping Systems - OMEGA FLEX, INC.; *pg.* 982, *pg.* 1532
TRACMASTER - Pipeline Pigging Product - T.D. WILLIAMSON, INC.; *pg.* 1380, *pg.* 1490
TRACNET - Satellite Communication Product - KVH INDUSTRIES INC; *pg.* 650, *pg.* 1602
TRACPHONE - Satellite Communication Product - KVH INDUSTRIES INC; *pg.* 650, *pg.* 1602
TRACPIPE - Gas Piping Systems - OMEGA FLEX, INC.; *pg.* 982, *pg.* 1532
TRACRITE - AXLE DIFFERENTIALS - AMERICAN AXLE & MANUFACTURING HOLDINGS, INC.; *pg.* 198, *pg.* 879
TRACRITE - Packaging Product - FLEXCON CORPORATION; *pg.* 1457, *pg.* 844
TRACS - Business Management Program - NATIONAL AUTOMOTIVE PARTS ASSOCIATION; *pg.* 213, *pg.* 515
TRACTION MAT - Plastic & Rubber - TEKNOR APEX COMPANY; *pg.* 1889, *pg.* 1605
TRACTION PLUS - Abrasive Films - SAINT-GOBAIN ABRASIVES, INC. - PHILADELPHIA; *pg.* 1180, *pg.* 1553
TRACTION-TRED - Ladder Product - WERNER HOLDING CO.; *pg.* 121, *pg.* 1534
TRACTIONTOWER - Medical Equipment - CONMED CORPORATION; *pg.* 1517, *pg.* 1347
TRACTOL - Coating & Finish - NOV AMERON; *pg.* 100, *pg.* 187
TRACVISION - Satellite Communication Product - KVH INDUSTRIES INC; *pg.* 650, *pg.* 1602
TRACY - Clothing - ABERCROMBIE & FITCH CO.; *pg.* 37, *pg.* 1466
TRACY - Furniture - AMISCO INDUSTRIES LTD.; *pg.* 913, *pg.* 1958
TRAD - Electronic Control Device - TASER INTERNATIONAL, INC.; *pg.* 677, *pg.* 24
TRADE DRESS - Shoes - SHOE CARNIVAL, INC.; *pg.* 1819, *pg.* 679
TRADE EAST - Spices & Seasonings - GORDON FOOD SERVICE INC.; *pg.* 1021, *pg.* 913
TRADE ENVELOPES - Envelopes - ENNIS, INC.; *pg.* 393, *pg.* 1727
TRADE EVENT MANAGEMENT - Software - JDA SOFTWARE GROUP, INC.; *pg.* 423, *pg.* 22
TRADE IN TRADE UP - Slogan - CALLAWAY GOLF COMPANY; *pg.* 1829, *pg.* 58
TRADE MARK - Vinyl Siding - PLY GEM SIDING GROUP; *pg.* 105, *pg.* 986
TRADE MATE - Tile & Ceramic Sealant - DOW CORNING CORPORATION; *pg.* 1159, *pg.* 900
TRADE SECRET - Hair Salons - REGIS CORPORATION; *pg.* 521, *pg.* 941
TRADE SHOWS USA DIRECTORY - Directory - SUMNER COMMUNICATIONS INC.; *pg.* 1690, *pg.* 338
TRADE TRIGGERS - Stock Trading Tool - TD AMERITRADE HOLDING CORPORATION; *pg.* 808, *pg.* 1018
TRADE UP POKER - Video Poker - INTERNATIONAL GAME TECHNOLOGY; *pg.* 957, *pg.* 1024
TRADEBOOK - Securities Trading System - BLOOMBERG L.P.; *pg.* 725, *pg.* 1204
TRADEBOOK - Paper - DOMTAR CORPORATION; *pg.* 1456, *pg.* 1954
TRADEDESK - Software - SS&C TECHNOLOGIES HOLDINGS, INC.; *pg.* 473, *pg.* 386
TRADEMARK - Steel Laboratory Cabinets - KEWAUNEE SCIENTIFIC CORPORATION; *pg.* 931, *pg.* 1391
TRADEMARKSCAN - Internet Service - THOMSON COMPUMARK; *pg.* 484, *pg.* 838

TRADEMASTER - Vehicles - SPARTAN MOTORS, INC.; pg. 217, pg. 874
THE TRADER - Financial Products - DOW JONES & COMPANY, INC.; pg. 1637, pg. 1225
TRADER VIC'S - Food Products & Beverages - TRADER VIC'S GOURMET PRODUCTS, INC.; pg. 901, pg. 69
TRADERONLINE.COM - Advertising Website - DOMINION ENTERPRISES; pg. 1636, pg. 1796
TRADEROUTE - Software - ARI NETWORK SERVICES, INC.; pg. 353, pg. 1873
THE TRADERS EXPO - Tradeshow - INVESTMENT SEMINARS, INC.; pg. 420, pg. 466
TRADES - Marker - LA-CO INDUSTRIES MARKAL CO., INC.; pg. 1170, pg. 610
TRADES MARKER - All Purpose Marker - LA-CO INDUSTRIES MARKAL CO., INC.; pg. 1170, pg. 610
TRADESMAN - Reel Stands - GREENLEE TEXTRON INC.; pg. 1048, pg. 655
TRADESMAN - Fall Protection Equipment - MINE SAFETY APPLIANCES COMPANY; pg. 1361, pg. 1525
TRADESTATION - Investment Analysis Software - TRADESTATION GROUP, INC.; pg. 811, pg. 459
TRADETHRU - Software - SS&C TECHNOLOGIES HOLDINGS, INC.; pg. 473, pg. 386
TRADEUPS - Software - MARKET VELOCITY, INC.; pg. 1265, pg. 527
TRADEWIND - Software - MICROS SYSTEMS, INC.; pg. 435, pg. 768
TRADEWIND - Eyewear - MINE SAFETY APPLIANCES COMPANY; pg. 1361, pg. 1525
TRADEWINDS - Furniture Collection - LANE VENTURE, INC.; pg. 933, pg. 1379
TRADEWINDS - Natural Shade - SPRINGS WINDOW FASHIONS LLC; pg. 943, pg. 1872
TRADEWINDS HIBISCUS - Flower Grower - ARIS HORTICULTURE, INC.; pg. 1793, pg. 1404
TRADEWORKS - Paint Sprayers - THE SHERWIN-WILLIAMS COMPANY; pg. 1447, pg. 1435
TRADING POINTS - Financial Products - DOW JONES & COMPANY, INC.; pg. 1637, pg. 1225
TRADIO - Roller & Fountain Pens - PENTEL OF AMERICA, LTD.; pg. 453, pg. 295
TRADITION - 3-Tab Roofing Shingles - BUILDING PRODUCTS OF CANADA CORP.; pg. 72, pg. 1951
TRADITION - Mattresses - KINGSDOWN, INC.; pg. 932, pg. 1383
TRADITION - Helmet - MINE SAFETY APPLIANCES COMPANY; pg. 1361, pg. 1525
TRADITION - Fabric - NEMSCHOFF, INC.; pg. 936, pg. 1890
TRADITION - Knee System - ZIMMER BIOMET HOLDINGS, INC.; pg. 1611, pg. 699
TRADITION, EXCELLENCE AND FUTURE PROMISE. - Slogan - SUPERVALU, INC.; pg. 1035, pg. 924
TRADITION, INNOVATION, PERFORMANCE. - Tagline - HSM SOLUTIONS; pg. 1884, pg. 1378
TRADITION OF EXCELLENCE - Slogan - HOLLAND AMERICA LINE INC.; pg. 1911, pg. 1836
TRADITIONAL - Ale - BIG ROCK BREWERY INCOME TRUST; pg. 239, pg. 1902
TRADITIONAL - Chimes - CRAFTMADE INTERNATIONAL, INC.; pg. 1295, pg. 1670
TRADITIONAL - Tables - JOFCO INC.; pg. 931, pg. 691
TRADITIONAL - Faucets - MOEN INCORPORATED; pg. 1056, pg. 1468
TRADITIONAL - Toy Scale Model Animal - REEVES INTERNATIONAL, INC.; pg. 966, pg. 1108
TRADITIONAL - Beverage Bottle - THERMOS L.L.C.; pg. 61, pg. 660
TRADITIONAL - Gas Grill - W.C. BRADLEY CO.; pg. 62, pg. 528
TRADITIONAL - Fan - WESTINGHOUSE LIGHTING CORPORATION; pg. 687, pg. 1571
TRADITIONAL 874 - Pant - WILLIAMSON-DICKIE MANUFACTURING COMPANY; pg. 50, pg. 1696
TRADITIONAL CLASSICS - Broadloom - COURISTAN INC.; pg. 921, pg. 1067
TRADITIONAL HOME - Magazine - MEREDITH CORPORATION; pg. 1663, pg. 705
TRADITIONAL IRA - Retirement Plans - PRINCIPAL FINANCIAL GROUP, INC.; pg. 796, pg. 706
TRADITIONAL LOUNGE - Waiting Seating - STEELCASE INC.; pg. 475, pg. 889
TRADITIONAL RECIPE - Cake Mixes & Base - DAWN FOOD PRODUCTS, INC.; pg. 1018, pg. 893
TRADITIONAL SELECT - Aluminum Siding - PLY GEM SIDING GROUP; pg. 105, pg. 986
TRADITIONAL STRIP - Laminated 2 1/4" Strip Flooring-Square Edge - ROBBINS, INC.; pg. 108, pg. 1425
TRADITIONAL STYLE MOTOMIRROR - Mirror - COMMERCIAL VEHICLE GROUP, INC.; pg. 203, pg. 1467
TRADITION.PASSION.EVOLUTION. - Tagline - SAPUTO, INC.; pg. 893, pg. 1956
TRADITIONS - Crochet Cotton Thread - THE DMC CORPORATION; pg. 692, pg. 1076
TRADITIONS - Stoves - LENNOX HEARTH PRODUCTS; pg. 93, pg. 1652
TRADITIONS: THE BREAKERS - Magazine - PALM BEACH MEDIA GROUP INC.; pg. 1674, pg. 457
TRADOS - Software - LIONBRIDGE TECHNOLOGIES INC.; pg. 428, pg. 851
TRAFALGER - Table - BLATT BOWLING & BILLIARD CORP.; pg. 1827, pg. 1203
TRAFFIC ACE - Accumulator - INTERNATIONAL ROAD DYNAMICS INC.; pg. 1912, pg. 1962
TRAFFIC BLAZER - Software Product - GO DADDY INC.; pg. 1249, pg. 21
TRAFFIC LINE - Traffic Paint - AKZONOBEL DECORATIVE PAINTS U.S.; pg. 1439, pg. 1474
TRAFFIC LINE WB - Waterborne Traffic Marking Paint - AKZONOBEL DECORATIVE PAINTS U.S.; pg. 1439, pg. 1474
TRAFFIC SERVER - Internet Services - YAHOO! INC.; pg. 1289, pg. 289
TRAFFIC TALLY PEGASUS - Traffic Counter - INTERNATIONAL ROAD DYNAMICS INC.; pg. 1912, pg. 1962
TRAFFIC TOP - Driveway Sealer - QUIKRETE COMPANIES; pg. 106, pg. 519
TRAFFIC WARNING SYSTEM - Detectors - COBRA ELECTRONICS CORPORATION; pg. 629, pg. 572
TRAFFIC WORLD - Logistics Publication - JOC GROUP INC.; pg. 1654, pg. 1096
TRAFFICALK-3G - Concrete System - L.M. SCOFIELD COMPANY; pg. 94, pg. 134
TRAFFICCAM - Webcam Software - EARTHCAM, INC.; pg. 1239, pg. 1072
TRAFFICLINK - Computer Application - NIELSEN AUDIO; pg. 446, pg. 768
TRAFFICPRO - Audio & Video Product - HARMAN INTERNATIONAL INDUSTRIES, INCORPORATED; pg. 641, pg. 374
TRAFFICSHIELD - Software - F5 NETWORKS, INC.; pg. 396, pg. 1835
TRAFFIDECK - Waterproofing - THE DOW CHEMICAL COMPANY; pg. 1157, pg. 898
TRAFLOW - Software - ASPEN TECHNOLOGY, INC.; pg. 354, pg. 804
TRAIL BUCK - Utility Vehicle - DEERE & COMPANY; pg. 703, pg. 632
TRAIL HAWK - Trademark & ATV Tires - CARLISLE TIRE & WHEEL COMPANY; pg. 1880, pg. 1612
TRAIL PRO - Trademark & ATV Tires - CARLISLE TIRE & WHEEL COMPANY; pg. 1880, pg. 1612
THE TRAIL RIDER - Horseback Riding Magazine - BELVOIR MEDIA GROUP, LLC; pg. 1620, pg. 360
TRAIL SCOUT - Trail Camera - BUSHNELL OUTDOOR PRODUCTS, INC.; pg. 1403, pg. 718
TRAIL WOLF - Trademark & ATV Tires - CARLISLE TIRE & WHEEL COMPANY; pg. 1880, pg. 1612
TRAILBACK - Bike Carrier - LUND INTERNATIONAL, INC.; pg. 211, pg. 526
TRAILBLAZER - Broadband System Equipment - BLONDER TONGUE LABORATORIES, INC.; pg. 625, pg. 1100
TRAILBLAZER - Sport Utility Vehicle - GENERAL MOTORS COMPANY; pg. 175, pg. 881
TRAILBLAZER - Headlamp - L.L. BEAN, INC.; pg. 1777, pg. 750
TRAILBLAZER - Welding & Cutting Equip. - MILLER ELECTRIC MANUFACTURING CO.; pg. 1361, pg. 1852
TRAILBLAZER - Surface Maintenance Machine - TENNANT COMPANY; pg. 1381, pg. 944
TRAILBLAZER - Food - WESTERN SIZZLIN CORPORATION; pg. 1755, pg. 1806
TRAILBLAZER LITE - Surface Maintenance Machine - TENNANT COMPANY; pg. 1381, pg. 944
TRAILER-BRITE - Automotive Cleaner - DELTA FOREMOST CHEMICAL CORPORATION; pg. 1155, pg. 1642
TRAILER PARK PARTY - Video Game - INTERNATIONAL GAME TECHNOLOGY; pg. 957, pg. 1024
TRAILER TONGUE - Toolbox - TRACTOR SUPPLY COMPANY; pg. 708, pg. 1627
TRAILERCOAT - Anti-Rust Primer For Boat Trailers - PETTIT PAINT COMPANY; pg. 1444, pg. 1116
TRAILERITE - Boat Cover - TAYLOR MADE GROUP; pg. 1711, pg. 1162
TRAILERS - Towing & Recovery Equipment - MILLER INDUSTRIES, INC.; pg. 185, pg. 1655
TRAILFINDER - Flashlight - ENERGIZER HOLDINGS, INC.; pg. 637, pg. 996
TRAILING STOPS - Application Service Provider - OPTIONSXPRESS HOLDINGS, INC.; pg. 790, pg. 586
TRAILMASTER - Fishing Equipment - WRIGHT & MCGILL CO.; pg. 1848, pg. 324
TRAILMAX - Storage Console - BESTOP, INC.; pg. 200, pg. 312
TRAILRUNNER - Aluminum Running Boards - LUND INTERNATIONAL, INC.; pg. 211, pg. 526
TRAILSTER WAGON - Bicycle - TREK BICYCLE CORPORATION; pg. 1847, pg. 1896
TRAIN - Office Furniture - STEELCASE INC.; pg. 475, pg. 889
TRAIN CHIEF - Wireless Control - CONTROL CHIEF HOLDINGS, INC.; pg. 630, pg. 1518
TRAINER - Test Electronic Device - TELEDYNE LECROY; pg. 1431, pg. 1153
TRAINING - Trade Publication - THE NIELSEN COMPANY B.V.; pg. 1671, pg. 1272
TRAINING BOARDSHORT - Clothing - K-SWISS; pg. 1837, pg. 306
TRAINING CAPRI - Clothing - K-SWISS; pg. 1837, pg. 306
TRAINING CAPSLEEVE - Clothing - K-SWISS; pg. 1837, pg. 306
TRAINING CREW - Clothing - K-SWISS; pg. 1837, pg. 306
TRAINING JACKET - Clothing - K-SWISS; pg. 1837, pg. 306
TRAINING PANT - Clothing - K-SWISS; pg. 1837, pg. 306
TRAINMASTER - Toy Train - LIONEL LLC; pg. 961, pg. 875
TRAINS - Magazine - KALMBACH PUBLISHING CO.; pg. 1656, pg. 1898
TRAINS - Fabric - NEMSCHOFF, INC.; pg. 936, pg. 1890
TRAINS.COM - Web Site - KALMBACH PUBLISHING CO.; pg. 1656, pg. 1898
TRAINSOUNDS - Toy Train - LIONEL LLC; pg. 961, pg. 875
TRAIT-TEX - Yarn - PACON CORPORATION; pg. 1466, pg. 1852
TRAJECTORY - Atmospheric Tool - BROOKS AUTOMATION, INC.; pg. 1320, pg. 813
TRAJECTORY - Metrology Module - NANOMETRICS INCORPORATED; pg. 1423, pg. 147
TRAK - Plasma System - NORDSON CORPORATION; pg. 1365, pg. 1480
TRAK - Software - R.R. DONNELLEY & SONS COMPANY; pg. 1682, pg. 589
TRAK - Bed Mill - SOUTHWESTERN INDUSTRIES, INC.; pg. 1429, pg. 69
TRAK AGE2 - Software - SOUTHWESTERN INDUSTRIES, INC.; pg. 1429, pg. 69
TRAK AGE3 - Software - SOUTHWESTERN INDUSTRIES, INC.; pg. 1429, pg. 69
TRAK-IT - Gas Fastening System - POWERS FASTENERS INC.; pg. 1059, pg. 1143
TRAKINAS - Sandwich Cookies - MONDELEZ INTERNATIONAL, INC.; pg. 878, pg. 601
TRAKLINE - Roll Door - RITE-HITE HOLDING CORPORATION; pg. 1372, pg. 1880
TRAKLINE PLUS - Fold Door - RITE-HITE HOLDING CORPORATION; pg. 1372, pg. 1880
TRAKLITE - Hands-Free Light - E.D. BULLARD COMPANY; pg. 1332, pg. 727
TRAKS MAX - Trademark & ATV Tires - CARLISLE TIRE & WHEEL COMPANY; pg. 1880, pg. 1612
TRAMATIC - Footwear - STEVEN MADDEN, LTD.; pg. 1819, pg. 1176
TRAN-COR - Electrical Steel Product - AK STEEL HOLDING CORPORATION; pg. 1311, pg. 1479
TRAN-STAY - Clear Polyester Layout Base Sheet - TRANSILWRAP COMPANY, INC.; pg. 1470, pg. 613
TRANCE - Trainer Shoe - BROOKS SPORTS INC.; pg. 1805, pg. 1818
TRANCEPORT - Fabric - NEMSCHOFF, INC.; pg. 936, pg. 1890
TRANDATE - Therapy System - PROMETHEUS LABORATORIES, INC.; pg. 1586, pg. 206
TRANE - Heating & Air Conditioning Equipment - TRANE INC.; pg. 116, pg. 1109

TRANQUIL - Pharmaceutical Product - ALVA/AMCO PHARMACAL COMPANIES, INC.; pg. 1492, pg. 637

TRANQUILITY - Gasoline Powertrain - CLUB CAR, INC.; pg. 1830, pg. 532

TRANQUILIZER - Pump Product - IDEX CORPORATION; pg. 1347, pg. 623

TRANS-AID - Stop Leak - TURTLE WAX, INC.; pg. 220, pg. 671

TRANS-BANNER I - Polyolefin - TRANSILWRAP COMPANY, INC.; pg. 1470, pg. 613

TRANS-BANNER II - Polyolefin - TRANSILWRAP COMPANY, INC.; pg. 1470, pg. 613

TRANS-BARRIER - Block Out Film - TRANSILWRAP COMPANY, INC.; pg. 1470, pg. 613

TRANS-BLOT - Software - BIO-RAD LABORATORIES, INC.; pg. 1504, pg. 101

TRANS-CLING - Printed Plastic Product - TRANSILWRAP COMPANY, INC.; pg. 1470, pg. 613

TRANS-CLING II - Low Tack Vinyl - TRANSILWRAP COMPANY, INC.; pg. 1470, pg. 613

TRANS-CORE - Laminating Film - TRANSILWRAP COMPANY, INC.; pg. 1470, pg. 613

TRANS-FLEX-CAST - Printable Plastic Product - TRANSILWRAP COMPANY, INC.; pg. 1470, pg. 613

TRANS-KOTE - Thermal Laminating Film - TRANSILWRAP COMPANY, INC.; pg. 1470, pg. 613

TRANS-KOTE TRANSGUARD - Laminating Film - TRANSILWRAP COMPANY, INC.; pg. 1470, pg. 613

TRANS-LC - Chemical Product - AIR PRODUCTS AND CHEMICALS, INC.; pg. 1145, pg. 1513

TRANS-MEDIC - Stops Transmission Trouble - RADIATOR SPECIALTY COMPANY; pg. 215, pg. 1380

TRANS NATIONAL GROUP SERVICES - Travel Agency; Special Membership Services - TNT VACATIONS; pg. 1925, pg. 801

TRANS-PAK - Solid Waste Compactor - HARRIS WASTE MANAGEMENT GROUP, INC.; pg. 1345, pg. 526

TRANS PAK - Antenna - TRIMBLE NAVIGATION LIMITED; pg. 1384, pg. 288

TRANS-RUPTER - Transformer Protector - S&C ELECTRIC COMPANY; pg. 1305, pg. 589

TRANS-RUPTER II - Transformer Protector - S&C ELECTRIC COMPANY; pg. 1305, pg. 589

TRANS-STICK - Printable Plastic Product - TRANSILWRAP COMPANY, INC.; pg. 1470, pg. 613

TRANS TEAR RESISTANT - Synthetic Paper - TRANSILWRAP COMPANY, INC.; pg. 1470, pg. 613

TRANS-TECH - Dielectric Resonator - SKYWORKS SOLUTIONS, INC.; pg. 674, pg. 862

TRANSACT - Software - CTI GROUP HOLDINGS INC.; pg. 381, pg. 684

TRANSACT - Software System - MENTOR GRAPHICS CORPORATION; pg. 432, pg. 1510

TRANSACT - Computer Printers - TRANSACT TECHNOLOGIES INCORPORATED; pg. 484, pg. 351

TRANSACT - Software - USA TECHNOLOGIES, INC.; pg. 815, pg. 1550

TRANSACTION MANAGEMENT - Software - BMC SOFTWARE, INC.; pg. 362, pg. 1701

TRANSACTION PERIODICALS CONSORTIUM - Periodicals - TRANSACTION PUBLISHERS, INC.; pg. 1695, pg. 1109

TRANSACTION PUBLISHERS - Books - TRANSACTION PUBLISHERS, INC.; pg. 1695, pg. 1109

TRANSACTION PUBLISHERS DISTRIBUTION - Warehousing & Distribution Service - TRANSACTION PUBLISHERS, INC.; pg. 1695, pg. 1109

TRANSACTION THAT COUNT - Slogan - EVERI HOLDINGS INC.; pg. 749, pg. 1023

TRANSACTIONAL MESSAGING - Marketing Tool - PREMIERE GLOBAL SERVICES, INC.; pg. 1275, pg. 518

TRANSAIR - Air Respirator - MINE SAFETY APPLIANCES COMPANY; pg. 1361, pg. 1525

TRANSALLOY - Card Stock - TRANSILWRAP COMPANY, INC.; pg. 1470, pg. 613

TRANSALLOY P-260EX - Multi-Polymer Alloy - TRANSILWRAP COMPANY, INC.; pg. 1470, pg. 613

TRANSAM DRX - Shoes - MASON COMPANIES, INC.; pg. 1811, pg. 1856

TRANSAMERICA FLOODMAP - Flood Rate Insurance Maps - PITNEY BOWES SOFTWARE INC.; pg. 455, pg. 1346

TRANSATLANTIC - Leather Product - COACH, INC.; pg. 3, pg. 1214

TRANSBELT - Belting Product - ALBANY INTERNATIONAL CORP.; pg. 691, pg. 1038

TRANSCABLE - Software System - MENTOR GRAPHICS CORPORATION; pg. 432, pg. 1510

TRANSCEIVER PIPELINE - Software Product Module - RIVERBED PERFORMANCE MANAGEMENT; pg. 462, pg. 765

TRANSCELL - Oral Delivery Alternative to Injections or Infusions - LUMARA HEALTH INC.; pg. 1557, pg. 973

TRANSCEND - Electronic Components - MOLEX INCORPORATED; pg. 655, pg. 628

TRANSCLONE - Clinical Diagnostic Product - BIO-RAD LABORATORIES, INC.; pg. 1504, pg. 101

TRANSCODE - Printer System - AVERY DENNISON CORPORATION; pg. 1452, pg. 95

TRANSCONFR - Shirts - ELBECO INCORPORATED; pg. 40, pg. 1584

TRANSCOURT - Portable Basketball Standards - LIFETIME PRODUCTS INC.; pg. 933, pg. 1751

TRANSCYT - Medical Product - HOLOGIC, INC.; pg. 1416, pg. 784

TRANSDUR - Pharmaceutical Product - ENDO PHARMACEUTICALS HOLDINGS, INC.; pg. 1528, pg. 1549

TRANSEAL - Transmission Sealer - RADIATOR SPECIALTY COMPANY; pg. 215, pg. 1380

TRANSEND - Medical Device - BOSTON SCIENTIFIC CORPORATION; pg. 1508, pg. 831

TRANSEND ADMINISTRATOR - Manipulate Directory - TRANSEND CORPORATION; pg. 485, pg. 178

TRANSEND MIGRATOR - Data Migration - TRANSEND CORPORATION; pg. 485, pg. 178

TRANSERVE II - Automatic Transmission Flush Product - WYNN OIL COMPANY; pg. 987, pg. 173

TRANSFECTIN - Software - BIO-RAD LABORATORIES, INC.; pg. 1504, pg. 101

TRANSFERITE - Tape - AMERICAN BILTRITE INC.; pg. 1878, pg. 856

TRANSFERMATE - Memory Card - SANDISK CORPORATION; pg. 465, pg. 147

TRANSFERTUBE - Labware - SPECTRUM LABORATORIES INC.; pg. 1595, pg. 69

TRANSFILM - Turf Product - PBI/GORDON CORPORATION; pg. 1176, pg. 985

TRANSFIX - Molecular Probe Product - THERMO FISHER SCIENTIFIC INC.; pg. 1602, pg. 61

TRANSFLASH - Memory Card - SANDISK CORPORATION; pg. 465, pg. 147

TRANSFLUOR - Reagent - MOLECULAR DEVICES CORPORATION; pg. 1568, pg. 287

TRANSFLUOSPHERES - Molecular Probe Product - THERMO FISHER SCIENTIFIC INC.; pg. 1602, pg. 61

TRANSFORM - Software - BOTTOMLINE TECHNOLOGIES (DE), INC.; pg. 727, pg. 1038

TRANSFORM - Cardiomyoplasty Pulse Generator - MEDTRONIC, INC.; pg. 1564, pg. 939

TRANSFORMATION - Carpet - INTERFACE, INC.; pg. 695, pg. 512

TRANSFORMER - Digital Mass Flow Product - ADVANCED ENERGY INDUSTRIES, INC.; pg. 613, pg. 328

TRANSFORMER - Construction Equipment - JLG INDUSTRIES, INC.; pg. 1351, pg. 1551

TRANSFORMER - Guitar Amplifier - PEAVEY ELECTRONICS CORPORATION; pg. 662, pg. 970

TRANSFORMER COUPLED PLASMA - Silicon Etch System - LAM RESEARCH CORPORATION; pg. 1354, pg. 91

TRANSFORMERS - Toys - FUNRISE TOY CORP.; pg. 549, pg. 300

TRANSFORMERS - Toy & Game - HASBRO, INC.; pg. 954, pg. 1603

TRANSFORMERS ARMADA - Toy & Game - HASBRO, INC.; pg. 954, pg. 1603

TRANSFORMERS ENERGON - Toy & Game - HASBRO, INC.; pg. 954, pg. 1603

TRANSFORMING DAILY LIFE - Slogan - KOCH INDUSTRIES, INC.; pg. 1463, pg. 724

TRANSFORMING IT MANAGEMENT. - Tagline - CA TECHNOLOGIES; pg. 366, pg. 1168

TRANSFORMING IT THROUGH AUTOMATION - Software - BMC SOFTWARE, INC.; pg. 362, pg. 1701

TRANSFORMING PATIENT CARE THROUGH NEUROTECHNOLOGY - Tagline - NEUROMETRIX, INC.; pg. 1572, pg. 852

TRANSFORMING TECHNOLOGY INTO RESULTS - Tagline - STEELCLOUD, INC.; pg. 476, pg. 1776

TRANSFORMING THE WAY THE WORLD COMMUNICATES - Slogan - TELLABS, INC.; pg. 678, pg. 637

TRANSFORMING THE WAYS PEOPLE WORK - Tag Line - STEELCASE INC.; pg. 475, pg. 889

TRANSGRIP - Printed Plastic Product - TRANSILWRAP COMPANY, INC.; pg. 1470, pg. 613

TRANSGUARD - Patch - TRANSILWRAP COMPANY, INC.; pg. 1470, pg. 613

TRANSHEET - Dental Product - DENTSPLY INTERNATIONAL INC.; pg. 1522, pg. 1596

TRANSIL - Reagent - MOLECULAR DEVICES CORPORATION; pg. 1568, pg. 287

TRANSIL-MASK - Vinyl Masking Film - TRANSILWRAP COMPANY, INC.; pg. 1470, pg. 613

TRANSIL-MATTE - Drafting Film - TRANSILWRAP COMPANY, INC.; pg. 1470, pg. 613

TRANSILENE - Film - TRANSILWRAP COMPANY, INC.; pg. 1470, pg. 613

TRANSILMASK - Orange Vinyl Masking Film - TRANSILWRAP COMPANY, INC.; pg. 1470, pg. 613

TRANSILMATTE - Matte Oriented Polyester - TRANSILWRAP COMPANY, INC.; pg. 1470, pg. 613

TRANSIT - Fabric - NEMSCHOFF, INC.; pg. 936, pg. 1890

TRANSIT CHECK - Tax Credit for Purchase of Transit Fares - REGIONAL TRANSPORTATION AUTHORITY; pg. 1921, pg. 588

TRANSITE-FLOR - Flooring Rubber - R.C.A. RUBBER COMPANY; pg. 1888, pg. 1402

TRANSITION PLUS - Dairy Premix - TROUW NUTRITION USA; pg. 1482, pg. 616

TRANSITIONS - Lenses - TRANSITIONS OPTICAL, INC.; pg. 1432, pg. 458

TRANSITIONS - Furniture - TROPITONE FURNITURE CO., INC.; pg. 945, pg. 118

TRANSITIONS - Lighting Product - WESTINGHOUSE LIGHTING CORPORATION; pg. 687, pg. 1571

TRANSITIONS - Distinctive Kitchen Designs with European, American & Asian Influences - WM OHS INC.; pg. 947, pg. 324

TRANSIVA - Catheter - ABBOTT LABORATORIES; pg. 1484, pg. 551

TRANSJUGULAR - Electrosurgical Devices - ANGIODYNAMICS, INC.; pg. 1495, pg. 1173

TRANSLATION - Furniture - STANLEY FURNITURE CO., INC.; pg. 943, pg. 1379

TRANSLAYOUT - Software System - MENTOR GRAPHICS CORPORATION; pg. 432, pg. 1510

TRANSLICER - Cutter - URSCHEL LABORATORIES INCORPORATED; pg. 1386, pg. 698

TRANSLICER 2000 - Slicer - URSCHEL LABORATORIES INCORPORATED; pg. 1386, pg. 698

TRANSLICER 2500 - Slicer - URSCHEL LABORATORIES INCORPORATED; pg. 1386, pg. 698

TRANSLINK - Pigment - BASF CATALYSTS LLC; pg. 1148, pg. 1074

TRANSLINK - Software - ELEMICA, INC.; pg. 1242, pg. 1591

TRANSLINK - Telecommunications Services - SPRINT CORPORATION; pg. 1874, pg. 719

TRANSLITE - Photo Film - EASTMAN KODAK COMPANY; pg. 1408, pg. 1333

TRANSLITE - Lighting Fixture & Control - PHILIPS LIGHTING; pg. 1303, pg. 806

TRANSLITE - Lighting - STEELCASE INC.; pg. 475, pg. 889

TRANSLUCENCE - Bathroom Design - DECOLAV, INC.; pg. 1123, pg. 411

TRANSMISSION TROUBLESHOOTER - Diagnostic Scan Tool Line - SNAP-ON INCORPORATED; pg. 1062, pg. 1862

TRANSMISSIVE REELS - Game - WMS INDUSTRIES INC.; pg. 593, pg. 666

TRANSOID - Battery Charging Product - CLORE AUTOMOTIVE LLC; pg. 202, pg. 716

TRANSOM - Fabric - NEMSCHOFF, INC.; pg. 936, pg. 1890

TRANSORB - Sorbent Packs - MULTISORB TECHNOLOGIES, INC.; pg. 1570, pg. 1150

TRANSPAC - Medical Device - HOSPIRA, INC.; pg. 1542, pg. 623

TRANSPAQUE - Film - TRANSILWRAP COMPANY, INC.; pg. 1470, pg. 613

TRANSPARENT CONTROL - Hosiery - KAYSER-ROTH CORPORATION; pg. 28, pg. 1374

TRANSPATH - Multiservice Software - CISCO SYSTEMS, INC.; pg. 372, pg. 240

TRANSPET - Approved Polyester - TRANSILWRAP COMPANY, INC.; pg. 1470, pg. 613

TRANSPLATE - Glass & Ceramic Material - CORNING INCORPORATED; pg. 1122, pg. 1154

First page reference indicates Business Class Edition
Second page reference indicates Geographic Edition

TRANSPLICE - Cable - COMMSCOPE, INC.; *pg.* 278, *pg.* 1378
TRANSPORT - Knife - BUCK KNIVES, INC.; *pg.* 1828, *pg.* 550
TRANSPORT - Basketball Equipment - LIFETIME PRODUCTS INC.; *pg.* 933, *pg.* 1751
TRANSPORT ADVANTAGE - Wireless Communication System - AT&T SOUTHEAST; *pg.* 1868, *pg.* 489
TRANSPORT MANAGER - Software - CISCO SYSTEMS, INC.; *pg.* 372, *pg.* 240
TRANSPORT TOPICS 100 - Business Newspaper - TRANSPORT TOPICS PUBLISHING GROUP; *pg.* 1696, *pg.* 1772
TRANSPORT TOPICS' LOGISTICS 50 - Business Newspaper - TRANSPORT TOPICS PUBLISHING GROUP; *pg.* 1696, *pg.* 1772
TRANSPORTATION MANAGEMENT SYSTEM - Automatic Train Supervision System for Traffic Control Centers - ALSTOM SIGNALING, INC.; *pg.* 1312, *pg.* 1350
TRANSPORTATION TELEPHONE TICKLER - Reference Guide - JOC GROUP INC.; *pg.* 1654, *pg.* 1096
TRANSPORTER - Hose - HBD INDUSTRIES, INC.; *pg.* 207, *pg.* 1449
TRANSPOWR - Bare Aluminum Overhead Cable - GENERAL CABLE CORPORATION; *pg.* 83, *pg.* 729
TRANSPROP - Clear Polypropylene - TRANSILWRAP COMPANY, INC.; *pg.* 1470, *pg.* 613
TRANSSECURE - Metallic Ink - TRANSILWRAP COMPANY, INC.; *pg.* 1470, *pg.* 613
TRANSTAR - Photo Paper, Sensitized Materials - EASTMAN KODAK COMPANY; *pg.* 1408, *pg.* 1333
TRANSTAR-96 - Glass & Ceramic Material - CORNING INCORPORATED; *pg.* 1122, *pg.* 1154
TRANSTAY II - Polyester - TRANSILWRAP COMPANY, INC.; *pg.* 1470, *pg.* 613
TRANSTEC - Aftermarket Rebuild Kit Distribution Division - FREUDENBERG-NOK; *pg.* 1882, *pg.* 904
TRANSTUBE - Guitar Amplifier - PEAVEY ELECTRONICS CORPORATION; *pg.* 662, *pg.* 970
TRANSVENE - Leads - MEDTRONIC, INC.; *pg.* 1564, *pg.* 939
TRANSVUE - Slide Trays - EASTMAN KODAK COMPANY; *pg.* 1408, *pg.* 1333
TRANSVY - Printable Plastic Product - TRANSILWRAP COMPANY, INC.; *pg.* 1470, *pg.* 613
TRANSWELL - Glass & Ceramic Material - CORNING INCORPORATED; *pg.* 1122, *pg.* 1154
TRANSWORLD BMX - Magazine - BONNIER ACTIVE MEDIA, INC.; *pg.* 1622, *pg.* 1205
TRANSWORLD BUSINESS - Magazine - BONNIER CORPORATION; *pg.* 1622, *pg.* 480
TRANSWORLD MOTOCROSS - Magazine - BONNIER ACTIVE MEDIA, INC.; *pg.* 1622, *pg.* 1205
TRANSWORLD MOTOCROSS - Magazine - BONNIER CORPORATION; *pg.* 1622, *pg.* 480
TRANSWORLD RIDE BMX - Magazine - BONNIER CORPORATION; *pg.* 1622, *pg.* 480
TRANSWORLD SKATEBOARDING - Magazine - BONNIER ACTIVE MEDIA, INC.; *pg.* 1622, *pg.* 1205
TRANSWORLD SKATEBOARDING - Magazine - BONNIER CORPORATION; *pg.* 1622, *pg.* 480
TRANSWORLD SNOWBOARDING - Magazine - BONNIER ACTIVE MEDIA, INC.; *pg.* 1622, *pg.* 1205
TRANSWORLD SNOWBOARDING - Magazine - BONNIER CORPORATION; *pg.* 1622, *pg.* 480
TRANSWORLD SURF - Magazine - BONNIER ACTIVE MEDIA, INC.; *pg.* 1622, *pg.* 1205
TRANSWORLD SURF - Magazine - BONNIER CORPORATION; *pg.* 1622, *pg.* 480
TRANSWORLDMOTOCROSS.COM - Web Site - BONNIER ACTIVE MEDIA, INC.; *pg.* 1622, *pg.* 1205
TRANSWORLDSNOWBOARDING.COM - Web Site - BONNIER ACTIVE MEDIA, INC.; *pg.* 1622, *pg.* 1205
TRANSWORLDSURF.COM - Web Site - BONNIER ACTIVE MEDIA, INC.; *pg.* 1622, *pg.* 1205
TRANXIT - Herbicide - E.I. DU PONT DE NEMOURS & COMPANY; *pg.* 1159, *pg.* 390
TRANZFECT - Biopharmaceutical Product - CYTRX CORPORATION; *pg.* 1521, *pg.* 129
TRANZPORT HOOD - Officer Training Aids - BAE SYSTEMS PRODUCTS GROUP; *pg.* 359, *pg.* 432
TRAP - Apparel - OAKLEY, INC.; *pg.* 1840, *pg.* 86
TRAP SHOOTER - Dispenser - HILLYARD, INC.; *pg.* 331, *pg.* 990
TRAPALERT - Remote Monitoring System - ARMSTRONG INTERNATIONAL, INC.; *pg.* 1069, *pg.* 909
TRAPBLASTER - Software - BMC SOFTWARE, INC.; *pg.* 362, *pg.* 1701
TRAPEZA - Fabric - NEMSCHOFF, INC.; *pg.* 936, *pg.* 1890
TRAPEZE - Commercial Lighting - SWIVELIER CO., INC.; *pg.* 1307, *pg.* 1142
TRAPP - Fragrance Product - FAULTLESS STARCH/BON AMI COMPANY; *pg.* 330, *pg.* 982
TRAPP PRIVATE GARDENS - Candles & Room Spray - FAULTLESS STARCH/BON AMI COMPANY; *pg.* 330, *pg.* 982
TRAPPER - Cleaner - BROOKFIELD ENGINEERING LABORATORIES, INC.; *pg.* 1403, *pg.* 833
TRAPPER - Dust Mop - HILLYARD, INC.; *pg.* 331, *pg.* 990
TRAPPER KEEPER - Office Product - WESTROCK COMPANY; *pg.* 1472, *pg.* 1805
TRAPPEY'S - Hot Sauces & Peppers - B&G FOODS, INC.; *pg.* 838, *pg.* 1102
TRASK - Leather Chukka - WOOLRICH, INC.; *pg.* 699, *pg.* 1595
TRASYS - Coating - E.I. DU PONT DE NEMOURS & COMPANY; *pg.* 1159, *pg.* 390
TRAUMACAL - High Nitrogen Liquid Formula for Burn Patients - MEAD JOHNSON NUTRITION COMPANY; *pg.* 1561, *pg.* 615
TRAUMACATH - Medical Device - INTEGRA LIFESCIENCES HOLDINGS CORPORATION; *pg.* 1545, *pg.* 1109
TRAV-A-DIAL - Measurement - SOUTHWESTERN INDUSTRIES, INC.; *pg.* 1429, *pg.* 69
TRAV-LER - Wagon - RADIO FLYER INC.; *pg.* 966, *pg.* 588
TRAV-LER - Interdental Brush - SUNSTAR AMERICAS INC.; *pg.* 1599, *pg.* 591
TRAV-O-LATORS - Elevator Product - OTIS ELEVATOR COMPANY; *pg.* 102, *pg.* 349
TRAVAN - Linear Tape Storage Media - IMATION CORP.; *pg.* 413, *pg.* 952
TRAVAN - Cartridges - QUANTUM CORPORATION; *pg.* 458, *pg.* 250
TRAVASAK - Backpacks - KELLWOOD COMPANY; *pg.* 28, *pg.* 975
TRAVASOL - Healthcare Product - BAXTER INTERNATIONAL INC.; *pg.* 1499, *pg.* 599
TRAVCORPS - Staffing Services - CROSS COUNTRY HEALTHCARE, INC.; *pg.* 1520, *pg.* 411
TRAVE - Liqueur - JIM BEAM BRANDS CO.; *pg.* 1965, *pg.* 601
TRAVEL - Telescope - MEADE INSTRUMENTS CORPORATION; *pg.* 1422, *pg.* 113
TRAVEL - Apparel - OAKLEY, INC.; *pg.* 1840, *pg.* 86
TRAVEL AGENT - Trade Publication - UBM ADVANSTAR; *pg.* 1697, *pg.* 1306
TRAVEL BOUND - Travel Services - TRAVELPORT LIMITED; *pg.* 1925, *pg.* 521
TRAVEL BUDDY - Baby Care Product - MUNCHKIN, INC.; *pg.* 964, *pg.* 300
THE TRAVEL CHANNEL - Television Station - DISCOVERY COMMUNICATIONS, INC.; *pg.* 282, *pg.* 777
TRAVEL-CORE - Medical & Aesthetic Product - DYNATRONICS CORPORATION; *pg.* 1526, *pg.* 1757
TRAVEL COUPON GUIDE - Advertising Publication - DOMINION ENTERPRISES; *pg.* 1636, *pg.* 1796
TRAVEL DOODLE SKETCH - Toy - THE OHIO ART COMPANY, INC.; *pg.* 965, *pg.* 1406
TRAVEL ETCH A SKETCH - Toy - THE OHIO ART COMPANY, INC.; *pg.* 965, *pg.* 1406
TRAVEL, LEARN. - Tag Line - EXPLORICA, INC.; *pg.* 1907, *pg.* 794
TRAVEL LITE - Clocks - HOWARD MILLER COMPANY; *pg.* 7, *pg.* 914
TRAVEL NORTH AMERICA AT HALF PRICE - Hotel Savings Book - ENTERTAINMENT PUBLICATIONS, INC.; *pg.* 1639, *pg.* 910
TRAVEL-READY - Blazer - HABAND COMPANY, INC.; *pg.* 1772, *pg.* 1099
TRAVEL RITE ANNUAL PROTECTION - Travel Insurance - TRAVEL GUARD GROUP, INC.; *pg.* 1925, *pg.* 1895
TRAVEL SAVER GUIDE - Advertising Publication - DOMINION ENTERPRISES; *pg.* 1636, *pg.* 1796
TRAVEL SMART - Travel Accessories - CONAIR CORPORATION; *pg.* 505, *pg.* 1055
TRAVEL TIPS - Newsletter - WEST MICHIGAN TOURIST ASSOCIATION; *pg.* 1930, *pg.* 891
TRAVEL+LEISURE - Media Publication - TIME INC.; *pg.* 1693, *pg.* 1300
TRAVELBAG - Travel Services - ORBITZ WORLDWIDE, INC.; *pg.* 1918, *pg.* 586
TRAVELCUBE - Surge Suppressor - TRIPPE MANUFACTURING COMPANY; *pg.* 220, *pg.* 592
TRAVELER - Healthcare Product - GF HEALTH PRODUCTS, INC.; *pg.* 1535, *pg.* 508
TRAVELER - Surge Suppressor - TRIPPE MANUFACTURING COMPANY; *pg.* 220, *pg.* 592
TRAVELER CREASE - Men's Clothing - JOS. A. BANK CLOTHIERS, INC.; *pg.* 42, *pg.* 771
TRAVELER DISCOUNT GUIDE - Advertising Publication - DOMINION ENTERPRISES; *pg.* 1636, *pg.* 1796
TRAVELER PLUS LID - Resealable Lid - SOLO CUP COMPANY; *pg.* 1469, *pg.* 625
TRAVELER SOS - Telephone Service - IDT CORPORATION; *pg.* 643, *pg.* 1096
TRAVELER XD - Medical Product - GF HEALTH PRODUCTS, INC.; *pg.* 1535, *pg.* 508
TRAVELERPLUS - Lid - SOLO CUP COMPANY; *pg.* 1469, *pg.* 625
TRAVELERS ADVANTAGE - Discount Travel Services - AFFINION GROUP, INC.; *pg.* 1225, *pg.* 372
TRAVELERS EXPRESS - Money Order - VIAD CORP.; *pg.* 816, *pg.* 20
TRAVELER'S RETREAT - Furniture - LEXINGTON HOME BRANDS; *pg.* 933, *pg.* 1391
TRAVELERSEXPRESS - Financial Payment Service - MONEYGRAM INTERNATIONAL, INC.; *pg.* 783, *pg.* 1684
TRAVELFUNDS - Traveler Service - AMERICAN EXPRESS COMPANY; *pg.* 712, *pg.* 1190
TRAVELFUNDS DIRECT - Traveler Services - AMERICAN EXPRESS COMPANY; *pg.* 712, *pg.* 1190
TRAVELHOST - Traveling Magazine - TRAVELHOST, INC.; *pg.* 1696, *pg.* 1689
TRAVELHOST TRAVEL REGISTRY - Online Gift Registry Service - TRAVELHOST, INC.; *pg.* 1696, *pg.* 1689
TRAVELING GNOMES - Video Game - INTERNATIONAL GAME TECHNOLOGY; *pg.* 957, *pg.* 1024
TRAVELING WILD - Video Game - INTERNATIONAL GAME TECHNOLOGY; *pg.* 957, *pg.* 1024
TRAVELITE - Stroller - GRACO CHILDREN'S PRODUCTS INC.; *pg.* 954, *pg.* 1531
TRAVELLER - Tires - TRACTOR SUPPLY COMPANY; *pg.* 708, *pg.* 1627
TRAVELMASTER - Acoustical Shell - WENGER CORPORATION; *pg.* 1307, *pg.* 952
TRAVELMATCH - Travel Agency - AMERICAN AUTOMOBILE ASSOCIATION; *pg.* 1190, *pg.* 429
TRAVELOCITY - Traveling Service - SABRE HOLDINGS CORPORATION; *pg.* 1922, *pg.* 1745
TRAVELOCITY.COM - Travel Website - EXPEDIA, INC.; *pg.* 1244, *pg.* 1814
TRAVELOCITY.COM - Website - TRAVELOCITY, INC.; *pg.* 1284, *pg.* 1745
TRAVELODGE - Hotels - WYNDHAM WORLDWIDE CORPORATION; *pg.* 1119, *pg.* 1107
TRAVELOGUE - Fabric - NEMSCHOFF, INC.; *pg.* 936, *pg.* 1890
TRAVELOK.COM - Website - OKLAHOMA TOURISM & RECREATION DEPARTMENT; *pg.* 1003, *pg.* 1487
TRAVELPORT CORPORATE MATRIX - Online Booking System - TRAVELPORT LIMITED; *pg.* 1925, *pg.* 521
TRAVELPORT FOR BUSINESS - Corporate Travel System - TRAVELPORT LIMITED; *pg.* 1925, *pg.* 521
TRAVELPOWER - Case - SCHNEIDER ELECTRIC; *pg.* 467, *pg.* 1609
TRAVELRIDE - Chassis - FORETRAVEL INC.; *pg.* 1909, *pg.* 1728
TRAVELSET - Pillows - TEMPUR SEALY INTERNATIONAL, INC.; *pg.* 944, *pg.* 731
TRAVELTRAX - Web-based Travel Reporting Tool - CONCUR TECHNOLOGIES; *pg.* 1903, *pg.* 501
TRAVELVIEW - Telescope - MEADE INSTRUMENTS CORPORATION; *pg.* 1422, *pg.* 113
TRAVELWARE - Baby Care Product - MUNCHKIN, INC.; *pg.* 964, *pg.* 300
TRAVERSE - Fabric - NEMSCHOFF, INC.; *pg.* 936, *pg.* 1890
TRAVERTINE - Ceramic, Glass, Stone Tiles & Slabs - WALKER & ZANGER, INC.; *pg.* 119, *pg.* 281
TRAVIOS - Medical Device - DEPUY SYNTHES; *pg.* 1523, *pg.* 1593
TRAVIS CLUB - Cigars - FINCK CIGAR CO.; *pg.* 1894, *pg.* 1740
TRAX - X-Ray Inspection Equipment - TERADYNE INC.; *pg.* 679, *pg.* 838
TRAXX - Software - MOREDIRECT; *pg.* 441, *pg.* 412

TRAXX - Medical Device - RESMED INC.; pg. 1589, pg. 207
TRAXX - Footwear - STEVEN MADDEN, LTD.; pg. 1819, pg. 1176
TRAXX - Tool Storage Products - WATERLOO INDUSTRIES, INC.; pg. 946, pg. 1885
TRAY HANDLER - Automated Material Handling - ATS AUTOMATION TOOLING SYSTEMS INC.; pg. 355, pg. 1919
TRAY-MATE - Food Containers - PACTIV CORPORATION; pg. 1466, pg. 624
TRAYBYTE - Dental Product - DENTSPLY INTERNATIONAL INC.; pg. 1522, pg. 1596
TRAZER - Exercise Equipment - CYBEX INTERNATIONAL, INC.; pg. 1521, pg. 832
TRBG1EXNXXMX - Transceivers - OPLINK COMMUNICATIONS, INC.; pg. 660, pg. 91
TRBG1LXDXXSX - Transceivers - OPLINK COMMUNICATIONS, INC.; pg. 660, pg. 91
TRBRITE - Film - THE DOW CHEMICAL COMPANY; pg. 1157, pg. 898
TRC - Paving Seal - TEXAS REFINERY CORP.; pg. 986, pg. 1696
TRC TEEN READERS CLUB - Books - SCHOLASTIC INC.; pg. 1683, pg. 1288
TRCE03KE2C000C3 - Transceivers - OPLINK COMMUNICATIONS, INC.; pg. 660, pg. 91
TRE - Test Technology - FORMFACTOR, INC.; pg. 1882, pg. 122
TRE VENTI - Furniture - STANLEY FURNITURE CO., INC.; pg. 943, pg. 1379
TREAD QUARTERS DISCOUNT TIRE - Auto Service - MONRO MUFFLER BRAKE, INC.; pg. 213, pg. 1336
TREADCLIMBER - Fitness Machine - NAUTILUS, INC.; pg. 1840, pg. 1846
TREADEASY - Footwear - P.W. MINOR & SON, INC.; pg. 1816, pg. 1140
TREADPRINT - Evidence Gathering Kit - BAE SYSTEMS PRODUCTS GROUP; pg. 359, pg. 432
TREASURA - Software - THOMSON REUTERS CORPORATION; pg. 1693, pg. 1944
TREASURE - Carpet - BEAULIEU GROUP, LLC; pg. 917, pg. 529
TREASURE CEREMONY - Game - WMS INDUSTRIES INC.; pg. 593, pg. 666
TREASURE CHEST CASINO - Casino - BOYD GAMING CORPORATION; pg. 1082, pg. 1022
TREASURE COVE - Video Game - INTERNATIONAL GAME TECHNOLOGY; pg. 957, pg. 1024
TREASURE DIVER - Game - WMS INDUSTRIES INC.; pg. 593, pg. 666
TREASURE HUNT - Animated Game - PENNSYLVANIA STATE LOTTERY; pg. 1003, pg. 1552
TREASURE KEEPER - Memory Frame Kit - E-Z BOWZ, LLC; pg. 692, pg. 1635
TREASURE SEEKER - Game - WMS INDUSTRIES INC.; pg. 593, pg. 666
TREASURE TALES - Game - WMS INDUSTRIES INC.; pg. 593, pg. 666
TREASURE TOUR USA - Game - WMS INDUSTRIES INC.; pg. 593, pg. 666
TREASURE TREE - Lottery Game - KENTUCKY LOTTERY CORPORATION; pg. 996, pg. 735
TREASURED MEMORIES - Figurines & Musicals - ENESCO, LLC; pg. 1124, pg. 620
TREASURED MEMORIES BOUQUET - Floral Bouquet - FTD GROUP, INC.; pg. 1795, pg. 608
TREASURES - Food & Beverage Product - NESTLE USA, INC.; pg. 883, pg. 96
TREASURES OF MACAU - Game - WMS INDUSTRIES INC.; pg. 593, pg. 666
TREASURES OF MACHU PICCHU - Game - WMS INDUSTRIES INC.; pg. 593, pg. 666
TREASURES OF SPARTA - Game - WMS INDUSTRIES INC.; pg. 593, pg. 666
TREASURES OF THE EARTH - Educational Materials - SCHOLASTIC INC.; pg. 1683, pg. 1288
TREASURES OF THE WORLD - Book - NOVICA UNITED, INC.; pg. 1271, pg. 137
TREASURES OF TROY - Video Game - INTERNATIONAL GAME TECHNOLOGY; pg. 957, pg. 1024
TREASURY MANAGER - Software - THOMSON REUTERS CORPORATION; pg. 1693, pg. 1944
TREASURYPOINT.COM - Software - SEI INVESTMENTS COMPANY; pg. 802, pg. 1558
TREAT SEAT - Doll And Toy - AMERICAN GIRL LLC; pg. 949, pg. 1871
TREAT YOURSELF - Shoe - AEROGROUP INTERNATIONAL, INC.; pg. 1803, pg. 1055
TREATED FAIRLY - Tagline - PROASSURANCE CORPORATION; pg. 1214, pg. 3
T.R.E.A.T.S. - Shoes - CALERES, INC.; pg. 1805, pg. 993
TREBOR - Pumps - IDEX CORPORATION; pg. 1347, pg. 623
TRECATOR - Tuberculosis Treatment Pharmaceutical Preparation - PFIZER INC.; pg. 1581, pg. 1278
TRECS - Transponder Reconfiguration System - INTEGRAL SYSTEMS, INC.; pg. 416, pg. 767
TREDAIR - Matting - THE BILTRITE CORPORATION; pg. 1879, pg. 850
TREE - Design - SCHOLASTIC INC.; pg. 1683, pg. 1288
TREE HUT - Cosmetic Product - NATERRA INTERNATIONAL INC.; pg. 59, pg. 1684
TREE OF KNOWLEDGE - Educational Materials - SCHOLASTIC INC.; pg. 1683, pg. 1288
TREE OF LIFE - Video Game - INTERNATIONAL GAME TECHNOLOGY; pg. 957, pg. 1024
TREE RIPE - Juices - JOHANNA FOODS INC.; pg. 866, pg. 1066
TREES - Tables - STEELCASE INC.; pg. 475, pg. 889
TREETOP - Fabric - NEMSCHOFF, INC.; pg. 936, pg. 1890
TREEVIEW - Software - FAIR ISAAC CORPORATION; pg. 1247, pg. 955
TREKK - Tents & Sleeping Bags - KELLWOOD COMPANY; pg. 28, pg. 975
TREKKER - Footwear - LACROSSE FOOTWEAR, INC.; pg. 1811, pg. 1503
TRELLIS - Textiles - BERNHARDT DESIGN; pg. 918, pg. 1381
TRELLIS - Fan - CRAFTMADE INTERNATIONAL, INC.; pg. 1295, pg. 1670
TRELLIS - Fabric - ETHAN ALLEN INTERIORS INC.; pg. 924, pg. 343
TRELLIS - Diamond Jewelry - LAZARE KAPLAN INTERNATIONAL, INC.; pg. 8, pg. 1250
TRELLIS - Fabric - NEMSCHOFF, INC.; pg. 936, pg. 1890
TRELSTAR - Medicine - PFIZER INC.; pg. 1581, pg. 1278
TRELSTAR LA 11.25 MG - Pharmaceutical Product - PFIZER INC.; pg. 1581, pg. 1278
TREMONTI SE - Guitar - PAUL REED SMITH GUITARS; pg. 574, pg. 779
TREN-SHORE - Aluminum Shoring System - ALLIED CONSTRUCTION PRODUCTS, LLC; pg. 1311, pg. 1427
TRENCH - Apparel - OAKLEY, INC.; pg. 1840, pg. 86
TRENCHCOAT - Film - THE DOW CHEMICAL COMPANY; pg. 1157, pg. 898
TRENCHWORK - Estimator - TRIMBLE NAVIGATION LIMITED; pg. 1384, pg. 288
TRENCOR - Paving Equipment - ASTEC INDUSTRIES, INC.; pg. 69, pg. 1628
TREND - Laundry Detergent - HENKEL CONSUMER GOODS; pg. 511, pg. 22
TREND - Kitchen Product - KOHLER CO.; pg. 91, pg. 1862
TREND ALARM LOG - Thermal Processing Equipment - SURFACE COMBUSTION, INC.; pg. 1077, pg. 1462
TRENDCAST - Coating Product - PPG INDUSTRIES, INC.; pg. 1445, pg. 1579
TRENDMASTERS - Toy & Leisure Product - JAKKS PACIFIC, INC.; pg. 960, pg. 142
TRENDS - Apparel - LANDAU UNIFORMS INCORPORATED; pg. 28, pg. 971
TRENDSETTER - Hair Dryer - ANDIS COMPANY; pg. 498, pg. 1895
TRENDSETTER - Commercial Printers - EASTMAN KODAK COMPANY; pg. 1408, pg. 1333
TRENDSPORT - Baby Strollers - BABY TREND, INC.; pg. 916, pg. 173
TRENDTRACK - Merchandise Analysis & Planning System - DESTINATION MATERNITY CORPORATION; pg. 23, pg. 1563
TRENDWALKER - Baby Walkers - BABY TREND, INC.; pg. 916, pg. 173
TRENDWALL - Furniture - TRENDWAY CORPORATION; pg. 945, pg. 892
TRENDWAY XPRESS - Quick Shipment Delivery - TRENDWAY CORPORATION; pg. 945, pg. 892
TRENDY - Knife - GERBER LEGENDARY BLADES; pg. 1834, pg. 1503
TRENET - Laundry Additives - THE CLOROX COMPANY; pg. 327, pg. 169
TRENTAL - Pharmaceutical Product - IMPAX LABORATORIES, INC.; pg. 1544, pg. 101
TRENTINO - Outdoor Fireplace - W.C. BRADLEY CO.; pg. 62, pg. 528
TRENZ - Vehicle Product - LUND INTERNATIONAL, INC.; pg. 211, pg. 526
TREON - Surgical Navigation System - MEDTRONIC, INC.; pg. 1564, pg. 939
TREQ-L - Colour Display Unit - OMNITRACS, LLC; pg. 449, pg. 1685
TRES CHIC - Shoe - AEROGROUP INTERNATIONAL, INC.; pg. 1803, pg. 1055
TRES CHIC - Faucets - MOEN INCORPORATED; pg. 1056, pg. 1468
TRES RICHES - Food Products - RICH PRODUCTS CORPORATION; pg. 892, pg. 1150
TRESCALA - Pharmaceutical Preparation - PFIZER INC.; pg. 1581, pg. 1278
TRESCERRO - Food Product - SHAMROCK FOODS COMPANY; pg. 895, pg. 20
TRESELLE - Beauty Product - AVON PRODUCTS, INC.; pg. 500, pg. 1198
TRESEMME - Hair Care Products - UNILEVER UNITED STATES, INC.; pg. 904, pg. 1061
TREVEALL - Records Management System - SMEAD MANUFACTURING COMPANY; pg. 470, pg. 926
TREVIGEL - Chemical Product - SPECTRUM CHEMICALS & LABORATORY PRODUCTS, INC.; pg. 1181, pg. 94
TREVISO - Furniture - JOFCO INC.; pg. 931, pg. 691
TREVISO - Bike - MARIN BIKES; pg. 1708, pg. 168
TREVISO - Community Name - WCI COMMUNITIES, INC.; pg. 1118, pg. 414
TREVOR - Ceiling Fan - WESTINGHOUSE LIGHTING CORPORATION; pg. 687, pg. 1571
TREVOR SORBIE OF AMERICA - Salon Product - THE STEPHAN COMPANY; pg. 1597, pg. 426
TREVORTON - Furniture - LA-Z-BOY INCORPORATED; pg. 932, pg. 901
TREWAX - Cleaning Product - ORECK CORPORATION; pg. 59, pg. 1653
TREX - Decking, Railing & Fencing Products - TREX COMPANY, INC.; pg. 116, pg. 1812
TREX ACCENTS - Decking & Railing - TREX COMPANY, INC.; pg. 116, pg. 1812
TREX ARTISAN SERIES RAILING - Railing System - TREX COMPANY, INC.; pg. 116, pg. 1812
TREX BRASILIA - Decking & Railing - TREX COMPANY, INC.; pg. 116, pg. 1812
TREX CONTOURS - Decking & Railing - TREX COMPANY, INC.; pg. 116, pg. 1812
TREX DESIGNER SERIES RAILING - Railing System - TREX COMPANY, INC.; pg. 116, pg. 1812
TREX HIDEAWAY - Decking & Railing - TREX COMPANY, INC.; pg. 116, pg. 1812
TREX ORIGINS - Decking & Railing - TREX COMPANY, INC.; pg. 116, pg. 1812
TREX SECLUSIONS - Decking & Railing - TREX COMPANY, INC.; pg. 116, pg. 1812
TREX SURROUNDINGS - Decking & Railing - TREX COMPANY, INC.; pg. 116, pg. 1812
TREXEXPRESS - Railing Assembly System - TREX COMPANY, INC.; pg. 116, pg. 1812
TREXTRIM - Decking & Railing - TREX COMPANY, INC.; pg. 116, pg. 1812
TRG - Title, Escrow & Other Settlement Services - REALOGY CORPORATION; pg. 1109, pg. 1081
TRI-AC - Bevel Product - GLEASON CORPORATION; pg. 1340, pg. 1335
TRI-CHEM - All Purpose Cleaners - ECOLAB INC.; pg. 329, pg. 960
TRI-CLAMP - Sanitary Transmitter - NOSHOK INC.; pg. 1366, pg. 1406
TRI-CLOVER - Ferrule - FIKE CORPORATION; pg. 1047, pg. 973
TRI-CO - Food Product - BUNGE LIMITED; pg. 842, pg. 1351
TRI-COLOR - Car Wash Equipment - D&S CAR WASH EQUIPMENT CO.; pg. 1327, pg. 979
TRI-COMFORT - Nursing Pads - EVENFLO COMPANY, INC.; pg. 924, pg. 1470
TRI-COOL - Metalworking Coolant - TRICO MFG. CORP.; pg. 219, pg. 1886
TRI-CORE - Medical & Aesthetic Product - DYNATRONICS CORPORATION; pg. 1526, pg. 1757
TRI-CORE - Insulated Commercial Door - RAYNOR GARAGE DOORS; pg. 106, pg. 607
TRI-CROSS - Bicycle Tire - SPECIALIZED BICYCLE

COMPONENTS, INC.; pg. 1711, pg. 152
TRI-CURVE - Sport Product - FRANKLIN SPORTS, INC.; pg. 1834, pg. 847
TRI-CUTTER - Carbide Drill Bit - POWERS FASTENERS INC.; pg. 1059, pg. 1143
TRI-ETHANE - Chemical Product - PPG INDUSTRIES, INC.; pg. 1445, pg. 1579
TRI-FLOW - Baby Care Product - MUNCHKIN, INC.; pg. 964, pg. 300
TRI-FLOW - Cleaners, Degreasers & Lubricants - THE SHERWIN-WILLIAMS COMPANY; pg. 1447, pg. 1435
TRI-HEART - Antiparasitic Preparation - MERCK & CO., INC.; pg. 1566, pg. 1077
TRI-HIST - Animal Safety Product - NEOGEN CORPORATION; pg. 883, pg. 896
TRI LINK - Microelectronics - AEROFLEX INCORPORATED; pg. 614, pg. 1321
TRI-LOGIC - Micro-Lubricant System - ITW FLUIDS NORTH AMERICA; pg. 980, pg. 614
TRI-LOKT - Clamping Systems - IDEX CORPORATION; pg. 1347, pg. 623
TRI-LUMA - Topical Drug - GALDERMA LABORATORIES, L.P.; pg. 1532, pg. 1695
TRI MARK - Triple Highlighter - DRI MARK PRODUCTS, INC.; pg. 388, pg. 1323
TRI-MARK - Cored Wire - HOBART BROTHERS COMPANY; pg. 1346, pg. 1477
TRI-MASTER - Blade - LENOX; pg. 1053, pg. 817
TRI-MAX - Cable - ELECTRIC EEL MANUFACTURING CO., INC.; pg. 80, pg. 1473
TRI-MERIT - Cattle Tool - MERCK & CO., INC.; pg. 1566, pg. 1077
TRI-MICRO - Oil Filter Gaskets - VILTER MANUFACTURING LLC; pg. 1078, pg. 1856
TRI-MODE - Medical Laser System - IRIDEX CORPORATION; pg. 648, pg. 160
TRI NI - Chemical Coating - ENTHONE INC.; pg. 1161, pg. 381
TRI-NORINYL - Pharmaceutical Product - ALLERGAN; pg. 1490, pg. 1101
TRI OMINOS - Game - PRESSMAN TOY CORPORATION; pg. 965, pg. 1734
TRI-ONIC - Low Voltage Fuse - MERSEN; pg. 1302, pg. 836
TRI-PHASIC WHITE - Skin Care Product - NU SKIN ENTERPRISES, INC.; pg. 518, pg. 1755
TRI-PLI - Barn Liner - FORTIFIBER CORPORATION; pg. 83, pg. 1021
TRI-POINT - Temperature & Pressure Switches - ASCO VALVE CANADA; pg. 619, pg. 1919
TRI-POWER - Selective Herbicide - NUFARM AMERICAS INC; pg. 1798, pg. 552
TRI SCENTS - Air Freshener - HENKEL CONSUMER GOODS; pg. 511, pg. 22
TRI-SEAL - Closure Liner - TEKNI-PLEX, INC.; pg. 1470, pg. 1122
TRI-SOURCE - Three Way Power Block - COLEMAN CABLE, INC.; pg. 1324, pg. 665
TRI-SOXSUPRINE - Animal Safety Product - NEOGEN CORPORATION; pg. 883, pg. 896
TRI-SPIKE ACETABULAR - Hip Product - ZIMMER BIOMET HOLDINGS, INC.; pg. 1611, pg. 699
TRI-SPORT - Bicycle Accessories - SPECIALIZED BICYCLE COMPONENTS, INC.; pg. 1711, pg. 152
TRI-STAR - In-Plant Laundry System - ECOLAB INC.; pg. 329, pg. 960
TRI-STAR - Disposable Cage Assembly - PALL CORPORATION; pg. 232, pg. 1323
TRI-STAR - Fastening Systems - TEXTRON INC.; pg. 235, pg. 1607
TRI-STAR L - 2000-Detergent Emulsion for Tough Fabric Soils - ECOLAB INC.; pg. 329, pg. 960
TRI-STATE HEADS OR TAILS - Lottery Game - VERMONT LOTTERY COMMISSION; pg. 1010, pg. 1764
TRI-STATE MEGABUCKS - Game - VERMONT LOTTERY COMMISSION; pg. 1010, pg. 1764
TRI-STATE PICK 3 - Game - VERMONT LOTTERY COMMISSION; pg. 1010, pg. 1764
TRI-STATE PICK 4 - Game - VERMONT LOTTERY COMMISSION; pg. 1010, pg. 1764
TRI-TEC - Three Spring Edge Support System-Patented Mattress Design - THERAPEDIC ASSOCIATES, INC.; pg. 945, pg. 1112
TRI TEX - Toilet Bowl Cleaner - SWISHER HYGIENE INC.; pg. 336, pg. 1507
TRI-TOWN NEWS - Newspaper - GREATER MEDIA NEWSPAPERS, INC.; pg. 1646, pg. 1071
TRI-VI-FLOR - Fluoride Vitamins - MEAD JOHNSON NUTRITION COMPANY; pg. 1561, pg. 615
TRI-VI-SOL - Vitamins for Children - MEAD JOHNSON NUTRITION COMPANY; pg. 1561, pg. 615
TRI-VI-SOL WITH IRON - Vitamins with Iron for Children - MEAD JOHNSON NUTRITION COMPANY; pg. 1561, pg. 615
TRI-WALL - Packaging - INTERNATIONAL PAPER COMPANY; pg. 1460, pg. 1644
TRI-WING - Truck Cover - PENDA CORPORATION; pg. 214, pg. 1887
TRI-X - Photo Film, Plates - EASTMAN KODAK COMPANY; pg. 1408, pg. 1333
TRIAC - Filtration System - SPECTRUM LABORATORIES INC.; pg. 1595, pg. 69
TRIACTIVE LASERDERMOLOGY - Cellulite Treatment System - CYNOSURE, INC.; pg. 1521, pg. 858
TRIAD - Sports Equipment - ALLIANCE SPORTS GROUP, L.P.; pg. 1825, pg. 1698
TRIAD - Dental Product - DENTSPLY INTERNATIONAL INC.; pg. 1522, pg. 1596
TRIAD - Car Seat - DOREL JUVENILE GROUP, INC.; pg. 923, pg. 676
TRIAD - Furniture - ETHAN ALLEN INTERIORS INC.; pg. 924, pg. 343
TRIAD - Adaptive Control System & Customer Management Solutions - FAIR ISAAC CORPORATION; pg. 1247, pg. 955
TRIAD - Medical Device - INTEGRA LIFESCIENCES HOLDINGS CORPORATION; pg. 1545, pg. 1109
TRIAD - Electronic Components - MOLEX INCORPORATED; pg. 655, pg. 628
TRIAD - Speaker Company - TRIAD SPEAKERS, INC.; pg. 682, pg. 1507
TRIAD - Electronic Ballasts - UNIVERSAL LIGHTING TECHNOLOGIES; pg. 1307, pg. 1655
TRIAD ACCREDIT - Electronic Instrument - KEITHLEY INSTRUMENTS, INC.; pg. 1418, pg. 1473
TRIAD PERSONNEL SERVICES - Contract Services Firm - GENERAL EMPLOYMENT ENTERPRISES, INC.; pg. 400, pg. 636
TRIADYNE - Percussion Therapy System - KINETIC CONCEPTS, INC.; pg. 1553, pg. 1741
TRIAGE - Pharmaceutical Product - ALERE INC.; pg. 1488, pg. 849
TRIAGE - Diagnostic Product - ALERE SAN DIEGO; pg. 1489, pg. 199
TRIAGE BNP TESTS - Quantitative Test - ALERE SAN DIEGO; pg. 1489, pg. 199
TRIAGE CARDIAC PANEL - Quantitative Test - ALERE SAN DIEGO; pg. 1489, pg. 199
TRIAGE CARDIAC SYSTEM - Cardiac System - ALERE SAN DIEGO; pg. 1489, pg. 199
TRIAGE CARDIOPROFILER - Quantitative Test - ALERE SAN DIEGO; pg. 1489, pg. 199
TRIAGE CENSUS - Pharmaceutical Product - ALERE INC.; pg. 1488, pg. 849
TRIAGE CENSUS - Software - ALERE SAN DIEGO; pg. 1489, pg. 199
TRIAGE METER - Quantitative Test - ALERE SAN DIEGO; pg. 1489, pg. 199
TRIAGE PROFILER SHORTNESS OF BREATH PANEL - Quantitative Test - ALERE SAN DIEGO; pg. 1489, pg. 199
TRIAGE SENSOR - Defense & Homeland Security Product - RADIANCE TECHNOLOGIES, INC.; pg. 1277, pg. 6
TRIAGE TOX DRUG SCREEN - Quantitative Test - ALERE SAN DIEGO; pg. 1489, pg. 199
TRIAGON - Laser Product - ROFIN-SINAR TECHNOLOGIES, INC.; pg. 668, pg. 904
TRIALMASTER - Computer Software - OMNICOMM SYSTEMS, INC.; pg. 1272, pg. 426
TRIALMAX - Software - FTI CONSULTING, INC.; pg. 760, pg. 478
TRIALONE - Computer Software - OMNICOMM SYSTEMS, INC.; pg. 1272, pg. 426
TRIAMINE - Herbicide - NUFARM AMERICAS INC; pg. 1798, pg. 552
TRIAMULOX - Veterinary Vaccine - PFIZER INC.; pg. 1581, pg. 1278
TRIANGLE - Cattle Vaccine - BOEHRINGER INGELHEIM VETMEDICA, INC.; pg. 1474, pg. 989
TRIANGLE - Copper Wire - COLEMAN CABLE, INC.; pg. 1324, pg. 665
TRIATHLON - Cable - COMMSCOPE, INC.; pg. 278, pg. 1378
TRIATHLON - Orthopaedic Product - STRYKER CORPORATION; pg. 1598, pg. 894
TRIAX - Paintballs - ALLIANCE SPORTS GROUP, L.P.; pg. 1825, pg. 1698
TRIAX - AS/R Systems - DAIFUKU WEBB; pg. 1327, pg. 885
TRIAX - Watch - NIKE, INC.; pg. 1812, pg. 1492
TRIAX SWIFT DIGITAL - Footwear - NIKE, INC.; pg. 1812, pg. 1492
TRIBAL - Furniture - ASHLEY FURNITURE INDUSTRIES, INC.; pg. 914, pg. 1852
TRIBAL SPORT - Golf Shoes - JOHNSTON & MURPHY CO.; pg. 1810, pg. 1651
TRIBE - Fabric - NEMSCHOFF, INC.; pg. 936, pg. 1890
TRIBECA - Guest Chairs - BERNHARDT DESIGN; pg. 918, pg. 1381
TRIBECA - Lighting - ETHAN ALLEN INTERIORS INC.; pg. 924, pg. 343
TRIBECA - Flatware - ONEIDA LTD; pg. 1129, pg. 1318
TRIBECA - Lighting Product - QUOIZEL INC.; pg. 1304, pg. 1616
TRIBECA - Car - SUBARU OF AMERICA, INC.; pg. 191, pg. 1050
TRIBECA - Ceramic, Glass, Stone Tiles & Slabs - WALKER & ZANGER, INC.; pg. 119, pg. 281
TRIBECCA - Carpet - BEAULIEU GROUP, LLC; pg. 917, pg. 529
TRIBOCOAT - Composite Electroless Coating - STANDEX INTERNATIONAL CORPORATION; pg. 60, pg. 1039
TRIBOGUARD - Hydraulic Filters - DONALDSON COMPANY, INC.; pg. 1329, pg. 917
TRIBOMATIC - Gun - NORDSON CORPORATION; pg. 1365, pg. 1480
TRIBONIC 20 - Steel Product - AK STEEL HOLDING CORPORATION; pg. 1311, pg. 1479
THE TRIBUNE - Indiana Newspaper - FREEDOM COMMUNICATIONS, INC.; pg. 1643, pg. 110
TRIBUNE - Media Services - TRIBUNE MEDIA COMPANY; pg. 1696, pg. 592
TRIBUNE CONNECTION - Friday Edition Newspaper - EAST VALLEY TRIBUNE; pg. 1638, pg. 25
THE TRIBUNE (FT. PIERCE) - Newspaper - THE E.W. SCRIPPS COMPANY; pg. 1639, pg. 1412
TRIBUNO - Vermouth - THE WINE GROUP, INC.; pg. 1972, pg. 234
TRIBUTE - Furniture - JASPER GROUP; pg. 930, pg. 691
TRIBUTE - Fabric - NEMSCHOFF, INC.; pg. 936, pg. 1890
TRIBUTE - Hotels - STARWOOD HOTELS & RESORTS WORLDWIDE, INC.; pg. 1114, pg. 378
TRIBUTE - Kitchenware - THE VOLLRATH COMPANY LLC; pg. 1139, pg. 1894
TRICALGOXYL - Skin Care Product - NU SKIN ENTERPRISES, INC.; pg. 518, pg. 1755
TRICAM - Optical Sensors - PERCEPTRON, INC.; pg. 215, pg. 904
TRICEP - Medical Device - BOSTON SCIENTIFIC CORPORATION; pg. 1508, pg. 831
TRICKY TREATS - Candy - R.M. PALMER COMPANY; pg. 1861, pg. 1585
TRICO - Windshield Wipers, Arms & Refills - TRICO PRODUCTS CORPORATION; pg. 220, pg. 905
TRICOLYTE - Chemical Coating - ENTHONE INC.; pg. 1161, pg. 381
TRICOOL - Power Supply Product - ANTEC INCORPORATED; pg. 350, pg. 90
TRICOR - Tablet - ABBOTT LABORATORIES; pg. 1484, pg. 551
TRICOR M FR - APP Modified Bitumen Sheet - JOHNS MANVILLE CORPORATION; pg. 89, pg. 320
TRICOR S - APP Modified Bitumen Sheet - JOHNS MANVILLE CORPORATION; pg. 89, pg. 320
TRICOT ST. RAPHAEL - Apparel - PERRY ELLIS INTERNATIONAL, INC.; pg. 45, pg. 445
TRIDAIR - Flotation System - CAMERON INTERNATIONAL; pg. 1151, pg. 1702
TRIDAIR HYDRAULIC - Water Separation Product - CAMERON INTERNATIONAL; pg. 1151, pg. 1702
TRIDAIR MECHANICAL - Water Separation Product - CAMERON INTERNATIONAL; pg. 1151, pg. 1702
TRIDAN - Fabrication Machinery - KAYDON CORPORATION; pg. 1352, pg. 866
TRIDENT - Plastics Product - AEP INDUSTRIES INC.; pg. 1878, pg. 1085
TRIDENT - Medical Equipment - CONMED CORPORATION; pg. 1517, pg. 1347

TRIDENT - Solid Dielectric Switchgear - G&W ELECTRIC COMPANY; *pg.* 1338, *pg.* 558
TRIDENT - Chart & Marking System - GRAPHIC CONTROLS LLC; *pg.* 401, *pg.* 1148
TRIDENT - Systems Integration & Aeronautics - LOCKHEED MARTIN CORPORATION; *pg.* 229, *pg.* 762
TRIDENT - Wrap Bug Shield - LUND INTERNATIONAL, INC.; *pg.* 211, *pg.* 526
TRIDENT - Sugarless Gum - MONDELEZ INTERNATIONAL, INC.; *pg.* 878, *pg.* 601
TRIDENT - Flashlight - STREAMLIGHT INC.; *pg.* 1306, *pg.* 1527
TRIDENT - Orthopaedic Product - STRYKER CORPORATION; *pg.* 1598, *pg.* 894
TRIDENT - Thermal Processing Equipment - SURFACE COMBUSTION, INC.; *pg.* 1077, *pg.* 1462
TRIDENT HP - Flashlight - STREAMLIGHT INC.; *pg.* 1306, *pg.* 1527
TRIDENT SEAFOODS - Logo - TRIDENT SEAFOODS CORPORATION; *pg.* 902, *pg.* 1842
TRIDEX - Detergent - TRION, INC.; *pg.* 682, *pg.* 1390
TRIDMAC - Pharmaceutical Preparations - TARGACEPT, INC.; *pg.* 1601, *pg.* 1395
TRIENDA - Injection Molded Product - TRIENDA, LLC; *pg.* 1890, *pg.* 1887
TRIENNIUM - Kitchenware - THE VOLLRATH COMPANY LLC; *pg.* 1139, *pg.* 1894
TRIESTE - Kitchen Product - KOHLER CO.; *pg.* 91, *pg.* 1862
TRIEX - Medical Device - COOK GROUP, INC.; *pg.* 1518, *pg.* 674
TRIFAB - Storefront Window Framing System - KAWNEER COMPANY, INC.; *pg.* 90, *pg.* 537
TRIFARI - Jewelry - KATE SPADE & COMPANY; *pg.* 27, *pg.* 1248
TRIFECTA - Cryogenic Product - CHART INDUSTRIES, INC.; *pg.* 1405, *pg.* 1454
TRIFLASH - Chip Device - SANDISK CORPORATION; *pg.* 465, *pg.* 147
TRIFLEX - Furniture - HERMAN MILLER, INC.; *pg.* 926, *pg.* 913
TRIFLEX - Musical Instrument - PEAVEY ELECTRONICS CORPORATION; *pg.* 662, *pg.* 970
TRIFLOW - Blower - GARDNER DENVER, INC.; *pg.* 1338, *pg.* 1592
TRIFLUOROACETIC ACID - Flurochemical - HALOCARBON PRODUCTS CORPORATION; *pg.* 978, *pg.* 1116
TRIFLUOROACETIC ACID-BIOGRADE - Flurochemical - HALOCARBON PRODUCTS CORPORATION; *pg.* 978, *pg.* 1116
TRIFLUOROACETIC ANHYDRIDE - Flurochemical - HALOCARBON PRODUCTS CORPORATION; *pg.* 978, *pg.* 1116
TRIFLUOROACETYL CHLORIDE - Flurochemical - HALOCARBON PRODUCTS CORPORATION; *pg.* 978, *pg.* 1116
TRIFLUOROETHANOL - Flurochemical - HALOCARBON PRODUCTS CORPORATION; *pg.* 978, *pg.* 1116
TRIFORCE I - Bait Casting Reels - DAIWA CORPORATION; *pg.* 1832, *pg.* 75
TRIFRESH - Vacuum Skin Packaging - SEALED AIR CORPORATION; *pg.* 1468, *pg.* 1058
TRIFURCON - Electronic Components - MOLEX INCORPORATED; *pg.* 655, *pg.* 628
TRIGARD - Protective Device - BOURNS, INC.; *pg.* 627, *pg.* 193
TRIGARD - Gas Monitoring System - MINE SAFETY APPLIANCES COMPANY; *pg.* 1361, *pg.* 1525
TRIGGER - Furniture - HOOKER FURNITURE CORPORATION; *pg.* 928, *pg.* 1788
TRIGGER PRO - Household Product - WD-40 COMPANY; *pg.* 337, *pg.* 210
TRIGGERFOAM - Foam - POWERS FASTENERS INC.; *pg.* 1059, *pg.* 1143
TRIGLO - Seatbelt Light - HONEYWELL INTERNATIONAL INC.; *pg.* 407, *pg.* 1088
TRIGLOSS - Foam Brush Carwash System - D&S CAR WASH EQUIPMENT CO.; *pg.* 1327, *pg.* 979
TRIGON - Packaging Product - SEALED AIR CORPORATION; *pg.* 1468, *pg.* 1058
TRIGRID - Oil Treater Product - CAMERON INTERNATIONAL; *pg.* 1151, *pg.* 1702
TRIGRIDMAX - Treater - CAMERON INTERNATIONAL; *pg.* 1151, *pg.* 1702
TRIGUARD - Gasket - W.L. GORE & ASSOCIATES, INC.; *pg.* 122, *pg.* 388
TRIHIBIT - Haemophilus b Conjugate Vaccine - SANOFI PASTEUR, INC; *pg.* 1591, *pg.* 1588
TRIHOT - Golf Equipment - CALLAWAY GOLF COMPANY; *pg.* 1829, *pg.* 58
TRIKESTER - Bicycle - TREK BICYCLE CORPORATION; *pg.* 1847, *pg.* 1896
TRIKO - Bath Product - KOHLER CO.; *pg.* 91, *pg.* 1862
TRILENE - Polymer Product - CHEMTURA CORPORATION; *pg.* 1152, *pg.* 355
TRILIPIX - Fenofibric Acid - ABBOTT LABORATORIES; *pg.* 1484, *pg.* 551
TRILL - Petcare Product - MARS, INCORPORATED; *pg.* 1858, *pg.* 1792
TRILLIANT HC - Thermoplastic Resins - POLYONE CORPORATION; *pg.* 1177, *pg.* 1404
TRILLION-AIR - Compressor - BADGER AIR BRUSH COMPANY; *pg.* 359, *pg.* 612
TRILLIUM - Sleeper & Recliner Seating - STEELCASE INC.; *pg.* 475, *pg.* 889
TRILOGY - Corporate Furniture - BERNHARDT DESIGN; *pg.* 918, *pg.* 1381
TRILOGY - Bicycle - G. JOANNOU CYCLE CO. INC.; *pg.* 1707, *pg.* 1098
TRILOGY - Cleaning Product - HILLYARD, INC.; *pg.* 331, *pg.* 990
TRILOGY - Paper - INTERNATIONAL PAPER COMPANY; *pg.* 1460, *pg.* 1644
TRILOGY - Kitchen Product - KOHLER CO.; *pg.* 91, *pg.* 1862
TRILOGY - Alarm Lock System - NAPCO SECURITY SYSTEMS, INC.; *pg.* 658, *pg.* 1138
TRILOGY - Chair - STEELCASE INC.; *pg.* 475, *pg.* 889
TRILOGY - Linear Accelerator - VARIAN MEDICAL SYSTEMS, INC.; *pg.* 1434, *pg.* 178
TRILOGY - Lens - YOUNGER OPTICS; *pg.* 1437, *pg.* 297
TRILYTE - Roof Prism Binoculars - SWIFT OPTICAL INSTRUMENTS, INC.; *pg.* 1430, *pg.* 1744
TRIM - Beverage - TREE TOP, INC.; *pg.* 901, *pg.* 1843
TRIM - Hair Cutting Kit - WAHL CLIPPER CORPORATION; *pg.* 524, *pg.* 662
TRIM - Nail Care Product - THE W.E. BASSETT COMPANY; *pg.* 524, *pg.* 371
TRIM CHIPS - Paint And Stain Product - BENJAMIN MOORE & CO.; *pg.* 1440, *pg.* 1085
TRIM CORE - Nutritional Product - NUTRACEUTICAL INTERNATIONAL CORPORATION; *pg.* 1576, *pg.* 1753
TRIM-CRAFT - Vehicle Trim Adhesives - PPG INDUSTRIES, INC.; *pg.* 1445, *pg.* 1579
TRIM-EASE - Lubricant - AMERICAN GREASE STICK CO.; *pg.* 971, *pg.* 902
TRIM-IT - Paint Trimming Tool - WAGNER SPRAY TECH CORPORATION; *pg.* 1449, *pg.* 954
TRIM MASTER - Cordless Angled Finish Nailer - PASLODE; *pg.* 1059, *pg.* 664
TRIM 'N VAC - Beard & Mustache Trimmer - WAHL CLIPPER CORPORATION; *pg.* 524, *pg.* 662
TRIM PLATE - Faucet Accessory - SLOAN VALVE COMPANY; *pg.* 1062, *pg.* 613
TRIM-PLEX - Nutritional Supplement - NATURAL ORGANICS, INC.; *pg.* 1571, *pg.* 1181
TRIM SHINE - Car Care Product - STONER INC.; *pg.* 985, *pg.* 1583
TRIM-TEX - Wide Strip - RIGIDIZED METALS CORP.; *pg.* 108, *pg.* 1151
TRIM-TO-SIZE - Air Conditioner Filter - RESEARCH PRODUCTS CORPORATION; *pg.* 1075, *pg.* 1867
TRIM TYTE - Fittings - UNITED STATES PIPE & FOUNDRY COMPANY, INC.; *pg.* 117, *pg.* 5
TRIM TYTON - Fittings - UNITED STATES PIPE & FOUNDRY COMPANY, INC.; *pg.* 117, *pg.* 5
TRIMAC - Transportation Service - TRIMAC CORPORATION; *pg.* 1926, *pg.* 1905
TRIMARK - Medical Product - HOLOGIC, INC.; *pg.* 1416, *pg.* 784
TRIMARK - Motion Pictures - LIONS GATE ENTERTAINMENT CORP.; *pg.* 296, *pg.* 274
TRIMBLE GEOMATICS OFFICE - Software - TRIMBLE NAVIGATION LIMITED; *pg.* 1384, *pg.* 288
TRIMBLE SURVEY CONTROLLER - Software - TRIMBLE NAVIGATION LIMITED; *pg.* 1384, *pg.* 288
TRIMBLE SURVEY PRO - Software - TRIMBLE NAVIGATION LIMITED; *pg.* 1384, *pg.* 288
TRIMBLE TOTAL CONTROL - Software - TRIMBLE NAVIGATION LIMITED; *pg.* 1384, *pg.* 288
TRIMBRITE - Tools - TRACTOR SUPPLY COMPANY; *pg.* 708, *pg.* 1627
TRIMCOMM - Radio - TRIMBLE NAVIGATION LIMITED; *pg.* 1384, *pg.* 288
TRIMEC - Turf Product - PBI/GORDON CORPORATION; *pg.* 1176, *pg.* 985
TRIMEC ENCORE - Turf Product - PBI/GORDON CORPORATION; *pg.* 1176, *pg.* 985
TRIMENE - Polymer Product - CHEMTURA CORPORATION; *pg.* 1152, *pg.* 355
TRIMENSIONAL - Medical Product - W.L. GORE & ASSOCIATES, INC.; *pg.* 122, *pg.* 388
TRIMESTER - Pharmaceutical Product - ALERE INC.; *pg.* 1488, *pg.* 849
TRIMFLIGHT - Navigation Aid - TRIMBLE NAVIGATION LIMITED; *pg.* 1384, *pg.* 288
TRIMLINE - Rectangular Beverage Dispensers - CARLISLE FOODSERVICE PRODUCTS INCORPORATED; *pg.* 1455, *pg.* 1485
TRIMLINE - Health & Fitness Product - NAUTILUS, INC.; *pg.* 1840, *pg.* 1846
TRIMLINE SERIES - Recessed Washroom Equipment & Toilet Partitions - BOBRICK WASHROOM EQUIPMENT, INC.; *pg.* 1043, *pg.* 166
TRIMLITE - Cameras, Microfilm Readers - EASTMAN KODAK COMPANY; *pg.* 1408, *pg.* 1333
TRIMMARK - Navigation Aid - TRIMBLE NAVIGATION LIMITED; *pg.* 1384, *pg.* 288
TRIMMATE - Lenses, Photographic Paper, Microfilm Equipment Accessories - EASTMAN KODAK COMPANY; *pg.* 1408, *pg.* 1333
TRIMOFIX - Fragrance Ingredient - INTERNATIONAL FLAVORS & FRAGRANCES INC.; *pg.* 512, *pg.* 1244
TRIMPACK - Navigation Aid - TRIMBLE NAVIGATION LIMITED; *pg.* 1384, *pg.* 288
TRIMPAK - Nutritional Supplement - NU SKIN ENTERPRISES, INC.; *pg.* 518, *pg.* 1755
TRIMPOT - Electrical Apparatus - BOURNS, INC.; *pg.* 627, *pg.* 193
TRIMPRINT - Instant Color Film & Cameras - EASTMAN KODAK COMPANY; *pg.* 1408, *pg.* 1333
TRIMPULSE - Software - GSI GROUP INC.; *pg.* 1415, *pg.* 784
TRIMRITE - Stainless Steel Product - CARPENTER TECHNOLOGY CORPORATION; *pg.* 73, *pg.* 1584
TRIMSHAKE - Nutritional Supplement - NU SKIN ENTERPRISES, INC.; *pg.* 518, *pg.* 1755
TRIMSMART - Laser System - GSI GROUP INC.; *pg.* 1415, *pg.* 784
TRIMSTAR - Mower Tractor - EXCEL INDUSTRIES, INC.; *pg.* 1795, *pg.* 715
TRIMSTIK - Nutritional Supplement - NU SKIN ENTERPRISES, INC.; *pg.* 518, *pg.* 1755
TRIMTRAC - Navigation Aid - TRIMBLE NAVIGATION LIMITED; *pg.* 1384, *pg.* 288
TRIMUNE - Nutritional Supplement - PHARMAVITE LLC; *pg.* 1584, *pg.* 167
TRINCHERO - Beverage - TRINCHERO FAMILY ESTATES; *pg.* 1971, *pg.* 197
TRINCOOL - Refrigerated Box Car - TRINITY INDUSTRIES, INC.; *pg.* 116, *pg.* 1690
TRINESSA - Pharmaceutical Product - ALLERGAN; *pg.* 1490, *pg.* 1101
TRINIDAD - Furniture - BASSETT FURNITURE INDUSTRIES, INCORPORATED; *pg.* 916, *pg.* 1776
TRINIDAD - Paints - PETTIT PAINT COMPANY; *pg.* 1444, *pg.* 1116
TRINIDING - Thermal Processing Equipment - SURFACE COMBUSTION, INC.; *pg.* 1077, *pg.* 1462
TRINITAR - Lenses - ALAN GORDON ENTERPRISES, INC.; *pg.* 1399, *pg.* 125
TRINITIE - Footwear - STEVEN MADDEN, LTD.; *pg.* 1819, *pg.* 1176
TRINITY - Anti-Perspirant - THE GILLETTE COMPANY; *pg.* 509, *pg.* 795
TRINITY - Furniture - JASPER GROUP; *pg.* 930, *pg.* 691
TRINITY - Women's Clothing & Accessories - WOODEN SHIPS OF HOBOKEN; *pg.* 35, *pg.* 1315
TRINITY OAKS - Beverage - TRINCHERO FAMILY ESTATES; *pg.* 1971, *pg.* 197
TRINIX - Routing Switchers - GRASS VALLEY, INC.; *pg.* 641, *pg.* 164
TRINKET - Footwear - P.W. MINOR & SON, INC.; *pg.* 1816, *pg.* 1140
TRIO - Hearing Aid - BELTONE ELECTRONICS LLC; *pg.* 1503, *pg.* 614
TRIO - Knife - BUCK KNIVES, INC.; *pg.* 1828, *pg.* 550

First page reference indicates Business Class Edition
Second page reference indicates Geographic Edition

TRIO - Patient Monitoring Device - MAQUET; *pg.* 1558, *pg.* 1082
TRIO - Food Products - NESTLE USA, INC.; *pg.* 883, *pg.* 96
TRIO - Apparel - OAKLEY, INC.; *pg.* 1840, *pg.* 86
TRIO - Spinal System - STRYKER CORPORATION; *pg.* 1598, *pg.* 894
TRIO PLUS - Office Furniture - JOFCO INC.; *pg.* 931, *pg.* 691
TRIO SUPREME - Food & Beverage Product - NESTLE USA, INC.; *pg.* 883, *pg.* 96
TRIOMPHE - Bath Accessory - CROSCILL, INC.; *pg.* 1122, *pg.* 1220
TRION - Electronic Air Cleaners - TRION, INC.; *pg.* 682, *pg.* 1390
TRION RX - Console HEPA Class II Medical Device Air Cleaner - TRION, INC.; *pg.* 682, *pg.* 1390
TRIOPTIC-S - Veterinary Ophthalmic Ointments - PFIZER INC.; *pg.* 1581, *pg.* 1278
TRIOX - Ultra Low NOx Gas Burner - HAUCK MANUFACTURING COMPANY, INC.; *pg.* 1345, *pg.* 1522
TRIP MAKER - Travel Planning Software - RAND MCNALLY & COMPANY; *pg.* 1679, *pg.* 661
TRIP REWARDS - Loyalty Program - WYNDHAM WORLDWIDE CORPORATION; *pg.* 1119, *pg.* 1107
TRIPACK - Water Separation Product - CAMERON INTERNATIONAL; *pg.* 1151, *pg.* 1702
TRIPADVISOR - Travel Information & Advice Services - EXPEDIA, INC.; *pg.* 1244, *pg.* 1814
TRIPADVISOR.COM - Travel Information & Advice Web Site - TRIPADVISOR, INC.; *pg.* 1926, *pg.* 835
TRIPAK - Container Grown Plant - MONROVIA GROWERS; *pg.* 1797, *pg.* 44
TRIPASSIST - Life & Health Insurance Administration Services - AMERICAN AUTOMOBILE ASSOCIATION; *pg.* 1190, *pg.* 429
TRIPCLIK - Disposable Photographic Camera - AMERICAN AUTOMOBILE ASSOCIATION; *pg.* 1190, *pg.* 429
TRIPEDIA - Diphtheria & Tetanus Toxoids & Acellular Pertussis Vaccine Adsorbed - SANOFI PASTEUR, INC; *pg.* 1591, *pg.* 1588
TRIPET - Grinding Machine - HARDINGE INC.; *pg.* 1344, *pg.* 1157
TRIPLAL - Fragrance Ingredient - INTERNATIONAL FLAVORS & FRAGRANCES INC.; *pg.* 512, *pg.* 1244
TRIPLE - Trolley - HILLYARD, INC.; *pg.* 331, *pg.* 990
TRIPLE-10 - Home & Farm Product - PBI/GORDON CORPORATION; *pg.* 1176, *pg.* 985
TRIPLE A - Auto Association Prints & Publications - AMERICAN AUTOMOBILE ASSOCIATION; *pg.* 1190, *pg.* 429
TRIPLE ACTION - Personal Defense Sprays - MACE SECURITY INTERNATIONAL, INC.; *pg.* 1172, *pg.* 1541
TRIPLE ATTACK - Pulper Machine - BOLTON-EMERSON AMERICAS, INC.; *pg.* 1318, *pg.* 827
TRIPLE BANKROLL - Game - MISSOURI LOTTERY; *pg.* 999, *pg.* 979
TRIPLE BINGO - Lottery Card - MISSOURI LOTTERY; *pg.* 999, *pg.* 979
TRIPLE BLACK TIE - Slots - INTERNATIONAL GAME TECHNOLOGY; *pg.* 957, *pg.* 1024
TRIPLE BLASTS - Candy-Coated Bubble Gum Pop - THE TOPPS COMPANY, INC.; *pg.* 588, *pg.* 1302
TRIPLE BLOCK - Animal Safety Product - NEOGEN CORPORATION; *pg.* 883, *pg.* 896
TRIPLE BONANZA - Slots - INTERNATIONAL GAME TECHNOLOGY; *pg.* 957, *pg.* 1024
TRIPLE BUCKS - Video Slots - INTERNATIONAL GAME TECHNOLOGY; *pg.* 957, *pg.* 1024
TRIPLE CASH - Slots - INTERNATIONAL GAME TECHNOLOGY; *pg.* 957, *pg.* 1024
TRIPLE CASH - Game - MISSOURI LOTTERY; *pg.* 999, *pg.* 979
TRIPLE CAST - Animal Safety Product - NEOGEN CORPORATION; *pg.* 883, *pg.* 896
TRIPLE CATS 'N' DOGS - Slots - INTERNATIONAL GAME TECHNOLOGY; *pg.* 957, *pg.* 1024
TRIPLE CHARMS - Game - WMS INDUSTRIES INC.; *pg.* 593, *pg.* 666
TRIPLE-CHIP - Saw Blade - THE DOALL COMPANY; *pg.* 1329, *pg.* 670
TRIPLE CHIP - Metal Cutting Saw Blade - SIMONDS INTERNATIONAL CORPORATION; *pg.* 1376, *pg.* 819
TRIPLE CLEANSE - Nutritional Supplement - GENERAL NUTRITION CENTERS, INC.; *pg.* 1534, *pg.* 1575
TRIPLE COVER - House Paint - AKZONOBEL DECORATIVE PAINTS U.S.; *pg.* 1439, *pg.* 1474
TRIPLE CROWN - Fence - CTB INTERNATIONAL CORP.; *pg.* 850, *pg.* 695
TRIPLE CROWN - Animal Safety Product - NEOGEN CORPORATION; *pg.* 883, *pg.* 896
TRIPLE CROWN - Horse Feed - SOUTHERN STATES COOPERATIVE, INC.; *pg.* 1482, *pg.* 1804
TRIPLE CROWN SERVICE - Intermodal Rail Service - NORFOLK SOUTHERN CORPORATION; *pg.* 1917, *pg.* 1797
TRIPLE CRYSTAL SEVENS - Slots - INTERNATIONAL GAME TECHNOLOGY; *pg.* 957, *pg.* 1024
TRIPLE DIAMOND - Slots - INTERNATIONAL GAME TECHNOLOGY; *pg.* 957, *pg.* 1024
TRIPLE DIAMOND DELUXE - Slots - INTERNATIONAL GAME TECHNOLOGY; *pg.* 957, *pg.* 1024
TRIPLE DIAMOND MINE - Slots - INTERNATIONAL GAME TECHNOLOGY; *pg.* 957, *pg.* 1024
TRIPLE DOLLARS - Slots - INTERNATIONAL GAME TECHNOLOGY; *pg.* 957, *pg.* 1024
TRIPLE DOUBLE - Slots - INTERNATIONAL GAME TECHNOLOGY; *pg.* 957, *pg.* 1024
TRIPLE DOUBLE - Portable Basketball Standards - LIFETIME PRODUCTS INC.; *pg.* 933, *pg.* 1751
TRIPLE DOUBLE CASH - Lottery Game - OHIO LOTTERY COMMISSION; *pg.* 1002, *pg.* 1433
TRIPLE DOUBLE DIAMOND - Game - INTERNATIONAL GAME TECHNOLOGY; *pg.* 957, *pg.* 1024
TRIPLE DOUBLE DIAMOND SLOT BINGO - Slots - INTERNATIONAL GAME TECHNOLOGY; *pg.* 957, *pg.* 1024
TRIPLE DOUBLE DOLLARS - Slots - INTERNATIONAL GAME TECHNOLOGY; *pg.* 957, *pg.* 1024
TRIPLE DOUBLE FIVE TIMES PAY - Slots - INTERNATIONAL GAME TECHNOLOGY; *pg.* 957, *pg.* 1024
TRIPLE DOUBLE LUCKY 7S - Slots - INTERNATIONAL GAME TECHNOLOGY; *pg.* 957, *pg.* 1024
TRIPLE DOUBLE RED WHITE & BLUE - Slots - INTERNATIONAL GAME TECHNOLOGY; *pg.* 957, *pg.* 1024
TRIPLE DOUBLE STARS - Game - INTERNATIONAL GAME TECHNOLOGY; *pg.* 957, *pg.* 1024
TRIPLE DOUBLE WILD CHERRY - Casino Game - INTERNATIONAL GAME TECHNOLOGY; *pg.* 957, *pg.* 1024
TRIPLE DOUGH - Game - MISSOURI LOTTERY; *pg.* 999, *pg.* 979
TRIPLE DYNAMITE 777 - Lottery Game - IDAHO LOTTERY; *pg.* 995, *pg.* 547
TRIPLE EDGE - Tri-Level Anti Sag Border - THERAPEDIC ASSOCIATES, INC.; *pg.* 945, *pg.* 1112
TRIPLE FIVE TIMES PAY - Slots - INTERNATIONAL GAME TECHNOLOGY; *pg.* 957, *pg.* 1024
TRIPLE FLEX - Nutritional Supplement - PHARMAVITE LLC; *pg.* 1584, *pg.* 167
TRIPLE FLEX - Cable - SHURE INCORPORATED; *pg.* 672, *pg.* 638
TRIPLE FORTUNE - Lottery Card - MISSOURI LOTTERY; *pg.* 999, *pg.* 979
TRIPLE FX - Nutritional Product - RBC LIFE SCIENCES, INC.; *pg.* 1588, *pg.* 1723
TRIPLE GOLD BARS - Slots - INTERNATIONAL GAME TECHNOLOGY; *pg.* 957, *pg.* 1024
TRIPLE GOLDEN CHERRIES - Game - WMS INDUSTRIES INC.; *pg.* 593, *pg.* 666
TRIPLE HEAT - Animal Safety Product - NEOGEN CORPORATION; *pg.* 883, *pg.* 896
TRIPLE I - Customer Computer System - LANDAUER, INC.; *pg.* 1554, *pg.* 615
TRIPLE IT - Game - INTERNATIONAL GAME TECHNOLOGY; *pg.* 420, *pg.* 1606
TRIPLE JACKPOT - Slots - INTERNATIONAL GAME TECHNOLOGY; *pg.* 957, *pg.* 1024
TRIPLE JACKPOT SLOT BINGO - Slots - INTERNATIONAL GAME TECHNOLOGY; *pg.* 957, *pg.* 1024
TRIPLE-L - Construction Equipment - JLG INDUSTRIES, INC.; *pg.* 1351, *pg.* 1551
TRIPLE LOCK - Electrosurgical Devices - ANGIODYNAMICS, INC.; *pg.* 1495, *pg.* 1173
TRIPLE LUCKY 7S - Slots - INTERNATIONAL GAME TECHNOLOGY; *pg.* 957, *pg.* 1024
TRIPLE LUNKER - Game - WMS INDUSTRIES INC.; *pg.* 593, *pg.* 666
TRIPLE LUXURY - Game - WMS INDUSTRIES INC.; *pg.* 593, *pg.* 666
TRIPLE M - Spiral Hams - KAYEM FOODS, INC.; *pg.* 867, *pg.* 814
TRIPLE MONEYBAGS - Game - MISSOURI LOTTERY; *pg.* 999, *pg.* 979
TRIPLE PLAY - Video Poker - INTERNATIONAL GAME TECHNOLOGY; *pg.* 957, *pg.* 1024
TRIPLE PLAY 2000 - Dry Cleaning & Laundry Product - ADCO, INC.; *pg.* 325, *pg.* 482
TRIPLE PLAY BOUQUET - Fruit Arrangements - EDIBLE ARRANGEMENTS INTERNATIONAL, INC.; *pg.* 1768, *pg.* 382
TRIPLE PLUS PAK - Cardboard Shipping & Packaging Materials - PPG INDUSTRIES, INC.; *pg.* 1445, *pg.* 1579
TRIPLE RED WHITE & BLUE - Slots - INTERNATIONAL GAME TECHNOLOGY; *pg.* 957, *pg.* 1024
TRIPLE RELIEF - Health Care Product - NATURE'S SUNSHINE PRODUCTS, INC.; *pg.* 1571, *pg.* 1754
TRIPLE SEAL - Plumbing Products - RADIATOR SPECIALTY COMPANY; *pg.* 215, *pg.* 1380
TRIPLE SHINE - Professional Wax - TURTLE WAX, INC.; *pg.* 220, *pg.* 671
TRIPLE STARS - Casino Game - INTERNATIONAL GAME TECHNOLOGY; *pg.* 957, *pg.* 1024
TRIPLE STRIKE - Slots - INTERNATIONAL GAME TECHNOLOGY; *pg.* 957, *pg.* 1024
TRIPLE TREAT - Game - WMS INDUSTRIES INC.; *pg.* 593, *pg.* 666
TRIPLE TRIPLE - Hamburger Sandwiches - IN-N-OUT BURGERS, INC.; *pg.* 1732, *pg.* 111
TRIPLE TWIST - Peanut Butter Chocolate Pretzels - BOYER CANDY COMPANY INC.; *pg.* 1851, *pg.* 1514
TRIPLE WHOPPER - Burger - BURGER KING CORPORATION; *pg.* 1719, *pg.* 440
TRIPLE WILD - Slots - INTERNATIONAL GAME TECHNOLOGY; *pg.* 957, *pg.* 1024
TRIPLE WIN - Lottery Card - MISSOURI LOTTERY; *pg.* 999, *pg.* 979
TRIPLE X - Dry Cleaning & Laundry Product - ADCO, INC.; *pg.* 325, *pg.* 482
TRIPLE X DRI-SHEEN - Charge Soap - ADCO, INC.; *pg.* 325, *pg.* 482
TRIPLE XXX - Musical Instrument - PEAVEY ELECTRONICS CORPORATION; *pg.* 662, *pg.* 970
TRIPLE XXX DUNGAREES - Apparel - LUCKY BRAND DUNGAREES, INC.; *pg.* 29, *pg.* 301
TRIPLE ZESTY HOT PEPPERS - Slots - INTERNATIONAL GAME TECHNOLOGY; *pg.* 957, *pg.* 1024
TRIPLELEAN - Vitamin & Dietary Supplement - NATROL, INC.; *pg.* 1570, *pg.* 64
TRIPLET - Selective Herbicide - NUFARM AMERICAS INC; *pg.* 1798, *pg.* 552
TRIPLET - Footwear - STEVEN MADDEN, LTD.; *pg.* 1819, *pg.* 1176
TRIPLETAKE - Fishing Equipment - CABELA'S INCORPORATED; *pg.* 535, *pg.* 1019
TRIPOD - Lighting - ETHAN ALLEN INTERIORS INC.; *pg.* 924, *pg.* 343
TRIPODS - Spotting Scope - BUSHNELL OUTDOOR PRODUCTS, INC.; *pg.* 1403, *pg.* 718
TRIPOLI - Furniture - HAWORTH, INC.; *pg.* 402, *pg.* 891
TRIPOLI - Door Glass - ODL INCORPORATED; *pg.* 101, *pg.* 914
TRIPOLI - Commercial Lighting - SWIVELIER CO., INC.; *pg.* 1307, *pg.* 1142
TRIPOLY - Homebuilding Services - KB HOME; *pg.* 90, *pg.* 134
TRIPORT - Audio Product - BOSE CORPORATION; *pg.* 626, *pg.* 820
TRIPP LITE - UPS System - TRIPPE MANUFACTURING COMPANY; *pg.* 220, *pg.* 592
TRIPP LITE OMNIPRO - UPS System - TRIPPE MANUFACTURING COMPANY; *pg.* 220, *pg.* 592
TRIPP LITE OMNISMART - UPS System - TRIPPE MANUFACTURING COMPANY; *pg.* 220, *pg.* 592
TRIPPEL - Beer - NEW BELGIUM BREWING COMPANY, INC.; *pg.* 258, *pg.* 328
TRIPS - Traveling Renal Patient Service; Treatment Facility Locator - FRESENIUS MEDICAL CARE NORTH AMERICA; *pg.* 1531, *pg.* 851
TRIPSAVER - Dropout Recloser - S&C ELECTRIC COMPANY; *pg.* 1305, *pg.* 589
TRIPTIK - Driving Directions & Maps - AMERICAN AUTOMOBILE ASSOCIATION; *pg.* 1190, *pg.* 429
TRIPTONE - Dive Travel Product - MCNETT CORPORATION;

pg. 1839, pg. 1817
TRIPWIRE VIA - Computer Software - TRIPWIRE, INC.; pg. 485, pg. 1507
TRIS NITRO - Biocide - THE DOW CHEMICAL COMPANY; pg. 1157, pg. 898
TRISACRYL - Chromatography Product - PALL CORPORATION; pg. 232, pg. 1323
TRISCOPE - Medical Instrument - WALLACH SURGICAL DEVICES, INC.; pg. 1436, pg. 381
TRISCUIT - Crackers - MONDELEZ INTERNATIONAL, INC.; pg. 878, pg. 601
TRISERT - Fasteners - YARDLEY PRODUCTS CORPORATION; pg. 1391, pg. 1596
TRISHA - Clothing - ABERCROMBIE & FITCH CO.; pg. 37, pg. 1466
TRISHA - Furniture - AMISCO INDUSTRIES LTD.; pg. 913, pg. 1958
TRISKELION - Lumpbreaker - WYSSMONT CO., INC.; pg. 1390, pg. 1068
TRISMAT - Chemical Product - SPECTRUM CHEMICALS & LABORATORY PRODUCTS, INC.; pg. 1181, pg. 94
TRISTAN - Furniture - LA-Z-BOY INCORPORATED; pg. 932, pg. 901
TRISTAR - Cutlery & Cutting Boards - LIFETIME BRANDS, INC.; pg. 1127, pg. 1161
TRISTAR - Headset - PLANTRONICS, INC.; pg. 663, pg. 270
TRISTAR - Medical Instrument - WALLACH SURGICAL DEVICES, INC.; pg. 1436, pg. 381
TRISTATE BOX - Computer/Communications Interface Analyzer - ELECTRO STANDARDS LABORATORIES INC.; pg. 390, pg. 1600
TRISTEN - Clothing - ABERCROMBIE & FITCH CO.; pg. 37, pg. 1466
TRITAN - Copolyester - EASTMAN CHEMICAL COMPANY; pg. 1159, pg. 1636
TRITOME - Medical Device - COOK GROUP, INC.; pg. 1518, pg. 674
TRITON - Carpet - BEAULIEU GROUP, LLC; pg. 917, pg. 529
TRITON - Orthopedic Device - DJO SURGICAL; pg. 1525, pg. 1661
TRITON - Surfactant - THE DOW CHEMICAL COMPANY; pg. 1157, pg. 898
TRITON - Furniture - FLEXSTEEL INDUSTRIES, INC.; pg. 925, pg. 707
TRITON - Air Spray & High Volume Low Pressure Sprayers - GRACO, INC.; pg. 1342, pg. 935
TRITON - Routing Switcher - GRASS VALLEY, INC.; pg. 641, pg. 164
TRITON - Kitchen Product - KOHLER CO.; pg. 91, pg. 1862
TRITON - Chemical Product - SPECTRUM CHEMICALS & LABORATORY PRODUCTS, INC.; pg. 1181, pg. 94
TRITON EXTREME - Music Workstation/Sampler - KORG USA, INC.; pg. 556, pg. 1180
TRITON HP-250 - Butterfly Valve - HENRY PRATT COMPANY; pg. 1049, pg. 555
TRITON LE - Music Workstation - KORG USA, INC.; pg. 556, pg. 1180
TRITON RACK - Expandable Module/Sampler - KORG USA, INC.; pg. 556, pg. 1180
TRITON STUDIO - Music Workstation/Sampler - KORG USA, INC.; pg. 556, pg. 1180
TRITON XL - Butterfly Valve - HENRY PRATT COMPANY; pg. 1049, pg. 555
TRITON XR-70 - Butterfly Valve - HENRY PRATT COMPANY; pg. 1049, pg. 555
TRITONPRO - 76 Key Music Workstation Sampler - KORG USA, INC.; pg. 556, pg. 1180
TRITOP - Veterinary Antibiotic & Steroid Preparation - PFIZER INC.; pg. 1581, pg. 1278
TRITTON - Gaming Audio Headsets - MAD CATZ INTERACTIVE INC.; pg. 429, pg. 204
TRIUMPH - Furniture - ASHLEY FURNITURE INDUSTRIES, INC.; pg. 914, pg. 1852
TRIUMPH - Fan - CRAFTMADE INTERNATIONAL, INC.; pg. 1295, pg. 1670
TRIUMPH - Seeds - DOW AGROSCIENCES LLC; pg. 1156, pg. 684
TRIUMPH - Disposables - GORDON FOOD SERVICE INC.; pg. 1021, pg. 913
TRIUMPH - Electrically-Operated Piston Pumps - GRACO, INC.; pg. 1342, pg. 935
TRIUMPH - Metal Security Locks - MASTER LOCK COMPANY LLC; pg. 1055, pg. 1884
TRIUMPH - Seat Cushion - THE ROHO GROUP; pg. 1591, pg. 556
TRIUMPH - Liquid Fry Shortening - VENTURA FOODS, LLC; pg. 908, pg. 49
TRIUMPH-1 - Electrosurgical Devices - ANGIODYNAMICS, INC.; pg. 1495, pg. 1173
TRIUMPH CONTOUR - Seat Cushion - THE ROHO GROUP; pg. 1591, pg. 556
TRIUMPH IMPERIAL - Writing Instruments - SHEAFFER PEN CORPORATION; pg. 469, pg. 371
TRIUMPH LEARNING - Publisher - HAIGHTS CROSS COMMUNICATIONS, INC.; pg. 1646, pg. 1237
TRIUMPH PICTURES - Motion Picture Production Company - SONY PICTURES ENTERTAINMENT INC.; pg. 309, pg. 72
TRIUMPH TUBULAR - Oil Country Tubular Goods - RUSSEL METALS INC.; pg. 1180, pg. 1928
TRIUS - Wine - ANDREW PELLER LIMITED; pg. 1956, pg. 1920
TRIVARIS Eye Care Product - ALLERGAN, INC.; pg. 1491, pg. 106
TRIVECTION - Ovens - GENERAL ELECTRIC COMPANY; pg. 1297, pg. 347
TRIVENTO - Wine - BANFI VINTNERS; pg. 1957, pg. 1161
TRIVERMICIDE - Pet Supplies - HAPPY JACK INC.; pg. 1476, pg. 1390
TRIVEX - Optical Product - PPG INDUSTRIES, INC.; pg. 1445, pg. 1579
TRIVIAL PURSUIT - Game - HASBRO, INC.; pg. 954, pg. 1603
TRIVIAL PURSUIT - Game - WINNING MOVES GAMES, INC.; pg. 970, pg. 816
TRIVIAL PURSUIT JUNIOR - Toy & Game - HASBRO, INC.; pg. 954, pg. 1603
TRIVOLT - Oil Treater Product - CAMERON INTERNATIONAL; pg. 1151, pg. 1702
TRIVOLTMAX - Treater - CAMERON INTERNATIONAL; pg. 1151, pg. 1702
TRIWAVE - Connector & Adapter - ALLIANCE FIBER OPTIC PRODUCTS, INC.; pg. 1399, pg. 283
TRIX - Cereal - GENERAL MILLS, INC.; pg. 828, pg. 933
TRIX - Yogurt - YOPLAIT USA, INC.; pg. 910, pg. 947
TRIX YOGURT - Yogurt - GENERAL MILLS, INC.; pg. 828, pg. 933
TRIXIE - Pony Puppet - GUND, INC.; pg. 954, pg. 1056
TRIZACT - Abrasive - 3M COMPANY; pg. 1142, pg. 956
TRIZOL - Molecular Biology Product - THERMO FISHER SCIENTIFIC INC.; pg. 1602, pg. 61
TRMODE - Torsional Resonance Mode Imaging - VEECO INSTRUMENTS INC.; pg. 1434, pg. 1322
TRO LUBE - Lubricants - MALLET & COMPANY, INC.; pg. 875, pg. 1521
TROFILE - Healthcare Product - MONOGRAM BIOSCIENCES, INC.; pg. 1569, pg. 280
TROGARD FINESSE - Medical Equipment - CONMED CORPORATION; pg. 1517, pg. 1347
TROIS PISTOLES - Beer - SLEEMAN UNIBROUE QUEBEC; pg. 265, pg. 1950
TROJAN - Condoms - CHURCH & DWIGHT CO., INC.; pg. 1153, pg. 1063
TROJAN - Lubricant and Process Oil - ROCK VALLEY OIL & CHEMICAL COMPANY; pg. 1179, pg. 631
TROJANOPTIVIEW - Water Treatment System - TROJAN TECHNOLOGIES, INC.; pg. 1384, pg. 1922
TROJANUV3000 - Wastewater Treatment - TROJAN TECHNOLOGIES, INC.; pg. 1384, pg. 1922
TROJANUV3000PLUS - Automatic Wastewater Cleaning Solution - TROJAN TECHNOLOGIES, INC.; pg. 1384, pg. 1922
TROJANUV3000PTP - Wastewater Treatment for Small Communities - TROJAN TECHNOLOGIES, INC.; pg. 1384, pg. 1922
TROJANUV4000PLUS - Wastewater Treatment System - TROJAN TECHNOLOGIES, INC.; pg. 1384, pg. 1922
TROJANUVLOGIC - Water Treatment System - TROJAN TECHNOLOGIES, INC.; pg. 1384, pg. 1922
TROJANUVMAX - Water Treatment System - TROJAN TECHNOLOGIES, INC.; pg. 1384, pg. 1922
TROJANUVPHOX - Water Treatment System - TROJAN TECHNOLOGIES, INC.; pg. 1384, pg. 1922
TROJANUVSWIFT - Water Treatment System - TROJAN TECHNOLOGIES, INC.; pg. 1384, pg. 1922
TROJANUVSWIFTECT - Environmental Contaminant Treatment - TROJAN TECHNOLOGIES, INC.; pg. 1384, pg. 1922
TROLLEZE - Lubricant - BIRKO CORPORATION; pg. 1149, pg. 332
TROLLI - Candy - FERRARA CANDY CO.; pg. 1852, pg. 612
TROM - Orthopedic Product - DJO INCORPORATED; pg. 1524, pg. 302
TRONIC - Crop Oil Replacement - KALO, INC.; pg. 1796, pg. 719
TROPARTIC - Oil - CONOCOPHILLIPS; pg. 975, pg. 1703
TROPEL - Glass & Ceramic Material - CORNING INCORPORATED; pg. 1122, pg. 1154
TROPHY - Aluminum Boat - ALUMACRAFT BOAT COMPANY; pg. 1705, pg. 964
TROPHY - Binocular - BUSHNELL OUTDOOR PRODUCTS, INC.; pg. 1403, pg. 718
TROPHY - Cleaning Product - HILLYARD, INC.; pg. 331, pg. 990
TROPHY - Horse Feed - MANNA PRO CORPORATION; pg. 1478, pg. 975
TROPHY IMAGE - Deer & Elk Products - KENT NUTRITION GROUP; pg. 1477, pg. 710
TROPI - Beverages - THE COCA-COLA COMPANY; pg. 240, pg. 493
TROPI-COOL - Hypo/Hyperthermia Equipment - CINCINNATI SUB-ZERO PRODUCTS, INC.; pg. 1070, pg. 1411
TROPI-KAI - Furniture - TROPITONE FURNITURE CO., INC.; pg. 945, pg. 118
TROPIC CRAFT - Furniture - BROWN JORDAN INTERNATIONAL COMPANY; pg. 919, pg. 740
TROPIC SEAS - Dinnerware - THE HOMER LAUGHLIN CHINA COMPANY; pg. 1125, pg. 1850
TROPICAL - Beverages - THE COCA-COLA COMPANY; pg. 240, pg. 493
TROPICAL CARNIVAL - Pet Product - PETSMART, INC.; pg. 1481, pg. 18
TROPICAL ESCAPE - Body Wash - HENKEL CONSUMER GOODS; pg. 511, pg. 22
TROPICAL FRUIT ZINGER - Tea Product - CELESTIAL SEASONINGS, INC.; pg. 846, pg. 310
TROPICAL PARADISE - Carpet - BEAULIEU GROUP, LLC; pg. 917, pg. 529
TROPICAL PARADISE - Blended Fruit Juices - CHIQUITA BRANDS INTERNATIONAL, INC.; pg. 847, pg. 1365
TROPICAL PUNCH - Nail Care Product - OPI PRODUCTS INC.; pg. 518, pg. 167
TROPICAL SMARTIES - Tropical Flavored Smarties Candies - SMARTIES CANDY COMPANY; pg. 1861, pg. 1127
TROPICAL SPLENDOR - Carpet - BEAULIEU GROUP, LLC; pg. 917, pg. 529
TROPICAL STORMZ POPS - Candy - TOOTSIE ROLL INDUSTRIES, INC.; pg. 1863, pg. 591
TROPICAL TREASURES - Container Grown Plant - MONROVIA GROWERS; pg. 1797, pg. 44
TROPICAN - Pet Product - PETSMART, INC.; pg. 1481, pg. 18
TROPICANA - Food & Beverage - PEPSICO, INC.; pg. 259, pg. 1327
TROPICANA 100 - Juice - TROPICANA PRODUCTS, INC.; pg. 902, pg. 592
TROPICANA COASTAL GROVES - Lemonade - TROPICANA PRODUCTS, INC.; pg. 902, pg. 592
TROPICANA LEMONADE & PUNCHES - Soft Drink - PEPSICO, INC.; pg. 259, pg. 1327
TROPICANA LIGHT LEMONADE & PUNCHES - Soft Drink - PEPSICO, INC.; pg. 259, pg. 1327
TROPICANA PURE PREMIUM - Juice - TROPICANA PRODUCTS, INC.; pg. 902, pg. 592
TROPICANA PURE TROPICS - Juice - TROPICANA PRODUCTS, INC.; pg. 902, pg. 592
TROPICANA SEASON'S BEST - Juice & Juice Drinks - TROPICANA PRODUCTS, INC.; pg. 902, pg. 592
TROPICANA SMOOTHIES - Juices - PEPSICO, INC.; pg. 259, pg. 1327
TROPICANA SMOOTHIES - Drink - TROPICANA PRODUCTS, INC.; pg. 902, pg. 592
TROPICANA TOUCHE DE LAIT - Drink - TROPICANA PRODUCTS, INC.; pg. 902, pg. 592
TROPICANA TWISTER - Juice Blends - PEPSICO, INC.; pg. 259, pg. 1327
TROPICANA TWISTER - Juice Drink - TROPICANA PRODUCTS, INC.; pg. 902, pg. 592
TROPICANA TWISTER SODAS - Soft Drink - PEPSICO, INC.; pg. 259, pg. 1327
TROPICOP - Antifouling Paint - PETTIT PAINT COMPANY; pg. 1444, pg. 1116
TROPIGRILL - Food Product - POLLO TROPICAL INC.; pg. 1745, pg. 445

TROPIKANE - Furniture - TROPITONE FURNITURE CO., INC.; *pg.* 945, *pg.* 118
TROPIQUE - Tile - ARTISTIC TILE INC.; *pg.* 914, *pg.* 1119
TROPOS - Image Generator - CAE INC.; *pg.* 226, *pg.* 1959
TROTTERS - Women's Shoes - PHOENIX FOOTWEAR GROUP, INC.; *pg.* 1815, *pg.* 60
TROUBLE - Toy & Game - HASBRO, INC.; *pg.* 954, *pg.* 1603
TROUBLESHOOTER - Cleaner - 3M COMPANY; *pg.* 1142, *pg.* 956
TROUGHVEYOR - Food Waste Disposer - THE SALVAJOR COMPANY; *pg.* 60, *pg.* 986
TROUPE MID - Footwear - NIKE, INC.; *pg.* 1812, *pg.* 1492
TROUPER - Stage & Riser - WENGER CORPORATION; *pg.* 1307, *pg.* 952
TROUPERETTE - Entertainment Lighting Product - BALLANTYNE STRONG, INC.; *pg.* 623, *pg.* 1013
TROWLEZE - Pressed & Monolithic Refractory - RESCO PRODUCTS, INC.; *pg.* 107, *pg.* 1581
TROXYMITE - Epoxy Resurfacer - TEXAS REFINERY CORP.; *pg.* 986, *pg.* 1696
TROY - Shoes - ALLEN-EDMONDS SHOE CORP.; *pg.* 1804, *pg.* 1887
TROY - Printer - BOTTOMLINE TECHNOLOGIES (DE), INC.; *pg.* 727, *pg.* 1038
TROY-BILT - Garden Equipment - MTD PRODUCTS, INC.; *pg.* 1057, *pg.* 1478
TROY CHECKWRITING SOFTWARE - Software - TROY GROUP INC.; *pg.* 485, *pg.* 71
TROY FORTRESS CHECK PAPER - Software - TROY GROUP INC.; *pg.* 485, *pg.* 71
TROY IRD PAPER - Paper - TROY GROUP INC.; *pg.* 485, *pg.* 71
TROY SECURITY CHECK PAPER - Paper - TROY GROUP INC.; *pg.* 485, *pg.* 71
TROY SECURITY PLUS CHECK PAPER - Paper - TROY GROUP INC.; *pg.* 485, *pg.* 71
TROY UNIFILM - Rheology Modifiers - TROY CORPORATION; *pg.* 1184, *pg.* 1067
TROY200 - Wireless Print Server - TROY GROUP INC.; *pg.* 485, *pg.* 71
TROYCHEM - Metal Carboxylate Product - TROY CORPORATION; *pg.* 1184, *pg.* 1067
TROYKYD - Metalworking Fluid Additive - TROY CORPORATION; *pg.* 1184, *pg.* 1067
TROYMAX - Metal Carboxylate Product - TROY CORPORATION; *pg.* 1184, *pg.* 1067
TROYSAN - Metalworking Fluid Additive - TROY CORPORATION; *pg.* 1184, *pg.* 1067
TROYSHIELD - Metalworking Fluid Additive - TROY CORPORATION; *pg.* 1184, *pg.* 1067
TROYSOL - Additive - TROY CORPORATION; *pg.* 1184, *pg.* 1067
TROYSPERSE - Additive - TROY CORPORATION; *pg.* 1184, *pg.* 1067
TROYTHIX - Additive - TROY CORPORATION; *pg.* 1184, *pg.* 1067
TRP-P8 - Medical Product - DENDREON CORPORATION; *pg.* 1522, *pg.* 1835
TRPA03E2 - Transceivers - OPLINK COMMUNICATIONS, INC.; *pg.* 660, *pg.* 91
TRPA03I1AXYS - Transceivers - OPLINK COMMUNICATIONS, INC.; *pg.* 660, *pg.* 91
TRPA03L1EXRS - Transceivers - OPLINK COMMUNICATIONS, INC.; *pg.* 660, *pg.* 91
TRPA03L2EXWS - Transceivers - OPLINK COMMUNICATIONS, INC.; *pg.* 660, *pg.* 91
TRPA03L2HXXXX - Transceivers - OPLINK COMMUNICATIONS, INC.; *pg.* 660, *pg.* 91
TRPA03L2IXXXX - Transceivers - OPLINK COMMUNICATIONS, INC.; *pg.* 660, *pg.* 91
TRPA03MM3XAS - Transceivers - OPLINK COMMUNICATIONS, INC.; *pg.* 660, *pg.* 91
TRPA12I1AXYM - Transceivers - OPLINK COMMUNICATIONS, INC.; *pg.* 660, *pg.* 91
TRPA12L1GXRM - Transceivers - OPLINK COMMUNICATIONS, INC.; *pg.* 660, *pg.* 91
TRPA12L2GXWM - Transceivers - OPLINK COMMUNICATIONS, INC.; *pg.* 660, *pg.* 91
TRPA12L2HXXXX - Transceivers - OPLINK COMMUNICATIONS, INC.; *pg.* 660, *pg.* 91
TRPA12L2IXXXX - Transceivers - OPLINK COMMUNICATIONS, INC.; *pg.* 660, *pg.* 91
TRPA12MM3XAS - Transceivers - OPLINK COMMUNICATIONS, INC.; *pg.* 660, *pg.* 91
TRPA12S1AXAM - Transceivers - OPLINK COMMUNICATIONS, INC.; *pg.* 660, *pg.* 91
TRPA48E2IXLMX - Transceivers - OPLINK COMMUNICATIONS, INC.; *pg.* 660, *pg.* 91
TRPA48E2IXXM - Transceivers - OPLINK COMMUNICATIONS, INC.; *pg.* 660, *pg.* 91
TRPA48E2ZXLMX - Transceivers - OPLINK COMMUNICATIONS, INC.; *pg.* 660, *pg.* 91
TRPA48I1 (ROHS) - Transceivers - OPLINK COMMUNICATIONS, INC.; *pg.* 660, *pg.* 91
TRPA48I1EXYM - Transceivers - OPLINK COMMUNICATIONS, INC.; *pg.* 660, *pg.* 91
TRPA48I2EXRM - Transceivers - OPLINK COMMUNICATIONS, INC.; *pg.* 660, *pg.* 91
TRPA48I2HXXXX - Transceivers - OPLINK COMMUNICATIONS, INC.; *pg.* 660, *pg.* 91
TRPA48I2IXXXX - Transceivers - OPLINK COMMUNICATIONS, INC.; *pg.* 660, *pg.* 91
TRPA48L1HXRM - Transceivers - OPLINK COMMUNICATIONS, INC.; *pg.* 660, *pg.* 91
TRPA48L2BXWM - Transceivers - OPLINK COMMUNICATIONS, INC.; *pg.* 660, *pg.* 91
TRPA48L2IXXXX - Transceivers - OPLINK COMMUNICATIONS, INC.; *pg.* 660, *pg.* 91
TRPA48S1 (ROHS) - Transceivers - OPLINK COMMUNICATIONS, INC.; *pg.* 660, *pg.* 91
TRPA48S1XXAM - Transceivers - OPLINK COMMUNICATIONS, INC.; *pg.* 660, *pg.* 91
TRPAFELXAXSS - Transceivers - OPLINK COMMUNICATIONS, INC.; *pg.* 660, *pg.* 91
TRPAFESMKXSS - Transceivers - OPLINK COMMUNICATIONS, INC.; *pg.* 660, *pg.* 91
TRPAG1EXJXNM - Transceivers - OPLINK COMMUNICATIONS, INC.; *pg.* 660, *pg.* 91
TRPAG1LXDXBM - Transceivers - OPLINK COMMUNICATIONS, INC.; *pg.* 660, *pg.* 91
TRPAG1SXLXES - Transceivers - OPLINK COMMUNICATIONS, INC.; *pg.* 660, *pg.* 91
TRPAG1VXIBMS - Transceivers - OPLINK COMMUNICATIONS, INC.; *pg.* 660, *pg.* 91
TRPAG1VXIXXXX - Transceivers - OPLINK COMMUNICATIONS, INC.; *pg.* 660, *pg.* 91
TRPAG1YXHXOM - Transceivers - OPLINK COMMUNICATIONS, INC.; *pg.* 660, *pg.* 91
TRPAG1YXHXXXX - Transceivers - OPLINK COMMUNICATIONS, INC.; *pg.* 660, *pg.* 91
TRPAG1YXZXAXMX - Transceivers - OPLINK COMMUNICATIONS, INC.; *pg.* 660, *pg.* 91
TRPAG1ZXIXGM - Transceivers - OPLINK COMMUNICATIONS, INC.; *pg.* 660, *pg.* 91
TRPAG1ZXIXXXX - Transceivers - OPLINK COMMUNICATIONS, INC.; *pg.* 660, *pg.* 91
TRPBFELXTXSX - Transceivers - OPLINK COMMUNICATIONS, INC.; *pg.* 660, *pg.* 91
TRPBG1LXDBXSX - Transceivers - OPLINK COMMUNICATIONS, INC.; *pg.* 660, *pg.* 91
TRPE03AI1C000E1 - Transceivers - OPLINK COMMUNICATIONS, INC.; *pg.* 660, *pg.* 91
TRPE03AI1I000E1 - Transceivers - OPLINK COMMUNICATIONS, INC.; *pg.* 660, *pg.* 91
TRPE03EL1C000E1 - Transceivers - OPLINK COMMUNICATIONS, INC.; *pg.* 660, *pg.* 91
TRPE03EL1I000E1 - Transceivers - OPLINK COMMUNICATIONS, INC.; *pg.* 660, *pg.* 91
TRPE03EL2C000E1 - Transceivers - OPLINK COMMUNICATIONS, INC.; *pg.* 660, *pg.* 91
TRPE03EL2I000E1 - Transceivers - OPLINK COMMUNICATIONS, INC.; *pg.* 660, *pg.* 91
TRPE12AI1C000E2 - Transceivers - OPLINK COMMUNICATIONS, INC.; *pg.* 660, *pg.* 91
TRPE12AI1I000E2 - Transceivers - OPLINK COMMUNICATIONS, INC.; *pg.* 660, *pg.* 91
TRPE12AS1C000E2 - Transceivers - OPLINK COMMUNICATIONS, INC.; *pg.* 660, *pg.* 91
TRPE12AS1I000E2 - Transceivers - OPLINK COMMUNICATIONS, INC.; *pg.* 660, *pg.* 91
TRPE12GL1C000E2 - Transceivers - OPLINK COMMUNICATIONS, INC.; *pg.* 660, *pg.* 91
TRPE12GL1I000E2 - Transceivers - OPLINK COMMUNICATIONS, INC.; *pg.* 660, *pg.* 91
TRPE12GL2C000E2 - Transceivers - OPLINK COMMUNICATIONS, INC.; *pg.* 660, *pg.* 91
TRPE12GL2I000E2 - Transceivers - OPLINK COMMUNICATIONS, INC.; *pg.* 660, *pg.* 91
TRPE48DS1C000E2 - Transceivers - OPLINK COMMUNICATIONS, INC.; *pg.* 660, *pg.* 91
TRPE48DS1I000E2 - Transceivers - OPLINK COMMUNICATIONS, INC.; *pg.* 660, *pg.* 91
TRPE48FI1C000E2 - Transceivers - OPLINK COMMUNICATIONS, INC.; *pg.* 660, *pg.* 91
TRPE48FI1I000E2 - Transceivers - OPLINK COMMUNICATIONS, INC.; *pg.* 660, *pg.* 91
TRPE48FI2C000E2 - Transceivers - OPLINK COMMUNICATIONS, INC.; *pg.* 660, *pg.* 91
TRPE48FI2I000E2 - Transceivers - OPLINK COMMUNICATIONS, INC.; *pg.* 660, *pg.* 91
TRPE48IL1C000E2 - Transceivers - OPLINK COMMUNICATIONS, INC.; *pg.* 660, *pg.* 91
TRPE48IL1I000E2 - Transceivers - OPLINK COMMUNICATIONS, INC.; *pg.* 660, *pg.* 91
TRPE48IL2C000E2 - Transceivers - OPLINK COMMUNICATIONS, INC.; *pg.* 660, *pg.* 91
TRPE48IL2I000E2 - Transceivers - OPLINK COMMUNICATIONS, INC.; *pg.* 660, *pg.* 91
TRPE48KE2C00010 - Transceivers - OPLINK COMMUNICATIONS, INC.; *pg.* 660, *pg.* 91
TRPE48KE2C00020 - Transceivers - OPLINK COMMUNICATIONS, INC.; *pg.* 660, *pg.* 91
TRPE48KE2C00030 - Transceivers - OPLINK COMMUNICATIONS, INC.; *pg.* 660, *pg.* 91
TRPE48KE2C00040 - Transceivers - OPLINK COMMUNICATIONS, INC.; *pg.* 660, *pg.* 91
TRPE48KE2C00050 - Transceivers - OPLINK COMMUNICATIONS, INC.; *pg.* 660, *pg.* 91
TRPE48KE2C00060 - Transceivers - OPLINK COMMUNICATIONS, INC.; *pg.* 660, *pg.* 91
TRPE48KE2C00070 - Transceivers - OPLINK COMMUNICATIONS, INC.; *pg.* 660, *pg.* 91
TRPE48KE2C00080 - Transceivers - OPLINK COMMUNICATIONS, INC.; *pg.* 660, *pg.* 91
TRPE48KE2C000E2 - Transceivers - OPLINK COMMUNICATIONS, INC.; *pg.* 660, *pg.* 91
TRPE48KE2E00010 - Transceivers - OPLINK COMMUNICATIONS, INC.; *pg.* 660, *pg.* 91
TRPE48KE2E00020 - Transceivers - OPLINK COMMUNICATIONS, INC.; *pg.* 660, *pg.* 91
TRPE48KE2E00030 - Transceivers - OPLINK COMMUNICATIONS, INC.; *pg.* 660, *pg.* 91
TRPE48KE2E00040 - Transceivers - OPLINK COMMUNICATIONS, INC.; *pg.* 660, *pg.* 91
TRPE48KE2E00050 - Transceivers - OPLINK COMMUNICATIONS, INC.; *pg.* 660, *pg.* 91
TRPE48KE2E00060 - Transceivers - OPLINK COMMUNICATIONS, INC.; *pg.* 660, *pg.* 91
TRPE48KE2E00070 - Transceivers - OPLINK COMMUNICATIONS, INC.; *pg.* 660, *pg.* 91
TRPE48KE2E00080 - Transceivers - OPLINK COMMUNICATIONS, INC.; *pg.* 660, *pg.* 91
TRPE48KE2E000E2 - Transceivers - OPLINK COMMUNICATIONS, INC.; *pg.* 660, *pg.* 91
TRPEG1CLXC000E2 - Transceivers - OPLINK COMMUNICATIONS, INC.; *pg.* 660, *pg.* 91
TRPEG1CLXI000E2 - Transceivers - OPLINK COMMUNICATIONS, INC.; *pg.* 660, *pg.* 91
TRPEG1EEXC000E2 - Transceivers - OPLINK COMMUNICATIONS, INC.; *pg.* 660, *pg.* 91
TRPEG1EEXI000E2 - Transceivers - OPLINK COMMUNICATIONS, INC.; *pg.* 660, *pg.* 91
TRPEG1HYXC000E2 - Transceivers - OPLINK COMMUNICATIONS, INC.; *pg.* 660, *pg.* 91
TRPEG1HYXI000E2 - Transceivers - OPLINK COMMUNICATIONS, INC.; *pg.* 660, *pg.* 91
TRPEG1JZXC000E2 - Transceivers - OPLINK COMMUNICATIONS, INC.; *pg.* 660, *pg.* 91
TRPEG1JZXI000E2 - Transceivers - OPLINK COMMUNICATIONS, INC.; *pg.* 660, *pg.* 91
TRPEG1KVXC000E1 - Transceivers - OPLINK COMMUNICATIONS, INC.; *pg.* 660, *pg.* 91
TRPEG1KVXE000E1 - Transceivers - OPLINK COMMUNICATIONS, INC.; *pg.* 660, *pg.* 91
TRPNFEMM3XSS - Transceivers - OPLINK COMMUNICATIONS, INC.; *pg.* 660, *pg.* 91
TRPW48E2OXXXX - Transceivers - OPLINK COMMUNICATIONS, INC.; *pg.* 660, *pg.* 91
TRPW48L2OXXXX - Transceivers - OPLINK COMMUNICATIONS, INC.; *pg.* 660, *pg.* 91
TRS - Software - TRIMBLE NAVIGATION LIMITED; *pg.* 1384, *pg.* 288
TRS ENVIRONMENTAL - Rents, Leases & Sells Environmental Test Equipment for Soil, Air & Water - MCGRATH RENTCORP; *pg.* 1104, *pg.* 122

TRS1 - Adapter - ANDREA ELECTRONICS CORPORATION; *pg.* 617, *pg.* 1143
TRSIV - Pure Non-Metallic Silicon-Based Thermoplastic Chemicals - DOW CORNING CORPORATION; *pg.* 1159, *pg.* 900
TRSRENTELCO - Electronic Test Equipment Rentals - MCGRATH RENTCORP; *pg.* 1104, *pg.* 122
TRU - French Restaurant - LETTUCE ENTERTAIN YOU ENTERPRISES, INC.; *pg.* 1735, *pg.* 580
TRU ALOE - Nutritional Product - RBC LIFE SCIENCES, INC.; *pg.* 1588, *pg.* 1723
TRU-BALLISTIC - Fiber - HONEYWELL INTERNATIONAL INC.; *pg.* 407, *pg.* 1088
TRU-BOND - Roofing Shingles with Sealant - OWENS CORNING; *pg.* 102, *pg.* 1476
TRU-BORE - Technology - CALLAWAY GOLF COMPANY; *pg.* 1829, *pg.* 58
TRU-C BIOCOMPLEX - Dietary Supplement - NOW HEALTH GROUP, INC.; *pg.* 1576, *pg.* 557
TRU-CHANNEL - Window & Door - HARVEY INDUSTRIES, INC.; *pg.* 86, *pg.* 851
TRU FACE - Skin Care Product - NU SKIN ENTERPRISES, INC.; *pg.* 518, *pg.* 1755
TRU-FEED 50 - Automatic Powdered Detergent Cleansing System - ECOLAB INC.; *pg.* 329, *pg.* 960
TRU-FIT - Home Care Product - BECTON, DICKINSON & COMPANY; *pg.* 1501, *pg.* 1068
TRU-FIT - Patient Handling Equipment - STRYKER CORPORATION; *pg.* 1598, *pg.* 894
TRU-FLATE - Air Accessories - PLEWS/EDELMANN; *pg.* 215, *pg.* 607
TRU-FLO - Mass Flow Control - MKS INSTRUMENTS, INC.; *pg.* 1362, *pg.* 781
TRU-FLOW - Data Traffic Management - SIERRA WIRELESS INCORPORATED; *pg.* 673, *pg.* 1909
TRU-FORM - Building Products - BOISE CASCADE HOLDINGS, L.L.C.; *pg.* 1453, *pg.* 546
TRU-GLAZE - Epoxy Coatings - AKZONOBEL DECORATIVE PAINTS U.S.; *pg.* 1439, *pg.* 1474
TRU-GLAZE 2 - Waterborne Epoxy Coatings - AKZONOBEL DECORATIVE PAINTS U.S.; *pg.* 1439, *pg.* 1474
TRU-GLAZE 4 - Epoxy Coatings - AKZONOBEL DECORATIVE PAINTS U.S.; *pg.* 1439, *pg.* 1474
TRU HOODIA COMPLEX - Dietary Supplement - NOW HEALTH GROUP, INC.; *pg.* 1576, *pg.* 557
TRU-INSTALL - Plug & Play Software - SIERRA WIRELESS INCORPORATED; *pg.* 673, *pg.* 1909
TRU-LEDE - Thread Forming Taps - KENNAMETAL IPG; *pg.* 1353, *pg.* 1615
TRU-LEVEL - Bath & Plumbing Product - JACUZZI BRANDS CORPORATION; *pg.* 554, *pg.* 65
TRU-LOCATE - Antenna Technology - SIERRA WIRELESS INCORPORATED; *pg.* 673, *pg.* 1909
TRU-LOK - Measuring Product - THE L.S. STARRETT COMPANY; *pg.* 1421, *pg.* 783
TRU-MARK - Cable - GENERAL CABLE CORPORATION; *pg.* 83, *pg.* 729
TRU-PLY - Building Products - BOISE CASCADE HOLDINGS, L.L.C.; *pg.* 1453, *pg.* 546
TRU POINTE - Refrigerant Leak Detector - BACHARACH INC.; *pg.* 1400, *pg.* 1556
TRU-POWERSAVE - Power Management - SIERRA WIRELESS INCORPORATED; *pg.* 673, *pg.* 1909
TRU-PULL - Orthopedic Product - DJO INCORPORATED; *pg.* 1524, *pg.* 302
TRU-TEST - Paint - TRUE VALUE COMPANY; *pg.* 1065, *pg.* 592
TRU-TINT - Carnations - DENVER WHOLESALE FLORISTS COMPANY; *pg.* 1794, *pg.* 319
TRU-TORQUE - Automatic Torque Control System - SMITH INTERNATIONAL, INC.; *pg.* 1377, *pg.* 1715
TRU-TRAC - Orthopedic Device - DJO SURGICAL; *pg.* 1525, *pg.* 1661
TRU-TUNE - Auto Tune - WATLOW ELECTRIC MANUFACTURING COMPANY; *pg.* 1078, *pg.* 1004
TRU-VAL - Beverage - GREEN SPOT, INC.; *pg.* 251, *pg.* 68
TRU VUE - Optical Glass - APOGEE ENTERPRISES, INC.; *pg.* 67, *pg.* 930
TRUBASE - Dental Product - DENTSPLY INTERNATIONAL INC.; *pg.* 1522, *pg.* 1596
TRUBLEND - Dental Product - DENTSPLY INTERNATIONAL INC.; *pg.* 1522, *pg.* 1596
TRUCK PAC - Battery Charging Product - CLORE AUTOMOTIVE LLC; *pg.* 202, *pg.* 716
TRUCKCARE - Services - PETERBILT MOTORS CO.; *pg.* 188, *pg.* 1691
TRUCKEX - Muffler - AP EXHAUST PRODUCTS, INC.; *pg.* 199, *pg.* 1373
TRUCKHYDE - Tonneau Cover - SHUR-CO, INC.; *pg.* 110, *pg.* 1626
TRUCKING - Magazine - RANDALL-REILLY PUBLISHING COMPANY LLC; *pg.* 1679, *pg.* 8
TRUCKING TIMES & SPORT UTILITY - Business-to-Business Magazine - WIESNER PUBLISHING, LLC; *pg.* 1702, *pg.* 328
TRUCKRAIL EXPRESS - Truck Transportation - SCHNEIDER; *pg.* 1922, *pg.* 1859
TRUCONVEC - Kitchen Appliance - VIKING RANGE CORPORATION; *pg.* 61, *pg.* 968
TRUE ACCESS - Software System - ALCATEL-LUCENT; *pg.* 615, *pg.* 1094
TRUE ALARM - Safety System - TYCO SIMPLEXGRINNELL LP; *pg.* 682, *pg.* 859
TRUE BALANCE - Bedding - JAMISON BEDDING, INC.; *pg.* 930, *pg.* 1651
TRUE BALANCE - Dietary Supplement - NOW HEALTH GROUP, INC.; *pg.* 1576, *pg.* 557
TRUE BLUE - Power Supply Product - ANTEC INCORPORATED; *pg.* 350, *pg.* 90
TRUE BLUE A CLAMP - Medical Clamp - DRAVON MEDICAL, INC.; *pg.* 1525, *pg.* 1497
TRUE BLUE T CLAMP - Medical Clamp - DRAVON MEDICAL, INC.; *pg.* 1525, *pg.* 1497
TRUE COLOR - Beauty Product - AVON PRODUCTS, INC.; *pg.* 500, *pg.* 1198
TRUE COLOR - Lighting - OTTLITE; *pg.* 1303, *pg.* 475
TRUE COST TO OWN - Pricing System - EDMUNDS, INC.; *pg.* 1241, *pg.* 273
TRUE CREDENTIALS FOR ADOBE - Online Transaction Security Product - VERISIGN, INC.; *pg.* 488, *pg.* 1799
TRUE DIGITAL - Digital Sensor - ION GEOPHYSICAL CORPORATION; *pg.* 1350, *pg.* 1708
TRUE EARNINGS - Credit Cards - AMERICAN EXPRESS COMPANY; *pg.* 712, *pg.* 1190
TRUE/FIX - Orthopedic Product - DJO SURGICAL; *pg.* 1525, *pg.* 1661
TRUE/FLEX - Orthopedic Product - DJO SURGICAL; *pg.* 1525, *pg.* 1661
TRUE FOCUS - Dietary Supplement - NOW HEALTH GROUP, INC.; *pg.* 1576, *pg.* 557
TRUE FRIENDS BOUQUET - Floral Bouquet - FTD GROUP, INC.; *pg.* 1795, *pg.* 608
TRUE GRACE - Platinum Credit Card - AMERICAN EXPRESS COMPANY; *pg.* 712, *pg.* 1190
TRUE GRIP - Ladder Product - WERNER HOLDING CO.; *pg.* 121, *pg.* 1534
TRUE GRIT - Nutshell - HAMMONS PRODUCTS COMPANY; *pg.* 1855, *pg.* 1007
TRUE ILLUSION - Concealer - MAYBELLINE LLC; *pg.* 516, *pg.* 1257
TRUE/LOK - Orthopedic Product - DJO SURGICAL; *pg.* 1525, *pg.* 1661
TRUE LOVE - Carpet - BEAULIEU GROUP, LLC; *pg.* 917, *pg.* 529
TRUE NORTH - Healthy Snacks - FRITO-LAY NORTH AMERICA, INC.; *pg.* 1853, *pg.* 1730
TRUE NORTH VODKA - Alcoholic Beverage - GRAND TRAVERSE DISTILLERY; *pg.* 1964, *pg.* 909
TRUE PINE - Household Product - BLUE CROSS LABORATORIES; *pg.* 326, *pg.* 277
TRUE PIXEL - Electronic Sign System - DAKTRONICS, INC.; *pg.* 633, *pg.* 1624
TRUE PORE-FECTION - Beauty Product - AVON PRODUCTS, INC.; *pg.* 500, *pg.* 1198
TRUE POTPURRI - Cleaner & Deodorizer - BLUE CROSS LABORATORIES; *pg.* 326, *pg.* 277
TRUE PROFESSIONAL - Cutting Tools - ACME UNITED CORPORATION; *pg.* 1040, *pg.* 346
TRUE RECIPE - Potatoes - J.R. SIMPLOT COMPANY; *pg.* 867, *pg.* 547
TRUE SHUTDOWN - Electronic Technology - MAXIM INTEGRATED PRODUCTS, INC.; *pg.* 653, *pg.* 247
TRUE SILVER - Mattress - SELECT COMFORT CORPORATION; *pg.* 942, *pg.* 942
TRUE SOA - Service Oriented Architecture - EPICOR SOFTWARE CORPORATION; *pg.* 393, *pg.* 110
TRUE SPOT - Smoke Test Kit - BACHARACH INC.; *pg.* 1400, *pg.* 1556
TRUE STORIES - Cable Television Channel - STARZ ENTERTAINMENT, LLC; *pg.* 310, *pg.* 327
TRUE VALUE HARDWARE STORES - Retail Stores - TRUE VALUE COMPANY; *pg.* 1065, *pg.* 592
TRUE WHITE GEL - Health Care Product - HEALTH PRODUCTS CORPORATION; *pg.* 1540, *pg.* 1356
TRUE WIND - Footwear - K-SWISS; *pg.* 1837, *pg.* 306
TRUE20 - In-Clinic Lab Systems - HESKA CORPORATION; *pg.* 1542, *pg.* 335
TRUE2GO - Blood Glucose Monitor - NIPRO DIAGNOSTICS, INC.; *pg.* 1573, *pg.* 426
TRUEADC - Software - RUDOLPH TECHNOLOGIES, INC.; *pg.* 669, *pg.* 918
TRUEALLOCATION - Software Solution - CALLIDUS SOFTWARE INC.; *pg.* 368, *pg.* 183
TRUEBLUE - Electronic Monitoring Services - BROOKS AUTOMATION, INC.; *pg.* 1320, *pg.* 813
TRUEBLUE - Air Transportation Service - JETBLUE AIRWAYS CORPORATION; *pg.* 1913, *pg.* 1174
TRUEBLUE - Blueberry Beverage - LEADING BRANDS, INC.; *pg.* 1026, *pg.* 1911
TRUEBLUE - Hot Melt Replacement Part - NORDSON CORPORATION; *pg.* 1365, *pg.* 1480
TRUECAREERS - Magazine - SLM CORPORATION; *pg.* 804, *pg.* 388
TRUECHANNEL - Software - CALLIDUS SOFTWARE INC.; *pg.* 368, *pg.* 183
TRUECOMP - Software - CALLIDUS SOFTWARE INC.; *pg.* 368, *pg.* 183
TRUECOMP ARCHITECTURE - Scalable Compensation Administration Module - CALLIDUS SOFTWARE INC.; *pg.* 368, *pg.* 183
TRUECOMP DATAMART - Software - CALLIDUS SOFTWARE INC.; *pg.* 368, *pg.* 183
TRUECOMP GRID - Software - CALLIDUS SOFTWARE INC.; *pg.* 368, *pg.* 183
TRUECOMP MANAGER - Software - CALLIDUS SOFTWARE INC.; *pg.* 368, *pg.* 183
TRUECONNECTION - Software Solution - CALLIDUS SOFTWARE INC.; *pg.* 368, *pg.* 183
TRUECONTROL - Power Supply Product - ANTEC INCORPORATED; *pg.* 350, *pg.* 90
TRUECW - Medical Laser System - IRIDEX CORPORATION; *pg.* 648, *pg.* 160
TRUEDGE - Manufacturing Process for Metal Seals - WEST PHARMACEUTICAL SERVICES, INC.; *pg.* 1472, *pg.* 1532
TRUEDRIVE - Electronic Products - TEXAS INSTRUMENTS INCORPORATED; *pg.* 679, *pg.* 1688
TRUEFFS - Software - SANDISK CORPORATION; *pg.* 465, *pg.* 147
TRUEFILL - First Test - NIPRO DIAGNOSTICS, INC.; *pg.* 1573, *pg.* 426
TRUEFINISH - Coating Product - PPG INDUSTRIES, INC.; *pg.* 1445, *pg.* 1579
TRUEFIRE - Integrated Circuits - AVAGO TECHNOLOGIES; *pg.* 358, *pg.* 238
TRUEFOUNDATION - Software Solution - CALLIDUS SOFTWARE INC.; *pg.* 368, *pg.* 183
TRUEIMAGE - Software - FEI COMPANY; *pg.* 1413, *pg.* 1498
TRUEINFORMATION - Software - CALLIDUS SOFTWARE INC.; *pg.* 368, *pg.* 183
TRUEINTEGRATION - Software - CALLIDUS SOFTWARE INC.; *pg.* 368, *pg.* 183
TRUELEAD - Network Monitoring Tool - LOOKSMART, LTD.; *pg.* 1265, *pg.* 221
TRUEMATCH - Office Product - HAWORTH, INC.; *pg.* 402, *pg.* 891
TRUEMBO - Software Solution - CALLIDUS SOFTWARE INC.; *pg.* 368, *pg.* 183
TRUENET - Office Product - HAWORTH, INC.; *pg.* 402, *pg.* 891
TRUEPERFORMANCE - Software - CALLIDUS SOFTWARE INC.; *pg.* 368, *pg.* 183
TRUEPERFORMANCE INDEX - Software Solution - CALLIDUS SOFTWARE INC.; *pg.* 368, *pg.* 183
TRUEPERFORMANCE INDICATOR - Software Solution - CALLIDUS SOFTWARE INC.; *pg.* 368, *pg.* 183
TRUEPHY - Integrated Circuits - AVAGO TECHNOLOGIES; *pg.* 358, *pg.* 238
TRUEPOWER - Line of PC Power Supplies - ANTEC INCORPORATED; *pg.* 350, *pg.* 90
TRUEPRODUCER - Software Solution - CALLIDUS SOFTWARE INC.; *pg.* 368, *pg.* 183
TRUEQUOTA - Software Solution - CALLIDUS SOFTWARE INC.; *pg.* 368, *pg.* 183
TRUEREAD - Blood Glucose Monitor - NIPRO

DIAGNOSTICS, INC.; *pg.* 1573, *pg.* 426
TRUEREFERRAL - Software - CALLIDUS SOFTWARE INC.; *pg.* 368, *pg.* 183
TRUERESOLUTION - Software - CALLIDUS SOFTWARE INC.; *pg.* 368, *pg.* 183
TRUERESULT - Blood Glucose Monitor - NIPRO DIAGNOSTICS, INC.; *pg.* 1573, *pg.* 426
TRUERH - Mechanical & Electrical System - JOHNSON CONTROLS, INC.; *pg.* 209, *pg.* 1876
TRUESAMPLE - Software - METRIXLAB; *pg.* 1266, *pg.* 223
TRUESCALE - Probe Technology - FORMFACTOR, INC.; *pg.* 1882, *pg.* 122
TRUESERIAL - Ethernet Connection - PERLE SYSTEMS LIMITED; *pg.* 454, *pg.* 1924
TRUESERVICE - Software - CALLIDUS SOFTWARE INC.; *pg.* 368, *pg.* 183
TRUESERVICE+ - Software Solution - CALLIDUS SOFTWARE INC.; *pg.* 368, *pg.* 183
TRUESTORE - Integrated Circuits - AVAGO TECHNOLOGIES; *pg.* 358, *pg.* 238
TRUESUPPORT - Software - CALLIDUS SOFTWARE INC.; *pg.* 368, *pg.* 183
TRUETARGET - Software Solution - CALLIDUS SOFTWARE INC.; *pg.* 368, *pg.* 183
TRUETEST - Blood Glucose Monitor - NIPRO DIAGNOSTICS, INC.; *pg.* 1573, *pg.* 426
TRUETOUCH - Touchscreen Solutions - CYPRESS SEMICONDUCTOR CORPORATION; *pg.* 1326, *pg.* 243
TRUETRACK - Diabetes Monitoring Product - NIPRO DIAGNOSTICS, INC.; *pg.* 1573, *pg.* 426
TRUETRACK SMART SYSTEM - Blood Glucose System - NIPRO DIAGNOSTICS, INC.; *pg.* 1573, *pg.* 426
TRUETRACKING - Software - PASSUR AEROSPACE, INC.; *pg.* 233, *pg.* 376
TRUETUBE - Analyzer Tubing - O'BRIEN CORPORATION; *pg.* 1366, *pg.* 1001
TRUETYPE - Font Technology - APPLE INC.; *pg.* 350, *pg.* 73
TRUEUSE - Fleet Utilization Analysis Tools - I.D. SYSTEMS, INC.; *pg.* 643, *pg.* 1134
TRUEWAVE - Programmable AC & DC Power - AMETEK PROGRAMMABLE POWER, INC.; *pg.* 616, *pg.* 200
TRUFLE - Footwear - STEVEN MADDEN, LTD.; *pg.* 1819, *pg.* 1176
TRUFLOW - Polymerized Asphalt Coating - OWENS CORNING; *pg.* 102, *pg.* 1476
TRUFOCUS - Medical Laser System - IRIDEX CORPORATION; *pg.* 648, *pg.* 160
TRUFORM - Graphics Card - ADVANCED MICRO DEVICES, INC.; *pg.* 613, *pg.* 282
TRUFORM - Coating Product - PPG INDUSTRIES, INC.; *pg.* 1445, *pg.* 1579
TRUGREEN - Lawn Care Products & Services - TRUGREEN-CHEMLAWN; *pg.* 1801, *pg.* 1647
TRUGREEN-CHEMLAWN - Lawn Care - THE SERVICEMASTER COMPANY, LLC; *pg.* 335, *pg.* 1646
TRUGREEN LANDCARE - Commercial Landscaping - THE SERVICEMASTER COMPANY, LLC; *pg.* 335, *pg.* 1646
TRUGUARD - Asphalt-Based Sealant for Pavements - OWENS CORNING; *pg.* 102, *pg.* 1476
TRULO - Asphalt - OWENS CORNING; *pg.* 102, *pg.* 1476
TRULY YOURS - Carpet - BEAULIEU GROUP, LLC; *pg.* 917, *pg.* 529
TRUMBLE GREETINGS - Greeting Cards & Gifts - LEANIN' TREE, INC.; *pg.* 1658, *pg.* 311
TRUMBULL - Asphalt - OWENS CORNING; *pg.* 102, *pg.* 1476
TRUMELT - Asphalt - OWENS CORNING; *pg.* 102, *pg.* 1476
TRUMOTIONHD - Image Processing Product - SEMTECH CORPORATION GENNUM PRODUCTS; *pg.* 671, *pg.* 1919
TRUMP MARINA - Hotel & Casino - TRUMP ENTERTAINMENT RESORTS, INC.; *pg.* 1117, *pg.* 1041
TRUMP ONE - Trump Card - TRUMP ENTERTAINMENT RESORTS, INC.; *pg.* 1117, *pg.* 1041
TRUMP PLAZA - Hotel & Casino - TRUMP ENTERTAINMENT RESORTS, INC.; *pg.* 1117, *pg.* 1041
TRUMP TAJ MAHAL - Hotel & Casino - TRUMP ENTERTAINMENT RESORTS, INC.; *pg.* 1117, *pg.* 1041
TRUMPET - Educational Materials - SCHOLASTIC INC.; *pg.* 1683, *pg.* 1288
TRUMPET CLUB SPECIAL EDITION - Educational Materials - SCHOLASTIC INC.; *pg.* 1683, *pg.* 1288
TRUMPF - Fabricating Machinery - TRUMPF INC.; *pg.* 1385, *pg.* 349
TRUNK 2000 - Fume Exhauster - DONALDSON COMPANY, INC.; *pg.* 1329, *pg.* 917
TRUNK & CO. - Backpacks, Body Bags & Duffles - SAMSONITE CORPORATION; *pg.* 11, *pg.* 830
TRUNZ - Meat Products - WORLDWIDE FOOD PRODUCTS INC.; *pg.* 910, *pg.* 1170
TRUPATH - Network Technology - APPNETA; *pg.* 352, *pg.* 1909
TRUPAVE - Paving Mat - OWENS CORNING; *pg.* 102, *pg.* 1476
TRUPOINT - Assay Kit - PERKINELMER, INC.; *pg.* 1426, *pg.* 853
TRUPWR - Detector - ANALOG DEVICES, INC.; *pg.* 617, *pg.* 839
TRUS BUT VERIFY - Slogan - OWENS ONLINE, INC.; *pg.* 1273, *pg.* 475
TRUSCAN - Software - SYMANTEC CORPORATION; *pg.* 478, *pg.* 161
TRUSCIENT - Veterinary Preparation - PFIZER INC.; *pg.* 1581, *pg.* 1278
TRUSCOTT - Wine - WEIBEL, INC.; *pg.* 1972, *pg.* 122
TRUSEAL - Plastics Product - AEP INDUSTRIES INC.; *pg.* 1878, *pg.* 1085
TRUSEAR - Kitchen Appliance - VIKING RANGE CORPORATION; *pg.* 61, *pg.* 968
TRUSPEC - Motor Vehicle Product - JASON INDUSTRIES, INC.; *pg.* 208, *pg.* 1875
TRUSPEC - Laboratory Equipment - LECO CORPORATION; *pg.* 1355, *pg.* 906
TRUSS-TECH - Commercial Lighting - SWIVELIER CO., INC.; *pg.* 1307, *pg.* 1142
TRUSS TROUPER - Entertainment Lighting Product - BALLANTYNE STRONG, INC.; *pg.* 623, *pg.* 1013
TRUSST - Footwear - STEVEN MADDEN, LTD.; *pg.* 1819, *pg.* 1176
TRUST - Track - COILCRAFT, INC.; *pg.* 1324, *pg.* 562
TRUST & CONFIDENCE - Tagline - MONRO MUFFLER BRAKE, INC.; *pg.* 213, *pg.* 1336
TRUST. COMMITMENT. RESULTS. - Slogan - KEY TRONIC CORPORATION; *pg.* 424, *pg.* 1844
TRUST INTERNATIONAL - Reservation System - TRAVELPORT LIMITED; *pg.* 1925, *pg.* 521
TRUST NETWORK - Telecommunication Product - VERISIGN, INC.; *pg.* 488, *pg.* 1799
TRUST. SCIENCE. INNOVATION - Tagline - TSI INCORPORATED; *pg.* 1432, *pg.* 965
TRUST THE MIDAS TOUCH - Slogan - MIDAS, INC.; *pg.* 212, *pg.* 620
TRUST THE PLUS - Slogan - LCA-VISION INC.; *pg.* 1419, *pg.* 1416
TRUSTCO - Financial Services - TRUSTCO BANK CORP NY; *pg.* 811, *pg.* 1162
TRUSTCONNECTOR - Software - PHOENIX TECHNOLOGIES LTD.; *pg.* 454, *pg.* 147
TRUSTED BY LEADERS - Slogan - ECAIN COMMUNICATIONS CORPORATION; *pg.* 1242, *pg.* 284
TRUSTED CHOICE - Relief Fund - INDEPENDENT INSURANCE AGENTS & BROKERS OF AMERICA, INC.; *pg.* 144, *pg.* 1770
THE TRUSTED CHOICE FOR ONLINE BUSINESS - Slogan - AKAMAI TECHNOLOGIES, INC.; *pg.* 1226, *pg.* 807
TRUSTED COMMERCE - Computer Software - TRUSTWAVE HOLDINGS, INC.; *pg.* 1285, *pg.* 593
TRUSTED NOTARY - Certification - NATIONAL NOTARY ASSOCIATION; *pg.* 150, *pg.* 64
TRUSTED. PROVEN. - Slogan - AUTONOMY PLEASANTON; *pg.* 358, *pg.* 183
TRUSTED TO BRING NETWORKS TOGETHER - Tag Line - NEUSTAR, INC.; *pg.* 1872, *pg.* 1807
TRUSTEDAPP - Computer Software - TRUSTWAVE HOLDINGS, INC.; *pg.* 1285, *pg.* 593
TRUSTEDCORE - Data Security Software - PHOENIX TECHNOLOGIES LTD.; *pg.* 454, *pg.* 147
TRUSTEDDWG - Functionality - AUTODESK INC.; *pg.* 356, *pg.* 257
TRUSTEDFLASH - Electronic Units - SANDISK CORPORATION; *pg.* 465, *pg.* 147
TRUSTEDSENTRY - Computer Software - TRUSTWAVE HOLDINGS, INC.; *pg.* 1285, *pg.* 593
TRUSTEDSIGNINS - Flash Memory Card - SANDISK CORPORATION; *pg.* 465, *pg.* 147
TRUSTKEEPER - Data Security Service - TRUSTWAVE HOLDINGS, INC.; *pg.* 1285, *pg.* 593
TRUSTMINDER - Software - TRUSTWAVE HOLDINGS, INC.; *pg.* 1285, *pg.* 593
TRUSTOR - Software - SYMANTEC CORPORATION; *pg.* 478, *pg.* 161
TRUSTPOINT - Software - CERTICOM CORP.; *pg.* 371, *pg.* 1925
TRUSTWATCH - Flash Drive - SANDISK CORPORATION; *pg.* 465, *pg.* 147
TRUSTWAVE - Computer Software - TRUSTWAVE HOLDINGS, INC.; *pg.* 1285, *pg.* 593
TRUSTWAVE SECURITY DATA WAREHOUSE - Computer Software - TRUSTWAVE HOLDINGS, INC.; *pg.* 1285, *pg.* 593
TRUTH - Campaign Against Smoking - TRUTH INITIATIVE; *pg.* 158, *pg.* 405
TRUTH IN ENGINEERING - Tagline - AUDI OF AMERICA, INC.; *pg.* 164, *pg.* 1784
TRUTH VALUE SERVICE - Tagline - INNODATA ISOGEN, INC.; *pg.* 1259, *pg.* 1072
TRUTIME - Time Reporting System - AMANO CINCINNATI, INC.; *pg.* 348, *pg.* 1117
TRUTIME - Software - DAKTRONICS, INC.; *pg.* 633, *pg.* 1624
TRUTINT - Flame Retardants - CHEMTURA CORPORATION; *pg.* 1152, *pg.* 355
TRUTRAK - GPS Receiver - L-3 INTERSTATE ELECTRONICS CORPORATION; *pg.* 650, *pg.* 43
TRUTV - Television Broadcasting - TURNER BROADCASTING SYSTEM, INC.; *pg.* 314, *pg.* 521
TRUVADA - Biopharmaceutical Product - GILEAD SCIENCES, INC.; *pg.* 1535, *pg.* 88
TRUVIA - Natural Sweetener - CARGILL, INC.; *pg.* 845, *pg.* 965
TRUVIEW - Software - BIO-RAD LABORATORIES, INC.; *pg.* 1504, *pg.* 101
TRUVIEW - Headlamp - FEDERAL-MOGUL HOLDINGS CORPORATION; *pg.* 205, *pg.* 907
TRUWAX - Dental Product - DENTSPLY INTERNATIONAL INC.; *pg.* 1522, *pg.* 1596
TRX-PROFESSIONAL SERVICES - Fixed-Cost Technical & Operational Assessments Applications - CONCUR TECHNOLOGIES; *pg.* 1903, *pg.* 501
TRX-TRAVEL ANALYTICS - Travel Management Programs - CONCUR TECHNOLOGIES; *pg.* 1903, *pg.* 501
TRXA03I1 (ROHS) - Transceivers - OPLINK COMMUNICATIONS, INC.; *pg.* 660, *pg.* 91
TRXA03L1 (ROHS) - Transceivers - OPLINK COMMUNICATIONS, INC.; *pg.* 660, *pg.* 91
TRXA03L2 (ROHS) - Transceivers - OPLINK COMMUNICATIONS, INC.; *pg.* 660, *pg.* 91
TRXA12I1 (ROHS) - Transceivers - OPLINK COMMUNICATIONS, INC.; *pg.* 660, *pg.* 91
TRXA12L1 (ROHS) - Transceivers - OPLINK COMMUNICATIONS, INC.; *pg.* 660, *pg.* 91
TRXA12L2 (ROHS) - Transceivers - OPLINK COMMUNICATIONS, INC.; *pg.* 660, *pg.* 91
TRXA12MM (ROHS) - Transceivers - OPLINK COMMUNICATIONS, INC.; *pg.* 660, *pg.* 91
TRXA12S1 (ROHS) - Transceivers - OPLINK COMMUNICATIONS, INC.; *pg.* 660, *pg.* 91
TRXA48I2 (ROHS) - Transceivers - OPLINK COMMUNICATIONS, INC.; *pg.* 660, *pg.* 91
TRXA48L1 (ROHS) - Transceivers - OPLINK COMMUNICATIONS, INC.; *pg.* 660, *pg.* 91
TRXA48L2 (ROHS) - Transceivers - OPLINK COMMUNICATIONS, INC.; *pg.* 660, *pg.* 91
TRXAFEEX ZX (ROHS) - Transceivers - OPLINK COMMUNICATIONS, INC.; *pg.* 660, *pg.* 91
TRXAFELX (ROHS) - Transceivers - OPLINK COMMUNICATIONS, INC.; *pg.* 660, *pg.* 91
TRXAG1 SM (ROHS) - Transceivers - OPLINK COMMUNICATIONS, INC.; *pg.* 660, *pg.* 91
TRXAG1 SM (ROHS) EX - Transceivers - OPLINK COMMUNICATIONS, INC.; *pg.* 660, *pg.* 91
TRXAG1 SM (ROHS) LX - Transceivers - OPLINK COMMUNICATIONS, INC.; *pg.* 660, *pg.* 91
TRXAG1 SM (ROHS) YX - Transceivers - OPLINK COMMUNICATIONS, INC.; *pg.* 660, *pg.* 91
TRXAG1SX (ROHS) - Transceivers - OPLINK COMMUNICATIONS, INC.; *pg.* 660, *pg.* 91
TRXAG1VXIXMS (ROHS) - Transceivers - OPLINK COMMUNICATIONS, INC.; *pg.* 660, *pg.* 91
TRXAG1ZXM (ROHS) - Transceivers - OPLINK COMMUNICATIONS, INC.; *pg.* 660, *pg.* 91
TRXBG1EXM (ROHS) - Transceivers - OPLINK COMMUNICATIONS, INC.; *pg.* 660, *pg.* 91
TRXBG1LXM (ROHS) - Transceivers - OPLINK COMMUNICATIONS, INC.; *pg.* 660, *pg.* 91

TRXNFEMM (ROHS) - Transceivers - OPLINK COMMUNICATIONS, INC.; pg. 660, pg. 91

TRY A LITTLE TENDERNESS - Retail Mail Order Service - OMAHA STEAKS INTERNATIONAL, INC.; pg. 1780, pg. 1017

TRY BEFORE YOU BUY - Slogan - MERLE NORMAN COSMETICS, INC.; pg. 517, pg. 136

TRY SOMETHING NEW - Slogan - STARTSAMPLING, INC.; pg. 1283, pg. 561

TRYAD - Animal Safety Product - NEOGEN CORPORATION; pg. 883, pg. 896

TRYCITE - Film - THE DOW CHEMICAL COMPANY; pg. 1157, pg. 898

TRYGLE - Toy & Game - HASBRO, INC.; pg. 954, pg. 1603

TRYMER - Insulation - THE DOW CHEMICAL COMPANY; pg. 1157, pg. 898

TRYPIO - Toy & Game - HASBRO, INC.; pg. 954, pg. 1603

TRYPLE - Cell Culture Product - THERMO FISHER SCIENTIFIC INC.; pg. 1602, pg. 61

TRYST - Fabric - NEMSCHOFF, INC.; pg. 936, pg. 1890

TS-LINK - Molecular Probe Product - THERMO FISHER SCIENTIFIC INC.; pg. 1602, pg. 61

TS800 - Home & Garden Product - WESTROCK COMPANY; pg. 1472, pg. 1805

TSA - Chromogenic & Fluorescent Signals - PERKINELMER, INC.; pg. 1426, pg. 853

TSA - Test Equipment - SPX THERMAL PRODUCT SOLUTIONS; pg. 1378, pg. 1555

TSARATANA - Chocolate Product - GUITTARD CHOCOLATE COMPANY; pg. 1855, pg. 55

TSC1 - Data Collector - TRIMBLE NAVIGATION LIMITED; pg. 1384, pg. 288

TSCAN - Carrier Serving Area - ADTRAN, INC.; pg. 344, pg. 6

TSCE - Software - TRIMBLE NAVIGATION LIMITED; pg. 1384, pg. 288

TSCHUDIN - Grinding Machine - HARDINGE INC.; pg. 1344, pg. 1157

TSCSP - Packaging Technology - AMKOR TECHNOLOGY, INC.; pg. 67, pg. 25

TSE - Spoken English Test - EDUCATIONAL TESTING SERVICE INC.; pg. 1394, pg. 1111

TSIP TALKER - Software - TRIMBLE NAVIGATION LIMITED; pg. 1384, pg. 288

TSL - Fluid Handling System - GRACO, INC.; pg. 1342, pg. 935

TSM - Software - TRIMBLE NAVIGATION LIMITED; pg. 1384, pg. 288

TSP - Steel Components - XTEK, INC.; pg. 1390, pg. 1427

TSRH-3D - Thoracolumbar System - MEDTRONIC, INC.; pg. 1564, pg. 939

TSS - All Stainless Steel Thermostatic Steam Trap - SPIRAX SARCO, INC.; pg. 1076, pg. 1612

TSU - Networking Product - ADTRAN, INC.; pg. 344, pg. 6

TSU - Fluid Handling System - GRACO, INC.; pg. 1342, pg. 935

TSU 100 - Networking Product - ADTRAN, INC.; pg. 344, pg. 6

TSU 100E - Networking Product - ADTRAN, INC.; pg. 344, pg. 6

TSU 120 - Networking Product - ADTRAN, INC.; pg. 344, pg. 6

TSU 120E - Networking Product - ADTRAN, INC.; pg. 344, pg. 6

TSU 600 - Networking Product - ADTRAN, INC.; pg. 344, pg. 6

TSU 600 VP24 E&M - Networking Product - ADTRAN, INC.; pg. 344, pg. 6

TSU 600 VP24 FXO - Networking Product - ADTRAN, INC.; pg. 344, pg. 6

TSU 600 VP24 FXS - Networking Product - ADTRAN, INC.; pg. 344, pg. 6

TSU 600E - Networking Product - ADTRAN, INC.; pg. 344, pg. 6

TSU ACE - Networking Product - ADTRAN, INC.; pg. 344, pg. 6

TSU ESP - Networking Product - ADTRAN, INC.; pg. 344, pg. 6

TSU IQ - Networking Product - ADTRAN, INC.; pg. 344, pg. 6

TSU IQ+ - Networking Product - ADTRAN, INC.; pg. 344, pg. 6

TSU LT - Networking Product - ADTRAN, INC.; pg. 344, pg. 6

TSUNAMI - Carpet - BEAULIEU GROUP, LLC; pg. 917, pg. 529

TSUNAMI - Laser - NEWPORT CORPORATION; pg. 1424, pg. 114

TSUNAMI GRILL - Restaurant - ARK RESTAURANTS CORP.; pg. 1715, pg. 1196

TSUPREM-4 - Software - SYNOPSYS, INC.; pg. 480, pg. 162

TSUS - Networking Products - ADTRAN, INC.; pg. 344, pg. 6

TSUYADASHI MYPET - Floor Cleaner - KAO BRANDS CO. INC.; pg. 513, pg. 1415

TSV - Sportswear - TAOS SKI VALLEY, INC.; pg. 1116, pg. 1136

TSV-2 - Bovine Rhinotracheitis Parainfluenza3 Vaccine - PFIZER INC.; pg. 1581, pg. 1278

TT - Medical Device - LEMAITRE VASCULAR, INC.; pg. 1555, pg. 805

TT - Sneakers - REEBOK INTERNATIONAL LTD.; pg. 1817, pg. 811

TT-100 - Viscometer - BROOKFIELD ENGINEERING LABORATORIES, INC.; pg. 1403, pg. 833

TT LITE XL - Golf Shaft - TRUE TEMPER SPORTS, INC.; pg. 1817, pg. 1647

TTB - Semiconductor Solution - CYPRESS SEMICONDUCTOR CORPORATION; pg. 1326, pg. 243

TTR - Transformer Turn Ratio Test Sets - MEGGER INC.; pg. 1422, pg. 1557

TTS - Survey Instrument - TRIMBLE NAVIGATION LIMITED; pg. 1384, pg. 288

TTW1 - Gas, Electric & Oil Powered Heaters - BRADFORD-WHITE CORPORATION; pg. 1069, pg. 1514

TTW2 - Gas, Electric & Oil Powered Heaters - BRADFORD-WHITE CORPORATION; pg. 1069, pg. 1514

TTX - Bicycle - TREK BICYCLE CORPORATION; pg. 1847, pg. 1896

TUACA - Liqueur - BROWN-FORMAN CORPORATION; pg. 1958, pg. 732

TUALATIN ESTATE - Wine - WILLAMETTE VALLEY VINEYARDS, INC.; pg. 1972, pg. 1510

TUB-GUARD - Medical Product - GF HEALTH PRODUCTS, INC.; pg. 1535, pg. 508

TUB-N-TILE - Sealant - OATEY SUPPLY CHAIN SERVICES; pg. 30, pg. 1433

TUB TATTOOS - Safety Product - VENTURI, INC.; pg. 1606, pg. 910

TUB TIME - Storage Bag - 1-800-FLOWERS.COM, INC.; pg. 1758, pg. 1151

TUBE 'N TILE - Bathroom Cleaner - METHOD PRODUCTS INC.; pg. 332, pg. 223

TUBE-O-FLAME - Burner - MAXON CORPORATION; pg. 1359, pg. 695

TUBE-O-THERM - Burner - MAXON CORPORATION; pg. 1359, pg. 695

TUBE ROSE - Tobacco Product - AMERICAN SNUFF COMPANY; pg. 1893, pg. 1641

TUBEJET - Dust Filter - SLY, INC.; pg. 1376, pg. 1475

TUBELITE - Aluminum Product - APOGEE ENTERPRISES, INC.; pg. 67, pg. 930

TUBEROSE MUSK - Fragrance - PARFUMS DE COEUR LTD.; pg. 519, pg. 376

TUBERSOL - Tuberculin Purfied Protein Derivative - SANOFI PASTEUR, INC; pg. 1591, pg. 1588

TUBESAND - Sand & Aggregate - QUIKRETE COMPANIES; pg. 106, pg. 519

TUBESTAR - Glass & Ceramic Material - CORNING INCORPORATED; pg. 1122, pg. 1154

TUBETRACE - Preinsulated Heat Traced Tubing - THERMON AMERICAS INC.; pg. 1077, pg. 1744

TUBI - Exhaust System - CHAMPION MOTORSPORT; pg. 168, pg. 459

TUBIGRIP - Wound Care Product - CONVATEC LTD.; pg. 1518, pg. 1121

TUBIPAD - Wound Care Product - CONVATEC LTD.; pg. 1518, pg. 1121

TUBSIDER - Infant Carrier - INFANTINO, LLC; pg. 957, pg. 203

TUBULAR - Heater - WATLOW ELECTRIC MANUFACTURING COMPANY; pg. 1078, pg. 1004

TUBULAR EXHAUST SYSTEMS - Exhaust Systems - EDELBROCK CORPORATION; pg. 204, pg. 293

TUBULAR-HP - Battery - EXIDE TECHNOLOGIES; pg. 204, pg. 483

TUBULAR LATTICE NETWORK - Golf Accessories - CALLAWAY GOLF COMPANY; pg. 1829, pg. 58

TUBULINTRACKER - Molecular Probe Product - THERMO FISHER SCIENTIFIC INC.; pg. 1602, pg. 61

TUC - Biscuits - MONDELEZ INTERNATIONAL, INC.; pg. 878, pg. 601

TUCCHETTI - Italian Food - LETTUCE ENTERTAIN YOU ENTERPRISES, INC.; pg. 1735, pg. 580

TUCCI BENUCCH - Italian Restaurant - LETTUCE ENTERTAIN YOU ENTERPRISES, INC.; pg. 1735, pg. 580

TUCHEL - Electronics - AMPHENOL CORPORATION; pg. 616, pg. 381

TUCKAWAY - Monitor - AKRON BRASS COMPANY; pg. 1311, pg. 1482

TUCKER - Furniture - AMERICAN LEATHER LP; pg. 912, pg. 1673

TUCKER - Casual Shoes - JOHNSTON & MURPHY CO.; pg. 1810, pg. 1651

TUCKER - Fabric - NEMSCHOFF, INC.; pg. 936, pg. 1890

TUCKS - Hemorrhoid Treatments - MCNEIL-PPC, INC.; pg. 1560, pg. 1533

TUCON - Business Information Seminars - TIBCO SOFTWARE INC.; pg. 484, pg. 178

TUCOPRIM - Veterinary Antibiotic Products - PFIZER INC.; pg. 1581, pg. 1278

TUDOR - Battery - EXIDE TECHNOLOGIES; pg. 204, pg. 483

TUDOR - Fabric - NEMSCHOFF, INC.; pg. 936, pg. 1890

TUDOR COURT - Embroidered Fleece Jacket - HABAND COMPANY, INC.; pg. 1772, pg. 1099

TUENS - Candy - WM. WRIGLEY JR. COMPANY; pg. 1863, pg. 596

TUESDAY - Women's Clothing & Accessories - WOODEN SHIPS OF HOBOKEN; pg. 35, pg. 1315

TUESDAY MORNING - Variety Stores - TUESDAY MORNING CORPORATION; pg. 1789, pg. 1690

TUEX - Polymer Product - CHEMTURA CORPORATION; pg. 1152, pg. 355

TUF-BASE - Gypsum Panel - USG CORPORATION; pg. 118, pg. 594

TUF-CAL - Gypsum Cement - USG CORPORATION; pg. 118, pg. 594

TUF-GRIP - Wire Slings & Assemblies - WIRECO WORLDGROUP; pg. 1389, pg. 987

TUF-KOTE/PFV - Wire Rope - WIRECO WORLDGROUP; pg. 1389, pg. 987

TUF-MAX - Shovel Hoist Wire Rope - WIRECO WORLDGROUP; pg. 1389, pg. 987

TUF-R - Linear Low Density Polyethylene Bags - ELKAY PLASTICS COMPANY, INC.; pg. 1882, pg. 68

TUF SEAL - Sealant - HILLYARD, INC.; pg. 331, pg. 990

TUF-SET - Joint Compound - USG CORPORATION; pg. 118, pg. 594

TUF-SET LITE - Joint Compound - USG CORPORATION; pg. 118, pg. 594

TUF-SPRAY - Ceiling Spray Texture - USG CORPORATION; pg. 118, pg. 594

TUF-STONE - Gypsum Cement - USG CORPORATION; pg. 118, pg. 594

TUF-STRAND - Structural Wire Assemblies - WIRECO WORLDGROUP; pg. 1389, pg. 987

TUF-TAPE - Joint Tape - USG CORPORATION; pg. 118, pg. 594

TUF-TEX - Balloon - MAPLE CITY RUBBER COMPANY; pg. 962, pg. 1468

TUF-TEX - Spray Texture - USG CORPORATION; pg. 118, pg. 594

TUFF - Furniture - THE COMMERCIAL FURNITURE GROUP; pg. 920, pg. 994

TUFF 1 - Ratchets - SK HAND TOOL CORPORATION; pg. 1062, pg. 663

TUFF-CUFF - Cuffs - CAS MEDICAL SYSTEMS, INC.; pg. 1513, pg. 339

TUFF CURE - Rubber Products Retread System - OLIVER RUBBER COMPANY; pg. 1887, pg. 1358

TUFF-GRIP - Tape - IDEAL INDUSTRIES, INC.; pg. 1051, pg. 662

TUFF GUARD - Non-Stick Coatings - JARDEN CONSUMER SOLUTIONS; pg. 57, pg. 412

TUFF-KOTE - Barn Paint - JONES-BLAIR COMPANY; pg. 1443, pg. 1682

TUFF-KRAFT - Protective Packaging Material - PACTIV CORPORATION; pg. 1466, pg. 624

TUFF KUT - Cutting Fluid - THE DOALL COMPANY; pg. 1329, pg. 670

TUFF LIL' SQUIRTZ - Bath Organizer - HOME PRODUCTS INTERNATIONAL, INC.; pg. 1125, pg. 577

TUFF-LINE - Linear Potentiometer Product - SENSOR SYSTEMS, LLC; pg. 672, pg. 464

TUFF-LITE - Lightning - AMERICAN GREASE STICK CO.; pg. 971, pg. 902

First page reference indicates Business Class Edition
Second page reference indicates Geographic Edition

TUFF-LITE - Couplings - DIXON VALVE & COUPLING COMPANY; *pg.* 1045, *pg.* 766
TUFF LUFF - Headstay System - SCHAEFER MARINE INC.; *pg.* 1373, *pg.* 835
TUFF POCKET - File Pockets - SMEAD MANUFACTURING COMPANY; *pg.* 470, *pg.* 926
TUFF-ROD - Tape - IDEAL INDUSTRIES, INC.; *pg.* 1051, *pg.* 662
TUFF-SEAL - Water Resistant Cable - WHITNEY BLAKE CO., INC.; *pg.* 1308, *pg.* 1764
TUFF SPORT - Scoreboard & Sports Product - DAKTRONICS, INC.; *pg.* 633, *pg.* 1624
TUFF-SPUN - Shred-Resistant Lightly Waxed & Unwaxed Dental Floss - SUNSTAR AMERICAS INC.; *pg.* 1599, *pg.* 591
TUFF-STACK - Fluid Handling System - GRACO, INC.; *pg.* 1342, *pg.* 935
TUFF STUFF - All-Purpose Cleaner - THE CLOROX COMPANY; *pg.* 327, *pg.* 169
TUFF STUFF - Pre-School Role-Play Toys - MATTEL, INC.; *pg.* 962, *pg.* 81
TUFF-TOTE - Durability Tote - GLOBE COMPOSITE SOLUTIONS, LTD.; *pg.* 1883, *pg.* 842
TUFF-TRAC - Vinyl Matting - THE BILTRITE CORPORATION; *pg.* 1879, *pg.* 850
TUFFBRAZE - Abrasion Resistant Liner Plate - RUSSEL METALS INC.; *pg.* 1180, *pg.* 1928
TUFFGARD - Mailing Envelopes - SEALED AIR CORPORATION; *pg.* 1468, *pg.* 1058
TUFFGARD EXTREME - Cushioned Mailers - SEALED AIR CORPORATION; *pg.* 1468, *pg.* 1058
TUFFHIDE - Primer - USG CORPORATION; *pg.* 118, *pg.* 594
TUFFKUSHION - Footwear - WELLCO ENTERPRISES, INC.; *pg.* 1822, *pg.* 1392
TUFFLAKE - Automotive Coating - SILBERLINE MANUFACTURING CO., INC.; *pg.* 110, *pg.* 1588
TUFFLEX - Cushioning & Padding - RSI HOME PRODUCTS; *pg.* 108, *pg.* 1381
TUFFLEX - Tape - XPEDX; *pg.* 1473, *pg.* 1377
TUFFLINK - Adapter - BECTON, DICKINSON & COMPANY; *pg.* 1501, *pg.* 1068
TUFFLITE - Insulated Wire - CARLISLE INTERCONNECT TECHNOLOGIES; *pg.* 1294, *pg.* 461
TUFFMATE - Wiper And Cleaning Cloth - GEORGIA-PACIFIC LLC; *pg.* 1458, *pg.* 507
TUFFRYN - Membrane - PALL CORPORATION; *pg.* 232, *pg.* 1323
TUFFTEAK - Decking Boards - LUMBER LIQUIDATORS HOLDINGS, INC.; *pg.* 94, *pg.* 1808
TUFFWEAR - Extended Life Carbide Scraper - YETTER MANUFACTURING CO., INC.; *pg.* 708, *pg.* 598
TUFFY - Mesh Scrubber - THE CLOROX COMPANY; *pg.* 327, *pg.* 169
TUFFY - Industrial Sewing Machine Motors - CONSEW; *pg.* 53, *pg.* 1049
TUFFY - Audio, Video & Computer Furniture - H. WILSON COMPANY; *pg.* 1415, *pg.* 666
TUFFY - Mufflers - TUFFY ASSOCIATES CORPORATION; *pg.* 220, *pg.* 1477
TUFFYLAND PRODUCTS - Furniture - H. WILSON COMPANY; *pg.* 1415, *pg.* 666
TUFLIN - Resin - THE DOW CHEMICAL COMPANY; *pg.* 1157, *pg.* 898
TUFRAM - Coating - GENERAL MAGNAPLATE CORPORATION; *pg.* 1164, *pg.* 1079
TUFTEX - Hose - HBD INDUSTRIES, INC.; *pg.* 207, *pg.* 1449
TUFTEX - Carpet - SHAW INDUSTRIES GROUP, INC.; *pg.* 942, *pg.* 530
TUFWITE - Paper & Nonwoven Material - FIBERMARK INC.; *pg.* 1457, *pg.* 1764
TUG ALONG - Dog Toy - THE HARTZ MOUNTAIN CORP.; *pg.* 1476, *pg.* 1120
TUGGER - Puller - GREENLEE TEXTRON INC.; *pg.* 1048, *pg.* 655
TUGIT - Hoist - COLUMBUS MCKINNON CORPORATION; *pg.* 1325, *pg.* 1138
TUGS! - Apparel - SUPERIOR UNIFORM GROUP, INC.; *pg.* 33, *pg.* 468
TUITION ANSWER - Student Loans - SLM CORPORATION; *pg.* 804, *pg.* 388
TUKON - Hardness Testing Instrument - INSTRON CORPORATION; *pg.* 1349, *pg.* 839
TULANE - Footwear - EASTLAND SHOE CORPORATION; *pg.* 1808, *pg.* 750
TULIP - Door & Wood Product - CONESTOGA WOOD SPECIALTIES CORP.; *pg.* 921, *pg.* 1527
TULIP - Window Treatment - HERITAGE LACE INC.; *pg.* 694, *pg.* 711
TULIP - Seafood - TRIDENT SEAFOODS CORPORATION; *pg.* 902, *pg.* 1842
TULIP DELI - Deli Displayware - CARLISLE FOODSERVICE PRODUCTS INCORPORATED; *pg.* 1455, *pg.* 1485
TULIP DRAGON - Hat - WOODEN SHIPS OF HOBOKEN; *pg.* 35, *pg.* 1315
TULIP GARDEN - Flower Arrangement - 1-800-FLOWERS.COM, INC.; *pg.* 1758, *pg.* 1151
TULIPS - Bedding - CROSCILL, INC.; *pg.* 1122, *pg.* 1220
TULIPSET - Engagement Ring - STULLER, INC.; *pg.* 13, *pg.* 745
TULI'S - Foot Care - MUELLER SPORTS MEDICINE, INC.; *pg.* 1570, *pg.* 1887
TULOPAN - White Spirit - THE DOW CHEMICAL COMPANY; *pg.* 1157, *pg.* 898
TUMBLE FORMS2 - Positioners - ALIMED, INC.; *pg.* 1490, *pg.* 816
TUMBLIN' MONKEYS - Toy - MATTEL, INC.; *pg.* 962, *pg.* 81
TUMBLING GNOMES - Toys - 1-800-FLOWERS.COM, INC.; *pg.* 1758, *pg.* 1151
TUMBLING REELS - Video Game - INTERNATIONAL GAME TECHNOLOGY; *pg.* 957, *pg.* 1024
TUMMY CARE - Vitamin & Dietary Supplement - NATROL, INC.; *pg.* 1570, *pg.* 64
TUMMY TUCK - Contouring Apparel Technology - NYDJ APPAREL, LLC; *pg.* 30, *pg.* 302
TUMT - Medical Device - UROLOGIX, INC.; *pg.* 1604, *pg.* 945
TUNA HELPER - Main Dish Mixes - GENERAL MILLS, INC.; *pg.* 828, *pg.* 933
TUNA SPIRALS - Food Product - ANNIE'S INC.; *pg.* 1760, *pg.* 45
TUNDRA - Truck - TOYOTA MOTOR NORTH AMERICA, INC.; *pg.* 192, *pg.* 1303
TUNED IN TO YOU. - Slogan - PRECISION AUTO CARE, INC.; *pg.* 215, *pg.* 1787
TUNES - Medicated Lozenges - MARS, INCORPORATED; *pg.* 1858, *pg.* 1792
TUNGSEAL - Tung Oil Stain - THE VALSPAR CORPORATION; *pg.* 1449, *pg.* 945
TUNGSTEN BEE - Gaming Product - GLD PRODUCTS, INC.; *pg.* 1835, *pg.* 1882
TUNGSWELD - Saw Blade - SIMONDS INTERNATIONAL CORPORATION; *pg.* 1376, *pg.* 819
TUNICOVER - Plant Protector - GARDENS ALIVE!, INC.; *pg.* 1796, *pg.* 693
TUNISIAN - Tile - ARTISTIC TILE INC.; *pg.* 914, *pg.* 1119
TUNITE - Alloy - CALLAWAY GOLF COMPANY; *pg.* 1829, *pg.* 58
TUNNEL WASH - Automotive Reconditioning Product - MOC PRODUCTS COMPANY, INC.; *pg.* 332, *pg.* 174
TUPELO BLOSSOM - Honey - MILLER'S HONEY COMPANY; *pg.* 1860, *pg.* 1759
TUPERSAN - Turf Product - PBI/GORDON CORPORATION; *pg.* 1176, *pg.* 985
TUPERSCAN - Turf & Ornamental - PBI/GORDON CORPORATION; *pg.* 1176, *pg.* 985
TUPPERCARE - Kids Feeding Line - TUPPERWARE BRANDS CORPORATION; *pg.* 1139, *pg.* 456
TUPPERKIDS - Kids Feeding Line - TUPPERWARE BRANDS CORPORATION; *pg.* 1139, *pg.* 456
TUPPERWAVE - Microwave - TUPPERWARE BRANDS CORPORATION; *pg.* 1139, *pg.* 456
TURANZA - Passenger Tires - BRIDGESTONE AMERICAS, INC.; *pg.* 201, *pg.* 1649
TURBO - Floor Care Product - BISSELL HOMECARE, INC.; *pg.* 52, *pg.* 887
TURBO - Textile Care Product - ECOLAB INC.; *pg.* 329, *pg.* 960
TURBO - Case Cleaning Media - LYMAN PRODUCTS CORPORATION; *pg.* 1839, *pg.* 356
TURBO-BOOSTER - Vascular Interventions - THE SPECTRANETICS CORPORATION; *pg.* 1595, *pg.* 315
TURBO CHARGED - Apparel - VANS, INC.; *pg.* 1821, *pg.* 76
TURBO CLASSIC - Gas Grill - BARBEQUES GALORE, INC.; *pg.* 51, *pg.* 173
TURBO DRAFT - Installation System - SCHUTTE & KOERTING INC.; *pg.* 1428, *pg.* 1589
TURBO-DRYER - Treating Units - WYSSMONT CO., INC.; *pg.* 1390, *pg.* 1068
TURBO ELITE - Gas Grill - BARBEQUES GALORE, INC.; *pg.* 51, *pg.* 173
TURBO ELITE - Excimer Laser System - THE SPECTRANETICS CORPORATION; *pg.* 1595, *pg.* 315
TURBO ENERGY - Nutritional Product - NUTRACEUTICAL INTERNATIONAL CORPORATION; *pg.* 1576, *pg.* 1753
TURBO EXTREME - Educational Toys - LEAPFROG ENTERPRISES, INC.; *pg.* 961, *pg.* 84
TURBO FILE 2400 - Nailcare Product - MEDICOOL, INC.; *pg.* 1562, *pg.* 294
TURBO FILE II - Nailcare Product - MEDICOOL, INC.; *pg.* 1562, *pg.* 294
TURBO-FLO - Process Automation System - KEY TECHNOLOGY, INC.; *pg.* 868, *pg.* 1847
TURBO HEATER - Oxygen Delivery Device - VITAL SIGNS, INC.; *pg.* 1607, *pg.* 1126
TURBO JAM - Fitness Video & DVD - BEACHBODY, LLC; *pg.* 271, *pg.* 272
TURBO REELETTE - Video Game - INTERNATIONAL GAME TECHNOLOGY; *pg.* 957, *pg.* 1024
TURBO SELECT - Gas Grill - BARBEQUES GALORE, INC.; *pg.* 51, *pg.* 173
TURBO SKYLANE - Aircraft - CESSNA AIRCRAFT COMPANY; *pg.* 226, *pg.* 723
TURBO-STATIC DISC - Water Heater - BRADFORD-WHITE CORPORATION; *pg.* 1069, *pg.* 1514
TURBO STATIONAIR - Aircraft - CESSNA AIRCRAFT COMPANY; *pg.* 226, *pg.* 723
TURBO STS - Gas Grill - BARBEQUES GALORE, INC.; *pg.* 51, *pg.* 173
TURBO SUPERTERM - Access Control System - NAPCO SECURITY SYSTEMS, INC.; *pg.* 658, *pg.* 1138
TURBO SWIRL - Ceiling Fan - WESTINGHOUSE LIGHTING CORPORATION; *pg.* 687, *pg.* 1571
TURBO TEAM - Bicycle Accessories - SPECIALIZED BICYCLE COMPONENTS, INC.; *pg.* 1711, *pg.* 152
TURBO-TECH - Tires - TBC CORPORATION; *pg.* 1889, *pg.* 457
TURBO TESTER - Bevel Product - GLEASON CORPORATION; *pg.* 1340, *pg.* 1335
TURBO-TILL - Tillage Product - GREAT PLAINS MANUFACTURING, INCORPORATED; *pg.* 704, *pg.* 721
TURBO-TOMATO - Weed Control - GARDENS ALIVE!, INC.; *pg.* 1796, *pg.* 693
TURBO TRANSIT - Pack - L.L. BEAN, INC.; *pg.* 1777, *pg.* 750
TURBO TURTLE - Ride-ons - RADIO FLYER INC.; *pg.* 966, *pg.* 588
TURBO TWIST - Educational Toys - LEAPFROG ENTERPRISES, INC.; *pg.* 961, *pg.* 84
TURBO-TWISTER - Kitchen Appliance - HAMILTON BEACH BRANDS, INC.; *pg.* 56, *pg.* 1783
TURBO VENTS - Simulated Air Intake Vents - LUND INTERNATIONAL, INC.; *pg.* 211, *pg.* 526
TURBOBRUSH - Floor Care Product - BISSELL HOMECARE, INC.; *pg.* 52, *pg.* 887
TURBOCACHE - Graphic System - NVIDIA CORPORATION; *pg.* 447, *pg.* 268
TURBOCAT - Floor Care Product - H-P PRODUCTS, INC.; *pg.* 85, *pg.* 1458
TURBOCHARGER - Water Heater - LOCHINVAR CORPORATION; *pg.* 1073, *pg.* 1640
TURBOCHEF - Cooking Equipment - THE MIDDLEBY CORPORATION; *pg.* 1361, *pg.* 610
TURBOCHEF - Company Name - TURBOCHEF TECHNOLOGIES, INC.; *pg.* 902, *pg.* 1670
TURBODISC - Semiconductor Material - EMCORE CORPORATION; *pg.* 636, *pg.* 39
TURBODISC - Epitaxial Equipment - VEECO INSTRUMENTS INC.; *pg.* 1434, *pg.* 1322
TURBODOG - Beer - ABITA BREWING COMPANY; *pg.* 237, *pg.* 741
TURBODOX - Computer Modem Software - TEXAS INSTRUMENTS INCORPORATED; *pg.* 679, *pg.* 1688
TURBOFORCE - Fluid Handling System - GRACO, INC.; *pg.* 1342, *pg.* 935
TURBOGIG - Computer Products - BROADCOM CORPORATION; *pg.* 364, *pg.* 108
TURBOHONE - Honing Tool - SUNNEN PRODUCTS COMPANY; *pg.* 1379, *pg.* 1004
TURBOJET - Nozzles - AKRON BRASS COMPANY; *pg.* 1311, *pg.* 1482
TURBOMATRIX - Thermal Desorber - PERKINELMER, INC.; *pg.* 1426, *pg.* 853
TURBOPADDLE - Paddle Game - SCHOOL-TECH, INC.; *pg.* 1844, *pg.* 866
TURBOPLUS - High Vacuum Pumping - BROOKS

AUTOMATION, INC.; *pg.* 1320, *pg.* 813
TURBOPREP - Liquid Chromatography Software - PPG INDUSTRIES, INC.; *pg.* 1445, *pg.* 1579
TURBOQAM - Computer Products - BROADCOM CORPORATION; *pg.* 364, *pg.* 108
TURBOTAX - Software - INTUIT INC.; *pg.* 769, *pg.* 158
TURBOTEAM - Vacuum Systems - H-P PRODUCTS, INC.; *pg.* 85, *pg.* 1458
TURBOTREATER - High Pressure Gas Quench Vacuum Furnace - IPSEN INTERNATIONAL, INC.; *pg.* 1073, *pg.* 562
TURBOTRON - Blower - GARDNER DENVER, INC.; *pg.* 1338, *pg.* 1592
TURBOTRONIC - Gas Turbine Product - SOLAR TURBINES INCORPORATED; *pg.* 1377, *pg.* 209
TURBOWASH - Washing Machine - MAC-GRAY CORPORATION; *pg.* 58, *pg.* 852
TURBULATOR - Axially-Placed Steel Bars Placed Inside Rotating Paper-Drying Cylinders - KADANT JOHNSON INC.; *pg.* 1073, *pg.* 909
TURBULENCE - Carpet - INTERFACE, INC.; *pg.* 695, *pg.* 512
TURF ALIVE! - Lawn Care Product - GARDENS ALIVE!, INC.; *pg.* 1796, *pg.* 693
TURF BUILDER - Lawn Fertilizer - THE SCOTTS MIRACLE-GRO COMPANY; *pg.* 1799, *pg.* 1459
TURF BUILDER PLUS 2 - Fertilizer - THE SCOTTS MIRACLE-GRO COMPANY; *pg.* 1799, *pg.* 1459
TURF BUILDER PLUS HALTS - Fertilizer - THE SCOTTS MIRACLE-GRO COMPANY; *pg.* 1799, *pg.* 1459
TURF BUILDER WITH WATER SMART - Fertilizer - THE SCOTTS MIRACLE-GRO COMPANY; *pg.* 1799, *pg.* 1459
TURF BUSTER - Trademark & ATV Tires - CARLISLE TIRE & WHEEL COMPANY; *pg.* 1880, *pg.* 1612
TURF MASTER - Trademark & Heavy Duty Lawn Mower Tires - CARLISLE TIRE & WHEEL COMPANY; *pg.* 1880, *pg.* 1612
TURF MATE - Trademark & Lawn Mower Tires - CARLISLE TIRE & WHEEL COMPANY; *pg.* 1880, *pg.* 1612
TURF PRO - Trademark & ATV Tires - CARLISLE TIRE & WHEEL COMPANY; *pg.* 1880, *pg.* 1612
TURF TAMER - Lawn Care Equipment - LAWN DOCTOR INC.; *pg.* 1796, *pg.* 1074
TURF TENDER - Lawn Spreader For Fertilizer, Seed, Topdressing - GANDY COMPANY; *pg.* 703, *pg.* 952
TURFCIDE - Polymer Product - CHEMTURA CORPORATION; *pg.* 1152, *pg.* 355
TURFGEAR - Fabric - UNDER ARMOUR, INC.; *pg.* 49, *pg.* 759
TURFLINER - Fluid Handling System - GRACO, INC.; *pg.* 1342, *pg.* 935
TURFSEED - Lawn & Garden Product - THE SCOTTS MIRACLE-GRO COMPANY; *pg.* 1799, *pg.* 1459
TURIN - Fabric - NEMSCHOFF, INC.; *pg.* 936, *pg.* 1890
TURKEY HILL - Dairy Products - TURKEY HILL DAIRY, INC.; *pg.* 902, *pg.* 1522
TURKEY TRIPLER - Lottery Game - ILLINOIS STATE LOTTERY; *pg.* 995, *pg.* 578
TURKLEEN - Scalding Product - BIRKO CORPORATION; *pg.* 1149, *pg.* 332
TURKUAZ - Beverages - THE COCA-COLA COMPANY; *pg.* 240, *pg.* 493
TURN 6 LC - Machining Center - ATS AUTOMATION TOOLING SYSTEMS INC.; *pg.* 355, *pg.* 1919
TURN CLEAN - Wing Pulley - VAN GORP CORPORATION; *pg.* 1387, *pg.* 711
TURN IT ON - Tag Line - ZAP; *pg.* 222, *pg.* 277
TURN IT ON. KEEP IT ON - Software - SYMANTEC CORPORATION; *pg.* 478, *pg.* 161
TURN LOCK - Briefcase - SANTA FE LEATHER CORPORATION; *pg.* 12, *pg.* 1059
TURN-O-MATIC - Control Unit - CHECKPOINT SYSTEMS, INC.; *pg.* 628, *pg.* 1559
TURN OF CHANCE - Video Game - INTERNATIONAL GAME TECHNOLOGY; *pg.* 957, *pg.* 1024
TURN OF FORTUNE - Video Game - INTERNATIONAL GAME TECHNOLOGY; *pg.* 957, *pg.* 1024
TURN SELECT - Polyurethane Foam - SPAN-AMERICA MEDICAL SYSTEMS, INC.; *pg.* 1595, *pg.* 1618
TURNBERRY - Fabric - NEMSCHOFF, INC.; *pg.* 936, *pg.* 1890
TURNBERRY: TURNBERRY ISLE RESORT & CLUB - Magazine - PALM BEACH MEDIA GROUP INC.; *pg.* 1674, *pg.* 457
TURNBRIDGE - Carpet - BEAULIEU GROUP, LLC; *pg.* 917, *pg.* 529
TURNER BROADCASTING SYSTEMS - Entertainment Product - TIME WARNER INC.; *pg.* 312, *pg.* 1302
TURNING INTEGRATION INTO INSIGHT - Software - INFORMATICA CORPORATION; *pg.* 414, *pg.* 190
TURNING LEAF - Wine - E&J GALLO WINERY; *pg.* 1962, *pg.* 149
TURNING MOMENTS INTO MEMORIES SINCE 1882 - Slogan - F. KORBEL BROS. INC.; *pg.* 1963, *pg.* 100
TURNKEY QC - Software - BIO-RAD LABORATORIES, INC.; *pg.* 1504, *pg.* 101
TURNLOK - Wiring Devices - PASS & SEYMOUR/LEGRAND; *pg.* 1303, *pg.* 1344
TURNSTONE - Furniture - STEELCASE INC.; *pg.* 475, *pg.* 889
TURNTABLE - Spreader - EASTMAN MACHINE COMPANY; *pg.* 1331, *pg.* 1148
TURPENOID - Turpentine Substitute - MARTIN/F. WEBER COMPANY; *pg.* 962, *pg.* 1567
TURPENOID NATURAL - Non-Toxic Cleaner - MARTIN/F. WEBER COMPANY; *pg.* 962, *pg.* 1567
TURPEX - Softeners - HUNTSMAN CORPORATION; *pg.* 1167, *pg.* 1758
TURQUOISE SPREADER - Container Grown Plant - MONROVIA GROWERS; *pg.* 1797, *pg.* 44
TURTLE - Media Case - NER HOLDINGS INC.; *pg.* 444, *pg.* 1071
TURTLE BAY - Eyewear - MAUI JIM, INC.; *pg.* 9, *pg.* 651
TURTLE BEACH - Gaming Audio Brand - HYPERSOUND; *pg.* 643, *pg.* 186
TURTLE CLUB - Membership of People Saved by Hard Hat - E.D. BULLARD COMPANY; *pg.* 1332, *pg.* 727
TURTLE TRACKS - Educational Materials - SCHOLASTIC INC.; *pg.* 1683, *pg.* 1288
TURTLEBACK - Vehicle Safety System - GROTE INDUSTRIES, INC.; *pg.* 206, *pg.* 693
TURTLEBACK II - High Count LED Lamp - GROTE INDUSTRIES, INC.; *pg.* 206, *pg.* 693
TURTOGA MEXICAN KITCHEN - Restaurant - MEXICAN RESTAURANTS, INC.; *pg.* 1741, *pg.* 1711
TUSCAN - Dairy Product - DEAN FOODS COMPANY; *pg.* 852, *pg.* 1679
TUSCAN COLLECTION - Grill - W.C. BRADLEY CO.; *pg.* 62, *pg.* 528
TUSCAN VILLA - Paint - PRATT & LAMBERT PAINTS; *pg.* 1446, *pg.* 1434
TUSCANO'S ITALIAN STYLE SUBS - Subs - NOBLE ROMAN'S, INC.; *pg.* 1741, *pg.* 689
TUSCANY - Furniture - ASHLEY FURNITURE INDUSTRIES, INC.; *pg.* 914, *pg.* 1852
TUSCANY - Rug - COURISTAN INC.; *pg.* 921, *pg.* 1067
TUSCANY - Furniture - ETHAN ALLEN INTERIORS INC.; *pg.* 924, *pg.* 343
TUSCANY - Furniture - HAWORTH, INC.; *pg.* 402, *pg.* 891
TUSCANY - Lighting Product - QUOIZEL INC.; *pg.* 1304, *pg.* 1616
TUSCANY - Pavers - WALKER & ZANGER, INC.; *pg.* 119, *pg.* 281
TUSCANY STEAKS & SEAFOOD - Games - PENN NATIONAL GAMING, INC.; *pg.* 574, *pg.* 1595
TUSCARORA GAS PIPELINE CO - Gas Service - NV ENERGY, INC.; *pg.* 1948, *pg.* 1028
TUSCON - Fabric - NEMSCHOFF, INC.; *pg.* 936, *pg.* 1890
TUSK - Fabric - NEMSCHOFF, INC.; *pg.* 936, *pg.* 1890
TUSK - Fabric - UNIROYAL ENGINEERED PRODUCTS; *pg.* 699, *pg.* 467
TUSSIGON - Pharmaceutical Product - KING PHARMACEUTICALS, INC.; *pg.* 1553, *pg.* 1627
TUTOR - Training Table System - HOWE FURNITURE CORPORATION; *pg.* 928, *pg.* 998
TUTOR TIME - Day Care Centers - LEARNING CARE GROUP INC.; *pg.* 604, *pg.* 903
TUTTI FRUTTI - Stuffed Turtle - GUND, INC.; *pg.* 954, *pg.* 1056
TUTTOROSSO - Tomato & Vegetable Juice - RED GOLD, INC.; *pg.* 891, *pg.* 677
TUXEDO - Furniture - BUSH INDUSTRIES INC.; *pg.* 919, *pg.* 1170
TUXEDO - Furniture - HAWORTH, INC.; *pg.* 402, *pg.* 891
TUXEDO - Accessories - THE MEN'S WEARHOUSE, INC.; *pg.* 44, *pg.* 1711
TUXEDO - Fabric - NEMSCHOFF, INC.; *pg.* 936, *pg.* 1890
TUXEDO - Footwear - OAKLEY, INC.; *pg.* 1840, *pg.* 86
TUXEDOS - Candy - PROMOTION IN MOTION, INC.; *pg.* 1861, *pg.* 1052
TUXXEDO - Footwear - STEVEN MADDEN, LTD.; *pg.* 1819, *pg.* 1176
TV ESSENTIALS - Software - RENTRAK CORPORATION; *pg.* 306, *pg.* 1506
TV GUIDE - Periodical - ROVI CORPORATION; *pg.* 463, *pg.* 269
TV GUIDE INTERACTIVE - Digital Directory - ROVI CORPORATION; *pg.* 463, *pg.* 269
TV GUIDE MOBILE - Digital Directory - ROVI CORPORATION; *pg.* 463, *pg.* 269
TV GUIDE NETWORK - Preview Channel Guide - TV GUIDE MAGAZINE GROUP, INC.; *pg.* 1697, *pg.* 1305
TV GUIDE ON SCREEN - Digital Directory - ROVI CORPORATION; *pg.* 463, *pg.* 269
TV GUIDE ULTIMATE CABLE - Magazine - TV GUIDE MAGAZINE GROUP, INC.; *pg.* 1697, *pg.* 1305
TV HITS - Video Game - INTERNATIONAL GAME TECHNOLOGY; *pg.* 957, *pg.* 1024
TV MAN - TV Antenna - WINEGARD COMPANY; *pg.* 688, *pg.* 702
TV-ON-CHIP - Graphics Card - ADVANCED MICRO DEVICES, INC.; *pg.* 613, *pg.* 282
TV-ON-DEMAND - Graphics Card - ADVANCED MICRO DEVICES, INC.; *pg.* 613, *pg.* 282
TV PAINT - Paint - ROSCO LABORATORIES, INC.; *pg.* 1782, *pg.* 378
TV TIME - Basket - THE LONGABERGER COMPANY; *pg.* 1127, *pg.* 1467
TV WONDER - 3D Graphical Technology - ADVANCED MICRO DEVICES, INC.-MARKHAM; *pg.* 345, *pg.* 1922
TVAC - Container - CHART INDUSTRIES, INC.; *pg.* 1405, *pg.* 1454
TVC - Protein Ingredient - ARCHER-DANIELS-MIDLAND COMPANY; *pg.* 825, *pg.* 565
TV.COM - Television & Related Media Website - CBS INTERACTIVE, INC.; *pg.* 369, *pg.* 215
TVG - Pharmaceutical Product - PDI, INC.; *pg.* 1580, *pg.* 1104
TVL - Medical Device - ST. JUDE MEDICAL, INC.; *pg.* 1596, *pg.* 963
TVP - Protein Ingredient - ARCHER-DANIELS-MIDLAND COMPANY; *pg.* 825, *pg.* 565
TVS - Window Glazing Units - PPG INDUSTRIES, INC.; *pg.* 1445, *pg.* 1579
TVSN - Retail Shopping Network - IAC/INTERACTIVECORP; *pg.* 292, *pg.* 1242
TV.TV - Telephone Service - IDT CORPORATION; *pg.* 643, *pg.* 1096
TV.TV BROADBAND NETWORK - Telephone Service - IDT CORPORATION; *pg.* 643, *pg.* 1096
TVUS/HSG-CATH - Uterine Assessment Catheters - UTAH MEDICAL PRODUCTS, INC.; *pg.* 1605, *pg.* 1752
TWARON - Fabric - HEXCEL CORPORATION; *pg.* 1884, *pg.* 375
TWAYNE PUBLISHERS - Critical Biographies & Studies on Literature - GALE CENGAGE LEARNING; *pg.* 1643, *pg.* 885
TWEAK - Fabric - NEMSCHOFF, INC.; *pg.* 936, *pg.* 1890
TWEED - Pillow - AMERICAN LEATHER LP; *pg.* 912, *pg.* 1673
TWEED - Fabric - NEMSCHOFF, INC.; *pg.* 936, *pg.* 1890
TWEETDECK - Social Media Dashboard - TWITTER, INC.; *pg.* 1285, *pg.* 228
TWEEZE - Home Products - HABAND COMPANY, INC.; *pg.* 1772, *pg.* 1099
TWEEZLIGHT - Healthcare Product - MEDICOOL, INC.; *pg.* 1562, *pg.* 294
TWELVE OAKS - Vinegar - NATIONAL FRUIT PRODUCT COMPANY, INC.; *pg.* 882, *pg.* 1811
TWICE AS NICE - Blouses - HABAND COMPANY, INC.; *pg.* 1772, *pg.* 1099
TWICE THE ICE - Game - WMS INDUSTRIES INC.; *pg.* 593, *pg.* 666
TWICE YOUR HONEY - Video Game - INTERNATIONAL GAME TECHNOLOGY; *pg.* 957, *pg.* 1024
TWICE YOUR MONKEY - Video Game - INTERNATIONAL GAME TECHNOLOGY; *pg.* 957, *pg.* 1024
TWICER - Agricultural Product - WILBUR-ELLIS COMPANY; *pg.* 1185, *pg.* 234
TWILIGHT - Mask - INVACARE CORPORATION; *pg.* 1546, *pg.* 1451
TWILIGHT - Fabric - NEMSCHOFF, INC.; *pg.* 936, *pg.* 1890
TWILIGHT - Fabric - UNIROYAL ENGINEERED PRODUCTS; *pg.* 699, *pg.* 467
THE TWILIGHT ZONE - Game - INTERNATIONAL GAME

First page reference indicates Business Class Edition
Second page reference indicates Geographic Edition

TECHNOLOGY; *pg.* 957, *pg.* 1024
TWILIGHTER - Family of Low Wattage HIP - CRESCENT/STONCO SUPPLY DIVISION; *pg.* 1295, *pg.* 1121
TWIN CAM - Engine - HARLEY-DAVIDSON, INC.; *pg.* 178, *pg.* 1874
TWIN CITY GRILL - Casual Dining Restaurant - LETTUCE ENTERTAIN YOU ENTERPRISES, INC.; *pg.* 1735, *pg.* 580
TWIN DIE - Hardware - MICRON TECHNOLOGY, INC.; *pg.* 435, *pg.* 547
TWIN-FLO - HVAC Equipment - MESTEK, INC.; *pg.* 1074, *pg.* 857
TWIN-FROST - Medical Product - PROPPER MANUFACTURING COMPANY, INC.; *pg.* 1586, *pg.* 1175
TWIN LUNCH KIT - Insulated Lunch Bag - IGLOO PRODUCTS CORPORATION; *pg.* 1126, *pg.* 1724
TWIN-PAC - Aircraft Engine - PRATT & WHITNEY CANADA CORP.; *pg.* 1370, *pg.* 1952
TWIN-PASS - Catheter - VASCULAR SOLUTIONS, INC.; *pg.* 1434, *pg.* 946
TWIN-PASS .023 - Catheter - VASCULAR SOLUTIONS, INC.; *pg.* 1434, *pg.* 946
TWIN PEAKS - Knife - BUCK KNIVES, INC.; *pg.* 1828, *pg.* 550
TWIN-SIX - Carton - PACTIV CORPORATION; *pg.* 1466, *pg.* 624
TWIN SPAR - Snowmobile - ARCTIC CAT INC.; *pg.* 1705, *pg.* 953
TWIN-STACK - Connector - MOLEX INCORPORATED; *pg.* 655, *pg.* 628
TWIN STAR - Broadband System Equipment - BLONDER TONGUE LABORATORIES, INC.; *pg.* 625, *pg.* 1100
TWIN STREAMS - Publishing Imprint - KENSINGTON PUBLISHING CORP.; *pg.* 1656, *pg.* 1248
TWIN-TASK - Flashlight - STREAMLIGHT INC.; *pg.* 1306, *pg.* 1527
TWIN-TEE - Metal Pipe Fitting - TACO INCORPORATED; *pg.* 1077, *pg.* 1601
TWIN TEMP - Air Conditioner - FRIEDRICH AIR CONDITIONING CO.; *pg.* 1072, *pg.* 1740
TWIN TRAVELER - Portable Coolers - THERMOS L.L.C.; *pg.* 61, *pg.* 660
TWIN-TURN - Machinery - HARDINGE INC.; *pg.* 1344, *pg.* 1157
TWIN WARRIORS - Video Game - INTERNATIONAL GAME TECHNOLOGY; *pg.* 957, *pg.* 1024
TWIN WIN - Video Game - INTERNATIONAL GAME TECHNOLOGY; *pg.* 957, *pg.* 1024
TWINAVR - Integrated Circuit - ATMEL CORPORATION; *pg.* 621, *pg.* 238
TWINCOOL - Dual Cooling Line System - GRACO, INC.; *pg.* 1342, *pg.* 935
TWINDICATOR - Sterilization Product - PROPPER MANUFACTURING COMPANY, INC.; *pg.* 1586, *pg.* 1175
TWINDOW - Fan - KAZ, INC.; *pg.* 58, *pg.* 844
TWINDOW - Insulating Glass Units - PPG INDUSTRIES, INC.; *pg.* 1445, *pg.* 1579
TWINDRIVE - Bicycle Component - SRAM CORPORATION; *pg.* 967, *pg.* 590
TWINFILE - Rotating File Cabinet - TAB PRODUCTS CO. LLC; *pg.* 481, *pg.* 1869
TWINFIX - Micro Implant System - STRYKER CORPORATION; *pg.* 1598, *pg.* 894
TWINFLOW - Fluid Handling System - GRACO, INC.; *pg.* 1342, *pg.* 935
TWINKIES - Snack Cakes - HOSTESS BRANDS LLC; *pg.* 1856, *pg.* 984
TWINKLETWIRLS DANCE STUDIO - Toy & Game - HASBRO, INC.; *pg.* 954, *pg.* 1603
TWINMIXER - Fluid Handling System - GRACO, INC.; *pg.* 1342, *pg.* 935
TWINNET - Business Services - TWIN DISC, INCORPORATED; *pg.* 220, *pg.* 1889
TWINSPLIT - Fiber Optic Transmission System - COMMUNICATIONS SPECIALTIES, INC.; *pg.* 377, *pg.* 1338
TWINSTAR - Model Helicopter - AIRBUS HELICOPTERS, INC.; *pg.* 223, *pg.* 1698
TWINVANE - Double Vane Pump Pressure Compensators - BOSCH REXROTH CORPORATION; *pg.* 1319, *pg.* 1516
TWINWIPES - Windshield Towels - WAUSAU PAPER BAY WEST; *pg.* 1471, *pg.* 1465
TWIRL - Bath Product - KOHLER CO.; *pg.* 91, *pg.* 1862
TWIRLIX - Chocolate Fudge - WELLS ENTERPRISES, INC.; *pg.* 909, *pg.* 709
TWIST - Furniture - THE COMMERCIAL FURNITURE GROUP; *pg.* 920, *pg.* 994
TWIST - Furniture - HERMAN MILLER, INC.; *pg.* 926, *pg.* 913
TWIST - Glove - KOMBI, LTD.; *pg.* 1838, *pg.* 1766
TWIST AND HOLD - Bath Organizer & Accessory - HOME PRODUCTS INTERNATIONAL, INC.; *pg.* 1125, *pg.* 577
TWIST & SHOUT - Educational Toys - LEAPFROG ENTERPRISES, INC.; *pg.* 961, *pg.* 84
TWIST-LOK - Pad Holder - 3M COMPANY; *pg.* 1142, *pg.* 956
TWIST-LOK - Plug - GENOVA PRODUCTS, INC.; *pg.* 83, *pg.* 875
TWIST-LOK - Bow Shank - SHUR-CO, INC.; *pg.* 110, *pg.* 1626
TWIST 'N FILL - Cleaning Chemical - 3M COMPANY; *pg.* 1142, *pg.* 956
TWIST-N-SET - Flange - OATEY SUPPLY CHAIN SERVICES; *pg.* 30, *pg.* 1433
TWIST N SHOUT - Carpet - BEAULIEU GROUP, LLC; *pg.* 917, *pg.* 529
TWIST OF FATE - Video Game - INTERNATIONAL GAME TECHNOLOGY; *pg.* 957, *pg.* 1024
TWIST-PROOF - Ladder Product - WERNER HOLDING CO.; *pg.* 121, *pg.* 1534
TWIST TIGHT - Baby Care Product - MUNCHKIN, INC.; *pg.* 964, *pg.* 300
TWISTED FROSTY - Ice Cream Drink - WENDY'S INTERNATIONAL, INC.; *pg.* 1755, *pg.* 1451
TWISTED PAIR - Pasta - EDEN FOODS INC.; *pg.* 1019, *pg.* 875
TWISTED SPINSTER - Video Game - INTERNATIONAL GAME TECHNOLOGY; *pg.* 957, *pg.* 1024
TWISTED TEA - Beverage - THE BOSTON BEER COMPANY, INC.; *pg.* 239, *pg.* 790
TWISTED TEA BREWING COMPANY - Brewer - THE BOSTON BEER COMPANY, INC.; *pg.* 239, *pg.* 790
TWISTER - Cleaning System - AMERICO MANUFACTURING CO., INC.; *pg.* 325, *pg.* 482
TWISTER - Rotating Rivet Tool - ARROW FASTENER COMPANY, INC.; *pg.* 1042, *pg.* 1118
TWISTER - Software - CHYRONHEGO; *pg.* 371, *pg.* 1179
TWISTER - Footwear - COBIAN CORP.; *pg.* 1806, *pg.* 253
TWISTER - Game - HASBRO, INC.; *pg.* 954, *pg.* 1603
TWISTER - Mop Handle - HILLYARD, INC.; *pg.* 331, *pg.* 990
TWISTER - Wire Connector - IDEAL INDUSTRIES, INC.; *pg.* 1051, *pg.* 662
TWISTER - Lottery Game - IOWA LOTTERY; *pg.* 996, *pg.* 705
TWISTER - Chicken Sandwich - KFC CORPORATION; *pg.* 1733, *pg.* 735
TWISTER - Fabric - NEMSCHOFF, INC.; *pg.* 936, *pg.* 1890
TWISTER DB PLUS - Connector - IDEAL INDUSTRIES, INC.; *pg.* 1051, *pg.* 662
TWISTER MOVES - Toy & Game - HASBRO, INC.; *pg.* 954, *pg.* 1603
TWISTER-PAK - Cans - SONOCO PRODUCTS COMPANY; *pg.* 1469, *pg.* 1619
TWISTER PRO - Connector - IDEAL INDUSTRIES, INC.; *pg.* 1051, *pg.* 662
TWISTFLEX - Drive Belting - FENNER DRIVES; *pg.* 1336, *pg.* 1551
TWISTHALER - Asthma Treatment - MERCK & CO., INC.; *pg.* 1566, *pg.* 1077
TWISTLOCK - Bicycle Accessories - SPECIALIZED BICYCLE COMPONENTS, INC.; *pg.* 1711, *pg.* 152
TWISTORK - Agitators - GRACO, INC.; *pg.* 1342, *pg.* 935
TWISTTIE - Bag - PACTIV CORPORATION; *pg.* 1466, *pg.* 624
TWISTY FISH - Baby Care Product - MUNCHKIN, INC.; *pg.* 964, *pg.* 300
TWISTY PUNCH - Candy Product - AMERICAN LICORICE CO. INC.; *pg.* 1850, *pg.* 692
TWITCHELL CREEK - Shirts - ABERCROMBIE & FITCH CO.; *pg.* 37, *pg.* 1466
TWITTER - Apparel - VANS, INC.; *pg.* 1821, *pg.* 76
TWIX - Candy Bar - MARS, INCORPORATED; *pg.* 1858, *pg.* 1792
TWIX JAVA - Candy Bar - MARS, INCORPORATED; *pg.* 1858, *pg.* 1792
TWIZZLERS - Candy - THE HERSHEY CO.; *pg.* 1855, *pg.* 1538
TWIZZLERS - Frozen Beverage - YOCREAM INTERNATIONAL INC.; *pg.* 1039, *pg.* 1508
TWIZZLERS PULL-N-PEEL - Candy - THE HERSHEY CO.; *pg.* 1855, *pg.* 1538
TWO BEST FRIENDS - Educational Materials - SCHOLASTIC INC.; *pg.* 1683, *pg.* 1288
TWO BY TWO - Hamburger Sandwiches - IN-N-OUT BURGERS, INC.; *pg.* 1732, *pg.* 111
TWO COOL - Beverage Coolers - IGLOO PRODUCTS CORPORATION; *pg.* 1126, *pg.* 1724
TWO FINGERS - Tequila - HEAVEN HILL DISTILLERIES, INC.; *pg.* 1964, *pg.* 725
TWO HEARTS - Maternity Apparel - DESTINATION MATERNITY CORPORATION; *pg.* 23, *pg.* 1563
TWO-IN-ONE - Blouses - HABAND COMPANY, INC.; *pg.* 1772, *pg.* 1099
TWO-PULL - Beer - GRANITE CITY FOOD & BREWERY LTD; *pg.* 1730, *pg.* 937
TWO STEP - Folding Two-Step Stool with Handle - DOREL JUVENILE GROUP, INC.; *pg.* 923, *pg.* 676
TWO-TIMIN. - Reversible Socks - SPANX INC.; *pg.* 32, *pg.* 520
TWO TOUCH - Integrated Circuit - ATMEL CORPORATION; *pg.* 621, *pg.* 238
TWO TOUGH - Cleaning Product - ORECK CORPORATION; *pg.* 59, *pg.* 1653
TWO-WAY - Fasteners - MACLEAN-FOGG COMPANY INC.; *pg.* 1358, *pg.* 635
TWO-WAY - Spinner - WRIGHT & MCGILL CO.; *pg.* 1848, *pg.* 324
TWOCAL - Nutritional Product - ABBOTT LABORATORIES; *pg.* 1484, *pg.* 551
TWOSE - Grass Boom Trimmers - ALAMO GROUP INC.; *pg.* 1311, *pg.* 1745
TX - Orthopedic Device - DJO SURGICAL; *pg.* 1525, *pg.* 1661
TX - Fluid Handling System - GRACO, INC.; *pg.* 1342, *pg.* 935
TX - Isolators - LIGHTPATH TECHNOLOGIES INC; *pg.* 1420, *pg.* 454
TX10 SEMIFLEX - Cable - TIMES FIBER COMMUNICATIONS, INC.; *pg.* 681, *pg.* 382
TX2 - Wood Product - STEELCASE INC.; *pg.* 475, *pg.* 889
TXP - Extruded Polyester - TRANSILWRAP COMPANY, INC.; *pg.* 1470, *pg.* 613
TY-D - Cable Tie-Mount - PENNENGINEERING FASTENING TECHNOLOGIES; *pg.* 1059, *pg.* 1526
TY-DUCT - Wiring Duct & Accessories - THOMAS & BETTS CORPORATION; *pg.* 680, *pg.* 1646
TY-FAST - Cable Tie - THOMAS & BETTS CORPORATION; *pg.* 680, *pg.* 1646
TY-GRIP - Fastener - THOMAS & BETTS CORPORATION; *pg.* 680, *pg.* 1646
TY-MET - Stainless Steel Ties - THOMAS & BETTS CORPORATION; *pg.* 680, *pg.* 1646
TY-RAP - Cable Tie - THOMAS & BETTS CORPORATION; *pg.* 680, *pg.* 1646
TYCHEM - Hood - E.D. BULLARD COMPANY; *pg.* 1332, *pg.* 727
TYCHEM - Protective Apparel - E.I. DU PONT DE NEMOURS & COMPANY; *pg.* 1159, *pg.* 390
TYCHEM - Clothing - LAKELAND INDUSTRIES, INC.; *pg.* 1354, *pg.* 1338
TYCO - Toy - MATTEL, INC.; *pg.* 962, *pg.* 81
TYCOS - Clinical Assessment - ALIMED, INC.; *pg.* 1490, *pg.* 816
TYCOS - Stethoscope - WELCH ALLYN INC.; *pg.* 1436, *pg.* 1342
TYDEN - Self Locking Seals - THE VIKING GROUP; *pg.* 119, *pg.* 891
TYDEX - Brake Fluid - THE DOW CHEMICAL COMPANY; *pg.* 1157, *pg.* 898
TYE - Tillage Equipment, Planters - AGCO CORPORATION; *pg.* 700, *pg.* 530
TYGACIL - Antibiotic - PFIZER INC.; *pg.* 1581, *pg.* 1278
TYLAN - Tylosin - ELANCO ANIMAL HEALTH; *pg.* 1475, *pg.* 681
TYLAN SULFA-G - Tylosin Phosphate - ELANCO ANIMAL HEALTH; *pg.* 1475, *pg.* 681
TYLENOL - Healthcare Product - JOHNSON & JOHNSON; *pg.* 1549, *pg.* 1091
TYLENOL - Pain Reliever - MCNEIL-PPC, INC.; *pg.* 1560, *pg.* 1533
TYLENOL COUGH/COLD/FLU - Cold Symptom Medication - MCNEIL-PPC, INC.; *pg.* 1560, *pg.* 1533
TYLENOL HEADACHE PLUS - Pain Reliever - MCNEIL-PPC, INC.; *pg.* 1560, *pg.* 1533

TYLENOL PM - Nighttime Pain Reliever - MCNEIL-PPC, INC.; *pg.* 1560, *pg.* 1533
TYLENOL SINUS/ALLERGY SINUS - Sinus Medication - MCNEIL-PPC, INC.; *pg.* 1560, *pg.* 1533
TYLER - Furniture - AMERICAN LEATHER LP; *pg.* 912, *pg.* 1673
TYLER - Agricultural Equipment - CNH AMERICA LLC; *pg.* 702, *pg.* 560
TYLER WENTWORTH - Armoires - TONNER DOLL COMPANY, INC.; *pg.* 968, *pg.* 1171
TYLOK PLUS - Dental Product - DENTSPLY INTERNATIONAL INC.; *pg.* 1522, *pg.* 1596
TYLOSIN - Sterile Antibiotic Injection - BOEHRINGER INGELHEIM VETMEDICA, INC.; *pg.* 1474, *pg.* 989
TYLOX - Healthcare Product - JOHNSON & JOHNSON; *pg.* 1549, *pg.* 1091
TYMOR - Adhesive & Sealant - DOW CHEMICAL; *pg.* 1156, *pg.* 1563
TYMOR - Tie Resins - THE DOW CHEMICAL COMPANY; *pg.* 1157, *pg.* 898
TYNA-MYTE - Electric Air Valve - HUMPHREY PRODUCTS CORPORATION; *pg.* 1300, *pg.* 894
TYNEX - Nylon Filaments - E.I. DU PONT DE NEMOURS & COMPANY; *pg.* 1159, *pg.* 390
TYPAR - Nonwoven Industrial Fabric - E.I. DU PONT DE NEMOURS & COMPANY; *pg.* 1159, *pg.* 390
TYPAR - Industrial Rainwear - LAKELAND INDUSTRIES, INC.; *pg.* 1354, *pg.* 1338
TYPE 30 - Glass Fiber Roving - OWENS CORNING; *pg.* 102, *pg.* 1476
TYPENNINGTON - Hardware Flooring - LUMBER LIQUIDATORS HOLDINGS, INC.; *pg.* 94, *pg.* 1808
TYPEPLEX - Reagents - SEQUENOM, INC.; *pg.* 1593, *pg.* 209
TYPESTYLER - Overhead Maker - VARITRONICS, LLC; *pg.* 487, *pg.* 954
TYPHIM VI - Typhoid Vi Polysaccharide Vaccine - SANOFI PASTEUR, INC; *pg.* 1591, *pg.* 1588
TYPHOON - Footwear - EASTLAND SHOE CORPORATION; *pg.* 1808, *pg.* 750
TYPHOON - Heavy Duty Bathroom Cleaner - HILLYARD, INC.; *pg.* 331, *pg.* 990
TYPHOON - Fire Pumps - IDEX CORPORATION; *pg.* 1347, *pg.* 623
TYPHOON - Eyewear - MAUI JIM, INC.; *pg.* 9, *pg.* 651
TYPHOON - Laser Printer - RICOH PRINTING SYSTEMS AMERICA, INC.; *pg.* 462, *pg.* 279
TYPHOON - Surface Maintenance Machine - TENNANT COMPANY; *pg.* 1381, *pg.* 944
TYRANT - Apparel - OAKLEY, INC.; *pg.* 1840, *pg.* 86
TYRE MARQUE - Rubber Marking Crayon - LA-CO INDUSTRIES MARKAL CO., INC.; *pg.* 1170, *pg.* 610
TYRE PRO - Tire And Rubber Product - THE GOODYEAR TIRE & RUBBER COMPANY; *pg.* 1883, *pg.* 1401
TYRIL - Chemical Product - THE DOW CHEMICAL COMPANY; *pg.* 1157, *pg.* 898
TYRIN - Chlorinated Polyethylene - THE DOW CHEMICAL COMPANY; *pg.* 1157, *pg.* 898
TYSON - Food Product - ELLENBEE-LEGGETT COMPANY INC.; *pg.* 854, *pg.* 1452
TYSON - Meat & Poultry Products - TYSON FOODS, INC.; *pg.* 902, *pg.* 35
TYSON DAY STARTS - Breakfast Products - TYSON FOODS, INC.; *pg.* 902, *pg.* 35
TYSON DELI ROTISSERIE - Chicken - TYSON FOODS, INC.; *pg.* 902, *pg.* 35
TYSON HOLLY FARMS - Fresh Poultry - TYSON FOODS, INC.; *pg.* 902, *pg.* 35
TYSON MARINATED RAW BREADED - Chicken - TYSON FOODS, INC.; *pg.* 902, *pg.* 35
TYSON'S PRIDE - Poultry Items - TYSON FOODS, INC.; *pg.* 902, *pg.* 35
TYTON - Fittings - UNITED STATES PIPE & FOUNDRY COMPANY, INC.; *pg.* 117, *pg.* 5
TYTON JOINT - Pipe - UNITED STATES PIPE & FOUNDRY COMPANY, INC.; *pg.* 117, *pg.* 5
TYTON JOINT - Pipe & Fitting - WALTER ENERGY, INC.; *pg.* 120, *pg.* 4
TYTRON - Material Test Systems - MTS SYSTEMS CORPORATION; *pg.* 442, *pg.* 923
TYVEC ATTICWRAP - Insulation - E.I. DU PONT DE NEMOURS & COMPANY; *pg.* 1159, *pg.* 390
TYVEK - High-Performance Material - E.I. DU PONT DE NEMOURS & COMPANY; *pg.* 1159, *pg.* 390
TYVEK - Clothing - LAKELAND INDUSTRIES, INC.; *pg.* 1354, *pg.* 1338
TYVEK - Package - MULTISORB TECHNOLOGIES, INC.; *pg.* 1570, *pg.* 1150
TYVEK - Medical Device - OLIVER PRODUCTS COMPANY INC.; *pg.* 1367, *pg.* 888
TYVEK - Strips & Tags - SENTRY TECHNOLOGY CORPORATION; *pg.* 672, *pg.* 1339
TYVEK - File Pocket - SMEAD MANUFACTURING COMPANY; *pg.* 470, *pg.* 926
TYVEK - Coated Lidding - TEKRA CORPORATION; *pg.* 1184, *pg.* 1884
TYVEK - Printable Plastic Product - TRANSILWRAP COMPANY, INC.; *pg.* 1470, *pg.* 613
TYVEK ASURON - Protective Material - E.I. DU PONT DE NEMOURS & COMPANY; *pg.* 1159, *pg.* 390
TYVEK BRILLION - Printing Paper - E.I. DU PONT DE NEMOURS & COMPANY; *pg.* 1159, *pg.* 390
TYVEK BRILLION - Spunbonded Olefin - TRANSILWRAP COMPANY, INC.; *pg.* 1470, *pg.* 613
TYVEK COMMERCIAL WRAP - Industrial Wrap - E.I. DU PONT DE NEMOURS & COMPANY; *pg.* 1159, *pg.* 390
TYVEK DRAINWRAP - Industrial Wrap - E.I. DU PONT DE NEMOURS & COMPANY; *pg.* 1159, *pg.* 390
TYVEK HOMEWRAP - Insulation - E.I. DU PONT DE NEMOURS & COMPANY; *pg.* 1159, *pg.* 390
TYVEK STUCCOWRAP - Insulation - E.I. DU PONT DE NEMOURS & COMPANY; *pg.* 1159, *pg.* 390
TYVEK THERMAWRAP - Insulation - E.I. DU PONT DE NEMOURS & COMPANY; *pg.* 1159, *pg.* 390
TYZOR - Organic Titanates - E.I. DU PONT DE NEMOURS & COMPANY; *pg.* 1159, *pg.* 390

U

U - Beer - SLEEMAN UNIBROUE QUEBEC; *pg.* 265, *pg.* 1950
U-2 - Systems Integration & Aeronautics - LOCKHEED MARTIN CORPORATION; *pg.* 229, *pg.* 762
U-505 SUBMARINE - Beverage Glassware - MUSEUM OF SCIENCE AND INDUSTRY; *pg.* 565, *pg.* 583
U BY UNGARO - Fragrance - AVON PRODUCTS, INC.; *pg.* 500, *pg.* 1198
U-CHARGE - Energy Storage System - VALENCE TECHNOLOGY, INC.; *pg.* 684, *pg.* 1667
U-CORD - Stem Cell - CRYO-CELL INTERNATIONAL, INC.; *pg.* 1520, *pg.* 452
U-DANCE - Toy & Game - HASBRO, INC.; *pg.* 954, *pg.* 1603
U-FREE - Office Furniture - STEELCASE INC.; *pg.* 475, *pg.* 889
U-HAUL - Moving Services - AMERCO; *pg.* 1898, *pg.* 1031
U-HAUL - Rental Trucks & Trailers - U-HAUL INTERNATIONAL, INC.; *pg.* 1926, *pg.* 20
U-NO - Milk Chocolate - ANNABELLE CANDY COMPANY, INC.; *pg.* 1850, *pg.* 100
U-NO BAR - Candy - ANNABELLE CANDY COMPANY, INC.; *pg.* 1850, *pg.* 100
U-PLEX - Aerospace Product - EATON CORPORATION; *pg.* 1331, *pg.* 1429
U-PRINT - Label - AVERY DENNISON CORPORATION; *pg.* 1452, *pg.* 95
U SEAL - Casing Seal - T.D. WILLIAMSON, INC.; *pg.* 1380, *pg.* 1490
U SERIES - Self Priming Centrifugal High Efficiency Pump - THE GORMAN-RUPP COMPANY; *pg.* 1341, *pg.* 1458
U-TEACH - Electric Instrument - UNIVERSAL INSTRUMENTS CORPORATION; *pg.* 683, *pg.* 1154
U-TWO - Designer Fragrance - PARFUMS DE COEUR LTD.; *pg.* 519, *pg.* 376
U-VIS - Software - AUTODESK INC.; *pg.* 356, *pg.* 257
U-YOU - Designer Fragrance - PARFUMS DE COEUR LTD.; *pg.* 519, *pg.* 376
U2 - Beer - SLEEMAN UNIBROUE QUEBEC; *pg.* 265, *pg.* 1950
UA ANTLER T - Apparels - UNDER ARMOUR, INC.; *pg.* 49, *pg.* 759
UA ATTACK - Apparels - UNDER ARMOUR, INC.; *pg.* 49, *pg.* 759
UA BASE - Apparels - UNDER ARMOUR, INC.; *pg.* 49, *pg.* 759
UA BREAKAWAY - Men's Footwear - UNDER ARMOUR, INC.; *pg.* 49, *pg.* 759
UA CAPTURE - Apparels - UNDER ARMOUR, INC.; *pg.* 49, *pg.* 759
UA CHIMIRA - Men's Footwear - UNDER ARMOUR, INC.; *pg.* 49, *pg.* 759
UA CUMBERLAND II - Apparels - UNDER ARMOUR, INC.; *pg.* 49, *pg.* 759
UA DEMOLISH - Men's Footwear - UNDER ARMOUR, INC.; *pg.* 49, *pg.* 759
UA ILLUSION - Men's Footwear - UNDER ARMOUR, INC.; *pg.* 49, *pg.* 759
UA METAL - Apparels - UNDER ARMOUR, INC.; *pg.* 49, *pg.* 759
UA MIRAGE - Apparels - UNDER ARMOUR, INC.; *pg.* 49, *pg.* 759
UA PLAYER POLO - Apparels - UNDER ARMOUR, INC.; *pg.* 49, *pg.* 759
UA POWER - Apparels - UNDER ARMOUR, INC.; *pg.* 49, *pg.* 759
UA PROXIMO - Apparels - UNDER ARMOUR, INC.; *pg.* 49, *pg.* 759
UA PULSE - Accessories - UNDER ARMOUR, INC.; *pg.* 49, *pg.* 759
UA REVENANT - Men's Footwear - UNDER ARMOUR, INC.; *pg.* 49, *pg.* 759
UA TECH - Fabric - UNDER ARMOUR, INC.; *pg.* 49, *pg.* 759
UAI - Pharmaceutical Product - ALERE INC.; *pg.* 1488, *pg.* 849
UB - LED - CREE INC.; *pg.* 631, *pg.* 1371
UBA - Medical Product - HOLOGIC, INC.; *pg.* 1416, *pg.* 784
UBAC - Chemical Coating - ENTHONE INC.; *pg.* 1161, *pg.* 381
UBERSOCIAL - Twitter Application - UBERMEDIA, INC.; *pg.* 1286, *pg.* 181
UBERTI - Firearm - BENELLI USA CORPORATION; *pg.* 1827, *pg.* 754
UBIQ SOFTWARE - Software - NBS TECHNOLOGIES INC.; *pg.* 786, *pg.* 1941
UBL - Semiconductor Solution - CYPRESS SEMICONDUCTOR CORPORATION; *pg.* 1326, *pg.* 243
UBZ - Software - BIO-RAD LABORATORIES, INC.; *pg.* 1504, *pg.* 101
UC EXPRESS - Claim Service - EQUIFAX WORKFORCE SOLUTIONS; *pg.* 394, *pg.* 997
UC STRIP - Nasal Tube Fastener - DERMA SCIENCES, INC.; *pg.* 1523, *pg.* 1111
UCAR - All-Acrylic, Styrene-Acrylic & Vinyl-Acrylic Resins - THE DOW CHEMICAL COMPANY; *pg.* 1157, *pg.* 898
UCARCIDE - Antimicrobial - THE DOW CHEMICAL COMPANY; *pg.* 1157, *pg.* 898
UCARHIDE - Opacifier - THE DOW CHEMICAL COMPANY; *pg.* 1157, *pg.* 898
UCARKLEAN - Solution - THE DOW CHEMICAL COMPANY; *pg.* 1157, *pg.* 898
UCARMAG - Binder Resins - THE DOW CHEMICAL COMPANY; *pg.* 1157, *pg.* 898
UCARSAN - Sanitizer - THE DOW CHEMICAL COMPANY; *pg.* 1157, *pg.* 898
UCARSEP - Amine Reclamation System - THE DOW CHEMICAL COMPANY; *pg.* 1157, *pg.* 898
UCARSOL - Gas Treating Solvent - THE DOW CHEMICAL COMPANY; *pg.* 1157, *pg.* 898
UCARTHERM - Heat Transfer Fluid - THE DOW CHEMICAL COMPANY; *pg.* 1157, *pg.* 898
UCAT - Catalyst - THE DOW CHEMICAL COMPANY; *pg.* 1157, *pg.* 898
UCECOAT - UV-Curable Resins - CYTEC INDUSTRIES, INC.; *pg.* 1155, *pg.* 1131
UCECRYL - Water-based Acrylic Polymers - CYTEC INDUSTRIES, INC.; *pg.* 1155, *pg.* 1131
UCERIS - Pharmaceutical Product - SALIX PHARMACEUTICALS, INC.; *pg.* 1591, *pg.* 1388
UCG-BETA SLIDE - Pharmaceutical Product - ALERE INC.; *pg.* 1488, *pg.* 849
UCG BETA-STAT - Pharmaceutical Product - ALERE INC.; *pg.* 1488, *pg.* 849
UCG-EARLY PROBE II - Pharmaceutical Product - ALERE INC.; *pg.* 1488, *pg.* 849
UCG-SLIDE TEST - Pharmaceutical Product - ALERE INC.; *pg.* 1488, *pg.* 849
UCG STICK - Pharmaceutical Product - ALERE INC.; *pg.* 1488, *pg.* 849
UCG-TEST - Pharmaceutical Product - ALERE INC.; *pg.* 1488, *pg.* 849
UCG-TITRATION SET - Pharmaceutical Product - ALERE INC.; *pg.* 1488, *pg.* 849
UCG TUBE TEST - Pharmaceutical Product - ALERE INC.; *pg.* 1488, *pg.* 849
UCON - Fluid - THE DOW CHEMICAL COMPANY; *pg.* 1157,

First page reference indicates Business Class Edition
Second page reference indicates Geographic Edition

pg. 898

UCONALL - Lubricants - THE DOW CHEMICAL COMPANY; *pg.* 1157, *pg.* 898

UCONEX - Antimicrobial - THE DOW CHEMICAL COMPANY; *pg.* 1157, *pg.* 898

UCSP - Chip Scale Package - MAXIM INTEGRATED PRODUCTS, INC.; *pg.* 653, *pg.* 247

UDDERDINE - Spray Wash - BOUMATIC LLC; *pg.* 701, *pg.* 1865

UDDERGUARD - Fabric Product - BELTON INDUSTRIES, INC.; *pg.* 691, *pg.* 1612

UDEL - Thermoplastic Product - WESTLAKE PLASTICS COMPANY; *pg.* 1892, *pg.* 1548

UDIMAR - Alloy - SPECIAL METALS CORPORATION; *pg.* 1377, *pg.* 1850

UDIMET - Alloy Product - SPECIAL METALS CORPORATION; *pg.* 1377, *pg.* 1850

UDIQUE - Chemical Coating - ENTHONE INC.; *pg.* 1161, *pg.* 381

UDI'S - Gluten-Free Bakery Products - BOULDER BRANDS, INC.; *pg.* 1016, *pg.* 310

UF-100 - Urine Cell Analyzer - IRIS INTERNATIONAL, INC.; *pg.* 1547, *pg.* 64

U.F. MAT - Fabric - KOPPERS HOLDINGS INC.; *pg.* 1170, *pg.* 1577

UFD - Storage System - HGST; *pg.* 406, *pg.* 260

UFO - Commercial Lighting - SWIVELIER CO., INC.; *pg.* 1307, *pg.* 1142

UFO-USER FRIENDLY OFFICE - Ergonomically Designed Computer Accessories - RUBBERMAID HOME PRODUCTS; *pg.* 1138, *pg.* 1453

UFOOD - Restaurants - UFOOD RESTAURANT GROUP, INC.; *pg.* 1754, *pg.* 837

UFT - United Farm Tool - AG-MEIER INDUSTRIES LLC; *pg.* 700, *pg.* 1668

UFWC 1X2 - Coupler - OPLINK COMMUNICATIONS, INC.; *pg.* 660, *pg.* 91

UFWC 2X2 - Coupler - OPLINK COMMUNICATIONS, INC.; *pg.* 660, *pg.* 91

UFX - Performance Knits - ELBECO INCORPORATED; *pg.* 40, *pg.* 1584

UGG - Boots, Apparel, Loungewear, Accessories & Handbags - DECKERS OUTDOOR CORPORATION; *pg.* 1807, *pg.* 100

UGI CORPORATION - Energy Product - UGI CORPORATION; *pg.* 1953, *pg.* 1544

UGI ENTERPRISES - Energy Services - UGI CORPORATION; *pg.* 1953, *pg.* 1544

UGI UTILITIES INC - Natural Gas & Electric Utility - UGI CORPORATION; *pg.* 1953, *pg.* 1544

UGLIES - Swim Wear - DOLFIN INTERNATIONAL CORPORATION; *pg.* 23, *pg.* 1553

UGLY'S - Fire Safety Book - NATIONAL FIRE PROTECTION ASSOCIATION; *pg.* 149, *pg.* 842

UGO BASILE THERMAL PLANTAR - Analgesia Instrument - STOELTING CO.; *pg.* 1430, *pg.* 671

UH-1Y - Military Helicopter - BELL HELICOPTER TEXTRON, INC.; *pg.* 224, *pg.* 1693

UHAUL.COM - Trailer - U-HAUL INTERNATIONAL, INC.; *pg.* 1926, *pg.* 20

UHF-R - Wireless Microphone System - SHURE INCORPORATED; *pg.* 672, *pg.* 638

UHTC - Telescope - MEADE INSTRUMENTS CORPORATION; *pg.* 1422, *pg.* 113

UICS - Electric Instrument - UNIVERSAL INSTRUMENTS CORPORATION; *pg.* 683, *pg.* 1154

UIL HOLDINGS CORPORATION - Commercial & Industrial Conservation - UIL HOLDINGS CORPORATION; *pg.* 1953, *pg.* 359

UJENA JAM - Publication - UJENA SWIMWEAR AND FASHIONS; *pg.* 34, *pg.* 163

ULBRASEAL - Stainless Steel & Special Metal Strips - ULBRICH STAINLESS STEEL & SPECIAL METALS, INC.; *pg.* 117, *pg.* 360

ULBRAVAR - Stainless Steel & Special Metal Strips - ULBRICH STAINLESS STEEL & SPECIAL METALS, INC.; *pg.* 117, *pg.* 360

ULBRICH - Stainless Steel & Special Metal Strips & Round & Flat Shaped Wire - ULBRICH STAINLESS STEEL & SPECIAL METALS, INC.; *pg.* 117, *pg.* 360

ULCETROL - Dietary Supplement - NOW HEALTH GROUP, INC.; *pg.* 1576, *pg.* 557

ULE - Glass & Ceramic Material - CORNING INCORPORATED; *pg.* 1122, *pg.* 1154

ULRICH SERIALS ANALYSIS SYSTEM - Online Database - R.R. BOWKER LLC; *pg.* 1682, *pg.* 1095

ULRICH'S INTERNATIONAL PERIODICALS DIRECTORY - Reference Book for Serials - R.R. BOWKER LLC; *pg.* 1682, *pg.* 1095

ULRICHSWEB.COM - Online Database - R.R. BOWKER LLC; *pg.* 1682, *pg.* 1095

ULTA BEAUTY - Cosmetics - ULTA SALON, COSMETICS & FRAGRANCE, INC.; *pg.* 524, *pg.* 559

ULTA PROFESSIONAL - Cosmetics - ULTA SALON, COSMETICS & FRAGRANCE, INC.; *pg.* 524, *pg.* 559

ULTA.COM - E-Commerce Website - ULTA SALON, COSMETICS & FRAGRANCE, INC.; *pg.* 524, *pg.* 559

ULTAMUS RAID - Data Protection Appliances - OVERLAND STORAGE, INC.; *pg.* 451, *pg.* 205

ULTAMUS RAID 1200 - Data Protection - OVERLAND STORAGE, INC.; *pg.* 451, *pg.* 205

ULTAMUS RAID 4800 - Data Protection - OVERLAND STORAGE, INC.; *pg.* 451, *pg.* 205

ULTANE - Drug - ABBOTT LABORATORIES; *pg.* 1484, *pg.* 551

ULTEM - Engineered Plastics - GENERAL ELECTRIC COMPANY; *pg.* 1297, *pg.* 347

ULTEM - Thermoplastic Product - WESTLAKE PLASTICS COMPANY; *pg.* 1892, *pg.* 1548

ULTI-MATE - Knife - BUCK KNIVES, INC.; *pg.* 1828, *pg.* 550

ULTI-MATE - Cushion - INVACARE CORPORATION; *pg.* 1546, *pg.* 1451

ULTI-MATE - Electronic Components - MOLEX INCORPORATED; *pg.* 655, *pg.* 628

ULTIKLEEN - Filter Assembly - PALL CORPORATION; *pg.* 232, *pg.* 1323

ULTIMA - Ceilings & Walls - ARMSTRONG WORLD INDUSTRIES, INC.; *pg.* 914, *pg.* 1545

ULTIMA - Carpet - BEAULIEU GROUP, LLC; *pg.* 917, *pg.* 529

ULTIMA - Laser Measurement Instrument - COHERENT, INC.; *pg.* 1406, *pg.* 265

ULTIMA - Flooring Product - CONGOLEUM CORPORATION; *pg.* 921, *pg.* 1084

ULTIMA - Medical & Aesthetic Product - DYNATRONICS CORPORATION; *pg.* 1526, *pg.* 1757

ULTIMA - Picture Paper - EASTMAN KODAK COMPANY; *pg.* 1408, *pg.* 1333

ULTIMA - Video Game - ELECTRONIC ARTS INC.; *pg.* 951, *pg.* 189

ULTIMA - Paper Towels, Soap & Bath Tissue - GEORGIA-PACIFIC LLC; *pg.* 1458, *pg.* 507

ULTIMA - Furniture - JASPER GROUP; *pg.* 930, *pg.* 691

ULTIMA - Truck Storage Boxes - LUND INTERNATIONAL, INC.; *pg.* 211, *pg.* 526

ULTIMA - Gas Monitor - MINE SAFETY APPLIANCES COMPANY; *pg.* 1361, *pg.* 1525

ULTIMA - Fabric - NEMSCHOFF, INC.; *pg.* 936, *pg.* 1890

ULTIMA - Tilt Mount - NEWPORT CORPORATION; *pg.* 1424, *pg.* 114

ULTIMA - Laptop Case - SAMSONITE CORPORATION; *pg.* 11, *pg.* 830

ULTIMA 1400 - Multi-purpose Cutting Plotter - MUTOH AMERICA INC.; *pg.* 443, *pg.* 18

ULTIMA 80 - Hearing Aid - BELTONE ELECTRONICS LLC; *pg.* 1503, *pg.* 614

ULTIMA 850 - Multi-purpose Cutting Plotter - MUTOH AMERICA INC.; *pg.* 443, *pg.* 18

ULTIMA COOK - Speed Oven - WHIRLPOOL CORPORATION; *pg.* 62, *pg.* 872

ULTIMA II - Cosmetics - REVLON, INC.; *pg.* 521, *pg.* 1286

ULTIMA LEATHER - Leather Textiles - BERNHARDT DESIGN; *pg.* 918, *pg.* 1381

ULTIMAGOLD - Cocktails - PERKINELMER, INC.; *pg.* 1426, *pg.* 853

ULTIMANET - Software - ULTIMATE TECHNOLOGY CORPORATION; *pg.* 486, *pg.* 1349

ULTIMATE - Screws - ATLAS BOLT & SCREW COMPANY; *pg.* 1042, *pg.* 1403

THE ULTIMATE - Banking Service - THE BANK OF NOVA SCOTIA; *pg.* 721, *pg.* 1935

ULTIMATE - Art Product - DANIEL SMITH INC.; *pg.* 1766, *pg.* 1835

ULTIMATE - Glove - ETONIC WORLDWIDE LLC; *pg.* 1808, *pg.* 857

ULTIMATE - Spray Gun Cleaning Kit - GRACO, INC.; *pg.* 1342, *pg.* 935

ULTIMATE - Soldering Flux - LA-CO INDUSTRIES MARKAL CO., INC.; *pg.* 1170, *pg.* 610

ULTIMATE - In-Ground Vinyl Pools - POOL CORPORATION; *pg.* 1843, *pg.* 743

ULTIMATE - Molecular Biology Product - THERMO FISHER SCIENTIFIC INC.; *pg.* 1602, *pg.* 61

ULTIMATE - Crosstrainer - WEINBRENNER SHOE COMPANY, INC.; *pg.* 1822, *pg.* 1871

ULTIMATE - Recreation Vehicle - WINNEBAGO INDUSTRIES, INC.; *pg.* 1712, *pg.* 707

ULTIMATE ACCOUNT - Account - SALEM FIVE CENTS SAVINGS BANK; *pg.* 800, *pg.* 843

ULTIMATE BIRTHDAY BUNDLE - Birthday Gifts - 1-800-FLOWERS.COM, INC.; *pg.* 1758, *pg.* 1151

ULTIMATE CHOICE - Golf Gifts - GOLF GIFTS & GALLERY; *pg.* 1835, *pg.* 1887

ULTIMATE CHOICE - Weight Loss Program - JENNY CRAIG OPERATIONS, INC.; *pg.* 1548, *pg.* 59

ULTIMATE CHORUS - Guitar Amplifier - FENDER MUSICAL INSTRUMENTS CORPORATION; *pg.* 547, *pg.* 21

ULTIMATE DOOM - Video Game - ID SOFTWARE, INC.; *pg.* 956, *pg.* 1727

ULTIMATE FAMILY WAGON - Wagon - RADIO FLYER INC.; *pg.* 966, *pg.* 588

ULTIMATE GREENZONE - Health Care Product - NATURE'S SUNSHINE PRODUCTS, INC.; *pg.* 1571, *pg.* 1754

ULTIMATE HEALTH - Body Tone Vitamin Formula - ADH HEALTH PRODUCTS, INC.; *pg.* 1487, *pg.* 1154

ULTIMATE ID - Cable Tie - PANDUIT CORP.; *pg.* 661, *pg.* 663

ULTIMATE KITCHEN GARDENER - Gardening Appliance Systems - AEROGROW INTERNATIONAL, INC.; *pg.* 1393, *pg.* 310

THE ULTIMATE LADDERED - Banking Service - THE BANK OF NOVA SCOTIA; *pg.* 721, *pg.* 1935

ULTIMATE LIGHT BEER BY DESIGN - Tagline - MILLERCOORS; *pg.* 254, *pg.* 1877

ULTIMATE LOVE BOUQUET - Flower Arrangement - 1-800-FLOWERS.COM, INC.; *pg.* 1758, *pg.* 1151

ULTIMATE MOIST - Hair & Skin Product - AUBREY ORGANICS INC.; *pg.* 499, *pg.* 470

ULTIMATE MX - Airless Paint Sprayer - GRACO, INC.; *pg.* 1342, *pg.* 935

ULTIMATE NOVA - Electric Airless Paint Sprayer - GRACO, INC.; *pg.* 1342, *pg.* 935

ULTIMATE NUTRIT - Nutritional Product - NUTRACEUTICAL INTERNATIONAL CORPORATION; *pg.* 1576, *pg.* 1753

ULTIMATE NUTRITION - Nutritional Product - NUTRACEUTICAL INTERNATIONAL CORPORATION; *pg.* 1576, *pg.* 1753

THE ULTIMATE OFFICE COFFEE - Coffee Service - KEURIG GREEN MOUNTAIN, INC.; *pg.* 868, *pg.* 1768

ULTIMATE PLUS - Airless Paint Sprayer - GRACO, INC.; *pg.* 1342, *pg.* 935

THE ULTIMATE POWER SOURCE - Slogan - JOHNSON CONTROLS, INC.; *pg.* 209, *pg.* 1876

THE ULTIMATE PROTECTIVE SYSTEM. - Slogan - PELICAN PRODUCTS; *pg.* 1467, *pg.* 843

ULTIMATE QUAKE - Game - ACTIVISION BLIZZARD, INC.; *pg.* 948, *pg.* 271

THE ULTIMATE REFRESHER - Sparkling Mineral Water - CRYSTAL GEYSER WATER COMPANY; *pg.* 248, *pg.* 57

THE ULTIMATE SAVINGS MEMBERSHIP - Coupon Books - ENTERTAINMENT PUBLICATIONS, INC.; *pg.* 1639, *pg.* 910

ULTIMATE SEVENS - Video Game - INTERNATIONAL GAME TECHNOLOGY; *pg.* 957, *pg.* 1024

ULTIMATE SPIDER-MAN - Game - ACTIVISION BLIZZARD, INC.; *pg.* 948, *pg.* 271

ULTIMATE STRATEGO - Game - WINNING MOVES GAMES, INC.; *pg.* 970, *pg.* 816

ULTIMATE SUEDE - Apparel - CABELA'S INCORPORATED; *pg.* 535, *pg.* 1019

ULTIMATE TEXTURE - Carpet - BEAULIEU GROUP, LLC; *pg.* 917, *pg.* 529

ULTIMATE TWIST - Carpet - BEAULIEU GROUP, LLC; *pg.* 917, *pg.* 529

THE ULTIMATE VISUAL EXPERIENCE - Graphics Card - ADVANCED MICRO DEVICES, INC.; *pg.* 613, *pg.* 282

ULTIMATE WEAR - Nail Enamel - MAYBELLINE LLC; *pg.* 516, *pg.* 1257

ULTIMATE X POKER - Video Game - INTERNATIONAL GAME TECHNOLOGY; *pg.* 957, *pg.* 1024

ULTIMATEBLUE - Radio Modem - RF MICRO DEVICES, INC.; *pg.* 667, *pg.* 1376

ULTIMATOUCH 1800 SERIES - Touch Screen Workstation - ULTIMATE TECHNOLOGY CORPORATION; *pg.* 486, *pg.* 1349

ULTIMATTE - Paint - ROSCO LABORATORIES, INC.; *pg.* 1782, *pg.* 378
ULTIMAX - Control Software - HURCO COMPANIES, INC.; *pg.* 409, *pg.* 686
ULTIMAX - Socks - WIGWAM MILLS, INC.; *pg.* 15, *pg.* 1894
ULTINET - Software - HURCO COMPANIES, INC.; *pg.* 409, *pg.* 686
ULTIPATH - Controllers - HURCO COMPANIES, INC.; *pg.* 409, *pg.* 686
ULTIPLEAT - Filter Cartridge - PALL CORPORATION; *pg.* 232, *pg.* 1323
ULTIPOCKET - Software - HURCO COMPANIES, INC.; *pg.* 409, *pg.* 686
ULTIPOR - Filter Cartridge - PALL CORPORATION; *pg.* 232, *pg.* 1323
ULTIPRO - Software - THE ULTIMATE SOFTWARE GROUP, INC.; *pg.* 486, *pg.* 479
ULTR-LOK - Clamping Systems - IDEX CORPORATION; *pg.* 1347, *pg.* 623
ULTRA - Protective Material - 3M COMPANY; *pg.* 1142, *pg.* 956
ULTRA - Paint - AKZONOBEL DECORATIVE PAINTS U.S.; *pg.* 1439, *pg.* 1474
ULTRA - Clipper Kit - ANDIS COMPANY; *pg.* 498, *pg.* 1895
ULTRA - Semiconductor Processing Equipment - AXCELIS TECHNOLOGIES, INC.; *pg.* 1400, *pg.* 787
ULTRA - Software - CYPRESS SEMICONDUCTOR CORPORATION; *pg.* 1326, *pg.* 243
ULTRA - Screen - DA-LITE SCREEN COMPANY; *pg.* 632, *pg.* 698
ULTRA - Dental Product - DENTSPLY INTERNATIONAL INC.; *pg.* 1522, *pg.* 1596
ULTRA - Photographic Paper - EASTMAN KODAK COMPANY; *pg.* 1408, *pg.* 1333
ULTRA - Gel Coats - FERRO CORPORATION; *pg.* 1162, *pg.* 1462
ULTRA - Thermal Imaging System - FLIR SYSTEMS, INC.; *pg.* 1413, *pg.* 1510
ULTRA - Wringer - GEERPRES INC.; *pg.* 1339, *pg.* 901
ULTRA - Electronic Sprayers - GRACO, INC.; *pg.* 1342, *pg.* 935
ULTRA - Fabric - POLYMER GROUP, INC.; *pg.* 698, *pg.* 1368
ULTRA - Medical Product - PROPPER MANUFACTURING COMPANY, INC.; *pg.* 1586, *pg.* 1175
ULTRA - Software - ROCKWELL AUTOMATION, INC.; *pg.* 668, *pg.* 1880
ULTRA - Suitcase - SAMSONITE CORPORATION; *pg.* 11, *pg.* 830
ULTRA - MP&G Accelerator - SIGMA DESIGNS, INC.; *pg.* 469, *pg.* 148
ULTRA - Automotive Coating - SILBERLINE MANUFACTURING CO., INC.; *pg.* 110, *pg.* 1588
ULTRA - Plastic Houseware Product - STERILITE CORPORATION; *pg.* 1138, *pg.* 848
ULTRA - Light - SUREFIRE, LLC; *pg.* 1307, *pg.* 90
ULTRA - Healthcare Product - SWANSON HEALTH PRODUCTS INC.; *pg.* 1600, *pg.* 1397
ULTRA - Lotion Soap - SWISHER HYGIENE INC.; *pg.* 336, *pg.* 1507
ULTRA - Label Product - SYSTEMAX, INC.; *pg.* 481, *pg.* 1324
ULTRA - Pipeline Pigging Product - T.D. WILLIAMSON, INC.; *pg.* 1380, *pg.* 1490
ULTRA - Software - VERINT SYSTEMS INC.; *pg.* 488, *pg.* 1182
ULTRA 7000 - Thermal Imaging System - FLIR SYSTEMS, INC.; *pg.* 1413, *pg.* 1510
ULTRA 8000 - Thermal Imager - FLIR SYSTEMS, INC.; *pg.* 1413, *pg.* 1510
ULTRA 8500 - Thermal Imager - FLIR SYSTEMS, INC.; *pg.* 1413, *pg.* 1510
ULTRA-ACTIVIN - Nutritional Supplement - NATURAL ORGANICS, INC.; *pg.* 1571, *pg.* 1181
ULTRA AIRE - Air Filter - DONALDSON COMPANY, INC.; *pg.* 1329, *pg.* 917
ULTRA-BASE - Gypsum Ceiling Board - USG CORPORATION; *pg.* 118, *pg.* 594
ULTRA BEAD - Paper Faced Metal Outside Corner Tape-On Trim - USG CORPORATION; *pg.* 118, *pg.* 594
ULTRA BLEND - Apparel - GILDAN ACTIVEWEAR INC.; *pg.* 1835, *pg.* 1955
ULTRA-BLUE-SEAL - Vehicle Safety System - GROTE INDUSTRIES, INC.; *pg.* 206, *pg.* 693
ULTRA/BOND - Adhesives - ROYAL ADHESIVES & SEALANTS LLC; *pg.* 1179, *pg.* 697
ULTRA-BOND QUIK - Dental Cement - DEN-MAT CORPORATION; *pg.* 1522, *pg.* 271
ULTRA BOUCLE - Rug - COURISTAN INC.; *pg.* 921, *pg.* 1067
ULTRA-BROW - Eyebrow Product - MAYBELLINE LLC; *pg.* 516, *pg.* 1257
ULTRA CAB - Cab/Sleeper Enhancement - PETERBILT MOTORS CO.; *pg.* 188, *pg.* 1691
ULTRA CABLE FEEDER - Cable Feeder - GREENLEE TEXTRON INC.; *pg.* 1048, *pg.* 655
ULTRA CARB INTERCEPT - Vitamin & Dietary Supplement - NATROL, INC.; *pg.* 1570, *pg.* 64
ULTRA CARE - Software - AMERICAN REPUBLIC INSURANCE COMPANY; *pg.* 1191, *pg.* 704
ULTRA CERAMIC MATTE - Interior Wall Paint - THE MURALO COMPANY; *pg.* 1444, *pg.* 1042
ULTRA-CHEM - Hose - HBD INDUSTRIES, INC.; *pg.* 207, *pg.* 1449
ULTRA-CHONDROITIN - Nutritional Supplement - NATURAL ORGANICS, INC.; *pg.* 1571, *pg.* 1181
ULTRA-CINCH - Cable Tie - PANDUIT CORP.; *pg.* 661, *pg.* 663
ULTRA CLASSIC - Motorcycles - HARLEY-DAVIDSON, INC.; *pg.* 178, *pg.* 1874
ULTRA CLEAR - Varnish - MOHAWK FINISHING PRODUCTS, INC.; *pg.* 1173, *pg.* 1378
ULTRA CLEAR - Cup - SOLO CUP COMPANY; *pg.* 1469, *pg.* 625
ULTRA CLOROX2 - Color Safe Bleach - THE CLOROX COMPANY; *pg.* 327, *pg.* 169
ULTRA COLOR - Beauty Product - AVON PRODUCTS, INC.; *pg.* 500, *pg.* 1198
ULTRA-COM - Microcontroller for Plastics Assembly - DUKANE CORPORATION; *pg.* 634, *pg.* 658
ULTRA COMPOSITE - Construction Material - CRANE PLASTICS HOLDING COMPANY; *pg.* 1881, *pg.* 1439
ULTRA COTE - Clays For Coating & Filling Paper & Board - BASF CATALYSTS LLC; *pg.* 1148, *pg.* 1074
ULTRA COTE - Automotive Reconditioning Product - MOC PRODUCTS COMPANY, INC.; *pg.* 332, *pg.* 174
ULTRA COTTON - Apparel - GILDAN ACTIVEWEAR INC.; *pg.* 1835, *pg.* 1955
ULTRA CRANBERRY - Nutritional Supplement - NATURAL ORGANICS, INC.; *pg.* 1571, *pg.* 1181
ULTRA CSP - Packaging System - AMKOR TECHNOLOGY, INC.; *pg.* 67, *pg.* 25
ULTRA CUT - Haircutting Kit - CONAIR CORPORATION; *pg.* 505, *pg.* 1055
ULTRA DEO BASE - Odor Counteractant Concentrate - SURCO PRODUCTS, INC.; *pg.* 336, *pg.* 1581
ULTRA DISH - Household Product - BLUE CROSS LABORATORIES; *pg.* 326, *pg.* 277
ULTRA DOLCE - Sauce - LIDESTRI FOODS, INC.; *pg.* 874, *pg.* 1159
ULTRA-DRY - Continuous Flow Drying System - CTB INTERNATIONAL CORP.; *pg.* 850, *pg.* 695
ULTRA-DUCT - Modular Wiring Management System - PASS & SEYMOUR/LEGRAND; *pg.* 1303, *pg.* 1344
ULTRA ELITE - Gas Mask - MINE SAFETY APPLIANCES COMPANY; *pg.* 1361, *pg.* 1525
ULTRA EPO - Nutritional Supplement - NATURAL ORGANICS, INC.; *pg.* 1571, *pg.* 1181
ULTRA ETCH - Etchant System - MACDERMID, INC.; *pg.* 1172, *pg.* 321
ULTRA-FIBER - Pharmaceutical Product - ALVA/AMCO PHARMACAL COMPANIES, INC.; *pg.* 1492, *pg.* 637
ULTRA FILTER - Gas Mask - MINE SAFETY APPLIANCES COMPANY; *pg.* 1361, *pg.* 1525
ULTRA-FIT - Face Mask - BAXTER INTERNATIONAL INC.; *pg.* 1499, *pg.* 599
ULTRA FIT CIRCLE - Accessories - BALANCED BODY, INC.; *pg.* 1826, *pg.* 195
ULTRA FLEX - Cable - GENERAL CABLE CORPORATION; *pg.* 83, *pg.* 729
ULTRA-FLEX - Fluid Handling System - GRACO, INC.; *pg.* 1342, *pg.* 935
ULTRA FLEX - Waste Bags - PACTIV CORPORATION; *pg.* 1466, *pg.* 624
ULTRA FLEX - Resin Mouldings - WHITE RIVER HARDWOODS-WOODWORKS, INC.; *pg.* 121, *pg.* 31
ULTRA FLEX HOME EQUITY - Banking Services - FIRST NIAGARA FINANCIAL GROUP, INC.; *pg.* 757, *pg.* 1148
ULTRA FLEXIBLE - Hose - TEKNOR APEX COMPANY; *pg.* 1889, *pg.* 1605
ULTRA-FLO - Shot Metering Dispenser - GRACO, INC.; *pg.* 1342, *pg.* 935
ULTRA FLOSS - Dental Floss - GILLETTE; *pg.* 1536, *pg.* 795
ULTRA FLUFFY - Fabric Softener Sheet - BLUE CROSS LABORATORIES; *pg.* 326, *pg.* 277
ULTRA FLUSH - Pressure-Assisted Toilet - GERBER PLUMBING FIXTURES CORPORATION; *pg.* 84, *pg.* 672
ULTRA-FOAM - Refrigerated Truck Insulation - KIDRON, INC.; *pg.* 181, *pg.* 1457
ULTRA FORCE - Mechanical Vibratory Feeder - ERIEZ MANUFACTURING CO. INC.; *pg.* 1335, *pg.* 1530
ULTRA FORM - Steel Product - AK STEEL HOLDING CORPORATION; *pg.* 1311, *pg.* 1479
ULTRA FORM - Grinder - BRYANT GRINDER; *pg.* 1320, *pg.* 1768
ULTRA FYRE GAS INSERTS - Ceramic Product - PORTLAND WILLAMETTE; *pg.* 1129, *pg.* 1505
ULTRA FYRE GAS LOGS - Ceramic Product - PORTLAND WILLAMETTE; *pg.* 1129, *pg.* 1505
ULTRA GAUZE - Surgical Gauze - CROSSTEX INTERNATIONAL INC.; *pg.* 1520, *pg.* 1164
ULTRA GEAR - Apparel - SPORT OBERMEYER LTD.; *pg.* 1846, *pg.* 310
ULTRA GINKGO - Nutritional Supplement - NATURAL ORGANICS, INC.; *pg.* 1571, *pg.* 1181
ULTRA GLOSS 90 - Clays For Coating & Filling Paper & Board - BASF CATALYSTS LLC; *pg.* 1148, *pg.* 1074
ULTRA-GLUCOSAMINE - Nutritional Supplement - NATURAL ORGANICS, INC.; *pg.* 1571, *pg.* 1181
ULTRA GOURMET ICE - Beverage - BUNN-O-MATIC CORPORATION; *pg.* 53, *pg.* 661
ULTRA-GRIP - Multi-Purpose Latex Primer - DUNN-EDWARDS CORPORATION; *pg.* 1442, *pg.* 129
ULTRA-HAIR - Nutritional Supplement - NATURAL ORGANICS, INC.; *pg.* 1571, *pg.* 1181
ULTRA-HIDE - Coating - AKZONOBEL DECORATIVE PAINTS U.S.; *pg.* 1439, *pg.* 1474
ULTRA HIT PROGRESSIVE - Game - WMS INDUSTRIES INC.; *pg.* 593, *pg.* 666
ULTRA-HYDE - Belt Pad - KLEIN TOOLS INC.; *pg.* 1052, *pg.* 627
ULTRA ICE - Medical Device - BOSTON SCIENTIFIC CORPORATION; *pg.* 1508, *pg.* 831
ULTRA II - Cable - COMMSCOPE, INC.; *pg.* 278, *pg.* 1378
ULTRA-ISOFLAVONE - Nutritional Supplement - NATURAL ORGANICS, INC.; *pg.* 1571, *pg.* 1181
ULTRA-JUICE - Nutritional Supplement - NATURAL ORGANICS, INC.; *pg.* 1571, *pg.* 1181
ULTRA LIFE - Cow Colostrum Supplement - TROUW NUTRITION USA; *pg.* 1482, *pg.* 616
ULTRA LIGHTWEIGHT - Rifle - WEATHERBY, INC.; *pg.* 1848, *pg.* 181
ULTRA LIP SHINE - Cosmetic Product - MERLE NORMAN COSMETICS, INC.; *pg.* 517, *pg.* 136
ULTRA-LITE - Spray Guns - GRACO, INC.; *pg.* 1342, *pg.* 935
ULTRA LO-SOX - Catalyst Additive - JOHNSON MATTHEY PROCESS TECHNOLOGIES; *pg.* 1169, *pg.* 1083
ULTRA-LOCK - Electronic Components - MOLEX INCORPORATED; *pg.* 655, *pg.* 628
ULTRA LOW - Chemical Product - NOVA CHEMICALS CORPORATION; *pg.* 1175, *pg.* 1904
ULTRA LOW ADAPTER - Adapter - BROOKFIELD ENGINEERING LABORATORIES, INC.; *pg.* 1403, *pg.* 833
ULTRA LOW BOOT 522 - Jean - LEVI STRAUSS & CO.; *pg.* 43, *pg.* 220
ULTRA-LUTEIN - Nutritional Supplement - NATURAL ORGANICS, INC.; *pg.* 1571, *pg.* 1181
ULTRA LUXURY - Beauty Product - AVON PRODUCTS, INC.; *pg.* 500, *pg.* 1198
ULTRA-MAG - Level Controls - DWYER INSTRUMENTS INC.; *pg.* 1330, *pg.* 694
ULTRA MARATHON - Low Maintenance Floor - ROCHESTER MIDLAND CORPORATION; *pg.* 334, *pg.* 1337
ULTRA MASTER - Software - ROCKWELL AUTOMATION, INC.; *pg.* 668, *pg.* 1880
ULTRA MAT - Plastic & Rubber - TEKNOR APEX COMPANY; *pg.* 1889, *pg.* 1605
ULTRA-MATIC - Pump Product - IDEX CORPORATION; *pg.* 1347, *pg.* 623
ULTRA MATTE - Adhesive Coated Paper - SPINNAKER COATING, LLC; *pg.* 1470, *pg.* 1477
ULTRA MEGA - Nutritional Supplement - GENERAL

First page reference indicates Business Class Edition
Second page reference indicates Geographic Edition

NUTRITION CENTERS, INC.; *pg.* 1534, *pg.* 1575
ULTRA-MINI - Switch - OPLINK COMMUNICATIONS, INC.; *pg.* 660, *pg.* 91
ULTRA MINTS - Mints - NEW ENGLAND CONFECTIONERY COMPANY INC.; *pg.* 1860, *pg.* 842
ULTRA MIRAGE - Diagnostic Product - RESMED INC.; *pg.* 1589, *pg.* 207
ULTRA MIRROR - Glass Product - GUARDIAN INDUSTRIES CORP.; *pg.* 85, *pg.* 869
ULTRA-MIX - Carbon Steel Pump - GRACO, INC.; *pg.* 1342, *pg.* 935
ULTRA-NAILS - Nutritional Supplement - NATURAL ORGANICS, INC.; *pg.* 1571, *pg.* 1181
ULTRA NATURAL RUN - Footwear - K-SWISS; *pg.* 1837, *pg.* 306
ULTRA NO-FOG - Face Mask - CROSSTEX INTERNATIONAL INC.; *pg.* 1520, *pg.* 1164
ULTRA-NOSE-BOX - Vehicle Safety System - GROTE INDUSTRIES, INC.; *pg.* 206, *pg.* 693
ULTRA NTRL RUN II S - Footwear - K-SWISS; *pg.* 1837, *pg.* 306
ULTRA OMEGA 3-6-9 - Nutritional Product - NUTRACEUTICAL INTERNATIONAL CORPORATION; *pg.* 1576, *pg.* 1753
ULTRA-ONE - Nutritional Supplement - NATURAL ORGANICS, INC.; *pg.* 1571, *pg.* 1181
ULTRA OXY - Dish Detergent - BLUE CROSS LABORATORIES; *pg.* 326, *pg.* 277
ULTRA PEP-BACK - Pharmaceutical Product - ALVA/AMCO PHARMACAL COMPANIES, INC.; *pg.* 1492, *pg.* 637
ULTRA-PIN - Vehicle Safety System - GROTE INDUSTRIES, INC.; *pg.* 206, *pg.* 693
ULTRA PLAS - Chemical Product - WESTROCK COMPANY; *pg.* 1472, *pg.* 1805
ULTRA PLUS - Glove - CROSSTEX INTERNATIONAL INC.; *pg.* 1520, *pg.* 1164
ULTRA-POUR - BB O&ES Concrete Form Plywood - PLUM CREEK TIMBER COMPANY, INC.; *pg.* 105, *pg.* 1838
ULTRA PRECISE - Eye Pencils - COVER GIRL COSMETICS; *pg.* 506, *pg.* 772
ULTRA PRENATAL - Nutritional Supplement - NATURAL ORGANICS, INC.; *pg.* 1571, *pg.* 1181
ULTRA/PRO - Brush - THE WOOSTER BRUSH COMPANY; *pg.* 1450, *pg.* 1482
ULTRA PROFESSIONAL - Steam Iron - ROWENTA (USA), INC.; *pg.* 60, *pg.* 1084
ULTRA PURE - Medical Device - INTEGRA LIFESCIENCES HOLDINGS CORPORATION; *pg.* 1545, *pg.* 1109
ULTRA PURE - Water Service - MILWAUKEE VALVE COMPANY, INC.; *pg.* 1361, *pg.* 1884
ULTRA-QUAT - Sanitizer - BIRKO CORPORATION; *pg.* 1149, *pg.* 332
ULTRA-RIDE - Seat - PETERBILT MOTORS CO.; *pg.* 188, *pg.* 1691
ULTRA RULE - Hand Tool - GENERAL TOOLS & INSTRUMENTS LLC; *pg.* 1048, *pg.* 1234
ULTRA-SEAL - Face Mask - BAXTER INTERNATIONAL INC.; *pg.* 1499, *pg.* 599
ULTRA-SEAL - Vehicle Safety System - GROTE INDUSTRIES, INC.; *pg.* 206, *pg.* 693
ULTRA-SEAL - Closure - SONOCO PRODUCTS COMPANY; *pg.* 1469, *pg.* 1619
ULTRA-SENSE - Sensor Faucets - SYMMONS INDUSTRIES, INC.; *pg.* 114, *pg.* 803
ULTRA SEVEN - Sleeper Mattresses - KINGSDOWN, INC.; *pg.* 932, *pg.* 1383
ULTRA SHAFTLINER - Building Product - GEORGIA-PACIFIC LLC; *pg.* 1458, *pg.* 507
ULTRA SIDE-GLOW - Fiber Optic Lighting Cables - REVOLUTION LIGHTING TECHNOLOGIES, INC.; *pg.* 1304, *pg.* 377
ULTRA-SKIN - Nutritional Supplement - NATURAL ORGANICS, INC.; *pg.* 1571, *pg.* 1181
ULTRA SLEEPER - Sleeper - PETERBILT MOTORS CO.; *pg.* 188, *pg.* 1691
ULTRA-SLIM - Hair Straightener - CONAIR CORPORATION; *pg.* 505, *pg.* 1055
ULTRA-SLIP - Stylet - VITAL SIGNS, INC.; *pg.* 1607, *pg.* 1126
ULTRA SOFT - Outerwear - UNIFIRST CORPORATION; *pg.* 50, *pg.* 860
ULTRA-SPAN - Steel Truss System - MITEK, INC.; *pg.* 1056, *pg.* 975
ULTRA SPARK - Automotive Spark Plug Wires - AUTOZONE, INC.; *pg.* 200, *pg.* 1641
ULTRA-SPEED - Film - EASTMAN KODAK COMPANY; *pg.* 1408, *pg.* 1333
ULTRA-SPHERES - Solder Spheres - KESTER, INC.; *pg.* 649, *pg.* 620
ULTRA-STABLE - Mirror Mount - OPTOSIGMA CORP.; *pg.* 1425, *pg.* 262
ULTRA-SUCKLE - Medicated Milk Replacer - MANNA PRO CORPORATION; *pg.* 1478, *pg.* 975
ULTRA-TECH - Shirt - CORTLAND LINE COMPANY; *pg.* 1831, *pg.* 1155
ULTRA-TEK - Industrial Filter - DONALDSON COMPANY, INC.; *pg.* 1329, *pg.* 917
ULTRA-TEMP - Truck Refrigeration System - KIDRON, INC.; *pg.* 181, *pg.* 1457
ULTRA-THIN - Medical Device - BOSTON SCIENTIFIC CORPORATION; *pg.* 1508, *pg.* 831
ULTRA TONER - Resistance Training - SCHOOL-TECH, INC.; *pg.* 1844, *pg.* 866
ULTRA TUGGER - Puller - GREENLEE TEXTRON INC.; *pg.* 1048, *pg.* 655
ULTRA-TWIN - Gas Mask - MINE SAFETY APPLIANCES COMPANY; *pg.* 1361, *pg.* 1525
ULTRA ULTIMATE - High-Strength & High Wet-Abrasion Resistant - SAMSON ROPE TECHNOLOGIES; *pg.* 1468, *pg.* 1820
ULTRA-V - Vertical Pressure Screen - KADANT BLACK CLAWSON INC.; *pg.* 1352, *pg.* 1460
ULTRA V SERIES - Centrifugal Trash Pumps - THE GORMAN-RUPP COMPANY; *pg.* 1341, *pg.* 1458
ULTRA VAC - Industrial Vacuum Cleaner - HI-VAC CORPORATION; *pg.* 56, *pg.* 1458
ULTRA-VIRILE-ACTIN - Nutritional Supplement - NATURAL ORGANICS, INC.; *pg.* 1571, *pg.* 1181
ULTRA WATERBORNE - Finishes - THE MURALO COMPANY; *pg.* 1444, *pg.* 1042
ULTRA-WEB - Air Filter - DONALDSON COMPANY, INC.; *pg.* 1329, *pg.* 917
ULTRA WHISPERS - Jewelry - ROMAN RESEARCH, INC.; *pg.* 11, *pg.* 824
ULTRA WHITE - Varnish - MOHAWK FINISHING PRODUCTS, INC.; *pg.* 1173, *pg.* 1378
ULTRA WHITE 90 - Pre Dispersed Coating Pigment - BASF CATALYSTS LLC; *pg.* 1148, *pg.* 1074
ULTRA WIDEBAND - Power Amplifier - KRATOS LANCASTER; *pg.* 1419, *pg.* 1546
ULTRA Z - Screws - ATLAS BOLT & SCREW COMPANY; *pg.* 1042, *pg.* 1403
ULTRA-ZYME - Nutritional Supplement - NATURAL ORGANICS, INC.; *pg.* 1571, *pg.* 1181
ULTRA+ - Electronic Components - MOLEX INCORPORATED; *pg.* 655, *pg.* 628
ULTRAAQUA - Oil & Water Separators - DONALDSON COMPANY, INC.; *pg.* 1329, *pg.* 917
ULTRABAC - Broadloom - MANNINGTON MILLS, INC.; *pg.* 934, *pg.* 1119
ULTRABAC - Veterinary Immunization Biologicals - PFIZER INC.; *pg.* 1581, *pg.* 1278
ULTRABAND - Ultra Low Elongation Plastic Strapping - DYNARIC, INC.; *pg.* 1882, *pg.* 1810
ULTRABEAT - Software Feature - APPLE INC.; *pg.* 350, *pg.* 73
ULTRABEV - Filter - DONALDSON COMPANY, INC.; *pg.* 1329, *pg.* 917
ULTRABIND - Affinity Membrane - PALL CORPORATION; *pg.* 232, *pg.* 1323
ULTRABIX - Chemical - SENSIENT COLORS INC.; *pg.* 1180, *pg.* 1003
ULTRABLATOR - Medical Equipment - CONMED CORPORATION; *pg.* 1517, *pg.* 1347
ULTRABLOCK - Bleached Cotton - BARNHARDT MANUFACTURING COMPANY; *pg.* 1498, *pg.* 1364
ULTRABOND - Perm - ZOTOS INTERNATIONAL, INC.; *pg.* 524, *pg.* 345
ULTRABOOK - Laptop Computer - INTEL CORPORATION; *pg.* 645, *pg.* 266
ULTRABRIGHT - Laser Detectors - COBRA ELECTRONICS CORPORATION; *pg.* 629, *pg.* 572
ULTRABRIGHT - Led - CREE INC.; *pg.* 631, *pg.* 1371
ULTRABRITE - Computer Monitor - VIEWSONIC CORPORATION; *pg.* 489, *pg.* 303
ULTRAC - Filter - DONALDSON COMPANY, INC.; *pg.* 1329, *pg.* 917
ULTRACAL - Tube Feeding Formula High in Fiber - MEAD JOHNSON NUTRITION COMPANY; *pg.* 1561, *pg.* 615
ULTRACAL - Gypsum Cement - USG CORPORATION; *pg.* 118, *pg.* 594
THE ULTRACAPACITOR COMPANY - Tagline - MAXWELL TECHNOLOGIES, INC.; *pg.* 653, *pg.* 204
ULTRACASE - Thermal Processing Equipment - SURFACE COMBUSTION, INC.; *pg.* 1077, *pg.* 1462
ULTRACAST - Coil Transformer - DYNAPOWER CORPORATION; *pg.* 1330, *pg.* 1768
ULTRACEL CREW - Clothing - K-SWISS; *pg.* 1837, *pg.* 306
ULTRACEL POLO - Clothing - K-SWISS; *pg.* 1837, *pg.* 306
ULTRACEL TEE - Clothing - K-SWISS; *pg.* 1837, *pg.* 306
ULTRACEROX - Precision Abrasive Product - SAINT-GOBAIN ABRASIVES, INC. - PHILADELPHIA; *pg.* 1180, *pg.* 1553
ULTRACET - Healthcare Product - JOHNSON & JOHNSON; *pg.* 1549, *pg.* 1091
ULTRACHECK - Cuffs - CAS MEDICAL SYSTEMS, INC.; *pg.* 1513, *pg.* 339
ULTRACHEM - Steel Product - AK STEEL HOLDING CORPORATION; *pg.* 1311, *pg.* 1479
ULTRACHOICE - Livestock Vaccine - PFIZER INC.; *pg.* 1581, *pg.* 1278
ULTRACINCH - Ablation Device - ST. JUDE MEDICAL, INC.; *pg.* 1596, *pg.* 963
ULTRACLEAN - Chemical Product - SPECTRUM CHEMICALS & LABORATORY PRODUCTS, INC.; *pg.* 1181, *pg.* 94
ULTRACLEANER - Air Cleaning - PNEUMATICSCALEANGELUS; *pg.* 1369, *pg.* 1445
ULTRACODE - Gypsum Panels - USG CORPORATION; *pg.* 118, *pg.* 594
ULTRACOLOR - Poly Products - SMEAD MANUFACTURING COMPANY; *pg.* 470, *pg.* 926
ULTRACOOL - Water Chiller - DONALDSON COMPANY, INC.; *pg.* 1329, *pg.* 917
ULTRACORR - Containerboard - GEORGIA-PACIFIC LLC; *pg.* 1458, *pg.* 507
ULTRACRAFT CABINETRY - Semi-custom Cabinetry - NORCRAFT HOLDINGS, LP; *pg.* 100, *pg.* 921
ULTRACROWN - Dental Product - DENTSPLY INTERNATIONAL INC.; *pg.* 1522, *pg.* 1596
ULTRACRUISE - Cruise Control - ROSTRA PRECISION CONTROLS, INC.; *pg.* 216, *pg.* 1381
ULTRACURE - Acrylic Coated Film & Foil Laminations - HAZEN PAPER COMPANY; *pg.* 1459, *pg.* 825
ULTRACYCLE - Linerboard - GEORGIA-PACIFIC LLC; *pg.* 1458, *pg.* 507
ULTRACYCLE PLUS - Linerboard - GEORGIA-PACIFIC LLC; *pg.* 1458, *pg.* 507
ULTRADENSE - Pharmaceutical Product - MISSION PHARMACAL COMPANY INC.; *pg.* 1568, *pg.* 1742
ULTRADEX - High-Precision Index Table - A.G. DAVIS/AA GAGE; *pg.* 1310, *pg.* 908
ULTRADEX - Skills Assessment Software - MANPOWER INC.; *pg.* 430, *pg.* 1877
ULTRADOME - Magnifier - ULTRAOPTIX, INC.; *pg.* 1433, *pg.* 346
ULTRADOSE - Germicidal Ultrasonic Cleaning Solution - L&R MANUFACTURING COMPANY; *pg.* 1419, *pg.* 1076
ULTRADRI - Filter - DONALDSON COMPANY, INC.; *pg.* 1329, *pg.* 917
ULTRADRIL - Drilling Fluid System - M-I SWACO; *pg.* 980, *pg.* 1710
ULTRADRIVE - Drive System - CARDIAC SCIENCE CORPORATION; *pg.* 1512, *pg.* 1897
ULTRADUR - Switchgear Enclosure Finishing System - S&C ELECTRIC COMPANY; *pg.* 1305, *pg.* 589
ULTRADURA - Industrial Safety Eyewear - UVEX SAFETY; *pg.* 1433, *pg.* 1608
ULTRAEASE - Glass & Ceramic Material - CORNING INCORPORATED; *pg.* 1122, *pg.* 1154
ULTRAEDGE - Cattle Clipper - ANDIS COMPANY; *pg.* 498, *pg.* 1895
ULTRAESSENCE - Rug - COURISTAN INC.; *pg.* 921, *pg.* 1067
ULTRAFAST - Laser & Laser System - COHERENT, INC.; *pg.* 1406, *pg.* 265
ULTRAFELT - Printing Paper - MOHAWK FINE PAPERS, INC.; *pg.* 1464, *pg.* 1153
ULTRAFINA - High Gloss Finish - 3M COMPANY; *pg.* 1142, *pg.* 956
ULTRAFINE - Cuprous Oxide - AMERICAN CHEMET CORPORATION; *pg.* 1147, *pg.* 599
ULTRAFINE - Flame Retardants - CHEMTURA CORPORATION; *pg.* 1152, *pg.* 355
ULTRAFINE - Ceramic & Plastic Product - COORSTEK, INC.; *pg.* 77, *pg.* 330

ULTRAFIT - PK System - SURGICAL SPECIALTIES CORPORATION; *pg.* 1600, *pg.* 1912
ULTRAFIX - Medical Equipment - CONMED CORPORATION; *pg.* 1517, *pg.* 1347
ULTRAFIX - Adhesive Dressing - DERMA SCIENCES, INC.; *pg.* 1523, *pg.* 1111
ULTRAFLEX - Scissors - ACME UNITED CORPORATION; *pg.* 1040, *pg.* 346
ULTRAFLEX - Medical Device - BOSTON SCIENTIFIC CORPORATION; *pg.* 1508, *pg.* 831
ULTRAFLEX - Software - EMC CORPORATION; *pg.* 391, *pg.* 825
ULTRAFLEX - Hose - HBD INDUSTRIES, INC.; *pg.* 207, *pg.* 1449
ULTRAFLEX - Male External Catheter - MEDLINE INDUSTRIES, INC.; *pg.* 1562, *pg.* 635
ULTRAFLO - Feeding System or Feeder - CTB INTERNATIONAL CORP.; *pg.* 850, *pg.* 695
ULTRAFLOOR - Acoustic Product - LEAR CORPORATION; *pg.* 229, *pg.* 907
ULTRAFORM - Poster - MONADNOCK PAPER MILLS, INC.; *pg.* 1464, *pg.* 1033
ULTRAFREEZE - Medical Instrument - WALLACH SURGICAL DEVICES, INC.; *pg.* 1436, *pg.* 381
ULTRAGARD - Towel - CROSSTEX INTERNATIONAL INC.; *pg.* 1520, *pg.* 1164
ULTRAGLIDE - Surface Maintenance Machine - TENNANT COMPANY; *pg.* 1381, *pg.* 944
ULTRAGRAFIX - Card Personalization System - DATACARD CORPORATION; *pg.* 382, *pg.* 948
ULTRAGRIP - Shoe & Boot Cover - ALPHA PRO TECH, LTD.; *pg.* 1492, *pg.* 1922
ULTRAGUARD - Industrial Goggles (Safety) - UVEX SAFETY; *pg.* 1433, *pg.* 1608
ULTRAHIDE - Poster - MONADNOCK PAPER MILLS, INC.; *pg.* 1464, *pg.* 1033
ULTRAHOME - Cable - COMMSCOPE, INC.; *pg.* 278, *pg.* 1378
ULTRAHYDROGEL - Guard Column - WATERS CORPORATION; *pg.* 1436, *pg.* 834
ULTRAIR - Filter - DONALDSON COMPANY, INC.; *pg.* 1329, *pg.* 917
ULTRAJAK - Jack - EMG, INC.; *pg.* 636, *pg.* 277
ULTRALAB - Tangential Flow System - PALL CORPORATION; *pg.* 232, *pg.* 1323
ULTRALAP - Lapping Film - SAINT-GOBAIN ABRASIVES, INC. - PHILADELPHIA; *pg.* 1180, *pg.* 1553
ULTRALAST - Wheel - HAMILTON CASTER & MFG. CO.; *pg.* 206, *pg.* 1454
ULTRALEATHER - Leather Textiles - BERNHARDT DESIGN; *pg.* 918, *pg.* 1381
ULTRALEC - Powdered Lecithin for Food Applications - ARCHER-DANIELS-MIDLAND COMPANY; *pg.* 825, *pg.* 565
ULTRALIFE - Pump Product - IDEX CORPORATION; *pg.* 1347, *pg.* 623
ULTRALIFE HIRATE - Lithium Battery - ULTRALIFE CORPORATION; *pg.* 1385, *pg.* 1317
ULTRALIFE POLYMER - Battery - ULTRALIFE CORPORATION; *pg.* 1385, *pg.* 1317
THE ULTRALIFE POWER SOURCE - Slogan - ULTRALIFE CORPORATION; *pg.* 1385, *pg.* 1317
ULTRALIFE THIN CELL - Lithium Battery - ULTRALIFE CORPORATION; *pg.* 1385, *pg.* 1317
ULTRALIGHT - Mining Lamp System - MINE SAFETY APPLIANCES COMPANY; *pg.* 1361, *pg.* 1525
ULTRALIGN - Fiber Optic Positioning System - NEWPORT CORPORATION; *pg.* 1424, *pg.* 114
ULTRALINE - Grinder - BRYANT GRINDER; *pg.* 1320, *pg.* 1768
ULTRALINE - Graphic Arts Films & Chemicals - EASTMAN KODAK COMPANY; *pg.* 1408, *pg.* 1333
ULTRALINE - High Strength Polyolefin Rope - SAMSON ROPE TECHNOLOGIES; *pg.* 1468, *pg.* 1820
ULTRALINK - Vehicle Safety System - GROTE INDUSTRIES, INC.; *pg.* 206, *pg.* 693
ULTRALITE - Glove - 180S, LLC; *pg.* 1824, *pg.* 754
ULTRALITE - Laptop Desk - LAPWORKS, INC.; *pg.* 426, *pg.* 187
ULTRALITE - Packaging Foam - SEALED AIR CORPORATION; *pg.* 1468, *pg.* 1058
ULTRALITE BEANIE - Hats - 180S, LLC; *pg.* 1824, *pg.* 754
ULTRALITE CARPAL TUNNEL WRIST BRACE - Light Wrist Splint Allowing Finger Flexibility - MUELLER SPORTS MEDICINE, INC.; *pg.* 1570, *pg.* 1887
ULTRALITE CRG - Glove - 180S, LLC; *pg.* 1824, *pg.* 754
ULTRALOK - Tooth System - ESCO CORPORATION; *pg.* 1335, *pg.* 1502
ULTRALOK - Locking Impact Fastener - JOHNS MANVILLE CORPORATION; *pg.* 89, *pg.* 320
ULTRALON - Fluoropolymer Coating - WHITFORD WORLDWIDE COMPANY; *pg.* 1185, *pg.* 1529
ULTRALOONS - Foil Balloons - CTI INDUSTRIES CORPORATION; *pg.* 1881, *pg.* 555
ULTRALUBE - Lubricant - BIRKO CORPORATION; *pg.* 1149, *pg.* 332
ULTRALUXE - Slacks & Shorts - HABAND COMPANY, INC.; *pg.* 1772, *pg.* 1099
ULTRALYTE COMPACT - Speed Enforcement Laser - LASER TECHNOLOGY, INC.; *pg.* 1419, *pg.* 314
ULTRALYTE LRB - Measurement Laser Product - LASER TECHNOLOGY, INC.; *pg.* 1419, *pg.* 314
ULTRAM - Healthcare Product - JOHNSON & JOHNSON; *pg.* 1549, *pg.* 1091
ULTRAM - Pharmaceutical Product - VALEANT PHARMACEUTICALS INTERNATIONAL, INC.; *pg.* 1605, *pg.* 1957
ULTRAM ER - Pharmaceutical Product - IMPAX LABORATORIES, INC.; *pg.* 1544, *pg.* 101
ULTRAMAPPER - Processors - AVAGO TECHNOLOGIES; *pg.* 358, *pg.* 238
ULTRAMAR - Gasoline Retail Outlets - VALERO ENERGY CORPORATION; *pg.* 986, *pg.* 1743
ULTRAMARK - Software - BIO-RAD LABORATORIES, INC.; *pg.* 1504, *pg.* 101
ULTRAMATE - Second-Stage Pump Addition - THE GORMAN-RUPP COMPANY; *pg.* 1341, *pg.* 1458
ULTRAMATE X - Roll Covering - VAIL RUBBER WORKS, INC.; *pg.* 1891, *pg.* 906
ULTRAMATIC - Equipment - ANDERSON & VREELAND, INC.; *pg.* 1616, *pg.* 1064
ULTRAMAX - High Purity Hydrochloric Acid - DETREX CORPORATION; *pg.* 1156, *pg.* 906
ULTRAMAX - Molecular Biology Product - THERMO FISHER SCIENTIFIC INC.; *pg.* 1602, *pg.* 61
ULTRAMAX - All-Welded Plate & Frame Heat Exchangers - TRANTER PHE, INC.; *pg.* 1383, *pg.* 1749
ULTRAMEDIA - Thermal Imaging System - FLIR SYSTEMS, INC.; *pg.* 1413, *pg.* 1510
ULTRAMEDIA - Interconnect Device - TEXAS INSTRUMENTS INCORPORATED; *pg.* 679, *pg.* 1688
ULTRAMESH - Filter - DONALDSON COMPANY, INC.; *pg.* 1329, *pg.* 917
ULTRAMET - Ultrasonic Cleaner - BUEHLER, LTD.; *pg.* 1403, *pg.* 622
ULTRAMET - Nanotechnology - ULTRATECH, INC.; *pg.* 1433, *pg.* 251
ULTRAMET-L - Filter Assembly - PALL CORPORATION; *pg.* 232, *pg.* 1323
ULTRAMIC - Advanced Ceramic Heater - WATLOW ELECTRIC MANUFACTURING COMPANY; *pg.* 1078, *pg.* 1004
ULTRAMOVABLE - Steel Wall Panel - CLESTRA HAUSERMAN, INC.; *pg.* 76, *pg.* 1526
ULTRAN - Cylinder - BIMBA MANUFACTURING COMPANY; *pg.* 1317, *pg.* 633
ULTRANET - Router & Extension - BROCADE CORPORATION; *pg.* 365, *pg.* 312
ULTRANOX - Polymer Product - CHEMTURA CORPORATION; *pg.* 1152, *pg.* 355
ULTRAOPT - Software - BMC SOFTWARE, INC.; *pg.* 362, *pg.* 1701
ULTRAOPTIX - Visual Aids - ULTRAOPTIX, INC.; *pg.* 1433, *pg.* 346
ULTRAPAC - Block Machine - BESSER COMPANY; *pg.* 1317, *pg.* 865
ULTRAPAC - Air Dryer - DONALDSON COMPANY, INC.; *pg.* 1329, *pg.* 917
ULTRAPAC II - Concrete Product Machine - BESSER COMPANY; *pg.* 1317, *pg.* 865
ULTRAPAK - Wafer Shipping Box - ENTEGRIS, INC.; *pg.* 1882, *pg.* 788
ULTRAPAK - Maximum Furniture Protection - INTERSTATE WORLDWIDE RELOCATION, INC.; *pg.* 1912, *pg.* 1807
ULTRAPC - Audio Entertainment - DTS, INC.; *pg.* 634, *pg.* 55
ULTRAPEEL - Membrane Closures - SONOCO PRODUCTS COMPANY; *pg.* 1469, *pg.* 1619
ULTRAPHIL - Moisture Management Agent - HUNTSMAN CORPORATION; *pg.* 1167, *pg.* 1758
ULTRAPHONE - Wireless Telecommunications System - INTERDIGITAL, INC.; *pg.* 1872, *pg.* 1543
ULTRAPINE - Wood & Building Material - WEYERHAEUSER COMPANY; *pg.* 121, *pg.* 1820
ULTRAPIPE - Cable - COMMSCOPE, INC.; *pg.* 278, *pg.* 1378
ULTRAPOINT - Software - EMC CORPORATION; *pg.* 391, *pg.* 825
ULTRAPOL - Filter & Lens - THE TIFFEN COMPANY LLC; *pg.* 1432, *pg.* 1165
ULTRAPRECISE - Toner - HURST CHEMICAL COMPANY; *pg.* 1168, *pg.* 174
ULTRAPRO - Adhesive - 3M COMPANY; *pg.* 1142, *pg.* 956
ULTRAPURE - Lead-Free Bar Solders - KESTER, INC.; *pg.* 649, *pg.* 620
ULTRAPURE - Air Purifier - ORANGE PEEL ENTERPRISES, INC.; *pg.* 1028, *pg.* 477
ULTRAPURE - Molecular Biology Product - THERMO FISHER SCIENTIFIC INC.; *pg.* 1602, *pg.* 61
ULTRAQ - Audio System - QSOUND LABS, INC.; *pg.* 666, *pg.* 1904
ULTRARANGE - Glass & Ceramic Material - CORNING INCORPORATED; *pg.* 1122, *pg.* 1154
ULTRARESERVOIR - Tangential Flow System - PALL CORPORATION; *pg.* 232, *pg.* 1323
ULTRAROCKER - Software - BIO-RAD LABORATORIES, INC.; *pg.* 1504, *pg.* 101
ULTRARON - Rotary Table - A.G. DAVIS/AA GAGE; *pg.* 1310, *pg.* 908
ULTRASCALE - Software - EMC CORPORATION; *pg.* 391, *pg.* 825
ULTRASCAN - Analytical Device - BRUKER CORPORATION; *pg.* 1511, *pg.* 788
ULTRASCAN - Monitor - DELL INC.; *pg.* 383, *pg.* 1737
ULTRASCENDOR - Athletic Shoes - K-SWISS; *pg.* 1837, *pg.* 306
ULTRASCENDOR MID - Footwear - K-SWISS; *pg.* 1837, *pg.* 306
ULTRASCENT - Bleached Cotton - BARNHARDT MANUFACTURING COMPANY; *pg.* 1498, *pg.* 1364
ULTRASCULPT - Medical Device - MENTOR CORPORATION; *pg.* 1565, *pg.* 263
ULTRASE - Pharmaceutical Product - IMPAX LABORATORIES, INC.; *pg.* 1544, *pg.* 101
ULTRASEAL - Glass & Ceramic Material - CORNING INCORPORATED; *pg.* 1122, *pg.* 1154
ULTRASEAL - Packaging System - SEALED AIR CORPORATION; *pg.* 1468, *pg.* 1058
ULTRASEAL - Membrane Closure for Cans - SONOCO PRODUCTS COMPANY; *pg.* 1469, *pg.* 1619
ULTRASEAL - Plastic Houseware Product - STERILITE CORPORATION; *pg.* 1138, *pg.* 848
ULTRASEAL - Zipper - ZIP-PAK; *pg.* 1473, *pg.* 631
ULTRASEEK - Software - AUTONOMY, INC.; *pg.* 358, *pg.* 212
ULTRASENSE - Molecular Biology Product - THERMO FISHER SCIENTIFIC INC.; *pg.* 1602, *pg.* 61
ULTRASETTE - Tangential Flow System - PALL CORPORATION; *pg.* 232, *pg.* 1323
ULTRASHADOW - Software - NVIDIA CORPORATION; *pg.* 447, *pg.* 268
ULTRASHIELD - Urethane Enamel - DUNN-EDWARDS CORPORATION; *pg.* 1442, *pg.* 129
ULTRASHIELD - Gel Protective Coating - FERRO CORPORATION; *pg.* 1162, *pg.* 1462
ULTRASHIELD - Fly Control Product - W.F. YOUNG, INC.; *pg.* 1610, *pg.* 817
ULTRASHINE - Surface Maintenance Machine - TENNANT COMPANY; *pg.* 1381, *pg.* 944
ULTRASIC - Ceramic & Plastic Product - COORSTEK, INC.; *pg.* 77, *pg.* 330
ULTRASKILL - Skill Assessment Program - MANPOWER INC.; *pg.* 430, *pg.* 1877
ULTRASLING - Orthopedic Product - DJO INCORPORATED; *pg.* 1524, *pg.* 302
ULTRASMOOTH - Steel Product - AK STEEL HOLDING CORPORATION; *pg.* 1311, *pg.* 1479
ULTRASOAK - Aqueous Cleaner - HUBBARD-HALL, INC.; *pg.* 1167, *pg.* 382
ULTRASOF - Foam Horseshoe - SCHOOL-TECH, INC.; *pg.* 1844, *pg.* 866
ULTRASOFT - Jewelry Cleaner - CONNOISSEURS PRODUCTS CORPORATION; *pg.* 329, *pg.* 861
ULTRASOLID - Paint Product - AKZO NOBEL; *pg.* 1439, *pg.* 1952

First page reference indicates Business Class Edition
Second page reference indicates Geographic Edition

ULTRASONIC - Cleaning Powder And Solution - L&R MANUFACTURING COMPANY; pg. 1419, pg. 1076
ULTRASONIK - Dental Product - DENTSPLY INTERNATIONAL INC.; pg. 1522, pg. 1596
ULTRASORB - Bleached Cotton - BARNHARDT MANUFACTURING COMPANY; pg. 1498, pg. 1364
ULTRASORB - Medical Equipment - CONMED CORPORATION; pg. 1517, pg. 1347
ULTRASORBS - Medical Product - MEDLINE INDUSTRIES, INC.; pg. 1562, pg. 635
ULTRASORP - Filter - DONALDSON COMPANY, INC.; pg. 1329, pg. 917
ULTRASORT 408 - Wafer Sorter - BROOKS AUTOMATION, INC.; pg. 1320, pg. 813
ULTRASOUND - Imaging Service - DIGIRAD CORPORATION; pg. 1524, pg. 185
ULTRASPARC - Hardware & Software - POLYWELL COMPUTERS, INC.; pg. 456, pg. 280
ULTRASPEC - Industrial Safety Eyewear - UVEX SAFETY; pg. 1433, pg. 1608
ULTRASPERSE - Boiler Treatment Products - GE WATER & PROCESS TECHNOLOGIES; pg. 1339, pg. 1588
ULTRASPOT - Fly Control Product - W.F. YOUNG, INC.; pg. 1610, pg. 817
ULTRASPUN - Commercial Knitting Yarn - NATIONAL SPINNING COMPANY, INC.; pg. 697, pg. 1265
ULTRASTACK - Furniture - VIRCO MANUFACTURING CORPORATION; pg. 946, pg. 297
ULTRASTAK - Packaging Materials & Container Board - GEORGIA-PACIFIC LLC; pg. 1458, pg. 507
ULTRASTAK PLUS - Linerboard - GEORGIA-PACIFIC LLC; pg. 1458, pg. 507
ULTRASTINGER - Flashlight - STREAMLIGHT INC.; pg. 1306, pg. 1527
ULTRASTREAM - Spray Product - SPRAYING SYSTEMS CO.; pg. 1063, pg. 670
ULTRASTRIP - Resist Stripper - MACDERMID, INC.; pg. 1172, pg. 321
ULTRASTRONG - High-Strength & High-Abrasion Resistant Rope - SAMSON ROPE TECHNOLOGIES; pg. 1468, pg. 1820
ULTRASTYRAGEL - Guard Column - WATERS CORPORATION; pg. 1436, pg. 834
ULTRASULFOMEM - Filter - DONALDSON COMPANY, INC.; pg. 1329, pg. 917
ULTRASWIM - Hair Shampoo Products - CHATTEM, INC.; pg. 1515, pg. 1628
ULTRASWITCH - Actuators - FLOWSERVE CORPORATION; pg. 82, pg. 1719
ULTRATANE - Butane - MASTER APPLIANCE CORP.; pg. 1055, pg. 1888
ULTRATANE BUTANE - Powered Butane Product - MASTER APPLIANCE CORP.; pg. 1055, pg. 1888
ULTRATEC - Graphic Arts Films - EASTMAN KODAK COMPANY; pg. 1408, pg. 1333
ULTRATEC - Hardwood Flooring - NYDREE FLOORING; pg. 939, pg. 1782
ULTRATEST - Hand Tool - GENERAL TOOLS & INSTRUMENTS LLC; pg. 1048, pg. 1234
ULTRATEX - Glove - CROSSTEX INTERNATIONAL INC.; pg. 1520, pg. 1164
ULTRATEX - Softeners - HUNTSMAN CORPORATION; pg. 1167, pg. 1758
ULTRATHANE - Percutaneous - COOK GROUP, INC.; pg. 1518, pg. 674
ULTRATHANE - Cleaning Product - HILLYARD, INC.; pg. 331, pg. 990
ULTRATHERM - Beverage Cooler - IGLOO PRODUCTS CORPORATION; pg. 1126, pg. 1724
ULTRATHICK - Cover & Pad - HOME PRODUCTS INTERNATIONAL, INC.; pg. 1125, pg. 577
ULTRATHIN - Led - CREE INC.; pg. 631, pg. 1371
ULTRATHON - Personal Safety Product - 3M COMPANY; pg. 1142, pg. 956
ULTRATIDE - Antibody - PDL BIOPHARMA INC.; pg. 1580, pg. 1022
ULTRATIP - Soldering Tip - MASTER APPLIANCE CORP.; pg. 1055, pg. 1888
ULTRATITE - Conduit - SOUTHWIRE COMPANY; pg. 1063, pg. 527
ULTRATORCH - Butane-Powered - MASTER APPLIANCE CORP.; pg. 1055, pg. 1888
ULTRATRACE - Medical Product - CONMED CORPORATION; pg. 1517, pg. 1347
ULTRAVAC - Heater - ROBERTS-GORDON INC.; pg. 1076, pg. 1151
ULTRAVAC - Coiled Tubing - STAAR SURGICAL COMPANY; pg. 1597, pg. 151
ULTRAVAND - Handheld Ablation Device - ST. JUDE MEDICAL, INC.; pg. 1596, pg. 963
ULTRAVIEW - Electron Microscope - FEI COMPANY; pg. 1413, pg. 1498
ULTRAVISION - Illuminated Assembly Magnifier - PROPHOTONIX LIMITED; pg. 1427, pg. 1039
ULTRAVON - Detergents - HUNTSMAN CORPORATION; pg. 1167, pg. 1758
ULTRAVS - Medical Device - INTEGRA LIFESCIENCES HOLDINGS CORPORATION; pg. 1545, pg. 1109
ULTRAVUE - Facepieces - MINE SAFETY APPLIANCES COMPANY; pg. 1361, pg. 1525
ULTRAWARE - Software - ROCKWELL AUTOMATION, INC.; pg. 668, pg. 1880
ULTRAWASH - Dishwasher - SEARS HOLDINGS CORPORATION; pg. 1784, pg. 618
ULTRAWHITE - Glass Product - GUARDIAN INDUSTRIES CORP.; pg. 85, pg. 869
ULTRAZORBE - Nutritional Supplement - GARDEN OF LIFE, INC.; pg. 1532, pg. 478
ULTRAZYME - Medical Device - ABBOTT MEDICAL OPTICS, INC.; pg. 1485, pg. 260
ULTREEN - Cleaning Solution - ALLSOP, INC.; pg. 347, pg. 1817
ULTRESS - Hair Coloring - P&G-CLAIROL, INC.; pg. 519, pg. 1418
ULTREX - Pigment - BASF CATALYSTS LLC; pg. 1148, pg. 1074
ULTREX - Filter - DONALDSON COMPANY, INC.; pg. 1329, pg. 917
ULTREX - Light Engine - VIAVI SOLUTIONS INC.; pg. 1435, pg. 148
ULTRIM PLUS - Nutritional Product - RELIV INTERNATIONAL, INC.; pg. 1589, pg. 975
ULTRO - Electrical Wire & Cable - GENERAL CABLE CORPORATION; pg. 83, pg. 384
ULTROGEL - Chromatography Product - PALL CORPORATION; pg. 232, pg. 1323
ULTROL - Nuclear Cables - GENERAL CABLE CORPORATION; pg. 83, pg. 729
ULTRON - Memory Cushion Inserts - DEER STAGS INC.; pg. 1807, pg. 1222
ULX PROFESSIONAL - Wireless System - SHURE INCORPORATED; pg. 672, pg. 638
ULYSIS - Molecular Probe Product - THERMO FISHER SCIENTIFIC INC.; pg. 1602, pg. 61
UM-SSD - Storage System - HGST; pg. 406, pg. 260
UMADD - Publication - MOTHERS AGAINST DRUNK DRIVING (MADD); pg. 147, pg. 1723
UMAX - Integrated Circuit Device - MAXIM INTEGRATED PRODUCTS, INC.; pg. 653, pg. 247
UMBILI-CATH - Umbilical Vessel Catheters - UTAH MEDICAL PRODUCTS, INC.; pg. 1605, pg. 1752
UMBPLEX - Computer Program - COMPUTER SCIENCES CORPORATION; pg. 378, pg. 1780
UMBRELLA - Valve - VERNAY LABORATORIES, INC.; pg. 1891, pg. 1482
UMBRIA - Rug - COURISTAN INC.; pg. 921, pg. 1067
UMBRIA - Fabric - NEMSCHOFF, INC.; pg. 936, pg. 1890
UMC - Software - GLEASON CORPORATION; pg. 1340, pg. 1335
UMC ULTIMA - Bevel Product - GLEASON CORPORATION; pg. 1340, pg. 1335
UMP - Alarms - ALIMED, INC.; pg. 1490, pg. 816
UMRBUS - Software - SYNOPSYS, INC.; pg. 480, pg. 162
UMTS (CONSUMER) - Mobile Solutions - SONUS NETWORKS INC.; pg. 1281, pg. 858
UMTS (ENTERPRISE) - Mobile Solutions - SONUS NETWORKS INC.; pg. 1281, pg. 858
UNADS - Accelerators - R.T. VANDERBILT COMPANY, INC.; pg. 1180, pg. 364
UNALON - Polishing Pad - UNIVERSAL PHOTONICS, INC.; pg. 1433, pg. 1167
UNASIL - Optical Product - UNIVERSAL PHOTONICS, INC.; pg. 1433, pg. 1167
UNASYN - Medicine - PFIZER INC.; pg. 1581, pg. 1278
UNBELIEVABLE PIE - Pie - BAKERS SQUARE; pg. 1715, pg. 316
UNBELIEVABLY SOFT BABY - Dolls - THE GOLDBERGER COMPANY, LLC; pg. 954, pg. 1235
UNBOUND - Perfume - ELIZABETH ARDEN, INC.; pg. 507, pg. 448
UNBOUND ENERGY - Energy Drinks - MONSTER BEVERAGE CORPORATION; pg. 257, pg. 69
UNCLE BEN'S - Food Products - MARS, INCORPORATED; pg. 1858, pg. 1792
UNCLE BURGER - Fast Food - A&W FOOD SERVICES OF CANADA INC.; pg. 1714, pg. 1908
UNCLE DAVE'S - Sauce - GOLD PURE FOOD PRODUCTS CO., INC.; pg. 858, pg. 1166
UNCLE SAM - Video Slots - INTERNATIONAL GAME TECHNOLOGY; pg. 957, pg. 1024
UNCLE WIGGILY - Game - WINNING MOVES GAMES, INC.; pg. 970, pg. 816
THE UNCOMMON DRUGSTORE - Tag Line - DRUGSTORE.COM, INC.; pg. 1239, pg. 1814
UNCOMPROMISED CHECK SOLUTIONS - Software - ENNIS, INC.; pg. 393, pg. 1727
UNCOPPER - PB Tubing & Fittings - GENOVA PRODUCTS, INC.; pg. 83, pg. 875
UNCOPPER PRO - Solvent & Roof Flashing - GENOVA PRODUCTS, INC.; pg. 83, pg. 875
UNCRUSTABLES - Sandwich - THE J.M. SMUCKER COMPANY; pg. 865, pg. 1468
UNDELETE - Software - CONDUSIV TECHNOLOGIES; pg. 379, pg. 51
UNDELETEPLUS - Software - PHOENIX TECHNOLOGIES LTD.; pg. 454, pg. 147
UNDER ARMOUR METAL - Fabric - UNDER ARMOUR, INC.; pg. 49, pg. 759
UNDER COVER - Skin Care Product - NEUTROGENA CORPORATION; pg. 517, pg. 137
UNDER-THE-COUNTER PERFECT CHOICE - Water Filter - BEE-ALIVE INC.; pg. 1503, pg. 1348
UNDERCARINFO.NET - Online Undercar Information Service - HUNTER ENGINEERING COMPANY; pg. 208, pg. 973
UNDERCOVER - Switchgear - S&C ELECTRIC COMPANY; pg. 1305, pg. 589
UNDERCOVER - Sealer - SWISHER HYGIENE INC.; pg. 336, pg. 1507
UNDERCURRENT - Carpet - INTERFACE, INC.; pg. 695, pg. 512
UNDERGEAR - Men's Activewear & Fashion Underwear Catalog - HANOVER DIRECT, INC.; pg. 1772, pg. 1130
UNDERGRADER - Under-Ground Grader - ARNOLD MACHINERY COMPANY; pg. 1314, pg. 1755
UNDERGROUND - Screw-On-Connector - IDEAL INDUSTRIES, INC.; pg. 1051, pg. 662
UNDERGROUND STATION - Shoes - GENESCO INC.; pg. 1809, pg. 1650
UNDERJAMS - Baby Care Product - THE PROCTER & GAMBLE COMPANY; pg. 1129, pg. 1418
UNDERLINE - Lighting - STEELCASE INC.; pg. 475, pg. 889
UNDERLOCK - Fluid Handling System - GRACO, INC.; pg. 1342, pg. 935
UNDERMOUNT - Sink - ELKAY MANUFACTURING COMPANY; pg. 80, pg. 645
UNDEROOS - Children's Underwear - FRUIT OF THE LOOM, INC.; pg. 41, pg. 725
UNDERS & OVERS - Body Liners - CAPEZIO BALLET MAKERS INC.; pg. 1805, pg. 1125
UNDERSEA UNIVERSITY - Educational Materials - SCHOLASTIC INC.; pg. 1683, pg. 1288
UNDERSEAL - Rubberized Undercoating - 3M COMPANY; pg. 1142, pg. 956
UNDERSPIN - Reels - DAIWA CORPORATION; pg. 1832, pg. 75
UNDERSTANDING WHAT'S IMPORTANT - Slogan - M&T BANK CORPORATION; pg. 777, pg. 1149
UNDERTONE - Kitchen Product - KOHLER CO.; pg. 91, pg. 1862
UNDERWAIR - Underwear - HABAND COMPANY, INC.; pg. 1772, pg. 1099
THE UNDERWEAR COMPANY - Slogan - STANFIELD'S LIMITED; pg. 48, pg. 1917
UNDERWOOD - Meat Spreads - B&G FOODS, INC.; pg. 838, pg. 1102
UNDIE-TECTABLE - Clothing - SPANX INC.; pg. 32, pg. 520
UNDO - Pet Odor Decontaminant - SURCO PRODUCTS, INC.; pg. 336, pg. 1581
UNEPOXY - Antifouling Paint - PETTIT PAINT COMPANY; pg. 1444, pg. 1116
UNERASE - Software - SYMANTEC CORPORATION; pg. 478, pg. 161
UNFORGETTABLE - Fragrance - REVLON, INC.; pg. 521, pg. 1286
UNFORTUNATE EVENTS - Game - ACTIVISION BLIZZARD,

INC.; *pg.* 948, *pg.* 271
UNFRANCHISE - Business Development System - MARKET AMERICA WORLDWIDE, INC.; *pg.* 1265, *pg.* 1375
UNGLASS - Polycarbonate Water Cooler Bottles - LIQUI-BOX CORPORATION; *pg.* 1464, *pg.* 1802
UNHINGED - Fabric - NEMSCHOFF, INC.; *pg.* 936, *pg.* 1890
UNI - Multiplexer - PMC-SIERRA, INC.; *pg.* 664, *pg.* 287
UNI-BLUE - Thermal Processing Equipment - SURFACE COMBUSTION, INC.; *pg.* 1077, *pg.* 1462
UNI-CER - Optical Product - UNIVERSAL PHOTONICS, INC.; *pg.* 1433, *pg.* 1167
UNI-CLEAR - Optical Product - UNIVERSAL PHOTONICS, INC.; *pg.* 1433, *pg.* 1167
UNI-CLIP - Medical Device - INTEGRA LIFESCIENCES HOLDINGS CORPORATION; *pg.* 1545, *pg.* 1109
UNI-CLOTH - Optical Product - UNIVERSAL PHOTONICS, INC.; *pg.* 1433, *pg.* 1167
UNI-DIE - Power & Grounding Connector - PANDUIT CORP.; *pg.* 661, *pg.* 663
UNI-DOT - Fiber Optic Sights - LYMAN PRODUCTS CORPORATION; *pg.* 1839, *pg.* 356
UNI-DRAW - Thermal Processing Equipment - SURFACE COMBUSTION, INC.; *pg.* 1077, *pg.* 1462
UNI-DRILL - Single Flute Solid Carbide Drill - REGAL BELOIT CORPORATION; *pg.* 106, *pg.* 1854
UNI-DROP - Thermal Processing Equipment - SURFACE COMBUSTION, INC.; *pg.* 1077, *pg.* 1462
UNI-F.I.T - Integrated Tags - CHECKPOINT SYSTEMS, INC.; *pg.* 628, *pg.* 1559
UNI-FIT - Air Conditioner - FRIEDRICH AIR CONDITIONING CO.; *pg.* 1072, *pg.* 1740
UNI-FIT - Couplers - RAIN BIRD CORPORATION; *pg.* 707, *pg.* 44
UNI-FLANGE - Restraints & Casing Spacers - THE FORD METER BOX COMPANY, INC.; *pg.* 1047, *pg.* 698
UNI-FLEX - Shoe And Glove - ACUSHNET COMPANY; *pg.* 1824, *pg.* 818
UNI-FLEX - Textured Coating - JONES-BLAIR COMPANY; *pg.* 1443, *pg.* 1682
UNI-FLO - Eye & Face Wash - HAWS CORPORATION; *pg.* 56, *pg.* 1032
UNI-FRAME - Cage System Floor Stand - CTB INTERNATIONAL CORP.; *pg.* 850, *pg.* 695
UNI-FRAME - Building Product - LESTER BUILDING SYSTEMS, LLC; *pg.* 93, *pg.* 927
UNI FUSE - Electrosurgical Devices - ANGIODYNAMICS, INC.; *pg.* 1495, *pg.* 1173
UNI-GRIP - Multi Surface Dry Fog - AKZONOBEL DECORATIVE PAINTS U.S.; *pg.* 1439, *pg.* 1474
UNI-GRIP - Disposable Radiography Holder - DENTSPLY INTERNATIONAL INC.; *pg.* 1522, *pg.* 1596
UNI-HARD - Neutral Salt - HEATBATH CORPORATION; *pg.* 1165, *pg.* 826
UNI-HOIST - Salt Bath System - AJAX ELECTRIC CO.; *pg.* 1068, *pg.* 1541
UNI KLEEN - Metal Finishing Product - HEATBATH CORPORATION; *pg.* 1165, *pg.* 826
UNI-KYD - Alkyd - ARIZONA CHEMICAL CO. LLC; *pg.* 1147, *pg.* 431
UNI-LECTA - Seating Product - IRWIN SEATING COMPANY INC.; *pg.* 929, *pg.* 887
UNI-LOK - Ripper System - ESCO CORPORATION; *pg.* 1335, *pg.* 1502
UNI MARKER - Electronic Marker - GREENLEE TEXTRON INC.; *pg.* 1048, *pg.* 655
UNI-MESH - Optical Product - UNIVERSAL PHOTONICS, INC.; *pg.* 1433, *pg.* 1167
UNI-MILK - Milk Replacer for All Farm Species - MANNA PRO CORPORATION; *pg.* 1478, *pg.* 975
UNI-PAD - Optical Product - UNIVERSAL PHOTONICS, INC.; *pg.* 1433, *pg.* 1167
UNI-PAK - Unit Heaters - ADAMS MFG. CO.; *pg.* 51, *pg.* 1427
UNI-PRIME - Paint - KELLY-MOORE PAINT COMPANY, INC.; *pg.* 1443, *pg.* 198
UNI-PRIME - Electrodeposition Coatings - PPG INDUSTRIES, INC.; *pg.* 1445, *pg.* 1579
UNI-RAD - Burner - MAXON CORPORATION; *pg.* 1359, *pg.* 695
UNI-REZ - Resin - ARIZONA CHEMICAL CO. LLC; *pg.* 1147, *pg.* 431
UNI-RUPTER - Single-Pole Load Switching Device - S&C ELECTRIC COMPANY; *pg.* 1305, *pg.* 589
UNI-SEMI-LEAF - Optical Product - UNIVERSAL PHOTONICS, INC.; *pg.* 1433, *pg.* 1167
UNI-SPAND - Bevel Product - GLEASON CORPORATION; *pg.* 1340, *pg.* 1335
UNI-SYN - Carburetor Synchronizer - EDELBROCK CORPORATION; *pg.* 204, *pg.* 293
UNI-TAC - Resin - ARIZONA CHEMICAL CO. LLC; *pg.* 1147, *pg.* 431
UNI-TAP - Nylon Drive Anchor - MKT FASTENING, LLC; *pg.* 1056, *pg.* 34
UNI-TECH - Shoe And Glove - ACUSHNET COMPANY; *pg.* 1824, *pg.* 818
UNI-TIP - Fluid Handling System - GRACO, INC.; *pg.* 1342, *pg.* 935
UNI-TRAC - Mobile Filing Cabinets - TAB PRODUCTS CO. LLC; *pg.* 481, *pg.* 1869
UNIBACK - Wheelchair Back - INVACARE CORPORATION; *pg.* 1546, *pg.* 1451
UNIBEACON - Warning Light - UNITY MANUFACTURING COMPANY; *pg.* 221, *pg.* 594
UNIBEAM - Conveyor Components - DAIFUKU WEBB; *pg.* 1327, *pg.* 885
UNIBILT - Conveyors, Enclosed Track - DAIFUKU WEBB; *pg.* 1327, *pg.* 885
UNIBILT - Cab Sleeper System - PETERBILT MOTORS CO.; *pg.* 188, *pg.* 1691
UNIBLATE - Electrosurgical Devices - ANGIODYNAMICS, INC.; *pg.* 1495, *pg.* 1173
UNIBLEND - Copper Tape Shield - GENERAL CABLE CORPORATION; *pg.* 83, *pg.* 729
UNIBRITE - Steel Product - AK STEEL HOLDING CORPORATION; *pg.* 1311, *pg.* 1479
UNICABLE - Adapter - RF INDUSTRIES, LTD.; *pg.* 461, *pg.* 208
UNICAM - Glass & Ceramic Material - CORNING INCORPORATED; *pg.* 1122, *pg.* 1154
UNICAN - Pushbutton Lock Mechanism - KABA ILCO CORP.; *pg.* 1052, *pg.* 1390
UNICAP - Nutritional Supplements - MCNEIL-PPC, INC.; *pg.* 1560, *pg.* 1533
UNICARB - Application Technology - THE DOW CHEMICAL COMPANY; *pg.* 1157, *pg.* 898
UNICARE - Health Care Plan - ANTHEM, INC.; *pg.* 1192, *pg.* 683
UNICARE - Pharmaceutical Product - VALEANT PHARMACEUTICALS INTERNATIONAL; *pg.* 1605, *pg.* 1047
UNICEL DXL - Testing Instrument System - BECKMAN COULTER, INC.; *pg.* 1402, *pg.* 48
UNICHEM - Chemical Delivery System - ATMI, INC.; *pg.* 1314, *pg.* 342
UNICHIP - Interchangeable Tolerance Chip Thermistor - MEASUREMENT SPECIALTIES/YSI TEMPERATURE; *pg.* 1074, *pg.* 1482
UNICIRCLE - Retread System - THE GOODYEAR TIRE & RUBBER COMPANY; *pg.* 1883, *pg.* 1401
UNICLEAN - Clean Room Services - UNIFIRST CORPORATION; *pg.* 50, *pg.* 860
UNICLEAR - Gellant - ARIZONA CHEMICAL CO. LLC; *pg.* 1147, *pg.* 431
UNICOMB - Type of Drill & Tap Combination - REGAL BELOIT CORPORATION; *pg.* 106, *pg.* 1854
UNICORD - Power Transmission Belt - HBD INDUSTRIES, INC.; *pg.* 207, *pg.* 1449
UNICORN LIMITED - Traffic Counter & Classifier - INTERNATIONAL ROAD DYNAMICS INC.; *pg.* 1912, *pg.* 1962
UNICORN MAGIC - Video Game - INTERNATIONAL GAME TECHNOLOGY; *pg.* 957, *pg.* 1024
UNICORN TALES - Video Game - INTERNATIONAL GAME TECHNOLOGY; *pg.* 957, *pg.* 1024
UNICOS - Supercomputing System - CRAY INC.; *pg.* 380, *pg.* 1834
UNICOS MAX - Supercomputing System - CRAY INC.; *pg.* 380, *pg.* 1834
UNICOVER - Dispensing Equipment - IDEX CORPORATION; *pg.* 1347, *pg.* 623
UNICREPE - Resins Used in the Manufacture of Paper - GEORGIA-PACIFIC LLC; *pg.* 1458, *pg.* 507
UNICUBE - Bulk Container - GREIF INC.; *pg.* 1459, *pg.* 1447
UNICURE - Polymer Product - CHEMTURA CORPORATION; *pg.* 1152, *pg.* 355
UNIDAPT - Adapter Cable Assemblies - RF INDUSTRIES, LTD.; *pg.* 461, *pg.* 208
UNIDEK - International Trade Forms - UNZ & COMPANY, INC.; *pg.* 1698, *pg.* 1084
UNIDEX - Glass & Ceramic Material - CORNING INCORPORATED; *pg.* 1122, *pg.* 1154
UNIDRUM - Air Operated Pumps - GRACO, INC.; *pg.* 1342, *pg.* 935
UNIDUCT 2700 - Nonmetallic Raceway - WIREMOLD/LEGRAND; *pg.* 689, *pg.* 383
UNIDUCT 2800 - Nonmetallic Raceway - WIREMOLD/LEGRAND; *pg.* 689, *pg.* 383
UNIDUCT 2900 - Nonmetallic Raceway - WIREMOLD/LEGRAND; *pg.* 689, *pg.* 383
UNIDYME - Dimer Acid Product - ARIZONA CHEMICAL CO. LLC; *pg.* 1147, *pg.* 431
UNIDYNE - Vocal Microphone - SHURE INCORPORATED; *pg.* 672, *pg.* 638
UNIFACE - Software - COMPUWARE CORPORATION; *pg.* 379, *pg.* 879
UNIFAX - Communication Product - J2 GLOBAL COMMUNICATIONS, INC.; *pg.* 1260, *pg.* 133
UNIFER - Pharmaceutical Product - VALEANT PHARMACEUTICALS INTERNATIONAL; *pg.* 1605, *pg.* 1047
UNIFIED ACCESS ARCHITECTURE - Software - EXTREME NETWORKS INC; *pg.* 287, *pg.* 245
UNIFIED AUTHENTIFICATION OTP - Internet Site Security Product - VERISIGN, INC.; *pg.* 488, *pg.* 1799
UNIFIED AUTHENTIFICATION PKI FOR WINDOWS - Online Transaction Security Product - VERISIGN, INC.; *pg.* 488, *pg.* 1799
UNIFIED COMMUNICATOR - Software System - MITEL NETWORKS, INC.; *pg.* 1872, *pg.* 13
UNIFIED DATA MANAGEMENT - Software Solution - COMMVAULT SYSTEMS, INC.; *pg.* 377, *pg.* 1125
UNIFIED SEAL ALIGNMENT - Seal - A.W. CHESTERTON COMPANY; *pg.* 1315, *pg.* 861
UNIFIT - Medical Device - LEMAITRE VASCULAR, INC.; *pg.* 1555, *pg.* 805
UNIFIX - Photographic Fixer - EASTMAN KODAK COMPANY; *pg.* 1408, *pg.* 1333
UNIFLAME - Grill - BLUE RHINO CORPORATION; *pg.* 1318, *pg.* 1393
UNIFLEX - Dimer Acid Product - ARIZONA CHEMICAL CO. LLC; *pg.* 1147, *pg.* 431
UNIFLEX - Flex Mount - PANAVISE PRODUCTS, INC.; *pg.* 1058, *pg.* 1032
UNIFLEX GRIDS - Metallic Grids Inside Mattresses - KINGSDOWN, INC.; *pg.* 932, *pg.* 1383
UNIFLOT - Sulfide Promoter - HUNTSMAN CORPORATION; *pg.* 1167, *pg.* 1758
UNIFLOW - Fume Hoods - HEMCO CORPORATION; *pg.* 1416, *pg.* 979
UNIFLUX - Surface Finish Product - DOW CHEMICAL; *pg.* 1156, *pg.* 1563
UNIFORM EMULSIFIER - Dry Cleaning & Laundry Product - ADCO, INC.; *pg.* 325, *pg.* 482
UNIFORM FIRE CODE - Fire Safety Book - NATIONAL FIRE PROTECTION ASSOCIATION; *pg.* 149, *pg.* 842
UNIFORM MECHANICAL CODE - Fire Safety Book - NATIONAL FIRE PROTECTION ASSOCIATION; *pg.* 149, *pg.* 842
THE UNIFORM PEOPLE - Uniform Programs - CINTAS CORPORATION; *pg.* 372, *pg.* 1411
UNIFORM PLUMBING CODE - Fire Safety Book - NATIONAL FIRE PROTECTION ASSOCIATION; *pg.* 149, *pg.* 842
UNIFORMANCE - Software System - HONEYWELL INTERNATIONAL INC.; *pg.* 407, *pg.* 1088
UNIFRAME - Vinyl Windows - NORTEK, INC.; *pg.* 100, *pg.* 1607
UNIFUSOR - Aneroid Gauge & Thumbwheel Valve - CAS MEDICAL SYSTEMS, INC.; *pg.* 1513, *pg.* 339
UNIGARD - Flame-Retardant Compounds - THE DOW CHEMICAL COMPANY; *pg.* 1157, *pg.* 898
UNIGRAIN - Steel Product - AK STEEL HOLDING CORPORATION; *pg.* 1311, *pg.* 1479
UNIGRAPHICS - Software - MSC SOFTWARE CORPORATION; *pg.* 441, *pg.* 262
UNIGROUP - Office Interior Systems Furniture - HAWORTH, INC.; *pg.* 402, *pg.* 891
UNIGY - Rotary Screw - INGERSOLL-RAND COMPANY; *pg.* 1349, *pg.* 1370
UNIHIB - Water Treatment Chemicals - LONZA INC.; *pg.* 1171, *pg.* 1041
UNIJET - Flow Cell - BIOANALYTICAL SYSTEMS, INC.; *pg.* 1402, *pg.* 700
UNIJET - Spray Product - SPRAYING SYSTEMS CO.; *pg.* 1063, *pg.* 670
UNIKOTE - Interior Acrylic Enamel Undercoater - DUNN-

First page reference indicates Business Class Edition
Second page reference indicates Geographic Edition

EDWARDS CORPORATION; pg. 1442, pg. 129

UNILAB - Modular Work Areas & Environmental Enclosures - HEMCO CORPORATION; pg. 1416, pg. 979

UNILAST - Wheel - HAMILTON CASTER & MFG. CO.; pg. 206, pg. 1454

UNILINE - Laboratory Furniture - HEMCO CORPORATION; pg. 1416, pg. 979

UNILINE - Wormgear Reducer Series - REGAL BELOIT CORPORATION; pg. 106, pg. 1854

UNILITE - Hand-Held Spotlight - UNITY MANUFACTURING COMPANY; pg. 221, pg. 594

UNILOCK - Medical Device - DEPUY SYNTHES; pg. 1523, pg. 1593

UNILOK - Batteries - UNIVERSAL POWER GROUP, INC.; pg. 683, pg. 1671

UNIMAC - On-Premise Laundry Equipment - ALLIANCE LAUNDRY HOLDINGS LLC; pg. 51, pg. 1890

UNIMAX - Mini Lab - HEMCO CORPORATION; pg. 1416, pg. 979

UNIMAX - Iron Sulfide - HUNTSMAN CORPORATION; pg. 1167, pg. 1758

UNIMESSAGE - Facsimile Equipment - MURATEC AMERICA, INC.; pg. 443, pg. 1733

UNIMODULE - One Piece Electric Clutch/Brake - WARNER ELECTRIC, INC.; pg. 221, pg. 661

UNINET - Email Tool - NOTIFIER CO.; pg. 659, pg. 360

UNIOIL - Surface Finish Product - DOW CHEMICAL; pg. 1156, pg. 1563

UNION - Fabric - NEMSCHOFF, INC.; pg. 936, pg. 1890

UNION - Apparel - OAKLEY, INC.; pg. 1840, pg. 86

UNION - Mens & Women's Wear - SEATTLE PACIFIC INDUSTRIES, INC.; pg. 48, pg. 1822

UNION - Non-Metallic Box - THOMAS & BETTS CORPORATION; pg. 680, pg. 1646

UNION - Power Transmission Product - U.S. TSUBAKI, INC.; pg. 221, pg. 670

UNION - Wire Rope - WIRECO WORLDGROUP; pg. 1389, pg. 987

UNION - Valves - THE WM. POWELL COMPANY; pg. 1389, pg. 1427

UNION LEAGUE - Table - BLATT BOWLING & BILLIARD CORP.; pg. 1827, pg. 1203

UNION MEMORIAL HOSPITAL - Hospital - MEDSTAR HEALTH INC.; pg. 1563, pg. 767

UNION WORKMAN - Tobacco Product - AMERICAN SNUFF COMPANY; pg. 1893, pg. 1641

UNIONBAY - Young Men's, Junior & Boys & Girls Sportswear - SEATTLE PACIFIC INDUSTRIES, INC.; pg. 48, pg. 1822

UNIPAC - Induction Melting Systems - INDUCTOTHERM CORP.; pg. 1348, pg. 1114

UNIPAC - Bearing - THE TIMKEN COMPANY; pg. 218, pg. 1408

UNIPAC-PLUS - Bearing - THE TIMKEN COMPANY; pg. 218, pg. 1408

UNIPAK - Software - DATA I/O CORPORATION; pg. 382, pg. 1824

UNIPAK - Ink - VAN SON HOLLAND INK CORPORATION OF AMERICA; pg. 487, pg. 1169

UNIPASS DRILL 'N' TAP - Drill & Tap on the Same Blank - REGAL BELOIT CORPORATION; pg. 106, pg. 1854

UNIPASS TAPER PIPE DRILL 'N' TAP - Drill & Tap on the Same Blank Tapered - REGAL BELOIT CORPORATION; pg. 106, pg. 1854

UNIPET NUTRITABS - Animal Vitamin & Mineral Supplement - PFIZER INC.; pg. 1581, pg. 1278

UNIPINE - Fragrance Ingredient - INTERNATIONAL FLAVORS & FRAGRANCES INC.; pg. 512, pg. 1244

UNIPISTON - Sealing Devices - FEDERAL-MOGUL HOLDINGS CORPORATION; pg. 205, pg. 907

UNIPIVOT - Audio & Video Product - HARMAN INTERNATIONAL INDUSTRIES, INCORPORATED; pg. 641, pg. 374

UNIPLANE - Audio & Video Product - HARMAN INTERNATIONAL INDUSTRIES, INCORPORATED; pg. 641, pg. 374

UNIPOINT - Audio & Video Product - HARMAN INTERNATIONAL INDUSTRIES, INCORPORATED; pg. 641, pg. 374

UNIPRENE - Plastic & Rubber - TEKNOR APEX COMPANY; pg. 1889, pg. 1605

UNIPRISE - Cable - COMMSCOPE, INC.; pg. 278, pg. 1378

UNIPRISE - Healthcare & Well-Being Services - UNITEDHEALTH GROUP INCORPORATED; pg. 1221, pg. 950

UNIPURGE - Purging Compounds - THE DOW CHEMICAL COMPANY; pg. 1157, pg. 898

UNIQ-PRINT - Carpet Chemicals - OMNOVA SOLUTIONS INC; pg. 1176, pg. 1453

UNIQUE - Laboratory Equipment - LECO CORPORATION; pg. 1355, pg. 906

UNIQUE - Floor Polish - SWISHER HYGIENE INC.; pg. 336, pg. 1507

UNIQUE HOMES - Real Estate Guide - NETWORK COMMUNICATIONS INC.; pg. 1271, pg. 534

UNIQUE SOLUTIONS... CUSTOM MADE DAILY - Slogan - TRIAD SPEAKERS, INC.; pg. 682, pg. 1507

UNIQUELY ME - Apparel - ALWAYS FOR ME INC.; pg. 17, pg. 1163

UNIQUELY YOURS - Technology Security System - CHECKPOINT SYSTEMS, INC.; pg. 628, pg. 1559

UNIQUESOLUTIONSTRIAD - Slogan - TRIAD SPEAKERS, INC.; pg. 682, pg. 1507

UNIQUEWARE - Identification Technique - MAXIM INTEGRATED PRODUCTS, INC.; pg. 653, pg. 247

UNIRACK - Tobacco Holding Racks - GAS-FIRED PRODUCTS, INC.; pg. 1338, pg. 1367

UNIROAM - Wireless Telecommunication Product - SYNIVERSE HOLDINGS, INC.; pg. 479, pg. 475

UNIROYAL - Passenger & Light Truck Tires - MICHELIN NORTH AMERICA INC.; pg. 1886, pg. 1618

UNIROYAL CHEMICAL - Chemical Product - CHEMTURA CORPORATION; pg. 1152, pg. 355

UNISAT - Paper - INTERNATIONAL PAPER COMPANY; pg. 1460, pg. 1644

UNISEA - Seafood Products - UNISEA FOODS, INC.; pg. 906, pg. 1829

UNISET - Press - MANROLAND INC.; pg. 430, pg. 669

UNISET - Anchor - MKT FASTENING, LLC; pg. 1056, pg. 34

UNISEX - Ear Warmer - 180S, LLC; pg. 1824, pg. 754

UNISHIELD - Copper Wire Shield - GENERAL CABLE CORPORATION; pg. 83, pg. 729

UNISIM - Software System - HONEYWELL INTERNATIONAL INC.; pg. 407, pg. 1088

UNISOIL - Additive - BASF CATALYSTS LLC; pg. 1148, pg. 1074

UNISOL - Fabric - NEMSCHOFF, INC.; pg. 936, pg. 1890

UNISOLV - Chemical Product - SPECTRUM CHEMICALS & LABORATORY PRODUCTS, INC.; pg. 1181, pg. 94

UNISOM - Sleep Aid Product - CHATTEM, INC.; pg. 1515, pg. 1628

UNISOM - Medicine - PFIZER INC.; pg. 1581, pg. 1278

UNISON - Dental Product - DENTSPLY INTERNATIONAL INC.; pg. 1522, pg. 1596

UNISON - Lighting Equipment - ELECTRONIC THEATRE CONTROLS, INC.; pg. 1296, pg. 1872

UNISON - Fabric - NEMSCHOFF, INC.; pg. 936, pg. 1890

UNISON - Office Furniture - STEELCASE INC.; pg. 475, pg. 889

UNISON - Aircraft Engine Electrical Components - UNISON INDUSTRIES, LLC; pg. 235, pg. 435

UNISPAN - Self Support System - HUFCOR INCORPORATED; pg. 87, pg. 1861

UNISPHERE - Software - EMC CORPORATION; pg. 391, pg. 825

UNISPHERE - Microphone - SHURE INCORPORATED; pg. 672, pg. 638

UNISPHERE - Pipeline Pigging Product - T.D. WILLIAMSON, INC.; pg. 1380, pg. 1490

UNISTACK - Concrete Batching Equipment - BESSER COMPANY; pg. 1317, pg. 865

UNISTEEL - Tire - THE GOODYEAR TIRE & RUBBER COMPANY; pg. 1883, pg. 1401

UNISTRUT - Metal Framing - UNISTRUT CORPORATION; pg. 117, pg. 913

UNISWITCH - Syringe Selector - BIOANALYTICAL SYSTEMS, INC.; pg. 1402, pg. 700

UNISYS - Computers & Data Processing Systems - UNISYS CORPORATION; pg. 487, pg. 1517

UNIT-BEARING - Bearing Product - THE TIMKEN COMPANY; pg. 218, pg. 1408

UNIT-DOSE - Packaging System - MTS MEDICATION TECHNOLOGIES, INC.; pg. 442, pg. 463

UNIT RIG - Truck - TEREX CORPORATION; pg. 1381, pg. 384

UNIT WALL - Window - ALCOA INC.; pg. 65, pg. 1188

UNITECH - Pumps - IDEX CORPORATION; pg. 1347, pg. 623

UNITED - Carbon Black - CABOT CORPORATION; pg. 1151, pg. 792

UNITED - Moving Company - UNITED VAN LINES, LLC; pg. 1929, pg. 978

UNITED AIRLINES - Commercial Airline - UNITED CONTINENTAL HOLDINGS, INC.; pg. 1927, pg. 593

UNITED CENTRIFUGAL - Pump - FLOWSERVE CORPORATION; pg. 82, pg. 1719

UNITED EASYACCESS - Wireless Technology - UNITED CONTINENTAL HOLDINGS, INC.; pg. 1927, pg. 593

UNITED EASYCHECK-IN - Airline Service - UNITED CONTINENTAL HOLDINGS, INC.; pg. 1927, pg. 593

UNITED EASYINFO - Airline Service - UNITED CONTINENTAL HOLDINGS, INC.; pg. 1927, pg. 593

UNITED EASYUPDATE - Airline Service - UNITED CONTINENTAL HOLDINGS, INC.; pg. 1927, pg. 593

UNITED ECONOMY - Airline Service - UNITED CONTINENTAL HOLDINGS, INC.; pg. 1927, pg. 593

UNITED ECONOMY PLUS - Airline Service - UNITED CONTINENTAL HOLDINGS, INC.; pg. 1927, pg. 593

UNITED FIRST - Airline Service - UNITED CONTINENTAL HOLDINGS, INC.; pg. 1927, pg. 593

UNITED FIRST SUITE - Airline Service - UNITED CONTINENTAL HOLDINGS, INC.; pg. 1927, pg. 593

UNITED INTERLOCK - Plank Grating - UNISTRUT CORPORATION; pg. 117, pg. 913

UNITED PARCEL SERVICE - Express Parcel Deliveries - UNITED PARCEL SERVICE, INC.; pg. 1928, pg. 522

UNITED POWER - Pledge - DANAHER CORPORATION; pg. 1044, pg. 397

UNITED SPACE ALLIANCE - Space Shuttle Missions, Launches, Flight & Ground Operations - LOCKHEED MARTIN CORPORATION; pg. 229, pg. 762

UNITED STATES COLD SOLUTIONS - Logistics Packages for Refrigerated Distribution - UNITED STATES COLD STORAGE, INC.; pg. 61, pg. 1051

UNITED STATES COLD STORAGE - Refrigerated Warehousing, Logistics & Related Services - UNITED STATES COLD STORAGE, INC.; pg. 61, pg. 1051

UNITED STATES MINT SILVER PROOF SET - Annual Proof Versions of All Circulating Coins Struck in Coin Silver - UNITED STATES MINT; pg. 814, pg. 406

UNITED STATES POSTAL SERVICE - Postal Service for the United States - UNITED STATES POSTAL SERVICE; pg. 1009, pg. 406

UNITED VAN LINES - Transportation System - UNIGROUP, INC.; pg. 1927, pg. 977

UNITEDCOMMUNITIES - Residential Communities - UNITED, INC.; pg. 1117, pg. 1905

UNITEK - Adhesive Coated Appliance System - 3M COMPANY; pg. 1142, pg. 956

UNITEK - Orthodontic Materials - 3M UNITEK CORPORATION; pg. 1483, pg. 150

UNITER - Plastics Product - AEP INDUSTRIES INC.; pg. 1878, pg. 1085

UNITHROID - Pharmaceutical Product - LANNETT COMPANY, INC.; pg. 1555, pg. 1566

UNITOL - Tall Oil - ARIZONA CHEMICAL CO. LLC; pg. 1147, pg. 431

UNITRAC - Pneumatic Retraction System - AESCULAP, INC.; pg. 1487, pg. 1521

UNITRAY - Heated & Refrigerated Cart - STANDEX INTERNATIONAL CORPORATION; pg. 60, pg. 1039

UNITRAY - Molecular Biology Product - THERMO FISHER SCIENTIFIC INC.; pg. 1602, pg. 61

UNITRODE - Semiconductors Products - TEXAS INSTRUMENTS INCORPORATED; pg. 679, pg. 1688

UNITRON 3 - Rethermalization System - STANDEX INTERNATIONAL CORPORATION; pg. 60, pg. 1039

UNITRON 5 - Rethermalization System - STANDEX INTERNATIONAL CORPORATION; pg. 60, pg. 1039

UNITRON 7 - Rethermalization System - STANDEX INTERNATIONAL CORPORATION; pg. 60, pg. 1039

UNITY - Software - BIO-RAD LABORATORIES, INC.; pg. 1504, pg. 101

UNITY - Dinnerware - THE HOMER LAUGHLIN CHINA COMPANY; pg. 1125, pg. 1850

UNITY - Flatware - ONEIDA LTD; pg. 1129, pg. 1318

UNITY - Satellite Receiver - WEGENER CORPORATION; pg. 687, pg. 533

UNITY DESKTOP - Software - BIO-RAD LABORATORIES, INC.; pg. 1504, pg. 101

UNITY PC - Software - BIO-RAD LABORATORIES, INC.; pg. 1504, pg. 101

UNITY PLATFORM - Semiconductor Device - ULTRATECH, INC.; pg. 1433, pg. 251

UNITY PLUS - Software - BIO-RAD LABORATORIES, INC.; pg. 1504, pg. 101

UNITY PLUS/PRO - Software - BIO-RAD LABORATORIES, INC.; *pg.* 1504, *pg.* 101
UNITY POST - Software - BIO-RAD LABORATORIES, INC.; *pg.* 1504, *pg.* 101
UNITY PRO - Software - BIO-RAD LABORATORIES, INC.; *pg.* 1504, *pg.* 101
UNITY REAL TIME - Software - BIO-RAD LABORATORIES, INC.; *pg.* 1504, *pg.* 101
UNITY SEATING - Pew Chair - SAUDER MANUFACTURING COMPANY; *pg.* 941, *pg.* 1403
UNITY WEB - Software - BIO-RAD LABORATORIES, INC.; *pg.* 1504, *pg.* 101
UNIVADINE - Levelling Agents - HUNTSMAN CORPORATION; *pg.* 1167, *pg.* 1758
UNIVAL - Resin - THE DOW CHEMICAL COMPANY; *pg.* 1157, *pg.* 898
UNIVEDER - Plastics Product - AEP INDUSTRIES INC.; *pg.* 1878, *pg.* 1085
UNIVER - Chemical Reagent - HACH COMPANY; *pg.* 1415, *pg.* 334
UNIVERSAL - Electric Motors - A.O. SMITH CORPORATION; *pg.* 1313, *pg.* 1872
UNIVERSAL - Catalytic Converter - AP EXHAUST PRODUCTS, INC.; *pg.* 199, *pg.* 1373
UNIVERSAL - Labeler - AVERY DENNISON CORPORATION; *pg.* 1452, *pg.* 95
UNIVERSAL - Air Brush - BADGER AIR BRUSH COMPANY; *pg.* 359, *pg.* 612
UNIVERSAL - Livestock Equipment - BEHLEN MFG. CO.; *pg.* 701, *pg.* 1010
UNIVERSAL - Furniture - BUSH INDUSTRIES INC.; *pg.* 919, *pg.* 1170
UNIVERSAL - Electrocardiograph - CARDIAC SCIENCE CORPORATION; *pg.* 1512, *pg.* 1897
UNIVERSAL - Quality & Classic Chafers - CARLISLE FOODSERVICE PRODUCTS INCORPORATED; *pg.* 1455, *pg.* 1485
UNIVERSAL - X-Ray Systems - DGT HOLDINGS; *pg.* 634, *pg.* 1223
UNIVERSAL - Fire Fighting Foam Concentrate - KIDDE FIRE FIGHTING; *pg.* 1170, *pg.* 1531
UNIVERSAL - Trimmer Power Adapter - LYMAN PRODUCTS CORPORATION; *pg.* 1839, *pg.* 356
UNIVERSAL - Medical Product - MEDLINE INDUSTRIES, INC.; *pg.* 1562, *pg.* 635
UNIVERSAL - Notary Certificates - NATIONAL NOTARY ASSOCIATION; *pg.* 150, *pg.* 64
UNIVERSAL - Hot Melt Adhesive Dispenser - NORDSON CORPORATION; *pg.* 1365, *pg.* 1480
UNIVERSAL - Fabric - UNIROYAL ENGINEERED PRODUCTS; *pg.* 699, *pg.* 467
UNIVERSAL - Electric Instrument - UNIVERSAL INSTRUMENTS CORPORATION; *pg.* 683, *pg.* 1154
UNIVERSAL - Ballasts - UNIVERSAL LIGHTING TECHNOLOGIES; *pg.* 1307, *pg.* 1655
UNIVERSAL - Optical Product - UNIVERSAL PHOTONICS, INC.; *pg.* 1433, *pg.* 1167
UNIVERSAL - Batteries - UNIVERSAL POWER GROUP, INC.; *pg.* 683, *pg.* 1671
UNIVERSAL - Security Instruments - UNIVERSAL SECURITY INSTRUMENTS, INC.; *pg.* 683, *pg.* 775
UNIVERSAL - Diesel Engine - WESTERBEKE CORPORATION; *pg.* 1388, *pg.* 847
UNIVERSAL 2 - Medical Device - INTEGRA LIFESCIENCES HOLDINGS CORPORATION; *pg.* 1545, *pg.* 1109
UNIVERSAL ACETABULAR - Hip Product - ZIMMER BIOMET HOLDINGS, INC.; *pg.* 1611, *pg.* 699
UNIVERSAL APPEAL - Slogan - EDEN FOODS INC.; *pg.* 1019, *pg.* 875
UNIVERSAL BUS LOGIC - Semiconductor Solution - CYPRESS SEMICONDUCTOR CORPORATION; *pg.* 1326, *pg.* 243
UNIVERSAL CAPACITIVE READOUT - Integrated Circuit - ISC8; *pg.* 1350, *pg.* 71
UNIVERSAL CRICKET - Kids Remote - UNIVERSAL ELECTRONICS, INC.; *pg.* 683, *pg.* 262
UNIVERSAL DIAGNOSTIC - Hardware System - MICRO 2000, INC.; *pg.* 434, *pg.* 96
UNIVERSAL FLEET CARD - Fuel Credit Card - WRIGHT EXPRESS CORPORATION; *pg.* 493, *pg.* 753
UNIVERSAL HUGGER - Fan - CRAFTMADE INTERNATIONAL, INC.; *pg.* 1295, *pg.* 1670
UNIVERSAL LID HOLDER - Chafer Lid Holders - CARLISLE FOODSERVICE PRODUCTS INCORPORATED; *pg.* 1455, *pg.* 1485
UNIVERSAL LIFE - Life Insurance - PAN-AMERICAN LIFE INSURANCE COMPANY; *pg.* 1213, *pg.* 747
UNIVERSAL LOWPRO - Mounting Bracket - ACR ELECTRONICS, INC.; *pg.* 612, *pg.* 422
UNIVERSAL MOLD RELEASE - Releasing Agent - SMOOTH-ON INC.; *pg.* 111, *pg.* 1528
UNIVERSAL NEURO - Fixation System - STRYKER CORPORATION; *pg.* 1598, *pg.* 894
UNIVERSAL NONVERBAL INTELLIGENCE TEST - Assessment Tool - HOUGHTON MIFFLIN HARCOURT PUBLISHING COMPANY; *pg.* 1651, *pg.* 796
UNIVERSAL PATCHING FRAME - Electronic Components - MOLEX INCORPORATED; *pg.* 655, *pg.* 628
UNIVERSAL PLUS - Medical Equipment - CONMED CORPORATION; *pg.* 1517, *pg.* 1347
UNIVERSAL S/I - Medical Equipment - CONMED CORPORATION; *pg.* 1517, *pg.* 1347
UNIVERSAL SURROUND - Orthopedic Product - DJO INCORPORATED; *pg.* 1524, *pg.* 302
UNIVERSAL TECHNICAL SERVICE - Health & Fitness Product - ICON HEALTH & FITNESS, INC.; *pg.* 1837, *pg.* 1752
UNIVERSAL TRIMMER - Precision Cartridge Case Trimmer - LYMAN PRODUCTS CORPORATION; *pg.* 1839, *pg.* 356
UNIVERSAL WORKSURFACES - Tables - STEELCASE INC.; *pg.* 475, *pg.* 889
UNIVERSALCUSHION - Cushion - TEMPUR SEALY INTERNATIONAL, INC.; *pg.* 944, *pg.* 731
UNIVERSALDSL - Software - TELLABS, INC.; *pg.* 678, *pg.* 637
UNIVERSALIGHT - Illumination Module - UNIVERSAL INSTRUMENTS CORPORATION; *pg.* 683, *pg.* 1154
UNIVERSE - Fabric - NEMSCHOFF, INC.; *pg.* 936, *pg.* 1890
UNIVERSITY CLUB - School Uniforms - LT APPAREL GROUP; *pg.* 29, *pg.* 1254
UNIVERSITY OF TOKYO PRESS - Publisher - COLUMBIA UNIVERSITY PRESS; *pg.* 1628, *pg.* 1216
UNIVEST CORPORATION OF PENNSYLVANIA - Banking Services - UNIVEST CORPORATION OF PENNSYLVANIA; *pg.* 814, *pg.* 1586
UNIVEX - Food Preparing Machine - UNIVEX CORPORATION; *pg.* 1386, *pg.* 1039
UNIVIEW - Scoreboard & Sports Product - DAKTRONICS, INC.; *pg.* 633, *pg.* 1624
UNIVISION - Spanish-Language Television Broadcaster - UNIVISION COMMUNICATIONS INC.; *pg.* 683, *pg.* 1307
UNIVIT - Carbon Steel Product - AK STEEL HOLDING CORPORATION; *pg.* 1311, *pg.* 1479
UNIVOGUE - Apparel - SUPERIOR UNIFORM GROUP, INC.; *pg.* 33, *pg.* 468
UNIWEAR - Outerwear - UNIFIRST CORPORATION; *pg.* 50, *pg.* 860
UNIWEAVE - Industrial Uniform Shirts - UNIFIRST CORPORATION; *pg.* 50, *pg.* 860
UNIWEB - Unidirectionally Oriented Continuous Carbon Filaments - TOHO TENAX AMERICA, INC.; *pg.* 1184, *pg.* 1655
UNIWRAP - Papers - DAUBERT INDUSTRIES, INC.; *pg.* 1155, *pg.* 561
UNIX - Software - LYNX SOFTWARE TECHNOLOGIES; *pg.* 429, *pg.* 247
UNKNOWN - Eyewear - OAKLEY, INC.; *pg.* 1840, *pg.* 86
UNLEADED - Apparel - OAKLEY, INC.; *pg.* 1840, *pg.* 86
UNLEASH THE BEAST! - Beverage - MONSTER BEVERAGE CORPORATION; *pg.* 257, *pg.* 69
UNLEASH THE NUT WITHIN. - Tagline - BEER NUTS, INC.; *pg.* 1850, *pg.* 557
UNLEASHED - Game - ACTIVISION BLIZZARD, INC.; *pg.* 948, *pg.* 271
UNLIMIT YOURSELF. - Tagline - METROPCS, INC.; *pg.* 1872, *pg.* 1683
UNLIMITED - Software System - AT&T COMMUNICATIONS CORP.; *pg.* 1866, *pg.* 1043
UNLIMITED ANSWERS - Wireless Communication System - AT&T SOUTHEAST; *pg.* 1868, *pg.* 489
UNLIMITED BOUNDARIES - Furniture - HERMAN MILLER, INC.; *pg.* 926, *pg.* 913
UNLOAD - Software - BMC SOFTWARE, INC.; *pg.* 362, *pg.* 1701
UNLOAD PLUS - IMS Database Utility - BMC SOFTWARE, INC.; *pg.* 362, *pg.* 1701
UNLOCK THE TREASURE - Game - WMS INDUSTRIES INC.; *pg.* 593, *pg.* 666
UNMISTAKABLE - Cologne Spray - ENESCO, LLC; *pg.* 1124, *pg.* 620
UNMP - Pharmaceutical Product - ALERE INC.; *pg.* 1488, *pg.* 849
UNNA-FLEX - Wound Care Product - CONVATEC LTD.; *pg.* 1518, *pg.* 1121
UNNA-PAK - Bandages - DERMA SCIENCES, INC.; *pg.* 1523, *pg.* 1111
UNNAPRESS - Bandage - DERMA SCIENCES, INC.; *pg.* 1523, *pg.* 1111
UNO - Furniture - AMERICAN LEATHER LP; *pg.* 912, *pg.* 1673
UNO - Software - BIO-RAD LABORATORIES, INC.; *pg.* 1504, *pg.* 101
UNO - Game - INTERNATIONAL GAME TECHNOLOGY; *pg.* 957, *pg.* 1024
UNO - Toy - MATTEL, INC.; *pg.* 962, *pg.* 81
UNO - Office Furniture - STEELCASE INC.; *pg.* 475, *pg.* 889
UNO 20 COMMEMORATIVE EDITION - Card Game - MATTEL GAMES/PUZZLES; *pg.* 962, *pg.* 80
UNO CHICAGO BAR & GRILL - Original Deep Dish Pizza - UNO RESTAURANT HOLDINGS CORPORATION; *pg.* 1754, *pg.* 856
UNO, DOS, SCRATCH - Lottery Game - MICHIGAN STATE LOTTERY BUREAU; *pg.* 999, *pg.* 895
UNOSPHERE - Software - BIO-RAD LABORATORIES, INC.; *pg.* 1504, *pg.* 101
UNOSPHERE SUPRA - Software - BIO-RAD LABORATORIES, INC.; *pg.* 1504, *pg.* 101
UNOXOL - Alcohol Solvents - THE DOW CHEMICAL COMPANY; *pg.* 1157, *pg.* 898
UNREEL - Wire & Cable Pack - BELDEN, INC.; *pg.* 624, *pg.* 993
UNSCENTED - Fragrance - PARFUMS DE COEUR LTD.; *pg.* 519, *pg.* 376
UNSCENTED ODOR BLOCK - Technology - PACTIV CORPORATION; *pg.* 1466, *pg.* 624
THE UNSCRAMBLER - Software - CAMO SOFTWARE, INC.; *pg.* 368, *pg.* 1133
UNSCRAMBLER CLASSIFIER - Software - CAMO SOFTWARE, INC.; *pg.* 368, *pg.* 1133
UNSCRAMBLER ONLINE - Software - CAMO SOFTWARE, INC.; *pg.* 368, *pg.* 1133
UNSCRAMBLER OPTIMIZER - Software - CAMO SOFTWARE, INC.; *pg.* 368, *pg.* 1133
UNSCRAMBLER PREDICTOR - Software - CAMO SOFTWARE, INC.; *pg.* 368, *pg.* 1133
UNSTALLABLE - Diaphragm Pump - INGERSOLL-RAND COMPANY; *pg.* 1349, *pg.* 1370
UNTRATECH 7000 - Leather Textiles - BERNHARDT DESIGN; *pg.* 918, *pg.* 1381
UNWRAP A SMILE - Slogan - MCKEE FOODS CORPORATION; *pg.* 1860, *pg.* 1630
UOP - Fuel - HONEYWELL INTERNATIONAL INC.; *pg.* 407, *pg.* 1088
UP AND DOWN WALL STREET - Financial Products - DOW JONES & COMPANY, INC.; *pg.* 1637, *pg.* 1225
UP & UP - Target Branded Products - TARGET CORPORATION; *pg.* 1786, *pg.* 942
UP IN THE AIR - Cat Toy - THE HARTZ MOUNTAIN CORP.; *pg.* 1476, *pg.* 1120
UP UP & AWAY - Game - WMS INDUSTRIES INC.; *pg.* 593, *pg.* 666
UP YOUR KILT - Game - WMS INDUSTRIES INC.; *pg.* 593, *pg.* 666
UP YOUR MASS - Nutritional Supplement - MAXIMUM HUMAN PERFORMANCE, INC.; *pg.* 1559, *pg.* 1065
UPAK - Packing Drums of Fiber or Fiber with Metallic Ends - SONOCO PRODUCTS COMPANY; *pg.* 1469, *pg.* 1619
UPBEAT - Fabric - NEMSCHOFF, INC.; *pg.* 936, *pg.* 1890
UPBEET - Herbicide - E.I. DU PONT DE NEMOURS & COMPANY; *pg.* 1159, *pg.* 390
UPCHURCH SCIENTIFIC - Pumps - IDEX CORPORATION; *pg.* 1347, *pg.* 623
UPCORE - Water Treatment Apparatus - THE DOW CHEMICAL COMPANY; *pg.* 1157, *pg.* 898
UPDATE - Robotic Product - HAMILTON CO., INC.; *pg.* 1415, *pg.* 1031
UPDATE SERVICE - Software - FLEXERA SOFTWARE INC.; *pg.* 398, *pg.* 658
UPDATE UTILITY - Software - DELL SOFTWARE; *pg.* 385, *pg.* 40
UPDATEEXPERT - Software - EDGEWAVE INC; *pg.* 390, *pg.* 202
UPES - Resin - NOVA CHEMICALS CORPORATION; *pg.* 1175, *pg.* 1904
UPFRONT - Software - EASTMAN KODAK COMPANY; *pg.*

1408, *pg.* 1333
UPFRONT - Educational Materials - SCHOLASTIC INC.; *pg.* 1683, *pg.* 1288
UPGRADE SERVICES - Mobile Solutions - SONUS NETWORKS INC.; *pg.* 1281, *pg.* 858
UPHOLD - Medical Device - BOSTON SCIENTIFIC CORPORATION; *pg.* 1508, *pg.* 831
UPHOLD - Cleaning Product - HILLYARD, INC.; *pg.* 331, *pg.* 990
UPI ARABIC SERVICE - News Reports to & from Arabic-Speaking Communities - UNITED PRESS INTERNATIONAL, INC.; *pg.* 1698, *pg.* 405
UPI NEWSTRACK - News Snapshot Service - UNITED PRESS INTERNATIONAL, INC.; *pg.* 1698, *pg.* 405
UPI PERSPECTIVES - News Reports - UNITED PRESS INTERNATIONAL, INC.; *pg.* 1698, *pg.* 405
UPI PHOTOS - Photograph Service - UNITED PRESS INTERNATIONAL, INC.; *pg.* 1698, *pg.* 405
UPI SPANISH - News Reports for & from Spanish-Speaking Communities - UNITED PRESS INTERNATIONAL, INC.; *pg.* 1698, *pg.* 405
UPLANDER - Footwear - LACROSSE FOOTWEAR, INC.; *pg.* 1811, *pg.* 1503
UPLINK - Communication Product - NUMEREX CORP.; *pg.* 660, *pg.* 517
UPPER DECK AUDIENCE SEATING SYSTEM - Chair - WENGER CORPORATION; *pg.* 1307, *pg.* 952
UPPER DECK AUTHENTICATED - Autograph Checking System - THE UPPER DECK COMPANY, LLC; *pg.* 969, *pg.* 62
THE UPPER ROOM - Daily Devotional Guide - THE UPPER ROOM; *pg.* 1698, *pg.* 1655
UPPER WOLF JAW - Clothing - ABERCROMBIE & FITCH CO.; *pg.* 37, *pg.* 1466
UPPERCUT - Fungicide - E.I. DU PONT DE NEMOURS & COMPANY; *pg.* 1159, *pg.* 390
UPPERCUTS - Boxing Accessories - ALLIANCE SPORTS GROUP, L.P.; *pg.* 1825, *pg.* 1698
THE UPRIGHT MRI - MRI Scanner - FONAR CORPORATION; *pg.* 1413, *pg.* 1179
UPRIGHT VERTICAL BRIEF - Briefcase - SANTA FE LEATHER CORPORATION; *pg.* 12, *pg.* 1059
UPRINT - 3D Printer - STRATASYS, INC.; *pg.* 476, *pg.* 923
UPROAR - Designer Fragrance - PARFUMS DE COEUR LTD.; *pg.* 519, *pg.* 376
UPROMISE - Store Program - CVS HEALTH CORPORATION; *pg.* 1765, *pg.* 1610
UPS 10 KG BOX - Software - UNITED PARCEL SERVICE, INC.; *pg.* 1928, *pg.* 522
UPS 25 KG BOX - Software - UNITED PARCEL SERVICE, INC.; *pg.* 1928, *pg.* 522
UPS 2ND DAY AIR - Software - UNITED PARCEL SERVICE, INC.; *pg.* 1928, *pg.* 522
UPS 2ND DAY AIR A.M. - Software - UNITED PARCEL SERVICE, INC.; *pg.* 1928, *pg.* 522
UPS AIR CARGO SERVICE - Software - UNITED PARCEL SERVICE, INC.; *pg.* 1928, *pg.* 522
UPS AIR FREIGHT DIRECT - Shipping Services - UNITED PARCEL SERVICE, INC.; *pg.* 1928, *pg.* 522
UPS AUTOGISTICS - Business Management - UNITED PARCEL SERVICE, INC.; *pg.* 1928, *pg.* 522
UPS BRAND EXCHANGE - Business Services - UNITED PARCEL SERVICE, INC.; *pg.* 1928, *pg.* 522
UPS CAMPUSSHIP - Shipping Services - UNITED PARCEL SERVICE, INC.; *pg.* 1928, *pg.* 522
UPS CAPITAL - Financial Services - UNITED PARCEL SERVICE, INC.; *pg.* 1928, *pg.* 522
UPS CAPITAL BUSINESS CREDIT - Financial Services - UNITED PARCEL SERVICE, INC.; *pg.* 1928, *pg.* 522
UPS DELIVER MORE - Software - UNITED PARCEL SERVICE, INC.; *pg.* 1928, *pg.* 522
UPS DELIVERY INTERCEPT - Business Services - UNITED PARCEL SERVICE, INC.; *pg.* 1928, *pg.* 522
UPS DELIVERY LINK - Software - UNITED PARCEL SERVICE, INC.; *pg.* 1928, *pg.* 522
UPS EARLY A.M. - Software - UNITED PARCEL SERVICE, INC.; *pg.* 1928, *pg.* 522
UPS EXCHANGE COLLECT - Finance Services - UNITED PARCEL SERVICE, INC.; *pg.* 1928, *pg.* 522
UPS EXPEDITE - Software - UNITED PARCEL SERVICE, INC.; *pg.* 1928, *pg.* 522
UPS EXPRESS - Shipping Services - UNITED PARCEL SERVICE, INC.; *pg.* 1928, *pg.* 522
UPS EXPRESS CRITICAL - Software - UNITED PARCEL SERVICE, INC.; *pg.* 1928, *pg.* 522
UPS FREIGHT OVER THE ROAD - Online Software - UNITED PARCEL SERVICE, INC.; *pg.* 1928, *pg.* 522
UPS GROUNDSAVER - Software - UNITED PARCEL SERVICE, INC.; *pg.* 1928, *pg.* 522
UPS HUNDREDWEIGHT SERVICE - Discounted Shipping Services - UNITED PARCEL SERVICE, INC.; *pg.* 1928, *pg.* 522
UPS INNOPLEX - Real Estate Management - UNITED PARCEL SERVICE, INC.; *pg.* 1928, *pg.* 522
UPS INTELLIVERSE - Business Management - UNITED PARCEL SERVICE, INC.; *pg.* 1928, *pg.* 522
UPS INTERNET TOOLS - Software - UNITED PARCEL SERVICE, INC.; *pg.* 1928, *pg.* 522
UPS MAIL INNOVATIONS - Electronic Bill - UNITED PARCEL SERVICE, INC.; *pg.* 1928, *pg.* 522
UPS MAIL LOGIC - Shipping Services - UNITED PARCEL SERVICE, INC.; *pg.* 1928, *pg.* 522
UPS NEXT DAY AIR SAVER - Software - UNITED PARCEL SERVICE, INC.; *pg.* 1928, *pg.* 522
UPS ONLINE - Online Services - UNITED PARCEL SERVICE, INC.; *pg.* 1928, *pg.* 522
UPS ONLINE COURIER - Software - UNITED PARCEL SERVICE, INC.; *pg.* 1928, *pg.* 522
UPS PREFERRED - Software - UNITED PARCEL SERVICE, INC.; *pg.* 1928, *pg.* 522
UPS SAVER - Software - UNITED PARCEL SERVICE, INC.; *pg.* 1928, *pg.* 522
UPS SIGNATURE TRACKING - Software - UNITED PARCEL SERVICE, INC.; *pg.* 1928, *pg.* 522
THE UPS STORE - Services - UNITED PARCEL SERVICE, INC.; *pg.* 1928, *pg.* 522
UPS TOTALTRACK - Software - UNITED PARCEL SERVICE, INC.; *pg.* 1928, *pg.* 522
UPS TRACKPAD - Software - UNITED PARCEL SERVICE, INC.; *pg.* 1928, *pg.* 522
UPS TRADE ABILITY - Computer Hardware - UNITED PARCEL SERVICE, INC.; *pg.* 1928, *pg.* 522
UPS TRADE DIRECT - Data Processing Services - UNITED PARCEL SERVICE, INC.; *pg.* 1928, *pg.* 522
UPS TRADE SENSE - Software - UNITED PARCEL SERVICE, INC.; *pg.* 1928, *pg.* 522
UPS VOICE NOTIFICATION - Voice Tracking - UNITED PARCEL SERVICE, INC.; *pg.* 1928, *pg.* 522
UPS WORLDWIDE EXPRESS - Shipping Services - UNITED PARCEL SERVICE, INC.; *pg.* 1928, *pg.* 522
UPS WORLDWIDE LOGISTICS - Software - UNITED PARCEL SERVICE, INC.; *pg.* 1928, *pg.* 522
UPSCALE - Software - SYMANTEC CORPORATION; *pg.* 478, *pg.* 161
UPS.COM - Online Tracking Services - UNITED PARCEL SERVICE, INC.; *pg.* 1928, *pg.* 522
UPSERS - Software - UNITED PARCEL SERVICE, INC.; *pg.* 1928, *pg.* 522
UPSIDE DOWN - Marking Paints - SHERWIN-WILLIAMS DIVERSIFIED BRANDS DIVISION; *pg.* 1448, *pg.* 1435
UPSIDE DOWN FRUIT AND WHITE CHOCLATE CAKE - Food Product - GAY LEA FOODS CO-OPERATIVE LIMITED; *pg.* 858, *pg.* 1926
UPSIDES - Side Dishes - J.R. SIMPLOT COMPANY; *pg.* 867, *pg.* 547
UPSNET - Software - UNITED PARCEL SERVICE, INC.; *pg.* 1928, *pg.* 522
UPSTART - Office Furniture - KNOLL, INC.; *pg.* 425, *pg.* 1527
UPSTATE FARMS - Dairy Products - UPSTATE NIAGARA COOPERATIVE, INC.; *pg.* 907, *pg.* 1151
UPSTREAM - Wafer Test Product - FORMFACTOR, INC.; *pg.* 1882, *pg.* 122
UPSTREAM - Water Disposal - WASTE MANAGEMENT, INC.; *pg.* 1954, *pg.* 1716
UPT - Phosphor Particles Detection of Various Substances - ORASURE TECHNOLOGIES INC; *pg.* 1578, *pg.* 1516
UPTIME 100 - Electric Instrument - UNIVERSAL INSTRUMENTS CORPORATION; *pg.* 683, *pg.* 1154
UPTON - Furniture - ASHLEY FURNITURE INDUSTRIES, INC.; *pg.* 914, *pg.* 1852
UPTOWN - Dinnerware - THE HOMER LAUGHLIN CHINA COMPANY; *pg.* 1125, *pg.* 1850
UPTOWN - Bakery Product - J&J SNACK FOODS CORPORATION; *pg.* 865, *pg.* 1107
UPTOWN - Fabric - NEMSCHOFF, INC.; *pg.* 936, *pg.* 1890
UPTOWN PRIME - Perishable Product - PROVIDE COMMERCE, INC.; *pg.* 1276, *pg.* 206
UPUBLISHER - Manual - XEROX CORPORATION; *pg.* 494, *pg.* 365
UPWARDLY MOBILE - Carpet - INTERFACE, INC.; *pg.* 695, *pg.* 512
UPWORDS - Game - HASBRO, INC.; *pg.* 954, *pg.* 1603
UR-X - Underground Residential Distribution Cable - THE OKONITE COMPANY; *pg.* 1302, *pg.* 1113
URALANE - Epoxy Laminating Product - HUNTSMAN CORPORATION; *pg.* 1167, *pg.* 1758
URAN - Fertilizer - POTASHCORP; *pg.* 1799, *pg.* 641
URBAN - Bag - SOLO; *pg.* 12, *pg.* 1165
URBAN COMFORT - Furniture - STANLEY FURNITURE CO., INC.; *pg.* 943, *pg.* 1379
URBAN DECAY - Cosmetics - L'OREAL USA; *pg.* 514, *pg.* 1252
URBAN EMISSIONS - Diesel Additive - POWER SERVICE PRODUCTS, INC.; *pg.* 983, *pg.* 1749
URBAN GRID - Carpet - INTERFACE, INC.; *pg.* 695, *pg.* 512
URBAN OUTFITTERS - Apparel - URBAN OUTFITTERS, INC.; *pg.* 1789, *pg.* 1571
URBAN PINE - Container Grown Plant - MONROVIA GROWERS; *pg.* 1797, *pg.* 44
URBAN REBOUNDING - Fitness Product - BALLY TOTAL FITNESS HOLDINGS CORPORATION; *pg.* 532, *pg.* 1200
URBANA - Lighting Product - QUOIZEL INC.; *pg.* 1304, *pg.* 1616
URBANBABY - Website for Expectant Mothers - CBS INTERACTIVE, INC.; *pg.* 369, *pg.* 215
URBANITE - Kitchen Product - KOHLER CO.; *pg.* 91, *pg.* 1862
URBANSPOON - Online Services - IAC/INTERACTIVECORP; *pg.* 292, *pg.* 1242
URBANVILLE - Furniture - ASHLEY FURNITURE INDUSTRIES, INC.; *pg.* 914, *pg.* 1852
URDATA - Rental Equipment - UNITED RENTALS, INC.; *pg.* 1386, *pg.* 350
URE-BOND - Urethane Adhesive - SMOOTH-ON INC.; *pg.* 111, *pg.* 1528
URE-FIL - Ceramic Product - SMOOTH-ON INC.; *pg.* 111, *pg.* 1528
URE-STAT - Static Dissipative Floor Finisher - WALTER G. LEGGE COMPANY, INC.; *pg.* 337, *pg.* 1321
URECHOLINE - Pharmaceutical Product - IMPAX LABORATORIES, INC.; *pg.* 1544, *pg.* 101
UREPRIME - Primer - JONES-BLAIR COMPANY; *pg.* 1443, *pg.* 1682
URETHANE - Industrial Hand Cleaner - THE DOW CHEMICAL COMPANY; *pg.* 1157, *pg.* 898
URETHANES TECHNOLOGY INTERNATIONAL - Trade Magazine - CRAIN COMMUNICATIONS, INC.; *pg.* 1631, *pg.* 879
URGE - Beverages - THE COCA-COLA COMPANY; *pg.* 240, *pg.* 493
URGE - Snacks, Candy & Nuts - KWIK TRIP INC.; *pg.* 1026, *pg.* 1864
URGE TO CONVERGE - Software - WIND RIVER SYSTEMS, INC.; *pg.* 493, *pg.* 38
URGENT - Neurostimulation Products - COGENTIX MEDICAL, INC.; *pg.* 1516, *pg.* 948
URGENT ACTION - Association Services - AMNESTY INTERNATIONAL USA; *pg.* 131, *pg.* 1194
URGENT EXCELLENCE - Tagline - LITTLEFIELD CORPORATION; *pg.* 558, *pg.* 1664
URI-CATH - Closed Urinary Drainage System for the Neonatal/Pediatric Patient - UTAH MEDICAL PRODUCTS, INC.; *pg.* 1605, *pg.* 1752
URICALM - Pharmaceutical Product - ALVA/AMCO PHARMACAL COMPANIES, INC.; *pg.* 1492, *pg.* 637
URICON - Animal Safety Product - NEOGEN CORPORATION; *pg.* 883, *pg.* 896
URIKARE - Animal Safety Product - NEOGEN CORPORATION; *pg.* 883, *pg.* 896
URISELECT - Software - BIO-RAD LABORATORIES, INC.; *pg.* 1504, *pg.* 101
URISPAS - Pharmaceutical Product - IMPAX LABORATORIES, INC.; *pg.* 1544, *pg.* 101
URISTAT - Healthcare Product - JOHNSON & JOHNSON; *pg.* 1549, *pg.* 1091
URO-FILL - Acrylic Urethane Primer Surfacer - ITW - EVERCOAT; *pg.* 1443, *pg.* 1415
URO-HYTRIN - Pharmaceutical Product - ABBOTT LABORATORIES; *pg.* 1484, *pg.* 551
URO-J - Underground Residential Distribution Okoguard Insulation - THE OKONITE COMPANY; *pg.* 1302, *pg.* 1113
URO-TEX - Medical Device - MENTOR CORPORATION; *pg.* 1565, *pg.* 263

UROBIOTIC - Medicine - PFIZER INC.; *pg.* 1581, *pg.* 1278
UROCIT - Pharmaceutical Product - MISSION PHARMACAL COMPANY INC.; *pg.* 1568, *pg.* 1742
UROCIT-K - Pharmaceutical Product - MISSION PHARMACAL COMPANY INC.; *pg.* 1568, *pg.* 1742
URODIE - Pharmaceutical Product - ABBOTT LABORATORIES; *pg.* 1484, *pg.* 551
UROFLO - Pharmaceutical Product - ABBOTT LABORATORIES; *pg.* 1484, *pg.* 551
UROLOGIX MOBILE - Treatment Service - UROLOGIX, INC.; *pg.* 1604, *pg.* 945
UROLUME - Medical Device - AMERICAN MEDICAL SYSTEMS HOLDINGS, INC.; *pg.* 1493, *pg.* 947
UROMAX ULTRA - Medical Device - BOSTON SCIENTIFIC CORPORATION; *pg.* 1508, *pg.* 831
UROPLASTY - Medical Devices - COGENTIX MEDICAL, INC.; *pg.* 1516, *pg.* 948
UROQID-ACID - Pharmaceuticals - BEACH PRODUCTS, INC.; *pg.* 1501, *pg.* 471
UROQID-ACID NO. 2 - Pharmaceuticals - BEACH PRODUCTS, INC.; *pg.* 1501, *pg.* 471
URORISK - Pharmaceutical Product - MISSION PHARMACAL COMPANY INC.; *pg.* 1568, *pg.* 1742
UROTEC - Epoxy & Polyurethane Topcoats - PPG INDUSTRIES, INC.; *pg.* 1445, *pg.* 1579
UROVYSION - Bladder Cancer Kit - ABBOTT LABORATORIES; *pg.* 1484, *pg.* 551
UROVYSION - Medical Test - QUEST DIAGNOSTICS INCORPORATED; *pg.* 1587, *pg.* 1080
URS - URS - TRIMBLE NAVIGATION LIMITED; *pg.* 1384, *pg.* 288
URSA - Oil Fuel - CHEVRON CORPORATION; *pg.* 974, *pg.* 259
URUKU - Cosmetics - AVEDA CORPORATION; *pg.* 499, *pg.* 917
URUN - Beverages - THE COCA-COLA COMPANY; *pg.* 240, *pg.* 493
U.S. 1 - Power Tool - MILWAUKEE ELECTRIC TOOL CORP.; *pg.* 1056, *pg.* 1855
U.S. BANCORP - Financial Services - U.S. BANCORP; *pg.* 815, *pg.* 945
U.S. CUSTOM HOUSE GUIDE - Directory - JOC GROUP INC.; *pg.* 1654, *pg.* 1096
U.S. DAIRY EXPORT COUNCIL - Dairy Product - DAIRY MANAGEMENT, INC.; *pg.* 138, *pg.* 656
US EDUCATION CORPORATION - Education Services - DEVRY EDUCATION GROUP INC.; *pg.* 600, *pg.* 607
US FIBER OPTICS - Household Products - ACS INDUSTRIES, INC.; *pg.* 1040, *pg.* 1602
U.S. LOCK - Security Hardware Products - INTERLINE BRANDS, INC.; *pg.* 1051, *pg.* 433
U.S. NEWS - Weekly - U.S. NEWS & WORLD REPORT, L.P.; *pg.* 1698, *pg.* 1308
U.S. NEWS & WORLD REPORT - Magazines & Books - U.S. NEWS & WORLD REPORT, L.P.; *pg.* 1698, *pg.* 1308
U.S. NEWS ONLINE - Web Site - U.S. NEWS & WORLD REPORT, L.P.; *pg.* 1698, *pg.* 1308
U.S. NEWS WASHINGTON BUSINESS REPORT - Report - U.S. NEWS & WORLD REPORT, L.P.; *pg.* 1698, *pg.* 1308
U.S. SILICA - Underground Silica - U.S. SILICA COMPANY; *pg.* 1185, *pg.* 1849
US TRAVEL GUIDE - Advertising Publication - DOMINION ENTERPRISES; *pg.* 1636, *pg.* 1796
US WEEKLY - Magazine - WENNER MEDIA LLC; *pg.* 1701, *pg.* 1314
US WEIGHT - Sporting Good Product - ESCALADE INC.; *pg.* 1833, *pg.* 678
USA EASY PAY - Insurance Product - SBLI USA LIFE INSURANCE COMPANY, INC.; *pg.* 1216, *pg.* 1288
USA LOADER - Trademark & Industrial Tires - CARLISLE TIRE & WHEEL COMPANY; *pg.* 1880, *pg.* 1612
USA LOGISTICS - Transportation Logistics Division - USA TRUCK, INC.; *pg.* 1929, *pg.* 36
USA OVERNIGHT - Domestic Express Delivery - DHL HOLDINGS (USA), INC.; *pg.* 1906, *pg.* 459
USA PEAR BUDDIES - Spokes Characters Who Teach Children About Pear Nutrition - PEAR BUREAU NORTHWEST; *pg.* 153, *pg.* 1500
USA POKER - Video Game - INTERNATIONAL GAME TECHNOLOGY; *pg.* 957, *pg.* 1024
USA TIME - Time, Temperature & Weather Announcement System - ELECTRONIC TELE-COMMUNICATIONS, INC.; *pg.* 390, *pg.* 1897
USA TODAY - Newspaper - GANNETT CO., INC.; *pg.* 1643, *pg.* 1790
USA TRAIL - Trademark & Industrial Tires - CARLISLE TIRE & WHEEL COMPANY; *pg.* 1880, *pg.* 1612
USA WEEKEND - Newspaper - GANNETT CO., INC.; *pg.* 1643, *pg.* 1790
USAG - Facom Tools - STANLEY BLACK & DECKER, INC.; *pg.* 1063, *pg.* 358
USAGE - Software - AXEDA SYSTEMS INC.; *pg.* 359, *pg.* 819
USANIMALS - Health Care Product - USANA HEALTH SCIENCES, INC.; *pg.* 1605, *pg.* 1761
USB - Molecular Biology Reagents - AFFYMETRIX, INC.; *pg.* 1487, *pg.* 263
USB - Software - WIND RIVER SYSTEMS, INC.; *pg.* 493, *pg.* 38
USB-511 - Electronic Component - EMCORE CORPORATION; *pg.* 636, *pg.* 39
USB-520 - Electronic Component - EMCORE CORPORATION; *pg.* 636, *pg.* 39
USB DEVELOPER'S KIT - Software - WIND RIVFR SYSTEMS, INC.; *pg.* 493, *pg.* 38
USB FLASH MODULE - Storage System - HGST; *pg.* 406, *pg.* 260
USB-LIVE - Digital Video Product - HAUPPAUGE DIGITAL, INC.; *pg.* 402, *pg.* 1164
USB MEMORY STICK - Digital Film Reader - LEXAR MEDIA, INC.; *pg.* 1262, *pg.* 146
USB-SCOPE - Hardware System - MICRO 2000, INC.; *pg.* 434, *pg.* 96
USBC COLLEGIATE - Bowling Promotional Services - UNITED STATES BOWLING CONGRESS; *pg.* 159, *pg.* 1660
USBC HIGH SCHOOL - Bowling Promotional Services - UNITED STATES BOWLING CONGRESS; *pg.* 159, *pg.* 1660
USBC JUNIOR TEAM USA - Bowling Promotional Services - UNITED STATES BOWLING CONGRESS; *pg.* 159, *pg.* 1660
USBC TEAM USA - Bowling Promotional Services - UNITED STATES BOWLING CONGRESS; *pg.* 159, *pg.* 1660
USBD-2A - Stereo Audio Adapter - ANDREA ELECTRONICS CORPORATION; *pg.* 617, *pg.* 1143
USBXPRESS - Development Kit - SILICON LABORATORIES INC.; *pg.* 674, *pg.* 1666
USCD - Storage System - HGST; *pg.* 406, *pg.* 260
USE DIAMOND - Anchor - MKT FASTENING, LLC; *pg.* 1056, *pg.* 34
USECO - Food Service Equipment - STANDEX INTERNATIONAL CORPORATION; *pg.* 60, *pg.* 1039
USED CARS - Video Slots - INTERNATIONAL GAME TECHNOLOGY; *pg.* 957, *pg.* 1024
USEDBOATS.COM - Website - BONNIER CORPORATION; *pg.* 1622, *pg.* 480
USER EXPERIENCE MONITOR - Software - DELL SOFTWARE; *pg.* 385, *pg.* 40
USER2USER - Software System - MENTOR GRAPHICS CORPORATION; *pg.* 432, *pg.* 1510
USF HOLLAND - Logistics - YRC WORLDWIDE INC.; *pg.* 1931, *pg.* 720
USG - Acoustical Finish Ceiling Spray - USG CORPORATION; *pg.* 118, *pg.* 594
USIFLEX - Ductile Iron Pipe - UNITED STATES PIPE & FOUNDRY COMPANY, INC.; *pg.* 117, *pg.* 5
USIP - Microcontroller - MAXIM INTEGRATED PRODUCTS, INC.; *pg.* 653, *pg.* 247
USKUDAR - Carpet - WOVEN LEGENDS INC.; *pg.* 947, *pg.* 1572
USLD - Communication Product - CENTURYLINK, INC; *pg.* 1870, *pg.* 317
USM-406 - Flight Test System - BAE SYSTEMS-INFORMATION WARFARE; *pg.* 623, *pg.* 1036
USM-458/NEWTS - Navy Electronic Warfare Test System - BAE SYSTEMS-INFORMATION WARFARE; *pg.* 623, *pg.* 1036
USM-464 - Flight Test System - BAE SYSTEMS-INFORMATION WARFARE; *pg.* 623, *pg.* 1036
USM-638 - Flight Test System - BAE SYSTEMS-INFORMATION WARFARE; *pg.* 623, *pg.* 1036
USM-639 - Flight Test System - BAE SYSTEMS-INFORMATION WARFARE; *pg.* 623, *pg.* 1036
USO - Electronic Components - MOLEX INCORPORATED; *pg.* 655, *pg.* 628
USP - Electronic Components - MOLEX INCORPORATED; *pg.* 655, *pg.* 628
USPDI - Medical Information - TRUVEN HEALTH ANALYTICS; *pg.* 486, *pg.* 331
USS - Encryption Devices - ITUS CORPORATION; *pg.* 422, *pg.* 1180
USTC - Testing Laboratory - SGS U.S. TESTING COMPANY INC.; *pg.* 1181, *pg.* 1065
UT - LED - CREE INC.; *pg.* 631, *pg.* 1371
UT SERIES - Wireless Microphones - SHURE INCORPORATED; *pg.* 672, *pg.* 638
UT230 - LED - CREE INC.; *pg.* 631, *pg.* 1371
UTAH JAZZ - Basketball Team - JAZZ BASKETBALL INVESTORS, INC.; *pg.* 554, *pg.* 1759
UTAH MEDICAL PRODUCTS INC - Medical Product - UTAH MEDICAL PRODUCTS, INC.; *pg.* 1605, *pg.* 1752
UTAH POWER - ABN - PACIFICORP; *pg.* 1949, *pg.* 1504
UTAHBALL - Gynecological Electrodes - UTAH MEDICAL PRODUCTS, INC.; *pg.* 1605, *pg.* 1752
UTAHLOOP - Gynecological Electrodes - UTAH MEDICAL PRODUCTS, INC.; *pg.* 1605, *pg.* 1752
UTC PD 1100 - Customer Displays - ULTIMATE TECHNOLOGY CORPORATION; *pg.* 486, *pg.* 1349
UTC PD 1200 - Customer Displays - ULTIMATE TECHNOLOGY CORPORATION; *pg.* 486, *pg.* 1349
UTC PD 220 - Customer Displays - ULTIMATE TECHNOLOGY CORPORATION; *pg.* 486, *pg.* 1349
UTE TAFFY - Candy - SWEET CANDY COMPANY; *pg.* 1862, *pg.* 1761
UTELL - Hotel - PEGASUS SOLUTIONS, INC.; *pg.* 452, *pg.* 1685
UTICA/GRAPHIC - Printers Insurance - UTICA MUTUAL INSURANCE COMPANY; *pg.* 1222, *pg.* 1183
UTICA NATIONAL - Insurance Group - UTICA MUTUAL INSURANCE COMPANY; *pg.* 1222, *pg.* 1183
UTILAC - Paint And Stain Product - BENJAMIN MOORE & CO.; *pg.* 1440, *pg.* 1085
UTILATUB - Tub & Sink - E.L. MUSTEE & SONS, INC.; *pg.* 1124, *pg.* 1430
UTILATWIN - Tub & Sink - E.L. MUSTEE & SONS, INC.; *pg.* 1124, *pg.* 1430
UTILI-FOAM - Spray System - THE DOW CHEMICAL COMPANY; *pg.* 1157, *pg.* 898
UTILIMASTER - Vehicles - SPARTAN MOTORS, INC.; *pg.* 217, *pg.* 874
UTILITY - Furniture - HOWE FURNITURE CORPORATION; *pg.* 928, *pg.* 998
UTILITY FIT - Foam - THE DOW CHEMICAL COMPANY; *pg.* 1157, *pg.* 898
UTILITY FLEET MANAGEMENT - Business Magazine - TRANSPORT TOPICS PUBLISHING GROUP; *pg.* 1696, *pg.* 1772
UTILITY LOCK - Security Device - WINNER INTERNATIONAL, LLC; *pg.* 222, *pg.* 1586
UTILITY SHEARS - Knife - BUCK KNIVES, INC.; *pg.* 1828, *pg.* 550
UTILITY SUITE ACCELERATORS - Software - BMC SOFTWARE, INC.; *pg.* 362, *pg.* 1701
UTILITY TOOL - Cable - THE RIPLEY COMPANY; *pg.* 1305, *pg.* 342
UTILITY TRAILER - Van - UTILITY TRAILER MANUFACTURING COMPANY; *pg.* 1712, *pg.* 68
UTILIVAN - Vehicles - SPARTAN MOTORS, INC.; *pg.* 217, *pg.* 874
UTMC - Integration Circuits - AEROFLEX INCORPORATED; *pg.* 614, *pg.* 1321
UTMS - Power Monitor - OPLINK COMMUNICATIONS, INC.; *pg.* 660, *pg.* 91
UTNE READER - Publication - OGDEN PUBLICATIONS, INC.; *pg.* 1672, *pg.* 722
UTOPIA - Flooring Product - CONGOLEUM CORPORATION; *pg.* 921, *pg.* 1084
UTOPIA - Software System - MENTOR GRAPHICS CORPORATION; *pg.* 432, *pg.* 1510
UTOPIA - Fabric - NEMSCHOFF, INC.; *pg.* 936, *pg.* 1890
UTOPIA - Slipper - R.G. BARRY CORPORATION; *pg.* 1818, *pg.* 1470
UTRAMAT - Drain Valve - DONALDSON COMPANY, INC.; *pg.* 1329, *pg.* 917
UULTRAZINE - Chemical Product - WESTROCK COMPANY; *pg.* 1472, *pg.* 1805
UV-CHEK - Light Stabilizers - FERRO CORPORATION; *pg.* 1162, *pg.* 1462
UV-FAST - UV Absorbers - HUNTSMAN CORPORATION; *pg.* 1167, *pg.* 1758
UV GEL BED - Software - BIO-RAD LABORATORIES, INC.; *pg.* 1504, *pg.* 101
UV MASTER - Offset Printing Blanket - ROTADYNE; *pg.* 1681, *pg.* 529

First page reference indicates Business Class Edition
Second page reference indicates Geographic Edition

UV-SUN - UV Absorbers - HUNTSMAN CORPORATION; *pg.* 1167, *pg.* 1758
UV TECH - Protectant - MCNETT CORPORATION; *pg.* 1839, *pg.* 1817
UV/ULTRA - Printing Paper - NEENAH PAPER, INC.; *pg.* 1465, *pg.* 484
UV/ULTRA II - Paper - NEENAH PAPER, INC.; *pg.* 1465, *pg.* 484
UV15-7LRI - Adhesive - MASTER BOND INC.; *pg.* 1172, *pg.* 1072
UVAR - Healthcare Product - JOHNSON & JOHNSON; *pg.* 1549, *pg.* 1091
UVECOAT - Curable Resins - CYTEC INDUSTRIES, INC.; *pg.* 1155, *pg.* 1131
UVEE STOPPERS - Lens Treatment Product - EMERGING VISION, INC.; *pg.* 1411, *pg.* 1227
UVEKOL - Glass Laminating System - CYTEC INDUSTRIES, INC.; *pg.* 1155, *pg.* 1131
UVEX BANDIT - Protective Eye-wear - ALIMED, INC.; *pg.* 1490, *pg.* 816
UVEX CLASSIC - Industrial Goggles - UVEX SAFETY; *pg.* 1433, *pg.* 1608
UVEX FITLOGIC - Safety Eyewear - UVEX SAFETY; *pg.* 1433, *pg.* 1608
UVEX FURY - Goggles - UVEX SAFETY; *pg.* 1433, *pg.* 1608
UVEX SKYPER - Safety Eyewear - UVEX SAFETY; *pg.* 1433, *pg.* 1608
UVEX SPITFIRE - Safety Eyewear - UVEX SAFETY; *pg.* 1433, *pg.* 1608
UVEXTREME AF - Anti-Fog Coating - UVEX SAFETY; *pg.* 1433, *pg.* 1608
UVISION - Wafer Inspection Tool - APPLIED MATERIALS, INC.; *pg.* 618, *pg.* 264
UVITEX - Fluorescent Whitening Agents - HUNTSMAN CORPORATION; *pg.* 1167, *pg.* 1758
UWATEC - Dive Computers & Other Electronic Equipment - JOHNSON OUTDOORS INC.; *pg.* 1837, *pg.* 1888
UWBTRACER - Analyzer - TELEDYNE LECROY; *pg.* 1431, *pg.* 1153
UWDM 59 - Fiber Optic Component - OPLINK COMMUNICATIONS, INC.; *pg.* 660, *pg.* 91
UWDM59 - Splitter - OPLINK COMMUNICATIONS, INC.; *pg.* 660, *pg.* 91
UWIN - Internet Wagering Platform - INTERNATIONAL GAME TECHNOLOGY; *pg.* 420, *pg.* 1606
UXL - Publisher - GALE CENGAGE LEARNING; *pg.* 1643, *pg.* 885

V

V-200 NOVABRIK - Splitter And Turnover - BESSER COMPANY; *pg.* 1317, *pg.* 865
V-22 - Tilt Rotor Aircraft Twin Engine - BELL HELICOPTER TEXTRON, INC.; *pg.* 224, *pg.* 1693
V-8 - Vegetable Juice - CAMPBELL SOUP COMPANY; *pg.* 844, *pg.* 1048
V&B - Tools - VAUGHAN & BUSHNELL MANUFACTURING COMPANY, INC.; *pg.* 1066, *pg.* 616
V-BALL - Elastomeric Ball - VERNAY LABORATORIES, INC.; *pg.* 1891, *pg.* 1482
V BAR - Saloon - ARK RESTAURANTS CORP.; *pg.* 1715, *pg.* 1196
V-BITE - Connector - BOMAR INTERCONNECT PRODUCTS, INC.; *pg.* 1318, *pg.* 1079
V CARBON MAX - Eyewear - NIKE, INC.; *pg.* 1812, *pg.* 1492
V-COMP - Spray System - GRACO, INC.; *pg.* 1342, *pg.* 935
V CONNECTORS - Microwave Components - ANRITSU COMPANY; *pg.* 618, *pg.* 152
V-COTE - Paint & Coating - DIAMOND VOGEL PAINT, INC.; *pg.* 1441, *pg.* 710
V-DAMP - Sound Deadener - DAUBERT INDUSTRIES, INC.; *pg.* 1155, *pg.* 561
V-DRIVE - Premium Roll Covers - VAIL RUBBER WORKS, INC.; *pg.* 1891, *pg.* 906
V-DRIVE II - Premium Roll Covers - VAIL RUBBER WORKS, INC.; *pg.* 1891, *pg.* 906
V-FACTOR - Musical Instrument - GIBSON GUITAR CORP.; *pg.* 550, *pg.* 1650
V-FLASH - Desktop Modeler - 3D SYSTEMS CORPORATION; *pg.* 339, *pg.* 1621
V-FLEX - Adhesive Weatherstrip - M-D BUILDING PRODUCTS, INC.; *pg.* 95, *pg.* 1486
V-FLEX - Curtain Release System - RITE-HITE HOLDING CORPORATION; *pg.* 1372, *pg.* 1880
V-FLEX - Construction Business Forms - THE STANDARD REGISTER COMPANY; *pg.* 473, *pg.* 1446
V-GARD - Headwear - MINE SAFETY APPLIANCES COMPANY; *pg.* 1361, *pg.* 1525
V/I PROBE - Analyzer & Software - MKS INSTRUMENTS, INC.; *pg.* 1362, *pg.* 781
V-JET - Cleaning Pig - T.D. WILLIAMSON, INC.; *pg.* 1380, *pg.* 1490
V-LINK - Video Product - DAKTRONICS, INC.; *pg.* 633, *pg.* 1624
V-LO - Professional Knives - DEXTER-RUSSELL INC.; *pg.* 1123, *pg.* 844
V-MAC - Automotive System - MACK TRUCKS, INC.; *pg.* 183, *pg.* 1375
V-MATE - Video Memory Card - SANDISK CORPORATION; *pg.* 465, *pg.* 147
V-MAX - Animal Health Product - PHIBROCHEM; *pg.* 1177, *pg.* 1124
V-MAX - Steel Product - RUSSEL METALS INC.; *pg.* 1180, *pg.* 1928
V-MAX - Synthetic Paper - VALERON STRENGTH FILMS; *pg.* 1891, *pg.* 1716
V-MAX BLUE - Fluid Handling System - GRACO, INC.; *pg.* 1342, *pg.* 935
V MDOT - Chemical Products - AIR PRODUCTS AND CHEMICALS, INC.; *pg.* 1145, *pg.* 1513
V. MUELLER - Surgical Instrumentation - CARDINAL HEALTH, INC.; *pg.* 1512, *pg.* 1448
V-NET - Video Product - DAKTRONICS, INC.; *pg.* 633, *pg.* 1624
V-OPTICS - Mass Analyzer System - WATERS CORPORATION; *pg.* 1436, *pg.* 834
V PAK - Electrode System - ZOLL MEDICAL CORPORATION; *pg.* 1612, *pg.* 814
V. PEARL - Food Product - GENERAL MILLS, INC.; *pg.* 828, *pg.* 933
V-PLAY - Video Product - DAKTRONICS, INC.; *pg.* 633, *pg.* 1624
V-PORTAL - Adapter - VONAGE HOLDINGS CORP.; *pg.* 686, *pg.* 1074
V-PRESS - Premium Roll Covers - VAIL RUBBER WORKS, INC.; *pg.* 1891, *pg.* 906
V-PRESS G - Premium Roll Covers - VAIL RUBBER WORKS, INC.; *pg.* 1891, *pg.* 906
V-PRESS G II - Premium Roll Covers - VAIL RUBBER WORKS, INC.; *pg.* 1891, *pg.* 906
V-PRESS G X - Premium Roll Covers - VAIL RUBBER WORKS, INC.; *pg.* 1891, *pg.* 906
V-PRESS II - Premium Roll Covers - VAIL RUBBER WORKS, INC.; *pg.* 1891, *pg.* 906
V-PRESS X - Premium Roll Covers - VAIL RUBBER WORKS, INC.; *pg.* 1891, *pg.* 906
V-READY - Sound Isolation System - WENGER CORPORATION; *pg.* 1307, *pg.* 952
V-ROD - Motorcycle - HARLEY-DAVIDSON, INC.; *pg.* 178, *pg.* 1874
V-ROOM - Sound Isolation System - WENGER CORPORATION; *pg.* 1307, *pg.* 952
V-SAFE - Wheel Valve Lockouts - HONEYWELL NORTH SAFETY PRODUCTS; *pg.* 42, *pg.* 1600
V-SEALS - Sealing Element - THE TIMKEN COMPANY; *pg.* 218, *pg.* 1408
V-SERIES - Gas Apparatus - THE HARRIS PRODUCTS GROUP; *pg.* 1345, *pg.* 533
V SERIES - Office Product - HAWORTH, INC.; *pg.* 402, *pg.* 891
V SERIES - Electronics - RENESAS ELECTRONICS AMERICA INC.; *pg.* 667, *pg.* 269
V-SHOK - Ammunition - FEDERAL PREMIUM AMMUNITION; *pg.* 1834, *pg.* 915
V-SIZE - Premium Roll Covers - VAIL RUBBER WORKS, INC.; *pg.* 1891, *pg.* 906
V-SIZE II - Premium Roll Covers - VAIL RUBBER WORKS, INC.; *pg.* 1891, *pg.* 906
V-SIZE III - Premium Roll Covers - VAIL RUBBER WORKS, INC.; *pg.* 1891, *pg.* 906
V-SLAM - Impactor - STEDMAN MACHINE COMPANY; *pg.* 1379, *pg.* 673
V-SORT - Vertical Merge/Sort, Conveyor Belt - DAIFUKU WEBB; *pg.* 1327, *pg.* 885
V-TECH - Paint & Coating - DIAMOND VOGEL PAINT, INC.; *pg.* 1441, *pg.* 710
V-THERNET - Computer Products - BROADCOM CORPORATION; *pg.* 364, *pg.* 108
V-TIP - Valve - VERNAY LABORATORIES, INC.; *pg.* 1891, *pg.* 1482
V-TOP - Security Product - BAE SYSTEMS PRODUCTS GROUP; *pg.* 359, *pg.* 432
V-TOUR - Video Product - DAKTRONICS, INC.; *pg.* 633, *pg.* 1624
V-TRAX - Sole - WELLCO ENTERPRISES, INC.; *pg.* 1822, *pg.* 1392
V-TWIN - Magazine - PAISANO PUBLICATIONS, LLC; *pg.* 1674, *pg.* 38
V-TWIN NEWS - Magazine - PAISANO PUBLICATIONS, LLC; *pg.* 1674, *pg.* 38
V-TYPE - Musical Instrument - PEAVEY ELECTRONICS CORPORATION; *pg.* 662, *pg.* 970
V VALVOLINE - Automobile Grille Emblems, Hitch Covers & Hitch Cover Locks - ASHLAND INC.; *pg.* 972, *pg.* 726
V VALVOLINE RACING - Automotive Oil Change Pans - ASHLAND INC.; *pg.* 972, *pg.* 726
V-WALL - Floor-to-Ceiling Partitions - HERMAN MILLER, INC.; *pg.* 926, *pg.* 913
V-WATCH - Electrical Test & Measurement - HD ELECTRIC COMPANY; *pg.* 1299, *pg.* 666
V-XTREME - Q-Switched Laser - NEWPORT CORPORATION; *pg.* 1424, *pg.* 114
V ZUH - Plastic Packaging Product - POLY PAK AMERICA, INC.; *pg.* 1467, *pg.* 138
V16 - Telecommunications Equipment - ALCATEL-LUCENT; *pg.* 615, *pg.* 1094
V2 - Human Resources & Recruitment Multimedia Software - LOCKHEED MARTIN CORPORATION; *pg.* 229, *pg.* 762
V2 MINI MOON - Torch - COAST CUTLERY COMPANY; *pg.* 1121, *pg.* 1501
V2 TRIPLEX - Torch - COAST CUTLERY COMPANY; *pg.* 1121, *pg.* 1501
V20 - Electronic Equipment - RENESAS ELECTRONICS AMERICA INC.; *pg.* 667, *pg.* 269
V20H - Electronic Equipment - RENESAS ELECTRONICS AMERICA INC.; *pg.* 667, *pg.* 269
V25 - Electronic Equipment - RENESAS ELECTRONICS AMERICA INC.; *pg.* 667, *pg.* 269
V2I - Software - SYMANTEC CORPORATION; *pg.* 478, *pg.* 161
V2I BUILDER - Software - SYMANTEC CORPORATION; *pg.* 478, *pg.* 161
V2I OBSERVER - Software - SYMANTEC CORPORATION; *pg.* 478, *pg.* 161
V2I PROTECTOR - Software - SYMANTEC CORPORATION; *pg.* 478, *pg.* 161
V3 - Wall Valance - LITECONTROL CORPORATION; *pg.* 1301, *pg.* 841
V3-12 VIBRAPAC - Concrete Product Machine - BESSER COMPANY; *pg.* 1317, *pg.* 865
V3 SOLAR - Semiconductor Batch-Immersion System - AKRION, INC.; *pg.* 1311, *pg.* 1513
V30 - Electronic Equipment - RENESAS ELECTRONICS AMERICA INC.; *pg.* 667, *pg.* 269
V30H - Electronic Equipment - RENESAS ELECTRONICS AMERICA INC.; *pg.* 667, *pg.* 269
V3100 SERIES - Software - NETAPP, INC.; *pg.* 444, *pg.* 287
V40 - Electronic Equipment - RENESAS ELECTRONICS AMERICA INC.; *pg.* 667, *pg.* 269
V5-DEST - Promoter - THERMO FISHER SCIENTIFIC INC.; *pg.* 1602, *pg.* 61
V50 - Electronic Equipment - RENESAS ELECTRONICS AMERICA INC.; *pg.* 667, *pg.* 269
V500 - Skate - ROLLER DERBY SKATE CORP.; *pg.* 966, *pg.* 630
V600 - Electron Microscope - FEI COMPANY; *pg.* 1413, *pg.* 1498
V6000 SERIES - Software - NETAPP, INC.; *pg.* 444, *pg.* 287
V8 - Food Product - CAMPBELL COMPANY OF CANADA LTD; *pg.* 844, *pg.* 1935
V8 SPLASH - Food Product - CAMPBELL COMPANY OF CANADA LTD; *pg.* 844, *pg.* 1935
V8-V-FUSION - Juice Drink - CAMPBELL SOUP COMPANY; *pg.* 844, *pg.* 1048
V800 - Electronic Equipment - RENESAS ELECTRONICS AMERICA INC.; *pg.* 667, *pg.* 269
V805 - Electronic Equipment - RENESAS ELECTRONICS AMERICA INC.; *pg.* 667, *pg.* 269
V810 - Electronic Equipment - RENESAS ELECTRONICS AMERICA INC.; *pg.* 667, *pg.* 269
V820 - Electronic Equipment - RENESAS ELECTRONICS AMERICA INC.; *pg.* 667, *pg.* 269
VAC - Sub-Atmospheric Gas Delivery - ATMI, INC.; *pg.* 1314, *pg.* 342

V.A.C. - Wound Care System - KINETIC CONCEPTS, INC.; *pg.* 1553, *pg.* 1741
VAC-407 - Vacuum Robot - BROOKS AUTOMATION, INC.; *pg.* 1320, *pg.* 813
VAC-A-SAMPLE - Pneumatic Sampling System - SEEDBURO EQUIPMENT CO.; *pg.* 707, *pg.* 590
VAC-CHECK - Vacuum Gauge - MKS INSTRUMENTS, INC.; *pg.* 1362, *pg.* 781
VAC CONNECT - Therapy System - KINETIC CONCEPTS, INC.; *pg.* 1553, *pg.* 1741
VAC FILE - Podiatry Machine - MEDICOOL, INC.; *pg.* 1562, *pg.* 294
VAC FREEDOM - Therapy System - KINETIC CONCEPTS, INC.; *pg.* 1553, *pg.* 1741
VAC GRANUFOAM - Dressing System - KINETIC CONCEPTS, INC.; *pg.* 1553, *pg.* 1741
VAC INSTILL - Wound Healing System - KINETIC CONCEPTS, INC.; *pg.* 1553, *pg.* 1741
VAC PAC - Cleaning Product - HILLYARD, INC.; *pg.* 331, *pg.* 990
VAC SIMPLACE - Therapy System - KINETIC CONCEPTS, INC.; *pg.* 1553, *pg.* 1741
VAC-U-NATE - Medical Product - UTAH MEDICAL PRODUCTS, INC.; *pg.* 1605, *pg.* 1752
VAC-U-RIG - Power Tools - MILWAUKEE ELECTRIC TOOL CORP.; *pg.* 1056, *pg.* 1855
VAC-U-VATOR - Pneumatic Conveyors - CHRISTIANSON SYSTEMS, INC.; *pg.* 1323, *pg.* 917
VACALL - Vacuum Street Sweepers - ALAMO GROUP INC.; *pg.* 1311, *pg.* 1745
VACATION - Fabric - NEMSCHOFF, INC.; *pg.* 936, *pg.* 1890
VACATION DESTINATION - Prerecorded Audio Tapes Containing Travel Information - AMERICAN AUTOMOBILE ASSOCIATION; *pg.* 1190, *pg.* 429
VACATION GUARANTEE - Cruise Line - CARNIVAL CRUISE LINES; *pg.* 1902, *pg.* 441
THE VACATION GUIDE - Annual Tourism Publication - TENNESSEE DEPARTMENT OF TOURIST DEVELOPMENT; *pg.* 1007, *pg.* 1654
VACATION IN PARADISE - Men's Clothing - JOS. A. BANK CLOTHIERS, INC.; *pg.* 42, *pg.* 771
VACATION OUTLET - Travel Company - WORLD TRAVEL HOLDINGS; *pg.* 1931, *pg.* 860
VACATIONSAVER.COM - Travel Website - DOMINION ENTERPRISES; *pg.* 1636, *pg.* 1796
VACBOSS - Pneumatic Conveyors - CHRISTIANSON SYSTEMS, INC.; *pg.* 1323, *pg.* 917
VACCASE - Thermal Processing Equipment - SURFACE COMBUSTION, INC.; *pg.* 1077, *pg.* 1462
VACCUM METALIZED FLAKE - Pigment - SILBERLINE MANUFACTURING CO., INC.; *pg.* 110, *pg.* 1588
VACHON - Bakery Products - SAPUTO, INC.; *pg.* 893, *pg.* 1956
VACHON - Snack Cakes - VACHON BAKERY INC.; *pg.* 907, *pg.* 1959
VACPAK - Stoker - DETROIT STOKER CO.; *pg.* 1070, *pg.* 900
VACREL - Dry Film Soldermask - E.I. DU PONT DE NEMOURS & COMPANY; *pg.* 1159, *pg.* 390
VACSTAR - Vacuum System - AIR TECHNIQUES, INC.; *pg.* 1487, *pg.* 1178
VACTOR - Municipal Vacuum Vehicles - FEDERAL SIGNAL CORPORATION; *pg.* 638, *pg.* 645
VACTOR HXX - Hydro-Excavator Vehicles - FEDERAL SIGNAL CORPORATION; *pg.* 638, *pg.* 645
VACU-CLEAN - Vacuum Cleaning System - HMI INDUSTRIES INC.; *pg.* 56, *pg.* 1475
VACU FLUSH - Wax - MOC PRODUCTS COMPANY, INC.; *pg.* 332, *pg.* 174
VACU/TROL - Pump - SPECTRUM LABORATORIES INC.; *pg.* 1595, *pg.* 69
VACUCAP - Vacuum Filtration Device - PALL CORPORATION; *pg.* 232, *pg.* 1323
VACUDRAW - Thermal Processing Equipment - SURFACE COMBUSTION, INC.; *pg.* 1077, *pg.* 1462
VACUDYNE - Process Control Equipment - ALTAIR CORPORATION; *pg.* 1312, *pg.* 910
VACUFLO - Vacuum Systems - H-P PRODUCTS, INC.; *pg.* 85, *pg.* 1458
VACUFLOW - Powder Fillers - PNEUMATICSCALEANGELUS; *pg.* 1369, *pg.* 1445
VACUFUGE - Laboratory Product - EPPENDORF NORTH AMERICA; *pg.* 1412, *pg.* 1164
VACUMET - Alloy - CARPENTER TECHNOLOGY CORPORATION; *pg.* 73, *pg.* 1584
VACUSEALED - Oceanographic Product - TELEDYNE BENTHOS, INC.; *pg.* 1431, *pg.* 838
VACUSHIELD - Vent & Air Filter - PALL CORPORATION; *pg.* 232, *pg.* 1323
VACUTEC - Healthcare Product - GF HEALTH PRODUCTS, INC.; *pg.* 1535, *pg.* 508
VACUTIGHT - Pumps - IDEX CORPORATION; *pg.* 1347, *pg.* 623
VACUTRON - Vacuum Regulator - ALLIED HEALTHCARE PRODUCTS, INC.; *pg.* 1491, *pg.* 990
VACUUM SENTRY - Vacuum Valve - MKS INSTRUMENTS, INC.; *pg.* 1362, *pg.* 781
VAD - Desuperheaters - SPX PROCESS EQUIPMENT; *pg.* 1378, *pg.* 1551
VADCARE - Pharmaceutical Product - ALERE INC.; *pg.* 1488, *pg.* 849
VADDIS - DVD Player - CSR; *pg.* 280, *pg.* 284
VADWATCH - Pharmaceutical Product - ALERE INC.; *pg.* 1488, *pg.* 849
VAGABOND - Wireless Microphone System - SHURE INCORPORATED; *pg.* 672, *pg.* 638
VAGABOND INN EXECUTIVE - Hotel - VAGABOND FRANCHISE SYSTEM, INC.; *pg.* 1117, *pg.* 141
VAGISIL - Feminine Itching Medication - COMBE INCORPORATED; *pg.* 1516, *pg.* 1351
VAGISITE - Bioadhesive Delivery System Used in Treatments for Vaginal Infections - LUMARA HEALTH INC.; *pg.* 1557, *pg.* 973
VAHINE - Dessert Products - MCCORMICK & COMPANY, INCORPORATED; *pg.* 1027, *pg.* 779
VAIL - Carpet - BEAULIEU GROUP, LLC; *pg.* 917, *pg.* 529
VAIL - Fabric - NEMSCHOFF, INC.; *pg.* 936, *pg.* 1890
VAIL - Resort - VAIL RESORTS, INC.; *pg.* 1117, *pg.* 313
VAIL CONVERSATION - Furniture - FLEXSTEEL INDUSTRIES, INC.; *pg.* 925, *pg.* 707
VAIL PRESS - Roller Cover - VAIL RUBBER WORKS, INC.; *pg.* 1891, *pg.* 906
VAIL-THERM - Resin Roll Covers - VAIL RUBBER WORKS, INC.; *pg.* 1891, *pg.* 906
VAL-AN - Aluminum Instrument - ZERO MANUFACTURING, INC.; *pg.* 1892, *pg.* 1752
VALARI - Footwear - STEVEN MADDEN, LTD.; *pg.* 1819, *pg.* 1176
VALBAZEN - Veterinary Anthelmintic - PFIZER INC.; *pg.* 1581, *pg.* 1278
VALBOND - Chemical Product - AIR PRODUCTS AND CHEMICALS, INC.; *pg.* 1145, *pg.* 1513
VALCALOX - Damper Regulator - YOUNG REGULATOR COMPANY; *pg.* 1078, *pg.* 1478
VALCYTE - Pharmaceutical Product - HOFFMANN-LA ROCHE INC.; *pg.* 1542, *pg.* 1099
VALDIVIESO - Chilean Wine - LAIRD & COMPANY, INC.; *pg.* 1966, *pg.* 1119
VALENCIA - Leather Textiles - BERNHARDT DESIGN; *pg.* 918, *pg.* 1381
VALENCIA - Footwear - COBIAN CORP.; *pg.* 1806, *pg.* 253
VALENCIA - Rug - COURISTAN INC.; *pg.* 921, *pg.* 1067
VALENCIA - Fan - CRAFTMADE INTERNATIONAL, INC.; *pg.* 1295, *pg.* 1670
VALENCIA - Office Furniture - STEELCASE INC.; *pg.* 475, *pg.* 889
VALENCIA - Bicycle - TREK BICYCLE CORPORATION; *pg.* 1847, *pg.* 1896
VALENTINA - Perfume ine - ENESCO, LLC; *pg.* 1124, *pg.* 620
VALENTINE'S DAY DOUBLER - Lottery Game - OHIO LOTTERY COMMISSION; *pg.* 1002, *pg.* 1433
VALENTINO - Furniture - AMISCO INDUSTRIES LTD.; *pg.* 913, *pg.* 1958
VALEO ROCKER SWITCH DPDT - Switch - COMMERCIAL VEHICLE GROUP, INC.; *pg.* 203, *pg.* 1467
VALEO ROCKER SWITCH SPST - Switch - COMMERCIAL VEHICLE GROUP, INC.; *pg.* 203, *pg.* 1467
VALEO SWITCH - Switch - COMMERCIAL VEHICLE GROUP, INC.; *pg.* 203, *pg.* 1467
VALEREX - Plastic Drum - GREIF INC.; *pg.* 1459, *pg.* 1447
VALERIA - Lighting Product - QUOIZEL INC.; *pg.* 1304, *pg.* 1616
VALERIAN - Herbal Formula - SHAKLEE CORPORATION; *pg.* 1593, *pg.* 184
VALERIE - Clothing - ABERCROMBIE & FITCH CO.; *pg.* 37, *pg.* 1466
VALERO - Gasoline Retail Outlets - VALERO ENERGY CORPORATION; *pg.* 986, *pg.* 1743
VALERON - Strength Film - VALERON STRENGTH FILMS; *pg.* 1891, *pg.* 1716
VALET - Mobile Electronics Equipment - DEI HOLDINGS, INC.; *pg.* 633, *pg.* 302
VALET - Fabric - NEMSCHOFF, INC.; *pg.* 936, *pg.* 1890
VALET AUTO-STROP - Blades - THE GILLETTE COMPANY; *pg.* 509, *pg.* 795
VALETHENE - Composite Steel Plastic Drum - GREIF INC.; *pg.* 1459, *pg.* 1447
VALFOR - Zeolite - PQ CORPORATION; *pg.* 1178, *pg.* 1515
VALHALLA - Video Game - INTERNATIONAL GAME TECHNOLOGY; *pg.* 957, *pg.* 1024
VALHALLA - Magazine - VIKING YACHT COMPANY; *pg.* 1712, *pg.* 1094
VALHALLA - Kitchenware - THE VOLLRATH COMPANY LLC; *pg.* 1139, *pg.* 1894
VALIANT - Systems Integration & Aeronautics - LOCKHEED MARTIN CORPORATION; *pg.* 229, *pg.* 762
VALIANT KNIGHT - Game - WMS INDUSTRIES INC.; *pg.* 593, *pg.* 666
VALIDATE - Security Product - FLEXCON CORPORATION; *pg.* 1457, *pg.* 844
VALIDATEIT - Software - BIO-RAD LABORATORIES, INC.; *pg.* 1504, *pg.* 101
VALIDIAN - Explosive Detection System - LOCKHEED MARTIN CORPORATION; *pg.* 229, *pg.* 762
VALISCREEN - Assays & Reagents - PERKINELMER, INC.; *pg.* 1426, *pg.* 853
VALIUM - Pharmaceutical Product - HOFFMANN-LA ROCHE INC.; *pg.* 1542, *pg.* 1099
VALLEY - Bowling Equipment - BRUNSWICK BOWLING & BILLIARDS CORP.; *pg.* 1828, *pg.* 622
VALLEY - Patio Covers - METALS USA, INC.; *pg.* 97, *pg.* 425
VALLEY - Irrigation Equipment - VALMONT INDUSTRIES, INC.; *pg.* 1387, *pg.* 1019
VALLEY ARTS - Guitars - GIBSON GUITAR CORP.; *pg.* 550, *pg.* 1650
VALLEY-DYNAMO - Bowling Equipment - BRUNSWICK BOWLING & BILLIARDS CORP.; *pg.* 1828, *pg.* 622
VALLEY FORGE - Lighting Product - QUOIZEL INC.; *pg.* 1304, *pg.* 1616
VALLEY FRESH - Poultry Product - HORMEL FOODS CORPORATION; *pg.* 863, *pg.* 915
VALLEY GREEN - Promotional Packet Seeds - THE PAGE SEED CO.; *pg.* 1798, *pg.* 1163
VALLEY II - Glove - KOMBI, LTD.; *pg.* 1838, *pg.* 1766
VALLEY LANE - Leather Slides - HABAND COMPANY, INC.; *pg.* 1772, *pg.* 1099
VALLEY MORNING STAR - Texas Newspaper - FREEDOM COMMUNICATIONS, INC.; *pg.* 1643, *pg.* 110
VALLEY OAKS - Wine - FETZER VINEYARDS; *pg.* 1963, *pg.* 104
VALLEY OF GOLD - Video Game - INTERNATIONAL GAME TECHNOLOGY; *pg.* 957, *pg.* 1024
VALLEYFAIR! - Amusement Park - CEDAR FAIR, L.P.; *pg.* 537, *pg.* 1471
VALOR VS. VENOM - Toy & Game - HASBRO, INC.; *pg.* 954, *pg.* 1603
VALORDATA BROWSER - Pricing Web Site - STANDARD & POOR'S RATINGS SERVICES; *pg.* 805, *pg.* 1296
VALORDATA FEED - Online Data Information - STANDARD & POOR'S RATINGS SERVICES; *pg.* 805, *pg.* 1296
VALOX IQ - Engineered Plastics - GENERAL ELECTRIC COMPANY; *pg.* 1297, *pg.* 347
VALPRE - Beverages - THE COCA-COLA COMPANY; *pg.* 240, *pg.* 493
VALRUST - Rust Preventive - ROCK VALLEY OIL & CHEMICAL COMPANY; *pg.* 1179, *pg.* 631
VALSER - Water - THE COCA-COLA COMPANY; *pg.* 240, *pg.* 493
VALSER VIVA - Beverages - THE COCA-COLA COMPANY; *pg.* 240, *pg.* 493
VALTAC - Chemical Products - AIR PRODUCTS AND CHEMICALS, INC.; *pg.* 1145, *pg.* 1513
VALTEK - Valve - FLOWSERVE CORPORATION; *pg.* 82, *pg.* 1719
VALTEK EMA - Pump - FLOWSERVE CORPORATION; *pg.* 82, *pg.* 1719
VALTEX - Paper & Nonwoven Material - FIBERMARK INC.; *pg.* 1457, *pg.* 1764
VALU-BILT - Tractor Accessories - ALAMO GROUP INC.; *pg.* 1311, *pg.* 1745
VALU LINE - Cleaner Sheet - HURST CHEMICAL COMPANY; *pg.* 1168, *pg.* 174
VALU-PAC - Saw Blade - THE DOALL COMPANY; *pg.* 1329,

First page reference indicates Business Class Edition
Second page reference indicates Geographic Edition

pg. 670
VALU PAK - Packaging Automation System - INLINE PLASTICS CORP.; *pg.* 1460, *pg.* 370
VALU-RITE - Retail Network - MCKESSON CORPORATION; *pg.* 1560, *pg.* 222
VALU-SOFT - Water, Waste Water & Processed Water Filtering & Treatment Equipment - DOW CHEMICAL; *pg.* 1156, *pg.* 1563
VALU TIME - Economy Brand Food Products - BASHAS' SUPERMARKETS; *pg.* 1015, *pg.* 12
VALUARC - Thermal Spray Wire - SULZER METCO (WESTBURY) INC.; *pg.* 1064, *pg.* 1350
VALUBAND - Pump - IDEX CORPORATION; *pg.* 1347, *pg.* 623
VALUCLIPS - Pump Product - IDEX CORPORATION; *pg.* 1347, *pg.* 623
VALUCRAFT - Automotive Hard Parts Including Starters, Alternators & Brakes - AUTOZONE, INC.; *pg.* 200, *pg.* 1641
VALUE - Scissors - ACME UNITED CORPORATION; *pg.* 1040, *pg.* 346
VALUE - Graphite Golf Shaft - ALDILA, INC.; *pg.* 1825, *pg.* 185
VALUE ASSURANCE PROCESS - Manual - XEROX CORPORATION; *pg.* 494, *pg.* 365
VALUE-CORE - Door - LARSON MANUFACTURING COMPANY; *pg.* 93, *pg.* 1624
VALUE DIFFERENCE - Insurance - FEDERATED MUTUAL INSURANCE COMPANY; *pg.* 1200, *pg.* 952
VALUE LINE - Investment Information Publisher & Money Manager - VALUE LINE, INC.; *pg.* 1699, *pg.* 1308
VALUE LINE ASSET MANAGEMENT - Management Services for Mutual Funds & Institutional Accounts - VALUE LINE, INC.; *pg.* 1699, *pg.* 1308
VALUE LINE INVESTMENT ANALYZER 3.0 - Publication - VALUE LINE, INC.; *pg.* 1699, *pg.* 1308
VALUE LINE INVESTMENT SURVEY - Stock Analysis Print Publication & Software - VALUE LINE, INC.; *pg.* 1699, *pg.* 1308
VALUE LINE MUTUAL FUND SURVEY - Publication - VALUE LINE, INC.; *pg.* 1699, *pg.* 1308
VALUE LINE SAFETY - Publication - VALUE LINE, INC.; *pg.* 1699, *pg.* 1308
VALUE LINE TIMELINESS - Publication - VALUE LINE, INC.; *pg.* 1699, *pg.* 1308
VALUE MAPPING - Methodology - SALES PERFORMANCE INTERNATIONAL, INC.; *pg.* 464, *pg.* 1368
VALUE OUR EXPERIENCE - Tagline - FEDERATED INVESTORS, INC.; *pg.* 752, *pg.* 1575
VALUE SUPPLEX - Apparel - ATTITUDES IN DRESSING INC.; *pg.* 19, *pg.* 1057
VALUECHROM - Software - BIO-RAD LABORATORIES, INC.; *pg.* 1504, *pg.* 101
VALUELAB - Internet Services - YAHOO! INC.; *pg.* 1289, *pg.* 289
VALUELOADER - Tape Autoloader - QUANTUM CORPORATION; *pg.* 458, *pg.* 250
VALUEMAG - Magnetic Material - BUNTING MAGNETICS CO.; *pg.* 1320, *pg.* 717
VALUEMESH - Joint Tape - USG CORPORATION; *pg.* 118, *pg.* 594
VALUEMIX - Plural Components Proportioners - GRACO, INC.; *pg.* 1342, *pg.* 935
VALUEPOINT - Optimized Productivity Services - LAM RESEARCH CORPORATION; *pg.* 1354, *pg.* 91
VALUEQUIX - Manual - XEROX CORPORATION; *pg.* 494, *pg.* 365
VALUERAM - Generic Memory Line - KINGSTON TECHNOLOGY COMPANY, INC.; *pg.* 425, *pg.* 90
VALUES - Coupon Books - ENTERTAINMENT PUBLICATIONS, INC.; *pg.* 1639, *pg.* 910
VALUESAFETY - Paper Product - BOISE CASCADE HOLDINGS, L.L.C.; *pg.* 1453, *pg.* 546
VALUFLEX - Hose - HBD INDUSTRIES, INC.; *pg.* 207, *pg.* 1449
VALUFLOR - Sheet Vinyl Flooring - CONGOLEUM CORPORATION; *pg.* 921, *pg.* 1084
VALULINE - Antenna - COMMSCOPE; *pg.* 630, *pg.* 668
VALULINE - Chemical Product - HURST CHEMICAL COMPANY; *pg.* 1168, *pg.* 174
VALUMAX - Prism - NEWPORT CORPORATION; *pg.* 1424, *pg.* 114
VALUPAK - Burner - MAXON CORPORATION; *pg.* 1359, *pg.* 695
VALUPERFCARD - Manual - XEROX CORPORATION; *pg.* 494, *pg.* 365
VALUPLAZ - Engineered Product And System - SULZER METCO (WESTBURY) INC.; *pg.* 1064, *pg.* 1350
VALUSCAN - Scanner - OMRON SCIENTIFIC TECHNOLOGIES INCORPORATED; *pg.* 1425, *pg.* 91
VALUSTRAP - Pump Product - IDEX CORPORATION; *pg.* 1347, *pg.* 623
VALUTIME - Food Products - SPARTANNASH CO; *pg.* 1034, *pg.* 889
VALVE - Eyewear - OAKLEY, INC.; *pg.* 1840, *pg.* 86
VALVE ACTION - Counter Display - LA-CO INDUSTRIES MARKAL CO., INC.; *pg.* 1170, *pg.* 610
VALVE-PAK - End Closures - SONOCO PRODUCTS COMPANY; *pg.* 1469, *pg.* 1619
VALVED ULTRASEAL - Membrane Closure - SONOCO PRODUCTS COMPANY; *pg.* 1469, *pg.* 1619
VALVEGUARD - Rupture Disc Product - FIKE CORPORATION; *pg.* 1047, *pg.* 973
VALVEKING - Musical Instrument - PEAVEY ELECTRONICS CORPORATION; *pg.* 662, *pg.* 970
VALVES FOR THE 21ST CENTURY - Tagline - HENRY PRATT COMPANY; *pg.* 1049, *pg.* 555
VALVOLINE - Lubricants - ASHLAND INC.; *pg.* 972, *pg.* 726
VALVOLINE INSTANT OIL CHANGE - Quick Lube Outlets - ASHLAND INC.; *pg.* 972, *pg.* 726
VAMA - Vehicular Warning & Police Equipment - FEDERAL SIGNAL CORPORATION; *pg.* 638, *pg.* 645
VAMAC - Synthetic Elastomer - E.I. DU PONT DE NEMOURS & COMPANY; *pg.* 1159, *pg.* 390
VAMPIRE - Game - ACTIVISION BLIZZARD, INC.; *pg.* 948, *pg.* 271
VAMPIRE HUNTER - Toy & Game - HASBRO, INC.; *pg.* 954, *pg.* 1603
VAN - Insulation Product - ALPHA ASSOCIATES, INC.; *pg.* 691, *pg.* 1078
VAN CLEEF & ARPELS - Jewelry - VAN CLEEF & ARPELS, INC.; *pg.* 15, *pg.* 1308
VAN-COUVERED IN SNOW - Nail Care Product - OPI PRODUCTS INC.; *pg.* 518, *pg.* 167
VAN DE KAMP'S - Frozen Seafood - PINNACLE FOODS GROUP LLC; *pg.* 889, *pg.* 1104
VAN HEUSEN - Apparel - PVH CORP.; *pg.* 46, *pg.* 1283
VAN KEUREN - Tools - KENNAMETAL INC.; *pg.* 1052, *pg.* 1547
VAN KEUREN - Tools - KENNAMETAL IPG; *pg.* 1353, *pg.* 1615
VAN-O-LUNCH - Snack Food - SNYDER'S-LANCE, INC.; *pg.* 896, *pg.* 1368
VANAX - Accelerators - R.T. VANDERBILT COMPANY, INC.; *pg.* 1180, *pg.* 364
VANCAMP - Food Product - CONAGRA FOODS, INC.; *pg.* 826, *pg.* 1014
VANCANZA - Fabric - NEMSCHOFF, INC.; *pg.* 936, *pg.* 1890
VANCHEM - Adhesion Promoters - R.T. VANDERBILT COMPANY, INC.; *pg.* 1180, *pg.* 364
VANCIDE - Industrial Preservative - R.T. VANDERBILT COMPANY, INC.; *pg.* 1180, *pg.* 364
VANCOCIN - Prescription Drug - SHIRE; *pg.* 1593, *pg.* 1532
VANCOUVER - Furniture - HAWORTH, INC.; *pg.* 402, *pg.* 891
VANCOUVER CANUCKS - Professional Hockey Team - CANUCKS SPORTS & ENTERTAINMENT; *pg.* 536, *pg.* 1910
VANCOUVER.COM - Travel Website - LIVE CURRENT MEDIA INC.; *pg.* 1263, *pg.* 1911
VANDAL LOW - Footwear - NIKE, INC.; *pg.* 1812, *pg.* 1492
VANDERBILT - Tire - TBC CORPORATION; *pg.* 1889, *pg.* 457
VANDOR - Fragrance Ingredient - INTERNATIONAL FLAVORS & FRAGRANCES INC.; *pg.* 512, *pg.* 1244
VANEE - Ventilation Systems - NORTEK, INC.; *pg.* 100, *pg.* 1607
VANEOMETER - Anemometer - DWYER INSTRUMENTS INC.; *pg.* 1330, *pg.* 694
VANESE - Furniture - TELESCOPE CASUAL FURNITURE INC.; *pg.* 944, *pg.* 1162
VANESE SLING COLLECTION - Furniture - TELESCOPE CASUAL FURNITURE INC.; *pg.* 944, *pg.* 1162
VANESSA - Footwear - EASTLAND SHOE CORPORATION; *pg.* 1808, *pg.* 750
VANESSA - Footwear - P.W. MINOR & SON, INC.; *pg.* 1816, *pg.* 1140
VANESSA - Lighting - SWIVELIER CO., INC.; *pg.* 1307, *pg.* 1142
VANFRE - Processing Aids - R.T. VANDERBILT COMPANY, INC.; *pg.* 1180, *pg.* 364
VANGARD - Recreational Van Conversion Fabrics - GUILFORD PERFORMANCE TEXTILES; *pg.* 693, *pg.* 1393
VANGUARD - Engine Type - BRIGGS & STRATTON CORPORATION; *pg.* 201, *pg.* 1899
VANGUARD - Knife - BUCK KNIVES, INC.; *pg.* 1828, *pg.* 550
VANGUARD - Variable Message Sign System - DAKTRONICS, INC.; *pg.* 633, *pg.* 1624
VANGUARD - Vanilla - DAVID MICHAEL & CO. INC.; *pg.* 852, *pg.* 1563
VANGUARD - Stroller - DOREL JUVENILE GROUP, INC.; *pg.* 923, *pg.* 676
VANGUARD - Office Furniture - JOFCO INC.; *pg.* 931, *pg.* 691
VANGUARD - Headwear - MINE SAFETY APPLIANCES COMPANY; *pg.* 1361, *pg.* 1525
VANGUARD - Quasi-CW Solid State UV Laser - NEWPORT CORPORATION; *pg.* 1424, *pg.* 114
VANGUARD - Mounting System - WEATHERBY, INC.; *pg.* 1848, *pg.* 181
VANGUARD - Knee System - ZIMMER BIOMET HOLDINGS, INC.; *pg.* 1611, *pg.* 699
VANGUARD BACK COUNTRY - Rifle - WEATHERBY, INC.; *pg.* 1848, *pg.* 181
VANGUARD DELUXE - Rifle - WEATHERBY, INC.; *pg.* 1848, *pg.* 181
VANGUARD ETF - Exchange Traded Funds - THE VANGUARD GROUP, INC.; *pg.* 816, *pg.* 1550
VANGUARD FINANCIAL ADVISOR SERVICES - Advisor Services - THE VANGUARD GROUP, INC.; *pg.* 816, *pg.* 1550
VANGUARD II - Lateral Protective Helmet - MINE SAFETY APPLIANCES COMPANY; *pg.* 1361, *pg.* 1525
VANGUARD IRA - Retirement Plan - THE VANGUARD GROUP, INC.; *pg.* 816, *pg.* 1550
VANGUARD LIFESTRATEGY - Fund - THE VANGUARD GROUP, INC.; *pg.* 816, *pg.* 1550
VANGUARD LIFETIME INCOME PROGRAM - Retirement Plan - THE VANGUARD GROUP, INC.; *pg.* 816, *pg.* 1550
VANGUARD PREDATOR - Rifle - WEATHERBY, INC.; *pg.* 1848, *pg.* 181
VANGUARD PREMIUM - Moving & Storage Blankets - SEALED AIR CORPORATION; *pg.* 1468, *pg.* 1058
VANGUARD SAGE COUNTRY - Rifle - WEATHERBY, INC.; *pg.* 1848, *pg.* 181
VANGUARD TOTAL BOND MARKET INDEX FUND SIGNAL - Shares - THE VANGUARD GROUP, INC.; *pg.* 816, *pg.* 1550
VANGUARDADVANTAGE - Brokerage Account - THE VANGUARD GROUP, INC.; *pg.* 816, *pg.* 1550
VANI-SOL - High Acid Bowl Cleanser - RECKITT BENCKISER INC.; *pg.* 1136, *pg.* 1105
VANILLA - Air Freshener - SWISHER HYGIENE INC.; *pg.* 336, *pg.* 1507
VANILLA COKE - Soft Drink - THE COCA-COLA COMPANY; *pg.* 240, *pg.* 493
VANILLA COKE ZERO - Beverages - THE COCA-COLA COMPANY; *pg.* 240, *pg.* 493
VANILLA FANTASY - Fragrance - PARFUMS DE COEUR LTD.; *pg.* 519, *pg.* 376
VANILLA FIELDS - Women's Fragrance - COTY, INC.; *pg.* 506, *pg.* 1219
VANILLA MUSK - Women's fragrance - COTY, INC.; *pg.* 506, *pg.* 1219
VANILLA OVER THE RAINBOW - Ice Cream - DIPPIN' DOTS LLC; *pg.* 853, *pg.* 739
VANILLA SLIM SHAKE - Nutritional Product - RBC LIFE SCIENCES, INC.; *pg.* 1588, *pg.* 1723
VANISH - Cleaning Product - S.C. JOHNSON & SON, INC.; *pg.* 334, *pg.* 1889
VANISHING POINT - Furniture - HERMAN MILLER, INC.; *pg.* 926, *pg.* 913
VANISPERSE - Chemical Product - WESTROCK COMPANY; *pg.* 1472, *pg.* 1805
VANITY - Gaming Product - GLD PRODUCTS, INC.; *pg.* 1835, *pg.* 1882
VANITY - Basket - THE LONGABERGER COMPANY; *pg.* 1127, *pg.* 1467
VANITY FAIR - Magazine - CONDE NAST PUBLICATIONS, INC.; *pg.* 1629, *pg.* 1217
VANITY FAIR - Tissue Product - GEORGIA-PACIFIC LLC; *pg.* 1458, *pg.* 507

VANITY FAIR - Intimate Apparel - V.F. CORPORATION; *pg.* 34, *pg.* 1376

VANNA - Furniture - AMISCO INDUSTRIES LTD.; *pg.* 913, *pg.* 1958

VANOCHA - Chocolate - BIGLARI HOLDINGS INC.; *pg.* 1015, *pg.* 1739

VANPAK - Seating - FLEXSTEEL INDUSTRIES, INC.; *pg.* 925, *pg.* 707

VANPLAST - Plasticizers - R.T. VANDERBILT COMPANY, INC.; *pg.* 1180, *pg.* 364

VANQUISH - Medicine - BAYER HEALTHCARE CONSUMER CARE DIVISION; *pg.* 1500, *pg.* 1087

VAN'S - Snack Foods & Frozen Breakfast Foods - VAN'S INTERNATIONAL FOODS, INC.; *pg.* 908, *pg.* 302

VANS - Footwear - V.F. CORPORATION; *pg.* 34, *pg.* 1376

VANSCURVES - Apparel - VANS, INC.; *pg.* 1821, *pg.* 76

VANSIL - Chemical Product - R.T. VANDERBILT COMPANY, INC.; *pg.* 1180, *pg.* 364

VANSTAAL - Electric Trolling Motors - ZEBCO; *pg.* 1848, *pg.* 1491

VANTAGE - Atmospheric RTP Application - APPLIED MATERIALS, INC.; *pg.* 618, *pg.* 264

VANTAGE - String - ASHAWAY LINE & TWINE MFG. CO.; *pg.* 1826, *pg.* 1600

VANTAGE - Knife - BUCK KNIVES, INC.; *pg.* 1828, *pg.* 550

VANTAGE - Furniture - BUSH INDUSTRIES INC.; *pg.* 919, *pg.* 1170

VANTAGE - Software - COMPUWARE CORPORATION; *pg.* 379, *pg.* 879

VANTAGE - Soft, Daily-Wear Contact Lens - THE COOPER COMPANIES, INC.; *pg.* 1518, *pg.* 183

VANTAGE - Software - EPICOR SOFTWARE CORPORATION; *pg.* 393, *pg.* 110

VANTAGE - DVD Encoder Chip - ESS TECHNOLOGY, INC.; *pg.* 395, *pg.* 90

VANTAGE - Furniture - HERMAN MILLER, INC.; *pg.* 926, *pg.* 913

VANTAGE - Wireless Camera - ITERIS, INC.; *pg.* 293, *pg.* 261

VANTAGE - Men's Shoe - JACK SCHWARTZ SHOES, INC.; *pg.* 1810, *pg.* 1245

VANTAGE - Bath & Plumbing Product - JACUZZI BRANDS CORPORATION; *pg.* 554, *pg.* 65

VANTAGE - Card Game - MATTEL GAMES/PUZZLES; *pg.* 962, *pg.* 80

VANTAGE - Spray Booth - NORDSON CORPORATION; *pg.* 1365, *pg.* 1480

VANTAGE - Heater - ROBERTS-GORDON INC.; *pg.* 1076, *pg.* 1151

VANTAGE - Transducer - SNAP-ON INCORPORATED; *pg.* 1062, *pg.* 1862

VANTAGE - Grass Killer - SOUTHERN AGRICULTURAL INSECTICIDES, INC.; *pg.* 1181, *pg.* 458

VANTAGE - Semi Finished Product - STANBEE COMPANY, INC.; *pg.* 1819, *pg.* 1050

VANTAGE - Flashlight - STREAMLIGHT INC.; *pg.* 1306, *pg.* 1527

VANTAGE - Pipeline Pigging Product - T.D. WILLIAMSON, INC.; *pg.* 1380, *pg.* 1490

VANTAGE - Computer Control - VILTER MANUFACTURING LLC; *pg.* 1078, *pg.* 1856

VANTAGE ACCENTS - Soft, Daily-Wear Contact Lens - THE COOPER COMPANIES, INC.; *pg.* 1518, *pg.* 183

VANTAGE FLOSSIN' - Men's Shoe - JACK SCHWARTZ SHOES, INC.; *pg.* 1810, *pg.* 1245

VANTAGE LASER CUTTING - Cutting & Burning Steel - RUSSEL METALS INC.; *pg.* 1180, *pg.* 1928

VANTAGE-ONE - Computer Program - COMPUTER SCIENCES CORPORATION; *pg.* 378, *pg.* 1780

VANTAGE PRO - Diagnostic Tool - SNAP-ON INCORPORATED; *pg.* 1062, *pg.* 1862

VANTAGE RADIANCE - Atmospheric RTP Application - APPLIED MATERIALS, INC.; *pg.* 618, *pg.* 264

VANTAGE RT - Product Name - MERCURY COMPUTER SYSTEMS, INC.; *pg.* 434, *pg.* 813

VANTAGE THIN - Soft, Flexible-Wear Contact Lens - THE COOPER COMPANIES, INC.; *pg.* 1518, *pg.* 183

VANTAGE THIN ACCENTS - Soft, Flexible-Wear Contact Lens - THE COOPER COMPANIES, INC.; *pg.* 1518, *pg.* 183

VANTAGE V - Cleaning Pig - T.D. WILLIAMSON, INC.; *pg.* 1380, *pg.* 1490

VANTAGEISI - Software - WIND RIVER SYSTEMS, INC.; *pg.* 493, *pg.* 38

VANTAGERT - Software - MERCURY COMPUTER SYSTEMS, INC.; *pg.* 434, *pg.* 813

VANTALC - Mineral Fillers - R.T. VANDERBILT COMPANY, INC.; *pg.* 1180, *pg.* 364

VANTIN - Medicine - PFIZER INC.; *pg.* 1581, *pg.* 1278

VANTIS - Electric Instrument - UNIVERSAL INSTRUMENTS CORPORATION; *pg.* 683, *pg.* 1154

VANWAX - Waxes - R.T. VANDERBILT COMPANY, INC.; *pg.* 1180, *pg.* 364

VAPAC - Steam Humidifiers - NORTEK, INC.; *pg.* 100, *pg.* 1607

VAPAM - Agricultural Chemical - AMERICAN VANGUARD CORPORATION; *pg.* 1793, *pg.* 165

VAPEX - Paint & Varnish - PRATT & LAMBERT PAINTS; *pg.* 1446, *pg.* 1434

VAPONA - Concentrate Insecticide - BOEHRINGER INGELHEIM VETMEDICA, INC.; *pg.* 1474, *pg.* 989

VAPONA - Homeowner Product - PBI/GORDON CORPORATION; *pg.* 1176, *pg.* 985

VAPOR - Refill - A. T. CROSS COMPANY; *pg.* 339, *pg.* 1602

VAPOR - Decorative Architectural Product - MASCO CORPORATION; *pg.* 96, *pg.* 909

VAPOR DRY - Fabric - BROOKS SPORTS INC.; *pg.* 1805, *pg.* 1818

VAPOR LINE - Sterilization Product - PROPPER MANUFACTURING COMPANY, INC.; *pg.* 1586, *pg.* 1175

VAPOR PAC - Carbon Adsorption System - CALGON CARBON CORPORATION; *pg.* 1151, *pg.* 1574

VAPOR PRO - Analyzer - ARIZONA INSTRUMENT LLC; *pg.* 1400, *pg.* 12

VAPOR-SHIELD - Primer - KELLY-MOORE PAINT COMPANY, INC.; *pg.* 1443, *pg.* 198

VAPOR WRAPPER - Papers - DAUBERT INDUSTRIES, INC.; *pg.* 1155, *pg.* 561

VAPORAIRE - LPG Air Mixer - ALGAS-SDI; *pg.* 1311, *pg.* 1831

VAPORBLOCK - Vapor Retarder - RAVEN INDUSTRIES, INC.; *pg.* 1888, *pg.* 1625

VAPORFLO - Test Equipment - SPX THERMAL PRODUCT SOLUTIONS; *pg.* 1378, *pg.* 1555

VAPORGARD - Anti-Transpirant - MILLER CHEMICAL & FERTILIZER CORPORATION; *pg.* 706, *pg.* 1535

VAPORPH3OS - Chemical Product - CYTEC INDUSTRIES, INC.; *pg.* 1155, *pg.* 1131

VAPORSTOP - Vapor Barrier - FORTIFIBER CORPORATION; *pg.* 83, *pg.* 1021

VAPOUR - Kitchen Product - KOHLER CO.; *pg.* 91, *pg.* 1862

VAPOURLUME - Specialty Lighting - JUNO LIGHTING, INC.; *pg.* 1300, *pg.* 606

VAPROX - Sterilant - STERIS CORPORATION; *pg.* 1597, *pg.* 1464

VAPURE - Vapor Compression Still - PAUL MUELLER COMPANY; *pg.* 706, *pg.* 1007

VAQUERO - Revolver - STURM, RUGER & COMPANY, INC.; *pg.* 1846, *pg.* 371

VARADOS - Footwear - K-SWISS; *pg.* 1837, *pg.* 306

VARAFINE - Filter Cartridge - PALL CORPORATION; *pg.* 232, *pg.* 1323

VARANASI - Rug - COURISTAN INC.; *pg.* 921, *pg.* 1067

VARASHIELD - Air Deflector - PETERBILT MOTORS CO.; *pg.* 188, *pg.* 1691

VARBUSINESS - Magazine - UNITED BUSINESS MEDIA LLC; *pg.* 1697, *pg.* 1177

VAREKAI - Show And Ticket - CIRQUE DU SOLEIL INC.; *pg.* 540, *pg.* 1954

VARI-BIT - Drill Bit - LENOX; *pg.* 1053, *pg.* 817

VARI-BRIGHT - Graphics Card - ADVANCED MICRO DEVICES, INC.; *pg.* 613, *pg.* 282

VARI-CELL - Electric Instrument - UNIVERSAL INSTRUMENTS CORPORATION; *pg.* 683, *pg.* 1154

VARI-FIT - Heel Cradle - ACUSHNET COMPANY; *pg.* 1824, *pg.* 818

VARI-GRIP - Machinery - HARDINGE INC.; *pg.* 1344, *pg.* 1157

VARI-LASE - Medical Device - VASCULAR SOLUTIONS, INC.; *pg.* 1434, *pg.* 946

VARI-LITE - Lighting Fixture & Control - PHILIPS LIGHTING; *pg.* 1303, *pg.* 806

VARI-SEAL - Filter Housing - PALL CORPORATION; *pg.* 232, *pg.* 1323

VARI-TAP - Transformers - ATLAS SOUND; *pg.* 621, *pg.* 1692

VARI-TEMP 2000 - Truck Refrigeration System - KIDRON, INC.; *pg.* 181, *pg.* 1457

VARI-X - Optical Product - LEUPOLD & STEVENS, INC.; *pg.* 1420, *pg.* 1492

VARIA - Furniture - ASHLEY FURNITURE INDUSTRIES, INC.; *pg.* 914, *pg.* 1852

VARIA - Furniture - HAWORTH, INC.; *pg.* 402, *pg.* 891

VARIABLE INCLINING POSITIONS BED - Electric Bed - KINGSDOWN, INC.; *pg.* 932, *pg.* 1383

VARIABLESPEED/BILEVEL - Fault Protection - MAXIM INTEGRATED PRODUCTS, INC.; *pg.* 653, *pg.* 247

VARIAIR - Gun - MASTER APPLIANCE CORP.; *pg.* 1055, *pg.* 1888

VARIAN - Implanter - IMPLANT SCIENCES CORPORATION; *pg.* 1348, *pg.* 860

VARIANT - Clinical Diagnostic Product - BIO-RAD LABORATORIES, INC.; *pg.* 1504, *pg.* 101

VARIANT - Adjustable Height Table - HOWE FURNITURE CORPORATION; *pg.* 928, *pg.* 998

VARIANT EXPRESS - Software - BIO-RAD LABORATORIES, INC.; *pg.* 1504, *pg.* 101

VARIANT II - Software - BIO-RAD LABORATORIES, INC.; *pg.* 1504, *pg.* 101

VARIANT ONLINE LIBRARY - Software - BIO-RAD LABORATORIES, INC.; *pg.* 1504, *pg.* 101

VARIATIONS - Magazine - FRIENDFINDER NETWORKS INC.; *pg.* 1643, *pg.* 411

VARIBEST - Vinyl Skirting - NORTEK, INC.; *pg.* 100, *pg.* 1607

VARICARE - Medical Device - C.R. BARD, INC.; *pg.* 1519, *pg.* 1094

VARICK - Leather Product - COACH, INC.; *pg.* 3, *pg.* 1214

VARIGRIP - Orthopedic Implant Product - DJO SURGICAL; *pg.* 1525, *pg.* 1661

VARILITE - Medical Laser System - IRIDEX CORPORATION; *pg.* 648, *pg.* 160

VARIMAC - Nondestructive Testing - MAGNETIC ANALYSIS CORPORATION; *pg.* 1421, *pg.* 1158

VARIO-RETINAR - Lenses - EASTMAN KODAK COMPANY; *pg.* 1408, *pg.* 1333

VARIOCLEAN - Aqueous Parts Cleaning System - IPSEN INTERNATIONAL, INC.; *pg.* 1073, *pg.* 562

VARIOCOOL - Gas Treatment System - LECHLER, INC.; *pg.* 1444, *pg.* 658

VARIOCROM - Plastic & Rubber - TEKNOR APEX COMPANY; *pg.* 1889, *pg.* 1605

VARIOLAS - UV Micromachining System - COHERENT, INC.; *pg.* 1406, *pg.* 265

VARIOMATCH - Matching Network - ADVANCED ENERGY INDUSTRIES, INC.; *pg.* 613, *pg.* 328

VARIS - Medical System - VARIAN MEDICAL SYSTEMS, INC.; *pg.* 1434, *pg.* 178

VARISIMMER - Kitchen Appliance - VIKING RANGE CORPORATION; *pg.* 61, *pg.* 968

VARISLICER - Medical Device - OLIVER PRODUCTS COMPANY INC.; *pg.* 1367, *pg.* 888

VARISORT - Mail Sorter - PITNEY BOWES INC.; *pg.* 454, *pg.* 376

VARISPEED A2000 - Motion Control Product - GRAHAM MOTORS AND CONTROLS; *pg.* 177, *pg.* 1692

VARISPEED R400 - Motion Control Product - GRAHAM MOTORS AND CONTROLS; *pg.* 177, *pg.* 1692

VARISPEED S1000 - Motion Control Product - GRAHAM MOTORS AND CONTROLS; *pg.* 177, *pg.* 1692

VARITEMP - Heat Gun - MASTER APPLIANCE CORP.; *pg.* 1055, *pg.* 1888

VARITESS - Paper - NEENAH PAPER, INC.; *pg.* 1465, *pg.* 484

VARITRONICS - Business Graphics Products - BRADY CORPORATION; *pg.* 363, *pg.* 1873

VARIVALVE - Radiator Air Vents - HEAT-TIMER CORPORATION; *pg.* 1072, *pg.* 1065

VARIWEB - Feeder - STANDARD DUPLICATING MACHINES CORPORATION; *pg.* 473, *pg.* 783

VARIZIG - Drug - EMERGENT BIOSOLUTIONS; *pg.* 1528, *pg.* 1914

VARIZONE - Digital Public Address System - ATLAS SOUND; *pg.* 621, *pg.* 1692

VARMOR - Clear Urethane Finishes - PRATT & LAMBERT PAINTS; *pg.* 1446, *pg.* 1434

VARTA - Battery - ENERSYS INC.; *pg.* 1334, *pg.* 1584

VARTA - Automotive Batteries - JOHNSON CONTROLS, INC.; *pg.* 209, *pg.* 1876

VARY EASY - Furniture - HERMAN MILLER, INC.; *pg.* 926, *pg.* 913

VAS - Bath Product - KOHLER CO.; *pg.* 91, *pg.* 1862

VASCADE - Optical Fiber - CORNING INCORPORATED; *pg.* 1122, *pg.* 1154

VASCUTAPE - Medical Tape Marked With Radiopaque Ink -

First page reference indicates Business Class Edition
Second page reference indicates Geographic Edition

LEMAITRE VASCULAR, INC.; *pg.* 1555, *pg.* 805
VASELINE - Petroleum Jelly - UNILEVER UNITED STATES, INC.; *pg.* 904, *pg.* 1061
VASERETIC - Pharmaceutical Product - VALEANT PHARMACEUTICALS INTERNATIONAL, INC.; *pg.* 1605, *pg.* 1957
VASO-PROPHIN - Health & Beauty Product - DIXIE HEALTH, INC.; *pg.* 1524, *pg.* 535
VASODERM - Health & Beauty Product - DIXIE HEALTH, INC.; *pg.* 1524, *pg.* 535
VASOPROPHIN RX - Health & Beauty Product - DIXIE HEALTH, INC.; *pg.* 1524, *pg.* 535
VASOSEAL - Vascular Hemostasis Device for Sealing of Wounds - MAQUET; *pg.* 1558, *pg.* 1082
VASOTEC - Pharmaceutical Product - VALEANT PHARMACEUTICALS INTERNATIONAL, INC.; *pg.* 1605, *pg.* 1957
VASQUE - Hiking, Mountaineering & Backpacking Shoes - RED WING SHOE COMPANY, INC.; *pg.* 1817, *pg.* 954
VASQUE OUTDOOR HIKING BOOTS - Footwear - RED WING SHOE COMPANY, INC.; *pg.* 1817, *pg.* 954
VASSARETTE - Intimate Apparel - V.F. CORPORATION; *pg.* 34, *pg.* 1376
VASTERBOTTEN - Cheese - A.V. OLSSON TRADING CO, INC.; *pg.* 838, *pg.* 372
VATMAN - Solid Imaging Material - 3D SYSTEMS CORPORATION; *pg.* 339, *pg.* 1621
VAUDREUIL - Milk & Chees Products - AGROPUR COOPERATIVE; *pg.* 836, *pg.* 1950
VAULT - Soft Drink - THE COCA-COLA COMPANY; *pg.* 240, *pg.* 493
THE VAULT - Eyewear - OAKLEY, INC.; *pg.* 1840, *pg.* 86
VAULT TRACKER - Software - COMMVAULT SYSTEMS, INC.; *pg.* 377, *pg.* 1125
VAULT ZERO - Beverages - THE COCA-COLA COMPANY; *pg.* 240, *pg.* 493
VAUXHALL - Vehicle - GENERAL MOTORS COMPANY; *pg.* 175, *pg.* 881
VAXA - Homeopathic Products - NUTRACEUTICAL INTERNATIONAL CORPORATION; *pg.* 1576, *pg.* 1753
VAXCAVATOR - Vacuum Excavation Equipment - MCLAUGHLIN BORING SYSTEMS; *pg.* 1360, *pg.* 1617
VAXCEL - Medical Device - BOSTON SCIENTIFIC CORPORATION; *pg.* 1508, *pg.* 831
VAZO - Free Radical Initiators - E.I. DU PONT DE NEMOURS & COMPANY; *pg.* 1159, *pg.* 390
VBEAM - Aesthetic Skin Treatment Laser - CANDELA CORPORATION; *pg.* 1404, *pg.* 855
VBOSS - Spinal System - STRYKER CORPORATION; *pg.* 1598, *pg.* 894
VBP - Converged Network Appliance - POLYCOM, INC.; *pg.* 664, *pg.* 249
VC SERIES - Compact Condensate Pumps - LITTLE GIANT PUMP COMPANY; *pg.* 1356, *pg.* 1486
VC1 - Lighting System - LITECONTROL CORPORATION; *pg.* 1301, *pg.* 841
VC7D1305T - Video Camera - BOSCH SECURITY SYSTEMS, INC.; *pg.* 626, *pg.* 1158
VCARE - Medical Equipment - CONMED CORPORATION; *pg.* 1517, *pg.* 1347
VCD - Drives - MAGNETEK, INC.; *pg.* 1301, *pg.* 1870
VCE - Video Conferencing Product - POLYCOM, INC.; *pg.* 664, *pg.* 249
VCLASS - Security Appliance - WATCHGUARD TECHNOLOGIES, INC.; *pg.* 491, *pg.* 1842
VCMA SERIES - Medium Condensate Pumps - LITTLE GIANT PUMP COMPANY; *pg.* 1356, *pg.* 1486
VCOM - VME Bus - NEONODE, INC.; *pg.* 659, *pg.* 268
VCOPTIC - Lighting System - LITECONTROL CORPORATION; *pg.* 1301, *pg.* 841
VCR - Plastic Tube - SWAGELOK COMPANY; *pg.* 1064, *pg.* 1473
VCR CO-PILOT - VCR Programming Device - JOSEPH ENTERPRISES, INC.; *pg.* 960, *pg.* 220
VCR PLUS+ - Video Recording Software - ROVI CORPORATION; *pg.* 463, *pg.* 269
VCS - Medical Device - LEMAITRE VASCULAR, INC.; *pg.* 1555, *pg.* 805
VCS - Software - SYNOPSYS, INC.; *pg.* 480, *pg.* 162
VCS - Surface Maintenance Machine - TENNANT COMPANY; *pg.* 1381, *pg.* 944
VCS EXPRESS - Software - SYNOPSYS, INC.; *pg.* 480, *pg.* 162
VCSEL TOSA - Electronic Component - EMCORE CORPORATION; *pg.* 636, *pg.* 39
VCSI - Software - SYNOPSYS, INC.; *pg.* 480, *pg.* 162
VCU-1600 - Two Piece All Aluminum Chassis Computer Designed for Rugged Environments - MILTOPE GROUP, INC.; *pg.* 440, *pg.* 6
VDARA CONDO HOTEL AT CITYCENTER - Resort & Casino - MGM RESORTS INTERNATIONAL; *pg.* 1105, *pg.* 1028
VDMS 2000 - Software - BIO-RAD LABORATORIES, INC.; *pg.* 1504, *pg.* 101
VDR - Vertical Blanking Interval Data Receiver for National Datacast - PUBLIC BROADCASTING SERVICE; *pg.* 305, *pg.* 1774
VEA 520 - Tipping Machine - STANDARD DUPLICATING MACHINES CORPORATION; *pg.* 473, *pg.* 783
VECO - Probe - YSI INCORPORATED; *pg.* 1438, *pg.* 1483
VECT SELECT - Pulse Configuration - ST. JUDE MEDICAL, INC.; *pg.* 1596, *pg.* 963
VECTA - Office Furniture - STEELCASE INC.; *pg.* 475, *pg.* 889
VECTA 2 - Direction Finder - ACR ELECTRONICS, INC.; *pg.* 612, *pg.* 422
VECTAFLEX - Seating - STEELCASE INC.; *pg.* 475, *pg.* 889
VECTIBIX - Treatment of Colorectal Carcinoma - AMGEN INC.; *pg.* 1493, *pg.* 291
VECTIS - Cameras - KONICA MINOLTA BUSINESS SOLUTIONS USA, INC.; *pg.* 1419, *pg.* 1113
VECTOR - Water Scrubber - ATMI, INC.; *pg.* 1314, *pg.* 342
VECTOR - Bowling Equipment - BRUNSWICK BOWLING & BILLIARDS CORP.; *pg.* 1828, *pg.* 622
VECTOR - Laser & Laser System - COHERENT, INC.; *pg.* 1406, *pg.* 265
VECTOR - Fire Helmet - E.D. BULLARD COMPANY; *pg.* 1332, *pg.* 727
VECTOR - Image Processor - ELECTROSONIC SYSTEMS, INC.; *pg.* 635, *pg.* 949
VECTOR - Wireless Product - HEMISPHERE GPS INC.; *pg.* 642, *pg.* 1903
VECTOR - Abrasive Flow Machine - KENNAMETAL EXTRUDE HONE; *pg.* 1352, *pg.* 1542
VECTOR - Automated Wafer Fabrication System - LAM RESEARCH CORPORATION; *pg.* 1354, *pg.* 246
VECTOR - Footwear - REEBOK INTERNATIONAL LTD.; *pg.* 1817, *pg.* 811
VECTOR - Video Viewing System - SWORDFISH FINANCIAL, INC.; *pg.* 1430, *pg.* 1737
VECTOR - Ceiling Fan - WESTINGHOUSE LIGHTING CORPORATION; *pg.* 687, *pg.* 1571
VECTOR 100 - Ice Hockey Stick - REEBOK-CCM HOCKEY, INC.; *pg.* 1844, *pg.* 1960
VECTOR 110 - Ice Hockey Stick - REEBOK-CCM HOCKEY, INC.; *pg.* 1844, *pg.* 1960
VECTOR BROADBAND - Single-Point Recording - ION GEOPHYSICAL CORPORATION; *pg.* 1350, *pg.* 1708
VECTOR DRIVE - Motor Drive - BALDOR ELECTRIC COMPANY; *pg.* 1316, *pg.* 32
VECTOR ELITE - Ceiling Fan - WESTINGHOUSE LIGHTING CORPORATION; *pg.* 687, *pg.* 1571
VECTOR FL52 - CTP Imaging System - PRESSTEK LLC; *pg.* 1678, *pg.* 1034
VECTOR NTI - Biomolecule Product - THERMO FISHER SCIENTIFIC INC.; *pg.* 1602, *pg.* 61
VECTORCAM - Line of Professional Products - VICON INDUSTRIES, INC.; *pg.* 685, *pg.* 1166
VECTORDESIGNER - Online Guide - THERMO FISHER SCIENTIFIC INC.; *pg.* 1602, *pg.* 61
VECTORSEIS - Cable And Connector - ION GEOPHYSICAL CORPORATION; *pg.* 1350, *pg.* 1708
VECTRA - Cervical Plating System - DEPUY SYNTHES; *pg.* 1523, *pg.* 1593
VECTRA - Orthopedic Implant Product - DJO SURGICAL; *pg.* 1525, *pg.* 1661
VECTRA - Flatware - ONEIDA LTD; *pg.* 1129, *pg.* 1318
VECTRA - Motor Homes - WINNEBAGO INDUSTRIES, INC.; *pg.* 1712, *pg.* 707
VECTRA GENISYS - Orthopedic Device - DJO SURGICAL; *pg.* 1525, *pg.* 1661
VECTRAVISION - Ion & Electron Beam - FEI COMPANY; *pg.* 1413, *pg.* 1498
VECTUS - Case Management Software - FAIR ISAAC CORPORATION; *pg.* 1247, *pg.* 955
VEDIT - Text Editor - GREENVIEW DATA, INC.; *pg.* 401, *pg.* 866
VEDIT PLUS - Text Editor - GREENVIEW DATA, INC.; *pg.* 401, *pg.* 866
VEE BLOCK - Refractory Product - RESCO PRODUCTS, INC.; *pg.* 107, *pg.* 1581
VEE PAC - Engine Air Filter - DONALDSON COMPANY, INC.; *pg.* 1329, *pg.* 917
VEEDER ROOT - Fuel Management System - DANAHER CORPORATION; *pg.* 1044, *pg.* 397
VEEGUM - Thickeners - R.T. VANDERBILT COMPANY, INC.; *pg.* 1180, *pg.* 364
VEEJET - Spray Product - SPRAYING SYSTEMS CO.; *pg.* 1063, *pg.* 670
VEELOS-V - Belts - FENNER DRIVES; *pg.* 1336, *pg.* 1551
VEET - Depilatory Products - RECKITT BENCKISER INC.; *pg.* 1136, *pg.* 1105
VEETHANE - Extruded Plastic V-Belting - SHINGLE BELTING COMPANY; *pg.* 1375, *pg.* 1544
VEG-E-GARDEN - Vegetable Growing Kits - AEROGROW INTERNATIONAL, INC.; *pg.* 1393, *pg.* 310
VEG-MIX - Process Automation System - KEY TECHNOLOGY, INC.; *pg.* 868, *pg.* 1847
VEGA - Airbrushes - BADGER AIR BRUSH COMPANY; *pg.* 359, *pg.* 612
VEGA - Fabric - NEMSCHOFF, INC.; *pg.* 936, *pg.* 1890
VEGA HARPOON - Systems Integration & Aeronautics - LOCKHEED MARTIN CORPORATION; *pg.* 229, *pg.* 762
VEGA VENTURA - Systems Integration & Aeronautics - LOCKHEED MARTIN CORPORATION; *pg.* 229, *pg.* 762
VEGALUBE - Pan Oil - MALLET & COMPANY, INC.; *pg.* 875, *pg.* 1521
VEGAMINE - Hydrolyzed Vegetable Protein - GRIFFITH LABORATORIES, INC.; *pg.* 860, *pg.* 552
VEGAN - Dairy Free Food Products - GALAXY NUTRITIONAL FOODS, INC.; *pg.* 857, *pg.* 1603
VEGAS - Fabric - NEMSCHOFF, INC.; *pg.* 936, *pg.* 1890
VEGAS - Bicycle Accessories - SPECIALIZED BICYCLE COMPONENTS, INC.; *pg.* 1711, *pg.* 152
VEGAS BOULEVARD - Lottery Game - MICHIGAN STATE LOTTERY BUREAU; *pg.* 999, *pg.* 895
VEGE-SAL - Food Products - MODERN PRODUCTS, INC.; *pg.* 1568, *pg.* 1871
VEGECELL - Hair & Skin Product - AUBREY ORGANICS INC.; *pg.* 499, *pg.* 470
VEGECOL - Hair & Skin Product - AUBREY ORGANICS INC.; *pg.* 499, *pg.* 470
VEGEFULL - Bean Ingredient - ARCHER-DANIELS-MIDLAND COMPANY; *pg.* 825, *pg.* 565
VEGEMEC - Turf Product - PBI/GORDON CORPORATION; *pg.* 1176, *pg.* 985
VEGETABLES ALIVE! - Vegetable Gardening - GARDENS ALIVE!, INC.; *pg.* 1796, *pg.* 693
VEGETARIAN - Healthcare Product - SWANSON HEALTH PRODUCTS INC.; *pg.* 1600, *pg.* 1397
VEGF TRAP - Therapeutic Medicine - REGENERON PHARMACEUTICALS, INC.; *pg.* 1588, *pg.* 1345
VEGGIE - Soy Nutritious Food Products - GALAXY NUTRITIONAL FOODS, INC.; *pg.* 857, *pg.* 1603
VEGGIE COMPLETE - Nutritional Product - NUTRACEUTICAL INTERNATIONAL CORPORATION; *pg.* 1576, *pg.* 1753
VEGGIE CORN DOGS - Veggie Hot Dogs - KELLOGG COMPANY; *pg.* 831, *pg.* 870
VEGGIE CRISPS - Vegetable Snack Chips - SNYDER'S OF HANOVER, INC.; *pg.* 1862, *pg.* 1536
VEGGIE DELITE - Lettuce, Tomato, Green Pepper, Onion, Olive & Pickle Sandwich - SUBWAY RESTAURANTS; *pg.* 1751, *pg.* 356
VEGGIE PATCH - Pizza - APPLEBEE'S INTERNATIONAL, INC.; *pg.* 1715, *pg.* 980
VEGGIE.COM - Advertising Website - LIVE CURRENT MEDIA INC.; *pg.* 1263, *pg.* 1911
VEGGIETALES - Video - BIG IDEA, INC.; *pg.* 271, *pg.* 1632
VEGGIETUNES - Music - BIG IDEA, INC.; *pg.* 271, *pg.* 1632
VEGGY - Soy Nutritious Food Products - GALAXY NUTRITIONAL FOODS, INC.; *pg.* 857, *pg.* 1603
VEGI MAC - Fast Food - MCDONALD'S CORPORATION; *pg.* 1737, *pg.* 645
VEGIT - Food Seasoning - MODERN PRODUCTS, INC.; *pg.* 1568, *pg.* 1871
VEGITABETA - Beverages - THE COCA-COLA COMPANY; *pg.* 240, *pg.* 493
VEGLIFE - Nutritional Product - NUTRACEUTICAL INTERNATIONAL CORPORATION; *pg.* 1576, *pg.* 1753
VEGY - Pizza - DONATOS PIZZERIA CORPORATION; *pg.* 1727, *pg.* 1439
VEHICLE ALERT - Environmental Security Product - WINLAND ELECTRONICS, INC.; *pg.* 688, *pg.* 928
VEHICLE ASSET COMMUNICATOR - Wireless Communication Equipment - I.D. SYSTEMS, INC.; *pg.* 643,

pg. 1134
VEHICLE HISTORY REPORT - Information Retrieval Services - CARFAX INC.; *pg.* 202, *pg.* 1777
VEIN AWAY - Sand Additive - HILL & GRIFFITH COMPANY; *pg.* 1167, *pg.* 1414
VEIN SUPREME - Herbal Product - NOW HEALTH GROUP, INC.; *pg.* 1576, *pg.* 557
VEKTOR - X-Ray Diffraction Metrology - NANOMETRICS INCORPORATED; *pg.* 1423, *pg.* 147
VELADISC - Filter Equipment - PALL CORPORATION; *pg.* 232, *pg.* 1323
VELCADE - Pharmaceutical Product - MILLENNIUM: THE TAKEDA ONCOLOGY COMPANY; *pg.* 1568, *pg.* 809
VELCRO - Cradle Arm Sling - ALIMED, INC.; *pg.* 1490, *pg.* 816
VELCRO - Medical & Aesthetic Product - DYNATRONICS CORPORATION; *pg.* 1526, *pg.* 1757
VELCRO - Healthcare Product - GF HEALTH PRODUCTS, INC.; *pg.* 1535, *pg.* 508
VELCRO - Footwear - P.W. MINOR & SON, INC.; *pg.* 1816, *pg.* 1140
VELEIRO - Soyabean Oil - CARGILL LIMITED; *pg.* 1475, *pg.* 1914
VELESE - Fabric - NEMSCHOFF, INC.; *pg.* 936, *pg.* 1890
VELFOAM - Medical & Aesthetic Product - DYNATRONICS CORPORATION; *pg.* 1526, *pg.* 1757
VELKET - Laboratory Product - PROPPER MANUFACTURING COMPANY, INC.; *pg.* 1586, *pg.* 1175
VELLA - Bathroom Accessories - SYMMONS INDUSTRIES, INC.; *pg.* 114, *pg.* 803
VELLUM - Printing Paper - MOHAWK FINE PAPERS, INC.; *pg.* 1464, *pg.* 1153
VELOCE 500 - Women's Apparel - A&E STORES, INC.; *pg.* 17, *pg.* 1124
VELOCICALC AIR VELOCITY METER - Air Velocity Meter - TSI INCORPORATED; *pg.* 1432, *pg.* 965
VELOCICALC MULTI FUNCTION VENTILATION METER - Multi-Function Ventilation Meter - TSI INCORPORATED; *pg.* 1432, *pg.* 965
VELOCICALC ROTATING VANE ANEMOMETER - Rotating Vane Anemometer - TSI INCORPORATED; *pg.* 1432, *pg.* 965
VELOCICUT - Cutting Head - URSCHEL LABORATORIES INCORPORATED; *pg.* 1386, *pg.* 698
VELOCIGENE - Genetic Engineering Services - REGENERON PHARMACEUTICALS, INC.; *pg.* 1588, *pg.* 1345
VELOCIIMMUNE - Antibody Preparations - REGENERON PHARMACEUTICALS, INC.; *pg.* 1588, *pg.* 1345
VELOCIMAB - Antibody Preparations - REGENERON PHARMACEUTICALS, INC.; *pg.* 1588, *pg.* 1345
VELOCIMOUSE - Genetic Engineering Services - REGENERON PHARMACEUTICALS, INC.; *pg.* 1588, *pg.* 1345
VELOCITI - Digital Signal Processor & Integrated Circuits - TEXAS INSTRUMENTS INCORPORATED; *pg.* 679, *pg.* 1688
VELOCITY - Semiconductor Batch-Immersion System - AKRION, INC.; *pg.* 1311, *pg.* 1513
VELOCITY - Sport Optical Product - BUSHNELL OUTDOOR PRODUCTS, INC.; *pg.* 1403, *pg.* 718
VELOCITY - Fan - CRAFTMADE INTERNATIONAL, INC.; *pg.* 1295, *pg.* 1670
VELOCITY - Orthopedic Product - DJO INCORPORATED; *pg.* 1524, *pg.* 302
VELOCITY - Automobile Races - DOVER MOTORSPORTS, INC.; *pg.* 545, *pg.* 387
VELOCITY - Printing Products - ELECTRONICS FOR IMAGING, INC.; *pg.* 390, *pg.* 88
VELOCITY - Software - EMC CORPORATION; *pg.* 391, *pg.* 825
VELOCITY - Software - INFORMATICA CORPORATION; *pg.* 414, *pg.* 190
VELOCITY - Paper - INTERNATIONAL PAPER COMPANY; *pg.* 1460, *pg.* 1644
VELOCITY - Urinalysis Workstation - IRIS INTERNATIONAL, INC.; *pg.* 1547, *pg.* 64
VELOCITY - Satellite Communication Product - KVH INDUSTRIES INC; *pg.* 650, *pg.* 1602
VELOCITY - Car Part Accessory - PRO-LINE, INC.; *pg.* 966, *pg.* 45
VELOCITY - Software - SMITH INTERNATIONAL, INC.; *pg.* 1377, *pg.* 1715
VELOCITY ACCELERATION - Satellite Communications Software - KVH INDUSTRIES INC; *pg.* 650, *pg.* 1602
VELOCITY ENGINE - Vector Processing Unit - APPLE INC.; *pg.* 350, *pg.* 73
VELOCITY POWERED BY CN - Non Downloadable Software - CANADIAN NATIONAL RAILWAY COMPANY; *pg.* 1902, *pg.* 1953
VELOCITY SPIKE DISTANCE - Footwear - SAUCONY, INC.; *pg.* 1818, *pg.* 828
VELOCITY-T - Tabletop Image Reader - FUJIFILM MEDICAL SYSTEMS USA, INC.; *pg.* 1531, *pg.* 374
VELOCITY-U - Upright Image Reader - FUJIFILM MEDICAL SYSTEMS USA, INC.; *pg.* 1531, *pg.* 374
VELOMETER - Thermal Anemometer - TSI INCORPORATED; *pg.* 1432, *pg.* 965
VELOMETER JR. - Measurement Device - TSI INCORPORATED; *pg.* 1432, *pg.* 965
VELOS - Home Appliance Product - WHIRLPOOL CORPORATION; *pg.* 62, *pg.* 872
VELOUR - Alkyd enamel - AKZONOBEL DECORATIVE PAINTS U.S.; *pg.* 1439, *pg.* 1474
VELPAR - Herbicide - E.I. DU PONT DE NEMOURS & COMPANY; *pg.* 1159, *pg.* 390
VELV-IT - Wood Stain - JONES-BLAIR COMPANY; *pg.* 1443, *pg.* 1682
VELVA-GLO - Enamel - JONES-BLAIR COMPANY; *pg.* 1443, *pg.* 1682
VELVA-GRAIN - Wood Stain - JONES-BLAIR COMPANY; *pg.* 1443, *pg.* 1682
VELVAPLAST - Refractory Coating - ASHLAND INC.; *pg.* 972, *pg.* 726
VELVEETA - Cheese Spreads - THE KRAFT HEINZ COMPANY; *pg.* 870, *pg.* 1577
VELVET - Semisweet Chocolate - CARGILL LIMITED; *pg.* 1475, *pg.* 1914
VELVET - Bathroom Tissue & Towel - ORCHIDS PAPER PRODUCTS COMPANY; *pg.* 1465, *pg.* 1488
VELVET - Footwear - P.W. MINOR & SON, INC.; *pg.* 1816, *pg.* 1140
VELVET DRIVE - Transmissions - REGAL BELOIT CORPORATION; *pg.* 106, *pg.* 1854
VELVET-RIDE - Shackle - LORD CORPORATION; *pg.* 1357, *pg.* 1360
VELVET TOUCH - Medical Product - UTAH MEDICAL PRODUCTS, INC.; *pg.* 1605, *pg.* 1752
VELVETEX - Amphoteric Betaine - HENKEL CORPORATION; *pg.* 1165, *pg.* 1535
VELVETOP - Icing And Filling - DAWN FOOD PRODUCTS, INC.; *pg.* 1018, *pg.* 893
VELVEX - Patterned Glass - AGC GLASS NORTH AMERICA, INC.; *pg.* 65, *pg.* 482
VENACURE EVLT - Varicose Vein Therapy - ANGIODYNAMICS, INC.; *pg.* 1495, *pg.* 1173
VENDARE MEDIA - Software - IDEALAB, INC.; *pg.* 1258, *pg.* 180
VENDETTA - Agricultural Product - WILBUR-ELLIS COMPANY; *pg.* 1185, *pg.* 234
VENDINGMISER - Software - USA TECHNOLOGIES, INC.; *pg.* 815, *pg.* 1550
VENDMAX - Software - CRANE CO.; *pg.* 227, *pg.* 373
VENDOME - Jewelry - AMERICAN BILTRITE INC.; *pg.* 1878, *pg.* 856
VENDOME - Lounge Chairs - BERNHARDT DESIGN; *pg.* 918, *pg.* 1381
VENDOR MANAGED INVENTORY - Software - JDA SOFTWARE GROUP, INC.; *pg.* 423, *pg.* 22
VENECIA - Furniture - ASHLEY FURNITURE INDUSTRIES, INC.; *pg.* 914, *pg.* 1852
VENECIN - Footwear - STEVEN MADDEN, LTD.; *pg.* 1819, *pg.* 1176
VENEER - Carpet - INTERFACE, INC.; *pg.* 695, *pg.* 512
VENEER MODEL B - Screen - DA-LITE SCREEN COMPANY; *pg.* 632, *pg.* 698
VENETIAN - Mirror - ETHAN ALLEN INTERIORS INC.; *pg.* 924, *pg.* 343
VENEZIA - Apparel - ASCENA RETAIL GROUP, INC.; *pg.* 18, *pg.* 1081
VENEZIA - Bike - MARIN BIKES; *pg.* 1708, *pg.* 168
VENEZIA - Ceramic, Glass, Stone Tiles & Slabs - WALKER & ZANGER, INC.; *pg.* 119, *pg.* 281
VENI-GARD - Medical Equipment - CONMED CORPORATION; *pg.* 1517, *pg.* 1347
VENICARE - Medical Device - HOSPIRA, INC.; *pg.* 1542, *pg.* 623
VENICE - Carpet - BEAULIEU GROUP, LLC; *pg.* 917, *pg.* 529
VENICE - Furniture Collection - CENTURY FURNITURE INDUSTRIES; *pg.* 920, *pg.* 1377
THE VENICE - Home Floor Plan - JACOBSEN MANUFACTURING, INC.; *pg.* 1098, *pg.* 460
VENICE - Italian Ice - TURKEY HILL DAIRY, INC.; *pg.* 902, *pg.* 1522
VENICE RICHES - Game - WMS INDUSTRIES INC.; *pg.* 593, *pg.* 666
VENICE VNZ - Footwear - K-SWISS; *pg.* 1837, *pg.* 306
VENICIA - Bath & Plumbing Product - JACUZZI BRANDS CORPORATION; *pg.* 554, *pg.* 65
VENICIA - Furniture - STANLEY FURNITURE CO., INC.; *pg.* 943, *pg.* 1379
VENISE - Food Product - PEPPERIDGE FARM, INC.; *pg.* 888, *pg.* 363
VENIX - Nutritional Supplement - NU SKIN ENTERPRISES, INC.; *pg.* 518, *pg.* 1755
VENMAT - Waste Water Treatment - DOW CHEMICAL; *pg.* 1156, *pg.* 1563
VENOFER - Iron Sucrose Injection - LUITPOLD PHARMACEUTICALS, INC.; *pg* 1557, *pg.* 1342
VENOM - Non-Carbonated Soft Drink - DR PEPPER SNAPPLE GROUP, INC.; *pg.* 250, *pg.* 1729
VENOM GT - Skate - ROLLER DERBY SKATE CORP.; *pg.* 966, *pg.* 630
VENPURE - Granule - DOW CHEMICAL; *pg.* 1156, *pg.* 1563
VENT DOWELS - Press Fit Fastener - DRIV-LOK, INC.; *pg.* 1046, *pg.* 662
VENT FOG/IMP - Oil Mist Filter - TRION, INC.; *pg.* 682, *pg.* 1390
VENTA-LATORS - Side Window Deflectors - LUND INTERNATIONAL, INC.; *pg.* 211, *pg.* 526
VENTABELT - Process Belt - ALBANY INTERNATIONAL CORP.; *pg.* 691, *pg.* 1038
VENTAIRE - Battery - ENERGIZER HOLDINGS, INC.; *pg.* 637, *pg.* 996
VENTANAS - Community Name - WCI COMMUNITIES, INC.; *pg.* 1118, *pg.* 414
VENTED ARRAY - Eyewear - OAKLEY, INC.; *pg.* 1840, *pg.* 86
VENTFAB - Ventilation Ducting - FLEXFAB HORIZONS INTERNATIONAL, LLC; *pg.* 1072, *pg.* 891
VENTGARD - Automatic Exhaust Air Dampers - YOUNG REGULATOR COMPANY; *pg.* 1078, *pg.* 1478
VENTIAL - Medical Device - RESMED INC.; *pg.* 1589, *pg.* 207
VENTIAN GOLD & RIVER CLUBS - Community Name - WCI COMMUNITIES, INC.; *pg.* 1118, *pg.* 414
VENTITE - Valve - MAXON CORPORATION; *pg.* 1359, *pg.* 695
VENTRA - Catheter - SMITHS MEDICAL MD, INC.; *pg.* 1594, *pg.* 963
VENTRILOQUIST - Shoe - AEROGROUP INTERNATIONAL, INC.; *pg.* 1803, *pg.* 1055
VENTRIX - Medical Device - INTEGRA LIFESCIENCES HOLDINGS CORPORATION; *pg.* 1545, *pg.* 1109
VENTROL - Levine Tube - MEDTRONIC; *pg.* 1563, *pg.* 183
VENTSANKE - Cleaning Laundry Dryer - MAC-GRAY CORPORATION; *pg.* 58, *pg.* 852
VENTSHADE - Truck Window Rain Deflectors - LUND INTERNATIONAL, INC.; *pg.* 211, *pg.* 526
VENTSORB - Carbon Adsorption System - CALGON CARBON CORPORATION; *pg.* 1151, *pg.* 1574
VENTSURE - Roofing System - OWENS CORNING; *pg.* 102, *pg.* 1476
VENTURA - Connector - AMPHENOL CORPORATION; *pg.* 616, *pg.* 381
VENTURA - Table - BLATT BOWLING & BILLIARD CORP.; *pg.* 1827, *pg.* 1203
VENTURA - Bicycles - G. JOANNOU CYCLE CO. INC.; *pg.* 1707, *pg.* 1098
VENTURA - Tire And Rubber Product - THE GOODYEAR TIRE & RUBBER COMPANY; *pg.* 1883, *pg.* 1401
VENTURA - Bathroom Fan - HUNTER FAN COMPANY; *pg.* 57, *pg.* 1631
VENTURA - Pan Coating - VENTURA FOODS, LLC; *pg.* 908, *pg.* 49
VENTURA COMP - Bicycle - G. JOANNOU CYCLE CO. INC.; *pg.* 1707, *pg.* 1098
VENTURA COUNTRY STAR - Newspaper - THE E.W. SCRIPPS COMPANY; *pg.* 1639, *pg.* 1412
VENTURA COUNTY STAR - Newspaper - THE E.W. SCRIPPS COMPANY; *pg.* 1639, *pg.* 1412
VENTURA SPORT - Bicycle - G. JOANNOU CYCLE CO. INC.; *pg.* 1707, *pg.* 1098
VENTURCOM - Software - INTERVALZERO INC.; *pg.* 420,

First page reference indicates Business Class Edition
Second page reference indicates Geographic Edition

pg. 851
VENTURE - Furniture - ASHLEY FURNITURE INDUSTRIES, INC.; *pg.* 914, *pg.* 1852
VENTURE - Compressor Unit - INVACARE CORPORATION; *pg.* 1546, *pg.* 1451
VENTURE - Truck Cover - PENDA CORPORATION; *pg.* 214, *pg.* 1887
VENTURE - Hearing Instrument - SEMTECH CORPORATION GENNUM PRODUCTS; *pg.* 671, *pg.* 1919
VENTURE - Wire Control Catheter - ST. JUDE MEDICAL, INC.; *pg.* 1596, *pg.* 963
VENTURE - Wireless Control Product - UNIVERSAL ELECTRONICS, INC.; *pg.* 683, *pg.* 262
VENTURE VISION - Human Resource & Recruitment Multimedia Software - LOCKHEED MARTIN CORPORATION; *pg.* 229, *pg.* 762
VENTURES - Investment Vehicle - ALPHABET INC.; *pg.* 347, *pg.* 153
VENTUREXPERT - Software - THOMSON REUTERS CORPORATION; *pg.* 1693, *pg.* 1944
VENTURI - 4 Week Stop Smoking System - VENTURI, INC.; *pg.* 1606, *pg.* 910
VENTVISOR - Side Window Deflector - LUND INTERNATIONAL, INC.; *pg.* 211, *pg.* 526
VENUE - Fabric - NEMSCHOFF, INC.; *pg.* 936, *pg.* 1890
VENUS - Laser System - AMERICAN MEDICAL SYSTEMS, INC.; *pg.* 1399, *pg.* 238
VENUS - Furniture - AMISCO INDUSTRIES LTD.; *pg.* 913, *pg.* 1958
VENUS - Saloon - ARK RESTAURANTS CORP.; *pg.* 1715, *pg.* 1196
VENUS - Video Product - DAKTRONICS, INC.; *pg.* 633, *pg.* 1624
VENUS - Foam Product - FXI; *pg.* 1163, *pg.* 1552
VENUS - Blade And Razor - THE GILLETTE COMPANY; *pg.* 509, *pg.* 795
VENUS - Routing Swticher - GRASS VALLEY, INC.; *pg.* 641, *pg.* 164
VENUS - Footwear - PHOENIX FOOTWEAR GROUP, INC.; *pg.* 1815, *pg.* 60
VENUS 2L - Women's Specific Hydration Pack - JANSPORT; *pg.* 1837, *pg.* 38
VENUS DIVINE - Blade & Razor - THE GILLETTE COMPANY; *pg.* 509, *pg.* 795
VENUS EMBRACE - Razor - THE GILLETTE COMPANY; *pg.* 509, *pg.* 795
VENUS-I - YAG Laser System - AMERICAN MEDICAL SYSTEMS, INC.; *pg.* 1399, *pg.* 238
VENUS-I - Medical Laser System - IRIDEX CORPORATION; *pg.* 648, *pg.* 160
VENZA - Sports Utility Vehicle - TOYOTA MOTOR NORTH AMERICA, INC.; *pg.* 192, *pg.* 1303
VEOVA - Chemical Product - HEXION; *pg.* 1166, *pg.* 1440
VEPRO - Hydraulic Equipment - IDEX CORPORATION; *pg.* 1347, *pg.* 623
VEPTR - Medical Device - DEPUY SYNTHES; *pg.* 1523, *pg.* 1593
VERA - Software - SYNOPSYS, INC.; *pg.* 480, *pg.* 162
VERA BRADLEY - Purses & Accessories - VERA BRADLEY, INC.; *pg.* 15, *pg.* 697
VERA WANG - Bridal Dresses & Accessories - VERA WANG BRIDAL HOUSE LTD.; *pg.* 34, *pg.* 1309
VERACODE - Universal Capture Bead Sets - ILLUMINA, INC.; *pg.* 412, *pg.* 203
VERACRUZ - Bath Product - KOHLER CO.; *pg.* 91, *pg.* 1862
VERAFLEX - Grille - SHURE INCORPORATED; *pg.* 672, *pg.* 638
VERANDA - Magazine - THE HEARST CORPORATION; *pg.* 1649, *pg.* 1239
VERANDA - Medical Equipment - INVACARE CORPORATION; *pg.* 1546, *pg.* 1451
VERANDA - Fabric - NEMSCHOFF, INC.; *pg.* 936, *pg.* 1890
VERANDAH BREEZE - Ceiling Fan - WESTINGHOUSE LIGHTING CORPORATION; *pg.* 687, *pg.* 1571
VERAQUIS - Pharmaceutical Preparation - PFIZER INC.; *pg.* 1581, *pg.* 1278
VERASEM - 3D Metrology SEM System - APPLIED MATERIALS, INC.; *pg.* 618, *pg.* 264
VERASMART - Web-Based Modular Solutions - CALERO SOFTWARE, LLC; *pg.* 368, *pg.* 1333
VERASTREAM - Software - ATTACHMATE CORPORATION; *pg.* 356, *pg.* 1833
VERATAG - Healthcare Product - MONOGRAM BIOSCIENCES, INC.; *pg.* 1569, *pg.* 280
VERATOX - Food Safety Product - NEOGEN CORPORATION; *pg.* 883, *pg.* 896
VERATTI - Safety & Protective Equipment - ENCON SAFETY PRODUCTS; *pg.* 1334, *pg.* 1705
VERDANT - Fabric - NEMSCHOFF, INC.; *pg.* 936, *pg.* 1890
VERDE PEACH MIST - Antioxidant Tea - CELESTIAL SEASONINGS, INC.; *pg.* 846, *pg.* 310
VERDI - Laser & Laser System - COHERENT, INC.; *pg.* 1406, *pg.* 265
VERDI - Flatware - ONEIDA LTD; *pg.* 1129, *pg.* 1318
VERDICT - Diagnostic Product - MEDTOX SCIENTIFIC, INC.; *pg.* 1422, *pg.* 962
VERDISEAL - Roofing Membrane - THE DOW CHEMICAL COMPANY; *pg.* 1157, *pg.* 898
VERDOX - Fragrance Ingredient - INTERNATIONAL FLAVORS & FRAGRANCES INC.; *pg.* 512, *pg.* 1244
VERGE - Multi-purpose Seating - STEELCASE INC.; *pg.* 475, *pg.* 889
VERI-CAL - Blood Pressure Monitoring Accessories - UTAH MEDICAL PRODUCTS, INC.; *pg.* 1605, *pg.* 1752
VERI-CHEX - Electrical Test Instruments - ASSOCIATED RESEARCH INC.; *pg.* 1400, *pg.* 622
VERI-KLEEN - Cleaning Product - SLIDE PRODUCTS, INC.; *pg.* 1181, *pg.* 670
VERI TEST - Destructive Machine Software - AVERY WEIGH-TRONIX, INC.; *pg.* 1315, *pg.* 925
VERIBROM - Photographic Developer - EASTMAN KODAK COMPANY; *pg.* 1408, *pg.* 1333
VERICAP - Capsule Weighing System - MOCON, INC.; *pg.* 1363, *pg.* 940
VERICEL - Membrane Disc Filter - PALL CORPORATION; *pg.* 232, *pg.* 1323
VERICENTRE - Appliance Management Applications - VERIFONE SYSTEMS, INC.; *pg.* 487, *pg.* 251
VERICHIP - Miniaturized Radio Frequency Identification Device - POSITIVEID CORPORATION; *pg.* 665, *pg.* 422
VERICHROME - Photo Film - EASTMAN KODAK COMPANY; *pg.* 1408, *pg.* 1333
VERICOLOR - Photo Color Film, Chemicals - EASTMAN KODAK COMPANY; *pg.* 1408, *pg.* 1333
VERICOLOR - Color Verification & Identification System - X-RITE, INCORPORATED; *pg.* 1437, *pg.* 891
VERIF-EYE - Reflectance Reader - PRESSURE BIOSCIENCES, INC.; *pg.* 1586, *pg.* 844
VERIFAX - Photocopying Equipment - EASTMAN KODAK COMPANY; *pg.* 1408, *pg.* 1333
VERIFICATION PROBE - Software - BIO-RAD LABORATORIES, INC.; *pg.* 1504, *pg.* 101
VERIFIER - Boring Machine System - MCLAUGHLIN BORING SYSTEMS; *pg.* 1360, *pg.* 1617
THE VERIFIER - Central Station Alarm Verification System - VICON INDUSTRIES, INC.; *pg.* 685, *pg.* 1166
VERIFIER VISION - Pipe & Cable Locator - MCLAUGHLIN BORING SYSTEMS; *pg.* 1360, *pg.* 1617
VERIFORM - Servo Device - PRECITECH, INC.; *pg.* 1427, *pg.* 1035
VERIFY - Software - EVOLVING SYSTEMS, INC.; *pg.* 395, *pg.* 326
VERIFY - Biological Indicator - STERIS CORPORATION; *pg.* 1597, *pg.* 1464
VERIGOOD - Paper & Nonwoven Material - FIBERMARK INC.; *pg.* 1457, *pg.* 1764
VERIKEY - Locker - AMERICAN LOCKER GROUP INCORPORATED; *pg.* 1041, *pg.* 1674
VERIMOVE - Software - PITNEY BOWES INC.; *pg.* 454, *pg.* 376
VERIPATH - Peripheral Guide Wire - ABBOTT LABORATORIES; *pg.* 1484, *pg.* 551
VERIPHY - Results Management Solution - NUANCE COMMUNICATIONS, INC.; *pg.* 447, *pg.* 806
VERIPHY - Cable Diagnostics - VITESSE SEMICONDUCTOR CORPORATION; *pg.* 686, *pg.* 57
VERIPORT - Software - EVOLVING SYSTEMS, INC.; *pg.* 395, *pg.* 326
VERISHIELD - Security Architecture - VERIFONE SYSTEMS, INC.; *pg.* 487, *pg.* 251
VERISIGN & DESIGN - Telecommunication Product - VERISIGN, INC.; *pg.* 488, *pg.* 1799
VERISIGN DESIGN - Telecommunication Product - VERISIGN, INC.; *pg.* 488, *pg.* 1799
VERISIGN IDEFENSE SECURITY - Online Transaction Security Product - VERISIGN, INC.; *pg.* 488, *pg.* 1799
VERISIGN IDENTITY PROTECTION - Internet Site Security Product - VERISIGN, INC.; *pg.* 488, *pg.* 1799
VERISIGN SECURED DESIGN - Telecommunication Product - VERISIGN, INC.; *pg.* 488, *pg.* 1799
VERISIGN SECURED SEAL - Internet Site Security Product - VERISIGN, INC.; *pg.* 488, *pg.* 1799
VERISIGN SSL CETIFICATES - Internet Site Security Product - VERISIGN, INC.; *pg.* 488, *pg.* 1799
VERISMO - Coffee Pods - STARBUCKS CORPORATION; *pg.* 897, *pg.* 1840
VERISURE - Pharmaceutical Container System - WEST PHARMACEUTICAL SERVICES, INC.; *pg.* 1472, *pg.* 1532
VERITAS - Software - SYMANTEC CORPORATION; *pg.* 478, *pg.* 161
VERITAS DATA CENTER FOUNDATION - Software - SYMANTEC CORPORATION; *pg.* 478, *pg.* 161
VERITAS SERVER FOUNDATION - Software - SYMANTEC CORPORATION; *pg.* 478, *pg.* 161
VERITAS STORAGE FOUNDATION - Software - SYMANTEC CORPORATION; *pg.* 478, *pg.* 161
VERITEST - Software - LIONBRIDGE TECHNOLOGIES INC.; *pg.* 428, *pg.* 851
VERITHERM - Paper Products - BOISE CASCADE HOLDINGS, L.L.C.; *pg.* 1453, *pg.* 546
VERITY - Kitchen Product - KOHLER CO.; *pg.* 91, *pg.* 1862
VERITY - Pacemakers - ST. JUDE MEDICAL, INC.; *pg.* 1596, *pg.* 963
VERITY RECORDS - Gospel Music Focused Record Label - SONY MUSIC ENTERTAINMENT; *pg.* 309, *pg.* 1294
VERITYSEM - Metrology System - APPLIED MATERIALS, INC.; *pg.* 618, *pg.* 264
VERIWISE - Fleet Tracking & Management System - I.D. SYSTEMS, INC.; *pg.* 643, *pg.* 1134
VERIX - Automation Equipment - VERIFONE SYSTEMS, INC.; *pg.* 487, *pg.* 251
VERIZON - Wireline Communications - VERIZON COMMUNICATIONS INC.; *pg.* 1875, *pg.* 1309
VERIZON FIVE CENTS PLAN - Communication Service - VERIZON COMMUNICATIONS INC.; *pg.* 1875, *pg.* 1309
VERIZON FREEDOM - Calling Plan - VERIZON COMMUNICATIONS INC.; *pg.* 1875, *pg.* 1309
VERIZON WIRELESS - Wireless Communications - VERIZON COMMUNICATIONS INC.; *pg.* 1875, *pg.* 1309
VERMATAINER - Bulk Container - GREIF INC.; *pg.* 1459, *pg.* 1447
VERMICULITE - Insulation Product - ALPHA ASSOCIATES, INC.; *pg.* 691, *pg.* 1078
VERMONT - Tools - KENNAMETAL INC.; *pg.* 1052, *pg.* 1547
VERMONT - Fabric - NEMSCHOFF, INC.; *pg.* 936, *pg.* 1890
VERMONT BEAR-GRAM - Teddy Bear - THE VERMONT TEDDY BEAR COMPANY; *pg.* 969, *pg.* 1767
VERMONT COUNTRY BLEND - Coffee - KEURIG GREEN MOUNTAIN, INC.; *pg.* 868, *pg.* 1768
THE VERMONT COUNTRY STORE - Catalog - VERMONT COUNTRY STORE, INC.; *pg.* 1789, *pg.* 1766
VERMONT MAID - Syrup - B&G FOODS, INC.; *pg.* 838, *pg.* 1102
VERMONT MAPLE SYRUP - Sausage - JOHNSONVILLE SAUSAGE, LLC; *pg.* 867, *pg.* 1894
VERMONT MATTERS - Slogan - MERCHANTS BANCSHARES, INC.; *pg.* 782, *pg.* 1768
VERMONT PURE - Bottled Water - CRYSTAL ROCK HOLDINGS, INC.; *pg.* 248, *pg.* 382
THE VERMONT TEDDY BEAR COMPANY - Stuffed Toys - THE VERMONT TEDDY BEAR COMPANY; *pg.* 969, *pg.* 1767
VERMOUTH - Apparel - VANS, INC.; *pg.* 1821, *pg.* 76
VERMOX - Healthcare Product - JOHNSON & JOHNSON; *pg.* 1549, *pg.* 1091
VERNAFLO - Flow Control - VERNAY LABORATORIES, INC.; *pg.* 1891, *pg.* 1482
VERNON SAWYER - Trucking Transportation Service - KLLM TRANSPORT SERVICES, INC.; *pg.* 1914, *pg.* 971
VERO BEACH PRESS JOURNAL - Newspaper - THE E.W. SCRIPPS COMPANY; *pg.* 1639, *pg.* 1412
VERONA - Furniture - ASHLEY FURNITURE INDUSTRIES, INC.; *pg.* 914, *pg.* 1852
VERONA - Furniture - BUSH INDUSTRIES INC.; *pg.* 919, *pg.* 1170
VERONA - Rug - COURISTAN INC.; *pg.* 921, *pg.* 1067
VERONA - Bike - MARIN BIKES; *pg.* 1708, *pg.* 168
VERONA - Cookies - PEPPERIDGE FARM, INC.; *pg.* 888, *pg.* 363
VERONA - Ceiling Fan - WESTINGHOUSE LIGHTING CORPORATION; *pg.* 687, *pg.* 1571
VERONIQUE - Furniture - HOOKER FURNITURE CORPORATION; *pg.* 928, *pg.* 1788
VERRO - Pool Cleaning Robot - IROBOT CORP.; *pg.* 1418, *pg.* 785

VERS-A-STRIPER - Display - AERVOE INDUSTRIES INCORPORATED; *pg.* 1439, *pg.* 1021
VERS-GRIP - Bevel Product - GLEASON CORPORATION; *pg.* 1340, *pg.* 1335
VERS L'UNIVERS - Systems Integration & Aeronautics - LOCKHEED MARTIN CORPORATION; *pg.* 229, *pg.* 762
VERSA - Extruder - DAVIS-STANDARD LLC; *pg.* 1328, *pg.* 368
VERSA-CAL - Thermocouple Calibrators - MEGGER INC.; *pg.* 1422, *pg.* 1557
VERSA-DECK - Building Products - BOISE CASCADE HOLDINGS, L.L.C.; *pg.* 1453, *pg.* 546
VERSA-DOME - Pump Product - IDEX CORPORATION; *pg.* 1347, *pg.* 623
VERSA-GLO - Interior & Exterior Latex Semi-Gloss Paint - DUNN-EDWARDS CORPORATION; *pg.* 1442, *pg.* 129
VERSA-GLOSS - Interior & Exterior Latex Gloss Paint - DUNN-EDWARDS CORPORATION; *pg.* 1442, *pg.* 129
VERSA-HOOD - Respirator - MINE SAFETY APPLIANCES COMPANY; *pg.* 1361, *pg.* 1525
VERSA-LAM - Wood Product - BOISE CASCADE HOLDINGS, L.L.C.; *pg.* 1453, *pg.* 546
VERSA-LAM PLUS - Laminated Veneer Lumber Beams - BOISE CASCADE HOLDINGS, L.L.C.; *pg.* 1453, *pg.* 546
VERSA-LITE - Lighting Product - HD ELECTRIC COMPANY; *pg.* 1299, *pg.* 666
VERSA-MATIC - Pump Product - IDEX CORPORATION; *pg.* 1347, *pg.* 623
VERSA-MOLE - Drilling Tool - MCLAUGHLIN BORING SYSTEMS; *pg.* 1360, *pg.* 1617
VERSA PIVOT - Roof & Wall Hinges - KAWNEER COMPANY, INC.; *pg.* 90, *pg.* 537
VERSA-RIM - Building Products - BOISE CASCADE HOLDINGS, L.L.C.; *pg.* 1453, *pg.* 546
VERSA-RIM 98 - Rimboard - BOISE CASCADE HOLDINGS, L.L.C.; *pg.* 1453, *pg.* 546
VERSA-RIM PLUS - Building Products - BOISE CASCADE HOLDINGS, L.L.C.; *pg.* 1453, *pg.* 546
VERSA-RUGGED - Pump Product - IDEX CORPORATION; *pg.* 1347, *pg.* 623
VERSA-SENSE - Pump Product - IDEX CORPORATION; *pg.* 1347, *pg.* 623
VERSA-SPRAY - Gun - NORDSON CORPORATION; *pg.* 1365, *pg.* 1480
VERSA-STRAND - Building Products - BOISE CASCADE HOLDINGS, L.L.C.; *pg.* 1453, *pg.* 546
VERSA-STUD - Laminated Veneer Lumber - BOISE CASCADE HOLDINGS, L.L.C.; *pg.* 1453, *pg.* 546
VERSA-TECH - Wheel - HAMILTON CASTER & MFG. CO.; *pg.* 206, *pg.* 1454
VERSA-TINT - Tinting Colors - JONES-BLAIR COMPANY; *pg.* 1443, *pg.* 1682
VERSA-TOGGLE - Plastic Screw Anchor - MKT FASTENING, LLC; *pg.* 1056, *pg.* 34
VERSA-TUFF - Pump Product - IDEX CORPORATION; *pg.* 1347, *pg.* 623
VERSA VAULT - Handgun Vault - SMITH & WESSON HOLDING CORPORATION; *pg.* 1845, *pg.* 846
VERSA WRAP II - Plastics Product - AEP INDUSTRIES INC.; *pg.* 1878, *pg.* 1085
VERSABACS - Carpet Backings - THE DOW CHEMICAL COMPANY; *pg.* 1157, *pg.* 898
VERSABLADE - Electronic Components - MOLEX INCORPORATED; *pg.* 655, *pg.* 628
VERSABLOCK - Glass & Ceramic Material - CORNING INCORPORATED; *pg.* 1122, *pg.* 1154
VERSABLUE - Adhesive Melter - NORDSON CORPORATION; *pg.* 1365, *pg.* 1480
VERSACACHE - Caching System - CAMBEX CORPORATION; *pg.* 368, *pg.* 844
VERSACAP - Capsule - PALL CORPORATION; *pg.* 232, *pg.* 1323
VERSACAT - Ethernet Product - VITESSE SEMICONDUCTOR CORPORATION; *pg.* 686, *pg.* 57
VERSACLAD - Varnish - MOHAWK FINISHING PRODUCTS, INC.; *pg.* 1173, *pg.* 1378
VERSACOLOR - Flooring System - THE VALSPAR CORPORATION; *pg.* 1449, *pg.* 945
VERSACOR - Coating System - CENTRIA, INC.; *pg.* 74, *pg.* 1554
VERSADIL - Diluent - NEVILLE CHEMICAL COMPANY; *pg.* 1174, *pg.* 1578
VERSADOC - Software - BIO-RAD LABORATORIES, INC.; *pg.* 1504, *pg.* 101
VERSADRUM - Melters - NORDSON CORPORATION; *pg.* 1365, *pg.* 1480
VERSADYME - Dimerized Fatty Acids - HENKEL CORPORATION; *pg.* 1165, *pg.* 1535
VERSAFLAT - Exterior Non-Acrylic Flat Paint - DUNN-EDWARDS CORPORATION; *pg.* 1442, *pg.* 129
VERSAFLEX - Leather Sneakers - REEBOK INTERNATIONAL LTD.; *pg.* 1817, *pg.* 811
VERSAFLO - Water Separation Product - CAMERON INTERNATIONAL; *pg.* 1151, *pg.* 1702
VERSAFLO - Photo Chemicals - EASTMAN KODAK COMPANY; *pg.* 1408, *pg.* 1333
VERSAFLUOR - Software - BIO-RAD LABORATORIES, INC.; *pg.* 1504, *pg.* 101
VERSAFOLD - Partition - MITY ENTERPRISES, INC.; *pg.* 935, *pg.* 1753
VERSAFORM - Microfilming Apparatus - EASTMAN KODAK COMPANY; *pg.* 1408, *pg.* 1333
VERSAGLAZE - Glass Applications - KAWNEER COMPANY, INC.; *pg.* 90, *pg.* 537
VERSAILLES - Furniture - HOOKER FURNITURE CORPORATION; *pg.* 928, *pg.* 1788
VERSAILLES - Video Game - INTERNATIONAL GAME TECHNOLOGY; *pg.* 957, *pg.* 1024
VERSAILLES - Fabric - NEMSCHOFF, INC.; *pg.* 936, *pg.* 1890
VERSAKRIMP - Electronic Components - MOLEX INCORPORATED; *pg.* 655, *pg.* 628
VERSALAC - Varnish - MOHAWK FINISHING PRODUCTS, INC.; *pg.* 1173, *pg.* 1378
VERSALITE - Photographic Film & Papers - EASTMAN KODAK COMPANY; *pg.* 1408, *pg.* 1333
VERSALITE - Vehicle Safety System - GROTE INDUSTRIES, INC.; *pg.* 206, *pg.* 693
VERSALITE - Shotshell Wads - HORNADY MANUFACTURING COMPANY; *pg.* 1836, *pg.* 1010
VERSALITE - Stage & Riser - WENGER CORPORATION; *pg.* 1307, *pg.* 952
VERSALOK - Mattress - RESTONIC MATTRESS CORPORATION; *pg.* 941, *pg.* 553
VERSALON - Polyamide Hot Melt Adhesive Resins - HENKEL CORPORATION; *pg.* 1165, *pg.* 1535
VERSAMAG - Salt - DOW CHEMICAL; *pg.* 1156, *pg.* 1563
VERSAMAT - Film Processor - EASTMAN KODAK COMPANY; *pg.* 1408, *pg.* 1333
VERSAMATIC - Carpet Vacuum - HILLYARD, INC.; *pg.* 331, *pg.* 990
VERSAMAX - Microplate Reader - MOLECULAR DEVICES CORPORATION; *pg.* 1568, *pg.* 287
VERSAMET - Metallograph - UNITRON INC.; *pg.* 1433, *pg.* 1153
VERSAMID - Polyamide Resins - HENKEL CORPORATION; *pg.* 1165, *pg.* 1535
VERSAMODE - Medical Product - GF HEALTH PRODUCTS, INC.; *pg.* 1535, *pg.* 508
VERSAMOUNT - Access Hatch - THE BILCO COMPANY; *pg.* 70, *pg.* 383
VERSAMOUNT - Dry Mounting Tissue - EASTMAN KODAK COMPANY; *pg.* 1408, *pg.* 1333
VERSANT - Data Management Software - ACTIAN CORPORATION; *pg.* 342, *pg.* 188
VERSAPACKER - Packaging Films & Equipment - SEALED AIR CORPORATION; *pg.* 1468, *pg.* 1058
VERSAPAIL - Bulk Melters - NORDSON CORPORATION; *pg.* 1365, *pg.* 1480
VERSAPANEL - Metal Building Product - CENTRIA, INC.; *pg.* 74, *pg.* 1554
VERSAPOR - Membrane Disc Filter - PALL CORPORATION; *pg.* 232, *pg.* 1323
VERSAPOT - Calibrators/Potentiometers - MEGGER INC.; *pg.* 1422, *pg.* 1557
VERSAPRIME - High Performance Primer - DUNN-EDWARDS CORPORATION; *pg.* 1442, *pg.* 129
VERSAPRO - Massage Product - RELAX THE BACK CORPORATION; *pg.* 940, *pg.* 120
VERSAPROBE - Meter Reading Device - BADGER METER, INC.; *pg.* 1401, *pg.* 1873
VERSAPULSE POWERSUITE - Medical Device - BOSTON SCIENTIFIC CORPORATION; *pg.* 1508, *pg.* 831
VERSAREST - Fixture - FONAR CORPORATION; *pg.* 1413, *pg.* 1179
VERSARRAY - Software - BIO-RAD LABORATORIES, INC.; *pg.* 1504, *pg.* 101
VERSARRAY CHIPREADER - Software - BIO-RAD LABORATORIES, INC.; *pg.* 1504, *pg.* 101
VERSASATIN - Interior & Exterior Low Sheen Paint - DUNN-EDWARDS CORPORATION; *pg.* 1442, *pg.* 129
VERSASCOPE - Software - RUDOLPH TECHNOLOGIES, INC.; *pg.* 669, *pg.* 918
VERSASHIELD - Fiberglass Roofing Underlayment - GAF MATERIALS CORP.; *pg.* 83, *pg.* 1681
VERSASTAND - Instrument Enclosure System - THERMON AMERICAS INC.; *pg.* 1077, *pg.* 1744
VERSASTAT - Laser Delivery Device - AMERICAN MEDICAL SYSTEMS, INC.; *pg.* 1399, *pg.* 238
VERSASTAT I - Handpiece for Laserscope Aesthetic Lasers - AMERICAN MEDICAL SYSTEMS, INC.; *pg.* 1399, *pg.* 238
VERSASTYLE - Wheel - MAXION WHEELS; *pg.* 212, *pg.* 903
VERSATECH - Keyboard Tray - ALIMED, INC.; *pg.* 1490, *pg.* 816
VERSATENN - Digital Programmer - SPX THERMAL PRODUCT SOLUTIONS; *pg.* 1378, *pg.* 1555
VERSATHANE - Polyurethane Product - AIR PRODUCTS AND CHEMICALS, INC.; *pg.* 1145, *pg.* 1513
VERSATHERM - Heaters - CHROMALOX, INC.; *pg.* 1070, *pg.* 1574
VERSATILE - Cleaning Product - VON SCHRADER COMPANY; *pg.* 62, *pg.* 1890
VERSATIP - Multipurpose Tool Kit - DREMEL; *pg.* 1046, *pg.* 634
VERSATIX - Bi-metal Blade - THE L.S. STARRETT COMPANY; *pg.* 1421, *pg.* 783
VERSATOL - Screen - DA-LITE SCREEN COMPANY; *pg.* 632, *pg.* 698
VERSATOL - Photo Developer - EASTMAN KODAK COMPANY; *pg.* 1408, *pg.* 1333
VERSATONE - Photo Processing Chemicals - EASTMAN KODAK COMPANY; *pg.* 1408, *pg.* 1333
VERSATRANS - Chemical Product - PPG INDUSTRIES, INC.; *pg.* 1445, *pg.* 1579
VERSATRYME - Trimer Acid - HENKEL CORPORATION; *pg.* 1165, *pg.* 1535
VERSATUFF - Food Safety Instrument - COOPER-ATKINS CORPORATION; *pg.* 1407, *pg.* 355
VERSAVENT - Closure - ATLAS BOLT & SCREW COMPANY; *pg.* 1042, *pg.* 1403
VERSAVENT - Kitchen Appliance - VIKING RANGE CORPORATION; *pg.* 61, *pg.* 968
VERSAVIEW - Computer - ROCKWELL AUTOMATION, INC.; *pg.* 668, *pg.* 1880
VERSAVISION - Graphics Card - ADVANCED MICRO DEVICES, INC.; *pg.* 613, *pg.* 282
VERSAWALL - Metal Building Product - CENTRIA, INC.; *pg.* 74, *pg.* 1554
VERSAWALL - Interior & Exterior Latex Flat Enamel - DUNN-EDWARDS CORPORATION; *pg.* 1442, *pg.* 129
VERSE - Bike - ELECTRA BICYCLE COMPANY; *pg.* 1706, *pg.* 303
VERSE - Kitchen Product - KOHLER CO.; *pg.* 91, *pg.* 1862
VERSE - Fabric - NEMSCHOFF, INC.; *pg.* 936, *pg.* 1890
VERSED - Pharmaceutical Product - HOFFMANN-LA ROCHE INC.; *pg.* 1542, *pg.* 1099
VERSENATE - Chelating Agent - THE DOW CHEMICAL COMPANY; *pg.* 1157, *pg.* 898
VERSENE - Chelating Agent - THE DOW CHEMICAL COMPANY; *pg.* 1157, *pg.* 898
VERSENEX - Chelating Agent - THE DOW CHEMICAL COMPANY; *pg.* 1157, *pg.* 898
VERSENOL - Chelating Agent - THE DOW CHEMICAL COMPANY; *pg.* 1157, *pg.* 898
VERSICON - Hose - HBD INDUSTRIES, INC.; *pg.* 207, *pg.* 1449
VERSICOPY - Cut Size Copy Paper - NETWORK SERVICES COMPANY; *pg.* 1465, *pg.* 659
VERSIFEEDER - Vibrating Screw Feeder - VIBRA SCREW INC.; *pg.* 1387, *pg.* 1126
VERSIFLEX - Bridge Product - THE D.S. BROWN COMPANY; *pg.* 79, *pg.* 1468
VERSIFY - Chemical Product - THE DOW CHEMICAL COMPANY; *pg.* 1157, *pg.* 898
VERSIL-PAK - Barrier Wrap - DAUBERT INDUSTRIES, INC.; *pg.* 1155, *pg.* 561
VERSILOK - Adhesive - LORD CORPORATION; *pg.* 1357, *pg.* 1360
VERSION MANAGER - Software - SERENA SOFTWARE, INC.; *pg.* 468, *pg.* 192
VERSITRON - Hardness Tester - NEWAGE TESTING INSTRUMENTS, INC.; *pg.* 1058, *pg.* 1532
VERSIVA - Wound Care Product - CONVATEC LTD.; *pg.* 1518, *pg.* 1121

First page reference indicates Business Class Edition
Second page reference indicates Geographic Edition

VERSTAD - Footwear - K-SWISS; pg. 1837, pg. 306
VERSUS GORE-TEX - Medical Device - INTEGRA LIFESCIENCES HOLDINGS CORPORATION; pg. 1545, pg. 1109
VERSYS - Conductor Etch - LAM RESEARCH CORPORATION; pg. 1354, pg. 91
VERT-I-PAK - Air Conditioner - FRIEDRICH AIR CONDITIONING CO.; pg. 1072, pg. 1740
VERTA-FLAME - Burner - SELAS HEAT TECHNOLOGY COMPANY LLC; pg. 1076, pg. 1553
VERTA-LOCK - Load Restraining Ceiling System - UTILITY TRAILER MANUFACTURING COMPANY; pg. 1712, pg. 68
VERTAK - Bonding Technology - E.I. DU PONT DE NEMOURS & COMPANY; pg. 1159, pg. 390
VERTENEX - Fragrance Ingredient - INTERNATIONAL FLAVORS & FRAGRANCES INC.; pg. 512, pg. 1244
VERTEX - Seal Technology - E.I. DU PONT DE NEMOURS & COMPANY; pg. 1159, pg. 390
VERTEX - Photoluminescence Mapping System - NANOMETRICS INCORPORATED; pg. 1423, pg. 147
VERTEX - Fasteners - VERTEX DISTRIBUTION; pg. 1066, pg. 784
VERTEX 80V - Analytical Device - BRUKER CORPORATION; pg. 1511, pg. 788
VERTEX TELLER AUTOMATION SYSTEM - Host-Based Teller Automation System - JACK HENRY & ASSOCIATES, INC.; pg. 422, pg. 988
VERTI-G - Cuttings Dryer - M-I SWACO; pg. 980, pg. 1710
VERTICADE - Vertical Barricade - UNITED RENTALS, INC.; pg. 1386, pg. 350
VERTICAL MAPPER - Software - PITNEY BOWES SOFTWARE INC.; pg. 455, pg. 1346
VERTICAL MASTER - Vest - SIMMS FISHING PRODUCTS CORP.; pg. 1845, pg. 1008
VERTICAL SERVICE PROVIDER - Online Transaction Security Product - VERISIGN, INC.; pg. 488, pg. 1799
VERTICELL - Blinds & Shades - SPRINGS WINDOW FASHIONS LLC; pg. 943, pg. 1872
VERTICENT - Software - ASA INTERNATIONAL LTD.; pg. 353, pg. 1036
VERTIFLEX - Cover - DYNATECT MANUFACTURING INC.; pg. 1330, pg. 1883
VERTIGAGE - Industrial Instrumentation - SIEMENS PROCESS INDUSTRIES AND DRIVE; pg. 1376, pg. 1587
VERTIGO - Book & Magazine Publishing Imprint - DC COMICS, INC.; pg. 1633, pg. 1221
VERTIGO - Rod Hanging System - POWERS FASTENERS INC.; pg. 1059, pg. 1143
VERTIGO - Candy - THE TOPPS COMPANY, INC.; pg. 588, pg. 1302
VERTITRAK - Vertical Drilling Service - BAKER HUGHES INTEQ; pg. 1316, pg. 1700
VERTO - Consumer Graphics Card & Memory - PNY TECHNOLOGIES, INC.; pg. 455, pg. 1105
VERTOFIX - Fragrance Ingredient - INTERNATIONAL FLAVORS & FRAGRANCES INC.; pg. 512, pg. 1244
VERTREL - Cleaning Agent - E.I. DU PONT DE NEMOURS & COMPANY; pg. 1159, pg. 390
VERUS - Diagnostic Tool - SNAP-ON INCORPORATED; pg. 1062, pg. 1862
VERVE - Pens - A. T. CROSS COMPANY; pg. 339, pg. 1602
VERVE - Footwear - CAPEZIO BALLET MAKERS INC.; pg. 1805, pg. 1125
VERVE - Molecular Biology Product - THERMO FISHER SCIENTIFIC INC.; pg. 1602, pg. 61
VERVESS - Pharmaceutical Preparation - PFIZER INC.; pg. 1581, pg. 1278
VERY BERRY - Nutritional Product - NUTRACEUTICAL INTERNATIONAL CORPORATION; pg. 1576, pg. 1753
VERY VEGGIE - Lettuce - DOLE FRESH VEGETABLES; pg. 854, pg. 198
VERYFINE - Beverage - SUNNY DELIGHT BEVERAGES CO.; pg. 899, pg. 1426
VES - Health Care Product - HEALTH PRODUCTS CORPORATION; pg. 1540, pg. 1356
VESA - LCD Display - VIEWSONIC CORPORATION; pg. 489, pg. 303
VESANOID - Pharmaceutical Product - HOFFMANN-LA ROCHE INC.; pg. 1542, pg. 1099
VESDA - Detection Systems - ANSUL, INCORPORATED; pg. 1147, pg. 1869
VESDA - Air Sampling System - FIKE CORPORATION; pg. 1047, pg. 973
VESDA LASERPLUS - Fire & Smoke Detection System - FIKE CORPORATION; pg. 1047, pg. 973
VESPA - Fabric - NEMSCHOFF, INC.; pg. 936, pg. 1890
VESPA - Hat - WOODEN SHIPS OF HOBOKEN; pg. 35, pg. 1315
VESPEL - Custom-Formed Resin Parts & Shapes - E.I. DU PONT DE NEMOURS & COMPANY; pg. 1159, pg. 390
VESPER - Footwear - EASTLAND SHOE CORPORATION; pg. 1808, pg. 750
VESPHENE - Phenolic Disinfectant - STERIS CORPORATION; pg. 1597, pg. 1464
VESSELS - Bath Product - KOHLER CO.; pg. 91, pg. 1862
VESSELS BOTTICELLI - Bath Product - KOHLER CO.; pg. 91, pg. 1862
VESTA-SYDE - Instrument Decontamination System - STERIS CORPORATION; pg. 1597, pg. 1464
VESTED INTEREST - Banking Services - THE PNC FINANCIAL SERVICES GROUP, INC.; pg. 795, pg. 1579
VESTEK - Software Tool And Application - THOMSON REUTERS MARKETS; pg. 810, pg. 1299
VESTIGE - Faucets - MOEN INCORPORATED; pg. 1056, pg. 1468
VESTITO - Carpet - INTERFACE, INC.; pg. 695, pg. 512
VESTYPE - Body Harness - MINE SAFETY APPLIANCES COMPANY; pg. 1361, pg. 1525
VESUVIO - Fabric - NEMSCHOFF, INC.; pg. 936, pg. 1890
VESUVIUS - Video Game - INTERNATIONAL GAME TECHNOLOGY; pg. 957, pg. 1024
VET/E-SIG - ECG Sensor - HESKA CORPORATION; pg. 1542, pg. 335
VET/IV - Pump - HESKA CORPORATION; pg. 1542, pg. 335
VET/OX - Digital Monitor - HESKA CORPORATION; pg. 1542, pg. 335
VET/OX G2 DIGITAL MONITOR - Digital Monitor - HESKA CORPORATION; pg. 1542, pg. 335
VETAUTOREAD - Analyzer - IDEXX LABORATORIES, INC.; pg. 1543, pg. 753
VETERANS MAKE THE BEST EMPLOYEES - Tag Line - VETJOBS, INC.; pg. 1287, pg. 535
VETERINARY HEALTHCARE COMMUNICATIONS - Veterinary Publications - TRUVEN HEALTH ANALYTICS; pg. 1696, pg. 867
VETERINARY PRACTICE-MANAGEMENT - Software - IDEXX LABORATORIES, INC.; pg. 1543, pg. 753
VETERINARY PRACTICE NEWS - Magazine - I-5 PUBLISHING LLC; pg. 1651, pg. 133
VETJOBS - Job Board - VETJOBS, INC.; pg. 1287, pg. 535
VETLAB - Analyzer - IDEXX LABORATORIES, INC.; pg. 1543, pg. 753
VETLINK - Analyzer - IDEXX LABORATORIES, INC.; pg. 1543, pg. 753
VETLYTE - Analyzer - IDEXX LABORATORIES, INC.; pg. 1543, pg. 753
VETMEDIN - Canine Medicine - BOEHRINGER INGELHEIM VETMEDICA, INC.; pg. 1474, pg. 980
VETO PRO PAC - Truck Equipment - AMERICAN VAN EQUIPMENT INC.; pg. 199, pg. 1078
VETSCAN - Blood Analysis System - ABAXIS, INC.; pg. 1483, pg. 298
VETSTAT - Analyzer - IDEXX LABORATORIES, INC.; pg. 1543, pg. 753
VETSULIN - Dog Treatment - MERCK & CO., INC.; pg. 1566, pg. 1077
VETTE PANEL ADHESIVE/FILLER - Polyester Body Filler - ITW - EVERCOAT; pg. 1443, pg. 1415
VETTER - Hydraulic Equipment - IDEX CORPORATION; pg. 1347, pg. 623
VETTEST - Analyzer - IDEXX LABORATORIES, INC.; pg. 1543, pg. 753
VEUVE CLICQUOT - Champagne - MOET HENNESSY; pg. 1966, pg. 1260
VF - Apparel - V.F. CORPORATION; pg. 34, pg. 1376
VF-45 - Fiber - 3M COMPANY; pg. 1142, pg. 956
VF SOLUTIONS - Apparel - V.F. CORPORATION; pg. 34, pg. 1376
VFC - Rock Crushers - TELSMITH, INC.; pg. 1381, pg. 1871
VFEND - Medicine - PFIZER INC.; pg. 1581, pg. 1278
VFHRM - Vertical Flow Treater - CAMERON INTERNATIONAL; pg. 1151, pg. 1702
VFRAME - Software - CISCO SYSTEMS, INC.; pg. 372, pg. 240
VFT - Golf Equipment - CALLAWAY GOLF COMPANY; pg. 1829, pg. 58
VFX - Filter - CAMERON INTERNATIONAL; pg. 1151, pg. 1702
VFX-250S - Video Over Frame Relay - LATTICE INC.; pg. 1872, pg. 1108
VG-2 ALERT - Signal Detection Feature - COBRA ELECTRONICS CORPORATION; pg. 629, pg. 572
VGAMMA9 - T Cell Receptors - BECKMAN COULTER, INC.; pg. 1402, pg. 48
VGDF - Telecommunications Modules - ALCATEL-LUCENT USA, INC.; pg. 615, pg. 1728
VGF STRENGTH. PERFORMANCE. INNOVATION - Tagline - AXT, INC.; pg. 1400, pg. 90
VH ISOSTATION - Vibration Isolation Workstations - NEWPORT CORPORATION; pg. 1424, pg. 114
VHALEN - Footwear - STEVEN MADDEN, LTD.; pg. 1819, pg. 1176
VHDL COMPILER - Software - SYNOPSYS, INC.; pg. 480, pg. 162
VHDM - Connector - AMPHENOL CORPORATION; pg. 616, pg. 381
VHDM-HSD - Connector - AMPHENOL CORPORATION; pg. 616, pg. 381
VHM - Vehicle Health Management - BAE SYSTEMS-INFORMATION WARFARE; pg. 623, pg. 1036
VHS-OPTISORT - Sorter - KEY TECHNOLOGY, INC.; pg. 868, pg. 1847
VI-CELL - Testing Instrument System - BECKMAN COULTER, INC.; pg. 1402, pg. 48
VI-CORR - Pump Product - IDEX CORPORATION; pg. 1347, pg. 623
VI-RAM - Ripple Attenuation Module - VICOR CORPORATION; pg. 1435, pg. 783
VIA - Paper - INTERNATIONAL PAPER COMPANY; pg. 1460, pg. 1644
VIA - Instant Coffee - STARBUCKS CORPORATION; pg. 897, pg. 1840
VIA COLORS - Printing Paper - MOHAWK FINE PAPERS, INC.; pg. 1464, pg. 1153
VIA FORTE - Ceramic, Glass, Stone Tiles & Slabs - WALKER & ZANGER, INC.; pg. 119, pg. 281
VIA NOVA - Shoes - SHOE CARNIVAL, INC.; pg. 1819, pg. 679
VIA PANERA - Bakery Product - PANERA BREAD COMPANY; pg. 1029, pg. 1001
VIA ROMA - Coffee Product - COFFEE HOLDING CO., INC.; pg. 849, pg. 1343
VIA XEROX - Software - XEROX CORPORATION; pg. 494, pg. 365
VIABAHN - Medical Product - W.L. GORE & ASSOCIATES, INC.; pg. 122, pg. 388
VIABIL - Medical Equipment - CONMED CORPORATION; pg. 1517, pg. 1347
VIABIL - Interventional & Endovascular Product - W.L. GORE & ASSOCIATES, INC.; pg. 122, pg. 388
VIACRYL - Waterborne - CYTEC INDUSTRIES, INC.; pg. 1155, pg. 1131
VIACTIV - Healthcare Product - JOHNSON & JOHNSON; pg. 1549, pg. 1091
VIADENT - Anti-Plaque Toothpaste, Gel & Oral Rinse - COLGATE ORAL PHARMACEUTICAL; pg. 1516, pg. 1214
VIAFLEX - Healthcare Product - BAXTER INTERNATIONAL INC.; pg. 1499, pg. 599
VIAFORM - Copper Integration - ATMI, INC.; pg. 1314, pg. 342
VIAGRA - Erectile Dysfunction Medication - PFIZER INC.; pg. 1581, pg. 1278
VIAGRAM - Molecular Probe Product - THERMO FISHER SCIENTIFIC INC.; pg. 1602, pg. 61
VIAKAL - Personal & Household Product - THE PROCTER & GAMBLE COMPANY; pg. 1129, pg. 1418
VIAL2BAG - Drug Administration System - WEST PHARMACEUTICAL SERVICES, INC.; pg. 1472, pg. 1532
VIALA - Premium Wine - THE DONUM ESTATE, INC; pg. 1962, pg. 279
VIALKYD - Solventborne - CYTEC INDUSTRIES, INC.; pg. 1155, pg. 1131
VIANET - Broadband - AIRSPAN NETWORKS INC.; pg. 346, pg. 410
VIANET - Identity Information Software - DATACARD CORPORATION; pg. 382, pg. 948
VIASAT-1 - Broadband Satellite Network - VIASAT, INC.; pg. 489, pg. 62
VIASYS - Respiratory Care Product - CARDINAL HEALTH, INC.; pg. 1512, pg. 1448
VIATORR - Endoprosthesis - W.L. GORE & ASSOCIATES, INC.; pg. 122, pg. 388
VIATRAC 14 PLUS - Catheter - ABBOTT LABORATORIES;

pg. 1484, *pg.* 551
VIAVIDEO - Video Conferencing Product - POLYCOM, INC.; *pg.* 664, *pg.* 249
VIB NET - Source Controller - ION GEOPHYSICAL CORPORATION; *pg.* 1350, *pg.* 1708
VIB PRO - Vibrator - ION GEOPHYSICAL CORPORATION; *pg.* 1350, *pg.* 1708
VIBE - Fabric - NEMSCHOFF, INC.; *pg.* 936, *pg.* 1890
VIBE - Entertainment & Lifestyle Brand - SPINMEDIA; *pg.* 1282, *pg.* 104
VIBE - Surface Material - STEELCASE INC.; *pg.* 475, *pg.* 889
VIBETONE - Software - IMMERSION CORPORATION; *pg.* 413, *pg.* 246
VIBETONZ - Hardware & Software - IMMERSION CORPORATION; *pg.* 413, *pg.* 246
THE VIBRA-BLENDER - Blender - VIBRA SCREW INC.; *pg.* 1387, *pg.* 1126
VIBRA-BLENDER - Continuous Blender - VIBRA SCREW INC.; *pg.* 1387, *pg.* 1126
VIBRA FLEX PIPE - Rubber Pipe - THE MERCER RUBBER COMPANY; *pg.* 1886, *pg.* 1165
VIBRA-KLEEN - Cleaner - HOUGHTON INTERNATIONAL INC.; *pg.* 1167, *pg.* 1589
VIBRA-METRIC - Weigh-Belt Feeder - VIBRA SCREW INC.; *pg.* 1387, *pg.* 1126
VIBRA-SEAL - Adhesive - HENKEL CORPORATION; *pg.* 1049, *pg.* 369
VIBRA-SERT - Threaded Insert - GROOV-PIN CORPORATION; *pg.* 1049, *pg.* 1608
VIBRACURE - Polymer Product - CHEMTURA CORPORATION; *pg.* 1152, *pg.* 355
VIBRAKRIMP - Electronic Components - MOLEX INCORPORATED; *pg.* 655, *pg.* 628
VIBRALINK - Rod End - TUTHILL CORPORATION; *pg.* 1385, *pg.* 561
VIBRAM - Footwear Product - DECKERS OUTDOOR CORPORATION; *pg.* 1807, *pg.* 100
VIBRAM - Fishing Gear Product - SIMMS FISHING PRODUCTS CORP.; *pg.* 1845, *pg.* 1008
VIBRAM - Enforcer Slip-Resisting Outsole - WEINBRENNER SHOE COMPANY, INC.; *pg.* 1822, *pg.* 1871
VIBRAMYCIN - Medicine - PFIZER INC.; *pg.* 1581, *pg.* 1278
VIBRANT - Bath Product - KOHLER CO.; *pg.* 91, *pg.* 1862
VIBRANT 3 - Footwear - K-SWISS; *pg.* 1837, *pg.* 306
VIBRANT-C - Juice - JAMBA, INC.; *pg.* 1024, *pg.* 84
VIBRANT-C BOOST - Boost - JAMBA, INC.; *pg.* 1024, *pg.* 84
VIBRAPAC - Block Machine - BESSER COMPANY; *pg.* 1317, *pg.* 865
VIBRATHANE - Polymer Product - CHEMTURA CORPORATION; *pg.* 1152, *pg.* 355
VIBRATTO - DVD Player - ESS TECHNOLOGY, INC.; *pg.* 395, *pg.* 90
VIBRO-KING - Screening - TELSMITH, INC.; *pg.* 1381, *pg.* 1871
VIBRO-MAC - Concrete Pipe Machinery - BESSER COMPANY; *pg.* 1317, *pg.* 865
VIBROCAST - Pressed & Monolithic Refractory - RESCO PRODUCTS, INC.; *pg.* 107, *pg.* 1581
VIBROMET - Polishing Machine - BUEHLER, LTD.; *pg.* 1403, *pg.* 622
VIBROXIDE - Polishing Grade Powders - FERRO CORPORATION; *pg.* 1162, *pg.* 1462
VIC - Piping System - VICTAULIC COMPANY; *pg.* 1066, *pg.* 1529
VIC-ADJUSTABLE - Tool for Cut Grooving Pipes - VICTAULIC COMPANY; *pg.* 1066, *pg.* 1529
VIC-BALL - Grooved End Ball Valve - VICTAULIC COMPANY; *pg.* 1066, *pg.* 1529
VIC-BOLTLESS - Pin Assembled Grooved Pipe Coupling - VICTAULIC COMPANY; *pg.* 1066, *pg.* 1529
VIC-EASY - Roll Grooving Tool - VICTAULIC COMPANY; *pg.* 1066, *pg.* 1529
VIC-FLANGE - Flange-to-Groove Adapter - VICTAULIC COMPANY; *pg.* 1066, *pg.* 1529
VIC-FLEX - Flexible Fire Protection Coupling - VICTAULIC COMPANY; *pg.* 1066, *pg.* 1529
VIC-GROOVER - Tool for Cut Grooving Individual Pipes - VICTAULIC COMPANY; *pg.* 1066, *pg.* 1529
VIC-LET - Hole Cutting Tool - VICTAULIC COMPANY; *pg.* 1066, *pg.* 1529
VIC-O-WELL - Hole Cutting Tool - VICTAULIC COMPANY; *pg.* 1066, *pg.* 1529
VIC-PLUG - Grooved End Eccentric Plug Valve - VICTAULIC COMPANY; *pg.* 1066, *pg.* 1529
VIC-PRESS 304 - Piping System - VICTAULIC COMPANY; *pg.* 1066, *pg.* 1529
VIC-STRAINER - Grooved End Tee-type Strainer - VICTAULIC COMPANY; *pg.* 1066, *pg.* 1529
VIC-TAP - Hole Cutting Tool - VICTAULIC COMPANY; *pg.* 1066, *pg.* 1529
VICA - Beverages - THE COCA-COLA COMPANY; *pg.* 240, *pg.* 493
VICAN - Pump Product - IDEX CORPORATION; *pg.* 1347, *pg.* 623
VICARD - Pharmaceutical Product - ABBOTT LABORATORIES; *pg.* 1484, *pg.* 551
VICCHIOMAGGIO - Italian Wine - LAIRD & COMPANY, INC.; *pg.* 1966, *pg.* 1119
VICE - Refill - A. T. CROSS COMPANY; *pg.* 339, *pg.* 1602
VICEROY - Cigarette - REYNOLDS AMERICAN INC.; *pg.* 1894, *pg.* 1395
VICHY - Cosmetics - L'OREAL USA; *pg.* 514, *pg.* 1252
VICIOUUS - Footwear - STEVEN MADDEN, LTD.; *pg.* 1819, *pg.* 1176
VICKERS - Pumps - EATON CORPORATION; *pg.* 1331, *pg.* 1429
VICKS - Air Purifier - KAZ, INC.; *pg.* 58, *pg.* 844
VICKS - Health Care Product - THE PROCTER & GAMBLE COMPANY; *pg.* 1129, *pg.* 1418
VICKS EARLY DEFENSE - Hand Sanitizer - THE PROCTER & GAMBLE COMPANY; *pg.* 1129, *pg.* 1418
VICKY - Footwear - BEBE STORES, INC.; *pg.* 19, *pg.* 49
VICOAX - Closed-Circuit Television Equipment - VICON INDUSTRIES, INC.; *pg.* 685, *pg.* 1166
VICODIN - Painkiller - ABBOTT LABORATORIES; *pg.* 1484, *pg.* 551
VICOL - Synthetic Polymer - HUNTSMAN CORPORATION; *pg.* 1167, *pg.* 1758
VICONNET - 6 Channel Video Server - VICON INDUSTRIES, INC.; *pg.* 685, *pg.* 1166
VICOPROFEN - Painkiller - ABBOTT LABORATORIES; *pg.* 1484, *pg.* 551
VICRYL - Healthcare Product - JOHNSON & JOHNSON; *pg.* 1549, *pg.* 1091
VIC'S - Gourmet Popcorn in Assorted Flavors - BARREL O'FUN SNACK FOODS CO.; *pg.* 1850, *pg.* 952
VICTIM IMPACT PANEL - Awareness Program - MOTHERS AGAINST DRUNK DRIVING (MADD); *pg.* 147, *pg.* 1723
VICTOR - Furniture - AMISCO INDUSTRIES LTD.; *pg.* 913, *pg.* 1958
VICTOR - Food Product - BUNGE LIMITED; *pg.* 842, *pg.* 1351
VICTOR - Books for Spiritual Growth - DAVID C. COOK; *pg.* 1633, *pg.* 315
VICTOR - Photographic Processors - EASTMAN KODAK COMPANY; *pg.* 1408, *pg.* 1333
VICTOR - Mining Equipment - FEDERAL SIGNAL CORPORATION; *pg.* 638, *pg.* 645
VICTOR - Plate Reader & Imager - PERKINELMER, INC.; *pg.* 1426, *pg.* 853
VICTOR - Pest Control - THE WOODSTREAM CORPORATION; *pg.* 1801, *pg.* 1549
VICTOR BLACK BOX - Trap - THE WOODSTREAM CORPORATION; *pg.* 1801, *pg.* 1549
VICTOR REINZ - Gaskets & Sealing Products - DANA HOLDING CORPORATION; *pg.* 203, *pg.* 1461
VICTOR SERIES - Manifolds - EDELBROCK CORPORATION; *pg.* 204, *pg.* 293
VICTORIA - Rug - COURISTAN INC.; *pg.* 921, *pg.* 1067
VICTORIA - Wall Decor - HERITAGE LACE INC.; *pg.* 694, *pg.* 711
VICTORIA - Fabric - NEMSCHOFF, INC.; *pg.* 936, *pg.* 1890
VICTORIA - Footwear - P.W. MINOR & SON, INC.; *pg.* 1816, *pg.* 1140
VICTORIA SPENSER - Shoes - SHOE CARNIVAL, INC.; *pg.* 1819, *pg.* 679
VICTORIAN - Semisweet Chocolate - CARGILL LIMITED; *pg.* 1475, *pg.* 1914
VICTORIAN - Concrete Lighting Pole - NOV AMERON; *pg.* 100, *pg.* 187
VICTORIAN CRYSTAL - Doors - THERMA-TRU CORP.; *pg.* 115, *pg.* 1462
VICTORIAN EARL GREY - Tea - CELESTIAL SEASONINGS, INC.; *pg.* 846, *pg.* 310
VICTORIAN ROSE - Scarf - HERITAGE LACE INC.; *pg.* 694, *pg.* 711
VICTORIAN SPLENDOR - Rose Plants - 1-800-FLOWERS.COM, INC.; *pg.* 1758, *pg.* 1151
VICTORIAN VIOLETS - Dinnerware - THE HOMER LAUGHLIN CHINA COMPANY; *pg.* 1125, *pg.* 1850
VICTORIA'S SECRET - Lingerie Shops - VICTORIA'S SECRET STORES, LLC; *pg.* 1789, *pg.* 1471
VICTORIA'S SECRET PINK - Collegiate Lifestyle Brand - VICTORIA'S SECRET STORES, LLC; *pg.* 1789, *pg.* 1471
VICTORINOX - Multi-Tools - VICTORINOX SWISS ARMY INC.; *pg.* 1139, *pg.* 357
VICTORY - Hoof Care Products - GEA FARM TECHNOLOGIES; *pg.* 704, *pg.* 636
VICTORY - Musical Instrument - GIBSON GUITAR CORP.; *pg.* 550, *pg.* 1650
VICTORY - Cast Iron Gas Boiler - SLANT/FIN CORPORATION; *pg.* 1076, *pg.* 1163
VICTORY - Pacemakers - ST. JUDE MEDICAL, INC.; *pg.* 1596, *pg.* 963
VICTORY - Commercial Refrigerators & Freezers - VICTORY REFRIGERATION COMPANY LLC; *pg.* 61, *pg.* 1051
VICTORY AT SEA VIDEO - Video Series - DIRECT HOLDINGS AMERICAS INC.; *pg.* 1636, *pg.* 1780
VICTORY GARDEN - Carpet - BEAULIEU GROUP, LLC; *pg.* 917, *pg.* 529
VICTORY LANE - Welding Helmet - SELLSTROM MANUFACTURING CO.; *pg.* 1428, *pg.* 659
VICTORY MOTORCYCLES - Vehicles - POLARIS INDUSTRIES INC.; *pg.* 1709, *pg.* 928
VICTORY WINGS - Food Product - TYSON FOODS, INC.; *pg.* 902, *pg.* 35
VIDA CRISTIANA - Magazine - CHARISMA MEDIA; *pg.* 1627, *pg.* 436
VIDA CUSH - Footwear - COBIAN CORP.; *pg.* 1806, *pg.* 253
VIDA23 - Multicultural Website - DR PEPPER SNAPPLE GROUP, INC.; *pg.* 250, *pg.* 1729
VIDAL SASSOON - Personal Care Electrical Product - HELEN OF TROY L.P.; *pg.* 511, *pg.* 1692
VIDAL SASSOON - Hair Care Products - THE PROCTER & GAMBLE COMPANY; *pg.* 1129, *pg.* 1418
VIDAL SASSOON - Chain of Beauty Salons - VIDAL SASSOON CO.; *pg.* 524, *pg.* 1426
VIDENE - Office Furniture - HAWORTH, INC.; *pg.* 402, *pg.* 891
VIDEO DISPLAY - Cathode Ray Tubes - VIDEO DISPLAY CORPORATION; *pg.* 685, *pg.* 542
VIDEO GAME ESSENTIALS - Software - RENTRAK CORPORATION; *pg.* 306, *pg.* 1506
VIDEO IMMERSION - Graphics Card - ADVANCED MICRO DEVICES, INC.; *pg.* 613, *pg.* 282
VIDEO MEDIA CENTER - Content Management Solution - POLYCOM, INC.; *pg.* 664, *pg.* 249
VIDEO NETWORK MANAGEMENT - Software - POLYCOM, INC.; *pg.* 664, *pg.* 249
VIDEO POKER PARLOUR & DESIGN - Games - PENN NATIONAL GAMING, INC.; *pg.* 574, *pg.* 1595
VIDEO SLOT KING - Video Game - INTERNATIONAL GAME TECHNOLOGY; *pg.* 957, *pg.* 1024
VIDEO STORE - Trade Publication - UBM ADVANSTAR; *pg.* 1697, *pg.* 1306
VIDEO TRANSPORT - Wireline Solutions - SONUS NETWORKS INC.; *pg.* 1281, *pg.* 858
VIDEO VRA - Hearing Screening Test - INTELLIGENT HEARING SYSTEMS CORP.; *pg.* 1546, *pg.* 443
VIDEOFILM NOTES - Technical Publication - EASTMAN KODAK COMPANY; *pg.* 1408, *pg.* 1333
VIDEOGENESIS - Software - ACD SYSTEMS INTERNATIONAL INC.; *pg.* 340, *pg.* 1913
VIDEOGUM - Visual Entertainment Commmentary Site - SPINMEDIA; *pg.* 1282, *pg.* 104
VIDEOJET - Printers - VIDEOJET TECHNOLOGIES INC.; *pg.* 489, *pg.* 671
VIDEOJET 10 - Video Encoder/Decoder - BOSCH SECURITY SYSTEMS, INC.; *pg.* 626, *pg.* 1158
VIDEOJET 1000 - Video Encoder/Decoder - BOSCH SECURITY SYSTEMS, INC.; *pg.* 626, *pg.* 1158
VIDEOJET 8000 - Video Encoder - BOSCH SECURITY SYSTEMS, INC.; *pg.* 626, *pg.* 1158
VIDEOJET EXCEL - Printers - VIDEOJET TECHNOLOGIES INC.; *pg.* 489, *pg.* 671
VIDEOJET FOCUS - Laser Printers - VIDEOJET TECHNOLOGIES INC.; *pg.* 489, *pg.* 671
VIDEOJET IPRO - Ink Jet Printers - VIDEOJET TECHNOLOGIES INC.; *pg.* 489, *pg.* 671
VIDEOJET TECHNOLOGIES - Coding Equipment - DANAHER CORPORATION; *pg.* 1044, *pg.* 397
VIDEOJET XPRO - Video Encoder - BOSCH SECURITY SYSTEMS, INC.; *pg.* 626, *pg.* 1158
VIDEOKEY - Digital Video Badging System - MAXXESS SYSTEMS, INC.; *pg.* 431, *pg.* 43

VIDEOLINK - Software - SMITH MICRO SOFTWARE, INC.; *pg.* 471, *pg.* 41
VIDEOLINK - Transmission System - VICON INDUSTRIES, INC.; *pg.* 685, *pg.* 1166
VIDEOMASK - Interdiction System - BLONDER TONGUE LABORATORIES, INC.; *pg.* 625, *pg.* 1100
VIDEONOW - Toy & Game - HASBRO, INC.; *pg.* 954, *pg.* 1603
VIDEOPATH - Veterinary Imaging System - WELCH ALLYN INC.; *pg.* 1436, *pg.* 1342
VIDEOPOINT - Video-Based Information Display System - THE ADT CORPORATION; *pg.* 612, *pg.* 409
VIDEOSCOPE - Periodical - PHANMEDIA L.L.C.; *pg.* 1677, *pg.* 1100
VIDEOSHADER - Graphics Card - ADVANCED MICRO DEVICES, INC.; *pg.* 613, *pg.* 282
VIDEOSITE - Business Unit - INTERNATIONAL GAME TECHNOLOGY; *pg.* 420, *pg.* 1606
VIDEOSOAP - Graphics Card - ADVANCED MICRO DEVICES, INC.; *pg.* 613, *pg.* 282
VIDEOTECH - Alignment System Software - HUNTER ENGINEERING COMPANY; *pg.* 208, *pg.* 973
VIDEOTENN - Touch Screen Programmer - SPX THERMAL PRODUCT SOLUTIONS; *pg.* 1378, *pg.* 1555
VIDEX - Health Care Product - BRISTOL-MYERS SQUIBB COMPANY; *pg.* 1509, *pg.* 1206
VIDIERA - Testing Instrument System - BECKMAN COULTER, INC.; *pg.* 1402, *pg.* 48
VIDIKRON - Video Product - PLANAR SYSTEMS, INC.; *pg.* 455, *pg.* 1495
VIDISIC - Lacrimal Fluid Substitute - BAUSCH & LOMB INCORPORATED; *pg.* 1401, *pg.* 1045
VIDITALK - Software - VIEWSONIC CORPORATION; *pg.* 489, *pg.* 303
VIDMAR - Modular Storage Systems - STANLEY BLACK & DECKER, INC.; *pg.* 1063, *pg.* 358
VIDOS-NVR - Video Management System - BOSCH SECURITY SYSTEMS, INC.; *pg.* 626, *pg.* 1158
VIDOS VIDEO MANAGEMENT SYSTEM - Software - BOSCH SECURITY SYSTEMS, INC.; *pg.* 626, *pg.* 1158
VIDSTER - Toy - MATTEL, INC.; *pg.* 962, *pg.* 81
VIDUX - Plastic & Rubber - TEKNOR APEX COMPANY; *pg.* 1889, *pg.* 1605
VIENNA - Leather Textiles - BERNHARDT DESIGN; *pg.* 918, *pg.* 1381
VIENNA CREMES - Snack Size Cookies - KELLOGG COMPANY; *pg.* 831, *pg.* 870
VIENNA ES - Ceiling Fan - WESTINGHOUSE LIGHTING CORPORATION; *pg.* 687, *pg.* 1571
VIENNA FINGERS - Cookies - KELLOGG COMPANY; *pg.* 831, *pg.* 870
VIENNA SWIRL - Carpet - INTERFACE, INC.; *pg.* 695, *pg.* 512
VIENNESE BLEND - Coffee - PEET'S COFFEE & TEA, INC.; *pg.* 1029, *pg.* 85
VIENNETTA - Ice Cream and Frozen Novelties - UNILEVER CANADA INC.; *pg.* 903, *pg.* 1946
VIERA - Food Product - A. DUDA & SONS INC.; *pg.* 835, *pg.* 457
VIETNAM VIDEO - Video Series - DIRECT HOLDINGS AMERICAS INC.; *pg.* 1636, *pg.* 1780
VIETNAM.COM - Travel Website - LIVE CURRENT MEDIA INC.; *pg.* 1263, *pg.* 1911
VIETTE - Wine - REMY COINTREAU USA INC.; *pg.* 1969, *pg.* 1285
VIEU STAR - Systems Integration & Aeronautics - LOCKHEED MARTIN CORPORATION; *pg.* 229, *pg.* 762
VIEW - Motor Homes - WINNEBAGO INDUSTRIES, INC.; *pg.* 1712, *pg.* 707
VIEWABLES - Labeling System - SMEAD MANUFACTURING COMPANY; *pg.* 470, *pg.* 926
VIEWBASE - Software System - MENTOR GRAPHICS CORPORATION; *pg.* 432, *pg.* 1510
VIEWBOOK - Computer Equipment - VIEWSONIC CORPORATION; *pg.* 489, *pg.* 303
VIEWCARE - Computer Monitor - VIEWSONIC CORPORATION; *pg.* 489, *pg.* 303
VIEWCUBE - 3D Navigation Tool - AUTODESK INC.; *pg.* 356, *pg.* 257
VIEWED TO BE THE BEST - Slogan - PELLA CORPORATION; *pg.* 104, *pg.* 711
VIEWFIRST - Sports Marketing System - CANDID COLOR SYSTEMS, INC.; *pg.* 1404, *pg.* 1485
VIEWFLEX - Catheter - ST. JUDE MEDICAL, INC.; *pg.* 1596, *pg.* 963
VIEWLETS - Software - EMC CORPORATION; *pg.* 391, *pg.* 825
VIEWLUX - Plate Reader & Imager - PERKINELMER, INC.; *pg.* 1426, *pg.* 853
VIEWMASTER - Direct-to-Host, Browser-Based Access Provider - ATTACHMATE CORPORATION; *pg.* 356, *pg.* 1833
VIEWMATCH - Computer Equipment - VIEWSONIC CORPORATION; *pg.* 489, *pg.* 303
VIEWMATE - Intracardiac Ultrasound System - ST. JUDE MEDICAL, INC.; *pg.* 1596, *pg.* 963
VIEWMATE - Mice Product - VIEWSONIC CORPORATION; *pg.* 489, *pg.* 303
VIEWMAX - Host-to-Web Integration Tool - CSPI TECHNOLOGY SOLUTIONS; *pg.* 381, *pg.* 421
VIEWMETER - Computer Equipment - VIEWSONIC CORPORATION; *pg.* 489, *pg.* 303
VIEWNIQUE - Wallcovering - OMNOVA SOLUTIONS INC; *pg.* 1176, *pg.* 1453
VIEWPAC - Recorder - SIEMENS PROCESS INDUSTRIES AND DRIVE; *pg.* 1376, *pg.* 1587
VIEWPANEL - Computer Equipment - VIEWSONIC CORPORATION; *pg.* 489, *pg.* 303
VIEWPOINT - Software - EMC CORPORATION; *pg.* 391, *pg.* 825
VIEWPOINT - Furniture - HERMAN MILLER, INC.; *pg.* 926, *pg.* 913
VIEWPOINT - Software - OPENTEXT; *pg.* 450, *pg.* 1665
VIEWPOINTS - Furniture - BASSETT FURNITURE INDUSTRIES, INCORPORATED; *pg.* 916, *pg.* 1776
VIEWPORT - Software - CRESTRON ELECTRONICS INC.; *pg.* 631, *pg.* 1116
VIEWSAVER - Door - SIMPSON DOOR COMPANY; *pg.* 110, *pg.* 1823
VIEWSIM - Software System - MENTOR GRAPHICS CORPORATION; *pg.* 432, *pg.* 1510
VIEWSTAR - Software - OPENTEXT; *pg.* 450, *pg.* 1665
VIEWSTATION - Video Conferencing Product - POLYCOM, INC.; *pg.* 664, *pg.* 249
VIFB - HVAC Equipment - MESTEK, INC.; *pg.* 1074, *pg.* 857
VIGILON - Primary Wound Dressing - C.R. BARD, INC.; *pg.* 1519, *pg.* 1094
VIGNE REGALI - Wine - BANFI VINTNERS; *pg.* 1957, *pg.* 1161
VIGNETTE - Soft Fabric Shades on Easy Operating Clutch System - HUNTER DOUGLAS, INC.; *pg.* 928, *pg.* 1320
VIGNETTE - Fabric - NEMSCHOFF, INC.; *pg.* 936, *pg.* 1890
VIGORA - Bath Product - KOHLER CO.; *pg.* 91, *pg.* 1862
VIGOROL - Gels & Mousses - INSPIRED BEAUTY BRANDS; *pg.* 512, *pg.* 1244
VIGOROX - Chemical - FMC CORPORATION; *pg.* 1163, *pg.* 1564
VIIIIVA - Heart Rate Monitor - 4IIII INNOVATIONS INC.; *pg.* 64, *pg.* 1905
VIKAN HYGIENE SYSTEM - Sanitation System - CHESHER EQUIPMENT LTD.; *pg.* 1323, *pg.* 1925
VIKANE - Structural Fumigant - DOW AGROSCIENCES LLC; *pg.* 1156, *pg.* 684
VIKING - Catheter - ABBOTT LABORATORIES; *pg.* 1484, *pg.* 551
VIKING - Pump Product - IDEX CORPORATION; *pg.* 1347, *pg.* 623
VIKING - Systems Integration & Aeronautics - LOCKHEED MARTIN CORPORATION; *pg.* 229, *pg.* 762
VIKING - Lattice Shad Covers & Screen Prods - METALS USA, INC.; *pg.* 97, *pg.* 425
VIKING - Adult Hardcover Books - PENGUIN RANDOM HOUSE; *pg.* 1675, *pg.* 1276
VIKING - Kitchen Appliance - VIKING RANGE CORPORATION; *pg.* 61, *pg.* 968
VIKING CROWN LOUNGE - Cruise Ship - ROYAL CARIBBEAN CRUISES LTD; *pg.* 1921, *pg.* 446
VIKING ELECTRONICS - Connectors - COOPER INTERCONNECT; *pg.* 630, *pg.* 1118
VIKING HANGING SCALES - Utility & Sportsman's Scales - JARDEN CONSUMER SOLUTIONS; *pg.* 57, *pg.* 412
VIKING KESTREL - Children's Hardcover Books - PENGUIN RANDOM HOUSE; *pg.* 1675, *pg.* 1276
VIKING MAG DRIVE - Pump Product - IDEX CORPORATION; *pg.* 1347, *pg.* 623
VIKING PUMP - Pumps - IDEX CORPORATION; *pg.* 1347, *pg.* 623
VIKING SHIP BRAND - Plant Nutrient - YARA N AMERICA, INC.; *pg.* 1802, *pg.* 477
VIKING WEAR - Apparel Materials - VIKING YACHT COMPANY; *pg.* 1712, *pg.* 1094
VIKTOR DREARY - Doll - TONNER DOLL COMPANY, INC.; *pg.* 968, *pg.* 1171
VIKUITI - Film - 3M COMPANY; *pg.* 1142, *pg.* 956
VILETTA - Bathroom Faucet - MOEN INCORPORATED; *pg.* 1056, *pg.* 1468
VILLA - Medical Imaging Systems - DGT HOLDINGS; *pg.* 634, *pg.* 1223
VILLA - Fan - HUNTER FAN COMPANY; *pg.* 57, *pg.* 1631
VILLA ANTICA - Furniture - STANLEY FURNITURE CO., INC.; *pg.* 943, *pg.* 1379
VILLA CERNA - Wine - BANFI VINTNERS; *pg.* 1957, *pg.* 1161
VILLA FRIZZONI - Food Product - SHAMROCK FOODS COMPANY; *pg.* 895, *pg.* 20
VILLA JOLADA ITALY - Wine and Spirits - LEONARD KREUSCH, INC.; *pg.* 254, *pg.* 1099
VILLA MARIE - Furniture - ASHLEY FURNITURE INDUSTRIES, INC.; *pg.* 914, *pg.* 1852
VILLA MASSA - Italian Liqueurs - LAIRD & COMPANY, INC.; *pg.* 1966, *pg.* 1119
VILLA RUSTICA - Stone - WALKER & ZANGER, INC.; *pg.* 119, *pg.* 281
VILLAGE - Fabric - F. SCHUMACHER & CO.; *pg.* 925, *pg.* 1230
VILLAGE CRAFTS BY MICHAELS - Crafts Stores - MICHAELS STORES, INC.; *pg.* 1127, *pg.* 1722
VILLAGE GARDEN - Salad Dressings - PERFORMANCE FOOD GROUP COMPANY, LLC; *pg.* 1030, *pg.* 1803
VILLAGE INN - Restaurants - AMERICAN BLUE RIBBON HOLDINGS; *pg.* 1714, *pg.* 1648
VILLAGE KNIT - Ear Warmer - 180S, LLC; *pg.* 1824, *pg.* 754
VILLAGE PRIDE - Bread - KLOSTERMAN BAKING COMPANY, INC.; *pg.* 869, *pg.* 1415
VILLAGE SQUARE - Carpet - BEAULIEU GROUP, LLC; *pg.* 917, *pg.* 529
THE VILLAGE VOICE - Newspaper - VILLAGE VOICE MEDIA HOLDINGS, LLC; *pg.* 1699, *pg.* 1311
VILLAGER - Table - BLATT BOWLING & BILLIARD CORP.; *pg.* 1827, *pg.* 1203
VILLAGER - Apparel - KATE SPADE & COMPANY; *pg.* 27, *pg.* 1248
VILLAGER - Bath Product - KOHLER CO.; *pg.* 91, *pg.* 1862
VILLAWARE - Kitchen Appliances - JARDEN CONSUMER SOLUTIONS; *pg.* 57, *pg.* 412
VIMEO - Online Video Platform - IAC/INTERACTIVECORP; *pg.* 292, *pg.* 1242
VIMMS - Software - VULCAN, INC.; *pg.* 687, *pg.* 5
VIN-L-STRIPE - Traffic Marking Paint - DUNN-EDWARDS CORPORATION; *pg.* 1442, *pg.* 129
VINA - Vehicle - IHS AUTOMOTIVE DRIVEN BY POLK; *pg.* 1652, *pg.* 907
VINAC - Vinyl Acetate Binder - AIR PRODUCTS AND CHEMICALS, INC.; *pg.* 1145, *pg.* 1513
VINCE & LARRY - Safety Belts - THE ADVERTISING COUNCIL, INC.; *pg.* 125, *pg.* 1187
VINCENT - Furniture - AMERICAN LEATHER LP; *pg.* 912, *pg.* 1673
VINCENT - Dispensing Equipment - IDEX CORPORATION; *pg.* 1347, *pg.* 623
VINCENT - Bath Product - ROHL LLC; *pg.* 1061, *pg.* 116
VINCENZO - Jewelry - UNCAS MANUFACTURING COMPANY; *pg.* 15, *pg.* 1608
VINCI - Writing Instruments - DIXON TICONDEROGA COMPANY; *pg.* 388, *pg.* 430
VINDICATOR - Cleaning Product - HILLYARD, INC.; *pg.* 331, *pg.* 990
VINDICATOR + - Hospital Disinfectant - HILLYARD, INC.; *pg.* 331, *pg.* 990
VINE - Video Sharing Service - TWITTER, INC.; *pg.* 1285, *pg.* 228
VINESS - Foam - HSM SOLUTIONS; *pg.* 1884, *pg.* 1378
VINETA - Fabric - NEMSCHOFF, INC.; *pg.* 936, *pg.* 1890
VINEYARD - Furniture - BROWN JORDAN INTERNATIONAL COMPANY; *pg.* 919, *pg.* 740
VINEYARD - Table Textile - HERITAGE LACE INC.; *pg.* 694, *pg.* 711
VINEYARD - Dinnerware - THE HOMER LAUGHLIN CHINA COMPANY; *pg.* 1125, *pg.* 1850
VINEYARD VINES - Clothing - VINEYARD VINES LLC; *pg.* 50, *pg.* 379
VINIKA - Plastic Compound & Resin - A. SCHULMAN, INC.; *pg.* 1144, *pg.* 1452
VINNATA - Kitchen Product - KOHLER CO.; *pg.* 91, *pg.* 1862
VINO - Dinnerware - THE HOMER LAUGHLIN CHINA

COMPANY; *pg.* 1125, *pg.* 1850
VINO - Fabric - NEMSCHOFF, INC.; *pg.* 936, *pg.* 1890
VINO E ORO - Tile - ARTISTIC TILE INC.; *pg.* 914, *pg.* 1119
VINOPHANE - Plastics Product - AEP INDUSTRIES INC.; *pg.* 1878, *pg.* 1085
VINSOL - Resin - HERCULES INCORPORATED; *pg.* 1166, *pg.* 392
VINTAGE - Rug - ETHAN ALLEN INTERIORS INC.; *pg.* 924, *pg.* 343
VINTAGE - Furniture - JASPER GROUP; *pg.* 930, *pg.* 691
VINTAGE - Bath Product - KOHLER CO.; *pg.* 91, *pg.* 1862
VINTAGE - Fabric - NEMSCHOFF, INC.; *pg.* 936, *pg.* 1890
VINTAGE - Bag - SOLO; *pg.* 12, *pg.* 1165
VINTAGE - Wood Product - TEMBEC INC.; *pg.* 114, *pg.* 1957
VINTAGE - Ceiling Fan - WESTINGHOUSE LIGHTING CORPORATION; *pg.* 687, *pg.* 1571
VINTAGE - Women's Clothing & Accessories - WOODEN SHIPS OF HOBOKEN; *pg.* 35, *pg.* 1315
VINTAGE ANCHOR - Book Imprint PENGUIN RANDOM HOUSE; *pg.* 1675, *pg.* 1276
VINTAGE BLUE - Sportswear & Dresses - KELLWOOD COMPANY; *pg.* 28, *pg.* 975
VINTAGE ELWAY - Furniture - BASSETT FURNITURE INDUSTRIES, INCORPORATED; *pg.* 916, *pg.* 1776
VINTAGE GLASS - Ceramic, Glass, Stone Tiles & Slabs - WALKER & ZANGER, INC.; *pg.* 119, *pg.* 281
VINTAGE NATURAL BEEF - Beef Products - NATIONAL BEEF PACKING COMPANY, LLC; *pg.* 882, *pg.* 985
VINTAGE RE-ISSUE - Guitar Strings - GIBSON GUITAR CORP.; *pg.* 550, *pg.* 1650
VINTAGE ROSE - Scarf - HERITAGE LACE INC.; *pg.* 694, *pg.* 711
VINTAGE SIXTY-SIX - Jewelry - ALEX AND ANI; *pg.* 1, *pg.* 1600
VINTAGE STRAIGHT 539 - Jean - LEVI STRAUSS & CO.; *pg.* 43, *pg.* 220
VINTAGE STUDIO - Misses' Sportswear & Dresses - KELLWOOD COMPANY; *pg.* 28, *pg.* 975
VINTELA - Software - DELL SOFTWARE; *pg.* 385, *pg.* 40
VINTELLIGENCE - VIN decoder - IHS AUTOMOTIVE DRIVEN BY POLK; *pg.* 1652, *pg.* 907
VINTNER'S RESERVE - Beverage - KENDALL-JACKSON WINE ESTATES, LTD.; *pg.* 1965, *pg.* 277
VINYL - Cushion - DYNATRONICS CORPORATION; *pg.* 1526, *pg.* 1757
VINYL-CLAD - Door - LARSON MANUFACTURING COMPANY; *pg.* 93, *pg.* 1624
VINYL DETAILS - Building Product - BLUELINX HOLDINGS, INC.; *pg.* 70, *pg.* 491
VINYL FLAT - Coating Product - PPG INDUSTRIES, INC.; *pg.* 1445, *pg.* 1579
VINYL-PANE - Window Material - WARP BROTHERS; *pg.* 1471, *pg.* 595
VINYL SUEDE - Ceiling Paint - PPG INDUSTRIES, INC.; *pg.* 1445, *pg.* 1579
VINYLASTIC - Interior Pigmented Sealer - DUNN-EDWARDS CORPORATION; *pg.* 1442, *pg.* 129
VINYLCIDE - Antifouling Paint - PETTIT PAINT COMPANY; *pg.* 1444, *pg.* 1116
VINYLEX - Automotive Protectant Cleaners - SUMMIT INDUSTRIES, INC.; *pg.* 1599, *pg.* 535
VINYLUBE - Plastic Additives - LONZA INC.; *pg.* 1171, *pg.* 1041
VIO - Beverages - THE COCA-COLA COMPANY; *pg.* 240, *pg.* 493
VIOGNIER - Wine - BILTMORE ESTATE WINE COMPANY; *pg.* 1958, *pg.* 1358
VIOGNIER - Wine - KENDALL-JACKSON WINE ESTATES, LTD.; *pg.* 1965, *pg.* 277
VIP - Power Supply System - INDUCTOTHERM CORP.; *pg.* 1348, *pg.* 1114
VIP - Mini-Terminals - INDUSTRIAL ELECTRONIC ENGINEERS, INC.; *pg.* 644, *pg.* 300
VIP - Seating Product - IRWIN SEATING COMPANY INC.; *pg.* 929, *pg.* 887
VIP - Medical Product - ST. JUDE MEDICAL, INC.; *pg.* 1596, *pg.* 963
VIP 10 - Video Encoder/Decoder - BOSCH SECURITY SYSTEMS, INC.; *pg.* 626, *pg.* 1158
VIP 1000 - Video Encoder/Decoder - BOSCH SECURITY SYSTEMS, INC.; *pg.* 626, *pg.* 1158
VIP AUTHENTICATION - Internet Site Security Product - VERISIGN, INC.; *pg.* 488, *pg.* 1799
VIP/BALBOA - Image Processor Board - ISC8; *pg.* 1350, *pg.* 71
VIP CLUB - Players Club - NEW JERSEY STATE LOTTERY; *pg.* 1000, *pg.* 1126
VIP CREDENTIAL - Online Transaction Security Product - VERISIGN, INC.; *pg.* 488, *pg.* 1799
VIP FILM HOLDER - Dental Product - DENTSPLY INTERNATIONAL INC.; *pg.* 1522, *pg.* 1596
VIP FRAUD DETECTION - Internet Site Security Product - VERISIGN, INC.; *pg.* 488, *pg.* 1799
VIP POWER TRAK - Induction Melting Systems - INDUCTOTHERM CORP.; *pg.* 1348, *pg.* 1114
VIP SEATING - Seating - IRWIN SEATING COMPANY INC.; *pg.* 929, *pg.* 887
VIP X1 - Video Encoder - BOSCH SECURITY SYSTEMS, INC.; *pg.* 626, *pg.* 1158
VIP X2 - Video Encoder - BOSCH SECURITY SYSTEMS, INC.; *pg.* 626, *pg.* 1158
VIP XD - Video Decoder - BOSCH SECURITY SYSTEMS, INC.; *pg.* 626, *pg.* 1158
VIPAC - Power Supply System - VICOR CORPORATION; *pg.* 1435, *pg.* 783
VIPAK - Enclosure System - O'BRIEN CORPORATION; *pg.* 1366, *pg.* 1001
VIPDESK CONNECT - Services - ASPIRE LIFESTYLES OF THE AMERICAS; *pg.* 1230, *pg.* 1770
VIPER - Solid Imaging Material - 3D SYSTEMS CORPORATION; *pg.* 339, *pg.* 1621
VIPER - Battery Charging Product - CLORE AUTOMOTIVE LLC; *pg.* 202, *pg.* 716
VIPER - Laser & Laser System - COHERENT, INC.; *pg.* 1406, *pg.* 265
VIPER - Automobile Electronics - DEI HOLDINGS, INC.; *pg.* 633, *pg.* 302
VIPER - Gaming Product - GLD PRODUCTS, INC.; *pg.* 1835, *pg.* 1882
VIPER - Hose - THE GOODYEAR TIRE & RUBBER COMPANY; *pg.* 1883, *pg.* 1401
VIPER - Pool Cleaner - HAYWARD POOL PRODUCTS; *pg.* 1049, *pg.* 1057
VIPER - Medical Device - INTEGRA LIFESCIENCES HOLDINGS CORPORATION; *pg.* 1545, *pg.* 1109
VIPER - Automated Macro-Defect Inspection System - KLA-TENCOR CORPORATION; *pg.* 1353, *pg.* 146
VIPER - Security & Law Enforcement Products - MACE SECURITY INTERNATIONAL, INC.; *pg.* 1172, *pg.* 1541
VIPER - Labeling Product - PANDUIT CORP.; *pg.* 661, *pg.* 663
VIPER - Firearms - REMINGTON ARMS COMPANY, LLC; *pg.* 1844, *pg.* 1382
VIPER - Software - THE VANGUARD GROUP, INC.; *pg.* 816, *pg.* 1550
VIPER - Coulter - YETTER MANUFACTURING CO., INC.; *pg.* 708, *pg.* 598
VIPER-G - Recloser Component - G&W ELECTRIC COMPANY; *pg.* 1338, *pg.* 558
VIPER M1 - Skate - ROLLER DERBY SKATE CORP.; *pg.* 966, *pg.* 630
VIPER-S - Solid Dielectric - G&W ELECTRIC COMPANY; *pg.* 1338, *pg.* 558
VIPER-ST - Solid Dielectric - G&W ELECTRIC COMPANY; *pg.* 1338, *pg.* 558
VIPFLEX2 - Plate Reader - X-RITE, INCORPORATED; *pg.* 1437, *pg.* 891
VIPP - Software - XEROX CORPORATION; *pg.* 494, *pg.* 365
VIPRION - Software - F5 NETWORKS, INC.; *pg.* 396, *pg.* 1835
VIQ SHUTTLE DRA - Software - VIQ SOLUTIONS INC.; *pg.* 490, *pg.* 1905
VIRACEPT - Medicine - PFIZER INC.; *pg.* 1581, *pg.* 1278
VIRACLE - Nutritional Supplement - LANELABS USA INC.; *pg.* 1554, *pg.* 1128
VIRACON - Glass Fabricating - APOGEE ENTERPRISES, INC.; *pg.* 67, *pg.* 930
VIRACON CURVLITE - Auto Replacement Glass - APOGEE ENTERPRISES, INC.; *pg.* 67, *pg.* 930
VIRAMIDINE - Pharmaceutical Product - VALEANT PHARMACEUTICALS INTERNATIONAL; *pg.* 1605, *pg.* 1047
VIRAPOWER - Molecular Biology Product - THERMO FISHER SCIENTIFIC INC.; *pg.* 1602, *pg.* 61
VIRATEC - Optical Glass - APOGEE ENTERPRISES, INC.; *pg.* 67, *pg.* 930
VIRAZOLE - Pharmaceutical Product - VALEANT PHARMACEUTICALS INTERNATIONAL; *pg.* 1605, *pg.* 1047
VIRCHEM - Chemical Product - CARUS CORPORATION; *pg.* 1152, *pg.* 652
VIREAD - Biopharmaceutical Product - GILEAD SCIENCES, INC.; *pg.* 1535, *pg.* 88
VIRGIN RIVER HOTEL - Resort, Casino & Bingo - MESQUITE GAMING, LLC; *pg.* 1104, *pg.* 1030
VIRGIN VINES - Wine - BROWN-FORMAN CORPORATION; *pg.* 1958, *pg.* 732
VIRGINIA BRAND - Honey & Salad Dressing - VITA FOOD PRODUCTS, INC.; *pg.* 909, *pg.* 595
VIRGINIA DARE - Flavors & Colors - VIRGINIA DARE EXTRACT CO., INC.; *pg.* 908, *pg.* 1147
VIRGINIA IS FOR LOVERS - Slogan - VIRGINIA TOURISM AUTHORITY; *pg.* 1010, *pg.* 1804
VIRGINIA LAWYERS WEEKLY - Newspaper - MASSACHUSETTS LAWYERS WEEKLY, INC.; *pg.* 1662, *pg.* 798
VIRGINIA POWER - Electric Utility - DOMINION VIRGINIA POWER; *pg.* 1939, *pg.* 1802
VIRGINIA REEL - Meat Products - BAR-S FOODS CO.; *pg.* 839, *pg.* 15
VIRGINIA SLIMS - Cigarettes - PHILIP MORRIS USA INC.; *pg.* 1894, *pg.* 1803
VIRGINIAN PILOT - Media Product Service - PILOT MEDIA; *pg.* 1677, *pg.* 1797
VIRIDIAN - Casegoods - STEELCASE INC.; *pg.* 475, *pg.* 889
VIRISORB - Minerals - MINERALS TECHNOLOGIES INC.; *pg.* 1173, *pg.* 617
VIROCLEAR - Software - BIO-RAD LABORATORIES, INC.; *pg.* 1504, *pg.* 101
VIROCLEAR MUMZ - Software - BIO-RAD LABORATORIES, INC.; *pg.* 1504, *pg.* 101
VIRODETECT - Software - BIO-RAD LABORATORIES, INC.; *pg.* 1504, *pg.* 101
VIROGEN - Pharmaceutical Product - ALERE INC.; *pg.* 1488, *pg.* 849
VIROPTIC - Pharmaceutical Product - KING PHARMACEUTICALS, INC.; *pg.* 1553, *pg.* 1627
VIROTROL - Software - BIO-RAD LABORATORIES, INC.; *pg.* 1504, *pg.* 101
VIRSIM - Software - SYNOPSYS, INC.; *pg.* 480, *pg.* 162
VIRTEK LASERCNC - Laser Projection System - VIRTEK VISION INTERNATIONAL, INC.; *pg.* 1435, *pg.* 1948
VIRTEK LASEREDGE - Laser Engraving Solution - VIRTEK VISION INTERNATIONAL, INC.; *pg.* 1435, *pg.* 1948
VIRTEK LASERMC - Laser Engraving Solution - VIRTEK VISION INTERNATIONAL, INC.; *pg.* 1435, *pg.* 1948
VIRTEK LPS7 - Laser Projector - VIRTEK VISION INTERNATIONAL, INC.; *pg.* 1435, *pg.* 1948
VIRTEK TRUSSLINE - Laser Engraving Solution - VIRTEK VISION INTERNATIONAL, INC.; *pg.* 1435, *pg.* 1948
VIRTEK VIP - Prefabricated Construction - VIRTEK VISION INTERNATIONAL, INC.; *pg.* 1435, *pg.* 1948
VIRTUAL AC - Neutralizer - MKS INSTRUMENTS, INC.; *pg.* 1362, *pg.* 781
VIRTUAL AUDIO - Audio System - QSOUND LABS, INC.; *pg.* 666, *pg.* 1904
VIRTUAL CHART - Computer Software - ASTRO-MED, INC.; *pg.* 619, *pg.* 1609
VIRTUAL COLLECTION AGENT - Online Financial Services - ACI WORLDWIDE; *pg.* 710, *pg.* 1777
VIRTUAL ENGINE - Simulator System - MTS SYSTEMS CORPORATION; *pg.* 442, *pg.* 923
VIRTUAL FILE MANAGER - Software - NETAPP, INC.; *pg.* 444, *pg.* 287
VIRTUAL MASTERCARD - Credit Card - MASTERCARD INCORPORATED; *pg.* 779, *pg.* 1325
VIRTUAL MATRIX - Software - EMC CORPORATION; *pg.* 391, *pg.* 825
VIRTUAL MATRIX ARCHITECTURE - Software - EMC CORPORATION; *pg.* 391, *pg.* 825
VIRTUAL NEGAWATT POWER PLAN - Demand Response System - SYNACOR, INC.; *pg.* 479, *pg.* 1380
VIRTUAL PEAKING CAPACITY - Software - COMVERGE, INC.; *pg.* 1325, *pg.* 536
VIRTUAL PIPELINE - Processors - AVAGO TECHNOLOGIES; *pg.* 358, *pg.* 238
VIRTUAL PROCESS ENGINEER - Electric Instrument - UNIVERSAL INSTRUMENTS CORPORATION; *pg.* 683, *pg.* 1154
VIRTUAL PROVISIONING - Software - EMC CORPORATION; *pg.* 391, *pg.* 825
VIRTUAL SIMULATOR - Software - EAGLE POINT SOFTWARE CORPORATION; *pg.* 389, *pg.* 707
VIRTUAL VIEW - Alignment System Software - HUNTER ENGINEERING COMPANY; *pg.* 208, *pg.* 973

VIRTUAL WALL - Nitrogen Barrier Device - MKS INSTRUMENTS, INC.; *pg.* 1362, *pg.* 781
VIRTUALHAND - Hardware & Software - IMMERSION CORPORATION; *pg.* 413, *pg.* 246
VIRTUALIZATION & GREEN IT - Event - TECHNOLOGY EXECUTIVES CLUB, LTD.; *pg.* 482, *pg.* 627
VIRTUALLY - Fabric - NEMSCHOFF, INC.; *pg.* 936, *pg.* 1890
VIRTUALLY ANYWHERE - Software - SYMANTEC CORPORATION; *pg.* 478, *pg.* 161
VIRTUALLY INVISIBLE - Audio Product - BOSE CORPORATION; *pg.* 626, *pg.* 820
VIRTUALWIRE - Multiplexing System - CIENA CORPORATION; *pg.* 628, *pg.* 771
VIRTUOSA 153 QE ALEX ANDERSON CLASSIC - Sewing Machines - BERNINA OF AMERICA INC.; *pg.* 51, *pg.* 554
VIRTUOSA 153 QUILTER'S EDITION - Quilting Machines - BERNINA OF AMERICA INC.; *pg.* 51, *pg.* 554
VIRTUOSA 155 - Sewing Machine - BERNINA OF AMERICA INC.; *pg.* 51, *pg.* 554
VIRTUOSO - Software - CADENCE DESIGN SYSTEMS, INC.; *pg.* 367, *pg.* 239
VIRTUOSO - Curing Light - DEN-MAT CORPORATION; *pg.* 1522, *pg.* 271
VIRTURAL DIME - Telephone Service - IDT CORPORATION; *pg.* 643, *pg.* 1096
VIRULIZIN - Cancer Treatment - APTOSE BIOSCIENCES; *pg.* 1495, *pg.* 1934
VIS-U-ALL - Heat Seal Pouch - STERIS CORPORATION; *pg.* 1597, *pg.* 1464
VISA - Cash Card - VISA U.S.A., INC.; *pg.* 817, *pg.* 231
VISA BUSINESS CARD - Bank-Issued Card for Business Use - VISA U.S.A., INC.; *pg.* 817, *pg.* 231
VISA BUXX - Stored Value Card for Teens - VISA U.S.A., INC.; *pg.* 817, *pg.* 231
VISA CLASSIC CARD - Standard Bank Issued Credit Card - VISA U.S.A., INC.; *pg.* 817, *pg.* 231
VISA DEBIT CARD - Bank-Issued Card That Pays From Customers' Deposit Account - VISA U.S.A., INC.; *pg.* 817, *pg.* 231
VISA GOLD CARD - Upscale Bank-Issued Card - VISA U.S.A., INC.; *pg.* 817, *pg.* 231
VISA INFINITE - Consumer Credit Card - VISA U.S.A., INC.; *pg.* 817, *pg.* 231
VISA-PAC - Passport & Visa Application Service - DHL HOLDINGS (USA), INC.; *pg.* 1906, *pg.* 459
VISA PLATINUM - Consumer Credit Card - VISA U.S.A., INC.; *pg.* 817, *pg.* 231
VISA SIGNATURE - Consumer Credit Card - VISA U.S.A., INC.; *pg.* 817, *pg.* 231
VISA SMART - Chip Cards - VISA U.S.A., INC.; *pg.* 817, *pg.* 231
VISA TRAVEL VOUCHERS - Travelers' Vouchers - VISA U.S.A., INC.; *pg.* 817, *pg.* 231
VISA TRAVELERS CHEQUES - Travelers' Checks - VISA U.S.A., INC.; *pg.* 817, *pg.* 231
VISAGE - Electronic Image Processing Apparatus - EASTMAN KODAK COMPANY; *pg.* 1408, *pg.* 1333
VISAGE - Cosmetics - REVLON, INC.; *pg.* 521, *pg.* 1286
VISAGERT - Software - MERCURY COMPUTER SYSTEMS, INC.; *pg.* 434, *pg.* 813
VISBA - DVD Encoder Chip - ESS TECHNOLOGY, INC.; *pg.* 395, *pg.* 90
VISCAL - Calibration Kit - BROOKFIELD ENGINEERING LABORATORIES, INC.; *pg.* 1403, *pg.* 833
VISCARIN - Food Ingredient - FMC CORPORATION; *pg.* 1163, *pg.* 1564
VISCO JET - MicroHydraulic Product - THE LEE COMPANY; *pg.* 1420, *pg.* 383
VISCO/MAX - Multi-shaft Dissolver - MOREHOUSE-COWLES; *pg.* 1363, *pg.* 66
VISCOFOAM - Wheelchair Cushions - INVACARE CORPORATION; *pg.* 1546, *pg.* 1451
VISCOGEL - Waxy Maize Starches - CARGILL LIMITED; *pg.* 1475, *pg.* 1914
VISCOLAS - Medical & Aesthetic Product - DYNATRONICS CORPORATION; *pg.* 1526, *pg.* 1757
VISCOLUX - Bedding Foam - CARPENTER CO.; *pg.* 920, *pg.* 1801
VISCOMAT - Motion Picture Photo Processing Apparatus & Chemicals - EASTMAN KODAK COMPANY; *pg.* 1408, *pg.* 1333
VISCON - Fluid Heaters - GRACO, INC.; *pg.* 1342, *pg.* 935
VISCONTI - Confectionery Products - THE HERSHEY CO.; *pg.* 1855, *pg.* 1538
VISCONTI - Carpet - INTERFACE, INC.; *pg.* 695, *pg.* 512
VISCOOL - Metalworking Fluid - ROCK VALLEY OIL & CHEMICAL COMPANY; *pg.* 1179, *pg.* 631
VISCOPHOBE - Polymers - THE DOW CHEMICAL COMPANY; *pg.* 1157, *pg.* 898
VISCOR - Calibration Fluid - ROCK VALLEY OIL & CHEMICAL COMPANY; *pg.* 1179, *pg.* 631
VISCOSEL - Laboratory Viscometer - BROOKFIELD ENGINEERING LABORATORIES, INC.; *pg.* 1403, *pg.* 833
VISCOSENSOR - Sensor - DYNISCO INSTRUMENTS LLC; *pg.* 1526, *pg.* 823
VISCOUNT - Pump - GRACO, INC.; *pg.* 1342, *pg.* 935
VISCTRONIC - Fan Drive - BORGWARNER INC.; *pg.* 167, *pg.* 867
VISE ACTION - Compression Latch - SOUTHCO, INC.; *pg.* 1063, *pg.* 1522
VISE BUDDY - Hand Tools - PANAVISE PRODUCTS, INC.; *pg.* 1058, *pg.* 1032
VISE-GRIP - Locking Pliers - NEWELL RUBBERMAID INC.; *pg.* 1128, *pg.* 515
VISEDGE - Inspection System - KLA-TENCOR CORPORATION; *pg.* 1353, *pg.* 146
VISENZA - Eyeglass Lenses & Blanks - PPG INDUSTRIES, INC.; *pg.* 1445, *pg.* 1579
VISFLEX - Plastic Casing - VISKASE COMPANIES, INC.; *pg.* 1471, *pg.* 599
VISFLO - Lane Conditioner And Cleaner - BOWLMOR AMF; *pg.* 1828, *pg.* 1206
VISHAY ANGSTROHM - Electronic Component - VISHAY INTERTECHNOLOGY, INC.; *pg.* 1435, *pg.* 1551
VISHAY AZTRONIC - Inductors - VISHAY INTERTECHNOLOGY, INC.; *pg.* 1435, *pg.* 1551
VISHAY BCCOMPONENTS - Electronic Component - VISHAY INTERTECHNOLOGY, INC.; *pg.* 1435, *pg.* 1551
VISHAY BEYSCHLAG - Electronic Component - VISHAY INTERTECHNOLOGY, INC.; *pg.* 1435, *pg.* 1551
VISHAY BLH - Load Cell Weighing Systems - VISHAY INTERTECHNOLOGY, INC.; *pg.* 1435, *pg.* 1551
VISHAY CELTRON - Electronic Component - VISHAY INTERTECHNOLOGY, INC.; *pg.* 1435, *pg.* 1551
VISHAY CERA-MITE - Electronic Component - VISHAY INTERTECHNOLOGY, INC.; *pg.* 1435, *pg.* 1551
VISHAY DALE - Resistors/Potentiometers - VISHAY INTERTECHNOLOGY, INC.; *pg.* 1435, *pg.* 1551
VISHAY DRALORIC - Resistors/Potentiometers - VISHAY INTERTECHNOLOGY, INC.; *pg.* 1435, *pg.* 1551
VISHAY ELECTRO-FILMS - Electronic Component - VISHAY INTERTECHNOLOGY, INC.; *pg.* 1435, *pg.* 1551
VISHAY ESTA - Electronic Component - VISHAY INTERTECHNOLOGY, INC.; *pg.* 1435, *pg.* 1551
VISHAY FOIL RESISTORS - Foil Resistors - VISHAY INTERTECHNOLOGY, INC.; *pg.* 1435, *pg.* 1551
VISHAY MICRO-MEASUREMENTS - Electronic Component - VISHAY INTERTECHNOLOGY, INC.; *pg.* 1435, *pg.* 1551
VISHAY NOBEL - Electronic Component - VISHAY INTERTECHNOLOGY, INC.; *pg.* 1435, *pg.* 1551
VISHAY PM ONBOARD - Weighing System - VISHAY INTERTECHNOLOGY, INC.; *pg.* 1435, *pg.* 1551
VISHAY REVERE - Weighing System - VISHAY INTERTECHNOLOGY, INC.; *pg.* 1435, *pg.* 1551
VISHAY ROEDERSTEIN - Film Capacitors - VISHAY INTERTECHNOLOGY, INC.; *pg.* 1435, *pg.* 1551
VISHAY SFERNICE - Resistors/Potentiometers - VISHAY INTERTECHNOLOGY, INC.; *pg.* 1435, *pg.* 1551
VISHAY SPECTROL - Resistors - VISHAY INTERTECHNOLOGY, INC.; *pg.* 1435, *pg.* 1551
VISHAY SPRAGUE - Tantalum Capacitors - VISHAY INTERTECHNOLOGY, INC.; *pg.* 1435, *pg.* 1551
VISHAY SYSTEMS - Test & Measurements - VISHAY INTERTECHNOLOGY, INC.; *pg.* 1435, *pg.* 1551
VISHAY TECHNO - Resistors/Potentiometers - VISHAY INTERTECHNOLOGY, INC.; *pg.* 1435, *pg.* 1551
VISHAY TEDEA-HUNTLEIGH - Electronic Component - VISHAY INTERTECHNOLOGY, INC.; *pg.* 1435, *pg.* 1551
VISHAY THIN FILM - Resistors - VISHAY INTERTECHNOLOGY, INC.; *pg.* 1435, *pg.* 1551
VISHAY TRANSDUCERS - Test & Measurements - VISHAY INTERTECHNOLOGY, INC.; *pg.* 1435, *pg.* 1551
VISHAY ULTRONIX - Resistors/Potentiometers - VISHAY INTERTECHNOLOGY, INC.; *pg.* 1435, *pg.* 1551
VISHAY VITRAMON - Electronic Component - VISHAY INTERTECHNOLOGY, INC.; *pg.* 1435, *pg.* 1551
VISI-BLUE - Transilluminator System - UVP, INC.; *pg.* 1434, *pg.* 298
VISI-FLOAT - Flowmeter - DWYER INSTRUMENTS INC.; *pg.* 1330, *pg.* 694
VISI/VAC - Circuit Interrupters - SCHNEIDER ELECTRIC USA, INC.; *pg.* 1306, *pg.* 650
VISIAN ICL - Implantable Collamer Lens - STAAR SURGICAL COMPANY; *pg.* 1597, *pg.* 151
VISIAN TORIC ICL - Implantable Collamer Lens - STAAR SURGICAL COMPANY; *pg.* 1597, *pg.* 151
VISIBEAD - Solid Glass Beads for Wet-Night Reflecting - POTTERS INDUSTRIES, INC.; *pg.* 105, *pg.* 1515
VISIBEAD - Glass Beads - PQ CORPORATION; *pg.* 1178, *pg.* 1515
VISIBILITY - Wireless Telecommunication Product - SYNIVERSE HOLDINGS, INC.; *pg.* 479, *pg.* 475
VISIBLE IMPACT - Firearm Targets - CROSMAN CORPORATION; *pg.* 951, *pg.* 1143
VISIBLE SOLUTIONS - Paint - THE SHERWIN-WILLIAMS COMPANY; *pg.* 1447, *pg.* 1435
VISIBLY BETTER - Slogan - PGT, INC.; *pg.* 104, *pg.* 452
VISIBLY EVEN - Skin Care Product - NEUTROGENA CORPORATION; *pg.* 517, *pg.* 137
VISICOL - Pharmaceutical Product - SALIX PHARMACEUTICALS, INC.; *pg.* 1591, *pg.* 1388
VISICONN - Software - DAKTRONICS, INC.; *pg.* 633, *pg.* 1624
VISIDOC-IT - Imaging System - UVP, INC.; *pg.* 1434, *pg.* 298
VISIFLEX SUREPASS - Delivery System - ENDOLOGIX, INC.; *pg.* 1528, *pg.* 109
VISIG - Software - RAYTHEON COMPANY; *pg.* 233, *pg.* 854
VISIGUN - Safety Marking Sphere Dispenser - POTTERS INDUSTRIES, INC.; *pg.* 105, *pg.* 1515
VISIGUN - Glass Beads - PQ CORPORATION; *pg.* 1178, *pg.* 1515
VISIKOM - Telephone Intercom - ATLAS SOUND; *pg.* 621, *pg.* 1692
VISILEX - Medical Device - C.R. BARD, INC.; *pg.* 1519, *pg.* 1094
VISIMATE - Labeling & Sign System - VARITRONICS, LLC; *pg.* 487, *pg.* 954
VISINE - Eye Drops - JOHNSON & JOHNSON; *pg.* 1549, *pg.* 1091
VISINE - Red & Dry Eye Relief - MCNEIL-PPC, INC.; *pg.* 1560, *pg.* 1533
VISIO - Beta Vario Light Unit - 3M COMPANY; *pg.* 1142, *pg.* 956
VISION - Diagnostic Products - ABBOTT LABORATORIES; *pg.* 1484, *pg.* 551
VISION - Carpet - BEAULIEU GROUP, LLC; *pg.* 917, *pg.* 529
VISION - Load Port Module - BROOKS AUTOMATION, INC.; *pg.* 1320, *pg.* 813
VISION - Holter Monitoring Device - CARDIAC SCIENCE CORPORATION; *pg.* 1512, *pg.* 1897
VISION - Software - DAEGIS INC; *pg.* 381, *pg.* 195
VISION - Software - DST SYSTEMS, INC.; *pg.* 388, *pg.* 982
VISION - Software System - FISERV, INC.; *pg.* 397, *pg.* 1855
VISION - Truck Cabs - MACK TRUCKS, INC.; *pg.* 183, *pg.* 1375
VISION - Sail Boats - MARLOW-HUNTER LLC; *pg.* 1709, *pg.* 409
VISION - Fabric - NEMSCHOFF, INC.; *pg.* 936, *pg.* 1890
VISION - Supplement & Food Product - NEW EARTH LIFE SCIENCES, INC.; *pg.* 1573, *pg.* 1499
VISION - Mid-priced Frameless Stock & Semi-custom Cabinets - NORCRAFT HOLDINGS, LP; *pg.* 100, *pg.* 921
VISION - Servers & Gateways - ONMOBILE LIVE, INC.; *pg.* 449, *pg.* 829
VISION - Motorhome - REXHALL INDUSTRIES, INC.; *pg.* 1710, *pg.* 121
VISION - Medical System - VARIAN MEDICAL SYSTEMS, INC.; *pg.* 1434, *pg.* 178
VISION AIRE - Rolling Grille - CORNELL IRON WORKS, INC.; *pg.* 77, *pg.* 1554
VISION & SOLUTION CENTER - Technology Evaluation Services - CACI INTERNATIONAL INC.; *pg.* 367, *pg.* 1773
VISION DELIVERED - Software Program - CENVEO INC.; *pg.* 1626, *pg.* 372
VISION DIRECT - Video Cameras - DIEBOLD, INCORPORATED; *pg.* 387, *pg.* 1407
VISION ESSENTIALS - Supplement & Food Product - NEW EARTH LIFE SCIENCES, INC.; *pg.* 1573, *pg.* 1499
VISION FIRST - Free Eye Exam Program - CLEVELAND BROWNS FOOTBALL COMPANY LLC; *pg.* 541, *pg.* 1406
VISION FIRST DESIGN - Ophthalmic Technology - SIGNET ARMORLITE, INC.; *pg.* 1429, *pg.* 60
VISION GLIDE - Side-Folding Grille - CORNELL IRON WORKS, INC.; *pg.* 77, *pg.* 1554

VISION HIP SYSTEM - Hip Product - ZIMMER BIOMET HOLDINGS, INC.; *pg.* 1611, *pg.* 699
VISION OF THE FUTURE - Tagline - STAAR SURGICAL COMPANY; *pg.* 1597, *pg.* 151
VISION OF THE SEAS - Cruise Ship - ROYAL CARIBBEAN CRUISES LTD; *pg.* 1921, *pg.* 446
VISION SERIES - Slot Machines - INTERNATIONAL GAME TECHNOLOGY; *pg.* 957, *pg.* 1024
VISION SHAPING TREATMENT - Overnight Orthokeratology - BAUSCH & LOMB INCORPORATED; *pg.* 1401, *pg.* 1045
VISION VOICE SERVER - Product - ONMOBILE LIVE, INC.; *pg.* 449, *pg.* 829
VISION WORLD - Eye Care Centers - VISIONWORKS OF AMERICA, INC.; *pg.* 1436, *pg.* 1744
VISION360 - Software - SYMANTEC CORPORATION; *pg.* 478, *pg.* 161
VISIONALL - Lens - DANKER LABORATORIES INC.; *pg.* 1408, *pg.* 465
VISIONALL MULTI - Lens - DANKER LABORATORIES INC.; *pg.* 1408, *pg.* 465
VISIONARY - Major Surgery Light - MEDLINE INDUSTRIES, INC.; *pg.* 1562, *pg.* 635
VISIONBANK - Computer Equipment - VIEWSONIC CORPORATION; *pg.* 489, *pg.* 303
VISIONCAST - Conferencing - PREMIERE GLOBAL SERVICES, INC.; *pg.* 1275, *pg.* 518
VISIONEX - Nutritional Supplement - USANA HEALTH SCIENCES, INC.; *pg.* 1605, *pg.* 1761
VISIONICE II - Software - WIND RIVER SYSTEMS, INC.; *pg.* 493, *pg.* 38
VISIONPAK - Packaging System - AMKOR TECHNOLOGY, INC.; *pg.* 67, *pg.* 25
VISIONPRO - Software - COGNEX CORPORATION; *pg.* 1406, *pg.* 834
VISIONPRO - Thermostat - HONEYWELL INTERNATIONAL INC.; *pg.* 407, *pg.* 1088
VISIONPROBE II - Software - WIND RIVER SYSTEMS, INC.; *pg.* 493, *pg.* 38
VISIONS - Corporate Furniture & Conference Tables - BERNHARDT DESIGN; *pg.* 918, *pg.* 1381
VISIONS - Furniture - BUSH INDUSTRIES INC.; *pg.* 919, *pg.* 1170
VISIONS - Rug - COURISTAN INC.; *pg.* 921, *pg.* 1067
VISIONSOFT - Software - ANC SPORTS ENTERPRISES, LLC; *pg.* 1825, *pg.* 1325
VISIONSTRIP - Roofing Material - TREMCO INCORPORATED; *pg.* 116, *pg.* 1405
VISIONTEC - Head Restraint Controls - LEAR CORPORATION; *pg.* 229, *pg.* 907
VISIONTOOLS - Software - CRESTRON ELECTRONICS INC.; *pg.* 631, *pg.* 1116
VISIONVIEW - Machine Vision System - COGNEX CORPORATION; *pg.* 1406, *pg.* 834
VISIONWARE - Software System - KRONOS INCORPORATED; *pg.* 425, *pg.* 813
VISIONWARE - Software - WIND RIVER SYSTEMS, INC.; *pg.* 493, *pg.* 38
VISIONWORKS - Eye Care Centers - VISIONWORKS OF AMERICA, INC.; *pg.* 1436, *pg.* 1744
VISIONWRITER - Electronic Display System - TRANS-LUX CORPORATION; *pg.* 681, *pg.* 365
VISIONXD - Software - WIND RIVER SYSTEMS, INC.; *pg.* 493, *pg.* 38
VISIPAQUE - Medical Device - GE HEALTHCARE TECHNOLOGIES; *pg.* 1533, *pg.* 1897
VISIPLUS - Optical Sensor - CHECKPOINT SYSTEMS, INC.; *pg.* 628, *pg.* 1559
VISLON - Zipper - YKK CORPORATION OF AMERICA; *pg.* 699, *pg.* 536
VISMAX - Sausage Casing - VISKASE COMPANIES, INC.; *pg.* 1471, *pg.* 599
VISOR - Ergonomic Seating - KNOLL, INC.; *pg.* 425, *pg.* 1527
VISOR SHELF-IT - Truck Equipment - AMERICAN VAN EQUIPMENT INC.; *pg.* 199, *pg.* 1078
VISPLAY - Wall System - MARLITE, INC.; *pg.* 95, *pg.* 1448
VISPLAY AIR - Wall System - MARLITE, INC.; *pg.* 95, *pg.* 1448
VISPLAY AREA - Wall System - MARLITE, INC.; *pg.* 95, *pg.* 1448
VISPLAY BEAM - Wall System - MARLITE, INC.; *pg.* 95, *pg.* 1448
VISPLAY INVISIBLE - Wall System - MARLITE, INC.; *pg.* 95, *pg.* 1448
VISPLAY MONO - Wall System - MARLITE, INC.; *pg.* 95, *pg.* 1448
VISPLAY STRIPES - Wall System - MARLITE, INC.; *pg.* 95, *pg.* 1448
VISQUEEN - Plastics Product - AEP INDUSTRIES INC.; *pg.* 1878, *pg.* 1085
VISSION - Computer Control - VILTER MANUFACTURING LLC; *pg.* 1078, *pg.* 1856
VISTA - Modern Occasional Tables - BERNHARDT DESIGN; *pg.* 918, *pg.* 1381
VISTA - Software - EPICOR SOFTWARE CORPORATION; *pg.* 393, *pg.* 110
VISTA - Account Management Risk Score Service - FAIR ISAAC CORPORATION; *pg.* 1247, *pg.* 955
VISTA - Towel Dispenser - GEORGIA-PACIFIC LLC; *pg.* 1458, *pg.* 507
VISTA - Medical Product - GF HEALTH PRODUCTS, INC.; *pg.* 1535, *pg.* 508
VISTA - Control Panel - HONEYWELL INTERNATIONAL INC.; *pg.* 407, *pg.* 1088
VISTA - Steel Office Furniture - INVINCIBLE OFFICE FURNITURE; *pg.* 420, *pg.* 1868
VISTA - Appliances - JARDEN CONSUMER SOLUTIONS; *pg.* 57, *pg.* 412
VISTA - Furniture - JASPER GROUP; *pg.* 930, *pg.* 691
VISTA - Systems Integration & Aeronautics - LOCKHEED MARTIN CORPORATION; *pg.* 229, *pg.* 762
VISTA - Personal Grooming Product - MILLERS FORGE INC.; *pg.* 1056, *pg.* 1733
VISTA - Gas Delivery Pressure Transducer - MKS INSTRUMENTS, INC.; *pg.* 1362, *pg.* 781
VISTA - Melter - NORDSON CORPORATION; *pg.* 1365, *pg.* 1480
VISTA - Skylights - ODL INCORPORATED; *pg.* 101, *pg.* 914
VISTA - Medical Device - RESMED INC.; *pg.* 1589, *pg.* 207
VISTA - Switchgear - S&C ELECTRIC COMPANY; *pg.* 1305, *pg.* 589
VISTA - Retractable Awnings - SUNSETTER PRODUCTS, LP; *pg.* 113, *pg.* 830
VISTA - Control System - VILTER MANUFACTURING LLC; *pg.* 1078, *pg.* 1856
VISTA - Motor Homes - WINNEBAGO INDUSTRIES, INC.; *pg.* 1712, *pg.* 707
VISTA 2000 EXTRA - Steel Office Furniture - INVINCIBLE OFFICE FURNITURE; *pg.* 420, *pg.* 1868
VISTA GLIDE - Side-Folding Closure - CORNELL IRON WORKS, INC.; *pg.* 77, *pg.* 1554
VISTA IC - Healthcare Product - GF HEALTH PRODUCTS, INC.; *pg.* 1535, *pg.* 508
VISTA PLUS - Software - DELL SOFTWARE; *pg.* 385, *pg.* 40
VISTA VIEW - Display System - EVANS & SUTHERLAND COMPUTER CORPORATION; *pg.* 638, *pg.* 1757
VISTABEL - Skin Care Product - ALLERGAN, INC.; *pg.* 1491, *pg.* 106
VISTACAM - Intraoral Video Camera System - AIR TECHNIQUES, INC.; *pg.* 1487, *pg.* 1178
VISTACAPTURE - Software - SCAN-OPTICS, LLC; *pg.* 467, *pg.* 354
VISTACOR - Glass & Ceramic Material - CORNING INCORPORATED; *pg.* 1122, *pg.* 1154
VISTACPG - Software - JDA SOFTWARE GROUP, INC.; *pg.* 423, *pg.* 22
VISTAGARD - Rolling Grille - CORNELL IRON WORKS, INC.; *pg.* 77, *pg.* 1554
VISTAGRAY - Glass Product - PPG INDUSTRIES, INC.; *pg.* 1445, *pg.* 1579
VISTAR - Closed Circuit Television Equipment - VICON INDUSTRIES, INC.; *pg.* 685, *pg.* 1166
VISTARIL - Medicine - PFIZER INC.; *pg.* 1581, *pg.* 1278
VISTAWALL - Architectural Product - BUTLER MANUFACTURING COMPANY; *pg.* 72, *pg.* 981
VISTCONNECT - Software - VISTEON CORPORATION; *pg.* 221, *pg.* 912
VISTEC - Analytical Technology - BAKER PETROLITE CORPORATION; *pg.* 1148, *pg.* 1745
VISTEON VOICE TECHNOLOGY - Voice Activation System - VISTEON CORPORATION; *pg.* 221, *pg.* 912
VISTIDE - Biopharmaceutical Product - GILEAD SCIENCES, INC.; *pg.* 1535, *pg.* 88
VISTIVE - Insecticides - MONSANTO COMPANY; *pg.* 1173, *pg.* 999
VISU-GLOW - Leak Detector - LA-CO INDUSTRIES MARKAL CO., INC.; *pg.* 1170, *pg.* 610
VISU-TEMP - Pressure Balanced Safety Shower Systems - SYMMONS INDUSTRIES, INC.; *pg.* 114, *pg.* 803
VISUAL 1040 TAX - Comprehensive Individual Tax Preparation Software - SAGE SOFTWARE, INC.; *pg.* 464, *pg.* 116
VISUAL ACCOUNTS PAYABLE - Payables Tracking & Cash Management Program - SAGE SOFTWARE, INC.; *pg.* 464, *pg.* 116
VISUAL ACCOUNTS RECEIVABLE - Sales Entry & Receivables Management Program - SAGE SOFTWARE, INC.; *pg.* 464, *pg.* 116
VISUAL APB - Software Suite - MOTOROLA SOLUTIONS, INC.; *pg.* 657, *pg.* 659
VISUAL AUTO TELLER - Remote Banking - DIEBOLD, INCORPORATED; *pg.* 387, *pg.* 1407
VISUAL COMMUNICATOR - Software - ADOBE SYSTEMS INCORPORATED; *pg.* 342, *pg.* 235
VISUAL COMMUNICATOR PRO - Digital Media System - REALNETWORKS, INC.; *pg.* 460, *pg.* 1839
VISUAL CONCERT PC - Video Conferencing Product - POLYCOM, INC.; *pg.* 664, *pg.* 249
VISUAL CONSTRUCTION - Software - AUTODESK INC.; *pg.* 356, *pg.* 257
VISUAL DEPRECIATION - Depreciation & Asset Management System - SAGE SOFTWARE, INC.; *pg.* 464, *pg.* 116
VISUAL DIRECTOR - Wireless Communication System - AT&T SOUTHEAST; *pg.* 1868, *pg.* 489
VISUAL EXCELLENCE PROCESSING - Image Processing Product - SEMTECH CORPORATION GENNUM PRODUCTS; *pg.* 671, *pg.* 1919
VISUAL FIXTURING - Measurement Evaluation - PERCEPTRON, INC.; *pg.* 215, *pg.* 904
VISUAL HD - Business Service Management Product - DATAWATCH CORPORATION; *pg.* 383, *pg.* 813
VISUAL HELP DESK - Business Service Management Product - DATAWATCH CORPORATION; *pg.* 383, *pg.* 813
VISUAL INSIGHT - Business Intelligence Product - DATAWATCH CORPORATION; *pg.* 383, *pg.* 813
VISUAL LATCH - Stroller Latching System - EVENFLO COMPANY, INC.; *pg.* 924, *pg.* 1470
VISUAL LISP - Software - AUTODESK INC.; *pg.* 356, *pg.* 257
VISUAL PREFECTION - Beauty Product - AVON PRODUCTS, INC.; *pg.* 500, *pg.* 1198
VISUAL RECALL - Manual - XEROX CORPORATION; *pg.* 494, *pg.* 365
VISUAL SURVEY - Software - AUTODESK INC.; *pg.* 356, *pg.* 257
VISUAL SYSTEM SIMULATOR - Computer Software - AWR CORPORATION; *pg.* 623, *pg.* 78
VISUAL TEST EXTENSIONS - Electronic Instrument - KEITHLEY INSTRUMENTS, INC.; *pg.* 1418, *pg.* 1473
VISUALFONE - Hardware & Software - ANALOG DEVICES, INC.; *pg.* 617, *pg.* 839
VISUALLYNUX - Software - LYNX SOFTWARE TECHNOLOGIES; *pg.* 429, *pg.* 247
VISUALLYNUX IDE - Development Tool - LYNX SOFTWARE TECHNOLOGIES; *pg.* 429, *pg.* 247
VISUALPAYMENTS - Software - VERIFONE SYSTEMS, INC.; *pg.* 487, *pg.* 251
VISUALSAN - Software System - EMC CORPORATION; *pg.* 391, *pg.* 825
VISUALSCOPE - Software - KEITHLEY INSTRUMENTS, INC.; *pg.* 1418, *pg.* 1473
VISUALSRM - Software System - EMC CORPORATION; *pg.* 391, *pg.* 825
VISUALWORKS - Software - CINCOM SYSTEMS, INC.; *pg.* 372, *pg.* 1411
VISUM - Surgical Light - STRYKER CORPORATION; *pg.* 1598, *pg.* 894
VISV - Container - HOSPIRA, INC.; *pg.* 1542, *pg.* 623
VISWISE - Wireless Telecommunication Product - SYNIVERSE HOLDINGS, INC.; *pg.* 479, *pg.* 475
VISX - Software Product - CLARY CORPORATION; *pg.* 226, *pg.* 150
VIT-PLUS - Carbon Steel Product - AK STEEL HOLDING CORPORATION; *pg.* 1311, *pg.* 1479
VITA - Soft Drink - THE COCA-COLA COMPANY; *pg.* 240, *pg.* 493
VITA - Dental Product - DENTSPLY INTERNATIONAL INC.; *pg.* 1522, *pg.* 1596
VITA - Fish Products - VITA FOOD PRODUCTS, INC.; *pg.* 909, *pg.* 595
VITA-15 - Animal Safety Product - NEOGEN CORPORATION; *pg.* 883, *pg.* 896
VITA BURST - Food Product - SUN-RYPE PRODUCTS LTD.; *pg.* 899, *pg.* 1908

First page reference indicates Business Class Edition
Second page reference indicates Geographic Edition

VITA COCO - Coconut Water - ALL MARKET, INC.; *pg.* 237, *pg.* 1189
VITA COCO KIDS - Coconut Water - ALL MARKET, INC.; *pg.* 237, *pg.* 1189
VITA-MIX - Blenders - CHESHER EQUIPMENT LTD.; *pg.* 1323, *pg.* 1925
VITA PEDIC - Innerspring Mattress - JAMISON BEDDING, INC.; *pg.* 930, *pg.* 1651
VITA-PREP - Chef's Power Tool - CHESHER EQUIPMENT LTD.; *pg.* 1323, *pg.* 1925
VITA-PRO - Chef's Power Tool - CHESHER EQUIPMENT LTD.; *pg.* 1323, *pg.* 1925
VITACHROME - Biological Supplies - CAROLINA BIOLOGICAL SUPPLY COMPANY; *pg.* 1513, *pg.* 1359
VITADVANCE - Wellness Product - AVON PRODUCTS, INC.; *pg.* 500, *pg.* 1198
VITAFREZE - Frozen Confections - CRYSTAL CREAM & BUTTER COMPANY; *pg.* 850, *pg.* 149
VITAJET - Injection System - BIOJECT MEDICAL TECHNOLOGIES INC.; *pg.* 1506, *pg.* 1509
VITAKRAFT - Pet Product - PETSMART, INC.; *pg.* 1481, *pg.* 18
VITAL - Nutritional Product - ABBOTT LABORATORIES; *pg.* 1484, *pg.* 551
VITAL - Beverages - THE COCA-COLA COMPANY; *pg.* 240, *pg.* 493
VITAL ANSWERS FOR BETTER HEALTH...NOW - Pharmaceutical Product - ALERE INC.; *pg.* 1488, *pg.* 849
VITAL CONNECT - Software - VITAL IMAGES, INC.; *pg.* 1607, *pg.* 950
VITAL CYCLE - Fertilizer Product - SYNAGRO TECHNOLOGIES, INC.; *pg.* 1800, *pg.* 759
VITAL GAUGE - Manometer - VITAL SIGNS, INC.; *pg.* 1607, *pg.* 1126
VITAL ISSUES MEDICINE - Medical Device - PDI, INC.; *pg.* 1580, *pg.* 1104
THE VITAL LINK TO A WIRELESS WORLD - Slogan - TESSCO TECHNOLOGIES, INC.; *pg.* 679, *pg.* 773
VITAL O - Beverages - THE COCA-COLA COMPANY; *pg.* 240, *pg.* 493
VITAL-PERFECTION - Skin Care - SHISEIDO COSMETICS AMERICA OF SAC; *pg.* 522, *pg.* 1291
VITAL RADIANCE - Cosmetics - REVLON, INC.; *pg.* 521, *pg.* 1286
VITAL SEAL - Laryngeal Mask Airway - VITAL SIGNS, INC.; *pg.* 1607, *pg.* 1126
VITAL SIGNS - Company Name - VITAL SIGNS, INC.; *pg.* 1607, *pg.* 1126
VITAL-T - Sports Drink - ENERGY BRANDS, INC.; *pg.* 854, *pg.* 1227
VITAL TEMP - Temperature Monitoring Device - VITAL SIGNS, INC.; *pg.* 1607, *pg.* 1126
VITAL VIEW - Laryngoscope Blade - VITAL SIGNS, INC.; *pg.* 1607, *pg.* 1126
VITAL VIEW II - Laryngoscope System - VITAL SIGNS, INC.; *pg.* 1607, *pg.* 1126
VITALACCESS - Software System - ALCATEL-LUCENT; *pg.* 615, *pg.* 1094
VITALAPPS - Telecommunications Equipment - ALCATEL-LUCENT; *pg.* 615, *pg.* 1094
VITALCARDIA - Software - VITAL IMAGES, INC.; *pg.* 1607, *pg.* 950
VITALEVENT - Telecommunications Equipment - ALCATEL-LUCENT; *pg.* 615, *pg.* 1094
VITALIS - Personal Care Electrical Product - HELEN OF TROY L.P.; *pg.* 511, *pg.* 1692
VITALITY - Medical Device - BOSTON SCIENTIFIC CORPORATION; *pg.* 1508, *pg.* 831
VITALITY - Fruit Juices - NESTLE PROFESSIONAL BEVERAGES; *pg.* 257, *pg.* 474
VITALIZER - Toothbrush - THE GILLETTE COMPANY; *pg.* 509, *pg.* 795
VITALNET - Telecommunications Equipment - ALCATEL-LUCENT; *pg.* 615, *pg.* 1094
VITALOK - Cooking Equipment Technology - AMWAY CORPORATION; *pg.* 326, *pg.* 864
VITALPERFORMANCE - Software Upgrades & Maintenance Program - VITAL IMAGES, INC.; *pg.* 1607, *pg.* 950
VITALQIP - Software System - ALCATEL-LUCENT; *pg.* 615, *pg.* 1094
VITALS - Magazine - FAIRCHILD FASHION GROUP; *pg.* 1640, *pg.* 1230
VITALSCREEN - Medical Display System - PLANAR SYSTEMS, INC.; *pg.* 455, *pg.* 1495
VITALSQM - Telecommunications Equipment - ALCATEL-LUCENT; *pg.* 615, *pg.* 1094
VITALSTIM - Orthopedic Device - DJO SURGICAL; *pg.* 1525, *pg.* 1661
VITALSUITE - Software System - ALCATEL-LUCENT; *pg.* 615, *pg.* 1094
VITALVIEW - Patient Monitoring System - CRITICARE SYSTEMS, INC.; *pg.* 1520, *pg.* 1897
VITAMAT - Juice Extractors - CHESHER EQUIPMENT LTD.; *pg.* 1323, *pg.* 1925
VITAMIN AND MINERAL SYSTEM - Nutritional Supplement - WHITEWING LABS, INC.; *pg.* 1610, *pg.* 99
VITAMIN C ABSOLUTE - Skin Care Products - REVLON, INC.; *pg.* 521, *pg.* 1286
VITAMIN CODE - Health Supplement - GARDEN OF LIFE, INC.; *pg.* 1532, *pg.* 478
VITAMIN E CLUSTERS - Nutritional Product - RBC LIFE SCIENCES, INC.; *pg.* 1588, *pg.* 1723
VITAMIN K FOOD DIARY - Pharmaceutical Product - ALERE INC.; *pg.* 1488, *pg.* 849
VITAMIN WORLD - Nutritional Supplements - NBTY, INC.; *pg.* 1572, *pg.* 1338
VITAMINSHOPPE.COM - Website - VITAMIN SHOPPE, INC.; *pg.* 1608, *pg.* 1098
VITAMINWATER - Beverage - THE COCA-COLA COMPANY; *pg.* 240, *pg.* 493
VITAMINWATER - Bottled Water - ENERGY BRANDS, INC.; *pg.* 854, *pg.* 1227
VITAMINWATER ZERO - Beverage - THE COCA-COLA COMPANY; *pg.* 240, *pg.* 493
VITAMINWATER10 - Beverage - THE COCA-COLA COMPANY; *pg.* 240, *pg.* 493
VITAS - Hospice Service - CHEMED CORPORATION; *pg.* 327, *pg.* 1410
VITASHURE - Nutrition & Food Product - BALCHEM CORPORATION; *pg.* 839, *pg.* 1183
VITASILK - Shampoo - BLUE CROSS LABORATORIES; *pg.* 326, *pg.* 277
VITASOY - Soya Drink - AMWAY CORPORATION; *pg.* 326, *pg.* 864
VITATRON - Pacemaker - MEDTRONIC, INC.; *pg.* 1564, *pg.* 939
VITAVAX - Polymer Product - CHEMTURA CORPORATION; *pg.* 1152, *pg.* 355
VITAWAVE - Health Care Product - NATURE'S SUNSHINE PRODUCTS, INC.; *pg.* 1571, *pg.* 1754
VITELLINO - Furniture - ASHLEY FURNITURE INDUSTRIES, INC.; *pg.* 914, *pg.* 1852
VITESSE - Laser & Laser System - COHERENT, INC.; *pg.* 1406, *pg.* 265
VITESSE - Excimer Laser System - THE SPECTRANETICS CORPORATION; *pg.* 1595, *pg.* 315
VITESSE - Semiconductor Products - VITESSE SEMICONDUCTOR CORPORATION; *pg.* 686, *pg.* 57
VITICURE - Polymer Product - CHEMTURA CORPORATION; *pg.* 1152, *pg.* 355
VITINGO - Beverages - THE COCA-COLA COMPANY; *pg.* 240, *pg.* 493
VITIVA PET - Polymer - EASTMAN CHEMICAL COMPANY; *pg.* 1159, *pg.* 1636
VITO - Food Product - BUNGE LIMITED; *pg.* 842, *pg.* 1351
VITON - Sealants - CONAX TECHNOLOGIES LLC; *pg.* 1325, *pg.* 1148
VITON - Power Equipment - ECHO INCORPORATED; *pg.* 1046, *pg.* 626
VITON - Chemical - MILLER-STEPHENSON CHEMICAL COMPANY, INC.; *pg.* 1172, *pg.* 344
VITOX - Nutritional Supplement - NU SKIN ENTERPRISES, INC.; *pg.* 518, *pg.* 1755
VITR-AU-LESS - Conductor Paste - FERRO CORPORATION; *pg.* 1162, *pg.* 1462
VITRASE - Ophthalmology Product - BAUSCH & LOMB INCORPORATED; *pg.* 1401, *pg.* 1045
VITRAVENE - Drug - ISIS PHARMACEUTICALS, INC.; *pg.* 1548, *pg.* 59
VITREA - Software - VITAL IMAGES, INC.; *pg.* 1607, *pg.* 950
VITREA 2 - Software - VITAL IMAGES, INC.; *pg.* 1607, *pg.* 950
VITREAACCESS - Software - VITAL IMAGES, INC.; *pg.* 1607, *pg.* 950
VITREBOND - Polymer Glass - 3M COMPANY; *pg.* 1142, *pg.* 956
VITREMER - Glass Ionomer System - 3M COMPANY; *pg.* 1142, *pg.* 956
VITRERIE - Fabric - NEMSCHOFF, INC.; *pg.* 936, *pg.* 1890
VITREX - Flooring Tool - Q.E.P. CO., INC.; *pg.* 1371, *pg.* 413
VITRIA - Company Name - VITRIA TECHNOLOGY, INC.; *pg.* 490, *pg.* 289
VITRIDE - Reducing Agent - DOW CHEMICAL; *pg.* 1156, *pg.* 1563
VITRIDE - Chemical Product - SPECTRUM CHEMICALS & LABORATORY PRODUCTS, INC.; *pg.* 1181, *pg.* 94
VITROBOT - Electron Microscope - FEI COMPANY; *pg.* 1413, *pg.* 1498
VITROS - Healthcare Product - JOHNSON & JOHNSON; *pg.* 1549, *pg.* 1091
VITROTRIM - Automotive Body Trim - 3M COMPANY; *pg.* 1142, *pg.* 956
VITRUVIUS - Pharmaceutical Product - ALERE INC.; *pg.* 1488, *pg.* 849
VITUGEN - Animal Nutrition Product - VITUSA CORP.; *pg.* 1482, *pg.* 1063
VITUPROP - Animal Nutrition Product - VITUSA CORP.; *pg.* 1482, *pg.* 1063
VIVA - Hot Air Balloon - CAMERON BALLOONS U.S.; *pg.* 1829, *pg.* 884
VIVA - Water - THE COCA-COLA COMPANY; *pg.* 240, *pg.* 493
VIVA - Paper Towels - KIMBERLY-CLARK CORPORATION; *pg.* 1461, *pg.* 1720
VIVA LAS VEGAS - Game - MISSOURI LOTTERY; *pg.* 999, *pg.* 979
VIVA MAMBO - Game - WMS INDUSTRIES INC.; *pg.* 593, *pg.* 666
VIVACI - Footwear - STEVEN MADDEN, LTD.; *pg.* 1819, *pg.* 1176
VIVALDI - Fabric - NEMSCHOFF, INC.; *pg.* 936, *pg.* 1890
VIVALDI'S SEASONS - Video Game - INTERNATIONAL GAME TECHNOLOGY; *pg.* 957, *pg.* 1024
VIVAXL - Health & Beauty Product - DIXIE HEALTH, INC.; *pg.* 1524, *pg.* 535
VIVE - Cereal - KASHI COMPANY; *pg.* 830, *pg.* 119
VIVELLE - Estradiol Transdermal System - NOVEN PHARMACEUTICALS, INC.; *pg.* 1576, *pg.* 445
VIVELLE-DOT - Estradiol Transdermal System - NOVEN PHARMACEUTICALS, INC.; *pg.* 1576, *pg.* 445
VIVI - Furniture - HOOKER FURNITURE CORPORATION; *pg.* 928, *pg.* 1788
VIVIA - Dry Cleaning & Laundry Product - ADCO, INC.; *pg.* 325, *pg.* 482
VIVIAN - Footwear - CAPEZIO BALLET MAKERS INC.; *pg.* 1805, *pg.* 1125
VIVID - Gene Array Slide - PALL CORPORATION; *pg.* 232, *pg.* 1323
VIVID - Color Safe Bleach - RECKITT BENCKISER INC.; *pg.* 1136, *pg.* 1105
VIVID - Paints - RPM INTERNATIONAL INC.; *pg.* 1447, *pg.* 1464
VIVID 3 - Medical Device - GE HEALTHCARE TECHNOLOGIES; *pg.* 1533, *pg.* 1897
VIVID 7 - Medical Device - GE HEALTHCARE TECHNOLOGIES; *pg.* 1533, *pg.* 1897
VIVID COLORS - Control Vector - THERMO FISHER SCIENTIFIC INC.; *pg.* 1602, *pg.* 61
VIVIDFX - Paint - ROSCO LABORATORIES, INC.; *pg.* 1782, *pg.* 378
VIVISTA - Software - SUNGARD DATA SYSTEMS INC.; *pg.* 477, *pg.* 1592
VIVITE - Skin Care Product - ALLERGAN, INC.; *pg.* 1491, *pg.* 106
VIVO! - Laser Color Printer - ASTRO-MED, INC.; *pg.* 619, *pg.* 1609
VIVO - Faucet - ELKAY MANUFACTURING COMPANY; *pg.* 80, *pg.* 645
VIVO INTERIORS - Furniture - HERMAN MILLER, INC.; *pg.* 926, *pg.* 913
VIVYPAK - Polyethylene Resin - THE DOW CHEMICAL COMPANY; *pg.* 1157, *pg.* 898
VIXEN - File Product - SIMONDS INTERNATIONAL CORPORATION; *pg.* 1376, *pg.* 819
VIZ-A-BALL - Bowling Equipment - BRUNSWICK BOWLING & BILLIARDS CORP.; *pg.* 1828, *pg.* 622
VIZEON - Medical Equipment - CONMED CORPORATION; *pg.* 1517, *pg.* 1347
VIZIA - Light Switch - LEVITON MANUFACTURING COMPANY, INC.; *pg.* 1301, *pg.* 1180
VIZION - Bath & Plumbing Product - JACUZZI BRANDS CORPORATION; *pg.* 554, *pg.* 65
VIZIR - Personal & Household Product - THE PROCTER & GAMBLE COMPANY; *pg.* 1129, *pg.* 1418
VL - Airbrush - PAASCHE AIRBRUSH COMPANY; *pg.* 1444,

pg. 587
VLA - Systems Integration & Aeronautics - LOCKHEED MARTIN CORPORATION; *pg.* 229, *pg.* 762
VLADIMIR - Vodka - MONTEBELLO BRANDS INC.; *pg.* 1967, *pg.* 758
VLASIC - Pickles, Peppers & Relish - PINNACLE FOODS GROUP LLC; *pg.* 889, *pg.* 1104
VLM - Computer Software - NOVELL INC.; *pg.* 446, *pg.* 852
VLSR - Virtual Line Switched Ring - CIENA CORPORATION; *pg.* 628, *pg.* 771
VLYNQ - Integrated Circuit Hardware - TEXAS INSTRUMENTS INCORPORATED; *pg.* 679, *pg.* 1688
VM2IQ - Software - USA TECHNOLOGIES, INC.; *pg.* 815, *pg.* 1550
VMAX - Software - EMC CORPORATION; *pg.* 391, *pg.* 825
VMAX - Software - MOLECULAR DEVICES CORPORATION; *pg.* 1568, *pg.* 287
VMC - Software - SYNOPSYS, INC.; *pg.* 480, *pg.* 162
VMC 600 Machining Center - KINGSBURY CORPORATION; *pg.* 1353, *pg.* 1035
VMD01-M60 - Motion Detector - BOSCH SECURITY SYSTEMS, INC.; *pg.* 626, *pg.* 1158
VMPILOT - Software - EMULEX CORPORATION; *pg.* 392, *pg.* 70
VMS - Processor Card - POLYCOM, INC.; *pg.* 664, *pg.* 249
VMS MOUNTING SYSTEM - Machinery Mounting System - ALLIED CONSTRUCTION PRODUCTS, LLC; *pg.* 1311, *pg.* 1427
VMWARE - Software System - EMC CORPORATION; *pg.* 391, *pg.* 825
VMWARE - Software - EMULEX CORPORATION; *pg.* 392, *pg.* 70
VMWARE ACE - Virtual Desktop Control Software - VMWARE, INC.; *pg.* 490, *pg.* 179
VMWARE ESXI - Datacenter Platform - VMWARE, INC.; *pg.* 490, *pg.* 179
VMWARE PLAYER - Virtual Operating System Management Software - VMWARE, INC.; *pg.* 490, *pg.* 179
VMWARE THINAPP - Application Virtualizer - VMWARE, INC.; *pg.* 490, *pg.* 179
VMWARE VCLOUD - Cloud Computing Software - VMWARE, INC.; *pg.* 490, *pg.* 179
VMWARE VIEW 4 - Desktop Management Software - VMWARE, INC.; *pg.* 490, *pg.* 179
VMWARE VSPHERE 4 - Datacenter Platform - VMWARE, INC.; *pg.* 490, *pg.* 179
VN-FLEX - Thermoplastic Control Cable - GENERAL CABLE CORPORATION; *pg.* 83, *pg.* 384
VN-TC - Thermoplastic Type TC Tray Cable - GENERAL CABLE CORPORATION; *pg.* 83, *pg.* 384
VN-VIEWER - Software - VICON INDUSTRIES, INC.; *pg.* 685, *pg.* 1166
VNESERVER - Software Product & Module - RIVERBED PERFORMANCE MANAGEMENT; *pg.* 462, *pg.* 765
VNPP - Lighting Control System - SYNACOR, INC.; *pg.* 479, *pg.* 1380
VNS CHOICE - Managed Long Term Care - VISITING NURSE SERVICE OF NEW YORK; *pg.* 1607, *pg.* 1311
VNS THERAPY - Medical Device - LIVANOVA; *pg.* 1557, *pg.* 1710
VNTC - Industrial Cables - GENERAL CABLE CORPORATION; *pg.* 83, *pg.* 729
VNX - Software - EMC CORPORATION; *pg.* 391, *pg.* 825
VNX5100 - Software - EMC CORPORATION; *pg.* 391, *pg.* 825
VNXE - Software - EMC CORPORATION; *pg.* 391, *pg.* 825
VNXE3100 - Software - EMC CORPORATION; *pg.* 391, *pg.* 825
VO - Canadian Whisky - DIAGEO CANADA, INC.; *pg.* 1961, *pg.* 1937
VO 11 - Desuperheaters - SPX PROCESS EQUIPMENT; *pg.* 1378, *pg.* 1551
VO 76 - Desuperheaters - SPX PROCESS EQUIPMENT; *pg.* 1378, *pg.* 1551
VO-POP - Popcorn Oil - VENTURA FOODS, LLC; *pg.* 908, *pg.* 49
VOC ABATOR - Air Pollution Control Equipment - DONALDSON COMPANY, INC.; *pg.* 1329, *pg.* 917
VOCALISE - Cosmetic Product - SHISEIDO COSMETICS AMERICA OF SAC; *pg.* 522, *pg.* 1291
VOCAT - Catalyst - BASF CATALYSTS LLC; *pg.* 1148, *pg.* 1074
VOCON - Speech Recognition Software - NUANCE COMMUNICATIONS, INC.; *pg.* 447, *pg.* 806
VOCUS PUBLIC RELATIONS 3.0 - Public Relations Automation Software - CISION, INC.; *pg.* 375, *pg.* 761
VODAVI - Business Communications System - VERTICAL COMMUNICATIONS, INC.; *pg.* 488, *pg.* 270
VODAVI STAR PLUS - Business Communications System - VERTICAL COMMUNICATIONS, INC.; *pg.* 488, *pg.* 270
VODAVI TELENIUM IP - Business Communications System - VERTICAL COMMUNICATIONS, INC.; *pg.* 488, *pg.* 270
VODAVI XTS IP - Telephone System - VERTICAL COMMUNICATIONS, INC.; *pg.* 488, *pg.* 270
VODCAST - Content Tools - SEACHANGE INTERNATIONAL, INC.; *pg.* 1279, *pg.* 781
VOGEL - Fluid Technology - ITT CORPORATION; *pg.* 1351, *pg.* 1354
VOGT - Valve - FLOWSERVE CORPORATION; *pg.* 82, *pg.* 1719
VOGUE - Magazine - CONDE NAST PUBLICATIONS, INC.; *pg.* 1629, *pg.* 1217
VOGUE - Rug - COURISTAN INC.; *pg.* 921, *pg.* 1067
VOGUE - Fashion Magazine - VOGUE MAGAZINE; *pg.* 1700, *pg.* 1311
VOGUE-LITE - Lighting Fixtures - SWIVELIER CO., INC.; *pg.* 1307, *pg.* 1142
VOICE - Magazine - FULL GOSPEL BUSINESS MEN'S FELLOWSHIP INTERNATIONAL; *pg.* 141, *pg.* 110
VOICE ALERT - Laser Detectors - COBRA ELECTRONICS CORPORATION; *pg.* 629, *pg.* 572
VOICE@WORK - Association Services - AMERICAN FEDERATION OF LABOR - CONGRESS OF INDUSTRIAL ORGANIZATIONS; *pg.* 128, *pg.* 394
VOICE CONNECTIONS - Pharmaceutical Product - ALERE INC.; *pg.* 1488, *pg.* 849
VOICE CONTROL - Loudspeakers - ATLAS SOUND; *pg.* 621, *pg.* 1692
VOICE DNA - Software System - AT&T COMMUNICATIONS CORP.; *pg.* 1866, *pg.* 1043
VOICE ENABLED MARKETPLACE - Voice Carrier Systems - TELECOMMUNICATION SYSTEMS INC.; *pg.* 483, *pg.* 754
VOICE ENHANCER - Hearing Device - BELTONE ELECTRONICS LLC; *pg.* 1503, *pg.* 614
VOICE OF EXPERIENCE - Slogan - PROGRESS SOFTWARE CORPORATION; *pg.* 457, *pg.* 786
THE VOICE OF THE INTERNET - Tag Line - MITEL NETWORKS, INC.; *pg.* 1872, *pg.* 13
THE VOICE OF THE NETWORK - Tagline - ELECTRONIC TELE-COMMUNICATIONS, INC.; *pg.* 390, *pg.* 1897
VOICE OVER BROADBAND - Wireline Solutions - SONUS NETWORKS INC.; *pg.* 1281, *pg.* 858
VOICE PORT - Cable - ARRIS GROUP, INC.; *pg.* 353, *pg.* 541
VOICE RADIESSE - Voice Gel - MERZ AESTHETICS; *pg.* 1567, *pg.* 255
VOICE REALITY - Device - AUTODESK INC.; *pg.* 356, *pg.* 257
VOICE/TONE - Emergency Loudspeakers - ATLAS SOUND; *pg.* 621, *pg.* 1692
VOICE VPN - Wireline Solutions - SONUS NETWORKS INC.; *pg.* 1281, *pg.* 858
VOICECENTER - Software - ANDREA ELECTRONICS CORPORATION; *pg.* 617, *pg.* 1143
VOICEMAIL PLUS - Telecommunication Services - VONAGE HOLDINGS CORP.; *pg.* 686, *pg.* 1074
VOICEPLUS - Network Conferencing System - POLYCOM, INC.; *pg.* 664, *pg.* 249
VOICEREACH - Telecom Product - PREMIERE GLOBAL SERVICES, INC.; *pg.* 1275, *pg.* 518
VOICESTATION - Voice Product - POLYCOM, INC.; *pg.* 664, *pg.* 249
VOICETONE - Speech Recognition Technology - ADVANCED TELECOM SERVICES; *pg.* 1865, *pg.* 1591
VOICEVOYAGER - Computer Software - TEXAS INSTRUMENTS INCORPORATED; *pg.* 679, *pg.* 1688
VOICEWING - Broadband Phone Service - VERIZON COMMUNICATIONS INC.; *pg.* 1875, *pg.* 1309
VOID - Apparel - OAKLEY, INC.; *pg.* 1840, *pg.* 86
VOID KRAFT - Recycled Paper Packaging Material - SEALED AIR CORPORATION; *pg.* 1468, *pg.* 1058
VOIP DEVELOPER MAGAZINE - Trade Publication - TECHNOLOGY MARKETING CORP.; *pg.* 1691, *pg.* 364
VOIPSWITCH - Desktop Application - TECHNOLOGY MARKETING CORP.; *pg.* 1691, *pg.* 364
VOISYS - Software - CIQ, INC.; *pg.* 1235, *pg.* 415
VOKEY DESIGN - Golf Clubs - ACUSHNET COMPANY; *pg.* 1824, *pg.* 818
VOL-CON - Electrical Tester - IDEAL INDUSTRIES, INC.; *pg.* 1051, *pg.* 662
VOL-TEST XL - Electrical Tester - IDEAL INDUSTRIES, INC.; *pg.* 1051, *pg.* 662
VOL-U-METER - Control Measurement - BROOKS INSTRUMENT, LLC; *pg.* 1403, *pg.* 1537
VOLATEX - Core Sheet Varnishes - E.I. DU PONT DE NEMOURS & COMPANY; *pg.* 1159, *pg.* 390
VOLCANO - Eyewear - MAUI JIM, INC.; *pg.* 9, *pg.* 651
VOLCANO TACOS - Tacos in Red Corn Tortilla Shells - TACO BELL CORP.; *pg.* 1752, *pg.* 117
VOLCARB - Minerals - MINERALS TECHNOLOGIES INC.; *pg.* 1173, *pg.* 617
VOLCLAY - Bentonite Clay - MINERALS TECHNOLOGIES INC.; *pg.* 1173, *pg.* 617
VOLERA - Computer Software - NOVELL INC.; *pg.* 446, *pg.* 852
VOLITION - Fiber Optic Cable - 3M COMPANY; *pg.* 1142, *pg.* 956
VOLLETTA - Dinnerware - THE HOMER LAUGHLIN CHINA COMPANY; *pg.* 1125, *pg.* 1850
VOLNAY - Fabric - SCALAMANDRE, INC.; *pg.* 941, *pg.* 1058
VOLO - Software - AUTODESK INC.; *pg.* 356, *pg.* 257
VOLOCIXMAB - Antibody - PDL BIOPHARMA INC.; *pg.* 1580, *pg.* 1022
VOLOY - Plastic Compound & Resin - A. SCHULMAN, INC.; *pg.* 1144, *pg.* 1452
VOLT - Automobile - GENERAL MOTORS COMPANY; *pg.* 175, *pg.* 881
THE VOLTA REVIEW - Periodical - ALEXANDER GRAHAM BELL ASSOCIATION FOR THE DEAF AND HARD OF HEARING; *pg.* 126, *pg.* 393
VOLTA VOICES - Periodical - ALEXANDER GRAHAM BELL ASSOCIATION FOR THE DEAF AND HARD OF HEARING; *pg.* 126, *pg.* 393
VOLTAGE - Fabric - NEMSCHOFF, INC.; *pg.* 936, *pg.* 1890
VOLTAGESTORM - Software - CADENCE DESIGN SYSTEMS, INC.; *pg.* 367, *pg.* 239
VOLTAIRE - Guest Chairs - BERNHARDT DESIGN; *pg.* 918, *pg.* 1381
VOLTALEF - Resin used in Oils & Greases - ARKEMA INC.; *pg.* 1147, *pg.* 1543
VOLTRON - Wire Enamels - E.I. DU PONT DE NEMOURS & COMPANY; *pg.* 1159, *pg.* 390
VOLTS - Software - SCHLUMBERGER LIMITED; *pg.* 801, *pg.* 1714
VOLUETTE - Chemical Standard Solution - HACH COMPANY; *pg.* 1415, *pg.* 334
VOLUME EXPRESS - Mascara - MAYBELLINE LLC; *pg.* 516, *pg.* 1257
VOLUMEKIND - Hair Care Product - NU SKIN ENTERPRISES, INC.; *pg.* 518, *pg.* 1755
VOLUMEMANAGER - Storage System - SYMANTEC CORPORATION; *pg.* 479, *pg.* 1753
VOLUMIZING SPRAY - Hair Care Product - JOHN PAUL MITCHELL SYSTEMS; *pg.* 512, *pg.* 133
VOLUNTEER CORPS - Event - CHICAGO WHITE SOX LTD.; *pg.* 539, *pg.* 570
VOLUSON 730 - Medical Device - GE HEALTHCARE TECHNOLOGIES; *pg.* 1533, *pg.* 1897
VOLUTE - Fabric - NEMSCHOFF, INC.; *pg.* 936, *pg.* 1890
VOLVIC - Non-Carbonated Water - NESTLE WATERS NORTH AMERICA INC.; *pg.* 257, *pg.* 375
VOLVO - Class 7 Truck & Tractors - VOLVO TRUCKS NORTH AMERICA, INC.; *pg.* 195, *pg.* 1377
VOLVO VN - Class 8 Truck & Tractors - VOLVO TRUCKS NORTH AMERICA, INC.; *pg.* 195, *pg.* 1377
VON DUPRIN - Door Hardware - INGERSOLL-RAND COMPANY; *pg.* 1349, *pg.* 1370
VON SCHRADER DETERGENT (BLUE LABEL) - Anti-Resoil, Low PH Carpet & Upholstery Detergent - VON SCHRADER COMPANY; *pg.* 62, *pg.* 1890
VON SCHRADER DETERGENT (RED LABEL) - Anti-Resoil, High PH Carpet Detergent - VON SCHRADER COMPANY; *pg.* 62, *pg.* 1890
VONAGE - Telecommunications - VONAGE HOLDINGS CORP.; *pg.* 686, *pg.* 1074
VONAGE SOFTPHONE - Software - VONAGE HOLDINGS CORP.; *pg.* 686, *pg.* 1074
VONAGE V-PHONE - Telecommunication Services - VONAGE HOLDINGS CORP.; *pg.* 686, *pg.* 1074
VONAGE VISUAL VOICEMAIL - Telecommunication Services - VONAGE HOLDINGS CORP.; *pg.* 686, *pg.* 1074
VONGO - Broadband Download Service - STARZ ENTERTAINMENT, LLC; *pg.* 310, *pg.* 327
VONG'S THAI KITCHEN - Thai Restaurant - LETTUCE

First page reference indicates Business Class Edition
Second page reference indicates Geographic Edition

ENTERTAIN YOU ENTERPRISES, INC.; pg. 1735, pg. 580
VONTU - Software - SYMANTEC CORPORATION; pg. 478, pg. 161
VOODOO - Golf Club Shafts - ALDILA, INC.; pg. 1825, pg. 185
VOODOO - Musical Instrument - GIBSON GUITAR CORP.; pg. 550, pg. 1650
VOODOO SPIN - Video Game - INTERNATIONAL GAME TECHNOLOGY; pg. 957, pg. 1024
VOORTMAN COOKIES - Cookies - VOORTMAN COOKIES LIMITED; pg. 1863, pg. 1919
VORACOR - Polyurethane Component - THE DOW CHEMICAL COMPANY; pg. 1157, pg. 898
VORACTIV - Polyether & Copolymer Polyols - THE DOW CHEMICAL COMPANY; pg. 1157, pg. 898
VORAD - Truck Component - EATON CORPORATION; pg. 1331, pg. 1429
VORAD EVT-300 - Collision Warning System for Automobile Drivers - EATON CORPORATION; pg. 1331, pg. 1429
VORALAST - Polyurethane Component - THE DOW CHEMICAL COMPANY; pg. 1157, pg. 898
VORALIFE - Polyols - THE DOW CHEMICAL COMPANY; pg. 1157, pg. 898
VORALUX - Polyurethane Component - THE DOW CHEMICAL COMPANY; pg. 1157, pg. 898
VORAMER - Adhesive - THE DOW CHEMICAL COMPANY; pg. 1157, pg. 898
VORANATE - Specialty Isocyanate - THE DOW CHEMICAL COMPANY; pg. 1157, pg. 898
VORANOL - Polyols - THE DOW CHEMICAL COMPANY; pg. 1157, pg. 898
VORANOL - Foam Seating Product - RENOSOL CORPORATION; pg. 1179, pg. 872
VORASTAR - Polymer - THE DOW CHEMICAL COMPANY; pg. 1157, pg. 898
VORASURF - Surfactant - THE DOW CHEMICAL COMPANY; pg. 1157, pg. 898
VORATEC - Polyurethane Component - THE DOW CHEMICAL COMPANY; pg. 1157, pg. 898
VORATRON - Adhesive - THE DOW CHEMICAL COMPANY; pg. 1157, pg. 898
VORAZ - Seal & Thermoplastic Component - GREENE, TWEED & CO.; pg. 1344, pg. 1544
VORTAX - Textiles - BERNHARDT DESIGN; pg. 918, pg. 1381
VORTEC - Air Filter - AMSOIL INC.; pg. 971, pg. 1896
VORTECH - Air Separator - TACO INCORPORATED; pg. 1077, pg. 1601
VORTEX - Electrosurgical Devices - ANGIODYNAMICS, INC.; pg. 1495, pg. 1173
VORTEX - Suspended Roller Coaster - CANADA'S WONDERLAND COMPANY; pg. 536, pg. 1947
VORTEX - Oil Fuel - CHEVRON CORPORATION; pg. 974, pg. 259
VORTEX - Coin Changer - COIN ACCEPTORS, INC.; pg. 1324, pg. 994
VORTEX - Tooth System - ESCO CORPORATION; pg. 1335, pg. 1502
VORTEX - Forage Harvest System - GEHL COMPANY; pg. 1339, pg. 1899
VORTEX - Stainless Steel Propeller - MICHIGAN WHEEL CORPORATION; pg. 1709, pg. 888
VORTEX - Fabric - NEMSCHOFF, INC.; pg. 936, pg. 1890
VORTEX - Valve - PELICAN PRODUCTS; pg. 1467, pg. 843
VORTEX - Voice Product - POLYCOM, INC.; pg. 664, pg. 249
VORTEX - Lighting Equipment - ROSCO LABORATORIES, INC.; pg. 1782, pg. 378
VORTEX - Regenerative Blower - THE SPENCER TURBINE CO.; pg. 1378, pg. 386
VORTEX - Chemical Cleaner Product - TECH SPRAY, L.P.; pg. 1183, pg. 1659
VORTEX - Connectionless Steamers - UNIFIED BRANDS INC.; pg. 1385, pg. 970
VORTEX - Media Packaging - WESTROCK COMPANY; pg. 1472, pg. 1805
VORTEX BLUE-RAY - Media Packaging - WESTROCK COMPANY; pg. 1472, pg. 1805
VORTEXML DESIGNER - Software - DATAWATCH CORPORATION; pg. 383, pg. 813
VORTEXML SERVER - Business Intelligence Product - DATAWATCH CORPORATION; pg. 383, pg. 813
VORTIFLARE - Burner - MAXON CORPORATION; pg. 1359, pg. 695
VORTX - Medical Device - BOSTON SCIENTIFIC CORPORATION; pg. 1508, pg. 831
VOSKY - Electronic Product - ACTIONTEC ELECTRONICS, INC.; pg. 342, pg. 282
VOSTRO - Computers - DELL INC.; pg. 383, pg. 1737
VOTRE PARTENAIRE CULINAIRE - Slogan - CUISINE SOLUTIONS, INC.; pg. 850, pg. 1770
VOUGHT - Systems Integration & Aeronautics - LOCKHEED MARTIN CORPORATION; pg. 229, pg. 762
VOV - Automatic & Fluid Control Valves - TEXAS INSTRUMENTS INCORPORATED; pg. 679, pg. 1688
VOX - Otolaryngology Tissue Bulking Products - COGENTIX MEDICAL, INC.; pg. 1516, pg. 948
VOX - Vodka - JIM BEAM BRANDS CO.; pg. 1965, pg. 601
VOX - Amplifiers - KORG USA, INC.; pg. 556, pg. 1180
VOX - Awareness Program - PLANNED PARENTHOOD FEDERATION OF AMERICA, INC.; pg. 154, pg. 1282
VOXELVIEW - Software - VITAL IMAGES, INC.; pg. 1607, pg. 950
VOXPRO - PC Voice Editing System - BROADCAST ELECTRONICS, INC.; pg. 627, pg. 653
VOYA - Journal - SCARECROW PRESS, INC.; pg. 1683, pg. 773
VOYAGE - Fabric - NEMSCHOFF, INC.; pg. 936, pg. 1890
VOYAGE - Hand-Held Electronic Devices - TEXAS INSTRUMENTS INCORPORATED; pg. 679, pg. 1688
VOYAGE THROUGH THE UNIVERSE - Book Series - DIRECT HOLDINGS AMERICAS INC.; pg. 1636, pg. 1780
VOYAGER - Catheter - ABBOTT LABORATORIES; pg. 1484, pg. 551
VOYAGER - Integrated Circuit - ATMEL CORPORATION; pg. 621, pg. 238
VOYAGER - Binocular - BUSHNELL OUTDOOR PRODUCTS, INC.; pg. 1403, pg. 718
VOYAGER - Microwave Synthesis Product - CEM CORPORATION; pg. 1405, pg. 1382
VOYAGER - Cameras - EASTMAN KODAK COMPANY; pg. 1408, pg. 1333
VOYAGER - Cleaning Product - HILLYARD, INC.; pg. 331, pg. 990
VOYAGER - Eyewear - MAUI JIM, INC.; pg. 9, pg. 651
VOYAGER - Wagon - RADIO FLYER INC.; pg. 966, pg. 588
VOYAGER - Software Development Tool - RECURSION SOFTWARE, INC.; pg. 460, pg. 1697
VOYAGER - Marine Lighting - SWIVELIER CO., INC.; pg. 1307, pg. 1142
VOYAGER - Molecular Biology Product - THERMO FISHER SCIENTIFIC INC.; pg. 1602, pg. 61
VOYAGER - Service - THE VANGUARD GROUP, INC.; pg. 816, pg. 1550
VOYAGER ADVENTURE SYSTEM - Toy - VTECH ELECTRONICS NORTH AMERICA, LLC; pg. 969, pg. 554
VOYAGER OF THE SEAS - Cruise Ship - ROYAL CARIBBEAN CRUISES LTD; pg. 1921, pg. 446
VOYAGER SELECT SERVICES - Service - THE VANGUARD GROUP, INC.; pg. 816, pg. 1550
VOYAGER SERVICES - Service - THE VANGUARD GROUP, INC.; pg. 816, pg. 1550
VOYAGES - Book - CONCORDIA PUBLISHING HOUSE; pg. 1629, pg. 995
VOYAGEUR - Hearing Instrument - SEMTECH CORPORATION GENNUM PRODUCTS; pg. 671, pg. 1919
VOYAGEUR ELITE - Building Products - BOISE CASCADE HOLDINGS, L.L.C.; pg. 1453, pg. 546
VOYENCE - Software - EMC CORPORATION; pg. 391, pg. 825
VOZ DEL LECTOR - Educational Materials - SCHOLASTIC INC.; pg. 1683, pg. 1288
VP - Manual - XEROX CORPORATION; pg. 494, pg. 365
VPAC - Emission Testing System - MISTRAS GROUP, INC.; pg. 1362, pg. 1113
VPAP - Comfort Bilevel Device - RESMED INC.; pg. 1589, pg. 207
VPAP ADAPT SV - Bilevel Device - RESMED INC.; pg. 1589, pg. 207
VPAP AUTO - Bilevel Device - RESMED INC.; pg. 1589, pg. 207
VPAP MALIBU - Bilevel Device - RESMED INC.; pg. 1589, pg. 207
VPAP MAX - Medical Device - RESMED INC.; pg. 1589, pg. 207
VPC - Gas Curing High-Performance Coating Systems - ASHLAND INC.; pg. 972, pg. 726
VPI - Vital Processor Interlocking Control System - ALSTOM SIGNALING, INC.; pg. 1312, pg. 1350
VPN FIREWALL BRICK - Software System - ALCATEL-LUCENT; pg. 615, pg. 1094
VPNMANAGER - Telecommunication Product - AVAYA INC.; pg. 621, pg. 264
VPON - Optical Networking Product - HARMONIC, INC.; pg. 402, pg. 246
VPR - Electronic Components - MOLEX INCORPORATED; pg. 655, pg. 628
VPS - Closed-Circuit Television Equipment - VICON INDUSTRIES, INC.; pg. 685, pg. 1166
VPT - Network Printer - RICOH PRINTING SYSTEMS AMERICA, INC.; pg. 462, pg. 279
VPX - Software - CITRIX SYSTEMS, INC.; pg. 375, pg. 424
VR - Photographic Film, Cameras & Flash Units - EASTMAN KODAK COMPANY; pg. 1408, pg. 1333
VR-G - Photographic Film - EASTMAN KODAK COMPANY; pg. 1408, pg. 1333
VR SERIES - Electronic Equipment - RENESAS ELECTRONICS AMERICA INC.; pg. 667, pg. 269
VR SOLAR - Battery - C&D TECHNOLOGIES, INC.; pg. 627, pg. 1517
VR/WESSON - Tools - AGI-VR/WESSON INC; pg. 1041, pg. 415
VR2 - Data Encoding Technology - OVERLAND STORAGE, INC.; pg. 451, pg. 205
VR4000 - Electronic Equipment - RENESAS ELECTRONICS AMERICA INC.; pg. 667, pg. 269
VR4000PC - Electronic Equipment - RENESAS ELECTRONICS AMERICA INC.; pg. 667, pg. 269
VR4000SC - Electronic Equipment - RENESAS ELECTRONICS AMERICA INC.; pg. 667, pg. 269
VR4200 - Electronic Equipment - RENESAS ELECTRONICS AMERICA INC.; pg. 667, pg. 269
VR4200LP - Electronic Equipment - RENESAS ELECTRONICS AMERICA INC.; pg. 667, pg. 269
VR4200PC - Electronic Equipment - RENESAS ELECTRONICS AMERICA INC.; pg. 667, pg. 269
VR4400 - Electronic Equipment - RENESAS ELECTRONICS AMERICA INC.; pg. 667, pg. 269
VR4400MC - Electronic Equipment - RENESAS ELECTRONICS AMERICA INC.; pg. 667, pg. 269
VR4400PC - Electronic Equipment - RENESAS ELECTRONICS AMERICA INC.; pg. 667, pg. 269
VR4400SC - Electronic Equipment - RENESAS ELECTRONICS AMERICA INC.; pg. 667, pg. 269
VRINGCARB - Thermal Processing Equipment - SURFACE COMBUSTION, INC.; pg. 1077, pg. 1462
VRS - Medical Device - NATUS MEDICAL INCORPORATED; pg. 1572, pg. 199
VRS - Virtual Reference Station System - TRIMBLE NAVIGATION LIMITED; pg. 1384, pg. 288
VRS NOW - Software - TRIMBLE NAVIGATION LIMITED; pg. 1384, pg. 288
VRSC - Motorcycles - HARLEY-DAVIDSON, INC.; pg. 178, pg. 1874
VS - Graphite Golf Shaft - ALDILA, INC.; pg. 1825, pg. 185
VS-C - Health Care Product - NATURE'S SUNSHINE PRODUCTS, INC.; pg. 1571, pg. 1754
VS EASYFIT - Ventilator - RESMED INC.; pg. 1589, pg. 207
VS INTEGRA - Ventilator - RESMED INC.; pg. 1589, pg. 207
VS PROTO - Golf Club Shafts - ALDILA, INC.; pg. 1825, pg. 185
VS SERENA - Sleep Devices - RESMED INC.; pg. 1589, pg. 207
VS ULTRA - Ventilator - RESMED INC.; pg. 1589, pg. 207
VS1 - Vibration Monitor - ELECTRO-SENSORS, INC.; pg. 1333, pg. 948
VS3 - Power Wall Cleaning System - VON SCHRADER COMPANY; pg. 62, pg. 1890
VSAM-ASSIST - Software - EMC CORPORATION; pg. 391, pg. 825
VSAM ASSISTANT - Software - EMC CORPORATION; pg. 391, pg. 825
VSCOPE - Embedded Waveform Viewing Technology - VITESSE SEMICONDUCTOR CORPORATION; pg. 686, pg. 57
VSCORE - Software - VITAL IMAGES, INC.; pg. 1607, pg. 950
VSE - Software - CYPRESS SEMICONDUCTOR CORPORATION; pg. 1326, pg. 243
VSE 1000 VOLT - Insulated Tools - SK HAND TOOL CORPORATION; pg. 1062, pg. 663
V.SERIES - Communications Product - MOTOROLA SOLUTIONS, INC.; pg. 657, pg. 659

VSG - Single-Screw Natural Gas Compressor - VILTER MANUFACTURING LLC; *pg.* 1078, *pg.* 1856
VSH - Kitchen Appliance - VIKING RANGE CORPORATION; *pg.* 61, *pg.* 968
VSIPL - Software - MERCURY COMPUTER SYSTEMS, INC.; *pg.* 434, *pg.* 813
VSM - Vehicle System Manager - DAIFUKU WEBB; *pg.* 1327, *pg.* 885
V.SMILE - Television Learning System - VTECH ELECTRONICS NORTH AMERICA, LLC; *pg.* 969, *pg.* 554
VSPHERE 4 - Software - EMULEX CORPORATION; *pg.* 392, *pg.* 70
VSPWORKS - Software - WIND RIVER SYSTEMS, INC.; *pg.* 493, *pg.* 38
VSR - Architectural Roof System - BUTLER MANUFACTURING COMPANY; *pg.* 72, *pg.* 981
VSR90 - Airbrush Design - PAASCHE AIRBRUSH COMPANY; *pg.* 1444, *pg.* 587
VSS - Vibration Monitoring & Control Service - BAKER HUGHES INTEQ; *pg.* 1316, *pg.* 1700
VSS - Automobile Storage Lifts - ROTARY LIFT; *pg.* 216, *pg.* 694
VSTAX - Semiconductor Solution - VITESSE SEMICONDUCTOR CORPORATION; *pg.* 686, *pg.* 57
VSX - Video Conferencing Product - POLYCOM, INC.; *pg.* 664, *pg.* 249
VSYNC - Medical Device - RESMED INC.; *pg.* 1589, *pg.* 207
VSYNC WITH TICONTROL - Medical Device - RESMED INC.; *pg.* 1589, *pg.* 207
VTC-3 - Vertical Turning System - KINGSBURY CORPORATION; *pg.* 1353, *pg.* 1035
VTC-4 - Vertical Turning System - KINGSBURY CORPORATION; *pg.* 1353, *pg.* 1035
VTC-400 - Vertical Turning System - KINGSBURY CORPORATION; *pg.* 1353, *pg.* 1035
VTC-5 - Vertical Turning System - KINGSBURY CORPORATION; *pg.* 1353, *pg.* 1035
VTD - Tool Line - KENNAMETAL IPG; *pg.* 1353, *pg.* 1615
VTE - Electric Viscosel - BROOKFIELD ENGINEERING LABORATORIES, INC.; *pg.* 1403, *pg.* 833
VTMIS - Systems Integration & Aeronautics - LOCKHEED MARTIN CORPORATION; *pg.* 229, *pg.* 762
VTOUR - Software - AUTODESK INC.; *pg.* 356, *pg.* 257
VU-STAT - Static Dissipative Acrylic Compound - EVONIK CYRO LLC; *pg.* 1162, *pg.* 1103
VU-TRON - Insulated Wire & Cable - GENERAL CABLE CORPORATION; *pg.* 83, *pg.* 729
VUALL CORMATIC - Tissue Dispenser - GEORGIA-PACIFIC LLC; *pg.* 1458, *pg.* 507
VULCALITE - Wheel - HAMILTON CASTER & MFG. CO.; *pg.* 206, *pg.* 1454
VULCAM - Dental Product - DENTSPLY INTERNATIONAL INC.; *pg.* 1522, *pg.* 1596
VULCAN - Carbon Black - CABOT CORPORATION; *pg.* 1151, *pg.* 792
VULCAN - Motorcycles - KAWASAKI MOTORS CORP., U.S.A.; *pg.* 1708, *pg.* 111
VULCAN - Thermoplastic Melting Kettles - M-B COMPANIES, INC.; *pg.* 1357, *pg.* 1884
VULCAN - Radiator - MESTEK, INC.; *pg.* 1074, *pg.* 857
VULCAN - Towing & Recovery Equipment - MILLER INDUSTRIES, INC.; *pg.* 185, *pg.* 1655
VULCAN - Rescue Harness - MINE SAFETY APPLIANCES COMPANY; *pg.* 1361, *pg.* 1525
VULCAN - Flashlight - STREAMLIGHT INC.; *pg.* 1306, *pg.* 1527
VULCAN - Traffic Control Signs - VULCAN, INC.; *pg.* 687, *pg.* 5
VULCAN CAL-STAT - Thermostat - VULCAN ELECTRIC COMPANY; *pg.* 1078, *pg.* 751
VULCHUR - Scavenger & Odor Control - QUAKER CHEMICAL CORP.; *pg.* 1178, *pg.* 1524
VULCRAFT - Steel Joist & Joist Girders, Steel Roof & Floor Decking - NUCOR CORPORATION; *pg.* 101, *pg.* 1368
VULKAN - Actuator - PRECISION VALVE CORPORATION; *pg.* 1060, *pg.* 1357
VULKEM - Polyurethane Sealant - RPM INTERNATIONAL INC.; *pg.* 1447, *pg.* 1464
VULKEM - Roofing Material - TREMCO INCORPORATED; *pg.* 116, *pg.* 1405
VUMAX - Bio-Microscope System - ESCALON MEDICAL CORP.; *pg.* 1412, *pg.* 1592
VUMON - Health Care Product - BRISTOL-MYERS SQUIBB COMPANY; *pg.* 1509, *pg.* 1206
VUTEK - Ink-Jet Printer - COOLEY GROUP, INC.; *pg.* 691, *pg.* 1603
VUTEK - UV Curing Digital Inkjet Printer - ELECTRONICS FOR IMAGING, INC.; *pg.* 390, *pg.* 88
VWIRE - Virtual Infrastructure Management - TRIPWIRE, INC.; *pg.* 485, *pg.* 1507
VWORKSPACE - Software - DELL SOFTWARE; *pg.* 385, *pg.* 40
VX - Riflescope - LEUPOLD & STEVENS, INC.; *pg.* 1420, *pg.* 1492
VX - Variable Carbon Potential Atmosphere Gas Generator - SURFACE COMBUSTION, INC.; *pg.* 1077, *pg.* 1462
VX-10 - Loudspeakers - VELODYNE ACOUSTICS, INC.; *pg.* 685, *pg.* 152
VX TECHNOLOGY - Multiphase Measurements - SCHLUMBERGER LIMITED; *pg.* 801, *pg.* 1714
VXA - Backup Tape Drive - TANDBERG DATA; *pg.* 481, *pg.* 311
VXDCOM - Software - WIND RIVER SYSTEMS, INC.; *pg.* 493, *pg.* 38
VXFUSION - Software - WIND RIVER SYSTEMS, INC.; *pg.* 493, *pg.* 38
VXGDB - Software - WIND RIVER SYSTEMS, INC.; *pg.* 493, *pg.* 38
VXGNU - Software - WIND RIVER SYSTEMS, INC.; *pg.* 493, *pg.* 38
VXMP - Software - WIND RIVER SYSTEMS, INC.; *pg.* 493, *pg.* 38
VXOPC - Software - WIND RIVER SYSTEMS, INC.; *pg.* 493, *pg.* 38
VXP - Video Processors - SIGMA DESIGNS, INC.; *pg.* 469, *pg.* 148
VXSIM - Software - WIND RIVER SYSTEMS, INC.; *pg.* 493, *pg.* 38
VXVMI - Software - WIND RIVER SYSTEMS, INC.; *pg.* 493, *pg.* 38
VXWORKS AE - Software - WIND RIVER SYSTEMS, INC.; *pg.* 493, *pg.* 38
VXXXX - Fluid Handling System - GRACO, INC.; *pg.* 1342, *pg.* 935
VY ELECTRIFY - Football Cleats - REEBOK INTERNATIONAL LTD.; *pg.* 1817, *pg.* 811
VYBEX - Polyester Compounds - FERRO CORPORATION; *pg.* 1162, *pg.* 1462
VYBRAN - Commercial Knitting Yarn - NATIONAL SPINNING COMPANY, INC.; *pg.* 697, *pg.* 1265
VYBRANT - Molecular Probe Product - THERMO FISHER SCIENTIFIC INC.; *pg.* 1602, *pg.* 61
VYCOM - Building Products - CPG INTERNATIONAL, INC.; *pg.* 1881, *pg.* 1586
VYCOR - Indus. & Laboratoryware - CORNING INCORPORATED; *pg.* 1122, *pg.* 1154
VYDATE - Insecticide - E.I. DU PONT DE NEMOURS & COMPANY; *pg.* 1159, *pg.* 390
VYSIS - Medical Test - QUEST DIAGNOSTICS INCORPORATED; *pg.* 1587, *pg.* 1080
VYSTAR - Natural Rubber Latex - VYSTAR CORPORATION; *pg.* 1891, *pg.* 532
VYTAFLEX - Urethane Liquid Rubber - SMOOTH-ON INC.; *pg.* 111, *pg.* 1528
VYTEX - Natural Rubber Latex - VYSTAR CORPORATION; *pg.* 1891, *pg.* 532
VYTORIN - Medicine - MERCK & CO., INC.; *pg.* 1566, *pg.* 1077
VZM - Video Zoom Microscope Lens - EDMUND INDUSTRIAL OPTICS INC.; *pg.* 1411, *pg.* 1041

W

W - Magazine - CONDE NAST PUBLICATIONS, INC.; *pg.* 1629, *pg.* 1217
W - Healthcare Products - WALGREEN CO.; *pg.* 1608, *pg.* 605
W-2 EXPRESS - Automated W-2 - EQUIFAX WORKFORCE SOLUTIONS; *pg.* 394, *pg.* 997
W-CLASS - Bar Code System - DATAMAX CORPORATION; *pg.* 1633, *pg.* 453
W HOTELS - Hotel Chain - STARWOOD HOTELS & RESORTS WORLDWIDE, INC.; *pg.* 1114, *pg.* 378
W-OPTICS - Mass Analyzer System - WATERS CORPORATION; *pg.* 1436, *pg.* 834
W-P FEEDS - Livestock Feeds & Feed Supplements - ALTAIR CORPORATION; *pg.* 1312, *pg.* 910
W PUBLISHING GROUP - Books - THOMAS NELSON INC.; *pg.* 1692, *pg.* 1654
W-SERIES - Software - TINIUS OLSEN, INC.; *pg.* 1432, *pg.* 1541
W-SNAKE - Belts - STEVEN MADDEN, LTD.; *pg.* 1819, *pg.* 1176
W-STUDS - Footwear - STEVEN MADDEN, LTD.; *pg.* 1819, *pg.* 1176
W-WOVEN - Belts - STEVEN MADDEN, LTD.; *pg.* 1819, *pg.* 1176
W900 - Trucks - KENWORTH TRUCK CO.; *pg.* 181, *pg.* 1822
WA - Desking System - KNOLL, INC.; *pg.* 425, *pg.* 1527
WAAS - Tracking Receivers - GARMIN INTERNATIONAL, INC.; *pg.* 1414, *pg.* 717
WAAS RECEIVER - Precision Landing & Approach Differential System Receiver - NOVATEL INC.; *pg.* 1424, *pg.* 1904
WABASH VALLEY - Furniture - BROWN JORDAN INTERNATIONAL COMPANY; *pg.* 919, *pg.* 740
WABASSO - Window - SPRINGS GLOBAL, INC.; *pg.* 698, *pg.* 1616
WABER - Power Strip - TRIPPE MANUFACTURING COMPANY; *pg.* 220, *pg.* 592
WABTEC - Air Brake System - WESTINGHOUSE AIR BRAKE TECHNOLOGIES CORPORATION; *pg.* 1388, *pg.* 1595
WAC - Dielectric Etch System - LAM RESEARCH CORPORATION; *pg.* 1354, *pg.* 91
WACAM - Market Research Services - MARITZ INC.; *pg.* 1914, *pg.* 977
WACK-O-WAX - Candy - TOOTSIE ROLL INDUSTRIES, INC.; *pg.* 1863, *pg.* 591
WACKY PACK - Food Product - SONIC CORP.; *pg.* 1750, *pg.* 1487
WADDA TOMATO - Tomato Plants - ARMSTRONG GARDEN CENTERS, INC.; *pg.* 1793, *pg.* 99
WADE - Truck Accessories - WESTIN AUTOMOTIVE PRODUCTS, INC.; *pg.* 222, *pg.* 211
WADE 3 - Shoe - CONVERSE INC.; *pg.* 1831, *pg.* 793
WADERWICK - Fishing Gear Product - SIMMS FISHING PRODUCTS CORP.; *pg.* 1845, *pg.* 1008
WADSWORTH - Educational Publications - THOMSON REUTERS CORPORATION; *pg.* 1693, *pg.* 1944
WAFER - Tables - HOWE FURNITURE CORPORATION; *pg.* 928, *pg.* 998
THE WAFER CUTTER - Tear Shaping Cutters & Replaceable Cutting Elements - GLEASON CORPORATION; *pg.* 1340, *pg.* 1335
WAFER-ENGINEERED - Semiconductor Material - KOPIN CORPORATION; *pg.* 425, *pg.* 847
THE WAFER-ENGINEERING COMPANY - Slogan - KOPIN CORPORATION; *pg.* 425, *pg.* 847
THE WAFER HOB - Gear Cutting Hobs - GLEASON CORPORATION; *pg.* 1340, *pg.* 1335
WAFERCARE - Services - ENTEGRIS, INC.; *pg.* 1882, *pg.* 788
WAFERCON - Electronic Components - MOLEX INCORPORATED; *pg.* 655, *pg.* 628
WAFERGARD - Filters & Pumps - ENTEGRIS, INC.; *pg.* 1882, *pg.* 788
WAFERGRIP - Semiconductor Dicing Equipment - DYNATEX INTERNATIONAL; *pg.* 635, *pg.* 277
WAFERLESS AUTOCLEAN - Cleaning System - LAM RESEARCH CORPORATION; *pg.* 1354, *pg.* 91
WAFERMARK - Laser System - GSI GROUP INC.; *pg.* 1415, *pg.* 784
WAFERPRO - Stud Bumper Product - KULICKE & SOFFA INDUSTRIES, INC.; *pg.* 650, *pg.* 1533
WAFERPURE - Purifiers - ENTEGRIS, INC.; *pg.* 1882, *pg.* 788
WAFERREPAIR - Laser System - GSI GROUP INC.; *pg.* 1415, *pg.* 784
WAFERS - Designer Kit - COILCRAFT, INC.; *pg.* 1324, *pg.* 562
WAFERSENSE - Auto Leveling Sensor - CYBEROPTICS CORPORATION; *pg.* 1408, *pg.* 925
WAFERSIGHT - Inspection System - KLA-TENCOR CORPORATION; *pg.* 1353, *pg.* 146
WAFERTRIM - Laser System - GSI GROUP INC.; *pg.* 1415, *pg.* 784
WAFFLE - Fabric - NEMSCHOFF, INC.; *pg.* 936, *pg.* 1890
WAFFLE BOWL - Ice Cream Sundae - INTERNATIONAL DAIRY QUEEN, INC.; *pg.* 1732, *pg.* 938
WAFFLE CRISP - Cereal - POST HOLDINGS, INC.; *pg.* 833, *pg.* 1002
WAG.COM - Pet Supplies - QUIDSI, INC.; *pg.* 1276, *pg.* 1076
WAGE-NET - Game - WMS INDUSTRIES INC.; *pg.* 593, *pg.* 666
WAGIND - Process Indicator Card - MEDLINE INDUSTRIES,

INC.; *pg.* 1562, *pg.* 635

WAGNER - Automotive Brakes & Lighting - FEDERAL-MOGUL HOLDINGS CORPORATION; *pg.* 205, *pg.* 907

WAGNER - Paint Spraying Equip. & Cordless Drills - WAGNER SPRAY TECH CORPORATION; *pg.* 1449, *pg.* 954

WAGON MASTER - Carts - GEERPRES INC.; *pg.* 1339, *pg.* 901

WAGON WHEEL - Tissue Dispenser - WAUSAU PAPER BAY WEST; *pg.* 1471, *pg.* 1465

WAHA - Cooking Oil - CARGILL LIMITED; *pg.* 1475, *pg.* 1914

WAHL CUSTOM SHAVE SYSTEM - Electric Shaver - WAHL CLIPPER CORPORATION; *pg.* 524, *pg.* 662

WAHL TRIM N VAC - Bread and Mustache Trimmer - WAHL CLIPPER CORPORATION; *pg.* 524, *pg.* 662

WAI LANA - Fitness Equipment - BALLY TOTAL FITNESS HOLDINGS CORPORATION; *pg.* 532, *pg.* 1200

WAILEA - Eyewear - MAUI JIM, INC.; *pg.* 9, *pg.* 651

WAIMEA BAY - Eyewear - MAUI JIM, INC.; *pg.* 9, *pg.* 651

WAINSCOT - Fabric - NEMSCHOFF, INC.; *pg.* 936, *pg.* 1890

WAINWRIGHT - Furniture - STANLEY FURNITURE CO., INC.; *pg.* 943, *pg.* 1379

WAKE FOREST - Guest Chairs - BERNHARDT DESIGN; *pg.* 918, *pg.* 1381

WAKE RUNNER - Engine Tune Supply Tool - BG PRODUCTS, INC.; *pg.* 200, *pg.* 722

WAKE-UP WRAP - Breakfast Sandwich - DUNKIN' BRANDS GROUP, INC.; *pg.* 1727, *pg.* 810

WAKEBOARDING - Magazine - BONNIER CORPORATION; *pg.* 1622, *pg.* 480

WAKEFIELD - Wines - BROWN-FORMAN CORPORATION; *pg.* 1958, *pg.* 732

WAKELY - Perfume - ABERCROMBIE & FITCH CO.; *pg.* 37, *pg.* 1466

WAL-MART SUPERCENTER - General Merchandise & Grocery - WAL-MART STORES, INC.; *pg.* 1790, *pg.* 29

WALDBAUM'S - Food Stores - THE GREAT ATLANTIC & PACIFIC TEA COMPANY, INC.; *pg.* 1021, *pg.* 1086

WALDEN - Shoes - ALLEN-EDMONDS SHOE CORP.; *pg.* 1804, *pg.* 1887

WALDEN - Office Furniture - JOFCO INC.; *pg.* 931, *pg.* 691

WALDEN - Office Furniture - STEELCASE INC.; *pg.* 475, *pg.* 889

WALDORF - Table - BLATT BOWLING & BILLIARD CORP.; *pg.* 1827, *pg.* 1203

WALDORF ASTORIA - Hotel - HILTON WORLDWIDE, INC.; *pg.* 1094, *pg.* 1791

WALEECO - Candy - F.B. WASHBURN CANDY CORP.; *pg.* 1852, *pg.* 803

WALGREENS - Drug Stores - WALGREEN CO.; *pg.* 1608, *pg.* 605

WALGREENS.COM - Website - WALGREEN CO.; *pg.* 1608, *pg.* 605

WALK-AND-TALK - Interactive Whiteboards - POLYVISION CORPORATION; *pg.* 665, *pg.* 531

WALK-AND-TALK - Office Furniture - STEELCASE INC.; *pg.* 475, *pg.* 889

WALK LIKE MADD - Awareness Program - MOTHERS AGAINST DRUNK DRIVING (MADD); *pg.* 147, *pg.* 1723

WALK MAKER - Building Form Product - QUIKRETE COMPANIES; *pg.* 106, *pg.* 519

WALK 'N CUT - Kitchen Appliance - HAMILTON BEACH BRANDS, INC.; *pg.* 56, *pg.* 1783

WALK THIS WHEY - Slogan - LEPRINO FOODS COMPANY; *pg.* 874, *pg.* 320

WALK-UP - Manual - XEROX CORPORATION; *pg.* 494, *pg.* 365

WALKABOUT - Treadmill - BATTLE CREEK EQUIPMENT CO.; *pg.* 1499, *pg.* 870

WALKABOUT - Orthopedic Product - DJO INCORPORATED; *pg.* 1524, *pg.* 302

WALKABOUT - Communications Management Software - NUANCE COMMUNICATIONS, INC.; *pg.* 447, *pg.* 806

WALKABOUT II - Glove - KOMBI, LTD.; *pg.* 1838, *pg.* 1766

WALKAMERICA - Fundraiser - MARCH OF DIMES BIRTH DEFECTS FOUNDATION; *pg.* 146, *pg.* 1354

WALKER - Reading Glass - A. T. CROSS COMPANY; *pg.* 339, *pg.* 1602

WALKER - Furniture - JASPER GROUP; *pg.* 930, *pg.* 691

WALKER - Communication Headset Product - PLANTRONICS, INC.; *pg.* 663, *pg.* 270

WALKER - Emission System - TENNECO, INC.; *pg.* 985, *pg.* 625

WALKER FRENCH - Potato Sticks - PEPSICO, INC.; *pg.* 259, *pg.* 1327

WALKER MONSTER - Snacks - PEPSICO, INC.; *pg.* 259, *pg.* 1327

WALKER ZANGER - Ceramic, Glass, Stone Tiles & Slabs - WALKER & ZANGER, INC.; *pg.* 119, *pg.* 281

WALKERCELL - Infloor Wiring System - WIREMOLD/LEGRAND; *pg.* 689, *pg.* 383

WALKERDECK - Infloor Wiring System - WIREMOLD/LEGRAND; *pg.* 689, *pg.* 383

WALKERDUCT - Infloor Wiring System - WIREMOLD/LEGRAND; *pg.* 689, *pg.* 383

WALKERDUCT PRO - Infloor Wiring System - WIREMOLD/LEGRAND; *pg.* 689, *pg.* 383

WALKERFLEX - Wiring System - WIREMOLD/LEGRAND; *pg.* 689, *pg.* 383

WALKERS - Food & Beverage - PEPSICO, INC.; *pg.* 259, *pg.* 1327

WALKERS SQUARE - Potato Snacks - PEPSICO, INC.; *pg.* 259, *pg.* 1327

WALKERTALK - Floor Graphics Display System - TRANSILWRAP COMPANY, INC.; *pg.* 1470, *pg.* 613

WALKERTALKER - Printed Plastic Product - TRANSILWRAP COMPANY, INC.; *pg.* 1470, *pg.* 613

WALKIE - Pallet Trucks - NISSAN FORKLIFT CORPORATION, NORTH AMERICA; *pg.* 186, *pg.* 631

WALKIE RIDER - Pallet Trucks - NISSAN FORKLIFT CORPORATION, NORTH AMERICA; *pg.* 186, *pg.* 631

THE WALKING COMPANY COLLECTION - Footwear - THE WALKING COMPANY, INC.; *pg.* 1822, *pg.* 307

WALKING ON AIR - Carpet - INTERFACE, INC.; *pg.* 695, *pg.* 512

WALKING ON CLOUDS - Carpet - INTERFACE, INC.; *pg.* 695, *pg.* 512

WALKING STRIKE PATH - Outsole - MASON COMPANIES, INC.; *pg.* 1811, *pg.* 1856

WALKING TREE - Wine - JIM BEAM BRANDS CO.; *pg.* 1965, *pg.* 601

WALKSTATION - Office Furniture - STEELCASE INC.; *pg.* 475, *pg.* 889

WALKWAYS - Fabric - NEMSCHOFF, INC.; *pg.* 936, *pg.* 1890

WALL - Lighting System - LITECONTROL CORPORATION; *pg.* 1301, *pg.* 841

WALL-A-BED - Bedding Products - SIMMONS COMPANY; *pg.* 943, *pg.* 520

WALL-DOG - Screw Anchor - POWERS FASTENERS INC.; *pg.* 1059, *pg.* 1143

WALL FARM - Display Furniture - AEROGROW INTERNATIONAL, INC.; *pg.* 1393, *pg.* 310

WALL GARDEN - Display Furniture - AEROGROW INTERNATIONAL, INC.; *pg.* 1393, *pg.* 310

WALL-GRIP - Paint And Stain Product - BENJAMIN MOORE & CO.; *pg.* 1440, *pg.* 1085

WALL HIDE - Coating Product - PPG INDUSTRIES, INC.; *pg.* 1445, *pg.* 1579

WALL HUGGER - Recliner Mechanisms - LEGGETT & PLATT, INCORPORATED; *pg.* 933, *pg.* 974

WALL-LUX - Security Lighting - JUNO LIGHTING, INC.; *pg.* 1300, *pg.* 606

WALL MATE - Wall Washing Kits - GEERPRES INC.; *pg.* 1339, *pg.* 901

WALL-MOUNT - Air Conditioner - BARD MANUFACTURING COMPANY; *pg.* 1069, *pg.* 1406

WALL-SATIN - Paint And Stain Product - BENJAMIN MOORE & CO.; *pg.* 1440, *pg.* 1085

WALL/SLOT - Lighting System - LITECONTROL CORPORATION; *pg.* 1301, *pg.* 841

WALL STREET & TECHNOLOGY - Publisher - UNITED BUSINESS MEDIA LLC; *pg.* 1697, *pg.* 1177

THE WALL STREET JOURNAL - Daily Business & Financial Publication - DOW JONES & COMPANY, INC.; *pg.* 1637, *pg.* 1225

THE WALL STREET JOURNAL SUNDAY - Bannered Journal Pages in More than 80 U.S. Newspapers - DOW JONES & COMPANY, INC.; *pg.* 1637, *pg.* 1225

WALL SUPREME - Coating Product - PPG INDUSTRIES, INC.; *pg.* 1445, *pg.* 1579

WALL SYSTEM - Curtain Walls - ALCOA INC.; *pg.* 65, *pg.* 1188

WALL/WASH - Lighting System - LITECONTROL CORPORATION; *pg.* 1301, *pg.* 841

WALLDUCT MEDICAL - Wiring System - WIREMOLD/LEGRAND; *pg.* 689, *pg.* 383

WALLFLEX - Medical Device - BOSTON SCIENTIFIC CORPORATION; *pg.* 1508, *pg.* 831

WALLFLOWER PRESS - Publisher - COLUMBIA UNIVERSITY PRESS; *pg.* 1628, *pg.* 1216

WALLGRAFT - Medical Device - BOSTON SCIENTIFIC CORPORATION; *pg.* 1508, *pg.* 831

WALLHIDE - Paints, Primers, Enamels, Lacquers, Shellacs, Stains, Varnishes & Thinners - PPG INDUSTRIES, INC.; *pg.* 1445, *pg.* 1579

WALLHUGGER - Adapter - ROSCO LABORATORIES, INC.; *pg.* 1782, *pg.* 378

WALLINGTON - Table - BLATT BOWLING & BILLIARD CORP.; *pg.* 1827, *pg.* 1203

WALLIS - Footwear - K-SWISS; *pg.* 1837, *pg.* 306

WALLITE SWIVEL - Hospital Lighting - SWIVELIER CO., INC.; *pg.* 1307, *pg.* 1142

WALLMASTER - Air Conditioner - FRIEDRICH AIR CONDITIONING CO.; *pg.* 1072, *pg.* 1740

WALLMATE - Insulation - THE DOW CHEMICAL COMPANY; *pg.* 1157, *pg.* 898

WALLMAX - Healthcare Product - GF HEALTH PRODUCTS, INC.; *pg.* 1535, *pg.* 508

WALLSAVER - Removable Poster Tape - 3M COMPANY; *pg.* 1142, *pg.* 956

WALLSAVER - Furniture - NEMSCHOFF, INC.; *pg.* 936, *pg.* 1890

WALLSTENT - Medical Device - BOSTON SCIENTIFIC CORPORATION; *pg.* 1508, *pg.* 831

WALLSTENT MONORAIL - Medical Device - BOSTON SCIENTIFIC CORPORATION; *pg.* 1508, *pg.* 831

WALLSTREET - Furniture - JOFCO INC.; *pg.* 931, *pg.* 691

WALLTONE - Interior Flat Wall Paint - DUNN-EDWARDS CORPORATION; *pg.* 1442, *pg.* 129

WALLY PARKS NHRA - Motorsports Museum - NATIONAL HOT ROD ASSOCIATION; *pg.* 149, *pg.* 99

WALLY WEST - Character - DC COMICS, INC.; *pg.* 1633, *pg.* 1221

WALNECK'S CLASSIC MOTORCYCLE - Photo Advertising Guide - DOMINION ENTERPRISES; *pg.* 1636, *pg.* 1796

WALNUT ACRES ORGANIC - Food Product - THE HAIN CELESTIAL GROUP, INC.; *pg.* 860, *pg.* 1172

THE WALNUT BREWERY - Brew Pub - ROCK BOTTOM RESTAURANTS, INC.; *pg.* 1748, *pg.* 334

WALNUT CREST - Varietal Wines - BANFI VINTNERS; *pg.* 1957, *pg.* 1161

WALOCEL - Cellulose Polymers - THE DOW CHEMICAL COMPANY; *pg.* 1157, *pg.* 898

WALSRODER - Nitrocellulose - THE DOW CHEMICAL COMPANY; *pg.* 1157, *pg.* 898

WALT DISNEY - Motion Picture & Television Production Company - THE WALT DISNEY COMPANY; *pg.* 317, *pg.* 52

WALT DISNEY COMICS - Books - THE WALT DISNEY COMPANY; *pg.* 317, *pg.* 52

WALT DISNEY MASTERPIECE COLLECTION - Video Cassettes - THE WALT DISNEY COMPANY; *pg.* 317, *pg.* 52

WALT DISNEY RECORDS - Soundtrack - THE WALT DISNEY COMPANY; *pg.* 317, *pg.* 52

WALT DISNEY WORLD - Amusement Park - THE WALT DISNEY COMPANY; *pg.* 317, *pg.* 52

WALTER - Medical Cabinet - BLICKMAN HEALTH INDUSTRIES, INC.; *pg.* 1506, *pg.* 1051

WALTER READE THEATRES - Motion Picture Theaters - CINEPLEX ENTERTAINMENT LP; *pg.* 275, *pg.* 1936

WALTHAM - Furniture - JOFCO INC.; *pg.* 931, *pg.* 691

WALTHAM - Petcare Product - MARS, INCORPORATED; *pg.* 1858, *pg.* 1792

WALTHAM - Watch - M.Z. BERGER & CO., INC.; *pg.* 10, *pg.* 1175

THE WALTON SUN - Florida Newspaper - FREEDOM COMMUNICATIONS, INC.; *pg.* 1643, *pg.* 110

WAM! - Cable Television Channel - STARZ ENTERTAINMENT, LLC; *pg.* 310, *pg.* 327

WAMPOLE - Rapid Membrane Test Products - ALERE INC.; *pg.* 1488, *pg.* 849

WAMSUTTA - Bed Linen - SPRINGS GLOBAL, INC.; *pg.* 698, *pg.* 1616

WAMSUTTA BABY - Bed Linen - SPRINGS GLOBAL, INC.; *pg.* 698, *pg.* 1616

WAN - Software - CISCO SYSTEMS, INC.; *pg.* 372, *pg.* 240

WAN FU - Wine - SHAW ROSS INTERNATIONAL IMPORTERS; *pg.* 1970, *pg.* 449

WANADAPT - Wan Adapters for PCI - NEONODE, INC.; *pg.* 659, *pg.* 268

WANCHAI FERRY - Food Product - GENERAL MILLS, INC.; *pg.* 828, *pg.* 933

THE WAND - Syringe - MILESTONE SCIENTIFIC, INC.; *pg.* 1568, *pg.* 1079
THE WAND PLUS - Syringe - MILESTONE SCIENTIFIC, INC.; *pg.* 1568, *pg.* 1079
WANDA - Fabric - NEMSCHOFF, INC.; *pg.* 936, *pg.* 1890
WANDA THE WHALE - Pool Cleaner - HAYWARD POOL PRODUCTS; *pg.* 1049, *pg.* 1057
WANDER - Textiles - BERNHARDT DESIGN; *pg.* 918, *pg.* 1381
WANDERGUARD - Security Products - STANLEY BLACK & DECKER, INC.; *pg.* 1063, *pg.* 358
WANG - Medical Equipment - CONMED CORPORATION; *pg.* 1517, *pg.* 1347
WANJET - Software - F5 NETWORKS, INC.; *pg.* 396, *pg.* 1835
WANNA PLAY? - Designer Fragrance - PARFUMS DE COEUR LTD.; *pg.* 519, *pg.* 376
WANPMC - Wan Adapters for PMC - NEONODE, INC.; *pg.* 659, *pg.* 268
WANPTMC - Software - NEONODE, INC.; *pg.* 659, *pg.* 268
WANSCALER - Software - CITRIX SYSTEMS, INC.; *pg.* 375, *pg.* 424
WANT - Apparel - OAKLEY, INC.; *pg.* 1840, *pg.* 86
WANTED: A HARD JOB - Tagline - GRAYCOR INC.; *pg.* 84, *pg.* 619
WAPSTR - Mobile Suite - CHYRONHEGO; *pg.* 371, *pg.* 1179
WAR - Apparel - OAKLEY, INC.; *pg.* 1840, *pg.* 86
WAR BIRD - Golf Ball - CALLAWAY GOLF COMPANY; *pg.* 1829, *pg.* 58
WAR HAWK - Apparel - OAKLEY, INC.; *pg.* 1840, *pg.* 86
WARBIRD - Golf Product - CALLAWAY GOLF COMPANY; *pg.* 1829, *pg.* 58
WARBIRDS - Fan - CRAFTMADE INTERNATIONAL, INC.; *pg.* 1295, *pg.* 1670
WARBIRDS - Online Game - IENTERTAINMENT NETWORK, INC.; *pg.* 1258, *pg.* 1360
WARBIRDS AIR COMBAT - Online Game - IENTERTAINMENT NETWORK, INC.; *pg.* 1258, *pg.* 1360
WARBY PARKER - Eyewear - JAND, INC.; *pg.* 1418, *pg.* 1245
WARD - Jacket - SANTA FE LEATHER CORPORATION; *pg.* 12, *pg.* 1059
WARDLEY - Fish Products - THE HARTZ MOUNTAIN CORP.; *pg.* 1476, *pg.* 1120
WARE - Glass & Ceramic Material - CORNING INCORPORATED; *pg.* 1122, *pg.* 1154
WARING - Small Kitchen Appliances - CONAIR CORPORATION; *pg.* 505, *pg.* 1055
WARING - Blenders & Mixers - WARING PRODUCTS, INC.; *pg.* 62, *pg.* 379
WARING BY CUISINART - Food Processers - WARING PRODUCTS, INC.; *pg.* 62, *pg.* 379
WARING PRO - Blender - WARING PRODUCTS, INC.; *pg.* 62, *pg.* 379
WARLI - Footwear - STEVEN MADDEN, LTD.; *pg.* 1819, *pg.* 1176
WARM AIR - Warming System - CINCINNATI SUB-ZERO PRODUCTS, INC.; *pg.* 1070, *pg.* 1411
WARM & GENTLE - Perm - ZOTOS INTERNATIONAL, INC.; *pg.* 524, *pg.* 345
WARM BLUSH - Blush - MERLE NORMAN COSMETICS, INC.; *pg.* 517, *pg.* 136
WARM DELIGHT MINIS - Dessert - GENERAL MILLS, INC.; *pg.* 828, *pg.* 933
WARM EMBRACE - Carpet - BEAULIEU GROUP, LLC; *pg.* 917, *pg.* 529
WARM FUZZIES - Pillow and Throw - HERITAGE LACE INC.; *pg.* 694, *pg.* 711
WARM GLOW - Warmer - MUNCHKIN, INC.; *pg.* 964, *pg.* 300
WARM SUGAR VANILLA - Fragrance - PARFUMS DE COEUR LTD.; *pg.* 519, *pg.* 376
WARM TECH - Blending System - HAWS CORPORATION; *pg.* 56, *pg.* 1032
WARM UP JACKET - Clothing - K-SWISS; *pg.* 1837, *pg.* 306
WARMAIR - Massage Product - HUMAN TOUCH; *pg.* 928, *pg.* 123
WARMFLO - Medical Device - MALLINCKRODT PHARMACEUTICALS; *pg.* 1557, *pg.* 978
WARMFLO - Fluid Warming System - MEDTRONIC; *pg.* 1563, *pg.* 183
WARMING TUBE - Medical Product - CINCINNATI SUB-ZERO PRODUCTS, INC.; *pg.* 1070, *pg.* 1411
WARMSPORT - Drivers - CALLAWAY GOLF COMPANY; *pg.* 1829, *pg.* 58
WARMTH & BRAWN - Jacket - HABAND COMPANY, INC.; *pg.* 1772, *pg.* 1099
WARMTH THROUGH INNOVATION - Tag Line - INDERA MILLS COMPANY; *pg.* 26, *pg.* 1396
WARMTOUCH - Convective Air Warming Systems - MEDTRONIC; *pg.* 1563, *pg.* 183
WARMTRACE - Domestic Hot Water Systems - THERMON AMERICAS INC.; *pg.* 1077, *pg.* 1744
WARN INDUSTRIAL - Industrial Winches, Hoists & Accessories - WARN INDUSTRIES, INC.; *pg.* 221, *pg.* 1497
WARN WARE - Clothing & Accessories - WARN INDUSTRIES, INC.; *pg.* 221, *pg.* 1497
WARN WORKS - Utilitarian Off-Road Product - WARN INDUSTRIES, INC.; *pg.* 221, *pg.* 1497
WARNE - Beatrix Potter Books - PENGUIN RANDOM HOUSE; *pg.* 1675, *pg.* 1276
WARNER ASPECT - Books - HBG BOOKS, INC.; *pg.* 1648, *pg.* 1238
WARNER BROS. - Entertainment Product - TIME WARNER INC.; *pg.* 312, *pg.* 1302
WARNER BROS. - Record Label - WARNER MUSIC GROUP CORP.; *pg.* 590, *pg.* 1313
WARNER ELECTRIC - Elec. & Mech. Brakes & Clutches, Precision Ball Bearing Screws, Step Motors - WARNER ELECTRIC, INC.; *pg.* 221, *pg.* 661
WARP - Software - CYPRESS SEMICONDUCTOR CORPORATION; *pg.* 1326, *pg.* 243
WARP - Internet Service - SHAW COMMUNICATIONS INC.; *pg.* 307, *pg.* 1904
WARP ENTERPRISE - Software - CYPRESS SEMICONDUCTOR CORPORATION; *pg.* 1326, *pg.* 243
WARP PROFESSIONAL - Software - CYPRESS SEMICONDUCTOR CORPORATION; *pg.* 1326, *pg.* 243
WARP SPEED - Power Semiconductor Device - INTERNATIONAL RECTIFIER CORPORATION; *pg.* 647, *pg.* 80
WARP2 - Software - CYPRESS SEMICONDUCTOR CORPORATION; *pg.* 1326, *pg.* 243
WARP2ISR - Software - CYPRESS SEMICONDUCTOR CORPORATION; *pg.* 1326, *pg.* 243
WARP2SIM - Software - CYPRESS SEMICONDUCTOR CORPORATION; *pg.* 1326, *pg.* 243
WARP3 - Software - CYPRESS SEMICONDUCTOR CORPORATION; *pg.* 1326, *pg.* 243
WARPISR - Software - CYPRESS SEMICONDUCTOR CORPORATION; *pg.* 1326, *pg.* 243
WARPLANES - Fan - CRAFTMADE INTERNATIONAL, INC.; *pg.* 1295, *pg.* 1670
WARPS - Window Material - FLEX-O-GLASS, INC.; *pg.* 1457, *pg.* 574
WARRANTY CHECK - Information Retrieval Services - CARFAX INC.; *pg.* 202, *pg.* 1777
WARREN - Tobacco Product - AMERICAN SNUFF COMPANY; *pg.* 1893, *pg.* 1641
WARREN - Commercial Printing Papers - SAPPI FINE PAPER NORTH AMERICA; *pg.* 1468, *pg.* 801
WARREN COUNTY - Twist Tobacco - AMERICAN SNUFF COMPANY; *pg.* 1893, *pg.* 1641
WARREN MILLER ENTERTAINMENT - Magazine - BONNIER CORPORATION; *pg.* 1622, *pg.* 480
WARREN RUPP - Pumps - IDEX CORPORATION; *pg.* 1347, *pg.* 623
WARRIOR - Tires - MICHELIN NORTH AMERICA INC.; *pg.* 1886, *pg.* 1618
WARRIOR - Athletic Equipment - NEW BALANCE ATHLETIC SHOE, INC.; *pg.* 1811, *pg.* 798
WARRIOR - Aircraft - PIPER AIRCRAFT, INC.; *pg.* 233, *pg.* 477
WARRIOR - Circular Cloth Cutter - THE WOLF MACHINE CO.; *pg.* 1389, *pg.* 1427
WARRIOR - All Terrain Vehicle - YAMAHA MOTOR CORPORATION USA; *pg.* 1713, *pg.* 76
WARSTEINER PREMIUM DUNKEL - Traditional German Dark Brown Lager - WARSTEINER IMPORTERS AGENCY, INC.; *pg.* 266, *pg.* 1479
WARSTEINER PREMIUM FRESH - Non-Alcoholic Beer - WARSTEINER IMPORTERS AGENCY, INC.; *pg.* 266, *pg.* 1479
WARSTEINER PREMIUM VERUM - Pilsner - WARSTEINER IMPORTERS AGENCY, INC.; *pg.* 266, *pg.* 1479
WART-OFF - Wart Remover - MCNEIL-PPC, INC.; *pg.* 1560, *pg.* 1533
WARTHOG - Cream Ale - BIG ROCK BREWERY INCOME TRUST; *pg.* 239, *pg.* 1902
WARTORN - Apparel - OAKLEY, INC.; *pg.* 1840, *pg.* 86
WARWICK - Semisweet Chocolate - CARGILL LIMITED; *pg.* 1475, *pg.* 1914
WARWICK - Fabric - NEMSCHOFF, INC.; *pg.* 936, *pg.* 1890
WASABI - Bicycle - TREK BICYCLE CORPORATION; *pg.* 1847, *pg.* 1896
THE WASH - Hair Care Product - JOHN PAUL MITCHELL SYSTEMS; *pg.* 512, *pg.* 133
WASH 'N CURL - Hair Care Product - CCA INDUSTRIES, INC.; *pg.* 503, *pg.* 1114
WASH 'N DRI - Premoistened Towelettes - THE CLOROX COMPANY; *pg.* 327, *pg.* 169
WASH 'N TINT - Hair Care Product - CCA INDUSTRIES, INC.; *pg.* 503, *pg.* 1114
WASH N' WAX - Automotive Reconditioning Product - MOC PRODUCTS COMPANY, INC.; *pg.* 332, *pg.* 174
WASH 'N WEAR - Enamel - JONES-BLAIR COMPANY; *pg.* 1443, *pg.* 1682
WASHALERT - Laundry Monitoring System - ALLIANCE LAUNDRY HOLDINGS LLC; *pg.* 51, *pg.* 1890
WASHAWAY - Bar-Code Labels - CHECKPOINT SYSTEMS, INC.; *pg.* 628, *pg.* 1559
WASHBOARD - Patterned Glass - AGC GLASS NORTH AMERICA, INC.; *pg.* 65, *pg.* 482
WASHBURN - Guitars - U.S. MUSIC CORPORATION; *pg.* 315, *pg.* 560
WASHDOWN DUTY - Motors - BALDOR ELECTRIC COMPANY; *pg.* 1316, *pg.* 32
WASHER SOLVENT - Wax - MOC PRODUCTS COMPANY, INC.; *pg.* 332, *pg.* 174
WASHI - Fabric - NEMSCHOFF, INC.; *pg.* 936, *pg.* 1890
WASHINGTON CIRCLE THEATRES - Motion Picture Theaters - CINEPLEX ENTERTAINMENT LP; *pg.* 275, *pg.* 1936
WASHINGTON FEDERAL - Investment Company - WASHINGTON FEDERAL INC.; *pg.* 818, *pg.* 1842
WASHINGTON FEDERAL SAVINGS - Savings Institution - WASHINGTON FEDERAL INC.; *pg.* 818, *pg.* 1842
WASHINGTON GAS - Natural Gas LCD Utility - WASHINGTON GAS LIGHT CO.; *pg.* 1954, *pg.* 407
WASHINGTON HOSPITAL CENTER - Hospital - MEDSTAR HEALTH INC.; *pg.* 1563, *pg.* 767
THE WASHINGTON POST - Daily & Sunday Newspaper - GRAHAM HOLDINGS COMPANY; *pg.* 1645, *pg.* 1773
THE WASHINGTON POST - Daily Newspaper - THE WASHINGTON POST; *pg.* 1701, *pg.* 407
WASHINGTON REDSKINS - Football Team - WASHINGTON FOOTBALL, INC.; *pg.* 591, *pg.* 1776
WASHINGTON SPORTS CLUBS - Fitness Center - TOWN SPORTS INTERNATIONAL HOLDINGS, INC.; *pg.* 589, *pg.* 1303
WASHINGTON SQUARE - Jewelry - LAGOS INC.; *pg.* 8, *pg.* 1566
THE WASHINGTON TIMES - Daily Newspaper - THE WASHINGTON TIMES, LLC; *pg.* 1701, *pg.* 408
THE WASHINGTONIAN MAGAZINE - Magazine - CAPITAL GAZETTE COMMUNICATIONS INC.; *pg.* 1625, *pg.* 754
WASHJET - Spray Nozzle - SPRAYING SYSTEMS CO.; *pg.* 1063, *pg.* 670
WASP & HORNET KILLER PLUS - Insecticide - CRC INDUSTRIES, INC.; *pg.* 329, *pg.* 1590
WAST SIDE COLLECTION - Pet Fashion - PETEDGE; *pg.* 1481, *pg.* 787
WASTE & RECYCLING NEWS - Newspaper - CRAIN COMMUNICATIONS, INC.; *pg.* 1631, *pg.* 879
WASTE KING - Hot Water Dispensers & Disposers - ANAHEIM MANUFACTURING COMPANY; *pg.* 51, *pg.* 48
WASTE NEWS - Newspaper - CRAIN COMMUNICATIONS, INC.; *pg.* 1631, *pg.* 879
WASTE-WAGON - Linen Cart - GEERPRES INC.; *pg.* 1339, *pg.* 901
WASTE WATCH - Community Safety Services - WASTE MANAGEMENT, INC.; *pg.* 1954, *pg.* 1716
WASTELAND - Game - ACTIVISION BLIZZARD, INC.; *pg.* 948, *pg.* 271
WASTEROUTE - Management Services - WASTE MANAGEMENT, INC.; *pg.* 1954, *pg.* 1716
WASTEWIZARD - Industrial Fluid Recycling Systems - GE WATER & PROCESS TECHNOLOGIES; *pg.* 1339, *pg.* 1588
WATCH GEAR - Watch - TOURNEAU INC.; *pg.* 14, *pg.* 1303
WATCH STATION - Watch Retailer - LUXOTTICA RETAIL; *pg.* 8, *pg.* 1460
WATCH WINDOW - Software Product - WOODWARD, INC.; *pg.* 122, *pg.* 329

First page reference indicates Business Class Edition
Second page reference indicates Geographic Edition

WATCH YOUR CHILD GROW,FLOURISH & EXCEL - Slogan - NOBEL LEARNING COMMUNITIES, INC.; *pg.* 605, *pg.* 1593
WATCH YOURSELF CHANGE - Slogan - WEIGHT WATCHERS INTERNATIONAL, INC.; *pg.* 1609, *pg.* 1313
WATCHALERT - Wireless Communication System - AT&T SOUTHEAST; *pg.* 1868, *pg.* 489
WATCHBAND INCISION - Healthcare Product - JOHNSON & JOHNSON; *pg.* 1549, *pg.* 1091
WATCHDOG - Oil Dryer - TRICO MFG. CORP.; *pg.* 219, *pg.* 1886
WATCHDOG - Software - TRIPPE MANUFACTURING COMPANY; *pg.* 220, *pg.* 592
WATCHDOG PUMP PROTECTION SYSTEM - Pumping System - GRACO, INC.; *pg.* 1342, *pg.* 935
WATCHGUARD - Laminated Safety Glass - PPG INDUSTRIES, INC.; *pg.* 1445, *pg.* 1579
WATCHMAN - Gas Monitor - MINE SAFETY APPLIANCES COMPANY; *pg.* 1361, *pg.* 1525
WATCHMASTER - Marine Clock - SWIFT OPTICAL INSTRUMENTS, INC.; *pg.* 1430, *pg.* 1744
WATCHMATE - Barometer & Thermometer - SWIFT OPTICAL INSTRUMENTS, INC.; *pg.* 1430, *pg.* 1744
WATCHPORT - Computer Peripheral Equipment - DIGI INTERNATIONAL INC.; *pg.* 387, *pg.* 948
WATCONNECT - Software - WATLOW ELECTRIC MANUFACTURING COMPANY; *pg.* 1078, *pg.* 1004
WATER BABIES - Sun Care Products - MERCK & CO., INC.; *pg.* 1566, *pg.* 1077
WATER BUFFALO - Leather Product - COACH, INC.; *pg.* 3, *pg.* 1214
WATER DANCE - Bathroom Accessories - SYMMONS INDUSTRIES, INC.; *pg.* 114, *pg.* 803
WATER EAGLE - Fishing Rods - WRIGHT & MCGILL CO.; *pg.* 1848, *pg.* 324
WATER FALL - Textiles - BERNHARDT DESIGN; *pg.* 918, *pg.* 1381
WATER-FINE - Filter Cartridge - PALL CORPORATION; *pg.* 232, *pg.* 1323
WATER FX - Acidifying Agent - KALO, INC.; *pg.* 1796, *pg.* 719
WATER GARDEN NEWS - Magazine - I-5 PUBLISHING LLC; *pg.* 1651, *pg.* 133
WATER GIRL INT'L - Women's Surf Clothing - LOST ARROW CORPORATION; *pg.* 44, *pg.* 301
WATER JACKET - Eyewear - OAKLEY, INC.; *pg.* 1840, *pg.* 86
THE WATER LIBRARY - Bookstore - AMERICAN WATER WORKS ASSOCIATION; *pg.* 131, *pg.* 316
WATER LINE - Textiles - BERNHARDT DESIGN; *pg.* 918, *pg.* 1381
WATER LOCK - Superabsorbent Polymers - GRAIN PROCESSING CORPORATION; *pg.* 859, *pg.* 709
WATER OUT - Herbal Product - NOW HEALTH GROUP, INC.; *pg.* 1576, *pg.* 557
WATER RAINBOW - Bath & Plumbing Product - JACUZZI BRANDS CORPORATION; *pg.* 554, *pg.* 65
WATER RHYTHM - Bath Product - KOHLER CO.; *pg.* 91, *pg.* 1862
WATER SENTRY - Lead, Cyst, Sediment & Odor Removal Water Filters - ELKAY MANUFACTURING COMPANY; *pg.* 80, *pg.* 645
WATER SMART. - Lawn Watering - THE SCOTTS MIRACLE-GRO COMPANY; *pg.* 1799, *pg.* 1459
WATER THAT MOVES YOU - Slogan - JACUZZI BRANDS CORPORATION; *pg.* 554, *pg.* 65
WATER WHITE - Dry Cleaning & Laundry Product - ADCO, INC.; *pg.* 325, *pg.* 482
WATER WORKS - Hair Color - AMERICAN INTERNATIONAL INDUSTRIES COMPANY; *pg.* 498, *pg.* 126
WATERBOY - Running Accessories - BROOKS SPORTS INC.; *pg.* 1805, *pg.* 1818
WATERBUG ALERT - Environmental Security Product - WINLAND ELECTRONICS, INC.; *pg.* 688, *pg.* 928
WATERBURY - Shoes - ALLEN-EDMONDS SHOE CORP.; *pg.* 1804, *pg.* 1887
WATERBURY - Header - SENECA FALLS MACHINES; *pg.* 1374, *pg.* 1341
WATERBURY HEADERS - Cold Heading or Threading Machines - SENECA FALLS MACHINES; *pg.* 1374, *pg.* 1341
WATERCAD - Software - BENTLEY SYSTEMS, INC.; *pg.* 361, *pg.* 1531
WATERCALK - Concrete System - L.M. SCOFIELD COMPANY; *pg.* 94, *pg.* 134
WATERCALK-3G - Concrete System - L.M. SCOFIELD COMPANY; *pg.* 94, *pg.* 134
WATERCALK-3S - Concrete System - L.M. SCOFIELD COMPANY; *pg.* 94, *pg.* 134
WATERCOLOR - Magazine - NIELSEN BUSINESS MEDIA; *pg.* 1671, *pg.* 1272
WATERCOLOR - Trade Publication - THE NIELSEN COMPANY B.V.; *pg.* 1671, *pg.* 1272
WATERCOLORS - Garden Hose - TEKNI-PLEX, INC.; *pg.* 1470, *pg.* 1122
WATERCOVE - Bath Product - KOHLER CO.; *pg.* 91, *pg.* 1862
THE WATERFALL - Gutter Protection - BENJAMIN OBDYKE, INC.; *pg.* 70, *pg.* 1540
WATERFALL - Roofing Ventilation Product - BENJAMIN OBDYKE, INC.; *pg.* 70, *pg.* 1540
WATERFALL - Personal Care Product - COLGATE-PALMOLIVE COMPANY; *pg.* 504, *pg.* 1215
WATERFALL - Bedding - CROSCILL, INC.; *pg.* 1122, *pg.* 1220
WATERFALL - Ceramic, Glass, Stone Tiles & Slabs - WALKER & ZANGER, INC.; *pg.* 119, *pg.* 281
WATERFORD - Glassworks - 1-800-FLOWERS.COM, INC.; *pg.* 1758, *pg.* 1151
WATERFORD - Wallcovering - YORK WALLCOVERINGS INC.; *pg.* 947, *pg.* 1598
WATERFRONT - Fabric - NEMSCHOFF, INC.; *pg.* 936, *pg.* 1890
WATERFRONT BISTRO - Frozen Seafood Products - SAFEWAY INC.; *pg.* 1032, *pg.* 184
WATERGEMS - Software - BENTLEY SYSTEMS, INC.; *pg.* 361, *pg.* 1531
WATERGIRL - Clothing Line - PATAGONIA; *pg.* 31, *pg.* 301
WATERHAVEN - Bath Product - KOHLER CO.; *pg.* 91, *pg.* 1862
WATERHILL - Faucets - MOEN INCORPORATED; *pg.* 1056, *pg.* 1468
WATERKID - Footwear - COBIAN CORP.; *pg.* 1806, *pg.* 253
WATERLASE - Dental Laser Product - BIOLASE TECHNOLOGY, INC.; *pg.* 1506, *pg.* 107
WATERLASE C100 - Dental Laser Product - BIOLASE TECHNOLOGY, INC.; *pg.* 1506, *pg.* 107
WATERLASE DENTISTRY - Dental Product - BIOLASE TECHNOLOGY, INC.; *pg.* 1506, *pg.* 107
WATERLASE MD - Dental Laser Product - BIOLASE TECHNOLOGY, INC.; *pg.* 1506, *pg.* 107
WATERLASE MD GOLD - Dental Laser Product - BIOLASE TECHNOLOGY, INC.; *pg.* 1506, *pg.* 107
WATERLASE MD TURBO - Dental Laser Product - BIOLASE TECHNOLOGY, INC.; *pg.* 1506, *pg.* 107
WATERLEFE - Community Name - WCI COMMUNITIES, INC.; *pg.* 1118, *pg.* 414
WATERLESS - Battery - ENERSYS INC.; *pg.* 1334, *pg.* 1584
WATERLOC - Outsole - ACUSHNET COMPANY; *pg.* 1824, *pg.* 818
WATERLOO - Hardware - FORTUNE BRANDS HOME & SECURITY, INC.; *pg.* 55, *pg.* 600
WATERLOO - Tool Storage Products - WATERLOO INDUSTRIES, INC.; *pg.* 946, *pg.* 1885
WATERMAID - Rice - RIVIANA FOODS INC.; *pg.* 892, *pg.* 1713
WATERMAN - Footwear - COBIAN CORP.; *pg.* 1806, *pg.* 253
WATERMAN - Fine Writing Instruments - NEWELL RUBBERMAID INC.; *pg.* 1128, *pg.* 515
WATERMARK - Chemical Product - GFS CHEMICALS, INC.; *pg.* 1164, *pg.* 1471
WATERMASTER - Fountain - RITCHIE INDUSTRIES, INC.; *pg.* 707, *pg.* 703
WATERMATIC - Fountain - RITCHIE INDUSTRIES, INC.; *pg.* 707, *pg.* 703
WATERMATIC 150S - Watering System for Sheep & Goats - RITCHIE INDUSTRIES, INC.; *pg.* 707, *pg.* 703
WATERMELON DAISY - Fruit Arrangements - EDIBLE ARRANGEMENTS INTERNATIONAL, INC.; *pg.* 1768, *pg.* 382
WATERMELON FESTIVAL - Fruit Arrangements - EDIBLE ARRANGEMENTS INTERNATIONAL, INC.; *pg.* 1768, *pg.* 382
WATERPACK - Fertilizer - SIMPLOT PARTNERS INC.; *pg.* 1800, *pg.* 548
WATERPIK SHOWERHEADS - Shower Heads - WATER PIK, INC.; *pg.* 1609, *pg.* 329
WATERPROOF - Color Proofing System - E.I. DU PONT DE NEMOURS & COMPANY; *pg.* 1159, *pg.* 390
WATERPROOF - Eye Liner - MERLE NORMAN COSMETICS, INC.; *pg.* 517, *pg.* 136
WATERPROOF MASCARA - Mascara - MERLE NORMAN COSMETICS, INC.; *pg.* 517, *pg.* 136
WATERS - Autosampler - HAMILTON CO., INC.; *pg.* 1415, *pg.* 1031
WATERS CRITICAL CLEAN - Quality Parts Component - WATERS CORPORATION; *pg.* 1436, *pg.* 834
WATER'S EDGE - Furniture - STANLEY FURNITURE CO., INC.; *pg.* 943, *pg.* 1379
WATERS 'EM RIGHT - Slogan - RITCHIE INDUSTRIES, INC.; *pg.* 707, *pg.* 703
WATER'S GROVE - Bath Product - KOHLER CO.; *pg.* 91, *pg.* 1862
WATERSABRE - Fluid-Jet Cutting System - TELEDYNE BROWN ENGINEERING, INC.; *pg.* 235, *pg.* 6
WATERSAFE - Software - BENTLEY SYSTEMS, INC.; *pg.* 361, *pg.* 1531
WATERSAVR - Evaporation Reduction Chemical - FLEXIBLE SOLUTIONS INTERNATIONAL, INC.; *pg.* 1163, *pg.* 1913
WATERSCAPE - Bath Product - KOHLER CO.; *pg.* 91, *pg.* 1862
WATERSENSE - Faucet - MOEN INCORPORATED; *pg.* 1056, *pg.* 1468
WATERSHED - Metal Finishing Product - HEATBATH CORPORATION; *pg.* 1165, *pg.* 826
WATERSHED - Water Repellant - JONES-BLAIR COMPANY; *pg.* 1443, *pg.* 1682
WATERSHED - Fabric - NEMSCHOFF, INC.; *pg.* 936, *pg.* 1890
WATERSKI - Magazine - BONNIER CORPORATION; *pg.* 1622, *pg.* 480
WATERSTOP-RX - Joint Sealant Product - MINERALS TECHNOLOGIES INC.; *pg.* 1173, *pg.* 617
WATERTILE - Bath Product - KOHLER CO.; *pg.* 91, *pg.* 1862
WATERTITE - Electronic Components - MOLEX INCORPORATED; *pg.* 655, *pg.* 628
WATERTITE - Sealant - RPM INTERNATIONAL INC.; *pg.* 1447, *pg.* 1464
WATERTOWN DAILY TIMES - Newspaper - JOHNSON NEWSPAPER CORPORATION; *pg.* 1655, *pg.* 1349
WATERVEYOR - Abrasive Removal System - FLOW INTERNATIONAL CORPORATION; *pg.* 1337, *pg.* 1821
WATERWISE - Water Filtration Products - WATERWISE INC.; *pg.* 1066, *pg.* 438
WATERWITCH - Wall Decor - ETHAN ALLEN INTERIORS INC.; *pg.* 924, *pg.* 343
WATERWIZARD - Water Heaters - AERCO INTERNATIONAL INC.; *pg.* 1068, *pg.* 1142
WATERWORKS - Economy Irrigation Injector - KALO, INC.; *pg.* 1796, *pg.* 719
WATERWORKS - Soluble Support System - STRATASYS, INC.; *pg.* 476, *pg.* 923
WATERWORKS - Garden Hose - TEKNI-PLEX, INC.; *pg.* 1470, *pg.* 1122
WATERWORKS - Game - WINNING MOVES GAMES, INC.; *pg.* 970, *pg.* 816
WATERWORLD CONCORD - Park - SIX FLAGS ENTERTAINMENT CORPORATION; *pg.* 583, *pg.* 1698
WATERWORLD SACRAMENTO - Park - SIX FLAGS ENTERTAINMENT CORPORATION; *pg.* 583, *pg.* 1698
WATKINS - Hot Tubs - MASCO CORPORATION; *pg.* 96, *pg.* 909
WATKINS GLEN INTERNATIONAL - Motorsports Facility - INTERNATIONAL SPEEDWAY CORPORATION; *pg.* 553, *pg.* 420
WATLOW.COM - Electric Heating Elements - WATLOW ELECTRIC MANUFACTURING COMPANY; *pg.* 1078, *pg.* 1004
WATS - Sterilization Product - PROPPER MANUFACTURING COMPANY, INC.; *pg.* 1586, *pg.* 1175
WATSON - Furniture - JASPER GROUP; *pg.* 930, *pg.* 691
WATSON ENGAGEMENT ADVISOR - Development Platform - INTERNATIONAL BUSINESS MACHINES CORPORATION; *pg.* 418, *pg.* 1138
WATSON-GUPTILL - Art Instructions Books - NIELSEN BUSINESS MEDIA; *pg.* 1671, *pg.* 1272
WATT - Publishing - WATT PUBLISHING COMPANY; *pg.* 1701, *pg.* 655
WATT POULTRY U.S.A. - USA Poultry Magazine - WATT PUBLISHING COMPANY; *pg.* 1701, *pg.* 655
WATTIE'S - Food Products - THE KRAFT HEINZ COMPANY; *pg.* 870, *pg.* 1577
WATTS CURRENT - Quarterly Publication - WATLOW ELECTRIC MANUFACTURING COMPANY; *pg.* 1078, *pg.*

1004
WATTSAVER - Wireless Communication System - AT&T SOUTHEAST; *pg.* 1868, *pg.* 489
WATVIEW - Software - WATLOW ELECTRIC MANUFACTURING COMPANY; *pg.* 1078, *pg.* 1004
WAUKESHA 88 - Nongalling Corrosion Resistant Alloy Used in Food & Chemical Industries - WAUKESHA FOUNDRY INC.; *pg.* 1388, *pg.* 1898
WAUKESHA 88 METAL - Anti-Gallery Alloy used where Gallery & Sizing are a Problem - WAUKESHA FOUNDRY INC.; *pg.* 1388, *pg.* 1898
WAUSAU - Window & Wall Systems - APOGEE ENTERPRISES, INC.; *pg.* 67, *pg.* 930
WAUSAU - Paper Product - WASAU PAPER CORP.; *pg.* 1471, *pg.* 1882
WAVE - Vinyl Emulsions - AIR PRODUCTS AND CHEMICALS, INC.; *pg.* 1145, *pg.* 1513
WAVE - Modern Occasional Tables - BERNHARDT DESIGN; *pg.* 918, *pg.* 1381
WAVE - Audio Product - BOSE CORPORATION; *pg.* 626, *pg.* 820
WAVE - Cutting Tool - LEATHERMAN TOOL GROUP, INC.; *pg.* 1053, *pg.* 1504
WAVE - Athletic Shoes - MIZUNO USA, INC.; *pg.* 1839, *pg.* 538
WAVE - Baseline Processing - TRIMBLE NAVIGATION LIMITED; *pg.* 1384, *pg.* 288
WAVE 400 - Lens - COSTA DEL MAR SUNGLASSES, INC.; *pg.* 1407, *pg.* 419
WAVE 580 - Lens - COSTA DEL MAR SUNGLASSES, INC.; *pg.* 1407, *pg.* 419
WAVE FORM - Ceiling Fan - WESTINGHOUSE LIGHTING CORPORATION; *pg.* 687, *pg.* 1571
WAVE FORM DELUXE - Fan - WESTINGHOUSE LIGHTING CORPORATION; *pg.* 687, *pg.* 1571
WAVE IP - Business Communications System - VERTICAL COMMUNICATIONS, INC.; *pg.* 488, *pg.* 270
WAVE MASTER - Marine Coatings - SEYMOUR OF SYCAMORE, INC.; *pg.* 1447, *pg.* 663
WAVE RAGE - Personal Care Electrical Product - HELEN OF TROY L.P.; *pg.* 511, *pg.* 1692
WAVE SPORT - Kayaks - CONFLUENCE WATERSPORTS CO. INC.; *pg.* 1706, *pg.* 1617
WAVE TECHNOLOGY - Ultraviolet Radiation Protection - COSTA DEL MAR SUNGLASSES, INC.; *pg.* 1407, *pg.* 419
WAVE TECHNOLOGY - Athletic Footwear Cushioning - MIZUNO USA, INC.; *pg.* 1839, *pg.* 538
WAVE-TY - Stainless Steel Product - PANDUIT CORP.; *pg.* 661, *pg.* 663
WAVEBRIDGE - Wireless Product - PLAINTREE SYSTEMS INC.; *pg.* 663, *pg.* 1918
WAVEBURNER - Application Program - APPLE INC.; *pg.* 350, *pg.* 73
WAVEDIRECTOR - Software - CIENA CORPORATION; *pg.* 628, *pg.* 771
WAVEEXPERT - Oscilloscope - TELEDYNE LECROY; *pg.* 1431, *pg.* 1153
WAVEFORM DATAPORT - Software System - MENTOR GRAPHICS CORPORATION; *pg.* 432, *pg.* 1510
WAVEFORM-READY - Processing Platforms - MERCURY COMPUTER SYSTEMS, INC.; *pg.* 434, *pg.* 813
WAVEJET 300A - Oscilloscopes - TELEDYNE LECROY; *pg.* 1431, *pg.* 1153
WAVELETS - Emission Testing System - MISTRAS GROUP, INC.; *pg.* 1362, *pg.* 1113
WAVELOCK - Software - CIENA CORPORATION; *pg.* 628, *pg.* 771
WAVELOGIC - Software - CIENA CORPORATION; *pg.* 628, *pg.* 771
WAVEMAKER - Eyewear - MAUI JIM, INC.; *pg.* 9, *pg.* 651
WAVEMASTER - Laser Measurement Instrument - COHERENT, INC.; *pg.* 1406, *pg.* 265
WAVE'N DRY - Towel Dispenser - WAUSAU PAPER BAY WEST; *pg.* 1471, *pg.* 1465
WAVEPRECISION - Precision Optics Product - GSI GROUP INC.; *pg.* 1415, *pg.* 784
WAVEREADY - Gigabit Ethernet Fiberoptic Extender - VIAVI SOLUTIONS INC.; *pg.* 1435, *pg.* 148
WAVERLY - Shoes - ALLEN-EDMONDS SHOE CORP.; *pg.* 1804, *pg.* 1887
WAVERLY - Carpet - BEAULIEU GROUP, LLC; *pg.* 917, *pg.* 529
WAVERLY - Guest Chairs - BERNHARDT DESIGN; *pg.* 918, *pg.* 1381
WAVERLY - Fabric - F. SCHUMACHER & CO.; *pg.* 925, *pg.* 1230
WAVERLY - Apparel - ICONIX BRAND GROUP, INC.; *pg.* 26, *pg.* 1243
WAVERUNNER - Personal Water Craft - YAMAHA MOTOR CORPORATION USA; *pg.* 1713, *pg.* 76
WAVESCAN WAVEFRONT - Medical Device - ABBOTT MEDICAL OPTICS, INC.; *pg.* 1485, *pg.* 260
WAVESPEED - Computer Peripheral Equipment - DIGI INTERNATIONAL INC.; *pg.* 387, *pg.* 948
WAVESTAR - Software System - ALCATEL-LUCENT; *pg.* 615, *pg.* 1094
WAVESTAR ADM 16/1 - Multiplexer & Transport System - ALCATEL-LUCENT; *pg.* 615, *pg.* 38
WAVESWITCH - Ethernet Switch - PLAINTREE SYSTEMS INC.; *pg.* 663, *pg.* 1918
WAVEWATCHER - Software - CIENA CORPORATION; *pg.* 628, *pg.* 771
WAVEX - Specialty Paper - APPVION INC.; *pg.* 1451, *pg.* 1852
WAVS - Automated Valve Station - WATERS CORPORATION; *pg.* 1436, *pg.* 834
WAVSTAT - Cancer Diagnostic Products - SPECTRASCIENCE, INC.; *pg.* 1595, *pg.* 210
WAVY-LAY'S - Potato Chips - FRITO-LAY NORTH AMERICA, INC.; *pg.* 1853, *pg.* 1730
WAVY LAY'S - Potato Chips - PEPSICO, INC.; *pg.* 259, *pg.* 1327
WAX AS-U-DRY - Automotive Waxes & Polishes - ASHLAND INC.; *pg.* 972, *pg.* 726
WAX AWAY - Earwax Removal Ear Drops - MCKEON PRODUCTS, INC.; *pg.* 1559, *pg.* 912
WAX-IT-DRY - Gel - THE CLOROX COMPANY; *pg.* 327, *pg.* 169
WAX WORKS - Hair Care Product - JOHN PAUL MITCHELL SYSTEMS; *pg.* 512, *pg.* 133
WAXCUT - Non-Flammable Aqueous Cleaner for Dissolving Wax, Oil, Soil & Grease - ACTON TECHNOLOGIES, INC.; *pg.* 1145, *pg.* 1582
WAXIMUM - Waxed Leather Protector - THE TIMBERLAND COMPANY; *pg.* 1821, *pg.* 1039
WAXY MAIZ - Seed Corn - MOEWS SEED CO., INC.; *pg.* 1797, *pg.* 616
THE WAY BANKING SHOULD BE - Slogan - MACATAWA BANK CORPORATION; *pg.* 778, *pg.* 892
THE WAY CAR BUYING SHOULD BE - Slogan - CARMAX, INC.; *pg.* 167, *pg.* 1800
THE WAY TO BETTER HEALTH - Health Plan & Publication - MEDICA, INC.; *pg.* 1208, *pg.* 949
THE WAY TO PAY - Slogan - VERIFONE SYSTEMS, INC.; *pg.* 487, *pg.* 251
WAY TO ROLL - Bike - ELECTRA BICYCLE COMPANY; *pg.* 1706, *pg.* 303
THE WAY YOU WANT IT - Slogan - FRONTIER COMMUNICATIONS OF NEW YORK, INC.; *pg.* 398, *pg.* 1335
WAYNE-DALTON - Garage Doors - WAYNE-DALTON CORP.; *pg.* 120, *pg.* 1465
WAYNE FARMS - Poultry - CONTINENTAL GRAIN COMPANY; *pg.* 1475, *pg.* 1218
WAYNEGARD - Garage Door - WAYNE-DALTON CORP.; *pg.* 120, *pg.* 1465
WB - Light - THE WILL-BURT CO., INC.; *pg.* 1437, *pg.* 1469
WB RECORDS - Lottery Game - CALIFORNIA LOTTERY; *pg.* 990, *pg.* 196
WB100 - Fluid Handling System - GRACO, INC.; *pg.* 1342, *pg.* 935
WBC - Cable - COMMSCOPE, INC.; *pg.* 278, *pg.* 1378
WBL - Motorsports Entertainment - SPEEDWAY MOTORSPORTS, INC.; *pg.* 584, *pg.* 1370
WCI COMMUNITIES,INC - Community Name - WCI COMMUNITIES, INC.; *pg.* 1118, *pg.* 414
WCI LIFESTYLES BEYOND EXPECTATIONS - Slogan - WCI COMMUNITIES, INC.; *pg.* 1118, *pg.* 414
WCMD - Systems Integration & Aeronautics - LOCKHEED MARTIN CORPORATION; *pg.* 229, *pg.* 762
WCPO, ABC (CINCINNATI) - Television Broadcasting Station - THE E.W. SCRIPPS COMPANY; *pg.* 1639, *pg.* 1412
WD-40 - Lubricant, Penetrant, Rust Preventative, Moisture Displacer & Cleaner - WD-40 COMPANY; *pg.* 337, *pg.* 210
WD-40 BIG BLAST - Lubricant - WD-40 COMPANY; *pg.* 337, *pg.* 210
WD-40 NO-MESS PEN - Stain Remover - WD-40 COMPANY; *pg.* 337, *pg.* 210
WD ANYWHERE ACCESS - Software - WESTERN DIGITAL CORPORATION; *pg.* 492, *pg.* 118
WD BACKUP - Software - WESTERN DIGITAL CORPORATION; *pg.* 492, *pg.* 118
WD CAVIAR - Hard Drive - WESTERN DIGITAL CORPORATION; *pg.* 492, *pg.* 118
WD CAVIAR BLACK - Hard Drive - WESTERN DIGITAL CORPORATION; *pg.* 492, *pg.* 118
WD CAVIAR BLUE - Hard Drive - WESTERN DIGITAL CORPORATION; *pg.* 492, *pg.* 118
WD CAVIAR GREEN - Hard Drive - WESTERN DIGITAL CORPORATION; *pg.* 492, *pg.* 118
WD DUAL-OPTION - External Hard Drive - WESTERN DIGITAL CORPORATION; *pg.* 492, *pg.* 118
WD ELEMENTS - External Hard Drive - WESTERN DIGITAL CORPORATION; *pg.* 492, *pg.* 118
WD GREENPOWER TECHNOLOGY - Hard Drive Platform - WESTERN DIGITAL CORPORATION; *pg.* 492, *pg.* 118
WD PERFORMER - Hard Drive - WESTERN DIGITAL CORPORATION; *pg.* 492, *pg.* 118
WD RAPTOR - Enterprise Drive - WESTERN DIGITAL CORPORATION; *pg.* 492, *pg.* 118
WD SCORPIO - Hard Drive - WESTERN DIGITAL CORPORATION; *pg.* 492, *pg.* 118
WD SCORPIO BLACK - Hard Drive - WESTERN DIGITAL CORPORATION; *pg.* 492, *pg.* 118
WD SCORPIO BLUE - Hard Drive - WESTERN DIGITAL CORPORATION; *pg.* 492, *pg.* 118
WD SYNC - Synchronization & Encryption Software - WESTERN DIGITAL CORPORATION; *pg.* 492, *pg.* 118
WD TV - Media Player - WESTERN DIGITAL CORPORATION; *pg.* 492, *pg.* 118
WD VELOCIRAPTOR - Hard Drive - WESTERN DIGITAL CORPORATION; *pg.* 492, *pg.* 118
WE - Women's Entertainment Network - AMC NETWORKS INC.; *pg.* 269, *pg.* 1189
W.E. ANDERSON - Flow and Level Controls - DWYER INSTRUMENTS INC.; *pg.* 1330, *pg.* 694
WE ARE ENTERTAINMENT - Tagline - TRANS WORLD ENTERTAINMENT CORPORATION; *pg.* 313, *pg.* 1137
WE ARE FOCUSED ON YOU - Tagline - RCN TELECOM SERVICES, LLC.; *pg.* 306, *pg.* 1785
WE ARE PEARLS. - Tag Line - IMPERIAL-DELTAH, INC.; *pg.* 7, *pg.* 1601
WE ARE THE GAME - Trademark - NATIONAL COLLEGIATE ATHLETIC ASSOCIATION; *pg.* 567, *pg.* 688
WE BRING COMFORT TO YOUR LIFE. - Slogan - CARPENTER CO.; *pg.* 920, *pg.* 1801
WE BRING LIFE TO PRODUCTS. - Slogan - SENSIENT TECHNOLOGIES CORPORATION; *pg.* 895, *pg.* 1881
WE BRING THE CARING HOME - Slogan - VISITING NURSE SERVICE OF NEW YORK; *pg.* 1607, *pg.* 1311
WE BUILD BRANDS - Tagline - LEADING BRANDS, INC.; *pg.* 1026, *pg.* 1911
WE BUILD PRODUCTIVITY - Tag Line - PARAGON TECHNOLOGIES, INC.; *pg.* 1367, *pg.* 1528
WE CAN HANDLE ANYTHING - All Products - NUPLA CORPORATION; *pg.* 101, *pg.* 281
WE CAN'T START BLAND - Tagline - BUFFALO WILD WINGS, INC.; *pg.* 1718, *pg.* 931
WE CARE. - Tag Line - ELDER MANUFACTURING COMPANY, INC.; *pg.* 40, *pg.* 996
WE CARE HAIR - Hair Service Center - REGIS CORPORATION; *pg.* 521, *pg.* 941
WE CHANGE LIVES! - Tagline - CREDIT ACCEPTANCE CORPORATION; *pg.* 742, *pg.* 906
WE CREATE GREAT TASTE - Slogan - WILD FLAVORS, INC.; *pg.* 910, *pg.* 728
WE DELIVER RESULTS - Pharmaceutical Product - ALERE INC.; *pg.* 1488, *pg.* 849
WE DELIVER, YOU SAVE. - Slogan - 1-800 CONTACTS, INC.; *pg.* 1758, *pg.* 1753
WE DESIGN IT. WE INSTALL IT. YOU ENJOY IT. - Slogan - GARAGETEK INC.; *pg.* 1457, *pg.* 1179
WE DO ENTERTAINMENT BIG - Tag Line - REGAL ENTERTAINMENT GROUP; *pg.* 579, *pg.* 1638
WE DON.T MAKE IT .TIL YOU ORDER IT. - Restaurant Service - JACK IN THE BOX INC.; *pg.* 1732, *pg.* 204
WE DON'T MAKE PROMISES, WE DELIVER RESULTS - Tagline - GENERAL EMPLOYMENT ENTERPRISES, INC.; *pg.* 400, *pg.* 636
WE FIND THEM BEFORE THEY FIND YOU - Slogan - WEBSENSE, INC.; *pg.* 491, *pg.* 210
WE FIT YOUR LIFE. - Tagline - V.F. CORPORATION; *pg.* 34, *pg.* 1376
W.E. GARRETT - Tobacco Product - AMERICAN SNUFF

COMPANY; pg. 1893, pg. 1641
WE GET YOU READY TO PLAY - Tagline - BIG 5 SPORTING GOODS CORPORATION; pg. 1827, pg. 78
WE GET YOUR BLOOD FLOWING - Slogan - THE SPECTRANETICS CORPORATION; pg. 1595, pg. 315
WE GREW UP HERE - Tagline - NORTHWEST NATURAL GAS COMPANY; pg. 1947, pg. 1504
WE HAVE GOT A SOLUTION FOR THAT - Slogan - SCANSOURCE, INC.; pg. 671, pg. 1618
WE HAVE YOUR BRAND - Slogan - PC CONNECTION, INC.; pg. 452, pg. 1036
WE HELP YOU INVENT THE FUTURE - Slogan - DOW CORNING CORPORATION; pg. 1159, pg. 900
WE INNOVATE HEALTHCARE - Tag Line - HOFFMANN-LA ROCHE LIMITED; pg. 1542, pg. 1926
WE INSPIRE. SHE MAKES IT HAPPEN - Tagline - MEREDITH CORPORATION; pg. 1663, pg. 705
WE KEEP IT GOING - Slogan - PRECISION AUTO CARE, INC.; pg. 215, pg. 1787
WE KEEP THE FUN IN BOATING - Tagline - ATTWOOD CORPORATION; pg. 1705, pg. 897
WE KEEP THE REGION MOVING! - Tagline - DELAWARE RIVER PORT AUTHORITY OF PENNSYLVANIA & NEW JERSEY; pg. 1905, pg. 1049
WE KNOW GIRLS - Doll And Toy - AMERICAN GIRL LLC; pg. 949, pg. 1871
WE KNOW SO MUCH ABOUT TAXES WE CAN HELP ANYBODY - Slogan - JACKSON HEWITT TAX SERVICE INC.; pg. 771, pg. 1103
WE KNOW THE NEIGHBORHOOD! - Tagline - WESTERN BEEF, INC.; pg. 1037, pg. 1333
WE LIGHT UP OUR CUSTOMERS' LIVES! - Slogan - TOPBULB.COM LLC; pg. 1307, pg. 677
WE LIKE YOU TOO - Tagline - JETBLUE AIRWAYS CORPORATION; pg. 1913, pg. 1174
WE LISTEN. WE UNDERSTAND. WE MAKE IT WORK - Slogan - COMERICA INCORPORATED; pg. 740, pg. 1677
WE LOVE HAVING YOU HERE - Tag Line - HILTON WORLDWIDE, INC.; pg. 1094, pg. 1791
WE MAJOR IN CAREERS - Slogan - DEVRY EDUCATION GROUP INC.; pg. 600, pg. 607
WE MAKE BOATING MORE FUN - Slogan - WEST MARINE, INC.; pg. 1712, pg. 305
WE MAKE EVERYDAY LIFE BETTER, EVERY DAY. - Tagline - THE CLOROX COMPANY; pg. 327, pg. 169
WE MAKE EVERYTHING CLICK - Slogan - THE SSI GROUP, INC.; pg. 473, pg. 7
WE MAKE HOME POSSIBLE - Slogan - FEDERAL HOME LOAN MORTGAGE CORPORATION; pg. 751, pg. 1790
WE MAKE INFORMATION INTELLIGENT - Slogan - ACXIOM CORPORATION; pg. 342, pg. 33
WE MAKE IT EASY - Tagline - SCHNUCK MARKETS, INC.; pg. 1033, pg. 1002
WE MAKE IT PERSONAL - Slogan - FINANCIAL ENGINES, INC.; pg. 753, pg. 285
WE MAKE IT SIMPLE, YOU MAKE IT BEAUTIFUL - Paint And Stain Product - BENJAMIN MOORE & CO.; pg. 1440, pg. 1085
WE MAKE NANOTECHNOLOGY WORK! - Tagline - NANOPHASE TECHNOLOGIES CORPORATION; pg. 1174, pg. 656
WE MAKE THE BRANDS YOU LOVE - Slogan - PROMOTION IN MOTION, INC.; pg. 1861, pg. 1052
WE MAKE THE WORLD'S BEST MATTRESS - Slogan - SERTA, INC.; pg. 942, pg. 619
WE MAKE YOUR IDEAS PROFITABLE - Slogan - SHOKAI FAR EAST LTD.; pg. 672, pg. 1155
WE MEAN BUSINESS IN SPACE - Slogan - ASTROTECH CORPORATION; pg. 1400, pg. 1660
WE MEAN CLEAN. - Slogan - BISSELL HOMECARE, INC.; pg. 52, pg. 887
WE NEVER FORGET WHAT WE'RE WORKING FOR - Slogan - LOCKHEED MARTIN CORPORATION; pg. 229, pg. 762
WE NEVER FORGET WHO WE'RE WORKING FOR - Slogan - LOCKHEED MARTIN CORPORATION; pg. 229, pg. 762
WE PUT HORSEPOWER TO WORK - Slogan - TWIN DISC, INCORPORATED; pg. 220, pg. 1889
WE PUT SOLAR TO WORK - Tagline - CARMANAH TECHNOLOGIES CORPORATION; pg. 628, pg. 1913
WE PUT YOUR MESSAGE IN MOTION! - Tagline - PERRYGRAF; pg. 454, pg. 561
WE RACK YOUR WORLD! - Tag Line - GREAT LAKES CASE & CABINET CO., INC.; pg. 401, pg. 1529
WE REPLACE THE IRREPLACEABLE - Slogan - REPLACEMENTS, LTD.; pg. 1138, pg. 1383
WE REVOLVE AROUND YOU - Slogan - EARTHLINK HOLDINGS CORP.; pg. 1240, pg. 504
WE RUN THE TIGHTEST SHIP IN THE SHIPPING BUSINESS - Software - UNITED PARCEL SERVICE, INC.; pg. 1928, pg. 522
WE SERVE THE PEOPLE WHO SERVE THE PEOPLE - Slogan - CSE INSURANCE GROUP; pg. 1199, pg. 304
WE SPECIALIZE. IN YOU. - Slogan - OAKWOOD HEALTHCARE, INC.; pg. 1577, pg. 878
WE STAND FOR SERVICE - Slogan - WSFS FINANCIAL CORPORATION; pg. 823, pg. 392
WE TAKE BANKING PERSONALLY. - Slogan - BAY STATE SAVINGS BANK; pg. 722, pg. 862
WE TAKE CARE - Slogan - MAPLE LEAF FOODS INC.; pg. 875, pg. 1927
WE TAKE CARE OF IT - Tag Line - THE SUDDATH COMPANIES INC.; pg. 1924, pg. 435
WE THINK LIKE BABIES - Slogan - INFANTINO, LLC; pg. 957, pg. 203
WE THINK YOU'LL LIKE THE CHEMISTRY - Slogan - CHEMICAL FINANCIAL CORPORATION; pg. 734, pg. 898
WE WANT YOU TO KNOW - Slogan - AETNA INC.; pg. 1187, pg. 351
WE WORK - Tagline - NET-TEMPS, INC.; pg. 1269, pg. 838
WE WORK HARD SO YOU DON'T HAVE TO! - Slogan - S.C. JOHNSON & SON, INC.; pg. 334, pg. 1889
WE WROTE THE BOOK ON RED MEAT - Cook Book - OMAHA STEAKS INTERNATIONAL, INC.; pg. 1780, pg. 1017
WE WROTE THE BOOK ON STEAK - Cook Book - OMAHA STEAKS INTERNATIONAL, INC.; pg. 1780, pg. 1017
WEA - Globe & Butterfly Control Valves - DWYER INSTRUMENTS INC.; pg. 1330, pg. 694
WEALTH CREATION THROUGH REAL ESTATE INVESTMENT - Tagline - TIGRENT INC.; pg. 608, pg. 415
WEALTH GENERATOR SYSTEM - Prerecorded Audio Discs - NIGHTINGALE-CONANT CORPORATION; pg. 152, pg. 670
WEALTH INTELLIGENCE ACADEMY - Training Organization - TIGRENT INC.; pg. 608, pg. 415
WEALTH INTELLIGENCE NETWORK - Magazine Publications - TIGRENT INC.; pg. 608, pg. 415
WEALTHLINE - Business Management Solutions - ADVENT SOFTWARE, INC.; pg. 345, pg. 211
WEALTHPOINT - Business Analysis Service - BLACKBAUD, INC.; pg. 361, pg. 1613
WEALTHSTATION - Software - SUNGARD DATA SYSTEMS INC.; pg. 477, pg. 1592
WEALTHWARE - Software - FIDELITY NATIONAL INFORMATION SERVICES; pg. 397, pg. 1549
WEALTHY WIZARD - Game - INTERNATIONAL GAME TECHNOLOGY; pg. 420, pg. 1606
WEAPONS & WARRIORS - Game - PRESSMAN TOY CORPORATION; pg. 965, pg. 1734
WEAPONWATCH - Defense & Homeland Security Product - RADIANCE TECHNOLOGIES, INC.; pg. 1277, pg. 6
WEAR IT LIKE NO ONE ELSE - Tagline - BOSTON PROPER, INC.; pg. 20, pg. 410
WEAR. LOVE. REPEAT. - Slogan - LANDAU UNIFORMS INCORPORATED; pg. 28, pg. 971
WEAR 'N GO - Lipcolor - MAYBELLINE LLC; pg. 516, pg. 1257
WEAREVER - Writing Instrument - DIXON TICONDEROGA COMPANY; pg. 388, pg. 430
WEAREVER - Commercial Cookware - LINCOLN FOODSERVICE PRODUCTS, LLC; pg. 1127, pg. 1432
WEARGUARD - Coating Product - PPG INDUSTRIES, INC.; pg. 1445, pg. 1579
WEARMAX - Fastening System - TEXTRON INC.; pg. 235, pg. 1607
WEARSHIELD - Electrode - LINCOLN ELECTRIC HOLDINGS, INC.; pg. 1355, pg. 1432
WEARWOLF - Switch - THE FROG, SWITCH & MANUFACTURING COMPANY; pg. 1338, pg. 1520
WEASEL YOUR WAY OUT OF YARD WORK - Tag Line - FAULTLESS STARCH/BON AMI COMPANY; pg. 330, pg. 982
WEATHER BEAK - Drum Handling Equipment - LIFTOMATIC MATERIAL HANDLING INC.; pg. 94, pg. 560
WEATHER-BLOCK - Apparel - CABELA'S INCORPORATED; pg. 535, pg. 1019
THE WEATHER CHANNEL - Cable Network Company - THE WEATHER CHANNEL LLC; pg. 320, pg. 523
WEATHER-PLATE - Paint & Coating - DIAMOND VOGEL PAINT, INC.; pg. 1441, pg. 710
WEATHER SHILED - Paint - KELLY-MOORE PAINT COMPANY, INC.; pg. 1443, pg. 198
WEATHER STATION - Weather Instruments - SWIFT OPTICAL INSTRUMENTS, INC.; pg. 1430, pg. 1744
WEATHER-TECH - Apparel - I. SPIEWAK & SONS, INC.; pg. 42, pg. 1242
WEATHER-TITE - 3-Tab Roofing Shingles - BUILDING PRODUCTS OF CANADA CORP.; pg. 72, pg. 1951
WEATHER TOUGH - Padlocks - MASTER LOCK COMPANY LLC; pg. 1055, pg. 1884
WEATHER UNDERGROUND - Weather Service - THE WEATHER CHANNEL LLC; pg. 320, pg. 523
WEATHERALL - Paint - TRUE VALUE COMPANY; pg. 1065, pg. 592
WEATHERBAN - Air Drying & Moisture Curing Liquid Sealants - 3M COMPANY; pg. 1142, pg. 956
WEATHERBEATER - Exterior Paints - SEARS HOLDINGS CORPORATION; pg. 1784, pg. 618
WEATHERBEST - Building Product - BLUELINX HOLDINGS, INC.; pg. 70, pg. 491
WEATHERBEST - Composite Decking - LOUISIANA-PACIFIC CORPORATION; pg. 94, pg. 1652
WEATHERBY - Magnum Ammunition - WEATHERBY, INC.; pg. 1848, pg. 181
WEATHER.COM - Weather Service - THE WEATHER CHANNEL LLC; pg. 320, pg. 523
WEATHERGARD - Weathered Rolling Door - CORNELL IRON WORKS, INC.; pg. 77, pg. 1554
WEATHERGARD - Metal Building Fastening Systems - SFS INTEC, INC.; pg. 1061, pg. 1596
WEATHERGEAR - Clothing - THE TIMBERLAND COMPANY; pg. 1821, pg. 1039
WEATHERGUARD - Covers, Curtains - REFRIGIWEAR, INC.; pg. 47, pg. 529
WEATHERGUARD MATS - Outdoor Mats - MOHAWK HOME; pg. 935, pg. 541
WEATHERHEAD - Hydraulic Components - EATON CORPORATION; pg. 1331, pg. 1429
WEATHERKING - In-Ground Vinyl Pools - POOL CORPORATION; pg. 1843, pg. 743
WEATHERLOCK - Roofing System - OWENS CORNING; pg. 102, pg. 1476
WEATHERMASTER - Outdoor Furniture - LANE VENTURE, INC.; pg. 933, pg. 1379
WEATHERMASTER - Weather Instrument - SWIFT OPTICAL INSTRUMENTS, INC.; pg. 1430, pg. 1744
WEATHERMASTER - Polyethylene Tarp - TRACTOR SUPPLY COMPANY; pg. 708, pg. 1627
WEATHERMATE - Building Product - BLUELINX HOLDINGS, INC.; pg. 70, pg. 491
WEATHERMATE - Weather Barrier Products - THE DOW CHEMICAL COMPANY; pg. 1157, pg. 898
WEATHERMATE - Wood & Building Material - WEYERHAEUSER COMPANY; pg. 121, pg. 1820
WEATHERMATIC - Underground Sprinkler System - TELSCO INDUSTRIES, INC.; pg. 1381, pg. 1698
WEATHERMATICA - Watertight 110 Camera - KONICA MINOLTA BUSINESS SOLUTIONS USA, INC.; pg. 1419, pg. 1113
WEATHERMAX - Technical Fabric - INTERNATIONAL TEXTILE GROUP, INC.; pg. 696, pg. 1374
WEATHERPAD - Felt - AMERICAN FELT & FILTER COMPANY; pg. 1312, pg. 1184
WEATHERPAK - Construction - GREIF INC.; pg. 1459, pg. 1447
WEATHERPANE - Multiple Glazed Window Units - PPG INDUSTRIES, INC.; pg. 1445, pg. 1579
WEATHERPROOF - Screw-On-Connector - IDEAL INDUSTRIES, INC.; pg. 1051, pg. 662
WEATHERRITE OUTDOOR - Sports Equipment - ALLIANCE SPORTS GROUP, L.P.; pg. 1825, pg. 1698
WEATHERSHED - Horse Feeds - SOUTHERN STATES COOPERATIVE, INC.; pg. 1482, pg. 1804
WEATHERSHIELD - Water Repellent Pressure Treated Wood - OSMOSE, INC.; pg. 102, pg. 533
WEATHERSLIP - Weather-Resistant Protective Coating - DOW CHEMICAL; pg. 1156, pg. 1563
WEATHERSMART - Barrier - FORTIFIBER CORPORATION; pg. 83, pg. 1021
WEATHERSOF - Golf Gloves - ACUSHNET COMPANY; pg. 1824, pg. 818
WEATHERTECH - Rubber Floor Mats - MACNEIL

AUTOMOTIVE PRODUCTS, LTD.; *pg.* 211, *pg.* 559

WEATHERTEL - Voice Processing Platform - ELECTRONIC TELE-COMMUNICATIONS, INC.; *pg.* 390, *pg.* 1897

WEATHERTYTE - Sign & Awning Product - COOLEY GROUP, INC.; *pg.* 691, *pg.* 1603

WEAVE - Glass Tile - WALKER & ZANGER, INC.; *pg.* 119, *pg.* 281

WEAVER - Chicken Products - TYSON FOODS, INC.; *pg.* 902, *pg.* 35

WEAVERS - Fabric - NEMSCHOFF, INC.; *pg.* 936, *pg.* 1890

WEAVEWARE - Platters & Baskets - CARLISLE FOODSERVICE PRODUCTS INCORPORATED; *pg.* 1455, *pg.* 1485

WEAVINGS - Journal of Christian Spiritual Life - THE UPPER ROOM; *pg.* 1698, *pg.* 1655

WEB - Bicycle Accessories - SPECIALIZED BICYCLE COMPONENTS, INC.; *pg.* 1711, *pg.* 152

WEB COMMANDER - Scheduling Software - POLYCOM, INC.; *pg.* 664, *pg.* 249

WEB DEFENCE - Software - WEBSENSE, INC.; *pg.* 491, *pg.* 210

WEB ID - Software - 3M; *pg.* 339, *pg.* 179

WEB OF SCIENCE - Science Publication - THOMSON REUTERS CORPORATION; *pg.* 1693, *pg.* 1944

WEB OUTPUT PAK - Software - ADOBE SYSTEMS INCORPORATED; *pg.* 342, *pg.* 235

WEB PARTS FOR SHAREPOINT - Software - DELL SOFTWARE; *pg.* 385, *pg.* 40

WEB PROTECTION SERVICES - Software - WEBSENSE, INC.; *pg.* 491, *pg.* 210

WEB PUBLISHER - Software - QVIDIAN; *pg.* 458, *pg.* 829

WEB-RADIO - Radio & Multimedia Service - BRS MEDIA INC.; *pg.* 1233, *pg.* 214

WEB ROUSER - Web Applications - EOLAS TECHNOLOGIES, INC.; *pg.* 1243, *pg.* 573

WEB SECURITY - Software - WEBSENSE, INC.; *pg.* 491, *pg.* 210

WEB SECURITY ECOSYSTEM - Software - WEBSENSE, INC.; *pg.* 491, *pg.* 210

WEB SECURITY SAAS - Software - WEBROOT SOFTWARE, INC.; *pg.* 1289, *pg.* 313

WEB SERVICES MANAGER - Distribution Services - BARRISTER GLOBAL SERVICES NETWORK, INC.; *pg.* 360, *pg.* 744

WEB SHELVING - Office Furniture - JOFCO INC.; *pg.* 931, *pg.* 691

WEB SHIPPING - Internet-Based Shipping - DHL HOLDINGS (USA), INC.; *pg.* 1906, *pg.* 459

WEB STINGER - Skate - ROLLER DERBY SKATE CORP.; *pg.* 966, *pg.* 630

WEB-SYNC - Computer Software - DAKTRONICS, INC.; *pg.* 633, *pg.* 1624

WEB TECHNIQUES - Magazine - UNITED BUSINESS MEDIA LLC; *pg.* 1697, *pg.* 1177

WEB TLC - Remote Library Management Web-Based - OVERLAND STORAGE, INC.; *pg.* 451, *pg.* 205

WEB WATCH - Publisher - BLOOMBERG BNA; *pg.* 1621, *pg.* 1772

WEB WHOLESALER MAGAZINE - Magazine - SUMNER COMMUNICATIONS INC.; *pg.* 1690, *pg.* 338

WEBACCELERATOR - Software - F5 NETWORKS, INC.; *pg.* 396, *pg.* 1835

WEBAF - Software - SAS INSTITUTE INC.; *pg.* 466, *pg.* 1361

WEBB - Conveyors & Corporate Name - DAIFUKU WEBB; *pg.* 1327, *pg.* 885

WEBB ALLOY II - Special Steel Track - DAIFUKU WEBB; *pg.* 1327, *pg.* 885

WEBB-KEY - Disconnect Conveyor Screws - DAIFUKU WEBB; *pg.* 1327, *pg.* 885

WEBB-X - Conveyor Chain - DAIFUKU WEBB; *pg.* 1327, *pg.* 885

WEBBALLOY - Special Steel, Double-Channel Track - DAIFUKU WEBB; *pg.* 1327, *pg.* 885

WEBBED - Belt - OAKLEY, INC.; *pg.* 1840, *pg.* 86

WEBBLAZER - Software - WEBSENSE, INC.; *pg.* 491, *pg.* 210

WEBBVIEW - Baggage Tracking & Control Software - DAIFUKU WEBB; *pg.* 1327, *pg.* 885

WEBCASTI AM/FM - Radio & Multimedia Service - BRS MEDIA INC.; *pg.* 1233, *pg.* 214

WEBCASTI.COM - Radio & Multimedia Service - BRS MEDIA INC.; *pg.* 1233, *pg.* 214

WEBCASTING & KNOWLEDGE MANAGEMENT - Tag Line - SONIC FOUNDRY, INC.; *pg.* 472, *pg.* 1867

WEBCATCHER - Software - WEBSENSE, INC.; *pg.* 491, *pg.* 210

WEBCHECK - Software - 3M; *pg.* 339, *pg.* 179

WEBCLIENT - Software - FIDELITY NATIONAL INFORMATION SERVICES; *pg.* 397, *pg.* 1549

WEBCLIENT - Software - PROGRESS SOFTWARE CORPORATION; *pg.* 457, *pg.* 786

WEBCONNECT - Software - BIO-RAD LABORATORIES, INC.; *pg.* 1504, *pg.* 101

WEBCONNECT - Web Tool - OPENCONNECT SYSTEMS, INC.; *pg.* 449, *pg.* 1685

WEBCONNECT SSO - Web Tool - OPENCONNECT SYSTEMS, INC.; *pg.* 449, *pg.* 1685

WEBCORE - Wallcovering - OMNOVA SOLUTIONS INC; *pg.* 1176, *pg.* 1453

WEBCRAWLER - Internet Search Engine - BLUCORA; *pg.* 1232, *pg.* 1813

WEBCSR - Software - FIDELITY NATIONAL INFORMATION SERVICES; *pg.* 397, *pg.* 1549

WEB.DATA - Web Application - AMKOR TECHNOLOGY, INC.; *pg.* 67, *pg.* 25

WEBDEFEND - Computer Software - TRUSTWAVE HOLDINGS, INC.; *pg.* 1285, *pg.* 593

WEBDNA - Software - SMITH MICRO SOFTWARE, INC.; *pg.* 471, *pg.* 41

WEBEIS - Software - SAS INSTITUTE INC.; *pg.* 466, *pg.* 1361

WEBER - Gas Grill - WEBER-STEPHEN PRODUCTS LLC; *pg.* 62, *pg.* 650

WEBER Q - Grill - WEBER-STEPHEN PRODUCTS LLC; *pg.* 62, *pg.* 650

WEBER SMOKEY JOE - Charcoal Grill - BARBEQUES GALORE, INC.; *pg.* 51, *pg.* 173

WEBER'S BREAD - Retail White Bread - BIMBO BAKERIES USA; *pg.* 840, *pg.* 151

WEBEVENT - Software - HEALTHSTREAM, INC.; *pg.* 1649, *pg.* 1651

WEBEX - Meeting Application - CISCO SYSTEMS, INC.; *pg.* 372, *pg.* 240

WEBEX EVENT CENTER - Software - WEBEX COMMUNICATIONS, INC.; *pg.* 491, *pg.* 270

WEBEX MEETING CENTER - Software - WEBEX COMMUNICATIONS, INC.; *pg.* 491, *pg.* 270

WEBEX SMARTTECH - Software - WEBEX COMMUNICATIONS, INC.; *pg.* 491, *pg.* 270

WEBFACTS - Internet Ad Tracking - ADVERTISING CHECKING BUREAU INCORPORATED; *pg.* 345, *pg.* 1187

WEBFETCH - Search Engine - BLUCORA; *pg.* 1232, *pg.* 1813

WEBFETTI - Online Services - IAC/INTERACTIVECORP; *pg.* 292, *pg.* 1242

WEBFITTER - Software - XILINX, INC.; *pg.* 496, *pg.* 252

WEBFOCUS - Internet Report Generator - INFORMATION BUILDERS INC.; *pg.* 415, *pg.* 1243

WEBGPI - Software - DANFOSS POWER SOLUTIONS COMPANY; *pg.* 1328, *pg.* 701

WEBHOUND - Web Technology Software - SAS INSTITUTE INC.; *pg.* 466, *pg.* 1361

WEBLINE - Furniture Seating Systems - LEGGETT & PLATT, INCORPORATED; *pg.* 933, *pg.* 974

WEBLOY - Iron with Additives - WEBSTER INDUSTRIES INC.; *pg.* 1388, *pg.* 1475

WEBMAIL - E-Mail Hosting - RACKSPACE HOSTING, INC.; *pg.* 1277, *pg.* 1742

WEBMD.COM - Consumer Web Site - WEBMD HEALTH CORPORATION; *pg.* 1288, *pg.* 1313

WEBMINDER - Conveyor Guide Rollers - HYDRALIGN; *pg.* 1257, *pg.* 833

WEBOBJECTS - Software - APPLE INC.; *pg.* 350, *pg.* 73

WEBONY - Telephone Service - IDT CORPORATION; *pg.* 643, *pg.* 1096

WEBONY.COM - Telephone Service - IDT CORPORATION; *pg.* 643, *pg.* 1096

WEBPAD - Handheld Device - ADVANCED MICRO DEVICES, INC.; *pg.* 613, *pg.* 282

WEBPASS - Security Technology - THE UPPER DECK COMPANY, LLC; *pg.* 969, *pg.* 62

WEBPDA - Software - WIND RIVER SYSTEMS, INC.; *pg.* 493, *pg.* 38

WEBPDM - Product Data Management Software - GERBER SCIENTIFIC, INC.; *pg.* 1414, *pg.* 380

WEBPHAGE - Software - DYAX CORP.; *pg.* 1525, *pg.* 805

WEBPLUS - Software - WIND RIVER SYSTEMS, INC.; *pg.* 493, *pg.* 38

WEBREVIEW.COM NETWORK - Magazine - UNITED BUSINESS MEDIA LLC; *pg.* 1697, *pg.* 1177

WEBROOT INTERNET SECURITY ESSENTIALS - Software - WEBROOT SOFTWARE, INC.; *pg.* 1289, *pg.* 313

WEBROOT PARENTAL CONTROLS - Software - WEBROOT SOFTWARE, INC.; *pg.* 1289, *pg.* 313

THE WEB'S HOTTEST JOBS - Internet Services - YAHOO! INC.; *pg.* 1289, *pg.* 289

WEBSCRIPT - Computer Software - APPLE INC.; *pg.* 350, *pg.* 73

WEBSENSE CONTENT GATEWAY - Software - WEBSENSE, INC.; *pg.* 491, *pg.* 210

WEBSENSE ENTERPRISE - Software - WEBSENSE, INC.; *pg.* 491, *pg.* 210

WEBSENSE EXPRESS - Software - WEBSENSE, INC.; *pg.* 491, *pg.* 210

WEBSERIES - Software System - BOTTOMLINE TECHNOLOGIES (DE), INC.; *pg.* 727, *pg.* 1038

WEBSITE - Fabric - NEMSCHOFF, INC.; *pg.* 936, *pg.* 1890

WEBSITE MAGAZINE - Magazine - WEBSITE MAGAZINE INCORPORATED; *pg.* 1701, *pg.* 607

WEBSITE TONIGHT - Software Product - GO DADDY INC.; *pg.* 1249, *pg.* 21

WEBSITESMART - Software - ARI NETWORK SERVICES, INC.; *pg.* 353, *pg.* 1873

WEBSITESMART PRO - Software - ARI NETWORK SERVICES, INC.; *pg.* 353, *pg.* 1873

WEBSPECS.NET - Online Alignment Service - HUNTER ENGINEERING COMPANY; *pg.* 208, *pg.* 973

WEBSPEED - Software - PROGRESS SOFTWARE CORPORATION; *pg.* 457, *pg.* 786

WEBSPIRATION - Tool - INSPIRATION SOFTWARE, INC.; *pg.* 1653, *pg.* 1503

WEBSTER - Film Cleaning Equipment - EASTMAN KODAK COMPANY; *pg.* 1408, *pg.* 1333

WEBSTER - Transmission Components - GARDNER DENVER, INC.; *pg.* 1338, *pg.* 1592

WEBSTER - Chains - WEBSTER INDUSTRIES INC.; *pg.* 1388, *pg.* 1475

WEBTA - Software System - KRONOS INCORPORATED; *pg.* 425, *pg.* 813

WEBTEL - Software - WIND RIVER SYSTEMS, INC.; *pg.* 493, *pg.* 38

WEBTHORITY - Software - DELL SOFTWARE; *pg.* 385, *pg.* 40

WEBTOX - Internet-Based Point-of-Care Reporting System - MEDTOX SCIENTIFIC, INC.; *pg.* 1422, *pg.* 962

WEBWHOLESALERMAGAZINE.COM - Website - SUMNER COMMUNICATIONS INC.; *pg.* 1690, *pg.* 338

WEBWORKZONE - Computer Software - NOVELL INC.; *pg.* 446, *pg.* 852

WEBXTENDER - Software System - EMC CORPORATION; *pg.* 391, *pg.* 825

WEBZ.NET - Radio & Multimedia Service - BRS MEDIA INC.; *pg.* 1233, *pg.* 214

WECOBEE - Chemical Product - STEPAN COMPANY; *pg.* 1182, *pg.* 643

WECOTE - Chemical Product - WESTROCK COMPANY; *pg.* 1472, *pg.* 1805

WEDAC - Detergent System - PENETONE CORPORATION; *pg.* 333, *pg.* 1050

WEDDING ANNOUNCEMENT - Packet Seeds - THE PAGE SEED CO.; *pg.* 1798, *pg.* 1163

WEDDING CHANNEL - Online Wedding Resource - XO GROUP INC.; *pg.* 1289, *pg.* 1316

WEDDINGMOON - Hotel Reservations - SANDALS RESORTS INTERNATIONAL; *pg.* 1111, *pg.* 446

WEDG-AC - Bevel Product - GLEASON CORPORATION; *pg.* 1340, *pg.* 1335

WEDGE - Glass Interlayer - E.I. DU PONT DE NEMOURS & COMPANY; *pg.* 1159, *pg.* 390

WEDGE-BOLT - Screw Anchor - POWERS FASTENERS INC.; *pg.* 1059, *pg.* 1143

WEDGE-LOCK - Vault Door - DIEBOLD, INCORPORATED; *pg.* 387, *pg.* 1407

WEDGE-LOCK - Pipeline Pigging Product - T.D. WILLIAMSON, INC.; *pg.* 1380, *pg.* 1490

WEDGEMASTER - Wedgers - LINCOLN FOODSERVICE PRODUCTS, LLC; *pg.* 1127, *pg.* 1432

WEDGIE - Bicycle Accessories - SPECIALIZED BICYCLE COMPONENTS, INC.; *pg.* 1711, *pg.* 152

WEDGIEE - Footwear - STEVEN MADDEN, LTD.; *pg.* 1819, *pg.* 1176

WEDGY - Palm Patches - WELLS LAMONT CORPORATION; *pg.* 15, *pg.* 638

First page reference indicates Business Class Edition
Second page reference indicates Geographic Edition

WEDLOCK - Bicycle Accessories - SPECIALIZED BICYCLE COMPONENTS, INC.; *pg.* 1711, *pg.* 152
WEE WAFFLE - Building Block Toys - RUBBERMAID HOME PRODUCTS; *pg.* 1138, *pg.* 1453
WEEBLES - Toy & Game - HASBRO, INC.; *pg.* 954, *pg.* 1603
WEEBOK - Childrens Clothing & Footwear Line - REEBOK INTERNATIONAL LTD.; *pg.* 1817, *pg.* 811
WEED-ASIDE - Herbicidal Soap - GARDENS ALIVE!, INC.; *pg.* 1796, *pg.* 693
WEED-B-GON - Lawn & Garden Products - THE SCOTTS MIRACLE-GRO COMPANY; *pg.* 1799, *pg.* 1459
WEED-B-GON MAX - Lawn & Garden Product - THE SCOTTS MIRACLE-GRO COMPANY; *pg.* 1799, *pg.* 1459
WEED BEATER - Household Insect Control - BONIDE PRODUCTS, INC.; *pg.* 1794, *pg.* 1320
WEED-NO-MORE - Homeowner Product - PBI/GORDON CORPORATION; *pg.* 1176, *pg.* 985
WEED POPPER - Gardening & Hardware Product - FAULTLESS STARCH/BON AMI COMPANY; *pg.* 330, *pg.* 982
WEED PRO - Insecticide - SOUTHERN AGRICULTURAL INSECTICIDES, INC.; *pg.* 1181, *pg.* 458
WEED ZAPPER - Herbicide - DELTA FOREMOST CHEMICAL CORPORATION; *pg.* 1155, *pg.* 1642
WEEDOL - Lawn & Garden Products - THE SCOTTS MIRACLE-GRO COMPANY; *pg.* 1799, *pg.* 1459
WEEDZOUT - Herbicide - DELTA FOREMOST CHEMICAL CORPORATION; *pg.* 1155, *pg.* 1642
WEEJUNS - Shoes - G.H. BASS & CO.; *pg.* 1809, *pg.* 1234
WEEKEND - Disposable Camera with Wider Lens - EASTMAN KODAK COMPANY; *pg.* 1408, *pg.* 1333
WEEKEND - Spray Paints - SHERWIN-WILLIAMS DIVERSIFIED BRANDS DIVISION; *pg.* 1448, *pg.* 1435
WEEKEND TAKEOFF - Weekend Fuel Pricing Program - SIGNATURE FLIGHT SUPPORT CORP.; *pg.* 234, *pg.* 456
WEEKENDER - Footwear - P.W. MINOR & SON, INC.; *pg.* 1816, *pg.* 1140
WEEKLY $1000 PAYDAY - Game - MISSOURI LOTTERY; *pg.* 999, *pg.* 979
WEFORIA.COM - Website - YELLOW BOOK USA, INC.; *pg.* 1703, *pg.* 1347
WEGE - Food Product - HANOVER FOODS CORPORATION; *pg.* 861, *pg.* 1535
WEGMANS PHARMACY - Medical Service - WEGMANS FOOD MARKETS, INC.; *pg.* 1037, *pg.* 1337
WEGMANS SMARTFILL - Automated Telephone Service - WEGMANS FOOD MARKETS, INC.; *pg.* 1037, *pg.* 1337
WEIBEL - Sparkling & Table Wines - WEIBEL, INC.; *pg.* 1972, *pg.* 122
WEIDER - Health & Fitness Product - ICON HEALTH & FITNESS, INC.; *pg.* 1837, *pg.* 1752
WEIGH BAR - Sensing Device - AVERY WEIGH-TRONIX, INC.; *pg.* 1315, *pg.* 925
WEIGH-MATIC - Weigh System, Bin, or Scale - CTB INTERNATIONAL CORP.; *pg.* 850, *pg.* 695
WEIGH SCALE FILLER - Liquid Filling - U.S. BOTTLERS MACHINERY COMPANY; *pg.* 1386, *pg.* 1369
WEIGHT ASSIST - Nutritional Supplement - PHARMAVITE LLC; *pg.* 1584, *pg.* 167
WEIGHT BURNER - Boost - JAMBA, INC.; *pg.* 1024, *pg.* 84
WEIGHT LOSS CENTERS - Slogan - FORM YOU 3 INTERNATIONAL, INC.; *pg.* 1531, *pg.* 1400
THE WEIGHT-LOSS PROFESSIONALS - Slogan - DIET CENTER WORLDWIDE, INC.; *pg.* 1524, *pg.* 1400
WEIGHT SENSE - Pharmaceutical Product - ALERE INC.; *pg.* 1488, *pg.* 849
WEIGHT WATCHERS - Low-Calorie Food - WEIGHT WATCHERS INTERNATIONAL, INC.; *pg.* 1609, *pg.* 1313
WEIGHT WATCHERS SMART - Dietary Frozen Foods - THE KRAFT HEINZ COMPANY; *pg.* 870, *pg.* 1577
WEIGHTLESS VOLUME - Skin Care Product - NEUTROGENA CORPORATION; *pg.* 517, *pg.* 137
WEIGHTWATCHERS - Mouth Watering Chocolate - RUSSELL STOVER CANDIES, INC.; *pg.* 1861, *pg.* 986
WEIGHTWATCHERS - Frozen Treats - WELLS ENTERPRISES, INC.; *pg.* 909, *pg.* 709
WEIMAR - Fabric - NEMSCHOFF, INC.; *pg.* 936, *pg.* 1890
WEINBERGER - Hand Traction Apparatus - STERIS CORPORATION; *pg.* 1597, *pg.* 1464
WEINBRENNER - Shoes - WEINBRENNER SHOE COMPANY, INC.; *pg.* 1822, *pg.* 1871
WEISS MONEY MANAGEMENT - Investment Advisors - WEISS RESEARCH; *pg.* 819, *pg.* 436
WEISS RATINGS - Rating Agency - WEISS RESEARCH; *pg.* 819, *pg.* 436
WEISS RESEARCH - Newsletter Publishing - WEISS RESEARCH; *pg.* 819, *pg.* 436
WELCH - Vacuum Pumps - GARDNER DENVER, INC.; *pg.* 1338, *pg.* 1592
WELCH ALLYN - Clinical Assessment - ALIMED, INC.; *pg.* 1490, *pg.* 816
WELCH ALLYN ACUITYLINK - Clinician Notifier - WELCH ALLYN INC.; *pg.* 1436, *pg.* 1342
WELCH ALLYN CARDIOPERFECT - Workstation - WELCH ALLYN INC.; *pg.* 1436, *pg.* 1342
WELCH ALLYN CP 100 - Electrocardiograph - WELCH ALLYN INC.; *pg.* 1436, *pg.* 1342
WELCH ALLYN CP 200 - Electrocardiograph - WELCH ALLYN INC.; *pg.* 1436, *pg.* 1342
WELCH ALLYN FLEXNET - Wireless Network - WELCH ALLYN INC.; *pg.* 1436, *pg.* 1342
WELCH ALLYN MACROVIEW - Otoscopes - WELCH ALLYN INC.; *pg.* 1436, *pg.* 1342
WELCH ALLYN PC-BASED SPIROPERFECT - Spirometer - WELCH ALLYN INC.; *pg.* 1436, *pg.* 1342
WELCH ALLYN PROXENON - Surgical Headlight - WELCH ALLYN INC.; *pg.* 1436, *pg.* 1342
WELCH DIRECTORR - Chemical Product - SPECTRUM CHEMICALS & LABORATORY PRODUCTS, INC.; *pg.* 1181, *pg.* 94
WELCHADE - Drink - WELCH FOODS INC.; *pg.* 909, *pg.* 815
WELCH'S - Juices, Drinks & Cocktails - WELCH FOODS INC.; *pg.* 909, *pg.* 815
WELCH'S CHILLED GRAPE JUICE - Chilled Grape Juice - WELCH FOODS INC.; *pg.* 909, *pg.* 815
WELCH'S FRUIT JUICE BARS - Frozen Juice Bars - WELCH FOODS INC.; *pg.* 909, *pg.* 815
WELCH'S FRUIT SNACKS - Fruit Snacks - PROMOTION IN MOTION, INC.; *pg.* 1861, *pg.* 1052
WELCH'S GRAPE & CRANBERRY CONCENTRATES - Grape & Cranberry Concentrates - WELCH FOODS INC.; *pg.* 909, *pg.* 815
WELCH'S GRAPE JELLY & JAM - Grape Jelly & Jam - WELCH FOODS INC.; *pg.* 909, *pg.* 815
WELCH'S JUICEMAKERS - Food Product - WELCH FOODS INC.; *pg.* 909, *pg.* 815
WELCH'S LIGHT JUICE COCKTAILS - Light Juice Cocktails - WELCH FOODS INC.; *pg.* 909, *pg.* 815
WELCH'S ORCHARD BLENDED JUICK COCKTAILS - Blended Juice Cocktails - WELCH FOODS INC.; *pg.* 909, *pg.* 815
WELCH'S PURPLE GRAPE JUICE - Purple Grape Juice - WELCH FOODS INC.; *pg.* 909, *pg.* 815
WELCH'S SPARKLING JUICE - Sparkling Juice - WELCH FOODS INC.; *pg.* 909, *pg.* 815
WELCH'S SQUEEZABLES - Squeezable Jellies, Jams & Preserves - WELCH FOODS INC.; *pg.* 909, *pg.* 815
WELCH'S TOMATO JUICE - Tomato Juice - WELCH FOODS INC.; *pg.* 909, *pg.* 815
WELCH'S TOTALLY FRUIT - Spreadable Fruit Spreads - WELCH FOODS INC.; *pg.* 909, *pg.* 815
WELCH'S WHITE GRAPE JUICE - White Grape Juice - WELCH FOODS INC.; *pg.* 909, *pg.* 815
WELCOME - Wall Decor - HERITAGE LACE INC.; *pg.* 694, *pg.* 711
WELCOME FRIENDS - Lace Flag - HERITAGE LACE INC.; *pg.* 694, *pg.* 711
WELCOME JOSEFINA - Dolls - AMERICAN GIRL LLC; *pg.* 949, *pg.* 1871
WELCOME TO ALBUQUERQUE-IT'S A TRIP - Tagline - ALBUQUERQUE CONVENTION & VISITORS BUREAU; *pg.* 988, *pg.* 1135
WELCOME TO BED - Slogan - TEMPUR SEALY INTERNATIONAL, INC.; *pg.* 944, *pg.* 731
WELCOME TO THE HUMAN NETWORK. - Tagline - CISCO SYSTEMS, INC.; *pg.* 372, *pg.* 240
WELCOMHOME - Computer Applications - DELTEK, INC.; *pg.* 386, *pg.* 1784
WELD-FLEX - Fabric - SELLSTROM MANUFACTURING CO.; *pg.* 1428, *pg.* 659
WELDALITE - Systems Integration & Aeronautics - LOCKHEED MARTIN CORPORATION; *pg.* 229, *pg.* 762
WELDANPOWER - Welder - LINCOLN ELECTRIC HOLDINGS, INC.; *pg.* 1355, *pg.* 1432
WELDFLEX - Insulation Product - ALPHA ASSOCIATES, INC.; *pg.* 691, *pg.* 1078
WELDGARD - Insulation Product - ALPHA ASSOCIATES, INC.; *pg.* 691, *pg.* 1078
WELDRAWN - Metal Tubing - SUPERIOR TUBE COMPANY INC.; *pg.* 113, *pg.* 1522
WELDY 2000 - Air Conditioning System - TRION, INC.; *pg.* 682, *pg.* 1390
WE'LL FIX YOU RIGHT UP - Tagline - AUBUCHON HARDWARE; *pg.* 1043, *pg.* 859
WELL FOCUS - Pharmaceutical Product - ALERE INC.; *pg.* 1488, *pg.* 849
WELL-GARD - Discharge Guard - CTB INTERNATIONAL CORP.; *pg.* 850, *pg.* 695
WE'LL GIVE YOU AN EDGE - Slogan - PRINCIPAL FINANCIAL GROUP, INC.; *pg.* 796, *pg.* 706
WE'LL PICK YOU UP - Rental & Leasing Services - ENTERPRISE HOLDINGS, INC.; *pg.* 1906, *pg.* 996
WELL-READ LIFE - Community - LEVENGER COMPANY; *pg.* 1776, *pg.* 421
WELL-VU - Video Viewing System - SWORDFISH FINANCIAL, INC.; *pg.* 1430, *pg.* 1737
WELLA - Personal & Household Product - THE PROCTER & GAMBLE COMPANY; *pg.* 1129, *pg.* 1418
WELLBROM - Chemical Product - ALBEMARLE CORPORATION; *pg.* 1146, *pg.* 741
WELLBUTRIN - Pharmaceutical Product - VALEANT PHARMACEUTICALS INTERNATIONAL, INC.; *pg.* 1605, *pg.* 1957
WELLBUTRIN SR - Pharmaceutical Product - IMPAX LABORATORIES, INC.; *pg.* 1544, *pg.* 101
WELLBUTRIN XL - Pharmaceutical Product - IMPAX LABORATORIES, INC.; *pg.* 1544, *pg.* 101
WELLCO - Footwear - WELLCO ENTERPRISES, INC.; *pg.* 1822, *pg.* 1392
WELLEN - Apparel - OAKLEY, INC.; *pg.* 1840, *pg.* 86
WELLESLEY - Bathroom Fan - HUNTER FAN COMPANY; *pg.* 57, *pg.* 1631
WELLFORM - Oilfield Chemicals - ALBEMARLE CORPORATION; *pg.* 1146, *pg.* 741
WELLGUARD - Chemical Product - ALBEMARLE CORPORATION; *pg.* 1146, *pg.* 741
WELLIE - Footwear - L.L. BEAN, INC.; *pg.* 1777, *pg.* 750
WELLINGTON - Fan - CRAFTMADE INTERNATIONAL, INC.; *pg.* 1295, *pg.* 1670
WELLINGTON - Office Furniture - JOFCO INC.; *pg.* 931, *pg.* 691
WELLMASTER - Pipe & Supply Company - WELLMASTER CARTS; *pg.* 1388, *pg.* 1934
WELLNESS 101 - Nutritional Supplement - PHARMAVITE LLC; *pg.* 1584, *pg.* 167
WELLNESS COLD & FLU - Vitamin & Herbal Supplement - SOURCE NATURALS; *pg.* 1595, *pg.* 278
WELLNESS COUGH SYRUP - Vitamin & Herbal Supplement - SOURCE NATURALS; *pg.* 1595, *pg.* 278
WELLNESS EARACHE - Vitamin & Herbal Supplement - SOURCE NATURALS; *pg.* 1595, *pg.* 278
WELLNESS FORMULA - Vitamin & Herbal Supplement - SOURCE NATURALS; *pg.* 1595, *pg.* 278
THE WELLNESS FROM COCA-COLA - Beverages - THE COCA-COLA COMPANY; *pg.* 240, *pg.* 493
WELLNESS MULTIPLE - Vitamin & Herbal Supplement - SOURCE NATURALS; *pg.* 1595, *pg.* 278
WELLNESS REWARDS - Nutritional Supplement - PHARMAVITE LLC; *pg.* 1584, *pg.* 167
WELLPATCH - Pain Relieving Pad - THE MENTHOLATUM COMPANY; *pg.* 1565, *pg.* 1320
WELLPRO.Z - Depth Filter With Z.Plex Technology - GE WATER & PROCESS TECHNOLOGIES; *pg.* 1339, *pg.* 1588
WELLS - Kitchen Equipment - THE MIDDLEBY CORPORATION; *pg.* 1361, *pg.* 610
WELLS - Automotive Prods. - WELLS MANUFACTURING, L.P.; *pg.* 222, *pg.* 1858
WELLS LAMONT - Company Name - WELLS LAMONT CORPORATION; *pg.* 15, *pg.* 638
WELLSEIS - Air Gun - BOLT TECHNOLOGY CORPORATION; *pg.* 1318, *pg.* 360
WELLSLEY - Furniture - HAWORTH, INC.; *pg.* 402, *pg.* 891
WELLSLEY FARMS - Prepared Foods - BJ'S WHOLESALE CLUB, INC.; *pg.* 1762, *pg.* 857
WELLSPRING - Kitchen Product - KOHLER CO.; *pg.* 91, *pg.* 1862
WELLWORTH - Bath Product - KOHLER CO.; *pg.* 91, *pg.* 1862
WEMSENSE WEB SECURITY ECOSYSTEM - Software - WEBSENSE, INC.; *pg.* 491, *pg.* 210
WEN-LOCK - Automatic Lock Available on Select JELD-WEN Vinyl Windows - JELD-WEN, INC.; *pg.* 1051, *pg.* 1499

WENDE - Footwear - STEVEN MADDEN, LTD.; *pg.* 1819, *pg.* 1176
WENDELL - Casual Shoes - JOHNSTON & MURPHY CO.; *pg.* 1810, *pg.* 1651
WENDY'S - Fast Food Restaurants - THE WENDY'S COMPANY; *pg.* 1755, *pg.* 1450
WENDY'S - Fast Food Restaurants - WENDY'S INTERNATIONAL, INC.; *pg.* 1755, *pg.* 1451
WENZEL - Sleeping Bags & Tents - EXXEL OUTDOORS LLC; *pg.* 1833, *pg.* 311
WE'RE BETTER THAN EVER - Tag Line - HOMELAND STORES, INC.; *pg.* 1023, *pg.* 1486
WE'RE IN YOUR KITCHEN - Slogan - EDLUND COMPANY, INC.; *pg.* 1123, *pg.* 1765
WE'RE LISTENING - Tag Line - EAGLEBANK; *pg.* 745, *pg.* 762
WE'RE ON YOUR SIDE - Slogan - J.R. SIMPLOT COMPANY; *pg.* 867, *pg.* 547
WE'RE READY IN ADVANCE - Tagline - ADVANCE AUTO PARTS, INC.; *pg.* 197, *pg.* 1805
WE'RE TALKING RENTS - Tag Line - MCGRATH RENTCORP; *pg.* 1104, *pg.* 122
WE'RE THE MOVIEST! - Slogan - MOVIES UNLIMITED INC.; *pg.* 1779, *pg.* 1567
WE'RE THE SILENT VIBRATOR GUYS - Slogan - VIBCO INC.; *pg.* 1387, *pg.* 1611
WE.RE THERE WHEN YOU NEED US. - Tag Line - TUCSON ELECTRIC POWER COMPANY; *pg.* 1953, *pg.* 27
WERE THERE'S PRINTING THERE'S BALDWIN - Tag Line - BALDWIN TECHNOLOGY COMPANY, INC.; *pg.* 1316, *pg.* 410
WE'RE WITH YOU EVERY STEP OF THE WAY - Tag Line - GERBER LIFE INSURANCE COMPANY; *pg.* 1201, *pg.* 1352
WERNDL - Office Furniture - STEELCASE INC.; *pg.* 475, *pg.* 889
WERNDL COMMUNICATOR - Storage Product - STEELCASE INC.; *pg.* 475, *pg.* 889
WERNDL CONFERENCE - Tables - STEELCASE INC.; *pg.* 475, *pg.* 889
WERNDL EMERGE - Office Furniture - STEELCASE INC.; *pg.* 475, *pg.* 889
WERNDL FLIP TOP - Office Furniture - STEELCASE INC.; *pg.* 475, *pg.* 889
WERNDL FREEWALL - Office Furniture - STEELCASE INC.; *pg.* 475, *pg.* 889
WERNDL INFOTAINER - Worktools - STEELCASE INC.; *pg.* 475, *pg.* 889
WERNDL MOBY - Storage Product - STEELCASE INC.; *pg.* 475, *pg.* 889
WERNDL TOUCHDOWN - Tables - STEELCASE INC.; *pg.* 475, *pg.* 889
WES MONTGOMERY - Guitars - GIBSON GUITAR CORP.; *pg.* 550, *pg.* 1650
WESBAR - Led Lighting Technology - TRIMAS CORPORATION; *pg.* 1383, *pg.* 874
WESCO BUYERS GUIDE - Buyers Guide - WESCO INTERNATIONAL INC.; *pg.* 687, *pg.* 1582
WESCODYNE - Detergent - STERIS CORPORATION; *pg.* 1597, *pg.* 1464
WESJET - Extrusion Air Ring - DAVIS-STANDARD LLC; *pg.* 1328, *pg.* 368
WESLEY - Footwear - VANS, INC.; *pg.* 1821, *pg.* 76
WESLO - Health & Fitness Product - ICON HEALTH & FITNESS, INC.; *pg.* 1837, *pg.* 1752
WESSON - Food Product - CONAGRA FOODS, INC.; *pg.* 826, *pg.* 1014
WEST - Furniture - BUSH INDUSTRIES INC.; *pg.* 919, *pg.* 1170
WEST - Control System - DYNAPAR; *pg.* 1408, *pg.* 616
WEST - Metal Caps, Lids, Closures & Liners for Containers - WEST PHARMACEUTICAL SERVICES, INC.; *pg.* 1472, *pg.* 1532
WEST ANALYTICAL SERVICES - Drug Testing - WEST PHARMACEUTICAL SERVICES, INC.; *pg.* 1472, *pg.* 1532
WEST BEND - Beverage - REGAL WARE, INC.; *pg.* 1137, *pg.* 1862
WEST BRIDGE - Peripheral Controllers - CYPRESS SEMICONDUCTOR CORPORATION; *pg.* 1326, *pg.* 243
WEST COAST - Uniforms - ELBECO INCORPORATED; *pg.* 40, *pg.* 1584
THE WEST COUNTY GAZETTE - Newspaper - CAPITAL GAZETTE COMMUNICATIONS INC.; *pg.* 1625, *pg.* 754
WEST CREEK - Food Related Products - PERFORMANCE FOOD GROUP COMPANY, LLC; *pg.* 1030, *pg.* 1803
WEST ELM - Furniture - WILLIAMS-SONOMA, INC.; *pg.* 1140, *pg.* 234
WEST GROUP - Software Tool And Application - THOMSON REUTERS CORPORATION; *pg.* 1693, *pg.* 1944
WEST INSTRUMENTS - Temperature Controller - DANAHER CORPORATION; *pg.* 1044, *pg.* 397
WEST-MEX - Food - TACO JOHN'S INTERNATIONAL, INC.; *pg.* 1753, *pg.* 1901
WEST MICHIGAN CAREFREE TRAVEL - Spring/Summer Travel Guide - WEST MICHIGAN TOURIST ASSOCIATION; *pg.* 1930, *pg.* 891
WEST-NILE INNOVATOR - Equine Vaccine - PFIZER INC.; *pg.* 1581, *pg.* 1278
WEST SPECTRA - Bottle Seals - WEST PHARMACEUTICAL SERVICES, INC.; *pg.* 1472, *pg.* 1532
WESTAR - Herbicide - E.I. DU PONT DE NEMOURS & COMPANY; *pg.* 1159, *pg.* 390
WESTAR - Ready-to-Sterilize Stoppers - WEST PHARMACEUTICAL SERVICES, INC.; *pg.* 1472, *pg.* 1532
WESTBOW PRESS - Books - THOMAS NELSON INC.; *pg.* 1692, *pg.* 1654
WESTBRAE NATURAL - Food Product - THE HAIN CELESTIAL GROUP, INC.; *pg.* 860, *pg.* 1172
WESTBROOK - Furniture - ASHLEY FURNITURE INDUSTRIES, INC.; *pg.* 914, *pg.* 1852
WESTBURY - Fabric - NEMSCHOFF, INC.; *pg.* 936, *pg.* 1890
WESTCOTT - Scissors - ACME UNITED CORPORATION; *pg.* 1040, *pg.* 346
WESTERBEKE - Rebuilding Services - FLIGHT SYSTEMS, INC.; *pg.* 1337, *pg.* 1548
WESTERLY SUN - Daily Newspaper - THE RECORD-JOURNAL PUBLISHING COMPANY; *pg.* 1680, *pg.* 354
WESTERN - Lattice Shade Covers & Screen Prods - METALS USA, INC.; *pg.* 97, *pg.* 425
WESTERN - Apparel - OAKLEY, INC.; *pg.* 1840, *pg.* 86
WESTERN - Restaurants & Food - WESTERN SIZZLIN CORPORATION; *pg.* 1755, *pg.* 1806
WESTERN COUNTRY PIES - Restaurant Quality Pie Products - THE SCHWAN FOOD COMPANY; *pg.* 894, *pg.* 928
WESTERN DIGITAL - Computer System - ALIENWARE CORPORATION; *pg.* 346, *pg.* 439
WESTERN FAMILY - Food Product - ASSOCIATED FOOD STORES, INC.; *pg.* 1014, *pg.* 1756
WESTERN FAMILY - Food Products - UNIFIED GROCERS, INC.; *pg.* 1036, *pg.* 66
WESTERN FAMILY - Grocery Wholesaler - WESTERN FAMILY HOLDING CO., INC.; *pg.* 1037, *pg.* 1509
WESTERN LAND ROLLER - Pump - FLOWSERVE CORPORATION; *pg.* 82, *pg.* 1719
WESTERN MERCHANDISER - Magazine - SUMNER COMMUNICATIONS INC.; *pg.* 1690, *pg.* 338
WESTERN METERS - Electronic Measurement Instrument - MESA LABORATORIES, INC.; *pg.* 1567, *pg.* 333
WESTERN SCHOOLS - Home Study Continuing Education for Health Care Professionals - SPECIALTY CATALOG CORPORATION; *pg.* 1786, *pg.* 856
WESTERN SIZZLIN COW - Restaurants & Food - WESTERN SIZZLIN CORPORATION; *pg.* 1755, *pg.* 1806
WESTERN SIZZLIN STEAK & MORE - Restaurants & Food - WESTERN SIZZLIN CORPORATION; *pg.* 1755, *pg.* 1806
WESTERN SIZZLIN STEAK HOUSE - Restaurants - WESTERN SIZZLIN CORPORATION; *pg.* 1755, *pg.* 1806
WESTERN SIZZLIN WOOD GRILL - Restaurants - WESTERN SIZZLIN CORPORATION; *pg.* 1755, *pg.* 1806
WESTERN SUN - Farm Supplies & Feeds - INTERMOUNTAIN FARMERS ASSOCIATION; *pg.* 705, *pg.* 1759
WESTERN TRADITIONS - Greeting Cards - LEANIN' TREE, INC.; *pg.* 1658, *pg.* 311
WESTERN UNION MONEY TRANSFER - Money Services - THE WESTERN UNION COMPANY; *pg.* 822, *pg.* 327
WESTERNBREEZE - Molecular Biology Product - THERMO FISHER SCIENTIFIC INC.; *pg.* 1602, *pg.* 61
WESTERNC - Software - BIO-RAD LABORATORIES, INC.; *pg.* 1504, *pg.* 101
WESTFALIASURGE - Farm Supplies - GEA FARM TECHNOLOGIES; *pg.* 704, *pg.* 636
WESTGARD ADVISOR - Software - BIO-RAD LABORATORIES, INC.; *pg.* 1504, *pg.* 101
THE WESTGATE HOTEL - Hotel - SINCLAIR OIL CORPORATION; *pg.* 984, *pg.* 1760
WESTGATE RESORTS - Resort - CENTRAL FLORIDA INVESTMENTS INC.; *pg.* 1085, *pg.* 452
WESTIN - Hotel Chain - STARWOOD HOTELS & RESORTS WORLDWIDE, INC.; *pg.* 1114, *pg.* 378
WESTIN - Automotive Product - WESTIN AUTOMOTIVE PRODUCTS, INC.; *pg.* 222, *pg.* 211
WESTIN - Food Products - WESTIN FOODS, INC.; *pg.* 909, *pg.* 1019
WESTINGHOUSE - Rebuilding Services - FLIGHT SYSTEMS, INC.; *pg.* 1337, *pg.* 1548
WESTINGHOUSE LIGHT BULBS - Line of Light Bulbs - WESTINGHOUSE LIGHTING CORPORATION; *pg.* 687, *pg.* 1571
WESTLAKE - Office Furniture - JOFCO INC.; *pg.* 931, *pg.* 691
WESTLAW - Legal Publications - THOMSON REUTERS CORPORATION; *pg.* 1693, *pg.* 1944
WESTLEY'S - Tire Cleaners - SHELL LUBRICANTS; *pg.* 217, *pg.* 1714
WESTMINSTER - Dinnerware - THE HOMER LAUGHLIN CHINA COMPANY; *pg.* 1125, *pg.* 1850
WESTMINSTER JOHN KNOX PRESS - Religious Books - PRESBYTERIAN PUBLISHING CORPORATION; *pg.* 1678, *pg.* 737
WESTMORELAND - Coal Mining & Power Production - WESTMORELAND COAL COMPANY; *pg.* 1955, *pg.* 328
WESTMORELAND ENERGY - Power Production - WESTMORELAND COAL COMPANY; *pg.* 1955, *pg.* 328
WESTMORELAND POWER - Power Development - WESTMORELAND COAL COMPANY; *pg.* 1955, *pg.* 328
WESTON - Furniture - BASSETT FURNITURE INDUSTRIES, INCORPORATED; *pg.* 916, *pg.* 1776
WESTON - Furniture - BUSH INDUSTRIES INC.; *pg.* 919, *pg.* 1170
WESTON - Polymer Product - CHEMTURA CORPORATION; *pg.* 1152, *pg.* 355
WESTON - Leather Product - COACH, INC.; *pg.* 3, *pg.* 1214
WESTON - Furniture - ETHAN ALLEN INTERIORS INC.; *pg.* 924, *pg.* 343
WESTON - Bakery Product - GEORGE WESTON LIMITED; *pg.* 858, *pg.* 1938
WESTON - Eye Protection - MCR SAFETY; *pg.* 1422, *pg.* 1630
THE WESTON GALLERIES - Picture Frames - WILTON PRODUCTS, INC.; *pg.* 1140, *pg.* 672
WESTON WOODS - Educational Materials - SCHOLASTIC INC.; *pg.* 1683, *pg.* 1288
WESTONESOURCE - Pharmaceutical Service - WEST PHARMACEUTICAL SERVICES, INC.; *pg.* 1472, *pg.* 1532
WESTOVER - Kitchen Product - KOHLER CO.; *pg.* 91, *pg.* 1862
WESTPINE - General Purpose Cleaner - PENETONE CORPORATION; *pg.* 333, *pg.* 1050
WESTPORT - Shoes - ALLEN-EDMONDS SHOE CORP.; *pg.* 1804, *pg.* 1887
WESTSHORE YACHT CLUB - Community Name - WCI COMMUNITIES, INC.; *pg.* 1118, *pg.* 414
WESTSOY - Food Product - THE HAIN CELESTIAL GROUP, INC.; *pg.* 860, *pg.* 1172
WESTWARD - Hand & Power Tools - W.W. GRAINGER, INC.; *pg.* 1390, *pg.* 625
WESTWAYS - Travel Magazine - AUTOMOBILE CLUB OF SOUTHERN CALIFORNIA; *pg.* 134, *pg.* 126
WESTWIND - Precision Motion System - GSI GROUP INC.; *pg.* 1415, *pg.* 784
WESTWIND - Portable Evaporative Cooler - SEELEY INTERNATIONAL AMERICAS; *pg.* 1076, *pg.* 19
WESVAR - Statistical Software - WESTAT INC.; *pg.* 161, *pg.* 776
WET & SET - Wall & Ceiling Repair Patch - HYDE TOOLS, INC.; *pg.* 1125, *pg.* 844
WET CEL - Fishing Lines - 3M COMPANY; *pg.* 1142, *pg.* 956
WET N' SET - Hook & Helper - HOME PRODUCTS INTERNATIONAL, INC.; *pg.* 1125, *pg.* 577
WET N WILD - Cosmetics - MARKWINS INTERNATIONAL CORP.; *pg.* 516, *pg.* 67
WET 'N WILD - Amusement Parks - WET 'N WILD, INC.; *pg.* 592, *pg.* 457
WET-NAP - Moist Towelettes - NICE-PAK PRODUCTS, INC.; *pg.* 1465, *pg.* 1319
WET ONES - Skincare - EDGEWELL PERSONAL CARE; *pg.* 1526, *pg.* 995
WET SEAL - Clothing Stores - THE WET SEAL, LLC; *pg.* 35, *pg.* 88
WET SHINE - Nail & Lip Color - MAYBELLINE LLC; *pg.* 516, *pg.* 1257
WET SUIT AND DRY SUIT - Cleaner & Conditioner - MCNETT CORPORATION; *pg.* 1839, *pg.* 1817

WET TIP - Sinking Tip - 3M COMPANY; *pg.* 1142, *pg.* 956
WET WHEELS - Baby Care Product - MUNCHKIN, INC.; *pg.* 964, *pg.* 300
WETAID - Metal Finishing Product - HEATBATH CORPORATION; *pg.* 1165, *pg.* 826
WETCLEANING - Dry Cleaning & Laundry Product - ADCO, INC.; *pg.* 325, *pg.* 482
WETFEET - Online Recruiting Services - UNIVERSUM USA; *pg.* 1286, *pg.* 1307
WETGUARD - Lighting Tool - LEVITON MANUFACTURING COMPANY, INC.; *pg.* 1301, *pg.* 1180
WET'N BLACK - Tire Dressing - TURTLE WAX, INC.; *pg.* 220, *pg.* 671
WETORDRY - Waterproof Resin Bonded Coated Abrasives - 3M COMPANY; *pg.* 1142, *pg.* 956
WETPAK - Suitcase - SAMSONITE CORPORATION; *pg.* 11, *pg.* 830
WETSPOT - Removal - ADCO, INC.; *pg.* 325, *pg.* 482
WETWOP - Evidence Collecting Tools - BAE SYSTEMS PRODUCTS GROUP; *pg.* 359, *pg.* 432
WETZELS PRETZELS - Logo - WETZEL'S PRETZELS LLC; *pg.* 910, *pg.* 181
WE'VE GOT A YOU ATTITUDE! - Slogan - PENN NATIONAL GAMING, INC.; *pg.* 574, *pg.* 1595
WE'VE GOT FUN DOWN TO A SCIENCE - Educational Services - MUSEUM OF SCIENCE AND INDUSTRY; *pg.* 565, *pg.* 583
WEVE GOT THE CRUNCH - Slogan - CHURCH'S CHICKEN, INC.; *pg.* 1722, *pg.* 493
WE'VE GOT YOU COVERED - Slogan - TOTES ISOTONER CORPORATION; *pg.* 14, *pg.* 1426
WE'VE GOT YOU UNDER OUR WING - Tag Line - AFLAC INCORPORATED; *pg.* 1188, *pg.* 527
WE'VE MADE AMERICAN GIRLS OUR BUSINESS - Slogan - AMERICAN GIRL LLC; *pg.* 949, *pg.* 1871
WEWS, ABC (CLEVELAND) - Television Broadcasting Station - THE E.W. SCRIPPS COMPANY; *pg.* 1639, *pg.* 1412
WEXFORD - Fabric - NEMSCHOFF, INC.; *pg.* 936, *pg.* 1890
WEXINDEX - Fleet Management & Costs System - WRIGHT EXPRESS CORPORATION; *pg.* 493, *pg.* 753
WEXONLINE - Fleet Management System - WRIGHT EXPRESS CORPORATION; *pg.* 493, *pg.* 753
WEXSMART - Mobile Reporting - WRIGHT EXPRESS CORPORATION; *pg.* 493, *pg.* 753
WF - Ferrous & Nonferrous Forgings - DAIFUKU WEBB; *pg.* 1327, *pg.* 885
WF REPCO - Furnace Fittings & Accessories - WAUKESHA FOUNDRY INC.; *pg.* 1388, *pg.* 1898
WF-XTRA - Steel Product - A. FINKL & SONS CO.; *pg.* 1309, *pg.* 563
WFA - Association - CITIZENS FOR GLOBAL SOLUTIONS; *pg.* 137, *pg.* 397
WFLA-TV - TV Station - MEDIA GENERAL, INC.; *pg.* 297, *pg.* 1803
WFMB SERIES - Floor Boxes - WIREMOLD/LEGRAND; *pg.* 689, *pg.* 383
WFTS, ABC (TAMPA) - Television Broadcasting Network - THE E.W. SCRIPPS COMPANY; *pg.* 1639, *pg.* 1412
WG&L - Software - THOMSON REUTERS TAX & ACCOUNTING; *pg.* 1693, *pg.* 1299
WGNY-AM - Radio Station - SUNRISE BROADCASTING OF NEW YORK, INC.; *pg.* 311, *pg.* 1184
WGNY-FM - Radio Station - SUNRISE BROADCASTING OF NEW YORK, INC.; *pg.* 311, *pg.* 1184
WHAC-A-MOLE - Toy & Game - HASBRO, INC.; *pg.* 954, *pg.* 1603
WHALER - Eyewear - MAUI JIM, INC.; *pg.* 9, *pg.* 651
WHAT A WAY TO GOYA - Slogan - GOYA FOODS, INC.; *pg.* 859, *pg.* 1075
WHAT EVERYBODY NEEDS - Tagline - CRYSTAL ROCK HOLDINGS, INC.; *pg.* 248, *pg.* 382
WHAT HEALTHY PETS ARE MADE OF. - Tag Line - IAMS COMPANY; *pg.* 1477, *pg.* 1633
WHAT IDEAS CAN DO - Tagline - APPVION INC.; *pg.* 1451, *pg.* 1852
WHAT IS SIX SIGMA - Business Management Textbook - PIVOTAL RESOURCES, INC.; *pg.* 455, *pg.* 304
WHAT PIZZA SHOULDBE - Slogan - DONATOS PIZZERIA CORPORATION; *pg.* 1727, *pg.* 1439
WHAT PLAYERS WANT - Slogan - WMS INDUSTRIES INC.; *pg.* 593, *pg.* 666
WHAT PUTS THE "VIRGIN" IN EXTRA VIRGIN OLIVE OIL? - Slogan - POMPEIAN, INC.; *pg.* 890, *pg.* 759
WHAT REALLY MATTERS - Slogan - THE NORTHERN TRUST COMPANY; *pg.* 787, *pg.* 585
WHAT THE BEST COMPANIES DO - Slogan - CEB INC.; *pg.* 733, *pg.* 1773
WHAT WE KNOW - Pillow and Throw - HERITAGE LACE INC.; *pg.* 694, *pg.* 711
WHAT WHITE TEA TASTES LIKE - Slogan - INKO'S WHITE ICED TEA; *pg.* 1023, *pg.* 1243
WHATABLENDER - Food Product - WHATABURGER, INC.; *pg.* 1755, *pg.* 1744
WHATABLENDERS - Food Product - WHATABURGER, INC.; *pg.* 1755, *pg.* 1744
WHATABURGER JR. - Food Product - WHATABURGER, INC.; *pg.* 1755, *pg.* 1744
WHATACATCH - Fish Sandwiches - WHATABURGER, INC.; *pg.* 1755, *pg.* 1744
WHATACHICK'N - Chicken Sandwiches - WHATABURGER, INC.; *pg.* 1755, *pg.* 1744
WHATAGUY - Food Product - WHATABURGER, INC.; *pg.* 1755, *pg.* 1744
WHATAKIDS - Food Product - WHATABURGER, INC.; *pg.* 1755, *pg.* 1744
WHATAMEAL - Food Product - WHATABURGER, INC.; *pg.* 1755, *pg.* 1744
WHATAPALS - Food Product - WHATABURGER, INC.; *pg.* 1755, *pg.* 1744
WHATASIZE IT! - Food Product - WHATABURGER, INC.; *pg.* 1755, *pg.* 1744
WHATCHAMACALLIT - Chocolate Candy - THE HERSHEY CO.; *pg.* 1855, *pg.* 1538
WHATEVER YOU ARE - Pillow and Throw - HERITAGE LACE INC.; *pg.* 694, *pg.* 711
WHATIS.COM - Website - TECHTARGET, INC.; *pg.* 482, *pg.* 837
WHAT'LL WE THINK OF NEXT? - Slogan - ANAREN, INC.; *pg.* 617, *pg.* 1157
WHAT'S HOT FROM MOTT - Monthly Media Publication - MASSACHUSETTS OFFICE OF TRAVEL & TOURISM; *pg.* 998, *pg.* 798
WHAT'S IN YOUR WALLET? - Slogan - CAPITAL ONE FINANCIAL CORPORATION; *pg.* 730, *pg.* 1789
WHAT'S NEWS - Column Heading - DOW JONES & COMPANY, INC.; *pg.* 1637, *pg.* 1225
WHAT'S NOT TO LOVE? - Slogan - BERTUCCI'S CORP.; *pg.* 1716, *pg.* 838
WHAT'S YOUR FAVOURITE THING? - Slogan - FRISCH'S RESTAURANTS, INC.; *pg.* 1729, *pg.* 1413
WHATSAPP - Messaging App - FACEBOOK, INC.; *pg.* 1245, *pg.* 143
WHAT'SWHAT - Women's Shoe - AEROGROUP INTERNATIONAL, INC.; *pg.* 1803, *pg.* 1055
WHEAT THINS - Crackers - MONDELEZ INTERNATIONAL, INC.; *pg.* 878, *pg.* 601
WHEATABLES - Crackers - KELLOGG COMPANY; *pg.* 831, *pg.* 870
WHEATEX - Food Product - MGP INGREDIENTS, INC.; *pg.* 877, *pg.* 714
WHEATIES - Cereal - GENERAL MILLS, INC.; *pg.* 828, *pg.* 933
WHEATON - Pediatric Orthotics - ALIMED, INC.; *pg.* 1490, *pg.* 816
WHEATON WORLDWIDE MOVING - Moving of Household Goods - WHEATON VAN LINES, INC.; *pg.* 1930, *pg.* 691
WHEEL BOSS - Bearing - THE TIMKEN COMPANY; *pg.* 218, *pg.* 1408
WHEEL DRAGON - Bucketwheel Dredge - ELLICOTT DREDGES, LLC; *pg.* 1333, *pg.* 757
WHEEL-LOK - Vehicle Restraint - RITE-HITE HOLDING CORPORATION; *pg.* 1372, *pg.* 1880
WHEEL OF FORTUNE - Game - HASBRO, INC.; *pg.* 954, *pg.* 1603
WHEEL OF FORTUNE - Game - INTERNATIONAL GAME TECHNOLOGY; *pg.* 957, *pg.* 1024
WHEEL OF FORTUNE - Lottery Game - OHIO LOTTERY COMMISSION; *pg.* 1002, *pg.* 1433
WHEEL OF GOLD - Game - INTERNATIONAL GAME TECHNOLOGY; *pg.* 957, *pg.* 1024
WHEEL-PAC - Bearing - THE TIMKEN COMPANY; *pg.* 218, *pg.* 1408
WHEEL PALS - Toy & Game - HASBRO, INC.; *pg.* 954, *pg.* 1603
WHEELBERT - Video Game - INTERNATIONAL GAME TECHNOLOGY; *pg.* 957, *pg.* 1024
WHEELEASY - Wheelbarrow - ALLSOP, INC.; *pg.* 347, *pg.* 1817
WHEELER PUBLISHING - Publisher - GALE CENGAGE LEARNING; *pg.* 1643, *pg.* 885
WHEELFINDER.COM - Auto Classified Website - TAMPA BAY TIMES; *pg.* 1691, *pg.* 464
WHEELIE COOL - Ice Chest - IGLOO PRODUCTS CORPORATION; *pg.* 1126, *pg.* 1724
WHEELOCK - Horn Strobe - COOPER WHEELOCK; *pg.* 630, *pg.* 1080
WHEELS - Sports Car Style Yo-Yo - DUNCAN TOYS COMPANY; *pg.* 951, *pg.* 1465
WHEELS FOR YOU - Classifieds Publication - MADISON NEWSPAPERS, INC.; *pg.* 1661, *pg.* 1866
WHEELS OF FIRE - Snap-Tite Model Kits - REVELL; *pg.* 966, *pg.* 611
WHEELS ON THE BUS - Toy & Game - HASBRO, INC.; *pg.* 954, *pg.* 1603
WHEELTRONIC - Hoists & Lifts for Vehicle Service Shops - SNAP-ON INCORPORATED; *pg.* 1062, *pg.* 1862
WHEELWORKS - Software - PERCEPTRON, INC.; *pg.* 215, *pg.* 904
WHEN A LITTLE IS EXACTLY ENOUGH - Slogan - CHIQUITA BRANDS INTERNATIONAL, INC.; *pg.* 847, *pg.* 1365
WHEN IMAGE EXPERIENCE MATTERS. - Tagline - PLANAR SYSTEMS, INC.; *pg.* 455, *pg.* 1495
WHEN OVERNIGHT JUST ISN'T FAST ENOUGH - Tagline - INTEGRATED BIOPHARMA, INC.; *pg.* 1546, *pg.* 1073
WHEN PERFORMANCE MATTERS MOST - Slogan - BRADY CORPORATION; *pg.* 363, *pg.* 1873
WHEN YOU GET THE FACTS...IT'S RE/MAX! - Slogan - RE/MAX INTERNATIONAL, INC.; *pg.* 1109, *pg.* 322
WHEN YOU NEED A BATH - Tagline - AJAX ELECTRIC CO.; *pg.* 1068, *pg.* 1541
WHEN YOU'RE READY TO PLAY - Slogan - PENN NATIONAL GAMING, INC.; *pg.* 574, *pg.* 1595
WHER MEDICINE LIVES - Tagline - UNIVERSITY OF ARKANSAS FOR MEDICAL SCIENCES; *pg.* 608, *pg.* 34
WHERE A KID CAN BE A KID - Slogan - CEC ENTERTAINMENT, INC.; *pg.* 1721, *pg.* 1717
WHERE A LOVE FOR LEARNING GROWS - Doll And Toy - AMERICAN GIRL LLC; *pg.* 949, *pg.* 1871
WHERE BEST FRIENDS ARE MADE - Slogan - BUILD-A-BEAR WORKSHOP, INC.; *pg.* 950, *pg.* 993
WHERE CANDY FAVORITES COME FROM - Tagline - TOOTSIE ROLL INDUSTRIES, INC.; *pg.* 1863, *pg.* 591
WHERE CHEMISTRY MAKES THE DIFFERENCE - Tagline - COOLEY GROUP, INC.; *pg.* 691, *pg.* 1603
WHERE COURTESY & COMFORT COUNT - Tagline - HOME PROPERTIES INC.; *pg.* 1096, *pg.* 1336
WHERE DO YOU WANT TO BE? - Slogan - RE/MAX INTERNATIONAL, INC.; *pg.* 1109, *pg.* 322
WHERE EXCELLENCE GROWS - Tag Line - THE PHOENIX COMPANIES, INC.; *pg.* 1214, *pg.* 352
WHERE FLORIDA LIVES - Slogan - WCI COMMUNITIES, INC.; *pg.* 1118, *pg.* 414
WHERE FLORIDA LIVES & PLAYS - Slogan - WCI COMMUNITIES, INC.; *pg.* 1118, *pg.* 414
WHERE FRESHNESS MATTERS - Slogan - WEIS MARKETS, INC.; *pg.* 1037, *pg.* 1588
WHERE GIRLS GROW STRONG - Slogan - GIRL SCOUTS OF THE UNITED STATES OF AMERICA; *pg.* 142, *pg.* 1235
WHERE GREAT IDEAS ARE SURFACING! - Tag Line - WILSONART INTERNATIONAL, INC.; *pg.* 1450, *pg.* 1746
WHERE HEALTH MEETS REAL LIFE - Pharmaceutical Product - PFIZER INC.; *pg.* 1581, *pg.* 1278
WHERE IDEAS BECOME REALITY - Slogan - PLEXUS CORP.; *pg.* 455, *pg.* 1883
WHERE INFORMATION LIVES - Slogan - EMC CORPORATION; *pg.* 391, *pg.* 825
WHERE IT ALL COMES TOGETHER - Slogan - MAGNA INTERNATIONAL INC.; *pg.* 211, *pg.* 1918
WHERE MANUFACTURING COMES TOGETHER - Tagline - SOCIETY OF MANUFACTURING ENGINEERS; *pg.* 157, *pg.* 878
WHERE MEDIA IS GOING - Slogan - PENTON MEDIA, INC.; *pg.* 1676, *pg.* 1277
WHERE MEDICINE MEETS TECHNOLOGY - Tag Line - ZOGENIX, INC.; *pg.* 1612, *pg.* 211
WHERE PEOPLE ARE WORTH MORE THAN MONEY - Slogan - CREDIT UNION NATIONAL ASSOCIATION; *pg.* 138, *pg.* 1865
WHERE PEOPLE CONNECT - Slogan - SPARK NETWORKS, INC.; *pg.* 472, *pg.* 140
WHERE PETS ARE FAMILY - Tagline - PETSMART, INC.; *pg.* 1481, *pg.* 18
WHERE PETS FIND FAMILIES - Tagline - PETSMART, INC.;

pg. 1481, pg. 18

WHERE QUALITY IS A TRADITION - Tagline - HERESITE PROTECTIVE COATINGS, INC.; pg. 1442, pg. 1868

WHERE QUALITY SERVICE IS STILL AVAILABLE - Tagline - HENRY BONA POOLS & SPAS; pg. 1836, pg. 1078

WHERE SIMPLE GOODNESS BEGINS - Tag Line - LAND O'LAKES, INC.; pg. 873, pg. 915

WHERE SMART CAR BUYERS START - Slogan - EDMUNDS, INC.; pg. 1241, pg. 273

WHERE SMART SOLUTIONS TAKE FLIGHT - Tag Line - PPG AEROSPACE; pg. 1178, pg. 290

WHERE SPEED & SOLUTIONS ARE THE DIFFERENCE - Tagline - POLYONE CORPORATION; pg. 1177, pg. 1404

WHERE STAYING IN TOUCH IS AFFORDABLE & FUN - Slogan - CURRENT USA, INC.; pg. 1765, pg. 315

WHERE THE EXPERIENCE IS EVERYTHING - Tagline - CANLAN ICE SPORTS CORPORATION; pg. 536, pg. 1907

WHERE THE NEWS IS FIRST - Slogan - TRUCKER PUBLICATIONS INC.; pg. 1696, pg. 1

WHERE THE POWER OF KNOWLEDGE SAVES LIVES - Slogan - CITY OF HOPE NATIONAL MEDICAL CENTER; pg. 1516, pg. 77

WHERE TO GO FOR PACKAGING AND FULFILLMENT - Tagline - COMPLEMAR PARTNERS; pg. 1455, pg. 1333

WHERE TRUST IS BUILT - Homebuilding Services - KB HOME; pg. 90, pg. 134

WHERE VALUES THRIVE - Slogan - THRIVENT FINANCIAL FOR LUTHERANS; pg. 1219, pg. 944

WHERE YOU CAN'T AFFORD TO COMPROMISE - Tagline - AMERICAN SCIENCE AND ENGINEERING, INC.; pg. 1399, pg. 787

WHERE YOU TURN - Tagline - THE TIMKEN COMPANY; pg. 218, pg. 1408

WHERE YOUR BEST MEALS BEGIN - Slogan - HAGGEN, INC.; pg. 1022, pg. 1817

WHERE YOUR FAMILY WANTS TO EAT! - Slogan - HOSS'S STEAK & SEA HOUSE, INC.; pg. 1731, pg. 1526

WHEREAWARE - Computer Software - NOVELL INC.; pg. 446, pg. 852

WHEREBOUTZ - Navigation & Location Systems - TELENAV, INC.; pg. 678, pg. 288

WHEREHOUSE MUSIC - Retail Music & Video Stores - TRANS WORLD ENTERTAINMENT CORPORATION; pg. 313, pg. 1137

WHERE'S MY WATER - Mobile Franchise - DISNEY INTERACTIVE MEDIA GROUP; pg. 1239, pg. 95

WHEREVER HEALTHCARE IS PROVIDED - Tagline - ATC HEALTHCARE, INC.; pg. 1497, pg. 1184

WHETPRO - Agricultural Product - ARCHER-DANIELS-MIDLAND COMPANY; pg. 825, pg. 565

WHETPRO 75 - Gluten - ARCHER-DANIELS-MIDLAND COMPANY; pg. 825, pg. 565

WHETPRO 80 - Gluten - ARCHER-DANIELS-MIDLAND COMPANY; pg. 825, pg. 565

WHETPRO 82 - Gluten - ARCHER-DANIELS-MIDLAND COMPANY; pg. 825, pg. 565

WHETSTAR - Agricultural Product - ARCHER-DANIELS-MIDLAND COMPANY; pg. 825, pg. 565

WHEY-HD - Whey Protein Powder - BPI SPORTS, LLC; pg. 842, pg. 430

WHEY POND - T-Shirts - ABERCROMBIE & FITCH CO.; pg. 37, pg. 1466

WHEY PROTEIN - Boost - JAMBA, INC.; pg. 1024, pg. 84

WHEY-TEIN - Nutritional Supplement - NATURAL ORGANICS, INC.; pg. 1571, pg. 1181

WHICH WAY USA - Activity Kit Series - HIGHLIGHTS FOR CHILDREN, INC.; pg. 1650, pg. 1440

WHILE SILTEX - Medical Device - MENTOR CORPORATION; pg. 1565, pg. 263

WHILTON - Furniture - ASHLEY FURNITURE INDUSTRIES, INC.; pg. 914, pg. 1852

WHIMS - Cookies - PEPPERIDGE FARM, INC.; pg. 888, pg. 363

WHIPPING WILD - Game - WMS INDUSTRIES INC.; pg. 593, pg. 666

WHIPS - Yogurt - YOPLAIT USA, INC.; pg. 910, pg. 947

WHIRL - Fabric - NEMSCHOFF, INC.; pg. 936, pg. 1890

WHIRL-A-WAY - Heat Treating Equipment - SECO/WARWICK CORPORATION; pg. 1076, pg. 1552

WHIRL BALL - Sport Product - FRANKLIN SPORTS, INC.; pg. 1834, pg. 847

WHIRLAMATIC - Cleaning Product - HILLYARD, INC.; pg. 331, pg. 990

WHIRLAWAY - Waste Disposer & Instant Hot Water Dispenser - ANAHEIM MANUFACTURING COMPANY; pg. 51, pg. 48

WHIRLBUSTER - Anti-Whirl PDC - BAKER HUGHES INTEQ; pg. 1316, pg. 1700

WHIRLJET - Spray Product - SPRAYING SYSTEMS CO.; pg. 1063, pg. 670

WHIRLOUT - Exhaust - SWARTWOUT DIVISION; pg. 114, pg. 978

WHIRLPOOL - Air Purifier - LOWE'S COMPANIES, INC.; pg. 1053, pg. 1383

WHIRLPOOL & YOU - Tagline - WHIRLPOOL CORPORATION; pg. 62, pg. 872

WHIRLWIND - Compressor - BADGER AIR BRUSH COMPANY; pg. 359, pg. 612

WHIRLWIND - Cotton Candy Machine - GOLD MEDAL PRODUCTS CO.; pg. 55, pg. 1414

WHIRLWIND - Submersible Pump - LITTLE GIANT PUMP COMPANY; pg. 1356, pg. 1486

WHIRLWIND - Fabric - NEMSCHOFF, INC.; pg. 936, pg. 1890

WHIRLWIND - Classifier - STURTEVANT INC.; pg. 1379, pg. 824

WHIRLWIND AIR SEPARATOR - Air Separator - STURTEVANT INC.; pg. 1379, pg. 824

WHISKAS - Petcare Product - MARS, INCORPORATED; pg. 1858, pg. 1792

WHISKAS - Cat Food - MARS PETCARE; pg. 1478, pg. 1633

WHISKAS TEMPTATIONS - Pet Food - MARS, INCORPORATED; pg. 1858, pg. 1792

WHISKAS TEMPTATIONS - Cat Treats - MARS PETCARE; pg. 1478, pg. 1633

WHISKER - Eyewear - OAKLEY, INC.; pg. 1840, pg. 86

WHISKER CITY - Pet Supplies - PETSMART, INC.; pg. 1481, pg. 18

WHISKY DYC - Whisky - JIM BEAM BRANDS CO.; pg. 1965, pg. 601

WHISKY PARTS CO. - Bicycle Components - QUALITY BICYCLE PRODUCTS; pg. 1710, pg. 918

WHISLER PLUS - Lip System - ESCO CORPORATION; pg. 1335, pg. 1502

WHISPER - Fabric - NEMSCHOFF, INC.; pg. 936, pg. 1890

WHISPER - Sanitary Pads - THE PROCTER & GAMBLE COMPANY; pg. 1129, pg. 1418

WHISPER - Air Freshener - SWISHER HYGIENE INC.; pg. 336, pg. 1507

WHISPER CONNECT - Baby Monitor - EVENFLO COMPANY, INC.; pg. 924, pg. 1470

WHISPER CONNECT DUAL - Nursery Monitor - EVENFLO COMPANY, INC.; pg. 924, pg. 1470

WHISPER CONNECT PRO - Nursery Monitor - EVENFLO COMPANY, INC.; pg. 924, pg. 1470

WHISPER CONNECT SENSA - Baby Monitor - EVENFLO COMPANY, INC.; pg. 924, pg. 1470

WHISPER CONNECT TRIA - Nursery Monitor - EVENFLO COMPANY, INC.; pg. 924, pg. 1470

WHISPER JET - Burners - ASTEC INDUSTRIES, INC.; pg. 69, pg. 1628

WHISPER JET - Mailing & Mailroom Systems, Machines & Software - HASLER, INC.; pg. 1459, pg. 356

WHISPER JET - Medication Nebulizer - VITAL SIGNS, INC.; pg. 1607, pg. 1126

WHISPERDRIVE - Connector - WESTERN DIGITAL CORPORATION; pg. 492, pg. 118

WHISPERDYNE - Centrifuge Components - WESTERN STATES MACHINE COMPANY; pg. 1388, pg. 1455

WHISPERFLO - Ovens - BKI; pg. 52, pg. 1621

WHISPERING - Furniture - ASHLEY FURNITURE INDUSTRIES, INC.; pg. 914, pg. 1852

WHISPERING WLLOW FAIRIES - Porcelain Dolls - CHARISMA BRANDS, LLC; pg. 2, pg. 120

WHISPERLITE - Healthcare Product - GF HEALTH PRODUCTS, INC.; pg. 1535, pg. 508

WHISPERS OF THE FOREST - Oil & Spray - AROMATIQUE INC.; pg. 499, pg. 32

WHISPERSTATION - Software - MICROWAY, INC.; pg. 1267, pg. 841

WHISPERTOUCH - Stereo Volume Control - ATLAS SOUND; pg. 621, pg. 1692

WHISTLE - Medical Equipment - CONMED CORPORATION; pg. 1517, pg. 1347

WHISTLE DOG - Fast Food - A&W FOOD SERVICES OF CANADA INC.; pg. 1714, pg. 1908

WHISTLE JUNCTION - Restaurant - STAR BUFFET, INC.; pg. 1751, pg. 24

WHISTLE POPS - Candy - SPANGLER CANDY COMPANY; pg. 1862, pg. 1407

WHISTLING STRAITS - Bath Product - KOHLER CO.; pg. 91, pg. 1862

WHITAKER R COLLECTION - Fabric - VICTOR INNOVATIVE TEXTILES; pg. 699, pg. 819

WHITE - Tractors - AGCO CORPORATION; pg. 700, pg. 530

WHITE & BUTTERY - Microwave Pop Corn - AMERICAN POP CORN COMPANY; pg. 825, pg. 712

WHITE CAMELLIA - Hair & Skin Product - AUBREY ORGANICS INC.; pg. 499, pg. 470

WHITE CAP - Aerosol Pan Coating - VENTURA FOODS, LLC; pg. 908, pg. 49

WHITE CAPE - Container Grown Plant - MONROVIA GROWERS; pg. 1797, pg. 44

WHITE CASTLE - Fast Food Restaurants - WHITE CASTLE MANAGEMENT CO.; pg. 1756, pg. 1444

WHITE CHEDDAR GENIUS FOOD - Popcorn - NEWMAN'S OWN, INC.; pg. 886, pg. 384

WHITE CHRISTMAS EXPRESS - Locomotive & Cars - BACHMANN INDUSTRIES, INC.; pg. 950, pg. 1559

WHITE CRANBERRY - Juice - OCEAN SPRAY CRANBERRIES, INC.; pg. 887, pg. 827

WHITE CROWN - Canned Meat & Fish - ATALANTA CORPORATION; pg. 838, pg. 1057

WHITE CRYSTAL - Salt - DOW CHEMICAL; pg. 1156, pg. 1563

WHITE DIAMONDS - Skin Care Products - ELIZABETH ARDEN, INC.; pg. 507, pg. 448

WHITE DOT - Writing Instrument - SHEAFFER PEN CORPORATION; pg. 469, pg. 371

WHITE ELECTRICAL - Electrical Construction - WHITE ELECTRICAL CONSTRUCTION CO.; pg. 688, pg. 524

WHITE FANG SCHNAPPS - Distilled Spirits - HOOD RIVER DISTILLERS INC.; pg. 1964, pg. 1498

WHITE FLOWER - Table Textile - HERITAGE LACE INC.; pg. 694, pg. 711

WHITE GINGER - Fragrance - PARFUMS DE COEUR LTD.; pg. 519, pg. 376

WHITE GOLD - Dental Product - DENTSPLY INTERNATIONAL INC.; pg. 1522, pg. 1596

WHITE HAWK SELECT IPA - Beer - MENDOCINO BREWING COMPANY; pg. 254, pg. 298

WHITE HORSE INN - Radio Broadcast - ALLIANCE OF CONFESSING EVANGELICALS, INC.; pg. 126, pg. 1545

WHITE HOT - Golf Equipment - CALLAWAY GOLF COMPANY; pg. 1829, pg. 58

WHITE HOT - Heat Alert Baby Care Product - MUNCHKIN, INC.; pg. 964, pg. 300

WHITE HOT ACES - Video Poker - INTERNATIONAL GAME TECHNOLOGY; pg. 957, pg. 1024

WHITE HOUSE BLACK MARKET - Private Branded Clothing for Women - CHICO'S FAS, INC.; pg. 21, pg. 427

WHITE ICE - Slots - INTERNATIONAL GAME TECHNOLOGY; pg. 957, pg. 1024

WHITE ICE 8S - Lottery Game - NEW YORK STATE LOTTERY; pg. 1001, pg. 1340

WHITE LIGHTNIN' - Container Grown Plant - MONROVIA GROWERS; pg. 1797, pg. 44

WHITE LIGHTNING - Conveyor Belting - HBD INDUSTRIES, INC.; pg. 207, pg. 1449

WHITE LIGHTNING - Spackling Compound - THE SHERWIN-WILLIAMS COMPANY; pg. 1447, pg. 1435

WHITE LILY - Corn Muffins - THE J.M. SMUCKER COMPANY; pg. 865, pg. 1468

WHITE MOCCA - Coffee Beverage - THE SECOND CUP LTD.; pg. 1749, pg. 1928

WHITE N BRITE - Dry Cleaning & Laundry Product - ADCO, INC.; pg. 325, pg. 482

WHITE OUTDOOR - Lawn & Garden Equipment - MTD PRODUCTS, INC.; pg. 1057, pg. 1478

WHITE PINE - Wall Decor - HERITAGE LACE INC.; pg. 694, pg. 711

WHITE RIVER FARMS - Catalog & Food Products - JARDEN CORPORATION; pg. 1885, pg. 412

WHITE ROSE - Table Textile - HERITAGE LACE INC.; pg. 694, pg. 711

WHITE SHOULDERS - Fragrance - ELIZABETH ARDEN, INC.; pg. 507, pg. 448

WHITE STAR - Heavyweight Body Filler - ITW - EVERCOAT; pg. 1443, pg. 1415

WHITE STAR - Valves - THE WM. POWELL COMPANY; pg. 1389, pg. 1427

WHITE STARS - Slots - INTERNATIONAL GAME TECHNOLOGY; pg. 957, pg. 1024

First page reference indicates Business Class Edition
Second page reference indicates Geographic Edition

WHITE-SUNDSTRAND - Machine Tool Product - BOURN & KOCH MACHINE TOOL COMPANY; *pg.* 1319, *pg.* 654
WHITE SWAN - Glace (Candied Fruit) - PARADISE, INC.; *pg.* 888, *pg.* 458
WHITE WATER - Water Park - HERSCHEND FAMILY ENTERTAINMENT CORP.; *pg.* 552, *pg.* 973
WHITE WATER - ATLANTA - Park - SIX FLAGS ENTERTAINMENT CORPORATION; *pg.* 583, *pg.* 1698
WHITE WATER BAY - Park - SIX FLAGS ENTERTAINMENT CORPORATION; *pg.* 583, *pg.* 1698
WHITE WAVE - Tempeh & Tofu - THE WHITEWAVE FOODS COMPANY; *pg.* 1037, *pg.* 324
WHITEGMC AERO SERIES - Class 8 Truck & Tractors - VOLVO TRUCKS NORTH AMERICA, INC.; *pg.* 195, *pg.* 1377
WHITEGMC CONVENTIONALS - Class 8 Truck & Tractors - VOLVO TRUCKS NORTH AMERICA, INC.; *pg.* 195, *pg.* 1377
WHITEHALL - Paper - DOMTAR CORPORATION; *pg.* 1456, *pg.* 1954
WHITEHAVEN - Wine - E&J GALLO WINERY; *pg.* 1962, *pg.* 149
WHITEHUNTER - Knife - COAST CUTLERY COMPANY; *pg.* 1121, *pg.* 1501
WHITENING GEL - Toothbrush - RANIR LLC; *pg.* 520, *pg.* 888
WHITENING GEL NIGHT - Toothbrush - RANIR LLC; *pg.* 520, *pg.* 888
WHITENING WRAPS - Whitening - RANIR LLC; *pg.* 520, *pg.* 888
WHITES - Medical Apparel - BARCO UNIFORMS, INC.; *pg.* 19, *pg.* 94
WHITE'S AUTOSCAN - Metal Detector - WHITE'S ELECTRONICS; *pg.* 688, *pg.* 1509
WHITESIDE - White PVC Fabric - STANDARD SAFETY EQUIPMENT CO.; *pg.* 1379, *pg.* 632
WHITESKIN - Foam Pig - T.D. WILLIAMSON, INC.; *pg.* 1380, *pg.* 1490
WHITESTAR - Medical Device - ABBOTT MEDICAL OPTICS, INC.; *pg.* 1485, *pg.* 260
WHITETAIL EXTREME - Apparel - CABELA'S INCORPORATED; *pg.* 535, *pg.* 1019
WHITEUV - Ultraviolet Curing System - NORDSON CORPORATION; *pg.* 1365, *pg.* 1480
WHITEUV+ - Ultraviolet Curing System - NORDSON CORPORATION; *pg.* 1365, *pg.* 1480
WHITEWAY - Lighting Fixture - HUBBELL INCORPORATED; *pg.* 1299, *pg.* 370
WHITEWHEAT - Food Product - FLOWERS FOODS, INC.; *pg.* 855, *pg.* 541
WHITEY - Plastic Tube - SWAGELOK COMPANY; *pg.* 1064, *pg.* 1473
WHITEY'S CHILI - Food Product - WINDSOR QUALITY FOOD CO., LTD.; *pg.* 910, *pg.* 1717
WHITFIELD - Furniture - ETHAN ALLEN INTERIORS INC.; *pg.* 924, *pg.* 343
WHITFIELD - Stoves & Chimney Inserts - LENNOX HEARTH PRODUCTS; *pg.* 93, *pg.* 1652
WHITFORD - Fluoropolymer Coating Company - WHITFORD WORLDWIDE COMPANY; *pg.* 1185, *pg.* 1529
WHITING - Cranes, Railroad Maintenance & Metallurgical Equipment - WHITING CORPORATION; *pg.* 1389, *pg.* 633
WHITMAN'S - Candy - RUSSELL STOVER CANDIES, INC.; *pg.* 1861, *pg.* 986
WHITMAN'S SAMPLER - Pecan Crown - RUSSELL STOVER CANDIES, INC.; *pg.* 1861, *pg.* 986
WHITNEY - Furniture - ETHAN ALLEN INTERIORS INC.; *pg.* 924, *pg.* 343
WHITNEY EDUCATION GROUP - Education Group - TIGRENT INC.; *pg.* 608, *pg.* 415
WHITNEY LIBRARY OF DESIGN - Books for Designers - NIELSEN BUSINESS MEDIA; *pg.* 1671, *pg.* 1272
WHITNEY'S - Seafood - TRIDENT SEAFOODS CORPORATION; *pg.* 902, *pg.* 1842
WHITNON - Spindle & Slide - SETCO SALES COMPANY; *pg.* 1061, *pg.* 1426
WHITTAKER SAFETY EQUIPMENT - Electronic & Fluid Controls - MEGGITT SAFETY SYSTEMS, INC.; *pg.* 653, *pg.* 279
WHIZ - Shampoo Bowl Spray - BELVEDERE USA CORPORATION; *pg.* 917, *pg.* 556
WHIZ - Automotive Chemicals - MALCO PRODUCTS, INC.; *pg.* 1172, *pg.* 1404
WHIZ BANG - Popcorn Machine - GOLD MEDAL PRODUCTS CO.; *pg.* 55, *pg.* 1414
WHIZKID - Software - SLM CORPORATION; *pg.* 804, *pg.* 388
WHIZLOCK - Fasteners - MACLEAN-FOGG COMPANY INC.; *pg.* 1358, *pg.* 635
WHIZZER - Mat & Equipment Disinfectant - MUELLER SPORTS MEDICINE, INC.; *pg.* 1570, *pg.* 1887
WHO DUNNIT? - Game - WMS INDUSTRIES INC.; *pg.* 593, *pg.* 666
WHO MAKES PROGRESS - Slogan - PROGRESS SOFTWARE CORPORATION; *pg.* 457, *pg.* 786
WHO-SONG & LARRY'S - Restaurants - REAL MEX RESTAURANTS, INC.; *pg.* 1746, *pg.* 75
WHO WANTS TO BE A MILLIONAIRE - Toy - MATTEL, INC.; *pg.* 962, *pg.* 81
WHO WAS WHO IN AMERICA - Biographical Reference Book - MARQUIS WHO'S WHO, LLC; *pg.* 1661, *pg.* 1044
WHOLE BODY CLEANSE - Natural Diet Plan - ENZYMATIC THERAPY INC.; *pg.* 1529, *pg.* 1859
WHOLE CLUSTER - Wine - WILLAMETTE VALLEY VINEYARDS, INC.; *pg.* 1972, *pg.* 1510
WHOLE DOG JOURNAL - Magazine - BELVOIR MEDIA GROUP, LLC; *pg.* 1620, *pg.* 360
THE WHOLE ENCHILADA - Game - WMS INDUSTRIES INC.; *pg.* 593, *pg.* 666
WHOLE FOODS - Food Product - WHOLE FOODS MARKET, INC.; *pg.* 1038, *pg.* 1667
WHOLE FRUIT - Fruit Sorbets - J&J SNACK FOODS CORPORATION; *pg.* 865, *pg.* 1107
WHOLE GRAIN - Pretzel Snacks - HERR FOODS INC.; *pg.* 861, *pg.* 1557
WHOLE GRAIN WHITE LIGHT STYLE - Bread - PEPPERIDGE FARM, INC.; *pg.* 888, *pg.* 363
WHOLE GRAIN WHITE SANDWICH - Bread - PEPPERIDGE FARM, INC.; *pg.* 888, *pg.* 363
WHOLE GRAIN WHITE VERY THIN - Bread - PEPPERIDGE FARM, INC.; *pg.* 888, *pg.* 363
WHOLE LIFE - Life Insurance - PAN-AMERICAN LIFE INSURANCE COMPANY; *pg.* 1213, *pg.* 747
WHOLE O'S - Cereal - NATURE'S PATH FOODS INC.; *pg.* 833, *pg.* 1908
WHOLE RICE TIME RELEASE SINGLE DAY - Chelated Multi-Vitamin & Mineral - SCHIFF NUTRITION INTERNATIONAL, INC.; *pg.* 1592, *pg.* 1760
WHOLEHOG - Software - HIGH END SYSTEMS, INC.; *pg.* 1299, *pg.* 1663
WHOLESALECENTRAL.COM - Website - SUMNER COMMUNICATIONS INC.; *pg.* 1690, *pg.* 338
WHOLESOME VALLEY - Food Products - GALAXY NUTRITIONAL FOODS, INC.; *pg.* 857, *pg.* 1603
WHOLESOME VALLEY ORGANIC - Cheese Product - GALAXY NUTRITIONAL FOODS, INC.; *pg.* 857, *pg.* 1603
WHOLEVIEW 2 - Technology Research Report - FORRESTER RESEARCH, INC.; *pg.* 1642, *pg.* 807
WHOPPER - Burger - BURGER KING CORPORATION; *pg.* 1719, *pg.* 440
WHOPPER JR - Sandwich - BURGER KING CORPORATION; *pg.* 1719, *pg.* 440
WHOPPERS - Chocolate Candy - THE HERSHEY CO.; *pg.* 1855, *pg.* 1538
WHO'S NEWS - Column Heading - DOW JONES & COMPANY, INC.; *pg.* 1637, *pg.* 1225
WHO'S WHO AMOUNG STUDENTS - Magazine - RANDALL-REILLY PUBLISHING COMPANY LLC; *pg.* 1679, *pg.* 8
WHO'S WHO IN AMERICA - Biographical Reference Book - MARQUIS WHO'S WHO, LLC; *pg.* 1661, *pg.* 1044
WHO'S WHO IN AMERICAN ART - Biographical Reference Book - MARQUIS WHO'S WHO, LLC; *pg.* 1661, *pg.* 1044
WHO'S WHO IN AMERICAN LAW - Biographical Reference Book - MARQUIS WHO'S WHO, LLC; *pg.* 1661, *pg.* 1044
WHO'S WHO IN AMERICAN POLITICS - Biographical Reference Book - MARQUIS WHO'S WHO, LLC; *pg.* 1661, *pg.* 1044
WHO'S WHO IN ASIA - Biographical Reference Book - MARQUIS WHO'S WHO, LLC; *pg.* 1661, *pg.* 1044
WHO'S WHO IN FINANCE AND INDUSTRY - Biographical Reference Book - MARQUIS WHO'S WHO, LLC; *pg.* 1661, *pg.* 1044
WHO'S WHO IN MEDICINE AND HEALTHCARE - Biographical Reference Book - MARQUIS WHO'S WHO, LLC; *pg.* 1661, *pg.* 1044
WHO'S WHO IN SCIENCE AND ENGINEERING - Biographical Reference Book - MARQUIS WHO'S WHO, LLC; *pg.* 1661, *pg.* 1044
WHO'S WHO IN THE EAST - Biographical Reference Book - MARQUIS WHO'S WHO, LLC; *pg.* 1661, *pg.* 1044
WHO'S WHO IN THE MIDWEST - Biographical Reference Book - MARQUIS WHO'S WHO, LLC; *pg.* 1661, *pg.* 1044
WHO'S WHO IN THE SOUTH AND SOUTHWEST - Biographical Reference Book - MARQUIS WHO'S WHO, LLC; *pg.* 1661, *pg.* 1044
WHO'S WHO IN THE WEST - Biographical Reference Book - MARQUIS WHO'S WHO, LLC; *pg.* 1661, *pg.* 1044
WHO'S WHO IN THE WORLD - Biographical Reference Book - MARQUIS WHO'S WHO, LLC; *pg.* 1661, *pg.* 1044
WHO'S WHO OF AMERICAN WOMEN - Biographical Reference Book - MARQUIS WHO'S WHO, LLC; *pg.* 1661, *pg.* 1044
WHS-100 - Weldable High Strength Steels - THE TIMKEN COMPANY; *pg.* 218, *pg.* 1408
WHS-130 - Weldable High Strength Steels - THE TIMKEN COMPANY; *pg.* 218, *pg.* 1408
WHUPPIN' STICK - Fishing Equipment - CABELA'S INCORPORATED; *pg.* 535, *pg.* 1019
WHY - Eyewear - OAKLEY, INC.; *pg.* 1840, *pg.* 86
WHY 8.0 - Sunglasses - OAKLEY, INC.; *pg.* 1840, *pg.* 86
WHY 8.1 - Sunglasses - OAKLEY, INC.; *pg.* 1840, *pg.* 86
WHY BUY A MATTRESS ANYWHERE ELSE - Slogan - SLEEP COUNTRY USA, INC.; *pg.* 943, *pg.* 1822
WHY PLAY ANYWHERE ELSE? - Slogan - PENN NATIONAL GAMING, INC.; *pg.* 574, *pg.* 1595
WI-105 - Indicators - AVERY WEIGH-TRONIX, INC.; *pg.* 1315, *pg.* 925
WI-125 GROUP - Indicators - AVERY WEIGH-TRONIX, INC.; *pg.* 1315, *pg.* 925
WI-125 LED - Indicators - AVERY WEIGH-TRONIX, INC.; *pg.* 1315, *pg.* 925
WI-127 - Indicators - AVERY WEIGH-TRONIX, INC.; *pg.* 1315, *pg.* 925
WI-130 - Indicators - AVERY WEIGH-TRONIX, INC.; *pg.* 1315, *pg.* 925
WI-150 LOW POWER - Indicators - AVERY WEIGH-TRONIX, INC.; *pg.* 1315, *pg.* 925
WI-152 BATTERY - Indicators - AVERY WEIGH-TRONIX, INC.; *pg.* 1315, *pg.* 925
WI-FI - Software - SOCKET MOBILE, INC.; *pg.* 471, *pg.* 164
WI-FI - Software - VIEWSONIC CORPORATION; *pg.* 489, *pg.* 303
WI-SYS - Antenna Products - PCTEL, INC.; *pg.* 452, *pg.* 557
WIBA - Inter-Facility Links - EMCORE CORPORATION; *pg.* 636, *pg.* 39
WIBOX - Electronic Device - LANTRONIX, INC.; *pg.* 426, *pg.* 112
WICH - Gear Shaving Machines & Tools - GLEASON CORPORATION; *pg.* 1340, *pg.* 1335
WICHITA - Orthopaedic Product - STRYKER CORPORATION; *pg.* 1598, *pg.* 894
WICHITA - Air Clutches & Brakes - WARNER ELECTRIC, INC.; *pg.* 221, *pg.* 661
WICHITA FALLS TIMES RECORD NEWS - Newspaper - THE E.W. SCRIPPS COMPANY; *pg.* 1639, *pg.* 1412
WICKED GOOD - Slippers - L.L. BEAN, INC.; *pg.* 1777, *pg.* 750
WICKED RICHES - Game - WMS INDUSTRIES INC.; *pg.* 593, *pg.* 666
WICKER - Fabric - NEMSCHOFF, INC.; *pg.* 936, *pg.* 1890
WICKER - Ceiling Fan - WESTINGHOUSE LIGHTING CORPORATION; *pg.* 687, *pg.* 1571
WICKERWEAVE - Plastic Product - THE STEP2 COMPANY LLC; *pg.* 1889, *pg.* 1474
WICKERWORK - Fabric - NEMSCHOFF, INC.; *pg.* 936, *pg.* 1890
WICKFORD COMBINATION - Weather Instruments - SWIFT OPTICAL INSTRUMENTS, INC.; *pg.* 1430, *pg.* 1744
WIDCOMM - Software - BROADCOM CORPORATION; *pg.* 364, *pg.* 108
WIDE BAND - Male External Catheter - MEDLINE INDUSTRIES, INC.; *pg.* 1562, *pg.* 635
WIDE BOY - Brush - THE WOOSTER BRUSH COMPANY; *pg.* 1450, *pg.* 1482
WIDE DUPLEX - Optical Product - LEUPOLD & STEVENS, INC.; *pg.* 1420, *pg.* 1492
WIDE ELCAMINO - Truck Seating - SEATS INCORPORATED; *pg.* 217, *pg.* 1890
WIDE EYES - Residential Lighting - SWIVELIER CO., INC.; *pg.* 1307, *pg.* 1142
WIDE GLIDE - Motorcycle - HARLEY-DAVIDSON, INC.; *pg.* 178, *pg.* 1874
WIDE-LITE - Lighting Fixture & Control - PHILIPS LIGHTING; *pg.* 1303, *pg.* 806

WIDE PARALLELOGRAM - Suspension - SEATS INCORPORATED; *pg.* 217, *pg.* 1890
WIDE/PLY - High-Beam Spiral Tube Paper - SONOCO PRODUCTS COMPANY; *pg.* 1469, *pg.* 1619
WIDE-RANGE - Gas Burner - MAXON CORPORATION; *pg.* 1359, *pg.* 695
WIDE SHOES FOR MEN - Tag Line - HITCHCOCK SHOES, INC.; *pg.* 1810, *pg.* 824
WIDE SHOT MAX - Power Painter - WAGNER SPRAY TECH CORPORATION; *pg.* 1449, *pg.* 954
WIDE SHOT PLUS - Power Painter - WAGNER SPRAY TECH CORPORATION; *pg.* 1449, *pg.* 954
WIDE SOCKS - Healthcare Product - MEDICOOL, INC.; *pg.* 1562, *pg.* 294
WIDE SPACES SWING - Childproof Indoor Gate - EVENFLO COMPANY, INC.; *pg.* 924, *pg.* 1470
WIDE TRACK - Cleaning Product - RUG DOCTOR, LP; *pg.* 1373, *pg.* 1734
WIDE WALE - Carpet - INTERFACE, INC.; *pg.* 695, *pg.* 512
WIDE WEB LAMINATING - Plastic Film - MULTI-PLASTICS, INC.; *pg.* 1886, *pg.* 1457
WIDEAZZ - Adjustable Wrench - CHANNELLOCK, INC.; *pg.* 1044, *pg.* 1551
WIDERAC - Fluid Handling System - GRACO, INC.; *pg.* 1342, *pg.* 935
WIDESIDE - Fabrics - HERCULITE PRODUCTS, INC.; *pg.* 694, *pg.* 1529
WIDESPAN - Structural System - BUTLER MANUFACTURING COMPANY; *pg.* 72, *pg.* 981
WIDESTRIKE - Insect Protection Products - DOW AGROSCIENCES LLC; *pg.* 1156, *pg.* 684
WIDETRACKER - Suitcase - SAMSONITE CORPORATION; *pg.* 11, *pg.* 830
WIDEWALL - Fiber Glass Plastic Continuous Flat Sheet - MOLDED FIBER GLASS COMPANIES; *pg.* 1886, *pg.* 1403
WIDGET - Scraper & Cutter - THE GILLETTE COMPANY; *pg.* 509, *pg.* 795
WIDIA - Tools - KENNAMETAL INC.; *pg.* 1052, *pg.* 1547
WIDIA MANCHESTER - Tools - KENNAMETAL INC.; *pg.* 1052, *pg.* 1547
WIDMER BROTHERS BREWING - Craft Brewery - CRAFT BREWERS ALLIANCE, INC; *pg.* 247, *pg.* 1502
WIDMER HEFEWEIZEN - Beer - CRAFT BREWERS ALLIANCE, INC; *pg.* 247, *pg.* 1502
WIEGMANN - Enclosure - HUBBELL INCORPORATED; *pg.* 1299, *pg.* 370
WIEJSKE WYROBY - Pickles, Peppers & Relish - PINNACLE FOODS GROUP LLC; *pg.* 889, *pg.* 1104
WIENERSCHNITZEL - Fast Food Restaurants - GALARDI GROUP, INC.; *pg.* 1729, *pg.* 110
WIFFLE - Game - THE WIFFLE BALL INC.; *pg.* 1848, *pg.* 371
WIFI CONVERGENCE (VCC) - Cable Solutions - SONUS NETWORKS INC.; *pg.* 1281, *pg.* 858
WIFI REVOLUTION - Online Publication - TECHNOLOGY MARKETING CORP.; *pg.* 1691, *pg.* 364
WIFI TELEPHONY MAGAZINE - Trade Publication - TECHNOLOGY MARKETING CORP.; *pg.* 1691, *pg.* 364
WIG-L-BUG - Dental Product - DENTSPLY INTERNATIONAL INC.; *pg.* 1522, *pg.* 1596
WIGEON - Furniture - ASHLEY FURNITURE INDUSTRIES, INC.; *pg.* 914, *pg.* 1852
WIGGLE- IN - Body Suit - CARTER'S, INC.; *pg.* 21, *pg.* 491
WIGGLE WORMS - Candies - JELLY BELLY CANDY COMPANY; *pg.* 1857, *pg.* 86
WIGGLEWORKS - Educational Materials - SCHOLASTIC INC.; *pg.* 1683, *pg.* 1288
WIGGLEWORKS SCHOLASTIC BEGINNING LITERACY SYSTEM - Educational Materials - SCHOLASTIC INC.; *pg.* 1683, *pg.* 1288
WIGGLY WORMS - Toy - MATTEL, INC.; *pg.* 962, *pg.* 81
WIGGY - Musical Instrument - PEAVEY ELECTRONICS CORPORATION; *pg.* 662, *pg.* 970
WIGO - Beauty Care Product - HELEN OF TROY L.P.; *pg.* 511, *pg.* 1692
WIGSHOP.COM - Online WIg Shop - SPECIALTY CATALOG CORPORATION; *pg.* 1786, *pg.* 856
WIGWAM - Socks - WIGWAM MILLS, INC.; *pg.* 15, *pg.* 1894
WIKIANSWERS - Search Engine - ANSWERS CORPORATION; *pg.* 1229, *pg.* 1195
WIKIANSWERS.COM - Free Search Engine Website - ANSWERS CORPORATION; *pg.* 1229, *pg.* 1195
WIKIPEDIA - Free Online Encyclopedia - WIKIMEDIA FOUNDATION INC.; *pg.* 161, *pg.* 234
WIKTOR - Stent - MEDTRONIC, INC.; *pg.* 1564, *pg.* 939
WILBANKS - Ceramic & Plastic Product - COORSTEK, INC.; *pg.* 77, *pg.* 330
WILBERT - Shoes - ALLEN-EDMONDS SHOE CORP.; *pg.* 1804, *pg.* 1887
WILBUR - Sweets - CARGILL, INC.; *pg.* 845, *pg.* 965
WILBUR BEANS - Side Order - FAMOUS DAVE'S OF AMERICA, INC.; *pg.* 1728, *pg.* 926
WILBUR BUDS - Chocolate Coating - CARGILL LIMITED; *pg.* 1475, *pg.* 1914
WILBUR COON - Shoes - P.W. MINOR & SON, INC.; *pg.* 1816, *pg.* 1140
WILCH - Frozen Beverage Dispensers - GRINDMASTER CORPORATION; *pg.* 56, *pg.* 734
WILCOID - Vegetable Tan Fabric - CHICAGO-WILCOX MFG. COMPANY, INC.; *pg.* 202, *pg.* 661
WILD 2'S POKER - Game - INTERNATIONAL GAME TECHNOLOGY; *pg.* 420, *pg.* 1606
WILD 8'S - Lottery Game - MISSOURI LOTTERY; *pg.* 999, *pg.* 979
WILD ABOUT CHOCOLATE - Ice Cream - DIPPIN' DOTS LLC; *pg.* 853, *pg.* 739
WILD & LOOSE - Game - WMS INDUSTRIES INC.; *pg.* 593, *pg.* 666
WILD & LUCKY - Slots - INTERNATIONAL GAME TECHNOLOGY; *pg.* 957, *pg.* 1024
WILD & WILDER - Game - WMS INDUSTRIES INC.; *pg.* 593, *pg.* 666
WILD ANIMALS - Flashlight - ENERGIZER HOLDINGS, INC.; *pg.* 637, *pg.* 996
WILD ASIA - Area Rugs & Broadloom - COURISTAN INC.; *pg.* 921, *pg.* 1067
WILD AT HEART - Fiction Series - AMERICAN GIRL LLC; *pg.* 949, *pg.* 1871
WILD AVALANCHE - Game - WMS INDUSTRIES INC.; *pg.* 593, *pg.* 666
WILD BEAR - Video Slots - INTERNATIONAL GAME TECHNOLOGY; *pg.* 957, *pg.* 1024
WILD BEAR SALMON RUN - Video Slots - INTERNATIONAL GAME TECHNOLOGY; *pg.* 957, *pg.* 1024
WILD BERRY SPLASH - Fruit Juices - CHIQUITA BRANDS INTERNATIONAL, INC.; *pg.* 847, *pg.* 1365
WILD BILL'S - Snack Stick - HATFIELD QUALITY MEATS, INC.; *pg.* 861, *pg.* 1537
WILD BONUS SEVENS - Video Game - BALLY TECHNOLOGIES, INC.; *pg.* 531, *pg.* 1022
WILD BUNCH - Beverage - TRINCHERO FAMILY ESTATES; *pg.* 1971, *pg.* 197
WILD CARD - Lottery Game - MONTANA LOTTERY; *pg.* 1000, *pg.* 1008
WILD CARD 2 - Lottery Game - IDAHO LOTTERY; *pg.* 995, *pg.* 547
WILD CHANCE - Game - WMS INDUSTRIES INC.; *pg.* 593, *pg.* 666
WILD CHERRY - Slots - INTERNATIONAL GAME TECHNOLOGY; *pg.* 957, *pg.* 1024
WILD CHERRY CASHWORD - Lottery Game - IDAHO LOTTERY; *pg.* 995, *pg.* 547
WILD CHERRY PEPSI - Soft Drink - PEPSICO, INC.; *pg.* 259, *pg.* 1327
WILD COUNTRY - Beauty Product - AVON PRODUCTS, INC.; *pg.* 500, *pg.* 1198
WILD COUNTRY - Game - WMS INDUSTRIES INC.; *pg.* 593, *pg.* 666
WILD DELIGHT - Pet Food - PETSMART, INC.; *pg.* 1481, *pg.* 18
WILD DEVILS - Game - WMS INDUSTRIES INC.; *pg.* 593, *pg.* 666
WILD DIAMONDS - Slots - INTERNATIONAL GAME TECHNOLOGY; *pg.* 957, *pg.* 1024
WILD DUCK - Handling Product - C.R. DANIELS, INC.; *pg.* 1456, *pg.* 769
WILD FIVE TIMES PAY - Slots - INTERNATIONAL GAME TECHNOLOGY; *pg.* 957, *pg.* 1024
WILD FLOWER PINE-SOL - All Purpose Cleaner - THE CLOROX COMPANY; *pg.* 327, *pg.* 169
WILD FLOWERS - Lace - HERITAGE LACE INC.; *pg.* 694, *pg.* 711
WILD FREESIA - Personal Care Product - COLGATE-PALMOLIVE COMPANY; *pg.* 504, *pg.* 1215
WILD FRONTIER - Game - WMS INDUSTRIES INC.; *pg.* 593, *pg.* 666
WILD HARVEST - Organic Foods - SUPERVALU, INC.; *pg.* 1035, *pg.* 924
WILD HONEY - Honey - MILLER'S HONEY COMPANY; *pg.* 1860, *pg.* 1759
WILD HORSE - Wine - JIM BEAM BRANDS CO.; *pg.* 1965, *pg.* 601
WILD KINGDOM - Adventure Tour - MUTUAL OF OMAHA INSURANCE COMPANY; *pg.* 1210, *pg.* 1016
WILD LIGHTNING - Game - WMS INDUSTRIES INC.; *pg.* 593, *pg.* 666
WILD MAN - Motorsports Entertainment - SPEEDWAY MOTORSPORTS, INC.; *pg.* 584, *pg.* 1370
WILD MILLIONS - Lottery Game - MASSACHUSETTS STATE LOTTERY; *pg.* 998, *pg.* 802
WILD MONEY - Lottery Game - RHODE ISLAND LOTTERY; *pg.* 1004, *pg.* 1600
WILD MOUNTAIN BLUEBERRY - Coffee - KEURIG GREEN MOUNTAIN, INC.; *pg.* 868, *pg.* 1768
WILD NEIGHBORS - Awareness Program - THE HUMANE SOCIETY OF THE UNITED STATES; *pg.* 143, *pg.* 400
WILD NUMBER BINGO - Lottery Game - OHIO LOTTERY COMMISSION; *pg.* 1002, *pg.* 1433
WILD ONES - Scissors - ACME UNITED CORPORATION; *pg.* 1040, *pg.* 346
WILD RAIN - Men's Cologne - THE GILLETTE COMPANY; *pg.* 509, *pg.* 795
WILD SAFARI - Game - WMS INDUSTRIES INC.; *pg.* 593, *pg.* 666
WILD SAPPHIRES - Slots - INTERNATIONAL GAME TECHNOLOGY; *pg.* 957, *pg.* 1024
WILD SHOT - Game - WMS INDUSTRIES INC.; *pg.* 593, *pg.* 666
WILD STAR RED WHITE & BLUE - Slots - INTERNATIONAL GAME TECHNOLOGY; *pg.* 957, *pg.* 1024
WILD STREAK - Game - WMS INDUSTRIES INC.; *pg.* 593, *pg.* 666
WILD TAXI - Video Slots - INTERNATIONAL GAME TECHNOLOGY; *pg.* 957, *pg.* 1024
WILD THING - Amusement & Water Park - CEDAR FAIR, L.P.; *pg.* 537, *pg.* 1471
WILD THING - Pulltab Game - IDAHO LOTTERY; *pg.* 995, *pg.* 547
WILD THING - Slots - INTERNATIONAL GAME TECHNOLOGY; *pg.* 957, *pg.* 1024
WILD THORNBERRYS - Toy - MATTEL, INC.; *pg.* 962, *pg.* 81
WILD-TILES - Video Game - INTERNATIONAL GAME TECHNOLOGY; *pg.* 957, *pg.* 1024
WILD VINES - Wine - E&J GALLO WINERY; *pg.* 1962, *pg.* 149
WILD WEST DOMAINS - Software - GO DADDY INC.; *pg.* 1249, *pg.* 21
WILD WILD SAFARI - Game - WMS INDUSTRIES INC.; *pg.* 593, *pg.* 666
WILD WILD WEST GAMBLING HALL AND HOTEL - Hotel & Casino - STATION CASINOS, INC.; *pg.* 585, *pg.* 1030
WILD WILDERNESS - Game - WMS INDUSTRIES INC.; *pg.* 593, *pg.* 666
WILD WIND - Hair & Skin Product - AUBREY ORGANICS INC.; *pg.* 499, *pg.* 470
WILD WING - Bird Feed - KENT NUTRITION GROUP; *pg.* 1477, *pg.* 710
WILD WINGS - Kitchen Accessories - CABELA'S INCORPORATED; *pg.* 535, *pg.* 1019
WILD WIZARD - Game - WMS INDUSTRIES INC.; *pg.* 593, *pg.* 666
WILD ZONE - Game - WMS INDUSTRIES INC.; *pg.* 593, *pg.* 666
WILDBIRD - Magazine - I-5 PUBLISHING LLC; *pg.* 1651, *pg.* 133
WILDCARD2 - Lotto Game - SOUTH DAKOTA LOTTERY; *pg.* 1006, *pg.* 1624
WILDCAT PLATESETTER - Four Page Broadsheet Platesetter - ECRM IMAGING SYSTEMS, INC.; *pg.* 1410, *pg.* 848
WILDCAT RUN - Community Name - WCI COMMUNITIES, INC.; *pg.* 1118, *pg.* 414
WILDCAT TRAIL - Bike - MARIN BIKES; *pg.* 1708, *pg.* 168
WILDERNESS - Kayaks - CONFLUENCE WATERSPORTS CO. INC.; *pg.* 1706, *pg.* 1617
WILDERNESS - Pie Fillings - PINNACLE FOODS GROUP LLC; *pg.* 889, *pg.* 1104
THE WILDERNESS EXPRESS - Cruise Ship - ROYAL CARIBBEAN CRUISES LTD; *pg.* 1921, *pg.* 446
WILDFINDER - Map-Driven Searchable Database of 26,000 Animal Species - WORLD WILDLIFE FUND, INC.; *pg.* 162, *pg.* 408
WILDFIRE - Fire Helmets - E.D. BULLARD COMPANY; *pg.*

First page reference indicates Business Class Edition
Second page reference indicates Geographic Edition

1332, *pg.* 727
WILDFIRE - Fine Dining Restaurant - LETTUCE ENTERTAIN YOU ENTERPRISES, INC.; *pg.* 1735, *pg.* 580
WILDFIRE RELEAF - Tree Planting Program - AMERICAN FORESTS; *pg.* 128, *pg.* 394
WILDFLOWER BLOSSOM - Honey - MILLER'S HONEY COMPANY; *pg.* 1860, *pg.* 1759
WILDFOWL - Magazine - RENTPATH, INC.; *pg.* 1680, *pg.* 538
WILDLAND - Headwear - MINE SAFETY APPLIANCES COMPANY; *pg.* 1361, *pg.* 1525
WILDLIFE ADVENTURE CARDS - Educational Materials - SCHOLASTIC INC.; *pg.* 1683, *pg.* 1288
WILDLIFE GALLERY - Deluxe Cards - LEANIN' TREE, INC.; *pg.* 1658, *pg.* 311
WILDLIFE TRACKS - Magazine - THE HUMANE SOCIETY OF THE UNITED STATES; *pg.* 143, *pg.* 400
WILDROOT - Hair Care Products - THE STEPHAN COMPANY; *pg.* 1597, *pg.* 426
WILDSTORM - Book & Magazine Publishing Imprint - DC COMICS, INC.; *pg.* 1633, *pg.* 1221
WILDWATER ADVENTURE - Waterpark - CEDAR FAIR, L.P.; *pg.* 537, *pg.* 1471
WILDWATER KINGDOM - Amusement & Water Park - CEDAR FAIR, L.P.; *pg.* 537, *pg.* 1471
WILDWOOD - Scarf - HERITAGE LACE INC.; *pg.* 694, *pg.* 711
WILDWOOD - Video Game - INTERNATIONAL GAME TECHNOLOGY; *pg.* 957, *pg.* 1024
WILEY INTERSCIENCE - Scientific Journals - JOHN WILEY & SONS, INC.; *pg.* 1655, *pg.* 1073
WILEY-VCH - Scientific, Technical & Medical Publications - JOHN WILEY & SONS, INC.; *pg.* 1655, *pg.* 1073
WILEY VIRTUAL - CPA Exam Review - SMARTPROS LTD.; *pg.* 1281, *pg.* 1166
WILFLEX - Lighting Product - H.E. WILLIAMS, INC.; *pg.* 1299, *pg.* 974
WILFLEX - Screen Printing Ink - POLYONE CORPORATION; *pg.* 1177, *pg.* 1404
WILIMGTON HEIGHTS - Furniture - ASHLEY FURNITURE INDUSTRIES, INC.; *pg.* 914, *pg.* 1852
WILINK - Semiconductors - TEXAS INSTRUMENTS INCORPORATED; *pg.* 679, *pg.* 1688
WILKINS - Water - THE COCA-COLA COMPANY; *pg.* 240, *pg.* 493
WILKINSON SWORD - Shaving Products - EDGEWELL PERSONAL CARE; *pg.* 1526, *pg.* 995
WILL-BURT - Masts, Telescoping, Stokers - THE WILL-BURT CO., INC.; *pg.* 1437, *pg.* 1469
WILL SNEAKER - Shoes - COACH, INC.; *pg.* 3, *pg.* 1214
WILLAMETTE VALLEY VINEYARDS - Wine - WILLAMETTE VALLEY VINEYARDS, INC.; *pg.* 1972, *pg.* 1510
WILLCOPY - Paper Product - WEYERHAEUSER COMPANY; *pg.* 121, *pg.* 1820
WILLETT - Software Product - DANAHER CORPORATION; *pg.* 1044, *pg.* 397
WILLETT - Printers - VIDEOJET TECHNOLOGIES INC.; *pg.* 489, *pg.* 671
WILLIAM HILL - Wine - JIM BEAM BRANDS CO.; *pg.* 1965, *pg.* 601
WILLIAM MORROW - Books - HARPERCOLLINS PUBLISHERS INC.; *pg.* 1647, *pg.* 1237
WILLIAM PENN - Blended Whiskey - LAIRD & COMPANY, INC.; *pg.* 1966, *pg.* 1119
WILLIAM RAST - Lifestyle Fashion Brand - SEQUENTIAL BRANDS GROUP, INC.; *pg.* 1395, *pg.* 1290
WILLIAM WORTHINGTON'S WHITE SHIELD - Beverages - MOLSON COORS BREWING COMPANY; *pg.* 256, *pg.* 321
WILLIAMS - Bulk Material Handling - ANVIL ATTACHMENTS, LLC; *pg.* 1313, *pg.* 748
WILLIAMS - Fluid Control Product - MILTON ROY COMPANY; *pg.* 1361, *pg.* 1542
WILLIAMS - Hand Tools - SNAP-ON INCORPORATED; *pg.* 1062, *pg.* 1862
WILLIAMS' - Breads - UNITED STATES BAKERY; *pg.* 907, *pg.* 1507
WILLIAMS - Slot Machines; Video Lottery Terminals - WMS INDUSTRIES INC.; *pg.* 593, *pg.* 666
WILLIAMS COUNTRY SAUSAGE - Pork Sausage - WILLIAMS SAUSAGE CO., INC.; *pg.* 910, *pg.* 1656
WILLIAMS MUG SHAVE SOAP - Powder And Cream - COMBE INCORPORATED; *pg.* 1516, *pg.* 1351
WILLIAMS OF VERMONT - Processed Food - KAYEM FOODS, INC.; *pg.* 867, *pg.* 814
WILLIAMS-SONOMA - Cookware & Tableware - WILLIAMS-SONOMA, INC.; *pg.* 1140, *pg.* 234
WILLIAMS-SONOMA HOME - Furniture - WILLIAMS-SONOMA, INC.; *pg.* 1140, *pg.* 234
WILLIAMSBURG - Museum & Related Merchandise - COLONIAL WILLIAMSBURG FOUNDATION; *pg.* 541, *pg.* 1811
THE WILLIAMSBURG - Natural Pine Swing Set - CREATIVE PLAYTHINGS LTD.; *pg.* 1831, *pg.* 820
WILLIAMSBURG - Paper - INTERNATIONAL PAPER COMPANY; *pg.* 1460, *pg.* 1644
WILLIAMSBURG - Decorative Flower - NATURAL DECORATIONS, INC.; *pg.* 936, *pg.* 5
WILLIAMSBURG - Paints - SHERWIN WILLIAMS; *pg.* 1448, *pg.* 1436
WILLIAMSBURG PURE SIMPLE TODAY - Brand Name - COLONIAL WILLIAMSBURG FOUNDATION; *pg.* 541, *pg.* 1811
WILLIAMSBURG RESERVE - Brand Name - COLONIAL WILLIAMSBURG FOUNDATION; *pg.* 541, *pg.* 1811
WILLIE G - Apparel - HARLEY-DAVIDSON, INC.; *pg.* 178, *pg.* 1874
WILLIS - Leather Product - COACH, INC.; *pg.* 3, *pg.* 1214
WILLMAR - Agricultural Sprayer - AGCO CORPORATION; *pg.* 700, *pg.* 530
WILLMAR - Windows - JELD-WEN, INC.; *pg.* 1051, *pg.* 1499
WILLOW - Textiles - BERNHARDT DESIGN; *pg.* 918, *pg.* 1381
WILLOW - Carpet - INTERFACE, INC.; *pg.* 695, *pg.* 512
WILLOW BREEZE - Ceiling Fan - WESTINGHOUSE LIGHTING CORPORATION; *pg.* 687, *pg.* 1571
WILLOW CREEK - Ceramic Tile - WALKER & ZANGER, INC.; *pg.* 119, *pg.* 281
WILLOW RIDGE - Apparel - ASCENA RETAIL GROUP, INC.; *pg.* 18, *pg.* 1081
WILLPACTOR - Impact Crusher - WILLIAMS PATENT CRUSHER & PULVERIZER CO., INC.; *pg.* 1389, *pg.* 1005
WILLY WONKA'S - Candy - NESTLE USA, INC.; *pg.* 883, *pg.* 96
WILMAR - Maintenance Products - INTERLINE BRANDS, INC.; *pg.* 1051, *pg.* 433
WILMINGTON - Table - BLATT BOWLING & BILLIARD CORP.; *pg.* 1827, *pg.* 1203
WILMINGTON - Furniture - FLEXSTEEL INDUSTRIES, INC.; *pg.* 925, *pg.* 707
WILMINGTON - Lighting Product - QUOIZEL INC.; *pg.* 1304, *pg.* 1616
WILSEAL - Teflon Tape - CHICAGO-WILCOX MFG. COMPANY, INC.; *pg.* 202, *pg.* 661
WILSHIRE - Furniture - ASHLEY FURNITURE INDUSTRIES, INC.; *pg.* 914, *pg.* 1852
WILSHIRE - Lounge Chairs - BERNHARDT DESIGN; *pg.* 918, *pg.* 1381
WILSHIRE - Beverage Dispenser - CORNELIUS INC; *pg.* 1326, *pg.* 952
WILSHIRE - Surface Material - STEELCASE INC.; *pg.* 475, *pg.* 889
WILSON - Hardness Products - INSTRON CORPORATION; *pg.* 1349, *pg.* 839
WILSON - Hardness Tester - NEWAGE TESTING INSTRUMENTS, INC.; *pg.* 1058, *pg.* 1532
WILSON - Deli Products - TYSON FOODS, INC.; *pg.* 902, *pg.* 35
WILSON - Athletic Equipment - WILSON SPORTING GOODS CO.; *pg.* 1848, *pg.* 596
WILSON JONES - Document Management - ACCO BRANDS CORPORATION; *pg.* 340, *pg.* 626
WILSON PUBLICATIONS - Publishing - PUBLICATIONS & COMMUNICATIONS, INC.; *pg.* 1678, *pg.* 1665
WILSONART - Laminates, Adhesives, Solid Surfaces & Flooring Products - WILSONART INTERNATIONAL, INC.; *pg.* 1450, *pg.* 1746
WILSON'S LEATHER - Leather Goods - G-III APPAREL GROUP, LTD.; *pg.* 41, *pg.* 1233
WILSONSNYDER - Pump - FLOWSERVE CORPORATION; *pg.* 82, *pg.* 1719
WILT-PRUF - Anti-Transpirant - WILT-PRUF PRODUCTS, INC.; *pg.* 1801, *pg.* 346
WILTON ENTERPRISES - Baking & Decorating Products - WILTON PRODUCTS, INC.; *pg.* 1140, *pg.* 672
WIMAX - Amplifiers - IXYS CORPORATION; *pg.* 422, *pg.* 146
WIMAX - Wireless Broadband - RICHARDSON ELECTRONICS, LTD.; *pg.* 667, *pg.* 622
WIMAX - Mobile Solutions - SONUS NETWORKS INC.; *pg.* 1281, *pg.* 858
WIMAX CONVERGENCE - Cable Solutions - SONUS NETWORKS INC.; *pg.* 1281, *pg.* 858
WIMAX FORUM - Wireless Network Product - AIRSPAN NETWORKS INC.; *pg.* 346, *pg.* 410
WIMAX MAGAZINE - Trade Publication - TECHNOLOGY MARKETING CORP.; *pg.* 1691, *pg.* 364
WIMEDIA - Analyzer - TELEDYNE LECROY; *pg.* 1431, *pg.* 1153
WIN 1,000 A WEEK FOR LIFE - Lottery Game - NEW YORK STATE LOTTERY; *pg.* 1001, *pg.* 1340
WIN 4 - Lottery Game - NEW YORK STATE LOTTERY; *pg.* 1001, *pg.* 1340
WIN A LATTE - Video Game - INTERNATIONAL GAME TECHNOLOGY; *pg.* 957, *pg.* 1024
WIN FOR LIFE - Lottery Game - GEORGIA LOTTERY CORPORATION; *pg.* 993, *pg.* 506
WIN FOR LIFE - Lottery Game - OHIO LOTTERY COMMISSION; *pg.* 1002, *pg.* 1433
WIN IT ALL - Lottery Game - ILLINOIS STATE LOTTERY; *pg.* 995, *pg.* 578
WIN-RECIPE - Thermal Processing Equipment - SURFACE COMBUSTION, INC.; *pg.* 1077, *pg.* 1462
WIN SCHULER'S - Food Products - WIN SCHULER FOODS; *pg.* 910, *pg.* 908
WIN-SHIELD - Shielded Windows - PARKER CHOMERICS; *pg.* 662, *pg.* 862
WINALIGN - Alignment System Software - HUNTER ENGINEERING COMPANY; *pg.* 208, *pg.* 973
WINBADGE - Photo ID System - IMAGEWARE SYSTEMS, INC.; *pg.* 412, *pg.* 203
WINBRYTE - Software - BIO-RAD LABORATORIES, INC.; *pg.* 1504, *pg.* 101
WINCAL - Software - CASCADE MICROTECH, INC.; *pg.* 1405, *pg.* 1492
WINCATS - Software Tool Displaying Database Information over Geographic Backgrounds - APPLIED GLOBAL TECHNOLOGIES; *pg.* 352, *pg.* 460
WINCHAP - Database Program - FRYE ELECTRONICS, INC.; *pg.* 1413, *pg.* 1509
WINCHESTER - Ammunition - OLIN CORPORATION; *pg.* 1176, *pg.* 976
WINCHESTER - Lighting Product - WESTINGHOUSE LIGHTING CORPORATION; *pg.* 687, *pg.* 1571
WINCON - Control Software - BTU INTERNATIONAL, INC.; *pg.* 1320, *pg.* 838
WINCONSOLE - Software System - ALCATEL-LUCENT; *pg.* 615, *pg.* 1094
WIND - Carpet - INTERFACE, INC.; *pg.* 695, *pg.* 512
WIND & WONDER - Catalog Order Services - 1-800-FLOWERS.COM, INC.; *pg.* 1758, *pg.* 1151
WIND CREST - Retirement Community - ERICKSON LIVING; *pg.* 1090, *pg.* 766
WIND DANCERS - Toy Model Horse - REEVES INTERNATIONAL, INC.; *pg.* 966, *pg.* 1108
WIND FOUNDATION CLASSES - Software - WIND RIVER SYSTEMS, INC.; *pg.* 493, *pg.* 38
WIND PRO - Fabric - 180S, LLC; *pg.* 1824, *pg.* 754
WIND RIVER - Optical Product - LEUPOLD & STEVENS, INC.; *pg.* 1420, *pg.* 1492
WIND RUNNER - Gaming Product - GLD PRODUCTS, INC.; *pg.* 1835, *pg.* 1882
WIND SONG - Fragrance - PARFUMS DE COEUR LTD.; *pg.* 519, *pg.* 376
WIND STAR - Turf Maintenance Machinery - SMITHCO, INC.; *pg.* 1377, *pg.* 1592
WIND WEB SERVER - Software - WIND RIVER SYSTEMS, INC.; *pg.* 493, *pg.* 38
WINDAU - Guard Tour Software - DETEX CORPORATION; *pg.* 633, *pg.* 1728
WINDBREAK - Apparel - SPORT OBERMEYER LTD.; *pg.* 1846, *pg.* 310
WINDBREAKER - Glove - KOMBI, LTD.; *pg.* 1838, *pg.* 1766
WINDCHILL - Software - PARAMETRIC TECHNOLOGY CORPORATION; *pg.* 452, *pg.* 835
WINDCONFIG - Software - WIND RIVER SYSTEMS, INC.; *pg.* 493, *pg.* 38
WINDCONNECT - Print Server Product - TROY GROUP INC.; *pg.* 485, *pg.* 71
WINDCONNECT II - Wireless Printer Adapter - TROY GROUP INC.; *pg.* 485, *pg.* 71
WINDEMERE - Wallcovering - YORK WALLCOVERINGS INC.; *pg.* 947, *pg.* 1598
WINDEO - Chipset - SIGMA DESIGNS, INC.; *pg.* 469, *pg.* 148

WINDEX - Cleaning Product - S.C. JOHNSON & SON, INC.; *pg.* 334, *pg.* 1889
WINDEX BEST ON GLASS - Cleaner - S.C. JOHNSON & SON, INC.; *pg.* 334, *pg.* 1889
WINDEX GLASS AND SURFACE WIPE - Cleaner - S.C. JOHNSON & SON, INC.; *pg.* 334, *pg.* 1889
WINDEX KITCHEN & GLASS - Cleaner - S.C. JOHNSON & SON, INC.; *pg.* 334, *pg.* 1889
WINDEX MOUNTAIN BERRY - Cleaner - S.C. JOHNSON & SON, INC.; *pg.* 334, *pg.* 1889
WINDEX NO DRIP - Cleaner - S.C. JOHNSON & SON, INC.; *pg.* 334, *pg.* 1889
WINDEX OUTDOOR - Cleaner - S.C. JOHNSON & SON, INC.; *pg.* 334, *pg.* 1889
WINDEX POWERIZED FOAMING - Cleaner - S.C. JOHNSON & SON, INC.; *pg.* 334, *pg.* 1889
WINDEX SPARKLING ORANGE - Cleaner - S.C. JOHNSON & SON, INC.; *pg.* 334, *pg.* 1889
WINDEX VINEGAR - Cleaner - S.C. JOHNSON & SON, INC.; *pg.* 334, *pg.* 1889
WINDEX VINEGAR WIPE - Cleaner - S.C. JOHNSON & SON, INC.; *pg.* 334, *pg.* 1889
WINDFLOW BLADE - Rear Air Deflector - LUND INTERNATIONAL, INC.; *pg.* 211, *pg.* 526
WINDHAM - Furniture - ASHLEY FURNITURE INDUSTRIES, INC.; *pg.* 914, *pg.* 1852
WINDHAM - Lighting - ETHAN ALLEN INTERIORS INC.; *pg.* 924, *pg.* 343
WINDHAM - Furniture - LA-Z-BOY INCORPORATED; *pg.* 932, *pg.* 901
WINDHAM - Furniture - TELESCOPE CASUAL FURNITURE INC.; *pg.* 944, *pg.* 1162
WINDHAM SLING - Indoor/Outdoor Casual Aluminum Furniture - TELESCOPE CASUAL FURNITURE INC.; *pg.* 944, *pg.* 1162
WINDJET - Spray Product - SPRAYING SYSTEMS CO.; *pg.* 1063, *pg.* 670
WINDLINK - Software - WIND RIVER SYSTEMS, INC.; *pg.* 493, *pg.* 38
WINDMANAGE - Software - WIND RIVER SYSTEMS, INC.; *pg.* 493, *pg.* 38
WINDMILL - Window Treatment - HERITAGE LACE INC.; *pg.* 694, *pg.* 711
WINDML - Software - WIND RIVER SYSTEMS, INC.; *pg.* 493, *pg.* 38
WINDNET - Software - WIND RIVER SYSTEMS, INC.; *pg.* 493, *pg.* 38
WINDO BRITE - Cleaning Preparation - WALTER G. LEGGE COMPANY, INC.; *pg.* 337, *pg.* 1321
WINDO-CLEAN - Cleaning Product - HILLYARD, INC.; *pg.* 331, *pg.* 990
WINDO-WELD - Auto Window Sealers & Primer, Sealant - 3M COMPANY; *pg.* 1142, *pg.* 956
WINDOGRAF - Chart & Marking System - GRAPHIC CONTROLS LLC; *pg.* 401, *pg.* 1148
WINDOW CLEAR - Window Cleaner - BLUE CROSS LABORATORIES; *pg.* 326, *pg.* 277
WINDOW JETKLEER - Window Cleaner - PENETONE CORPORATION; *pg.* 333, *pg.* 1050
WINDOW OF CARE - Pharmaceutical Product - ALERE INC.; *pg.* 1488, *pg.* 849
WINDOW WASHER - Software - WEBROOT SOFTWARE, INC.; *pg.* 1289, *pg.* 313
WINDOWGRIP - Telescoping Mount - PANAVISE PRODUCTS, INC.; *pg.* 1058, *pg.* 1032
WINDOWPANE - Women's Clothing & Accessories - WOODEN SHIPS OF HOBOKEN; *pg.* 35, *pg.* 1315
WINDOWRITER - Electronic Display System - TRANS-LUX CORPORATION; *pg.* 681, *pg.* 365
WINDOWS 7 - Operating System - MICROSOFT CORPORATION; *pg.* 435, *pg.* 1824
WINDOWS 8.1 - Computer Operating System - MICROSOFT CORPORATION; *pg.* 435, *pg.* 1824
WINDOWS AZURE - Application Development & Hosting - MICROSOFT CORPORATION; *pg.* 435, *pg.* 1824
WINDOWS COMPATIBILITY CENTER - Software - MICROSOFT CORPORATION; *pg.* 435, *pg.* 1824
WINDOWS DEVELOPER'S JOURNAL - Magazine - UNITED BUSINESS MEDIA LLC; *pg.* 1697, *pg.* 1177
WINDOWS - HEALING AND HELPING THROUGH LOSS - Educational Program - ACTIVE PARENTING PUBLISHERS; *pg.* 1613, *pg.* 535
WINDOWS INTUNE - Computer Software - MICROSOFT CORPORATION; *pg.* 435, *pg.* 1824
WINDOWS MEDIA CENTER - Software - MICROSOFT CORPORATION; *pg.* 435, *pg.* 1824
WINDOWS MEDIA PLAYER - Software - MICROSOFT CORPORATION; *pg.* 435, *pg.* 1824
WINDOWS PHONE - Smart Phone - MICROSOFT CORPORATION; *pg.* 435, *pg.* 1824
WINDOWS RT 8.1 - Operating System - MICROSOFT CORPORATION; *pg.* 435, *pg.* 1824
WINDOWS SERVER - Operating System - MICROSOFT CORPORATION; *pg.* 435, *pg.* 1824
WINDPORT - Wireless Printer Adapter - TROY GROUP INC.; *pg.* 485, *pg.* 71
WINDPOWER - Software - WIND RIVER SYSTEMS, INC.; *pg.* 493, *pg.* 38
WINDS - Computer Software - LCC INTERNATIONAL, INC.; *pg.* 651, *pg.* 1792
WINDSCAPES - Food Product - SHAMROCK FOODS COMPANY; *pg.* 895, *pg.* 20
WINDSH - Software - WIND RIVER SYSTEMS, INC.; *pg.* 493, *pg.* 38
WINDSHEAR - Carpet Dryer - TORNADO INDUSTRIES, INC.; *pg.* 1383, *pg.* 591
WINDSOR - Table - BLATT BOWLING & BILLIARD CORP.; *pg.* 1827, *pg.* 1203
WINDSOR - Medical Cabinet - BLICKMAN HEALTH INDUSTRIES, INC.; *pg.* 1506, *pg.* 1051
WINDSOR - Saw Chain - BLOUNT INTERNATIONAL, INC.; *pg.* 1043, *pg.* 1501
WINDSOR - Flavour - CARGILL LIMITED; *pg.* 1475, *pg.* 1914
WINDSOR - Brick & Tile Product - CHEROKEE BRICK & TILE COMPANY; *pg.* 75, *pg.* 535
WINDSOR - Salt - DOW CHEMICAL; *pg.* 1156, *pg.* 1563
WINDSOR - Footwear - EASTLAND SHOE CORPORATION; *pg.* 1808, *pg.* 750
WINDSOR - Furniture - ETHAN ALLEN INTERIORS INC.; *pg.* 924, *pg.* 343
WINDSOR - Scarf - HERITAGE LACE INC.; *pg.* 694, *pg.* 711
WINDSOR - Whiskey - JIM BEAM BRANDS CO.; *pg.* 1965, *pg.* 601
WINDSOR - Furniture - JOFCO INC.; *pg.* 931, *pg.* 691
WINDSOR - Fabric - NEMSCHOFF, INC.; *pg.* 936, *pg.* 1890
WINDSOR - In-Ground Vinyl Pools - POOL CORPORATION; *pg.* 1843, *pg.* 743
WINDSOR - Footwear - P.W. MINOR & SON, INC.; *pg.* 1816, *pg.* 1140
WINDSOR FROZEN FOODS - Food Product - WINDSOR QUALITY FOOD CO., LTD.; *pg.* 910, *pg.* 1717
WINDSOR SALT - Industrial Material - DOW CHEMICAL; *pg.* 1156, *pg.* 1563
WINDSPOILER - Premium Design Wiper Blades - TRICO PRODUCTS CORPORATION; *pg.* 220, *pg.* 905
WINDSPORT - Golf Accessories - CALLAWAY GOLF COMPANY; *pg.* 1829, *pg.* 58
WINDSTOPPER - Glove Liner - KOMBI, LTD.; *pg.* 1838, *pg.* 1766
WINDSTOPPER - Fishing Gear Product - SIMMS FISHING PRODUCTS CORP.; *pg.* 1845, *pg.* 1008
WINDSTOPPER - Fabric - W.L. GORE & ASSOCIATES, INC.; *pg.* 122, *pg.* 388
WINDSTOPPER N2S - Fabric - W.L. GORE & ASSOCIATES, INC.; *pg.* 122, *pg.* 388
WINDSTORM - Software - WIND RIVER SYSTEMS, INC.; *pg.* 493, *pg.* 38
WINDSURF - Software - WIND RIVER SYSTEMS, INC.; *pg.* 493, *pg.* 38
WINDSURFING - Magazine - BONNIER CORPORATION; *pg.* 1622, *pg.* 480
WINDTRICITY - Utility Program - CPS ENERGY; *pg.* 1939, *pg.* 1739
WINDVIEW - Software - WIND RIVER SYSTEMS, INC.; *pg.* 493, *pg.* 38
WINDWARD - Eyewear - MAUI JIM, INC.; *pg.* 9, *pg.* 651
WINDWARD - Furniture - TELESCOPE CASUAL FURNITURE INC.; *pg.* 944, *pg.* 1162
WINDWAY - Kitchenware - THE VOLLRATH COMPANY LLC; *pg.* 1139, *pg.* 1894
WINDY CITY PRETTY - Nail Care Product - OPI PRODUCTS INC.; *pg.* 518, *pg.* 167
WINE AWAY - Red Wine Stain Remover - EVERGREEN LABS, INC.; *pg.* 330, *pg.* 1847
WINE COUNTRY - Video Game - INTERNATIONAL GAME TECHNOLOGY; *pg.* 957, *pg.* 1024
WINE CUBE - Wine - TARGET CORPORATION; *pg.* 1786, *pg.* 942
WINE FOR THE SPIRIT - Fund Raising Services - OAKWOOD HEALTHCARE, INC.; *pg.* 1577, *pg.* 878
WINELINE - Hose - THE GOODYEAR TIRE & RUBBER COMPANY; *pg.* 1883, *pg.* 1401
WINERGY - Petcare Product - MARS, INCORPORATED; *pg.* 1858, *pg.* 1792
WINESTEWARD - Cooler - DACOR; *pg.* 54, *pg.* 67
WINETASTING NETWORK - Wines Network - 1-800-FLOWERS.COM, INC.; *pg.* 1758, *pg.* 1151
WINETASTING.COM - Website - 1-800-FLOWERS.COM, INC.; *pg.* 1758, *pg.* 1151
WINFAX - Software - SYMANTEC CORPORATION; *pg.* 478, *pg.* 161
WING - Heat Recovery Equipment - MESTEK, INC.; *pg.* 1074, *pg.* 857
WING COMMAND - Pest Elimination System - ECOLAB INC.; *pg.* 329, *pg.* 960
WING COMMANDER - Video Game - ELECTRONIC ARTS INC.; *pg.* 951, *pg.* 189
WING DEFENSER - Toy & Game - HASBRO, INC.; *pg.* 954, *pg.* 1603
WING-DINGS - Poultry Products - PILGRIM'S PRIDE CORPORATION; *pg.* 889, *pg.* 330
WING-FIL - Tire Filling Compound - THE GOODYEAR TIRE & RUBBER COMPANY; *pg.* 1883, *pg.* 1401
WING NUT - Wire Connectors - IDEAL INDUSTRIES, INC.; *pg.* 1051, *pg.* 662
WING-SHOK - Ammunition - FEDERAL PREMIUM AMMUNITION; *pg.* 1834, *pg.* 915
WING ZINGS - Poultry Product - PILGRIM'S PRIDE CORPORATION; *pg.* 889, *pg.* 330
WINGAMAJIG - Food Kiosk Services - TYSON FOODS, INC.; *pg.* 902, *pg.* 35
WINGATE - Hotels - WYNDHAM WORLDWIDE CORPORATION; *pg.* 1119, *pg.* 1107
WINGATE INN - Hotels - WYNDHAM WORLDWIDE CORPORATION; *pg.* 1119, *pg.* 1107
WINGATHER - Software - BROOKFIELD ENGINEERING LABORATORIES, INC.; *pg.* 1403, *pg.* 833
WINGCURE - Cure Blend For SBR - THE GOODYEAR TIRE & RUBBER COMPANY; *pg.* 1883, *pg.* 1401
WINGFOOT - Tire - THE GOODYEAR TIRE & RUBBER COMPANY; *pg.* 1883, *pg.* 1401
WINGHAM - Shoes - ALLEN-EDMONDS SHOE CORP.; *pg.* 1804, *pg.* 1887
WINGMASTER - Ammunition - REMINGTON ARMS COMPANY, LLC; *pg.* 1844, *pg.* 1382
WINGS - Fragrance - ELIZABETH ARDEN, INC.; *pg.* 507, *pg.* 448
WINGS - Chicken Wings - KFC CORPORATION; *pg.* 1733, *pg.* 735
WINGS - Protective Eyewear - SELLSTROM MANUFACTURING CO.; *pg.* 1428, *pg.* 659
WINGS - Polyurethane Foam - SPAN-AMERICA MEDICAL SYSTEMS, INC.; *pg.* 1595, *pg.* 1618
WINGS BEERS SPORTS ALL THE ESSENTIALS - Tagline - BUFFALO WILD WINGS, INC.; *pg.* 1718, *pg.* 931
WINGS BOOKS - Publishing Imprint - PENGUIN RANDOM HOUSE; *pg.* 1675, *pg.* 1276
WINGS OF FIRE - Further-Processed Poultry Items - TYSON FOODS, INC.; *pg.* 902, *pg.* 35
WINGS ON THE FLY - Service Mark - TYSON FOODS, INC.; *pg.* 902, *pg.* 35
WINGSATIONS - Chicken Wings - PILGRIM'S PRIDE CORPORATION; *pg.* 889, *pg.* 330
WINGSTAY - Rubber Products - THE GOODYEAR TIRE & RUBBER COMPANY; *pg.* 1883, *pg.* 1401
WINGSTOP - Polymar Short Stop - THE GOODYEAR TIRE & RUBBER COMPANY; *pg.* 1883, *pg.* 1401
WINGTACK - C-5 Hydrocarbon Resin - THE GOODYEAR TIRE & RUBBER COMPANY; *pg.* 1883, *pg.* 1401
WINGTWIST - Screw-On Connector - IDEAL INDUSTRIES, INC.; *pg.* 1051, *pg.* 662
WINGUARD - Frame - PGT, INC.; *pg.* 104, *pg.* 452
WINHEAT - Software - GULF PUBLISHING COMPANY; *pg.* 1646, *pg.* 1707
WINK - Beverages - THE COCA-COLA COMPANY; *pg.* 240, *pg.* 493
WINKLER BAKERY - Dry Ingredient - OLD SALEM, INCORPORATED; *pg.* 572, *pg.* 1395
WINKS - Convenience Store & Gas Station - ALIMENTATION COUCHE-TARD INC.; *pg.* 1013, *pg.* 1951
WINMARK BUSINESS SOLUTIONS - Online Resource - WINMARK CORPORATION; *pg.* 1792, *pg.* 946
WINMARK CAPITAL - Finance Services - WINMARK CORPORATION; *pg.* 1792, *pg.* 946
WINMAU - Sporting Good Product - ESCALADE INC.; *pg.*

First page reference indicates Business Class Edition
Second page reference indicates Geographic Edition

1833, *pg.* 678
WINMELT - Software - BIO-RAD LABORATORIES, INC.; *pg.* 1504, *pg.* 101
WINMON - Graphical User Interface - S&C ELECTRIC COMPANY; *pg.* 1305, *pg.* 589
WINN-DIXIE - Supermarkets - WINN DIXIE STORES, INC.; *pg.* 1038, *pg.* 435
WINNAT - Software - WIND RIVER SYSTEMS, INC.; *pg.* 493, *pg.* 38
WINNEBAGO - Recreation Vehicle - WINNEBAGO INDUSTRIES, INC.; *pg.* 1712, *pg.* 707
WINNER - Cameras - EASTMAN KODAK COMPANY; *pg.* 1408, *pg.* 1333
WINNER GOLD - Printing Plates - EASTMAN KODAK COMPANY; *pg.* 1408, *pg.* 1333
WINNER GREEN - Lottery Game - MASSACHUSETTS STATE LOTTERY; *pg.* 998, *pg.* 802
WINNER TAKE ALL - Lottery Game - MASSACHUSETTS STATE LOTTERY; *pg.* 998, *pg.* 802
WINNERS CIRCLE - Rewards Program - CAESARS ENTERTAINMENT CORPORATION; *pg.* 1083, *pg.* 1023
WINNERS NETWORK - Game - WMS INDUSTRIES INC.; *pg.* 593, *pg.* 666
WINNING BID - Game - WMS INDUSTRIES INC.; *pg.* 593, *pg.* 666
WINNING STREAK - Game - WMS INDUSTRIES INC.; *pg.* 593, *pg.* 666
WINNING TARGET - Video Game - INTERNATIONAL GAME TECHNOLOGY; *pg.* 957, *pg.* 1024
WINNING THE FIGHT AGAINST CANCER, EVERYDAY - Slogan - CANCER TREATMENT CENTERS OF AMERICA; *pg.* 1511, *pg.* 410
WINNING THROUGH INNOVATION - Tagline - ARI NETWORK SERVICES, INC.; *pg.* 353, *pg.* 1873
WINNING TOUCH - Video Game - INTERNATIONAL GAME TECHNOLOGY; *pg.* 957, *pg.* 1024
WINNING VALUE - Wireless Communication System - AT&T SOUTHEAST; *pg.* 1868, *pg.* 489
WINNOX - Burner - ECLIPSE INC.; *pg.* 1332, *pg.* 655
WINNOZL - Software - BENTLEY SYSTEMS, INC.; *pg.* 361, *pg.* 1531
WINOMS CS - Software - EASTMAN KODAK COMPANY; *pg.* 1408, *pg.* 1333
WINPATH - Hardware Product - INTERPHASE CORPORATION; *pg.* 420, *pg.* 1732
WINPHLASH - Software - PHOENIX TECHNOLOGIES LTD.; *pg.* 454, *pg.* 147
WINPLATE - Software - IDEXX LABORATORIES, INC.; *pg.* 1543, *pg.* 753
WINPOET - Software - WIND RIVER SYSTEMS, INC.; *pg.* 493, *pg.* 38
WINRACE DATABASE - Software - ASPEN TECHNOLOGY, INC.; *pg.* 354, *pg.* 804
WINS-FIS - Financial Information System - AVEMCO INSURANCE COMPANY; *pg.* 1194, *pg.* 769
WINSIGHT - Computer Applications - DELTEK, INC.; *pg.* 386, *pg.* 1784
WINSLET - Lighting Product - QUOIZEL INC.; *pg.* 1304, *pg.* 1616
WINSLET - Bathroom Accessories - SYMMONS INDUSTRIES, INC.; *pg.* 114, *pg.* 803
WINSLOW - Furniture - ASHLEY FURNITURE INDUSTRIES, INC.; *pg.* 914, *pg.* 1852
WINSLOW - Fabric - NEMSCHOFF, INC.; *pg.* 936, *pg.* 1890
WINSMITH - Software - GULF PUBLISHING COMPANY; *pg.* 1646, *pg.* 1707
WINSOR PILATES - Fitness Program - GUTHY-RENKER LLC; *pg.* 289, *pg.* 273
WINSTON - Furniture - BROWN JORDAN INTERNATIONAL COMPANY; *pg.* 919, *pg.* 740
WINSTON-SALEM JOURNAL - Daily Newspaper - MEDIA GENERAL, INC.; *pg.* 297, *pg.* 1803
WINTEGRA - Hardware Product - INTERPHASE CORPORATION; *pg.* 420, *pg.* 1732
WINTER ALE - Seasonal Beer - THE BROOKLYN BREWERY; *pg.* 239, *pg.* 1145
WINTER BREW - Beverage - SPRECHER BREWING COMPANY; *pg.* 265, *pg.* 1858
WINTER DOUBLE DOUBLER - Scratch Lottery Game - IDAHO LOTTERY; *pg.* 995, *pg.* 547
WINTER GARDEN - Seating Product - IRWIN SEATING COMPANY INC.; *pg.* 929, *pg.* 887
WINTER-GLO - Red PVC Fabric - STANDARD SAFETY EQUIPMENT CO.; *pg.* 1379, *pg.* 632
WINTER-GLO-20 - Heavyweight Red PVC Fabric - STANDARD SAFETY EQUIPMENT CO.; *pg.* 1379, *pg.* 632
WINTER GREENS - Scarf - HERITAGE LACE INC.; *pg.* 694, *pg.* 711
WINTER HARVEST - Paintbrushes - MARTIN/F. WEBER COMPANY; *pg.* 962, *pg.* 1567
WINTER PRO 250 - Glove - 180S, LLC; *pg.* 1824, *pg.* 754
WINTER PRO 475 - Glove - 180S, LLC; *pg.* 1824, *pg.* 754
WINTER PRO 475 HV - Glove - 180S, LLC; *pg.* 1824, *pg.* 754
WINTER PRO 650X - Glove - 180S, LLC; *pg.* 1824, *pg.* 754
WINTER PRO 850X - Glove - 180S, LLC; *pg.* 1824, *pg.* 754
WINTER PRO 875 - Glove - 180S, LLC; *pg.* 1824, *pg.* 754
WINTER-SLIX - Silicone Fluid - DELTA FOREMOST CHEMICAL CORPORATION; *pg.* 1155, *pg.* 1642
WINTER WALKER - Snowshoes - L.L. BEAN, INC.; *pg.* 1777, *pg.* 750
WINTER WELLNESS - Nutritional Supplement - PHARMAVITE LLC; *pg.* 1584, *pg.* 167
WINTER X GAMES - Extreme Winter Sports Tournament - ESPN, INC.; *pg.* 285, *pg.* 340
WINTERFRESH - Gum - WM. WRIGLEY JR. COMPANY; *pg.* 1863, *pg.* 596
WINTERGREEN - Scent - PETEDGE; *pg.* 1481, *pg.* 787
WINTERGREEN XTREME - Moist Tobacco - AMERICAN SNUFF COMPANY; *pg.* 1893, *pg.* 1641
WINTERHAVEN - Furniture - STANLEY FURNITURE CO., INC.; *pg.* 943, *pg.* 1379
WINTERHOOK - Beverage - CRAFT BREWERS ALLIANCE, INC; *pg.* 247, *pg.* 1502
WINTERIZER - Lawn Fertilizer - THE SCOTTS MIRACLE-GRO COMPANY; *pg.* 1799, *pg.* 1459
WINTERMINT - Fabric - NEMSCHOFF, INC.; *pg.* 936, *pg.* 1890
WINTERSHIELD - Grille Cover - LUND INTERNATIONAL, INC.; *pg.* 211, *pg.* 526
WINTERSOF - Glove - ACUSHNET COMPANY; *pg.* 1824, *pg.* 818
WINTHROPE - Guest Chairs - BERNHARDT DESIGN; *pg.* 918, *pg.* 1381
WINTOMS - Software - KENNAMETAL INC.; *pg.* 1052, *pg.* 1547
WINTUK - Commercial Knitting Yarn - NATIONAL SPINNING COMPANY, INC.; *pg.* 697, *pg.* 1265
WINTV - Digital Video Product - HAUPPAUGE DIGITAL, INC.; *pg.* 402, *pg.* 1164
WINTV-D - TV Receiver - HAUPPAUGE DIGITAL, INC.; *pg.* 402, *pg.* 1164
WINTV-DBX - TV Receiver - HAUPPAUGE DIGITAL, INC.; *pg.* 402, *pg.* 1164
WINTV-GO - TV Receiver - HAUPPAUGE DIGITAL, INC.; *pg.* 402, *pg.* 1164
WINTV-GO-FM - Digital Video Product - HAUPPAUGE DIGITAL, INC.; *pg.* 402, *pg.* 1164
WINTV-GO-PLUS - Digital Video Product - HAUPPAUGE DIGITAL, INC.; *pg.* 402, *pg.* 1164
WINTV-HD - Video Product - HAUPPAUGE DIGITAL, INC.; *pg.* 402, *pg.* 1164
WINTV HVR - Digital Video Product - HAUPPAUGE DIGITAL, INC.; *pg.* 402, *pg.* 1164
WINTV-HVR-950Q - Digital Video Product - HAUPPAUGE DIGITAL, INC.; *pg.* 402, *pg.* 1164
WINTV-NEXUS-S - TV Receiver - HAUPPAUGE DIGITAL, INC.; *pg.* 402, *pg.* 1164
WINTV-NOVA-S PCI - TV Receiver - HAUPPAUGE DIGITAL, INC.; *pg.* 402, *pg.* 1164
WINTV-NOVA-S USB - TV Receiver - HAUPPAUGE DIGITAL, INC.; *pg.* 402, *pg.* 1164
WINTV-NOVA-T PCI - TV Receiver - HAUPPAUGE DIGITAL, INC.; *pg.* 402, *pg.* 1164
WINTV-PVR - Digital Video Product - HAUPPAUGE DIGITAL, INC.; *pg.* 402, *pg.* 1164
WINTV-PVR-250 - Video Recorder - HAUPPAUGE DIGITAL, INC.; *pg.* 402, *pg.* 1164
WINTV-PVR-250MCE - Video Recorder - HAUPPAUGE DIGITAL, INC.; *pg.* 402, *pg.* 1164
WINTV-PVR-350 - Video Recorder - HAUPPAUGE DIGITAL, INC.; *pg.* 402, *pg.* 1164
WINTV-PVR-USB - TV Receiver - HAUPPAUGE DIGITAL, INC.; *pg.* 402, *pg.* 1164
WINTV-RADIO - Digital Video Product - HAUPPAUGE DIGITAL, INC.; *pg.* 402, *pg.* 1164
WINTV-THEATER - TV Receiver - HAUPPAUGE DIGITAL, INC.; *pg.* 402, *pg.* 1164
WINTV-USB - Digital Video Product - HAUPPAUGE DIGITAL, INC.; *pg.* 402, *pg.* 1164
WINTV-USB-FM - Digital Video Product - HAUPPAUGE DIGITAL, INC.; *pg.* 402, *pg.* 1164
WINTV-USB2 - Digital Video Product - HAUPPAUGE DIGITAL, INC.; *pg.* 402, *pg.* 1164
WINVPN - Software - WIND RIVER SYSTEMS, INC.; *pg.* 493, *pg.* 38
WINX - Toy - MATTEL, INC.; *pg.* 962, *pg.* 81
WIP - Integrated RFID System - BROOKS AUTOMATION, INC.; *pg.* 1320, *pg.* 813
WIP BALM - Sandals - AEROGROUP INTERNATIONAL, INC.; *pg.* 1803, *pg.* 1055
WIPEDISK - Software - SYMANTEC CORPORATION; *pg.* 478, *pg.* 161
WIPEFILE - Software - SYMANTEC CORPORATION; *pg.* 478, *pg.* 161
WIPEOUT - Cleaning Preparation - STAGESTEP INC.; *pg.* 1688, *pg.* 1570
WIPING WOOD - Stain - MOHAWK FINISHING PRODUCTS, INC.; *pg.* 1173, *pg.* 1378
WIPLL - Wireless Network Product - AIRSPAN NETWORKS INC.; *pg.* 346, *pg.* 410
WIPMANAGE - Wireless Network Product - AIRSPAN NETWORKS INC.; *pg.* 346, *pg.* 410
WIPORT - Electronic Device - LANTRONIX, INC.; *pg.* 426, *pg.* 112
WIRE - Networking Software - AUTODESK INC.; *pg.* 356, *pg.* 257
THE WIRE - Cable Television Show - HOME BOX OFFICE, INC.; *pg.* 290, *pg.* 1240
WIRE BASKET TRAY - Wiring System - WIREMOLD/LEGRAND; *pg.* 689, *pg.* 383
WIRE GEM - Commercial Lighting - SWIVELIER CO., INC.; *pg.* 1307, *pg.* 1142
WIRE LUBE - Wire Pulling Lubricant - IDEAL INDUSTRIES, INC.; *pg.* 1051, *pg.* 662
WIRE-NUT - Wire Connector - IDEAL INDUSTRIES, INC.; *pg.* 1051, *pg.* 662
WIRE SKULL - Apparel - OAKLEY, INC.; *pg.* 1840, *pg.* 86
WIRE TAP - Frames - OAKLEY, INC.; *pg.* 1840, *pg.* 86
WIRE TRAP-LITE - Electronic Components - MOLEX INCORPORATED; *pg.* 655, *pg.* 628
WIRE TWIST - Screw-On-Connector - IDEAL INDUSTRIES, INC.; *pg.* 1051, *pg.* 662
WIREBOUND BOOK - Design - SCHOLASTIC INC.; *pg.* 1683, *pg.* 1288
WIRECO - Wire Rope - WIRECO WORLDGROUP; *pg.* 1389, *pg.* 987
WIRED - Magazine - CONDE NAST PUBLICATIONS, INC.; *pg.* 1629, *pg.* 1217
WIREDSCHOLAR - Magazine - SLM CORPORATION; *pg.* 804, *pg.* 388
WIREHAWK - Circuit Tester - THEXTON MANUFACTURING COMPANY, INC.; *pg.* 218, *pg.* 925
WIRELESS ADAPTIVE - Dual Sensor - NAPCO SECURITY SYSTEMS, INC.; *pg.* 658, *pg.* 1138
WIRELESS & EMAIL ALERTS - Software - MONEY.NET, INC.; *pg.* 1268, *pg.* 1261
WIRELESS ASSET NET - Software - I.D. SYSTEMS, INC.; *pg.* 643, *pg.* 1134
WIRELESS DESIGN & DEVELOPMENT - Trade Magazine - ADVANTAGE BUSINESS MEDIA; *pg.* 1613, *pg.* 1116
THE WIRELESS GUIDE - Knowledge Tool - TESSCO TECHNOLOGIES, INC.; *pg.* 679, *pg.* 773
WIRELESS INTELLIGENT GATEWAY - Multimedia Messaging - TELECOMMUNICATION SYSTEMS INC.; *pg.* 483, *pg.* 754
WIRELESS INTERACTION CLIENT - Software - INTERACTIVE INTELLIGENCE, INC.; *pg.* 417, *pg.* 687
THE WIRELESS JOURNAL - Journal - TESSCO TECHNOLOGIES, INC.; *pg.* 679, *pg.* 773
WIRELESS SOLUTIONS - Wireless Networking Applications - TESSCO TECHNOLOGIES, INC.; *pg.* 679, *pg.* 773
WIRELESS TECHNOLOGIES TO MOVE YOUR IDEAS - Tag Line - INTERDIGITAL, INC.; *pg.* 1872, *pg.* 1543
WIRELESS TETHER - Toy Train - LIONEL LLC; *pg.* 961, *pg.* 875
THE WIRELESS UPDATE - E-Newsletter - TESSCO TECHNOLOGIES, INC.; *pg.* 679, *pg.* 773
WIRELESS WEEK - Trade Magazine - ADVANTAGE BUSINESS MEDIA; *pg.* 1613, *pg.* 1116
WIRELESSAIR - Advanced Integrated Remote - AIR LIFT COMPANY; *pg.* 198, *pg.* 895
WIRELESSHID - Wireless Solution - CYPRESS SEMICONDUCTOR CORPORATION; *pg.* 1326, *pg.* 243

WIRELESSINFO - PCS, Paging, SMR & Data Provider Map - PITNEY BOWES SOFTWARE INC.; *pg.* 455, *pg.* 1346
WIRELESSLON - Wireless Solution - CYPRESS SEMICONDUCTOR CORPORATION; *pg.* 1326, *pg.* 243
WIRELESSUSB - Wireless Solution - CYPRESS SEMICONDUCTOR CORPORATION; *pg.* 1326, *pg.* 243
WIRELESSUSB LR - Wireless Solution - CYPRESS SEMICONDUCTOR CORPORATION; *pg.* 1326, *pg.* 243
WIRELESSUSB LS - Wireless Solution - CYPRESS SEMICONDUCTOR CORPORATION; *pg.* 1326, *pg.* 243
WIRELINK - Automatic Connection Equipment - MACLEAN-FOGG COMPANY INC.; *pg.* 1358, *pg.* 635
WIREMASTER - Plier - CHANNELLOCK, INC.; *pg.* 1044, *pg.* 1551
WIREPROTECT - Insurance - PAN-AMERICAN LIFE INSURANCE COMPANY; *pg.* 1213, *pg.* 747
WIRETAP - Client Server Access Protocol - AUTODESK INC.; *pg.* 356, *pg.* 257
WIRETAP - Eyewear - OAKLEY, INC.; *pg.* 1840, *pg.* 86
WIRETAPCENTRAL - Software - AUTODESK INC.; *pg.* 356, *pg.* 257
WIREUP - Upgrade Wiring Products - PASS & SEYMOUR/LEGRAND; *pg.* 1303, *pg.* 1344
WIREVISE - Automatic Connection Equipment - MACLEAN-FOGG COMPANY INC.; *pg.* 1358, *pg.* 635
WIREWAY - Wiring System - WIREMOLD/LEGRAND; *pg.* 689, *pg.* 383
WIRTH - Steel Products - RUSSEL METALS INC.; *pg.* 1180, *pg.* 1928
WIRTH BUSINESS CREDIT - Finance Services - WINMARK CORPORATION; *pg.* 1792, *pg.* 946
WISCO - Window Envelopes - CENVEO INC.; *pg.* 1626, *pg.* 372
WISCONSIN DELLS EVENTS - Publication - MADISON NEWSPAPERS, INC.; *pg.* 1661, *pg.* 1866
WISCONSIN ENERGY - Water System - WEC ENERGY GROUP, INC.; *pg.* 1954, *pg.* 1881
WISCONSIN FORMULA - Personal Defense Sprays - MACE SECURITY INTERNATIONAL, INC.; *pg.* 1172, *pg.* 1541
WISCONSIN PUBLIC RADIO - Telecommunication Service - WISCONSIN EDUCATIONAL COMMUNICATIONS BOARD; *pg.* 321, *pg.* 1868
WISCONSIN PUBLIC TELEVISION - Telecommunication Service - WISCONSIN EDUCATIONAL COMMUNICATIONS BOARD; *pg.* 321, *pg.* 1868
WISCONSIN STATE JOURNAL - Newspaper - MADISON NEWSPAPERS, INC.; *pg.* 1661, *pg.* 1866
WISDOM - Liposomal Technology - IDEXX LABORATORIES, INC.; *pg.* 1543, *pg.* 753
WISDOM - Fabric - NEMSCHOFF, INC.; *pg.* 936, *pg.* 1890
WISDOM - Goggle - OAKLEY, INC.; *pg.* 1840, *pg.* 86
WISDOM - Healthcare Product - SWANSON HEALTH PRODUCTS INC.; *pg.* 1600, *pg.* 1397
WISDOM & WARTER - Sherry - BANFI VINTNERS; *pg.* 1957, *pg.* 1161
WISDOM GOLD - Software - OWENS & MINOR, INC.; *pg.* 1579, *pg.* 1795
WISE - Software - SYMANTEC CORPORATION; *pg.* 478, *pg.* 161
W.I.S.E. - WorkPlace Insurance For Employees - UTICA MUTUAL INSURANCE COMPANY; *pg.* 1222, *pg.* 1183
WISE EYES - Program - DEVON ENERGY CORPORATION; *pg.* 975, *pg.* 1485
WISE PACKAGE STUDIO - Software - SYMANTEC CORPORATION; *pg.* 478, *pg.* 161
WISE SOLUTIONS - Software - SYMANTEC CORPORATION; *pg.* 478, *pg.* 161
WISEGUIDE - Medical Device - BOSTON SCIENTIFIC CORPORATION; *pg.* 1508, *pg.* 831
WISENUT - Web Technology - LOOKSMART, LTD.; *pg.* 1265, *pg.* 221
WISER'S - Vodka - CORBY DISTILLERIES LTD.; *pg.* 1961, *pg.* 1937
WISER'S DE LUXE - Whisky - CORBY DISTILLERIES LTD.; *pg.* 1961, *pg.* 1937
WISER'S SPECIAL BLEND - Whisky - CORBY DISTILLERIES LTD.; *pg.* 1961, *pg.* 1937
WISER'S VERY OLD - Whisky - CORBY DISTILLERIES LTD.; *pg.* 1961, *pg.* 1937
WISH - Apparel - BEBE STORES, INC.; *pg.* 19, *pg.* 49
WISH BIG - Bouquet - 1-800-FLOWERS.COM, INC.; *pg.* 1758, *pg.* 1151
WISH-BONE - Salad Dressing - PINNACLE FOODS GROUP LLC; *pg.* 889, *pg.* 1104
WISH BOOK - Holiday Gift Catalog - SEARS HOLDINGS CORPORATION; *pg.* 1784, *pg.* 618
WISH YOU WERE HERE - Game - WMS INDUSTRIES INC.; *pg.* 593, *pg.* 666
WISHBONE - Office Equipment - KNOLL, INC.; *pg.* 425, *pg.* 1527
WISHBONE - Fabric - NEMSCHOFF, INC.; *pg.* 936, *pg.* 1890
WISHES - Fabric - NEMSCHOFF, INC.; *pg.* 936, *pg.* 1890
WISHLIST - Category Search - TIVO INC.; *pg.* 313, *pg.* 251
WISK - Laundry Detergent - THE SUN PRODUCTS CORPORATION; *pg.* 336, *pg.* 385
WISMATIC - Metal Cutting Equipment & Machinery - WISCONSIN MACHINE TOOL CORPORATION; *pg.* 1389, *pg.* 1855
WISP - Autosampler - HAMILTON CO., INC.; *pg.* 1415, *pg.* 1031
WISP - Software - WIND RIVER SYSTEMS, INC.; *pg.* 493, *pg.* 38
WISPATHINS - Lens - EMERGING VISION, INC.; *pg.* 1411, *pg.* 1227
WISPI - Semiconductor Solution - CYPRESS SEMICONDUCTOR CORPORATION; *pg.* 1326, *pg.* 243
WISTERIA - Carpet - BEAULIEU GROUP, LLC; *pg.* 917, *pg.* 529
WISTERIA - Bedding - CROSCILL, INC.; *pg.* 1122, *pg.* 1220
WITCH - Skin Care Product - FLEET LABORATORIES; *pg.* 1531, *pg.* 1787
WITCH-HAZEL - Soap - GRANDPA BRANDS COMPANY; *pg.* 1538, *pg.* 727
WITCHES BREW - Game - WMS INDUSTRIES INC.; *pg.* 593, *pg.* 666
WITCO - Chemical Product - CHEMTURA CORPORATION; *pg.* 1152, *pg.* 355
WITCOBOND - Polymer Product - CHEMTURA CORPORATION; *pg.* 1152, *pg.* 355
WITCOTHANE - Polymer Product - CHEMTURA CORPORATION; *pg.* 1152, *pg.* 355
WITH A NAME LIKE SMUCKER'S, IT HAS TO BE GOOD - Slogan - THE J.M. SMUCKER COMPANY; *pg.* 865, *pg.* 1468
WITH US, IT'S PERSONAL - Tag Line - RITE AID CORPORATION; *pg.* 1590, *pg.* 1519
WITH YOU EVERY DAY, EVERY POUND OF THE WAY - Slogan - PHYSICIANS WEIGHT LOSS CENTERS, INC.; *pg.* 1585, *pg.* 1402
WITH YOU. FOR LIFE. - Tagline - SUTTER HEALTH; *pg.* 1600, *pg.* 197
WITHCES BROOM - Video Game - INTERNATIONAL GAME TECHNOLOGY; *pg.* 957, *pg.* 1024
WITHOUT IT, NO INSURANCE IS COMPLETE - Tag Line - AFLAC INCORPORATED; *pg.* 1188, *pg.* 527
WITHSTAND - Mar & Scuff Resistant Paints for Wood, Metal & Concrete - PRATT & LAMBERT PAINTS; *pg.* 1446, *pg.* 1434
WITNEY - Footwear - STEVEN MADDEN, LTD.; *pg.* 1819, *pg.* 1176
WITT PRINTING - Business Forms - ENNIS, INC.; *pg.* 393, *pg.* 1727
WITTIG - Rotary Sliding Vane Compressors & Vacuum Pumps - GARDNER DENVER, INC.; *pg.* 1338, *pg.* 1592
WITTNAUER - Watch & Clock - BULOVA CORPORATION; *pg.* 2, *pg.* 1356
WIVIEW - Business Planning Tool - LCC INTERNATIONAL, INC.; *pg.* 651, *pg.* 1792
WIZARD - Testing Instrument System - BECKMAN COULTER, INC.; *pg.* 1402, *pg.* 48
WIZARD - Billing Service - CONVERGYS CORPORATION; *pg.* 379, *pg.* 1412
WIZARD - Gaming Product - GLD PRODUCTS, INC.; *pg.* 1835, *pg.* 1882
WIZARD - Desk Stand - LAPWORKS, INC.; *pg.* 426, *pg.* 187
WIZARD - Nutritional Product - NUTRACEUTICAL INTERNATIONAL CORPORATION; *pg.* 1576, *pg.* 1753
WIZARD - Automatic Gamma Counter - PERKINELMER, INC.; *pg.* 1426, *pg.* 853
WIZARD - Electric Display Panels - STEELCASE INC.; *pg.* 475, *pg.* 889
WIZARD GLASS - Video Game - INTERNATIONAL GAME TECHNOLOGY; *pg.* 957, *pg.* 1024
WIZARD SPINS - Game - WMS INDUSTRIES INC.; *pg.* 593, *pg.* 666
WIZARDS - Professional Basketball Team - WASHINGTON WIZARDS; *pg.* 591, *pg.* 408
WIZARDS OF THE COAST - Toy & Game - HASBRO, INC.; *pg.* 954, *pg.* 1603
WIZCOM - Hotel & Car Rental Reservation System - TRAVELPORT LIMITED; *pg.* 1925, *pg.* 521
WL WELLER - Bourbon - SAZERAC COMPANY, INC.; *pg.* 1969, *pg.* 745
WM. F. COMLY & SON - Auctioneers - WM. F. COMLY & SON, INC.; *pg.* 1792, *pg.* 1572
WMAR, ABC (BALTIMORE) - Television Broadcasting Station - THE E.W. SCRIPPS COMPANY; *pg.* 1639, *pg.* 1412
WMAX - Movie Channel - HOME BOX OFFICE, INC.; *pg.* 290, *pg.* 1240
WMF/USA - Stainless Steel Hollow & Flatware - WMF OF AMERICA, INC.; *pg.* 1140, *pg.* 1380
WMI - Socks & Knitted Headwear - WIGWAM MILLS, INC.; *pg.* 15, *pg.* 1894
WMS AUDIO CHIME - Game - WMS INDUSTRIES INC.; *pg.* 593, *pg.* 666
WMS GAMING - Slot Machines - WMS INDUSTRIES INC.; *pg.* 593, *pg.* 666
WMTA - West Michigan Tourist Association - WEST MICHIGAN TOURIST ASSOCIATION; *pg.* 1930, *pg.* 891
WMVP - Digital Video Product - HAUPPAUGE DIGITAL, INC.; *pg.* 402, *pg.* 1164
WNBA - Game - WNBA ENTERPRISES, LLC; *pg.* 594, *pg.* 1314
W'NG-ITS - Food Product - MURRY'S, INC.; *pg.* 882, *pg.* 780
WNYT - News Channel - WNYT-TV; *pg.* 322, *pg.* 1137
WOBBLE - Fabric - NEMSCHOFF, INC.; *pg.* 936, *pg.* 1890
WOBBLE - Surface Material - STEELCASE INC.; *pg.* 475, *pg.* 889
WOCOSEN - Plastic Product - TROY CORPORATION; *pg.* 1184, *pg.* 1067
WOLBORG - Toy & Game - HASBRO, INC.; *pg.* 954, *pg.* 1603
WOLCOTT - Shoes - ALLEN-EDMONDS SHOE CORP.; *pg.* 1804, *pg.* 1887
WOLED - Organic Light Emitting Device - UNIVERSAL DISPLAY CORPORATION; *pg.* 683, *pg.* 1064
WOLF - Food Product - CONAGRA FOODS, INC.; *pg.* 826, *pg.* 1014
WOLF - Cooking - SUB ZERO WOLF; *pg.* 60, *pg.* 1867
WOLF-BOSCH - Foam Rubber Cutter - THE WOLF MACHINE CO.; *pg.* 1389, *pg.* 1427
WOLF CREEK - T-Shirts - ABERCROMBIE & FITCH CO.; *pg.* 37, *pg.* 1466
WOLF MOUNTAIN - Hat - KEY INDUSTRIES, INC.; *pg.* 43, *pg.* 714
WOLF PACK - Firework Product - B.J. ALAN COMPANY; *pg.* 1150, *pg.* 1483
WOLF RIDGE - Bike - MARIN BIKES; *pg.* 1708, *pg.* 168
WOLF SPIRIT - Game - WMS INDUSTRIES INC.; *pg.* 593, *pg.* 666
WOLFE - Biological Products - CAROLINA BIOLOGICAL SUPPLY COMPANY; *pg.* 1513, *pg.* 1359
WOLFENSTEIN - Game - ACTIVISION BLIZZARD, INC.; *pg.* 948, *pg.* 271
WOLFENSTEIN 3D - Video Game - ID SOFTWARE, INC.; *pg.* 956, *pg.* 1727
WOLFERMAN'S - Specialty Breakfast Products - HARRY & DAVID HOLDINGS, INC.; *pg.* 1022, *pg.* 1499
WOLFF'S - Buckwheat Food Product - THE BIRKETT MILLS; *pg.* 826, *pg.* 1321
WOLFGANG - Guitar - PEAVEY ELECTRONICS CORPORATION; *pg.* 662, *pg.* 970
WOLFGANG - Advisory Council - SEATTLE SYMPHONY ORCHESTRA; *pg.* 582, *pg.* 1840
WOLFPAC - Software - NETWOLVES CORPORATION; *pg.* 1271, *pg.* 474
WOLFSCHMIDT - Vodka - JIM BEAM BRANDS CO.; *pg.* 1965, *pg.* 601
WOLTRA - Bodycare & Skincare - AMERICAN INTERNATIONAL INDUSTRIES COMPANY; *pg.* 498, *pg.* 126
WOLVERINE SPORTS - Athletic Equipment - SCHOOL-TECH, INC.; *pg.* 1844, *pg.* 866
WOLVERINE'S - Game - ACTIVISION BLIZZARD, INC.; *pg.* 948, *pg.* 271
WOLVERTON - Game - WMS INDUSTRIES INC.; *pg.* 593, *pg.* 666
WOMAN - Fragrance - HERBALIFE INTERNATIONAL OF AMERICA, INC.; *pg.* 1541, *pg.* 132
WOMAN TO WOMAN - Radio Program - INTERNATIONAL LUTHERAN LAYMEN'S LEAGUE; *pg.* 293, *pg.* 998
WOMAN WITH EXTENDED HAIR DESIGN - Games - PENN NATIONAL GAMING, INC.; *pg.* 574, *pg.* 1595
WOMAN'S DAY - Women's Network - THE HEARST CORPORATION; *pg.* 1649, *pg.* 1239

First page reference indicates Business Class Edition
Second page reference indicates Geographic Edition

WOMEN & CO. - Membership Program - CITIGROUP INC.; *pg.* 735, *pg.* 1212
WOMEN OF EARTH - Fragrance - AVON PRODUCTS, INC.; *pg.* 500, *pg.* 1198
WOMEN OF FAITH - Online Community - THOMAS NELSON INC.; *pg.* 1692, *pg.* 1654
WOMENENTREPRENEUR.COM - Website - ENTREPRENEUR MEDIA, INC.; *pg.* 1639, *pg.* 110
WOMEN'S ARGINMAX - Nutritional Supplement - GENERAL NUTRITION CENTERS, INC.; *pg.* 1534, *pg.* 1575
WOMEN'S CIRCLE - Nutritional Supplement - PHARMAVITE LLC; *pg.* 1584, *pg.* 167
WOMEN'S COLLEGE CUP - Trademark (Div. I Women's Soccer) - NATIONAL COLLEGIATE ATHLETIC ASSOCIATION; *pg.* 567, *pg.* 688
WOMEN'S COLLEGE WORLD SERIES - Trademark (Div. I Women's Softball) - NATIONAL COLLEGIATE ATHLETIC ASSOCIATION; *pg.* 567, *pg.* 688
WOMEN'S ELITE EIGHT - Trademark - NATIONAL COLLEGIATE ATHLETIC ASSOCIATION; *pg.* 567, *pg.* 688
WOMEN'S FINAL 4 - Trademark (Div. I Women's Basketball) - NATIONAL COLLEGIATE ATHLETIC ASSOCIATION; *pg.* 567, *pg.* 688
WOMEN'S FINAL FOUR - Trademark (Div. I Women's Basketball) - NATIONAL COLLEGIATE ATHLETIC ASSOCIATION; *pg.* 567, *pg.* 688
WOMEN'S FROZEN FOUR - Trademark (Div. I Women's Ice Hockey) - NATIONAL COLLEGIATE ATHLETIC ASSOCIATION; *pg.* 567, *pg.* 688
WOMEN'S HEALTH - Magazine - RODALE, INC.; *pg.* 1681, *pg.* 1530
WOMEN'S TYLENOL - Pain Reliever - MCNEIL-PPC, INC.; *pg.* 1560, *pg.* 1533
WOMENSHEALTHMAG.COM - Website - RODALE, INC.; *pg.* 1681, *pg.* 1530
WONDER - Graphics Card - ADVANCED MICRO DEVICES, INC.; *pg.* 613, *pg.* 282
WONDER - Rice - AMERICAN RICE, INC.; *pg.* 837, *pg.* 1700
WONDER - Cleaning Product - THE LIBMAN COMPANY; *pg.* 331, *pg.* 553
WONDER - Bread Tray - MOLDED FIBER GLASS COMPANIES; *pg.* 1886, *pg.* 1403
WONDER BOND - Bonding Coat - AKZONOBEL DECORATIVE PAINTS U.S.; *pg.* 1439, *pg.* 1474
WONDER BOX - Device Controller Kit - LORD CORPORATION; *pg.* 1357, *pg.* 1360
WONDER CLEANER - Automotive Cleaner - DELTA FOREMOST CHEMICAL CORPORATION; *pg.* 1155, *pg.* 1642
WONDER CURL - Mascara - MAYBELLINE LLC; *pg.* 516, *pg.* 1257
WONDER FINISH - Foundation - MAYBELLINE LLC; *pg.* 516, *pg.* 1257
WONDER GEL - Personal Care Product - LIFEPLUS INTERNATIONAL; *pg.* 1556, *pg.* 29
WONDER GIRL - Character - DC COMICS, INC.; *pg.* 1633, *pg.* 1221
WONDER GUARD - House & Masonry Paint - AKZONOBEL DECORATIVE PAINTS U.S.; *pg.* 1439, *pg.* 1474
WONDER HIDE - Interior Latex Semi-Gloss Enamel - AKZONOBEL DECORATIVE PAINTS U.S.; *pg.* 1439, *pg.* 1474
THE WONDER OF BROADBAND - Tag Line - IDT CORPORATION; *pg.* 643, *pg.* 1096
WONDER PINE TAR - Soap - GRANDPA BRANDS COMPANY; *pg.* 1538, *pg.* 727
WONDER-PRIME - Interior Latex Primer-Sealer - AKZONOBEL DECORATIVE PAINTS U.S.; *pg.* 1439, *pg.* 1474
WONDER-PRUF - Waterproofing Coating - AKZONOBEL DECORATIVE PAINTS U.S.; *pg.* 1439, *pg.* 1474
WONDER SHIELD - House Paint - AKZONOBEL DECORATIVE PAINTS U.S.; *pg.* 1439, *pg.* 1474
WONDER-SPEED - Interior Latex Paint - AKZONOBEL DECORATIVE PAINTS U.S.; *pg.* 1439, *pg.* 1474
WONDER-STICK - Wallcovering Adhesive & Primer - AKZONOBEL DECORATIVE PAINTS U.S.; *pg.* 1439, *pg.* 1474
WONDER TINT - Colorants - AKZONOBEL DECORATIVE PAINTS U.S.; *pg.* 1439, *pg.* 1474
WONDER TONES - Interior Primer & Paint - AKZONOBEL DECORATIVE PAINTS U.S.; *pg.* 1439, *pg.* 1474
WONDER-WICK - Socks & Knitted Headwear - WIGWAM MILLS, INC.; *pg.* 15, *pg.* 1894
WONDER WOMAN - Character - DC COMICS, INC.; *pg.* 1633, *pg.* 1221
WONDER WOODTONES - Wall Paint - AKZONOBEL DECORATIVE PAINTS U.S.; *pg.* 1439, *pg.* 1474
WONDERBAR - Displaying Bar - VARITRONICS, LLC; *pg.* 487, *pg.* 954
WONDERBOX - Device Controller Kit - LORD CORPORATION; *pg.* 1357, *pg.* 1360
WONDERBRA - Intimate Apparel - HANESBRANDS INC.; *pg.* 26, *pg.* 1394
WONDERFLEX - Lined Silicone Gel - ALIMED, INC.; *pg.* 1490, *pg.* 816
WONDERFOAM - Pillow - RELAX THE BACK CORPORATION; *pg.* 940, *pg.* 120
WONDERFUL COUNSELOR - Wall Decor - HERITAGE LACE INC.; *pg.* 694, *pg.* 711
WONDERGLASS - Insulated Glass Panel - FOUR SEASONS SUNROOM; *pg.* 83, *pg.* 1167
WONDERLIER - Kitchenware - TUPPERWARE BRANDS CORPORATION; *pg.* 1139, *pg.* 456
WONDERMAS - Chemical Cleaner Product - TECH SPRAY, L.P.; *pg.* 1183, *pg.* 1659
WONDERMASK - Cleaning Product - TECH SPRAY, L.P.; *pg.* 1183, *pg.* 1659
WONDERPETS! - Fruit Flavored Snacks - KELLOGG COMPANY; *pg.* 831, *pg.* 870
WONDERWASH - Cleaning Products - CLAYTON INDUSTRIES CO.; *pg.* 1323, *pg.* 66
WONDERWIRE - Bra & Shapewear - GLAMORISE FOUNDATIONS, INC.; *pg.* 25, *pg.* 1235
WONDRA - Flour - GENERAL MILLS, INC.; *pg.* 828, *pg.* 933
WONT CHIP - Topcoats - ORLY INTERNATIONAL, INC.; *pg.* 518, *pg.* 137
WOOD - Magazine - MEREDITH CORPORATION; *pg.* 1663, *pg.* 705
WOOD & WOOD PRODUCTS - Magazine - VANCE PUBLISHING CORPORATION; *pg.* 1699, *pg.* 627
WOOD & WOOD PRODUCTS RED BOOK - Magazine - VANCE PUBLISHING CORPORATION; *pg.* 1699, *pg.* 627
WOOD BLEACH - Sealer - THE SAVOGRAN COMPANY; *pg.* 1447, *pg.* 840
WOOD CLASSICS - Hardwood & Rattan Products for Traditional Cabinets - REV-A-SHELF; *pg.* 1060, *pg.* 738
WOOD CLASSICS - Stain - THE SHERWIN-WILLIAMS COMPANY; *pg.* 1447, *pg.* 1435
WOOD FOR GOLD - Surface Cleaner - METHOD PRODUCTS INC.; *pg.* 332, *pg.* 223
WOOD GUARDIAN - Coating Product - PPG INDUSTRIES, INC.; *pg.* 1445, *pg.* 1579
WOOD I BEAM - Building Product - BLUELINX HOLDINGS, INC.; *pg.* 70, *pg.* 491
WOOD I BEAM - Joists - GEORGIA-PACIFIC LLC; *pg.* 1458, *pg.* 507
WOOD IMAGES - Wood Blinds - SPRINGS WINDOW FASHIONS LLC; *pg.* 943, *pg.* 1872
WOOD-KNOCKER - Rod Hanging System - POWERS FASTENERS INC.; *pg.* 1059, *pg.* 1143
WOOD-KOR - Bulkhead Panel - GREIF INC.; *pg.* 1459, *pg.* 1447
WOOD N' STREAM - Outdoor/Casual Shoes - WEINBRENNER SHOE COMPANY, INC.; *pg.* 1822, *pg.* 1871
WOOD SPLENDOR - Cleaning Product - ORECK CORPORATION; *pg.* 59, *pg.* 1653
WOOD STONE - Ovens - CHESHER EQUIPMENT LTD.; *pg.* 1323, *pg.* 1925
WOOD SWELL & LOCK - Repair Product - DAP PRODUCTS, INC.; *pg.* 1441, *pg.* 756
WOOD-TO-STEEL - Secures Wood Sheathing & Decking Material to Steel Studs - PASLODE; *pg.* 1059, *pg.* 664
WOOD VIOLET - Fabric - NEMSCHOFF, INC.; *pg.* 936, *pg.* 1890
WOODARD - Furniture - CRAFTMADE INTERNATIONAL, INC.; *pg.* 1295, *pg.* 1670
WOODBOARD PUZZLES - Toy & Game - HASBRO, INC.; *pg.* 954, *pg.* 1603
WOODBRIDGE - Wine - CONSTELLATION BRANDS, INC.; *pg.* 1960, *pg.* 1348
WOODBRIDGE - Corporate Apparel - L.A. T SPORTSWEAR, LLC; *pg.* 1838, *pg.* 526
WOODCOCK-JOHNSON - Tests - HOUGHTON MIFFLIN HARCOURT PUBLISHING COMPANY; *pg.* 1651, *pg.* 796
WOODCRAFT - Paint Product - KELLY-MOORE PAINT COMPANY, INC.; *pg.* 1443, *pg.* 198
WOODCRAFTS - Basket - THE LONGABERGER COMPANY; *pg.* 1127, *pg.* 1467
WOODFIELD - Kitchen Product - KOHLER CO.; *pg.* 91, *pg.* 1862
WOODFIELD SUITES - Hotel Chain - LA QUINTA CORPORATION; *pg.* 1099, *pg.* 1722
WOODFORD RESERVE - Kentucky Straight Bourbon Whiskey - BROWN-FORMAN CORPORATION; *pg.* 1958, *pg.* 732
WOODGRAIN - Pillow - AMERICAN LEATHER LP; *pg.* 912, *pg.* 1673
WOODGRIP - Metal Building Wood-Frame Fasteners - SFS INTEC, INC.; *pg.* 1061, *pg.* 1596
WOODHULL LAKE - Clothing - ABERCROMBIE & FITCH CO.; *pg.* 37, *pg.* 1466
WOODIE - Roofing Fastener - POWERS FASTENERS INC.; *pg.* 1059, *pg.* 1143
WOODLAND - Nutritional Product - NUTRACEUTICAL INTERNATIONAL CORPORATION; *pg.* 1576, *pg.* 1753
WOODLAND - Lighting Product - QUOIZEL INC.; *pg.* 1304, *pg.* 1616
WOODLAND PUBLISHING - Publication - NUTRACEUTICAL INTERNATIONAL CORPORATION; *pg.* 1576, *pg.* 1753
WOODLAND WAY - Carpet - INTERFACE, INC.; *pg.* 695, *pg.* 512
WOODLAND WHISPER - Video Viewing System - SWORDFISH FINANCIAL, INC.; *pg.* 1430, *pg.* 1737
WOODLANDS - Tents - L.L. BEAN, INC.; *pg.* 1777, *pg.* 750
WOODLINE - Garage Door - MARTIN DOOR MANUFACTURING, INC.; *pg.* 96, *pg.* 1759
WOODLINES - Horizontal Blinds - SPRINGS GLOBAL, INC.; *pg.* 698, *pg.* 1616
WOODMARK - Upholstered Furniture - HOWARD MILLER COMPANY; *pg.* 7, *pg.* 914
WOODMASTER - Interior Stains - AKZONOBEL DECORATIVE PAINTS U.S.; *pg.* 1439, *pg.* 1474
WOODMAT - Fibreboard - CANFOR CORPORATION; *pg.* 1454, *pg.* 1910
WOODMERE - Faucets - MOEN INCORPORATED; *pg.* 1056, *pg.* 1468
WOODPAK - Water-Cooled Stoker for the Forestry & Wood Working Industries - DETROIT STOKER CO.; *pg.* 1070, *pg.* 900
WOODPECKER - Band Saw Blades - THE L.S. STARRETT COMPANY; *pg.* 1421, *pg.* 783
WOODPECKER XF - Band Saw Blades - THE L.S. STARRETT COMPANY; *pg.* 1421, *pg.* 783
WOODPECKERS' PICK - Bird Seed - INTERMOUNTAIN FARMERS ASSOCIATION; *pg.* 705, *pg.* 1759
WOODPLAY - Sporting Good Product - ESCALADE INC.; *pg.* 1833, *pg.* 678
WOODPLUS - Wood Blinds - SPRINGS WINDOW FASHIONS LLC; *pg.* 943, *pg.* 1872
WOODS PUMP - Medical Product - CAS MEDICAL SYSTEMS, INC.; *pg.* 1513, *pg.* 339
WOODSCAPES - Exterior Stains - THE SHERWIN-WILLIAMS COMPANY; *pg.* 1447, *pg.* 1435
WOODSHADES - Pre-Stained Pressure Treated Wood - OSMOSE, INC.; *pg.* 102, *pg.* 533
WOODSHOP NEWS - Editorial Publication - DOMINION ENTERPRISES; *pg.* 1636, *pg.* 1796
WOODSIDE - Footwear - EASTLAND SHOE CORPORATION; *pg.* 1808, *pg.* 750
WOODSIDE - Over-and-Under Shotgun - STURM, RUGER & COMPANY, INC.; *pg.* 1846, *pg.* 371
WOODSMAN - Knife - BUCK KNIVES, INC.; *pg.* 1828, *pg.* 550
WOODSMITHS - Furniture - BROWN JORDAN INTERNATIONAL COMPANY; *pg.* 919, *pg.* 740
WOODSTALK - BioProduct - THE DOW CHEMICAL COMPANY; *pg.* 1157, *pg.* 898
WOODSTEP - Flooring Product - STAGESTEP INC.; *pg.* 1688, *pg.* 1570
WOODSTEP PLUS - Flooring Product - STAGESTEP INC.; *pg.* 1688, *pg.* 1570
WOODSTEP ULTRA - Flooring Product - STAGESTEP INC.; *pg.* 1688, *pg.* 1570
WOODSTOCK - Shoes - ALLEN-EDMONDS SHOE CORP.; *pg.* 1804, *pg.* 1887
WOODSTOCK - Furniture - ETHAN ALLEN INTERIORS INC.; *pg.* 924, *pg.* 343
WOODSTOCK - Dinnerware - THE HOMER LAUGHLIN CHINA COMPANY; *pg.* 1125, *pg.* 1850
WOODTRUDER - Extruder - DAVIS-STANDARD LLC; *pg.* 1328, *pg.* 368
WOODWELD - Pressed Wood Resins - GEORGIA-PACIFIC

LLC; *pg.* 1458, *pg.* 507
WOODWORKING - Magazine - RANDALL-REILLY PUBLISHING COMPANY LLC; *pg.* 1679, *pg.* 8
WOODWORKS - Ceilings & Walls - ARMSTRONG WORLD INDUSTRIES, INC.; *pg.* 914, *pg.* 1545
WOODWRIGHT - Window - ANDERSEN CORPORATION; *pg.* 67, *pg.* 916
WOOH! - Tagline - IDAHO LOTTERY; *pg.* 995, *pg.* 547
WOOL-EASE - Yarn - LION BRAND YARN COMPANY; *pg.* 696, *pg.* 1050
WOOL 'N CARE - Household Product - BLUE CROSS LABORATORIES; *pg.* 326, *pg.* 277
WOOL SQUARES - Rug - COURISTAN INC.; *pg.* 921, *pg.* 1067
WOOL TONES - Rug - COURISTAN INC.; *pg.* 921, *pg.* 1067
WOOLITE - Laundry Detergent - RECKITT BENCKISER INC.; *pg.* 1136, *pg.* 1105
WORCESTER - Valve - FLOWSERVE CORPORATION; *pg.* 82, *pg.* 1719
WORCESTER TELEGRAM & GAZETTE - Publication - WORCESTER TELEGRAM & GAZETTE CORP.; *pg.* 1702, *pg.* 863
WORD - Record Label - WARNER MUSIC GROUP CORP.; *pg.* 590, *pg.* 1313
WORD BY WORD FIRST READERS - Educational Materials - SCHOLASTIC INC.; *pg.* 1683, *pg.* 1288
WORD FAMILY TALES - Educational Materials - SCHOLASTIC INC.; *pg.* 1683, *pg.* 1288
WORD GIRL - Educational Materials - SCHOLASTIC INC.; *pg.* 1683, *pg.* 1288
WORD WHAMMER - Educational Toys - LEAPFROG ENTERPRISES, INC.; *pg.* 961, *pg.* 84
WORDMASTER - Thesaurus & Phonetic Speller - FRANKLIN ELECTRONIC PUBLISHERS, INC.; *pg.* 398, *pg.* 1048
WORDPERFECT 12 PRODUCTIVITY - Software - COREL CORPORATION; *pg.* 380, *pg.* 1931
WORDPERFECT MAIL - Software - COREL CORPORATION; *pg.* 380, *pg.* 1931
WORDPERFECT OFFICE 12 - Software - COREL CORPORATION; *pg.* 380, *pg.* 1931
WORDS ON CASSETTE - Guide to Audiocassette Collections - R.R. BOWKER LLC; *pg.* 1682, *pg.* 1095
WORK-A-ROUND - Basket - THE LONGABERGER COMPANY; *pg.* 1127, *pg.* 1467
WORK BIG - Projector - INFOCUS CORPORATION; *pg.* 644, *pg.* 1503
WORK. BUILD. CREATE. - Slogan - BOISE CASCADE HOLDINGS, L.L.C.; *pg.* 1453, *pg.* 546
WORK-DRY - T-Shirt - CARHARTT, INC.; *pg.* 39, *pg.* 875
WORK FORCE - Footwear - LACROSSE FOOTWEAR, INC.; *pg.* 1811, *pg.* 1503
WORK FORCE - Grease Gun - TRACTOR SUPPLY COMPANY; *pg.* 708, *pg.* 1627
WORK MANAGER - Office Furniture & Accessories - RUBBERMAID HOME PRODUCTS; *pg.* 1138, *pg.* 1453
WORK MATE - Trademark & ATV Tires - CARLISLE TIRE & WHEEL COMPANY; *pg.* 1880, *pg.* 1612
THE WORK NUMBER - Technologies to Serve Human Resources, Benefits & Payroll Markets - EQUIFAX WORKFORCE SOLUTIONS; *pg.* 394, *pg.* 997
THE WORK NUMBER EPAYROLL SERVICES - Calculator - EQUIFAX WORKFORCE SOLUTIONS; *pg.* 394, *pg.* 997
WORK ONE - Industrial Foot Wear - WEINBRENNER SHOE COMPANY, INC.; *pg.* 1822, *pg.* 1871
WORK VIRTUALLY ANYWHERE - Software - SYMANTEC CORPORATION; *pg.* 478, *pg.* 161
WORKCAMO - Jacket - CARHARTT, INC.; *pg.* 39, *pg.* 875
WORKCENTRE - Software - XEROX CORPORATION; *pg.* 494, *pg.* 365
WORKCOMFORT - Cargo Short - CARHARTT, INC.; *pg.* 39, *pg.* 875
WORKER BEE - Syringe Pump Controller - BIOANALYTICAL SYSTEMS, INC.; *pg.* 1402, *pg.* 700
WORKERBEE - Cutting Room Equipment - EASTMAN MACHINE COMPANY; *pg.* 1331, *pg.* 1148
WORKFLEX - Coat - CARHARTT, INC.; *pg.* 39, *pg.* 875
WORKFLOW - Document File Trays - STEELCASE INC.; *pg.* 475, *pg.* 889
WORKFLOWRX - Software - OMNICELL INC.; *pg.* 1578, *pg.* 161
WORKFORCE CENTRAL - Software System - KRONOS INCORPORATED; *pg.* 425, *pg.* 813
WORKFORCE CONNECT - Data Integration & Modification Solution - KRONOS INCORPORATED; *pg.* 425, *pg.* 813
WORKFORCE HR - Human Resources Application - KRONOS INCORPORATED; *pg.* 425, *pg.* 813
WORKFORCE MANAGEMENT - Human Resources Magazine - CRAIN COMMUNICATIONS, INC.; *pg.* 1631, *pg.* 879
WORKFORCE MOBILETIME - Portable Time & Labor Data Collection Application - KRONOS INCORPORATED; *pg.* 425, *pg.* 813
WORKFORCE PAYROLL - Payroll Processing Application - KRONOS INCORPORATED; *pg.* 425, *pg.* 813
WORKFORCE RECRUITER - Web-Based Recruiting Application - KRONOS INCORPORATED; *pg.* 425, *pg.* 813
WORKFORCE SCHEDULER - Staff Scheduling Software - KRONOS INCORPORATED; *pg.* 425, *pg.* 813
WORKFORCE TELETIME - Telephone-Based Interactive Voice Response Application - KRONOS INCORPORATED; *pg.* 425, *pg.* 813
WORKFORCE TIMEKEEPER - Automation Solution for Employee Time & Attendance Data Management - KRONOS INCORPORATED; *pg.* 425, *pg.* 813
WORKHOG - Battery - ENERSYS INC.; *pg.* 1334, *pg.* 1584
WORKHORSE - Electrosurgical Devices - ANGIODYNAMICS, INC.; *pg.* 1495, *pg.* 1173
WORKHORSE - Electronic Instrument - KEITHLEY INSTRUMENTS, INC.; *pg.* 1418, *pg.* 1473
WORKHORSE - Fabric - NEMSCHOFF, INC.; *pg.* 936, *pg.* 1890
WORKHORSE - Sectional Doors - RITE-HITE HOLDING CORPORATION; *pg.* 1372, *pg.* 1880
WORKHORSE 1000 - Sectional Dock Door - RITE-HITE HOLDING CORPORATION; *pg.* 1372, *pg.* 1880
WORKING CLASS - Carpet - INTERFACE, INC.; *pg.* 695, *pg.* 512
WORKING MODEL - Software - MSC SOFTWARE CORPORATION; *pg.* 441, *pg.* 262
WORKING MOTHER - Magazine - WORKING MOTHER MEDIA, INC.; *pg.* 1702, *pg.* 1315
WORKING TO SAVE LIVES - Tagline - UTAH MEDICAL PRODUCTS, INC.; *pg.* 1605, *pg.* 1752
WORKING TOGETHER FOR A HEALTHIER WORLD - Slogan - PFIZER INC.; *pg.* 1581, *pg.* 1278
WORKINGFAMILIES.COM - Online Consumer Services - AMERICAN FEDERATION OF LABOR - CONGRESS OF INDUSTRIAL ORGANIZATIONS; *pg.* 128, *pg.* 394
WORKKEYS - Skill Requirements System - ACT INC.; *pg.* 597, *pg.* 708
WORKLON - Apparel - SUPERIOR UNIFORM GROUP, INC.; *pg.* 33, *pg.* 468
WORKMAN - Fall Protection Equipment - MINE SAFETY APPLIANCES COMPANY; *pg.* 1361, *pg.* 1525
WORKMASTER - Technical Furniture - IAC INDUSTRIES, INC.; *pg.* 929, *pg.* 48
WORKMASTER - Flat Back Encapsulating Garment - STANDARD SAFETY EQUIPMENT CO.; *pg.* 1379, *pg.* 632
WORKOUT PANT - Clothing - K-SWISS; *pg.* 1837, *pg.* 306
THE WORKPLACE ROLLING STORAGE - Drawer System for Home or Office - HOME PRODUCTS INTERNATIONAL, INC.; *pg.* 1125, *pg.* 577
WORKPRO - Apparel - MARKS WORK WEARHOUSE LTD.; *pg.* 44, *pg.* 1903
WORKQWEST - Web-Based Technology - MAXIMUS, INC.; *pg.* 780, *pg.* 1799
WORKRITE - Ergonomic Office Products - KNAPE & VOGT MANUFACTURING COMPANY; *pg.* 1052, *pg.* 913
THE WORKS - Pizza - DONATOS PIZZERIA CORPORATION; *pg.* 1727, *pg.* 1439
THE WORKS - Lottery Game - IDAHO LOTTERY; *pg.* 995, *pg.* 547
WORKS TO YOUR ADVANTAGE - Tag Line - GRAYBAR ELECTRIC COMPANY, INC.; *pg.* 1299, *pg.* 997
WORKS Z 4 - Skate - ROLLER DERBY SKATE CORP.; *pg.* 966, *pg.* 630
WORKSBASE - Software - BIO-RAD LABORATORIES, INC.; *pg.* 1504, *pg.* 101
WORKSHITE PRO - Attachments - DEERE & COMPANY; *pg.* 703, *pg.* 632
WORKSPACE EXCHANGE - Office Product - HAWORTH, INC.; *pg.* 402, *pg.* 891
WORKSTATION - Information Processing Products - FELLOWES, INC.; *pg.* 397, *pg.* 620
WORKSTATION+ - Software Product - PEGASYSTEMS INC.; *pg.* 453, *pg.* 809
WORKSTREAM - Manufacturing Execution System - APPLIED MATERIALS, INC.; *pg.* 618, *pg.* 264
WORKWEAR - Work Clothing - SEARS HOLDINGS CORPORATION; *pg.* 1784, *pg.* 618
WORKWORLD - Internet Services - YAHOO! INC.; *pg.* 1289, *pg.* 289
WORKXPERT - Software System - MENTOR GRAPHICS CORPORATION; *pg.* 432, *pg.* 1510
WORLD - Game - ACTIVISION BLIZZARD, INC.; *pg.* 948, *pg.* 271
WORLD - Hand & Hair Dryers, Faucets, Hand Wash Station - WORLD DRYER CORPORATION; *pg.* 63, *pg.* 556
THE WORLD ACCORDING TO KLUTZ - Educational Materials - SCHOLASTIC INC.; *pg.* 1683, *pg.* 1288
WORLD CENTER OF RACING - Motorsports Event - INTERNATIONAL SPEEDWAY CORPORATION; *pg.* 553, *pg.* 420
WORLD CHAMPIONSHIP WRESTLING - Wrestling Production - WORLD WRESTLING ENTERTAINMENT, INC.; *pg.* 595, *pg.* 380
WORLD CLASS - Software - ATEX MEDIA COMMAND, INC.; *pg.* 355, *pg.* 848
WORLD CLASS MARKET - Slogan - BIG Y FOODS, INC.; *pg.* 1015, *pg.* 845
WORLD CLASS SNOWMOBILES - Snowmobile - ARCTIC CAT INC.; *pg.* 1705, *pg.* 953
WORLD CLASS SUPPORT FOR SCIENCE & MATH - Tagline - CAROLINA BIOLOGICAL SUPPLY COMPANY; *pg.* 1513, *pg.* 1359
WORLD DISCOVERY SCIENCE READERS - Educational Materials - SCHOLASTIC INC.; *pg.* 1683, *pg.* 1288
WORLD ELITE MASTERCARD - Credit Card - MASTERCARD INCORPORATED; *pg.* 779, *pg.* 1325
WORLD ENTERTAINMENT SERVICES - Magazine - BONNIER CORPORATION; *pg.* 1622, *pg.* 480
WORLD-FAMOUS - Wooden Director Chairs - TELESCOPE CASUAL FURNITURE INC.; *pg.* 944, *pg.* 1162
WORLD FAMOUS FISH TACO - Restaurant Services - RUBIO'S RESTAURANTS, INC.; *pg.* 1748, *pg.* 60
THE WORLD IS OPEN TO YOU. EXPERIENCE IT! - Slogan - TRAVEL-BY-NET, INC.; *pg.* 1925, *pg.* 1183
THE WORLD IS OUR HOMETOWN - Company Slogan - BROOKFIELD GLOBAL RELOCATION SERVICES; *pg.* 1083, *pg.* 560
THE WORLD LEADER IN SERVING SCIENCE - Tagline - THERMO FISHER SCIENTIFIC INC.; *pg.* 1431, *pg.* 854
WORLD-LITE - Lamp - DAZOR MANUFACTURING CORP.; *pg.* 1296, *pg.* 995
WORLD MASTERCARD - Credit Card - MASTERCARD INCORPORATED; *pg.* 779, *pg.* 1325
THE WORLD MONEY SHOW - Tradeshow - INVESTMENT SEMINARS, INC.; *pg.* 420, *pg.* 466
WORLD OF CARE - Tagline - COLGATE-PALMOLIVE COMPANY; *pg.* 504, *pg.* 1215
WORLD OF GOLF - Golf Gifts & Accessories - GOLF GIFTS & GALLERY; *pg.* 1835, *pg.* 1887
WORLD OF MAGIC - Video Game - INTERNATIONAL GAME TECHNOLOGY; *pg.* 957, *pg.* 1024
WORLD OF WARCRAFT - Game - ACTIVISION BLIZZARD, INC.; *pg.* 948, *pg.* 271
WORLD OIL - Trade Journal - GULF PUBLISHING COMPANY; *pg.* 1646, *pg.* 1707
WORLD PETROLEUM INDUSTRY - Trade Journal - GULF PUBLISHING COMPANY; *pg.* 1646, *pg.* 1707
THE WORLD RUNS BETTER WITH ROGERS - Slogan - ROGERS CORPORATION; *pg.* 1305, *pg.* 369
THE WORLD SERIES OF HANDICAPPING - Slogan - PENN NATIONAL GAMING, INC.; *pg.* 574, *pg.* 1595
WORLD SERIES OF POKER - Game - CAESARS ENTERTAINMENT CORPORATION; *pg.* 1083, *pg.* 1023
WORLD SPORTS & MARKETING - Magazine - BONNIER CORPORATION; *pg.* 1622, *pg.* 480
WORLD TIMER - Watch - TOURNEAU INC.; *pg.* 14, *pg.* 1303
WORLD WAR II VIDEO - Video Series - DIRECT HOLDINGS AMERICAS INC.; *pg.* 1636, *pg.* 1780
WORLD WEEK - Educational Materials - SCHOLASTIC INC.; *pg.* 1683, *pg.* 1288
WORLD WIDE MOVERS - Tag Line - AMERICAN RED BALL TRANSIT CO. INC.; *pg.* 1899, *pg.* 682
WORLD WIDE WORSHIP - Christian Music Station - EDUCATIONAL MEDIA FOUNDATION; *pg.* 284, *pg.* 194
WORLD WRESTLING ENTERTAINMENT - World Wrestling - WORLD WRESTLING ENTERTAINMENT, INC.; *pg.* 595, *pg.* 380
WORLDFREIGHT - Shipments of 220 lbs. & Above - DHL HOLDINGS (USA), INC.; *pg.* 1906, *pg.* 459

First page reference indicates Business Class Edition
Second page reference indicates Geographic Edition

WORLDINFO - Digital Map Database of the World - PITNEY BOWES SOFTWARE INC.; *pg.* 455, *pg.* 1346
WORLDLY - Fabric - NEMSCHOFF, INC.; *pg.* 936, *pg.* 1890
WORLDMAIL - Re-Mail Service - DHL HOLDINGS (USA), INC.; *pg.* 1906, *pg.* 459
WORLDNET - Software System - AT&T COMMUNICATIONS CORP.; *pg.* 1866, *pg.* 1043
WORLDOFWATCHES.COM - Watch Store - DIAMOND.COM; *pg.* 1238, *pg.* 1954
WORLDPOINTS - Credit Card - HUNTINGTON BANCSHARES INCORPORATED; *pg.* 767, *pg.* 1440
WORLDPORT - Services - UNITED PARCEL SERVICE, INC.; *pg.* 1928, *pg.* 522
WORLDREACH - Insurance Engineering Services - FACTORY MUTUAL INSURANCE COMPANY; *pg.* 1199, *pg.* 1601
THE WORLD'S CHOCOLATIER - Tagline - ROCKY MOUNTAIN CHOCOLATE FACTORY, INC.; *pg.* 1032, *pg.* 324
THE WORLD'S CLEANEST GARAGE - Tagline - GARAGETEK INC.; *pg.* 1457, *pg.* 1179
WORLD'S FAVORITE FLORIST - Slogan - 1-800-FLOWERS.COM, INC.; *pg.* 1758, *pg.* 1151
THE WORLD'S FINEST CRYSTAL - Slogan - CRYSTAL WORLD, INC.; *pg.* 4, *pg.* 1122
THE WORLD'S FINEST CUTLERY - Slogan - CUTCO CORPORATION; *pg.* 1123, *pg.* 1318
WORLD'S FOREMOST BANK - Bank - CABELA'S INCORPORATED; *pg.* 535, *pg.* 1019
WORLD'S FOREMOST OUTFITTER - Slogan - CABELA'S INCORPORATED; *pg.* 535, *pg.* 1019
WORLD'S FRIENDLIEST - Slogan - CALLAWAY GOLF COMPANY; *pg.* 1829, *pg.* 58
THE WORLD'S LARGEST HOTEL CHAIN - Slogan - BEST WESTERN INTERNATIONAL, INC.; *pg.* 1081, *pg.* 15
THE WORLD'S MOST BEAUTIFUL DIAMOND - Slogan - LAZARE KAPLAN INTERNATIONAL, INC.; *pg.* 8, *pg.* 1250
THE WORLD.S MOST HUGGABLE... - Tag Line - GUND, INC.; *pg.* 954, *pg.* 1056
THE WORLD'S MOST HUGGABLE SINCE 1898 - Slogan - GUND, INC.; *pg.* 954, *pg.* 1056
THE WORLD'S MOST PERFECTLY CUT DIAMOND - Tag Line - HEARTS ON FIRE COMPANY; *pg.* 6, *pg.* 796
THE WORLDS MOST PERFECTLY DEVELOPED MAN. - Tagline - CHARLES ATLAS, LTD.; *pg.* 538, *pg.* 1211
THE WORLD'S MOST POWERFUL MAGNETIC FIELD - Slogan - COILCRAFT, INC.; *pg.* 1324, *pg.* 562
THE WORLD'S MOST RELIABLE ARRIVAL SYSTEM - Software - PASSUR AEROSPACE, INC.; *pg.* 233, *pg.* 376
THE WORLD'S NETWORKING COMPANY - Slogan - AT&T COMMUNICATIONS CORP.; *pg.* 1866, *pg.* 1043
WORLDS OF CURLS - Ethnic Hair Care Products - J. STRICKLAND & COMPANY; *pg.* 512, *pg.* 970
WORLDS OF FUN - Amusement Park - CEDAR FAIR, L.P.; *pg.* 537, *pg.* 1471
THE WORLD'S ONLINE MARKETPLACE - Slogan - EBAY INC.; *pg.* 1240, *pg.* 243
THE WORLD'S ONLY TRULY GLOBAL VALUATION FIRM - Slogan - AMERICAN APPRAISAL ASSOCIATES, INC.; *pg.* 349, *pg.* 1872
THE WORLD'S TOUGHEST ATVS - Slogan - POLARIS INDUSTRIES INC.; *pg.* 1709, *pg.* 928
THE WORLD'S WEATHER AUTHORITY - Slogan - ACCUWEATHER, INC.; *pg.* 268, *pg.* 1587
WORLDSCOPE - Financial Publications - THOMSON REUTERS CORPORATION; *pg.* 1693, *pg.* 1944
WORLDSHIP - Shipping Services - UNITED PARCEL SERVICE, INC.; *pg.* 1928, *pg.* 522
WORLDVANE - Vane Pump with International Mounting Capability - BOSCH REXROTH CORPORATION; *pg.* 1319, *pg.* 1516
WORLDWIDE DATACHECK - Data Management System for Blood Gas Quality Control - RADIOMETER AMERICA INC.; *pg.* 1588, *pg.* 1481
WORLDWIDE EXPRESS - Logistics - DHL HOLDINGS (USA), INC.; *pg.* 1906, *pg.* 459
THE WORLDWIDE LEADER IN CRYSTAL GROWTH TECHNOLOGY - Tagline - II-VI INCORPORATED; *pg.* 1417, *pg.* 1585
WORLDWIDE PRIORITY EXPRESS - Express Package Delivery Service - DHL HOLDINGS (USA), INC.; *pg.* 1906, *pg.* 459
WORLDWIDE SOLUTIONS IN FLAKE ICE TECHNOLOGY - Tag Line - NORTH STAR ICE EQUIPMENT CORPORATION; *pg.* 1366, *pg.* 1838
WORLDWIDE SPORT NUTRITION - Nutritional Supplements - NBTY, INC.; *pg.* 1572, *pg.* 1338
WORSTERWARM - Blazer/Slacks - HABAND COMPANY, INC.; *pg.* 1772, *pg.* 1099
WORTH - Convenience Stores - THE PANTRY, INC.; *pg.* 1029, *pg.* 1360
WORTH - Diameter Fixture - THE WORTH COMPANY; *pg.* 1848, *pg.* 1895
WORTHINGTON - Pump - FLOWSERVE CORPORATION; *pg.* 82, *pg.* 1719
WORTHINGTON - Meat Alternatives - KELLOGG COMPANY; *pg.* 831, *pg.* 870
WORTHINGTON'S CREAMFLOW - Beverages - MOLSON COORS BREWING COMPANY; *pg.* 256, *pg.* 321
WORTHY OF THE INVESTMENT - Slogan - COMSTOCK HOLDING COMPANIES INC.; *pg.* 1087, *pg.* 1798
WORX - Drug Therapy Management System - MEDIWARE INFORMATION SYSTEMS, INC.; *pg.* 431, *pg.* 716
WORX - Work & Steel Toe Footwear - RED WING SHOE COMPANY, INC.; *pg.* 1817, *pg.* 954
WORX ENERGY - Beverage - MONSTER BEVERAGE CORPORATION; *pg.* 257, *pg.* 69
WORX UNIVERSAL - Internet Based Pharmacy Management System - MEDIWARE INFORMATION SYSTEMS, INC.; *pg.* 431, *pg.* 716
WOTSITS - Corn Snack - FRITO-LAY NORTH AMERICA, INC.; *pg.* 1853, *pg.* 1730
WOTSITS - Snack Food - PEPSICO, INC.; *pg.* 259, *pg.* 1327
WOUND CARE PROTOCOLS - Healthcare Product - GENTIVA HEALTH SERVICES, INC.; *pg.* 1534, *pg.* 506
WOVEN DAISY CUTTER - Footwear - OAKLEY, INC.; *pg.* 1840, *pg.* 86
WOVEN ELEGANCE - Carpet - BEAULIEU GROUP, LLC; *pg.* 917, *pg.* 529
WOVEN RATTAN - Carpet - BEAULIEU GROUP, LLC; *pg.* 917, *pg.* 529
WOVEN TRADITIONS - Basket - THE LONGABERGER COMPANY; *pg.* 1127, *pg.* 1467
WOVO - Serveware Product - WILTON PRODUCTS, INC.; *pg.* 1140, *pg.* 672
WOW! - Lawn Care Product - GARDENS ALIVE!, INC.; *pg.* 1796, *pg.* 693
WOW - Flashlight - STREAMLIGHT INC.; *pg.* 1306, *pg.* 1527
WOW BAO - Asian Take Away Restaurant - LETTUCE ENTERTAIN YOU ENTERPRISES, INC.; *pg.* 1735, *pg.* 580
WOW BARS - Candy - SORBEE INTERNATIONAL, LLC; *pg.* 1862, *pg.* 1570
WOW COW - Ice Cream - UNITED DAIRY FARMERS, INC.; *pg.* 906, *pg.* 1426
WOWER - Recognition Award - BARKER CREEK PUBLISHING INC.; *pg.* 1619, *pg.* 1818
WOWY - Support Community Website - BEACHBODY, LLC; *pg.* 271, *pg.* 272
WP - Water-Resistant Chain - U.S. TSUBAKI, INC.; *pg.* 221, *pg.* 670
WP-233 IMPACT - Printers - AVERY WEIGH-TRONIX, INC.; *pg.* 1315, *pg.* 925
WP-234 IMPACT - Printers - AVERY WEIGH-TRONIX, INC.; *pg.* 1315, *pg.* 925
WPI CABLE SYSTEMS - Cable Assemblies - COOPER INTERCONNECT; *pg.* 630, *pg.* 1118
WPI SARASOTA - Cable Assemblies - COOPER INTERCONNECT; *pg.* 630, *pg.* 1118
WPT TEXAS HOLD 'EM - Lottery Game - MINNESOTA STATE LOTTERY; *pg.* 999, *pg.* 956
WPTV, NBC (WEST PALM BEACH) - Television Broadcasting Station - THE E.W. SCRIPPS COMPANY; *pg.* 1639, *pg.* 1412
WR - Pump Component - GREENE, TWEED & CO.; *pg.* 1344, *pg.* 1544
WRANGLE - Apparel - VANS, INC.; *pg.* 1821, *pg.* 76
WRANGLER - Tire - THE GOODYEAR TIRE & RUBBER COMPANY; *pg.* 1883, *pg.* 1401
WRANGLER - Floor Cleaning Product - NSS ENTERPRISES, INC.; *pg.* 59, *pg.* 1476
WRANGLER - Apparel - V.F. CORPORATION; *pg.* 34, *pg.* 1376
WRANGLER HERO - Jeanswear - V.F. CORPORATION; *pg.* 34, *pg.* 1376
WRANGLER HOME - Furniture - FLEXSTEEL INDUSTRIES, INC.; *pg.* 925, *pg.* 707
WRANGLERS - Smoked Franks - HORMEL FOODS CORPORATION; *pg.* 863, *pg.* 915
WRAP-A-DAX - Computer Software And An Electronic Switch - ALCATEL-LUCENT USA, INC.; *pg.* 615, *pg.* 1728
WRAP & RIBBON - Shears - ACME UNITED CORPORATION; *pg.* 1040, *pg.* 346
WRAP AROUND PAYS - Game - WMS INDUSTRIES INC.; *pg.* 593, *pg.* 666
WRAP-CAP - Crimp Connector - IDEAL INDUSTRIES, INC.; *pg.* 1051, *pg.* 662
WRAP CARDIGAN - Women's Clothing & Accessories - WOODEN SHIPS OF HOBOKEN; *pg.* 35, *pg.* 1315
WRAP-ON - Orthopedic Product - DJO INCORPORATED; *pg.* 1524, *pg.* 302
WRAP SEAM SKIRT - Clothing - K-SWISS; *pg.* 1837, *pg.* 306
WRAP/UP - Plastics Product - AEP INDUSTRIES INC.; *pg.* 1878, *pg.* 1085
WRAP'N CRAFT - Box to Store Wrapping, Cards, Bows etc. - RUBBERMAID HOME PRODUCTS; *pg.* 1138, *pg.* 1453
WRAPONS - Cold or Hot Therapy Pads - MUELLER SPORTS MEDICINE, INC.; *pg.* 1570, *pg.* 1887
WRAPPED RIBBON - Cheese - LEPRINO FOODS COMPANY; *pg.* 874, *pg.* 320
WRAPPERS - Side Bed Rail Protectors - LUND INTERNATIONAL, INC.; *pg.* 211, *pg.* 526
WRAPPP - Footwear - STEVEN MADDEN, LTD.; *pg.* 1819, *pg.* 1176
WRAPS - Educational Materials - SCHOLASTIC INC.; *pg.* 1683, *pg.* 1288
WRAPTURE - Body Tights - ATTITUDES IN DRESSING INC.; *pg.* 19, *pg.* 1057
WRATH OF HEAVEN - Game - ACTIVISION BLIZZARD, INC.; *pg.* 948, *pg.* 271
WRATTEN - Light Filter - EASTMAN KODAK COMPANY; *pg.* 1408, *pg.* 1333
WRESTLEMANIA - Wrestling - WORLD WRESTLING ENTERTAINMENT, INC.; *pg.* 595, *pg.* 380
WRESTLING.COM - Advertising Website - LIVE CURRENT MEDIA INC.; *pg.* 1263, *pg.* 1911
WRIGHT - Bacon Products - TYSON FOODS, INC.; *pg.* 902, *pg.* 35
WRIGHT MOUNTAIN - Clothing - ABERCROMBIE & FITCH CO.; *pg.* 37, *pg.* 1466
WRIGHT PREFILL - Healthcare Product - MEDICOOL, INC.; *pg.* 1562, *pg.* 294
THE WRIGHT WING! - Processed Chicken - TYSON FOODS, INC.; *pg.* 902, *pg.* 35
WRIGHT'S - Liquid Smoke - B&G FOODS, INC.; *pg.* 838, *pg.* 1102
WRIGHT'S - Cleaning Product - WEIMAN PRODUCTS, LLC; *pg.* 337, *pg.* 616
WRIGLEY'S SPEARMINT - Gum - WM. WRIGLEY JR. COMPANY; *pg.* 1863, *pg.* 596
WRIST-O-TWIST - Excavator Accessory - BADGER EQUIPMENT COMPANY; *pg.* 1315, *pg.* 966
WRIST-TOP - Digital Compass - BUSHNELL OUTDOOR PRODUCTS, INC.; *pg.* 1403, *pg.* 718
WRIST WRAPS - Orthopedic Product - DJO INCORPORATED; *pg.* 1524, *pg.* 302
WRISTAT - Anti-Static Device - WALTER G. LEGGE COMPANY, INC.; *pg.* 337, *pg.* 1321
WRITE 180 - Educational Materials - SCHOLASTIC INC.; *pg.* 1683, *pg.* 1288
WRITE LYRICS - Educational Materials - SCHOLASTIC INC.; *pg.* 1683, *pg.* 1288
WRITE ON! - Educational Materials - RENAISSANCE LEARNING, INC.; *pg.* 607, *pg.* 1899
WRITE SOURCE - Language Arts Programs - HOUGHTON MIFFLIN HARCOURT PUBLISHING COMPANY; *pg.* 1651, *pg.* 796
WRITE TO SANTA KIT - Toy And Game - INNOVATIVE USA, INC.; *pg.* 957, *pg.* 363
WRITEQUEST - Educational Test - QUESTAR ASSESSMENT, INC.; *pg.* 1679, *pg.* 1143
THE WRITER - Magazine - KALMBACH PUBLISHING CO.; *pg.* 1656, *pg.* 1898
WRITING ADVANTAGE - Workshop - FRANKLIN COVEY CO.; *pg.* 1642, *pg.* 1758
WRITING RENAISSANCE - Educational Materials - RENAISSANCE LEARNING, INC.; *pg.* 607, *pg.* 1899
WRQX-FM - Radio Station - WRQX-FM RADIO; *pg.* 323, *pg.* 408
WRS - Automotive Electrical Product - WAIGLOBAL; *pg.* 221, *pg.* 1585
W.S. - Valves - THE WM. POWELL COMPANY; *pg.* 1389, *pg.* 1427

WS-FTP PROFESSIONAL - Software - IPSWITCH, INC.; *pg.* 421, *pg.* 828
WS-FTP SERVER - Software - IPSWITCH, INC.; *pg.* 421, *pg.* 828
WSE - Software - WEBSENSE, INC.; *pg.* 491, *pg.* 210
WSFS - Banking - WSFS FINANCIAL CORPORATION; *pg.* 823, *pg.* 392
WSJ.COM - Business News & Information Website - DOW JONES & COMPANY, INC.; *pg.* 1637, *pg.* 1225
WSPA-TV - TV Station - MEDIA GENERAL, INC.; *pg.* 297, *pg.* 1803
WSX - Software - WEBSENSE, INC.; *pg.* 491, *pg.* 210
WTO REPORTER - Publisher - BLOOMBERG BNA; *pg.* 1621, *pg.* 1772
WTVD - TV Station - WTVD-TV INC.; *pg.* 323, *pg.* 1372
WU XING SEVENS - Video Game - INTERNATIONAL GAME TECHNOLOGY; *pg.* 957, *pg.* 1024
WUNDERBAR - Bologna Products - TYSON FOODS, INC.; *pg.* 902, *pg.* 35
WURLITZER - Musical Instrument - GIBSON GUITAR CORP.; *pg.* 550, *pg.* 1650
W.W. FLYERS - Foodservice Poultry Items - TYSON FOODS, INC.; *pg.* 902, *pg.* 35
W.W. NORTON - Books - W.W. NORTON & COMPANY, INC.; *pg.* 1702, *pg.* 1316
WWD - Women's Wear Daily - FAIRCHILD FASHION GROUP; *pg.* 1640, *pg.* 1230
WWDLUXURY - Newspaper - FAIRCHILD FASHION GROUP; *pg.* 1640, *pg.* 1230
WWE NEW YORK - Entertainment Complex - WORLD WRESTLING ENTERTAINMENT, INC.; *pg.* 595, *pg.* 380
WWE RACING - Media & Entertainment Services - WORLD WRESTLING ENTERTAINMENT, INC.; *pg.* 595, *pg.* 380
WWE RAW - TV Show - WORLD WRESTLING ENTERTAINMENT, INC.; *pg.* 595, *pg.* 380
WWE SMACKDOWN - TV Show - WORLD WRESTLING ENTERTAINMENT, INC.; *pg.* 595, *pg.* 380
WWE SUPERSTARS - TV Show - WORLD WRESTLING ENTERTAINMENT, INC.; *pg.* 595, *pg.* 380
W.W.SPECIAL - Automotive Reconditioning Product - MOC PRODUCTS COMPANY, INC.; *pg.* 332, *pg.* 174
WWTDD - Celebrity News & Opinion Site - SPINMEDIA; *pg.* 1282, *pg.* 104
WWW.DELL.COM - Website - DELL INC.; *pg.* 383, *pg.* 1737
WWW.HATSHACK.COM - Website - HAT WORLD, INC.; *pg.* 42, *pg.* 686
WWW.HATWORLD.COM - Website - HAT WORLD, INC.; *pg.* 42, *pg.* 686
WWW.LIDS.COM - Website - HAT WORLD, INC.; *pg.* 42, *pg.* 686
WWW.LIDSKIDS.COM - Website - HAT WORLD, INC.; *pg.* 42, *pg.* 686
WWW.MAPLELEAFS.COM - Maple Leafs Fan Web Site - MAPLE LEAF SPORTS & ENTERTAINMENT LTD.; *pg.* 560, *pg.* 1940
WWW.MESDA.ORG - Museum - OLD SALEM, INCORPORATED; *pg.* 572, *pg.* 1395
WWW.OLDSALEM.ORG - Museum - OLD SALEM, INCORPORATED; *pg.* 572, *pg.* 1395
WWW.RAPTORS.COM - Raptors Fan Web Site - MAPLE LEAF SPORTS & ENTERTAINMENT LTD.; *pg.* 560, *pg.* 1940
WWW.RUE21.COM - Website - RUE21, INC.; *pg.* 32, *pg.* 1591
WXYZ, ABC (DETROIT) - Television Broadcasting Station - THE E.W. SCRIPPS COMPANY; *pg.* 1639, *pg.* 1412
WYANDOT LAKE - Park - SIX FLAGS ENTERTAINMENT CORPORATION; *pg.* 583, *pg.* 1698
WYATT - Furniture - HOOKER FURNITURE CORPORATION; *pg.* 928, *pg.* 1788
WYKO - Metrology Systems - VEECO INSTRUMENTS INC.; *pg.* 1434, *pg.* 1322
WYKO HD8000 - Magnetic Head Profiling System - VEECO INSTRUMENTS INC.; *pg.* 1434, *pg.* 1322
WYKO NT1100 - Optical Profiler - VEECO INSTRUMENTS INC.; *pg.* 1434, *pg.* 1322
WYKO NT3300 - Optical Profiler - VEECO INSTRUMENTS INC.; *pg.* 1434, *pg.* 1322
WYLER'S - Food Product - THE JEL SERT COMPANY; *pg.* 865, *pg.* 668
WYLER'S - Bouillons & Soups - THE KRAFT HEINZ COMPANY; *pg.* 870, *pg.* 1577
WYNDHAM - Ceiling Fan - WESTINGHOUSE LIGHTING CORPORATION; *pg.* 687, *pg.* 1571
WYNDHAM HOTELS & RESORTS - Hotels & Resorts - WYNDHAM WORLDWIDE CORPORATION; *pg.* 1119, *pg.* 1107
WYNDTELL - Wireless Communication Product - PURPLE COMMUNICATIONS, INC.; *pg.* 457, *pg.* 194
WYNN LAS VEGAS - Casino - WYNN RESORTS LIMITED; *pg.* 1119, *pg.* 1030
WYNN MACAU - Casino - WYNN RESORTS LIMITED; *pg.* 1119, *pg.* 1030
WYNN'S - Auto Chemical Additives - WYNN OIL COMPANY; *pg.* 987, *pg.* 173
WYNWOOD - All Products - DMI FURNITURE, INC.; *pg.* 923, *pg.* 733
WYOMING BOOK - Paper Products - BOISE CASCADE HOLDINGS, L.L.C.; *pg.* 1453, *pg.* 546
WYPALL - Commercial Wipe - KIMBERLY-CLARK CORPORATION; *pg.* 1461, *pg.* 1720
WYSH - Footwear - STEVEN MADDEN, LTD.; *pg.* 1819, *pg.* 1176
WYTOX - Polymer Product - CHEMTURA CORPORATION; *pg.* 1152, *pg.* 355

X

X - Project Building - ALPHABET INC.; *pg.* 347, *pg.* 153
X - Fragrance - PARFUMS DE COEUR LTD.; *pg.* 519, *pg.* 376
X-12 - Irons - CALLAWAY GOLF COMPANY; *pg.* 1829, *pg.* 58
X-14 - Irons - CALLAWAY GOLF COMPANY; *pg.* 1829, *pg.* 58
X-16 - Irons - CALLAWAY GOLF COMPANY; *pg.* 1829, *pg.* 58
X-18 - Irons - CALLAWAY GOLF COMPANY; *pg.* 1829, *pg.* 58
X-18 PRO - Golf Product - CALLAWAY GOLF COMPANY; *pg.* 1829, *pg.* 58
X-20 - Irons - CALLAWAY GOLF COMPANY; *pg.* 1829, *pg.* 58
X-20TOUR - Irons - CALLAWAY GOLF COMPANY; *pg.* 1829, *pg.* 58
X-35 - Systems Integration & Aeronautics - LOCKHEED MARTIN CORPORATION; *pg.* 229, *pg.* 762
X-ACTION - Health Care Product - NATURE'S SUNSHINE PRODUCTS, INC.; *pg.* 1571, *pg.* 1754
X-AIR - Compressor - BADGER AIR BRUSH COMPANY; *pg.* 359, *pg.* 612
X-CALIBUR - Suitcase - SAMSONITE CORPORATION; *pg.* 11, *pg.* 830
X-CAPE - Specialty Chemicals - OMNOVA SOLUTIONS INC; *pg.* 1176, *pg.* 1453
X-CEL - Synthetic Fleece - ALIMED, INC.; *pg.* 1490, *pg.* 816
X-CELL - Egg Filler Flat - PACTIV CORPORATION; *pg.* 1466, *pg.* 624
X-CLYPS - Software System - CHYRONHEGO; *pg.* 371, *pg.* 1179
X CORE - Security Appliance - WATCHGUARD TECHNOLOGIES, INC.; *pg.* 491, *pg.* 1842
X-FACTOR - Musical Instrument - GIBSON GUITAR CORP.; *pg.* 550, *pg.* 1650
X-FORGED - Irons - CALLAWAY GOLF COMPANY; *pg.* 1829, *pg.* 58
X-FRAME - Software - TERADYNE INC.; *pg.* 679, *pg.* 838
X GAMES - Extreme Sports Tournament - ESPN, INC.; *pg.* 285, *pg.* 340
X-HALE - Header Bag - OLIVER PRODUCTS COMPANY INC.; *pg.* 1367, *pg.* 888
X-HYDRA - Anti-Perspirant - THE GILLETTE COMPANY; *pg.* 509, *pg.* 795
X-JUMBO - Biological Supplies - CAROLINA BIOLOGICAL SUPPLY COMPANY; *pg.* 1513, *pg.* 1359
X-LINK - Electronic Components - MOLEX INCORPORATED; *pg.* 655, *pg.* 628
X MACHINE - Staple & Brad Nailer - ARROW FASTENER COMPANY, INC.; *pg.* 1042, *pg.* 1118
X MARKS THE SPOT - Video Game - WMS INDUSTRIES INC.; *pg.* 593, *pg.* 666
X-MEN - Game - ACTIVISION BLIZZARD, INC.; *pg.* 948, *pg.* 271
X METAL - Sunglasses - OAKLEY, INC.; *pg.* 1840, *pg.* 86
X-OLENE - Electrical Wire & Cable - THE OKONITE COMPANY; *pg.* 1302, *pg.* 1113
X-OMAT - Processors - EASTMAN KODAK COMPANY; *pg.* 1408, *pg.* 1333
X-OMATIC - Intensifying Screens, X-ray Film, Cassettes - EASTMAN KODAK COMPANY; *pg.* 1408, *pg.* 1333
X-PACK - Fluid Handling System - GRACO, INC.; *pg.* 1342, *pg.* 935
X-PAL - Optical Product - UNIVERSAL PHOTONICS, INC.; *pg.* 1433, *pg.* 1167
X-PANDER - Suitcase - SAMSONITE CORPORATION; *pg.* 11, *pg.* 830
X-PANDISK - Bevel Product - GLEASON CORPORATION; *pg.* 1340, *pg.* 1335
X PEAK - Security Appliance - WATCHGUARD TECHNOLOGIES, INC.; *pg.* 491, *pg.* 1842
X-PHY - Electronic Components - BROADCOM CORPORATION; *pg.* 364, *pg.* 108
X-PLEX - Software - BIO-RAD LABORATORIES, INC.; *pg.* 1504, *pg.* 101
X-PLORER - Musical Instrument - GIBSON GUITAR CORP.; *pg.* 550, *pg.* 1650
X-PLUS - Fluid Handling System - GRACO, INC.; *pg.* 1342, *pg.* 935
X-PRESS MILL - Processing System - HOSOKAWA MICRON POWDER SYSTEMS; *pg.* 1347, *pg.* 1124
X-PUMP BLOCK - Radiant Systems - TACO INCORPORATED; *pg.* 1077, *pg.* 1601
X-RAID - Wireless Networking Product - NETGEAR, INC.; *pg.* 444, *pg.* 247
X-RAID2 - Wireless Networking Product - NETGEAR, INC.; *pg.* 444, *pg.* 247
X-RAIL - Electronic Control Device - TASER INTERNATIONAL, INC.; *pg.* 677, *pg.* 24
X-RAY - Ice Hockey Helmet - REEBOK-CCM HOCKEY, INC.; *pg.* 1844, *pg.* 1960
X-RITECOLOR - Spectrophotometer - X-RITE, INCORPORATED; *pg.* 1437, *pg.* 891
X SERIES - Furniture - HAWORTH, INC.; *pg.* 402, *pg.* 891
X-SOLE - Irons - CALLAWAY GOLF COMPANY; *pg.* 1829, *pg.* 58
X-SPANN - Irons - CALLAWAY GOLF COMPANY; *pg.* 1829, *pg.* 58
X-STACK - Furniture - STEELCASE INC.; *pg.* 475, *pg.* 889
X-STAND - Notebook Riser - LAPWORKS, INC.; *pg.* 426, *pg.* 187
X-STAR - Air Conditioner - FRIEDRICH AIR CONDITIONING CO.; *pg.* 1072, *pg.* 1740
X-STEP - Fiberglass Custom Truck & SUV Steps - LUND INTERNATIONAL, INC.; *pg.* 211, *pg.* 526
X-STREAM - Digital Crosspoint Switch - ANALOG DEVICES, INC.; *pg.* 617, *pg.* 839
X-STREAM - Test Electronic Device - TELEDYNE LECROY; *pg.* 1431, *pg.* 1153
X-TENSE - Synthetic Rubber - THE DOW CHEMICAL COMPANY; *pg.* 1157, *pg.* 898
X-TENZ - Patient Seating - STEELCASE INC.; *pg.* 475, *pg.* 889
X-TERMINATOR - Wrap Bug Shields - LUND INTERNATIONAL, INC.; *pg.* 211, *pg.* 526
X-TOUR - Golf Product - CALLAWAY GOLF COMPANY; *pg.* 1829, *pg.* 58
X-TRA - Utility Cart - HILLYARD, INC.; *pg.* 331, *pg.* 990
X-TRA-EDGE - Tooth System - ESCO CORPORATION; *pg.* 1335, *pg.* 1502
X-TRA HOT 777 DESIGN - Game - WMS INDUSTRIES INC.; *pg.* 593, *pg.* 666
X-TRACT - Knife - BUCK KNIVES, INC.; *pg.* 1828, *pg.* 550
X-TRACT ESSENTIAL - Knife - BUCK KNIVES, INC.; *pg.* 1828, *pg.* 550
X-TRACT FIN - Knife - BUCK KNIVES, INC.; *pg.* 1828, *pg.* 550
X TRANS - Composite Sheet - TRANSILWRAP COMPANY, INC.; *pg.* 1470, *pg.* 613
X-TREL - Implantable Electrode - MEDTRONIC, INC.; *pg.* 1564, *pg.* 939
X-TREME - Toaster - APW WYOTT FOOD SERVICE EQUIPMENT, INC.; *pg.* 1314, *pg.* 1658
X-TREME - Magnetic Die Cutting Cylinder - BUNTING MAGNETICS CO.; *pg.* 1320, *pg.* 717
X-TREME - Gaming Product - GLD PRODUCTS, INC.; *pg.* 1835, *pg.* 1882
X-TREME - Metal Locks - MASTER LOCK COMPANY LLC; *pg.* 1055, *pg.* 1884
X-TREME - Fabric Cleaner - MCNETT CORPORATION; *pg.* 1839, *pg.* 1817
X-TREME BOX - Power Distribution Center - COLEMAN CABLE, INC.; *pg.* 1324, *pg.* 665
X-TREME DENSITY SYSTEMS - Supplemental Cooling Systems - EMERSON NETWORK POWER LIEBERT; *pg.*

First page reference indicates Business Class Edition
Second page reference indicates Geographic Edition

1071, *pg.* 1439

X-TREME GULP - Fountain Soft Drink - 7-ELEVEN, INC.; *pg.* 1012, *pg.* 1672

X-TREME REELS - Game - WMS INDUSTRIES INC.; *pg.* 593, *pg.* 666

X-TREME SOUR SMARTIES - Sour Smarties Candies - SMARTIES CANDY COMPANY; *pg.* 1861, *pg.* 1127

X-TREME WASH - Fabric Cleaner - MCNETT CORPORATION; *pg.* 1839, *pg.* 1817

X-TREME WINNINGS - Lottery Game - NEW JERSEY STATE LOTTERY; *pg.* 1000, *pg.* 1126

X-TRU - Coating Products - RUSSEL METALS INC.; *pg.* 1180, *pg.* 1928

X-TRUDE - Food Product - BUNGE LIMITED; *pg.* 842, *pg.* 1351

X-TUNE - Surf Boards - THE DOW CHEMICAL COMPANY; *pg.* 1157, *pg.* 898

X UVEX - Goggles/Spectacles - UVEX SAFETY; *pg.* 1433, *pg.* 1608

X-VAC - Vacuum Excavator - HI-VAC CORPORATION; *pg.* 56, *pg.* 1458

X-WAV - Conveyor Oven - APW WYOTT FOOD SERVICE EQUIPMENT, INC.; *pg.* 1314, *pg.* 1658

X-WORD - Lottery Game - CALIFORNIA LOTTERY; *pg.* 990, *pg.* 196

X-TREME FILLING - Printer - XEROX CORPORATION; *pg.* 494, *pg.* 365

X1 TECHNOLOGIES - Software - IDEALAB, INC.; *pg.* 1258, *pg.* 180

X100 - Protective Eyewear - SELLSTROM MANUFACTURING CO.; *pg.* 1428, *pg.* 659

X11 - Lined Cut-Resistant Gloves - BAE SYSTEMS PRODUCTS GROUP; *pg.* 359, *pg.* 432

X12 - Protective Eyewear - SELLSTROM MANUFACTURING CO.; *pg.* 1428, *pg.* 659

X2 - Transceiver - FINISAR CORPORATION; *pg.* 639, *pg.* 285

X2 - Projector - INFOCUS CORPORATION; *pg.* 644, *pg.* 1503

X2 ADVENTURE - Personal Transporter - SEGWAY INC.; *pg.* 1923, *pg.* 1033

X2 GOLF - Personal Transporter - SEGWAY INC.; *pg.* 1923, *pg.* 1033

X2 TURF - Personal Transporter - SEGWAY INC.; *pg.* 1923, *pg.* 1033

X200 - Protective Eyewear - SELLSTROM MANUFACTURING CO.; *pg.* 1428, *pg.* 659

X26 - Electronic Control Device - TASER INTERNATIONAL, INC.; *pg.* 677, *pg.* 24

X300 - Protective Eyewear - SELLSTROM MANUFACTURING CO.; *pg.* 1428, *pg.* 659

X5D - 61 Key Synthesizer - KORG USA, INC.; *pg.* 556, *pg.* 1180

X8 PROSPECTOR - X-Ray System - BRUKER CORPORATION; *pg.* 1511, *pg.* 788

X8 PROTEUM - X-Ray System - BRUKER CORPORATION; *pg.* 1511, *pg.* 788

X99 - Furniture - HAWORTH, INC.; *pg.* 402, *pg.* 891

XACT - Stent System - ABBOTT LABORATORIES; *pg.* 1484, *pg.* 551

XACT - Steering - VOLVO PENTA OF THE AMERICAS, INC.; *pg.* 1712, *pg.* 1778

XACTA - System Security - TELOS CORPORATION; *pg.* 483, *pg.* 1776

XACTA COMMERCE TRUST - System Security - TELOS CORPORATION; *pg.* 483, *pg.* 1776

XACTA IA MANAGER - System Security - TELOS CORPORATION; *pg.* 483, *pg.* 1776

XACTA WEBC&A - System Security - TELOS CORPORATION; *pg.* 483, *pg.* 1776

XACTACPAK - Gasket - GREENE, TWEED & CO.; *pg.* 1344, *pg.* 1544

XACTEMP - Hand-Held Temperature Probes - WATLOW ELECTRIC MANUFACTURING COMPANY; *pg.* 1078, *pg.* 1004

XACTPAK - Cable - WATLOW ELECTRIC MANUFACTURING COMPANY; *pg.* 1078, *pg.* 1004

XAD - Resin - DOW CHEMICAL; *pg.* 1156, *pg.* 1563

XAD - Computer Software - NOVELL INC.; *pg.* 446, *pg.* 852

XALATAN - Prescription Eyedrops - PFIZER INC.; *pg.* 1581, *pg.* 1278

XALCOM - Glaucoma Treatment - PFIZER INC.; *pg.* 1581, *pg.* 1278

XAMIN - Software - SUNGARD DATA SYSTEMS INC.; *pg.* 477, *pg.* 1592

XANADU - Fabric - NEMSCHOFF, INC.; *pg.* 936, *pg.* 1890

XANAX - Medicine - PFIZER INC.; *pg.* 1581, *pg.* 1278

XANAX XR - Pharmaceutical Product - IMPAX LABORATORIES, INC.; *pg.* 1544, *pg.* 101

XANAX XR - Pharmaceutical Product - PFIZER INC.; *pg.* 1581, *pg.* 1278

XANGO - Dietary Supplement Juice - XANGO, LLC; *pg.* 1610, *pg.* 1751

XANTOS - Seating - TRENDWAY CORPORATION; *pg.* 945, *pg.* 892

XANTOS XS - Excimer Lasers - COHERENT, INC.; *pg.* 1406, *pg.* 265

XAP - Audio Conferencing System - CLEARONE COMMUNICATIONS, INC.; *pg.* 629, *pg.* 1756

XAPWARE PLUS - Software - DIEBOLD, INCORPORATED; *pg.* 387, *pg.* 1407

XARD-B-LOONS - Foil Balloons - CTI INDUSTRIES CORPORATION; *pg.* 1881, *pg.* 555

XATANET - Communication System - OMNITRACS, LLC; *pg.* 449, *pg.* 1685

XAUI - Channel - BROADCOM CORPORATION; *pg.* 364, *pg.* 108

XB - LED - CREE INC.; *pg.* 631, *pg.* 1371

XB PLUS - LED - CREE INC.; *pg.* 631, *pg.* 1371

XB500 - LED - CREE INC.; *pg.* 631, *pg.* 1371

XB900 - LED - CREE INC.; *pg.* 631, *pg.* 1371

XBB - Computer Hardware - AVAGO TECHNOLOGIES; *pg.* 358, *pg.* 238

XBEAM - Shoe Cushioning Technology - REEBOK INTERNATIONAL LTD.; *pg.* 1817, *pg.* 811

XBEE - Computer Peripheral Equipment - DIGI INTERNATIONAL INC.; *pg.* 387, *pg.* 948

XBEE-PRO - RF ModuleComputer Peripheral Equipment - DIGI INTERNATIONAL INC.; *pg.* 387, *pg.* 948

XBOX - Entertainment Console - MICROSOFT CORPORATION; *pg.* 435, *pg.* 1824

XBRIDGE - Analytical Column - WATERS CORPORATION; *pg.* 1436, *pg.* 834

XBRIGHT - Led - CREE INC.; *pg.* 631, *pg.* 1371

XBRIGHTPLUS - Led - CREE INC.; *pg.* 631, *pg.* 1371

XC1255 - Photocopier - XEROX CORPORATION; *pg.* 494, *pg.* 365

XC1875 - Photocopier - XEROX CORPORATION; *pg.* 494, *pg.* 365

XC33 - Photocopier - XEROX CORPORATION; *pg.* 494, *pg.* 365

XC540 - Photocopier - XEROX CORPORATION; *pg.* 494, *pg.* 365

XC580 - Photocopier - XEROX CORPORATION; *pg.* 494, *pg.* 365

XC820 - Photocopier - XEROX CORPORATION; *pg.* 494, *pg.* 365

XC830 - Photocopier - XEROX CORPORATION; *pg.* 494, *pg.* 365

XC865 - Photocopier - XEROX CORPORATION; *pg.* 494, *pg.* 365

XCALIBRE - Software System - MENTOR GRAPHICS CORPORATION; *pg.* 432, *pg.* 1510

XCALIBUR - Footwear - STEVEN MADDEN, LTD.; *pg.* 1819, *pg.* 1176

XCALIBUR - Software - THERMO FISHER SCIENTIFIC INC.; *pg.* 1431, *pg.* 854

XCDA - Purge Gas - ENTEGRIS, INC.; *pg.* 1882, *pg.* 788

XCEDA - Chemical Mechanical Planarization Product - LAM RESEARCH CORPORATION; *pg.* 1354, *pg.* 246

XCEDE - Connector Platform - AMPHENOL CORPORATION; *pg.* 616, *pg.* 381

XCEED - Stent System - ABBOTT LABORATORIES; *pg.* 1484, *pg.* 551

XCEEDER - Conveyor Chain - U.S. TSUBAKI, INC.; *pg.* 221, *pg.* 670

XCEL - Suture Anchor - STRYKER CORPORATION; *pg.* 1598, *pg.* 894

XCEL ENERGY CENTER - Sports Arena - MINNESOTA WILD HOCKEY CLUB, LP; *pg.* 563, *pg.* 962

XCELERATOR IP - Business Communications System - VERTICAL COMMUNICATIONS, INC.; *pg.* 488, *pg.* 270

XCELL - Molecular Biology Product - THERMO FISHER SCIENTIFIC INC.; *pg.* 1602, *pg.* 61

XCELL SURELOCK - Biomolecule Product - THERMO FISHER SCIENTIFIC INC.; *pg.* 1602, *pg.* 61

XCELSORT - Sliding Shoe Sorter - PARAGON TECHNOLOGIES, INC.; *pg.* 1367, *pg.* 1528

XCESS - Deodorant - BLUE CROSS LABORATORIES; *pg.* 326, *pg.* 277

XCHANGE - Robotic Collimator Exchange - ACCURAY INCORPORATED; *pg.* 1486, *pg.* 282

XCHANGE - Publication - INFORMA EXHIBITIONS LLC; *pg.* 1653, *pg.* 17

XCHANGE - Publisher - UNITED BUSINESS MEDIA LLC; *pg.* 1697, *pg.* 1177

XCHANGE POINT - Computer Software - ENERGY & POWER SOLUTIONS, INC.; *pg.* 392, *pg.* 71

XCHANGENOW - Warranty Replacement Program - OVERLAND STORAGE, INC.; *pg.* 451, *pg.* 205

XCHECKER - Universal Download Cable that Supplies XL2000, 3000 and 4000 FPGA Families - XILINX, INC.; *pg.* 496, *pg.* 252

XCHEK - Diagnostic Software - IDEXX LABORATORIES, INC.; *pg.* 1543, *pg.* 753

XCHIP - Electronic Device - LANTRONIX, INC.; *pg.* 426, *pg.* 112

XCHIP DIRECT - Electronic Device - LANTRONIX, INC.; *pg.* 426, *pg.* 112

XCI - Software - WELOCALIZE, INC.; *pg.* 1289, *pg.* 769

XCITABLUE - Software - BIO-RAD LABORATORIES, INC.; *pg.* 1504, *pg.* 101

XCITE - Computer Peripheral Equipment - DIGI INTERNATIONAL INC.; *pg.* 387, *pg.* 948

XCITE - Sailboat - MARLOW-HUNTER LLC; *pg.* 1709, *pg.* 409

XCLAIM - Video Card - ADVANCED MICRO DEVICES, INC.; *pg.* 613, *pg.* 282

XCLUDA - Software - BIO-RAD LABORATORIES, INC.; *pg.* 1504, *pg.* 101

XCODE - Developer Software - APPLE INC.; *pg.* 350, *pg.* 73

XCON - Cable Instrument - PEAVEY ELECTRONICS CORPORATION; *pg.* 662, *pg.* 970

XCONFIG - Software System - MENTOR GRAPHICS CORPORATION; *pg.* 432, *pg.* 1510

XCORE - Software - WATCHGUARD TECHNOLOGIES, INC.; *pg.* 491, *pg.* 1842

XCOUNTER - Software - XEROX CORPORATION; *pg.* 494, *pg.* 365

XCP-DS - Dental Product - DENTSPLY INTERNATIONAL INC.; *pg.* 1522, *pg.* 1596

XD - Systems Integration & Aeronautics - LOCKHEED MARTIN CORPORATION; *pg.* 229, *pg.* 762

XD-PICTURE CARD - Memory Card - LEXAR MEDIA, INC.; *pg.* 1262, *pg.* 146

XD-PICTURE CARD - Digital Camera - PNY TECHNOLOGIES, INC.; *pg.* 455, *pg.* 1105

XD-PICTURE CARD - Memory Card - SANDISK CORPORATION; *pg.* 465, *pg.* 147

XDEV - Software - TELEDYNE LECROY; *pg.* 1431, *pg.* 1153

XDIMENSION - Golf Shoe - ACUSHNET COMPANY; *pg.* 1824, *pg.* 818

XDR - Memory Interface Systems for Graphic Applications - RAMBUS INC.; *pg.* 459, *pg.* 288

XDR 2 - Chip Interface System - RAMBUS INC.; *pg.* 459, *pg.* 288

XDS - Emulator Systems & Software - TEXAS INSTRUMENTS INCORPORATED; *pg.* 679, *pg.* 1688

XDS510 - Printed Circuit Boards - TEXAS INSTRUMENTS INCORPORATED; *pg.* 679, *pg.* 1688

XDS5100 - Printed Circuit Boards - TEXAS INSTRUMENTS INCORPORATED; *pg.* 679, *pg.* 1688

XDS560 - Electronic Components - TEXAS INSTRUMENTS INCORPORATED; *pg.* 679, *pg.* 1688

XEBRA - Electric Car - ZAP; *pg.* 222, *pg.* 277

XELCORE - Software - BROADCOM CORPORATION; *pg.* 364, *pg.* 108

XELODA - Pharmaceutical Product - HOFFMANN-LA ROCHE INC.; *pg.* 1542, *pg.* 1099

XEMT2100 / 3980 - Electronic Component - EMCORE CORPORATION; *pg.* 636, *pg.* 39

XEN - Software - CITRIX SYSTEMS, INC.; *pg.* 375, *pg.* 424

XEN CORPORATION - Systems, Software & Integration Consulting Services - CACI INTERNATIONAL INC.; *pg.* 367, *pg.* 1773

XEN DATA CENTER - Software - CITRIX SYSTEMS, INC.; *pg.* 375, *pg.* 424

XEN SOURCE - Software - CITRIX SYSTEMS, INC.; *pg.* 375, *pg.* 424

XENCENTER - Software - CITRIX SYSTEMS, INC.; *pg.* 375, *pg.* 424

XENDESKTOP - Software - CITRIX SYSTEMS, INC.; *pg.* 375, *pg.* 424

XENENTERPRISE - Software - CITRIX SYSTEMS, INC.; *pg.* 375, *pg.* 424

XENEREX - Therapeutic Product - AVANIR PHARMACEUTICALS; *pg.* 1498, *pg.* 40
XENFORM - Medical Device - BOSTON SCIENTIFIC CORPORATION; *pg.* 1508, *pg.* 831
XENICAL - Pharmaceutical Product - HOFFMANN-LA ROCHE INC.; *pg.* 1542, *pg.* 1099
XENIT - Car Care Product - STONER INC.; *pg.* 985, *pg.* 1583
XENITH - Bicycles - G. JOANNOU CYCLE CO. INC.; *pg.* 1707, *pg.* 1098
XENITH - Packaging Films - SEALED AIR CORPORATION; *pg.* 1468, *pg.* 1058
XENITH PRO - Bicycle - G. JOANNOU CYCLE CO. INC.; *pg.* 1707, *pg.* 1098
XENITH TEAM - Bicycle - G. JOANNOU CYCLE CO. INC.; *pg.* 1707, *pg.* 1098
XENIUM - Hemodialysis Dialyzer - BAXTER INTERNATIONAL INC.; *pg.* 1499, *pg.* 599
XENMOTION - Software - CITRIX SYSTEMS, INC.; *pg.* 375, *pg.* 424
XENON - High Intensity Lamp - BALLANTYNE STRONG, INC.; *pg.* 623, *pg.* 1013
XENONICS - Illumination Device - XENONICS HOLDINGS, INC.; *pg.* 1308, *pg.* 62
XENOPRESSURE - Automatic Conveyor System - PARAGON TECHNOLOGIES, INC.; *pg.* 1367, *pg.* 1528
XENOROL - Roller Conveyor - PARAGON TECHNOLOGIES, INC.; *pg.* 1367, *pg.* 1528
XENOS ENTERPRISE SERVER - Software - ACTUATE CANADA; *pg.* 1225, *pg.* 1933
XENOSORT - Automatic Conveyor System - PARAGON TECHNOLOGIES, INC.; *pg.* 1367, *pg.* 1528
XENOTECH - Entertainment Lighting Product - BALLANTYNE STRONG, INC.; *pg.* 623, *pg.* 1013
XENOTRACTION - Automatic Conveyor System - PARAGON TECHNOLOGIES, INC.; *pg.* 1367, *pg.* 1528
XENOWORKS - Software - BIO-RAD LABORATORIES, INC.; *pg.* 1504, *pg.* 101
XENOY IQ - Engineered Plastics - GENERAL ELECTRIC COMPANY; *pg.* 1297, *pg.* 347
XENPAK - Fiber Optic Product - EMCORE CORPORATION; *pg.* 636, *pg.* 39
XENPAK - Transceiver - FINISAR CORPORATION; *pg.* 639, *pg.* 285
XENPAK - Network Testing System - IXIA; *pg.* 422, *pg.* 56
XENSERVER - Software - CITRIX SYSTEMS, INC.; *pg.* 375, *pg.* 424
XENSUMMIT - Software - CITRIX SYSTEMS, INC.; *pg.* 375, *pg.* 424
XENSUPPORT - Software - CITRIX SYSTEMS, INC.; *pg.* 375, *pg.* 424
XEO - Light-Based Aesthetic System - CUTERA, INC.; *pg.* 1521, *pg.* 49
XERCISE BANDS - Resistance Training - SCHOOL-TECH, INC.; *pg.* 1844, *pg.* 866
XERI-BIRD - Emission Device - RAIN BIRD CORPORATION; *pg.* 707, *pg.* 44
XERI-MAN - Tool - RAIN BIRD CORPORATION; *pg.* 707, *pg.* 44
XERIGATION - Sprinklers - RAIN BIRD CORPORATION; *pg.* 707, *pg.* 44
XEROPAQUE - Paper Products - BOISE CASCADE HOLDINGS, L.L.C.; *pg.* 1453, *pg.* 546
XEROX - Business Products - XEROX CORPORATION; *pg.* 494, *pg.* 365
XEROX CAPITAL SERVICES AND DESIGN - Manual - XEROX CORPORATION; *pg.* 494, *pg.* 365
THE XEROX COMPANY STORE - Manual - XEROX CORPORATION; *pg.* 494, *pg.* 365
XEROX CONNECT AND DESIGN - Manual - XEROX CORPORATION; *pg.* 494, *pg.* 365
XEROX INTELLIGENT BARCODE UTILITY - Manual - XEROX CORPORATION; *pg.* 494, *pg.* 365
XEROX MAKES YOUR WORK. . .FLOW - Manual - XEROX CORPORATION; *pg.* 494, *pg.* 365
XEROX PROFESSIONAL DOCUMENT SERVICES - Manual - XEROX CORPORATION; *pg.* 494, *pg.* 365
XEROX SCAN MANAGER - Manual - XEROX CORPORATION; *pg.* 494, *pg.* 365
XEROX VALUE ASSURANCE PROCESS - Manual - XEROX CORPORATION; *pg.* 494, *pg.* 365
XERTUBE - Resistance Training - SCHOOL-TECH, INC.; *pg.* 1844, *pg.* 866
XERXES - Game - WMS INDUSTRIES INC.; *pg.* 593, *pg.* 666
XEVO - Mass Spectrometer - WATERS CORPORATION; *pg.* 1436, *pg.* 834
XFACTOR - SAASM-based GPS Receiver - L-3 INTERSTATE ELECTRONICS CORPORATION; *pg.* 650, *pg.* 43
XFACTOR - Game - WMS INDUSTRIES INC.; *pg.* 593, *pg.* 666
XFER - Software Product - WOODWARD, INC.; *pg.* 122, *pg.* 329
XFINITY - Cable Television Broadcasting Service - COMCAST CORPORATION; *pg.* 276, *pg.* 1560
XFL - TV Show - WORLD WRESTLING ENTERTAINMENT, INC.; *pg.* 595, *pg.* 380
XFLASH QUAD - Detector - BRUKER CORPORATION; *pg.* 1511, *pg.* 788
XFP - Transceiver - FINISAR CORPORATION; *pg.* 639, *pg.* 285
XFP PRO - Semiconductor Solution - VITESSE SEMICONDUCTOR CORPORATION; *pg.* 686, *pg.* 57
XFP2000 - Com System - ANACOMP, INC.; *pg.* 350, *pg.* 1777
XG - Reels - WRIGHT & MCGILL CO.; *pg.* 1848, *pg.* 324
XGIG - Analyzer - FINISAR CORPORATION; *pg.* 639, *pg.* 285
XGLRRXM - Transceivers - OPLINK COMMUNICATIONS, INC.; *pg.* 660, *pg.* 91
XGRID - Application Program - APPLE INC.; *pg.* 350, *pg.* 73
XHALE - Medical Device - OLIVER PRODUCTS COMPANY INC.; *pg.* 1367, *pg.* 888
XHS - Stainless Steel Propeller - MICHIGAN WHEEL CORPORATION; *pg.* 1709, *pg.* 888
XI BLADERAIDER - Workstation - @XI COMPUTER CORPORATION; *pg.* 355, *pg.* 199
XI GROUP - Advertising Publication - DOMINION ENTERPRISES; *pg.* 1636, *pg.* 1796
XI MTOWER - CAD System - @XI COMPUTER CORPORATION; *pg.* 355, *pg.* 199
XI NETRAIDER - Workstation - @XI COMPUTER CORPORATION; *pg.* 355, *pg.* 199
XI NTOWER - Workstation - @XI COMPUTER CORPORATION; *pg.* 355, *pg.* 199
XI POWERGO - Workstation - @XI COMPUTER CORPORATION; *pg.* 355, *pg.* 199
XI WEBRAIDER - Workstation - @XI COMPUTER CORPORATION; *pg.* 355, *pg.* 199
XIA - Spinal System - STRYKER CORPORATION; *pg.* 1598, *pg.* 894
XIAMETER - Silicon-Based Chemical Products - DOW CORNING CORPORATION; *pg.* 1159, *pg.* 900
XIENCE V - Stent System - ABBOTT LABORATORIES; *pg.* 1484, *pg.* 551
XIFAXAN - Pharmaceutical Product - SALIX PHARMACEUTICALS, INC.; *pg.* 1591, *pg.* 1388
XIGRIS - Pharmaceutical Product - ELI LILLY AND COMPANY; *pg.* 1527, *pg.* 684
XILINX SPARTAN-IIE - Circuit Board - XILINX, INC.; *pg.* 496, *pg.* 252
XILINX VIRTEX-II - Circuit Board - XILINX, INC.; *pg.* 496, *pg.* 252
XILLEON - Video Card - ADVANCED MICRO DEVICES, INC.; *pg.* 613, *pg.* 282
XILLEON - 3D Graphical Technology - ADVANCED MICRO DEVICES, INC.-MARKHAM; *pg.* 345, *pg.* 1922
XILO - Tile - ARTISTIC TILE INC.; *pg.* 914, *pg.* 1119
XILO - Ceramic, Glass, Stone Tiles & Slabs - WALKER & ZANGER, INC.; *pg.* 119, *pg.* 281
XIMAVISION - Medical System - VARIAN MEDICAL SYSTEMS, INC.; *pg.* 1434, *pg.* 178
XIMIAN - Computer Software - NOVELL INC.; *pg.* 446, *pg.* 852
XINGER - Microwave & Surface Components - ANAREN, INC.; *pg.* 617, *pg.* 1157
XIO - Software - ELEKTA; *pg.* 391, *pg.* 987
XIP CAVIAR - Seafood - OCEAN BEAUTY SEAFOODS, INC.; *pg.* 1028, *pg.* 1838
XIP-LIGHT - Manual - XEROX CORPORATION; *pg.* 494, *pg.* 365
XIV - Software - INTERNATIONAL BUSINESS MACHINES CORPORATION; *pg.* 418, *pg.* 1138
XIVE - Dental Product - DENTSPLY INTERNATIONAL INC.; *pg.* 1522, *pg.* 1596
XL - Post Hole Diggers - AG-MEIER INDUSTRIES LLC; *pg.* 700, *pg.* 1668
XL - Regulator Bypass Switch - S&C ELECTRIC COMPANY; *pg.* 1305, *pg.* 589
XL-2000 - Sonicators - MISONIX INC.; *pg.* 1568, *pg.* 1159
XL-2000 - Cast Iron Oil Boiler - SLANT/FIN CORPORATION; *pg.* 1076, *pg.* 1163
XL LAPTOP - Briefcase - SANTA FE LEATHER CORPORATION; *pg.* 12, *pg.* 1059
XL-MCL - Flow Cytometer - BECKMAN COULTER, INC.; *pg.* 1402, *pg.* 48
XL POWER-PISTON - Pump - GRACO, INC.; *pg.* 1342, *pg.* 935
XL PRO - Metal Detector - WHITE'S ELECTRONICS; *pg.* 688, *pg.* 1509
XL-TC - Electrical Wire & Cable - GENERAL CABLE CORPORATION; *pg.* 83, *pg.* 384
XLAMP - Led - CREE INC.; *pg.* 631, *pg.* 1371
XLERATOR - Muffler - AP EXHAUST PRODUCTS, INC.; *pg.* 199, *pg.* 1373
XLERATOR - Hide Processing Agent - BIRKO CORPORATION; *pg.* 1149, *pg.* 332
XLERATOR - Plumbing Product - SLOAN VALVE COMPANY; *pg.* 1062, *pg.* 613
XLERATOR BIG MAX - Muffler - AP EXHAUST PRODUCTS, INC.; *pg.* 199, *pg.* 1373
XLERATOR ENFORCER - Glasspack & Turbopack - AP EXHAUST PRODUCTS, INC.; *pg.* 199, *pg.* 1373
XLERATOR XSS - Muffler - AP EXHAUST PRODUCTS, INC.; *pg.* 199, *pg.* 1373
XLIF - Surgical Procedure - NUVASIVE, INC.; *pg.* 1577, *pg.* 205
XLO - Sponges - THE CLOROX COMPANY; *pg.* 327, *pg.* 169
XLR - Light Source - CYMER, INC.; *pg.* 1296, *pg.* 202
XLR-12-3-PP - Patch Panel - EMCORE CORPORATION; *pg.* 636, *pg.* 39
XLR8 - High Performance Consumer Graphics Card & High Performance Memory - PNY TECHNOLOGIES, INC.; *pg.* 455, *pg.* 1105
XLR8R - Music & Culture Site - SPINMEDIA; *pg.* 1282, *pg.* 104
XLT - Truck Seating - SEATS INCORPORATED; *pg.* 217, *pg.* 1890
XLTEK - Medical Device - NATUS MEDICAL INCORPORATED; *pg.* 1572, *pg.* 199
XM - Software - ROCKWELL AUTOMATION, INC.; *pg.* 668, *pg.* 1880
XM SERIES END MILL - M42 Cobalt End Mill - REGAL BELOIT CORPORATION; *pg.* 106, *pg.* 1854
XMAP - Testing Technology - LUMINEX CORPORATION; *pg.* 1421, *pg.* 1664
XMAP - Software - TELEDYNE LECROY; *pg.* 1431, *pg.* 1153
XMARK - Software - BIO-RAD LABORATORIES, INC.; *pg.* 1504, *pg.* 101
XMATE - Insecticides, Fungicides, Herbicides & Pesticides - DOW CHEMICAL; *pg.* 1156, *pg.* 1563
XMATH - Software - TELEDYNE LECROY; *pg.* 1431, *pg.* 1153
XMC - Fiber Glass Reinforced Compositions & Fibers - PPG INDUSTRIES, INC.; *pg.* 1445, *pg.* 1579
XMEGA - Integrated Circuit - ATMEL CORPORATION; *pg.* 621, *pg.* 238
XML CONNECT - Web Tool - OPENCONNECT SYSTEMS, INC.; *pg.* 449, *pg.* 1685
XML SOLUTION KIT - Software - BOTTOMLINE TECHNOLOGIES INC.; *pg.* 363, *pg.* 483
XML THREAT MANAGER - Software - AVAGO TECHNOLOGIES; *pg.* 358, *pg.* 238
XML2PDF MERGE - Software - ACTUATE CANADA; *pg.* 1225, *pg.* 1933
XMP - Paper Products - BOISE CASCADE HOLDINGS, L.L.C.; *pg.* 1453, *pg.* 546
XMP-2 - Remote Control Protocol - UNIVERSAL ELECTRONICS, INC.; *pg.* 683, *pg.* 262
XO LAGER - Beer - BIG ROCK BREWERY INCOME TRUST; *pg.* 239, *pg.* 1902
XODUST - Dust Control Products - 3M COMPANY; *pg.* 1142, *pg.* 956
XOHM - Mobile Internet Service - SPRINT CORPORATION; *pg.* 1874, *pg.* 719
XOI BAR - Food Energy Bar - NU SKIN ENTERPRISES, INC.; *pg.* 518, *pg.* 1755
XOOM - Integrated Circuits - AVAGO TECHNOLOGIES; *pg.* 358, *pg.* 238
XOOM - Valve & Actuator - XOOM CORPORATION; *pg.* 1289, *pg.* 234
XOOMERANG - Mobile Solution - VERISIGN, INC.; *pg.* 488, *pg.* 1799
XOPENEX - Pharmaceutical Product - SUNOVION PHARMACEUTICALS INC.; *pg.* 1599, *pg.* 832

XOPENEX HFA - Inhaler - SUNOVION PHARMACEUTICALS INC.; *pg.* 1599, *pg.* 832
XOS - Switch - EXTREME NETWORKS INC; *pg.* 287, *pg.* 245
XOXO - Footwear - COBIAN CORP.; *pg.* 1806, *pg.* 253
XP - Bearing - THE TIMKEN COMPANY; *pg.* 218, *pg.* 1408
XP BOND - Dental Product - DENTSPLY INTERNATIONAL INC.; *pg.* 1522, *pg.* 1596
XP/PM - Particle Metal End Mill - REGAL BELOIT CORPORATION; *pg.* 106, *pg.* 1854
XP/PMC - Particle Metal End Mill with Cobalt - REGAL BELOIT CORPORATION; *pg.* 106, *pg.* 1854
XP5000 - Narrow Web Press - MARK ANDY, INC.; *pg.* 1359, *pg.* 975
XPAK - Transceiver - FINISAR CORPORATION; *pg.* 639, *pg.* 285
XPAK - Mailer Product - POLYAIR INTER PACK INC.; *pg.* 1467, *pg.* 1941
XPANEL - Software - CRESTRON ELECTRONICS INC.; *pg.* 631, *pg.* 1116
XPANZ - Office Product - WESTROCK COMPANY; *pg.* 1472, *pg.* 1805
XPEAK - Software - WATCHGUARD TECHNOLOGIES, INC.; *pg.* 491, *pg.* 1842
XPEDITER - Software - COMPUWARE CORPORATION; *pg.* 379, *pg.* 879
XPEDITION - Cruise Ship - ROYAL CARIBBEAN CRUISES LTD; *pg.* 1921, *pg.* 446
XPEDITOR - Refuse Vehicle - VOLVO TRUCKS NORTH AMERICA, INC.; *pg.* 195, *pg.* 1377
XPEDX - Paper - INTERNATIONAL PAPER COMPANY; *pg.* 1460, *pg.* 1644
XPEL - Nutritional Supplement - MAXIMUM HUMAN PERFORMANCE, INC.; *pg.* 1559, *pg.* 1065
XPERT - Stent System - ABBOTT LABORATORIES; *pg.* 1484, *pg.* 551
XPERT - Paint - AKZONOBEL DECORATIVE PAINTS U.S.; *pg.* 1439, *pg.* 1474
XPERTDOC CONTACT GADGET - Report Generator - PROCESS ACADEMY, INC.; *pg.* 456, *pg.* 1951
XPERTDOC DATA GADGET - Report Generator - PROCESS ACADEMY, INC.; *pg.* 456, *pg.* 1951
XPERTDOC STUDIO 2006 - Report Generator - PROCESS ACADEMY, INC.; *pg.* 456, *pg.* 1951
XPERTDOC STUDIO 2007 - Report Generator - PROCESS ACADEMY, INC.; *pg.* 456, *pg.* 1951
XPG - Apparel - CABELA'S INCORPORATED; *pg.* 535, *pg.* 1019
XPHASE - Power Semiconductor Device - INTERNATIONAL RECTIFIER CORPORATION; *pg.* 647, *pg.* 80
XPIG - Tool - T.D. WILLIAMSON, INC.; *pg.* 1380, *pg.* 1490
XPLEAT - Pleated Cartridge Filters - GE WATER & PROCESS TECHNOLOGIES; *pg.* 1339, *pg.* 1588
XPLORE3D - Software Product - FEI COMPANY; *pg.* 1413, *pg.* 1498
XPO2 - Medical Equipment - INVACARE CORPORATION; *pg.* 1546, *pg.* 1451
XPOGRAPH - Foam Display Board - THE DOW CHEMICAL COMPANY; *pg.* 1157, *pg.* 898
XPONENT - Software - LUMINEX CORPORATION; *pg.* 1421, *pg.* 1664
XPORTER - Pickup Truck Rack - THULE, INC.; *pg.* 218, *pg.* 369
XPOSURE - Aldehyde Sampler Cartridge - WATERS CORPORATION; *pg.* 1436, *pg.* 834
XPP - Book Projects - CENVEO INC.; *pg.* 1626, *pg.* 372
XPR - Software - BIO-RAD LABORATORIES, INC.; *pg.* 1504, *pg.* 101
XPR - Two Way Radios - MOTOROLA SOLUTIONS, INC.; *pg.* 657, *pg.* 659
XPRESS - Specialty Lighting - BALLANTYNE STRONG, INC.; *pg.* 623, *pg.* 1013
XPRESS - Wireless Technology - BROADCOM CORPORATION; *pg.* 364, *pg.* 108
XPRESS - Computer Peripheral Equipment - DIGI INTERNATIONAL INC.; *pg.* 387, *pg.* 948
XPRESS - Software - FIDELITY NATIONAL INFORMATION SERVICES; *pg.* 397, *pg.* 1549
XPRESS - Pre-Engineered Metal Buildings - KIRBY BUILDING SYSTEMS, INC.; *pg.* 91, *pg.* 1655
XPRESS - Electronic Components - MOLEX INCORPORATED; *pg.* 655, *pg.* 628
XPRESS - Fabric - NEMSCHOFF, INC.; *pg.* 936, *pg.* 1890
XPRESS - Leader Peptide - THERMO FISHER SCIENTIFIC INC.; *pg.* 1602, *pg.* 61
XPRESS-IT - Automobile Cleaning Preparations - ASHLAND INC.; *pg.* 972, *pg.* 726
XPRESS-LOCK - Electronic Components - MOLEX INCORPORATED; *pg.* 655, *pg.* 628
XPRESS LUBE - Oil Fuel - CHEVRON CORPORATION; *pg.* 974, *pg.* 259
XPRESS PRO - Software - AMX CORPORATION; *pg.* 349, *pg.* 1735
XPRESSAUDIO - Microprocessor - ADVANCED MICRO DEVICES, INC.; *pg.* 613, *pg.* 282
XPRESSGRAPHICS - Microprocessor System - ADVANCED MICRO DEVICES, INC.; *pg.* 613, *pg.* 282
XPRESSHUB - Microprocessor - ADVANCED MICRO DEVICES, INC.; *pg.* 613, *pg.* 282
XPRESSION - Software - EMC CORPORATION; *pg.* 391, *pg.* 825
XPRESSNET - Wireless Communication Product - IPMOBILENET, LLC; *pg.* 648, *pg.* 261
XPRESSO - Software - EMC CORPORATION; *pg.* 391, *pg.* 825
XPRESSO - Manual - XEROX CORPORATION; *pg.* 494, *pg.* 365
XPRESSRAM - Microprocessor - ADVANCED MICRO DEVICES, INC.; *pg.* 613, *pg.* 282
XPRESSWAY - Milking Parlor Systems - BOUMATIC LLC; *pg.* 701, *pg.* 1865
XPRINT - Printer - XEROX CORPORATION; *pg.* 494, *pg.* 365
XPRT - Patient Handling Equipment - STRYKER CORPORATION; *pg.* 1598, *pg.* 894
XPS - Manual - XEROX CORPORATION; *pg.* 494, *pg.* 365
XPSIM - Software - GULF PUBLISHING COMPANY; *pg.* 1646, *pg.* 1707
THE XQ - Core Offerings - FRANKLIN COVEY CO.; *pg.* 1642, *pg.* 1758
XQUEST - Wallcovering - OMNOVA SOLUTIONS INC; *pg.* 1176, *pg.* 1453
XR - Electronic Targeting Apparatus - LOCKHEED MARTIN CORPORATION; *pg.* 229, *pg.* 762
XR - Wire Welding Module - MILLER ELECTRIC MANUFACTURING CO.; *pg.* 1361, *pg.* 1852
XR 4286 - Pentaerythritol Ester - ARIZONA CHEMICAL CO. LLC; *pg.* 1147, *pg.* 431
XRAY - Software System - MENTOR GRAPHICS CORPORATION; *pg.* 432, *pg.* 1510
XRAY-PAK - Radiation Shielding Technology - MAXWELL TECHNOLOGIES, INC.; *pg.* 653, *pg.* 204
XRC - Electronic Components - MOLEX INCORPORATED; *pg.* 655, *pg.* 628
XRE - Medical Product - HOLOGIC, INC.; *pg.* 1416, *pg.* 784
XRT - Software - DELL SOFTWARE; *pg.* 385, *pg.* 40
XS - Glass & Ceramic Material - CORNING INCORPORATED; *pg.* 1122, *pg.* 1154
XS - Power Fuse - S&C ELECTRIC COMPANY; *pg.* 1305, *pg.* 589
XS-100-B - Universal Stringing Block - SHERMAN & REILLY, INC.; *pg.* 1062, *pg.* 1629
XSAN - Application Program - APPLE INC.; *pg.* 350, *pg.* 73
XSELLERATOR - Software Program - QUORUM INFORMATION TECHNOLOGIES INC.; *pg.* 458, *pg.* 1904
XSENSOR - Pressure Measurement System - THE ROHO GROUP; *pg.* 1591, *pg.* 556
XSERVE - Server - APPLE INC.; *pg.* 350, *pg.* 73
XSFLOOD - Flood Coverage in Excess of Federal Government Limits - THE SEIBELS BRUCE GROUP, INC.; *pg.* 1216, *pg.* 1614
XSI - Software - AUTODESK INC.; *pg.* 356, *pg.* 257
XSIGHT - Lung & Spine Tracking System - ACCURAY INCORPORATED; *pg.* 1486, *pg.* 282
X.SPOT - Lighting Product - HIGH END SYSTEMS, INC.; *pg.* 1299, *pg.* 1663
XST - Synthesizer - XILINX, INC.; *pg.* 496, *pg.* 252
XSTAT - X-Ray Inspection Equipment - TERADYNE INC.; *pg.* 679, *pg.* 838
XSTATIC - Video Game - INTERNATIONAL GAME TECHNOLOGY; *pg.* 957, *pg.* 1024
XSTATION - X-Ray Inspection Equipment - TERADYNE INC.; *pg.* 679, *pg.* 838
XSTREAM - Remote Plasma Source - ADVANCED ENERGY INDUSTRIES, INC.; *pg.* 613, *pg.* 328
XSTREAM - Computer Peripheral Equipment - DIGI INTERNATIONAL INC.; *pg.* 387, *pg.* 948
XSTREAM - Filter - HAYWARD POOL PRODUCTS; *pg.* 1049, *pg.* 1057
XT - LED - CREE INC.; *pg.* 631, *pg.* 1371
XT - Hubs & Bushings - VAN GORP CORPORATION; *pg.* 1387, *pg.* 711
XT-12 - LED - CREE INC.; *pg.* 631, *pg.* 1371
XT-16 - LED - CREE INC.; *pg.* 631, *pg.* 1371
XT-18 - LED - CREE INC.; *pg.* 631, *pg.* 1371
XT-21 - LED - CREE INC.; *pg.* 631, *pg.* 1371
XT-24 - LED - CREE INC.; *pg.* 631, *pg.* 1371
XT-27 - LED - CREE INC.; *pg.* 631, *pg.* 1371
XT POLYMER - Acrylic Based Multipolymer Compound - EVONIK CYRO LLC; *pg.* 1162, *pg.* 1103
XT-REME - Drum Pulley - VAN GORP CORPORATION; *pg.* 1387, *pg.* 711
XT3 MULTI-PURPOSE DUMP BODIES - Dump Body - HIGHWAY EQUIPMENT COMPANY; *pg.* 704, *pg.* 702
XTAG - Respiratory Viral Panel - LUMINEX CORPORATION; *pg.* 1421, *pg.* 1664
XTC TRANSMITTER - Controller - SIEMENS PROCESS INDUSTRIES AND DRIVE; *pg.* 1376, *pg.* 1587
XTEND - Plastic & Rubber Material - AXEL PLASTICS RESEARCH LABORATORIES, INC.; *pg.* 326, *pg.* 1356
XTEND - Natural Sweetener - CARGILL, INC.; *pg.* 845, *pg.* 965
XTEND - Computer Peripheral Equipment - DIGI INTERNATIONAL INC.; *pg.* 387, *pg.* 948
XTEND - Software - OPTIONSXPRESS HOLDINGS, INC.; *pg.* 790, *pg.* 586
XTEND - Globalization Technology - WELOCALIZE, INC.; *pg.* 1289, *pg.* 769
XTEND-IT - Resin - SMOOTH-ON INC.; *pg.* 111, *pg.* 1528
XTENDER IMAGING - Data Manager - PEARSON ASSESSMENTS; *pg.* 1674, *pg.* 918
XTENSIONS - Software - QUARK, INC.; *pg.* 458, *pg.* 322
XTERRA - Analytical Column - WATERS CORPORATION; *pg.* 1436, *pg.* 834
XTG - Hair Care Product - JOHN PAUL MITCHELL SYSTEMS; *pg.* 512, *pg.* 133
XTHIN - Led - CREE INC.; *pg.* 631, *pg.* 1371
XTK - Technology Kit - WELOCALIZE, INC.; *pg.* 1289, *pg.* 769
XTM - Software & Firmware - AVAGO TECHNOLOGIES; *pg.* 358, *pg.* 238
XTNDCONNECT PC - Software - SAP; *pg.* 465, *pg.* 78
XTOL - Photographic Developer - EASTMAN KODAK COMPANY; *pg.* 1408, *pg.* 1333
XTOL - Tall Oil Fatty Acids & Tall Oil Byproducts - GEORGIA-PACIFIC LLC; *pg.* 1458, *pg.* 507
XTOLUBE - Oxidation Stable Esters - GEORGIA-PACIFIC LLC; *pg.* 1458, *pg.* 507
XTP - Pistol Bullet - HORNADY MANUFACTURING COMPANY; *pg.* 1836, *pg.* 1010
XTR - Diagnostic System - BECTON, DICKINSON & COMPANY; *pg.* 1501, *pg.* 1068
XTRA - Backboard - ALLIED HEALTHCARE PRODUCTS, INC.; *pg.* 1491, *pg.* 990
XTRA - Laundry Detergent - CHURCH & DWIGHT CO., INC.; *pg.* 1153, *pg.* 1063
XTRA ACTION - Video Game - INTERNATIONAL GAME TECHNOLOGY; *pg.* 957, *pg.* 1024
XTRA-CAL - Calcium Supplement - HERBALIFE INTERNATIONAL OF AMERICA, INC.; *pg.* 1541, *pg.* 132
XTRA CREDIT - Video Game - INTERNATIONAL GAME TECHNOLOGY; *pg.* 957, *pg.* 1024
XTRA DEPTH - Shoes - P.W. MINOR & SON, INC.; *pg.* 1816, *pg.* 1140
XTRA DRAIN - Cleaning Product - ALEN AMERICAS INC.; *pg.* 325, *pg.* 1699
XTRA FLEX - Fittings - UNITED STATES PIPE & FOUNDRY COMPANY, INC.; *pg.* 117, *pg.* 5
XTRA-GUARD - Wire & Cable Products - BELDEN, INC.; *pg.* 624, *pg.* 993
XTRA LEMON - Cleaning Product - ALEN AMERICAS INC.; *pg.* 325, *pg.* 1699
XTRA LINE - Video Game - INTERNATIONAL GAME TECHNOLOGY; *pg.* 957, *pg.* 1024
XTRA NICE'N FLUFFY - Fabric Softener - CHURCH & DWIGHT CO., INC.; *pg.* 1153, *pg.* 1063
XTRA PINE - Cleaning Product - ALEN AMERICAS INC.; *pg.* 325, *pg.* 1699
XTRA TRACTION TECHNOLOGY - Foot Wear - CALLAWAY GOLF COMPANY; *pg.* 1829, *pg.* 58
XTRA-WIDE - Binocular - BUSHNELL OUTDOOR PRODUCTS, INC.; *pg.* 1403, *pg.* 718
XTRA WIDTH TECHNOLOGY - Slogan - CALLAWAY GOLF COMPANY; *pg.* 1829, *pg.* 58
XTRABROM - Chemical Product - ALBEMARLE

CORPORATION; *pg.* 1146, *pg.* 741

XTRACLEAN - Chemical Product - SPECTRUM CHEMICALS & LABORATORY PRODUCTS, INC.; *pg.* 1181, *pg.* 94

XTRACTOR - Metal Separator - BUNTING MAGNETICS CO.; *pg.* 1320, *pg.* 717

XTRACTOR VENT - Roofing Ventilation Product - BENJAMIN OBDYKE, INC.; *pg.* 70, *pg.* 1540

XTRAGLOS - Adhesive Coated Paper - SPINNAKER COATING, LLC; *pg.* 1470, *pg.* 1477

XTRALIFE - Fiber - BEAULIEU GROUP, LLC; *pg.* 917, *pg.* 529

XTRALIFE - Batteries - EASTMAN KODAK COMPANY; *pg.* 1408, *pg.* 1333

XTRALOK - Medical Equipment - CONMED CORPORATION; *pg.* 1517, *pg.* 1347

XTRASORB - Medical Dressing Product - DERMA SCIENCES, INC.; *pg.* 1523, *pg.* 1111

XTRASTRETCH - Terry Thumbs - WELLS LAMONT CORPORATION; *pg.* 15, *pg.* 638

XTRATIME - Firelog - DURAFLAME, INC.; *pg.* 1123, *pg.* 280

XTREME - Moist Smokeless Tobacco - AMERICAN SNUFF COMPANY; *pg.* 1893, *pg.* 1641

XTREME - Body Armor - BAE SYSTEMS PRODUCTS GROUP; *pg.* 359, *pg.* 432

XTREME - Color Change Environment - GEMA USA INC.; *pg.* 1339, *pg.* 686

XTREME - Reciprocating Piston Pumps - GRACO, INC.; *pg.* 1342, *pg.* 935

XTREME - High Efficiency Reverse Cleaner - KADANT BLACK CLAWSON INC.; *pg.* 1352, *pg.* 1460

XTREME - Toothbrush - RANIR LLC; *pg.* 520, *pg.* 888

XTREME - Food Product - SHAMROCK FOODS COMPANY; *pg.* 895, *pg.* 20

XTREME-1 - Software - SHAW COMMUNICATIONS INC.; *pg.* 307, *pg.* 1904

XTREME ICE - Beverage Dispensing System - CORNELIUS INC.; *pg.* 54, *pg.* 614

XTREME LIGHT - Flashlight - STREAMLIGHT INC.; *pg.* 1306, *pg.* 1527

XTREME MASSAGE - Toothbrush - RANIR LLC; *pg.* 520, *pg.* 888

XTREME MONITOR - Computer Equipment - VIEWSONIC CORPORATION; *pg.* 489, *pg.* 303

XTREME PACK - Defibrillator - ZOLL MEDICAL CORPORATION; *pg.* 1612, *pg.* 814

XTREME POWER-PISTON - Fluid Handling System - GRACO, INC.; *pg.* 1342, *pg.* 935

XTREME RANGE SUPERHETERODYNE - Laser Detectors - COBRA ELECTRONICS CORPORATION; *pg.* 629, *pg.* 572

XTREME SPORT - Spark Plugs - HONEYWELL INTERNATIONAL INC.; *pg.* 407, *pg.* 1088

XTREME START - Spark Plugs - HONEYWELL INTERNATIONAL INC.; *pg.* 407, *pg.* 1088

XTREMEMIX - Fluid Handling System - GRACO, INC.; *pg.* 1342, *pg.* 935

XTREMEPCB - Software System - MENTOR GRAPHICS CORPORATION; *pg.* 432, *pg.* 1510

XTREMESEALS - Fluid Handling System - GRACO, INC.; *pg.* 1342, *pg.* 935

XTREMEVIEW - LCD Display - VIEWSONIC CORPORATION; *pg.* 489, *pg.* 303

XUSAL - Pharmaceutical Product - SUNOVION PHARMACEUTICALS INC.; *pg.* 1599, *pg.* 832

XVIB - Energy Sources - ION GEOPHYSICAL CORPORATION; *pg.* 1350, *pg.* 1708

XWIRE - Medical Equipment - CONMED CORPORATION; *pg.* 1517, *pg.* 1347

XX-CLONE - High Efficiency Through Flow Tailing Cleaner - KADANT BLACK CLAWSON INC.; *pg.* 1352, *pg.* 1460

XX LARGE - Frozen Mexican Food - RUIZ FOOD PRODUCTS, INC.; *pg.* 893, *pg.* 77

XX2 - Protective Eyewear - SELLSTROM MANUFACTURING CO.; *pg.* 1428, *pg.* 659

XXL - Musical Instrument - PEAVEY ELECTRONICS CORPORATION; *pg.* 662, *pg.* 970

XY ZIN - Wine - JIM BEAM BRANDS CO.; *pg.* 1965, *pg.* 601

XYCOMP - Seal & Thermoplastic Component - GREENE, TWEED & CO.; *pg.* 1344, *pg.* 1544

XYFLEXPRO - Dispensing Equipment - SPEEDLINE TECHNOLOGIES, INC.; *pg.* 1378, *pg.* 823

XYFLUOR - Seal & Thermoplastic Component - GREENE, TWEED & CO.; *pg.* 1344, *pg.* 1544

XYFORCE - Wireless Communication Product - TELECOMMUNICATION SYSTEMS INC.; *pg.* 483, *pg.* 754

XYLAC - Fluoropolymer Coating System - WHITFORD WORLDWIDE COMPANY; *pg.* 1185, *pg.* 1529

XYLAN - Fluoropolymer Coating System - WHITFORD WORLDWIDE COMPANY; *pg.* 1185, *pg.* 1529

XYLAR - Fluoropolymer Coating System - WHITFORD WORLDWIDE COMPANY; *pg.* 1185, *pg.* 1529

XYLIWHITE - Toothpaste - NOW HEALTH GROUP, INC.; *pg.* 1576, *pg.* 557

XYMARK - Laser System - GSI GROUP INC.; *pg.* 1415, *pg.* 784

XYNTHA - Hemophilia Treatment Pharmaceutical Preparation - PFIZER INC.; *pg.* 1581, *pg.* 1278

XYPAGES - Location Enabled Mobile Search - TELECOMMUNICATION SYSTEMS INC.; *pg.* 483, *pg.* 754

XYPOINT - Wireless Communication Product - TELECOMMUNICATION SYSTEMS INC.; *pg.* 483, *pg.* 754

XYZAL - Pharmaceutical Product - SUNOVION PHARMACEUTICALS INC.; *pg.* 1599, *pg.* 832

Y

Y! - Internet Services - YAHOO! INC.; *pg.* 1289, *pg.* 289

Y&C - Pens & Markers - YASUTOMO & CO.; *pg.* 497, *pg.* 280

Y-BALL MESURFLO SYSTEM - Valve & Strainer - HAYS FLUID CONTROLS; *pg.* 1049, *pg.* 1370

Y! BUZZ - Internet Services - YAHOO! INC.; *pg.* 1289, *pg.* 289

Y-FLEX - Shoe And Glove - ACUSHNET COMPANY; *pg.* 1824, *pg.* 818

Y! ONESEARCH - Internet Services - YAHOO! INC.; *pg.* 1289, *pg.* 289

Y-SERIES - Mill Grinder Blender - STEDMAN MACHINE COMPANY; *pg.* 1379, *pg.* 673

YA-HOO! - Internet Services - YAHOO! INC.; *pg.* 1289, *pg.* 289

YACHT PREFERENCE - Commercial Insurance - THE CHUBB CORPORATION; *pg.* 1196, *pg.* 1128

YACHT TRADER - Magazine - DOMINION ENTERPRISES; *pg.* 1636, *pg.* 1796

YACHTBROKER.COM - Website - BONNIER CORPORATION; *pg.* 1622, *pg.* 480

YACHTING - Magazine - BONNIER ACTIVE MEDIA, INC.; *pg.* 1622, *pg.* 1205

YACHTING - Magazine - BONNIER CORPORATION; *pg.* 1622, *pg.* 480

YACHTINGNET.COM - Web Site - BONNIER ACTIVE MEDIA, INC.; *pg.* 1622, *pg.* 1205

THE YACHTS OF SEABOURN - Passenger Cruises & Tours - CARNIVAL CORPORATION; *pg.* 1902, *pg.* 441

YACHTSMAN - Brush - THE WOOSTER BRUSH COMPANY; *pg.* 1450, *pg.* 1482

YACHTWORLD.COM - Advertising Website - DOMINION ENTERPRISES; *pg.* 1636, *pg.* 1796

YAHOO! - Internet Search Engine - YAHOO! INC.; *pg.* 1289, *pg.* 289

YAHOO! 360 - Internet Services - YAHOO! INC.; *pg.* 1289, *pg.* 289

YAHOO! BUZZ - Internet Services - YAHOO! INC.; *pg.* 1289, *pg.* 289

YAHOO! GEOPLANET - Internet Services - YAHOO! INC.; *pg.* 1289, *pg.* 289

YAHOO! GO - Internet Services - YAHOO! INC.; *pg.* 1289, *pg.* 289

YAHOO! GROUPS - Internet Services - YAHOO! INC.; *pg.* 1289, *pg.* 289

YAHOO! ONECONNECT - Internet Services - YAHOO! INC.; *pg.* 1289, *pg.* 289

YAHOO! ONESEARCH - Internet Services - YAHOO! INC.; *pg.* 1289, *pg.* 289

YAHOO! SEARCH BOSS - Internet Services - YAHOO! INC.; *pg.* 1289, *pg.* 289

YAHTZEE - Toy & Game - HASBRO, INC.; *pg.* 954, *pg.* 1603

YAHTZEE GAME FOLIO - Game - HASBRO, INC.; *pg.* 954, *pg.* 1603

YAKIMA DOOR - Doors - JELD-WEN, INC.; *pg.* 1051, *pg.* 1499

YALE - Hoist - COLUMBUS MCKINNON CORPORATION; *pg.* 1325, *pg.* 1138

YALE - Furniture - HOOKER FURNITURE CORPORATION; *pg.* 928, *pg.* 1788

YALE - Lift Truck - NACCO INDUSTRIES, INC.; *pg.* 1174, *pg.* 1433

YALE PRESS LOG - News - YALE UNIVERSITY PRESS; *pg.* 1703, *pg.* 359

YALE PRESS PODCAST - Monthly Show - YALE UNIVERSITY PRESS; *pg.* 1703, *pg.* 359

YAMMER - Enterprise Social Network - MICROSOFT CORPORATION; *pg.* 435, *pg.* 1824

YAMON - Software - IMAGINATION TECHNOLOGIES; *pg.* 412, *pg.* 285

YANAGI - Fabric - NEMSCHOFF, INC.; *pg.* 936, *pg.* 1890

YANG TZE - Fabric - SCALAMANDRE, INC.; *pg.* 941, *pg.* 1058

YANGGUANG - Beverages - THE COCA-COLA COMPANY; *pg.* 240, *pg.* 493

YANGGUANG JUICY T - Beverages - THE COCA-COLA COMPANY; *pg.* 240, *pg.* 493

YANKEE - Monthly Magazine, New England Region - YANKEE PUBLISHING INC.; *pg.* 1703, *pg.* 1033

YANKEE DOODLE DOLLARS - Lottery Game - OHIO LOTTERY COMMISSION; *pg.* 1002, *pg.* 1433

YANKEE MAGAZINE TRAVEL GUIDE TO NEW ENGLAND - Magazine - YANKEE PUBLISHING INC.; *pg.* 1703, *pg.* 1033

YANKEES MAGAZINE - Magazine - NEW YORK YANKEES; *pg.* 570, *pg.* 1144

YANKEES YEARBOOK - Annual - NEW YORK YANKEES; *pg.* 570, *pg.* 1144

YANKTON DAILY PROCESSING & DAKOTAN - Magazine - YANKTON DAILY PRESS & DAKOTAN; *pg.* 1703, *pg.* 1626

YANMAR - Diesel Engines, Pumps, Generators - YANMAR AMERICA CORPORATION; *pg.* 196, *pg.* 482

YARD CARE - Organic Ground Covers - MOUNTAIN WEST, LLC; *pg.* 98, *pg.* 550

YARD MACHINES - Garden Equipment - MTD PRODUCTS, INC.; *pg.* 1057, *pg.* 1478

YARD-MAN - Power Mowers/Snow Equipment - MTD PRODUCTS, INC.; *pg.* 1057, *pg.* 1478

THE YARD MASTER - Packaging Product - GRAPHIC PACKAGING HOLDING COMPANY; *pg.* 1459, *pg.* 509

YARDAGE PRO - Laser Rangefinder - BUSHNELL OUTDOOR PRODUCTS, INC.; *pg.* 1403, *pg.* 718

YARDLEY PRODUCTS - Manufacturer of Threaded Inserts for a Wide Range of Fastening Applications - YARDLEY PRODUCTS CORPORATION; *pg.* 1391, *pg.* 1596

YARDWORKS - Garden Shredder - CANADIAN TIRE CORPORATION LIMITED; *pg.* 202, *pg.* 1936

YARIS - Car - TOYOTA MOTOR NORTH AMERICA, INC.; *pg.* 192, *pg.* 1303

YARN - Fabric - NEMSCHOFF, INC.; *pg.* 936, *pg.* 1890

YARN PAK - Injection Molded Product - TRIENDA, LLC; *pg.* 1890, *pg.* 1887

YASARGIL TITANIUM ANEURYSM CLIP SYSTEM - Titanium Aneurysm Clip System - AESCULAP, INC.; *pg.* 1487, *pg.* 1521

YATAK - Carpet - WOVEN LEGENDS INC.; *pg.* 947, *pg.* 1572

YAUN - Bulk Material Handling - ANVIL ATTACHMENTS, LLC; *pg.* 1313, *pg.* 748

YAZI GINGER VODKA - Distilled Spirits - HOOD RIVER DISTILLERS INC.; *pg.* 1964, *pg.* 1498

Y.COM - Internet Services - YAHOO! INC.; *pg.* 1289, *pg.* 289

YEAH, IT TASTES THAT GOOD - Tagline - PEPSICO, INC.; *pg.* 259, *pg.* 1327

YEAR OF THE OX - Lottery Game - CALIFORNIA LOTTERY; *pg.* 990, *pg.* 196

YEARBOOK OF INTERNATIONAL ORGANIZATIONS - Index of Worldwide Organizations - R.R. BOWKER LLC; *pg.* 1682, *pg.* 1095

YEARLING - Publishing Imprint - PENGUIN RANDOM HOUSE CHILDREN'S BOOKS; *pg.* 1676, *pg.* 1277

YEBISU STOUT - Lager Beer - SAPPORO U.S.A., INC.; *pg.* 1969, *pg.* 295

YELKIN - High-Quality Lecithin for Food Applications - ARCHER-DANIELS-MIDLAND COMPANY; *pg.* 825, *pg.* 565

YELKIN 1018 - Lecithin - ARCHER-DANIELS-MIDLAND COMPANY; *pg.* 825, *pg.* 565

YELKIN DS - Lecithin - ARCHER-DANIELS-MIDLAND COMPANY; *pg.* 825, *pg.* 565

YELKIN GOLD - Lecithin - ARCHER-DANIELS-MIDLAND COMPANY; *pg.* 825, *pg.* 565

YELKIN SS - Lecithin - ARCHER-DANIELS-MIDLAND COMPANY; *pg.* 825, *pg.* 565

YELKIN T - Lecithin - ARCHER-DANIELS-MIDLAND COMPANY; *pg.* 825, *pg.* 565
YELKIN TS - Lecithin - ARCHER-DANIELS-MIDLAND COMPANY; *pg.* 825, *pg.* 565
YELKINOL AC - Agricultural Product - ARCHER-DANIELS-MIDLAND COMPANY; *pg.* 825, *pg.* 565
YELLO-BOWL - Safety & Protective Equipment - ENCON SAFETY PRODUCTS; *pg.* 1334, *pg.* 1705
YELLOW 77 - Wire Pulling Lubricant - IDEAL INDUSTRIES, INC.; *pg.* 1051, *pg.* 662
YELLOW BOOK - Telephone Directory - YELLOW BOOK USA, INC.; *pg.* 1703, *pg.* 1347
YELLOW BOOK USA - Telephone Directory - YELLOW BOOK USA, INC.; *pg.* 1703, *pg.* 1347
THE YELLOW IRIS - Urinalysis Workstation - IRIS INTERNATIONAL, INC.; *pg.* 1547, *pg.* 64
YELLOW JACKET - Lashing Strap - CUSTOM ACCESSORIES INC.; *pg.* 203, *pg.* 653
YELLOW JACKET - Cleaning Products - KATY INDUSTRIES, INC.; *pg.* 1126, *pg.* 973
YELLOW JACKET - Glass Fiber Insulation - OWENS CORNING; *pg.* 102, *pg.* 1476
YELLOW JACKET - Firearms - REMINGTON ARMS COMPANY, LLC; *pg.* 1844, *pg.* 1382
YELLOW LABEL - Honey Flavored Syrups - WHITFIELD FOODS, INC.; *pg.* 910, *pg.* 8
YELLOW ROADWAY - Global Transportation Service - YRC WORLDWIDE INC.; *pg.* 1931, *pg.* 720
YELLOW-SEVEN - Chemical Product - SPECTRUM CHEMICALS & LABORATORY PRODUCTS, INC.; *pg.* 1181, *pg.* 94
YELLOW SHEETS - OTC Public Company Quotation Products - OTC MARKETS GROUP INC.; *pg.* 791, *pg.* 1275
YELLOW TAG - Clearance Event - BEST BUY CO., INC.; *pg.* 1761, *pg.* 954
YELLOW TRANSPORTATION - Global Transportation Services - YRC WORLDWIDE INC.; *pg.* 1931, *pg.* 720
YELLOWBOOK.COM - Website - YELLOW BOOK USA, INC.; *pg.* 1703, *pg.* 1347
YELLOWGO - Stain Remover - A.L. WILSON CHEMICAL CO.; *pg.* 325, *pg.* 1076
YELLOWJACKET - Foldable Safety Road Marker - EAGLE MANUFACTURING COMPANY; *pg.* 79, *pg.* 1851
YELOMINE - Mine Piping - CERTAINTEED CORPORATION; *pg.* 74, *pg.* 1589
YEN.COM - Advertising Website - LIVE CURRENT MEDIA INC.; *pg.* 1263, *pg.* 1911
YENKIN-MAJESTIC - Paints, Polymers, Varnishes & Enamels - YENKIN-MAJESTIC PAINT CORPORATION; *pg.* 1450, *pg.* 1445
YERVOY - Cancer Medication - BRISTOL-MYERS SQUIBB COMPANY; *pg.* 1509, *pg.* 1206
YES - Trademark - NATIONAL COLLEGIATE ATHLETIC ASSOCIATION; *pg.* 567, *pg.* 688
YES! - Tag Line - THE WESTERN UNION COMPANY; *pg.* 822, *pg.* 327
YES ESSENTIALS - Stain-Resistant Automotive Products - MILLIKEN & COMPANY; *pg.* 696, *pg.* 1622
YES NETWORK - Television Station - NEW YORK YANKEES; *pg.* 570, *pg.* 1144
YES, YOU CAN. - Slogan - INVACARE CORPORATION; *pg.* 1546, *pg.* 1451
YES YOU CAN. YES WE CAN. - Slogan - COMMUNITYONE BANCORP; *pg.* 741, *pg.* 1358
YETTER - Planter Unit - YETTER MANUFACTURING CO., INC.; *pg.* 708, *pg.* 598
YF-VAX - Yellow Fever Vaccine - SANOFI PASTEUR, INC; *pg.* 1591, *pg.* 1588
YHL (YOUTH HOCKEY LEAGUE) - Recreational Ice Sport League - CANLAN ICE SPORTS CORPORATION; *pg.* 536, *pg.* 1907
YIELD BASE - Data Management Technology - MKS INSTRUMENTS, INC.; *pg.* 1362, *pg.* 781
YIELD DYNAMICS - Software - MKS INSTRUMENTS, INC.; *pg.* 1362, *pg.* 781
YIELD MINE - Decision-making Technology - MKS INSTRUMENTS, INC.; *pg.* 1362, *pg.* 781
YIELDASSIST - Software System - MENTOR GRAPHICS CORPORATION; *pg.* 432, *pg.* 1510
YIELDGARD - Insect Resistant Seeds - MONSANTO COMPANY; *pg.* 1173, *pg.* 999
YIELDGARD - Grain Seed Product - TERRAL SEED, INC.; *pg.* 1801, *pg.* 748
YIELDGARD VT - Insecticides - MONSANTO COMPANY; *pg.* 1173, *pg.* 999
YIELDINSIGHT - Software System - MENTOR GRAPHICS CORPORATION; *pg.* 432, *pg.* 1510
YIELDIRECTOR - Software - SYNOPSYS, INC.; *pg.* 480, *pg.* 162
YIELDMASTER - Film Lamination - E.I. DU PONT DE NEMOURS & COMPANY; *pg.* 1159, *pg.* 390
YIN & YANG - Game - WMS INDUSTRIES INC.; *pg.* 593, *pg.* 666
YKK - Fastening & Architectural Product - YKK CORPORATION OF AMERICA; *pg.* 699, *pg.* 536
YKK AP - Fastening & Architectural Product - YKK CORPORATION OF AMERICA; *pg.* 699, *pg.* 536
Y!MUSIC - Music - YAHOO! INC.; *pg.* 1289, *pg.* 289
YNGWIE MALMSTEEN STRATOCASTER - Electric Guitar - FENDER MUSICAL INSTRUMENTS CORPORATION; *pg.* 547, *pg.* 21
YO BABY - Cereal - STONYFIELD FARM, INC.; *pg.* 899, *pg.* 1035
YO CAFFE - Coffee-flavored Yogurt Drink - YOCREAM INTERNATIONAL INC.; *pg.* 1039, *pg.* 1508
YO-FLEX - Diary Product - CHR. HANSEN; *pg.* 847, *pg.* 1873
YO GABBA GABBA - Toy - SPIN MASTER LTD.; *pg.* 967, *pg.* 1943
YO-PRO - Molecular Probe Product - THERMO FISHER SCIENTIFIC INC.; *pg.* 1602, *pg.* 61
YO-YO DOUGH - Lottery Game - IDAHO LOTTERY; *pg.* 995, *pg.* 547
YOCAFFE LATTE - Coffee - YOCREAM INTERNATIONAL INC.; *pg.* 1039, *pg.* 1508
YOCREAM FROZEN CUSTARD - Soft Serve Yogurt Products - YOCREAM INTERNATIONAL INC.; *pg.* 1039, *pg.* 1508
YOGA BOOTY BALLET - Fitness Video & DVD - BEACHBODY, LLC; *pg.* 271, *pg.* 272
YOGADOT - Treadtowel - HUGGER MUGGER YOGA PRODUCTS LLC; *pg.* 1836, *pg.* 1758
YOGAFIT - Yoga Studio Franchise - LIFT BRANDS; *pg.* 557, *pg.* 920
YOGAKIDS - DVD - GAIAM, INC.; *pg.* 1532, *pg.* 334
YOGATARD - Clothing - HUGGER MUGGER YOGA PRODUCTS LLC; *pg.* 1836, *pg.* 1758
YOGI BERRA CASH - Lottery Game - NEW JERSEY STATE LOTTERY; *pg.* 1000, *pg.* 1126
YOGOPAK - Paperboard Packaging Product - WESTROCK COMPANY; *pg.* 1472, *pg.* 1805
YOGOS - Yogurt-Covered Fruity Dots - KELLOGG COMPANY; *pg.* 831, *pg.* 870
YOGURT STAND - Frozen Yogurt - YOCREAM INTERNATIONAL INC.; *pg.* 1039, *pg.* 1508
YOGURTNESS - Software - BIO-RAD LABORATORIES, INC.; *pg.* 1504, *pg.* 101
YOHIMBE ACTION FOR MEN - Nutritional Product - NUTRACEUTICAL INTERNATIONAL CORPORATION; *pg.* 1576, *pg.* 1753
YOKES - Food Store - URM STORES, INC.; *pg.* 1036, *pg.* 1844
YOKOHAMA TIRES-PASSENGER AND COMMERCIAL - Tires - YOKOHAMA TIRE CORPORATION; *pg.* 1892, *pg.* 94
YOKOZUMA - Video Game - INTERNATIONAL GAME TECHNOLOGY; *pg.* 957, *pg.* 1024
YOLINK - Internet Search Enhancement Tool - TIGERLOGIC CORPORATION; *pg.* 484, *pg.* 117
YOLITE - Diary Product - ANDERSON ERICKSON DAIRY COMPANY; *pg.* 837, *pg.* 704
YOPLAIT - Dairy Products - AGROPUR COOPERATIVE; *pg.* 836, *pg.* 1950
YOPLAIT - Yogurt - GENERAL MILLS, INC.; *pg.* 828, *pg.* 933
YOPLAIT - Yogurt - YOPLAIT USA, INC.; *pg.* 910, *pg.* 947
YOPLAIT/COLOMBO - Food Product - GENERAL MILLS, INC.; *pg.* 828, *pg.* 933
YOPLAIT DELIGHTS - Yogurt - GENERAL MILLS, INC.; *pg.* 828, *pg.* 933
YOPLAIT KIDS - Refrigerated Yogurt - GENERAL MILLS, INC.; *pg.* 828, *pg.* 933
YOPLAIT YO-PLUS - Dairy Drink - GENERAL MILLS, INC.; *pg.* 828, *pg.* 933
YOPLUS LIGHT - Yogurt - GENERAL MILLS, INC.; *pg.* 828, *pg.* 933
YORK - Peppermint Patty - THE HERSHEY CO.; *pg.* 1855, *pg.* 1538
YORK - Chiller Product - JOHNSON CONTROLS, INC.; *pg.* 209, *pg.* 1876
YORK - Air Conditioners & Furnaces - JOHNSON CONTROLS UNITARY PRODUCTS; *pg.* 1073, *pg.* 1484
YORK ISOFLOW - Absorption Chillers - JOHNSON CONTROLS, INC.; *pg.* 209, *pg.* 1876
YORK LATITUDE - Air-cooled Screw Chiller - JOHNSON CONTROLS, INC.; *pg.* 209, *pg.* 1876
YORK MAXE - Compound Centrifugal Chillers - JOHNSON CONTROLS, INC.; *pg.* 209, *pg.* 1876
YORK PARAFLOW - Absorption Chillers - JOHNSON CONTROLS, INC.; *pg.* 209, *pg.* 1876
YORK STREET - Furniture - ASHLEY FURNITURE INDUSTRIES, INC.; *pg.* 914, *pg.* 1852
YORK TITAN - Centrifugal Chillers - JOHNSON CONTROLS, INC.; *pg.* 209, *pg.* 1876
YORKCALC - Software - JOHNSON CONTROLS, INC.; *pg.* 209, *pg.* 1876
YORKER - Plastic Closures - JARDEN CORPORATION; *pg.* 1885, *pg.* 412
YORKSHIRE - Gooseneck Server - THE VOLLRATH COMPANY LLC; *pg.* 1139, *pg.* 1894
YORKSHIRE - Ceiling Fan - WESTINGHOUSE LIGHTING CORPORATION; *pg.* 687, *pg.* 1571
YORKTOWNE - Fabric - NEMSCHOFF, INC.; *pg.* 936, *pg.* 1890
YORKWORKSCE - Software - JOHNSON CONTROLS, INC.; *pg.* 209, *pg.* 1876
YOSHE - Fabric - NEMSCHOFF, INC.; *pg.* 936, *pg.* 1890
YOTTAYOTTA - Software - EMC CORPORATION; *pg.* 391, *pg.* 825
YOU ALWAYS HAVE LEGGE TO STAND ON - Tagline - WALTER G. LEGGE COMPANY, INC.; *pg.* 337, *pg.* 1321
YOU BET IT'S FUN - Tag Line - FINGER LAKES RACING ASSOCIATION INC.; *pg.* 548, *pg.* 1160
YOU BRING THE FAMILY AND WE'LL PACK THE FUN - Tag Line - HILTON WORLDWIDE, INC.; *pg.* 1094, *pg.* 1791
YOU BY CROCS - Womens Footwear - CROCS, INC.; *pg.* 1806, *pg.* 335
YOU CAN REALIZE YOUR POWER - Slogan - SBLI USA LIFE INSURANCE COMPANY, INC.; *pg.* 1216, *pg.* 1288
YOU CAN SCRATCH OFF - Educational Materials - SCHOLASTIC INC.; *pg.* 1683, *pg.* 1288
YOU CAN'T ARGUE WITH PHYSICS - Slogan - CALLAWAY GOLF COMPANY; *pg.* 1829, *pg.* 58
YOU CAN'T BEAT THE SYSTEM - Slogan - CHARLOTTE PIPE & FOUNDRY COMPANY; *pg.* 1044, *pg.* 1365
YOU CAN'T GET FROM I TO P WITHOUT IP - Slogan - AT&T SOUTHEAST; *pg.* 1868, *pg.* 489
YOU CAN'T PREDICT. YOU CAN PREPARE - Tag Line - MASSACHUSETTS MUTUAL LIFE INSURANCE COMPANY; *pg.* 1207, *pg.* 845
YOU COULD USE SOME BASEBALL - Tagline - RANGERS BASEBALL LLC; *pg.* 578, *pg.* 1659
YOU DESERVE A CRUISE - Tagline - CRUISE LINES INTERNATIONAL ASSOCIATION, INC.; *pg.* 138, *pg.* 424
YOU DRIVE OUR INNOVATION - Tagline - BALLY TECHNOLOGIES, INC.; *pg.* 531, *pg.* 1022
YOU FIT. YOUR STYLE. YOUR NECESSITIES - Tagline - BARE NECESSITIES, INC.; *pg.* 19, *pg.* 1056
YOU GOT 30 MINUTES - Slogan - DOMINO'S PIZZA, INC.; *pg.* 1726, *pg.* 865
YOU GOTTA EAT - Slogan - CHECKERS DRIVE-IN RESTAURANTS, INC.; *pg.* 1017, *pg.* 472
YOU HAVE TO BE HERE - Tagline - BUFFALO WILD WINGS, INC.; *pg.* 1718, *pg.* 931
YOU PICK TWO - Bakery Product - PANERA BREAD COMPANY; *pg.* 1029, *pg.* 1001
YOU SUPPLY THE PRESS. WE'LL SUPPLY THE REST - Tagline - P/A INDUSTRIES, INC.; *pg.* 1367, *pg.* 339
YOU! THE EXPERIENCE - Museum Exhibition Services - MUSEUM OF SCIENCE AND INDUSTRY; *pg.* 565, *pg.* 583
YOU WITNESS NEWS - Internet Services - YAHOO! INC.; *pg.* 1289, *pg.* 289
YOUKI - Beverages - THE COCA-COLA COMPANY; *pg.* 240, *pg.* 493
YOU.LL FIND IT WITH US. - Slogan - AIRGAS, INC.; *pg.* 1146, *pg.* 1583
YOU.LL FIND US IN ALL THE RIGHT PLACES. - Slogan - DAP PRODUCTS, INC.; *pg.* 1441, *pg.* 756
YOUNG AMERICA - Youth Furniture - STANLEY FURNITURE CO., INC.; *pg.* 943, *pg.* 1379
YOUNG AMERICAN - Studio Beds - KINGSDOWN, INC.; *pg.* 932, *pg.* 1383
YOUNG & SMYLIE - Sugar Confectionary - THE HERSHEY CO.; *pg.* 1855, *pg.* 1538

YOUNG CHANG - Piano - YOUNG CHANG NORTH AMERICA; *pg.* 595, *pg.* 77
YOUNG EASTSIDER - Women's Contemporary Clothing - BLOOMINGDALE'S, INC.; *pg.* 1763, *pg.* 1204
YOUNG FRANKENSTEIN - Game - INTERNATIONAL GAME TECHNOLOGY; *pg.* 957, *pg.* 1024
YOUNG PEOPLE'S CONCERTS - Publisher - PHILHARMONIC SYMPHONY SOCIETY OF NEW YORK INC.; *pg.* 575, *pg.* 1282
YOUNG RIDER - Magazine - I-5 PUBLISHING LLC; *pg.* 1651, *pg.* 133
YOUNGER (THINNER) YOU DIET - Book - RODALE, INC.; *pg.* 1681, *pg.* 1530
YOUNG'S GOLD SWEET - Bagged Shell Pecan - YOUNG PECAN, INC.; *pg.* 1864, *pg.* 1615
YOUNIQUELY 4 U - Providing Marketing Service - CHECKPOINT SYSTEMS, INC.; *pg.* 628, *pg.* 1559
YOUR AGRICULTURE COMPANY - Tagline - AGCO CORPORATION; *pg.* 700, *pg.* 530
YOUR ALL DRY BAKERY CAFE - Tagline - BAB, INC.; *pg.* 1715, *pg.* 599
YOUR ASSISTANT - Computer Software - MITEL NETWORKS CORPORATION; *pg.* 654, *pg.* 1921
YOUR BODY'S OWN MOOD ENHANCER - Nutritional Supplement - PHARMAVITE LLC; *pg.* 1584, *pg.* 167
YOUR BROADBAND EQUIPMENT SOURCE VOICE.VIDEO.DATA - Tagline - BLONDER TONGUE LABORATORIES, INC.; *pg.* 625, *pg.* 1100
YOUR BUSINESS HAS ARRIVED - Tagline - EQUINIX, INC.; *pg.* 394, *pg.* 190
YOUR CALLING IS CALLING - Slogan - MONSTER WORLDWIDE, INC.; *pg.* 1268, *pg.* 859
YOUR CHURCH - Magazine - CHRISTIANITY TODAY INTERNATIONAL; *pg.* 1627, *pg.* 561
YOUR CLEANING SOLUTIONS RESOURCE - Tag Line - PENETONE CORPORATION; *pg.* 333, *pg.* 1050
YOUR COMMUNITY BANKER - Slogan - WESTAMERICA BANCORPORATION; *pg.* 821, *pg.* 258
YOUR COMMUNITY, NOT-FOR-PROFIT HEALTH CENTER - Tagline - SENTARA HEALTHCARE; *pg.* 1593, *pg.* 1797
YOUR COMPETITIVE ADVANTAGE! - Tagline - BELL FLAVORS & FRAGRANCES, INC.; *pg.* 501, *pg.* 640
YOUR COMPLETE CABLE SOLUTION - Slogan - COLEMAN CABLE, INC.; *pg.* 1324, *pg.* 665
YOUR COMPLETE LEAD GENERATION EXPERT - Tagline - CIQ, INC.; *pg.* 1235, *pg.* 415
YOUR CRITICAL LIFT EXPERTS - Tagline - AMERICAN CRANE & EQUIPMENT CORPORATION; *pg.* 1312, *pg.* 1526
YOUR CULINARY PARTNER - Slogan - CUISINE SOLUTIONS, INC.; *pg.* 850, *pg.* 1770
YOUR CURVES WILL AMAZE YOU. - Slogan - CURVES INTERNATIONAL INC.; *pg.* 542, *pg.* 1748
YOUR DESIGN & OMS PARTNER - Slogan - OPLINK COMMUNICATIONS, INC.; *pg.* 660, *pg.* 91
YOUR DRIVE EN ESPANOL - Monthly Automotive Guide - DAILY NEWS, L.P.; *pg.* 1632, *pg.* 1221
YOUR ENVIRONMENTAL SECURITY - Environmental Security - WINLAND ELECTRONICS, INC.; *pg.* 688, *pg.* 928
YOUR EXTENDED FAMILY - Slogan - MOLINA HEALTHCARE, INC.; *pg.* 1569, *pg.* 123
YOUR FAMILY DESERVES THE FRESHEST - Tag Line - HATFIELD QUALITY MEATS, INC.; *pg.* 861, *pg.* 1537
YOUR FLORIST OF CHOICE - Slogan - 1-800-FLOWERS.COM, INC.; *pg.* 1758, *pg.* 1151
YOUR FRIEND IN THE DIGITAL AGE - Slogan - COX COMMUNICATIONS, INC.; *pg.* 279, *pg.* 501
YOUR FRIEND IN THE MORTGAGE BUSINESS - Slogan - CRESTLINE FUNDING CORP.; *pg.* 742, *pg.* 109
YOUR FUTURE. YOUR WAY. - Tagline - AXA EQUITABLE LIFE INSURANCE COMPANY; *pg.* 1194, *pg.* 1199
YOUR GENETIC COMPASS - Educational Publications - GENELINK, INC.; *pg.* 1533, *pg.* 438
YOUR HEALTH, OUR PASSION. - Tagline - VERMILLION, INC.; *pg.* 1435, *pg.* 1667
YOUR HEALTH. YOUR PARTNER. - Slogan - HEALTHPARTNERS, INC.; *pg.* 1203, *pg.* 918
YOUR HOME IS WHERE OUR HEART IS - Slogan - ZIPREALTY, INC.; *pg.* 1120, *pg.* 85
YOUR HOME TOWN BANK - Slogan - TRUSTCO BANK CORP NY; *pg.* 811, *pg.* 1162
YOUR IN-HOME OUTLET MALL - Slogan - SIERRA TRADING POST INC.; *pg.* 1819, *pg.* 1901
YOUR INTELLIGENT ROBOTICS PARTNER - Tagline - ADEPT TECHNOLOGY, INC.; *pg.* 1310, *pg.* 182
YOUR INTERCONNECTION ADVANTAGE - Wireless Communication System - AT&T SOUTHEAST; *pg.* 1868, *pg.* 489
YOUR LICENSE TO SPEED - Slogan - RAMBUS INC.; *pg.* 459, *pg.* 288
YOUR LIFE'S TILE RESOURCE - Slogan - WALKER & ZANGER, INC.; *pg.* 119, *pg.* 281
YOUR LINK TO A BRIGHTER FUTURE - Slogan - ONEIDA SAVINGS BANK; *pg.* 790, *pg.* 1319
YOUR LUCKY PLACE - Games - PENN NATIONAL GAMING, INC.; *pg.* 574, *pg.* 1595
YOUR ONE STOP SOURCE FOR QUALITY CLEANING PRODUCTS - Slogan - ZEPHYR MANUFACTURING COMPANY INC.; *pg.* 1141, *pg.* 1006
YOUR ONLINE OUTLET - Slogan - OVERSTOCK.COM, INC.; *pg.* 1273, *pg.* 1760
YOUR PARTNER FOR A HEALTHY ENVIRONMENT - Tagline - SMITHEREEN PEST MANAGEMENT SERVICES; *pg.* 1800, *pg.* 638
YOUR PARTNER FOR SEATING SOLUTIONS - Slogan - HUSSEY SEATING CO.; *pg.* 929, *pg.* 751
YOUR PARTNER IN GROWTH. - Tagline - DELUXE CORPORATION; *pg.* 1634, *pg.* 964
YOUR PARTNER IN TANNING - Slogan - ETS, LLC; *pg.* 54, *pg.* 685
YOUR PASSION. OUR PROMISE - Tag Line - LAND O'LAKES, INC.; *pg.* 873, *pg.* 915
YOUR PERFECT SECOND HOME - Tag Line - HILTON WORLDWIDE, INC.; *pg.* 1094, *pg.* 1791
YOUR PLAN FOR LIFE - Slogan - BLUE CROSS & BLUE SHIELD OF RHODE ISLAND; *pg.* 1195, *pg.* 1606
YOUR REAL NEIGHBOR! - Tag Line - BARLEYCORN'S; *pg.* 1716, *pg.* 726
YOUR SCIENTIFIC CONNECTION - Tagline - BIOANALYTICAL SYSTEMS, INC.; *pg.* 1402, *pg.* 700
YOUR SOLUTION TO PARTICLE SIZE REDUCTION - Slogan - STEDMAN MACHINE COMPANY; *pg.* 1379, *pg.* 673
YOUR SOLUTIONS PARTNER - Slogan - DUKE MANUFACTURING COMPANY, INC.; *pg.* 54, *pg.* 995
YOUR SOLUTIONS SOURCE - Tagline - HDI SOLUTIONS, INC.; *pg.* 403, *pg.* 1
YOUR STORAGE SOLUTION - Slogan - ROUSSEAU METAL, INC.; *pg.* 463, *pg.* 1960
YOUR SUCCESS IS OUR BUSINESS - Tagline - INGRAM MICRO MOBILITY; *pg.* 415, *pg.* 697
YOUR SUITE CHOICE - Slogan - INNSUITES HOSPITALITY TRUST; *pg.* 1097, *pg.* 17
YOUR TELEPHONE JUST GOT SMARTER - Slogan - MICROSTRATEGY, INC.; *pg.* 1266, *pg.* 1809
YOUR TOTAL SOURCE - Slogan - TESSCO TECHNOLOGIES, INC.; *pg.* 679, *pg.* 773
YOUR TRANSFORMATION - Skincare - CANYON RANCH MANAGEMENT, LLC; *pg.* 1084, *pg.* 27
YOUR TRUSTED GUIDE TO GIFTING - Slogan - 1-800-FLOWERS.COM, INC.; *pg.* 1758, *pg.* 1151
YOUR TRUSTED SOURCE FOR QUALITY SEAFOOD SINCE 1947 - Slogan - F.W. BRYCE, INC.; *pg.* 857, *pg.* 823
YOUR VIRTUAL INVENTORY - Configured Solution - TESSCO TECHNOLOGIES, INC.; *pg.* 679, *pg.* 773
YOUR VISION, OUR SOFTWARE - Tag Line - INTERVALZERO INC.; *pg.* 420, *pg.* 851
YOUR WIRELESS SUCCESS, NOTHING LESS - Tag Line - TESSCO TECHNOLOGIES, INC.; *pg.* 679, *pg.* 773
YOUR WORDS, YOUR PICTURES - Manual - XEROX CORPORATION; *pg.* 494, *pg.* 365
YOUR WORLD. DELIVERED - Slogan - AT&T INC.; *pg.* 1867, *pg.* 1674
YOUR WORLD. YOUR SOA. - Slogan - PROGRESS SOFTWARE CORPORATION; *pg.* 457, *pg.* 786
YOU'RE A PISA WORK - Nail Care Product - OPI PRODUCTS INC.; *pg.* 518, *pg.* 167
YOU'RE BERRY SPECIAL - Fruit Arrangements - EDIBLE ARRANGEMENTS INTERNATIONAL, INC.; *pg.* 1768, *pg.* 382
YOU'RE SUCH A KABUKI QUEEN - Nail Care Product - OPI PRODUCTS INC.; *pg.* 518, *pg.* 167
YOU'RE THE GREATEST - Flower Arrangement - 1-800-FLOWERS.COM, INC.; *pg.* 1758, *pg.* 1151
YOU'RE VIRTUALLY THERE - Slogan - CLEARONE COMMUNICATIONS, INC.; *pg.* 629, *pg.* 1756
YOURSELF - Apparel - OAKLEY, INC.; *pg.* 1840, *pg.* 86
YOURVILLAORMINE - Nail Care Product - OPI PRODUCTS INC.; *pg.* 518, *pg.* 167
YOUTH ACTIVISM - Educational Programs - TRUTH INITIATIVE; *pg.* 158, *pg.* 405
YOUTH IN ACTION - Awareness Program - MOTHERS AGAINST DRUNK DRIVING (MADD); *pg.* 147, *pg.* 1723
YOUTH OUTLAST - Socks - WIGWAM MILLS, INC.; *pg.* 15, *pg.* 1894
YOUTH PETITE - Furniture - ETHAN ALLEN INTERIORS INC.; *pg.* 924, *pg.* 343
YOUTH SUPER SPECS - Safety Goggle - SCHOOL-TECH, INC.; *pg.* 1844, *pg.* 866
YOUTHAIR - Male Grooming Product - AMERICAN INTERNATIONAL INDUSTRIES COMPANY; *pg.* 498, *pg.* 126
YOUTHFUL ESSENCE - Beauty Product - GUTHY-RENKER LLC; *pg.* 289, *pg.* 273
YOUTHOLOGY - Anti-Aging Skincare - CAPITAL BRANDS, LLC; *pg.* 53, *pg.* 127
YOUTUBE - Video-Sharing Website - GOOGLE INC.; *pg.* 1249, *pg.* 153
YOUTUBE - Online Broadcasting Services - YOUTUBE, LLC; *pg.* 1291, *pg.* 198
YOU'VE EARNED IT. YOU DESERVE IT. WE HAVE IT! - Tagline - OFF ROAD UNLIMITED CORP.; *pg.* 214, *pg.* 52
YOU'VE GOT A GIANT ON YOUR SIDE - Tag Line - GIANT OF MARYLAND LLC; *pg.* 1021, *pg.* 773
YOYO - Molecular Probe Product - THERMO FISHER SCIENTIFIC INC.; *pg.* 1602, *pg.* 61
YR-1 - Yield Rheometer - BROOKFIELD ENGINEERING LABORATORIES, INC.; *pg.* 1403, *pg.* 833
YSI - Multiparameter - YSI INCORPORATED; *pg.* 1438, *pg.* 1483
YST-SW1500 - Subwoofer - YAMAHA ELECTRONICS CORPORATION USA; *pg.* 689, *pg.* 51
YST-SW215 - Subwoofer - YAMAHA ELECTRONICS CORPORATION USA; *pg.* 689, *pg.* 51
YU SING - Frozen Food - BELLISIO FOODS, INC.; *pg.* 840, *pg.* 931
YUCATAN - Coating - ARCHER-DANIELS-MIDLAND COMPANY; *pg.* 825, *pg.* 565
YUCATAN - Fabric - NEMSCHOFF, INC.; *pg.* 936, *pg.* 1890
YUCATAN IF U WANT - Nail Care Product - OPI PRODUCTS INC.; *pg.* 518, *pg.* 167
YUE SAI - Cosmetics - L'OREAL USA; *pg.* 514, *pg.* 1252
YUHANROX - Bleach - THE CLOROX COMPANY; *pg.* 327, *pg.* 169
YUKON - Aluminum Boat - ALUMACRAFT BOAT COMPANY; *pg.* 1705, *pg.* 964
YUKON - 3-Tab Roofing Shingles - BUILDING PRODUCTS OF CANADA CORP.; *pg.* 72, *pg.* 1951
YUKON - Footwear - EASTLAND SHOE CORPORATION; *pg.* 1808, *pg.* 750
YUKON - Sport Utility Vehicle - GENERAL MOTORS COMPANY; *pg.* 175, *pg.* 881
YUKON - Gaming Product - GLD PRODUCTS, INC.; *pg.* 1835, *pg.* 1882
YUKON - Hose - THE GOODYEAR TIRE & RUBBER COMPANY; *pg.* 1883, *pg.* 1401
YUKON BANNER - Vinyl - TRANSILWRAP COMPANY, INC.; *pg.* 1470, *pg.* 613
YUKON BELLE - Container Grown Plant - MONROVIA GROWERS; *pg.* 1797, *pg.* 44
YUKON BLEND - Coffee - STARBUCKS CORPORATION; *pg.* 897, *pg.* 1840
YUKON DENALI - Sport Utility Vehicle - GENERAL MOTORS COMPANY; *pg.* 175, *pg.* 881
YUKON GOLD - Game - WMS INDUSTRIES INC.; *pg.* 593, *pg.* 666
YUKON JACK CANADIAN LIQUEUR - Liqueur - DIAGEO NORTH AMERICA, INC.; *pg.* 1961, *pg.* 361
YUKON XL - Sport Utility Vehicle - GENERAL MOTORS COMPANY; *pg.* 175, *pg.* 881
YUKON XL DENALI - Sport Utility Vehicle - GENERAL MOTORS COMPANY; *pg.* 175, *pg.* 881
YUMA - Lighting Product - QUOIZEL INC.; *pg.* 1304, *pg.* 1616
THE YUMA DAILY SUN - Arizona Newspaper - FREEDOM COMMUNICATIONS, INC.; *pg.* 1643, *pg.* 110
YUMMY BEARS - Fruit Snack Candy - SWEET CANDY COMPANY; *pg.* 1862, *pg.* 1761
YUMMY CHEESE - Food Product - ANNIE'S INC.; *pg.* 1760, *pg.* 45
YUMSTERS - Yogurt - YOPLAIT USA, INC.; *pg.* 910, *pg.* 947
YURI'S REVENGE - Video Game - ELECTRONIC ARTS INC.; *pg.* 951, *pg.* 189

YUZU - Air Freshener - SWISHER HYGIENE INC.; *pg.* 336, *pg.* 1507
YVES - Soy Protein Meat Alternatives - THE HAIN CELESTIAL GROUP, INC.; *pg.* 860, *pg.* 1172
YVES ROCHE - Wine & Spirits - LEONARD KREUSCH, INC.; *pg.* 254, *pg.* 1099
YVES VEGGIE CUISINE - Food Product - THE HAIN CELESTIAL GROUP, INC.; *pg.* 860, *pg.* 1172
YZ SYSTEMS - Fluid Control Product - MILTON ROY COMPANY; *pg.* 1361, *pg.* 1542

Z

Z - Snowmobile - ARCTIC CAT INC.; *pg.* 1705, *pg.* 953
Z-14 - Fragrance - ELIZABETH ARDEN, INC.; *pg.* 507, *pg.* 448
Z BACKSCATTER - Proprietary X-Ray Imaging Technology - AMERICAN SCIENCE AND ENGINEERING, INC.; *pg.* 1399, *pg.* 787
Z BACKSCATTER VAN - Mobile Security - AMERICAN SCIENCE AND ENGINEERING, INC.; *pg.* 1399, *pg.* 787
Z-BEC - Zinc Supplement - ALERE INC.; *pg.* 1488, *pg.* 849
Z-BIND - Membrane - PALL CORPORATION; *pg.* 232, *pg.* 1323
Z-CAT HP - Enhancement Additive - JOHNSON MATTHEY PROCESS TECHNOLOGIES; *pg.* 1169, *pg.* 1083
Z-CAT PLUS - Enhancement Additive - JOHNSON MATTHEY PROCESS TECHNOLOGIES; *pg.* 1169, *pg.* 1083
Z-CLOTH - Fabric - THE ZIPPERTUBING COMPANY; *pg.* 1892, *pg.* 12
Z-DECK - Truck Leveler - RITE-HITE HOLDING CORPORATION; *pg.* 1372, *pg.* 1880
Z-FLEX - Flat Jacket - THE ZIPPERTUBING COMPANY; *pg.* 1892, *pg.* 12
Z-FLUTE - Packaging Product - GRAPHIC PACKAGING HOLDING COMPANY; *pg.* 1459, *pg.* 509
Z GARD - Gas Monitoring System - MINE SAFETY APPLIANCES COMPANY; *pg.* 1361, *pg.* 1525
Z-GRIP - Clog-Free Lightweight Body Filler - ITW - EVERCOAT; *pg.* 1443, *pg.* 1415
Z-LIFT - Desk Stand - LAPWORKS, INC.; *pg.* 426, *pg.* 187
Z-LIGHT SPHERES - Microspheres - 3M COMPANY; *pg.* 1142, *pg.* 956
Z-LINK - Integrated Circuit - ATMEL CORPORATION; *pg.* 621, *pg.* 238
Z-MAX - Electronic Component - LEVITON MANUFACTURING COMPANY, INC.; *pg.* 1301, *pg.* 1180
Z PORTAL - Inspection System - AMERICAN SCIENCE AND ENGINEERING, INC.; *pg.* 1399, *pg.* 787
Z RIDGE - Hip & Ridge Shingles - GAF MATERIALS CORP.; *pg.* 83, *pg.* 1681
Z SEAL - Casing Seal - T.D. WILLIAMSON, INC.; *pg.* 1380, *pg.* 1490
Z SERIES - Marine Transmissions - REGAL BELOIT CORPORATION; *pg.* 106, *pg.* 1854
Z-SERIES - Elastomeric Roll Covering - VAIL RUBBER WORKS, INC.; *pg.* 1891, *pg.* 906
Z-SERIES CV - Elastomeric Roll Covering - VAIL RUBBER WORKS, INC.; *pg.* 1891, *pg.* 906
Z-SHIELD - Foil Shielding - THE ZIPPERTUBING COMPANY; *pg.* 1892, *pg.* 12
Z-SPAR - Marine Paints - PETTIT PAINT COMPANY; *pg.* 1444, *pg.* 1116
Z-SPEXX - Bearing - THE TIMKEN COMPANY; *pg.* 218, *pg.* 1408
Z-STAR - Air Conditioner - FRIEDRICH AIR CONDITIONING CO.; *pg.* 1072, *pg.* 1740
Z-TRAK - Mowers - DEERE & COMPANY; *pg.* 703, *pg.* 632
Z-TYPE - Hot Air Balloon - CAMERON BALLOONS U.S.; *pg.* 1829, *pg.* 884
Z-WAVE - Controller - SIGMA DESIGNS, INC.; *pg.* 469, *pg.* 148
Z-WRAP - Jacket - THE ZIPPERTUBING COMPANY; *pg.* 1892, *pg.* 12
Z-ZONE - Electronic Components - MOLEX INCORPORATED; *pg.* 655, *pg.* 628
Z1 - Snowmobile - ARCTIC CAT INC.; *pg.* 1705, *pg.* 953
Z1 - Particle Counter - BECKMAN COULTER, INC.; *pg.* 1402, *pg.* 48
Z100 - Dental Adhesive - 3M COMPANY; *pg.* 1142, *pg.* 956
Z16F - Software - ZILOG INC.; *pg.* 497, *pg.* 252
Z2 - Particle Counter - BECKMAN COULTER, INC.; *pg.* 1402, *pg.* 48
Z3MS - Chemical Products - AIR PRODUCTS AND CHEMICALS, INC.; *pg.* 1145, *pg.* 1513
Z3MS - Trimethylsilane in Gaseous State - DOW CORNING CORPORATION; *pg.* 1159, *pg.* 900
Z4MS - Chemical Product - AIR PRODUCTS AND CHEMICALS, INC.; *pg.* 1145, *pg.* 1513
Z8 ENCORE! MC - Micrologic Semiconductor Device - ZILOG INC.; *pg.* 497, *pg.* 252
Z8 GP - Micrologic Semiconductor Device - ZILOG INC.; *pg.* 497, *pg.* 252
ZA STENT - Medical Device - COOK GROUP, INC.; *pg.* 1518, *pg.* 674
ZABIHA HALAL - Chicken Product - MAPLE LODGE FARMS LTD.; *pg.* 876, *pg.* 1918
ZABRINA - Ballerina Puppet - GUND, INC.; *pg.* 954, *pg.* 1056
ZABUTONS - Cushion - HUGGER MUGGER YOGA PRODUCTS LLC; *pg.* 1836, *pg.* 1758
ZAC - Metal Building Long-Life Fasteners - SFS INTEC, INC.; *pg.* 1061, *pg.* 1596
ZACKY FARMS - Chicken Turkey Further Processed - ZACKY FARMS, INC.; *pg.* 911, *pg.* 93
ZAFUS - Fabric - HUGGER MUGGER YOGA PRODUCTS LLC; *pg.* 1836, *pg.* 1758
ZAG - Consumer Mechanics Tools - STANLEY BLACK & DECKER, INC.; *pg.* 1063, *pg.* 358
ZAGAM - Antibiotic - MYLAN, INC.; *pg.* 1570, *pg.* 1520
ZAGNUT - Chocolate Candy - THE HERSHEY CO.; *pg.* 1855, *pg.* 1538
ZAINET - Software - SUNGARD DATA SYSTEMS INC.; *pg.* 477, *pg.* 1592
ZALADS - Food Product - ZAXBY'S FRANCHISING, INC.; *pg.* 1756, *pg.* 486
ZAMAC HAMMER-SCREW - Pin Anchor - POWERS FASTENERS INC.; *pg.* 1059, *pg.* 1143
ZAMAC NAILIN - Pin Anchor - POWERS FASTENERS INC.; *pg.* 1059, *pg.* 1143
ZAMAK FIBER-SERT - Self-Tapping Inserts - YARDLEY PRODUCTS CORPORATION; *pg.* 1391, *pg.* 1596
ZAMBONI - Toy Train - LIONEL LLC; *pg.* 961, *pg.* 875
ZAMKOWE - Beer - UNITED STATES BEVERAGE LLC; *pg.* 266, *pg.* 379
ZANAFLEX - Spasticity Management - ACORDA THERAPEUTICS, INC.; *pg.* 1486, *pg.* 1138
ZAND - Nutritional Product - NUTRACEUTICAL INTERNATIONAL CORPORATION; *pg.* 1576, *pg.* 1753
ZANE - Furniture - AMERICAN LEATHER LP; *pg.* 912, *pg.* 1673
ZANIES - Pet Toys - PETEDGE; *pg.* 1481, *pg.* 787
ZANTAC - Heartburn Relief Medicine - BOEHRINGER INGELHEIM PHARMACEUTICALS, INC.; *pg.* 1507, *pg.* 368
ZAP - Adhesive Product - SUPER GLUE CORPORATION; *pg.* 1183, *pg.* 187
ZAP DUDE - Electric Vehicle - ZAP; *pg.* 222, *pg.* 277
ZAP-IT - Masonry Drive Anchor - MKT FASTENING, LLC; *pg.* 1056, *pg.* 34
ZAP-LOK - Pipes - RUSSEL METALS INC.; *pg.* 1180, *pg.* 1928
ZAP SCIENCE - Educational Materials - SCHOLASTIC INC.; *pg.* 1683, *pg.* 1288
ZAPATA WHITE & GOLD - Tequila - LAIRD & COMPANY, INC.; *pg.* 1966, *pg.* 1119
ZAP'EMS - Frozen Food - BELLISIO FOODS, INC.; *pg.* 840, *pg.* 931
ZAPI - Lighting System - PHILIPS SOLID-STATE LIGHTING SOLUTIONS; *pg.* 1303, *pg.* 806
ZAPINO - Electric Scooter - ZAP; *pg.* 222, *pg.* 277
ZAPPER - Wireless Control Product - UNIVERSAL ELECTRONICS, INC.; *pg.* 683, *pg.* 262
ZAPPETIZERS - Food Product - ZAXBY'S FRANCHISING, INC.; *pg.* 1756, *pg.* 486
ZAPPY - Electric Scooter - ZAP; *pg.* 222, *pg.* 277
ZAPTRUCK XL - Electric Car - ZAP; *pg.* 222, *pg.* 277
ZAPVAN SHUTTLE - Electric Car - ZAP; *pg.* 222, *pg.* 277
ZAR - Wood Finishing Product - UNITED GILSONITE LABORATORIES; *pg.* 1449, *pg.* 1527
ZARA - Footwear - COBIAN CORP.; *pg.* 1806, *pg.* 253
ZARAFINA - Tea Maker - JARDEN CONSUMER SOLUTIONS; *pg.* 57, *pg.* 412
ZARCO TEQUILA - Spirits - PROXIMO SPIRITS, INC.; *pg.* 1969, *pg.* 1076
ZARIS - Reticle Automation System - BROOKS AUTOMATION, INC.; *pg.* 1320, *pg.* 813
ZARONTIN - Medicine - PFIZER INC.; *pg.* 1581, *pg.* 1278
ZATARAIN'S - Seafood, Sauces & Rice Mixes - ZATARAIN'S BRANDS, INC.; *pg.* 911, *pg.* 744
ZAV - Detergents - KAO BRANDS CO. INC.; *pg.* 513, *pg.* 1415
ZAX SUACE - Food Product - ZAXBY'S FRANCHISING, INC.; *pg.* 1756, *pg.* 486
ZBAR - Food Product - CLIF BAR INC.; *pg.* 848, *pg.* 83
ZBC - Patented Technology - SANMINA-SCI CORPORATION; *pg.* 671, *pg.* 250
ZBL - Semiconductor Solution - CYPRESS SEMICONDUCTOR CORPORATION; *pg.* 1326, *pg.* 243
ZBT - Cymbals - AVEDIS ZILDJIAN COMPANY; *pg.* 531, *pg.* 839
ZDNET - Website for Business Technology Professionals - CBS INTERACTIVE, INC.; *pg.* 369, *pg.* 215
ZDOTS - Development Tool - ZILOG INC.; *pg.* 497, *pg.* 252
ZDXMODEMRACK - Rackmount Chassis - MULTI-TECH SYSTEMS INC.; *pg.* 442, *pg.* 951
ZEBCO - Fishing Tackle - ZEBCO; *pg.* 1848, *pg.* 1491
ZEBRA - Medical Device - BOSTON SCIENTIFIC CORPORATION; *pg.* 1508, *pg.* 831
ZEBRA - Footwear - COBIAN CORP.; *pg.* 1806, *pg.* 253
ZEBRA - Furniture - ETHAN ALLEN INTERIORS INC.; *pg.* 924, *pg.* 343
ZEBRA - Publishing Imprint - KENSINGTON PUBLISHING CORP.; *pg.* 1656, *pg.* 1248
ZEBU - Fabric - NEMSCHOFF, INC.; *pg.* 936, *pg.* 1890
ZECLAR - Pharmaceutical Product - ABBOTT LABORATORIES; *pg.* 1484, *pg.* 551
ZED451 - Restaurants - TAVISTOCK RESTAURANT GROUP; *pg.* 1753, *pg.* 803
ZEE - Napkins - GEORGIA-PACIFIC LLC; *pg.* 1458, *pg.* 507
ZEELAN - Software System - MENTOR GRAPHICS CORPORATION; *pg.* 432, *pg.* 1510
ZEEMS - Electronic Fuel Injection - ZENITH FUEL SYSTEMS LLC; *pg.* 222, *pg.* 1776
ZEEOSPHERES - Hollow Spheres - 3M COMPANY; *pg.* 1142, *pg.* 956
ZEEVO - Semiconductors - BROADCOM CORPORATION; *pg.* 364, *pg.* 108
ZEGERID - Pharmaceutical Product - SALIX PHARMACEUTICALS, INC.; *pg.* 1591, *pg.* 1388
ZEINA - Personal Care Ingredient - GRAIN PROCESSING CORPORATION; *pg.* 859, *pg.* 709
ZELAPAR - Pharmaceutical Product - VALEANT PHARMACEUTICALS INTERNATIONAL; *pg.* 1605, *pg.* 1047
ZELDOX - Antipsychotic Drug - PFIZER INC.; *pg.* 1581, *pg.* 1278
ZELEC - Chemical Product - STEPAN COMPANY; *pg.* 1182, *pg.* 643
ZELLERS - Merchandise Store - HUDSON'S BAY COMPANY; *pg.* 1773, *pg.* 1938
ZELUX - Compression Molded Product - WESTLAKE PLASTICS COMPANY; *pg.* 1892, *pg.* 1548
ZEMAC - Surface Modifier - VERTELLUS SPECIALTIES INC.; *pg.* 1185, *pg.* 690
ZEMAIRA - Pharmaceutical Product - CSL BEHRING LLC; *pg.* 1520, *pg.* 1543
ZEMDRAIN - Fabric - E.I. DU PONT DE NEMOURS & COMPANY; *pg.* 1159, *pg.* 390
ZEMMOUR - Rug - ETHAN ALLEN INTERIORS INC.; *pg.* 924, *pg.* 343
ZEMPLAR - Tablet - ABBOTT LABORATORIES; *pg.* 1484, *pg.* 551
ZEMURON - Neuromuscular Blocking Agent - MERCK & CO., INC.; *pg.* 1566, *pg.* 1077
ZEN - Pillow - HUGGER MUGGER YOGA PRODUCTS LLC; *pg.* 1836, *pg.* 1758
ZEN AGAIN - Shoe - AEROGROUP INTERNATIONAL, INC.; *pg.* 1803, *pg.* 1055
ZEN GARDEN - Video Game - INTERNATIONAL GAME TECHNOLOGY; *pg.* 957, *pg.* 1024
ZEN GARDEN - Ceramic, Glass, Stone Tiles & Slabs - WALKER & ZANGER, INC.; *pg.* 119, *pg.* 281
ZENACIOUS - Sandals - AEROGROUP INTERNATIONAL, INC.; *pg.* 1803, *pg.* 1055
ZENAPAX - Pharmaceutical Product - HOFFMANN-LA ROCHE INC.; *pg.* 1542, *pg.* 1099
ZENERGEN - Nutritional Product - NUTRITION 21, INC.; *pg.* 1577, *pg.* 1327
ZENIQUIN - Veterinary Antibiotic - PFIZER INC.; *pg.* 1581, *pg.* 1278
ZENITE - Liquid Crystal Polymer Resin - E.I. DU PONT DE NEMOURS & COMPANY; *pg.* 1159, *pg.* 390
ZENITH - Sandals - AEROGROUP INTERNATIONAL, INC.;

pg. 1803, *pg.* 1055
ZENITH - Lounge Chairs - BERNHARDT DESIGN; *pg.* 918, *pg.* 1381
ZENITH - Medical Device - COOK GROUP, INC.; *pg.* 1518, *pg.* 674
ZENITH - Healthcare Product - GF HEALTH PRODUCTS, INC.; *pg.* 1535, *pg.* 508
ZENITH - Cruise Ship - ROYAL CARIBBEAN CRUISES LTD; *pg.* 1921, *pg.* 446
ZENIX - Contaminant Control Technology - HERCULES INCORPORATED; *pg.* 1166, *pg.* 392
ZENON - Molecular Probe Product - THERMO FISHER SCIENTIFIC INC.; *pg.* 1602, *pg.* 61
ZENTRON - High Strength Glass Fiber - OWENS CORNING; *pg.* 102, *pg.* 1476
ZENVIA - Pharmaceutical Preparations - AVANIR PHARMACEUTICALS; *pg.* 1498, *pg.* 40
ZENWORKS - Computer Operations - NOVELL INC.; *pg.* 446, *pg.* 852
ZEO! - Color Inkjet Label - ASTRO-MED, INC.; *pg.* 619, *pg.* 1609
ZEO TABS - Salt Product - CARGILL LIMITED; *pg.* 1475, *pg.* 1914
ZEOCASSETTE - Molecular Biology Product - THERMO FISHER SCIENTIFIC INC.; *pg.* 1602, *pg.* 61
ZEOCIN - Cell Culture Product - THERMO FISHER SCIENTIFIC INC.; *pg.* 1602, *pg.* 61
ZEOTHIX - Silica - J.M. HUBER CORPORATION; *pg.* 1169, *pg.* 1056
ZEP - Chemical Product - ACUITY BRANDS, INC.; *pg.* 1294, *pg.* 487
ZEP - Specialty Chemicals - ZEP INC.; *pg.* 338, *pg.* 524
ZEP AUTOMOTIVE - Specialty Chemicals - ZEP INC.; *pg.* 338, *pg.* 524
ZEP COMMERCIAL - Specialty Chemicals - ZEP INC.; *pg.* 338, *pg.* 524
ZEP PROFESSIONAL - Specialty Chemicals - ZEP INC.; *pg.* 338, *pg.* 524
ZEP VEHICLE CARE - Vehicle Care - ZEP INC.; *pg.* 338, *pg.* 524
ZEPHYR - Track Systems for Light Weight Sliding Doors - AIR-LEC INDUSTRIES LLC; *pg.* 1041, *pg.* 1864
ZEPHYR - Hose - HBD INDUSTRIES, INC.; *pg.* 207, *pg.* 1449
ZEPHYR - Gasoline - J.D. STREETT & CO., INC.; *pg.* 980, *pg.* 988
ZEPHYR - Lighting Product - QUOIZEL INC.; *pg.* 1304, *pg.* 1616
ZEPHYR - Pacemakers - ST. JUDE MEDICAL, INC.; *pg.* 1596, *pg.* 963
ZEPHYR - Antenna - TRIMBLE NAVIGATION LIMITED; *pg.* 1384, *pg.* 288
ZEPHYR GEODETIC - Antenna - TRIMBLE NAVIGATION LIMITED; *pg.* 1384, *pg.* 288
ZEPPELIN - Microphone Windscreens - ALAN GORDON ENTERPRISES, INC.; *pg.* 1399, *pg.* 125
ZEPTOCLOCK - Semiconductor Solution - CYPRESS SEMICONDUCTOR CORPORATION; *pg.* 1326, *pg.* 243
ZEPURE - Oral Care Products - VERTELLUS SPECIALTIES INC.; *pg.* 1185, *pg.* 690
ZEREX - Automotive Antifreeze - ASHLAND INC.; *pg.* 972, *pg.* 726
ZERIT - Health Care Product - BRISTOL-MYERS SQUIBB COMPANY; *pg.* 1509, *pg.* 1206
ZERO - Soft Drink - THE COCA-COLA COMPANY; *pg.* 240, *pg.* 493
ZERO - Chocolate Candy - THE HERSHEY CO.; *pg.* 1855, *pg.* 1538
ZERO - Eyewear - OAKLEY, INC.; *pg.* 1840, *pg.* 86
ZERO BACKGROUND - Biomolecule Product - THERMO FISHER SCIENTIFIC INC.; *pg.* 1602, *pg.* 61
ZERO BLUNT - Biomolecule Product - THERMO FISHER SCIENTIFIC INC.; *pg.* 1602, *pg.* 61
ZERO BUS LATENCY - Semiconductor Solution - CYPRESS SEMICONDUCTOR CORPORATION; *pg.* 1326, *pg.* 243
ZERO CHARGE - Chemical Cleaner Product - TECH SPRAY, L.P.; *pg.* 1183, *pg.* 1659
ZERO DUPLICATION - Program - THE TIMKEN COMPANY; *pg.* 218, *pg.* 1408
ZERO-FLEX - Rigid Grooved Pipe Coupling - VICTAULIC COMPANY; *pg.* 1066, *pg.* 1529
ZERO FLUSH - Vitamin & Dietary Supplement - NATROL, INC.; *pg.* 1570, *pg.* 64
ZERO-G - Body Armor - BAE SYSTEMS PRODUCTS GROUP; *pg.* 359, *pg.* 432
ZERO GRAVITY - Health Supplement - GARDEN OF LIFE, INC.; *pg.* 1532, *pg.* 478
ZERO GRAVITY SPORTS - Sport Product - FRANKLIN SPORTS, INC.; *pg.* 1834, *pg.* 847
ZERO L - Sunglasses - OAKLEY, INC.; *pg.* 1840, *pg.* 86
ZERO LANDFILL - Manual - XEROX CORPORATION; *pg.* 494, *pg.* 365
ZERO-MAX - Speed Transmission - ZERO-MAX, INC.; *pg.* 222, *pg.* 954
ZERO-MIST - Chemical Coating - ENTHONE INC.; *pg.* 1161, *pg.* 381
ZERO RECOVERY - Rectifier - CREE INC.; *pg.* 631, *pg.* 1371
ZERO TRANS - Specialty Oils - CARGILL LIMITED; *pg.* 1475, *pg.* 1914
ZERO WASTE BOTTLES - Water Bottles - PRIMO WATER CORPORATION; *pg.* 1030, *pg.* 1395
ZEROCLEARANCE - Automotive Thermal & Acoustical Barrier - LYDALL, INC.; *pg.* 1357, *pg.* 354
ZEROCOPY - Software - WIND RIVER SYSTEMS, INC.; *pg.* 493, *pg.* 38
ZERODINERO - Telephone Service - IDT CORPORATION; *pg.* 643, *pg.* 1096
ZEROMATIC - Commercial Lighting - SWIVELIER CO., INC.; *pg.* 1307, *pg.* 1142
ZEROPACK - Hot Melt Adhesive - H.B. FULLER COMPANY; *pg.* 1165, *pg.* 961
ZEROSE - Natural Sweetener - CARGILL, INC.; *pg.* 845, *pg.* 965
ZEROSTAT - Aristatic Agents - HUNTSMAN CORPORATION; *pg.* 1167, *pg.* 1758
ZEROTIP - Medical Device - BOSTON SCIENTIFIC CORPORATION; *pg.* 1508, *pg.* 831
ZEROTONDO - Infant's Clothing - BENETTON U.S.A. CORPORATION; *pg.* 19, *pg.* 1202
ZERTO - Packaged Foods - ATALANTA CORPORATION; *pg.* 838, *pg.* 1057
ZEST - Dental Implant System - LIFECORE BIOMEDICAL, LLC; *pg.* 1556, *pg.* 920
ZEST - Personal & Beauty Product - THE PROCTER & GAMBLE COMPANY; *pg.* 1129, *pg.* 1418
ZESTA - Snacks - KELLOGG COMPANY; *pg.* 831, *pg.* 870
ZESTIE - Footwear - STEVEN MADDEN, LTD.; *pg.* 1819, *pg.* 1176
ZESTIMATE - Home Valuation - ZILLOW GROUP, INC.; *pg.* 1292, *pg.* 1843
ZESTY HORSERADISH - Mustard - PLOCHMAN, INC.; *pg.* 890, *pg.* 631
ZESTY ITALIAN COTTAGE CHEESE SALAD TOPPER - Food Product - GAY LEA FOODS CO-OPERATIVE LIMITED; *pg.* 858, *pg.* 1926
ZETA - Furniture - THE COMMERCIAL FURNITURE GROUP; *pg.* 920, *pg.* 994
ZETA-PROBE - Software - BIO-RAD LABORATORIES, INC.; *pg.* 1504, *pg.* 101
ZETABON - Coated Metal - THE DOW CHEMICAL COMPANY; *pg.* 1157, *pg.* 898
ZETAJET - Injection Therapy System - BIOJECT MEDICAL TECHNOLOGIES INC.; *pg.* 1506, *pg.* 1509
ZETAX - Accelerators - R.T. VANDERBILT COMPANY, INC.; *pg.* 1180, *pg.* 364
ZETIA - Medicine - MERCK & CO., INC.; *pg.* 1566, *pg.* 1077
ZEUS - Grooming Switch - AVAGO TECHNOLOGIES; *pg.* 358, *pg.* 238
ZEUS - Surgical System - INTUITIVE SURGICAL, INC.; *pg.* 1546, *pg.* 286
ZEUS - Glove - KOMBI, LTD.; *pg.* 1838, *pg.* 1766
ZEUSIOPS - Storage System - HGST; *pg.* 406, *pg.* 260
ZEUSIOPS SSD - Storage System - HGST; *pg.* 406, *pg.* 260
ZEVO - Golf Equipment - GOLFSMITH INTERNATIONAL HOLDINGS, INC.; *pg.* 1835, *pg.* 1662
ZFR - Pump Product - IDEX CORPORATION; *pg.* 1347, *pg.* 623
ZHCR - Pumps - IDEX CORPORATION; *pg.* 1347, *pg.* 623
ZHERMACK - Dental Product - DENTSPLY INTERNATIONAL INC.; *pg.* 1522, *pg.* 1596
ZHIVAGO - Fabric - NEMSCHOFF, INC.; *pg.* 936, *pg.* 1890
ZI-BLAK - Black Oxide - HEATBATH CORPORATION; *pg.* 1165, *pg.* 826
ZIA NATURAL SKINCARE - Skin Care Products - THE HAIN CELESTIAL GROUP, INC.; *pg.* 860, *pg.* 1172
ZIACOTE - Metallic Container - THE PROTECTOSEAL COMPANY; *pg.* 1370, *pg.* 556
ZICAM COLD REMEDY - Cold Remedy Lozenges, Nasal Spray, Oral Mists & Tablets - MATRIXX INITIATIVES, INC.; *pg.* 1559, *pg.* 23
ZIDO - Furniture - ANTHRO CORPORATION; *pg.* 913, *pg.* 1509
ZIEBART - Rust Protection, Paint Protection & Interior Protection - ZIEBART INTERNATIONAL CORPORATION; *pg.* 222, *pg.* 912
ZIEGEN LIGHT - Beer - ANHEUSER-BUSCH COMPANIES, LLC; *pg.* 237, *pg.* 991
ZIEGENBOCK - Beer - ANHEUSER-BUSCH COMPANIES, LLC; *pg.* 237, *pg.* 991
ZIEGLER - Rug - ETHAN ALLEN INTERIORS INC.; *pg.* 924, *pg.* 343
ZIEGLER - Financial Services - THE ZIEGLER COMPANIES, INC.; *pg.* 824, *pg.* 597
ZIESTA - Sleep Wear & Accessories - MCNETT CORPORATION; *pg.* 1839, *pg.* 1817
ZIFCON - Electronic Components - MOLEX INCORPORATED; *pg.* 655, *pg.* 628
ZIGBEE - Wireless Control - CRESTRON ELECTRONICS INC.; *pg.* 631, *pg.* 1116
ZIGBEE - Computer Peripheral Equipment - DIGI INTERNATIONAL INC.; *pg.* 387, *pg.* 948
ZIGBEE - Semiconductor Product - FREESCALE SEMICONDUCTOR, INC.; *pg.* 398, *pg.* 1662
ZIGBEE - Integrated Circuit Product - SILICON LABORATORIES INC.; *pg.* 674, *pg.* 1666
ZIGBEE - RF Software - TEXAS INSTRUMENTS INCORPORATED; *pg.* 679, *pg.* 1688
ZIGBIT - Integrated Circuit - ATMEL CORPORATION; *pg.* 621, *pg.* 238
ZIGG - Cough Lozenges - PROPHASE LABS, INC.; *pg.* 1586, *pg.* 1526
ZIGZAGZ - Scissors - ACME UNITED CORPORATION; *pg.* 1040, *pg.* 346
ZIKO - Health Care Product - HEALTH PRODUCTS CORPORATION; *pg.* 1540, *pg.* 1356
ZIL-BEL - Bells - AVEDIS ZILDJIAN COMPANY; *pg.* 531, *pg.* 839
ZILCO NEW BEAT - Musical Instrument - AVEDIS ZILDJIAN COMPANY; *pg.* 531, *pg.* 839
ZILDJIAN - Cymbals - AVEDIS ZILDJIAN COMPANY; *pg.* 531, *pg.* 839
ZILLA - Pet Product - PETSMART, INC.; *pg.* 1481, *pg.* 18
ZILLOW.COM - Online Real Estate Service - ZILLOW GROUP, INC.; *pg.* 1292, *pg.* 1843
ZIMMATIC - Center Pivot - LINDSAY CORPORATION; *pg.* 1356, *pg.* 1016
ZIMMER - Electric LPG Vaporizer - ALGAS-SDI; *pg.* 1311, *pg.* 1831
ZIMMER - Dress Shoes - JOHNSTON & MURPHY CO.; *pg.* 1810, *pg.* 1651
ZIMMERMAN - Ergonomic Handling Product - INGERSOLL-RAND COMPANY; *pg.* 1349, *pg.* 1370
ZINC - Textiles - BERNHARDT DESIGN; *pg.* 918, *pg.* 1381
ZINC - Software - WIND RIVER SYSTEMS, INC.; *pg.* 493, *pg.* 38
ZINC RICH - Paint & Coating - AERVOE INDUSTRIES INCORPORATED; *pg.* 1439, *pg.* 1021
ZINC-RIG - Fluid Handling System - GRACO, INC.; *pg.* 1342, *pg.* 935
ZINCGRIP - Carbon Steel Product - AK STEEL HOLDING CORPORATION; *pg.* 1311, *pg.* 1479
ZINCOVER - Chemical Reagent - HACH COMPANY; *pg.* 1415, *pg.* 334
ZINCPRIME 100 - Zinc Rich Primers - AKZONOBEL DECORATIVE PAINTS U.S.; *pg.* 1439, *pg.* 1474
ZINCROLYTE - Chemical Coating - ENTHONE INC.; *pg.* 1161, *pg.* 381
ZINDEX - Home Valuation - ZILLOW GROUP, INC.; *pg.* 1292, *pg.* 1843
ZINECARD - Medicine - PFIZER INC.; *pg.* 1581, *pg.* 1278
ZING - Carpet Cleaner - SWISHER HYGIENE INC.; *pg.* 336, *pg.* 1507
ZING - Filter & Lens - THE TIFFEN COMPANY LLC; *pg.* 1432, *pg.* 1165
ZING - Chewing Gum Flavor - WM. WRIGLEY JR. COMPANY; *pg.* 1863, *pg.* 596
ZINGER - Horizontal Media Mill - MOREHOUSE-COWLES; *pg.* 1363, *pg.* 66
ZINGERS - Snack Cakes - HOSTESS BRANDS LLC; *pg.* 1856, *pg.* 984
ZINGO - Net Carb - BROWN & HALEY; *pg.* 1851, *pg.* 1820
ZINGOS - Mints - BROWN & HALEY; *pg.* 1851, *pg.* 1820
ZINGS - Ethnic Inspired Appetizers - THE SCHWAN FOOD COMPANY; *pg.* 894, *pg.* 928

First page reference indicates Business Class Edition
Second page reference indicates Geographic Edition

ZINIO - Software - VIEWSONIC CORPORATION; *pg.* 489, *pg.* 303
ZINMAX - Nutritional Product - NUTRITION 21, INC.; *pg.* 1577, *pg.* 1327
ZINOL - Metal Finishing Product - HEATBATH CORPORATION; *pg.* 1165, *pg.* 826
ZINOX 350 - Zinc Oxide - AMERICAN CHEMET CORPORATION; *pg.* 1147, *pg.* 599
ZINSSER - Shellac - RPM INTERNATIONAL INC.; *pg.* 1447, *pg.* 1464
ZIP-A-DEE MINI POP - Candy - TOOTSIE ROLL INDUSTRIES, INC.; *pg.* 1863, *pg.* 591
ZIP CARE - Cleaner & Lubricant - MCNETT CORPORATION; *pg.* 1839, *pg.* 1817
ZIP-CLEAN - Fluid Handling System - GRACO, INC.; *pg.* 1342, *pg.* 935
ZIP-CLIP - Fluid Handling System - GRACO, INC.; *pg.* 1342, *pg.* 935
ZIP DATA - Software - MELISSA DATA CORP.; *pg.* 432, *pg.* 188
ZIP FRONT POLO - Clothing - K-SWISS; *pg.* 1837, *pg.* 306
ZIP FRONT TANK - Clothing - K-SWISS; *pg.* 1837, *pg.* 306
ZIP-IT - Wall Anchor - POWERS FASTENERS INC.; *pg.* 1059, *pg.* 1143
ZIP-ITY DO-DOLLY - Dolls - THE GOLDBERGER COMPANY, LLC; *pg.* 954, *pg.* 1235
ZIP-KLIP - Hard Hat Attachment - SELLSTROM MANUFACTURING CO.; *pg.* 1428, *pg.* 659
ZIP-MESH - Wire & Cable - THE ZIPPERTUBING COMPANY; *pg.* 1892, *pg.* 12
ZIP 'N GO - Outerwear - HABAND COMPANY, INC.; *pg.* 1772, *pg.* 1099
ZIP 'N VAC - Storage Bags - HABAND COMPANY, INC.; *pg.* 1772, *pg.* 1099
ZIP-PAK - Packaging Products - ZIP-PAK; *pg.* 1473, *pg.* 631
ZIP-PAK SLIDER - Sliding Device - ZIP-PAK; *pg.* 1473, *pg.* 631
ZIP POWER - Hand Cleaner - DELTA FOREMOST CHEMICAL CORPORATION; *pg.* 1155, *pg.* 1642
ZIP-RIB - Roofing System - MERCHANT & EVANS, INC.; *pg.* 97, *pg.* 1048
ZIP-ROLL - Pressure Rollers - GRACO, INC.; *pg.* 1342, *pg.* 935
ZIP SEAL - Systems Integration & Aeronautics - LOCKHEED MARTIN CORPORATION; *pg.* 229, *pg.* 762
ZIP SELECT - Software - MELISSA DATA CORP.; *pg.* 432, *pg.* 188
ZIP-SLICK - Dry Cleaning & Laundry Product - ADCO, INC.; *pg.* 325, *pg.* 482
ZIP-SLIP - Release Agent - ASHLAND INC.; *pg.* 972, *pg.* 726
ZIP SORTER - Package Conveying Machinery - INTELLIGRATED SYSTEMS LLC; *pg.* 1350, *pg.* 998
ZIP-SPRAY - Sprayers - GRACO, INC.; *pg.* 1342, *pg.* 935
ZIP SPRAY-N-ROLL - Sprayers - GRACO, INC.; *pg.* 1342, *pg.* 935
ZIP-STRIP - Removable Urethane Compound Sealant Strips - LOCKHEED MARTIN CORPORATION; *pg.* 229, *pg.* 762
ZIP SWITCH - Package Conveying Machinery - INTELLIGRATED SYSTEMS LLC; *pg.* 1350, *pg.* 998
ZIP TECH - Lubricant & Protectant - MCNETT CORPORATION; *pg.* 1839, *pg.* 1817
ZIP-TEX - Fluid Handling System - GRACO, INC.; *pg.* 1342, *pg.* 935
ZIP-TIGHT - Suitcase - SAMSONITE CORPORATION; *pg.* 11, *pg.* 830
ZIP-TIP - Fluid Handling System - GRACO, INC.; *pg.* 1342, *pg.* 935
ZIP-TOGGLE - Wall Anchor - POWERS FASTENERS INC.; *pg.* 1059, *pg.* 1143
ZIP USA - Software - MELISSA DATA CORP.; *pg.* 432, *pg.* 188
ZIP WAX - Car Wash - TURTLE WAX, INC.; *pg.* 220, *pg.* 671
ZIP+4 MAPINFO MAPMARKER - Mapping Tool - PITNEY BOWES SOFTWARE INC.; *pg.* 455, *pg.* 1346
ZIPAGENT - Real Estate Solutions - ZIPREALTY, INC.; *pg.* 1120, *pg.* 85
ZIPCAR - Car Sharing Services - ZIPCAR, INC.; *pg.* 1931, *pg.* 810
ZIPCARD - Forms - THE STANDARD REGISTER COMPANY; *pg.* 473, *pg.* 1446
ZIPCON - Electronic Components - MOLEX INCORPORATED; *pg.* 655, *pg.* 628
ZIPCONNECT - Wireless Communication System - AT&T SOUTHEAST; *pg.* 1868, *pg.* 489
ZIPLOC - Storage Bags - S.C. JOHNSON & SON, INC.; *pg.* 334, *pg.* 1889
ZIPLOC CONTAINERS - Home Cleaner - S.C. JOHNSON & SON, INC.; *pg.* 334, *pg.* 1889
ZIPLOC DOUBLE-GUARD - Freezer Storage Bags - S.C. JOHNSON & SON, INC.; *pg.* 334, *pg.* 1889
ZIPLON - Zipper - YKK CORPORATION OF AMERICA; *pg.* 699, *pg.* 536
ZIPMAGIC - Software - SMITH MICRO SOFTWARE, INC.; *pg.* 471, *pg.* 41
ZIPMAILER - Business Forms - THE STANDARD REGISTER COMPANY; *pg.* 473, *pg.* 1446
ZIPNOTIFY - Real Estate Solutions - ZIPREALTY, INC.; *pg.* 1120, *pg.* 85
ZIPPAK - Forms Holder - THE STANDARD REGISTER COMPANY; *pg.* 473, *pg.* 1446
ZIPPER - Cutlery - BUCK KNIVES, INC.; *pg.* 1828, *pg.* 550
ZIPPER - Fabric - NEMSCHOFF, INC.; *pg.* 936, *pg.* 1890
ZIPPER - Beanie - OAKLEY, INC.; *pg.* 1840, *pg.* 86
ZIPPER-LIP - Lip Systems - ESCO CORPORATION; *pg.* 1335, *pg.* 1502
ZIPPER-MESH - Shielding - THE ZIPPERTUBING COMPANY; *pg.* 1892, *pg.* 12
ZIPPER TAPE - Resealable Packaging Solution - ZIP-PAK; *pg.* 1473, *pg.* 631
ZIPPERTUBING - Wire & Cable - THE ZIPPERTUBING COMPANY; *pg.* 1892, *pg.* 12
ZIPPING ALONG - Dresses & Sets - HABAND COMPANY, INC.; *pg.* 1772, *pg.* 1099
ZIPPO - Cigarette Lighters - ZIPPO MANUFACTURING COMPANY, INC.; *pg.* 1895, *pg.* 1518
ZIPPY MART - Convenience Stores - CROWN CENTRAL LLC; *pg.* 975, *pg.* 756
ZIPPY PRINT - Quick Printing Services - ALLEGRA NETWORK LLC; *pg.* 1614, *pg.* 904
ZIPSAFE - Slidecutter - AEP INDUSTRIES INC.; *pg.* 1878, *pg.* 1085
ZIPSET - Business Forms - THE STANDARD REGISTER COMPANY; *pg.* 473, *pg.* 1446
ZIPUP - Footwear - STEVEN MADDEN, LTD.; *pg.* 1819, *pg.* 1176
ZIPWIRE - Medical Device - BOSTON SCIENTIFIC CORPORATION; *pg.* 1508, *pg.* 831
ZIRAMIC - Coatings - ENTEGRIS, INC.; *pg.* 1882, *pg.* 788
ZIRCADYNE - Zirconium & Zirconium Alloy Mill Products - ATI WAH CHANG; *pg.* 1314, *pg.* 1492
ZIRCATE - Dental Product - DENTSPLY INTERNATIONAL INC.; *pg.* 1522, *pg.* 1596
ZITHRO - Pharmaceutical Product - PFIZER INC.; *pg.* 1581, *pg.* 1278
ZITHRO COMPLETE - Pharmaceutical Product - PFIZER INC.; *pg.* 1581, *pg.* 1278
ZITHROMAX - Pharmaceutical Product - CUBIST PHARMACEUTICALS, INC.; *pg.* 1521, *pg.* 828
ZITHROMAX - Medicine - PFIZER INC.; *pg.* 1581, *pg.* 1278
ZIXAUDITOR - Software - ZIX CORPORATION; *pg.* 497, *pg.* 1691
ZIXCONNECT - Transport Security - ZIX CORPORATION; *pg.* 497, *pg.* 1691
ZIXDIRECT - Email Delivery - ZIX CORPORATION; *pg.* 497, *pg.* 1691
ZIXDIRECTORY - Email Encryption Service - ZIX CORPORATION; *pg.* 497, *pg.* 1691
ZIXIT - Application Based on Digital Signature & Encryption Technology - ZIX CORPORATION; *pg.* 497, *pg.* 1691
ZIXMAIL - Software - ZIX CORPORATION; *pg.* 497, *pg.* 1691
ZIXMESSAGE - Electronic Tool - ZIX CORPORATION; *pg.* 497, *pg.* 1691
ZIXPORT - Software - ZIX CORPORATION; *pg.* 497, *pg.* 1691
ZIXRESEARCH CENTER - Research Tool - ZIX CORPORATION; *pg.* 497, *pg.* 1691
ZIXSECURE CENTER - Electronic Tool - ZIX CORPORATION; *pg.* 497, *pg.* 1691
ZIXVPM - Virtual Private Messenger - ZIX CORPORATION; *pg.* 497, *pg.* 1691
ZIXWORKS - Software - ZIX CORPORATION; *pg.* 497, *pg.* 1691
ZIZ-O - Cleaning Product - HILLYARD, INC.; *pg.* 331, *pg.* 990
ZLIBS - Software System - MENTOR GRAPHICS CORPORATION; *pg.* 432, *pg.* 1510
ZLINER - Spray on Liner - ZIEBART INTERNATIONAL CORPORATION; *pg.* 222, *pg.* 912
ZMAP - Web Applications - EOLAS TECHNOLOGIES, INC.; *pg.* 1243, *pg.* 573
ZMAX - Medicine - PFIZER INC.; *pg.* 1581, *pg.* 1278
ZMAX - Engine Lubricant - SPEEDWAY MOTORSPORTS, INC.; *pg.* 584, *pg.* 1370
ZMAX SOLO - Medicine - PFIZER INC.; *pg.* 1581, *pg.* 1278
ZMP - LED - CREE INC.; *pg.* 631, *pg.* 1371
ZMX - Catalyst Additive - JOHNSON MATTHEY PROCESS TECHNOLOGIES; *pg.* 1169, *pg.* 1083
ZNBRITE - Plating Process System - A BRITE COMPANY; *pg.* 1144, *pg.* 1697
ZNEO - Software - ZILOG INC.; *pg.* 497, *pg.* 252
ZOCOR - Medicine - MERCK & CO., INC.; *pg.* 1566, *pg.* 1077
ZODIAC - Watch - FOSSIL GROUP, INC.; *pg.* 5, *pg.* 1735
ZODIAC - Lottery Game - NEW JERSEY STATE LOTTERY; *pg.* 1000, *pg.* 1126
ZODIAC - Fabric - UNIROYAL ENGINEERED PRODUCTS; *pg.* 699, *pg.* 467
ZODIAC CASHWORD - Lottery Game - MICHIGAN STATE LOTTERY BUREAU; *pg.* 999, *pg.* 895
ZODIAC PRODUCTS - Aviation Engine Line Cleaners - FINE ORGANICS CORPORATION; *pg.* 330, *pg.* 1052
ZODIAC RICHES - Video Game - INTERNATIONAL GAME TECHNOLOGY; *pg.* 957, *pg.* 1024
ZODIAK - Digital Production Switcher - GRASS VALLEY, INC.; *pg.* 641, *pg.* 164
ZODIAQ - Quartz Surfaces - E.I. DU PONT DE NEMOURS & COMPANY; *pg.* 1159, *pg.* 390
ZODY - Office Product - HAWORTH, INC.; *pg.* 402, *pg.* 891
ZOE - Clothing - ABERCROMBIE & FITCH CO.; *pg.* 37, *pg.* 1466
ZOE - Furniture - AMISCO INDUSTRIES LTD.; *pg.* 913, *pg.* 1958
ZOE - Lounge Chairs - BERNHARDT DESIGN; *pg.* 918, *pg.* 1381
ZOE - Leather Product - COACH, INC.; *pg.* 3, *pg.* 1214
ZOE - Furniture - ETHAN ALLEN INTERIORS INC.; *pg.* 924, *pg.* 343
ZOE - Chair - LA-Z-BOY INCORPORATED; *pg.* 932, *pg.* 901
ZOE B AND T - Dental Product - DENTSPLY INTERNATIONAL INC.; *pg.* 1522, *pg.* 1596
ZOEII - Footwear - STEVEN MADDEN, LTD.; *pg.* 1819, *pg.* 1176
ZOLL E SERIES - Full Featured Defibrillator - ZOLL MEDICAL CORPORATION; *pg.* 1612, *pg.* 814
ZOLOFT - Depression & High Anxiety Medication - PFIZER INC.; *pg.* 1581, *pg.* 1278
ZOLVSTAT - Enzymatic Detergent - STERIS CORPORATION; *pg.* 1597, *pg.* 1464
ZON - Computer Software - NOVELL INC.; *pg.* 446, *pg.* 852
ZONARE - Ultrasound Systems - ZONARE MEDICAL SYSTEMS, INC.; *pg.* 1612, *pg.* 163
ZONATAC - Terpene Resin - ARIZONA CHEMICAL CO. LLC; *pg.* 1147, *pg.* 431
ZONDERVAN - Books - HARPERCOLLINS PUBLISHERS INC.; *pg.* 1647, *pg.* 1237
ZONE - Bowling Equipment - BRUNSWICK BOWLING & BILLIARDS CORP.; *pg.* 1828, *pg.* 622
Z.ONE - Ultrasound Systems - ZONARE MEDICAL SYSTEMS, INC.; *pg.* 1612, *pg.* 163
ZONE CONTROL - Conveyor - SHUTTLEWORTH, INC.; *pg.* 1375, *pg.* 682
ZONE OF MAXIMUM USE - Ophthalmic Technology - SIGNET ARMORLITE, INC.; *pg.* 1429, *pg.* 60
ZONE SONOGRAPHY - Ultrasound Systems - ZONARE MEDICAL SYSTEMS, INC.; *pg.* 1612, *pg.* 163
ZONED COMFORT CONTROL - Cooling System - RESEARCH PRODUCTS CORPORATION; *pg.* 1075, *pg.* 1867
ZONEMASTER - Surge Protector - WIREMOLD/LEGRAND; *pg.* 689, *pg.* 383
ZONEPERFECT - Nutritional Product - ABBOTT LABORATORIES; *pg.* 1484, *pg.* 551
ZONERUNNER - Software - F5 NETWORKS, INC.; *pg.* 396, *pg.* 1835
ZONNEBLOEM - South African Wines - DREYFUS ASHBY INC.; *pg.* 1962, *pg.* 1226
ZONYL - Fluoridizer - E.I. DU PONT DE NEMOURS & COMPANY; *pg.* 1159, *pg.* 390
ZOO - Search Engine - BLUCORA; *pg.* 1232, *pg.* 1813
ZOO MED - Pet Product - PETSMART, INC.; *pg.* 1481, *pg.* 18
ZOO MIX - Polyurethane Compound - CHASE CORPORATION; *pg.* 1152, *pg.* 803
ZOO PALS - Children's Tableware - PACTIV CORPORATION; *pg.* 1466, *pg.* 624
ZOOBILEE - Educational Product - BARKER CREEK

PUBLISHING INC.; *pg.* 1619, *pg.* 1818
ZOOLOGIC - Software - SS&C TECHNOLOGIES HOLDINGS, INC.; *pg.* 473, *pg.* 386
ZOOM - Character - DC COMICS, INC.; *pg.* 1633, *pg.* 1221
ZOOM - Tape - IDEAL INDUSTRIES, INC.; *pg.* 1051, *pg.* 662
ZOOM - Molecular Biology Product - THERMO FISHER SCIENTIFIC INC.; *pg.* 1602, *pg.* 61
ZOOM BLUR - Footwear - NIKE, INC.; *pg.* 1812, *pg.* 1492
ZOOM GROOM - Natural Rubber Brushes - PETEDGE; *pg.* 1481, *pg.* 787
ZOOM KOBE IV - Footwear - NIKE, INC.; *pg.* 1812, *pg.* 1492
ZOOM SHARKLEY - Footwear - NIKE, INC.; *pg.* 1812, *pg.* 1492
ZOOM SPOUT - Lubricant - LA-CO INDUSTRIES MARKAL CO., INC.; *pg.* 1170, *pg.* 610
ZOOM STAR - Colposcope - WALLACH SURGICAL DEVICES, INC.; *pg.* 1436, *pg.* 381
ZOOM STRUCTURE TRIAX - Footwear - NIKE, INC.; *pg.* 1812, *pg.* 1492
ZOOM T-5 - Footwear - NIKE, INC.; *pg.* 1812, *pg.* 1492
ZOOM TRAINER ESSENTIAL - Footwear - NIKE, INC.; *pg.* 1812, *pg.* 1492
ZOOM VICTORY+ - Footwear - NIKE, INC.; *pg.* 1812, *pg.* 1492
ZOOMAIR - Network Interface Cards - ZOOM TECHNOLOGIES, INC.; *pg.* 497, *pg.* 1317
ZOOMATES - Educational Materials - SCHOLASTIC INC.; *pg.* 1683, *pg.* 1288
ZOOMCAM - Video Camera - ZOOM TECHNOLOGIES, INC.; *pg.* 497, *pg.* 1317
ZOOMERANG - Software - METRIXLAB; *pg.* 1266, *pg.* 223
ZOOMGUARD - Lightening Protection - ZOOM TECHNOLOGIES, INC.; *pg.* 497, *pg.* 1317
ZOOMOBILE - Toy - INFANTINO, LLC; *pg.* 957, *pg.* 203
ZOOMPANEL - Software - METRIXLAB; *pg.* 1266, *pg.* 223
ZOOMS - Lawn Product - ARIENS COMPANY INC.; *pg.* 700, *pg.* 1855
ZOOMSCOPE - Medical Instrument - WALLACH SURGICAL DEVICES, INC.; *pg.* 1436, *pg.* 381
ZOOMSTAR - Medical Instrument - WALLACH SURGICAL DEVICES, INC.; *pg.* 1436, *pg.* 381
ZOOMSTREAM IMAGES - Software - VENDIO, INC.; *pg.* 1287, *pg.* 256
ZOOMTEL - VoIP Product - ZOOM TECHNOLOGIES, INC.; *pg.* 497, *pg.* 1317
ZOOSEQ - Animal Gene Sequence Database - INCYTE CORPORATION; *pg.* 1545, *pg.* 392
ZORB-IT-ALL - Hygienic Fluid Absorber - SURCO PRODUCTS, INC.; *pg.* 336, *pg.* 1581
ZORBA - Apparel - HANESBRANDS INC.; *pg.* 26, *pg.* 1394
ZORBAX - Cartridge - AGILENT TECHNOLOGIES, INC.; *pg.* 614, *pg.* 264
ZORBITALL - Absorbent - DELTA FOREMOST CHEMICAL CORPORATION; *pg.* 1155, *pg.* 1642
ZORCAINE - Dental Anesthetics - EASTMAN KODAK COMPANY; *pg.* 1408, *pg.* 1333
ZORFLEX - Activated Carbon Cloth - CALGON CARBON CORPORATION; *pg.* 1151, *pg.* 1574
ZORIASIS - Health & Beauty Product - DIXIE HEALTH, INC.; *pg.* 1524, *pg.* 535
ZORIEN - Health & Nutrition Product - NOVUS INTERNATIONAL, INC.; *pg.* 706, *pg.* 1001
ZOSTAVAX - Medicine - MERCK & CO., INC.; *pg.* 1566, *pg.* 1077
ZOSTRIX - Diabetic Topical Foot Pain Cream - AKORN; *pg.* 1488, *pg.* 1138
ZOSYN - Antibiotic - PFIZER INC.; *pg.* 1581, *pg.* 1278
ZOURS - Candy - JUST BORN, INC.; *pg.* 1857, *pg.* 1516
ZOUT - Stain Remover - HENKEL CONSUMER GOODS; *pg.* 511, *pg.* 22
ZOUZOU - Fabric - NEMSCHOFF, INC.; *pg.* 936, *pg.* 1890
ZOVIA - Pharmaceutical Product - ALLERGAN; *pg.* 1490, *pg.* 1101
ZOVIRAX - Pharmaceutical Product - VALEANT PHARMACEUTICALS INTERNATIONAL, INC.; *pg.* 1605, *pg.* 1957
ZOX - Glass & Plastic Polish - FERRO CORPORATION; *pg.* 1162, *pg.* 1462
Z.PLEX - High Performance Depth Filter Technology - GE WATER & PROCESS TECHNOLOGIES; *pg.* 1339, *pg.* 1588
ZPLZ - Zebra Programming Language - ZEBRA TECHNOLOGIES CORPORATION; *pg.* 690, *pg.* 628
ZQ - Instrument Control Software - WATERS CORPORATION; *pg.* 1436, *pg.* 834
ZR - Snowmobile - ARCTIC CAT INC.; *pg.* 1705, *pg.* 953
Z'SCAN - Sensor - ADVANCED ENERGY INDUSTRIES, INC.; *pg.* 613, *pg.* 328
ZSPRAY - Mass Detector - WATERS CORPORATION; *pg.* 1436, *pg.* 834
ZT - Jacketing For Cables - THE ZIPPERTUBING COMPANY; *pg.* 1892, *pg.* 12
ZT-TAPE - Polyurethane - THE ZIPPERTUBING COMPANY; *pg.* 1892, *pg.* 12
ZTELLIGENCE - Software - METRIXLAB; *pg.* 1266, *pg.* 223
ZTJ - Space Solar Cell - EMCORE CORPORATION; *pg.* 636, *pg.* 39
ZTJM - Space Solar Cell - EMCORE CORPORATION; *pg.* 636, *pg.* 39
ZTOMCATS - Chemical Product - AIR PRODUCTS AND CHEMICALS, INC.; *pg.* 1145, *pg.* 1513
ZUBRIN - Medicine - MERCK & CO., INC.; *pg.* 1566, *pg.* 1077
ZUGIBEAST - Postable Equipment - HUDSON TECHNOLOGIES, INC.; *pg.* 1073, *pg.* 1320
ZULU KINGDOM - Video Game - INTERNATIONAL GAME TECHNOLOGY; *pg.* 957, *pg.* 1024
ZUMA - Guiding Catheter - MEDTRONIC, INC.; *pg.* 1564, *pg.* 939
ZUMA - Furniture - VIRCO MANUFACTURING CORPORATION; *pg.* 946, *pg.* 297
ZUMAFRD - Furniture - VIRCO MANUFACTURING CORPORATION; *pg.* 946, *pg.* 297
ZUMANITY - Show And Ticket - CIRQUE DU SOLEIL INC.; *pg.* 540, *pg.* 1954
ZUMBA - Fitness Product - BALLY TOTAL FITNESS HOLDINGS CORPORATION; *pg.* 532, *pg.* 1200
ZUMFOOT - Footwear - ROCKY BRANDS, INC.; *pg.* 1818, *pg.* 1466
ZUPREEM - Pet Product - PETSMART, INC.; *pg.* 1481, *pg.* 18
ZURI - Cosmetics - J. STRICKLAND & COMPANY; *pg.* 512, *pg.* 970
ZURICH - Furniture - AMERICAN LEATHER LP; *pg.* 912, *pg.* 1673
ZURION - Health Care Product - HEALTH PRODUCTS CORPORATION; *pg.* 1540, *pg.* 1356
Z'WARE - Software - ADVANCED ENERGY INDUSTRIES, INC.; *pg.* 613, *pg.* 328
ZWINKY - Online Services - IAC/INTERACTIVECORP; *pg.* 292, *pg.* 1242
ZWINKY CUTIES - Online Services - IAC/INTERACTIVECORP; *pg.* 292, *pg.* 1242
ZX - Gasoline - J.D. STREETT & CO., INC.; *pg.* 980, *pg.* 988
ZX002 - Pharmaceutical Product - ZOGENIX, INC.; *pg.* 1612, *pg.* 211
ZXP - Electronic Components - MOLEX INCORPORATED; *pg.* 655, *pg.* 628
ZYBAN - Pharmaceutical Product - IMPAX LABORATORIES, INC.; *pg.* 1544, *pg.* 101
ZYBAN - Pharmaceutical Product - VALEANT PHARMACEUTICALS INTERNATIONAL, INC.; *pg.* 1605, *pg.* 1957
ZYDERM - Skin Care Product - ALLERGAN, INC.; *pg.* 1491, *pg.* 106
ZYDIS - Pharmaceutical Product - CARDINAL HEALTH, INC.; *pg.* 1512, *pg.* 1448
ZYDONE - Pharmaceutical Product - ENDO PHARMACEUTICALS HOLDINGS, INC.; *pg.* 1528, *pg.* 1549
ZYFLO - Pharmaceutical Product - CHIESI USA, INC.; *pg.* 1515, *pg.* 1359
ZYFLO CR - Pharmaceutical Product - CHIESI USA, INC.; *pg.* 1515, *pg.* 1359
ZYGLO - Fluorescent Penetrant - ITW MAGNAFLUX; *pg.* 1418, *pg.* 615
ZYLAR - High Performance Styrenics - NOVA CHEMICALS CORPORATION; *pg.* 1175, *pg.* 1904
ZYLET - Pharmaceutical Product - BAUSCH & LOMB INCORPORATED; *pg.* 1401, *pg.* 1045
ZYLEXIS - Medicine - PFIZER INC.; *pg.* 1581, *pg.* 1278
ZYLOPRIM - Therapy System - PROMETHEUS LABORATORIES, INC.; *pg.* 1586, *pg.* 206
ZYMAR - Eye Care Product - ALLERGAN, INC.; *pg.* 1491, *pg.* 106
ZYMAX - Lab Dialysis Product - SPECTRUM LABORATORIES INC.; *pg.* 1595, *pg.* 69
ZYME - Health Supplement - GARDEN OF LIFE, INC.; *pg.* 1532, *pg.* 478
ZYNTAR - Chemical Product - NOVA CHEMICALS CORPORATION; *pg.* 1175, *pg.* 1904
ZYOPTIX - Refractive Surgery System - BAUSCH & LOMB INCORPORATED; *pg.* 1401, *pg.* 1045
ZYPLAST - Skin Care Product - ALLERGAN, INC.; *pg.* 1491, *pg.* 106
ZYPLEX - Lightweight Laminate - ARCELORMITTAL DOFASCO INC.; *pg.* 68, *pg.* 1921
ZYPREXA - Pharmaceutical Product - ELI LILLY AND COMPANY; *pg.* 1527, *pg.* 684
ZYRON - Electronic Etching System - E.I. DU PONT DE NEMOURS & COMPANY; *pg.* 1159, *pg.* 390
ZYRTEC - Allergy Relief Medicine - MCNEIL-PPC, INC.; *pg.* 1560, *pg.* 1533
ZYRTEC - Allergy Medication - PFIZER INC.; *pg.* 1581, *pg.* 1278
ZYTEL - Resins - E.I. DU PONT DE NEMOURS & COMPANY; *pg.* 1159, *pg.* 390
ZYTON - Electronic Components - MOLEX INCORPORATED; *pg.* 655, *pg.* 628
ZYVOX - Staph Infection Treatment - PFIZER INC.; *pg.* 1581, *pg.* 1278
ZYWAVE - Wavefront Aberrometer - BAUSCH & LOMB INCORPORATED; *pg.* 1401, *pg.* 1045

S.I.C. INDEX

0115 - Corn Production

THE ANDERSONS INCORPORATED, *pg.* 1793, *pg.* 1461
INGREDION, *pg.* 864, *pg.* 669
MOEWS SEED CO., INC., *pg.* 1797, *pg.* 616

0116 - Soybean Production

MONSANTO, *pg.* 1798, *pg.* 971

0119 - Cash Grains, NEC

ALLIANCE ONE INTERNATIONAL, INC., *pg.* 1893, *pg.* 1384
AMANA SOCIETY, INC., *pg.* 836, *pg.* 701
THE ANDERSONS INCORPORATED, *pg.* 1793, *pg.* 1461
BURROUGHS & CHAPIN CO. INC., *pg.* 72, *pg.* 1621
CARGILL LIMITED, *pg.* 1475, *pg.* 1914
CHIQUITA BRANDS INTERNATIONAL, INC., *pg.* 847, *pg.* 1365
COOPERATIVE REGIONS OF ORGANIC PRODUCER POOLS, *pg.* 850, *pg.* 1864
D'ARRIGO BROS. COMPANY, *pg.* 852, *pg.* 197
GOLDEN PEANUT COMPANY, L.L.C., *pg.* 1854, *pg.* 484
LIMONEIRA COMPANY, *pg.* 705, *pg.* 276
MONSANTO COMPANY, *pg.* 1173, *pg.* 999
PREMIER TECH LTD., *pg.* 1799, *pg.* 1959
PRT FOREST REGENERATION INCOME FUND, *pg.* 1799, *pg.* 1913

0131 - Cotton & Cottonseed Production

MONSANTO, *pg.* 1798, *pg.* 971

0132 - Tobacco Production

ALTADIS USA, INC., *pg.* 1893, *pg.* 423

0133 - Sugarcane & Sugar Beet Production

UNITED STATES SUGAR CORPORATION, *pg* 907, *pg.* 417

0161 - Vegetable & Melon Production

BOLTHOUSE FARMS, *pg.* 841, *pg.* 44
CHIQUITA BRANDS INTERNATIONAL, INC., *pg.* 847, *pg.* 1365
D'ARRIGO BROS. COMPANY, *pg.* 852, *pg.* 197
DOLE FOOD COMPANY, INC., *pg.* 853, *pg.* 306
FRESH DEL MONTE PRODUCE INC., *pg.* 856, *pg.* 418
NATURAL SELECTION FOODS, LLC, *pg.* 882, *pg.* 252

0171 - Berry Farms

FRESH DEL MONTE PRODUCE INC., *pg.* 856, *pg.* 418
OCEAN SPRAY CRANBERRIES, INC., *pg.* 887, *pg.* 827

0172 - Production of Grapes

DELICATO FAMILY VINEYARDS, *pg.* 1961, *pg.* 163
F. KORBEL BROS. INC., *pg.* 1963, *pg.* 100
GIUMARRA VINEYARDS CORPORATION, *pg.* 1964, *pg.* 45
SCHEID VINEYARDS INC., *pg.* 1970, *pg.* 198
TREASURY WINE ESTATES, *pg.* 1971, *pg.* 164
TRINCHERO FAMILY ESTATES, *pg.* 1971, *pg.* 197

0173 - Production of Tree Nuts

BLUE DIAMOND GROWERS, *pg.* 840, *pg.* 195
JOHN B. SANFILIPPO & SON, INC., *pg.* 1024, *pg.* 610
YOUNG PECAN, INC., *pg.* 1864, *pg.* 1615

0174 - Citrus Fruits Production

CHIQUITA BRANDS INTERNATIONAL, INC., *pg.* 847, *pg.* 1365
DOLE FOOD COMPANY, INC., *pg.* 853, *pg.* 306
FRESH DEL MONTE PRODUCE INC., *pg.* 856, *pg.* 418

0175 - Deciduous Tree Fruits Production

DOLE FOOD COMPANY, INC., *pg.* 853, *pg.* 306
FRESH DEL MONTE PRODUCE INC., *pg.* 856, *pg.* 418
KNOUSE FOODS COOPERATIVE INC., *pg.* 869, *pg.* 1558

0179 - Production of Fruits & Tree Nuts, NEC

CHIQUITA BRANDS INTERNATIONAL, INC., *pg.* 847, *pg.* 1365
DOLE FOOD COMPANY, INC., *pg.* 853, *pg.* 306
DUNDEE CITRUS GROWERS ASSOCIATION, *pg.* 854, *pg.* 422
FRESH DEL MONTE PRODUCE INC., *pg.* 856, *pg.* 418
MAUI LAND & PINEAPPLE COMPANY, INC., *pg.* 876, *pg.* 545
POINSETTIA GROVES INC., *pg.* 890, *pg.* 478

0181 - Ornamental Floriculture & Nursery Products Production

ARIS HORTICULTURE, INC., *pg.* 1793, *pg.* 1404
BALL HORTICULTURAL COMPANY, *pg.* 1793, *pg.* 668
THE CONARD-PYLE COMPANY, *pg.* 1794, *pg.* 1594
FORREST KEELING NURSERY, INC., *pg.* 1795, *pg.* 977
HARRIS MORAN SEED CO., *pg.* 1796, *pg.* 150
MONROVIA GROWERS, *pg.* 1797, *pg.* 44
PANAMERICAN SEED CO., *pg.* 1798, *pg.* 668
PLUM CREEK TIMBER COMPANY, INC., *pg.* 105, *pg.* 1838
POTLATCH CORPORATION, *pg.* 1467, *pg.* 1844
SIMPSON LUMBER COMPANY, LLC, *pg.* 110, *pg.* 1845
SPEEDLING INCORPORATED, *pg.* 1800, *pg.* 468
W. ATLEE BURPEE & CO., *pg.* 1801, *pg.* 1590
WAYNESBORO NURSERIES, INC., *pg.* 1801, *pg.* 1811

0182 - Food Crops Grown Under Cover

CONAGRA FOODS, INC., *pg.* 826, *pg.* 1014
MONSANTO, *pg.* 1798, *pg.* 971
MONTEREY MUSHROOMS, INC., *pg.* 881, *pg.* 305
SYLVAN INC., *pg.* 900, *pg.* 1544

0211 - Beef Cattle Feedlots

TEXAS BEEF COUNCIL, *pg.* 158, *pg.* 1666

0212 - Beef Cattle, Except Feedlots

CHOBANI LLC, *pg.* 847, *pg.* 1318
CLOVER STORNETTA FARMS INC., *pg.* 848, *pg.* 182
DAIRYLEA COOPERATIVE INC., *pg.* 851, *pg.* 1157
FOREMOST FARMS USA COOPERATIVE, *pg.* 856, *pg.* 1854
GAY LEA FOODS CO-OPERATIVE LIMITED, *pg.* 858, *pg.* 1926
LAND O'LAKES, INC., *pg.* 873, *pg.* 915
LIFEWAY FOODS, INC., *pg.* 874, *pg.* 634
MIDWEST MICROSYSTEMS, LLC, *pg.* 1267, *pg.* 1012
SHAMROCK FOODS COMPANY, *pg.* 895, *pg.* 20
SMITHFIELD FOODS, INC., *pg.* 896, *pg.* 1806
TEXAS BEEF COUNCIL, *pg.* 158, *pg.* 1666
U.S. PREMIUM BEEF, LLC, *pg.* 907, *pg.* 987

0213 - Hog Production

SMITHFIELD FOODS, INC., *pg.* 896, *pg.* 1806

0251 - Broiler, Fryer & Roaster Chickens Production

PECO FOODS INC., *pg.* 888, *pg.* 8
PILGRIM'S PRIDE CORPORATION, *pg.* 889, *pg.* 330
SANDERSON FARMS, INC., *pg.* 893, *pg.* 970

0252 - Chicken Eggs Production

CAL-MAINE FOODS, INC., *pg.* 843, *pg.* 969
LAND O'LAKES, INC., *pg.* 873, *pg.* 915
MICHAEL FOODS, INC., *pg.* 877, *pg.* 949

0253 - Turkeys & Turkey Eggs Production

BUTTERBALL, LLC, *pg.* 843, *pg.* 1385
CARGILL TURKEY PRODUCTS, *pg.* 846, *pg.* 1784
JENNIE-O TURKEY STORE, LLC, *pg.* 865, *pg.* 966
KAUFFMAN POULTRY FARMS, INC., *pg.* 867, *pg.* 665
SMITHFIELD FOODS, INC., *pg.* 896, *pg.* 1806
ZACKY FARMS, INC., *pg.* 911, *pg.* 93

0254 - Poultry Hatcheries Production

BUTTERBALL, LLC, *pg.* 843, *pg.* 1385
FOSTER FARMS, *pg.* 856, *pg.* 122
PECO FOODS INC., *pg.* 888, *pg.* 8
TYSON FOODS, INC., *pg.* 902, *pg.* 35

0259 - Poultry & Eggs Production, NEC

HORMEL FOODS CORPORATION, *pg.* 863, *pg.* 915
TYSON FOODS, INC., *pg.* 902, *pg.* 35

0271 - Fur-Bearing Animals & Rabbits Production

AMERICAN LEGEND COOPERATIVE, *pg.* 18, *pg.* 1833

0273 - Animal Aquaculture

AMANA SOCIETY, INC., *pg.* 836, *pg.* 701
ELANCO ANIMAL HEALTH, *pg.* 1475, *pg.* 681
SEAWORLD TEXAS, *pg.* 583, *pg.* 1742
SMITHFIELD FOODS, INC., *pg.* 896, *pg.* 1806

0279 - Animal Specialties, NEC

AMANA SOCIETY, INC., *pg.* 836, *pg.* 701
ELANCO ANIMAL HEALTH, *pg.* 1475, *pg.* 681
SMITHFIELD FOODS, INC., *pg.* 896, *pg.* 1806

0711 - Soil Preparation Services

THE ANDERSONS INCORPORATED, *pg.* 1793, *pg.* 1461
CHIQUITA BRANDS INTERNATIONAL, INC., *pg.* 847, *pg.* 1365
EASYTURF, *pg.* 1833, *pg.* 302
GREEN EARTH TECHNOLOGIES, INC., *pg.* 704, *pg.* 1352
SPEEDLING INCORPORATED, *pg.* 1800, *pg.* 468
VCA INC., *pg.* 1606, *pg.* 141

0723 - Crop Preparation Services for Market, Except Cotton Ginning

THE ANDERSONS INCORPORATED, *pg.* 1793, *pg.* 1461
DIAMOND FOODS, INC., *pg.* 1851, *pg.* 216
DOLE FRESH VEGETABLES, *pg.* 854, *pg.* 198
NATURAL SELECTION FOODS, LLC, *pg.* 882, *pg.* 252
OCEAN MIST FARMS CORP., *pg.* 887, *pg.* 64
OREGON CHERRY GROWERS, INC., *pg.* 1028, *pg.* 1508
SYNGENTA SEEDS, INC., *pg.* 1801, *pg.* 950
VALLEY FIG GROWERS, INC., *pg.* 908, *pg.* 93

0742 - Veterinary Services for Animal Specialties

AMERICAN SOCIETY FOR THE PREVENTION OF CRUELTY TO ANIMALS, *pg.* 131, *pg.* 1193
BIO-REFERENCE LABORATORIES, INC., *pg.* 1402, *pg.* 1058
BIOANALYTICAL SYSTEMS, INC., *pg.* 1402, *pg.* 700
BIOCLINICA, INC., *pg.* 1506, *pg.* 1556
CORRPRO COMPANIES, INC., *pg.* 631, *pg.* 1464
ECOLOGY AND ENVIRONMENT, INC., *pg.* 1410, *pg.* 1173
ERESEARCH TECHNOLOGY INC., *pg.* 1243, *pg.* 1564
FINISAR CORPORATION, *pg.* 639, *pg.* 285
INDIANA CROP IMPROVEMENT ASSOCIATION, INC., *pg.* 144, *pg.* 693
LABORATORY CORPORATION OF AMERICA HOLDINGS, *pg.* 1554, *pg.* 1359
LANDAUER, INC., *pg.* 1554, *pg.* 615
MEDTOX SCIENTIFIC, INC., *pg.* 1422, *pg.* 962
MISTRAS GROUP, INC., *pg.* 1362, *pg.* 1113
MWI VETERINARY SUPPLY, INC., *pg.* 1570, *pg.* 548
NATIONAL TECHNICAL SYSTEMS INC., *pg.* 99, *pg.* 56
PERKINELMER, INC., *pg.* 1426, *pg.* 853
PETMED EXPRESS, INC., *pg.* 1781, *pg.* 460
RESPONSE GENETICS, INC., *pg.* 1590, *pg.* 139
SGS U.S. TESTING COMPANY INC., *pg.* 1181, *pg.* 1065
TERADYNE INC., *pg.* 679, *pg.* 838
UNDERWRITERS LABORATORIES INC., *pg.* 1396, *pg.* 641
VCA INC., *pg.* 1606, *pg.* 141

0751 - Livestock Services, Except Veterinary

ADM ALLIANCE NUTRITION, INC., *pg.* 1474, *pg.* 653
AJINOMOTO HEARTLAND LLC, *pg.* 1488, *pg.* 563
AMERICAN FOODS GROUP, LLC, *pg.* 837, *pg.* 1859
BAKER COMMODITIES, INC., *pg.* 839, *pg.* 301
CARGILL ANIMAL NUTRITION, *pg.* 1475, *pg.* 965
CARGILL, INC., *pg.* 845, *pg.* 965
CLEAR SPRINGS FOODS, INC., *pg.* 848, *pg.* 548
CLOUGHERTY PACKING COMPANY, *pg.* 848, *pg.* 128
DIETZ & WATSON INC., *pg.* 853, *pg.* 1563
FROMM FAMILY PET FOODS, INC., *pg.* 1476, *pg.* 1870
FURST-MCNESS COMPANY, *pg.* 1476, *pg.* 613
HATFIELD QUALITY MEATS, INC., *pg.* 861, *pg.* 1537
HILL'S PET NUTRITION, INC., *pg.* 1476, *pg.* 721
HORMEL FOODS CORPORATION, *pg.* 863, *pg.* 915
HOUSE OF RAEFORD FARMS, INC., *pg.* 864, *pg.* 1386
HUBBARD FEEDS INC., *pg.* 1477, *pg.* 928
IAMS COMPANY, *pg.* 1477, *pg.* 1633
JOHN MORRELL & CO., *pg.* 866, *pg.* 1415
KAYEM FOODS, INC., *pg.* 867, *pg.* 814
KENT NUTRITION GROUP, *pg.* 1477, *pg.* 710
KRAFT FOODS OSCAR MAYER, *pg.* 870, *pg.* 1866
KUNZLER & COMPANY, INC., *pg.* 1026, *pg.* 1546
MANNA PRO CORPORATION, *pg.* 1478, *pg.* 975
MARS, INCORPORATED, *pg.* 1858, *pg.* 1792
NATIONAL BEEF PACKING COMPANY, LLC, *pg.* 882, *pg.* 985
NESTLE PURINA PETCARE CANADA, *pg.* 1479, *pg.* 1928
NOVUS INTERNATIONAL, INC., *pg.* 706, *pg.* 1001
SMITHFIELD FOODS, INC., *pg.* 896, *pg.* 1806
THE SMITHFIELD PACKING CO., INC., *pg.* 896, *pg.* 1807
SOUTHERN STATES COOPERATIVE, INC., *pg.* 1482, *pg.* 1804
SPECIALTY FOODS GROUP-FIELD PACKING DIV., *pg.* 897, *pg.* 739
SUGAR CREEK PACKING CO., *pg.* 899, *pg.* 1478
TROUW NUTRITION USA, *pg.* 1482, *pg.* 616
TYSON FOODS, INC., *pg.* 902, *pg.* 35
U.S. PREMIUM BEEF, LLC, *pg.* 907, *pg.* 987
VITUSA CORP., *pg.* 1482, *pg.* 1063

0752 - Animal Specialty Services, Except Veterinary

AMERICAN HEREFORD ASSOCIATION, *pg.* 129, *pg.* 980
AMERICAN QUARTER HORSE ASSOCIATION, *pg.* 130, *pg.* 1658
AMERICAN SOCIETY FOR THE PREVENTION OF CRUELTY TO ANIMALS, *pg.* 131, *pg.* 1193
ANIMAL HEALTH INTERNATIONAL, INC., *pg.* 1474, *pg.* 1749
BUTTE HUMANE SOCIETY, *pg.* 135, *pg.* 65
THE CLOROX COMPANY, *pg.* 327, *pg.* 169
ECOLAB INC., *pg.* 329, *pg.* 960
ECOLAB INC.-FOOD & BEVERAGE DIVISION, *pg.* 330, *pg.* 960
H.W. NAYLOR COMPANY, INC., *pg.* 1477, *pg.* 1183
MAC-GRAY CORPORATION, *pg.* 58, *pg.* 852
MERCK ANIMAL HEALTH, *pg.* 1479, *pg.* 387
PETCO ANIMAL SUPPLIES, INC., *pg.* 1480, *pg.* 206
PETSMART, INC., *pg.* 1481, *pg.* 18
VCA INC., *pg.* 1606, *pg.* 141
VETERINARY PET INSURANCE CO., *pg.* 1222, *pg.* 49
VIRBAC CORPORATION, *pg.* 1606, *pg.* 1696

0762 - Farm Management Services

EXPRESS SCRIPTS, INC., *pg.* 1530, *pg.* 997
FARMERS NATIONAL COMPANY, *pg.* 703, *pg.* 1015
INTERACTIVE DATA CORPORATION, *pg.* 769, *pg.* 785
KNOUSE FOODS COOPERATIVE INC., *pg.* 869, *pg.* 1558

0781 - Landscape Counseling & Planning

THE DAVEY TREE EXPERT COMPANY, *pg.* 1794, *pg.* 1456

0782 - Lawn & Garden Services

ARBOR MASTERS TREE SERVICE, *pg.* 68, *pg.* 721
ARMSTRONG GARDEN CENTERS, INC., *pg.* 1793, *pg.* 99
THE DAVEY TREE EXPERT COMPANY, *pg.* 1794, *pg.* 1456
THE F.A. BARTLETT TREE EXPERT COMPANY, *pg.* 1795, *pg.* 373
ORKIN, INC., *pg.* 1798, *pg.* 517
THE SERVICEMASTER COMPANY, LLC, *pg.* 335, *pg.* 1646
THE SIEBENTHALER CO., *pg.* 1800, *pg.* 1446
SPRING-GREEN LAWN CARE CORPORATION, *pg.* 1800, *pg.* 652
TRUGREEN-CHEMLAWN, *pg.* 1801, *pg.* 1647

0811 - Timber Tracts

PLUM CREEK TIMBER COMPANY, INC., *pg.* 105, *pg.* 1838
POTLATCH CORPORATION, *pg.* 1467, *pg.* 1844

0921 - Fish Hatcheries & Preserves

THE CATFISH INSTITUTE, *pg.* 136, *pg.* 969

0971 - Hunting & Trapping & Game Propagation

DUCKS UNLIMITED, INC., *pg.* 139, *pg.* 1642

1011 - Iron Ores Mining

ARCELORMITTAL STEEL USA INC., *pg.* 68, *pg.* 564
TURQUOISE HILL RESOURCES LTD., *pg.* 1385, *pg.* 1913

1021 - Copper Ores Mining

ASARCO INCORPORATED, *pg.* 69, *pg.* 15
CANADIAN ROYALTIES INC., *pg.* 73, *pg.* 1960
FREEPORT-MCMORAN COPPER & GOLD, INC., *pg.* 1163, *pg.* 16
KENNECOTT UTAH COPPER CORPORATION, *pg.* 1170, *pg.* 1763
RED METAL RESOURCES LTD., *pg.* 106, *pg.* 1934
TECK RESOURCES LIMITED, *pg.* 1183, *pg.* 1912
TURQUOISE HILL RESOURCES LTD., *pg.* 1385, *pg.* 1913
YAMANA GOLD INC., *pg.* 1396, *pg.* 1947

1031 - Lead & Zinc Ores Mining

KENNECOTT UTAH COPPER CORPORATION, *pg.* 1170, *pg.* 1763
TECK RESOURCES LIMITED, *pg.* 1183, *pg.* 1912

1041 - Gold Ores Mining

AGNICO-EAGLE MINES LIMITED, *pg.* 971, *pg.* 1934
CADILLAC VENTURES INC., *pg.* 1393, *pg.* 1935
COEUR D'ALENE MINES CORPORATION, *pg.* 1154, *pg.* 549
FREEPORT-MCMORAN COPPER & GOLD, INC., *pg.* 1163, *pg.* 16
IAMGOLD, *pg.* 7, *pg.* 1952
RED METAL RESOURCES LTD., *pg.* 106, *pg.* 1934
ROYAL GOLD, INC., *pg.* 11, *pg.* 323
TECK RESOURCES LIMITED, *pg.* 1183, *pg.* 1912
TURQUOISE HILL RESOURCES LTD., *pg.* 1385, *pg.* 1913
YAMANA GOLD INC., *pg.* 1396, *pg.* 1947

1044 - Silver Ores Mining

ASARCO INCORPORATED, *pg.* 69, *pg.* 15
COEUR D'ALENE MINES CORPORATION, *pg.* 1154, *pg.* 549
ROYAL GOLD, INC., *pg.* 11, *pg.* 323

1081 - Metal Mining Services

TECK RESOURCES LIMITED, *pg.* 1183, *pg.* 1912
YAMANA GOLD INC., *pg.* 1396, *pg.* 1947

1094 - Uranium-Radium-Vanadium Ores

DEJOUR ENERGY, *pg.* 975, *pg.* 1910

1099 - Miscellaneous Metal Ores Mining, NEC

FREEPORT-MCMORAN COPPER & GOLD, INC., *pg.* 1163, *pg.* 16
KAISER ALUMINUM CORPORATION, *pg.* 90, *pg.* 86
ROYAL GOLD, INC., *pg.* 11, *pg.* 323
YAMANA GOLD INC., *pg.* 1396, *pg.* 1947

1221 - Surface Mining-Bituminous Coal & Lignite

ARCH COAL, INC., *pg.* 68, *pg.* 992
CONSOL ENERGY INC., *pg.* 1154, *pg.* 1520
THE NORTH AMERICAN COAL CORPORATION, *pg.* 1175, *pg.* 1733
PEABODY ENERGY CORPORATION, *pg.* 1176, *pg.* 1001
WESTMORELAND COAL COMPANY, *pg.* 1955, *pg.* 328

1222 - Underground Mining-Bituminous Coal

ALLETE, INC., *pg.* 1933, *pg.* 921
ARCH COAL, INC., *pg.* 68, *pg.* 992
CONSOL ENERGY INC., *pg.* 1154, *pg.* 1520
THE NORTH AMERICAN COAL CORPORATION, *pg.* 1175, *pg.* 1733
PEABODY ENERGY CORPORATION, *pg.* 1176, *pg.* 1001
TECK RESOURCES LIMITED, *pg.* 1183, *pg.* 1912
WALTER ENERGY, INC., *pg.* 120, *pg.* 4

1231 - Anthracite Mining

ARCH COAL, INC., *pg.* 68, *pg.* 992
READING ANTHRACITE COMPANY, *pg.* 1179, *pg.* 1583

1241 - Coal Mining Services

First page reference indicates Business Class Edition
Second page reference indicates Geographic Edition

ARCH COAL, INC., pg. 68, pg. 992
READING ANTHRACITE COMPANY, pg. 1179, pg. 1583
TECK RESOURCES LIMITED, pg. 1183, pg. 1912
YAMANA GOLD INC., pg. 1396, pg. 1947

1311 - Crude Petroleum & Natural Gas

ANADARKO PETROLEUM CORPORATION, pg. 971, pg. 1746
APACHE CORPORATION, pg. 1934, pg. 1700
BASIN ELECTRIC POWER COOPERATIVE, pg. 1936, pg. 1397
BLUE DOLPHIN ENERGY COMPANY, pg. 972, pg. 1701
BP AMERICA INC., pg. 972, pg. 1702
BP EXPLORATION (ALASKA) INC., pg. 973, pg. 10
CENTURION ENERGY INTERNATIONAL INC., pg. 973, pg. 1903
CHESAPEAKE ENERGY CORPORATION, pg. 1937, pg. 1485
CONOCOPHILLIPS, pg. 975, pg. 1703
CROSSTEX ENERGY, L.P., pg. 975, pg. 1678
DEJOUR ENERGY, pg. 975, pg. 1910
DELEK US HOLDINGS, INC., pg. 975, pg. 1627
DEVON ENERGY CORPORATION, pg. 976, pg. 1704
DEVON ENERGY CORPORATION, pg. 975, pg. 1485
DRIL-QUIP, INC., pg. 1330, pg. 1704
ENCANA CORP., pg. 976, pg. 1903
ENERPLUS CORPORATION, pg. 976, pg. 1903
ENTERPRISE PRODUCTS PARTNERS L.P., pg. 976, pg. 1705
EPL OIL & GAS, INC., pg. 976, pg. 746
ERGON, INC., pg. 976, pg. 969
EXXON MOBIL CORPORATION, pg. 977, pg. 1718
GEOKINETICS INC., pg. 978, pg. 1706
HESS CORPORATION, pg. 979, pg. 1240
HKN, INC., pg. 979, pg. 1745
HYPERDYNAMICS CORPORATION, pg. 979, pg. 1708
IMPERIAL OIL LIMITED, pg. 979, pg. 1903
KINDER MORGAN, pg. 1945, pg. 1709
M-D BUILDING PRODUCTS, INC., pg. 95, pg. 1486
MAGELLAN PETROLEUM CORPORATION, pg. 981, pg. 321
MARATHON OIL CORPORATION, pg. 981, pg. 1710
MARKWEST ENERGY PARTNERS, L.P., pg. 981, pg. 321
MURPHY OIL CORPORATION, pg. 982, pg. 31
NATIONAL FUEL GAS COMPANY, pg. 982, pg. 1355
NEWFIELD EXPLORATION COMPANY, pg. 45, pg. 1747
NEXEN INC., pg. 1174, pg. 1904
OCCIDENTAL OIL & GAS CORPORATION, pg. 982, pg. 1712
OCCIDENTAL PETROLEUM CORPORATION, pg. 1175, pg. 137
PENGROWTH ENERGY CORP., pg. 983, pg. 1904
PLANAR SYSTEMS, INC., pg. 455, pg. 1495
QUICKSILVER RESOURCES INC., pg. 983, pg. 1696
RENEWABLE ENERGY GROUP, INC., pg. 984, pg. 701
ROYALE ENERGY, INC., pg. 984, pg. 208
SOUTHWEST GAS CORPORATION, pg. 984, pg. 1029
SUNCOR ENERGY INC., pg. 985, pg. 1905
SUNOCO INC., pg. 985, pg. 1571
TERVITA CORPORATION, pg. 986, pg. 1905
TRANSMONTAIGNE, INC., pg. 986, pg. 323
ZION OIL & GAS, INC., pg. 987, pg. 1691

1321 - Natural Gas Liquids

AMERICAN CHEMET CORPORATION, pg. 1147, pg. 599
ANADARKO PETROLEUM CORPORATION, pg. 971, pg. 1746
APACHE CORPORATION, pg. 1934, pg. 1700
ASHLAND INC., pg. 972, pg. 726
ASHLAND PERFORMANCE MATERIALS, pg. 1147, pg. 1448
AVANTOR PERFORMANCE MATERIALS, INC., pg. 1148, pg. 1521
BASF CATALYSTS LLC, pg. 1148, pg. 1074
BIRKO CORPORATION, pg. 1149, pg. 332
BUCKMAN, pg. 1150, pg. 1641
BURGESS PIGMENT COMPANY, pg. 1150, pg. 535
CARUS CORPORATION, pg. 1152, pg. 652
CENTURION ENERGY INTERNATIONAL INC., pg. 973, pg. 1903
CERAMIC COLOR & CHEMICAL MFG. CO., pg. 1441, pg. 1555
CHART INDUSTRIES, INC., pg. 1405, pg. 1454
CHURCH & DWIGHT CO., INC., pg. 1153, pg. 1063
COMPASS MINERALS INTERNATIONAL, INC., pg. 1154, pg. 718
CROSSTEX ENERGY, L.P., pg. 975, pg. 1678
DEEPWATER CHEMICALS, INC., pg. 1155, pg. 1491
DETREX CORPORATION, pg. 1156, pg. 906
DOVER CHEMICAL CORPORATION, pg. 1156, pg. 1447
THE DOW CHEMICAL COMPANY, pg. 1157, pg. 898
DOW CORNING CORPORATION, pg. 1159, pg. 900
ENERGEN CORPORATION, pg. 1941, pg. 2
EVONIK CORPORATION, pg. 1162, pg. 1103
EXXON MOBIL CORPORATION, pg. 977, pg. 1718
FMC LITHIUM DIVISION, pg. 1163, pg. 1366
GFS CHEMICALS, INC., pg. 1164, pg. 1471
HEATBATH CORPORATION, pg. 1165, pg. 826
HERCULES INCORPORATED, pg. 1166, pg. 392
HUNTSMAN CORPORATION, pg. 1167, pg. 1758
IMPERIAL OIL LIMITED, pg. 979, pg. 1903
INTERNATIONAL FLAVORS & FRAGRANCES INC., pg. 512, pg. 1244
J.M. HUBER CORPORATION, pg. 1169, pg. 1056
JOHNSON MATTHEY PROCESS TECHNOLOGIES, pg. 1169, pg. 1083
JONES-HAMILTON CO., pg. 1169, pg. 1478
KAISER ALUMINUM CORPORATION, pg. 90, pg. 86
KING INDUSTRIES, INC., pg. 1443, pg. 363
KOPPERS HOLDINGS INC., pg. 1170, pg. 1577
LANDEC CORPORATION, pg. 1419, pg. 145
LOCKHART COMPANY, pg. 1171, pg. 1534
LYONDELLBASELL INDUSTRIES, pg. 980, pg. 1710
MARKWEST ENERGY PARTNERS, L.P., pg. 981, pg. 321
MATERION ADVANCED CHEMICALS, pg. 1172, pg. 1877
MCGEAN-ROHCO, INC., pg. 1172, pg. 1432
MERICHEM COMPANY, pg. 1172, pg. 1711
MULTI-METALS, pg. 1363, pg. 737
MULTISORB TECHNOLOGIES, INC., pg. 1570, pg. 1150
NATIONAL FUEL GAS COMPANY, pg. 982, pg. 1355
NOAH TECHNOLOGIES CORPORATION, pg. 1175, pg. 1742
NOVA CHEMICALS CORPORATION, pg. 1175, pg. 1904
OCCIDENTAL PETROLEUM CORPORATION, pg. 1175, pg. 137
ONEOK, INC., pg. 982, pg. 1490
PIEDMONT NATURAL GAS COMPANY, INC., pg. 1949, pg. 1368
PQ CORPORATION, pg. 1178, pg. 1515
QUAKER CHEMICAL CORP., pg. 1178, pg. 1524
QUICKSILVER RESOURCES INC., pg. 983, pg. 1696
RHODIA INC., pg. 1179, pg. 1053
RIO TINTO BORAX, pg. 334, pg. 331
SENSIENT TECHNOLOGIES CORPORATION, pg. 895, pg. 1881
SIGMA-ALDRICH CORPORATION, pg. 1181, pg. 1881
SILBERLINE MANUFACTURING CO., INC., pg. 110, pg. 1588
TETRA TECHNOLOGIES, INC., pg. 986, pg. 1747
UOP LLC, pg. 1386, pg. 606
VELSICOL CHEMICAL CORPORATION, pg. 1185, pg. 657
THE WILLIAMS COMPANIES, INC., pg. 987, pg. 1491

1381 - Drilling Oil & Gas Wells

ALBERTA STAR DEVELOPMENT CORP., pg. 971, pg. 1909
BADGER DAYLIGHTING LTD., pg. 1315, pg. 1902
BP AMERICA INC., pg. 972, pg. 1702
DEVON ENERGY CORPORATION, pg. 976, pg. 1704
DEVON ENERGY CORPORATION, pg. 975, pg. 1485
EXXON MOBIL CORPORATION, pg. 977, pg. 1718
HALLIBURTON COMPANY, pg. 978, pg. 1707
MARATHON OIL CORPORATION, pg. 981, pg. 1710
PARKER DRILLING COMPANY, pg. 982, pg. 1712
ROWAN COMPANIES, INC., pg. 984, pg. 1713
STALLION OILFIELD SERVICES, INC., pg. 985, pg. 1715
TERVITA CORPORATION, pg. 986, pg. 1905

1389 - Oil & Gas Field Services, NEC

ANADARKO PETROLEUM CORPORATION, pg. 971, pg. 1746
BADGER DAYLIGHTING LTD., pg. 1315, pg. 1902
BLUE DOLPHIN ENERGY COMPANY, pg. 972, pg. 1701
BP AMERICA INC., pg. 972, pg. 1702
CENTURION ENERGY INTERNATIONAL INC., pg. 973, pg. 1903
CGGVERITAS SERVICES (U.S.) INC., pg. 973, pg. 1703
CHEVRON CORPORATION, pg. 974, pg. 259
DAWSON GEOPHYSICAL COMPANY, pg. 383, pg. 1727
DIRECT ENERGY, pg. 1939, pg. 1704
ECHELON CORPORATION, pg. 389, pg. 245
EGPI FIRECREEK, INC., pg. 976, pg. 21
ENERGEN CORPORATION, pg. 1941, pg. 2
EPL OIL & GAS, INC., pg. 976, pg. 746
EXTERRAN HOLDINGS, INC., pg. 977, pg. 1705
EXXON MOBIL CORPORATION, pg. 977, pg. 1718
GEOKINETICS INC., pg. 978, pg. 1706
GEOSPATIAL HOLDINGS, INC., pg. 84, pg. 1585
GIBSONS ENERGY, pg. 1340, pg. 743
HALLIBURTON COMPANY, pg. 978, pg. 1707
HESS CORPORATION, pg. 979, pg. 1240
HKN, INC., pg. 979, pg. 1745
HUNTING COMPANY, US OFFICE, pg. 979, pg. 1708
INCOMING INC., pg. 979, pg. 1243
THE KENAN ADVANTAGE GROUP, INC., pg. 1914, pg. 1408
M-I SWACO, pg. 980, pg. 1710
MACFADDEN COMMUNICATIONS GROUP, LLC, pg. 1660, pg. 1254
MAGELLAN PETROLEUM CORPORATION, pg. 981, pg. 321
NATIONAL OILHEAT RESEARCH ALLIANCE, pg. 150, pg. 1771
NEWPARK RESOURCES, INC., pg. 982, pg. 1747
NORTHERN ILLINOIS GAS COMPANY, pg. 1947, pg. 637
PARKER DRILLING COMPANY, pg. 982, pg. 1712
POWERSECURE INTERNATIONAL, INC., pg. 105, pg. 1392
PURADYN FILTER TECHNOLOGIES, INC., pg. 215, pg. 414
QUESTAR CORPORATION, pg. 983, pg. 1760
QUICKSILVER RESOURCES INC., pg. 983, pg. 1696
ROYALE ENERGY, INC., pg. 984, pg. 208
RPC, INC., pg. 984, pg. 519
SCHLUMBERGER LIMITED, pg. 801, pg. 1714
SCHLUMBERGER WELL COMPLETIONS, pg. 1373, pg. 1714
STALLION OILFIELD SERVICES, INC., pg. 985, pg. 1715
STEWART & STEVENSON, LLC, pg. 985, pg. 1715
SUNCOR ENERGY INC., pg. 985, pg. 1905
TETRA TECHNOLOGIES, INC., pg. 986, pg. 1747
UNITED STATES OIL & GAS CORPORATION, pg. 986, pg. 1147

1411 - Dimension Stone

POLYCOR INC., pg. 105, pg. 1950
ROCK OF AGES CORPORATION, pg. 108, pg. 1766
VULCAN MATERIALS COMPANY, pg. 119, pg. 4

1422 - Crushed & Broken Limestone

CARMEUSE NORTH AMERICA, pg. 73, pg. 1574

1423 - Crushed & Broken Granite

ROCK OF AGES CORPORATION, pg. 108, pg. 1766

1429 - Crushed & Broken Stone, NEC

AMERICAN GILSONITE CO., pg. 1313, pg. 1700
BARTON MINES COMPANY LLC, pg. 1148, pg. 1171
COMPASS MINERALS INTERNATIONAL, INC., pg. 1154, pg. 718
MDU RESOURCES GROUP, INC., pg. 981, pg. 1397
MOUNTAIN WEST, LLC, pg. 98, pg. 550
PQ CORPORATION, pg. 1178, pg. 1515
U.S. PUMICE COMPANY, pg. 1185, pg. 65
VULCAN MATERIALS COMPANY, pg. 119, pg. 4

1442 - Construction Sand & Gravel

MDU RESOURCES GROUP, INC., pg. 981, pg. 1397
PARAGON TECHNOLOGIES, INC., pg. 1367, pg. 1528

VULCAN MATERIALS COMPANY, pg. 119, pg. 4

1446 - Industrial Sand

FAIRMOUNT SANTROL, pg. 1162, pg. 1409
U.S. SILICA COMPANY, pg. 1185, pg. 1849

1455 - Kaolin & Ball Clay

AMERICAN ART CLAY CO., INC., pg. 1759, pg. 682
BURGESS PIGMENT COMPANY, pg. 1150, pg. 535
HILL & GRIFFITH COMPANY, pg. 1167, pg. 1414
MULTISORB TECHNOLOGIES, INC., pg. 1570, pg. 1150
OIL-DRI CORPORATION OF AMERICA, pg. 1480, pg. 586
RESCO PRODUCTS GREENSBORO, pg. 107, pg. 1375
SILBRICO CORPORATION, pg. 110, pg. 617
U.S. SILICA COMPANY, pg. 1185, pg. 1849

1459 - Clay, Ceramic & Refractory Minerals, NEC

AMERICAN ART CLAY CO., INC., pg. 1759, pg. 682
BURGESS PIGMENT COMPANY, pg. 1150, pg. 535
HILL & GRIFFITH COMPANY, pg. 1167, pg. 1414
KYANITE MINING CORPORATION, pg. 1170, pg. 1779
MINERALS TECHNOLOGIES INC., pg. 1173, pg. 617
MOMENTIVE PERFORMANCE MATERIALS, INC., pg. 1464, pg. 1349
MULTISORB TECHNOLOGIES, INC., pg. 1570, pg. 1150
OIL-DRI CORPORATION OF AMERICA, pg. 1480, pg. 586
RESCO PRODUCTS GREENSBORO, pg. 107, pg. 1375
SILBRICO CORPORATION, pg. 110, pg. 617

1474 - Potash, Soda & Borate Minerals

ANADARKO PETROLEUM CORPORATION, pg. 971, pg. 1746
CHURCH & DWIGHT CO., INC., pg. 1153, pg. 1063
COMPASS MINERALS INTERNATIONAL, INC., pg. 1154, pg. 718
OLIN CORPORATION, pg. 1176, pg. 976
POTASH CORP., pg. 1177, pg. 641
RIO TINTO BORAX, pg. 334, pg. 331

1479 - Chemical & Fertilizer Mineral Mining, NEC

AMERICAN ART CLAY CO., INC., pg. 1759, pg. 682
BURGESS PIGMENT COMPANY, pg. 1150, pg. 535
COMPASS MINERALS INTERNATIONAL, INC., pg. 1154, pg. 718
FMC LITHIUM DIVISION, pg. 1163, pg. 1366
HILL & GRIFFITH COMPANY, pg. 1167, pg. 1414
MULTISORB TECHNOLOGIES, INC., pg. 1570, pg. 1150
OIL-DRI CORPORATION OF AMERICA, pg. 1480, pg. 586
RESCO PRODUCTS GREENSBORO, pg. 107, pg. 1375
SILBRICO CORPORATION, pg. 110, pg. 617
TERRABIOGEN TECHNOLOGIES INC., pg. 1890, pg. 1908
TOR MINERALS INTERNATIONAL INC., pg. 1184, pg. 1672

1499 - Miscellaneous Nonmetallic Minerals, Except Fuels

AMERICAN ART CLAY CO., INC., pg. 1759, pg. 682
AMERICAN GILSONITE CO., pg. 1313, pg. 1700
BARTON MINES COMPANY LLC, pg. 1148, pg. 1171
BURGESS PIGMENT COMPANY, pg. 1150, pg. 535
COMPASS MINERALS INTERNATIONAL, INC., pg. 1154, pg. 718
HILL & GRIFFITH COMPANY, pg. 1167, pg. 1414
MULTISORB TECHNOLOGIES, INC., pg. 1570, pg. 1150
OIL-DRI CORPORATION OF AMERICA, pg. 1480, pg. 586
PQ CORPORATION, pg. 1178, pg. 1515
RESCO PRODUCTS GREENSBORO, pg. 107, pg. 1375
SILBRICO CORPORATION, pg. 110, pg. 617
U.S. PUMICE COMPANY, pg. 1185, pg. 65

1521 - General Contractors-Single Family Houses

ALVAREZ HOMES, INC., pg. 66, pg. 470
ARCS INVESTMENTS, LLC, pg. 68, pg. 450
BEAZER HOMES USA, INC., pg. 1081, pg. 491
BROOKFIELD HOMES, pg. 71, pg. 77
BROOKFIELD HOMES CORPORATION, pg. 72, pg. 1779
COASTAL CONSTRUCTION GROUP OF SOUTH FLORIDA INC., pg. 1087, pg. 441
COMSTOCK HOLDING COMPANIES INC., pg. 1087, pg. 1798
DAVID WEEKLEY HOMES, LP, pg. 78, pg. 1704
DOMINION HOMES, INC., pg. 79, pg. 1449
D.R. HORTON, INC., pg. 1090, pg. 1694
FLEXI-VAN LEASING, INC., pg. 1909, pg. 1077
HERITAGE HOMES INC., pg. 87, pg. 857
THE HUNT CORPORATION, pg. 88, pg. 22
JOHN CANNON HOMES INC., pg. 89, pg. 466
LAMPERT YARDS, INC., pg. 1053, pg. 962
LENNAR CORPORATION, pg. 1100, pg. 443
LENNAR HOMES, INC., pg. 1101, pg. 443
LENNAR HOMES, INC., pg. 93, pg. 1710
LIBERTY GROUP OF COMPANIES, pg. 1101, pg. 416
M/I HOMES, INC., pg. 95, pg. 1441
M.D.C. HOLDINGS, INC., pg. 1104, pg. 321
MERITAGE HOMES CORPORATION, pg. 97, pg. 23
NATIONWIDE HOMES, INC., pg. 99, pg. 1788
PURCELL CO., INC., pg. 1109, pg. 968
SOUTH FLORIDA DESIGN, pg. 112, pg. 413
TOLL BROTHERS, INC., pg. 115, pg. 1541
WALTER ENERGY, INC., pg. 120, pg. 4
WAUSAU HOMES, INC., pg. 120, pg. 1890

1522 - General Contractors-Residential Buildings, other than Single-Family

AG-MEIER INDUSTRIES LLC, pg. 700, pg. 1668
ANTHEM, INC., pg. 1192, pg. 683
THE AUSTIN COMPANY, pg. 69, pg. 1428
AV HOMES INC., pg. 1080, pg. 20
THE BECK GROUP, pg. 70, pg. 1676
BOSTON MEDICAL CENTER, pg. 1508, pg. 791
BRASFIELD & GORRIE, LLC, pg. 71, pg. 2
CALATLANTIC GROUP, INC., pg. 1084, pg. 108
COASTAL CONSTRUCTION GROUP OF SOUTH FLORIDA INC., pg. 1087, pg. 441
COMSTOCK HOLDING COMPANIES INC., pg. 1087, pg. 1798
CUNNINGHAM-LIMP COMPANY, pg. 77, pg. 885
DENHOLTZ MANAGEMENT CORP., pg. 78, pg. 1083
DOMINION HOMES, INC., pg. 79, pg. 1449
DPR CONSTRUCTION, INC., pg. 79, pg. 189
D.R. HORTON, INC., pg. 1090, pg. 1694
DUGAN & MEYERS CONSTRUCTION CO., INC., pg. 79, pg. 1412
EXTERRAN HOLDINGS, INC., pg. 977, pg. 1705
FISHER DEVELOPMENT INC., pg. 81, pg. 218
THE FLATLEY COMPANY, pg. 1092, pg. 802
FLORIDA EAST COAST INDUSTRIES, INC., pg. 1909, pg. 433
FLUOR CORPORATION, pg. 82, pg. 1719
FOREST CITY ENTERPRISES, INC., pg. 1092, pg. 1430
GIBRALTAR INDUSTRIES, INC., pg. 1340, pg. 1148
GILBANE BUILDING COMPANY, pg. 84, pg. 1606
GRAYCOR INC., pg. 84, pg. 619
H&E EQUIPMENT SERVICES, INC., pg. 85, pg. 742
HERITAGE HOMES INC., pg. 87, pg. 857
HIBBETT SPORTS, INC., pg. 1836, pg. 3
HOVNANIAN ENTERPRISES, INC., pg. 1096, pg. 1114
HUNT BUILDING COMPANY LIMITED, pg. 87, pg. 1692
HUNT CONSTRUCTION GROUP, INC., pg. 87, pg. 686
JACOBS ENGINEERING GROUP, INC., pg. 88, pg. 180
J.E. DUNN CONSTRUCTION GROUP, INC., pg. 89, pg. 984
JERSEY MIKE'S SUBS, pg. 1733, pg. 1083
KB HOME, pg. 90, pg. 134
KITCHELL CORPORATION, pg. 1099, pg. 17
LARKEN ASSOCIATES, pg. 93, pg. 1073
LENNAR CORPORATION, pg. 1100, pg. 443
LENNAR HOMES, INC., pg. 1101, pg. 443
LESTER BUILDING SYSTEMS, LLC, pg. 93, pg. 927
M/I HOMES, INC., pg. 95, pg. 1441
MARNELL COMPANIES, pg. 95, pg. 1028
MCCARTHY BUILDING COMPANIES, INC., pg. 96, pg. 999
M.D.C. HOLDINGS, INC., pg. 1104, pg. 321
MERITAGE HOMES CORPORATION, pg. 97, pg. 23
MET-CON CONSTRUCTION INC., pg. 97, pg. 925
MILLER AND SMITH HOMES, INC., pg. 97, pg. 1794
MINAEAN INTERNATIONAL CORPORATION, pg. 97, pg. 1911
NEWGROUND RESOURCES, pg. 99, pg. 975
OMEGA FLEX, INC., pg. 982, pg. 1532
OPUS CORPORATION, pg. 101, pg. 949
OVERTON MOORE PROPERTIES, pg. 1107, pg. 94
PACIFIC NATIONAL GROUP INC., pg. 103, pg. 119
PHILLIPS DEVELOPMENT & REALTY, LLC, pg. 1108, pg. 475
P.J. DICK-TRUMBULL-LINDY, pg. 104, pg. 1579
PULTEGROUP, INC., pg. 1109, pg. 873
RAMPART CAPITAL CORPORATION, pg. 798, pg. 1672
RITCHIE BROS. AUCTIONEERS INCORPORATED, pg. 1372, pg. 1907
ROUGH BROTHERS, INC., pg. 108, pg. 1425
SAMUELS GROUP, INC., pg. 109, pg. 1898
SCHUMACHER HOMES, INC., pg. 109, pg. 1408
SCOTTSDALE COMPANY, pg. 1111, pg. 451
SCS ENGINEERS, pg. 109, pg. 124
STILES CORPORATION, pg. 1115, pg. 427
TOLL BROTHERS, INC., pg. 115, pg. 1541
UNITED STATES AWNING COMPANY, pg. 117, pg. 467
U.S. PHYSICAL THERAPY, INC., pg. 1604, pg. 1716
WCI COMMUNITIES, INC., pg. 1118, pg. 414
THE WEITZ COMPANY, pg. 121, pg. 707
WILLIAM LYON HOMES, pg. 122, pg. 166
W.M. JORDAN COMPANY INC., pg. 122, pg. 1796
WYNN RESORTS LIMITED, pg. 1119, pg. 1030

1531 - Operative Builders

ALVAREZ HOMES, INC., pg. 66, pg. 470
ANTHEM, INC., pg. 1192, pg. 683
ARCS INVESTMENTS, LLC, pg. 68, pg. 450
AV HOMES INC., pg. 1080, pg. 20
BEAZER HOMES USA, INC., pg. 1081, pg. 491
THE BECK GROUP, pg. 70, pg. 1676
BRASFIELD & GORRIE, LLC, pg. 71, pg. 2
BROOKFIELD HOMES, pg. 71, pg. 77
BROOKFIELD HOMES CORPORATION, pg. 72, pg. 1779
CALATLANTIC GROUP, INC., pg. 1084, pg. 108
COASTAL CONSTRUCTION GROUP OF SOUTH FLORIDA INC., pg. 1087, pg. 441
COMSTOCK HOLDING COMPANIES INC., pg. 1087, pg. 1798
CUNNINGHAM-LIMP COMPANY, pg. 77, pg. 885
DAVID WEEKLEY HOMES, LP, pg. 78, pg. 1704
DENHOLTZ MANAGEMENT CORP., pg. 78, pg. 1083
DOMINION HOMES, INC., pg. 79, pg. 1449
DPR CONSTRUCTION, INC., pg. 79, pg. 189
D.R. HORTON, INC., pg. 1090, pg. 1694
DUGAN & MEYERS CONSTRUCTION CO., INC., pg. 79, pg. 1412
FISHER DEVELOPMENT INC., pg. 81, pg. 218
FLEXI-VAN LEASING, INC., pg. 1909, pg. 1077
FLORIDA EAST COAST INDUSTRIES, INC., pg. 1909, pg. 433
FLUOR CORPORATION, pg. 82, pg. 1719
FOREST CITY ENTERPRISES, INC., pg. 1092, pg. 1430
GIBRALTAR INDUSTRIES, INC., pg. 1340, pg. 1148
GILBANE BUILDING COMPANY, pg. 84, pg. 1606
GRAYCOR INC., pg. 84, pg. 619
HERITAGE HOMES INC., pg. 87, pg. 857
HIBBETT SPORTS, INC., pg. 1836, pg. 3
HOVNANIAN ENTERPRISES, INC., pg. 1096, pg. 1114
HUNT BUILDING COMPANY LIMITED, pg. 87, pg. 1692
HUNT CONSTRUCTION GROUP, INC., pg. 87, pg. 686
THE HUNT CORPORATION, pg. 88, pg. 22
JACOBS ENGINEERING GROUP, INC., pg. 88, pg. 180
J.E. DUNN CONSTRUCTION GROUP, INC., pg. 89, pg. 984
JERSEY MIKE'S SUBS, pg. 1733, pg. 1083
JOHN CANNON HOMES INC., pg. 89, pg. 466
KB HOME, pg. 90, pg. 134
KITCHELL CORPORATION, pg. 1099, pg. 17
LAMPERT YARDS, INC., pg. 1053, pg. 962
LARKEN ASSOCIATES, pg. 93, pg. 1073
LENNAR CORPORATION, pg. 1100, pg. 443
LENNAR HOMES, INC., pg. 1101, pg. 443
LENNAR HOMES, INC., pg. 93, pg. 1710
LESTER BUILDING SYSTEMS, LLC, pg. 93, pg. 927
LIBERTY GROUP OF COMPANIES, pg. 1101, pg. 416

First page reference indicates Business Class Edition
Second page reference indicates Geographic Edition

M/I HOMES, INC., pg. 95, pg. 1441
MARNELL COMPANIES, pg. 95, pg. 1028
MCCARTHY BUILDING COMPANIES, INC., pg. 96, pg. 999
M.D.C. HOLDINGS, INC., pg. 1104, pg. 321
MERITAGE HOMES CORPORATION, pg. 97, pg. 23
MET-CON CONSTRUCTION INC., pg. 97, pg. 925
MILLER AND SMITH HOMES, INC., pg. 97, pg. 1794
MINAEAN INTERNATIONAL CORPORATION, pg. 97, pg. 1911
NATIONWIDE HOMES, INC., pg. 99, pg. 1788
NEWGROUND RESOURCES, pg. 99, pg. 975
OMEGA FLEX, INC., pg. 982, pg. 1532
OPUS CORPORATION, pg. 101, pg. 949
OVERTON MOORE PROPERTIES, pg. 1107, pg. 94
PACIFIC NATIONAL GROUP INC., pg. 103, pg. 119
PHILLIPS DEVELOPMENT & REALTY, LLC, pg. 1108, pg. 475
P.J. DICK-TRUMBULL-LINDY, pg. 104, pg. 1579
PULTEGROUP, INC., pg. 1109, pg. 873
PURCELL CO., INC., pg. 1109, pg. 968
RAMPART CAPITAL CORPORATION, pg. 798, pg. 1672
ROUGH BROTHERS, INC., pg. 108, pg. 1425
SAMUELS GROUP, INC., pg. 109, pg. 1898
SCHUMACHER HOMES, INC., pg. 109, pg. 1408
SCOTTSDALE COMPANY, pg. 1111, pg. 451
SOUTH FLORIDA DESIGN, pg. 112, pg. 413
STILES CORPORATION, pg. 1115, pg. 427
TOLL BROTHERS, INC., pg. 115, pg. 1541
UNITED STATES AWNING COMPANY, pg. 117, pg. 467
U.S. PHYSICAL THERAPY, INC., pg. 1604, pg. 1716
WALTER ENERGY, INC., pg. 120, pg. 4
WAUSAU HOMES, INC., pg. 120, pg. 1890
WCI COMMUNITIES, INC., pg. 1118, pg. 414
WILLIAM LYON HOMES, pg. 122, pg. 166
W.M. JORDAN COMPANY INC., pg. 122, pg. 1796
WYNN RESORTS LIMITED, pg. 1119, pg. 1030

1541 - General Contractors-Industrial Buildings & Warehouses

AG-MEIER INDUSTRIES LLC, pg. 700, pg. 1668
THE AUSTIN COMPANY, pg. 69, pg. 1428
AV HOMES INC., pg. 1080, pg. 20
THE BECK GROUP, pg. 70, pg. 1676
BOSTON MEDICAL CENTER, pg. 1508, pg. 791
BRASFIELD & GORRIE, LLC, pg. 71, pg. 2
CALATLANTIC GROUP, INC., pg. 1084, pg. 108
CAMBRIDGE BRASS, pg. 73, pg. 1919
CDM SMITH, pg. 74, pg. 807
DOMINION HOMES, INC., pg. 79, pg. 1449
D.R. HORTON, INC., pg. 1090, pg. 1694
DUGAN & MEYERS CONSTRUCTION CO., INC., pg. 79, pg. 1412
EXTERRAN HOLDINGS, INC., pg. 977, pg. 1705
THE FLATLEY COMPANY, pg. 1092, pg. 802
FOREST CITY ENTERPRISES, INC., pg. 1092, pg. 1430
GRANITE CONSTRUCTION INCORPORATED, pg. 84, pg. 305
GRAYCOR INC., pg. 84, pg. 619
GREAT LAKES DREDGE & DOCK CORPORATION, pg. 84, pg. 645
H&E EQUIPMENT SERVICES, INC., pg. 85, pg. 742
HALLIBURTON COMPANY, pg. 978, pg. 1707
HARROP INDUSTRIES, INC., pg. 86, pg. 1440
HOVNANIAN ENTERPRISES, INC., pg. 1096, pg. 1114
HUNT CONSTRUCTION GROUP, INC., pg. 87, pg. 686
INSITUFORM TECHNOLOGIES INC, pg. 88, pg. 974
JACOBS ENGINEERING GROUP, INC., pg. 88, pg. 180
KB HOME, pg. 90, pg. 134
KBR, INC., pg. 90, pg. 1709
KITCHELL CORPORATION, pg. 1099, pg. 17
LENNAR CORPORATION, pg. 1100, pg. 443
LENNAR HOMES, INC., pg. 1101, pg. 443
MASTEC, INC., pg. 430, pg. 418
MCCARTHY BUILDING COMPANIES, INC., pg. 96, pg. 999
MCCAULEY PROPELLER SYSTEMS, pg. 231, pg. 724
M.D.C. HOLDINGS, INC., pg. 1104, pg. 321
MDU RESOURCES GROUP, INC., pg. 981, pg. 1397
MERITAGE HOMES CORPORATION, pg. 97, pg. 23
MINAEAN INTERNATIONAL CORPORATION, pg. 97, pg. 1911
MWH GLOBAL, INC., pg. 98, pg. 312
MYR GROUP INC., pg. 98, pg. 656
OPUS CORPORATION, pg. 101, pg. 949
OVERTON MOORE PROPERTIES, pg. 1107, pg. 94
PARSONS CORPORATION, pg. 103, pg. 180
PULTEGROUP, INC., pg. 1109, pg. 873
RAMPART CAPITAL CORPORATION, pg. 798, pg. 1672
THE REINFORCED EARTH COMPANY, pg. 106, pg. 1799
RITCHIE BROS. AUCTIONEERS INCORPORATED, pg. 1372, pg. 1907
SCHUMACHER HOMES, INC., pg. 109, pg. 1408
SCS ENGINEERS, pg. 109, pg. 124
STILES CORPORATION, pg. 1115, pg. 427
TOLL BROTHERS, INC., pg. 115, pg. 1541
WCI COMMUNITIES, INC., pg. 1118, pg. 414
THE WEITZ COMPANY, pg. 121, pg. 707
WILLIAM LYON HOMES, pg. 122, pg. 166

1622 - Bridge, Tunnel & Elevated Highway Construction

ACE ASPHALT OF ARIZONA, INC., pg. 64, pg. 13
BAKER CONCRETE CONSTRUCTION, INC., pg. 69, pg. 1465
THE BLOOMFIELD MANUFACTURING CO., INC., pg. 70, pg. 674
CENTURY FENCE COMPANY, pg. 74, pg. 1886
DCK WORLDWIDE, LLC, pg. 78, pg. 1574
E.V. WILLIAMS, INC., pg. 81, pg. 1810
FOX CONTRACTORS CORP., pg. 1337, pg. 680
GRANITE CONSTRUCTION INCORPORATED, pg. 84, pg. 305
MCCARTHY BUILDING COMPANIES, INC., pg. 96, pg. 999
MDU RESOURCES GROUP, INC., pg. 981, pg. 1397
PARSONS CORPORATION, pg. 103, pg. 180
THE SHERWIN-WILLIAMS COMPANY, pg. 1447, pg. 1435
WINDOWS AND WALLS UNLIMITED, INC., pg. 946, pg. 1343

1623 - Water, Sewer, Pipeline, Communications & Power Line Construction

ARIZONA PUBLIC SERVICE COMPANY, pg. 1935, pg. 14
BATAVIA DOWNS GAMING, pg. 533, pg. 1140
CAMBRIDGE BRASS, pg. 73, pg. 1919
CDM SMITH, pg. 74, pg. 807
GE WATER & PROCESS TECHNOLOGIES, pg. 1339, pg. 1588
THE GOLDFIELD CORPORATION, pg. 84, pg. 439
GRANITE CONSTRUCTION INCORPORATED, pg. 84, pg. 305
GREAT LAKES DREDGE & DOCK CORPORATION, pg. 84, pg. 645
HALLIBURTON COMPANY, pg. 978, pg. 1707
HARROP INDUSTRIES, INC., pg. 86, pg. 1440
HENKELS & MCCOY, INC., pg. 86, pg. 1517
INSITUFORM TECHNOLOGIES INC, pg. 88, pg. 974
JACOBS ENGINEERING GROUP, INC., pg. 88, pg. 180
KBR, INC., pg. 90, pg. 1709
MASTEC, INC., pg. 430, pg. 418
MCCARTHY BUILDING COMPANIES, INC., pg. 96, pg. 999
MCCAULEY PROPELLER SYSTEMS, pg. 231, pg. 724
MDU RESOURCES GROUP, INC., pg. 981, pg. 1397
MICHELS CORPORATION, pg. 97, pg. 1855
MINAEAN INTERNATIONAL CORPORATION, pg. 97, pg. 1911
MWH GLOBAL, INC., pg. 98, pg. 312
MYR GROUP INC., pg. 98, pg. 656
NEWPARK RESOURCES, INC., pg. 982, pg. 1747
PARSONS CORPORATION, pg. 103, pg. 180
PIKE ELECTRIC CORPORATION, pg. 104, pg. 1385
PLAINS ALL AMERICAN PIPELINE, L.P., pg. 983, pg. 1712
PREFORMED LINE PRODUCTS COMPANY, pg. 1370, pg. 1434
THE REINFORCED EARTH COMPANY, pg. 106, pg. 1799
SABRE INDUSTRIES, INC., pg. 669, pg. 1658
SBA COMMUNICATIONS CORPORATION, pg. 671, pg. 413
SCHLUMBERGER LIMITED, pg. 801, pg. 1714
THE SERVICEMASTER COMPANY, LLC, pg. 335, pg. 1646
TETRA TECHNOLOGIES, INC., pg. 986, pg. 1747
TRANSMONTAIGNE, INC., pg. 986, pg. 323
WESTINGHOUSE SOLAR, pg. 688, pg. 58

1629 - Heavy Construction, NEC

ACE ASPHALT OF ARIZONA, INC., pg. 64, pg. 13
BAKER CONCRETE CONSTRUCTION, INC., pg. 69, pg. 1465
CAMBRIDGE BRASS, pg. 73, pg. 1919
CDM SMITH, pg. 74, pg. 807
DCK WORLDWIDE, LLC, pg. 78, pg. 1574
E.V. WILLIAMS, INC., pg. 81, pg. 1810
FOX CONTRACTORS CORP., pg. 1337, pg. 680
GRANITE CONSTRUCTION INCORPORATED, pg. 84, pg. 305
GREAT LAKES DREDGE & DOCK CORPORATION, pg. 84, pg. 645
HALLIBURTON COMPANY, pg. 978, pg. 1707
HARROP INDUSTRIES, INC., pg. 86, pg. 1440
INSITUFORM TECHNOLOGIES INC, pg. 88, pg. 974
JACOBS ENGINEERING GROUP, INC., pg. 88, pg. 180
KBR, INC., pg. 90, pg. 1709
MASTEC, INC., pg. 430, pg. 418
MCCARTHY BUILDING COMPANIES, INC., pg. 96, pg. 999
MCCAULEY PROPELLER SYSTEMS, pg. 231, pg. 724
MDU RESOURCES GROUP, INC., pg. 981, pg. 1397
MWH GLOBAL, INC., pg. 98, pg. 312
MYR GROUP INC., pg. 98, pg. 656
PARSONS CORPORATION, pg. 103, pg. 180
THE REINFORCED EARTH COMPANY, pg. 106, pg. 1799

1711 - Plumbing, Heating & Air Conditioning Contractors

AAON, INC., pg. 1068, pg. 1488
ACCO ENGINEERED SYSTEMS, pg. 1068, pg. 95
AMERICAN DG ENERGY INC., pg. 1068, pg. 850
AQUATIC, pg. 68, pg. 42
BRADFORD-WHITE CORPORATION, pg. 1069, pg. 1514
CHEMED CORPORATION, pg. 327, pg. 1410
CIRCOR INTERNATIONAL, INC., pg. 76, pg. 805
COGENIC MECHANICAL, pg. 76, pg. 1333
EDD HELMS GROUP, INC., pg. 1071, pg. 442
EMBASSY INDUSTRIES, INC., pg. 1071, pg. 1164
EMCOR SERVICES NORTHEAST COMMAIR/BALCO, pg. 1071, pg. 847
FRIEDRICH AIR CONDITIONING CO., pg. 1072, pg. 1740
HUDSON TECHNOLOGIES, INC., pg. 1073, pg. 1320
INTERLINE BRANDS, INC., pg. 1051, pg. 433
JUSTRITE MANUFACTURING COMPANY, LLC, pg. 1394, pg. 606
MARLEY ENGINEERED PRODUCTS, pg. 1074, pg. 1612
MINAEAN INTERNATIONAL CORPORATION, pg. 97, pg. 1911
MR. ROOTER CORPORATION, pg. 1057, pg. 1749
N&M COOL TODAY, INC., pg. 1074, pg. 466
NIXCO PLUMBING INC., pg. 99, pg. 1461
PLIBRICO CO. LLC, pg. 104, pg. 587
ROBERTS-GORDON INC., pg. 1076, pg. 1151
ROTO-ROOTER, INC., pg. 108, pg. 1425
SANDEN INTERNATIONAL (USA), INC., pg. 217, pg. 1750
S.T. JOHNSON CO., pg. 1077, pg. 173
STANLEY BLACK & DECKER, INC., pg. 1063, pg. 358
TD INDUSTRIES, INC., pg. 1077, pg. 1688
TRI COUNTY AIR CONDITIONING-HEATING, INC., pg. 116, pg. 451
YOUNG REGULATOR COMPANY, pg. 1078, pg. 1478

1721 - Painting & Paper Hanging Contractors

THE BLOOMFIELD MANUFACTURING CO., INC., pg. 70, pg. 674
CENTURY FENCE COMPANY, pg. 74, pg. 1886
THE SHERWIN-WILLIAMS COMPANY, pg. 1447, pg. 1435
WINDOWS AND WALLS UNLIMITED, INC., pg. 946, pg. 1343

1731 - Electrical Work Contractors

AAON, INC., pg. 1068, pg. 1488
ACCO ENGINEERED SYSTEMS, pg. 1068, pg. 95
ALCATEL-LUCENT USA, INC., pg. 615, pg. 1728
AMERICAN DG ENERGY INC., pg. 1068, pg. 850
AQUATIC, pg. 68, pg. 42
AUDIO COMMAND SYSTEMS, INC., pg. 621, pg. 1350
BRADFORD-WHITE CORPORATION, pg. 1069, pg. 1514
CENTRAL HUDSON GAS & ELECTRIC CORPORATION, pg.

1937, *pg.* 1324
CHEMED CORPORATION, *pg.* 327, *pg.* 1410
CIRCOR INTERNATIONAL, INC., *pg.* 76, *pg.* 805
COGENIC MECHANICAL, *pg.* 76, *pg.* 1333
DON BELL SIGNS LLC, *pg.* 388, *pg.* 460
ECHELON CORPORATION, *pg.* 389, *pg.* 245
EDD HELMS GROUP, INC., *pg.* 1071, *pg.* 442
EMBASSY INDUSTRIES, INC., *pg.* 1071, *pg.* 1164
EMCOR GROUP, INC., *pg.* 80, *pg.* 361
EMCOR SERVICES NORTHEAST COMMAIR/BALCO, *pg.* 1071, *pg.* 847
EVERGREEN ELECTRIC, INC., *pg.* 1071, *pg.* 1048
FRIEDRICH AIR CONDITIONING CO., *pg.* 1072, *pg.* 1740
HUDSON TECHNOLOGIES, INC., *pg.* 1073, *pg.* 1320
INTEGRATED ELECTRICAL SERVICES, INC., *pg.* 88, *pg.* 1708
INTEGRATED SYSTEMS ANALYSTS, INC., *pg.* 416, *pg.* 1771
INTERLINE BRANDS, INC., *pg.* 1051, *pg.* 433
MARLEY ENGINEERED PRODUCTS, *pg.* 1074, *pg.* 1612
MR. ROOTER CORPORATION, *pg.* 1057, *pg.* 1749
MYR GROUP INC., *pg.* 98, *pg.* 656
N&M COOL TODAY, INC., *pg.* 1074, *pg.* 466
NIXCO PLUMBING INC., *pg.* 99, *pg.* 1461
PHILIPS SOLID-STATE LIGHTING SOLUTIONS, *pg.* 1303, *pg.* 806
PIKE ELECTRIC CORPORATION, *pg.* 104, *pg.* 1385
PLIBRICO CO. LLC, *pg.* 104, *pg.* 587
PROTECTION ONE, INC., *pg.* 665, *pg.* 715
ROBERTS-GORDON INC., *pg.* 1076, *pg.* 1151
ROTO-ROOTER, INC., *pg.* 108, *pg.* 1425
SANDEN INTERNATIONAL (USA), INC., *pg.* 217, *pg.* 1750
SL INDUSTRIES, INC., *pg.* 674, *pg.* 1090
S.T. JOHNSON CO., *pg.* 1077, *pg.* 173
TD INDUSTRIES, INC., *pg.* 1077, *pg.* 1688
TRI-CITY ELECTRICAL CONTRACTORS, INC., *pg.* 116, *pg.* 409
TRI COUNTY AIR CONDITIONING-HEATING, INC., *pg.* 116, *pg.* 451
UIL HOLDINGS CORPORATION, *pg.* 1953, *pg.* 359
WESTINGHOUSE SOLAR, *pg.* 688, *pg.* 58
WHITE ELECTRICAL CONSTRUCTION CO., *pg.* 688, *pg.* 524
YOUNG REGULATOR COMPANY, *pg.* 1078, *pg.* 1478

1741 - Masonry, Stone Setting & other Stone Work Contractors

BAKER CONCRETE CONSTRUCTION, INC., *pg.* 69, *pg.* 1465
BRAND ENERGY, INC., *pg.* 71, *pg.* 533
USG CORPORATION, *pg.* 118, *pg.* 594

1742 - Plastering, Drywall, Acoustical & Insulation Work Contractors

ARTISTIC TILE INC., *pg.* 914, *pg.* 1119
TOPBUILD CORPORATION, *pg.* 116, *pg.* 421

1743 - Terrazzo, Tile, Marble & Mosaic Work Contractors

ARTISTIC TILE INC., *pg.* 914, *pg.* 1119

1751 - Carpentry Work

APOGEE ENTERPRISES, INC., *pg.* 67, *pg.* 930
FRANK B. RHODES FURNITURE MAKER, *pg.* 925, *pg.* 766
STANLEY ACCESS TECHNOLOGIES, LLC, *pg.* 112, *pg.* 349

1752 - Floor Laying & other Floor Work, NEC

CARLISLE WIDE PLANK FLOORS, INC., *pg.* 919, *pg.* 1039
FLOOR CONCEPTS INC., *pg.* 925, *pg.* 391

1761 - Roofing, Siding & Sheet Metal Work

CENTRIA ARCHITECTURAL SYSTEMS, *pg.* 74, *pg.* 1554
CENTRIA, INC., *pg.* 74, *pg.* 1554
ROOFING BY CURRY, *pg.* 108, *pg.* 467

1771 - Concrete Work

BAKER CONCRETE CONSTRUCTION, INC., *pg.* 69, *pg.* 1465
BRAND ENERGY, INC., *pg.* 71, *pg.* 533
USG CORPORATION, *pg.* 118, *pg.* 594

1791 - Structural Steel Erection

JUSTRITE MANUFACTURING COMPANY, LLC, *pg.* 1394, *pg.* 606
MINAEAN INTERNATIONAL CORPORATION, *pg.* 97, *pg.* 1911
STANLEY BLACK & DECKER, INC., *pg.* 1063, *pg.* 358

1796 - Installation or Erection of Building Equipment, NEC

COGENIC MECHANICAL, *pg.* 76, *pg.* 1333
HUDSON TECHNOLOGIES, INC., *pg.* 1073, *pg.* 1320
INDUSTRIAL DISTRIBUTION GROUP, INC., *pg.* 413, *pg.* 1358
KAMAN CORPORATION, *pg.* 229, *pg.* 338
LAWSON PRODUCTS, INC., *pg.* 1355, *pg.* 580
MCCORMICK & COMPANY, INCORPORATED, *pg.* 1027, *pg.* 779
OTIS ELEVATOR COMPANY, *pg.* 102, *pg.* 349
PARAGON TECHNOLOGIES, INC., *pg.* 1367, *pg.* 1528
TWIN DISC, INCORPORATED, *pg.* 220, *pg.* 1889

1799 - Special Trade Contractors, NEC

AAON, INC., *pg.* 1068, *pg.* 1488
ACCO ENGINEERED SYSTEMS, *pg.* 1068, *pg.* 95
AMERICAN DG ENERGY INC., *pg.* 1068, *pg.* 850
AQUATIC, *pg.* 68, *pg.* 42
ARCH COAL, INC., *pg.* 68, *pg.* 992
BAKER CONCRETE CONSTRUCTION, INC., *pg.* 69, *pg.* 1465
BRADFORD-WHITE CORPORATION, *pg.* 1069, *pg.* 1514
BRAND ENERGY, INC., *pg.* 71, *pg.* 533
CENTRIA ARCHITECTURAL SYSTEMS, *pg.* 74, *pg.* 1554
CENTRIA, INC., *pg.* 74, *pg.* 1554
CHEMED CORPORATION, *pg.* 327, *pg.* 1410
CIRCOR INTERNATIONAL, INC., *pg.* 76, *pg.* 805
COGENIC MECHANICAL, *pg.* 76, *pg.* 1333
EDD HELMS GROUP, INC., *pg.* 1071, *pg.* 442
EMBASSY INDUSTRIES, INC., *pg.* 1071, *pg.* 1164
EMCOR SERVICES NORTHEAST COMMAIR/BALCO, *pg.* 1071, *pg.* 847
FRIEDRICH AIR CONDITIONING CO., *pg.* 1072, *pg.* 1740
HUDSON TECHNOLOGIES, INC., *pg.* 1073, *pg.* 1320
INTERLINE BRANDS, INC., *pg.* 1051, *pg.* 433
JUSTRITE MANUFACTURING COMPANY, LLC, *pg.* 1394, *pg.* 606
MARLEY ENGINEERED PRODUCTS, *pg.* 1074, *pg.* 1612
MINAEAN INTERNATIONAL CORPORATION, *pg.* 97, *pg.* 1911
MR. ROOTER CORPORATION, *pg.* 1057, *pg.* 1749
N&M COOL TODAY, INC., *pg.* 1074, *pg.* 466
NIXCO PLUMBING INC., *pg.* 99, *pg.* 1461
PLIBRICO CO. LLC, *pg.* 104, *pg.* 587
ROBERTS-GORDON INC., *pg.* 1076, *pg.* 1151
ROOFING BY CURRY, *pg.* 108, *pg.* 467
ROTO-ROOTER, INC., *pg.* 108, *pg.* 1425
SANDEN INTERNATIONAL (USA), INC., *pg.* 217, *pg.* 1750
S.T. JOHNSON CO., *pg.* 1077, *pg.* 173
STANLEY BLACK & DECKER, INC., *pg.* 1063, *pg.* 358
TD INDUSTRIES, INC., *pg.* 1077, *pg.* 1688
TECK RESOURCES LIMITED, *pg.* 1183, *pg.* 1912
TRI COUNTY AIR CONDITIONING-HEATING, INC., *pg.* 116, *pg.* 451
USG CORPORATION, *pg.* 118, *pg.* 594
YOUNG REGULATOR COMPANY, *pg.* 1078, *pg.* 1478

2013 - Sausages & other Prepared Meat Products

AMERICAN FOODS GROUP, LLC, *pg.* 837, *pg.* 1859
BAKER COMMODITIES, INC., *pg.* 839, *pg.* 301
DARLING INGREDIENTS, INC., *pg.* 852, *pg.* 1718
HORMEL FOODS CORPORATION, *pg.* 863, *pg.* 915
JBS USA HOLDING, INC., *pg.* 865, *pg.* 330
MAPLE LODGE FARMS LTD., *pg.* 876, *pg.* 1918
SMITHFIELD FOODS, INC., *pg.* 896, *pg.* 1806
SPECIALTY FOODS GROUP-FIELD PACKING DIV., *pg.* 897, *pg.* 739
TYSON FOODS, INC., *pg.* 902, *pg.* 35

2015 - Poultry Slaughtering & Processing

ADVANCEPIERRE FOODS, INC., *pg.* 1714, *pg.* 1409
BARBER FOODS, INC., *pg.* 839, *pg.* 751
BUTTERBALL, LLC, *pg.* 843, *pg.* 1385
CONAGRA FOODS, INC., *pg.* 826, *pg.* 1014
CONTINENTAL GRAIN COMPANY, *pg.* 1475, *pg.* 1218
EMPIRE KOSHER POULTRY, INC., *pg.* 854, *pg.* 1553
FARMERS PRIDE, INC., *pg.* 855, *pg.* 1534
FOSTER FARMS, *pg.* 856, *pg.* 122
GOLD'N PLUMP POULTRY, INC., *pg.* 858, *pg.* 956
HORMEL FOODS CORPORATION, *pg.* 863, *pg.* 915
HOUSE OF RAEFORD FARMS, INC., *pg.* 864, *pg.* 1386
JENNIE-O TURKEY STORE, LLC, *pg.* 865, *pg.* 966
MAPLE LODGE FARMS LTD., *pg.* 876, *pg.* 1918
OREGON FREEZE DRY, INC., *pg.* 888, *pg.* 1492
PERDUE FARMS INCORPORATED, *pg.* 889, *pg.* 777
PILGRIM'S PRIDE CORPORATION, *pg.* 889, *pg.* 330
SANDERSON FARMS, INC., *pg.* 893, *pg.* 970
SIMMONS FOODS INC., *pg.* 895, *pg.* 35
SMITHFIELD FOODS, INC., *pg.* 896, *pg.* 1806
TYSON FOODS, INC., *pg.* 902, *pg.* 35

2021 - Creamery Butter

ASSOCIATED MILK PRODUCERS INC., *pg.* 838, *pg.* 951
CLOVER STORNETTA FARMS INC., *pg.* 848, *pg.* 182
CRYSTAL CREAM & BUTTER COMPANY, *pg.* 850, *pg.* 149
LAND O'LAKES, INC., *pg.* 873, *pg.* 915

2022 - Natural, Processed & Imitation Cheese

ADVANCED FOOD PRODUCTS LLC, *pg.* 835, *pg.* 1555
AGRI-MARK, INC., *pg.* 1012, *pg.* 833
AGROPUR COOPERATIVE, *pg.* 836, *pg.* 1950
ASSOCIATED MILK PRODUCERS INC., *pg.* 838, *pg.* 951
BAR-S FOODS CO., *pg.* 839, *pg.* 15
BEL BRANDS USA, *pg.* 839, *pg.* 566
BONGRAIN NORTH AMERICA, *pg.* 841, *pg.* 1556
CALIFORNIA MILK ADVISORY BOARD, *pg.* 843, *pg.* 149
CARL BUDDIG & COMPANY, *pg.* 846, *pg.* 619
COLONNA BROS., INC., *pg.* 849, *pg.* 1098
GALAXY NUTRITIONAL FOODS, INC., *pg.* 857, *pg.* 1603
THE GREAT LAKES CHEESE CO., INC., *pg.* 859, *pg.* 1455
KEMPS LLC, *pg.* 867, *pg.* 961
LACTALIS AMERICAN GROUP, *pg.* 873, *pg.* 1149
LAND O'LAKES, INC., *pg.* 873, *pg.* 915
LEPRINO FOODS COMPANY, *pg.* 874, *pg.* 320
LIFEWAY FOODS, INC., *pg.* 874, *pg.* 634
MONDELEZ INTERNATIONAL, INC., *pg.* 878, *pg.* 601
SAPUTO CHEESE USA INC., *pg.* 893, *pg.* 627
SARGENTO FOODS INC., *pg.* 894, *pg.* 1886
SCHREIBER FOODS, INC., *pg.* 894, *pg.* 1859
TILLAMOOK COUNTY CREAMERY ASSOCIATION, *pg.* 901, *pg.* 1509
V&V SUPREMO FOODS, INC., *pg.* 907, *pg.* 595
WIN SCHULER FOODS, *pg.* 910, *pg.* 908

2023 - Dry, Condensed & Evaporated Dairy Products

AGRI-MARK, INC., *pg.* 1012, *pg.* 833
AGROPUR COOPERATIVE, *pg.* 836, *pg.* 1950
ANDERSON ERICKSON DAIRY COMPANY, *pg.* 837, *pg.* 704
ASSOCIATED MILK PRODUCERS INC., *pg.* 838, *pg.* 951
BRISTOL-MYERS SQUIBB COMPANY, *pg.* 1509, *pg.* 1206
BROUGHTON FOODS COMPANY, *pg.* 842, *pg.* 1458

CCA INDUSTRIES, INC., *pg.* 503, *pg.* 1114
CLOVER STORNETTA FARMS INC., *pg.* 848, *pg.* 182
CRYSTAL CREAM & BUTTER COMPANY, *pg.* 850, *pg.* 149
DAIRY FARMERS OF AMERICA, INC., *pg.* 851, *pg.* 982
THE DANNON COMPANY, INC., *pg.* 851, *pg.* 1351
DARIGOLD, INC., *pg.* 852, *pg.* 1835
DEAN FOODS COMPANY, *pg.* 852, *pg.* 1679
FOREMOST FARMS USA COOPERATIVE, *pg.* 856, *pg.* 1854
FRIENDSHIP DAIRIES, INC., *pg.* 857, *pg.* 1171
GARELICK FARMS, LLC, *pg.* 858, *pg.* 823
GAY LEA FOODS CO-OPERATIVE LIMITED, *pg.* 858, *pg.* 1926
HILAND DAIRY FOODS COMPANY, *pg.* 862, *pg.* 1006
HP HOOD LLC, *pg.* 864, *pg.* 829
JOHANNA FOODS INC., *pg.* 866, *pg.* 1066
LIFEWAY FOODS, INC., *pg.* 874, *pg.* 634
MICHIGAN MILK PRODUCERS ASSOCIATION, *pg.* 147, *pg.* 903
NESTLE USA, INC., *pg.* 883, *pg.* 96
NOW HEALTH GROUP, INC., *pg.* 1576, *pg.* 557
OAK FARMS DAIRY, *pg.* 887, *pg.* 1685
OAKHURST DAIRY, *pg.* 887, *pg.* 752
OBERWEIS DAIRY, INC., *pg.* 887, *pg.* 638
PARMALAT CANADA INC., *pg.* 888, *pg.* 1941
PRAIRIE FARMS DAIRY, INC., *pg.* 890, *pg.* 561
PURITY DAIRIES, LLC, *pg.* 891, *pg.* 1653
SAPUTO, INC., *pg.* 893, *pg.* 1956
SCHREIBER FOODS, INC., *pg.* 894, *pg.* 1859
STONYFIELD FARM, INC., *pg.* 899, *pg.* 1035
SUBCO FOODS OF WISCONSIN, *pg.* 899, *pg.* 1894
SYNUTRA INTERNATIONAL, INC., *pg.* 1600, *pg.* 776
TURKEY HILL DAIRY, INC., *pg.* 902, *pg.* 1522
UPSTATE NIAGARA COOPERATIVE, INC., *pg.* 907, *pg.* 1151
WELLS ENTERPRISES, INC., *pg.* 909, *pg.* 709

2024 - Ice Cream & Frozen Desserts

AMERICAN DAIRY QUEEN CORPORATION, *pg.* 1714, *pg.* 930
BALDWIN RICHARDSON FOODS COMPANY, *pg.* 1850, *pg.* 612
BEN & JERRY'S HOMEMADE, INC., *pg.* 1850, *pg.* 1767
BLUE BELL CREAMERIES, L.P., *pg.* 1851, *pg.* 1668
CARVEL CORPORATION, *pg.* 846, *pg.* 492
DEAN FOODS COMPANY, *pg.* 852, *pg.* 1679
DIPPIN' DOTS LLC, *pg.* 853, *pg.* 739
DREYER'S GRAND ICE CREAM HOLDINGS, INC., *pg.* 1852, *pg.* 171
FIELDBROOK FOODS INC., *pg.* 1852, *pg.* 1156
FRIENDLY ICE CREAM, LLC, *pg.* 1853, *pg.* 859
GENERAL MILLS, INC., *pg.* 828, *pg.* 933
GRAETER'S, INC., *pg.* 1854, *pg.* 1414
HILAND DAIRY FOODS COMPANY, *pg.* 862, *pg.* 1006
HP HOOD LLC, *pg.* 864, *pg.* 829
J&J SNACK FOODS CORPORATION, *pg.* 865, *pg.* 1107
THE JEL SERT COMPANY, *pg.* 865, *pg.* 668
PERRY'S ICE CREAM CO., INC., *pg.* 1861, *pg.* 1137
PURITY DAIRIES, LLC, *pg.* 891, *pg.* 1653
REDCO FOODS, INC., *pg.* 891, *pg.* 1174
REED'S, INC., *pg.* 264, *pg.* 139
THE SCHWAN FOOD COMPANY, *pg.* 894, *pg.* 928
STONYFIELD FARM, INC., *pg.* 899, *pg.* 1035
TURKEY HILL DAIRY, INC., *pg.* 902, *pg.* 1522
WELLS ENTERPRISES, INC., *pg.* 909, *pg.* 709
YOCREAM INTERNATIONAL INC., *pg.* 1039, *pg.* 1508

2026 - Fluid Milk

AGRI-MARK, INC., *pg.* 1012, *pg.* 833
AGROPUR COOPERATIVE, *pg.* 836, *pg.* 1950
ANDERSON ERICKSON DAIRY COMPANY, *pg.* 837, *pg.* 704
ASSOCIATED MILK PRODUCERS INC., *pg.* 838, *pg.* 951
BRISTOL-MYERS SQUIBB COMPANY, *pg.* 1509, *pg.* 1206
BROUGHTON FOODS COMPANY, *pg.* 842, *pg.* 1458
CCA INDUSTRIES, INC., *pg.* 503, *pg.* 1114
CLOVER STORNETTA FARMS INC., *pg.* 848, *pg.* 182
CRYSTAL CREAM & BUTTER COMPANY, *pg.* 850, *pg.* 149
DAIRY FARMERS OF AMERICA, INC., *pg.* 851, *pg.* 982
THE DANNON COMPANY, INC., *pg.* 851, *pg.* 1351
DARIGOLD, INC., *pg.* 852, *pg.* 1835
DEAN FOODS COMPANY, *pg.* 852, *pg.* 1679
FOREMOST FARMS USA COOPERATIVE, *pg.* 856, *pg.* 1854
FRIENDSHIP DAIRIES, INC., *pg.* 857, *pg.* 1171
GARELICK FARMS, LLC, *pg.* 858, *pg.* 823
GAY LEA FOODS CO-OPERATIVE LIMITED, *pg.* 858, *pg.* 1926
HILAND DAIRY FOODS COMPANY, *pg.* 862, *pg.* 1006
HP HOOD LLC, *pg.* 864, *pg.* 829
JOHANNA FOODS INC., *pg.* 866, *pg.* 1066
LIFEWAY FOODS, INC., *pg.* 874, *pg.* 634
MICHIGAN MILK PRODUCERS ASSOCIATION, *pg.* 147, *pg.* 903
NESTLE USA, INC., *pg.* 883, *pg.* 96
NOW HEALTH GROUP, INC., *pg.* 1576, *pg.* 557
OAK FARMS DAIRY, *pg.* 887, *pg.* 1685
OAKHURST DAIRY, *pg.* 887, *pg.* 752
OBERWEIS DAIRY, INC., *pg.* 887, *pg.* 638
PARMALAT CANADA INC., *pg.* 888, *pg.* 1941
PRAIRIE FARMS DAIRY, INC., *pg.* 890, *pg.* 561
PURITY DAIRIES, LLC, *pg.* 891, *pg.* 1653
SAPUTO, INC., *pg.* 893, *pg.* 1956
SCHREIBER FOODS, INC., *pg.* 894, *pg.* 1859
STONYFIELD FARM, INC., *pg.* 899, *pg.* 1035
SUBCO FOODS OF WISCONSIN, *pg.* 899, *pg.* 1894
SYNUTRA INTERNATIONAL, INC., *pg.* 1600, *pg.* 776
TURKEY HILL DAIRY, INC., *pg.* 902, *pg.* 1522
UPSTATE NIAGARA COOPERATIVE, INC., *pg.* 907, *pg.* 1151
WELLS ENTERPRISES, INC., *pg.* 909, *pg.* 709

2032 - Canned Specialties

BUSH BROTHERS & COMPANY, *pg.* 843, *pg.* 1636
CAMPBELL COMPANY OF CANADA LTD, *pg.* 844, *pg.* 1935
CAMPBELL SOUP COMPANY, *pg.* 844, *pg.* 1048
DIAMOND FOODS, INC., *pg.* 1851, *pg.* 216
EINSTEIN NOAH RESTAURANT GROUP, INC., *pg.* 1019, *pg.* 332
HANOVER FOODS CORPORATION, *pg.* 861, *pg.* 1535
MORGAN FOODS, INC., *pg.* 881, *pg.* 673
NESTLE HEALTHCARE NUTRITION, *pg.* 1572, *pg.* 941

2033 - Canned Fruits, Vegetables, Preserves, Jams & Jellies

ALGOOD FOOD COMPANY, *pg.* 836, *pg.* 731
B&G FOODS, INC., *pg.* 838, *pg.* 1102
BELL-CARTER FOODS, INC., *pg.* 839, *pg.* 120
BOULDER BRANDS, INC., *pg.* 1016, *pg.* 310
BUSH BROTHERS & COMPANY, *pg.* 843, *pg.* 1636
CAINS FOODS, L.P., *pg.* 843, *pg.* 784
CAMPBELL SOUP COMPANY, *pg.* 844, *pg.* 1048
THE C.F. SAUER COMPANY, *pg.* 847, *pg.* 1801
COFFEE HOLDING CO., INC., *pg.* 849, *pg.* 1343
COUNTRY PURE FOODS, INC., *pg.* 247, *pg.* 1400
DEL MONTE FOODS, INC., *pg.* 852, *pg.* 304
DOLE FOOD COMPANY, INC., *pg.* 853, *pg.* 306
FARIBAULT FOODS, INC., *pg.* 855, *pg.* 925
FLORIDA'S NATURAL GROWERS, *pg.* 855, *pg.* 437
THE FREMONT COMPANY, *pg.* 856, *pg.* 1454
FRESH DEL MONTE PRODUCE INC., *pg.* 856, *pg.* 418
FURMANO FOODS, INC., *pg.* 857, *pg.* 1557
GLK FOODS, LLC, *pg.* 858, *pg.* 1852
GOLD PURE FOOD PRODUCTS CO., INC., *pg.* 858, *pg.* 1166
GRAY & COMPANY, *pg.* 859, *pg.* 1503
HANOVER FOODS CORPORATION, *pg.* 861, *pg.* 1535
H.J. HEINZ CO. OF CANADA LTD., *pg.* 863, *pg.* 1929
THE J.M. SMUCKER COMPANY, *pg.* 865, *pg.* 1468
JOHANNA FOODS INC., *pg.* 866, *pg.* 1066
JOHN B. SANFILIPPO & SON, INC., *pg.* 1024, *pg.* 610
KEN'S FOODS, INC., *pg.* 867, *pg.* 832
KIKKOMAN INTERNATIONAL INC., *pg.* 868, *pg.* 220
KNOTT'S BERRY FARM, *pg.* 556, *pg.* 50
KNOUSE FOODS COOPERATIVE INC., *pg.* 869, *pg.* 1558
THE KRAFT HEINZ COMPANY, *pg.* 870, *pg.* 1577
KRIER FOODS, INC., *pg.* 253, *pg.* 1890
LANCASTER COLONY CORPORATION, *pg.* 873, *pg.* 1441
LIDESTRI FOODS, INC., *pg.* 874, *pg.* 1159
LOUIS MAULL COMPANY, *pg.* 875, *pg.* 999
MAUI LAND & PINEAPPLE COMPANY, INC., *pg.* 876, *pg.* 545
MCILHENNY COMPANY, *pg.* 876, *pg.* 741
MEGAMEX FOODS, LLC, *pg.* 833, *pg.* 66
MIZKAN AMERICAS, INC., *pg.* 877, *pg.* 634
MONTEREY GOURMET FOODS, INC., *pg.* 881, *pg.* 94
MOODY DUNBAR INC., *pg.* 1028, *pg.* 1635
MUSCO FAMILY OLIVE COMPANY, *pg.* 882, *pg.* 297
NAKED JUICE COMPANY, INC., *pg.* 882, *pg.* 150
NATIONAL FRUIT PRODUCT COMPANY, INC., *pg.* 882, *pg.* 1811
NESTLE USA, INC., *pg.* 883, *pg.* 96
NEWMAN'S OWN, INC., *pg.* 886, *pg.* 384
OCEAN SPRAY CRANBERRIES, INC., *pg.* 887, *pg.* 827
OREGON CHERRY GROWERS, INC., *pg.* 1028, *pg.* 1508
PLOCHMAN, INC., *pg.* 890, *pg.* 631
Q&B FOODS, INC., *pg.* 891, *pg.* 119
RECKITT BENCKISER INC., *pg.* 1136, *pg.* 1105
RED GOLD, INC., *pg.* 891, *pg.* 677
REILY FOODS COMPANY, *pg.* 891, *pg.* 747
SAN-J INTERNATIONAL, INC., *pg.* 893, *pg.* 1803
SENECA FOODS CORPORATION, *pg.* 895, *pg.* 1177
SOKOL & COMPANY, *pg.* 1862, *pg.* 598
T. MARZETTI COMPANY, *pg.* 900, *pg.* 1444
TRADER VIC'S GOURMET PRODUCTS, INC., *pg.* 901, *pg.* 69
TREEHOUSE FOODS, INC., *pg.* 901, *pg.* 649
TROPICANA PRODUCTS, INC., *pg.* 902, *pg.* 592
UNILEVER UNITED STATES, INC., *pg.* 904, *pg.* 1061
UPSTATE NIAGARA COOPERATIVE, INC., *pg.* 907, *pg.* 1151
VALLEY FIG GROWERS, INC., *pg.* 908, *pg.* 93
WELCH FOODS INC., *pg.* 909, *pg.* 815
WELCH'S INTERNATIONAL, *pg.* 909, *pg.* 816
WESTIN FOODS, INC., *pg.* 909, *pg.* 1019
ZATARAIN'S BRANDS, INC., *pg.* 911, *pg.* 744

2034 - Dried & Dehydrated Fruits & Vegetables & Soup Mixes

4C FOODS CORPORATION, *pg.* 835, *pg.* 1145
ABBOTT NUTRITION, *pg.* 1485, *pg.* 1437
ACH FOOD COMPANIES, INC., *pg.* 835, *pg.* 1631
ADAMS EXTRACT & SPICE LLC, *pg.* 835, *pg.* 1698
ADVANCED FOOD PRODUCTS LLC, *pg.* 835, *pg.* 1555
ADVANCEPIERRE FOODS, INC., *pg.* 1714, *pg.* 1409
ALLIED OLD ENGLISH, INC., *pg.* 836, *pg.* 1110
AMERICAN ITALIAN PASTA COMPANY, *pg.* 837, *pg.* 980
AMERICAN LICORICE CO. INC., *pg.* 1850, *pg.* 692
AMERICAN POP CORN COMPANY, *pg.* 825, *pg.* 712
AMY'S KITCHEN, INC., *pg.* 837, *pg.* 276
ANNIE'S INC., *pg.* 1760, *pg.* 45
ATEECO, INC., *pg.* 838, *pg.* 1586
ATKINS NUTRITIONALS, INC., *pg.* 1498, *pg.* 316
AZTECA FOODS, INCORPORATED, *pg.* 838, *pg.* 566
B&G FOODS, INC., *pg.* 838, *pg.* 1102
BASIC AMERICAN FOODS, INC., *pg.* 839, *pg.* 303
BESTSWEET INC., *pg.* 1851, *pg.* 1383
BIG BOY RESTAURANTS INTERNATIONAL, LLC, *pg.* 1716, *pg.* 912
BKI, *pg.* 52, *pg.* 1621
BOULDER BRANDS, INC., *pg.* 1016, *pg.* 310
BROWN & HALEY, *pg.* 1851, *pg.* 1820
BRUCE FOODS CORPORATION, *pg.* 842, *pg.* 743
CAL-MAINE FOODS, INC., *pg.* 843, *pg.* 969
CAMPBELL SOUP COMPANY, *pg.* 844, *pg.* 1048
CARGILL, INC., *pg.* 845, *pg.* 965
CARGILL SALT, *pg.* 846, *pg.* 926
THE C.F. SAUER COMPANY, *pg.* 847, *pg.* 1801
CHATTANOOGA BAKERY INC., *pg.* 847, *pg.* 1628
CHR. HANSEN, *pg.* 847, *pg.* 1873
COLONNA BROS., INC., *pg.* 849, *pg.* 1098
CONAGRA FOODS, *pg.* 826, *pg.* 994
CONAGRA FOODS, INC., *pg.* 826, *pg.* 1014
COOPERATIVE REGIONS OF ORGANIC PRODUCER POOLS, *pg.* 850, *pg.* 1864
CP KELCO, *pg.* 1154, *pg.* 201
CUISINE SOLUTIONS, INC., *pg.* 850, *pg.* 1770
CUSTOM CULINARY, INC., *pg.* 851, *pg.* 644
DEAN FOODS COMPANY, *pg.* 852, *pg.* 1679
DOLE FOOD COMPANY, INC., *pg.* 853, *pg.* 306
DOLE FRESH VEGETABLES, *pg.* 854, *pg.* 198
DUTCH GOLD HONEY INC., *pg.* 854, *pg.* 1546
EXXON MOBIL CORPORATION, *pg.* 977, *pg.* 1718
FARMER BROTHERS COMPANY, *pg.* 855, *pg.* 293
F.B. WASHBURN CANDY CORP., *pg.* 1852, *pg.* 803
FERRARA CANDY CO., *pg.* 1852, *pg.* 612

FERRERO U.S.A., INC., *pg.* 1852, *pg.* 1121
FONA INTERNATIONAL INC., *pg.* 855, *pg.* 613
FRONTIER NATURAL PRODUCTS CO-OP, *pg.* 509, *pg.* 710
FUCHS NORTH AMERICA., *pg.* 857, *pg.* 774
GENERAL MILLS, INC., *pg.* 828, *pg.* 933
GIORDANO'S ENTERPRISES, INC., *pg.* 1729, *pg.* 575
GOLD PURE FOOD PRODUCTS CO., INC., *pg.* 858, *pg.* 1166
GOLD STAR CHILI INC., *pg.* 1021, *pg.* 1414
GOLDEN ENTERPRISES INC., *pg.* 1854, *pg.* 2
GRECIAN DELIGHT FOODS INC., *pg.* 859, *pg.* 610
GRIFFIN FOOD COMPANY, *pg.* 860, *pg.* 1484
GRIFFITH LABORATORIES, INC., *pg.* 860, *pg.* 552
GRIFFITH LABORATORIES LTD., *pg.* 860, *pg.* 1934
GRINDMASTER CORPORATION, *pg.* 56, *pg.* 734
GRUMA CORPORATION, *pg.* 860, *pg.* 951
GRUMA CORPORATION, *pg.* 860, *pg.* 1720
GUITTARD CHOCOLATE COMPANY, *pg.* 1855, *pg.* 55
THE HAIN CELESTIAL GROUP, INC., *pg.* 860, *pg.* 1172
HERR FOODS INC., *pg.* 861, *pg.* 1557
THE HERSHEY CO., *pg.* 1855, *pg.* 1538
HORMEL FOODS CORPORATION, *pg.* 863, *pg.* 915
HULMAN & COMPANY, *pg.* 864, *pg.* 698
IDAHO FRESH-PAK INC., *pg.* 864, *pg.* 549
INGREDION, *pg.* 864, *pg.* 669
INVENTURE FOODS, INC., *pg.* 1023, *pg.* 17
JELLY BELLY CANDY COMPANY, *pg.* 1857, *pg.* 86
THE J.M. SMUCKER COMPANY, *pg.* 865, *pg.* 1468
JOHN B. SANFILIPPO & SON, INC., *pg.* 1024, *pg.* 610
JOYVA CORPORATION, *pg.* 1857, *pg.* 1146
JUST BORN, INC., *pg.* 1857, *pg.* 1516
KANAN ENTERPRISES, INC., *pg.* 1857, *pg.* 1473
KNOUSE FOODS COOPERATIVE INC., *pg.* 869, *pg.* 1558
KOSTO FOOD PRODUCTS CO., *pg.* 869, *pg.* 665
KOZY SHACK INC., *pg.* 869, *pg.* 1167
KRAFT CANADA INC., *pg.* 869, *pg.* 1939
THE KRAFT HEINZ COMPANY, *pg.* 870, *pg.* 1577
LA CIE MCCORMICK CANADA CO., *pg.* 872, *pg.* 1922
LANCASTER COLONY CORPORATION, *pg.* 873, *pg.* 1441
LEON'S FINE FOODS, INC., *pg.* 874, *pg.* 1727
LIBERTY ORCHARDS CO., INC., *pg.* 1857, *pg.* 1819
LIFEWAY FOODS, INC., *pg.* 874, *pg.* 634
LITTLE LADY FOODS, INC., *pg.* 875, *pg.* 611
MACANDREWS & FORBES HOLDINGS INC., *pg.* 777, *pg.* 1254
MAFCO WORLDWIDE CORPORATION, *pg.* 1858, *pg.* 1049
MALLET & COMPANY, INC., *pg.* 875, *pg.* 1521
MAPLE LEAF FOODS INC., *pg.* 875, *pg.* 1927
MARS, INCORPORATED, *pg.* 1858, *pg.* 1792
MASSIMO ZANETTI BEVERAGE USA, *pg.* 876, *pg.* 1808
THE MASTERSON COMPANY, INC., *pg.* 876, *pg.* 1877
MCCORMICK & COMPANY, INCORPORATED, *pg.* 1027, *pg.* 779
MCILHENNY COMPANY, *pg.* 876, *pg.* 741
MEAD JOHNSON NUTRITION COMPANY, *pg.* 1561, *pg.* 615
MEGAMEX FOODS, LLC, *pg.* 833, *pg.* 66
MICHAEL FOODS, INC., *pg.* 877, *pg.* 949
MILLER'S HONEY COMPANY, *pg.* 1860, *pg.* 1759
MIZKAN AMERICAS, INC., *pg.* 877, *pg.* 634
MODERN PRODUCTS, INC., *pg.* 1568, *pg.* 1871
MONDELEZ NORTH AMERICA, *pg.* 881, *pg.* 1054
MONTEREY GOURMET FOODS, INC., *pg.* 881, *pg.* 94
MONTEREY MUSHROOMS, INC., *pg.* 881, *pg.* 305
MORGAN FOODS, INC., *pg.* 881, *pg.* 673
NATIONAL FRUIT PRODUCT COMPANY, INC., *pg.* 882, *pg.* 1811
NESTLE HEALTHCARE NUTRITION, *pg.* 1572, *pg.* 941
NEW ENGLAND CONFECTIONERY COMPANY INC., *pg.* 1860, *pg.* 842
NEW WORLD PASTA COMPANY, *pg.* 885, *pg.* 1537
OLD DUTCH FOODS, INC., *pg.* 888, *pg.* 956
PARADISE, INC., *pg.* 888, *pg.* 458
PARMALAT CANADA INC., *pg.* 888, *pg.* 1941
PERFETTI VAN MELLE USA, INC., *pg.* 1860, *pg.* 727
PINNACLE FOODS GROUP LLC, *pg.* 889, *pg.* 1104
THE PROCTER & GAMBLE COMPANY, *pg.* 1129, *pg.* 1418
PROMOTION IN MOTION, INC., *pg.* 1861, *pg.* 1052
REED'S, INC., *pg.* 264, *pg.* 139
REIDCO, INC., *pg.* 891, *pg.* 675
REILY FOODS COMPANY, *pg.* 891, *pg.* 747
RESER'S FINE FOODS INC., *pg.* 1032, *pg.* 1496
RUDOLPH FOODS COMPANY, *pg.* 892, *pg.* 1458
RUIZ FOOD PRODUCTS, INC., *pg.* 893, *pg.* 77
SENSIENT TECHNOLOGIES CORPORATION, *pg.* 895, *pg.* 1881
SLIM-FAST FOODS COMPANY, *pg.* 896, *pg.* 1061
SMARTIES CANDY COMPANY, *pg.* 1861, *pg.* 1127
SMUCKER FOODS OF CANADA CO., *pg.* 896, *pg.* 1924
SOKOL & COMPANY, *pg.* 1862, *pg.* 598
SORBEE INTERNATIONAL, LLC, *pg.* 1862, *pg.* 1570
SPANGLER CANDY COMPANY, *pg.* 1862, *pg.* 1407
SPECTRUM ORGANIC PRODUCTS, INC., *pg.* 1596, *pg.* 182
SUBCO FOODS, INC., *pg.* 899, *pg.* 668
SUN-RYPE PRODUCTS LTD., *pg.* 899, *pg.* 1908
SUNOPTA INGREDIENTS, INC., *pg.* 900, *pg.* 942
SUNSWEET GROWERS, INC., *pg.* 900, *pg.* 309
SWEET CANDY COMPANY, *pg.* 1862, *pg.* 1761
TOOTSIE ROLL INDUSTRIES, INC., *pg.* 1863, *pg.* 591
THE TOPPS COMPANY, INC., *pg.* 588, *pg.* 1302
TOTAL NUTRACEUTICAL SOLUTIONS, INC., *pg.* 1603, *pg.* 1509
TRADER VIC'S GOURMET PRODUCTS, INC., *pg.* 901, *pg.* 69
TYSON FOODS, INC., *pg.* 902, *pg.* 35
UNILEVER CANADA INC., *pg.* 903, *pg.* 1946
UNILEVER UNITED STATES, INC., *pg.* 904, *pg.* 1061
WATKINS INCORPORATED, *pg.* 909, *pg.* 967
WESTIN FOODS, INC., *pg.* 909, *pg.* 1019
WHITFIELD FOODS, INC., *pg.* 910, *pg.* 8
WILD FLAVORS, INC., *pg.* 910, *pg.* 728
WM. WRIGLEY JR. COMPANY, *pg.* 1863, *pg.* 596
ZATARAIN'S BRANDS, INC., *pg.* 911, *pg.* 744

2035 - Pickled Fruits & Vegetables, Vegetable Sauces & Seasonings & Salad Dressings

ALGOOD FOOD COMPANY, *pg.* 836, *pg.* 731
B&G FOODS, INC., *pg.* 838, *pg.* 1102
CAINS FOODS, L.P., *pg.* 843, *pg.* 784
CAMPBELL SOUP COMPANY, *pg.* 844, *pg.* 1048
THE C.F. SAUER COMPANY, *pg.* 847, *pg.* 1801
GOLD PURE FOOD PRODUCTS CO., INC., *pg.* 858, *pg.* 1166
JOHN B. SANFILIPPO & SON, INC., *pg.* 1024, *pg.* 610
KEN'S FOODS, INC., *pg.* 867, *pg.* 832
KIKKOMAN INTERNATIONAL INC., *pg.* 868, *pg.* 220
THE KRAFT HEINZ COMPANY, *pg.* 870, *pg.* 1577
LANCASTER COLONY CORPORATION, *pg.* 873, *pg.* 1441
LIDESTRI FOODS, INC., *pg.* 874, *pg.* 1159
MCILHENNY COMPANY, *pg.* 876, *pg.* 741
MEGAMEX FOODS, LLC, *pg.* 833, *pg.* 66
MIZKAN AMERICAS, INC., *pg.* 877, *pg.* 634
NEWMAN'S OWN, INC., *pg.* 886, *pg.* 384
PLOCHMAN, INC., *pg.* 890, *pg.* 631
Q&B FOODS, INC., *pg.* 891, *pg.* 119
RECKITT BENCKISER INC., *pg.* 1136, *pg.* 1105
REILY FOODS COMPANY, *pg.* 891, *pg.* 747
SAN-J INTERNATIONAL, INC., *pg.* 893, *pg.* 1803
T. MARZETTI COMPANY, *pg.* 900, *pg.* 1444
TRADER VIC'S GOURMET PRODUCTS, INC., *pg.* 901, *pg.* 69
TREEHOUSE FOODS, INC., *pg.* 901, *pg.* 649
UNILEVER UNITED STATES, INC., *pg.* 904, *pg.* 1061
WESTIN FOODS, INC., *pg.* 909, *pg.* 1019
ZATARAIN'S BRANDS, INC., *pg.* 911, *pg.* 744

2037 - Frozen Fruits, Fruit Juices & Vegetables

CAMPBELL SOUP COMPANY, *pg.* 844, *pg.* 1048
CELSIUS HOLDINGS, INC., *pg.* 239, *pg.* 411
CHIQUITA BRANDS INTERNATIONAL, INC., *pg.* 847, *pg.* 1365
COCA-COLA NORTH AMERICA, *pg.* 848, *pg.* 500
COUNTRY PURE FOODS, INC., *pg.* 247, *pg.* 1400
CUISINE SOLUTIONS, INC., *pg.* 850, *pg.* 1770
FLORIDA'S NATURAL GROWERS, *pg.* 855, *pg.* 437
GOLDEN ENTERPRISES INC., *pg.* 1854, *pg.* 2
HEINZ FROZEN FOOD COMPANY, *pg.* 861, *pg.* 1576
J.R. SIMPLOT COMPANY, *pg.* 867, *pg.* 547
KNOUSE FOODS COOPERATIVE INC., *pg.* 869, *pg.* 1558
MILNE FOOD PRODUCTS, INC., *pg.* 877, *pg.* 1824
PEPSI BEVERAGES COMPANY, *pg.* 258, *pg.* 1342
PINNACLE FOODS GROUP LLC, *pg.* 889, *pg.* 1104
POM WONDERFUL, LLC, *pg.* 890, *pg.* 139
REED'S, INC., *pg.* 264, *pg.* 139
SENECA FOODS CORPORATION, *pg.* 895, *pg.* 1177
SUN-RYPE PRODUCTS LTD., *pg.* 899, *pg.* 1908
SUNNY DELIGHT BEVERAGES CO., *pg.* 899, *pg.* 1426
SUNSWEET GROWERS, INC., *pg.* 900, *pg.* 309
TREE TOP, INC., *pg.* 901, *pg.* 1843
VENTURA COASTAL LLC, *pg.* 908, *pg.* 301
WELCH FOODS INC., *pg.* 909, *pg.* 815
WELCH'S INTERNATIONAL, *pg.* 909, *pg.* 816
XANGO, LLC, *pg.* 1610, *pg.* 1751

2038 - Frozen Specialties, NEC

ARMANINO FOODS OF DISTINCTION, INC., *pg.* 837, *pg.* 100
ATEECO, INC., *pg.* 838, *pg.* 1586
BARBER FOODS, INC., *pg.* 839, *pg.* 751
BELLISIO FOODS, INC., *pg.* 840, *pg.* 931
BERNATELLO'S PIZZA INC., *pg.* 840, *pg.* 928
BRIDGFORD FOODS CORPORATION, *pg.* 842, *pg.* 42
CONAGRA FOODS LAMB WESTON, INC., *pg.* 850, *pg.* 549
CONTINENTAL MILLS, INC., *pg.* 827, *pg.* 1845
CUISINE SOLUTIONS, INC., *pg.* 850, *pg.* 1770
THE HAIN CELESTIAL GROUP, INC., *pg.* 860, *pg.* 1172
HEINZ FROZEN FOOD COMPANY, *pg.* 861, *pg.* 1576
INVENTURE FOODS, INC., *pg.* 1023, *pg.* 17
THE KRAFT HEINZ COMPANY, *pg.* 870, *pg.* 1577
LANCASTER COLONY CORPORATION, *pg.* 873, *pg.* 1441
LITTLE LADY FOODS, INC., *pg.* 875, *pg.* 611
MCCAIN FOODS LIMITED, *pg.* 876, *pg.* 1915
RUIZ FOOD PRODUCTS, INC., *pg.* 893, *pg.* 77
THE SCHWAN FOOD COMPANY, *pg.* 894, *pg.* 928
SKYLINE CHILI, INC., *pg.* 1033, *pg.* 1452
TABATCHNICK FINE FOODS, INC., *pg.* 900, *pg.* 1122
WIN SCHULER FOODS, *pg.* 910, *pg.* 908
WINDSOR QUALITY FOOD CO., LTD., *pg.* 910, *pg.* 1717

2041 - Flour & other Grain Mill Products

ADM MILLING, *pg.* 825, *pg.* 718
ARCHER-DANIELS-MIDLAND COMPANY, *pg.* 825, *pg.* 565
BETTY CROCKER PRODUCTS, *pg.* 840, *pg.* 931
THE BIRKETT MILLS, *pg.* 826, *pg.* 1321
BOB'S RED MILL NATURAL FOODS, INC., *pg.* 841, *pg.* 1500
CONAGRA FOODS, INC., *pg.* 826, *pg.* 1014
CONTINENTAL GRAIN COMPANY, *pg.* 1475, *pg.* 1218
GENERAL MILLS, INC., *pg.* 828, *pg.* 933
HODGSON MILL, INC., *pg.* 830, *pg.* 609
HULMAN & COMPANY, *pg.* 864, *pg.* 698
KASHI COMPANY, *pg.* 830, *pg.* 119
KELLOGG COMPANY, *pg.* 831, *pg.* 870
THE KING ARTHUR FLOUR COMPANY, INC., *pg.* 833, *pg.* 1767
MGP INGREDIENTS, INC., *pg.* 877, *pg.* 714
NORTH DAKOTA MILL & ELEVATOR ASSOCIATION, *pg.* 833, *pg.* 1398
PENFORD CORPORATION, *pg.* 1177, *pg.* 314
THE UHLMANN CO., *pg.* 834, *pg.* 986

2043 - Cereal Breakfast Foods

BETTY CROCKER PRODUCTS, *pg.* 840, *pg.* 931
CONAGRA FOODS, *pg.* 826, *pg.* 994
GENERAL MILLS, INC., *pg.* 828, *pg.* 933
GILSTER-MARY LEE CORPORATION, *pg.* 858, *pg.* 563
THE HAIN CELESTIAL GROUP, INC., *pg.* 860, *pg.* 1172
HILLSHIRE BRANDS, *pg.* 862, *pg.* 576
KELLOGG COMPANY, *pg.* 831, *pg.* 870
MONDELEZ INTERNATIONAL, INC., *pg.* 878, *pg.* 601
NATURE'S PATH FOODS INC., *pg.* 833, *pg.* 1908
POST CONSUMER BRANDS, *pg.* 833, *pg.* 927
POST HOLDINGS, INC., *pg.* 833, *pg.* 1002
THE QUAKER OATS COMPANY, *pg.* 834, *pg.* 588

2044 - Rice Milling

AMERICAN LICORICE CO. INC., *pg.* 1850, *pg.* 692
AMERICAN RICE, INC., *pg.* 837, *pg.* 1700
FARMERS RICE COOPERATIVE, *pg.* 855, *pg.* 196
GRIFFITH LABORATORIES LTD., *pg.* 860, *pg.* 1934
MAFCO WORLDWIDE CORPORATION, *pg.* 1858, *pg.* 1049
RICELAND FOODS, INC., *pg.* 892, *pg.* 36

First page reference indicates Business Class Edition
Second page reference indicates Geographic Edition

RIVIANA FOODS INC., *pg.* 892, *pg.* 1713
SAGE V FOODS, LLC, *pg.* 893, *pg.* 139

2045 - Prepared Flour Mixes & Doughs

BRIDGFORD FOODS CORPORATION, *pg.* 842, *pg.* 42
CONTINENTAL MILLS, INC., *pg.* 827, *pg.* 1845
COOKIE TREE BAKERIES, *pg.* 1851, *pg.* 1756
DAWN FOOD PRODUCTS, INC., *pg.* 1018, *pg.* 893
FRY KRISP COMPANY, *pg.* 857, *pg.* 893
GENERAL MILLS, INC., *pg.* 828, *pg.* 933
HODGSON MILL, INC., *pg.* 830, *pg.* 609
THE KING ARTHUR FLOUR COMPANY, INC., *pg.* 833, *pg.* 1767
MANISCHEWITZ COMPANY, *pg.* 875, *pg.* 1097
NEWLY WEDS FOODS, INC., *pg.* 886, *pg.* 585

2046 - Wet Corn Milling

ARCHER-DANIELS-MIDLAND COMPANY, *pg.* 825, *pg.* 565
BUNGE LIMITED, *pg.* 842, *pg.* 1351
GRAIN PROCESSING CORPORATION, *pg.* 859, *pg.* 709
HULMAN & COMPANY, *pg.* 864, *pg.* 698
INGREDION, *pg.* 864, *pg.* 669
PENFORD CORPORATION, *pg.* 1177, *pg.* 314

2047 - Dog & Cat Food

ALL AMERICAN PET COMPANY, INC., *pg.* 1474, *pg.* 125
THE BLUE BUFFALO CO., *pg.* 1474, *pg.* 385
BUMBLE BEE FOODS LLC, *pg.* 842, *pg.* 201
FROMM FAMILY PET FOODS, INC., *pg.* 1476, *pg.* 1870
THE HARTZ MOUNTAIN CORP., *pg.* 1476, *pg.* 1120
HEINZ NORTH AMERICA, *pg.* 861, *pg.* 1576
IAMS COMPANY, *pg.* 1477, *pg.* 1633
MARS CANADA INC., *pg.* 1478, *pg.* 1918
MARS NORTH AMERICA, *pg.* 1859, *pg.* 1072
MARS PETCARE, *pg.* 1478, *pg.* 1633
NESTLE PURINA PETCARE COMPANY, *pg.* 1479, *pg.* 1000
THE PROCTER & GAMBLE COMPANY, *pg.* 1129, *pg.* 1418
STARKIST FOODS INC., *pg.* 898, *pg.* 1581

2051 - Bread & other Bakery Products, Except Cookies & Crackers

ALFRED NICKLES BAKERY, INC., *pg.* 836, *pg.* 1466
AMERICAN BLUE RIBBON HOLDINGS, *pg.* 1714, *pg.* 1648
THE ATLANTA BREAD COMPANY, *pg.* 1715, *pg.* 540
AUNT MILLIE'S BAKERIES, *pg.* 838, *pg.* 680
AWREY BAKERIES, INC., *pg.* 1015, *pg.* 896
BAB, INC., *pg.* 1715, *pg.* 599
BENSON'S, INC., *pg.* 1850, *pg.* 526
BIMBO BAKERIES USA, *pg.* 840, *pg.* 151
CAMPBELL SOUP COMPANY, *pg.* 844, *pg.* 1048
CHATTANOOGA BAKERY INC., *pg.* 847, *pg.* 1628
CHEESECAKE FACTORY INCORPORATED, *pg.* 1017, *pg.* 56
CLIF BAR INC., *pg.* 848, *pg.* 83
COLLIN STREET BAKERY, *pg.* 1851, *pg.* 1672
CONAGRA FOODS, *pg.* 826, *pg.* 994
COOKIE TREE BAKERIES, *pg.* 1851, *pg.* 1756
FLOWERS FOODS BAKERIES GROUP, LLC, *pg.* 855, *pg.* 541
FLOWERS FOODS, INC., *pg.* 855, *pg.* 541
FRITO-LAY NORTH AMERICA, INC., *pg.* 1853, *pg.* 1730
GEORGE WESTON LIMITED, *pg.* 858, *pg.* 1938
GONNELLA BAKING COMPANY, *pg.* 859, *pg.* 575
GRAETER'S, INC., *pg.* 1854, *pg.* 1414
GRECIAN DELIGHT FOODS INC., *pg.* 859, *pg.* 610
THE HAIN CELESTIAL GROUP, INC., *pg.* 860, *pg.* 1172
HOSTESS BRANDS LLC, *pg.* 1856, *pg.* 984
J&J SNACK FOODS CORPORATION, *pg.* 865, *pg.* 1107
KING'S HAWAIIAN BAKERY WEST, INC., *pg.* 869, *pg.* 293
KLOSTERMAN BAKING COMPANY, INC., *pg.* 869, *pg.* 1415
KRONOS PRODUCTS, INC., *pg.* 872, *pg.* 614
LATE JULY SNACKS LLC, *pg.* 1026, *pg.* 784
MANISCHEWITZ COMPANY, *pg.* 875, *pg.* 1097
MCKEE FOODS CORPORATION, *pg.* 1860, *pg.* 1630
MRS. BAIRD'S BAKERIES, INC., *pg.* 1860, *pg.* 1695
NATURE'S PATH FOODS INC., *pg.* 833, *pg.* 1908
NEWLY WEDS FOODS, INC., *pg.* 886, *pg.* 585
NONNI'S FOOD COMPANY INC., *pg.* 886, *pg.* 1490
NORSE DAIRY SYSTEMS LLC, *pg.* 886, *pg.* 1442
NORTH DAKOTA MILL & ELEVATOR ASSOCIATION, *pg.* 833, *pg.* 1398
PEPPERIDGE FARM, INC., *pg.* 888, *pg.* 363
RAPALA VMC CORPORATION, *pg.* 1843, *pg.* 949
RHODES INTERNATIONAL, INC., *pg.* 891, *pg.* 1760
RIVIANA FOODS INC., *pg.* 892, *pg.* 1713
ROTELLAS ITALIAN BAKERY, INC., *pg.* 892, *pg.* 1018
SCHMIDT BAKING CO., INC., *pg.* 894, *pg.* 759
SCHULZE & BURCH BISCUIT COMPANY, *pg.* 894, *pg.* 589
SNYDER'S-LANCE, INC., *pg.* 896, *pg.* 1368
SORBEE INTERNATIONAL, LLC, *pg.* 1862, *pg.* 1570
TASTY BAKING COMPANY, *pg.* 1862, *pg.* 1571
UNILEVER UNITED STATES, INC., *pg.* 904, *pg.* 1061
UNITED STATES BAKERY, *pg.* 907, *pg.* 1507
VACHON BAKERY INC., *pg.* 907, *pg.* 1959
VOORTMAN COOKIES LIMITED, *pg.* 1863, *pg.* 1919
WESTON BAKERIES LIMITED, *pg.* 909, *pg.* 1932

2052 - Cookies & Crackers

CAMPBELL SOUP COMPANY, *pg.* 844, *pg.* 1048
CHATTANOOGA BAKERY INC., *pg.* 847, *pg.* 1628
CLIF BAR INC., *pg.* 848, *pg.* 83
CONAGRA FOODS, *pg.* 826, *pg.* 994
COOKIE TREE BAKERIES, *pg.* 1851, *pg.* 1756
FLOWERS FOODS, INC., *pg.* 855, *pg.* 541
FRITO-LAY NORTH AMERICA, INC., *pg.* 1853, *pg.* 1730
THE HAIN CELESTIAL GROUP, INC., *pg.* 860, *pg.* 1172
J&J SNACK FOODS CORPORATION, *pg.* 865, *pg.* 1107
LATE JULY SNACKS LLC, *pg.* 1026, *pg.* 784
MANISCHEWITZ COMPANY, *pg.* 875, *pg.* 1097
MCKEE FOODS CORPORATION, *pg.* 1860, *pg.* 1630
NEWLY WEDS FOODS, INC., *pg.* 886, *pg.* 585
NONNI'S FOOD COMPANY INC., *pg.* 886, *pg.* 1490
NORSE DAIRY SYSTEMS LLC, *pg.* 886, *pg.* 1442
NORTH DAKOTA MILL & ELEVATOR ASSOCIATION, *pg.* 833, *pg.* 1398
PEPPERIDGE FARM, INC., *pg.* 888, *pg.* 363
RIVIANA FOODS INC., *pg.* 892, *pg.* 1713
SCHULZE & BURCH BISCUIT COMPANY, *pg.* 894, *pg.* 589
SNYDER'S-LANCE, INC., *pg.* 896, *pg.* 1368
SORBEE INTERNATIONAL, LLC, *pg.* 1862, *pg.* 1570
TASTY BAKING COMPANY, *pg.* 1862, *pg.* 1571
UNILEVER UNITED STATES, INC., *pg.* 904, *pg.* 1061
VOORTMAN COOKIES LIMITED, *pg.* 1863, *pg.* 1919

2053 - Frozen Baking Products, Except Bread

CAMPBELL SOUP COMPANY, *pg.* 844, *pg.* 1040
ELI'S CHEESECAKE COMPANY, *pg.* 1852, *pg.* 572
HILLSHIRE BRANDS, *pg.* 862, *pg.* 576
J&J SNACK FOODS CORPORATION, *pg.* 865, *pg.* 1107
KELLOGG COMPANY, *pg.* 831, *pg.* 870
RICH PRODUCTS CORPORATION, *pg.* 892, *pg.* 1150

2061 - Cane Sugar, Except Refining

AMERICAN CRYSTAL SUGAR COMPANY, *pg.* 837, *pg.* 951
BUNGE LIMITED, *pg.* 842, *pg.* 1351
IMPERIAL SUGAR COMPANY, *pg.* 864, *pg.* 1746
TOOTSIE ROLL INDUSTRIES, INC., *pg.* 1863, *pg.* 591
UNITED STATES SUGAR CORPORATION, *pg.* 907, *pg.* 417

2062 - Cane Sugar Refining

C&H SUGAR COMPANY, INC., *pg.* 843, *pg.* 71
IMPERIAL SUGAR COMPANY, *pg.* 864, *pg.* 1746

2063 - Beet Sugar Manufacturing

AMERICAN CRYSTAL SUGAR COMPANY, *pg.* 837, *pg.* 951
MINN-DAK FARMERS COOPERATIVE, *pg.* 877, *pg.* 1399

2064 - Candy & other Confectionery Products

ANNABELLE CANDY COMPANY, INC., *pg.* 1850, *pg.* 100
BLOMMER CHOCOLATE COMPANY, *pg.* 1851, *pg.* 566
BOYER CANDY COMPANY INC., *pg.* 1851, *pg.* 1514
CAMPBELL SOUP COMPANY, *pg.* 844, *pg.* 1048
GHIRARDELLI CHOCOLATE COMPANY, *pg.* 1854, *pg.* 252
GODIVA CHOCOLATIER, INC., *pg.* 1854, *pg.* 1235
GUITTARD CHOCOLATE COMPANY, *pg.* 1855, *pg.* 55
HERSHEY CANADA, INC., *pg.* 1855, *pg.* 1926
THE HERSHEY CO., *pg.* 1855, *pg.* 1538
JOHN B. SANFILIPPO & SON, INC., *pg.* 1024, *pg.* 610
JUST BORN, INC., *pg.* 1857, *pg.* 1516
LINDT & SPRUNGLI (USA) INC., *pg.* 1857, *pg.* 1039
MARS, INCORPORATED, *pg.* 1858, *pg.* 1792
MARS NORTH AMERICA, *pg.* 1859, *pg.* 1072
NESTLE CANADA INC., *pg.* 883, *pg.* 1929
NEW ENGLAND CONFECTIONERY COMPANY INC., *pg.* 1860, *pg.* 842
PROMOTION IN MOTION, INC., *pg.* 1861, *pg.* 1052
RAMMKERR, INC., *pg.* 1746, *pg.* 986
R.M. PALMER COMPANY, *pg.* 1861, *pg.* 1585
ROCKY MOUNTAIN CHOCOLATE FACTORY, INC., *pg.* 1032, *pg.* 324
RUSSELL STOVER CANDIES, INC., *pg.* 1861, *pg.* 986
SNYDER'S-LANCE, INC., *pg.* 896, *pg.* 1368
SORBEE INTERNATIONAL, LLC, *pg.* 1862, *pg.* 1570
SPANGLER CANDY COMPANY, *pg.* 1862, *pg.* 1407
STANDARD FUNCTIONAL FOODS GROUP(SFFG), *pg.* 1862, *pg.* 1654
TOOTSIE ROLL INDUSTRIES, INC., *pg.* 1863, *pg.* 591
WORLD'S FINEST CHOCOLATE, INC., *pg.* 1864, *pg.* 597

2066 - Chocolate & Cocoa Products

BLOMMER CHOCOLATE COMPANY, *pg.* 1851, *pg.* 566
CAMPBELL SOUP COMPANY, *pg.* 844, *pg.* 1048
GHIRARDELLI CHOCOLATE COMPANY, *pg.* 1854, *pg.* 252
GODIVA CHOCOLATIER, INC., *pg.* 1854, *pg.* 1235
GUITTARD CHOCOLATE COMPANY, *pg.* 1855, *pg.* 55
THE HERSHEY CO., *pg.* 1855, *pg.* 1538
LINDT & SPRUNGLI (USA) INC., *pg.* 1857, *pg.* 1039
MARS NORTH AMERICA, *pg.* 1859, *pg.* 1072
NEW ENGLAND CONFECTIONERY COMPANY INC., *pg.* 1860, *pg.* 842
R.M. PALMER COMPANY, *pg.* 1861, *pg.* 1585
ROCKY MOUNTAIN CHOCOLATE FACTORY, INC., *pg.* 1032, *pg.* 324
SPANGLER CANDY COMPANY, *pg.* 1862, *pg.* 1407
WORLD'S FINEST CHOCOLATE, INC., *pg.* 1864, *pg.* 597

2068 - Salted & Roasted Nuts & Seeds

ALGOOD FOOD COMPANY, *pg.* 836, *pg.* 731
BEER NUTS, INC., *pg.* 1850, *pg.* 557
BIRDSONG CORPORATION, *pg.* 1851, *pg.* 1808
DIAMOND FOODS, INC., *pg.* 1851, *pg.* 216
GOLDEN ENTERPRISES INC., *pg.* 1854, *pg.* 2
HAMMONS PRODUCTS COMPANY, *pg.* 1855, *pg.* 1007
JOHN B. SANFILIPPO & SON, INC., *pg.* 1024, *pg.* 610
KANAN ENTERPRISES, INC., *pg.* 1857, *pg.* 1473
THE LEAVITT CORPORATION, *pg.* 874, *pg.* 818
REILY FOODS COMPANY, *pg.* 891, *pg.* 747

2075 - Soybean Oil Mills

ACH FOOD COMPANIES, INC., *pg.* 835, *pg.* 1631
AG PROCESSING INC., *pg.* 835, *pg.* 1013
ARCHER-DANIELS-MIDLAND COMPANY, *pg.* 825, *pg.* 565
BUNGE LIMITED, *pg.* 842, *pg.* 1351
CHS INC., *pg.* 702, *pg.* 926
CONAGRA FOODS, INC., *pg.* 826, *pg.* 1014
DARLING INGREDIENTS, INC., *pg.* 852, *pg.* 1718
THE HAIN CELESTIAL GROUP, INC., *pg.* 860, *pg.* 1172
MALLET & COMPANY, INC., *pg.* 875, *pg.* 1521
OWENSBORO GRAIN COMPANY, INC., *pg.* 706, *pg.* 739
PERDUE FARMS INCORPORATED, *pg.* 889, *pg.* 777
POMPEIAN, INC., *pg.* 890, *pg.* 759
PYCO INDUSTRIES, INC., *pg.* 706, *pg.* 1726
RICELAND FOODS, INC., *pg.* 892, *pg.* 36
SPECTRUM ORGANIC PRODUCTS, INC., *pg.* 1596, *pg.* 182
SUNRISE SOYA FOODS, *pg.* 900, *pg.* 1912
VENTURA FOODS, LLC, *pg.* 908, *pg.* 49

2079 - Shortening, Table Oils, Margarine & other Edible Fats & Oils, NEC

ACH FOOD COMPANIES, INC., *pg.* 835, *pg.* 1631
AG PROCESSING INC., *pg.* 835, *pg.* 1013
ARCHER-DANIELS-MIDLAND COMPANY, *pg.* 825, *pg.* 565
BUNGE LIMITED, *pg.* 842, *pg.* 1351
CHS INC., *pg.* 702, *pg.* 926
CONAGRA FOODS, INC., *pg.* 826, *pg.* 1014
DARLING INGREDIENTS, INC., *pg.* 852, *pg.* 1718
GRAIN PROCESSING CORPORATION, *pg.* 859, *pg.* 709
THE HAIN CELESTIAL GROUP, INC., *pg.* 860, *pg.* 1172
HULMAN & COMPANY, *pg.* 864, *pg.* 698
INGREDION, *pg.* 864, *pg.* 669
MALLET & COMPANY, INC., *pg.* 875, *pg.* 1521
OWENSBORO GRAIN COMPANY, INC., *pg.* 706, *pg.* 739
PENFORD CORPORATION, *pg.* 1177, *pg.* 314
PERDUE FARMS INCORPORATED, *pg.* 889, *pg.* 777
POMPEIAN, INC., *pg.* 890, *pg.* 759
PYCO INDUSTRIES, INC., *pg.* 706, *pg.* 1726
RICELAND FOODS, INC., *pg.* 892, *pg.* 36
SPECTRUM ORGANIC PRODUCTS, INC., *pg.* 1596, *pg.* 182
SUNRISE SOYA FOODS, *pg.* 900, *pg.* 1912
VENTURA FOODS, LLC, *pg.* 908, *pg.* 49

2082 - Malt Beverages

ABITA BREWING COMPANY, *pg.* 237, *pg.* 741
ANHEUSER-BUSCH COMPANIES, LLC, *pg.* 237, *pg.* 991
BIG ROCK BREWERY INCOME TRUST, *pg.* 239, *pg.* 1902
BJ'S RESTAURANTS, INC., *pg.* 1716, *pg.* 104
THE BOSTON BEER COMPANY, INC., *pg.* 239, *pg.* 790
THE BROOKLYN BREWERY, *pg.* 239, *pg.* 1145
CAPITAL BREWERY CO., INC., *pg.* 239, *pg.* 1872
COASTAL EXTREME BREWING COMPANY, *pg.* 240, *pg.* 1602
CRAFT BREWERS ALLIANCE, INC, *pg.* 247, *pg.* 1502
DESCHUTES BREWERY INC., *pg.* 248, *pg.* 1496
D.G. YUENGLING & SON INCORPORATED, *pg.* 248, *pg.* 1582
DOGFISH HEAD CRAFT BREWERY, INC., *pg.* 249, *pg.* 388
FLYING DOG BREWERY, *pg.* 251, *pg.* 319
THE GREAT WESTERN BREWING COMPANY, *pg.* 251, *pg.* 1962
JACOB LEINENKUGEL BREWING CO., *pg.* 253, *pg.* 1856
LABATT BREWING COMPANY LIMITED, *pg.* 253, *pg.* 1939
THE LION BREWERY, INC., *pg.* 254, *pg.* 1594
MARNIER-LAPOSTOLLE INC., *pg.* 1966, *pg.* 1256
MENDOCINO BREWING COMPANY, *pg.* 254, *pg.* 298
MILLERCOORS, *pg.* 254, *pg.* 1877
MILLERCOORS LLC, *pg.* 255, *pg.* 582
MOLSON COORS BREWING COMPANY, *pg.* 256, *pg.* 321
MOLSON COORS CANADA INC., *pg.* 256, *pg.* 1955
MOLSON INC., *pg.* 256, *pg.* 1955
NEW BELGIUM BREWING COMPANY, INC., *pg.* 258, *pg.* 328
NEW ENGLAND BREWING COMPANY, *pg.* 1967, *pg.* 386
PABST BREWING COMPANY, *pg.* 258, *pg.* 137
PHILIP MORRIS USA INC., *pg.* 1894, *pg.* 1803
SIERRA NEVADA BREWING CO., *pg.* 265, *pg.* 65
SLEEMAN BREWERIES, LTD., *pg.* 265, *pg.* 1920
SPRECHER BREWING COMPANY, *pg.* 265, *pg.* 1858
SUMMIT BREWING CO., *pg.* 265, *pg.* 963
UNITED STATES BEVERAGE LLC, *pg.* 266, *pg.* 379

2083 - Malt

ARCHER-DANIELS-MIDLAND COMPANY, *pg.* 825, *pg.* 565

2084 - Wines, Brandy & Brandy Spirits

ANDREW PELLER LIMITED, *pg.* 1956, *pg.* 1920
BEAM SUNTORY INC., *pg.* 1957, *pg.* 599
BILTMORE ESTATE WINE COMPANY, *pg.* 1958, *pg.* 1358
BROWN-FORMAN BEVERAGES, *pg.* 1958, *pg.* 731
BROWN-FORMAN CORPORATION, *pg.* 1958, *pg.* 732
CAMERON HUGHES WINE, *pg.* 1960, *pg.* 214
CAMPARI AMERICA, *pg.* 1960, *pg.* 214
CONSTELLATION BRANDS CANADA, *pg.* 1960, *pg.* 1925
CONSTELLATION BRANDS, INC., *pg.* 1960, *pg.* 1348
CORBY DISTILLERIES LTD., *pg.* 1961, *pg.* 1937
DIAGEO CANADA, INC., *pg.* 1961, *pg.* 1937
DIAGEO NORTH AMERICA, INC., *pg.* 1961, *pg.* 361
DOMAINE CHANDON, INC., *pg.* 1962, *pg.* 308
THE DONUM ESTATE, INC, *pg.* 1962, *pg.* 279
E&J GALLO WINERY, *pg.* 1962, *pg.* 149
F. KORBEL BROS. INC., *pg.* 1963, *pg.* 100
FETZER VINEYARDS, *pg.* 1963, *pg.* 104
FIFTH GENERATION, INC., *pg.* 1963, *pg.* 1662
FORTUNE BRANDS HOME & SECURITY, INC., *pg.* 55, *pg.* 600
GEYSER PEAK WINERY, *pg.* 1964, *pg.* 101
GIUMARRA VINEYARDS CORPORATION, *pg.* 1964, *pg.* 45
GLOBAL WINE COMPANY, *pg.* 1964, *pg.* 278
GRAIN PROCESSING CORPORATION, *pg.* 859, *pg.* 709
HEAVEN HILL DISTILLERIES, INC., *pg.* 1964, *pg.* 725
HOOD RIVER DISTILLERS INC., *pg.* 1964, *pg.* 1498
JACK DANIEL'S DISTILLERY, *pg.* 1964, *pg.* 1640
JIM BEAM BRANDS CO., *pg.* 1965, *pg.* 601
KENDALL-JACKSON WINE ESTATES, LTD., *pg.* 1965, *pg.* 277
KING ESTATE OREGON WINES, *pg.* 1965, *pg.* 1497
LAIRD & COMPANY, INC., *pg.* 1966, *pg.* 1119
MAGNET ENTERPRISES, INC., *pg.* 1966, *pg.* 581
MAKER'S MARK DISTILLERY, INC., *pg.* 1966, *pg.* 731
MCCORMICK DISTILLING CO., INC., *pg.* 1966, *pg.* 1007
MGP INGREDIENTS, INC., *pg.* 877, *pg.* 714
MONTEBELLO BRANDS INC., *pg.* 1967, *pg.* 758
M.S. WALKER, INC., *pg.* 1967, *pg.* 843
NOLET SPIRITS USA INC., *pg.* 1967, *pg.* 41
THE PATRON SPIRITS COMPANY, *pg.* 1967, *pg.* 1029
PERNOD RICARD USA, INC., *pg.* 1968, *pg.* 1332
REX HILL VINEYARDS, *pg.* 1969, *pg.* 1500
ROBERT MONDAVI WINERY, *pg.* 1969, *pg.* 173
SAZERAC COMPANY, INC., *pg.* 1969, *pg.* 745
SCHEID VINEYARDS INC., *pg.* 1970, *pg.* 198
STE. MICHELLE WINE ESTATES LTD., *pg.* 1970, *pg.* 1847
STONE BRIDGE CELLARS INC., *pg.* 1971, *pg.* 197
TREASURY WINE ESTATES, *pg.* 1971, *pg.* 164
TRINCHERO FAMILY ESTATES, *pg.* 1971, *pg.* 197
WEIBEL, INC., *pg.* 1972, *pg.* 122
WENTE VINEYARDS, *pg.* 1972, *pg.* 122
WILLAMETTE VALLEY VINEYARDS, INC., *pg.* 1972, *pg.* 1510
WILLIAM GRANT & SONS, INC., *pg.* 1972, *pg.* 1057

2086 - Bottled & Canned Soft Drinks & Carbonated Waters

4C FOODS CORPORATION, *pg.* 835, *pg.* 1145
ALL MARKET, INC., *pg.* 237, *pg.* 1189
ANDERSON ERICKSON DAIRY COMPANY, *pg.* 837, *pg.* 704
ARROWHEAD MOUNTAIN SPRING WATER COMPANY, *pg.* 238, *pg.* 349
CAROLINA BEVERAGE CORPORATION, *pg.* 239, *pg.* 1390
COCA-COLA BOTTLING CO. CONSOLIDATED, *pg.* 240, *pg.* 1365
THE COCA-COLA COMPANY, *pg.* 240, *pg.* 493
COCA-COLA REFRESHMENTS USA, INC., *pg.* 247, *pg.* 500
CRYSTAL GEYSER WATER COMPANY, *pg.* 248, *pg.* 57
CRYSTAL ROCK HOLDINGS, INC., *pg.* 248, *pg.* 382
DR PEPPER SNAPPLE GROUP, INC., *pg.* 250, *pg.* 1729
DS WATERS OF AMERICA, INC., *pg.* 250, *pg.* 504
ENERGY BRANDS, INC., *pg.* 854, *pg.* 1227
FIJI WATER, *pg.* 251, *pg.* 130
THE GATORADE COMPANY, *pg.* 251, *pg.* 574
HONEST TEA, *pg.* 253, *pg.* 762
JONES SODA CO., *pg.* 253, *pg.* 1836
KNOUSE FOODS COOPERATIVE INC., *pg.* 869, *pg.* 1558
KRIER FOODS, INC., *pg.* 253, *pg.* 1890
LEADING BRANDS, INC., *pg.* 1026, *pg.* 1911
THE LION BREWERY, INC., *pg.* 254, *pg.* 1594
THE MONARCH BEVERAGE COMPANY, INC., *pg.* 257, *pg.* 514
MONDELEZ INTERNATIONAL, *pg.* 877, *pg.* 1344
MONSTER BEVERAGE CORPORATION, *pg.* 257, *pg.* 69
MOUNTAIN VALLEY SPRING COMPANY, *pg.* 257, *pg.* 33
NATIONAL BEVERAGE CORP., *pg.* 257, *pg.* 425
NESTLE WATERS NORTH AMERICA INC., *pg.* 257, *pg.* 375
NOR-CAL BEVERAGE CO., INC., *pg.* 258, *pg.* 305
PEPSI BEVERAGES COMPANY, *pg.* 258, *pg.* 1342
PEPSI-COLA BOTTLING OF CENTRAL NEW ENGLAND, *pg.* 259, *pg.* 824
PEPSICO, INC., *pg.* 259, *pg.* 1327
POLAR BEVERAGES, *pg.* 264, *pg.* 862
PRIMO WATER CORPORATION, *pg.* 1030, *pg.* 1395
RED BULL NORTH AMERICA, INC., *pg.* 264, *pg.* 275
REED'S, INC., *pg.* 264, *pg.* 139
ROCKSTAR, INC., *pg.* 265, *pg.* 1029
SPRECHER BREWING COMPANY, *pg.* 265, *pg.* 1858
TREE TOP, INC., *pg.* 901, *pg.* 1843
TROPICANA PRODUCTS, INC., *pg.* 902, *pg.* 592
VITUSA CORP., *pg.* 1482, *pg.* 1063
WHITE ROCK PRODUCTS CORP., *pg.* 266, *pg.* 1355

2087 - Flavoring Extracts & Flavoring Syrups, NEC

CHR. HANSEN, *pg.* 847, *pg.* 1873
THE COCA-COLA COMPANY, *pg.* 240, *pg.* 493
COCA-COLA REFRESHMENTS USA, INC., *pg.* 247, *pg.* 500
DAVID MICHAEL & CO. INC., *pg.* 852, *pg.* 1563
DOUBLE-COLA CO.-USA, *pg.* 249, *pg.* 1629
FUCHS NORTH AMERICA., *pg.* 857, *pg.* 774
THE JEL SERT COMPANY, *pg.* 865, *pg.* 668
JOHN B. SANFILIPPO & SON, INC., *pg.* 1024, *pg.* 610
LA CIE MCCORMICK CANADA CO., *pg.* 872, *pg.* 1922
MACANDREWS & FORBES HOLDINGS INC., *pg.* 777, *pg.* 1254
PURECIRCLE USA INC., *pg.* 1861, *pg.* 648
SENSIENT COLORS INC., *pg.* 1180, *pg.* 1003
SENSIENT FLAVORS INC., *pg.* 895, *pg.* 690
SENSIENT TECHNOLOGIES CORPORATION, *pg.* 895, *pg.* 1881
SORBEE INTERNATIONAL, LLC, *pg.* 1862, *pg.* 1570
UNGERER & COMPANY, *pg.* 524, *pg.* 1079
UNILEVER UNITED STATES, INC., *pg.* 904, *pg.* 1061
VENTURA COASTAL LLC, *pg.* 908, *pg.* 301
VIRGINIA DARE EXTRACT CO., INC., *pg.* 908, *pg.* 1147
WILD FLAVORS, INC., *pg.* 910, *pg.* 728

2091 - Canned & Cured Fish & Seafoods

BUMBLE BEE FOODS LLC, *pg.* 842, *pg.* 201
CONSOLIDATED CATFISH COMPANIES, LLC, *pg.* 850, *pg.* 969
THE GORTON GROUP, *pg.* 859, *pg.* 823
ICICLE SEAFOODS, INC., *pg.* 864, *pg.* 1836
OCEAN BEAUTY SEAFOODS, INC., *pg.* 1028, *pg.* 1838
PETER PAN SEAFOODS, INC., *pg.* 889, *pg.* 1838
SEA WATCH INTERNATIONAL, LTD., *pg.* 895, *pg.* 769
STARKIST FOODS INC., *pg.* 898, *pg.* 1581
UNISEA FOODS, INC., *pg.* 906, *pg.* 1829
VITA FOOD PRODUCTS, INC., *pg.* 909, *pg.* 595

2092 - Prepared Fresh or Frozen Fish & Seafoods

AMERICAN SEAFOODS, LP, *pg.* 837, *pg.* 1833
BON SECOUR FISHERIES INC., *pg.* 841, *pg.* 5
CONSOLIDATED CATFISH COMPANIES, LLC, *pg.* 850, *pg.* 969
GEORGE WESTON LIMITED, *pg.* 858, *pg.* 1938
THE GORTON GROUP, *pg.* 859, *pg.* 823
HIGH LINER FOODS, *pg.* 862, *pg.* 1796
HIGH LINER FOODS (USA) INCORPORATED, *pg.* 862, *pg.* 816
ICICLE SEAFOODS, INC., *pg.* 864, *pg.* 1836
OCEAN BEAUTY SEAFOODS, INC., *pg.* 1028, *pg.* 1838
PAMLICO PACKING COMPANY INCORPORATED, *pg.* 888, *pg.* 1374
PETER PAN SEAFOODS, INC., *pg.* 889, *pg.* 1838
PHILLIPS FOODS INC., *pg.* 1030, *pg.* 758
RICH PRODUCTS CORPORATION, *pg.* 892, *pg.* 1150
SEA WATCH INTERNATIONAL, LTD., *pg.* 895, *pg.* 769
TABATCHNICK FINE FOODS, INC., *pg.* 900, *pg.* 1122
TRIDENT SEAFOODS CORPORATION, *pg.* 902, *pg.* 1842
UNISEA FOODS, INC., *pg.* 906, *pg.* 1829

2095 - Roasted Coffee

4C FOODS CORPORATION, *pg.* 835, *pg.* 1145
CELESTIAL SEASONINGS, INC., *pg.* 846, *pg.* 310

First page reference indicates Business Class Edition
Second page reference indicates Geographic Edition

COFFEE HOLDING CO., INC., *pg.* 849, *pg.* 1343
COMMUNITY COFFEE COMPANY LLC, *pg.* 849, *pg.* 741
DUNKIN' BRANDS GROUP, INC., *pg.* 1727, *pg.* 810
EIGHT O'CLOCK COFFEE, *pg.* 250, *pg.* 1086
FARMER BROTHERS COMPANY, *pg.* 855, *pg.* 293
FRESHBREW COFFEE, LLC, *pg.* 857, *pg.* 1706
THE HAIN CELESTIAL GROUP, INC., *pg.* 860, *pg.* 1172
HAWAII COFFEE COMPANY, *pg.* 861, *pg.* 543
KEURIG GREEN MOUNTAIN, INC., *pg.* 868, *pg.* 1768
KRAFT FOODS GEVALIA, *pg.* 253, *pg.* 387
MASSIMO ZANETTI BEVERAGE USA, *pg.* 876, *pg.* 1808
MELITTA USA INC., *pg.* 781, *pg.* 416
MONDELEZ INTERNATIONAL, INC., *pg.* 878, *pg.* 601
NESTLE USA - BEVERAGE DIVISION, INC., *pg.* 883, *pg.* 96
PEET'S COFFEE & TEA, INC., *pg.* 1029, *pg.* 85
PEPSI BEVERAGES COMPANY, *pg.* 258, *pg.* 1342
R.C. BIGELOW, INC., *pg.* 891, *pg.* 348
REDCO FOODS, INC., *pg.* 891, *pg.* 1174
REILY FOODS COMPANY, *pg.* 891, *pg.* 747
SEATTLE COFFEE COMPANY, *pg.* 265, *pg.* 1839
STARBUCKS CORPORATION, *pg.* 897, *pg.* 1840
SWISS WATER DECAFFEINATED COFFEE INCOME FUND, *pg.* 900, *pg.* 1907
TAZO TEA COMPANY, *pg.* 1036, *pg.* 1507
TETLEY USA INC., *pg.* 901, *pg.* 1095
VAN HOUTTE, INC., *pg.* 908, *pg.* 1957

2096 - Potato Chips, Corn Chips & Similar Snacks

ATKINS NUTRITIONALS, INC., *pg.* 1498, *pg.* 316
AZTECA FOODS, INCORPORATED, *pg.* 838, *pg.* 566
BARREL O'FUN SNACK FOODS CO., *pg.* 1850, *pg.* 952
CAMPBELL SOUP COMPANY, *pg.* 844, *pg.* 1048
CAPE COD POTATO CHIP COMPANY, *pg.* 845, *pg.* 826
CHATTANOOGA BAKERY INC., *pg.* 847, *pg.* 1628
C.J. VITNER CO., *pg.* 848, *pg.* 571
CLIF BAR INC., *pg.* 848, *pg.* 83
CONAGRA FOODS, *pg.* 826, *pg.* 994
COOKIE TREE BAKERIES, *pg.* 1851, *pg.* 1756
DIAMOND FOODS, INC., *pg.* 1851, *pg.* 216
FLOWERS FOODS, INC., *pg.* 855, *pg.* 541
FRITO-LAY NORTH AMERICA, INC., *pg.* 1853, *pg.* 1730
GENERAL MILLS, INC., *pg.* 828, *pg.* 933
GOLDEN ENTERPRISES INC., *pg.* 1854, *pg.* 2
GOLDEN FLAKE SNACK FOODS, INC., *pg.* 1854, *pg.* 3
THE HAIN CELESTIAL GROUP, INC., *pg.* 860, *pg.* 1172
HERR FOODS INC., *pg.* 861, *pg.* 1557
INVENTURE FOODS, INC., *pg.* 1023, *pg.* 17
J&J SNACK FOODS CORPORATION, *pg.* 865, *pg.* 1107
JOHN B. SANFILIPPO & SON, INC., *pg.* 1024, *pg.* 610
THE KRAFT HEINZ COMPANY, *pg.* 870, *pg.* 1577
LATE JULY SNACKS LLC, *pg.* 1026, *pg.* 784
LEADING BRANDS, INC., *pg.* 1026, *pg.* 1911
MANISCHEWITZ COMPANY, *pg.* 875, *pg.* 1097
MCKEE FOODS CORPORATION, *pg.* 1860, *pg.* 1630
MIKE-SELL'S POTATO CHIP COMPANY, *pg.* 1860, *pg.* 1446
MONDELEZ INTERNATIONAL, INC., *pg.* 878, *pg.* 601
NEW YORK FRIES, *pg.* 1028, *pg.* 1941
NEWLY WEDS FOODS, INC., *pg.* 886, *pg.* 585
NONNI'S FOOD COMPANY INC., *pg.* 886, *pg.* 1490
NORSE DAIRY SYSTEMS LLC, *pg.* 886, *pg.* 1442
NORTH DAKOTA MILL & ELEVATOR ASSOCIATION, *pg.* 833, *pg.* 1398
OLD DUTCH FOODS, INC., *pg.* 888, *pg.* 956
PEPPERIDGE FARM, INC., *pg.* 888, *pg.* 363
PEPSICO, INC., *pg.* 259, *pg.* 1327
PINNACLE FOODS GROUP LLC, *pg.* 889, *pg.* 1104
THE POPCORN FACTORY, *pg.* 1861, *pg.* 625
RIVIANA FOODS INC., *pg.* 892, *pg.* 1713
RUDOLPH FOODS COMPANY, *pg.* 892, *pg.* 1458
SABRA DIPPING COMPANY LLC, *pg.* 893, *pg.* 1686
SCHULZE & BURCH BISCUIT COMPANY, *pg.* 894, *pg.* 589
SNYDER'S-LANCE, INC., *pg.* 896, *pg.* 1368
SNYDER'S OF HANOVER, INC., *pg.* 1862, *pg.* 1536
SORBEE INTERNATIONAL, LLC, *pg.* 1862, *pg.* 1570
STACY'S PITA CHIP COMPANY, INC., *pg.* 1034, *pg.* 842
SUN-RYPE PRODUCTS LTD., *pg.* 899, *pg.* 1908
TASTY BAKING COMPANY, *pg.* 1862, *pg.* 1571
TIM HORTONS, INC., *pg.* 1754, *pg.* 1930
UNILEVER UNITED STATES, INC., *pg.* 904, *pg.* 1061
UTZ QUALITY FOODS, INC., *pg.* 907, *pg.* 1536
VOORTMAN COOKIES LIMITED, *pg.* 1863, *pg.* 1919
ZAPP'S POTATO CHIPS, INC., *pg.* 1864, *pg.* 743

2097 - Manufactured Ice

BON SECOUR FISHERIES INC., *pg.* 841, *pg.* 5
UNITED STATES COLD STORAGE, INC., *pg.* 61, *pg.* 1051

2098 - Macaroni, Spaghetti, Vermicelli & Noodles

4C FOODS CORPORATION, *pg.* 835, *pg.* 1145
ABBOTT NUTRITION, *pg.* 1485, *pg.* 1437
ACH FOOD COMPANIES, INC., *pg.* 835, *pg.* 1631
ADAMS EXTRACT & SPICE LLC, *pg.* 835, *pg.* 1698
ADVANCED FOOD PRODUCTS LLC, *pg.* 835, *pg.* 1555
ADVANCEPIERRE FOODS, INC., *pg.* 1714, *pg.* 1409
ALLIED OLD ENGLISH, INC., *pg.* 836, *pg.* 1110
AMERICAN ITALIAN PASTA COMPANY, *pg.* 837, *pg.* 980
AMERICAN LICORICE CO. INC., *pg.* 1850, *pg.* 692
AMERICAN POP CORN COMPANY, *pg.* 825, *pg.* 712
AMY'S KITCHEN, INC., *pg.* 837, *pg.* 276
ANNIE'S INC., *pg.* 1760, *pg.* 45
ATEECO, INC., *pg.* 838, *pg.* 1586
ATKINS NUTRITIONALS, INC., *pg.* 1498, *pg.* 316
AZTECA FOODS, INCORPORATED, *pg.* 838, *pg.* 566
B&G FOODS, INC., *pg.* 838, *pg.* 1102
BARILLA AMERICA, INC., *pg.* 839, *pg.* 555
BASIC AMERICAN FOODS, INC., *pg.* 839, *pg.* 303
BESTSWEET INC., *pg.* 1851, *pg.* 1383
BIG BOY RESTAURANTS INTERNATIONAL, LLC, *pg.* 1716, *pg.* 912
BKI, *pg.* 52, *pg.* 1621
BOULDER BRANDS, INC., *pg.* 1016, *pg.* 310
BROWN & HALEY, *pg.* 1851, *pg.* 1820
BRUCE FOODS CORPORATION, *pg.* 842, *pg.* 743
CAL-MAINE FOODS, INC., *pg.* 843, *pg.* 969
CAMPBELL SOUP COMPANY, *pg.* 844, *pg.* 1048
CARGILL, INC., *pg.* 845, *pg.* 965
CARGILL SALT, *pg.* 846, *pg.* 926
THE C.F. SAUER COMPANY, *pg.* 847, *pg.* 1801
CHATTANOOGA BAKERY INC., *pg.* 847, *pg.* 1628
CHR. HANSEN, *pg.* 847, *pg.* 1873
COLONNA BROS., INC., *pg.* 849, *pg.* 1098
CONAGRA FOODS, INC., *pg.* 826, *pg.* 1014
COOPERATIVE REGIONS OF ORGANIC PRODUCER POOLS, *pg.* 850, *pg.* 1864
CP KELCO, *pg.* 1154, *pg.* 201
CUISINE SOLUTIONS, INC., *pg.* 850, *pg.* 1770
CUSTOM CULINARY, INC., *pg.* 851, *pg.* 644
DEAN FOODS COMPANY, *pg.* 852, *pg.* 1679
DOLE FOOD COMPANY, INC., *pg.* 853, *pg.* 306
DOLE FRESH VEGETABLES, *pg.* 854, *pg.* 198
DUTCH GOLD HONEY INC., *pg.* 854, *pg.* 1546
EDEN FOODS INC., *pg.* 1019, *pg.* 875
EXXON MOBIL CORPORATION, *pg.* 977, *pg.* 1718
FARMER BROTHERS COMPANY, *pg.* 855, *pg.* 293
F.B. WASHBURN CANDY CORP., *pg.* 1852, *pg.* 803
FERRARA CANDY CO., *pg.* 1852, *pg.* 612
FERRERO U.S.A., INC., *pg.* 1852, *pg.* 1121
FONA INTERNATIONAL INC., *pg.* 855, *pg.* 613
FRONTIER NATURAL PRODUCTS CO-OP, *pg.* 509, *pg.* 710
FUCHS NORTH AMERICA., *pg.* 857, *pg.* 774
GENERAL MILLS, INC., *pg.* 828, *pg.* 933
GILSTER-MARY LEE CORPORATION, *pg.* 858, *pg.* 563
GIORDANO'S ENTERPRISES, INC., *pg.* 1729, *pg.* 575
GOLD PURE FOOD PRODUCTS CO., INC., *pg.* 858, *pg.* 1166
GOLD STAR CHILI INC., *pg.* 1021, *pg.* 1414
GOLDEN ENTERPRISES INC., *pg.* 1854, *pg.* 2
GRECIAN DELIGHT FOODS INC., *pg.* 859, *pg.* 610
GRIFFIN FOOD COMPANY, *pg.* 860, *pg.* 1484
GRIFFITH LABORATORIES, INC., *pg.* 860, *pg.* 552
GRIFFITH LABORATORIES LTD., *pg.* 860, *pg.* 1934
GRINDMASTER CORPORATION, *pg.* 56, *pg.* 734
GRUMA CORPORATION, *pg.* 860, *pg.* 951
GRUMA CORPORATION, *pg.* 860, *pg.* 1720
GUITTARD CHOCOLATE COMPANY, *pg.* 1855, *pg.* 55
THE HAIN CELESTIAL GROUP, INC., *pg.* 860, *pg.* 1172
HERR FOODS INC., *pg.* 861, *pg.* 1557
THE HERSHEY CO., *pg.* 1855, *pg.* 1538
HORMEL FOODS CORPORATION, *pg.* 863, *pg.* 915
HULMAN & COMPANY, *pg.* 864, *pg.* 698
IDAHO FRESH-PAK INC., *pg.* 864, *pg.* 549
INGREDION, *pg.* 864, *pg.* 669
JELLY BELLY CANDY COMPANY, *pg.* 1857, *pg.* 86
THE J.M. SMUCKER COMPANY, *pg.* 865, *pg.* 1468
JOHN B. SANFILIPPO & SON, INC., *pg.* 1024, *pg.* 610
JOYVA CORPORATION, *pg.* 1857, *pg.* 1146
JUST BORN, INC., *pg.* 1857, *pg.* 1516
KOSTO FOOD PRODUCTS CO., *pg.* 869, *pg.* 665
KOZY SHACK INC., *pg.* 869, *pg.* 1167
KRAFT CANADA INC., *pg.* 869, *pg.* 1939
THE KRAFT HEINZ COMPANY, *pg.* 870, *pg.* 1577
LA CIE MCCORMICK CANADA CO., *pg.* 872, *pg.* 1922
LANCASTER COLONY CORPORATION, *pg.* 873, *pg.* 1441
LEON'S FINE FOODS, INC., *pg.* 874, *pg.* 1727
LIBERTY ORCHARDS CO., INC., *pg.* 1857, *pg.* 1819
LITTLE LADY FOODS, INC., *pg.* 875, *pg.* 611
MACANDREWS & FORBES HOLDINGS INC., *pg.* 777, *pg.* 1254
MAFCO WORLDWIDE CORPORATION, *pg.* 1858, *pg.* 1049
MALLET & COMPANY, INC., *pg.* 875, *pg.* 1521
MAPLE LEAF FOODS INC., *pg.* 875, *pg.* 1927
MARS, INCORPORATED, *pg.* 1858, *pg.* 1792
MASSIMO ZANETTI BEVERAGE USA, *pg.* 876, *pg.* 1808
THE MASTERSON COMPANY, INC., *pg.* 876, *pg.* 1877
MCCORMICK & COMPANY, INCORPORATED, *pg.* 1027, *pg.* 779
MCILHENNY COMPANY, *pg.* 876, *pg.* 741
MEAD JOHNSON NUTRITION COMPANY, *pg.* 1561, *pg.* 615
MEGAMEX FOODS, LLC, *pg.* 833, *pg.* 66
MICHAEL FOODS, INC., *pg.* 877, *pg.* 949
MILLER'S HONEY COMPANY, *pg.* 1860, *pg.* 1759
MIZKAN AMERICAS, INC., *pg.* 877, *pg.* 634
MODERN PRODUCTS, INC., *pg.* 1568, *pg.* 1871
MONDELEZ NORTH AMERICA, *pg.* 881, *pg.* 1054
MONTEREY GOURMET FOODS, INC., *pg.* 881, *pg.* 94
MORGAN FOODS, INC., *pg.* 881, *pg.* 673
NATIONAL FRUIT PRODUCT COMPANY, INC., *pg.* 882, *pg.* 1811
NESTLE HEALTHCARE NUTRITION, *pg.* 1572, *pg.* 941
NEW ENGLAND CONFECTIONERY COMPANY INC., *pg.* 1860, *pg.* 842
NEW WORLD PASTA COMPANY, *pg.* 885, *pg.* 1537
OLD DUTCH FOODS, INC., *pg.* 888, *pg.* 956
PARADISE, INC., *pg.* 888, *pg.* 458
PARMALAT CANADA INC., *pg.* 888, *pg.* 1941
PERFETTI VAN MELLE USA, INC., *pg.* 1860, *pg.* 727
PINNACLE FOODS GROUP LLC, *pg.* 889, *pg.* 1104
THE PROCTER & GAMBLE COMPANY, *pg.* 1129, *pg.* 1418
PROMOTION IN MOTION, INC., *pg.* 1861, *pg.* 1052
REED'S, INC., *pg.* 264, *pg.* 139
REIDCO, INC., *pg.* 891, *pg.* 675
REILY FOODS COMPANY, *pg.* 891, *pg.* 747
RESER'S FINE FOODS INC., *pg.* 1032, *pg.* 1496
RUDOLPH FOODS COMPANY, *pg.* 892, *pg.* 1458
RUIZ FOOD PRODUCTS, INC., *pg.* 893, *pg.* 77
SENSIENT TECHNOLOGIES CORPORATION, *pg.* 895, *pg.* 1881
SLIM-FAST FOODS COMPANY, *pg.* 896, *pg.* 1061
SMARTIES CANDY COMPANY, *pg.* 1861, *pg.* 1127
SMUCKER FOODS OF CANADA CO., *pg.* 896, *pg.* 1924
SOKOL & COMPANY, *pg.* 1862, *pg.* 598
SORBEE INTERNATIONAL, LLC, *pg.* 1862, *pg.* 1570
SPANGLER CANDY COMPANY, *pg.* 1862, *pg.* 1407
SPECTRUM ORGANIC PRODUCTS, INC., *pg.* 1596, *pg.* 182
SUBCO FOODS, INC., *pg.* 899, *pg.* 668
SUN-RYPE PRODUCTS LTD., *pg.* 899, *pg.* 1908
SUNOPTA INGREDIENTS, INC., *pg.* 900, *pg.* 942
SWEET CANDY COMPANY, *pg.* 1862, *pg.* 1761
T. MARZETTI COMPANY, *pg.* 900, *pg.* 1444
TOOTSIE ROLL INDUSTRIES, INC., *pg.* 1863, *pg.* 591
THE TOPPS COMPANY, INC., *pg.* 588, *pg.* 1302
TOTAL NUTRACEUTICAL SOLUTIONS, INC., *pg.* 1603, *pg.* 1509
TRADER VIC'S GOURMET PRODUCTS, INC., *pg.* 901, *pg.* 69
TYSON FOODS, INC., *pg.* 902, *pg.* 35
UNILEVER CANADA INC., *pg.* 903, *pg.* 1946
UNILEVER UNITED STATES, INC., *pg.* 904, *pg.* 1061
WATKINS INCORPORATED, *pg.* 909, *pg.* 967
WESTIN FOODS, INC., *pg.* 909, *pg.* 1019
WHITFIELD FOODS, INC., *pg.* 910, *pg.* 8
WILD FLAVORS, INC., *pg.* 910, *pg.* 728
WM. WRIGLEY JR. COMPANY, *pg.* 1863, *pg.* 596
ZATARAIN'S BRANDS, INC., *pg.* 911, *pg.* 744

2099 - Food Preparations, NEC

ABITA BREWING COMPANY, *pg.* 237, *pg.* 741
ADAMS EXTRACT & SPICE LLC, *pg.* 835, *pg.* 1698
AMERICAN ITALIAN PASTA COMPANY, *pg.* 837, *pg.* 980
ANHEUSER-BUSCH COMPANIES, LLC, *pg.* 237, *pg.* 991
AZTECA FOODS, INCORPORATED, *pg.* 838, *pg.* 566
B&G FOODS, INC., *pg.* 838, *pg.* 1102
BASIC AMERICAN FOODS, INC., *pg.* 839, *pg.* 303
BIG ROCK BREWERY INCOME TRUST, *pg.* 239, *pg.* 1902
BJ'S RESTAURANTS, INC., *pg.* 1716, *pg.* 104
BKI, *pg.* 52, *pg.* 1621
THE BOSTON BEER COMPANY, INC., *pg.* 239, *pg.* 790
THE BROOKLYN BREWERY, *pg.* 239, *pg.* 1145
CAPITAL BREWERY CO., INC., *pg.* 239, *pg.* 1872
THE C.F. SAUER COMPANY, *pg.* 847, *pg.* 1801
CHR. HANSEN, *pg.* 847, *pg.* 1873
COASTAL EXTREME BREWING COMPANY, *pg.* 240, *pg.* 1602
THE COCA-COLA COMPANY, *pg.* 240, *pg.* 493
COCA-COLA REFRESHMENTS USA, INC., *pg.* 247, *pg.* 500
COLONNA BROS., INC., *pg.* 849, *pg.* 1098
CONAGRA FOODS, *pg.* 826, *pg.* 994
CONAGRA FOODS, INC., *pg.* 826, *pg.* 1014
CRAFT BREWERS ALLIANCE, INC, *pg.* 247, *pg.* 1502
CUSTOM CULINARY, INC., *pg.* 851, *pg.* 644
DAVID MICHAEL & CO. INC., *pg.* 852, *pg.* 1563
DESCHUTES BREWERY INC., *pg.* 248, *pg.* 1496
D.G. YUENGLING & SON INCORPORATED, *pg.* 248, *pg.* 1582
DOGFISH HEAD CRAFT BREWERY, INC., *pg.* 249, *pg.* 388
DOUBLE-COLA CO.-USA, *pg.* 249, *pg.* 1629
DOW CHEMICAL, *pg.* 1156, *pg.* 1563
EXXON MOBIL CORPORATION, *pg.* 977, *pg.* 1718
FARMER BROTHERS COMPANY, *pg.* 855, *pg.* 293
FLYING DOG BREWERY, *pg.* 251, *pg.* 319
FRONTIER NATURAL PRODUCTS CO-OP, *pg.* 509, *pg.* 710
FUCHS NORTH AMERICA., *pg.* 857, *pg.* 774
GENERAL MILLS, INC., *pg.* 828, *pg.* 933
THE GREAT WESTERN BREWING COMPANY, *pg.* 251, *pg.* 1962
GRIFFITH LABORATORIES LTD., *pg.* 860, *pg.* 1934
GRUMA CORPORATION, *pg.* 860, *pg.* 951
GRUMA CORPORATION, *pg.* 860, *pg.* 1720
THE HAIN CELESTIAL GROUP, INC., *pg.* 860, *pg.* 1172
IDAHO FRESH-PAK INC., *pg.* 864, *pg.* 549
INVENTURE FOODS, INC., *pg.* 1023, *pg.* 17
JACOB LEINENKUGEL BREWING CO., *pg.* 253, *pg.* 1856
THE JEL SERT COMPANY, *pg.* 865, *pg.* 668
JOHN B. SANFILIPPO & SON, INC., *pg.* 1024, *pg.* 610
KANAN ENTERPRISES, INC., *pg.* 1857, *pg.* 1473
KNOUSE FOODS COOPERATIVE INC., *pg.* 869, *pg.* 1558
THE KRAFT HEINZ COMPANY, *pg.* 870, *pg.* 1577
LA CIE MCCORMICK CANADA CO., *pg.* 872, *pg.* 1922
LABATT BREWING COMPANY LIMITED, *pg.* 253, *pg.* 1939
LIFEWAY FOODS, INC., *pg.* 874, *pg.* 634
THE LION BREWERY, INC., *pg.* 254, *pg.* 1594
MACANDREWS & FORBES HOLDINGS INC., *pg.* 777, *pg.* 1254
MARNIER-LAPOSTOLLE INC., *pg.* 1966, *pg.* 1256
MEGAMEX FOODS, LLC, *pg.* 833, *pg.* 66
MENDOCINO BREWING COMPANY, *pg.* 254, *pg.* 298
MICHAEL FOODS, INC., *pg.* 877, *pg.* 949
MILLERCOORS, *pg.* 254, *pg.* 1877
MILLERCOORS LLC, *pg.* 255, *pg.* 582
MOLSON COORS BREWING COMPANY, *pg.* 256, *pg.* 321
MOLSON COORS CANADA INC., *pg.* 256, *pg.* 1955
MOLSON INC., *pg.* 256, *pg.* 1955
MONTEREY MUSHROOMS, INC., *pg.* 881, *pg.* 305
NEW BELGIUM BREWING COMPANY, INC., *pg.* 258, *pg.* 328
NEW ENGLAND BREWING COMPANY, *pg.* 1967, *pg.* 386
PABST BREWING COMPANY, *pg.* 258, *pg.* 137
PARMALAT CANADA INC., *pg.* 888, *pg.* 1941
PHILIP MORRIS USA INC., *pg.* 1894, *pg.* 1803
PLUM ORGANICS, *pg.* 890, *pg.* 85
PURECIRCLE USA INC., *pg.* 1861, *pg.* 648
REIDCO, INC., *pg.* 891, *pg.* 675
SENSIENT COLORS INC., *pg.* 1180, *pg.* 1003
SENSIENT FLAVORS INC., *pg.* 895, *pg.* 690
SENSIENT TECHNOLOGIES CORPORATION, *pg.* 895, *pg.* 1881
SIERRA NEVADA BREWING CO., *pg.* 265, *pg.* 65
SLEEMAN BREWERIES, LTD., *pg.* 265, *pg.* 1920
SORBEE INTERNATIONAL, LLC, *pg.* 1862, *pg.* 1570
SPRECHER BREWING COMPANY, *pg.* 265, *pg.* 1858
SUMMIT BREWING CO., *pg.* 265, *pg.* 963
SUNSWEET GROWERS, INC., *pg.* 900, *pg.* 309
TOOTSIE ROLL INDUSTRIES, INC., *pg.* 1863, *pg.* 591
TYSON FOODS, INC., *pg.* 902, *pg.* 35
UNGERER & COMPANY, *pg.* 524, *pg.* 1079
UNILEVER UNITED STATES, INC., *pg.* 904, *pg.* 1061
UNITED STATES BEVERAGE LLC, *pg.* 266, *pg.* 379
VENTURA COASTAL LLC, *pg.* 908, *pg.* 301
VIRGINIA DARE EXTRACT CO., INC., *pg.* 908, *pg.* 1147
WATKINS INCORPORATED, *pg.* 909, *pg.* 967
WILD FLAVORS, INC., *pg.* 910, *pg.* 728
WM. WRIGLEY JR. COMPANY, *pg.* 1863, *pg.* 596

2111 - Cigarettes

ALTADIS USA, INC., *pg.* 1893, *pg.* 423
ALTRIA GROUP, INC., *pg.* 1893, *pg.* 1800
PHILIP MORRIS INTERNATIONAL INC., *pg.* 1894, *pg.* 1282
PHILIP MORRIS USA INC., *pg.* 1894, *pg.* 1803
REYNOLDS AMERICAN INC., *pg.* 1894, *pg.* 1395
R.J. REYNOLDS TOBACCO CO., *pg.* 1895, *pg.* 1395
ROCK CREEK PHARMACEUTICALS, INC., *pg.* 1895, *pg.* 466
VECTOR GROUP LTD., *pg.* 1895, *pg.* 447
ZIPPO MANUFACTURING COMPANY, INC., *pg.* 1895, *pg.* 1518

2141 - Tobacco Stemming & Redrying

ALTADIS USA, INC., *pg.* 1893, *pg.* 423
AMERICAN SNUFF COMPANY, *pg.* 1893, *pg.* 1641
AVANTI CIGAR CORPORATION, *pg.* 1894, *pg.* 1527
FINCK CIGAR CO., *pg.* 1894, *pg.* 1740
LIVEWORLD, INC., *pg.* 1264, *pg.* 246
REYNOLDS AMERICAN INC., *pg.* 1894, *pg.* 1395
R.J. REYNOLDS TOBACCO CO., *pg.* 1895, *pg.* 1395
ROCK CREEK PHARMACEUTICALS, INC., *pg.* 1895, *pg.* 466
SWISHER INTERNATIONAL, INC., *pg.* 1895, *pg.* 345
U.S. SMOKELESS TOBACCO COMPANY, *pg.* 1895, *pg.* 1804

2211 - Broad Woven Fabric Mills, Cotton

ALBANY INTERNATIONAL CORP., *pg.* 691, *pg.* 1038
ASSOCIATED FABRICS CORPORATION, *pg.* 691, *pg.* 1064
BELTON INDUSTRIES, INC., *pg.* 691, *pg.* 1612
THE BEN SILVER CORPORATION, *pg.* 38, *pg.* 1613
BLOCKSOM & COMPANY, *pg.* 691, *pg.* 694
CARPENTER CO., *pg.* 920, *pg.* 1801
CARTER'S, INC., *pg.* 21, *pg.* 491
COLUMBIA SPORTSWEAR COMPANY, *pg.* 1830, *pg.* 1501
COPLAND FABRICS, INC., *pg.* 692, *pg.* 1359
COUNTRY CURTAINS RETAIL INC., *pg.* 921, *pg.* 827
CROWN CRAFTS INFANT PRODUCTS, INC., *pg.* 922, *pg.* 68
CYTEC INDUSTRIES, INC., *pg.* 1155, *pg.* 1131
DELTA APPAREL, INC., *pg.* 39, *pg.* 1617
DURA UNDERCUSHIONS LTD., *pg.* 923, *pg.* 1954
F. SCHUMACHER & CO., *pg.* 925, *pg.* 1230
FAB INDUSTRIES CORP., *pg.* 692, *pg.* 1162
FEDERAL FOAM TECHNOLOGIES INC., *pg.* 692, *pg.* 1884
FENNER DRIVES, *pg.* 1336, *pg.* 1551
G-III APPAREL GROUP, LTD., *pg.* 41, *pg.* 1233
GALEY & LORD LLC, *pg.* 693, *pg.* 1621
GILDAN ACTIVEWEAR INC., *pg.* 1835, *pg.* 1955
GLEN RAVEN, INC., *pg.* 693, *pg.* 1373
GREENWOOD MILLS, INC., *pg.* 693, *pg.* 1619
GUILFORD PERFORMANCE TEXTILES, *pg.* 693, *pg.* 1393
HAMPSHIRE GROUP LIMITED, *pg.* 25, *pg.* 1237
HANESBRANDS INC., *pg.* 26, *pg.* 1394
HARODITE INDUSTRIES, INC., *pg.* 693, *pg.* 847
HOLLISTON LLC, *pg.* 1460, *pg.* 1630
INTERNATIONAL FIBER CORP., *pg.* 865, *pg.* 1317
INTERNATIONAL TEXTILE GROUP, INC., *pg.* 696, *pg.* 1374
JPS INDUSTRIES, INC., *pg.* 1169, *pg.* 1617
KNOLL, INC., *pg.* 425, *pg.* 1527
LEIGH FIBERS, INC., *pg.* 93, *pg.* 1623
MILLIKEN & COMPANY, *pg.* 696, *pg.* 1622
MOMENTUM TEXTILES INC., *pg.* 697, *pg.* 114
MOUNT VERNON MILLS, INC., *pg.* 697, *pg.* 1620
NAME MAKER INC., *pg.* 697, *pg.* 515
NATIONAL SPINNING COMPANY, INC., *pg.* 697, *pg.* 1265
THE PENN COMPANIES, *pg.* 10, *pg.* 1568
PLAINS COTTON COOPERATIVE ASSOCIATION, *pg.* 697, *pg.* 1726
POLARTEC LLC, *pg.* 697, *pg.* 827
POLYMER GROUP, INC., *pg.* 698, *pg.* 1368
THE PORT CANVAS COMPANY, *pg.* 11, *pg.* 750
RALPH PUCCI INTERNATIONAL LTD., *pg.* 940, *pg.* 1285
RHODE ISLAND TEXTILE COMPANY, INC., *pg.* 698, *pg.* 1605
RUSSELL BRANDS LLC, *pg.* 698, *pg.* 726
SAFER PRINTS INC., *pg.* 32, *pg.* 1098
SCALAMANDRE, INC., *pg.* 941, *pg.* 1058
SPRINGS GLOBAL, INC., *pg.* 698, *pg.* 1616
TRIMTEX CO. INC., *pg.* 699, *pg.* 1055
VELCRO USA INC., *pg.* 699, *pg.* 1036
VICTOR INNOVATIVE TEXTILES, *pg.* 699, *pg.* 819
VOLCOM, INC., *pg.* 1847, *pg.* 71
XERIUM TECHNOLOGIES, INC., *pg.* 1703, *pg.* 1389

2241 - Narrow Fabrics & other Smallwares Mills: Cotton, Wool, Silk & Man-Made Fiber

ASSOCIATED FABRICS CORPORATION, *pg.* 691, *pg.* 1064
BELTON INDUSTRIES, INC., *pg.* 691, *pg.* 1612
THE BEN SILVER CORPORATION, *pg.* 38, *pg.* 1613
BLOCKSOM & COMPANY, *pg.* 691, *pg.* 694
CARTER'S, INC., *pg.* 21, *pg.* 491
COLUMBIA SPORTSWEAR COMPANY, *pg.* 1830, *pg.* 1501
COUNTRY CURTAINS RETAIL INC., *pg.* 921, *pg.* 827
CROWN CRAFTS INFANT PRODUCTS, INC., *pg.* 922, *pg.* 68
CYTEC INDUSTRIES, INC., *pg.* 1155, *pg.* 1131
DELTA APPAREL, INC., *pg.* 39, *pg.* 1617
DURA UNDERCUSHIONS LTD., *pg.* 923, *pg.* 1954
FEDERAL FOAM TECHNOLOGIES INC., *pg.* 692, *pg.* 1884
FENNER DRIVES, *pg.* 1336, *pg.* 1551
G-III APPAREL GROUP, LTD., *pg.* 41, *pg.* 1233
GILDAN ACTIVEWEAR INC., *pg.* 1835, *pg.* 1955
GUILFORD PERFORMANCE TEXTILES, *pg.* 693, *pg.* 1393
HAMPSHIRE GROUP LIMITED, *pg.* 25, *pg.* 1237
HANESBRANDS INC., *pg.* 26, *pg.* 1394
HOLLISTON LLC, *pg.* 1460, *pg.* 1630
INTERNATIONAL FIBER CORP., *pg.* 865, *pg.* 1317
INTERNATIONAL TEXTILE GROUP, INC., *pg.* 696, *pg.* 1374
KNOLL, INC., *pg.* 425, *pg.* 1527
LEIGH FIBERS, INC., *pg.* 93, *pg.* 1623
NAME MAKER INC., *pg.* 697, *pg.* 515
NATIONAL SPINNING COMPANY, INC., *pg.* 697, *pg.* 1265
THE PENN COMPANIES, *pg.* 10, *pg.* 1568
RALPH PUCCI INTERNATIONAL LTD., *pg.* 940, *pg.* 1285
RHODE ISLAND TEXTILE COMPANY, INC., *pg.* 698, *pg.* 1605
RUSSELL BRANDS LLC, *pg.* 698, *pg.* 726
SAFER PRINTS INC., *pg.* 32, *pg.* 1098
SCALAMANDRE, INC., *pg.* 941, *pg.* 1058
TRIMTEX CO. INC., *pg.* 699, *pg.* 1055
VELCRO USA INC., *pg.* 699, *pg.* 1036
VICTOR INNOVATIVE TEXTILES, *pg.* 699, *pg.* 819

2251 - Women's Full-Length & Knee-Length Hosiery, Except Socks

HAMPSHIRE GROUP LIMITED, *pg.* 25, *pg.* 1237
KAYSER-ROTH CORPORATION, *pg.* 28, *pg.* 1374
RELIABLE OF MILWAUKEE, *pg.* 698, *pg.* 1879
WIGWAM MILLS, INC., *pg.* 15, *pg.* 1894

2252 - Hosiery, NEC

HAMPSHIRE GROUP LIMITED, *pg.* 25, *pg.* 1237
KAYSER-ROTH CORPORATION, *pg.* 28, *pg.* 1374
RELIABLE OF MILWAUKEE, *pg.* 698, *pg.* 1879
WIGWAM MILLS, INC., *pg.* 15, *pg.* 1894

2253 - Knit Outerwear Mills

First page reference indicates Business Class Edition
Second page reference indicates Geographic Edition

CARTER'S, INC., *pg.* 21, *pg.* 491
CHEROKEE GLOBAL BRANDS, *pg.* 21, *pg.* 278
FAB INDUSTRIES CORP., *pg.* 692, *pg.* 1162
FRUIT OF THE LOOM, INC., *pg.* 41, *pg.* 725
GILDAN ACTIVEWEAR INC., *pg.* 1835, *pg.* 1955
GUESS?, INC., *pg.* 25, *pg.* 132
HAMPSHIRE GROUP LIMITED, *pg.* 25, *pg.* 1237
HERITAGE SPORTSWEAR, LLC, *pg.* 26, *pg.* 1455
KELLWOOD COMPANY, *pg.* 28, *pg.* 975
PARIS ACCESSORIES, INC., *pg.* 10, *pg.* 1276
RELIABLE OF MILWAUKEE, *pg.* 698, *pg.* 1879
RUSSELL BRANDS LLC, *pg.* 698, *pg.* 726
ST. JOHN KNITS INTERNATIONAL, INC., *pg.* 33, *pg.* 116
WIGWAM MILLS, INC., *pg.* 15, *pg.* 1894

2254 - Knit Underwear & Nightwear Mills

ALGY TRIMMING COMPANY, *pg.* 17, *pg.* 429
CARTER'S, INC., *pg.* 21, *pg.* 491
CHEROKEE GLOBAL BRANDS, *pg.* 21, *pg.* 278
CUPID FOUNDATIONS, INC., *pg.* 22, *pg.* 1220
FAB INDUSTRIES CORP., *pg.* 692, *pg.* 1162
FRUIT OF THE LOOM, INC., *pg.* 41, *pg.* 725
GARAN, INCORPORATED, *pg.* 24, *pg.* 1234
GILDAN ACTIVEWEAR INC., *pg.* 1835, *pg.* 1955
GLAMORISE FOUNDATIONS, INC., *pg.* 25, *pg.* 1235
GUESS?, INC., *pg.* 25, *pg.* 132
HAMPSHIRE GROUP LIMITED, *pg.* 25, *pg.* 1237
HANESBRANDS INC., *pg.* 26, *pg.* 1394
HERITAGE SPORTSWEAR, LLC, *pg.* 26, *pg.* 1455
INDERA MILLS COMPANY, *pg.* 26, *pg.* 1396
JOCKEY INTERNATIONAL, INC., *pg.* 27, *pg.* 1861
KELLWOOD COMPANY, *pg.* 28, *pg.* 975
KIYONNA CLOTHING, INC., *pg.* 28, *pg.* 42
NAUTICA APPAREL, INC., *pg.* 45, *pg.* 1265
PARIS ACCESSORIES, INC., *pg.* 10, *pg.* 1276
PLAYTEX APPAREL, INC., *pg.* 31, *pg.* 1395
RELIABLE OF MILWAUKEE, *pg.* 698, *pg.* 1879
RUSSELL BRANDS LLC, *pg.* 698, *pg.* 726
SPANX INC., *pg.* 32, *pg.* 520
ST. JOHN KNITS INTERNATIONAL, INC., *pg.* 33, *pg.* 116
TOMMY HILFIGER USA, *pg.* 48, *pg.* 1302
V.F. CORPORATION, *pg.* 34, *pg.* 1376
WACOAL AMERICA INC., *pg.* 35, *pg.* 1312
WEISSMAN THEATRICAL SUPPLY, INC., *pg.* 35, *pg.* 1004
WIGWAM MILLS, INC., *pg.* 15, *pg.* 1894

2257 - Circular Knit Fabric Mills

DRAPER KNITTING CO., INC., *pg.* 692, *pg.* 810
TRIMTEX CO. INC., *pg.* 699, *pg.* 1055

2258 - Lace & Warp Knit Fabric Mills

FAB INDUSTRIES CORP., *pg.* 692, *pg.* 1162
GILDAN ACTIVEWEAR INC., *pg.* 1835, *pg.* 1955
GUILFORD PERFORMANCE TEXTILES, *pg.* 693, *pg.* 1393
HOLLANDER SLEEP PRODUCTS, *pg.* 927, *pg.* 411
LYDALL, INC., *pg.* 1357, *pg.* 354
WESTCHESTER LACE & TEXTILES INC., *pg.* 699, *pg.* 1098

2261 - Finishers of Broad Woven Fabrics of Cotton

ASSOCIATED FABRICS CORPORATION, *pg.* 691, *pg.* 1064
BEMIDJI WOOLEN MILLS, *pg.* 38, *pg.* 916
CALICO CORNERS, *pg.* 691, *pg.* 1543
CONRAD INDUSTRIES, INC., *pg.* 691, *pg.* 1392
CRUISIN' USA/BOWLINGSHIRT.COM., *pg.* 1765, *pg.* 995
DELTA APPAREL, INC., *pg.* 39, *pg.* 1617
DESIGNTEX GROUP INC., *pg.* 692, *pg.* 1223
EBSCO INDUSTRIES, INC., *pg.* 1638, *pg.* 2
F. SCHUMACHER & CO., *pg.* 925, *pg.* 1230
GALEY & LORD LLC, *pg.* 693, *pg.* 1621
HARODITE INDUSTRIES, INC., *pg.* 693, *pg.* 847
INTERNATIONAL TEXTILE GROUP, INC., *pg.* 696, *pg.* 1374
ITOCHU INTERNATIONAL INC., *pg.* 1351, *pg.* 1245
J. ROBERT SCOTT INC., *pg.* 930, *pg.* 105
JANLYNN CORPORATION, *pg.* 696, *pg.* 815
JHB INTERNATIONAL, INC., *pg.* 696, *pg.* 320
KRAVET FABRICS INC., *pg.* 932, *pg.* 1142
THE LIFE IS GOOD COMPANY, *pg.* 44, *pg.* 1034
LION BROTHERS COMPANY, INC., *pg.* 696, *pg.* 774
MOMENTUM TEXTILES INC., *pg.* 697, *pg.* 114
ONTARIO WALL COVERINGS, *pg.* 940, *pg.* 1941
THE PENN COMPANIES, *pg.* 10, *pg.* 1568
PRYM CONSUMER USA, *pg.* 698, *pg.* 1622
STARK CARPET CORPORATION, *pg.* 944, *pg.* 1296
WOODEN SHIPS OF HOBOKEN, *pg.* 35, *pg.* 1315

2273 - Carpets & Rugs

BACOVA GUILD, LTD., *pg.* 916, *pg.* 1779
BEAULIEU GROUP, LLC, *pg.* 917, *pg.* 529
COURISTAN INC., *pg.* 921, *pg.* 1067
THE DIXIE GROUP, INC., *pg.* 692, *pg.* 1629
INTERFACE FLOORING SYSTEMS INC., *pg.* 929, *pg.* 534
INTERFACE, INC., *pg.* 695, *pg.* 512
MOHAWK HOME, *pg.* 935, *pg.* 541
MOHAWK INDUSTRIES, INC., *pg.* 935, *pg.* 527
RALPH PUCCI INTERNATIONAL LTD., *pg.* 940, *pg.* 1285
SHAW INDUSTRIES GROUP, INC., *pg.* 942, *pg.* 530
SONOCO PRODUCTS COMPANY, *pg.* 1469, *pg.* 1619
SPRINGS GLOBAL, INC., *pg.* 698, *pg.* 1616

2281 - Yarn Spinning Mills: Cotton, Man-Made Fibers, Silk, Wool, Mohair & Animal Fibers

ASSOCIATED FABRICS CORPORATION, *pg.* 691, *pg.* 1064
BEAULIEU GROUP, LLC, *pg.* 917, *pg.* 529
BELTON INDUSTRIES, INC., *pg.* 691, *pg.* 1612
THE BEN SILVER CORPORATION, *pg.* 38, *pg.* 1613
BLOCKSOM & COMPANY, *pg.* 691, *pg.* 694
COUNTRY CURTAINS RETAIL INC., *pg.* 921, *pg.* 827
CROWN CRAFTS INFANT PRODUCTS, INC., *pg.* 922, *pg.* 68
CYTEC INDUSTRIES, INC., *pg.* 1155, *pg.* 1131
DELTA APPAREL, INC., *pg.* 39, *pg.* 1617
THE DIXIE GROUP, INC., *pg.* 692, *pg.* 1629
DURA UNDERCUSHIONS LTD., *pg.* 923, *pg.* 1954
FEDERAL FOAM TECHNOLOGIES INC., *pg.* 692, *pg.* 1884
FENNER DRIVES, *pg.* 1336, *pg.* 1551
G-III APPAREL GROUP, LTD., *pg.* 41, *pg.* 1233
GLEN RAVEN, INC., *pg.* 693, *pg.* 1373
GUILFORD PERFORMANCE TEXTILES, *pg.* 693, *pg.* 1393
HAMPSHIRE GROUP LIMITED, *pg.* 25, *pg.* 1237
HANESBRANDS INC., *pg.* 26, *pg.* 1394
HOLLISTON LLC, *pg.* 1460, *pg.* 1630
INTERNATIONAL FIBER CORP., *pg.* 865, *pg.* 1317
INTERNATIONAL TEXTILE GROUP, INC., *pg.* 696, *pg.* 1374
KNOLL, INC., *pg.* 425, *pg.* 1527
LEIGH FIBERS, INC., *pg.* 93, *pg.* 1623
MOUNT VERNON MILLS, INC., *pg.* 697, *pg.* 1620
NAME MAKER INC., *pg.* 697, *pg.* 515
NATIONAL SPINNING COMPANY, INC., *pg.* 697, *pg.* 1265
PARKDALE MILLS INC., *pg.* 697, *pg.* 1373
THE PENN COMPANIES, *pg.* 10, *pg.* 1568
RALPH PUCCI INTERNATIONAL LTD., *pg.* 940, *pg.* 1285
RUSSELL BRANDS LLC, *pg.* 698, *pg.* 726
SAFER PRINTS INC., *pg.* 32, *pg.* 1098
VICTOR INNOVATIVE TEXTILES, *pg.* 699, *pg.* 819

2284 - Thread Mills

ASSOCIATED FABRICS CORPORATION, *pg.* 691, *pg.* 1064
BELTON INDUSTRIES, INC., *pg.* 691, *pg.* 1612
THE BEN SILVER CORPORATION, *pg.* 38, *pg.* 1613
BLOCKSOM & COMPANY, *pg.* 691, *pg.* 694
COUNTRY CURTAINS RETAIL INC., *pg.* 921, *pg.* 827
CROWN CRAFTS INFANT PRODUCTS, INC., *pg.* 922, *pg.* 68
CYTEC INDUSTRIES, INC., *pg.* 1155, *pg.* 1131
DELTA APPAREL, INC., *pg.* 39, *pg.* 1617
DURA UNDERCUSHIONS LTD., *pg.* 923, *pg.* 1954
FEDERAL FOAM TECHNOLOGIES INC., *pg.* 692, *pg.* 1884
FENNER DRIVES, *pg.* 1336, *pg.* 1551
G-III APPAREL GROUP, LTD., *pg.* 41, *pg.* 1233
GUILFORD PERFORMANCE TEXTILES, *pg.* 693, *pg.* 1393
HAMPSHIRE GROUP LIMITED, *pg.* 25, *pg.* 1237
HANESBRANDS INC., *pg.* 26, *pg.* 1394
HOLLISTON LLC, *pg.* 1460, *pg.* 1630
INTERNATIONAL FIBER CORP., *pg.* 865, *pg.* 1317
INTERNATIONAL TEXTILE GROUP, INC., *pg.* 696, *pg.* 1374
KNOLL, INC., *pg.* 425, *pg.* 1527
LEIGH FIBERS, INC., *pg.* 93, *pg.* 1623
MAKE IT COATS, *pg.* 696, *pg.* 1367
NAME MAKER INC., *pg.* 697, *pg.* 515
NATIONAL SPINNING COMPANY, INC., *pg.* 697, *pg.* 1265
THE PENN COMPANIES, *pg.* 10, *pg.* 1568
RALPH PUCCI INTERNATIONAL LTD., *pg.* 940, *pg.* 1285
RUSSELL BRANDS LLC, *pg.* 698, *pg.* 726
SAFER PRINTS INC., *pg.* 32, *pg.* 1098
VICTOR INNOVATIVE TEXTILES, *pg.* 699, *pg.* 819

2295 - Coated Fabrics, Not Rubberized

ALPHA ASSOCIATES, INC., *pg.* 691, *pg.* 1078
HERCULITE PRODUCTS, INC., *pg.* 694, *pg.* 1529
HOLLISTON LLC, *pg.* 1460, *pg.* 1630
OMNOVA SOLUTIONS INC, *pg.* 1176, *pg.* 1453
OXFORD INDUSTRIES, INC., *pg.* 30, *pg.* 517
SCHNELLER, INC., *pg.* 234, *pg.* 1456
SUPERIOR UNIFORM GROUP, INC., *pg.* 33, *pg.* 468
SWANK, INC., *pg.* 13, *pg.* 1297
UNIROYAL ENGINEERED PRODUCTS, *pg.* 699, *pg.* 467

2296 - Tire Cord & Fabric

INVISTA B.V., *pg.* 1168, *pg.* 723
PIRELLI TIRE NORTH AMERICA, *pg.* 1887, *pg.* 539

2297 - Nonwoven Fabrics

CRANE & CO., INC., *pg.* 1456, *pg.* 816
DRAPER KNITTING CO., INC., *pg.* 692, *pg.* 810
FREUDENBERG NONWOVENS LIMITED PARTNERSHIP, *pg.* 693, *pg.* 1371
JASON INDUSTRIES, INC., *pg.* 208, *pg.* 1875
POLYMER GROUP, INC., *pg.* 698, *pg.* 1368

2298 - Cordage & Twine

ASHAWAY LINE & TWINE MFG. CO., *pg.* 1826, *pg.* 1600
CARRON NET COMPANY, INC., *pg.* 1830, *pg.* 1896
CORTLAND LINE COMPANY, *pg.* 1831, *pg.* 1155
RHODE ISLAND TEXTILE COMPANY, INC., *pg.* 698, *pg.* 1605
SAMSON ROPE TECHNOLOGIES, *pg.* 1468, *pg.* 1820

2299 - Textile Goods, NEC

AERO SYSTEMS ENGINEERING INC., *pg.* 223, *pg.* 959
ALGAS-SDI, *pg.* 1311, *pg.* 1831
AMERICAN FELT & FILTER COMPANY, *pg.* 1312, *pg.* 1184
ASSOCIATED FABRICS CORPORATION, *pg.* 691, *pg.* 1064
AUTOMATION DEVICES, INC., *pg.* 1315, *pg.* 1532
BACOVA GUILD, LTD., *pg.* 916, *pg.* 1779
BELTON INDUSTRIES, INC., *pg.* 691, *pg.* 1612
BEMIDJI WOOLEN MILLS, *pg.* 38, *pg.* 916
THE BEN SILVER CORPORATION, *pg.* 38, *pg.* 1613
BLOCKSOM & COMPANY, *pg.* 691, *pg.* 694
BRIGHT OF AMERICA, INC., *pg.* 1121, *pg.* 1851
CALICO CORNERS, *pg.* 691, *pg.* 1543
CARTER'S, INC., *pg.* 21, *pg.* 491
CC INDUSTRIES, INC., *pg.* 920, *pg.* 569
CHEROKEE GLOBAL BRANDS, *pg.* 21, *pg.* 278
CLAYTON INDUSTRIES CO., *pg.* 1323, *pg.* 66
COHESANT, INC., *pg.* 1154, *pg.* 1405
COUNTRY CURTAINS RETAIL INC., *pg.* 921, *pg.* 827
CROLL-REYNOLDS COMPANY, INC., *pg.* 1326, *pg.* 1103
CROSCILL, INC., *pg.* 1122, *pg.* 1220
CROWN CRAFTS INFANT PRODUCTS, INC., *pg.* 922, *pg.* 68
CYTEC INDUSTRIES, INC., *pg.* 1155, *pg.* 1131
DANAHER MOTION, *pg.* 1327, *pg.* 1593
DELTA APPAREL, INC., *pg.* 39, *pg.* 1617
DESIGNTEX GROUP INC., *pg.* 692, *pg.* 1223
DONALDSON COMPANY, INC., *pg.* 1329, *pg.* 917
DRAPER KNITTING CO., INC., *pg.* 692, *pg.* 810
DUFF-NORTON, *pg.* 204, *pg.* 1365
DURA UNDERCUSHIONS LTD., *pg.* 923, *pg.* 1954
EAGLE TECHNOLOGIES GROUP, *pg.* 1331, *pg.* 874
EAST CHICAGO MACHINE TOOL CORPORATION, *pg.* 1331, *pg.* 676

THE ENTWISTLE CO., *pg.* 637, *pg.* 826
F. SCHUMACHER & CO., *pg.* 925, *pg.* 1230
FAB INDUSTRIES CORP., *pg.* 692, *pg.* 1162
FEDERAL FOAM TECHNOLOGIES INC., *pg.* 692, *pg.* 1884
FENNER DRIVES, *pg.* 1336, *pg.* 1551
FIKE CORPORATION, *pg.* 1047, *pg.* 973
FLEXFAB HORIZONS INTERNATIONAL, LLC, *pg.* 1072, *pg.* 891
FRUIT OF THE LOOM, INC., *pg.* 41, *pg.* 725
G-III APPAREL GROUP, LTD., *pg.* 41, *pg.* 1233
GALEY & LORD LLC, *pg.* 693, *pg.* 1621
GILDAN ACTIVEWEAR INC., *pg.* 1835, *pg.* 1955
GUESS?, INC., *pg.* 25, *pg.* 132
GUILFORD PERFORMANCE TEXTILES, *pg.* 693, *pg.* 1393
HAMPSHIRE GROUP LIMITED, *pg.* 25, *pg.* 1237
HANESBRANDS INC., *pg.* 26, *pg.* 1394
HARRIS WASTE MANAGEMENT GROUP, INC., *pg.* 1345, *pg.* 526
HAYWARD POOL PRODUCTS, *pg.* 1049, *pg.* 1067
HERITAGE LACE INC., *pg.* 694, *pg.* 711
HERITAGE SPORTSWEAR, LLC, *pg.* 26, *pg.* 1455
HOLLANDER SLEEP PRODUCTS, *pg.* 927, *pg.* 411
HOLLISTON LLC, *pg.* 1460, *pg.* 1630
HOLMATRO, INC., *pg.* 1346, *pg.* 771
ILLINOIS TOOL WORKS INC., *pg.* 1348, *pg.* 614
INGERSOLL-RAND COMPANY, *pg.* 1349, *pg.* 1370
INTERNATIONAL FIBER CORP., *pg.* 865, *pg.* 1317
INTERNATIONAL TEXTILE GROUP, INC., *pg.* 696, *pg.* 1374
ITOCHU INTERNATIONAL INC., *pg.* 1351, *pg.* 1245
J. ROBERT SCOTT INC., *pg.* 930, *pg.* 105
JHB INTERNATIONAL, INC., *pg.* 696, *pg.* 320
JOCKEY INTERNATIONAL, INC., *pg.* 27, *pg.* 1861
KAYDON CORPORATION, *pg.* 1352, *pg.* 866
KAYSER-ROTH CORPORATION, *pg.* 28, *pg.* 1374
KELLWOOD COMPANY, *pg.* 28, *pg.* 975
KIDDE FIRE FIGHTING, *pg.* 1170, *pg.* 1531
KNOLL, INC., *pg.* 425, *pg.* 1527
KRAVET FABRICS INC., *pg.* 932, *pg.* 1142
LEIGH FIBERS, INC., *pg.* 93, *pg.* 1623
LINDE GAS LLC, *pg.* 1356, *pg.* 1095
LYDALL, INC., *pg.* 1357, *pg.* 354
MAKE IT COATS, *pg.* 696, *pg.* 1367
MCNEIL & NRM INC., *pg.* 1360, *pg.* 1402
MOMENTUM TEXTILES INC., *pg.* 697, *pg.* 114
NAME MAKER INC., *pg.* 697, *pg.* 515
NATIONAL BULK EQUIPMENT, INC., *pg.* 1479, *pg.* 892
NATIONAL METAL FINISHING CORP., *pg.* 1363, *pg.* 1084
NATIONAL SPINNING COMPANY, INC., *pg.* 697, *pg.* 1265
NORDSON CORPORATION, *pg.* 1365, *pg.* 1480
PALL CORPORATION, *pg.* 232, *pg.* 1323
PANGBORN CORPORATION, *pg.* 1367, *pg.* 532
PARIS ACCESSORIES, INC., *pg.* 10, *pg.* 1276
PENFLEX, INC., *pg.* 104, *pg.* 1534
THE PENN COMPANIES, *pg.* 10, *pg.* 1568
PMFG, INC., *pg.* 1369, *pg.* 1685
POLYMER GROUP, INC., *pg.* 698, *pg.* 1368
PRAXAIR, INC., *pg.* 1178, *pg.* 344
PRYM CONSUMER USA, *pg.* 698, *pg.* 1622
RALPH PUCCI INTERNATIONAL LTD., *pg.* 940, *pg.* 1285
REEL-O-MATIC, INC., *pg.* 1371, *pg.* 1487
RELIABLE AUTOMATIC SPRINKLER CO., INC., *pg.* 1137, *pg.* 1158
RELIABLE OF MILWAUKEE, *pg.* 698, *pg.* 1879
RUSSELL BRANDS LLC, *pg.* 698, *pg.* 726
SAFER PRINTS INC., *pg.* 32, *pg.* 1098
SERFILCO, LTD., *pg.* 1375, *pg.* 641
SHEEX, INC., *pg.* 1138, *pg.* 1614
ST. JOHN KNITS INTERNATIONAL, INC., *pg.* 33, *pg.* 116
STARK CARPET CORPORATION, *pg.* 944, *pg.* 1296
SULLAIR CORPORATION, *pg.* 1379, *pg.* 695
TENNANT COMPANY, *pg.* 1381, *pg.* 944
THERMOTRON INDUSTRIES, *pg.* 235, *pg.* 892
TRANSACT TECHNOLOGIES INCORPORATED, *pg.* 484, *pg.* 351
TRICO MFG. CORP., *pg.* 219, *pg.* 1886
TRIMTEX CO. INC., *pg.* 699, *pg.* 1055
VICTOR INNOVATIVE TEXTILES, *pg.* 699, *pg.* 819
WESTCHESTER LACE & TEXTILES INC., *pg.* 699, *pg.* 1098
WESTERN STATES MACHINE COMPANY, *pg.* 1388, *pg.* 1455
WIGWAM MILLS, INC., *pg.* 15, *pg.* 1894
WILLIAMS PATENT CRUSHER & PULVERIZER CO., INC., *pg.* 1389, *pg.* 1005
WOODEN SHIPS OF HOBOKEN, *pg.* 35, *pg.* 1315

2311 - Men's & Boys' Suits, Coats & Overcoats

AEROPOSTALE, INC., *pg.* 17, *pg.* 1188
AMERICAN APPAREL, INC., *pg.* 18, *pg.* 126
ANN INC., *pg.* 18, *pg.* 1195
ARMY & NAVY DEPARTMENT STORES LIMITED, *pg.* 38, *pg.* 1909
BAKERS FOOTWEAR GROUP, INC., *pg.* 19, *pg.* 992
BOB'S STORES CORP., *pg.* 38, *pg.* 354
BOSTON PROPER, INC., *pg.* 20, *pg.* 410
BURLINGTON COAT FACTORY, *pg.* 1764, *pg.* 1047
CAVENDER'S STORES LIMITED, *pg.* 39, *pg.* 1748
CHAMPS SPORTS, *pg.* 1806, *pg.* 414
CHARLOTTE RUSSE, INC., *pg.* 21, *pg.* 201
CITI TRENDS INC., *pg.* 22, *pg.* 539
CITY SPORTS, *pg.* 1830, *pg.* 860
CLAIRE'S STORES, INC., *pg.* 1764, *pg.* 617
DICK'S SPORTING GOODS, INC., *pg.* 1832, *pg.* 1524
DOROTHY GRANT LTD., *pg.* 24, *pg.* 1910
THE DRESS BARN, INC., *pg.* 1767, *pg.* 1343
DRYSDALES INC., *pg.* 1767, *pg.* 1489
EDDIE BAUER, INC., *pg.* 40, *pg.* 1814
THE FINISH LINE, INC., *pg.* 1769, *pg.* 686
FISHMAN & TOBIN, INC., *pg.* 41, *pg.* 1582
FLYNN & O'HARA UNIFORMS INC., *pg.* 1769, *pg.* 1564
G-III APPAREL GROUP, LTD., *pg.* 41, *pg.* 1233
THE GAP, INC., *pg.* 1770, *pg.* 218
GORDMANS STORES INC., *pg.* 1771, *pg.* 1016
GROUPE BIKINI VILLAGE INC., *pg.* 25, *pg.* 1950
HANNA ANDERSSON CORPORATION, *pg.* 1772, *pg.* 1503
HAPPY JACK INC., *pg.* 1476, *pg.* 1390
HARDWICK CLOTHES INC., *pg.* 42, *pg.* 1630
HAT WORLD, INC., *pg.* 42, *pg.* 686
HICKEY-FREEMAN CO., INC., *pg.* 42, *pg.* 1336
HOT TOPIC, INC., *pg.* 42, *pg.* 67
J. CREW GROUP, INC., *pg.* 1773, *pg.* 1245
KATE SPADE LLC, *pg.* 28, *pg.* 1248
L BRANDS, INC., *pg.* 1776, *pg.* 1441
LADY GRACE STORES INC., *pg.* 28, *pg.* 861
LANDS' END, INC., *pg.* 1776, *pg.* 1857
LAURA ASHLEY, INC., *pg.* 29, *pg.* 1615
LOEHMANN'S HOLDINGS INC., *pg.* 29, *pg.* 1144
LORD & TAYLOR LLC, *pg.* 1777, *pg.* 1252
LULULEMON ATHLETICA INC., *pg.* 44, *pg.* 1911
LUSKEY'S WESTERN STORES, INC., *pg.* 44, *pg.* 1657
MARKS WORK WEARHOUSE LTD., *pg.* 44, *pg.* 1903
MAYER/BERKSHIRE CORPORATION, *pg.* 29, *pg.* 1129
THE MEN'S WEARHOUSE, INC., *pg.* 44, *pg.* 1711
MICHAEL KORS (USA), INC., *pg.* 29, *pg.* 1260
OXFORD INDUSTRIES, INC., *pg.* 30, *pg.* 517
PACIFIC SUNWEAR OF CALIFORNIA, INC., *pg.* 1781, *pg.* 43
PENDLETON WOOLEN MILLS, INC., *pg.* 697, *pg.* 1505
PVH CORP., *pg.* 46, *pg.* 1283
RECREATIONAL EQUIPMENT, INC., *pg.* 1843, *pg.* 1821
RON JON SURF SHOP OF FLORIDA INC., *pg.* 1844, *pg.* 417
RUE21, INC., *pg.* 32, *pg.* 1591
SCHEELS, *pg.* 47, *pg.* 1397
SCREAMER INC., *pg.* 12, *pg.* 1839
SCRUBS & BEYOND, *pg.* 32, *pg.* 1003
SHEPLERS, INC., *pg.* 1785, *pg.* 724
SOUTHWICK CLOTHING LLC, *pg.* 48, *pg.* 824
SPANX INC., *pg.* 32, *pg.* 520
SPORT CHALET, INC., *pg.* 1846, *pg.* 119
THE SPORTS AUTHORITY, INC., *pg.* 1846, *pg.* 326
STEVEN MADDEN, LTD., *pg.* 1819, *pg.* 1176
SUN PRECAUTIONS, INC., *pg.* 33, *pg.* 1820
TRUE RELIGION BRAND JEANS, *pg.* 49, *pg.* 143
UJENA SWIMWEAR AND FASHIONS, *pg.* 34, *pg.* 163
ULLA POPKEN LTD., *pg.* 1789, *pg.* 771
UNDER ARMOUR, INC., *pg.* 49, *pg.* 759
VERA BRADLEY, INC., *pg.* 15, *pg.* 697
VICTORIA'S SECRET STORES, LLC, *pg.* 1789, *pg.* 1471
WEISSMAN THEATRICAL SUPPLY, INC., *pg.* 35, *pg.* 1004
WEST COAST LEATHER, *pg.* 35, *pg.* 233
THE WET SEAL, LLC, *pg.* 35, *pg.* 88
WOOLRICH, INC., *pg.* 699, *pg.* 1595
ZUMIEZ INC., *pg.* 16, *pg.* 1822

2321 - Men's & Boys' Shirts, Except Work Shirts

AEROPOSTALE, INC., *pg.* 17, *pg.* 1188
AMERICAN APPAREL, INC., *pg.* 18, *pg.* 126
ANN INC., *pg.* 18, *pg.* 1195
ARMY & NAVY DEPARTMENT STORES LIMITED, *pg.* 38, *pg.* 1909
BAKERS FOOTWEAR GROUP, INC., *pg.* 19, *pg.* 992
BOB'S STORES CORP., *pg.* 38, *pg.* 354
BOSTON PROPER, INC., *pg.* 20, *pg.* 410
BURLINGTON COAT FACTORY, *pg.* 1764, *pg.* 1047
CARTER'S, INC., *pg.* 21, *pg.* 491
CAVENDER'S STORES LIMITED, *pg.* 39, *pg.* 1748
CHAMPS SPORTS, *pg.* 1806, *pg.* 414
CHARLOTTE RUSSE, INC., *pg.* 21, *pg.* 201
CITI TRENDS INC., *pg.* 22, *pg.* 539
CITY SPORTS, *pg.* 1830, *pg.* 860
CLAIRE'S STORES, INC., *pg.* 1764, *pg.* 617
DELTA APPAREL, INC., *pg.* 39, *pg.* 1617
DICK'S SPORTING GOODS, INC., *pg.* 1832, *pg.* 1524
DOROTHY GRANT LTD., *pg.* 24, *pg.* 1910
THE DRESS BARN, INC., *pg.* 1767, *pg.* 1343
DRYSDALES INC., *pg.* 1767, *pg.* 1489
EDDIE BAUER, INC., *pg.* 40, *pg.* 1814
ELDER MANUFACTURING COMPANY, INC., *pg.* 40, *pg.* 996
THE FINISH LINE, INC., *pg.* 1769, *pg.* 686
FISHMAN & TOBIN, INC., *pg.* 41, *pg.* 1582
FLYNN & O'HARA UNIFORMS INC., *pg.* 1769, *pg.* 1564
THE GAP, INC., *pg.* 1770, *pg.* 218
GARAN, INCORPORATED, *pg.* 24, *pg.* 1234
GORDMANS STORES INC., *pg.* 1771, *pg.* 1016
GROUPE BIKINI VILLAGE INC., *pg.* 25, *pg.* 1950
HANNA ANDERSSON CORPORATION, *pg.* 1772, *pg.* 1503
HAPPY JACK INC., *pg.* 1476, *pg.* 1390
HAT WORLD, INC., *pg.* 42, *pg.* 686
HOT TOPIC, INC., *pg.* 42, *pg.* 67
J. CREW GROUP, INC., *pg.* 1773, *pg.* 1245
KATE SPADE LLC, *pg.* 28, *pg.* 1248
KELLWOOD COMPANY, *pg.* 28, *pg.* 975
L BRANDS, INC., *pg.* 1776, *pg.* 1441
LADY GRACE STORES INC., *pg.* 28, *pg.* 861
LANDS' END, INC., *pg.* 1776, *pg.* 1857
LAURA ASHLEY, INC., *pg.* 29, *pg.* 1615
LOEHMANN'S HOLDINGS INC., *pg.* 29, *pg.* 1144
LORD & TAYLOR LLC, *pg.* 1777, *pg.* 1252
LULULEMON ATHLETICA INC., *pg.* 44, *pg.* 1911
LUSKEY'S WESTERN STORES, INC., *pg.* 44, *pg.* 1657
MARKS WORK WEARHOUSE LTD., *pg.* 44, *pg.* 1903
MAYER/BERKSHIRE CORPORATION, *pg.* 29, *pg.* 1129
THE MEN'S WEARHOUSE, INC., *pg.* 44, *pg.* 1711
MICHAEL KORS (USA), INC., *pg.* 29, *pg.* 1260
PACIFIC SUNWEAR OF CALIFORNIA, INC., *pg.* 1781, *pg.* 43
PERRY ELLIS INTERNATIONAL, INC., *pg.* 45, *pg.* 445
PVH CORP., *pg.* 46, *pg.* 1283
RALPH LAUREN CORPORATION, *pg.* 46, *pg.* 1284
RECREATIONAL EQUIPMENT, INC., *pg.* 1843, *pg.* 1821
RIVER'S END TRADING COMPANY, *pg.* 47, *pg.* 1867
RON JON SURF SHOP OF FLORIDA INC., *pg.* 1844, *pg.* 417
RUE21, INC., *pg.* 32, *pg.* 1591
SCHEELS, *pg.* 47, *pg.* 1397
SCREAMER INC., *pg.* 12, *pg.* 1839
SCRUBS & BEYOND, *pg.* 32, *pg.* 1003
SHEPLERS, INC., *pg.* 1785, *pg.* 724
SPANX INC., *pg.* 32, *pg.* 520
SPORT CHALET, INC., *pg.* 1846, *pg.* 119
THE SPORTS AUTHORITY, INC., *pg.* 1846, *pg.* 326
STEVEN MADDEN, LTD., *pg.* 1819, *pg.* 1176
SUN PRECAUTIONS, INC., *pg.* 33, *pg.* 1820
SUNRISE BRANDS, LLC, *pg.* 33, *pg.* 140
TOMMY BAHAMA, *pg.* 48, *pg.* 1842
TRUE RELIGION BRAND JEANS, *pg.* 49, *pg.* 143
UJENA SWIMWEAR AND FASHIONS, *pg.* 34, *pg.* 163
ULLA POPKEN LTD., *pg.* 1789, *pg.* 771
UNDER ARMOUR, INC., *pg.* 49, *pg.* 759
VERA BRADLEY, INC., *pg.* 15, *pg.* 697
V.F. CORPORATION, *pg.* 34, *pg.* 1376
VF JEANSWEAR LIMITED PARTNERSHIP, *pg.* 50, *pg.* 1377
VICTORIA'S SECRET STORES, LLC, *pg.* 1789, *pg.* 1471
WEISSMAN THEATRICAL SUPPLY, INC., *pg.* 35, *pg.* 1004
WEST COAST LEATHER, *pg.* 35, *pg.* 233
THE WET SEAL, LLC, *pg.* 35, *pg.* 88
ZUMIEZ INC., *pg.* 16, *pg.* 1822

2322 - Men's & Boys' Underwear & Nightwear

ALGY TRIMMING COMPANY, *pg.* 17, *pg.* 429
CUPID FOUNDATIONS, INC., *pg.* 22, *pg.* 1220
GLAMORISE FOUNDATIONS, INC., *pg.* 25, *pg.* 1235
HANESBRANDS INC., *pg.* 26, *pg.* 1394
INDERA MILLS COMPANY, *pg.* 26, *pg.* 1396
JHANE BARNES, INC., *pg.* 42, *pg.* 1246
JOCKEY INTERNATIONAL, INC., *pg.* 27, *pg.* 1861
KELLWOOD COMPANY, *pg.* 28, *pg.* 975
KIYONNA CLOTHING, INC., *pg.* 28, *pg.* 42
NAUTICA APPAREL, INC., *pg.* 45, *pg.* 1265
PLAYTEX APPAREL, INC., *pg.* 31, *pg.* 1395
PVH CORP., *pg.* 46, *pg.* 1283
SEAN JOHN CLOTHING, INC., *pg.* 48, *pg.* 1290
SPANX INC., *pg.* 32, *pg.* 520
TOMMY HILFIGER USA, *pg.* 48, *pg.* 1302
UNDER ARMOUR, INC., *pg.* 49, *pg.* 759
V.F. CORPORATION, *pg.* 34, *pg.* 1376
WACOAL AMERICA INC., *pg.* 35, *pg.* 1312
WEISSMAN THEATRICAL SUPPLY, INC., *pg.* 35, *pg.* 1004

2323 - Men's & Boys' Neckwear

BEAU TIES LTD., *pg.* 38, *pg.* 1766
COUNTESS MARA, INC., *pg.* 39, *pg.* 1219
PVH CORP., *pg.* 46, *pg.* 1283
PVH NECKWEAR GROUP, *pg.* 46, *pg.* 139
RANDA CORP., *pg.* 47, *pg.* 1285

2325 - Men's & Boys' Trousers & Slacks

CARHARTT, INC., *pg.* 39, *pg.* 875
GUESS?, INC., *pg.* 25, *pg.* 132
HICKEY-FREEMAN CO., INC., *pg.* 42, *pg.* 1336
JORDACHE ENTERPRISES, INC., *pg.* 27, *pg.* 1246
KELLWOOD COMPANY, *pg.* 28, *pg.* 975
LEE JEANS, *pg.* 43, *pg.* 721
LEVI STRAUSS & CO., *pg.* 43, *pg.* 220
OXFORD INDUSTRIES, INC., *pg.* 30, *pg.* 517
PERRY ELLIS INTERNATIONAL, INC., *pg.* 45, *pg.* 445
PVH CORP., *pg.* 46, *pg.* 1283
RALPH LAUREN CORPORATION, *pg.* 46, *pg.* 1284
SOUTHWICK CLOTHING LLC, *pg.* 48, *pg.* 824
STANFIELD'S LIMITED, *pg.* 48, *pg.* 1917
TRUE RELIGION BRAND JEANS, *pg.* 49, *pg.* 143
V.F. CORPORATION, *pg.* 34, *pg.* 1376
VF JEANSWEAR LIMITED PARTNERSHIP, *pg.* 50, *pg.* 1377

2326 - Men's & Boys' Work Clothing

BARCO UNIFORMS, INC., *pg.* 19, *pg.* 94
BLAUER MANUFACTURING COMPANY, INC., *pg.* 20, *pg.* 789
CARHARTT, INC., *pg.* 39, *pg.* 875
CINTAS CORPORATION, *pg.* 372, *pg.* 1411
ELBECO INCORPORATED, *pg.* 40, *pg.* 1584
THE FECHHEIMER BROTHERS COMPANY, *pg.* 41, *pg.* 1412
HAGGAR CORPORATION, *pg.* 41, *pg.* 1682
ICONIX BRAND GROUP, INC., *pg.* 26, *pg.* 1243
KAZOO, INC., *pg.* 43, *pg.* 894
KEY INDUSTRIES, INC., *pg.* 43, *pg.* 714
POINT BLANK SOLUTIONS, INC., *pg.* 1467, *pg.* 460
PVH CORP., *pg.* 46, *pg.* 1283
QUIKSILVER, INC., *pg.* 31, *pg.* 104
RALPH LAUREN CORPORATION, *pg.* 46, *pg.* 1284
RIVERSIDE MANUFACTURING COMPANY, *pg.* 32, *pg.* 536
THE SALK COMPANY, *pg.* 1591, *pg.* 800
SEAN JOHN CLOTHING, INC., *pg.* 48, *pg.* 1290
SUPERIOR UNIFORM GROUP, INC., *pg.* 33, *pg.* 468
TRUE RELIGION BRAND JEANS, *pg.* 49, *pg.* 143
VINEYARD VINES LLC, *pg.* 50, *pg.* 379
WILLIAMSON-DICKIE MANUFACTURING COMPANY, *pg.* 50, *pg.* 1696

2329 - Men's & Boys' Clothing, NEC

ACUSHNET COMPANY, *pg.* 1824, *pg.* 818
A.H. SCHREIBER CO., INC., *pg.* 17, *pg.* 1188
ALGY TRIMMING COMPANY, *pg.* 17, *pg.* 429
ALLESON OF ROCHESTER, INC., *pg.* 37, *pg.* 1333
ALYCE PARIS, *pg.* 18, *pg.* 634
AMERICAN APPAREL, INC., *pg.* 18, *pg.* 126
ASCENA RETAIL GROUP, INC., *pg.* 18, *pg.* 1081
BAD BOY WORLDWIDE ENTERTAINMENT GROUP, *pg.* 270, *pg.* 1199
BARCO UNIFORMS, INC., *pg.* 19, *pg.* 94
BE AEROSPACE, INC., *pg.* 224, *pg.* 478
BEAU TIES LTD., *pg.* 38, *pg.* 1766
BENETTON U.S.A. CORPORATION, *pg.* 19, *pg.* 1202
BLAUER MANUFACTURING COMPANY, INC., *pg.* 20, *pg.* 789
BROOKS SPORTS INC., *pg.* 1805, *pg.* 1818
BUYSEASONS, INC., *pg.* 20, *pg.* 1883
CANNONDALE BICYCLE CORPORATION, *pg.* 1705, *pg.* 1515
CARHARTT, INC., *pg.* 39, *pg.* 875
CARTER'S, INC., *pg.* 21, *pg.* 491
CHAMPION ATHLETICWEAR INC., *pg.* 39, *pg.* 1394
CINTAS CORPORATION, *pg.* 372, *pg.* 1411
COLUMBIA SPORTSWEAR COMPANY, *pg.* 1830, *pg.* 1501
COMMERCIAL VEHICLE GROUP, INC., *pg.* 203, *pg.* 1467
COUNTESS MARA, INC., *pg.* 39, *pg.* 1219
CROWN CRAFTS INFANT PRODUCTS, INC., *pg.* 922, *pg.* 68
CUPID FOUNDATIONS, INC., *pg.* 22, *pg.* 1220
CUSTOMINK, LLC, *pg.* 22, *pg.* 1780
CUTTER & BUCK, INC., *pg.* 39, *pg.* 1835
DANIER LEATHER, INC., *pg.* 22, *pg.* 1937
DELTA APPAREL, INC., *pg.* 39, *pg.* 1617
DOLFIN INTERNATIONAL CORPORATION, *pg.* 23, *pg.* 1553
DOROTHY GRANT LTD., *pg.* 24, *pg.* 1910
DURA UNDERCUSHIONS LTD., *pg.* 923, *pg.* 1954
EL CHARRO LLC, *pg.* 1808, *pg.* 1691
ELBECO INCORPORATED, *pg.* 40, *pg.* 1584
ELDER MANUFACTURING COMPANY, INC., *pg.* 40, *pg.* 996
EMERGENCY MEDICAL SERVICES CORPORATION, *pg.* 1528, *pg.* 331
THE FECHHEIMER BROTHERS COMPANY, *pg.* 41, *pg.* 1412
FISHMAN & TOBIN, INC., *pg.* 41, *pg.* 1582
FLEXSTEEL INDUSTRIES, INC., *pg.* 925, *pg.* 707
FOSSIL GROUP, INC., *pg.* 5, *pg.* 1735
G-III APPAREL GROUP, LTD., *pg.* 41, *pg.* 1233
GARAN, INCORPORATED, *pg.* 24, *pg.* 1234
GEM-DANDY, INC., *pg.* 41, *pg.* 1382
GEORGE GLOVE CO., INC., *pg.* 5, *pg.* 1084
GILDAN ACTIVEWEAR INC., *pg.* 1835, *pg.* 1955
GLAMORISE FOUNDATIONS, INC., *pg.* 25, *pg.* 1235
GUESS?, INC., *pg.* 25, *pg.* 132
HAGGAR CORPORATION, *pg.* 41, *pg.* 1682
HANESBRANDS INC., *pg.* 26, *pg.* 1394
HARDWICK CLOTHES INC., *pg.* 42, *pg.* 1630
HATCO, INC., *pg.* 6, *pg.* 1698
HELLY-HANSEN (US), INC., *pg.* 26, *pg.* 1813
HICKEY-FREEMAN CO., INC., *pg.* 42, *pg.* 1336
HONEYWELL NORTH SAFETY PRODUCTS, *pg.* 42, *pg.* 1600
I. SPIEWAK & SONS, INC., *pg.* 42, *pg.* 1242
ICONIX BRAND GROUP, INC., *pg.* 26, *pg.* 1243
INDERA MILLS COMPANY, *pg.* 26, *pg.* 1396
IZOD, *pg.* 42, *pg.* 1046
JANLYNN CORPORATION, *pg.* 696, *pg.* 815
JHANE BARNES, INC., *pg.* 42, *pg.* 1246
JOCKEY INTERNATIONAL, INC., *pg.* 27, *pg.* 1861
JOHNSON CONTROLS, INC., *pg.* 209, *pg.* 1876
JORDACHE ENTERPRISES, INC., *pg.* 27, *pg.* 1246
KATE SPADE & COMPANY, *pg.* 27, *pg.* 1248
KAZOO, INC., *pg.* 43, *pg.* 894
KELLWOOD COMPANY, *pg.* 28, *pg.* 975
KEY INDUSTRIES, INC., *pg.* 43, *pg.* 714
KIYONNA CLOTHING, INC., *pg.* 28, *pg.* 42
LACROSSE FOOTWEAR, INC., *pg.* 1811, *pg.* 1503
LAKELAND INDUSTRIES, INC., *pg.* 1354, *pg.* 1338
LANDAU UNIFORMS INCORPORATED, *pg.* 28, *pg.* 971
LEAR CORPORATION, *pg.* 229, *pg.* 907
LEE JEANS, *pg.* 43, *pg.* 721
LEHIGH OUTFITTERS, LLC, *pg.* 43, *pg.* 1466
LEVI STRAUSS & CO., *pg.* 43, *pg.* 220
L.L. BEAN, INC., *pg.* 1777, *pg.* 750
LUCKY BRAND DUNGAREES, INC., *pg.* 29, *pg.* 301
MICHAEL KORS (USA), INC., *pg.* 29, *pg.* 1260
MOUNTAIN HARDWEAR, INC., *pg.* 1839, *pg.* 193
NAUTICA APPAREL, INC., *pg.* 45, *pg.* 1265
NEW ERA CAP COMPANY INC., *pg.* 1840, *pg.* 1155
NIKE, INC., *pg.* 1812, *pg.* 1492
THE NORTH FACE, INC., *pg.* 1840, *pg.* 252
OXFORD INDUSTRIES, INC., *pg.* 30, *pg.* 517
PARIS ACCESSORIES, INC., *pg.* 10, *pg.* 1276
PATAGONIA, *pg.* 31, *pg.* 301
PAULA LISHMAN LIMITED, *pg.* 31, *pg.* 1932
PENDLETON WOOLEN MILLS, INC., *pg.* 697, *pg.* 1505
PERFORM GROUP, LLC, *pg.* 31, *pg.* 1597
PERRY ELLIS INTERNATIONAL, INC., *pg.* 45, *pg.* 445
PHOENIX FOOTWEAR GROUP, INC., *pg.* 1815, *pg.* 60
PLAYTEX APPAREL, INC., *pg.* 31, *pg.* 1395
POINT BLANK SOLUTIONS, INC., *pg.* 1467, *pg.* 460
POLARIS INDUSTRIES INC., *pg.* 1709, *pg.* 928
PVH CORP., *pg.* 46, *pg.* 1283
PVH NECKWEAR GROUP, *pg.* 46, *pg.* 139
QUIKSILVER, INC., *pg.* 31, *pg.* 104
RALPH LAUREN CORPORATION, *pg.* 46, *pg.* 1284
RALPH PUCCI INTERNATIONAL LTD., *pg.* 940, *pg.* 1285
RANDA ACCESSORIES, LLC, *pg.* 47, *pg.* 657
RANDA CORP., *pg.* 47, *pg.* 1285
RAWLINGS SPORTING GOODS CO., INC., *pg.* 1843, *pg.* 1002
RECARO NORTH AMERICA, INC., *pg.* 216, *pg.* 869
REFRIGIWEAR, INC., *pg.* 47, *pg.* 529
RIVER'S END TRADING COMPANY, *pg.* 47, *pg.* 1867
RIVERSIDE MANUFACTURING COMPANY, *pg.* 32, *pg.* 536
ROCKY BRANDS, INC., *pg.* 1818, *pg.* 1466
THE SALK COMPANY, *pg.* 1591, *pg.* 800
SEAN JOHN CLOTHING, INC., *pg.* 48, *pg.* 1290
SELLSTROM MANUFACTURING CO., *pg.* 1428, *pg.* 659
SKINNYCORP L.L.C., *pg.* 1280, *pg.* 590
SMARTWOOL, *pg.* 32, *pg.* 335
SOUTHWICK CLOTHING LLC, *pg.* 48, *pg.* 824
SPANX INC., *pg.* 32, *pg.* 520
SPORT HALEY, INC., *pg.* 33, *pg.* 333
STANDARD SAFETY EQUIPMENT CO., *pg.* 1379, *pg.* 632
STANFIELD'S LIMITED, *pg.* 48, *pg.* 1917
STEVEN MADDEN, LTD., *pg.* 1819, *pg.* 1176
SUNRISE BRANDS, LLC, *pg.* 33, *pg.* 140
SUPERIOR UNIFORM GROUP, INC., *pg.* 33, *pg.* 468
SWANK, INC., *pg.* 13, *pg.* 1297
TANDY LEATHER FACTORY, INC., *pg.* 48, *pg.* 1696
THERAPEDIC ASSOCIATES, INC., *pg.* 945, *pg.* 1112
THE TIMBERLAND COMPANY, *pg.* 1821, *pg.* 1039
TOMMY BAHAMA, *pg.* 48, *pg.* 1842
TOMMY HILFIGER USA, *pg.* 48, *pg.* 1302
TOTES ISOTONER CORPORATION, *pg.* 14, *pg.* 1426
TRUE RELIGION BRAND JEANS, *pg.* 49, *pg.* 143
UNDER ARMOUR, INC., *pg.* 49, *pg.* 759
VANS, INC., *pg.* 1821, *pg.* 76
VERA BRADLEY, INC., *pg.* 15, *pg.* 697
V.F. CORPORATION, *pg.* 34, *pg.* 1376
VF IMAGEWEAR, *pg.* 50, *pg.* 476
VF JEANSWEAR LIMITED PARTNERSHIP, *pg.* 50, *pg.* 1377
VINEYARD VINES LLC, *pg.* 50, *pg.* 379
VOLCOM, INC., *pg.* 1847, *pg.* 71
WACOAL AMERICA INC., *pg.* 35, *pg.* 1312
WEISSMAN THEATRICAL SUPPLY, INC., *pg.* 35, *pg.* 1004
WELLS LAMONT CORPORATION, *pg.* 15, *pg.* 638
WILLIAMSON-DICKIE MANUFACTURING COMPANY, *pg.* 50, *pg.* 1696
WOLVERINE WORLD WIDE, INC., *pg.* 1822, *pg.* 905
WOOLRICH, INC., *pg.* 699, *pg.* 1595

2331 - Women's, Misses' & Juniors' Blouses & Shirts

CAPEZIO BALLET MAKERS INC., *pg.* 1805, *pg.* 1125
CARTER'S, INC., *pg.* 21, *pg.* 491
ELDER MANUFACTURING COMPANY, INC., *pg.* 40, *pg.* 996
GARAN, INCORPORATED, *pg.* 24, *pg.* 1234
KATE SPADE & COMPANY, *pg.* 27, *pg.* 1248
KELLWOOD COMPANY, *pg.* 28, *pg.* 975
KIYONNA CLOTHING, INC., *pg.* 28, *pg.* 42
MICHAEL KORS (USA), INC., *pg.* 29, *pg.* 1260
NYDJ APPAREL, LLC, *pg.* 30, *pg.* 302
OXFORD INDUSTRIES, INC., *pg.* 30, *pg.* 517

SUGARTOWN WORLDWIDE INC., pg. 33, pg. 1544
SUNRISE BRANDS, LLC, pg. 33, pg. 140
TORY BURCH LLC, pg. 34, pg. 1302

2335 - Women's, Misses' & Juniors' Dresses

AEROPOSTALE, INC., pg. 17, pg. 1188
ALFRED ANGELO, INC., pg. 17, pg. 1532
ALYCE PARIS, pg. 18, pg. 634
AMERICAN APPAREL, INC., pg. 18, pg. 126
ANN INC., pg. 18, pg. 1195
ARMY & NAVY DEPARTMENT STORES LIMITED, pg. 38, pg. 1909
BAKERS FOOTWEAR GROUP, INC., pg. 19, pg. 992
BOB'S STORES CORP., pg. 38, pg. 354
BOSTON PROPER, INC., pg. 20, pg. 410
BURLINGTON COAT FACTORY, pg. 1764, pg. 1047
CARTER'S, INC., pg. 21, pg. 491
CAVENDER'S STORES LIMITED, pg. 39, pg. 1748
CHAMPS SPORTS, pg. 1806, pg. 414
CHARLOTTE RUSSE, INC., pg. 21, pg. 201
CITI TRENDS INC., pg. 22, pg. 539
CITY SPORTS, pg. 1830, pg. 860
CLAIRE'S STORES, INC., pg. 1764, pg. 617
DICK'S SPORTING GOODS, INC., pg. 1832, pg. 1524
THE DONNA KARAN COMPANY LLC, pg. 23, pg. 1225
DOROTHY GRANT LTD., pg. 24, pg. 1910
THE DRESS BARN, INC., pg. 1767, pg. 1343
DRYSDALES INC., pg. 1767, pg. 1489
EDDIE BAUER, INC., pg. 40, pg. 1814
THE FINISH LINE, INC., pg. 1769, pg. 686
FLYNN & O'HARA UNIFORMS INC., pg. 1769, pg. 1564
THE GAP, INC., pg. 1770, pg. 218
GARAN, INCORPORATED, pg. 24, pg. 1234
GORDMANS STORES INC., pg. 1771, pg. 1016
GROUPE BIKINI VILLAGE INC., pg. 25, pg. 1950
HANNA ANDERSSON CORPORATION, pg. 1772, pg. 1503
HAPPY JACK INC., pg. 1476, pg. 1390
HAT WORLD, INC., pg. 42, pg. 686
HOT TOPIC, INC., pg. 42, pg. 67
J. CREW GROUP, INC., pg. 1773, pg. 1245
JLM COUTURE, INC., pg. 27, pg. 1246
KATE SPADE & COMPANY, pg. 27, pg. 1248
KATE SPADE LLC, pg. 28, pg. 1248
KIYONNA CLOTHING, INC., pg. 28, pg. 42
L BRANDS, INC., pg. 1776, pg. 1441
LADY GRACE STORES INC., pg. 28, pg. 861
LANDS' END, INC., pg. 1776, pg. 1857
LAURA ASHLEY, INC., pg. 29, pg. 1615
LOEHMANN'S HOLDINGS INC., pg. 29, pg. 1144
LORD & TAYLOR LLC, pg. 1777, pg. 1252
LULULEMON ATHLETICA INC., pg. 44, pg. 1911
LUSKEY'S WESTERN STORES, INC., pg. 44, pg. 1657
MARKS WORK WEARHOUSE LTD., pg. 44, pg. 1903
MAYER/BERKSHIRE CORPORATION, pg. 29, pg. 1129
THE MEN'S WEARHOUSE, INC., pg. 44, pg. 1711
MICHAEL KORS (USA), INC., pg. 29, pg. 1260
OSCAR DE LA RENTA LTD., pg. 30, pg. 1274
OXFORD INDUSTRIES, INC., pg. 30, pg. 517
PACIFIC SUNWEAR OF CALIFORNIA, INC., pg. 1781, pg. 43
PRADA U.S.A. CORP., pg. 31, pg. 1283
RECREATIONAL EQUIPMENT, INC., pg. 1843, pg. 1821
RON JON SURF SHOP OF FLORIDA INC., pg. 1844, pg. 417
RUE21, INC., pg. 32, pg. 1591
SCHEELS, pg. 47, pg. 1397
SCREAMER INC., pg. 12, pg. 1839
SCRUBS & BEYOND, pg. 32, pg. 1003
SHEPLERS, INC., pg. 1785, pg. 724
SIONI APPAREL GROUP, pg. 32, pg. 1292
SPANX INC., pg. 32, pg. 520
SPORT CHALET, INC., pg. 1846, pg. 119
THE SPORTS AUTHORITY, INC., pg. 1846, pg. 326
STEVEN MADDEN, LTD., pg. 1819, pg. 1176
SUN PRECAUTIONS, INC., pg. 33, pg. 1820
SUNRISE BRANDS, LLC, pg. 33, pg. 140
TANNER COMPANIES, LP, pg. 34, pg. 1390
TRUE RELIGION BRAND JEANS, pg. 49, pg. 143
UJENA SWIMWEAR AND FASHIONS, pg. 34, pg. 163
ULLA POPKEN LTD., pg. 1789, pg. 771
VERA BRADLEY, INC., pg. 15, pg. 697
VERA WANG BRIDAL HOUSE LTD., pg. 34, pg. 1309
VICTORIA'S SECRET STORES, LLC, pg. 1789, pg. 1471
WEISSMAN THEATRICAL SUPPLY, INC., pg. 35, pg. 1004
WEST COAST LEATHER, pg. 35, pg. 233
THE WET SEAL, LLC, pg. 35, pg. 88
ZUMIEZ INC., pg. 16, pg. 1822

2337 - Women's, Misses' & Juniors' Suits, Skirts & Coats

HAMRICK INC., pg. 41, pg. 1616
KIYONNA CLOTHING, INC., pg. 28, pg. 42
MICHAEL KORS (USA), INC., pg. 29, pg. 1260
NYDJ APPAREL, LLC, pg. 30, pg. 302
PENDLETON WOOLEN MILLS, INC., pg. 697, pg. 1505
TRUE RELIGION BRAND JEANS, pg. 49, pg. 143
WEISSMAN THEATRICAL SUPPLY, INC., pg. 35, pg. 1004

2339 - Women's, Misses' & Juniors' Outerwear, NEC

ACUSHNET COMPANY, pg. 1824, pg. 818
A.H. SCHREIBER CO., INC., pg. 17, pg. 1188
ALFRED ANGELO, INC., pg. 17, pg. 1532
ALGY TRIMMING COMPANY, pg. 17, pg. 429
ALLESON OF ROCHESTER, INC., pg. 37, pg. 1333
ALYCE PARIS, pg. 18, pg. 634
AMERICAN APPAREL, INC., pg. 18, pg. 126
ASCENA RETAIL GROUP, INC., pg. 18, pg. 1081
ATHLETA, pg. 19, pg. 181
ATTITUDES IN DRESSING INC., pg. 19, pg. 1057
BARCO UNIFORMS, INC., pg. 19, pg. 94
BEBE STORES, INC., pg. 19, pg. 49
BENETTON U.S.A. CORPORATION, pg. 19, pg. 1202
BLAUER MANUFACTURING COMPANY, INC., pg. 20, pg. 789
BROOKS SPORTS INC., pg. 1805, pg. 1818
BUYSEASONS, INC., pg. 20, pg. 1883
CAPEZIO BALLET MAKERS INC., pg. 1805, pg. 1125
CARTER'S, INC., pg. 21, pg. 491
CHAMPION ATHLETICWEAR INC., pg. 39, pg. 1394
CHANEL, INC., pg. 503, pg. 1211
COLUMBIA SPORTSWEAR COMPANY, pg. 1830, pg. 1501
CROWN CRAFTS INFANT PRODUCTS, INC., pg. 922, pg. 68
CUPID FOUNDATIONS, INC., pg. 22, pg. 1220
CUSTOMINK, LLC, pg. 22, pg. 1780
CUTTER & BUCK, INC., pg. 39, pg. 1835
DANIER LEATHER, INC., pg. 22, pg. 1937
DELIA'S, INC., pg. 23, pg. 1222
DELTA APPAREL, INC., pg. 39, pg. 1617
DESTINATION MATERNITY CORPORATION, pg. 23, pg. 1563
DOLFIN INTERNATIONAL CORPORATION, pg. 23, pg. 1553
THE DONNA KARAN COMPANY LLC, pg. 23, pg. 1225
DURA UNDERCUSHIONS LTD., pg. 923, pg. 1954
EILEEN FISHER, INC., pg. 24, pg. 1168
EL CHARRO LLC, pg. 1808, pg. 1691
ELDER MANUFACTURING COMPANY, INC., pg. 40, pg. 996
THE FECHHEIMER BROTHERS COMPANY, pg. 41, pg. 1412
FLEXSTEEL INDUSTRIES, INC., pg. 925, pg. 707
FOSSIL GROUP, INC., pg. 5, pg. 1735
G-III APPAREL GROUP, LTD., pg. 41, pg. 1233
GARAN, INCORPORATED, pg. 24, pg. 1234
GEM-DANDY, INC., pg. 41, pg. 1382
GILDAN ACTIVEWEAR INC., pg. 1835, pg. 1955
GLAMORISE FOUNDATIONS, INC., pg. 25, pg. 1235
GUESS?, INC., pg. 25, pg. 132
HAMRICK INC., pg. 41, pg. 1616
HANESBRANDS INC., pg. 26, pg. 1394
HATCO, INC., pg. 6, pg. 1698
HELLY-HANSEN (US), INC., pg. 26, pg. 1813
HONEYWELL NORTH SAFETY PRODUCTS, pg. 42, pg. 1600
ICONIX BRAND GROUP, INC., pg. 26, pg. 1243
INDERA MILLS COMPANY, pg. 26, pg. 1396
IZOD, pg. 42, pg. 1046
JACQUES MORET, INC., pg. 27, pg. 1245
JANLYNN CORPORATION, pg. 696, pg. 815
JLM COUTURE, INC., pg. 27, pg. 1246
JOCKEY INTERNATIONAL, INC., pg. 27, pg. 1861
JORDACHE ENTERPRISES, INC., pg. 27, pg. 1246
JUNONIA LTD., pg. 27, pg. 929
KATE SPADE & COMPANY, pg. 27, pg. 1248
KELLWOOD COMPANY, pg. 28, pg. 975
KIYONNA CLOTHING, INC., pg. 28, pg. 42
LACROSSE FOOTWEAR, INC., pg. 1811, pg. 1503
LAKELAND INDUSTRIES, INC., pg. 1354, pg. 1338
LANDAU UNIFORMS INCORPORATED, pg. 28, pg. 971
LEHIGH OUTFITTERS, LLC, pg. 43, pg. 1466
LEVI STRAUSS & CO., pg. 43, pg. 220
L.L. BEAN, INC., pg. 1777, pg. 750
LOST ARROW CORPORATION, pg. 44, pg. 301
LT APPAREL GROUP, pg. 29, pg. 1254
LUCKY BRAND DUNGAREES, INC., pg. 29, pg. 301
MICHAEL KORS (USA), INC., pg. 29, pg. 1260
MOUNTAIN HARDWEAR, INC., pg. 1839, pg. 193
NAUTICA APPAREL, INC., pg. 45, pg. 1265
NEW ERA CAP COMPANY INC., pg. 1840, pg. 1155
NIKE, INC., pg. 1812, pg. 1492
THE NORTH FACE, INC., pg. 1840, pg. 252
NYDJ APPAREL, LLC, pg. 30, pg. 302
OSCAR DE LA RENTA LTD., pg. 30, pg. 1274
OXFORD INDUSTRIES, INC., pg. 30, pg. 517
PARIS ACCESSORIES, INC., pg. 10, pg. 1276
PATAGONIA, pg. 31, pg. 301
PAULA LISHMAN LIMITED, pg. 31, pg. 1932
PENDLETON WOOLEN MILLS, INC., pg. 697, pg. 1505
PERFORM GROUP, LLC, pg. 31, pg. 1597
PHOENIX FOOTWEAR GROUP, INC., pg. 1815, pg. 60
PLAYTEX APPAREL, INC., pg. 31, pg. 1395
POINT BLANK SOLUTIONS, INC., pg. 1467, pg. 460
PRADA U.S.A. CORP., pg. 31, pg. 1283
PVH CORP., pg. 46, pg. 1283
RALPH LAUREN CORPORATION, pg. 46, pg. 1284
RANDA ACCESSORIES, LLC, pg. 47, pg. 657
RAWLINGS SPORTING GOODS CO., INC., pg. 1843, pg. 1002
REFRIGIWEAR, INC., pg. 47, pg. 529
RIVERSIDE MANUFACTURING COMPANY, pg. 32, pg. 536
ROCKY BRANDS, INC., pg. 1818, pg. 1466
SELLSTROM MANUFACTURING CO., pg. 1428, pg. 659
SIONI APPAREL GROUP, pg. 32, pg. 1292
SKINNYCORP L.L.C., pg. 1280, pg. 590
SMARTWOOL, pg. 32, pg. 335
SPANX INC., pg. 32, pg. 520
SPORT HALEY, INC., pg. 33, pg. 333
ST. JOHN KNITS INTERNATIONAL, INC., pg. 33, pg. 116
STANDARD SAFETY EQUIPMENT CO., pg. 1379, pg. 632
STEVEN MADDEN, LTD., pg. 1819, pg. 1176
SUGARTOWN WORLDWIDE INC., pg. 33, pg. 1544
SUNRISE BRANDS, LLC, pg. 33, pg. 140
SUPERIOR UNIFORM GROUP, INC., pg. 33, pg. 468
SWANK, INC., pg. 13, pg. 1297
TANDY LEATHER FACTORY, INC., pg. 48, pg. 1696
TANNER COMPANIES, LP, pg. 34, pg. 1390
THERAPEDIC ASSOCIATES, INC., pg. 945, pg. 1112
THE TIMBERLAND COMPANY, pg. 1821, pg. 1039
TOMMY HILFIGER USA, pg. 48, pg. 1302
TORY BURCH LLC, pg. 34, pg. 1302
TRUE RELIGION BRAND JEANS, pg. 49, pg. 143
UNDER ARMOUR, INC., pg. 49, pg. 759
VARSITY BRANDS, INC., pg. 1847, pg. 1647
VERA BRADLEY, INC., pg. 15, pg. 697
VERA WANG BRIDAL HOUSE LTD., pg. 34, pg. 1309
V.F. CORPORATION, pg. 34, pg. 1376
VF IMAGEWEAR, pg. 50, pg. 476
VOLCOM, INC., pg. 1847, pg. 71
WACOAL AMERICA INC., pg. 35, pg. 1312
WEISSMAN THEATRICAL SUPPLY, INC., pg. 35, pg. 1004

2341 - Women's, Misses', Children's & Infants' Underwear & Nightwear

ACUSHNET COMPANY, pg. 1824, pg. 818
ALGY TRIMMING COMPANY, pg. 17, pg. 429
ALYCE PARIS, pg. 18, pg. 634
AMERICAN APPAREL, INC., pg. 18, pg. 126
ASCENA RETAIL GROUP, INC., pg. 18, pg. 1081
BARCO UNIFORMS, INC., pg. 19, pg. 94
BROOKS SPORTS INC., pg. 1805, pg. 1818
BUYSEASONS, INC., pg. 20, pg. 1883
CARTER'S, INC., pg. 21, pg. 491
CROWN CRAFTS INFANT PRODUCTS, INC., pg. 922, pg.

First page reference indicates Business Class Edition
Second page reference indicates Geographic Edition

68
CUPID FOUNDATIONS, INC., pg. 22, pg. 1220
CUSTOMINK, LLC, pg. 22, pg. 1780
DURA UNDERCUSHIONS LTD., pg. 923, pg. 1954
EL CHARRO LLC, pg. 1808, pg. 1691
THE FECHHEIMER BROTHERS COMPANY, pg. 41, pg. 1412
FLEXSTEEL INDUSTRIES, INC., pg. 925, pg. 707
FOSSIL GROUP, INC., pg. 5, pg. 1735
GARAN, INCORPORATED, pg. 24, pg. 1234
GEM-DANDY, INC., pg. 41, pg. 1382
GILDAN ACTIVEWEAR INC., pg. 1835, pg. 1955
GLAMORISE FOUNDATIONS, INC., pg. 25, pg. 1235
HANESBRANDS INC., pg. 26, pg. 1394
HONEYWELL NORTH SAFETY PRODUCTS, pg. 42, pg. 1600
INDERA MILLS COMPANY, pg. 26, pg. 1396
IZOD, pg. 42, pg. 1046
JANLYNN CORPORATION, pg. 696, pg. 815
JOCKEY INTERNATIONAL, INC., pg. 27, pg. 1861
KATE SPADE & COMPANY, pg. 27, pg. 1248
KELLWOOD COMPANY, pg. 28, pg. 975
KIYONNA CLOTHING, INC., pg. 28, pg. 42
LAKELAND INDUSTRIES, INC., pg. 1354, pg. 1338
LANDAU UNIFORMS INCORPORATED, pg. 28, pg. 971
LEHIGH OUTFITTERS, LLC, pg. 43, pg. 1466
L.L. BEAN, INC., pg. 1777, pg. 750
LUCKY BRAND DUNGAREES, INC., pg. 29, pg. 301
MICHAEL KORS (USA), INC., pg. 29, pg. 1260
NAUTICA APPAREL, INC., pg. 45, pg. 1265
THE NORTH FACE, INC., pg. 1840, pg. 252
PARIS ACCESSORIES, INC., pg. 10, pg. 1276
PERFORM GROUP, LLC, pg. 31, pg. 1597
PHOENIX FOOTWEAR GROUP, INC., pg. 1815, pg. 60
PLAYTEX APPAREL, INC., pg. 31, pg. 1395
POINT BLANK SOLUTIONS, INC., pg. 1467, pg. 460
PVH CORP., pg. 46, pg. 1283
RANDA ACCESSORIES, LLC, pg. 47, pg. 657
RAWLINGS SPORTING GOODS CO., INC., pg. 1843, pg. 1002
REFRIGIWEAR, INC., pg. 47, pg. 529
RIVERSIDE MANUFACTURING COMPANY, pg. 32, pg. 536
ROCKY BRANDS, INC., pg. 1818, pg. 1466
SELLSTROM MANUFACTURING CO., pg. 1428, pg. 659
SKINNYCORP L.L.C., pg. 1280, pg. 590
SMARTWOOL, pg. 32, pg. 335
SPANX INC., pg. 32, pg. 520
STANDARD SAFETY EQUIPMENT CO., pg. 1379, pg. 632
STEVEN MADDEN, LTD., pg. 1819, pg. 1176
SUNRISE BRANDS, LLC, pg. 33, pg. 140
SUPERIOR UNIFORM GROUP, INC., pg. 33, pg. 468
SWANK, INC., pg. 13, pg. 1297
THERAPEDIC ASSOCIATES, INC., pg. 945, pg. 1112
THE TIMBERLAND COMPANY, pg. 1821, pg. 1039
TOMMY HILFIGER USA, pg. 48, pg. 1302
VERA BRADLEY, INC., pg. 15, pg. 697
V.F. CORPORATION, pg. 34, pg. 1376
VOLCOM, INC., pg. 1847, pg. 71
WACOAL AMERICA INC., pg. 35, pg. 1312
WEISSMAN THEATRICAL SUPPLY, INC., pg. 35, pg. 1004

2353 - Hats, Caps & Millinery

HATCO, INC., pg. 6, pg. 1698
NEW ERA CAP COMPANY INC., pg. 1840, pg. 1155
UNDER ARMOUR, INC., pg. 49, pg. 759

2361 - Girls', Children's & Infants' Dresses, Blouses & Shirts

ALGY TRIMMING COMPANY, pg. 17, pg. 429
CARTER'S, INC., pg. 21, pg. 491
CUPID FOUNDATIONS, INC., pg. 22, pg. 1220
GARAN, INCORPORATED, pg. 24, pg. 1234
GLAMORISE FOUNDATIONS, INC., pg. 25, pg. 1235
HANESBRANDS INC., pg. 26, pg. 1394
INDERA MILLS COMPANY, pg. 26, pg. 1396
JOCKEY INTERNATIONAL, INC., pg. 27, pg. 1861
KELLWOOD COMPANY, pg. 28, pg. 975
KIYONNA CLOTHING, INC., pg. 28, pg. 42
NAUTICA APPAREL, INC., pg. 45, pg. 1265
PLAYTEX APPAREL, INC., pg. 31, pg. 1395
SPANX INC., pg. 32, pg. 520
TOMMY HILFIGER USA, pg. 48, pg. 1302
V.F. CORPORATION, pg. 34, pg. 1376
WACOAL AMERICA INC., pg. 35, pg. 1312
WEISSMAN THEATRICAL SUPPLY, INC., pg. 35, pg. 1004

2371 - Fur Goods

DANIER LEATHER, INC., pg. 22, pg. 1937
G-III APPAREL GROUP, LTD., pg. 41, pg. 1233
PAULA LISHMAN LIMITED, pg. 31, pg. 1932
TANDY LEATHER FACTORY, INC., pg. 48, pg. 1696

2389 - Apparel & Accessories, NEC

ACUSHNET COMPANY, pg. 1824, pg. 818
AEROJET ROCKETDYNE HOLDINGS, INC., pg. 1145, pg. 186
A.H. SCHREIBER CO., INC., pg. 17, pg. 1188
ALGY TRIMMING COMPANY, pg. 17, pg. 429
ALLESON OF ROCHESTER, INC., pg. 37, pg. 1333
ALYCE PARIS, pg. 18, pg. 634
AMERICAN APPAREL, INC., pg. 18, pg. 126
AMERICAN BILTRITE INC., pg. 1878, pg. 856
ANSELL, pg. 1495, pg. 1114
ASCENA RETAIL GROUP, INC., pg. 18, pg. 1081
ATHLETA, pg. 19, pg. 181
ATTITUDES IN DRESSING INC., pg. 19, pg. 1057
BARCO UNIFORMS, INC., pg. 19, pg. 94
BE AEROSPACE, INC., pg. 224, pg. 478
BEBE STORES, INC., pg. 19, pg. 49
BENETTON U.S.A. CORPORATION, pg. 19, pg. 1202
THE BILTRITE CORPORATION, pg. 1879, pg. 850
BLAUER MANUFACTURING COMPANY, INC., pg. 20, pg. 789
BROOKS SPORTS INC., pg. 1805, pg. 1818
BUYSEASONS, INC., pg. 20, pg. 1883
CARTER'S, INC., pg. 21, pg. 491
CHAMPION ATHLETICWEAR INC., pg. 39, pg. 1394
CHANEL, INC., pg. 503, pg. 1211
CHASE CORPORATION, pg. 1152, pg. 803
CHURCH & DWIGHT CO., INC., pg. 1153, pg. 1063
COLUMBIA SPORTSWEAR COMPANY, pg. 1830, pg. 1501
COMMERCIAL VEHICLE GROUP, INC., pg. 203, pg. 1467
CONTINENTAL AMERICAN CORP., pg. 1880, pg. 723
COOPER-STANDARD AUTOMOTIVE INC., pg. 1880, pg. 903
COOPER TIRE & RUBBER COMPANY, pg. 1881, pg. 1453
CROWN CRAFTS INFANT PRODUCTS, INC., pg. 922, pg. 68
CTI INDUSTRIES CORPORATION, pg. 1881, pg. 555
CUSTOMINK, LLC, pg. 22, pg. 1780
CUTTER & BUCK, INC., pg. 39, pg. 1835
DARNELL-ROSE, pg. 1045, pg. 67
DELIA'S, INC., pg. 23, pg. 1222
DELTA APPAREL, INC., pg. 39, pg. 1617
DESTINATION MATERNITY CORPORATION, pg. 23, pg. 1563
DOLFIN INTERNATIONAL CORPORATION, pg. 23, pg. 1553
DOREL JUVENILE GROUP, INC., pg. 923, pg. 676
DURA UNDERCUSHIONS LTD., pg. 923, pg. 1954
EILEEN FISHER, INC., pg. 24, pg. 1168
EL CHARRO LLC, pg. 1808, pg. 1691
FABREEKA INTERNATIONAL, INC., pg. 1882, pg. 847
THE FECHHEIMER BROTHERS COMPANY, pg. 41, pg. 1412
FLEXSTEEL INDUSTRIES, INC., pg. 925, pg. 707
FOSSIL GROUP, INC., pg. 5, pg. 1735
GARAN, INCORPORATED, pg. 24, pg. 1234
GEM-DANDY, INC., pg. 41, pg. 1382
GILDAN ACTIVEWEAR INC., pg. 1835, pg. 1955
GUESS?, INC., pg. 25, pg. 132
HANESBRANDS INC., pg. 26, pg. 1394
HELLY-HANSEN (US), INC., pg. 26, pg. 1813
HONEYWELL NORTH SAFETY PRODUCTS, pg. 42, pg. 1600
HONEYWELL SALISBURY ELECTRICAL SAFETY, pg. 1884, pg. 558
HSM SOLUTIONS, pg. 1884, pg. 1378
ICONIX BRAND GROUP, INC., pg. 26, pg. 1243
INDUSTRIAL RUBBER PRODUCTS, INC., pg. 1349, pg. 926
IZOD, pg. 42, pg. 1046
JACQUES MORET, INC., pg. 27, pg. 1245
JANLYNN CORPORATION, pg. 696, pg. 815
JOHNSON CONTROLS, INC., pg. 209, pg. 1876
JORDACHE ENTERPRISES, INC., pg. 27, pg. 1246
JUNONIA LTD., pg. 27, pg. 929
KATE SPADE & COMPANY, pg. 27, pg. 1248
KIYONNA CLOTHING, INC., pg. 28, pg. 42
KRACO ENTERPRISES, LLC, pg. 210, pg. 68
LACROSSE FOOTWEAR, INC., pg. 1811, pg. 1503
LAKELAND INDUSTRIES, INC., pg. 1354, pg. 1338
LANDAU UNIFORMS INCORPORATED, pg. 28, pg. 971
LAVELLE INDUSTRIES INC., pg. 1053, pg. 1856
LEAR CORPORATION, pg. 229, pg. 907
LEHIGH OUTFITTERS, LLC, pg. 43, pg. 1466
LEVI STRAUSS & CO., pg. 43, pg. 220
L.L. BEAN, INC., pg. 1777, pg. 750
LOST ARROW CORPORATION, pg. 44, pg. 301
LT APPAREL GROUP, pg. 29, pg. 1254
LUCKY BRAND DUNGAREES, INC., pg. 29, pg. 301
MAPA PROFESSIONAL, pg. 1885, pg. 555
MAPLE CITY RUBBER COMPANY, pg. 962, pg. 1468
MARYLAND PLASTICS, INC., pg. 1885, pg. 769
THE MERCER RUBBER COMPANY, pg. 1886, pg. 1165
MICHAEL KORS (USA), INC., pg. 29, pg. 1260
MOUNTAIN HARDWEAR, INC., pg. 1839, pg. 193
MUNCHKIN, INC., pg. 964, pg. 300
NIKE, INC., pg. 1812, pg. 1492
THE NORTH FACE, INC., pg. 1840, pg. 252
NUSIL TECHNOLOGY LLC, pg. 1887, pg. 63
NYDJ APPAREL, LLC, pg. 30, pg. 302
OMNOVA SOLUTIONS INC, pg. 1176, pg. 1453
O'NEILL INC., pg. 1842, pg. 270
OSCAR DE LA RENTA LTD., pg. 30, pg. 1274
PARIS ACCESSORIES, INC., pg. 10, pg. 1276
PATAGONIA, pg. 31, pg. 301
PAULA LISHMAN LIMITED, pg. 31, pg. 1932
PERFORM GROUP, LLC, pg. 31, pg. 1597
PHOENIX FOOTWEAR GROUP, INC., pg. 1815, pg. 60
POINT BLANK SOLUTIONS, INC., pg. 1467, pg. 460
POLARIS INDUSTRIES INC., pg. 1709, pg. 928
PVH CORP., pg. 46, pg. 1283
QUADION CORPORATION, pg. 1888, pg. 941
RADIATOR SPECIALTY COMPANY, pg. 215, pg. 1380
RALPH LAUREN CORPORATION, pg. 46, pg. 1284
RANDA ACCESSORIES, LLC, pg. 47, pg. 657
RAWLINGS SPORTING GOODS CO., INC., pg. 1843, pg. 1002
R.C.A. RUBBER COMPANY, pg. 1888, pg. 1402
RECARO NORTH AMERICA, INC., pg. 216, pg. 869
REESE ENTERPRISES, INC., pg. 1888, pg. 955
REFRIGIWEAR, INC., pg. 47, pg. 529
RIVERSIDE MANUFACTURING COMPANY, pg. 32, pg. 536
ROCKY BRANDS, INC., pg. 1818, pg. 1466
SCHLEGEL SYSTEMS, INC., pg. 109, pg. 1337
SELLSTROM MANUFACTURING CO., pg. 1428, pg. 659
SKINNYCORP L.L.C., pg. 1280, pg. 590
SMARTWOOL, pg. 32, pg. 335
SPORT HALEY, INC., pg. 33, pg. 333
ST. JOHN KNITS INTERNATIONAL, INC., pg. 33, pg. 116
STANDARD SAFETY EQUIPMENT CO., pg. 1379, pg. 632
STEVEN MADDEN, LTD., pg. 1819, pg. 1176
SUGARTOWN WORLDWIDE INC., pg. 33, pg. 1544
SUNRISE BRANDS, LLC, pg. 33, pg. 140
SUPERIOR UNIFORM GROUP, INC., pg. 33, pg. 468
SWANK, INC., pg. 13, pg. 1297
TANNER COMPANIES, LP, pg. 34, pg. 1390
TEKNOR APEX COMPANY, pg. 1889, pg. 1605
TEXTILE RUBBER & CHEMICAL COMPANY, pg. 1890, pg. 530
THERAPEDIC ASSOCIATES, INC., pg. 945, pg. 1112
THE TIMBERLAND COMPANY, pg. 1821, pg. 1039
TOMMY HILFIGER USA, pg. 48, pg. 1302
TRICO PRODUCTS CORPORATION, pg. 220, pg. 905
UNDER ARMOUR, INC., pg. 49, pg. 759
VAIL RUBBER WORKS, INC., pg. 1891, pg. 906
VARSITY BRANDS, INC., pg. 1847, pg. 1647
VERA BRADLEY, INC., pg. 15, pg. 697
VESTA INC., pg. 1435, pg. 1858
VF IMAGEWEAR, pg. 50, pg. 476
VICTUS, INC., pg. 1606, pg. 447
VOLCOM, INC., pg. 1847, pg. 71
VYSTAR CORPORATION, pg. 1891, pg. 532
WEISSMAN THEATRICAL SUPPLY, INC., pg. 35, pg. 1004
WEST PHARMACEUTICAL SERVICES, INC., pg. 1472, pg. 1532
XERIUM TECHNOLOGIES, INC., pg. 1703, pg. 1389

2391 - Curtains & Draperies

3 DAY BLINDS, INC., *pg.* 912, *pg.* 105
CROSCILL, INC., *pg.* 1122, *pg.* 1220

2392 - Housefurnishings, Except Curtains & Draperies

3 DAY BLINDS, INC., *pg.* 912, *pg.* 105
BACOVA GUILD, LTD., *pg.* 916, *pg.* 1779
BRIGHT OF AMERICA, INC., *pg.* 1121, *pg.* 1851
CC INDUSTRIES, INC., *pg.* 920, *pg.* 569
CROSCILL, INC., *pg.* 1122, *pg.* 1220
CROWN CRAFTS INFANT PRODUCTS, INC., *pg.* 922, *pg.* 68
GUILFORD PERFORMANCE TEXTILES, *pg.* 693, *pg.* 1393
HERITAGE LACE INC., *pg.* 694, *pg.* 711
HOLLANDER SLEEP PRODUCTS, *pg.* 927, *pg.* 411
INTERNATIONAL TEXTILE GROUP, INC., *pg.* 696, *pg.* 1374
POLYMER GROUP, INC., *pg.* 698, *pg.* 1368
SHEEX, INC., *pg.* 1138, *pg.* 1614

2393 - Textile Bags

ACUSHNET COMPANY, *pg.* 1824, *pg.* 818
AEROJET ROCKETDYNE HOLDINGS, INC., *pg.* 1145, *pg.* 186
AMERICAN BILTRITE INC., *pg.* 1878, *pg.* 856
ANSELL, *pg.* 1495, *pg.* 1114
BACOVA GUILD, LTD., *pg.* 916, *pg.* 1779
THE BILTRITE CORPORATION, *pg.* 1879, *pg.* 850
BRIGHT OF AMERICA, INC., *pg.* 1121, *pg.* 1851
CC INDUSTRIES, INC., *pg.* 920, *pg.* 569
CHASE CORPORATION, *pg.* 1152, *pg.* 803
CHURCH & DWIGHT CO., INC., *pg.* 1153, *pg.* 1063
CONTINENTAL AMERICAN CORP., *pg.* 1880, *pg.* 723
COOPER-STANDARD AUTOMOTIVE INC., *pg.* 1880, *pg.* 903
COOPER TIRE & RUBBER COMPANY, *pg.* 1881, *pg.* 1453
CROSCILL, INC., *pg.* 1122, *pg.* 1220
CROWN CRAFTS INFANT PRODUCTS, INC., *pg.* 922, *pg.* 68
CTI INDUSTRIES CORPORATION, *pg.* 1881, *pg.* 555
DARNELL-ROSE, *pg.* 1045, *pg.* 67
DOREL JUVENILE GROUP, INC., *pg.* 923, *pg.* 676
DURA UNDERCUSHIONS LTD., *pg.* 923, *pg.* 1954
THE EVERCARE COMPANY, *pg.* 1124, *pg.* 483
FABREEKA INTERNATIONAL, INC., *pg.* 1882, *pg.* 847
GUILFORD PERFORMANCE TEXTILES, *pg.* 693, *pg.* 1393
HERITAGE LACE INC., *pg.* 694, *pg.* 711
HOLLANDER SLEEP PRODUCTS, *pg.* 927, *pg.* 411
HONEYWELL SALISBURY ELECTRICAL SAFETY, *pg.* 1884, *pg.* 558
HORIZON DESIGNS, INC., *pg.* 695, *pg.* 1011
HOSOKAWA MICRON POWDER SYSTEMS, *pg.* 1347, *pg.* 1124
HSM SOLUTIONS, *pg.* 1884, *pg.* 1378
INDUSTRIAL RUBBER PRODUCTS, INC., *pg.* 1349, *pg.* 926
INTERNATIONAL TEXTILE GROUP, INC., *pg.* 696, *pg.* 1374
JANDD MOUNTAINEERING, INC., *pg.* 1837, *pg.* 204
KRACO ENTERPRISES, LLC, *pg.* 210, *pg.* 68
LAVELLE INDUSTRIES INC., *pg.* 1053, *pg.* 1856
MAPA PROFESSIONAL, *pg.* 1885, *pg.* 555
MAPLE CITY RUBBER COMPANY, *pg.* 962, *pg.* 1468
MARYLAND PLASTICS, INC., *pg.* 1885, *pg.* 769
THE MERCER RUBBER COMPANY, *pg.* 1886, *pg.* 1165
MUNCHKIN, INC., *pg.* 964, *pg.* 300
NUSIL TECHNOLOGY LLC, *pg.* 1887, *pg.* 63
OMNOVA SOLUTIONS INC, *pg.* 1176, *pg.* 1453
O'NEILL INC., *pg.* 1842, *pg.* 270
POLYMER GROUP, INC., *pg.* 698, *pg.* 1368
QUADION CORPORATION, *pg.* 1888, *pg.* 941
RADIATOR SPECIALTY COMPANY, *pg.* 215, *pg.* 1380
R.C.A. RUBBER COMPANY, *pg.* 1888, *pg.* 1402
REESE ENTERPRISES, INC., *pg.* 1888, *pg.* 955
SCHLEGEL SYSTEMS, INC., *pg.* 109, *pg.* 1337
SHEEX, INC., *pg.* 1138, *pg.* 1614
TEKNOR APEX COMPANY, *pg.* 1889, *pg.* 1605
TEXTILE RUBBER & CHEMICAL COMPANY, *pg.* 1890, *pg.* 530
THERAPEDIC ASSOCIATES, INC., *pg.* 945, *pg.* 1112
TRICO PRODUCTS CORPORATION, *pg.* 220, *pg.* 905
VAIL RUBBER WORKS, INC., *pg.* 1891, *pg.* 906
VESTA INC., *pg.* 1435, *pg.* 1858
VICTUS, INC., *pg.* 1606, *pg.* 447
VYSTAR CORPORATION, *pg.* 1891, *pg.* 532
WEST PHARMACEUTICAL SERVICES, INC., *pg.* 1472, *pg.* 1532
XERIUM TECHNOLOGIES, INC., *pg.* 1703, *pg.* 1389

2394 - Canvas & Related Products

ANCHOR INDUSTRIES, INC., *pg.* 1825, *pg.* 678
C.R. DANIELS, INC., *pg.* 1456, *pg.* 769
DIAMOND BRAND CANVAS PRODUCTS CO., INC., *pg.* 1832, *pg.* 1372
DURASOL AWNINGS, INC., *pg.* 79, *pg.* 1153
IRT, INC., *pg.* 1169, *pg.* 771
OHIO AWNING & MANUFACTURING CO., *pg.* 1842, *pg.* 1433
SUNSETTER PRODUCTS, LP, *pg.* 113, *pg.* 830
TAYLOR MADE GROUP, *pg.* 1711, *pg.* 1162

2396 - Automotive Trimmings, Apparel Findings & Related Products

JOHNSON CONTROLS, INC., *pg.* 209, *pg.* 1876
RECARO NORTH AMERICA, INC., *pg.* 216, *pg.* 869

2411 - Logging Camps & Logging Contractors

TIMBERWEST FOREST CORP., *pg.* 1470, *pg.* 1912

2421 - Sawmills & Planing Mills, General

ANTHONY FOREST PRODUCTS CO., INC., *pg.* 67, *pg.* 31
AQUARION WATER COMPANY, *pg.* 1935, *pg.* 357
BOISE CASCADE HOLDINGS, L.L.C., *pg.* 1453, *pg.* 546
CANFOR CORPORATION, *pg.* 1454, *pg.* 1910
CEDAR SHAKE & SHINGLE BUREAU, *pg.* 74, *pg.* 1908
JOHN BOOS & CO., *pg.* 1126, *pg.* 609
LOUISIANA-PACIFIC CORPORATION, *pg.* 94, *pg.* 1652
PLUM CREEK TIMBER COMPANY, INC., *pg.* 105, *pg.* 1838
RAYONIER INC., *pg.* 1179, *pg.* 434
SIERRA PACIFIC INDUSTRIES, *pg.* 110, *pg.* 43
SIMPSON LUMBER COMPANY, LLC, *pg.* 110, *pg.* 1845
TEMBEC INC., *pg.* 114, *pg.* 1957
UNIVERSAL FOREST PRODUCTS, INC., *pg.* 117, *pg.* 890
WEYERHAEUSER COMPANY, *pg.* 121, *pg.* 1820

2431 - Millwork

ADVANCED ENVIRONMENTAL RECYCLING TECHNOLOGIES, INC., *pg.* 1310, *pg.* 35
ANDERSEN CORPORATION, *pg.* 67, *pg.* 916
ANDERSON HARDWOOD FLOORS, *pg.* 67, *pg.* 1613
ANTHONY FOREST PRODUCTS CO., INC., *pg.* 67, *pg.* 31
AQUARION WATER COMPANY, *pg.* 1935, *pg.* 357
ARMSTRONG WORLD INDUSTRIES, INC., *pg.* 914, *pg.* 1545
ATRIUM COMPANIES, INC., *pg.* 69, *pg.* 1676
BACOVA GUILD, LTD., *pg.* 916, *pg.* 1779
BOISE CASCADE HOLDINGS, L.L.C., *pg.* 1453, *pg.* 546
CANFOR CORPORATION, *pg.* 1454, *pg.* 1910
CEDAR SHAKE & SHINGLE BUREAU, *pg.* 74, *pg.* 1908
CLOPAY BUILDING PRODUCTS COMPANY, *pg.* 76, *pg.* 1459
CONESTOGA WOOD SPECIALTIES CORP., *pg.* 921, *pg.* 1527
HURD WINDOWS & DOORS INC, *pg.* 88, *pg.* 1869
JOHN BOOS & CO., *pg.* 1126, *pg.* 609
LOEWEN, *pg.* 934, *pg.* 1914
LOUISIANA-PACIFIC CORPORATION, *pg.* 94, *pg.* 1652
MARLITE, INC., *pg.* 95, *pg.* 1448
MARVIN WINDOWS & DOORS, *pg.* 934, *pg.* 965
MASONITE INTERNATIONAL CORPORATION, *pg.* 1054, *pg.* 1920
NYDREE FLOORING, *pg.* 939, *pg.* 1782
ODL INCORPORATED, *pg.* 101, *pg.* 914
OVERHEAD DOOR CORPORATION, *pg.* 102, *pg.* 1725
PELLA CORPORATION, *pg.* 104, *pg.* 711
PLUM CREEK TIMBER COMPANY, INC., *pg.* 105, *pg.* 1838
RAYONIER INC., *pg.* 1179, *pg.* 434
ROBBINS, INC., *pg.* 108, *pg.* 1425
SHAW INDUSTRIES GROUP, INC., *pg.* 942, *pg.* 530
SIERRA PACIFIC INDUSTRIES, *pg.* 110, *pg.* 43
SIMPSON DOOR COMPANY, *pg.* 110, *pg.* 1823
SIMPSON LUMBER COMPANY, LLC, *pg.* 110, *pg.* 1845
TEMBEC INC., *pg.* 114, *pg.* 1957
THERMA-TRU CORP., *pg.* 115, *pg.* 1462
UNIVERSAL FOREST PRODUCTS, INC., *pg.* 117, *pg.* 890
VIKING DOOR & WINDOW, *pg.* 119, *pg.* 251
WAYNE-DALTON CORP., *pg.* 120, *pg.* 1465
WEYERHAEUSER COMPANY, *pg.* 121, *pg.* 1820
WINDOWS AND WALLS UNLIMITED, INC., *pg.* 946, *pg.* 1343

2434 - Wood Kitchen Cabinets

AMERICAN WOODMARK CORPORATION, *pg.* 913, *pg.* 1811
ARMSTRONG WORLD INDUSTRIES, INC., *pg.* 914, *pg.* 1545
THE ENKEBOLL COMPANY, *pg.* 923, *pg.* 63
EUROTECH CABINETRY, INC., *pg.* 924, *pg.* 466
FOREIGN TRADERS, INC., *pg.* 1769, *pg.* 1135
FORTUNE BRANDS HOME & SECURITY, INC., *pg.* 55, *pg.* 600
GAF MATERIALS CORP., *pg.* 83, *pg.* 1681
HOOKER FURNITURE CORPORATION, *pg.* 928, *pg.* 1788
ICON DESIGN & DISPLAY, INC., *pg.* 1460, *pg.* 277
JEREMIAH CAMPBELL & COMPANY, *pg.* 931, *pg.* 749
JOHN BOOS & CO., *pg.* 1126, *pg.* 609
KITCHEN KOMPACT, INC., *pg.* 91, *pg.* 692
KRAFTMAID CABINETRY, INC., *pg.* 1053, *pg.* 1465
LEGGETT & PLATT, INCORPORATED, *pg.* 933, *pg.* 974
LINDAL CEDAR HOMES, INC., *pg.* 94, *pg.* 1837
LOZIER CORPORATION, *pg.* 94, *pg.* 1016
MANHATTAN ASSOCIATES, INC., *pg.* 430, *pg.* 513
MASCO CORPORATION, *pg.* 96, *pg.* 909
MASTERBRAND CABINETS, INC., *pg.* 96, *pg.* 692
MELE COMPANIES, INC., *pg.* 9, *pg.* 1347
MILLER MULTIPLEX DISPLAY FIXTURE CO., *pg.* 935, *pg.* 609
NORCRAFT HOLDINGS, LP, *pg.* 100, *pg.* 921
PACIFIC COLUMNS, INC., *pg.* 103, *pg.* 49
PARISI INCORPORATED, *pg.* 103, *pg.* 1556
POGGENPOHL U.S., INC., *pg.* 105, *pg.* 1065
RESTORATION HARDWARE HOLDINGS, INC., *pg.* 1060, *pg.* 70
THE SERAPH, *pg.* 942, *pg.* 847
WILSONART INTERNATIONAL, INC., *pg.* 1450, *pg.* 1746
WITH HEART & HAND, *pg.* 946, *pg.* 837
WM OHS INC., *pg.* 947, *pg.* 324

2435 - Hardwood Veneer & Plywood

ADVANCED ENVIRONMENTAL RECYCLING TECHNOLOGIES, INC., *pg.* 1310, *pg.* 35
ANDERSON HARDWOOD FLOORS, *pg.* 67, *pg.* 1613
LEGGETT & PLATT, INCORPORATED, *pg.* 933, *pg.* 974
NORTEK, INC., *pg.* 100, *pg.* 1607
RICHELIEU HARDWARE LTD., *pg.* 1060, *pg.* 1961

2436 - Softwood Veneer & Plywood

UNIVERSAL FOREST PRODUCTS, INC., *pg.* 117, *pg.* 890
ZYNGA INC., *pg.* 1292, *pg.* 235

2439 - Structural Wood Members, NEC

THE EASTERN COMPANY, *pg.* 1331, *pg.* 357
NAPLES LUMBER & SUPPLY INC., *pg.* 99, *pg.* 451
REDBUILT LLC, *pg.* 106, *pg.* 548
UNADILLA SILO COMPANY INC., *pg.* 117, *pg.* 1346
UNIVERSAL FOREST PRODUCTS, INC., *pg.* 117, *pg.* 890

2449 - Wood Containers, NEC

ADELPHI PAPER HANGINGS LLC, *pg.* 912, *pg.* 1342
ANTHONY FOREST PRODUCTS CO., INC., *pg.* 67, *pg.* 31

First page reference indicates Business Class Edition
Second page reference indicates Geographic Edition

AQUARION WATER COMPANY, *pg.* 1935, *pg.* 357
BOISE CASCADE HOLDINGS, L.L.C., *pg.* 1453, *pg.* 546
CANFOR CORPORATION, *pg.* 1454, *pg.* 1910
CEDAR SHAKE & SHINGLE BUREAU, *pg.* 74, *pg.* 1908
THE GREAT AMERICAN HANGER COMPANY INC., *pg.* 926, *pg.* 442
IFCO SYSTEMS NORTH AMERICA, *pg.* 411, *pg.* 1708
JELD-WEN, INC., *pg.* 1051, *pg.* 1499
JOHN BOOS & CO., *pg.* 1126, *pg.* 609
THE LONGABERGER COMPANY, *pg.* 1127, *pg.* 1467
LOUISIANA-PACIFIC CORPORATION, *pg.* 94, *pg.* 1652
MASCO CORPORATION, *pg.* 96, *pg.* 909
OMEGA NATIONAL PRODUCTS, *pg.* 939, *pg.* 737
PLUM CREEK TIMBER COMPANY, INC., *pg.* 105, *pg.* 1838
RAYONIER INC., *pg.* 1179, *pg.* 434
SCOTT'S LIQUID GOLD-INC., *pg.* 335, *pg.* 323
SIERRA PACIFIC INDUSTRIES, *pg.* 110, *pg.* 43
SIMPSON LUMBER COMPANY, LLC, *pg.* 110, *pg.* 1845
TEMBEC INC., *pg.* 114, *pg.* 1957
UNIVERSAL FOREST PRODUCTS, INC., *pg.* 117, *pg.* 890
VAUGHAN & BUSHNELL MANUFACTURING COMPANY, INC., *pg.* 1066, *pg.* 616
WALPOLE WOODWORKERS, INC., *pg.* 120, *pg.* 849
WEYERHAEUSER COMPANY, *pg.* 121, *pg.* 1820
WHITE RIVER HARDWOODS-WOODWORKS, INC., *pg.* 121, *pg.* 31
WMS INDUSTRIES INC., *pg.* 593, *pg.* 666

2451 - Mobile Homes

AMERICAN HOMESTAR CORPORATION, *pg.* 67, *pg.* 1725
CAVCO INDUSTRIES, INC., *pg.* 74, *pg.* 16
CHAMPION ENTERPRISES HOLDINGS, LLC, *pg.* 75, *pg.* 910
CHIEF INDUSTRIES, INC., *pg.* 1323, *pg.* 1010
CLAYTON HOMES, INC., *pg.* 1086, *pg.* 1640
JACOBSEN MANUFACTURING, INC., *pg.* 1098, *pg.* 460
LIBERTY HOMES, INC., *pg.* 93, *pg.* 681
MINAEAN INTERNATIONAL CORPORATION, *pg.* 97, *pg.* 1911
SKYLINE CORPORATION, *pg.* 1711, *pg.* 677

2452 - Prefabricated Wood Buildings & Components

CLAYTON HOMES, INC., *pg.* 1086, *pg.* 1640
FIBERESIN INDUSTRIES, INC., *pg.* 81, *pg.* 1885
GEORGIA-PACIFIC LLC, *pg.* 1458, *pg.* 507
LIBERTY HOMES, INC., *pg.* 93, *pg.* 681
LINDAL CEDAR HOMES, INC., *pg.* 94, *pg.* 1837
MENARD, INC., *pg.* 1055, *pg.* 1857
NATIONWIDE HOMES, INC., *pg.* 99, *pg.* 1788
OMEGA NATIONAL PRODUCTS, *pg.* 939, *pg.* 737
PALM HARBOR HOMES, INC., *pg.* 1107, *pg.* 1658
ROCKY MOUNTAIN LOG HOMES, *pg.* 108, *pg.* 1008
TREX COMPANY, INC., *pg.* 116, *pg.* 1812
WAUSAU HOMES, INC., *pg.* 120, *pg.* 1890

2491 - Wood Preserving

J.H. BAXTER & COMPANY, *pg.* 89, *pg.* 255
KOPPERS HOLDINGS INC., *pg.* 1170, *pg.* 1577
OSMOSE, INC., *pg.* 102, *pg.* 533
OSMOSE, INC., *pg.* 102, *pg.* 1150
ROBBINS, INC., *pg.* 108, *pg.* 1425
UNIVERSAL FOREST PRODUCTS, INC., *pg.* 117, *pg.* 890

2493 - Reconstituted Wood Products

ADVANCED ENVIRONMENTAL RECYCLING TECHNOLOGIES, INC., *pg.* 1310, *pg.* 35
AMERICAN EXCELSIOR COMPANY, *pg.* 1451, *pg.* 1659
FIBERESIN INDUSTRIES, INC., *pg.* 81, *pg.* 1885
HOMASOTE COMPANY, *pg.* 87, *pg.* 1126
LOUISIANA-PACIFIC CORPORATION, *pg.* 94, *pg.* 1652
PANOLAM INDUSTRIES INTERNATIONAL, INC., *pg.* 103, *pg.* 370
TREX COMPANY, INC., *pg.* 116, *pg.* 1812
UNIBOARD CANADA INC., *pg.* 117, *pg.* 1952
UNIVERSAL FOREST PRODUCTS, INC., *pg.* 117, *pg.* 890

2499 - Wood Products, NEC

ADELPHI PAPER HANGINGS LLC, *pg.* 912, *pg.* 1342
ALPHA PRO TECH, LTD., *pg.* 1492, *pg.* 1922
ANDIS COMPANY, *pg.* 498, *pg.* 1895
ANTHONY FOREST PRODUCTS CO., INC., *pg.* 67, *pg.* 31
AQUARION WATER COMPANY, *pg.* 1935, *pg.* 357
AROMATIQUE INC., *pg.* 499, *pg.* 32
BD MEDICAL, *pg.* 1501, *pg.* 1762
BLYTH, INC., *pg.* 502, *pg.* 349
BOISE CASCADE HOLDINGS, L.L.C., *pg.* 1453, *pg.* 546
BRADY CORPORATION, *pg.* 363, *pg.* 1873
BRIGHT OF AMERICA, INC., *pg.* 1121, *pg.* 1851
BUZTRONICS, INC., *pg.* 1294, *pg.* 683
CANFOR CORPORATION, *pg.* 1454, *pg.* 1910
CEDAR SHAKE & SHINGLE BUREAU, *pg.* 74, *pg.* 1908
EDUCATIONAL INSIGHTS, INC., *pg.* 951, *pg.* 187
ENERGIZER HOLDINGS, INC., *pg.* 637, *pg.* 996
FOLKMANIS, INC., *pg.* 953, *pg.* 83
THE HARTZ MOUNTAIN CORP., *pg.* 1476, *pg.* 1120
HELEN OF TROY L.P., *pg.* 511, *pg.* 1692
HYDRALIGN, *pg.* 1257, *pg.* 833
IGT, *pg.* 412, *pg.* 1031
INTERNATIONAL GAME TECHNOLOGY, *pg.* 957, *pg.* 1024
JASON INDUSTRIES, INC., *pg.* 208, *pg.* 1875
JOHN BOOS & CO., *pg.* 1126, *pg.* 609
JOHNSON & JOHNSON BABY PRODUCTS, INC., *pg.* 1552, *pg.* 1094
LAKELAND INDUSTRIES, INC., *pg.* 1354, *pg.* 1338
LARSON-JUHL US LLC, *pg.* 933, *pg.* 537
LOUISIANA-PACIFIC CORPORATION, *pg.* 94, *pg.* 1652
MINE SAFETY APPLIANCES COMPANY, *pg.* 1361, *pg.* 1525
MULTIMEDIA GAMES INC., *pg.* 442, *pg.* 1664
NATURAL DECORATIONS, INC., *pg.* 936, *pg.* 5
OIL-DRI CORPORATION OF AMERICA, *pg.* 1480, *pg.* 586
OSBORN INTERNATIONAL, *pg.* 1367, *pg.* 1406
OTTERBOX PRODUCTS LLC, *pg.* 451, *pg.* 329
PLUM CREEK TIMBER COMPANY, INC., *pg.* 105, *pg.* 1838
RAUCH INDUSTRIES, INC., *pg.* 940, *pg.* 1373
RAYONIER INC., *pg.* 1179, *pg.* 434
REPLOGLE GLOBES, INC., *pg.* 461, *pg.* 559
SCOTT'S LIQUID GOLD-INC., *pg.* 335, *pg.* 323
SEALY CORPORATION, *pg.* 942, *pg.* 1391
SIERRA PACIFIC INDUSTRIES, *pg.* 110, *pg.* 43
SIMPSON LUMBER COMPANY, LLC, *pg.* 110, *pg.* 1845
ST. JUDE MEDICAL, INC., *pg.* 1596, *pg.* 963
TELEDYNE BENTHOS, INC., *pg.* 1431, *pg.* 838
TEMBEC INC., *pg.* 114, *pg.* 1957
TRANS-LUX CORPORATION, *pg.* 681, *pg.* 365
UNIVERSAL FOREST PRODUCTS, INC., *pg.* 117, *pg.* 890
WAHL CLIPPER CORPORATION, *pg.* 524, *pg.* 662
WEYERHAEUSER COMPANY, *pg.* 121, *pg.* 1820
WMS INDUSTRIES INC., *pg.* 593, *pg.* 666
THE WOODSTREAM CORPORATION, *pg.* 1801, *pg.* 1549
THE YANKEE CANDLE COMPANY, INC., *pg.* 1792, *pg.* 843

2512 - Wood Household Furniture, Upholstered

AMERICAN LEATHER LP, *pg.* 912, *pg.* 1673
ASHLEY FURNITURE INDUSTRIES, INC., *pg.* 914, *pg.* 1852
BASSETT FURNITURE INDUSTRIES, INCORPORATED, *pg.* 916, *pg.* 1776
BERNHARDT DESIGN, *pg.* 918, *pg.* 1381
BRIDON AMERICAN CORP., *pg.* 1319, *pg.* 1594
BROWN JORDAN INTERNATIONAL COMPANY, *pg.* 919, *pg.* 740
BROYHILL FURNITURE INDUSTRIES, INC., *pg.* 919, *pg.* 1381
CENTURY FURNITURE INDUSTRIES, *pg.* 920, *pg.* 1377
CROWN CRAFTS INFANT PRODUCTS, INC., *pg.* 922, *pg.* 68
ETHAN ALLEN INTERIORS INC., *pg.* 924, *pg.* 343
FLEXSTEEL INDUSTRIES, INC., *pg.* 925, *pg.* 707
HARDEN FURNITURE INC., *pg.* 926, *pg.* 1177
HERITAGE HOME GROUP, *pg.* 926, *pg.* 1379
HICKORY CHAIR COMPANY, *pg.* 927, *pg.* 1378
HOME MERIDIAN INTERNATIONAL, INC., *pg.* 928, *pg.* 1379
HOOKER FURNITURE CORPORATION, *pg.* 928, *pg.* 1788
J. ROBERT SCOTT INC., *pg.* 930, *pg.* 105
JAMISON BEDDING, INC., *pg.* 930, *pg.* 1651
JENNIFER CONVERTIBLES INC., *pg.* 931, *pg.* 1355
THE KARGES FURNITURE COMPANY, INC., *pg.* 931, *pg.* 679
KING KOIL LICENSING COMPANY INC., *pg.* 932, *pg.* 671
KINGSDOWN, INC., *pg.* 932, *pg.* 1383
LA-Z-BOY INCORPORATED, *pg.* 932, *pg.* 901
LANE VENTURE, INC., *pg.* 933, *pg.* 1379
LASALLE BRISTOL CORP., *pg.* 1053, *pg.* 677
LEGGETT & PLATT, INCORPORATED, *pg.* 933, *pg.* 974
LEXINGTON HOME BRANDS, *pg.* 933, *pg.* 1391
MITCHELL GOLD & BOB WILLIAMS, *pg.* 935, *pg.* 1391
NATIONAL BEDDING CO., *pg.* 935, *pg.* 618
NEUTRAL POSTURE, INC., *pg.* 939, *pg.* 1669
RELAX THE BACK CORPORATION, *pg.* 940, *pg.* 120
RESTONIC MATTRESS CORPORATION, *pg.* 941, *pg.* 553
SEALY CORPORATION, *pg.* 942, *pg.* 1391
SELECT COMFORT CORPORATION, *pg.* 942, *pg.* 942
THE SERAPH, *pg.* 942, *pg.* 847
SERTA, INC., *pg.* 942, *pg.* 619
SHEEX, INC., *pg.* 1138, *pg.* 1614
SIMMONS COMPANY, *pg.* 943, *pg.* 520
THE STANDARD MATTRESS COMPANY, *pg.* 943, *pg.* 352
STEARNS & FOSTER BEDDING COMPANY, *pg.* 944, *pg.* 1392
TEMPUR SEALY INTERNATIONAL, INC., *pg.* 944, *pg.* 731
THERAPEDIC ASSOCIATES, INC., *pg.* 945, *pg.* 1112
THOMASVILLE FURNITURE INDUSTRIES, INC., *pg.* 945, *pg.* 1391
TOMLINSON/ERWIN-LAMBETH, INC., *pg.* 945, *pg.* 1391
WHITE LOTUS HOME, *pg.* 946, *pg.* 1073
WINDOWS AND WALLS UNLIMITED, INC., *pg.* 946, *pg.* 1343

2514 - Metal Household Furniture

AMISCO INDUSTRIES LTD., *pg.* 913, *pg.* 1958
BROWN JORDAN INTERNATIONAL COMPANY, *pg.* 919, *pg.* 740
CC INDUSTRIES, INC., *pg.* 920, *pg.* 569
INVACARE CORPORATION, *pg.* 1546, *pg.* 1451
JARDEN CONSUMER SOLUTIONS, *pg.* 57, *pg.* 412
JOHN BOOS & CO., *pg.* 1126, *pg.* 609
LASALLE BRISTOL CORP., *pg.* 1053, *pg.* 677
LEGGETT & PLATT, INCORPORATED, *pg.* 933, *pg.* 974
MURPHY BED CO., INC., *pg.* 935, *pg.* 1159
RIO BRANDS, INC., *pg.* 941, *pg.* 1570
TELESCOPE CASUAL FURNITURE INC., *pg.* 944, *pg.* 1162
TROPITONE FURNITURE CO., INC., *pg.* 945, *pg.* 118
WILLIAMS-SONOMA, INC., *pg.* 1140, *pg.* 234

2515 - Mattresses, Foundations & Convertible Beds

BRIDON AMERICAN CORP., *pg.* 1319, *pg.* 1594
CROWN CRAFTS INFANT PRODUCTS, INC., *pg.* 922, *pg.* 68
JAMISON BEDDING, INC., *pg.* 930, *pg.* 1651
KING KOIL LICENSING COMPANY INC., *pg.* 932, *pg.* 671
KINGSDOWN, INC., *pg.* 932, *pg.* 1383
LEGGETT & PLATT, INCORPORATED, *pg.* 933, *pg.* 974
NATIONAL BEDDING CO., *pg.* 935, *pg.* 618
RELAX THE BACK CORPORATION, *pg.* 940, *pg.* 120
RESTONIC MATTRESS CORPORATION, *pg.* 941, *pg.* 553
SEALY CORPORATION, *pg.* 942, *pg.* 1391
SELECT COMFORT CORPORATION, *pg.* 942, *pg.* 942
SERTA, INC., *pg.* 942, *pg.* 619
SHEEX, INC., *pg.* 1138, *pg.* 1614
SIMMONS COMPANY, *pg.* 943, *pg.* 520
THE STANDARD MATTRESS COMPANY, *pg.* 943, *pg.* 352
STEARNS & FOSTER BEDDING COMPANY, *pg.* 944, *pg.* 1392
TEMPUR SEALY INTERNATIONAL, INC., *pg.* 944, *pg.* 731
THERAPEDIC ASSOCIATES, INC., *pg.* 945, *pg.* 1112
WHITE LOTUS HOME, *pg.* 946, *pg.* 1073

2517 - Wood Television, Radio, Phonograph & Sewing Machine Cabinets

BERNINA OF AMERICA INC., *pg.* 51, *pg.* 554
H. WILSON COMPANY, *pg.* 1415, *pg.* 666
LASALLE BRISTOL CORP., *pg.* 1053, *pg.* 677

2519 - Household Furniture, NEC

ADELPHI PAPER HANGINGS LLC, *pg.* 912, *pg.* 1342
AMERICAN LOCKER GROUP INCORPORATED, *pg.* 1041, *pg.* 1674
CANNON EQUIPMENT COMPANY, *pg.* 1321, *pg.* 920
CEDAR SHAKE & SHINGLE BUREAU, *pg.* 74, *pg.* 1908
EVENFLO COMPANY, INC., *pg.* 924, *pg.* 1470
FLEXSTEEL INDUSTRIES, INC., *pg.* 925, *pg.* 707
GRACO CHILDREN'S PRODUCTS INC., *pg.* 954, *pg.* 1531
THE GREAT AMERICAN HANGER COMPANY INC., *pg.* 926, *pg.* 442
HEAT SEAL LLC, *pg.* 1345, *pg.* 1431
HUFCOR INCORPORATED, *pg.* 87, *pg.* 1861
JELD-WEN, INC., *pg.* 1051, *pg.* 1499
JOHN BOOS & CO., *pg.* 1126, *pg.* 609
LASALLE BRISTOL CORP., *pg.* 1053, *pg.* 677
LEGGETT & PLATT, INCORPORATED, *pg.* 933, *pg.* 974
LEON'S FURNITURE LIMITED, *pg.* 933, *pg.* 1948
LIFETIME PRODUCTS INC., *pg.* 933, *pg.* 1751
LISTA INTERNATIONAL CORPORATION, *pg.* 934, *pg.* 825
THE LONGABERGER COMPANY, *pg.* 1127, *pg.* 1467
LOZIER CORPORATION, *pg.* 94, *pg.* 1016
MASCO CORPORATION, *pg.* 96, *pg.* 909
MEG, *pg.* 97, *pg.* 675
MODERNFOLD, INC., *pg.* 98, *pg.* 681
OMEGA NATIONAL PRODUCTS, *pg.* 939, *pg.* 737
RELAX THE BACK CORPORATION, *pg.* 940, *pg.* 120
SCOTT'S LIQUID GOLD-INC., *pg.* 335, *pg.* 323
VAUGHAN & BUSHNELL MANUFACTURING COMPANY, INC., *pg.* 1066, *pg.* 616
WALPOLE WOODWORKERS, INC., *pg.* 120, *pg.* 849
WENGER CORPORATION, *pg.* 1307, *pg.* 952
WEYERHAEUSER COMPANY, *pg.* 121, *pg.* 1820
WHITE RIVER HARDWOODS-WOODWORKS, INC., *pg.* 121, *pg.* 31
WMS INDUSTRIES INC., *pg.* 593, *pg.* 666
YETTER MANUFACTURING CO., INC., *pg.* 708, *pg.* 598

2521 - Wood Office Furniture

ANTHRO CORPORATION, *pg.* 913, *pg.* 1509
BUSH INDUSTRIES INC., *pg.* 919, *pg.* 1170
CONESTOGA WOOD SPECIALTIES CORP., *pg.* 921, *pg.* 1527
F.E. HALE MANUFACTURING COMPANY, *pg.* 925, *pg.* 1160
THE GUNLOCKE COMPANY, *pg.* 926, *pg.* 1349
HAWORTH, INC., *pg.* 402, *pg.* 891
HERMAN MILLER, INC., *pg.* 926, *pg.* 913
HOME MERIDIAN INTERNATIONAL, INC., *pg.* 928, *pg.* 1379
THE HON COMPANY, *pg.* 928, *pg.* 709
JASPER GROUP, *pg.* 930, *pg.* 691
JOFCO INC., *pg.* 931, *pg.* 691
KIMBALL INTERNATIONAL, INC., *pg.* 931, *pg.* 692
KNOLL, INC., *pg.* 425, *pg.* 1527
LUXOR CORP., *pg.* 428, *pg.* 666
MARTIN UNIVERSAL DESIGN, INC., *pg.* 430, *pg.* 884
MARTIN'S CHAIR, INC., *pg.* 934, *pg.* 1556
POLYVISION CORPORATION, *pg.* 665, *pg.* 531
STEELCASE INC., *pg.* 475, *pg.* 889
STONE CREEK FURNITURE INC., *pg.* 944, *pg.* 20
TRENDWAY CORPORATION, *pg.* 945, *pg.* 892
ZONGKERS CUSTOM FURNITURE, INC., *pg.* 947, *pg.* 1019

2522 - Metal Office Furniture

ANTHRO CORPORATION, *pg.* 913, *pg.* 1509
CHAMPION INDUSTRIES, INC., *pg.* 1626, *pg.* 1849
THE COMMERCIAL FURNITURE GROUP, *pg.* 920, *pg.* 994
FELLOWES, INC., *pg.* 397, *pg.* 620
FIRE KING SECURITY GROUP, *pg.* 1336, *pg.* 696
GREAT LAKES CASE & CABINET CO., INC., *pg.* 401, *pg.* 1529
HAWORTH, INC., *pg.* 402, *pg.* 891
HNI CORPORATION, *pg.* 927, *pg.* 709
THE HON COMPANY, *pg.* 928, *pg.* 709
HOWE FURNITURE CORPORATION, *pg.* 928, *pg.* 998
INVINCIBLE OFFICE FURNITURE, *pg.* 420, *pg.* 1868
KNOLL, INC., *pg.* 425, *pg.* 1527
LUXOR CORP., *pg.* 428, *pg.* 666
MARTIN UNIVERSAL DESIGN, INC., *pg.* 430, *pg.* 884
MITY ENTERPRISES, INC., *pg.* 935, *pg.* 1753
MODERNFOLD, INC., *pg.* 98, *pg.* 681
NEUTRAL POSTURE, INC., *pg.* 939, *pg.* 1669
NL INDUSTRIES, INC., *pg.* 1174, *pg.* 1684
POLYVISION CORPORATION, *pg.* 665, *pg.* 531
RELAX THE BACK CORPORATION, *pg.* 940, *pg.* 120
STEELCASE INC., *pg.* 475, *pg.* 889
TRENDWAY CORPORATION, *pg.* 945, *pg.* 892
VIRCO MANUFACTURING CORPORATION, *pg.* 946, *pg.* 297

2531 - Public Building & Related Furniture

ACOUSTIC INNOVATIONS INC., *pg.* 912, *pg.* 409
ADELPHI PAPER HANGINGS LLC, *pg.* 912, *pg.* 1342
ALL STAR CARTS AND VEHICLES CORP., *pg.* 163, *pg.* 1141
ALPHA PRO TECH, LTD., *pg.* 1492, *pg.* 1922
AMERICAN DREW, *pg.* 912, *pg.* 1374
AMERICAN LOCKER GROUP INCORPORATED, *pg.* 1041, *pg.* 1674
AMERICAN LOCKER SECURITY SYSTEMS, INC., *pg.* 1042, *pg.* 1674
ANDIS COMPANY, *pg.* 498, *pg.* 1895
AROMATIQUE INC., *pg.* 499, *pg.* 32
BD MEDICAL, *pg.* 1501, *pg.* 1762
BELVEDERE USA CORPORATION, *pg.* 917, *pg.* 556
BLANC INDUSTRIES SIGNAGE & DISPLAY GROUP, *pg.* 1621, *pg.* 1053
BLYTH, INC., *pg.* 502, *pg.* 349
BRADY CORPORATION, *pg.* 363, *pg.* 1873
BRIGHT OF AMERICA, INC., *pg.* 1121, *pg.* 1851
BUZTRONICS, INC., *pg.* 1294, *pg.* 683
CLOSETMAID CORPORATION, *pg.* 920, *pg.* 452
THE COMMERCIAL FURNITURE GROUP, *pg.* 920, *pg.* 994
DEMCO INC., *pg.* 386, *pg.* 1865
EDUCATIONAL INSIGHTS, INC., *pg.* 951, *pg.* 187
ENERGIZER HOLDINGS, INC., *pg.* 637, *pg.* 996
THE ENKEBOLL COMPANY, *pg.* 923, *pg.* 63
EUROTECH CABINETRY, INC., *pg.* 924, *pg.* 466
FOLKMANIS, INC., *pg.* 953, *pg.* 83
FOREIGN TRADERS, INC., *pg.* 1769, *pg.* 1135
FORTUNE BRANDS HOME & SECURITY, INC., *pg.* 55, *pg.* 600
GAF MATERIALS CORP., *pg.* 83, *pg.* 1681
GRACO CHILDREN'S PRODUCTS INC., *pg.* 954, *pg.* 1531
THE GUNLOCKE COMPANY, *pg.* 926, *pg.* 1349
THE HARTZ MOUNTAIN CORP., *pg.* 1476, *pg.* 1120
HELEN OF TROY L.P., *pg.* 511, *pg.* 1692
HICKORY CHAIR COMPANY, *pg.* 927, *pg.* 1378
HOME MERIDIAN INTERNATIONAL, INC., *pg.* 928, *pg.* 1379
HUSSEY SEATING CO., *pg.* 929, *pg.* 751
HYDRALIGN, *pg.* 1257, *pg.* 833
IAC INDUSTRIES, INC., *pg.* 929, *pg.* 48
ICON DESIGN & DISPLAY, INC., *pg.* 1460, *pg.* 277
IGT, *pg.* 412, *pg.* 1031
IMPERIAL WOODWORKS, INC., *pg.* 929, *pg.* 1749
INTERNATIONAL GAME TECHNOLOGY, *pg.* 957, *pg.* 1024
IRWIN SEATING COMPANY INC., *pg.* 929, *pg.* 887
JASON INDUSTRIES, INC., *pg.* 208, *pg.* 1875
JASPER GROUP, *pg.* 930, *pg.* 691
JBI, INC., *pg.* 930, *pg.* 123
JEREMIAH CAMPBELL & COMPANY, *pg.* 931, *pg.* 749
JOHN BOOS & CO., *pg.* 1126, *pg.* 609
JOHNSON & JOHNSON BABY PRODUCTS, INC., *pg.* 1552, *pg.* 1094
KENNAMETAL INC., *pg.* 1052, *pg.* 1547
KEWAUNEE SCIENTIFIC CORPORATION, *pg.* 931, *pg.* 1391
KNAPE & VOGT MANUFACTURING COMPANY, *pg.* 1052, *pg.* 913
KNOLL, INC., *pg.* 425, *pg.* 1527
KRAFTMAID CABINETRY, INC., *pg.* 1053, *pg.* 1465
LAKELAND INDUSTRIES, INC., *pg.* 1354, *pg.* 1338
LARSON-JUHL US LLC, *pg.* 933, *pg.* 537
LINDAL CEDAR HOMES, INC., *pg.* 94, *pg.* 1837
LISTA INTERNATIONAL CORPORATION, *pg.* 934, *pg.* 825
LOZIER CORPORATION, *pg.* 94, *pg.* 1016
MANHATTAN ASSOCIATES, INC., *pg.* 430, *pg.* 513
MINE SAFETY APPLIANCES COMPANY, *pg.* 1361, *pg.* 1525
MIRACLE RECREATION EQUIPMENT COMPANY, *pg.* 1839, *pg.* 988
MITY ENTERPRISES, INC., *pg.* 935, *pg.* 1753
MULTIMEDIA GAMES INC., *pg.* 442, *pg.* 1664
NATURAL DECORATIONS, INC., *pg.* 936, *pg.* 5
NEMSCHOFF, INC., *pg.* 936, *pg.* 1890
OIL-DRI CORPORATION OF AMERICA, *pg.* 1480, *pg.* 586
OSBORN INTERNATIONAL, *pg.* 1367, *pg.* 1406
OTTERBOX PRODUCTS LLC, *pg.* 451, *pg.* 329
PACIFIC COLUMNS, INC., *pg.* 103, *pg.* 49
PARISI INCORPORATED, *pg.* 103, *pg.* 1556
POLYVISION CORPORATION, *pg.* 665, *pg.* 531
RAUCH INDUSTRIES, INC., *pg.* 940, *pg.* 1373
REPLOGLE GLOBES, INC., *pg.* 461, *pg.* 559
SAUDER MANUFACTURING COMPANY, *pg.* 941, *pg.* 1403
SAUDER WOODWORKING CO., *pg.* 941, *pg.* 1403
SCOTT'S LIQUID GOLD-INC., *pg.* 335, *pg.* 323
SEALY CORPORATION, *pg.* 942, *pg.* 1391
SEATS INCORPORATED, *pg.* 217, *pg.* 1890
THE SERAPH, *pg.* 942, *pg.* 847
ST. JUDE MEDICAL, INC., *pg.* 1596, *pg.* 963
TELEDYNE BENTHOS, INC., *pg.* 1431, *pg.* 838
THOMASVILLE FURNITURE INDUSTRIES, INC., *pg.* 945, *pg.* 1391
TRANS-LUX CORPORATION, *pg.* 681, *pg.* 365
UMF MEDICAL, *pg.* 946, *pg.* 1542
VANSAN CORPORATION, *pg.* 685, *pg.* 68
VIRCO MANUFACTURING CORPORATION, *pg.* 946, *pg.* 297
WAHL CLIPPER CORPORATION, *pg.* 524, *pg.* 662
WATERLOO INDUSTRIES, INC., *pg.* 946, *pg.* 1885
WENGER CORPORATION, *pg.* 1307, *pg.* 952
WITH HEART & HAND, *pg.* 946, *pg.* 837
WMS INDUSTRIES INC., *pg.* 593, *pg.* 666
THE WOODSTREAM CORPORATION, *pg.* 1801, *pg.* 1549
THE YANKEE CANDLE COMPANY, INC., *pg.* 1792, *pg.* 843
ZONGKERS CUSTOM FURNITURE, INC., *pg.* 947, *pg.* 1019

2541 - Wood Partitions, Shelving, Lockers & Office & Store Fixtures

THE ENKEBOLL COMPANY, *pg.* 923, *pg.* 63
EUROTECH CABINETRY, INC., *pg.* 924, *pg.* 466
FOREIGN TRADERS, INC., *pg.* 1769, *pg.* 1135
GAF MATERIALS CORP., *pg.* 83, *pg.* 1681
ICON DESIGN & DISPLAY, INC., *pg.* 1460, *pg.* 277
JEREMIAH CAMPBELL & COMPANY, *pg.* 931, *pg.* 749
LINDAL CEDAR HOMES, INC., *pg.* 94, *pg.* 1837
LOZIER CORPORATION, *pg.* 94, *pg.* 1016
MANHATTAN ASSOCIATES, INC., *pg.* 430, *pg.* 513
PACIFIC COLUMNS, INC., *pg.* 103, *pg.* 49
THE SERAPH, *pg.* 942, *pg.* 847
WITH HEART & HAND, *pg.* 946, *pg.* 837

2542 - Office & Store Fixtures, Partitions, Shelving & Lockers, Except Wood

AIR-LEC INDUSTRIES LLC, *pg.* 1041, *pg.* 1864
A.L. HANSEN MANUFACTURING CO., *pg.* 1041, *pg.* 665
ALLFAST FASTENING SYSTEMS, INC., *pg.* 1041, *pg.* 66
AMATOM ELECTRONIC HARDWARE, INC., *pg.* 1041, *pg.* 342
AMERICAN DREW, *pg.* 912, *pg.* 1374
AMERICAN LOCKER GROUP INCORPORATED, *pg.* 1041, *pg.* 1674
AMERICAN LOCKER SECURITY SYSTEMS, INC., *pg.* 1042, *pg.* 1674
AMERICAN VAN EQUIPMENT INC., *pg.* 199, *pg.* 1078
AMISCO INDUSTRIES LTD., *pg.* 913, *pg.* 1958
APTARGROUP, INC., *pg.* 1451, *pg.* 598
ASCO SINTERING CO., *pg.* 1042, *pg.* 126
ASHLEY FURNITURE INDUSTRIES, INC., *pg.* 914, *pg.* 1852
ATTWOOD CORPORATION, *pg.* 1705, *pg.* 897
AUTOMATIC EQUIPMENT CORPORATION, *pg.* 1315, *pg.* 1410
BAKER KNAPP & TUBBS INC., *pg.* 916, *pg.* 566
BALL & BALL HARDWARE REPRODUCTIONS, *pg.* 916, *pg.* 1531
BARNES GROUP INC., *pg.* 1317, *pg.* 340
BASSETT FURNITURE INDUSTRIES, INCORPORATED, *pg.* 916, *pg.* 1776
BERNHARDT DESIGN, *pg.* 918, *pg.* 1381
BLACK & DECKER, *pg.* 1043, *pg.* 1907
BOBRICK WASHROOM EQUIPMENT, INC., *pg.* 1043, *pg.* 166
BROWN JORDAN INTERNATIONAL COMPANY, *pg.* 919, *pg.* 740

BROYHILL FURNITURE INDUSTRIES, INC., *pg.* 919, *pg.* 1381
BRYCE CORPORATION, *pg.* 1879, *pg.* 1641
BTM CORPORATION, *pg.* 1320, *pg.* 898
BUCKEYE CORRUGATED INC., *pg.* 1454, *pg.* 1400
BUSH INDUSTRIES INC., *pg.* 919, *pg.* 1170
BWAY HOLDING COMPANY, *pg.* 1454, *pg.* 491
CASCADE CORPORATION, *pg.* 1321, *pg.* 1497
CC INDUSTRIES, INC., *pg.* 920, *pg.* 569
CENTURY FURNITURE INDUSTRIES, *pg.* 920, *pg.* 1377
CHF INDUSTRIES, INC., *pg.* 920, *pg.* 1211
CHICAGO-WILCOX MFG. COMPANY, INC., *pg.* 202, *pg.* 661
CHILD CRAFT INDUSTRIES, INC., *pg.* 920, *pg.* 1463
CLOSETMAID CORPORATION, *pg.* 920, *pg.* 452
COMPX INTERNATIONAL INC., *pg.* 1044, *pg.* 1678
CROSMAN CORPORATION, *pg.* 951, *pg.* 1143
CUSTOM PAK, INC., *pg.* 1881, *pg.* 703
DARNELL-ROSE, *pg.* 1045, *pg.* 67
DECO PRODUCTS CO., *pg.* 1045, *pg.* 704
DMI FURNITURE, INC., *pg.* 923, *pg.* 733
DREMEL, *pg.* 1046, *pg.* 634
DRIV-LOK, INC., *pg.* 1046, *pg.* 662
THE EASTERN COMPANY, *pg.* 1331, *pg.* 357
EBERHARD MANUFACTURING DIVISION, *pg.* 1046, *pg.* 1475
THE ENKEBOLL COMPANY, *pg.* 923, *pg.* 63
E.R. WAGNER CASTERS AND WHEELS DIV., *pg.* 1047, *pg.* 1874
ERICO INTERNATIONAL CORPORATION, *pg.* 1335, *pg.* 1472
ESCO CORPORATION, *pg.* 1335, *pg.* 1502
ETHAN ALLEN INTERIORS INC., *pg.* 924, *pg.* 343
EUROTECH CABINETRY, INC., *pg.* 924, *pg.* 466
FEDERAL HOSE MANUFACTURING INC., *pg.* 1047, *pg.* 1469
FLEXIBLE STEEL LACING COMPANY, *pg.* 1337, *pg.* 608
FOREIGN TRADERS, INC., *pg.* 1769, *pg.* 1135
FORTUNE BRANDS HOME & SECURITY, INC., *pg.* 55, *pg.* 600
GAF MATERIALS CORP., *pg.* 83, *pg.* 1681
GIBRALTAR INDUSTRIES, INC., *pg.* 1340, *pg.* 1148
GREAT LAKES CASE & CABINET CO., INC., *pg.* 401, *pg.* 1529
GREIF INC., *pg.* 1459, *pg.* 1447
GRIPNAIL CORPORATION, *pg.* 1048, *pg.* 1601
GROOV-PIN CORPORATION, *pg.* 1049, *pg.* 1608
GROUPE DUTAILIER INC., *pg.* 926, *pg.* 1960
HANNAY REELS INC., *pg.* 1344, *pg.* 1351
HARDEN FURNITURE INC., *pg.* 926, *pg.* 1177
HERITAGE HOME GROUP, *pg.* 926, *pg.* 1379
HICKORY CHAIR COMPANY, *pg.* 927, *pg.* 1378
HOME MERIDIAN INTERNATIONAL, INC., *pg.* 928, *pg.* 1379
HOOKER FURNITURE CORPORATION, *pg.* 928, *pg.* 1788
HOWARD MILLER COMPANY, *pg.* 7, *pg.* 914
ICON DESIGN & DISPLAY, INC., *pg.* 1460, *pg.* 277
INVACARE CORPORATION, *pg.* 1546, *pg.* 1451
JARDEN CONSUMER SOLUTIONS, *pg.* 57, *pg.* 412
JEREMIAH CAMPBELL & COMPANY, *pg.* 931, *pg.* 749
JOHN BOOS & CO., *pg.* 1126, *pg.* 609
KABA ILCO CORP., *pg.* 1052, *pg.* 1390
THE KARGES FURNITURE COMPANY, INC., *pg.* 931, *pg.* 679
KENNAMETAL INC., *pg.* 1052, *pg.* 1547
KINDEL FURNITURE COMPANY, *pg.* 931, *pg.* 887
KINGSLEY-BATE, LTD., *pg.* 932, *pg.* 1787
KNAPE & VOGT MANUFACTURING COMPANY, *pg.* 1052, *pg.* 913
KRAFTMAID CABINETRY, INC., *pg.* 1053, *pg.* 1465
KURZ TRANSFER PRODUCTS, L.P., *pg.* 1354, *pg.* 1367
LARSON-JUHL US LLC, *pg.* 933, *pg.* 537
LASALLE BRISTOL CORP., *pg.* 1053, *pg.* 677
LEGGETT & PLATT, INCORPORATED, *pg.* 933, *pg.* 974
LEXINGTON HOME BRANDS, *pg.* 933, *pg.* 1391
LINDAL CEDAR HOMES, INC., *pg.* 94, *pg.* 1837
LOZIER CORPORATION, *pg.* 94, *pg.* 1016
LYDALL, INC., *pg.* 1357, *pg.* 354
MANHATTAN ASSOCIATES, INC., *pg.* 430, *pg.* 513
MANITOWOC CRANE SHADY GROVE, *pg.* 1359, *pg.* 1586
MARTIN'S CHAIR, INC., *pg.* 934, *pg.* 1556
MASTER LOCK COMPANY LLC, *pg.* 1055, *pg.* 1884
MATCO TOOLS CORPORATION, *pg.* 1055, *pg.* 1474
MATERION CORPORATION, *pg.* 1359, *pg.* 1463
MATERION MICROELECTRONICS & SERVICES, *pg.* 1559, *pg.* 1149
MCGUIRE FAMILY FURNITURE MAKERS, *pg.* 935, *pg.* 1766
MEDECO HIGH SECURITY LOCKS, INC., *pg.* 1055, *pg.* 1806
MITEK, INC., *pg.* 1056, *pg.* 975
MURPHY BED CO., INC., *pg.* 935, *pg.* 1159
NACCO INDUSTRIES, INC., *pg.* 1174, *pg.* 1433
OMG, INC., *pg.* 1367, *pg.* 781
OXO, *pg.* 1058, *pg.* 1275
PACIFIC COLUMNS, INC., *pg.* 103, *pg.* 49
PACTIV CORPORATION, *pg.* 1466, *pg.* 624
PASLODE, *pg.* 1059, *pg.* 664
PENN ENGINEERING & MANUFACTURING CORP., *pg.* 1059, *pg.* 1525
PENNENGINEERING FASTENING TECHNOLOGIES, *pg.* 1059, *pg.* 1526
PORTLAND WILLAMETTE, *pg.* 1129, *pg.* 1505
PRECISION VALVE CORPORATION, *pg.* 1060, *pg.* 1357
REV-A-SHELF, *pg.* 1060, *pg.* 738
RICHELIEU HARDWARE LTD., *pg.* 1060, *pg.* 1961
RIO BRANDS, INC., *pg.* 941, *pg.* 1570
ROCKY MOUNTAIN HARDWARE INC., *pg.* 1061, *pg.* 549
RONA, INC., *pg.* 216, *pg.* 1950
ROUSSEAU METAL, INC., *pg.* 463, *pg.* 1960
RUSSEL METALS INC., *pg.* 1180, *pg.* 1928
RYERSON INC., *pg.* 1373, *pg.* 589
SARGENT & GREENLEAF, INC., *pg.* 1061, *pg.* 739
SARGENT MANUFACTURING COMPANY, *pg.* 1061, *pg.* 359
SCHAEFER MARINE INC., *pg.* 1373, *pg.* 835
SENIOR FLEXONICS INC., *pg.* 1375, *pg.* 556
SENTRY GROUP, INC., *pg.* 468, *pg.* 1337
THE SERAPH, *pg.* 942, *pg.* 847
SHILOH INDUSTRIES, INC., *pg.* 1375, *pg.* 1478
SHUR-CO, INC., *pg.* 110, *pg.* 1626
SIMPSON MANUFACTURING COMPANY, INC., *pg.* 1376, *pg.* 185
SOLIDSCAPE, INC., *pg.* 1063, *pg.* 1037
SOUTHERN FOLGER DETENTION EQUIPMENT COMPANY, *pg.* 1063, *pg.* 1743
SPIROL INTERNATIONAL CORPORATION, *pg.* 1378, *pg.* 345
STANLEY BLACK & DECKER, INC., *pg.* 1063, *pg.* 358
STANLEY FURNITURE CO., INC., *pg.* 943, *pg.* 1379
TCI PRECISION METALS, INC., *pg.* 1380, *pg.* 95
TELESCOPE CASUAL FURNITURE INC., *pg.* 944, *pg.* 1162
THERMOS L.L.C., *pg.* 61, *pg.* 660
THOMASVILLE FURNITURE INDUSTRIES, INC., *pg.* 945, *pg.* 1391
TIDEL ENGINEERING, L.P., *pg.* 1382, *pg.* 1670
TRINITY INDUSTRIES, INC., *pg.* 116, *pg.* 1690
TROPITONE FURNITURE CO., INC., *pg.* 945, *pg.* 118
TRUTH HARDWARE CORP., *pg.* 1066, *pg.* 952
UNIVERSAL INDUSTRIAL PRODUCTS CO., *pg.* 1066, *pg.* 1470
WENGER CORPORATION, *pg.* 1307, *pg.* 952
WHITE LOTUS HOME, *pg.* 946, *pg.* 1073
THE WICKER WORKS, *pg.* 946, *pg.* 233
WILLIAMS-SONOMA, INC., *pg.* 1140, *pg.* 234
WINNER INTERNATIONAL, LLC, *pg.* 222, *pg.* 1586
WITH HEART & HAND, *pg.* 946, *pg.* 837
WITT INDUSTRIES, INC., *pg.* 1140, *pg.* 1461
WORTHINGTON INDUSTRIES, INC., *pg.* 123, *pg.* 1444
YARDLEY PRODUCTS CORPORATION, *pg.* 1391, *pg.* 1596
ZIM-AMERICAN ISRAELI SHIPPING CO., *pg.* 1931, *pg.* 1798
ZIPPO MANUFACTURING COMPANY, INC., *pg.* 1895, *pg.* 1518

2591 - Drapery Hardware & Window Blinds & Shades

3 DAY BLINDS, INC., *pg.* 912, *pg.* 105
BLINDS TO GO INC., *pg.* 918, *pg.* 1953
HUNTER DOUGLAS, INC., *pg.* 928, *pg.* 1320
JS INTERNATIONAL, INC., *pg.* 931, *pg.* 818
KENNEY MANUFACTURING COMPANY, *pg.* 1052, *pg.* 1609
SPRINGS WINDOW FASHIONS LLC, *pg.* 943, *pg.* 1872

2611 - Pulp Mills

CANFOR CORPORATION, *pg.* 1454, *pg.* 1910
GEORGIA-PACIFIC CELLULOSE, *pg.* 1164, *pg.* 1644
NEENAH PAPER, INC., *pg.* 1465, *pg.* 484
PARSONS & WHITTEMORE, INC., *pg.* 103, *pg.* 1339
PLUM CREEK TIMBER COMPANY, INC., *pg.* 105, *pg.* 1838
TEMBEC INC., *pg.* 114, *pg.* 1957

2621 - Paper Mills

APPVION INC., *pg.* 1451, *pg.* 1852
BPM INC., *pg.* 1454, *pg.* 1886
CANFOR CORPORATION, *pg.* 1454, *pg.* 1910
CENVEO INC., *pg.* 1626, *pg.* 372
CRANE & CO., INC., *pg.* 1456, *pg.* 816
DOMTAR CORPORATION, *pg.* 1456, *pg.* 1954
FIBERMARK INC., *pg.* 1457, *pg.* 1764
FINCH PAPER LLC, *pg.* 1457, *pg.* 1161
GEORGIA-PACIFIC CELLULOSE, *pg.* 1164, *pg.* 1644
GEORGIA-PACIFIC LLC, *pg.* 1458, *pg.* 507
INTERNATIONAL PAPER-BLEACHED BOARD DIV., *pg.* 1460, *pg.* 1644
INTERNATIONAL PAPER COMPANY, *pg.* 1460, *pg.* 1644
KIMBERLY-CLARK CORPORATION, *pg.* 1461, *pg.* 1720
MEADWESTVACO PACKAGING SYSTEMS, LLC, *pg.* 1464, *pg.* 514
MOHAWK FINE PAPERS, INC., *pg.* 1464, *pg.* 1153
MONADNOCK PAPER MILLS, INC., *pg.* 1464, *pg.* 1033
THE MORNING CALL, INC., *pg.* 1665, *pg.* 1513
NEENAH PAPER, INC., *pg.* 1465, *pg.* 484
NICE-PAK PRODUCTS, INC., *pg.* 1465, *pg.* 1319
ORCHIDS PAPER PRODUCTS COMPANY, *pg.* 1465, *pg.* 1488
PARSONS & WHITTEMORE, INC., *pg.* 103, *pg.* 1339
PLUM CREEK TIMBER COMPANY, INC., *pg.* 105, *pg.* 1838
POTLATCH CORPORATION, *pg.* 1467, *pg.* 1844
RESOLUTE FOREST PRODUCTS, *pg.* 1468, *pg.* 968
SOUTHWORTH COMPANY INC., *pg.* 1470, *pg.* 781
SWM, *pg.* 1895, *pg.* 485
TEMBEC INC., *pg.* 114, *pg.* 1957
WASAU PAPER CORP., *pg.* 1471, *pg.* 1882
WAUSAU PAPER, *pg.* 1471, *pg.* 1855
WAUSAU PAPER BAY WEST, *pg.* 1471, *pg.* 1465
WESTROCK COMPANY, *pg.* 1472, *pg.* 1805
XPEDX, *pg.* 1472, *pg.* 1458

2631 - Paperboard Mills

ARVCO CONTAINER CORPORATION, *pg.* 1452, *pg.* 894
CANFOR CORPORATION, *pg.* 1454, *pg.* 1910
CARAUSTAR INDUSTRIES, INC., *pg.* 1455, *pg.* 525
CASCADES, INC., *pg.* 73, *pg.* 1950
FIBERMARK INC., *pg.* 1457, *pg.* 1764
GEORGIA-PACIFIC CELLULOSE, *pg.* 1164, *pg.* 1644
GRAPHIC PACKAGING HOLDING COMPANY, *pg.* 1459, *pg.* 509
GREIF INC., *pg.* 1459, *pg.* 1447
MELE COMPANIES, INC., *pg.* 9, *pg.* 1347
NEENAH PAPER, INC., *pg.* 1465, *pg.* 484
PARSONS & WHITTEMORE, INC., *pg.* 103, *pg.* 1339
PLUM CREEK TIMBER COMPANY, INC., *pg.* 105, *pg.* 1838
POTLATCH CORPORATION, *pg.* 1467, *pg.* 1844
SONOCO PRODUCTS COMPANY, *pg.* 1469, *pg.* 1619
SOUTHWEST BINDING & LAMINATING, *pg.* 1377, *pg.* 988
TEMBEC INC., *pg.* 114, *pg.* 1957
THE UNION GROUP, *pg.* 487, *pg.* 819
UNITED STATES BOX CORP., *pg.* 1471, *pg.* 1098
WESTROCK COMPANY, *pg.* 1472, *pg.* 1805
WEYERHAEUSER COMPANY, *pg.* 121, *pg.* 1820

2652 - Set-Up Paperboard Boxes

GREIF INC., *pg.* 1459, *pg.* 1447
PACKAGING CORPORATION OF AMERICA, *pg.* 1466, *pg.* 624
UNITED STATES BOX CORP., *pg.* 1471, *pg.* 1098

2653 - Corrugated & Solid Fiber Boxes

ACCO BRANDS CORPORATION, *pg.* 340, *pg.* 626
AMERICAN STATIONERY CO., INC., *pg.* 349, *pg.* 696
APPVION INC., *pg.* 1451, *pg.* 1852
ARVCO CONTAINER CORPORATION, *pg.* 1452, *pg.* 894
ATLANTIC CORPORATION, *pg.* 1452, *pg.* 1392
BPM INC., *pg.* 1454, *pg.* 1886

BUCKEYE CORRUGATED INC., *pg.* 1454, *pg.* 1400
CALUMET CARTON COMPANY, *pg.* 1454, *pg.* 661
CANSON INC., *pg.* 1625, *pg.* 844
CARAUSTAR INDUSTRIES, INC., *pg.* 1455, *pg.* 525
CASCADES, INC., *pg.* 73, *pg.* 1950
CENVEO INC., *pg.* 1626, *pg.* 372
CRESCENT CARDBOARD COMPANY, L.L.C., *pg.* 1456, *pg.* 670
DOMTAR CORPORATION, *pg.* 1456, *pg.* 1954
FINCH PAPER LLC, *pg.* 1457, *pg.* 1161
GRAPHIC PACKAGING HOLDING COMPANY, *pg.* 1459, *pg.* 509
GREIF INC., *pg.* 1459, *pg.* 1447
KOCH INDUSTRIES, INC., *pg.* 1463, *pg.* 724
LAWRENCE PAPER COMPANY, *pg.* 1463, *pg.* 715
MCCOURT LABEL COMPANY, *pg.* 1464, *pg.* 1548
MITCHEL-LINCOLN PACKAGING LTD, *pg.* 1464, *pg.* 1960
ONTARIO WALL COVERINGS, *pg.* 940, *pg.* 1941
PACKAGING CORPORATION OF AMERICA, *pg.* 1466, *pg.* 624
PACON CORPORATION, *pg.* 1466, *pg.* 1852
SAPPI FINE PAPER NORTH AMERICA, *pg.* 1468, *pg.* 801
SMEAD MANUFACTURING COMPANY, *pg.* 470, *pg.* 926
TECUMSEH PACKAGING SOLUTIONS, *pg.* 1470, *pg.* 909
TUFCO TECHNOLOGIES, INC., *pg.* 1697, *pg.* 1860
VARITRONICS, LLC, *pg.* 487, *pg.* 954
WESTROCK COMPANY, *pg.* 1472, *pg.* 1805
XPEDX, *pg.* 1473, *pg.* 1377

2655 - Fiber Cans, Tubes, Drums & Similar Products

GIBRALTAR PACKAGING GROUP, INC., *pg.* 1459, *pg.* 1011
GREIF INC., *pg.* 1459, *pg.* 1447
SONOCO PRODUCTS COMPANY, *pg.* 1469, *pg.* 1619

2656 - Sanitary Food Containers, Except Folding

AMCOR PET PACKAGING INC., *pg.* 1451, *pg.* 898
CLARCOR, INC., *pg.* 1455, *pg.* 1632
GEORGIA-PACIFIC LLC, *pg.* 1458, *pg.* 507
IFCO SYSTEMS NORTH AMERICA, *pg.* 411, *pg.* 1708
SCHREIBER FOODS, INC., *pg.* 894, *pg.* 1859

2657 - Folding Paperboard Boxes, Including Sanitary

GIBRALTAR PACKAGING GROUP, INC., *pg.* 1459, *pg.* 1011
GRAPHIC PACKAGING HOLDING COMPANY, *pg.* 1459, *pg.* 509
GREIF INC., *pg.* 1459, *pg.* 1447
GUNTHER MELE LIMITED, *pg.* 6, *pg.* 1919
MOD-PAC CORP., *pg.* 1665, *pg.* 1150
PACKAGING CORPORATION OF AMERICA, *pg.* 1466, *pg.* 624

2671 - Coated & Laminated Paper & Plastics Film

AEP INDUSTRIES INC., *pg.* 1878, *pg.* 1085
ALLIED SECURITY INNOVATIONS, INC., *pg.* 1041, *pg.* 1066
AMERICAN PACKAGING CORPORATION, *pg.* 1451, *pg.* 1333
APPVION INC., *pg.* 1451, *pg.* 1852
ATMI, INC., *pg.* 1314, *pg.* 342
AVERY DENNISON CORPORATION, *pg.* 1452, *pg.* 95
BEMIS COMPANY, INC., *pg.* 1453, *pg.* 1882
BEMIS HEALTHCARE PACKAGING, *pg.* 1453, *pg.* 1885
BRYCE CORPORATION, *pg.* 1879, *pg.* 1641
BUCKEYE CORRUGATED INC., *pg.* 1454, *pg.* 1400
ELKAY PLASTICS COMPANY, INC., *pg.* 1882, *pg.* 68
FORTIFIBER CORPORATION, *pg.* 83, *pg.* 1021
GEORGIA-PACIFIC LLC, *pg.* 1458, *pg.* 507
GIBRALTAR PACKAGING GROUP, INC., *pg.* 1459, *pg.* 1011
HOLO-SOURCE CORPORATION, *pg.* 1416, *pg.* 896
H.S. CROCKER CO., INC., *pg.* 1651, *pg.* 619
INNOVATIVE PLASTICS CORPORATION, *pg.* 1460, *pg.* 1319
INTERTAPE POLYMER GROUP INC., *pg.* 1885, *pg.* 1960
LANGSTON COMPANIES, INC., *pg.* 1463, *pg.* 1645
MONOSOL, LLC, *pg.* 59, *pg.* 694
POLYAIR INTER PACK INC., *pg.* 1467, *pg.* 1941
RAYONIER INC., *pg.* 1179, *pg.* 434
REYNOLDS CONSUMER PRODUCTS, *pg.* 1138, *pg.* 625
SEALED AIR CORPORATION, *pg.* 1468, *pg.* 1058
SONOCO PRODUCTS COMPANY, *pg.* 1469, *pg.* 1619
SURFACE COATINGS LLC, *pg.* 1470, *pg.* 1737
TEKNI-PLEX, INC., *pg.* 1470, *pg.* 1122
THERMWELL PRODUCTS CO., INC., *pg.* 1065, *pg.* 1082
TREDEGAR CORPORATION, *pg.* 1890, *pg.* 1804
TUFCO TECHNOLOGIES, INC., *pg.* 1697, *pg.* 1860
WESTROCK COMPANY, *pg.* 1472, *pg.* 1805
ZAGG INCORPORATED, *pg.* 690, *pg.* 1762
ZIP-PAK, *pg.* 1473, *pg.* 631

2672 - Coated & Laminated Paper, NEC

AMERICAN BILTRITE INC., *pg.* 1878, *pg.* 856
AVERY DENNISON CORPORATION, *pg.* 1452, *pg.* 95
BRADY CORPORATION, *pg.* 363, *pg.* 1873
HAZEN PAPER COMPANY, *pg.* 1459, *pg.* 825
HENKEL CONSUMER ADHESIVES, INC., *pg.* 403, *pg.* 1480
H.S. CROCKER CO., INC., *pg.* 1651, *pg.* 619
MOHAWK FINE PAPERS, INC., *pg.* 1464, *pg.* 1153
OLIVER PRODUCTS COMPANY INC., *pg.* 1367, *pg.* 888
PINNACLE COATING & CONVERTING, INC., *pg.* 1467, *pg.* 1622
SCHNELLER, INC., *pg.* 234, *pg.* 1456
SPINNAKER COATING, LLC, *pg.* 1470, *pg.* 1477
THE STANDARD REGISTER COMPANY, *pg.* 473, *pg.* 1446
THERMWELL PRODUCTS CO., INC., *pg.* 1065, *pg.* 1082
TOPFLIGHT CORPORATION, *pg.* 681, *pg.* 1534
VARITRONICS, LLC, *pg.* 487, *pg.* 954
WEBER PACKAGING SOLUTIONS, INC., *pg.* 491, *pg.* 554
WESTERN STATES ENVELOPE & LABEL, *pg.* 492, *pg.* 1856
YORK WALLCOVERINGS INC., *pg.* 947, *pg.* 1598
ZEBRA TECHNOLOGIES CORPORATION, *pg.* 690, *pg.* 628

2673 - Plastics, Foil & Coated Paper Bags

AUTOMATED PACKAGING SYSTEMS INC., *pg.* 1452, *pg.* 1474
DRAVON MEDICAL, INC., *pg.* 1525, *pg.* 1497
LIQUI-BOX CORPORATION, *pg.* 1464, *pg.* 1802
NEXUS PLASTICS, INC., *pg.* 1465, *pg.* 1073
PACTIV CORPORATION, *pg.* 1466, *pg.* 624
REYNOLDS CONSUMER PRODUCTS, *pg.* 1138, *pg.* 625
SEALED AIR CORPORATION, *pg.* 1468, *pg.* 1058

2674 - Uncoated Paper & Multiwall Bags

AMERICAN PACKAGING CORPORATION, *pg.* 1451, *pg.* 1333
BROWN PAPER GOODS COMPANY, *pg.* 1454, *pg.* 665
LANGSTON COMPANIES, INC., *pg.* 1463, *pg.* 1645
SAPPI FINE PAPER NORTH AMERICA, *pg.* 1468, *pg.* 801
SEALED AIR CORPORATION, *pg.* 1468, *pg.* 1058

2675 - Die-Cut Paper, Paperboard & Cardboard

AMERICAN STATIONERY CO., INC., *pg.* 349, *pg.* 696
APPVION INC., *pg.* 1451, *pg.* 1852
ATLANTIC CORPORATION, *pg.* 1452, *pg.* 1392
BEMIS COMPANY, INC., *pg.* 1453, *pg.* 1882
BPM INC., *pg.* 1454, *pg.* 1886
CANSON INC., *pg.* 1625, *pg.* 844
CARAUSTAR INDUSTRIES, INC., *pg.* 1455, *pg.* 525
CASCADES, INC., *pg.* 73, *pg.* 1950
THE COLAD GROUP, INC., *pg.* 377, *pg.* 1147
CRESCENT CARDBOARD COMPANY, L.L.C., *pg.* 1456, *pg.* 670
DOMTAR CORPORATION, *pg.* 1456, *pg.* 1954
ESSELTE BUSINESS CORP, *pg.* 395, *pg.* 1179
FINCH PAPER LLC, *pg.* 1457, *pg.* 1161
MCCOURT LABEL COMPANY, *pg.* 1464, *pg.* 1548
ONTARIO WALL COVERINGS, *pg.* 940, *pg.* 1941
PACON CORPORATION, *pg.* 1466, *pg.* 1852
SAPPI FINE PAPER NORTH AMERICA, *pg.* 1468, *pg.* 801
SMEAD MANUFACTURING COMPANY, *pg.* 470, *pg.* 926
TUFCO TECHNOLOGIES, INC., *pg.* 1697, *pg.* 1860
VARITRONICS, LLC, *pg.* 487, *pg.* 954
WESTROCK COMPANY, *pg.* 1472, *pg.* 1805
XPEDX, *pg.* 1473, *pg.* 1377

2676 - Sanitary Paper Products

A-T SURGICAL MFG. CO., INC., *pg.* 1483, *pg.* 825
ACUSHNET COMPANY, *pg.* 1824, *pg.* 818
ALIMED, INC., *pg.* 1490, *pg.* 816
ALLIED HEALTHCARE PRODUCTS, INC., *pg.* 1491, *pg.* 990
ALPHA PRO TECH, LTD., *pg.* 1492, *pg.* 1922
AMERICAN BILTRITE INC., *pg.* 1878, *pg.* 856
AMERICAN MEDICAL SYSTEMS HOLDINGS, INC., *pg.* 1493, *pg.* 947
ASSOCIATED HYGIENIC PRODUCTS LLC, *pg.* 1496, *pg.* 531
BAE SYSTEMS PRODUCTS GROUP, *pg.* 359, *pg.* 432
BARNHARDT MANUFACTURING COMPANY, *pg.* 1498, *pg.* 1364
BAXTER INTERNATIONAL INC., *pg.* 1499, *pg.* 599
BD MEDICAL, *pg.* 1501, *pg.* 1762
BECTON, DICKINSON & COMPANY, *pg.* 1501, *pg.* 1068
BOSTON SCIENTIFIC CORPORATION, *pg.* 1508, *pg.* 831
CARDINAL HEALTH, INC., *pg.* 1512, *pg.* 1448
CAS MEDICAL SYSTEMS, INC., *pg.* 1513, *pg.* 339
CONGOLEUM CORPORATION, *pg.* 921, *pg.* 1084
THE COOPER COMPANIES, INC., *pg.* 1518, *pg.* 183
CORDIS CORPORATION, *pg.* 1519, *pg.* 430
CORE MOLDING TECHNOLOGIES, INC., *pg.* 1881, *pg.* 1439
CRYOLIFE, INC., *pg.* 1520, *pg.* 534
DAVID CLARK COMPANY INCORPORATED, *pg.* 633, *pg.* 862
DEPUY SYNTHES, *pg.* 1523, *pg.* 1593
DEPUYSYNTHES, *pg.* 1523, *pg.* 699
DJO INCORPORATED, *pg.* 1524, *pg.* 302
DJO SURGICAL, *pg.* 1525, *pg.* 1661
DURA UNDERCUSHIONS LTD., *pg.* 923, *pg.* 1954
E.D. BULLARD COMPANY, *pg.* 1332, *pg.* 727
ENCON SAFETY PRODUCTS, *pg.* 1334, *pg.* 1705
ENDOLOGIX, INC., *pg.* 1528, *pg.* 109
ENERGIZER HOLDINGS, INC., *pg.* 637, *pg.* 996
EXACTECH, INC., *pg.* 1529, *pg.* 428
FEMPRO CONSUMER PRODUCTS ULC., *pg.* 1530, *pg.* 1950
FGX INTERNATIONAL, INC., *pg.* 5, *pg.* 1608
GEORGIA-PACIFIC CELLULOSE, *pg.* 1164, *pg.* 1644
HANGER INC., *pg.* 1539, *pg.* 1663
HEMCO CORPORATION, *pg.* 1416, *pg.* 979
HEMCON MEDICAL TECHNOLOGIES, INC., *pg.* 1541, *pg.* 1503
HOVEROUND CORP., *pg.* 1543, *pg.* 466
INTUITIVE SURGICAL, INC., *pg.* 1546, *pg.* 286
INVACARE CORPORATION, *pg.* 1546, *pg.* 1451
JAMES ALEXANDER CORPORATION, *pg.* 1461, *pg.* 1044
JOHNSON & JOHNSON, *pg.* 1549, *pg.* 1091
JOHNSON & JOHNSON BABY PRODUCTS, INC., *pg.* 1552, *pg.* 1094
KIMBERLY-CLARK CORPORATION, *pg.* 1461, *pg.* 1720
KIMBERLY-CLARK INC., *pg.* 1463, *pg.* 1927
KRUGER PAPER PRODUCTS LP, *pg.* 1463, *pg.* 1927
LAKELAND INDUSTRIES, INC., *pg.* 1354, *pg.* 1338
LIFECELL CORPORATION, *pg.* 1556, *pg.* 1045
LIFECORE BIOMEDICAL, LLC, *pg.* 1556, *pg.* 920
LIVANOVA, *pg.* 1557, *pg.* 1710
MAURICE J. MARKELL SHOE CO., INC., *pg.* 1811, *pg.* 1356
MCKEON PRODUCTS, INC., *pg.* 1559, *pg.* 912
MCR SAFETY, *pg.* 1422, *pg.* 1630
MEDLINE INDUSTRIES, INC., *pg.* 1562, *pg.* 635
MEDPORT, LLC, *pg.* 1563, *pg.* 1607
MEDTRONIC, *pg.* 1563, *pg.* 830
MEDTRONIC, INC., *pg.* 1564, *pg.* 939
MENTOR CORPORATION, *pg.* 1565, *pg.* 263
MICROAIRE SURGICAL INSTRUMENTS INC., *pg.* 1423, *pg.* 1778
MILESTONE SCIENTIFIC, INC., *pg.* 1568, *pg.* 1079
MUELLER SPORTS MEDICINE, INC., *pg.* 1570, *pg.* 1887
NUVASIVE, INC., *pg.* 1577, *pg.* 205
OAKLEY, INC., *pg.* 1840, *pg.* 86
ORCHIDS PAPER PRODUCTS COMPANY, *pg.* 1465, *pg.* 1488

OSTEOMED CORPORATION, *pg.* 1425, *pg.* 1658
PALL CORPORATION, *pg.* 232, *pg.* 1323
PHILIPS RESPIRONICS, *pg.* 1585, *pg.* 1555
POINT BLANK SOLUTIONS, INC., *pg.* 1467, *pg.* 460
ROCHESTER MIDLAND CORPORATION, *pg.* 334, *pg.* 1337
THE SALK COMPANY, *pg.* 1591, *pg.* 800
SOLO CUP COMPANY, *pg.* 1469, *pg.* 625
SPAN-AMERICA MEDICAL SYSTEMS, INC., *pg.* 1595, *pg.* 1618
ST. JUDE MEDICAL, INC., *pg.* 1596, *pg.* 963
STAAR SURGICAL COMPANY, *pg.* 1597, *pg.* 151
STERIS CORPORATION, *pg.* 1597, *pg.* 1464
STRYKER CORPORATION, *pg.* 1598, *pg.* 894
STRYKER MAKO, *pg.* 1598, *pg.* 427
STRYKER ORTHOPAEDICS, *pg.* 1599, *pg.* 1082
SURGICAL SPECIALTIES CORPORATION, *pg.* 1600, *pg.* 1912
SYMMETRY MEDICAL INC., *pg.* 1600, *pg.* 699
SYSCO GUEST SUPPLY, LLC, *pg.* 336, *pg.* 1085
TELEFLEX INCORPORATED, *pg.* 48, *pg.* 1548
THERAGENICS CORPORATION, *pg.* 1431, *pg.* 527
THERAPEDIC ASSOCIATES, INC., *pg.* 945, *pg.* 1112
TUFCO TECHNOLOGIES, INC., *pg.* 1697, *pg.* 1860
UTAH MEDICAL PRODUCTS, INC., *pg.* 1605, *pg.* 1752
UVEX SAFETY, *pg.* 1433, *pg.* 1608
VITAL SIGNS, INC., *pg.* 1607, *pg.* 1126
WASAU PAPER CORP., *pg.* 1471, *pg.* 1882
WAUSAU PAPER BAY WEST, *pg.* 1471, *pg.* 1465
WEST PHARMACEUTICAL SERVICES, INC., *pg.* 1472, *pg.* 1532
WISCONSIN PHARMACAL COMPANY, LLC, *pg.* 1610, *pg.* 1861
ZIMMER BIOMET HOLDINGS, INC., *pg.* 1611, *pg.* 699

2677 - Envelopes

B&W PRESS, INC., *pg.* 1619, *pg.* 823
CALUMET CARTON COMPANY, *pg.* 1454, *pg.* 661
MEADWESTVACO PACKAGING SYSTEMS, LLC, *pg.* 1464, *pg.* 514
POLY PAK AMERICA, INC., *pg.* 1467, *pg.* 138
TAYLOR CORPORATION, *pg.* 1691, *pg.* 952
TENSION ENVELOPE CORPORATION, *pg.* 483, *pg.* 986
WESTERN STATES ENVELOPE & LABEL, *pg.* 492, *pg.* 1856

2678 - Stationery, Tablets & Related Products

AMERICAN GREETINGS CORPORATION, *pg.* 1615, *pg.* 1428
AMERICAN STATIONERY CO., INC., *pg.* 349, *pg.* 696
BIC CORPORATION, *pg.* 501, *pg.* 369
CRANE & CO., INC., *pg.* 1456, *pg.* 816
CSS INDUSTRIES, INC., *pg.* 1631, *pg.* 1562
MEADWESTVACO CONSUMER & OFFICE PRODUCTS, *pg.* 431, *pg.* 1456
TAB PRODUCTS CO. LLC, *pg.* 481, *pg.* 1869
WAUSAU PAPER, *pg.* 1471, *pg.* 1855

2679 - Converted Paper & Paperboard Products, NEC

BEMIS COMPANY, INC., *pg.* 1453, *pg.* 1882
THE COLAD GROUP, INC., *pg.* 377, *pg.* 1147
ESSELTE BUSINESS CORP, *pg.* 395, *pg.* 1179
ONTARIO WALL COVERINGS, *pg.* 940, *pg.* 1941
WESTROCK COMPANY, *pg.* 1472, *pg.* 1805

2711 - Newspapers: Publishing, or Publishing & Printing

ABILENE REPORTER NEWS, *pg.* 1613, *pg.* 1657
ADVANCE PUBLICATIONS, INC., *pg.* 1613, *pg.* 1343
ADVERTISING AGE, *pg.* 1613, *pg.* 1187
ADVISOR-SOURCE NEWSPAPERS, *pg.* 1614, *pg.* 902
A.H. BELO CORPORATION, *pg.* 1614, *pg.* 1673
AMARILLO GLOBE-NEWS, *pg.* 1614, *pg.* 1658
AMERICAN LAWYER MEDIA, INC., *pg.* 1615, *pg.* 1193
AMERICAN MEDIA, INC., *pg.* 1615, *pg.* 410
AMESBURY NEWS, *pg.* 1616, *pg.* 787
AMOS PRESS, INC., *pg.* 1616, *pg.* 1472
ANTELOPE VALLEY NEWSPAPER INC., *pg.* 1617, *pg.* 174
THE ARIZONA REPUBLIC, *pg.* 1617, *pg.* 14
THE ARKANSAS CITY TRAVELER, *pg.* 1617, *pg.* 714
THE ARLINGTON ADVOCATE, *pg.* 1617, *pg.* 828
ARMADA TIMES, *pg.* 1617, *pg.* 902
ASBURY PARK PRESS INC., *pg.* 1617, *pg.* 1090
ASHLAND DAILY TIDINGS, *pg.* 1617, *pg.* 1499
ASIAN WEEK FOUNDATION, *pg.* 1617, *pg.* 212
ATHENS BANNER-HERALD, *pg.* 1618, *pg.* 486
THE ATLANTA JOURNAL-CONSTITUTION, *pg.* 1618, *pg.* 490
AUTOMOTIVE NEWS, *pg.* 1618, *pg.* 879
THE BALTIMORE SUN COMPANY, *pg.* 1619, *pg.* 755
THE BENNINGTON BANNER, *pg.* 1620, *pg.* 1764
BEVERLY CITIZEN, *pg.* 1620, *pg.* 816
BILLERICA MINUTEMAN, *pg.* 1621, *pg.* 815
THE BLADE CO., *pg.* 1621, *pg.* 1476
BLISS COMMUNICATIONS INC., *pg.* 1621, *pg.* 1861
BLOCK COMMUNICATIONS, INC., *pg.* 1621, *pg.* 1476
BLOOMBERG BNA, *pg.* 1621, *pg.* 1772
BNP MEDIA, *pg.* 1622, *pg.* 910
THE BOSTON GLOBE, *pg.* 1623, *pg.* 790
BREHM COMMUNICATIONS INC., *pg.* 1623, *pg.* 201
BROWN CITY BANNER, *pg.* 1624, *pg.* 874
THE BROWNSVILLE HERALD, *pg.* 1624, *pg.* 1668
THE CALGARY SUN, *pg.* 1625, *pg.* 1903
CALKINS MEDIA INC., *pg.* 1625, *pg.* 1548
THE CANTON REPOSITORY, *pg.* 1625, *pg.* 1407
CAPE COD TIMES, *pg.* 1625, *pg.* 826
CAPE CODDER, *pg.* 1625, *pg.* 840
CAPITAL CITY PRESS, *pg.* 1625, *pg.* 741
CAPITAL GAZETTE COMMUNICATIONS INC., *pg.* 1625, *pg.* 754
CARROLL COUNTY TIMES, *pg.* 1626, *pg.* 780
THE CHARLOTTE OBSERVER PUBLISHING CO., *pg.* 1627, *pg.* 1364
CHELMSFORD INDEPENDENT, *pg.* 1627, *pg.* 815
CHICAGO READER, INC., *pg.* 1627, *pg.* 570
CHICAGO SUN TIMES, *pg.* 1627, *pg.* 570
CHICAGO TRIBUNE COMPANY, *pg.* 1627, *pg.* 570
CINCINNATI BUSINESS COURIER, *pg.* 1627, *pg.* 1411
THE CINCINNATI ENQUIRER, INC., *pg.* 1628, *pg.* 1411
CITRUS COUNTY CHRONICLE, *pg.* 1628, *pg.* 419
CLOVIS NEWS JOURNAL, *pg.* 1628, *pg.* 1135
COLORADO COMMUNITY NEWSPAPERS, *pg.* 1628, *pg.* 332
COMMUNITY NEWSPAPERS INC., *pg.* 1628, *pg.* 486
CONCORD JOURNAL, *pg.* 1629, *pg.* 815
CORPUS CHRISTI CALLER-TIMES, *pg.* 1630, *pg.* 1671
COUNTRY GAZETTE, *pg.* 1630, *pg.* 833
CQ ROLL CALL, *pg.* 1631, *pg.* 397
CRAIN COMMUNICATIONS, INC., *pg.* 1631, *pg.* 879
CRAIN'S CHICAGO BUSINESS, *pg.* 1631, *pg.* 572
CRAIN'S NEW YORK BUSINESS, *pg.* 1631, *pg.* 1220
CREATIVE LOAFING, INC., *pg.* 1631, *pg.* 472
CYNTHIANA PUBLISHING CO., *pg.* 1632, *pg.* 726
THE DAILY ARDMOREITE, *pg.* 1632, *pg.* 1484
THE DAILY BREEZE, *pg.* 1632, *pg.* 293
THE DAILY HERALD CO., *pg.* 1632, *pg.* 1819
THE DAILY ITEM, *pg.* 1632, *pg.* 829
THE DAILY ITEM, *pg.* 1632, *pg.* 1588
DAILY NEWS, L.P., *pg.* 1632, *pg.* 1221
THE DAILY OAKLAND PRESS, *pg.* 1632, *pg.* 905
DAILY PRESS, *pg.* 1632, *pg.* 302
DAILY RACING FORM, LLC, *pg.* 1632, *pg.* 1221
DAILY RECORD, *pg.* 1633, *pg.* 1103
DAILY REPUBLICAN REGISTER, *pg.* 1633, *pg.* 634
THE DAILY STAR, *pg.* 1633, *pg.* 1319
DAILY TIMES LEADER, *pg.* 1633, *pg.* 972
THE DALLAS MORNING NEWS CO., *pg.* 1633, *pg.* 1679
DELTA FARM PRESS, *pg.* 1634, *pg.* 968
THE DEMOCRAT CO., *pg.* 1634, *pg.* 708
DENTON PUBLISHING COMPANY, *pg.* 1634, *pg.* 1691
DERRICK PUBLISHING CO., *pg.* 1635, *pg.* 1558
DERRY PUBLISHING CO. INC., *pg.* 1635, *pg.* 1033
DESERT DISPATCH, *pg.* 1635, *pg.* 45
DETROIT LEGAL NEWS PUBLISHING LLC, *pg.* 1635, *pg.* 880
THE DETROIT NEWS, INC., *pg.* 1635, *pg.* 880
THE DISPATCH PRINTING COMPANY, *pg.* 1636, *pg.* 1439
DODGE CITY DAILY GLOBE, *pg.* 1636, *pg.* 714
THE DOLAN COMPANY, *pg.* 1636, *pg.* 932
DOVER-SHERBORN PRESS, *pg.* 1636, *pg.* 835
DOW JONES & COMPANY, INC., *pg.* 1637, *pg.* 1225
EAGLE-TRIBUNE PUBLISHING COMPANY INC., *pg.* 1638, *pg.* 837
EAST OREGONIAN PUBLISHING CO., *pg.* 1638, *pg.* 1500
EAST VALLEY TRIBUNE, *pg.* 1638, *pg.* 25
EAU CLAIRE PRESS COMPANY, *pg.* 1638, *pg.* 1857
THE EVANSVILLE COURIER & PRESS, *pg.* 1639, *pg.* 678
THE E.W. SCRIPPS COMPANY, *pg.* 1639, *pg.* 1412
THE EXAMINER, *pg.* 1640, *pg.* 979
FAYETTEVILLE PUBLISHING CO., *pg.* 1641, *pg.* 1372
THE FLORIDA TIMES-UNION, *pg.* 1641, *pg.* 433
THE FORT MORGAN TIMES, *pg.* 1642, *pg.* 329
FORT WORTH STAR-TELEGRAM, *pg.* 1642, *pg.* 1694
FORUM COMMUNICATIONS COMPANY, *pg.* 1642, *pg.* 1397
FRANK MAYBORN ENTERPRISES, *pg.* 1642, *pg.* 1746
THE FREE LANCE-STAR PUBLISHING CO., *pg.* 1643, *pg.* 1782
FREEDOM COMMUNICATIONS, INC., *pg.* 1643, *pg.* 110
THE FREELANCE-STAR RADIO GROUPS, *pg.* 1643, *pg.* 1782
GANNETT CO., INC., *pg.* 289, *pg.* 1681
GANNETT CO., INC., *pg.* 1643, *pg.* 1790
THE GASTON GAZETTE, *pg.* 1644, *pg.* 1373
GATEHOUSE MEDIA, INC., *pg.* 1644, *pg.* 1159
THE GAZETTE, *pg.* 1644, *pg.* 315
GAZETTE COMMUNICATIONS, INC., *pg.* 1644, *pg.* 702
GEORGE J. FOSTER CO. INC., *pg.* 1644, *pg.* 1033
GRAHAM HOLDINGS COMPANY, *pg.* 1645, *pg.* 1773
THE GRAND ISLAND DAILY INDEPENDENT, *pg.* 1646, *pg.* 1010
GRASSROOTS ENTERPRISE, INC., *pg.* 1255, *pg.* 400
GRAY TELEVISION, INC., *pg.* 289, *pg.* 509
GREATER MEDIA NEWSPAPERS, INC., *pg.* 1646, *pg.* 1071
THE HAMILTON SPECTATOR, *pg.* 1647, *pg.* 1921
HAMILTON-WENHAM CHRONICLE, *pg.* 1647, *pg.* 816
HANNIBAL COURIER-POST, *pg.* 1647, *pg.* 978
HAVELOCK NEWS, *pg.* 1648, *pg.* 1377
HAVERHILL GAZETTE, *pg.* 1648, *pg.* 837
THE HEARST CORPORATION, *pg.* 1649, *pg.* 1239
HI-DESERT PUBLISHING CO. INC., *pg.* 1650, *pg.* 309
HILLSDALE DAILY NEWS, *pg.* 1650, *pg.* 891
THE HOLLYWOOD REPORTER INC., *pg.* 1650, *pg.* 133
HOMETOWN COMMUNICATIONS NETWORK, INC., *pg.* 1650, *pg.* 904
THE HONOLULU STAR-ADVERTISER, *pg.* 1650, *pg.* 544
HOUR PUBLISHING COMPANY, *pg.* 1651, *pg.* 362
INDIANAPOLIS STAR, *pg.* 1652, *pg.* 687
THE INQUIRER & MIRROR, *pg.* 1653, *pg.* 834
INSIDE BUSINESS INC., *pg.* 1653, *pg.* 1797
INVESTORS BUSINESS DAILY, INC., *pg.* 1653, *pg.* 133
IOWA FARMER TODAY, *pg.* 1653, *pg.* 702
JACKSONVILLE BUSINESS JOURNAL, *pg.* 1654, *pg.* 433
THE JACKSONVILLE DAILY NEWS CO., *pg.* 1654, *pg.* 1380
JACKSONVILLE JOURNAL-COURIER, *pg.* 1654, *pg.* 621
JERSEY JOURNAL NEWSPAPER, *pg.* 1654, *pg.* 1120
JOHNSON NEWSPAPER CORPORATION, *pg.* 1655, *pg.* 1349
THE JOURNAL GAZETTE, *pg.* 1655, *pg.* 680
JOURNAL INC., *pg.* 1655, *pg.* 972
JOURNAL MEDIA GROUP, INC., *pg.* 1655, *pg.* 1876
JOURNAL SENTINEL, INC., *pg.* 1655, *pg.* 1876
JOURNAL STAR, INC., *pg.* 1656, *pg.* 651
JUNEAU EMPIRE, *pg.* 1656, *pg.* 10
THE JUPITER COURIER JOURNAL, *pg.* 1656, *pg.* 468
THE KANSAS CITY STAR COMPANY, *pg.* 1656, *pg.* 985
KINSTON FREE PRESS, *pg.* 1656, *pg.* 1380
KITSAP SUN, *pg.* 1657, *pg.* 1819
KNOXVILLE NEWS-SENTINEL COMPANY, *pg.* 1657, *pg.* 1637
LAKE CITY REPORTER, *pg.* 1657, *pg.* 436
LANCASTER NEWSPAPERS INC., *pg.* 1657, *pg.* 1546
LANDMARK MEDIA ENTERPRISES LLC, *pg.* 295, *pg.* 1797
LAPEER COUNTY PRESS, *pg.* 1657, *pg.* 896
LAS VEGAS SUN, INC., *pg.* 1657, *pg.* 1021
LEBHAR-FRIEDMAN INC., *pg.* 1658, *pg.* 1250
LEE ENTERPRISES, INCORPORATED, *pg.* 1658, *pg.* 704
LEWISTON DAILY SUN, *pg.* 1658, *pg.* 751
THE LIMA NEWS, *pg.* 1659, *pg.* 1457
LINCOLN NEWS MESSENGER, *pg.* 1659, *pg.* 122
LOG CABIN DEMOCRAT, LLC, *pg.* 1660, *pg.* 31
LOS ANGELES DAILY NEWS PUBLISHING COMPANY, *pg.* 1660, *pg.* 308
LOS ANGELES TIMES COMMUNICATIONS, LLC, *pg.* 1660, *pg.* 135
THE LUBBOCK AVALANCHE-JOURNAL, *pg.* 1660, *pg.* 1726
MACOMB COUNTY LEGAL NEWS, *pg.* 1660, *pg.* 901

MADISON NEWSPAPERS, INC., *pg.* 1661, *pg.* 1866
MARIN INDEPENDENT JOURNAL, *pg.* 1661, *pg.* 258
MASSACHUSETTS LAWYERS WEEKLY, INC., *pg.* 1662, *pg.* 798
THE MCCLATCHY COMPANY, *pg.* 1662, *pg.* 196
MCCLATCHY NEWSPAPERS, INC., *pg.* 1662, *pg.* 197
MEDIA GENERAL, INC., *pg.* 297, *pg.* 1803
MEDICINE HAT NEWS, *pg.* 1663, *pg.* 1906
METROWEST DAILY NEWS, *pg.* 1665, *pg.* 821
THE MIAMI HERALD, *pg.* 1665, *pg.* 444
MICHIGAN.COM, *pg.* 1665, *pg.* 884
MILLER GROUP MEDIA, *pg.* 1665, *pg.* 621
MLIVE MEDIA GROUP, *pg.* 1665, *pg.* 888
THE MONITOR, *pg.* 1665, *pg.* 1726
THE MORNING CALL, INC., *pg.* 1665, *pg.* 1513
THE MORNING SUN, *pg.* 1666, *pg.* 720
MORRIS COMMUNICATIONS COMPANY LLC, *pg.* 1666, *pg.* 525
MORRIS MULTIMEDIA, INC., *pg.* 1666, *pg.* 540
MORRIS PUBLISHING GROUP, LLC, *pg.* 1666, *pg.* 525
NAPLES DAILY NEWS, *pg.* 1666, *pg.* 451
NATIONAL HOT ROD ASSOCIATION, *pg.* 149, *pg.* 99
NEW JERSEY HILLS MEDIA GROUP, *pg.* 1667, *pg.* 1044
THE NEW YORK OBSERVER, LLC, *pg.* 1668, *pg.* 1269
THE NEW YORK POST, *pg.* 1668, *pg.* 1269
THE NEW YORK TIMES, *pg.* 1668, *pg.* 1270
THE NEW YORK TIMES COMPANY, *pg.* 1668, *pg.* 1270
THE NEWARK ADVOCATE, *pg.* 1669, *pg.* 1467
NEWS AMERICA INCORPORATED, *pg.* 1669, *pg.* 1271
NEWS & RECORD, *pg.* 1669, *pg.* 1375
NEWS CHIEF, *pg.* 1669, *pg.* 480
NEWS CORPORATION, *pg.* 1669, *pg.* 1271
THE NEWS-ENTERPRISE, *pg.* 1669, *pg.* 727
THE NEWS-HERALD, *pg.* 1670, *pg.* 908
NEWS-LEADER, *pg.* 1670, *pg.* 422
NEWS MEDIA CORPORATION, *pg.* 1670, *pg.* 654
THE NEWS-SENTINEL, *pg.* 1670, *pg.* 681
NEWS-SUN, INC., *pg.* 1670, *pg.* 467
THE NEWS-TIMES, *pg.* 1670, *pg.* 344
THE NEWS TRIBUNE, *pg.* 1670, *pg.* 1845
NEWS TRIBUNE CO., *pg.* 1670, *pg.* 980
NEWS WEST PUBLISHING COMPANY INC., *pg.* 1670, *pg.* 12
NEWSDAY MEDIA GROUP, *pg.* 1670, *pg.* 1181
THE NEWTON KANSAN, *pg.* 1671, *pg.* 717
NJBIZ, *pg.* 1671, *pg.* 1122
NOLA MEDIA GROUP, *pg.* 1671, *pg.* 747
NORTH JERSEY MEDIA GROUP INC., *pg.* 1672, *pg.* 1072
NORTHWEST FLORIDA DAILY NEWS, *pg.* 1672, *pg.* 428
NORTHWEST GEORGIA NEWS, *pg.* 1672, *pg.* 539
THE OAK RIDGER, LLC, *pg.* 1672, *pg.* 1655
OBSERVER PUBLISHING COMPANY, *pg.* 1672, *pg.* 1591
OCONEE PUBLISHING INC., *pg.* 1672, *pg.* 1621
ODESSA AMERICAN, *pg.* 1672, *pg.* 1728
OGDEN NEWSPAPERS, INC., *pg.* 1672, *pg.* 1851
OGDEN PUBLISHING CORPORATION, *pg.* 1672, *pg.* 1753
ONION, INC., *pg.* 1673, *pg.* 586
THE ORANGE COUNTY REGISTER, *pg.* 1673, *pg.* 262
OREGONIAN PUBLISHING CO., *pg.* 1673, *pg.* 1504
THE OTTAWA CITIZEN, *pg.* 1673, *pg.* 1932
PACIFIC PALISADES POST INC., *pg.* 1673, *pg.* 174
PADDOCK PUBLICATIONS, INC., *pg.* 1674, *pg.* 554
PALATKA DAILY NEWS, *pg.* 1674, *pg.* 457
PAMPLIN MEDIA GROUP, *pg.* 1674, *pg.* 1504
PARADE PUBLICATIONS INC., *pg.* 1674, *pg.* 1276
THE PENINSULA CLARION, *pg.* 1676, *pg.* 11
PHILADELPHIA DAILY NEWS, *pg.* 1677, *pg.* 1569
THE PHILADELPHIA INQUIRER, *pg.* 1677, *pg.* 1569
PILOT MEDIA, *pg.* 1677, *pg.* 1797
PLAIN DEALER PUBLISHING CO., *pg.* 1677, *pg.* 1434
PORTERVILLE RECORDER, *pg.* 1677, *pg.* 185
THE POST COMPANY, *pg.* 1677, *pg.* 549
PRESS-REPUBLICAN, *pg.* 1678, *pg.* 1322
THE PRINCE GEORGE CITIZEN, *pg.* 1678, *pg.* 1908
THE PROVIDENCE JOURNAL, *pg.* 1678, *pg.* 1607
QUEBECOR MEDIA INC., *pg.* 1679, *pg.* 1956
THE RECORD, *pg.* 1680, *pg.* 1922
THE RECORD, *pg.* 1680, *pg.* 281
THE RECORD-JOURNAL PUBLISHING COMPANY, *pg.* 1680, *pg.* 354
THE ROANOKE TIMES, *pg.* 1680, *pg.* 1806
SAN ANGELO STANDARD, INC., *pg.* 1682, *pg.* 1739
SAN ANTONIO EXPRESS NEWS, *pg.* 1682, *pg.* 1742
THE SAN DIEGO UNION-TRIBUNE, LLC, *pg.* 1682, *pg.* 208
SAN FRANCISCO CHRONICLE, *pg.* 1683, *pg.* 226
SAN JOSE MERCURY NEWS, *pg.* 1683, *pg.* 250
SANDUSKY NEWSPAPERS INC., *pg.* 1683, *pg.* 1472
SANTA CRUZ SENTINEL, *pg.* 1683, *pg.* 278
SAVANNAH MORNING NEWS, *pg.* 1683, *pg.* 540
SEATTLE POST-INTELLIGENCER, *pg.* 1685, *pg.* 1839
SEATTLE TIMES COMPANY, *pg.* 1685, *pg.* 1840
THE SEDALIA DEMOCRAT, *pg.* 1685, *pg.* 1005
SF NEWSPAPER COMPANY, LLC, *pg.* 1686, *pg.* 227
SHAWNEE NEWS-STAR, *pg.* 1686, *pg.* 1488
SNOWMASS VILLAGE SUN, *pg.* 1687, *pg.* 335
SOUND PUBLISHING, INC., *pg.* 1687, *pg.* 1823
THE SPOKESMAN-REVIEW, *pg.* 1687, *pg.* 1844
THE SPORTING NEWS, *pg.* 1688, *pg.* 1295
THE ST. AUGUSTINE RECORD, *pg.* 1688, *pg.* 461
ST. LOUIS POST-DISPATCH LLC, *pg.* 1688, *pg.* 1004
STAR COURIER, *pg.* 1689, *pg.* 621
THE STAR TRIBUNE COMPANY, *pg.* 1689, *pg.* 942
THE STARPHOENIX, *pg.* 1689, *pg.* 1962
THE STATE JOURNAL-REGISTER, *pg.* 1689, *pg.* 662
STYLE WEEKLY INC., *pg.* 1690, *pg.* 1804
THE SUN, *pg.* 1690, *pg.* 198
THE SUN, *pg.* 1690, *pg.* 28
SUN JOURNAL, *pg.* 1690, *pg.* 1386
SUN-TIMES MEDIA GROUP, INC., *pg.* 1690, *pg.* 591
SWIFT NEWSPAPERS, INC., *pg.* 1690, *pg.* 1032
TAMPA BAY BUSINESS JOURNAL, *pg.* 1691, *pg.* 476
TAMPA BAY NEWSPAPERS, INC., *pg.* 1691, *pg.* 468
TAMPA BAY TIMES, *pg.* 1691, *pg.* 464
THE TAMPA TRIBUNE, *pg.* 1691, *pg.* 476
THE TELEGRAM, *pg.* 1691, *pg.* 1916
THE TELEGRAPH, *pg.* 1691, *pg.* 553
TIMES HERALD-RECORD, *pg.* 1694, *pg.* 1182
THE TIMES-NEWS, *pg.* 1694, *pg.* 1359
THE TIMES PUBLISHING CO., *pg.* 1695, *pg.* 464
TIMES PUBLISHING CO. INC., *pg.* 1695, *pg.* 1530
TIMES RECORD NEWS, *pg.* 1695, *pg.* 1749
TORONTO STAR NEWSPAPERS LTD., *pg.* 1695, *pg.* 1945
TRANSCONTINENTAL INC., *pg.* 1695, *pg.* 1957
TRANSPORT TOPICS PUBLISHING GROUP, *pg.* 1696, *pg.* 1772
TRAVERSE CITY RECORD-EAGLE, *pg.* 1696, *pg.* 910
TRIBUNE MEDIA COMPANY, *pg.* 1696, *pg.* 592
TRUCKER PUBLICATIONS INC., *pg.* 1696, *pg.* 1
UNITED PRESS INTERNATIONAL, INC., *pg.* 1698, *pg.* 405
VALLEY MORNING STAR, *pg.* 1699, *pg.* 1699
VENTURA COUNTY STAR, *pg.* 1699, *pg.* 57
VICTORIA ADVOCATE PUBLISHING COMPANY, *pg.* 1699, *pg.* 1748
VILLAGE SOUP, *pg.* 1699, *pg.* 752
VILLAGE VOICE MEDIA HOLDINGS, LLC, *pg.* 1699, *pg.* 1311
VOICE COMMUNICATIONS CORP., *pg.* 1700, *pg.* 902
THE WALL STREET JOURNAL, *pg.* 1700, *pg.* 1312
THE WALTON SUN, *pg.* 1701, *pg.* 465
WARRICK PUBLISHING CO. INC., *pg.* 1701, *pg.* 675
THE WASHINGTON POST, *pg.* 1701, *pg.* 407
WEISS RESEARCH, *pg.* 819, *pg.* 436
WESTERN COMMUNICATIONS INC., *pg.* 1701, *pg.* 1496
WESTERN NEWSPAPERS, INC., *pg.* 1702, *pg.* 28
THE WICHITA EAGLE, *pg.* 1702, *pg.* 724
WORCESTER TELEGRAM & GAZETTE CORP., *pg.* 1702, *pg.* 863
YANKTON DAILY PRESS & DAKOTAN, *pg.* 1703, *pg.* 1626
THE YORK NEWS-TIMES, *pg.* 1703, *pg.* 1020

2721 - Periodicals: Publishing, or Publishing & Printing

AARP, *pg.* 124, *pg.* 393
ABILENE REPORTER NEWS, *pg.* 1613, *pg.* 1657
ADVANCE PUBLICATIONS, INC., *pg.* 1613, *pg.* 1343
ADVANTAGE BUSINESS MEDIA, *pg.* 1613, *pg.* 1116
ADVERTISING AGE, *pg.* 1613, *pg.* 1187
ADVISOR-SOURCE NEWSPAPERS, *pg.* 1614, *pg.* 902
A.H. BELO CORPORATION, *pg.* 1614, *pg.* 1673
ALLEN PRESS INC., *pg.* 1614, *pg.* 715
A.M. BEST COMPANY, *pg.* 1614, *pg.* 1101
AMARILLO GLOBE-NEWS, *pg.* 1614, *pg.* 1658
AMERICAN BABY MAGAZINE, *pg.* 1614, *pg.* 1190
AMERICAN COLLEGE OF NURSE-MIDWIVES, *pg.* 127, *pg.* 777
AMERICAN CONFERENCE OF GOVERNMENTAL INDUSTRIAL HYGIENISTS, *pg.* 127, *pg.* 1409
THE AMERICAN DENTAL ASSOCIATION, *pg.* 127, *pg.* 564
AMERICAN DIABETES ASSOCIATION, *pg.* 127, *pg.* 1770
AMERICAN HEART ASSOCIATION INC., *pg.* 128, *pg.* 1673
AMERICAN INSTITUTE OF CERTIFIED PUBLIC ACCOUNTANTS INC., *pg.* 129, *pg.* 1192
AMERICAN INSTITUTE OF CHEMICAL ENGINEERS, *pg.* 129, *pg.* 1193
AMERICAN KENNEL CLUB, INC., *pg.* 129, *pg.* 1193
AMERICAN LAWYER MEDIA, INC., *pg.* 1615, *pg.* 1193
AMERICAN MATHEMATICAL SOCIETY, INC., *pg.* 129, *pg.* 1605
AMERICAN MEDIA, INC., *pg.* 1615, *pg.* 410
AMERICAN MEDICAL ASSOCIATION, *pg.* 130, *pg.* 564
AMERICAN METEOROLOGICAL SOCIETY, *pg.* 1616, *pg.* 789
AMERICAN RADIO RELAY LEAGUE, INC., *pg.* 130, *pg.* 359
AMERICA'S TEST KITCHEN, *pg.* 1616, *pg.* 803
AMESBURY NEWS, *pg.* 1616, *pg.* 787
AMOS PRESS, INC., *pg.* 1616, *pg.* 1472
ANCESTRY.COM LLC, *pg.* 1228, *pg.* 1754
ANCIENT AMERICAN, *pg.* 1616, *pg.* 1856
ANNIE'S, *pg.* 1617, *pg.* 673
ANTARCTIC PRESS, *pg.* 1617, *pg.* 1739
ANTELOPE VALLEY NEWSPAPER INC., *pg.* 1617, *pg.* 174
ARCHITECTURAL DIGEST, *pg.* 1617, *pg.* 1196
THE ARIZONA REPUBLIC, *pg.* 1617, *pg.* 14
THE ARKANSAS CITY TRAVELER, *pg.* 1617, *pg.* 714
THE ARLINGTON ADVOCATE, *pg.* 1617, *pg.* 828
ARMADA TIMES, *pg.* 1617, *pg.* 902
ASBURY PARK PRESS INC., *pg.* 1617, *pg.* 1090
ASHLAND DAILY TIDINGS, *pg.* 1617, *pg.* 1499
ASIAN WEEK FOUNDATION, *pg.* 1617, *pg.* 212
ASIMOV'S SCIENCE FICTION MAGAZINE, *pg.* 1618, *pg.* 1197
ATHENS BANNER-HERALD, *pg.* 1618, *pg.* 486
ATHLON SPORTS, INC., *pg.* 1618, *pg.* 1648
THE ATLANTA JOURNAL-CONSTITUTION, *pg.* 1618, *pg.* 490
THE ATLANTIC MONTHLY GROUP, *pg.* 1618, *pg.* 396
AUDUBON MAGAZINE, *pg.* 1618, *pg.* 1198
AUTOMOTIVE NEWS, *pg.* 1618, *pg.* 879
BABCOX MEDIA, *pg.* 1619, *pg.* 1400
BACK TO THE BIBLE, *pg.* 270, *pg.* 1011
THE BALTIMORE SUN COMPANY, *pg.* 1619, *pg.* 755
BARRON'S, *pg.* 1620, *pg.* 1201
B.A.S.S., L.L.C., *pg.* 270, *pg.* 1
BAUER PUBLISHING USA, *pg.* 1620, *pg.* 1059
BELVOIR MEDIA GROUP, LLC, *pg.* 1620, *pg.* 360
THE BENNINGTON BANNER, *pg.* 1620, *pg.* 1764
BETTER HOMES & GARDENS BOOKS, *pg.* 1620, *pg.* 704
BEVERLY CITIZEN, *pg.* 1620, *pg.* 816
BILLERICA MINUTEMAN, *pg.* 1621, *pg.* 815
BIZBASH MEDIA INC., *pg.* 1621, *pg.* 1203
THE BLADE CO., *pg.* 1621, *pg.* 1476
BLISS COMMUNICATIONS INC., *pg.* 1621, *pg.* 1861
BLOCK COMMUNICATIONS, INC., *pg.* 1621, *pg.* 1476
BLOOMBERG BNA, *pg.* 1621, *pg.* 1772
BLOOMBERG BUSINESSWEEK, *pg.* 1621, *pg.* 1204
BNP MEDIA, *pg.* 1622, *pg.* 910
BOBIT BUSINESS MEDIA, *pg.* 1622, *pg.* 293
BONNIER ACTIVE MEDIA, INC., *pg.* 1622, *pg.* 1205
BONNIER CORPORATION, *pg.* 1622, *pg.* 480
THE BOSTON GLOBE, *pg.* 1623, *pg.* 790
BOYS' LIFE MAGAZINE, *pg.* 1623, *pg.* 1206
BRAINERD DAILY DISPATCH, *pg.* 1623, *pg.* 919
BRANT PUBLICATIONS, INC., *pg.* 1623, *pg.* 1206
BREHM COMMUNICATIONS INC., *pg.* 1623, *pg.* 201
BROWN CITY BANNER, *pg.* 1624, *pg.* 874
THE BROWNSVILLE HERALD, *pg.* 1624, *pg.* 1668
BUSINESS & LEGAL REPORTS INC., *pg.* 1624, *pg.* 367
THE CALGARY SUN, *pg.* 1625, *pg.* 1903
CALKINS MEDIA INC., *pg.* 1625, *pg.* 1548
THE CANTON REPOSITORY, *pg.* 1625, *pg.* 1407
CAPE COD TIMES, *pg.* 1625, *pg.* 826
CAPE CODDER, *pg.* 1625, *pg.* 840
CAPITAL CITY PRESS, *pg.* 1625, *pg.* 741
CAPITAL GAZETTE COMMUNICATIONS INC., *pg.* 1625, *pg.* 754
CARROLL COUNTY TIMES, *pg.* 1626, *pg.* 780
CCH INC., *pg.* 1626, *pg.* 653
CHARISMA MEDIA, *pg.* 1627, *pg.* 436
THE CHARLOTTE OBSERVER PUBLISHING CO., *pg.* 1627, *pg.* 1364
CHELMSFORD INDEPENDENT, *pg.* 1627, *pg.* 815
CHICAGO READER, INC., *pg.* 1627, *pg.* 570
CHICAGO SUN TIMES, *pg.* 1627, *pg.* 570

CHICAGO TRIBUNE COMPANY, *pg.* 1627, *pg.* 570
CHRISTIAN HERALD ASSOCIATION, *pg.* 1627, *pg.* 1212
CHRISTIANITY TODAY INTERNATIONAL, *pg.* 1627, *pg.* 561
CINCINNATI BUSINESS COURIER, *pg.* 1627, *pg.* 1411
THE CINCINNATI ENQUIRER, INC., *pg.* 1628, *pg.* 1411
CITRUS COUNTY CHRONICLE, *pg.* 1628, *pg.* 419
CITY GUIDE MAGAZINE, *pg.* 1628, *pg.* 1214
CLIPPER MAGAZINE INC., *pg.* 1628, *pg.* 1555
CLOVIS NEWS JOURNAL, *pg.* 1628, *pg.* 1135
COLORADO COMMUNITY NEWSPAPERS, *pg.* 1628, *pg.* 332
COMMUNITY NEWSPAPERS INC., *pg.* 1628, *pg.* 486
COMPLEX MEDIA, INC., *pg.* 1628, *pg.* 1217
COMPUTERWORLD, INC., *pg.* 1629, *pg.* 820
CONCORD JOURNAL, *pg.* 1629, *pg.* 815
CONDE NAST PUBLICATIONS, INC., *pg.* 1629, *pg.* 1217
CONDE NAST PUBLICATIONS, INC., *pg.* 1630, *pg.* 128
CONDE NAST TRAVELER, *pg.* 1630, *pg.* 1218
CORPUS CHRISTI CALLER-TIMES, *pg.* 1630, *pg.* 1671
COSMOPOLITAN, *pg.* 1630, *pg.* 1218
COUNCIL ON FOREIGN RELATIONS, *pg.* 138, *pg.* 1219
COUNTRY GAZETTE, *pg.* 1630, *pg.* 833
COUNTRY SAMPLER INC., *pg.* 1630, *pg.* 658
CQ ROLL CALL, *pg.* 1631, *pg.* 397
CRAIN COMMUNICATIONS, INC., *pg.* 1631, *pg.* 879
CRAIN'S CHICAGO BUSINESS, *pg.* 1631, *pg.* 572
CRAIN'S NEW YORK BUSINESS, *pg.* 1631, *pg.* 1220
CREATIVE LOAFING, INC., *pg.* 1631, *pg.* 472
CRM MEDIA, LLC, *pg.* 1631, *pg.* 1220
CYNTHIANA PUBLISHING CO., *pg.* 1632, *pg.* 726
THE DAILY ARDMOREITE, *pg.* 1632, *pg.* 1484
THE DAILY BREEZE, *pg.* 1632, *pg.* 293
THE DAILY HERALD CO., *pg.* 1632, *pg.* 1819
THE DAILY ITEM, *pg.* 1632, *pg.* 829
THE DAILY ITEM, *pg.* 1632, *pg.* 1588
DAILY NEWS, L.P., *pg.* 1632, *pg.* 1221
THE DAILY OAKLAND PRESS, *pg.* 1632, *pg.* 905
DAILY PRESS, *pg.* 1632, *pg.* 302
DAILY RACING FORM, LLC, *pg.* 1632, *pg.* 1221
DAILY RECORD, *pg.* 1633, *pg.* 1103
DAILY REPUBLICAN REGISTER, *pg.* 1633, *pg.* 634
THE DAILY STAR, *pg.* 1633, *pg.* 1319
DAILY TIMES LEADER, *pg.* 1633, *pg.* 972
THE DALLAS MORNING NEWS CO., *pg.* 1633, *pg.* 1679
DANCE MAGAZINE, *pg.* 1633, *pg.* 1221
DARK HORSE COMICS, INC., *pg.* 1633, *pg.* 1500
DAVID C. COOK, *pg.* 1633, *pg.* 315
DC COMICS, INC., *pg.* 1633, *pg.* 1221
DELTA FARM PRESS, *pg.* 1634, *pg.* 968
THE DEMOCRAT CO., *pg.* 1634, *pg.* 708
DENTON PUBLISHING COMPANY, *pg.* 1634, *pg.* 1691
DERRICK PUBLISHING CO., *pg.* 1635, *pg.* 1558
DERRY PUBLISHING CO. INC., *pg.* 1635, *pg.* 1033
DESERT DISPATCH, *pg.* 1635, *pg.* 45
DESERT PUBLICATIONS INC., *pg.* 1635, *pg.* 174
DETAILS MAGAZINE, *pg.* 1635, *pg.* 1223
DETROIT LEGAL NEWS PUBLISHING LLC, *pg.* 1635, *pg.* 880
THE DETROIT NEWS, INC., *pg.* 1635, *pg.* 880
THE DISPATCH PRINTING COMPANY, *pg.* 1636, *pg.* 1439
DODGE CITY DAILY GLOBE, *pg.* 1636, *pg.* 714
THE DOLAN COMPANY, *pg.* 1636, *pg.* 932
DOMINION ENTERPRISES, *pg.* 1636, *pg.* 1796
DOVER-SHERBORN PRESS, *pg.* 1636, *pg.* 835
DOW JONES & COMPANY, INC., *pg.* 1637, *pg.* 1225
DUPONT PUBLISHING, INC., *pg.* 1637, *pg.* 462
DUPONT REGISTRY, *pg.* 1637, *pg.* 462
EAGLE-TRIBUNE PUBLISHING COMPANY INC., *pg.* 1638, *pg.* 837
EAST OREGONIAN PUBLISHING CO., *pg.* 1638, *pg.* 1500
EAST VALLEY TRIBUNE, *pg.* 1638, *pg.* 25
EAU CLAIRE PRESS COMPANY, *pg.* 1638, *pg.* 1857
EDITORIAL TELEVISA INTERNATIONAL, *pg.* 1638, *pg.* 442
EDMENTUM, INC., *pg.* 390, *pg.* 917
ELLE.COM, *pg.* 1242, *pg.* 1227
ELSEVIER HEALTH SCIENCES, *pg.* 1638, *pg.* 1564
EMMIS COMMUNICATIONS CORPORATION, *pg.* 285, *pg.* 685
ENTERTAINMENT WEEKLY INC., *pg.* 1639, *pg.* 1228
ENTREPRENEUR MEDIA, INC., *pg.* 1639, *pg.* 110
ESPN, INC., *pg.* 285, *pg.* 340
ESSENCE MAGAZINE, *pg.* 1639, *pg.* 1229
THE EVANSVILLE COURIER & PRESS, *pg.* 1639, *pg.* 678
THE E.W. SCRIPPS COMPANY, *pg.* 1639, *pg.* 1412
THE EXAMINER, *pg.* 1640, *pg.* 979
FAIRCHILD FASHION GROUP, *pg.* 1640, *pg.* 1230
THE FAMILY CIRCLE, INC., *pg.* 1640, *pg.* 1230
FARM JOURNAL MEDIA, *pg.* 1640, *pg.* 1564
FASTLINE PUBLICATIONS INC., *pg.* 1641, *pg.* 726
FAYETTEVILLE PUBLISHING CO., *pg.* 1641, *pg.* 1372
FLASHES PUBLISHERS, *pg.* 1641, *pg.* 864
FLORIDA FAMILY MAGAZINE, *pg.* 1641, *pg.* 466
THE FLORIDA TIMES-UNION, *pg.* 1641, *pg.* 433
FORBES, INC., *pg.* 1641, *pg.* 1232
THE FORT MORGAN TIMES, *pg.* 1642, *pg.* 329
FORT WORTH STAR-TELEGRAM, *pg.* 1642, *pg.* 1694
FORTUNE, *pg.* 1642, *pg.* 1232
FORUM COMMUNICATIONS COMPANY, *pg.* 1642, *pg.* 1397
FRANK MAYBORN ENTERPRISES, *pg.* 1642, *pg.* 1746
THE FREE LANCE-STAR PUBLISHING CO., *pg.* 1643, *pg.* 1782
FREEDOM COMMUNICATIONS, INC., *pg.* 1643, *pg.* 110
THE FREELANCE-STAR RADIO GROUPS, *pg.* 1643, *pg.* 1782
FRIENDFINDER NETWORKS INC., *pg.* 1643, *pg.* 411
FULL GOSPEL BUSINESS MEN'S FELLOWSHIP INTERNATIONAL, *pg.* 141, *pg.* 110
GALE CENGAGE LEARNING, *pg.* 1643, *pg.* 885
THE GALLUP ORGANIZATION-PRINCETON, *pg.* 1643, *pg.* 1111
GANNETT CO., INC., *pg.* 289, *pg.* 1681
GANNETT CO., INC., *pg.* 1643, *pg.* 1790
GANNETT HEALTHCARE GROUP, *pg.* 1644, *pg.* 617
GARDNER PUBLICATIONS, INC., *pg.* 1644, *pg.* 1413
GARLINGHOUSE COMPANY, *pg.* 1644, *pg.* 1612
THE GASTON GAZETTE, *pg.* 1644, *pg.* 1373
GATEHOUSE MEDIA, INC, *pg.* 1644, *pg.* 1159
THE GAZETTE, *pg.* 1644, *pg.* 315
GAZETTE COMMUNICATIONS, INC., *pg.* 1644, *pg.* 702
GEORGE J. FOSTER CO. INC., *pg.* 1644, *pg.* 1033
GLAMOUR, *pg.* 1645, *pg.* 1235
GOOD HOUSEKEEPING, *pg.* 1645, *pg.* 1236
GRAHAM HOLDINGS COMPANY, *pg.* 1645, *pg.* 1773
THE GRAND ISLAND DAILY INDEPENDENT, *pg.* 1646, *pg.* 1010
GRASSROOTS ENTERPRISE, INC., *pg.* 1255, *pg.* 400
GRAY TELEVISION, INC., *pg.* 289, *pg.* 509
GREAT LAKES PUBLISHING COMPANY, *pg.* 1646, *pg.* 1431
GREATER MEDIA NEWSPAPERS, INC., *pg.* 1646, *pg.* 1071
GUARDSMARK, LLC, *pg.* 401, *pg.* 1237
GULF PUBLISHING COMPANY, *pg.* 1646, *pg.* 1707
HAIGHTS CROSS COMMUNICATIONS, INC., *pg.* 1646, *pg.* 1237
THE HAMILTON SPECTATOR, *pg.* 1647, *pg.* 1921
HAMILTON-WENHAM CHRONICLE, *pg.* 1647, *pg.* 816
HANNIBAL COURIER-POST, *pg.* 1647, *pg.* 978
HARLEQUIN MAGAZINES INC, *pg.* 1647, *pg.* 1237
HARPER'S MAGAZINE FOUNDATION, *pg.* 1648, *pg.* 1238
HARPO, INC., *pg.* 290, *pg.* 576
HAVELOCK NEWS, *pg.* 1648, *pg.* 1377
HAVERHILL GAZETTE, *pg.* 1648, *pg.* 837
HEALTH MAGAZINE, *pg.* 1648, *pg.* 1238
THE HEARST CORPORATION, *pg.* 1649, *pg.* 1239
HEARST MAGAZINES, *pg.* 1649, *pg.* 1239
HERE MEDIA INC., *pg.* 290, *pg.* 132
HI-DESERT PUBLISHING CO. INC., *pg.* 1650, *pg.* 309
HIGHLIGHTS FOR CHILDREN, INC., *pg.* 1650, *pg.* 1440
HILLSDALE DAILY NEWS, *pg.* 1650, *pg.* 891
THE HOLLYWOOD REPORTER INC., *pg.* 1650, *pg.* 133
HOMETOWN COMMUNICATIONS NETWORK, INC., *pg.* 1650, *pg.* 904
THE HONOLULU STAR-ADVERTISER, *pg.* 1650, *pg.* 544
HORIZON HOUSE PUBLICATIONS INC., *pg.* 1650, *pg.* 839
HOUR PUBLISHING COMPANY, *pg.* 1651, *pg.* 362
HOUSE BEAUTIFUL, *pg.* 1651, *pg.* 1241
I-5 PUBLISHING LLC, *pg.* 1651, *pg.* 133
IN STYLE MAGAZINE, *pg.* 1652, *pg.* 1243
INDEPENDENT INSURANCE AGENTS & BROKERS OF AMERICA, INC., *pg.* 144, *pg.* 1770
INDIANAPOLIS STAR, *pg.* 1652, *pg.* 687
INFORMA EXHIBITIONS LLC, *pg.* 1653, *pg.* 17
INFORMATION TODAY INC., *pg.* 1653, *pg.* 1084
THE INQUIRER & MIRROR, *pg.* 1653, *pg.* 834
INSIDE BUSINESS INC., *pg.* 1653, *pg.* 1797
INSTITUTIONAL INVESTOR, INC., *pg.* 1653, *pg.* 1244
INTERNATIONAL DATA GROUP, *pg.* 1653, *pg.* 796
INVESTORS BUSINESS DAILY, INC., *pg.* 1653, *pg.* 133
IOWA FARMER TODAY, *pg.* 1653, *pg.* 702
ISLANDS MAGAZINE, *pg.* 1654, *pg.* 480
JACKSONVILLE BUSINESS JOURNAL, *pg.* 1654, *pg.* 433
THE JACKSONVILLE DAILY NEWS CO., *pg.* 1654, *pg.* 1380
JACKSONVILLE JOURNAL-COURIER, *pg.* 1654, *pg.* 621
JAMESON PUBLISHING INC., *pg.* 1654, *pg.* 1530
JENKINS GROUP, INC., *pg.* 1654, *pg.* 909
JERSEY JOURNAL NEWSPAPER, *pg.* 1654, *pg.* 1120
JOBSON HEALTHCARE INFORMATION LLC, *pg.* 1654, *pg.* 1246
JOC GROUP INC., *pg.* 1654, *pg.* 1096
JOHN WILEY & SONS, INC., *pg.* 1655, *pg.* 1073
JOHNSON NEWSPAPER CORPORATION, *pg.* 1655, *pg.* 1349
JOHNSON PUBLISHING COMPANY, INC., *pg.* 1655, *pg.* 579
THE JOURNAL GAZETTE, *pg.* 1655, *pg.* 680
JOURNAL INC., *pg.* 1655, *pg.* 972
JOURNAL MEDIA GROUP, INC., *pg.* 1655, *pg.* 1876
JOURNAL OF COMMERCE, INC., *pg.* 1655, *pg.* 1097
JOURNAL SENTINEL, INC., *pg.* 1655, *pg.* 1876
JOURNAL STAR, INC., *pg.* 1656, *pg.* 651
JUNEAU EMPIRE, *pg.* 1656, *pg.* 10
THE JUPITER COURIER JOURNAL, *pg.* 1656, *pg.* 468
KALMBACH PUBLISHING CO., *pg.* 1656, *pg.* 1898
THE KANSAS CITY STAR COMPANY, *pg.* 1656, *pg.* 985
KELLEY BLUE BOOK CO., INC., *pg.* 1656, *pg.* 112
KINSTON FREE PRESS, *pg.* 1656, *pg.* 1380
THE KIPLINGER WASHINGTON EDITORS, INC., *pg.* 1657, *pg.* 401
KITSAP SUN, *pg.* 1657, *pg.* 1819
KMWORLD, *pg.* 1657, *pg.* 749
KNOXVILLE NEWS-SENTINEL COMPANY, *pg.* 1657, *pg.* 1637
KRAUSE PUBLICATIONS, INC., *pg.* 1657, *pg.* 1861
LADIES' HOME JOURNAL, *pg.* 1657, *pg.* 1250
LAKE CITY REPORTER, *pg.* 1657, *pg.* 436
LANCASTER NEWSPAPERS INC., *pg.* 1657, *pg.* 1546
LANDMARK MEDIA ENTERPRISES LLC, *pg.* 295, *pg.* 1797
LAPEER COUNTY PRESS, *pg.* 1657, *pg.* 896
LAS VEGAS SUN, INC., *pg.* 1657, *pg.* 1021
LATINA MEDIA VENTURES, LLC, *pg.* 1657, *pg.* 1250
LAURIN PUBLISHING CO., INC., *pg.* 1658, *pg.* 841
LEBHAR-FRIEDMAN INC., *pg.* 1658, *pg.* 1250
LEE ENTERPRISES, INCORPORATED, *pg.* 1658, *pg.* 704
LEWISTON DAILY SUN, *pg.* 1658, *pg.* 751
THE LIMA NEWS, *pg.* 1659, *pg.* 1457
LINCOLN NEWS MESSENGER, *pg.* 1659, *pg.* 122
LINE PUBLICATIONS, INC., *pg.* 1659, *pg.* 134
LIPPINCOTT WILLIAMS & WILKINS, INC., *pg.* 1659, *pg.* 1567
LLEWELLYN WORLDWIDE LIMITED, *pg.* 1660, *pg.* 967
LOG CABIN DEMOCRAT, LLC, *pg.* 1660, *pg.* 31
LOS ANGELES DAILY NEWS PUBLISHING COMPANY, *pg.* 1000, *pg.* 308
LOS ANGELES MAGAZINE, *pg.* 1660, *pg.* 135
LOS ANGELES TIMES COMMUNICATIONS, LLC, *pg.* 1660, *pg.* 135
LRP PUBLICATIONS, *pg.* 1660, *pg.* 1540
THE LUBBOCK AVALANCHE-JOURNAL, *pg.* 1660, *pg.* 1726
MACFADDEN COMMUNICATIONS GROUP, LLC, *pg.* 1660, *pg.* 1254
MACOMB COUNTY LEGAL NEWS, *pg.* 1660, *pg.* 901
MADISON NEWSPAPERS, INC., *pg.* 1661, *pg.* 1866
MANSUETO VENTURES LLC, *pg.* 1661, *pg.* 1256
MARIN INDEPENDENT JOURNAL, *pg.* 1661, *pg.* 258
MARKETING MAGAZINE, *pg.* 1661, *pg.* 1940
MARTHA STEWART LIVING OMNIMEDIA, INC., *pg.* 1661, *pg.* 1256
MARVEL ENTERTAINMENT, LLC, *pg.* 1662, *pg.* 1257
MASSACHUSETTS LAWYERS WEEKLY, INC., *pg.* 1662, *pg.* 798
MASSACHUSETTS MEDICAL SOCIETY, *pg.* 1559, *pg.* 852
THE MCCLATCHY COMPANY, *pg.* 1662, *pg.* 196
MCCLATCHY NEWSPAPERS, INC., *pg.* 1662, *pg.* 197
THE MCGRAW-HILL COMPANIES INC., *pg.* 1663, *pg.* 1257
MEDIA GENERAL, INC., *pg.* 297, *pg.* 1803
MEDICINE HAT NEWS, *pg.* 1663, *pg.* 1906
MEREDITH CORPORATION, *pg.* 1663, *pg.* 705
MERION MATTERS, *pg.* 1664, *pg.* 1544
METROWEST DAILY NEWS, *pg.* 1665, *pg.* 821
THE MIAMI HERALD, *pg.* 1665, *pg.* 444
MICHIGAN.COM, *pg.* 1665, *pg.* 884
MILLER GROUP MEDIA, *pg.* 1665, *pg.* 621
MLIVE MEDIA GROUP, *pg.* 1665, *pg.* 888
THE MONITOR, *pg.* 1665, *pg.* 1726

MOODY PUBLISHERS, pg. 1665, pg. 583
THE MORNING CALL, INC., pg. 1665, pg. 1513
THE MORNING SUN, pg. 1666, pg. 720
MORNINGSTAR, INC., pg. 784, pg. 583
MORRIS COMMUNICATIONS COMPANY LLC, pg. 1666, pg. 525
MORRIS MULTIMEDIA, INC., pg. 1666, pg. 540
MORRIS PUBLISHING GROUP, LLC, pg. 1666, pg. 525
MOTHER EARTH NEWS, pg. 1666, pg. 722
MSCI INC., pg. 785, pg. 1262
NAPLES DAILY NEWS, pg. 1666, pg. 451
NATIONAL ASSOCIATION OF ORTHOPAEDIC NURSES, pg. 148, pg. 584
NATIONAL ASSOCIATION OF REALTORS, pg. 1666, pg. 584
NATIONAL AUDUBON SOCIETY, pg. 148, pg. 1263
NATIONAL FIRE PROTECTION ASSOCIATION, pg. 149, pg. 842
NATIONAL GEOGRAPHIC SOCIETY, pg. 1667, pg. 402
NATIONAL HOT ROD ASSOCIATION, pg. 149, pg. 99
NATIONAL JOURNAL GROUP, pg. 1667, pg. 402
NATIONAL PARKS CONSERVATION ASSOCIATION, pg. 150, pg. 403
NATIONAL REVIEW, INC., pg. 1667, pg. 1265
NATIONAL SPORTING GOODS ASSOCIATION, pg. 151, pg. 634
NETWORK COMMUNICATIONS INC., pg. 1271, pg. 534
THE NEW ENGLAND JOURNAL OF MEDICINE, pg. 1667, pg. 799
NEW JERSEY HILLS MEDIA GROUP, pg. 1667, pg. 1044
NEW JERSEY MONTHLY, pg. 1667, pg. 1089
THE NEW REPUBLIC INC., pg. 1667, pg. 403
NEW YORK MAGAZINE, pg. 1667, pg. 1269
THE NEW YORK POST, pg. 1668, pg. 1269
THE NEW YORK TIMES, pg. 1668, pg. 1270
THE NEW YORK TIMES COMPANY, pg. 1668, pg. 1270
THE NEW YORKER MAGAZINE, INC., pg. 1669, pg. 1271
THE NEWARK ADVOCATE, pg. 1669, pg. 1467
NEWS AMERICA INCORPORATED, pg. 1669, pg. 1271
NEWS & RECORD, pg. 1669, pg. 1375
NEWS CHIEF, pg. 1669, pg. 480
NEWS CORPORATION, pg. 1669, pg. 1271
THE NEWS-ENTERPRISE, pg. 1669, pg. 727
THE NEWS-HERALD, pg. 1670, pg. 908
NEWS-LEADER, pg. 1670, pg. 422
NEWS MEDIA CORPORATION, pg. 1670, pg. 654
THE NEWS-SENTINEL, pg. 1670, pg. 681
NEWS-SUN, INC., pg. 1670, pg. 467
THE NEWS-TIMES, pg. 1670, pg. 344
THE NEWS TRIBUNE, pg. 1670, pg. 1845
NEWS TRIBUNE CO., pg. 1670, pg. 980
NEWS WEST PUBLISHING COMPANY INC., pg. 1670, pg. 12
NEWSDAY MEDIA GROUP, pg. 1670, pg. 1181
NEWSMAX MEDIA, INC., pg. 1271, pg. 479
NEWSWEEK DAILY BEAST CO., pg. 1670, pg. 1271
THE NEWTON KANSAN, pg. 1671, pg. 717
NIELSEN BUSINESS MEDIA, pg. 1671, pg. 1272
NJBIZ, pg. 1671, pg. 1122
NOLA MEDIA GROUP, pg. 1671, pg. 747
NORTH AMERICAN PUBLISHING COMPANY, pg. 1671, pg. 1567
NORTH JERSEY MEDIA GROUP INC., pg. 1672, pg. 1072
NORTHWEST FLORIDA DAILY NEWS, pg. 1672, pg. 428
NORTHWEST GEORGIA NEWS, pg. 1672, pg. 539
THE OAK RIDGER, LLC, pg. 1672, pg. 1655
OBSERVER PUBLISHING COMPANY, pg. 1672, pg. 1591
OCONEE PUBLISHING INC., pg. 1672, pg. 1621
ODESSA AMERICAN, pg. 1672, pg. 1728
OGDEN NEWSPAPERS, INC., pg. 1672, pg. 1851
OGDEN PUBLICATIONS, INC., pg. 1672, pg. 722
OGDEN PUBLISHING CORPORATION, pg. 1672, pg. 1753
O'MEARA-BROWN PUBLICATIONS, INC., pg. 1673, pg. 586
OPEN SKY MEDIA, pg. 1673, pg. 451
THE ORANGE COUNTY REGISTER, pg. 1673, pg. 262
OREGONIAN PUBLISHING CO., pg. 1673, pg. 1504
THE OTTAWA CITIZEN, pg. 1673, pg. 1932
OUR SUNDAY VISITOR, INC., pg. 1673, pg. 682
PACIFIC PALISADES POST INC., pg. 1673, pg. 174
PACIFIC PRESS PUBLISHING ASSOCIATION, pg. 1674, pg. 550
PADDOCK PUBLICATIONS, INC., pg. 1674, pg. 554
PAISANO PUBLICATIONS, LLC, pg. 1674, pg. 38
PALATKA DAILY NEWS, pg. 1674, pg. 457
PALM BEACH MEDIA GROUP INC., pg. 1674, pg. 457
PAMPLIN MEDIA GROUP, pg. 1674, pg. 1504
PARADE MAGAZINE, pg. 1674, pg. 1275
PARADE PUBLICATIONS INC., pg. 1674, pg. 1276
PAZDUR PUBLISHING CO., pg. 1674, pg. 115
PC MAGAZINE, pg. 1674, pg. 1276
THE PENINSULA CLARION, pg. 1676, pg. 11
PENNWELL PUBLISHING COMPANY INC., pg. 1676, pg. 1490
PENTON MEDIA, INC., pg. 1676, pg. 719
PENTON MEDIA, INC., pg. 1676, pg. 1277
PEOPLE MAGAZINE, pg. 1676, pg. 1278
PERSONAL SELLING POWER INC., pg. 1677, pg. 1782
PHANMEDIA L.L.C., pg. 1677, pg. 1100
PHILADELPHIA DAILY NEWS, pg. 1677, pg. 1569
THE PHILADELPHIA INQUIRER, pg. 1677, pg. 1569
PILOT MEDIA, pg. 1677, pg. 1797
PLAIN DEALER PUBLISHING CO., pg. 1677, pg. 1434
PLAYBILL INCORPORATED, pg. 1677, pg. 1282
PORTERVILLE RECORDER, pg. 1677, pg. 185
THE POST COMPANY, pg. 1677, pg. 549
PRESBYTERIAN PUBLISHING CORPORATION, pg. 1678, pg. 737
PRESS-REPUBLICAN, pg. 1678, pg. 1322
THE PRINCE GEORGE CITIZEN, pg. 1678, pg. 1908
PRINCETON UNIVERSITY PRESS, pg. 1678, pg. 1112
THE PROVIDENCE JOURNAL, pg. 1678, pg. 1607
PUBLIC UTILITIES REPORTS, INC., pg. 1678, pg. 1809
PUBLICATIONS & COMMUNICATIONS, INC., pg. 1678, pg. 1665
PUBLICATIONS INTERNATIONAL, LTD., pg. 1679, pg. 628
PUTMAN MEDIA, INC., pg. 1679, pg. 621
QUANTURO PUBLISHING, INC., pg. 1679, pg. 445
QUEBECOR MEDIA INC., pg. 1679, pg. 1956
RANDALL-REILLY PUBLISHING COMPANY LLC, pg. 1679, pg. 8
THE READER'S DIGEST ASSOCIATION, INC., pg. 1679, pg. 1322
THE RECORD, pg. 1680, pg. 1922
THE RECORD, pg. 1680, pg. 281
THE RECORD-JOURNAL PUBLISHING COMPANY, pg. 1680, pg. 354
RENTPATH, INC., pg. 1680, pg. 538
RICHMOND SYMPHONY, pg. 579, pg. 1803
THE ROANOKE TIMES, pg. 1680, pg. 1806
ROBB REPORT, pg. 1681, pg. 142
RODALE, INC., pg. 1681, pg. 1530
ROGERS MEDIA INC., pg. 1681, pg. 1942
ROLLING STONE MAGAZINE, pg. 1681, pg. 1287
ROSEBUD ENTERTAINMENT LLC, pg. 1681, pg. 759
THE ROUGH NOTES COMPANY, INC., pg. 1681, pg. 675
SAN ANGELO STANDARD, INC., pg. 1682, pg. 1739
SAN ANTONIO EXPRESS NEWS, pg. 1682, pg. 1742
SAN DIEGO BUSINESS JOURNAL, pg. 1682, pg. 208
THE SAN DIEGO UNION-TRIBUNE, LLC, pg. 1682, pg. 208
SAN FRANCISCO CHRONICLE, pg. 1683, pg. 226
SAN JOSE MERCURY NEWS, pg. 1683, pg. 250
SANDUSKY NEWSPAPERS INC., pg. 1683, pg. 1472
SANTA CRUZ SENTINEL, pg. 1683, pg. 278
SATURDAY EVENING POST SOCIETY, pg. 1683, pg. 690
SAVANNAH MORNING NEWS, pg. 1683, pg. 540
SCHOLASTIC CORPORATION, pg. 1683, pg. 1288
SCHOLASTIC INC., pg. 1683, pg. 1288
SCHROEDER PUBLISHING COMPANY, pg. 1685, pg. 739
SCIENTIFIC AMERICAN, INC., pg. 1685, pg. 1290
SCRANTON GILLETTE COMMUNICATIONS, pg. 1685, pg. 554
SEATTLE POST-INTELLIGENCER, pg. 1685, pg. 1839
SEATTLE TIMES COMPANY, pg. 1685, pg. 1840
THE SEDALIA DEMOCRAT, pg. 1685, pg. 1005
SELF MAGAZINE, pg. 1686, pg. 1290
SEVENTEEN MAGAZINE, pg. 1686, pg. 1290
SF NEWSPAPER COMPANY, LLC, pg. 1686, pg. 227
SHAWNEE NEWS-STAR, pg. 1686, pg. 1488
SIMMONS-BOARDMAN PUBLISHING CORP., pg. 1686, pg. 1292
SMITHSONIAN MAGAZINE, pg. 1687, pg. 404
SNOWMASS VILLAGE SUN, pg. 1687, pg. 335
SOUND PUBLISHING, INC., pg. 1687, pg. 1823
THE SOUTHERN POVERTY LAW CENTER, pg. 157, pg. 7
SPA FINDER, INC., pg. 1113, pg. 1295
THE SPOKESMAN-REVIEW, pg. 1687, pg. 1844
THE SPORTING NEWS, pg. 1688, pg. 1295
SPORTS ILLUSTRATED, pg. 1688, pg. 1295
SPRINGER SCIENCE+BUSINESS MEDIA, LLC, pg. 1688, pg. 1295
THE ST. AUGUSTINE RECORD, pg. 1688, pg. 461
ST. LOUIS POST-DISPATCH LLC, pg. 1688, pg. 1004
STANDARD PUBLISHING GROUP LLC, pg. 1689, pg. 1426
STAR COURIER, pg. 1689, pg. 621
THE STAR TRIBUNE COMPANY, pg. 1689, pg. 942
STARLOG GROUP, INC., pg. 1689, pg. 1296
THE STARPHOENIX, pg. 1689, pg. 1962
THE STATE JOURNAL-REGISTER, pg. 1689, pg. 662
STYLE WEEKLY INC., pg. 1690, pg. 1804
SUMNER COMMUNICATIONS INC., pg. 1690, pg. 338
THE SUN, pg. 1690, pg. 198
THE SUN, pg. 1690, pg. 28
SUN JOURNAL, pg. 1690, pg. 1386
SUN-TIMES MEDIA GROUP, INC., pg. 1690, pg. 591
SUPERMARKET NEWS, pg. 1690, pg. 1297
SWIFT NEWSPAPERS, INC., pg. 1690, pg. 1032
SYS-CON MEDIA, INC., pg. 1690, pg. 1134
TAMPA BAY BUSINESS JOURNAL, pg. 1691, pg. 476
TAMPA BAY MAGAZINE, pg. 1691, pg. 416
TAMPA BAY NEWSPAPERS, INC., pg. 1691, pg. 468
TAMPA BAY PUBLICATIONS, INC., pg. 1691, pg. 416
TAMPA BAY TIMES, pg. 1691, pg. 464
THE TAMPA TRIBUNE, pg. 1691, pg. 476
TECHNOLOGY MARKETING CORP., pg. 1691, pg. 364
THE TELEGRAM, pg. 1691, pg. 1916
THE TELEGRAPH, pg. 1691, pg. 553
TEN: THE ENTHUSIAST NETWORK, pg. 1691, pg. 1298
TENNIS MAGAZINE, pg. 1692, pg. 1298
TEXAS MONTHLY, pg. 1692, pg. 1666
THOMAS PUBLISHING COMPANY LLC, pg. 1692, pg. 1299
THOMSON REUTERS - CORPORATE HEADQUARTERS, pg. 1693, pg. 1299
THOMSON REUTERS CORPORATION, pg. 1693, pg. 1944
TIME INC., pg. 1693, pg. 1300
TIME OUT NEW YORK, pg. 1694, pg. 1301
TIME WARNER INC., pg. 312, pg. 1302
TIMES HERALD-RECORD, pg. 1694, pg. 1182
THE TIMES-NEWS, pg. 1694, pg. 1359
THE TIMES PUBLISHING CO., pg. 1695, pg. 464
TIMES PUBLISHING CO. INC., pg. 1695, pg. 1530
TIMES RECORD NEWS, pg. 1695, pg. 1749
THE TOPEKA CAPITAL-JOURNAL, pg. 1695, pg. 722
TORONTO STAR NEWSPAPERS LTD., pg. 1695, pg. 1945
TOWN & COUNTRY, pg. 1695, pg. 1303
TPR EDUCATION, LLC, pg. 1695, pg. 822
TRADE PRESS MEDIA GROUP, pg. 1695, pg. 1881
TRANSACTION PUBLISHERS, INC., pg. 1695, pg. 1109
TRANSCONTINENTAL INC., pg. 1695, pg. 1957
TRANSPORT TOPICS PUBLISHING GROUP, pg. 1696, pg. 1772
TRAVERSE CITY RECORD-EAGLE, pg. 1696, pg. 910
TREND MAGAZINES, INC., pg. 1696, pg. 465
TRIBUNE MEDIA COMPANY, pg. 1696, pg. 592
TRUCKER PUBLICATIONS INC., pg. 1696, pg. 1
TV GUIDE MAGAZINE GROUP, INC., pg. 1697, pg. 1305
TWELVE SIGNS, INC., pg. 1697, pg. 141
UBM ADVANSTAR, pg. 1697, pg. 1306
UNITED PRESS INTERNATIONAL, INC., pg. 1698, pg. 405
THE UPPER ROOM, pg. 1698, pg. 1655
U.S. NAVAL INSTITUTE, pg. 1698, pg. 754
U.S. NEWS & WORLD REPORT, L.P., pg. 1698, pg. 1308
US WEEKLY LLC, pg. 1698, pg. 1308
VALLEY MORNING STAR, pg. 1699, pg. 1699
VALUE LINE, INC., pg. 1699, pg. 1308
VANCE PUBLISHING CORPORATION, pg. 1699, pg. 627
VANITY FAIR, pg. 1699, pg. 1308
VENTURA COUNTY STAR, pg. 1699, pg. 57
VICTORIA ADVOCATE PUBLISHING COMPANY, pg. 1699, pg. 1748
VILLAGE SOUP, pg. 1699, pg. 752
VILLAGE VOICE MEDIA HOLDINGS, LLC, pg. 1699, pg. 1311
VOGUE MAGAZINE, pg. 1700, pg. 1311
VOICE COMMUNICATIONS CORP., pg. 1700, pg. 902
THE WALL STREET JOURNAL, pg. 1700, pg. 1312
THE WALTON SUN, pg. 1701, pg. 465
WARRICK PUBLISHING CO. INC., pg. 1701, pg. 675
THE WASHINGTON POST, pg. 1701, pg. 407
WATT PUBLISHING COMPANY, pg. 1701, pg. 655
WEBSITE MAGAZINE INCORPORATED, pg. 1701, pg. 607
WEISS RESEARCH, pg. 819, pg. 436
WENNER MEDIA LLC, pg. 1701, pg. 1314
WESTERN COMMUNICATIONS INC., pg. 1701, pg. 1496
WESTERN NEWSPAPERS, INC., pg. 1702, pg. 28
THE WICHITA EAGLE, pg. 1702, pg. 724

First page reference indicates Business Class Edition
Second page reference indicates Geographic Edition

WIESNER PUBLISHING, LLC, pg. 1702, pg. 328
WORCESTER TELEGRAM & GAZETTE CORP., pg. 1702, pg. 863
WORKING MOTHER MEDIA, INC., pg. 1702, pg. 1315
WORTH, pg. 1702, pg. 1315
XBOX, pg. 970, pg. 1829
YACHTING MAGAZINE, pg. 1703, pg. 1602
YANKEE PUBLISHING INC., pg. 1703, pg. 1033
YANKTON DAILY PRESS & DAKOTAN, pg. 1703, pg. 1626
THE YORK NEWS-TIMES, pg. 1703, pg. 1020
YOUNG MONEY, pg. 1703, pg. 773
ZIFF DAVIS, LLC, pg. 1703, pg. 1316

2731 - Books: Publishing, or Publishing & Printing

ABOUT, INC., pg. 1225, pg. 1186
ACADEMIC COMMUNICATION ASSOCIATES, INC., pg. 1613, pg. 173
ACADEMIC INNOVATIONS, pg. 1613, pg. 262
ACTIVE PARENTING PUBLISHERS, pg. 1613, pg. 535
ADVANCE PUBLICATIONS, INC., pg. 1613, pg. 1343
ADVANTAGE BUSINESS MEDIA, pg. 1613, pg. 1116
ADVERTISING AGE, pg. 1613, pg. 1187
ALFRED A. KNOPF, INC., pg. 1614, pg. 1189
ALLEN ORGAN COMPANY, pg. 527, pg. 1549
ALLIANCE DATA SYSTEMS CORPORATION, pg. 347, pg. 1729
ALLRECIPES.COM, pg. 1226, pg. 1831
A.M. BEST COMPANY, pg. 1614, pg. 1101
AMERICAN GIRL LLC, pg. 949, pg. 1871
AMERICAN HERITAGE PUBLISHING, pg. 1615, pg. 775
AMERICAN MATHEMATICAL SOCIETY, INC., pg. 129, pg. 1605
AMERICAN MEDIA, INC., pg. 1615, pg. 410
AMERICAN PUBLIC EDUCATION, INC., pg. 597, pg. 1849
AMERICAN TECHNICAL PUBLISHERS, INC., pg. 1616, pg. 649
AMERICA'S TEST KITCHEN, pg. 1616, pg. 803
ANCESTRY.COM LLC, pg. 1228, pg. 1754
ANDREWS MCMEEL UNIVERSAL, pg. 1616, pg. 980
ANNIE'S, pg. 1617, pg. 673
AOL INC., pg. 1229, pg. 1195
ASIAN WEEK FOUNDATION, pg. 1617, pg. 212
ASSOCIATION OF AMERICAN PUBLISHERS, INC., pg. 133, pg. 1197
ASTARA, INC., pg. 1618, pg. 186
AT&T INC., pg. 1867, pg. 1674
AUDIBLE, INC., pg. 1230, pg. 1095
AUGSBURG FORTRESS, pg. 1618, pg. 931
AUTHOR SOLUTIONS, INC., pg. 1618, pg. 674
AUTOBYTEL INC., pg. 1230, pg. 107
AUTOMOTIVE NEWS, pg. 1618, pg. 879
AVENTION, pg. 1230, pg. 815
AVVO, INC., pg. 1231, pg. 1833
AWARE RECORDS, pg. 531, pg. 611
B-SCADA, INC., pg. 1231, pg. 419
BAKER PUBLISHING GROUP, pg. 1619, pg. 864
BANKRATE, INC., pg. 1231, pg. 451
BARKER CREEK PUBLISHING INC., pg. 1619, pg. 1818
BARNES & NOBLE, INC., pg. 1619, pg. 1201
BARRON'S EDUCATIONAL SERIES, INC., pg. 1620, pg. 1164
BELVOIR MEDIA GROUP, LLC, pg. 1620, pg. 360
THE BERRY COMPANY LLC, pg. 1869, pg. 1445
BEYOND.COM, INC., pg. 1231, pg. 1543
BIOSPACE, INC., pg. 1231, pg. 1082
BIZBASH MEDIA INC., pg. 1621, pg. 1203
BLOOMBERG BNA, pg. 1621, pg. 1772
BLUE MAN PRODUCTIONS, INC., pg. 533, pg. 1205
BODYBUILDING.COM LLC, pg. 1232, pg. 549
BOFI HOLDING, INC., pg. 726, pg. 200
BONNIER ACTIVE MEDIA, INC., pg. 1622, pg. 1205
BONNIER CORPORATION, pg. 1622, pg. 480
BOOKAZINE COMPANY, INC., pg. 1622, pg. 1042
BOYDS MILLS PRESS, INC., pg. 1623, pg. 1539
BRIDGE PUBLICATIONS INC., pg. 1623, pg. 127
BRILLIANT DIGITAL, pg. 1233, pg. 281
BROADVIEW PRESS INC., pg. 1623, pg. 1902
BUSINESS & LEGAL REPORTS INC., pg. 1624, pg. 367
CALIFORNIA OFFSET PRINTERS, INC., pg. 1625, pg. 95
CAMBIUM LEARNING GROUP, INC., pg. 599, pg. 1677
CAMBRIDGE INFORMATION GROUP, INC., pg. 1625, pg. 761
CAPSTONE PRESS, INC., pg. 1625, pg. 951
CAREERBUILDER, LLC, pg. 1234, pg. 568
CARL FISCHER, LLC, pg. 1625, pg. 1209
CASTLE CONNOLLY MEDICAL LTD., pg. 1626, pg. 1210
CBS CORPORATION, pg. 273, pg. 1210
CBS INTERACTIVE, INC., pg. 369, pg. 215
CBS SPORTSLINE.COM, INC., pg. 1234, pg. 423
CCH, pg. 1626, pg. 569
CCH INC., pg. 1626, pg. 653
CENGAGE LEARNING, pg. 1626, pg. 215
CHARISMA MEDIA, pg. 1627, pg. 436
CHARITY NAVIGATOR, pg. 136, pg. 1071
CINCINNATI BUSINESS COURIER, pg. 1627, pg. 1411
CIRQUE DU SOLEIL INC., pg. 540, pg. 1954
CLASSMATES ONLINE, INC., pg. 1235, pg. 1834
COLLECTORS EDITIONS, pg. 1628, pg. 58
COLUMBIA UNIVERSITY PRESS, pg. 1628, pg. 1216
COMCAST INTERACTIVE MEDIA, LLC, pg. 1236, pg. 1562
COMSCORE, INC, pg. 1236, pg. 1798
CONCORDIA PUBLISHING HOUSE, pg. 1629, pg. 995
CONDE NAST DIGITAL, pg. 1237, pg. 1217
CONDE NAST PUBLICATIONS, INC., pg. 1629, pg. 1217
CONSOLIDATED COMMUNICATIONS HOLDINGS, INC., pg. 630, pg. 631
CONSUMERREVIEW, INC., pg. 1237, pg. 193
CONSUMERS UNION OF THE UNITED STATES, INC., pg. 1630, pg. 1356
COOKING.COM, pg. 1237, pg. 143
COPERNIC INC., pg. 1237, pg. 1958
CORNELL UNIVERSITY PRESS, pg. 1630, pg. 1169
CORNERWORLD CORPORATION, pg. 1237, pg. 1678
CORT BUSINESS SERVICES CORPORATION, pg. 921, pg. 1777
CPP, INC., pg. 1631, pg. 153
CQ ROLL CALL, pg. 1631, pg. 397
CRAIN COMMUNICATIONS, INC., pg. 1631, pg. 879
CRAIN'S CHICAGO BUSINESS, pg. 1631, pg. 572
CRAIN'S NEW YORK BUSINESS, pg. 1631, pg. 1220
CREDITCARDS.COM, INC., pg. 1237, pg. 1661
CREDITRISKMONITOR.COM, INC., pg. 1631, pg. 1348
DEX MEDIA INC, pg. 1635, pg. 1680
DEX ONE CORPORATION, pg. 1635, pg. 1360
DK PUBLISHING, pg. 1636, pg. 1224
THE DOLAN COMPANY, pg. 1636, pg. 932
DOMINION ENTERPRISES, pg. 1636, pg. 1796
DOVER PUBLICATIONS, INC., pg. 1636, pg. 1182
DOW JONES & COMPANY, INC., pg. 1637, pg. 1225
THE DUN & BRADSTREET CORP., pg. 1637, pg. 1120
DYNAMIC RESOURCE GROUP, pg. 1637, pg. 674
EDGAR ONLINE, INC., pg. 746, pg. 776
EDITORIAL TELEVISA INTERNATIONAL, pg. 1638, pg. 442
EDMUNDS, INC., pg. 1241, pg. 273
EDUCATIONAL DEVELOPMENT CORPORATION, pg. 1638, pg. 1490
ELLIE MAE, INC., pg. 1243, pg. 183
ELSEVIER HEALTH SCIENCES, pg. 1638, pg. 1564
EMUSIC.COM, INC., pg. 1243, pg. 1227
ENCYCLOPAEDIA BRITANNICA, INC., pg. 1638, pg. 573
ENTERTAINMENT PUBLICATIONS, INC., pg. 1639, pg. 910
ENVESTNET, INC., pg. 748, pg. 573
EPOCRATES, INC., pg. 1529, pg. 254
ESM SOLUTIONS CORPORATION, pg. 1243, pg. 1591
ESPIAL GROUP INC., pg. 1243, pg. 1932
EXCELLIGENCE LEARNING CORP., pg. 1768, pg. 151
EXPEDIA, INC., pg. 1244, pg. 1814
EXPERIAN CONSUMER DIRECT, pg. 1245, pg. 71
F.A. DAVIS PUBLISHING COMPANY, pg. 1640, pg. 1564
FACEBOOK, INC., pg. 1245, pg. 143
FACTSET RESEARCH SYSTEMS INC., pg. 1247, pg. 361
FAIRCHILD FASHION GROUP, pg. 1640, pg. 1230
FARRAR, STRAUS & GIROUX, INC., pg. 1640, pg. 1231
FILM SCORE MONTHLY, pg. 1641, pg. 103
FINANCIAL ENGINES, INC., pg. 753, pg. 285
FIRST DATABANK, INC., pg. 397, pg. 217
FLASHES PUBLISHERS, pg. 1641, pg. 864
FORBES.COM LLC, pg. 1247, pg. 1232
FRANKLIN ELECTRONIC PUBLISHERS, INC., pg. 398, pg. 1048
FREDERICK FELL PUBLISHERS, INC., pg. 1643, pg. 431
FRIENDFINDER NETWORKS INC., pg. 1643, pg. 411
GAIN CAPITAL HOLDINGS, INC., pg. 760, pg. 1043
GALE CENGAGE LEARNING, pg. 1643, pg. 885
GARDNER PUBLICATIONS, INC., pg. 1644, pg. 1413
GATEHOUSE MEDIA, INC., pg. 1644, pg. 1159
GAWKER MEDIA LLC, pg. 1248, pg. 1234
GEORGE BRAZILLER PUBLISHERS, INC., pg. 1644, pg. 1234
GLAMOUR, pg. 1645, pg. 1235
THE GLOBE PEQUOT PRESS, INC., pg. 1645, pg. 350
GOOD HOUSEKEEPING, pg. 1645, pg. 1236
THE GOODHEART-WILLCOX CO., INC., pg. 1645, pg. 663
GOOGLE INC., pg. 1249, pg. 153
GRAHAM HOLDINGS COMPANY, pg. 1645, pg. 1773
GREAT LAKES PUBLISHING COMPANY, pg. 1646, pg. 1431
GREY HOUSE PUBLISHING CORP., pg. 1646, pg. 1137
GROVE/ATLANTIC, INC., pg. 1646, pg. 1236
GULF PUBLISHING COMPANY, pg. 1646, pg. 1707
HAIGHTS CROSS COMMUNICATIONS, INC., pg. 1646, pg. 1237
HAINES & COMPANY, INC., pg. 1646, pg. 1468
HARLEQUIN ENTERPRISES LIMITED, pg. 1647, pg. 1938
HARMONIC, INC., pg. 402, pg. 246
HARPERCOLLINS PUBLISHERS INC., pg. 1647, pg. 1237
HARPO, INC., pg. 290, pg. 576
HARRIS CONNECT LLC, pg. 1648, pg. 1143
HARVARD UNIVERSITY PRESS, pg. 1648, pg. 808
HBG BOOKS, INC., pg. 1648, pg. 1238
HEALTHCENTRAL, pg. 1256, pg. 1773
HEALTHPORT, INC., pg. 403, pg. 484
HEALTHY DIRECTIONS, pg. 1649, pg. 775
THE HEARST CORPORATION, pg. 1649, pg. 1239
HEARST MAGAZINES, pg. 1649, pg. 1239
HERE MEDIA INC., pg. 290, pg. 132
HERFF JONES, INC., pg. 7, pg. 686
HOLLYWOOD MEDIA CORP., pg. 1256, pg. 412
HOME SCHOOL HOLDINGS, INC., pg. 1256, pg. 606
HOMEAWAY, INC., pg. 1911, pg. 1663
HOMES.COM, INC., pg. 1256, pg. 203
HOOKED MEDIA GROUP, pg. 1256, pg. 219
HORIZON HOUSE PUBLICATIONS INC., pg. 1650, pg. 839
HOT OFF THE PRESS, INC., pg. 1650, pg. 1497
HOTWIRE, INC., pg. 1912, pg. 219
HOUGHTON MIFFLIN HARCOURT, pg. 1650, pg. 611
HOUGHTON MIFFLIN HARCOURT PUBLISHING COMPANY, pg. 1651, pg. 796
HOUGHTON MIFFLIN HARCOURT PUBLISHING COMPANY, pg. 1651, pg. 454
HOUR PUBLISHING COMPANY, pg. 1651, pg. 362
HULU LLC, pg. 1257, pg. 274
HUMAN KINETICS PUBLISHERS INC., pg. 1651, pg. 562
HYPERION BOOKS, pg. 1651, pg. 1242
IAC/INTERACTIVECORP, pg. 292, pg. 1242
IDEALAB, INC., pg. 1258, pg. 180
IGN ENTERTAINMENT, INC., pg. 1258, pg. 220
IHS AUTOMOTIVE DRIVEN BY POLK, pg. 1652, pg. 907
IHS INC., pg. 1652, pg. 326
IN TOUCH WEEKLY, pg. 1652, pg. 1060
INFOGROUP INC., pg. 1652, pg. 1016
INFORMA EXHIBITIONS LLC, pg. 1653, pg. 17
INFORMATION TODAY INC., pg. 1653, pg. 1084
INNER TRADITIONS INTERNATIONAL, pg. 1653, pg. 1767
INNOVATIVE USA, INC., pg. 957, pg. 363
INSTITUTIONAL INVESTOR, INC., pg. 1653, pg. 1244
INSWEB CORPORATION, pg. 1205, pg. 186
INTELIMAX MEDIA INC., pg. 1259, pg. 1911
INTERNET MEDIA SERVICES, INC., pg. 1259, pg. 274
ISLANDS MAGAZINE, pg. 1654, pg. 480
IUNIVERSE, INC., pg. 1259, pg. 674
J.J. KELLER & ASSOCIATES, INC., pg. 1654, pg. 1883
JOBSON HEALTHCARE INFORMATION LLC, pg. 1654, pg. 1246
JOHN WILEY & SONS, INC., pg. 1655, pg. 1073
THE JOHNS HOPKINS UNIVERSITY PRESS, pg. 1655, pg. 757
JOHNSON PUBLISHING COMPANY, INC., pg. 1655, pg. 579
JOURNAL OF COMMERCE, INC., pg. 1655, pg. 1097
K-TEL INTERNATIONAL, INC., pg. 1052, pg. 953
K12, INC., pg. 1260, pg. 1785
KALMBACH PUBLISHING CO., pg. 1656, pg. 1898
KAYAK, pg. 1260, pg. 363
KCNC-TV, pg. 293, pg. 320
KELLEY BLUE BOOK CO., INC., pg. 1656, pg. 112
KENSINGTON PUBLISHING CORP., pg. 1656, pg. 1248
THE KNOPF DOUBLEDAY GROUP, pg. 1657, pg. 1249
KORG USA, INC., pg. 556, pg. 1180
KRAUSE PUBLICATIONS, INC., pg. 1657, pg. 1861
LABELQUEST, INC., pg. 1463, pg. 611
LAURA DAMIANO DESIGNS, pg. 1658, pg. 1354

LAURIN PUBLISHING CO., INC., pg. 1658, pg. 841
LAW BULLETIN PUBLISHING COMPANY, pg. 1658, pg. 580
LEGALZOOM.COM, INC., pg. 1261, pg. 96
LEXISNEXIS CORPORATE AFFILIATIONS, pg. 1658, pg. 1095
LEXISNEXIS GROUP, pg. 1658, pg. 1446
LEXISNEXIS LITIGATION SOLUTIONS, pg. 1659, pg. 1446
LIMELIGHT NETWORKS, INC., pg. 1262, pg. 26
LINKEDIN CORPORATION, pg. 1262, pg. 160
LIPPINCOTT WILLIAMS & WILKINS, INC., pg. 1659, pg. 1567
LITERARY CLASSICS OF THE UNITED STATES, INC., pg. 1659, pg. 1251
LITTLE, BROWN & COMPANY, pg. 1660, pg. 1251
LIVE CURRENT MEDIA INC., pg. 1263, pg. 1911
LIVEPERSON, INC., pg. 1264, pg. 1252
LLEWELLYN WORLDWIDE LIMITED, pg. 1660, pg. 967
LOOPNET, INC., pg. 1265, pg. 222
MANUFACTURERS' NEWS, INC., pg. 1661, pg. 612
MARKET LEADER, INC., pg. 1102, pg. 1822
MARKETWATCH, INC., pg. 1265, pg. 222
MARQUIS WHO'S WHO, LLC, pg. 1661, pg. 1044
MARTHA STEWART LIVING OMNIMEDIA, INC., pg. 1661, pg. 1256
MARTINDALE-HUBBELL, INC., pg. 1662, pg. 1095
MARVEL ENTERTAINMENT, LLC, pg. 1662, pg. 1257
MASTERBEAT CORPORATION, pg. 1265, pg. 1257
MAX SOUND CORPORATION, pg. 1266, pg. 1711
MCBOOKS PRESS INC., pg. 1662, pg. 1170
MCFARLAND & COMPANY, INC., pg. 1662, pg. 1380
THE MCGRAW-HILL COMPANIES INC., pg. 1663, pg. 1257
MEDIA GENERAL, pg. 297, pg. 1607
MEDIABISTRO, INC., pg. 1266, pg. 1258
MEN'S JOURNAL, pg. 1663, pg. 1258
MEREDITH CORPORATION, pg. 1663, pg. 705
MERGENT, INC., pg. 1664, pg. 1616
MERRIAM-WEBSTER, INC., pg. 1664, pg. 846
MICHELIN NORTH AMERICA INC., pg. 1886, pg. 1618
MIDNIGHT MARQUEE PRESS, INC., pg. 1665, pg. 758
MIQ LOGISTICS, LLC, pg. 1267, pg. 719
MORNINGSTAR, INC., pg. 784, pg. 583
MORRIS CERULLO WORLD EVANGELISM, pg. 147, pg. 205
MORRIS PUBLISHING GROUP, LLC, pg. 1666, pg. 525
THE MOTLEY FOOL, INC., pg. 784, pg. 1771
MOVE, INC., pg. 1268, pg. 247
MULTI-AD, INC., pg. 1666, pg. 652
MUSIC SALES CORPORATION, pg. 1666, pg. 1263
MYLIFE.COM, INC., pg. 1268, pg. 137
NAMEMEDIA, INC., pg. 1269, pg. 852
THE NATIONAL ENQUIRER, pg. 1667, pg. 412
NATIONAL GEOGRAPHIC SOCIETY, pg. 1667, pg. 402
NETWORK COMMUNICATIONS INC., pg. 1271, pg. 534
NEULION, INC., pg. 302, pg. 1321
NEW DIMENSIONS WORLD BROADCASTING NETWORK, pg. 302, pg. 298
NEWS AMERICA INCORPORATED, pg. 1669, pg. 1271
NEWS CORPORATION, pg. 1669, pg. 1271
NEWSMAX MEDIA, INC., pg. 1271, pg. 479
NIELSEN BUSINESS MEDIA, pg. 1671, pg. 1272
THE NIELSEN COMPANY B.V., pg. 1671, pg. 1272
NTN BUZZTIME, INC., pg. 659, pg. 60
OAG WORLDWIDE LIMITED, pg. 1672, pg. 609
OGDEN PUBLISHING CORPORATION, pg. 1672, pg. 1753
OMNICOMM SYSTEMS, INC., pg. 1272, pg. 426
ON24, INC., pg. 1272, pg. 224
OPTIMIZERX CORPORATION, pg. 1673, pg. 905
ORBITZ WORLDWIDE, INC., pg. 1918, pg. 586
THE ORCHARD ENTERPRISES, INC., pg. 572, pg. 1274
O'REILLY MEDIA, INC., pg. 1673, pg. 278
OXFORD UNIVERSITY PRESS, INC., pg. 1673, pg. 1275
PACIFIC PRESS PUBLISHING ASSOCIATION, pg. 1674, pg. 550
PANDORA MEDIA INC., pg. 1273, pg. 172
PASSKEY INTERNATIONAL, INC., pg. 1274, pg. 853
PEARSON ASSESSMENT & INFORMATION, pg. 1674, pg. 1742
PEARSON EDUCATION, pg. 1675, pg. 800
PENGUIN RANDOM HOUSE, pg. 1675, pg. 1276
PENGUIN RANDOM HOUSE, pg. 1675, pg. 1276
PENGUIN RANDOM HOUSE CHILDREN'S BOOKS, pg. 1676, pg. 1277
PENNWELL PUBLISHING COMPANY INC., pg. 1676, pg. 1490
PENTON MEDIA, INC., pg. 1676, pg. 719
PENTON MEDIA, INC., pg. 1676, pg. 1277
PEOPLE2PEOPLE GROUP INC., pg. 1676, pg. 800
THE PERSEUS BOOKS GROUP, pg. 1676, pg. 1278
PERSONAL SELLING POWER INC., pg. 1677, pg. 1782
PHILANTHROPEDIA, pg. 153, pg. 1811
PIKSEL, pg. 1275, pg. 1282
THE PLANNING SHOP, pg. 1677, pg. 178
PRESBYTERIAN PUBLISHING CORPORATION, pg. 1678, pg. 737
PRINCETON UNIVERSITY PRESS, pg. 1678, pg. 1112
PRUDENT PUBLISHING COMPANY, INC., pg. 1678, pg. 1115
PUBLIC UTILITIES REPORTS, INC., pg. 1678, pg. 1809
PUBLICATIONS INTERNATIONAL, LTD., pg. 1679, pg. 628
PUTMAN MEDIA, INC., pg. 1679, pg. 621
QUEBECOR MEDIA INC., pg. 1679, pg. 1956
QUESTAR ASSESSMENT, INC., pg. 1679, pg. 1143
QUOTEMEDIA, INC., pg. 797, pg. 13
RAND MCNALLY & COMPANY, pg. 1679, pg. 661
THE READER'S DIGEST ASSOCIATION, INC., pg. 1679, pg. 1322
RENTPATH, INC., pg. 1680, pg. 538
REPLOGLE GLOBES, INC., pg. 461, pg. 559
RODALE, INC., pg. 1681, pg. 1530
ROLLING STONE MAGAZINE, pg. 1681, pg. 1287
ROSEBUD ENTERTAINMENT LLC, pg. 1681, pg. 759
ROSETTA STONE INC., pg. 462, pg. 1774
THE ROUGH NOTES COMPANY, INC., pg. 1681, pg. 675
R.R. BOWKER LLC, pg. 1682, pg. 1095
RR DONNELLEY, pg. 1682, pg. 838
RUNNING PRESS, pg. 1682, pg. 1570
SABRE HOLDINGS CORPORATION, pg. 1922, pg. 1745
SALESFORCE.COM, INC., pg. 1278, pg. 226
SAN DIEGO BUSINESS JOURNAL, pg. 1682, pg. 208
SCARECROW PRESS, INC., pg. 1683, pg. 773
SCHOLASTIC CORPORATION, pg. 1683, pg. 1288
SCHOLASTIC INC., pg. 1683, pg. 1288
SCHROEDER PUBLISHING COMPANY, pg. 1685, pg. 739
SCIENTIFIC AMERICAN, INC., pg. 1685, pg. 1290
SCRIPPS NETWORKS INTERACTIVE, INC., pg. 1279, pg. 1638
SELF MAGAZINE, pg. 1686, pg. 1290
SESAME WORKSHOP, pg. 307, pg. 1290
SF NEWSPAPER COMPANY, LLC, pg. 1686, pg. 227
SHAMBHALA PUBLICATIONS INC., pg. 1686, pg. 801
SHAREDBOOK INC., pg. 1686, pg. 1291
SIERRA CLUB, pg. 156, pg. 227
SIMMONS-BOARDMAN PUBLISHING CORP., pg. 1686, pg. 1292
SIMON & SCHUSTER CHILDREN'S PUBLISHING, pg. 1686, pg. 1292
SIMON & SCHUSTER, INC., pg. 1687, pg. 1292
SKINNYCORP L.L.C., pg. 1280, pg. 590
SMARTER TRAVEL MEDIA LLC, pg. 1687, pg. 801
SPA FINDER, INC., pg. 1113, pg. 1295
SPARK NETWORKS, INC., pg. 472, pg. 140
THE SPORTING NEWS, pg. 1688, pg. 1295
SPORTSDIRECT INC., pg. 1282, pg. 1917
SPRINGER SCIENCE+BUSINESS MEDIA, LLC, pg. 1688, pg. 1295
SRDS, INC., pg. 1688, pg. 657
ST. MARTINS PRESS, INC., pg. 1688, pg. 1295
STANDARD PUBLISHING GROUP LLC, pg. 1689, pg. 1426
STENHOUSE PUBLISHERS, pg. 1689, pg. 752
STERLING PUBLISHING CO., INC., pg. 1689, pg. 1296
STREAMING MEDIA HOSTING, INC., pg. 1283, pg. 166
THE STREET, INC., pg. 1283, pg. 1296
STUBHUB, INC., pg. 586, pg. 228
SUMNER COMMUNICATIONS INC., pg. 1690, pg. 338
SUN-TIMES MEDIA GROUP, INC., pg. 1690, pg. 591
SYNACOR, INC., pg. 1283, pg. 1151
SYRACUSE UNIVERSITY PRESS, pg. 1690, pg. 1344
TECHNOLOGY MARKETING CORP., pg. 1691, pg. 364
TECHTARGET, INC., pg. 482, pg. 837
TEN: THE ENTHUSIAST NETWORK, pg. 1691, pg. 1298
THEATRE COMMUNICATIONS GROUP, INC., pg. 587, pg. 1298
THEHUFFINGTONPOST.COM, INC., pg. 1692, pg. 1298
THEODORE PRESSER CO., pg. 1692, pg. 1544
THOMAS NELSON INC., pg. 1692, pg. 1654
THOMAS NELSON PUBLISHERS, pg. 1692, pg. 1654
THOMAS PUBLISHING COMPANY LLC, pg. 1692, pg. 1299
THOMSON ELITE, pg. 484, pg. 72
THOMSON REUTERS - CORPORATE HEADQUARTERS, pg. 1693, pg. 1299
THOMSON REUTERS CORPORATION, pg. 1693, pg. 1944
THOMSON REUTERS MARKETS, pg. 810, pg. 1299
THOMSON REUTERS TAX & ACCOUNTING, pg. 1693, pg. 1299
THE TOPPS COMPANY, INC., pg. 588, pg. 1302
TPR EDUCATION, LLC, pg. 1695, pg. 822
TRACK DATA CORPORATION, pg. 1284, pg. 1147
TRANSCONTINENTAL INC., pg. 1695, pg. 1957
TRAVELHOST, INC., pg. 1696, pg. 1689
TRAVELZOO INC, pg. 1926, pg. 1304
TRUVEN HEALTH ANALYTICS, pg. 1696, pg. 867
TV GUIDE MAGAZINE GROUP, INC., pg. 1697, pg. 1305
TWELVE SIGNS, INC., pg. 1697, pg. 141
TYNDALE HOUSE PUBLISHERS, INC., pg. 1697, pg. 561
UNIGUEST, pg. 1697, pg. 1655
UNITED ONLINE, INC., pg. 1286, pg. 308
UNIVERSITY OF CHICAGO PRESS, pg. 1698, pg. 594
UNIVISION COMMUNICATIONS INC., pg. 683, pg. 1307
UNZ & COMPANY, INC., pg. 1698, pg. 1084
U.S. NAVAL INSTITUTE, pg. 1698, pg. 754
VACATION.COM, INC., pg. 1287, pg. 1772
VALASSIS, pg. 1698, pg. 386
VARESE SARABANDE RECORDS, INC., pg. 1789, pg. 281
VERISIGN, INC., pg. 488, pg. 1799
VOGUE MAGAZINE, pg. 1700, pg. 1311
WALDEN MEDIA, LLC, pg. 317, pg. 141
WAND, INC., pg. 1288, pg. 324
WARNER MUSIC GROUP CORP., pg. 590, pg. 1313
WARNER PRESS, INC., pg. 1701, pg. 673
WEBMD HEALTH CORPORATION, pg. 1288, pg. 1313
WEBSITE MAGAZINE INCORPORATED, pg. 1701, pg. 607
WESTERN COMMUNICATIONS INC., pg. 1701, pg. 1496
WHITE HOUSE HISTORICAL ASSOCIATION, pg. 1702, pg. 408
WHITEPAGES.COM INC., pg. 1289, pg. 1842
WIKIMEDIA FOUNDATION INC., pg. 161, pg. 234
WILLIAM H. SADLIER, INC., pg. 1702, pg. 1314
WILLIAM S. HEIN & CO., INC., pg. 1702, pg. 1151
WILTON PRODUCTS, INC., pg. 1140, pg. 672
WIND-UP RECORDS, pg. 592, pg. 1314
WORDEN BROTHERS, INC., pg. 823, pg. 1372
WORKMAN PUBLISHING COMPANY, pg. 1702, pg. 1315
W.W. NORTON & COMPANY, INC., pg. 1702, pg. 1316
XO GROUP INC., pg. 1289, pg. 1316
YANKEE PUBLISHING INC., pg. 1703, pg. 1033
YELLOW BOOK USA, INC., pg. 1703, pg. 1347
YOUTUBE, LLC, pg. 1291, pg. 198
ZAGAT, pg. 1703, pg. 1316
ZIFF DAVIS, LLC, pg. 1703, pg. 1316
ZILLOW GROUP, INC., pg. 1292, pg. 1843
ZIX CORPORATION, pg. 497, pg. 1691
THE ZONDERVAN CORPORATION, pg. 1703, pg. 891

2732 - Book Printing

EBSCO INDUSTRIES, INC., pg. 1638, pg. 2
JENKINS GROUP, INC., pg. 1654, pg. 909
LITERARY CLASSICS OF THE UNITED STATES, INC., pg. 1659, pg. 1251
THE PERSEUS BOOKS GROUP, pg. 1676, pg. 1278
QUAD/GRAPHICS, INC., pg. 1468, pg. 1896
RR DONNELLEY, pg. 1682, pg. 838
THE SHERIDAN GROUP, INC., pg. 1686, pg. 772
STANDARD PUBLISHING GROUP LLC, pg. 1689, pg. 1426

2741 - Miscellaneous Publishing

ABOUT, INC., pg. 1225, pg. 1186
ACXIOM CORPORATION, pg. 342, pg. 607
ADVANCE PUBLICATIONS, INC., pg. 1613, pg. 1343
ADVANTAGE BUSINESS MEDIA, pg. 1613, pg. 1116
ADVERTISING AGE, pg. 1613, pg. 1187
ADVERTISING DISTRIBUTORS OF AMERICA INC., pg. 345, pg. 1338
ALLEN ORGAN COMPANY, pg. 527, pg. 1549
ALLIANCE DATA SYSTEMS CORPORATION, pg. 347, pg. 1729
ALLRECIPES.COM, pg. 1226, pg. 1831
AMERICAN HERITAGE PUBLISHING, pg. 1615, pg. 775
AMERICAN LIST COUNSEL, INC., pg. 349, pg. 1110
AMERICAN MATHEMATICAL SOCIETY, INC., pg. 129, pg. 1605
AMERICAN MEDIA, INC., pg. 1615, pg. 410
AMERICAN PUBLIC EDUCATION, INC., pg. 597, pg. 1849

First page reference indicates Business Class Edition
Second page reference indicates Geographic Edition

AMERICA'S TEST KITCHEN, *pg.* 1616, *pg.* 803
AMERIMARK DIRECT, LLC, *pg.* 1759, *pg.* 1428
ANCESTRY.COM LLC, *pg.* 1228, *pg.* 1754
ANDREWS MCMEEL UNIVERSAL, *pg.* 1616, *pg.* 980
ANNIE'S, *pg.* 1617, *pg.* 673
AOL INC., *pg.* 1229, *pg.* 1195
ASIAN WEEK FOUNDATION, *pg.* 1617, *pg.* 212
ASSOCIATION OF AMERICAN PUBLISHERS, INC., *pg.* 133, *pg.* 1197
AT&T INC., *pg.* 1867, *pg.* 1674
AUDIBLE, INC., *pg.* 1230, *pg.* 1095
AUTHOR SOLUTIONS, INC., *pg.* 1618, *pg.* 674
AUTOBYTEL INC., *pg.* 1230, *pg.* 107
AUTOMOTIVE NEWS, *pg.* 1618, *pg.* 879
AVENTION, *pg.* 1230, *pg.* 815
AVVO, INC., *pg.* 1231, *pg.* 1833
AWARE RECORDS, *pg.* 531, *pg.* 611
B-SCADA, INC., *pg.* 1231, *pg.* 419
BANKRATE, INC., *pg.* 1231, *pg.* 451
THE BERRY COMPANY LLC, *pg.* 1869, *pg.* 1445
BEYOND.COM, INC., *pg.* 1231, *pg.* 1543
BIOSPACE, INC., *pg.* 1231, *pg.* 1082
BIZBASH MEDIA INC., *pg.* 1621, *pg.* 1203
BLOOMBERG BNA, *pg.* 1621, *pg.* 1772
BLUE MAN PRODUCTIONS, INC., *pg.* 533, *pg.* 1205
BODYBUILDING.COM LLC, *pg.* 1232, *pg.* 549
BOFI HOLDING, INC., *pg.* 726, *pg.* 200
BONNIER ACTIVE MEDIA, INC., *pg.* 1622, *pg.* 1205
BONNIER CORPORATION, *pg.* 1622, *pg.* 480
BOOKAZINE COMPANY, INC., *pg.* 1622, *pg.* 1042
BRILLIANT DIGITAL, *pg.* 1233, *pg.* 281
CALIFORNIA OFFSET PRINTERS, INC., *pg.* 1625, *pg.* 95
CAMBRIDGE INFORMATION GROUP, INC., *pg.* 1625, *pg.* 761
CAREERBUILDER, LLC, *pg.* 1234, *pg.* 568
CARL FISCHER, LLC, *pg.* 1625, *pg.* 1209
CASTLE CONNOLLY MEDICAL LTD., *pg.* 1626, *pg.* 1210
CBS CORPORATION, *pg.* 273, *pg.* 1210
CBS INTERACTIVE, INC., *pg.* 369, *pg.* 215
CBS SPORTSLINE.COM, INC., *pg.* 1234, *pg.* 423
CCH, *pg.* 1626, *pg.* 569
CHARITY NAVIGATOR, *pg.* 136, *pg.* 1071
CINCINNATI BUSINESS COURIER, *pg.* 1627, *pg.* 1411
CIRQUE DU SOLEIL INC., *pg.* 540, *pg.* 1954
CLASSMATES ONLINE, INC., *pg.* 1235, *pg.* 1834
COLLECTORS EDITIONS, *pg.* 1628, *pg.* 58
COMCAST INTERACTIVE MEDIA, LLC, *pg.* 1236, *pg.* 1562
COMSCORE, INC, *pg.* 1236, *pg.* 1798
CONCLUSIVE ANALYTICS, *pg.* 1236, *pg.* 1380
CONCORDIA PUBLISHING HOUSE, *pg.* 1629, *pg.* 995
CONDE NAST DIGITAL, *pg.* 1237, *pg.* 1217
CONDE NAST PUBLICATIONS, INC., *pg.* 1629, *pg.* 1217
CONSOLIDATED COMMUNICATIONS HOLDINGS, INC., *pg.* 630, *pg.* 631
CONSUMERREVIEW, INC., *pg.* 1237, *pg.* 193
CONSUMERS UNION OF THE UNITED STATES, INC., *pg.* 1630, *pg.* 1356
COOKING.COM, *pg.* 1237, *pg.* 143
COPERNIC INC., *pg.* 1237, *pg.* 1958
CORNERWORLD CORPORATION, *pg.* 1237, *pg.* 1678
CORT BUSINESS SERVICES CORPORATION, *pg.* 921, *pg.* 1777
CPP, INC., *pg.* 1631, *pg.* 153
CRAIN COMMUNICATIONS, INC., *pg.* 1631, *pg.* 879
CRAIN'S CHICAGO BUSINESS, *pg.* 1631, *pg.* 572
CRAIN'S NEW YORK BUSINESS, *pg.* 1631, *pg.* 1220
CREDITCARDS.COM, INC., *pg.* 1237, *pg.* 1661
CREDITRISKMONITOR.COM, INC., *pg.* 1631, *pg.* 1348
DEX MEDIA INC, *pg.* 1635, *pg.* 1680
DEX ONE CORPORATION, *pg.* 1635, *pg.* 1360
THE DOLAN COMPANY, *pg.* 1636, *pg.* 932
DOMINION ENTERPRISES, *pg.* 1636, *pg.* 1796
DOMO RECORDS, INC., *pg.* 1767, *pg.* 129
DOW JONES & COMPANY, INC., *pg.* 1637, *pg.* 1225
THE DUN & BRADSTREET CORP., *pg.* 1637, *pg.* 1120
DYNAMIC RESOURCE GROUP, *pg.* 1637, *pg.* 674
EDGAR ONLINE, INC., *pg.* 746, *pg.* 776
EDMUNDS, INC., *pg.* 1241, *pg.* 273
ELLIE MAE, INC., *pg.* 1243, *pg.* 183
ELSEVIER HEALTH SCIENCES, *pg.* 1638, *pg.* 1564
EMUSIC.COM, INC., *pg.* 1243, *pg.* 1227
ENVESTNET, INC., *pg.* 748, *pg.* 573
EPOCRATES, INC., *pg.* 1529, *pg.* 254
ESM SOLUTIONS CORPORATION, *pg.* 1243, *pg.* 1591
ESPIAL GROUP INC., *pg.* 1243, *pg.* 1932
EXCELLIGENCE LEARNING CORP., *pg.* 1768, *pg.* 151
EXPEDIA, INC., *pg.* 1244, *pg.* 1814
EXPERIAN CONSUMER DIRECT, *pg.* 1245, *pg.* 71
FACEBOOK, INC., *pg.* 1245, *pg.* 143
FACTSET RESEARCH SYSTEMS INC., *pg.* 1247, *pg.* 361
FAIRCHILD FASHION GROUP, *pg.* 1640, *pg.* 1230
FILM SCORE MONTHLY, *pg.* 1641, *pg.* 103
FINANCIAL ENGINES, INC., *pg.* 753, *pg.* 285
FIRST DATABANK, INC., *pg.* 397, *pg.* 217
FLASHES PUBLISHERS, *pg.* 1641, *pg.* 864
FORBES.COM LLC, *pg.* 1247, *pg.* 1232
FOURSQUARE LABS, INC, *pg.* 1248, *pg.* 1232
FRANKLIN ELECTRONIC PUBLISHERS, INC., *pg.* 398, *pg.* 1048
FRIENDFINDER NETWORKS INC., *pg.* 1643, *pg.* 411
GAIN CAPITAL HOLDINGS, INC., *pg.* 760, *pg.* 1043
GALE CENGAGE LEARNING, *pg.* 1643, *pg.* 885
GATEHOUSE MEDIA, INC., *pg.* 1644, *pg.* 1159
GAWKER MEDIA LLC, *pg.* 1248, *pg.* 1234
GLAMOUR, *pg.* 1645, *pg.* 1235
GOOGLE INC., *pg.* 1249, *pg.* 153
GRAHAM HOLDINGS COMPANY, *pg.* 1645, *pg.* 1773
GREY HOUSE PUBLISHING CORP., *pg.* 1646, *pg.* 1137
GULF PUBLISHING COMPANY, *pg.* 1646, *pg.* 1707
HAINES & COMPANY, INC., *pg.* 1646, *pg.* 1468
HARMONIC, INC., *pg.* 402, *pg.* 246
HARPO, INC., *pg.* 290, *pg.* 576
HARRIS CONNECT LLC, *pg.* 1648, *pg.* 1143
HARVARD UNIVERSITY PRESS, *pg.* 1648, *pg.* 808
HEALTHCENTRAL, *pg.* 1256, *pg.* 1773
HEALTHPORT, INC., *pg.* 403, *pg.* 484
HEALTHY DIRECTIONS, *pg.* 1649, *pg.* 775
THE HEARST CORPORATION, *pg.* 1649, *pg.* 1239
HERFF JONES, INC., *pg.* 7, *pg.* 686
THE HIBBERT GROUP, *pg.* 407, *pg.* 1126
HOLLYWOOD MEDIA CORP., *pg.* 1256, *pg.* 412
HOME SCHOOL HOLDINGS, INC., *pg.* 1256, *pg.* 606
HOMEAWAY, INC., *pg.* 1911, *pg.* 1663
HOMES.COM, INC., *pg.* 1256, *pg.* 203
HOOKED MEDIA GROUP, *pg.* 1256, *pg.* 219
HOTWIRE, INC., *pg.* 1912, *pg.* 219
HOUR PUBLISHING COMPANY, *pg.* 1651, *pg.* 362
HULU LLC, *pg.* 1257, *pg.* 274
IAC/INTERACTIVECORP, *pg.* 292, *pg.* 1242
IDEALAB, INC., *pg.* 1258, *pg.* 180
IDG ENTERPRISE, *pg.* 1258, *pg.* 821
IGN ENTERTAINMENT, INC., *pg.* 1258, *pg.* 220
IHS AUTOMOTIVE DRIVEN BY POLK, *pg.* 1652, *pg.* 907
IHS INC., *pg.* 1652, *pg.* 326
INFOGROUP, *pg.* 414, *pg.* 350
INFOGROUP, *pg.* 769, *pg.* 1038
INFOGROUP INC., *pg.* 1652, *pg.* 1016
INFORMA EXHIBITIONS LLC, *pg.* 1653, *pg.* 17
INFORMATION TODAY INC., *pg.* 1653, *pg.* 1084
INSTITUTIONAL INVESTOR, INC., *pg.* 1653, *pg.* 1244
INSWEB CORPORATION, *pg.* 1205, *pg.* 186
INTELIMAX MEDIA INC., *pg.* 1259, *pg.* 1911
INTERNET MEDIA SERVICES, INC., *pg.* 1259, *pg.* 274
ISLANDS MAGAZINE, *pg.* 1654, *pg.* 480
IUNIVERSE, INC., *pg.* 1259, *pg.* 674
JAPS-OLSON COMPANY, *pg.* 1654, *pg.* 956
J.J. KELLER & ASSOCIATES, INC., *pg.* 1654, *pg.* 1883
JOBSON HEALTHCARE INFORMATION LLC, *pg.* 1654, *pg.* 1246
JOHN WILEY & SONS, INC., *pg.* 1655, *pg.* 1073
THE JOHNS HOPKINS UNIVERSITY PRESS, *pg.* 1655, *pg.* 757
JOURNAL OF COMMERCE, INC., *pg.* 1655, *pg.* 1097
K-TEL INTERNATIONAL, INC., *pg.* 1052, *pg.* 953
K12, INC., *pg.* 1260, *pg.* 1785
KAYAK, *pg.* 1260, *pg.* 363
KCNC-TV, *pg.* 293, *pg.* 320
KELLEY BLUE BOOK CO., INC., *pg.* 1656, *pg.* 112
KLOUT, INC., *pg.* 1261, *pg.* 220
KORG USA, INC., *pg.* 556, *pg.* 1180
LABELQUEST, INC., *pg.* 1463, *pg.* 611
LAURA DAMIANO DESIGNS, *pg.* 1658, *pg.* 1354
LAURIN PUBLISHING CO., INC., *pg.* 1658, *pg.* 841
LAW BULLETIN PUBLISHING COMPANY, *pg.* 1658, *pg.* 580
LEGALZOOM.COM, INC., *pg.* 1261, *pg.* 96
LEXISNEXIS CORPORATE AFFILIATIONS, *pg.* 1658, *pg.* 1095
LEXISNEXIS GROUP, *pg.* 1658, *pg.* 1446
LEXISNEXIS LITIGATION SOLUTIONS, *pg.* 1659, *pg.* 1446
LIMELIGHT NETWORKS, INC., *pg.* 1262, *pg.* 26
LINKEDIN CORPORATION, *pg.* 1262, *pg.* 160
LIVE CURRENT MEDIA INC., *pg.* 1263, *pg.* 1911
LIVEPERSON, INC., *pg.* 1264, *pg.* 1252
LOOPNET, INC., *pg.* 1265, *pg.* 222
MANUFACTURERS' NEWS, INC., *pg.* 1661, *pg.* 612
MARKET LEADER, INC., *pg.* 1102, *pg.* 1822
MARKETWATCH, INC., *pg.* 1265, *pg.* 222
MARQUIS WHO'S WHO, LLC, *pg.* 1661, *pg.* 1044
MARTHA STEWART LIVING OMNIMEDIA, INC., *pg.* 1661, *pg.* 1256
MARTINDALE-HUBBELL, INC., *pg.* 1662, *pg.* 1095
MASTERBEAT CORPORATION, *pg.* 1265, *pg.* 1257
MAX SOUND CORPORATION, *pg.* 1266, *pg.* 1711
MEDIA GENERAL, *pg.* 297, *pg.* 1607
MEDIABISTRO, INC., *pg.* 1266, *pg.* 1258
MEETUP INC., *pg.* 1266, *pg.* 1258
MEN'S JOURNAL, *pg.* 1663, *pg.* 1258
MEREDITH CORPORATION, *pg.* 1663, *pg.* 705
MERGENT, INC., *pg.* 1664, *pg.* 1616
MERRIAM-WEBSTER, INC., *pg.* 1664, *pg.* 846
MICHELIN NORTH AMERICA INC., *pg.* 1886, *pg.* 1618
MIQ LOGISTICS, LLC, *pg.* 1267, *pg.* 719
MORNINGSTAR, INC., *pg.* 784, *pg.* 583
MORRIS CERULLO WORLD EVANGELISM, *pg.* 147, *pg.* 205
MORRIS PUBLISHING GROUP, LLC, *pg.* 1666, *pg.* 525
THE MOTLEY FOOL, INC., *pg.* 784, *pg.* 1771
MOVE, INC., *pg.* 1268, *pg.* 247
MULTI-AD, INC., *pg.* 1666, *pg.* 652
MUSIC SALES CORPORATION, *pg.* 1666, *pg.* 1263
MYLIFE.COM, INC., *pg.* 1268, *pg.* 137
NAMEMEDIA, INC., *pg.* 1269, *pg.* 852
NETWORK COMMUNICATIONS INC., *pg.* 1271, *pg.* 534
NEULION, INC., *pg.* 302, *pg.* 1321
NEWSMAX MEDIA, INC., *pg.* 1271, *pg.* 479
NIELSEN BUSINESS MEDIA, *pg.* 1671, *pg.* 1272
THE NIELSEN COMPANY B.V., *pg.* 1671, *pg.* 1272
NTN BUZZTIME, INC., *pg.* 659, *pg.* 60
OAG WORLDWIDE LIMITED, *pg.* 1672, *pg.* 609
OGDEN PUBLISHING CORPORATION, *pg.* 1672, *pg.* 1753
OMNICOMM SYSTEMS, INC., *pg.* 1272, *pg.* 426
ON24, INC., *pg.* 1272, *pg.* 224
ONION, INC., *pg.* 1673, *pg.* 586
OPTIMIZERX CORPORATION, *pg.* 1673, *pg.* 905
ORBITZ WORLDWIDE, INC., *pg.* 1918, *pg.* 586
THE ORCHARD ENTERPRISES, INC., *pg.* 572, *pg.* 1274
O'REILLY MEDIA, INC., *pg.* 1673, *pg.* 278
PANDORA MEDIA INC., *pg.* 1273, *pg.* 172
PASSKEY INTERNATIONAL, INC., *pg.* 1274, *pg.* 853
PEARSON ASSESSMENT & INFORMATION, *pg.* 1674, *pg.* 1742
PENTON MEDIA, INC., *pg.* 1676, *pg.* 719
PENTON MEDIA, INC., *pg.* 1676, *pg.* 1277
PEOPLE2PEOPLE GROUP INC., *pg.* 1676, *pg.* 800
PHILANTHROPEDIA, *pg.* 153, *pg.* 1811
PIKSEL, *pg.* 1275, *pg.* 1282
PRUDENT PUBLISHING COMPANY, INC., *pg.* 1678, *pg.* 1115
Q INTERACTIVE INC., *pg.* 1276, *pg.* 588
QUEBECOR MEDIA INC., *pg.* 1679, *pg.* 1956
QUESTAR ASSESSMENT, INC., *pg.* 1679, *pg.* 1143
QUIDSI, INC., *pg.* 1276, *pg.* 1076
QUOTEMEDIA, INC., *pg.* 797, *pg.* 13
RAND MCNALLY & COMPANY, *pg.* 1679, *pg.* 661
THE READER'S DIGEST ASSOCIATION, INC., *pg.* 1679, *pg.* 1322
RENTPATH, INC., *pg.* 1680, *pg.* 538
REPLOGLE GLOBES, INC., *pg.* 461, *pg.* 559
ROLLING STONE MAGAZINE, *pg.* 1681, *pg.* 1287
ROSETTA STONE INC., *pg.* 462, *pg.* 1774
THE ROUGH NOTES COMPANY, INC., *pg.* 1681, *pg.* 675
R.R. BOWKER LLC, *pg.* 1682, *pg.* 1095
RR DONNELLEY, *pg.* 1682, *pg.* 838
SABRE HOLDINGS CORPORATION, *pg.* 1922, *pg.* 1745
SALESFORCE.COM, INC., *pg.* 1278, *pg.* 226
SAN DIEGO BUSINESS JOURNAL, *pg.* 1682, *pg.* 208
SCRIPPS NETWORKS INTERACTIVE, INC., *pg.* 1279, *pg.* 1638
SELF MAGAZINE, *pg.* 1686, *pg.* 1290
SF NEWSPAPER COMPANY, LLC, *pg.* 1686, *pg.* 227
SHAREDBOOK INC., *pg.* 1686, *pg.* 1291
SIERRA CLUB, *pg.* 156, *pg.* 227
SIMON & SCHUSTER, INC., *pg.* 1687, *pg.* 1292
SKINNYCORP L.L.C., *pg.* 1280, *pg.* 590
SMARTER TRAVEL MEDIA LLC, *pg.* 1687, *pg.* 801

SONY MUSIC ENTERTAINMENT, *pg.* 309, *pg.* 1294
SPA FINDER, INC., *pg.* 1113, *pg.* 1295
SPARK NETWORKS, INC., *pg.* 472, *pg.* 140
SPINMEDIA, *pg.* 1282, *pg.* 104
SPORTSDIRECT INC., *pg.* 1282, *pg.* 1917
SPOTIFY, *pg.* 1282, *pg.* 1295
SRDS, INC., *pg.* 1688, *pg.* 657
STANDARD PUBLISHING GROUP LLC, *pg.* 1689, *pg.* 1426
STAT RESOURCE GROUP, INC., *pg.* 1689, *pg.* 345
STREAMING MEDIA HOSTING, INC., *pg.* 1283, *pg.* 166
THE STREET, INC., *pg.* 1283, *pg.* 1296
STUBHUB, INC., *pg.* 586, *pg.* 228
SUMNER COMMUNICATIONS INC., *pg.* 1690, *pg.* 338
SUN-TIMES MEDIA GROUP, INC., *pg.* 1690, *pg.* 591
SYNACOR, INC., *pg.* 1283, *pg.* 1151
TAYLOR CORPORATION, *pg.* 1691, *pg.* 952
TECHNOLOGY MARKETING CORP., *pg.* 1691, *pg.* 364
TECHTARGET, INC., *pg.* 482, *pg.* 837
TEN: THE ENTHUSIAST NETWORK, *pg.* 1691, *pg.* 1298
THEHUFFINGTONPOST.COM, INC., *pg.* 1692, *pg.* 1298
THEODORE PRESSER CO., *pg.* 1692, *pg.* 1544
THOMAS PUBLISHING COMPANY LLC, *pg.* 1692, *pg.* 1299
THOMSON ELITE, *pg.* 484, *pg.* 72
THOMSON REUTERS - CORPORATE HEADQUARTERS, *pg.* 1693, *pg.* 1299
THOMSON REUTERS CORPORATION, *pg.* 1693, *pg.* 1944
TIME OUT NEW YORK, *pg.* 1694, *pg.* 1301
THE TOPPS COMPANY, INC., *pg.* 588, *pg.* 1302
TRACK DATA CORPORATION, *pg.* 1284, *pg.* 1147
TRANSCONTINENTAL INC., *pg.* 1695, *pg.* 1957
TRAVELHOST, INC., *pg.* 1696, *pg.* 1689
TRAVELZOO INC, *pg.* 1926, *pg.* 1304
TRUVEN HEALTH ANALYTICS, *pg.* 1696, *pg.* 867
TUMBLR, INC., *pg.* 1285, *pg.* 1305
TV GUIDE MAGAZINE GROUP, INC., *pg.* 1697, *pg.* 1305
TWELVE SIGNS, INC., *pg.* 1697, *pg.* 141
TWITTER, INC., *pg.* 1285, *pg.* 228
UNIGUEST, *pg.* 1697, *pg.* 1655
UNITED ONLINE, INC., *pg.* 1286, *pg.* 308
UNIVERSITY OF CHICAGO PRESS, *pg.* 1698, *pg.* 594
UNIVISION COMMUNICATIONS INC., *pg.* 683, *pg.* 1307
VACATION.COM, INC., *pg.* 1287, *pg.* 1772
VALASSIS, *pg.* 1698, *pg.* 386
VALPAK DIRECT MARKETING SYSTEMS, INC., *pg.* 1699, *pg.* 438
VARESE SARABANDE RECORDS, INC., *pg.* 1789, *pg.* 281
VERISIGN, INC., *pg.* 488, *pg.* 1799
VERTICALRESPONSE, INC., *pg.* 489, *pg.* 230
VOGUE MAGAZINE, *pg.* 1700, *pg.* 1311
WAND, INC., *pg.* 1288, *pg.* 324
WARNER MUSIC GROUP CORP., *pg.* 590, *pg.* 1313
WEBMD HEALTH CORPORATION, *pg.* 1288, *pg.* 1313
WEBSITE MAGAZINE INCORPORATED, *pg.* 1701, *pg.* 607
WESTERN COMMUNICATIONS INC., *pg.* 1701, *pg.* 1496
WHITEPAGES.COM INC., *pg.* 1289, *pg.* 1842
WIKIMEDIA FOUNDATION INC., *pg.* 161, *pg.* 234
WIND-UP RECORDS, *pg.* 592, *pg.* 1314
XO GROUP INC., *pg.* 1289, *pg.* 1316
YANKEE PUBLISHING INC., *pg.* 1703, *pg.* 1033
YELLOW BOOK USA, INC., *pg.* 1703, *pg.* 1347
YELP! INC., *pg.* 1291, *pg.* 235
YOUTUBE, LLC, *pg.* 1291, *pg.* 198
ZAGAT, *pg.* 1703, *pg.* 1316
ZILLOW GROUP, INC., *pg.* 1292, *pg.* 1843
ZIX CORPORATION, *pg.* 497, *pg.* 1691

2752 - Commercial Printing, Lithographic

ABNOTE NORTH AMERICA, *pg.* 1878, *pg.* 789
ALLEGRA NETWORK LLC, *pg.* 1614, *pg.* 904
ALPHA CTP SYSTEM, *pg.* 347, *pg.* 848
AMERICAN BANKNOTE CORPORATION, *pg.* 1615, *pg.* 1067
AMERICAN REPROGRAPHICS COMPANY, *pg.* 1616, *pg.* 303
AMERICAN VANGUARD CORPORATION, *pg.* 1793, *pg.* 165
ANACOMP, INC., *pg.* 350, *pg.* 1777
ARCADE MARKETING, INC., *pg.* 352, *pg.* 1196
B&W PRESS, INC., *pg.* 1619, *pg.* 823
BACOVA GUILD, LTD., *pg.* 916, *pg.* 1779
BEL-ART PRODUCTS, INC., *pg.* 1879, *pg.* 1129
BREHM COMMUNICATIONS INC., *pg.* 1623, *pg.* 201
BROWN & BIGELOW, INC., *pg.* 1624, *pg.* 959
CALIFORNIA OFFSET PRINTERS, INC., *pg.* 1625, *pg.* 95
CAPITAL CITY PRESS, *pg.* 1625, *pg.* 741
CARROLL COUNTY TIMES, *pg.* 1626, *pg.* 780
CARTA MUNDI, INC., *pg.* 951, *pg.* 1677
THE CAXTON PRINTERS LTD., *pg.* 1626, *pg.* 548
CCPRESS.NET INC., *pg.* 1626, *pg.* 756
CENVEO INC., *pg.* 1626, *pg.* 372
CHAMPION INDUSTRIES, INC., *pg.* 1626, *pg.* 1849
CHICAGO SUN TIMES, *pg.* 1627, *pg.* 570
THE COLAD GROUP, INC., *pg.* 377, *pg.* 1147
COMMENTARY, *pg.* 1628, *pg.* 1216
CONCORD PRINTING, *pg.* 1629, *pg.* 974
CONTINENTAL AMERICAN CORP., *pg.* 1880, *pg.* 723
COSMOPOLITAN, *pg.* 1630, *pg.* 1218
CRANE & CO., INC., *pg.* 1456, *pg.* 816
DAILY PRESS, *pg.* 1632, *pg.* 302
DAILY REPUBLICAN REGISTER, *pg.* 1633, *pg.* 634
DAY-TIMERS, INC., *pg.* 1766, *pg.* 1528
DELUXE CORPORATION, *pg.* 1634, *pg.* 964
DEX ONE CORPORATION, *pg.* 1635, *pg.* 1360
EAGLE-TRIBUNE PUBLISHING COMPANY INC., *pg.* 1638, *pg.* 837
EAGLE:XM, *pg.* 1239, *pg.* 319
FASTSIGNS INTERNATIONAL, INC., *pg.* 81, *pg.* 1669
FEDEX OFFICE & PRINT SERVICES, INC., *pg.* 396, *pg.* 1681
FIRST FINANCIAL BANKSHARES, INC., *pg.* 755, *pg.* 1657
FLEXSTEEL INDUSTRIES, INC., *pg.* 925, *pg.* 707
GRAPHIC CONTROLS LLC, *pg.* 401, *pg.* 1148
GROSSMAN MARKETING GROUP, *pg.* 401, *pg.* 843
HARLAND CLARKE HOLDINGS CORP., *pg.* 1647, *pg.* 1741
HORIZON DESIGNS, INC., *pg.* 695, *pg.* 1011
I/D/E/A/ INC., *pg.* 1460, *pg.* 548
INDEPENDENT CAN COMPANY, *pg.* 1460, *pg.* 760
INDIANAPOLIS STAR, *pg.* 1652, *pg.* 687
INTEGRACORE, INC., *pg.* 416, *pg.* 1763
ITC PRINTING & PROMOTIONS, *pg.* 1654, *pg.* 1124
JAPS-OLSON COMPANY, *pg.* 1654, *pg.* 956
JOHNSON NEWSPAPER CORPORATION, *pg.* 1655, *pg.* 1349
THE KIPLINGER WASHINGTON EDITORS, INC., *pg.* 1657, *pg.* 401
LUNA IMAGING LTD., *pg.* 1421, *pg.* 136
MATRIX INTEGRATION LLC, *pg.* 430, *pg.* 692
MCCLATCHY NEWSPAPERS, INC., *pg.* 1662, *pg.* 197
MCCOURT LABEL COMPANY, *pg.* 1464, *pg.* 1548
MEADWESTVACO CORP. - OFFICE PRODUCTS GROUP, *pg.* 431, *pg.* 1342
MERRILL CORPORATION, *pg.* 1664, *pg.* 962
MONOTYPE IMAGING HOLDINGS, INC., *pg.* 656, *pg.* 861
OBSERVER PUBLISHING COMPANY, *pg.* 1672, *pg.* 1591
OPENTEXT, *pg.* 1272, *pg.* 1956
OUR SUNDAY VISITOR, INC., *pg.* 1673, *pg.* 682
POPULAR MECHANICS, *pg.* 1677, *pg.* 1282
PRINTINGFORLESS.COM, INC., *pg.* 456, *pg.* 1009
PRINTRONIX, INC., *pg.* 456, *pg.* 115
QUAD/GRAPHICS, INC., *pg.* 1468, *pg.* 1896
REDBOOK, *pg.* 1680, *pg.* 1285
RESEARCH SOLUTIONS, INC., *pg.* 1680, *pg.* 85
R.R. DONNELLEY & SONS COMPANY, *pg.* 1682, *pg.* 589
SCANTRON CORPORATION, *pg.* 467, *pg.* 922
SCHWARZ PAPER COMPANY, *pg.* 1468, *pg.* 634
SERIGRAPH, INC., *pg.* 1686, *pg.* 1899
THE SHERIDAN GROUP, INC., *pg.* 1686, *pg.* 772
SIR SPEEDY, INC., *pg.* 1687, *pg.* 149
SOUTHEASTERN PRINTING COMPANY INC., *pg.* 1687, *pg.* 468
THE STANDARD REGISTER COMPANY, *pg.* 473, *pg.* 1446
TAYLOR CORPORATION, *pg.* 1691, *pg.* 952
THAYER PUBLISHING, *pg.* 1692, *pg.* 928
TIMES PUBLISHING CO. INC., *pg.* 1695, *pg.* 1530
THE TOPPS COMPANY, INC., *pg.* 588, *pg.* 1302
TRANSCONTINENTAL INC., *pg.* 1695, *pg.* 1957
TUFCO TECHNOLOGIES, INC., *pg.* 1697, *pg.* 1860
UNIGUEST, *pg.* 1697, *pg.* 1655
THE UPPER DECK COMPANY, LLC, *pg.* 969, *pg.* 62
VALASSIS COMMUNICATIONS, INC., *pg.* 1287, *pg.* 897
VISTAPRINT USA, INCORPORATED, *pg.* 1700, *pg.* 829
THE WASHINGTON TIMES, LLC, *pg.* 1701, *pg.* 408
WORKMAN PUBLISHING COMPANY, *pg.* 1702, *pg.* 1315

2754 - Commercial Printing, Gravure

123GREETINGS.COM, INC., *pg.* 1225, *pg.* 1184
AMERICAN BANKNOTE CORPORATION, *pg.* 1615, *pg.* 1067
AMERICAN GREETINGS CORPORATION, *pg.* 1615, *pg.* 1428
CLIPPER MAGAZINE INC., *pg.* 1628, *pg.* 1555
CSS INDUSTRIES, INC., *pg.* 1631, *pg.* 1562
DATAMAX CORPORATION, *pg.* 1633, *pg.* 453
HALLMARK CARDS, INC., *pg.* 1646, *pg.* 983
LEANIN' TREE, INC., *pg.* 1658, *pg.* 311
QUAD/GRAPHICS, INC., *pg.* 1468, *pg.* 1896
R.R. DONNELLEY & SONS COMPANY, *pg.* 1682, *pg.* 589
SILVER STAR BRANDS, *pg.* 1785, *pg.* 1886
SPS STUDIOS, INC., *pg.* 1688, *pg.* 311
TAYLOR CORPORATION, *pg.* 1691, *pg.* 952
THAYER PUBLISHING, *pg.* 1692, *pg.* 928

2759 - Commercial Printing, NEC

123GREETINGS.COM, INC., *pg.* 1225, *pg.* 1184
ALPHA CTP SYSTEM, *pg.* 347, *pg.* 848
AMERICAN BANKNOTE CORPORATION, *pg.* 1615, *pg.* 1067
AMERICAN GREETINGS CORPORATION, *pg.* 1615, *pg.* 1428
ANACOMP, INC., *pg.* 350, *pg.* 1777
BACOVA GUILD, LTD., *pg.* 916, *pg.* 1779
BE AEROSPACE, INC., *pg.* 224, *pg.* 478
CHAMPION INDUSTRIES, INC., *pg.* 1626, *pg.* 1849
THE COLAD GROUP, INC., *pg.* 377, *pg.* 1147
COMMENTARY, *pg.* 1628, *pg.* 1216
COMMERCIAL VEHICLE GROUP, INC., *pg.* 203, *pg.* 1467
CONCORD PRINTING, *pg.* 1629, *pg.* 974
CONTINENTAL AMERICAN CORP., *pg.* 1880, *pg.* 723
COSMOPOLITAN, *pg.* 1630, *pg.* 1218
CRANE & CO., INC., *pg.* 1456, *pg.* 816
CSS INDUSTRIES, INC., *pg.* 1631, *pg.* 1562
DELUXE CORPORATION, *pg.* 1634, *pg.* 964
FASTSIGNS INTERNATIONAL, INC., *pg.* 81, *pg.* 1669
FEDEX OFFICE & PRINT SERVICES, INC., *pg.* 396, *pg.* 1681
FIRST FINANCIAL BANKSHARES, INC., *pg.* 755, *pg.* 1657
FLEXSTEEL INDUSTRIES, INC., *pg.* 925, *pg.* 707
GROSSMAN MARKETING GROUP, *pg.* 401, *pg.* 843
HALLMARK CARDS, INC., *pg.* 1646, *pg.* 983
HORIZON DESIGNS, INC., *pg.* 695, *pg.* 1011
ITC PRINTING & PROMOTIONS, *pg.* 1654, *pg.* 1124
JOHNSON CONTROLS, INC., *pg.* 209, *pg.* 1876
LEANIN' TREE, INC., *pg.* 1658, *pg.* 311
LEAR CORPORATION, *pg.* 229, *pg.* 907
LUNA IMAGING LTD., *pg.* 1421, *pg.* 136
MATRIX INTEGRATION LLC, *pg.* 430, *pg.* 692
MCCLATCHY NEWSPAPERS, INC., *pg.* 1662, *pg.* 197
MERRILL CORPORATION, *pg.* 1664, *pg.* 962
MONOTYPE IMAGING HOLDINGS, INC., *pg.* 656, *pg.* 861
OBSERVER PUBLISHING COMPANY, *pg.* 1672, *pg.* 1591
OPENTEXT, *pg.* 1272, *pg.* 1956
OUR SUNDAY VISITOR, INC., *pg.* 1673, *pg.* 682
POLARIS INDUSTRIES INC., *pg.* 1709, *pg.* 928
POPULAR MECHANICS, *pg.* 1677, *pg.* 1282
PRINTRONIX, INC., *pg.* 456, *pg.* 115
QUAD/GRAPHICS, INC., *pg.* 1468, *pg.* 1896
RECARO NORTH AMERICA, INC., *pg.* 216, *pg.* 869
REDBOOK, *pg.* 1680, *pg.* 1285
RESEARCH SOLUTIONS, INC., *pg.* 1680, *pg.* 85
R.R. DONNELLEY & SONS COMPANY, *pg.* 1682, *pg.* 589
SERIGRAPH, INC., *pg.* 1686, *pg.* 1899
THE SHERIDAN GROUP, INC., *pg.* 1686, *pg.* 772
SILVER STAR BRANDS, *pg.* 1785, *pg.* 1886
SOUTHEASTERN PRINTING COMPANY INC., *pg.* 1687, *pg.* 468
SPS STUDIOS, INC., *pg.* 1688, *pg.* 311
TAYLOR CORPORATION, *pg.* 1691, *pg.* 952
THAYER PUBLISHING, *pg.* 1692, *pg.* 928
THE TOPPS COMPANY, INC., *pg.* 588, *pg.* 1302
TRANSCONTINENTAL INC., *pg.* 1695, *pg.* 1957
TUFCO TECHNOLOGIES, INC., *pg.* 1697, *pg.* 1860
VISTAPRINT USA, INCORPORATED, *pg.* 1700, *pg.* 829
WORKMAN PUBLISHING COMPANY, *pg.* 1702, *pg.* 1315

2761 - Manifold Business Forms

ACCO BRANDS CORPORATION, *pg.* 340, *pg.* 626
AMERICAN THERMOPLASTIC COMPANY, *pg.* 349, *pg.*

1573
BOULDER BRANDS, INC., pg. 1016, pg. 310
CHAMPION INDUSTRIES, INC., pg. 1626, pg. 1849
ENNIS, INC., pg. 393, pg. 1727
FORWARD INDUSTRIES, INC., pg. 5, pg. 478
HARLAND CLARKE HOLDINGS CORP., pg. 1647, pg. 1741
IMPRESO, INC., pg. 413, pg. 1671
MEADWESTVACO CORP. - OFFICE PRODUCTS GROUP, pg. 431, pg. 1342
PEARSON ASSESSMENTS, pg. 1674, pg. 918
PIP PRINTING, INC., pg. 1677, pg. 149
RANDA CORP., pg. 47, pg. 1285
SAFEGUARD BUSINESS SYSTEMS, INC., pg. 464, pg. 1686
SCANTRON CORPORATION, pg. 467, pg. 922
STANDARD DUPLICATING MACHINES CORPORATION, pg. 473, pg. 783
THE STANDARD REGISTER COMPANY, pg. 473, pg. 1446
THE UNION GROUP, pg. 487, pg. 819
VIATECH PUBLISHING SOLUTIONS, pg. 489, pg. 1141

2771 - Greeting Card Publishing & Printing

123GREETINGS.COM, INC., pg. 1225, pg. 1184
AMERICAN GREETINGS CORPORATION, pg. 1615, pg. 1428
CSS INDUSTRIES, INC., pg. 1631, pg. 1562
HALLMARK CARDS, INC., pg. 1646, pg. 983
LEANIN' TREE, INC., pg. 1658, pg. 311
SILVER STAR BRANDS, pg. 1785, pg. 1886
SPS STUDIOS, INC., pg. 1688, pg. 311
TAYLOR CORPORATION, pg. 1691, pg. 952
THAYER PUBLISHING, pg. 1692, pg. 928

2782 - Blankbooks, Loose Leaf Binders & Devices

ACCO BRANDS CORPORATION, pg. 340, pg. 626
AMERICAN THERMOPLASTIC COMPANY, pg. 349, pg. 1573
BOULDER BRANDS, INC., pg. 1016, pg. 310
FORWARD INDUSTRIES, INC., pg. 5, pg. 478
HARLAND CLARKE HOLDINGS CORP., pg. 1647, pg. 1741
MEADWESTVACO CORP. - OFFICE PRODUCTS GROUP, pg. 431, pg. 1342
RANDA CORP., pg. 47, pg. 1285
STANDARD DUPLICATING MACHINES CORPORATION, pg. 473, pg. 783
THE UNION GROUP, pg. 487, pg. 819
VIATECH PUBLISHING SOLUTIONS, pg. 489, pg. 1141

2789 - Bookbinding & Related Work

KURZ TRANSFER PRODUCTS, L.P., pg. 1354, pg. 1367
QUAD/GRAPHICS, INC., pg. 1468, pg. 1896
SOUTHWEST BINDING & LAMINATING, pg. 1377, pg. 988
TAYLOR CORPORATION, pg. 1691, pg. 952
VIATECH PUBLISHING SOLUTIONS, pg. 489, pg. 1141

2791 - Typesetting

AMERICAN REPROGRAPHICS COMPANY, pg. 1616, pg. 303
CYNTHIANA PUBLISHING CO., pg. 1632, pg. 726
THE DEMOCRAT CO., pg. 1634, pg. 708
THE EVANSVILLE COURIER & PRESS, pg. 1639, pg. 678
FAYETTEVILLE PUBLISHING CO., pg. 1641, pg. 1372
I/D/E/A/ INC., pg. 1460, pg. 548
NEWS & RECORD, pg. 1669, pg. 1375
PRINTINGFORLESS.COM, INC., pg. 456, pg. 1009
SATURDAY EVENING POST SOCIETY, pg. 1683, pg. 690
SGK, pg. 1686, pg. 590
THE STATE JOURNAL-REGISTER, pg. 1689, pg. 662
TRADE PRESS MEDIA GROUP, pg. 1695, pg. 1881

2812 - Alkalies & Chlorine

ARM & HAMMER CONSUMER PRODUCTS, pg. 326, pg. 1110
AXIALL CORPORATION, pg. 69, pg. 491
CORAL CHEMICAL COMPANY, pg. 1154, pg. 666
NL INDUSTRIES, INC., pg. 1174, pg. 1684
OCCIDENTAL CHEMICAL CORPORATION, pg. 1175, pg. 1685
OLIN CORPORATION, pg. 1176, pg. 976
PPG INDUSTRIES, INC., pg. 1445, pg. 1579
RHODIA INC., pg. 1179, pg. 1053

2813 - Industrial Gases

ABENGOA BIOENERGY CORP., pg. 971, pg. 974
ACETO CORPORATION, pg. 1145, pg. 1323
AIR PRODUCTS AND CHEMICALS, INC., pg. 1145, pg. 1513
AKZO NOBEL INC., pg. 1146, pg. 563
ANGUS CHEMICAL COMPANY, pg. 1147, pg. 560
ASHLAND INC., pg. 972, pg. 726
ASHLAND PERFORMANCE MATERIALS, pg. 1147, pg. 1448
BAKER HUGHES INCORPORATED, pg. 1315, pg. 1700
BAKER PETROLITE CORPORATION, pg. 1148, pg. 1745
BALCHEM CORPORATION, pg. 839, pg. 1183
BELL FLAVORS & FRAGRANCES, INC., pg. 501, pg. 640
BIOSAFE SYSTEMS, LLC, pg. 1149, pg. 345
BOULDER SCIENTIFIC COMPANY, pg. 1150, pg. 335
BUCKMAN, pg. 1150, pg. 1641
CARGILL, INC., pg. 845, pg. 965
CHEM-TREND LIMITED PARTNERSHIP, pg. 973, pg. 892
CHEMTURA CORPORATION, pg. 1152, pg. 355
CLARIANT CORPORATION, pg. 1153, pg. 1365
CUMBERLAND PACKING CORP., pg. 851, pg. 1146
DAVID MICHAEL & CO. INC., pg. 852, pg. 1563
DOVER CHEMICAL CORPORATION, pg. 1156, pg. 1447
THE DOW CHEMICAL COMPANY, pg. 1157, pg. 898
EVONIK CORPORATION, pg. 1162, pg. 1103
EXXON MOBIL CORPORATION, pg. 977, pg. 1718
FIRMENICH INCORPORATED, pg. 509, pg. 1109
FMC CORPORATION, pg. 1163, pg. 1564
GAGE PRODUCTS COMPANY, pg. 1164, pg. 886
GRAIN PROCESSING CORPORATION, pg. 859, pg. 709
HARSCO CORPORATION, pg. 86, pg. 1519
HEADWATERS INCORPORATED, pg. 978, pg. 1763
HENKEL CORPORATION, pg. 1166, pg. 897
HENKEL CORPORATION, pg. 1165, pg. 1535
HERCULES INCORPORATED, pg. 1166, pg. 392
HEXION, pg. 1166, pg. 1440
HOUGHTON INTERNATIONAL INC., pg. 1167, pg. 1589
HUNTSMAN CORPORATION, pg. 1167, pg. 1758
INOLEX GROUP INC., pg. 1168, pg. 1566
INTERNATIONAL FLAVORS & FRAGRANCES INC., pg. 512, pg. 1244
JARCHEM INDUSTRIES, INC., pg. 1169, pg. 1096
LINCOLN ELECTRIC HOLDINGS, INC., pg. 1355, pg. 1432
LINDE GAS LLC, pg. 1350, pg. 1095
LINDSAY CORPORATION, pg. 1356, pg. 1016
LIPO CHEMICALS INC., pg. 1171, pg. 1107
LONZA INC., pg. 1171, pg. 1041
THE LUBRIZOL CORPORATION, pg. 1171, pg. 1481
LYONDELLBASELL INDUSTRIES, pg. 980, pg. 1710
MACANDREWS & FORBES HOLDINGS INC., pg. 777, pg. 1254
MERICHEM COMPANY, pg. 1172, pg. 1711
MERISANT COMPANY, pg. 876, pg. 581
MGP INGREDIENTS, INC., pg. 877, pg. 714
NATIONAL ENZYME COMPANY, pg. 882, pg. 978
NEVILLE CHEMICAL COMPANY, pg. 1174, pg. 1578
NEWMARKET CORPORATION, pg. 982, pg. 1803
NOVA CHEMICALS CORPORATION, pg. 1175, pg. 1904
NUFARM AMERICAS INC, pg. 1798, pg. 552
THE NUTRASWEET COMPANY, pg. 1860, pg. 585
OCCIDENTAL CHEMICAL CORPORATION, pg. 1175, pg. 1685
OXYSURE SYSTEMS, INC., pg. 1579, pg. 1697
PACIFIC ETHANOL, INC., pg. 982, pg. 197
PHARMCO-AAPER, pg. 1177, pg. 740
PRAXAIR, INC., pg. 1178, pg. 344
QUAKER CHEMICAL CORP., pg. 1178, pg. 1524
R.T. VANDERBILT COMPANY, INC., pg. 1180, pg. 364
SACHEM INC., pg. 1180, pg. 1665
SASOL NORTH AMERICA INC., pg. 984, pg. 1713
SI GROUP, INC., pg. 1181, pg. 1341
SIGMA-ALDRICH CORPORATION, pg. 1181, pg. 1881
SIGMA-ALDRICH CORPORATION, pg. 1181, pg. 1003
SLIDE PRODUCTS, INC., pg. 1181, pg. 670
SPURRIER CHEMICAL COMPANIES, INC., pg. 1182, pg. 724
SUNOCO CHEMICALS, pg. 1182, pg. 1570
SYMRISE, INC., pg. 1183, pg. 1125
TOTAL PETROCHEMICALS USA, INC., pg. 1184, pg. 1716
TROY CORPORATION, pg. 1184, pg. 1067
VERTELLUS SPECIALTIES INC., pg. 1185, pg. 690
WILLERT HOME PRODUCTS, INC., pg. 1140, pg. 1005

2816 - Inorganic Pigments

ALTAIR NANOTECHNOLOGIES INC., pg. 1147, pg. 1031
AMERICAN CHEMET CORPORATION, pg. 1147, pg. 599
ASHLAND INC., pg. 972, pg. 726
ASHLAND PERFORMANCE MATERIALS, pg. 1147, pg. 1448
AVANTOR PERFORMANCE MATERIALS, INC., pg. 1148, pg. 1521
BASF CATALYSTS LLC, pg. 1148, pg. 1074
BIRKO CORPORATION, pg. 1149, pg. 332
BUCKMAN, pg. 1150, pg. 1641
BURGESS PIGMENT COMPANY, pg. 1150, pg. 535
CABOT CORPORATION, pg. 1151, pg. 792
CARUS CORPORATION, pg. 1152, pg. 652
CERAMIC COLOR & CHEMICAL MFG. CO., pg. 1441, pg. 1555
CHURCH & DWIGHT CO., INC., pg. 1153, pg. 1063
COMPASS MINERALS INTERNATIONAL, INC., pg. 1154, pg. 718
DAY-GLO COLOR CORP., pg. 1441, pg. 1429
DEEPWATER CHEMICALS, INC., pg. 1155, pg. 1491
DETREX CORPORATION, pg. 1156, pg. 906
DOVER CHEMICAL CORPORATION, pg. 1156, pg. 1447
THE DOW CHEMICAL COMPANY, pg. 1157, pg. 898
DOW CORNING CORPORATION, pg. 1159, pg. 900
EVONIK CORPORATION, pg. 1162, pg. 1103
EXXON MOBIL CORPORATION, pg. 977, pg. 1718
FMC LITHIUM DIVISION, pg. 1163, pg. 1366
GFS CHEMICALS, INC., pg. 1164, pg. 1471
HEATBATH CORPORATION, pg. 1165, pg. 826
HERCULES INCORPORATED, pg. 1166, pg. 392
HUNTSMAN CORPORATION, pg. 1167, pg. 1758
IMPERIAL OIL LIMITED, pg. 979, pg. 1903
INTERNATIONAL FLAVORS & FRAGRANCES INC., pg. 512, pg. 1244
J.M. HUBER CORPORATION, pg. 1169, pg. 1056
JOHNSON MATTHEY PROCESS TECHNOLOGIES, pg. 1169, pg. 1083
JONES-HAMILTON CO., pg. 1169, pg. 1478
KAISER ALUMINUM CORPORATION, pg. 90, pg. 86
KING INDUSTRIES, INC., pg. 1443, pg. 363
KOPPERS HOLDINGS INC., pg. 1170, pg. 1577
KRONOS WORLDWIDE, INC., pg. 980, pg. 1053
LANDEC CORPORATION, pg. 1419, pg. 145
L.M. SCOFIELD COMPANY, pg. 94, pg. 134
LOCKHART COMPANY, pg. 1171, pg. 1534
LYONDELLBASELL INDUSTRIES, pg. 980, pg. 1710
MATERION ADVANCED CHEMICALS, pg. 1172, pg. 1877
MCGEAN-ROHCO, INC., pg. 1172, pg. 1432
MERICHEM COMPANY, pg. 1172, pg. 1711
MULTI-METALS, pg. 1363, pg. 737
MULTISORB TECHNOLOGIES, INC., pg. 1570, pg. 1150
NL INDUSTRIES, INC., pg. 1174, pg. 1684
NOAH TECHNOLOGIES CORPORATION, pg. 1175, pg. 1742
NOVA CHEMICALS CORPORATION, pg. 1175, pg. 1904
OCCIDENTAL PETROLEUM CORPORATION, pg. 1175, pg. 137
PQ CORPORATION, pg. 1178, pg. 1515
QUAKER CHEMICAL CORP., pg. 1178, pg. 1524
RHODIA INC., pg. 1179, pg. 1053
RIO TINTO BORAX, pg. 334, pg. 331
SIGMA-ALDRICH CORPORATION, pg. 1181, pg. 1881
SILBERLINE MANUFACTURING CO., INC., pg. 110, pg. 1588
TETRA TECHNOLOGIES, INC., pg. 986, pg. 1747
TOR MINERALS INTERNATIONAL INC., pg. 1184, pg. 1672
UOP LLC, pg. 1386, pg. 606
VALHI, INC., pg. 1185, pg. 1690
THE VALSPAR CORPORATION, pg. 1449, pg. 945
VELSICOL CHEMICAL CORPORATION, pg. 1185, pg. 657

2819 - Industrial Inorganic Chemicals, NEC

ABENGOA BIOENERGY CORP., *pg.* 971, *pg.* 974
ACETO CORPORATION, *pg.* 1145, *pg.* 1323
AIR PRODUCTS AND CHEMICALS, INC., *pg.* 1145, *pg.* 1513
AKZO NOBEL INC., *pg.* 1146, *pg.* 563
AMERICAN CHEMET CORPORATION, *pg.* 1147, *pg.* 599
ANGUS CHEMICAL COMPANY, *pg.* 1147, *pg.* 560
ASHLAND INC., *pg.* 972, *pg.* 726
ASHLAND PERFORMANCE MATERIALS, *pg.* 1147, *pg.* 1448
AVANTOR PERFORMANCE MATERIALS, INC., *pg.* 1148, *pg.* 1521
BAKER HUGHES INCORPORATED, *pg.* 1315, *pg.* 1700
BAKER PETROLITE CORPORATION, *pg.* 1148, *pg.* 1745
BALCHEM CORPORATION, *pg.* 839, *pg.* 1183
BASF CATALYSTS LLC, *pg.* 1148, *pg.* 1074
BELL FLAVORS & FRAGRANCES, INC., *pg.* 501, *pg.* 640
BIOSAFE SYSTEMS, LLC, *pg.* 1149, *pg.* 345
BIRKO CORPORATION, *pg.* 1149, *pg.* 332
BOULDER SCIENTIFIC COMPANY, *pg.* 1150, *pg.* 335
BUCKMAN, *pg.* 1150, *pg.* 1641
BURGESS PIGMENT COMPANY, *pg.* 1150, *pg.* 535
CARGILL, INC., *pg.* 845, *pg.* 965
CARUS CORPORATION, *pg.* 1152, *pg.* 652
CERAMIC COLOR & CHEMICAL MFG. CO., *pg.* 1441, *pg.* 1555
CHEM-TREND LIMITED PARTNERSHIP, *pg.* 973, *pg.* 892
CHEMTURA CORPORATION, *pg.* 1152, *pg.* 355
CHURCH & DWIGHT CO., INC., *pg.* 1153, *pg.* 1063
CLARIANT CORPORATION, *pg.* 1153, *pg.* 1365
COMPASS MINERALS INTERNATIONAL, INC., *pg.* 1154, *pg.* 718
CUMBERLAND PACKING CORP., *pg.* 851, *pg.* 1146
DAVID MICHAEL & CO. INC., *pg.* 852, *pg.* 1563
DEEPWATER CHEMICALS, INC., *pg.* 1155, *pg.* 1491
DETREX CORPORATION, *pg.* 1156, *pg.* 906
DOVER CHEMICAL CORPORATION, *pg.* 1156, *pg.* 1447
THE DOW CHEMICAL COMPANY, *pg.* 1157, *pg.* 898
DOW CORNING CORPORATION, *pg.* 1159, *pg.* 900
EVONIK CORPORATION, *pg.* 1162, *pg.* 1103
EXXON MOBIL CORPORATION, *pg.* 977, *pg.* 1718
FIRMENICH INCORPORATED, *pg.* 509, *pg.* 1109
FMC CORPORATION, *pg.* 1163, *pg.* 1564
FMC LITHIUM DIVISION, *pg.* 1163, *pg.* 1366
GAGE PRODUCTS COMPANY, *pg.* 1164, *pg.* 886
GFS CHEMICALS, INC., *pg.* 1164, *pg.* 1471
GRAIN PROCESSING CORPORATION, *pg.* 859, *pg.* 709
HEADWATERS INCORPORATED, *pg.* 978, *pg.* 1763
HEATBATH CORPORATION, *pg.* 1165, *pg.* 826
HENKEL CORPORATION, *pg.* 1166, *pg.* 897
HENKEL CORPORATION, *pg.* 1165, *pg.* 1535
HERCULES INCORPORATED, *pg.* 1166, *pg.* 392
HEXION, *pg.* 1166, *pg.* 1440
HOUGHTON INTERNATIONAL INC., *pg.* 1167, *pg.* 1589
HUNTSMAN CORPORATION, *pg.* 1167, *pg.* 1758
IMPERIAL OIL LIMITED, *pg.* 979, *pg.* 1903
INOLEX GROUP INC., *pg.* 1168, *pg.* 1566
INTERNATIONAL FLAVORS & FRAGRANCES INC., *pg.* 512, *pg.* 1244
JARCHEM INDUSTRIES, INC., *pg.* 1169, *pg.* 1096
J.M. HUBER CORPORATION, *pg.* 1169, *pg.* 1056
JOHNSON MATTHEY PROCESS TECHNOLOGIES, *pg.* 1169, *pg.* 1083
JONES-HAMILTON CO., *pg.* 1169, *pg.* 1478
KAISER ALUMINUM CORPORATION, *pg.* 90, *pg.* 86
KING INDUSTRIES, INC., *pg.* 1443, *pg.* 363
KOPPERS HOLDINGS INC., *pg.* 1170, *pg.* 1577
LANDEC CORPORATION, *pg.* 1419, *pg.* 145
LIPO CHEMICALS INC., *pg.* 1171, *pg.* 1107
LOCKHART COMPANY, *pg.* 1171, *pg.* 1534
LONZA INC., *pg.* 1171, *pg.* 1041
THE LUBRIZOL CORPORATION, *pg.* 1171, *pg.* 1481
LYONDELLBASELL INDUSTRIES, *pg.* 980, *pg.* 1710
MACANDREWS & FORBES HOLDINGS INC., *pg.* 777, *pg.* 1254
MATERION ADVANCED CHEMICALS, *pg.* 1172, *pg.* 1877
MCGEAN-ROHCO, INC., *pg.* 1172, *pg.* 1432
MERICHEM COMPANY, *pg.* 1172, *pg.* 1711
MERISANT COMPANY, *pg.* 876, *pg.* 581
MGP INGREDIENTS, INC., *pg.* 877, *pg.* 714
MULTI-METALS, *pg.* 1363, *pg.* 737
MULTISORB TECHNOLOGIES, INC., *pg.* 1570, *pg.* 1150
NATIONAL ENZYME COMPANY, *pg.* 882, *pg.* 978
NEVILLE CHEMICAL COMPANY, *pg.* 1174, *pg.* 1578
NEWMARKET CORPORATION, *pg.* 982, *pg.* 1803
NOAH TECHNOLOGIES CORPORATION, *pg.* 1175, *pg.* 1742
NOVA CHEMICALS CORPORATION, *pg.* 1175, *pg.* 1904
NUFARM AMERICAS INC, *pg.* 1798, *pg.* 552
THE NUTRASWEET COMPANY, *pg.* 1860, *pg.* 585
OCCIDENTAL CHEMICAL CORPORATION, *pg.* 1175, *pg.* 1685
OCCIDENTAL PETROLEUM CORPORATION, *pg.* 1175, *pg.* 137
PACIFIC ETHANOL, INC., *pg.* 982, *pg.* 197
PHARMCO-AAPER, *pg.* 1177, *pg.* 740
PQ CORPORATION, *pg.* 1178, *pg.* 1515
QUAKER CHEMICAL CORP., *pg.* 1178, *pg.* 1524
RHODIA INC., *pg.* 1179, *pg.* 1053
RIO TINTO BORAX, *pg.* 334, *pg.* 331
R.T. VANDERBILT COMPANY, INC., *pg.* 1180, *pg.* 364
SACHEM INC., *pg.* 1180, *pg.* 1665
SASOL NORTH AMERICA INC., *pg.* 984, *pg.* 1713
SI GROUP, INC., *pg.* 1181, *pg.* 1341
SIGMA-ALDRICH CORPORATION, *pg.* 1181, *pg.* 1881
SIGMA-ALDRICH CORPORATION, *pg.* 1181, *pg.* 1003
SILBERLINE MANUFACTURING CO., INC., *pg.* 110, *pg.* 1588
SPURRIER CHEMICAL COMPANIES, INC., *pg.* 1182, *pg.* 724
SUNOCO CHEMICALS, *pg.* 1182, *pg.* 1570
SYMRISE, INC., *pg.* 1183, *pg.* 1125
TETRA TECHNOLOGIES, INC., *pg.* 986, *pg.* 1747
TOTAL PETROCHEMICALS USA, INC., *pg.* 1184, *pg.* 1716
TROY CORPORATION, *pg.* 1184, *pg.* 1067
UOP LLC, *pg.* 1386, *pg.* 606
VELSICOL CHEMICAL CORPORATION, *pg.* 1185, *pg.* 657
VERTELLUS SPECIALTIES INC., *pg.* 1185, *pg.* 690
WILLERT HOME PRODUCTS, INC., *pg.* 1140, *pg.* 1005

2821 - Plastics Materials, Synthetic Resins & Nonvulcanizable Elastomers

3M COMPANY, *pg.* 1142, *pg.* 956
A. SCHULMAN, INC., *pg.* 1144, *pg.* 1452
ALBEMARLE CORPORATION, *pg.* 1146, *pg.* 741
AMERICAN GILSONITE CO., *pg.* 1313, *pg.* 1700
ASHLAND INC., *pg.* 972, *pg.* 726
ASHLAND PERFORMANCE MATERIALS, *pg.* 1147, *pg.* 1448
AXEL PLASTICS RESEARCH LABORATORIES, INC., *pg.* 326, *pg.* 1356
AXIALL CORPORATION, *pg.* 69, *pg.* 491
BURKE INDUSTRIES, INC., *pg.* 919, *pg.* 239
CARPENTER CO., *pg.* 920, *pg.* 1801
CHEMTURA CORPORATION, *pg.* 1152, *pg.* 355
CRANE CO., *pg.* 227, *pg.* 373
CYTEC INDUSTRIES, INC., *pg.* 1155, *pg.* 1131
DOW CHEMICAL, *pg.* 1156, *pg.* 1563
THE DOW CHEMICAL COMPANY, *pg.* 1157, *pg.* 898
DOW CORNING CORPORATION, *pg.* 1159, *pg.* 900
EASTMAN CHEMICAL COMPANY, *pg.* 1159, *pg.* 1636
E.I. DU PONT DE NEMOURS & COMPANY, *pg.* 1159, *pg.* 390
E.V. ROBERTS & ASSOCIATES, INC., *pg.* 1161, *pg.* 63
EVONIK CYRO LLC, *pg.* 1162, *pg.* 1103
HAHL INC., *pg.* 1299, *pg.* 1620
HERESITE PROTECTIVE COATINGS, INC., *pg.* 1442, *pg.* 1868
HEXCEL CORPORATION, *pg.* 1884, *pg.* 375
HEXION, *pg.* 1166, *pg.* 1440
INOLEX CHEMICAL COMPANY, *pg.* 1168, *pg.* 1566
INOLEX GROUP INC., *pg.* 1168, *pg.* 1566
INTERPLASTIC CORPORATION, *pg.* 1168, *pg.* 961
INVISTA B.V., *pg.* 1168, *pg.* 723
ITW - EVERCOAT, *pg.* 1443, *pg.* 1415
KOPPERS HOLDINGS INC., *pg.* 1170, *pg.* 1577
LANDEC CORPORATION, *pg.* 1419, *pg.* 145
LUCITE INTERNATIONAL, INC., *pg.* 94, *pg.* 1631
MILLER-STEPHENSON CHEMICAL COMPANY, INC., *pg.* 1172, *pg.* 344
MOMENTIVE PERFORMANCE MATERIALS, INC., *pg.* 1464, *pg.* 1349
NEVILLE CHEMICAL COMPANY, *pg.* 1174, *pg.* 1578
OLIN CORPORATION, *pg.* 1176, *pg.* 976
PECORA CORPORATION, *pg.* 1444, *pg.* 1536
POLYONE CORPORATION, *pg.* 1177, *pg.* 1404
REICHHOLD, INC., *pg.* 1179, *pg.* 1372
ROCHLING GLASTIC COMPOSITES, *pg.* 1889, *pg.* 1435
ROGERS CORPORATION, *pg.* 1305, *pg.* 369
SASOL NORTH AMERICA INC., *pg.* 984, *pg.* 1713
SMOOTH-ON INC., *pg.* 111, *pg.* 1528
STEPAN COMPANY, *pg.* 1182, *pg.* 643
THE VALSPAR CORPORATION, *pg.* 1449, *pg.* 945
WILSONART INTERNATIONAL, INC., *pg.* 1450, *pg.* 1746
W.L. GORE & ASSOCIATES, INC., *pg.* 122, *pg.* 388
YENKIN-MAJESTIC PAINT CORPORATION, *pg.* 1450, *pg.* 1445

2822 - Synthetic Rubber (Vulcanizable Elastomers)

CTI INDUSTRIES CORPORATION, *pg.* 1881, *pg.* 555
REICHHOLD, INC., *pg.* 1179, *pg.* 1372
THE ROHO GROUP, *pg.* 1591, *pg.* 556
SMOOTH-ON INC., *pg.* 111, *pg.* 1528

2823 - Cellulosic Man-Made Fibers

CARPENTER CO., *pg.* 920, *pg.* 1801
INTERNATIONAL FIBER CORP., *pg.* 865, *pg.* 1317

2824 - Synthetic Organic Fibers Except Cellulosic

A. SCHULMAN, INC., *pg.* 1144, *pg.* 1452
LEIGH FIBERS, INC., *pg.* 93, *pg.* 1623
QUADRANT ENGINEERING PLASTIC PRODUCTS, *pg.* 1178, *pg.* 1585
TEXON MATERIALS INC., *pg.* 1820, *pg.* 843
TOHO TENAX AMERICA, INC., *pg.* 1184, *pg.* 1655

2833 - Medicinal Chemical & Botanical Products

AKORN, *pg.* 1488, *pg.* 1138
BACTOLAC PHARMACEUTICAL, INC., *pg.* 1498, *pg.* 1163
BAXTER INTERNATIONAL INC., *pg.* 1499, *pg.* 599
BAZI INTERNATIONAL, INC., *pg.* 1501, *pg.* 107
BIOTECH CORPORATION, *pg.* 1506, *pg.* 349
BOIRON USA INC., *pg.* 1507, *pg.* 1556
CYANOTECH CORPORATION, *pg.* 1154, *pg.* 545
DEPOMED, INC., *pg.* 1523, *pg.* 143
DESIGNING HEALTH, INC., *pg.* 1523, *pg.* 299
ENDO PHARMACEUTICALS HOLDINGS, INC., *pg.* 1528, *pg.* 1549
ENZYMATIC THERAPY INC., *pg.* 1529, *pg.* 1859
FITLIFE BRANDS, *pg.* 1531, *pg.* 1015
FLORA MANUFACTURING & DISTRIBUTING LTD., *pg.* 1531, *pg.* 1907
GENENTECH, INC., *pg.* 1533, *pg.* 279
GENERAL NUTRITION CENTERS, INC., *pg.* 1534, *pg.* 1575
THE HAIN CELESTIAL GROUP, INC., *pg.* 860, *pg.* 1172
HEALTH PRODUCTS CORPORATION, *pg.* 1540, *pg.* 1356
JANSSEN PHARMACEUTICA PRODUCTS, L.P., *pg.* 1548, *pg.* 1125
LANDEC CORPORATION, *pg.* 1419, *pg.* 145
LANELABS USA INC., *pg.* 1554, *pg.* 1128
LIFECORE BIOMEDICAL, LLC, *pg.* 1556, *pg.* 920
LIFEVANTAGE CORPORATION, *pg.* 1556, *pg.* 1762
MANNATECH, INCORPORATED, *pg.* 1558, *pg.* 1671
MATRIXX INITIATIVES, INC., *pg.* 1559, *pg.* 23
MEDIFAST, INC., *pg.* 1562, *pg.* 774
MEDIMMUNE LLC, *pg.* 1562, *pg.* 770
MERA PHARMACEUTICALS, INC., *pg.* 1566, *pg.* 545
NATROL, INC., *pg.* 1570, *pg.* 64
NATURAL ALTERNATIVES INTERNATIONAL, INC., *pg.* 1571, *pg.* 253
NATURE'S SUNSHINE PRODUCTS, INC., *pg.* 1571, *pg.* 1754
NBTY, INC., *pg.* 1572, *pg.* 1338
NEW EARTH LIFE SCIENCES, INC., *pg.* 1573, *pg.* 1499
NUTRACEUTICAL INTERNATIONAL CORPORATION, *pg.* 1576, *pg.* 1753
NUTRITION 21, INC., *pg.* 1577, *pg.* 1327
OBAGI MEDICAL PRODUCTS, INC., *pg.* 1577, *pg.* 123
PACIFICHEALTH LABORATORIES, INC., *pg.* 1579, *pg.* 1083
PFIZER INC., *pg.* 1581, *pg.* 1278

First page reference indicates Business Class Edition
Second page reference indicates Geographic Edition

PHARMAVITE LLC, *pg.* 1584, *pg.* 167
PURETEK CORPORATION, *pg.* 1587, *pg.* 211
RELIV INTERNATIONAL, INC., *pg.* 1589, *pg.* 975
SCHIFF NUTRITION INTERNATIONAL, INC., *pg.* 1592, *pg.* 1760
SCIENTIFIC PROTEIN LABORATORIES, INC., *pg.* 1593, *pg.* 1898
SHIRE, *pg.* 1593, *pg.* 1532
TWINLAB CORPORATION, *pg.* 1603, *pg.* 1306
USANA HEALTH SCIENCES, INC., *pg.* 1605, *pg.* 1761
VALEANT PHARMACEUTICALS INTERNATIONAL, INC., *pg.* 1605, *pg.* 1957
VITATECH INTERNATIONAL, INC., *pg.* 1608, *pg.* 298
XANGO, LLC, *pg.* 1610, *pg.* 1751

2834 - Pharmaceutical Preparations

ABBOTT DIABETES CARE, INC., *pg.* 1483, *pg.* 38
ABBOTT LABORATORIES, *pg.* 1484, *pg.* 551
ABBOTT MEDICAL OPTICS, INC., *pg.* 1485, *pg.* 260
ACORDA THERAPEUTICS, INC., *pg.* 1486, *pg.* 1138
ADH HEALTH PRODUCTS, INC., *pg.* 1487, *pg.* 1154
AFEXA LIFE SCIENCES INC., *pg.* 1487, *pg.* 1905
AFFYMAX, INC., *pg.* 1487, *pg.* 73
AFFYMETRIX, INC., *pg.* 1487, *pg.* 263
AKORN, *pg.* 1488, *pg.* 1138
AKORN, INC., *pg.* 1488, *pg.* 622
ALBEMARLE CORPORATION, *pg.* 1146, *pg.* 741
ALERE INC., *pg.* 1488, *pg.* 849
ALEXION PHARMACEUTICALS, INC., *pg.* 1489, *pg.* 341
ALIMERA SCIENCES, INC., *pg.* 1490, *pg.* 482
ALLERGAN, *pg.* 1490, *pg.* 1101
ALLERGAN, INC., *pg.* 1491, *pg.* 106
ALLIQUA, INC., *pg.* 1492, *pg.* 1189
ALLOS THERAPEUTICS, INC., *pg.* 1492, *pg.* 336
ALVA/AMCO PHARMACAL COMPANIES, INC., *pg.* 1492, *pg.* 637
AMAG PHARMACEUTICALS, INC., *pg.* 1492, *pg.* 827
ANIMAL HEALTH INTERNATIONAL, INC., *pg.* 1474, *pg.* 1749
APTOSE BIOSCIENCES, *pg.* 1495, *pg.* 1934
ARDEA BIOSCIENCES, INC., *pg.* 1495, *pg.* 200
ARENA PHARMACEUTICALS, INC., *pg.* 1495, *pg.* 200
ARIAD PHARMACEUTICALS, INC., *pg.* 1496, *pg.* 807
ASTELLAS PHARMA US, INC., *pg.* 1496, *pg.* 640
ASTEX PHARMACEUTICALS, INC, *pg.* 1497, *pg.* 77
ASTRAZENECA PHARMACEUTICALS LP, *pg.* 1497, *pg.* 389
AT LAST NATURALS, INC., *pg.* 499, *pg.* 1347
AVANIR PHARMACEUTICALS, *pg.* 1498, *pg.* 40
AVEO PHARMACEUTICALS, INC., *pg.* 1498, *pg.* 807
BACTOLAC PHARMACEUTICAL, INC., *pg.* 1498, *pg.* 1163
BAUSCH & LOMB INCORPORATED, *pg.* 1401, *pg.* 1045
BAXTER INTERNATIONAL INC., *pg.* 1499, *pg.* 599
BAYER HEALTHCARE PHARMACEUTICAL DIVISION, *pg.* 1500, *pg.* 1132
BAZI INTERNATIONAL, INC., *pg.* 1501, *pg.* 107
BD DIAGNOSTICS - TRIPATH, *pg.* 1402, *pg.* 1358
BEACH PRODUCTS, INC., *pg.* 1501, *pg.* 471
BELLUS HEALTH INC., *pg.* 1503, *pg.* 1951
BEUTLICH PHARMACEUTICALS LP, *pg.* 1503, *pg.* 665
BIO-PATH HOLDINGS, INC., *pg.* 1504, *pg.* 1752
BIOMERICA, INC., *pg.* 1506, *pg.* 107
BLISTEX, INC., *pg.* 502, *pg.* 644
BOEHRINGER INGELHEIM PHARMACEUTICALS, INC., *pg.* 1507, *pg.* 368
BOEHRINGER INGELHEIM VETMEDICA, INC., *pg.* 1474, *pg.* 989
BRACCO DIAGNOSTICS, INC., *pg.* 1509, *pg.* 1085
BRISTOL-MYERS SQUIBB COMPANY, *pg.* 1509, *pg.* 1206
BRISTOL-MYERS SQUIBB U.S. PHARMACEUTICAL GROUP, *pg.* 1511, *pg.* 1110
CARDINAL HEALTH, INC., *pg.* 1512, *pg.* 1448
CARGILL, INC., *pg.* 845, *pg.* 965
CELL THERAPEUTICS, INC., *pg.* 1514, *pg.* 1834
CHATTEM, INC., *pg.* 1515, *pg.* 1628
CHIESI USA, INC., *pg.* 1515, *pg.* 1359
CHURCH & DWIGHT CO., INC., *pg.* 1153, *pg.* 1063
CODEXIS, INC., *pg.* 1154, *pg.* 189
COLGATE ORAL PHARMACEUTICAL, *pg.* 1516, *pg.* 1214
COMPUMED, INC., *pg.* 378, *pg.* 128
CORD BLOOD AMERICA, INC., *pg.* 1519, *pg.* 1023
CORGENIX MEDICAL CORPORATION, *pg.* 1519, *pg.* 312
CUBIST PHARMACEUTICALS, INC., *pg.* 1521, *pg.* 828
CUMBERLAND PHARMACEUTICALS, INC., *pg.* 1521, *pg.* 1650
CYCLACEL PHARMACEUTICALS, INC., *pg.* 1521, *pg.* 1044
DENDREON CORPORATION, *pg.* 1522, *pg.* 1835
DEPOMED, INC., *pg.* 1523, *pg.* 143
DERMA SCIENCES, INC., *pg.* 1523, *pg.* 1111
DUSA PHARMACEUTICALS, INC., *pg.* 1525, *pg.* 860
DYAX CORP., *pg.* 1525, *pg.* 805
DYMATIZE ENTERPRISES, INC., *pg.* 1525, *pg.* 1692
EISAI INC., *pg.* 1526, *pg.* 1133
ELI LILLY AND COMPANY, *pg.* 1527, *pg.* 684
EMISPHERE TECHNOLOGIES, INC., *pg.* 1528, *pg.* 1118
ENCORIUM GROUP, INC., *pg.* 1528, *pg.* 1591
ENDO PHARMACEUTICALS HOLDINGS, INC., *pg.* 1528, *pg.* 1549
ENZYMATIC THERAPY INC., *pg.* 1529, *pg.* 1859
EXACT SCIENCES CORPORATION, *pg.* 1529, *pg.* 1865
FIBROCELL SCIENCE, INC., *pg.* 1530, *pg.* 1531
FIRST SURGICAL PARTNERS INC., *pg.* 1531, *pg.* 1668
FITLIFE BRANDS, *pg.* 1531, *pg.* 1015
FLEET LABORATORIES, *pg.* 1531, *pg.* 1787
FLORA MANUFACTURING & DISTRIBUTING LTD., *pg.* 1531, *pg.* 1907
FRESENIUS KABI USA, *pg.* 1531, *pg.* 626
G&W LABORATORIES INC., *pg.* 1532, *pg.* 1123
GALDERMA LABORATORIES, L.P., *pg.* 1532, *pg.* 1695
GANEDEN BIOTECH, INC., *pg.* 1532, *pg.* 1463
GARDEN OF LIFE, INC., *pg.* 1532, *pg.* 478
GENELINK, INC., *pg.* 1533, *pg.* 438
GENENTECH, INC., *pg.* 1533, *pg.* 279
GENEREX BIOTECHNOLOGY CORPORATION, *pg.* 1534, *pg.* 1938
GENZYME CORPORATION, *pg.* 1534, *pg.* 808
GILEAD SCIENCES, INC., *pg.* 1535, *pg.* 88
GLAXO SMITH KLINE INC., *pg.* 1536, *pg.* 1926
GLAXOSMITHKLINE, *pg.* 1536, *pg.* 1389
GLAXOSMITHKLINE, *pg.* 1537, *pg.* 776
GLAXOSMITHKLINE, *pg.* 1536, *pg.* 1565
GLAXOSMITHKLINE CONSUMER HEALTHCARE, *pg.* 510, *pg.* 1554
GRANDPA BRANDS COMPANY, *pg.* 1538, *pg.* 727
HALOZYME THERAPEUTICS, INC., *pg.* 1539, *pg.* 203
HAPPY JACK INC., *pg.* 1476, *pg.* 1390
HESKA CORPORATION, *pg.* 1542, *pg.* 335
HOFFMANN-LA ROCHE INC., *pg.* 1542, *pg.* 1099
HOFFMANN-LA ROCHE LIMITED, *pg.* 1542, *pg.* 1926
HOSPIRA, INC., *pg.* 1542, *pg.* 623
IDERA PHARMACEUTICALS, INC., *pg.* 1543, *pg.* 808
IDEXX LABORATORIES, INC., *pg.* 1543, *pg.* 753
IMAGING DIAGNOSTIC SYSTEMS, INC., *pg.* 1544, *pg.* 425
IMMUCOR, INC., *pg.* 1544, *pg.* 537
IMMUNOGEN, INC., *pg.* 1544, *pg.* 851
IMMUNOMEDICS, INC., *pg.* 1544, *pg.* 1087
IMPAX LABORATORIES, INC., *pg.* 1544, *pg.* 101
INCYTE CORPORATION, *pg.* 1545, *pg.* 392
INTEGRATED BIOPHARMA, INC., *pg.* 1546, *pg.* 1073
INTERLEUKIN GENETICS, INC., *pg.* 1546, *pg.* 851
IRIS INTERNATIONAL, INC., *pg.* 1547, *pg.* 64
ISIS PHARMACEUTICALS, INC., *pg.* 1548, *pg.* 59
ISORAY, INC., *pg.* 1548, *pg.* 1830
JANSSEN BIOTECH, INC., *pg.* 1548, *pg.* 1540
JANSSEN PHARMACEUTICA PRODUCTS, L.P., *pg.* 1548, *pg.* 1125
JOHNSON & JOHNSON, *pg.* 1549, *pg.* 1091
JOHNSON & JOHNSON BABY PRODUCTS, INC., *pg.* 1552, *pg.* 1094
JOHNSON & JOHNSON - MERCK CONSUMER PHARMACEUTICALS CO., *pg.* 1552, *pg.* 1533
JUNIPER PHARMACEUTICALS, *pg.* 1552, *pg.* 797
KERYX BIOPHARMACEUTICALS, INC., *pg.* 1553, *pg.* 1248
KING PHARMACEUTICALS, INC., *pg.* 1553, *pg.* 1627
KYOWA HAKKO U.S.A., INC., *pg.* 1554, *pg.* 1249
LA JOLLA PHARMACEUTICAL COMPANY, *pg.* 1554, *pg.* 204
LANNETT COMPANY, INC., *pg.* 1555, *pg.* 1566
LEXICON PHARMACEUTICALS, INC., *pg.* 1555, *pg.* 1747
LIFESCAN INC, *pg.* 1556, *pg.* 146
LIFEVANTAGE CORPORATION, *pg.* 1556, *pg.* 1762
LIGAND PHARMACEUTICALS INC., *pg.* 1556, *pg.* 119
LUITPOLD PHARMACEUTICALS, INC., *pg.* 1557, *pg.* 1342
LUMARA HEALTH INC., *pg.* 1557, *pg.* 973
MANNKIND CORPORATION, *pg.* 1558, *pg.* 299
MATRIXX INITIATIVES, INC., *pg.* 1559, *pg.* 23
MCNEIL-PPC, INC., *pg.* 1560, *pg.* 1533
MEAD JOHNSON NUTRITION COMPANY, *pg.* 1561, *pg.* 615
MEDICINE SHOPPE INTERNATIONAL, INC., *pg.* 1561, *pg.* 976
THE MEDICINES COMPANY, *pg.* 1561, *pg.* 1104
MEDIFAST, INC., *pg.* 1562, *pg.* 774
MEDIMMUNE LLC, *pg.* 1562, *pg.* 770
MEDTOX SCIENTIFIC, INC., *pg.* 1422, *pg.* 962
MEDWELL CAPITAL CORP., *pg.* 781, *pg.* 1906
THE MENTHOLATUM COMPANY, *pg.* 1565, *pg.* 1320
MERCK & CO., INC., *pg.* 1566, *pg.* 1077
MERCK ANIMAL HEALTH, *pg.* 1479, *pg.* 387
MERCK ANIMAL HEALTH, *pg.* 1478, *pg.* 1124
MERIDIAN BIOSCIENCE INC., *pg.* 1422, *pg.* 1417
MERZ AESTHETICS, *pg.* 1567, *pg.* 255
MILLENNIUM: THE TAKEDA ONCOLOGY COMPANY, *pg.* 1568, *pg.* 809
MISSION PHARMACAL COMPANY INC., *pg.* 1568, *pg.* 1742
MONOGRAM BIOSCIENCES, INC., *pg.* 1569, *pg.* 280
MONTICELLO DRUG CO., *pg.* 1569, *pg.* 434
MTS MEDICATION TECHNOLOGIES, INC., *pg.* 442, *pg.* 463
MUELLER SPORTS MEDICINE, INC., *pg.* 1570, *pg.* 1887
MYLAN, INC., *pg.* 1570, *pg.* 1520
NATROL, INC., *pg.* 1570, *pg.* 64
NATURAL ORGANICS, INC., *pg.* 1571, *pg.* 1181
NATURE MADE NUTRITIONAL PRODUCTS INC., *pg.* 883, *pg.* 148
NATURE'S SUNSHINE PRODUCTS, INC., *pg.* 1571, *pg.* 1754
NBTY, INC., *pg.* 1572, *pg.* 1338
NEKTAR THERAPEUTICS, *pg.* 1572, *pg.* 224
NEOGEN CORPORATION, *pg.* 883, *pg.* 896
NEW EARTH LIFE SCIENCES, INC., *pg.* 1573, *pg.* 1499
NORDIC NATURALS, INC., *pg.* 1573, *pg.* 305
NORDION INC., *pg.* 1573, *pg.* 1932
NOVARTIS CORPORATION, *pg.* 1574, *pg.* 1273
NOVARTIS PHARMACEUTICALS CORP., *pg.* 1575, *pg.* 1054
NOVARTIS VACCINES & DIAGNOSTICS, INC., *pg.* 1575, *pg.* 809
NOVEN PHARMACEUTICALS, INC., *pg.* 1576, *pg.* 445
NPS PHARMACEUTICALS, INC., *pg.* 1576, *pg.* 1043
NUTRACEUTICAL INTERNATIONAL CORPORATION, *pg.* 1576, *pg.* 1753
NUTRICIA NORTH AMERICA, *pg.* 1577, *pg.* 776
NUTRITION 21, INC., *pg.* 1577, *pg.* 1327
OBAGI MEDICAL PRODUCTS, INC., *pg.* 1577, *pg.* 123
OCULUS INNOVATIVE SCIENCES, *pg.* 1577, *pg.* 182
OMNICELL INC., *pg.* 1578, *pg.* 161
ONCOGENEX PHARMACEUTICALS, INC., *pg.* 1578, *pg.* 1818
ONCOTHYREON INC., *pg.* 1578, *pg.* 1838
ORAGENICS, INC., *pg.* 1578, *pg.* 475
ORASURE TECHNOLOGIES INC, *pg.* 1578, *pg.* 1516
OXIS INTERNATIONAL, INC., *pg.* 1579, *pg.* 47
PACIFICHEALTH LABORATORIES, INC., *pg.* 1579, *pg.* 1083
PACIRA PHARMACEUTICALS, INC., *pg.* 1579, *pg.* 1104
PAIN THERAPEUTICS, INC., *pg.* 1579, *pg.* 1665
PALADIN LABS, INC., *pg.* 1579, *pg.* 1956
PDL BIOPHARMA INC., *pg.* 1580, *pg.* 1022
PFIZER INC., *pg.* 1581, *pg.* 1278
PHARMACEUTICAL PRODUCT DEVELOPMENT, INC., *pg.* 1584, *pg.* 1393
PHARMAVITE LLC, *pg.* 1584, *pg.* 167
PRESSURE BIOSCIENCES, INC., *pg.* 1586, *pg.* 844
PRESTIGE BRANDS HOLDINGS, INC., *pg.* 520, *pg.* 1345
THE PROCTER & GAMBLE COMPANY, *pg.* 1129, *pg.* 1418
PROMETHEUS LABORATORIES, INC., *pg.* 1586, *pg.* 206
PROPHASE LABS, INC., *pg.* 1586, *pg.* 1526
PURDUE PHARMA LP, *pg.* 1587, *pg.* 377
PURETEK CORPORATION, *pg.* 1587, *pg.* 211
QIAGEN GAITHERSBURG INC., *pg.* 1587, *pg.* 771
QUIDEL CORPORATION, *pg.* 1588, *pg.* 207
REGENERON PHARMACEUTICALS, INC., *pg.* 1588, *pg.* 1345
REPLIGEN CORPORATION, *pg.* 1589, *pg.* 854
SAGENT HOLDING CO., *pg.* 1591, *pg.* 659
SALIX PHARMACEUTICALS, INC., *pg.* 1591, *pg.* 1388
SANOFI PASTEUR, INC, *pg.* 1591, *pg.* 1588
SANOFI US, *pg.* 1592, *pg.* 1046
SCHIFF NUTRITION INTERNATIONAL, INC., *pg.* 1592, *pg.* 1760
SCIENTIFIC PROTEIN LABORATORIES, INC., *pg.* 1593, *pg.* 1898

SERACARE LIFE SCIENCES, INC., *pg.* 1593, *pg.* 833
SHEFFIELD LABORATORIES, *pg.* 1375, *pg.* 359
SHIRE, *pg.* 1593, *pg.* 1532
SIEMENS HEALTHCARE DIAGNOSTICS, *pg.* 673, *pg.* 604
SIGA TECHNOLOGIES, INC., *pg.* 1594, *pg.* 1292
SIMILASAN CORPORATION, *pg.* 1594, *pg.* 332
SIMULATIONS PLUS, INC., *pg.* 470, *pg.* 121
SOURCE NATURALS, *pg.* 1595, *pg.* 278
SPECTRUM CHEMICALS & LABORATORY PRODUCTS, INC., *pg.* 1181, *pg.* 94
SPHERIX INC., *pg.* 1596, *pg.* 1808
STRAIGHT ARROW PRODUCTS, INC., *pg.* 523, *pg.* 1517
SUCAMPO PHARMACEUTICALS, INC., *pg.* 1599, *pg.* 765
SUMMIT INDUSTRIES, INC., *pg.* 1599, *pg.* 535
SUNOVION PHARMACEUTICALS INC., *pg.* 1599, *pg.* 832
TAKEDA PHARMACEUTICALS USA, INC., *pg.* 1600, *pg.* 605
TARGACEPT, INC., *pg.* 1601, *pg.* 1395
TECHNE CORPORATION, *pg* 1601, *pg.* 944
TENDER CORPORATION, *pg.* 1601, *pg.* 1035
THERAGENICS CORPORATION, *pg.* 1431, *pg.* 527
TWINLAB CORPORATION, *pg.* 1603, *pg.* 1306
ULURU INC., *pg.* 1603, *pg.* 1658
UNITED-GUARDIAN, INC., *pg.* 1184, *pg.* 1165
UNITED THERAPEUTICS CORPORATION, *pg.* 1604, *pg.* 778
VALEANT PHARMACEUTICALS INTERNATIONAL, *pg.* 1605, *pg.* 1047
VALEANT PHARMACEUTICALS INTERNATIONAL, INC., *pg.* 1605, *pg.* 1957
VERTEX PHARMACEUTICALS INCORPORATED, *pg.* 1606, *pg.* 801
VICTUS, INC., *pg.* 1606, *pg.* 447
VIRBAC CORPORATION, *pg.* 1606, *pg.* 1696
VITAL IMAGES, INC., *pg.* 1607, *pg.* 950
VITAL PHARMACEUTICALS, INC., *pg.* 1607, *pg.* 479
VITATECH INTERNATIONAL, INC., *pg.* 1608, *pg.* 298
VIVUS, INC., *pg.* 1608, *pg.* 163
WELCH ALLYN INC., *pg.* 1436, *pg.* 1342
W.F. YOUNG, INC., *pg.* 1610, *pg.* 817
WHITEWING LABS, INC., *pg.* 1610, *pg.* 99
XOMA CORPORATION, *pg.* 1611, *pg.* 46
ZOGENIX, INC., *pg.* 1612, *pg.* 211

2835 - In Vitro & In Vivo Diagnostic Substances

ABBOTT DIABETES CARE, INC., *pg.* 1483, *pg.* 38
AFFYMETRIX, INC., *pg.* 1487, *pg.* 263
ALERE INC., *pg.* 1488, *pg.* 849
ALLIQUA, INC., *pg.* 1492, *pg.* 1189
BD DIAGNOSTICS - TRIPATH, *pg.* 1402, *pg.* 1358
BIOMERICA, INC., *pg.* 1506, *pg.* 107
CHURCH & DWIGHT CO., INC., *pg.* 1153, *pg.* 1063
COMPUMED, INC., *pg.* 378, *pg.* 128
CORD BLOOD AMERICA, INC., *pg.* 1519, *pg.* 1023
CORGENIX MEDICAL CORPORATION, *pg.* 1519, *pg.* 312
EXACT SCIENCES CORPORATION, *pg.* 1529, *pg.* 1865
GLAXOSMITHKLINE, *pg.* 1537, *pg.* 776
HALOZYME THERAPEUTICS, INC., *pg.* 1539, *pg.* 203
IDEXX LABORATORIES, INC., *pg.* 1543, *pg.* 753
IMAGING DIAGNOSTIC SYSTEMS, INC., *pg.* 1544, *pg.* 425
INTERLEUKIN GENETICS, INC., *pg.* 1546, *pg.* 851
JANSSEN BIOTECH, INC., *pg.* 1548, *pg.* 1540
NEOGEN CORPORATION, *pg.* 883, *pg.* 896
ORASURE TECHNOLOGIES INC, *pg.* 1578, *pg.* 1516
QUIDEL CORPORATION, *pg.* 1588, *pg.* 207

2836 - Biological Products, Except Diagnostic Substances

ACORDA THERAPEUTICS, INC., *pg.* 1486, *pg.* 1138
ALERE INC., *pg.* 1488, *pg.* 849
ALLIQUA, INC., *pg.* 1492, *pg.* 1189
AMGEN INC., *pg.* 1493, *pg.* 291
APPLIED DNA SCIENCES, INC., *pg.* 1393, *pg.* 1343
ARIAD PHARMACEUTICALS, INC., *pg.* 1496, *pg.* 807
BAXTER INTERNATIONAL INC., *pg.* 1499, *pg.* 599
BELLUS HEALTH INC., *pg.* 1503, *pg.* 1951
BOEHRINGER INGELHEIM PHARMACEUTICALS, INC., *pg.* 1507, *pg.* 368
BOEHRINGER INGELHEIM VETMEDICA, INC., *pg.* 1474, *pg.* 989
BRAINSTORM CELL THERAPEUTICS INC., *pg.* 1509, *pg.* 1072
CAROLINA BIOLOGICAL SUPPLY COMPANY, *pg.* 1513, *pg.* 1359
COLORADO SERUM CO., *pg.* 1516, *pg.* 318
CSL BEHRING LLC, *pg.* 1520, *pg.* 1543
CYTRX CORPORATION, *pg.* 1521, *pg.* 129
EMERGENT BIOSOLUTIONS, *pg.* 1528, *pg.* 1914
FIBROCELL SCIENCE, INC., *pg.* 1530, *pg.* 1531
GENZYME CORPORATION, *pg.* 1534, *pg.* 808
GILEAD SCIENCES, INC., *pg.* 1535, *pg.* 88
GLAXOSMITHKLINE, *pg.* 1536, *pg.* 1565
HESKA CORPORATION, *pg.* 1542, *pg.* 335
IDERA PHARMACEUTICALS, INC., *pg.* 1543, *pg.* 808
INTEGRA LIFESCIENCES HOLDINGS CORPORATION, *pg.* 1545, *pg.* 1109
INTERNATIONAL AIDS VACCINE INITIATIVE, *pg.* 145, *pg.* 1244
JANSSEN BIOTECH, INC., *pg.* 1548, *pg.* 1540
LA JOLLA PHARMACEUTICAL COMPANY, *pg.* 1554, *pg.* 204
LEXICON PHARMACEUTICALS, INC., *pg.* 1555, *pg.* 1747
LIFE TECHNOLOGIES, *pg.* 1420, *pg.* 1497
LIFECELL CORPORATION, *pg.* 1556, *pg.* 1045
LIFECORE BIOMEDICAL, LLC, *pg.* 1556, *pg.* 920
MEAD JOHNSON NUTRITION COMPANY, *pg.* 1561, *pg.* 615
THE MEDICINES COMPANY, *pg.* 1561, *pg.* 1104
MEDIMMUNE LLC, *pg.* 1562, *pg.* 770
MEDWELL CAPITAL CORP., *pg.* 781, *pg.* 1906
MERCK & CO., INC., *pg.* 1566, *pg.* 1077
MILLIPORE CORPORATION, *pg.* 1423, *pg.* 788
MONOGRAM BIOSCIENCES, INC., *pg.* 1569, *pg.* 280
NEOGEN CORPORATION, *pg.* 883, *pg.* 896
NPS PHARMACEUTICALS, INC., *pg.* 1576, *pg.* 1043
NUTRITION 21, INC., *pg.* 1577, *pg.* 1327
OCULUS INNOVATIVE SCIENCES, *pg.* 1577, *pg.* 182
ONCOTHYREON INC., *pg.* 1578, *pg.* 1838
PDL BIOPHARMA INC., *pg.* 1580, *pg.* 1022
PHARMACEUTICAL PRODUCT DEVELOPMENT, INC., *pg.* 1584, *pg.* 1393
POSITIVEID CORPORATION, *pg.* 665, *pg.* 422
PURETEK CORPORATION, *pg.* 1587, *pg.* 211
REPLIGEN CORPORATION, *pg.* 1589, *pg.* 854
ROCHE NIMBLEGEN, INC., *pg.* 667, *pg.* 1867
SIGMA-ALDRICH CORPORATION, *pg.* 1181, *pg.* 1003
SURMODICS, INC., *pg.* 1600, *pg.* 924
TECHNE CORPORATION, *pg.* 1601, *pg.* 944
THERMO FISHER SCIENTIFIC INC., *pg.* 1602, *pg.* 61
UNITED THERAPEUTICS CORPORATION, *pg.* 1604, *pg.* 778
XANGO, LLC, *pg.* 1610, *pg.* 1751
XOMA CORPORATION, *pg.* 1611, *pg.* 46
ZEPTOMETRIX CORPORATION, *pg.* 1611, *pg.* 1151

2841 - Soap & other Detergents, Except Specialty Cleaners

ACTIVE ORGANICS, INC., *pg.* 498, *pg.* 1725
AERVOE INDUSTRIES INCORPORATED, *pg.* 1439, *pg.* 1021
A.L. WILSON CHEMICAL CO., *pg.* 325, *pg.* 1076
ALCONOX, INC., *pg.* 325, *pg.* 1351
AMERICAN CREW, INC., *pg.* 498, *pg.* 316
AMERICAN INTERNATIONAL INDUSTRIES COMPANY, *pg.* 498, *pg.* 126
ANNIE OAKLEY ENTERPRISES, INC., *pg.* 499, *pg.* 693
ARM & HAMMER CONSUMER PRODUCTS, *pg.* 326, *pg.* 1110
AROMATIQUE INC., *pg.* 499, *pg.* 32
AT LAST NATURALS, INC., *pg.* 499, *pg.* 1347
AUBREY ORGANICS INC., *pg.* 499, *pg.* 470
AVEDA CORPORATION, *pg.* 499, *pg.* 917
AVON PRODUCTS, INC., *pg.* 500, *pg.* 1198
BARE ESCENTUALS, INC., *pg.* 500, *pg.* 213
BATH & BODY WORKS, LLC, *pg.* 500, *pg.* 1471
BEAUTICONTROL COSMETICS, INC., *pg.* 501, *pg.* 1669
BEIERSDORF NORTH AMERICA INC., *pg.* 501, *pg.* 385
BELL FLAVORS & FRAGRANCES, INC., *pg.* 501, *pg.* 640
BLISTEX, INC., *pg.* 502, *pg.* 644
BLYTH, INC., *pg.* 502, *pg.* 349
THE BONNE BELL COMPANY, *pg.* 502, *pg.* 1480
BRISTOL-MYERS SQUIBB COMPANY, *pg.* 1509, *pg.* 1206
BURT'S BEES INC., *pg.* 502, *pg.* 1370
CCA INDUSTRIES, INC., *pg.* 503, *pg.* 1114
CHANEL, INC., *pg.* 503, *pg.* 1211
CHATTEM, INC., *pg.* 1515, *pg.* 1628
CHURCH & DWIGHT CANADA CORP., *pg.* 503, *pg.* 1925
CHURCH & DWIGHT CO., INC., *pg.* 1153, *pg.* 1063
CLINIQUE LABORATORIES LLC, *pg.* 503, *pg.* 1214
COLGATE-PALMOLIVE CANADA INC., *pg.* 503, *pg.* 1937
COLGATE-PALMOLIVE COMPANY, *pg.* 504, *pg.* 1215
THE COLOR FACTORY, INC., *pg.* 505, *pg.* 281
COMBE INCORPORATED, *pg.* 1516, *pg.* 1351
COTY, INC., *pg.* 506, *pg.* 1219
COVER GIRL COSMETICS, *pg.* 506, *pg.* 772
CREATIVE NAIL DESIGN, INC., *pg.* 506, *pg.* 302
DERMA SCIENCES, INC., *pg.* 1523, *pg.* 1111
DHC USA INC., *pg.* 507, *pg.* 216
DIVERSEY, INC., *pg.* 1123, *pg.* 1896
DS LABORATORIES, INC., *pg.* 507, *pg.* 442
ECOLAB INC., *pg.* 329, *pg.* 960
ECOLAB INC.-FOOD & BEVERAGE DIVISION, *pg.* 330, *pg.* 960
ELIZABETH ARDEN, INC., *pg.* 507, *pg.* 448
EMINENCE ORGANIC SKIN CARE INC., *pg.* 508, *pg.* 1910
ER'GO CANDLES INC., *pg.* 508, *pg.* 1680
THE ESTEE LAUDER COMPANIES INC., *pg.* 508, *pg.* 1229
E.T. BROWNE DRUG COMPANY, INC., *pg.* 509, *pg.* 1060
THE FEMALE HEALTH COMPANY, *pg.* 1530, *pg.* 573
FLEET LABORATORIES, *pg.* 1531, *pg.* 1787
GILLETTE, *pg.* 1536, *pg.* 795
THE GILLETTE COMPANY, *pg.* 509, *pg.* 795
GLAXOSMITHKLINE CONSUMER HEALTHCARE, *pg.* 510, *pg.* 1554
GOJO INDUSTRIES, INC., *pg.* 330, *pg.* 1401
GRANDPA BRANDS COMPANY, *pg.* 1538, *pg.* 727
THE HAIN CELESTIAL GROUP, INC., *pg.* 860, *pg.* 1172
THE HAPPY COMPANY, *pg.* 954, *pg.* 101
HENKEL CONSUMER GOODS, *pg.* 511, *pg.* 22
INSPIRED BEAUTY BRANDS, *pg.* 512, *pg.* 1244
INTER PARFUMS, INC., *pg.* 512, *pg.* 1244
J. STRICKLAND & COMPANY, *pg.* 512, *pg.* 970
JOHNSON & JOHNSON, *pg.* 1549, *pg.* 1091
KAO BRANDS CO. INC., *pg.* 513, *pg.* 1415
KERSTIN FLORIAN, INC., *pg.* 513, *pg.* 121
KOLMAR LABS GROUP, *pg.* 513, *pg.* 1322
LADY PRIMROSE'S, INC., *pg.* 513, *pg.* 1683
LANMAN & KEMP-BARCLAY CO., INC., *pg.* 514, *pg.* 1132
L'OREAL USA, *pg.* 514, *pg.* 1252
LUSTER PRODUCTS INC., *pg.* 515, *pg.* 581
LUZIER PERSONALIZED COSMETICS, INC., *pg.* 515, *pg.* 978
M.A.C. COSMETICS, *pg.* 516, *pg.* 1924
MACANDREWS & FORBES HOLDINGS INC., *pg.* 777, *pg.* 1254
MARIETTA HOSPITALITY, *pg.* 1464, *pg.* 1155
MARKWINS INTERNATIONAL CORP., *pg.* 516, *pg.* 67
MARY KAY INC., *pg.* 516, *pg.* 1657
MARY KAY INC., *pg.* 516, *pg.* 1657
MAYBELLINE LLC, *pg.* 516, *pg.* 1257
THE MENTHOLATUM COMPANY, *pg.* 1565, *pg.* 1320
MERLE NORMAN COSMETICS, INC., *pg.* 517, *pg.* 136
METHOD PRODUCTS INC., *pg.* 332, *pg.* 223
NATERRA INTERNATIONAL INC., *pg.* 59, *pg.* 1684
NATUROPATHICA LTD., *pg.* 517, *pg.* 1156
NEUTROGENA CORPORATION, *pg.* 517, *pg.* 137
NORTHERN LABS, INC., *pg.* 517, *pg.* 1869
NU SKIN ENTERPRISES, INC., *pg.* 518, *pg.* 1755
OPI PRODUCTS INC., *pg.* 518, *pg.* 167
ORLY INTERNATIONAL, INC., *pg.* 518, *pg.* 137
P&G-CLAIROL, INC., *pg.* 519, *pg.* 1418
PARFUMS DE COEUR LTD., *pg.* 519, *pg.* 376
PARLUX FRAGRANCES, INC., *pg.* 519, *pg.* 426
PETER THOMAS ROTH LABS LLC, *pg.* 520, *pg.* 1278
THE PROCTER & GAMBLE COMPANY, *pg.* 1129, *pg.* 1418
PROCTER & GAMBLE INC., *pg.* 333, *pg.* 1929
RBC LIFE SCIENCES, INC., *pg.* 1588, *pg.* 1723
REDKEN LABORATORIES LLC, *pg.* 520, *pg.* 1285
REVLON CONSUMER PRODUCTS CORPORATION, *pg.* 521, *pg.* 1286
REVLON, INC., *pg.* 521, *pg.* 1286
ROBERTET, INC., *pg.* 522, *pg.* 1100
RUE21, INC., *pg.* 32, *pg.* 1591
S.C. JOHNSON & SON, INC., *pg.* 334, *pg.* 1889
SCOTT'S LIQUID GOLD-INC., *pg.* 335, *pg.* 323
SHEFFIELD LABORATORIES, *pg.* 1375, *pg.* 359
STEARNS PRODUCTS INC., *pg.* 523, *pg.* 279
STEPAN COMPANY, *pg.* 1182, *pg.* 643

THE STEPHAN COMPANY, pg. 1597, pg. 426
STILA COSMETICS, pg. 523, pg. 99
STRAIGHT ARROW PRODUCTS, INC., pg. 523, pg. 1517
THE SUN PRODUCTS CORPORATION, pg. 336, pg. 385
SURCO PRODUCTS, INC., pg. 336, pg. 1581
SWISHER HYGIENE INC., pg. 336, pg. 1507
SYSCO GUEST SUPPLY, LLC, pg. 336, pg. 1085
THEOCHEM LABORATORIES, INC., pg. 1184, pg. 476
TOM'S OF MAINE, INC., pg. 523, pg. 750
UNGERER & COMPANY, pg. 524, pg. 1079
UNITED-GUARDIAN, INC., pg. 1184, pg. 1165
VIDAL SASSOON CO., pg. 524, pg. 1426
WATKINS INCORPORATED, pg. 909, pg. 967
THE W.E. BASSETT COMPANY, pg. 524, pg. 371
ZEP INC., pg. 338, pg. 524
ZOTOS INTERNATIONAL, INC., pg. 524, pg. 345

2842 - Specialty Cleaning, Polishing & Sanitation Preparations

ADCO, INC., pg. 325, pg. 482
A.L. WILSON CHEMICAL CO., pg. 325, pg. 1076
ANCHOR PAINT MANUFACTURING CO. INC., pg. 1440, pg. 1489
BISSELL HOMECARE, INC., pg. 52, pg. 887
BLUE CROSS LABORATORIES, pg. 326, pg. 277
BRONDOW, INC., pg. 327, pg. 1346
CHURCH & DWIGHT CO., INC., pg. 1153, pg. 1063
THE CLOROX COMPANY, pg. 327, pg. 169
CONNOISSEURS PRODUCTS CORPORATION, pg. 329, pg. 861
COPPER-BRITE, INC., pg. 329, pg. 263
CORAL CHEMICAL COMPANY, pg. 1154, pg. 666
CRITZAS INDUSTRIES, INC., pg. 329, pg. 995
CUSTOM CHEMICAL FORMULATORS, INC., pg. 329, pg. 271
DELTA FOREMOST CHEMICAL CORPORATION, pg. 1155, pg. 1642
DIVERSEY, INC., pg. 1123, pg. 1896
DOBER CHEMICAL CORP., pg. 1156, pg. 671
DURACLEAN INTERNATIONAL, INC., pg. 329, pg. 553
EARTH FRIENDLY PRODUCTS, pg. 329, pg. 552
FAULTLESS STARCH/BON AMI COMPANY, pg. 330, pg. 982
FINE ORGANICS CORPORATION, pg. 330, pg. 1052
THE FULLER BRUSH COMPANY, pg. 330, pg. 715
GAGE PRODUCTS COMPANY, pg. 1164, pg. 886
GREEN EARTH TECHNOLOGIES, INC., pg. 704, pg. 1352
KYZEN CORPORATION, pg. 331, pg. 1652
L&R MANUFACTURING COMPANY, pg. 1419, pg. 1076
MACDERMID, INC., pg. 1172, pg. 321
MALCO PRODUCTS, INC., pg. 1172, pg. 1404
MAPA PROFESSIONAL, pg. 1885, pg. 555
METHOD PRODUCTS INC., pg. 332, pg. 223
MILLER-STEPHENSON CHEMICAL COMPANY, INC., pg. 1172, pg. 344
MOC PRODUCTS COMPANY, INC., pg. 332, pg. 174
NCH CORPORATION, pg. 1174, pg. 1723
NILODOR, INC., pg. 332, pg. 1406
NORTHERN LABS, INC., pg. 517, pg. 1869
OCEAN BIO CHEM, INC., pg. 1444, pg. 426
PENETONE CORPORATION, pg. 333, pg. 1050
RECKITT BENCKISER INC., pg. 1136, pg. 1105
ROCHESTER MIDLAND CORPORATION, pg. 334, pg. 1337
S.C. JOHNSON & SON, INC., pg. 334, pg. 1889
SENORET CHEMICAL COMPANY, pg. 335, pg. 1548
STARBRITE CORP., pg. 336, pg. 426
STONER INC., pg. 985, pg. 1583
SUMMIT INDUSTRIES, INC., pg. 1599, pg. 535
SUNSHINE MAKERS, INC., pg. 336, pg. 105
SYSCO GUEST SUPPLY, LLC, pg. 336, pg. 1085
THEOCHEM LABORATORIES, INC., pg. 1184, pg. 476
TURTLE WAX, INC., pg. 220, pg. 671
WALTER G. LEGGE COMPANY, INC., pg. 337, pg. 1321
WEIMAN PRODUCTS, LLC, pg. 337, pg. 616
ZEP INC., pg. 338, pg. 524

2843 - Surface Active Agents, Finishing Agents, Sulfonated Oils & Assistants

ACTON TECHNOLOGIES, INC., pg. 1145, pg. 1582
ATLAS REFINERY, INC., pg. 1148, pg. 1095
CHEMTURA CORPORATION, pg. 1152, pg. 355
HENKEL CORPORATION, pg. 1165, pg. 1535
HUNTSMAN CORPORATION, pg. 1167, pg. 1758
STEPAN COMPANY, pg. 1182, pg. 643

2844 - Perfumes, Cosmetics & other Toilet Preparations

ACTIVE ORGANICS, INC., pg. 498, pg. 1725
AMERICAN CREW, INC., pg. 498, pg. 316
AMERICAN INTERNATIONAL INDUSTRIES COMPANY, pg. 498, pg. 126
ANNIE OAKLEY ENTERPRISES, INC., pg. 499, pg. 693
AT LAST NATURALS, INC., pg. 499, pg. 1347
AUBREY ORGANICS INC., pg. 499, pg. 470
AVEDA CORPORATION, pg. 499, pg. 917
AVON PRODUCTS, INC., pg. 500, pg. 1198
BARE ESCENTUALS, INC., pg. 500, pg. 213
BATH & BODY WORKS, LLC, pg. 500, pg. 1471
BEAUTICONTROL COSMETICS, INC., pg. 501, pg. 1669
BEIERSDORF NORTH AMERICA INC., pg. 501, pg. 385
BELL FLAVORS & FRAGRANCES, INC., pg. 501, pg. 640
BLISTEX, INC., pg. 502, pg. 644
BLYTH, INC., pg. 502, pg. 349
THE BONNE BELL COMPANY, pg. 502, pg. 1480
BRISTOL-MYERS SQUIBB COMPANY, pg. 1509, pg. 1206
BURT'S BEES INC., pg. 502, pg. 1370
CCA INDUSTRIES, INC., pg. 503, pg. 1114
CHANEL, INC., pg. 503, pg. 1211
CHATTEM, INC., pg. 1515, pg. 1628
CHURCH & DWIGHT CANADA CORP., pg. 503, pg. 1925
CLINIQUE LABORATORIES LLC, pg. 503, pg. 1214
COLGATE-PALMOLIVE CANADA INC., pg. 503, pg. 1937
THE COLOR FACTORY, INC., pg. 505, pg. 281
COMBE INCORPORATED, pg. 1516, pg. 1351
COTY, INC., pg. 506, pg. 1219
COVER GIRL COSMETICS, pg. 506, pg. 772
CREATIVE NAIL DESIGN, INC., pg. 506, pg. 302
DERMA SCIENCES, INC., pg. 1523, pg. 1111
DHC USA INC., pg. 507, pg. 216
DS LABORATORIES, INC., pg. 507, pg. 442
ELIZABETH ARDEN, INC., pg. 507, pg. 448
EMINENCE ORGANIC SKIN CARE INC., pg. 508, pg. 1910
ER'GO CANDLES INC., pg. 508, pg. 1680
THE ESTEE LAUDER COMPANIES INC., pg. 508, pg. 1229
E.T. BROWNE DRUG COMPANY, INC., pg. 509, pg. 1060
THE FEMALE HEALTH COMPANY, pg. 1530, pg. 573
FLEET LABORATORIES, pg. 1531, pg. 1787
GILLETTE, pg. 1536, pg. 795
THE GILLETTE COMPANY, pg. 509, pg. 795
GLAXOSMITHKLINE CONSUMER HEALTHCARE, pg. 510, pg. 1554
THE HAIN CELESTIAL GROUP, INC., pg. 860, pg. 1172
THE HAPPY COMPANY, pg. 954, pg. 101
HENKEL CONSUMER GOODS, pg. 511, pg. 22
INSPIRED BEAUTY BRANDS, pg. 512, pg. 1244
INTER PARFUMS, INC., pg. 512, pg. 1244
J. STRICKLAND & COMPANY, pg. 512, pg. 970
KERSTIN FLORIAN, INC., pg. 513, pg. 121
KOLMAR LABS GROUP, pg. 513, pg. 1322
LADY PRIMROSE'S, INC., pg. 513, pg. 1683
LANMAN & KEMP-BARCLAY CO., INC., pg. 514, pg. 1132
L'OREAL USA, pg. 514, pg. 1252
LUSTER PRODUCTS INC., pg. 515, pg. 581
LUZIER PERSONALIZED COSMETICS, INC., pg. 515, pg. 978
M.A.C. COSMETICS, pg. 516, pg. 1924
MACANDREWS & FORBES HOLDINGS INC., pg. 777, pg. 1254
MARKWINS INTERNATIONAL CORP., pg. 516, pg. 67
MARY KAY INC., pg. 516, pg. 1657
MARY KAY INC., pg. 516, pg. 1657
MAYBELLINE LLC, pg. 516, pg. 1257
THE MENTHOLATUM COMPANY, pg. 1565, pg. 1320
MERLE NORMAN COSMETICS, INC., pg. 517, pg. 136
NATERRA INTERNATIONAL INC., pg. 59, pg. 1684
NATUROPATHICA LTD., pg. 517, pg. 1156
NEUTROGENA CORPORATION, pg. 517, pg. 137
NORTHERN LABS, INC., pg. 517, pg. 1869
NU SKIN ENTERPRISES, INC., pg. 518, pg. 1755
OPI PRODUCTS INC., pg. 518, pg. 167
ORLY INTERNATIONAL, INC., pg. 518, pg. 137
P&G-CLAIROL, INC., pg. 519, pg. 1418
PARFUMS DE COEUR LTD., pg. 519, pg. 376
PARLUX FRAGRANCES, INC., pg. 519, pg. 426
PETER THOMAS ROTH LABS LLC, pg. 520, pg. 1278
THE PROCTER & GAMBLE COMPANY, pg. 1129, pg. 1418
PROCTER & GAMBLE INC., pg. 333, pg. 1929
RBC LIFE SCIENCES, INC., pg. 1588, pg. 1723
REDKEN LABORATORIES LLC, pg. 520, pg. 1285
REVLON CONSUMER PRODUCTS CORPORATION, pg. 521, pg. 1286
REVLON, INC., pg. 521, pg. 1286
ROBERTET, INC., pg. 522, pg. 1100
RUE21, INC., pg. 32, pg. 1591
S.C. JOHNSON & SON, INC., pg. 334, pg. 1889
SCOTT'S LIQUID GOLD-INC., pg. 335, pg. 323
SHEFFIELD LABORATORIES, pg. 1375, pg. 359
STEARNS PRODUCTS INC., pg. 523, pg. 279
THE STEPHAN COMPANY, pg. 1597, pg. 426
STILA COSMETICS, pg. 523, pg. 99
STRAIGHT ARROW PRODUCTS, INC., pg. 523, pg. 1517
SURCO PRODUCTS, INC., pg. 336, pg. 1581
SYSCO GUEST SUPPLY, LLC, pg. 336, pg. 1085
TOM'S OF MAINE, INC., pg. 523, pg. 750
UNGERER & COMPANY, pg. 524, pg. 1079
UNITED-GUARDIAN, INC., pg. 1184, pg. 1165
VIDAL SASSOON CO., pg. 524, pg. 1426
THE W.E. BASSETT COMPANY, pg. 524, pg. 371
ZOTOS INTERNATIONAL, INC., pg. 524, pg. 345

2851 - Paints, Varnishes, Lacquers, Enamels & Allied Products

3M COMPANY, pg. 1142, pg. 956
ABBOTT LABORATORIES, pg. 1484, pg. 551
AERVOE INDUSTRIES INCORPORATED, pg. 1439, pg. 1021
AIRGAS, INC., pg. 1146, pg. 1583
AKZO NOBEL, pg. 1439, pg. 1952
AKZO NOBEL COATINGS INC., pg. 1439, pg. 1437
AKZO NOBEL DECORATIVE PAINTS, USA, pg. 1439, pg. 1474
AKZO NOBEL INC., pg. 1146, pg. 563
AKZONOBEL DECORATIVE PAINTS U.S., pg. 1439, pg. 1474
ALTAIR NANOTECHNOLOGIES INC., pg. 1147, pg. 1031
ANACHEMIA CANADA, INC., pg. 1147, pg. 1951
ANCHOR PAINT MANUFACTURING CO. INC., pg. 1440, pg. 1489
ANDERSON DEVELOPMENT COMPANY, pg. 1147, pg. 864
ANGUS CHEMICAL COMPANY, pg. 1147, pg. 560
APYRON TECHNOLOGIES, INC., pg. 1495, pg. 488
ARKEMA INC., pg. 1147, pg. 1543
AROMALAND INC., pg. 499, pg. 1135
ASHLAND INC., pg. 972, pg. 726
ASHLAND PERFORMANCE MATERIALS, pg. 1147, pg. 1448
ATLAS REFINERY, INC., pg. 1148, pg. 1095
ATMI, INC., pg. 1314, pg. 342
AVERY DENNISON CORPORATION, pg. 1452, pg. 95
A.W. CHESTERTON COMPANY, pg. 1315, pg. 861
BAKER PETROLITE CORPORATION, pg. 1148, pg. 1745
BENJAMIN MOORE & CO., pg. 1440, pg. 1085
BG PRODUCTS, INC., pg. 200, pg. 722
BIC CORPORATION, pg. 501, pg. 369
BIO-RAD LABORATORIES, INC., pg. 1504, pg. 101
BIOSAFE SYSTEMS, LLC, pg. 1149, pg. 345
BISSELL HOMECARE, INC., pg. 52, pg. 887
BOEHRINGER INGELHEIM PHARMACEUTICALS, INC., pg. 1507, pg. 368
BONIDE PRODUCTS, INC., pg. 1794, pg. 1320
BREWER SCIENCE, INC., pg. 1150, pg. 989
BROOKTRONICS ENGINEERING CORPORATION, pg. 1320, pg. 299
BURGESS PIGMENT COMPANY, pg. 1150, pg. 535
CALGON CARBON CORPORATION, pg. 1151, pg. 1574
CALIFORNIA PRODUCTS CORPORATION, pg. 1441, pg. 781
CARBOLINE CO., pg. 1152, pg. 994
CHEMTURA CORPORATION, pg. 1152, pg. 355
CHROMA CORPORATION, pg. 1441, pg. 632
CODEXIS, INC., pg. 1154, pg. 189
COHESANT, INC., pg. 1154, pg. 1405
COMPLEX CHEMICALS COMPANY, INC., pg. 974, pg. 748
CYTEC INDUSTRIES, INC., pg. 1155, pg. 1131
DAP PRODUCTS, INC., pg. 1441, pg. 756

DAVIS PAINT COMPANY, *pg.* 1441, *pg.* 982
DAY-GLO COLOR CORP., *pg.* 1441, *pg.* 1429
DEEPWATER CHEMICALS, INC., *pg.* 1155, *pg.* 1491
DETREX CORPORATION, *pg.* 1156, *pg.* 906
DIAMOND VOGEL PAINT, INC., *pg.* 1441, *pg.* 710
DOBER CHEMICAL CORP., *pg.* 1156, *pg.* 671
DOW CHEMICAL, *pg.* 1156, *pg.* 1563
THE DOW CHEMICAL COMPANY, *pg.* 1157, *pg.* 898
DUNN-EDWARDS CORPORATION, *pg.* 1442, *pg.* 129
EASTMAN CHEMICAL COMPANY, *pg.* 1159, *pg.* 1636
E.I. DU PONT DE NEMOURS & COMPANY, *pg.* 1159, *pg.* 390
EMERALD PERFORMANCE MATERIALS, LLC, *pg.* 1161, *pg.* 1445
ENERGIZER HOLDINGS, INC., *pg.* 637, *pg.* 996
ENTHONE INC., *pg.* 1161, *pg.* 381
THE EUCLID CHEMICAL COMPANY, *pg.* 81, *pg.* 1430
EUREKA CHEMICAL COMPANY, *pg.* 1161, *pg.* 279
EXXON MOBIL CORPORATION, *pg.* 977, *pg.* 1718
FERRO CORPORATION, *pg.* 1162, *pg.* 1462
FIRMENICH INCORPORATED, *pg.* 509, *pg.* 1109
THE FLAMEMASTER CORPORATION, *pg.* 1162, *pg.* 174
FLEXIBLE SOLUTIONS INTERNATIONAL, INC., *pg.* 1163, *pg.* 1913
FMC CORPORATION, *pg.* 1163, *pg.* 1564
FMC LITHIUM DIVISION, *pg.* 1163, *pg.* 1366
FRAGRANCE RESOURCES, INC., *pg.* 509, *pg.* 1052
GEORGIA-PACIFIC LLC, *pg.* 1458, *pg.* 507
HALOCARBON PRODUCTS CORPORATION, *pg.* 978, *pg.* 1116
HAR ADHESIVE TECHNOLOGIES, *pg.* 1442, *pg.* 1405
H.B. FULLER COMPANY, *pg.* 1165, *pg.* 961
HENKEL CORPORATION, *pg.* 1166, *pg.* 897
HERCULES INCORPORATED, *pg.* 1166, *pg.* 392
HOMAX PRODUCTS INC., *pg.* 1442, *pg.* 1817
HONEYWELL CONSUMER PRODUCTS GROUP, *pg.* 208, *pg.* 344
HUNTSMAN CORPORATION, *pg.* 1167, *pg.* 1758
INTERNATIONAL FLAVORS & FRAGRANCES INC., *pg.* 512, *pg.* 1244
ITW - EVERCOAT, *pg.* 1443, *pg.* 1415
JBI, INC., *pg.* 293, *pg.* 1317
JOHNSON MANUFACTURING COMPANY, *pg.* 1169, *pg.* 712
JONES-BLAIR COMPANY, *pg.* 1443, *pg.* 1682
JOTUN PAINTS, INC., *pg.* 1443, *pg.* 742
KELLY-MOORE PAINT COMPANY, INC., *pg.* 1443, *pg.* 198
KIDDE FIRE FIGHTING, *pg.* 1170, *pg.* 1531
KILGORE FLARES, *pg.* 1170, *pg.* 1656
KING INDUSTRIES, INC., *pg.* 1443, *pg.* 363
KOCH INDUSTRIES, INC., *pg.* 1463, *pg.* 724
KOP-COAT, INC., *pg.* 1444, *pg.* 1576
KOPPERS HOLDINGS INC., *pg.* 1170, *pg.* 1577
KRONOS INTERNATIONAL, INC., *pg.* 980, *pg.* 1683
KRONOS WORLDWIDE, INC., *pg.* 980, *pg.* 1053
KYOWA HAKKO U.S.A., INC., *pg.* 1554, *pg.* 1249
LA-CO INDUSTRIES MARKAL CO., INC., *pg.* 1170, *pg.* 610
LAPOLLA INDUSTRIES, INC., *pg.* 1444, *pg.* 1710
L.M. SCOFIELD COMPANY, *pg.* 94, *pg.* 134
LONZA INC., *pg.* 1171, *pg.* 1041
THE LUBRIZOL CORPORATION, *pg.* 1171, *pg.* 1481
LUSTER-ON PRODUCTS, INC., *pg.* 1171, *pg.* 845
MACDERMID, INC., *pg.* 1172, *pg.* 321
MARTIN/F. WEBER COMPANY, *pg.* 962, *pg.* 1567
MASTER BOND INC., *pg.* 1172, *pg.* 1072
MASTERCHEM INDUSTRIES, LLC, *pg.* 1444, *pg.* 979
MCGEAN-ROHCO, INC., *pg.* 1172, *pg.* 1432
MCLAUGHLIN GORMLEY KING COMPANY, *pg.* 1797, *pg.* 939
MILLIKEN & COMPANY, *pg.* 696, *pg.* 1622
MOHAWK FINISHING PRODUCTS, INC., *pg.* 1173, *pg.* 1378
MORGAN ADVANCED MATERIALS, *pg.* 1363, *pg.* 835
MORGRO, INC., *pg.* 1798, *pg.* 1759
NALCO CO., *pg.* 1174, *pg.* 636
NCH CORPORATION, *pg.* 1174, *pg.* 1723
NL INDUSTRIES, INC., *pg.* 1174, *pg.* 1684
NOAH TECHNOLOGIES CORPORATION, *pg.* 1175, *pg.* 1742
NOVA CHEMICALS CORPORATION, *pg.* 1175, *pg.* 1904
NUCO2 INC., *pg.* 1175, *pg.* 468
OIL-DRI CORPORATION OF AMERICA, *pg.* 1480, *pg.* 586
OLD WORLD INDUSTRIES, INC., *pg.* 1175, *pg.* 641
OMNOVA SOLUTIONS INC, *pg.* 1176, *pg.* 1453
OXYSURE SYSTEMS, INC., *pg.* 1579, *pg.* 1697
P. KAY METAL SUPPLY INC., *pg.* 1176, *pg.* 137
PETROFERM INC., *pg.* 1177, *pg.* 616
PETTIT PAINT COMPANY, *pg.* 1444, *pg.* 1116
POWER SERVICE PRODUCTS, INC., *pg.* 983, *pg.* 1749
PPG AEROSPACE, *pg.* 1178, *pg.* 290
PPG AEROSPACE DEFT FACILITY, *pg.* 1445, *pg.* 115
PPG INDUSTRIES, INC., *pg.* 1445, *pg.* 1579
THE PROCTER & GAMBLE COMPANY, *pg.* 1129, *pg.* 1418
QUAKER CHEMICAL CORP., *pg.* 1178, *pg.* 1524
RADIATOR SPECIALTY COMPANY, *pg.* 215, *pg.* 1380
THE REAL MILK PAINT CO., *pg.* 1446, *pg.* 1583
RED SPOT PAINT & VARNISH CO., INC., *pg.* 1446, *pg.* 679
RENTECH, INC., *pg.* 1179, *pg.* 139
RPM INTERNATIONAL INC., *pg.* 1447, *pg.* 1464
RUST-OLEUM CORPORATION, *pg.* 1447, *pg.* 664
SACHEM INC., *pg.* 1180, *pg.* 1665
THE SAVOGRAN COMPANY, *pg.* 1447, *pg.* 840
SEYMOUR OF SYCAMORE, INC., *pg.* 1447, *pg.* 663
THE SHERWIN-WILLIAMS COMPANY, *pg.* 1447, *pg.* 1435
SHERWIN-WILLIAMS DIVERSIFIED BRANDS DIVISION, *pg.* 1448, *pg.* 1435
SIGMA-ALDRICH CORPORATION, *pg.* 1181, *pg.* 1003
SIKA CORPORATION, *pg.* 110, *pg.* 1080
SPECTRUM CHEMICALS & LABORATORY PRODUCTS, INC., *pg.* 1181, *pg.* 94
STANCHEM, INC., *pg.* 1449, *pg.* 345
STEPAN COMPANY, *pg.* 1182, *pg.* 643
SUNOCO CHEMICALS, *pg.* 1182, *pg.* 1570
TECHNIC INCORPORATED, *pg.* 1183, *pg.* 1601
THE TESTOR CORPORATION, *pg.* 968, *pg.* 655
TEXTILE RUBBER & CHEMICAL COMPANY, *pg.* 1890, *pg.* 530
TREMCO INCORPORATED, *pg.* 116, *pg.* 1405
UNITED GILSONITE LABORATORIES, *pg.* 1449, *pg.* 1527
UNITED-GUARDIAN, INC., *pg.* 1184, *pg.* 1165
VALENT U.S.A. CORP., *pg.* 708, *pg.* 305
VALHI, INC., *pg.* 1185, *pg.* 1690
THE VALSPAR CORPORATION, *pg.* 1449, *pg.* 945
VERTELLUS SPECIALTIES INC., *pg.* 1185, *pg.* 690
WD-40 COMPANY, *pg.* 337, *pg.* 210
WEIMAN PRODUCTS, LLC, *pg.* 337, *pg.* 616
THE WILLAMETTE VALLEY COMPANY, *pg.* 1186, *pg.* 1497
WISCONSIN PHARMACAL COMPANY, LLC, *pg.* 1610, *pg.* 1861
W.M. BARR & COMPANY, INC., *pg.* 338, *pg.* 1647
W.R. GRACE & CO., *pg.* 123, *pg.* 810
WYNN OIL COMPANY, *pg.* 987, *pg.* 173
YENKIN-MAJESTIC PAINT CORPORATION, *pg.* 1450, *pg.* 1445
ZEP INC., *pg.* 338, *pg.* 524

2861 - Gum & Wood Chemicals

ARIZONA CHEMICAL CO. LLC, *pg.* 1147, *pg.* 431
HERCULES INCORPORATED, *pg.* 1166, *pg.* 392
KOPPERS HOLDINGS INC., *pg.* 1170, *pg.* 1577
RAYONIER INC., *pg.* 1179, *pg.* 434

2865 - Cyclic Organic Crudes & Intermediates, Organic Dyes & Pigments

ABENGOA BIOENERGY CORP., *pg.* 971, *pg.* 974
ACETO CORPORATION, *pg.* 1145, *pg.* 1323
AIR PRODUCTS AND CHEMICALS, INC., *pg.* 1145, *pg.* 1513
AKZO NOBEL INC., *pg.* 1146, *pg.* 563
ANGUS CHEMICAL COMPANY, *pg.* 1147, *pg.* 560
ASHLAND INC., *pg.* 972, *pg.* 726
ASHLAND PERFORMANCE MATERIALS, *pg.* 1147, *pg.* 1448
BAKER HUGHES INCORPORATED, *pg.* 1315, *pg.* 1700
BAKER PETROLITE CORPORATION, *pg.* 1148, *pg.* 1745
BALCHEM CORPORATION, *pg.* 839, *pg.* 1183
BELL FLAVORS & FRAGRANCES, INC., *pg.* 501, *pg.* 640
BIOSAFE SYSTEMS, LLC, *pg.* 1149, *pg.* 345
BOULDER SCIENTIFIC COMPANY, *pg.* 1150, *pg.* 335
BUCKMAN, *pg.* 1150, *pg.* 1641
CARGILL, INC., *pg.* 845, *pg.* 965
CHEM-TREND LIMITED PARTNERSHIP, *pg.* 973, *pg.* 892
CHEMTURA CORPORATION, *pg.* 1152, *pg.* 355
CLARIANT CORPORATION, *pg.* 1153, *pg.* 1365
CUMBERLAND PACKING CORP., *pg.* 851, *pg.* 1146
DAVID MICHAEL & CO. INC., *pg.* 852, *pg.* 1563
DOVER CHEMICAL CORPORATION, *pg.* 1156, *pg.* 1447
THE DOW CHEMICAL COMPANY, *pg.* 1157, *pg.* 898
EVONIK CORPORATION, *pg.* 1162, *pg.* 1103
EXXON MOBIL CORPORATION, *pg.* 977, *pg.* 1718
FIRMENICH INCORPORATED, *pg.* 509, *pg.* 1109
FMC CORPORATION, *pg.* 1163, *pg.* 1564
GAGE PRODUCTS COMPANY, *pg.* 1164, *pg.* 886
GRAIN PROCESSING CORPORATION, *pg.* 859, *pg.* 709
HEADWATERS INCORPORATED, *pg.* 978, *pg.* 1763
HENKEL CORPORATION, *pg.* 1166, *pg.* 897
HENKEL CORPORATION, *pg.* 1165, *pg.* 1535
HERCULES INCORPORATED, *pg.* 1166, *pg.* 392
HEXION, *pg.* 1166, *pg.* 1440
HOUGHTON INTERNATIONAL INC., *pg.* 1167, *pg.* 1589
HUNTSMAN CORPORATION, *pg.* 1167, *pg.* 1758
INCOMING INC., *pg.* 979, *pg.* 1243
INOLEX CHEMICAL COMPANY, *pg.* 1168, *pg.* 1566
INOLEX GROUP INC., *pg.* 1168, *pg.* 1566
INTERNATIONAL FLAVORS & FRAGRANCES INC., *pg.* 512, *pg.* 1244
JARCHEM INDUSTRIES, INC., *pg.* 1169, *pg.* 1096
KOPPERS HOLDINGS INC., *pg.* 1170, *pg.* 1577
LIPO CHEMICALS INC., *pg.* 1171, *pg.* 1107
LONZA INC., *pg.* 1171, *pg.* 1041
THE LUBRIZOL CORPORATION, *pg.* 1171, *pg.* 1481
LYONDELLBASELL INDUSTRIES, *pg.* 980, *pg.* 1710
MACANDREWS & FORBES HOLDINGS INC., *pg.* 777, *pg.* 1254
MERICHEM COMPANY, *pg.* 1172, *pg.* 1711
MERISANT COMPANY, *pg.* 876, *pg.* 581
MGP INGREDIENTS, INC., *pg.* 877, *pg.* 714
NATIONAL ENZYME COMPANY, *pg.* 882, *pg.* 978
NEVILLE CHEMICAL COMPANY, *pg.* 1174, *pg.* 1578
NEWMARKET CORPORATION, *pg.* 982, *pg.* 1803
NL INDUSTRIES, INC., *pg.* 1174, *pg.* 1684
NOVA CHEMICALS CORPORATION, *pg.* 1175, *pg.* 1904
NUFARM AMERICAS INC, *pg.* 1798, *pg.* 552
THE NUTRASWEET COMPANY, *pg.* 1860, *pg.* 585
OCCIDENTAL CHEMICAL CORPORATION, *pg.* 1175, *pg.* 1685
PACIFIC ETHANOL, INC., *pg.* 982, *pg.* 197
PHARMCO-AAPER, *pg.* 1177, *pg.* 740
QUAKER CHEMICAL CORP., *pg.* 1178, *pg.* 1524
R.T. VANDERBILT COMPANY, INC., *pg.* 1180, *pg.* 364
SACHEM INC., *pg.* 1180, *pg.* 1665
SASOL NORTH AMERICA INC., *pg.* 984, *pg.* 1713
SI GROUP, INC., *pg.* 1181, *pg.* 1341
SIGMA-ALDRICH CORPORATION, *pg.* 1181, *pg.* 1881
SIGMA-ALDRICH CORPORATION, *pg.* 1181, *pg.* 1003
SPURRIER CHEMICAL COMPANIES, INC., *pg.* 1182, *pg.* 724
SUNOCO CHEMICALS, *pg.* 1182, *pg.* 1570
SYMRISE, INC., *pg.* 1183, *pg.* 1125
TOTAL PETROCHEMICALS USA, INC., *pg.* 1184, *pg.* 1716
TROY CORPORATION, *pg.* 1184, *pg.* 1067
THE VALSPAR CORPORATION, *pg.* 1449, *pg.* 945
VERTELLUS SPECIALTIES INC., *pg.* 1185, *pg.* 690
WILLERT HOME PRODUCTS, INC., *pg.* 1140, *pg.* 1005

2869 - Industrial Organic Chemicals, NEC

3M COMPANY, *pg.* 1142, *pg.* 956
ABBOTT LABORATORIES, *pg.* 1484, *pg.* 551
ABENGOA BIOENERGY CORP., *pg.* 971, *pg.* 974
ACETO CORPORATION, *pg.* 1145, *pg.* 1323
AIR PRODUCTS AND CHEMICALS, INC., *pg.* 1145, *pg.* 1513
AIRGAS, INC., *pg.* 1146, *pg.* 1583
AKZO NOBEL INC., *pg.* 1146, *pg.* 563
ALTAIR NANOTECHNOLOGIES INC., *pg.* 1147, *pg.* 1031
ANACHEMIA CANADA, INC., *pg.* 1147, *pg.* 1951
ANDERSON DEVELOPMENT COMPANY, *pg.* 1147, *pg.* 864
ANGUS CHEMICAL COMPANY, *pg.* 1147, *pg.* 560
APYRON TECHNOLOGIES, INC., *pg.* 1495, *pg.* 488
ARKEMA INC., *pg.* 1147, *pg.* 1543
AROMALAND INC., *pg.* 499, *pg.* 1135
ASHLAND INC., *pg.* 972, *pg.* 726
ASHLAND PERFORMANCE MATERIALS, *pg.* 1147, *pg.* 1448
ATLAS REFINERY, INC., *pg.* 1148, *pg.* 1095
ATMI, INC., *pg.* 1314, *pg.* 342
AVERY DENNISON CORPORATION, *pg.* 1452, *pg.* 95
BAKER HUGHES INCORPORATED, *pg.* 1315, *pg.* 1700

First page reference indicates Business Class Edition
Second page reference indicates Geographic Edition

BAKER PETROLITE CORPORATION, *pg.* 1148, *pg.* 1745
BALCHEM CORPORATION, *pg.* 839, *pg.* 1183
BELL FLAVORS & FRAGRANCES, INC., *pg.* 501, *pg.* 640
BG PRODUCTS, INC., *pg.* 200, *pg.* 722
BIC CORPORATION, *pg.* 501, *pg.* 369
BIO-RAD LABORATORIES, INC., *pg.* 1504, *pg.* 101
BIOSAFE SYSTEMS, LLC, *pg.* 1149, *pg.* 345
BISSELL HOMECARE, INC., *pg.* 52, *pg.* 887
BOEHRINGER INGELHEIM PHARMACEUTICALS, INC., *pg.* 1507, *pg.* 368
BONIDE PRODUCTS, INC., *pg.* 1794, *pg.* 1320
BOULDER SCIENTIFIC COMPANY, *pg.* 1150, *pg.* 335
BROOKTRONICS ENGINEERING CORPORATION, *pg.* 1320, *pg.* 299
BUCKMAN, *pg.* 1150, *pg.* 1641
BURGESS PIGMENT COMPANY, *pg.* 1150, *pg.* 535
CALGON CARBON CORPORATION, *pg.* 1151, *pg.* 1574
CARGILL, INC., *pg.* 845, *pg.* 965
CHEM-TREND LIMITED PARTNERSHIP, *pg.* 973, *pg.* 892
CHEMTURA CORPORATION, *pg.* 1152, *pg.* 355
CLARIANT CORPORATION, *pg.* 1153, *pg.* 1365
CODEXIS, INC., *pg.* 1154, *pg.* 189
COMPLEX CHEMICALS COMPANY, INC., *pg.* 974, *pg.* 748
CUMBERLAND PACKING CORP., *pg.* 851, *pg.* 1146
CYTEC INDUSTRIES, INC., *pg.* 1155, *pg.* 1131
DAVID MICHAEL & CO. INC., *pg.* 852, *pg.* 1563
DEEPWATER CHEMICALS, INC., *pg.* 1155, *pg.* 1491
DETREX CORPORATION, *pg.* 1156, *pg.* 906
DOBER CHEMICAL CORP., *pg.* 1156, *pg.* 671
DOVER CHEMICAL CORPORATION, *pg.* 1156, *pg.* 1447
DOW CHEMICAL, *pg.* 1156, *pg.* 1563
THE DOW CHEMICAL COMPANY, *pg.* 1157, *pg.* 898
EASTMAN CHEMICAL COMPANY, *pg.* 1159, *pg.* 1636
E.I. DU PONT DE NEMOURS & COMPANY, *pg.* 1159, *pg.* 390
EMERALD PERFORMANCE MATERIALS, LLC, *pg.* 1161, *pg.* 1445
ENERGIZER HOLDINGS, INC., *pg.* 637, *pg.* 996
ENTHONE INC., *pg.* 1161, *pg.* 381
EUREKA CHEMICAL COMPANY, *pg.* 1161, *pg.* 279
EVONIK CORPORATION, *pg.* 1162, *pg.* 1103
EXXON MOBIL CORPORATION, *pg.* 977, *pg.* 1718
FIRMENICH INCORPORATED, *pg.* 509, *pg.* 1109
THE FLAMEMASTER CORPORATION, *pg.* 1162, *pg.* 174
FLEXIBLE SOLUTIONS INTERNATIONAL, INC., *pg.* 1163, *pg.* 1913
FMC CORPORATION, *pg.* 1163, *pg.* 1564
FMC LITHIUM DIVISION, *pg.* 1163, *pg.* 1366
FRAGRANCE RESOURCES, INC., *pg.* 509, *pg.* 1052
GAGE PRODUCTS COMPANY, *pg.* 1164, *pg.* 886
GEORGIA-PACIFIC LLC, *pg.* 1458, *pg.* 507
GRAIN PROCESSING CORPORATION, *pg.* 859, *pg.* 709
HALOCARBON PRODUCTS CORPORATION, *pg.* 978, *pg.* 1116
HEADWATERS INCORPORATED, *pg.* 978, *pg.* 1763
HENKEL CORPORATION, *pg.* 1166, *pg.* 897
HENKEL CORPORATION, *pg.* 1165, *pg.* 1535
HERCULES INCORPORATED, *pg.* 1166, *pg.* 392
HEXION, *pg.* 1166, *pg.* 1440
HONEYWELL CONSUMER PRODUCTS GROUP, *pg.* 208, *pg.* 344
HOUGHTON INTERNATIONAL INC., *pg.* 1167, *pg.* 1589
HUNTSMAN CORPORATION, *pg.* 1167, *pg.* 1758
INCOMING INC., *pg.* 979, *pg.* 1243
INOLEX CHEMICAL COMPANY, *pg.* 1168, *pg.* 1566
INOLEX GROUP INC., *pg.* 1168, *pg.* 1566
INTERNATIONAL FLAVORS & FRAGRANCES INC., *pg.* 512, *pg.* 1244
JARCHEM INDUSTRIES, INC., *pg.* 1169, *pg.* 1096
JBI, INC., *pg.* 293, *pg.* 1317
JOHNSON MANUFACTURING COMPANY, *pg.* 1169, *pg.* 712
KIDDE FIRE FIGHTING, *pg.* 1170, *pg.* 1531
KILGORE FLARES, *pg.* 1170, *pg.* 1656
KING INDUSTRIES, INC., *pg.* 1443, *pg.* 363
KOCH INDUSTRIES, INC., *pg.* 1463, *pg.* 724
KOPPERS HOLDINGS INC., *pg.* 1170, *pg.* 1577
KRONOS INTERNATIONAL, INC., *pg.* 980, *pg.* 1683
KYOWA HAKKO U.S.A., INC., *pg.* 1554, *pg.* 1249
LA-CO INDUSTRIES MARKAL CO., INC., *pg.* 1170, *pg.* 610
LIPO CHEMICALS INC., *pg.* 1171, *pg.* 1107
L.M. SCOFIELD COMPANY, *pg.* 94, *pg.* 134
LONZA INC., *pg.* 1171, *pg.* 1041
THE LUBRIZOL CORPORATION, *pg.* 1171, *pg.* 1481
LUSTER-ON PRODUCTS, INC., *pg.* 1171, *pg.* 845
LYONDELLBASELL INDUSTRIES, *pg.* 980, *pg.* 1710
MACANDREWS & FORBES HOLDINGS INC., *pg.* 777, *pg.* 1254
MACDERMID, INC., *pg.* 1172, *pg.* 321
MCGEAN-ROHCO, INC., *pg.* 1172, *pg.* 1432
MCLAUGHLIN GORMLEY KING COMPANY, *pg.* 1797, *pg.* 939
MERICHEM COMPANY, *pg.* 1172, *pg.* 1711
MERISANT COMPANY, *pg.* 876, *pg.* 581
MGP INGREDIENTS, INC., *pg.* 877, *pg.* 714
MILLIKEN & COMPANY, *pg.* 696, *pg.* 1622
MORGAN ADVANCED MATERIALS, *pg.* 1363, *pg.* 835
MORGRO, INC., *pg.* 1798, *pg.* 1759
NALCO CO., *pg.* 1174, *pg.* 636
NATIONAL ENZYME COMPANY, *pg.* 882, *pg.* 978
NCH CORPORATION, *pg.* 1174, *pg.* 1723
NEVILLE CHEMICAL COMPANY, *pg.* 1174, *pg.* 1578
NEWMARKET CORPORATION, *pg.* 982, *pg.* 1803
NL INDUSTRIES, INC., *pg.* 1174, *pg.* 1684
NOAH TECHNOLOGIES CORPORATION, *pg.* 1175, *pg.* 1742
NOVA CHEMICALS CORPORATION, *pg.* 1175, *pg.* 1904
NUCO2 INC., *pg.* 1175, *pg.* 468
NUFARM AMERICAS INC, *pg.* 1798, *pg.* 552
THE NUTRASWEET COMPANY, *pg.* 1860, *pg.* 585
OCCIDENTAL CHEMICAL CORPORATION, *pg.* 1175, *pg.* 1685
OIL-DRI CORPORATION OF AMERICA, *pg.* 1480, *pg.* 586
OLD WORLD INDUSTRIES, INC., *pg.* 1175, *pg.* 641
OMNOVA SOLUTIONS INC, *pg.* 1176, *pg.* 1453
OXYSURE SYSTEMS, INC., *pg.* 1579, *pg.* 1697
P. KAY METAL SUPPLY INC., *pg.* 1176, *pg.* 137
PACIFIC ETHANOL, INC., *pg.* 982, *pg.* 197
PETROFERM INC., *pg.* 1177, *pg.* 616
PHARMCO-AAPER, *pg.* 1177, *pg.* 740
POWER SERVICE PRODUCTS, INC., *pg.* 983, *pg.* 1749
THE PROCTER & GAMBLE COMPANY, *pg.* 1129, *pg.* 1418
QUAKER CHEMICAL CORP., *pg.* 1178, *pg.* 1524
RADIATOR SPECIALTY COMPANY, *pg.* 215, *pg.* 1380
RENTECH, INC., *pg.* 1179, *pg.* 139
R.T. VANDERBILT COMPANY, INC., *pg.* 1180, *pg.* 364
RUST-OLEUM CORPORATION, *pg.* 1447, *pg.* 664
SACHEM INC., *pg.* 1180, *pg.* 1665
SASOL NORTH AMERICA INC., *pg.* 984, *pg.* 1713
SEYMOUR OF SYCAMORE, INC., *pg.* 1447, *pg.* 663
SI GROUP, INC., *pg.* 1181, *pg.* 1341
SIGMA-ALDRICH CORPORATION, *pg.* 1181, *pg.* 1881
SIGMA-ALDRICH CORPORATION, *pg.* 1181, *pg.* 1003
SPECTRUM CHEMICALS & LABORATORY PRODUCTS, INC., *pg.* 1181, *pg.* 94
SPURRIER CHEMICAL COMPANIES, INC., *pg.* 1182, *pg.* 724
STANCHEM, INC., *pg.* 1449, *pg.* 345
STEPAN COMPANY, *pg.* 1182, *pg.* 643
SUNOCO CHEMICALS, *pg.* 1182, *pg.* 1570
SYMRISE, INC., *pg.* 1183, *pg.* 1125
TECHNIC INCORPORATED, *pg.* 1183, *pg.* 1601
TEXTILE RUBBER & CHEMICAL COMPANY, *pg.* 1890, *pg.* 530
TOTAL PETROCHEMICALS USA, INC., *pg.* 1184, *pg.* 1716
TROY CORPORATION, *pg.* 1184, *pg.* 1067
UNITED-GUARDIAN, INC., *pg.* 1184, *pg.* 1165
VALENT U.S.A. CORP., *pg.* 708, *pg.* 305
VALHI, INC., *pg.* 1185, *pg.* 1690
THE VALSPAR CORPORATION, *pg.* 1449, *pg.* 945
VERTELLUS SPECIALTIES INC., *pg.* 1185, *pg.* 690
WD-40 COMPANY, *pg.* 337, *pg.* 210
WEIMAN PRODUCTS, LLC, *pg.* 337, *pg.* 616
WILLERT HOME PRODUCTS, INC., *pg.* 1140, *pg.* 1005
WISCONSIN PHARMACAL COMPANY, LLC, *pg.* 1610, *pg.* 1861
W.R. GRACE & CO., *pg.* 123, *pg.* 810
WYNN OIL COMPANY, *pg.* 987, *pg.* 173
ZEP INC., *pg.* 338, *pg.* 524

2873 - Nitrogenous Fertilizers

MILLER CHEMICAL & FERTILIZER CORPORATION, *pg.* 706, *pg.* 1535
MORGRO, INC., *pg.* 1798, *pg.* 1759
PLANTABBS PRODUCTS COMPANY, *pg.* 1799, *pg.* 758
POTASHCORP, *pg.* 1799, *pg.* 641
THE SCOTTS MIRACLE-GRO COMPANY, *pg.* 1799, *pg.* 1459

2874 - Phosphatic Fertilizers

J.R. SIMPLOT COMPANY, AGRI BUSINESS, *pg.* 1796, *pg.* 547
PLANTABBS PRODUCTS COMPANY, *pg.* 1799, *pg.* 758
POTASH CORP., *pg.* 1177, *pg.* 641
POTASHCORP, *pg.* 1799, *pg.* 641
THE SCOTTS MIRACLE-GRO COMPANY, *pg.* 1799, *pg.* 1459
SIMPLOT PARTNERS INC., *pg.* 1800, *pg.* 548

2875 - Fertilizers, Mixing Only

LEBANON SEABOARD CORPORATION, *pg.* 1797, *pg.* 1547
MFA INCORPORATED, *pg.* 1479, *pg.* 976

2879 - Pesticides & Agricultural Chemicals, NEC

AMERICAN VANGUARD CORPORATION, *pg.* 1793, *pg.* 165
BASF, *pg.* 1793, *pg.* 992
BAYER CORPORATION, *pg.* 1499, *pg.* 1573
BAYER CROPSCIENCE, *pg.* 1149, *pg.* 981
BIOSAFE SYSTEMS, LLC, *pg.* 1149, *pg.* 345
BONIDE PRODUCTS, INC., *pg.* 1794, *pg.* 1320
COPPER-BRITE, INC., *pg.* 329, *pg.* 263
DOW AGROSCIENCES LLC, *pg.* 1156, *pg.* 684
THE DOW CHEMICAL COMPANY, *pg.* 1157, *pg.* 898
ECOLAB INC., *pg.* 329, *pg.* 960
E.I. DU PONT DE NEMOURS & COMPANY, *pg.* 1159, *pg.* 390
FMC CORPORATION, *pg.* 1163, *pg.* 1564
KALO, INC., *pg.* 1796, *pg.* 719
MCLAUGHLIN GORMLEY KING COMPANY, *pg.* 1797, *pg.* 939
MILLER CHEMICAL & FERTILIZER CORPORATION, *pg.* 706, *pg.* 1535
MONSANTO COMPANY, *pg.* 1173, *pg.* 999
NUFARM AMERICAS INC, *pg.* 1798, *pg.* 552
PBI/GORDON CORPORATION, *pg.* 1176, *pg.* 985
SENORET CHEMICAL COMPANY, *pg.* 335, *pg.* 1548
SMITHEREEN PEST MANAGEMENT SERVICES, *pg.* 1800, *pg.* 638
SOUTHERN AGRICULTURAL INSECTICIDES, INC., *pg.* 1181, *pg.* 458
SYNGENTA PROFESSIONAL PRODUCTS, *pg.* 1183, *pg.* 1376
WD-40 COMPANY, *pg.* 337, *pg.* 210
WILLERT HOME PRODUCTS, INC., *pg.* 1140, *pg.* 1005
WILT-PRUF PRODUCTS, INC., *pg.* 1801, *pg.* 346
WISCONSIN PHARMACAL COMPANY, LLC, *pg.* 1610, *pg.* 1861
ZEP INC., *pg.* 338, *pg.* 524

2891 - Adhesives & Sealants

3M COMPANY, *pg.* 1142, *pg.* 956
ASHLAND PERFORMANCE MATERIALS, *pg.* 1147, *pg.* 1448
ATLAS MINERALS & CHEMICALS, INC., *pg.* 69, *pg.* 1552
AVERY DENNISON CORPORATION, *pg.* 1452, *pg.* 95
BOSTIK INC., *pg.* 1150, *pg.* 1899
BOSTIK INC., *pg.* 1150, *pg.* 833
CHEMTURA CORPORATION, *pg.* 1152, *pg.* 355
DAP PRODUCTS, INC., *pg.* 1441, *pg.* 756
DAUBERT INDUSTRIES, INC., *pg.* 1155, *pg.* 561
THE DOW CHEMICAL COMPANY, *pg.* 1157, *pg.* 898
ELMER'S PRODUCTS, INC., *pg.* 1442, *pg.* 1479
THE EUCLID CHEMICAL COMPANY, *pg.* 81, *pg.* 1430
EVANS ADHESIVE CORPORATION, LTD., *pg.* 1161, *pg.* 1440
THE FLAMEMASTER CORPORATION, *pg.* 1162, *pg.* 174
FLEXCON CORPORATION, *pg.* 1457, *pg.* 844
GENOVA PRODUCTS, INC., *pg.* 83, *pg.* 875
GLUEFAST COMPANY, INC., *pg.* 1459, *pg.* 1090
HAR ADHESIVE TECHNOLOGIES, *pg.* 1442, *pg.* 1405
H.B. FULLER COMPANY, *pg.* 1165, *pg.* 961
HELLERMANNTYTON, *pg.* 642, *pg.* 1875
HENKEL CORPORATION, *pg.* 1049, *pg.* 369
ITW DYNATEC, *pg.* 1351, *pg.* 1635
LA-CO INDUSTRIES MARKAL CO., INC., *pg.* 1170, *pg.* 610
LAPOLLA INDUSTRIES, INC., *pg.* 1444, *pg.* 1710

LORD CORPORATION, pg. 1357, pg. 1360
MASTER BOND INC., pg. 1172, pg. 1072
MASTERCHEM INDUSTRIES, LLC, pg. 1444, pg. 979
MITSUBISHI RAYON CARBON FIBER AND COMPOSITES, INC.,, pg. 1173, pg. 113
NUSIL TECHNOLOGY LLC, pg. 1887, pg. 63
PARKER CHOMERICS, pg. 662, pg. 862
PECORA CORPORATION, pg. 1444, pg. 1536
PETTIT PAINT COMPANY, pg. 1444, pg. 1116
PPG AEROSPACE DEFT FACILITY, pg. 1445, pg. 115
ROYAL ADHESIVES & SEALANTS LLC, pg. 1179, pg. 697
RPM INTERNATIONAL INC., pg. 1447, pg. 1464
SIKA CORPORATION, pg. 110, pg. 1080
SUPER GLUE CORPORATION, pg. 1183, pg. 187
SURMODICS, INC., pg. 1600, pg. 924
THE TESTOR CORPORATION, pg. 968, pg. 655
TEXTILE RUBBER & CHEMICAL COMPANY, pg. 1890, pg. 530
TREMCO INCORPORATED, pg. 116, pg. 1405
TYCO INTERNATIONAL (US) INC., pg. 1891, pg. 1113
UNITED GILSONITE LABORATORIES, pg. 1449, pg. 1527
WHITFORD WORLDWIDE COMPANY, pg. 1185, pg. 1529
W.J. RUSCOE COMPANY, pg. 122, pg. 1403
ZEP INC., pg. 338, pg. 524

2892 - Explosives

AUSTIN POWDER COMPANY, pg. 1148, pg. 1428
BLASTGARD INTERNATIONAL INC., pg. 1150, pg. 415

2893 - Printing Ink

COLOR IMAGING INC., pg. 1407, pg. 536
FLINT GROUP, INC., pg. 1163, pg. 904
HEWLETT-PACKARD COMPANY, pg. 404, pg. 175
INX INTERNATIONAL INK CO., pg. 421, pg. 658
LIQUIDMETAL TECHNOLOGIES, INC., pg. 1356, pg. 188
SUN CHEMICAL INK, pg. 1182, pg. 643

2895 - Carbon Black

ALTAIR NANOTECHNOLOGIES INC., pg. 1147, pg. 1031
AMERICAN CHEMET CORPORATION, pg. 1147, pg. 599
BASF CATALYSTS LLC, pg. 1148, pg. 1074
CABOT CORPORATION, pg. 1151, pg. 792
CERAMIC COLOR & CHEMICAL MFG. CO., pg. 1441, pg. 1555
DAY-GLO COLOR CORP., pg. 1441, pg. 1429
DETREX CORPORATION, pg. 1156, pg. 906
FMC LITHIUM DIVISION, pg. 1163, pg. 1366
HUNTSMAN CORPORATION, pg. 1167, pg. 1758
KOPPERS HOLDINGS INC., pg. 1170, pg. 1577
KRONOS WORLDWIDE, INC., pg. 980, pg. 1053
L.M. SCOFIELD COMPANY, pg. 94, pg. 134
MASTER SILICON CARBIDE INDUSTRIES, INC., pg. 1172, pg. 353
NL INDUSTRIES, INC., pg. 1174, pg. 1684
SILBERLINE MANUFACTURING CO., INC., pg. 110, pg. 1588
TETRA TECHNOLOGIES, INC., pg. 986, pg. 1747
TOR MINERALS INTERNATIONAL INC., pg. 1184, pg. 1672
VALHI, INC., pg. 1185, pg. 1690
THE VALSPAR CORPORATION, pg. 1449, pg. 945

2899 - Chemicals & Chemical Preparations, NEC

3M COMPANY, pg. 1142, pg. 956
ABBOTT LABORATORIES, pg. 1484, pg. 551
ABENGOA BIOENERGY CORP., pg. 971, pg. 974
ACETO CORPORATION, pg. 1145, pg. 1323
ACME STAPLE COMPANY, INC., pg. 341, pg. 1034
AIR PRODUCTS AND CHEMICALS, INC., pg. 1145, pg. 1513
AIRGAS, INC., pg. 1146, pg. 1583
AKZO NOBEL INC., pg. 1146, pg. 563
ALTAIR NANOTECHNOLOGIES INC., pg. 1147, pg. 1031
AMERICAN CHEMET CORPORATION, pg. 1147, pg. 599
AMERICAN MOLD REMOVAL, INC., pg. 1393, pg. 436
ANACHEMIA CANADA, INC., pg. 1147, pg. 1951
ANDERSON DEVELOPMENT COMPANY, pg. 1147, pg. 864
ANGUS CHEMICAL COMPANY, pg. 1147, pg. 560
APYRON TECHNOLOGIES, INC., pg. 1495, pg. 488
ARKEMA INC., pg. 1147, pg. 1543
AROMALAND INC., pg. 499, pg. 1135
ASHLAND INC., pg. 972, pg. 726
ASHLAND PERFORMANCE MATERIALS, pg. 1147, pg. 1448
ATLAS REFINERY, INC., pg. 1148, pg. 1095
ATMI, INC., pg. 1314, pg. 342
AVANTOR PERFORMANCE MATERIALS, INC., pg. 1148, pg. 1521
AVERY DENNISON CORPORATION, pg. 1452, pg. 95
BADGER AIR BRUSH COMPANY, pg. 359, pg. 612
BAKER HUGHES INCORPORATED, pg. 1315, pg. 1700
BAKER PETROLITE CORPORATION, pg. 1148, pg. 1745
BALCHEM CORPORATION, pg. 839, pg. 1183
BASF CATALYSTS LLC, pg. 1148, pg. 1074
BELL FLAVORS & FRAGRANCES, INC., pg. 501, pg. 640
BG PRODUCTS, INC., pg. 200, pg. 722
BIC CORPORATION, pg. 501, pg. 369
BIO-RAD LABORATORIES, INC., pg. 1504, pg. 101
BIOSAFE SYSTEMS, LLC, pg. 1149, pg. 345
BIRKO CORPORATION, pg. 1149, pg. 332
BISSELL HOMECARE, INC., pg. 52, pg. 887
BOEHRINGER INGELHEIM PHARMACEUTICALS, INC., pg. 1507, pg. 368
BONIDE PRODUCTS, INC., pg. 1794, pg. 1320
BOULDER SCIENTIFIC COMPANY, pg. 1150, pg. 335
BROOKTRONICS ENGINEERING CORPORATION, pg. 1320, pg. 299
BUCKMAN, pg. 1150, pg. 1641
BURGESS PIGMENT COMPANY, pg. 1150, pg. 535
CALGON CARBON CORPORATION, pg. 1151, pg. 1574
CARGILL, INC., pg. 845, pg. 965
CARUS CORPORATION, pg. 1152, pg. 652
CERAMIC COLOR & CHEMICAL MFG. CO., pg. 1441, pg. 1555
CHEM-TREND LIMITED PARTNERSHIP, pg. 973, pg. 892
CHEMTURA CORPORATION, pg. 1152, pg. 355
CHURCH & DWIGHT CO., INC., pg. 1153, pg. 1063
CLARIANT CORPORATION, pg. 1153, pg. 1365
CODEXIS, INC., pg. 1154, pg. 189
COMPASS MINERALS INTERNATIONAL, INC., pg. 1154, pg. 718
COMPLEX CHEMICALS COMPANY, INC., pg. 974, pg. 748
CRAYOLA CANADA, pg. 951, pg. 1922
CRAYOLA LLC, pg. 951, pg. 1528
CUMBERLAND PACKING CORP., pg. 851, pg. 1146
CYTEC INDUSTRIES, INC., pg. 1155, pg. 1131
DAVID MICHAEL & CO. INC., pg. 852, pg. 1563
DEEPWATER CHEMICALS, INC., pg. 1155, pg. 1491
DETREX CORPORATION, pg. 1156, pg. 906
DIXON TICONDEROGA COMPANY, pg. 388, pg. 430
DOBER CHEMICAL CORP., pg. 1156, pg. 671
DOVER CHEMICAL CORPORATION, pg. 1156, pg. 1447
DOW CHEMICAL, pg. 1156, pg. 1563
THE DOW CHEMICAL COMPANY, pg. 1157, pg. 898
DOW CORNING CORPORATION, pg. 1159, pg. 900
DRIVESAVERS DATA RECOVERY, INC., pg. 388, pg. 168
EASTMAN CHEMICAL COMPANY, pg. 1159, pg. 1636
E.I. DU PONT DE NEMOURS & COMPANY, pg. 1159, pg. 390
EMERALD PERFORMANCE MATERIALS, LLC, pg. 1161, pg. 1445
ENERGIZER HOLDINGS, INC., pg. 637, pg. 996
ENGLOBAL CORPORATION, pg. 81, pg. 1705
ENTHONE INC., pg. 1161, pg. 381
EUREKA CHEMICAL COMPANY, pg. 1161, pg. 279
EVONIK CORPORATION, pg. 1162, pg. 1103
EXXON MOBIL CORPORATION, pg. 977, pg. 1718
FIRMENICH INCORPORATED, pg. 509, pg. 1109
THE FLAMEMASTER CORPORATION, pg. 1162, pg. 174
FLEXIBLE SOLUTIONS INTERNATIONAL, INC., pg. 1163, pg. 1913
FMC CORPORATION, pg. 1163, pg. 1564
FMC LITHIUM DIVISION, pg. 1163, pg. 1366
FRAGRANCE RESOURCES, INC., pg. 509, pg. 1052
GAGE PRODUCTS COMPANY, pg. 1164, pg. 886
GEORGIA-PACIFIC LLC, pg. 1458, pg. 507
GFS CHEMICALS, INC., pg. 1164, pg. 1471
GRAIN PROCESSING CORPORATION, pg. 859, pg. 709
HALOCARBON PRODUCTS CORPORATION, pg. 978, pg. 1116
HEADWATERS INCORPORATED, pg. 978, pg. 1763
HEATBATH CORPORATION, pg. 1165, pg. 826
HENKEL CORPORATION, pg. 1166, pg. 897
HENKEL CORPORATION, pg. 1165, pg. 1535
HERCULES INCORPORATED, pg. 1166, pg. 392
HEXION, pg. 1166, pg. 1440
HONEYWELL CONSUMER PRODUCTS GROUP, pg. 208, pg. 344
HOUGHTON INTERNATIONAL INC., pg. 1167, pg. 1589
HUNTSMAN CORPORATION, pg. 1167, pg. 1758
IMPERIAL OIL LIMITED, pg. 979, pg. 1903
INOLEX GROUP INC., pg. 1168, pg. 1566
INTERNATIONAL FLAVORS & FRAGRANCES INC., pg. 512, pg. 1244
JARCHEM INDUSTRIES, INC., pg. 1169, pg. 1096
JBI, INC., pg. 293, pg. 1317
J.M. HUBER CORPORATION, pg. 1169, pg. 1056
JOHNSON MANUFACTURING COMPANY, pg. 1169, pg. 712
JOHNSON MATTHEY PROCESS TECHNOLOGIES, pg. 1169, pg. 1083
JONES-HAMILTON CO., pg. 1169, pg. 1478
KAISER ALUMINUM CORPORATION, pg. 90, pg. 86
KIDDE FIRE FIGHTING, pg. 1170, pg. 1531
KILGORE FLARES, pg. 1170, pg. 1656
KING INDUSTRIES, INC., pg. 1443, pg. 363
KOCH INDUSTRIES, INC., pg. 1463, pg. 724
KOPPERS HOLDINGS INC., pg. 1170, pg. 1577
KRONOS INTERNATIONAL, INC., pg. 980, pg. 1683
KYOWA HAKKO U.S.A., INC., pg. 1554, pg. 1249
LA-CO INDUSTRIES MARKAL CO., INC., pg. 1170, pg. 610
LANDEC CORPORATION, pg. 1419, pg. 145
LIPO CHEMICALS INC., pg. 1171, pg. 1107
L.M. SCOFIELD COMPANY, pg. 94, pg. 134
LOCKHART COMPANY, pg. 1171, pg. 1534
LONZA INC., pg. 1171, pg. 1041
THE LUBRIZOL CORPORATION, pg. 1171, pg. 1481
LUSTER-ON PRODUCTS, INC., pg. 1171, pg. 845
LYONDELLBASELL INDUSTRIES, pg. 980, pg. 1710
MACANDREWS & FORBES HOLDINGS INC., pg. 777, pg. 1254
MACDERMID, INC., pg. 1172, pg. 321
MARTIN/F. WEBER COMPANY, pg. 962, pg. 1567
MATERION ADVANCED CHEMICALS, pg. 1172, pg. 1877
MCGEAN-ROHCO, INC., pg. 1172, pg. 1432
MCLAUGHLIN GORMLEY KING COMPANY, pg. 1797, pg. 939
MERICHEM COMPANY, pg. 1172, pg. 1711
MERISANT COMPANY, pg. 876, pg. 581
MGP INGREDIENTS, INC., pg. 877, pg. 714
MILLIKEN & COMPANY, pg. 696, pg. 1622
MORGAN ADVANCED MATERIALS, pg. 1363, pg. 835
MORGRO, INC., pg. 1798, pg. 1759
MULTI-METALS, pg. 1363, pg. 737
MULTISORB TECHNOLOGIES, INC., pg. 1570, pg. 1150
NALCO CO., pg. 1174, pg. 636
NATIONAL ENZYME COMPANY, pg. 882, pg. 978
NCH CORPORATION, pg. 1174, pg. 1723
NEOPOST CANADA LIMITED, pg. 1364, pg. 1924
NEVILLE CHEMICAL COMPANY, pg. 1174, pg. 1578
NEWMARKET CORPORATION, pg. 982, pg. 1803
NL INDUSTRIES, INC., pg. 1174, pg. 1684
NOAH TECHNOLOGIES CORPORATION, pg. 1175, pg. 1742
NOVA CHEMICALS CORPORATION, pg. 1175, pg. 1904
NUCO2 INC., pg. 1175, pg. 468
NUFARM AMERICAS INC, pg. 1798, pg. 552
THE NUTRASWEET COMPANY, pg. 1860, pg. 585
OCCIDENTAL CHEMICAL CORPORATION, pg. 1175, pg. 1685
OCCIDENTAL PETROLEUM CORPORATION, pg. 1175, pg. 137
OIL-DRI CORPORATION OF AMERICA, pg. 1480, pg. 586
OLD WORLD INDUSTRIES, INC., pg. 1175, pg. 641
OMNOVA SOLUTIONS INC, pg. 1176, pg. 1453
OXYSURE SYSTEMS, INC., pg. 1579, pg. 1697
P. KAY METAL SUPPLY INC., pg. 1176, pg. 137
PAASCHE AIRBRUSH COMPANY, pg. 1444, pg. 587
PACIFIC ETHANOL, INC., pg. 982, pg. 197
PAR TECHNOLOGY CORPORATION, pg. 452, pg. 1183
PEACE INDUSTRIES INC., pg. 1368, pg. 656
PETROFERM INC., pg. 1177, pg. 616
PHARMCO-AAPER, pg. 1177, pg. 740
PITNEY BOWES INC., pg. 454, pg. 376
POWER SERVICE PRODUCTS, INC., pg. 983, pg. 1749
PQ CORPORATION, pg. 1178, pg. 1515
PRESSTEK, INC., pg. 456, pg. 606
THE PROCTER & GAMBLE COMPANY, pg. 1129, pg. 1418
QUAKER CHEMICAL CORP., pg. 1178, pg. 1524

First page reference indicates Business Class Edition
Second page reference indicates Geographic Edition

RADIATOR SPECIALTY COMPANY, *pg.* 215, *pg.* 1380
RENTECH, INC., *pg.* 1179, *pg.* 139
RHODIA INC., *pg.* 1179, *pg.* 1053
RIO TINTO BORAX, *pg.* 334, *pg.* 331
R.T. VANDERBILT COMPANY, INC., *pg.* 1180, *pg.* 364
RUST-OLEUM CORPORATION, *pg.* 1447, *pg.* 664
SACHEM INC., *pg.* 1180, *pg.* 1665
SASOL NORTH AMERICA INC., *pg.* 984, *pg.* 1713
SEYMOUR OF SYCAMORE, INC., *pg.* 1447, *pg.* 663
SI GROUP, INC., *pg.* 1181, *pg.* 1341
SIGMA-ALDRICH CORPORATION, *pg.* 1181, *pg.* 1881
SIGMA-ALDRICH CORPORATION, *pg.* 1181, *pg.* 1003
SILBERLINE MANUFACTURING CO., INC., *pg.* 110, *pg.* 1588
SPECTRUM CHEMICALS & LABORATORY PRODUCTS, INC., *pg.* 1181, *pg.* 94
SPURRIER CHEMICAL COMPANIES, INC., *pg.* 1182, *pg.* 724
STANCHEM, INC., *pg.* 1449, *pg.* 345
THE STAPLEX COMPANY, INC., *pg.* 474, *pg.* 1146
STEPAN COMPANY, *pg.* 1182, *pg.* 643
SUNOCO CHEMICALS, *pg.* 1182, *pg.* 1570
SYMRISE, INC., *pg.* 1183, *pg.* 1125
TECHNIC INCORPORATED, *pg.* 1183, *pg.* 1601
TETRA TECHNOLOGIES, INC., *pg.* 986, *pg.* 1747
TEXTILE RUBBER & CHEMICAL COMPANY, *pg.* 1890, *pg.* 530
TOTAL PETROCHEMICALS USA, INC., *pg.* 1184, *pg.* 1716
TROY CORPORATION, *pg.* 1184, *pg.* 1067
UNITED-GUARDIAN, INC., *pg.* 1184, *pg.* 1165
UOP LLC, *pg.* 1386, *pg.* 606
VALENT U.S.A. CORP., *pg.* 708, *pg.* 305
VALHI, INC., *pg.* 1185, *pg.* 1690
VELSICOL CHEMICAL CORPORATION, *pg.* 1185, *pg.* 657
VERTELLUS SPECIALTIES INC., *pg.* 1185, *pg.* 690
WD-40 COMPANY, *pg.* 337, *pg.* 210
WEIMAN PRODUCTS, LLC, *pg.* 337, *pg.* 616
WESTROCK COMPANY, *pg.* 1472, *pg.* 1805
WILLERT HOME PRODUCTS, INC., *pg.* 1140, *pg.* 1005
WISCONSIN PHARMACAL COMPANY, LLC, *pg.* 1610, *pg.* 1861
W.R. GRACE & CO., *pg.* 123, *pg.* 810
WYNN OIL COMPANY, *pg.* 987, *pg.* 173
ZEP INC., *pg.* 338, *pg.* 524

2911 - Petroleum Refining

ALON USA ENERGY, INC., *pg.* 971, *pg.* 1673
ASHLAND INC., *pg.* 972, *pg.* 726
BARDAHL MANUFACTURING CORPORATION, *pg.* 972, *pg.* 1833
CHEVRON CORPORATION, *pg.* 974, *pg.* 259
CITGO PETROLEUM CORPORATION, *pg.* 974, *pg.* 1703
CONOCOPHILLIPS, *pg.* 975, *pg.* 1703
CROWN CENTRAL LLC, *pg.* 975, *pg.* 756
ERGON, INC., *pg.* 976, *pg.* 969
EXXON MOBIL CORPORATION, *pg.* 977, *pg.* 1718
FJ MANAGEMENT, INC., *pg.* 978, *pg.* 1758
HESS CORPORATION, *pg.* 979, *pg.* 1240
HUNT REFINING COMPANY INC., *pg.* 979, *pg.* 8
IMPERIAL OIL LIMITED, *pg.* 979, *pg.* 1903
KOCH INDUSTRIES, INC., *pg.* 1463, *pg.* 724
LIQUIDMETAL TECHNOLOGIES, INC., *pg.* 1356, *pg.* 188
MARATHON OIL CORPORATION, *pg.* 981, *pg.* 1710
MARATHON PETROLEUM COMPANY LLC, *pg.* 981, *pg.* 1454
MURPHY OIL CORPORATION, *pg.* 982, *pg.* 31
NEWFIELD EXPLORATION COMPANY, *pg.* 45, *pg.* 1747
POWER SERVICE PRODUCTS, INC., *pg.* 983, *pg.* 1749
SINCLAIR OIL CORPORATION, *pg.* 984, *pg.* 1760
SUNCOR ENERGY INC., *pg.* 985, *pg.* 1905
SUNOCO INC., *pg.* 985, *pg.* 1571
TERVITA CORPORATION, *pg.* 986, *pg.* 1905
UNITED REFINING COMPANY, *pg.* 986, *pg.* 1590
VALERO ENERGY CORPORATION, *pg.* 986, *pg.* 1743
WD-40 COMPANY, *pg.* 337, *pg.* 210

2951 - Asphalt Paving Mixtures & Blocks

ERGON, INC., *pg.* 976, *pg.* 969
MITSUBISHI RAYON CARBON FIBER AND COMPOSITES, INC.,, *pg.* 1173, *pg.* 113
SYAR INDUSTRIES, INC., *pg.* 114, *pg.* 163

2952 - Asphalt Felts & Coatings

ATLAS MINERALS & CHEMICALS, INC., *pg.* 69, *pg.* 1552
BUILDING MATERIALS CORPORATION OF AMERICA, *pg.* 72, *pg.* 1129
BUILDING PRODUCTS OF CANADA CORP., *pg.* 72, *pg.* 1951
GAF MATERIALS CORP., *pg.* 83, *pg.* 1681
JOHNS MANVILLE CORPORATION, *pg.* 89, *pg.* 320
OWENS CORNING, *pg.* 102, *pg.* 1476
RED SPOT PAINT & VARNISH CO., INC., *pg.* 1446, *pg.* 679
REVERE PRODUCTS, *pg.* 107, *pg.* 1435
TEXAS REFINERY CORP., *pg.* 986, *pg.* 1696
TREMCO INCORPORATED, *pg.* 116, *pg.* 1405

2992 - Lubricating Oils & Greases

AERVOE INDUSTRIES INCORPORATED, *pg.* 1439, *pg.* 1021
AMERICAN GREASE STICK CO., *pg.* 971, *pg.* 902
AMSOIL INC., *pg.* 971, *pg.* 1896
ASHLAND INC., *pg.* 972, *pg.* 726
AXEL PLASTICS RESEARCH LABORATORIES, INC., *pg.* 326, *pg.* 1356
BARDAHL MANUFACTURING CORPORATION, *pg.* 972, *pg.* 1833
BEL-RAY COMPANY, INC., *pg.* 972, *pg.* 1128
BG PRODUCTS, INC., *pg.* 200, *pg.* 722
CASTROL NORTH AMERICA INC., *pg.* 973, *pg.* 1129
CHEM-TREND LIMITED PARTNERSHIP, *pg.* 973, *pg.* 892
CITGO PETROLEUM CORPORATION, *pg.* 974, *pg.* 1703
COMPLEX CHEMICALS COMPANY, INC., *pg.* 974, *pg.* 748
CRC INDUSTRIES, INC., *pg.* 329, *pg.* 1590
D-A LUBRICANT COMPANY, *pg.* 975, *pg.* 693
DETREX CORPORATION, *pg.* 1156, *pg.* 906
EXXON MOBIL CORPORATION, *pg.* 977, *pg.* 1718
FISKE BROTHERS REFINING COMPANY, *pg.* 978, *pg.* 1096
GOLD EAGLE COMPANY, *pg.* 206, *pg.* 575
HESS CORPORATION, *pg.* 979, *pg.* 1240
HOUGHTON INTERNATIONAL INC., *pg.* 1167, *pg.* 1589
HYDROTEX PARTNERS LTD., *pg.* 979, *pg.* 1602
JIG-A-WORLD, *pg.* 980, *pg.* 1951
LUBRIPLATE LUBRICANTS, *pg.* 980, *pg.* 1097
M-I SWACO, *pg.* 980, *pg.* 1710
MAINTENANCE, INC., *pg.* 95, *pg.* 1482
NALCO CO., *pg.* 1174, *pg.* 636
OLD WORLD INDUSTRIES, INC., *pg.* 1175, *pg.* 641
PENETONE CORPORATION, *pg.* 333, *pg.* 1050
ROCK VALLEY OIL & CHEMICAL COMPANY, *pg.* 1179, *pg.* 631
SHELL LUBRICANTS, *pg.* 217, *pg.* 1714
SLIDE PRODUCTS, INC., *pg.* 1181, *pg.* 670
STONER INC., *pg.* 985, *pg.* 1583
TEXAS REFINERY CORP., *pg.* 986, *pg.* 1696
TROY CORPORATION, *pg.* 1184, *pg.* 1067
WD-40 COMPANY, *pg.* 337, *pg.* 210
WYNN OIL COMPANY, *pg.* 987, *pg.* 173
ZEP INC., *pg.* 338, *pg.* 524

2999 - Products of Petroleum & Coal, NEC

A&A GLOBAL INDUSTRIES INC., *pg.* 948, *pg.* 767
A. FINKL & SONS CO., *pg.* 1309, *pg.* 563
ABBOTT BALL COMPANY, *pg.* 1040, *pg.* 383
AK STEEL HOLDING CORPORATION, *pg.* 1311, *pg.* 1479
ALLEGHENY TECHNOLOGIES INCORPORATED, *pg.* 66, *pg.* 1572
ANCHOR DANLY, *pg.* 67, *pg.* 1948
ARCELORMITTAL DOFASCO INC., *pg.* 68, *pg.* 1921
ARCELORMITTAL STEEL USA INC., *pg.* 68, *pg.* 564
ARCH COAL, INC., *pg.* 68, *pg.* 992
ASHLAND INC., *pg.* 972, *pg.* 726
CANADA FORGINGS INC., *pg.* 1321, *pg.* 1948
CARPENTER TECHNOLOGY CORPORATION, *pg.* 73, *pg.* 1584
CITIZENS ENERGY GROUP, *pg.* 1937, *pg.* 683
COMMERCIAL METALS COMPANY, *pg.* 76, *pg.* 1718
ELLWOOD CITY FORGE, *pg.* 1333, *pg.* 1529
ESSAR STEEL ALGOMA INC., *pg.* 81, *pg.* 1933
EXXON MOBIL CORPORATION, *pg.* 977, *pg.* 1718
GERDAU AMERISTEEL JOLIET STEEL MILL, *pg.* 1048, *pg.* 621
GERDAU AMERISTEEL SAND SPRINGS STEEL MILL, *pg.* 1048, *pg.* 1488
GIBRALTAR INDUSTRIES, INC., *pg.* 1340, *pg.* 1148
HANDY & HARMAN LTD., *pg.* 85, *pg.* 1352
HEADWATERS INCORPORATED, *pg.* 978, *pg.* 1763
ITW FLUIDS NORTH AMERICA, *pg.* 980, *pg.* 614
KEYSTONE CONSOLIDATED INDUSTRIES, INC., *pg.* 90, *pg.* 1683
KEYSTONE STEEL & WIRE CO., *pg.* 91, *pg.* 651
KOCH INDUSTRIES, INC., *pg.* 1463, *pg.* 724
NEWMARKET CORPORATION, *pg.* 982, *pg.* 1803
NUCOR CORPORATION, *pg.* 101, *pg.* 1368
SHELL OIL COMPANY, *pg.* 984, *pg.* 1714
STEEL DYNAMICS, INC., *pg.* 113, *pg.* 681
WALTER ENERGY, INC., *pg.* 120, *pg.* 4
WORTHINGTON INDUSTRIES, INC., *pg.* 123, *pg.* 1444
XTEK, INC., *pg.* 1390, *pg.* 1427

3011 - Tires & Inner Tubes

AMERITYRE CORPORATION, *pg.* 1879, *pg.* 1021
BRIDGESTONE AMERICAS, INC., *pg.* 1879, *pg.* 1648
BRIDGESTONE AMERICAS, INC., *pg.* 201, *pg.* 1649
CARLISLE TIRE & WHEEL COMPANY, *pg.* 1880, *pg.* 1612
CONTINENTAL GENERAL TIRE INC., *pg.* 1880, *pg.* 1925
CONTINENTAL TIRE NORTH AMERICA, INC., *pg.* 1880, *pg.* 1615
COOPER TIRE & RUBBER COMPANY, *pg.* 1881, *pg.* 1453
THE GOODYEAR TIRE & RUBBER COMPANY, *pg.* 1883, *pg.* 1401
THE HERCULES TIRE & RUBBER COMPANY, *pg.* 1884, *pg.* 1454
MICHELIN AMERICAS SMALL TIRES (MAST), *pg.* 1886, *pg.* 1618
MICHELIN NORTH AMERICA INC., *pg.* 1886, *pg.* 1618
PIRELLI TIRE NORTH AMERICA, *pg.* 1887, *pg.* 539
TITAN INTERNATIONAL, INC., *pg.* 219, *pg.* 653
YOKOHAMA TIRE CORPORATION, *pg.* 1892, *pg.* 94

3021 - Rubber & Plastics Footwear

THE BILTRITE CORPORATION, *pg.* 1879, *pg.* 850
BROOKS SPORTS INC., *pg.* 1805, *pg.* 1818
CALERES, INC., *pg.* 1805, *pg.* 993
CROCS, INC., *pg.* 1806, *pg.* 335
DECKERS OUTDOOR CORPORATION, *pg.* 1807, *pg.* 100
ENPRO INDUSTRIES, INC., *pg.* 1334, *pg.* 1366
ICONIX BRAND GROUP, INC., *pg.* 26, *pg.* 1243
K-SWISS, *pg.* 1837, *pg.* 306
KENNETH COLE PRODUCTIONS, INC., *pg.* 1810, *pg.* 1248
LACROSSE FOOTWEAR, INC., *pg.* 1811, *pg.* 1503
PHOENIX FOOTWEAR GROUP, INC., *pg.* 1815, *pg.* 60
PRINCIPLE PLASTICS, INC., *pg.* 1816, *pg.* 94
STEVEN MADDEN, LTD., *pg.* 1819, *pg.* 1176
WELLCO ENTERPRISES, INC., *pg.* 1822, *pg.* 1392

3052 - Rubber & Plastics Hose & Belting

AIRBOSS OF AMERICA CORP., *pg.* 1878, *pg.* 1929
CTP TRANSPORTATION PRODUCTS, *pg.* 203, *pg.* 1006
FLEXFAB HORIZONS INTERNATIONAL, LLC, *pg.* 1072, *pg.* 891
THE GATES CORPORATION, *pg.* 205, *pg.* 319
HBD INDUSTRIES, INC., *pg.* 207, *pg.* 1449
KIDDE FIRE FIGHTING, *pg.* 1170, *pg.* 1531
THE MERCER RUBBER COMPANY, *pg.* 1886, *pg.* 1165
SHINGLE BELTING COMPANY, *pg.* 1375, *pg.* 1544

3053 - Gaskets, Packing & Sealing Devices

AEROJET ROCKETDYNE HOLDINGS, INC., *pg.* 1145, *pg.* 186
A.W. CHESTERTON COMPANY, *pg.* 1315, *pg.* 861
BUCKEYE CORRUGATED INC., *pg.* 1454, *pg.* 1400
CHICAGO-WILCOX MFG. COMPANY, INC., *pg.* 202, *pg.* 661
DANA HOLDING CORPORATION, *pg.* 203, *pg.* 1461
ENPRO INDUSTRIES, INC., *pg.* 1334, *pg.* 1366
FEDERAL-MOGUL HOLDINGS CORPORATION, *pg.* 205,

pg. 907
THE FLEXITALLIC GROUP, *pg.* 1337, *pg.* 1691
FREUDENBERG-NOK, *pg.* 1882, *pg.* 904
GARLOCK SEALING TECHNOLOGIES, *pg.* 205, *pg.* 1320
GREENE, TWEED & CO., *pg.* 1344, *pg.* 1544
ILPEA INDUSTRIES, INC., *pg.* 1348, *pg.* 697
JASON INDUSTRIES, INC., *pg.* 208, *pg.* 1875
LAPOLLA INDUSTRIES, INC., *pg.* 1444, *pg.* 1710
LYDALL, INC., *pg.* 1357, *pg.* 354
PARKER CHOMERICS, *pg.* 662, *pg.* 862
SEALING DEVICES INC., *pg.* 1889, *pg.* 1173
SKF SEALING SOLUTIONS, *pg.* 217, *pg.* 610
SKF USA, *pg.* 217, *pg.* 1535
SURFACE COATINGS LLC, *pg.* 1470, *pg.* 1737
THE VIKING GROUP, *pg.* 119, *pg.* 891
WIKA INSTRUMENT CORPORATION, *pg.* 1437, *pg.* 534

3061 - Molded, Extruded & Lathe-Cut Rubber Goods

AEROJET ROCKETDYNE HOLDINGS, INC., *pg.* 1145, *pg.* 186
AVON RUBBER & PLASTICS INC., *pg.* 1879, *pg.* 874
COOPER-STANDARD AUTOMOTIVE INC., *pg.* 1880, *pg.* 903
THE D.S. BROWN COMPANY, *pg.* 79, *pg.* 1468
HONEYWELL SALISBURY ELECTRICAL SAFETY, *pg.* 1884, *pg.* 558
LAVELLE INDUSTRIES INC., *pg.* 1053, *pg.* 1856
MYERS INDUSTRIES, INC., *pg.* 1887, *pg.* 1402
OLIVER RUBBER COMPANY, *pg.* 1887, *pg.* 1358
R.C.A. RUBBER COMPANY, *pg.* 1888, *pg.* 1402
VERNAY LABORATORIES, INC., *pg.* 1891, *pg.* 1482

3069 - Fabricated Rubber Products, NEC

ACUSHNET COMPANY, *pg.* 1824, *pg.* 818
AEROJET ROCKETDYNE HOLDINGS, INC., *pg.* 1145, *pg.* 186
AMERICAN BILTRITE INC., *pg.* 1878, *pg.* 856
ANSELL, *pg.* 1495, *pg.* 1114
THE BILTRITE CORPORATION, *pg.* 1879, *pg.* 850
CHASE CORPORATION, *pg.* 1152, *pg.* 803
CHURCH & DWIGHT CO., INC., *pg.* 1153, *pg.* 1063
CONTINENTAL AMERICAN CORP., *pg.* 1880, *pg.* 723
COOPER-STANDARD AUTOMOTIVE INC., *pg.* 1880, *pg.* 903
COOPER TIRE & RUBBER COMPANY, *pg.* 1881, *pg.* 1453
CTI INDUSTRIES CORPORATION, *pg.* 1881, *pg.* 555
DARNELL-ROSE, *pg.* 1045, *pg.* 67
DOREL JUVENILE GROUP, INC., *pg.* 923, *pg.* 676
DURA UNDERCUSHIONS LTD., *pg.* 923, *pg.* 1954
FABREEKA INTERNATIONAL, INC., *pg.* 1882, *pg.* 847
HONEYWELL SALISBURY ELECTRICAL SAFETY, *pg.* 1884, *pg.* 558
HSM SOLUTIONS, *pg.* 1884, *pg.* 1378
INDUSTRIAL RUBBER PRODUCTS, INC., *pg.* 1349, *pg.* 926
KRACO ENTERPRISES, LLC, *pg.* 210, *pg.* 68
LAVELLE INDUSTRIES INC., *pg.* 1053, *pg.* 1856
MAPA PROFESSIONAL, *pg.* 1885, *pg.* 555
MAPLE CITY RUBBER COMPANY, *pg.* 962, *pg.* 1468
MARYLAND PLASTICS, INC., *pg.* 1885, *pg.* 769
THE MERCER RUBBER COMPANY, *pg.* 1886, *pg.* 1165
MUNCHKIN, INC., *pg.* 964, *pg.* 300
NUSIL TECHNOLOGY LLC, *pg.* 1887, *pg.* 63
OMNOVA SOLUTIONS INC, *pg.* 1176, *pg.* 1453
O'NEILL INC., *pg.* 1842, *pg.* 270
QUADION CORPORATION, *pg.* 1888, *pg.* 941
RADIATOR SPECIALTY COMPANY, *pg.* 215, *pg.* 1380
R.C.A. RUBBER COMPANY, *pg.* 1888, *pg.* 1402
REESE ENTERPRISES, INC., *pg.* 1888, *pg.* 955
SCHLEGEL SYSTEMS, INC., *pg.* 109, *pg.* 1337
TEKNOR APEX COMPANY, *pg.* 1889, *pg.* 1605
TEXTILE RUBBER & CHEMICAL COMPANY, *pg.* 1890, *pg.* 530
THERAPEDIC ASSOCIATES, INC., *pg.* 945, *pg.* 1112
TRICO PRODUCTS CORPORATION, *pg.* 220, *pg.* 905
VAIL RUBBER WORKS, INC., *pg.* 1891, *pg.* 906
VESTA INC., *pg.* 1435, *pg.* 1858
VICTUS, INC., *pg.* 1606, *pg.* 447
VYSTAR CORPORATION, *pg.* 1891, *pg.* 532
WEST PHARMACEUTICAL SERVICES, INC., *pg.* 1472, *pg.* 1532
XERIUM TECHNOLOGIES, INC., *pg.* 1703, *pg.* 1389

3081 - Unsupported Plastics Film & Sheet

ABNOTE NORTH AMERICA, *pg.* 1878, *pg.* 789
ACTON TECHNOLOGIES, INC., *pg.* 1145, *pg.* 1582
AEP INDUSTRIES INC., *pg.* 1878, *pg.* 1085
BEMIS COMPANY, INC., *pg.* 1453, *pg.* 1882
CABOT CORPORATION, *pg.* 1151, *pg.* 792
CONGOLEUM CORPORATION, *pg.* 921, *pg.* 1084
THE DOW CHEMICAL COMPANY, *pg.* 1157, *pg.* 898
DUNMORE CORPORATION, *pg.* 1456, *pg.* 1518
FLEX-O-GLASS, INC., *pg.* 1457, *pg.* 574
FLEXCON CORPORATION, *pg.* 1457, *pg.* 844
GSE LINING TECHNOLOGY, INC., *pg.* 1164, *pg.* 1706
JPS INDUSTRIES, INC., *pg.* 1169, *pg.* 1617
KLOCKNER PENTAPLAST OF AMERICA, INC., *pg.* 1885, *pg.* 1783
NEXUS PLASTICS, INC., *pg.* 1465, *pg.* 1073
PLASTIC SUPPLIERS, INC., *pg.* 1888, *pg.* 1443
PLY GEM SIDING GROUP, *pg.* 105, *pg.* 986
POLY PAK AMERICA, INC., *pg.* 1467, *pg.* 138
RAVEN INDUSTRIES, INC., *pg.* 1888, *pg.* 1625
SPORT COURT INTERNATIONAL INC., *pg.* 1846, *pg.* 1761
SUMMIT PLASTIC CO., *pg.* 1470, *pg.* 1403
TEKRA CORPORATION, *pg.* 1184, *pg.* 1884
TRANSILWRAP COMPANY, INC., *pg.* 1470, *pg.* 613
TRIENDA, LLC, *pg.* 1890, *pg.* 1887
VALERON STRENGTH FILMS, *pg.* 1891, *pg.* 1716
WARP BROTHERS, *pg.* 1471, *pg.* 595
WESTLAKE PLASTICS COMPANY, *pg.* 1892, *pg.* 1548

3082 - Unsupported Plastics Profile Shapes

AIRLITE PLASTICS COMPANY, *pg.* 1451, *pg.* 1013
ALLFLEX USA, INC., *pg.* 1878, *pg.* 1717
ALPHA PACKAGING, *pg.* 1451, *pg.* 990
AMERICAN BILTRITE INC., *pg.* 1878, *pg.* 856
AMERICAN CASTING & MANUFACTURING CORPORATION, *pg.* 1312, *pg.* 1321
ANCHOR HOCKING COMPANY, *pg.* 1121, *pg.* 1457
APTAR OF STRATFORD, *pg.* 1313, *pg.* 380
APTARGROUP, INC., *pg.* 1451, *pg.* 598
ARMALY BRANDS, *pg.* 326, *pg.* 912
ARTUS CORPORATION, *pg.* 1314, *pg.* 1059
AVON RUBBER & PLASTICS INC., *pg.* 1879, *pg.* 874
BALL CORPORATION, *pg.* 1452, *pg.* 311
BEDFORD INDUSTRIES, INC., *pg.* 1453, *pg.* 967
BEL-ART PRODUCTS, INC., *pg.* 1879, *pg.* 1129
BERRY PLASTICS, *pg.* 1879, *pg.* 678
BERRY PLASTICS LANCASTER, *pg.* 1453, *pg.* 1546
BRADY CORPORATION, *pg.* 363, *pg.* 1873
CANADIAN PLASTICS INDUSTRY ASSOCIATION, *pg.* 136, *pg.* 1925
CAPSONIC GROUP LLC, *pg.* 1880, *pg.* 609
CARLISLE FOODSERVICE PRODUCTS INCORPORATED, *pg.* 1455, *pg.* 1485
CASCADES, INC., *pg.* 73, *pg.* 1950
CHANNELL COMMERCIAL CORP., *pg.* 1870, *pg.* 291
CHASE CORPORATION, *pg.* 1152, *pg.* 803
CHEM-TAINER INDUSTRIES, INC., *pg.* 1455, *pg.* 1349
COMAR INC., *pg.* 1455, *pg.* 1047
CONGOLEUM CORPORATION, *pg.* 921, *pg.* 1084
CORE MOLDING TECHNOLOGIES, INC., *pg.* 1881, *pg.* 1439
CPG INTERNATIONAL, INC., *pg.* 1881, *pg.* 1586
C.R. DANIELS, INC., *pg.* 1456, *pg.* 769
CRANE PLASTICS HOLDING COMPANY, *pg.* 1881, *pg.* 1439
CUSTOM PAK, INC., *pg.* 1881, *pg.* 703
DATACARD CORPORATION, *pg.* 382, *pg.* 948
DELSTAR TECHNOLOGIES, INC., *pg.* 1881, *pg.* 387
DIMCO-GRAY COMPANY, *pg.* 1881, *pg.* 1409
DIPCRAFT MANUFACTURING COMPANY, *pg.* 79, *pg.* 1518
DOLBY LABORATORIES, INC., *pg.* 284, *pg.* 217
DOREL JUVENILE GROUP, INC., *pg.* 923, *pg.* 676
THE DOW CHEMICAL COMPANY, *pg.* 1157, *pg.* 898
DYNARIC, INC., *pg.* 1882, *pg.* 1810
EASYTURF, *pg.* 1833, *pg.* 302
ENTEGRIS, INC., *pg.* 1882, *pg.* 788
ESSENTRA COMPONENTS, *pg.* 1047, *pg.* 612
FLAMBEAU, INC., *pg.* 1336, *pg.* 1854
FLEX-O-GLASS, INC., *pg.* 1457, *pg.* 574
FLEXIBLE SOLUTIONS INTERNATIONAL, INC., *pg.* 1163, *pg.* 1913
FORWARD INDUSTRIES, INC., *pg.* 5, *pg.* 478
THE GATES CORPORATION, *pg.* 205, *pg.* 319
GE CANADA COMPANY, *pg.* 1296, *pg.* 1926
GENOVA PRODUCTS, INC., *pg.* 83, *pg.* 875
GLOBE COMPOSITE SOLUTIONS, LTD., *pg.* 1883, *pg.* 842
GRACO CHILDREN'S PRODUCTS INC., *pg.* 954, *pg.* 1531
THE GREAT AMERICAN HANGER COMPANY INC., *pg.* 926, *pg.* 442
GREAT LAKES WINDOW, INC., *pg.* 85, *pg.* 1478
GRIFFON CORPORATION, *pg.* 641, *pg.* 1236
HAMILTON CASTER & MFG. CO., *pg.* 206, *pg.* 1454
HARRINGTON & KING PERFORATING COMPANY, INC., *pg.* 1164, *pg.* 576
HELLERMANNTYTON, *pg.* 642, *pg.* 1875
HEXCEL CORPORATION, *pg.* 1004, *pg.* 376
ILLINOIS TOOL WORKS INC., *pg.* 1348, *pg.* 614
ILPEA INDUSTRIES, INC., *pg.* 1348, *pg.* 697
INLINE PLASTICS CORP., *pg.* 1460, *pg.* 370
INNOVATIVE PLASTICS CORPORATION, *pg.* 1460, *pg.* 1319
KLW PLASTICS, INC., *pg.* 1463, *pg.* 1465
LOOP-LOC LTD., *pg.* 1838, *pg.* 1165
LUCITE INTERNATIONAL, INC., *pg.* 94, *pg.* 1631
MARYLAND PLASTICS, INC., *pg.* 1885, *pg.* 769
MOLDED FIBER GLASS COMPANIES, *pg.* 1886, *pg.* 1403
MOMENTIVE PERFORMANCE MATERIALS, INC., *pg.* 1464, *pg.* 1349
MYERS INDUSTRIES, INC., *pg.* 1887, *pg.* 1402
NATIONAL MOLDING, LLC, *pg.* 1887, *pg.* 430
NEWELL RUBBERMAID INC., *pg.* 1128, *pg.* 515
NORANDEX/REYNOLDS DISTRIBUTION, INC., *pg.* 99, *pg.* 1455
NORTHLAND ALUMINUM PRODUCTS INC., *pg.* 1129, *pg.* 941
THE OHIO ART COMPANY, INC., *pg.* 965, *pg.* 1406
PANOLAM INDUSTRIES INTERNATIONAL, INC., *pg.* 103, *pg.* 370
PARKER HANNIFIN - WEBSTER PLASTICS INC, *pg.* 1887, *pg.* 1159
PELICAN PRODUCTS, *pg.* 1467, *pg.* 843
PELICAN PRODUCTS, INC., *pg.* 1842, *pg.* 295
PENDA CORPORATION, *pg.* 214, *pg.* 1887
PERMALITH PLASTICS LLC, *pg.* 1887, *pg.* 1108
PLANO MOLDING COMPANY, *pg.* 1887, *pg.* 652
PLASKOLITE, INC., *pg.* 1888, *pg.* 1443
PLASTI-FAB LTD., *pg.* 1888, *pg.* 1904
PLASTICS.COM, INC., *pg.* 1275, *pg.* 819
POLYONE CORPORATION, *pg.* 1177, *pg.* 1404
POWERS FASTENERS INC., *pg.* 1059, *pg.* 1143
PTA CORPORATION, *pg.* 1888, *pg.* 368
PURE FISHING, INC., *pg.* 1843, *pg.* 1614
QUADRANT ENGINEERING PLASTIC PRODUCTS, *pg.* 1178, *pg.* 1585
RAVEN INDUSTRIES, INC., *pg.* 1888, *pg.* 1625
REESE ENTERPRISES, INC., *pg.* 1888, *pg.* 955
RENOSOL CORPORATION, *pg.* 1179, *pg.* 872
REYNOLDS CONSUMER PRODUCTS, *pg.* 1138, *pg.* 625
ROCHLING GLASTIC COMPOSITES, *pg.* 1889, *pg.* 1435
RUBBERMAID HOME PRODUCTS, *pg.* 1138, *pg.* 1453
SAFE-HIT CORPORATION, *pg.* 1889, *pg.* 589
SCHLEGEL SYSTEMS, INC., *pg.* 109, *pg.* 1337
SENTRY GROUP, INC., *pg.* 468, *pg.* 1337
THE SHERWIN-WILLIAMS COMPANY, *pg.* 1447, *pg.* 1435
SNYDER INDUSTRIES, INC., *pg.* 1377, *pg.* 1012
SOLO CUP COMPANY, *pg.* 1469, *pg.* 625
SPX PROCESS EQUIPMENT, *pg.* 1378, *pg.* 1337
STANBEE COMPANY, INC., *pg.* 1819, *pg.* 1050
THE STEP2 COMPANY LLC, *pg.* 1889, *pg.* 1474
STERILITE CORPORATION, *pg.* 1138, *pg.* 848
STULL TECHNOLOGIES INC., *pg.* 1889, *pg.* 1122
SUPER GLUE CORPORATION, *pg.* 1183, *pg.* 187
TEKNI-PLEX, INC., *pg.* 1470, *pg.* 1122
TEKRA CORPORATION, *pg.* 1184, *pg.* 1884
TERVIS TUMBLER COMPANY, *pg.* 1890, *pg.* 477
THETFORD CORPORATION, *pg.* 337, *pg.* 867
TREDEGAR CORPORATION, *pg.* 1890, *pg.* 1804
TREX COMPANY, INC., *pg.* 116, *pg.* 1812
TRIENDA, LLC, *pg.* 1890, *pg.* 1887
TRUE HOME VALUE, INC., *pg.* 117, *pg.* 738
TUPPERWARE BRANDS CORPORATION, *pg.* 1139, *pg.*

First page reference indicates Business Class Edition
Second page reference indicates Geographic Edition

456
TYCO INTERNATIONAL (US) INC., pg. 1891, pg. 1113
UNETTE CORPORATION, pg. 1184, pg. 1114
VISKASE COMPANIES, INC., pg. 1471, pg. 599
WARP BROTHERS, pg. 1471, pg. 595
WASCO PRODUCTS, INC., pg. 120, pg. 752
WENTWORTH TECHNOLOGIES CO. LTD., pg. 1891, pg. 1919
WESTLAKE PLASTICS COMPANY, pg. 1892, pg. 1548
WHIRLEY INDUSTRIES, INC., pg. 1892, pg. 1590
THE WIFFLE BALL INC., pg. 1848, pg. 371
WINZELER GEAR, pg. 1892, pg. 616
WISCO PRODUCTS, INC., pg. 1389, pg. 1447
ZCL COMPOSITES INC., pg. 1892, pg. 1906
ZERO MANUFACTURING, INC., pg. 1892, pg. 1752
THE ZIPPERTUBING COMPANY, pg. 1892, pg. 12

3083 - Laminated Plastics, Plate, Sheet & Profile Shapes

ADVANCED DRAINAGE SYSTEMS, INC., pg. 1878, pg. 1455
BUILDING MATERIALS CORPORATION OF AMERICA, pg. 72, pg. 1129
CHROMA CORPORATION, pg. 1441, pg. 632
DUNMORE CORPORATION, pg. 1456, pg. 1518
EVONIK CYRO LLC, pg. 1162, pg. 1103
HENKEL CONSUMER ADHESIVES, INC., pg. 403, pg. 1480
MOLDED FIBER GLASS COMPANIES, pg. 1886, pg. 1403
PILGRIM PLASTIC PRODUCTS COMPANY, pg. 1887, pg. 803
PLASKOLITE, INC., pg. 1888, pg. 1443
ROGERS CORPORATION, pg. 1305, pg. 369

3084 - Plastics Pipe

ADVANCED DRAINAGE SYSTEMS, INC., pg. 1878, pg. 1455
AIRLITE PLASTICS COMPANY, pg. 1451, pg. 1013
ALLFLEX USA, INC., pg. 1878, pg. 1717
ALPHA PACKAGING, pg. 1451, pg. 990
AMERICAN BILTRITE INC., pg. 1878, pg. 856
AMERICAN CASTING & MANUFACTURING CORPORATION, pg. 1312, pg. 1321
ANCHOR HOCKING COMPANY, pg. 1121, pg. 1457
APTAR OF STRATFORD, pg. 1313, pg. 380
APTARGROUP, INC., pg. 1451, pg. 598
ARMALY BRANDS, pg. 326, pg. 912
ARTUS CORPORATION, pg. 1314, pg. 1059
AVON RUBBER & PLASTICS INC., pg. 1879, pg. 874
BALL CORPORATION, pg. 1452, pg. 311
BEDFORD INDUSTRIES, INC., pg. 1453, pg. 967
BEL-ART PRODUCTS, INC., pg. 1879, pg. 1129
BERRY PLASTICS, pg. 1879, pg. 678
BERRY PLASTICS LANCASTER, pg. 1453, pg. 1546
BRADY CORPORATION, pg. 363, pg. 1873
CANADIAN PLASTICS INDUSTRY ASSOCIATION, pg. 136, pg. 1925
CANTEX INC., pg. 73, pg. 1727
CAPSONIC GROUP LLC, pg. 1880, pg. 609
CARLISLE FOODSERVICE PRODUCTS INCORPORATED, pg. 1455, pg. 1485
CASCADES, INC., pg. 73, pg. 1950
CHANNELL COMMERCIAL CORP., pg. 1870, pg. 291
CHARLOTTE PIPE & FOUNDRY COMPANY, pg. 1044, pg. 1365
CHASE CORPORATION, pg. 1152, pg. 803
CHEM-TAINER INDUSTRIES, INC., pg. 1455, pg. 1349
COMAR INC., pg. 1455, pg. 1047
CONTINENTAL INDUSTRIES INC., pg. 1880, pg. 1489
CORE MOLDING TECHNOLOGIES, INC., pg. 1881, pg. 1439
CPG INTERNATIONAL, INC., pg. 1881, pg. 1586
C.R. DANIELS, INC., pg. 1456, pg. 769
CRANE CHEMPHARMA & ENERGY, pg. 1044, pg. 1382
CRANE PLASTICS HOLDING COMPANY, pg. 1881, pg. 1439
CRESLINE PLASTIC PIPE CO., INC., pg. 1881, pg. 678
CUSTOM PAK, INC., pg. 1881, pg. 703
DATACARD CORPORATION, pg. 382, pg. 948
DELSTAR TECHNOLOGIES, INC., pg. 1881, pg. 387
DETREX CORPORATION, pg. 1156, pg. 906
DIMCO-GRAY COMPANY, pg. 1881, pg. 1409
DIPCRAFT MANUFACTURING COMPANY, pg. 79, pg. 1518
DOLBY LABORATORIES, INC., pg. 284, pg. 217
DOREL JUVENILE GROUP, INC., pg. 923, pg. 676
THE DOW CHEMICAL COMPANY, pg. 1157, pg. 898
DYNARIC, INC., pg. 1882, pg. 1810
EASYTURF, pg. 1833, pg. 302
ESSENTRA COMPONENTS, pg. 1047, pg. 612
FLAMBEAU, INC., pg. 1336, pg. 1854
FLEXIBLE SOLUTIONS INTERNATIONAL, INC., pg. 1163, pg. 1913
FORWARD INDUSTRIES, INC., pg. 5, pg. 478
THE GATES CORPORATION, pg. 205, pg. 319
GE CANADA COMPANY, pg. 1296, pg. 1926
GENOVA PRODUCTS, INC., pg. 83, pg. 875
GLOBE COMPOSITE SOLUTIONS, LTD., pg. 1883, pg. 842
GRACO CHILDREN'S PRODUCTS INC., pg. 954, pg. 1531
THE GREAT AMERICAN HANGER COMPANY INC., pg. 926, pg. 442
GREAT LAKES WINDOW, INC., pg. 85, pg. 1478
GRIFFON CORPORATION, pg. 641, pg. 1236
HAMILTON CASTER & MFG. CO., pg. 206, pg. 1454
HARRINGTON & KING PERFORATING COMPANY, INC., pg. 1164, pg. 576
HELLERMANNTYTON, pg. 642, pg. 1875
HEXCEL CORPORATION, pg. 1884, pg. 375
ILLINOIS TOOL WORKS INC., pg. 1348, pg. 614
ILPEA INDUSTRIES, INC., pg. 1348, pg. 697
INLINE PLASTICS CORP., pg. 1460, pg. 370
INNOVATIVE PLASTICS CORPORATION, pg. 1460, pg. 1319
KLW PLASTICS, INC., pg. 1463, pg. 1465
LOOP-LOC LTD., pg. 1838, pg. 1165
LUCITE INTERNATIONAL, INC., pg. 94, pg. 1631
MARYLAND PLASTICS, INC., pg. 1885, pg. 769
MOLDED FIBER GLASS COMPANIES, pg. 1886, pg. 1403
MOMENTIVE PERFORMANCE MATERIALS, INC., pg. 1464, pg. 1349
NATIONAL MOLDING, LLC, pg. 1887, pg. 430
NEWELL RUBBERMAID INC., pg. 1128, pg. 515
NORANDEX/REYNOLDS DISTRIBUTION, INC., pg. 99, pg. 1455
NORTHLAND ALUMINUM PRODUCTS INC., pg. 1129, pg. 941
THE OHIO ART COMPANY, INC., pg. 965, pg. 1406
PANOLAM INDUSTRIES INTERNATIONAL, INC., pg. 103, pg. 370
PARKER HANNIFIN - WEBSTER PLASTICS INC, pg. 1887, pg. 1159
PELICAN PRODUCTS, pg. 1467, pg. 843
PELICAN PRODUCTS, INC., pg. 1842, pg. 295
PENDA CORPORATION, pg. 214, pg. 1887
PERMALITH PLASTICS LLC, pg. 1887, pg. 1108
PLANO MOLDING COMPANY, pg. 1887, pg. 652
PLASKOLITE, INC., pg. 1888, pg. 1443
PLASTI-FAB LTD., pg. 1888, pg. 1904
PLASTICS.COM, INC., pg. 1275, pg. 819
POLYONE CORPORATION, pg. 1177, pg. 1404
POWERS FASTENERS INC., pg. 1059, pg. 1143
PTA CORPORATION, pg. 1888, pg. 368
PURE FISHING, INC., pg. 1843, pg. 1614
RAVEN INDUSTRIES, INC., pg. 1888, pg. 1625
REESE ENTERPRISES, INC., pg. 1888, pg. 955
RENOSOL CORPORATION, pg. 1179, pg. 872
REYNOLDS CONSUMER PRODUCTS, pg. 1138, pg. 625
ROCHLING GLASTIC COMPOSITES, pg. 1889, pg. 1435
RUBBERMAID HOME PRODUCTS, pg. 1138, pg. 1453
SAFE-HIT CORPORATION, pg. 1889, pg. 589
SCHLEGEL SYSTEMS, INC., pg. 109, pg. 1337
SENTRY GROUP, INC., pg. 468, pg. 1337
THE SHERWIN-WILLIAMS COMPANY, pg. 1447, pg. 1435
SNYDER INDUSTRIES, INC., pg. 1377, pg. 1012
SOLO CUP COMPANY, pg. 1469, pg. 625
SPX PROCESS EQUIPMENT, pg. 1378, pg. 1337
STANBEE COMPANY, INC., pg. 1819, pg. 1050
THE STEP2 COMPANY LLC, pg. 1889, pg. 1474
STERILITE CORPORATION, pg. 1138, pg. 848
STULL TECHNOLOGIES INC., pg. 1889, pg. 1122
SUPER GLUE CORPORATION, pg. 1183, pg. 187
TEKNI-PLEX, INC., pg. 1470, pg. 1122
TEKRA CORPORATION, pg. 1184, pg. 1884
TERVIS TUMBLER COMPANY, pg. 1890, pg. 477
THETFORD CORPORATION, pg. 337, pg. 867
TREDEGAR CORPORATION, pg. 1890, pg. 1804
TREX COMPANY, INC., pg. 116, pg. 1812
TRIENDA, LLC, pg. 1890, pg. 1887
TRUE HOME VALUE, INC., pg. 117, pg. 738
TUPPERWARE BRANDS CORPORATION, pg. 1139, pg. 456
TYCO INTERNATIONAL (US) INC., pg. 1891, pg. 1113
UNETTE CORPORATION, pg. 1184, pg. 1114
VISKASE COMPANIES, INC., pg. 1471, pg. 599
WASCO PRODUCTS, INC., pg. 120, pg. 752
WATTS WATER TECHNOLOGIES, INC., pg. 1078, pg. 837
WENTWORTH TECHNOLOGIES CO. LTD., pg. 1891, pg. 1919
WHIRLEY INDUSTRIES, INC., pg. 1892, pg. 1590
THE WIFFLE BALL INC., pg. 1848, pg. 371
WINZELER GEAR, pg. 1892, pg. 616
WISCO PRODUCTS, INC., pg. 1389, pg. 1447
ZCL COMPOSITES INC., pg. 1892, pg. 1906
ZERO MANUFACTURING, INC., pg. 1892, pg. 1752
THE ZIPPERTUBING COMPANY, pg. 1892, pg. 12

3085 - Plastics Bottles

BWAY HOLDING COMPANY, pg. 1454, pg. 491
HANDI-CRAFT COMPANY, pg. 954, pg. 998
MUNCHKIN, INC., pg. 964, pg. 300
WHIRLEY INDUSTRIES, INC., pg. 1892, pg. 1590

3086 - Plastics Foam Products

AMERICAN EXCELSIOR COMPANY, pg. 1451, pg. 1659
BARNHARDT MANUFACTURING COMPANY, pg. 1498, pg. 1364
CARPENTER CO., pg. 920, pg. 1801
CLAYTON CORPORATION, pg. 1154, pg. 977
CRYOVAC, INC., pg. 1456, pg. 1615
THE DOW CHEMICAL COMPANY, pg. 1157, pg. 898
FEDERAL FOAM TECHNOLOGIES INC., pg. 692, pg. 1884
FXI, pg. 1163, pg. 1552
HOMASOTE COMPANY, pg. 87, pg. 1126
HUNTSMAN CORPORATION, pg. 1167, pg. 1758
IGLOO PRODUCTS CORPORATION, pg. 1126, pg. 1724
JANESVILLE ACOUSTICS, pg. 1885, pg. 907
LAPOLLA INDUSTRIES, INC., pg. 1444, pg. 1710
MYERS INDUSTRIES, INC., pg. 1887, pg. 1402
POLYAIR INTER PACK INC., pg. 1467, pg. 1941
POLYONE CORPORATION, pg. 1177, pg. 1404
SPAN-AMERICA MEDICAL SYSTEMS, INC., pg. 1595, pg. 1618
TEKNI-PLEX, INC., pg. 1470, pg. 1122
THERMOS L.L.C., pg. 61, pg. 660
TOTAL PETROCHEMICALS USA, INC., pg. 1184, pg. 1716
UFP TECHNOLOGIES, INC., pg. 1891, pg. 823

3087 - Custom Compounding of Purchased Plastics Resins

RENOSOL CORPORATION, pg. 1179, pg. 872
SI GROUP, INC., pg. 1181, pg. 1341
TEKNOR APEX COMPANY, pg. 1889, pg. 1605

3088 - Plastics Plumbing Fixtures

AQUATIC, pg. 68, pg. 42
E.L. MUSTEE & SONS, INC., pg. 1124, pg. 1430
FORTUNE BRANDS HOME & SECURITY, INC., pg. 55, pg. 600
MAAX INC.-MINNEAPOLIS, pg. 1885, pg. 938
METPAR CORP., pg. 97, pg. 1350
WATKINS MANUFACTURING CORPORATION, pg. 120, pg. 303

3089 - Plastics Products, NEC

AIRLITE PLASTICS COMPANY, pg. 1451, pg. 1013
ALLFLEX USA, INC., pg. 1878, pg. 1717
ALPHA PACKAGING, pg. 1451, pg. 990
AMERICAN CASTING & MANUFACTURING CORPORATION, pg. 1312, pg. 1321
ANCHOR HOCKING COMPANY, pg. 1121, pg. 1457
APTAR OF STRATFORD, pg. 1313, pg. 380
APTARGROUP, INC., pg. 1451, pg. 598
ARMALY BRANDS, pg. 326, pg. 912
ARTUS CORPORATION, pg. 1314, pg. 1059
AVON RUBBER & PLASTICS INC., pg. 1879, pg. 874
BALL CORPORATION, pg. 1452, pg. 311
BEDFORD INDUSTRIES, INC., pg. 1453, pg. 967

BEL-ART PRODUCTS, INC., *pg.* 1879, *pg.* 1129
BERRY PLASTICS, *pg.* 1879, *pg.* 678
BERRY PLASTICS LANCASTER, *pg.* 1453, *pg.* 1546
BRADY CORPORATION, *pg.* 363, *pg.* 1873
BUZTRONICS, INC., *pg.* 1294, *pg.* 683
CANADIAN PLASTICS INDUSTRY ASSOCIATION, *pg.* 136, *pg.* 1925
CAPSONIC GROUP LLC, *pg.* 1880, *pg.* 609
CARLISLE FOODSERVICE PRODUCTS INCORPORATED, *pg.* 1455, *pg.* 1485
CASCADES, INC., *pg.* 73, *pg.* 1950
CHANNELL COMMERCIAL CORP., *pg.* 1870, *pg.* 291
CHASE CORPORATION, *pg.* 1152, *pg.* 803
CHEM-TAINER INDUSTRIES, INC., *pg.* 1455, *pg.* 1349
COMAR INC., *pg.* 1455, *pg.* 1047
CORE MOLDING TECHNOLOGIES, INC., *pg.* 1881, *pg.* 1439
CPG INTERNATIONAL, INC., *pg.* 1881, *pg.* 1586
C.R. DANIELS, INC., *pg.* 1456, *pg.* 769
CRANE PLASTICS HOLDING COMPANY, *pg.* 1881, *pg.* 1439
CUSTOM PAK, INC., *pg.* 1881, *pg.* 703
DATACARD CORPORATION, *pg.* 382, *pg.* 948
DELSTAR TECHNOLOGIES, INC., *pg.* 1881, *pg.* 387
DIMCO-GRAY COMPANY, *pg.* 1881, *pg.* 1409
DIPCRAFT MANUFACTURING COMPANY, *pg.* 79, *pg.* 1518
DOLBY LABORATORIES, INC., *pg.* 284, *pg.* 217
DOREL JUVENILE GROUP, INC., *pg.* 923, *pg.* 676
THE DOW CHEMICAL COMPANY, *pg.* 1157, *pg.* 898
DYNARIC, INC., *pg.* 1882, *pg.* 1810
EASYTURF, *pg.* 1833, *pg.* 302
ESSENTRA COMPONENTS, *pg.* 1047, *pg.* 612
FLAMBEAU, INC., *pg.* 1336, *pg.* 1854
FLEXIBLE SOLUTIONS INTERNATIONAL, INC., *pg.* 1163, *pg.* 1913
THE GATES CORPORATION, *pg.* 205, *pg.* 319
GE CANADA COMPANY, *pg.* 1296, *pg.* 1926
GENOVA PRODUCTS, INC., *pg.* 83, *pg.* 875
GLOBE COMPOSITE SOLUTIONS, LTD., *pg.* 1883, *pg.* 842
GRACO CHILDREN'S PRODUCTS INC., *pg.* 954, *pg.* 1531
THE GREAT AMERICAN HANGER COMPANY INC., *pg.* 926, *pg.* 442
GREAT LAKES WINDOW, INC., *pg.* 85, *pg.* 1478
GRIFFON CORPORATION, *pg.* 641, *pg.* 1236
HAMILTON CASTER & MFG. CO., *pg.* 206, *pg.* 1454
HARRINGTON & KING PERFORATING COMPANY, INC., *pg.* 1164, *pg.* 576
HELLERMANNTYTON, *pg.* 642, *pg.* 1875
HEXCEL CORPORATION, *pg.* 1884, *pg.* 375
ILLINOIS TOOL WORKS INC., *pg.* 1348, *pg.* 614
ILPEA INDUSTRIES, INC., *pg.* 1348, *pg.* 697
INLINE PLASTICS CORP., *pg.* 1460, *pg.* 370
INNOVATIVE PLASTICS CORPORATION, *pg.* 1460, *pg.* 1319
KLW PLASTICS, INC., *pg.* 1463, *pg.* 1465
LOOP-LOC LTD., *pg.* 1838, *pg.* 1165
LUCITE INTERNATIONAL, INC., *pg.* 94, *pg.* 1631
MARYLAND PLASTICS, INC., *pg.* 1885, *pg.* 769
MOLDED FIBER GLASS COMPANIES, *pg.* 1886, *pg.* 1403
MOMENTIVE PERFORMANCE MATERIALS, INC., *pg.* 1464, *pg.* 1349
NATIONAL MOLDING, LLC, *pg.* 1887, *pg.* 430
NEWELL RUBBERMAID INC., *pg.* 1128, *pg.* 515
NORANDEX/REYNOLDS DISTRIBUTION, INC., *pg.* 99, *pg.* 1455
NORTHLAND ALUMINUM PRODUCTS INC., *pg.* 1129, *pg.* 941
THE OHIO ART COMPANY, INC., *pg.* 965, *pg.* 1406
PANOLAM INDUSTRIES INTERNATIONAL, INC., *pg.* 103, *pg.* 370
PARKER HANNIFIN - WEBSTER PLASTICS INC, *pg.* 1887, *pg.* 1159
PELICAN PRODUCTS, *pg.* 1467, *pg.* 843
PELICAN PRODUCTS, INC., *pg.* 1842, *pg.* 295
PENDA CORPORATION, *pg.* 214, *pg.* 1887
PERMALITH PLASTICS LLC, *pg.* 1887, *pg.* 1108
PLANO MOLDING COMPANY, *pg.* 1887, *pg.* 652
PLASKOLITE, INC., *pg.* 1888, *pg.* 1443
PLASTI-FAB LTD., *pg.* 1888, *pg.* 1904
PLASTICS.COM, INC., *pg.* 1275, *pg.* 819
POLYONE CORPORATION, *pg.* 1177, *pg.* 1404
POWERS FASTENERS INC., *pg.* 1059, *pg.* 1143
PTA CORPORATION, *pg.* 1888, *pg.* 368
PURE FISHING, INC., *pg.* 1843, *pg.* 1614
RAVEN INDUSTRIES, INC., *pg.* 1888, *pg.* 1625
REESE ENTERPRISES, INC., *pg.* 1888, *pg.* 955
RENOSOL CORPORATION, *pg.* 1179, *pg.* 872
REYNOLDS CONSUMER PRODUCTS, *pg.* 1138, *pg.* 625
ROCHLING GLASTIC COMPOSITES, *pg.* 1889, *pg.* 1435
RUBBERMAID HOME PRODUCTS, *pg.* 1138, *pg.* 1453
SAFE-HIT CORPORATION, *pg.* 1889, *pg.* 589
SCHLEGEL SYSTEMS, INC., *pg.* 109, *pg.* 1337
SENTRY GROUP, INC., *pg.* 468, *pg.* 1337
THE SHERWIN-WILLIAMS COMPANY, *pg.* 1447, *pg.* 1435
SNYDER INDUSTRIES, INC., *pg.* 1377, *pg.* 1012
SOLO CUP COMPANY, *pg.* 1469, *pg.* 625
SPX PROCESS EQUIPMENT, *pg.* 1378, *pg.* 1337
STANBEE COMPANY, INC., *pg.* 1819, *pg.* 1050
THE STEP2 COMPANY LLC, *pg.* 1889, *pg.* 1474
STERILITE CORPORATION, *pg.* 1138, *pg.* 848
STULL TECHNOLOGIES INC., *pg.* 1889, *pg.* 1122
SUPER GLUE CORPORATION, *pg.* 1183, *pg.* 187
TEKNI-PLEX, INC., *pg.* 1470, *pg.* 1122
TEKRA CORPORATION, *pg.* 1184, *pg.* 1884
TERVIS TUMBLER COMPANY, *pg.* 1890, *pg.* 477
THETFORD CORPORATION, *pg.* 337, *pg.* 867
TREDEGAR CORPORATION, *pg.* 1890, *pg.* 1804
TREX COMPANY, INC., *pg.* 116, *pg.* 1812
TRIENDA, LLC, *pg.* 1890, *pg.* 1887
TRUE HOME VALUE, INC., *pg.* 117, *pg.* 738
TUPPERWARE BRANDS CORPORATION, *pg.* 1139, *pg.* 456
TYCO INTERNATIONAL (US) INC., *pg.* 1891, *pg.* 1113
UNETTE CORPORATION, *pg.* 1184, *pg.* 1114
VISKASE COMPANIES, INC., *pg.* 1471, *pg.* 599
WASCO PRODUCTS, INC., *pg.* 120, *pg.* 752
WENTWORTH TECHNOLOGIES CO. LTD., *pg.* 1891, *pg.* 1919
WHIRLEY INDUSTRIES, INC., *pg.* 1892, *pg.* 1590
THE WIFFLE BALL INC., *pg.* 1848, *pg.* 371
WINZELER GEAR, *pg.* 1892, *pg.* 616
WISCO PRODUCTS, INC., *pg.* 1389, *pg.* 1447
ZCL COMPOSITES INC., *pg.* 1892, *pg.* 1906
ZERO MANUFACTURING, INC., *pg.* 1892, *pg.* 1752
THE ZIPPERTUBING COMPANY, *pg.* 1892, *pg.* 12

3111 - Leather Tanning & Finishing

EDELMAN LEATHER, LLC, *pg.* 923, *pg.* 359
SCOTT'S LIQUID GOLD-INC., *pg.* 335, *pg.* 323
SEALY CORPORATION, *pg.* 942, *pg.* 1391

3142 - House Slippers

R.G. BARRY CORPORATION, *pg.* 1818, *pg.* 1470

3143 - Men's Footwear, Except Athletic

THE ALDEN SHOE COMPANY, *pg.* 1804, *pg.* 833
ALLEN-EDMONDS SHOE CORP., *pg.* 1804, *pg.* 1887
GENFOOT INC., *pg.* 1809, *pg.* 1951
JUSTIN BRANDS, INC., *pg.* 1810, *pg.* 1695
K-SWISS, *pg.* 1837, *pg.* 306
KENNETH COLE PRODUCTIONS, INC., *pg.* 1810, *pg.* 1248
L.A. GEAR, INC., *pg.* 1811, *pg.* 134
LACROSSE FOOTWEAR, INC., *pg.* 1811, *pg.* 1503
LEHIGH OUTFITTERS, LLC, *pg.* 43, *pg.* 1466
PHOENIX FOOTWEAR GROUP, INC., *pg.* 1815, *pg.* 60
P.W. MINOR & SON, INC., *pg.* 1816, *pg.* 1140
RED WING SHOE COMPANY, INC., *pg.* 1817, *pg.* 954
THE ROCKPORT GROUP, *pg.* 1818, *pg.* 812
ROCKY BRANDS, INC., *pg.* 1818, *pg.* 1466
STEVEN MADDEN, LTD., *pg.* 1819, *pg.* 1176
THE TIMBERLAND COMPANY, *pg.* 1821, *pg.* 1039
WEINBRENNER SHOE COMPANY, INC., *pg.* 1822, *pg.* 1871
WELLCO ENTERPRISES, INC., *pg.* 1822, *pg.* 1392
WEYCO GROUP, INC., *pg.* 1822, *pg.* 1858
WOLVERINE WORLD WIDE, INC., *pg.* 1822, *pg.* 905

3144 - Women's Footwear, Except Athletic

BCBG MAX AZRIA GROUP LLC, *pg.* 19, *pg.* 301
CALERES, *pg.* 1805, *pg.* 1932
COLE-HAAN LLC, *pg.* 1806, *pg.* 1034
DEER STAGS INC., *pg.* 1807, *pg.* 1222
HI-TEC SPORTS USA, INC., *pg.* 1809, *pg.* 150
ICONIX BRAND GROUP, INC., *pg.* 26, *pg.* 1243
JUSTIN BRANDS, INC., *pg.* 1810, *pg.* 1695
KENNETH COLE PRODUCTIONS, INC., *pg.* 1810, *pg.* 1248
LACROSSE FOOTWEAR, INC., *pg.* 1811, *pg.* 1503
LEHIGH OUTFITTERS, LLC, *pg.* 43, *pg.* 1466
MASON COMPANIES, INC., *pg.* 1811, *pg.* 1856
PHOENIX FOOTWEAR GROUP, INC., *pg.* 1815, *pg.* 60
P.W. MINOR & SON, INC., *pg.* 1816, *pg.* 1140
THE ROCKPORT GROUP, INC., *pg.* 1818, *pg.* 812
ROCKY BRANDS, INC., *pg.* 1818, *pg.* 1466
STEVEN MADDEN, LTD., *pg.* 1819, *pg.* 1176
THE TIMBERLAND COMPANY, *pg.* 1821, *pg.* 1039
WEINBRENNER SHOE COMPANY, INC., *pg.* 1822, *pg.* 1871

3149 - Footwear, Except Rubber, NEC

ADIDAS AMERICA INC., *pg.* 1803, *pg.* 1500
CALERES, INC., *pg.* 1805, *pg.* 993
CAPEZIO BALLET MAKERS INC., *pg.* 1805, *pg.* 1125
CROCS, INC., *pg.* 1806, *pg.* 335
L.A. GEAR, INC., *pg.* 1811, *pg.* 134
LACROSSE FOOTWEAR, INC., *pg.* 1811, *pg.* 1503
LEHIGH OUTFITTERS, LLC, *pg.* 43, *pg.* 1466
MAURICE J. MARKELL SHOE CO., INC., *pg.* 1811, *pg.* 1356
NEW BALANCE ATHLETIC SHOE, INC., *pg.* 1811, *pg.* 798
NIKE, INC., *pg.* 1812, *pg.* 1492
RED WING SHOE COMPANY, INC., *pg.* 1817, *pg.* 954
REEBOK INTERNATIONAL LTD., *pg.* 1817, *pg.* 811
ROCKY BRANDS, INC., *pg.* 1818, *pg.* 1466
SAUCONY, INC., *pg.* 1818, *pg.* 828
STANBEE COMPANY, INC., *pg.* 1819, *pg.* 1050

3151 - Leather Gloves & Mittens

GEORGE GLOVE CO., INC., *pg.* 5, *pg.* 1084
TOTES ISOTONER CORPORATION, *pg.* 14, *pg.* 1426
WELLS LAMONT CORPORATION, *pg.* 15, *pg.* 638

3161 - Luggage

FORWARD INDUSTRIES, INC., *pg.* 5, *pg.* 478
JANSPORT, *pg.* 1837, *pg.* 38
MERCURY LUGGAGE/SEWARD TRUNK, *pg.* 9, *pg.* 434
THE PORT CANVAS COMPANY, *pg.* 11, *pg.* 750
SAMSONITE CORPORATION, *pg.* 11, *pg.* 830
SEALED AIR CORPORATION, *pg.* 1468, *pg.* 1058
SOLO, *pg.* 12, *pg.* 1165
SWANK, INC., *pg.* 13, *pg.* 1297
TANDY LEATHER FACTORY, INC., *pg.* 48, *pg.* 1696
TILLEY OF CANADA LIMITED, *pg.* 14, *pg.* 1920
TUMI, INC., *pg.* 15, *pg.* 1123
VERA BRADLEY, INC., *pg.* 15, *pg.* 697
ZERO MANUFACTURING, INC., *pg.* 1892, *pg.* 1752

3171 - Women's Handbags & Purses

COACH, INC., *pg.* 3, *pg.* 1214
DOONEY & BOURKE, INC., *pg.* 24, *pg.* 361
FORWARD INDUSTRIES, INC., *pg.* 5, *pg.* 478
TANO, INC., *pg.* 13, *pg.* 1183
TILLEY OF CANADA LIMITED, *pg.* 14, *pg.* 1920
TUMI, INC., *pg.* 15, *pg.* 1123
VERA BRADLEY, INC., *pg.* 15, *pg.* 697

3172 - Personal Leather Goods, Except Women's Handbags & Purses

BARRINGTON GROUP LTD., *pg.* 1, *pg.* 1676
CHARLES & COLVARD LTD, *pg.* 3, *pg.* 1384
COACH, INC., *pg.* 3, *pg.* 1214
DOONEY & BOURKE, INC., *pg.* 24, *pg.* 361
FOSSIL GROUP, INC., *pg.* 5, *pg.* 1735
ROOTS CANADA LTD., *pg.* 47, *pg.* 1942
SWANK, INC., *pg.* 13, *pg.* 1297
TILLEY OF CANADA LIMITED, *pg.* 14, *pg.* 1920
TUMI, INC., *pg.* 15, *pg.* 1123

3199 - Leather Goods, NEC

BARRINGTON GROUP LTD., pg. 1, pg. 1676
CHARLES & COLVARD LTD, pg. 3, pg. 1384
COACH, INC., pg. 3, pg. 1214
DOONEY & BOURKE, INC., pg. 24, pg. 361
EDELMAN LEATHER, LLC, pg. 923, pg. 359
FOSSIL GROUP, INC., pg. 5, pg. 1735
KLEIN TOOLS INC., pg. 1052, pg. 627
LAM RESEARCH CORPORATION, pg. 1354, pg. 246
ROOTS CANADA LTD., pg. 47, pg. 1942
SWANK, INC., pg. 13, pg. 1297
TANDY LEATHER FACTORY, INC., pg. 48, pg. 1696
TILLEY OF CANADA LIMITED, pg. 14, pg. 1920
TUMI, INC., pg. 15, pg. 1123

3211 - Flat Glass

AGC GLASS NORTH AMERICA, INC., pg. 65, pg. 482
APOGEE ENTERPRISES, INC., pg. 67, pg. 930
GUARDIAN INDUSTRIES CORP., pg. 85, pg. 869
PILKINGTON NORTH AMERICA, INC., pg. 215, pg. 1477
PPG CANADA INC., pg. 1178, pg. 1928
PPG INDUSTRIES, INC., pg. 1445, pg. 1579
SCHOTT GEMTRON CORPORATION, pg. 109, pg. 1656
VIRGINIA GLASS PRODUCTS CORPORATION, pg. 119, pg. 1788
WASCO PRODUCTS, INC., pg. 120, pg. 752

3221 - Glass Containers

ARDAGH GROUP, pg. 1452, pg. 470
CERTAINTEED CORPORATION, pg. 74, pg. 1589
E&J GALLO WINERY, pg. 1962, pg. 149
JARDEN HOME BRANDS, pg. 1126, pg. 920
OWENS CORNING, pg. 102, pg. 1476
OWENS-ILLINOIS, INC., pg. 1466, pg. 1470
REXAM BEVERAGE CAN NORTH AMERICA, pg. 1468, pg. 588

3229 - Pressed & Blown Glass & Glassware, NEC

ANCHOR HOCKING COMPANY, pg. 1121, pg. 1457
CORNING INCORPORATED, pg. 1122, pg. 1154
CRYSTAL WORLD, INC., pg. 4, pg. 1122
ENERGY FOCUS, INC., pg. 1411, pg. 1472
THE FENTON ART GLASS COMPANY, pg. 1124, pg. 1851
LENOX CORPORATION, pg. 1126, pg. 1518
LIBBEY, INC., pg. 1126, pg. 1476
LOOS & COMPANY, INC., pg. 1356, pg. 368
REVOLUTION LIGHTING TECHNOLOGIES, INC., pg. 1304, pg. 377
ROCKY MOUNTAIN INSTRUMENT, INC., pg. 1428, pg. 332
STEFAN SYDOR OPTICS, INC., pg. 1430, pg. 1337
TRANSITIONS OPTICAL, INC., pg. 1432, pg. 458

3231 - Glass Products, Made of Purchased Glass

AGC GLASS NORTH AMERICA, INC., pg. 65, pg. 482
AMERICAN LOUVER COMPANY, pg. 1294, pg. 660
ANDERSEN CORPORATION, pg. 67, pg. 916
COMAR INC., pg. 1455, pg. 1047
COMMERCIAL VEHICLE GROUP, INC., pg. 203, pg. 1467
DORMAN PRODUCTS, INC., pg. 204, pg. 1522
THE FENTON ART GLASS COMPANY, pg. 1124, pg. 1851
GENTEX CORPORATION, pg. 206, pg. 913
GLASS FAB INC., pg. 1414, pg. 1335
GROTE INDUSTRIES, INC., pg. 206, pg. 693
HCS CORPORATION, pg. 86, pg. 1821
INTERNATIONAL REVOLVING DOORS, pg. 88, pg. 679
ONEIDA LTD, pg. 1129, pg. 1318
POTTERS INDUSTRIES, INC., pg. 105, pg. 1515
PQ CORPORATION, pg. 1178, pg. 1515
RAUCH INDUSTRIES, INC., pg. 940, pg. 1373
SCHOTT NORTH AMERICA, INC., pg. 109, pg. 698
VIRGINIA GLASS PRODUCTS CORPORATION, pg. 119, pg. 1788

3241 - Cement, Hydraulic

HOLCIM (U.S.) INC., pg. 1346, pg. 885
LAFARGE NORTH AMERICA INC., pg. 93, pg. 779
LAFARGE NORTH AMERICA INC., pg. 93, pg. 579
LEHIGH HANSON, INC., pg. 93, pg. 1513

3251 - Brick & Structural Clay Tile

BORAL ROOFING, pg. 71, pg. 107
CHEROKEE BRICK & TILE COMPANY, pg. 75, pg. 535
ELGIN-BUTLER BRICK COMPANY, pg. 80, pg. 1662
GLEN-GERY CORPORATION, pg. 84, pg. 1595
MORGAN ADVANCED MATERIALS, pg. 1363, pg. 835
PRAXAIR, INC., pg. 1178, pg. 344
UNIQUE TILE, pg. 117, pg. 988

3253 - Ceramic Wall & Floor Tile

AMERICAN BILTRITE INC., pg. 1878, pg. 856
CROSSVILLE, INC., pg. 77, pg. 1632
DAL-TILE CORPORATION, pg. 78, pg. 1678
FLORIDA TILE INDUSTRIES, INC., pg. 82, pg. 730
MANNINGTON MILLS, INC., pg. 934, pg. 1119
MANNINGTON RESILIENT FLOORS, pg. 934, pg. 1119
MOHAWK INDUSTRIES, INC., pg. 935, pg. 527
SUMMITVILLE TILES, INC., pg. 113, pg. 1475

3255 - Clay Refractories

CHEROKEE BRICK & TILE COMPANY, pg. 75, pg. 535
QUIKRETE COMPANIES, pg. 106, pg. 519
RESCO PRODUCTS, INC., pg. 107, pg. 1581
THERMAL CERAMICS INC., pg. 1382, pg. 525

3261 - Vitreous China Plumbing Fixtures & China & Earthenware Fittings & Bathroom Accessories

AS AMERICA, INC., pg. 68, pg. 1108
DIAMOND SPAS, INC., pg. 79, pg. 329
JACUZZI BRANDS CORPORATION, pg. 554, pg. 65
SLOAN VALVE COMPANY, pg. 1062, pg. 613

3262 - Vitreous China Table & Kitchen Articles

ABC CARPET & HOME INC., pg. 912, pg. 1185
ACTIVE ELECTRICAL SUPPLY COMPANY, pg. 612, pg. 563
ANADARKO PETROLEUM CORPORATION, pg. 971, pg. 1746
ANNA'S LINEN COMPANY INC., pg. 1760, pg. 70
APPLIANCE RECYCLING CENTERS OF AMERICA, INC., pg. 51, pg. 930
ARMSTRONG WORLD INDUSTRIES, INC., pg. 914, pg. 1545
AT HOME STORES LLC, pg. 1760, pg. 1729
BEALL'S, INC., pg. 1760, pg. 414
BED BATH & BEYOND INC., pg. 1121, pg. 1127
BELLACOR INC., pg. 917, pg. 929
THE BEN SILVER CORPORATION, pg. 38, pg. 1613
BLINDS TO GO INC., pg. 918, pg. 1101
CAPITOL LIGHTING, pg. 1294, pg. 1053
CARLISLE FOODSERVICE PRODUCTS INCORPORATED, pg. 1455, pg. 1485
CERAMTEC NORTH AMERICA ELECTRONIC APPLICATIONS, INC., pg. 628, pg. 1620
CERTAINTEED CORPORATION, pg. 74, pg. 1589
COUNTRY CURTAINS RETAIL INC., pg. 921, pg. 827
CRATE & BARREL, INC., pg. 922, pg. 640
CUISINART INC., pg. 1123, pg. 373
ENESCO, LLC, pg. 1124, pg. 620
EUROMARKET DESIGNS, INC., pg. 1124, pg. 640
FARREY'S WHOLESALE HARDWARE CO., INC., pg. 1047, pg. 442
GORDMANS STORES INC., pg. 1771, pg. 1016
THE GUILD INC., pg. 1255, pg. 1866
GUMP'S CORP., pg. 1772, pg. 219
HOMEGOODS, INC., pg. 1125, pg. 821
THE HOMER LAUGHLIN CHINA COMPANY, pg. 1125, pg. 1850
HUDSON'S BAY COMPANY, pg. 1773, pg. 1938
KIRKWOOD HOLDING, INC., pg. 649, pg. 1469
LAMPS PLUS INC., pg. 1300, pg. 64
LENOX CORPORATION, pg. 1126, pg. 1518
LIBBEY, INC., pg. 1126, pg. 1476
THE LONGABERGER COMPANY, pg. 1127, pg. 1467
MATTRESS HOLDING CORP., pg. 935, pg. 1711
MOMENTIVE PERFORMANCE MATERIALS, INC., pg. 1464, pg. 1349
ONEIDA LTD, pg. 1129, pg. 1318
OTTLITE, pg. 1303, pg. 475
PIER 1 IMPORTS, INC., pg. 940, pg. 1695
PQ CORPORATION, pg. 1178, pg. 1515
QUIKRETE COMPANIES, pg. 106, pg. 519
RESTORATION HARDWARE HOLDINGS, INC., pg. 1060, pg. 70
SELECT COMFORT CORPORATION, pg. 942, pg. 942
SMOKY MOUNTAIN KNIFE WORKS INC., pg. 1786, pg. 1655
SURE FIT INC., pg. 944, pg. 1514
THERMAL CERAMICS INC., pg. 1382, pg. 525
TUESDAY MORNING CORPORATION, pg. 1789, pg. 1690
UNIFRAX CORPORATION, pg. 220, pg. 1317
U.S. PUMICE COMPANY, pg. 1185, pg. 65
VILLEROY & BOCH TABLEWARE, LTD., pg. 1139, pg. 1085
WILLIAM-WAYNE & COMPANY, pg. 946, pg. 1314
WITH HEART & HAND, pg. 946, pg. 837

3264 - Porcelain Electrical Supplies

BUNTING MAGNETICS CO., pg. 1320, pg. 717
COORSTEK, INC., pg. 77, pg. 330
CORNING INCORPORATED, pg. 1122, pg. 1154
LAPP INSULATOR COMPANY, LLC, pg. 1946, pg. 1173

3271 - Concrete Block & Brick

BORAL ROOFING, pg. 71, pg. 107
CEMEX, INC., pg. 74, pg. 1703
CHEROKEE BRICK & TILE COMPANY, pg. 75, pg. 535
ELGIN-BUTLER BRICK COMPANY, pg. 80, pg. 1662
GLEN-GERY CORPORATION, pg. 84, pg. 1595
LEHIGH HANSON, INC., pg. 93, pg. 1513
MORGAN ADVANCED MATERIALS, pg. 1363, pg. 835
PRAXAIR, INC., pg. 1178, pg. 344
UNIQUE TILE, pg. 117, pg. 988

3272 - Concrete Products, Except Block & Brick

BORAL ROOFING, pg. 71, pg. 107
BRADLEY CORPORATION, pg. 71, pg. 1870
CONCRETE TECHNOLOGY INCORPORATED, pg. 921, pg. 438
DAYTON SUPERIOR CORPORATION, pg. 1328, pg. 1464
THE EUCLID CHEMICAL COMPANY, pg. 81, pg. 1430
GLEN-GERY CORPORATION, pg. 84, pg. 1595
HOLCIM (U.S.) INC., pg. 1346, pg. 885
L.B. FOSTER COMPANY, pg. 1355, pg. 1578
LEHIGH HANSON, INC., pg. 93, pg. 1513
LENNOX HEARTH PRODUCTS, pg. 93, pg. 1652
NOV AMERON, pg. 100, pg. 187
SMITH-MIDLAND CORPORATION, pg. 111, pg. 1795
TREMCO INCORPORATED, pg. 116, pg. 1405
VULCAN MATERIALS COMPANY, pg. 119, pg. 4

3273 - Ready-Mixed Concrete

CEMEX, INC., pg. 74, pg. 1703
LAFARGE NORTH AMERICA INC., pg. 93, pg. 579
LEHIGH HANSON, INC., pg. 93, pg. 1513
MDU RESOURCES GROUP, INC., pg. 981, pg. 1397
SAKRETE OF NORTH AMERICA, LLC, pg. 109, pg. 1425

3274 - Lime

CARMEUSE NORTH AMERICA, pg. 73, pg. 1574

3275 - Gypsum Products

ANADARKO PETROLEUM CORPORATION, pg. 971, pg. 1746

ARMSTRONG WORLD INDUSTRIES, INC., pg. 914, pg. 1545
THE BEN SILVER CORPORATION, pg. 38, pg. 1613
CERAMTEC NORTH AMERICA ELECTRONIC APPLICATIONS, INC., pg. 628, pg. 1620
CERTAINTEED CORPORATION, pg. 74, pg. 1589
CGC INC., pg. 75, pg. 1925
G-P GYPSUM CORPORATION, pg. 978, pg. 505
KIRKWOOD HOLDING, INC., pg. 649, pg. 1469
MOMENTIVE PERFORMANCE MATERIALS, INC., pg. 1464, pg. 1349
PQ CORPORATION, pg. 1178, pg. 1515
QUIKRETE COMPANIES, pg. 106, pg. 519
THERMAL CERAMICS INC., pg. 1382, pg. 525
UNIFRAX CORPORATION, pg. 220, pg. 1317
U.S. PUMICE COMPANY, pg. 1185, pg. 65
USG CORPORATION, pg. 118, pg. 594

3281 - Cut Stone & Stone Products

COLD SPRING GRANITE COMPANY, pg. 76, pg. 920
COSENTINO USA, pg. 77, pg. 1745
HEADWATERS INCORPORATED, pg. 978, pg. 1763
ROCK OF AGES CORPORATION, pg. 108, pg. 1766
RSI HOME PRODUCTS, pg. 108, pg. 1381

3291 - Abrasive Products

AMERICO MANUFACTURING CO., INC., pg. 325, pg. 482
ARTNET WORLDWIDE CORPORATION, pg. 353, pg. 1197
BARNES INTERNATIONAL INC., pg. 1317, pg. 654
BARTON MINES COMPANY LLC, pg. 1148, pg. 1171
CONNOISSEURS PRODUCTS CORPORATION, pg. 329, pg. 861
CRATEX MANUFACTURING CO., INC., pg. 77, pg. 85
FLOW INTERNATIONAL CORPORATION, pg. 1337, pg. 1821
HERMES ABRASIVES LTD., pg. 1166, pg. 1810
IMERYS FUSED MINERALS, pg. 1348, pg. 1317
SAINT-GOBAIN ABRASIVES, INC. - PHILADELPHIA, pg. 1180, pg. 1553

3295 - Minerals & Earths, Ground or Otherwise Treated

AMERICAN ART CLAY CO., INC., pg. 1759, pg. 682
BURGESS PIGMENT COMPANY, pg. 1150, pg. 535
HILL & GRIFFITH COMPANY, pg. 1167, pg. 1414
MULTISORB TECHNOLOGIES, INC., pg. 1570, pg. 1150
OIL-DRI CORPORATION OF AMERICA, pg. 1480, pg. 586
RESCO PRODUCTS GREENSBORO, pg. 107, pg. 1375
SILBRICO CORPORATION, pg. 110, pg. 617

3296 - Mineral Wool

ACOUSTIC INNOVATIONS INC., pg. 912, pg. 409
JOHNS MANVILLE CORPORATION, pg. 89, pg. 320
OWENS CORNING, pg. 102, pg. 1476
SILBRICO CORPORATION, pg. 110, pg. 617
UNIFRAX CORPORATION, pg. 220, pg. 1317

3297 - Nonclay Refractories

CORNING INCORPORATED, pg. 1122, pg. 1154
RESCO PRODUCTS, INC., pg. 107, pg. 1581

3299 - Nonmetallic Mineral Products, NEC

ANADARKO PETROLEUM CORPORATION, pg. 971, pg. 1746
ARMSTRONG WORLD INDUSTRIES, INC., pg. 914, pg. 1545
THE BEN SILVER CORPORATION, pg. 38, pg. 1613
BORAL ROOFING, pg. 71, pg. 107
BRADLEY CORPORATION, pg. 71, pg. 1870
CERAMTEC NORTH AMERICA ELECTRONIC APPLICATIONS, INC., pg. 628, pg. 1620
CERTAINTEED CORPORATION, pg. 74, pg. 1589
CONCRETE TECHNOLOGY INCORPORATED, pg. 921, pg. 438
DAYTON SUPERIOR CORPORATION, pg. 1328, pg. 1464
THE EUCLID CHEMICAL COMPANY, pg. 81, pg. 1430
GLEN-GERY CORPORATION, pg. 84, pg. 1595
HOLCIM (U.S.) INC., pg. 1346, pg. 885
KIRKWOOD HOLDING, INC., pg. 649, pg. 1469
L.B. FOSTER COMPANY, pg. 1355, pg. 1578
LEHIGH HANSON, INC., pg. 93, pg. 1513
LENNOX HEARTH PRODUCTS, pg. 93, pg. 1652
MOMENTIVE PERFORMANCE MATERIALS, INC., pg. 1464, pg. 1349
NOV AMERON, pg. 100, pg. 187
PQ CORPORATION, pg. 1178, pg. 1515
QUIKRETE COMPANIES, pg. 106, pg. 519
SMITH-MIDLAND CORPORATION, pg. 111, pg. 1795
THERMAL CERAMICS INC., pg. 1382, pg. 525
TREMCO INCORPORATED, pg. 116, pg. 1405
UNIFRAX CORPORATION, pg. 220, pg. 1317
U.S. PUMICE COMPANY, pg. 1185, pg. 65
VULCAN MATERIALS COMPANY, pg. 119, pg. 4

3312 - Steel Works, Blast Furnaces, Including Coke Ovens & Rolling Mills

A&A GLOBAL INDUSTRIES INC., pg. 948, pg. 767
A. FINKL & SONS CO., pg. 1309, pg. 563
ABBOTT BALL COMPANY, pg. 1040, pg. 383
AK STEEL HOLDING CORPORATION, pg. 1311, pg. 1479
ALLEGHENY TECHNOLOGIES INCORPORATED, pg. 66, pg. 1572
ANCHOR DANLY, pg. 67, pg. 1948
ARCELORMITTAL DOFASCO INC., pg. 68, pg. 1921
ARCELORMITTAL STEEL USA INC., pg. 68, pg. 564
CANADA FORGINGS INC., pg. 1321, pg. 1948
CARPENTER TECHNOLOGY CORPORATION, pg. 73, pg. 1584
COMMERCIAL METALS COMPANY, pg. 76, pg. 1718
ELLWOOD CITY FORGE, pg. 1333, pg. 1529
ESSAR STEEL ALGOMA INC., pg. 81, pg. 1933
GERDAU AMERISTEEL JOLIET STEEL MILL, pg. 1048, pg. 621
GERDAU AMERISTEEL SAND SPRINGS STEEL MILL, pg. 1048, pg. 1488
GIBRALTAR INDUSTRIES, INC., pg. 1340, pg. 1148
HANDY & HARMAN LTD., pg. 85, pg. 1352
KEYSTONE CONSOLIDATED INDUSTRIES, INC., pg. 90, pg. 1683
KEYSTONE STEEL & WIRE CO., pg. 91, pg. 651
NUCOR CORPORATION, pg. 101, pg. 1368
STEEL DYNAMICS, INC., pg. 113, pg. 681
WALTER ENERGY, INC., pg. 120, pg. 4
WORTHINGTON INDUSTRIES, INC., pg. 123, pg. 1444
XTEK, INC., pg. 1390, pg. 1427

3313 - Electrometallurgical Products, Except Steel

GLOBE SPECIALTY METALS INC., pg. 1164, pg. 1235
MATERION CORPORATION, pg. 1359, pg. 1463

3315 - Steel Wiredrawing & Steel Nails & Spikes

ASSOCIATED MATERIALS LLC, pg. 69, pg. 1445
KEYSTONE CONSOLIDATED INDUSTRIES, INC., pg. 90, pg. 1683
MASTER HALCO, pg. 96, pg. 474
MEADOW BURKE, pg. 96, pg. 474
NUCOR CORPORATION, pg. 101, pg. 1368
SENECA WIRE & MANUFACTURING COMPANY, pg. 1061, pg. 1454
WIRECO WORLDGROUP, pg. 1389, pg. 987
WIRECO WORLDGROUP, pg. 1389, pg. 721

3316 - Cold Rolled Steel Sheet, Strip & Bars

A&A GLOBAL INDUSTRIES INC., pg. 948, pg. 767
A. FINKL & SONS CO., pg. 1309, pg. 563
ABBOTT BALL COMPANY, pg. 1040, pg. 383
AK STEEL HOLDING CORPORATION, pg. 1311, pg. 1479
ALL-CLAD METALCRAFTERS LLC, pg. 1121, pg. 1519
ALLEGHENY TECHNOLOGIES INCORPORATED, pg. 66, pg. 1572
ANCHOR DANLY, pg. 67, pg. 1948
ARCELORMITTAL DOFASCO INC., pg. 68, pg. 1921
ARCELORMITTAL STEEL USA INC., pg. 68, pg. 564
CANADA FORGINGS INC., pg. 1321, pg. 1948
CARPENTER TECHNOLOGY CORPORATION, pg. 73, pg. 1584
CLARK GRAVE VAULT COMPANY, pg. 76, pg. 1438
COMMERCIAL METALS COMPANY, pg. 76, pg. 1718
CONSOLIDATED METAL PRODUCTS, INC., pg. 1325, pg. 1412
ELLWOOD CITY FORGE, pg. 1333, pg. 1529
ESSAR STEEL ALGOMA INC., pg. 81, pg. 1933
GERDAU AMERISTEEL JOLIET STEEL MILL, pg. 1048, pg. 621
GERDAU AMERISTEEL SAND SPRINGS STEEL MILL, pg. 1048, pg. 1488
GIBRALTAR INDUSTRIES, INC., pg. 1340, pg. 1148
GREER STEEL COMPANY, pg. 85, pg. 1447
HANDY & HARMAN LTD., pg. 85, pg. 1352
KEYSTONE CONSOLIDATED INDUSTRIES, INC., pg. 90, pg. 1683
KEYSTONE POWDERED METAL COMPANY, pg. 1353, pg. 1585
KEYSTONE STEEL & WIRE CO., pg. 91, pg. 651
NORWALK POWDERED METALS, INC., pg. 1058, pg. 340
NUCOR CORPORATION, pg. 101, pg. 1368
PETERSEN ALUMINUM CORPORATION, pg. 104, pg. 611
STEEL DYNAMICS, INC., pg. 113, pg. 681
SULZER METCO (WESTBURY) INC., pg. 1064, pg. 1350
ULBRICH STAINLESS STEEL & SPECIAL METALS, INC., pg. 117, pg. 360
VALMONT INDUSTRIES, INC., pg. 1387, pg. 1019
WALL COLMONOY CORPORATION, pg. 1185, pg. 898
WALTER ENERGY, INC., pg. 120, pg. 4
WORTHINGTON INDUSTRIES, INC., pg. 123, pg. 1444
XTEK, INC., pg. 1390, pg. 1427

3317 - Steel Pipe & Tubes

AFC CABLE SYSTEMS, INC., pg. 1294, pg. 835
AK STEEL HOLDING CORPORATION, pg. 1311, pg. 1479
ALLEGHENY TECHNOLOGIES INCORPORATED, pg. 66, pg. 1572
CHARLOTTE PIPE & FOUNDRY COMPANY, pg. 1044, pg. 1365
DAYTON SUPERIOR CORPORATION, pg. 1328, pg. 1464
L.B. FOSTER COMPANY, pg. 1355, pg. 1578
NAYLOR PIPE COMPANY, pg. 1364, pg. 584
NORTHWEST PIPE COMPANY, pg. 100, pg. 1846
PTC ALLIANCE CORP., pg. 1370, pg. 1594
STEEL DYNAMICS, INC., pg. 113, pg. 681
SUPERIOR TUBE COMPANY INC., pg. 113, pg. 1522
SWEPCO TUBE CORPORATION, pg. 114, pg. 1052
WHEATLAND TUBE COMPANY, pg. 121, pg. 1594

3321 - Gray & Ductile Iron Foundries

ANVIL INTERNATIONAL, INC., pg. 1879, pg. 1038
ARMSTRONG INTERNATIONAL, INC., pg. 1069, pg. 909
BRADKEN, pg. 1150, pg. 714
ELYRIA FOUNDRY COMPANY, pg. 1046, pg. 1451
NEENAH FOUNDRY COMPANY, pg. 99, pg. 1883
T&S PERFECTION CHAIN PRODUCTS, INC., pg. 1065, pg. 5
UNITED STATES PIPE & FOUNDRY COMPANY, INC., pg. 117, pg. 5
WALTER ENERGY, INC., pg. 120, pg. 4

3324 - Steel Investment Foundries

HITCHINER MANUFACTURING COMPANY INC., pg. 87, pg. 1037
MICHIGAN WHEEL CORPORATION, pg. 1709, pg. 888

3325 - Steel Foundries, NEC

ASSOCIATED MATERIALS LLC, pg. 69, pg. 1445
BRADKEN, pg. 1150, pg. 714
CARPENTER TECHNOLOGY CORPORATION, pg. 73, pg. 1584

THE FROG, SWITCH & MANUFACTURING COMPANY, pg. 1338, pg. 1520
HENSLEY INDUSTRIES, INC., pg. 1166, pg. 1682
PRECISION CASTPARTS CORP., pg. 105, pg. 1506
WAUKESHA FOUNDRY INC., pg. 1388, pg. 1898

3331 - Primary Smelting & Refining of Copper

LIQUIDMETAL TECHNOLOGIES, INC., pg. 1356, pg. 188
TECK RESOURCES LIMITED, pg. 1183, pg. 1912

3334 - Primary Production of Aluminum

CENTURY ALUMINUM OF WEST VIRGINIA, INC., pg. 74, pg. 1851
CONNELL LIMITED PARTNERSHIP, pg. 1325, pg. 793
KAISER ALUMINUM CORPORATION, pg. 90, pg. 86

3339 - Primary Smelting & Refining of Nonferrous Metals, Except Copper & Aluminum

ALLEGHENY TECHNOLOGIES INCORPORATED, pg. 66, pg. 1572
ATI WAH CHANG, pg. 1314, pg. 1492
BELMONT METALS, INC., pg. 1317, pg. 1145
COEUR D'ALENE MINES CORPORATION, pg. 1154, pg. 549
ENCORE WIRE CORPORATION, pg. 637, pg. 1726
KESTER, INC., pg. 649, pg. 620
NANOPHASE TECHNOLOGIES CORPORATION, pg. 1174, pg. 656
NOVELIS INC., pg. 100, pg. 516
STERN-LEACH, pg. 1064, pg. 783
TECK RESOURCES LIMITED, pg. 1183, pg. 1912

3341 - Secondary Smelting & Refining of Nonferrous Metals

ALERIS RECYCLING & SPECIFICATION ALLOYS AMERICAS, pg. 66, pg. 1405
ALPHA, pg. 1146, pg. 1123
BELMONT METALS, INC., pg. 1317, pg. 1145
COMPX INTERNATIONAL INC., pg. 1044, pg. 1678
HARSCO CORPORATION, pg. 86, pg. 1519
MATERION CORPORATION, pg. 1359, pg. 1463
MATERION MICROELECTRONICS & SERVICES, pg. 1559, pg. 1149
METALICO INC., pg. 97, pg. 1053

3351 - Rolling, Drawing & Extruding of Copper

ENCORE WIRE CORPORATION, pg. 637, pg. 1726
LITTLE FALLS ALLOYS, INC., pg. 1171, pg. 1107
OLIN CORPORATION, pg. 1176, pg. 976
SOUTHWIRE COMPANY, pg. 1063, pg. 527

3353 - Aluminum Sheet, Plate & Foil

ALCOA INC., pg. 65, pg. 1188
PETERSEN ALUMINUM CORPORATION, pg. 104, pg. 611
PLY GEM SIDING GROUP, pg. 105, pg. 986
REYNOLDS CONSUMER PRODUCTS, pg. 1138, pg. 625

3354 - Aluminum Extruded Products

ALCOA INC., pg. 65, pg. 1188
ASSOCIATED MATERIALS LLC, pg. 69, pg. 1445
CENTURY ALUMINUM OF WEST VIRGINIA, INC., pg. 74, pg. 1851
DELAIR GROUP, LLC, pg. 78, pg. 1053
HYGRADE METAL MOULDING MANUFACTURING CORP., pg. 1884, pg. 1516
MESTEK, INC., pg. 1074, pg. 857
TREDEGAR CORPORATION, pg. 1890, pg. 1804
WORTHINGTON INDUSTRIES, INC., pg. 123, pg. 1444
ZERO MANUFACTURING, INC., pg. 1892, pg. 1752

3355 - Aluminum Rolling & Drawing, NEC

AESP, INC., pg. 345, pg. 439
AFC CABLE SYSTEMS, INC., pg. 1294, pg. 835
AGILTRON, INC., pg. 1398, pg. 860
ALCOA INC., pg. 65, pg. 1188
AMPHENOL FIBER SYSTEMS INTERNATIONAL, INC., pg. 617, pg. 1658
ASSOCIATED MATERIALS LLC, pg. 69, pg. 1445
BELDEN, INC., pg. 624, pg. 993
COLEMAN CABLE, INC., pg. 1324, pg. 665
COMMSCOPE, pg. 630, pg. 668
COMMSCOPE, INC., pg. 278, pg. 1378
COOPER INTERCONNECT, pg. 630, pg. 1118
CORNING CABLE SYSTEMS LLC, pg. 1407, pg. 1378
CORNING INCORPORATED, pg. 1122, pg. 1154
DPL INC., pg. 1939, pg. 1445
ENCORE WIRE CORPORATION, pg. 637, pg. 1726
ESSEX GROUP, INC., pg. 638, pg. 680
FUSHI COPPERWELD, pg. 1296, pg. 1632
GENERAL CABLE CORPORATION, pg. 83, pg. 729
LIGHTPATH TECHNOLOGIES INC, pg. 1420, pg. 454
MATRIX INTEGRATION LLC, pg. 430, pg. 692
NOVELIS INC., pg. 100, pg. 516
OPLINK COMMUNICATIONS, INC., pg. 660, pg. 91
ORTRONICS/LEGRAND, pg. 451, pg. 359
RADIO FREQUENCY SYSTEMS, INC., pg. 666, pg. 354
REVOLUTION LIGHTING TECHNOLOGIES, INC., pg. 1304, pg. 377
THE RIPLEY COMPANY, pg. 1305, pg. 342
SENECA WIRE & MANUFACTURING COMPANY, pg. 1061, pg. 1454
SOURCE PHOTONICS, INC., pg. 1429, pg. 305
SOUTHWIRE COMPANY, pg. 1063, pg. 527
STANDARD WIRE & CABLE CO., pg. 1306, pg. 187
SUPERIOR ESSEX, INC., pg. 676, pg. 521
TIMES FIBER COMMUNICATIONS, INC., pg. 681, pg. 382
WERNER HOLDING CO., pg. 121, pg. 1534
W.L. GORE & ASSOCIATES, INC., pg. 122, pg. 388

3356 - Rolling, Drawing & Extruding of Nonferrous Metals, Except Copper & Aluminum

AAR CORP., pg. 223, pg. 671
AESP, INC., pg. 345, pg. 439
AFC CABLE SYSTEMS, INC., pg. 1294, pg. 835
AGILTRON, INC., pg. 1398, pg. 860
ALPHA, pg. 1146, pg. 1123
AMPHENOL FIBER SYSTEMS INTERNATIONAL, INC., pg. 617, pg. 1658
ASSOCIATED MATERIALS LLC, pg. 69, pg. 1445
BELDEN, INC., pg. 624, pg. 993
COLEMAN CABLE, INC., pg. 1324, pg. 665
COMMSCOPE, pg. 630, pg. 668
COMMSCOPE, INC., pg. 278, pg. 1378
COOPER INTERCONNECT, pg. 630, pg. 1118
CORNING CABLE SYSTEMS LLC, pg. 1407, pg. 1378
CORNING INCORPORATED, pg. 1122, pg. 1154
DPL INC., pg. 1939, pg. 1445
ENCORE WIRE CORPORATION, pg. 637, pg. 1726
ESSEX GROUP, INC., pg. 638, pg. 680
FUSHI COPPERWELD, pg. 1296, pg. 1632
GENERAL CABLE CORPORATION, pg. 83, pg. 729
HYGRADE METAL MOULDING MANUFACTURING CORP., pg. 1884, pg. 1516
LIGHTPATH TECHNOLOGIES INC, pg. 1420, pg. 454
MATRIX INTEGRATION LLC, pg. 430, pg. 692
METALICO INC., pg. 97, pg. 1053
NL INDUSTRIES, INC., pg. 1174, pg. 1684
OPLINK COMMUNICATIONS, INC., pg. 660, pg. 91
ORTRONICS/LEGRAND, pg. 451, pg. 359
RADIO FREQUENCY SYSTEMS, INC., pg. 666, pg. 354
REVOLUTION LIGHTING TECHNOLOGIES, INC., pg. 1304, pg. 377
THE RIPLEY COMPANY, pg. 1305, pg. 342
SIGMUND COHN CORP., pg. 1062, pg. 1183
SOURCE PHOTONICS, INC., pg. 1429, pg. 305
SOUTHWIRE COMPANY, pg. 1063, pg. 527
SPECIAL METALS CORPORATION, pg. 1377, pg. 1850
STANDARD WIRE & CABLE CO., pg. 1306, pg. 187
SUPERIOR ESSEX, INC., pg. 676, pg. 521
SWEPCO TUBE CORPORATION, pg. 114, pg. 1052
TIMES FIBER COMMUNICATIONS, INC., pg. 681, pg. 382
ULBRICH STAINLESS STEEL & SPECIAL METALS, INC., pg. 117, pg. 360
W.L. GORE & ASSOCIATES, INC., pg. 122, pg. 388
WORTHINGTON INDUSTRIES, INC., pg. 123, pg. 1444

3357 - Drawing & Insulating of Nonferrous Wire

AESP, INC., pg. 345, pg. 439
AFC CABLE SYSTEMS, INC., pg. 1294, pg. 835
AGILTRON, INC., pg. 1398, pg. 860
AMPHENOL FIBER SYSTEMS INTERNATIONAL, INC., pg. 617, pg. 1658
ASSOCIATED MATERIALS LLC, pg. 69, pg. 1445
BELDEN, INC., pg. 624, pg. 993
COLEMAN CABLE, INC., pg. 1324, pg. 665
COMMSCOPE, pg. 630, pg. 668
COMMSCOPE, INC., pg. 278, pg. 1378
COOPER INTERCONNECT, pg. 630, pg. 1118
CORNING CABLE SYSTEMS LLC, pg. 1407, pg. 1378
CORNING INCORPORATED, pg. 1122, pg. 1154
DPL INC., pg. 1939, pg. 1445
ENCORE WIRE CORPORATION, pg. 637, pg. 1726
ESSEX GROUP, INC., pg. 638, pg. 680
FUSHI COPPERWELD, pg. 1296, pg. 1632
GENERAL CABLE CORPORATION, pg. 83, pg. 729
LIGHTPATH TECHNOLOGIES INC, pg. 1420, pg. 454
MATRIX INTEGRATION LLC, pg. 430, pg. 692
OPLINK COMMUNICATIONS, INC., pg. 660, pg. 91
ORTRONICS/LEGRAND, pg. 451, pg. 359
RADIO FREQUENCY SYSTEMS, INC., pg. 666, pg. 354
REVOLUTION LIGHTING TECHNOLOGIES, INC., pg. 1304, pg. 377
THE RIPLEY COMPANY, pg. 1305, pg. 342
SOURCE PHOTONICS, INC., pg. 1429, pg. 305
SOUTHWIRE COMPANY, pg. 1063, pg. 527
STANDARD WIRE & CABLE CO., pg. 1306, pg. 187
SUPERIOR ESSEX, INC., pg. 676, pg. 521
TIMES FIBER COMMUNICATIONS, INC., pg. 681, pg. 382
W.L. GORE & ASSOCIATES, INC., pg. 122, pg. 388

3363 - Aluminum Die-Castings

ATI LADISH FORGING, pg. 69, pg. 1856
CHICAGO WHITE METAL CASTING, INC., pg. 1153, pg. 556
CONSOLIDATED METCO INC., pg. 1325, pg. 1846
HITCHINER MANUFACTURING COMPANY INC., pg. 87, pg. 1037
KITCHEN-QUIP, INC., pg. 1885, pg. 699
KOCH ENTERPRISES, INC., pg. 91, pg. 679
MADISON-KIPP CORPORATION, pg. 1358, pg. 1866
PECO, INC., pg. 1368, pg. 1505
TWIN CITY DIE CASTINGS CO., pg. 1066, pg. 945

3364 - Nonferrous Die-Castings, Except Aluminum

AMERICAN CASTING & MANUFACTURING CORPORATION, pg. 1312, pg. 1321
CHICAGO WHITE METAL CASTING, INC., pg. 1153, pg. 556
DECO PRODUCTS CO., pg. 1045, pg. 704
MADISON-KIPP CORPORATION, pg. 1358, pg. 1866
MATTHEWS INTERNATIONAL CORPORATION, pg. 1662, pg. 1578
PECO, INC., pg. 1368, pg. 1505
PRECISION CASTPARTS CORP., pg. 105, pg. 1506
TWIN CITY DIE CASTINGS CO., pg. 1066, pg. 945
WORTHINGTON INDUSTRIES, INC., pg. 123, pg. 1444

3365 - Aluminum Foundries

CALPHALON CORPORATION, pg. 1121, pg. 1470
CONSOLIDATED METCO INC., pg. 1325, pg. 1846
MAXION WHEELS, pg. 212, pg. 903
NORTHLAND ALUMINUM PRODUCTS INC., pg. 1129, pg.

941
RANGE KLEEN MANUFACTURING INC., *pg.* 60, *pg.* 1458
THE VOLLRATH COMPANY LLC, *pg.* 1139, *pg.* 1894

3369 - Nonferrous Foundries, Except Aluminum & Copper

ELYRIA FOUNDRY COMPANY, *pg.* 1046, *pg.* 1451
HELMICK CORPORATION, *pg.* 1346, *pg.* 1849
KITCHEN-QUIP, INC., *pg.* 1885, *pg.* 699
PFISTER, INC., *pg.* 1059, *pg.* 88
WAUKESHA FOUNDRY INC., *pg.* 1388, *pg.* 1898

3398 - Metal Heat Treating

BODYCOTE THERMAL PROCESSING, *pg.* 71, *pg.* 632
GIBRALTAR INDUSTRIES, INC., *pg.* 1340, *pg.* 1148
KARSTEN MANUFACTURING CORPORATION, *pg.* 1838, *pg.* 17
KENNAMETAL INC., *pg.* 1052, *pg.* 1547
STIHL, INC., *pg.* 1064, *pg.* 1810
WALL COLMONOY CORPORATION, *pg.* 1185, *pg.* 898

3411 - Metal Cans

BALL CORPORATION, *pg.* 1452, *pg.* 311
BWAY HOLDING COMPANY, *pg.* 1454, *pg.* 491
CROWN HOLDINGS, INC., *pg.* 1456, *pg.* 1562
EAGLE MANUFACTURING COMPANY, *pg.* 79, *pg.* 1851
INDEPENDENT CAN COMPANY, *pg.* 1460, *pg.* 760
REXAM BEVERAGE CAN NORTH AMERICA, *pg.* 1468, *pg.* 588

3421 - Cutlery

ACME UNITED CORPORATION, *pg.* 1040, *pg.* 346
ANDIS COMPANY, *pg.* 498, *pg.* 1895
BEAR & SON CUTLERY, INC., *pg.* 1827, *pg.* 7
BIRKS & MAYORS INC., *pg.* 1, *pg.* 1953
BUCK KNIVES, INC., *pg.* 1828, *pg.* 550
COMPX INTERNATIONAL INC., *pg.* 1044, *pg.* 1678
CUTCO CORPORATION, *pg.* 1123, *pg.* 1318
DEXTER-RUSSELL INC., *pg.* 1123, *pg.* 844
FISKARS BRANDS, INC., *pg.* 1124, *pg.* 1866
GERBER LEGENDARY BLADES, *pg.* 1834, *pg.* 1503
THE GILLETTE COMPANY, *pg.* 509, *pg.* 795
HYDE TOOLS, INC., *pg.* 1125, *pg.* 844
LIBBEY, INC., *pg.* 1126, *pg.* 1476
LIFETIME BRANDS, INC., *pg.* 1127, *pg.* 1161
ONEIDA LTD, *pg.* 1129, *pg.* 1318
THE VOLLRATH COMPANY LLC, *pg.* 1139, *pg.* 1894
WAHL CLIPPER CORPORATION, *pg.* 524, *pg.* 662
THE W.E. BASSETT COMPANY, *pg.* 524, *pg.* 371
W.R. CASE & SONS CUTLERY COMPANY, *pg.* 1141, *pg.* 1518

3423 - Hand & Edge Tools, Except Machine Tools & Hand Saws

ACME UNITED CORPORATION, *pg.* 1040, *pg.* 346
A.G. DAVIS/AA GAGE, *pg.* 1310, *pg.* 908
AGCO CORPORATION, *pg.* 700, *pg.* 530
AGI-VR/WESSON INC, *pg.* 1041, *pg.* 415
ALAMO GROUP INC., *pg.* 1311, *pg.* 1745
AMEREQUIP CORPORATION, *pg.* 700, *pg.* 1862
ARIENS COMPANY INC., *pg.* 700, *pg.* 1855
ARROW FASTENER COMPANY, INC., *pg.* 1042, *pg.* 1118
ART'S-WAY MANUFACTURING CO., INC., *pg.* 701, *pg.* 701
A.T. FERRELL COMPANY, INC., *pg.* 701, *pg.* 674
ATT HOLDING CO., *pg.* 1043, *pg.* 1519
AUSCO PRODUCTS, INC., *pg.* 199, *pg.* 872
BARRY CONTROLS, *pg.* 1317, *pg.* 825
BEAR & SON CUTLERY, INC., *pg.* 1827, *pg.* 7
BEHLEN MFG. CO., *pg.* 701, *pg.* 1010
BLOUNT INTERNATIONAL, INC., *pg.* 1043, *pg.* 1501
BOUMATIC LLC, *pg.* 701, *pg.* 1865
BOURN & KOCH MACHINE TOOL COMPANY, *pg.* 1319, *pg.* 654
BRADY CORPORATION, *pg.* 363, *pg.* 1873
BRIGGS & STRATTON CORPORATION, *pg.* 201, *pg.* 1899
BUCK KNIVES, INC., *pg.* 1828, *pg.* 550
BUSH HOG, INC., *pg.* 702, *pg.* 8
THE CHALLENGE MACHINERY COMPANY, *pg.* 1322, *pg.* 902
CHANNELLOCK, INC., *pg.* 1044, *pg.* 1551
CHARLES & COLVARD LTD, *pg.* 3, *pg.* 1384
CHARLES MACHINE WORKS, INC., *pg.* 1322, *pg.* 1488
CHASE CORPORATION, *pg.* 1152, *pg.* 803
THE CINCINNATI GILBERT MACHINE TOOL COMPANY, L.L.C., *pg.* 1323, *pg.* 1411
CNH AMERICA LLC, *pg.* 702, *pg.* 560
COMPX INTERNATIONAL INC., *pg.* 1044, *pg.* 1678
CTB INTERNATIONAL CORP., *pg.* 850, *pg.* 695
CUTCO CORPORATION, *pg.* 1123, *pg.* 1318
DANAHER CORPORATION, *pg.* 1044, *pg.* 397
DANUSER MACHINE COMPANY, INC., *pg.* 703, *pg.* 978
DEERE & COMPANY, *pg.* 703, *pg.* 632
DEGELMAN INDUSTRIES LTD., *pg.* 703, *pg.* 1962
DEXTER-RUSSELL INC., *pg.* 1123, *pg.* 844
DORMER PRAMET, *pg.* 1329, *pg.* 609
DYNATECT MANUFACTURING INC., *pg.* 1330, *pg.* 1883
DYNATEX INTERNATIONAL, *pg.* 635, *pg.* 277
EASTMAN INDUSTRIES, *pg.* 1046, *pg.* 751
ECHO INCORPORATED, *pg.* 1046, *pg.* 626
EDAC TECHNOLOGIES CORPORATION, *pg.* 1332, *pg.* 342
EDLUND COMPANY, INC., *pg.* 1123, *pg.* 1765
ELECTRIC EEL MANUFACTURING CO., INC., *pg.* 80, *pg.* 1473
EMERSON INDUSTRIAL AUTOMATION, *pg.* 1296, *pg.* 657
EXCEL INDUSTRIES, INC., *pg.* 1795, *pg.* 715
FISCHER SPINDLE GROUP, *pg.* 1047, *pg.* 1888
FISKARS BRANDS, INC., *pg.* 1124, *pg.* 1866
FLEXBAR MACHINE CORP., *pg.* 1337, *pg.* 1169
FLOWTRON OUTDOOR PRODUCTS, *pg.* 639, *pg.* 830
GANDY COMPANY, *pg.* 703, *pg.* 952
GAS-FIRED PRODUCTS, INC., *pg.* 1338, *pg.* 1367
GEA FARM TECHNOLOGIES, *pg.* 704, *pg.* 636
GEHL COMPANY, *pg.* 1339, *pg.* 1899
GENERAL TOOLS & INSTRUMENTS LLC, *pg.* 1048, *pg.* 1234
GERBER LEGENDARY BLADES, *pg.* 1834, *pg.* 1503
THE GILLETTE COMPANY, *pg.* 509, *pg.* 795
GORILLA GLUE CO., *pg.* 1048, *pg.* 1414
GREAT PLAINS MANUFACTURING, INCORPORATED, *pg.* 704, *pg.* 721
GSI GROUP INC., *pg.* 1415, *pg.* 784
HARDINGE INC., *pg.* 1344, *pg.* 1157
HARIG MANUFACTURING CORPORATION, *pg.* 1345, *pg.* 637
HARPER INDUSTRIES, INC., *pg.* 704, *pg.* 715
HARRIS WASTE MANAGEMENT GROUP, INC., *pg.* 1345, *pg.* 526
HARSH INTERNATIONAL, INC., *pg.* 1345, *pg.* 324
HAWKEYE STEEL PRODUCTS, INC., *pg.* 704, *pg.* 708
HENNESSY INDUSTRIES, INC., *pg.* 207, *pg.* 1639
HIGHWAY EQUIPMENT COMPANY, *pg.* 704, *pg.* 702
HILTI, INC., *pg.* 1346, *pg.* 1490
HINIKER COMPANY, *pg.* 704, *pg.* 927
HONEYWELL SENSING & CONTROL, *pg.* 229, *pg.* 926
HOUGEN MANUFACTURING INC., *pg.* 1347, *pg.* 908
HUBBELL INCORPORATED, *pg.* 1299, *pg.* 370
HYDE TOOLS, INC., *pg.* 1125, *pg.* 844
IDI COMPOSITES INTERNATIONAL, *pg.* 57, *pg.* 696
JACOBSEN TEXTRON, *pg.* 1708, *pg.* 1367
JOHN DEERE CONSUMER & COMMERCIAL EQUIPMENT, INC., *pg.* 705, *pg.* 1360
JOHN DEERE LTD., *pg.* 705, *pg.* 1920
KELLY-MOORE PAINT COMPANY, INC., *pg.* 1443, *pg.* 198
KELLY RYAN EQUIPMENT COMPANY, *pg.* 705, *pg.* 1010
KENNAMETAL INC., *pg.* 1052, *pg.* 1547
KENNAMETAL IPG, *pg.* 1353, *pg.* 1615
KILLARK ELECTRIC, *pg.* 1300, *pg.* 998
KLEIN TOOLS INC., *pg.* 1052, *pg.* 627
LAM RESEARCH CORPORATION, *pg.* 1354, *pg.* 91
LAPP INSULATOR COMPANY, LLC, *pg.* 1946, *pg.* 1173
LEATHERMAN TOOL GROUP, INC., *pg.* 1053, *pg.* 1504
LIBBEY, INC., *pg.* 1126, *pg.* 1476
LIFETIME BRANDS, INC., *pg.* 1127, *pg.* 1161
LINDSAY CORPORATION, *pg.* 1356, *pg.* 1016
LISLE CORPORATION, *pg.* 1356, *pg.* 703
LOWELL CORPORATION, *pg.* 1053, *pg.* 856
THE L.S. STARRETT COMPANY, *pg.* 1421, *pg.* 783
LUNDELL ENTERPRISES, INC., *pg.* 706, *pg.* 703
MATCO TOOLS CORPORATION, *pg.* 1055, *pg.* 1474
MCLAUGHLIN BORING SYSTEMS, *pg.* 1360, *pg.* 1617
MELNOR, INC., *pg.* 1055, *pg.* 1811
MILLER MANUFACTURING COMPANY, *pg.* 706, *pg.* 921
MOORE TOOL COMPANY, INC., *pg.* 1057, *pg.* 339
MTD PRODUCTS, INC., *pg.* 1057, *pg.* 1478
MULBERRY METAL PRODUCTS, INC., *pg.* 1302, *pg.* 1127
MULTI-METALS, *pg.* 1363, *pg.* 737
MY-D HAN-D MFG. INC., *pg.* 706, *pg.* 714
NEWELL RUBBERMAID INC., *pg.* 1128, *pg.* 515
NUPLA CORPORATION, *pg.* 101, *pg.* 281
O'BRIEN CORPORATION, *pg.* 1366, *pg.* 1001
ONEIDA LTD, *pg.* 1129, *pg.* 1318
PANDUIT CORP., *pg.* 661, *pg.* 663
THE PERRY COMPANY, *pg.* 706, *pg.* 1749
POWERS FASTENERS INC., *pg.* 1059, *pg.* 1143
PRECITECH, INC., *pg.* 1427, *pg.* 1035
PREFORMED LINE PRODUCTS COMPANY, *pg.* 1370, *pg.* 1434
Q.E.P. CO., INC., *pg.* 1371, *pg.* 413
REINKE MANUFACTURING COMPANY, INC., *pg.* 707, *pg.* 1010
RIDGE TOOL COMPANY, *pg.* 1372, *pg.* 1452
RITCHIE INDUSTRIES, INC., *pg.* 707, *pg.* 703
ROBERT BOSCH TOOL CORP, *pg.* 1060, *pg.* 634
S-T INDUSTRIES, INC., *pg.* 1428, *pg.* 956
SCHILLER-PFEIFFER, INC., *pg.* 1061, *pg.* 1587
SEEDBURO EQUIPMENT CO., *pg.* 707, *pg.* 590
SENECA FALLS MACHINES, *pg.* 1374, *pg.* 1341
SHERMAN & REILLY, INC., *pg.* 1062, *pg.* 1629
SIMONDS INTERNATIONAL CORPORATION, *pg.* 1376, *pg.* 819
SIOUX STEEL COMPANY, *pg.* 707, *pg.* 1625
SK HAND TOOL CORPORATION, *pg.* 1062, *pg.* 663
SNAP-ON INCORPORATED, *pg.* 1062, *pg.* 1862
SOUTHWESTERN INDUSTRIES, INC., *pg.* 1429, *pg.* 69
SPEEDGRIP CHUCK, INC., *pg.* 1377, *pg.* 677
STANLEY BLACK & DECKER, INC., *pg.* 1063, *pg.* 358
STARRETT, *pg.* 1064, *pg.* 1621
THE STEP2 COMPANY LLC, *pg.* 1889, *pg.* 1474
THEXTON MANUFACTURING COMPANY, INC., *pg.* 218, *pg.* 925
THE TORO COMPANY, *pg.* 1065, *pg.* 918
VAUGHAN & BUSHNELL MANUFACTURING COMPANY, INC., *pg.* 1066, *pg.* 616
VERMEER MANUFACTURING COMPANY, *pg.* 708, *pg.* 711
THE W.E. BASSETT COMPANY, *pg.* 524, *pg.* 371
WEATHERTEC CORPORATION, *pg.* 708, *pg.* 93
WIREMOLD/LEGRAND, *pg.* 689, *pg.* 383
WISCONSIN MACHINE TOOL CORPORATION, *pg.* 1389, *pg.* 1855
WOODCRAFT SUPPLY CORP., *pg.* 1390, *pg.* 1850
W.R. CASE & SONS CUTLERY COMPANY, *pg.* 1141, *pg.* 1518
YETTER MANUFACTURING CO., INC., *pg.* 708, *pg.* 598
ZEPHYR MANUFACTURING CO., INC., *pg.* 1391, *pg.* 105

3425 - Hand Saws & Saw Blades

LENOX, *pg.* 1053, *pg.* 817
MILWAUKEE ELECTRIC TOOL CORP., *pg.* 1056, *pg.* 1855

3429 - Hardware, NEC

AIR-LEC INDUSTRIES LLC, *pg.* 1041, *pg.* 1864
A.L. HANSEN MANUFACTURING CO., *pg.* 1041, *pg.* 665
ALLFAST FASTENING SYSTEMS, INC., *pg.* 1041, *pg.* 66
AMATOM ELECTRONIC HARDWARE, INC., *pg.* 1041, *pg.* 342
AMERICAN LOCKER GROUP INCORPORATED, *pg.* 1041, *pg.* 1674
AMERICAN VAN EQUIPMENT INC., *pg.* 199, *pg.* 1078
APTARGROUP, INC., *pg.* 1451, *pg.* 598
ASCO SINTERING CO., *pg.* 1042, *pg.* 126
ATTWOOD CORPORATION, *pg.* 1705, *pg.* 897
AUTOMATIC EQUIPMENT CORPORATION, *pg.* 1315, *pg.* 1410
BALL & BALL HARDWARE REPRODUCTIONS, *pg.* 916, *pg.* 1531
BARNES GROUP INC., *pg.* 1317, *pg.* 340
BLACK & DECKER, *pg.* 1043, *pg.* 1907
BOBRICK WASHROOM EQUIPMENT, INC., *pg.* 1043, *pg.* 166
BRYCE CORPORATION, *pg.* 1879, *pg.* 1641
BTM CORPORATION, *pg.* 1320, *pg.* 898
BUCKEYE CORRUGATED INC., *pg.* 1454, *pg.* 1400
BWAY HOLDING COMPANY, *pg.* 1454, *pg.* 491
CASCADE CORPORATION, *pg.* 1321, *pg.* 1497

CHICAGO-WILCOX MFG. COMPANY, INC., *pg.* 202, *pg.* 661
COMPX INTERNATIONAL INC., *pg.* 1044, *pg.* 1678
CROSMAN CORPORATION, *pg.* 951, *pg.* 1143
DARNELL-ROSE, *pg.* 1045, *pg.* 67
DECO PRODUCTS CO., *pg.* 1045, *pg.* 704
DREMEL, *pg.* 1046, *pg.* 634
DRIV-LOK, INC., *pg.* 1046, *pg.* 662
THE EASTERN COMPANY, *pg.* 1331, *pg.* 357
EBERHARD MANUFACTURING DIVISION, *pg.* 1046, *pg.* 1475
E.R. WAGNER CASTERS AND WHEELS DIV., *pg.* 1047, *pg.* 1874
ERICO INTERNATIONAL CORPORATION, *pg.* 1335, *pg.* 1472
ESCO CORPORATION, *pg.* 1335, *pg.* 1502
FEDERAL HOSE MANUFACTURING INC., *pg.* 1047, *pg.* 1469
FLEXIBLE STEEL LACING COMPANY, *pg.* 1337, *pg.* 608
FORTUNE BRANDS HOME & SECURITY, INC., *pg.* 55, *pg.* 600
GIBRALTAR INDUSTRIES, INC., *pg.* 1340, *pg.* 1148
GREAT LAKES CASE & CABINET CO., INC., *pg.* 401, *pg.* 1529
GREIF INC., *pg.* 1459, *pg.* 1447
GRIPNAIL CORPORATION, *pg.* 1048, *pg.* 1601
GROOV-PIN CORPORATION, *pg.* 1049, *pg.* 1608
HANNAY REELS INC., *pg.* 1344, *pg.* 1351
KABA ILCO CORP., *pg.* 1052, *pg.* 1390
KENNAMETAL INC., *pg.* 1052, *pg.* 1547
KNAPE & VOGT MANUFACTURING COMPANY, *pg.* 1052, *pg.* 913
KURZ TRANSFER PRODUCTS, L.P., *pg.* 1354, *pg.* 1367
LARSON-JUHL US LLC, *pg.* 933, *pg.* 537
LYDALL, INC., *pg.* 1357, *pg.* 354
MANITOWOC CRANE SHADY GROVE, *pg.* 1359, *pg.* 1586
MASTER LOCK COMPANY LLC, *pg.* 1055, *pg.* 1884
MATCO TOOLS CORPORATION, *pg.* 1055, *pg.* 1474
MATERION CORPORATION, *pg.* 1359, *pg.* 1463
MATERION MICROELECTRONICS & SERVICES, *pg.* 1559, *pg.* 1149
MEDECO HIGH SECURITY LOCKS, INC., *pg.* 1055, *pg.* 1806
MITEK, INC., *pg.* 1056, *pg.* 975
NACCO INDUSTRIES, INC., *pg.* 1174, *pg.* 1433
OMG, INC., *pg.* 1367, *pg.* 781
OXO, *pg.* 1058, *pg.* 1275
PACTIV CORPORATION, *pg.* 1466, *pg.* 624
PASLODE, *pg.* 1059, *pg.* 664
PENN ENGINEERING & MANUFACTURING CORP., *pg.* 1059, *pg.* 1525
PENNENGINEERING FASTENING TECHNOLOGIES, *pg.* 1059, *pg.* 1526
PORTLAND WILLAMETTE, *pg.* 1129, *pg.* 1505
PRECISION VALVE CORPORATION, *pg.* 1060, *pg.* 1357
REV-A-SHELF, *pg.* 1060, *pg.* 738
RICHELIEU HARDWARE LTD., *pg.* 1060, *pg.* 1961
ROCKY MOUNTAIN HARDWARE INC., *pg.* 1061, *pg.* 549
RONA, INC., *pg.* 216, *pg.* 1950
ROUSSEAU METAL, INC., *pg.* 463, *pg.* 1960
RUSSEL METALS INC., *pg.* 1180, *pg.* 1928
RYERSON INC., *pg.* 1373, *pg.* 589
SARGENT & GREENLEAF, INC., *pg.* 1061, *pg.* 739
SARGENT MANUFACTURING COMPANY, *pg.* 1061, *pg.* 359
SCHAEFER MARINE INC., *pg.* 1373, *pg.* 835
SENIOR FLEXONICS INC., *pg.* 1375, *pg.* 556
SENTRY GROUP, INC., *pg.* 468, *pg.* 1337
SHILOH INDUSTRIES, INC., *pg.* 1375, *pg.* 1478
SHUR-CO, INC., *pg.* 110, *pg.* 1626
SIMPSON MANUFACTURING COMPANY, INC., *pg.* 1376, *pg.* 185
SOLIDSCAPE, INC., *pg.* 1063, *pg.* 1037
SOUTHERN FOLGER DETENTION EQUIPMENT COMPANY, *pg.* 1063, *pg.* 1743
SPIROL INTERNATIONAL CORPORATION, *pg.* 1378, *pg.* 345
STANLEY BLACK & DECKER, INC., *pg.* 1063, *pg.* 358
TCI PRECISION METALS, INC., *pg.* 1380, *pg.* 95
THERMOS L.L.C., *pg.* 61, *pg.* 660
TIDEL ENGINEERING, L.P., *pg.* 1382, *pg.* 1670
TRINITY INDUSTRIES, INC., *pg.* 116, *pg.* 1690
TRUTH HARDWARE CORP., *pg.* 1066, *pg.* 952
UNIVERSAL INDUSTRIAL PRODUCTS CO., *pg.* 1066, *pg.* 1470
WINNER INTERNATIONAL, LLC, *pg.* 222, *pg.* 1586
WITT INDUSTRIES, INC., *pg.* 1140, *pg.* 1461
WORTHINGTON INDUSTRIES, INC., *pg.* 123, *pg.* 1444
YARDLEY PRODUCTS CORPORATION, *pg.* 1391, *pg.* 1596
ZIM-AMERICAN ISRAELI SHIPPING CO., *pg.* 1931, *pg.* 1798
ZIPPO MANUFACTURING COMPANY, INC., *pg.* 1895, *pg.* 1518

3431 - Enameled Iron & Metal Sanitary Ware

AMERICAN SPECIALTIES INC., *pg.* 325, *pg.* 1356
BOBRICK WASHROOM EQUIPMENT, INC., *pg.* 1043, *pg.* 166
BRADLEY CORPORATION, *pg.* 71, *pg.* 1870
DECOLAV, INC., *pg.* 1123, *pg.* 411
ELKAY MANUFACTURING COMPANY, *pg.* 80, *pg.* 645
HAWS CORPORATION, *pg.* 56, *pg.* 1032
JOHN BOOS & CO., *pg.* 1126, *pg.* 609
JOSAM COMPANY, *pg.* 89, *pg.* 695
KOHLER CO., *pg.* 91, *pg.* 1862
METPAR CORP., *pg.* 97, *pg.* 1350
MOEN INCORPORATED, *pg.* 1056, *pg.* 1468
MURDOCK, INC., *pg.* 98, *pg.* 67
POLAR WARE COMPANY, *pg.* 1129, *pg.* 1862
SPEAKMAN COMPANY, *pg.* 112, *pg.* 388
TELSCO INDUSTRIES, INC., *pg.* 1381, *pg.* 1698

3432 - Plumbing Fixture Fittings & Trim

AS AMERICA, INC., *pg.* 68, *pg.* 1108
BEAD INDUSTRIES INC., *pg.* 200, *pg.* 356
BRASSCRAFT MANUFACTURING COMPANY, *pg.* 1043, *pg.* 902
THE CHICAGO FAUCET COMPANY, *pg.* 1044, *pg.* 606
DELTA FAUCET COMPANY, *pg.* 78, *pg.* 684
D'VONTZ, *pg.* 1123, *pg.* 1489
E.L. MUSTEE & SONS, INC., *pg.* 1124, *pg.* 1430
FALCON WATERFREE TECHNOLOGIES, LLC, *pg.* 81, *pg.* 912
FISHER MANUFACTURING COMPANY, *pg.* 81, *pg.* 297
THE FORD METER BOX COMPANY, INC., *pg.* 1047, *pg.* 698
GERBER PLUMBING FIXTURES CORPORATION, *pg.* 84, *pg.* 672
GROHE AMERICA, INC., *pg.* 1048, *pg.* 557
JACUZZI BRANDS CORPORATION, *pg.* 554, *pg.* 65
JOSAM COMPANY, *pg.* 89, *pg.* 695
KEENEY MANUFACTURING COMPANY, *pg.* 90, *pg.* 360
KOHLER CO., *pg.* 91, *pg.* 1862
MASCO CORPORATION, *pg.* 96, *pg.* 909
MOEN INCORPORATED, *pg.* 1056, *pg.* 1468
PFISTER, INC., *pg.* 1059, *pg.* 88
RAIN BIRD CORPORATION, *pg.* 707, *pg.* 44
SPEAKMAN COMPANY, *pg.* 112, *pg.* 388
SYMMONS INDUSTRIES, INC., *pg.* 114, *pg.* 803
T&S BRASS & BRONZE WORKS, INC., *pg.* 114, *pg.* 1623
TELSCO INDUSTRIES, INC., *pg.* 1381, *pg.* 1698

3433 - Heating Equipment, Except Electric & Warm Air Furnaces

AERO SYSTEMS ENGINEERING INC., *pg.* 223, *pg.* 959
ALGAS-SDI, *pg.* 1311, *pg.* 1831
AMERICAN ELECTRIC TECHNOLOGIES, INC., *pg.* 349, *pg.* 1700
AMERICAN FELT & FILTER COMPANY, *pg.* 1312, *pg.* 1184
A.O. SMITH CORPORATION, *pg.* 1313, *pg.* 1872
AUTOMATION DEVICES, INC., *pg.* 1315, *pg.* 1532
BARD MANUFACTURING COMPANY, *pg.* 1069, *pg.* 1406
BRADFORD-WHITE CORPORATION, *pg.* 1069, *pg.* 1514
BROAN-NUTONE LLC, *pg.* 1069, *pg.* 1860
BURNHAM HOLDINGS, INC., *pg.* 1069, *pg.* 1546
CHROMALOX, INC., *pg.* 1070, *pg.* 1574
C.I. HAYES, *pg.* 1070, *pg.* 1600
CLAYTON INDUSTRIES CO., *pg.* 1323, *pg.* 66
COHESANT, INC., *pg.* 1154, *pg.* 1405
CONAIR CORPORATION, *pg.* 505, *pg.* 1055
CROLL-REYNOLDS COMPANY, INC., *pg.* 1326, *pg.* 1103
DANAHER MOTION, *pg.* 1327, *pg.* 1593
DETROIT STOKER CO., *pg.* 1070, *pg.* 900
DIMPLEX NORTH AMERICA LIMITED, *pg.* 54, *pg.* 1920
DONALDSON COMPANY, INC., *pg.* 1329, *pg.* 917
DUFF-NORTON, *pg.* 204, *pg.* 1365
EAGLE TECHNOLOGIES GROUP, *pg.* 1331, *pg.* 874
EAST CHICAGO MACHINE TOOL CORPORATION, *pg.* 1331, *pg.* 676
ECLIPSE INC., *pg.* 1332, *pg.* 655
ECODYNE HEAT EXCHANGERS, INC., *pg.* 1071, *pg.* 1705
EMBASSY INDUSTRIES, INC., *pg.* 1071, *pg.* 1164
THE ENTWISTLE CO., *pg.* 637, *pg.* 826
FAFCO INC., *pg.* 1071, *pg.* 65
FIELD CONTROLS LLC, *pg.* 1071, *pg.* 1380
FIKE CORPORATION, *pg.* 1047, *pg.* 973
FLEXFAB HORIZONS INTERNATIONAL, LLC, *pg.* 1072, *pg.* 891
GAS-FIRED PRODUCTS, INC., *pg.* 1338, *pg.* 1367
THE GILLETTE COMPANY, *pg.* 509, *pg.* 795
HAMILTON BEACH BRANDS, INC., *pg.* 56, *pg.* 1783
HARRIS WASTE MANAGEMENT GROUP, INC., *pg.* 1345, *pg.* 526
HAUCK MANUFACTURING COMPANY, INC., *pg.* 1345, *pg.* 1522
HAYWARD POOL PRODUCTS, *pg.* 1049, *pg.* 1057
HELEN OF TROY L.P., *pg.* 511, *pg.* 1692
HOLMATRO, INC., *pg.* 1346, *pg.* 771
HUBBELL LIGHTING - PROGRESS LIGHTING DIVISION, *pg.* 1300, *pg.* 1617
HUMAN TOUCH, *pg.* 928, *pg.* 123
HUNTER FAN COMPANY, *pg.* 57, *pg.* 1631
ILLINOIS TOOL WORKS INC., *pg.* 1348, *pg.* 614
INGERSOLL-RAND COMPANY, *pg.* 1349, *pg.* 1370
INSTANTRON CO., INC., *pg.* 512, *pg.* 1608
JARDEN CORPORATION, *pg.* 1885, *pg.* 412
KAYDON CORPORATION, *pg.* 1352, *pg.* 866
KAZ, INC., *pg.* 58, *pg.* 844
KIDDE FIRE FIGHTING, *pg.* 1170, *pg.* 1531
LINDE GAS LLC, *pg.* 1356, *pg.* 1095
MAXON CORPORATION, *pg.* 1359, *pg.* 695
MCNEIL & NRM INC., *pg.* 1360, *pg.* 1402
MELITTA USA INC., *pg.* 781, *pg.* 416
MELNOR, INC., *pg.* 1055, *pg.* 1811
MESTEK, INC., *pg.* 1074, *pg.* 857
NACCO INDUSTRIES, INC., *pg.* 1174, *pg.* 1433
NATIONAL BULK EQUIPMENT, INC., *pg.* 1479, *pg.* 892
NATIONAL METAL FINISHING CORP., *pg.* 1363, *pg.* 1084
NATIONAL PRESTO INDUSTRIES, INC, *pg.* 1128, *pg.* 1857
NORDSON CORPORATION, *pg.* 1365, *pg.* 1480
P&F INDUSTRIES, INC., *pg.* 1075, *pg.* 1182
PALL CORPORATION, *pg.* 232, *pg.* 1323
PANGBORN CORPORATION, *pg.* 1367, *pg.* 532
PENFLEX, INC., *pg.* 104, *pg.* 1534
PHILIPS LIGHTING, *pg.* 1303, *pg.* 806
PMFG, INC., *pg.* 1369, *pg.* 1685
PRAXAIR, INC., *pg.* 1178, *pg.* 344
PREFERRED UTILITIES MANUFACTURING CORPORATION, *pg.* 1075, *pg.* 344
REEL-O-MATIC, INC., *pg.* 1371, *pg.* 1487
REGAL WARE, INC., *pg.* 1137, *pg.* 1862
RELIABLE AUTOMATIC SPRINKLER CO., INC., *pg.* 1137, *pg.* 1158
RHEEM MANUFACTURING - AIR CONDITIONING DIV, *pg.* 1075, *pg.* 32
RHEEM MANUFACTURING COMPANY, *pg.* 1075, *pg.* 519
ROBERTS-GORDON INC., *pg.* 1076, *pg.* 1151
SERFILCO, LTD., *pg.* 1375, *pg.* 641
SLANT/FIN CORPORATION, *pg.* 1076, *pg.* 1163
S.T. JOHNSON CO., *pg.* 1077, *pg.* 173
SULLAIR CORPORATION, *pg.* 1379, *pg.* 695
TACO INCORPORATED, *pg.* 1077, *pg.* 1601
TENNANT COMPANY, *pg.* 1381, *pg.* 944
THERMOTRON INDUSTRIES, *pg.* 235, *pg.* 892
TRANE INC., *pg.* 116, *pg.* 1109
TRANSACT TECHNOLOGIES INCORPORATED, *pg.* 484, *pg.* 351
TRICO MFG. CORP., *pg.* 219, *pg.* 1886
VAPOR CORP., *pg.* 61, *pg.* 427
WAHL CLIPPER CORPORATION, *pg.* 524, *pg.* 662
WESTERN STATES MACHINE COMPANY, *pg.* 1388, *pg.* 1455
WHIRLPOOL CORPORATION, *pg.* 62, *pg.* 872
WILLIAMS PATENT CRUSHER & PULVERIZER CO., INC., *pg.* 1389, *pg.* 1005

3441 - Fabricated Structural Metal

ALLEGHENY TECHNOLOGIES INCORPORATED, *pg.* 66, *pg.* 1572
AMERICAN ELECTRIC TECHNOLOGIES, INC., *pg.* 349, *pg.* 1700
ARCHITECTURAL ART MFG. INC., *pg.* 68, *pg.* 775
BLICKMAN HEALTH INDUSTRIES, INC., *pg.* 1506, *pg.* 1051
BROADWIND ENERGY, INC., *pg.* 1319, *pg.* 598
DAYTON SUPERIOR CORPORATION, *pg.* 1328, *pg.* 1464
DELAIR GROUP, LLC, *pg.* 78, *pg.* 1053
THE D.S. BROWN COMPANY, *pg.* 79, *pg.* 1468
ESCO CORPORATION, *pg.* 1335, *pg.* 1502
HIRSCHFELD INDUSTRIES, INC., *pg.* 87, *pg.* 1739
LAYSTROM MANUFACTURING CO., *pg.* 1355, *pg.* 580
METALS USA, INC., *pg.* 97, *pg.* 425
MITEK, INC., *pg.* 1056, *pg.* 975
MOBILE MINI, INC., *pg.* 1362, *pg.* 26
OWEN INDUSTRIES, INC., *pg.* 102, *pg.* 702
PYRAMID MOULDINGS, *pg.* 105, *pg.* 429
RODNEY HUNT COMPANY, *pg.* 1372, *pg.* 840
SIMPSON MANUFACTURING COMPANY, INC., *pg.* 1376, *pg.* 185
STEEL DYNAMICS, INC., *pg.* 113, *pg.* 681
STINGER MEDICAL LLC, *pg.* 476, *pg.* 1648
TRITON INDUSTRIES, INC., *pg.* 1384, *pg.* 592
VALMONT INDUSTRIES, INC., *pg.* 1387, *pg.* 1019

3442 - Metal Doors, Sash, Frames, Molding & Trim

AMERICAN ELECTRIC TECHNOLOGIES, INC., *pg.* 349, *pg.* 1700
AMUNEAL MANUFACTURING CORPORATION, *pg.* 617, *pg.* 1558
ARTUS CORPORATION, *pg.* 1314, *pg.* 1059
ASSA ABLOY DOOR SECURITY SOLUTIONS, *pg.* 1042, *pg.* 358
ATIS GROUP INC., *pg.* 1042, *pg.* 1952
ATRIUM COMPANIES, INC., *pg.* 69, *pg.* 1676
THE BILCO COMPANY, *pg.* 70, *pg.* 383
BUTLER MANUFACTURING COMPANY, *pg.* 72, *pg.* 981
CENTRIA ARCHITECTURAL SYSTEMS, *pg.* 74, *pg.* 1554
CENTRIA, INC., *pg.* 74, *pg.* 1554
CHILDERS CARPORTS AND STRUCTURES, INC., *pg.* 76, *pg.* 1703
CLOPAY BUILDING PRODUCTS COMPANY, *pg.* 76, *pg.* 1459
CORNELL IRON WORKS, INC., *pg.* 77, *pg.* 1554
CURRIES COMPANY, *pg.* 77, *pg.* 709
THE CYCLONE MFG. CO., *pg.* 78, *pg.* 698
EAGLE MANUFACTURING COMPANY, *pg.* 79, *pg.* 1851
THE EASTERN COMPANY, *pg.* 1331, *pg.* 357
FOUR SEASONS SUNROOM, *pg.* 83, *pg.* 1167
GASSER & SONS, INC., *pg.* 83, *pg.* 1153
HENDRICK MANUFACTURING COMPANY, *pg.* 86, *pg.* 1520
HMT LLC, *pg.* 979, *pg.* 1747
HUFCOR INCORPORATED, *pg.* 87, *pg.* 1861
HUNTER DOUGLAS, INC., *pg.* 928, *pg.* 1320
INTERNATIONAL REVOLVING DOORS, *pg.* 88, *pg.* 679
JAMISON DOOR COMPANY, *pg.* 89, *pg.* 771
KAWNEER COMPANY, INC., *pg.* 90, *pg.* 537
LARSON MANUFACTURING COMPANY, *pg.* 93, *pg.* 1624
LOUIS BERKMAN CO., *pg.* 1357, *pg.* 1473
M&G DURA-VENT, INC., *pg.* 95, *pg.* 298
MARTIN DOOR MANUFACTURING, INC., *pg.* 96, *pg.* 1759
MARVIN WINDOWS & DOORS, *pg.* 934, *pg.* 965
MATERION CORPORATION, *pg.* 1359, *pg.* 1463
METALFAB, INC., *pg.* 1360, *pg.* 1127
MIDDLE ATLANTIC PRODUCTS INC., *pg.* 1360, *pg.* 1065
NABCO ENTRANCES, INC., *pg.* 99, *pg.* 1882
NORTEK, INC., *pg.* 100, *pg.* 1607
ODL INCORPORATED, *pg.* 101, *pg.* 914
OVERHEAD DOOR CORPORATION, *pg.* 102, *pg.* 1725
OVERLY MANUFACTURING COMPANY, *pg.* 102, *pg.* 1534
PELLA CORPORATION, *pg.* 104, *pg.* 711
PENTAIR WATER POOL AND SPA, INC., *pg.* 104, *pg.* 1171
PGT, INC., *pg.* 104, *pg.* 452
PHANTOM MFG. (INTL.) LTD., *pg.* 104, *pg.* 1907
RAYNOR GARAGE DOORS, *pg.* 106, *pg.* 607
RIGIDIZED METALS CORP., *pg.* 108, *pg.* 1151
SIMPSON MANUFACTURING COMPANY, INC., *pg.* 1376, *pg.* 185
SPEEDRACK PRODUCTS GROUP, LTD., *pg.* 112, *pg.* 908
STARRCO COMPANY INC., *pg.* 113, *pg.* 988
SUPER SKY PRODUCTS, INC., *pg.* 113, *pg.* 1871
THERMA-TRU CORP., *pg.* 115, *pg.* 1462
THERMAL INDUSTRIES, INC., *pg.* 115, *pg.* 1555
TREDEGAR CORPORATION, *pg.* 1890, *pg.* 1804
TRINITY INDUSTRIES, INC., *pg.* 116, *pg.* 1690
UMF MEDICAL, *pg.* 946, *pg.* 1542
VIKING RANGE CORPORATION, *pg.* 61, *pg.* 968
WAYNE-DALTON CORP., *pg.* 120, *pg.* 1465

3443 - Fabricated Plate Work (Boiler Shops)

AERCO INTERNATIONAL INC., *pg.* 1068, *pg.* 1142
AEROFIN CORP., *pg.* 1068, *pg.* 1787
THE BOARDMAN INC., *pg.* 71, *pg.* 1484
BOILER TUBE COMPANY OF AMERICA, *pg.* 1318, *pg.* 1620
CMI-SCHNEIBLE COMPANY, *pg.* 1324, *pg.* 906
HARSCO CORPORATION, *pg.* 86, *pg.* 1519
HARSCO RAIL, *pg.* 1345, *pg.* 1623
JUSTRITE MANUFACTURING COMPANY, LLC, *pg.* 1394, *pg.* 606
MODERN WELDING COMPANY, INC., *pg.* 1363, *pg.* 739
PAUL MUELLER COMPANY, *pg.* 706, *pg.* 1007
PERRY VIDEX LLC, *pg.* 1368, *pg.* 1072
STANDEX INTERNATIONAL CORPORATION, *pg.* 60, *pg.* 1039
STEBBINS ENGINEERING & MANUFACTURING COMPANY, *pg.* 113, *pg.* 1349
SUPERIOR DIE SET CORP., *pg.* 1379, *pg.* 1885
VILTER MANUFACTURING LLC, *pg.* 1078, *pg.* 1856
WASHINGTON PRODUCTS INC., *pg.* 1387, *pg.* 1461
THE WILL-BURT CO., INC., *pg.* 1437, *pg.* 1469
WORTHINGTON INDUSTRIES, INC., *pg.* 123, *pg.* 1444
WSF INDUSTRIES, INC., *pg.* 1390, *pg.* 1346
XYLEM INC., *pg.* 1078, *pg.* 1339

3444 - Sheet Metal Work

AMERICAN ELECTRIC TECHNOLOGIES, INC., *pg.* 349, *pg.* 1700
AMUNEAL MANUFACTURING CORPORATION, *pg.* 617, *pg.* 1558
ARTUS CORPORATION, *pg.* 1314, *pg.* 1059
CENTRIA ARCHITECTURAL SYSTEMS, *pg.* 74, *pg.* 1554
CENTRIA, INC., *pg.* 74, *pg.* 1554
CHILDERS CARPORTS AND STRUCTURES, INC., *pg.* 76, *pg.* 1703
THE CYCLONE MFG. CO., *pg.* 78, *pg.* 698
EAGLE MANUFACTURING COMPANY, *pg.* 79, *pg.* 1851
THE EASTERN COMPANY, *pg.* 1331, *pg.* 357
FOUR SEASONS SUNROOM, *pg.* 83, *pg.* 1167
GASSER & SONS, INC., *pg.* 83, *pg.* 1153
HENDRICK MANUFACTURING COMPANY, *pg.* 86, *pg.* 1520
HMT LLC, *pg.* 979, *pg.* 1747
HUNTER DOUGLAS, INC., *pg.* 928, *pg.* 1320
LOUIS BERKMAN CO., *pg.* 1357, *pg.* 1473
M&G DURA-VENT, INC., *pg.* 95, *pg.* 298
MATERION CORPORATION, *pg.* 1359, *pg.* 1463
METALFAB, INC., *pg.* 1360, *pg.* 1127
MIDDLE ATLANTIC PRODUCTS INC., *pg.* 1360, *pg.* 1065
NORTEK, INC., *pg.* 100, *pg.* 1607
ODL INCORPORATED, *pg.* 101, *pg.* 914
PENTAIR WATER POOL AND SPA, INC., *pg.* 104, *pg.* 1171
RIGIDIZED METALS CORP., *pg.* 108, *pg.* 1151
SIMPSON MANUFACTURING COMPANY, INC., *pg.* 1376, *pg.* 185
SPEEDRACK PRODUCTS GROUP, LTD., *pg.* 112, *pg.* 908
STARRCO COMPANY INC., *pg.* 113, *pg.* 988
SUPER SKY PRODUCTS, INC., *pg.* 113, *pg.* 1871
TRINITY INDUSTRIES, INC., *pg.* 116, *pg.* 1690
UMF MEDICAL, *pg.* 946, *pg.* 1542
VIKING RANGE CORPORATION, *pg.* 61, *pg.* 968

3446 - Architectural & Ornamental Metal Work

AGCO CORPORATION, *pg.* 700, *pg.* 530
ALABAMA METAL INDUSTRIES CORPORATION, *pg.* 65, *pg.* 1
ALAMO GROUP INC., *pg.* 1311, *pg.* 1745
AMEREQUIP CORPORATION, *pg.* 700, *pg.* 1862
AMERICAN SPECIALTIES INC., *pg.* 325, *pg.* 1356
ARCHITECTURAL ART MFG. INC., *pg.* 68, *pg.* 775
ART'S-WAY MANUFACTURING CO., INC., *pg.* 701, *pg.* 701
A.T. FERRELL COMPANY, INC., *pg.* 701, *pg.* 674
AUSCO PRODUCTS, INC., *pg.* 199, *pg.* 872
BEHLEN MFG. CO., *pg.* 701, *pg.* 1010
THE BILCO COMPANY, *pg.* 70, *pg.* 383
BOUMATIC LLC, *pg.* 701, *pg.* 1865
BUSH HOG, INC., *pg.* 702, *pg.* 8
CNH AMERICA LLC, *pg.* 702, *pg.* 560
CORNELL IRON WORKS, INC., *pg.* 77, *pg.* 1554
CTB INTERNATIONAL CORP., *pg.* 850, *pg.* 695
DANUSER MACHINE COMPANY, INC., *pg.* 703, *pg.* 978
DEERE & COMPANY, *pg.* 703, *pg.* 632
DEGELMAN INDUSTRIES LTD., *pg.* 703, *pg.* 1962
THE ENKEBOLL COMPANY, *pg.* 923, *pg.* 63
EXCEL INDUSTRIES, INC., *pg.* 1795, *pg.* 715
GANDY COMPANY, *pg.* 703, *pg.* 952
GAS-FIRED PRODUCTS, INC., *pg.* 1338, *pg.* 1367
GEA FARM TECHNOLOGIES, *pg.* 704, *pg.* 636
GEHL COMPANY, *pg.* 1339, *pg.* 1899
GIBRALTAR INDUSTRIES, INC., *pg.* 1340, *pg.* 1148
GREAT PLAINS MANUFACTURING, INCORPORATED, *pg.* 704, *pg.* 721
HARPER INDUSTRIES, INC., *pg.* 704, *pg.* 715
HARRIS WASTE MANAGEMENT GROUP, INC., *pg.* 1345, *pg.* 526
HARSH INTERNATIONAL, INC., *pg.* 1345, *pg.* 324
HAWKEYE STEEL PRODUCTS, INC., *pg.* 704, *pg.* 708
HIGHWAY EQUIPMENT COMPANY, *pg.* 704, *pg.* 702
HINIKER COMPANY, *pg.* 704, *pg.* 927
JOHN DEERE LTD., *pg.* 705, *pg.* 1920
KAWNEER COMPANY, INC., *pg.* 90, *pg.* 537
KELLY RYAN EQUIPMENT COMPANY, *pg.* 705, *pg.* 1010
LAM RESEARCH CORPORATION, *pg.* 1354, *pg.* 91
LAVI INDUSTRIES INC., *pg.* 93, *pg.* 299
LINDSAY CORPORATION, *pg.* 1356, *pg.* 1016
LUNDELL ENTERPRISES, INC., *pg.* 706, *pg.* 703
MERCHANT & EVANS, INC., *pg.* 97, *pg.* 1048
MILLER MANUFACTURING COMPANY, *pg.* 706, *pg.* 921
MY-D HAN-D MFG. INC., *pg.* 706, *pg.* 714
OVERLY MANUFACTURING COMPANY, *pg.* 102, *pg.* 1534
PENTAIR WATER POOL AND SPA, INC., *pg.* 104, *pg.* 1171
THE PERRY COMPANY, *pg.* 706, *pg.* 1749
PYRAMID MOULDINGS, *pg.* 105, *pg.* 429
REINKE MANUFACTURING COMPANY, INC., *pg.* 707, *pg.* 1010
RITCHIE INDUSTRIES, INC., *pg.* 707, *pg.* 703
SEEDBURO EQUIPMENT CO., *pg.* 707, *pg.* 590
SIOUX STEEL COMPANY, *pg.* 707, *pg.* 1625
SUNSETTER PRODUCTS, LP, *pg.* 113, *pg.* 830
UNISTRUT CORPORATION, *pg.* 117, *pg.* 913
VERMEER MANUFACTURING COMPANY, *pg.* 708, *pg.* 711
WEATHERTEC CORPORATION, *pg.* 708, *pg.* 93
WHITE RIVER HARDWOODS-WOODWORKS, INC., *pg.* 121, *pg.* 31
YETTER MANUFACTURING CO., INC., *pg.* 708, *pg.* 598

3448 - Prefabricated Metal Buildings & Components

ARMSTRONG WORLD INDUSTRIES, INC., *pg.* 914, *pg.* 1545
BEHLEN MFG. CO., *pg.* 701, *pg.* 1010
BROADWIND ENERGY, INC., *pg.* 1319, *pg.* 598
BUTLER MANUFACTURING COMPANY, *pg.* 72, *pg.* 981
CHIEF INDUSTRIES, INC., *pg.* 1323, *pg.* 1010
CHILDERS CARPORTS AND STRUCTURES, INC., *pg.* 76, *pg.* 1703
FOUR SEASONS SUNROOM, *pg.* 83, *pg.* 1167
GULF STATES MANUFACTURERS, INC., *pg.* 85, *pg.* 971
JACK WALTERS & SONS CORP., *pg.* 88, *pg.* 1852
JACOBSEN MANUFACTURING, INC., *pg.* 1098, *pg.* 460
KIRBY BUILDING SYSTEMS, INC., *pg.* 91, *pg.* 1655
MOBILE MINI, INC., *pg.* 1362, *pg.* 26
NCI BUILDING SYSTEMS, INC., *pg.* 1364, *pg.* 1712
ROUGH BROTHERS, INC., *pg.* 108, *pg.* 1425
STAR BUILDING SYSTEMS, *pg.* 112, *pg.* 1488
STARRCO COMPANY INC., *pg.* 113, *pg.* 988
SUNPORCH STRUCTURES INC., *pg.* 113, *pg.* 384
UNISTRUT CORPORATION, *pg.* 117, *pg.* 913
VARCO PRUDEN BUILDINGS, INC., *pg.* 118, *pg.* 1647

3449 - Miscellaneous Structural

Metal Work

PYRAMID MOULDINGS, pg. 105, pg. 429

3451 - Screw Machine Products

AMERICAN JEBCO CORPORATION, pg. 1041, pg. 612
THE EASTERN COMPANY, pg. 1331, pg. 357
SCHMITT INDUSTRIES, INC., pg. 1374, pg. 1506
TSI INCORPORATED, pg. 1432, pg. 965

3452 - Bolts, Nuts, Screws, Rivets & Washers

AIR-LEC INDUSTRIES LLC, pg. 1041, pg. 1864
A.L. HANSEN MANUFACTURING CO., pg. 1041, pg. 665
ALLFAST FASTENING SYSTEMS, INC., pg. 1041, pg. 66
AMATOM ELECTRONIC HARDWARE, INC., pg. 1041, pg. 342
AMERICAN JEBCO CORPORATION, pg. 1041, pg. 612
AMERICAN LOCKER GROUP INCORPORATED, pg. 1041, pg. 1674
AMERICAN VAN EQUIPMENT INC., pg. 199, pg. 1078
ASCO SINTERING CO., pg. 1042, pg. 126
ATLAS BOLT & SCREW COMPANY, pg. 1042, pg. 1403
ATTWOOD CORPORATION, pg. 1705, pg. 897
BALL & BALL HARDWARE REPRODUCTIONS, pg. 916, pg. 1531
BLACK & DECKER, pg. 1043, pg. 1907
BTM CORPORATION, pg. 1320, pg. 898
CHICAGO RIVET & MACHINE COMPANY, pg. 1323, pg. 636
COMPX INTERNATIONAL INC., pg. 1044, pg. 1678
CONSOLIDATED METAL PRODUCTS, INC., pg. 1325, pg. 1412
DAYTON SUPERIOR CORPORATION, pg. 1328, pg. 1464
DECO PRODUCTS CO., pg. 1045, pg. 704
DFCI SOLUTIONS INC., pg. 1328, pg. 1350
DREMEL, pg. 1046, pg. 634
DRIV-LOK, INC., pg. 1046, pg. 662
THE EASTERN COMPANY, pg. 1331, pg. 357
EBERHARD MANUFACTURING DIVISION, pg. 1046, pg. 1475
E.R. WAGNER CASTERS AND WHEELS DIV., pg. 1047, pg. 1874
FASTENAL COMPANY, pg. 396, pg. 966
THE FERRY CAP & SET SCREW COMPANY, pg. 1047, pg. 1457
FLEXIBLE STEEL LACING COMPANY, pg. 1337, pg. 608
FORTUNE BRANDS HOME & SECURITY, INC., pg. 55, pg. 600
FREEWAY CORPORATION, pg. 1338, pg. 1431
GREIF INC., pg. 1459, pg. 1447
GRIPNAIL CORPORATION, pg. 1048, pg. 1601
GROOV-PIN CORPORATION, pg. 1049, pg. 1608
HINDLEY MANUFACTURING COMPANY, INC., pg. 1049, pg. 1601
JOHN HASSALL, INC., pg. 1052, pg. 1350
KABA ILCO CORP., pg. 1052, pg. 1390
KENNAMETAL INC., pg. 1052, pg. 1547
KNAPE & VOGT MANUFACTURING COMPANY, pg. 1052, pg. 913
LONG-LOK FASTENERS CORP., pg. 1053, pg. 1416
MASTER LOCK COMPANY LLC, pg. 1055, pg. 1884
MATCO TOOLS CORPORATION, pg. 1055, pg. 1474
MEDECO HIGH SECURITY LOCKS, INC., pg. 1055, pg. 1806
MITEK, INC., pg. 1056, pg. 975
NATIONAL RIVET & MANUFACTURING COMPANY, pg. 1364, pg. 1898
OXO, pg. 1058, pg. 1275
PASLODE, pg. 1059, pg. 664
PCC SPS FASTENER DIVISION, pg. 1059, pg. 1542
PENN ENGINEERING & MANUFACTURING CORP., pg. 1059, pg. 1525
PENNENGINEERING FASTENING TECHNOLOGIES, pg. 1059, pg. 1526
PORTLAND WILLAMETTE, pg. 1129, pg. 1505
PRECISION CASTPARTS CORP., pg. 105, pg. 1506
REV-A-SHELF, pg. 1060, pg. 738
RICHELIEU HARDWARE LTD., pg. 1060, pg. 1961
ROBERTSON INC., pg. 1372, pg. 1924
ROCKFORD PRODUCTS CORP., pg. 1372, pg. 655
ROCKY MOUNTAIN HARDWARE INC., pg. 1061, pg. 549
RONA, INC., pg. 216, pg. 1950
ROUSSEAU METAL, INC., pg. 463, pg. 1960
SARGENT & GREENLEAF, INC., pg. 1061, pg. 739
SARGENT MANUFACTURING COMPANY, pg. 1061, pg. 359
SCHAEFER MARINE INC., pg. 1373, pg. 835
SFS INTEC, INC., pg. 1061, pg. 1596
SHUR-CO, INC., pg. 110, pg. 1626
SHUR-LOK COMPANY, pg. 1375, pg. 116
SIMPSON MANUFACTURING COMPANY, INC., pg. 1376, pg. 185
SOLIDSCAPE, INC., pg. 1063, pg. 1037
SOUTHERN FOLGER DETENTION EQUIPMENT COMPANY, pg. 1063, pg. 1743
SPIROL INTERNATIONAL CORPORATION, pg. 1378, pg. 345
STANLEY BLACK & DECKER, INC., pg. 1063, pg. 358
THE STIMPSON COMPANY, INC., pg. 1182, pg. 460
SUPPLY TECHNOLOGIES LLC, pg. 1064, pg. 1436
TCI PRECISION METALS, INC., pg. 1380, pg. 95
TRIMAS CORPORATION, pg. 1383, pg. 874
TRUTH HARDWARE CORP., pg. 1066, pg. 952
UNIVERSAL INDUSTRIAL PRODUCTS CO., pg. 1066, pg. 1470
UNIVERSAL THREAD GRINDING COMPANY, pg. 1066, pg. 349
VERTEX DISTRIBUTION, pg. 1066, pg. 784
WINNER INTERNATIONAL, LLC, pg. 222, pg. 1586
YARDLEY PRODUCTS CORPORATION, pg. 1391, pg. 1596

3462 - Iron & Steel Forgings

A. FINKL & SONS CO., pg. 1309, pg. 563
AMERICAN AXLE & MANUFACTURING HOLDINGS, INC., pg. 198, pg. 879
AMPCO-PITTSBURGH CORPORATION, pg. 1313, pg. 1573
ATI LADISH FORGING, pg. 69, pg. 1856
ELLWOOD CITY FORGE, pg. 1333, pg. 1529
ELLWOOD NATIONAL FORGE COMPANY, LLC, pg. 1333, pg. 1542
L.B. FOSTER COMPANY, pg. 1355, pg. 1578
MASTER LOCK COMPANY LLC, pg. 1055, pg. 1884
MEADVILLE FORGING COMPANY INC., pg. 1360, pg. 1552
MKT FASTENING, LLC, pg. 1056, pg. 34
MODERNFORGECOMPANIES, LLC, pg. 98, pg. 558
NUCOR CORPORATION, pg. 101, pg. 1368
PEERLESS CHAIN COMPANY, pg. 1887, pg. 967
ZCL COMPOSITES INC., pg. 1892, pg. 1906

3463 - Nonferrous Forgings

ALCOA WHEEL & FORGED PRODUCTS, pg. 66, pg. 1427
ATI LADISH FORGING, pg. 69, pg. 1856
MATERION CORPORATION, pg. 1359, pg. 1463
TRIMAS CORPORATION, pg. 1383, pg. 874

3465 - Automotive Stampings

BORGWARNER INC., pg. 167, pg. 867
JASON INDUSTRIES, INC., pg. 208, pg. 1875
TOWER INTERNATIONAL, INC., pg. 219, pg. 897

3466 - Metal Crowns & Closures

APTARGROUP, INC., pg. 1451, pg. 598
WEST PHARMACEUTICAL SERVICES, INC., pg. 1472, pg. 1532

3469 - Metal Stampings, NEC

ACCURATE PERFORATING COMPANY, INC., pg. 1309, pg. 563
ACME METAL CAP CO., INC., pg. 1310, pg. 1356
ACME STAPLE COMPANY, INC., pg. 341, pg. 1034
ACS INDUSTRIES, INC., pg. 1040, pg. 1602
ADMIRAL TOOL & MANUFACTURING COMPANY INC., pg. 1310, pg. 896
AFC CABLE SYSTEMS, INC., pg. 1294, pg. 835
ALL-CLAD METALCRAFTERS LLC, pg. 1121, pg. 1519
APW WYOTT FOOD SERVICE EQUIPMENT, INC., pg. 1314, pg. 1658
BARNES GROUP INC., pg. 1317, pg. 340
BAYLOFF STAMPED PRODUCTS, pg. 1317, pg. 1457
BELDEN, INC., pg. 624, pg. 993
BRIDON AMERICAN CORP., pg. 1319, pg. 1594
BUD INDUSTRIES, INC., pg. 627, pg. 1482
BUFFALO WIRE WORKS CO., INC., pg. 72, pg. 1147
CALPHALON CORPORATION, pg. 1121, pg. 1470
CANNON EQUIPMENT COMPANY, pg. 1321, pg. 920
CARLISLE INTERCONNECT TECHNOLOGIES, pg. 1294, pg. 461
CHAMPLAIN CABLE CORP., pg. 1044, pg. 1765
CHASE CORPORATION, pg. 1152, pg. 803
CHICAGO METAL FABRICATORS, INC., pg. 1323, pg. 569
CLOSETMAID CORPORATION, pg. 920, pg. 452
COLEMAN CABLE, INC., pg. 1324, pg. 665
COLUMBUS MCKINNON CORPORATION, pg. 1325, pg. 1138
CORNING INCORPORATED, pg. 1122, pg. 1154
CRENLO, LLC, pg. 77, pg. 955
DAYTON SUPERIOR CORPORATION, pg. 1328, pg. 1464
ERICO INTERNATIONAL CORPORATION, pg. 1335, pg. 1472
ESSENTRA COMPONENTS, pg. 1047, pg. 612
ESSEX GROUP, INC., pg. 638, pg. 680
ESTAD STAMPING & MANUFACTURING COMPANY, pg. 1336, pg. 598
FORTUNE BRANDS HOME & SECURITY, INC., pg. 55, pg. 600
FREEWAY CORPORATION, pg. 1338, pg. 1431
FUSHI COPPERWELD, pg. 1296, pg. 1632
GASSER & SONS, INC., pg. 83, pg. 1153
GENERAL CABLE CORPORATION, pg. 83, pg. 384
GLOBE SPECIALTY METALS INC., pg. 1164, pg. 1235
GRC ENTERPRISES, INC., pg. 1344, pg. 677
THE GREAT AMERICAN HANGER COMPANY INC., pg. 926, pg. 442
GREENLEE TEXTRON INC., pg. 1048, pg. 655
HANDY & HARMAN LTD., pg. 85, pg. 1352
HARRINGTON & KING PERFORATING COMPANY, INC., pg. 1164, pg. 576
HENDRICK MANUFACTURING COMPANY, pg. 86, pg. 1520
HILTI, INC., pg. 1346, pg. 1490
HINDLEY MANUFACTURING COMPANY, INC., pg. 1049, pg. 1601
HOUSTON WIRE & CABLE COMPANY, pg. 643, pg. 1708
JOHN HASSALL, INC., pg. 1052, pg. 1350
KEYSTONE CONSOLIDATED INDUSTRIES, INC., pg. 90, pg. 1683
KEYSTONE STEEL & WIRE CO., pg. 91, pg. 651
LAYSTROM MANUFACTURING CO., pg. 1355, pg. 580
LEVITON MANUFACTURING COMPANY, INC., pg. 1301, pg. 1180
LIFETIME BRANDS, INC., pg. 1127, pg. 1161
LITTLE FALLS ALLOYS, INC., pg. 1171, pg. 1107
MACCAFERRI, INC., pg. 95, pg. 780
MATERION CORPORATION, pg. 1359, pg. 1463
METAL TEXTILES CORPORATION, pg. 654, pg. 1057
MICRO CORP., pg. 1056, pg. 1122
NATIONAL BAND & TAG CO., pg. 1479, pg. 739
NEWARK WIRE CLOTH CO., pg. 99, pg. 1052
THE OKONITE COMPANY, pg. 1302, pg. 1113
PEACE INDUSTRIES INC., pg. 1368, pg. 656
PEERLESS CHAIN COMPANY, pg. 1887, pg. 967
POLAR WARE COMPANY, pg. 1129, pg. 1862
QUALITY PERFORATING, INC., pg. 1468, pg. 1520
RADIX WIRE COMPANY, pg. 1304, pg. 1434
RANGE KLEEN MANUFACTURING INC., pg. 60, pg. 1458
REGAL WARE, INC., pg. 1137, pg. 1862
RIGIDIZED METALS CORP., pg. 108, pg. 1151
RSCC AEROSPACE & DEFENSE, pg. 1373, pg. 1036
SALSBURY INDUSTRIES, pg. 464, pg. 139
SEFAR AMERICA, INC., pg. 698, pg. 1080
SENCO PRODUCTS, INC., pg. 1374, pg. 1425
SHILOH INDUSTRIES, INC., pg. 1375, pg. 1478
SIGMUND COHN CORP., pg. 1062, pg. 1183
SOMMER METALCRAFT CORPORATION, pg. 112, pg. 676
SUPERIOR ESSEX, INC., pg. 676, pg. 521
T&S PERFECTION CHAIN PRODUCTS, INC., pg. 1065, pg. 5
TORRMETAL CORPORATION, pg. 1383, pg. 1436
TRITON INDUSTRIES, INC., pg. 1384, pg. 592
UNIVERSAL INDUSTRIAL PRODUCTS CO., pg. 1066, pg. 1470
VULCAN, INC., pg. 687, pg. 5
WASHINGTON PRODUCTS INC., pg. 1387, pg. 1461

WEBSTER INDUSTRIES INC., pg. 1388, pg. 1475
W.H. MAZE COMPANY, pg. 1389, pg. 652
WIRECO WORLDGROUP, pg. 1389, pg. 987
WIRECO WORLDGROUP, pg. 1389, pg. 721
WISCO PRODUCTS, INC., pg. 1389, pg. 1447
THE WOODSTREAM CORPORATION, pg. 1801, pg. 1549
WORLD KITCHEN LLC, pg. 1141, pg. 657

3471 - Electroplating, Plating, Polishing, Anodizing & Coloring

ADVANCED PLATING INC., pg. 197, pg. 1648
ALLEN AIRCRAFT PRODUCTS, INC., pg. 223, pg. 1471
THE BRON SHOE COMPANY, pg. 1440, pg. 1438
BROOKTRONICS ENGINEERING CORPORATION, pg. 1320, pg. 299
CRC INDUSTRIES, INC., pg. 329, pg. 1590
GENERAL MAGNAPLATE CORPORATION, pg. 1164, pg. 1079
HUBBARD-HALL, INC., pg. 1167, pg. 382
NATIONAL METAL FINISHING CORP., pg. 1363, pg. 1084
ORBEL CORPORATION, pg. 1058, pg. 1528
PRECISION ROLL GRINDERS, INC., pg. 1370, pg. 1514
SAPORITO FINISHING COMPANY, pg. 466, pg. 598
SUMMIT CORPORATION OF AMERICA, pg. 1182, pg. 380

3479 - Coating, Engraving & Allied Services, NEC

BUZTRONICS, INC., pg. 1294, pg. 683
CERAMTEC NORTH AMERICA ELECTRONIC APPLICATIONS, INC., pg. 628, pg. 1620
CHASE CORPORATION, pg. 1152, pg. 803
THE DOW CHEMICAL COMPANY, pg. 1157, pg. 898
EVAPORATED METAL FILMS CORP., pg. 1412, pg. 1170
GENERAL MAGNAPLATE CORPORATION, pg. 1164, pg. 1079
HANDY & HARMAN LTD., pg. 85, pg. 1352
LIQUIDMETAL TECHNOLOGIES, INC., pg. 1356, pg. 188
MATERION CORPORATION, pg. 1359, pg. 1463
MATERION MICROELECTRONICS & SERVICES, pg. 1559, pg. 1149
MERITOR, INC., pg. 212, pg. 911
NCI BUILDING SYSTEMS, INC., pg. 1364, pg. 1712
NORDSON CORPORATION, pg. 1365, pg. 1480
NOV AMERON, pg. 100, pg. 187
SEQUA CORPORATION, pg. 1180, pg. 1290
SULZER METCO (WESTBURY) INC., pg. 1064, pg. 1350
SUMMIT CORPORATION OF AMERICA, pg. 1182, pg. 380
VIRTEK VISION INTERNATIONAL, INC., pg. 1435, pg. 1948
WATTS WATER TECHNOLOGIES, INC., pg. 1078, pg. 837

3482 - Small Arms Ammunition

DAISY MANUFACTURING COMPANY, pg. 1831, pg. 35
FEDERAL PREMIUM AMMUNITION, pg. 1834, pg. 915
FREEDOM GROUP, INC., pg. 1834, pg. 1382
HORNADY MANUFACTURING COMPANY, pg. 1836, pg. 1010
REMINGTON ARMS COMPANY, LLC, pg. 1844, pg. 1382
SMITH & WESSON HOLDING CORPORATION, pg. 1845, pg. 846
STURM, RUGER & COMPANY, INC., pg. 1846, pg. 371

3483 - Ammunition, Except Small Arms, NEC

THE DEWEY ELECTRONICS CORPORATION, pg. 1328, pg. 1099
TEXTRON SYSTEMS CORPORATION, pg. 235, pg. 860

3484 - Small Arms

DAISY MANUFACTURING COMPANY, pg. 1831, pg. 35
FREEDOM GROUP, INC., pg. 1834, pg. 1382
O.F. MOSSBERG & SONS, INC., pg. 1842, pg. 360
REMINGTON ARMS COMPANY, LLC, pg. 1844, pg. 1382
SMITH & WESSON HOLDING CORPORATION, pg. 1845, pg. 846
STURM, RUGER & COMPANY, INC., pg. 1846, pg. 371
WEATHERBY, INC., pg. 1848, pg. 181

3489 - Ordnance & Accessories, NEC

BLOUNT INTERNATIONAL, INC., pg. 1043, pg. 1501
THE DEWEY ELECTRONICS CORPORATION, pg. 1328, pg. 1099
THE ENTWISTLE CO., pg. 637, pg. 826
NORTHROP GRUMMAN CORPORATION, pg. 231, pg. 1781
REMINGTON ARMS COMPANY, LLC, pg. 1844, pg. 1382
SMITH & WESSON HOLDING CORPORATION, pg. 1845, pg. 846
STURM, RUGER & COMPANY, INC., pg. 1846, pg. 371
TASER INTERNATIONAL, INC., pg. 677, pg. 24

3491 - Industrial Valves

AMOT CONTROLS CORPORATION, pg. 1068, pg. 1700
ARMSTRONG INTERNATIONAL, INC., pg. 1069, pg. 909
BADGER METER, INC., pg. 1401, pg. 1873
BARKSDALE, INC., pg. 1317, pg. 126
BRAY INTERNATIONAL, INC., pg. 52, pg. 1702
CASHCO, INC., pg. 1044, pg. 714
CIRCOR AEROSPACE, INC., pg. 226, pg. 69
CIRCOR INTERNATIONAL, INC., pg. 76, pg. 805
CLAYTON CORPORATION, pg. 1154, pg. 977
CRANE CO., pg. 227, pg. 373
DANFOSS POWER SOLUTIONS COMPANY, pg. 1328, pg. 701
ENGINEERED CONTROLS INTERNATIONAL LLC, pg. 1334, pg. 1372
FABCO-AIR, INC., pg. 1336, pg. 429
FLOWSERVE CORPORATION, pg. 82, pg. 1719
THE GORMAN-RUPP COMPANY, pg. 1341, pg. 1458
HENRY PRATT COMPANY, pg. 1049, pg. 555
MKS INSTRUMENTS, INC., pg. 1362, pg. 781
MODERN EQUIPMENT COMPANY, pg. 1363, pg. 1887
MOOG INC., pg. 231, pg. 1156
MUELLER WATER PRODUCTS, INC., pg. 98, pg. 515
RICHARDS INDUSTRIES VALVE GROUP, pg. 107, pg. 1425
RODNEY HUNT COMPANY, pg. 1372, pg. 840
ROPER TECHNOLOGIES, INC., pg. 1372, pg. 467
S.A. ARMSTRONG LIMITED, pg. 1373, pg. 1934
SMC CORPORATION OF AMERICA, pg. 1376, pg. 696
SPIRAX SARCO, INC., pg. 1076, pg. 1612
SPX PROCESS EQUIPMENT, pg. 1378, pg. 1551
SWAGELOK COMPANY, pg. 1064, pg. 1473
UNITED STATES PIPE & FOUNDRY COMPANY, INC., pg. 117, pg. 5
VICTAULIC COMPANY, pg. 1066, pg. 1529
WATEROUS COMPANY, pg. 1387, pg. 965
WATTS WATER TECHNOLOGIES, INC., pg. 1078, pg. 837
WEATHERFORD PRODUCTION OPTIMIZATION, pg. 987, pg. 1725
THE WM. POWELL COMPANY, pg. 1389, pg. 1427

3492 - Fluid Power Valves & Hose Fittings

AERCO INTERNATIONAL INC., pg. 1068, pg. 1142
BOSCH REXROTH CORPORATION, pg. 1319, pg. 1516
CIRCOR INTERNATIONAL, INC., pg. 76, pg. 805
COLFAX CORPORATION, pg. 1324, pg. 770
CRANE CO., pg. 227, pg. 373
DANFOSS POWER SOLUTIONS COMPANY, pg. 1328, pg. 701
DEUBLIN COMPANY, pg. 78, pg. 666
DIXON VALVE & COUPLING COMPANY, pg. 1045, pg. 766
HAMMOND VALVE CORP., pg. 1049, pg. 1883
HUMPHREY PRODUCTS CORPORATION, pg. 1300, pg. 894
KIDDE FIRE FIGHTING, pg. 1170, pg. 1531
MILWAUKEE VALVE COMPANY, INC., pg. 1361, pg. 1884
NORGREN, INC., pg. 231, pg. 333
OMEGA FLEX, INC., pg. 982, pg. 1532
POLYFLON COMPANY, pg. 1369, pg. 364
SERVOTRONICS, INC., pg. 1375, pg. 1157
TUTHILL CORPORATION, pg. 1385, pg. 561
WOODWARD HRT, pg. 236, pg. 270
YOUNG & FRANKLIN, INC., pg. 1391, pg. 1174

3493 - Steel Springs, Except Wire

AIR LIFT COMPANY, pg. 198, pg. 895
BRIDGESTONE AMERICAS, INC., pg. 1879, pg. 1648
FIRESTONE INDUSTRIAL PRODUCTS DIVISION, pg. 1882, pg. 686
MERITOR, INC., pg. 212, pg. 911

3494 - Valves & Pipe Fittings, NEC

AIR-LEC INDUSTRIES LLC, pg. 1041, pg. 1864
A.L. HANSEN MANUFACTURING CO., pg. 1041, pg. 665
ALLFAST FASTENING SYSTEMS, INC., pg. 1041, pg. 66
AMATOM ELECTRONIC HARDWARE, INC., pg. 1041, pg. 342
AMERICAN LOCKER GROUP INCORPORATED, pg. 1041, pg. 1674
AMERICAN VAN EQUIPMENT INC., pg. 199, pg. 1078
APTAR OF STRATFORD, pg. 1313, pg. 380
APTARGROUP, INC., pg. 1451, pg. 598
AS AMERICA, INC., pg. 68, pg. 1108
ASCO SINTERING CO., pg. 1042, pg. 126
ATTWOOD CORPORATION, pg. 1705, pg. 097
AUTOMATIC EQUIPMENT CORPORATION, pg. 1315, pg. 1410
BADGER METER, INC., pg. 1401, pg. 1873
BALL & BALL HARDWARE REPRODUCTIONS, pg. 916, pg. 1531
BARNES GROUP INC., pg. 1317, pg. 340
BEAD INDUSTRIES INC., pg. 200, pg. 356
BLACK & DECKER, pg. 1043, pg. 1907
BOBRICK WASHROOM EQUIPMENT, INC., pg. 1043, pg. 166
BRASSCRAFT MANUFACTURING COMPANY, pg. 1043, pg. 902
BRYCE CORPORATION, pg. 1879, pg. 1641
BTM CORPORATION, pg. 1320, pg. 898
BUCKEYE CORRUGATED INC., pg. 1454, pg. 1400
BWAY HOLDING COMPANY, pg. 1454, pg. 491
CAMERON DRILLING & PRODUCTION SYSTEMS, pg. 1321, pg. 1702
CAMERON VALVES & MEASUREMENT, pg. 1321, pg. 1703
CASCADE CORPORATION, pg. 1321, pg. 1497
THE CHICAGO FAUCET COMPANY, pg. 1044, pg. 606
CHICAGO-WILCOX MFG. COMPANY, INC., pg. 202, pg. 661
CIRCOR AEROSPACE, INC., pg. 226, pg. 69
CIRCOR INTERNATIONAL, INC., pg. 76, pg. 805
COMPX INTERNATIONAL INC., pg. 1044, pg. 1678
CONBRACO INDUSTRIES INC., pg. 1325, pg. 1382
CONTINENTAL INDUSTRIES INC., pg. 1880, pg. 1489
CROSMAN CORPORATION, pg. 951, pg. 1143
DARNELL-ROSE, pg. 1045, pg. 67
DECO PRODUCTS CO., pg. 1045, pg. 704
DELTA FAUCET COMPANY, pg. 78, pg. 684
DREMEL, pg. 1046, pg. 634
DRIV-LOK, INC., pg. 1046, pg. 662
D'VONTZ, pg. 1123, pg. 1489
THE EASTERN COMPANY, pg. 1331, pg. 357
EBERHARD MANUFACTURING DIVISION, pg. 1046, pg. 1475
E.L. MUSTEE & SONS, INC., pg. 1124, pg. 1430
ENGINEERED CONTROLS INTERNATIONAL LLC, pg. 1334, pg. 1372
E.R. WAGNER CASTERS AND WHEELS DIV., pg. 1047, pg. 1874
ERICO INTERNATIONAL CORPORATION, pg. 1335, pg. 1472
ESCO CORPORATION, pg. 1335, pg. 1502
FALCON WATERFREE TECHNOLOGIES, LLC, pg. 81, pg. 912
FEDERAL HOSE MANUFACTURING INC., pg. 1047, pg. 1469
FIKE CORPORATION, pg. 1047, pg. 973
FISHER MANUFACTURING COMPANY, pg. 81, pg. 297
FLEXIBLE STEEL LACING COMPANY, pg. 1337, pg. 608
THE FORD METER BOX COMPANY, INC., pg. 1047, pg. 698
FORTUNE BRANDS HOME & SECURITY, INC., pg. 55, pg. 600
GERBER PLUMBING FIXTURES CORPORATION, pg. 84, pg. 672
GIBRALTAR INDUSTRIES, INC., pg. 1340, pg. 1148
GREAT LAKES CASE & CABINET CO., INC., pg. 401, pg. 1529
GREIF INC., pg. 1459, pg. 1447
GRIPNAIL CORPORATION, pg. 1048, pg. 1601

First page reference indicates Business Class Edition
Second page reference indicates Geographic Edition

GROHE AMERICA, INC., pg. 1048, pg. 557
GROOV-PIN CORPORATION, pg. 1049, pg. 1608
HAMMOND VALVE CORP., pg. 1049, pg. 1883
HANNAY REELS INC., pg. 1344, pg. 1351
HAYS FLUID CONTROLS, pg. 1049, pg. 1370
JACUZZI BRANDS CORPORATION, pg. 554, pg. 65
JOSAM COMPANY, pg. 89, pg. 695
KABA ILCO CORP., pg. 1052, pg. 1390
KADANT JOHNSON INC., pg. 1073, pg. 909
KEENEY MANUFACTURING COMPANY, pg. 90, pg. 360
KENNAMETAL INC., pg. 1052, pg. 1547
KNAPE & VOGT MANUFACTURING COMPANY, pg. 1052, pg. 913
KOHLER CO., pg. 91, pg. 1862
KURZ TRANSFER PRODUCTS, L.P., pg. 1354, pg. 1367
LARSON-JUHL US LLC, pg. 933, pg. 537
LECHLER, INC., pg. 1444, pg. 658
LYDALL, INC., pg. 1357, pg. 354
MANITOWOC CRANE SHADY GROVE, pg. 1359, pg. 1586
MASCO CORPORATION, pg. 96, pg. 909
MASTER LOCK COMPANY LLC, pg. 1055, pg. 1884
MATCO TOOLS CORPORATION, pg. 1055, pg. 1474
MATERION CORPORATION, pg. 1359, pg. 1463
MATERION MICROELECTRONICS & SERVICES, pg. 1559, pg. 1149
MEDECO HIGH SECURITY LOCKS, INC., pg. 1055, pg. 1806
MILWAUKEE VALVE COMPANY, INC., pg. 1361, pg. 1884
MITEK, INC., pg. 1056, pg. 975
MOEN INCORPORATED, pg. 1056, pg. 1468
NACCO INDUSTRIES, INC., pg. 1174, pg. 1433
NEWARK WIRE CLOTH CO., pg. 99, pg. 1052
OMG, INC., pg. 1367, pg. 781
OXO, pg. 1058, pg. 1275
PACTIV CORPORATION, pg. 1466, pg. 624
PASLODE, pg. 1059, pg. 664
PENN ENGINEERING & MANUFACTURING CORP., pg. 1059, pg. 1525
PENNENGINEERING FASTENING TECHNOLOGIES, pg. 1059, pg. 1526
PFISTER, INC., pg. 1059, pg. 88
POLYFLON COMPANY, pg. 1369, pg. 364
PORTLAND WILLAMETTE, pg. 1129, pg. 1505
PRECISION VALVE CORPORATION, pg. 1060, pg. 1357
RAIN BIRD CORPORATION, pg. 707, pg. 44
REV-A-SHELF, pg. 1060, pg. 738
RICHARDS INDUSTRIES VALVE GROUP, pg. 107, pg. 1425
RICHELIEU HARDWARE LTD., pg. 1060, pg. 1961
ROCKY MOUNTAIN HARDWARE INC., pg. 1061, pg. 549
ROMAC INDUSTRIES, INC., pg. 1061, pg. 1818
RONA, INC., pg. 216, pg. 1950
ROUSSEAU METAL, INC., pg. 463, pg. 1960
RUSSEL METALS INC., pg. 1180, pg. 1928
RYERSON INC., pg. 1373, pg. 589
SARGENT & GREENLEAF, INC., pg. 1061, pg. 739
SARGENT MANUFACTURING COMPANY, pg. 1061, pg. 359
SCHAEFER MARINE INC., pg. 1373, pg. 835
SENIOR FLEXONICS INC., pg. 1375, pg. 556
SENTRY GROUP, INC., pg. 468, pg. 1337
SHILOH INDUSTRIES, INC., pg. 1375, pg. 1478
SHUR-CO, INC., pg. 110, pg. 1626
SIMPSON MANUFACTURING COMPANY, INC., pg. 1376, pg. 185
SLOAN VALVE COMPANY, pg. 1062, pg. 613
SOLIDSCAPE, INC., pg. 1063, pg. 1037
SOUTHERN FOLGER DETENTION EQUIPMENT COMPANY, pg. 1063, pg. 1743
SPEAKMAN COMPANY, pg. 112, pg. 388
SPIRAX SARCO, INC., pg. 1076, pg. 1612
SPIROL INTERNATIONAL CORPORATION, pg. 1378, pg. 345
STANLEY BLACK & DECKER, INC., pg. 1063, pg. 358
STRAHMAN VALVES, INC., pg. 1379, pg. 1517
SWAGELOK COMPANY, pg. 1064, pg. 1473
SYMMONS INDUSTRIES, INC., pg. 114, pg. 803
T&S BRASS & BRONZE WORKS, INC., pg. 114, pg. 1623
TCI PRECISION METALS, INC., pg. 1380, pg. 95
TELSCO INDUSTRIES, INC., pg. 1381, pg. 1698
THERMOS L.L.C., pg. 61, pg. 660
TIDEL ENGINEERING, L.P., pg. 1382, pg. 1670
TRINITY INDUSTRIES, INC., pg. 116, pg. 1690
TRUTH HARDWARE CORP., pg. 1066, pg. 952
UNIVERSAL INDUSTRIAL PRODUCTS CO., pg. 1066, pg. 1470
VICTAULIC COMPANY, pg. 1066, pg. 1529
WATTS WATER TECHNOLOGIES, INC., pg. 1078, pg. 837
WEATHERTEC CORPORATION, pg. 708, pg. 93
WINNER INTERNATIONAL, LLC, pg. 222, pg. 1586
WITT INDUSTRIES, INC., pg. 1140, pg. 1461
THE WM. POWELL COMPANY, pg. 1389, pg. 1427
WORTHINGTON INDUSTRIES, INC., pg. 123, pg. 1444
YARDLEY PRODUCTS CORPORATION, pg. 1391, pg. 1596
ZIM-AMERICAN ISRAELI SHIPPING CO., pg. 1931, pg. 1798
ZIPPO MANUFACTURING COMPANY, INC., pg. 1895, pg. 1518

3495 - Wire Springs

BARNES GROUP INC., pg. 1317, pg. 340
DE-STA-CO INDUSTRIES, pg. 1045, pg. 867
HSM SOLUTIONS, pg. 1884, pg. 1378

3496 - Miscellaneous Fabricated Wire Products

ACME STAPLE COMPANY, INC., pg. 341, pg. 1034
ACS INDUSTRIES, INC., pg. 1040, pg. 1602
AFC CABLE SYSTEMS, INC., pg. 1294, pg. 835
ASSOCIATED MATERIALS LLC, pg. 69, pg. 1445
BELDEN, INC., pg. 624, pg. 993
BRIDON AMERICAN CORP., pg. 1319, pg. 1594
BUFFALO WIRE WORKS CO., INC., pg. 72, pg. 1147
CANNON EQUIPMENT COMPANY, pg. 1321, pg. 920
CARLISLE INTERCONNECT TECHNOLOGIES, pg. 1294, pg. 461
CHAMPLAIN CABLE CORP., pg. 1044, pg. 1765
CHASE CORPORATION, pg. 1152, pg. 803
CLOSETMAID CORPORATION, pg. 920, pg. 452
COLEMAN CABLE, INC., pg. 1324, pg. 665
COLUMBUS MCKINNON CORPORATION, pg. 1325, pg. 1138
CORNING INCORPORATED, pg. 1122, pg. 1154
DAYTON SUPERIOR CORPORATION, pg. 1328, pg. 1464
ERICO INTERNATIONAL CORPORATION, pg. 1335, pg. 1472
ESSENTRA COMPONENTS, pg. 1047, pg. 612
ESSEX GROUP, INC., pg. 638, pg. 680
ESTAD STAMPING & MANUFACTURING COMPANY, pg. 1336, pg. 598
FORTUNE BRANDS HOME & SECURITY, INC., pg. 55, pg. 600
FUSHI COPPERWELD, pg. 1296, pg. 1632
GENERAL CABLE CORPORATION, pg. 83, pg. 384
GRC ENTERPRISES, INC., pg. 1344, pg. 677
THE GREAT AMERICAN HANGER COMPANY INC., pg. 926, pg. 442
GREENLEE TEXTRON INC., pg. 1048, pg. 655
HANDY & HARMAN LTD., pg. 85, pg. 1352
HILTI, INC., pg. 1346, pg. 1490
HINDLEY MANUFACTURING COMPANY, INC., pg. 1049, pg. 1601
HOUSTON WIRE & CABLE COMPANY, pg. 643, pg. 1708
JOHN HASSALL, INC., pg. 1052, pg. 1350
KEYSTONE CONSOLIDATED INDUSTRIES, INC., pg. 90, pg. 1683
KEYSTONE STEEL & WIRE CO., pg. 91, pg. 651
LEVITON MANUFACTURING COMPANY, INC., pg. 1301, pg. 1180
LITTLE FALLS ALLOYS, INC., pg. 1171, pg. 1107
MACCAFERRI, INC., pg. 95, pg. 780
MASTER HALCO, pg. 96, pg. 474
MEADOW BURKE, pg. 96, pg. 474
METAL TEXTILES CORPORATION, pg. 654, pg. 1057
NEWARK WIRE CLOTH CO., pg. 99, pg. 1052
NUCOR CORPORATION, pg. 101, pg. 1368
THE OKONITE COMPANY, pg. 1302, pg. 1113
PEACE INDUSTRIES INC., pg. 1368, pg. 656
PEERLESS CHAIN COMPANY, pg. 1887, pg. 967
QUALITY PERFORATING, INC., pg. 1468, pg. 1520
RADIX WIRE COMPANY, pg. 1304, pg. 1434
RSCC AEROSPACE & DEFENSE, pg. 1373, pg. 1036
SEFAR AMERICA, INC., pg. 698, pg. 1080
SENCO PRODUCTS, INC., pg. 1374, pg. 1425
SENECA WIRE & MANUFACTURING COMPANY, pg. 1061, pg. 1454
SIGMUND COHN CORP., pg. 1062, pg. 1183
SOMMER METALCRAFT CORPORATION, pg. 112, pg. 676
SUPERIOR ESSEX, INC., pg. 676, pg. 521
T&S PERFECTION CHAIN PRODUCTS, INC., pg. 1065, pg. 5
WEBSTER INDUSTRIES INC., pg. 1388, pg. 1475
W.H. MAZE COMPANY, pg. 1389, pg. 652
WIRECO WORLDGROUP, pg. 1389, pg. 987
WIRECO WORLDGROUP, pg. 1389, pg. 721
THE WOODSTREAM CORPORATION, pg. 1801, pg. 1549

3497 - Metal Foil & Leaf

BPM INC., pg. 1454, pg. 1886
HAZEN PAPER COMPANY, pg. 1459, pg. 825
NOVELIS INC., pg. 100, pg. 516
REYNOLDS CONSUMER PRODUCTS, pg. 1138, pg. 625

3498 - Fabricated Pipe & Fabricated Pipe Fittings

ANVIL INTERNATIONAL, INC., pg. 1879, pg. 1038
CHICAGO TUBE & IRON CO., pg. 1323, pg. 656
CRANE CHEMPHARMA & ENERGY, pg. 1044, pg. 1382
DEUBLIN COMPANY, pg. 78, pg. 666
FIBER GLASS SYSTEMS L.P., pg. 1162, pg. 34
H-P PRODUCTS, INC., pg. 85, pg. 1458
MFRI INC., pg. 1074, pg. 637
MORRIS COUPLING COMPANY, pg. 1057, pg. 1530
OMEGA FLEX, INC., pg. 982, pg. 1532
SUPERIOR TUBE COMPANY INC., pg. 113, pg. 1522
WALTER ENERGY, INC., pg. 120, pg. 4

3499 - Fabricated Metal Products, NEC

ACCURATE PERFORATING COMPANY, INC., pg. 1309, pg. 563
ACME METAL CAP CO., INC., pg. 1310, pg. 1356
ADMIRAL TOOL & MANUFACTURING COMPANY INC., pg. 1310, pg. 896
AFC CABLE SYSTEMS, INC., pg. 1294, pg. 835
AIR-LEC INDUSTRIES LLC, pg. 1041, pg. 1864
A.L. HANSEN MANUFACTURING CO., pg. 1041, pg. 665
ALAMO GROUP INC., pg. 1311, pg. 1745
ALL-CLAD METALCRAFTERS LLC, pg. 1121, pg. 1519
ALLFAST FASTENING SYSTEMS, INC., pg. 1041, pg. 66
AMATOM ELECTRONIC HARDWARE, INC., pg. 1041, pg. 342
AMEREQUIP CORPORATION, pg. 700, pg. 1862
AMERICAN ELECTRIC TECHNOLOGIES, INC., pg. 349, pg. 1700
AMERICAN LOCKER GROUP INCORPORATED, pg. 1041, pg. 1674
AMERICAN VAN EQUIPMENT INC., pg. 199, pg. 1078
AMUNEAL MANUFACTURING CORPORATION, pg. 617, pg. 1558
APTARGROUP, INC., pg. 1451, pg. 598
APW WYOTT FOOD SERVICE EQUIPMENT, INC., pg. 1314, pg. 1658
ARTUS CORPORATION, pg. 1314, pg. 1059
ASCO SINTERING CO., pg. 1042, pg. 126
A.T. FERRELL COMPANY, INC., pg. 701, pg. 674
ATTWOOD CORPORATION, pg. 1705, pg. 897
AUTOMATIC EQUIPMENT CORPORATION, pg. 1315, pg. 1410
BALL & BALL HARDWARE REPRODUCTIONS, pg. 916, pg. 1531
BARNES GROUP INC., pg. 1317, pg. 340
BAYLOFF STAMPED PRODUCTS, pg. 1317, pg. 1457
BLACK & DECKER, pg. 1043, pg. 1907
BOBRICK WASHROOM EQUIPMENT, INC., pg. 1043, pg. 166
BRYCE CORPORATION, pg. 1879, pg. 1641
BTM CORPORATION, pg. 1320, pg. 898
BUCKEYE CORRUGATED INC., pg. 1454, pg. 1400
BUD INDUSTRIES, INC., pg. 627, pg. 1482
BUFFALO WIRE WORKS CO., INC., pg. 72, pg. 1147
BWAY HOLDING COMPANY, pg. 1454, pg. 491
CALPHALON CORPORATION, pg. 1121, pg. 1470
CASCADE CORPORATION, pg. 1321, pg. 1497
CENTRIA ARCHITECTURAL SYSTEMS, pg. 74, pg. 1554
CENTRIA, INC., pg. 74, pg. 1554
CHICAGO METAL FABRICATORS, INC., pg. 1323, pg. 569
CHICAGO-WILCOX MFG. COMPANY, INC., pg. 202, pg.

661
CHILDERS CARPORTS AND STRUCTURES, INC., *pg.* 76, *pg.* 1703
COMPX INTERNATIONAL INC., *pg.* 1044, *pg.* 1678
CRENLO, LLC, *pg.* 77, *pg.* 955
CROSMAN CORPORATION, *pg.* 951, *pg.* 1143
THE CYCLONE MFG. CO., *pg.* 78, *pg.* 698
DARNELL-ROSE, *pg.* 1045, *pg.* 67
DECO PRODUCTS CO., *pg.* 1045, *pg.* 704
DOVER CORPORATION, *pg.* 1329, *pg.* 608
DREMEL, *pg.* 1046, *pg.* 634
DRIV-LOK, INC., *pg.* 1046, *pg.* 662
EAGLE MANUFACTURING COMPANY, *pg.* 79, *pg.* 1851
THE EASTERN COMPANY, *pg.* 1331, *pg.* 357
EBERHARD MANUFACTURING DIVISION, *pg.* 1046, *pg.* 1475
E.R. WAGNER CASTERS AND WHEELS DIV., *pg.* 1047, *pg.* 1874
ERICO INTERNATIONAL CORPORATION, *pg.* 1335, *pg.* 1472
ESCO CORPORATION, *pg.* 1335, *pg.* 1502
ESTAD STAMPING & MANUFACTURING COMPANY, *pg.* 1336, *pg.* 598
FEDERAL HOSE MANUFACTURING INC., *pg.* 1047, *pg.* 1469
FLEXIBLE STEEL LACING COMPANY, *pg.* 1337, *pg.* 608
FORTUNE BRANDS HOME & SECURITY, INC., *pg.* 55, *pg.* 600
FOUR SEASONS SUNROOM, *pg.* 83, *pg.* 1167
FREEWAY CORPORATION, *pg.* 1338, *pg.* 1431
FULL VISION, INC., *pg.* 1163, *pg.* 717
GASSER & SONS, INC., *pg.* 83, *pg.* 1153
GEHL COMPANY, *pg.* 1339, *pg.* 1899
GIBRALTAR INDUSTRIES, INC., *pg.* 1340, *pg.* 1148
GLOBE SPECIALTY METALS INC., *pg.* 1164, *pg.* 1235
GREAT LAKES CASE & CABINET CO., INC., *pg.* 401, *pg.* 1529
GREENLEE TEXTRON INC., *pg.* 1048, *pg.* 655
GREIF INC., *pg.* 1459, *pg.* 1447
GRIPNAIL CORPORATION, *pg.* 1048, *pg.* 1601
GROOV-PIN CORPORATION, *pg.* 1049, *pg.* 1608
HAMILTON CASTER & MFG. CO., *pg.* 206, *pg.* 1454
HANNAY REELS INC., *pg.* 1344, *pg.* 1351
HANSLER MANUTENTION, INC, *pg.* 178, *pg.* 1950
HARRINGTON & KING PERFORATING COMPANY, INC., *pg.* 1164, *pg.* 576
HENDRICK MANUFACTURING COMPANY, *pg.* 86, *pg.* 1520
HMT LLC, *pg.* 979, *pg.* 1747
HUNTER DOUGLAS, INC., *pg.* 928, *pg.* 1320
HYSTER-YALE MATERIALS HANDLING, *pg.* 1347, *pg.* 1503
INTELLIGRATED SYSTEMS LLC, *pg.* 1350, *pg.* 998
J.B. POINDEXTER & CO., INC., *pg.* 209, *pg.* 1709
KABA ILCO CORP., *pg.* 1052, *pg.* 1390
KENNAMETAL INC., *pg.* 1052, *pg.* 1547
KEYSTONE STEEL & WIRE CO., *pg.* 91, *pg.* 651
KNAPE & VOGT MANUFACTURING COMPANY, *pg.* 1052, *pg.* 913
KURZ TRANSFER PRODUCTS, L.P., *pg.* 1354, *pg.* 1367
LARSON-JUHL US LLC, *pg.* 933, *pg.* 537
LAYSTROM MANUFACTURING CO., *pg.* 1355, *pg.* 580
LIFETIME BRANDS, INC., *pg.* 1127, *pg.* 1161
LIFTOMATIC MATERIAL HANDLING INC., *pg.* 94, *pg.* 560
LOUIS BERKMAN CO., *pg.* 1357, *pg.* 1473
LYDALL, INC., *pg.* 1357, *pg.* 354
M&G DURA-VENT, INC., *pg.* 95, *pg.* 298
MAGLINE, INC., *pg.* 1358, *pg.* 908
MANITEX INTERNATIONAL, INC., *pg.* 1358, *pg.* 559
MANITOWOC CRANE SHADY GROVE, *pg.* 1359, *pg.* 1586
MASTER LOCK COMPANY LLC, *pg.* 1055, *pg.* 1884
MATCO TOOLS CORPORATION, *pg.* 1055, *pg.* 1474
MATERION CORPORATION, *pg.* 1359, *pg.* 1463
MATERION MICROELECTRONICS & SERVICES, *pg.* 1559, *pg.* 1149
MEDECO HIGH SECURITY LOCKS, INC., *pg.* 1055, *pg.* 1806
METALFAB, INC., *pg.* 1360, *pg.* 1127
MICRO CORP., *pg.* 1056, *pg.* 1122
MIDDLE ATLANTIC PRODUCTS INC., *pg.* 1360, *pg.* 1065
MITEK, INC., *pg.* 1056, *pg.* 975
MOTAN, INC., *pg.* 1886, *pg.* 903
NACCO INDUSTRIES, INC., *pg.* 1174, *pg.* 1433
NATIONAL BAND & TAG CO., *pg.* 1479, *pg.* 739
NISSAN FORKLIFT CORPORATION, NORTH AMERICA, *pg.* 186, *pg.* 631
NORTEK, INC., *pg.* 100, *pg.* 1607
NUTTING, *pg.* 1366, *pg.* 1626
ODL INCORPORATED, *pg.* 101, *pg.* 914
OMG, INC., *pg.* 1367, *pg.* 781
OXO, *pg.* 1058, *pg.* 1275
PACTIV CORPORATION, *pg.* 1466, *pg.* 624
PASLODE, *pg.* 1059, *pg.* 664
PENN ENGINEERING & MANUFACTURING CORP., *pg.* 1059, *pg.* 1525
PENNENGINEERING FASTENING TECHNOLOGIES, *pg.* 1059, *pg.* 1526
PENTAIR WATER POOL AND SPA, INC., *pg.* 104, *pg.* 1171
PETERBILT MOTORS CO., *pg.* 188, *pg.* 1691
PETTIBONE, LLC, *pg.* 1368, *pg.* 609
POLAR WARE COMPANY, *pg.* 1129, *pg.* 1862
PORTLAND WILLAMETTE, *pg.* 1129, *pg.* 1505
PRECISION VALVE CORPORATION, *pg.* 1060, *pg.* 1357
QUALITY PERFORATING, INC., *pg.* 1468, *pg.* 1520
RANGE KLEEN MANUFACTURING INC., *pg.* 60, *pg.* 1458
REGAL WARE, INC., *pg.* 1137, *pg.* 1862
REV-A-SHELF, *pg.* 1060, *pg.* 738
RICHELIEU HARDWARE LTD., *pg.* 1060, *pg.* 1961
RIGIDIZED METALS CORP., *pg.* 108, *pg.* 1151
RITE-HITE HOLDING CORPORATION, *pg.* 1372, *pg.* 1880
ROCKY MOUNTAIN HARDWARE INC., *pg.* 1061, *pg.* 549
RONA, INC., *pg.* 216, *pg.* 1950
ROUSSEAU METAL, INC., *pg.* 463, *pg.* 1960
RUSSEL METALS INC., *pg.* 1180, *pg.* 1928
RYERSON INC., *pg.* 1373, *pg.* 589
SALSBURY INDUSTRIES, *pg.* 464, *pg.* 139
SARGENT & GREENLEAF, INC., *pg.* 1061, *pg.* 739
SARGENT MANUFACTURING COMPANY, *pg.* 1061, *pg.* 359
SCHAEFER MARINE INC., *pg.* 1373, *pg.* 835
SENIOR FLEXONICS INC., *pg.* 1375, *pg.* 556
SENTRY GROUP, INC., *pg.* 468, *pg.* 1337
SHILOH INDUSTRIES, INC., *pg.* 1375, *pg.* 1478
SHUR-CO, INC., *pg.* 110, *pg.* 1626
SIMPSON MANUFACTURING COMPANY, INC., *pg.* 1376, *pg.* 185
SOLIDSCAPE, INC., *pg.* 1063, *pg.* 1037
SOUTHERN FOLGER DETENTION EQUIPMENT COMPANY, *pg.* 1063, *pg.* 1743
SPEEDRACK PRODUCTS GROUP, LTD., *pg.* 112, *pg.* 908
SPIROL INTERNATIONAL CORPORATION, *pg.* 1378, *pg.* 345
STANLEY BLACK & DECKER, INC., *pg.* 1063, *pg.* 358
STARRCO COMPANY INC., *pg.* 113, *pg.* 988
SUPER SKY PRODUCTS, INC., *pg.* 113, *pg.* 1871
TCI PRECISION METALS, INC., *pg.* 1380, *pg.* 95
TEREX CORPORATION, *pg.* 1381, *pg.* 384
THERMOS L.L.C., *pg.* 61, *pg.* 660
TIDEL ENGINEERING, L.P., *pg.* 1382, *pg.* 1670
TORRMETAL CORPORATION, *pg.* 1383, *pg.* 1436
TRINITY INDUSTRIES, INC., *pg.* 116, *pg.* 1690
TRITON INDUSTRIES, INC., *pg.* 1384, *pg.* 592
TRUTH HARDWARE CORP., *pg.* 1066, *pg.* 952
UMF MEDICAL, *pg.* 946, *pg.* 1542
UNIVERSAL INDUSTRIAL PRODUCTS CO., *pg.* 1066, *pg.* 1470
VIKING RANGE CORPORATION, *pg.* 61, *pg.* 968
VULCAN, INC., *pg.* 687, *pg.* 5
WASHINGTON PRODUCTS INC., *pg.* 1387, *pg.* 1461
WINNER INTERNATIONAL, LLC, *pg.* 222, *pg.* 1586
WISCO PRODUCTS, INC., *pg.* 1389, *pg.* 1447
WITT INDUSTRIES, INC., *pg.* 1140, *pg.* 1461
WORLD KITCHEN LLC, *pg.* 1141, *pg.* 657
WORTHINGTON INDUSTRIES, *pg.* 222, *pg.* 1626
WORTHINGTON INDUSTRIES, INC., *pg.* 123, *pg.* 1444
YARDLEY PRODUCTS CORPORATION, *pg.* 1391, *pg.* 1596
ZIM-AMERICAN ISRAELI SHIPPING CO., *pg.* 1931, *pg.* 1798
ZIPPO MANUFACTURING COMPANY, INC., *pg.* 1895, *pg.* 1518

3511 - Steam, Gas & Hydraulic Turbines & Turbine Generator Set Units

BARBOUR STOCKWELL INCORPORATED, *pg.* 1316, *pg.* 861
BRIGGS & STRATTON CORPORATION, *pg.* 201, *pg.* 1899
ELLIOTT COMPANY, *pg.* 1333, *pg.* 1542
GENERAC POWER SYSTEMS INC., *pg.* 1340, *pg.* 1898
GENERAL ELECTRIC COMPANY, *pg.* 1297, *pg.* 347
MERCURY MARINE, *pg.* 1709, *pg.* 1857
PRECISION CASTPARTS CORP., *pg.* 105, *pg.* 1506
SIEMENS, *pg.* 1376, *pg.* 1466
SIEMENS CANADA LTD., *pg.* 1306, *pg.* 1921
SOLAR TURBINES INCORPORATED, *pg.* 1377, *pg.* 209
STS TURBO, INC., *pg.* 218, *pg.* 1753
TUTHILL CORPORATION, *pg.* 1385, *pg.* 561
VOITH HYDRO INC., *pg.* 1387, *pg.* 1598
VOLVO PENTA OF THE AMERICAS, INC., *pg.* 1712, *pg.* 1778
WOODWARD, INC., *pg.* 122, *pg.* 329
XZERES WIND CORP., *pg.* 1396, *pg.* 1512

3519 - Internal Combustion Engines, NEC

THE ADT CORPORATION, *pg.* 612, *pg.* 409
ADVANCED ENERGY INDUSTRIES, INC., *pg.* 613, *pg.* 328
BAE SYSTEMS PRODUCTS GROUP, *pg.* 359, *pg.* 432
BALLARD POWER SYSTEMS, INC., *pg.* 70, *pg.* 1907
BLONDER TONGUE LABORATORIES, INC., *pg.* 625, *pg.* 1100
BRADY CORPORATION, *pg.* 363, *pg.* 1873
BRANSON ULTRASONICS CORPORATION, *pg.* 1319, *pg.* 342
BRANSON ULTRASONICS CORPORATION-PRECISION CLEANING DIV, *pg.* 1319, *pg.* 343
BROAN-NUTONE LLC, *pg.* 1069, *pg.* 1860
BRUNSWICK CORPORATION, *pg.* 1828, *pg.* 623
C&D TECHNOLOGIES, INC., *pg.* 627, *pg.* 1517
CATERPILLAR, INC., *pg.* 1321, *pg.* 650
THE CHAMBERLAIN GROUP, INC., *pg.* 75, *pg.* 611
CHASE CORPORATION, *pg.* 1152, *pg.* 803
CHECKPOINT SYSTEMS, INC., *pg.* 628, *pg.* 1559
CLORE AUTOMOTIVE LLC, *pg.* 202, *pg.* 716
CONDUCTIX INC., *pg.* 1295, *pg.* 1015
CTS VALPEY CORPORATION, *pg.* 632, *pg.* 825
CUMMINS INC., *pg.* 1326, *pg.* 676
CUMMINS POWER GENERATION, *pg.* 1326, *pg.* 932
CVI MELLES GRIOT, *pg.* 1407, *pg.* 59
DETEX CORPORATION, *pg.* 633, *pg.* 1728
EATON CORPORATION, *pg.* 1331, *pg.* 1429
ELECTRO-MOTIVE DIESEL, INC., *pg.* 1333, *pg.* 621
ENERGIZER HOLDINGS, INC., *pg.* 637, *pg.* 996
ENPRO INDUSTRIES, INC., *pg.* 1334, *pg.* 1366
GENERAL ELECTRIC COMPANY, *pg.* 1297, *pg.* 347
THE GENIE COMPANY, *pg.* 55, *pg.* 1403
GLOBAL EPOINT INC., *pg.* 400, *pg.* 67
GSI GROUP INC., *pg.* 1415, *pg.* 784
HIGHFIELD MANUFACTURING CO., *pg.* 1346, *pg.* 339
HUBBELL INCORPORATED, *pg.* 1299, *pg.* 370
HUBBELL POWER SYSTEMS, INC., *pg.* 643, *pg.* 1614
IMPCO TECHNOLOGIES, INC., *pg.* 208, *pg.* 261
INTERNATIONAL COMPONENTS CORPORATION, *pg.* 647, *pg.* 669
INVISIBLE FENCE, INC., *pg.* 648, *pg.* 1637
ISOMET CORPORATION, *pg.* 1418, *pg.* 1807
IXIA, *pg.* 422, *pg.* 56
JACOBS VEHICLE SYSTEMS, *pg.* 1351, *pg.* 338
L-3 MAS CANADA, *pg.* 229, *pg.* 1952
LA MARCHE MANUFACTURING COMPANY, *pg.* 1300, *pg.* 606
LASER TECHNOLOGY, INC., *pg.* 1419, *pg.* 314
LIND ELECTRONICS, INC., *pg.* 1355, *pg.* 938
MASTER APPLIANCE CORP., *pg.* 1055, *pg.* 1888
MATEC INSTRUMENT COMPANIES, INC., *pg.* 1421, *pg.* 839
MAXXESS SYSTEMS, INC., *pg.* 431, *pg.* 43
MERCURY MARINE, *pg.* 1709, *pg.* 1857
MORSE WATCHMANS INC., *pg.* 656, *pg.* 368
NABCO ENTRANCES, INC., *pg.* 99, *pg.* 1882
NEW WAVE RESEARCH INCORPORATED, *pg.* 1423, *pg.* 91
NEWPORT CORPORATION, *pg.* 1424, *pg.* 114
NISSAN FORKLIFT CORPORATION, NORTH AMERICA, *pg.* 186, *pg.* 631
PERCEPTICS, LLC, *pg.* 1426, *pg.* 1637
PROPHOTONIX LIMITED, *pg.* 1427, *pg.* 1039
QUINCY COMPRESSOR INC., *pg.* 1371, *pg.* 653
ROCKWELL AUTOMATION, INC., *pg.* 668, *pg.* 1880
ROFIN-SINAR TECHNOLOGIES, INC., *pg.* 668, *pg.* 904
SCHNEIDER CANADA, INC., *pg.* 1374, *pg.* 1928
SCHNEIDER ELECTRIC, *pg.* 467, *pg.* 1609

First page reference indicates Business Class Edition
Second page reference indicates Geographic Edition

SEASTAR SOLUTIONS, pg. 1374, pg. 1548
SILICON GRAPHICS INTERNATIONAL CORP, pg. 470, pg. 148
SL INDUSTRIES, INC., pg. 674, pg. 1090
SUREFIRE, LLC, pg. 1307, pg. 90
TDK-LAMBDA HIGH POWER DIVISION, pg. 1380, pg. 1090
TECHNIBUS LLC, pg. 1380, pg. 1408
TECUMSEH PRODUCTS COMPANY, pg. 1381, pg. 866
VISHAY INTERTECHNOLOGY, INC., pg. 1435, pg. 1551
WESTERBEKE CORPORATION, pg. 1388, pg. 847
WOODWARD, INC., pg. 122, pg. 329

3523 - Farm Machinery & Equipment

AGCO CORPORATION, pg. 700, pg. 530
ALAMO GROUP INC., pg. 1311, pg. 1745
AMEREQUIP CORPORATION, pg. 700, pg. 1862
ART'S-WAY MANUFACTURING CO., INC., pg. 701, pg. 701
A.T. FERRELL COMPANY, INC., pg. 701, pg. 674
AUSCO PRODUCTS, INC., pg. 199, pg. 872
BEHLEN MFG. CO., pg. 701, pg. 1010
BOUMATIC LLC, pg. 701, pg. 1865
BUSH HOG, INC., pg. 702, pg. 8
CNH AMERICA LLC, pg. 702, pg. 560
CTB INTERNATIONAL CORP., pg. 850, pg. 695
DANUSER MACHINE COMPANY, INC., pg. 703, pg. 978
DEERE & COMPANY, pg. 703, pg. 632
DEGELMAN INDUSTRIES LTD., pg. 703, pg. 1962
EXCEL INDUSTRIES, INC., pg. 1795, pg. 715
GANDY COMPANY, pg. 703, pg. 952
GAS-FIRED PRODUCTS, INC., pg. 1338, pg. 1367
GEA FARM TECHNOLOGIES, pg. 704, pg. 636
GEHL COMPANY, pg. 1339, pg. 1899
GREAT PLAINS MANUFACTURING, INCORPORATED, pg. 704, pg. 721
HARPER INDUSTRIES, INC., pg. 704, pg. 715
HARRIS WASTE MANAGEMENT GROUP, INC., pg. 1345, pg. 526
HARSH INTERNATIONAL, INC., pg. 1345, pg. 324
HAWKEYE STEEL PRODUCTS, INC., pg. 704, pg. 708
HIGHWAY EQUIPMENT COMPANY, pg. 704, pg. 702
HINIKER COMPANY, pg. 704, pg. 927
JOHN DEERE LTD., pg. 705, pg. 1920
KELLY RYAN EQUIPMENT COMPANY, pg. 705, pg. 1010
LAM RESEARCH CORPORATION, pg. 1354, pg. 91
LINDSAY CORPORATION, pg. 1356, pg. 1016
LUNDELL ENTERPRISES, INC., pg. 706, pg. 703
MILLER MANUFACTURING COMPANY, pg. 706, pg. 921
MY-D HAN-D MFG. INC., pg. 706, pg. 714
THE PERRY COMPANY, pg. 706, pg. 1749
REINKE MANUFACTURING COMPANY, INC., pg. 707, pg. 1010
RITCHIE INDUSTRIES, INC., pg. 707, pg. 703
SEEDBURO EQUIPMENT CO., pg. 707, pg. 590
SIOUX STEEL COMPANY, pg. 707, pg. 1625
VERMEER MANUFACTURING COMPANY, pg. 708, pg. 711
WEATHERTEC CORPORATION, pg. 708, pg. 93
YETTER MANUFACTURING CO., INC., pg. 708, pg. 598

3524 - Lawn & Garden Tractors & Home Lawn & Garden Equipment

ARIENS COMPANY INC., pg. 700, pg. 1855
ATT HOLDING CO., pg. 1043, pg. 1519
BLOUNT INTERNATIONAL, INC., pg. 1043, pg. 1501
BRIGGS & STRATTON CORPORATION, pg. 201, pg. 1899
EASTMAN INDUSTRIES, pg. 1046, pg. 751
ECHO INCORPORATED, pg. 1046, pg. 626
FLOWTRON OUTDOOR PRODUCTS, pg. 639, pg. 830
GANDY COMPANY, pg. 703, pg. 952
JACOBSEN TEXTRON, pg. 1708, pg. 1367
JOHN DEERE CONSUMER & COMMERCIAL EQUIPMENT, INC., pg. 705, pg. 1360
MELNOR, INC., pg. 1055, pg. 1811
MTD PRODUCTS, INC., pg. 1057, pg. 1478
SCHILLER-PFEIFFER, INC., pg. 1061, pg. 1587
THE STEP2 COMPANY LLC, pg. 1889, pg. 1474
THE TORO COMPANY, pg. 1065, pg. 918

3531 - Construction Machinery & Equipment

AIR-LEC INDUSTRIES LLC, pg. 1041, pg. 1864
ALAMO GROUP INC., pg. 1311, pg. 1745
ALLIED CONSTRUCTION PRODUCTS, LLC, pg. 1311, pg. 1427
ALTEC INDUSTRIES INC., pg. 1312, pg. 1
ANVIL ATTACHMENTS, LLC, pg. 1313, pg. 748
ASTEC INDUSTRIES, INC., pg. 69, pg. 1628
BADGER EQUIPMENT COMPANY, pg. 1315, pg. 966
BESSER COMPANY, pg. 1317, pg. 865
BOMAG AMERICAS, INC., pg. 1318, pg. 621
CASHCO, INC., pg. 1044, pg. 714
CATERPILLAR, INC., pg. 1321, pg. 650
CHARLES MACHINE WORKS, INC., pg. 1322, pg. 1488
CNH AMERICA LLC, pg. 702, pg. 560
COLUMBUS MCKINNON CORPORATION, pg. 1325, pg. 1138
THE CYCLONE MFG. CO., pg. 78, pg. 698
DANUSER MACHINE COMPANY, INC., pg. 703, pg. 978
DEERE & COMPANY, pg. 703, pg. 632
EXCEL INDUSTRIES, INC., pg. 1795, pg. 715
THE FROG, SWITCH & MANUFACTURING COMPANY, pg. 1338, pg. 1520
FULL VISION, INC., pg. 1163, pg. 717
GEHL COMPANY, pg. 1339, pg. 1899
GENCOR INDUSTRIES, INC., pg. 1339, pg. 453
HENSLEY INDUSTRIES, INC., pg. 1166, pg. 1682
HIGHWAY EQUIPMENT COMPANY, pg. 704, pg. 702
INDUSTRIAL DISTRIBUTION GROUP, INC., pg. 413, pg. 1358
JLG INDUSTRIES, INC., pg. 1351, pg. 1551
KOMATSU AMERICA CORP., pg. 92, pg. 655
KPI-JCI, pg. 1354, pg. 1626
MARINE TRAVELIFT, INC., pg. 1359, pg. 1895
MITEK, INC., pg. 1056, pg. 975
P&H MINING EQUIPMENT, pg. 103, pg. 1879
PETTIBONE, LLC, pg. 1368, pg. 609
TELSMITH, INC., pg. 1381, pg. 1871
TEREX CEDARAPIDS, pg. 1381, pg. 703
TEREX CORPORATION, pg. 1381, pg. 384
TOROMONT CAT, pg. 192, pg. 1914
VERMEER MANUFACTURING COMPANY, pg. 708, pg. 711
VIBCO INC., pg. 1387, pg. 1611

3532 - Mining Machinery & Equipment, Except Oil & Gas Field Machinery Equipment

ASTEC INDUSTRIES, INC., pg. 69, pg. 1628
BLUE OX, pg. 701, pg. 1019
BRUNNER & LAY, INC., pg. 1320, pg. 35
CATERPILLAR, INC., pg. 1321, pg. 650
CENTRIFUGAL & MECHANICAL INDUSTRIES, INC., pg. 1322, pg. 994
ESCO CORPORATION, pg. 1335, pg. 1502
FEDERAL SIGNAL CORPORATION, pg. 638, pg. 645
HUTCHINSON/MAYRATH INDUSTRIES INC., pg. 704, pg. 714
JOY GLOBAL, INC., pg. 1351, pg. 1876
JOY MINING MACHINERY, pg. 1352, pg. 1591
KENNAMETAL INC., pg. 1052, pg. 1547
MINE SAFETY APPLIANCES COMPANY, pg. 1361, pg. 1525
MOOG INC., pg. 231, pg. 1156
THE NOLAN COMPANY, pg. 1365, pg. 1408
STEDMAN MACHINE COMPANY, pg. 1379, pg. 673
TELSMITH, INC., pg. 1381, pg. 1871
WILLIAMS PATENT CRUSHER & PULVERIZER CO., INC., pg. 1389, pg. 1005

3533 - Oil & Gas Field Machinery & Equipment

BAKER HUGHES INCORPORATED, pg. 1315, pg. 1700
BAKER HUGHES INTEQ, pg. 1316, pg. 1700
BOLT TECHNOLOGY CORPORATION, pg. 1318, pg. 360
CAMERON DRILLING & PRODUCTION SYSTEMS, pg. 1321, pg. 1702
CAMERON INTERNATIONAL, pg. 1151, pg. 1702
DRIL-QUIP, INC., pg. 1330, pg. 1704
EXXON MOBIL CORPORATION, pg. 977, pg. 1718
GARDNER DENVER, INC., pg. 1338, pg. 1592
GE ENERGY, pg. 1338, pg. 506
THE GEORGE E. FAILING COMPANY, pg. 1340, pg. 1484
LUFKIN INDUSTRIES, INC., pg. 1357, pg. 1726
NATIONAL OILWELL VARCO, INC., pg. 1364, pg. 1712
POWERSECURE INTERNATIONAL, INC., pg. 105, pg. 1392
SMITH INTERNATIONAL, INC., pg. 1377, pg. 1715
STEWART & STEVENSON, LLC, pg. 985, pg. 1715
T.D. WILLIAMSON, INC., pg. 1380, pg. 1490
WELLMASTER CARTS, pg. 1388, pg. 1934

3534 - Elevators & Moving Stairways

THE FLINCHBAUGH CO., INC., pg. 82, pg. 1551
INCLINATOR COMPANY OF AMERICA, pg. 88, pg. 1536
KONE INC., pg. 1353, pg. 633
OTIS ELEVATOR COMPANY, pg. 102, pg. 349
SAVARIA CONCORD LIFTS INC., pg. 1592, pg. 1919
SAVARIA CORPORATION, pg. 1592, pg. 1951
UNITED TECHNOLOGIES CORPORATION, pg. 235, pg. 353

3535 - Conveyors & Conveying Equipment

AGCO CORPORATION, pg. 700, pg. 530
ALAMO GROUP INC., pg. 1311, pg. 1745
AMEREQUIP CORPORATION, pg. 700, pg. 1862
ART'S-WAY MANUFACTURING CO., INC., pg. 701, pg. 701
A.T. FERRELL COMPANY, INC., pg. 701, pg. 674
AUSCO PRODUCTS, INC., pg. 199, pg. 872
BEHLEN MFG. CO., pg. 701, pg. 1010
BOUMATIC LLC, pg. 701, pg. 1865
BROOKS AUTOMATION, INC., pg. 1320, pg. 813
BUSH HOG, INC., pg. 702, pg. 8
BW CONTAINER SYSTEMS, pg. 1321, pg. 656
CHRISTIANSON SYSTEMS, INC., pg. 1323, pg. 917
CNH AMERICA LLC, pg. 702, pg. 560
CTB INTERNATIONAL CORP., pg. 850, pg. 695
DANUSER MACHINE COMPANY, INC., pg. 703, pg. 978
DEERE & COMPANY, pg. 703, pg. 632
DEGELMAN INDUSTRIES LTD., pg. 703, pg. 1962
DORNER MANUFACTURING CORP., pg. 1329, pg. 1861
EXCEL INDUSTRIES, INC., pg. 1795, pg. 715
GANDY COMPANY, pg. 703, pg. 952
GAS-FIRED PRODUCTS, INC., pg. 1338, pg. 1367
GEA FARM TECHNOLOGIES, pg. 704, pg. 636
GEHL COMPANY, pg. 1339, pg. 1899
GREAT PLAINS MANUFACTURING, INCORPORATED, pg. 704, pg. 721
HARPER INDUSTRIES, INC., pg. 704, pg. 715
HARRIS WASTE MANAGEMENT GROUP, INC., pg. 1345, pg. 526
HARSH INTERNATIONAL, INC., pg. 1345, pg. 324
HAWKEYE STEEL PRODUCTS, INC., pg. 704, pg. 708
HIGHWAY EQUIPMENT COMPANY, pg. 704, pg. 702
HINIKER COMPANY, pg. 704, pg. 927
INTELLIGRATED, INC., pg. 1349, pg. 1460
INTELLIGRATED SYSTEMS INC., pg. 1349, pg. 1414
INTERROLL ENGINEERING WEST INC., pg. 1350, pg. 314
INTERSYSTEMS, pg. 1350, pg. 1016
INTRALOX LLC, pg. 1350, pg. 744
JLG INDUSTRIES, INC., pg. 1351, pg. 1551
JOHN DEERE LTD., pg. 705, pg. 1920
JOY MINING MACHINERY, pg. 1352, pg. 1591
KELLY RYAN EQUIPMENT COMPANY, pg. 705, pg. 1010
KPI-JCI, pg. 1354, pg. 1626
THE LAITRAM LLC, pg. 1354, pg. 744
LAM RESEARCH CORPORATION, pg. 1354, pg. 91
LINDSAY CORPORATION, pg. 1356, pg. 1016
LUNDELL ENTERPRISES, INC., pg. 706, pg. 703
MAC EQUIPMENT, INC., pg. 1357, pg. 985
MAYFRAN INTERNATIONAL, INC., pg. 1359, pg. 1432
METALFAB, INC., pg. 1360, pg. 1127
METZGAR CONVEYOR COMPANY, pg. 1360, pg. 875
MILLER MANUFACTURING COMPANY, pg. 706, pg. 921
MOTAN, INC., pg. 1886, pg. 903
MY-D HAN-D MFG. INC., pg. 706, pg. 714
NORTH STAR ICE EQUIPMENT CORPORATION, pg. 1366, pg. 1838
PARAGON TECHNOLOGIES, INC., pg. 1367, pg. 1528
THE PERRY COMPANY, pg. 706, pg. 1749
PNEUMATICSCALEANGELUS, pg. 1369, pg. 1445
PRAB, INC., pg. 1369, pg. 894
PUTZMEISTER AMERICA, pg. 1371, pg. 1896

REINKE MANUFACTURING COMPANY, INC., pg. 707, pg. 1010
RENOLD, INC., pg. 1371, pg. 1351
RITCHIE INDUSTRIES, INC., pg. 707, pg. 703
SCREW CONVEYOR INDUSTRIES, pg. 1374, pg. 682
SEEDBURO EQUIPMENT CO., pg. 707, pg. 590
SHINGLE BELTING COMPANY, pg. 1375, pg. 1544
SHUTTLEWORTH, INC., pg. 1375, pg. 682
SIOUX STEEL COMPANY, pg. 707, pg. 1625
SWISSLOG LOGISTICS, pg. 1380, pg. 1796
UNEX MANUFACTURING, INC., pg. 1385, pg. 1075
VAN GORP CORPORATION, pg. 1387, pg. 711
VERMEER MANUFACTURING COMPANY, pg. 708, pg. 711
WEATHERTEC CORPORATION, pg. 708, pg. 93
WEBSTER INDUSTRIES INC., pg. 1388, pg. 1475
WES-TECH AUTOMATION SOLUTIONS, pg. 1388, pg. 560
YETTER MANUFACTURING CO., INC., pg. 708, pg. 598

3536 - Overhead Traveling Cranes, Hoists & Monorail Systems

AIR-LEC INDUSTRIES LLC, pg. 1041, pg. 1864
A.L. HANSEN MANUFACTURING CO., pg. 1041, pg. 665
ALAMO GROUP INC., pg. 1311, pg. 1745
ALLFAST FASTENING SYSTEMS, INC., pg. 1041, pg. 66
ALLIED CONSTRUCTION PRODUCTS, LLC, pg. 1311, pg. 1427
ALTEC INDUSTRIES INC., pg. 1312, pg. 1
AMATOM ELECTRONIC HARDWARE, INC., pg. 1041, pg. 342
AMERICAN CRANE & EQUIPMENT CORPORATION, pg. 1312, pg. 1526
AMERICAN LOCKER GROUP INCORPORATED, pg. 1041, pg. 1674
AMERICAN VAN EQUIPMENT INC., pg. 199, pg. 1078
ANVIL ATTACHMENTS, LLC, pg. 1313, pg. 748
ASCO SINTERING CO., pg. 1042, pg. 126
ASTEC INDUSTRIES, INC., pg. 69, pg. 1628
ATTWOOD CORPORATION, pg. 1705, pg. 897
BADGER EQUIPMENT COMPANY, pg. 1315, pg. 966
BALL & BALL HARDWARE REPRODUCTIONS, pg. 916, pg. 1531
BESSER COMPANY, pg. 1317, pg. 865
BLACK & DECKER, pg. 1043, pg. 1907
BLOOM MANUFACTURING, INC., pg. 701, pg. 708
BOMAG AMERICAS, INC., pg. 1318, pg. 621
BTM CORPORATION, pg. 1320, pg. 898
CASHCO, INC., pg. 1044, pg. 714
CATERPILLAR, INC., pg. 1321, pg. 650
CHARLES MACHINE WORKS, INC., pg. 1322, pg. 1488
CNH AMERICA LLC, pg. 702, pg. 560
COLUMBUS MCKINNON CORPORATION, pg. 1325, pg. 1138
COMPX INTERNATIONAL INC., pg. 1044, pg. 1678
THE CYCLONE MFG. CO., pg. 78, pg. 698
DAIFUKU WEBB, pg. 1327, pg. 885
DANUSER MACHINE COMPANY, INC., pg. 703, pg. 978
DECO PRODUCTS CO., pg. 1045, pg. 704
DEERE & COMPANY, pg. 703, pg. 632
DOWNS CRANE & HOIST CO, INC., pg. 1330, pg. 129
DREMEL, pg. 1046, pg. 634
DRIV-LOK, INC., pg. 1046, pg. 662
THE EASTERN COMPANY, pg. 1331, pg. 357
EBERHARD MANUFACTURING DIVISION, pg. 1046, pg. 1475
E.R. WAGNER CASTERS AND WHEELS DIV., pg. 1047, pg. 1874
EXCEL INDUSTRIES, INC., pg. 1795, pg. 715
FLEXIBLE STEEL LACING COMPANY, pg. 1337, pg. 608
FORTUNE BRANDS HOME & SECURITY, INC., pg. 55, pg. 600
THE FROG, SWITCH & MANUFACTURING COMPANY, pg. 1338, pg. 1520
FULL VISION, INC., pg. 1163, pg. 717
GEHL COMPANY, pg. 1339, pg. 1899
GENCOR INDUSTRIES, INC., pg. 1339, pg. 453
GREIF INC., pg. 1459, pg. 1447
GRIPNAIL CORPORATION, pg. 1048, pg. 1601
GROOV-PIN CORPORATION, pg. 1049, pg. 1608
HARRINGTON HOISTS, INC., pg. 1345, pg. 1551
HARSH INTERNATIONAL, INC., pg. 1345, pg. 324
HENSLEY INDUSTRIES, INC., pg. 1166, pg. 1682
HIGHWAY EQUIPMENT COMPANY, pg. 704, pg. 702
INDUSTRIAL DISTRIBUTION GROUP, INC., pg. 413, pg. 1358
JLG INDUSTRIES, INC., pg. 1351, pg. 1551
KABA ILCO CORP., pg. 1052, pg. 1390
KENNAMETAL INC., pg. 1052, pg. 1547
KNAPE & VOGT MANUFACTURING COMPANY, pg. 1052, pg. 913
KOMATSU AMERICA CORP., pg. 92, pg. 655
KPI-JCI, pg. 1354, pg. 1626
MANITEX INTERNATIONAL, INC., pg. 1358, pg. 559
THE MANITOWOC COMPANY, INC., pg. 1358, pg. 1868
MARINE TRAVELIFT, INC., pg. 1359, pg. 1895
MASTER LOCK COMPANY LLC, pg. 1055, pg. 1884
MATCO TOOLS CORPORATION, pg. 1055, pg. 1474
MEDECO HIGH SECURITY LOCKS, INC., pg. 1055, pg. 1806
MIDWEST INDUSTRIES, INC., pg. 185, pg. 708
MITEK, INC., pg. 1056, pg. 975
OMAHA STANDARD PALFINGER, pg. 706, pg. 704
OXO, pg. 1058, pg. 1275
P&H MINING EQUIPMENT, pg. 103, pg. 1879
PASLODE, pg. 1059, pg. 664
PENN ENGINEERING & MANUFACTURING CORP., pg. 1059, pg. 1525
PENNENGINEERING FASTENING TECHNOLOGIES, pg. 1059, pg. 1526
PETTIBONE, LLC, pg. 1368, pg. 609
PORTLAND WILLAMETTE, pg. 1129, pg. 1505
REV-A-SHELF, pg. 1060, pg. 738
RICHELIEU HARDWARE LTD., pg. 1060, pg. 1961
ROCKY MOUNTAIN HARDWARE INC., pg. 1061, pg. 549
RONA, INC., pg. 216, pg. 1950
ROUSSEAU METAL, INC., pg. 463, pg. 1960
SARGENT & GREENLEAF, INC., pg. 1061, pg. 739
SARGENT MANUFACTURING COMPANY, pg. 1061, pg. 359
SCHAEFER MARINE INC., pg. 1373, pg. 835
SHUR-CO, INC., pg. 110, pg. 1626
SIMPSON MANUFACTURING COMPANY, INC., pg. 1376, pg. 185
SOLIDSCAPE, INC., pg. 1063, pg. 1037
SOUTHERN FOLGER DETENTION EQUIPMENT COMPANY, pg. 1063, pg. 1743
STANLEY BLACK & DECKER, INC., pg. 1063, pg. 358
TCI PRECISION METALS, INC., pg. 1380, pg. 95
TELSMITH, INC., pg. 1381, pg. 1871
TEREX CEDARAPIDS, pg. 1381, pg. 703
TEREX CORPORATION, pg. 1381, pg. 384
TOROMONT CAT, pg. 192, pg. 1914
TRUTH HARDWARE CORP., pg. 1066, pg. 952
UNIVERSAL INDUSTRIAL PRODUCTS CO., pg. 1066, pg. 1470
VERMEER MANUFACTURING COMPANY, pg. 708, pg. 711
VIBCO INC., pg. 1387, pg. 1611
WARN INDUSTRIES, INC., pg. 221, pg. 1497
WINNER INTERNATIONAL, LLC, pg. 222, pg. 1586
YARDLEY PRODUCTS CORPORATION, pg. 1391, pg. 1596

3537 - Industrial Trucks, Tractors, Trailers & Stackers

ACME STAPLE COMPANY, INC., pg. 341, pg. 1034
ACS INDUSTRIES, INC., pg. 1040, pg. 1602
AFC CABLE SYSTEMS, INC., pg. 1294, pg. 835
ALAMO GROUP INC., pg. 1311, pg. 1745
AMEREQUIP CORPORATION, pg. 700, pg. 1862
ARCTIC CAT INC., pg. 1705, pg. 953
A.T. FERRELL COMPANY, INC., pg. 701, pg. 674
AUTOMATIC EQUIPMENT CORPORATION, pg. 1315, pg. 1410
BELDEN, INC., pg. 624, pg. 993
BLUE OX, pg. 701, pg. 1019
BOMBARDIER RECREATIONAL PRODUCTS, INC., pg. 201, pg. 1960
BRIDON AMERICAN CORP., pg. 1319, pg. 1594
BUFFALO WIRE WORKS CO., INC., pg. 72, pg. 1147
CANNON EQUIPMENT COMPANY, pg. 1321, pg. 920
CARLISLE INTERCONNECT TECHNOLOGIES, pg. 1294, pg. 461
CASCADE CORPORATION, pg. 1321, pg. 1497
CHAMPLAIN CABLE CORP., pg. 1044, pg. 1765
CHASE CORPORATION, pg. 1152, pg. 803
CLOSETMAID CORPORATION, pg. 920, pg. 452
CLUB CAR, INC., pg. 1830, pg. 532
COLEMAN CABLE, INC., pg. 1324, pg. 665
COLUMBUS MCKINNON CORPORATION, pg. 1325, pg. 1138
CORNING INCORPORATED, pg. 1122, pg. 1154
DAYTON SUPERIOR CORPORATION, pg. 1328, pg. 1464
DOVER CORPORATION, pg. 1329, pg. 608
E-Z-GO TEXTRON, pg. 1706, pg. 525
ERICO INTERNATIONAL CORPORATION, pg. 1335, pg. 1472
ESSENTRA COMPONENTS, pg. 1047, pg. 612
ESSEX GROUP, INC., pg. 638, pg. 680
ESTAD STAMPING & MANUFACTURING COMPANY, pg. 1336, pg. 598
FEDERAL SIGNAL CORPORATION, pg. 638, pg. 645
FORTUNE BRANDS HOME & SECURITY, INC., pg. 55, pg. 600
FULL VISION, INC., pg. 1163, pg. 717
FUSHI COPPERWELD, pg. 1296, pg. 1632
GEHL COMPANY, pg. 1339, pg. 1899
GENERAL CABLE CORPORATION, pg. 83, pg. 384
GRC ENTERPRISES, INC., pg. 1344, pg. 677
THE GREAT AMERICAN HANGER COMPANY INC., pg. 926, pg. 442
GREENLEE TEXTRON INC., pg. 1048, pg. 655
HAMILTON CASTER & MFG. CO., pg. 206, pg. 1454
HANDY & HARMAN LTD., pg. 85, pg. 1352
HANSLER MANUTENTION, INC, pg. 178, pg. 1950
HILTI, INC., pg. 1346, pg. 1490
HINDLEY MANUFACTURING COMPANY, INC., pg. 1049, pg. 1601
HOUSTON WIRE & CABLE COMPANY, pg. 643, pg. 1708
HYSTER-YALE MATERIALS HANDLING, pg. 1347, pg. 1503
INTELLIGRATED SYSTEMS LLC, pg. 1350, pg. 998
J.B. POINDEXTER & CO., INC., pg. 209, pg. 1709
JOHN HASSALL, INC., pg. 1052, pg. 1350
KEYSTONE CONSOLIDATED INDUSTRIES, INC., pg. 90, pg. 1683
KEYSTONE STEEL & WIRE CO., pg. 91, pg. 651
LEVITON MANUFACTURING COMPANY, INC., pg. 1301, pg. 1180
LIFTOMATIC MATERIAL HANDLING INC., pg. 94, pg. 560
LITTLE FALLS ALLOYS, INC., pg. 1171, pg. 1107
MACCAFERRI, INC., pg. 95, pg. 780
MAGLINE, INC., pg. 1358, pg. 908
MANITEX INTERNATIONAL, INC., pg. 1358, pg. 559
METAL TEXTILES CORPORATION, pg. 654, pg. 1057
MOTAN, INC., pg. 1886, pg. 903
NACCO INDUSTRIES, INC., pg. 1174, pg. 1433
NEWARK WIRE CLOTH CO., pg. 99, pg. 1052
NISSAN FORKLIFT CORPORATION, NORTH AMERICA, pg. 186, pg. 631
NUTTING, pg. 1366, pg. 1626
THE OKONITE COMPANY, pg. 1302, pg. 1113
PEACE INDUSTRIES INC., pg. 1368, pg. 656
PEERLESS CHAIN COMPANY, pg. 1887, pg. 967
PERCEPTICS, LLC, pg. 1426, pg. 1637
PETERBILT MOTORS CO., pg. 188, pg. 1691
PETTIBONE, LLC, pg. 1368, pg. 609
POLARIS INDUSTRIES INC., pg. 1709, pg. 928
QUALITY PERFORATING, INC., pg. 1468, pg. 1520
RADIX WIRE COMPANY, pg. 1304, pg. 1434
RITE-HITE HOLDING CORPORATION, pg. 1372, pg. 1880
RSCC AEROSPACE & DEFENSE, pg. 1373, pg. 1036
SEFAR AMERICA, INC., pg. 698, pg. 1080
SENCO PRODUCTS, INC., pg. 1374, pg. 1425
SIGMUND COHN CORP., pg. 1062, pg. 1183
SOMMER METALCRAFT CORPORATION, pg. 112, pg. 676
SUPERIOR ESSEX, INC., pg. 676, pg. 521
T&S PERFECTION CHAIN PRODUCTS, INC., pg. 1065, pg. 5
TEREX CORPORATION, pg. 1381, pg. 384
TRIMAS CORPORATION, pg. 1383, pg. 874
WEBSTER INDUSTRIES INC., pg. 1388, pg. 1475
WESTINGHOUSE AIR BRAKE TECHNOLOGIES CORPORATION, pg. 1388, pg. 1595
W.H. MAZE COMPANY, pg. 1389, pg. 652
WIRECO WORLDGROUP, pg. 1389, pg. 987
WIRECO WORLDGROUP, pg. 1389, pg. 721
THE WOODSTREAM CORPORATION, pg. 1801, pg. 1549
WORTHINGTON INDUSTRIES, pg. 222, pg. 1626

3541 - Machine Tools, Metal Cutting Types

ACME UNITED CORPORATION, pg. 1040, pg. 346

AGI-VR/WESSON INC, *pg.* 1041, *pg.* 415
BARDONS & OLIVER, INC., *pg.* 1316, *pg.* 1472
BARNES INTERNATIONAL INC., *pg.* 1317, *pg.* 654
CHARLES MACHINE WORKS, INC., *pg.* 1322, *pg.* 1488
THE CINCINNATI GILBERT MACHINE TOOL COMPANY, L.L.C., *pg.* 1323, *pg.* 1411
DUMORE CORPORATION, *pg.* 1330, *pg.* 1869
EASTMAN MACHINE COMPANY, *pg.* 1331, *pg.* 1148
EDAC TECHNOLOGIES CORPORATION, *pg.* 1332, *pg.* 342
ELECTRON BEAM TECHNOLOGIES, INC., *pg.* 1046, *pg.* 621
ESAB WELDING & CUTTING PRODUCTS, *pg.* 1335, *pg.* 1615
ESTERLINE TECHNOLOGIES CORPORATION, *pg.* 1412, *pg.* 1814
HARDINGE INC., *pg.* 1344, *pg.* 1157
HITACHI KOKI USA, LTD., *pg.* 1050, *pg.* 537
HURCO COMPANIES, INC., *pg.* 409, *pg.* 686
II-VI INCORPORATED, *pg.* 1417, *pg.* 1585
KAUFMAN MFG. COMPANY, *pg.* 1352, *pg.* 1868
KENNAMETAL EXTRUDE HONE, *pg.* 1352, *pg.* 1542
KENNAMETAL INC., *pg.* 1052, *pg.* 1547
KINGSBURY CORPORATION, *pg.* 1353, *pg.* 1035
MAKINO INC., *pg.* 1358, *pg.* 1461
MCDONOUGH MANUFACTURING COMPANY, *pg.* 1360, *pg.* 1857
MOORE TOOL COMPANY, INC., *pg.* 1057, *pg.* 339
NETZSCH PUMPS NORTH AMERICA, LLC, *pg.* 1364, *pg.* 1532
OKUMA AMERICA CORPORATION, *pg.* 1366, *pg.* 1368
RIDGE TOOL COMPANY, *pg.* 1372, *pg.* 1452
ROMAC INDUSTRIES, INC., *pg.* 1061, *pg.* 1818
SANTINELLI INTERNATIONAL INC., *pg.* 1395, *pg.* 1165
SENECA FALLS MACHINES, *pg.* 1374, *pg.* 1341
SETCO SALES COMPANY, *pg.* 1061, *pg.* 1426
SPX PRECISION COMPONENTS - FENN DIVISION, *pg.* 1378, *pg.* 360
SUNNEN PRODUCTS COMPANY, *pg.* 1379, *pg.* 1004
THERMWOOD CORPORATION, *pg.* 1382, *pg.* 676
TIMESAVERS INC., *pg.* 1382, *pg.* 928
UNIVERSAL PHOTONICS, INC., *pg.* 1433, *pg.* 1167
WELDON SOLUTIONS, *pg.* 1388, *pg.* 1598
WISCONSIN MACHINE TOOL CORPORATION, *pg.* 1389, *pg.* 1855
YARDLEY PRODUCTS CORPORATION, *pg.* 1391, *pg.* 1596

3542 - Machine Tools, Metal Forming Types

BOURN & KOCH MACHINE TOOL COMPANY, *pg.* 1319, *pg.* 654
BRYANT GRINDER, *pg.* 1320, *pg.* 1768
BTM CORPORATION, *pg.* 1320, *pg.* 898
CHICAGO RIVET & MACHINE COMPANY, *pg.* 1323, *pg.* 636
FABCO-AIR, INC., *pg.* 1336, *pg.* 429
GEORGE T. SCHMIDT, INC., *pg.* 1340, *pg.* 637
NATIONAL MACHINERY LLC, *pg.* 1363, *pg.* 1475
NATIONAL RIVET & MANUFACTURING COMPANY, *pg.* 1364, *pg.* 1898
PANAVISE PRODUCTS, INC., *pg.* 1058, *pg.* 1032
RING PRECISION COMPONENTS, *pg.* 1372, *pg.* 1170
ROYLE SYSTEMS GROUP, *pg.* 1373, *pg.* 1100
SCOTCHMAN INDUSTRIES, INC., *pg.* 1374, *pg.* 1624
TRUMPF INC., *pg.* 1385, *pg.* 349

3544 - Special Dies & Tools, Die Sets, Jigs & Fixtures & Industrial Molds

ADMIRAL TOOL & MANUFACTURING COMPANY INC., *pg.* 1310, *pg.* 896
ANCHOR DANLY, *pg.* 67, *pg.* 1948
CONNELL LIMITED PARTNERSHIP, *pg.* 1325, *pg.* 793
FANCORT INDUSTRIES, INC., *pg.* 1336, *pg.* 1131
GEORGE T. SCHMIDT, INC., *pg.* 1340, *pg.* 637
HARIG MANUFACTURING CORPORATION, *pg.* 1345, *pg.* 637
KENNAMETAL IPG, *pg.* 1353, *pg.* 1615
MILACRON LLC, *pg.* 1361, *pg.* 1405
MODERNFORGECOMPANIES, LLC, *pg.* 98, *pg.* 558
OMG, INC., *pg.* 1367, *pg.* 781
PRECISION CASTPARTS CORP., *pg.* 105, *pg.* 1506
RING PRECISION COMPONENTS, *pg.* 1372, *pg.* 1170
SPX CORPORATION, *pg.* 218, *pg.* 1369
SUPERIOR DIE SET CORP., *pg.* 1379, *pg.* 1885
TORRMETAL CORPORATION, *pg.* 1383, *pg.* 1436
WENTWORTH TECHNOLOGIES CO. LTD., *pg.* 1891, *pg.* 1919

3545 - Cutting Tools, Machine Tool Accessories & Machinists Precision Measuring Devices

A.G. DAVIS/AA GAGE, *pg.* 1310, *pg.* 908
AGI-VR/WESSON INC, *pg.* 1041, *pg.* 415
BARRY CONTROLS, *pg.* 1317, *pg.* 825
BLOUNT INTERNATIONAL, INC., *pg.* 1043, *pg.* 1501
BOURN & KOCH MACHINE TOOL COMPANY, *pg.* 1319, *pg.* 654
CHARLES & COLVARD LTD, *pg.* 3, *pg.* 1384
CHARLES MACHINE WORKS, INC., *pg.* 1322, *pg.* 1488
THE CINCINNATI GILBERT MACHINE TOOL COMPANY, L.L.C., *pg.* 1323, *pg.* 1411
DANAHER CORPORATION, *pg.* 1044, *pg.* 397
DORMER PRAMET, *pg.* 1329, *pg.* 609
DYNATECT MANUFACTURING INC., *pg.* 1330, *pg.* 1883
DYNATEX INTERNATIONAL, *pg.* 635, *pg.* 277
EDAC TECHNOLOGIES CORPORATION, *pg.* 1332, *pg.* 342
FLEXBAR MACHINE CORP., *pg.* 1337, *pg.* 1169
HARDINGE INC., *pg.* 1344, *pg.* 1157
HARIG MANUFACTURING CORPORATION, *pg.* 1345, *pg.* 637
HENNESSY INDUSTRIES, INC., *pg.* 207, *pg.* 1639
HILTI, INC., *pg.* 1346, *pg.* 1490
HOUGEN MANUFACTURING INC., *pg.* 1347, *pg.* 908
KENNAMETAL INC., *pg.* 1052, *pg.* 1547
KENNAMETAL IPG, *pg.* 1353, *pg.* 1615
THE L.S. STARRETT COMPANY, *pg.* 1421, *pg.* 783
MCLAUGHLIN BORING SYSTEMS, *pg.* 1360, *pg.* 1617
MOORE TOOL COMPANY, INC., *pg.* 1057, *pg.* 339
MULTI-METALS, *pg.* 1363, *pg.* 737
POWERS FASTENERS INC., *pg.* 1059, *pg.* 1143
Q.E.P. CO., INC., *pg.* 1371, *pg.* 413
ROBERT BOSCH TOOL CORP, *pg.* 1060, *pg.* 634
SENECA FALLS MACHINES, *pg.* 1374, *pg.* 1341
SIMONDS INTERNATIONAL CORPORATION, *pg.* 1376, *pg.* 819
SPEEDGRIP CHUCK, INC., *pg.* 1377, *pg.* 677
WISCONSIN MACHINE TOOL CORPORATION, *pg.* 1389, *pg.* 1855
WOODCRAFT SUPPLY CORP., *pg.* 1390, *pg.* 1850
ZEPHYR MANUFACTURING CO., INC., *pg.* 1391, *pg.* 105

3546 - Power Driven Hand Tools

ARROW FASTENER COMPANY, INC., *pg.* 1042, *pg.* 1118
BRUNNER & LAY, INC., *pg.* 1320, *pg.* 35
CHARLES MACHINE WORKS, INC., *pg.* 1322, *pg.* 1488
DANAHER CORPORATION, *pg.* 1044, *pg.* 397
MCLAUGHLIN BORING SYSTEMS, *pg.* 1360, *pg.* 1617
MILWAUKEE ELECTRIC TOOL CORP., *pg.* 1056, *pg.* 1855
MKT FASTENING, LLC, *pg.* 1056, *pg.* 34
P&F INDUSTRIES, INC., *pg.* 1075, *pg.* 1182
ROBERT BOSCH TOOL CORP, *pg.* 1060, *pg.* 634
SENCO PRODUCTS, INC., *pg.* 1374, *pg.* 1425
SNAP-ON INCORPORATED, *pg.* 1062, *pg.* 1862
STANLEY BLACK & DECKER, INC., *pg.* 1063, *pg.* 358
STIHL, INC., *pg.* 1064, *pg.* 1810
THOMPSON INTERNATIONAL INC., *pg.* 1382, *pg.* 729
TRUMPF INC., *pg.* 1385, *pg.* 349
ZEPHYR MANUFACTURING CO., INC., *pg.* 1391, *pg.* 105

3547 - Rolling Mill Machinery & Equipment

SCOTCHMAN INDUSTRIES, INC., *pg.* 1374, *pg.* 1624

3548 - Electric & Gas Welding & Soldering Equipment

THE ADT CORPORATION, *pg.* 612, *pg.* 409
ADVANCED ENERGY INDUSTRIES, INC., *pg.* 613, *pg.* 328
BAE SYSTEMS PRODUCTS GROUP, *pg.* 359, *pg.* 432
BALLARD POWER SYSTEMS, INC., *pg.* 70, *pg.* 1907
BLONDER TONGUE LABORATORIES, INC., *pg.* 625, *pg.* 1100
BRADY CORPORATION, *pg.* 363, *pg.* 1873
BRANSON ULTRASONICS CORPORATION, *pg.* 1319, *pg.* 342
BRANSON ULTRASONICS CORPORATION - PLASTICS JOINING DIVISION, *pg.* 1403, *pg.* 343
BRANSON ULTRASONICS CORPORATION-PRECISION CLEANING DIV, *pg.* 1319, *pg.* 343
BROAN-NUTONE LLC, *pg.* 1069, *pg.* 1860
C&D TECHNOLOGIES, INC., *pg.* 627, *pg.* 1517
THE CHAMBERLAIN GROUP, INC., *pg.* 75, *pg.* 611
CHASE CORPORATION, *pg.* 1152, *pg.* 803
CHECKPOINT SYSTEMS, INC., *pg.* 628, *pg.* 1559
CLORE AUTOMOTIVE LLC, *pg.* 202, *pg.* 716
CONDUCTIX INC., *pg.* 1295, *pg.* 1015
CTS VALPEY CORPORATION, *pg.* 632, *pg.* 825
CVI MELLES GRIOT, *pg.* 1407, *pg.* 59
DETEX CORPORATION, *pg.* 633, *pg.* 1728
EATON CORPORATION, *pg.* 1331, *pg.* 1429
ELECTRON BEAM TECHNOLOGIES, INC., *pg.* 1046, *pg.* 621
ENERGIZER HOLDINGS, INC., *pg.* 637, *pg.* 996
ESAB WELDING & CUTTING PRODUCTS, *pg.* 1335, *pg.* 1615
THE GENIE COMPANY, *pg.* 55, *pg.* 1403
GLOBAL EPOINT INC., *pg.* 400, *pg.* 67
GSI GROUP INC., *pg.* 1415, *pg.* 784
THE HARRIS PRODUCTS GROUP, *pg.* 1345, *pg.* 533
HIGHFIELD MANUFACTURING CO., *pg.* 1346, *pg.* 339
HOBART BROTHERS COMPANY, *pg.* 1346, *pg.* 1477
HUBBELL INCORPORATED, *pg.* 1299, *pg.* 370
HUBBELL POWER SYSTEMS, INC., *pg.* 643, *pg.* 1614
INTERNATIONAL COMPONENTS CORPORATION, *pg.* 647, *pg.* 669
INVISIBLE FENCE, INC., *pg.* 648, *pg.* 1637
ISOMET CORPORATION, *pg.* 1418, *pg.* 1807
IXIA, *pg.* 422, *pg.* 56
LA MARCHE MANUFACTURING COMPANY, *pg.* 1300, *pg.* 606
LASER TECHNOLOGY, INC., *pg.* 1419, *pg.* 314
LINCOLN ELECTRIC HOLDINGS, INC., *pg.* 1355, *pg.* 1432
LIND ELECTRONICS, INC., *pg.* 1355, *pg.* 938
MASTER APPLIANCE CORP., *pg.* 1055, *pg.* 1888
MATEC INSTRUMENT COMPANIES, INC., *pg.* 1421, *pg.* 839
MAXXESS SYSTEMS, INC., *pg.* 431, *pg.* 43
MILLER ELECTRIC MANUFACTURING CO., *pg.* 1361, *pg.* 1852
MORSE WATCHMANS INC., *pg.* 656, *pg.* 368
NABCO ENTRANCES, INC., *pg.* 99, *pg.* 1882
NEW WAVE RESEARCH INCORPORATED, *pg.* 1423, *pg.* 91
NEWPORT CORPORATION, *pg.* 1424, *pg.* 114
PERCEPTICS, LLC, *pg.* 1426, *pg.* 1637
PROPHOTONIX LIMITED, *pg.* 1427, *pg.* 1039
ROCKWELL AUTOMATION, INC., *pg.* 668, *pg.* 1880
ROFIN-SINAR TECHNOLOGIES, INC., *pg.* 668, *pg.* 904
SCHNEIDER CANADA, INC., *pg.* 1374, *pg.* 1928
SCHNEIDER ELECTRIC, *pg.* 467, *pg.* 1609
SILICON GRAPHICS INTERNATIONAL CORP, *pg.* 470, *pg.* 148
SL INDUSTRIES, INC., *pg.* 674, *pg.* 1090
SUREFIRE, LLC, *pg.* 1307, *pg.* 90
TDK-LAMBDA HIGH POWER DIVISION, *pg.* 1380, *pg.* 1090
TECHNIBUS LLC, *pg.* 1380, *pg.* 1408
VISHAY INTERTECHNOLOGY, INC., *pg.* 1435, *pg.* 1551
WOODWARD, INC., *pg.* 122, *pg.* 329

3549 - Metalworking Machinery, NEC

BALDOR ELECTRIC COMPANY, *pg.* 1316, *pg.* 32
BARDONS & OLIVER, INC., *pg.* 1316, *pg.* 1472
BLACK BROTHERS COMPANY, *pg.* 70, *pg.* 632
DAVIS-STANDARD LLC, *pg.* 1328, *pg.* 368
LEVER MANUFACTURING CORP., *pg.* 1355, *pg.* 1082
LINCOLN ELECTRIC HOLDINGS, INC., *pg.* 1355, *pg.* 1432
METRO MACHINE & ENGINEERING CORP., *pg.* 1360, *pg.* 923
P/A INDUSTRIES, INC., *pg.* 1367, *pg.* 339
ROYLE SYSTEMS GROUP, *pg.* 1373, *pg.* 1100
SUNNEN PRODUCTS COMPANY, *pg.* 1379, *pg.* 1004
WES-TECH AUTOMATION SOLUTIONS, *pg.* 1388, *pg.* 560

3552 - Textile Machinery

EASTMAN MACHINE COMPANY, *pg.* 1331, *pg.* 1148
FLETCHER INDUSTRIES, INC., *pg.* 1337, *pg.* 1390
THE HANDY/KENLIN GROUP, *pg.* 86, *pg.* 670
LEVER MANUFACTURING CORP., *pg.* 1355, *pg.* 1082
PELLERIN MILNOR CORPORATION, *pg.* 1368, *pg.* 744
PRECITECH, INC., *pg.* 1427, *pg.* 1035
THE WOLF MACHINE CO., *pg.* 1389, *pg.* 1427

3553 - Woodworking Machinery

AMUNEAL MANUFACTURING CORPORATION, *pg.* 617, *pg.* 1558
BLACK BROTHERS COMPANY, *pg.* 70, *pg.* 632
BLOUNT INTERNATIONAL, INC., *pg.* 1043, *pg.* 1501
CORLEY MANUFACTURING CO., *pg.* 1326, *pg.* 1628
DIEHL WOODWORKING MACHINERY, INC., *pg.* 1328, *pg.* 698
INGERSOLL-RAND COMPANY, *pg.* 1349, *pg.* 1370
SHOPSMITH, INC., *pg.* 1375, *pg.* 1446
WOODCRAFT SUPPLY CORP., *pg.* 1390, *pg.* 1850
ZEBRA TECHNOLOGIES CORPORATION, *pg.* 690, *pg.* 628

3554 - Paper Industries Machinery

BAUMFOLDER CORPORATION, *pg.* 360, *pg.* 1472
BOLTON-EMERSON AMERICAS, INC., *pg.* 1318, *pg.* 827
THE CHALLENGE MACHINERY COMPANY, *pg.* 1322, *pg.* 902
DAHLE USA, *pg.* 382, *pg.* 1038
KADANT BLACK CLAWSON INC., *pg.* 1352, *pg.* 1460
KADANT INC., *pg.* 1352, *pg.* 858
KEMPSMITH MACHINE COMPANY, *pg.* 1352, *pg.* 1876
PINNACLE COATING & CONVERTING, INC., *pg.* 1467, *pg.* 1622

3555 - Printing Trades Machinery & Equipment

ANDERSON & VREELAND, INC., *pg.* 1616, *pg.* 1064
BALDWIN TECHNOLOGY COMPANY, INC., *pg.* 1316, *pg.* 410
BUTLER AUTOMATIC, INC., *pg.* 1320, *pg.* 833
COLOR IMAGING INC., *pg.* 1407, *pg.* 536
DELPHAX TECHNOLOGIES INC., *pg.* 386, *pg.* 917
DOYLE SYSTEMS, *pg.* 1330, *pg.* 1404
ECRM IMAGING SYSTEMS, INC., *pg.* 1410, *pg.* 848
GRAVOGRAPH-NEW HERMES, *pg.* 1344, *pg.* 531
GSI GROUP INC., *pg.* 1415, *pg.* 784
HARLAND CLARKE HOLDINGS CORP., *pg.* 1647, *pg.* 1741
HEWLETT-PACKARD COMPANY, *pg.* 404, *pg.* 175
IKONICS CORPORATION, *pg.* 1168, *pg.* 921
MANROLAND INC., *pg.* 430, *pg.* 669
MARK ANDY, INC., *pg.* 1359, *pg.* 975
NCR CORPORATION, *pg.* 443, *pg.* 531
NEWS TRIBUNE CO., *pg.* 1670, *pg.* 980
OKI DATA AMERICAS, INC., *pg.* 449, *pg.* 1090
PIERCE EQUIPMENT, *pg.* 1369, *pg.* 1640
PRESSTEK, INC., *pg.* 456, *pg.* 606
PRESSTEK LLC, *pg.* 1678, *pg.* 1034
PRINTRONIX, INC., *pg.* 456, *pg.* 115
RICOH AMERICAS CORP., *pg.* 462, *pg.* 538
ROTADYNE, *pg.* 1681, *pg.* 529
SCANTRON CORPORATION, *pg.* 467, *pg.* 922
SPEEDLINE TECHNOLOGIES, INC., *pg.* 1378, *pg.* 823
WEBER PACKAGING SOLUTIONS, INC., *pg.* 491, *pg.* 554
XEIKON AMERICA, INC., *pg.* 1390, *pg.* 621

3556 - Food Products Machinery

ALFA LAVAL INC., *pg.* 700, *pg.* 1800
AMF BAKERY SYSTEMS, *pg.* 1313, *pg.* 1800
ANDERSON INTERNATIONAL CORP., *pg.* 1313, *pg.* 1474
APW WYOTT FOOD SERVICE EQUIPMENT, INC., *pg.* 1314, *pg.* 1658
BELSHAW ADAMATIC BAKERY GROUP, *pg.* 1317, *pg.* 1813
BUHLER AEROGLIDE, *pg.* 1069, *pg.* 1359
CRES-COR, *pg.* 1326, *pg.* 1464
CREST FOODS CO. INC., *pg.* 850, *pg.* 554
DEDERT CORPORATION, *pg.* 1408, *pg.* 649
DUKE MANUFACTURING COMPANY, INC., *pg.* 54, *pg.* 995
EDLUND COMPANY, INC., *pg.* 1123, *pg.* 1765
FRYMASTER LLC, *pg.* 55, *pg.* 748
GLOBAL SMOOTHIE SUPPLY, INC., *pg.* 858, *pg.* 1681
GOLD MEDAL PRODUCTS CO., *pg.* 55, *pg.* 1414
GRINDMASTER CORPORATION, *pg.* 56, *pg.* 734
HAWKEYE STEEL PRODUCTS, INC., *pg.* 704, *pg.* 708
HOBART CORPORATION, *pg.* 1346, *pg.* 1477
HOLLYMATIC CORPORATION, *pg.* 1346, *pg.* 598
HUTCHINSON/MAYRATH INDUSTRIES INC., *pg.* 704, *pg.* 714
KEY TECHNOLOGY, INC., *pg.* 868, *pg.* 1847
THE LAITRAM LLC, *pg.* 1354, *pg.* 744
LINCOLN FOODSERVICE PRODUCTS, LLC, *pg.* 1127, *pg.* 1432
LITTLEFORD DAY INC., *pg.* 1356, *pg.* 728
THE MANITOWOC COMPANY, INC., *pg.* 1358, *pg.* 1868
MARS, INCORPORATED, *pg.* 1858, *pg.* 1792
THE MIDDLEBY CORPORATION, *pg.* 1361, *pg.* 610
MOREHOUSE-COWLES, *pg.* 1363, *pg.* 66
NATIONAL PRESTO INDUSTRIES, INC, *pg.* 1128, *pg.* 1857
NORSE DAIRY SYSTEMS LLC, *pg.* 886, *pg.* 1442
NU-VU FOODSERVICE SYSTEMS, *pg.* 887, *pg.* 898
OLIVER PRODUCTS COMPANY INC., *pg.* 1367, *pg.* 888
PAUL MUELLER COMPANY, *pg.* 706, *pg.* 1007
PERFORMANCE FOOD GROUP COMPANY, LLC, *pg.* 1030, *pg.* 1803
PLANET PRODUCTS CORPORATION, *pg.* 1369, *pg.* 1418
THE SALVAJOR COMPANY, *pg.* 60, *pg.* 986
SANISERV, *pg.* 1373, *pg.* 695
SCHREIBER FOODS, INC., *pg.* 894, *pg.* 1859
STANDEX INTERNATIONAL CORPORATION, *pg.* 60, *pg.* 1039
TAYLOR COMPANY, *pg.* 901, *pg.* 655
TIPPER TIE, INC., *pg.* 1382, *pg.* 1358
UNIFIED BRANDS INC., *pg.* 1385, *pg.* 970
UNIVEX CORPORATION, *pg.* 1386, *pg.* 1039
URSCHEL LABORATORIES INCORPORATED, *pg.* 1386, *pg.* 698

3559 - Special Industry Machinery, NEC

A BRITE COMPANY, *pg.* 1144, *pg.* 1697
ADEPT TECHNOLOGY, INC., *pg.* 1310, *pg.* 182
AERCO INTERNATIONAL INC., *pg.* 1068, *pg.* 1142
AEROFIN CORP., *pg.* 1068, *pg.* 1787
AIXTRON INC., *pg.* 1310, *pg.* 283
ALTAIR CORPORATION, *pg.* 1312, *pg.* 910
AMANO CINCINNATI, INC., *pg.* 348, *pg.* 1117
AMERICAN ART CLAY CO., INC., *pg.* 1759, *pg.* 682
AMKOR TECHNOLOGY, INC., *pg.* 67, *pg.* 25
ANDERSON INTERNATIONAL CORP., *pg.* 1313, *pg.* 1474
A.O. SMITH CORPORATION, *pg.* 1313, *pg.* 1872
APPLIED MATERIALS, INC, *pg.* 618, *pg.* 1009
APPLIED MATERIALS, INC., *pg.* 618, *pg.* 264
AUTOLIV NORTH AMERICA, AMERICAN TECHNICAL CENTER, *pg.* 200, *pg.* 867
AVIALL, INC., *pg.* 224, *pg.* 1676
AXCELIS TECHNOLOGIES, INC., *pg.* 1400, *pg.* 787
AXT, INC., *pg.* 1400, *pg.* 90
BABCOCK & WILCOX POWER GENERATION GROUP, INC., *pg.* 1069, *pg.* 1404
BALDOR ELECTRIC COMPANY, *pg.* 1316, *pg.* 32
BALTIMORE AIRCOIL COMPANY, *pg.* 1069, *pg.* 773
BEE LINE COMPANY, *pg.* 200, *pg.* 701
BESSER COMPANY, *pg.* 1317, *pg.* 865
BLOUNT INTERNATIONAL, INC., *pg.* 1043, *pg.* 1501
THE BOARDMAN INC., *pg.* 71, *pg.* 1484
BOILER TUBE COMPANY OF AMERICA, *pg.* 1318, *pg.* 1620
BROOKS AUTOMATION, INC., *pg.* 1320, *pg.* 813
BTU INTERNATIONAL, INC., *pg.* 1320, *pg.* 838
BURNHAM HOLDINGS, INC., *pg.* 1069, *pg.* 1546
CEMTREX, INC., *pg.* 1322, *pg.* 1159
CHART INDUSTRIES, INC., *pg.* 1405, *pg.* 1454
CLEAVER-BROOKS, *pg.* 76, *pg.* 1874
CLINTON INDUSTRIES, INC., *pg.* 1324, *pg.* 1079
CMI-SCHNEIBLE COMPANY, *pg.* 1324, *pg.* 906
COHESANT, INC., *pg.* 1154, *pg.* 1405
CONNELL LIMITED PARTNERSHIP, *pg.* 1325, *pg.* 793
CVD EQUIPMENT CORPORATION, *pg.* 632, *pg.* 1152
CYMER, INC., *pg.* 1296, *pg.* 202
DAIFUKU WEBB, *pg.* 1327, *pg.* 885
DANAHER CORPORATION, *pg.* 1044, *pg.* 397
DAVIS-STANDARD LLC, *pg.* 1328, *pg.* 368
DEDERT CORPORATION, *pg.* 1408, *pg.* 649
DIAMOND POWER INTERNATIONAL, INC., *pg.* 1070, *pg.* 1457
DOVER CORPORATION, *pg.* 1329, *pg.* 608
ELGIN NATIONAL INDUSTRIES, INC., *pg.* 1333, *pg.* 608
EMCORE CORPORATION, *pg.* 636, *pg.* 39
ENERFAB, INC., *pg.* 81, *pg.* 1412
ENERGY RECOVERY, INC., *pg.* 1334, *pg.* 252
ENVIRONMENTAL TECTONICS CORPORATION, *pg.* 1411, *pg.* 1587
EPILOG CORPORATION, *pg.* 1412, *pg.* 330
ERIEZ MANUFACTURING CO. INC., *pg.* 1335, *pg.* 1530
EXTERRAN HOLDINGS, INC., *pg.* 977, *pg.* 1705
FAIRCHILD SEMICONDUCTOR CORPORATION, *pg.* 638, *pg.* 245
FARREL CORPORATION, *pg.* 1336, *pg.* 337
FLUID MANAGEMENT, *pg.* 1442, *pg.* 670
GENCOR INDUSTRIES, INC., *pg.* 1339, *pg.* 453
GERBER SCIENTIFIC, INC., *pg.* 1414, *pg.* 380
GIW INDUSTRIES, INC., *pg.* 1340, *pg.* 533
GLOUCESTER ENGINEERING, CO., *pg.* 1341, *pg.* 823
GRAVER TECHNOLOGIES LLC, *pg.* 1343, *pg.* 387
GSI GROUP INC., *pg.* 1415, *pg.* 784
HARSCO CORPORATION, *pg.* 86, *pg.* 1519
HARSCO RAIL, *pg.* 1345, *pg.* 1623
HOBART BROTHERS COMPANY, *pg.* 1346, *pg.* 1477
HORNADY MANUFACTURING COMPANY, *pg.* 1836, *pg.* 1010
HOSOKAWA MICRON POWDER SYSTEMS, *pg.* 1347, *pg.* 1124
HUNTER ENGINEERING COMPANY, *pg.* 208, *pg.* 973
IDEX CORPORATION, *pg.* 1347, *pg.* 623
ILLINOIS TOOL WORKS INC., *pg.* 1348, *pg.* 614
INDUSTRIAL DISTRIBUTION GROUP, INC., *pg.* 413, *pg.* 1358
INGERSOLL-RAND COMPANY, *pg.* 1349, *pg.* 1370
INTERNATIONAL BALER CORP., *pg.* 1350, *pg.* 433
INTERNATIONAL ROAD DYNAMICS INC., *pg.* 1912, *pg.* 1962
ITW DYNATEC, *pg.* 1351, *pg.* 1635
JUSTRITE MANUFACTURING COMPANY, LLC, *pg.* 1394, *pg.* 606
KATY INDUSTRIES, INC., *pg.* 1126, *pg.* 973
KEY TECHNOLOGY, INC., *pg.* 868, *pg.* 1847
KINGSBURY CORPORATION, *pg.* 1353, *pg.* 1035
KLA-TENCOR CORPORATION, *pg.* 1353, *pg.* 146
KULICKE & SOFFA INDUSTRIES, INC., *pg.* 650, *pg.* 1533
KYZEN CORPORATION, *pg.* 331, *pg.* 1652
LAM RESEARCH CORPORATION, *pg.* 1354, *pg.* 91
LAPOLLA INDUSTRIES, INC., *pg.* 1444, *pg.* 1710
LITTLEFORD DAY INC., *pg.* 1356, *pg.* 728
LOCHINVAR CORPORATION, *pg.* 1073, *pg.* 1640
LUNDELL ENTERPRISES, INC., *pg.* 706, *pg.* 703
LYMAN PRODUCTS CORPORATION, *pg.* 1839, *pg.* 356
LYNCH TECHNOLOGIES, INC., *pg.* 1357, *pg.* 526
MANITEX INTERNATIONAL, INC., *pg.* 1358, *pg.* 559
MCDONOUGH MANUFACTURING COMPANY, *pg.* 1360, *pg.* 1857
MCNEIL & NRM INC., *pg.* 1360, *pg.* 1402
MERROW MACHINE COMPANY, *pg.* 58, *pg.* 819
MICROFLUIDICS INTERNATIONAL CORPORATION, *pg.* 58, *pg.* 836
MILACRON LLC, *pg.* 1361, *pg.* 1405
MODERN EQUIPMENT COMPANY, *pg.* 1363, *pg.* 1887
MODERN WELDING COMPANY, INC., *pg.* 1363, *pg.* 739
MOOG INC., *pg.* 231, *pg.* 1156
MOREHOUSE-COWLES, *pg.* 1363, *pg.* 66
NANOMETRICS INCORPORATED, *pg.* 1423, *pg.* 147
NOBLES MANUFACTURING, INC., *pg.* 59, *pg.* 1890
NORDSON CORPORATION, *pg.* 1365, *pg.* 1480
ON SEMICONDUCTOR CORPORATION, *pg.* 101, *pg.* 18
P&F INDUSTRIES, INC., *pg.* 1075, *pg.* 1182
PAUL MUELLER COMPANY, *pg.* 706, *pg.* 1007
PERCEPTRON, INC., *pg.* 215, *pg.* 904
PERRY PRODUCTS CORPORATION, *pg.* 1368, *pg.* 1072
PERRY VIDEX LLC, *pg.* 1368, *pg.* 1072
PMFG, INC., *pg.* 1369, *pg.* 1685
PROCESS CONTROL CORPORATION, *pg.* 1370, *pg.* 518
ROCKWELL AUTOMATION, INC., *pg.* 668, *pg.* 1880
ROTARY LIFT, *pg.* 216, *pg.* 694
S. HOWES, INC., *pg.* 1373, *pg.* 1342
S.A. ARMSTRONG LIMITED, *pg.* 1373, *pg.* 1934
SELAS HEAT TECHNOLOGY COMPANY LLC, *pg.* 1076, *pg.* 1553

First page reference indicates Business Class Edition
Second page reference indicates Geographic Edition

SIMPSON TECHNOLOGIES CORPORATION, *pg.* 111, *pg.* 555
SINGER SEWING COMPANY, *pg.* 698, *pg.* 1639
SPEEDLINE TECHNOLOGIES, INC., *pg.* 1378, *pg.* 823
SPP PROCESS TECHNOLOGY SYSTEMS LIMITED-THERMAL DIVISION, *pg.* 472, *pg.* 250
STANDEX INTERNATIONAL CORPORATION, *pg.* 60, *pg.* 1039
STEBBINS ENGINEERING & MANUFACTURING COMPANY, *pg.* 113, *pg.* 1349
STURTEVANT INC., *pg.* 1379, *pg.* 824
SUPERIOR DIE SET CORP., *pg.* 1379, *pg.* 1885
SWECO, *pg.* 1380, *pg.* 728
TECHNIC INCORPORATED, *pg.* 1183, *pg.* 1601
THOMAS ENGINEERING INC., *pg.* 1382, *pg.* 619
TOPPAN PHOTOMASKS, INC., *pg.* 1432, *pg.* 1739
TRANTER PHE, INC., *pg.* 1383, *pg.* 1749
TRIO-TECH INTERNATIONAL, *pg.* 1384, *pg.* 300
ULTRATECH, INC., *pg.* 1433, *pg.* 251
UNIVERSAL INSTRUMENTS CORPORATION, *pg.* 683, *pg.* 1154
VILTER MANUFACTURING LLC, *pg.* 1078, *pg.* 1856
WAKEFIELD-VETTE, *pg.* 119, *pg.* 1038
WASHINGTON PRODUCTS INC., *pg.* 1387, *pg.* 1461
WELLCO ENTERPRISES, INC., *pg.* 1822, *pg.* 1392
WEYERHAEUSER COMPANY LIMITED, *pg.* 121, *pg.* 1913
WHITING CORPORATION, *pg.* 1389, *pg.* 633
THE WILL-BURT CO., INC., *pg.* 1437, *pg.* 1469
WORTHINGTON INDUSTRIES, INC., *pg.* 123, *pg.* 1444
WSF INDUSTRIES, INC., *pg.* 1390, *pg.* 1346
WYSSMONT CO., INC., *pg.* 1390, *pg.* 1068
XYLEM INC., *pg.* 1078, *pg.* 1339

3561 - Pumps & Pumping Equipment

ACF INDUSTRIES LLC, *pg.* 1310, *pg.* 989
ADAMS RITE AEROSPACE INC., *pg.* 1041, *pg.* 93
AKRON BRASS COMPANY, *pg.* 1311, *pg.* 1482
AMERICAN MACHINE & TOOL COMPANY, INC., *pg.* 1042, *pg.* 1585
ANSALDO STS, *pg.* 618, *pg.* 1573
COLFAX CORPORATION, *pg.* 1324, *pg.* 770
CONERGY, INC., *pg.* 1325, *pg.* 318
CORKEN, INC., *pg.* 1325, *pg.* 1485
CRANE CO., *pg.* 227, *pg.* 373
DANFOSS POWER SOLUTIONS COMPANY, *pg.* 1328, *pg.* 701
DOVER CORPORATION, *pg.* 1329, *pg.* 608
FLOW INTERNATIONAL CORPORATION, *pg.* 1337, *pg.* 1821
FLOWSERVE CORPORATION, *pg.* 82, *pg.* 1719
GARDNER DENVER, INC., *pg.* 1338, *pg.* 1592
GIW INDUSTRIES, INC., *pg.* 1340, *pg.* 533
THE GORMAN-RUPP COMPANY, *pg.* 1341, *pg.* 1458
GORMAN-RUPP OF CANADA LTD., *pg.* 1341, *pg.* 1933
GOULDS PUMPS, INCORPORATED, *pg.* 1342, *pg.* 1341
GRACO, INC., *pg.* 1342, *pg.* 935
GUSHER PUMPS, INC., *pg.* 1344, *pg.* 727
HARSCO RAIL, *pg.* 1345, *pg.* 1623
HYPRO, *pg.* 705, *pg.* 951
IDEX CORPORATION, *pg.* 1347, *pg.* 623
ITT CORPORATION, *pg.* 1351, *pg.* 1354
LINCOLN INDUSTRIAL CORP., *pg.* 1355, *pg.* 999
LITTLE GIANT PUMP COMPANY, *pg.* 1356, *pg.* 1486
MARCH MANUFACTURING INC., *pg.* 1359, *pg.* 615
MICO, INCORPORATED, *pg.* 212, *pg.* 951
MILTON ROY COMPANY, *pg.* 1361, *pg.* 1542
NETZSCH PUMPS NORTH AMERICA, LLC, *pg.* 1364, *pg.* 1532
THE NOLAN COMPANY, *pg.* 1365, *pg.* 1408
NORDCO, INC., *pg.* 1365, *pg.* 1884
PLEWS/EDELMANN, *pg.* 215, *pg.* 607
PUTZMEISTER AMERICA, *pg.* 1371, *pg.* 1896
S.A. ARMSTRONG LIMITED, *pg.* 1373, *pg.* 1934
SERFILCO, LTD., *pg.* 1375, *pg.* 641
TACO INCORPORATED, *pg.* 1077, *pg.* 1601
TECUMSEH PRODUCTS COMPANY, *pg.* 1381, *pg.* 866
TRINITY INDUSTRIES, INC., *pg.* 116, *pg.* 1690
TUTHILL CORPORATION PUMP GROUP, *pg.* 1385, *pg.* 553
TUTHILL VACUUM & BLOWER SYSTEMS, *pg.* 1385, *pg.* 1007
VIKING PUMP, INC., *pg.* 1387, *pg.* 702
VOSSLOH TRACK MATERIAL, INC., *pg.* 1387, *pg.* 1585
WATEROUS COMPANY, *pg.* 1387, *pg.* 965
WESTINGHOUSE AIR BRAKE TECHNOLOGIES CORPORATION, *pg.* 1388, *pg.* 1595
XYLEM INC., *pg.* 1078, *pg.* 1339

3562 - Ball And Roller Bearings

DEL-TRON PRECISION, INC., *pg.* 1328, *pg.* 337
DIAMOND CHAIN COMPANY, *pg.* 1328, *pg.* 684
GENERAL BEARING CORPORATION, *pg.* 205, *pg.* 1350
KAYDON CORPORATION, *pg.* 1352, *pg.* 866
NEW HAMPSHIRE BALL BEARINGS, INC., *pg.* 1058, *pg.* 1038
NL INDUSTRIES, INC., *pg.* 1174, *pg.* 1684
NN, INC., *pg.* 1365, *pg.* 1635
PAYSON CASTERS, INC., *pg.* 1059, *pg.* 616
REGAL POWER TRANSMISSION SOLUTIONS, *pg.* 216, *pg.* 698
SKF USA, *pg.* 217, *pg.* 1535
THE TIMKEN COMPANY, *pg.* 218, *pg.* 1408

3563 - Air & Gas Compressors

ATLAS COPCO COMPTEC LLC, *pg.* 1314, *pg.* 1349
CHART INDUSTRIES, INC., *pg.* 1405, *pg.* 1454
COHESANT, INC., *pg.* 1154, *pg.* 1405
CORKEN, INC., *pg.* 1325, *pg.* 1485
DEWALT INDUSTRIAL TOOL COMPANY, *pg.* 1328, *pg.* 757
EDWARDS VACUUM, INC., *pg.* 1332, *pg.* 1340
ELLIOTT COMPANY, *pg.* 1333, *pg.* 1542
GARDNER DENVER, INC., *pg.* 1338, *pg.* 1592
GARDNER DENVER NASH, *pg.* 1338, *pg.* 381
GRACO, INC., *pg.* 1342, *pg.* 935
INGERSOLL-RAND COMPANY, *pg.* 1349, *pg.* 1370
MARINE & OFFSHORE CANADA, *pg.* 1359, *pg.* 1933
NORWALK COMPRESSOR COMPANY, INC., *pg.* 1366, *pg.* 380
PAASCHE AIRBRUSH COMPANY, *pg.* 1444, *pg.* 587
PARKER HANNIFIN CORPORATION, *pg.* 1368, *pg.* 1434
PRAXAIR-TAFA, *pg.* 1370, *pg.* 1033
QUINCY COMPRESSOR INC., *pg.* 1371, *pg.* 653
SULLAIR CORPORATION, *pg.* 1379, *pg.* 695
TECUMSEH PRODUCTS COMPANY, *pg.* 1381, *pg.* 866
TITAN TOOL, INC., *pg.* 1383, *pg.* 1100
WAGNER SPRAY TECH CORPORATION, *pg.* 1449, *pg.* 954
XEBEC ADSORPTION INC., *pg.* 236, *pg.* 1950

3564 - Industrial & Commercial Fans & Blowers & Air Purification Equipment

AMETEK ROTRON, *pg.* 1068, *pg.* 1356
BALDWIN FILTERS, *pg.* 1316, *pg.* 1011
BOBRICK WASHROOM EQUIPMENT, INC., *pg.* 1043, *pg.* 166
BROAN-NUTONE LLC, *pg.* 1069, *pg.* 1860
CLARCOR, INC., *pg.* 1455, *pg.* 1632
CMI-SCHNEIBLE COMPANY, *pg.* 1324, *pg.* 906
DONALDSON COMPANY, INC., *pg.* 1329, *pg.* 917
ECLIPSE INC., *pg.* 1332, *pg.* 655
E.D. BULLARD COMPANY, *pg.* 1332, *pg.* 727
FIELD CONTROLS LLC, *pg.* 1071, *pg.* 1380
FLANDERS CORPORATION, *pg.* 1336, *pg.* 1392
GARDNER DENVER, INC., *pg.* 1338, *pg.* 1592
GENERAL FILTERS, INC., *pg.* 1072, *pg.* 903
GRAVER TECHNOLOGIES LLC, *pg.* 1343, *pg.* 387
H-P PRODUCTS, INC., *pg.* 85, *pg.* 1458
HAUCK MANUFACTURING COMPANY, INC., *pg.* 1345, *pg.* 1522
HF GROUP INC., *pg.* 1346, *pg.* 68
IRT, INC., *pg.* 1169, *pg.* 771
M&G DURA-VENT, INC., *pg.* 95, *pg.* 298
MAC EQUIPMENT, INC., *pg.* 1357, *pg.* 985
MFRI INC., *pg.* 1074, *pg.* 637
MIDWESCO FILTER RESOURCES INC., *pg.* 1464, *pg.* 1811
MOORE FANS LLC, *pg.* 1363, *pg.* 987
PANGBORN CORPORATION, *pg.* 1367, *pg.* 532
PARKER HANNIFIN CORPORATION, *pg.* 1368, *pg.* 1434
PURAFIL, INC., *pg.* 333, *pg.* 530
RESEARCH PRODUCTS CORPORATION, *pg.* 1075, *pg.* 1867
SLY, INC., *pg.* 1376, *pg.* 1475
THE SPENCER TURBINE CO., *pg.* 1378, *pg.* 386
SURCO PRODUCTS, INC., *pg.* 336, *pg.* 1581
TRION, INC., *pg.* 682, *pg.* 1390
WORLD DRYER CORPORATION, *pg.* 63, *pg.* 556

3565 - Packaging Machinery

ABC PACKAGING MACHINE CORPORATION, *pg.* 1309, *pg.* 477
AUTOMATED PACKAGING SYSTEMS INC., *pg.* 1452, *pg.* 1474
AVERY DENNISON CORPORATION, *pg.* 1452, *pg.* 95
B.H. BUNN COMPANY, *pg.* 1453, *pg.* 437
BUTLER AUTOMATIC, INC., *pg.* 1320, *pg.* 833
CAMPBELL WRAPPER CORPORATION, *pg.* 1454, *pg.* 1856
DOUGLAS MACHINE, INC., *pg.* 1456, *pg.* 915
DOVER CORPORATION, *pg.* 1329, *pg.* 608
HASLER, INC., *pg.* 1459, *pg.* 356
HEAT SEAL LLC, *pg.* 1345, *pg.* 1431
ITW HI-CONE, *pg.* 1461, *pg.* 620
LABEL-AIRE, INC., *pg.* 426, *pg.* 93
MARK ANDY, INC., *pg.* 1359, *pg.* 975
METRO MACHINE & ENGINEERING CORP., *pg.* 1360, *pg.* 923
NEW ENGLAND MACHINERY, INC., *pg.* 1364, *pg.* 415
PNEUMATICSCALEANGELUS, *pg.* 1369, *pg.* 1445
POTDEVIN MACHINE COMPANY, *pg.* 1369, *pg.* 1131
R.A. JONES & CO., *pg.* 1371, *pg.* 704
S. HOWES, INC., *pg.* 1373, *pg.* 1342
SEALED AIR CORPORATION, *pg.* 1468, *pg.* 1058
TIPPER TIE, INC., *pg.* 1382, *pg.* 1358
TRIANGLE PACKAGE MACHINERY CO., *pg.* 1383, *pg.* 592
U.S. BOTTLERS MACHINERY COMPANY, *pg.* 1386, *pg.* 1369

3566 - Speed Changers, Industrial High Speed Drives & Gears

ASCO SINTERING CO., *pg.* 1042, *pg.* 126
BOSTON GEAR, *pg.* 201, *pg.* 802
BREEZE-EASTERN CORPORATION, *pg.* 1319, *pg.* 1132
DANFOSS GRAHAM, *pg.* 203, *pg.* 1874
PHILADELPHIA GEAR CORPORATION, *pg.* 1368, *pg.* 1544
REGAL BELOIT CORPORATION, *pg.* 106, *pg.* 1854
REULAND ELECTRIC COMPANY, *pg.* 1304, *pg.* 68
ROCKWELL AUTOMATION, INC., *pg.* 668, *pg.* 1880
ZERO-MAX, INC., *pg.* 222, *pg.* 954

3567 - Industrial Process Furnaces & Ovens

AJAX ELECTRIC CO., *pg.* 1068, *pg.* 1541
BTU INTERNATIONAL, INC., *pg.* 1320, *pg.* 838
C.I. HAYES, *pg.* 1070, *pg.* 1600
DESPATCH INDUSTRIES, *pg.* 1070, *pg.* 927
GENCOR INDUSTRIES, INC., *pg.* 1339, *pg.* 453
THE GRIEVE CORPORATION, *pg.* 1072, *pg.* 657
HARROP INDUSTRIES, INC., *pg.* 86, *pg.* 1440
INDUCTOTHERM CORP., *pg.* 1348, *pg.* 1114
IPSEN INTERNATIONAL, INC., *pg.* 1073, *pg.* 562
NSS ENTERPRISES, INC., *pg.* 59, *pg.* 1476
PRECISION CONTROL SYSTEMS, INC./ RESEARCH INC., *pg.* 1427, *pg.* 923
SECO/WARWICK CORPORATION, *pg.* 1076, *pg.* 1552
SPX THERMAL PRODUCT SOLUTIONS, *pg.* 1378, *pg.* 1555
SURFACE COMBUSTION, INC., *pg.* 1077, *pg.* 1462
TENOVA, *pg.* 114, *pg.* 1525
VULCAN ELECTRIC COMPANY, *pg.* 1078, *pg.* 751
WATLOW ELECTRIC MANUFACTURING COMPANY, *pg.* 1078, *pg.* 1004
WYSSMONT CO., INC., *pg.* 1390, *pg.* 1068

3568 - Mechanical Power Transmission Equipment, NEC

ALTRA HOLDINGS, INC., *pg.* 198, *pg.* 802
ALTRIA INDUSTRIAL MOTION CORP., *pg.* 1312, *pg.* 802
BALDOR ELECTRIC COMPANY, *pg.* 1316, *pg.* 32
THE CARLYLE JOHNSON MACHINE COMPANY, L.L.C., *pg.* 1321, *pg.* 339
DANFOSS POWER SOLUTIONS COMPANY, *pg.* 1328, *pg.* 701
DIAMOND CHAIN COMPANY, *pg.* 1328, *pg.* 684

FALLBROOK TECHNOLOGIES INC., pg. 1336, pg. 203
FENNER DRIVES, pg. 1336, pg. 1551
KADANT JOHNSON INC., pg. 1073, pg. 909
KEYSTONE POWDERED METAL COMPANY, pg. 1353, pg. 1585
MIETHER BEARING PRODUCTS, INC., pg. 1361, pg. 1728
MORRIS COUPLING COMPANY, pg. 1057, pg. 1530
NEAPCO, INC., pg. 214, pg. 1582
PAYSON CASTERS, INC., pg. 1059, pg. 616
RBS GLOBAL, INC., pg. 1371, pg. 1879
REGAL BELOIT CORPORATION, pg. 106, pg. 1854
RENOLD, INC., pg. 1371, pg. 1351
THE TIMKEN COMPANY, pg. 218, pg. 1408
TWIN DISC, INCORPORATED, pg. 220, pg. 1889
U.S. TSUBAKI, INC., pg. 221, pg. 670
XTEK, INC., pg. 1390, pg. 1427
ZERO-MAX, INC., pg. 222, pg. 954

3569 - General Industrial Machinery & Equipment, NEC

AERO SYSTEMS ENGINEERING INC., pg. 223, pg. 959
ALGAS-SDI, pg. 1311, pg. 1831
AMERICAN AXLE & MANUFACTURING HOLDINGS, INC., pg. 198, pg. 879
AMERICAN FELT & FILTER COMPANY, pg. 1312, pg. 1184
ATEK, pg. 620, pg. 919
AUTOMATION DEVICES, INC., pg. 1315, pg. 1532
AUTOSWAGE PRODUCTS, INC., pg. 200, pg. 369
BLOOM MANUFACTURING, INC., pg. 701, pg. 708
CLAYTON INDUSTRIES CO., pg. 1323, pg. 66
COHESANT, INC., pg. 1154, pg. 1405
CROLL-REYNOLDS COMPANY, INC., pg. 1326, pg. 1103
DANAHER MOTION, pg. 1327, pg. 1593
DONALDSON COMPANY, INC., pg. 1329, pg. 917
DUFF-NORTON, pg. 204, pg. 1365
EAGLE TECHNOLOGIES GROUP, pg. 1331, pg. 874
EAST CHICAGO MACHINE TOOL CORPORATION, pg. 1331, pg. 676
ELLWOOD NATIONAL FORGE COMPANY, LLC, pg. 1333, pg. 1542
THE ENTWISTLE CO., pg. 637, pg. 826
FIKE CORPORATION, pg. 1047, pg. 973
FLEXFAB HORIZONS INTERNATIONAL, LLC, pg. 1072, pg. 891
THE FLINCHBAUGH CO., INC., pg. 82, pg. 1551
HARRIS WASTE MANAGEMENT GROUP, INC., pg. 1345, pg. 526
HAYWARD POOL PRODUCTS, pg. 1049, pg. 1057
HELMICK CORPORATION, pg. 1346, pg. 1849
HOLMATRO, INC., pg. 1346, pg. 771
ILLINOIS TOOL WORKS INC., pg. 1348, pg. 614
INGERSOLL-RAND COMPANY, pg. 1349, pg. 1370
KAYDON CORPORATION, pg. 1352, pg. 866
KEMPSMITH MACHINE COMPANY, pg. 1352, pg. 1876
KIDDE FIRE FIGHTING, pg. 1170, pg. 1531
LINDE GAS LLC, pg. 1356, pg. 1095
MCNEIL & NRM INC., pg. 1360, pg. 1402
MIETHER BEARING PRODUCTS, INC., pg. 1361, pg. 1728
NATIONAL BULK EQUIPMENT, INC., pg. 1479, pg. 892
NATIONAL METAL FINISHING CORP., pg. 1363, pg. 1084
NORDSON CORPORATION, pg. 1365, pg. 1480
PALL CORPORATION, pg. 232, pg. 1323
PANGBORN CORPORATION, pg. 1367, pg. 532
PENFLEX, INC., pg. 104, pg. 1534
PLANET PRODUCTS CORPORATION, pg. 1369, pg. 1418
PMFG, INC., pg. 1369, pg. 1685
PRAXAIR, INC., pg. 1178, pg. 344
REEL-O-MATIC, INC., pg. 1371, pg. 1487
RELIABLE AUTOMATIC SPRINKLER CO., INC., pg. 1137, pg. 1158
SERFILCO, LTD., pg. 1375, pg. 641
SULLAIR CORPORATION, pg. 1379, pg. 695
TENNANT COMPANY, pg. 1381, pg. 944
THERMOTRON INDUSTRIES, pg. 235, pg. 892
TRANSACT TECHNOLOGIES INCORPORATED, pg. 484, pg. 351
TRICO MFG. CORP., pg. 219, pg. 1886
U.S. AXLE, INC., pg. 221, pg. 1582
WESTERN STATES MACHINE COMPANY, pg. 1388, pg. 1455
THE WILL-BURT CO., INC., pg. 1437, pg. 1469
WILLIAMS PATENT CRUSHER & PULVERIZER CO., INC., pg. 1389, pg. 1005

3571 - Electronic Computers

ABSOLUTE SOFTWARE CORPORATION, pg. 340, pg. 1909
ACER AMERICA CORPORATION, pg. 341, pg. 235
ALIENWARE CORPORATION, pg. 346, pg. 439
AMX CORPORATION, pg. 349, pg. 1735
APPLE INC., pg. 350, pg. 73
THE ASCII GROUP, INC., pg. 132, pg. 761
ASTRONAUTICS CORPORATION OF AMERICA, pg. 224, pg. 1873
AUDIO COMMAND SYSTEMS, INC., pg. 621, pg. 1350
BROCADE COMMUNICATIONS SYSTEMS, INC., pg. 365, pg. 239
CONCURRENT COMPUTER CORPORATION, pg. 379, pg. 531
CRAY INC., pg. 380, pg. 1834
CRESTRON ELECTRONICS INC., pg. 631, pg. 1116
DELL FORCE10 NETWORKS, INC., pg. 383, pg. 243
DELL INC., pg. 383, pg. 1737
DIGI INTERNATIONAL INC., pg. 387, pg. 948
ECHELON CORPORATION, pg. 389, pg. 245
ELMA ELECTRONIC INC., pg. 391, pg. 90
EVANS & SUTHERLAND COMPUTER CORPORATION - DIGITAL THEATER DIVISION, pg. 395, pg. 1757
EXAR CORPORATION, pg. 395, pg. 91
EZENIA! INC., pg. 396, pg. 1039
GE INTELLIGENT PLATFORMS, pg. 400, pg. 1135
GE INTELLIGENT PLATFORMS, pg. 1339, pg. 1777
HEWLETT-PACKARD COMPANY, pg. 404, pg. 175
IGO, INC., pg. 644, pg. 22
INTERNATIONAL BUSINESS MACHINES CORPORATION, pg. 418, pg. 1138
INTRUSION INC., pg. 1259, pg. 1736
ITRON INC., pg. 422, pg. 1822
LEXMARK INTERNATIONAL, INC., pg. 427, pg. 730
MAXWELL TECHNOLOGIES, INC., pg. 653, pg. 204
MEGGITT TRAINING SYSTEMS, pg. 1839, pg. 541
MERCURY COMPUTER SYSTEMS, INC., pg. 434, pg. 813
MICROWAY, INC., pg. 1267, pg. 841
NEONODE, INC., pg. 659, pg. 268
POLYWELL COMPUTERS, INC., pg. 456, pg. 280
RADISYS CORPORATION, pg. 458, pg. 1498
SILICON GRAPHICS INTERNATIONAL CORP, pg. 470, pg. 148
SOCKET MOBILE, INC., pg. 471, pg. 164
STRATUS TECHNOLOGIES, INC., pg. 477, pg. 832
TEXAS INSTRUMENTS INCORPORATED, pg. 679, pg. 1688
VOLT INFORMATION SCIENCES, INC., pg. 490, pg. 1312

3572 - Computer Storage Devices

ADVANCED MICRO DEVICES, INC., pg. 613, pg. 282
ALACRITECH, INC., pg. 346, pg. 237
ALANCO TECHNOLOGIES, INC., pg. 346, pg. 20
ALCATEL-LUCENT, pg. 615, pg. 38
ALLSOP, INC., pg. 347, pg. 1817
AUTONOMY PLEASANTON, pg. 358, pg. 183
BLUE COAT SYSTEMS, INC., pg. 362, pg. 284
BROCADE COMMUNICATIONS SYSTEMS, INC., pg. 365, pg. 239
CAMBEX CORPORATION, pg. 368, pg. 844
CANDELIS, INC., pg. 368, pg. 165
DATARAM CORPORATION, pg. 383, pg. 1111
DELL STORAGE, pg. 386, pg. 922
DOT HILL SYSTEMS CORP., pg. 388, pg. 333
EMC CORPORATION, pg. 391, pg. 825
EN POINTE TECHNOLOGIES, INC., pg. 1243, pg. 94
HGST, pg. 406, pg. 260
IMATION CORP., pg. 413, pg. 952
IMATION NEXSAN SOLUTIONS, pg. 413, pg. 292
INTEGRAL SYSTEMS, INC., pg. 416, pg. 767
INTEL CORPORATION, pg. 645, pg. 266
INTERPOINT CORPORATION, pg. 647, pg. 1824
KINGSTON TECHNOLOGY COMPANY, INC., pg. 425, pg. 90
MICROBOARDS TECHNOLOGY, LLC, pg. 434, pg. 920
MILTOPE GROUP, INC., pg. 440, pg. 6
NCR CORPORATION, pg. 443, pg. 531
NETAPP, INC., pg. 444, pg. 287
OCZ STORAGE SOLUTIONS, pg. 448, pg. 248
OVERLAND STORAGE, INC., pg. 451, pg. 205
PRESILIENT, LLC, pg. 456, pg. 313
QUALSTAR CORPORATION, pg. 458, pg. 279
QUANTUM CORPORATION, pg. 458, pg. 250
SANDISK CORPORATION, pg. 465, pg. 147
STRUCTURED COMMUNICATION SYSTEMS, INC., pg. 477, pg. 1497
UNIFIEDONLINE, INC., pg. 486, pg. 1780
WESTERN DIGITAL CORPORATION, pg. 492, pg. 118

3575 - Computer Terminals

ACER AMERICA CORPORATION, pg. 341, pg. 235
ADVANCED MICRO DEVICES, INC.-MARKHAM, pg. 345, pg. 1922
DIEBOLD, INCORPORATED, pg. 387, pg. 1407
EZENIA! INC., pg. 396, pg. 1039
GEORGE RISK INDUSTRIES, INC., pg. 1298, pg. 1011
INDUSTRIAL ELECTRONIC ENGINEERS, INC., pg. 644, pg. 300
LENOVO GROUP LTD, pg. 427, pg. 1384
NORTECH SYSTEMS INCORPORATED, pg. 659, pg. 966
PLANAR SYSTEMS, INC., pg. 455, pg. 1495
RICOH PRINTING SYSTEMS AMERICA, INC., pg. 462, pg. 279
SYSTEMAX, INC., pg. 481, pg. 1324
VERIFONE SYSTEMS, INC., pg. 487, pg. 251
WMS INDUSTRIES INC., pg. 593, pg. 666

3577 - Computer Peripheral Equipment, NEC

3D SYSTEMS CORPORATION, pg. 339, pg. 1621
3M TOUCH SYSTEMS, INC., pg. 339, pg. 833
A. T. CROSS COMPANY, pg. 339, pg. 1602
ACCO BRANDS CORPORATION, pg. 340, pg. 626
ACER AMERICA CORPORATION, pg. 341, pg. 235
AHEARN & SOPER INC., pg. 345, pg. 1932
ANALOGIC CORPORATION, pg. 1399, pg. 840
ANDREA ELECTRONICS CORPORATION, pg. 617, pg. 1143
ANTEC INCORPORATED, pg. 350, pg. 90
APPLE INC., pg. 350, pg. 73
ASANTE TECHNOLOGIES, INC., pg. 619, pg. 238
ASTRO-MED, INC., pg. 619, pg. 1609
AUDIOCODES USA, pg. 356, pg. 1121
AVID TECHNOLOGY, INC., pg. 622, pg. 804
BLACK BOX CORPORATION, pg. 361, pg. 1547
BLUE COAT SYSTEMS, INC., pg. 362, pg. 284
THE BOEING COMPANY, pg. 225, pg. 567
BRADY CORPORATION, pg. 363, pg. 1873
BROCADE COMMUNICATIONS SYSTEMS, INC., pg. 365, pg. 239
CADENCE DESIGN SYSTEMS, INC., pg. 367, pg. 239
CAPCOM USA, INC., pg. 950, pg. 254
CHYRONHEGO, pg. 371, pg. 1179
CISCO SYSTEMS, INC., pg. 372, pg. 240
COMMUNICATIONS SPECIALTIES, INC., pg. 377, pg. 1338
CORSAIR COMPONENTS, INC., pg. 380, pg. 90
CUSTOM SENSORS & TECHNOLOGIES, pg. 1407, pg. 152
D-LINK SYSTEMS, INC., pg. 381, pg. 89
DATALOGIC, pg. 382, pg. 1588
DATAMAX CORPORATION, pg. 1633, pg. 453
DIEBOLD, INCORPORATED, pg. 387, pg. 1407
DIGI INTERNATIONAL INC., pg. 387, pg. 948
EASTMAN KODAK COMPANY, pg. 1408, pg. 1333
ECRM IMAGING SYSTEMS, INC., pg. 1410, pg. 848
EFAX.COM INC., pg. 1242, pg. 129
ELECTRONICS FOR IMAGING, INC., pg. 390, pg. 88
ELEKTA, pg. 391, pg. 987
ELO TOUCH SOLUTIONS, pg. 635, pg. 145
EMC CORPORATION, pg. 391, pg. 825
EMTEC, INC., pg. 392, pg. 1123
EMULEX CORPORATION, pg. 392, pg. 70
EPSON AMERICA INC., pg. 394, pg. 122
ERGOTRON, INC., pg. 395, pg. 960
EVANS & SUTHERLAND COMPUTER CORPORATION, pg. 638, pg. 1757
EVANS & SUTHERLAND COMPUTER CORPORATION - DIGITAL THEATER DIVISION, pg. 395, pg. 1757
F5 NETWORKS, INC., pg. 396, pg. 1835
GE INTELLIGENT PLATFORMS, pg. 400, pg. 1135
GLORY GLOBAL SOLUTIONS, pg. 401, pg. 628
HARLAND CLARKE HOLDINGS CORP., pg. 1647, pg. 1741
HAUPPAUGE DIGITAL, INC., pg. 402, pg. 1164
HEWLETT-PACKARD COMPANY, pg. 404, pg. 175

ICAD, INC., *pg.* 643, *pg.* 1037
IGO, INC., *pg.* 644, *pg.* 22
INDUSTRIAL ELECTRONIC ENGINEERS, INC., *pg.* 644, *pg.* 300
INFOCUS CORPORATION, *pg.* 644, *pg.* 1503
INTELLICHECK MOBILISA, INC., *pg.* 416, *pg.* 1823
INTERLINK ELECTRONICS, INC., *pg.* 417, *pg.* 57
INTERNATIONAL BUSINESS MACHINES CORPORATION, *pg.* 418, *pg.* 1138
INTERPHASE CORPORATION, *pg.* 420, *pg.* 1732
INTRUSION INC., *pg.* 1259, *pg.* 1736
ITUS CORPORATION, *pg.* 422, *pg.* 1180
JUNIPER NETWORKS, INC., *pg.* 1260, *pg.* 286
KENSINGTON TECHNOLOGY GROUP, *pg.* 424, *pg.* 191
KEY TRONIC CORPORATION, *pg.* 424, *pg.* 1844
KINGSTON TECHNOLOGY COMPANY, INC., *pg.* 425, *pg.* 90
KOFAX IMAGE PRODUCTS, INC., *pg.* 1419, *pg.* 112
KRONOS INCORPORATED, *pg.* 425, *pg.* 813
LANTRONIX, INC., *pg.* 426, *pg.* 112
LEXMARK INTERNATIONAL, INC., *pg.* 427, *pg.* 730
LOGITECH INC., *pg.* 1264, *pg.* 164
MAD CATZ INTERACTIVE INC., *pg.* 429, *pg.* 204
MEGGITT TRAINING SYSTEMS, *pg.* 1839, *pg.* 541
MICROBOARDS TECHNOLOGY, LLC, *pg.* 434, *pg.* 920
MICROVISION, INC., *pg.* 654, *pg.* 1828
MICROWAY, INC., *pg.* 1267, *pg.* 841
MILTOPE GROUP, INC., *pg.* 440, *pg.* 6
MITEK SYSTEMS, INC., *pg.* 440, *pg.* 204
MORSE WATCHMANS INC., *pg.* 656, *pg.* 368
MOTOROLA ENTERPRISE MOBILITY, *pg.* 441, *pg.* 1167
MOTOROLA SOLUTIONS, INC., *pg.* 657, *pg.* 659
NCR CORPORATION, *pg.* 443, *pg.* 531
NEONODE, INC., *pg.* 659, *pg.* 268
NER HOLDINGS INC., *pg.* 444, *pg.* 1071
NETGEAR, INC., *pg.* 444, *pg.* 247
NETSCOUT SYSTEMS, INC., *pg.* 1270, *pg.* 858
OKI DATA AMERICAS, INC., *pg.* 449, *pg.* 1090
OPENCONNECT SYSTEMS, INC., *pg.* 449, *pg.* 1685
ORTRONICS/LEGRAND, *pg.* 451, *pg.* 359
OVERLAND STORAGE, INC., *pg.* 451, *pg.* 205
PASSUR AEROSPACE, INC., *pg.* 233, *pg.* 376
PEARSON ASSESSMENTS, *pg.* 1674, *pg.* 918
PERLE SYSTEMS LIMITED, *pg.* 454, *pg.* 1924
PLAINTREE SYSTEMS INC., *pg.* 663, *pg.* 1918
PRESSTEK LLC, *pg.* 1678, *pg.* 1034
PRINTRONIX, INC., *pg.* 456, *pg.* 115
PROGRESS DATADIRECT, *pg.* 457, *pg.* 1385
RADISYS CORPORATION, *pg.* 458, *pg.* 1498
RAYTHEON, *pg.* 459, *pg.* 115
RELAX TECHNOLOGY, INC., *pg.* 461, *pg.* 298
RICOH PRINTING SYSTEMS AMERICA, INC., *pg.* 462, *pg.* 279
RSA SECURITY INC., *pg.* 463, *pg.* 786
SCAN-OPTICS, LLC, *pg.* 467, *pg.* 354
SCANTRON CORPORATION, *pg.* 467, *pg.* 922
SIGMA DESIGNS, INC., *pg.* 469, *pg.* 148
SOCKET MOBILE, INC., *pg.* 471, *pg.* 164
STEELCLOUD, INC., *pg.* 476, *pg.* 1776
STRATASYS, INC., *pg.* 476, *pg.* 923
SUPER MICRO COMPUTER, INC., *pg.* 478, *pg.* 251
TECH DATA CORPORATION, *pg.* 482, *pg.* 416
TECSYS, INC., *pg.* 482, *pg.* 1956
TELEGENIX INC., *pg.* 678, *pg.* 1051
TIDEL ENGINEERING, L.P., *pg.* 1382, *pg.* 1670
TROY GROUP INC., *pg.* 485, *pg.* 71
ULTIMATE TECHNOLOGY CORPORATION, *pg.* 486, *pg.* 1349
UNICOM ENGINEERING, *pg.* 1286, *pg.* 812
VALVE CORPORATION, *pg.* 487, *pg.* 1817
VERIFONE SYSTEMS, INC., *pg.* 487, *pg.* 251
VIEW SYSTEMS, INC., *pg.* 489, *pg.* 760
VIEWSONIC CORPORATION, *pg.* 489, *pg.* 303
WIZZARD SPEECH LLC., *pg.* 493, *pg.* 1582
ZEBRA TECHNOLOGIES CORPORATION, *pg.* 690, *pg.* 628
ZOOM TECHNOLOGIES, INC., *pg.* 497, *pg.* 1317

3582 - Commercial Laundry, Dry Cleaning & Pressing Machines

1-800-VENDING, INC., *pg.* 1759, *pg.* 1751
ADCO, INC., *pg.* 325, *pg.* 482
ALLIANCE LAUNDRY HOLDINGS LLC, *pg.* 51, *pg.* 1890
COIN ACCEPTORS, INC., *pg.* 1324, *pg.* 994
EZCORP, INC., *pg.* 750, *pg.* 1662
HAPP CONTROLS INC., *pg.* 641, *pg.* 634
KEY TECHNOLOGY, INC., *pg.* 868, *pg.* 1847
MAC-GRAY CORPORATION, *pg.* 58, *pg.* 852
NCR CORPORATION, *pg.* 443, *pg.* 531
NORDSON CORPORATION, *pg.* 1365, *pg.* 1480
OUTERWALL INC., *pg.* 1367, *pg.* 1816
PAR TECHNOLOGY CORPORATION, *pg.* 452, *pg.* 1183
PELLERIN MILNOR CORPORATION, *pg.* 1368, *pg.* 744
ROTARY LIFT, *pg.* 216, *pg.* 694

3585 - Air Conditioning & Warm Air Heating Equipment & Commercial & Industrial Refrigeration Equipment

AAON, INC., *pg.* 1068, *pg.* 1488
ADAMS MFG. CO., *pg.* 51, *pg.* 1427
AEROFIN CORP., *pg.* 1068, *pg.* 1787
BALTIMORE AIRCOIL COMPANY, *pg.* 1069, *pg.* 773
BARD MANUFACTURING COMPANY, *pg.* 1069, *pg.* 1406
BROAN-NUTONE LLC, *pg.* 1069, *pg.* 1860
BUHLER AEROGLIDE, *pg.* 1069, *pg.* 1359
CARRIER CORPORATION, *pg.* 1070, *pg.* 349
C.I. HAYES, *pg.* 1070, *pg.* 1600
CORNELIUS INC., *pg.* 54, *pg.* 614
CORNELIUS INC, *pg.* 1326, *pg.* 952
DANAHER CORPORATION, *pg.* 1044, *pg.* 397
DOMETIC CORPORATION, *pg.* 1070, *pg.* 677
DORMAN PRODUCTS, INC., *pg.* 204, *pg.* 1522
DOVER CORPORATION, *pg.* 1329, *pg.* 608
ECODYNE HEAT EXCHANGERS, INC., *pg.* 1071, *pg.* 1705
ELKAY MANUFACTURING COMPANY, *pg.* 80, *pg.* 645
EMERSON CLIMATE TECHNOLOGIES, INC., *pg.* 1333, *pg.* 1472
EMERSON NETWORK POWER LIEBERT, *pg.* 1071, *pg.* 1439
FIELD CONTROLS LLC, *pg.* 1071, *pg.* 1380
FRIEDRICH AIR CONDITIONING CO., *pg.* 1072, *pg.* 1740
FUJITSU GENERAL AMERICA, INC., *pg.* 55, *pg.* 1065
GEA REFRIGERATION NORTH AMERICA, INC., *pg.* 1072, *pg.* 1597
GENERAL FILTERS, INC., *pg.* 1072, *pg.* 903
GOODMAN GROUP, INC., *pg.* 1072, *pg.* 1706
HEAT CONTROLLER, INC., *pg.* 1072, *pg.* 893
HILL PHOENIX INC., *pg.* 1072, *pg.* 528
HUSSMANN INTERNATIONAL, INC., *pg.* 1347, *pg.* 973
JOHNSON CONTROLS, INC., *pg.* 209, *pg.* 1876
JOHNSON CONTROLS, INC., *pg.* 1073, *pg.* 1597
LENNOX INTERNATIONAL INC., *pg.* 1073, *pg.* 1736
LYTRON INCORPORATED, *pg.* 1074, *pg.* 861
THE MANITOWOC COMPANY, INC., *pg.* 1358, *pg.* 1000
MANITOWOC ICE, INC., *pg.* 58, *pg.* 1868
MESTEK, INC., *pg.* 1074, *pg.* 857
MODINE MANUFACTURING COMPANY, *pg.* 1074, *pg.* 1888
NORTEK GLOBAL HVAC, *pg.* 1075, *pg.* 989
NORTEK, INC., *pg.* 100, *pg.* 1607
NORTH STAR ICE EQUIPMENT CORPORATION, *pg.* 1366, *pg.* 1838
PARKER HANNIFIN CORPORATION, *pg.* 1368, *pg.* 1434
RESEARCH PRODUCTS CORPORATION, *pg.* 1075, *pg.* 1867
RHEEM MANUFACTURING - AIR CONDITIONING DIV, *pg.* 1075, *pg.* 32
RHEEM MANUFACTURING COMPANY, *pg.* 1075, *pg.* 519
SCOTSMAN GROUP LLC, *pg.* 1374, *pg.* 665
SLANT/FIN CORPORATION, *pg.* 1076, *pg.* 1163
STANDEX INTERNATIONAL CORPORATION, *pg.* 60, *pg.* 1039
TEI STRUTHERS WELLS, *pg.* 1381, *pg.* 1590
THERMO KING CORPORATION, *pg.* 1077, *pg.* 918
TRANE INC., *pg.* 116, *pg.* 1109
TRION, INC., *pg.* 682, *pg.* 1390
TRIUMPH THERMAL SYSTEMS, INC., *pg.* 235, *pg.* 1454
UNITED TECHNOLOGIES CORPORATION, *pg.* 235, *pg.* 353
VICTORY REFRIGERATION COMPANY LLC, *pg.* 61, *pg.* 1051
VILTER MANUFACTURING LLC, *pg.* 1078, *pg.* 1856
WATSCO INC., *pg.* 1078, *pg.* 417
WESTERBEKE CORPORATION, *pg.* 1388, *pg.* 847
WHIRLPOOL CORPORATION, *pg.* 62, *pg.* 872
WORLD DRYER CORPORATION, *pg.* 63, *pg.* 556

3586 - Measuring & Dispensing Pumps

BELSHAW ADAMATIC BAKERY GROUP, *pg.* 1317, *pg.* 1813
CORNELIUS INC, *pg.* 1326, *pg.* 952
EARTH FRIENDLY PRODUCTS, *pg.* 329, *pg.* 552
THE GORMAN-RUPP COMPANY, *pg.* 1341, *pg.* 1458
IDEX CORPORATION, *pg.* 1347, *pg.* 623
LINCOLN INDUSTRIAL CORP., *pg.* 1355, *pg.* 999
MARCH MANUFACTURING INC., *pg.* 1359, *pg.* 615
MY-D HAN-D MFG. INC., *pg.* 706, *pg.* 714
NESTLE PROFESSIONAL BEVERAGES, *pg.* 257, *pg.* 474
NORWALK COMPRESSOR COMPANY, INC., *pg.* 1366, *pg.* 380
POWERSECURE INTERNATIONAL, INC., *pg.* 105, *pg.* 1392

3589 - Service Industry Machines, NEC

A BRITE COMPANY, *pg.* 1144, *pg.* 1697
ADELPHI PAPER HANGINGS LLC, *pg.* 912, *pg.* 1342
ADEPT TECHNOLOGY, INC., *pg.* 1310, *pg.* 182
THE ADT CORPORATION, *pg.* 612, *pg.* 409
ADVANCED ENERGY INDUSTRIES, INC., *pg.* 613, *pg.* 328
AIXTRON INC., *pg.* 1310, *pg.* 283
ALPHA PRO TECH, LTD., *pg.* 1492, *pg.* 1922
ALTAIR CORPORATION, *pg.* 1312, *pg.* 910
ALTO-SHAAM INC., *pg.* 836, *pg.* 1869
AMANO CINCINNATI, INC., *pg.* 348, *pg.* 1117
AMERICAN ART CLAY CO., INC., *pg.* 1759, *pg.* 682
AMERICAN AXLE & MANUFACTURING HOLDINGS, INC., *pg.* 198, *pg.* 879
AMKOR TECHNOLOGY, INC., *pg.* 67, *pg.* 25
AMSOIL INC., *pg.* 971, *pg.* 1896
ANDERSON INTERNATIONAL CORP., *pg.* 1313, *pg.* 1474
ANDIS COMPANY, *pg.* 498, *pg.* 1895
A.O. SMITH CORPORATION, *pg.* 1313, *pg.* 1872
APPLIED MATERIALS, INC, *pg.* 618, *pg.* 1009
APPLIED MATERIALS, INC., *pg.* 618, *pg.* 264
THE ARISTOTLE CORPORATION, *pg.* 1496, *pg.* 372
AROMATIQUE INC., *pg.* 499, *pg.* 32
ATEK, *pg.* 620, *pg.* 919
AUTOLIV NORTH AMERICA, AMERICAN TECHNICAL CENTER, *pg.* 200, *pg.* 867
AUTOSWAGE PRODUCTS, INC., *pg.* 200, *pg.* 369
AVIALL, INC., *pg.* 224, *pg.* 1676
AXCELIS TECHNOLOGIES, INC., *pg.* 1400, *pg.* 787
AXT, INC., *pg.* 1400, *pg.* 90
BABCOCK & WILCOX POWER GENERATION GROUP, INC., *pg.* 1069, *pg.* 1404
BAE SYSTEMS PRODUCTS GROUP, *pg.* 359, *pg.* 432
BALDOR ELECTRIC COMPANY, *pg.* 1316, *pg.* 32
BALLARD POWER SYSTEMS, INC., *pg.* 70, *pg.* 1907
BALTIMORE AIRCOIL COMPANY, *pg.* 1069, *pg.* 773
BD MEDICAL, *pg.* 1501, *pg.* 1762
BEE LINE COMPANY, *pg.* 200, *pg.* 701
BELSHAW ADAMATIC BAKERY GROUP, *pg.* 1317, *pg.* 1813
BELVEDERE USA CORPORATION, *pg.* 917, *pg.* 556
BESSER COMPANY, *pg.* 1317, *pg.* 865
BLONDER TONGUE LABORATORIES, INC., *pg.* 625, *pg.* 1100
BLOOM MANUFACTURING, INC., *pg.* 701, *pg.* 708
BLOUNT INTERNATIONAL, INC., *pg.* 1043, *pg.* 1501
BLYTH, INC., *pg.* 502, *pg.* 349
BRADY CORPORATION, *pg.* 363, *pg.* 1873
BRANSON ULTRASONICS CORPORATION, *pg.* 1319, *pg.* 342
BRANSON ULTRASONICS CORPORATION - PLASTICS JOINING DIVISION, *pg.* 1403, *pg.* 343
BRANSON ULTRASONICS CORPORATION-PRECISION CLEANING DIV, *pg.* 1319, *pg.* 343
BRIGHT OF AMERICA, INC., *pg.* 1121, *pg.* 1851
BROAN-NUTONE LLC, *pg.* 1069, *pg.* 1860
BROOKS AUTOMATION, INC., *pg.* 1320, *pg.* 813
BTU INTERNATIONAL, INC., *pg.* 1320, *pg.* 838
BUNN-O-MATIC CORPORATION, *pg.* 53, *pg.* 661
BURNHAM HOLDINGS, INC., *pg.* 1069, *pg.* 1546
BUZTRONICS, INC., *pg.* 1294, *pg.* 683
C&D TECHNOLOGIES, INC., *pg.* 627, *pg.* 1517
CAE USA, INC., *pg.* 226, *pg.* 472

CEMTREX, INC., *pg.* 1322, *pg.* 1159
THE CHAMBERLAIN GROUP, INC., *pg.* 75, *pg.* 611
CHART INDUSTRIES, INC., *pg.* 1405, *pg.* 1454
CHASE CORPORATION, *pg.* 1152, *pg.* 803
CHECKPOINT SYSTEMS, INC., *pg.* 628, *pg.* 1559
CLEAVER-BROOKS, *pg.* 76, *pg.* 1874
CLINTON INDUSTRIES, INC., *pg.* 1324, *pg.* 1079
CLORE AUTOMOTIVE LLC, *pg.* 202, *pg.* 716
COHERENT, INC., *pg.* 1406, *pg.* 265
COHESANT, INC., *pg.* 1154, *pg.* 1405
CONDUCTIX INC., *pg.* 1295, *pg.* 1015
CONNELL LIMITED PARTNERSHIP, *pg.* 1325, *pg.* 793
CTS VALPEY CORPORATION, *pg.* 632, *pg.* 825
CUBIC CORPORATION, *pg.* 632, *pg.* 201
CULLIGAN INTERNATIONAL COMPANY, *pg.* 54, *pg.* 656
CVD EQUIPMENT CORPORATION, *pg.* 632, *pg.* 1152
CVI MELLES GRIOT, *pg.* 1407, *pg.* 59
CYMER, INC., *pg.* 1296, *pg.* 202
D&S CAR WASH EQUIPMENT CO., *pg.* 1327, *pg.* 979
DAHLE USA, *pg.* 382, *pg.* 1038
DAIFUKU WEBB, *pg.* 1327, *pg.* 885
DANAHER CORPORATION, *pg.* 1044, *pg.* 397
DANFOSS POWER SOLUTIONS COMPANY, *pg.* 1328, *pg.* 701
DAVIS-STANDARD LLC, *pg.* 1328, *pg.* 368
DEDERT CORPORATION, *pg.* 1408, *pg.* 649
DETEX CORPORATION, *pg.* 633, *pg.* 1728
DIAMOND POWER INTERNATIONAL, INC., *pg.* 1070, *pg.* 1457
DOVER CORPORATION, *pg.* 1329, *pg.* 608
DUKE MANUFACTURING COMPANY, INC., *pg.* 54, *pg.* 995
EAST CHICAGO MACHINE TOOL CORPORATION, *pg.* 1331, *pg.* 676
EATON CORPORATION, *pg.* 1331, *pg.* 1429
EDUCATIONAL INSIGHTS, INC., *pg.* 951, *pg.* 187
ELECTRIC EEL MANUFACTURING CO., INC., *pg.* 80, *pg.* 1473
ELGIN NATIONAL INDUSTRIES, INC., *pg.* 1333, *pg.* 608
ELLWOOD NATIONAL FORGE COMPANY, LLC, *pg.* 1333, *pg.* 1542
EMCORE CORPORATION, *pg.* 636, *pg.* 39
ENERFAB, INC., *pg.* 81, *pg.* 1412
ENERGIZER HOLDINGS, INC., *pg.* 637, *pg.* 996
ENERGY RECOVERY, INC., *pg.* 1334, *pg.* 252
ENVIRONMENTAL TECTONICS CORPORATION, *pg.* 1411, *pg.* 1587
EPILOG CORPORATION, *pg.* 1412, *pg.* 330
ERIEZ MANUFACTURING CO. INC., *pg.* 1335, *pg.* 1530
EXTERRAN HOLDINGS, INC., *pg.* 977, *pg.* 1705
FAIRCHILD SEMICONDUCTOR CORPORATION, *pg.* 638, *pg.* 245
FARREL CORPORATION, *pg.* 1336, *pg.* 337
FLIGHTSAFETY INTERNATIONAL, INC., *pg.* 601, *pg.* 1160
THE FLINCHBAUGH CO., INC., *pg.* 82, *pg.* 1551
FLOW INTERNATIONAL CORPORATION, *pg.* 1337, *pg.* 1821
FLUID MANAGEMENT, *pg.* 1442, *pg.* 670
FOLKMANIS, INC., *pg.* 953, *pg.* 83
FRANKE INC., *pg.* 55, *pg.* 1656
GARLAND COMMERCIAL RANGES, LTD., *pg.* 1124, *pg.* 1925
GEERPRES INC., *pg.* 1339, *pg.* 901
GENCOR INDUSTRIES, INC., *pg.* 1339, *pg.* 453
THE GENIE COMPANY, *pg.* 55, *pg.* 1403
GERBER SCIENTIFIC, INC., *pg.* 1414, *pg.* 380
GIW INDUSTRIES, INC., *pg.* 1340, *pg.* 533
GLOBAL EPOINT INC., *pg.* 400, *pg.* 67
GLOUCESTER ENGINEERING, CO., *pg.* 1341, *pg.* 823
GOLD MEDAL PRODUCTS CO., *pg.* 55, *pg.* 1414
GOODWAY TECHNOLOGIES CORPORATION, *pg.* 1341, *pg.* 374
GRAVER TECHNOLOGIES LLC, *pg.* 1343, *pg.* 387
GSI GROUP INC., *pg.* 1415, *pg.* 784
HARSCO CORPORATION, *pg.* 86, *pg.* 1519
HARSCO RAIL, *pg.* 1345, *pg.* 1623
THE HARTZ MOUNTAIN CORP., *pg.* 1476, *pg.* 1120
HELEN OF TROY L.P., *pg.* 511, *pg.* 1692
HELMICK CORPORATION, *pg.* 1346, *pg.* 1849
HI-VAC CORPORATION, *pg.* 56, *pg.* 1458
HIGHFIELD MANUFACTURING CO., *pg.* 1346, *pg.* 339
HOBART BROTHERS COMPANY, *pg.* 1346, *pg.* 1477
HOBART CORPORATION, *pg.* 1346, *pg.* 1477
HORNADY MANUFACTURING COMPANY, *pg.* 1836, *pg.* 1010
HOSOKAWA MICRON POWDER SYSTEMS, *pg.* 1347, *pg.* 1124
HUBBELL INCORPORATED, *pg.* 1299, *pg.* 370
HUBBELL POWER SYSTEMS, INC., *pg.* 643, *pg.* 1614
HUNTER ENGINEERING COMPANY, *pg.* 208, *pg.* 973
HYDRALIGN, *pg.* 1257, *pg.* 833
IDEX CORPORATION, *pg.* 1347, *pg.* 623
IGT, *pg.* 412, *pg.* 1031
ILLINOIS TOOL WORKS INC., *pg.* 1348, *pg.* 614
INDUSTRIAL DISTRIBUTION GROUP, INC., *pg.* 413, *pg.* 1358
INGERSOLL-RAND COMPANY, *pg.* 1349, *pg.* 1370
INTERNATIONAL BALER CORP., *pg.* 1350, *pg.* 433
INTERNATIONAL COMPONENTS CORPORATION, *pg.* 647, *pg.* 669
INTERNATIONAL GAME TECHNOLOGY, *pg.* 957, *pg.* 1024
INTERNATIONAL ROAD DYNAMICS INC., *pg.* 1912, *pg.* 1962
INVISIBLE FENCE, INC., *pg.* 648, *pg.* 1637
IROBOT CORP., *pg.* 1418, *pg.* 705
ISOMET CORPORATION, *pg.* 1418, *pg.* 1807
ITW DYNATEC, *pg.* 1351, *pg.* 1635
IXIA, *pg.* 422, *pg.* 56
JASON INDUSTRIES, INC., *pg.* 208, *pg.* 1875
JENNY PRODUCTS, INC., *pg.* 331, *pg.* 1586
JOHNSON & JOHNSON BABY PRODUCTS, INC., *pg.* 1552, *pg.* 1094
KATY INDUSTRIES, INC., *pg.* 1126, *pg.* 973
KEMPSMITH MACHINE COMPANY, *pg.* 1352, *pg.* 1876
KEY TECHNOLOGY, INC., *pg.* 868, *pg.* 1847
KINGSBURY CORPORATION, *pg.* 1353, *pg.* 1035
KLA-TENCOR CORPORATION, *pg.* 1353, *pg.* 146
KULICKE & SOFFA INDUSTRIES, INC., *pg.* 650, *pg.* 1533
KYZEN CORPORATION, *pg.* 331, *pg.* 1652
LA MARCHE MANUFACTURING COMPANY, *pg.* 1300, *pg.* 606
LAKELAND INDUSTRIES, INC., *pg.* 1354, *pg.* 1338
LAM RESEARCH CORPORATION, *pg.* 1354, *pg.* 91
LAPOLLA INDUSTRIES, INC., *pg.* 1444, *pg.* 1710
LARSON-JUHL US LLC, *pg.* 933, *pg.* 537
LASER TECHNOLOGY, INC., *pg.* 1419, *pg.* 314
LIND ELECTRONICS, INC., *pg.* 1355, *pg.* 938
LITTLEFORD DAY INC., *pg.* 1356, *pg.* 728
LOCHINVAR CORPORATION, *pg.* 1073, *pg.* 1640
LUNDELL ENTERPRISES, INC., *pg.* 706, *pg.* 703
LYMAN PRODUCTS CORPORATION, *pg.* 1839, *pg.* 356
LYNCH TECHNOLOGIES, INC., *pg.* 1357, *pg.* 526
MANITEX INTERNATIONAL, INC., *pg.* 1358, *pg.* 559
MASTER APPLIANCE CORP., *pg.* 1055, *pg.* 1888
MATEC INSTRUMENT COMPANIES, INC., *pg.* 1421, *pg.* 839
MAXXESS SYSTEMS, INC., *pg.* 431, *pg.* 43
MCDONOUGH MANUFACTURING COMPANY, *pg.* 1360, *pg.* 1857
MCNEIL & NRM INC., *pg.* 1360, *pg.* 1402
MERROW MACHINE COMPANY, *pg.* 58, *pg.* 819
MICROFLUIDICS INTERNATIONAL CORPORATION, *pg.* 58, *pg.* 836
THE MIDDLEBY CORPORATION, *pg.* 1361, *pg.* 610
MIETHER BEARING PRODUCTS, INC., *pg.* 1361, *pg.* 1728
MILACRON LLC, *pg.* 1361, *pg.* 1405
MINE SAFETY APPLIANCES COMPANY, *pg.* 1361, *pg.* 1525
MINUTEMAN INTERNATIONAL, INC., *pg.* 332, *pg.* 652
MODERN EQUIPMENT COMPANY, *pg.* 1363, *pg.* 1887
MOOG INC., *pg.* 231, *pg.* 1156
MOREHOUSE-COWLES, *pg.* 1363, *pg.* 66
MORSE WATCHMANS INC., *pg.* 656, *pg.* 368
MULTIMEDIA GAMES INC., *pg.* 442, *pg.* 1664
NABCO ENTRANCES, INC., *pg.* 99, *pg.* 1882
NANOMETRICS INCORPORATED, *pg.* 1423, *pg.* 147
NATURAL DECORATIONS, INC., *pg.* 936, *pg.* 5
NEW WAVE RESEARCH INCORPORATED, *pg.* 1423, *pg.* 91
NEWPORT CORPORATION, *pg.* 1424, *pg.* 114
NILFISK-ADVANCE, INC., *pg.* 332, *pg.* 953
NOBLES MANUFACTURING, INC., *pg.* 59, *pg.* 1890
NORDSON CORPORATION, *pg.* 1365, *pg.* 1480
NSS ENTERPRISES, INC., *pg.* 59, *pg.* 1476
OIL-DRI CORPORATION OF AMERICA, *pg.* 1480, *pg.* 586
ON SEMICONDUCTOR CORPORATION, *pg.* 101, *pg.* 18
OSBORN INTERNATIONAL, *pg.* 1367, *pg.* 1406
OTTERBOX PRODUCTS LLC, *pg.* 451, *pg.* 329
P&F INDUSTRIES, INC., *pg.* 1075, *pg.* 1182
PARKER HANNIFIN CORPORATION, *pg.* 1368, *pg.* 1434
PERCEPTICS, LLC, *pg.* 1426, *pg.* 1637
PERCEPTRON, INC., *pg.* 215, *pg.* 904
PERRY PRODUCTS CORPORATION, *pg.* 1368, *pg.* 1072
PLANET PRODUCTS CORPORATION, *pg.* 1369, *pg.* 1418
PMFG, INC., *pg.* 1369, *pg.* 1685
PROCESS CONTROL CORPORATION, *pg.* 1370, *pg.* 518
PROPHOTONIX LIMITED, *pg.* 1427, *pg.* 1039
PULLMAN-HOLT CORPORATION, *pg.* 333, *pg.* 475
RAUCH INDUSTRIES, INC., *pg.* 940, *pg.* 1373
REPLOGLE GLOBES, INC., *pg.* 461, *pg.* 559
ROCKWELL AUTOMATION, INC., *pg.* 668, *pg.* 1880
ROFIN-SINAR TECHNOLOGIES, INC., *pg.* 668, *pg.* 904
ROTARY LIFT, *pg.* 216, *pg.* 694
RUG DOCTOR, LP, *pg.* 1373, *pg.* 1734
S. HOWES, INC., *pg.* 1373, *pg.* 1342
S.A. ARMSTRONG LIMITED, *pg.* 1373, *pg.* 1934
THE SALVAJOR COMPANY, *pg.* 60, *pg.* 986
SANISERV, *pg.* 1373, *pg.* 695
SCANTRON CORPORATION, *pg.* 467, *pg.* 922
SCHNEIDER CANADA, INC., *pg.* 1374, *pg.* 1928
SCHNEIDER ELECTRIC, *pg.* 467, *pg.* 1609
SCOTT'S LIQUID GOLD-INC., *pg.* 335, *pg.* 323
SEALY CORPORATION, *pg.* 942, *pg.* 1391
SELAS HEAT TECHNOLOGY COMPANY LLC, *pg.* 1076, *pg.* 1553
SHOP-VAC CORPORATION, *pg.* 1375, *pg.* 1595
SILICON GRAPHICS INTERNATIONAL CORP, *pg.* 470, *pg.* 148
SIMPSON TECHNOLOGIES CORPORATION, *pg.* 111, *pg.* 555
SINGER SEWING COMPANY, *pg.* 698, *pg.* 1639
SL INDUSTRIES, INC., *pg.* 674, *pg.* 1090
SPEEDLINE TECHNOLOGIES, INC., *pg.* 1378, *pg.* 823
THE SPENCER TURBINE CO., *pg.* 1378, *pg.* 386
SPP PROCESS TECHNOLOGY SYSTEMS LIMITED-THERMAL DIVISION, *pg.* 472, *pg.* 250
ST. JUDE MEDICAL, INC., *pg.* 1596, *pg.* 963
STURTEVANT INC., *pg.* 1379, *pg.* 824
SUREFIRE, LLC, *pg.* 1307, *pg.* 90
SWECO, *pg.* 1380, *pg.* 728
TDK-LAMBDA HIGH POWER DIVISION, *pg.* 1380, *pg.* 1090
TECHNIBUS LLC, *pg.* 1380, *pg.* 1408
TECHNIC INCORPORATED, *pg.* 1183, *pg.* 1601
TELEDYNE BENTHOS, INC., *pg.* 1431, *pg.* 838
TENNANT COMPANY, *pg.* 1381, *pg.* 944
THOMAS ENGINEERING INC., *pg.* 1382, *pg.* 619
TOPPAN PHOTOMASKS, INC., *pg.* 1432, *pg.* 1739
TORNADO INDUSTRIES, INC., *pg.* 1383, *pg.* 591
TRANS-LUX CORPORATION, *pg.* 681, *pg.* 365
TRANTER PHE, INC., *pg.* 1383, *pg.* 1749
TRIO-TECH INTERNATIONAL, *pg.* 1384, *pg.* 300
TURBOCHEF TECHNOLOGIES, INC., *pg.* 902, *pg.* 1670
ULTRATECH, INC., *pg.* 1433, *pg.* 251
UNIVERSAL INSTRUMENTS CORPORATION, *pg.* 683, *pg.* 1154
U.S. AXLE, INC., *pg.* 221, *pg.* 1582
VICTORY REFRIGERATION COMPANY LLC, *pg.* 61, *pg.* 1051
VIDAL SASSOON CO., *pg.* 524, *pg.* 1426
VILTER MANUFACTURING LLC, *pg.* 1078, *pg.* 1856
VISHAY INTERTECHNOLOGY, INC., *pg.* 1435, *pg.* 1551
WAHL CLIPPER CORPORATION, *pg.* 524, *pg.* 662
WAKEFIELD-VETTE, *pg.* 119, *pg.* 1038
WELLCO ENTERPRISES, INC., *pg.* 1822, *pg.* 1392
WEYERHAEUSER COMPANY LIMITED, *pg.* 121, *pg.* 1913
WHITING CORPORATION, *pg.* 1389, *pg.* 633
THE WILL-BURT CO., INC., *pg.* 1437, *pg.* 1469
WMS INDUSTRIES INC., *pg.* 593, *pg.* 666
THE WOODSTREAM CORPORATION, *pg.* 1801, *pg.* 1549
WOODWARD, INC., *pg.* 122, *pg.* 329
WYSSMONT CO., INC., *pg.* 1390, *pg.* 1068
THE YANKEE CANDLE COMPANY, INC., *pg.* 1792, *pg.* 843

3592 - Carburetors, Pistons, Piston Rings & Valves

DANFOSS POWER SOLUTIONS COMPANY, *pg.* 1328, *pg.* 701
FEDERAL-MOGUL HOLDINGS CORPORATION, *pg.* 205, *pg.* 907
HASTINGS MANUFACTURING COMPANY, LLC, *pg.* 207, *pg.* 891
ZENITH FUEL SYSTEMS LLC, *pg.* 222, *pg.* 1776

3593 - Fluid Power Cylinders &

Actuators

BIMBA MANUFACTURING COMPANY, *pg.* 1317, *pg.* 633
CASCADE CORPORATION, *pg.* 1321, *pg.* 1497
DE-STA-CO INDUSTRIES, *pg.* 1045, *pg.* 867
FLUIDIGM CORPORATION, *pg.* 1413, *pg.* 279
IDEX CORPORATION, *pg.* 1347, *pg.* 623
INDIAN HEAD INDUSTRIES, INC., *pg.* 208, *pg.* 1367
PARKER HANNIFIN CORPORATION, *pg.* 1368, *pg.* 1434
QUANTUM FUEL SYSTEMS TECHNOLOGIES WORLDWIDE, INC., *pg.* 1371, *pg.* 115
SERVOTRONICS, INC., *pg.* 1375, *pg.* 1157
SONO-TEK CORPORATION, *pg.* 112, *pg.* 1182
WEBER-HYDRAULIK, *pg.* 1388, *pg.* 524

3594 - Fluid Power Pumps & Motors

BOSCH REXROTH CORPORATION, *pg.* 1319, *pg.* 1516
COLFAX CORPORATION, *pg.* 1324, *pg.* 770
CRANE CO., *pg.* 227, *pg.* 373
DANFOSS POWER SOLUTIONS COMPANY, *pg.* 1328, *pg.* 701
ENERGY RECOVERY, INC., *pg.* 1334, *pg.* 252
FEDERAL SIGNAL CORPORATION, *pg.* 638, *pg.* 645
THE GORMAN-RUPP COMPANY, *pg.* 1341, *pg.* 1458
GRACO, INC., *pg.* 1342, *pg.* 935
HARPER INDUSTRIES, INC., *pg.* 704, *pg.* 715
IDEX CORPORATION, *pg.* 1347, *pg.* 623
LINDE HYDRAULICS CORPORATION, *pg.* 1356, *pg.* 1407
NLB CORP., *pg.* 1365, *pg.* 913
PARKER HANNIFIN CORPORATION, *pg.* 1368, *pg.* 1434
SERVOTRONICS, INC., *pg.* 1375, *pg.* 1157
TECUMSEH PRODUCTS COMPANY, *pg.* 1381, *pg.* 866
YOUNG & FRANKLIN, INC., *pg.* 1391, *pg.* 1174

3596 - Scales & Balances, Except Laboratory

AVERY WEIGH-TRONIX, INC., *pg.* 1315, *pg.* 925
DETECTO SCALE COMPANY, *pg.* 1045, *pg.* 1007
EMERY WINSLOW SCALE COMPANY, *pg.* 1411, *pg.* 369
HYER INDUSTRIES INC., *pg.* 1051, *pg.* 841
MEASUREMENT SPECIALTIES INC., *pg.* 1360, *pg.* 1783
METTLER-TOLEDO INC., *pg.* 1056, *pg.* 1441
PENNSYLVANIA SCALE COMPANY, *pg.* 1059, *pg.* 1546
STAPLES, INC., *pg.* 474, *pg.* 821

3599 - Industrial & Commercial Machinery & Equipment, NEC

AMERICAN AXLE & MANUFACTURING HOLDINGS, INC., *pg.* 198, *pg.* 879
ATEK, *pg.* 620, *pg.* 919
AUTOSWAGE PRODUCTS, INC., *pg.* 200, *pg.* 369
BLOOM MANUFACTURING, INC., *pg.* 701, *pg.* 708
ELLWOOD NATIONAL FORGE COMPANY, LLC, *pg.* 1333, *pg.* 1542
THE FLINCHBAUGH CO., INC., *pg.* 82, *pg.* 1551
HELMICK CORPORATION, *pg.* 1346, *pg.* 1849
KEMPSMITH MACHINE COMPANY, *pg.* 1352, *pg.* 1876
MIETHER BEARING PRODUCTS, INC., *pg.* 1361, *pg.* 1728
PLANET PRODUCTS CORPORATION, *pg.* 1369, *pg.* 1418
U.S. AXLE, INC., *pg.* 221, *pg.* 1582
THE WILL-BURT CO., INC., *pg.* 1437, *pg.* 1469

3612 - Power, Distribution & Specialty Transformers

ABB INC., *pg.* 1309, *pg.* 1359
ABB INC., *pg.* 64, *pg.* 1959
BADGER MAGNETICS INC., *pg.* 623, *pg.* 927
BASLER ELECTRIC COMPANY, *pg.* 623, *pg.* 616
BEACON POWER, LLC, *pg.* 1936, *pg.* 848
BRANSON ULTRASONICS CORPORATION, *pg.* 1319, *pg.* 342
BRANSON ULTRASONICS CORPORATION - PLASTICS JOINING DIVISION, *pg.* 1403, *pg.* 343
BRANSON ULTRASONICS CORPORATION-PRECISION CLEANING DIV, *pg.* 1319, *pg.* 343
C&D TECHNOLOGIES, INC., *pg.* 627, *pg.* 1517
CARMANAH TECHNOLOGIES CORPORATION, *pg.* 628, *pg.* 1913
CLORE AUTOMOTIVE LLC, *pg.* 202, *pg.* 716
DYNAPOWER CORPORATION, *pg.* 1330, *pg.* 1768
ELECTRON BEAM TECHNOLOGIES, INC., *pg.* 1046, *pg.* 621
ENTECH SOLAR, INC., *pg.* 1335, *pg.* 1694
ESAB WELDING & CUTTING PRODUCTS, *pg.* 1335, *pg.* 1615
GENERAC HOLDINGS INC., *pg.* 1340, *pg.* 1897
THE GEORGE E. FAILING COMPANY, *pg.* 1340, *pg.* 1484
THE HARRIS PRODUCTS GROUP, *pg.* 1345, *pg.* 533
HOBART BROTHERS COMPANY, *pg.* 1346, *pg.* 1477
IMPULSE NC LLC, *pg.* 1051, *pg.* 1385
LINCOLN ELECTRIC HOLDINGS, INC., *pg.* 1355, *pg.* 1432
LITTELFUSE, INC., *pg.* 1301, *pg.* 580
MARSH BELLOFRAM CORPORATION, *pg.* 1885, *pg.* 1850
MILLER ELECTRIC MANUFACTURING CO., *pg.* 1361, *pg.* 1852
MKS INSTRUMENTS, INC., *pg.* 1362, *pg.* 781
NIAGARA TRANSFORMER CORP., *pg.* 1302, *pg.* 1150
OHMITE MANUFACTURING COMPANY, *pg.* 660, *pg.* 553
PREMIER POWER RENEWABLE ENERGY, INC., *pg.* 1075, *pg.* 78
SIEMENS CORPORATION, *pg.* 803, *pg.* 1291
SL INDUSTRIES, INC., *pg.* 674, *pg.* 1090
SOLAR POWER, INC., *pg.* 675, *pg.* 195
THERMON AMERICAS INC., *pg.* 1077, *pg.* 1744
TII NETWORK TECHNOLOGIES, INC., *pg.* 680, *pg.* 1157
UNIVERSAL LIGHTING TECHNOLOGIES, *pg.* 1307, *pg.* 1655
UQM TECHNOLOGIES, INC., *pg.* 684, *pg.* 334
WAUKESHA ELECTRIC SYSTEMS, *pg.* 687, *pg.* 1898

3613 - Switchgear & Switchboard Apparatus

ABB INC., *pg.* 1309, *pg.* 1359
AJAX ELECTRIC CO., *pg.* 1068, *pg.* 1541
ASCO VALVE CANADA, *pg.* 619, *pg.* 1919
BEL FUSE INC., *pg.* 624, *pg.* 1075
COLE HERSEE COMPANY, *pg.* 202, *pg.* 792
COOPER WIRING DEVICES, *pg.* 1295, *pg.* 538
CTS CORPORATION, *pg.* 631, *pg.* 677
EATON BUSSMANN, INC., *pg.* 1331, *pg.* 977
EMERSON NETWORK POWER LIEBERT, *pg.* 1071, *pg.* 1439
ERGON, INC., *pg.* 976, *pg.* 969
G&W ELECTRIC COMPANY, *pg.* 1338, *pg.* 558
HONEYWELL SENSING & CONTROL, *pg.* 229, *pg.* 926
JEWELL INSTRUMENTS, LLC, *pg.* 1418, *pg.* 1036
LEVITON MANUFACTURING COMPANY, INC., *pg.* 1301, *pg.* 1180
LITTELFUSE, INC., *pg.* 1301, *pg.* 580
MECHANICAL PRODUCTS INC., *pg.* 1302, *pg.* 894
MERSEN, *pg.* 1302, *pg.* 836
NUMEREX CORP., *pg.* 660, *pg.* 517
S&C ELECTRIC COMPANY, *pg.* 1305, *pg.* 589
SCHNEIDER ELECTRIC USA, INC., *pg.* 1306, *pg.* 650
SIEMENS PROCESS INDUSTRIES AND DRIVES, *pg.* 673, *pg.* 485
TEXAS INSTRUMENTS INCORPORATED, *pg.* 679, *pg.* 1688
TII NETWORK TECHNOLOGIES, INC., *pg.* 680, *pg.* 1157
TRICO MFG. CORP., *pg.* 219, *pg.* 1886

3621 - Motors & Generators

AEROFLEX INCORPORATED, *pg.* 614, *pg.* 1321
ALLIED MOTION TECHNOLOGIES INC., *pg.* 616, *pg.* 1137
AMETEK FLOORCARE SPECIALTY MOTORS DIVISION, *pg.* 616, *pg.* 1456
BALDOR ELECTRIC COMPANY, *pg.* 1316, *pg.* 32
BODINE ELECTRIC COMPANY, *pg.* 1318, *pg.* 641
CARTER MOTOR COMPANY, *pg.* 1321, *pg.* 665
CUMMINS INC., *pg.* 1326, *pg.* 676
CUMMINS POWER GENERATION, *pg.* 1326, *pg.* 932
DUMORE CORPORATION, *pg.* 1330, *pg.* 1869
EATON CORPORATION - INDUSTRIAL CONTROLS, *pg.* 1296, *pg.* 1874
ELECTROCRAFT, INC, *pg.* 1333, *pg.* 1033
ELECTROID CO, *pg.* 1333, *pg.* 1123
FRANKLIN ELECTRIC CO., INC., *pg.* 1337, *pg.* 680
GENERAC HOLDINGS INC., *pg.* 1340, *pg.* 1897
GENERAC POWER SYSTEMS INC., *pg.* 1340, *pg.* 1898
GENERAL ELECTRIC COMPANY, *pg.* 1297, *pg.* 347
HBD INDUSTRIES, INC., *pg.* 207, *pg.* 1449
IN-SINK-ERATOR, *pg.* 57, *pg.* 1888
KIRKWOOD HOLDING, INC., *pg.* 649, *pg.* 1469
LENNOX INTERNATIONAL INC., *pg.* 1073, *pg.* 1736
MOLE-RICHARDSON CO., *pg.* 1302, *pg.* 103
PENN ENGINEERING & MANUFACTURING CORP., *pg.* 1059, *pg.* 1525
REGAL BELOIT CORPORATION, *pg.* 106, *pg.* 1854
REULAND ELECTRIC COMPANY, *pg.* 1304, *pg.* 68
SAG HARBOR INDUSTRIES, *pg.* 1305, *pg.* 1340
SIEMENS PROCESS INDUSTRIES AND DRIVES, *pg.* 673, *pg.* 485
SPX CORPORATION, *pg.* 218, *pg.* 1369
TOLEDO COMMUTATOR CO., *pg.* 1383, *pg.* 903
UQM TECHNOLOGIES, INC., *pg.* 684, *pg.* 334
WESTERBEKE CORPORATION, *pg.* 1388, *pg.* 847
ZAP, *pg.* 222, *pg.* 277

3624 - Carbon & Graphite Products

ALDILA, INC., *pg.* 1825, *pg.* 185
GRAPHITE METALLIZING CORPORATION, *pg.* 1343, *pg.* 1356
HELWIG CARBON PRODUCTS, INC., *pg.* 1346, *pg.* 1875
ZOLTEK COMPANIES, INC., *pg.* 123, *pg.* 974

3625 - Relays & Industrial Controls

ADAMS RITE AEROSPACE INC., *pg.* 1041, *pg.* 93
ALLIED MOTION TECHNOLOGIES INC., *pg.* 616, *pg.* 1137
ALTAIR CORPORATION, *pg.* 1312, *pg.* 910
ALTRIA INDUSTRIAL MOTION CORP., *pg.* 1312, *pg.* 802
AMATOM ELECTRONIC HARDWARE, INC., *pg.* 1041, *pg.* 342
AUTOMATION DEVICES, INC., *pg.* 1315, *pg.* 1532
BADGER MAGNETICS INC., *pg.* 623, *pg.* 927
BALDOR ELECTRIC COMPANY, *pg.* 1316, *pg.* 32
BODINE ELECTRIC COMPANY, *pg.* 1318, *pg.* 641
THE CARLYLE JOHNSON MACHINE COMPANY, L.L.C., *pg.* 1321, *pg.* 339
CONBRACO INDUSTRIES INC., *pg.* 1325, *pg.* 1382
CONTROL CHIEF HOLDINGS, INC., *pg.* 630, *pg.* 1518
CORBY INDUSTRIES, INC., *pg.* 380, *pg.* 1513
CORLEY MANUFACTURING CO., *pg.* 1326, *pg.* 1628
D&S CAR WASH EQUIPMENT CO., *pg.* 1327, *pg.* 979
DANAHER CORPORATION, *pg.* 1044, *pg.* 397
DANFOSS GRAHAM, *pg.* 203, *pg.* 1874
DEVAR, INC., *pg.* 633, *pg.* 339
DUFF-NORTON, *pg.* 204, *pg.* 1365
EATON CORPORATION, *pg.* 1331, *pg.* 1429
EATON HYDRAULICS INC., *pg.* 1332, *pg.* 922
EMERSON WHITE-RODGERS, *pg.* 1071, *pg.* 996
FLIGHT SYSTEMS, INC., *pg.* 1337, *pg.* 1548
GUARDIAN ELECTRIC MANUFACTURING COMPANY, *pg.* 641, *pg.* 672
INTERNATIONAL CONTROLS & MEASUREMENTS CORP., *pg.* 1350, *pg.* 1317
ITERIS, INC., *pg.* 293, *pg.* 261
ITT CORPORATION, *pg.* 1351, *pg.* 1354
LA MARCHE MANUFACTURING COMPANY, *pg.* 1300, *pg.* 606
LITTELFUSE, INC., *pg.* 1301, *pg.* 580
MOOG FLO-TORK, *pg.* 1363, *pg.* 1469
MOTORCAR PARTS OF AMERICA, INC., *pg.* 213, *pg.* 295
OHMITE MANUFACTURING COMPANY, *pg.* 660, *pg.* 553
P/A INDUSTRIES, INC., *pg.* 1367, *pg.* 339
PANASONIC ELECTRIC WORKS CORPORATION OF AMERICA, *pg.* 661, *pg.* 1095
RETZLAFF INCORPORATED, *pg.* 667, *pg.* 258
ROCKWELL AUTOMATION, INC., *pg.* 668, *pg.* 1880
SOR, INC., *pg.* 1306, *pg.* 716
SOUTHWESTERN INDUSTRIES, INC., *pg.* 1429, *pg.* 69
TRANSICO INCORPORATED, *pg.* 682, *pg.* 49
TUFFALOY PRODUCTS, INC., *pg.* 1385, *pg.* 1619
UNIVERSAL ELECTRONICS, INC., *pg.* 683, *pg.* 262
VALCOR ENGINEERING CORPORATION, *pg.* 1386, *pg.* 1123
WARD LEONARD ELECTRIC COMPANY, INC., *pg.* 687, *pg.* 380
WOODWARD HRT, *pg.* 236, *pg.* 270

3631 - Household Cooking

Equipment

BARBEQUES GALORE, INC., *pg.* 51, *pg.* 173
BSH HOME APPLIANCES CORPORATION, *pg.* 53, *pg.* 108
DACOR, *pg.* 54, *pg.* 67
GE CONSUMER & INDUSTRIAL, *pg.* 55, *pg.* 733
HOBART FOOD EQUIPMENT GROUP CANADA, *pg.* 56, *pg.* 1929
JARDEN CONSUMER SOLUTIONS, *pg.* 57, *pg.* 412
JARDEN CORPORATION, *pg.* 1885, *pg.* 412
MACANDREWS & FORBES HOLDINGS INC., *pg.* 777, *pg.* 1254
NEWELL RUBBERMAID INC., *pg.* 1128, *pg.* 515
TOSHIBA AMERICA, INC., *pg.* 681, *pg.* 1302
TURBOCHEF TECHNOLOGIES, INC., *pg.* 902, *pg.* 1670
VIKING RANGE CORPORATION, *pg.* 61, *pg.* 968
VITA-MIX CORPORATION, *pg.* 1139, *pg.* 1436
W.C. BRADLEY CO., *pg.* 62, *pg.* 528
WEBER-STEPHEN PRODUCTS LLC, *pg.* 62, *pg.* 650

3632 - Household Refrigerators & Home & Farm Freezers

GE CONSUMER & INDUSTRIAL, *pg.* 55, *pg.* 733
SUB ZERO WOLF, *pg.* 60, *pg.* 1867
THETFORD CORPORATION, *pg.* 337, *pg.* 867

3633 - Household Laundry Equipment

ALLIANCE LAUNDRY HOLDINGS LLC, *pg.* 51, *pg.* 1890
WHIRLPOOL CORPORATION, *pg.* 62, *pg.* 872

3634 - Electric Housewares & Fans

BROAN-NUTONE LLC, *pg.* 1069, *pg.* 1860
CONAIR CORPORATION, *pg.* 505, *pg.* 1055
DIMPLEX NORTH AMERICA LIMITED, *pg.* 54, *pg.* 1920
HAMILTON BEACH BRANDS, INC., *pg.* 56, *pg.* 1783
HELEN OF TROY L.P., *pg.* 511, *pg.* 1692
HUBBELL LIGHTING - PROGRESS LIGHTING DIVISION, *pg.* 1300, *pg.* 1617
HUMAN TOUCH, *pg.* 928, *pg.* 123
HUNTER FAN COMPANY, *pg.* 57, *pg.* 1631
INSTANTRON CO., INC., *pg.* 512, *pg.* 1608
JARDEN CORPORATION, *pg.* 1885, *pg.* 412
KAZ, INC., *pg.* 58, *pg.* 844
MELITTA USA INC., *pg.* 781, *pg.* 416
MELNOR, INC., *pg.* 1055, *pg.* 1811
NACCO INDUSTRIES, INC., *pg.* 1174, *pg.* 1433
NATIONAL PRESTO INDUSTRIES, INC, *pg.* 1128, *pg.* 1857
PHILIPS LIGHTING, *pg.* 1303, *pg.* 806
REGAL WARE, INC., *pg.* 1137, *pg.* 1862
VAPOR CORP., *pg.* 61, *pg.* 427
WAHL CLIPPER CORPORATION, *pg.* 524, *pg.* 662
WHIRLPOOL CORPORATION, *pg.* 62, *pg.* 872

3635 - Household Vacuum Cleaners

AERUS LLC, *pg.* 51, *pg.* 1673
BISSELL HOMECARE, INC., *pg.* 52, *pg.* 887
THE GENIE COMPANY, *pg.* 55, *pg.* 1403
HMI INDUSTRIES INC., *pg.* 56, *pg.* 1475
IROBOT CORP., *pg.* 1418, *pg.* 785
MACANDREWS & FORBES HOLDINGS INC., *pg.* 777, *pg.* 1254
ORECK CORPORATION, *pg.* 59, *pg.* 1653
STANLEY STEEMER INTERNATIONAL, INC., *pg.* 944, *pg.* 1450

3639 - Household Appliances, NEC

ANAHEIM MANUFACTURING COMPANY, *pg.* 51, *pg.* 48
ELECTROLUX HOME PRODUCTS NORTH AMERICA, *pg.* 54, *pg.* 1366
GE CANADA COMPANY, *pg.* 1296, *pg.* 1926
GE CONSUMER & INDUSTRIAL, *pg.* 55, *pg.* 733
GENERAL ELECTRIC COMPANY, *pg.* 1297, *pg.* 347
HOBART FOOD EQUIPMENT GROUP CANADA, *pg.* 56, *pg.* 1929
HUMAN TOUCH, *pg.* 928, *pg.* 123
IN-SINK-ERATOR, *pg.* 57, *pg.* 1888
JARDEN CORPORATION, *pg.* 1885, *pg.* 412
LOCHINVAR CORPORATION, *pg.* 1073, *pg.* 1640
NORTEK, INC., *pg.* 100, *pg.* 1607
SPECTRUM BRANDS HOLDINGS, INC., *pg.* 60, *pg.* 1867
TTI FLOOR CARE NORTH AMERICA, *pg.* 61, *pg.* 1473
WARING PRODUCTS, INC., *pg.* 62, *pg.* 379

3641 - Electric Lamp Bulbs & Tubes

ENERGY FOCUS, INC., *pg.* 1411, *pg.* 1472
GENERAL ELECTRIC COMPANY, *pg.* 1297, *pg.* 347
MAGELLAN HEALTH SERVICES, INC., *pg.* 1557, *pg.* 337
OSRAM SYLVANIA, INC., *pg.* 1302, *pg.* 816
PHILIPS LIGHTING, *pg.* 1303, *pg.* 806
ROYAL HAEGER LAMP COMPANY, *pg.* 1305, *pg.* 631
XENONICS HOLDINGS, INC., *pg.* 1308, *pg.* 62

3643 - Current-Carrying Wiring Devices

AESP, INC., *pg.* 345, *pg.* 439
ALLIED MOTION TECHNOLOGIES INC., *pg.* 616, *pg.* 1137
AMPHENOL CORPORATION, *pg.* 616, *pg.* 381
BOMAR INTERCONNECT PRODUCTS, INC., *pg.* 1318, *pg.* 1079
CARLISLE INTERCONNECT TECHNOLOGIES, *pg.* 1294, *pg.* 461
COLE HERSEE COMPANY, *pg.* 202, *pg.* 792
CONTROL PRODUCTS, INC., *pg.* 1407, *pg.* 1054
COOPER WIRING DEVICES, *pg.* 1295, *pg.* 538
EMERSON INDUSTRIAL AUTOMATION, *pg.* 1296, *pg.* 657
G&W ELECTRIC COMPANY, *pg.* 1338, *pg.* 558
HARRIS HOLDINGS INC., *pg.* 1345, *pg.* 541
HUBBELL INCORPORATED, *pg.* 1299, *pg.* 370
IDEAL INDUSTRIES, INC., *pg.* 1051, *pg.* 662
LUNA INNOVATIONS INC., *pg.* 1557, *pg.* 1806
PANDUIT CORP., *pg.* 661, *pg.* 663
PASS & SEYMOUR/LEGRAND, *pg.* 1303, *pg.* 1344
REGAL POWER TRANSMISSION SOLUTIONS, *pg.* 216, *pg.* 698
RF INDUSTRIES, LTD., *pg.* 461, *pg.* 208
S&C ELECTRIC COMPANY, *pg.* 1305, *pg.* 589
SCHNEIDER ELECTRIC USA, INC., *pg.* 1306, *pg.* 650
SENSOR SYSTEMS, LLC, *pg.* 672, *pg.* 464
SL INDUSTRIES, INC., *pg.* 674, *pg.* 1090
TE CONNECTIVITY LTD., *pg.* 677, *pg.* 1515
THERMON AMERICAS INC., *pg.* 1077, *pg.* 1744
THOMAS & BETTS CORPORATION, *pg.* 680, *pg.* 1646
WHITNEY BLAKE CO., INC., *pg.* 1308, *pg.* 1764
WIREMOLD/LEGRAND, *pg.* 689, *pg.* 383

3644 - Noncurrent-Carrying Wiring Devices

CHASE CORPORATION, *pg.* 1152, *pg.* 803
EMERSON INDUSTRIAL AUTOMATION, *pg.* 1296, *pg.* 657
HONEYWELL SENSING & CONTROL, *pg.* 229, *pg.* 926
HUBBELL INCORPORATED, *pg.* 1299, *pg.* 370
IDI COMPOSITES INTERNATIONAL, *pg.* 57, *pg.* 696
KILLARK ELECTRIC, *pg.* 1300, *pg.* 998
LAPP INSULATOR COMPANY, LLC, *pg.* 1946, *pg.* 1173
MULBERRY METAL PRODUCTS, INC., *pg.* 1302, *pg.* 1127
O'BRIEN CORPORATION, *pg.* 1366, *pg.* 1001
PANDUIT CORP., *pg.* 661, *pg.* 663
PREFORMED LINE PRODUCTS COMPANY, *pg.* 1370, *pg.* 1434
SHERMAN & REILLY, INC., *pg.* 1062, *pg.* 1629
WIREMOLD/LEGRAND, *pg.* 689, *pg.* 383

3645 - Residential Electric Lighting Fixtures

ACUITY BRANDS, INC., *pg.* 1294, *pg.* 487
AMERICAN PERIOD LIGHTING, INC., *pg.* 1294, *pg.* 1545
ENERGY FOCUS, INC., *pg.* 1411, *pg.* 1472
JUNO LIGHTING, INC., *pg.* 1300, *pg.* 606
LIGHTOLIER, *pg.* 1301, *pg.* 819
PHILIPS LIGHTING, *pg.* 1303, *pg.* 806
PRESCOLITE INC., *pg.* 1304, *pg.* 1622
QUOIZEL INC., *pg.* 1304, *pg.* 1616
ROYAL HAEGER LAMP COMPANY, *pg.* 1305, *pg.* 631
SCHNEIDER ELECTRIC USA, INC., *pg.* 1306, *pg.* 650
SWIVELIER CO., INC., *pg.* 1307, *pg.* 1142
THE TORO COMPANY, *pg.* 1065, *pg.* 918
WESTINGHOUSE LIGHTING CORPORATION, *pg.* 687, *pg.* 1571

3646 - Commercial, Industrial & Institutional Electric Lighting Fixtures

ACUITY BRANDS, INC., *pg.* 1294, *pg.* 487
AMERICAN LOUVER COMPANY, *pg.* 1294, *pg.* 660
AMERICAN PERIOD LIGHTING, INC., *pg.* 1294, *pg.* 1545
CIRCA LIGHTING, INC., *pg.* 1295, *pg.* 539
CRAFTMADE INTERNATIONAL, INC., *pg.* 1295, *pg.* 1670
CREE INC., *pg.* 1295, *pg.* 1888
CRESCENT/STONCO SUPPLY DIVISION, *pg.* 1295, *pg.* 1121
CYALUME TECHNOLOGIES HOLDINGS, INC., *pg.* 1295, *pg.* 856
DAZOR MANUFACTURING CORP., *pg.* 1296, *pg.* 995
ELECTRONIC THEATRE CONTROLS, INC., *pg.* 1296, *pg.* 1872
FEDERAL SIGNAL CORPORATION, *pg.* 638, *pg.* 645
GE CONSUMER & INDUSTRIAL, *pg.* 55, *pg.* 733
H.E. WILLIAMS, INC., *pg.* 1299, *pg.* 974
HINKLEY LIGHTING INC., *pg.* 1299, *pg.* 1404
JOHNSON CONTROLS, INC., *pg.* 209, *pg.* 1876
JUNO LIGHTING GROUP, *pg.* 648, *pg.* 679
LITECONTROL CORPORATION, *pg.* 1301, *pg.* 841
LSI INDUSTRIES INC., *pg.* 58, *pg.* 1416
OTTLITE, *pg.* 1303, *pg.* 475
PHILIPS LIGHTING, *pg.* 1303, *pg.* 806
PHILIPS SOLID-STATE LIGHTING SOLUTIONS, *pg.* 1303, *pg.* 806
PHOENIX PRODUCTS COMPANY, *pg.* 1304, *pg.* 1879
REVOLUTION LIGHTING TECHNOLOGIES, INC., *pg.* 1304, *pg.* 377
SCHNEIDER ELECTRIC USA, INC., *pg.* 1306, *pg.* 650
SWIVELIER CO., INC., *pg.* 1307, *pg.* 1142

3647 - Vehicular Lighting Equipment

FEDERAL SIGNAL CORPORATION, *pg.* 638, *pg.* 645
GROTE INDUSTRIES, INC., *pg.* 206, *pg.* 693
OSRAM SYLVANIA, INC., *pg.* 1302, *pg.* 816
PROGRESSIVE DYNAMICS, INC., *pg.* 665, *pg.* 898
UNITY MANUFACTURING COMPANY, *pg.* 221, *pg.* 594

3648 - Lighting Equipment, NEC

ACR ELECTRONICS, INC., *pg.* 612, *pg.* 422
ACUITY BRANDS, INC., *pg.* 1294, *pg.* 487
THE ADT CORPORATION, *pg.* 612, *pg.* 409
ADVANCED ENERGY INDUSTRIES, INC., *pg.* 613, *pg.* 328
BAE SYSTEMS PRODUCTS GROUP, *pg.* 359, *pg.* 432
BALLANTYNE STRONG, INC., *pg.* 623, *pg.* 1013
BALLARD POWER SYSTEMS, INC., *pg.* 70, *pg.* 1907
BIG BEAM EMERGENCY SYSTEMS, INC., *pg.* 1294, *pg.* 598
BLONDER TONGUE LABORATORIES, INC., *pg.* 625, *pg.* 1100
BRADY CORPORATION, *pg.* 363, *pg.* 1873
BRANSON ULTRASONICS CORPORATION, *pg.* 1319, *pg.* 342
BRANSON ULTRASONICS CORPORATION-PRECISION CLEANING DIV, *pg.* 1319, *pg.* 343
BROAN-NUTONE LLC, *pg.* 1069, *pg.* 1860
C&D TECHNOLOGIES, INC., *pg.* 627, *pg.* 1517
CARMANAH TECHNOLOGIES CORPORATION, *pg.* 628, *pg.* 1913
THE CHAMBERLAIN GROUP, INC., *pg.* 75, *pg.* 611
CHASE CORPORATION, *pg.* 1152, *pg.* 803
CHECKPOINT SYSTEMS, INC., *pg.* 628, *pg.* 1559
CLORE AUTOMOTIVE LLC, *pg.* 202, *pg.* 716
CONDUCTIX INC., *pg.* 1295, *pg.* 1015
CTS VALPEY CORPORATION, *pg.* 632, *pg.* 825
CVI MELLES GRIOT, *pg.* 1407, *pg.* 59
CYALUME TECHNOLOGIES HOLDINGS, INC., *pg.* 1295, *pg.* 856

DETEX CORPORATION, *pg.* 633, *pg.* 1728
EATON CORPORATION, *pg.* 1331, *pg.* 1429
EATON'S CROUSE-HINDS, *pg.* 1296, *pg.* 1344
ELECTRONIC THEATRE CONTROLS, INC., *pg.* 1296, *pg.* 1872
ENERGIZER HOLDINGS, INC., *pg.* 637, *pg.* 996
ENERGY FOCUS, INC., *pg.* 1411, *pg.* 1472
FEDERAL SIGNAL CORPORATION, *pg.* 638, *pg.* 645
GE CANADA COMPANY, *pg.* 1296, *pg.* 1926
GE CONSUMER & INDUSTRIAL, *pg.* 55, *pg.* 733
THE GENIE COMPANY, *pg.* 55, *pg.* 1403
GLOBAL EPOINT INC., *pg.* 400, *pg.* 67
GSI GROUP INC., *pg.* 1415, *pg.* 784
HARRIS HOLDINGS INC., *pg.* 1345, *pg.* 541
HIGH END SYSTEMS, INC., *pg.* 1299, *pg.* 1663
HIGHFIELD MANUFACTURING CO., *pg.* 1346, *pg.* 339
HINKLEY LIGHTING INC., *pg.* 1299, *pg.* 1404
HUBBELL INCORPORATED, *pg.* 1299, *pg.* 370
HUBBELL POWER SYSTEMS, INC., *pg.* 643, *pg.* 1614
INTERNATIONAL COMPONENTS CORPORATION, *pg.* 647, *pg.* 669
INVISIBLE FENCE, INC., *pg.* 648, *pg.* 1637
ISOMET CORPORATION, *pg.* 1418, *pg.* 1807
IXIA, *pg.* 422, *pg.* 56
LA MARCHE MANUFACTURING COMPANY, *pg.* 1300, *pg.* 606
LASER TECHNOLOGY, INC., *pg.* 1419, *pg.* 314
LIGHTING SCIENCE GROUP CORPORATION, *pg.* 1301, *pg.* 467
LIGHTOLIER, *pg.* 1301, *pg.* 819
LIND ELECTRONICS, INC., *pg.* 1355, *pg.* 938
LSI INDUSTRIES INC., *pg.* 58, *pg.* 1416
MASTER APPLIANCE CORP., *pg.* 1055, *pg.* 1888
MATEC INSTRUMENT COMPANIES, INC., *pg.* 1421, *pg.* 839
MAXXESS SYSTEMS, INC., *pg.* 431, *pg.* 43
MOLE-RICHARDSON CO., *pg.* 1302, *pg.* 103
MORSE WATCHMANS INC., *pg.* 656, *pg.* 368
NABCO ENTRANCES, INC., *pg.* 99, *pg.* 1882
NEW WAVE RESEARCH INCORPORATED, *pg.* 1423, *pg.* 91
NEWPORT CORPORATION, *pg.* 1424, *pg.* 114
PELICAN PRODUCTS, INC., *pg.* 1842, *pg.* 295
PERCEPTICS, LLC, *pg.* 1426, *pg.* 1637
PHILIPS EMERGENCY LIGHTING, *pg.* 1303, *pg.* 1631
PHILIPS LIGHTING, *pg.* 1303, *pg.* 806
PHILIPS SOLID-STATE LIGHTING SOLUTIONS, *pg.* 1303, *pg.* 806
PROPHOTONIX LIMITED, *pg.* 1427, *pg.* 1039
REJUVENATION INC., *pg.* 1304, *pg.* 1506
REVOLUTION LIGHTING TECHNOLOGIES, INC., *pg.* 1304, *pg.* 377
ROCKWELL AUTOMATION, INC., *pg.* 668, *pg.* 1880
ROFIN SINAR TECHNOLOGIES, INC., *pg.* 668, *pg.* 904
SCHNEIDER CANADA, INC., *pg.* 1374, *pg.* 1928
SCHNEIDER ELECTRIC, *pg.* 467, *pg.* 1609
SILICON GRAPHICS INTERNATIONAL CORP, *pg.* 470, *pg.* 148
SL INDUSTRIES, INC., *pg.* 674, *pg.* 1090
STREAMLIGHT INC., *pg.* 1306, *pg.* 1527
SUREFIRE, LLC, *pg.* 1307, *pg.* 90
TDK-LAMBDA HIGH POWER DIVISION, *pg.* 1380, *pg.* 1090
TECHNIBUS LLC, *pg.* 1380, *pg.* 1408
TROJAN TECHNOLOGIES, INC., *pg.* 1384, *pg.* 1922
UNILUX, INC., *pg.* 682, *pg.* 1118
UNIVERSAL DISPLAY CORPORATION, *pg.* 683, *pg.* 1064
UNIVERSAL LIGHTING TECHNOLOGIES, *pg.* 1307, *pg.* 1655
VISHAY INTERTECHNOLOGY, INC., *pg.* 1435, *pg.* 1551
WOODWARD, INC., *pg.* 122, *pg.* 329
XENONICS HOLDINGS, INC., *pg.* 1308, *pg.* 62

3651 - Household Audio & Video Equipment

8X8, INC., *pg.* 1865, *pg.* 282
AAVID THERMALLOY, LLC, *pg.* 612, *pg.* 1035
ACACIA RESEARCH CORPORATION, *pg.* 1398, *pg.* 165
ACOPIAN TECHNICAL COMPANY, *pg.* 612, *pg.* 1528
ACTIVE POWER, INC., *pg.* 1310, *pg.* 1660
ADVANCED ENERGY INDUSTRIES, INC., *pg.* 613, *pg.* 328
ALLSOP, INC., *pg.* 347, *pg.* 1817
ALPHA VIDEO & AUDIO, INC., *pg.* 269, *pg.* 924
ALPINE ELECTRONICS OF AMERICA, INC., *pg.* 616, *pg.* 292
ALTEC LANSING LLC, *pg.* 348, *pg.* 1553
AMERICAN ELECTRIC TECHNOLOGIES, INC., *pg.* 349, *pg.* 1700
AMERICAN TECHNICAL CERAMICS CORP., *pg.* 616, *pg.* 1168
AMETEK PROGRAMMABLE POWER, INC., *pg.* 616, *pg.* 200
ANAREN, INC., *pg.* 617, *pg.* 1157
API TECHNOLOGIES CORP., *pg.* 618, *pg.* 452
ASCO POWER TECHNOLOGIES, L.P., *pg.* 1314, *pg.* 1066
ASTRO-MED, INC., *pg.* 619, *pg.* 1609
ATEK, *pg.* 620, *pg.* 919
ATLAS SOUND, *pg.* 621, *pg.* 1692
AUDIO RESEARCH CORPORATION, *pg.* 621, *pg.* 953
AVX CORPORATION, *pg.* 623, *pg.* 1616
AWR CORPORATION, *pg.* 623, *pg.* 78
BALL CORPORATION, *pg.* 1452, *pg.* 311
BASLER ELECTRIC COMPANY, *pg.* 623, *pg.* 616
BEAD INDUSTRIES INC., *pg.* 200, *pg.* 356
BEL FUSE INC., *pg.* 624, *pg.* 1075
BENCHMARK ELECTRONICS, INC., *pg.* 624, *pg.* 1659
BOGEN COMMUNICATIONS INTERNATIONAL INC., *pg.* 625, *pg.* 1113
BOSE CORPORATION, *pg.* 626, *pg.* 820
BROADCOM CORPORATION, *pg.* 364, *pg.* 108
CHROMALOX, INC., *pg.* 1070, *pg.* 1574
CHYRONHEGO, *pg.* 371, *pg.* 1179
CLARION CORPORATION OF AMERICA, *pg.* 629, *pg.* 75
CLARY CORPORATION, *pg.* 226, *pg.* 150
CLEARPLAY, *pg.* 541, *pg.* 1756
COBRA ELECTRONICS CORPORATION, *pg.* 629, *pg.* 572
CODA OCTOPUS GROUP, INC., *pg.* 629, *pg.* 437
COHERENT, INC., *pg.* 1406, *pg.* 265
COLLABRX, INC., *pg.* 1324, *pg.* 216
COMMUNICATIONS SYSTEMS, INC., *pg.* 630, *pg.* 948
COOPER INTERCONNECT, *pg.* 630, *pg.* 1118
CRANE AEROSPACE & ELECTRONICS, KELTEC OPERATION, *pg.* 631, *pg.* 428
CREATIVE VISTAS INC., *pg.* 1044, *pg.* 1948
CRESTRON ELECTRONICS INC., *pg.* 631, *pg.* 1116
CTS CORPORATION, *pg.* 631, *pg.* 677
CUSTOM SENSORS & TECHNOLOGIES, *pg.* 1407, *pg.* 152
DATA I/O CORPORATION, *pg.* 382, *pg.* 1824
DEI HOLDINGS, INC., *pg.* 633, *pg.* 302
DGT HOLDINGS, *pg.* 634, *pg.* 1223
DIGITAL VIDEO SYSTEMS, INC., *pg.* 634, *pg.* 153
DOVER CORPORATION, *pg.* 1329, *pg.* 608
DOW ELECTRONIC MATERIALS, *pg.* 1159, *pg.* 832
DTS, INC., *pg.* 634, *pg.* 55
DYNAVOX INC., *pg.* 635, *pg.* 1574
EATON BUSSMANN, INC., *pg.* 1331, *pg.* 977
ELECTROCUBE INCORPORATED, *pg.* 635, *pg.* 185
ELENCO ELECTRONICS, INC., *pg.* 953, *pg.* 670
ELO TOUCH SOLUTIONS, *pg.* 635, *pg.* 145
EMERSON RADIO CORP., *pg.* 636, *pg.* 1087
EMG, INC., *pg.* 636, *pg.* 277
EMPOWER RF SYSTEMS, INC., *pg.* 637, *pg.* 105
EMRISE CORPORATION, *pg.* 637, *pg.* 1371
FINISAR CORPORATION, *pg.* 639, *pg.* 285
FLEXTRONICS INTERNATIONAL LTD., *pg.* 81, *pg.* 245
FOX ELECTRONICS, *pg.* 639, *pg.* 428
FUSION UV SYSTEMS, INC., *pg.* 640, *pg.* 770
GALE CENGAGE LEARNING, *pg.* 1643, *pg.* 885
GE INTELLIGENT PLATFORMS, *pg.* 400, *pg.* 1135
GIGA-TRONICS INCORPORATED, *pg.* 640, *pg.* 260
GIGOPTIX, INC., *pg.* 400, *pg.* 245
GUARDIAN ELECTRIC MANUFACTURING COMPANY, *pg.* 641, *pg.* 672
HAPP CONTROLS INC., *pg.* 641, *pg.* 634
HARMAN CONSUMER, INC., *pg.* 641, *pg.* 1355
HARMAN INTERNATIONAL INDUSTRIES, INCORPORATED, *pg.* 641, *pg.* 374
HARMONIC, INC., *pg.* 402, *pg.* 246
HAUPPAUGE DIGITAL, INC., *pg.* 402, *pg.* 1164
HITTITE MICROWAVE CORPORATION, *pg.* 642, *pg.* 813
HUTCHINSON TECHNOLOGY INC., *pg.* 409, *pg.* 926
HYPERSOUND, *pg.* 643, *pg.* 186
I.D. SYSTEMS, INC., *pg.* 643, *pg.* 1134
IEC ELECTRONICS CORP., *pg.* 643, *pg.* 1317
II-VI INCORPORATED, *pg.* 1417, *pg.* 1585
INFINEON TECHNOLOGIES NORTH AMERICA CORP., *pg.* 644, *pg.* 145
INFINERA CORPORATION, *pg.* 644, *pg.* 286
INFOCUS CORPORATION, *pg.* 644, *pg.* 1503
INTERPOINT CORPORATION, *pg.* 647, *pg.* 1824
ITERIS, INC., *pg.* 293, *pg.* 261
IVEDA SOLUTIONS, INC., *pg.* 88, *pg.* 13
JABIL CIRCUIT, INC., *pg.* 422, *pg.* 463
KEVLIN CORPORATION, *pg.* 649, *pg.* 1034
KEY TRONIC CORPORATION, *pg.* 424, *pg.* 1844
KIMBALL INTERNATIONAL, INC., *pg.* 931, *pg.* 692
KLIPSCH GROUP, INC., *pg.* 649, *pg.* 688
KOSS CORPORATION, *pg.* 649, *pg.* 1877
KRATOS-GENERAL MICROWAVE, *pg.* 650, *pg.* 1344
KRATOS LANCASTER, *pg.* 1419, *pg.* 1546
KRELL INDUSTRIES, INC., *pg.* 650, *pg.* 367
LAW ENFORCEMENT ASSOCIATES CORPORATION, *pg.* 651, *pg.* 1387
THE LGL GROUP, INC., *pg.* 652, *pg.* 454
LIGHTPATH TECHNOLOGIES INC, *pg.* 1420, *pg.* 454
LOUD TECHNOLOGIES INC., *pg.* 652, *pg.* 1847
LRAD CORPORATION, *pg.* 652, *pg.* 204
LSI SACO TECHNOLOGIES, INC., *pg.* 652, *pg.* 1955
MACLEAN-FOGG COMPANY INC., *pg.* 1358, *pg.* 635
MAD CATZ INTERACTIVE INC., *pg.* 429, *pg.* 204
MARTEK POWER ABBOTT, INC., *pg.* 652, *pg.* 294
MATERION MICROELECTRONICS & SERVICES, *pg.* 1559, *pg.* 1149
MEGGITT TRAINING SYSTEMS, *pg.* 1839, *pg.* 541
MERCURY COMPUTER SYSTEMS, INC., *pg.* 434, *pg.* 813
MICRON TECHNOLOGY, INC., *pg.* 435, *pg.* 547
MICROSEMI CORPORATION, *pg.* 435, *pg.* 41
MICROVISION, INC., *pg.* 654, *pg.* 1828
MICROWAVE FILTER COMPANY, INC., *pg.* 654, *pg.* 1157
MILESTONE AV TECHNOLOGIES, INC., *pg.* 654, *pg.* 964
MITSUBISHI DIGITAL ELECTRONICS AMERICA, INC., *pg.* 655, *pg.* 113
MOLEX INCORPORATED, *pg.* 655, *pg.* 628
MRV COMMUNICATIONS, INC., *pg.* 441, *pg.* 64
NHT AUDIO, LLC, *pg.* 659, *pg.* 45
NORTECH SYSTEMS INCORPORATED, *pg.* 659, *pg.* 966
NORTEK SECURITY & CONTROL LLC, *pg.* 659, *pg.* 59
NORTHROP GRUMMAN CORPORATION, *pg.* 231, *pg.* 1781
NOVATEL INC., *pg.* 1424, *pg.* 1904
ORACLE CORPORATION, *pg.* 1272, *pg.* 786
PALOMAR TECHNOLOGIES INC., *pg.* 661, *pg.* 60
PARKERVISION, INC., *pg.* 1426, *pg.* 434
PEAVEY ELECTRONICS CORPORATION, *pg.* 662, *pg.* 970
PERCEPTRON, INC., *pg.* 215, *pg.* 904
PHILIPS ELECTRONICS NORTH AMERICA, *pg.* 662, *pg.* 782
PLANAR SYSTEMS, INC., *pg.* 455, *pg.* 1495
PLAYNETWORK, INC., *pg.* 577, *pg.* 1829
PLEXUS CORP., *pg.* 455, *pg.* 1883
POLK AUDIO, INC., *pg.* 664, *pg.* 758
POST GLOVER RESISTORS INC., *pg.* 1585, *pg.* 727
PROGRESSIVE DYNAMICS, INC., *pg.* 665, *pg.* 898
PROJECTS UNLIMITED, INC., *pg.* 665, *pg.* 1446
PROVISION HOLDING, INC., *pg.* 665, *pg.* 65
PULSE ELECTRONICS CORPORATION, *pg.* 666, *pg.* 206
Q-TECH CORPORATION, *pg.* 666, *pg.* 72
QSOUND LABS, INC., *pg.* 666, *pg.* 1904
QUAM-NICHOLS COMPANY, *pg.* 666, *pg.* 588
RICOH PRINTING SYSTEMS AMERICA, INC., *pg.* 462, *pg.* 279
ROCKFORD CORPORATION, *pg.* 667, *pg.* 26
ROSTRA PRECISION CONTROLS, INC., *pg.* 216, *pg.* 1381
ROWE INTERNATIONAL CORP, *pg.* 669, *pg.* 889
SANMINA-SCI CORPORATION, *pg.* 671, *pg.* 250
SDI TECHNOLOGIES, INC., *pg.* 671, *pg.* 1113
SHURE INCORPORATED, *pg.* 672, *pg.* 638
SILICON GRAPHICS INTERNATIONAL CORP, *pg.* 470, *pg.* 148
SKULLCANDY, INC., *pg.* 674, *pg.* 1754
SKYWORKS SOLUTIONS, INC., *pg.* 674, *pg.* 862
SL INDUSTRIES, INC., *pg.* 674, *pg.* 1090
SONY ELECTRONICS, INC., *pg.* 676, *pg.* 209
SOURCE PHOTONICS, INC., *pg.* 1429, *pg.* 305
SPACEDEV INC., *pg.* 234, *pg.* 186
SPARTON CORPORATION, *pg.* 1377, *pg.* 660
STANDEX INTERNATIONAL CORPORATION, *pg.* 60, *pg.* 1039
TDK-LAMBDA HIGH POWER DIVISION, *pg.* 1380, *pg.* 1090
TECHNICOLOR, INC., *pg.* 311, *pg.* 57
TELEGENIX INC., *pg.* 678, *pg.* 1051
TELENAV, INC., *pg.* 678, *pg.* 288
TELLABS, INC., *pg.* 678, *pg.* 637
TOSHIBA AMERICA CONSUMER PRODUCTS, LLC, *pg.* 681, *pg.* 1130
TOSHIBA AMERICA, INC., *pg.* 681, *pg.* 1302

TRANS-LUX CORPORATION, *pg.* 681, *pg.* 365
TRIAD SPEAKERS, INC., *pg.* 682, *pg.* 1507
TRIPPE MANUFACTURING COMPANY, *pg.* 220, *pg.* 592
TYCO INTERNATIONAL (US) INC., *pg.* 1891, *pg.* 1113
UNILUX, INC., *pg.* 682, *pg.* 1118
UNIVERSAL DISPLAY CORPORATION, *pg.* 683, *pg.* 1064
UNIVERSAL ELECTRONICS, INC., *pg.* 683, *pg.* 262
UNIVERSAL SECURITY INSTRUMENTS, INC., *pg.* 683, *pg.* 775
UQM TECHNOLOGIES, INC., *pg.* 684, *pg.* 334
U.S. MUSIC CORPORATION, *pg.* 315, *pg.* 560
VEECO INSTRUMENTS INC., *pg.* 1434, *pg.* 1322
VELODYNE ACOUSTICS, INC., *pg.* 685, *pg.* 152
VIAVI SOLUTIONS INC., *pg.* 1435, *pg.* 148
VICOR CORPORATION, *pg.* 1435, *pg.* 783
VIDEO DISPLAY CORPORATION, *pg.* 685, *pg.* 542
VUZIX CORPORATION, *pg.* 687, *pg.* 1337
WEGENER CORPORATION, *pg.* 687, *pg.* 533
WEST CORPORATION, *pg.* 492, *pg.* 1019
WINEGARD COMPANY, *pg.* 688, *pg.* 702
WINLAND ELECTRONICS, INC., *pg.* 688, *pg.* 928
WOODWARD, INC., *pg.* 122, *pg.* 329
ZAGG INCORPORATED, *pg.* 690, *pg.* 1762
ZOOM TECHNOLOGIES, INC., *pg.* 497, *pg.* 1317

3652 - Phonograph Records & Pre-Recorded Audio Tapes & Discs

BMG/MUSIC, *pg.* 533, *pg.* 1205
BRIDGE PUBLICATIONS INC., *pg.* 1623, *pg.* 127
DOMO RECORDS, INC., *pg.* 1767, *pg.* 129
DRG RECORDS INCORPORATED, *pg.* 1767, *pg.* 1226
E1 ENTERTAINMENT U.S. LP, *pg.* 284, *pg.* 1323
ENTERTAINMENT ONE LTD., *pg.* 546, *pg.* 1937
FOCUS FEATURES, *pg.* 287, *pg.* 273
HUMAN KINETICS PUBLISHERS INC., *pg.* 1651, *pg.* 562
INGRAM ENTERTAINMENT INC., *pg.* 292, *pg.* 1639
INTERSCOPE GEFFEN & A&M RECORDS, *pg.* 293, *pg.* 274
INTRADA INC., *pg.* 1773, *pg.* 171
K-TEL INTERNATIONAL, INC., *pg.* 1052, *pg.* 953
MAXELL CORPORATION OF AMERICA, *pg.* 652, *pg.* 1079
NAXOS OF AMERICA INC., *pg.* 1779, *pg.* 1633
POINT.360, INC., *pg.* 305, *pg.* 52
POWER MUSIC, INC., *pg.* 305, *pg.* 1751
RLJ ENTERTAINMENT, INC., *pg.* 306, *pg.* 778
ROUNDER RECORDS CORPORATION, *pg.* 307, *pg.* 807
SF GLOBAL SOURCING, *pg.* 307, *pg.* 227
THE SINGING MACHINE COMPANY, INC., *pg.* 674, *pg.* 426
SONY MUSIC ENTERTAINMENT, *pg.* 309, *pg.* 1294
TECHNICOLOR, INC., *pg.* 311, *pg.* 57
UNIVERSAL STUDIOS, INC., *pg.* 315, *pg.* 298
WARNER MUSIC GROUP CORP., *pg.* 590, *pg.* 1313

3661 - Telephone & Telegraph Apparatus

ADTRAN, INC., *pg.* 344, *pg.* 6
AESP, INC., *pg.* 345, *pg.* 439
AIRVANA, INC., *pg.* 268, *pg.* 812
ALCATEL-LUCENT, *pg.* 615, *pg.* 1094
ALCATEL-LUCENT, *pg.* 615, *pg.* 38
ALCATEL-LUCENT USA, INC., *pg.* 615, *pg.* 1728
ALLIANCE FIBER OPTIC PRODUCTS, INC., *pg.* 1399, *pg.* 283
AMERICAN ELECTRIC TECHNOLOGIES, INC., *pg.* 349, *pg.* 1700
ARRIS GROUP, INC., *pg.* 353, *pg.* 541
AVAYA INC., *pg.* 621, *pg.* 264
BLACKBERRY LIMITED, *pg.* 625, *pg.* 1947
BOGEN COMMUNICATIONS INTERNATIONAL INC., *pg.* 625, *pg.* 1113
CHANNELL COMMERCIAL CORP., *pg.* 1870, *pg.* 291
CLEARONE COMMUNICATIONS, INC., *pg.* 629, *pg.* 1756
COMMUNICATIONS SPECIALTIES, INC., *pg.* 377, *pg.* 1338
COMMUNICATIONS SYSTEMS, INC., *pg.* 630, *pg.* 948
CORNING CABLE SYSTEMS LLC, *pg.* 1407, *pg.* 1378
DIGITAL LIGHTWAVE, INC., *pg.* 634, *pg.* 462
ELECTRO STANDARDS LABORATORIES INC., *pg.* 390, *pg.* 1600
ELECTRONIC TELE-COMMUNICATIONS, INC., *pg.* 390, *pg.* 1897
EMULEX CORPORATION, *pg.* 392, *pg.* 70
EXTREME NETWORKS INC, *pg.* 287, *pg.* 245
EZENIA! INC., *pg.* 396, *pg.* 1039
GENERAL DATACOMM INDUSTRIES, INC., *pg.* 400, *pg.* 357
GN NETCOM INC., *pg.* 640, *pg.* 1037
INTERDIGITAL, INC., *pg.* 1872, *pg.* 1543
JUNIPER NETWORKS, INC., *pg.* 1260, *pg.* 286
KOSS CORPORATION, *pg.* 649, *pg.* 1877
LANTRONIX, INC., *pg.* 426, *pg.* 112
LATTICE INC., *pg.* 1872, *pg.* 1108
LEVEL 3 COMMUNICATIONS, INC., *pg.* 1262, *pg.* 1664
LIGHTPATH TECHNOLOGIES INC, *pg.* 1420, *pg.* 454
LOJACK CORPORATION, *pg.* 210, *pg.* 811
MITEL NETWORKS CORPORATION, *pg.* 654, *pg.* 1921
MITEL NETWORKS, INC., *pg.* 1872, *pg.* 13
MOTOROLA SOLUTIONS, INC., *pg.* 657, *pg.* 659
MPHASE TECHNOLOGIES, INC., *pg.* 441, *pg.* 363
MULTI-TECH SYSTEMS INC., *pg.* 442, *pg.* 951
MURATEC AMERICA, INC., *pg.* 443, *pg.* 1733
NEC CORPORATION OF AMERICA, INC., *pg.* 658, *pg.* 1723
NETGEAR, INC., *pg.* 444, *pg.* 247
NEUSTAR, INC., *pg.* 1872, *pg.* 1807
NUMEREX CORP., *pg.* 660, *pg.* 517
ONMOBILE LIVE, INC., *pg.* 449, *pg.* 829
OPLINK COMMUNICATIONS, INC., *pg.* 660, *pg.* 91
PLAINTREE SYSTEMS INC., *pg.* 663, *pg.* 1918
PLANTRONICS, INC., *pg.* 663, *pg.* 270
POLYCOM, INC., *pg.* 664, *pg.* 249
PREFORMED LINE PRODUCTS COMPANY, *pg.* 1370, *pg.* 1434
QUALCOMM INCORPORATED, *pg.* 1873, *pg.* 207
RAULAND-BORG CORPORATION, *pg.* 666, *pg.* 634
RICOH PRINTING SYSTEMS AMERICA, INC., *pg.* 462, *pg.* 279
SDI TECHNOLOGIES, INC., *pg.* 671, *pg.* 1113
SHORETEL, INC., *pg.* 469, *pg.* 288
SIQURA, *pg.* 308, *pg.* 771
SONUS NETWORKS INC., *pg.* 1281, *pg.* 858
TELEBYTE, INC., *pg.* 482, *pg.* 1165
TELLABS, INC., *pg.* 678, *pg.* 637
ZOOM TECHNOLOGIES, INC., *pg.* 497, *pg.* 1317

3663 - Radio & Television Broadcasting & Communications Equipment

AAVID THERMALLOY, LLC, *pg.* 612, *pg.* 1035
ACACIA RESEARCH CORPORATION, *pg.* 1398, *pg.* 165
ACOPIAN TECHNICAL COMPANY, *pg.* 612, *pg.* 1528
ACTIVE POWER, INC., *pg.* 1310, *pg.* 1660
ADDVANTAGE TECHNOLOGIES GROUP, INC., *pg.* 612, *pg.* 1484
ADTRAN, INC., *pg.* 344, *pg.* 6
ADVANCED ENERGY INDUSTRIES, INC., *pg.* 613, *pg.* 328
AESP, INC., *pg.* 345, *pg.* 439
AIRSPAN NETWORKS INC., *pg.* 346, *pg.* 410
AIRVANA, INC., *pg.* 268, *pg.* 812
ALIEN TECHNOLOGY CORPORATION, *pg.* 269, *pg.* 152
AMERICAN ELECTRIC TECHNOLOGIES, INC., *pg.* 349, *pg.* 1700
AMERICAN TECHNICAL CERAMICS CORP., *pg.* 616, *pg.* 1168
AMETEK PROGRAMMABLE POWER, INC., *pg.* 616, *pg.* 200
ANAREN, INC., *pg.* 617, *pg.* 1157
ANDREA ELECTRONICS CORPORATION, *pg.* 617, *pg.* 1143
ANTENNA PRODUCTS CORPORATION, *pg.* 618, *pg.* 1727
API TECHNOLOGIES CORP., *pg.* 618, *pg.* 452
APPLE INC., *pg.* 350, *pg.* 73
ARRIS GROUP, INC., *pg.* 353, *pg.* 541
ASCO POWER TECHNOLOGIES, L.P., *pg.* 1314, *pg.* 1066
ASTRO-MED, INC., *pg.* 619, *pg.* 1609
ATEK, *pg.* 620, *pg.* 919
AVX CORPORATION, *pg.* 623, *pg.* 1616
AWR CORPORATION, *pg.* 623, *pg.* 78
AXIA NETMEDIA CORPORATION, *pg.* 623, *pg.* 1902
AXXCELERA BROADBAND WIRELESS INC., *pg.* 623, *pg.* 263
BALL CORPORATION, *pg.* 1452, *pg.* 311
BASLER ELECTRIC COMPANY, *pg.* 623, *pg.* 616
BEAD INDUSTRIES INC., *pg.* 200, *pg.* 356
BEL FUSE INC., *pg.* 624, *pg.* 1075
BENCHMARK ELECTRONICS, INC., *pg.* 624, *pg.* 1659
BLACKBERRY LIMITED, *pg.* 625, *pg.* 1947
BLONDER TONGUE LABORATORIES, INC., *pg.* 625, *pg.* 1100
BOGEN COMMUNICATIONS INTERNATIONAL INC., *pg.* 625, *pg.* 1113
BOSCH COMMUNICATIONS INC., *pg.* 626, *pg.* 919
BROADCAST ELECTRONICS, INC., *pg.* 627, *pg.* 653
BROADCOM CORPORATION, *pg.* 364, *pg.* 108
CBC (AMERICA) CORP., *pg.* 273, *pg.* 293
CHROMALOX, INC., *pg.* 1070, *pg.* 1574
CHYRONHEGO, *pg.* 371, *pg.* 1179
CLARY CORPORATION, *pg.* 226, *pg.* 150
CLEARONE COMMUNICATIONS, INC., *pg.* 629, *pg.* 1756
COBRA ELECTRONICS CORPORATION, *pg.* 629, *pg.* 572
CODA OCTOPUS GROUP, INC., *pg.* 629, *pg.* 437
COHERENT, INC., *pg.* 1406, *pg.* 265
COLLABRX, INC., *pg.* 1324, *pg.* 216
COMMSCOPE, *pg.* 630, *pg.* 668
COMMSCOPE, INC., *pg.* 278, *pg.* 1378
COMMUNICATIONS SYSTEMS, INC., *pg.* 630, *pg.* 948
COMTECH TELECOMMUNICATIONS CORP., *pg.* 379, *pg.* 1179
CONTINENTAL ELECTRONICS CORPORATION, *pg.* 630, *pg.* 1678
COOPER INTERCONNECT, *pg.* 630, *pg.* 1118
CPI INTERNATIONAL, INC., *pg.* 631, *pg.* 175
CRANE AEROSPACE & ELECTRONICS, KELTEC OPERATION, *pg.* 631, *pg.* 428
CREATIVE VISTAS INC., *pg.* 1044, *pg.* 1948
CTS CORPORATION, *pg.* 631, *pg.* 677
CUSTOM SENSORS & TECHNOLOGIES, *pg.* 1407, *pg.* 152
DATA I/O CORPORATION, *pg.* 382, *pg.* 1824
DAVID CLARK COMPANY INCORPORATED, *pg.* 633, *pg.* 862
DEI HOLDINGS, INC., *pg.* 633, *pg.* 302
DGT HOLDINGS, *pg.* 634, *pg.* 1223
DIALOGIC INC., *pg.* 281, *pg.* 243
DIGITAL LIGHTWAVE, INC., *pg.* 634, *pg.* 462
DOLBY LABORATORIES, INC., *pg.* 284, *pg.* 217
DOVER CORPORATION, *pg.* 1329, *pg.* 608
DOW ELECTRONIC MATERIALS, *pg.* 1159, *pg.* 832
DUKANE CORPORATION, *pg.* 634, *pg.* 658
DURA-LINE HOLDINGS, *pg.* 389, *pg.* 1636
DYNAVOX INC., *pg.* 635, *pg.* 1574
EATON BUSSMANN, INC., *pg.* 1331, *pg.* 977
ECESSA CORPORATION, *pg.* 635, *pg.* 953
EF JOHNSON TECHNOLOGIES, INC., *pg.* 390, *pg.* 1718
ELECSYS CORPORATION, *pg.* 635, *pg.* 717
ELECTROCUBE INCORPORATED, *pg.* 635, *pg.* 185
ELENCO ELECTRONICS, INC., *pg.* 953, *pg.* 670
ELO TOUCH SOLUTIONS, *pg.* 635, *pg.* 145
EMG, INC., *pg.* 636, *pg.* 277
EMPOWER RF SYSTEMS, INC., *pg.* 637, *pg.* 105
EMRISE CORPORATION, *pg.* 637, *pg.* 1371
ERICSSON, INC., *pg.* 638, *pg.* 1730
EXTREME NETWORKS INC, *pg.* 287, *pg.* 245
FINISAR CORPORATION, *pg.* 639, *pg.* 285
FLEXTRONICS INTERNATIONAL LTD., *pg.* 81, *pg.* 245
FOX ELECTRONICS, *pg.* 639, *pg.* 428
FUSION UV SYSTEMS, INC., *pg.* 640, *pg.* 770
GALE CENGAGE LEARNING, *pg.* 1643, *pg.* 885
GATESAIR, INC., *pg.* 640, *pg.* 1460
GE INTELLIGENT PLATFORMS, *pg.* 400, *pg.* 1135
GIGA-TRONICS INCORPORATED, *pg.* 640, *pg.* 260
GIGOPTIX, INC., *pg.* 400, *pg.* 245
GLENTEL INC., *pg.* 1944, *pg.* 1907
GLOBECOMM SYSTEMS INC., *pg.* 640, *pg.* 1164
GRASS VALLEY, INC., *pg.* 641, *pg.* 164
GUARDIAN ELECTRIC MANUFACTURING COMPANY, *pg.* 641, *pg.* 672
HAPP CONTROLS INC., *pg.* 641, *pg.* 634
HARMONIC, INC., *pg.* 402, *pg.* 246
HARRIS CORPORATION, *pg.* 642, *pg.* 439
HARRIS CORP. RF COMMUNICATIONS DIVISION, *pg.* 642, *pg.* 1336
HAUPPAUGE DIGITAL, INC., *pg.* 402, *pg.* 1164
HITTITE MICROWAVE CORPORATION, *pg.* 642, *pg.* 813
HUTCHINSON TECHNOLOGY INC., *pg.* 409, *pg.* 926
HYPERSOUND, *pg.* 643, *pg.* 186
IBIQUITY DIGITAL CORPORATION, *pg.* 409, *pg.* 767
I.D. SYSTEMS, INC., *pg.* 643, *pg.* 1134
IEC ELECTRONICS CORP., *pg.* 643, *pg.* 1317
II-VI INCORPORATED, *pg.* 1417, *pg.* 1585
INCONTACT, INC., *pg.* 413, *pg.* 1752
INFINEON TECHNOLOGIES NORTH AMERICA CORP., *pg.* 644, *pg.* 145
INFINERA CORPORATION, *pg.* 644, *pg.* 286

INTERMEDIA, *pg.* 417, *pg.* 1815
INTERPOINT CORPORATION, *pg.* 647, *pg.* 1824
ITRON INC., *pg.* 422, *pg.* 1822
ITUS CORPORATION, *pg.* 422, *pg.* 1180
JABIL CIRCUIT, INC., *pg.* 422, *pg.* 463
JBI, INC., *pg.* 293, *pg.* 1317
KEVLIN CORPORATION, *pg.* 649, *pg.* 1034
KEY TRONIC CORPORATION, *pg.* 424, *pg.* 1844
KIMBALL INTERNATIONAL, INC., *pg.* 931, *pg.* 692
KRATOS-GENERAL MICROWAVE, *pg.* 650, *pg.* 1344
KRATOS LANCASTER, *pg.* 1419, *pg.* 1546
KVH INDUSTRIES INC, *pg.* 650, *pg.* 1602
L-3 COMMUNICATIONS HOLDINGS INC., *pg.* 650, *pg.* 1250
L-3 COMMUNICATIONS NARDA MICROWAVE-EAST, *pg.* 650, *pg.* 1165
LATTICE INC., *pg.* 1872, *pg.* 1108
THE LGL GROUP, INC., *pg.* 652, *pg.* 454
LIGHTPATH TECHNOLOGIES INC, *pg.* 1420, *pg.* 454
LOJACK CORPORATION, *pg.* 210, *pg.* 811
LORAL SPACE & COMMUNICATIONS INC., *pg.* 231, *pg.* 1252
LOUD TECHNOLOGIES INC., *pg.* 652, *pg.* 1847
MACLEAN-FOGG COMPANY INC., *pg.* 1358, *pg.* 635
MAD CATZ INTERACTIVE INC., *pg.* 429, *pg.* 204
MARTEK POWER ABBOTT, INC., *pg.* 652, *pg.* 294
MARTHA STEWART LIVING OMNIMEDIA, INC., *pg.* 1661, *pg.* 1256
MATERION MICROELECTRONICS & SERVICES, *pg.* 1559, *pg.* 1149
MEGGITT TRAINING SYSTEMS, *pg.* 1839, *pg.* 541
MERCURY COMPUTER SYSTEMS, INC., *pg.* 434, *pg.* 813
MICRON TECHNOLOGY, INC., *pg.* 435, *pg.* 547
MICROSEMI CORPORATION, *pg.* 435, *pg.* 41
MICROVISION, INC., *pg.* 654, *pg.* 1828
MICROWAVE FILTER COMPANY, INC., *pg.* 654, *pg.* 1157
MITEL NETWORKS CORPORATION, *pg.* 654, *pg.* 1921
MITSUBISHI DIGITAL ELECTRONICS AMERICA, INC., *pg.* 655, *pg.* 113
MOLEX INCORPORATED, *pg.* 655, *pg.* 628
MOTOROLA ENTERPRISE MOBILITY, *pg.* 441, *pg.* 1167
MOTOROLA MOBILITY LLC, *pg.* 657, *pg.* 627
MOTOROLA SOLUTIONS, INC., *pg.* 657, *pg.* 659
MPHASE TECHNOLOGIES, INC., *pg.* 441, *pg.* 363
MRV COMMUNICATIONS, INC., *pg.* 441, *pg.* 64
MULTI-TECH SYSTEMS INC., *pg.* 442, *pg.* 951
NETWORKFLEET, INC., *pg.* 445, *pg.* 205
NORTECH SYSTEMS INCORPORATED, *pg.* 659, *pg.* 966
NORTEK SECURITY & CONTROL LLC, *pg.* 659, *pg.* 59
NORTHROP GRUMMAN CORPORATION, *pg.* 231, *pg.* 1781
NOVATEL INC., *pg.* 1424, *pg.* 1904
ORACLE CORPORATION, *pg.* 1272, *pg.* 786
ORBITAL ATK, *pg.* 1425, *pg.* 1779
PALOMAR TECHNOLOGIES INC., *pg.* 661, *pg.* 60
PARKERVISION, INC., *pg.* 1426, *pg.* 434
PERCEPTRON, INC., *pg.* 215, *pg.* 904
PLANAR SYSTEMS, INC., *pg.* 455, *pg.* 1495
PLEXUS CORP., *pg.* 455, *pg.* 1883
POST GLOVER RESISTORS INC., *pg.* 1585, *pg.* 727
PROGRESSIVE DYNAMICS, INC., *pg.* 665, *pg.* 898
PROJECTS UNLIMITED, INC., *pg.* 665, *pg.* 1446
PROVISION HOLDING, INC., *pg.* 665, *pg.* 65
PULSE ELECTRONICS CORPORATION, *pg.* 666, *pg.* 206
Q-TECH CORPORATION, *pg.* 666, *pg.* 72
RADIO FREQUENCY SYSTEMS, INC., *pg.* 666, *pg.* 354
RAULAND-BORG CORPORATION, *pg.* 666, *pg.* 634
RAYTHEON APPLIED SIGNAL TECHNOLOGY, INC., *pg.* 667, *pg.* 288
RAYTHEON COMPANY, *pg.* 233, *pg.* 854
RF INDUSTRIES, LTD., *pg.* 461, *pg.* 208
RICOH PRINTING SYSTEMS AMERICA, INC., *pg.* 462, *pg.* 279
ROCKFORD CORPORATION, *pg.* 667, *pg.* 26
ROSTRA PRECISION CONTROLS, INC., *pg.* 216, *pg.* 1381
SABRE INDUSTRIES, INC., *pg.* 669, *pg.* 1658
SANMINA-SCI CORPORATION, *pg.* 671, *pg.* 250
SDI TECHNOLOGIES, INC., *pg.* 671, *pg.* 1113
SEACHANGE INTERNATIONAL, INC., *pg.* 1279, *pg.* 781
SENTRY TECHNOLOGY CORPORATION, *pg.* 672, *pg.* 1339
SEURA, INC., *pg.* 672, *pg.* 1860
SHURE INCORPORATED, *pg.* 672, *pg.* 638
SILICON GRAPHICS INTERNATIONAL CORP, *pg.* 470, *pg.* 148
SIQURA, *pg.* 308, *pg.* 771
SKYWORKS SOLUTIONS, INC., *pg.* 674, *pg.* 862
SL INDUSTRIES, INC., *pg.* 674, *pg.* 1090
SONIC FOUNDRY, INC., *pg.* 472, *pg.* 1867
SONIFI SOLUTIONS, *pg.* 1281, *pg.* 1625
SONUS NETWORKS INC., *pg.* 1281, *pg.* 858
SOURCE PHOTONICS, INC., *pg.* 1429, *pg.* 305
SPACEDEV INC., *pg.* 234, *pg.* 186
SPARTON CORPORATION, *pg.* 1377, *pg.* 660
STANDEX INTERNATIONAL CORPORATION, *pg.* 60, *pg.* 1039
TDK-LAMBDA HIGH POWER DIVISION, *pg.* 1380, *pg.* 1090
TELEGENIX INC., *pg.* 678, *pg.* 1051
TELENAV, INC., *pg.* 678, *pg.* 288
TELLABS, INC., *pg.* 678, *pg.* 637
THE TELX GROUP, INC., *pg.* 483, *pg.* 1298
TRANS-LUX CORPORATION, *pg.* 681, *pg.* 365
TRIPPE MANUFACTURING COMPANY, *pg.* 220, *pg.* 592
TYCO INTERNATIONAL (US) INC., *pg.* 1891, *pg.* 1113
UNIVERSAL DISPLAY CORPORATION, *pg.* 683, *pg.* 1064
UNIVERSAL SECURITY INSTRUMENTS, INC., *pg.* 683, *pg.* 775
UQM TECHNOLOGIES, INC., *pg.* 684, *pg.* 334
VEECO INSTRUMENTS INC., *pg.* 1434, *pg.* 1322
VELATEL GLOBAL COMMUNICATIONS, INC., *pg.* 685, *pg.* 210
VIASAT, INC., *pg.* 489, *pg.* 62
VIAVI SOLUTIONS INC., *pg.* 1435, *pg.* 148
VICON INDUSTRIES, INC., *pg.* 685, *pg.* 1166
VICOR CORPORATION, *pg.* 1435, *pg.* 783
VIDEO DISPLAY CORPORATION, *pg.* 685, *pg.* 542
VIEWSONIC CORPORATION, *pg.* 489, *pg.* 303
VUZIX CORPORATION, *pg.* 687, *pg.* 1337
WEGENER CORPORATION, *pg.* 687, *pg.* 533
WINEGARD COMPANY, *pg.* 688, *pg.* 702
WINLAND ELECTRONICS, INC., *pg.* 688, *pg.* 928
WOODWARD, INC., *pg.* 122, *pg.* 329
WTVC-TV, *pg.* 323, *pg.* 1630
XENTRIS WIRELESS, LLC, *pg.* 494, *pg.* 552
XPLORE TECHNOLOGIES CORP., *pg.* 497, *pg.* 1667
ZAGG INCORPORATED, *pg.* 690, *pg.* 1762
ZOOM TECHNOLOGIES, INC., *pg.* 497, *pg.* 1317

3669 - Communications Equipment, NEC

8X8, INC., *pg.* 1865, *pg.* 282
ALSTOM SIGNALING, INC., *pg.* 1312, *pg.* 1350
ARRIS GROUP, INC., *pg.* 353, *pg.* 541
ASURE SOFTWARE, INC., *pg.* 355, *pg.* 1660
BOSCH COMMUNICATIONS INC., *pg.* 626, *pg.* 919
BOSCH SECURITY SYSTEMS, INC., *pg.* 626, *pg.* 1158
BRK BRANDS, INC., *pg.* 627, *pg.* 554
BROCADE CORPORATION, *pg.* 365, *pg.* 312
CHANNELL COMMERCIAL CORP., *pg.* 1870, *pg.* 291
CHECKPOINT SYSTEMS, INC., *pg.* 628, *pg.* 1559
CISCO SYSTEMS, INC., *pg.* 372, *pg.* 240
COMMSCOPE, *pg.* 630, *pg.* 668
COMTECH TELECOMMUNICATIONS CORP., *pg.* 379, *pg.* 1179
COOPER WHEELOCK, *pg.* 630, *pg.* 1080
DAKTRONICS, INC., *pg.* 633, *pg.* 1624
ECHELON CORPORATION, *pg.* 389, *pg.* 245
ELECTRONIC TELE-COMMUNICATIONS, INC., *pg.* 390, *pg.* 1897
EMULEX CORPORATION, *pg.* 392, *pg.* 70
EZENIA! INC., *pg.* 396, *pg.* 1039
FARADAY, *pg.* 638, *pg.* 1066
FEDERAL SIGNAL CORPORATION, *pg.* 638, *pg.* 645
FINISAR CORPORATION, *pg.* 639, *pg.* 285
GEORGE RISK INDUSTRIES, INC., *pg.* 1298, *pg.* 1011
HARRIS CORPORATION, *pg.* 642, *pg.* 439
HAUPPAUGE DIGITAL, INC., *pg.* 402, *pg.* 1164
HEMISPHERE GPS INC., *pg.* 642, *pg.* 1903
HITTITE MICROWAVE CORPORATION, *pg.* 642, *pg.* 813
HOCHIKI AMERICA CORPORATION, *pg.* 1050, *pg.* 50
INTERPHASE CORPORATION, *pg.* 420, *pg.* 1732
INTRUSION INC., *pg.* 1259, *pg.* 1736
IPMOBILENET, LLC, *pg.* 648, *pg.* 261
ITERIS, INC., *pg.* 293, *pg.* 261
L-3 COMMUNICATIONS HOLDINGS INC., *pg.* 650, *pg.* 1250
LANTRONIX, INC., *pg.* 426, *pg.* 112
LOJACK CORPORATION, *pg.* 210, *pg.* 811
MEGGITT SAFETY SYSTEMS, INC., *pg.* 653, *pg.* 279
MONOTYPE IMAGING HOLDINGS, INC., *pg.* 656, *pg.* 861
NEONODE, INC., *pg.* 659, *pg.* 268
NETGEAR, INC., *pg.* 444, *pg.* 247
NETSCOUT SYSTEMS, INC., *pg.* 1270, *pg.* 858
NOTIFIER CO., *pg.* 659, *pg.* 360
NUMEREX CORP., *pg.* 660, *pg.* 517
OCLARO, INC., *pg.* 1425, *pg.* 248
ONMOBILE LIVE, INC., *pg.* 449, *pg.* 829
PCTEL, INC., *pg.* 452, *pg.* 557
POSITIVEID CORPORATION, *pg.* 665, *pg.* 422
RAYTHEON APPLIED SIGNAL TECHNOLOGY, INC., *pg.* 667, *pg.* 288
ROCKWELL COLLINS, INC., *pg.* 234, *pg.* 702
SAVOX COMMUNICATIONS LTD, *pg.* 671, *pg.* 1909
SENTRY TECHNOLOGY CORPORATION, *pg.* 672, *pg.* 1339
SHORETEL, INC., *pg.* 469, *pg.* 288
SILICON GRAPHICS INTERNATIONAL CORP, *pg.* 470, *pg.* 148
SILICON LABORATORIES INC., *pg.* 674, *pg.* 1666
SYSTEM SENSOR, *pg.* 676, *pg.* 658
TALK-A-PHONE CO., *pg.* 481, *pg.* 638
TANGOE, INC., *pg.* 481, *pg.* 368
TELEBYTE, INC., *pg.* 482, *pg.* 1165
TELEGENIX INC., *pg.* 678, *pg.* 1051
TELENAV, INC., *pg.* 678, *pg.* 288
TELKONET, INC., *pg.* 678, *pg.* 1881
TELLABS, INC., *pg.* 678, *pg.* 637
VERINT SYSTEMS INC., *pg.* 488, *pg.* 1182
VERITEQ, *pg.* 488, *pg.* 422
VICON INDUSTRIES, INC., *pg.* 685, *pg.* 1166
THE VIKING GROUP, *pg.* 119, *pg.* 891
WINLAND ELECTRONICS, INC., *pg.* 688, *pg.* 928
WIRELESS RONIN TECHNOLOGIES INC., *pg.* 689, *pg.* 951
ZAGG INCORPORATED, *pg.* 690, *pg.* 1762
ZOOM TECHNOLOGIES, INC., *pg.* 497, *pg.* 1317

3671 - Electron Tubes

CTS CORPORATION, *pg.* 631, *pg.* 677
HAMAMATSU CORPORATION, *pg.* 1415, *pg.* 1046
MAXWELL TECHNOLOGIES, INC., *pg.* 653, *pg.* 204
PHOTONIS USA PENNSYLVANIA, *pg.* 663, *pg.* 1547
VARIAN MEDICAL SYSTEMS X-RAY PRODUCTS, *pg.* 1434, *pg.* 1761
VIDEO DISPLAY CORPORATION, *pg.* 685, *pg.* 542

3672 - Printed Circuit Boards

ACTIONTEC ELECTRONICS, INC., *pg.* 342, *pg.* 282
BENCHMARK ELECTRONICS, INC., *pg.* 624, *pg.* 1659
BROCADE CORPORATION, *pg.* 365, *pg.* 312
BUD INDUSTRIES, INC., *pg.* 627, *pg.* 1482
CTS ELECTRONICS MANUFACTURING SOLUTIONS, *pg.* 632, *pg.* 151
ERGON, INC., *pg.* 976, *pg.* 969
IEC ELECTRONICS CORP., *pg.* 643, *pg.* 1317
JABIL CIRCUIT, INC., *pg.* 422, *pg.* 463
KEY TRONIC CORPORATION, *pg.* 424, *pg.* 1844
MICRON CORPORATION, *pg.* 654, *pg.* 840
MULTI-FINELINE ELECTRONIX, INC., *pg.* 658, *pg.* 114
NEONODE, INC., *pg.* 659, *pg.* 268
PLEXUS CORP., *pg.* 455, *pg.* 1883
PROJECTS UNLIMITED, INC., *pg.* 665, *pg.* 1446
ROGERS CORPORATION, *pg.* 1305, *pg.* 369
SAE ENGINEERING, INC., *pg.* 669, *pg.* 269
SANMINA-SCI CORPORATION, *pg.* 671, *pg.* 250
SPARTON CORPORATION, *pg.* 1377, *pg.* 660

3674 - Semiconductors & Related Devices

8X8, INC., *pg.* 1865, *pg.* 282
ADVANCED MICRO DEVICES, INC., *pg.* 613, *pg.* 282
ADVANCED PHOTONIX, INC., *pg.* 1398, *pg.* 865
AEROFLEX INCORPORATED, *pg.* 614, *pg.* 1321
AGILENT TECHNOLOGIES, INC., *pg.* 614, *pg.* 264
AIXTRON INC., *pg.* 1310, *pg.* 283
AKRION, INC., *pg.* 1311, *pg.* 1513
ALLIANCE FIBER OPTIC PRODUCTS, INC., *pg.* 1399, *pg.* 283
ALTERA CORPORATION, *pg.* 348, *pg.* 237
AMBERWAVE INC, *pg.* 348, *pg.* 1039
AMKOR TECHNOLOGY, INC., *pg.* 67, *pg.* 25
ANADIGICS, INC., *pg.* 617, *pg.* 1128

ANALOG DEVICES, INC., *pg.* 617, *pg.* 839
API TECHNOLOGIES CORP., *pg.* 618, *pg.* 452
APPLIED MATERIALS, INC., *pg.* 618, *pg.* 264
APPLIED MICRO CIRCUITS CORPORATION, *pg.* 618, *pg.* 283
ATMEL CORPORATION, *pg.* 621, *pg.* 238
ATMI, INC., *pg.* 1314, *pg.* 342
AVAGO TECHNOLOGIES, *pg.* 358, *pg.* 238
AXT, INC., *pg.* 1400, *pg.* 90
BALLARD POWER SYSTEMS, INC., *pg.* 70, *pg.* 1907
BROADCOM CORPORATION, *pg.* 364, *pg.* 108
CABOT MICROELECTRONICS CORPORATION, *pg.* 1151, *pg.* 554
CARMANAH TECHNOLOGIES CORPORATION, *pg.* 628, *pg.* 1913
CAVIUM NETWORKS, INC., *pg.* 369, *pg.* 240
CEVA, INC., *pg.* 628, *pg.* 153
CIRRUS LOGIC, INC., *pg.* 629, *pg.* 1661
CODA OCTOPUS GROUP, INC., *pg.* 629, *pg.* 437
COLLABRX, INC., *pg.* 1324, *pg.* 216
CONEXANT SYSTEMS, INC., *pg.* 379, *pg.* 165
CONVERSANT INTELLECTUAL PROPERTY MANAGEMENT INC., *pg.* 630, *pg.* 1931
CREE INC., *pg.* 631, *pg.* 1371
CSR, *pg.* 280, *pg.* 284
CYPRESS SEMICONDUCTOR CORPORATION, *pg.* 1326, *pg.* 243
DATA I/O CORPORATION, *pg.* 382, *pg.* 1824
DAW TECHNOLOGIES, INC., *pg.* 78, *pg.* 1756
DIODES INCORPORATED, *pg.* 634, *pg.* 1729
DOW ELECTRONIC MATERIALS, *pg.* 1159, *pg.* 832
EMCORE CORPORATION, *pg.* 636, *pg.* 39
ENTEGRIS, INC., *pg.* 1882, *pg.* 788
ESS TECHNOLOGY, INC., *pg.* 395, *pg.* 90
EXAR CORPORATION, *pg.* 395, *pg.* 91
FAIRCHILD SEMICONDUCTOR CORPORATION, *pg.* 638, *pg.* 245
FEI COMPANY, *pg.* 1413, *pg.* 1498
FINISAR CORPORATION, *pg.* 639, *pg.* 285
FIRST SOLAR, INC., *pg.* 639, *pg.* 26
FORMFACTOR, INC., *pg.* 1882, *pg.* 122
FREESCALE SEMICONDUCTOR, INC., *pg.* 398, *pg.* 1662
GIGOPTIX, INC., *pg.* 400, *pg.* 245
HITTITE MICROWAVE CORPORATION, *pg.* 642, *pg.* 813
HYNIX SEMICONDUCTOR AMERICA INC., *pg.* 409, *pg.* 246
II-VI INCORPORATED, *pg.* 1417, *pg.* 1585
IMAGINATION TECHNOLOGIES, *pg.* 412, *pg.* 285
INFINEON TECHNOLOGIES NORTH AMERICA CORP., *pg.* 644, *pg.* 145
INFINERA CORPORATION, *pg.* 644, *pg.* 286
INTEGRATED SILICON SOLUTION, INC., *pg.* 645, *pg.* 145
INTEL CORPORATION, *pg.* 645, *pg.* 266
INTERDIGITAL, INC., *pg.* 1872, *pg.* 1543
INTERNATIONAL RECTIFIER CORPORATION, *pg.* 647, *pg.* 80
INTERSIL CORPORATION, *pg.* 647, *pg.* 146
ISC8, *pg.* 1350, *pg.* 71
IXYS CORPORATION, *pg.* 422, *pg.* 146
JOHNSON SMITH COMPANY, *pg.* 1774, *pg.* 414
KEY SAFETY SYSTEMS, INC., *pg.* 210, *pg.* 908
KLA-TENCOR CORPORATION, *pg.* 1353, *pg.* 146
KOPIN CORPORATION, *pg.* 425, *pg.* 847
LAM RESEARCH CORPORATION, *pg.* 1354, *pg.* 246
LATTICE SEMICONDUCTOR CORPORATION, *pg.* 651, *pg.* 1498
LIGHTING SCIENCE GROUP CORPORATION, *pg.* 1301, *pg.* 467
LIGHTPATH TECHNOLOGIES INC, *pg.* 1420, *pg.* 454
LINEAR TECHNOLOGY CORP., *pg.* 652, *pg.* 147
LUNA INNOVATIONS INC., *pg.* 1557, *pg.* 1806
MARKTIME, *pg.* 1421, *pg.* 371
MAXIM INTEGRATED PRODUCTS, INC., *pg.* 653, *pg.* 247
MCT WORLDWIDE LLC, *pg.* 653, *pg.* 939
METHODE ELECTRONICS, INC., *pg.* 654, *pg.* 581
MICREL, INC., *pg.* 654, *pg.* 247
MICRON TECHNOLOGY, INC., *pg.* 435, *pg.* 547
MICROPAC INDUSTRIES INC., *pg.* 654, *pg.* 1698
MICROSEMI CORPORATION, *pg.* 435, *pg.* 41
MINI-SYSTEMS, INC., *pg.* 654, *pg.* 837
MOSYS INC., *pg.* 657, *pg.* 268
MRV COMMUNICATIONS, INC., *pg.* 441, *pg.* 64
NEOMAGIC CORPORATION, *pg.* 1364, *pg.* 247
NEXTEST SYSTEMS CORPORATION, *pg.* 445, *pg.* 248
NVE CORPORATION, *pg.* 447, *pg.* 923
NVIDIA CORPORATION, *pg.* 447, *pg.* 268
NXP SEMICONDUCTORS, *pg.* 660, *pg.* 248
ON SEMICONDUCTOR CORPORATION, *pg.* 101, *pg.* 18
OSI OPTOELECTRONICS, *pg.* 1425, *pg.* 100
PARKERVISION, INC., *pg.* 1426, *pg.* 434
PMC-SIERRA, INC., *pg.* 664, *pg.* 287
PNY TECHNOLOGIES, INC., *pg.* 455, *pg.* 1105
POWER INTEGRATIONS, INC., *pg.* 1369, *pg.* 249
PULSE ELECTRONICS CORPORATION, *pg.* 666, *pg.* 206
QUALITAU, INC., *pg.* 666, *pg.* 161
RAMBUS INC., *pg.* 459, *pg.* 288
RENESAS ELECTRONICS AMERICA INC., *pg.* 667, *pg.* 269
RF MICRO DEVICES, INC., *pg.* 667, *pg.* 1376
SEMTECH CORPORATION, *pg.* 671, *pg.* 57
SIGMA DESIGNS, INC., *pg.* 469, *pg.* 148
SILICON LABORATORIES INC., *pg.* 674, *pg.* 1666
SKYWORKS SOLUTIONS, INC., *pg.* 674, *pg.* 862
SONICS, INC., *pg.* 675, *pg.* 148
SPARTON CORPORATION, *pg.* 1377, *pg.* 660
SPIRE CORPORATION, *pg.* 1378, *pg.* 786
SPP PROCESS TECHNOLOGY SYSTEMS LIMITED-THERMAL DIVISION, *pg.* 472, *pg.* 250
STMICROELECTRONICS, INC., *pg.* 676, *pg.* 1671
TELEDYNE MICROELECTRONIC TECHNOLOGIES, *pg.* 678, *pg.* 140
TERADYNE INC., *pg.* 679, *pg.* 838
TESSERA TECHNOLOGIES INC., *pg.* 1382, *pg.* 251
TEXAS INSTRUMENTS INCORPORATED, *pg.* 679, *pg.* 1688
TOWERJAZZ U.S., *pg.* 1383, *pg.* 166
TRIO-TECH INTERNATIONAL, *pg.* 1384, *pg.* 300
UNIVERSAL DISPLAY CORPORATION, *pg.* 683, *pg.* 1064
VEECO INSTRUMENTS INC., *pg.* 1434, *pg.* 1322
VIAVI SOLUTIONS INC., *pg.* 1435, *pg.* 148
VISHAY INTERTECHNOLOGY, INC., *pg.* 1435, *pg.* 1551
VITESSE SEMICONDUCTOR CORPORATION, *pg.* 686, *pg.* 57
XILINX, INC., *pg.* 496, *pg.* 252
ZILOG INC., *pg.* 497, *pg.* 252

3675 - Electronic Capacitors

AMERICAN SHIZUKI CORPORATION, *pg.* 616, *pg.* 1013
AMERICAN TECHNICAL CERAMICS CORP., *pg.* 616, *pg.* 1168
AVX CORPORATION, *pg.* 623, *pg.* 1616
CORNELL DUBILIER ELECTRONICS, *pg.* 630, *pg.* 1620
ELECTROCUBE INCORPORATED, *pg.* 635, *pg.* 185
JOHANSON MANUFACTURING CORPORATION, *pg.* 648, *pg.* 1045
KEMET CORPORATION, *pg.* 649, *pg.* 1621
MAXWELL TECHNOLOGIES, INC., *pg.* 653, *pg.* 204
VISHAY AMERICAS, *pg.* 686, *pg.* 371
VISHAY INTERTECHNOLOGY, INC., *pg.* 1435, *pg.* 1551

3676 - Electronic Resistors

MICRO-OHM CORPORATION, *pg.* 1360, *pg.* 77
MINI-SYSTEMS, INC., *pg.* 654, *pg.* 837
POST GLOVER RESISTORS INC., *pg.* 1585, *pg.* 727
VISHAY INTERTECHNOLOGY, INC., *pg.* 1435, *pg.* 1551

3677 - Electronic Coils, Transformers & other Inductors

BEL FUSE INC., *pg.* 624, *pg.* 1075
BOURNS, INC., *pg.* 627, *pg.* 193
COILCRAFT, INC., *pg.* 1324, *pg.* 562
CORNELL DUBILIER ELECTRONICS, *pg.* 630, *pg.* 1620
DEXTER MAGNETIC TECHNOLOGIES, INC., *pg.* 634, *pg.* 610
HENKEL CORPORATION, *pg.* 1049, *pg.* 369
HUMPHREY PRODUCTS CORPORATION, *pg.* 1300, *pg.* 894
MESTEK, INC., *pg.* 1074, *pg.* 857
MICROWAVE FILTER COMPANY, INC., *pg.* 654, *pg.* 1157
SIGMATRON INTERNATIONAL, INC., *pg.* 674, *pg.* 611
TII NETWORK TECHNOLOGIES, INC., *pg.* 680, *pg.* 1157
VICOR CORPORATION, *pg.* 1435, *pg.* 783
VISHAY INTERTECHNOLOGY, INC., *pg.* 1435, *pg.* 1551

3678 - Electronic Connectors

AMPHENOL CORPORATION, *pg.* 616, *pg.* 381
AUTOSWAGE PRODUCTS, INC., *pg.* 200, *pg.* 369
BOMAR INTERCONNECT PRODUCTS, INC., *pg.* 1318, *pg.* 1079
CTS CORPORATION, *pg.* 631, *pg.* 677
CVD EQUIPMENT CORPORATION, *pg.* 632, *pg.* 1152
EVERETT CHARLES TECHNOLOGIES, *pg.* 638, *pg.* 185
METHODE ELECTRONICS, INC., *pg.* 654, *pg.* 581
MOLEX INCORPORATED, *pg.* 655, *pg.* 628
RF INDUSTRIES, LTD., *pg.* 461, *pg.* 208
TE CONNECTIVITY LTD., *pg.* 677, *pg.* 1515
THOMAS & BETTS CORPORATION, *pg.* 680, *pg.* 1646

3679 - Electronic Components, NEC

3D SYSTEMS CORPORATION, *pg.* 339, *pg.* 1621
3M TOUCH SYSTEMS, INC., *pg.* 339, *pg.* 833
A. T. CROSS COMPANY, *pg.* 339, *pg.* 1602
AAVID THERMALLOY, LLC, *pg.* 612, *pg.* 1035
ACACIA RESEARCH CORPORATION, *pg.* 1398, *pg.* 165
ACCO BRANDS CORPORATION, *pg.* 340, *pg.* 626
ACER AMERICA CORPORATION, *pg.* 341, *pg.* 235
ACOPIAN TECHNICAL COMPANY, *pg.* 612, *pg.* 1528
ACTIVE POWER, INC., *pg.* 1310, *pg.* 1660
ADTRAN, INC., *pg.* 344, *pg.* 6
ADVANCED ENERGY INDUSTRIES, INC., *pg.* 613, *pg.* 328
AESP, INC., *pg.* 345, *pg.* 439
AHEARN & SOPER INC., *pg.* 345, *pg.* 1932
AIRVANA, INC., *pg.* 268, *pg.* 812
ALCATEL-LUCENT, *pg.* 615, *pg.* 1094
ALCATEL-LUCENT, *pg.* 615, *pg.* 38
ALCATEL-LUCENT USA, INC., *pg.* 615, *pg.* 1728
ALLIANCE FIBER OPTIC PRODUCTS, INC., *pg.* 1399, *pg.* 283
AMERICAN ELECTRIC TECHNOLOGIES, INC., *pg.* 349, *pg.* 1700
AMERICAN TECHNICAL CERAMICS CORP., *pg.* 616, *pg.* 1168
AMETEK PROGRAMMABLE POWER, INC., *pg.* 616, *pg.* 200
ANALOGIC CORPORATION, *pg.* 1399, *pg.* 840
ANAREN, INC., *pg.* 617, *pg.* 1157
ANDREA ELECTRONICS CORPORATION, *pg.* 617, *pg.* 1143
ANTEC INCORPORATED, *pg.* 350, *pg.* 90
API TECHNOLOGIES CORP., *pg.* 618, *pg.* 452
APPLE INC., *pg.* 350, *pg.* 73
ARRIS GROUP, INC., *pg.* 353, *pg.* 541
ASANTE TECHNOLOGIES, INC., *pg.* 619, *pg.* 238
ASCO POWER TECHNOLOGIES, L.P., *pg.* 1314, *pg.* 1066
ASTRO-MED, INC., *pg.* 619, *pg.* 1609
ATEK, *pg.* 620, *pg.* 919
AUDIOCODES USA, *pg.* 356, *pg.* 1121
AVAYA INC., *pg.* 621, *pg.* 264
AVID TECHNOLOGY, INC., *pg.* 622, *pg.* 804
AVX CORPORATION, *pg.* 623, *pg.* 1616
AWR CORPORATION, *pg.* 623, *pg.* 78
BALL CORPORATION, *pg.* 1452, *pg.* 311
BASLER ELECTRIC COMPANY, *pg.* 623, *pg.* 616
BEAD INDUSTRIES INC., *pg.* 200, *pg.* 356
BEL FUSE INC., *pg.* 624, *pg.* 1075
BENCHMARK ELECTRONICS, INC., *pg.* 624, *pg.* 1659
BLACK BOX CORPORATION, *pg.* 361, *pg.* 1547
BLACKBERRY LIMITED, *pg.* 625, *pg.* 1947
BLUE COAT SYSTEMS, INC., *pg.* 362, *pg.* 284
THE BOEING COMPANY, *pg.* 225, *pg.* 567
BOGEN COMMUNICATIONS INTERNATIONAL INC., *pg.* 625, *pg.* 1113
BRADY CORPORATION, *pg.* 363, *pg.* 1873
BROADCOM CORPORATION, *pg.* 364, *pg.* 108
BROCADE COMMUNICATIONS SYSTEMS, INC., *pg.* 365, *pg.* 239
CADENCE DESIGN SYSTEMS, INC., *pg.* 367, *pg.* 239
CAPCOM USA, INC., *pg.* 950, *pg.* 254
CHANNELL COMMERCIAL CORP., *pg.* 1870, *pg.* 291
CHROMALOX, INC., *pg.* 1070, *pg.* 1574
CHYRONHEGO, *pg.* 371, *pg.* 1179
CISCO SYSTEMS, INC., *pg.* 372, *pg.* 240
CLARY CORPORATION, *pg.* 226, *pg.* 150
CLEARONE COMMUNICATIONS, INC., *pg.* 629, *pg.* 1756
CODA OCTOPUS GROUP, INC., *pg.* 629, *pg.* 437
COHERENT, INC., *pg.* 1406, *pg.* 265
COLLABRX, INC., *pg.* 1324, *pg.* 216
COMMUNICATIONS SPECIALTIES, INC., *pg.* 377, *pg.* 1338
COMMUNICATIONS SYSTEMS, INC., *pg.* 630, *pg.* 948

First page reference indicates Business Class Edition
Second page reference indicates Geographic Edition

COOPER INTERCONNECT, pg. 630, pg. 1118
CORNING CABLE SYSTEMS LLC, pg. 1407, pg. 1378
CORSAIR COMPONENTS, INC., pg. 380, pg. 90
CRANE AEROSPACE & ELECTRONICS, KELTEC OPERATION, pg. 631, pg. 428
CREATIVE VISTAS INC., pg. 1044, pg. 1948
CTS CORPORATION, pg. 631, pg. 677
CUSTOM SENSORS & TECHNOLOGIES, pg. 1407, pg. 152
D-LINK SYSTEMS, INC., pg. 381, pg. 89
DATA I/O CORPORATION, pg. 382, pg. 1824
DATALOGIC, pg. 382, pg. 1588
DATAMAX CORPORATION, pg. 1633, pg. 453
DGT HOLDINGS, pg. 634, pg. 1223
DIEBOLD, INCORPORATED, pg. 387, pg. 1407
DIGI INTERNATIONAL INC., pg. 387, pg. 948
DIGITAL LIGHTWAVE, INC., pg. 634, pg. 462
DOVER CORPORATION, pg. 1329, pg. 608
DOW ELECTRONIC MATERIALS, pg. 1159, pg. 832
DYNAVOX INC., pg. 635, pg. 1574
EASTMAN KODAK COMPANY, pg. 1408, pg. 1333
EATON BUSSMANN, INC., pg. 1331, pg. 977
ECRM IMAGING SYSTEMS, INC., pg. 1410, pg. 848
EFAX.COM INC., pg. 1242, pg. 129
ELECTRO STANDARDS LABORATORIES INC., pg. 390, pg. 1600
ELECTROCUBE INCORPORATED, pg. 635, pg. 185
ELECTRONIC TELE-COMMUNICATIONS, INC., pg. 390, pg. 1897
ELECTRONICS FOR IMAGING, INC., pg. 390, pg. 88
ELEKTA, pg. 391, pg. 987
ELENCO ELECTRONICS, INC., pg. 953, pg. 670
ELO TOUCH SOLUTIONS, pg. 635, pg. 145
EMC CORPORATION, pg. 391, pg. 825
EMG, INC., pg. 636, pg. 277
EMPOWER RF SYSTEMS, INC., pg. 637, pg. 105
EMRISE CORPORATION, pg. 637, pg. 1371
EMTEC, INC., pg. 392, pg. 1123
EMULEX CORPORATION, pg. 392, pg. 70
EPSON AMERICA INC., pg. 394, pg. 122
ERGOTRON, INC., pg. 395, pg. 960
EVANS & SUTHERLAND COMPUTER CORPORATION, pg. 638, pg. 1757
EVANS & SUTHERLAND COMPUTER CORPORATION - DIGITAL THEATER DIVISION, pg. 395, pg. 1757
EXTREME NETWORKS INC, pg. 287, pg. 245
EZENIA! INC., pg. 396, pg. 1039
F5 NETWORKS, INC., pg. 396, pg. 1835
FINISAR CORPORATION, pg. 639, pg. 285
FLEXTRONICS INTERNATIONAL LTD., pg. 81, pg. 245
FOX ELECTRONICS, pg. 639, pg. 428
FUSION UV SYSTEMS, INC., pg. 640, pg. 770
GALE CENGAGE LEARNING, pg. 1643, pg. 885
GE INTELLIGENT PLATFORMS, pg. 400, pg. 1135
GENERAL DATACOMM INDUSTRIES, INC., pg. 400, pg. 357
GIGA-TRONICS INCORPORATED, pg. 640, pg. 260
GIGOPTIX, INC., pg. 400, pg. 245
GLORY GLOBAL SOLUTIONS, pg. 401, pg. 628
GN NETCOM INC., pg. 640, pg. 1037
GUARDIAN ELECTRIC MANUFACTURING COMPANY, pg. 641, pg. 672
HAPP CONTROLS INC., pg. 641, pg. 634
HARLAND CLARKE HOLDINGS CORP., pg. 1647, pg. 1741
HAUPPAUGE DIGITAL, INC., pg. 402, pg. 1164
HEWLETT-PACKARD COMPANY, pg. 404, pg. 175
HITTITE MICROWAVE CORPORATION, pg. 642, pg. 813
HUTCHINSON TECHNOLOGY INC., pg. 409, pg. 926
HYPERSOUND, pg. 643, pg. 186
ICAD, INC., pg. 643, pg. 1037
I.D. SYSTEMS, INC., pg. 643, pg. 1134
IEC ELECTRONICS CORP., pg. 643, pg. 1317
IGO, INC., pg. 644, pg. 22
II-VI INCORPORATED, pg. 1417, pg. 1585
INDUSTRIAL ELECTRONIC ENGINEERS, INC., pg. 644, pg. 300
INFINEON TECHNOLOGIES NORTH AMERICA CORP., pg. 644, pg. 145
INFINERA CORPORATION, pg. 644, pg. 286
INFOCUS CORPORATION, pg. 644, pg. 1503
INTELLICHECK MOBILISA, INC., pg. 416, pg. 1823
INTERDIGITAL, INC., pg. 1872, pg. 1543
INTERLINK ELECTRONICS, INC., pg. 417, pg. 57
INTERNATIONAL BUSINESS MACHINES CORPORATION, pg. 418, pg. 1138
INTERPHASE CORPORATION, pg. 420, pg. 1732
INTERPOINT CORPORATION, pg. 647, pg. 1824
INTRUSION INC., pg. 1259, pg. 1736
ITUS CORPORATION, pg. 422, pg. 1180
JABIL CIRCUIT, INC., pg. 422, pg. 463
JUNIPER NETWORKS, INC., pg. 1260, pg. 286
KENSINGTON TECHNOLOGY GROUP, pg. 424, pg. 191
KEVLIN CORPORATION, pg. 649, pg. 1034
KEY TRONIC CORPORATION, pg. 424, pg. 1844
KIMBALL INTERNATIONAL, INC., pg. 931, pg. 692
KINGSTON TECHNOLOGY COMPANY, INC., pg. 425, pg. 90
KOFAX IMAGE PRODUCTS, INC., pg. 1419, pg. 112
KOSS CORPORATION, pg. 649, pg. 1877
KRATOS-GENERAL MICROWAVE, pg. 650, pg. 1344
KRATOS LANCASTER, pg. 1419, pg. 1546
KRONOS INCORPORATED, pg. 425, pg. 813
LANTRONIX, INC., pg. 426, pg. 112
LATTICE INC., pg. 1872, pg. 1108
LEVEL 3 COMMUNICATIONS, INC., pg. 1262, pg. 1664
LEXMARK INTERNATIONAL, INC., pg. 427, pg. 730
THE LGL GROUP, INC., pg. 652, pg. 454
LIGHTPATH TECHNOLOGIES INC, pg. 1420, pg. 454
LOGITECH INC., pg. 1264, pg. 164
LOJACK CORPORATION, pg. 210, pg. 811
MACLEAN-FOGG COMPANY INC., pg. 1358, pg. 635
MAD CATZ INTERACTIVE INC., pg. 429, pg. 204
MARTEK POWER ABBOTT, INC., pg. 652, pg. 294
MATERION MICROELECTRONICS & SERVICES, pg. 1559, pg. 1149
MEGGITT TRAINING SYSTEMS, pg. 1839, pg. 541
MERCURY COMPUTER SYSTEMS, INC., pg. 434, pg. 813
MICROBOARDS TECHNOLOGY, LLC, pg. 434, pg. 920
MICRON TECHNOLOGY, INC., pg. 435, pg. 547
MICROSEMI CORPORATION, pg. 435, pg. 41
MICROVISION, INC., pg. 654, pg. 1828
MICROWAVE FILTER COMPANY, INC., pg. 654, pg. 1157
MICROWAY, INC., pg. 1267, pg. 841
MILTOPE GROUP, INC., pg. 440, pg. 6
MITEK SYSTEMS, INC., pg. 440, pg. 204
MITEL NETWORKS CORPORATION, pg. 654, pg. 1921
MITEL NETWORKS, INC., pg. 1872, pg. 13
MOLEX INCORPORATED, pg. 655, pg. 628
MORSE WATCHMANS INC., pg. 656, pg. 368
MOTOROLA ENTERPRISE MOBILITY, pg. 441, pg. 1167
MOTOROLA SOLUTIONS, INC., pg. 657, pg. 659
MPHASE TECHNOLOGIES, INC., pg. 441, pg. 363
MRV COMMUNICATIONS, INC., pg. 441, pg. 64
MULTI-TECH SYSTEMS INC., pg. 442, pg. 951
MURATEC AMERICA, INC., pg. 443, pg. 1733
NCR CORPORATION, pg. 443, pg. 531
NEC CORPORATION OF AMERICA, INC., pg. 658, pg. 1723
NEONODE, INC., pg. 659, pg. 268
NER HOLDINGS INC., pg. 444, pg. 1071
NETGEAR, INC., pg. 444, pg. 247
NETSCOUT SYSTEMS, INC., pg. 1270, pg. 858
NEUSTAR, INC., pg. 1872, pg. 1807
NORTECH SYSTEMS INCORPORATED, pg. 659, pg. 966
NORTEK SECURITY & CONTROL LLC, pg. 659, pg. 59
NORTHROP GRUMMAN CORPORATION, pg. 231, pg. 1781
NOVATEL INC., pg. 1424, pg. 1904
NUMEREX CORP., pg. 660, pg. 517
OKI DATA AMERICAS, INC., pg. 449, pg. 1090
ONMOBILE LIVE, INC., pg. 449, pg. 829
OPENCONNECT SYSTEMS, INC., pg. 449, pg. 1685
OPLINK COMMUNICATIONS, INC., pg. 660, pg. 91
ORACLE CORPORATION, pg. 1272, pg. 786
ORTRONICS/LEGRAND, pg. 451, pg. 359
OVERLAND STORAGE, INC., pg. 451, pg. 205
PALOMAR TECHNOLOGIES INC., pg. 661, pg. 60
PASSUR AEROSPACE, INC., pg. 233, pg. 376
PEARSON ASSESSMENTS, pg. 1674, pg. 918
PERCEPTRON, INC., pg. 215, pg. 904
PERLE SYSTEMS LIMITED, pg. 454, pg. 1924
PLAINTREE SYSTEMS INC., pg. 663, pg. 1918
PLANAR SYSTEMS, INC., pg. 455, pg. 1495
PLANTRONICS, INC., pg. 663, pg. 270
PLEXUS CORP., pg. 455, pg. 1883
POLYCOM, INC., pg. 664, pg. 249
POST GLOVER RESISTORS INC., pg. 1585, pg. 727
PREFORMED LINE PRODUCTS COMPANY, pg. 1370, pg. 1434
PRESSTEK LLC, pg. 1678, pg. 1034
PRINTRONIX, INC., pg. 456, pg. 115
PROGRESS DATADIRECT, pg. 457, pg. 1385
PROGRESSIVE DYNAMICS, INC., pg. 665, pg. 898
PROJECTS UNLIMITED, INC., pg. 665, pg. 1446
PROVISION HOLDING, INC., pg. 665, pg. 65
PULSE ELECTRONICS CORPORATION, pg. 666, pg. 206
Q-TECH CORPORATION, pg. 666, pg. 72
QUALCOMM INCORPORATED, pg. 1873, pg. 207
RADISYS CORPORATION, pg. 458, pg. 1498
RAULAND-BORG CORPORATION, pg. 666, pg. 634
RAYTHEON, pg. 459, pg. 115
RELAX TECHNOLOGY, INC., pg. 461, pg. 298
RICOH PRINTING SYSTEMS AMERICA, INC., pg. 462, pg. 279
ROSTRA PRECISION CONTROLS, INC., pg. 216, pg. 1381
RSA SECURITY INC., pg. 463, pg. 786
SANMINA-SCI CORPORATION, pg. 671, pg. 250
SCAN-OPTICS, LLC, pg. 467, pg. 354
SCANTRON CORPORATION, pg. 467, pg. 922
SDI TECHNOLOGIES, INC., pg. 671, pg. 1113
SHORETEL, INC., pg. 469, pg. 288
SHURE INCORPORATED, pg. 672, pg. 638
SIGMA DESIGNS, INC., pg. 469, pg. 148
SILICON GRAPHICS INTERNATIONAL CORP, pg. 470, pg. 148
SIQURA, pg. 308, pg. 771
SKYWORKS SOLUTIONS, INC., pg. 674, pg. 862
SL INDUSTRIES, INC., pg. 674, pg. 1090
SOCKET MOBILE, INC., pg. 471, pg. 164
SONUS NETWORKS INC., pg. 1281, pg. 858
SOURCE PHOTONICS, INC., pg. 1429, pg. 305
SPACEDEV INC., pg. 234, pg. 186
SPARTON CORPORATION, pg. 1377, pg. 660
STANDEX INTERNATIONAL CORPORATION, pg. 60, pg. 1039
STEELCLOUD, INC., pg. 476, pg. 1776
STRATASYS, INC., pg. 476, pg. 923
SUPER MICRO COMPUTER, INC., pg. 478, pg. 251
TDK-LAMBDA HIGH POWER DIVISION, pg. 1380, pg. 1090
TECH DATA CORPORATION, pg. 482, pg. 416
TECSYS, INC., pg. 482, pg. 1956
TELEBYTE, INC., pg. 482, pg. 1165
TELEGENIX INC., pg. 678, pg. 1051
TELENAV, INC., pg. 678, pg. 288
TELLABS, INC., pg. 678, pg. 637
TIDEL ENGINEERING, L.P., pg. 1382, pg. 1670
TRANS-LUX CORPORATION, pg. 681, pg. 365
TRIPPE MANUFACTURING COMPANY, pg. 220, pg. 592
TROY GROUP INC., pg. 485, pg. 71
TYCO INTERNATIONAL (US) INC., pg. 1891, pg. 1113
ULTIMATE TECHNOLOGY CORPORATION, pg. 486, pg. 1349
UNICOM ENGINEERING, pg. 1286, pg. 812
UNIVERSAL DISPLAY CORPORATION, pg. 683, pg. 1064
UNIVERSAL SECURITY INSTRUMENTS, INC., pg. 683, pg. 775
UQM TECHNOLOGIES, INC., pg. 684, pg. 334
VALVE CORPORATION, pg. 487, pg. 1817
VEECO INSTRUMENTS INC., pg. 1434, pg. 1322
VERIFONE SYSTEMS, INC., pg. 487, pg. 251
VIAVI SOLUTIONS INC., pg. 1435, pg. 148
VICOR CORPORATION, pg. 1435, pg. 783
VIDEO DISPLAY CORPORATION, pg. 685, pg. 542
VIEW SYSTEMS, INC., pg. 489, pg. 760
VIEWSONIC CORPORATION, pg. 489, pg. 303
VUZIX CORPORATION, pg. 687, pg. 1337
WEGENER CORPORATION, pg. 687, pg. 533
WINLAND ELECTRONICS, INC., pg. 688, pg. 928
WIZZARD SPEECH LLC., pg. 493, pg. 1582
WOODWARD, INC., pg. 122, pg. 329
ZAGG INCORPORATED, pg. 690, pg. 1762
ZEBRA TECHNOLOGIES CORPORATION, pg. 690, pg. 628
ZOOM TECHNOLOGIES, INC., pg. 497, pg. 1317

3691 - Storage Batteries

C&D TECHNOLOGIES, INC., pg. 627, pg. 1517
DURACELL, pg. 635, pg. 337
ENERSYS INC., pg. 1334, pg. 1584
EXIDE TECHNOLOGIES, pg. 204, pg. 483
INTERSTATE BATTERY SYSTEM OF AMERICA INC., pg. 208, pg. 1682
JOHNSON CONTROLS, INC., pg. 209, pg. 1876
LIND ELECTRONICS, INC., pg. 1355, pg. 938
MAGNETIC METALS CORP., pg. 1358, pg. 1049
ULTRALIFE CORPORATION, pg. 1385, pg. 1317
YARDNEY TECHNICAL PRODUCTS, INC., pg. 690, pg.

1601

3692 - Primary Batteries, Dry & Wet

A123 SYSTEMS INC., *pg.* 1309, *pg.* 855
DURACELL, *pg.* 635, *pg.* 337
ENERGIZER HOLDINGS, INC., *pg.* 637, *pg.* 996
ENERSYS INC., *pg.* 1334, *pg.* 1584
INTERSTATE BATTERY SYSTEM OF AMERICA INC., *pg.* 208, *pg.* 1682
JOHNSON CONTROLS, INC., *pg.* 209, *pg.* 1876
ULTRALIFE CORPORATION, *pg.* 1385, *pg.* 1317
VALENCE TECHNOLOGY, INC., *pg.* 684, *pg.* 1667
VARTA MICROBATTERY, INC., *pg.* 221, *pg.* 1339
YARDNEY TECHNICAL PRODUCTS, INC., *pg.* 690, *pg.* 1601

3695 - Magnetic & Optical Recording Media

DEXTER MAGNETIC TECHNOLOGIES, INC., *pg.* 634, *pg.* 610
IMATION CORP., *pg.* 413, *pg.* 952
IMMERSION CORPORATION, *pg.* 413, *pg.* 246
INTERLINK ELECTRONICS, INC., *pg.* 417, *pg.* 57
OCLARO, INC., *pg.* 1425, *pg.* 248
QUALSTAR CORPORATION, *pg.* 458, *pg.* 279

3699 - Electrical Machinery, Equipment & Supplies, NEC

THE ADT CORPORATION, *pg.* 612, *pg.* 409
ADVANCED ENERGY INDUSTRIES, INC., *pg.* 613, *pg.* 328
BAE SYSTEMS PRODUCTS GROUP, *pg.* 359, *pg.* 432
BALLARD POWER SYSTEMS, INC., *pg.* 70, *pg.* 1907
BLONDER TONGUE LABORATORIES, INC., *pg.* 625, *pg.* 1100
BRADY CORPORATION, *pg.* 363, *pg.* 1873
BRANSON ULTRASONICS CORPORATION, *pg.* 1319, *pg.* 342
BRANSON ULTRASONICS CORPORATION-PRECISION CLEANING DIV, *pg.* 1319, *pg.* 343
BROAN-NUTONE LLC, *pg.* 1069, *pg.* 1860
C&D TECHNOLOGIES, INC., *pg.* 627, *pg.* 1517
THE CHAMBERLAIN GROUP, INC., *pg.* 75, *pg.* 611
CHASE CORPORATION, *pg.* 1152, *pg.* 803
CHECKPOINT SYSTEMS, INC., *pg.* 628, *pg.* 1559
CLORE AUTOMOTIVE LLC, *pg.* 202, *pg.* 716
CONDUCTIX INC., *pg.* 1295, *pg.* 1015
CTS VALPEY CORPORATION, *pg.* 632, *pg.* 825
CVI MELLES GRIOT, *pg.* 1407, *pg.* 59
DETEX CORPORATION, *pg.* 633, *pg.* 1728
EATON CORPORATION, *pg.* 1331, *pg.* 1429
ENERGIZER HOLDINGS, INC., *pg.* 637, *pg.* 996
THE GENIE COMPANY, *pg.* 55, *pg.* 1403
GLOBAL EPOINT INC., *pg.* 400, *pg.* 67
GSI GROUP INC., *pg.* 1415, *pg.* 784
HIGHFIELD MANUFACTURING CO., *pg.* 1346, *pg.* 339
HUBBELL INCORPORATED, *pg.* 1299, *pg.* 370
HUBBELL POWER SYSTEMS, INC., *pg.* 643, *pg.* 1614
INTERNATIONAL COMPONENTS CORPORATION, *pg.* 647, *pg.* 669
INVISIBLE FENCE, INC., *pg.* 648, *pg.* 1637
ISOMET CORPORATION, *pg.* 1418, *pg.* 1807
IXIA, *pg.* 422, *pg.* 56
LA MARCHE MANUFACTURING COMPANY, *pg.* 1300, *pg.* 606
LASER TECHNOLOGY, INC., *pg.* 1419, *pg.* 314
LIND ELECTRONICS, INC., *pg.* 1355, *pg.* 938
MASTER APPLIANCE CORP., *pg.* 1055, *pg.* 1888
MATEC INSTRUMENT COMPANIES, INC., *pg.* 1421, *pg.* 839
MAXXESS SYSTEMS, INC., *pg.* 431, *pg.* 43
MORSE WATCHMANS INC., *pg.* 656, *pg.* 368
NABCO ENTRANCES, INC., *pg.* 99, *pg.* 1882
NEW WAVE RESEARCH INCORPORATED, *pg.* 1423, *pg.* 91
NEWPORT CORPORATION, *pg.* 1424, *pg.* 114
PERCEPTICS, LLC, *pg.* 1426, *pg.* 1637
PROPHOTONIX LIMITED, *pg.* 1427, *pg.* 1039
ROCKWELL AUTOMATION, INC., *pg.* 668, *pg.* 1880
ROFIN-SINAR TECHNOLOGIES, INC., *pg.* 668, *pg.* 904
SCHNEIDER CANADA, INC., *pg.* 1374, *pg.* 1928
SCHNEIDER ELECTRIC, *pg.* 467, *pg.* 1609
SILICON GRAPHICS INTERNATIONAL CORP, *pg.* 470, *pg.* 148
SL INDUSTRIES, INC., *pg.* 674, *pg.* 1090
SUREFIRE, LLC, *pg.* 1307, *pg.* 90
TDK-LAMBDA HIGH POWER DIVISION, *pg.* 1380, *pg.* 1090
TECHNIBUS LLC, *pg.* 1380, *pg.* 1408
VISHAY INTERTECHNOLOGY, INC., *pg.* 1435, *pg.* 1551
WOODWARD, INC., *pg.* 122, *pg.* 329

3711 - Motor Vehicles & Passenger Car Bodies

AEROJET ROCKETDYNE, *pg.* 223, *pg.* 1782
AFFINIA WIX FILTRATION PRODUCTS, *pg.* 198, *pg.* 1373
AIR LIFT COMPANY, *pg.* 198, *pg.* 895
A.L. HANSEN MANUFACTURING CO., *pg.* 1041, *pg.* 665
ALLISON TRANSMISSION, INC., *pg.* 198, *pg.* 682
ALLOMATIC PRODUCTS COMPANY, *pg.* 198, *pg.* 1160
AM GENERAL, LLC, *pg.* 163, *pg.* 697
AMBAC INTERNATIONAL CORPORATION, *pg.* 198, *pg.* 1615
AMERICAN AXLE & MANUFACTURING HOLDINGS, INC., *pg.* 198, *pg.* 879
AMERICAN HONDA MOTOR CO., INC., *pg.* 163, *pg.* 292
AMP HOLDING INC., *pg.* 164, *pg.* 1406
AP EXHAUST PRODUCTS, INC., *pg.* 199, *pg.* 1373
AUSCO PRODUCTS, INC., *pg.* 199, *pg.* 872
AUTOLIV NORTH AMERICA, AMERICAN TECHNICAL CENTER, *pg.* 200, *pg.* 867
BALDWIN FILTERS, *pg.* 1316, *pg.* 1011
BESTOP, INC., *pg.* 200, *pg.* 312
BLUE BIRD CORPORATION, *pg.* 1705, *pg.* 532
BORGWARNER INC., *pg.* 167, *pg.* 867
BSM TECHNOLOGIES INC., *pg.* 627, *pg.* 1949
CAPSONIC GROUP LLC, *pg.* 1880, *pg.* 609
CARLISLE TIRE & WHEEL COMPANY, *pg.* 1880, *pg.* 1612
THE CARLSON COMPANY INC., *pg.* 167, *pg.* 722
CATERPILLAR, INC., *pg.* 1321, *pg.* 650
CLARCOR, INC., *pg.* 1455, *pg.* 1632
COLE HERSEE COMPANY, *pg.* 202, *pg.* 792
COMMERCIAL VEHICLE GROUP, INC., *pg.* 203, *pg.* 1467
CONSUMER PORTFOLIO SERVICES, INC., *pg.* 741, *pg.* 109
CORE MOLDING TECHNOLOGIES, INC., *pg.* 1881, *pg.* 1439
CPI HOLDINGS, LLC, *pg.* 203, *pg.* 32
CRANE CARRIER COMPANY, *pg.* 168, *pg.* 1489
CUMMINS INC., *pg.* 1326, *pg.* 676
CWC TEXTRON, *pg.* 1326, *pg.* 901
DANA HOLDING CORPORATION, *pg.* 203, *pg.* 1461
DANFOSS POWER SOLUTIONS COMPANY, *pg.* 1328, *pg.* 701
DELPHI AUTOMOTIVE LLP, *pg.* 204, *pg.* 910
DELPHI ELECTRONICS & SAFETY, *pg.* 633, *pg.* 692
DONALDSON COMPANY, INC., *pg.* 1329, *pg.* 917
DORMAN PRODUCTS, INC., *pg.* 204, *pg.* 1522
DOUGLAS DYNAMICS, INC., *pg.* 204, *pg.* 1874
EATON CORPORATION, *pg.* 1331, *pg.* 1429
EATON HYDRAULICS INC., *pg.* 1332, *pg.* 922
EDELBROCK CORPORATION, *pg.* 204, *pg.* 293
ELECTROID CO, *pg.* 1333, *pg.* 1123
FCA CANADA INC., *pg.* 170, *pg.* 1948
FCA US LLC, *pg.* 170, *pg.* 868
FEDERAL-MOGUL HOLDINGS CORPORATION, *pg.* 205, *pg.* 907
FEDERAL SIGNAL CORPORATION, *pg.* 638, *pg.* 645
FLOWTRON OUTDOOR PRODUCTS, *pg.* 639, *pg.* 830
FORD MOTOR COMPANY, *pg.* 172, *pg.* 876
FORD MOTOR COMPANY OF CANADA, LIMITED, *pg.* 174, *pg.* 1930
FRANKLIN ELECTRIC CO., INC., *pg.* 1337, *pg.* 680
FREIGHTLINER TRUCKS, *pg.* 174, *pg.* 1502
FREUDENBERG-NOK, *pg.* 1882, *pg.* 904
GENERAL DYNAMICS CORPORATION, *pg.* 228, *pg.* 1781
GENERAL MOTORS COMPANY, *pg.* 175, *pg.* 881
GENERAL MOTORS OF CANADA LTD., *pg.* 177, *pg.* 1931
GENTEX CORPORATION, *pg.* 206, *pg.* 913
GKN AUTOMOTIVE INC., *pg.* 206, *pg.* 869
THE GLEASON WORKS, *pg.* 1341, *pg.* 1336
GRAHAM MOTORS AND CONTROLS, *pg.* 177, *pg.* 1692
HACKNEY INTERNATIONAL, *pg.* 178, *pg.* 1392
HECKETHORN MANUFACTURING COMPANY, INC., *pg.* 207, *pg.* 1632
HEIL ENVIRONMENTAL INDUSTRIES, LTD., *pg.* 207, *pg.* 1629
HENDRICKSON INTERNATIONAL, *pg.* 207, *pg.* 672
HENNESSY INDUSTRIES, INC., *pg.* 207, *pg.* 1639
HONEYWELL CONSUMER PRODUCTS GROUP, *pg.* 208, *pg.* 344
HONEYWELL INTERNATIONAL INC., *pg.* 407, *pg.* 1088
HUTCHENS INDUSTRIES INC., *pg.* 208, *pg.* 1006
INDIAN HEAD INDUSTRIES, INC., *pg.* 208, *pg.* 1367
JACOBS VEHICLE SYSTEMS, *pg.* 1351, *pg.* 338
JANESVILLE ACOUSTICS, *pg.* 1885, *pg.* 907
J.B. POINDEXTER & CO., INC., *pg.* 209, *pg.* 1709
JOHN DEERE COFFEYVILLE WORKS INC, *pg.* 1351, *pg.* 714
JOHNSON CONTROLS, INC., *pg.* 209, *pg.* 1876
K&N ENGINEERING INC., *pg.* 210, *pg.* 194
KENWORTH TRUCK CO., *pg.* 181, *pg.* 1822
KEY SAFETY SYSTEMS, INC., *pg.* 210, *pg.* 908
KYB AMERICA LLC, *pg.* 210, *pg.* 681
LEAR CORPORATION, *pg.* 229, *pg.* 907
LEXUS DIVISION, *pg.* 182, *pg.* 294
LINGENFELTER PERFORMANCE ENGINEERING, INC., *pg.* 94, *pg.* 677
LISLE CORPORATION, *pg.* 1356, *pg.* 703
LKQ CORP., *pg.* 210, *pg.* 185
LOUIS BERKMAN CO., *pg.* 1357, *pg.* 1473
LUND INTERNATIONAL, INC., *pg.* 211, *pg.* 526
MACK TRUCKS, INC., *pg.* 183, *pg.* 1375
MAGNA INTERNATIONAL INC., *pg.* 211, *pg.* 1918
MAHLE BEHR USA INC., TROY, *pg.* 212, *pg.* 911
MAXION WHEELS, *pg.* 212, *pg.* 903
MERITOR, INC., *pg.* 212, *pg.* 911
MICHIGAN WHEEL CORPORATION, *pg.* 1709, *pg.* 888
MICO, INCORPORATED, *pg.* 212, *pg.* 951
MILE MARKER INTERNATIONAL INC., *pg.* 213, *pg.* 459
MILLER INDUSTRIES, INC., *pg.* 185, *pg.* 1655
MODINE MANUFACTURING COMPANY, *pg.* 1074, *pg.* 1888
MOTORCAR PARTS OF AMERICA, INC., *pg.* 213, *pg.* 295
MR. GASKET INC., *pg.* 213, *pg.* 1406
NATIONAL AUTOMOTIVE PARTS ASSOCIATION, *pg.* 213, *pg.* 515
NAVISTAR INTERNATIONAL CORPORATION, *pg.* 186, *pg.* 630
NEAPCO, INC., *pg.* 214, *pg.* 1582
NETWORKFLEET, INC., *pg.* 445, *pg.* 205
NISSAN NORTH AMERICA, INC., *pg.* 186, *pg.* 1633
OMAHA STANDARD PALFINGER, *pg.* 706, *pg.* 704
OSHKOSH CORPORATION, *pg.* 187, *pg.* 1885
OSHKOSH SPECIALTY VEHICLES, *pg.* 1918, *pg.* 561
PACCAR INC., *pg.* 187, *pg.* 1816
PARKER HANNIFIN WATTS FLUID AIR, *pg.* 1368, *pg.* 750
PARKHURST MANUFACTURING CO., INC., *pg.* 214, *pg.* 1005
PENDA CORPORATION, *pg.* 214, *pg.* 1887
PERCEPTRON, INC., *pg.* 215, *pg.* 904
THE PERRY COMPANY, *pg.* 706, *pg.* 1749
PIERCE MANUFACTURING, INC., *pg.* 188, *pg.* 1852
PLEWS/EDELMANN, *pg.* 215, *pg.* 607
POLARIS INDUSTRIES INC., *pg.* 1709, *pg.* 928
PURADYN FILTER TECHNOLOGIES, INC., *pg.* 215, *pg.* 414
QUANTUM FUEL SYSTEMS TECHNOLOGIES WORLDWIDE, INC., *pg.* 1371, *pg.* 115
REMY INTERNATIONAL, INC., *pg.* 216, *pg.* 696
RIETER AUTOMOTIVE NORTH AMERICA, INC., *pg.* 216, *pg.* 886
ROSTRA PRECISION CONTROLS, INC., *pg.* 216, *pg.* 1381
SAF-HOLLAND INTERNATIONAL, INC., *pg.* 217, *pg.* 902
SANDEN INTERNATIONAL (USA), INC., *pg.* 217, *pg.* 1750
SEASTAR SOLUTIONS, *pg.* 1374, *pg.* 1548
SHUR-CO, INC., *pg.* 110, *pg.* 1626
SPARTAN MOTORS, INC., *pg.* 217, *pg.* 874
SPARTON CORPORATION, *pg.* 1377, *pg.* 660
SPEEDWAY MOTORS INC., *pg.* 218, *pg.* 1012
STANDARD MOTOR PRODUCTS, INC., *pg.* 218, *pg.* 1176
STANDEX INTERNATIONAL CORPORATION, *pg.* 60, *pg.* 1039
STEMCO INC, *pg.* 1182, *pg.* 1726
STRUT, LLC, *pg.* 190, *pg.* 199
STS TURBO, INC., *pg.* 218, *pg.* 1753
SUPREME INDUSTRIES, INC., *pg.* 191, *pg.* 681
TELEFLEX INCORPORATED, *pg.* 48, *pg.* 1548
TENNECO, INC., *pg.* 985, *pg.* 625
TESLA MOTORS, INC., *pg.* 191, *pg.* 178
TEXTRON INC., *pg.* 235, *pg.* 1607
THOMAS BUILT BUSES, INC., *pg.* 191, *pg.* 1379

THULE, INC., *pg.* 218, *pg.* 369
TI AUTOMOTIVE LIMITED, *pg.* 191, *pg.* 869
TITAN INTERNATIONAL, INC., *pg.* 219, *pg.* 653
TOWER INTERNATIONAL, INC., *pg.* 219, *pg.* 897
TRICO PRODUCTS CORPORATION, *pg.* 220, *pg.* 905
TRUECAR INC., *pg.* 1284, *pg.* 276
TWIN DISC, INCORPORATED, *pg.* 220, *pg.* 1889
UNITED COMPONENTS, INC., *pg.* 220, *pg.* 679
UQM TECHNOLOGIES, INC., *pg.* 684, *pg.* 334
U.S. AXLE, INC., *pg.* 221, *pg.* 1582
UTILITY TRAILER MANUFACTURING COMPANY, *pg.* 1712, *pg.* 68
VAPOR BUS INTERNATIONAL, *pg.* 221, *pg.* 560
VISTEON CORPORATION, *pg.* 221, *pg.* 912
VOLKSWAGEN CANADA, INC., *pg.* 194, *pg.* 1918
VOLKSWAGEN GROUP OF AMERICA, INC., *pg.* 194, *pg.* 1785
VOLVO TRUCKS NORTH AMERICA, INC., *pg.* 195, *pg.* 1377
WAIGLOBAL, *pg.* 221, *pg.* 1585
WARN INDUSTRIES, INC., *pg.* 221, *pg.* 1497
WARNER ELECTRIC, INC., *pg.* 221, *pg.* 661
WELLS MANUFACTURING, L.P., *pg.* 222, *pg.* 1858
WILLIAMS CONTROLS, INC., *pg.* 222, *pg.* 1508
WINNEBAGO INDUSTRIES, INC., *pg.* 1712, *pg.* 707
WOODWARD, INC., *pg.* 122, *pg.* 329
WORTHINGTON INDUSTRIES, *pg.* 222, *pg.* 1626
ZF TRW, *pg.* 222, *pg.* 897

3714 - Motor Vehicle Parts & Accessories

AEROJET ROCKETDYNE, *pg.* 223, *pg.* 1782
AFFINIA WIX FILTRATION PRODUCTS, *pg.* 198, *pg.* 1373
AIR-LEC INDUSTRIES LLC, *pg.* 1041, *pg.* 1864
AIR LIFT COMPANY, *pg.* 198, *pg.* 895
A.L. HANSEN MANUFACTURING CO., *pg.* 1041, *pg.* 665
ALLFAST FASTENING SYSTEMS, INC., *pg.* 1041, *pg.* 66
ALLISON TRANSMISSION, INC., *pg.* 198, *pg.* 682
ALLOMATIC PRODUCTS COMPANY, *pg.* 198, *pg.* 1160
AM GENERAL, LLC, *pg.* 163, *pg.* 697
AMATOM ELECTRONIC HARDWARE, INC., *pg.* 1041, *pg.* 342
AMBAC INTERNATIONAL CORPORATION, *pg.* 198, *pg.* 1615
AMERICAN AXLE & MANUFACTURING HOLDINGS, INC., *pg.* 198, *pg.* 879
AMERICAN LOCKER GROUP INCORPORATED, *pg.* 1041, *pg.* 1674
AMERICAN VAN EQUIPMENT INC., *pg.* 199, *pg.* 1078
AP EXHAUST PRODUCTS, INC., *pg.* 199, *pg.* 1373
ARCTIC CAT INC., *pg.* 1705, *pg.* 953
ASCO SINTERING CO., *pg.* 1042, *pg.* 126
ATTWOOD CORPORATION, *pg.* 1705, *pg.* 897
AUSCO PRODUCTS, INC., *pg.* 199, *pg.* 872
AUTOLIV NORTH AMERICA, AMERICAN TECHNICAL CENTER, *pg.* 200, *pg.* 867
BALDWIN FILTERS, *pg.* 1316, *pg.* 1011
BALL & BALL HARDWARE REPRODUCTIONS, *pg.* 916, *pg.* 1531
BESTOP, INC., *pg.* 200, *pg.* 312
BLACK & DECKER, *pg.* 1043, *pg.* 1907
BLUE OX, *pg.* 701, *pg.* 1019
BOMBARDIER RECREATIONAL PRODUCTS, INC., *pg.* 201, *pg.* 1960
BORGWARNER INC., *pg.* 167, *pg.* 867
BSM TECHNOLOGIES INC., *pg.* 627, *pg.* 1949
BTM CORPORATION, *pg.* 1320, *pg.* 898
CAPSONIC GROUP LLC, *pg.* 1880, *pg.* 609
CARLISLE TIRE & WHEEL COMPANY, *pg.* 1880, *pg.* 1612
THE CARLSON COMPANY INC., *pg.* 167, *pg.* 722
CATERPILLAR, INC., *pg.* 1321, *pg.* 650
CLARCOR, INC., *pg.* 1455, *pg.* 1632
CLUB CAR, INC., *pg.* 1830, *pg.* 532
COLE HERSEE COMPANY, *pg.* 202, *pg.* 792
COMMERCIAL VEHICLE GROUP, INC., *pg.* 203, *pg.* 1467
COMPX INTERNATIONAL INC., *pg.* 1044, *pg.* 1678
CORE MOLDING TECHNOLOGIES, INC., *pg.* 1881, *pg.* 1439
CPI HOLDINGS, LLC, *pg.* 203, *pg.* 32
CUMMINS INC., *pg.* 1326, *pg.* 676
CWC TEXTRON, *pg.* 1326, *pg.* 901
DANA HOLDING CORPORATION, *pg.* 203, *pg.* 1461
DANFOSS POWER SOLUTIONS COMPANY, *pg.* 1328, *pg.* 701
DECO PRODUCTS CO., *pg.* 1045, *pg.* 704
DELPHI AUTOMOTIVE LLP, *pg.* 204, *pg.* 910
DELPHI ELECTRONICS & SAFETY, *pg.* 633, *pg.* 692
DONALDSON COMPANY, INC., *pg.* 1329, *pg.* 917
DORMAN PRODUCTS, INC., *pg.* 204, *pg.* 1522
DOUGLAS DYNAMICS, INC., *pg.* 204, *pg.* 1874
DREMEL, *pg.* 1046, *pg.* 634
DRIV-LOK, INC., *pg.* 1046, *pg.* 662
E-Z-GO TEXTRON, *pg.* 1706, *pg.* 525
THE EASTERN COMPANY, *pg.* 1331, *pg.* 357
EATON CORPORATION, *pg.* 1331, *pg.* 1429
EATON HYDRAULICS INC., *pg.* 1332, *pg.* 922
EBERHARD MANUFACTURING DIVISION, *pg.* 1046, *pg.* 1475
EDELBROCK CORPORATION, *pg.* 204, *pg.* 293
ELECTROID CO, *pg.* 1333, *pg.* 1123
E.R. WAGNER CASTERS AND WHEELS DIV., *pg.* 1047, *pg.* 1874
FEDERAL-MOGUL HOLDINGS CORPORATION, *pg.* 205, *pg.* 907
FEDERAL SIGNAL CORPORATION, *pg.* 638, *pg.* 645
FLEXIBLE STEEL LACING COMPANY, *pg.* 1337, *pg.* 608
FLOWTRON OUTDOOR PRODUCTS, *pg.* 639, *pg.* 830
FORD MOTOR COMPANY, *pg.* 172, *pg.* 876
FORTUNE BRANDS HOME & SECURITY, INC., *pg.* 55, *pg.* 600
FRANKLIN ELECTRIC CO., INC., *pg.* 1337, *pg.* 680
FREIGHTLINER TRUCKS, *pg.* 174, *pg.* 1502
FREUDENBERG-NOK, *pg.* 1882, *pg.* 904
GENERAL MOTORS COMPANY, *pg.* 175, *pg.* 881
GENTEX CORPORATION, *pg.* 206, *pg.* 913
GKN AUTOMOTIVE INC., *pg.* 206, *pg.* 869
THE GLEASON WORKS, *pg.* 1341, *pg.* 1336
GRAHAM MOTORS AND CONTROLS, *pg.* 177, *pg.* 1692
GREIF INC., *pg.* 1459, *pg.* 1447
GRIPNAIL CORPORATION, *pg.* 1048, *pg.* 1601
GROOV-PIN CORPORATION, *pg.* 1049, *pg.* 1608
HECKETHORN MANUFACTURING COMPANY, INC., *pg.* 207, *pg.* 1632
HENDRICKSON INTERNATIONAL, *pg.* 207, *pg.* 672
HENNESSY INDUSTRIES, INC., *pg.* 207, *pg.* 1639
HONEYWELL CONSUMER PRODUCTS GROUP, *pg.* 208, *pg.* 344
HONEYWELL INTERNATIONAL INC., *pg.* 407, *pg.* 1088
HUTCHENS INDUSTRIES INC., *pg.* 208, *pg.* 1006
INDIAN HEAD INDUSTRIES, INC., *pg.* 208, *pg.* 1367
JACOBS VEHICLE SYSTEMS, *pg.* 1351, *pg.* 338
JANESVILLE ACOUSTICS, *pg.* 1885, *pg.* 907
JOHN DEERE COFFEYVILLE WORKS INC, *pg.* 1351, *pg.* 714
JOHNSON CONTROLS, INC., *pg.* 209, *pg.* 1876
K&N ENGINEERING INC., *pg.* 210, *pg.* 194
KABA ILCO CORP., *pg.* 1052, *pg.* 1390
KENNAMETAL INC., *pg.* 1052, *pg.* 1547
KENWORTH TRUCK CO., *pg.* 181, *pg.* 1822
KEY SAFETY SYSTEMS, INC., *pg.* 210, *pg.* 908
KNAPE & VOGT MANUFACTURING COMPANY, *pg.* 1052, *pg.* 913
KYB AMERICA LLC, *pg.* 210, *pg.* 681
LINGENFELTER PERFORMANCE ENGINEERING, INC., *pg.* 94, *pg.* 677
LISLE CORPORATION, *pg.* 1356, *pg.* 703
LKQ CORP., *pg.* 210, *pg.* 185
LUND INTERNATIONAL, INC., *pg.* 211, *pg.* 526
MACK TRUCKS, INC., *pg.* 183, *pg.* 1375
MAGNA INTERNATIONAL INC., *pg.* 211, *pg.* 1918
MAHLE BEHR USA INC., TROY, *pg.* 212, *pg.* 911
MASTER LOCK COMPANY LLC, *pg.* 1055, *pg.* 1884
MATCO TOOLS CORPORATION, *pg.* 1055, *pg.* 1474
MAXION WHEELS, *pg.* 212, *pg.* 903
MEDECO HIGH SECURITY LOCKS, INC., *pg.* 1055, *pg.* 1806
MERITOR, INC., *pg.* 212, *pg.* 911
MICHIGAN WHEEL CORPORATION, *pg.* 1709, *pg.* 888
MICO, INCORPORATED, *pg.* 212, *pg.* 951
MILE MARKER INTERNATIONAL INC., *pg.* 213, *pg.* 459
MITEK, INC., *pg.* 1056, *pg.* 975
MODINE MANUFACTURING COMPANY, *pg.* 1074, *pg.* 1888
MOTORCAR PARTS OF AMERICA, INC., *pg.* 213, *pg.* 295
MR. GASKET INC., *pg.* 213, *pg.* 1406
NATIONAL AUTOMOTIVE PARTS ASSOCIATION, *pg.* 213, *pg.* 515
NAVISTAR INTERNATIONAL CORPORATION, *pg.* 186, *pg.* 630
NEAPCO, INC., *pg.* 214, *pg.* 1582
NETWORKFLEET, INC., *pg.* 445, *pg.* 205
OSHKOSH SPECIALTY VEHICLES, *pg.* 1918, *pg.* 561
OXO, *pg.* 1058, *pg.* 1275
PACCAR INC., *pg.* 187, *pg.* 1816
PARKER HANNIFIN WATTS FLUID AIR, *pg.* 1368, *pg.* 750
PASLODE, *pg.* 1059, *pg.* 664
PENDA CORPORATION, *pg.* 214, *pg.* 1887
PENN ENGINEERING & MANUFACTURING CORP., *pg.* 1059, *pg.* 1525
PENNENGINEERING FASTENING TECHNOLOGIES, *pg.* 1059, *pg.* 1526
PERCEPTICS, LLC, *pg.* 1426, *pg.* 1637
PERCEPTRON, INC., *pg.* 215, *pg.* 904
THE PERRY COMPANY, *pg.* 706, *pg.* 1749
PLEWS/EDELMANN, *pg.* 215, *pg.* 607
POLARIS INDUSTRIES INC., *pg.* 1709, *pg.* 928
PORTLAND WILLAMETTE, *pg.* 1129, *pg.* 1505
PURADYN FILTER TECHNOLOGIES, INC., *pg.* 215, *pg.* 414
REMY INTERNATIONAL, INC., *pg.* 216, *pg.* 696
REV-A-SHELF, *pg.* 1060, *pg.* 738
RICHELIEU HARDWARE LTD., *pg.* 1060, *pg.* 1961
RIETER AUTOMOTIVE NORTH AMERICA, INC., *pg.* 216, *pg.* 886
ROCKY MOUNTAIN HARDWARE INC., *pg.* 1061, *pg.* 549
RONA, INC., *pg.* 216, *pg.* 1950
ROSTRA PRECISION CONTROLS, INC., *pg.* 216, *pg.* 1381
ROUSSEAU METAL, INC., *pg.* 463, *pg.* 1960
SAF-HOLLAND INTERNATIONAL, INC., *pg.* 217, *pg.* 902
SANDEN INTERNATIONAL (USA), INC., *pg.* 217, *pg.* 1750
SARGENT & GREENLEAF, INC., *pg.* 1061, *pg.* 739
SARGENT MANUFACTURING COMPANY, *pg.* 1061, *pg.* 359
SCHAEFER MARINE INC., *pg.* 1373, *pg.* 835
SEASTAR SOLUTIONS, *pg.* 1374, *pg.* 1548
SHUR-CO, INC., *pg.* 110, *pg.* 1626
SIMPSON MANUFACTURING COMPANY, INC., *pg.* 1376, *pg.* 185
SOLIDSCAPE, INC., *pg.* 1063, *pg.* 1037
SOUTHERN FOLGER DETENTION EQUIPMENT COMPANY, *pg.* 1063, *pg.* 1743
SPARTAN MOTORS, INC., *pg.* 217, *pg.* 874
SPEEDWAY MOTORS INC., *pg.* 218, *pg.* 1012
STANDARD MOTOR PRODUCTS, INC., *pg.* 218, *pg.* 1176
STANDEX INTERNATIONAL CORPORATION, *pg.* 60, *pg.* 1039
STANLEY BLACK & DECKER, INC., *pg.* 1063, *pg.* 358
STEMCO INC, *pg.* 1182, *pg.* 1726
STRUT, LLC, *pg.* 190, *pg.* 199
STS TURBO, INC., *pg.* 218, *pg.* 1753
TCI PRECISION METALS, INC., *pg.* 1380, *pg.* 95
TELEFLEX INCORPORATED, *pg.* 48, *pg.* 1548
TENNECO, INC., *pg.* 985, *pg.* 625
TEXTRON INC., *pg.* 235, *pg.* 1607
THULE, INC., *pg.* 218, *pg.* 369
TI AUTOMOTIVE LIMITED, *pg.* 191, *pg.* 869
TITAN INTERNATIONAL, INC., *pg.* 219, *pg.* 653
TOWER INTERNATIONAL, INC., *pg.* 219, *pg.* 897
TRICO PRODUCTS CORPORATION, *pg.* 220, *pg.* 905
TRIMAS CORPORATION, *pg.* 1383, *pg.* 874
TRUTH HARDWARE CORP., *pg.* 1066, *pg.* 952
TWIN DISC, INCORPORATED, *pg.* 220, *pg.* 1889
UNITED COMPONENTS, INC., *pg.* 220, *pg.* 679
UNIVERSAL INDUSTRIAL PRODUCTS CO., *pg.* 1066, *pg.* 1470
UQM TECHNOLOGIES, INC., *pg.* 684, *pg.* 334
U.S. AXLE, INC., *pg.* 221, *pg.* 1582
UTILITY TRAILER MANUFACTURING COMPANY, *pg.* 1712, *pg.* 68
VISTEON CORPORATION, *pg.* 221, *pg.* 912
WAIGLOBAL, *pg.* 221, *pg.* 1585
WARN INDUSTRIES, INC., *pg.* 221, *pg.* 1497
WARNER ELECTRIC, INC., *pg.* 221, *pg.* 661
WELLS MANUFACTURING, L.P., *pg.* 222, *pg.* 1858
WESTINGHOUSE AIR BRAKE TECHNOLOGIES CORPORATION, *pg.* 1388, *pg.* 1595
WILLIAMS CONTROLS, INC., *pg.* 222, *pg.* 1508
WINNEBAGO INDUSTRIES, INC., *pg.* 1712, *pg.* 707
WINNER INTERNATIONAL, LLC, *pg.* 222, *pg.* 1586
WOODWARD, INC., *pg.* 122, *pg.* 329
WORTHINGTON INDUSTRIES, *pg.* 222, *pg.* 1626
YARDLEY PRODUCTS CORPORATION, *pg.* 1391, *pg.* 1596
ZF TRW, *pg.* 222, *pg.* 897

3715 - Truck Trailers

GENERAL ENGINES COMPANY INC., *pg.* 174, *pg.* 437
GREAT DANE TRAILERS, *pg.* 1707, *pg.* 539
HEIL ENVIRONMENTAL INDUSTRIES, LTD., *pg.* 207, *pg.* 1629
KIDRON, INC., *pg.* 181, *pg.* 1457
LUFKIN INDUSTRIES, INC., *pg.* 1357, *pg.* 1726
SAF-HOLLAND INTERNATIONAL, INC., *pg.* 217, *pg.* 902
UTILITY TRAILER MANUFACTURING COMPANY, *pg.* 1712, *pg.* 68

3716 - Motor Homes

AIRSTREAM, INC., *pg.* 163, *pg.* 1456
FORETRAVEL INC., *pg.* 1909, *pg.* 1728
JAYCO INC., *pg.* 1708, *pg.* 695
REXHALL INDUSTRIES, INC., *pg.* 1710, *pg.* 121
THOR INDUSTRIES, INC., *pg.* 1711, *pg.* 1456
WINNEBAGO INDUSTRIES, INC., *pg.* 1712, *pg.* 707

3721 - Aircraft

AEROVIRONMENT, INC., *pg.* 223, *pg.* 150
AIR INDUSTRIES GROUP, INC., *pg.* 223, *pg.* 1141
AIRBUS HELICOPTERS, INC., *pg.* 223, *pg.* 1698
AIRBUS NORTH AMERICA HOLDINGS, INC., *pg.* 1897, *pg.* 1784
ALLEN AIRCRAFT PRODUCTS, INC., *pg.* 223, *pg.* 1471
AMBAC INTERNATIONAL CORPORATION, *pg.* 198, *pg.* 1615
AVIALL, INC., *pg.* 224, *pg.* 1676
BE AEROSPACE, INC., *pg.* 224, *pg.* 478
BELL HELICOPTER TEXTRON, INC., *pg.* 224, *pg.* 1693
THE BOEING COMPANY, *pg.* 225, *pg.* 567
THE BOEING COMPANY - HELICOPTER DIVISION, *pg.* 226, *pg.* 13
BOMBARDIER INC., *pg.* 1318, *pg.* 1953
BOSTON GEAR, *pg.* 201, *pg.* 802
BREEZE-EASTERN CORPORATION, *pg.* 1319, *pg.* 1132
CAMERON BALLOONS U.S., *pg.* 1829, *pg.* 884
CESSNA AIRCRAFT COMPANY, *pg.* 226, *pg.* 723
CIRRUS DESIGN CORPORATION, *pg.* 226, *pg.* 921
CMC ELECTRONICS INC., *pg.* 376, *pg.* 1959
CRANE CO., *pg.* 227, *pg.* 373
DASSAULT FALCON JET CORP., *pg.* 227, *pg.* 1122
DUCOMMUN TECHNOLOGIES, INC., *pg.* 634, *pg.* 63
FIRST AVIATION SERVICES INC., *pg.* 227, *pg.* 384
GE AVIATION, *pg.* 227, *pg.* 1413
THE GLEASON WORKS, *pg.* 1341, *pg.* 1336
GULFSTREAM AEROSPACE CORPORATION, *pg.* 228, *pg.* 540
HEICO CORPORATION, *pg.* 228, *pg.* 431
HEXCEL CORPORATION, *pg.* 1884, *pg.* 375
KAMAN CORPORATION, *pg.* 229, *pg.* 338
KILGORE FLARES, *pg.* 1170, *pg.* 1656
LOCKHEED MARTIN CORPORATION, *pg.* 229, *pg.* 762
MEGGITT SAFETY SYSTEMS, INC., *pg.* 653, *pg.* 279
THE MISTRAL INC., *pg.* 1173, *pg.* 765
MOOG INC., *pg.* 231, *pg.* 1156
NOBLES MANUFACTURING, INC., *pg.* 59, *pg.* 1890
NORTHROP GRUMMAN CORPORATION, *pg.* 231, *pg.* 1781
NORTHSTAR AEROSPACE, INC., *pg.* 232, *pg.* 1941
ONE AVIATION CORPORATION, *pg.* 232, *pg.* 1135
PIPER AIRCRAFT, INC., *pg.* 233, *pg.* 477
PPG AEROSPACE, *pg.* 1178, *pg.* 290
PPG INDUSTRIES, INC., *pg.* 1445, *pg.* 1579
PRECISION CASTPARTS CORP., *pg.* 105, *pg.* 1506
RAYTHEON COMPANY, *pg.* 233, *pg.* 854
ROBINSON HELICOPTER COMPANY, *pg.* 234, *pg.* 295
ROGERSON AIRCRAFT CORPORATION, *pg.* 234, *pg.* 115
TELEFLEX INCORPORATED, *pg.* 48, *pg.* 1548
TEXTRON INC., *pg.* 235, *pg.* 1607
TEXTRON SYSTEMS CORPORATION, *pg.* 235, *pg.* 860
TRIUMPH THERMAL SYSTEMS, INC., *pg.* 235, *pg.* 1454
UNISON INDUSTRIES, LLC, *pg.* 235, *pg.* 435
UTC AEROSPACE SYSTEMS, *pg.* 236, *pg.* 1369
WOODWARD, INC., *pg.* 122, *pg.* 329
ZODIAC WATER & WASTE SYSTEMS, *pg.* 236, *pg.* 64

3724 - Aircraft Engines & Engine Parts

AAR CORP., *pg.* 223, *pg.* 671
ATI LADISH FORGING, *pg.* 69, *pg.* 1856
THE BOEING COMPANY, *pg.* 225, *pg.* 567
CONTINENTAL MOTORS, *pg.* 227, *pg.* 7
EDAC TECHNOLOGIES CORPORATION, *pg.* 1332, *pg.* 342
ENGINE COMPONENTS, INC., *pg.* 227, *pg.* 1740
FIRST AVIATION SERVICES INC., *pg.* 227, *pg.* 384
GE AVIATION, *pg.* 227, *pg.* 1413
GENERAL ELECTRIC COMPANY, *pg.* 1297, *pg.* 347
HEICO CORPORATION, *pg.* 228, *pg.* 431
HONEYWELL INTERNATIONAL INC., *pg.* 407, *pg.* 1088
LORD CORPORATION, *pg.* 1357, *pg.* 1360
NORTHROP GRUMMAN CORPORATION, *pg.* 231, *pg.* 1781
PRATT & WHITNEY, *pg.* 233, *pg.* 345
PRATT & WHITNEY CANADA CORP., *pg.* 1370, *pg.* 1952
PRECISION CASTPARTS CORP., *pg.* 105, *pg.* 1506
RAYTHEON COMPANY, *pg.* 233, *pg.* 854
ROLLS-ROYCE CORPORATION, *pg.* 216, *pg.* 689
TEXTRON INC., *pg.* 235, *pg.* 1607
UNISON INDUSTRIES, LLC, *pg.* 235, *pg.* 435
UNITED TECHNOLOGIES CORPORATION, *pg.* 235, *pg.* 353
UTC AEROSPACE SYSTEMS, *pg.* 236, *pg.* 1369
WOODWARD, INC., *pg.* 122, *pg.* 329

3728 - Aircraft Parts & Auxiliary Equipment, NEC

AIR INDUSTRIES GROUP, INC., *pg.* 223, *pg.* 1141
ALLEN AIRCRAFT PRODUCTS, INC., *pg.* 223, *pg.* 1471
AMBAC INTERNATIONAL CORPORATION, *pg.* 198, *pg.* 1615
AVIALL, INC., *pg.* 224, *pg.* 1676
BE AEROSPACE, INC., *pg.* 224, *pg.* 478
BELL HELICOPTER TEXTRON, INC., *pg.* 224, *pg.* 1693
BOSTON GEAR, *pg.* 201, *pg.* 802
BREEZE-EASTERN CORPORATION, *pg.* 1319, *pg.* 1132
CAMERON BALLOONS U.S., *pg.* 1829, *pg.* 884
CMC ELECTRONICS INC., *pg.* 376, *pg.* 1959
CRANE CO., *pg.* 227, *pg.* 373
DUCOMMUN TECHNOLOGIES, INC., *pg.* 634, *pg.* 63
FIRST AVIATION SERVICES INC., *pg.* 227, *pg.* 384
GE AVIATION, *pg.* 227, *pg.* 1413
THE GLEASON WORKS, *pg.* 1341, *pg.* 1336
HEICO CORPORATION, *pg.* 228, *pg.* 431
HEXCEL CORPORATION, *pg.* 1884, *pg.* 375
KILGORE FLARES, *pg.* 1170, *pg.* 1656
MEGGITT SAFETY SYSTEMS, INC., *pg.* 653, *pg.* 279
THE MISTRAL INC., *pg.* 1173, *pg.* 765
MOOG INC., *pg.* 231, *pg.* 1156
NOBLES MANUFACTURING, INC., *pg.* 59, *pg.* 1890
NORTHROP GRUMMAN CORPORATION, *pg.* 231, *pg.* 1781
NORTHSTAR AEROSPACE, INC., *pg.* 232, *pg.* 1941
PIPER AIRCRAFT, INC., *pg.* 233, *pg.* 477
PPG AEROSPACE, *pg.* 1178, *pg.* 290
PPG INDUSTRIES, INC., *pg.* 1445, *pg.* 1579
PRECISION CASTPARTS CORP., *pg.* 105, *pg.* 1506
RAYTHEON COMPANY, *pg.* 233, *pg.* 854
ROGERSON AIRCRAFT CORPORATION, *pg.* 234, *pg.* 115
TELEFLEX INCORPORATED, *pg.* 48, *pg.* 1548
TRIUMPH THERMAL SYSTEMS, INC., *pg.* 235, *pg.* 1454
UNISON INDUSTRIES, LLC, *pg.* 235, *pg.* 435
UTC AEROSPACE SYSTEMS, *pg.* 236, *pg.* 1369
WOODWARD, INC., *pg.* 122, *pg.* 329
ZODIAC WATER & WASTE SYSTEMS, *pg.* 236, *pg.* 64

3731 - Ship Building & Repairing

ALION SCIENCE AND TECHNOLOGY CORPORATION, *pg.* 615, *pg.* 1788
ELLICOTT DREDGES, LLC, *pg.* 1333, *pg.* 757
GENERAL DYNAMICS CORPORATION, *pg.* 228, *pg.* 1781
NASSCO HOLDINGS INCORPORATED, *pg.* 99, *pg.* 205
NORTHROP GRUMMAN CORPORATION, *pg.* 231, *pg.* 1781
RAYTHEON COMPANY, *pg.* 233, *pg.* 854

3732 - Boat Building & Repairing

ALUMACRAFT BOAT COMPANY, *pg.* 1705, *pg.* 964
BOMBARDIER RECREATIONAL PRODUCTS, INC., *pg.* 201, *pg.* 1960
BOSTON WHALER, INC., *pg.* 1705, *pg.* 422
BRISTOL MARINE, *pg.* 1705, *pg.* 1600
BRUNSWICK CORPORATION, *pg.* 1828, *pg.* 623
CATALINA YACHTS, INC., *pg.* 1706, *pg.* 307
CHRIS-CRAFT CORPORATION, *pg.* 1706, *pg.* 465
CONFLUENCE WATERSPORTS CO. INC., *pg.* 1706, *pg.* 1617
CORRECT CRAFT, INC., *pg.* 1706, *pg.* 452
GRADY-WHITE BOATS, INC., *pg.* 1707, *pg.* 1377
HATTERAS YACHTS, *pg.* 1708, *pg.* 1386
HOBIE CAT COMPANY, *pg.* 1708, *pg.* 173
HUCKINS YACHT CORPORATION, *pg.* 1708, *pg.* 433
JOHNSON OUTDOORS INC., *pg.* 1837, *pg.* 1888
KCS INTERNATIONAL, INC., *pg.* 556, *pg.* 1885
MARLOW-HUNTER LLC, *pg.* 1709, *pg.* 409
MASTERCRAFT BOAT COMPANY LLC, *pg.* 1709, *pg.* 1656
PALMER JOHNSON INCORPORATED, *pg.* 1709, *pg.* 1895
POLARIS INDUSTRIES INC., *pg.* 1709, *pg.* 928
S2 YACHTS, INC., *pg.* 1710, *pg.* 892
SABRE CORPORATION, *pg.* 1710, *pg.* 752
SEA RAY BOATS, INC., *pg.* 1710, *pg.* 1638
SILVER SHIPS, INC., *pg.* 1923, *pg.* 8
SKIER'S CHOICE INC., *pg.* 1711, *pg.* 1640
TAYLOR MADE GROUP, *pg.* 1711, *pg.* 1162
TRINITY YACHTS, LLC, *pg.* 1712, *pg.* 968
VIKING YACHT COMPANY, *pg.* 1712, *pg.* 1094

3743 - Railroad Equipment

ACF INDUSTRIES LLC, *pg.* 1310, *pg.* 989
ADAMS RITE AEROSPACE INC., *pg.* 1041, *pg.* 93
AIR-LEC INDUSTRIES LLC, *pg.* 1041, *pg.* 1864
ALAMO GROUP INC., *pg.* 1311, *pg.* 1745
ALLIED CONSTRUCTION PRODUCTS, LLC, *pg.* 1311, *pg.* 1427
ALTEC INDUSTRIES INC., *pg.* 1312, *pg.* 1
ANSALDO STS, *pg.* 618, *pg.* 1573
ANVIL ATTACHMENTS, LLC, *pg.* 1313, *pg.* 748
ASTEC INDUSTRIES, INC., *pg.* 69, *pg.* 1628
BADGER EQUIPMENT COMPANY, *pg.* 1315, *pg.* 966
BESSER COMPANY, *pg.* 1317, *pg.* 865
BOMAG AMERICAS, INC., *pg.* 1318, *pg.* 621
CASHCO, INC., *pg.* 1044, *pg.* 714
CATERPILLAR, INC., *pg.* 1321, *pg.* 650
CHARLES MACHINE WORKS, INC., *pg.* 1322, *pg.* 1488
CNH AMERICA LLC, *pg.* 702, *pg.* 560
COLUMBUS MCKINNON CORPORATION, *pg.* 1325, *pg.* 1138
THE CYCLONE MFG. CO., *pg.* 78, *pg.* 698
DANUSER MACHINE COMPANY, INC., *pg.* 703, *pg.* 978
DEERE & COMPANY, *pg.* 703, *pg.* 632
EXCEL INDUSTRIES, INC., *pg.* 1795, *pg.* 715
THE FROG, SWITCH & MANUFACTURING COMPANY, *pg.* 1338, *pg.* 1520
FULL VISION, INC., *pg.* 1163, *pg.* 717
GEHL COMPANY, *pg.* 1339, *pg.* 1899
GENCOR INDUSTRIES, INC., *pg.* 1339, *pg.* 453
HARSCO RAIL, *pg.* 1345, *pg.* 1623
HENSLEY INDUSTRIES, INC., *pg.* 1166, *pg.* 1682
HIGHWAY EQUIPMENT COMPANY, *pg.* 704, *pg.* 702
INDUSTRIAL DISTRIBUTION GROUP, INC., *pg.* 413, *pg.* 1358
JLG INDUSTRIES, INC., *pg.* 1351, *pg.* 1551
KOMATSU AMERICA CORP., *pg.* 92, *pg.* 655
KPI-JCI, *pg.* 1354, *pg.* 1626
MARINE TRAVELIFT, INC., *pg.* 1359, *pg.* 1895
MITEK, INC., *pg.* 1056, *pg.* 975
THE NOLAN COMPANY, *pg.* 1365, *pg.* 1408
NORDCO, INC., *pg.* 1365, *pg.* 1884
P&H MINING EQUIPMENT, *pg.* 103, *pg.* 1879
PETTIBONE, LLC, *pg.* 1368, *pg.* 609
TELSMITH, INC., *pg.* 1381, *pg.* 1871
TEREX CEDARAPIDS, *pg.* 1381, *pg.* 703
TEREX CORPORATION, *pg.* 1381, *pg.* 384
TOROMONT CAT, *pg.* 192, *pg.* 1914
TRINITY INDUSTRIES, INC., *pg.* 116, *pg.* 1690
VERMEER MANUFACTURING COMPANY, *pg.* 708, *pg.* 711
VIBCO INC., *pg.* 1387, *pg.* 1611
VOSSLOH TRACK MATERIAL, INC., *pg.* 1387, *pg.* 1585
WESTINGHOUSE AIR BRAKE TECHNOLOGIES CORPORATION, *pg.* 1388, *pg.* 1595

3751 - Motorcycles, Bicycles & Parts

ALVIMAR GENESIS, *pg.* 1825, *pg.* 886

First page reference indicates Business Class Edition
Second page reference indicates Geographic Edition

ARCTIC CAT INC., pg. 1705, pg. 953
ATLUS USA, INC., pg. 949, pg. 107
B. DAZZLE, INC., pg. 949, pg. 188
THE BABY JOGGER COMPANY, pg. 949, pg. 1800
BACHMANN INDUSTRIES, INC., pg. 950, pg. 1559
CANNONDALE BICYCLE CORPORATION, pg. 1705, pg. 1515
CARTA MUNDI, INC., pg. 951, pg. 1677
CONFEDERATE MOTORS, INC., pg. 168, pg. 2
DIAMONDBACK BICYCLES, pg. 1706, pg. 1821
E-Z BOWZ, LLC, pg. 692, pg. 1635
EDELBROCK CORPORATION, pg. 204, pg. 293
EDUCATIONAL INSIGHTS, INC., pg. 951, pg. 187
ELECTRA BICYCLE COMPANY, pg. 1706, pg. 303
ELECTRONIC ARTS INC., pg. 951, pg. 189
ELENCO ELECTRONICS, INC., pg. 953, pg. 670
FACTORY X DISTRIBUTION, pg. 953, pg. 532
FELT RACING LLC, pg. 1707, pg. 110
FORTUNET, INC., pg. 953, pg. 1024
FRACTILES, INC., pg. 953, pg. 311
FUNRISE TOY CORP., pg. 549, pg. 300
GAMEWRIGHT, pg. 953, pg. 836
GAMING PARTNERS INTERNATIONAL CORPORATION, pg. 954, pg. 1024
GIANT BICYCLE INC., pg. 1707, pg. 164
GLD PRODUCTS, INC., pg. 1835, pg. 1882
GUND, INC., pg. 954, pg. 1056
HARLEY-DAVIDSON, INC., pg. 178, pg. 1874
HASBRO, INC., pg. 954, pg. 1603
HUFFY CORPORATION, pg. 1836, pg. 1409
IMPERIAL TOY CORPORATION, pg. 957, pg. 166
JADA TOYS, INC., pg. 960, pg. 67
JAKKS PACIFIC, INC., pg. 960, pg. 142
JOSEPH ENTERPRISES, INC., pg. 960, pg. 220
LEAPFROG ENTERPRISES, INC., pg. 961, pg. 84
LEGO SYSTEMS, INC., pg. 961, pg. 346
LEHMAN TRIKES INC., pg. 1708, pg. 1626
LIFOAM INDUSTRIES INC., pg. 961, pg. 772
LIONEL LLC, pg. 961, pg. 875
MARIN BIKES, pg. 1708, pg. 168
MATTEL GAMES/PUZZLES, pg. 962, pg. 80
MATTEL, INC., pg. 962, pg. 81
MICROSOFT GAME STUDIOS, pg. 964, pg. 1828
MOOTS CYCLES, pg. 1709, pg. 335
THE OHIO ART COMPANY, INC., pg. 965, pg. 1406
OOZ & OZ INC., pg. 965, pg. 1838
PACIFIC CYCLE INC., pg. 1709, pg. 1867
PIAGGIO USA, INC., pg. 188, pg. 1282
POLARIS INDUSTRIES INC., pg. 1709, pg. 928
PRO-LINE, INC., pg. 966, pg. 45
QUALITY BICYCLE PRODUCTS, pg. 1710, pg. 918
RADIO FLYER INC., pg. 966, pg. 588
REEVES INTERNATIONAL, INC., pg. 966, pg. 1108
REVELL, pg. 966, pg. 611
SANTA CRUZ BICYCLES, pg. 1710, pg. 271
SASSY, INC., pg. 966, pg. 895
SDI TECHNOLOGIES, INC., pg. 671, pg. 1113
SEGWAY INC., pg. 1923, pg. 1033
SONY COMPUTER ENTERTAINMENT AMERICA LLC, pg. 966, pg. 256
SPECIALIZED BICYCLE COMPONENTS, INC., pg. 1711, pg. 152
SRAM CORPORATION, pg. 967, pg. 590
THE STEP2 COMPANY LLC, pg. 1889, pg. 1474
THINKWAY TOYS, pg. 968, pg. 1924
TREK BICYCLE CORPORATION, pg. 1847, pg. 1896
UBISOFT INC., pg. 589, pg. 229
THE UNITED STATES PLAYING CARD COMPANY, pg. 969, pg. 727
UNIVERSITY GAMES CORPORATION, pg. 969, pg. 230
VALLEY CASTING, INC., pg. 1891, pg. 928
WHAM-O, INC., pg. 969, pg. 308
THE WIFFLE BALL INC., pg. 1848, pg. 371
WINNING MOVES GAMES, INC., pg. 970, pg. 816
WIZARDS OF THE COAST, INC., pg. 970, pg. 1830
XBOX, pg. 970, pg. 1829
ZAP, pg. 222, pg. 277

3761 - Guided Missiles & Space Vehicles

ASTROTECH CORPORATION, pg. 1400, pg. 1660
THE BOEING COMPANY, pg. 225, pg. 567
GENERAL DYNAMICS CORPORATION, pg. 228, pg. 1781
LOCKHEED MARTIN CORPORATION, pg. 229, pg. 762
NORTHROP GRUMMAN CORPORATION, pg. 231, pg. 1781
ORBITAL ATK, pg. 1425, pg. 1779
RAYTHEON COMPANY, pg. 233, pg. 854
SPACEDEV INC., pg. 234, pg. 186

3764 - Guided Missile & Space Vehicle Propulsion Units & Propulsion Unit Parts

AEROJET ROCKETDYNE, pg. 223, pg. 1782
AEROJET ROCKETDYNE HOLDINGS, INC., pg. 1145, pg. 186
AEROJET ROCKETDYNE INC, pg. 614, pg. 186
THE BOEING COMPANY, pg. 225, pg. 567
THE MISTRAL INC., pg. 1173, pg. 765
MOOG INC., pg. 231, pg. 1156
NORTHROP GRUMMAN CORPORATION, pg. 231, pg. 1781
RAYTHEON COMPANY, pg. 233, pg. 854
SEQUA CORPORATION, pg. 1180, pg. 1290
SPACEDEV INC., pg. 234, pg. 186

3769 - Guided Missile & Space Vehicle Parts & Auxiliary Equipment, NEC

ALCOA WHEEL & FORGED PRODUCTS, pg. 66, pg. 1427
ASTROTECH CORPORATION, pg. 1400, pg. 1660
BALL CORPORATION, pg. 1452, pg. 311
DIGITALGLOBE, pg. 227, pg. 1785
L-3 COMMUNICATIONS HOLDINGS INC., pg. 650, pg. 1250
NORTHROP GRUMMAN CORPORATION, pg. 231, pg. 1781
RAYTHEON COMPANY, pg. 233, pg. 854
SPACEDEV INC., pg. 234, pg. 186

3792 - Travel Trailers & Campers

AIRSTREAM, INC., pg. 163, pg. 1456
ALL STAR CARTS AND VEHICLES CORP., pg. 163, pg. 1141
ARCTIC CAT INC., pg. 1705, pg. 953
BLUE OX, pg. 701, pg. 1019
BOMBARDIER RECREATIONAL PRODUCTS, INC., pg. 201, pg. 1960
CLUB CAR, INC., pg. 1830, pg. 532
DUTCHMEN MANUFACTURING, INC., pg. 1706, pg. 681
E-Z-GO TEXTRON, pg. 1706, pg. 525
EVELAND'S INC., pg. 169, pg. 916
FEATHERLITE, INC., pg. 1707, pg. 704
FEDERAL SIGNAL CORPORATION, pg. 638, pg. 645
JAYCO INC., pg. 1708, pg. 695
J.B. POINDEXTER & CO., INC., pg. 209, pg. 1709
MASTERCRAFT BOAT COMPANY LLC, pg. 1709, pg. 1656
MIDWEST INDUSTRIES, INC., pg. 185, pg. 708
PERCEPTICS, LLC, pg. 1426, pg. 1637
POLARIS INDUSTRIES INC., pg. 1709, pg. 928
THOR INDUSTRIES, INC., pg. 1711, pg. 1456
TRIMAS CORPORATION, pg. 1383, pg. 874
WESTINGHOUSE AIR BRAKE TECHNOLOGIES CORPORATION, pg. 1388, pg. 1595

3795 - Tanks & Tank Components

AM GENERAL, LLC, pg. 163, pg. 697
AMERICAN HONDA MOTOR CO., INC., pg. 163, pg. 292
AMP HOLDING INC., pg. 164, pg. 1406
BLUE BIRD CORPORATION, pg. 1705, pg. 532
CARLISLE TIRE & WHEEL COMPANY, pg. 1880, pg. 1612
COMMERCIAL VEHICLE GROUP, INC., pg. 203, pg. 1467
CONSUMER PORTFOLIO SERVICES, INC., pg. 741, pg. 109
CPI HOLDINGS, LLC, pg. 203, pg. 32
CRANE CARRIER COMPANY, pg. 168, pg. 1489
DANA HOLDING CORPORATION, pg. 203, pg. 1461
DELPHI AUTOMOTIVE LLP, pg. 204, pg. 910
FCA CANADA INC., pg. 170, pg. 1948
FCA US LLC, pg. 170, pg. 868
FEDERAL-MOGUL HOLDINGS CORPORATION, pg. 205, pg. 907
FEDERAL SIGNAL CORPORATION, pg. 638, pg. 645
FLOWTRON OUTDOOR PRODUCTS, pg. 639, pg. 830
FORD MOTOR COMPANY, pg. 172, pg. 876
FORD MOTOR COMPANY OF CANADA, LIMITED, pg. 174, pg. 1930
FREIGHTLINER TRUCKS, pg. 174, pg. 1502
GENERAL DYNAMICS CORPORATION, pg. 228, pg. 1781
GENERAL MOTORS COMPANY, pg. 175, pg. 881
GENERAL MOTORS OF CANADA LTD., pg. 177, pg. 1931
HACKNEY INTERNATIONAL, pg. 178, pg. 1392
HEIL ENVIRONMENTAL INDUSTRIES, LTD., pg. 207, pg. 1629
HUTCHENS INDUSTRIES INC., pg. 208, pg. 1006
J.B. POINDEXTER & CO., INC., pg. 209, pg. 1709
KENWORTH TRUCK CO., pg. 181, pg. 1822
LEAR CORPORATION, pg. 229, pg. 907
LEXUS DIVISION, pg. 182, pg. 294
LOUIS BERKMAN CO., pg. 1357, pg. 1473
MACK TRUCKS, INC., pg. 183, pg. 1375
MAGNA INTERNATIONAL INC., pg. 211, pg. 1918
MAXION WHEELS, pg. 212, pg. 903
MERITOR, INC., pg. 212, pg. 911
MILLER INDUSTRIES, INC., pg. 185, pg. 1655
NAVISTAR INTERNATIONAL CORPORATION, pg. 186, pg. 630
NISSAN NORTH AMERICA, INC., pg. 186, pg. 1633
OMAHA STANDARD PALFINGER, pg. 706, pg. 704
OSHKOSH CORPORATION, pg. 187, pg. 1885
OSHKOSH SPECIALTY VEHICLES, pg. 1918, pg. 561
PACCAR INC., pg. 187, pg. 1816
PARKHURST MANUFACTURING CO., INC., pg. 214, pg. 1005
PIERCE MANUFACTURING, INC., pg. 188, pg. 1852
POLARIS INDUSTRIES INC., pg. 1709, pg. 928
QUANTUM FUEL SYSTEMS TECHNOLOGIES WORLDWIDE, INC., pg. 1371, pg. 115
SHUR-CO, INC., pg. 110, pg. 1626
SPARTAN MOTORS, INC., pg. 217, pg. 874
SPARTON CORPORATION, pg. 1377, pg. 660
SUPREME INDUSTRIES, INC., pg. 191, pg. 681
TENNECO, INC., pg. 985, pg. 625
TESLA MOTORS, INC., pg. 191, pg. 178
TEXTRON INC., pg. 235, pg. 1607
THOMAS BUILT BUSES, INC., pg. 191, pg. 1379
TOWER INTERNATIONAL, INC., pg. 219, pg. 897
TRUECAR INC., pg. 1284, pg. 276
VAPOR BUS INTERNATIONAL, pg. 221, pg. 560
VOLKSWAGEN CANADA, INC., pg. 194, pg. 1918
VOLKSWAGEN GROUP OF AMERICA, INC., pg. 194, pg. 1785
VOLVO TRUCKS NORTH AMERICA, INC., pg. 195, pg. 1377
WILLIAMS CONTROLS, INC., pg. 222, pg. 1508
ZF TRW, pg. 222, pg. 897

3799 - Transportation Equipment, NEC

ARCTIC CAT INC., pg. 1705, pg. 953
BLUE OX, pg. 701, pg. 1019
BOMBARDIER RECREATIONAL PRODUCTS, INC., pg. 201, pg. 1960
CLUB CAR, INC., pg. 1830, pg. 532
E-Z-GO TEXTRON, pg. 1706, pg. 525
FEDERAL SIGNAL CORPORATION, pg. 638, pg. 645
PERCEPTICS, LLC, pg. 1426, pg. 1637
POLARIS INDUSTRIES INC., pg. 1709, pg. 928
TRIMAS CORPORATION, pg. 1383, pg. 874
WESTINGHOUSE AIR BRAKE TECHNOLOGIES CORPORATION, pg. 1388, pg. 1595

3812 - Navigation, Guidance, Search & Detection Systems & Instruments

ACORN ENERGY, INC., pg. 341, pg. 389
AEROFLEX INCORPORATED, pg. 614, pg. 1321
ASTRONAUTICS CORPORATION OF AMERICA, pg. 224, pg. 1873
BAE SYSTEMS-COMMUNICATION, NAVIGATION, IDENTIFICATION & RECONNAISSANCE, pg. 359, pg. 1163
BAE SYSTEMS-INFORMATION WARFARE, pg. 623, pg. 1036
BALL CORPORATION, pg. 1452, pg. 311
BENMAR MARINE ELECTRONICS, INC., pg. 624, pg. 105

THE BOEING COMPANY, pg. 225, pg. 567
BRIMROSE CORPORATION, pg. 1403, pg. 756
CHECKPOINT SYSTEMS, INC., pg. 628, pg. 1559
CMC ELECTRONICS INC., pg. 376, pg. 1959
CODA OCTOPUS GROUP, INC., pg. 629, pg. 437
COGNEX CORPORATION, pg. 1406, pg. 834
CONMED CORPORATION, pg. 1517, pg. 1347
THE DEWEY ELECTRONICS CORPORATION, pg. 1328, pg. 1099
DIGITALGLOBE, pg. 227, pg. 1785
ELECSYS CORPORATION, pg. 635, pg. 717
EMRISE CORPORATION, pg. 637, pg. 1371
ESCORT, INC., pg. 1412, pg. 1479
FLIR SYSTEMS, INC., pg. 1413, pg. 1510
GARMIN INTERNATIONAL, INC., pg. 1414, pg. 717
HEMISPHERE GPS INC., pg. 642, pg. 1903
HONEYWELL INTERNATIONAL INC., pg. 407, pg. 1088
II-VI INCORPORATED, pg. 1417, pg. 1585
IMPLANT SCIENCES CORPORATION, pg. 1348, pg. 860
IRT, INC., pg. 1169, pg. 771
KRATOS LANCASTER, pg. 1419, pg. 1546
KVH INDUSTRIES INC, pg. 650, pg. 1602
L-3 AVIONICS SYSTEMS, INC., pg. 650, pg. 888
L-3 COMMUNICATIONS ELECTRONIC SYSTEMS, pg. 229, pg. 1939
L-3 COMMUNICATIONS HOLDINGS INC., pg. 650, pg. 1250
L-3 INTERSTATE ELECTRONICS CORPORATION, pg. 650, pg. 43
LOCKHEED MARTIN CORPORATION, pg. 229, pg. 762
MOOG INC., pg. 231, pg. 1156
MOTOROLA CANADA LIMITED, pg. 657, pg. 1924
NAVCOM DEFENSE ELECTRONICS, INC., pg. 658, pg. 70
NORDSON CORPORATION, pg. 1365, pg. 1480
NORTHROP GRUMMAN CORPORATION, pg. 231, pg. 1781
NOVATEL INC., pg. 1424, pg. 1904
ORBITAL ATK, pg. 1425, pg. 1779
PHOTONIS USA PENNSYLVANIA, pg. 663, pg. 1547
PROPHOTONIX LIMITED, pg. 1427, pg. 1039
RANTEC MICROWAVE SYSTEMS, INC., pg. 666, pg. 307
RAYTHEON COMPANY, pg. 233, pg. 854
ROCKWELL COLLINS, INC., pg. 234, pg. 702
ROGERSON AIRCRAFT CORPORATION, pg. 234, pg. 115
SENTRY TECHNOLOGY CORPORATION, pg. 672, pg. 1339
SPARTON CORPORATION, pg. 1377, pg. 660
SPERRY MARINE INC., pg. 1430, pg. 1778
SYSTRON DONNER INERTIAL DIVISION, pg. 1430, pg. 69
TELEDYNE BENTHOS, INC., pg. 1431, pg. 838
TELEFLEX INCORPORATED, pg. 48, pg. 1548
TEXTRON SYSTEMS CORPORATION, pg. 235, pg. 860
TRIMBLE NAVIGATION LIMITED, pg. 1384, pg. 288
VICON INDUSTRIES, INC., pg. 685, pg. 1166
WHITE'S ELECTRONICS, pg. 688, pg. 1509

3821 - Laboratory Apparatus & Furniture

3M DETECTION SOLUTIONS, pg. 1398, pg. 1885
ABAXIS, INC., pg. 1483, pg. 298
ABBOTT LABORATORIES, pg. 1484, pg. 551
ABBOTT MEDICAL OPTICS, INC., pg. 1485, pg. 260
ABBOTT POINT OF CARE, INC., pg. 1486, pg. 1110
ACCURAY, pg. 1486, pg. 1864
ACCURAY INCORPORATED, pg. 1486, pg. 282
ALERE INC., pg. 1488, pg. 849
ALERE SAN DIEGO, pg. 1489, pg. 199
ALLERGAN, INC., pg. 1491, pg. 106
ALLIED HEALTHCARE PRODUCTS, INC., pg. 1491, pg. 990
ALLIED MOTION TECHNOLOGIES INC., pg. 616, pg. 1137
AMERICAN BIO MEDICA CORPORATION, pg. 1493, pg. 1171
AMERICAN MEDICAL SYSTEMS HOLDINGS, INC., pg. 1493, pg. 947
ANGIODYNAMICS, INC., pg. 1495, pg. 1173
ANIMAS CORPORATION, pg. 1495, pg. 1593
THE ARISTOTLE CORPORATION, pg. 1496, pg. 372
ARIZONA INSTRUMENT LLC, pg. 1400, pg. 12
ARKRAY USA, INC., pg. 1496, pg. 924
ASPEN SURGICAL PRODUCTS, INC., pg. 1400, pg. 874
ASSOCIATED RESEARCH INC., pg. 1400, pg. 622
ATRION CORPORATION, pg. 1400, pg. 1658
AVALIGN TECHNOLOGIES, pg. 1400, pg. 622
AXCELIS TECHNOLOGIES, INC., pg. 1400, pg. 787
AZONIX CORPORATION, pg. 1400, pg. 788
BACHARACH INC., pg. 1400, pg. 1556
BARKSDALE, INC., pg. 1317, pg. 126
BAUSCH & LOMB INCORPORATED, pg. 1401, pg. 1045
BAXTER INTERNATIONAL INC., pg. 1499, pg. 599
BD MEDICAL, pg. 1501, pg. 1762
BECKMAN COULTER, INC., pg. 1402, pg. 48
BECTON, DICKINSON & COMPANY, pg. 1501, pg. 1068
BIO-RAD LABORATORIES, INC., pg. 1504, pg. 101
BIOJECT MEDICAL TECHNOLOGIES INC., pg. 1506, pg. 1509
BMC INDUSTRIAL EDUCATIONAL SERVICES, pg. 362, pg. 902
BOLT TECHNOLOGY CORPORATION, pg. 1318, pg. 360
BOSTON SCIENTIFIC CORPORATION, pg. 1508, pg. 831
BOVIE MEDICAL CORPORATION, pg. 1402, pg. 1178
BRACCO DIAGNOSTICS, INC., pg. 1509, pg. 1085
BRISTOL-MYERS SQUIBB COMPANY, pg. 1509, pg. 1206
BRK BRANDS, INC., pg. 627, pg. 554
BRUKER CORPORATION, pg. 1511, pg. 788
BUEHLER, LTD., pg. 1403, pg. 622
CANTEL MEDICAL CORP., pg. 1405, pg. 1079
CARDIAC SCIENCE CORPORATION, pg. 1512, pg. 1897
CARDIACASSIST, INC., pg. 1405, pg. 1574
CAREFUSION CORPORATION, pg. 1513, pg. 201
CAS MEDICAL SYSTEMS, INC., pg. 1513, pg. 339
CASCADE MICROTECH, INC., pg. 1405, pg. 1492
CEM CORPORATION, pg. 1405, pg. 1382
CEPHEID, pg. 1514, pg. 284
CHARLES MACHINE WORKS, INC., pg. 1322, pg. 1488
CINCINNATI SUB-ZERO PRODUCTS, INC., pg. 1070, pg. 1411
CLAYTON INDUSTRIES CO., pg. 1323, pg. 66
COGENTIX MEDICAL, INC., pg. 1516, pg. 948
COGNEX CORPORATION, pg. 1406, pg. 834
COLORADO SERUM CO., pg. 1516, pg. 318
COMPUMED, INC., pg. 378, pg. 128
CONMED CORPORATION, pg. 1517, pg. 1347
CONVATEC LTD., pg. 1518, pg. 1121
COOK GROUP, INC., pg. 1518, pg. 674
COOPER-ATKINS CORPORATION, pg. 1407, pg. 355
THE COOPER COMPANIES, INC., pg. 1518, pg. 183
CORBY INDUSTRIES, INC., pg. 380, pg. 1513
CORDIS CORPORATION, pg. 1519, pg. 430
CORGENIX MEDICAL CORPORATION, pg. 1519, pg. 312
C.R. BARD, INC., pg. 1519, pg. 1094
CRANE CO., pg. 227, pg. 373
CRH MEDICAL CORPORATION, pg. 1520, pg. 1910
CRITICARE SYSTEMS, INC., pg. 1520, pg. 1897
CRYOLIFE, INC., pg. 1520, pg. 534
CTS VALPEY CORPORATION, pg. 632, pg. 825
CUBIC TRANSPORTATION SYSTEMS, INC., pg. 1905, pg. 202
CUTERA, INC., pg. 1521, pg. 49
CYBEROPTICS CORPORATION, pg. 1408, pg. 925
CYNOSURE, INC., pg. 1521, pg. 858
DAXOR CORPORATION, pg. 1522, pg. 1221
DEPUY SYNTHES, pg. 1523, pg. 1593
DERMA SCIENCES, INC., pg. 1523, pg. 1111
DESPATCH INDUSTRIES, pg. 1070, pg. 927
DEXCOM INC, pg. 1524, pg. 202
DIGIRAD CORPORATION, pg. 1524, pg. 185
DIGITAL LIGHTWAVE, INC., pg. 634, pg. 462
DIT-MCO INTERNATIONAL CORPORATION, pg. 634, pg. 982
DJO SURGICAL, pg. 1525, pg. 1661
DRAVON MEDICAL, INC., pg. 1525, pg. 1497
DYNATRONICS CORPORATION, pg. 1526, pg. 1757
DYNISCO INSTRUMENTS LLC, pg. 1526, pg. 823
EAGLE TECHNOLOGIES GROUP, pg. 1331, pg. 874
ELECTRO-SENSORS, INC., pg. 1333, pg. 948
ELECTROMED, INC., pg. 1527, pg. 951
ELEKTA, pg. 391, pg. 987
ELSTER AMERICAN METER COMPANY, pg. 1411, pg. 1387
EMERSON PROCESS MANAGEMENT, pg. 1334, pg. 1636
EMERSON PROCESS MANAGEMENT ROSEMOUNT INC., pg. 1334, pg. 920
ENCISION INC., pg. 1528, pg. 310
ENDOLOGIX, INC., pg. 1528, pg. 109
EXACTECH, INC., pg. 1529, pg. 428
FIELD CONTROLS LLC, pg. 1071, pg. 1380
FLEXBAR MACHINE CORP., pg. 1337, pg. 1169
THE FORD METER BOX COMPANY, INC., pg. 1047, pg. 698
FRANKLIN ELECTRIC CO., INC., pg. 1337, pg. 680
FREQUENCY ELECTRONICS, INC., pg. 639, pg. 1182
GAMMEX RMI INC., pg. 1532, pg. 1872
GE HEALTHCARE TECHNOLOGIES, pg. 1533, pg. 1897
GE INTELLIGENT PLATFORMS, pg. 1339, pg. 1777
GENERAL ELECTRIC COMPANY, pg. 1297, pg. 347
GF HEALTH PRODUCTS, INC., pg. 1535, pg. 508
GFS CHEMICALS, INC., pg. 1164, pg. 1471
GILSON COMPANY, INC., pg. 1414, pg. 1457
GLEASON - M&M PRECISION SYSTEMS CORPORATION, pg. 1341, pg. 1479
THE GRIEVE CORPORATION, pg. 1072, pg. 657
HAEMONETICS CORPORATION, pg. 1538, pg. 802
HEALTHTRONICS, INC., pg. 1540, pg. 1663
HEMCO CORPORATION, pg. 1416, pg. 979
HINDS INSTRUMENTS, INC., pg. 1416, pg. 1498
HOFFMANN-LA ROCHE INC., pg. 1542, pg. 1099
HOLOGIC, INC., pg. 1416, pg. 784
HOSPIRA, INC., pg. 1542, pg. 623
HUNTER ENGINEERING COMPANY, pg. 208, pg. 973
HUTCHINSON TECHNOLOGY INC., pg. 409, pg. 926
HYPERTENSION DIAGNOSTICS, INC., pg. 1543, pg. 921
IMAGE SENSING SYSTEMS, INC., pg. 412, pg. 961
IMPLANT SCIENCES CORPORATION, pg. 1348, pg. 860
INDUSTRIAL DISTRIBUTION GROUP, INC., pg. 413, pg. 1358
INSTRON CORPORATION, pg. 1349, pg. 839
INSULET CORPORATION, pg. 644, pg. 785
INTEGRA LIFESCIENCES HOLDINGS CORPORATION, pg. 1545, pg. 1109
INTELLIGENT HEARING SYSTEMS CORP., pg. 1546, pg. 443
INTUITIVE SURGICAL, INC., pg. 1546, pg. 286
INVACARE CORPORATION, pg. 1546, pg. 1451
INVERNESS CORPORATION, pg. 512, pg. 783
ION GEOPHYSICAL CORPORATION, pg. 1350, pg. 1708
IRIS INTERNATIONAL, INC., pg. 1547, pg. 64
ISORAY, INC., pg. 1548, pg. 1830
JEWELL INSTRUMENTS, LLC, pg. 1418, pg. 1036
JOHNSON & JOHNSON, pg. 1549, pg. 1091
JOHNSON & JOHNSON BABY PRODUCTS, INC., pg. 1552, pg. 1094
JOHNSON & JOHNSON INC., pg. 1552, pg. 1923
KAZ, INC., pg. 58, pg. 844
KEWAUNEE SCIENTIFIC CORPORATION, pg. 931, pg. 1391
KINETIC CONCEPTS, INC., pg. 1553, pg. 1741
L&R MANUFACTURING COMPANY, pg. 1419, pg. 1076
LAKE REGION MEDICAL, pg. 1554, pg. 860
LASER TECHNOLOGY, INC., pg. 1419, pg. 314
LECO CORPORATION, pg. 1355, pg. 906
THE LEE COMPANY, pg. 1420, pg. 383
LEMAITRE VASCULAR, INC., pg. 1555, pg. 805
LIFELOC TECHNOLOGIES, INC., pg. 1556, pg. 336
LIFESCAN INC, pg. 1556, pg. 146
THE L.S. STARRETT COMPANY, pg. 1421, pg. 783
LUMINEX CORPORATION, pg. 1421, pg. 1664
LUNA INNOVATIONS INC., pg. 1557, pg. 1806
MAGNETEK, INC., pg. 1301, pg. 1870
MAGNETIC ANALYSIS CORPORATION, pg. 1421, pg. 1158
MALLINCKRODT PHARMACEUTICALS, pg. 1557, pg. 978
MAQUET, pg. 1558, pg. 1082
MARSH BELLOFRAM CORPORATION, pg. 1885, pg. 1850
MASIMO CORPORATION, pg. 1558, pg. 113
MEASUREMENT SPECIALTIES INC., pg. 1360, pg. 1783
MECHANICAL TECHNOLOGY, INCORPORATED, pg. 1422, pg. 1137
MEDICOOL, INC., pg. 1562, pg. 294
MEDRAD, INC., pg. 1563, pg. 1591
MEDTRONIC, pg. 1563, pg. 830
MEDTRONIC, pg. 1563, pg. 183
MELA SCIENCES, INC., pg. 1422, pg. 1168
MEMRY CORPORATION, pg. 1565, pg. 337
MERIDIAN BIOSCIENCE INC., pg. 1422, pg. 1417
MESA LABORATORIES, INC., pg. 1567, pg. 333
MICRO CORP., pg. 1056, pg. 1122
MICROAIRE SURGICAL INSTRUMENTS INC., pg. 1423, pg. 1778
MICROFLUIDICS INTERNATIONAL CORPORATION, pg. 58, pg. 836
MILESTONE SCIENTIFIC, INC., pg. 1568, pg. 1079
MISONIX INC., pg. 1568, pg. 1159
MISTRAS GROUP, INC., pg. 1362, pg. 1113
MOCON, INC., pg. 1363, pg. 940
MOLECULAR DEVICES CORPORATION, pg. 1568, pg. 287
MTI INSTRUMENTS INC., pg. 658, pg. 1137

MTS SYSTEMS CORPORATION, *pg.* 442, *pg.* 923
MUELLER WATER PRODUCTS, INC., *pg.* 98, *pg.* 515
NATUS MEDICAL INCORPORATED, *pg.* 1572, *pg.* 199
NDC TECHNOLOGIES, *pg.* 1423, *pg.* 118
NEKTAR THERAPEUTICS, *pg.* 1572, *pg.* 224
NEOGEN CORPORATION, *pg.* 883, *pg.* 896
NEUROMETRIX, INC., *pg.* 1572, *pg.* 852
NEWAGE TESTING INSTRUMENTS, INC., *pg.* 1058, *pg.* 1532
NEWPORT CORPORATION, *pg.* 1424, *pg.* 114
NIPRO DIAGNOSTICS, INC., *pg.* 1573, *pg.* 426
NORDION INC., *pg.* 1573, *pg.* 1932
NORTH ATLANTIC INDUSTRIES INC., *pg.* 1424, *pg.* 1143
NUCLETRON CORPORATION, *pg.* 1424, *pg.* 516
NUVASIVE, INC., *pg.* 1577, *pg.* 205
OCULUS INNOVATIVE SCIENCES, *pg.* 1577, *pg.* 182
OSTEOMED CORPORATION, *pg.* 1425, *pg.* 1658
OXYSURE SYSTEMS, INC., *pg.* 1579, *pg.* 1697
PALL CORPORATION, *pg.* 232, *pg.* 1323
PARKER HANNIFIN CORPORATION, *pg.* 1368, *pg.* 1434
PATIENT SAFETY TECHNOLOGIES, INC., *pg.* 1580, *pg.* 114
PENTAX MEDICAL COMPANY, *pg.* 1580, *pg.* 1086
PERRYGRAF, *pg.* 454, *pg.* 561
PERSEON CORPORATION, *pg.* 1581, *pg.* 1760
POLAR ELECTRO INC., *pg.* 664, *pg.* 1173
PREFERRED UTILITIES MANUFACTURING CORPORATION, *pg.* 1075, *pg.* 344
PRESSCO TECHNOLOGY INC., *pg.* 1370, *pg.* 1434
PRESSURE BIOSCIENCES, INC., *pg.* 1586, *pg.* 844
PROPPER MANUFACTURING COMPANY, INC., *pg.* 1586, *pg.* 1175
QUALMARK CORPORATION, *pg.* 1427, *pg.* 322
QUIDEL CORPORATION, *pg.* 1588, *pg.* 207
RELIANCE MEDICAL PRODUCTS, INC., *pg.* 1589, *pg.* 1461
RESMED INC., *pg.* 1589, *pg.* 207
RETRACTABLE TECHNOLOGIES INC., *pg.* 1590, *pg.* 1725
ROCHE DIAGNOSTICS CORPORATION, *pg.* 1590, *pg.* 689
ROCKWELL MEDICAL TECHNOLOGIES, INC., *pg.* 1590, *pg.* 913
RUDOLPH TECHNOLOGIES, INC., *pg.* 669, *pg.* 918
S-T INDUSTRIES, INC., *pg.* 1428, *pg.* 956
SCINTREX LTD., *pg.* 1374, *pg.* 1920
SEASTAR SOLUTIONS, *pg.* 1374, *pg.* 1548
SECHRIST INDUSTRIES, INC., *pg.* 1593, *pg.* 43
SETRA SYSTEMS, INC., *pg.* 1428, *pg.* 802
SIEMENS MEDICAL SOLUTIONS USA, INC., *pg.* 469, *pg.* 1550
SMITH & NEPHEW, INC., ENDOSCOPY DIVISION, *pg.* 1594, *pg.* 783
SMITHS MEDICAL MD, INC., *pg.* 1594, *pg.* 963
SONOSITE, INC., *pg.* 1429, *pg.* 1818
SPACELABS HEALTHCARE, *pg.* 1595, *pg.* 1821
SPECTRAL DIAGNOSTICS INC., *pg.* 1430, *pg.* 1943
THE SPECTRANETICS CORPORATION, *pg.* 1595, *pg.* 315
SPECTRASCIENCE, INC., *pg.* 1595, *pg.* 210
SPECTRUM LABORATORIES INC., *pg.* 1595, *pg.* 69
SPIRE CORPORATION, *pg.* 1378, *pg.* 786
SPX CORPORATION, *pg.* 218, *pg.* 1369
SPX THERMAL PRODUCT SOLUTIONS, *pg.* 1378, *pg.* 1555
ST. JUDE MEDICAL, INC., *pg.* 1596, *pg.* 963
STAAR SURGICAL COMPANY, *pg.* 1597, *pg.* 151
THE STAPLEX COMPANY, INC., *pg.* 474, *pg.* 1146
STARRETT, *pg.* 1064, *pg.* 1621
STEREOTAXIS, INC., *pg.* 1597, *pg.* 1004
STERIS CORPORATION, *pg.* 1597, *pg.* 1464
STRYKER CORPORATION, *pg.* 1598, *pg.* 894
STRYKER MAKO, *pg.* 1598, *pg.* 427
SURGICAL SPECIALTIES CORPORATION, *pg.* 1600, *pg.* 1912
SYMMETRY MEDICAL INC., *pg.* 1600, *pg.* 699
TASER INTERNATIONAL, INC., *pg.* 677, *pg.* 24
TEKTRONIX, INC., *pg.* 1431, *pg.* 1496
TELEDYNE BENTHOS, INC., *pg.* 1431, *pg.* 838
TELEDYNE LECROY, *pg.* 1431, *pg.* 1153
TELEFLEX INCORPORATED, *pg.* 48, *pg.* 1548
THERMO FISHER SCIENTIFIC INC., *pg.* 1431, *pg.* 854
THWING-ALBERT INSTRUMENT COMPANY, *pg.* 1432, *pg.* 1131
TINIUS OLSEN, INC., *pg.* 1432, *pg.* 1541
TRIMEDYNE, INC., *pg.* 1432, *pg.* 121
TSI INCORPORATED, *pg.* 1432, *pg.* 965
TYCO INTERNATIONAL (US) INC., *pg.* 1891, *pg.* 1113
UNILIFE CORPORATION, *pg.* 1603, *pg.* 1597
UTAH MEDICAL PRODUCTS, INC., *pg.* 1605, *pg.* 1752
UVP, INC., *pg.* 1434, *pg.* 298
VACUUM TECHNOLOGY ASSOCIATES, INC., *pg.* 1386, *pg.* 824
VARIAN MEDICAL SYSTEMS, INC., *pg.* 1434, *pg.* 178
VASCULAR SOLUTIONS, INC., *pg.* 1434, *pg.* 946
VESTA INC., *pg.* 1435, *pg.* 1858
VIBCO INC., *pg.* 1387, *pg.* 1611
VITAL SIGNS, INC., *pg.* 1607, *pg.* 1126
VIVUS, INC., *pg.* 1608, *pg.* 163
WALLACH SURGICAL DEVICES, INC., *pg.* 1436, *pg.* 381
WATERS CORPORATION, *pg.* 1436, *pg.* 834
WELCH ALLYN INC., *pg.* 1436, *pg.* 1342
WIRELESS TELECOM GROUP, INC., *pg.* 689, *pg.* 1106
WOODWARD, INC., *pg.* 122, *pg.* 329
ZIMMER BIOMET HOLDINGS, INC., *pg.* 1611, *pg.* 699
ZONARE MEDICAL SYSTEMS, INC., *pg.* 1612, *pg.* 163

3822 - Automatic Controls for Regulating Residential & Commercial Environments & Appliances

ADAMS MFG. CO., *pg.* 51, *pg.* 1427
BROOKS INSTRUMENT, LLC, *pg.* 1403, *pg.* 1537
COMVERGE, INC., *pg.* 1325, *pg.* 536
CONTROL PRODUCTS, INC., *pg.* 1407, *pg.* 1054
DANAHER CORPORATION, *pg.* 1044, *pg.* 397
EMERSON WHITE-RODGERS, *pg.* 1071, *pg.* 996
GENERAL ELECTRIC COMPANY, *pg.* 1297, *pg.* 347
HEAT-TIMER CORPORATION, *pg.* 1072, *pg.* 1065
HONEYWELL INTERNATIONAL INC., *pg.* 407, *pg.* 1088
HUNTER FAN COMPANY, *pg.* 57, *pg.* 1631
INTERNATIONAL CONTROLS & MEASUREMENTS CORP., *pg.* 1350, *pg.* 1317
JOHNSON CONTROLS, INC., *pg.* 209, *pg.* 1876
PECO, INC., *pg.* 1368, *pg.* 1505
SIEMENS BUILDING TECHNOLOGIES, INC., *pg.* 1376, *pg.* 560
SOR, INC., *pg.* 1306, *pg.* 716
TSI INCORPORATED, *pg.* 1432, *pg.* 965
UNITED TECHNOLOGIES CORPORATION, *pg.* 235, *pg.* 353
WATLOW ELECTRIC MANUFACTURING COMPANY, *pg.* 1078, *pg.* 1004
YOUNG REGULATOR COMPANY, *pg.* 1078, *pg.* 1478

3823 - Industrial Instruments for Measurement, Display & Control of Process Variables & Related Products

ABB INC. - AUTOMATION TECHNOLOGIES INSTRUMENTATION PRODUCTS, *pg.* 1398, *pg.* 1590
ACRISON, INC., *pg.* 1310, *pg.* 1087
ADEPT TECHNOLOGY, INC., *pg.* 1310, *pg.* 182
AEROFLEX INCORPORATED, *pg.* 614, *pg.* 1321
ALFA LAVAL INC., *pg.* 700, *pg.* 1800
AMOT CONTROLS CORPORATION, *pg.* 1068, *pg.* 1700
ARIZONA INSTRUMENT LLC, *pg.* 1400, *pg.* 12
AZONIX CORPORATION, *pg.* 1400, *pg.* 788
BROOKFIELD ENGINEERING LABORATORIES, INC., *pg.* 1403, *pg.* 833
BROOKS INSTRUMENT, LLC, *pg.* 1403, *pg.* 1537
CINCINNATI SUB-ZERO PRODUCTS, INC., *pg.* 1070, *pg.* 1411
COGNEX CORPORATION, *pg.* 1406, *pg.* 834
CONAX TECHNOLOGIES LLC, *pg.* 1325, *pg.* 1148
CRANE CO., *pg.* 227, *pg.* 373
CTS VALPEY CORPORATION, *pg.* 632, *pg.* 825
DANAHER CORPORATION, *pg.* 1044, *pg.* 397
DOVER CORPORATION, *pg.* 1329, *pg.* 608
DWYER INSTRUMENTS INC., *pg.* 1330, *pg.* 694
ELECTRO-OPTIX, INC., *pg.* 1046, *pg.* 459
ELECTRO-SENSORS, INC., *pg.* 1333, *pg.* 948
EMERSON PROCESS MANAGEMENT ROSEMOUNT INC., *pg.* 1334, *pg.* 920
EMRISE CORPORATION, *pg.* 637, *pg.* 1371
ENTECH SOLAR, INC., *pg.* 1335, *pg.* 1694
ESTERLINE TECHNOLOGIES CORPORATION, *pg.* 1412, *pg.* 1814
FLUKE CORPORATION, *pg.* 1413, *pg.* 1819
GERBER SCIENTIFIC, INC., *pg.* 1414, *pg.* 380
GLEASON - M&M PRECISION SYSTEMS CORPORATION, *pg.* 1341, *pg.* 1479
HACH COMPANY, *pg.* 1415, *pg.* 334
HARMONIC, INC., *pg.* 402, *pg.* 246
HONEYWELL INTERNATIONAL INC., *pg.* 407, *pg.* 1088
HOWELL INSTRUMENTS INC., *pg.* 1417, *pg.* 1695
ITT CORPORATION, *pg.* 1351, *pg.* 1354
ITW MAGNAFLUX, *pg.* 1418, *pg.* 615
KEITHLEY INSTRUMENTS, INC., *pg.* 1418, *pg.* 1473
L-3 COMMUNICATIONS HOLDINGS INC., *pg.* 650, *pg.* 1250
THE LEE COMPANY, *pg.* 1420, *pg.* 383
LYNCH TECHNOLOGIES, INC., *pg.* 1357, *pg.* 526
MAHR FEDERAL, INC., *pg.* 1358, *pg.* 1606
MARINE ELECTRIC SYSTEMS, INC., *pg.* 652, *pg.* 1123
MARKTIME, *pg.* 1421, *pg.* 371
MATEC INSTRUMENT COMPANIES, INC., *pg.* 1421, *pg.* 839
MEASUREMENT SPECIALTIES/YSI TEMPERATURE, *pg.* 1074, *pg.* 1482
MESA LABORATORIES, INC., *pg.* 1567, *pg.* 333
MKS INSTRUMENTS, INC., *pg.* 1362, *pg.* 781
MOOG INC., *pg.* 231, *pg.* 1156
NANOMETRICS INCORPORATED, *pg.* 1423, *pg.* 147
NAO, INC., *pg.* 1074, *pg.* 1567
NATIONAL INSTRUMENTS CORPORATION, *pg.* 443, *pg.* 1664
NDC TECHNOLOGIES, *pg.* 1423, *pg.* 118
NORTEK SECURITY & CONTROL LLC, *pg.* 659, *pg.* 59
NOSHOK INC., *pg.* 1366, *pg.* 1406
NOVATEL INC., *pg.* 1424, *pg.* 1904
OMRON SCIENTIFIC TECHNOLOGIES INCORPORATED, *pg.* 1425, *pg.* 91
PLANAR SYSTEMS, INC., *pg.* 455, *pg.* 1495
PMFG, INC., *pg.* 1369, *pg.* 1685
PRECISION CONTROL SYSTEMS, INC./ RESEARCH INC., *pg.* 1427, *pg.* 923
PRO-DEX, INC., *pg.* 1586, *pg.* 115
QUALMARK CORPORATION, *pg.* 1427, *pg.* 322
QUANTUM FUEL SYSTEMS TECHNOLOGIES WORLDWIDE, INC., *pg.* 1371, *pg.* 115
REGAL POWER TRANSMISSION SOLUTIONS, *pg.* 216, *pg.* 698
ROCKWELL AUTOMATION, INC., *pg.* 668, *pg.* 1880
ROPER TECHNOLOGIES, INC., *pg.* 1372, *pg.* 467
SCHMITT INDUSTRIES, INC., *pg.* 1374, *pg.* 1506
SCHUTTE & KOERTING INC., *pg.* 1428, *pg.* 1589
SIEMENS PROCESS INDUSTRIES AND DRIVE, *pg.* 1376, *pg.* 1587
TEKTRONIX, INC., *pg.* 1431, *pg.* 1496
TSI INCORPORATED, *pg.* 1432, *pg.* 965
VEEDER-ROOT COMPANY, *pg.* 61, *pg.* 371
WIKA INSTRUMENT CORPORATION, *pg.* 1437, *pg.* 534
WINLAND ELECTRONICS, INC., *pg.* 688, *pg.* 928
YSI INCORPORATED, *pg.* 1438, *pg.* 1483

3824 - Totalizing Fluid Meters & Counting Devices

3M DETECTION SOLUTIONS, *pg.* 1398, *pg.* 1885
AGILENT TECHNOLOGIES, INC., *pg.* 614, *pg.* 264
ALLIED MOTION TECHNOLOGIES INC., *pg.* 616, *pg.* 1137
AMKOR TECHNOLOGY, INC., *pg.* 67, *pg.* 25
ANALOGIC CORPORATION, *pg.* 1399, *pg.* 840
ANRITSU COMPANY, *pg.* 618, *pg.* 152
ARIZONA INSTRUMENT LLC, *pg.* 1400, *pg.* 12
ASSOCIATED RESEARCH INC., *pg.* 1400, *pg.* 622
AXCELIS TECHNOLOGIES, INC., *pg.* 1400, *pg.* 787
AZONIX CORPORATION, *pg.* 1400, *pg.* 788
BACHARACH INC., *pg.* 1400, *pg.* 1556
BADGER METER, INC., *pg.* 1401, *pg.* 1873
BARKSDALE, INC., *pg.* 1317, *pg.* 126
BOLT TECHNOLOGY CORPORATION, *pg.* 1318, *pg.* 360
BOURNS, INC., *pg.* 627, *pg.* 193
BRK BRANDS, INC., *pg.* 627, *pg.* 554
CARTER MOTOR COMPANY, *pg.* 1321, *pg.* 665
CASCADE MICROTECH, INC., *pg.* 1405, *pg.* 1492
CEM CORPORATION, *pg.* 1405, *pg.* 1382
CHARLES MACHINE WORKS, INC., *pg.* 1322, *pg.* 1488
CLAYTON INDUSTRIES CO., *pg.* 1323, *pg.* 66
COGNEX CORPORATION, *pg.* 1406, *pg.* 834
COMVERGE, INC., *pg.* 1325, *pg.* 536
CORBY INDUSTRIES, INC., *pg.* 380, *pg.* 1513
CRANE CO., *pg.* 227, *pg.* 373
CTS VALPEY CORPORATION, *pg.* 632, *pg.* 825

CUBIC TRANSPORTATION SYSTEMS, INC., *pg.* 1905, *pg.* 202
CXR LARUS CORPORATION, *pg.* 632, *pg.* 243
CYBEROPTICS CORPORATION, *pg.* 1408, *pg.* 925
DANAHER CORPORATION, *pg.* 1044, *pg.* 397
DATA I/O CORPORATION, *pg.* 382, *pg.* 1824
DIGIRAD CORPORATION, *pg.* 1524, *pg.* 185
DIGITAL LIGHTWAVE, INC., *pg.* 634, *pg.* 462
DIT-MCO INTERNATIONAL CORPORATION, *pg.* 634, *pg.* 982
DOVER CORPORATION, *pg.* 1329, *pg.* 608
DWYER INSTRUMENTS INC., *pg.* 1330, *pg.* 694
DYNAPAR, *pg.* 1408, *pg.* 616
DYNISCO INSTRUMENTS LLC, *pg.* 1526, *pg.* 823
EAGLE TECHNOLOGIES GROUP, *pg.* 1331, *pg.* 874
EDWARDS VACUUM, INC., *pg.* 1332, *pg.* 1340
ELECTRO-SENSORS, INC., *pg.* 1333, *pg.* 948
ELECTROCRAFT, INC, *pg.* 1333, *pg.* 1033
ELENCO ELECTRONICS, INC., *pg.* 953, *pg.* 670
ELSTER AMCO WATER, INC., *pg.* 1411, *pg.* 452
ELSTER AMERICAN METER COMPANY, *pg.* 1411, *pg.* 1387
EMERSON PROCESS MANAGEMENT, *pg.* 1334, *pg.* 1636
EMERSON PROCESS MANAGEMENT ROSEMOUNT INC., *pg.* 1334, *pg.* 920
EVERETT CHARLES TECHNOLOGIES, *pg.* 638, *pg.* 185
FIELD CONTROLS LLC, *pg.* 1071, *pg.* 1380
FLUKE CORPORATION, *pg.* 1413, *pg.* 1819
THE FORD METER BOX COMPANY, INC., *pg.* 1047, *pg.* 698
FRANKLIN ELECTRIC CO., INC., *pg.* 1337, *pg.* 680
FREQUENCY ELECTRONICS, INC., *pg.* 639, *pg.* 1182
FRYE ELECTRONICS, INC., *pg.* 1413, *pg.* 1509
GAMMEX RMI INC., *pg.* 1532, *pg.* 1872
GE INTELLIGENT PLATFORMS, *pg.* 1339, *pg.* 1777
GIGA-TRONICS INCORPORATED, *pg.* 640, *pg.* 260
GILSON COMPANY, INC., *pg.* 1414, *pg.* 1457
GLEASON - M&M PRECISION SYSTEMS CORPORATION, *pg.* 1341, *pg.* 1479
HAYS FLUID CONTROLS, *pg.* 1049, *pg.* 1370
HD ELECTRIC COMPANY, *pg.* 1299, *pg.* 666
HID GLOBAL CORPORATION, *pg.* 1416, *pg.* 111
HINDS INSTRUMENTS, INC., *pg.* 1416, *pg.* 1498
HINIKER COMPANY, *pg.* 704, *pg.* 927
HUNTER ENGINEERING COMPANY, *pg.* 208, *pg.* 973
IDEAL INDUSTRIES, INC., *pg.* 1051, *pg.* 662
IMAGE SENSING SYSTEMS, INC., *pg.* 412, *pg.* 961
IMPLANT SCIENCES CORPORATION, *pg.* 1348, *pg.* 860
INSTRON CORPORATION, *pg.* 1349, *pg.* 839
ION GEOPHYSICAL CORPORATION, *pg.* 1350, *pg.* 1708
ITRON INC., *pg.* 422, *pg.* 1822
IXIA, *pg.* 422, *pg.* 56
JEWELL INSTRUMENTS, LLC, *pg.* 1418, *pg.* 1036
KEITHLEY INSTRUMENTS, INC., *pg.* 1418, *pg.* 1473
KLA-TENCOR CORPORATION, *pg.* 1353, *pg.* 146
L-3 COMMUNICATIONS HOLDINGS INC., *pg.* 650, *pg.* 1250
L-3 COMMUNICATIONS NARDA MICROWAVE-EAST, *pg.* 650, *pg.* 1165
L-3 INTERSTATE ELECTRONICS CORPORATION, *pg.* 650, *pg.* 43
LANDAUER, INC., *pg.* 1554, *pg.* 615
LASER TECHNOLOGY, INC., *pg.* 1419, *pg.* 314
LIQUID CONTROLS, INC., *pg.* 1356, *pg.* 622
THE L.S. STARRETT COMPANY, *pg.* 1421, *pg.* 783
LUMINEX CORPORATION, *pg.* 1421, *pg.* 1664
LUNA INNOVATIONS INC., *pg.* 1557, *pg.* 1806
MAGNETEK, INC., *pg.* 1301, *pg.* 1870
MAGNETIC ANALYSIS CORPORATION, *pg.* 1421, *pg.* 1158
MALLINCKRODT PHARMACEUTICALS, *pg.* 1557, *pg.* 978
MARINE ELECTRIC SYSTEMS, INC., *pg.* 652, *pg.* 1123
MARSH BELLOFRAM CORPORATION, *pg.* 1885, *pg.* 1850
MATEC INSTRUMENT COMPANIES, INC., *pg.* 1421, *pg.* 839
MCT WORLDWIDE LLC, *pg.* 653, *pg.* 939
MEASUREMENT SPECIALTIES INC., *pg.* 1360, *pg.* 1783
MECHANICAL TECHNOLOGY, INCORPORATED, *pg.* 1422, *pg.* 1137
MEGGER INC., *pg.* 1422, *pg.* 1557
MISTRAS GROUP, INC., *pg.* 1362, *pg.* 1113
MOCON, INC., *pg.* 1363, *pg.* 940
MTI INSTRUMENTS INC., *pg.* 658, *pg.* 1137
MTS SYSTEMS CORPORATION, *pg.* 442, *pg.* 923
MUELLER WATER PRODUCTS, INC., *pg.* 98, *pg.* 515
NANOMETRICS INCORPORATED, *pg.* 1423, *pg.* 147
NDC TECHNOLOGIES, *pg.* 1423, *pg.* 118
NEWAGE TESTING INSTRUMENTS, INC., *pg.* 1058, *pg.* 1532
NEXTEST SYSTEMS CORPORATION, *pg.* 445, *pg.* 248
NORTH ATLANTIC INDUSTRIES INC., *pg.* 1424, *pg.* 1143
O'BRIEN CORPORATION, *pg.* 1366, *pg.* 1001
PALL CORPORATION, *pg.* 232, *pg.* 1323
PARKER HANNIFIN CORPORATION, *pg.* 1368, *pg.* 1434
PERRYGRAF, *pg.* 454, *pg.* 561
POLAR ELECTRO INC., *pg.* 664, *pg.* 1173
PREFERRED UTILITIES MANUFACTURING CORPORATION, *pg.* 1075, *pg.* 344
PRESSCO TECHNOLOGY INC., *pg.* 1370, *pg.* 1434
Q-TECH CORPORATION, *pg.* 666, *pg.* 72
ROCKWELL MEDICAL TECHNOLOGIES, INC., *pg.* 1590, *pg.* 913
ROPER TECHNOLOGIES, INC., *pg.* 1372, *pg.* 467
RUDOLPH TECHNOLOGIES, INC., *pg.* 669, *pg.* 918
S-T INDUSTRIES, INC., *pg.* 1428, *pg.* 956
SCINTREX LTD., *pg.* 1374, *pg.* 1920
SEASTAR SOLUTIONS, *pg.* 1374, *pg.* 1548
SEMTECH CORPORATION GENNUM PRODUCTS, *pg.* 671, *pg.* 1919
SETRA SYSTEMS, INC., *pg.* 1428, *pg.* 802
SPX CORPORATION, *pg.* 218, *pg.* 1369
STARRETT, *pg.* 1064, *pg.* 1621
STOELTING CO., *pg.* 1430, *pg.* 671
SYNACOR, INC., *pg.* 479, *pg.* 1380
TASER INTERNATIONAL, INC., *pg.* 677, *pg.* 24
TEKTRONIX, INC., *pg.* 1431, *pg.* 1496
TELEDYNE BENTHOS, INC., *pg.* 1431, *pg.* 838
TELEDYNE LECROY, *pg.* 1431, *pg.* 1153
TELEFLEX INCORPORATED, *pg.* 48, *pg.* 1548
TERADYNE INC., *pg.* 679, *pg.* 838
THERAGENICS CORPORATION, *pg.* 1431, *pg.* 527
THERMO FISHER SCIENTIFIC INC., *pg.* 1431, *pg.* 854
THWING-ALBERT INSTRUMENT COMPANY, *pg.* 1432, *pg.* 1131
TINIUS OLSEN, INC., *pg.* 1432, *pg.* 1541
TRANSCAT, INC., *pg.* 682, *pg.* 1337
TRIMBLE NAVIGATION LIMITED, *pg.* 1384, *pg.* 288
TSI INCORPORATED, *pg.* 1432, *pg.* 965
VEEDER-ROOT COMPANY, *pg.* 61, *pg.* 371
VIBCO INC., *pg.* 1387, *pg.* 1611
WATERS CORPORATION, *pg.* 1436, *pg.* 834
WIRELESS TELECOM GROUP, INC., *pg.* 689, *pg.* 1106
WOODWARD, INC., *pg.* 122, *pg.* 329

3825 - Instruments for Measuring & Testing of Electricity & Electrical Signals

AGILENT TECHNOLOGIES, INC., *pg.* 614, *pg.* 264
AMKOR TECHNOLOGY, INC., *pg.* 67, *pg.* 25
ANALOGIC CORPORATION, *pg.* 1399, *pg.* 840
ANRITSU COMPANY, *pg.* 618, *pg.* 152
ASSOCIATED RESEARCH INC., *pg.* 1400, *pg.* 622
BOURNS, INC., *pg.* 627, *pg.* 193
CARTER MOTOR COMPANY, *pg.* 1321, *pg.* 665
CASCADE MICROTECH, INC., *pg.* 1405, *pg.* 1492
COMVERGE, INC., *pg.* 1325, *pg.* 536
CXR LARUS CORPORATION, *pg.* 632, *pg.* 243
DANAHER CORPORATION, *pg.* 1044, *pg.* 397
DIT-MCO INTERNATIONAL CORPORATION, *pg.* 634, *pg.* 982
DOVER CORPORATION, *pg.* 1329, *pg.* 608
EDWARDS VACUUM, INC., *pg.* 1332, *pg.* 1340
ELECTROCRAFT, INC, *pg.* 1333, *pg.* 1033
ELENCO ELECTRONICS, INC., *pg.* 953, *pg.* 670
EVERETT CHARLES TECHNOLOGIES, *pg.* 638, *pg.* 185
FLUKE CORPORATION, *pg.* 1413, *pg.* 1819
FREQUENCY ELECTRONICS, INC., *pg.* 639, *pg.* 1182
FRYE ELECTRONICS, INC., *pg.* 1413, *pg.* 1509
GIGA-TRONICS INCORPORATED, *pg.* 640, *pg.* 260
HD ELECTRIC COMPANY, *pg.* 1299, *pg.* 666
HID GLOBAL CORPORATION, *pg.* 1416, *pg.* 111
IDEAL INDUSTRIES, INC., *pg.* 1051, *pg.* 662
ITRON INC., *pg.* 422, *pg.* 1822
IXIA, *pg.* 422, *pg.* 56
KEITHLEY INSTRUMENTS, INC., *pg.* 1418, *pg.* 1473
KLA-TENCOR CORPORATION, *pg.* 1353, *pg.* 146
L-3 COMMUNICATIONS HOLDINGS INC., *pg.* 650, *pg.* 1250
L-3 COMMUNICATIONS NARDA MICROWAVE-EAST, *pg.* 650, *pg.* 1165
L-3 INTERSTATE ELECTRONICS CORPORATION, *pg.* 650, *pg.* 43
MAGNETIC ANALYSIS CORPORATION, *pg.* 1421, *pg.* 1158
MARINE ELECTRIC SYSTEMS, INC., *pg.* 652, *pg.* 1123
MATEC INSTRUMENT COMPANIES, INC., *pg.* 1421, *pg.* 839
MCT WORLDWIDE LLC, *pg.* 653, *pg.* 939
MEGGER INC., *pg.* 1422, *pg.* 1557
NEXTEST SYSTEMS CORPORATION, *pg.* 445, *pg.* 248
NORTH ATLANTIC INDUSTRIES INC., *pg.* 1424, *pg.* 1143
O'BRIEN CORPORATION, *pg.* 1366, *pg.* 1001
PRESSCO TECHNOLOGY INC., *pg.* 1370, *pg.* 1434
Q-TECH CORPORATION, *pg.* 666, *pg.* 72
SEMTECH CORPORATION GENNUM PRODUCTS, *pg.* 671, *pg.* 1919
STOELTING CO., *pg.* 1430, *pg.* 671
SYNACOR, INC., *pg.* 479, *pg.* 1380
TELEDYNE LECROY, *pg.* 1431, *pg.* 1153
TERADYNE INC., *pg.* 679, *pg.* 838
THERAGENICS CORPORATION, *pg.* 1431, *pg.* 527

3826 - Laboratory Analytical Instruments

ABAXIS, INC., *pg.* 1483, *pg.* 298
AFFYMETRIX, INC., *pg.* 1487, *pg.* 263
AMERICAN SCIENCE AND ENGINEERING, INC., *pg.* 1399, *pg.* 787
BACHARACH INC., *pg.* 1400, *pg.* 1556
BECKMAN COULTER, INC., *pg.* 1402, *pg.* 48
BIO-RAD LABORATORIES, INC., *pg.* 1504, *pg.* 101
BIOANALYTICAL SYSTEMS, INC., *pg.* 1402, *pg.* 700
BOULDER SCIENTIFIC COMPANY, *pg.* 1150, *pg.* 335
BROOKFIELD ENGINEERING LABORATORIES, INC., *pg.* 1403, *pg.* 833
BRUKER CORPORATION, *pg.* 1511, *pg.* 788
CEM CORPORATION, *pg.* 1405, *pg.* 1382
CEPHEID, *pg.* 1514, *pg.* 284
CLARIENT INC., *pg.* 1516, *pg.* 40
CLEARFIELD, INC., *pg.* 1406, *pg.* 953
COHERENT, INC., *pg.* 1406, *pg.* 265
COMBIMATRIX CORPORATION, *pg.* 1407, *pg.* 109
CYBEROPTICS CORPORATION, *pg.* 1408, *pg.* 925
DYNEX TECHNOLOGIES, INC., *pg.* 1408, *pg.* 1777
EXERGEN CORPORATION, *pg.* 1412, *pg.* 855
FEI COMPANY, *pg.* 1413, *pg.* 1498
FLUIDIGM CORPORATION, *pg.* 1413, *pg.* 279
HACH COMPANY, *pg.* 1415, *pg.* 334
HAMILTON CO., INC., *pg.* 1415, *pg.* 1031
HARVARD BIOSCIENCE, INC., *pg.* 1539, *pg.* 824
HUTCHINSON TECHNOLOGY INC., *pg.* 409, *pg.* 926
II-VI INCORPORATED, *pg.* 1417, *pg.* 1585
ILLUMINA, INC., *pg.* 412, *pg.* 203
ILX LIGHTWAVE CORPORATION, *pg.* 1417, *pg.* 1008
INTEGRA LIFESCIENCES HOLDINGS CORPORATION, *pg.* 1545, *pg.* 1109
IRIS INTERNATIONAL, INC., *pg.* 1547, *pg.* 64
ISOMET CORPORATION, *pg.* 1418, *pg.* 1807
ITT CORPORATION, *pg.* 1351, *pg.* 1354
LEICA MICROSYSTEMS, INC., *pg.* 1420, *pg.* 555
LUMINEX CORPORATION, *pg.* 1421, *pg.* 1664
MEASUREMENT SPECIALTIES/YSI TEMPERATURE, *pg.* 1074, *pg.* 1482
METTLER-TOLEDO INTERNATIONAL INC., *pg.* 1423, *pg.* 1441
MICROWAVE FILTER COMPANY, INC., *pg.* 654, *pg.* 1157
MILLIPORE CORPORATION, *pg.* 1423, *pg.* 788
MILTON ROY COMPANY, *pg.* 1361, *pg.* 1542
MOCON, INC., *pg.* 1363, *pg.* 940
MOLECULAR DEVICES CORPORATION, *pg.* 1568, *pg.* 287
NATUS MEDICAL INCORPORATED, *pg.* 1572, *pg.* 199
NIPRO DIAGNOSTICS, INC., *pg.* 1573, *pg.* 426
PERKINELMER, INC., *pg.* 1426, *pg.* 853
RANTEC MICROWAVE SYSTEMS, INC., *pg.* 666, *pg.* 307
ROCHE DIAGNOSTICS CORPORATION, *pg.* 1590, *pg.* 689
STOELTING CO., *pg.* 1430, *pg.* 671
THERMO FISHER SCIENTIFIC INC., *pg.* 1602, *pg.* 61
THERMO FISHER SCIENTIFIC INC., *pg.* 1431, *pg.* 854
THERMOTRON INDUSTRIES, *pg.* 235, *pg.* 892
THORLABS INC., *pg.* 1432, *pg.* 1098
TSI INCORPORATED, *pg.* 1432, *pg.* 965
ULTRATECH, INC., *pg.* 1433, *pg.* 251
UVP, INC., *pg.* 1434, *pg.* 298
VERMILLION, INC., *pg.* 1435, *pg.* 1667
WATERS CORPORATION, *pg.* 1436, *pg.* 834

First page reference indicates Business Class Edition
Second page reference indicates Geographic Edition

YSI INCORPORATED, *pg.* 1438, *pg.* 1483

3827 - Optical Instruments & Lenses

ABBOTT MEDICAL OPTICS, INC., *pg.* 1485, *pg.* 260
ANALOGIC CORPORATION, *pg.* 1399, *pg.* 840
BUSHNELL OUTDOOR PRODUCTS, INC., *pg.* 1403, *pg.* 718
CARL ZEISS, INC., *pg.* 1405, *pg.* 1345
CLEARFIELD, INC., *pg.* 1406, *pg.* 953
COGNEX CORPORATION, *pg.* 1406, *pg.* 834
CORNING INCORPORATED, *pg.* 1122, *pg.* 1154
CVI MELLES GRIOT, *pg.* 1407, *pg.* 59
CYBEROPTICS CORPORATION, *pg.* 1408, *pg.* 925
EDMUND INDUSTRIAL OPTICS INC., *pg.* 1411, *pg.* 1041
ELECTRO-OPTIX, INC., *pg.* 1046, *pg.* 459
EPILOG CORPORATION, *pg.* 1412, *pg.* 330
ESSILOR OF AMERICA, INC., *pg.* 1412, *pg.* 1680
FGX INTERNATIONAL, INC., *pg.* 5, *pg.* 1608
GLASS FAB INC., *pg.* 1414, *pg.* 1335
THE HILSINGER CO., *pg.* 1416, *pg.* 841
HINDS INSTRUMENTS, INC., *pg.* 1416, *pg.* 1498
HUTCHINSON TECHNOLOGY INC., *pg.* 409, *pg.* 926
II-VI INCORPORATED, *pg.* 1417, *pg.* 1585
ILX LIGHTWAVE CORPORATION, *pg.* 1417, *pg.* 1008
ISOMET CORPORATION, *pg.* 1418, *pg.* 1807
KAISER OPTICAL SYSTEMS, INC., *pg.* 229, *pg.* 866
L-3 WESCAM INC., *pg.* 1419, *pg.* 1919
LEICA CAMERA, INC., *pg.* 1420, *pg.* 1041
LEICA MICROSYSTEMS, INC., *pg.* 1420, *pg.* 555
LEUPOLD & STEVENS, INC., *pg.* 1420, *pg.* 1492
LIGHTPATH TECHNOLOGIES INC, *pg.* 1420, *pg.* 454
MEADE INSTRUMENTS CORPORATION, *pg.* 1422, *pg.* 113
NCR CORPORATION, *pg.* 443, *pg.* 531
NEWPORT CORPORATION, *pg.* 1424, *pg.* 114
OCLARO, INC., *pg.* 1425, *pg.* 248
OMRON SCIENTIFIC TECHNOLOGIES INCORPORATED, *pg.* 1425, *pg.* 91
OPLINK COMMUNICATIONS, INC., *pg.* 660, *pg.* 91
OPTOSIGMA CORP., *pg.* 1425, *pg.* 262
OSI OPTOELECTRONICS, *pg.* 1425, *pg.* 100
OZ OPTICS LIMTED, *pg.* 1426, *pg.* 1920
PHOTONIS USA PENNSYLVANIA, *pg.* 663, *pg.* 1547
POLAROID CORPORATION, *pg.* 1426, *pg.* 815
PROPHOTONIX LIMITED, *pg.* 1427, *pg.* 1039
REALD INC., *pg.* 1427, *pg.* 47
ROCKY MOUNTAIN INSTRUMENT, INC., *pg.* 1428, *pg.* 332
ROFIN-SINAR TECHNOLOGIES, INC., *pg.* 668, *pg.* 904
RUDOLPH TECHNOLOGIES, INC., *pg.* 669, *pg.* 918
SIGNATURE EYEWEAR, INC., *pg.* 1429, *pg.* 105
SIQURA, *pg.* 308, *pg.* 771
STEFAN SYDOR OPTICS, INC., *pg.* 1430, *pg.* 1337
SWIFT OPTICAL INSTRUMENTS, INC., *pg.* 1430, *pg.* 1744
THORLABS INC., *pg.* 1432, *pg.* 1098
TOPPAN PHOTOMASKS, INC., *pg.* 1432, *pg.* 1739
ULTRAOPTIX, INC., *pg.* 1433, *pg.* 346
ULTRATECH, INC., *pg.* 1433, *pg.* 251
UNILENS VISION INC., *pg.* 1433, *pg.* 438
VISION-EASE LENS CORPORATION, *pg.* 1436, *pg.* 954
VUZIX CORPORATION, *pg.* 687, *pg.* 1337
X-RITE, INCORPORATED, *pg.* 1437, *pg.* 891

3829 - Measuring & Controlling Devices, NEC

3M DETECTION SOLUTIONS, *pg.* 1398, *pg.* 1885
ALLIED MOTION TECHNOLOGIES INC., *pg.* 616, *pg.* 1137
ARIZONA INSTRUMENT LLC, *pg.* 1400, *pg.* 12
ASSOCIATED RESEARCH INC., *pg.* 1400, *pg.* 622
AXCELIS TECHNOLOGIES, INC., *pg.* 1400, *pg.* 787
AZONIX CORPORATION, *pg.* 1400, *pg.* 788
BACHARACH INC., *pg.* 1400, *pg.* 1556
BARKSDALE, INC., *pg.* 1317, *pg.* 126
BOLT TECHNOLOGY CORPORATION, *pg.* 1318, *pg.* 360
BRK BRANDS, INC., *pg.* 627, *pg.* 554
CASCADE MICROTECH, INC., *pg.* 1405, *pg.* 1492
CEM CORPORATION, *pg.* 1405, *pg.* 1382
CHARLES MACHINE WORKS, INC., *pg.* 1322, *pg.* 1488
CLAYTON INDUSTRIES CO., *pg.* 1323, *pg.* 66
COGNEX CORPORATION, *pg.* 1406, *pg.* 834
CORBY INDUSTRIES, INC., *pg.* 380, *pg.* 1513
CRANE CO., *pg.* 227, *pg.* 373
CTS VALPEY CORPORATION, *pg.* 632, *pg.* 825
CUBIC TRANSPORTATION SYSTEMS, INC., *pg.* 1905, *pg.* 202
CYBEROPTICS CORPORATION, *pg.* 1408, *pg.* 925
DIGIRAD CORPORATION, *pg.* 1524, *pg.* 185
DIGITAL LIGHTWAVE, INC., *pg.* 634, *pg.* 462
DIT-MCO INTERNATIONAL CORPORATION, *pg.* 634, *pg.* 982
DYNISCO INSTRUMENTS LLC, *pg.* 1526, *pg.* 823
EAGLE TECHNOLOGIES GROUP, *pg.* 1331, *pg.* 874
ELECTRO-SENSORS, INC., *pg.* 1333, *pg.* 948
ELSTER AMERICAN METER COMPANY, *pg.* 1411, *pg.* 1387
EMERSON PROCESS MANAGEMENT, *pg.* 1334, *pg.* 1636
EMERSON PROCESS MANAGEMENT ROSEMOUNT INC., *pg.* 1334, *pg.* 920
FIELD CONTROLS LLC, *pg.* 1071, *pg.* 1380
THE FORD METER BOX COMPANY, INC., *pg.* 1047, *pg.* 698
FRANKLIN ELECTRIC CO., INC., *pg.* 1337, *pg.* 680
FREQUENCY ELECTRONICS, INC., *pg.* 639, *pg.* 1182
GAMMEX RMI INC., *pg.* 1532, *pg.* 1872
GE INTELLIGENT PLATFORMS, *pg.* 1339, *pg.* 1777
GILSON COMPANY, INC., *pg.* 1414, *pg.* 1457
GLEASON - M&M PRECISION SYSTEMS CORPORATION, *pg.* 1341, *pg.* 1479
HINDS INSTRUMENTS, INC., *pg.* 1416, *pg.* 1498
HUNTER ENGINEERING COMPANY, *pg.* 208, *pg.* 973
IMAGE SENSING SYSTEMS, INC., *pg.* 412, *pg.* 961
IMPLANT SCIENCES CORPORATION, *pg.* 1348, *pg.* 860
INSTRON CORPORATION, *pg.* 1349, *pg.* 839
ION GEOPHYSICAL CORPORATION, *pg.* 1350, *pg.* 1708
JEWELL INSTRUMENTS, LLC, *pg.* 1418, *pg.* 1036
LASER TECHNOLOGY, INC., *pg.* 1419, *pg.* 314
THE L.S. STARRETT COMPANY, *pg.* 1421, *pg.* 783
LUMINEX CORPORATION, *pg.* 1421, *pg.* 1664
LUNA INNOVATIONS INC., *pg.* 1557, *pg.* 1806
MAGNETEK, INC., *pg.* 1301, *pg.* 1870
MAGNETIC ANALYSIS CORPORATION, *pg.* 1421, *pg.* 1158
MALLINCKRODT PHARMACEUTICALS, *pg.* 1557, *pg.* 978
MARSH BELLOFRAM CORPORATION, *pg.* 1885, *pg.* 1850
MEASUREMENT SPECIALTIES INC., *pg.* 1360, *pg.* 1783
MECHANICAL TECHNOLOGY, INCORPORATED, *pg.* 1422, *pg.* 1137
MISTRAS GROUP, INC., *pg.* 1362, *pg.* 1113
MOCON, INC., *pg.* 1363, *pg.* 940
MTI INSTRUMENTS INC., *pg.* 658, *pg.* 1137
MTS SYSTEMS CORPORATION, *pg.* 442, *pg.* 923
MUELLER WATER PRODUCTS, INC., *pg.* 98, *pg.* 515
NDC TECHNOLOGIES, *pg.* 1423, *pg.* 118
NEWAGE TESTING INSTRUMENTS, INC., *pg.* 1058, *pg.* 1532
NORTH ATLANTIC INDUSTRIES INC., *pg.* 1424, *pg.* 1143
PARKER HANNIFIN CORPORATION, *pg.* 1368, *pg.* 1434
PERRYGRAF, *pg.* 454, *pg.* 561
POLAR ELECTRO INC., *pg.* 664, *pg.* 1173
PREFERRED UTILITIES MANUFACTURING CORPORATION, *pg.* 1075, *pg.* 344
PRESSCO TECHNOLOGY INC., *pg.* 1370, *pg.* 1434
ROCKWELL MEDICAL TECHNOLOGIES, INC., *pg.* 1590, *pg.* 913
RUDOLPH TECHNOLOGIES, INC., *pg.* 669, *pg.* 918
S-T INDUSTRIES, INC., *pg.* 1428, *pg.* 956
SCINTREX LTD., *pg.* 1374, *pg.* 1920
SEASTAR SOLUTIONS, *pg.* 1374, *pg.* 1548
SETRA SYSTEMS, INC., *pg.* 1428, *pg.* 802
SPX CORPORATION, *pg.* 218, *pg.* 1369
STARRETT, *pg.* 1064, *pg.* 1621
TASER INTERNATIONAL, INC., *pg.* 677, *pg.* 24
TEKTRONIX, INC., *pg.* 1431, *pg.* 1496
TELEDYNE BENTHOS, INC., *pg.* 1431, *pg.* 838
TELEDYNE LECROY, *pg.* 1431, *pg.* 1153
TELEFLEX INCORPORATED, *pg.* 48, *pg.* 1548
THERMO FISHER SCIENTIFIC INC., *pg.* 1431, *pg.* 854
THWING-ALBERT INSTRUMENT COMPANY, *pg.* 1432, *pg.* 1131
TINIUS OLSEN, INC., *pg.* 1432, *pg.* 1541
TSI INCORPORATED, *pg.* 1432, *pg.* 965
VIBCO INC., *pg.* 1387, *pg.* 1611
WATERS CORPORATION, *pg.* 1436, *pg.* 834
WIRELESS TELECOM GROUP, INC., *pg.* 689, *pg.* 1106
WOODWARD, INC., *pg.* 122, *pg.* 329

3842 - Orthopedic, Prosthetic & Surgical Appliances & Supplies

A-T SURGICAL MFG. CO., INC., *pg.* 1483, *pg.* 825
ACUSHNET COMPANY, *pg.* 1824, *pg.* 818
AEROJET ROCKETDYNE HOLDINGS, INC., *pg.* 1145, *pg.* 186
ALCON, *pg.* 1399, *pg.* 530
ALIMED, INC., *pg.* 1490, *pg.* 816
ALIMERA SCIENCES, INC., *pg.* 1490, *pg.* 482
ALLIED HEALTHCARE PRODUCTS, INC., *pg.* 1491, *pg.* 990
ALPHA PRO TECH, LTD., *pg.* 1492, *pg.* 1922
AMERICAN BILTRITE INC., *pg.* 1878, *pg.* 856
AMERICAN MEDICAL SYSTEMS HOLDINGS, INC., *pg.* 1493, *pg.* 947
ANSELL, *pg.* 1495, *pg.* 1114
BAE SYSTEMS PRODUCTS GROUP, *pg.* 359, *pg.* 432
BARNHARDT MANUFACTURING COMPANY, *pg.* 1498, *pg.* 1364
BAUSCH & LOMB INCORPORATED, *pg.* 1401, *pg.* 1045
BAXTER INTERNATIONAL INC., *pg.* 1499, *pg.* 599
BD MEDICAL, *pg.* 1501, *pg.* 1762
BECTON, DICKINSON & COMPANY, *pg.* 1501, *pg.* 1068
THE BILTRITE CORPORATION, *pg.* 1879, *pg.* 850
BOSTON SCIENTIFIC CORPORATION, *pg.* 1508, *pg.* 831
BUSHNELL OUTDOOR PRODUCTS, INC., *pg.* 1403, *pg.* 718
CARDINAL HEALTH, INC., *pg.* 1512, *pg.* 1448
CARL ZEISS OPTICAL, INC., *pg.* 1405, *pg.* 1778
CAS MEDICAL SYSTEMS, INC., *pg.* 1513, *pg.* 339
CHASE CORPORATION, *pg.* 1152, *pg.* 803
CHURCH & DWIGHT CO., INC., *pg.* 1153, *pg.* 1063
CONGOLEUM CORPORATION, *pg.* 921, *pg.* 1084
CONTINENTAL AMERICAN CORP., *pg.* 1880, *pg.* 723
THE COOPER COMPANIES, INC., *pg.* 1518, *pg.* 183
COOPER-STANDARD AUTOMOTIVE INC., *pg.* 1880, *pg.* 903
COOPER TIRE & RUBBER COMPANY, *pg.* 1881, *pg.* 1453
COOPERVISION, INC., *pg.* 1407, *pg.* 1159
CORDIS CORPORATION, *pg.* 1519, *pg.* 430
CORE MOLDING TECHNOLOGIES, INC., *pg.* 1881, *pg.* 1439
CRYOLIFE, INC., *pg.* 1520, *pg.* 534
CTI INDUSTRIES CORPORATION, *pg.* 1881, *pg.* 555
DANKER LABORATORIES INC., *pg.* 1408, *pg.* 465
DARNELL-ROSE, *pg.* 1045, *pg.* 67
DAVID CLARK COMPANY INCORPORATED, *pg.* 633, *pg.* 862
DEPUY SYNTHES, *pg.* 1523, *pg.* 1593
DEPUYSYNTHES, *pg.* 1523, *pg.* 699
DJO INCORPORATED, *pg.* 1524, *pg.* 302
DJO SURGICAL, *pg.* 1525, *pg.* 1661
DOREL JUVENILE GROUP, INC., *pg.* 923, *pg.* 676
DURA UNDERCUSHIONS LTD., *pg.* 923, *pg.* 1954
E.D. BULLARD COMPANY, *pg.* 1332, *pg.* 727
EDROY PRODUCTS CO., INC., *pg.* 1411, *pg.* 1318
ENCON SAFETY PRODUCTS, *pg.* 1334, *pg.* 1705
ENDOLOGIX, INC., *pg.* 1528, *pg.* 109
ESSILOR OF AMERICA, INC., *pg.* 1412, *pg.* 1680
EXACTECH, INC., *pg.* 1529, *pg.* 428
FABREEKA INTERNATIONAL, INC., *pg.* 1882, *pg.* 847
FGX INTERNATIONAL, INC., *pg.* 5, *pg.* 1608
HANGER INC., *pg.* 1539, *pg.* 1663
HEMCO CORPORATION, *pg.* 1416, *pg.* 979
HEMCON MEDICAL TECHNOLOGIES, INC., *pg.* 1541, *pg.* 1503
THE HILSINGER CO., *pg.* 1416, *pg.* 841
HONEYWELL NORTH SAFETY PRODUCTS, *pg.* 42, *pg.* 1600
HONEYWELL SALISBURY ELECTRICAL SAFETY, *pg.* 1884, *pg.* 558
HOVEROUND CORP., *pg.* 1543, *pg.* 466
HSM SOLUTIONS, *pg.* 1884, *pg.* 1378
ICARE INDUSTRIES, INC., *pg.* 1417, *pg.* 463
INDUSTRIAL RUBBER PRODUCTS, INC., *pg.* 1349, *pg.* 926
INTUITIVE SURGICAL, INC., *pg.* 1546, *pg.* 286
INVACARE CORPORATION, *pg.* 1546, *pg.* 1451
JAMES ALEXANDER CORPORATION, *pg.* 1461, *pg.* 1044
JOHNSON & JOHNSON, *pg.* 1549, *pg.* 1091
JOHNSON & JOHNSON BABY PRODUCTS, INC., *pg.* 1552, *pg.* 1094
JOHNSON & JOHNSON VISION CARE, INC., *pg.* 1552, *pg.* 434
KIMBERLY-CLARK CORPORATION, *pg.* 1461, *pg.* 1720
KRACO ENTERPRISES, LLC, *pg.* 210, *pg.* 68

LAKELAND INDUSTRIES, INC., *pg.* 1354, *pg.* 1338
LAVELLE INDUSTRIES INC., *pg.* 1053, *pg.* 1856
LENSCRAFTERS, INC., *pg.* 1420, *pg.* 1460
LIFECELL CORPORATION, *pg.* 1556, *pg.* 1045
LIFECORE BIOMEDICAL, LLC, *pg.* 1556, *pg.* 920
LIVANOVA, *pg.* 1557, *pg.* 1710
LUXOTTICA GROUP, *pg.* 8, *pg.* 1323
MAPA PROFESSIONAL, *pg.* 1885, *pg.* 555
MAPLE CITY RUBBER COMPANY, *pg.* 962, *pg.* 1468
MARYLAND PLASTICS, INC., *pg.* 1885, *pg.* 769
MAURICE J. MARKELL SHOE CO., INC., *pg.* 1811, *pg.* 1356
MCKEON PRODUCTS, INC., *pg.* 1559, *pg.* 912
MCR SAFETY, *pg.* 1422, *pg.* 1630
MEDLINE INDUSTRIES, INC., *pg.* 1562, *pg.* 635
MEDPORT, LLC, *pg.* 1563, *pg.* 1607
MEDTRONIC, *pg.* 1563, *pg.* 830
MEDTRONIC, INC., *pg.* 1564, *pg.* 939
MENTOR CORPORATION, *pg.* 1565, *pg.* 263
THE MERCER RUBBER COMPANY, *pg.* 1886, *pg.* 1165
MICROAIRE SURGICAL INSTRUMENTS INC., *pg.* 1423, *pg.* 1778
MILESTONE SCIENTIFIC, INC., *pg.* 1568, *pg.* 1079
MUELLER SPORTS MEDICINE, INC., *pg.* 1570, *pg.* 1887
MUNCHKIN, INC., *pg.* 964, *pg.* 300
NOVARTIS CORPORATION, *pg.* 1574, *pg.* 1273
NUSIL TECHNOLOGY LLC, *pg.* 1887, *pg.* 63
NUVASIVE, INC., *pg.* 1577, *pg.* 205
OAKLEY, INC., *pg.* 1840, *pg.* 86
OMNOVA SOLUTIONS INC, *pg.* 1176, *pg.* 1453
O'NEILL INC., *pg.* 1842, *pg.* 270
OSTEOMED CORPORATION, *pg.* 1425, *pg.* 1658
PALL CORPORATION, *pg.* 232, *pg.* 1323
PHILIPS RESPIRONICS, *pg.* 1585, *pg.* 1555
QUADION CORPORATION, *pg.* 1888, *pg.* 941
RADIATOR SPECIALTY COMPANY, *pg.* 215, *pg.* 1380
R.C.A. RUBBER COMPANY, *pg.* 1888, *pg.* 1402
REESE ENTERPRISES, INC., *pg.* 1888, *pg.* 955
SAFILO USA INC., *pg.* 11, *pg.* 1106
THE SALK COMPANY, *pg.* 1591, *pg.* 800
SCHLEGEL SYSTEMS, INC., *pg.* 109, *pg.* 1337
SELLSTROM MANUFACTURING CO., *pg.* 1428, *pg.* 659
SIGNATURE EYEWEAR, INC., *pg.* 1429, *pg.* 105
SIGNET ARMORLITE, INC., *pg.* 1429, *pg.* 60
ST. JUDE MEDICAL, INC., *pg.* 1596, *pg.* 963
STAAR SURGICAL COMPANY, *pg.* 1597, *pg.* 151
STERIS CORPORATION, *pg.* 1597, *pg.* 1464
STRYKER CORPORATION, *pg.* 1598, *pg.* 894
STRYKER MAKO, *pg.* 1598, *pg.* 427
STRYKER ORTHOPAEDICS, *pg.* 1599, *pg.* 1082
SURGICAL SPECIALTIES CORPORATION, *pg.* 1600, *pg.* 1912
SYMMETRY MEDICAL INC., *pg.* 1600, *pg.* 699
TEKNOR APEX COMPANY, *pg.* 1889, *pg.* 1605
TELEFLEX INCORPORATED, *pg.* 48, *pg.* 1548
TEXTILE RUBBER & CHEMICAL COMPANY, *pg.* 1890, *pg.* 530
THERAGENICS CORPORATION, *pg.* 1431, *pg.* 527
THERAPEDIC ASSOCIATES, INC., *pg.* 945, *pg.* 1112
TRICO PRODUCTS CORPORATION, *pg.* 220, *pg.* 905
UTAH MEDICAL PRODUCTS, INC., *pg.* 1605, *pg.* 1752
UVEX SAFETY, *pg.* 1433, *pg.* 1608
VAIL RUBBER WORKS, INC., *pg.* 1891, *pg.* 906
VESTA INC., *pg.* 1435, *pg.* 1858
VICTUS, INC., *pg.* 1606, *pg.* 447
VITAL SIGNS, INC., *pg.* 1607, *pg.* 1126
VYSTAR CORPORATION, *pg.* 1891, *pg.* 532
WEST PHARMACEUTICAL SERVICES, INC., *pg.* 1472, *pg.* 1532
WISCONSIN PHARMACAL COMPANY, LLC, *pg.* 1610, *pg.* 1861
XERIUM TECHNOLOGIES, INC., *pg.* 1703, *pg.* 1389
YOUNGER OPTICS, *pg.* 1437, *pg.* 297
ZIMMER BIOMET HOLDINGS, INC., *pg.* 1611, *pg.* 699

3843 - Dental Equipment & Supplies

3M UNITEK CORPORATION, *pg.* 1483, *pg.* 150
A-DEC, INC., *pg.* 1483, *pg.* 1500
AIR TECHNIQUES, INC., *pg.* 1487, *pg.* 1178
ALIGN TECHNOLOGY, INC., *pg.* 1489, *pg.* 237
BIOHORIZONS, INC., *pg.* 1506, *pg.* 2
BIOLASE TECHNOLOGY, INC., *pg.* 1506, *pg.* 107
BIOMERICA, INC., *pg.* 1506, *pg.* 107
CHURCH & DWIGHT CO., INC., *pg.* 1153, *pg.* 1063
CROSSTEX INTERNATIONAL INC., *pg.* 1520, *pg.* 1164
DEN-MAT CORPORATION, *pg.* 1522, *pg.* 271
DENTSPLY INTERNATIONAL INC., *pg.* 1522, *pg.* 1596
HENRY SCHEIN, INC., *pg.* 1541, *pg.* 1180
MILESTONE SCIENTIFIC, INC., *pg.* 1568, *pg.* 1079
NATIONAL DENTEX CORPORATION, *pg.* 1570, *pg.* 834
PRO-DEX, INC., *pg.* 1586, *pg.* 115
RANIR LLC, *pg.* 520, *pg.* 888
SIRONA DENTAL SYSTEMS, INC., *pg.* 1429, *pg.* 1175
SUNSTAR AMERICAS INC., *pg.* 1599, *pg.* 591
WATER PIK, INC., *pg.* 1609, *pg.* 329
YOUNG INNOVATIONS, INC., *pg.* 1611, *pg.* 977

3844 - X-Ray Apparatus, Tubes & Equipment

ABBOTT DIABETES CARE, INC., *pg.* 1483, *pg.* 38
ABBOTT LABORATORIES, *pg.* 1484, *pg.* 551
ACCURAY, *pg.* 1486, *pg.* 1864
ACORN ENERGY, INC., *pg.* 341, *pg.* 389
ALLIANCE SPORTS GROUP, L.P., *pg.* 1825, *pg.* 1698
ALLIED HEALTHCARE PRODUCTS, INC., *pg.* 1491, *pg.* 990
AMERICAN MEDICAL SYSTEMS, INC., *pg.* 1399, *pg.* 238
AMERICAN SCIENCE AND ENGINEERING, INC., *pg.* 1399, *pg.* 787
ANGIODYNAMICS, INC., *pg.* 1495, *pg.* 1173
ARRHYTHMIA RESEARCH TECHNOLOGY, INC., *pg.* 1496, *pg.* 819
ATRION CORPORATION, *pg.* 1400, *pg.* 1658
BD MEDICAL, *pg.* 1501, *pg.* 1762
BELTONE ELECTRONICS LLC, *pg.* 1503, *pg.* 614
BOSTON SCIENTIFIC CORPORATION, *pg.* 1508, *pg.* 831
CANDELA CORPORATION, *pg.* 1404, *pg.* 855
CANTEL MEDICAL CORP., *pg.* 1405, *pg.* 1079
CARDIAC SCIENCE CORPORATION, *pg.* 1512, *pg.* 1897
CARDIONET, INC., *pg.* 1513, *pg.* 1523
COHERENT, INC., *pg.* 1406, *pg.* 265
CONMED CORPORATION, *pg.* 1517, *pg.* 1347
C.R. BARD, INC., *pg.* 1519, *pg.* 1094
CRITICARE SYSTEMS, INC., *pg.* 1520, *pg.* 1897
CUTERA, INC., *pg.* 1521, *pg.* 49
CYNOSURE, INC., *pg.* 1521, *pg.* 858
DENTSPLY INTERNATIONAL INC., *pg.* 1522, *pg.* 1596
DGT HOLDINGS, *pg.* 634, *pg.* 1223
DIGIRAD CORPORATION, *pg.* 1524, *pg.* 185
DJO SURGICAL, *pg.* 1525, *pg.* 1661
DYNATRONICS CORPORATION, *pg.* 1526, *pg.* 1757
ESCALON MEDICAL CORP., *pg.* 1412, *pg.* 1592
FONAR CORPORATION, *pg.* 1413, *pg.* 1179
GAMMEX RMI INC., *pg.* 1532, *pg.* 1872
GE HEALTHCARE TECHNOLOGIES, *pg.* 1533, *pg.* 1897
GENERAL ELECTRIC COMPANY, *pg.* 1297, *pg.* 347
GF HEALTH PRODUCTS, INC., *pg.* 1535, *pg.* 508
HAEMONETICS CORPORATION, *pg.* 1538, *pg.* 802
HEALTHTRONICS, INC., *pg.* 1540, *pg.* 1663
HUTCHINSON TECHNOLOGY INC., *pg.* 409, *pg.* 926
II-VI INCORPORATED, *pg.* 1417, *pg.* 1585
IRIDEX CORPORATION, *pg.* 648, *pg.* 160
JOHNSON & JOHNSON BABY PRODUCTS, INC., *pg.* 1552, *pg.* 1094
KINETIC CONCEPTS, INC., *pg.* 1553, *pg.* 1741
LANDAUER, INC., *pg.* 1554, *pg.* 615
LIVANOVA, *pg.* 1557, *pg.* 1710
MAQUET, *pg.* 1558, *pg.* 1082
MASIMO CORPORATION, *pg.* 1558, *pg.* 113
MEDRAD, INC., *pg.* 1563, *pg.* 1591
MEDTRONIC, *pg.* 1563, *pg.* 183
MEDTRONIC, INC., *pg.* 1564, *pg.* 939
MENTOR CORPORATION, *pg.* 1565, *pg.* 263
MIRACLE-EAR, INC., *pg.* 1568, *pg.* 940
MISONIX INC., *pg.* 1568, *pg.* 1159
NIPRO DIAGNOSTICS, INC., *pg.* 1573, *pg.* 426
PHILIPS RESPIRONICS, *pg.* 1585, *pg.* 1555
PHONAK LLC, *pg.* 1585, *pg.* 665
POSITRON CORP., *pg.* 665, *pg.* 680
RELIANCE MEDICAL PRODUCTS, INC., *pg.* 1589, *pg.* 1461
ROCKWELL MEDICAL TECHNOLOGIES, INC., *pg.* 1590, *pg.* 913
ROFIN-SINAR TECHNOLOGIES, INC., *pg.* 668, *pg.* 904
SIEMENS CORPORATION, *pg.* 803, *pg.* 1291
SIEMENS MEDICAL SOLUTIONS USA, INC., *pg.* 469, *pg.* 1550
SONOSITE, INC., *pg.* 1429, *pg.* 1818
SPACELABS HEALTHCARE, *pg.* 1595, *pg.* 1821
THE SPECTRANETICS CORPORATION, *pg.* 1595, *pg.* 315
ST. JUDE MEDICAL, INC., *pg.* 1596, *pg.* 963
STARKEY LABORATORIES, INC., *pg.* 1597, *pg.* 923
STEREOTAXIS, INC., *pg.* 1597, *pg.* 1004
SYMMETRY MEDICAL INC., *pg.* 1600, *pg.* 699
TELEFLEX INCORPORATED, *pg.* 48, *pg.* 1548
THERMO FISHER SCIENTIFIC INC., *pg.* 1431, *pg.* 854
TRIMEDYNE, INC., *pg.* 1432, *pg.* 121
TYCO INTERNATIONAL (US) INC., *pg.* 1891, *pg.* 1113
UROLOGIX, INC., *pg.* 1604, *pg.* 945
US ONCOLOGY, INC., *pg.* 1604, *pg.* 1747
VARIAN MEDICAL SYSTEMS, INC., *pg.* 1434, *pg.* 178
VARIAN MEDICAL SYSTEMS X-RAY PRODUCTS, *pg.* 1434, *pg.* 1761
VASCULAR SOLUTIONS, INC., *pg.* 1434, *pg.* 946
ZIMMER BIOMET HOLDINGS, INC., *pg.* 1611, *pg.* 699
ZOLL MEDICAL CORPORATION, *pg.* 1612, *pg.* 814
ZYNEX, INC., *pg.* 690, *pg.* 333

3845 - Electromedical & Electrotherapeutic Apparatus

A-T SURGICAL MFG. CO., INC., *pg.* 1483, *pg.* 825
ABBOTT DIABETES CARE, INC., *pg.* 1483, *pg.* 38
ABBOTT LABORATORIES, *pg.* 1484, *pg.* 551
ACORN ENERGY, INC., *pg.* 341, *pg.* 389
ACUSHNET COMPANY, *pg.* 1824, *pg.* 818
ALIMED, INC., *pg.* 1490, *pg.* 816
ALLIANCE SPORTS GROUP, L.P., *pg.* 1825, *pg.* 1698
ALLIED HEALTHCARE PRODUCTS, INC., *pg.* 1491, *pg.* 990
ALPHA PRO TECH, LTD., *pg.* 1492, *pg.* 1922
AMERICAN BILTRITE INC., *pg.* 1878, *pg.* 856
AMERICAN MEDICAL SYSTEMS HOLDINGS, INC., *pg.* 1493, *pg.* 947
AMERICAN MEDICAL SYSTEMS, INC., *pg.* 1399, *pg.* 238
ANGIODYNAMICS, INC., *pg.* 1495, *pg.* 1173
ARRHYTHMIA RESEARCH TECHNOLOGY, INC., *pg.* 1496, *pg.* 819
ATRION CORPORATION, *pg.* 1400, *pg.* 1658
BAE SYSTEMS PRODUCTS GROUP, *pg.* 359, *pg.* 432
BARNHARDT MANUFACTURING COMPANY, *pg.* 1498, *pg.* 1364
BAXTER INTERNATIONAL INC., *pg.* 1499, *pg.* 599
BD MEDICAL, *pg.* 1501, *pg.* 1762
BECTON, DICKINSON & COMPANY, *pg.* 1501, *pg.* 1068
BELTONE ELECTRONICS LLC, *pg.* 1503, *pg.* 614
BOSTON SCIENTIFIC CORPORATION, *pg.* 1508, *pg.* 831
CANDELA CORPORATION, *pg.* 1404, *pg.* 855
CANTEL MEDICAL CORP., *pg.* 1405, *pg.* 1079
CARDIAC SCIENCE CORPORATION, *pg.* 1512, *pg.* 1897
CARDINAL HEALTH, INC., *pg.* 1512, *pg.* 1448
CARDIONET, INC., *pg.* 1513, *pg.* 1523
CAS MEDICAL SYSTEMS, INC., *pg.* 1513, *pg.* 339
COHERENT, INC., *pg.* 1406, *pg.* 265
CONGOLEUM CORPORATION, *pg.* 921, *pg.* 1084
CONMED CORPORATION, *pg.* 1517, *pg.* 1347
THE COOPER COMPANIES, INC., *pg.* 1518, *pg.* 183
CORDIS CORPORATION, *pg.* 1519, *pg.* 430
CORE MOLDING TECHNOLOGIES, INC., *pg.* 1881, *pg.* 1439
C.R. BARD, INC., *pg.* 1519, *pg.* 1094
CRITICARE SYSTEMS, INC., *pg.* 1520, *pg.* 1897
CRYOLIFE, INC., *pg.* 1520, *pg.* 534
CUTERA, INC., *pg.* 1521, *pg.* 49
CYNOSURE, INC., *pg.* 1521, *pg.* 858
DAVID CLARK COMPANY INCORPORATED, *pg.* 633, *pg.* 862
DEPUY SYNTHES, *pg.* 1523, *pg.* 1593
DEPUYSYNTHES, *pg.* 1523, *pg.* 699
DGT HOLDINGS, *pg.* 634, *pg.* 1223
DIGIRAD CORPORATION, *pg.* 1524, *pg.* 185
DJO INCORPORATED, *pg.* 1524, *pg.* 302
DJO SURGICAL, *pg.* 1525, *pg.* 1661
DURA UNDERCUSHIONS LTD., *pg.* 923, *pg.* 1954
DYNATRONICS CORPORATION, *pg.* 1526, *pg.* 1757
E.D. BULLARD COMPANY, *pg.* 1332, *pg.* 727
ENCON SAFETY PRODUCTS, *pg.* 1334, *pg.* 1705
ENDOLOGIX, INC., *pg.* 1528, *pg.* 109
ESCALON MEDICAL CORP., *pg.* 1412, *pg.* 1592
EXACTECH, INC., *pg.* 1529, *pg.* 428
FGX INTERNATIONAL, INC., *pg.* 5, *pg.* 1608
FONAR CORPORATION, *pg.* 1413, *pg.* 1179
GE HEALTHCARE TECHNOLOGIES, *pg.* 1533, *pg.* 1897

GENERAL ELECTRIC COMPANY, *pg.* 1297, *pg.* 347
GF HEALTH PRODUCTS, INC., *pg.* 1535, *pg.* 508
HAEMONETICS CORPORATION, *pg.* 1538, *pg.* 802
HANGER INC., *pg.* 1539, *pg.* 1663
HEALTHTRONICS, INC., *pg.* 1540, *pg.* 1663
HEMCO CORPORATION, *pg.* 1416, *pg.* 979
HEMCON MEDICAL TECHNOLOGIES, INC., *pg.* 1541, *pg.* 1503
HOVEROUND CORP., *pg.* 1543, *pg.* 466
HUTCHINSON TECHNOLOGY INC., *pg.* 409, *pg.* 926
II-VI INCORPORATED, *pg.* 1417, *pg.* 1585
INTUITIVE SURGICAL, INC., *pg.* 1546, *pg.* 286
INVACARE CORPORATION, *pg.* 1546, *pg.* 1451
IRIDEX CORPORATION, *pg.* 648, *pg.* 160
JAMES ALEXANDER CORPORATION, *pg.* 1461, *pg.* 1044
JOHNSON & JOHNSON, *pg.* 1549, *pg.* 1091
JOHNSON & JOHNSON BABY PRODUCTS, INC., *pg.* 1552, *pg.* 1094
KIMBERLY-CLARK CORPORATION, *pg.* 1461, *pg.* 1720
KINETIC CONCEPTS, INC., *pg.* 1553, *pg.* 1741
LAKELAND INDUSTRIES, INC., *pg.* 1354, *pg.* 1338
LANDAUER, INC., *pg.* 1554, *pg.* 615
LIFECELL CORPORATION, *pg.* 1556, *pg.* 1045
LIFECORE BIOMEDICAL, LLC, *pg.* 1556, *pg.* 920
LIVANOVA, *pg.* 1557, *pg.* 1710
MAQUET, *pg.* 1558, *pg.* 1082
MAURICE J. MARKELL SHOE CO., INC., *pg.* 1811, *pg.* 1356
MCKEON PRODUCTS, INC., *pg.* 1559, *pg.* 912
MCR SAFETY, *pg.* 1422, *pg.* 1630
MEDLINE INDUSTRIES, INC., *pg.* 1562, *pg.* 635
MEDPORT, LLC, *pg.* 1563, *pg.* 1607
MEDRAD, INC., *pg.* 1563, *pg.* 1591
MEDTRONIC, *pg.* 1563, *pg.* 830
MEDTRONIC, *pg.* 1563, *pg.* 183
MEDTRONIC, INC., *pg.* 1564, *pg.* 939
MENTOR CORPORATION, *pg.* 1565, *pg.* 263
MICROAIRE SURGICAL INSTRUMENTS INC., *pg.* 1423, *pg.* 1778
MILESTONE SCIENTIFIC, INC., *pg.* 1568, *pg.* 1079
MIRACLE-EAR, INC., *pg.* 1568, *pg.* 940
MISONIX INC., *pg.* 1568, *pg.* 1159
MUELLER SPORTS MEDICINE, INC., *pg.* 1570, *pg.* 1887
NIPRO DIAGNOSTICS, INC., *pg.* 1573, *pg.* 426
NUVASIVE, INC., *pg.* 1577, *pg.* 205
OAKLEY, INC., *pg.* 1840, *pg.* 86
OSTEOMED CORPORATION, *pg.* 1425, *pg.* 1658
PALL CORPORATION, *pg.* 232, *pg.* 1323
PHILIPS RESPIRONICS, *pg.* 1585, *pg.* 1555
PHONAK LLC, *pg.* 1585, *pg.* 665
POSITRON CORP., *pg.* 665, *pg.* 680
RELIANCE MEDICAL PRODUCTS, INC., *pg.* 1589, *pg.* 1461
ROCKWELL MEDICAL TECHNOLOGIES, INC., *pg.* 1590, *pg.* 913
ROFIN-SINAR TECHNOLOGIES, INC., *pg.* 668, *pg.* 904
THE SALK COMPANY, *pg.* 1591, *pg.* 800
SIEMENS MEDICAL SOLUTIONS USA, INC., *pg.* 469, *pg.* 1550
SONOSITE, INC., *pg.* 1429, *pg.* 1818
SPACELABS HEALTHCARE, *pg.* 1595, *pg.* 1821
THE SPECTRANETICS CORPORATION, *pg.* 1595, *pg.* 315
ST. JUDE MEDICAL, INC., *pg.* 1596, *pg.* 963
STAAR SURGICAL COMPANY, *pg.* 1597, *pg.* 151
STARKEY LABORATORIES, INC., *pg.* 1597, *pg.* 923
STEREOTAXIS, INC., *pg.* 1597, *pg.* 1004
STERIS CORPORATION, *pg.* 1597, *pg.* 1464
STRYKER CORPORATION, *pg.* 1598, *pg.* 894
STRYKER MAKO, *pg.* 1598, *pg.* 427
STRYKER ORTHOPAEDICS, *pg.* 1599, *pg.* 1082
SURGICAL SPECIALTIES CORPORATION, *pg.* 1600, *pg.* 1912
SYMMETRY MEDICAL INC., *pg.* 1600, *pg.* 699
TELEFLEX INCORPORATED, *pg.* 48, *pg.* 1548
THERAGENICS CORPORATION, *pg.* 1431, *pg.* 527
THERAPEDIC ASSOCIATES, INC., *pg.* 945, *pg.* 1112
THERMO FISHER SCIENTIFIC INC., *pg.* 1431, *pg.* 854
TRIMEDYNE, INC., *pg.* 1432, *pg.* 121
TYCO INTERNATIONAL (US) INC., *pg.* 1891, *pg.* 1113
UROLOGIX, INC., *pg.* 1604, *pg.* 945
US ONCOLOGY, INC., *pg.* 1604, *pg.* 1747
UTAH MEDICAL PRODUCTS, INC., *pg.* 1605, *pg.* 1752
UVEX SAFETY, *pg.* 1433, *pg.* 1608
VARIAN MEDICAL SYSTEMS, INC., *pg.* 1434, *pg.* 178
VASCULAR SOLUTIONS, INC., *pg.* 1434, *pg.* 946
VITAL SIGNS, INC., *pg.* 1607, *pg.* 1126
WEST PHARMACEUTICAL SERVICES, INC., *pg.* 1472, *pg.* 1532
WISCONSIN PHARMACAL COMPANY, LLC, *pg.* 1610, *pg.* 1861
ZIMMER BIOMET HOLDINGS, INC., *pg.* 1611, *pg.* 699
ZOLL MEDICAL CORPORATION, *pg.* 1612, *pg.* 814
ZYNEX, INC., *pg.* 690, *pg.* 333

3851 - Ophthalmic Goods

1-800 CONTACTS, INC., *pg.* 1758, *pg.* 1753
COHEN'S FASHION OPTICAL INC., *pg.* 1406, *pg.* 1161
EMERGING VISION, INC., *pg.* 1411, *pg.* 1227
HORNER RAUSCH OPTICAL COMPANY EAST, INC., *pg.* 1417, *pg.* 1651
ICARE INDUSTRIES, INC., *pg.* 1417, *pg.* 463
LENSCRAFTERS, INC., *pg.* 1420, *pg.* 1460
LUXOTTICA RETAIL, *pg.* 8, *pg.* 1460
NATIONAL VISION, INC., *pg.* 1423, *pg.* 534
OPTICIANS ASSOCIATION OF AMERICA, *pg.* 152, *pg.* 1639
SOLSTICE MARKETING CONCEPTS, LLC, *pg.* 1429, *pg.* 1293
U.S. VISION, INC., *pg.* 1433, *pg.* 1071
VISIONWORKS OF AMERICA, INC., *pg.* 1436, *pg.* 1744

3861 - Photographic Equipment & Supplies

AGFA CORPORATION, *pg.* 1398, *pg.* 1114
ALAN GORDON ENTERPRISES, INC., *pg.* 1399, *pg.* 125
ANACOMP, INC., *pg.* 350, *pg.* 1777
AVID TECHNOLOGY, INC., *pg.* 622, *pg.* 804
BALLANTYNE STRONG, INC., *pg.* 623, *pg.* 1013
BOSCH SECURITY SYSTEMS, INC., *pg.* 626, *pg.* 1158
BRADY CORPORATION, *pg.* 363, *pg.* 1873
CANON U.S.A., INC., *pg.* 1404, *pg.* 1178
CODA INC., *pg.* 1406, *pg.* 1081
CODA OCTOPUS GROUP, INC., *pg.* 629, *pg.* 437
COLOR IMAGING INC., *pg.* 1407, *pg.* 536
DA-LITE SCREEN COMPANY, *pg.* 632, *pg.* 698
DUKANE CORPORATION, *pg.* 634, *pg.* 658
EASTMAN KODAK COMPANY, *pg.* 1408, *pg.* 1333
FLIR SYSTEMS, INC., *pg.* 1413, *pg.* 1510
IKONICS CORPORATION, *pg.* 1168, *pg.* 921
IMAGEWORKS, *pg.* 1544, *pg.* 1158
IMAX CORPORATION, *pg.* 1417, *pg.* 1926
INFOCUS CORPORATION, *pg.* 644, *pg.* 1503
KYOCERA DOCUMENT SOLUTIONS AMERICA, *pg.* 426, *pg.* 1065
LEICA CAMERA, INC., *pg.* 1420, *pg.* 1041
LEXAR MEDIA, INC., *pg.* 1262, *pg.* 146
PHOTOGENIC PROFESSIONAL LIGHTING, *pg.* 1426, *pg.* 556
PLUS VISION CORP. OF AMERICA, *pg.* 1275, *pg.* 1496
POLAROID CORPORATION, *pg.* 1426, *pg.* 815
ROSCO LABORATORIES, INC., *pg.* 1782, *pg.* 378
THE TIFFEN COMPANY LLC, *pg.* 1432, *pg.* 1165
X-RITE, INCORPORATED, *pg.* 1437, *pg.* 891
XEROX CORPORATION, *pg.* 494, *pg.* 365

3873 - Watches, Clocks, Clockwork Operated Devices & Parts

3M DETECTION SOLUTIONS, *pg.* 1398, *pg.* 1885
ACCO BRANDS CORPORATION, *pg.* 340, *pg.* 626
ACME STAPLE COMPANY, INC., *pg.* 341, *pg.* 1034
ALLIED MOTION TECHNOLOGIES INC., *pg.* 616, *pg.* 1137
AMANO CINCINNATI, INC., *pg.* 348, *pg.* 1117
ARIZONA INSTRUMENT LLC, *pg.* 1400, *pg.* 12
ARMITRON WATCH DIVISION, *pg.* 1, *pg.* 1174
ASSOCIATED RESEARCH INC., *pg.* 1400, *pg.* 622
AUDEMARS PIGUET (NORTH AMERICA), *pg.* 1, *pg.* 1198
AXCELIS TECHNOLOGIES, INC., *pg.* 1400, *pg.* 787
AZONIX CORPORATION, *pg.* 1400, *pg.* 788
BACHARACH INC., *pg.* 1400, *pg.* 1556
BARKSDALE, INC., *pg.* 1317, *pg.* 126
BARNES GROUP INC., *pg.* 1317, *pg.* 340
BAUME & MERCIER, INC., *pg.* 1, *pg.* 1201
BAUMFOLDER CORPORATION, *pg.* 360, *pg.* 1472
BIRKS & MAYORS INC., *pg.* 1, *pg.* 470
BOLT TECHNOLOGY CORPORATION, *pg.* 1318, *pg.* 360
BRK BRANDS, INC., *pg.* 627, *pg.* 554
BROTHER INTERNATIONAL CORPORATION - USA, *pg.* 53, *pg.* 1046
BULOVA CORPORATION, *pg.* 2, *pg.* 1356
BULOVA WATCH COMPANY LIMITED, *pg.* 2, *pg.* 1935
CASCADE MICROTECH, INC., *pg.* 1405, *pg.* 1492
CEM CORPORATION, *pg.* 1405, *pg.* 1382
CHARLES MACHINE WORKS, INC., *pg.* 1322, *pg.* 1488
CHASE-DURER LTD., *pg.* 3, *pg.* 46
CHELSEA CLOCK CO., INC., *pg.* 3, *pg.* 814
CHRISTOPHER DESIGNS, INC., *pg.* 3, *pg.* 1212
CLAYTON INDUSTRIES CO., *pg.* 1323, *pg.* 66
COGNEX CORPORATION, *pg.* 1406, *pg.* 834
CORBY INDUSTRIES, INC., *pg.* 380, *pg.* 1513
CRANE CO., *pg.* 227, *pg.* 373
CROTON WATCH COMPANY & NATIONWIDE TIME, *pg.* 4, *pg.* 1350
CTS VALPEY CORPORATION, *pg.* 632, *pg.* 825
CUBIC TRANSPORTATION SYSTEMS, INC., *pg.* 1905, *pg.* 202
CYBEROPTICS CORPORATION, *pg.* 1408, *pg.* 925
DATACARD CORPORATION, *pg.* 382, *pg.* 948
DE-STA-CO INDUSTRIES, *pg.* 1045, *pg.* 867
DIGIRAD CORPORATION, *pg.* 1524, *pg.* 185
DIGITAL LIGHTWAVE, INC., *pg.* 634, *pg.* 462
DIMCO-GRAY COMPANY, *pg.* 1881, *pg.* 1409
DIT-MCO INTERNATIONAL CORPORATION, *pg.* 634, *pg.* 982
DYNISCO INSTRUMENTS LLC, *pg.* 1526, *pg.* 823
EAGLE TECHNOLOGIES GROUP, *pg.* 1331, *pg.* 874
ELECTRIC TIME CO., INC., *pg.* 4, *pg.* 832
ELECTRO-OPTIX, INC., *pg.* 1046, *pg.* 459
ELECTRO-SENSORS, INC., *pg.* 1333, *pg.* 948
ELSTER AMERICAN METER COMPANY, *pg.* 1411, *pg.* 1387
EMERSON PROCESS MANAGEMENT, *pg.* 1334,. *pg.* 1636
EMERSON PROCESS MANAGEMENT ROSEMOUNT INC., *pg.* 1334, *pg.* 920
EUGENE BIRO CORP., *pg.* 5, *pg.* 1230
FARADAY, *pg.* 638, *pg.* 1066
FELLOWES, INC., *pg.* 397, *pg.* 620
FIELD CONTROLS LLC, *pg.* 1071, *pg.* 1380
THE FORD METER BOX COMPANY, INC., *pg.* 1047, *pg.* 698
FOSSIL GROUP, INC., *pg.* 5, *pg.* 1735
FRANKLIN ELECTRIC CO., INC., *pg.* 1337, *pg.* 680
FRANKLIN ELECTRONIC PUBLISHERS, INC., *pg.* 398, *pg.* 1048
FREQUENCY ELECTRONICS, INC., *pg.* 639, *pg.* 1182
GAMMEX RMI INC., *pg.* 1532, *pg.* 1872
GE INTELLIGENT PLATFORMS, *pg.* 1339, *pg.* 1777
GENEVA WATCH GROUP, *pg.* 5, *pg.* 1174
GEVRIL USA, *pg.* 6, *pg.* 1348
GILSON COMPANY, INC., *pg.* 1414, *pg.* 1457
GLEASON - M&M PRECISION SYSTEMS CORPORATION, *pg.* 1341, *pg.* 1479
GLORY GLOBAL SOLUTIONS, *pg.* 401, *pg.* 628
HINDS INSTRUMENTS, INC., *pg.* 1416, *pg.* 1498
HOWARD MILLER COMPANY, *pg.* 7, *pg.* 914
HSM SOLUTIONS, *pg.* 1884, *pg.* 1378
HUNTER ENGINEERING COMPANY, *pg.* 208, *pg.* 973
IMAGE SENSING SYSTEMS, INC., *pg.* 412, *pg.* 961
IMPLANT SCIENCES CORPORATION, *pg.* 1348, *pg.* 860
INSTRON CORPORATION, *pg.* 1349, *pg.* 839
INTERNATIONAL BUSINESS MACHINES CORPORATION, *pg.* 418, *pg.* 1138
ION GEOPHYSICAL CORPORATION, *pg.* 1350, *pg.* 1708
JEWELL INSTRUMENTS, LLC, *pg.* 1418, *pg.* 1036
KWIAT INC., *pg.* 8, *pg.* 1249
LASER TECHNOLOGY, INC., *pg.* 1419, *pg.* 314
LAZARE KAPLAN INTERNATIONAL, INC., *pg.* 8, *pg.* 1250
THE L.S. STARRETT COMPANY, *pg.* 1421, *pg.* 783
LUMINEX CORPORATION, *pg.* 1421, *pg.* 1664
LUNA INNOVATIONS INC., *pg.* 1557, *pg.* 1806
LYMAN PRODUCTS CORPORATION, *pg.* 1839, *pg.* 356
MAGNETEK, INC., *pg.* 1301, *pg.* 1870
MAGNETIC ANALYSIS CORPORATION, *pg.* 1421, *pg.* 1158
MALLINCKRODT PHARMACEUTICALS, *pg.* 1557, *pg.* 978
MARSH BELLOFRAM CORPORATION, *pg.* 1885, *pg.* 1850
MEASUREMENT SPECIALTIES INC., *pg.* 1360, *pg.* 1783
MECHANICAL TECHNOLOGY, INCORPORATED, *pg.* 1422, *pg.* 1137
MISTRAS GROUP, INC., *pg.* 1362, *pg.* 1113
MOCON, INC., *pg.* 1363, *pg.* 940
MOVADO GROUP, INC., *pg.* 10, *pg.* 1101
MTI INSTRUMENTS INC., *pg.* 658, *pg.* 1137
MTS SYSTEMS CORPORATION, *pg.* 442, *pg.* 923
MUELLER WATER PRODUCTS, INC., *pg.* 98, *pg.* 515

M.Z. BERGER & CO., INC., pg. 10, pg. 1175
NDC TECHNOLOGIES, pg. 1423, pg. 118
NEWAGE TESTING INSTRUMENTS, INC., pg. 1058, pg. 1532
NORTH ATLANTIC INDUSTRIES INC., pg. 1424, pg. 1143
OPEX CORPORATION, pg. 450, pg. 1087
PAR TECHNOLOGY CORPORATION, pg. 452, pg. 1183
PARKER HANNIFIN CORPORATION, pg. 1368, pg. 1434
PERRYGRAF, pg. 454, pg. 561
PIERCE EQUIPMENT, pg. 1369, pg. 1640
PITNEY BOWES INC., pg. 454, pg. 376
POINT BLANK SOLUTIONS, INC., pg. 1467, pg. 460
POLAR ELECTRO INC., pg. 664, pg. 1173
PREFERRED UTILITIES MANUFACTURING CORPORATION, pg. 1075, pg. 344
PRESSCO TECHNOLOGY INC., pg. 1370, pg. 1434
PRESSTEK, INC., pg. 456, pg. 606
PRESSURE BIOSCIENCES, INC., pg. 1586, pg. 844
ROCKWELL MEDICAL TECHNOLOGIES, INC., pg. 1590, pg. 913
ROWE INTERNATIONAL CORP, pg. 669, pg. 889
RUDOLPH TECHNOLOGIES, INC., pg. 669, pg. 918
S-T INDUSTRIES, INC., pg. 1428, pg. 956
SCINTREX LTD., pg. 1374, pg. 1920
SDI TECHNOLOGIES, INC., pg. 671, pg. 1113
SEASTAR SOLUTIONS, pg. 1374, pg. 1548
SETRA SYSTEMS, INC., pg. 1428, pg. 802
SPX CORPORATION, pg. 218, pg. 1369
STARRETT, pg. 1064, pg. 1621
TASER INTERNATIONAL, INC., pg. 677, pg. 24
TEKTRONIX, INC., pg. 1431, pg. 1496
TELEDYNE BENTHOS, INC., pg. 1431, pg. 838
TELEDYNE LECROY, pg. 1431, pg. 1153
TELEFLEX INCORPORATED, pg. 48, pg. 1548
THERMO FISHER SCIENTIFIC INC., pg. 1431, pg. 854
THWING-ALBERT INSTRUMENT COMPANY, pg. 1432, pg. 1131
TIFFANY & CO., pg. 13, pg. 1299
TIMEX CORPORATION, pg. 14, pg. 355
TINIUS OLSEN, INC., pg. 1432, pg. 1541
TOURNEAU INC., pg. 14, pg. 1303
TSI INCORPORATED, pg. 1432, pg. 965
VIBCO INC., pg. 1387, pg. 1611
VIDEOJET TECHNOLOGIES INC., pg. 489, pg. 671
WATERS CORPORATION, pg. 1436, pg. 834
WIRELESS TELECOM GROUP, INC., pg. 689, pg. 1106
WOODWARD, INC., pg. 122, pg. 329
W.R. COBB COMPANY, pg. 15, pg. 1601

3911 - Jewelry, Precious Metal

AUDEMARS PIGUET (NORTH AMERICA), pg. 1, pg. 1198
BERGIO INTERNATIONAL, INC., pg. 1, pg. 1065
BIRKS & MAYORS INC., pg. 1, pg. 470
BIRKS & MAYORS INC., pg. 1, pg. 1953
CERAMTEC NORTH AMERICA ELECTRONIC APPLICATIONS, INC., pg. 628, pg. 1620
CHARLES & COLVARD LTD, pg. 3, pg. 1384
CHASE CORPORATION, pg. 1152, pg. 803
CHRISTOPHER DESIGNS, INC., pg. 3, pg. 1212
CRAIGER DRAKE DESIGNS, pg. 4, pg. 1562
DANECRAFT INC., pg. 4, pg. 1606
DE HAGO, INC., pg. 4, pg. 1222
THE DOW CHEMICAL COMPANY, pg. 1157, pg. 898
EVAPORATED METAL FILMS CORP., pg. 1412, pg. 1170
GENERAL MAGNAPLATE CORPORATION, pg. 1164, pg. 1079
HANDY & HARMAN LTD., pg. 85, pg. 1352
HARRY KOTLAR & CO., INC., pg. 6, pg. 132
HARRY WINSTON, INC., pg. 6, pg. 1238
HEARTS ON FIRE COMPANY, pg. 6, pg. 796
IMPERIAL-DELTAH, INC., pg. 7, pg. 1601
KARAT PLATINUM LLC, pg. 7, pg. 1168
LAGOS INC., pg. 8, pg. 1566
LIQUIDMETAL TECHNOLOGIES, INC., pg. 1356, pg. 188
MARTIN FLYER INC., pg. 9, pg. 1257
MATERION CORPORATION, pg. 1359, pg. 1463
MATERION MICROELECTRONICS & SERVICES, pg. 1559, pg. 1149
MERITOR, INC., pg. 212, pg. 911
MICHAEL ANTHONY JEWELERS, INC., pg. 10, pg. 1183
NCI BUILDING SYSTEMS, INC., pg. 1364, pg. 1712
NORDSON CORPORATION, pg. 1365, pg. 1480
NOV AMERON, pg. 100, pg. 187
ONEIDA LTD, pg. 1129, pg. 1318
RICHLINE GROUP, INC., pg. 11, pg. 470
SEQUA CORPORATION, pg. 1180, pg. 1290
STULLER, INC., pg. 13, pg. 745
SULZER METCO (WESTBURY) INC., pg. 1064, pg. 1350
SUMMIT CORPORATION OF AMERICA, pg. 1182, pg. 380
VALLEY CASTING, INC., pg. 1891, pg. 928
VAN CLEEF & ARPELS, INC., pg. 15, pg. 1308
VIRTEK VISION INTERNATIONAL, INC., pg. 1435, pg. 1948
WATTS WATER TECHNOLOGIES, INC., pg. 1078, pg. 837
YURMAN DESIGN, INC., pg. 15, pg. 1316

3914 - Silverware, Plated Ware & Stainless Steel Ware

BIRKS & MAYORS INC., pg. 1, pg. 1953
CERAMTEC NORTH AMERICA ELECTRONIC APPLICATIONS, INC., pg. 628, pg. 1620
CHASE CORPORATION, pg. 1152, pg. 803
THE DOW CHEMICAL COMPANY, pg. 1157, pg. 898
EVAPORATED METAL FILMS CORP., pg. 1412, pg. 1170
GENERAL MAGNAPLATE CORPORATION, pg. 1164, pg. 1079
HANDY & HARMAN LTD., pg. 85, pg. 1352
LIQUIDMETAL TECHNOLOGIES, INC., pg. 1356, pg. 188
MATERION CORPORATION, pg. 1359, pg. 1463
MATERION MICROELECTRONICS & SERVICES, pg. 1559, pg. 1149
MERITOR, INC., pg. 212, pg. 911
NCI BUILDING SYSTEMS, INC., pg. 1364, pg. 1712
NORDSON CORPORATION, pg. 1365, pg. 1480
NOV AMERON, pg. 100, pg. 187
ONEIDA LTD, pg. 1129, pg. 1318
SEQUA CORPORATION, pg. 1180, pg. 1290
SULZER METCO (WESTBURY) INC., pg. 1064, pg. 1350
SUMMIT CORPORATION OF AMERICA, pg. 1182, pg. 380
VIRTEK VISION INTERNATIONAL, INC., pg. 1435, pg. 1948
THE VOLLRATH COMPANY LLC, pg. 1139, pg. 1894
WATTS WATER TECHNOLOGIES, INC., pg. 1078, pg. 837

3915 - Jewelers Findings & Materials & Lapidary Work

CHRISTOPHER DESIGNS, INC., pg. 3, pg. 1212
EUGENE BIRO CORP., pg. 5, pg. 1230
KWIAT INC., pg. 8, pg. 1249
LAZARE KAPLAN INTERNATIONAL, INC., pg. 8, pg. 1250
LYMAN PRODUCTS CORPORATION, pg. 1839, pg. 356
W.R. COBB COMPANY, pg. 15, pg. 1601

3931 - Musical Instruments

ALLEN ORGAN COMPANY, pg. 527, pg. 1549
AVEDIS ZILDJIAN COMPANY, pg. 531, pg. 839
AXL MUSICAL INSTRUMENTS CO., LTD., CORP., pg. 531, pg. 145
CONN-SELMER, INC., pg. 542, pg. 677
DEAN MARKLEY STRINGS, INC., pg. 543, pg. 265
EMG, INC., pg. 636, pg. 277
ERNIE BALL INC., pg. 1768, pg. 68
FENDER MUSICAL INSTRUMENTS CORPORATION, pg. 547, pg. 21
GIBSON GUITAR CORP., pg. 550, pg. 1650
PAUL REED SMITH GUITARS, pg. 574, pg. 779
PEAVEY ELECTRONICS CORPORATION, pg. 662, pg. 970
RICHMOND PHILHARMONIC INC., pg. 579, pg. 1803
STEINWAY & SONS, pg. 586, pg. 1176
STEINWAY MUSICAL INSTRUMENTS, INC., pg. 586, pg. 854
TAYLOR-LISTUG INC., pg. 587, pg. 78
U.S. MUSIC CORPORATION, pg. 315, pg. 560
YAMAHA CORPORATION OF AMERICA, pg. 595, pg. 51
YOUNG CHANG NORTH AMERICA, pg. 595, pg. 77

3942 - Dolls & Stuffed Toys

ALEXANDER DOLL COMPANY, INC., pg. 949, pg. 1545
FACTORY X DISTRIBUTION, pg. 953, pg. 532
FOLKMANIS, INC., pg. 953, pg. 83
GUND, INC., pg. 954, pg. 1056
HASBRO, INC., pg. 954, pg. 1603
MATTEL GAMES/PUZZLES, pg. 962, pg. 80
MATTEL, INC., pg. 962, pg. 81
THINKWAY TOYS, pg. 968, pg. 1924
TONNER DOLL COMPANY, INC., pg. 968, pg. 1171
THE VERMONT TEDDY BEAR COMPANY, pg. 969, pg. 1767
THE WORLD OF MINIATURE BEARS, INC., pg. 970, pg. 448

3944 - Games, Toys & Children's Vehicles; Except Dolls & Bicycles

ALVIMAR GENESIS, pg. 1825, pg. 886
ATLUS USA, INC., pg. 949, pg. 107
B. DAZZLE, INC., pg. 949, pg. 188
THE BABY JOGGER COMPANY, pg. 949, pg. 1800
BACHMANN INDUSTRIES, INC., pg. 950, pg. 1559
CARTA MUNDI, INC., pg. 951, pg. 1677
E-Z BOWZ, LLC, pg. 692, pg. 1635
EDUCATIONAL INSIGHTS, INC., pg. 951, pg. 187
ELECTRONIC ARTS INC., pg. 951, pg. 189
ELENCO ELECTRONICS, INC., pg. 953, pg. 670
FACTORY X DISTRIBUTION, pg. 953, pg. 532
FORTUNET, INC., pg. 953, pg. 1024
FRACTILES, INC., pg. 953, pg. 311
FUNRISE TOY CORP., pg. 549, pg. 300
GAMEWRIGHT, pg. 953, pg. 836
GAMING PARTNERS INTERNATIONAL CORPORATION, pg. 954, pg. 1024
GLD PRODUCTS, INC., pg. 1835, pg. 1882
GUND, INC., pg. 954, pg. 1056
HASBRO, INC., pg. 954, pg. 1603
IMPERIAL TOY CORPORATION, pg. 957, pg. 166
JADA TOYS, INC., pg. 960, pg. 67
JAKKS PACIFIC, INC., pg. 960, pg. 142
JOSEPH ENTERPRISES, INC., pg. 960, pg. 220
LEAPFROG ENTERPRISES, INC., pg. 961, pg. 84
LEGO SYSTEMS, INC., pg. 961, pg. 346
LIFOAM INDUSTRIES INC., pg. 961, pg. 772
LIONEL LLC, pg. 961, pg. 875
MAPLE CITY RUBBER COMPANY, pg. 962, pg. 1468
MATTEL GAMES/PUZZLES, pg. 962, pg. 80
MATTEL, INC., pg. 962, pg. 81
MICROSOFT GAME STUDIOS, pg. 964, pg. 1828
THE OHIO ART COMPANY, INC., pg. 965, pg. 1406
OOZ & OZ INC., pg. 965, pg. 1838
PRO-LINE, INC., pg. 966, pg. 45
RADIO FLYER INC., pg. 966, pg. 588
REEVES INTERNATIONAL, INC., pg. 966, pg. 1108
REVELL, pg. 966, pg. 611
SASSY, INC., pg. 966, pg. 895
SDI TECHNOLOGIES, INC., pg. 671, pg. 1113
SONY COMPUTER ENTERTAINMENT AMERICA LLC, pg. 966, pg. 256
THE STEP2 COMPANY LLC, pg. 1889, pg. 1474
THINKWAY TOYS, pg. 968, pg. 1924
UBISOFT INC., pg. 589, pg. 229
THE UNITED STATES PLAYING CARD COMPANY, pg. 969, pg. 727
UNIVERSITY GAMES CORPORATION, pg. 969, pg. 230
VALLEY CASTING, INC., pg. 1891, pg. 928
WHAM-O, INC., pg. 969, pg. 308
THE WIFFLE BALL INC., pg. 1848, pg. 371
WINNING MOVES GAMES, INC., pg. 970, pg. 816
WIZARDS OF THE COAST, INC., pg. 970, pg. 1830
XBOX, pg. 970, pg. 1829

3949 - Sporting & Athletic Goods, NEC

ACUSHNET COMPANY, pg. 1824, pg. 818
ADIDAS AMERICA INC., pg. 1803, pg. 1500
AEROJET ROCKETDYNE HOLDINGS, INC., pg. 1145, pg. 186
ALDILA, INC., pg. 1825, pg. 185
AMERICAN BILTRITE INC., pg. 1878, pg. 856
AMPAC ENTERPRISES, INC., pg. 1825, pg. 843
ANSELL, pg. 1495, pg. 1114
ANVIL HOLDINGS, INC., pg. 18, pg. 1195
ASHAWAY LINE & TWINE MFG. CO., pg. 1826, pg. 1600
BALANCED BODY, INC., pg. 1826, pg. 195
BASS PRO SHOPS, INC., pg. 1826, pg. 1006
BATTLE CREEK EQUIPMENT CO., pg. 1499, pg. 870
THE BILTRITE CORPORATION, pg. 1879, pg. 850
BLACK DIAMOND, INC., pg. 1827, pg. 1756

BOWLMOR AMF, *pg.* 1828, *pg.* 1206
BRIDGESTONE GOLF, INC., *pg.* 1828, *pg.* 528
BRUNSWICK BOWLING & BILLIARDS CORP., *pg.* 1828, *pg.* 622
BRUNSWICK CORPORATION, *pg.* 1828, *pg.* 623
BURNHAM BROTHERS, INC., *pg.* 1829, *pg.* 1727
BURTON SNOWBOARD COMPANY, *pg.* 1829, *pg.* 1765
CALLAWAY GOLF COMPANY, *pg.* 1829, *pg.* 58
CARRON NET COMPANY, INC., *pg.* 1830, *pg.* 1896
CHASE CORPORATION, *pg.* 1152, *pg.* 803
CHURCH & DWIGHT CO., INC., *pg.* 1153, *pg.* 1063
CLUB CAR, INC., *pg.* 1830, *pg.* 532
THE COLEMAN COMPANY, INC., *pg.* 1830, *pg.* 723
CONTINENTAL AMERICAN CORP., *pg.* 1880, *pg.* 723
COOPER-STANDARD AUTOMOTIVE INC., *pg.* 1880, *pg.* 903
COOPER TIRE & RUBBER COMPANY, *pg.* 1881, *pg.* 1453
CREATIVE PLAYTHINGS LTD., *pg.* 1831, *pg.* 820
CROSMAN CORPORATION, *pg.* 951, *pg.* 1143
CTI INDUSTRIES CORPORATION, *pg.* 1881, *pg.* 555
CYBEX INTERNATIONAL, INC., *pg.* 1521, *pg.* 832
DAIWA CORPORATION, *pg.* 1832, *pg.* 75
DARNELL-ROSE, *pg.* 1045, *pg.* 67
DATREK GOLF, *pg.* 1832, *pg.* 1801
DETROIT RED WINGS, INC., *pg.* 544, *pg.* 880
DOREL JUVENILE GROUP, INC., *pg.* 923, *pg.* 676
DURA UNDERCUSHIONS LTD., *pg.* 923, *pg.* 1954
E-Z-GO TEXTRON, *pg.* 1706, *pg.* 525
ENDLESS POOLS, INC., *pg.* 1833, *pg.* 1515
EPPINGER MANUFACTURING CO., *pg.* 1833, *pg.* 876
ESCALADE INC., *pg.* 1833, *pg.* 678
EVERLAST WORLDWIDE INC., *pg.* 1833, *pg.* 1230
EXERCYCLE CORPORATION, *pg.* 1833, *pg.* 823
EXXEL OUTDOORS LLC, *pg.* 1833, *pg.* 311
FABREEKA INTERNATIONAL, INC., *pg.* 1882, *pg.* 847
FEDERAL PREMIUM AMMUNITION, *pg.* 1834, *pg.* 915
FEEL GOLF CO., INC., *pg.* 1834, *pg.* 465
FILA USA, *pg.* 1808, *pg.* 779
THE FINISH LINE, INC., *pg.* 1769, *pg.* 686
FLAMBEAU, INC., *pg.* 1336, *pg.* 1854
FORTUNE BRANDS HOME & SECURITY, INC., *pg.* 55, *pg.* 600
FRANKLIN SPORTS, INC., *pg.* 1834, *pg.* 847
GILL ATHLETICS, INC., *pg.* 1835, *pg.* 562
GLD PRODUCTS, INC., *pg.* 1835, *pg.* 1882
GOLFSMITH INTERNATIONAL HOLDINGS, INC., *pg.* 1835, *pg.* 1662
HILLERICH & BRADSBY CO., INC., *pg.* 1836, *pg.* 576
HONEYWELL SALISBURY ELECTRICAL SAFETY, *pg.* 1884, *pg.* 558
HSM SOLUTIONS, *pg.* 1884, *pg.* 1378
HUFFY CORPORATION, *pg.* 1836, *pg.* 1409
HUGGER MUGGER YOGA PRODUCTS LLC, *pg.* 1836, *pg.* 1758
ICON HEALTH & FITNESS, INC., *pg.* 1837, *pg.* 1752
INDUSTRIAL RUBBER PRODUCTS, INC., *pg.* 1349, *pg.* 926
INNOVATIVE DESIGNS, INC., *pg.* 1837, *pg.* 1576
JANSPORT, *pg.* 1837, *pg.* 38
JOHNSON OUTDOORS INC., *pg.* 1837, *pg.* 1888
KARSTEN MANUFACTURING CORPORATION, *pg.* 1838, *pg.* 17
KRACO ENTERPRISES, LLC, *pg.* 210, *pg.* 68
LAVELLE INDUSTRIES INC., *pg.* 1053, *pg.* 1856
LIFETIME PRODUCTS INC., *pg.* 933, *pg.* 1751
LOOP-LOC LTD., *pg.* 1838, *pg.* 1165
LULULEMON ATHLETICA INC., *pg.* 44, *pg.* 1911
MACANDREWS & FORBES HOLDINGS INC., *pg.* 777, *pg.* 1254
MAPA PROFESSIONAL, *pg.* 1885, *pg.* 555
MAPLE CITY RUBBER COMPANY, *pg.* 962, *pg.* 1468
MARYLAND PLASTICS, INC., *pg.* 1885, *pg.* 769
MCKEON PRODUCTS, INC., *pg.* 1559, *pg.* 912
MCNETT CORPORATION, *pg.* 1839, *pg.* 1817
THE MERCER RUBBER COMPANY, *pg.* 1886, *pg.* 1165
MIRACLE RECREATION EQUIPMENT COMPANY, *pg.* 1839, *pg.* 988
MIZUNO USA, INC., *pg.* 1839, *pg.* 538
MUNCHKIN, INC., *pg.* 964, *pg.* 300
NAUTILUS, INC., *pg.* 1840, *pg.* 1846
NEW BALANCE ATHLETIC SHOE, INC., *pg.* 1811, *pg.* 798
NEW ERA CAP COMPANY INC., *pg.* 1840, *pg.* 1155
NIKE, INC., *pg.* 1812, *pg.* 1492
NUSIL TECHNOLOGY LLC, *pg.* 1887, *pg.* 63
OLHAUSEN BILLIARD MFG, INC., *pg.* 1842, *pg.* 1655
OMNOVA SOLUTIONS INC, *pg.* 1176, *pg.* 1453
O'NEILL INC., *pg.* 1842, *pg.* 270
PARAMOUNT FITNESS CORP., *pg.* 1842, *pg.* 138
PRECOR, INC., *pg.* 1843, *pg.* 1847
PRINCIPLE PLASTICS, INC., *pg.* 1816, *pg.* 94
PURE FISHING, INC., *pg.* 1843, *pg.* 1614
QUADION CORPORATION, *pg.* 1888, *pg.* 941
QUBICAAMF, *pg.* 1843, *pg.* 1795
RADIATOR SPECIALTY COMPANY, *pg.* 215, *pg.* 1380
RAPALA VMC CORPORATION, *pg.* 1843, *pg.* 949
RAWLINGS SPORTING GOODS CO., INC., *pg.* 1843, *pg.* 1002
R.C.A. RUBBER COMPANY, *pg.* 1888, *pg.* 1402
REEBOK-CCM HOCKEY, INC., *pg.* 1844, *pg.* 1960
REEBOK INTERNATIONAL LTD., *pg.* 1817, *pg.* 811
REESE ENTERPRISES, INC., *pg.* 1888, *pg.* 955
REMINGTON ARMS COMPANY, LLC, *pg.* 1844, *pg.* 1382
REVOLUTION MFG., *pg.* 1844, *pg.* 1753
ROGER CLEVELAND GOLF COMPANY, INC., *pg.* 1844, *pg.* 105
ROLLER DERBY SKATE CORP., *pg.* 966, *pg.* 630
SCHAEFER MARINE INC., *pg.* 1373, *pg.* 835
SCHLEGEL SYSTEMS, INC., *pg.* 109, *pg.* 1337
SCHOOL-TECH, INC., *pg.* 1844, *pg.* 866
SMITH & WESSON HOLDING CORPORATION, *pg.* 1845, *pg.* 846
SOLOFLEX, INC., *pg.* 1845, *pg.* 1498
SPALDING, *pg.* 1845, *pg.* 846
SPORT COURT INTERNATIONAL INC., *pg.* 1846, *pg.* 1761
SPORT HALEY, INC., *pg.* 33, *pg.* 333
SUPERCOACH, LLC, *pg.* 1847, *pg.* 24
TAYLORMADE-ADIDAS GOLF, *pg.* 1847, *pg.* 60
TEKNOR APEX COMPANY, *pg.* 1889, *pg.* 1605
TEXTILE RUBBER & CHEMICAL COMPANY, *pg.* 1890, *pg.* 530
THERAPEDIC ASSOCIATES, INC., *pg.* 945, *pg.* 1112
TRICO PRODUCTS CORPORATION, *pg.* 220, *pg.* 905
TRUE TEMPER SPORTS, INC., *pg.* 1847, *pg.* 1647
UNDER ARMOUR, INC., *pg.* 49, *pg.* 759
VAIL RUBBER WORKS, INC., *pg.* 1891, *pg.* 906
VARSITY BRANDS, INC., *pg.* 1847, *pg.* 1647
VESTA INC., *pg.* 1435, *pg.* 1858
VICTUS, INC., *pg.* 1606, *pg.* 447
VOLCOM, INC., *pg.* 1847, *pg.* 71
VYSTAR CORPORATION, *pg.* 1891, *pg.* 532
W.C. BRADLEY CO., *pg.* 62, *pg.* 528
WEST PHARMACEUTICAL SERVICES, INC., *pg.* 1472, *pg.* 1532
THE WIFFLE BALL INC., *pg.* 1848, *pg.* 371
WILSON SPORTING GOODS CO., *pg.* 1848, *pg.* 596
THE WORTH COMPANY, *pg.* 1848, *pg.* 1895
WRIGHT & MCGILL CO., *pg.* 1848, *pg.* 324
XERIUM TECHNOLOGIES, INC., *pg.* 1703, *pg.* 1389

3951 - Pens, Mechanical Pencils & Parts

A. T. CROSS COMPANY, *pg.* 339, *pg.* 1602
BARRINGTON GROUP LTD., *pg.* 1, *pg.* 1676
BIC CORPORATION, *pg.* 501, *pg.* 369
DIXON TICONDEROGA COMPANY, *pg.* 388, *pg.* 430
DRI MARK PRODUCTS, INC., *pg.* 388, *pg.* 1323
GRAPHIC CONTROLS LLC, *pg.* 401, *pg.* 1148
PENTEL OF AMERICA, LTD., *pg.* 453, *pg.* 295
SHEAFFER PEN CORPORATION, *pg.* 469, *pg.* 371

3952 - Lead Pencils, Crayons & Artists' Materials

ACCO BRANDS CORPORATION, *pg.* 340, *pg.* 626
ACME STAPLE COMPANY, INC., *pg.* 341, *pg.* 1034
ACOUSTIC INNOVATIONS INC., *pg.* 912, *pg.* 409
ADELPHI PAPER HANGINGS LLC, *pg.* 912, *pg.* 1342
ALL STAR CARTS AND VEHICLES CORP., *pg.* 163, *pg.* 1141
BADGER AIR BRUSH COMPANY, *pg.* 359, *pg.* 612
BAUMFOLDER CORPORATION, *pg.* 360, *pg.* 1472
BELVEDERE USA CORPORATION, *pg.* 917, *pg.* 556
BLANC INDUSTRIES SIGNAGE & DISPLAY GROUP, *pg.* 1621, *pg.* 1053
BROTHER INTERNATIONAL CORPORATION - USA, *pg.* 53, *pg.* 1046
THE COMMERCIAL FURNITURE GROUP, *pg.* 920, *pg.* 994
CRAYOLA CANADA, *pg.* 951, *pg.* 1922
CRAYOLA LLC, *pg.* 951, *pg.* 1528
DATACARD CORPORATION, *pg.* 382, *pg.* 948
DEMCO INC., *pg.* 386, *pg.* 1865
DIXON TICONDEROGA COMPANY, *pg.* 388, *pg.* 430
FELLOWES, INC., *pg.* 397, *pg.* 620
FRANKLIN ELECTRONIC PUBLISHERS, INC., *pg.* 398, *pg.* 1048
GLORY GLOBAL SOLUTIONS, *pg.* 401, *pg.* 628
GRACO CHILDREN'S PRODUCTS INC., *pg.* 954, *pg.* 1531
THE GUNLOCKE COMPANY, *pg.* 926, *pg.* 1349
HALLMARK CARDS, INC., *pg.* 1646, *pg.* 983
HOME MERIDIAN INTERNATIONAL, INC., *pg.* 928, *pg.* 1379
HUSSEY SEATING CO., *pg.* 929, *pg.* 751
IAC INDUSTRIES, INC., *pg.* 929, *pg.* 48
IMPERIAL WOODWORKS, INC., *pg.* 929, *pg.* 1749
INTERNATIONAL BUSINESS MACHINES CORPORATION, *pg.* 418, *pg.* 1138
IRWIN SEATING COMPANY INC., *pg.* 929, *pg.* 887
JASPER GROUP, *pg.* 930, *pg.* 691
JBI, INC., *pg.* 930, *pg.* 123
JOHN BOOS & CO., *pg.* 1126, *pg.* 609
KEWAUNEE SCIENTIFIC CORPORATION, *pg.* 931, *pg.* 1391
KNOLL, INC., *pg.* 425, *pg.* 1527
LISTA INTERNATIONAL CORPORATION, *pg.* 934, *pg.* 825
MARTIN/F. WEBER COMPANY, *pg.* 962, *pg.* 1567
MIRACLE RECREATION EQUIPMENT COMPANY, *pg.* 1839, *pg.* 988
MITY ENTERPRISES, INC., *pg.* 935, *pg.* 1753
NEMSCHOFF, INC., *pg.* 936, *pg.* 1890
NEOPOST CANADA LIMITED, *pg.* 1364, *pg.* 1924
OPEX CORPORATION, *pg.* 450, *pg.* 1087
PAASCHE AIRBRUSH COMPANY, *pg.* 1444, *pg.* 587
PAR TECHNOLOGY CORPORATION, *pg.* 452, *pg.* 1183
PARISI INCORPORATED, *pg.* 103, *pg.* 1556
PEACE INDUSTRIES INC., *pg.* 1368, *pg.* 656
PERRYGRAF, *pg.* 454, *pg.* 561
PIERCE EQUIPMENT, *pg.* 1369, *pg.* 1640
PITNEY BOWES INC., *pg.* 454, *pg.* 376
POINT BLANK SOLUTIONS, INC., *pg.* 1467, *pg.* 460
POLYVISION CORPORATION, *pg.* 665, *pg.* 531
PRESSTEK, INC., *pg.* 456, *pg.* 606
ROWE INTERNATIONAL CORP, *pg.* 669, *pg.* 889
SAUDER MANUFACTURING COMPANY, *pg.* 941, *pg.* 1403
SAUDER WOODWORKING CO., *pg.* 941, *pg.* 1403
SCOTT'S LIQUID GOLD-INC., *pg.* 335, *pg.* 323
SEATS INCORPORATED, *pg.* 217, *pg.* 1890
THE STAPLEX COMPANY, INC., *pg.* 474, *pg.* 1146
UMF MEDICAL, *pg.* 946, *pg.* 1542
VANSAN CORPORATION, *pg.* 685, *pg.* 68
VIDEOJET TECHNOLOGIES INC., *pg.* 489, *pg.* 671
VIRCO MANUFACTURING CORPORATION, *pg.* 946, *pg.* 297
WATERLOO INDUSTRIES, INC., *pg.* 946, *pg.* 1885
WMS INDUSTRIES INC., *pg.* 593, *pg.* 666
ZONGKERS CUSTOM FURNITURE, INC., *pg.* 947, *pg.* 1019

3953 - Marking Devices

AMERICAN MARKING SYSTEMS, INC., *pg.* 349, *pg.* 1051
C.H. HANSON COMPANY, *pg.* 1322, *pg.* 636
DIAGRAPH, *pg.* 387, *pg.* 989

3955 - Carbon Paper & Inked Ribbons

COLOR IMAGING INC., *pg.* 1407, *pg.* 536
SWM, *pg.* 1895, *pg.* 485

3961 - Costume Jewelry & Costume Novelties, Except Precious Metal

AMINCO INTERNATIONAL (USA) INC., *pg.* 1, *pg.* 120
BUZTRONICS, INC., *pg.* 1294, *pg.* 683
FGX INTERNATIONAL, INC., *pg.* 5, *pg.* 1608
HERFF JONES, INC., *pg.* 7, *pg.* 686
MARY KAY INC., *pg.* 516, *pg.* 1657
ROMAN RESEARCH, INC., *pg.* 11, *pg.* 824
SWAROVSKI NORTH AMERICA LIMITED INC., *pg.* 13, *pg.* 1600
UNCAS MANUFACTURING COMPANY, *pg.* 15, *pg.* 1608

3965 - Fasteners, Buttons, Needles & Pins

DFCI SOLUTIONS INC., *pg.* 1328, *pg.* 1350
THE HANDY/KENLIN GROUP, *pg.* 86, *pg.* 670
ILLINOIS TOOL WORKS INC., *pg.* 1348, *pg.* 614
MITEK, INC., *pg.* 1056, *pg.* 975
MOORE PUSH PIN CO., *pg.* 441, *pg.* 1595
PASLODE, *pg.* 1059, *pg.* 664
SOUTHCO, INC., *pg.* 1063, *pg.* 1522
STA-RITE GINNIE LOU, INC., *pg.* 523, *pg.* 660
THE STIMPSON COMPANY, INC., *pg.* 1182, *pg.* 460
VELCRO USA INC., *pg.* 699, *pg.* 1036
YKK CORPORATION OF AMERICA, *pg.* 699, *pg.* 536

3991 - Brooms & Brushes

BACOVA GUILD, LTD., *pg.* 916, *pg.* 1779
BRIGHT OF AMERICA, INC., *pg.* 1121, *pg.* 1851
CC INDUSTRIES, INC., *pg.* 920, *pg.* 569
COLGATE-PALMOLIVE COMPANY, *pg.* 504, *pg.* 1215
CROSCILL, INC., *pg.* 1122, *pg.* 1220
CROWN CRAFTS INFANT PRODUCTS, INC., *pg.* 922, *pg.* 68
THE EVERCARE COMPANY, *pg.* 1124, *pg.* 483
FOAMPRO MANUFACTURING, INC., *pg.* 1442, *pg.* 110
THE FULLER BRUSH COMPANY, *pg.* 330, *pg.* 715
GUILFORD PERFORMANCE TEXTILES, *pg.* 693, *pg.* 1393
HERITAGE LACE INC., *pg.* 694, *pg.* 711
HOLLANDER SLEEP PRODUCTS, *pg.* 927, *pg.* 411
INTERNATIONAL TEXTILE GROUP, INC., *pg.* 696, *pg.* 1374
JARDEN CORPORATION, *pg.* 1885, *pg.* 412
THE LIBMAN COMPANY, *pg.* 331, *pg.* 553
POLYMER GROUP, INC., *pg.* 698, *pg.* 1368
SHEEX, INC., *pg.* 1138, *pg.* 1614
SUNSTAR AMERICAS INC., *pg.* 1599, *pg.* 591
THE VALSPAR CORPORATION, *pg.* 1449, *pg.* 945
THE WOOSTER BRUSH COMPANY, *pg.* 1450, *pg.* 1482
ZEPHYR MANUFACTURING COMPANY INC., *pg.* 1141, *pg.* 1006

3993 - Signs & Advertising Displays

AMD INDUSTRIES, INC., *pg.* 66, *pg.* 598
BLANC INDUSTRIES SIGNAGE & DISPLAY GROUP, *pg.* 1621, *pg.* 1053
BRADY CORPORATION, *pg.* 363, *pg.* 1873
BUZTRONICS, INC., *pg.* 1294, *pg.* 683
CARMANAH TECHNOLOGIES CORPORATION, *pg.* 628, *pg.* 1913
CHICAGO SHOW INC., *pg.* 371, *pg.* 560
CUMMINGS INCORPORATED, *pg.* 77, *pg.* 1636
DAKTRONICS, INC., *pg.* 633, *pg.* 1624
DEE SIGN COMPANY, *pg.* 383, *pg.* 1479
DON BELL SIGNS LLC, *pg.* 388, *pg.* 460
ELECSYS CORPORATION, *pg.* 635, *pg.* 717
LEWTAN INDUSTRIES CORP., *pg.* 1658, *pg.* 352
LSI INDUSTRIES INC., *pg.* 58, *pg.* 1416
MAGNA VISUAL, INC., *pg.* 429, *pg.* 999
NATIONAL BANNER COMPANY, INC., *pg.* 697, *pg.* 1684
OHIO AWNING & MANUFACTURING CO., *pg.* 1842, *pg.* 1433
PERMALITH PLASTICS LLC, *pg.* 1887, *pg.* 1108
PILGRIM PLASTIC PRODUCTS COMPANY, *pg.* 1887, *pg.* 803
PROVISION HOLDING, INC., *pg.* 665, *pg.* 65
STERLING CUT GLASS COMPANY, INC., *pg.* 1138, *pg.* 727
TRANS-LUX CORPORATION, *pg.* 681, *pg.* 365
THE VERNON COMPANY, *pg.* 488, *pg.* 710
VULCAN, INC., *pg.* 687, *pg.* 5
YOUNG ELECTRIC SIGN COMPANY, *pg.* 1308, *pg.* 1762

3995 - Burial Caskets

AURORA CASKET COMPANY, INC., *pg.* 1393, *pg.* 673
CLARK GRAVE VAULT COMPANY, *pg.* 76, *pg.* 1438
HILL-ROM HOLDINGS, INC., *pg.* 1542, *pg.* 673
MATTHEWS INTERNATIONAL CORPORATION, *pg.* 1662, *pg.* 1578

3996 - Linoleum, Asphalted-Felt-Base & other Hard Surface Floor Coverings, NEC

ALESSCO INC., *pg.* 1878, *pg.* 563
ARMSTRONG WORLD INDUSTRIES, INC., *pg.* 914, *pg.* 1545
BURKE INDUSTRIES, INC., *pg.* 919, *pg.* 239
CONGOLEUM CORPORATION, *pg.* 921, *pg.* 1084
MANNINGTON MILLS, INC., *pg.* 934, *pg.* 1119
MANNINGTON RESILIENT FLOORS, *pg.* 934, *pg.* 1119
NYDREE FLOORING, *pg.* 939, *pg.* 1782
SHAW INDUSTRIES GROUP, INC., *pg.* 942, *pg.* 530

3999 - Manufacturing Industries, NEC

A-T SURGICAL MFG. CO., INC., *pg.* 1483, *pg.* 825
ACUSHNET COMPANY, *pg.* 1824, *pg.* 818
ADELPHI PAPER HANGINGS LLC, *pg.* 912, *pg.* 1342
ALIMED, INC., *pg.* 1490, *pg.* 816
ALLIED HEALTHCARE PRODUCTS, INC., *pg.* 1491, *pg.* 990
ALPHA PRO TECH, LTD., *pg.* 1492, *pg.* 1922
AMERICAN BILTRITE INC., *pg.* 1878, *pg.* 856
AMERICAN MEDICAL SYSTEMS HOLDINGS, INC., *pg.* 1493, *pg.* 947
ANDIS COMPANY, *pg.* 498, *pg.* 1895
AROMATIQUE INC., *pg.* 499, *pg.* 32
BAE SYSTEMS PRODUCTS GROUP, *pg.* 359, *pg.* 432
BARNHARDT MANUFACTURING COMPANY, *pg.* 1498, *pg.* 1364
BAXTER INTERNATIONAL INC., *pg.* 1499, *pg.* 599
BD MEDICAL, *pg.* 1501, *pg.* 1762
BECTON, DICKINSON & COMPANY, *pg.* 1501, *pg.* 1068
BLYTH, INC., *pg.* 502, *pg.* 349
BOSTON SCIENTIFIC CORPORATION, *pg.* 1508, *pg.* 831
BRADY CORPORATION, *pg.* 363, *pg.* 1873
BRIGHT OF AMERICA, INC., *pg.* 1121, *pg.* 1851
BUZTRONICS, INC., *pg.* 1294, *pg.* 683
CARDINAL HEALTH, INC., *pg.* 1512, *pg.* 1448
CAS MEDICAL SYSTEMS, INC., *pg.* 1513, *pg.* 339
CONGOLEUM CORPORATION, *pg.* 921, *pg.* 1084
THE COOPER COMPANIES, INC., *pg.* 1518, *pg.* 183
CORDIS CORPORATION, *pg.* 1519, *pg.* 430
CORE MOLDING TECHNOLOGIES, INC., *pg.* 1881, *pg.* 1439
CRYOLIFE, INC., *pg.* 1520, *pg.* 534
DAVID CLARK COMPANY INCORPORATED, *pg.* 633, *pg.* 862
DEPUY SYNTHES, *pg.* 1523, *pg.* 1593
DEPUYSYNTHES, *pg.* 1523, *pg.* 699
DJO INCORPORATED, *pg.* 1524, *pg.* 302
DJO SURGICAL, *pg.* 1525, *pg.* 1661
DURA UNDERCUSHIONS LTD., *pg.* 923, *pg.* 1954
E.D. BULLARD COMPANY, *pg.* 1332, *pg.* 727
EDUCATIONAL INSIGHTS, INC., *pg.* 951, *pg.* 187
ENCON SAFETY PRODUCTS, *pg.* 1334, *pg.* 1705
ENDOLOGIX, INC., *pg.* 1528, *pg.* 109
ENERGIZER HOLDINGS, INC., *pg.* 637, *pg.* 996
EXACTECH, INC., *pg.* 1529, *pg.* 428
FGX INTERNATIONAL, INC., *pg.* 5, *pg.* 1608
FOLKMANIS, INC., *pg.* 953, *pg.* 83
HANGER INC., *pg.* 1539, *pg.* 1663
THE HARTZ MOUNTAIN CORP., *pg.* 1476, *pg.* 1120
HELEN OF TROY L.P., *pg.* 511, *pg.* 1692
HEMCO CORPORATION, *pg.* 1416, *pg.* 979
HEMCON MEDICAL TECHNOLOGIES, INC., *pg.* 1541, *pg.* 1503
HOVEROUND CORP., *pg.* 1543, *pg.* 466
HYDRALIGN, *pg.* 1257, *pg.* 833
IGT, *pg.* 412, *pg.* 1031
INTERNATIONAL GAME TECHNOLOGY, *pg.* 957, *pg.* 1024
INTUITIVE SURGICAL, INC., *pg.* 1546, *pg.* 286
INVACARE CORPORATION, *pg.* 1546, *pg.* 1451
JAMES ALEXANDER CORPORATION, *pg.* 1461, *pg.* 1044
JASON INDUSTRIES, INC., *pg.* 208, *pg.* 1875
JOHNSON & JOHNSON, *pg.* 1549, *pg.* 1091
JOHNSON & JOHNSON BABY PRODUCTS, INC., *pg.* 1552, *pg.* 1094
KIMBERLY-CLARK CORPORATION, *pg.* 1461, *pg.* 1720
LAKELAND INDUSTRIES, INC., *pg.* 1354, *pg.* 1338
LARSON-JUHL US LLC, *pg.* 933, *pg.* 537
LIFECELL CORPORATION, *pg.* 1556, *pg.* 1045
LIFECORE BIOMEDICAL, LLC, *pg.* 1556, *pg.* 920
LIVANOVA, *pg.* 1557, *pg.* 1710
MAURICE J. MARKELL SHOE CO., INC., *pg.* 1811, *pg.* 1356
MCKEON PRODUCTS, INC., *pg.* 1559, *pg.* 912
MCR SAFETY, *pg.* 1422, *pg.* 1630
MEDLINE INDUSTRIES, INC., *pg.* 1562, *pg.* 635
MEDPORT, LLC, *pg.* 1563, *pg.* 1607
MEDTRONIC, *pg.* 1563, *pg.* 830
MEDTRONIC, INC., *pg.* 1564, *pg.* 939
MENTOR CORPORATION, *pg.* 1565, *pg.* 263
MICROAIRE SURGICAL INSTRUMENTS INC., *pg.* 1423, *pg.* 1778
MILESTONE SCIENTIFIC, INC., *pg.* 1568, *pg.* 1079
MINE SAFETY APPLIANCES COMPANY, *pg.* 1361, *pg.* 1525
MUELLER SPORTS MEDICINE, INC., *pg.* 1570, *pg.* 1887
MULTIMEDIA GAMES INC., *pg.* 442, *pg.* 1664
NATURAL DECORATIONS, INC., *pg.* 936, *pg.* 5
NUVASIVE, INC., *pg.* 1577, *pg.* 205
OAKLEY, INC., *pg.* 1840, *pg.* 86
OIL-DRI CORPORATION OF AMERICA, *pg.* 1480, *pg.* 586
OSBORN INTERNATIONAL, *pg.* 1367, *pg.* 1406
OSTEOMED CORPORATION, *pg.* 1425, *pg.* 1658
OTTERBOX PRODUCTS LLC, *pg.* 451, *pg.* 329
PALL CORPORATION, *pg.* 232, *pg.* 1323
PHILIPS RESPIRONICS, *pg.* 1585, *pg.* 1555
RAUCH INDUSTRIES, INC., *pg.* 940, *pg.* 1373
REPLOGLE GLOBES, INC., *pg.* 461, *pg.* 559
THE SALK COMPANY, *pg.* 1591, *pg.* 800
SCOTT'S LIQUID GOLD-INC., *pg.* 335, *pg.* 323
SEALY CORPORATION, *pg.* 942, *pg.* 1391
ST. JUDE MEDICAL, INC., *pg.* 1596, *pg.* 963
STAAR SURGICAL COMPANY, *pg.* 1597, *pg.* 151
STERIS CORPORATION, *pg.* 1597, *pg.* 1464
STRYKER CORPORATION, *pg.* 1598, *pg.* 894
STRYKER MAKO, *pg.* 1598, *pg.* 427
STRYKER ORTHOPAEDICS, *pg.* 1599, *pg.* 1082
SURGICAL SPECIALTIES CORPORATION, *pg.* 1600, *pg.* 1912
SYMMETRY MEDICAL INC., *pg.* 1600, *pg.* 699
TELEDYNE BENTHOS, INC., *pg.* 1431, *pg.* 838
TELEFLEX INCORPORATED, *pg.* 48, *pg.* 1548
THERAGENICS CORPORATION, *pg.* 1431, *pg.* 527
THERAPEDIC ASSOCIATES, INC., *pg.* 945, *pg.* 1112
TRANS-LUX CORPORATION, *pg.* 681, *pg.* 365
UTAH MEDICAL PRODUCTS, INC., *pg.* 1605, *pg.* 1752
UVEX SAFETY, *pg.* 1433, *pg.* 1608
VITAL SIGNS, INC., *pg.* 1607, *pg.* 1126
WAHL CLIPPER CORPORATION, *pg.* 524, *pg.* 662
WEST PHARMACEUTICAL SERVICES, INC., *pg.* 1472, *pg.* 1532
WISCONSIN PHARMACAL COMPANY, LLC, *pg.* 1610, *pg.* 1861
WMS INDUSTRIES INC., *pg.* 593, *pg.* 666
THE WOODSTREAM CORPORATION, *pg.* 1801, *pg.* 1549
THE YANKEE CANDLE COMPANY, INC., *pg.* 1792, *pg.* 843
ZIMMER BIOMET HOLDINGS, INC., *pg.* 1611, *pg.* 699

4011 - Railroads, Line-Haul Operating

BURLINGTON NORTHERN SANTA FE, LLC, *pg.* 1901, *pg.* 1694
CANADIAN NATIONAL RAILWAY COMPANY, *pg.* 1902, *pg.* 1953
CONSOLIDATED RAIL CORPORATION, *pg.* 1903, *pg.* 1562
CSX CORPORATION, *pg.* 1904, *pg.* 432
CSX TRANSPORTATION, INC., *pg.* 1904, *pg.* 432
FLORIDA EAST COAST INDUSTRIES, INC., *pg.* 1909, *pg.* 433
THE KANSAS CITY SOUTHERN RAILWAY COMPANY, *pg.* 1913, *pg.* 985
NATIONAL RAILROAD PASSENGER CORPORATION, *pg.* 1916, *pg.* 403
NORFOLK SOUTHERN CORPORATION, *pg.* 1917, *pg.* 1797
SCHNEIDER, *pg.* 1922, *pg.* 1859
UNION PACIFIC CORPORATION, *pg.* 1927, *pg.* 1018
UNION PACIFIC RAILROAD COMPANY, *pg.* 1927, *pg.* 1019

4013 - Railroad Switching & Terminal Establishments

ACF INDUSTRIES LLC, *pg.* 1310, *pg.* 989
ACP MARKETING, INC., *pg.* 1896, *pg.* 1953

First page reference indicates Business Class Edition
Second page reference indicates Geographic Edition

AMERICAN AIRLINES INC., *pg.* 1898, *pg.* 1693
BURLINGTON NORTHERN SANTA FE, LLC, *pg.* 1901, *pg.* 1694
CSX CORPORATION, *pg.* 1904, *pg.* 432
L.B. FOSTER COMPANY, *pg.* 1355, *pg.* 1578
NJ TRANSIT CORPORATION, *pg.* 1917, *pg.* 1097
RAILSERVE INC., *pg.* 1921, *pg.* 519
VIAD CORP., *pg.* 816, *pg.* 20
WESTINGHOUSE AIR BRAKE TECHNOLOGIES CORPORATION, *pg.* 1388, *pg.* 1595

4111 - Local & Suburban Transit

BOMBARDIER INC., *pg.* 1318, *pg.* 1953
CENTRAL FLORIDA REGIONAL TRANSPORT AUTHORITY, *pg.* 1903, *pg.* 452
GREATER CLEVELAND REGIONAL TRANSIT AUTHORITY, *pg.* 1909, *pg.* 1431
GREYHOUND LINES, INC., *pg.* 1910, *pg.* 1681
LONG ISLAND RAIL ROAD, *pg.* 1914, *pg.* 1170
LOS ANGELES COUNTY METROPOLITAN TRANSPORTATION AUTHORITY, *pg.* 1914, *pg.* 135
METROPOLITAN TRANSPORTATION AUTHORITY, *pg.* 1915, *pg.* 1260
NJ TRANSIT CORPORATION, *pg.* 1917, *pg.* 1097
PACE, *pg.* 1918, *pg.* 553
SOUTHEASTERN PENNSYLVANIA TRANSPORTATION AUTHORITY, *pg.* 1923, *pg.* 1570
WASHINGTON METROPOLITAN AREA TRANSIT AUTHORITY, *pg.* 1930, *pg.* 407
WESTINGHOUSE AIR BRAKE TECHNOLOGIES CORPORATION, *pg.* 1388, *pg.* 1595

4119 - Local Passenger Transportation, NEC (land ambulance)

A-1 LIMOUSINE INC., *pg.* 163, *pg.* 1110
BOMBARDIER INC., *pg.* 1318, *pg.* 1953
CAREY INTERNATIONAL, INC., *pg.* 1902, *pg.* 397
CENTRAL FLORIDA REGIONAL TRANSPORT AUTHORITY, *pg.* 1903, *pg.* 452
EMERGENCY MEDICAL SERVICES CORPORATION, *pg.* 1528, *pg.* 331
GREATER CLEVELAND REGIONAL TRANSIT AUTHORITY, *pg.* 1909, *pg.* 1431
GREYHOUND LINES, INC., *pg.* 1910, *pg.* 1681
LONG ISLAND RAIL ROAD, *pg.* 1914, *pg.* 1170
LOS ANGELES COUNTY METROPOLITAN TRANSPORTATION AUTHORITY, *pg.* 1914, *pg.* 135
METROPOLITAN TRANSPORTATION AUTHORITY, *pg.* 1915, *pg.* 1260
NJ TRANSIT CORPORATION, *pg.* 1917, *pg.* 1097
PACE, *pg.* 1918, *pg.* 553
ROYAL COACHMAN WORLDWIDE, *pg.* 1922, *pg.* 1053
SOUTHEASTERN PENNSYLVANIA TRANSPORTATION AUTHORITY, *pg.* 1923, *pg.* 1570
WASHINGTON METROPOLITAN AREA TRANSIT AUTHORITY, *pg.* 1930, *pg.* 407
WESTINGHOUSE AIR BRAKE TECHNOLOGIES CORPORATION, *pg.* 1388, *pg.* 1595

4121 - Taxicabs

SIRIUS XM HOLDINGS INC., *pg.* 308, *pg.* 1292

4131 - Intercity & Rural Bus Transportation

GREYHOUND CANADA TRANSPORTATION CORP., *pg.* 1910, *pg.* 1903
PETER PAN BUS LINES, INC., *pg.* 1919, *pg.* 846
PINELLAS SUNCOAST TRANSIT AUTHORITY, *pg.* 1919, *pg.* 463

4142 - Bus Charter Service, Except Local

FUGAZY INTERNATIONAL CORPORATION, *pg.* 1909, *pg.* 1233
PETER PAN BUS LINES, INC., *pg.* 1919, *pg.* 846

4212 - Local Trucking without Storage

AMERICAN RED BALL TRANSIT CO. INC., *pg.* 1899, *pg.* 682
THE ANDREWS MOVING & STORAGE COMPANY INC., *pg.* 1899, *pg.* 1474
ARKANSAS BEST CORPORATION, *pg.* 1899, *pg.* 32
ATLAS VAN LINES, INC., *pg.* 1900, *pg.* 678
BULLDOG MOVERS, INC., *pg.* 1901, *pg.* 491
CELADON GROUP, INC., *pg.* 1903, *pg.* 683
CLEAN HARBORS, INC., *pg.* 376, *pg.* 839
COOK MOVING SYSTEMS, INC., *pg.* 1904, *pg.* 1148
DIRECTORY DISTRIBUTING ASSOCIATES, INC., *pg.* 388, *pg.* 978
ENERGYSOLUTIONS INC., *pg.* 1941, *pg.* 1757
FEDEX CORPORATION, *pg.* 1907, *pg.* 1642
HEARTLAND EXPRESS, INC., *pg.* 1910, *pg.* 710
JOHNSON STORAGE & MOVING COMPANY, *pg.* 1913, *pg.* 320
THE KENAN ADVANTAGE GROUP, INC., *pg.* 1914, *pg.* 1408
MAVERICK TRANSPORTATION, INC., *pg.* 1915, *pg.* 35
MAY TRUCKING COMPANY INC., *pg.* 1915, *pg.* 1508
MILAN EXPRESS CO., INC., *pg.* 1916, *pg.* 1647
NATIONAL VAN LINES, INC., *pg.* 1916, *pg.* 559
NFI INDUSTRIES INC., *pg.* 1917, *pg.* 1127
PAUL ARPIN VAN LINES, INC., *pg.* 1919, *pg.* 1610
PLANES MOVING & STORAGE, INC., *pg.* 1919, *pg.* 1479
REPUBLIC SERVICES, INC., *pg.* 107, *pg.* 19
STEVENS GROUP, INC., *pg.* 1924, *pg.* 906
THE SUDDATH COMPANIES INC., *pg.* 1924, *pg.* 435
TRIMAC CORPORATION, *pg.* 1926, *pg.* 1905
TWO MEN AND A TRUCK INTERNATIONAL, INC., *pg.* 1926, *pg.* 896
UNIGROUP, INC., *pg.* 1927, *pg.* 977
WAGNER INDUSTRIES, INC., *pg.* 1930, *pg.* 987
WASTE CONNECTIONS, INC., *pg.* 1954, *pg.* 1747
WASTE MANAGEMENT, INC., *pg.* 1954, *pg.* 1716
WHEATON VAN LINES, INC., *pg.* 1930, *pg.* 691
YRC WORLDWIDE INC., *pg.* 1931, *pg.* 720

4213 - Trucking, Except Local

ABF FREIGHT SYSTEM, INC., *pg.* 1896, *pg.* 31
ARKANSAS BEST CORPORATION, *pg.* 1899, *pg.* 32
CELADON GROUP, INC., *pg.* 1903, *pg.* 683
CR ENGLAND, INC., *pg.* 1904, *pg.* 1756
DART TRANSIT COMPANY, *pg.* 1905, *pg.* 921
ERGON, INC., *pg.* 976, *pg.* 969
FEDEX CORPORATION, *pg.* 1907, *pg.* 1642
FRONTIER LOGISTICS, LP, *pg.* 1909, *pg.* 1728
GAINES MOTOR LINES INCORPORATED, *pg.* 1338, *pg.* 1378
GRAMMER INDUSTRIES INC., *pg.* 1909, *pg.* 681
GROENDYKE TRANSPORT, INC., *pg.* 1910, *pg.* 1484
HEARTLAND EXPRESS, INC., *pg.* 1910, *pg.* 710
J.B. HUNT TRANSPORT SERVICES, INC., *pg.* 1913, *pg.* 34
THE KANSAS CITY SOUTHERN RAILWAY COMPANY, *pg.* 1913, *pg.* 985
KLLM TRANSPORT SERVICES, INC., *pg.* 1914, *pg.* 971
LANDSTAR SYSTEM, INC., *pg.* 1914, *pg.* 434
MAVERICK TRANSPORTATION, INC., *pg.* 1915, *pg.* 35
MAY TRUCKING COMPANY INC., *pg.* 1915, *pg.* 1508
MILAN EXPRESS CO., INC., *pg.* 1916, *pg.* 1647
NFI INDUSTRIES INC., *pg.* 1917, *pg.* 1127
OLD DOMINION FREIGHT LINE, INC., *pg.* 1918, *pg.* 1391
P.A.M. TRANSPORTATION SERVICES, INC., *pg.* 1919, *pg.* 36
PAUL ARPIN VAN LINES, INC., *pg.* 1919, *pg.* 1610
PENSKE LOGISTICS, LLC, *pg.* 188, *pg.* 1584
PLANES MOVING & STORAGE, INC., *pg.* 1919, *pg.* 1479
SAIA, INC., *pg.* 1922, *pg.* 533
SCHNEIDER, *pg.* 1922, *pg.* 1859
SIRVA, INC., *pg.* 1923, *pg.* 669
TRI-STATE MOTOR TRANSIT CO., *pg.* 1926, *pg.* 980
UNITED PARCEL SERVICE, INC., *pg.* 1928, *pg.* 522
UNITED VAN LINES, LLC, *pg.* 1929, *pg.* 978
UPS GROUND FREIGHT, INC., *pg.* 1929, *pg.* 1804
US 1 INDUSTRIES, INC., *pg.* 1929, *pg.* 698
U.S. XPRESS ENTERPRISES, INC., *pg.* 1929, *pg.* 1630
USA TRUCK, INC., *pg.* 1929, *pg.* 36
WERNER ENTERPRISES, INC., *pg.* 1930, *pg.* 1019
XPO LOGISTICS, INC., *pg.* 1931, *pg.* 350
YRC WORLDWIDE INC., *pg.* 1931, *pg.* 720

4214 - Local Trucking with Storage

AMERICAN RED BALL TRANSIT CO. INC., *pg.* 1899, *pg.* 682
CELADON GROUP, INC., *pg.* 1903, *pg.* 683
CLEAN HARBORS, INC., *pg.* 376, *pg.* 839
COOK MOVING SYSTEMS, INC., *pg.* 1904, *pg.* 1148
DIRECTORY DISTRIBUTING ASSOCIATES, INC., *pg.* 388, *pg.* 978
ENERGYSOLUTIONS INC., *pg.* 1941, *pg.* 1757
FEDEX CORPORATION, *pg.* 1907, *pg.* 1642
HEARTLAND EXPRESS, INC., *pg.* 1910, *pg.* 710
JOHNSON STORAGE & MOVING COMPANY, *pg.* 1913, *pg.* 320
THE KENAN ADVANTAGE GROUP, INC., *pg.* 1914, *pg.* 1408
MAVERICK TRANSPORTATION, INC., *pg.* 1915, *pg.* 35
MAY TRUCKING COMPANY INC., *pg.* 1915, *pg.* 1508
MILAN EXPRESS CO., INC., *pg.* 1916, *pg.* 1647
NATIONAL VAN LINES, INC., *pg.* 1916, *pg.* 559
NFI INDUSTRIES INC., *pg.* 1917, *pg.* 1127
PAUL ARPIN VAN LINES, INC., *pg.* 1919, *pg.* 1610
PLANES MOVING & STORAGE, INC., *pg.* 1919, *pg.* 1479
PODS ENTERPRISES, INC., *pg.* 1919, *pg.* 416
REPUBLIC SERVICES, INC., *pg.* 107, *pg.* 19
THE SUDDATH COMPANIES INC., *pg.* 1924, *pg.* 435
TRIMAC CORPORATION, *pg.* 1926, *pg.* 1905
TWO MEN AND A TRUCK INTERNATIONAL, INC., *pg.* 1926, *pg.* 896
WAGNER INDUSTRIES, INC., *pg.* 1930, *pg.* 987
WASTE CONNECTIONS, INC., *pg.* 1954, *pg.* 1747
WASTE MANAGEMENT, INC., *pg.* 1954, *pg.* 1716
YRC WORLDWIDE INC., *pg.* 1931, *pg.* 720

4215 - Courier Services, Except by Air

DHL HOLDINGS (USA), INC., *pg.* 1906, *pg.* 459
FEDEX OFFICE & PRINT SERVICES, INC., *pg.* 396, *pg.* 1681
FEDEX SMARTPOST, INC., *pg.* 1909, *pg.* 1883
FRESHDIRECT, LLC, *pg.* 857, *pg.* 1174
UNITED PARCEL SERVICE, INC., *pg.* 1928, *pg.* 522

4221 - Farm Product Warehousing & Storage

BUNGE LIMITED, *pg.* 842, *pg.* 1351

4222 - Refrigerated Warehousing & Storage

BURRIS LOGISTICS, *pg.* 843, *pg.* 387
KIDRON, INC., *pg.* 181, *pg.* 1457
UNITED STATES COLD STORAGE, INC., *pg.* 61, *pg.* 1051

4225 - General Warehousing & Storage

CASESTACK, INC., *pg.* 369, *pg.* 272
COOK MOVING SYSTEMS, INC., *pg.* 1904, *pg.* 1148
CUBESMART, *pg.* 1088, *pg.* 1591
EDISON PROPERTIES, LLC, *pg.* 1906, *pg.* 1096
EXTRA SPACE STORAGE, INC., *pg.* 1091, *pg.* 1757
J.C. WHITNEY & CO., *pg.* 209, *pg.* 621
MOBILE MINI, INC., *pg.* 1362, *pg.* 26
NFI INDUSTRIES INC., *pg.* 1917, *pg.* 1127
PUBLIC STORAGE, *pg.* 1467, *pg.* 98
SCHNEIDER, *pg.* 1922, *pg.* 1859
SOVRAN SELF STORAGE, INC., *pg.* 472, *pg.* 1355
UNCLE BOBS SELF-STORAGE, *pg.* 1471, *pg.* 1151

4226 - Special Warehousing & Storage, NEC

BUXTON ACQUISITION CO., LLC, *pg.* 2, *pg.* 845
MOBILE MINI, INC., *pg.* 1362, *pg.* 26
PODS ENTERPRISES, INC., *pg.* 1919, *pg.* 416

STERILITE CORPORATION, *pg.* 1138, *pg.* 848

4311 - U.S. Postal Service

LIVEWORLD, INC., *pg.* 1264, *pg.* 246
ONVIA, INC., *pg.* 1272, *pg.* 1838
PFSWEB, INC., *pg.* 1275, *pg.* 1733
POINTS INTERNATIONAL LTD., *pg.* 1275, *pg.* 1941
POSTNET INTERNATIONAL FRANCHISE CORPORATION, *pg.* 456, *pg.* 322
QUOTEMEDIA, INC., *pg.* 797, *pg.* 13
SPARK NETWORKS, INC., *pg.* 472, *pg.* 140
STAMPS.COM INC., *pg.* 1282, *pg.* 82
UNITED STATES POSTAL SERVICE, *pg.* 1009, *pg.* 406

4412 - Deep Sea Freight Transportation-Foreign

ALEXANDER & BALDWIN, INC., *pg.* 1079, *pg.* 543
CROWLEY MARITIME CORPORATION, *pg.* 1904, *pg.* 170
CSX CORPORATION, *pg.* 1904, *pg.* 432
ERGON, INC., *pg.* 976, *pg.* 969
INTERNATIONAL SHIPHOLDING CORPORATION, *pg.* 1912, *pg.* 7
MATSON NAVIGATION COMPANY, INC., *pg.* 1915, *pg.* 172
NICOR GAS AN AGL RESOURCES COMPANY, *pg.* 1947, *pg.* 636
SEACOR HOLDINGS INC., *pg.* 1923, *pg.* 426

4432 - Great Lakes Freight Transportation

CROWLEY MARITIME CORPORATION, *pg.* 1904, *pg.* 170
INTERNATIONAL SHIPHOLDING CORPORATION, *pg.* 1912, *pg.* 7
ROWAN COMPANIES, INC., *pg.* 984, *pg.* 1713
SEACOR HOLDINGS INC., *pg.* 1923, *pg.* 426
UPS SUPPLY CHAIN SOLUTIONS, INC., *pg.* 1929, *pg.* 485

4449 - Freight Transportation-Water, NEC

ALGOMA CENTRAL CORPORATION, *pg.* 1898, *pg.* 1933
CARNIVAL CORPORATION, *pg.* 1902, *pg.* 441
CSX CORPORATION, *pg.* 1904, *pg.* 432
ERGON, INC., *pg.* 976, *pg.* 969
GREAT LAKES DREDGE & DOCK CORPORATION, *pg.* 84, *pg.* 645
ODYSSEY MARINE EXPLORATION, INC., *pg.* 1918, *pg.* 475
PORT AUTHORITY OF NEW YORK & NEW JERSEY, *pg.* 1919, *pg.* 1283

4481 - Passenger Transportation-Deep Sea

CARNIVAL CORPORATION, *pg.* 1902, *pg.* 441
CARNIVAL CRUISE LINES, *pg.* 1902, *pg.* 441
COSTA CRUISE LINES N.V., *pg.* 1904, *pg.* 431
CRYSTAL CRUISES LLC, *pg.* 1904, *pg.* 128
CUNARD LINE LTD., *pg.* 1905, *pg.* 299
NCL CORPORATION LTD., *pg.* 1916, *pg.* 444
NORWEGIAN CRUISE LINE, *pg.* 1917, *pg.* 444
ODYSSEY MARINE EXPLORATION, INC., *pg.* 1918, *pg.* 475
PACIFIC MARINE & SUPPLY CO. LTD. INC., *pg.* 1918, *pg.* 544
PRINCESS CRUISE LINES LTD., *pg.* 1920, *pg.* 270
ROYAL CARIBBEAN CRUISES LTD, *pg.* 1921, *pg.* 446

4482 - Ferries

CARNIVAL CORPORATION, *pg.* 1902, *pg.* 441
CARNIVAL CRUISE LINES, *pg.* 1902, *pg.* 441
COSTA CRUISE LINES N.V., *pg.* 1904, *pg.* 431
CRYSTAL CRUISES LLC, *pg.* 1904, *pg.* 128
CUNARD LINE LTD., *pg.* 1905, *pg.* 299
NCL CORPORATION LTD., *pg.* 1916, *pg.* 444
NORWEGIAN CRUISE LINE, *pg.* 1917, *pg.* 444
ODYSSEY MARINE EXPLORATION, INC., *pg.* 1918, *pg.* 475
PACIFIC MARINE & SUPPLY CO. LTD. INC., *pg.* 1918, *pg.* 544
PRINCESS CRUISE LINES LTD., *pg.* 1920, *pg.* 270
ROYAL CARIBBEAN CRUISES LTD, *pg.* 1921, *pg.* 446

4491 - Marine Cargo Handling

CSX CORPORATION, *pg.* 1904, *pg.* 432
MAERSK INC., *pg.* 1914, *pg.* 1080
MATSON NAVIGATION COMPANY, INC., *pg.* 1915, *pg.* 172
PORT OF GALVESTON, *pg.* 1919, *pg.* 1697
PORT OF MIAMI TERMINAL OPERATING COMPANY, LC, *pg.* 1920, *pg.* 445
VIRGINIA PORT AUTHORITY, *pg.* 1930, *pg.* 1797

4493 - Marinas

LECO CORPORATION, *pg.* 1355, *pg.* 906
PALMER JOHNSON INCORPORATED, *pg.* 1709, *pg.* 1895

4499 - Water Transportation Services, NEC

ACP MARKETING, INC., *pg.* 1896, *pg.* 1953
ALGOMA CENTRAL CORPORATION, *pg.* 1898, *pg.* 1933
ALION SCIENCE AND TECHNOLOGY CORPORATION, *pg.* 615, *pg.* 1788
AMERICAN AIRLINES INC., *pg.* 1898, *pg.* 1693
CARNIVAL CORPORATION, *pg.* 1902, *pg.* 441
CSX CORPORATION, *pg.* 1904, *pg.* 432
ELLICOTT DREDGES, LLC, *pg.* 1333, *pg.* 757
GENERAL DYNAMICS CORPORATION, *pg.* 228, *pg.* 1781
GREAT LAKES DREDGE & DOCK CORPORATION, *pg.* 84, *pg.* 645
MAERSK INC., *pg.* 1914, *pg.* 1080
MATSON NAVIGATION COMPANY, INC., *pg.* 1915, *pg.* 172
NASSCO HOLDINGS INCORPORATED, *pg.* 99, *pg.* 205
NJ TRANSIT CORPORATION, *pg.* 1917, *pg.* 1097
NORTHROP GRUMMAN CORPORATION, *pg.* 231, *pg.* 1781
ODYSSEY MARINE EXPLORATION, INC., *pg.* 1918, *pg.* 475
PORT AUTHORITY OF NEW YORK & NEW JERSEY, *pg.* 1919, *pg.* 1283
PORT OF GALVESTON, *pg.* 1919, *pg.* 1697
PORT OF MIAMI TERMINAL OPERATING COMPANY, LC, *pg.* 1920, *pg.* 445
RAYTHEON COMPANY, *pg.* 233, *pg.* 854
VIAD CORP., *pg.* 816, *pg.* 20
VIRGINIA PORT AUTHORITY, *pg.* 1930, *pg.* 1797

4512 - Air Transportation, Scheduled

ACE AVIATION HOLDINGS INC., *pg.* 1896, *pg.* 1953
AER LINGUS, *pg.* 1896, *pg.* 1171
AEROLINEAS ARGENTINAS, *pg.* 1896, *pg.* 439
AIR CANADA, *pg.* 1896, *pg.* 1902
AIR CHARTERS, INC., *pg.* 1897, *pg.* 1124
AIR FRANCE, USA, *pg.* 1897, *pg.* 1188
AIR NEW ZEALAND LTD. (U.S.A.), *pg.* 1897, *pg.* 78
ALASKA AIR GROUP, INC., *pg.* 1897, *pg.* 1830
ALASKA AIRLINES, INC., *pg.* 1897, *pg.* 1830
ALLEGIANT TRAVEL COMPANY, *pg.* 346, *pg.* 1022
AMERICAN AIRLINES GROUP INC., *pg.* 224, *pg.* 1693
AMERICAN AIRLINES INC., *pg.* 1898, *pg.* 1693
BRITISH AIRWAYS, *pg.* 1901, *pg.* 1207
DAYTON INTERNATIONAL AIRPORT, *pg.* 227, *pg.* 1478
DELTA AIR LINES, INC., *pg.* 1905, *pg.* 503
EL AL ISRAEL AIRLINES, LTD., *pg.* 1906, *pg.* 1226
FEDEX CORPORATION, *pg.* 1907, *pg.* 1642
FINNAIR OYJ-NEW YORK, *pg.* 1909, *pg.* 1231
FRONTIER AIRLINES, INC., *pg.* 1909, *pg.* 319
GREAT LAKES AVIATION, LTD., *pg.* 1909, *pg.* 1901
HAWAIIAN AIRLINES, INC., *pg.* 1910, *pg.* 543
HAWAIIAN HOLDINGS, INC., *pg.* 1910, *pg.* 544
HORIZON AIR INDUSTRIES, *pg.* 1912, *pg.* 1836
ICELANDAIR NORTH AMERICA, *pg.* 1912, *pg.* 841
JETBLUE AIRWAYS CORPORATION, *pg.* 1913, *pg.* 1174
KIMBERLY-CLARK CORPORATION, *pg.* 1461, *pg.* 1720
KLM ROYAL DUTCH AIRLINES, *pg.* 1914, *pg.* 1158
KUWAIT AIRWAYS CORP., *pg.* 1914, *pg.* 1068
MESA AIR GROUP, INC., *pg.* 1915, *pg.* 18
QANTAS AIRWAYS - USA, *pg.* 1920, *pg.* 139
SENTIENT JET, LLC, *pg.* 1923, *pg.* 859
SINGAPORE AIRLINES, *pg.* 1923, *pg.* 82
SKYWEST INC., *pg.* 1923, *pg.* 1755
SOUTHWEST AIRLINES CO., *pg.* 1923, *pg.* 1687
SPIRIT AIRLINES, INC., *pg.* 234, *pg.* 449
TAP PORTUGAL, *pg.* 1925, *pg.* 1098
THAI AIRWAYS INTERNATIONAL LTD., *pg.* 1925, *pg.* 83
UNITED AIRLINES, INC., *pg.* 1927, *pg.* 593
UNITED CONTINENTAL HOLDINGS, INC., *pg.* 1927, *pg.* 593
VIRGIN AMERICA INC., *pg.* 1930, *pg.* 55
VITRAN CORPORATION, INC., *pg.* 1930, *pg.* 1946
XPO LOGISTICS, INC., *pg.* 1931, *pg.* 350

4513 - Air Courier Services

AMERICAN AIRLINES GROUP INC., *pg.* 224, *pg.* 1693
DHL HOLDINGS (USA), INC., *pg.* 1906, *pg.* 459
DYNAMEX, INC., *pg.* 1906, *pg.* 1680
FEDEX OFFICE & PRINT SERVICES, INC., *pg.* 396, *pg.* 1681
FEDEX SMARTPOST, INC., *pg.* 1909, *pg.* 1883
FRESHDIRECT, LLC, *pg.* 857, *pg.* 1174
UNITED PARCEL SERVICE, INC., *pg.* 1928, *pg.* 522
UPS SUPPLY CHAIN SOLUTIONS, INC., *pg.* 1929, *pg.* 485

4522 - Air Transportation, Non-Scheduled

THE ALDERMAN COMPANY, *pg.* 1614, *pg.* 1379
AMERICAN ASSOCIATION FOR THE ADVANCEMENT OF SCIENCE, *pg.* 126, *pg.* 394
CITATIONAIR, *pg.* 1903, *pg.* 350
CORBIS CORPORATION, *pg.* 380, *pg.* 1834
DIGITALGLOBE, INC., *pg.* 1408, *pg.* 333
GETTY IMAGES, INC., *pg.* 1645, *pg.* 1836
HORIZON AIR INDUSTRIES, *pg.* 1912, *pg.* 1836
JOSTENS, INC., *pg.* 7, *pg.* 938
MARQUIS JET PARTNERS INC., *pg.* 1915, *pg.* 1256
MESA AIR GROUP, INC., *pg.* 1915, *pg.* 18
NETJETS INC., *pg.* 1917, *pg.* 1442
PORTRAIT INNOVATIONS HOLDING COMPANY, *pg.* 1427, *pg.* 1368
SENTIENT JET, LLC, *pg.* 1923, *pg.* 859
SHUTTERSTOCK, INC., *pg.* 1280, *pg.* 1291
VIACORD, *pg.* 1606, *pg.* 810
ZUMA PRESS, INC., *pg.* 1704, *pg.* 199

4581 - Airports, Flying Fields & Airport Terminal Services

AAR CORP., *pg.* 223, *pg.* 671
AMERICAN AIRLINES INC., *pg.* 1898, *pg.* 1693
ATLANTIC AVIATION, *pg.* 224, *pg.* 1772
ATLANTIC AVIATION CORPORATION, *pg.* 224, *pg.* 1729
CITATIONAIR, *pg.* 1903, *pg.* 350
DAYTON INTERNATIONAL AIRPORT, *pg.* 227, *pg.* 1478
EL AL ISRAEL AIRLINES, LTD., *pg.* 1906, *pg.* 1226
ENGINE COMPONENTS, INC., *pg.* 227, *pg.* 1740
GULFSTREAM AEROSPACE CORPORATION, *pg.* 228, *pg.* 540
HAECO AMERICAS, *pg.* 228, *pg.* 1374
HERTZ GLOBAL HOLDINGS, INC., *pg.* 179, *pg.* 450
HONEYWELL AEROSPACE, *pg.* 228, *pg.* 16
JAPAN AIRLINES COMPANY, LTD., *pg.* 1913, *pg.* 1245
JETBLUE AIRWAYS CORPORATION, *pg.* 1913, *pg.* 1174
MIAMI INTERNATIONAL AIRPORT, *pg.* 1916, *pg.* 444
PASSUR AEROSPACE, INC., *pg.* 233, *pg.* 376
SENTIENT JET, LLC, *pg.* 1923, *pg.* 859
SIGNATURE FLIGHT SUPPORT CORP., *pg.* 234, *pg.* 456
TAP PORTUGAL, *pg.* 1925, *pg.* 1098
ULTIMATE JETCHARTERS, INC., *pg.* 1927, *pg.* 1409
UNITED AIRLINES, INC., *pg.* 1927, *pg.* 593

4612 - Crude Petroleum Pipe Lines

ALON USA ENERGY, INC., *pg.* 971, *pg.* 1673
BLUE DOLPHIN ENERGY COMPANY, *pg.* 972, *pg.* 1701
MARATHON OIL CORPORATION, *pg.* 981, *pg.* 1710
MARATHON PETROLEUM COMPANY LLC, *pg.* 981, *pg.* 1454
PLAINS ALL AMERICAN PIPELINE, L.P., *pg.* 983, *pg.* 1712
SINCLAIR OIL CORPORATION, *pg.* 984, *pg.* 1760
TRANSMONTAIGNE, INC., *pg.* 986, *pg.* 323

4613 - Refined Petroleum Pipe

First page reference indicates Business Class Edition
Second page reference indicates Geographic Edition

Lines

FJ MANAGEMENT, INC., *pg.* 978, *pg.* 1758
MARATHON OIL CORPORATION, *pg.* 981, *pg.* 1710
MARATHON PETROLEUM COMPANY LLC, *pg.* 981, *pg.* 1454
PLAINS ALL AMERICAN PIPELINE, L.P., *pg.* 983, *pg.* 1712
TRANSCANADA CORPORATION, *pg.* 1953, *pg.* 1905
VALERO ENERGY CORPORATION, *pg.* 986, *pg.* 1743

4724 - Travel Agencies

AAA AUTO CLUB SOUTH, *pg.* 1187, *pg.* 470
ABERCROMBIE & KENT USA, LLC, *pg.* 1896, *pg.* 607
AIR INDIA, *pg.* 1897, *pg.* 1188
AIR NEW ZEALAND LTD. (U.S.A.), *pg.* 1897, *pg.* 78
ALEXANDER+ROBERTS, *pg.* 1898, *pg.* 1034
ALLEGIANT TRAVEL COMPANY, *pg.* 346, *pg.* 1022
AMERICAN EXPRESS COMPANY, *pg.* 712, *pg.* 1190
ANDREW HARPER, INC., *pg.* 1899, *pg.* 1660
APPLE VACATIONS INC., *pg.* 1899, *pg.* 1556
BARBADOS TOURISM AUTHORITY, *pg.* 1900, *pg.* 1200
BERMUDA DEPARTMENT OF TOURISM, *pg.* 989, *pg.* 1202
BUFFALO NIAGARA CONVENTION & VISITORS BUREAU, INC., *pg.* 1901, *pg.* 1147
CALIFORNIA TRAVEL & TOURISM COMMISSION, *pg.* 990, *pg.* 196
CARAVAN TOURS, INC., *pg.* 1902, *pg.* 568
CARLSON COMPANIES INC., *pg.* 1084, *pg.* 947
CARLSON WAGONLIT TRAVEL, *pg.* 1902, *pg.* 948
CLASSIC VACATIONS, LLC, *pg.* 1903, *pg.* 242
CLUB MED SALES, INC., *pg.* 1903, *pg.* 441
CRYSTAL CRUISES LLC, *pg.* 1904, *pg.* 128
DOWN UNDER ANSWERS, LLC, *pg.* 1906, *pg.* 1814
FRENCH GOVERNMENT TOURIST OFFICE, *pg.* 992, *pg.* 1233
GROUP VOYAGERS, INC., *pg.* 1910, *pg.* 333
HOLLAND AMERICA LINE INC., *pg.* 1911, *pg.* 1836
HOTWIRE, INC., *pg.* 1912, *pg.* 219
ICRUISE.COM CORP., *pg.* 1258, *pg.* 421
INDIA TOURISM, *pg.* 995, *pg.* 1243
JAMAICA TOURIST BOARD, *pg.* 996, *pg.* 443
LIBERTY TRAVEL, INC., *pg.* 1914, *pg.* 1113
MARITZ INC., *pg.* 1914, *pg.* 977
MARK TRAVEL CORPORATION, *pg.* 1915, *pg.* 1877
NORWEGIAN CRUISE LINE, *pg.* 1917, *pg.* 444
ORBITZ WORLDWIDE, INC., *pg.* 1918, *pg.* 586
OUTRIGGER ENTERPRISES, INC., *pg.* 1107, *pg.* 544
PLEASANT HOLIDAYS LLC, *pg.* 1919, *pg.* 307
RAIL EUROPE INC., *pg.* 1920, *pg.* 1354
SKYAUCTION.COM, INC., *pg.* 1281, *pg.* 1293
TAHITI TOURISME NORTH AMERICA, INC., *pg.* 1007, *pg.* 83
TRAVEL LEADERS, *pg.* 1925, *pg.* 1426
TRAVELCENTERS OF AMERICA, LLC, *pg.* 1925, *pg.* 1481
TRAVELPORT LIMITED, *pg.* 1925, *pg.* 521
TRAVELZOO INC, *pg.* 1926, *pg.* 1304
VACATION.COM, INC., *pg.* 1287, *pg.* 1772
VIRTUOSO LTD., *pg.* 1930, *pg.* 1696
VISIT FLORIDA INC., *pg.* 1010, *pg.* 470
WINDSTAR CRUISES, *pg.* 1931, *pg.* 1843
WORLD TRAVEL HOLDINGS, *pg.* 1931, *pg.* 860
YMT VACATIONS, *pg.* 1931, *pg.* 83

4725 - Tour Operators

ACADEMIC TRAVEL ABROAD, INC., *pg.* 1896, *pg.* 393
ALEXANDER+ROBERTS, *pg.* 1898, *pg.* 1034
APPLE VACATIONS INC., *pg.* 1899, *pg.* 1556
BAHAMAS TOURISM CENTER, *pg.* 1900, *pg.* 459
BARBADOS TOURISM AUTHORITY, *pg.* 1900, *pg.* 1200
CARAVAN TOURS, INC., *pg.* 1902, *pg.* 568
CARNIVAL CRUISE LINES, *pg.* 1902, *pg.* 441
CLASSIC VACATIONS, LLC, *pg.* 1903, *pg.* 242
CLUB MED SALES, INC., *pg.* 1903, *pg.* 441
EXPLORICA, INC., *pg.* 1907, *pg.* 794
GROUP VOYAGERS, INC., *pg.* 1910, *pg.* 333
HOLLAND AMERICA LINE INC., *pg.* 1911, *pg.* 1836
ISRAM WHOLESALE TOURS & TRAVEL LTD., *pg.* 1913, *pg.* 1244
NEW ORLEANS TOURISM MARKETING CORPORATION, *pg.* 1001, *pg.* 747
OUTER BANKS VISITORS BUREAU, *pg.* 1918, *pg.* 1382
PLAN ASIA, INC, *pg.* 1919, *pg.* 82
PLEASANT HOLIDAYS LLC, *pg.* 1919, *pg.* 307
PUERTO RICO TOURISM COMPANY, *pg.* 1004, *pg.* 1599
SANDALS RESORTS INTERNATIONAL, *pg.* 1111, *pg.* 446
TNT VACATIONS, *pg.* 1925, *pg.* 801
TRANSAT A.T., INC., *pg.* 1925, *pg.* 1957
WISCONSIN DEPARTMENT OF TOURISM, *pg.* 1011, *pg.* 1868
YMT VACATIONS, *pg.* 1931, *pg.* 83

4729 - Arrangement of Passenger Transportation, NEC

AAA AUTO CLUB SOUTH, *pg.* 1187, *pg.* 470
AIR INDIA, *pg.* 1897, *pg.* 1188
AMBASSADORS GROUP, INC., *pg.* 1898, *pg.* 1843
AMERICAN AIRLINES INC., *pg.* 1898, *pg.* 1693
AMERICAN AUTOMOBILE ASSOCIATION, *pg.* 1190, *pg.* 429
AMERICAN EXPRESS TRAVEL RELATED SERVICES COMPANY, INC., *pg.* 1079, *pg.* 1192
AMERICAN FILM INSTITUTE, *pg.* 528, *pg.* 126
AMERICAN RADIO RELAY LEAGUE, INC., *pg.* 130, *pg.* 359
AMNESTY INTERNATIONAL USA, *pg.* 131, *pg.* 1194
ATLANTA SYMPHONY ORCHESTRA, *pg.* 531, *pg.* 490
AUTO EUROPE, LLC, *pg.* 1900, *pg.* 751
AUTOMOBILE CLUB OF SOUTHERN CALIFORNIA, *pg.* 134, *pg.* 126
BAHAMAS TOURISM CENTER, *pg.* 1900, *pg.* 459
BERKSHIRE HATHAWAY HOME SERVICES, *pg.* 1081, *pg.* 469
BEST WESTERN INTERNATIONAL, INC., *pg.* 1081, *pg.* 15
BLUEGREEN CORPORATION, *pg.* 1082, *pg.* 410
BOAT OWNERS ASSOCIATION OF THE UNITED STATES, *pg.* 134, *pg.* 1770
CANADIAN PARKS AND WILDERNESS SOCIETY, *pg.* 136, *pg.* 1931
CARLSON WAGONLIT TRAVEL, *pg.* 1902, *pg.* 948
CENTER THEATRE GROUP OF LOS ANGELES, INC., *pg.* 538, *pg.* 128
CHEAPCARIBBEAN.COM, *pg.* 1903, *pg.* 1526
CONSUMER HEALTHCARE PRODUCTS ASSOCIATION, *pg.* 138, *pg.* 397
DATA LISTING SERVICE LLC, *pg.* 382, *pg.* 919
EMPIRE STATE DEVELOPMENT-DIVISION OF TOURISM, *pg.* 992, *pg.* 1227
EXPEDIA, INC., *pg.* 1244, *pg.* 1814
FLORIDA FRUIT & VEGETABLE ASSOCIATION, *pg.* 140, *pg.* 438
HOLLYWOOD MEDIA CORP., *pg.* 1256, *pg.* 412
HOLSTEIN ASSOCIATION USA, INC., *pg.* 143, *pg.* 1764
HOMEAWAY, INC., *pg.* 1911, *pg.* 1663
HOTELS.COM, L.P., *pg.* 1257, *pg.* 1682
IAC/INTERACTIVECORP, *pg.* 292, *pg.* 1242
INTERVAL LEISURE GROUP, INC., *pg.* 1912, *pg.* 443
KAYAK, *pg.* 1260, *pg.* 363
KNOXVILLE SYMPHONY SOCIETY INC., *pg.* 556, *pg.* 1637
LENOX HILL NEIGHBORHOOD HOUSE, *pg.* 146, *pg.* 1251
LIBERTY TRAVEL, INC., *pg.* 1914, *pg.* 1113
MAJOR LEAGUE BASEBALL, *pg.* 560, *pg.* 1255
MARITZ INC., *pg.* 1914, *pg.* 977
MARYLAND OFFICE OF TOURISM DEVELOPMENT, *pg.* 998, *pg.* 758
MCO PROPERTIES INC., *pg.* 1104, *pg.* 13
MISSISSIPPI MUSEUM OF ART, *pg.* 563, *pg.* 969
MOTHERS AGAINST DRUNK DRIVING (MADD), *pg.* 147, *pg.* 1723
NATIONAL ASSOCIATION FOR STOCK CAR AUTO RACING, *pg.* 566, *pg.* 420
NATIONAL ASSOCIATION OF PROFESSIONAL BASEBALL LEAGUES, INC., *pg.* 566, *pg.* 463
NATIONAL BASKETBALL ASSOCIATION, *pg.* 566, *pg.* 1264
NATIONAL COUNCIL ON PROBLEM GAMBLING, *pg.* 148, *pg.* 401
NATIONAL FOOTBALL LEAGUE, *pg.* 567, *pg.* 1264
NATIONAL HOCKEY LEAGUE, *pg.* 568, *pg.* 1265
NEW YORK ROAD RUNNERS CLUB, INC., *pg.* 152, *pg.* 1269
THE OPIUM GROUP, *pg.* 572, *pg.* 448
ORBITZ WORLDWIDE, INC., *pg.* 1918, *pg.* 586
PASSKEY INTERNATIONAL, INC., *pg.* 1274, *pg.* 853
THE PRICELINE GROUP INC., *pg.* 1276, *pg.* 364
PRUDENTIAL REAL ESTATE AFFILIATES, INC., *pg.* 1108, *pg.* 115
ROYAL CARIBBEAN CRUISES LTD, *pg.* 1921, *pg.* 446
SABRE HOLDINGS CORPORATION, *pg.* 1922, *pg.* 1745
SAN LUIS OBISPO COUNTY VISITORS & CONFERENCE BUREAU, *pg.* 1922, *pg.* 253
SAVE THE MANATEE CLUB, INC., *pg.* 156, *pg.* 439
SKYWEST INC., *pg.* 1923, *pg.* 1755
SMARTER TRAVEL MEDIA LLC, *pg.* 1687, *pg.* 801
SNOHOMISH COUNTY MUSIC PROJECT, *pg.* 584, *pg.* 1819
SOUTH AFRICAN TOURISM, *pg.* 1005, *pg.* 1294
STOWE AREA ASSOCIATION, INC., *pg.* 1115, *pg.* 1768
SUNDANCE INSTITUTE, *pg.* 311, *pg.* 1754
THAI AIRWAYS INTERNATIONAL LTD., *pg.* 1925, *pg.* 83
TICKETMASTER ENTERTAINMENT LLC, *pg.* 1284, *pg.* 48
TOURISM IRELAND, *pg.* 1007, *pg.* 1303
TRAVEL-BY-NET, INC., *pg.* 1925, *pg.* 1183
TRAVEL INDUSTRY ASSOCIATION OF AMERICA, *pg.* 158, *pg.* 405
TRAVELOCITY, INC., *pg.* 1284, *pg.* 1745
TRAVELPORT LIMITED, *pg.* 1925, *pg.* 521
TRAVELZOO INC, *pg.* 1926, *pg.* 1304
UNITED STATES OLYMPIC COMMITTEE, *pg.* 589, *pg.* 315
UPSPRING, *pg.* 160, *pg.* 1426
WORLD TRAVEL HOLDINGS, *pg.* 1931, *pg.* 860

4731 - Arrangement of Transportation of Freight & Cargo

ALBA WHEELS UP INTERNATIONAL, INC., *pg.* 1898, *pg.* 1170
ALEXANDER & BALDWIN, INC., *pg.* 1079, *pg.* 543
ALLSTATES WORLDCARGO, INC., *pg.* 1898, *pg.* 1042
AMERICAN RED BALL TRANSIT CO. INC., *pg.* 1899, *pg.* 682
ARKANSAS BEST CORPORATION, *pg.* 1899, *pg.* 32
ASSOCIATED GLOBAL SYSTEMS, INC., *pg.* 1899, *pg.* 1184
ATLAS VAN LINES, INC., *pg.* 1900, *pg.* 678
BDP INTERNATIONAL INC., *pg.* 1900, *pg.* 1559
CANADIAN NATIONAL RAILWAY COMPANY, *pg.* 1902, *pg.* 1953
CASESTACK, INC., *pg.* 369, *pg.* 272
CSX CORPORATION, *pg.* 1904, *pg.* 432
FEDEX CORPORATION, *pg.* 1907, *pg.* 1642
GAINES MOTOR LINES INCORPORATED, *pg.* 1338, *pg.* 1378
INTERSTATE WORLDWIDE RELOCATION, INC., *pg.* 1912, *pg.* 1807
MAERSK INC., *pg.* 1914, *pg.* 1080
MENLO WORLDWIDE, LLC, *pg.* 1915, *pg.* 255
MIQ LOGISTICS, LLC, *pg.* 1267, *pg.* 719
NATIONAL VAN LINES, INC., *pg.* 1916, *pg.* 559
OLD DOMINION FREIGHT LINE, INC., *pg.* 1918, *pg.* 1391
RYDER SYSTEM, INC., *pg.* 1922, *pg.* 446
SCHNEIDER, *pg.* 1922, *pg.* 1859
STEVENS GROUP, INC., *pg.* 1924, *pg.* 906
THE SUDDATH COMPANIES INC., *pg.* 1924, *pg.* 435
TRI-STATE MOTOR TRANSIT CO., *pg.* 1926, *pg.* 980
UNITED CONTINENTAL HOLDINGS, INC., *pg.* 1927, *pg.* 593
US 1 INDUSTRIES, INC., *pg.* 1929, *pg.* 698
U.S. XPRESS ENTERPRISES, INC., *pg.* 1929, *pg.* 1630
VITRAN CORPORATION, INC., *pg.* 1930, *pg.* 1946
WEICHERT RELOCATION RESOURCES INC., *pg.* 1118, *pg.* 1087
WERNER ENTERPRISES, INC., *pg.* 1930, *pg.* 1019
WHEATON VAN LINES, INC., *pg.* 1930, *pg.* 691
YRC WORLDWIDE INC., *pg.* 1931, *pg.* 720
ZIM-AMERICAN ISRAELI SHIPPING CO., *pg.* 1931, *pg.* 1798

4789 - Transportation Services, NEC

AAA AUTO CLUB SOUTH, *pg.* 1187, *pg.* 470
ACP MARKETING, INC., *pg.* 1896, *pg.* 1953
AIR INDIA, *pg.* 1897, *pg.* 1188
AMBASSADORS GROUP, INC., *pg.* 1898, *pg.* 1843
AMERICAN AIRLINES INC., *pg.* 1898, *pg.* 1693
AMERICAN AUTOMOBILE ASSOCIATION, *pg.* 1190, *pg.* 429
AMERICAN EXPRESS TRAVEL RELATED SERVICES COMPANY, INC., *pg.* 1079, *pg.* 1192
AUTO EUROPE, LLC, *pg.* 1900, *pg.* 751
AUTOMOBILE CLUB OF SOUTHERN CALIFORNIA, *pg.* 134,

pg. 126
BAHAMAS TOURISM CENTER, *pg.* 1900, *pg.* 459
BEST WESTERN INTERNATIONAL, INC., *pg.* 1081, *pg.* 15
CARLSON WAGONLIT TRAVEL, *pg.* 1902, *pg.* 948
CHEAPCARIBBEAN.COM, *pg.* 1903, *pg.* 1526
DATA LISTING SERVICE LLC, *pg.* 382, *pg.* 919
EMPIRE STATE DEVELOPMENT-DIVISION OF TOURISM, *pg.* 992, *pg.* 1227
EXPEDIA, INC., *pg.* 1244, *pg.* 1814
FLORIDA FRUIT & VEGETABLE ASSOCIATION, *pg.* 140, *pg.* 438
HOMEAWAY, INC., *pg.* 1911, *pg.* 1663
HOTELS.COM, L.P., *pg.* 1257, *pg.* 1682
IAC/INTERACTIVECORP, *pg.* 292, *pg.* 1242
INTERVAL LEISURE GROUP, INC., *pg.* 1912, *pg.* 443
KAYAK, *pg.* 1260, *pg.* 363
LIBERTY TRAVEL, INC., *pg.* 1914, *pg.* 1113
MARITZ INC., *pg.* 1914, *pg.* 977
MARYLAND OFFICE OF TOURISM DEVELOPMENT, *pg.* 998, *pg.* 758
NJ TRANSIT CORPORATION, *pg.* 1917, *pg.* 1097
ORBITZ WORLDWIDE, INC., *pg.* 1918, *pg.* 586
PASSKEY INTERNATIONAL, INC., *pg.* 1274, *pg.* 853
THE PRICELINE GROUP INC., *pg.* 1276, *pg.* 364
ROYAL CARIBBEAN CRUISES LTD, *pg.* 1921, *pg.* 446
SABRE HOLDINGS CORPORATION, *pg.* 1922, *pg.* 1745
SAN LUIS OBISPO COUNTY VISITORS & CONFERENCE BUREAU, *pg.* 1922, *pg.* 253
SKYWEST INC., *pg.* 1923, *pg.* 1755
SMARTER TRAVEL MEDIA LLC, *pg.* 1687, *pg.* 801
SOUTH AFRICAN TOURISM, *pg.* 1005, *pg.* 1294
STOWE AREA ASSOCIATION, INC., *pg.* 1115, *pg.* 1768
THAI AIRWAYS INTERNATIONAL LTD., *pg.* 1925, *pg.* 83
TOURISM IRELAND, *pg.* 1007, *pg.* 1303
TRAVEL-BY-NET, INC., *pg.* 1925, *pg.* 1183
TRAVELOCITY, INC., *pg.* 1284, *pg.* 1745
TRAVELPORT LIMITED, *pg.* 1925, *pg.* 521
TRAVELZOO INC, *pg.* 1926, *pg.* 1304
VIAD CORP., *pg.* 816, *pg.* 20
WORLD TRAVEL HOLDINGS, *pg.* 1931, *pg.* 860

4812 - Radio Telephone Communications

AIRSPAN NETWORKS INC., *pg.* 346, *pg.* 410
AIRVANA, INC., *pg.* 268, *pg.* 812
ALASKA COMMUNICATIONS SYSTEMS GROUP, INC., *pg.* 269, *pg.* 10
ALION SCIENCE AND TECHNOLOGY CORPORATION, *pg.* 615, *pg.* 1788
ALLTEL WIRELESS COMMUNICATIONS CORPORATION, *pg.* 1865, *pg.* 33
AMERICAN TOWER CORPORATION, *pg.* 164, *pg.* 789
ARUBA NETWORKS, INC., *pg.* 353, *pg.* 284
AT&T INC., *pg.* 1867, *pg.* 1674
AT&T MOBILITY LLC, *pg.* 619, *pg.* 488
AT&T MOBILITY LLC, *pg.* 620, *pg.* 1824
AT&T MOBILITY LLC, *pg.* 620, *pg.* 1152
AT&T SOUTHEAST, *pg.* 1868, *pg.* 489
ATLANTIC TELE-NETWORK, INC., *pg.* 620, *pg.* 787
BANDSINTOWN, *pg.* 1231, *pg.* 1200
BANDWIDTH.COM, INC., *pg.* 360, *pg.* 1386
BCE INC., *pg.* 1936, *pg.* 1960
BLACKBERRY LIMITED, *pg.* 625, *pg.* 1947
BOINGO WIRELESS, INC., *pg.* 625, *pg.* 127
BOOST MOBILE, *pg.* 1869, *pg.* 107
BRIGHTSTAR CORPORATION, *pg.* 627, *pg.* 440
BSM TECHNOLOGIES INC., *pg.* 627, *pg.* 1949
BULLSEYE TELECOM INC., *pg.* 366, *pg.* 906
C SPIRE WIRELESS, *pg.* 628, *pg.* 971
CELLCO PARTNERSHIP, *pg.* 1869, *pg.* 1042
CINCINNATI BELL INC., *pg.* 1871, *pg.* 1410
CONSOLIDATED COMMUNICATIONS HOLDINGS, INC., *pg.* 630, *pg.* 631
CRICKET WIRELESS LLC, *pg.* 381, *pg.* 483
DIRECTV GROUP HOLDINGS, LLC, *pg.* 281, *pg.* 79
EF JOHNSON TECHNOLOGIES, INC., *pg.* 390, *pg.* 1718
ENVENTIS, *pg.* 637, *pg.* 927
FUNMOBILITY, INC., *pg.* 640, *pg.* 183
FUSION TELECOMMUNICATIONS INTERNATIONAL, INC., *pg.* 1248, *pg.* 1233
GDT TEK, INC., *pg.* 399, *pg.* 453
GLOBALSTAR, INC., *pg.* 401, *pg.* 743
GOOD TECHNOLOGY, INC., *pg.* 1249, *pg.* 285
HAWAIIAN TELCOM COMMUNICATIONS, INC., *pg.* 1872, *pg.* 544
INTERCALL, INC., *pg.* 417, *pg.* 578
INTERMEDIA, *pg.* 417, *pg.* 1815
LCC INTERNATIONAL, INC., *pg.* 651, *pg.* 1792
LOGMEIN, INC., *pg.* 428, *pg.* 861
MATRIX INTEGRATION LLC, *pg.* 430, *pg.* 692
MERU NETWORKS, INC., *pg.* 434, *pg.* 286
METROPCS, INC., *pg.* 1872, *pg.* 1683
MONEXA TECHNOLOGIES CORPORATION, *pg.* 1268, *pg.* 1911
MOTOROLA SOLUTIONS, INC., *pg.* 657, *pg.* 659
MTONE WIRELESS CORPORATION, *pg.* 658, *pg.* 268
NET TALK.COM, INC., *pg.* 444, *pg.* 448
NET2PHONE, INC., *pg.* 1269, *pg.* 1097
NETMOTION WIRELESS, INC., *pg.* 445, *pg.* 1837
NII HOLDINGS, INC., *pg.* 659, *pg.* 1799
NTELOS HOLDINGS CORP., *pg.* 659, *pg.* 1811
PCTEL, INC., *pg.* 452, *pg.* 557
PLAINTREE SYSTEMS INC., *pg.* 663, *pg.* 1918
PURPLE COMMUNICATIONS, INC., *pg.* 457, *pg.* 194
QUALCOMM INCORPORATED, *pg.* 1873, *pg.* 207
QUEBECOR MEDIA INC., *pg.* 1679, *pg.* 1956
QUICKPLAY MEDIA INC., *pg.* 666, *pg.* 1941
ROGERS COMMUNICATIONS INC., *pg.* 668, *pg.* 1942
SAVOX COMMUNICATIONS LTD, *pg.* 671, *pg.* 1909
SBA COMMUNICATIONS CORPORATION, *pg.* 671, *pg.* 413
SHORETEL, INC., *pg.* 469, *pg.* 288
SIERRA WIRELESS INCORPORATED, *pg.* 673, *pg.* 1909
SONUS NETWORKS INC., *pg.* 1281, *pg.* 858
SPOK, *pg.* 1873, *pg.* 1807
SPRINT CORPORATION, *pg.* 1874, *pg.* 719
T-MOBILE US, INC., *pg.* 676, *pg.* 1816
TELEPHONE & DATA SYSTEMS, INC., *pg.* 1875, *pg.* 591
TELETOUCH COMMUNICATIONS, INC., *pg.* 483, *pg.* 1696
TELUS CORPORATION, *pg.* 1952, *pg.* 1912
TERAGO INC., *pg.* 1284, *pg.* 1934
TRACFONE WIRELESS, INC., *pg.* 681, *pg.* 447
TRACK GROUP, *pg.* 1603, *pg.* 1761
TRIMBLE NAVIGATION LIMITED, *pg.* 1384, *pg.* 288
UNIFIED SIGNAL, INC., *pg.* 682, *pg.* 1822
UNITED STATES CELLULAR CORPORATION, *pg.* 1875, *pg.* 594
USA TECHNOLOGIES, INC., *pg.* 815, *pg.* 1550
VERISIGN, INC., *pg.* 488, *pg.* 1799
VERIZON COMMUNICATIONS INC., *pg.* 1875, *pg.* 1309
VIDEOTRON LTD., *pg.* 317, *pg.* 1957
VIRGIN MOBILE USA, LP, *pg.* 685, *pg.* 1129
VISAGE MOBILE, INC., *pg.* 266, *pg.* 232
WIRELESS RONIN TECHNOLOGIES INC., *pg.* 689, *pg.* 951
WIRELESS XCESSORIES GROUP, INC., *pg.* 689, *pg.* 1541
ZAYO GROUP, LLC, *pg.* 1877, *pg.* 334

4813 - Telephone Communications, Except Radio Telephone

ADVANCED TELECOM SERVICES, *pg.* 1865, *pg.* 1591
AIRSPAN NETWORKS INC., *pg.* 346, *pg.* 410
AIRVANA, INC., *pg.* 268, *pg.* 812
ALASKA COMMUNICATIONS SYSTEMS GROUP, INC., *pg.* 269, *pg.* 10
ALION SCIENCE AND TECHNOLOGY CORPORATION, *pg.* 615, *pg.* 1788
ALLTEL WIRELESS COMMUNICATIONS CORPORATION, *pg.* 1865, *pg.* 33
AMERICAN TOWER CORPORATION, *pg.* 164, *pg.* 789
ARUBA NETWORKS, INC., *pg.* 353, *pg.* 284
AT&T, *pg.* 1865, *pg.* 258
AT&T COMMUNICATIONS CORP., *pg.* 1866, *pg.* 1043
AT&T INC., *pg.* 1867, *pg.* 1674
AT&T INC., *pg.* 1868, *pg.* 358
AT&T MOBILITY LLC, *pg.* 619, *pg.* 488
AT&T MOBILITY LLC, *pg.* 620, *pg.* 1824
AT&T MOBILITY LLC, *pg.* 620, *pg.* 1152
AT&T SOUTHEAST, *pg.* 1868, *pg.* 489
AT&T WEST, *pg.* 1869, *pg.* 212
ATLANTIC TELE-NETWORK, INC., *pg.* 620, *pg.* 787
BANDSINTOWN, *pg.* 1231, *pg.* 1200
BANDWIDTH.COM, INC., *pg.* 360, *pg.* 1386
BCE INC., *pg.* 1936, *pg.* 1960
BELL CANADA, *pg.* 1936, *pg.* 1960
BLACKBERRY LIMITED, *pg.* 625, *pg.* 1947
BOINGO WIRELESS, INC., *pg.* 625, *pg.* 127
BOOST MOBILE, *pg.* 1869, *pg.* 107
BRIGHTSTAR CORPORATION, *pg.* 627, *pg.* 440
BROADVIEW NETWORKS, INC., *pg.* 365, *pg.* 1339
BSM TECHNOLOGIES INC., *pg.* 627, *pg.* 1949
BULLSEYE TELECOM INC., *pg.* 366, *pg.* 906
C SPIRE WIRELESS, *pg.* 628, *pg.* 971
CELLCO PARTNERSHIP, *pg.* 1869, *pg.* 1042
CENTURYLINK, INC, *pg.* 1870, *pg.* 317
CENTURYLINK, INC., *pg.* 1870, *pg.* 746
CHARTER COMMUNICATIONS, INC., *pg.* 274, *pg.* 372
CINCINNATI BELL INC., *pg.* 1871, *pg.* 1410
CONSOLIDATED COMMUNICATIONS HOLDINGS, INC., *pg.* 630, *pg.* 631
CONSOLIDATED COMMUNICATIONS, INC., *pg.* 1871, *pg.* 1534
COX COMMUNICATIONS, INC., *pg.* 279, *pg.* 501
CRICKET WIRELESS LLC, *pg.* 381, *pg.* 483
DELTATHREE, INC., *pg.* 1238, *pg.* 1068
DIRECTV GROUP HOLDINGS, LLC, *pg.* 281, *pg.* 79
EARTHLINK HOLDINGS CORP., *pg.* 1240, *pg.* 504
EDD HELMS GROUP, INC., *pg.* 1071, *pg.* 442
EF JOHNSON TECHNOLOGIES, INC., *pg.* 390, *pg.* 1718
ENVENTIS, *pg.* 637, *pg.* 927
EQUINIX, INC., *pg.* 394, *pg.* 190
FAIRPOINT COMMUNICATIONS, INC., *pg.* 1871, *pg.* 1366
FRONTIER COMMUNICATIONS CORPORATION, *pg.* 1871, *pg.* 362
FRONTIER COMMUNICATIONS OF NEW YORK, INC., *pg.* 398, *pg.* 1335
FUNMOBILITY, INC., *pg.* 640, *pg.* 183
FUSION TELECOMMUNICATIONS INTERNATIONAL, INC., *pg.* 1248, *pg.* 1233
GDT TEK, INC., *pg.* 399, *pg.* 453
GENERAL COMMUNICATION, INC., *pg.* 1871, *pg.* 10
GLOBALSTAR, INC., *pg.* 401, *pg.* 743
GLOWPOINT, INC., *pg.* 401, *pg.* 1094
GOOD TECHNOLOGY, INC., *pg.* 1249, *pg.* 285
HAWAIIAN TELCOM COMMUNICATIONS, INC., *pg.* 1872, *pg.* 544
IDT CORPORATION, *pg.* 643, *pg.* 1096
INCONTACT, INC., *pg.* 413, *pg.* 1752
INTEGRA TELECOM, INC., *pg.* 644, *pg.* 938
INTERCALL, INC., *pg.* 417, *pg.* 578
INTERMEDIA, *pg.* 417, *pg.* 1815
J2 GLOBAL COMMUNICATIONS, INC., *pg.* 1260, *pg.* 133
LAUNCHFAX.COM INC., *pg.* 1261, *pg.* 1064
LCC INTERNATIONAL, INC., *pg.* 651, *pg.* 1792
LEVEL 3 COMMUNICATIONS, INC., *pg.* 1262, *pg.* 312
LOGMEIN, INC., *pg.* 428, *pg.* 861
MATRIX INTEGRATION LLC, *pg.* 430, *pg.* 692
MBLOX INC., *pg.* 1266, *pg.* 286
MERU NETWORKS, INC., *pg.* 434, *pg.* 286
METROPCS, INC., *pg.* 1872, *pg.* 1683
MONEXA TECHNOLOGIES CORPORATION, *pg.* 1268, *pg.* 1911
MOTOROLA SOLUTIONS, INC., *pg.* 657, *pg.* 659
MTONE WIRELESS CORPORATION, *pg.* 658, *pg.* 268
MTS ALLSTREAM, INC., *pg.* 1946, *pg.* 1940
MULTIBAND CORPORATION, *pg.* 442, *pg.* 940
NET TALK.COM, INC., *pg.* 444, *pg.* 448
NET2PHONE, INC., *pg.* 1269, *pg.* 1097
NETMOTION WIRELESS, INC., *pg.* 445, *pg.* 1837
NII HOLDINGS, INC., *pg.* 659, *pg.* 1799
NORTHWESTEL INC., *pg.* 1947, *pg.* 1963
NTELOS HOLDINGS CORP., *pg.* 659, *pg.* 1811
PCTEL, INC., *pg.* 452, *pg.* 557
PLAINTREE SYSTEMS INC., *pg.* 663, *pg.* 1918
PRIMUS TELECOMMUNICATIONS GROUP, INCORPORATED, *pg.* 665, *pg.* 1794
PURPLE COMMUNICATIONS, INC., *pg.* 457, *pg.* 194
QUALCOMM INCORPORATED, *pg.* 1873, *pg.* 207
QUEBECOR MEDIA INC., *pg.* 1679, *pg.* 1956
QUICKPLAY MEDIA INC., *pg.* 666, *pg.* 1941
RCN TELECOM SERVICES, LLC., *pg.* 306, *pg.* 1785
RETURN PATH, INC., *pg.* 461, *pg.* 1285
ROGERS COMMUNICATIONS INC., *pg.* 668, *pg.* 1942
SAVOX COMMUNICATIONS LTD, *pg.* 671, *pg.* 1909
SBA COMMUNICATIONS CORPORATION, *pg.* 671, *pg.* 413
SHENANDOAH TELECOMMUNICATIONS CO., *pg.* 672, *pg.* 1779
SHORETEL, INC., *pg.* 469, *pg.* 288
SIERRA WIRELESS INCORPORATED, *pg.* 673, *pg.* 1909
SONUS NETWORKS INC., *pg.* 1281, *pg.* 858
SPOK, *pg.* 1873, *pg.* 1807
SPRINT CORPORATION, *pg.* 1874, *pg.* 719

SRT COMMUNICATIONS INC., *pg.* 1282, *pg.* 1398
STARTEC GLOBAL COMMUNICATIONS CORPORATION, *pg.* 1874, *pg.* 768
T-MOBILE US, INC., *pg.* 676, *pg.* 1816
TELCOIQ, INC., *pg.* 1284, *pg.* 773
TELEPHONE & DATA SYSTEMS, INC., *pg.* 1875, *pg.* 591
TELETOUCH COMMUNICATIONS, INC., *pg.* 483, *pg.* 1696
TELUS CORPORATION, *pg.* 1952, *pg.* 1912
TERAGO INC., *pg.* 1284, *pg.* 1934
TRACFONE WIRELESS, INC., *pg.* 681, *pg.* 447
TRACK GROUP, *pg.* 1603, *pg.* 1761
TRIMBLE NAVIGATION LIMITED, *pg.* 1384, *pg.* 288
UNIFIED SIGNAL, INC., *pg.* 682, *pg.* 1822
UNITED STATES CELLULAR CORPORATION, *pg.* 1875, *pg.* 594
USA TECHNOLOGIES, INC., *pg.* 815, *pg.* 1550
VELATEL GLOBAL COMMUNICATIONS, INC., *pg.* 685, *pg.* 210
VERISIGN, INC., *pg.* 488, *pg.* 1799
VERIZON COMMUNICATIONS INC., *pg.* 1875, *pg.* 1309
VIDEOTRON LTD., *pg.* 317, *pg.* 1957
VIRGIN MOBILE USA, LP, *pg.* 685, *pg.* 1129
VISAGE MOBILE, INC., *pg.* 266, *pg.* 232
VONAGE HOLDINGS CORP., *pg.* 686, *pg.* 1074
WARWICK VALLEY TELEPHONE CO., *pg.* 1877, *pg.* 1349
WINDSTREAM CORPORATION, *pg.* 321, *pg.* 34
WIRELESS RONIN TECHNOLOGIES INC., *pg.* 689, *pg.* 951
WIRELESS XCESSORIES GROUP, INC., *pg.* 689, *pg.* 1541
XO HOLDINGS, INC., *pg.* 689, *pg.* 1786
ZAYO GROUP, LLC, *pg.* 1877, *pg.* 334

4832 - Radio Broadcasting Stations

1070 WIBC, *pg.* 267, *pg.* 682
ABC, INC., *pg.* 268, *pg.* 1185
AMERICAN URBAN RADIO NETWORKS, *pg.* 269, *pg.* 1573
BACK TO THE BIBLE, *pg.* 270, *pg.* 1011
BEASLEY BROADCAST GROUP, INC., *pg.* 271, *pg.* 450
BET HOLDINGS LLC, *pg.* 271, *pg.* 396
BLISS COMMUNICATIONS INC., *pg.* 1621, *pg.* 1861
CAPITOL BROADCASTING COMPANY, INC., *pg.* 272, *pg.* 1386
CBS CORPORATION, *pg.* 273, *pg.* 1210
CONNECTICUT PUBLIC BROADCASTING CORP., *pg.* 279, *pg.* 351
CORUS ENTERTAINMENT INC., *pg.* 279, *pg.* 1937
COX MEDIA GROUP, *pg.* 280, *pg.* 502
CUMULUS BROADCASTING INC, *pg.* 280, *pg.* 502
CUMULUS MEDIA INC., *pg.* 280, *pg.* 503
CURTIS MEDIA GROUP, *pg.* 281, *pg.* 1387
DERRICK PUBLISHING CO., *pg.* 1635, *pg.* 1558
EAGLE COMMUNICATIONS INC., *pg.* 284, *pg.* 715
EDUCATIONAL MEDIA FOUNDATION, *pg.* 284, *pg.* 194
EMMIS COMMUNICATIONS CORPORATION, *pg.* 285, *pg.* 685
ENTRAVISION COMMUNICATIONS CORPORATION, *pg.* 285, *pg.* 273
ESPN, INC., *pg.* 285, *pg.* 340
THE FREE LANCE-STAR PUBLISHING CO., *pg.* 1643, *pg.* 1782
THE FREELANCE-STAR RADIO GROUPS, *pg.* 1643, *pg.* 1782
GOODRICH QUALITY THEATERS, *pg.* 289, *pg.* 887
HALL COMMUNICATIONS INC., *pg.* 290, *pg.* 367
HARPO, INC., *pg.* 290, *pg.* 576
THE HEARST CORPORATION, *pg.* 1649, *pg.* 1239
IDEASTREAM, *pg.* 292, *pg.* 1431
INNER CITY BROADCASTING CORPORATION, *pg.* 292, *pg.* 1243
KCRG TV STATION, *pg.* 293, *pg.* 702
KLOS-FM RADIO, LLC, *pg.* 294, *pg.* 134
KPWR-FM, *pg.* 294, *pg.* 52
KQED INC., *pg.* 294, *pg.* 220
KSHE-FM, *pg.* 295, *pg.* 999
KSTP-FM, LLC, *pg.* 295, *pg.* 962
LARRY H. MILLER GROUP OF COMPANIES, *pg.* 182, *pg.* 1762
LIBERMAN BROADCASTING CORPORATION, *pg.* 296, *pg.* 52
LIVE365, INC., *pg.* 1264, *pg.* 89
MILLENNIUM RADIO NEW JERSEY, *pg.* 298, *pg.* 1126
NATIONAL AMUSEMENTS, INC., *pg.* 299, *pg.* 840
NETWORK CHICAGO, *pg.* 302, *pg.* 585
NEW DIMENSIONS WORLD BROADCASTING NETWORK, *pg.* 302, *pg.* 298
THE NEW YORK TIMES, *pg.* 1668, *pg.* 1270
THE NEW YORK TIMES COMPANY, *pg.* 1668, *pg.* 1270
NEWS CORPORATION, *pg.* 1669, *pg.* 1271
PAMAL BROADCASTING LTD., *pg.* 304, *pg.* 1173
PANDORA MEDIA INC., *pg.* 1273, *pg.* 172
PIKES PEAK TELEVISION INC., *pg.* 304, *pg.* 315
PRESS COMMUNICATIONS, LLC, *pg.* 305, *pg.* 1090
RADIO ONE, INC., *pg.* 305, *pg.* 778
RENDA BROADCASTING CORPORATION, *pg.* 306, *pg.* 1581
SALEM MEDIA GROUP, INC., *pg.* 307, *pg.* 57
SANDUSKY NEWSPAPERS INC., *pg.* 1683, *pg.* 1472
SARKES TARZIAN INC., *pg.* 307, *pg.* 674
SIRIUS CANADA INC., *pg.* 308, *pg.* 1943
SIRIUS XM HOLDINGS INC., *pg.* 308, *pg.* 1292
SOUTH CAROLINA EDUCATIONAL TELEVISION COMMISSION, *pg.* 310, *pg.* 1614
SOUTH CENTRAL COMMUNICATIONS CORPORATION, *pg.* 310, *pg.* 679
SPANISH BROADCASTING SYSTEM INC., *pg.* 310, *pg.* 446
SUNRISE BROADCASTING OF NEW YORK, INC., *pg.* 311, *pg.* 1184
TALK RADIO NETWORK, *pg.* 311, *pg.* 1497
TIMES-SHAMROCK, INC., *pg.* 313, *pg.* 1586
TOWNSQUARE MEDIA, INC., *pg.* 313, *pg.* 350
TRANS WORLD RADIO INC., *pg.* 313, *pg.* 1361
TRIBUNE MEDIA COMPANY, *pg.* 1696, *pg.* 592
UNIVISION COMMUNICATIONS INC., *pg.* 683, *pg.* 1307
VERSTANDIG BROADCASTING, *pg.* 316, *pg.* 1784
WABC-TV INC., *pg.* 317, *pg.* 1312
THE WALT DISNEY COMPANY, *pg.* 317, *pg.* 52
WASHINGTON EDUCATIONAL TELECOMMUNICATIONS ASSOCIATION, *pg.* 320, *pg.* 1775
WEGENER CORPORATION, *pg.* 687, *pg.* 533
WGBR-AM, *pg.* 321, *pg.* 1373
WHYY INC., *pg.* 321, *pg.* 1572
WISCONSIN EDUCATIONAL COMMUNICATIONS BOARD, *pg.* 321, *pg.* 1868
WJR-AM RADIO, *pg.* 322, *pg.* 884
WMAL-AM RADIO, *pg.* 322, *pg.* 408
WORD OF LIFE FELLOWSHIP, INC., *pg.* 161, *pg.* 1341
WPLJ RADIO, LLC, *pg.* 322, *pg.* 1316
WQDR-FM, *pg.* 323, *pg.* 1389
WQXR FM, *pg.* 595, *pg.* 1316
WRQX-FM RADIO, *pg.* 323, *pg.* 408
WTHI TV, *pg.* 323, *pg.* 698

4833 - Television Broadcasting Stations

ABC, INC., *pg.* 268, *pg.* 1185
ACME COMMUNICATIONS, INC., *pg.* 268, *pg.* 260
AT&T ALASCOM, *pg.* 619, *pg.* 10
BET HOLDINGS LLC, *pg.* 271, *pg.* 396
THE CANADIAN BROADCASTING CORPORATION, *pg.* 272, *pg.* 1931
CAPITOL BROADCASTING COMPANY, INC., *pg.* 272, *pg.* 1386
THE CARTOON NETWORK, *pg.* 273, *pg.* 492
CBS BROADCASTING INC., *pg.* 273, *pg.* 1210
CBS CORPORATION, *pg.* 273, *pg.* 1210
CBS ENTERTAINMENT DIVISION, *pg.* 274, *pg.* 1211
CBS SPORTS DIVISION, *pg.* 274, *pg.* 1211
THE CHRISTIAN BROADCASTING NETWORK INC., *pg.* 275, *pg.* 1810
CLOVIS NEWS JOURNAL, *pg.* 1628, *pg.* 1135
COMCAST SPORTSNET, *pg.* 278, *pg.* 1562
COMMUNITY TELEVISION FOUNDATION OF SOUTH FLORIDA, INC., *pg.* 278, *pg.* 441
COMMUNITY TELEVISION OF SOUTHERN CALIFORNIA, *pg.* 279, *pg.* 51
CONNECTICUT PUBLIC BROADCASTING CORP., *pg.* 279, *pg.* 351
CORUS ENTERTAINMENT INC., *pg.* 279, *pg.* 1937
CTV INC., *pg.* 280, *pg.* 1937
THE CW TELEVISION NETWORK, *pg.* 632, *pg.* 52
CWK NETWORK, INC., *pg.* 281, *pg.* 503
DETROIT PUBLIC TV, *pg.* 281, *pg.* 880
DICK CLARK PRODUCTIONS, INC., *pg.* 281, *pg.* 273
THE DISCOVERY CHANNEL, *pg.* 282, *pg.* 1933
THE DISPATCH PRINTING COMPANY, *pg.* 1636, *pg.* 1439
DIVERSIFIED COMMUNICATIONS, *pg.* 284, *pg.* 751
EMMIS COMMUNICATIONS CORPORATION, *pg.* 285, *pg.* 685
ENTRAVISION COMMUNICATIONS CORPORATION, *pg.* 285, *pg.* 273
EPIX, *pg.* 285, *pg.* 1228
THE E.W. SCRIPPS COMPANY, *pg.* 1639, *pg.* 1412
FLORIDA WEST COAST PUBLIC BROADCASTING, INC., *pg.* 287, *pg.* 473
FOX BROADCASTING COMPANY, *pg.* 287, *pg.* 130
FOX SPORTS NET, *pg.* 288, *pg.* 131
FOX TELEVISION STATIONS INC., *pg.* 288, *pg.* 131
FREEDOM COMMUNICATIONS, INC., *pg.* 1643, *pg.* 110
GANNETT CO., INC., *pg.* 289, *pg.* 1681
GANNETT CO., INC., *pg.* 1643, *pg.* 1790
GOLF CHANNEL, *pg.* 551, *pg.* 454
GRAHAM HOLDINGS COMPANY, *pg.* 1645, *pg.* 1773
GRANITE BROADCASTING CORPORATION, *pg.* 289, *pg.* 1236
GRAY TELEVISION, INC., *pg.* 289, *pg.* 509
HARPO, INC., *pg.* 290, *pg.* 576
THE HEARST CORPORATION, *pg.* 1649, *pg.* 1239
HLN, *pg.* 290, *pg.* 510
HSN, INC., *pg.* 291, *pg.* 462
HUBBARD BROADCASTING, INC., *pg.* 291, *pg.* 961
IAC/INTERACTIVECORP, *pg.* 292, *pg.* 1242
IDEASTREAM, *pg.* 292, *pg.* 1431
ION MEDIA NETWORKS, INC., *pg.* 293, *pg.* 479
JOURNAL MEDIA GROUP, INC., *pg.* 1655, *pg.* 1876
KCNC-TV, *pg.* 293, *pg.* 320
KCRA-TV, *pg.* 293, *pg.* 196
KCRG TV STATION, *pg.* 293, *pg.* 702
KENS-TV, *pg.* 294, *pg.* 1741
KFDM-TV, *pg.* 294, *pg.* 1668
KFOR-TV, *pg.* 294, *pg.* 1486
KGO TELEVISION, INC., *pg.* 294, *pg.* 220
KHON-TV, *pg.* 294, *pg.* 544
KHOU-TV, INC., *pg.* 294, *pg.* 1709
KJRH, *pg.* 294, *pg.* 1490
KNXV-TV, *pg.* 294, *pg.* 17
KOB-TV, INC., *pg.* 294, *pg.* 1135
KQED INC., *pg.* 294, *pg.* 220
KRQE-TV, *pg.* 294, *pg.* 1135
KSCI-TV, *pg.* 295, *pg.* 134
KSTC-TV CHANNEL 45, *pg.* 295, *pg.* 962
KSTP-TV, LLC, *pg.* 295, *pg.* 962
KTRK TELEVISION, INC., *pg.* 295, *pg.* 1709
KTVE-TV, *pg.* 295, *pg.* 748
KTVI-TV, *pg.* 295, *pg.* 999
KTVK-TV, INC., *pg.* 295, *pg.* 17
KTVL-TV, *pg.* 295, *pg.* 1499
KTVT BROADCASTING COMPANY LP, *pg.* 295, *pg.* 1683
KVUE-TV, *pg.* 295, *pg.* 1663
KWWL-TV, *pg.* 295, *pg.* 712
LANDMARK MEDIA ENTERPRISES LLC, *pg.* 295, *pg.* 1797
LARRY H. MILLER GROUP OF COMPANIES, *pg.* 182, *pg.* 1762
LIONS GATE ENTERTAINMENT CORP., *pg.* 296, *pg.* 274
LOUISIANA PUBLIC BROADCASTING, *pg.* 296, *pg.* 742
LOUISIANA TELEVISION BROADCASTING CORPORATION, *pg.* 296, *pg.* 742
MADISON SQUARE GARDEN NETWORK, *pg.* 297, *pg.* 1255
MAINE PUBLIC BROADCASTING NETWORK, *pg.* 297, *pg.* 751
MARTHA STEWART LIVING OMNIMEDIA, INC., *pg.* 1661, *pg.* 1256
MEDIA GENERAL, *pg.* 297, *pg.* 1607
MEDIA GENERAL, INC., *pg.* 297, *pg.* 1803
MEREDITH CORPORATION, *pg.* 1663, *pg.* 705
MORRIS MULTIMEDIA, INC., *pg.* 1666, *pg.* 540
MOUNT MANSFIELD TELEVISION INC., *pg.* 298, *pg.* 1768
NATIONAL AMUSEMENTS, INC., *pg.* 299, *pg.* 840
NATIONAL GEOGRAPHIC CHANNEL, *pg.* 299, *pg.* 402
NBC NEWS, *pg.* 300, *pg.* 1265
NBC UNIVERSAL, INC., *pg.* 300, *pg.* 1266
NBC UNIVERSAL TELEVISION NETWORKS GROUP, *pg.* 302, *pg.* 1267
NETWORK CHICAGO, *pg.* 302, *pg.* 585
NEULION, INC., *pg.* 302, *pg.* 1321
NEWS CORPORATION, *pg.* 1669, *pg.* 1271
NEWSCHANNEL 5, *pg.* 303, *pg.* 1653
NEXSTAR BROADCASTING, *pg.* 303, *pg.* 93
NEXSTAR BROADCASTING GROUP, INC., *pg.* 303, *pg.* 1723
NTN BUZZTIME, INC., *pg.* 659, *pg.* 60

NY 1 NEWS, pg. 303, pg. 1273
PIKES PEAK TELEVISION INC., pg. 304, pg. 315
PILOT MEDIA, pg. 1677, pg. 1797
PRESS COMMUNICATIONS, LLC, pg. 305, pg. 1090
PROGRAM PARTNERS, INC., pg. 305, pg. 301
PUBLIC BROADCASTING SERVICE, pg. 305, pg. 1774
RADIO ONE, INC., pg. 305, pg. 778
RENTPATH, INC., pg. 1680, pg. 538
ROGERS COMMUNICATIONS INC., pg. 668, pg. 1942
ROVI CORPORATION, pg. 463, pg. 269
SARKES TARZIAN INC., pg. 307, pg. 674
SHAW MEDIA INC., pg. 308, pg. 1943
SINCLAIR BROADCAST GROUP, INC., pg. 308, pg. 773
SOUTH CAROLINA EDUCATIONAL TELEVISION COMMISSION, pg. 310, pg. 1614
SOUTH CENTRAL COMMUNICATIONS CORPORATION, pg. 310, pg. 679
SPORTSNET NEW YORK, LLC, pg. 585, pg. 1295
SPORTVISION, INC., pg. 1282, pg. 590
STARZ ENTERTAINMENT, LLC, pg. 310, pg. 327
THE STREET, INC., pg. 1283, pg. 1296
SUNBEAM TELEVISION CORP., pg. 311, pg. 447
TELEMUNDO NETWORK INC., pg. 311, pg. 430
TRAVEL CHANNEL LLC, pg. 313, pg. 766
TRIBUNE MEDIA COMPANY, pg. 1696, pg. 592
TRUTV, pg. 314, pg. 1305
TURNER BROADCASTING SYSTEM, INC., pg. 314, pg. 521
TVA GROUP, INC., pg. 315, pg. 1957
TWIN CITIES PUBLIC TELEVISION, INC., pg. 315, pg. 964
UNIVISION COMMUNICATIONS INC., pg. 683, pg. 1307
VIACOM INC., pg. 316, pg. 1310
WABC-TV INC., pg. 317, pg. 1312
THE WALT DISNEY COMPANY, pg. 317, pg. 52
WASHINGTON EDUCATIONAL TELECOMMUNICATIONS ASSOCIATION, pg. 320, pg. 1775
WBNS TELEVISION, pg. 320, pg. 1444
WCCO-TV, pg. 591, pg. 946
WCPO-TV, pg. 320, pg. 1427
WDIO-TV, pg. 320, pg. 921
WEIGEL BROADCASTING CO., pg. 320, pg. 595
WEWS-TV, pg. 320, pg. 1437
WFAA-TV, pg. 320, pg. 1690
WFOR-TV, pg. 320, pg. 447
WGME, INC., pg. 321, pg. 752
WHAM-TV, pg. 321, pg. 1338
WHBF-TV, pg. 321, pg. 654
WHEC-TV LLC, pg. 321, pg. 1338
WHYY INC., pg. 321, pg. 1572
WICD-TV, pg. 321, pg. 562
WISCONSIN EDUCATIONAL COMMUNICATIONS BOARD, pg. 321, pg. 1868
WJBF-TV, pg. 321, pg. 525
WJLA & TBD, pg. 322, pg. 1775
WJZ-TV, pg. 322, pg. 760
WLNE-TV, pg. 322, pg. 1608
WLS TELEVISION, INC., pg. 322, pg. 596
WLUK-TV, pg. 322, pg. 1860
WMAR-TV, pg. 322, pg. 760
WNET.ORG, pg. 322, pg. 1315
WNYT-TV, pg. 322, pg. 1137
WPEC-TV, pg. 322, pg. 479
WPIX, INC., pg. 322, pg. 1316
WPVI-TV INC., pg. 323, pg. 1572
WRGB-TV, pg. 323, pg. 1341
WSAZ-TV, pg. 323, pg. 1850
WTVC-TV, pg. 323, pg. 1630
WTVD-TV INC., pg. 323, pg. 1372
WTVG 13ABC, pg. 323, pg. 1477
WTWC NBC 40, pg. 323, pg. 470
WVEC-TELEVISION, INC., pg. 323, pg. 1798
WWL-TV, INC., pg. 323, pg. 747
WWMT-TV, pg. 323, pg. 895
WXYZ-TV, pg. 323, pg. 908
WZVN TV ABC 7, pg. 323, pg. 428

4841 - Cable & other Pay Television Services

A&E TELEVISION NETWORKS, LLC, pg. 267, pg. 1185
ABC CABLE NETWORKS GROUP, pg. 268, pg. 51
ABC FAMILY CHANNEL, pg. 268, pg. 51
AMC NETWORKS INC., pg. 269, pg. 1189
ANIMAL PLANET, LLC, pg. 270, pg. 777
BET HOLDINGS LLC, pg. 271, pg. 396
BIO, pg. 1621, pg. 1202
BLOCK COMMUNICATIONS, INC., pg. 1621, pg. 1476
BRAVO MEDIA LLC, pg. 271, pg. 1206
BRIGHT HOUSE NETWORKS LLC, pg. 272, pg. 461
THE CABLE CENTER, pg. 535, pg. 317
CABLE IN THE CLASSROOM, pg. 272, pg. 397
CABLE NEWS NETWORK LP, pg. 1624, pg. 1208
CABLEVISION SYSTEMS CORPORATION, pg. 272, pg. 1141
CHARTER COMMUNICATIONS, INC., pg. 274, pg. 372
CHICAGOLAND TELEVISION NEWS, INC., pg. 275, pg. 570
CNBC, pg. 275, pg. 1059
COMCAST CABLE COMMUNICATIONS, INC., pg. 276, pg. 1560
COMCAST CORPORATION, pg. 276, pg. 1560
COMEDY PARTNERS, pg. 278, pg. 1216
COUNTRY MUSIC TELEVISION, INC., pg. 279, pg. 1649
COX COMMUNICATIONS, INC., pg. 279, pg. 501
CROWN MEDIA HOLDINGS INC., pg. 280, pg. 281
DIRECTV GROUP HOLDINGS, LLC, pg. 281, pg. 79
DISCOVERY COMMUNICATIONS, INC., pg. 282, pg. 777
DISH NETWORK CORPORATION, pg. 283, pg. 325
DIVERSIFIED COMMUNICATIONS, pg. 284, pg. 751
EAGLE COMMUNICATIONS INC., pg. 284, pg. 715
ESPN, INC., pg. 285, pg. 340
FOOD NETWORK, pg. 287, pg. 1231
FRONTIER COMMUNICATIONS CORPORATION, pg. 1871, pg. 362
FUSE NETWORKS LLC, pg. 288, pg. 1233
FX NETWORKS, LLC, pg. 288, pg. 131
G4 MEDIA, INC., pg. 289, pg. 132
GANNETT CO., INC., pg. 289, pg. 1681
GENERAL COMMUNICATION, INC., pg. 1871, pg. 10
GOLF CHANNEL, pg. 551, pg. 454
GRANDE COMMUNICATIONS NETWORKS LLC, pg. 1871, pg. 1744
THE HEARST CORPORATION, pg. 1649, pg. 1239
HERE MEDIA INC., pg. 290, pg. 132
THE HISTORY CHANNEL, pg. 290, pg. 1240
HOME & GARDEN TELEVISION, pg. 290, pg. 1637
HOME BOX OFFICE, INC., pg. 290, pg. 1240
HSN, INC., pg. 291, pg. 462
INNER CITY BROADCASTING CORPORATION, pg. 292, pg. 1243
THE JIM HENSON COMPANY, pg. 293, pg. 103
LIFETIME ENTERTAINMENT SERVICES LLC, pg. 296, pg. 1251
MEDIACOM COMMUNICATIONS CORPORATION, pg. 653, pg. 1182
MEDIACOM LLC, pg. 297, pg. 1182
MIDCONTINENT COMMUNICATIONS CO., pg. 298, pg. 1625
MTV NETWORKS COMPANY, pg. 298, pg. 1262
MTVN VIDEO HITS INC., pg. 299, pg. 1263
NATIONAL AMUSEMENTS, INC., pg. 299, pg. 840
NBC SPORTS NETWORK, pg. 300, pg. 375
NBC UNIVERSAL, INC., pg. 300, pg. 1266
NEW FRONTIER MEDIA, INC., pg. 302, pg. 311
NICKELODEON DIRECT INC., pg. 303, pg. 1271
THE OUTDOOR CHANNEL, pg. 303, pg. 291
OXYGEN MEDIA LLC, pg. 303, pg. 1275
QUEBECOR MEDIA INC., pg. 1679, pg. 1956
RCN TELECOM SERVICES, LLC., pg. 306, pg. 1785
ROGERS COMMUNICATIONS INC., pg. 668, pg. 1942
ROVI CORPORATION, pg. 463, pg. 269
SHAW COMMUNICATIONS INC., pg. 307, pg. 1904
SHOWTIME NETWORKS INC., pg. 308, pg. 1291
SONIFI SOLUTIONS, pg. 1281, pg. 1625
SPIKE TV, pg. 310, pg. 1295
SPORTSNET NEW YORK, LLC, pg. 585, pg. 1295
SRT COMMUNICATIONS INC., pg. 1282, pg. 1398
STARZ ENTERTAINMENT, LLC, pg. 310, pg. 327
SYFY, pg. 311, pg. 1297
TIME WARNER CABLE INC., pg. 312, pg. 1301
TIME WARNER INC., pg. 312, pg. 1302
TIVO INC., pg. 313, pg. 251
TURNER BROADCASTING SYSTEM, INC., pg. 314, pg. 521
UNIVISION COMMUNICATIONS INC., pg. 683, pg. 1307
USA NETWORKS, pg. 315, pg. 1308
VIACOM INC., pg. 316, pg. 1310
VIDEOTRON LTD., pg. 317, pg. 1957
WARNER BROS. ENTERTAINMENT INC., pg. 319, pg. 54
THE WEATHER CHANNEL LLC, pg. 320, pg. 523
YANKEES ENTERTAINMENT & SPORTS NETWORK, LLC, pg. 324, pg. 1316
YOUTOO TECHNOLOGIES, pg. 324, pg. 1724

4911 - Electric Services

ACTIVE POWER, INC., pg. 1310, pg. 1660
AEP OHIO, pg. 1933, pg. 1454
ALABAMA POWER COMPANY, pg. 1933, pg. 1
ALLETE, INC., pg. 1933, pg. 921
ALLIANT ENERGY CORPORATION, pg. 1933, pg. 1864
AMEREN CORPORATION, pg. 1934, pg. 990
AMEREN ILLINOIS COMPANY, pg. 1934, pg. 650
AMERICAN DG ENERGY INC., pg. 1068, pg. 850
AMERICAN ELECTRIC POWER COMPANY, INC., pg. 1934, pg. 1437
AMERICAN ELECTRIC POWER SERVICE CORPORATION, pg. 1934, pg. 1437
AMETEK PROGRAMMABLE POWER, INC., pg. 616, pg. 200
ARIZONA PUBLIC SERVICE COMPANY, pg. 1935, pg. 14
ATCO LTD., pg. 1935, pg. 1902
ATMOS ENERGY CORPORATION, pg. 1935, pg. 1675
AVISTA CORPORATION, pg. 1935, pg. 1843
BABCOCK & WILCOX POWER GENERATION GROUP, INC., pg. 1069, pg. 1404
BALTIMORE GAS AND ELECTRIC COMPANY, pg. 1936, pg. 755
BASIN ELECTRIC POWER COOPERATIVE, pg. 1936, pg. 1397
BEACON POWER, LLC, pg. 1936, pg. 848
CALPINE CORPORATION, pg. 1936, pg. 1702
CASS COUNTY ELECTRIC COOPERATIVE, INC., pg. 1937, pg. 1397
CENTRAL HUDSON GAS & ELECTRIC CORPORATION, pg. 1937, pg. 1324
CENTRAL MAINE POWER COMPANY, pg. 1937, pg. 749
CH ENERGY GROUP, INC., pg. 973, pg. 1324
CLECO CORPORATION, pg. 1937, pg. 748
CMS ENERGY CORPORATION, pg. 1937, pg. 893
CONSOLIDATED EDISON, INC., pg. 1938, pg. 1218
CONSTELLATION, pg. 1938, pg. 373
CONSTELLATION ENERGY RESOURCES, LLC, pg. 1938, pg. 756
CONSUMERS ENERGY COMPANY, pg. 1938, pg. 893
CPS ENERGY, pg. 1939, pg. 1739
DAIRYLAND POWER COOPERATIVE, pg. 1939, pg. 1864
DAKOTA ELECTRIC ASSOCIATION, pg. 1939, pg. 925
DOMINION RESOURCES, INC., pg. 1939, pg. 1802
DOMINION VIRGINIA POWER, pg. 1939, pg. 1802
DPL INC., pg. 1939, pg. 1445
DTE ENERGY COMPANY, pg. 1940, pg. 880
DUKE ENERGY INDIANA, INC., pg. 1940, pg. 696
DUKE ENERGY CORPORATION, pg. 1940, pg. 1366
DUKE ENERGY PROGRESS, pg. 1940, pg. 462
DUKE ENERGY PROGRESS, pg. 1940, pg. 1387
DUQUESNE LIGHT COMPANY, pg. 1940, pg. 1574
DYNEGY, INC., pg. 976, pg. 1705
EDISON INTERNATIONAL, pg. 1941, pg. 194
THE EMPIRE DISTRICT ELECTRIC COMPANY, pg. 1941, pg. 980
ENERGY FUTURE HOLDINGS CORP., pg. 1941, pg. 1680
ENERNOC, INC., pg. 976, pg. 794
ENTECH SOLAR, INC., pg. 1335, pg. 1694
ENTERGY CORPORATION, pg. 1941, pg. 746
ENTERGY NEW ORLEANS, INC., pg. 1942, pg. 746
EVERSOURCE, pg. 1942, pg. 337
EVERSOURCE, pg. 1942, pg. 1035
EVERSOURCE, pg. 977, pg. 794
EVERSOURCE, pg. 1942, pg. 845
EXELON CORPORATION, pg. 1942, pg. 573
FIRSTENERGY CORP., pg. 1942, pg. 1400
FLORIDA POWER & LIGHT COMPANY, pg. 1943, pg. 435
FLORIDA PUBLIC UTILITIES, pg. 1943, pg. 422
GAINESVILLE REGIONAL UTILITIES INC., pg. 1943, pg. 429
GDF SUEZ ENERGY NORTH AMERICA, INC., pg. 1164, pg. 1706
GEORGIA POWER COMPANY, pg. 1943, pg. 508
GREAT PLAINS ENERGY INCORPORATED, pg. 1944, pg. 983
GREEN MOUNTAIN ENERGY COMPANY, pg. 1944, pg. 1663
GREEN MOUNTAIN POWER CORPORATION, pg. 1944, pg. 1765
GULF POWER COMPANY, pg. 1944, pg. 458
HAWAIIAN ELECTRIC COMPANY, INC., pg. 1944, pg. 544

HOOSIER ENERGY RURAL ELECTRIC COOPERATIVE INC., *pg.* 1944, *pg.* 674
HYDRO-QUEBEC, *pg.* 1944, *pg.* 1955
IDACORP, INC., *pg.* 1944, *pg.* 546
INDIANAPOLIS POWER & LIGHT COMPANY, *pg.* 1945, *pg.* 687
ITC HOLDINGS CORP., *pg.* 1945, *pg.* 903
JERSEY CENTRAL POWER & LIGHT COMPANY, *pg.* 1945, *pg.* 1402
KANSAS CITY POWER & LIGHT COMPANY, *pg.* 1945, *pg.* 985
KENTUCKY UTILITIES COMPANY, *pg.* 1945, *pg.* 730
LG&E AND KU ENERGY LLC, *pg.* 1946, *pg.* 736
LIMONEIRA COMPANY, *pg.* 705, *pg.* 276
LONG ISLAND POWER AUTHORITY, *pg.* 1946, *pg.* 1346
LUFKIN INDUSTRIES, INC., *pg.* 1357, *pg.* 1726
MAGNETEK, INC., *pg.* 1301, *pg.* 1870
MDU RESOURCES GROUP, INC., *pg.* 981, *pg.* 1397
MEMPHIS LIGHT, GAS & WATER, *pg.* 1946, *pg.* 1645
MIDAMERICAN ENERGY HOLDINGS COMPANY, *pg.* 1946, *pg.* 706
NATIONAL GRID USA, *pg.* 1946, *pg.* 852
NEBRASKA PUBLIC POWER DISTRICT, *pg.* 1947, *pg.* 1010
NEW BRUNSWICK POWER CORPORATION, *pg.* 1947, *pg.* 1915
NORTHERN INDIANA PUBLIC SERVICE COMPANY, *pg.* 1947, *pg.* 694
NORTHWESTERN CORPORATION, *pg.* 1947, *pg.* 1625
NORTHWESTERN ENERGY, *pg.* 1947, *pg.* 1008
NRG ENERGY, INC., *pg.* 1366, *pg.* 1112
NRG ENERGY, INC., *pg.* 1948, *pg.* 1712
NV ENERGY, *pg.* 1948, *pg.* 1032
NV ENERGY, INC., *pg.* 1948, *pg.* 1028
OCEAN POWER TECHNOLOGIES, INC., *pg.* 1948, *pg.* 1107
OGE ENERGY CORP., *pg.* 1948, *pg.* 1486
OMAHA PUBLIC POWER DISTRICT, *pg.* 1948, *pg.* 1017
ORANGE & ROCKLAND UTILITIES, INC., *pg.* 1949, *pg.* 1321
P2 SOLAR INC., *pg.* 661, *pg.* 1909
PACIFIC ETHANOL, INC., *pg.* 982, *pg.* 197
PACIFICORP, *pg.* 1949, *pg.* 1504
PECO ENERGY COMPANY, *pg.* 1949, *pg.* 1568
PEPCO HOLDINGS, INC., *pg.* 1949, *pg.* 404
PG&E CORPORATION, *pg.* 1949, *pg.* 224
PNM RESOURCES, INC., *pg.* 1949, *pg.* 1135
PORTLAND GENERAL ELECTRIC COMPANY, *pg.* 1950, *pg.* 1505
POTOMAC ELECTRIC POWER COMPANY, *pg.* 1950, *pg.* 404
PPL CORPORATION, *pg.* 1950, *pg.* 1514
PREMIER POWER RENEWABLE ENERGY, INC., *pg.* 1075, *pg.* 78
PUBLIC SERVICE COMPANY OF OKLAHOMA, *pg.* 1950, *pg.* 1443
PUBLIC SERVICE ENTERPRISE GROUP INCORPORATED, *pg.* 1950, *pg.* 1097
PUGET ENERGY, INC., *pg.* 1950, *pg.* 1816
RGS ENERGY, *pg.* 1951, *pg.* 1322
SALT RIVER PROJECT, *pg.* 707, *pg.* 26
SANTEE COOPER, *pg.* 1951, *pg.* 1620
SASKPOWER, *pg.* 1951, *pg.* 1962
SCANA CORPORATION, *pg.* 1951, *pg.* 1612
SEATTLE CITY LIGHT, *pg.* 1951, *pg.* 1839
SEMPRA ENERGY, *pg.* 1951, *pg.* 209
SOUTHERN CALIFORNIA EDISON COMPANY, *pg.* 1952, *pg.* 194
SOUTHERN COMPANY, *pg.* 1952, *pg.* 520
SUNPOWER CORPORATION, *pg.* 1952, *pg.* 250
SYNACOR, INC., *pg.* 479, *pg.* 1380
TAMPA ELECTRIC COMPANY, *pg.* 1952, *pg.* 476
TRANSALTA CORPORATION, *pg.* 1953, *pg.* 1905
TUCSON ELECTRIC POWER COMPANY, *pg.* 1953, *pg.* 27
TXU ENERGY RETAIL COMPANY LLC, *pg.* 1953, *pg.* 1690
UGI CORPORATION, *pg.* 1953, *pg.* 1544
UIL HOLDINGS CORPORATION, *pg.* 1953, *pg.* 359
UNS ENERGY CORPORATION, *pg.* 1954, *pg.* 27
VERENDRYE ELECTRIC COOPERATIVE, *pg.* 1954, *pg.* 1398
WASHINGTON GAS LIGHT CO., *pg.* 1954, *pg.* 407
WEC ENERGY GROUP, INC., *pg.* 1954, *pg.* 1881
WESTMORELAND COAL COMPANY, *pg.* 1955, *pg.* 328
XCEL ENERGY INC., *pg.* 1955, *pg.* 946

4922 - Natural Gas Transmission

ATMOS ENERGY CORPORATION, *pg.* 1935, *pg.* 1675
BLUE DOLPHIN ENERGY COMPANY, *pg.* 972, *pg.* 1701
CROSSTEX ENERGY, L.P., *pg.* 975, *pg.* 1678
DEVON ENERGY CORPORATION, *pg.* 976, *pg.* 1704
DEVON ENERGY CORPORATION, *pg.* 975, *pg.* 1485
DOMINION EAST OHIO ENERGY, *pg.* 1939, *pg.* 1801
DUKE ENERGY CORPORATION, *pg.* 1940, *pg.* 1366
ENERGY TRANSFER EQUITY, L.P., *pg.* 1941, *pg.* 1680
ENTERPRISE PRODUCTS PARTNERS L.P., *pg.* 976, *pg.* 1705
EVERSOURCE, *pg.* 977, *pg.* 794
EXXON MOBIL CORPORATION, *pg.* 977, *pg.* 1718
KINDER MORGAN, *pg.* 1945, *pg.* 1709
LACLEDE GAS COMPANY, *pg.* 1945, *pg.* 999
THE LACLEDE GROUP, INC., *pg.* 980, *pg.* 999
MARATHON OIL CORPORATION, *pg.* 981, *pg.* 1710
OGE ENERGY CORP., *pg.* 1948, *pg.* 1486
ONEOK, INC., *pg.* 982, *pg.* 1490
PLAINS ALL AMERICAN PIPELINE, L.P., *pg.* 983, *pg.* 1712
SOUTHERN CALIFORNIA GAS COMPANY, *pg.* 1952, *pg.* 140
SOUTHWEST GAS CORPORATION, *pg.* 984, *pg.* 1029
TRANSCANADA CORPORATION, *pg.* 1953, *pg.* 1905
THE WILLIAMS COMPANIES, INC., *pg.* 987, *pg.* 1491

4924 - Natural Gas Distribution

ACTIVE POWER, INC., *pg.* 1310, *pg.* 1660
AEP OHIO, *pg.* 1933, *pg.* 1454
AGL RESOURCES INC., *pg.* 1933, *pg.* 487
ALABAMA GAS CORPORATION, *pg.* 1933, *pg.* 1
ALABAMA POWER COMPANY, *pg.* 1933, *pg.* 1
ALLETE, INC., *pg.* 1933, *pg.* 921
ALLIANT ENERGY CORPORATION, *pg.* 1933, *pg.* 1864
AMEREN CORPORATION, *pg.* 1934, *pg.* 990
AMEREN ILLINOIS COMPANY, *pg.* 1934, *pg.* 650
AMERICAN DG ENERGY INC., *pg.* 1068, *pg.* 850
AMERICAN ELECTRIC POWER COMPANY, INC., *pg.* 1934, *pg.* 1437
AMERICAN ELECTRIC POWER SERVICE CORPORATION, *pg.* 1934, *pg.* 1437
AMETEK PROGRAMMABLE POWER, INC., *pg.* 616, *pg.* 200
ANADARKO PETROLEUM CORPORATION, *pg.* 971, *pg.* 1746
ARIZONA PUBLIC SERVICE COMPANY, *pg.* 1935, *pg.* 14
ATCO LTD., *pg.* 1935, *pg.* 1902
ATMOS ENERGY CORPORATION, *pg.* 1935, *pg.* 1675
AVISTA CORPORATION, *pg.* 1935, *pg.* 1843
BABCOCK & WILCOX POWER GENERATION GROUP, INC., *pg.* 1069, *pg.* 1404
BALTIMORE GAS AND ELECTRIC COMPANY, *pg.* 1936, *pg.* 755
BASIN ELECTRIC POWER COOPERATIVE, *pg.* 1936, *pg.* 1397
BEACON POWER, LLC, *pg.* 1936, *pg.* 848
CALPINE CORPORATION, *pg.* 1936, *pg.* 1702
CASS COUNTY ELECTRIC COOPERATIVE, INC., *pg.* 1937, *pg.* 1397
CENTRAL HUDSON GAS & ELECTRIC CORPORATION, *pg.* 1937, *pg.* 1324
CENTRAL MAINE POWER COMPANY, *pg.* 1937, *pg.* 749
CH ENERGY GROUP, INC., *pg.* 973, *pg.* 1324
CHESAPEAKE UTILITIES CORPORATION, *pg.* 1937, *pg.* 387
CITIZENS ENERGY GROUP, *pg.* 1937, *pg.* 683
CLEAN ENERGY FUELS CORP., *pg.* 974, *pg.* 165
CLECO CORPORATION, *pg.* 1937, *pg.* 748
CMS ENERGY CORPORATION, *pg.* 1937, *pg.* 893
COLUMBIA GAS OF OHIO, INC., *pg.* 1938, *pg.* 1438
CONOCOPHILLIPS, *pg.* 975, *pg.* 1703
CONSOLIDATED EDISON, INC., *pg.* 1938, *pg.* 1218
CONSTELLATION, *pg.* 1938, *pg.* 373
CONSTELLATION ENERGY RESOURCES, LLC, *pg.* 1938, *pg.* 756
CONSUMERS ENERGY COMPANY, *pg.* 1938, *pg.* 893
CPS ENERGY, *pg.* 1939, *pg.* 1739
DAIRYLAND POWER COOPERATIVE, *pg.* 1939, *pg.* 1864
DAKOTA ELECTRIC ASSOCIATION, *pg.* 1939, *pg.* 925
DOMINION EAST OHIO ENERGY, *pg.* 1939, *pg.* 1801
DOMINION RESOURCES, INC., *pg.* 1939, *pg.* 1802
DOMINION VIRGINIA POWER, *pg.* 1939, *pg.* 1802
DPL INC., *pg.* 1939, *pg.* 1445
DTE ENERGY COMPANY, *pg.* 1940, *pg.* 880
DUKE ENERGY INDIANA, INC., *pg.* 1940, *pg.* 696
DUKE ENERGY CORPORATION, *pg.* 1940, *pg.* 1366
DUKE ENERGY PROGRESS, *pg.* 1940, *pg.* 462
DUKE ENERGY PROGRESS, *pg.* 1940, *pg.* 1387
DUQUESNE LIGHT COMPANY, *pg.* 1940, *pg.* 1574
DYNEGY, INC., *pg.* 976, *pg.* 1705
EDISON INTERNATIONAL, *pg.* 1941, *pg.* 194
THE EMPIRE DISTRICT ELECTRIC COMPANY, *pg.* 1941, *pg.* 980
ENERGEN CORPORATION, *pg.* 1941, *pg.* 2
ENERGY FUTURE HOLDINGS CORP., *pg.* 1941, *pg.* 1680
ENERGY TRANSFER EQUITY, L.P., *pg.* 1941, *pg.* 1680
ENERNOC, INC., *pg.* 976, *pg.* 794
ENTECH SOLAR, INC., *pg.* 1335, *pg.* 1694
ENTERGY CORPORATION, *pg.* 1941, *pg.* 746
ENTERGY NEW ORLEANS, INC., *pg.* 1942, *pg.* 746
ENTERPRISE PRODUCTS PARTNERS L.P., *pg.* 976, *pg.* 1705
EVERSOURCE, *pg.* 1942, *pg.* 337
EVERSOURCE, *pg.* 1942, *pg.* 1035
EVERSOURCE, *pg.* 977, *pg.* 794
EVERSOURCE, *pg.* 1942, *pg.* 845
EXELON CORPORATION, *pg.* 1942, *pg.* 573
EXXON MOBIL CORPORATION, *pg.* 977, *pg.* 1718
FERRELLGAS PARTNERS, L.P., *pg.* 977, *pg.* 718
FIRSTENERGY CORP., *pg.* 1942, *pg.* 1400
FLORIDA POWER & LIGHT COMPANY, *pg.* 1943, *pg.* 435
FLORIDA PUBLIC UTILITIES, *pg.* 1943, *pg.* 422
GAINESVILLE REGIONAL UTILITIES INC., *pg.* 1943, *pg.* 429
THE GAS COMPANY LLC, *pg.* 1943, *pg.* 543
GAZ METRO LIMITED PARTNERSHIP, *pg.* 1943, *pg.* 1955
GDF SUEZ ENERGY NORTH AMERICA, INC., *pg.* 1164, *pg.* 1706
GEORGIA POWER COMPANY, *pg.* 1943, *pg.* 508
GREAT PLAINS ENERGY INCORPORATED, *pg.* 1944, *pg.* 983
GREEN MOUNTAIN ENERGY COMPANY, *pg.* 1944, *pg.* 1663
GREEN MOUNTAIN POWER CORPORATION, *pg.* 1944, *pg.* 1765
GULF POWER COMPANY, *pg.* 1944, *pg.* 458
HAWAIIAN ELECTRIC COMPANY, INC., *pg.* 1944, *pg.* 544
HESS CORPORATION, *pg.* 979, *pg.* 1240
HKN, INC., *pg.* 979, *pg.* 1745
HOOSIER ENERGY RURAL ELECTRIC COOPERATIVE INC., *pg.* 1944, *pg.* 674
HYDRO-QUEBEC, *pg.* 1944, *pg.* 1955
IDACORP, INC., *pg.* 1944, *pg.* 546
INDIANAPOLIS POWER & LIGHT COMPANY, *pg.* 1945, *pg.* 687
INTERMOUNTAIN GAS COMPANY, *pg.* 1945, *pg.* 547
JERSEY CENTRAL POWER & LIGHT COMPANY, *pg.* 1945, *pg.* 1402
KANSAS CITY POWER & LIGHT COMPANY, *pg.* 1945, *pg.* 985
KENTUCKY UTILITIES COMPANY, *pg.* 1945, *pg.* 730
LACLEDE GAS COMPANY, *pg.* 1945, *pg.* 999
THE LACLEDE GROUP, INC., *pg.* 980, *pg.* 999
LG&E AND KU ENERGY LLC, *pg.* 1946, *pg.* 736
LIMONEIRA COMPANY, *pg.* 705, *pg.* 276
LONG ISLAND POWER AUTHORITY, *pg.* 1946, *pg.* 1346
LUFKIN INDUSTRIES, INC., *pg.* 1357, *pg.* 1726
MAGNETEK, INC., *pg.* 1301, *pg.* 1870
MARKWEST ENERGY PARTNERS, L.P., *pg.* 981, *pg.* 321
MDU RESOURCES GROUP, INC., *pg.* 981, *pg.* 1397
MEMPHIS LIGHT, GAS & WATER, *pg.* 1946, *pg.* 1645
MIDAMERICAN ENERGY HOLDINGS COMPANY, *pg.* 1946, *pg.* 706
NATIONAL FUEL GAS COMPANY, *pg.* 982, *pg.* 1355
NATIONAL FUEL GAS DISTRIBUTION CORP., *pg.* 1946, *pg.* 1355
NATIONAL GRID USA, *pg.* 1946, *pg.* 852
NEBRASKA PUBLIC POWER DISTRICT, *pg.* 1947, *pg.* 1010
NEW BRUNSWICK POWER CORPORATION, *pg.* 1947, *pg.* 1915
NORTHERN ILLINOIS GAS COMPANY, *pg.* 1947, *pg.* 637
NORTHERN INDIANA PUBLIC SERVICE COMPANY, *pg.* 1947, *pg.* 694
NORTHWEST NATURAL GAS COMPANY, *pg.* 1947, *pg.* 1504
NORTHWESTERN CORPORATION, *pg.* 1947, *pg.* 1625
NORTHWESTERN ENERGY, *pg.* 1947, *pg.* 1008
NRG ENERGY, INC., *pg.* 1366, *pg.* 1112
NRG ENERGY, INC., *pg.* 1948, *pg.* 1712

4931 - Electric & other Services Combined

4939 - Combination Utilities, NEC

DUKE ENERGY CORPORATION, *pg.* 1940, *pg.* 1366
DUKE ENERGY PROGRESS, *pg.* 1940, *pg.* 462
DUKE ENERGY PROGRESS, *pg.* 1940, *pg.* 1387
DUQUESNE LIGHT COMPANY, *pg.* 1940, *pg.* 1574
DYNEGY, INC., *pg.* 976, *pg.* 1705
EDISON INTERNATIONAL, *pg.* 1941, *pg.* 194
THE EMPIRE DISTRICT ELECTRIC COMPANY, *pg.* 1941, *pg.* 980
ENERGY FUTURE HOLDINGS CORP., *pg.* 1941, *pg.* 1680
ENERNOC, INC., *pg.* 976, *pg.* 794
ENTECH SOLAR, INC., *pg.* 1335, *pg.* 1694
ENTERGY CORPORATION, *pg.* 1941, *pg.* 746
ENTERGY NEW ORLEANS, INC., *pg.* 1942, *pg.* 746
EVERSOURCE, *pg.* 1942, *pg.* 337
EVERSOURCE, *pg.* 1942, *pg.* 1035
EVERSOURCE, *pg.* 977, *pg.* 794
EVERSOURCE, *pg.* 1942, *pg.* 845
EXELON CORPORATION, *pg.* 1942, *pg.* 573
FIRSTENERGY CORP., *pg.* 1942, *pg.* 1400
FLORIDA POWER & LIGHT COMPANY, *pg.* 1943, *pg.* 435
FLORIDA PUBLIC UTILITIES, *pg.* 1943, *pg.* 422
GAINESVILLE REGIONAL UTILITIES INC., *pg.* 1943, *pg.* 429
GDF SUEZ ENERGY NORTH AMERICA, INC., *pg.* 1164, *pg.* 1706
GEORGIA POWER COMPANY, *pg.* 1943, *pg.* 508
GREAT PLAINS ENERGY INCORPORATED, *pg.* 1944, *pg.* 983
GREEN MOUNTAIN ENERGY COMPANY, *pg.* 1944, *pg.* 1663
GREEN MOUNTAIN POWER CORPORATION, *pg.* 1944, *pg.* 1765
GULF POWER COMPANY, *pg.* 1944, *pg.* 458
HAWAIIAN ELECTRIC COMPANY, INC., *pg.* 1944, *pg.* 544
HOOSIER ENERGY RURAL ELECTRIC COOPERATIVE INC., *pg.* 1944, *pg.* 674
HYDRO-QUEBEC, *pg.* 1944, *pg.* 1955
IDACORP, INC., *pg.* 1944, *pg.* 546
INDIANAPOLIS POWER & LIGHT COMPANY, *pg.* 1945, *pg.* 687
ITC HOLDINGS CORP., *pg.* 1945, *pg.* 903
JERSEY CENTRAL POWER & LIGHT COMPANY, *pg.* 1945, *pg.* 1402
KANSAS CITY POWER & LIGHT COMPANY, *pg.* 1945, *pg.* 985
KENTUCKY UTILITIES COMPANY, *pg.* 1945, *pg.* 730
LG&E AND KU ENERGY LLC, *pg.* 1946, *pg.* 736
LIMONEIRA COMPANY, *pg.* 705, *pg.* 276
LONG ISLAND POWER AUTHORITY, *pg.* 1946, *pg.* 1346
LUFKIN INDUSTRIES, INC., *pg.* 1357, *pg.* 1726
MAGNETEK, INC., *pg.* 1301, *pg.* 1870
MDU RESOURCES GROUP, INC., *pg.* 981, *pg.* 1397
MEMPHIS LIGHT, GAS & WATER, *pg.* 1946, *pg.* 1645
MIDAMERICAN ENERGY HOLDINGS COMPANY, *pg.* 1946, *pg.* 706
NATIONAL GRID USA, *pg.* 1946, *pg.* 852
NEBRASKA PUBLIC POWER DISTRICT, *pg.* 1947, *pg.* 1010
NEW BRUNSWICK POWER CORPORATION, *pg.* 1947, *pg.* 1915
NORTHERN INDIANA PUBLIC SERVICE COMPANY, *pg.* 1947, *pg.* 694
NORTHWESTERN CORPORATION, *pg.* 1947, *pg.* 1625
NORTHWESTERN ENERGY, *pg.* 1947, *pg.* 1008
NRG ENERGY, INC., *pg.* 1366, *pg.* 1112
NRG ENERGY, INC., *pg.* 1948, *pg.* 1712
NV ENERGY, *pg.* 1948, *pg.* 1032
NV ENERGY, INC., *pg.* 1948, *pg.* 1028
OCEAN POWER TECHNOLOGIES, INC., *pg.* 1948, *pg.* 1107
OGE ENERGY CORP., *pg.* 1948, *pg.* 1486
OMAHA PUBLIC POWER DISTRICT, *pg.* 1948, *pg.* 1017
ORANGE & ROCKLAND UTILITIES, INC., *pg.* 1949, *pg.* 1321
P2 SOLAR INC., *pg.* 661, *pg.* 1909
PACIFIC ETHANOL, INC., *pg.* 982, *pg.* 197
PACIFICORP, *pg.* 1949, *pg.* 1504
PECO ENERGY COMPANY, *pg.* 1949, *pg.* 1568
PEPCO HOLDINGS, INC., *pg.* 1949, *pg.* 404
PG&E CORPORATION, *pg.* 1949, *pg.* 224
PNM RESOURCES, INC., *pg.* 1949, *pg.* 1135
PORTLAND GENERAL ELECTRIC COMPANY, *pg.* 1950, *pg.* 1505
POTOMAC ELECTRIC POWER COMPANY, *pg.* 1950, *pg.* 404
PPL CORPORATION, *pg.* 1950, *pg.* 1514
PREMIER POWER RENEWABLE ENERGY, INC., *pg.* 1075, *pg.* 78
PUBLIC SERVICE COMPANY OF OKLAHOMA, *pg.* 1950, *pg.* 1443
PUBLIC SERVICE ENTERPRISE GROUP INCORPORATED, *pg.* 1950, *pg.* 1097
PUGET ENERGY, INC., *pg.* 1950, *pg.* 1816
RGS ENERGY, *pg.* 1951, *pg.* 1322
SALT RIVER PROJECT, *pg.* 707, *pg.* 26
SANTEE COOPER, *pg.* 1951, *pg.* 1620
SASKPOWER, *pg.* 1951, *pg.* 1962
SCANA CORPORATION, *pg.* 1951, *pg.* 1612
SEATTLE CITY LIGHT, *pg.* 1951, *pg.* 1839
SEMPRA ENERGY, *pg.* 1951, *pg.* 209
SOUTHERN CALIFORNIA EDISON COMPANY, *pg.* 1952, *pg.* 194
SOUTHERN COMPANY, *pg.* 1952, *pg.* 520
SUNPOWER CORPORATION, *pg.* 1952, *pg.* 250
SYNACOR, INC., *pg.* 479, *pg.* 1380
TAMPA ELECTRIC COMPANY, *pg.* 1952, *pg.* 476
TRANSALTA CORPORATION, *pg.* 1953, *pg.* 1905
TUCSON ELECTRIC POWER COMPANY, *pg.* 1953, *pg.* 27
TXU ENERGY RETAIL COMPANY LLC, *pg.* 1953, *pg.* 1690
UGI CORPORATION, *pg.* 1953, *pg.* 1544
UIL HOLDINGS CORPORATION, *pg.* 1953, *pg.* 359
UNS ENERGY CORPORATION, *pg.* 1954, *pg.* 27
VERENDRYE ELECTRIC COOPERATIVE, *pg.* 1954, *pg.* 1398
WASHINGTON GAS LIGHT CO., *pg.* 1954, *pg.* 407
WEC ENERGY GROUP, INC., *pg.* 1954, *pg.* 1881
WESTMORELAND COAL COMPANY, *pg.* 1955, *pg.* 328
XCEL ENERGY INC., *pg.* 1955, *pg.* 946

4941 - Water Supply

ALLETE, INC., *pg.* 1933, *pg.* 921
AMERICAN WATER WORKS COMPANY, INC., *pg.* 1934, *pg.* 1128
AQUA AMERICA, INC., *pg.* 1935, *pg.* 1518
AQUARION WATER COMPANY, *pg.* 1935, *pg.* 357
BLUE EARTH, INC., *pg.* 70, *pg.* 1021
CONNECTICUT WATER SERVICE, INC., *pg.* 1938, *pg.* 342
THE EMPIRE DISTRICT ELECTRIC COMPANY, *pg.* 1941, *pg.* 980
ENERGY RECOVERY, INC., *pg.* 1334, *pg.* 252
ENTECH SOLAR, INC., *pg.* 1335, *pg.* 1694
ENVIROGEN TECHNOLOGIES, INC., *pg.* 1942, *pg.* 1724
GAINESVILLE REGIONAL UTILITIES INC., *pg.* 1943, *pg.* 429
GE WATER & PROCESS TECHNOLOGIES, *pg.* 1339, *pg.* 1588
LIMONEIRA COMPANY, *pg.* 705, *pg.* 276
LINDSAY CORPORATION, *pg.* 1356, *pg.* 1016
MIDDLESEX WATER COMPANY, *pg.* 1946, *pg.* 1075
PURESAFE WATER SYSTEMS, INC., *pg.* 333, *pg.* 1322
RELIABLE AUTOMATIC SPRINKLER CO., INC., *pg.* 1137, *pg.* 1158
THE TORO COMPANY IRRIGATION PRODUCTS, *pg.* 1065, *pg.* 194
TWO RIVERS WATER COMPANY, *pg.* 1286, *pg.* 323
UNITED WATER RESOURCES INC., *pg.* 1954, *pg.* 1073

4953 - Refuse Systems

AECOM, *pg.* 64, *pg.* 812
APPLIANCE RECYCLING CENTERS OF AMERICA, INC., *pg.* 51, *pg.* 930
CH2M HILL COMPANIES, LTD., *pg.* 75, *pg.* 325
COMMERCIAL METALS COMPANY, *pg.* 76, *pg.* 1718
ENERGYSOLUTIONS INC., *pg.* 1941, *pg.* 1757
EVOQUA WATER TECHNOLOGIES, *pg.* 1162, *pg.* 541
EXIDE TECHNOLOGIES, *pg.* 204, *pg.* 483
HARSCO CORPORATION, *pg.* 86, *pg.* 1519
INDUSTRIAL SERVICES OF AMERICA, INC., *pg.* 1884, *pg.* 734
INTERNATIONAL BALER CORP., *pg.* 1350, *pg.* 433
IRON MOUNTAIN INCORPORATED, *pg.* 421, *pg.* 796
ITRONICS INC., *pg.* 1169, *pg.* 1031
NUCOR CORPORATION, *pg.* 101, *pg.* 1368
PACIFIC MARINE & SUPPLY CO. LTD. INC., *pg.* 1918, *pg.* 544
PROGRESSIVE WASTE SOLUTIONS, *pg.* 796, *pg.* 1947
REPUBLIC SERVICES, INC., *pg.* 107, *pg.* 19
SAFETY-KLEEN HOLDCO, INC., *pg.* 1180, *pg.* 1734
SIMS METAL MANAGEMENT, *pg.* 1396, *pg.* 590
SONORO ENERGY LTD., *pg.* 112, *pg.* 1905
SYNAGRO TECHNOLOGIES, INC., *pg.* 1800, *pg.* 759
TERVITA CORPORATION, *pg.* 986, *pg.* 1905
WASTE CONNECTIONS, INC., *pg.* 1954, *pg.* 1747
WASTE MANAGEMENT, INC., *pg.* 1954, *pg.* 1716

4959 - Sanitary Services, NEC

ANTHONY & SYLVAN POOLS CORPORATION, *pg.* 1826, *pg.* 1428
APOGEE ENTERPRISES, INC., *pg.* 67, *pg.* 930
ATIS GROUP INC., *pg.* 1042, *pg.* 1952
BRAND ENERGY, INC., *pg.* 71, *pg.* 533
CENTURY FENCE COMPANY, *pg.* 74, *pg.* 1886
CLEAN HARBORS, INC., *pg.* 376, *pg.* 839
CLESTRA HAUSERMAN, INC., *pg.* 76, *pg.* 1526
DESIGN WITHIN REACH, INC., *pg.* 923, *pg.* 216
DUALITE SALES & SERVICE, INC., *pg.* 1296, *pg.* 1482
ECOLAB INC., *pg.* 329, *pg.* 960
ECOLAB INC.-FOOD & BEVERAGE DIVISION, *pg.* 330, *pg.* 960
E.L. WAGNER CO., INC., *pg.* 80, *pg.* 339
ELCAR FENCE & SUPPLY CO., *pg.* 80, *pg.* 319
ENERFAB, INC., *pg.* 81, *pg.* 1412
EVOQUA, *pg.* 1336, *pg.* 1590
FLUOR CORPORATION, *pg.* 82, *pg.* 1719
THE GOLDFIELD CORPORATION, *pg.* 84, *pg.* 439
HENRY BONA POOLS & SPAS, *pg.* 1836, *pg.* 1078
HERMAN MILLER, INC., *pg.* 926, *pg.* 913
KIMMINS CORP., *pg.* 91, *pg.* 473
MIDDLESEX WATER COMPANY, *pg.* 1946, *pg.* 1075
MINAEAN INTERNATIONAL CORPORATION, *pg.* 97, *pg.* 1911
PROGRESSIVE WASTE SOLUTIONS, *pg.* 796, *pg.* 1947
PURESAFE WATER SYSTEMS, INC., *pg.* 333, *pg.* 1322
REAL GOODS SOLAR, INC., *pg.* 1075, *pg.* 334
STEBBINS ENGINEERING & MANUFACTURING COMPANY, *pg.* 113, *pg.* 1349
SWARTWOUT DIVISION, *pg.* 114, *pg.* 978
WASTE MANAGEMENT, INC., *pg.* 1954, *pg.* 1716

5012 - Wholesale Distribution of Automobiles & other Motor Vehicles

AMERICAN HONDA MOTOR CO., INC., *pg.* 163, *pg.* 292
AMERICAN TIRE DISTRIBUTORS HOLDINGS, INC., *pg.* 199, *pg.* 1379
AUDI OF AMERICA, INC., *pg.* 164, *pg.* 1784
BELLA GROUP, *pg.* 166, *pg.* 1599
BMW OF NORTH AMERICA, LLC, *pg.* 166, *pg.* 1133
FERRARI NORTH AMERICA, INC., *pg.* 171, *pg.* 1060
GULF STATES TOYOTA, INC., *pg.* 177, *pg.* 1707
HONDA CANADA INC., *pg.* 179, *pg.* 1938
HYUNDAI MOTOR AMERICA, *pg.* 179, *pg.* 89
JAGUAR LAND ROVER NORTH AMERICA LLC, *pg.* 180, *pg.* 1081
JENKINS AUTO SALES OF FLORIDA, *pg.* 180, *pg.* 459
JM FAMILY ENTERPRISES INC., *pg.* 180, *pg.* 421
KAWASAKI MOTORS CORP., U.S.A., *pg.* 1708, *pg.* 111
KIA MOTORS AMERICA INC., *pg.* 181, *pg.* 112
LEXUS DIVISION, *pg.* 182, *pg.* 294
MASERATI NORTH AMERICA, INC., *pg.* 183, *pg.* 1060
MAZDA NORTH AMERICAN OPERATIONS, *pg.* 183, *pg.* 113
MERCEDES-BENZ USA, LLC, *pg.* 184, *pg.* 514
MIDAS INTERNATIONAL, INC., *pg.* 212, *pg.* 620
MIKE KASHTAN'S SUPERIOR AUTO SALES, *pg.* 185, *pg.* 458
MILE MARKER INTERNATIONAL INC., *pg.* 213, *pg.* 459
MITSUBISHI FUSO TRUCK OF AMERICA, INC., *pg.* 185, *pg.* 1045
MITSUBISHI MOTORS NORTH AMERICA, INC., *pg.* 185, *pg.* 75
O'BRIEN AUTOMOTIVE TEAM, *pg.* 187, *pg.* 663
O'GARA COACH LA JOLLA, *pg.* 187, *pg.* 120
PORSCHE CARS NORTH AMERICA, INC., *pg.* 189, *pg.* 518
RICHMOND FORD, *pg.* 189, *pg.* 1803
RUSH ENTERPRISES INC., *pg.* 189, *pg.* 1728
SOUTHEAST TOYOTA DISTRIBUTORS, LLC, *pg.* 190, *pg.* 421
SUBARU OF AMERICA, INC., *pg.* 191, *pg.* 1050
TESLA MOTORS, INC., *pg.* 191, *pg.* 178

First page reference indicates Business Class Edition
Second page reference indicates Geographic Edition

TOYOTA MOTOR SALES, U.S.A., INC., *pg.* 193, *pg.* 296
VOLKSWAGEN GROUP OF AMERICA, INC., *pg.* 194, *pg.* 1785
VOLVO CARS OF NORTH AMERICA LLC, *pg.* 195, *pg.* 1117
W.W. WALLWORK, INC., *pg.* 195, *pg.* 1398

5013 - Motor Vehicle Supplies & New Parts-Wholesale

ABT ELECTRONICS, INC., *pg.* 612, *pg.* 614
ACKLANDS-GRAINGER INC., *pg.* 197, *pg.* 1933
ADVANCE AUTO PARTS, INC., *pg.* 197, *pg.* 1805
AHERN RENTALS, INC., *pg.* 345, *pg.* 1022
AIRTEX PRODUCTS, *pg.* 198, *pg.* 612
AL & ED'S CORPORATION, *pg.* 615, *pg.* 299
AMERICAN GREASE STICK CO., *pg.* 971, *pg.* 902
AMERICAN VAN EQUIPMENT INC., *pg.* 199, *pg.* 1078
AUTOMOTIVE SUPPLY ASSOCIATES, INC., *pg.* 200, *pg.* 1033
AUTOZONE, INC., *pg.* 200, *pg.* 1641
BAND PRO FILM & DIGITAL INC., *pg.* 623, *pg.* 51
BATTERIES PLUS BULBS LLC, *pg.* 360, *pg.* 1860
BELL INDUSTRIES, INC., *pg.* 624, *pg.* 683
BEST BUY CO., INC., *pg.* 1761, *pg.* 954
BEXEL CORPORATION, *pg.* 624, *pg.* 51
BMW OF NORTH AMERICA, LLC, *pg.* 166, *pg.* 1133
BRANDSMART USA, *pg.* 627, *pg.* 430
CAMBRIDGE SOUNDWORKS, INC., *pg.* 1234, *pg.* 781
CANADIAN TIRE CORPORATION LIMITED, *pg.* 202, *pg.* 1936
CARMAX, INC., *pg.* 167, *pg.* 1800
CARQUEST CORPORATION, *pg.* 168, *pg.* 1386
CASEY'S GENERAL STORES, INC., *pg.* 1017, *pg.* 701
CHAMPION MOTORSPORT, *pg.* 168, *pg.* 459
CLAUS ETTENSBERGER CORPORATION, *pg.* 202, *pg.* 305
THE COAST DISTRIBUTION SYSTEM, INC., *pg.* 1706, *pg.* 152
COMPETITION SPECIALTIES INC., *pg.* 203, *pg.* 1813
CONN'S, INC., *pg.* 630, *pg.* 1668
CRANE CARRIER COMPANY, *pg.* 168, *pg.* 1489
CUSTOM ACCESSORIES INC., *pg.* 203, *pg.* 653
DOUGLAS DYNAMICS, INC., *pg.* 204, *pg.* 1874
EMERSON NETWORK POWER, *pg.* 1071, *pg.* 1479
EMERY-WATERHOUSE COMPANY, *pg.* 1047, *pg.* 751
ETRONICS, INC., *pg.* 1244, *pg.* 1146
FLEETPRIDE, INC., *pg.* 205, *pg.* 1747
FRY'S ELECTRONICS, INC., *pg.* 640, *pg.* 245
GENUINE PARTS COMPANY, *pg.* 206, *pg.* 506
GKN AUTOMOTIVE INC., *pg.* 206, *pg.* 869
GLEASON INDUSTRIAL PRODUCTS INC., *pg.* 1341, *pg.* 1874
GROUP 1 AUTOMOTIVE, INC., *pg.* 177, *pg.* 1706
GUARDIAN INDUSTRIES CORP., *pg.* 85, *pg.* 869
GUITAR CENTER, INC., *pg.* 1771, *pg.* 306
GULF STATES TOYOTA, INC., *pg.* 177, *pg.* 1707
HAHN AUTOMOTIVE WAREHOUSE, INC., *pg.* 206, *pg.* 1336
HHGREGG, INC., *pg.* 56, *pg.* 686
HYUNDAI AUTO CANADA, *pg.* 179, *pg.* 1923
HYUNDAI MOTOR AMERICA, *pg.* 179, *pg.* 89
INFOSONICS CORPORATION, *pg.* 644, *pg.* 203
INTERNATIONAL PLAZA & BAY STREET, *pg.* 1773, *pg.* 473
J&R MUSIC WORLD, *pg.* 554, *pg.* 1245
JASPER ENGINE & TRANSMISSION EXCHANGE, *pg.* 209, *pg.* 691
J.C. WHITNEY & CO., *pg.* 209, *pg.* 621
JM FAMILY ENTERPRISES INC., *pg.* 180, *pg.* 421
KAWASAKI MOTORS CORP., U.S.A., *pg.* 1708, *pg.* 111
KEYSTONE AUTOMOTIVE OPERATIONS, INC., *pg.* 210, *pg.* 1531
KIA MOTORS AMERICA INC., *pg.* 181, *pg.* 112
KRACO ENTERPRISES, LLC, *pg.* 210, *pg.* 68
KRELL INDUSTRIES, INC., *pg.* 650, *pg.* 367
KYB AMERICA LLC, *pg.* 210, *pg.* 681
LEAR CORPORATION, *pg.* 229, *pg.* 907
LES SCHWAB TIRE CENTERS OF OREGON, INC., *pg.* 210, *pg.* 1508
LKQ CORP., *pg.* 210, *pg.* 185
LONG MOTOR CORPORATION, *pg.* 211, *pg.* 716
LONNIE MCCURRY'S FOUR WHEEL DRIVE CENTER, INC., *pg.* 211, *pg.* 748
MACNEIL AUTOMOTIVE PRODUCTS, LTD., *pg.* 211, *pg.* 559
MAGNOLIA AUDIO VIDEO, *pg.* 652, *pg.* 1821
MARINEMAX, INC., *pg.* 1709, *pg.* 416
MASERATI NORTH AMERICA, INC., *pg.* 183, *pg.* 1060
MAZDA NORTH AMERICAN OPERATIONS, *pg.* 183, *pg.* 113
MERCEDES-BENZ USA, LLC, *pg.* 184, *pg.* 514
MIGHTY DISTRIBUTING SYSTEM OF AMERICA, *pg.* 213, *pg.* 538
MITSUBISHI FUSO TRUCK OF AMERICA, INC., *pg.* 185, *pg.* 1045
MR. GASKET INC., *pg.* 213, *pg.* 1406
MYERS INDUSTRIES, INC., *pg.* 1887, *pg.* 1402
NATIONAL AUTOMOTIVE PARTS ASSOCIATION, *pg.* 213, *pg.* 515
NEW AGE ELECTRONICS, INC., *pg.* 659, *pg.* 63
NISSAN NORTH AMERICA, INC., *pg.* 186, *pg.* 1633
OFF ROAD UNLIMITED CORP., *pg.* 214, *pg.* 52
O'REILLY AUTO PARTS, *pg.* 214, *pg.* 872
O'REILLY AUTOMOTIVE, INC., *pg.* 214, *pg.* 1006
P.C. RICHARD & SON, *pg.* 59, *pg.* 1159
PENDA CORPORATION, *pg.* 214, *pg.* 1887
THE PEP BOYS - MANNY, MOE & JACK, *pg.* 215, *pg.* 1568
PORSCHE CARS NORTH AMERICA, INC., *pg.* 189, *pg.* 518
PURVIS BEARING SERVICE LTD., *pg.* 1371, *pg.* 1686
REMY INTERNATIONAL, INC., *pg.* 216, *pg.* 696
SAM ASH MUSIC CORPORATION, *pg.* 669, *pg.* 1167
SEARS HOLDINGS CORPORATION, *pg.* 1784, *pg.* 618
SHENANDOAH TELECOMMUNICATIONS CO., *pg.* 672, *pg.* 1779
SUBARU CANADA, INC., *pg.* 190, *pg.* 1929
SUBARU OF AMERICA, INC., *pg.* 191, *pg.* 1050
THULE, INC., *pg.* 218, *pg.* 369
TODCO, INC., *pg.* 115, *pg.* 1459
TOYOTA CANADA, INC., *pg.* 192, *pg.* 1934
TRACTOR SUPPLY COMPANY, *pg.* 708, *pg.* 1627
TRANSTAR INDUSTRIES, INC., *pg.* 219, *pg.* 1478
TRIMAS CORPORATION, *pg.* 1383, *pg.* 874
UNI-SELECT INC., *pg.* 220, *pg.* 1950
UNITED COMPONENTS, INC., *pg.* 220, *pg.* 679
UNIVERSAL COOPERATIVES, INC., *pg.* 1482, *pg.* 922
U.S. AUTO PARTS NETWORK, INC., *pg.* 221, *pg.* 64
VALENTINO HOME ENTERTAINMENT, *pg.* 684, *pg.* 742
VALLEY TRUCK PARTS, INC., *pg.* 221, *pg.* 913
VAPOR BUS INTERNATIONAL, *pg.* 221, *pg.* 560
VELODYNE ACOUSTICS, INC., *pg.* 685, *pg.* 152
VOLKSWAGEN GROUP OF AMERICA, INC., *pg.* 194, *pg.* 1785
VOLVO CARS OF CANADA LTD., *pg.* 195, *pg.* 1946
VOLVO TRUCKS NORTH AMERICA, INC., *pg.* 195, *pg.* 1377
WAIGLOBAL, *pg.* 221, *pg.* 1585
WESTIN AUTOMOTIVE PRODUCTS, INC., *pg.* 222, *pg.* 211
THE W.W. WILLIAMS COMPANY, *pg.* 1390, *pg.* 1444
YAMAHA MOTOR CORPORATION USA, *pg.* 1713, *pg.* 76
ZIEBART INTERNATIONAL CORPORATION, *pg.* 222, *pg.* 912

5014 - Tires & Tubes-Wholesale

AKH COMPANY, INC., *pg.* 198, *pg.* 42
AMERICAN TIRE DISTRIBUTORS HOLDINGS, INC., *pg.* 199, *pg.* 1379
BELLE TIRE INC., *pg.* 200, *pg.* 864
BIG O TIRES, INC., *pg.* 201, *pg.* 314
BRIDGESTONE AMERICAS, INC., *pg.* 201, *pg.* 1649
COKER TIRE COMPANY, *pg.* 1880, *pg.* 1628
COLONY TIRE CORPORATION, *pg.* 203, *pg.* 1372
FREE SERVICE TIRE COMPANY, INC., *pg.* 205, *pg.* 1635
THE HERCULES TIRE & RUBBER COMPANY, *pg.* 1884, *pg.* 1454
JEFFERSON CHEVROLET CO., *pg.* 180, *pg.* 883
KAUFFMAN TIRE INC., *pg.* 1885, *pg.* 532
LES SCHWAB TIRE CENTERS OF OREGON, INC., *pg.* 210, *pg.* 1508
MICHELIN AMERICAS SMALL TIRES (MAST), *pg.* 1886, *pg.* 1618
MICHELIN NORTH AMERICA INC., *pg.* 1886, *pg.* 1618
MYERS INDUSTRIES, INC., *pg.* 1887, *pg.* 1402
REMA TIP TOP/NORTH AMERICA, INC., *pg.* 1889, *pg.* 1099
SOMERSET TIRE SERVICE, INC., *pg.* 217, *pg.* 1047
TBC CORPORATION, *pg.* 1889, *pg.* 457
TIRE KINGDOM, INC., *pg.* 219, *pg.* 436
THE TIRE RACK INC., *pg.* 1890, *pg.* 697
TIRES PLUS TOTAL CAR CARE, *pg.* 219, *pg.* 417
TOYO TIRE (U.S.A.) CORPORATION, *pg.* 1890, *pg.* 76
UNIVERSAL COOPERATIVES, INC., *pg.* 1482, *pg.* 922
YOKOHAMA TIRE CORPORATION, *pg.* 1892, *pg.* 94

5043 - Photographic Equipment & Supplies-Wholesale

CALUMET PHOTOGRAPHIC, INC., *pg.* 1404, *pg.* 568
CINEQUIPT INC., *pg.* 629, *pg.* 932
DISTRICT PHOTO INC., *pg.* 1408, *pg.* 761
FILM EMPORIUM INC., *pg.* 639, *pg.* 1173
FUJIFILM CANADA INC., *pg.* 1414, *pg.* 1925
FUJIFILM MEDICAL SYSTEMS USA, INC., *pg.* 1531, *pg.* 374
FUJIFILM U.S.A., INC., *pg.* 1414, *pg.* 1348
HASSELBLAD USA, INC., *pg.* 1416, *pg.* 1065
ICAD, INC., *pg.* 643, *pg.* 1037
NIKON INC., *pg.* 1424, *pg.* 1181
OLYMPUS AMERICA INC., *pg.* 1425, *pg.* 1521
SCHNEIDER OPTICS INC., *pg.* 1428, *pg.* 1165
THE TIFFEN COMPANY LLC, *pg.* 1432, *pg.* 1165

5045 - Computers & Computer Peripheral Equipment & Software-Wholesale

3M COMPANY, *pg.* 1142, *pg.* 956
A&K RAILROAD MATERIALS INC., *pg.* 1896, *pg.* 1755
A BRITE COMPANY, *pg.* 1144, *pg.* 1697
A. M. CASTLE & CO., *pg.* 64, *pg.* 644
A. SCHULMAN, INC., *pg.* 1144, *pg.* 1452
ABATIX CORP., *pg.* 1309, *pg.* 1672
ACCURATE FASTENERS INC., *pg.* 1309, *pg.* 789
ACE HARDWARE CORPORATION, *pg.* 1040, *pg.* 644
ADDVANTAGE TECHNOLOGIES GROUP, INC., *pg.* 612, *pg.* 1484
AERO CONTROLS, INC., *pg.* 223, *pg.* 439
AFFILIATED FOODS MIDWEST INC., *pg.* 1012, *pg.* 1013
A.G. DAVIS/AA GAGE, *pg.* 1310, *pg.* 908
AHERN RENTALS, INC., *pg.* 345, *pg.* 1022
AIRBUS HELICOPTERS, INC., *pg.* 223, *pg.* 1698
AIRCRAFT SPRUCE & SPECIALTY CO., *pg.* 1759, *pg.* 69
A.J. JERSEY INC., *pg.* 1310, *pg.* 1123
ALAMO IRON WORKS, *pg.* 1311, *pg.* 1739
ALIMAK HEK INC, *pg.* 66, *pg.* 1749
ALIMERA SCIENCES, INC., *pg.* 1490, *pg.* 482
ALLIED RUBBER & RIGGING SUPPLY, *pg.* 1878, *pg.* 1519
ALTAIR CORPORATION, *pg.* 1312, *pg.* 910
AMERICAN HONDA MOTOR CO., INC., *pg.* 163, *pg.* 292
AMERICAN TIRE DISTRIBUTORS HOLDINGS, INC., *pg.* 199, *pg.* 1379
AMPCO-PITTSBURGH CORPORATION, *pg.* 1313, *pg.* 1573
ANDERSON & VREELAND, INC., *pg.* 1616, *pg.* 1064
ANIXTER PENTACON, INC., *pg.* 1313, *pg.* 64
APPLIED INDUSTRIAL TECHNOLOGIES, INC., *pg.* 199, *pg.* 1428
ARBURG, INC., *pg.* 1314, *pg.* 359
ARGO INTERNATIONAL CORPORATION, *pg.* 1314, *pg.* 1196
ARNOLD MACHINERY COMPANY, *pg.* 1314, *pg.* 1755
AROTECH CORPORATION, *pg.* 1042, *pg.* 865
ASHLAND INC., *pg.* 972, *pg.* 726
ASTEC INDUSTRIES, INC., *pg.* 69, *pg.* 1628
ATLANTIC CORPORATION, *pg.* 1452, *pg.* 1392
ATLAS BOLT & SCREW COMPANY, *pg.* 1042, *pg.* 1403
ATMOS ENERGY CORPORATION, *pg.* 1935, *pg.* 1675
AUDI OF AMERICA, INC., *pg.* 164, *pg.* 1784
AUTOMATION MAILING AND SHIPPING SOLUTIONS, INC., *pg.* 358, *pg.* 1428
AVIALL, INC., *pg.* 224, *pg.* 1676
AWISCO NY CORPORATION, *pg.* 1315, *pg.* 1177
B&G FOODS, INC., *pg.* 838, *pg.* 1102
BAMBERGER POLYMERS, INC., *pg.* 1148, *pg.* 1171
BAUSCH & LOMB INCORPORATED, *pg.* 1401, *pg.* 1045
BEHLEN MFG. CO., *pg.* 701, *pg.* 1010
BELL-MARK CORPORATION, *pg.* 1620, *pg.* 1108
BELLA GROUP, *pg.* 166, *pg.* 1599
BENJAMIN OBDYKE, INC., *pg.* 70, *pg.* 1540
BMW OF NORTH AMERICA, LLC, *pg.* 166, *pg.* 1133
BOB EVANS FARMS, LLC, *pg.* 841, *pg.* 1467
BOLTON-EMERSON AMERICAS, INC., *pg.* 1318, *pg.* 827
BOSCH INSPECTION TECHNOLOGY INC., *pg.* 1319, *pg.* 1041
BP CORPORATION NORTH AMERICA INC., *pg.* 973, *pg.*

First page reference indicates Business Class Edition
Second page reference indicates Geographic Edition

665
BRENNAN INDUSTRIES INC., *pg.* 1319, *pg.* 1429
BROCK-MCVEY COMPANY, *pg.* 1043, *pg.* 729
BROTHER INTERNATIONAL CORPORATION - USA, *pg.* 53, *pg.* 1046
BRUNSWICK CORPORATION, *pg.* 1828, *pg.* 623
BRYANT GRINDER, *pg.* 1320, *pg.* 1768
BTU INTERNATIONAL, INC., *pg.* 1320, *pg.* 838
BURRIS LOGISTICS, *pg.* 843, *pg.* 387
BUTLER MACHINERY COMPANY, *pg.* 1321, *pg.* 1397
C&D TECHNOLOGIES, INC., *pg.* 627, *pg.* 1517
C&H DISTRIBUTORS, LLC, *pg.* 1044, *pg.* 1873
C&S WHOLESALE GROCERS, INC., *pg.* 1016, *pg.* 1035
CALAVO GROWERS, INC., *pg.* 843, *pg.* 276
CALUMET PHOTOGRAPHIC, INC., *pg.* 1404, *pg.* 568
CAMERON VALVES & MEASUREMENT, *pg.* 1321, *pg.* 1703
CARLSON JPM STORE FIXTURES, *pg.* 369, *pg.* 919
CASE PAPER COMPANY INC., *pg.* 1455, *pg.* 1163
CENTRAL STEEL & WIRE COMPANY, *pg.* 74, *pg.* 569
C.H. HANSON COMPANY, *pg.* 1322, *pg.* 636
CHERRY CENTRAL COOPERATIVE, INC., *pg.* 847, *pg.* 909
CHICAGO METAL FABRICATORS, INC., *pg.* 1323, *pg.* 569
CHICAGO TUBE & IRON CO., *pg.* 1323, *pg.* 656
CINEQUIPT INC., *pg.* 629, *pg.* 932
CITATIONAIR, *pg.* 1903, *pg.* 350
CLARK MATERIAL HANDLING COMPANY, *pg.* 1323, *pg.* 729
CO-EX CORP., *pg.* 76, *pg.* 382
COMMERCIAL METALS COMPANY, *pg.* 76, *pg.* 1718
CONAGRA FOODS LAMB WESTON, INC., *pg.* 850, *pg.* 549
CONSEW, *pg.* 53, *pg.* 1049
CRYOVAC, INC., *pg.* 1456, *pg.* 1615
CUTTER AVIATION, INC., *pg.* 227, *pg.* 16
D&S CAR WASH EQUIPMENT CO., *pg.* 1327, *pg.* 979
DANAHER MOTION, *pg.* 1327, *pg.* 1593
DANKER LABORATORIES INC., *pg.* 1408, *pg.* 465
DASSAULT FALCON JET CORP., *pg.* 227, *pg.* 1122
DAWN FOOD PRODUCTS, INC., *pg.* 1018, *pg.* 893
DEDERT CORPORATION, *pg.* 1408, *pg.* 649
DEL-TRON PRECISION, INC., *pg.* 1328, *pg.* 337
DE'LONGHI AMERICA INC., *pg.* 54, *pg.* 1118
DEUTZ CORPORATION, *pg.* 1328, *pg.* 536
DEVAR, INC., *pg.* 633, *pg.* 339
DEVON ENERGY CORPORATION, *pg.* 975, *pg.* 1485
DIEHL WOODWORKING MACHINERY, INC., *pg.* 1328, *pg.* 698
DISTRICT PHOTO INC., *pg.* 1408, *pg.* 761
DIXON VALVE & COUPLING COMPANY, *pg.* 1045, *pg.* 766
THE DOALL COMPANY, *pg.* 1329, *pg.* 670
DOUGLAS DYNAMICS, INC., *pg.* 204, *pg.* 1874
THE DOW CHEMICAL COMPANY, *pg.* 1157, *pg.* 898
DOWNS CRANE & HOIST CO, INC., *pg.* 1330, *pg.* 129
DREMEL, *pg.* 1046, *pg.* 634
DYNISCO INSTRUMENTS LLC, *pg.* 1526, *pg.* 823
EARLE M. JORGENSEN COMPANY, *pg.* 80, *pg.* 142
EATON'S CROUSE-HINDS, *pg.* 1296, *pg.* 1344
EDWARD DON & COMPANY, *pg.* 54, *pg.* 672
ELKAY PLASTICS COMPANY, INC., *pg.* 1882, *pg.* 68
EMBRAER AIRCRAFT HOLDING INC., *pg.* 227, *pg.* 425
EMERY-WATERHOUSE COMPANY, *pg.* 1047, *pg.* 751
ENCON SAFETY PRODUCTS, *pg.* 1334, *pg.* 1705
ENERFAB, INC., *pg.* 81, *pg.* 1412
ENGLISH COLOR & SUPPLY INC., *pg.* 1442, *pg.* 1735
ENTHONE INC., *pg.* 1161, *pg.* 381
EQUIPMENT DEPOT LTD., *pg.* 1335, *pg.* 1749
ESSENTRA COMPONENTS, *pg.* 1335, *pg.* 901
ESSILOR OF AMERICA, INC., *pg.* 1412, *pg.* 1680
E.V. ROBERTS & ASSOCIATES, INC., *pg.* 1161, *pg.* 63
EXTERRAN HOLDINGS, INC., *pg.* 977, *pg.* 1705
EXXON MOBIL CORPORATION, *pg.* 977, *pg.* 1718
FABREEKA INTERNATIONAL, INC., *pg.* 1882, *pg.* 847
FASTENAL COMPANY, *pg.* 396, *pg.* 966
FEDERAL HOSE MANUFACTURING INC., *pg.* 1047, *pg.* 1469
FERRARI NORTH AMERICA, INC., *pg.* 171, *pg.* 1060
FILM EMPORIUM INC., *pg.* 639, *pg.* 1173
FLOWERS FOODS, INC., *pg.* 855, *pg.* 541
FOOD SERVICES OF AMERICA, INC., *pg.* 856, *pg.* 21
FORKLIFTS OF MINNESOTA, INC., *pg.* 174, *pg.* 918
FORTUNET, INC., *pg.* 953, *pg.* 1024
FRANKE INC., *pg.* 55, *pg.* 1656
FROSTY ACRES BRANDS, INC., *pg.* 1020, *pg.* 484
FRYMASTER LLC, *pg.* 55, *pg.* 748
FUJIFILM CANADA INC., *pg.* 1414, *pg.* 1925
FUJIFILM MEDICAL SYSTEMS USA, INC., *pg.* 1531, *pg.* 374
FUJIFILM U.S.A., INC., *pg.* 1414, *pg.* 1348
FUJINON INC., *pg.* 1414, *pg.* 1129
FURUNO USA, INC., *pg.* 640, *pg.* 1819
F.W. BRYCE, INC., *pg.* 857, *pg.* 823
GARDNER DENVER NASH, *pg.* 1338, *pg.* 381
GEMA USA INC., *pg.* 1339, *pg.* 686
GENERAL BEARING CORPORATION, *pg.* 205, *pg.* 1350
GENERAL MILLS CANADA CORP., *pg.* 828, *pg.* 1926
GENERAL MOTORS COMPANY, *pg.* 175, *pg.* 881
GEORGIA-PACIFIC LLC, *pg.* 1458, *pg.* 507
GERBER SCIENTIFIC, INC., *pg.* 1414, *pg.* 380
GIBBS WIRE & STEEL COMPANY, INC., *pg.* 1048, *pg.* 371
GLEASON CORPORATION, *pg.* 1340, *pg.* 1335
GOLDEN CORRAL CORPORATION, *pg.* 1730, *pg.* 1387
GORDON FOOD SERVICE INC., *pg.* 1021, *pg.* 913
GOULDS PUMPS, INCORPORATED, *pg.* 1342, *pg.* 1341
GRAVOGRAPH-NEW HERMES, *pg.* 1344, *pg.* 531
GREGORY POOLE EQUIPMENT COMPANY INC., *pg.* 85, *pg.* 1387
GULF OIL LIMITED PARTNERSHIP, *pg.* 978, *pg.* 814
GULF STATES TOYOTA, INC., *pg.* 177, *pg.* 1707
H&E EQUIPMENT SERVICES, INC., *pg.* 85, *pg.* 742
HACO-ATLANTIC, INC., *pg.* 1344, *pg.* 1707
HAECO AMERICAS, *pg.* 228, *pg.* 1374
HARBORMASTER MARINE, INC., *pg.* 1707, *pg.* 896
HARLAND CLARKE HOLDINGS CORP., *pg.* 1647, *pg.* 1741
HARSCO CORPORATION, *pg.* 86, *pg.* 1519
HARWICK STANDARD DISTRIBUTION CORPORATION, *pg.* 1164, *pg.* 1402
HASSELBLAD USA, INC., *pg.* 1416, *pg.* 1065
HAWKINS, INC., *pg.* 1165, *pg.* 937
HD SUPPLY, INC., *pg.* 86, *pg.* 509
HEADWATERS INCORPORATED, *pg.* 978, *pg.* 1763
HI-VAC CORPORATION, *pg.* 56, *pg.* 1458
HICKMAN, WILLIAMS & COMPANY, *pg.* 87, *pg.* 1414
HIGH LINER FOODS, *pg.* 862, *pg.* 1796
HILL & GRIFFITH COMPANY, *pg.* 1167, *pg.* 1414
HIRSCH INTERNATIONAL CORP., *pg.* 694, *pg.* 1164
HIRSHFIELD'S INC., *pg.* 1442, *pg.* 937
HITACHI KOKI USA, LTD., *pg.* 1050, *pg.* 537
HKN, INC., *pg.* 979, *pg.* 1745
HOLLYMATIC CORPORATION, *pg.* 1346, *pg.* 598
HOLMATRO, INC., *pg.* 1346, *pg.* 771
HONDA CANADA INC., *pg.* 179, *pg.* 1938
HOUGEN MANUFACTURING INC., *pg.* 1347, *pg.* 908
THE H.T. HACKNEY COMPANY, *pg.* 1023, *pg.* 1637
HUBBARD-HALL, INC., *pg.* 1167, *pg.* 382
HUDSON TECHNOLOGIES, INC., *pg.* 1073, *pg.* 1320
HYUNDAI MOTOR AMERICA, *pg.* 179, *pg.* 89
ICAD, INC., *pg.* 643, *pg.* 1037
IFCO SYSTEMS NORTH AMERICA, *pg.* 411, *pg.* 1708
INDUSTRIAL DISTRIBUTION GROUP, INC., *pg.* 413, *pg.* 1358
INDUSTRIAL SERVICES OF AMERICA, INC., *pg.* 1884, *pg.* 734
INSTITUTION FOOD HOUSE, INC., *pg.* 864, *pg.* 1378
INTELLIGRATED, INC., *pg.* 1349, *pg.* 1460
INTELLIGRATED SYSTEMS LLC, *pg.* 1350, *pg.* 998
IRONPLANET, INC., *pg.* 1259, *pg.* 183
IRVING OIL CORPORATION, *pg.* 980, *pg.* 1038
ITOCHU INTERNATIONAL INC., *pg.* 1351, *pg.* 1245
ITT CORPORATION, *pg.* 1351, *pg.* 1354
JAGUAR LAND ROVER NORTH AMERICA LLC, *pg.* 180, *pg.* 1081
JBI, INC., *pg.* 930, *pg.* 123
JENKINS AUTO SALES OF FLORIDA, *pg.* 180, *pg.* 459
JM FAMILY ENTERPRISES INC., *pg.* 180, *pg.* 421
JOHNSON MANUFACTURING COMPANY, *pg.* 1169, *pg.* 712
JONES-BLAIR COMPANY, *pg.* 1443, *pg.* 1682
JOY GLOBAL, INC., *pg.* 1351, *pg.* 1876
JURA-CAPRESSO INC., *pg.* 58, *pg.* 1052
KAMAN CORPORATION, *pg.* 229, *pg.* 338
KAWASAKI MOTORS CORP., U.S.A., *pg.* 1708, *pg.* 111
KEENELAND ASSOCIATION INC., *pg.* 1477, *pg.* 730
KIA MOTORS AMERICA INC., *pg.* 181, *pg.* 112
KOCH ENTERPRISES, INC., *pg.* 91, *pg.* 679
KOMATSU AMERICA INDUSTRIES, LLC, *pg.* 1353, *pg.* 656
KOMORI AMERICA CORPORATION, *pg.* 1353, *pg.* 656
THE KRAFT HEINZ COMPANY, *pg.* 870, *pg.* 1577
KRAVET FABRICS INC., *pg.* 932, *pg.* 1142
KSB INC., *pg.* 1354, *pg.* 1802
LAWSON PRODUCTS, INC., *pg.* 1355, *pg.* 580
L.B. FOSTER COMPANY, *pg.* 1355, *pg.* 1578
LEXUS DIVISION, *pg.* 182, *pg.* 294
LIPPINCOTT WILLIAMS & WILKINS, *pg.* 1659, *pg.* 1514
LITTLE GIANT PUMP COMPANY, *pg.* 1356, *pg.* 1486
LOCAL & WESTERN OF TEXAS, INC., *pg.* 1026, *pg.* 1683
LUFKIN INDUSTRIES, INC., *pg.* 1357, *pg.* 1726
LUSTER-ON PRODUCTS, INC., *pg.* 1171, *pg.* 845
LUXOTTICA GROUP, *pg.* 8, *pg.* 1323
MACDERMID, INC., *pg.* 1172, *pg.* 321
MAKINO INC., *pg.* 1358, *pg.* 1461
MANITEX INTERNATIONAL, INC., *pg.* 1358, *pg.* 559
THE MANITOWOC COMPANY, INC., *pg.* 1358, *pg.* 1868
MANITOWOC ICE, INC., *pg.* 58, *pg.* 1868
MARCHON EYEWEAR, INC., *pg.* 1421, *pg.* 1180
MARCOLIN USA INC., *pg.* 1421, *pg.* 23
MARLEY ENGINEERED PRODUCTS, *pg.* 1074, *pg.* 1612
MARMON/KEYSTONE CORPORATION, *pg.* 1359, *pg.* 1519
MASERATI NORTH AMERICA, INC., *pg.* 183, *pg.* 1060
MATHESON VALLEY, *pg.* 981, *pg.* 1456
MAYFRAN INTERNATIONAL, INC., *pg.* 1359, *pg.* 1432
MAZDA NORTH AMERICAN OPERATIONS, *pg.* 183, *pg.* 113
MERCEDES-BENZ USA, LLC, *pg.* 184, *pg.* 514
MERCHANT & EVANS, INC., *pg.* 97, *pg.* 1048
MESTEK, INC., *pg.* 1074, *pg.* 857
METALS USA, INC., *pg.* 97, *pg.* 425
METZGAR CONVEYOR COMPANY, *pg.* 1360, *pg.* 875
MHI INJECTION MOLDING MACHINERY, INC., *pg.* 1886, *pg.* 620
MICHIGAN BLUEBERRY GROWERS ASSOCIATION, *pg.* 147, *pg.* 886
MIDAS, INC., *pg.* 212, *pg.* 620
MIDAS INTERNATIONAL, INC., *pg.* 212, *pg.* 620
MIKE KASHTAN'S SUPERIOR AUTO SALES, *pg.* 185, *pg.* 458
MILE MARKER INTERNATIONAL INC., *pg.* 213, *pg.* 459
MITSUBISHI FUSO TRUCK OF AMERICA, INC., *pg.* 185, *pg.* 1045
MITSUBISHI INTERNATIONAL CORPORATION, *pg.* 185, *pg.* 1260
MITSUBISHI MOTORS NORTH AMERICA, INC., *pg.* 185, *pg.* 75
MODERN TRACK MACHINERY, *pg.* 98, *pg.* 610
MODERN WELDING COMPANY, INC., *pg.* 1363, *pg.* 739
MOTION INDUSTRIES, INC., *pg.* 213, *pg.* 3
MOTORCAR PARTS OF AMERICA, INC., *pg.* 213, *pg.* 295
MSC INDUSTRIAL DIRECT CO., INC., *pg.* 1057, *pg.* 1181
MULTI-PLASTICS, INC., *pg.* 1886, *pg.* 1457
THE MURALO COMPANY, *pg.* 1444, *pg.* 1042
MURRY'S, INC., *pg.* 882, *pg.* 780
NACCO INDUSTRIES, INC., *pg.* 1174, *pg.* 1433
NATIONAL BULK EQUIPMENT, INC., *pg.* 1479, *pg.* 892
NATIONAL OILWELL VARCO, INC., *pg.* 1364, *pg.* 1712
NETJETS INC., *pg.* 1917, *pg.* 1442
NETWORK SERVICES COMPANY, *pg.* 1465, *pg.* 659
NEW ENGLAND MACHINERY, INC., *pg.* 1364, *pg.* 415
NIKON INC., *pg.* 1424, *pg.* 1181
NOSHOK INC., *pg.* 1366, *pg.* 1406
NRG ENERGY, INC., *pg.* 1948, *pg.* 1712
NUCOR CORPORATION, *pg.* 101, *pg.* 1368
NUTTING, *pg.* 1366, *pg.* 1626
O.A. NEWTON & SON CO, *pg.* 1366, *pg.* 387
O'BRIEN AUTOMOTIVE TEAM, *pg.* 187, *pg.* 663
OERLIKON BALZERS COATING USA, INC., *pg.* 1444, *pg.* 610
O'GARA COACH LA JOLLA, *pg.* 187, *pg.* 120
OHARA CORPORATION, *pg.* 1425, *pg.* 188
OIL-DRI CORPORATION OF AMERICA, *pg.* 1480, *pg.* 586
OKUMA AMERICA CORPORATION, *pg.* 1366, *pg.* 1368
OLYMPIC STEEL INC., *pg.* 101, *pg.* 1433
OLYMPUS AMERICA INC., *pg.* 1425, *pg.* 1521
OWEN INDUSTRIES, INC., *pg.* 102, *pg.* 702
P. KAY METAL SUPPLY INC., *pg.* 1176, *pg.* 137
PARAGON TECHNOLOGIES, INC., *pg.* 1367, *pg.* 1528
PEIRCE-PHELPS, INC., *pg.* 1075, *pg.* 1568
PENFLEX, INC., *pg.* 104, *pg.* 1534
PERCEPTICS, LLC, *pg.* 1426, *pg.* 1637
PERFORMANCE FOOD GROUP COMPANY, LLC, *pg.* 1030, *pg.* 1803
PERRY VIDEX LLC, *pg.* 1368, *pg.* 1072
PING INC., *pg.* 1842, *pg.* 19
PLAINS ALL AMERICAN PIPELINE, L.P., *pg.* 983, *pg.* 1712
PORSCHE CARS NORTH AMERICA, INC., *pg.* 189, *pg.* 518
POWER EQUIPMENT COMPANY INC, *pg.* 1369, *pg.* 1637
POWIN CORPORATION, *pg.* 1369, *pg.* 1509
PRAB, INC., *pg.* 1369, *pg.* 894

PRECIPART, *pg.* 1370, *pg.* 1160
PRECISION VALVE CORPORATION, *pg.* 1060, *pg.* 1357
PRESSTEK, INC., *pg.* 456, *pg.* 606
PROFESSIONAL PLASTICS, INC., *pg.* 1888, *pg.* 94
PURAFIL, INC., *pg.* 333, *pg.* 530
PURVIS BEARING SERVICE LTD., *pg.* 1371, *pg.* 1686
Q A GROUP LLC., *pg.* 1427, *pg.* 89
QUAKER VALLEY FOODS INC., *pg.* 1031, *pg.* 1570
QUEST SAFETY PRODUCTS, INC., *pg.* 1371, *pg.* 689
RACETRAC PETROLEUM, INC., *pg.* 983, *pg.* 519
R.D. BITZER CO. INC., *pg.* 106, *pg.* 1515
RELIANCE STEEL & ALUMINUM CO., *pg.* 1371, *pg.* 139
REMA TIP TOP/NORTH AMERICA, INC., *pg.* 1889, *pg.* 1099
RENTZEL PUMP MANUFACTURING, LP, *pg.* 707, *pg.* 1726
RESCO PRODUCTS GREENSBORO, *pg.* 107, *pg.* 1375
RICHMOND FORD, *pg.* 189, *pg.* 1803
RINNAI AMERICA CORP., *pg.* 1076, *pg.* 538
RITE-HITE HOLDING CORPORATION, *pg.* 1372, *pg.* 1880
ROFIN-SINAR TECHNOLOGIES, INC., *pg.* 668, *pg.* 904
ROLLEM CORPORATION OF AMERICA, *pg.* 1372, *pg.* 43
RUSH ENTERPRISES INC., *pg.* 189, *pg.* 1728
RUSSEL METALS INC., *pg.* 1180, *pg.* 1928
RYAN HERCO PRODUCTS CORPORATION, *pg.* 1889, *pg.* 52
RYERSON INC., *pg.* 1373, *pg.* 589
SAFWAY SERVICES, LLC, *pg.* 109, *pg.* 1898
SAMMONS ENTERPRISES, INC., *pg.* 1373, *pg.* 1686
THE SCHMIDT GROUP, INC., *pg.* 1374, *pg.* 1618
SCHNEIDER OPTICS INC., *pg.* 1428, *pg.* 1165
SCHOOL SPECIALTY, INC., *pg.* 467, *pg.* 1860
SCHWARZ PAPER COMPANY, *pg.* 1468, *pg.* 634
SEALING DEVICES INC., *pg.* 1889, *pg.* 1173
SECO/WARWICK CORPORATION, *pg.* 1076, *pg.* 1552
SEELEY INTERNATIONAL AMERICAS, *pg.* 1076, *pg.* 19
SEQUA CORPORATION, *pg.* 1180, *pg.* 1290
SETCO SALES COMPANY, *pg.* 1061, *pg.* 1426
SGK, *pg.* 1686, *pg.* 590
SHELL OIL COMPANY, *pg.* 984, *pg.* 1714
SIEMENS, *pg.* 1376, *pg.* 1466
SIGNATURE EYEWEAR, INC., *pg.* 1429, *pg.* 105
SIMS METAL MANAGEMENT, *pg.* 1396, *pg.* 590
SINGER SEWING COMPANY, *pg.* 698, *pg.* 1639
SMITH INTERNATIONAL, INC., *pg.* 1377, *pg.* 1715
SOUTHEAST TOYOTA DISTRIBUTORS, LLC, *pg.* 190, *pg.* 421
SOUTHERN PIPE & SUPPLY CO., INC., *pg.* 112, *pg.* 970
SPENCER FLUID POWER, *pg.* 1889, *pg.* 1822
SPRAYING SYSTEMS CO., *pg.* 1063, *pg.* 670
SPX PROCESS EQUIPMENT, *pg.* 1378, *pg.* 1337
STANDARD MOTOR PRODUCTS, INC., *pg.* 218, *pg.* 1176
SUBARU OF AMERICA, INC., *pg.* 191, *pg.* 1050
SUBURBAN PROPANE PARTNERS, L.P., *pg.* 113, *pg.* 1132
SUNCOR ENERGY INC., *pg.* 985, *pg.* 1905
SUPPLY TECHNOLOGIES LLC, *pg.* 1064, *pg.* 1436
SYSTEMAX, INC., *pg.* 481, *pg.* 1324
TCI PRECISION METALS, INC., *pg.* 1380, *pg.* 95
TECK RESOURCES LIMITED, *pg.* 1183, *pg.* 1912
TEREX CORPORATION, *pg.* 1381, *pg.* 384
TESLA MOTORS, INC., *pg.* 191, *pg.* 178
THOMAS ENGINEERING INC., *pg.* 1382, *pg.* 619
THOMPSON INTERNATIONAL INC., *pg.* 1382, *pg.* 729
THYBONY WALLCOVERINGS INC., *pg.* 945, *pg.* 591
THE TIFFEN COMPANY LLC, *pg.* 1432, *pg.* 1165
TITAN MACHINERY INC., *pg.* 1383, *pg.* 1398
TOYOTA MOTOR SALES, U.S.A., INC., *pg.* 193, *pg.* 296
TRAMMO, *pg.* 986, *pg.* 1304
TRANSILWRAP COMPANY, INC., *pg.* 1470, *pg.* 613
TRI STAR ENERGY, LLC, *pg.* 986, *pg.* 1655
TRICORBRAUN, *pg.* 1471, *pg.* 1004
TUBULAR STEEL INC., *pg.* 117, *pg.* 1004
TURA L.P., *pg.* 1433, *pg.* 1555
TWIN DISC, INCORPORATED, *pg.* 220, *pg.* 1889
UBERMEDIA, INC., *pg.* 1286, *pg.* 181
ULINE SHIPPING SUPPLIES, *pg.* 1385, *pg.* 666
UNITED REFINING COMPANY, *pg.* 986, *pg.* 1590
UNITED RENTALS, INC., *pg.* 1386, *pg.* 350
U.S. TSUBAKI, INC., *pg.* 221, *pg.* 670
VALERO ENERGY CORPORATION, *pg.* 986, *pg.* 1743
VALMONT INDUSTRIES, INC., *pg.* 1387, *pg.* 1019
THE VALSPAR CORPORATION, *pg.* 1449, *pg.* 945
VAN SON HOLLAND INK CORPORATION OF AMERICA, *pg.* 487, *pg.* 1169
VIBRA SCREW INC., *pg.* 1387, *pg.* 1126
VINTAGE PARTS, *pg.* 119, *pg.* 1854
VIP FOODSERVICE, *pg.* 908, *pg.* 545
VOLKSWAGEN GROUP OF AMERICA, INC., *pg.* 194, *pg.* 1785
VOLVO CARS OF NORTH AMERICA LLC, *pg.* 195, *pg.* 1117
VOLVO PENTA OF THE AMERICAS, INC., *pg.* 1712, *pg.* 1778
WATSCO INC., *pg.* 1078, *pg.* 417
WEATHERFORD PRODUCTION OPTIMIZATION, *pg.* 987, *pg.* 1725
WESCO FINANCIAL CORPORATION, *pg.* 821, *pg.* 181
WESCO INTERNATIONAL INC., *pg.* 687, *pg.* 1582
WESTERN FAMILY HOLDING CO., INC., *pg.* 1037, *pg.* 1509
WEYERHAEUSER COMPANY, *pg.* 121, *pg.* 1820
WHITE CASTLE MANAGEMENT CO., *pg.* 1756, *pg.* 1444
THE WILLAMETTE VALLEY COMPANY, *pg.* 1186, *pg.* 1497
WMS INDUSTRIES INC., *pg.* 593, *pg.* 666
THE WOLF MACHINE CO., *pg.* 1389, *pg.* 1427
W.W. GRAINGER, INC., *pg.* 1390, *pg.* 625
W.W. WALLWORK, INC., *pg.* 195, *pg.* 1398
THE W.W. WILLIAMS COMPANY, *pg.* 1390, *pg.* 1444
XPEDX, *pg.* 1473, *pg.* 1377
YAMAHA MOTOR CORPORATION USA, *pg.* 1713, *pg.* 76
YANMAR AMERICA CORPORATION, *pg.* 196, *pg.* 482
ZIMMERMAN-MCDONALD MACHINERY, INC., *pg.* 1391, *pg.* 1005

5046 - Commercial Equipment-Wholesale, NEC

ADDVANTAGE TECHNOLOGIES GROUP, INC., *pg.* 612, *pg.* 1484
CARLSON JPM STORE FIXTURES, *pg.* 369, *pg.* 919
DAWN FOOD PRODUCTS, INC., *pg.* 1018, *pg.* 893
EDWARD DON & COMPANY, *pg.* 54, *pg.* 672
FRANKE INC., *pg.* 55, *pg.* 1656
FRYMASTER LLC, *pg.* 55, *pg.* 748
GOLDEN CORRAL CORPORATION, *pg.* 1730, *pg.* 1387
JBI, INC., *pg.* 930, *pg.* 123
JURA-CAPRESSO INC., *pg.* 58, *pg.* 1052
THE MANITOWOC COMPANY, INC., *pg.* 1358, *pg.* 1868
PERCEPTICS, LLC, *pg.* 1426, *pg.* 1637
PERFORMANCE FOOD GROUP COMPANY, LLC, *pg.* 1030, *pg.* 1803
PING INC., *pg.* 1842, *pg.* 19
PRESSTEK, INC., *pg.* 456, *pg.* 606
SPX PROCESS EQUIPMENT, *pg.* 1378, *pg.* 1337
SYSTEMAX, INC., *pg.* 481, *pg.* 1324

5048 - Ophthalmic Goods-Wholesale

ALIMERA SCIENCES, INC., *pg.* 1490, *pg.* 482
BAUSCH & LOMB INCORPORATED, *pg.* 1401, *pg.* 1045
DANKER LABORATORIES INC., *pg.* 1408, *pg.* 465
ESSILOR OF AMERICA, INC., *pg.* 1412, *pg.* 1680
FUJINON INC., *pg.* 1414, *pg.* 1129
LUXOTTICA GROUP, *pg.* 8, *pg.* 1323
MARCHON EYEWEAR, INC., *pg.* 1421, *pg.* 1180
MARCOLIN USA INC., *pg.* 1421, *pg.* 23
OHARA CORPORATION, *pg.* 1425, *pg.* 188
SIGNATURE EYEWEAR, INC., *pg.* 1429, *pg.* 105
TURA L.P., *pg.* 1433, *pg.* 1555

5051 - Metals Service Centers & Offices

A. M. CASTLE & CO., *pg.* 64, *pg.* 644
ALAMO IRON WORKS, *pg.* 1311, *pg.* 1739
CENTRAL STEEL & WIRE COMPANY, *pg.* 74, *pg.* 569
CHICAGO TUBE & IRON CO., *pg.* 1323, *pg.* 656
COMMERCIAL METALS COMPANY, *pg.* 76, *pg.* 1718
EARLE M. JORGENSEN COMPANY, *pg.* 80, *pg.* 142
GIBBS WIRE & STEEL COMPANY, INC., *pg.* 1048, *pg.* 371
HARSCO CORPORATION, *pg.* 86, *pg.* 1519
HICKMAN, WILLIAMS & COMPANY, *pg.* 87, *pg.* 1414
L.B. FOSTER COMPANY, *pg.* 1355, *pg.* 1578
MARMON/KEYSTONE CORPORATION, *pg.* 1359, *pg.* 1519
MERCHANT & EVANS, INC., *pg.* 97, *pg.* 1048
METALS USA, INC., *pg.* 97, *pg.* 425
MITSUBISHI INTERNATIONAL CORPORATION, *pg.* 185, *pg.* 1260
MODERN WELDING COMPANY, INC., *pg.* 1363, *pg.* 739
NUCOR CORPORATION, *pg.* 101, *pg.* 1368
OLYMPIC STEEL INC., *pg.* 101, *pg.* 1433
OWEN INDUSTRIES, INC., *pg.* 102, *pg.* 702
P. KAY METAL SUPPLY INC., *pg.* 1176, *pg.* 137
RELIANCE STEEL & ALUMINUM CO., *pg.* 1371, *pg.* 139
RUSSEL METALS INC., *pg.* 1180, *pg.* 1928
RYERSON INC., *pg.* 1373, *pg.* 589
SIMS METAL MANAGEMENT, *pg.* 1396, *pg.* 590
TCI PRECISION METALS, INC., *pg.* 1380, *pg.* 95
TUBULAR STEEL INC., *pg.* 117, *pg.* 1004
WESCO FINANCIAL CORPORATION, *pg.* 821, *pg.* 181

5052 - Coal & other Minerals & Ores-Wholesale

HICKMAN, WILLIAMS & COMPANY, *pg.* 87, *pg.* 1414
TECK RESOURCES LIMITED, *pg.* 1183, *pg.* 1912

5075 - Warm Air Heating & Air Conditioning Equipment & Supplies-Wholesale

BENJAMIN OBDYKE, INC., *pg.* 70, *pg.* 1540
BROCK-MCVEY COMPANY, *pg.* 1043, *pg.* 729
DE'LONGHI AMERICA INC., *pg.* 54, *pg.* 1118
KOCH ENTERPRISES, INC., *pg.* 91, *pg.* 679
MARLEY ENGINEERED PRODUCTS, *pg.* 1074, *pg.* 1612
MESTEK, INC., *pg.* 1074, *pg.* 857
PEIRCE-PHELPS, INC., *pg.* 1075, *pg.* 1568
RINNAI AMERICA CORP., *pg.* 1076, *pg.* 538
SEELEY INTERNATIONAL AMERICAS, *pg.* 1076, *pg.* 19
SOUTHERN PIPE & SUPPLY CO., INC., *pg.* 112, *pg.* 970
WATSCO INC., *pg.* 1078, *pg.* 417

5078 - Refrigeration Equipment & Supplies-Wholesale

DOUGLAS DYNAMICS, INC., *pg.* 204, *pg.* 1874
HUDSON TECHNOLOGIES, INC., *pg.* 1073, *pg.* 1320
MANITOWOC ICE, INC., *pg.* 58, *pg.* 1868

5082 - Construction & Mining Machinery & Equipment, Except Petroleum-Wholesale

AHERN RENTALS, INC., *pg.* 345, *pg.* 1022
APPLIED INDUSTRIAL TECHNOLOGIES, INC., *pg.* 199, *pg.* 1428
ARNOLD MACHINERY COMPANY, *pg.* 1314, *pg.* 1755
ASTEC INDUSTRIES, INC., *pg.* 69, *pg.* 1628
BUTLER MACHINERY COMPANY, *pg.* 1321, *pg.* 1397
DOWNS CRANE & HOIST CO, INC., *pg.* 1330, *pg.* 129
H&E EQUIPMENT SERVICES, INC., *pg.* 85, *pg.* 742
IRONPLANET, INC., *pg.* 1259, *pg.* 183
JOY GLOBAL, INC., *pg.* 1351, *pg.* 1876
THE MANITOWOC COMPANY, INC., *pg.* 1358, *pg.* 1868
PARAGON TECHNOLOGIES, INC., *pg.* 1367, *pg.* 1528
POWER EQUIPMENT COMPANY INC, *pg.* 1369, *pg.* 1637
SAFWAY SERVICES, LLC, *pg.* 109, *pg.* 1898
TITAN MACHINERY INC., *pg.* 1383, *pg.* 1398
VINTAGE PARTS, *pg.* 119, *pg.* 1854

5083 - Farm & Garden Machinery & Equipment-Wholesale

A. DUDA & SONS INC., *pg.* 835, *pg.* 457
ACCO ENGINEERED SYSTEMS, *pg.* 1068, *pg.* 95
AERO CONTROLS, INC., *pg.* 223, *pg.* 439
AEROGROW INTERNATIONAL, INC., *pg.* 1393, *pg.* 310
AG-MEIER INDUSTRIES LLC, *pg.* 700, *pg.* 1668
AGCO CORPORATION, *pg.* 700, *pg.* 530
AHERN RENTALS, INC., *pg.* 345, *pg.* 1022
ALIMAK HEK INC, *pg.* 66, *pg.* 1749
AMERICAN CRYSTAL SUGAR COMPANY, *pg.* 837, *pg.* 951
AMPCO-PITTSBURGH CORPORATION, *pg.* 1313, *pg.* 1573
APSCO APPLIANCE CENTERS, *pg.* 51, *pg.* 415
ARCHER-DANIELS-MIDLAND COMPANY, *pg.* 825, *pg.* 565
ARIS HORTICULTURE, INC., *pg.* 1793, *pg.* 1404
ARMSTRONG GARDEN CENTERS, INC., *pg.* 1793, *pg.* 99
ATT HOLDING CO., *pg.* 1043, *pg.* 1519
AVERY WEIGH-TRONIX, INC., *pg.* 1315, *pg.* 925
AVIALL, INC., *pg.* 224, *pg.* 1676

First page reference indicates Business Class Edition
Second page reference indicates Geographic Edition

BALL HORTICULTURAL COMPANY, *pg.* 1793, *pg.* 668
BAYLOFF STAMPED PRODUCTS, *pg.* 1317, *pg.* 1457
BENJAMIN MOORE & CO., *pg.* 1440, *pg.* 1085
BLAIN SUPPLY, INC., *pg.* 701, *pg.* 1861
BRAUNSCHWEIGER JEWELERS, *pg.* 2, *pg.* 1088
CALIFORNIA PRODUCTS CORPORATION, *pg.* 1441, *pg.* 781
CALLOWAY'S NURSERY, INC., *pg.* 1794, *pg.* 1694
CENTRAL GARDEN & PET COMPANY, *pg.* 1475, *pg.* 303
THE CHAS. C. HART SEED CO., *pg.* 1794, *pg.* 384
CHEMED CORPORATION, *pg.* 327, *pg.* 1410
THE CIVIC GARDEN CENTER OF GREATER CINCINNATI, *pg.* 1794, *pg.* 1412
CONN'S, INC., *pg.* 630, *pg.* 1668
CORNELIUS NURSERIES, *pg.* 1794, *pg.* 1694
CROSMAN SEED CORPORATION, *pg.* 1794, *pg.* 1156
CRUSTBUSTER-SPEED KING, INC., *pg.* 702, *pg.* 714
DAVIS PAINT COMPANY, *pg.* 1441, *pg.* 982
DEERE & COMPANY, *pg.* 703, *pg.* 632
DIAMOND VOGEL PAINT, INC., *pg.* 1441, *pg.* 710
DUNN-EDWARDS CORPORATION, *pg.* 1442, *pg.* 129
THE DWYER GROUP, INC., *pg.* 79, *pg.* 1748
EARL MAY SEED & NURSERY L.C., *pg.* 1795, *pg.* 712
EMERY-WATERHOUSE COMPANY, *pg.* 1047, *pg.* 751
ENGLISH COLOR & SUPPLY INC., *pg.* 1442, *pg.* 1735
EXIDE TECHNOLOGIES, *pg.* 204, *pg.* 483
EXTERRAN HOLDINGS, INC., *pg.* 977, *pg.* 1705
FERRY-MORSE SEED COMPANY, *pg.* 1795, *pg.* 728
FLORIDA WEST COAST PUBLIC BROADCASTING, INC., *pg.* 287, *pg.* 473
GE CONSUMER & INDUSTRIAL, *pg.* 55, *pg.* 733
GEA FARM TECHNOLOGIES, *pg.* 704, *pg.* 636
GLOBAL EPOINT INC., *pg.* 400, *pg.* 67
GRIFFIN GREENHOUSE & NURSERY SUPPLIES, INC., *pg.* 704, *pg.* 848
GROSSENBURG IMPLEMENT, INC., *pg.* 1344, *pg.* 1626
HIRSHFIELD'S INC., *pg.* 1442, *pg.* 937
HOBART FOOD EQUIPMENT GROUP CANADA, *pg.* 56, *pg.* 1929
HUDSON TECHNOLOGIES, INC., *pg.* 1073, *pg.* 1320
JASPER ELECTRIC MOTORS, *pg.* 209, *pg.* 691
JVC AMERICAS CORP., *pg.* 648, *pg.* 1129
KONE INC., *pg.* 1353, *pg.* 633
KUBOTA TRACTOR CORPORATION, *pg.* 705, *pg.* 294
LILYPONS WATER GARDENS INC., *pg.* 1797, *pg.* 766
LURIE GLASS COMPANY, *pg.* 95, *pg.* 1877
MAXONS RESTORATIONS, *pg.* 332, *pg.* 1257
MONROVIA GROWERS, *pg.* 1797, *pg.* 44
MTD PRODUCTS, INC., *pg.* 1057, *pg.* 1478
NASCO INTERNATIONAL, INC., *pg.* 1779, *pg.* 1858
O.A. NEWTON & SON CO, *pg.* 1366, *pg.* 387
ORCHARD SUPPLY HARDWARE STORES CORP., *pg.* 1058, *pg.* 248
PANAMERICAN SEED CO., *pg.* 1798, *pg.* 668
PARAGON TECHNOLOGIES, INC., *pg.* 1367, *pg.* 1528
PLANTATION PRODUCTS INC, *pg.* 1799, *pg.* 839
RITCHIE BROS. AUCTIONEERS INCORPORATED, *pg.* 1372, *pg.* 1907
SCHILLER-PFEIFFER, INC., *pg.* 1061, *pg.* 1587
SEEDBURO EQUIPMENT CO., *pg.* 707, *pg.* 590
THE SHERWIN-WILLIAMS COMPANY, *pg.* 1447, *pg.* 1435
SHERWIN-WILLIAMS DIVERSIFIED BRANDS DIVISION, *pg.* 1448, *pg.* 1435
SHERWIN-WILLIAMS WOOD CARE GROUP, *pg.* 1448, *pg.* 1127
SHIVVERS INC., *pg.* 707, *pg.* 704
SMITH & HAWKEN, LTD., *pg.* 1786, *pg.* 168
SMITHCO, INC., *pg.* 1377, *pg.* 1592
STRANGE'S FLORIST & GREENHOUSES, *pg.* 1283, *pg.* 1804
TD INDUSTRIES, INC., *pg.* 1077, *pg.* 1688
TITAN MACHINERY INC., *pg.* 1383, *pg.* 1398
TRACTOR SUPPLY COMPANY, *pg.* 708, *pg.* 1627
TRUE VALUE COMPANY, *pg.* 1065, *pg.* 592
WALLPAPERS-TO-GO, INC., *pg.* 1791, *pg.* 1744
THE W.W. WILLIAMS COMPANY, *pg.* 1390, *pg.* 1444
YANMAR AMERICA CORPORATION, *pg.* 196, *pg.* 482

5084 - Industrial Machinery & Equipment-Wholesale

3M COMPANY, *pg.* 1142, *pg.* 956
A BRITE COMPANY, *pg.* 1144, *pg.* 1697
ABATIX CORP., *pg.* 1309, *pg.* 1672
ACCURATE FASTENERS INC., *pg.* 1309, *pg.* 789
A.G. DAVIS/AA GAGE, *pg.* 1310, *pg.* 908
A.J. JERSEY INC., *pg.* 1310, *pg.* 1123
ALAMO IRON WORKS, *pg.* 1311, *pg.* 1739
ALIMAK HEK INC, *pg.* 66, *pg.* 1749
ALLIED RUBBER & RIGGING SUPPLY, *pg.* 1878, *pg.* 1519
ALTAIR CORPORATION, *pg.* 1312, *pg.* 910
AMPCO-PITTSBURGH CORPORATION, *pg.* 1313, *pg.* 1573
ANDERSON & VREELAND, INC., *pg.* 1616, *pg.* 1064
ANIXTER PENTACON, INC., *pg.* 1313, *pg.* 64
APPLIED INDUSTRIAL TECHNOLOGIES, INC., *pg.* 199, *pg.* 1428
ARBURG, INC., *pg.* 1314, *pg.* 359
ARGO INTERNATIONAL CORPORATION, *pg.* 1314, *pg.* 1196
ARNOLD MACHINERY COMPANY, *pg.* 1314, *pg.* 1755
AROTECH CORPORATION, *pg.* 1042, *pg.* 865
ATLAS BOLT & SCREW COMPANY, *pg.* 1042, *pg.* 1403
AUTOMATION MAILING AND SHIPPING SOLUTIONS, INC., *pg.* 358, *pg.* 1428
AWISCO NY CORPORATION, *pg.* 1315, *pg.* 1177
BEHLEN MFG. CO., *pg.* 701, *pg.* 1010
BELL-MARK CORPORATION, *pg.* 1620, *pg.* 1108
BOLTON-EMERSON AMERICAS, INC., *pg.* 1318, *pg.* 827
BOSCH INSPECTION TECHNOLOGY INC., *pg.* 1319, *pg.* 1041
BRENNAN INDUSTRIES INC., *pg.* 1319, *pg.* 1429
BROTHER INTERNATIONAL CORPORATION - USA, *pg.* 53, *pg.* 1046
BRYANT GRINDER, *pg.* 1320, *pg.* 1768
BTU INTERNATIONAL, INC., *pg.* 1320, *pg.* 838
C&D TECHNOLOGIES, INC., *pg.* 627, *pg.* 1517
C&H DISTRIBUTORS, LLC, *pg.* 1044, *pg.* 1873
CAMERON VALVES & MEASUREMENT, *pg.* 1321, *pg.* 1703
C.H. HANSON COMPANY, *pg.* 1322, *pg.* 636
CHICAGO METAL FABRICATORS, INC., *pg.* 1323, *pg.* 569
CLARK MATERIAL HANDLING COMPANY, *pg.* 1323, *pg.* 729
CONSEW, *pg.* 53, *pg.* 1049
CRYOVAC, INC., *pg.* 1456, *pg.* 1615
D&S CAR WASH EQUIPMENT CO., *pg.* 1327, *pg.* 979
DANAHER MOTION, *pg.* 1327, *pg.* 1593
DEDERT CORPORATION, *pg.* 1408, *pg.* 649
DEL-TRON PRECISION, INC., *pg.* 1328, *pg.* 337
DEUTZ CORPORATION, *pg.* 1328, *pg.* 536
DEVAR, INC., *pg.* 633, *pg.* 339
DIEHL WOODWORKING MACHINERY, INC., *pg.* 1328, *pg.* 698
DIXON VALVE & COUPLING COMPANY, *pg.* 1045, *pg.* 766
THE DOALL COMPANY, *pg.* 1329, *pg.* 670
DREMEL, *pg.* 1046, *pg.* 634
DYNISCO INSTRUMENTS LLC, *pg.* 1526, *pg.* 823
EATON'S CROUSE-HINDS, *pg.* 1296, *pg.* 1344
EMERY-WATERHOUSE COMPANY, *pg.* 1047, *pg.* 751
ENCON SAFETY PRODUCTS, *pg.* 1334, *pg.* 1705
ENERFAB, INC., *pg.* 81, *pg.* 1412
ENTHONE INC., *pg.* 1161, *pg.* 381
EQUIPMENT DEPOT LTD., *pg.* 1335, *pg.* 1749
ESSENTRA COMPONENTS, *pg.* 1335, *pg.* 901
EXTERRAN HOLDINGS, INC., *pg.* 977, *pg.* 1705
FABREEKA INTERNATIONAL, INC., *pg.* 1882, *pg.* 847
FASTENAL COMPANY, *pg.* 396, *pg.* 966
FEDERAL HOSE MANUFACTURING INC., *pg.* 1047, *pg.* 1469
FORKLIFTS OF MINNESOTA, INC., *pg.* 174, *pg.* 918
FORTUNET, INC., *pg.* 953, *pg.* 1024
GARDNER DENVER NASH, *pg.* 1338, *pg.* 381
GEMA USA INC., *pg.* 1339, *pg.* 686
GENERAL BEARING CORPORATION, *pg.* 205, *pg.* 1350
GENERAL MOTORS COMPANY, *pg.* 175, *pg.* 881
GERBER SCIENTIFIC, INC., *pg.* 1414, *pg.* 380
GLEASON CORPORATION, *pg.* 1340, *pg.* 1335
GOULDS PUMPS, INCORPORATED, *pg.* 1342, *pg.* 1341
GREGORY POOLE EQUIPMENT COMPANY INC., *pg.* 85, *pg.* 1387
HACO-ATLANTIC, INC., *pg.* 1344, *pg.* 1707
HARLAND CLARKE HOLDINGS CORP., *pg.* 1647, *pg.* 1741
HAWKINS, INC., *pg.* 1165, *pg.* 937
HI-VAC CORPORATION, *pg.* 56, *pg.* 1458
HILL & GRIFFITH COMPANY, *pg.* 1167, *pg.* 1414
HIRSCH INTERNATIONAL CORP., *pg.* 694, *pg.* 1164
HITACHI KOKI USA, LTD., *pg.* 1050, *pg.* 537
HOLMATRO, INC., *pg.* 1346, *pg.* 771
HOUGEN MANUFACTURING INC., *pg.* 1347, *pg.* 908
IFCO SYSTEMS NORTH AMERICA, *pg.* 411, *pg.* 1708
INDUSTRIAL DISTRIBUTION GROUP, INC., *pg.* 413, *pg.* 1358
INTELLIGRATED, INC., *pg.* 1349, *pg.* 1460
INTELLIGRATED SYSTEMS LLC, *pg.* 1350, *pg.* 998
ITOCHU INTERNATIONAL INC., *pg.* 1351, *pg.* 1245
ITT CORPORATION, *pg.* 1351, *pg.* 1354
JOHNSON MANUFACTURING COMPANY, *pg.* 1169, *pg.* 712
KAMAN CORPORATION, *pg.* 229, *pg.* 338
KOMATSU AMERICA INDUSTRIES, LLC, *pg.* 1353, *pg.* 656
KOMORI AMERICA CORPORATION, *pg.* 1353, *pg.* 656
KSB INC., *pg.* 1354, *pg.* 1802
LAWSON PRODUCTS, INC., *pg.* 1355, *pg.* 580
LITTLE GIANT PUMP COMPANY, *pg.* 1356, *pg.* 1486
LUFKIN INDUSTRIES, INC., *pg.* 1357, *pg.* 1726
LUSTER-ON PRODUCTS, INC., *pg.* 1171, *pg.* 845
MAKINO INC., *pg.* 1358, *pg.* 1461
MANITEX INTERNATIONAL, INC., *pg.* 1358, *pg.* 559
MATHESON VALLEY, *pg.* 981, *pg.* 1456
MAYFRAN INTERNATIONAL, INC., *pg.* 1359, *pg.* 1432
METZGAR CONVEYOR COMPANY, *pg.* 1360, *pg.* 875
MHI INJECTION MOLDING MACHINERY, INC., *pg.* 1886, *pg.* 620
MOTION INDUSTRIES, INC., *pg.* 213, *pg.* 3
MOTORCAR PARTS OF AMERICA, INC., *pg.* 213, *pg.* 295
MSC INDUSTRIAL DIRECT CO., INC., *pg.* 1057, *pg.* 1181
NACCO INDUSTRIES, INC., *pg.* 1174, *pg.* 1433
NATIONAL BULK EQUIPMENT, INC., *pg.* 1479, *pg.* 892
NATIONAL OILWELL VARCO, INC., *pg.* 1364, *pg.* 1712
NEW ENGLAND MACHINERY, INC., *pg.* 1364, *pg.* 415
NOSHOK INC., *pg.* 1366, *pg.* 1406
NUTTING, *pg.* 1366, *pg.* 1626
O.A. NEWTON & SON CO, *pg.* 1366, *pg.* 387
OIL-DRI CORPORATION OF AMERICA, *pg.* 1480, *pg.* 586
OKUMA AMERICA CORPORATION, *pg.* 1366, *pg.* 1368
PENFLEX, INC., *pg.* 104, *pg.* 1534
PERRY VIDEX LLC, *pg.* 1368, *pg.* 1072
POWIN CORPORATION, *pg.* 1369, *pg.* 1509
PRAB, INC., *pg.* 1369, *pg.* 894
PRECIPART, *pg.* 1370, *pg.* 1160
PRECISION VALVE CORPORATION, *pg.* 1060, *pg.* 1357
PURAFIL, INC., *pg.* 333, *pg.* 530
PURVIS BEARING SERVICE LTD., *pg.* 1371, *pg.* 1686
Q A GROUP LLC., *pg.* 1427, *pg.* 89
QUEST SAFETY PRODUCTS, INC., *pg.* 1371, *pg.* 689
R.D. BITZER CO. INC., *pg.* 106, *pg.* 1515
REMA TIP TOP/NORTH AMERICA, INC., *pg.* 1889, *pg.* 1099
RENTZEL PUMP MANUFACTURING, LP, *pg.* 707, *pg.* 1726
RESCO PRODUCTS GREENSBORO, *pg.* 107, *pg.* 1375
RITE-HITE HOLDING CORPORATION, *pg.* 1372, *pg.* 1880
ROFIN-SINAR TECHNOLOGIES, INC., *pg.* 668, *pg.* 904
ROLLEM CORPORATION OF AMERICA, *pg.* 1372, *pg.* 43
SAMMONS ENTERPRISES, INC., *pg.* 1373, *pg.* 1686
THE SCHMIDT GROUP, INC., *pg.* 1374, *pg.* 1618
SEALING DEVICES INC., *pg.* 1889, *pg.* 1173
SECO/WARWICK CORPORATION, *pg.* 1076, *pg.* 1552
SEQUA CORPORATION, *pg.* 1180, *pg.* 1290
SETCO SALES COMPANY, *pg.* 1061, *pg.* 1426
SGK, *pg.* 1686, *pg.* 590
SIEMENS, *pg.* 1376, *pg.* 1466
SINGER SEWING COMPANY, *pg.* 698, *pg.* 1639
SPENCER FLUID POWER, *pg.* 1889, *pg.* 1822
SPRAYING SYSTEMS CO., *pg.* 1063, *pg.* 670
STANDARD MOTOR PRODUCTS, INC., *pg.* 218, *pg.* 1176
SUPPLY TECHNOLOGIES LLC, *pg.* 1064, *pg.* 1436
TEREX CORPORATION, *pg.* 1381, *pg.* 384
THOMAS ENGINEERING INC., *pg.* 1382, *pg.* 619
THOMPSON INTERNATIONAL INC., *pg.* 1382, *pg.* 729
TRICORBRAUN, *pg.* 1471, *pg.* 1004
TWIN DISC, INCORPORATED, *pg.* 220, *pg.* 1889
UNITED RENTALS, INC., *pg.* 1386, *pg.* 350
U.S. TSUBAKI, INC., *pg.* 221, *pg.* 670
VALMONT INDUSTRIES, INC., *pg.* 1387, *pg.* 1019
VAN SON HOLLAND INK CORPORATION OF AMERICA, *pg.* 487, *pg.* 1169
VIBRA SCREW INC., *pg.* 1387, *pg.* 1126
VINTAGE PARTS, *pg.* 119, *pg.* 1854
WEATHERFORD PRODUCTION OPTIMIZATION, *pg.* 987, *pg.* 1725
WESCO INTERNATIONAL INC., *pg.* 687, *pg.* 1582
THE WILLAMETTE VALLEY COMPANY, *pg.* 1186, *pg.* 1497
WMS INDUSTRIES INC., *pg.* 593, *pg.* 666
THE WOLF MACHINE CO., *pg.* 1389, *pg.* 1427
W.W. GRAINGER, INC., *pg.* 1390, *pg.* 625
THE W.W. WILLIAMS COMPANY, *pg.* 1390, *pg.* 1444

YANMAR AMERICA CORPORATION, pg. 196, pg. 482
ZIMMERMAN-MCDONALD MACHINERY, INC., pg. 1391, pg. 1005

5085 - Industrial Supplies-Wholesale

3M COMPANY, pg. 1142, pg. 956
ABATIX CORP., pg. 1309, pg. 1672
ACCURATE FASTENERS INC., pg. 1309, pg. 789
ALLIED RUBBER & RIGGING SUPPLY, pg. 1878, pg. 1519
ANIXTER PENTACON, INC., pg. 1313, pg. 64
APPLIED INDUSTRIAL TECHNOLOGIES, INC., pg. 199, pg. 1428
ATLAS BOLT & SCREW COMPANY, pg. 1042, pg. 1403
AUTOMATION MAILING AND SHIPPING SOLUTIONS, INC., pg. 358, pg. 1428
CAMERON VALVES & MEASUREMENT, pg. 1321, pg. 1703
C.H. HANSON COMPANY, pg. 1322, pg. 636
CRYOVAC, INC., pg. 1456, pg. 1615
DIXON VALVE & COUPLING COMPANY, pg. 1045, pg. 766
THE DOALL COMPANY, pg. 1329, pg. 670
DREMEL, pg. 1046, pg. 634
EMERY-WATERHOUSE COMPANY, pg. 1047, pg. 751
ENCON SAFETY PRODUCTS, pg. 1334, pg. 1705
ESSENTRA COMPONENTS, pg. 1335, pg. 901
FABREEKA INTERNATIONAL, INC., pg. 1882, pg. 847
FASTENAL COMPANY, pg. 396, pg. 966
FEDERAL HOSE MANUFACTURING INC., pg. 1047, pg. 1469
FORKLIFTS OF MINNESOTA, INC., pg. 174, pg. 918
GENERAL BEARING CORPORATION, pg. 205, pg. 1350
GERBER SCIENTIFIC, INC., pg. 1414, pg. 380
HILL & GRIFFITH COMPANY, pg. 1167, pg. 1414
IFCO SYSTEMS NORTH AMERICA, pg. 411, pg. 1708
INDUSTRIAL DISTRIBUTION GROUP, INC., pg. 413, pg. 1358
JOHNSON MANUFACTURING COMPANY, pg. 1169, pg. 712
KAMAN CORPORATION, pg. 229, pg. 338
LAWSON PRODUCTS, INC., pg. 1355, pg. 580
MATHESON VALLEY, pg. 981, pg. 1456
MOTION INDUSTRIES, INC., pg. 213, pg. 3
MSC INDUSTRIAL DIRECT CO., INC., pg. 1057, pg. 1181
PRECISION VALVE CORPORATION, pg. 1060, pg. 1357
PURVIS BEARING SERVICE LTD., pg. 1371, pg. 1686
Q A GROUP LLC., pg. 1427, pg. 89
QUEST SAFETY PRODUCTS, INC., pg. 1371, pg. 689
REMA TIP TOP/NORTH AMERICA, INC., pg. 1889, pg. 1099
RESCO PRODUCTS GREENSBORO, pg. 107, pg. 1375
SEALING DEVICES INC., pg. 1889, pg. 1173
SUPPLY TECHNOLOGIES LLC, pg. 1064, pg. 1436
TRICORBRAUN, pg. 1471, pg. 1004
U.S. TSUBAKI, INC., pg. 221, pg. 670
VAN SON HOLLAND INK CORPORATION OF AMERICA, pg. 487, pg. 1169
THE WILLAMETTE VALLEY COMPANY, pg. 1186, pg. 1497
W.W. GRAINGER, INC., pg. 1390, pg. 625

5088 - Transportation Equipment & Supplies, Except Motor Vehicles-Wholesale

A&K RAILROAD MATERIALS INC., pg. 1896, pg. 1755
AERO CONTROLS, INC., pg. 223, pg. 439
AIRBUS HELICOPTERS, INC., pg. 223, pg. 1698
AIRCRAFT SPRUCE & SPECIALTY CO., pg. 1759, pg. 69
ARGO INTERNATIONAL CORPORATION, pg. 1314, pg. 1196
AVIALL, INC., pg. 224, pg. 1676
BRUNSWICK CORPORATION, pg. 1828, pg. 623
CITATIONAIR, pg. 1903, pg. 350
CUTTER AVIATION, INC., pg. 227, pg. 16
DASSAULT FALCON JET CORP., pg. 227, pg. 1122
EMBRAER AIRCRAFT HOLDING INC., pg. 227, pg. 425
FURUNO USA, INC., pg. 640, pg. 1819
HAECO AMERICAS, pg. 228, pg. 1374
HARBORMASTER MARINE, INC., pg. 1707, pg. 896
L.B. FOSTER COMPANY, pg. 1355, pg. 1578
MIDAS, INC., pg. 212, pg. 620
MIDAS INTERNATIONAL, INC., pg. 212, pg. 620
MODERN TRACK MACHINERY, pg. 98, pg. 610
NETJETS INC., pg. 1917, pg. 1442
PLAINS ALL AMERICAN PIPELINE, L.P., pg. 983, pg. 1712
RUSH ENTERPRISES INC., pg. 189, pg. 1728
VOLVO PENTA OF THE AMERICAS, INC., pg. 1712, pg. 1778
YAMAHA MOTOR CORPORATION USA, pg. 1713, pg. 76

5093 - Scrap & Waste Materials

COMMERCIAL METALS COMPANY, pg. 76, pg. 1718
INDUSTRIAL SERVICES OF AMERICA, INC., pg. 1884, pg. 734
SIMS METAL MANAGEMENT, pg. 1396, pg. 590
WEYERHAEUSER COMPANY, pg. 121, pg. 1820

5113 - Industrial & Personal Service Paper-Wholesale

3M COMPANY, pg. 1142, pg. 956
ATLANTIC CORPORATION, pg. 1452, pg. 1392
AUTOMATION MAILING AND SHIPPING SOLUTIONS, INC., pg. 358, pg. 1428
C&H DISTRIBUTORS, LLC, pg. 1044, pg. 1873
CASE PAPER COMPANY INC., pg. 1455, pg. 1163
ELKAY PLASTICS COMPANY, INC., pg. 1882, pg. 68
GEORGIA-PACIFIC LLC, pg. 1458, pg. 507
HOLLYMATIC CORPORATION, pg. 1346, pg. 598
LIPPINCOTT WILLIAMS & WILKINS, pg. 1659, pg. 1514
NETWORK SERVICES COMPANY, pg. 1465, pg. 659
SCHOOL SPECIALTY, INC., pg. 467, pg. 1860
SCHWARZ PAPER COMPANY, pg. 1468, pg. 634
ULINE SHIPPING SUPPLIES, pg. 1385, pg. 666
XPEDX, pg. 1473, pg. 1377

5122 - Drugs, Drug Proprietaries & Druggists' Sundries-Wholesale

ADH HEALTH PRODUCTS, INC., pg. 1487, pg. 1154
AKORN, pg. 1488, pg. 1138
ALOETTE COSMETICS, INC., pg. 498, pg. 487
AMAG PHARMACEUTICALS, INC., pg. 1492, pg. 827
AMERICAN INTERNATIONAL INDUSTRIES COMPANY, pg. 498, pg. 126
AMERICO MANUFACTURING CO., INC., pg. 325, pg. 482
AMERISOURCEBERGEN CORPORATION, pg. 1493, pg. 1522
AMWAY CORPORATION, pg. 326, pg. 864
ANIMAL HEALTH INTERNATIONAL, INC., pg. 1474, pg. 1749
ANNIE OAKLEY ENTERPRISES, INC., pg. 499, pg. 693
ASD HEALTHCARE, pg. 1496, pg. 1697
BACTOLAC PHARMACEUTICAL, INC., pg. 1498, pg. 1163
BARE ESCENTUALS, INC., pg. 500, pg. 213
BATH & BODY WORKS, LLC, pg. 500, pg. 1471
BAYER HEALTHCARE CONSUMER CARE DIVISION, pg. 1500, pg. 1087
BEE-ALIVE INC., pg. 1503, pg. 1348
BEIERSDORF NORTH AMERICA INC., pg. 501, pg. 385
BENEFIT COSMETICS LLC, pg. 501, pg. 213
BI-O-KLEEN INDUSTRIES, INC., pg. 326, pg. 1845
BIOSCRIP, INC., pg. 1506, pg. 1158
BLISSWORLD LLC, pg. 501, pg. 1204
BORGHESE, INC., pg. 502, pg. 1205
BURT'S BEES INC., pg. 502, pg. 1370
CAREMARK PHARMACY SERVICES, pg. 1513, pg. 1649
CENTRIC GROUP LLC, pg. 1514, pg. 994
CHESHER EQUIPMENT LTD., pg. 1323, pg. 1925
COLGATE ORAL PHARMACEUTICAL, pg. 1516, pg. 1214
COLOR ME BEAUTIFUL, INC., pg. 505, pg. 1787
COSMETIQUE, INC., pg. 1765, pg. 664
DELTA FOREMOST CHEMICAL CORPORATION, pg. 1155, pg. 1642
DHC USA INC., pg. 507, pg. 216
DIXIE HEALTH, INC., pg. 1524, pg. 535
DS LABORATORIES, INC., pg. 507, pg. 442
EBY-BROWN CO., pg. 1767, pg. 636
EDEN COMPANY, pg. 1768, pg. 1050
ELIZABETH ARDEN, INC., pg. 507, pg. 448
THE ESTEE LAUDER COMPANIES INC., pg. 508, pg. 1229
EXPRESS SCRIPTS, pg. 1530, pg. 1070
FASHION FAIR COSMETICS, LLC, pg. 509, pg. 573
FRAGRANCENET.COM, INC., pg. 1248, pg. 1155
FRONTIER NATURAL PRODUCTS CO-OP, pg. 509, pg. 710
GOODY PRODUCTS, INC., pg. 510, pg. 509
HAELAN PRODUCTS, INC., pg. 860, pg. 1847
HEALTH PRODUCTS CORPORATION, pg. 1540, pg. 1356
HEALTHY DIRECTIONS, pg. 1649, pg. 775
HENRY SCHEIN, INC., pg. 1541, pg. 1180
HERBALIFE INTERNATIONAL OF AMERICA, INC., pg. 1541, pg. 132
HESKA CORPORATION, pg. 1542, pg. 335
HILLYARD, INC., pg. 331, pg. 990
INSPIRED BEAUTY BRANDS, pg. 512, pg. 1244
INTER PARFUMS, INC., pg. 512, pg. 1244
INTERCHEM CORPORATION, pg. 1168, pg. 1101
J. STRICKLAND & COMPANY, pg. 512, pg. 970
JEFFERS, INC., pg. 1477, pg. 5
JOHN PAUL MITCHELL SYSTEMS, pg. 512, pg. 133
JOHNSON & JOHNSON, pg. 1549, pg. 1091
JOLEN CREME BLEACH CORP., pg. 513, pg. 348
LANELABS USA INC., pg. 1554, pg. 1128
LIVING PROOF, INC., pg. 514, pg. 809
LORD & TAYLOR LLC, pg. 1777, pg. 1252
LUITPOLD PHARMACEUTICALS, INC., pg. 1557, pg. 1342
LUMARA HEALTH INC., pg. 1557, pg. 973
MAC-GRAY CORPORATION, pg. 58, pg. 852
MAJESTIC DRUG COMPANY, INC., pg. 516, pg. 1343
MARIETTA HOSPITALITY, pg. 1464, pg. 1155
MARILYN MIGLIN, L.P., pg. 516, pg. 581
MARTIN FRANCHISES INC., pg. 332, pg. 1458
MARY KAY INC., pg. 516, pg. 1657
MAYBELLINE LLC, pg. 516, pg. 1257
MCKESSON CORPORATION, pg. 1560, pg. 222
MEDICINE SHOPPE INTERNATIONAL, INC., pg. 1561, pg. 976
MERLE NORMAN COSMETICS, INC., pg. 517, pg. 136
MWI VETERINARY SUPPLY, INC., pg. 1570, pg. 548
NILFISK-ADVANCE, INC., pg. 332, pg. 953
NORTH AMERICAN CORP., pg. 446, pg. 615
NU SKIN ENTERPRISES, INC., pg. 518, pg. 1755
NUNATURALS, INC., pg. 1576, pg. 1497
NUTRICIA NORTH AMERICA, pg. 1577, pg. 776
OMNICARE, INC, pg. 1578, pg. 1418
OPI PRODUCTS INC., pg. 518, pg. 167
PACIFICHEALTH LABORATORIES, INC., pg. 1579, pg. 1083
PALM BEACH TAN, INC., pg. 519, pg. 1671
PARFUMS CHRISTIAN DIOR, INC, pg. 519, pg. 1276
PARLUX FRAGRANCES, INC., pg. 519, pg. 426
PERFUMANIA HOLDINGS, INC., pg. 520, pg. 1141
PERFUMANIA, INC., pg. 520, pg. 469
PRADA U.S.A. CORP., pg. 31, pg. 1283
PURDUE PHARMA LP, pg. 1587, pg. 377
QUALITY KING DISTRIBUTORS INC., pg. 1587, pg. 1339
RBC LIFE SCIENCES, INC., pg. 1588, pg. 1723
REDKEN LABORATORIES LLC, pg. 520, pg. 1285
REGIS CORPORATION, pg. 521, pg. 941
RESTAURANT DEPOT, LLC, pg. 1782, pg. 1153
REVERE PRODUCTS, pg. 107, pg. 1435
RICOLA USA, INC., pg. 1590, pg. 1106
RUE21, INC., pg. 32, pg. 1591
RUG DOCTOR, LP, pg. 1373, pg. 1734
SALLY BEAUTY HOLDINGS, INC., pg. 522, pg. 1691
SANOFI US, pg. 1592, pg. 1046
SCANDINAVIAN FORMULAS, INC., pg. 1592, pg. 1586
SEPHORA USA INC, pg. 522, pg. 227
SHAKLEE CORPORATION, pg. 1593, pg. 184
SHAMROCK FOODS COMPANY, pg. 895, pg. 20
SHISEIDO COSMETICS AMERICA OF SAC, pg. 522, pg. 1291
SMARTPAK EQUINE, LLC, pg. 1482, pg. 834
SPURRIER CHEMICAL COMPANIES, INC., pg. 1182, pg. 724
STEPAN COMPANY, pg. 1182, pg. 643
TONI & GUY USA, INC., pg. 523, pg. 1689
TOTAL NUTRACEUTICAL SOLUTIONS, INC., pg. 1603, pg. 1509
TRI-K INDUSTRIES, INC., pg. 523, pg. 1099
TWEEZERMAN INTERNATIONAL, pg. 524, pg. 1324
ULTA SALON, COSMETICS & FRAGRANCE, INC., pg. 524, pg. 559
UNITED NATURAL FOODS, INC., pg. 907, pg. 1608
VIDAL SASSOON CO., pg. 524, pg. 1426
VITACOST.COM, INC., pg. 1607, pg. 414
VON SCHRADER COMPANY, pg. 62, pg. 1890
WELLQUEST MEDICAL & WELLNESS CORPORATION, pg. 1610, pg. 31

5142 - Packaged Frozen Foods-Wholesale

AFFILIATED FOODS MIDWEST INC., pg. 1012, pg. 1013
B&G FOODS, INC., pg. 838, pg. 1102
BOB EVANS FARMS, LLC, pg. 841, pg. 1467
BURRIS LOGISTICS, pg. 843, pg. 387
C&S WHOLESALE GROCERS, INC., pg. 1016, pg. 1035
CALAVO GROWERS, INC., pg. 843, pg. 276
CHERRY CENTRAL COOPERATIVE, INC., pg. 847, pg. 909
CONAGRA FOODS LAMB WESTON, INC., pg. 850, pg. 549
FLOWERS FOODS, INC., pg. 855, pg. 541
FOOD SERVICES OF AMERICA, INC., pg. 856, pg. 21
FROSTY ACRES BRANDS, INC., pg. 1020, pg. 484
F.W. BRYCE, INC., pg. 857, pg. 823
GENERAL MILLS CANADA CORP., pg. 828, pg. 1926
GORDON FOOD SERVICE INC., pg. 1021, pg. 913
HIGH LINER FOODS, pg. 862, pg. 1796
INSTITUTION FOOD HOUSE, INC., pg. 864, pg. 1378
THE KRAFT HEINZ COMPANY, pg. 870, pg. 1577
THE KRAFT HEINZ COMPANY, pg. 871, pg. 641
LOCAL & WESTERN OF TEXAS, INC., pg. 1026, pg. 1683
MICHIGAN BLUEBERRY GROWERS ASSOCIATION, pg. 147, pg. 886
MURRY'S, INC., pg. 882, pg. 780
PERFORMANCE FOOD GROUP COMPANY, LLC, pg. 1030, pg. 1803
QUAKER VALLEY FOODS INC., pg. 1031, pg. 1570
VIP FOODSERVICE, pg. 908, pg. 545
WESTERN FAMILY HOLDING CO., INC., pg. 1037, pg. 1509
WHITE CASTLE MANAGEMENT CO., pg. 1756, pg. 1444

5146 - Fish & Seafoods-Wholesale

CANADIAN FISH EXPORTERS, INC., pg. 845, pg. 784
EASTERN FISH COMPANY, pg. 854, pg. 1124
H&N FOODS INTERNATIONAL, INC., pg. 1022, pg. 132
HIGH LINER FOODS INCORPORATED, pg. 862, pg. 1917
HOSS'S STEAK & SEA HOUSE, INC., pg. 1731, pg. 1526
KENNETH COLE PRODUCTIONS, INC., pg. 1810, pg. 1248
KEY FOOD STORES CO-OPERATIVE, INC., pg. 1025, pg. 1343
LEGAL SEA FOODS INC., pg. 1735, pg. 797
SAU-SEA FOODS, INC., pg. 894, pg. 1349
TRIDENT SEAFOODS CORPORATION, pg. 902, pg. 1842
VITA FOOD PRODUCTS, INC., pg. 909, pg. 595
WORLDWIDE FOOD PRODUCTS INC., pg. 910, pg. 1170

5147 - Meats & Meat Products-Wholesale

ADVANCEPIERRE FOODS, INC., pg. 1714, pg. 1409
AMERICAN FOODS GROUP, LLC, pg. 837, pg. 1859
ASSOCIATED FOOD STORES, INC., pg. 1014, pg. 1756
BAKER COMMODITIES, INC., pg. 839, pg. 301
BAR-S FOODS CO., pg. 839, pg. 15
BOAR'S HEAD PROVISIONS CO., INC., pg. 841, pg. 465
BOB EVANS FARMS, LLC, pg. 841, pg. 1467
BOZZUTO'S INC., pg. 1016, pg. 342
CARL BUDDIG & COMPANY, pg. 846, pg. 619
CLOUGHERTY PACKING COMPANY, pg. 848, pg. 128
DARLING INGREDIENTS, INC., pg. 852, pg. 1718
DIETZ & WATSON INC., pg. 853, pg. 1563
ELLENBEE-LEGGETT COMPANY INC., pg. 854, pg. 1452
FRED USINGER, INC., pg. 856, pg. 1874
FRESH MARK, INC., pg. 856, pg. 1461
HATFIELD QUALITY MEATS, INC., pg. 861, pg. 1537
HILLSHIRE BRANDS, pg. 862, pg. 576
HORMEL FOODS CORPORATION, pg. 863, pg. 915
JACMAR COMPANIES, INC., pg. 1733, pg. 67
JBS, pg. 865, pg. 1751
JBS USA HOLDING, INC., pg. 865, pg. 330
JOHN MORRELL FOOD GROUP, pg. 866, pg. 628
JOHNSONVILLE SAUSAGE, LLC, pg. 867, pg. 1894
JONES DAIRY FARM, pg. 867, pg. 1858
KAYEM FOODS, INC., pg. 867, pg. 814
KRONOS PRODUCTS, INC., pg. 872, pg. 614
KUNZLER & COMPANY, INC., pg. 1026, pg. 1546
LEON'S FINE FOODS, INC., pg. 874, pg. 1727
LES TROIS PETITS COCHONS, INC., pg. 874, pg. 1146
LINK SNACKS, INC., pg. 874, pg. 1881
LOCAL & WESTERN OF TEXAS, INC., pg. 1026, pg. 1683
LOPEZ FOODS INC., pg. 1026, pg. 1486
MAPLE LEAF CONSUMER FOODS, pg. 875, pg. 1922
MAPLE LODGE FARMS LTD., pg. 876, pg. 1918
MEAT & SEAFOOD SOLUTIONS, LLC, pg. 1027, pg. 1375
NEW ZEALAND LAMB COOPERATIVE, INC., pg. 886, pg. 385
ODOM'S TENNESSEE PRIDE SAUSAGE, INC., pg. 887, pg. 1640
OMAHA STEAKS INTERNATIONAL, INC., pg. 1780, pg. 1017
OREGON FREEZE DRY, INC., pg. 888, pg. 1492
PATRICK CUDAHY INC., pg. 888, pg. 1856
PEER FOODS INC., pg. 888, pg. 587
QUANTUM FOODS, INC., pg. 891, pg. 559
RESTAURANT DEPOT, LLC, pg. 1782, pg. 1153
ROSE PACKING COMPANY, pg. 892, pg. 556
SHERWOOD FOOD DISTRIBUTORS, pg. 1033, pg. 884
SMITHFIELD FOODS, INC., pg. 896, pg. 1806
THE SMITHFIELD PACKING CO., INC., pg. 896, pg. 1807
SPECIALTY FOODS GROUP-FIELD PACKING DIV., pg. 897, pg. 739
SUGAR CREEK PACKING CO., pg. 899, pg. 1478
SUPERVALU, INC., pg. 1035, pg. 924
TREEHOUSE FOODS, INC., pg. 901, pg. 649
TYSON FOODS, INC., pg. 902, pg. 35
UNIFIED GROCERS, INC., pg. 1036, pg. 1842
URM STORES, INC., pg. 1036, pg. 1844
WILLIAMS SAUSAGE CO., INC., pg. 910, pg. 1656
WINN DIXIE STORES, INC., pg. 1038, pg. 435

5154 - Livestock-Buying & Marketing

KEENELAND ASSOCIATION INC., pg. 1477, pg. 730

5162 - Plastics Materials & Basic Forms & Shapes-Wholesale

A. M. CASTLE & CO., pg. 64, pg. 644
A. SCHULMAN, INC., pg. 1144, pg. 1452
ASHLAND INC., pg. 972, pg. 726
BAMBERGER POLYMERS, INC., pg. 1148, pg. 1171
CO-EX CORP., pg. 76, pg. 382
THE DOW CHEMICAL COMPANY, pg. 1157, pg. 898
E.V. ROBERTS & ASSOCIATES, INC., pg. 1161, pg. 63
GRAVOGRAPH-NEW HERMES, pg. 1344, pg. 531
HARWICK STANDARD DISTRIBUTION CORPORATION, pg. 1164, pg. 1402
HD SUPPLY, INC., pg. 86, pg. 509
MACDERMID, INC., pg. 1172, pg. 321
MULTI-PLASTICS, INC., pg. 1886, pg. 1457
PROFESSIONAL PLASTICS, INC., pg. 1888, pg. 94
RYAN HERCO PRODUCTS CORPORATION, pg. 1889, pg. 52
SMITH INTERNATIONAL, INC., pg. 1377, pg. 1715
TRANSILWRAP COMPANY, INC., pg. 1470, pg. 613

5169 - Chemicals & Allied Products-Wholesale, NEC

ACCURATE CHEMICAL & SCIENTIFIC CORPORATION, pg. 1145, pg. 1350
ACETO CORPORATION, pg. 1145, pg. 1323
ACUITY BRANDS, INC., pg. 1294, pg. 487
AIR PRODUCTS AND CHEMICALS, INC., pg. 1145, pg. 1513
AIRGAS, INC., pg. 1146, pg. 1583
ALEN AMERICAS INC., pg. 325, pg. 1699
AMWAY CORPORATION, pg. 326, pg. 864
ASHLAND INC., pg. 972, pg. 726
AVENUE INDUSTRIAL SUPPLY CO. LTD., pg. 1043, pg. 1923
AWISCO NY CORPORATION, pg. 1315, pg. 1177
AXIALL CORPORATION, pg. 69, pg. 491
BALCHEM CORPORATION, pg. 839, pg. 1183
BASF CATALYSTS LLC, pg. 1148, pg. 1074
BIRKO CORPORATION, pg. 1149, pg. 332
CABOT CORPORATION, pg. 1151, pg. 792
CALGON CARBON CORPORATION, pg. 1151, pg. 1574
CHEMISPHERE CORPORATION, pg. 1152, pg. 994
CHEMTURA CORPORATION, pg. 1152, pg. 355
DAUBERT INDUSTRIES, INC., pg. 1155, pg. 561
THE DOW CHEMICAL COMPANY, pg. 1157, pg. 898
EVERGREEN LABS, INC., pg. 330, pg. 1847
FLEXIBLE SOLUTIONS INTERNATIONAL, INC., pg. 1163, pg. 1913
HARWICK STANDARD DISTRIBUTION CORPORATION, pg. 1164, pg. 1402
HAVILAND ENTERPRISES INC., pg. 1165, pg. 887
HAWKINS, INC., pg. 1165, pg. 937
HEATBATH CORPORATION, pg. 1165, pg. 826
HILLYARD, INC., pg. 331, pg. 990
HOMAX PRODUCTS INC., pg. 1442, pg. 1817
HUBBARD-HALL, INC., pg. 1167, pg. 382
HUNTSMAN CORPORATION, pg. 1167, pg. 1758
HURST CHEMICAL COMPANY, pg. 1168, pg. 174
INTERCHEM CORPORATION, pg. 1168, pg. 1101
INTERPLASTIC CORPORATION, pg. 1168, pg. 961
JELMAR COMPANY, pg. 331, pg. 660
KRAFT CHEMICAL COMPANY, pg. 1170, pg. 632
KRONOS INTERNATIONAL, INC., pg. 980, pg. 1683
KRONOS WORLDWIDE, INC., pg. 980, pg. 1053
THE LUBRIZOL CORPORATION, pg. 1171, pg. 1481
MAINTENANCE, INC., pg. 95, pg. 1482
MASTER SILICON CARBIDE INDUSTRIES, INC., pg. 1172, pg. 353
MATHESON VALLEY, pg. 981, pg. 1456
MAYS CHEMICAL COMPANY, pg. 1172, pg. 688
MERISANT COMPANY, pg. 876, pg. 581
MOC PRODUCTS COMPANY, INC., pg. 332, pg. 174
MULTICHEM, INC., pg. 1174, pg. 1950
NEWMARKET CORPORATION, pg. 982, pg. 1803
NL INDUSTRIES, INC., pg. 1174, pg. 1684
NOVA CHEMICALS CORPORATION, pg. 1175, pg. 1904
NUCO2 INC., pg. 1175, pg. 468
THE NUTRASWEET COMPANY, pg. 1860, pg. 585
PACIFIC ETHANOL, INC., pg. 982, pg. 197
PHARMCO-AAPER, pg. 1177, pg. 740
PHIBROCHEM, pg. 1177, pg. 1124
PRAXAIR, INC., pg. 1178, pg. 344
PREISER SCIENTIFIC, INC., pg. 1427, pg. 1851
PVS CHEMICALS, INC., pg. 1178, pg. 884
ROCK VALLEY OIL & CHEMICAL COMPANY, pg. 1179, pg. 631
R.T. VANDERBILT COMPANY, INC., pg. 1180, pg. 364
THE SAVOGRAN COMPANY, pg. 1447, pg. 840
SUMITOMO ELECTRIC, pg. 1599, pg. 1297
SWISHER INTERNATIONAL, INC., pg. 1600, pg. 1369
TECH SPRAY, L.P., pg. 1183, pg. 1659
TOR MINERALS INTERNATIONAL INC., pg. 1184, pg. 1672
TRI-K INDUSTRIES, INC., pg. 523, pg. 1099
UNIVAR INC., pg. 1184, pg. 1829
VALENT U.S.A. CORP., pg. 708, pg. 305
VALHI, INC., pg. 1185, pg. 1690
VON SCHRADER COMPANY, pg. 62, pg. 1890
WD-40 COMPANY, pg. 337, pg. 210
WILBUR-ELLIS COMPANY, pg. 1185, pg. 234
YARA N AMERICA, INC., pg. 1802, pg. 477
ZEP INC., pg. 338, pg. 524

5172 - Petroleum & Petroleum Products Wholesalers, Except Bulk Stations & Terminals

ASHLAND INC., pg. 972, pg. 726
ATMOS ENERGY CORPORATION, pg. 1935, pg. 1675
BP CORPORATION NORTH AMERICA INC., pg. 973, pg. 665
DEVON ENERGY CORPORATION, pg. 975, pg. 1485
EXXON MOBIL CORPORATION, pg. 977, pg. 1718
GULF OIL LIMITED PARTNERSHIP, pg. 978, pg. 814
HEADWATERS INCORPORATED, pg. 978, pg. 1763
HKN, INC., pg. 979, pg. 1745
THE H.T. HACKNEY COMPANY, pg. 1023, pg. 1637
IRVING OIL CORPORATION, pg. 980, pg. 1038
MITSUBISHI INTERNATIONAL CORPORATION, pg. 185, pg. 1260
NRG ENERGY, INC., pg. 1948, pg. 1712
PLAINS ALL AMERICAN PIPELINE, L.P., pg. 983, pg. 1712
RACETRAC PETROLEUM, INC., pg. 983, pg. 519
SHELL OIL COMPANY, pg. 984, pg. 1714
SUBURBAN PROPANE PARTNERS, L.P., pg. 113, pg. 1132
SUNCOR ENERGY INC., pg. 985, pg. 1905
TRAMMO, pg. 986, pg. 1304
TRI STAR ENERGY, LLC, pg. 986, pg. 1655
UNITED REFINING COMPANY, pg. 986, pg. 1590
VALERO ENERGY CORPORATION, pg. 986, pg. 1743

5182 - Wines & Distilled Alcoholic Beverages-Wholesale

MIKE'S HARD LEMONADE CO., *pg.* 1966, *pg.* 582

5198 - Paints, Varnishes & Supplies-Wholesale

ACE HARDWARE CORPORATION, *pg.* 1040, *pg.* 644
EMERY-WATERHOUSE COMPANY, *pg.* 1047, *pg.* 751
ENGLISH COLOR & SUPPLY INC., *pg.* 1442, *pg.* 1735
FASTENAL COMPANY, *pg.* 396, *pg.* 966
HIRSHFIELD'S INC., *pg.* 1442, *pg.* 937
JONES-BLAIR COMPANY, *pg.* 1443, *pg.* 1682
KRAVET FABRICS INC., *pg.* 932, *pg.* 1142
THE MURALO COMPANY, *pg.* 1444, *pg.* 1042
OERLIKON BALZERS COATING USA, INC., *pg.* 1444, *pg.* 610
THYBONY WALLCOVERINGS INC., *pg.* 945, *pg.* 591
THE VALSPAR CORPORATION, *pg.* 1449, *pg.* 945

5199 - Nondurable Goods-Wholesale, NEC

CLAVEL, LTD., *pg.* 376, *pg.* 823
E. MISHAN & SONS, INC., *pg.* 1767, *pg.* 1226
LION BRAND YARN COMPANY, *pg.* 696, *pg.* 1050
THE SARUT GROUP, *pg.* 12, *pg.* 1146
SEVENTH GENERATION, INC., *pg.* 335, *pg.* 1765
WARNER BROS. WORLDWIDE CONSUMER PRODUCTS, *pg.* 490, *pg.* 55

5211 - Lumber & other Building Materials Dealers

ACTIVE ELECTRICAL SUPPLY COMPANY, *pg.* 612, *pg.* 563
ADDVANTAGE TECHNOLOGIES GROUP, INC., *pg.* 612, *pg.* 1484
ALTEX ELECTRONICS, LTD., *pg.* 348, *pg.* 1739
AMERICAN BUILDERS & CONTRACTORS SUPPLY CO., INC., *pg.* 66, *pg.* 1854
AMERICAN WOODMARK CORPORATION, *pg.* 913, *pg.* 1811
AMETEK FLOORCARE SPECIALTY MOTORS DIVISION, *pg.* 616, *pg.* 1456
ANIXTER INTERNATIONAL INC., *pg.* 1313, *pg.* 614
ANIXTER PENTACON, INC., *pg.* 1313, *pg.* 64
ARMSTRONG WORLD INDUSTRIES, INC., *pg.* 914, *pg.* 1545
ARTISTIC TILE INC., *pg.* 914, *pg.* 1119
ASSOCIATED MATERIALS LLC, *pg.* 69, *pg.* 1445
AUBUCHON HARDWARE, *pg.* 1043, *pg.* 859
BATEMAN BROTHERS LUMBER CO., INC., *pg.* 70, *pg.* 1555
BEACON ROOFING SUPPLY, INC., *pg.* 70, *pg.* 840
BELDEN, INC., *pg.* 624, *pg.* 993
BENJAMIN MOORE & CO., *pg.* 1440, *pg.* 1085
BIG BEAM EMERGENCY SYSTEMS, INC., *pg.* 1294, *pg.* 598
BLUELINX HOLDINGS, INC., *pg.* 70, *pg.* 491
BMC SELECT, *pg.* 71, *pg.* 546
BOISE CASCADE, *pg.* 1453, *pg.* 788
BOISE CASCADE HOLDINGS, L.L.C., *pg.* 1453, *pg.* 546
BORAL ROOFING, *pg.* 71, *pg.* 107
BROCK-MCVEY COMPANY, *pg.* 1043, *pg.* 729
BUILDING MATERIALS CORPORATION OF AMERICA, *pg.* 72, *pg.* 1129
BUILDING PRODUCTS OF CANADA CORP., *pg.* 72, *pg.* 1951
CAE INC., *pg.* 226, *pg.* 1959
CAESARSTONE, *pg.* 919, *pg.* 299
CALIFORNIA PRODUCTS CORPORATION, *pg.* 1441, *pg.* 781
CARLISLE WIDE PLANK FLOORS, INC., *pg.* 919, *pg.* 1039
CASCADE MICROTECH, INC., *pg.* 1405, *pg.* 1492
CEDARBROOK SAUNA & STEAM, *pg.* 1830, *pg.* 1819
CHASE CORPORATION, *pg.* 1152, *pg.* 803
CLARY CORPORATION, *pg.* 226, *pg.* 150
CONSUMERS KITCHENS & BATHS, *pg.* 77, *pg.* 1167
CONTINENTAL MARKETING, *pg.* 1831, *pg.* 66
COSENTINO USA, *pg.* 77, *pg.* 1745
CPG INTERNATIONAL, INC., *pg.* 1881, *pg.* 1586
CRAFTMADE INTERNATIONAL, INC., *pg.* 1295, *pg.* 1670
DAVIS PAINT COMPANY, *pg.* 1441, *pg.* 982
DIAMOND VOGEL PAINT, INC., *pg.* 1441, *pg.* 710
DO IT BEST CORP., *pg.* 1045, *pg.* 680
DORCY INTERNATIONAL INC., *pg.* 1046, *pg.* 1439
DUNN-EDWARDS CORPORATION, *pg.* 1442, *pg.* 129
EAO SWITCH CORPORATION, *pg.* 1046, *pg.* 356
EATON CORPORATION - INDUSTRIAL CONTROLS, *pg.* 1296, *pg.* 1874
E.C. BARTON & COMPANY, *pg.* 80, *pg.* 33
EIS, INC., *pg.* 80, *pg.* 504
EMERY-WATERHOUSE COMPANY, *pg.* 1047, *pg.* 751
ENERGIZER HOLDINGS, INC., *pg.* 637, *pg.* 996
ENGLISH COLOR & SUPPLY INC., *pg.* 1442, *pg.* 1735
FASTENAL COMPANY, *pg.* 396, *pg.* 966
FISHER HOUSE FOUNDATION, INC., *pg.* 81, *pg.* 776
FLORIDA TILE INDUSTRIES, INC., *pg.* 82, *pg.* 730
FOXWORTH-GALBRAITH LUMBER COMPANY, *pg.* 1047, *pg.* 1730
FUJI ELECTRIC CORPORATION OF AMERICA, *pg.* 640, *pg.* 1118
GRAHAM MOTORS AND CONTROLS, *pg.* 177, *pg.* 1692
GRAYBAR ELECTRIC COMPANY, INC., *pg.* 1299, *pg.* 997
GREAT LAKES WINDOW, INC., *pg.* 85, *pg.* 1478
GROHE AMERICA, INC., *pg.* 1048, *pg.* 557
GROSSMANS BARGAIN OUTLET, *pg.* 85, *pg.* 847
GUARDIAN BUILDING PRODUCTS DISTRIBUTION, *pg.* 85, *pg.* 1619
GUARDIAN INDUSTRIES CORP., *pg.* 85, *pg.* 869
HARVEY INDUSTRIES, INC., *pg.* 86, *pg.* 851
HD SUPPLY, INC., *pg.* 86, *pg.* 509
H.E. WILLIAMS, INC., *pg.* 1299, *pg.* 974
HEADWATERS INCORPORATED, *pg.* 978, *pg.* 1763
HIGH END SYSTEMS, INC., *pg.* 1299, *pg.* 1663
HIRSHFIELD'S INC., *pg.* 1442, *pg.* 937
HOCHIKI AMERICA CORPORATION, *pg.* 1050, *pg.* 50
THE HOME DEPOT, INC., *pg.* 1050, *pg.* 510
HOME HARDWARE STORES LIMITED, *pg.* 1051, *pg.* 1933
HOUSTON WIRE & CABLE COMPANY, *pg.* 643, *pg.* 1708
HUTTIG BUILDING PRODUCTS, INC., *pg.* 88, *pg.* 998
INTERLINE BRANDS, INC., *pg.* 1051, *pg.* 433
JASPER ELECTRIC MOTORS, *pg.* 209, *pg.* 691
JELD-WEN, INC., *pg.* 1051, *pg.* 1499
KATY INDUSTRIES, INC., *pg.* 1126, *pg.* 973
KEENEY MANUFACTURING COMPANY, *pg.* 90, *pg.* 360
LAFARGE CANADA INC., *pg.* 92, *pg.* 1958
LAMPERT YARDS, INC., *pg.* 1053, *pg.* 962
LAMPS PLUS INC., *pg.* 1300, *pg.* 64
LARSON MANUFACTURING COMPANY, *pg.* 93, *pg.* 1624
LEADER INSTRUMENTS CORPORATION, *pg.* 1419, *pg.* 75
LOWE'S COMPANIES, INC., *pg.* 1053, *pg.* 1383
LSI INDUSTRIES INC., *pg.* 58, *pg.* 1416
LUMBER LIQUIDATORS HOLDINGS, INC., *pg.* 94, *pg.* 1808
LURIE GLASS COMPANY, *pg.* 95, *pg.* 1877
LYDALL, INC., *pg.* 1357, *pg.* 354
MARLITE, INC., *pg.* 95, *pg.* 1448
MARTIN DOOR MANUFACTURING, INC., *pg.* 96, *pg.* 1759
MAYER ELECTRIC SUPPLY COMPANY INC., *pg.* 653, *pg.* 3
MCCOY'S BUILDING SUPPLY CENTERS, *pg.* 1055, *pg.* 1744
MEEK'S BUILDING CENTERS, *pg.* 1055, *pg.* 1006
MENARD, INC., *pg.* 1055, *pg.* 1857
MERSEN, *pg.* 1302, *pg.* 836
MG BUILDING MATERIALS, *pg.* 1056, *pg.* 1741
MID-CAPE HOME CENTERS, *pg.* 1056, *pg.* 844
MINERALS TECHNOLOGIES INC., *pg.* 1173, *pg.* 617
NAPLES LUMBER & SUPPLY INC., *pg.* 99, *pg.* 451
NIAGARA TRANSFORMER CORP., *pg.* 1302, *pg.* 1150
NKK SWITCHES, *pg.* 1302, *pg.* 23
NORANDEX/REYNOLDS DISTRIBUTION, INC., *pg.* 99, *pg.* 1455
NORCRAFT HOLDINGS, LP, *pg.* 100, *pg.* 921
NORTEK, INC., *pg.* 100, *pg.* 1607
OATEY SUPPLY CHAIN SERVICES, *pg.* 30, *pg.* 1433
OCEAN POWER TECHNOLOGIES, INC., *pg.* 1948, *pg.* 1107
OLSON RUG COMPANY, *pg.* 939, *pg.* 586
OMEGA FLEX, INC., *pg.* 982, *pg.* 1532
OMEGA WATCH COMPANY, *pg.* 10, *pg.* 1131
OREPAC HOLDING COMPANY INC., *pg.* 102, *pg.* 1512
PACIFIC NATIONAL GROUP INC., *pg.* 103, *pg.* 119
PALM HARBOR HOMES, INC., *pg.* 1107, *pg.* 1658
PASS & SEYMOUR/LEGRAND, *pg.* 1303, *pg.* 1344
PHILIPS LIGHTING, *pg.* 1303, *pg.* 806
POWER & TELEPHONE SUPPLY COMPANY, *pg.* 665, *pg.* 1646
PRIMESOURCE BUILDING PRODUCTS, INC., *pg.* 105, *pg.* 1723
PURCELL MURRAY COMPANY INC., *pg.* 59, *pg.* 50
RAND WORLDWIDE, INC., *pg.* 459, *pg.* 821
R.D. BITZER CO. INC., *pg.* 106, *pg.* 1515
ROCK OF AGES CORPORATION, *pg.* 108, *pg.* 1766
ROCKY MOUNTAIN LOG HOMES, *pg.* 108, *pg.* 1008
ROHL LLC, *pg.* 1061, *pg.* 116
R.P. WILLIAMS & SONS, INC., *pg.* 108, *pg.* 1033
RSI HOME PRODUCTS, *pg.* 108, *pg.* 1381
RYAN HERCO PRODUCTS CORPORATION, *pg.* 1889, *pg.* 52
SANFORD & HAWLEY, INC., *pg.* 109, *pg.* 381
SCHNEIDER ELECTRIC, *pg.* 467, *pg.* 1609
SELKIRK CORPORATION, *pg.* 1076, *pg.* 1736
THE SHERWIN-WILLIAMS COMPANY, *pg.* 1447, *pg.* 1435
SHERWIN-WILLIAMS DIVERSIFIED BRANDS DIVISION, *pg.* 1448, *pg.* 1435
SHERWIN-WILLIAMS WOOD CARE GROUP, *pg.* 1448, *pg.* 1127
SIEMENS BUILDING TECHNOLOGIES, INC., *pg.* 1376, *pg.* 560
SIERRA PACIFIC INDUSTRIES, *pg.* 110, *pg.* 43
SL INDUSTRIES, INC., *pg.* 674, *pg.* 1090
SOUTHERN LUMBER & MILLWORK CORP., *pg.* 112, *pg.* 1613
SOUTHERN PIPE & SUPPLY CO., INC., *pg.* 112, *pg.* 970
STANDARD WIRE & CABLE CO., *pg.* 1306, *pg.* 187
STANLEY ACCESS TECHNOLOGIES, LLC, *pg.* 112, *pg.* 349
STAR LUMBER & SUPPLY COMPANY, INC., *pg.* 113, *pg.* 724
SUMMITVILLE TILES, INC., *pg.* 113, *pg.* 1475
SYAR INDUSTRIES, INC., *pg.* 114, *pg.* 163
TAMURA CORPORATION OF AMERICA, *pg.* 1380, *pg.* 291
TECHNIBUS LLC, *pg.* 1380, *pg.* 1408
THOMAS & BETTS CORPORATION, *pg.* 680, *pg.* 1646
TOPBULB.COM LLC, *pg.* 1307, *pg.* 677
TOTO USA, INC., *pg.* 1065, *pg.* 536
TRUE HOME VALUE, INC., *pg.* 117, *pg.* 738
UNIVERSAL FOREST PRODUCTS, INC., *pg.* 117, *pg.* 890
USG CORPORATION, *pg.* 118, *pg.* 594
W.A. ROOSEVELT COMPANY, *pg.* 119, *pg.* 1864
WALKER & ZANGER, INC., *pg.* 119, *pg.* 281
WALLPAPERS-TO-GO, INC., *pg.* 1791, *pg.* 1744
WALPOLE WOODWORKERS, INC., *pg.* 120, *pg.* 849
WATERWISE INC., *pg.* 1066, *pg.* 438
WATTS WATER TECHNOLOGIES, INC., *pg.* 1078, *pg.* 837
WAXMAN INDUSTRIES, INC., *pg.* 120, *pg.* 1406
WESCO INTERNATIONAL INC., *pg.* 687, *pg.* 1582
WESTINGHOUSE LIGHTING CORPORATION, *pg.* 687, *pg.* 1571
WM OHS INC., *pg.* 947, *pg.* 324
WOODWARD, INC., *pg.* 122, *pg.* 329
ZOLTEK COMPANIES, INC., *pg.* 123, *pg.* 974

5231 - Paint, Glass & Wallpaper Stores

BENJAMIN MOORE & CO., *pg.* 1440, *pg.* 1085
CALIFORNIA PRODUCTS CORPORATION, *pg.* 1441, *pg.* 781
DAVIS PAINT COMPANY, *pg.* 1441, *pg.* 982
DIAMOND VOGEL PAINT, INC., *pg.* 1441, *pg.* 710
DUNN-EDWARDS CORPORATION, *pg.* 1442, *pg.* 129
ENGLISH COLOR & SUPPLY INC., *pg.* 1442, *pg.* 1735
HIRSHFIELD'S INC., *pg.* 1442, *pg.* 937
LURIE GLASS COMPANY, *pg.* 95, *pg.* 1877
THE SHERWIN-WILLIAMS COMPANY, *pg.* 1447, *pg.* 1435
SHERWIN-WILLIAMS DIVERSIFIED BRANDS DIVISION, *pg.* 1448, *pg.* 1435
SHERWIN-WILLIAMS WOOD CARE GROUP, *pg.* 1448, *pg.* 1127
WALLPAPERS-TO-GO, INC., *pg.* 1791, *pg.* 1744

5251 - Hardware Stores

ACE HARDWARE CORPORATION, *pg.* 1040, *pg.* 644
ACO HARDWARE, INC., *pg.* 1040, *pg.* 885
ALASKA INDUSTRIAL HARDWARE INC., *pg.* 1041, *pg.* 10
AUBUCHON HARDWARE, *pg.* 1043, *pg.* 859
BENJAMIN OBDYKE, INC., *pg.* 70, *pg.* 1540
BLACK & DECKER CANADA INC., *pg.* 1043, *pg.* 1933
BLAIN SUPPLY, INC., *pg.* 701, *pg.* 1861

First page reference indicates Business Class Edition
Second page reference indicates Geographic Edition

COAST CUTLERY COMPANY, pg. 1121, pg. 1501
DARNELL-ROSE, pg. 1045, pg. 67
DO IT BEST CORP., pg. 1045, pg. 680
DORMER PRAMET, pg. 1329, pg. 609
EMERY-WATERHOUSE COMPANY, pg. 1047, pg. 751
FARREY'S WHOLESALE HARDWARE CO., INC., pg. 1047, pg. 442
FASTENAL COMPANY, pg. 396, pg. 966
HARBOR FREIGHT TOOLS, pg. 1772, pg. 55
INTERLINE BRANDS, INC., pg. 1051, pg. 433
LAWSON PRODUCTS, INC., pg. 1355, pg. 580
LIFETIME BRANDS, INC., pg. 1127, pg. 1161
MAKITA U.S.A., INC., pg. 1358, pg. 120
MATCO TOOLS CORPORATION, pg. 1055, pg. 1474
MCCOY'S BUILDING SUPPLY CENTERS, pg. 1055, pg. 1744
MOHAWK FINISHING PRODUCTS, INC., pg. 1173, pg. 1378
NORTHERN TOOL + EQUIPMENT, pg. 1366, pg. 919
ORCHARD SUPPLY HARDWARE STORES CORP., pg. 1058, pg. 248
OUTWATER PLASTIC INDUSTRIES, INC., pg. 1058, pg. 1044
PRO GROUP, INC., pg. 1782, pg. 331
Q.E.P. CO., INC., pg. 1371, pg. 413
RESTORATION HARDWARE HOLDINGS, INC., pg. 1060, pg. 70
ROCKFORD PRODUCTS CORP., pg. 1372, pg. 655
SNAP-ON INCORPORATED, pg. 1062, pg. 1862
SPENCER FLUID POWER, pg. 1889, pg. 1822
TRUE VALUE COMPANY, pg. 1065, pg. 592
VICTORINOX SWISS ARMY INC., pg. 1139, pg. 357
WAXMAN INDUSTRIES, INC., pg. 120, pg. 1406
WESTLAKE ACE HARDWARE, INC., pg. 1067, pg. 717

5261 - Retail Nurseries, Lawn & Garden Supply Stores

A. DUDA & SONS INC., pg. 835, pg. 457
AG PROCESSING INC., pg. 835, pg. 1013
AJINOMOTO HEARTLAND LLC, pg. 1488, pg. 563
ALLIANCE ONE INTERNATIONAL, INC., pg. 1893, pg. 1384
AMERICAN CRYSTAL SUGAR COMPANY, pg. 837, pg. 951
AMERICAN VANGUARD CORPORATION, pg. 1793, pg. 165
THE ANDERSONS INCORPORATED, pg. 1793, pg. 1461
ARCHER-DANIELS-MIDLAND COMPANY, pg. 825, pg. 565
ARETT SALES CORPORATION, pg. 700, pg. 1107
ARIS HORTICULTURE, INC., pg. 1793, pg. 1404
ARMSTRONG GARDEN CENTERS, INC., pg. 1793, pg. 99
BALL HORTICULTURAL COMPANY, pg. 1793, pg. 668
BIRDSONG CORPORATION, pg. 1851, pg. 1808
BUNGE LIMITED, pg. 842, pg. 1351
CALLOWAY'S NURSERY, INC., pg. 1794, pg. 1694
CENTRAL GARDEN & PET COMPANY, pg. 1475, pg. 303
THE CHAS. C. HART SEED CO., pg. 1794, pg. 384
CHS INC., pg. 702, pg. 926
THE CIVIC GARDEN CENTER OF GREATER CINCINNATI, pg. 1794, pg. 1412
CONRAD FAFARD, INC., pg. 702, pg. 781
CORNELIUS NURSERIES, pg. 1794, pg. 1694
CROSMAN SEED CORPORATION, pg. 1794, pg. 1156
DENVER WHOLESALE FLORISTS COMPANY, pg. 1794, pg. 319
DOW AGROSCIENCES LLC, pg. 1156, pg. 684
DUPONT PIONEER, pg. 1795, pg. 708
EARL MAY SEED & NURSERY L.C., pg. 1795, pg. 712
FERRY-MORSE SEED COMPANY, pg. 1795, pg. 728
FLORIDA WEST COAST PUBLIC BROADCASTING, INC., pg. 287, pg. 473
FORREST KEELING NURSERY, INC., pg. 1795, pg. 977
FTD GROUP, INC., pg. 1795, pg. 608
FURST-MCNESS COMPANY, pg. 1476, pg. 613
GILBERT H. WILD & SON, LLC, pg. 1796, pg. 1005
GRIFFIN GREENHOUSE & NURSERY SUPPLIES, INC., pg. 704, pg. 848
HARRIS MORAN SEED CO., pg. 1796, pg. 150
HARRY & DAVID HOLDINGS, INC., pg. 1022, pg. 1499
HAWKINS, INC., pg. 1165, pg. 937
INTERMOUNTAIN FARMERS ASSOCIATION, pg. 705, pg. 1759
J.D. HEISKELL & CO., pg. 1477, pg. 297
LANCASTER LEAF TOBACCO CO., pg. 1796, pg. 1786
LEBANON SEABOARD CORPORATION, pg. 1797, pg. 1547
LILYPONS WATER GARDENS INC., pg. 1797, pg. 766
MOEWS SEED CO., INC., pg. 1797, pg. 616
MONROVIA GROWERS, pg. 1797, pg. 44
MONSANTO, pg. 1798, pg. 971
MONSANTO, pg. 1798, pg. 1399
MONSANTO COMPANY, pg. 1173, pg. 999
MORINAGA NUTRITIONAL FOODS, INC., pg. 1028, pg. 295
N.K. HURST CO., INC., pg. 886, pg. 689
ORCHARD SUPPLY HARDWARE STORES CORP., pg. 1058, pg. 248
OWENSBORO GRAIN COMPANY, INC., pg. 706, pg. 739
THE PAGE SEED CO., pg. 1798, pg. 1163
PANAMERICAN SEED CO., pg. 1798, pg. 668
PHIBROCHEM, pg. 1177, pg. 1124
PLAINS COTTON COOPERATIVE ASSOCIATION, pg. 697, pg. 1726
PLANTATION PRODUCTS INC, pg. 1799, pg. 839
PREMIER TECH HORTICULTURE LTD., pg. 1799, pg. 1958
PYCO INDUSTRIES, INC., pg. 706, pg. 1726
THE SCOTTS MIRACLE-GRO COMPANY, pg. 1799, pg. 1459
THE SCOULAR COMPANY, pg. 1481, pg. 1018
THE SIEBENTHALER CO., pg. 1800, pg. 1446
SMITH & HAWKEN, LTD., pg. 1786, pg. 168
SOUTHERN AGRICULTURAL INSECTICIDES, INC., pg. 1181, pg. 458
STRANGE'S FLORIST & GREENHOUSES, pg. 1283, pg. 1804
SUN BULB COMPANY, INC., pg. 1800, pg. 409
SYNGENTA SEEDS, INC., pg. 1801, pg. 950
SYNGENTA SEEDS, INC., pg. 1801, pg. 630
TERRAL SEED, INC., pg. 1801, pg. 748
TILLAMOOK COUNTY CREAMERY ASSOCIATION, pg. 901, pg. 1509
TRACTOR SUPPLY COMPANY, pg. 708, pg. 1627
THE UHLMANN CO., pg. 834, pg. 986
VITERRA INC., pg. 834, pg. 1962
WAYNESBORO NURSERIES, INC., pg. 1801, pg. 1811
WHITE RIVER COOPERATIVE INC., pg. 708, pg. 693
WILBUR-ELLIS COMPANY, pg. 1185, pg. 234
YARA N AMERICA, INC., pg. 1802, pg. 477
YOUNG PECAN, INC., pg. 1864, pg. 1615

5271 - Mobile Home Dealers

AMERICAN HOMESTAR CORPORATION, pg. 67, pg. 1725
CAVCO INDUSTRIES, INC., pg. 74, pg. 16
CHAMPION ENTERPRISES HOLDINGS, LLC, pg. 75, pg. 910
CLAYTON HOMES, INC., pg. 1086, pg. 1640

5311 - Department Stores

BELK, INC., pg. 1760, pg. 1364
BIG LOTS, INC., pg. 1762, pg. 1438
BLOOMINGDALE'S, INC., pg. 1763, pg. 1204
BON TON STORES, INC., pg. 1763, pg. 1596
BOSCOV'S DEPARTMENT STORE, LLC, pg. 1763, pg. 1583
BURLINGTON COAT FACTORY, pg. 1764, pg. 1047
COSTA DEL MAR SUNGLASSES, INC., pg. 1407, pg. 419
DILLARD'S, INC., pg. 1766, pg. 34
FRED MEYER STORES, INC., pg. 1769, pg. 1502
THE GLIK COMPANY, pg. 1771, pg. 615
GORDMANS STORES INC., pg. 1771, pg. 1016
HART STORES INC., pg. 1773, pg. 1951
HUDSON'S BAY COMPANY, pg. 1773, pg. 1938
J.C. PENNEY COMPANY, INC., pg. 1774, pg. 1732
KMART CORPORATION, pg. 1775, pg. 617
KOHL'S CORPORATION, pg. 1775, pg. 1870
THE KROGER CO., pg. 1025, pg. 1416
LOEHMANN'S HOLDINGS INC., pg. 29, pg. 1144
LORD & TAYLOR LLC, pg. 1777, pg. 1252
MACY'S EAST, pg. 1777, pg. 1254
MACY'S FLORIDA, pg. 1777, pg. 444
MACY'S, INC., pg. 1778, pg. 1417
MARSHALLS OF MA, INC., pg. 1778, pg. 821
MEIJER, INC., pg. 1779, pg. 888
NEIMAN MARCUS, INC., pg. 30, pg. 1684
ROSS STORES, INC., pg. 1783, pg. 78
SAKS FIFTH AVENUE, INC., pg. 1783, pg. 1287
SAKS INCORPORATED, pg. 1783, pg. 1288
SAM'S CLUB, pg. 1783, pg. 29
SEARS HOLDINGS CORPORATION, pg. 1784, pg. 618
SHARPE DRY GOODS CO., INC., pg. 1785, pg. 1484
SHOPKO, pg. 1785, pg. 1860
STAGE STORES, INC., pg. 33, pg. 1715
STEIN MART, INC., pg. 1786, pg. 435
TARGET CORPORATION, pg. 1786, pg. 942
T.J. MAXX, pg. 1788, pg. 822
THE TJX COMPANIES, INC., pg. 1788, pg. 822
WAL-MART CANADA CORP., pg. 1790, pg. 1929
WAL-MART STORES, INC., pg. 1790, pg. 29
WAL-MART.COM, pg. 1287, pg. 50

5399 - Miscellaneous General Merchandise Stores

7-ELEVEN CANADA, INC., pg. 237, pg. 1909
7-ELEVEN, INC., pg. 1012, pg. 1672
99 CENTS ONLY STORES LLC, pg. 1759, pg. 66
ACME MARKETS, INC., pg. 1012, pg. 1549
AFFILIATED FOODS, INC., pg. 1012, pg. 1658
AHOLD USA, INC., pg. 1013, pg. 1520
ALBERTSON'S LLC, pg. 1013, pg. 546
ALDI FOOD INC., pg. 1013, pg. 556
ALIMENTATION COUCHE-TARD INC., pg. 1013, pg. 1951
ALLEGRO COFFEE CO., pg. 836, pg. 336
ALON BRANDS, INC., pg. 1013, pg. 1673
ARDEN GROUP, INC., pg. 1014, pg. 68
B&B CORPORATE HOLDINGS, INC., pg. 1015, pg. 471
BASHAS' SUPERMARKETS, pg. 1015, pg. 12
BI-LO, LLC, pg. 1015, pg. 1617
BIG LOTS, INC., pg. 1762, pg. 1438
BIG Y FOODS, INC., pg. 1015, pg. 845
BJ'S WHOLESALE CLUB, INC., pg. 1762, pg. 857
BROOKSHIRE GROCERY COMPANY, pg. 1016, pg. 1748
BUTERA MARKET, pg. 1016, pg. 609
C&K MARKET, INC., pg. 1016, pg. 1496
CASEY'S GENERAL STORES, INC., pg. 1017, pg. 701
CITARELLA, pg. 1017, pg. 1212
THE COPPS CORPORATION, pg. 1017, pg. 1895
COSTCO WHOLESALE CORPORATION, pg. 1765, pg. 1820
CUMBERLAND FARMS, INC., pg. 1018, pg. 820
D'AGOSTINO SUPERMARKETS INC., pg. 1018, pg. 1173
DEMOULAS SUPER MARKETS INC., pg. 1018, pg. 848
DIERBERGS MARKETS INC., pg. 1018, pg. 974
DIRECTBUY, INC., pg. 1766, pg. 694
DISCOUNT DRUG MART INC., pg. 1524, pg. 1464
DOLLAR GENERAL CORPORATION, pg. 1767, pg. 1635
DOMINICK'S FINER FOODS, LLC, pg. 1019, pg. 644
EMPIRE COMPANY LIMITED, pg. 1019, pg. 1917
FAMILY DOLLAR STORES, INC., pg. 1768, pg. 1382
FAREWAY STORES, INC., pg. 1019, pg. 702
FARM FRESH INC., pg. 1019, pg. 1810
FARM STORES, pg. 1019, pg. 417
FIESTA MART LLC, pg. 1019, pg. 1705
FOOD LION, LLC, pg. 1019, pg. 1390
THE FRED W. ALBRECHT GROCERY CO., pg. 1020, pg. 1400
FRED'S INC., pg. 1769, pg. 1644
FRESH & EASY NEIGHBORHOOD MARKET INC, pg. 1020, pg. 80
THE FRESH MARKET, INC., pg. 1020, pg. 1374
FRESHDIRECT, LLC, pg. 857, pg. 1174
GELSON'S MARKETS, pg. 1020, pg. 85
GEORGE WESTON LIMITED, pg. 858, pg. 1938
GERLAND CORPORATION, pg. 1020, pg. 1706
GIANT EAGLE AMERICAN SEAWAY FOODS, pg. 1020, pg. 1405
GIANT EAGLE, INC., pg. 1020, pg. 1575
GIANT FOOD STORES, LLC, pg. 1021, pg. 1520
GIANT OF MARYLAND LLC, pg. 1021, pg. 773
GO-MART INC., pg. 1021, pg. 1849
GOLUB CORPORATION, pg. 1021, pg. 1340
GOODWILL INDUSTRIES INTERNATIONAL, INC., pg. 1771, pg. 776
GRADE A MARKET INC., pg. 1021, pg. 362
THE GREAT ATLANTIC & PACIFIC TEA COMPANY, INC., pg. 1021, pg. 1086
GREENWICH VILLAGE ORCHESTRA, pg. 551, pg. 1236
H-E-B, pg. 1022, pg. 1740
HAGGEN, INC., pg. 1022, pg. 1817
HAMMACHER SCHLEMMER & CO., INC., pg. 1124, pg. 637
HANNAFORD BROTHERS CO., pg. 1022, pg. 752
HARPS FOOD STORES, INC., pg. 1022, pg. 35
HARRIS TEETER, INC., pg. 1022, pg. 1383
HOMELAND STORES, INC., pg. 1023, pg. 1486
HOUCHENS INDUSTRIES INC., pg. 1023, pg. 726
HY-VEE, INC., pg. 1023, pg. 713

5411 - Grocery Stores

First page reference indicates Business Class Edition
Second page reference indicates Geographic Edition

WINN DIXIE STORES, INC., pg. 1038, pg. 435
YOPLAIT USA, INC., pg. 910, pg. 947

5421 - Meat & Fish Markets, Including Freezer Provisions

ADVANCEPIERRE FOODS, INC., pg. 1714, pg. 1409
AMERICAN FOODS GROUP, LLC, pg. 837, pg. 1859
ASSOCIATED FOOD STORES, INC., pg. 1014, pg. 1756
BAR-S FOODS CO., pg. 839, pg. 15
BOAR'S HEAD PROVISIONS CO., INC., pg. 841, pg. 465
BOB EVANS FARMS, LLC, pg. 841, pg. 1467
BOZZUTO'S INC., pg. 1016, pg. 342
CARGILL MEAT SOLUTIONS, pg. 846, pg. 722
CARL BUDDIG & COMPANY, pg. 846, pg. 619
CEDAR FARMS COMPANY, INC., pg. 846, pg. 1559
CHARLES RIVER LABORATORIES, INC., pg. 1475, pg. 360
CLOUGHERTY PACKING COMPANY, pg. 848, pg. 128
DIETZ & WATSON INC., pg. 853, pg. 1563
ELLENBEE-LEGGETT COMPANY INC., pg. 854, pg. 1452
FRED USINGER, INC., pg. 856, pg. 1874
FRESH MARK, INC., pg. 856, pg. 1461
HATFIELD QUALITY MEATS, INC., pg. 861, pg. 1537
HILLSHIRE BRANDS, pg. 862, pg. 576
HORMEL FOODS CORPORATION, pg. 863, pg. 915
JACMAR COMPANIES, INC., pg. 1733, pg. 67
JBS, pg. 865, pg. 1751
JBS USA HOLDING, INC., pg. 865, pg. 330
JOHN MORRELL FOOD GROUP, pg. 866, pg. 628
JOHNSONVILLE SAUSAGE, LLC, pg. 867, pg. 1894
JONES DAIRY FARM, pg. 867, pg. 1858
KAYEM FOODS, INC., pg. 867, pg. 814
KEY FOOD STORES CO-OPERATIVE, INC., pg. 1025, pg. 1343
KRONOS PRODUCTS, INC., pg. 872, pg. 614
KUNZLER & COMPANY, INC., pg. 1026, pg. 1546
LANCASTER COLONY CORPORATION, pg. 873, pg. 1441
LEON'S FINE FOODS, INC., pg. 874, pg. 1727
LES TROIS PETITS COCHONS, INC., pg. 874, pg. 1146
LINK SNACKS, INC., pg. 874, pg. 1881
LOCAL & WESTERN OF TEXAS, INC., pg. 1026, pg. 1683
LOPEZ FOODS INC., pg. 1026, pg. 1486
MAPLE LEAF CONSUMER FOODS, pg. 875, pg. 1922
MEAT & SEAFOOD SOLUTIONS, LLC, pg. 1027, pg. 1375
NEW ZEALAND LAMB COOPERATIVE, INC., pg. 886, pg. 385
NULAID FOODS INC., pg. 887, pg. 193
ODOM'S TENNESSEE PRIDE SAUSAGE, INC., pg. 887, pg. 1640
OMAHA STEAKS INTERNATIONAL, INC., pg. 1780, pg. 1017
OREGON FREEZE DRY, INC., pg. 888, pg. 1492
PATRICK CUDAHY INC., pg. 888, pg. 1856
PEER FOODS INC., pg. 888, pg. 587
PERDUE FARMS INCORPORATED, pg. 889, pg. 777
QUANTUM FOODS, INC., pg. 891, pg. 559
RESTAURANT DEPOT, LLC, pg. 1782, pg. 1153
ROSE PACKING COMPANY, pg. 892, pg. 556
SHERWOOD FOOD DISTRIBUTORS, pg. 1033, pg. 884
SIMMONS FOODS INC., pg. 895, pg. 35
SMITHFIELD FOODS, INC., pg. 896, pg. 1806
THE SMITHFIELD PACKING CO., INC., pg. 896, pg. 1807
SPECIALTY FOODS GROUP-FIELD PACKING DIV., pg. 897, pg. 739
SUGAR CREEK PACKING CO., pg. 899, pg. 1478
SUPERVALU, INC., pg. 1035, pg. 924
SYSCO CORPORATION, pg. 1035, pg. 1716
TREEHOUSE FOODS, INC., pg. 901, pg. 649
UNIFIED GROCERS, INC., pg. 1036, pg. 1842
URM STORES, INC., pg. 1036, pg. 1844
WESTERN BEEF, INC., pg. 1037, pg. 1333
WILLIAMS SAUSAGE CO., INC., pg. 910, pg. 1656
WINN DIXIE STORES, INC., pg. 1038, pg. 435

5431 - Fruit Stores & Vegetable Markets

B.C. TREE FRUITS LTD., pg. 1015, pg. 1908
CALAVO GROWERS, INC., pg. 843, pg. 276
COSTA FRUIT & PRODUCE INC., pg. 850, pg. 793
DOLE FOOD COMPANY, INC., pg. 853, pg. 306
DRISCOLL STRAWBERRY ASSOCIATES INC., pg. 854, pg. 305
FRESH DEL MONTE PRODUCE INC., pg. 856, pg. 418
KEY FOOD STORES CO-OPERATIVE, INC., pg. 1025, pg. 1343
LA PREFERIDA, INC., pg. 873, pg. 579
MICHIGAN BLUEBERRY GROWERS ASSOCIATION, pg. 147, pg. 886
PERFORMANCE FOOD GROUP COMPANY, LLC, pg. 1030, pg. 1803
RESTAURANT DEPOT, LLC, pg. 1782, pg. 1153
SPARTANNASH CO., pg. 1034, pg. 925
SUNKIST GROWERS, INC., pg. 899, pg. 299
WASHINGTON STATE FRUIT COMMISSION, pg. 161, pg. 1847

5441 - Candy, Nut & Confectionery Stores

BROWN & HALEY, pg. 1851, pg. 1820
C.J. VITNER CO., pg. 848, pg. 571
EBY-BROWN CO., pg. 1767, pg. 636
FERRERO U.S.A., INC., pg. 1852, pg. 1121
GHIRARDELLI CHOCOLATE COMPANY, pg. 1854, pg. 252
THE HERSHEY CO., pg. 1855, pg. 1538
INTERNATIONAL DAIRY QUEEN, INC., pg. 1732, pg. 938
INVENTURE FOODS, INC., pg. 1023, pg. 17
MARS, INCORPORATED, pg. 1858, pg. 1792
MIKE-SELL'S POTATO CHIP COMPANY, pg. 1860, pg. 1446
PERFETTI VAN MELLE USA, INC., pg. 1860, pg. 727
PEZ CANDY, INC., pg. 1861, pg. 367
PROMOTION IN MOTION, INC., pg. 1861, pg. 1052
RAMMKERR, INC., pg. 1746, pg. 986
RUSSELL STOVER CANDIES, INC., pg. 1861, pg. 986
STORCK USA, L.P., pg. 1862, pg. 591
WHITMAN'S CANDIES, INC., pg. 1863, pg. 987

5461 - Retail Bakeries

AUNTIE ANNE'S INC., pg. 1715, pg. 1546
BAB, INC., pg. 1715, pg. 599
BIMBO BAKERIES USA INC., pg. 840, pg. 1540
BRUEGGER'S CORPORATION, pg. 1718, pg. 1764
CINNABON, INC., pg. 1723, pg. 493
DUNKIN' BRANDS GROUP, INC., pg. 1727, pg. 810
EINSTEIN NOAH RESTAURANT GROUP, INC., pg. 1019, pg. 332
HOSTESS BRANDS LLC, pg. 1856, pg. 984
KRISPY KREME DOUGHNUTS, INC., pg. 1734, pg. 1394
OLD SALEM, INCORPORATED, pg. 572, pg. 1395
WETZEL'S PRETZELS LLC, pg. 910, pg. 181

5499 - Miscellaneous Food Stores

ACTIVE ORGANICS, INC., pg. 498, pg. 1725
ADAMS EXTRACT & SPICE LLC, pg. 835, pg. 1698
ADH HEALTH PRODUCTS, INC., pg. 1487, pg. 1154
AKORN, pg. 1488, pg. 1138
ALOETTE COSMETICS, INC., pg. 498, pg. 487
ALPHA BAKING COMPANY, pg. 836, pg. 564
AMAG PHARMACEUTICALS, INC., pg. 1492, pg. 827
AMERICAN CRYSTAL SUGAR COMPANY, pg. 837, pg. 951
AMERICAN INTERNATIONAL INDUSTRIES COMPANY, pg. 498, pg. 126
AMERISOURCEBERGEN CORPORATION, pg. 1493, pg. 1522
AMWAY CORPORATION, pg. 326, pg. 864
ANIMAL HEALTH INTERNATIONAL, INC., pg. 1474, pg. 1749
ANNIE OAKLEY ENTERPRISES, INC., pg. 499, pg. 693
ARROWHEAD MOUNTAIN SPRING WATER COMPANY, pg. 238, pg. 349
ASD HEALTHCARE, pg. 1496, pg. 1697
ATALANTA CORPORATION, pg. 838, pg. 1057
ATKINS NUTRITIONALS, INC., pg. 1498, pg. 316
A.V. OLSSON TRADING CO. INC., pg. 838, pg. 372
BACTOLAC PHARMACEUTICAL, INC., pg. 1498, pg. 1163
BARE ESCENTUALS, INC., pg. 500, pg. 213
BASHAS' SUPERMARKETS, pg. 1015, pg. 12
BATH & BODY WORKS, LLC, pg. 500, pg. 1471
BAYER HEALTHCARE CONSUMER CARE DIVISION, pg. 1500, pg. 1087
BEE-ALIVE INC., pg. 1503, pg. 1348
BEIERSDORF NORTH AMERICA INC., pg. 501, pg. 385
BENEFIT COSMETICS LLC, pg. 501, pg. 213
BIOSCRIP, INC., pg. 1506, pg. 1158
BLISSWORLD LLC, pg. 501, pg. 1204
BORGHESE, INC., pg. 502, pg. 1205
BOSTON PIZZA INTERNATIONAL, INC., pg. 1016, pg. 1908
BURT'S BEES INC., pg. 502, pg. 1370
CAMERICAN INTERNATIONAL, pg. 844, pg. 1101
CAREMARK PHARMACY SERVICES, pg. 1513, pg. 1649
CARGILL SALT, pg. 846, pg. 926
CASEY'S GENERAL STORES, INC., pg. 1017, pg. 701
CEDAR FARMS COMPANY, INC., pg. 846, pg. 1559
CENTRIC GROUP LLC, pg. 1514, pg. 994
CHERRY CENTRAL COOPERATIVE, INC., pg. 847, pg. 909
CHOBANI LLC, pg. 847, pg. 1318
CIAO BELLA GELATO COMPANY, pg. 1851, pg. 1066
CLIF BAR INC., pg. 848, pg. 83
CLOVER STORNETTA FARMS INC., pg. 848, pg. 182
THE COFFEE BEANERY LTD., pg. 849, pg. 886
COFFEE HOLDING CO., INC., pg. 849, pg. 1343
COLAVITA USA, INC., pg. 849, pg. 1056
COLGATE ORAL PHARMACEUTICAL, pg. 1516, pg. 1214
COLONY BRANDS INC., pg. 849, pg. 1881
COLOR ME BEAUTIFUL, INC., pg. 505, pg. 1787
COSMETIQUE, INC., pg. 1765, pg. 664
COSTA FRUIT & PRODUCE INC., pg. 850, pg. 793
CROWN PRINCE, INC., pg. 850, pg. 67
CRYSTAL ROCK HOLDINGS, INC., pg. 248, pg. 382
CYTOSPORT, INC., pg. 1018, pg. 45
DEAN & DELUCA, INC., pg. 1018, pg. 723
DEAN FOODS COMPANY, pg. 852, pg. 1679
DEL MONTE FOODS, INC., pg. 852, pg. 304
DHC USA INC., pg. 507, pg. 216
DIXIE HEALTH, INC., pg. 1524, pg. 535
DREYER'S GRAND ICE CREAM HOLDINGS, INC., pg. 1852, pg. 171
DS LABORATORIES, INC., pg. 507, pg. 442
DUTCH GOLD HONEY INC., pg. 854, pg. 1546
EBY-BROWN CO., pg. 1767, pg. 636
EDEN COMPANY, pg. 1768, pg. 1050
EDEN FOODS INC., pg. 1019, pg. 875
EDIBLE ARRANGEMENTS INTERNATIONAL, INC., pg. 1768, pg. 382
ELIZABETH ARDEN, INC., pg. 507, pg. 448
ENZYMATIC THERAPY INC., pg. 1529, pg. 1859
THE ESTEE LAUDER COMPANIES INC., pg. 508, pg. 1229
EXPRESS SCRIPTS, pg. 1530, pg. 1070
FARMER BROTHERS COMPANY, pg. 855, pg. 293
FASHION FAIR COSMETICS, LLC, pg. 509, pg. 573
FORM YOU 3 INTERNATIONAL, INC., pg. 1531, pg. 1400
FRAGRANCENET.COM, INC., pg. 1248, pg. 1155
FRONTIER NATURAL PRODUCTS CO-OP, pg. 509, pg. 710
GAIAM, INC., pg. 1532, pg. 334
GALAXY NUTRITIONAL FOODS, INC., pg. 857, pg. 1603
GAY LEA FOODS CO-OPERATIVE LIMITED, pg. 858, pg. 1926
GENERAL NUTRITION CENTERS, INC., pg. 1534, pg. 1575
GERBER PRODUCTS COMPANY, pg. 858, pg. 1067
GNC HOLDINGS INC., pg. 1537, pg. 1576
GOODY PRODUCTS, INC., pg. 510, pg. 509
GORDON FOOD SERVICE INC., pg. 1021, pg. 913
GRAY & COMPANY, pg. 859, pg. 1503
THE GREAT LAKES CHEESE CO., INC., pg. 859, pg. 1455
GREEN SPOT, INC., pg. 251, pg. 68
HAELAN PRODUCTS, INC., pg. 860, pg. 1847
HAWAII COFFEE COMPANY, pg. 861, pg. 543
HAYDENERGY, INC., pg. 861, pg. 1238
HEALTH PRODUCTS CORPORATION, pg. 1540, pg. 1356
HEALTHY DIRECTIONS, pg. 1649, pg. 775
HENRY SCHEIN, INC., pg. 1541, pg. 1180
HERBALIFE INTERNATIONAL OF AMERICA, INC., pg. 1541, pg. 132
HESKA CORPORATION, pg. 1542, pg. 335
HICKORY FARMS, INC., pg. 862, pg. 1462
HILL'S PET NUTRITION, INC., pg. 1476, pg. 721
HILLSHIRE BRANDS, pg. 862, pg. 576
HOSTESS BRANDS LLC, pg. 1856, pg. 984
INKO'S WHITE ICED TEA, pg. 1023, pg. 1243
INSPIRED BEAUTY BRANDS, pg. 512, pg. 1244
INTER PARFUMS, INC., pg. 512, pg. 1244
INTERCHEM CORPORATION, pg. 1168, pg. 1101
J. STRICKLAND & COMPANY, pg. 512, pg. 970
THE JEAN COUTU GROUP (PJC) INC., pg. 1548, pg. 1952
JEFFERS, INC., pg. 1477, pg. 5
JENNY CRAIG OPERATIONS, INC., pg. 1548, pg. 59
JOHN PAUL MITCHELL SYSTEMS, pg. 512, pg. 133

JOHNSON & JOHNSON, *pg.* 1549, *pg.* 1091
JOHNSON BROTHERS LIQUOR COMPANY, *pg.* 1965, *pg.* 961
JOHNSON CONTROLS UNITARY PRODUCTS, *pg.* 1073, *pg.* 1484
JOLEN CREME BLEACH CORP., *pg.* 513, *pg.* 348
JURA-CAPRESSO INC., *pg.* 58, *pg.* 1052
KEURIG GREEN MOUNTAIN, INC., *pg.* 868, *pg.* 1768
KIKKOMAN INTERNATIONAL INC., *pg.* 868, *pg.* 220
KOZY SHACK INC., *pg.* 869, *pg.* 1167
KRAFT FOOD INGREDIENTS, *pg.* 870, *pg.* 1645
LA PREFERIDA, INC., *pg.* 873, *pg.* 579
LANCASTER LEAF TOBACCO CO., *pg.* 1796, *pg.* 1786
LAND O'LAKES, INC., *pg.* 873, *pg.* 915
LANELABS USA INC., *pg.* 1554, *pg.* 1128
LAVAZZA PREMIUM COFFEES CORP., *pg.* 874, *pg.* 1250
LIFEPLUS INTERNATIONAL, *pg.* 1556, *pg.* 29
LINDT & SPRUNGLI (USA) INC., *pg.* 1857, *pg.* 1039
LIVING PROOF, INC., *pg.* 514, *pg.* 009
LORD & TAYLOR LLC, *pg.* 1777, *pg.* 1252
LUITPOLD PHARMACEUTICALS, INC., *pg.* 1557, *pg.* 1342
LUMARA HEALTH INC., *pg.* 1557, *pg.* 973
MAJESTIC DRUG COMPANY, INC., *pg.* 516, *pg.* 1343
MARIETTA HOSPITALITY, *pg.* 1464, *pg.* 1155
MARILYN MIGLIN, L.P., *pg.* 516, *pg.* 581
MARY KAY INC., *pg.* 516, *pg.* 1657
MASSIMO ZANETTI BEVERAGE USA, *pg.* 876, *pg.* 1808
MAXIMUM HUMAN PERFORMANCE, INC., *pg.* 1559, *pg.* 1065
MAYBELLINE LLC, *pg.* 516, *pg.* 1257
MCKESSON CORPORATION, *pg.* 1560, *pg.* 222
MEAT & SEAFOOD SOLUTIONS, LLC, *pg.* 1027, *pg.* 1375
MEDICINE SHOPPE INTERNATIONAL, INC., *pg.* 1561, *pg.* 976
MERLE NORMAN COSMETICS, INC., *pg.* 517, *pg.* 136
MICHIGAN MILK PRODUCERS ASSOCIATION, *pg.* 147, *pg.* 903
MOUNTAIN VALLEY SPRING COMPANY, *pg.* 257, *pg.* 33
MWI VETERINARY SUPPLY, INC., *pg.* 1570, *pg.* 548
NATIONAL ENZYME COMPANY, *pg.* 882, *pg.* 978
NATIONAL WINE & SPIRITS, INC., *pg.* 1967, *pg.* 689
NESTLE PROFESSIONAL BEVERAGES, *pg.* 257, *pg.* 474
NESTLE WATERS NORTH AMERICA INC., *pg.* 257, *pg.* 375
N.K. HURST CO., INC., *pg.* 886, *pg.* 689
NORSELAND, INC., *pg.* 886, *pg.* 376
NORTH AMERICAN CORP., *pg.* 446, *pg.* 615
NU SKIN ENTERPRISES, INC., *pg.* 518, *pg.* 1755
NUNATURALS, INC., *pg.* 1576, *pg.* 1497
NUTRICIA NORTH AMERICA, *pg.* 1577, *pg.* 776
NUTRISYSTEM, INC., *pg.* 1577, *pg.* 1533
OAKHURST DAIRY, *pg.* 887, *pg.* 752
OMNICARE, INC, *pg.* 1578, *pg.* 1418
ORANGE PEEL ENTERPRISES, INC., *pg.* 1028, *pg.* 477
PACIFICHEALTH LABORATORIES, INC., *pg.* 1579, *pg.* 1083
PALM BEACH TAN, INC., *pg.* 519, *pg.* 1671
PARFUMS CHRISTIAN DIOR, INC, *pg.* 519, *pg.* 1276
PARLUX FRAGRANCES, INC., *pg.* 519, *pg.* 426
PEET'S COFFEE & TEA, INC., *pg.* 1029, *pg.* 85
PEPE'S INC., *pg.* 1744, *pg.* 587
PERFUMANIA HOLDINGS, INC., *pg.* 520, *pg.* 1141
PERFUMANIA, INC., *pg.* 520, *pg.* 469
POLAR BEVERAGES, *pg.* 264, *pg.* 862
PRADA U.S.A. CORP., *pg.* 31, *pg.* 1283
PRIMO WATER CORPORATION, *pg.* 1030, *pg.* 1395
PURDUE PHARMA LP, *pg.* 1587, *pg.* 377
QUALITY KING DISTRIBUTORS INC., *pg.* 1587, *pg.* 1339
RBC LIFE SCIENCES, INC., *pg.* 1588, *pg.* 1723
RED BULL NORTH AMERICA, INC., *pg.* 264, *pg.* 275
REDKEN LABORATORIES LLC, *pg.* 520, *pg.* 1285
REGIS CORPORATION, *pg.* 521, *pg.* 941
RESTAURANT DEPOT, LLC, *pg.* 1782, *pg.* 1153
RICOLA USA, INC., *pg.* 1590, *pg.* 1106
ROBERTET, INC., *pg.* 522, *pg.* 1100
ROMAN MEAL COMPANY, *pg.* 834, *pg.* 1845
ROUNDY'S SUPERMARKETS INC., *pg.* 1032, *pg.* 1880
RUE21, INC., *pg.* 32, *pg.* 1591
SALLY BEAUTY HOLDINGS, INC., *pg.* 522, *pg.* 1691
SANOFI US, *pg.* 1592, *pg.* 1046
SAU-SEA FOODS, INC., *pg.* 894, *pg.* 1349
SCANDINAVIAN FORMULAS, INC., *pg.* 1592, *pg.* 1586
SCHREIBER FOODS, INC., *pg.* 894, *pg.* 1859
THE SECOND CUP LTD., *pg.* 1749, *pg.* 1928
SEPHORA USA INC, *pg.* 522, *pg.* 227
SHAKLEE CORPORATION, *pg.* 1593, *pg.* 184
SHAMROCK FOODS COMPANY, *pg.* 895, *pg.* 20
SHISEIDO COSMETICS AMERICA OF SAC, *pg.* 522, *pg.* 1291
SLIM-FAST FOODS COMPANY, *pg.* 896, *pg.* 1061
SMARTPAK EQUINE, LLC, *pg.* 1482, *pg.* 834
SOBEYS INC., *pg.* 1034, *pg.* 1917
SPARTANNASH CO., *pg.* 1034, *pg.* 925
STAR FINE FOODS-BORGES USA, *pg.* 897, *pg.* 93
STARBUCKS CORPORATION, *pg.* 897, *pg.* 1840
STEPAN COMPANY, *pg.* 1182, *pg.* 643
STROHMEYER & ARPE COMPANY, *pg.* 899, *pg.* 1042
SUN-MAID GROWERS OF CALIFORNIA, *pg.* 899, *pg.* 119
SWANSON HEALTH PRODUCTS INC., *pg.* 1600, *pg.* 1397
SYSCO FOOD SERVICES OF ALBANY, LLC, *pg.* 1035, *pg.* 1163
TIM HORTONS, INC., *pg.* 1754, *pg.* 1930
TOTAL NUTRACEUTICAL SOLUTIONS, INC., *pg.* 1603, *pg.* 1509
TRI-K INDUSTRIES, INC., *pg.* 523, *pg.* 1099
TWEEZERMAN INTERNATIONAL, *pg.* 524, *pg.* 1324
ULTA SALON, COSMETICS & FRAGRANCE, INC., *pg.* 524, *pg.* 559
UNITED DAIRY FARMERS, INC., *pg.* 906, *pg.* 1426
UNITED NATURAL FOODS, INC., *pg.* 907, *pg.* 1608
UPTON TEA IMPORTS, *pg.* 1036, *pg.* 825
U.S. DAIRY EXPORT COUNCIL, *pg.* 160, *pg.* 1775
US FOODS, *pg.* 1036, *pg.* 703
V&V SUPREMO FOODS, INC., *pg.* 907, *pg.* 595
VENTURA FOODS, LLC, *pg.* 908, *pg.* 49
VIDAL SASSOON CO., *pg.* 524, *pg.* 1426
VITACOST.COM, INC., *pg.* 1607, *pg.* 414
VITAMIN SHOPPE, INC., *pg.* 1608, *pg.* 1098
VITASOY USA INC., *pg.* 62, *pg.* 784
VITUSA CORP., *pg.* 1482, *pg.* 1063
WELLQUEST MEDICAL & WELLNESS CORPORATION, *pg.* 1610, *pg.* 31
WESTIN FOODS, INC., *pg.* 909, *pg.* 1019
WHITE ROCK PRODUCTS CORP., *pg.* 266, *pg.* 1355
WHITE ROSE FOODS, *pg.* 910, *pg.* 1050
THE WHITEWAVE FOODS COMPANY, *pg.* 1037, *pg.* 324
WHOLE FOODS MARKET, INC., *pg.* 1038, *pg.* 1667
WM. WRIGLEY JR. COMPANY, *pg.* 1863, *pg.* 596
WORLD FINER FOODS, INC., *pg.* 910, *pg.* 1044
YOPLAIT USA, INC., *pg.* 910, *pg.* 947

5511 - Motor Vehicle Dealers (New & Used Cars)

ADELPHI ENTERPRISES L.P., *pg.* 163, *pg.* 614
ANCIRA ENTERPRISES INC., *pg.* 164, *pg.* 1739
ASBURY AUTOMOTIVE GROUP, INC., *pg.* 164, *pg.* 531
AUTONATION, *pg.* 165, *pg.* 773
AUTONATION, INC., *pg.* 165, *pg.* 423
BEECHMONT AUTOMOTIVE GROUP, *pg.* 166, *pg.* 1410
BELLA GROUP, *pg.* 166, *pg.* 1599
BERGSTROM AUTOMOTIVE, *pg.* 166, *pg.* 1883
BEUCKMAN FORD INC., *pg.* 166, *pg.* 973
BMW OF EL PASO, *pg.* 166, *pg.* 1691
BRAMAN MOTORS, INC., *pg.* 167, *pg.* 478
BRICKNER MOTORS, INC., *pg.* 167, *pg.* 1869
BUD DAVIS CADILLAC, INC., *pg.* 167, *pg.* 1641
CARMAX, INC., *pg.* 167, *pg.* 1800
THE COLLECTION, INC., *pg.* 168, *pg.* 418
CROWLEY AUTO GROUP, *pg.* 168, *pg.* 340
CURRY ACURA, *pg.* 168, *pg.* 1340
DARLING'S INC., *pg.* 168, *pg.* 749
DAVE SYVERSON INC., *pg.* 168, *pg.* 915
DAYTON ANDREWS FIVE STAR CHRYSLER PLYMOUTH JEEP, INC., *pg.* 169, *pg.* 415
DEAN ARBOUR CHEVROLET CADILLAC, *pg.* 169, *pg.* 885
DESERT EUROPEAN MOTORCARS, LTD., *pg.* 169, *pg.* 187
DIMMITT LUXURY MOTORS, *pg.* 169, *pg.* 416
DOWNTOWN FORD SALES INC., *pg.* 169, *pg.* 196
DRIVER'S MART, *pg.* 169, *pg.* 480
EARNHARDT HONDA, *pg.* 169, *pg.* 12
EWALD AUTOMOTIVE GROUP, LLC, *pg.* 170, *pg.* 1858
FAIRWAY FORD LINCOLN, *pg.* 170, *pg.* 1617
FCA CANADA INC., *pg.* 170, *pg.* 1948
FERMAN MOTOR CAR CO., INC., *pg.* 171, *pg.* 473
GALPIN MOTORS, INC., *pg.* 174, *pg.* 166
GARBER MANAGEMENT GROUP INC., *pg.* 174, *pg.* 906
GARFF ENTERPRISES INC., *pg.* 174, *pg.* 1758
GATOR FORD TRUCK SALES INC., *pg.* 174, *pg.* 467
GROUP 1 AUTOMOTIVE, INC., *pg.* 177, *pg.* 1706
GUARANTY CHEVROLET-PONTIAC, *pg.* 177, *pg.* 1498
GUARANTY RV CENTERS, *pg.* 1707, *pg.* 1499
HAROLD MATTHEWS NISSAN INC., *pg.* 178, *pg.* 1630
HEISER AUTOMOTIVE GROUP INC., *pg.* 179, *pg.* 1858
JEFFERSON CHEVROLET CO., *pg.* 180, *pg.* 883
JENKINS AUTO SALES OF FLORIDA, *pg.* 180, *pg.* 459
JERRY BIGGERS CHEVROLET - ISUZU INC., *pg.* 180, *pg.* 610
JOE MACHENS FORD INC., *pg.* 180, *pg.* 976
JOHN EAGLE HONDA OF HOUSTON, *pg.* 180, *pg.* 1709
JOYCE MOTORS CORP., *pg.* 181, *pg.* 1053
KELLEY AUTOMOTIVE GROUP, *pg.* 181, *pg.* 680
KUNI ENTERPRISES INC., *pg.* 182, *pg.* 1846
LARRY H. MILLER GROUP OF COMPANIES, *pg.* 182, *pg.* 1762
THE LINCOLN MOTOR COMPANY, *pg.* 182, *pg.* 878
LITHIA MOTORS INC, *pg.* 183, *pg.* 1499
LOU LARICHE CHEVROLET INC., *pg.* 183, *pg.* 904
MAGUIRE CHEVROLET-CADILLAC, *pg.* 183, *pg.* 1170
MAITA ENTERPRISES INC., *pg.* 183, *pg.* 196
MCINERNEY INC., *pg.* 184, *pg.* 903
MECHANICAL PROTECTION PLAN, *pg.* 184, *pg.* 717
MERCEDES-BENZ CANADA INC., *pg.* 184, *pg.* 1940
NAPLETON SCHAUMBURG MOTORS, INC., *pg.* 185, *pg.* 659
NEW COUNTRY MOTOR CAR GROUP INC., *pg.* 186, *pg.* 1340
NISSAN CANADA INC., *pg.* 214, *pg.* 1928
PACIFICO ENTERPRISES, INC., *pg.* 188, *pg.* 1568
PENSKE AUTOMOTIVE GROUP, INC., *pg.* 188, *pg.* 873
POTAMKIN AUTOMOTIVE, *pg.* 189, *pg.* 445
RANDALL REED'S PRESTIGE LINCOLN MERCURY, *pg.* 189, *pg.* 1698
REEDMAN TOLL AUTO WORLD, *pg.* 189, *pg.* 1547
REEVES IMPORT MOTORCARS INC., *pg.* 189, *pg.* 475
RELIABLE CHEVROLET, *pg.* 189, *pg.* 1736
RIVERSIDE FORD, *pg.* 189, *pg.* 885
RUSSELL & SMITH FORD INC., *pg.* 190, *pg.* 1713
SANDERSON FORD INC., *pg.* 190, *pg.* 13
SERVCO PACIFIC INC., *pg.* 190, *pg.* 544
SEWELL AUTOMOTIVE COMPANIES, *pg.* 190, *pg.* 1686
SONIC AUTOMOTIVE, INC., *pg.* 190, *pg.* 1369
STEVE FOLEY CADILLAC, *pg.* 190, *pg.* 641
TOM BUSH REGENCY MOTORS INC., *pg.* 192, *pg.* 435
TOWNE HYUNDAI, *pg.* 192, *pg.* 1053
TOYOTA OF MORRISTOWN, *pg.* 194, *pg.* 1089
W.W. WALLWORK, INC., *pg.* 195, *pg.* 1398

5521 - Motor Vehicle Dealers (Used Cars Only)

AMERICA'S CAR-MART, INC., *pg.* 164, *pg.* 29
AUTONATION, INC., *pg.* 165, *pg.* 423
BERGSTROM AUTOMOTIVE, *pg.* 166, *pg.* 1883
BEUCKMAN FORD INC., *pg.* 166, *pg.* 973
BMW OF EL PASO, *pg.* 166, *pg.* 1691
BRAMAN MOTORS, INC., *pg.* 167, *pg.* 478
BUD DAVIS CADILLAC, INC., *pg.* 167, *pg.* 1641
CARMAX, INC., *pg.* 167, *pg.* 1800
COPART, INC., *pg.* 168, *pg.* 86
DEAN ARBOUR CHEVROLET CADILLAC, *pg.* 169, *pg.* 885
DRIVER'S MART, *pg.* 169, *pg.* 480
DRIVETIME AUTOMOTIVE GROUP, INC., *pg.* 169, *pg.* 16
EARNHARDT'S AUTO CENTERS, *pg.* 169, *pg.* 12
ENTERPRISE HOLDINGS, INC., *pg.* 1906, *pg.* 996
FAIRWAY FORD LINCOLN, *pg.* 170, *pg.* 1617
GALPIN MOTORS, INC., *pg.* 174, *pg.* 166
GARBER MANAGEMENT GROUP INC., *pg.* 174, *pg.* 906
GATOR FORD TRUCK SALES INC., *pg.* 174, *pg.* 467
HEISER AUTOMOTIVE GROUP INC., *pg.* 179, *pg.* 1858
INSURANCE AUTO AUCTIONS, INC., *pg.* 180, *pg.* 669
JEFFERSON CHEVROLET CO., *pg.* 180, *pg.* 883
JERRY BIGGERS CHEVROLET - ISUZU INC., *pg.* 180, *pg.* 610
JOHN EAGLE HONDA OF HOUSTON, *pg.* 180, *pg.* 1709
LITHIA MOTORS INC, *pg.* 183, *pg.* 1499
MAITA ENTERPRISES INC., *pg.* 183, *pg.* 196
THE MAJOR AUTOMOTIVE COMPANIES, INC., *pg.* 183, *pg.* 1175
NAPLETON SCHAUMBURG MOTORS, INC., *pg.* 185, *pg.* 659
O'GARA COACH LA JOLLA, *pg.* 187, *pg.* 120
PENSKE AUTOMOTIVE GROUP, INC., *pg.* 188, *pg.* 873
REEDMAN TOLL AUTO WORLD, *pg.* 189, *pg.* 1547

First page reference indicates Business Class Edition
Second page reference indicates Geographic Edition

REEVES IMPORT MOTORCARS INC., *pg.* 189, *pg.* 475
SEWELL AUTOMOTIVE COMPANIES, *pg.* 190, *pg.* 1686

5541 - Gasoline Service Stations

7-ELEVEN CANADA, INC., *pg.* 237, *pg.* 1909
7-ELEVEN, INC., *pg.* 1012, *pg.* 1672
ACME MARKETS, INC., *pg.* 1012, *pg.* 1549
AFFILIATED FOODS, INC., *pg.* 1012, *pg.* 1658
AHOLD USA, INC., *pg.* 1013, *pg.* 1520
ALBERTSON'S LLC, *pg.* 1013, *pg.* 546
ALDI FOOD INC., *pg.* 1013, *pg.* 556
ALIMENTATION COUCHE-TARD INC., *pg.* 1013, *pg.* 1951
ALLEGRO COFFEE CO., *pg.* 836, *pg.* 336
ALON BRANDS, INC., *pg.* 1013, *pg.* 1673
ALON USA ENERGY, INC., *pg.* 971, *pg.* 1673
ARDEN GROUP, INC., *pg.* 1014, *pg.* 68
B&B CORPORATE HOLDINGS, INC., *pg.* 1015, *pg.* 471
BASHAS' SUPERMARKETS, *pg.* 1015, *pg.* 12
BI-LO, LLC, *pg.* 1015, *pg.* 1617
BIG Y FOODS, INC., *pg.* 1015, *pg.* 845
BROOKSHIRE GROCERY COMPANY, *pg.* 1016, *pg.* 1748
BUTERA MARKET, *pg.* 1016, *pg.* 609
C&K MARKET, INC., *pg.* 1016, *pg.* 1496
CASEY'S GENERAL STORES, INC., *pg.* 1017, *pg.* 701
CITARELLA, *pg.* 1017, *pg.* 1212
CONOCOPHILLIPS, *pg.* 975, *pg.* 1703
THE COPPS CORPORATION, *pg.* 1017, *pg.* 1895
CUMBERLAND FARMS, INC., *pg.* 1018, *pg.* 820
D'AGOSTINO SUPERMARKETS INC., *pg.* 1018, *pg.* 1173
DEMOULAS SUPER MARKETS INC., *pg.* 1018, *pg.* 848
DIERBERGS MARKETS INC., *pg.* 1018, *pg.* 974
DOMINICK'S FINER FOODS, LLC, *pg.* 1019, *pg.* 644
EMPIRE COMPANY LIMITED, *pg.* 1019, *pg.* 1917
ENGLEFIELD OIL COMPANY, *pg.* 976, *pg.* 1455
EXXON MOBIL CORPORATION, *pg.* 977, *pg.* 1718
FAREWAY STORES, INC., *pg.* 1019, *pg.* 702
FARM FRESH INC., *pg.* 1019, *pg.* 1810
FARM STORES, *pg.* 1019, *pg.* 417
FIESTA MART LLC, *pg.* 1019, *pg.* 1705
FJ MANAGEMENT, INC., *pg.* 978, *pg.* 1758
FOOD LION, LLC, *pg.* 1019, *pg.* 1390
THE FRED W. ALBRECHT GROCERY CO., *pg.* 1020, *pg.* 1400
FRESH & EASY NEIGHBORHOOD MARKET INC, *pg.* 1020, *pg.* 80
THE FRESH MARKET, INC., *pg.* 1020, *pg.* 1374
FRESHDIRECT, LLC, *pg.* 857, *pg.* 1174
GELSON'S MARKETS, *pg.* 1020, *pg.* 85
GEORGE WESTON LIMITED, *pg.* 858, *pg.* 1938
GERLAND CORPORATION, *pg.* 1020, *pg.* 1706
GIANT EAGLE AMERICAN SEAWAY FOODS, *pg.* 1020, *pg.* 1405
GIANT EAGLE, INC., *pg.* 1020, *pg.* 1575
GIANT FOOD STORES, LLC, *pg.* 1021, *pg.* 1520
GIANT OF MARYLAND LLC, *pg.* 1021, *pg.* 773
GO-MART INC., *pg.* 1021, *pg.* 1849
GOLUB CORPORATION, *pg.* 1021, *pg.* 1340
GRADE A MARKET INC., *pg.* 1021, *pg.* 362
THE GREAT ATLANTIC & PACIFIC TEA COMPANY, INC., *pg.* 1021, *pg.* 1086
GREENWICH VILLAGE ORCHESTRA, *pg.* 551, *pg.* 1236
H-E-B, *pg.* 1022, *pg.* 1740
HAGGEN, INC., *pg.* 1022, *pg.* 1817
HANNAFORD BROTHERS CO., *pg.* 1022, *pg.* 752
HARPS FOOD STORES, INC., *pg.* 1022, *pg.* 35
HARRIS TEETER, INC., *pg.* 1022, *pg.* 1383
HOMELAND STORES, INC., *pg.* 1023, *pg.* 1486
HOUCHENS INDUSTRIES INC., *pg.* 1023, *pg.* 726
HY-VEE, INC., *pg.* 1023, *pg.* 713
IGA, INC., *pg.* 1023, *pg.* 578
INGLES MARKETS, INCORPORATED, *pg.* 1023, *pg.* 1358
IRVING OIL CORPORATION, *pg.* 980, *pg.* 1038
JACK IN THE BOX INC., *pg.* 1732, *pg.* 204
JEWEL-OSCO, *pg.* 1024, *pg.* 620
K-VA-T FOOD STORES, INC., *pg.* 1025, *pg.* 1770
KEY FOOD STORES CO-OPERATIVE, INC., *pg.* 1025, *pg.* 1343
KING KULLEN GROCERY COMPANY, INC., *pg.* 1025, *pg.* 1141
KINGS FOOD MARKETS, INC., *pg.* 1025, *pg.* 1103
THE KROGER CO., *pg.* 1025, *pg.* 1416
KUM & GO, *pg.* 1775, *pg.* 713
KWIK TRIP INC., *pg.* 1026, *pg.* 1864
LOBLAW COMPANIES LIMITED, *pg.* 1026, *pg.* 1918
LOWE'S FOOD STORES, INC., *pg.* 1026, *pg.* 1394
LUND FOOD HOLDINGS, INC., *pg.* 875, *pg.* 924
MARSH SUPERMARKETS, INC., *pg.* 1027, *pg.* 688
MAVERIK COUNTRY STORES, INC., *pg.* 1027, *pg.* 1752
MEIJER, INC., *pg.* 1779, *pg.* 888
MFA OIL COMPANY, *pg.* 981, *pg.* 976
MORAN FOODS, INC., *pg.* 1028, *pg.* 976
NIEMANN FOODS INC., *pg.* 1028, *pg.* 653
THE PANTRY, INC., *pg.* 1029, *pg.* 1360
PEAPOD, LLC, *pg.* 1029, *pg.* 661
PILOT CORPORATION, *pg.* 983, *pg.* 1637
PRICE CHOPPER OPERATING CO., INC., *pg.* 1030, *pg.* 1341
PROVIGO INC., *pg.* 1030, *pg.* 1959
PUBLIX SUPER MARKETS, INC., *pg.* 1031, *pg.* 437
QUICK CHEK FOOD STORES INC., *pg.* 1031, *pg.* 1132
QUIKTRIP CORPORATION, *pg.* 1031, *pg.* 1490
RACETRAC PETROLEUM, INC., *pg.* 983, *pg.* 519
RALEY'S INC., *pg.* 1031, *pg.* 305
RALPHS GROCERY COMPANY, *pg.* 1031, *pg.* 69
RICE EPICUREAN MARKET, *pg.* 1032, *pg.* 1713
ROSAUERS SUPERMARKETS, INC., *pg.* 1032, *pg.* 1844
SAFEWAY INC., *pg.* 1032, *pg.* 184
SAVE-A-LOT, LTD., *pg.* 894, *pg.* 977
SAVE MART SUPERMARKETS, *pg.* 1033, *pg.* 150
SCHNUCK MARKETS, INC., *pg.* 1033, *pg.* 1002
SEDANO'S MANAGEMENT, INC., *pg.* 1033, *pg.* 430
SHEETZ, INC., *pg.* 1033, *pg.* 1514
SHOPRITE SUPERMARKETS, INC., *pg.* 1033, *pg.* 1160
SINCLAIR OIL CORPORATION, *pg.* 984, *pg.* 1760
SMITH'S FOOD & DRUG CENTERS, INC., *pg.* 1034, *pg.* 1761
SPARTANNASH CO, *pg.* 1034, *pg.* 889
SPEEDWAY LLC, *pg.* 985, *pg.* 1452
STATER BROS. MARKETS, *pg.* 1034, *pg.* 198
STATER BROTHERS HOLDINGS, *pg.* 1034, *pg.* 198
THE STOP & SHOP SUPERMARKET COMPANY LLC, *pg.* 1034, *pg.* 842
SUNOCO INC., *pg.* 985, *pg.* 1571
SUPERVALU, INC., *pg.* 1035, *pg.* 924
SUPERVALU, INC., FOOD MARKETING DIVISION, *pg.* 1035, *pg.* 681
SUPERVALU, INC., HARRISBURG DIVISION, *pg.* 1035, *pg.* 1526
SUSSER HOLDINGS CORPORATION, *pg.* 985, *pg.* 1671
SYSCO CORPORATION, *pg.* 1035, *pg.* 1716
TARGET CORPORATION, *pg.* 1786, *pg.* 942
TOPS HOLDING CORPORATION, *pg.* 1036, *pg.* 1355
TOPS MARKETS, LLC, *pg.* 1036, *pg.* 1355
TRADER JOE'S CO., *pg.* 1789, *pg.* 151
UNIFIED GROCERS, INC., *pg.* 1036, *pg.* 66
UNITED DAIRY FARMERS, INC., *pg.* 906, *pg.* 1426
UNITED REFINING COMPANY, *pg.* 986, *pg.* 1590
UNITED SUPERMARKETS, L.L.C., *pg.* 1036, *pg.* 1726
VALERO ENERGY CORPORATION, *pg.* 986, *pg.* 1743
VONS A SAFEWAY COMPANY, *pg.* 1036, *pg.* 43
WAKEFERN FOOD CORPORATION, *pg.* 1037, *pg.* 1058
WAL-MART STORES, INC., *pg.* 1790, *pg.* 29
WAWA, INC., *pg.* 1037, *pg.* 1552
WAYFIELD FOODS INC., *pg.* 1037, *pg.* 523
WEGMANS FOOD MARKETS, INC., *pg.* 1037, *pg.* 1337
WEIS MARKETS, INC., *pg.* 1037, *pg.* 1588
WESTERN BEEF, INC., *pg.* 1037, *pg.* 1333
WHOLE FOODS MARKET, INC., *pg.* 1038, *pg.* 1667
WINCO FOODS, INC., *pg.* 1038, *pg.* 548
WINN DIXIE STORES, INC., *pg.* 1038, *pg.* 435

5551 - Boat Dealers

BRISTOL MARINE, *pg.* 1705, *pg.* 1600
CATALINA YACHTS, INC., *pg.* 1706, *pg.* 307
CHRIS-CRAFT CORPORATION, *pg.* 1706, *pg.* 465
THE COAST DISTRIBUTION SYSTEM, INC., *pg.* 1706, *pg.* 152
GILMAN YACHTS OF FORT LAUDERDALE, INC., *pg.* 1707, *pg.* 425
MARINEMAX, INC., *pg.* 1709, *pg.* 416
TRINITY YACHTS, LLC, *pg.* 1712, *pg.* 968
WEST MARINE, INC., *pg.* 1712, *pg.* 305

5561 - Recreational Vehicle Dealers

CAMPING WORLD, INC., *pg.* 1830, *pg.* 725
GUARANTY CHEVROLET-PONTIAC, *pg.* 177, *pg.* 1498
GUARANTY RV CENTERS, *pg.* 1707, *pg.* 1499
LAZY DAYS R.V. CENTER, INC., *pg.* 182, *pg.* 467

5571 - Motorcycle Dealers

YAMAHA MOTOR CANADA LTD., *pg.* 1712, *pg.* 1947

5599 - Automotive Dealers, NEC

ADVANTAGE BMW CLEAR LAKE, *pg.* 163, *pg.* 1725
ADVANTAGE BMW MIDTOWN, *pg.* 163, *pg.* 1699
AIRCRAFT SPRUCE & SPECIALTY CO., *pg.* 1759, *pg.* 69
AMP HOLDING INC., *pg.* 164, *pg.* 1406
ASBURY AUTOMOTIVE GROUP, INC., *pg.* 164, *pg.* 531
BRUCKNER TRUCK SALES, INC., *pg.* 167, *pg.* 1659
CUTTER AVIATION, INC., *pg.* 227, *pg.* 16
GATOR FORD TRUCK SALES INC., *pg.* 174, *pg.* 467
INSURANCE AUTO AUCTIONS, INC., *pg.* 180, *pg.* 669
TODCO, INC., *pg.* 115, *pg.* 1459
WOLFINGTON BODY COMPANY, INC., *pg.* 195, *pg.* 1532
WORLD TOYOTA, *pg.* 195, *pg.* 524

5611 - Men's & Boys' Clothing & Accessory Stores

ABERCROMBIE & FITCH CO., *pg.* 37, *pg.* 1466
AEROPOSTALE, INC., *pg.* 17, *pg.* 1188
AMERICAN EAGLE OUTFITTERS, INC., *pg.* 37, *pg.* 1572
ASICS AMERICA CORPORATION, *pg.* 1826, *pg.* 106
BANANA REPUBLIC, *pg.* 1760, *pg.* 212
BARNEYS NEW YORK, INC., *pg.* 38, *pg.* 1201
BEN SHERMAN USA, *pg.* 19, *pg.* 1202
BERMO ENTERPRISES INC., *pg.* 20, *pg.* 906
BJ'S WHOLESALE CLUB, INC., *pg.* 1762, *pg.* 857
BLUEFLY, INC., *pg.* 1232, *pg.* 1205
BOY SCOUTS OF AMERICA, *pg.* 134, *pg.* 1717
BRODER BROS., CO., *pg.* 1828, *pg.* 1588
BROOKS BROTHERS GROUP, INC., *pg.* 39, *pg.* 1208
BURBERRY LIMITED, *pg.* 20, *pg.* 1208
CALVIN KLEIN, INC., *pg.* 20, *pg.* 1209
CENTURY 21 PROMOTIONS, INC., *pg.* 2, *pg.* 1834
CITI TRENDS INC., *pg.* 22, *pg.* 539
COLUMBIA SPORTSWEAR COMPANY, *pg.* 1830, *pg.* 1501
CUTTER & BUCK, INC., *pg.* 39, *pg.* 1835
CYTEC INDUSTRIES, INC., *pg.* 1155, *pg.* 1131
DESTINATION XL GROUP, INC., *pg.* 40, *pg.* 810
DOCKERS BRAND, *pg.* 40, *pg.* 217
DOLCE & GABBANA USA, INC., *pg.* 23, *pg.* 1225
DR. JAY'S INC., *pg.* 40, *pg.* 1085
DRYSDALES INC., *pg.* 1767, *pg.* 1489
THE ECHO DESIGN GROUP, INC., *pg.* 4, *pg.* 1226
EDDIE BAUER, INC., *pg.* 40, *pg.* 1814
EX OFFICIO, LLC, *pg.* 40, *pg.* 1835
EXPRESS, INC., *pg.* 24, *pg.* 1440
FOWNES BROTHERS & CO., INC., *pg.* 5, *pg.* 1233
THE GAP, INC., *pg.* 1770, *pg.* 218
GIORGIO ARMANI CORPORATION, *pg.* 25, *pg.* 1234
GORDMANS STORES INC., *pg.* 1771, *pg.* 1016
GTFM LLC, *pg.* 41, *pg.* 1236
HABAND COMPANY, INC., *pg.* 1772, *pg.* 1099
HAGGAR CORPORATION, *pg.* 41, *pg.* 1682
HANNA ANDERSSON CORPORATION, *pg.* 1772, *pg.* 1503
HUGO BOSS FASHIONS INC., *pg.* 42, *pg.* 1242
J. CREW GROUP, INC., *pg.* 1773, *pg.* 1245
JOS. A. BANK CLOTHIERS, INC., *pg.* 42, *pg.* 771
L.A. T SPORTSWEAR, LLC, *pg.* 1838, *pg.* 526
LANDS' END, INC., *pg.* 1776, *pg.* 1857
LOEHMANN'S HOLDINGS INC., *pg.* 29, *pg.* 1144
LORD & TAYLOR LLC, *pg.* 1777, *pg.* 1252
MCCUBBIN HOSIERY, INC., *pg.* 9, *pg.* 1486
THE MEN'S WEARHOUSE, INC., *pg.* 44, *pg.* 1711
MICHAEL KORS (USA), INC., *pg.* 29, *pg.* 1260
NORM THOMPSON OUTFITTERS INC., *pg.* 1780, *pg.* 1498
OLEG CASSINI, INC., *pg.* 30, *pg.* 1274
OSHKOSH B'GOSH, INC., *pg.* 45, *pg.* 1885
OTOMIX, INC., *pg.* 30, *pg.* 105
PACIFIC SUNWEAR OF CALIFORNIA, INC., *pg.* 1781, *pg.* 43
PAUL STUART, INC., *pg.* 1781, *pg.* 1276
PUMA NORTH AMERICA, INC., *pg.* 1816, *pg.* 858
PVH CORP., *pg.* 46, *pg.* 1283

QUIKSILVER, INC., pg. 31, pg. 104
ROYTEX, INC., pg. 47, pg. 1287
RUE21, INC., pg. 32, pg. 1591
SEATTLE PACIFIC INDUSTRIES, INC., pg. 48, pg. 1822
SIMMS FISHING PRODUCTS CORP., pg. 1845, pg. 1008
SPORT OBERMEYER LTD., pg. 1846, pg. 310
SPORTIF USA INC., pg. 33, pg. 1032
SUN PRECAUTIONS, INC., pg. 33, pg. 1820
UNIFIRST CORPORATION, pg. 50, pg. 860
URBAN OUTFITTERS, INC., pg. 1789, pg. 1571
V.F. CORPORATION, pg. 34, pg. 1376
VINEYARD VINES LLC, pg. 50, pg. 379
WEST COAST LEATHER, pg. 35, pg. 233
ZUMIEZ INC., pg. 16, pg. 1822

5621 - Women's Clothing Stores

A&E STORES, INC., pg. 17, pg. 1124
ABERCROMBIE & FITCH CO., pg. 37, pg. 1466
AEROPOSTALE, INC., pg. 17, pg. 1188
AIDAN INDUSTRIES, INC., pg. 17, pg. 1188
ALWAYS FOR ME INC., pg. 17, pg. 1163
AMERICAN EAGLE OUTFITTERS, INC., pg. 37, pg. 1572
ANN INC., pg. 18, pg. 1195
ANTHROPOLOGIE, INC., pg. 18, pg. 1558
ANVIL HOLDINGS, INC., pg. 18, pg. 1195
ASCENA RETAIL GROUP, INC., pg. 18, pg. 1081
ATTITUDES IN DRESSING INC., pg. 19, pg. 1057
BANANA REPUBLIC, pg. 1760, pg. 212
BARE NECESSITIES, INC., pg. 19, pg. 1056
BARNEYS NEW YORK, INC., pg. 38, pg. 1201
BCBG MAX AZRIA GROUP LLC, pg. 19, pg. 301
BEBE STORES, INC., pg. 19, pg. 49
BERGDORF GOODMAN, INC., pg. 1761, pg. 1202
BJ'S WHOLESALE CLUB, INC., pg. 1762, pg. 857
BLUE CANOE BODYWEAR, pg. 20, pg. 94
BLUEFLY, INC., pg. 1232, pg. 1205
THE BOPPY COMPANY, LLC, pg. 20, pg. 329
BOSTON PROPER, INC., pg. 20, pg. 410
BRODER BROS., CO., pg. 1828, pg. 1588
BURBERRY LIMITED, pg. 20, pg. 1208
CALVIN KLEIN, INC., pg. 20, pg. 1209
THE CATO CORPORATION, pg. 21, pg. 1364
CENTURY 21 PROMOTIONS, INC., pg. 2, pg. 1834
CHARLOTTE RUSSE, INC., pg. 21, pg. 201
CHICO'S FAS, INC., pg. 21, pg. 427
CHRISTOPHER & BANKS CORPORATION, pg. 22, pg. 953
CITI TRENDS INC., pg. 22, pg. 539
CUTTER & BUCK, INC., pg. 39, pg. 1835
DAVID'S BRIDAL, INC., pg. 23, pg. 1523
DEB SHOPS, INC., pg. 23, pg. 1563
DELIA'S, INC., pg. 23, pg. 1222
DESTINATION MATERNITY CORPORATION, pg. 23, pg. 1563
DOCKERS BRAND, pg. 40, pg. 217
DOLCE & GABBANA USA, INC., pg. 23, pg. 1225
DOROTHY GRANT LTD., pg. 24, pg. 1910
DRAPER'S & DAMON'S, INC., pg. 24, pg. 109
THE DRESS BARN, INC., pg. 1767, pg. 1343
THE ECHO DESIGN GROUP, INC., pg. 4, pg. 1226
EDDIE BAUER, INC., pg. 40, pg. 1814
EX OFFICIO, LLC, pg. 40, pg. 1835
EXPRESS, INC., pg. 24, pg. 1440
FLORENCE EISEMAN COMPANY LLC, pg. 24, pg. 1874
FOREVER 21, INC., pg. 24, pg. 130
FOWNES BROTHERS & CO., INC., pg. 5, pg. 1233
THE GAP, INC., pg. 1770, pg. 218
GARNET HILL, pg. 1771, pg. 1034
GILT GROUPE INC., pg. 24, pg. 1234
GIORGIO ARMANI CORPORATION, pg. 25, pg. 1234
GIRL SCOUTS OF THE UNITED STATES OF AMERICA, pg. 142, pg. 1235
GORDMANS STORES INC., pg. 1771, pg. 1016
GROUPE BIKINI VILLAGE INC., pg. 25, pg. 1950
GTFM LLC, pg. 41, pg. 1236
GUCCI AMERICA INC., pg. 6, pg. 1237
HABAND COMPANY, INC., pg. 1772, pg. 1099
HAGGAR CORPORATION, pg. 41, pg. 1682
HANNA ANDERSSON CORPORATION, pg. 1772, pg. 1503
HERITAGE SPORTSWEAR, LLC, pg. 26, pg. 1455
HOT TOPIC, INC., pg. 42, pg. 67
HOUSE OF Z LLC, pg. 26, pg. 1241
J. CREW GROUP, INC., pg. 1773, pg. 1245
THE J. JILL GROUP, INC., pg. 1774, pg. 842
JACQUES MORET, INC., pg. 27, pg. 1245
KATE SPADE LLC, pg. 28, pg. 1248
L BRANDS, INC., pg. 1776, pg. 1441
L.A. T SPORTSWEAR, LLC, pg. 1838, pg. 526
LANE BRYANT, pg. 1776, pg. 1441
LOEHMANN'S HOLDINGS INC., pg. 29, pg. 1144
LORD & TAYLOR LLC, pg. 1777, pg. 1252
LT APPAREL GROUP, pg. 29, pg. 1254
MAYER/BERKSHIRE CORPORATION, pg. 29, pg. 1129
MCCUBBIN HOSIERY, INC., pg. 9, pg. 1486
MICHAEL KORS (USA), INC., pg. 29, pg. 1260
MICHAEL STARS, INC., pg. 29, pg. 100
NATIONAL WHOLESALE COMPANY INC., pg. 30, pg. 1381
NEW YORK & COMPANY, INC., pg. 1779, pg. 1268
NORDSTROM, INC., pg. 1779, pg. 1837
NORM THOMPSON OUTFITTERS INC., pg. 1780, pg. 1498
NYDJ APPAREL, LLC, pg. 30, pg. 302
OLEG CASSINI, INC., pg. 30, pg. 1274
ORCHARD BRANDS CORPORATION, pg. 1780, pg. 1590
OTOMIX, INC., pg. 30, pg. 105
PACIFIC SUNWEAR OF CALIFORNIA, INC., pg. 1781, pg. 43
PAUL STUART, INC., pg. 1781, pg. 1276
PERRY ELLIS INTERNATIONAL, INC., pg. 45, pg. 445
RUE21, INC., pg. 32, pg. 1591
SAN FRANCISCO MERCANTILE COMPANY, INC., pg. 32, pg. 227
SIONI APPAREL GROUP, pg. 32, pg. 1292
SPORT HALEY, INC., pg. 33, pg. 333
SPORT OBERMEYER LTD., pg. 1846, pg. 310
SPORTIF USA INC., pg. 33, pg. 1032
THE TALBOTS, INC., pg. 34, pg. 824
TANO, INC., pg. 13, pg. 1183
TOMMY BAHAMA, pg. 48, pg. 1842
TWEEN BRANDS INC., pg. 34, pg. 1467
ULLA POPKEN LTD., pg. 1789, pg. 771
UNIFIRST CORPORATION, pg. 50, pg. 860
UNIQUE VINTAGE, pg. 34, pg. 52
URBAN OUTFITTERS, INC., pg. 1789, pg. 1571
VERA BRADLEY, INC., pg. 15, pg. 697
VERA WANG BRIDAL HOUSE LTD., pg. 34, pg. 1309
VICTORIA'S SECRET STORES, LLC, pg. 1789, pg. 1471
WEISSMAN THEATRICAL SUPPLY, INC., pg. 35, pg. 1004
THE WET SEAL, LLC, pg. 35, pg. 88
ZUMIEZ INC., pg. 16, pg. 1822

5641 - Children's & Infants' Wear Stores

AIDAN INDUSTRIES, INC., pg. 17, pg. 1188
ANVIL HOLDINGS, INC., pg. 18, pg. 1195
ATTITUDES IN DRESSING INC., pg. 19, pg. 1057
BJ'S WHOLESALE CLUB, INC., pg. 1762, pg. 857
BLUE CANOE BODYWEAR, pg. 20, pg. 94
THE BOPPY COMPANY, LLC, pg. 20, pg. 329
BRODER BROS., CO., pg. 1828, pg. 1588
CALVIN KLEIN, INC., pg. 20, pg. 1209
CENTURY 21 PROMOTIONS, INC., pg. 2, pg. 1834
THE CHILDREN'S PLACE, INC., pg. 22, pg. 1119
CUTTER & BUCK, INC., pg. 39, pg. 1835
DOLCE & GABBANA USA, INC., pg. 23, pg. 1225
DOROTHY GRANT LTD., pg. 24, pg. 1910
THE ECHO DESIGN GROUP, INC., pg. 4, pg. 1226
EDDIE BAUER, INC., pg. 40, pg. 1814
EX OFFICIO, LLC, pg. 40, pg. 1835
FLORENCE EISEMAN COMPANY LLC, pg. 24, pg. 1874
FOWNES BROTHERS & CO., INC., pg. 5, pg. 1233
THE GAP, INC., pg. 1770, pg. 218
GIORGIO ARMANI CORPORATION, pg. 25, pg. 1234
GIRL SCOUTS OF THE UNITED STATES OF AMERICA, pg. 142, pg. 1235
GORDMANS STORES INC., pg. 1771, pg. 1016
GTFM LLC, pg. 41, pg. 1236
THE GYMBOREE CORPORATION, pg. 25, pg. 77
HANNA ANDERSSON CORPORATION, pg. 1772, pg. 1503
HERITAGE SPORTSWEAR, LLC, pg. 26, pg. 1455
HOUSE OF Z LLC, pg. 26, pg. 1241
JACQUES MORET, INC., pg. 27, pg. 1245
KATE SPADE LLC, pg. 28, pg. 1248
L.A. T SPORTSWEAR, LLC, pg. 1838, pg. 526
LT APPAREL GROUP, pg. 29, pg. 1254
MAYER/BERKSHIRE CORPORATION, pg. 29, pg. 1129
MCCUBBIN HOSIERY, INC., pg. 9, pg. 1486
MICHAEL STARS, INC., pg. 29, pg. 100
NATIONAL WHOLESALE COMPANY INC., pg. 30, pg. 1381
NORM THOMPSON OUTFITTERS INC., pg. 1780, pg. 1498
NYDJ APPAREL, LLC, pg. 30, pg. 302
OLD NAVY, pg. 45, pg. 224
OLEG CASSINI, INC., pg. 30, pg. 1274
OSHKOSH B'GOSH, INC., pg. 45, pg. 1885
OTOMIX, INC., pg. 30, pg. 105
SAN FRANCISCO MERCANTILE COMPANY, INC., pg. 32, pg. 227
SIONI APPAREL GROUP, pg. 32, pg. 1292
SPORT OBERMEYER LTD., pg. 1846, pg. 310
SPORTIF USA INC., pg. 33, pg. 1032
TANO, INC., pg. 13, pg. 1183
TOMMY BAHAMA, pg. 48, pg. 1842
TOYS "R" US, INC., pg. 968, pg. 1130
TWEEN BRANDS INC., pg. 34, pg. 1467
UNIFIRST CORPORATION, pg. 50, pg. 860
WEISSMAN THEATRICAL SUPPLY, INC., pg. 35, pg. 1004

5651 - Family Clothing Stores

ABERCROMBIE & FITCH CO., pg. 37, pg. 1466
AMERICAN EAGLE OUTFITTERS, INC., pg. 37, pg. 1572
BEALL'S, INC., pg. 1760, pg. 414
BEMIDJI WOOLEN MILLS, pg. 38, pg. 916
BERMO ENTERPRISES INC., pg. 20, pg. 906
BOB'S STORES CORP., pg. 38, pg. 354
THE BUCKLE, INC., pg. 1764, pg. 1011
BURLINGTON COAT FACTORY, pg. 1764, pg. 1047
THE CHILDREN'S PLACE, INC., pg. 22, pg. 1119
CITI TRENDS INC., pg. 22, pg. 539
DEB SHOPS, INC., pg. 23, pg. 1563
ERICA TANOV INC., pg. 24, pg. 46
THE GAP, INC., pg. 1770, pg. 218
THE GLIK COMPANY, pg. 1771, pg. 615
GORDMANS STORES INC., pg. 1771, pg. 1016
HAMRICK INC., pg. 41, pg. 1616
HANNA ANDERSSON CORPORATION, pg. 1772, pg. 1503
KOHL'S CORPORATION, pg. 1775, pg. 1870
MACY'S FLORIDA, pg. 1777, pg. 444
NORDSTROM, INC., pg. 1779, pg. 1837
OLD NAVY, pg. 45, pg. 224
ROSS STORES, INC., pg. 1783, pg. 78
SABAS BUNCH LIMITED PARTNERSHIP, pg. 47, pg. 12
SIERRA TRADING POST INC., pg. 1819, pg. 1901
SKINNYCORP L.L.C., pg. 1280, pg. 590
STAGE STORES, INC., pg. 33, pg. 1715
STEIN MART, INC., pg. 1786, pg. 435
THE TIMBERLAND COMPANY, pg. 1821, pg. 1039
T.J. MAXX, pg. 1788, pg. 822
THE TJX COMPANIES, INC., pg. 1788, pg. 822
TOMMY BAHAMA, pg. 48, pg. 1842
URBAN OUTFITTERS, INC., pg. 1789, pg. 1571
WINMARK CORPORATION, pg. 1792, pg. 946

5661 - Shoe Stores

AEROGROUP INTERNATIONAL, INC., pg. 1803, pg. 1055
ALDO GROUP, pg. 1804, pg. 1959
ALLEN-EDMONDS SHOE CORP., pg. 1804, pg. 1887
ASICS AMERICA CORPORATION, pg. 1826, pg. 106
BAKERS FOOTWEAR GROUP, INC., pg. 19, pg. 992
BIRKENSTOCK DISTRIBUTION USA INC., pg. 1805, pg. 168
THE BUCKLE, INC., pg. 1764, pg. 1011
CALERES, INC., pg. 1805, pg. 993
CAPEZIO BALLET MAKERS INC., pg. 1805, pg. 1125
CAVENDER'S STORES LIMITED, pg. 39, pg. 1748
CHAMPS SPORTS, pg. 1806, pg. 414
CITY SPORTS, pg. 1830, pg. 860
CLARKS COMPANIES, pg. 1806, pg. 836
COBIAN CORP., pg. 1806, pg. 253
COLE-HAAN LLC, pg. 1806, pg. 1034
CONVERSE INC., pg. 1831, pg. 793
DANSKO INC., pg. 1807, pg. 1594
DEER STAGS INC., pg. 1807, pg. 1222
DSW, INC., pg. 1807, pg. 1439
EASTLAND SHOE CORPORATION, pg. 1808, pg. 750
FAMOUS FOOTWEAR, pg. 1808, pg. 997
FILA USA, pg. 1808, pg. 779
FOOT LOCKER, INC., pg. 1808, pg. 1231
GENESCO INC., pg. 1809, pg. 1650
G.H. BASS & CO., pg. 1809, pg. 1234
HENRY MODELL & COMPANY, INC., pg. 1836, pg. 1240

First page reference indicates Business Class Edition
Second page reference indicates Geographic Edition

HI-TEC SPORTS USA, INC., *pg.* 1809, *pg.* 150
HIBBETT SPORTS, INC., *pg.* 1836, *pg.* 3
HITCHCOCK SHOES, INC., *pg.* 1810, *pg.* 824
ICONIX BRAND GROUP, INC., *pg.* 26, *pg.* 1243
JACK SCHWARTZ SHOES, INC., *pg.* 1810, *pg.* 1245
JIMLAR CORPORATION, *pg.* 1810, *pg.* 1246
JOHNSTON & MURPHY CO., *pg.* 1810, *pg.* 1651
LEHIGH OUTFITTERS, LLC, *pg.* 43, *pg.* 1466
LOEHMANN'S HOLDINGS INC., *pg.* 29, *pg.* 1144
LORD & TAYLOR LLC, *pg.* 1777, *pg.* 1252
MERCURY INTERNATIONAL TRADING CORP., *pg.* 1811, *pg.* 837
NIKE CANADA LTD., *pg.* 1840, *pg.* 1934
NINE WEST HOLDINGS, INC., *pg.* 1815, *pg.* 1272
NORDSTROM, INC., *pg.* 1779, *pg.* 1837
PACIFIC SUNWEAR OF CALIFORNIA, INC., *pg.* 1781, *pg.* 43
PAYLESS SHOESOURCE, INC., *pg.* 31, *pg.* 722
PUMA NORTH AMERICA, INC., *pg.* 1816, *pg.* 858
RALPH LAUREN CORPORATION, *pg.* 46, *pg.* 1284
R.G. BARRY CORPORATION, *pg.* 1818, *pg.* 1470
RICHLEE SHOE COMPANY, *pg.* 1818, *pg.* 769
ROCKY BRANDS, INC., *pg.* 1818, *pg.* 1466
SABAS BUNCH LIMITED PARTNERSHIP, *pg.* 47, *pg.* 12
SALOMON NORTH AMERICA, INC., *pg.* 1844, *pg.* 1753
SCRUBS & BEYOND, *pg.* 32, *pg.* 1003
SHEPLERS, INC., *pg.* 1785, *pg.* 724
SHOE CARNIVAL, INC., *pg.* 1819, *pg.* 679
SKECHERS U.S.A., INC., *pg.* 1819, *pg.* 143
THE STRIDE RITE CORPORATION, *pg.* 1820, *pg.* 828
TOMS SHOE'S INC, *pg.* 1821, *pg.* 276
VANS, INC., *pg.* 1821, *pg.* 76
THE WALKING COMPANY HOLDINGS, INC., *pg.* 50, *pg.* 263
THE WALKING COMPANY, INC., *pg.* 1822, *pg.* 307
WEYCO GROUP, INC., *pg.* 1822, *pg.* 1858
WOLVERINE WORLD WIDE, INC., *pg.* 1822, *pg.* 905
ZAPPOS.COM, INC., *pg.* 1291, *pg.* 1030

5699 - Miscellaneous Apparel & Accessory Stores

A&E STORES, INC., *pg.* 17, *pg.* 1124
ABERCROMBIE & FITCH CO., *pg.* 37, *pg.* 1466
AEROPOSTALE, INC., *pg.* 17, *pg.* 1188
AIDAN INDUSTRIES, INC., *pg.* 17, *pg.* 1188
ALWAYS FOR ME INC., *pg.* 17, *pg.* 1163
AMERICAN APPAREL, INC., *pg.* 18, *pg.* 126
AMERICAN EAGLE OUTFITTERS, INC., *pg.* 37, *pg.* 1572
ANN INC., *pg.* 18, *pg.* 1195
ANTHROPOLOGIE, INC., *pg.* 18, *pg.* 1558
ANVIL HOLDINGS, INC., *pg.* 18, *pg.* 1195
ARMY & NAVY DEPARTMENT STORES LIMITED, *pg.* 38, *pg.* 1909
ASCENA RETAIL GROUP, INC., *pg.* 18, *pg.* 1081
ASICS AMERICA CORPORATION, *pg.* 1826, *pg.* 106
ATTITUDES IN DRESSING INC., *pg.* 19, *pg.* 1057
BAKERS FOOTWEAR GROUP, INC., *pg.* 19, *pg.* 992
BANANA REPUBLIC, *pg.* 1760, *pg.* 212
BARE NECESSITIES, INC., *pg.* 19, *pg.* 1056
BARNEYS NEW YORK, INC., *pg.* 38, *pg.* 1201
BCBG MAX AZRIA GROUP LLC, *pg.* 19, *pg.* 301
BEBE STORES, INC., *pg.* 19, *pg.* 49
BEN SHERMAN USA, *pg.* 19, *pg.* 1202
BERGDORF GOODMAN, INC., *pg.* 1761, *pg.* 1202
BERMO ENTERPRISES INC., *pg.* 20, *pg.* 906
BJ'S WHOLESALE CLUB, INC., *pg.* 1762, *pg.* 857
BLUE CANOE BODYWEAR, *pg.* 20, *pg.* 94
BLUEFLY, INC., *pg.* 1232, *pg.* 1205
BOB'S STORES CORP., *pg.* 38, *pg.* 354
THE BOPPY COMPANY, LLC, *pg.* 20, *pg.* 329
BOSTON PROPER, INC., *pg.* 20, *pg.* 410
BOY SCOUTS OF AMERICA, *pg.* 134, *pg.* 1717
BRODER BROS., CO., *pg.* 1828, *pg.* 1588
BROOKS BROTHERS GROUP, INC., *pg.* 39, *pg.* 1208
BURBERRY LIMITED, *pg.* 20, *pg.* 1208
BURLINGTON COAT FACTORY, *pg.* 1764, *pg.* 1047
CALVIN KLEIN, INC., *pg.* 20, *pg.* 1209
THE CATO CORPORATION, *pg.* 21, *pg.* 1364
CAVENDER'S STORES LIMITED, *pg.* 39, *pg.* 1748
CENTURY 21 PROMOTIONS, INC., *pg.* 2, *pg.* 1834
CHAMPS SPORTS, *pg.* 1806, *pg.* 414
CHARLOTTE RUSSE, INC., *pg.* 21, *pg.* 201
CHICO'S FAS, INC., *pg.* 21, *pg.* 427
CHRISTOPHER & BANKS CORPORATION, *pg.* 22, *pg.* 953
CITI TRENDS INC., *pg.* 22, *pg.* 539
CITY SPORTS, *pg.* 1830, *pg.* 860
CLAIRE'S STORES, INC., *pg.* 1764, *pg.* 617
COLUMBIA SPORTSWEAR COMPANY, *pg.* 1830, *pg.* 1501
CUTTER & BUCK, INC., *pg.* 39, *pg.* 1835
CYTEC INDUSTRIES, INC., *pg.* 1155, *pg.* 1131
DAVID'S BRIDAL, INC., *pg.* 23, *pg.* 1523
DEB SHOPS, INC., *pg.* 23, *pg.* 1563
DELIA'S, INC., *pg.* 23, *pg.* 1222
DESTINATION MATERNITY CORPORATION, *pg.* 23, *pg.* 1563
DESTINATION XL GROUP, INC., *pg.* 40, *pg.* 810
DICK'S SPORTING GOODS, INC., *pg.* 1832, *pg.* 1524
DOCKERS BRAND, *pg.* 40, *pg.* 217
DOLCE & GABBANA USA, INC., *pg.* 23, *pg.* 1225
DOROTHY GRANT LTD., *pg.* 24, *pg.* 1910
DR. JAY'S INC., *pg.* 40, *pg.* 1085
DRAPER'S & DAMON'S, INC., *pg.* 24, *pg.* 109
THE DRESS BARN, INC., *pg.* 1767, *pg.* 1343
DRYSDALES INC., *pg.* 1767, *pg.* 1489
THE ECHO DESIGN GROUP, INC., *pg.* 4, *pg.* 1226
EDDIE BAUER, INC., *pg.* 40, *pg.* 1814
EX OFFICIO, LLC, *pg.* 40, *pg.* 1835
EXPRESS, INC., *pg.* 24, *pg.* 1440
THE FINISH LINE, INC., *pg.* 1769, *pg.* 686
FLORENCE EISEMAN COMPANY LLC, *pg.* 24, *pg.* 1874
FLYNN & O'HARA UNIFORMS INC., *pg.* 1769, *pg.* 1564
FOREVER 21, INC., *pg.* 24, *pg.* 130
FOWNES BROTHERS & CO., INC., *pg.* 5, *pg.* 1233
THE GAP, INC., *pg.* 1770, *pg.* 218
GARNET HILL, *pg.* 1771, *pg.* 1034
GILT GROUPE INC., *pg.* 24, *pg.* 1234
GIORGIO ARMANI CORPORATION, *pg.* 25, *pg.* 1234
GIRL SCOUTS OF THE UNITED STATES OF AMERICA, *pg.* 142, *pg.* 1235
GORDMANS STORES INC., *pg.* 1771, *pg.* 1016
GROUPE BIKINI VILLAGE INC., *pg.* 25, *pg.* 1950
GTFM LLC, *pg.* 41, *pg.* 1236
GUCCI AMERICA INC., *pg.* 6, *pg.* 1237
HABAND COMPANY, INC., *pg.* 1772, *pg.* 1099
HAGGAR CORPORATION, *pg.* 41, *pg.* 1682
HANNA ANDERSSON CORPORATION, *pg.* 1772, *pg.* 1503
HAPPY JACK INC., *pg.* 1476, *pg.* 1390
HAT WORLD, INC., *pg.* 42, *pg.* 686
HERITAGE SPORTSWEAR, LLC, *pg.* 26, *pg.* 1455
HOT TOPIC, INC., *pg.* 42, *pg.* 67
HOUSE OF Z LLC, *pg.* 26, *pg.* 1241
HUGO BOSS FASHIONS INC., *pg.* 42, *pg.* 1242
J. CREW GROUP, INC., *pg.* 1773, *pg.* 1245
THE J. JILL GROUP, INC., *pg.* 1774, *pg.* 842
JACQUES MORET, INC., *pg.* 27, *pg.* 1245
JOS. A. BANK CLOTHIERS, INC., *pg.* 42, *pg.* 771
KATE SPADE LLC, *pg.* 28, *pg.* 1248
L BRANDS, INC., *pg.* 1776, *pg.* 1441
L.A. T SPORTSWEAR, LLC, *pg.* 1838, *pg.* 526
LADY GRACE STORES INC., *pg.* 28, *pg.* 861
LANDS' END, INC., *pg.* 1776, *pg.* 1857
LANE BRYANT, *pg.* 1776, *pg.* 1441
LAURA ASHLEY, INC., *pg.* 29, *pg.* 1615
LOEHMANN'S HOLDINGS INC., *pg.* 29, *pg.* 1144
LORD & TAYLOR LLC, *pg.* 1777, *pg.* 1252
LT APPAREL GROUP, *pg.* 29, *pg.* 1254
LULULEMON ATHLETICA INC., *pg.* 44, *pg.* 1911
LUSKEY'S WESTERN STORES, INC., *pg.* 44, *pg.* 1657
MARKS WORK WEARHOUSE LTD., *pg.* 44, *pg.* 1903
MAYER/BERKSHIRE CORPORATION, *pg.* 29, *pg.* 1129
MCCUBBIN HOSIERY, INC., *pg.* 9, *pg.* 1486
THE MEN'S WEARHOUSE, INC., *pg.* 44, *pg.* 1711
MICHAEL KORS (USA), INC., *pg.* 29, *pg.* 1260
MICHAEL STARS, INC., *pg.* 29, *pg.* 100
NATIONAL WHOLESALE COMPANY INC., *pg.* 30, *pg.* 1381
NEW YORK & COMPANY, INC., *pg.* 1779, *pg.* 1268
NORDSTROM, INC., *pg.* 1779, *pg.* 1837
NORM THOMPSON OUTFITTERS INC., *pg.* 1780, *pg.* 1498
NYDJ APPAREL, LLC, *pg.* 30, *pg.* 302
OLEG CASSINI, INC., *pg.* 30, *pg.* 1274
ORCHARD BRANDS CORPORATION, *pg.* 1780, *pg.* 1590
OSHKOSH B'GOSH, INC., *pg.* 45, *pg.* 1885
OTOMIX, INC., *pg.* 30, *pg.* 105
PACIFIC SUNWEAR OF CALIFORNIA, INC., *pg.* 1781, *pg.* 43
PAUL STUART, INC., *pg.* 1781, *pg.* 1276
PERRY ELLIS INTERNATIONAL, INC., *pg.* 45, *pg.* 445
PUMA NORTH AMERICA, INC., *pg.* 1816, *pg.* 858
PVH CORP., *pg.* 46, *pg.* 1283
QUIKSILVER, INC., *pg.* 31, *pg.* 104
RECREATIONAL EQUIPMENT, INC., *pg.* 1843, *pg.* 1821
RON JON SURF SHOP OF FLORIDA INC., *pg.* 1844, *pg.* 417
ROYTEX, INC., *pg.* 47, *pg.* 1287
RUE21, INC., *pg.* 32, *pg.* 1591
SAN FRANCISCO MERCANTILE COMPANY, INC., *pg.* 32, *pg.* 227
SCHEELS, *pg.* 47, *pg.* 1397
SCREAMER INC., *pg.* 12, *pg.* 1839
SCRUBS & BEYOND, *pg.* 32, *pg.* 1003
SEATTLE PACIFIC INDUSTRIES, INC., *pg.* 48, *pg.* 1822
SHEPLERS, INC., *pg.* 1785, *pg.* 724
SIMMS FISHING PRODUCTS CORP., *pg.* 1845, *pg.* 1008
SIONI APPAREL GROUP, *pg.* 32, *pg.* 1292
SPANX INC., *pg.* 32, *pg.* 520
SPORT CHALET, INC., *pg.* 1846, *pg.* 119
SPORT HALEY, INC., *pg.* 33, *pg.* 333
SPORT OBERMEYER LTD., *pg.* 1846, *pg.* 310
SPORTIF USA INC., *pg.* 33, *pg.* 1032
THE SPORTS AUTHORITY, INC., *pg.* 1846, *pg.* 326
STEVEN MADDEN, LTD., *pg.* 1819, *pg.* 1176
SUN PRECAUTIONS, INC., *pg.* 33, *pg.* 1820
THE TALBOTS, INC., *pg.* 34, *pg.* 824
TANO, INC., *pg.* 13, *pg.* 1183
TOMMY BAHAMA, *pg.* 48, *pg.* 1842
TRUE RELIGION BRAND JEANS, *pg.* 49, *pg.* 143
TWEEN BRANDS INC., *pg.* 34, *pg.* 1467
UJENA SWIMWEAR AND FASHIONS, *pg.* 34, *pg.* 163
ULLA POPKEN LTD., *pg.* 1789, *pg.* 771
UNIFIRST CORPORATION, *pg.* 50, *pg.* 860
UNIQUE VINTAGE, *pg.* 34, *pg.* 52
URBAN OUTFITTERS, INC., *pg.* 1789, *pg.* 1571
VERA BRADLEY, INC., *pg.* 15, *pg.* 697
VERA WANG BRIDAL HOUSE LTD., *pg.* 34, *pg.* 1309
V.F. CORPORATION, *pg.* 34, *pg.* 1376
VICTORIA'S SECRET STORES, LLC, *pg.* 1789, *pg.* 1471
VINEYARD VINES LLC, *pg.* 50, *pg.* 379
WEISSMAN THEATRICAL SUPPLY, INC., *pg.* 35, *pg.* 1004
WEST COAST LEATHER, *pg.* 35, *pg.* 233
THE WET SEAL, LLC, *pg.* 35, *pg.* 88
ZUMIEZ INC., *pg.* 16, *pg.* 1822

5712 - Furniture Stores

AARON'S, INC., *pg.* 912, *pg.* 486
ABC CARPET & HOME INC., *pg.* 912, *pg.* 1185
AFD CONTRACT FURNITURE, INC., *pg.* 912, *pg.* 1188
AMERICAN LEATHER LP, *pg.* 912, *pg.* 1673
ART VAN FURNITURE, INC., *pg.* 914, *pg.* 912
BABY TREND, INC., *pg.* 916, *pg.* 173
BAKER KNAPP & TUBBS INC., *pg.* 916, *pg.* 566
BASSETT FURNITURE INDUSTRIES, INCORPORATED, *pg.* 916, *pg.* 1776
BED BATH & BEYOND INC., *pg.* 1121, *pg.* 1127
BESTWAY, INC., *pg.* 52, *pg.* 1676
BINW, *pg.* 918, *pg.* 1833
BLU DOT DESIGN & MANUFACTURING, INC., *pg.* 918, *pg.* 931
BOB'S DISCOUNT FURNITURE INC., *pg.* 1763, *pg.* 354
BROOKSTONE, INC., *pg.* 1764, *pg.* 1036
BUSINESS FURNISHINGS LLC, *pg.* 919, *pg.* 697
CAPITOL LIGHTING, *pg.* 1294, *pg.* 1053
CHAMPION INDUSTRIES, INC., *pg.* 1626, *pg.* 1849
CHILD CRAFT INDUSTRIES, INC., *pg.* 920, *pg.* 1463
COLORTYME, INC., *pg.* 1765, *pg.* 1729
COST PLUS WORLD MARKET, *pg.* 921, *pg.* 170
DEMCO INC., *pg.* 386, *pg.* 1865
DESIGN WITHIN REACH, INC., *pg.* 923, *pg.* 216
DIRECTBUY, INC., *pg.* 1766, *pg.* 694
DMI FURNITURE, INC., *pg.* 923, *pg.* 733
EDWARD DON & COMPANY, *pg.* 54, *pg.* 672
EL DORADO FURNITURE CORP., *pg.* 923, *pg.* 452
FIRESIDE ANTIQUES, *pg.* 925, *pg.* 742
FISHER-PRICE, INC., *pg.* 953, *pg.* 1156
FOREIGN TRADERS, INC., *pg.* 1769, *pg.* 1135
FORSHAW OF ST. LOUIS, *pg.* 1124, *pg.* 997
FRANK B. RHODES FURNITURE MAKER, *pg.* 925, *pg.* 766
GALLERY MODEL HOMES, INC., *pg.* 926, *pg.* 1706
GUMP'S CORP., *pg.* 1772, *pg.* 219
HAVERTY FURNITURE COMPANIES, INC., *pg.* 926, *pg.* 509
HERITAGE HOME GROUP, *pg.* 926, *pg.* 1379

HHGREGG, INC., pg. 56, pg. 686
HOM FURNITURE, INC., pg. 927, pg. 938
HOME MERIDIAN INTERNATIONAL, INC., pg. 928, pg. 1379
HUMAN TOUCH, pg. 928, pg. 123
IKEA NORTH AMERICA SERVICES LLC, pg. 929, pg. 1523
JAMISON BEDDING, INC., pg. 930, pg. 1651
JENNIFER CONVERTIBLES INC., pg. 931, pg. 1355
JOFCO INC., pg. 931, pg. 691
KANE FURNITURE CORPORATION, pg. 931, pg. 458
KINGSLEY-BATE, LTD., pg. 932, pg. 1787
LA-Z-BOY INCORPORATED, pg. 932, pg. 901
LEE JOFA, INC., pg. 933, pg. 1142
LEON'S FURNITURE LIMITED, pg. 933, pg. 1948
MARLO FURNITURE CO., INC., pg. 934, pg. 769
THE MATTRESS FIRM, INC., pg. 934, pg. 1711
MATTRESS HOLDING CORP., pg. 935, pg. 1711
NATIONAL BUSINESS FURNITURE INC, pg. 1269, pg. 1879
OFFICE RESOURCES INC., pg. 939, pg. 737
PIER 1 IMPORTS, INC., pg. 940, pg. 1695
RALPH PUCCI INTERNATIONAL LTD., pg. 940, pg. 1285
RAYMOUR & FLANIGAN FURNITURE CO., pg. 940, pg. 1174
RELAX THE BACK CORPORATION, pg. 940, pg. 120
RESTORATION HARDWARE HOLDINGS, INC., pg. 1060, pg. 70
RIO BRANDS, INC., pg. 941, pg. 1570
ROBB & STUCKY, LTD., pg. 941, pg. 428
ROOMS TO GO.COM, INC., pg. 941, pg. 468
SAUDER MANUFACTURING COMPANY, pg. 941, pg. 1403
SCAN DESIGN OF FLORIDA INC., pg. 109, pg. 438
SCHOOL SPECIALTY, INC., pg. 467, pg. 1860
SIMMONS COMPANY, pg. 943, pg. 520
SLEEP COUNTRY USA, INC., pg. 943, pg. 1822
SLEEPY'S, INC., pg. 943, pg. 1167
THE STANDARD MATTRESS COMPANY, pg. 943, pg. 352
STAR FURNITURE COMPANY, pg. 944, pg. 1715
SUBURBAN FURNITURE CORP., pg. 944, pg. 1123
TEMPUR SEALY INTERNATIONAL, INC., pg. 944, pg. 731
THULE, INC., pg. 218, pg. 369
W.B. MASON COMPANY, pg. 491, pg. 803
WILLIAMS-SONOMA, INC., pg. 1140, pg. 234
W.S. BADCOCK CORPORATION, pg. 947, pg. 449

5713 - Floor Covering Stores

BIG LOTS, INC., pg. 1762, pg. 1438
BLINDS TO GO INC., pg. 918, pg. 1101
BR-111 IMPORT & EXPORT, INC., pg. 919, pg. 439
BUTLER CARPET COMPANY INC., pg. 919, pg. 415
CARPET FAIR, INC., pg. 920, pg. 756
CENTURY SUPPLY CO. INC., pg. 920, pg. 631
CERAMIC DEVELOPMENT CORP., pg. 1764, pg. 193
CHF INDUSTRIES, INC., pg. 920, pg. 1211
CONGOLEUM CORPORATION, pg. 921, pg. 1084
CONKLIN BROS, pg. 921, pg. 242
CONN'S, INC., pg. 630, pg. 1668
COST PLUS WORLD MARKET, pg. 921, pg. 170
COURISTAN INC., pg. 921, pg. 1067
CUTCO CORPORATION, pg. 1123, pg. 1318
EMERY-WATERHOUSE COMPANY, pg. 1047, pg. 751
EMPIRE TODAY, LLC, pg. 923, pg. 643
FARREY'S WHOLESALE HARDWARE CO., INC., pg. 1047, pg. 442
FORSHAW OF ST. LOUIS, pg. 1124, pg. 997
FREUDENBERG NONWOVENS LIMITED PARTNERSHIP, pg. 693, pg. 1371
GORDON INDUSTRIES LTD., pg. 6, pg. 1184
THE GREAT AMERICAN HANGER COMPANY INC., pg. 926, pg. 442
HERITAGE LACE INC., pg. 694, pg. 711
HOME PRODUCTS INTERNATIONAL, INC., pg. 1125, pg. 577
INTERNATIONAL WINE ACCESSORIES, INC., pg. 1964, pg. 71
KENNEY MANUFACTURING COMPANY, pg. 1052, pg. 1609
LALIQUE NORTH AMERICA, pg. 1126, pg. 1054
LENOX CORPORATION, pg. 1126, pg. 1518
LIFETIME BRANDS, INC., pg. 1127, pg. 1161
LUMBER LIQUIDATORS HOLDINGS, INC., pg. 94, pg. 1808
MOHAWK HOME, pg. 935, pg. 541
OLSON RUG COMPANY, pg. 939, pg. 586
ORCHARD BRANDS CORPORATION, pg. 1780, pg. 1590
RALPH LAUREN CORPORATION, pg. 46, pg. 1284
ROBB & STUCKY, LTD., pg. 941, pg. 428
THE ROBERT ALLEN GROUP, INC., pg. 698, pg. 819
ROBINSON HOME PRODUCTS INC., pg. 1060, pg. 1355
SEALY CORPORATION, pg. 942, pg. 1391
SHEEX, INC., pg. 1138, pg. 1614
STAGESTEP INC., pg. 1688, pg. 1570
STARK CARPET CORPORATION, pg. 944, pg. 1296
STERLING CUT GLASS COMPANY, INC., pg. 1138, pg. 727
SURE FIT INC., pg. 944, pg. 1514
SWAROVSKI NORTH AMERICA LIMITED INC., pg. 13, pg. 1600
TELEBRANDS, INC., pg. 1396, pg. 1066
THYBONY WALLCOVERINGS INC., pg. 945, pg. 591
TOWNECRAFT, INC., pg. 1139, pg. 1071
VECTOR MARKETING CORPORATION, pg. 1139, pg. 1318
VICTORINOX SWISS ARMY INC., pg. 1139, pg. 357
WAYNE TILE CO., pg. 946, pg. 1130
THE WICKER WORKS, pg. 946, pg. 233
WILTON PRODUCTS, INC., pg. 1140, pg. 672
WINDOWS OF THE WORLD, INC., pg. 946, pg. 419
WITH HEART & HAND, pg. 946, pg. 837
WMF OF AMERICA, INC., pg. 1140, pg. 1380
WOVEN LEGENDS INC., pg. 947, pg. 1572
W.S. BADCOCK CORPORATION, pg. 947, pg. 449

5714 - Drapery, Curtain & Upholstery Stores

BIG LOTS, INC., pg. 1762, pg. 1438
BLINDS TO GO INC., pg. 918, pg. 1101
BR-111 IMPORT & EXPORT, INC., pg. 919, pg. 439
BUTLER CARPET COMPANY INC., pg. 919, pg. 415
CARPET FAIR, INC., pg. 920, pg. 756
CENTURY SUPPLY CO. INC., pg. 920, pg. 631
CERAMIC DEVELOPMENT CORP., pg. 1764, pg. 193
CHF INDUSTRIES, INC., pg. 920, pg. 1211
CONGOLEUM CORPORATION, pg. 921, pg. 1084
CONKLIN BROS, pg. 921, pg. 242
CONN'S, INC., pg. 630, pg. 1668
COST PLUS WORLD MARKET, pg. 921, pg. 170
COURISTAN INC., pg. 921, pg. 1067
CUTCO CORPORATION, pg. 1123, pg. 1318
EMERY-WATERHOUSE COMPANY, pg. 1047, pg. 751
EMPIRE TODAY, LLC, pg. 923, pg. 643
FARREY'S WHOLESALE HARDWARE CO., INC., pg. 1047, pg. 442
FORSHAW OF ST. LOUIS, pg. 1124, pg. 997
FREUDENBERG NONWOVENS LIMITED PARTNERSHIP, pg. 693, pg. 1371
GORDON INDUSTRIES LTD., pg. 6, pg. 1184
THE GREAT AMERICAN HANGER COMPANY INC., pg. 926, pg. 442
HERITAGE LACE INC., pg. 694, pg. 711
HOME PRODUCTS INTERNATIONAL, INC., pg. 1125, pg. 577
INTERNATIONAL WINE ACCESSORIES, INC., pg. 1964, pg. 71
KENNEY MANUFACTURING COMPANY, pg. 1052, pg. 1609
LALIQUE NORTH AMERICA, pg. 1126, pg. 1054
LENOX CORPORATION, pg. 1126, pg. 1518
LIFETIME BRANDS, INC., pg. 1127, pg. 1161
LUMBER LIQUIDATORS HOLDINGS, INC., pg. 94, pg. 1808
MOHAWK HOME, pg. 935, pg. 541
OLSON RUG COMPANY, pg. 939, pg. 586
ORCHARD BRANDS CORPORATION, pg. 1780, pg. 1590
RALPH LAUREN CORPORATION, pg. 46, pg. 1284
ROBB & STUCKY, LTD., pg. 941, pg. 428
THE ROBERT ALLEN GROUP, INC., pg. 698, pg. 819
ROBINSON HOME PRODUCTS INC., pg. 1060, pg. 1355
SEALY CORPORATION, pg. 942, pg. 1391
SHEEX, INC., pg. 1138, pg. 1614
STAGESTEP INC., pg. 1688, pg. 1570
STARK CARPET CORPORATION, pg. 944, pg. 1296
STERLING CUT GLASS COMPANY, INC., pg. 1138, pg. 727
SURE FIT INC., pg. 944, pg. 1514
SWAROVSKI NORTH AMERICA LIMITED INC., pg. 13, pg. 1600
TELEBRANDS, INC., pg. 1396, pg. 1066
THYBONY WALLCOVERINGS INC., pg. 945, pg. 591
TOWNECRAFT, INC., pg. 1139, pg. 1071
VECTOR MARKETING CORPORATION, pg. 1139, pg. 1318
VICTORINOX SWISS ARMY INC., pg. 1139, pg. 357
WAYNE TILE CO., pg. 946, pg. 1130
THE WICKER WORKS, pg. 946, pg. 233
WILTON PRODUCTS, INC., pg. 1140, pg. 672
WINDOWS OF THE WORLD, INC., pg. 946, pg. 419
WITH HEART & HAND, pg. 946, pg. 837
WMF OF AMERICA, INC., pg. 1140, pg. 1380
WOVEN LEGENDS INC., pg. 947, pg. 1572
W.S. BADCOCK CORPORATION, pg. 947, pg. 449

5719 - Miscellaneous Homefurnishing Stores

3 DAY BLINDS, INC., pg. 912, pg. 105
ABC CARPET & HOME INC., pg. 912, pg. 1185
ACTIVE ELECTRICAL SUPPLY COMPANY, pg. 612, pg. 563
ANNA'S LINEN COMPANY INC., pg. 1760, pg. 70
APPLIANCE RECYCLING CENTERS OF AMERICA, INC., pg. 51, pg. 930
AT HOME STORES LLC, pg. 1760, pg. 1729
BEALL'S, INC., pg. 1760, pg. 414
BED BATH & BEYOND INC., pg. 1121, pg. 1127
BELLACOR INC., pg. 917, pg. 929
BLINDS TO GO INC., pg. 918, pg. 1101
CAPITOL LIGHTING, pg. 1294, pg. 1053
COUNTRY CURTAINS RETAIL INC., pg. 921, pg. 827
CRATE & BARREL, INC., pg. 922, pg. 640
CUISINART INC., pg. 1123, pg. 373
EUROMARKET DESIGNS, INC., pg. 1124, pg. 640
FARREY'S WHOLESALE HARDWARE CO., INC., pg. 1047, pg. 442
GORDMANS STORES INC., pg. 1771, pg. 1016
THE GUILD INC., pg. 1255, pg. 1866
GUMP'S CORP., pg. 1772, pg. 219
HOMEGOODS, INC., pg. 1125, pg. 821
THE HOMER LAUGHLIN CHINA COMPANY, pg. 1125, pg. 1850
HUDSON'S BAY COMPANY, pg. 1773, pg. 1938
LAMPS PLUS INC., pg. 1300, pg. 64
MATTRESS HOLDING CORP., pg. 935, pg. 1711
OTTLITE, pg. 1303, pg. 475
PIER 1 IMPORTS, INC., pg. 940, pg. 1695
RESTORATION HARDWARE HOLDINGS, INC., pg. 1060, pg. 70
SELECT COMFORT CORPORATION, pg. 942, pg. 942
SMOKY MOUNTAIN KNIFE WORKS INC., pg. 1786, pg. 1655
SURE FIT INC., pg. 944, pg. 1514
TUESDAY MORNING CORPORATION, pg. 1789, pg. 1690
WILLIAM-WAYNE & COMPANY, pg. 946, pg. 1314
WITH HEART & HAND, pg. 946, pg. 837

5722 - Household Appliance Stores

AESCULAP, INC., pg. 1487, pg. 1521
ALPINE ELECTRONICS OF AMERICA, INC., pg. 616, pg. 292
ANDIS COMPANY, pg. 498, pg. 1895
APPLIANCE RECYCLING CENTERS OF AMERICA, INC., pg. 51, pg. 930
APSCO APPLIANCE CENTERS, pg. 51, pg. 415
ARIZONA WHOLESALE SUPPLY COMPANY, pg. 914, pg. 15
ARROW ELECTRONICS, INC., pg. 619, pg. 325
AVIALL, INC., pg. 224, pg. 1676
BED BATH & BEYOND INC., pg. 1121, pg. 1127
BEST BUY CANADA LTD., pg. 1761, pg. 1907
BEST BUY CO., INC., pg. 1761, pg. 954
BLACK BOX CORPORATION, pg. 361, pg. 1547
BRANDSMART USA, pg. 627, pg. 430
BRAUN NORTH AMERICA, pg. 52, pg. 792
BROTHER INTERNATIONAL CORPORATION - USA, pg. 53, pg. 1046
C&D TECHNOLOGIES, INC., pg. 627, pg. 1517
CALGON CARBON CORPORATION, pg. 1151, pg. 1574
CHESHER EQUIPMENT LTD., pg. 1323, pg. 1925
CITIZEN SYSTEMS AMERICA CORPORATION, pg. 375, pg. 293
CLARION CORPORATION OF AMERICA, pg. 629, pg. 75
COLORTYME, INC., pg. 1765, pg. 1729
CONN'S, INC., pg. 630, pg. 1668
CONSUMERS KITCHENS & BATHS, pg. 77, pg. 1167
CPI INTERNATIONAL, INC., pg. 631, pg. 175
CRAFTMADE INTERNATIONAL, INC., pg. 1295, pg. 1670
DEI HOLDINGS, INC., pg. 633, pg. 302

First page reference indicates Business Class Edition
Second page reference indicates Geographic Edition

DE'LONGHI AMERICA INC., *pg.* 54, *pg.* 1118
DELPHAX TECHNOLOGIES INC., *pg.* 386, *pg.* 917
DIRECTBUY, INC., *pg.* 1766, *pg.* 694
THE DWYER GROUP, INC., *pg.* 79, *pg.* 1748
EMERSON RADIO CORP., *pg.* 636, *pg.* 1087
ETS, LLC, *pg.* 54, *pg.* 685
FEINTOOL EQUIPMENT CORP., *pg.* 1336, *pg.* 1413
FONAR CORPORATION, *pg.* 1413, *pg.* 1179
GENERAL DATACOMM INDUSTRIES, INC., *pg.* 400, *pg.* 357
GRC ENTERPRISES, INC., *pg.* 1344, *pg.* 677
HAVERTY FURNITURE COMPANIES, INC., *pg.* 926, *pg.* 509
HHGREGG, INC., *pg.* 56, *pg.* 686
HMI INDUSTRIES INC., *pg.* 56, *pg.* 1475
HOBART FOOD EQUIPMENT GROUP CANADA, *pg.* 56, *pg.* 1929
HONEYWELL AEROSPACE, *pg.* 228, *pg.* 16
INSTRON CORPORATION, *pg.* 1349, *pg.* 839
JANOME AMERICA, INC., *pg.* 57, *pg.* 1081
KEMET CORPORATION, *pg.* 649, *pg.* 1621
KOMATSU AMERICA INDUSTRIES, LLC, *pg.* 1353, *pg.* 656
KSB INC., *pg.* 1354, *pg.* 1802
LG ELECTRONICS U.S.A., INC., *pg.* 651, *pg.* 1060
LRAD CORPORATION, *pg.* 652, *pg.* 204
MEGGER INC., *pg.* 1422, *pg.* 1557
METTLER-TOLEDO INTERNATIONAL INC., *pg.* 1423, *pg.* 1441
MIELE INC., *pg.* 59, *pg.* 1112
MILESTONE AV TECHNOLOGIES, INC., *pg.* 654, *pg.* 964
MINT TURBINES LLC, *pg.* 231, *pg.* 1488
MOVADO GROUP, INC., *pg.* 10, *pg.* 1101
MULTIBAND CORPORATION, *pg.* 442, *pg.* 940
NACCO INDUSTRIES, INC., *pg.* 1174, *pg.* 1433
NANOMETRICS INCORPORATED, *pg.* 1423, *pg.* 147
NORTEK GLOBAL HVAC, *pg.* 1075, *pg.* 989
NORTEK, INC., *pg.* 100, *pg.* 1607
NORTHROP GRUMMAN CORPORATION, *pg.* 231, *pg.* 1781
ORBOTECH INC., *pg.* 1367, *pg.* 788
ORECK CORPORATION, *pg.* 59, *pg.* 1653
PANASONIC CORPORATION OF NORTH AMERICA, *pg.* 661, *pg.* 1120
P.C. RICHARD & SON, *pg.* 59, *pg.* 1159
PEIRCE-PHELPS, INC., *pg.* 1075, *pg.* 1568
PHILADELPHIA GEAR CORPORATION, *pg.* 1368, *pg.* 1544
PHILIPS ELECTRONICS NORTH AMERICA, *pg.* 662, *pg.* 782
PIONEER ELECTRONICS (USA) INC., *pg.* 663, *pg.* 124
PURCELL MURRAY COMPANY INC., *pg.* 59, *pg.* 50
RED PEACOCK INTERNATIONAL, INC., *pg.* 667, *pg.* 168
ROWENTA (USA), INC., *pg.* 60, *pg.* 1084
SAMSUNG ELECTRONICS AMERICA, INC., *pg.* 669, *pg.* 1115
SDI TECHNOLOGIES, INC., *pg.* 671, *pg.* 1113
SERVCO PACIFIC INC., *pg.* 190, *pg.* 544
SINGER SEWING COMPANY, *pg.* 698, *pg.* 1639
SNYDER-DIAMOND, *pg.* 1062, *pg.* 276
SPECTRUM BRANDS HOLDINGS, INC., *pg.* 60, *pg.* 1867
STARKEY LABORATORIES, INC., *pg.* 1597, *pg.* 923
T.D. WILLIAMSON, INC., *pg.* 1380, *pg.* 1490
TEAC AMERICA, INC., *pg.* 678, *pg.* 151
TELETOUCH COMMUNICATIONS, INC., *pg.* 483, *pg.* 1696
TOPBULB.COM LLC, *pg.* 1307, *pg.* 677
TOSHIBA AMERICA CONSUMER PRODUCTS, LLC, *pg.* 681, *pg.* 1130
TRANSCAT, INC., *pg.* 682, *pg.* 1337
VAPOR CORP., *pg.* 61, *pg.* 427
VIZIO, INC., *pg.* 686, *pg.* 118
VOITH HYDRO INC., *pg.* 1387, *pg.* 1598
VOXX INTERNATIONAL, *pg.* 686, *pg.* 1166
WARNER'S STELLIAN CO., INC., *pg.* 62, *pg.* 964
WATERWISE INC., *pg.* 1066, *pg.* 438
WAUKESHA ELECTRIC SYSTEMS, *pg.* 687, *pg.* 1898
WIRELESS XCESSORIES GROUP, INC., *pg.* 689, *pg.* 1541
WOODWARD, INC., *pg.* 122, *pg.* 329
YAMAHA ELECTRONICS CORPORATION USA, *pg.* 689, *pg.* 51

5731 - Radio, Television & Consumer Electronic Stores

1-800-FLOWERS.COM, INC., *pg.* 1758, *pg.* 1151
ABT ELECTRONICS, INC., *pg.* 612, *pg.* 614
ADDVANTAGE TECHNOLOGIES GROUP, INC., *pg.* 612, *pg.* 1484
ADVANCED BEAUTY SYSTEMS INC., *pg.* 498, *pg.* 1672
AGILYSYS, INC., *pg.* 614, *pg.* 1409
AL & ED'S CORPORATION, *pg.* 615, *pg.* 299
ALPINE ELECTRONICS OF AMERICA, INC., *pg.* 616, *pg.* 292
ALTEX ELECTRONICS, LTD., *pg.* 348, *pg.* 1739
ANDIS COMPANY, *pg.* 498, *pg.* 1895
ANRITSU COMPANY, *pg.* 618, *pg.* 152
ANTHONY & SYLVAN POOLS CORPORATION, *pg.* 1826, *pg.* 1428
ARIZONA WHOLESALE SUPPLY COMPANY, *pg.* 914, *pg.* 15
ARROW ELECTRONICS, INC., *pg.* 619, *pg.* 325
ART.COM, *pg.* 1229, *pg.* 83
ARTNET WORLDWIDE CORPORATION, *pg.* 353, *pg.* 1197
AT HOME STORES LLC, *pg.* 1760, *pg.* 1729
AVNET ELECTRONICS MARKETING, *pg.* 622, *pg.* 15
AVNET, INC., *pg.* 622, *pg.* 15
AVX CORPORATION, *pg.* 623, *pg.* 1616
BALLY NORTH AMERICA, INC., *pg.* 1804, *pg.* 1200
BAND PRO FILM & DIGITAL INC., *pg.* 623, *pg.* 51
BELL INDUSTRIES, INC., *pg.* 624, *pg.* 683
BEST BUY CANADA LTD., *pg.* 1761, *pg.* 1907
BEST BUY CO., INC., *pg.* 1761, *pg.* 954
BEXEL CORPORATION, *pg.* 624, *pg.* 51
BIOLASE TECHNOLOGY, INC., *pg.* 1506, *pg.* 107
THE BIRKETT MILLS, *pg.* 826, *pg.* 1321
BOXLIGHT CORPORATION, *pg.* 627, *pg.* 1813
BRANDSMART USA, *pg.* 627, *pg.* 430
BRAUN NORTH AMERICA, *pg.* 52, *pg.* 792
BROOKSTONE, INC., *pg.* 1764, *pg.* 1036
BROTHER INTERNATIONAL CORPORATION - USA, *pg.* 53, *pg.* 1046
BURDEN SALES COMPANY, *pg.* 702, *pg.* 1011
C&D TECHNOLOGIES, INC., *pg.* 627, *pg.* 1517
CAMBRIDGE SOUNDWORKS, INC., *pg.* 1234, *pg.* 781
CANON U.S.A., INC., *pg.* 1404, *pg.* 1178
CEDARBROOK SAUNA & STEAM, *pg.* 1830, *pg.* 1819
CENTRAL GARDEN & PET COMPANY, *pg.* 1475, *pg.* 303
CHAMPS SPORTS, *pg.* 1806, *pg.* 414
CHESHER EQUIPMENT LTD., *pg.* 1323, *pg.* 1925
CITIZEN SYSTEMS AMERICA CORPORATION, *pg.* 375, *pg.* 293
CLARION CORPORATION OF AMERICA, *pg.* 629, *pg.* 75
CMC ELECTRONICS INC., *pg.* 376, *pg.* 1959
COILCRAFT, INC., *pg.* 1324, *pg.* 562
COLORTYME, INC., *pg.* 1765, *pg.* 1729
COMMERCE SCIENCE CORPORATION, *pg.* 1236, *pg.* 501
COMPLEMAR PARTNERS, *pg.* 1455, *pg.* 1333
CONN'S, INC., *pg.* 630, *pg.* 1668
CONSOLIDATED COMMUNICATIONS, INC., *pg.* 1871, *pg.* 1534
CPI INTERNATIONAL, INC., *pg.* 631, *pg.* 175
CRAFTMADE INTERNATIONAL, INC., *pg.* 1295, *pg.* 1670
CRUCIAL TECHNOLOGY DIV OF MICRON, *pg.* 1237, *pg.* 550
D-A LUBRICANT COMPANY, *pg.* 975, *pg.* 693
D&H DISTRIBUTING CO., INC., *pg.* 381, *pg.* 1536
DEI HOLDINGS, INC., *pg.* 633, *pg.* 302
DE'LONGHI AMERICA INC., *pg.* 54, *pg.* 1118
DETECTO SCALE COMPANY, *pg.* 1045, *pg.* 1007
DICK BLICK COMPANY, *pg.* 1766, *pg.* 617
DIRECTBUY, INC., *pg.* 1766, *pg.* 694
DUCOMMUN TECHNOLOGIES, INC., *pg.* 634, *pg.* 63
EARL MAY SEED & NURSERY L.C., *pg.* 1795, *pg.* 712
EIS, INC., *pg.* 80, *pg.* 504
ELMA ELECTRONIC INC., *pg.* 391, *pg.* 90
EMERGING VISION, INC., *pg.* 1411, *pg.* 1227
EMERSON NETWORK POWER, *pg.* 1071, *pg.* 1479
EMERSON RADIO CORP., *pg.* 636, *pg.* 1087
EMPOWER RF SYSTEMS, INC., *pg.* 637, *pg.* 105
EMRISE CORPORATION, *pg.* 637, *pg.* 1371
ENDLESS POOLS, INC., *pg.* 1833, *pg.* 1515
EPSON ELECTRONICS AMERICA, *pg.* 638, *pg.* 658
ETRONICS, INC., *pg.* 1244, *pg.* 1146
EZCORP, INC., *pg.* 750, *pg.* 1662
THE FANTASY GALLERY, *pg.* 925, *pg.* 1705
FLAX ARTIST'S MATERIALS, *pg.* 1769, *pg.* 49
FLETCHER CHICAGO INC., *pg.* 1413, *pg.* 574
FLEXTRONICS INTERNATIONAL LTD., *pg.* 81, *pg.* 245
FRANCHISE CONCEPTS, INC., *pg.* 1769, *pg.* 1005
FRANKLIN ELECTRONIC PUBLISHERS, INC., *pg.* 398, *pg.* 1048
FREESCALE SEMICONDUCTOR, INC., *pg.* 398, *pg.* 1662
FRY'S ELECTRONICS, INC., *pg.* 640, *pg.* 245
FURUNO USA, INC., *pg.* 640, *pg.* 1819
GENERAL NUTRITION CENTERS, INC., *pg.* 1534, *pg.* 1575
GRAYBAR ELECTRIC COMPANY, INC., *pg.* 1299, *pg.* 997
HAMAMATSU CORPORATION, *pg.* 1415, *pg.* 1046
HEARUSA, INC., *pg.* 1541, *pg.* 457
HHGREGG, INC., *pg.* 56, *pg.* 686
HITACHI AMERICA, LTD., *pg.* 642, *pg.* 1344
HOBART FOOD EQUIPMENT GROUP CANADA, *pg.* 56, *pg.* 1929
HOUCHENS INDUSTRIES INC., *pg.* 1023, *pg.* 726
IKEGAMI ELECTRONICS (U.S.A.), INC., *pg.* 644, *pg.* 1083
INFOSONICS CORPORATION, *pg.* 644, *pg.* 203
INGRAM MICRO MOBILITY, *pg.* 415, *pg.* 697
INSTANTRON CO., INC., *pg.* 512, *pg.* 1608
INTERMOUNTAIN FARMERS ASSOCIATION, *pg.* 705, *pg.* 1759
INTERNATIONAL PLAZA & BAY STREET, *pg.* 1773, *pg.* 473
J&R MUSIC WORLD, *pg.* 554, *pg.* 1245
JACO ELECTRONICS, INC., *pg.* 648, *pg.* 1165
JANOME AMERICA, INC., *pg.* 57, *pg.* 1081
JEFFERS, INC., *pg.* 1477, *pg.* 5
JESSUP'S APPLIANCES, *pg.* 58, *pg.* 477
KATY INDUSTRIES, INC., *pg.* 1126, *pg.* 973
KEITHLEY INSTRUMENTS, INC., *pg.* 1418, *pg.* 1473
KEMET CORPORATION, *pg.* 649, *pg.* 1621
KIRKLAND'S INC., *pg.* 1126, *pg.* 1652
KONICA MINOLTA BUSINESS SOLUTIONS USA, INC., *pg.* 1419, *pg.* 1113
KRATOS-GENERAL MICROWAVE, *pg.* 650, *pg.* 1344
KRELL INDUSTRIES, INC., *pg.* 650, *pg.* 367
KYOCERA DOCUMENT SOLUTIONS AMERICA, *pg.* 426, *pg.* 1065
LARRY H. MILLER GROUP OF COMPANIES, *pg.* 182, *pg.* 1762
LESLIE'S POOLMART, INC., *pg.* 1838, *pg.* 17
LG ELECTRONICS U.S.A., INC., *pg.* 651, *pg.* 1060
LIBERATOR, INC., *pg.* 1395, *pg.* 513
LIGHTING SCIENCE GROUP CORPORATION, *pg.* 1301, *pg.* 467
LRAD CORPORATION, *pg.* 652, *pg.* 204
MAGNOLIA AUDIO VIDEO, *pg.* 652, *pg.* 1821
MAYER ELECTRIC SUPPLY COMPANY INC., *pg.* 653, *pg.* 3
THE METROPOLITAN MUSEUM OF ART, *pg.* 561, *pg.* 1259
MFA INCORPORATED, *pg.* 1479, *pg.* 976
MICHAELS STORES, INC., *pg.* 1127, *pg.* 1722
MIELE INC., *pg.* 59, *pg.* 1112
MILESTONE AV TECHNOLOGIES, INC., *pg.* 654, *pg.* 964
MIRACLE-EAR, INC., *pg.* 1568, *pg.* 940
MPHASE TECHNOLOGIES, INC., *pg.* 441, *pg.* 363
MULBERRY METAL PRODUCTS, INC., *pg.* 1302, *pg.* 1127
MURATA ELECTRONICS NORTH AMERICA, INC., *pg.* 658, *pg.* 540
MURATEC AMERICA, INC., *pg.* 443, *pg.* 1733
NAGRA USA, *pg.* 443, *pg.* 223
NEW AGE ELECTRONICS, INC., *pg.* 659, *pg.* 63
NKK SWITCHES, *pg.* 1302, *pg.* 23
NORTEK GLOBAL HVAC, *pg.* 1075, *pg.* 989
NORTEK, INC., *pg.* 100, *pg.* 1607
NOVICA UNITED, INC., *pg.* 1271, *pg.* 137
ORBOTECH INC., *pg.* 1367, *pg.* 788
PANASONIC CORPORATION OF NORTH AMERICA, *pg.* 661, *pg.* 1120
PANASONIC ELECTRIC WORKS CORPORATION OF AMERICA, *pg.* 661, *pg.* 1095
PARTY CITY CORPORATION, *pg.* 1781, *pg.* 1116
P.C. RICHARD & SON, *pg.* 59, *pg.* 1159
PEIRCE-PHELPS, INC., *pg.* 1075, *pg.* 1568
PERFUMANIA HOLDINGS, INC., *pg.* 520, *pg.* 1141
PET SUPPLIES PLUS, *pg.* 1781, *pg.* 897
PET VALU CANADA, INC., *pg.* 1480, *pg.* 1924
PETCO ANIMAL SUPPLIES, INC., *pg.* 1480, *pg.* 206
PETEDGE, *pg.* 1481, *pg.* 787
PETFOODDIRECT.COM, *pg.* 1481, *pg.* 1536
PETSMART, INC., *pg.* 1481, *pg.* 18
PHILIPS ELECTRONICS NORTH AMERICA, *pg.* 662, *pg.* 782
PHONAK LLC, *pg.* 1585, *pg.* 665
PIONEER ELECTRONICS (USA) INC., *pg.* 663, *pg.* 124
POWER & TELEPHONE SUPPLY COMPANY, *pg.* 665, *pg.* 1646
POWERMAT USA, LLC, *pg.* 665, *pg.* 875
PROGRESSIVE MEDICAL, INC., *pg.* 1586, *pg.* 1480
THE PROTECTOSEAL COMPANY, *pg.* 1370, *pg.* 556
PURCELL MURRAY COMPANY INC., *pg.* 59, *pg.* 50

RED PEACOCK INTERNATIONAL, INC., *pg.* 667, *pg.* 168
RICHARDSON ELECTRONICS, LTD., *pg.* 667, *pg.* 622
RICOH AMERICAS CORPORATION, *pg.* 461, *pg.* 1131
ROHDE & SCHWARZ, INC., *pg.* 1428, *pg.* 768
ROWENTA (USA), INC., *pg.* 60, *pg.* 1084
ROYAL CONSUMER INFORMATION PRODUCTS INC., *pg.* 463, *pg.* 1122
SAG HARBOR INDUSTRIES, *pg.* 1305, *pg.* 1340
SALLY BEAUTY HOLDINGS, INC., *pg.* 522, *pg.* 1691
SAM ASH MUSIC CORPORATION, *pg.* 669, *pg.* 1167
SAMSUNG ELECTRONICS AMERICA, INC., *pg.* 669, *pg.* 1115
SAMSUNG SEMICONDUCTOR, INC., *pg.* 670, *pg.* 250
SAMSUNG TELECOMMUNICATIONS AMERICA, LLC, *pg.* 670, *pg.* 1736
SCANSOURCE, INC., *pg.* 671, *pg.* 1618
SDI TECHNOLOGIES, INC., *pg.* 671, *pg.* 1113
SECUREEYE SYSTEMS, INC., *pg.* 1280, *pg.* 1822
SED INTERNATIONAL HOLDINGS, INC., *pg.* 400, *pg.* 534
SERVCO PACIFIC INC., *pg.* 190, *pg.* 544
SHARP ELECTRONICS CORPORATION, *pg.* 672, *pg.* 1082
SHENANDOAH TELECOMMUNICATIONS CO., *pg.* 672, *pg.* 1779
SHOKAI FAR EAST LTD., *pg.* 672, *pg.* 1155
SIGMATRON INTERNATIONAL, INC., *pg.* 674, *pg.* 611
SIMON PROPERTY GROUP, INC., *pg.* 1112, *pg.* 690
SINGER SEWING COMPANY, *pg.* 698, *pg.* 1639
THE SINGING MACHINE COMPANY, INC., *pg.* 674, *pg.* 426
SKULLCANDY, INC., *pg.* 674, *pg.* 1754
SNYDER-DIAMOND, *pg.* 1062, *pg.* 276
SPECTRUM BRANDS HOLDINGS, INC., *pg.* 60, *pg.* 1867
SPECTRUM GROUP INTERNATIONAL, INC., *pg.* 472, *pg.* 116
THE SPORTS AUTHORITY, INC., *pg.* 1846, *pg.* 326
THE STEPHAN COMPANY, *pg.* 1597, *pg.* 426
SUSSER HOLDINGS CORPORATION, *pg.* 985, *pg.* 1671
TAITRON COMPONENTS INCORPORATED, *pg.* 677, *pg.* 299
TAIYO YUDEN (U.S.A.), INC., *pg.* 1380, *pg.* 279
TAMURA CORPORATION OF AMERICA, *pg.* 1380, *pg.* 291
TEAC AMERICA, INC., *pg.* 678, *pg.* 151
TESSCO TECHNOLOGIES, INC., *pg.* 679, *pg.* 773
TITAN MACHINERY INC., *pg.* 1383, *pg.* 1398
TOPBULB.COM LLC, *pg.* 1307, *pg.* 677
TOSHIBA AMERICA CONSUMER PRODUCTS, LLC, *pg.* 681, *pg.* 1130
TRACTOR SUPPLY COMPANY, *pg.* 708, *pg.* 1627
UNILEVER UNITED STATES, INC., *pg.* 904, *pg.* 1061
UNIVERSAL COIN & BULLION LTD., *pg.* 1789, *pg.* 1668
UNIVERSAL POWER GROUP, INC., *pg.* 683, *pg.* 1671
UNIVERSAL SECURITY INSTRUMENTS, INC., *pg.* 683, *pg.* 775
VALENTINO HOME ENTERTAINMENT, *pg.* 684, *pg.* 742
VAPOR CORP., *pg.* 61, *pg.* 427
VELODYNE ACOUSTICS, INC., *pg.* 685, *pg.* 152
VERMONT CLOCK COMPANY, *pg.* 946, *pg.* 1766
VIZIO, INC., *pg.* 686, *pg.* 118
VOXX INTERNATIONAL, *pg.* 686, *pg.* 1166
WARNER'S STELLIAN CO., INC., *pg.* 62, *pg.* 964
WEIS MARKETS, INC., *pg.* 1037, *pg.* 1588
WILLIAMS-SONOMA, INC., *pg.* 1140, *pg.* 234
WINCHESTER ELECTRONICS CORP., *pg.* 688, *pg.* 382
WIRELESS XCESSORIES GROUP, INC., *pg.* 689, *pg.* 1541
WORLD WIDE TECHNOLOGY HOLDING CO., INC., *pg.* 493, *pg.* 988
YAMAHA CORPORATION OF AMERICA, *pg.* 595, *pg.* 51
YAMAHA ELECTRONICS CORPORATION USA, *pg.* 689, *pg.* 51
THE YANKEE CANDLE COMPANY, INC., *pg.* 1792, *pg.* 843
ZACK ELECTRONICS, INC., *pg.* 690, *pg.* 77
ZAGG INCORPORATED, *pg.* 690, *pg.* 1762

5734 - Computer & Computer Software Stores

ACI WORLDWIDE INC., *pg.* 341, *pg.* 1010
ADDVANTAGE TECHNOLOGIES GROUP, INC., *pg.* 612, *pg.* 1484
AGILYSYS, INC., *pg.* 614, *pg.* 1409
AHEARN & SOPER INC., *pg.* 345, *pg.* 1932
ALTEX ELECTRONICS, LTD., *pg.* 348, *pg.* 1739
ANRITSU COMPANY, *pg.* 618, *pg.* 152
ANTEC INCORPORATED, *pg.* 350, *pg.* 90
APACHE SOFTWARE FOUNDATION, *pg.* 132, *pg.* 769
APPLE INC., *pg.* 350, *pg.* 73
APPLIED SYSTEMS INC., *pg.* 352, *pg.* 663
ARIZONA WHOLESALE SUPPLY COMPANY, *pg.* 914, *pg.* 15
ARROW ELECTRONICS, INC., *pg.* 619, *pg.* 325
THE ASCII GROUP, INC., *pg.* 132, *pg.* 761
ASI CORPORATION, *pg.* 354, *pg.* 90
ASPYRA, INC., *pg.* 355, *pg.* 306
@XI COMPUTER CORPORATION, *pg.* 355, *pg.* 199
ATARI, INC., *pg.* 355, *pg.* 1198
ATLUS USA, INC., *pg.* 949, *pg.* 107
AVNET ELECTRONICS MARKETING, *pg.* 622, *pg.* 15
AVNET, INC., *pg.* 622, *pg.* 15
AVNET TECHNOLOGY SOLUTIONS, *pg.* 359, *pg.* 25
AVX CORPORATION, *pg.* 623, *pg.* 1616
BAND PRO FILM & DIGITAL INC., *pg.* 623, *pg.* 51
BD DIAGNOSTICS - TRIPATH, *pg.* 1402, *pg.* 1358
BELKIN INTERNATIONAL, INC., *pg.* 361, *pg.* 182
BELL INDUSTRIES, INC., *pg.* 624, *pg.* 683
BOB EVANS FARMS, LLC, *pg.* 841, *pg.* 1467
BUYERZONE.COM, LLC, *pg.* 1233, *pg.* 850
CANON U.S.A., INC., *pg.* 1404, *pg.* 1178
CAVIUM NETWORKS, INC., *pg.* 369, *pg.* 240
CDS GLOBAL, INC., *pg.* 370, *pg.* 704
CDW CORPORATION, *pg.* 370, *pg.* 663
CMC ELECTRONICS INC., *pg.* 376, *pg.* 1959
COILCRAFT, INC., *pg.* 1324, *pg.* 562
COMMERCE SCIENCE CORPORATION, *pg.* 1236, *pg.* 501
COMPUTER MART, *pg.* 1236, *pg.* 542
CONDUSIV TECHNOLOGIES, *pg.* 379, *pg.* 51
CONNECTUS SOFTWARE, *pg.* 379, *pg.* 772
CONSOLIDATED COMMUNICATIONS, INC., *pg.* 1871, *pg.* 1534
CORSAIR COMPONENTS, INC., *pg.* 380, *pg.* 90
CRUCIAL TECHNOLOGY DIV OF MICRON, *pg.* 1237, *pg.* 550
CSPI TECHNOLOGY SOLUTIONS, *pg.* 381, *pg.* 421
CURVATURE, *pg.* 381, *pg.* 263
CYBERRESEARCH INC., *pg.* 381, *pg.* 339
D-A LUBRICANT COMPANY, *pg.* 975, *pg.* 693
D&H DISTRIBUTING CO., INC., *pg.* 381, *pg.* 1536
D-LINK SYSTEMS, INC., *pg.* 381, *pg.* 89
DELL INC., *pg.* 383, *pg.* 1737
DETECTO SCALE COMPANY, *pg.* 1045, *pg.* 1007
DUCOMMUN TECHNOLOGIES, INC., *pg.* 634, *pg.* 63
EDUPOINT EDUCATIONAL SYSTEMS, LLC, *pg.* 390, *pg.* 109
EIS, INC., *pg.* 80, *pg.* 504
ELMA ELECTRONIC INC., *pg.* 391, *pg.* 90
EMERSON NETWORK POWER, *pg.* 1071, *pg.* 1479
EMPOWER RF SYSTEMS, INC., *pg.* 637, *pg.* 105
EMRISE CORPORATION, *pg.* 637, *pg.* 1371
EN POINTE TECHNOLOGIES, INC., *pg.* 1243, *pg.* 94
ENVIRONMENTAL SYSTEMS RESEARCH INSTITUTE INC., *pg.* 393, *pg.* 188
EPSON AMERICA INC., *pg.* 394, *pg.* 122
EPSON CANADA LIMITED, *pg.* 394, *pg.* 1933
EPSON ELECTRONICS AMERICA, *pg.* 638, *pg.* 658
EQUINIX, INC., *pg.* 394, *pg.* 190
EVANS & SUTHERLAND COMPUTER CORPORATION, *pg.* 638, *pg.* 1757
FLEXTRONICS INTERNATIONAL LTD., *pg.* 81, *pg.* 245
FRANKLIN ELECTRONIC PUBLISHERS, INC., *pg.* 398, *pg.* 1048
FREESCALE SEMICONDUCTOR, INC., *pg.* 398, *pg.* 1662
FRY'S ELECTRONICS, INC., *pg.* 640, *pg.* 245
FURUNO USA, INC., *pg.* 640, *pg.* 1819
GAMESTOP CORP., *pg.* 399, *pg.* 1699
GLOBAL EPOINT INC., *pg.* 400, *pg.* 67
GLOBAL IMAGING SYSTEMS, INC., *pg.* 400, *pg.* 473
GRAYBAR ELECTRIC COMPANY, INC., *pg.* 1299, *pg.* 997
HAMAMATSU CORPORATION, *pg.* 1415, *pg.* 1046
HARSCO CORPORATION, *pg.* 86, *pg.* 1519
HITACHI AMERICA, LTD., *pg.* 642, *pg.* 1344
HITACHI DATA SYSTEMS CORPORATION, *pg.* 407, *pg.* 265
HYNIX SEMICONDUCTOR AMERICA INC., *pg.* 409, *pg.* 246
IBM, *pg.* 410, *pg.* 1449
IBM CANADA LIMITED, *pg.* 411, *pg.* 1923
IKEGAMI ELECTRONICS (U.S.A.), INC., *pg.* 644, *pg.* 1083
IMAKENEWS, INC., *pg.* 413, *pg.* 851
INC.COM LLC, *pg.* 1258, *pg.* 1243
INFOR, *pg.* 414, *pg.* 484
INFOSONICS CORPORATION, *pg.* 644, *pg.* 203
INGRAM MICRO INC., *pg.* 415, *pg.* 261
INGRAM MICRO MOBILITY, *pg.* 415, *pg.* 697
INSIGHT ENTERPRISES, INC., *pg.* 415, *pg.* 26
INSIGHT ENTERPRISES, INC., *pg.* 415, *pg.* 557
INSIGHT ENTERPRISES, INC., *pg.* 416, *pg.* 1732
INTELLIGENT HEARING SYSTEMS CORP., *pg.* 1546, *pg.* 443
IOGEAR, INC., *pg.* 421, *pg.* 86
IRONPLANET, INC., *pg.* 1259, *pg.* 183
JACK HENRY & ASSOCIATES, INC., *pg.* 422, *pg.* 988
JACO ELECTRONICS, INC., *pg.* 648, *pg.* 1165
JOURNEY EDUCATION MARKETING, INC., *pg.* 1775, *pg.* 1683
JVC AMERICAS CORP., *pg.* 648, *pg.* 1129
KATY INDUSTRIES, INC., *pg.* 1126, *pg.* 973
KEITHLEY INSTRUMENTS, INC., *pg.* 1418, *pg.* 1473
KONICA MINOLTA BUSINESS SOLUTIONS USA, INC., *pg.* 1419, *pg.* 1113
KRATOS-GENERAL MICROWAVE, *pg.* 650, *pg.* 1344
KYOCERA DOCUMENT SOLUTIONS AMERICA, *pg.* 426, *pg.* 1065
LAPWORKS, INC., *pg.* 426, *pg.* 187
LEXMARK INTERNATIONAL, INC., *pg.* 427, *pg.* 730
LG ELECTRONICS U.S.A., INC., *pg.* 651, *pg.* 1060
LIGHTING SCIENCE GROUP CORPORATION, *pg.* 1301, *pg.* 467
LOCAL.COM CORPORATION, *pg.* 1264, *pg.* 113
LOWRY COMPUTER PRODUCTS, INC., *pg.* 428, *pg.* 874
LUFKIN INDUSTRIES, INC., *pg.* 1357, *pg.* 1726
MATRIX INTEGRATION LLC, *pg.* 430, *pg.* 692
MAYER ELECTRIC SUPPLY COMPANY INC., *pg.* 653, *pg.* 3
MEDIAGRIF INTERACTIVE TECHNOLOGIES, INC., *pg.* 431, *pg.* 1952
MEDICAL INFORMATION TECHNOLOGY, INC., *pg.* 431, *pg.* 859
MELISSA DATA CORP., *pg.* 432, *pg.* 188
MICRO 2000, INC., *pg.* 434, *pg.* 96
MICROS SYSTEMS, INC., *pg.* 435, *pg.* 768
MITEL NETWORKS, INC., *pg.* 1872, *pg.* 13
MOREDIRECT, *pg.* 441, *pg.* 412
MPHASE TECHNOLOGIES, INC., *pg.* 441, *pg.* 363
MSC SOFTWARE CORPORATION, *pg.* 441, *pg.* 262
MULBERRY METAL PRODUCTS, INC., *pg.* 1302, *pg.* 1127
MURATA ELECTRONICS NORTH AMERICA, INC., *pg.* 658, *pg.* 540
MURATEC AMERICA, INC., *pg.* 443, *pg.* 1733
MUTOH AMERICA INC., *pg.* 443, *pg.* 18
NAGRA USA, *pg.* 443, *pg.* 223
NAMEMEDIA, INC., *pg.* 1269, *pg.* 852
NEW AGE ELECTRONICS, INC., *pg.* 659, *pg.* 63
NEW RELIC, INC., *pg.* 445, *pg.* 224
NEWEGG INC., *pg.* 1271, *pg.* 67
NKK SWITCHES, *pg.* 1302, *pg.* 23
NTI CORPORATION, *pg.* 446, *pg.* 114
ORBOTECH INC., *pg.* 1367, *pg.* 788
PANASONIC CORPORATION OF NORTH AMERICA, *pg.* 661, *pg.* 1120
PANASONIC ELECTRIC WORKS CORPORATION OF AMERICA, *pg.* 661, *pg.* 1095
PC CONNECTION, INC., *pg.* 452, *pg.* 1036
PC MALL, INC., *pg.* 452, *pg.* 295
PCTEL, INC., *pg.* 452, *pg.* 557
PLUS VISION CORP. OF AMERICA, *pg.* 1275, *pg.* 1496
POLYWELL COMPUTERS, INC., *pg.* 456, *pg.* 280
POWER & TELEPHONE SUPPLY COMPANY, *pg.* 665, *pg.* 1646
POWERMAT USA, LLC, *pg.* 665, *pg.* 875
PRECISION DATA PRODUCTS, INC., *pg.* 456, *pg.* 895
PRESIDIO, *pg.* 456, *pg.* 1725
PRESSTEK, INC., *pg.* 456, *pg.* 606
PROFESSIONAL CONTROL CORPORATION, *pg.* 456, *pg.* 1858
PROGRESS SOFTWARE CORPORATION, *pg.* 457, *pg.* 786
RAND WORLDWIDE, INC., *pg.* 459, *pg.* 821
RECURSION SOFTWARE, INC., *pg.* 460, *pg.* 1697
REPLY! INC., *pg.* 1277, *pg.* 260
RICHARDSON ELECTRONICS, LTD., *pg.* 667, *pg.* 622
RICOH AMERICA, *pg.* 461, *pg.* 1550
RICOH AMERICAS CORPORATION, *pg.* 461, *pg.* 1131
ROHDE & SCHWARZ, INC., *pg.* 1428, *pg.* 768
ROYAL CONSUMER INFORMATION PRODUCTS INC., *pg.* 463, *pg.* 1122
SAG HARBOR INDUSTRIES, *pg.* 1305, *pg.* 1340
SAMSUNG ELECTRONICS AMERICA, INC., *pg.* 669, *pg.* 1115
SAMSUNG SEMICONDUCTOR, INC., *pg.* 670, *pg.* 250

First page reference indicates Business Class Edition
Second page reference indicates Geographic Edition

SAMSUNG TELECOMMUNICATIONS AMERICA, LLC, *pg.* 670, *pg.* 1736
SAP AMERICA, INC., *pg.* 466, *pg.* 1557
SCANSOURCE, INC., *pg.* 671, *pg.* 1618
SCANTRON CORPORATION, *pg.* 467, *pg.* 922
SECUREEYE SYSTEMS, INC., *pg.* 1280, *pg.* 1822
SED INTERNATIONAL HOLDINGS, INC., *pg.* 468, *pg.* 534
SEGA OF AMERICA INC., *pg.* 966, *pg.* 227
SHARP ELECTRONICS CORPORATION, *pg.* 672, *pg.* 1082
SHOKAI FAR EAST LTD., *pg.* 672, *pg.* 1155
SIGMATRON INTERNATIONAL, INC., *pg.* 674, *pg.* 611
THE SINGING MACHINE COMPANY, INC., *pg.* 674, *pg.* 426
SKULLCANDY, INC., *pg.* 674, *pg.* 1754
SOFTWARE HOUSE INTERNATIONAL, INC. (SHI), *pg.* 471, *pg.* 1122
SONY ELECTRONICS, INC., *pg.* 676, *pg.* 209
SPEED COMMERCE, INC., *pg.* 967, *pg.* 1737
SPS COMMERCE, INC., *pg.* 472, *pg.* 942
SPX PROCESS EQUIPMENT, *pg.* 1378, *pg.* 1337
SRA INTERNATIONAL, INC., *pg.* 473, *pg.* 1780
STEELCLOUD, INC., *pg.* 476, *pg.* 1776
SUMITOMO ELECTRIC, *pg.* 1599, *pg.* 1297
SYNNEX CORPORATION, *pg.* 480, *pg.* 92
TAITRON COMPONENTS INCORPORATED, *pg.* 677, *pg.* 299
TAIYO YUDEN (U.S.A.), INC., *pg.* 1380, *pg.* 279
TAMURA CORPORATION OF AMERICA, *pg.* 1380, *pg.* 291
TEAC AMERICA, INC., *pg.* 678, *pg.* 151
TECH DATA CORPORATION, *pg.* 482, *pg.* 416
TECHTARGET, INC., *pg.* 482, *pg.* 837
TESSCO TECHNOLOGIES, INC., *pg.* 679, *pg.* 773
TRANSCORE HOLDINGS INC., *pg.* 485, *pg.* 1541
UBISOFT INC., *pg.* 589, *pg.* 229
UNIVERSAL POWER GROUP, INC., *pg.* 683, *pg.* 1671
UNIVERSAL SECURITY INSTRUMENTS, INC., *pg.* 683, *pg.* 775
VOXX INTERNATIONAL, *pg.* 686, *pg.* 1166
WAUSAU FINANCIAL SYSTEMS INC., *pg.* 819, *pg.* 1882
WAYSIDE TECHNOLOGY GROUP, INC., *pg.* 491, *pg.* 1121
WESCO INTERNATIONAL INC., *pg.* 687, *pg.* 1582
WESTCON GROUP, INC., *pg.* 492, *pg.* 1345
WINCHESTER ELECTRONICS CORP., *pg.* 688, *pg.* 382
WMS INDUSTRIES INC., *pg.* 593, *pg.* 666
WORLD WIDE TECHNOLOGY HOLDING CO., INC., *pg.* 493, *pg.* 988
YAMAHA CORPORATION OF AMERICA, *pg.* 595, *pg.* 51
ZACK ELECTRONICS, INC., *pg.* 690, *pg.* 77
ZAGG INCORPORATED, *pg.* 690, *pg.* 1762

5735 - Record & Prerecorded Tape Stores

AMAZON.COM, INC., *pg.* 1226, *pg.* 1831
ATLANTIC RECORDS GROUP, *pg.* 270, *pg.* 1198
CD BABY, INC., *pg.* 1764, *pg.* 1501
DEP DISTRIBUTION EXCLUSIVE LTD, *pg.* 1766, *pg.* 1954
DIRECT HOLDINGS AMERICAS INC., *pg.* 1636, *pg.* 1780
HASTINGS ENTERTAINMENT, INC., *pg.* 1773, *pg.* 1659
INTRADA INC., *pg.* 1773, *pg.* 171
J&R MUSIC WORLD, *pg.* 554, *pg.* 1245
MOVIES UNLIMITED INC., *pg.* 1779, *pg.* 1567
POWER MUSIC, INC., *pg.* 305, *pg.* 1751
TLA ENTERTAINMENT GROUP, INC., *pg.* 313, *pg.* 1571
TRANS WORLD ENTERTAINMENT CORPORATION, *pg.* 313, *pg.* 1137
UNIVERSAL MOTOWN RECORDS, *pg.* 315, *pg.* 1307

5736 - Musical Instrument Stores

CARL FISCHER, LLC, *pg.* 1625, *pg.* 1209
CONN-SELMER, INC., *pg.* 542, *pg.* 677
ERNIE BALL INC., *pg.* 1768, *pg.* 68
FENDER MUSICAL INSTRUMENTS CORPORATION, *pg.* 547, *pg.* 21
GIBSON GUITAR CORP., *pg.* 550, *pg.* 1650
GUITAR CENTER, INC., *pg.* 1771, *pg.* 306
KAMAN MUSIC CORPORATION, *pg.* 555, *pg.* 339
KORG USA, INC., *pg.* 556, *pg.* 1180
MEGATRAX PRODUCTION MUSIC, INC., *pg.* 297, *pg.* 167
MUSICNOTES, INC., *pg.* 1268, *pg.* 1866
SAM ASH MUSIC CORPORATION, *pg.* 669, *pg.* 1167
STEINWAY & SONS, *pg.* 586, *pg.* 1176
STEINWAY MUSICAL INSTRUMENTS, INC., *pg.* 586, *pg.* 854
WINMARK CORPORATION, *pg.* 1792, *pg.* 946

5812 - Eating Places

A&W ALL-AMERICAN FOOD RESTAURANTS, INC., *pg.* 1714, *pg.* 731
A&W FOOD SERVICES OF CANADA INC., *pg.* 1714, *pg.* 1908
ABP CORPORATION, *pg.* 1714, *pg.* 789
ALLIED OLD ENGLISH, INC., *pg.* 836, *pg.* 1110
AMERICAN BLUE RIBBON HOLDINGS, *pg.* 1714, *pg.* 1648
AMERICAN DAIRY QUEEN CORPORATION, *pg.* 1714, *pg.* 930
AMERICAN RESTAURANT CONCEPTS, INC., *pg.* 1715, *pg.* 431
AMERISTAR CASINOS, INC., *pg.* 528, *pg.* 1022
ARAMARK, *pg.* 1013, *pg.* 1558
ARAMARK CANADA LTD., *pg.* 1014, *pg.* 1935
ARBY'S RESTAURANT GROUP, INC., *pg.* 1014, *pg.* 488
ARCHON CORPORATION, *pg.* 1080, *pg.* 1030
ARK RESTAURANTS CORP., *pg.* 1715, *pg.* 1196
THE ATLANTA BREAD COMPANY, *pg.* 1715, *pg.* 540
ATTITASH, *pg.* 531, *pg.* 1033
AUNTIE ANNE'S INC., *pg.* 1715, *pg.* 1546
BAB, INC., *pg.* 1715, *pg.* 599
BACK YARD BURGERS, INC., *pg.* 1715, *pg.* 1648
BAD BOY WORLDWIDE ENTERTAINMENT GROUP, *pg.* 270, *pg.* 1199
BAKERS SQUARE, *pg.* 1715, *pg.* 316
BARLEYCORN'S, *pg.* 1716, *pg.* 726
BEN & JERRY'S HOMEMADE, INC., *pg.* 1850, *pg.* 1767
BENIHANA INC., *pg.* 1716, *pg.* 409
BERTUCCI'S CORP., *pg.* 1716, *pg.* 838
THE BEVERLY HILLS HOTEL, *pg.* 1082, *pg.* 46
BIG BOY RESTAURANTS INTERNATIONAL, LLC, *pg.* 1716, *pg.* 912
BIGLARI HOLDINGS INC., *pg.* 1015, *pg.* 1739
BIMBO BAKERIES USA INC., *pg.* 840, *pg.* 1540
BISCUITVILLE, INC., *pg.* 1015, *pg.* 1374
BJ'S RESTAURANTS, INC., *pg.* 1716, *pg.* 104
BLOOMIN' BRANDS, INC., *pg.* 1716, *pg.* 471
BOB EVANS FARMS, LLC, *pg.* 841, *pg.* 1467
BOB EVANS RESTAURANTS, INC., *pg.* 1717, *pg.* 1438
BOJANGLES' RESTAURANTS, INC., *pg.* 1717, *pg.* 1364
BOMBAY PALACE COMPANY, *pg.* 1717, *pg.* 1205
BONEFISH GRILL, *pg.* 1717, *pg.* 471
BOSTON MARKET CORPORATION, *pg.* 1717, *pg.* 329
BOSTON RESTAURANT ASSOCIATES, INC., *pg.* 1717, *pg.* 829
BRAVO BRIO RESTAURANT GROUP, INC., *pg.* 1717, *pg.* 1438
BRIDGEMAN'S RESTAURANTS INC., *pg.* 1718, *pg.* 919
BRINKER INTERNATIONAL, INC., *pg.* 1718, *pg.* 1676
BRUEGGER'S CORPORATION, *pg.* 1718, *pg.* 1764
BUBBA GUMP SHRIMP COMPANY RESTAURANT & MARKET, *pg.* 1718, *pg.* 1702
BUCA, INC., *pg.* 1718, *pg.* 931
BUFFALO WILD WINGS, INC., *pg.* 1718, *pg.* 931
BURGER KING CORPORATION, *pg.* 1719, *pg.* 440
BURGERVILLE USA, *pg.* 1720, *pg.* 1845
CAESARS ENTERTAINMENT CORPORATION, *pg.* 1083, *pg.* 1023
CALIFORNIA PIZZA KITCHEN INC., *pg.* 1720, *pg.* 127
CAPTAIN D'S, LLC, *pg.* 1720, *pg.* 1649
CARA OPERATIONS LIMITED, *pg.* 1720, *pg.* 1947
CARIBOU COFFEE COMPANY, INC., *pg.* 1764, *pg.* 932
CARL KARCHER ENTERPRISES, INC., *pg.* 1720, *pg.* 63
CARLSON COMPANIES INC., *pg.* 1084, *pg.* 947
CARRABBA'S ITALIAN GRILL, LLC, *pg.* 1720, *pg.* 472
CARROLS CORPORATION, *pg.* 1720, *pg.* 1344
CARROLS RESTAURANT GROUP, INC., *pg.* 1721, *pg.* 1344
CBOCS, INC., *pg.* 1721, *pg.* 1639
CEC ENTERTAINMENT, INC., *pg.* 1721, *pg.* 1717
CENTERPLATE, INC., *pg.* 1017, *pg.* 372
CHATTANOOGA CHOO-CHOO HOLIDAY INN, *pg.* 1086, *pg.* 1628
CHECKERS DRIVE-IN RESTAURANTS, INC., *pg.* 1017, *pg.* 472
CHEDDAR'S, INC, *pg.* 1721, *pg.* 1718
CHEESECAKE FACTORY INCORPORATED, *pg.* 1017, *pg.* 56
CHEF'S INTERNATIONAL, INC., *pg.* 1721, *pg.* 1110
CHICK-FIL-A, INC., *pg.* 1721, *pg.* 492
CHILI'S, INC., *pg.* 1722, *pg.* 1677
CHIPOTLE MEXICAN GRILL, INC., *pg.* 1722, *pg.* 317
CHURCH'S CHICKEN, INC., *pg.* 1722, *pg.* 493
CICI ENTERPRISES LP, *pg.* 1723, *pg.* 1670
CINNABON, INC., *pg.* 1723, *pg.* 493
CKE RESTAURANTS INC., *pg.* 1723, *pg.* 63
COCO PAZZO OF ILLINOIS LLC, *pg.* 1723, *pg.* 572
COLUMBIA RESTAURANT GROUP, *pg.* 1723, *pg.* 472
CORKY'S BAR-B-Q, *pg.* 1723, *pg.* 1642
COSI, INC., *pg.* 1723, *pg.* 600
COUNTRY KITCHEN INTERNATIONAL, INC., *pg.* 1723, *pg.* 1865
COUSINS SUBMARINES, INC., *pg.* 1017, *pg.* 1870
CRACKER BARREL OLD COUNTRY STORE, INC., *pg.* 1723, *pg.* 1639
CRES-COR, *pg.* 1326, *pg.* 1464
CULINART, INC., *pg.* 1017, *pg.* 1321
DAIRY QUEEN CORPORATE STORE, *pg.* 1724, *pg.* 932
DARDEN RESTAURANTS, INC., *pg.* 1724, *pg.* 453
DAVCO RESTAURANTS INC., *pg.* 1724, *pg.* 768
DAVE & BUSTER'S ENTERTAINMENT, INC., *pg.* 1724, *pg.* 1679
DEAN & DELUCA, INC., *pg.* 1018, *pg.* 723
DEL FRISCO'S RESTAURANT GROUP, LLC, *pg.* 1018, *pg.* 1680
DEL TACO RESTAURANTS, INC., *pg.* 1725, *pg.* 121
DELAWARE NORTH COMPANIES, INC., *pg.* 1089, *pg.* 1148
DELI MANAGEMENT INC., *pg.* 1725, *pg.* 1668
DENNY'S CORPORATION, *pg.* 1725, *pg.* 1622
DENNY'S, INC., *pg.* 1725, *pg.* 1622
DESCHUTES BREWERY INC., *pg.* 248, *pg.* 1496
DINEEQUITY, INC., *pg.* 1725, *pg.* 95
DOCTOR'S ASSOCIATES INC., *pg.* 1726, *pg.* 356
DOGFISH HEAD CRAFT BREWERY, INC., *pg.* 249, *pg.* 388
DOMAINE CHANDON, INC., *pg.* 1962, *pg.* 308
DOMINO'S PIZZA, INC., *pg.* 1726, *pg.* 865
DONATOS PIZZERIA CORPORATION, *pg.* 1727, *pg.* 1439
DORAKU CORP., *pg.* 1727, *pg.* 448
DUNKIN' BRANDS GROUP, INC., *pg.* 1727, *pg.* 810
DYNAMIC MANAGEMENT COMPANY LLC, *pg.* 1727, *pg.* 1635
EAT'N PARK HOSPITALITY GROUP, *pg.* 1728, *pg.* 1539
EINSTEIN NOAH RESTAURANT GROUP, INC., *pg.* 1019, *pg.* 332
EL POLLO LOCO, INC., *pg.* 1728, *pg.* 70
ELI'S CHEESECAKE COMPANY, *pg.* 1852, *pg.* 572
ELMER'S RESTAURANTS, INC., *pg.* 1728, *pg.* 1502
EMPIRE KOSHER POULTRY, INC., *pg.* 854, *pg.* 1553
FAMIGLIA - DEBARTOLO, LLC, *pg.* 1728, *pg.* 1352
FAMOUS DAVE'S OF AMERICA, INC., *pg.* 1728, *pg.* 926
FAZOLI'S MANAGEMENT INC., *pg.* 1728, *pg.* 729
FLANIGAN'S ENTERPRISES, INC., *pg.* 1963, *pg.* 425
FOX & HOUND RESTAURANT GROUP, *pg.* 1729, *pg.* 723
FRED USINGER, INC., *pg.* 856, *pg.* 1874
FRESH ENTERPRISES, LLC, *pg.* 1729, *pg.* 110
FRIENDLY ICE CREAM, LLC, *pg.* 1853, *pg.* 859
FRISCH'S RESTAURANTS, INC., *pg.* 1729, *pg.* 1413
GARDEN FRESH RESTAURANT CORP., *pg.* 1729, *pg.* 203
GIORDANO'S ENTERPRISES, INC., *pg.* 1729, *pg.* 575
GODFATHER'S PIZZA, INC., *pg.* 1729, *pg.* 1015
GOLD STAR CHILI INC., *pg.* 1021, *pg.* 1414
GOLDEN CORRAL CORPORATION, *pg.* 1730, *pg.* 1387
GOLDEN NUGGET HOTEL, *pg.* 550, *pg.* 1024
GONNELLA BAKING COMPANY, *pg.* 859, *pg.* 575
GOOD TIMES RESTAURANTS, INC., *pg.* 1730, *pg.* 330
GORDON FOOD SERVICE INC., *pg.* 1021, *pg.* 913
GOSH ENTERPRISES, INC., *pg.* 1730, *pg.* 1440
GRANITE CITY FOOD & BREWERY LTD, *pg.* 1730, *pg.* 937
GRILL CONCEPTS, INC., *pg.* 1730, *pg.* 308
GRUBHUB INC., *pg.* 1255, *pg.* 576
GUCKENHEIMER ENTERPRISES, INC., *pg.* 1730, *pg.* 190
H&N FOODS INTERNATIONAL, INC., *pg.* 1022, *pg.* 132
HAMMONS PRODUCTS COMPANY, *pg.* 1855, *pg.* 1007
HARD ROCK CAFE INTERNATIONAL, INC., *pg.* 1730, *pg.* 454
HARDEES FOOD SYSTEMS, INC., *pg.* 1731, *pg.* 998
HONEY DEW ASSOCIATES, INC., *pg.* 1731, *pg.* 841
HOOTERS OF AMERICA LLC, *pg.* 1731, *pg.* 511
HORMEL FOODS CORPORATION - FOODSERVICE DIVISION, *pg.* 864, *pg.* 916
HOSS'S STEAK & SEA HOUSE, INC., *pg.* 1731, *pg.* 1526
HOSTESS BRANDS LLC, *pg.* 1856, *pg.* 984
HOULIHAN'S RESTAURANTS, INC., *pg.* 1731, *pg.* 716
HUNGRY HOWIE'S PIZZA & SUBS INC., *pg.* 1023, *pg.* 897
IL FORNAIO (AMERICA) CORPORATION, *pg.* 1731, *pg.* 70
IN-N-OUT BURGERS, INC., *pg.* 1732, *pg.* 111

INTERNATIONAL HOUSE OF PANCAKES, INC., *pg.* 1732, *pg.* 96
J. ALEXANDER'S CORPORATION, *pg.* 1732, *pg.* 1651
JACK IN THE BOX INC., *pg.* 1732, *pg.* 204
JACMAR COMPANIES, INC., *pg.* 1733, *pg.* 67
JAMBA, INC., *pg.* 1024, *pg.* 84
JERRY'S FAMOUS DELI, INC., *pg.* 1733, *pg.* 281
JIMMY JOHNS FRANCHISE, LLC, *pg.* 1024, *pg.* 562
THE JOHNNY ROCKETS GROUP, INC., *pg.* 1733, *pg.* 41
JRN, INC., *pg.* 1733, *pg.* 1631
KAHALA FRANCHISING LLC, *pg.* 1025, *pg.* 23
KER, INC., *pg.* 1733, *pg.* 438
KFC CORPORATION, *pg.* 1733, *pg.* 735
KIMPTON HOTEL & RESTAURANT GROUP, *pg.* 1099, *pg.* 220
KING'S HAWAIIAN BAKERY WEST, INC., *pg.* 869, *pg.* 293
KOBRAND CORPORATION, *pg.* 1965, *pg.* 1325
KONA GRILL INC., *pg.* 1734, *pg.* 23
KRISPY KREME DOUGHNUTS, INC., *pg.* 1734, *pg.* 1394
THE KRYSTAL COMPANY, *pg.* 1734, *pg.* 1629
LA ROSA'S, INC., *pg.* 1735, *pg.* 1416
LACKMANN CULINARY SERVICES, *pg.* 1026, *pg.* 1356
LAGO MAR PROPERTIES, INC., *pg.* 1100, *pg.* 425
LANDRY'S, INC., *pg.* 1735, *pg.* 1709
LARRY H. MILLER GROUP OF COMPANIES, *pg.* 182, *pg.* 1762
LAWRY'S RESTAURANTS, INC., *pg.* 1735, *pg.* 180
LEGAL SEA FOODS INC., *pg.* 1735, *pg.* 797
LETTUCE ENTERTAIN YOU ENTERPRISES, INC., *pg.* 1735, *pg.* 580
LEVY RESTAURANTS, INC., *pg.* 1736, *pg.* 580
LITTLE CAESARS ENTERPRISES, INC., *pg.* 1736, *pg.* 883
LOGAN'S ROADHOUSE, INC., *pg.* 1736, *pg.* 1652
LONE STAR STEAKHOUSE & SALOON, INC., *pg.* 1736, *pg.* 1733
LONG JOHN SILVER'S, LLC, *pg.* 1736, *pg.* 736
LOUIS PAPPAS RESTAURANT GROUP, LLC, *pg.* 1736, *pg.* 477
LUBY'S FUDDRUCKERS RESTAURANTS, LLC, *pg.* 1736, *pg.* 1710
LUBY'S, INC., *pg.* 1736, *pg.* 1710
MAMMA ILARDO'S CORP., *pg.* 1737, *pg.* 779
MARCOS PIZZA INC., *pg.* 1737, *pg.* 1476
MARSH SUPERMARKETS, INC., *pg.* 1027, *pg.* 688
MAX & ERMA'S RESTAURANTS, INC., *pg.* 1737, *pg.* 1652
MAZZIO'S CORPORATION, *pg.* 1737, *pg.* 1490
MCCORMICK & SCHMICK'S SEAFOOD RESTAURANTS, INC., *pg.* 1737, *pg.* 1711
MCDONALD'S CORPORATION, *pg.* 1737, *pg.* 645
MCDONALD'S RESTAURANTS OF CANADA LTD., *pg.* 1740, *pg.* 1940
MCGONIGAL'S PUB, *pg.* 1741, *pg.* 555
MERITAGE HOSPITALITY GROUP, INC., *pg.* 1741, *pg.* 888
MEXICAN RESTAURANTS, INC., *pg.* 1741, *pg.* 1711
MIMI'S CAFE, LLC, *pg.* 1741, *pg.* 297
MOE'S SOUTHWEST GRILL, LLC, *pg.* 1027, *pg.* 514
MORGAN'S FOODS, INC., *pg.* 1741, *pg.* 1432
MORTON'S RESTAURANT GROUP, INC., *pg.* 1741, *pg.* 583
MR. GATTI'S, LP, *pg.* 1741, *pg.* 1664
NATHAN'S FAMOUS INC., *pg.* 1741, *pg.* 1171
NATIONAL HONEY BOARD, *pg.* 149, *pg.* 328
NEW BOSTON GARDEN CORP., *pg.* 569, *pg.* 799
NEW YORK FRIES, *pg.* 1028, *pg.* 1941
NOBLE ROMAN'S, INC., *pg.* 1741, *pg.* 689
NOODLES & COMPANY, *pg.* 1742, *pg.* 313
NORTHCOTT HOSPITALITY INTERNATIONAL, LLC, *pg.* 1742, *pg.* 920
NPC INTERNATIONAL, INC., *pg.* 1742, *pg.* 719
NUTRITION MANAGEMENT SERVICES COMPANY, *pg.* 1742, *pg.* 1543
O'CHARLEY'S INC., *pg.* 1742, *pg.* 1653
OLD SALEM, INCORPORATED, *pg.* 572, *pg.* 1395
OLIVE GARDEN ITALIAN RESTAURANT, *pg.* 1742, *pg.* 454
THE OMNI HOMESTEAD RESORT, *pg.* 1106, *pg.* 1786
OVATION BRANDS, *pg.* 1743, *pg.* 921
PANDA RESTAURANT GROUP, INC., *pg.* 1743, *pg.* 194
PANERA BREAD COMPANY, *pg.* 1029, *pg.* 1001
PAPA GINOS-DEANGELO HOLDING CORPORATION, INC., *pg.* 1743, *pg.* 817
PAPA JOHN'S INTERNATIONAL, INC., *pg.* 1743, *pg.* 737
PAPA MURPHY'S INTERNATIONAL, LLC, *pg.* 1743, *pg.* 1846
PARASOLE RESTAURANT HOLDINGS, INC., *pg.* 1744, *pg.* 925
THE PASTA HOUSE CO., *pg.* 1744, *pg.* 1001
PEDDLER'S VILLAGE, INC., *pg.* 1107, *pg.* 1545
PEER FOODS INC., *pg.* 888, *pg.* 587
PERKINS & MARIE CALLENDER'S INC., *pg.* 1744, *pg.* 1645
PERRY'S ICE CREAM CO., INC., *pg.* 1861, *pg.* 1137
PETER PIPER, INC., *pg.* 1744, *pg.* 18
P.F. CHANG'S CHINA BISTRO, INC., *pg.* 1030, *pg.* 24
PHILLIPS FOODS INC., *pg.* 1030, *pg.* 758
PICCADILLY RESTAURANTS, LLC, *pg.* 1744, *pg.* 742
PINKBERRY INC., *pg.* 1744, *pg.* 275
PITA PIT USA, INC., *pg.* 1744, *pg.* 549
PIZZA HUT, INC., *pg.* 1744, *pg.* 1733
PIZZA INN, INC., *pg.* 1745, *pg.* 1746
POLLO TROPICAL INC., *pg.* 1745, *pg.* 445
POLYNESIAN CULTURAL CENTER, *pg.* 577, *pg.* 545
POPEYE'S CHICKEN & BISCUITS, *pg.* 1745, *pg.* 517
POPEYES LOUISIANA KITCHEN, INC., *pg.* 1745, *pg.* 517
PORT OF SUBS INC., *pg.* 1746, *pg.* 1032
POTBELLY SANDWICH WORKS LLC, *pg.* 1746, *pg.* 587
PRET A MANGER, *pg.* 1746, *pg.* 1283
PRODUCE MARKETING ASSOCIATION, *pg.* 154, *pg.* 388
QDOBA MEXICAN GRILL INC., *pg.* 1031, *pg.* 336
QUALITY DINING, INC., *pg.* 1746, *pg.* 695
THE QUIZNO'S MASTER LLC, *pg.* 1746, *pg.* 322
RAISING CANE'S USA, *pg.* 1746, *pg.* 742
REAL MEX RESTAURANTS, INC., *pg.* 1746, *pg.* 75
RED LION HOTELS CORP., *pg.* 1110, *pg.* 1844
RED LOBSTER, *pg.* 1747, *pg.* 455
RED MANGO INC., *pg.* 1747, *pg.* 1686
RED ROBIN GOURMET BURGERS, INC., *pg.* 1747, *pg.* 331
RESORTS ATLANTIC CITY, *pg.* 1110, *pg.* 1041
RESTAURANT ASSOCIATES CORPORATION, *pg.* 1747, *pg.* 1285
RESTAURANT DEVELOPERS CORP., *pg.* 1747, *pg.* 1464
RESTAURANTS UNLIMITED, INC., *pg.* 1748, *pg.* 1839
RHODES INTERNATIONAL, INC., *pg.* 891, *pg.* 1760
RIB CITY GRILL, INC., *pg.* 1748, *pg.* 428
RICE EPICUREAN MARKET, *pg.* 1032, *pg.* 1713
ROCK BOTTOM RESTAURANTS, INC., *pg.* 1748, *pg.* 334
ROCKY ROCOCO CORPORATION, *pg.* 1748, *pg.* 1885
ROMACORP, INC., *pg.* 1748, *pg.* 1734
ROUND TABLE PIZZA, *pg.* 1748, *pg.* 69
RUBIO'S RESTAURANTS, INC., *pg.* 1748, *pg.* 60
RUBY TUESDAY, INC., *pg.* 1748, *pg.* 1640
RUTH'S HOSPITALITY GROUP, INC., *pg.* 1748, *pg.* 480
SACRAMENTO KINGS, *pg.* 579, *pg.* 197
SANDELLA'S FLATBREAD CAFE, *pg.* 1749, *pg.* 383
SARGENTO FOODS INC., *pg.* 894, *pg.* 1886
SBARRO, INC., *pg.* 1749, *pg.* 1182
SCHLOTZSKY'S, LTD., *pg.* 1749, *pg.* 1665
SEMINOLE TRIBE OF FLORIDA, INC., *pg.* 156, *pg.* 431
SHAKEY'S USA, INC., *pg.* 1749, *pg.* 40
SHAMROCK FOODS COMPANY, *pg.* 895, *pg.* 20
SHONEY'S NORTH AMERICA, LLC, *pg.* 1749, *pg.* 1654
SILVER DINER, INC., *pg.* 1750, *pg.* 776
SKYLINE CHILI, INC., *pg.* 1033, *pg.* 1452
SMASHBURGER MASTER LLC, *pg.* 1750, *pg.* 323
SMITH & SONS FOODS, INC., *pg.* 1750, *pg.* 535
THE SMITH & WOLLENSKY RESTAURANT GROUP, INC., *pg.* 1750, *pg.* 1293
SMOKEY BONES BARBEQUE & GRILL, *pg.* 1750, *pg.* 456
SMOOTHIE KING FRANCHISES, INC., *pg.* 1750, *pg.* 743
SONIC CORP., *pg.* 1750, *pg.* 1487
SONNY'S FRANCHISE COMPANY INC., *pg.* 1751, *pg.* 480
SONNY'S REAL PIT BAR-B-QUE, *pg.* 1751, *pg.* 461
SOUTH ST BURGER CO, *pg.* 1751, *pg.* 1943
SPAGHETTI WAREHOUSE, INC., *pg.* 1751, *pg.* 1724
SPICY PICKLE FRANCHISING, INC., *pg.* 1751, *pg.* 323
STAR BUFFET, INC., *pg.* 1751, *pg.* 24
STARBUCKS CORPORATION, *pg.* 897, *pg.* 1840
STRANG CORPORATION, *pg.* 1751, *pg.* 1436
STRAW HAT COOPERATIVE CORPORATION, *pg.* 1751, *pg.* 260
SUBWAY RESTAURANTS, *pg.* 1751, *pg.* 356
SUNDAY RIVER SKIWAY CORP., *pg.* 586, *pg.* 749
SYSCO CORPORATION, *pg.* 1035, *pg.* 1716
TACO BELL CORP., *pg.* 1752, *pg.* 117
TACO BUENO RESTAURANTS, L.P., *pg.* 1753, *pg.* 1692
TACO CABANA, INC., *pg.* 1753, *pg.* 1743
TACO JOHN'S INTERNATIONAL, INC., *pg.* 1753, *pg.* 1901
TAVISTOCK RESTAURANT GROUP, *pg.* 1753, *pg.* 803
TEXAS ROADHOUSE, INC., *pg.* 1753, *pg.* 738
T.G.I. FRIDAY'S INC., *pg.* 1754, *pg.* 1669
TRUFOODS LLC, *pg.* 1754, *pg.* 1305
U-SWIRL, INC., *pg.* 903, *pg.* 1021
UFOOD RESTAURANT GROUP, INC., *pg.* 1754, *pg.* 837
UNO RESTAURANT HOLDINGS CORPORATION, *pg.* 1754, *pg.* 856
VCG HOLDING CORP., *pg.* 590, *pg.* 333
WAFFLE HOUSE, INCORPORATED, *pg.* 1754, *pg.* 538
WAL-MART STORES, INC., *pg.* 1790, *pg.* 29
WEBER-STEPHEN PRODUCTS LLC, *pg.* 62, *pg.* 650
THE WENDY'S COMPANY, *pg.* 1755, *pg.* 1450
WENDY'S INTERNATIONAL, INC., *pg.* 1755, *pg.* 1451
WESTERN SIZZLIN CORPORATION, *pg.* 1755, *pg.* 1806
WETZEL'S PRETZELS LLC, *pg.* 910, *pg.* 181
WHATABURGER, INC., *pg.* 1755, *pg.* 1744
WHITE CASTLE MANAGEMENT CO., *pg.* 1756, *pg.* 1444
YARD HOUSE USA, INC., *pg.* 1756, *pg.* 118
YUM! BRANDS, INC., *pg.* 1756, *pg.* 738
ZAXBY'S FRANCHISING, INC., *pg.* 1756, *pg.* 486
ZIPPY'S, INC., *pg.* 1757, *pg.* 545

5813 - Drinking Places (Alcoholic Beverages)

ARK RESTAURANTS CORP., *pg.* 1715, *pg.* 1196
BARLEYCORN'S, *pg.* 1716, *pg.* 726
BJ'S RESTAURANTS, INC., *pg.* 1716, *pg.* 104
BUBBA GUMP SHRIMP COMPANY RESTAURANT & MARKET, *pg.* 1718, *pg.* 1702
CAESARS ENTERTAINMENT CORPORATION, *pg.* 1083, *pg.* 1023
CENTURY CASINOS INC., *pg.* 538, *pg.* 315
CHEDDAR'S, INC, *pg.* 1721, *pg.* 1718
CHEESECAKE FACTORY INCORPORATED, *pg.* 1017, *pg.* 56
DAVE & BUSTER'S ENTERTAINMENT, INC., *pg.* 1724, *pg.* 1679
GRANITE CITY FOOD & BREWERY LTD, *pg.* 1730, *pg.* 937
HARD ROCK CAFE INTERNATIONAL, INC., *pg.* 1730, *pg.* 454
HOULIHAN'S RESTAURANTS, INC., *pg.* 1731, *pg.* 716
LAWRY'S RESTAURANTS, INC., *pg.* 1735, *pg.* 180
P.F. CHANG'S CHINA BISTRO, INC., *pg.* 1030, *pg.* 24
QUALITY DINING, INC., *pg.* 1746, *pg.* 695
RESTAURANT ASSOCIATES CORPORATION, *pg.* 1747, *pg.* 1285
ROGER SMITH HOTELS CORP., *pg.* 1111, *pg.* 1286
RUBY TUESDAY, INC., *pg.* 1748, *pg.* 1640
SEMINOLE TRIBE OF FLORIDA, INC., *pg.* 156, *pg.* 431
STRANG CORPORATION, *pg.* 1751, *pg.* 1436
T.G.I. FRIDAY'S INC., *pg.* 1754, *pg.* 1669
VCG HOLDING CORP., *pg.* 590, *pg.* 333

5912 - Drug Stores & Proprietary Stores

ADH HEALTH PRODUCTS, INC., *pg.* 1487, *pg.* 1154
AKORN, *pg.* 1488, *pg.* 1138
ALBERTSON'S LLC, *pg.* 1013, *pg.* 546
ALOETTE COSMETICS, INC., *pg.* 498, *pg.* 487
AMAG PHARMACEUTICALS, INC., *pg.* 1492, *pg.* 827
AMERICAN INTERNATIONAL INDUSTRIES COMPANY, *pg.* 498, *pg.* 126
AMERISOURCEBERGEN CORPORATION, *pg.* 1493, *pg.* 1522
AMWAY CORPORATION, *pg.* 326, *pg.* 864
ANIMAL HEALTH INTERNATIONAL, INC., *pg.* 1474, *pg.* 1749
ANNIE OAKLEY ENTERPRISES, INC., *pg.* 499, *pg.* 693
APRIA HEALTHCARE GROUP INC., *pg.* 1495, *pg.* 120
ASD HEALTHCARE, *pg.* 1496, *pg.* 1697
BACTOLAC PHARMACEUTICAL, INC., *pg.* 1498, *pg.* 1163
BARE ESCENTUALS, INC., *pg.* 500, *pg.* 213
THE BARTELL DRUG COMPANY, *pg.* 1499, *pg.* 1833
BATH & BODY WORKS, LLC, *pg.* 500, *pg.* 1471
BAYER HEALTHCARE CONSUMER CARE DIVISION, *pg.* 1500, *pg.* 1087
BEE-ALIVE INC., *pg.* 1503, *pg.* 1348
BEIERSDORF NORTH AMERICA INC., *pg.* 501, *pg.* 385
BENEFIT COSMETICS LLC, *pg.* 501, *pg.* 213
BIOSCRIP, INC., *pg.* 1506, *pg.* 1158
BLISSWORLD LLC, *pg.* 501, *pg.* 1204
BORGHESE, INC., *pg.* 502, *pg.* 1205
BURT'S BEES INC., *pg.* 502, *pg.* 1370
CANADA DRUGS LTD., *pg.* 1511, *pg.* 1914
CAREMARK PHARMACY SERVICES, *pg.* 1513, *pg.* 1649
CENTRIC GROUP LLC, *pg.* 1514, *pg.* 994

CIGNA TEL-DRUG, INC., *pg.* 1515, *pg.* 1625
COLGATE ORAL PHARMACEUTICAL, *pg.* 1516, *pg.* 1214
COLOR ME BEAUTIFUL, INC., *pg.* 505, *pg.* 1787
CONMED HEALTHCARE MANAGEMENT, INC., *pg.* 1518, *pg.* 772
COSMETIQUE, INC., *pg.* 1765, *pg.* 664
CVS HEALTH CORPORATION, *pg.* 1765, *pg.* 1610
DHC USA INC., *pg.* 507, *pg.* 216
DISCOUNT DRUG MART INC., *pg.* 1524, *pg.* 1464
DIXIE HEALTH, INC., *pg.* 1524, *pg.* 535
DRUGSTORE.COM, INC., *pg.* 1239, *pg.* 1814
DS LABORATORIES, INC., *pg.* 507, *pg.* 442
DUANE READE, INC., *pg.* 1525, *pg.* 1226
EBY-BROWN CO., *pg.* 1767, *pg.* 636
EDEN COMPANY, *pg.* 1768, *pg.* 1050
ELIZABETH ARDEN, INC., *pg.* 507, *pg.* 448
THE ESTEE LAUDER COMPANIES INC., *pg.* 508, *pg.* 1229
EXPRESS SCRIPTS, *pg.* 1530, *pg.* 1070
EXPRESS SCRIPTS, INC., *pg.* 1530, *pg.* 997
THE F. DOHMEN CO., *pg.* 1530, *pg.* 1858
FASHION FAIR COSMETICS, LLC, *pg.* 509, *pg.* 573
FITNESS RX, *pg.* 1641, *pg.* 1342
FRAGRANCENET.COM, INC., *pg.* 1248, *pg.* 1155
FRED'S INC., *pg.* 1769, *pg.* 1644
FRONTIER NATURAL PRODUCTS CO-OP, *pg.* 509, *pg.* 710
GIANT OF MARYLAND LLC, *pg.* 1021, *pg.* 773
GOODY PRODUCTS, INC., *pg.* 510, *pg.* 509
HAELAN PRODUCTS, INC., *pg.* 860, *pg.* 1847
HAGGEN, INC., *pg.* 1022, *pg.* 1817
HANNAFORD BROTHERS CO., *pg.* 1022, *pg.* 752
HEALTH PRODUCTS CORPORATION, *pg.* 1540, *pg.* 1356
HEALTHWAREHOUSE.COM, INC., *pg.* 403, *pg.* 728
HEALTHY DIRECTIONS, *pg.* 1649, *pg.* 775
HENRY SCHEIN, INC., *pg.* 1541, *pg.* 1180
HERBALIFE INTERNATIONAL OF AMERICA, INC., *pg.* 1541, *pg.* 132
HESKA CORPORATION, *pg.* 1542, *pg.* 335
HY-VEE, INC., *pg.* 1023, *pg.* 713
INSPIRED BEAUTY BRANDS, *pg.* 512, *pg.* 1244
INTER PARFUMS, INC., *pg.* 512, *pg.* 1244
INTERCHEM CORPORATION, *pg.* 1168, *pg.* 1101
J. STRICKLAND & COMPANY, *pg.* 512, *pg.* 970
THE JEAN COUTU GROUP (PJC) INC., *pg.* 1548, *pg.* 1952
JEFFERS, INC., *pg.* 1477, *pg.* 5
JOHN PAUL MITCHELL SYSTEMS, *pg.* 512, *pg.* 133
JOHNSON & JOHNSON, *pg.* 1549, *pg.* 1091
JOLEN CREME BLEACH CORP., *pg.* 513, *pg.* 348
KING KULLEN GROCERY COMPANY, INC., *pg.* 1025, *pg.* 1141
THE KROGER CO., *pg.* 1025, *pg.* 1416
LANELABS USA INC., *pg.* 1554, *pg.* 1128
LIBERTY MEDICAL SUPPLY, INC., *pg.* 1555, *pg.* 460
LIVING PROOF, INC., *pg.* 514, *pg.* 809
LORD & TAYLOR LLC, *pg.* 1777, *pg.* 1252
LUITPOLD PHARMACEUTICALS, INC., *pg.* 1557, *pg.* 1342
LUMARA HEALTH INC., *pg.* 1557, *pg.* 973
MAJESTIC DRUG COMPANY, INC., *pg.* 516, *pg.* 1343
MARIETTA HOSPITALITY, *pg.* 1464, *pg.* 1155
MARILYN MIGLIN, L.P., *pg.* 516, *pg.* 581
MARY KAY INC., *pg.* 516, *pg.* 1657
MAYBELLINE LLC, *pg.* 516, *pg.* 1257
MCKESSON CORPORATION, *pg.* 1560, *pg.* 222
MEDICINE SHOPPE INTERNATIONAL, INC., *pg.* 1561, *pg.* 976
MERLE NORMAN COSMETICS, INC., *pg.* 517, *pg.* 136
MWI VETERINARY SUPPLY, INC., *pg.* 1570, *pg.* 548
NORTH AMERICAN CORP., *pg.* 446, *pg.* 615
NU SKIN ENTERPRISES, INC., *pg.* 518, *pg.* 1755
NUNATURALS, INC., *pg.* 1576, *pg.* 1497
NUTRICIA NORTH AMERICA, *pg.* 1577, *pg.* 776
OMNICARE, INC, *pg.* 1578, *pg.* 1418
PACIFICHEALTH LABORATORIES, INC., *pg.* 1579, *pg.* 1083
PALM BEACH TAN, INC., *pg.* 519, *pg.* 1671
PARFUMS CHRISTIAN DIOR, INC, *pg.* 519, *pg.* 1276
PARLUX FRAGRANCES, INC., *pg.* 519, *pg.* 426
PERFUMANIA HOLDINGS, INC., *pg.* 520, *pg.* 1141
PERFUMANIA, INC., *pg.* 520, *pg.* 469
PRADA U.S.A. CORP., *pg.* 31, *pg.* 1283
PURDUE PHARMA LP, *pg.* 1587, *pg.* 377
QUALITY KING DISTRIBUTORS INC., *pg.* 1587, *pg.* 1339
RBC LIFE SCIENCES, INC., *pg.* 1588, *pg.* 1723
REDKEN LABORATORIES LLC, *pg.* 520, *pg.* 1285
REGIS CORPORATION, *pg.* 521, *pg.* 941
RICOLA USA, INC., *pg.* 1590, *pg.* 1106
RITE AID CORPORATION, *pg.* 1590, *pg.* 1519
RUE21, INC., *pg.* 32, *pg.* 1591
SALLY BEAUTY HOLDINGS, INC., *pg.* 522, *pg.* 1691
SANOFI US, *pg.* 1592, *pg.* 1046
SCANDINAVIAN FORMULAS, INC., *pg.* 1592, *pg.* 1586
SCHNUCK MARKETS, INC., *pg.* 1033, *pg.* 1002
SEDANO'S MANAGEMENT, INC., *pg.* 1033, *pg.* 430
SEPHORA USA INC, *pg.* 522, *pg.* 227
SHAKLEE CORPORATION, *pg.* 1593, *pg.* 184
SHISEIDO COSMETICS AMERICA OF SAC, *pg.* 522, *pg.* 1291
SHOPKO, *pg.* 1785, *pg.* 1860
SHOPPERS DRUG MART CORPORATION, *pg.* 1594, *pg.* 1943
SMARTPAK EQUINE, LLC, *pg.* 1482, *pg.* 834
SMITH'S FOOD & DRUG CENTERS, INC., *pg.* 1034, *pg.* 1761
STEPAN COMPANY, *pg.* 1182, *pg.* 643
TOTAL NUTRACEUTICAL SOLUTIONS, INC., *pg.* 1603, *pg.* 1509
TRI-K INDUSTRIES, INC., *pg.* 523, *pg.* 1099
TWEEZERMAN INTERNATIONAL, *pg.* 524, *pg.* 1324
ULTA SALON, COSMETICS & FRAGRANCE, INC., *pg.* 524, *pg.* 559
UNITED NATURAL FOODS, INC., *pg.* 907, *pg.* 1608
VIDAL SASSOON CO., *pg.* 524, *pg.* 1426
VITACOST.COM, INC., *pg.* 1607, *pg.* 414
VITAMIN SHOPPE, INC., *pg.* 1608, *pg.* 1098
VONS A SAFEWAY COMPANY, *pg.* 1036, *pg.* 43
WAL-MART STORES, INC., *pg.* 1790, *pg.* 29
WALGREEN CO., *pg.* 1608, *pg.* 605
WELLQUEST MEDICAL & WELLNESS CORPORATION, *pg.* 1610, *pg.* 31
WINN DIXIE STORES, INC., *pg.* 1038, *pg.* 435

5921 - Liquor Stores

THE ABSOLUT SPIRITS COMPANY INC., *pg.* 1956, *pg.* 1325
ADAMBA IMPORTS INTERNATIONAL, *pg.* 1956, *pg.* 1145
ANDREW PELLER LIMITED, *pg.* 1956, *pg.* 1920
ANHEUSER-BUSCH COMPANIES, LLC, *pg.* 237, *pg.* 991
B-21 FINE WINE & SPIRITS INC., *pg.* 1956, *pg.* 477
BACARDI GLOBAL BRANDS INC., *pg.* 1956, *pg.* 417
BACARDI USA, INC., *pg.* 1956, *pg.* 417
BANFI VINTNERS, *pg.* 1957, *pg.* 1161
BEAM SUNTORY INC., *pg.* 1957, *pg.* 599
BEN E. KEITH COMPANY, *pg.* 840, *pg.* 1676
THE BROOKLYN BREWERY, *pg.* 239, *pg.* 1145
BROWN-FORMAN CORPORATION, *pg.* 1958, *pg.* 732
CAMPARI AMERICA, *pg.* 1960, *pg.* 214
CASTLE BRANDS INC., *pg.* 239, *pg.* 1209
CENTRAL EUROPEAN DISTRIBUTION CORPORATION, *pg.* 240, *pg.* 1090
CROWN IMPORTS LLC, *pg.* 248, *pg.* 572
DIAGEO NORTH AMERICA, INC., *pg.* 1961, *pg.* 361
DIAGEO NORTH AMERICA INC., *pg.* 248, *pg.* 1223
DREYFUS ASHBY INC., *pg.* 1962, *pg.* 1226
EMPIRE DISTRIBUTORS, INC., *pg.* 251, *pg.* 504
FLANIGAN'S ENTERPRISES, INC., *pg.* 1963, *pg.* 425
FORTUNE BRANDS HOME & SECURITY, INC., *pg.* 55, *pg.* 600
FREDERICK WILDMAN & SONS LTD., *pg.* 1963, *pg.* 1233
FREIXENET U.S.A., *pg.* 1963, *pg.* 279
GARY'S WINE & MARKETPLACE, *pg.* 1964, *pg.* 1080
GRAND TRAVERSE DISTILLERY, *pg.* 1964, *pg.* 909
HEAVEN HILL DISTILLERIES, INC., *pg.* 1964, *pg.* 725
HEINEKEN USA INC., *pg.* 252, *pg.* 1352
JIM BEAM BRANDS CO., *pg.* 1965, *pg.* 601
JOHNSON BROTHERS LIQUOR COMPANY, *pg.* 1965, *pg.* 961
JORDANO'S, INC., *pg.* 1024, *pg.* 263
KIRIN BREWERY OF AMERICA, LLC, *pg.* 253, *pg.* 134
KOBRAND CORPORATION, *pg.* 1965, *pg.* 1325
LABATT USA LLC, *pg.* 254, *pg.* 1149
LAIRD & COMPANY, INC., *pg.* 1966, *pg.* 1119
LEONARD KREUSCH, INC., *pg.* 254, *pg.* 1099
MARNIER-LAPOSTOLLE INC., *pg.* 1966, *pg.* 1256
MENDOCINO BREWING COMPANY, *pg.* 254, *pg.* 298
MILLERCOORS LLC, *pg.* 255, *pg.* 582
MOET HENNESSY, *pg.* 1966, *pg.* 1260
M.S. WALKER, INC., *pg.* 1967, *pg.* 843
NATIONAL WINE & SPIRITS, INC., *pg.* 1967, *pg.* 689
NOLET SPIRITS USA INC., *pg.* 1967, *pg.* 41
NOR-CAL BEVERAGE CO., INC., *pg.* 258, *pg.* 305
OPICI WINE GROUP INC., *pg.* 1967, *pg.* 1071
PARTIDA TEQUILA, LLC, *pg.* 1967, *pg.* 224
THE PASTENE COMPANIES, LTD., *pg.* 1029, *pg.* 811
THE PATRON SPIRITS COMPANY, *pg.* 1967, *pg.* 1029
PHOENIX VINTNERS, LLC, *pg.* 1968, *pg.* 182
PINE STATE TRADING COMPANY, *pg.* 1781, *pg.* 749
PROXIMO SPIRITS, INC., *pg.* 1969, *pg.* 1076
REMY COINTREAU USA INC., *pg.* 1969, *pg.* 1285
REPUBLIC NATIONAL DISTRIBUTING COMPANY, *pg.* 264, *pg.* 1713
REX HILL VINEYARDS, *pg.* 1969, *pg.* 1500
SAPPORO U.S.A., INC., *pg.* 1969, *pg.* 295
SAZERAC COMPANY, INC., *pg.* 1969, *pg.* 745
SHAW ROSS INTERNATIONAL IMPORTERS, *pg.* 1970, *pg.* 449
SIDNEY FRANK IMPORTING CO., INC., *pg.* 1970, *pg.* 1184
SLEEMAN UNIBROUE QUEBEC, *pg.* 265, *pg.* 1950
SPEC'S FAMILY PARTNERS LTD., *pg.* 1970, *pg.* 1715
THE TERLATO WINE GROUP, *pg.* 1971, *pg.* 555
TRADER JOE'S CO., *pg.* 1789, *pg.* 151
UNITED DISTRIBUTORS, INC., *pg.* 1971, *pg.* 540
UNITED STATES BEVERAGE LLC, *pg.* 266, *pg.* 379
VEEV ACAI SPIRITS, *pg.* 1972, *pg.* 141
WARSTEINER IMPORTERS AGENCY, INC., *pg.* 266, *pg.* 1479
WILLAMETTE VALLEY VINEYARDS, INC., *pg.* 1972, *pg.* 1510
WILLIAM GRANT & SONS, INC., *pg.* 1972, *pg.* 1057
THE WINE GROUP, INC., *pg.* 1972, *pg.* 234
WINE.COM, INC., *pg.* 1972, *pg.* 234

5932 - Used Merchandise Stores

BACKUPWORKS.COM INC., *pg.* 359, *pg.* 120
BALL & BALL HARDWARE REPRODUCTIONS, *pg.* 916, *pg.* 1531
GOODWILL INDUSTRIES-SUNCOAST, INC., *pg.* 142, *pg.* 462
POWELL'S BOOKS INC., *pg.* 1677, *pg.* 1505
RED BARON ANTIQUES INCORPORATED, *pg.* 940, *pg.* 519
THE SALVATION ARMY, *pg.* 155, *pg.* 1771
WINMARK CORPORATION, *pg.* 1792, *pg.* 946

5941 - Sporting Goods & Bicycle Shops

ACADEMY SPORTS & OUTDOORS, LTD., *pg.* 1824, *pg.* 1724
ALLEGRO CORPORATION, *pg.* 1759, *pg.* 1501
ALLIANCE SPORTS GROUP, L.P., *pg.* 1825, *pg.* 1698
ALLSTAR PRODUCTS GROUP LLC, *pg.* 17, *pg.* 1166
AMINCO INTERNATIONAL (USA) INC., *pg.* 1, *pg.* 120
AMPAC ENTERPRISES, INC., *pg.* 1825, *pg.* 843
BATTLE CREEK EQUIPMENT CO., *pg.* 1499, *pg.* 870
BENELLI USA CORPORATION, *pg.* 1827, *pg.* 754
BIANCHI U.S.A., INC., *pg.* 1827, *pg.* 100
BIG 5 SPORTING GOODS CORPORATION, *pg.* 1827, *pg.* 78
BLACK DIAMOND, INC., *pg.* 1827, *pg.* 1756
BLATT BOWLING & BILLIARD CORP., *pg.* 1827, *pg.* 1203
BMG/MUSIC, *pg.* 533, *pg.* 1205
BRIDGESTONE GOLF, INC., *pg.* 1828, *pg.* 528
BURNHAM BROTHERS, INC., *pg.* 1829, *pg.* 1727
CABELA'S INCORPORATED, *pg.* 535, *pg.* 1019
CALLAWAY GOLF BALL OPERATIONS, INC., *pg.* 1829, *pg.* 814
CHAMPS SPORTS, *pg.* 1806, *pg.* 414
THE COAST DISTRIBUTION SYSTEM, INC., *pg.* 1706, *pg.* 152
COASTAL AMUSEMENTS INC., *pg.* 951, *pg.* 1078
THE COLEMAN COMPANY, INC., *pg.* 1830, *pg.* 723
CONCORD MUSIC GROUP, INC., *pg.* 1765, *pg.* 46
CREATIVE PLAYTHINGS LTD., *pg.* 1831, *pg.* 820
DAIWA CORPORATION, *pg.* 1832, *pg.* 75
DICK'S SPORTING GOODS, INC., *pg.* 1832, *pg.* 1524
DOVER SADDLERY, INC., *pg.* 1833, *pg.* 829
DUALITE SALES & SERVICE, INC., *pg.* 1296, *pg.* 1482
DURAFLAME, INC., *pg.* 1123, *pg.* 280
E1 ENTERTAINMENT U.S. LP, *pg.* 284, *pg.* 1323
EASTON SPORTS, INC., *pg.* 1833, *pg.* 299
ENERGIZER HOLDINGS, INC., *pg.* 637, *pg.* 996
ETONIC WORLDWIDE LLC, *pg.* 1808, *pg.* 857

ETS, LLC, *pg.* 54, *pg.* 685
EVERLAST WORLDWIDE INC., *pg.* 1833, *pg.* 1230
FITNESS RESOURCE, INC., *pg.* 1834, *pg.* 1807
FOOT LOCKER, INC., *pg.* 1808, *pg.* 1231
G. JOANNOU CYCLE CO. INC., *pg.* 1707, *pg.* 1098
GAMING PARTNERS INTERNATIONAL CORPORATION, *pg.* 954, *pg.* 1024
GANDER MOUNTAIN COMPANY, *pg.* 1834, *pg.* 960
GERBER LEGENDARY BLADES, *pg.* 1834, *pg.* 1503
GOLF GALAXY, INC., *pg.* 1835, *pg.* 1525
GOLFBALLS.COM, INC., *pg.* 1249, *pg.* 744
GOLFSMITH INTERNATIONAL HOLDINGS, INC., *pg.* 1835, *pg.* 1662
GUITAR CENTER, INC., *pg.* 1771, *pg.* 306
HEELYS, INC., *pg.* 1809, *pg.* 1669
HENRY MODELL & COMPANY, INC., *pg.* 1836, *pg.* 1240
HIBBETT SPORTS, INC., *pg.* 1836, *pg.* 3
IGT, *pg.* 412, *pg.* 1031
IMPERIAL INTERNATIONAL, *pg.* 1837, *pg.* 1050
INFANTINO, LLC, *pg.* 957, *pg.* 203
INTELITEK, INC., *pg.* 1349, *pg.* 1036
KOMBI, LTD., *pg.* 1838, *pg.* 1766
LALIQUE NORTH AMERICA, *pg.* 1126, *pg.* 1054
LESLIE'S POOLMART, INC., *pg.* 1838, *pg.* 17
LOST ARROW CORPORATION, *pg.* 44, *pg.* 301
LVMH INC., *pg.* 9, *pg.* 1254
MARINELAND OF FLORIDA, *pg.* 561, *pg.* 461
MAUI JIM, INC., *pg.* 9, *pg.* 651
MCNETT CORPORATION, *pg.* 1839, *pg.* 1817
MERCURY LUGGAGE/SEWARD TRUNK, *pg.* 9, *pg.* 434
MIZUNO USA, INC., *pg.* 1839, *pg.* 538
MOUNTAIN HARDWEAR, INC., *pg.* 1839, *pg.* 193
NIKE, INC., *pg.* 1812, *pg.* 1492
NLC PRODUCTS INC., *pg.* 99, *pg.* 34
THE NORTH FACE, INC., *pg.* 1840, *pg.* 252
O'NEILL INC., *pg.* 1842, *pg.* 270
THE ORVIS COMPANY, INC., *pg.* 1781, *pg.* 1764
OTTERBOX PRODUCTS LLC, *pg.* 451, *pg.* 329
OVERTON'S INC., *pg.* 1781, *pg.* 1377
PACIFIC CYCLE INC., *pg.* 1709, *pg.* 1867
PELICAN PRODUCTS, *pg.* 1467, *pg.* 843
PERFORMANCE DIRECT, INC., *pg.* 1781, *pg.* 1361
POOL CORPORATION, *pg.* 1843, *pg.* 743
QUBICAAMF, *pg.* 1843, *pg.* 1795
RAPALA VMC CORPORATION, *pg.* 1843, *pg.* 949
RECREATIONAL EQUIPMENT, INC., *pg.* 1843, *pg.* 1821
REGAL LAGER, INC., *pg.* 32, *pg.* 534
RLJ ENTERTAINMENT, INC., *pg.* 306, *pg.* 778
ROLLER DERBY SKATE CORP., *pg.* 966, *pg.* 630
RON JON SURF SHOP OF FLORIDA INC., *pg.* 1844, *pg.* 417
SALOMON NORTH AMERICA, INC., *pg.* 1844, *pg.* 1753
SCHOOL-TECH, INC., *pg.* 1844, *pg.* 866
SEA EAGLE BOATS, *pg.* 1845, *pg.* 1322
SEA EAGLE DIVISION OF HARRISON HOGE INDUSTRIES, INC., *pg.* 1710, *pg.* 1322
SHIMANO AMERICAN CORPORATION, *pg.* 1845, *pg.* 116
SIMMS FISHING PRODUCTS CORP., *pg.* 1845, *pg.* 1008
SPEED COMMERCE, INC., *pg.* 967, *pg.* 1737
SPORT CHALET, INC., *pg.* 1846, *pg.* 119
SPORT SUPPLY GROUP, INC., *pg.* 1846, *pg.* 1687
THE SPORTS AUTHORITY, INC., *pg.* 1846, *pg.* 326
SRAM CORPORATION, *pg.* 967, *pg.* 590
STEAMBOAT SKI & RESORT CORPORATION, *pg.* 1115, *pg.* 336
TAOS SKI VALLEY, INC., *pg.* 1116, *pg.* 1136
TARGUS GROUP INTERNATIONAL, INC., *pg.* 482, *pg.* 43
TRAVELPRO INTERNATIONAL, INC., *pg.* 14, *pg.* 413
TREK BICYCLE CORPORATION, *pg.* 1847, *pg.* 1896
VANS, INC., *pg.* 1821, *pg.* 76
VENTURI, INC., *pg.* 1606, *pg.* 910
VOLCOM, INC., *pg.* 1847, *pg.* 71
WATKINS MANUFACTURING CORPORATION, *pg.* 120, *pg.* 303
WEATHERBY, INC., *pg.* 1848, *pg.* 181
WILSON SPORTING GOODS CO., *pg.* 1848, *pg.* 596
WINMARK CORPORATION, *pg.* 1792, *pg.* 946
ZAP, *pg.* 222, *pg.* 277
ZEBCO, *pg.* 1848, *pg.* 1491

5942 - Book Stores

A BOOK COMPANY, LLC, *pg.* 1225, *pg.* 729
ABEBOOKS INC., *pg.* 1613, *pg.* 1913
ALIBRIS, INC., *pg.* 1759, *pg.* 83
AUGSBURG FORTRESS, *pg.* 1618, *pg.* 931
BAKER & TAYLOR, INC., *pg.* 1619, *pg.* 1362
BAKER PUBLISHING GROUP, *pg.* 1619, *pg.* 864
BARNES & NOBLE, INC., *pg.* 1619, *pg.* 1201
BARRON'S EDUCATIONAL SERIES, INC., *pg.* 1620, *pg.* 1164
BOOKAZINE COMPANY, INC., *pg.* 1622, *pg.* 1042
BOOKS-A-MILLION, INC., *pg.* 1623, *pg.* 2
BRODART CO., *pg.* 366, *pg.* 1594
THE CAXTON PRINTERS LTD., *pg.* 1626, *pg.* 548
COLUMBIA UNIVERSITY PRESS, *pg.* 1628, *pg.* 1216
DAEDALUS BOOKS, INC., *pg.* 1632, *pg.* 767
DIAMOND COMIC DISTRIBUTORS, INC., *pg.* 1635, *pg.* 772
DIRECT HOLDINGS AMERICAS INC., *pg.* 1636, *pg.* 1780
DIRECTORY DISTRIBUTING ASSOCIATES, INC., *pg.* 388, *pg.* 978
DIXIE HEALTH, INC., *pg.* 1524, *pg.* 535
EBSCO INFORMATION SERVICES WALPOLE, *pg.* 1638, *pg.* 849
EDUCATIONAL DEVELOPMENT CORPORATION, *pg.* 1638, *pg.* 1490
THE ELYSIAN FIELDS, INC., *pg.* 1768, *pg.* 466
FOLLETT CORPORATION, *pg.* 1641, *pg.* 669
FOLLETT HIGHER EDUCATION GROUP, *pg.* 1769, *pg.* 669
HARPERCOLLINS PUBLISHERS INC., *pg.* 1647, *pg.* 1237
HARVARD BUSINESS REVIEW, *pg.* 1648, *pg.* 1238
HASTINGS ENTERTAINMENT, INC., *pg.* 1773, *pg.* 1659
HOUSTON CHRONICLE, *pg.* 1651, *pg.* 1707
INDEPENDENT PUBLISHERS GROUP, *pg.* 1652, *pg.* 578
KENSINGTON PUBLISHING CORP., *pg.* 1656, *pg.* 1248
METRO NEWSPAPER ADVERTISING SERVICES, INC., *pg.* 1664, *pg.* 1259
METRO NEWSPAPERS ADVERTISING SERVICES, INC., *pg.* 1665, *pg.* 223
PENGUIN RANDOM HOUSE, *pg.* 1675, *pg.* 1276
THE PERSEUS BOOKS GROUP, *pg.* 1676, *pg.* 1278
POWELL'S BOOKS INC., *pg.* 1677, *pg.* 1505
PUBLISHERS GROUP WEST, *pg.* 1679, *pg.* 46
QUEBECOR MEDIA INC., *pg.* 1679, *pg.* 1956
THE RECORD SEARCHLIGHT, *pg.* 1680, *pg.* 188
ST. MARTINS PRESS, INC., *pg.* 1688, *pg.* 1295
STARLOG GROUP, INC., *pg.* 1689, *pg.* 1296
STERLING PUBLISHING CO., INC., *pg.* 1689, *pg.* 1296
SYRACUSE UNIVERSITY PRESS, *pg.* 1690, *pg.* 1344
WHITE HOUSE HISTORICAL ASSOCIATION, *pg.* 1702, *pg.* 408
WILLIAM S. HEIN & CO., INC., *pg.* 1702, *pg.* 1151
W.W. NORTON & COMPANY, INC., *pg.* 1702, *pg.* 1316
ZANER-BLOSER, INC., *pg.* 970, *pg.* 1445

5943 - Stationery Stores

A. T. CROSS COMPANY, *pg.* 339, *pg.* 1602
ACCO BRANDS CORPORATION, *pg.* 340, *pg.* 626
ACME STAPLE COMPANY, INC., *pg.* 341, *pg.* 1034
BELL-MARK CORPORATION, *pg.* 1620, *pg.* 1108
BOXLIGHT CORPORATION, *pg.* 627, *pg.* 1813
BROTHER INTERNATIONAL CORPORATION - USA, *pg.* 53, *pg.* 1046
BRUKER CORPORATION, *pg.* 1511, *pg.* 788
BUEHLER, LTD., *pg.* 1403, *pg.* 622
CANON U.S.A., INC., *pg.* 1404, *pg.* 1178
CAROLINA BIOLOGICAL SUPPLY COMPANY, *pg.* 1513, *pg.* 1359
CAROLINA WHOLESALE OFFICE MACHINE COMPANY, INC., *pg.* 369, *pg.* 1364
CARTRIDGE WORLD NORTH AMERICA, LLC., *pg.* 369, *pg.* 661
CASE PAPER COMPANY INC., *pg.* 1455, *pg.* 1163
CITIZEN SYSTEMS AMERICA CORPORATION, *pg.* 375, *pg.* 293
THE COLAD GROUP, INC., *pg.* 377, *pg.* 1147
COLE-PARMER INSTRUMENT COMPANY, *pg.* 1406, *pg.* 664
C.R. GIBSON, LLC, *pg.* 1631, *pg.* 1650
DRI MARK PRODUCTS, INC., *pg.* 388, *pg.* 1323
EMERY-WATERHOUSE COMPANY, *pg.* 1047, *pg.* 751
EPPENDORF NORTH AMERICA, *pg.* 1412, *pg.* 1164
EPSON AMERICA INC., *pg.* 394, *pg.* 122
ESM SOLUTIONS CORPORATION, *pg.* 1243, *pg.* 1591
ESSENDANT INC., *pg.* 1907, *pg.* 600
EVERI HOLDINGS INC., *pg.* 749, *pg.* 1023
FEDEX OFFICE & PRINT SERVICES, INC., *pg.* 396, *pg.* 1681
FIRE KING SECURITY GROUP, *pg.* 1336, *pg.* 696
FOLLETT HIGHER EDUCATION GROUP, *pg.* 1769, *pg.* 669
FRANKLIN COVEY CO., *pg.* 1642, *pg.* 1758
FUJINON INC., *pg.* 1414, *pg.* 1129
GENEVA WATCH GROUP, *pg.* 5, *pg.* 1174
GILSON COMPANY, INC., *pg.* 1414, *pg.* 1457
GLOBAL IMAGING SYSTEMS, INC., *pg.* 400, *pg.* 473
GROSSMAN MARKETING GROUP, *pg.* 401, *pg.* 843
HACKER INSTRUMENTS & INDUSTRIES INC., *pg.* 1415, *pg.* 1623
HASLER, INC., *pg.* 1459, *pg.* 356
INGRAM MICRO INC., *pg.* 415, *pg.* 261
KOMORI AMERICA CORPORATION, *pg.* 1353, *pg.* 656
KONICA MINOLTA BUSINESS SOLUTIONS USA, INC., *pg.* 1419, *pg.* 1113
LINDENMEYR MUNROE, *pg.* 1464, *pg.* 1325
MARUDAS PRINT SERVICES & PROMOTIONAL PRODUCTS, INC., *pg.* 430, *pg.* 962
MEADE INSTRUMENTS CORPORATION, *pg.* 1422, *pg.* 113
METTLER-TOLEDO INC., *pg.* 1056, *pg.* 1441
MICROS SYSTEMS, INC., *pg.* 435, *pg.* 768
MONROE SYSTEMS FOR BUSINESS, *pg.* 441, *pg.* 1518
MRV COMMUNICATIONS, INC., *pg.* 441, *pg.* 64
NEW AGE ELECTRONICS, INC., *pg.* 659, *pg.* 63
NIKON INC., *pg.* 1424, *pg.* 1181
OFFICE DEPOT, INC., *pg.* 448, *pg.* 412
OLYMPIA SALES, INC., *pg.* 1780, *pg.* 346
PACON CORPORATION, *pg.* 1466, *pg.* 1852
PATTERSON COMPANIES, INC., *pg.* 1580, *pg.* 962
PENTEL OF AMERICA, LTD., *pg.* 453, *pg.* 295
PREISER SCIENTIFIC, INC., *pg.* 1427, *pg.* 1851
QUALSTAR CORPORATION, *pg.* 458, *pg.* 279
RICOH AMERICA, *pg.* 461, *pg.* 1550
RICOH AMERICAS CORP., *pg.* 462, *pg.* 538
RICOH AMERICAS CORPORATION, *pg.* 461, *pg.* 1131
ROYAL CONSUMER INFORMATION PRODUCTS INC., *pg.* 463, *pg.* 1122
SANTINELLI INTERNATIONAL INC., *pg.* 1395, *pg.* 1165
SCHOOL SPECIALTY, INC., *pg.* 467, *pg.* 1860
SHARP ELECTRONICS CORPORATION, *pg.* 672, *pg.* 1082
SHEAFFER PEN CORPORATION, *pg.* 469, *pg.* 371
SHIMADZU SCIENTIFIC INSTRUMENTS, INC., *pg.* 1428, *pg.* 768
STAMPS.COM INC., *pg.* 1282, *pg.* 82
STANDARD DUPLICATING MACHINES CORPORATION, *pg.* 473, *pg.* 783
STAPLES, *pg.* 474, *pg.* 313
STAPLES, INC., *pg.* 474, *pg.* 821
SURPLUS CENTER, *pg.* 1380, *pg.* 1012
TAB PRODUCTS CO. LLC, *pg.* 481, *pg.* 1869
TENSION ENVELOPE CORPORATION, *pg.* 483, *pg.* 986
TRANSCAT, INC., *pg.* 682, *pg.* 1337
TROWBRIDGE ENTERPRISES, *pg.* 485, *pg.* 271
UNITRON INC., *pg.* 1433, *pg.* 1153
UNIVERSAL PHOTONICS, INC., *pg.* 1433, *pg.* 1167
U.S. TOY CO., INC., *pg.* 969, *pg.* 978
VICTORIAN TRADING COMPANY, *pg.* 1789, *pg.* 717
WARNER PRESS, INC., *pg.* 1701, *pg.* 673
WATERS CORPORATION, *pg.* 1185, *pg.* 1599
W.B. MASON COMPANY, *pg.* 491, *pg.* 803
XEROX CANADA INC., *pg.* 494, *pg.* 1930
YASUTOMO & CO., *pg.* 497, *pg.* 280
ZANER-BLOSER, INC., *pg.* 970, *pg.* 1445

5944 - Jewelry Stores

ARMITRON WATCH DIVISION, *pg.* 1, *pg.* 1174
ASCH/GROSSBARDT, INC., *pg.* 1, *pg.* 1197
AUDEMARS PIGUET (NORTH AMERICA), *pg.* 1, *pg.* 1198
BAUME & MERCIER, INC., *pg.* 1, *pg.* 1201
BIRKS & MAYORS INC., *pg.* 1, *pg.* 470
BLUE NILE, INC., *pg.* 2, *pg.* 1834
BRAUNSCHWEIGER JEWELERS, *pg.* 2, *pg.* 1088
BULGARI CORPORATION OF AMERICA, *pg.* 2, *pg.* 1208
BULOVA CORPORATION, *pg.* 2, *pg.* 1356
BULOVA WATCH COMPANY LIMITED, *pg.* 2, *pg.* 1935
CARELLE LTD., *pg.* 2, *pg.* 1209
CHASE-DURER LTD., *pg.* 3, *pg.* 46
CITIZEN WATCH CO. OF AMERICA, INC., *pg.* 3, *pg.* 293
CROTON WATCH COMPANY & NATIONWIDE TIME, *pg.* 4, *pg.* 1350
DANECRAFT INC., *pg.* 4, *pg.* 1606
DAVID BIRNBAUM/RARE 1 CORPORATION, *pg.* 4, *pg.*

1221
DGSE COMPANIES, INC., pg. 4, pg. 1680
EDUCATIONAL COIN COMPANY, pg. 746, pg. 1167
ELISA ILANA CUSTOM DESIGNS, pg. 4, pg. 1015
EMPIRE DIAMOND CORPORATION, pg. 4, pg. 1227
EUGENE BIRO CORP., pg. 5, pg. 1230
FOSSIL GROUP, INC., pg. 5, pg. 1735
THE FRANKLIN MINT, LLC, pg. 1769, pg. 1533
GUMP'S CORP., pg. 1772, pg. 219
HARRY KOTLAR & CO., INC., pg. 6, pg. 132
HARRY WINSTON, INC., pg. 6, pg. 1238
HARTGERS DIAMONDS, LTD., pg. 6, pg. 1134
HEARTS ON FIRE COMPANY, pg. 6, pg. 796
HELZBERG'S DIAMOND SHOPS, INC., pg. 6, pg. 984
HERITAGE GALLERIES & AUCTIONEER, pg. 143, pg. 1682
HERMES OF PARIS, INC., pg. 7, pg. 1240
ICE.COM, INC., pg. 1258, pg. 1955
JOHN HARDY USA, INC., pg. 7, pg. 1246
JUDITH RIPKA COMPANIES INC., pg. 7, pg. 1247
KWIAT INC., pg. 8, pg. 1249
LAURA PEARCE, LTD., pg. 8, pg. 513
LAZARE KAPLAN INTERNATIONAL, INC., pg. 8, pg. 1250
LONG'S JEWELERS LTD., pg. 8, pg. 805
LORD & TAYLOR LLC, pg. 1777, pg. 1252
LOU MADDALONI JEWELERS INC., pg. 8, pg. 1168
MICHAEL ANTHONY JEWELERS, INC., pg. 10, pg. 1183
MIKIMOTO (AMERICA) CO. LTD., pg. 10, pg. 1260
MONEX DEPOSIT COMPANY, pg. 10, pg. 165
MOVADO GROUP, INC., pg. 10, pg. 1101
M.Z. BERGER & CO., INC., pg. 10, pg. 1175
NIKAIA, INC., pg. 10, pg. 765
OMEGA WATCH COMPANY, pg. 10, pg. 1131
PLATINUM GUILD INTERNATIONAL (USA) JEWELRY, INC., pg. 10, pg. 1282
REEDS JEWELERS, INC., pg. 11, pg. 1393
RICHLINE GROUP, INC., pg. 11, pg. 470
ROGERS & HOLLANDS ENTERPRISES INC., pg. 11, pg. 631
ROLEX WATCH U.S.A., INC., pg. 11, pg. 1286
ROSS-SIMONS INC., pg. 1783, pg. 1600
SAMUELS JEWELERS, INC., pg. 12, pg. 1665
SEIKO CORPORATION OF AMERICA, pg. 12, pg. 1082
STERLING JEWELERS INC., pg. 13, pg. 1402
STS JEWELS, pg. 1283, pg. 1297
STULLER, INC., pg. 13, pg. 745
SWATCH GROUP USA, pg. 13, pg. 1131
TACORI ENTERPRISES, pg. 13, pg. 99
TIFFANY & CO., pg. 13, pg. 1299
TOURNEAU INC., pg. 14, pg. 1303
UNIVERSAL COIN & BULLION LTD., pg. 1789, pg. 1668
UNIVERSAL WATCH CO., INC., pg. 15, pg. 1030
VAN CLEEF & ARPELS, INC., pg. 15, pg. 1308
VERMONT CLOCK COMPANY, pg. 946, pg. 1766
WOODEN SHIPS OF HOBOKEN, pg. 35, pg. 1315
W.R. COBB COMPANY, pg. 15, pg. 1601
ZALE CORPORATION, pg. 16, pg. 1724

5945 - Hobby, Toy & Game Shops

A.C. MOORE ARTS & CRAFTS, INC., pg. 691, pg. 1044
ALLEGRO CORPORATION, pg. 1759, pg. 1501
ALLSTAR PRODUCTS GROUP LLC, pg. 17, pg. 1166
AMINCO INTERNATIONAL (USA) INC., pg. 1, pg. 120
ANTARCTIC PRESS, pg. 1617, pg. 1739
BACHMANN INDUSTRIES, INC., pg. 950, pg. 1559
BANDAI AMERICA INCORPORATED, pg. 950, pg. 75
BENELLI USA CORPORATION, pg. 1827, pg. 754
B.J. ALAN COMPANY, pg. 1150, pg. 1483
BMG/MUSIC, pg. 533, pg. 1205
BUILD-A-BEAR WORKSHOP, INC., pg. 950, pg. 993
CAPCOM USA, INC., pg. 950, pg. 254
CARTA MUNDI, INC., pg. 951, pg. 1677
COASTAL AMUSEMENTS INC., pg. 951, pg. 1078
CONCORD MUSIC GROUP, INC., pg. 1765, pg. 46
DANIEL SMITH INC., pg. 1766, pg. 1835
DISCOUNT SCHOOL SUPPLY, pg. 1238, pg. 151
DUALITE SALES & SERVICE, INC., pg. 1296, pg. 1482
DUNCAN TOYS COMPANY, pg. 951, pg. 1465
DURAFLAME, INC., pg. 1123, pg. 280
E-Z BOWZ, LLC, pg. 692, pg. 1635
E1 ENTERTAINMENT U.S. LP, pg. 284, pg. 1323
ENERGIZER HOLDINGS, INC., pg. 637, pg. 996
ETS, LLC, pg. 54, pg. 685
FISHER-PRICE, INC., pg. 953, pg. 1156
GAMESTOP CORP., pg. 399, pg. 1699
THE GOLDBERGER COMPANY, LLC, pg. 954, pg. 1235
GUITAR CENTER, INC., pg. 1771, pg. 306
GUND, INC., pg. 954, pg. 1056
HOB-LOB LIMITED PARTNERSHIP, pg. 552, pg. 1486
HOBBICO, INC., pg. 956, pg. 562
HOBBY LOBBY STORES INC., pg. 927, pg. 1486
HOT OFF THE PRESS, INC., pg. 1650, pg. 1497
IGT, pg. 412, pg. 1031
INFANTINO, LLC, pg. 957, pg. 203
INNOVATIVE USA, INC., pg. 957, pg. 363
INTELITEK, INC., pg. 1349, pg. 1036
LALIQUE NORTH AMERICA, pg. 1126, pg. 1054
LEGO SYSTEMS, INC., pg. 961, pg. 346
LIFOAM INDUSTRIES INC., pg. 961, pg. 772
LVMH INC., pg. 9, pg. 1254
MAUI JIM, INC., pg. 9, pg. 651
MERCURY LUGGAGE/SEWARD TRUNK, pg. 9, pg. 434
MGA ENTERTAINMENT, INC., pg. 964, pg. 300
MICHAELS STORES, INC., pg. 1127, pg. 1722
MULTIMEDIA GAMES INC., pg. 442, pg. 1664
NINTENDO OF AMERICA, INC., pg. 965, pg. 1829
OTTERBOX PRODUCTS LLC, pg. 451, pg. 329
PELICAN PRODUCTS, pg. 1467, pg. 843
PLAYMATES TOYS INC., pg. 965, pg. 82
PRESSMAN TOY CORPORATION, pg. 965, pg. 1734
REEVES INTERNATIONAL, INC., pg. 966, pg. 1108
REGAL LAGER, INC., pg. 32, pg. 534
RLJ ENTERTAINMENT, INC., pg. 306, pg. 778
SEGA OF AMERICA INC., pg. 966, pg. 227
SONY COMPUTER ENTERTAINMENT AMERICA LLC, pg. 966, pg. 256
SPEED COMMERCE, INC., pg. 967, pg. 1737
SPIN MASTER LTD., pg. 967, pg. 1943
STRAT-O-MATIC GAME CO., INC., pg. 968, pg. 1161
TARGUS GROUP INTERNATIONAL, INC., pg. 482, pg. 43
THINKWAY TOYS, pg. 968, pg. 1924
TOYS "R" US, INC., pg. 968, pg. 1130
TRAVELPRO INTERNATIONAL, INC., pg. 14, pg. 413
U.S. TOY CO., INC., pg. 969, pg. 978
VENTURI, INC., pg. 1606, pg. 910
VTECH ELECTRONICS NORTH AMERICA, LLC, pg. 969, pg. 554
WHAM-O, INC., pg. 969, pg. 308
WINMARK CORPORATION, pg. 1792, pg. 946

5946 - Camera & Photographic Supply Stores

ADORAMA CAMERA INC., pg. 1398, pg. 1187
CALUMET PHOTOGRAPHIC, INC., pg. 1404, pg. 568

5947 - Gift, Novelty & Souvenir Shops

BLYTH, INC., pg. 502, pg. 349
BROOKSTONE, INC., pg. 1764, pg. 1036
BUYSEASONS, INC., pg. 20, pg. 1883
CBOCS, INC., pg. 1721, pg. 1639
CELEBRATE EXPRESS, INC., pg. 1764, pg. 1883
COLONIAL WILLIAMSBURG FOUNDATION, pg. 541, pg. 1811
C.R. GIBSON, LLC, pg. 1631, pg. 1650
CRYSTAL WORLD, INC., pg. 4, pg. 1122
CURRENT USA, INC., pg. 1765, pg. 315
ELVIS PRESLEY ENTERPRISES, INC., pg. 1090, pg. 1642
ENESCO, LLC, pg. 1124, pg. 620
EUROMARKET DESIGNS, INC., pg. 1124, pg. 640
FRANCHISE CONCEPTS, INC., pg. 1769, pg. 1005
THE FRANKLIN MINT, LLC, pg. 1769, pg. 1533
GOLF GIFTS & GALLERY, pg. 1835, pg. 1887
GUMP'S CORP., pg. 1772, pg. 219
HALLMARK BUSINESS CONNECTIONS, pg. 402, pg. 937
HANOVER DIRECT, INC., pg. 1772, pg. 1130
HARRY & DAVID HOLDINGS, INC., pg. 1022, pg. 1499
HARTGERS DIAMONDS, LTD., pg. 6, pg. 1134
KIRKLAND'S INC., pg. 1126, pg. 1652
LILLIAN VERNON CORPORATION, pg. 1776, pg. 315
NAPLES ZOO INC., pg. 565, pg. 451
NATIONAL BASEBALL HALL OF FAME & MUSEUM, INC., pg. 566, pg. 1154
NORM THOMPSON OUTFITTERS INC., pg. 1780, pg. 1498
OLD SALEM, INCORPORATED, pg. 572, pg. 1395
PARTY CITY CORPORATION, pg. 1781, pg. 1116
PROVIDE COMMERCE, INC., pg. 1276, pg. 206
ROSS-SIMONS INC., pg. 1783, pg. 1600
SAVE THE CHILDREN FEDERATION, INC., pg. 156, pg. 384
SENDONLINE.COM, INC., pg. 1280, pg. 1112
SPENCER GIFTS LLC, pg. 1786, pg. 1057
THINGS REMEMBERED, INC., pg. 1788, pg. 1455
TUESDAY MORNING CORPORATION, pg. 1789, pg. 1690
THE UPPER DECK COMPANY, LLC, pg. 969, pg. 62
THE VERMONT TEDDY BEAR COMPANY, pg. 969, pg. 1767
WITH HEART & HAND, pg. 946, pg. 837
WORLD'S FINEST CHOCOLATE, INC., pg. 1864, pg. 597
ZOOLOGICAL SOCIETY OF SAN DIEGO, pg. 595, pg. 211

5948 - Luggage & Leather Goods Stores

BRIGGS & RILEY TRAVELWARE, pg. 2, pg. 1164
EBAGS, INC., pg. 1240, pg. 331
GUCCI AMERICA INC., pg. 6, pg. 1237
LVMH INC., pg. 9, pg. 1254
SOLO, pg. 12, pg. 1165
TUESDAY MORNING CORPORATION, pg. 1789, pg. 1690
TUMI, INC., pg. 15, pg. 1123
VERA BRADLEY, INC., pg. 15, pg. 697

5949 - Sewing, Needlework & Piece Goods Stores

3 DAY BLINDS, INC., pg. 912, pg. 105
ASSOCIATED FABRICS CORPORATION, pg. 691, pg. 1064
BEMIDJI WOOLEN MILLS, pg. 38, pg. 916
CALICO CORNERS, pg. 691, pg. 1543
DELTA APPAREL, INC., pg. 39, pg. 1617
DESIGNTEX GROUP INC., pg. 692, pg. 1223
THE DMC CORPORATION, pg. 692, pg. 1076
F. SCHUMACHER & CO., pg. 925, pg. 1230
GALEY & LORD LLC, pg. 693, pg. 1621
HANCOCK FABRICS, INC., pg. 693, pg. 968
HERRSCHNERS, INC., pg. 694, pg. 1895
HOB-LOB LIMITED PARTNERSHIP, pg. 552, pg. 1486
HOBBY LOBBY STORES INC., pg. 927, pg. 1486
ITOCHU INTERNATIONAL INC., pg. 1351, pg. 1245
J. ROBERT SCOTT INC., pg. 930, pg. 105
JANOME AMERICA, INC., pg. 57, pg. 1081
JHB INTERNATIONAL, INC., pg. 696, pg. 320
JO-ANN STORES LLC, pg. 696, pg. 1455
KRAVET FABRICS INC., pg. 932, pg. 1142
MARY MAXIM, INC., pg. 696, pg. 905
MICHAELS STORES, INC., pg. 1127, pg. 1722
MOMENTUM TEXTILES INC., pg. 697, pg. 114
PRYM CONSUMER USA, pg. 698, pg. 1622
STARK CARPET CORPORATION, pg. 944, pg. 1296
WOODEN SHIPS OF HOBOKEN, pg. 35, pg. 1315

5961 - Catalog & Mail Order Houses

1-800 CONTACTS, INC., pg. 1758, pg. 1753
1-800-FLOWERS.COM, INC., pg. 1758, pg. 1151
ABT ELECTRONICS, INC., pg. 612, pg. 614
ACCURATE MOTORCARS, pg. 1705, pg. 422
ADORAMA CAMERA INC., pg. 1398, pg. 1187
ALIBRIS, INC., pg. 1759, pg. 83
ALLEGRO CORPORATION, pg. 1759, pg. 1501
AMAZON.COM, INC., pg. 1226, pg. 1831
AMERICAN GIRL LLC, pg. 949, pg. 1871
AMERIMARK DIRECT, LLC, pg. 1759, pg. 1428
AUDIBLE, INC., pg. 1230, pg. 1095
AUTOTRADER, INC., pg. 1230, pg. 490
BARKER CREEK PUBLISHING INC., pg. 1619, pg. 1818
BARNES & NOBLE, INC., pg. 1619, pg. 1201
BEAU TIES LTD., pg. 38, pg. 1766
BIOSCRIP, INC., pg. 1506, pg. 1158
BLAIR CORPORATION, pg. 1762, pg. 1590
BLUE NILE, INC., pg. 2, pg. 1834
BLUEFLY, INC., pg. 1232, pg. 1205
BRA SMYTH OF CALIFORNIA, INC., pg. 20, pg. 265
THE BRADFORD GROUP, pg. 1763, pg. 637
BRODER BROS., CO., pg. 1828, pg. 1588
BROOKSTONE, INC., pg. 1764, pg. 1036

CABELA'S INCORPORATED, *pg.* 535, *pg.* 1019
CAFEPRESS.COM, INC., *pg.* 1234, *pg.* 254
CALUMET PHOTOGRAPHIC, INC., *pg.* 1404, *pg.* 568
CAMBRIDGE SOUNDWORKS, INC., *pg.* 1234, *pg.* 781
CAMPING WORLD, INC., *pg.* 1830, *pg.* 725
CANADA DRUGS LTD., *pg.* 1511, *pg.* 1914
CAREMARK PHARMACY SERVICES, *pg.* 1513, *pg.* 1649
CDW CORPORATION, *pg.* 370, *pg.* 663
CELEBRATE EXPRESS, INC., *pg.* 1764, *pg.* 1883
CHARISMA BRANDS, LLC, *pg.* 2, *pg.* 120
CHEAPCARIBBEAN.COM, *pg.* 1903, *pg.* 1526
CHILDREN'S WEAR DIGEST INC., *pg.* 22, *pg.* 1801
CHRISTIAN HERALD ASSOCIATION, *pg.* 1627, *pg.* 1212
THE COLEMAN COMPANY, INC., *pg.* 1830, *pg.* 723
COLONY BRANDS INC., *pg.* 849, *pg.* 1881
COPART, INC., *pg.* 168, *pg.* 86
COSMETIQUE, INC., *pg.* 1765, *pg.* 664
CRATE & BARREL, INC., *pg.* 922, *pg.* 640
CRUTCHFIELD CORPORATION, *pg.* 1237, *pg.* 1777
CURRENT USA, INC., *pg.* 1765, *pg.* 315
DANIEL SMITH INC., *pg.* 1766, *pg.* 1835
DAY-TIMERS, INC., *pg.* 1766, *pg.* 1528
DELIA'S, INC., *pg.* 23, *pg.* 1222
DESIGNING HEALTH, INC., *pg.* 1523, *pg.* 299
DESTINATION XL GROUP, INC., *pg.* 40, *pg.* 810
DHC USA INC., *pg.* 507, *pg.* 216
DIABETICSUPPLIES.COM, INC., *pg.* 1238, *pg.* 1846
DIAMOND.COM, *pg.* 1238, *pg.* 1954
DICK BLICK COMPANY, *pg.* 1766, *pg.* 617
DICK'S SPORTING GOODS, INC., *pg.* 1832, *pg.* 1524
DIRECT HOLDINGS AMERICAS INC., *pg.* 1636, *pg.* 1780
DIRECTBUY, INC., *pg.* 1766, *pg.* 694
DOLLARSTORE, INC., *pg.* 1239, *pg.* 109
DOVER SADDLERY, INC., *pg.* 1833, *pg.* 829
DRAPER'S & DAMON'S, INC., *pg.* 24, *pg.* 109
DRG RECORDS INCORPORATED, *pg.* 1767, *pg.* 1226
DRG TEXAS LP, *pg.* 1637, *pg.* 1668
DRUGSTORE.COM, INC., *pg.* 1239, *pg.* 1814
EBATES.COM, *pg.* 1240, *pg.* 217
EBAY INC., *pg.* 1240, *pg.* 243
ECOMPANYSTORE, INC., *pg.* 1241, *pg.* 483
EDDIE BAUER, INC., *pg.* 40, *pg.* 1814
EDIBLE ARRANGEMENTS INTERNATIONAL, INC., *pg.* 1768, *pg.* 382
EDMUND INDUSTRIAL OPTICS INC., *pg.* 1411, *pg.* 1041
ETSY, INC., *pg.* 1768, *pg.* 1230
EVINE LIVE INC., *pg.* 1768, *pg.* 922
EXCELLIGENCE LEARNING CORP., *pg.* 1768, *pg.* 151
EXPRESS SCRIPTS, *pg.* 1530, *pg.* 1070
EXPRESS SCRIPTS, INC., *pg.* 1530, *pg.* 997
FACETS MULTI-MEDIA, INC., *pg.* 547, *pg.* 573
FANCL INTERNATIONAL, INC., *pg.* 509, *pg.* 110
FASIG-TIPTON CO. INC., *pg.* 750, *pg.* 729
FINCK CIGAR CO., *pg.* 1894, *pg.* 1740
FISHER AUCTION COMPANY, INC., *pg.* 1092, *pg.* 459
FRAGRANCENET.COM, INC., *pg.* 1248, *pg.* 1155
THE FRANKLIN MINT, LLC, *pg.* 1769, *pg.* 1533
FTD.COM INC., *pg.* 1770, *pg.* 608
FULLBEAUTY BRANDS, *pg.* 1770, *pg.* 1233
GAIAM, INC., *pg.* 1532, *pg.* 334
GAMESTOP CORP., *pg.* 399, *pg.* 1699
GANDER MOUNTAIN COMPANY, *pg.* 1834, *pg.* 960
GARDENS ALIVE!, INC., *pg.* 1796, *pg.* 693
GARLINGHOUSE COMPANY, *pg.* 1644, *pg.* 1612
GARNET HILL, *pg.* 1771, *pg.* 1034
GILBERT H. WILD & SON, LLC, *pg.* 1796, *pg.* 1005
GOINDUSTRY-DOVEBID, INC., *pg.* 1249, *pg.* 255
GOLF GALAXY, INC., *pg.* 1835, *pg.* 1525
THE GUILD INC., *pg.* 1255, *pg.* 1866
HABAND COMPANY, INC., *pg.* 1772, *pg.* 1099
HAMMACHER SCHLEMMER & CO., INC., *pg.* 1124, *pg.* 637
HANCOCK FABRICS, INC., *pg.* 693, *pg.* 968
HANOVER DIRECT, INC., *pg.* 1772, *pg.* 1130
HARRIET CARTER GIFTS, INC., *pg.* 1773, *pg.* 1553
HARRY & DAVID HOLDINGS, INC., *pg.* 1022, *pg.* 1499
HASTINGS ENTERTAINMENT, INC., *pg.* 1773, *pg.* 1659
HEALTHWAREHOUSE.COM, INC., *pg.* 403, *pg.* 728
HERRSCHNERS, INC., *pg.* 694, *pg.* 1895
HICKORY FARMS, INC., *pg.* 862, *pg.* 1462
HISTORIC HOUSEFITTERS CO., INC., *pg.* 927, *pg.* 354
HOB-LOB LIMITED PARTNERSHIP, *pg.* 552, *pg.* 1486
HOBBICO, INC., *pg.* 956, *pg.* 562
HOBBY LOBBY STORES INC., *pg.* 927, *pg.* 1486
HSN, INC., *pg.* 291, *pg.* 462
IAC/INTERACTIVECORP, *pg.* 292, *pg.* 1242
INTERNATIONAL WINE ACCESSORIES, INC., *pg.* 1964, *pg.* 71
INTRADA INC., *pg.* 1773, *pg.* 171
IRONPLANET, INC., *pg.* 1259, *pg.* 183
J. CREW GROUP, INC., *pg.* 1773, *pg.* 1245
THE J. JILL GROUP, INC., *pg.* 1774, *pg.* 842
JAZZERCISE, INC., *pg.* 554, *pg.* 59
J.C. PENNEY COMPANY, INC., *pg.* 1774, *pg.* 1732
J.L. TODD AUCTION CO., *pg.* 1774, *pg.* 539
JOHNSON SMITH COMPANY, *pg.* 1774, *pg.* 414
JOS. A. BANK CLOTHIERS, INC., *pg.* 42, *pg.* 771
JUNONIA LTD., *pg.* 27, *pg.* 929
THE KING ARTHUR FLOUR COMPANY, INC., *pg.* 833, *pg.* 1767
KRUSE ENERGY & EQUIPMENT, *pg.* 182, *pg.* 1728
LADY GRACE STORES INC., *pg.* 28, *pg.* 861
LANDS' END, INC., *pg.* 1776, *pg.* 1857
LANTERN LANE ENTERTAINMENT LTD., *pg.* 296, *pg.* 56
LENOX CORPORATION, *pg.* 1126, *pg.* 1518
LEVENGER COMPANY, *pg.* 1776, *pg.* 421
LIBERATOR, INC., *pg.* 1395, *pg.* 513
LIBERATOR MEDICAL HOLDINGS, INC., *pg.* 1555, *pg.* 468
LIBERTY MEDICAL SUPPLY, INC., *pg.* 1555, *pg.* 460
LIBERTY ORCHARDS CO., INC., *pg.* 1857, *pg.* 1819
LILLIAN VERNON CORPORATION, *pg.* 1776, *pg.* 315
LIQUIDITY SERVICES, INC., *pg.* 1263, *pg.* 401
LITTLETON COIN CO., INC., *pg.* 1776, *pg.* 1035
LONG MOTOR CORPORATION, *pg.* 211, *pg.* 716
MACE SECURITY INTERNATIONAL, INC., *pg.* 1172, *pg.* 1541
MACY'S, INC., *pg.* 1778, *pg.* 1417
MAGAZINES.COM INC., *pg.* 1265, *pg.* 1633
MARKET AMERICA WORLDWIDE, INC., *pg.* 1265, *pg.* 1375
MARTHA STEWART LIVING OMNIMEDIA, INC., *pg.* 1661, *pg.* 1256
MARY MAXIM, INC., *pg.* 696, *pg.* 905
MASON COMPANIES, INC., *pg.* 1811, *pg.* 1856
MASTERBEAT CORPORATION, *pg.* 1265, *pg.* 1257
MBI INC., *pg.* 1778, *pg.* 363
MOVIES UNLIMITED INC., *pg.* 1779, *pg.* 1567
MUSICNOTES, INC., *pg.* 1268, *pg.* 1866
NASCO INTERNATIONAL, INC., *pg.* 1779, *pg.* 1858
NATIONAL FFA ORGANIZATION, *pg.* 149, *pg.* 688
NATIONAL VISION, INC., *pg.* 1423, *pg.* 534
NATIONAL WHOLESALE COMPANY INC., *pg.* 30, *pg.* 1381
NEIMAN MARCUS, INC., *pg.* 30, *pg.* 1684
NEWEGG INC., *pg.* 1271, *pg.* 67
NLC PRODUCTS INC., *pg.* 99, *pg.* 34
NORM THOMPSON OUTFITTERS INC., *pg.* 1780, *pg.* 1498
NORTHERN TOOL + EQUIPMENT, *pg.* 1366, *pg.* 919
NUTRISYSTEM, INC., *pg.* 1577, *pg.* 1533
OLYMPIA SALES, INC., *pg.* 1780, *pg.* 346
ONE STEP AHEAD, *pg.* 1780, *pg.* 1881
ORCHARD BRANDS CORPORATION, *pg.* 1780, *pg.* 1590
THE ORVIS COMPANY, INC., *pg.* 1781, *pg.* 1764
OVERSTOCK.COM, INC., *pg.* 1273, *pg.* 1760
OVERTON'S INC., *pg.* 1781, *pg.* 1377
OXFORD UNIVERSITY PRESS, INC., *pg.* 1673, *pg.* 1275
PAUL FREDRICK MENSTYLE INC., *pg.* 45, *pg.* 1532
PC CONNECTION, INC., *pg.* 452, *pg.* 1036
PC MALL, INC., *pg.* 452, *pg.* 295
PERFORMANCE DIRECT, INC., *pg.* 1781, *pg.* 1361
PETEDGE, *pg.* 1481, *pg.* 787
PETMED EXPRESS, INC., *pg.* 1781, *pg.* 460
PHILLIPS DE PURY & COMPANY, *pg.* 576, *pg.* 1282
PHOENIX VINTNERS, LLC, *pg.* 1968, *pg.* 182
POINSETTIA GROVES INC., *pg.* 890, *pg.* 478
THE POPCORN FACTORY, *pg.* 1861, *pg.* 625
PRESCRIPTIONS PLUS, INC., *pg.* 1782, *pg.* 479
PROVIDE COMMERCE, INC., *pg.* 1276, *pg.* 206
PUBLISHERS CLEARING HOUSE, *pg.* 1782, *pg.* 1324
QVC INC, *pg.* 305, *pg.* 1593
RABIN WORLDWIDE, INC., *pg.* 797, *pg.* 225
RAKUTEN.COM SHOPPING, *pg.* 1277, *pg.* 41
REIDCO, INC., *pg.* 891, *pg.* 675
REJUVENATION INC., *pg.* 1304, *pg.* 1506
REPLACEMENTS, LTD., *pg.* 1138, *pg.* 1383
REPLY! INC., *pg.* 1277, *pg.* 260
RICHLEE SHOE COMPANY, *pg.* 1818, *pg.* 769
RITCHIE BROS. AUCTIONEERS INCORPORATED, *pg.* 1372, *pg.* 1907
ROMAN RESEARCH, INC., *pg.* 11, *pg.* 824
SAKS INCORPORATED, *pg.* 1783, *pg.* 1288
SEA EAGLE BOATS, *pg.* 1845, *pg.* 1322
SEA EAGLE DIVISION OF HARRISON HOGE INDUSTRIES, INC., *pg.* 1710, *pg.* 1322
SHOPLOCAL, LLC, *pg.* 1280, *pg.* 590
SIERRA TRADING POST INC., *pg.* 1819, *pg.* 1901
SILVER STAR BRANDS, *pg.* 1785, *pg.* 1886
SKINNYCORP L.L.C., *pg.* 1280, *pg.* 590
SMARTPAK EQUINE, LLC, *pg.* 1482, *pg.* 834
SMITH & HAWKEN, LTD., *pg.* 1786, *pg.* 168
SMOKY MOUNTAIN KNIFE WORKS INC., *pg.* 1786, *pg.* 1655
SOLOFLEX, INC., *pg.* 1845, *pg.* 1498
SOTHEBY'S INC., *pg.* 472, *pg.* 1294
SOUTHWORTH COMPANY INC., *pg.* 1470, *pg.* 781
SPA FINDER, INC., *pg.* 1113, *pg.* 1295
SPECIALTY CATALOG CORPORATION, *pg.* 1786, *pg.* 856
SPEEDWAY MOTORS INC., *pg.* 218, *pg.* 1012
SPORT SUPPLY GROUP, INC., *pg.* 1846, *pg.* 1687
THE SPORTSMAN'S GUIDE, INC., *pg.* 1846, *pg.* 965
STAMPS.COM INC., *pg.* 1282, *pg.* 82
STARCREST PRODUCTS OF CALIFORNIA, *pg.* 1786, *pg.* 181
STRAT-O-MATIC GAME CO., INC., *pg.* 968, *pg.* 1161
STUBHUB, INC., *pg.* 586, *pg.* 228
SUNDANCE CATALOG CO., LTD., *pg.* 1786, *pg.* 1761
SURE FIT INC., *pg.* 944, *pg.* 1514
SWANSON HEALTH PRODUCTS INC., *pg.* 1600, *pg.* 1397
SYSTEMAX, INC., *pg.* 481, *pg.* 1324
THE TALBOTS, INC., *pg.* 34, *pg.* 824
TECHNOBRANDS, INC., *pg.* 1788, *pg.* 1778
TECHTARGET, INC., *pg.* 482, *pg.* 837
TOYS "R" US, INC., *pg.* 968, *pg.* 1130
TRANSACTION PUBLISHERS, INC., *pg.* 1695, *pg.* 1109
UBID.COM, *pg.* 1286, *pg.* 621
UJENA SWIMWEAR AND FASHIONS, *pg.* 34, *pg.* 163
UMSI INCORPORATED, *pg.* 1789, *pg.* 1084
UPTON TEA IMPORTS, *pg.* 1036, *pg.* 825
U.S. AUTO PARTS NETWORK, INC., *pg.* 221, *pg.* 64
VERMONT COUNTRY STORE, INC., *pg.* 1789, *pg.* 1766
THE VERMONT TEDDY BEAR COMPANY, *pg.* 969, *pg.* 1767
VERSTANDIG BROADCASTING, *pg.* 316, *pg.* 1784
VICTORIAN TRADING COMPANY, *pg.* 1789, *pg.* 717
VITA-MIX CORPORATION, *pg.* 1139, *pg.* 1436
VITACOST.COM, INC., *pg.* 1607, *pg.* 414
VITAMIN SHOPPE, INC., *pg.* 1608, *pg.* 1098
W. ATLEE BURPEE & CO., *pg.* 1801, *pg.* 1590
WAL-MART.COM, *pg.* 1287, *pg.* 50
THE WALKING COMPANY HOLDINGS, INC., *pg.* 50, *pg.* 263
WAYSIDE TECHNOLOGY GROUP, INC., *pg.* 491, *pg.* 1121
WEISSMAN THEATRICAL SUPPLY, INC., *pg.* 35, *pg.* 1004
WEST MARINE, INC., *pg.* 1712, *pg.* 305
WILLIAMS-SONOMA, INC., *pg.* 1140, *pg.* 234
WM. F. COMLY & SON, INC., *pg.* 1792, *pg.* 1572
XO GROUP INC., *pg.* 1289, *pg.* 1316
ZONES, INC., *pg.* 1292, *pg.* 1813

5962 - Automatic Merchandising Machine Operators

1-800-VENDING, INC., *pg.* 1759, *pg.* 1751
OLD FASHION FOODS, INC., *pg.* 1028, *pg.* 525
OUTERWALL INC., *pg.* 1367, *pg.* 1816
REDBOX AUTOMATED RETAIL, LLC, *pg.* 306, *pg.* 649

5963 - Direct Selling Establishments

AFFINION GROUP, INC., *pg.* 1225, *pg.* 372
BAZI INTERNATIONAL, INC., *pg.* 1501, *pg.* 107
B.C. TREE FRUITS LTD., *pg.* 1015, *pg.* 1908
CAMERICAN INTERNATIONAL, *pg.* 844, *pg.* 1101
CDW CORPORATION, *pg.* 370, *pg.* 663
DRISCOLL STRAWBERRY ASSOCIATES INC., *pg.* 854, *pg.* 305
EOS INTERNATIONAL, INC., *pg.* 1243, *pg.* 59
THE FRANKLIN MINT, LLC, *pg.* 1769, *pg.* 1533
GIFTCERTIFICATES.COM, *pg.* 1249, *pg.* 1015
HORMEL FOODS CORPORATION - FOODSERVICE DIVISION, *pg.* 864, *pg.* 916
HOVEROUND CORP., *pg.* 1543, *pg.* 466
KEY FOOD STORES CO-OPERATIVE, INC., *pg.* 1025, *pg.* 1343
MARKET AMERICA WORLDWIDE, INC., *pg.* 1265, *pg.* 1375

First page reference indicates Business Class Edition
Second page reference indicates Geographic Edition

MURRY'S, INC., *pg.* 882, *pg.* 780
NUTRISYSTEM, INC., *pg.* 1577, *pg.* 1533
OBERWEIS DAIRY, INC., *pg.* 887, *pg.* 638
PUBLISHERS CLEARING HOUSE, *pg.* 1782, *pg.* 1324
SMARTPAK EQUINE, LLC, *pg.* 1482, *pg.* 834
THE TIRE RACK INC., *pg.* 1890, *pg.* 697
TRUE NORTH NUTRITION LTD., *pg.* 1603, *pg.* 1933
VECTOR MARKETING CORPORATION, *pg.* 1139, *pg.* 1318
XANGO, LLC, *pg.* 1610, *pg.* 1751

5983 - Fuel Oil Dealers

CROWN CENTRAL LLC, *pg.* 975, *pg.* 756
DELEK US HOLDINGS, INC., *pg.* 975, *pg.* 1627
ENGLEFIELD OIL COMPANY, *pg.* 976, *pg.* 1455
EXXON MOBIL CORPORATION, *pg.* 977, *pg.* 1718
FJ MANAGEMENT, INC., *pg.* 978, *pg.* 1758
GULF OIL LIMITED PARTNERSHIP, *pg.* 978, *pg.* 814
HESS CORPORATION, *pg.* 979, *pg.* 1240
J.D. STREETT & CO., INC., *pg.* 980, *pg.* 988
MARATHON PETROLEUM COMPANY LLC, *pg.* 981, *pg.* 1454
MFA OIL COMPANY, *pg.* 981, *pg.* 976
RACETRAC PETROLEUM, INC., *pg.* 983, *pg.* 519
SLOMIN'S INC., *pg.* 1076, *pg.* 1167
WHITE RIVER COOPERATIVE INC., *pg.* 708, *pg.* 693

5984 - Bottled or Bulk Liquified Petroleum (LP) Gas Dealers

BLUE RHINO CORPORATION, *pg.* 1318, *pg.* 1393
CHESAPEAKE UTILITIES CORPORATION, *pg.* 1937, *pg.* 387
CROWN CENTRAL LLC, *pg.* 975, *pg.* 756
DELEK US HOLDINGS, INC., *pg.* 975, *pg.* 1627
ENERGY TRANSFER EQUITY, L.P., *pg.* 1941, *pg.* 1680
ENGLEFIELD OIL COMPANY, *pg.* 976, *pg.* 1455
EXXON MOBIL CORPORATION, *pg.* 977, *pg.* 1718
FERRELLGAS PARTNERS, L.P., *pg.* 977, *pg.* 718
FJ MANAGEMENT, INC., *pg.* 978, *pg.* 1758
GULF OIL LIMITED PARTNERSHIP, *pg.* 978, *pg.* 814
HESS CORPORATION, *pg.* 979, *pg.* 1240
J.D. STREETT & CO., INC., *pg.* 980, *pg.* 988
MARATHON PETROLEUM COMPANY LLC, *pg.* 981, *pg.* 1454
MATHESON VALLEY, *pg.* 981, *pg.* 1456
MFA OIL COMPANY, *pg.* 981, *pg.* 976
RACETRAC PETROLEUM, INC., *pg.* 983, *pg.* 519
SUBURBAN PROPANE PARTNERS, L.P., *pg.* 113, *pg.* 1132
WHITE RIVER COOPERATIVE INC., *pg.* 708, *pg.* 693

5992 - Florists

1-800-FLOWERS.COM, INC., *pg.* 1758, *pg.* 1151
EDIBLE ARRANGEMENTS INTERNATIONAL, INC., *pg.* 1768, *pg.* 382
FLOWERBUD.COM, *pg.* 1247, *pg.* 1499
FTD GROUP, INC., *pg.* 1795, *pg.* 608
FTD.COM INC., *pg.* 1770, *pg.* 608
NATURAL DECORATIONS, INC., *pg.* 936, *pg.* 5
PROVIDE COMMERCE, INC., *pg.* 1276, *pg.* 206
ROSE HILLS COMPANY, *pg.* 1395, *pg.* 307
STRANGE'S FLORIST & GREENHOUSES, *pg.* 1283, *pg.* 1804
TELEFLORA LLC, *pg.* 1801, *pg.* 140

5993 - Tobacco Stores & Stands

ALLIANCE ONE INTERNATIONAL, INC., *pg.* 1893, *pg.* 1384
ALTRIA GROUP, INC., *pg.* 1893, *pg.* 1800
EBY-BROWN CO., *pg.* 1767, *pg.* 636
GEORGETOWN TOBACCO & PIPE STORES INC., *pg.* 1771, *pg.* 400
PINE STATE TRADING COMPANY, *pg.* 1781, *pg.* 749
PREMIER TECH HORTICULTURE LTD., *pg.* 1799, *pg.* 1958
REPUBLIC TOBACCO LP, *pg.* 1894, *pg.* 615
U.S. SMOKELESS TOBACCO COMPANY, *pg.* 1895, *pg.* 1804

5994 - News Dealers & Newsstands

MCCOLLA ENTERPRISES LTD., *pg.* 1737, *pg.* 722
NEW BOSTON GARDEN CORP., *pg.* 569, *pg.* 799

5999 - Miscellaneous Retail Stores, NEC

1-800-FLOWERS.COM, INC., *pg.* 1758, *pg.* 1151
ACCURAY, *pg.* 1486, *pg.* 1864
ADVANCED BEAUTY SYSTEMS INC., *pg.* 498, *pg.* 1672
AESCULAP, INC., *pg.* 1487, *pg.* 1521
AL & ED'S CORPORATION, *pg.* 615, *pg.* 299
ALADDIN TEMP-RITE, LLC, *pg.* 1013, *pg.* 1635
ALIMED, INC., *pg.* 1490, *pg.* 816
ALPHA PRO TECH, LTD., *pg.* 1492, *pg.* 1922
AMERISOURCEBERGEN CORPORATION, *pg.* 1493, *pg.* 1522
ANTHONY & SYLVAN POOLS CORPORATION, *pg.* 1826, *pg.* 1428
APRIA HEALTHCARE GROUP INC., *pg.* 1495, *pg.* 120
ARKRAY USA, INC., *pg.* 1496, *pg.* 924
ART.COM, *pg.* 1229, *pg.* 83
ARTNET WORLDWIDE CORPORATION, *pg.* 353, *pg.* 1197
AT HOME STORES LLC, *pg.* 1760, *pg.* 1729
BAG BORROW OR STEAL, INC., *pg.* 1, *pg.* 1833
BALLY NORTH AMERICA, INC., *pg.* 1804, *pg.* 1200
BELTONE ELECTRONICS LLC, *pg.* 1503, *pg.* 614
BEST BUY CO., INC., *pg.* 1761, *pg.* 954
BIOHORIZONS, INC., *pg.* 1506, *pg.* 2
BIOLASE TECHNOLOGY, INC., *pg.* 1506, *pg.* 107
THE BIRKETT MILLS, *pg.* 826, *pg.* 1321
BMC INDUSTRIAL EDUCATIONAL SERVICES, *pg.* 362, *pg.* 902
BOSCH INSPECTION TECHNOLOGY INC., *pg.* 1319, *pg.* 1041
BOSLEY INC., *pg.* 1508, *pg.* 46
BOXLIGHT CORPORATION, *pg.* 627, *pg.* 1813
BRISTOL-MYERS SQUIBB COMPANY, *pg.* 1509, *pg.* 1206
BROOKSTONE, INC., *pg.* 1764, *pg.* 1036
BURDEN SALES COMPANY, *pg.* 702, *pg.* 1011
CANDELA CORPORATION, *pg.* 1404, *pg.* 855
CARDIONET, INC., *pg.* 1513, *pg.* 1523
CARL ZEISS, INC., *pg.* 1405, *pg.* 1345
CEDARBROOK SAUNA & STEAM, *pg.* 1830, *pg.* 1819
CENTRAL GARDEN & PET COMPANY, *pg.* 1475, *pg.* 303
CHAMPS SPORTS, *pg.* 1806, *pg.* 414
COMPLEMAR PARTNERS, *pg.* 1455, *pg.* 1333
DEL MONTE FOODS, INC., *pg.* 852, *pg.* 304
DICK BLICK COMPANY, *pg.* 1766, *pg.* 617
DYNEX TECHNOLOGIES, INC., *pg.* 1408, *pg.* 1777
EARL MAY SEED & NURSERY L.C., *pg.* 1795, *pg.* 712
EMERGING VISION, INC., *pg.* 1411, *pg.* 1227
ENDLESS POOLS, INC., *pg.* 1833, *pg.* 1515
EPPENDORF NORTH AMERICA, *pg.* 1412, *pg.* 1164
EZCORP, INC., *pg.* 750, *pg.* 1662
THE FANTASY GALLERY, *pg.* 925, *pg.* 1705
FLAX ARTIST'S MATERIALS, *pg.* 1769, *pg.* 49
FLETCHER CHICAGO INC., *pg.* 1413, *pg.* 574
FRANCHISE CONCEPTS, INC., *pg.* 1769, *pg.* 1005
FRESENIUS MEDICAL CARE NORTH AMERICA, *pg.* 1531, *pg.* 851
FUJIFILM MEDICAL SYSTEMS USA, INC., *pg.* 1531, *pg.* 374
FUJIREBIO DIAGNOSTICS INC., *pg.* 1531, *pg.* 1550
GENERAL NUTRITION CENTERS, INC., *pg.* 1534, *pg.* 1575
GF HEALTH PRODUCTS, INC., *pg.* 1535, *pg.* 508
HEALTHTRONICS, INC., *pg.* 1540, *pg.* 1663
HEARUSA, INC., *pg.* 1541, *pg.* 457
HENRY SCHEIN, INC., *pg.* 1541, *pg.* 1180
HILL'S PET NUTRITION, INC., *pg.* 1476, *pg.* 721
HOUCHENS INDUSTRIES INC., *pg.* 1023, *pg.* 726
INSTANTRON CO., INC., *pg.* 512, *pg.* 1608
INTEGRA MILTEX, INC., *pg.* 1546, *pg.* 1597
INTERMOUNTAIN FARMERS ASSOCIATION, *pg.* 705, *pg.* 1759
INTERNATIONAL PLAZA & BAY STREET, *pg.* 1773, *pg.* 473
JEFFERS, INC., *pg.* 1477, *pg.* 5
JESSUP'S APPLIANCES, *pg.* 58, *pg.* 477
KINETIC CONCEPTS, INC., *pg.* 1553, *pg.* 1741
KIRKLAND'S INC., *pg.* 1126, *pg.* 1652
LARRY H. MILLER GROUP OF COMPANIES, *pg.* 182, *pg.* 1762
LESLIE'S POOLMART, INC., *pg.* 1838, *pg.* 17
LIBERATOR, INC., *pg.* 1395, *pg.* 513
LIBERATOR MEDICAL HOLDINGS, INC., *pg.* 1555, *pg.* 468
LIFELOC TECHNOLOGIES, INC., *pg.* 1556, *pg.* 336
MCKESSON CORPORATION, *pg.* 1560, *pg.* 222
MEDASSETS INC., *pg.* 1561, *pg.* 484
MEDLINE INDUSTRIES, INC., *pg.* 1562, *pg.* 635
THE METROPOLITAN MUSEUM OF ART, *pg.* 561, *pg.* 1259
MFA INCORPORATED, *pg.* 1479, *pg.* 976
MICHAELS STORES, INC., *pg.* 1127, *pg.* 1722
MILESTONE SCIENTIFIC, INC., *pg.* 1568, *pg.* 1079
MILLERS FORGE INC., *pg.* 1056, *pg.* 1733
MIRACLE-EAR, INC., *pg.* 1568, *pg.* 940
MTS MEDICATION TECHNOLOGIES, INC., *pg.* 442, *pg.* 463
MWI VETERINARY SUPPLY, INC., *pg.* 1570, *pg.* 548
NET32, INC., *pg.* 1269, *pg.* 1360
NIPRO DIAGNOSTICS, INC., *pg.* 1573, *pg.* 426
NOVATION LLC, *pg.* 446, *pg.* 1723
NOVICA UNITED, INC., *pg.* 1271, *pg.* 137
OMNICARE, INC, *pg.* 1578, *pg.* 1418
OWENS & MINOR, INC., *pg.* 1579, *pg.* 1795
PARTY CITY CORPORATION, *pg.* 1781, *pg.* 1116
PATTERSON COMPANIES, INC., *pg.* 1580, *pg.* 962
PATTERSON DENTAL SUPPLY, INC., *pg.* 1580, *pg.* 963
PERFUMANIA HOLDINGS, INC., *pg.* 520, *pg.* 1141
PET SUPPLIES PLUS, *pg.* 1781, *pg.* 897
PET VALU CANADA, INC., *pg.* 1480, *pg.* 1924
PETCO ANIMAL SUPPLIES, INC., *pg.* 1480, *pg.* 206
PETEDGE, *pg.* 1481, *pg.* 787
PETFOODDIRECT.COM, *pg.* 1481, *pg.* 1536
PETSMART, INC., *pg.* 1481, *pg.* 18
PHILIPS HEALTHCARE, *pg.* 1585, *pg.* 783
PHONAK LLC, *pg.* 1585, *pg.* 665
PRO-DEX, INC., *pg.* 1586, *pg.* 115
PROGRESSIVE MEDICAL, INC., *pg.* 1586, *pg.* 1480
THE PROTECTOSEAL COMPANY, *pg.* 1370, *pg.* 556
PUPPYPAWS, INC., *pg.* 11, *pg.* 1463
QUALMARK CORPORATION, *pg.* 1427, *pg.* 322
RADIOMETER AMERICA INC., *pg.* 1588, *pg.* 1481
RESMED INC., *pg.* 1589, *pg.* 207
RETRACTABLE TECHNOLOGIES INC., *pg.* 1590, *pg.* 1725
THE ROHO GROUP, *pg.* 1591, *pg.* 556
RUE LA LA, *pg.* 1278, *pg.* 800
SALLY BEAUTY HOLDINGS, INC., *pg.* 522, *pg.* 1691
SIMON PROPERTY GROUP, INC., *pg.* 1112, *pg.* 690
SNYDER-DIAMOND, *pg.* 1062, *pg.* 276
SPECTRAL DIAGNOSTICS INC., *pg.* 1430, *pg.* 1943
SPECTRUM GROUP INTERNATIONAL, INC., *pg.* 472, *pg.* 116
THE SPORTS AUTHORITY, INC., *pg.* 1846, *pg.* 326
THE STEPHAN COMPANY, *pg.* 1597, *pg.* 426
SUSSER HOLDINGS CORPORATION, *pg.* 985, *pg.* 1671
TITAN MACHINERY INC., *pg.* 1383, *pg.* 1398
TRACTOR SUPPLY COMPANY, *pg.* 708, *pg.* 1627
UNILEVER UNITED STATES, INC., *pg.* 904, *pg.* 1061
UNIVERSAL COIN & BULLION LTD., *pg.* 1789, *pg.* 1668
UNIVERSAL HOSPITAL SERVICES, INC., *pg.* 1604, *pg.* 945
VERMONT CLOCK COMPANY, *pg.* 946, *pg.* 1766
VESTA INC., *pg.* 1435, *pg.* 1858
VWR FUNDING, INC., *pg.* 1608, *pg.* 1583
WEIS MARKETS, INC., *pg.* 1037, *pg.* 1588
WILLIAMS-SONOMA, INC., *pg.* 1140, *pg.* 234
THE YANKEE CANDLE COMPANY, INC., *pg.* 1792, *pg.* 843
YOUNG INNOVATIONS, INC., *pg.* 1611, *pg.* 977
ZIMMER BIOMET HOLDINGS, INC., *pg.* 1611, *pg.* 699

6011 - Federal Reserve Banks

FIFTH THIRD BANCORP, *pg.* 752, *pg.* 1413
SOUTHEASTERN BANK FINANCIAL CORPORATION, *pg.* 804, *pg.* 525

6022 - State Commercial Banks & Trust Companies

ALLY FINANCIAL INC., *pg.* 711, *pg.* 878
CATHAY GENERAL BANCORP, INC., *pg.* 732, *pg.* 127
CYBERSOURCE CORPORATION, *pg.* 381, *pg.* 216
EQUIFAX INC., *pg.* 748, *pg.* 504
FARMERS NATIONAL BANC CORP., *pg.* 750, *pg.* 1407
GERMAN AMERICAN BANCORP, INC., *pg.* 762, *pg.* 691
MERCHANTS BANCSHARES, INC., *pg.* 782, *pg.* 1768
OPUS BANK, *pg.* 790, *pg.* 1819
UNITY BANCORP, INC., *pg.* 814, *pg.* 1052
VIST FINANCIAL CORP., *pg.* 818, *pg.* 1596

6029 - Commercial Banks, NEC

First page reference indicates Business Class Edition
Second page reference indicates Geographic Edition

1ST SOURCE BANK, *pg.* 710, *pg.* 697
ACNB CORPORATION, *pg.* 710, *pg.* 1534
ADAMS COUNTY NATIONAL BANK INC., *pg.* 710, *pg.* 1534
ALMA BANK, *pg.* 711, *pg.* 1140
AMEGY BANK, N.A., *pg.* 711, *pg.* 1700
AMERICAN BANK INCORPORATED, *pg.* 711, *pg.* 1513
AMERICAN NATIONAL BANKSHARES INC., *pg.* 714, *pg.* 1779
AMERICAN RIVER BANKSHARES, *pg.* 714, *pg.* 186
AMERIS BANCORP, *pg.* 715, *pg.* 536
ARROW FINANCIAL CORPORATION, *pg.* 716, *pg.* 1161
ASSOCIATED BANC-CORP, *pg.* 716, *pg.* 1859
ASTORIA FINANCIAL CORPORATION, *pg.* 717, *pg.* 1172
ATHENS BANCSHARES CORPORATION, *pg.* 717, *pg.* 1627
BAKER BOYER BANCORP, *pg.* 717, *pg.* 1846
BANCFIRST CORPORATION, *pg.* 717, *pg.* 1484
BANCO POPULAR NORTH AMERICA - CALIFORNIA REGIONAL OFFICE, *pg.* 717, *pg.* 42
BANCORPSOUTH, INC., *pg.* 717, *pg.* 971
BANK LEUMI USA, *pg.* 718, *pg.* 1200
BANK OF AMERICA CORPORATION, *pg.* 718, *pg.* 1362
BANK OF AMERICAN FORK, *pg.* 720, *pg.* 1751
BANK OF CHARLES TOWN, *pg.* 720, *pg.* 1849
BANK OF HAWAII CORPORATION, *pg.* 720, *pg.* 543
BANK OF MARIN BANCORP, *pg.* 720, *pg.* 168
BANK OF MCKENNEY, *pg.* 720, *pg.* 1788
BANK OF NASHVILLE, *pg.* 720, *pg.* 1648
THE BANK OF NEW YORK MELLON CORPORATION, *pg.* 720, *pg.* 1200
THE BANK OF NOVA SCOTIA, *pg.* 721, *pg.* 1935
BANK OF SOUTH CAROLINA CORPORATION, *pg.* 721, *pg.* 1613
BANK OF THE CASCADES, *pg.* 721, *pg.* 1496
BANK OF THE OZARKS, INC., *pg.* 721, *pg.* 33
BANK OF THE SIERRA, INC., *pg.* 721, *pg.* 185
BANK OF THE WEST, *pg.* 721, *pg.* 213
BANK OF TUSCALOOSA, *pg.* 722, *pg.* 8
BANK OF UTAH, *pg.* 722, *pg.* 1752
BANK RHODE ISLAND, *pg.* 722, *pg.* 1605
BANKRATE, INC., *pg.* 1231, *pg.* 451
BANNER CORPORATION, *pg.* 722, *pg.* 1846
BAR HARBOR BANK & TRUST, *pg.* 722, *pg.* 749
BAY BANKS OF VIRGINIA, INC., *pg.* 722, *pg.* 1787
BAY STATE SAVINGS BANK, *pg.* 722, *pg.* 862
BAYLAKE CORP., *pg.* 722, *pg.* 1895
BB&T CORPORATION, *pg.* 723, *pg.* 1393
BBCN BANCORP, INC., *pg.* 723, *pg.* 126
BBVA COMPASS BANK, *pg.* 723, *pg.* 2
BCB BANCORP, INC., *pg.* 723, *pg.* 1042
BENEFICIAL BANK, *pg.* 724, *pg.* 1559
THE BERKSHIRE BANK, *pg.* 724, *pg.* 1202
BLUE VALLEY BAN CORP, *pg.* 725, *pg.* 718
BMO HARRIS BANK N.A., *pg.* 725, *pg.* 567
BNC BANCORP, *pg.* 726, *pg.* 1379
BOK FINANCIAL CORPORATION, *pg.* 726, *pg.* 1489
THE BOSTON COMPANY ASSET MANAGEMENT, LLC, *pg.* 726, *pg.* 790
BOSTON PRIVATE, *pg.* 726, *pg.* 791
BOSTON PRIVATE, *pg.* 726, *pg.* 254
BOTETOURT BANKSHARES, INC., *pg.* 726, *pg.* 1777
BRIDGE BANCORP, INC., *pg.* 727, *pg.* 1144
BRIDGEHAMPTON NATIONAL BANK, *pg.* 727, *pg.* 1144
BRITTON & KOONTZ FIRST NATIONAL BANK, *pg.* 727, *pg.* 970
BRUNSWICK BANCORP, *pg.* 727, *pg.* 1091
BRYN MAWR BANK CORPORATION, *pg.* 728, *pg.* 1519
BUSINESS DEVELOPMENT BANK OF CANADA, *pg.* 72, *pg.* 1953
C&F FINANCIAL CORPORATION, *pg.* 728, *pg.* 1811
CADENCE FINANCIAL CORPORATION, *pg.* 728, *pg.* 971
CALIFORNIA BANK & TRUST, *pg.* 728, *pg.* 201
CALIFORNIA FIRST NATIONAL BANCORP, *pg.* 728, *pg.* 109
CALVIN B. TAYLOR BANKSHARES, INC., *pg.* 728, *pg.* 761
CAMDEN NATIONAL BANK, INC., *pg.* 729, *pg.* 749
CANADIAN IMPERIAL BANK OF COMMERCE, *pg.* 729, *pg.* 1935
CAPE BANCORP, INC., *pg.* 730, *pg.* 1049
CAPITAL BANK, *pg.* 730, *pg.* 1393
CAPITAL BANK CORPORATION, *pg.* 730, *pg.* 1386
CAPITAL ONE BANK (USA), N.A., *pg.* 730, *pg.* 1789
CAPITAL ONE FINANCIAL CORPORATION, *pg.* 730, *pg.* 1789
CAPITOL FEDERAL FINANCIAL, INC., *pg.* 731, *pg.* 721
CARDINAL BANK N.A., *pg.* 732, *pg.* 1790
CARDINAL FINANCIAL CORP., *pg.* 732, *pg.* 1790
CAROLINA BANK HOLDINGS, INC., *pg.* 732, *pg.* 1374
CASCADE BANCORP, *pg.* 732, *pg.* 1496
CATHAY GENERAL BANCORP, INC., *pg.* 732, *pg.* 127
CB&S BANK, *pg.* 732, *pg.* 8
CCFNB BANCORP, INC., *pg.* 733, *pg.* 1517
CENTRAL FEDERAL CORPORATION, *pg.* 733, *pg.* 1453
CENTRAL PACIFIC FINANCIAL CORPORATION, *pg.* 733, *pg.* 543
CENTRAL VALLEY COMMUNITY BANCORP, *pg.* 733, *pg.* 93
CENTRUE FINANCIAL CORPORATION, *pg.* 733, *pg.* 994
CENTURY BANK & TRUST, *pg.* 733, *pg.* 875
CFG COMMUNITY BANK, *pg.* 734, *pg.* 756
CHARTER FINANCIAL CORPORATION, *pg.* 734, *pg.* 542
CHEMICAL FINANCIAL CORPORATION, *pg.* 734, *pg.* 898
CHESAPEAKE FINANCIAL SHARES, INC., *pg.* 735, *pg.* 1787
CHEVIOT FINANCIAL CORP., *pg.* 735, *pg.* 1409
CHICOPEE BANCORP, INC., *pg.* 735, *pg.* 815
CHOICEONE FINANCIAL SERVICES, INC., *pg.* 735, *pg.* 908
CIB MARINE BANCSHARES, INC., *pg.* 735, *pg.* 1897
CITIGROUP INC., *pg.* 735, *pg.* 1212
CITIZENS BANK & TRUST, *pg.* 737, *pg.* 976
CITIZENS FIRST CORPORATION, *pg.* 737, *pg.* 725
CITIZENS HOLDING COMPANY, *pg.* 737, *pg.* 971
CITY HOLDING COMPANY, *pg.* 737, *pg.* 1849
CITY NATIONAL CORPORATION, *pg.* 738, *pg.* 128
CNB FINANCIAL CORPORATION, *pg.* 739, *pg.* 1522
COCC, *pg.* 376, *pg.* 337
COLONY BANKCORP, INC., *pg.* 739, *pg.* 532
THE COLUMBIA BANK, *pg.* 739, *pg.* 767
COLUMBIA BANKING SYSTEM, INC., *pg.* 739, *pg.* 1844
COLUMBUS BANK AND TRUST COMPANY, *pg.* 739, *pg.* 528
COMERICA INCORPORATED, *pg.* 740, *pg.* 1677
COMMERCE BANCSHARES, INC., *pg.* 740, *pg.* 982
COMMERCEBANK HOLDING CORPORATION, *pg.* 740, *pg.* 418
COMMERCIAL BANCSHARES, INC., *pg.* 740, *pg.* 1477
COMMERCIAL BANK & TRUST OF PENNSYLVANIA, *pg.* 740, *pg.* 1547
COMMERCIAL NATIONAL FINANCIAL CORPORATION, *pg.* 740, *pg.* 1547
COMMUNITY BANK, N.A., *pg.* 741, *pg.* 1155
COMMUNITY BANK SYSTEM, INC., *pg.* 741, *pg.* 1155
COMMUNITY PARTNERS BANCORP, *pg.* 741, *pg.* 1084
COMMUNITY STATE BANK, *pg.* 741, *pg.* 1896
COMMUNITY WEST BANCSHARES, *pg.* 741, *pg.* 99
COMMUNITYONE BANCORP, *pg.* 741, *pg.* 1358
CORTLAND SAVINGS & BANKING CO., *pg.* 742, *pg.* 1445
CROGHAN BANCSHARES, INC., *pg.* 742, *pg.* 1454
CULLEN/FROST BANKERS, INC., *pg.* 742, *pg.* 1740
DCB FINANCIAL CORP., *pg.* 743, *pg.* 1457
DORAL FINANCIAL CORPORATION, *pg.* 744, *pg.* 1599
EAGLE BANCORP, INC., *pg.* 745, *pg.* 762
EAGLEBANK, *pg.* 745, *pg.* 762
EASTERN VIRGINIA BANKSHARES, INC., *pg.* 746, *pg.* 1808
THE ELMIRA SAVINGS BANK, FSB, *pg.* 746, *pg.* 1157
EMCLAIRE FINANCIAL CORP., *pg.* 747, *pg.* 1529
EMPRISE BANK, *pg.* 747, *pg.* 723
ENTERPRISE BANCORP INC., *pg.* 747, *pg.* 829
ESB FINANCIAL CORPORATION, *pg.* 749, *pg.* 1529
ESSA BANCORP, INC., *pg.* 749, *pg.* 1587
ESSEX BANK, *pg.* 749, *pg.* 1808
EVANS BANCORP, INC., *pg.* 749, *pg.* 1138
EXTRACO BANKS, *pg.* 750, *pg.* 1749
F&M BANK CORP., *pg.* 750, *pg.* 1808
FARMERS & MERCHANTS BANCORP, *pg.* 750, *pg.* 1403
FARMERS CAPITAL BANK CORPORATION, *pg.* 750, *pg.* 728
FARMERS NATIONAL BANC CORP., *pg.* 750, *pg.* 1407
THE FAUQUIER BANK, *pg.* 751, *pg.* 1810
FAUQUIER BANKSHARES INC, *pg.* 751, *pg.* 1810
FENTURA FINANCIAL, INC., *pg.* 752, *pg.* 886
FIDELITY BANK, *pg.* 752, *pg.* 505
FIDELITY D & D BANCORP INC., *pg.* 752, *pg.* 1527
FIDELITY SOUTHERN CORPORATION, *pg.* 752, *pg.* 505
FIFTH THIRD BANCORP, *pg.* 752, *pg.* 1413
FIFTH THIRD BANK, INDIANA (SOUTHERN), *pg.* 753, *pg.* 678
FINANCIAL INSTITUTIONS, INC., *pg.* 753, *pg.* 1349
FIRST BANCORP OF INDIANA, INC., *pg.* 753, *pg.* 678
FIRST BANK, *pg.* 753, *pg.* 1808
FIRST BANKS, INC., *pg.* 754, *pg.* 976
FIRST BUSEY CORPORATION, *pg.* 754, *pg.* 562
FIRST CAPITAL BANCORP, INC., *pg.* 754, *pg.* 1782
FIRST CITIZENS BANK, *pg.* 754, *pg.* 483
FIRST COMMONWEALTH FINANCIAL CORPORATION, *pg.* 754, *pg.* 1541
FIRST COMMUNITY BANCSHARES, INC., *pg.* 754, *pg.* 1776
FIRST COMMUNITY CORPORATION, *pg.* 754, *pg.* 1620
FIRST FINANCIAL BANKSHARES, INC., *pg.* 755, *pg.* 1657
FIRST HORIZON NATIONAL CORPORATION, *pg.* 755, *pg.* 1644
FIRST INTERSTATE BANCSYSTEM, INC., *pg.* 755, *pg.* 1008
FIRST KEYSTONE COMMUNITY BANK, *pg.* 756, *pg.* 1515
FIRST MARINER BANCORP, *pg.* 756, *pg.* 757
FIRST MARINER BANK, *pg.* 756, *pg.* 757
FIRST MIDWEST BANCORP INC., *pg.* 756, *pg.* 620
FIRST NATIONAL COMMUNITY BANCORP, INC., *pg.* 756, *pg.* 1527
FIRST NIAGARA BANK, *pg.* 757, *pg.* 358
FIRST NIAGARA BANK, *pg.* 756, *pg.* 1174
FIRST NIAGARA FINANCIAL GROUP, INC., *pg.* 757, *pg.* 1148
FIRST PREMIER BANK, *pg.* 757, *pg.* 1625
FIRST SECURITY GROUP, INC., *pg.* 757, *pg.* 1629
FIRST SOUTH BANCORP, INC., *pg.* 757, *pg.* 1392
FIRST WEST VIRGINIA BANCORP, INC., *pg.* 757, *pg.* 1851
FIRST WESTERN BANK & TRUST, *pg.* 757, *pg.* 1398
FIRSTRUST SAVINGS BANK, *pg.* 758, *pg.* 1523
FLORIDA COMMUNITY BANKS, INC., *pg.* 758, *pg.* 431
FNBH BANCORP, INC., *pg.* 759, *pg.* 893
GERMAN AMERICAN BANCORP, INC., *pg.* 762, *pg.* 691
GLACIER BANK, *pg.* 762, *pg.* 1009
GLEN BURNIE BANCORP, *pg.* 762, *pg.* 771
GRAYSON BANKSHARES, INC., *pg.* 763, *pg.* 1786
GREAT SOUTHERN BANCORP, INC., *pg.* 763, *pg.* 1006
GREATER HUDSON BANK, N.A., *pg.* 763, *pg.* 1182
GUARANTY BANCSHARES, INC., *pg.* 764, *pg.* 1728
GUARANTY BANK, *pg.* 764, *pg.* 1006
HAMPTON ROADS BANKSHARES, INC., *pg.* 765, *pg.* 1796
HANCOCK BANK, *pg.* 765, *pg.* 968
HANCOCK HOLDING COMPANY, *pg.* 765, *pg.* 968
HAWTHORN BANCSHARES, INC., *pg.* 765, *pg.* 987
HEARTLAND FINANCIAL USA, INC., *pg.* 765, *pg.* 707
HERITAGE COMMERCE CORP., *pg.* 765, *pg.* 246
HERITAGE FINANCIAL CORPORATION, *pg.* 765, *pg.* 1823
HF FINANCIAL CORP., *pg.* 766, *pg.* 1625
HILLCREST BANK, N.A., *pg.* 766, *pg.* 719
HINGHAM INSTITUTION FOR SAVINGS, *pg.* 766, *pg.* 824
HOME BANCSHARES, INC., *pg.* 766, *pg.* 31
HOPFED BANCORP, INC., *pg.* 766, *pg.* 729
HORIZON BANCORP, *pg.* 767, *pg.* 694
HSBC BANK CANADA, *pg.* 767, *pg.* 1911
HUNTINGTON BANCSHARES INCORPORATED, *pg.* 767, *pg.* 1440
THE HUNTINGTON NATIONAL BANK, *pg.* 767, *pg.* 1440
IBERIABANK CORPORATION, *pg.* 768, *pg.* 744
IBW FINANCIAL CORP., *pg.* 768, *pg.* 401
INDEPENDENT BANK CORPORATION, *pg.* 768, *pg.* 893
INDEPENDENT BANK CORP., *pg.* 768, *pg.* 843
INTERACTIVE DATA CORPORATION, *pg.* 769, *pg.* 785
INTERNATIONAL BANCSHARES CORPORATION, *pg.* 769, *pg.* 1725
IOWA FIRST BANCSHARES CORP., *pg.* 771, *pg.* 710
ISABELLA BANK CORPORATION, *pg.* 771, *pg.* 901
JACKSONVILLE BANCORP, INC., *pg.* 771, *pg.* 433
JEFFERSONVILLE BANCORP, *pg.* 772, *pg.* 1170
JPMORGAN CHASE & CO., *pg.* 772, *pg.* 1246
JUNIATA VALLEY FINANCIAL CORP., *pg.* 773, *pg.* 1553
KENTUCKY BANCSHARES, INC., *pg.* 773, *pg.* 739
KEYBANK, *pg.* 773, *pg.* 1319
KEYCORP, *pg.* 774, *pg.* 1432
LAKE SHORE BANCORP, INC., *pg.* 775, *pg.* 1156
LAKELAND FINANCIAL CORPORATION, *pg.* 775, *pg.* 699
LANDMARK BANCORP, INC., *pg.* 775, *pg.* 717
LIBERTY BANCORP, INC., *pg.* 775, *pg.* 987
LOUISIANA BANCORP, INC., *pg.* 777, *pg.* 745
THE LYONS NATIONAL BANK, *pg.* 777, *pg.* 1177
M&T BANK CORPORATION, *pg.* 777, *pg.* 1149
MACATAWA BANK CORPORATION, *pg.* 778, *pg.* 892
MACKINAC FINANCIAL CORPORATION, *pg.* 778, *pg.* 898
MECHANICS BANK, *pg.* 781, *pg.* 193
MERCANTILE BANK CORPORATION, *pg.* 782, *pg.* 888
MERCHANTS BANCSHARES, INC., *pg.* 782, *pg.* 1768

First page reference indicates Business Class Edition
Second page reference indicates Geographic Edition

METRO BANCORP, INC., *pg.* 782, *pg.* 1537
MID PENN BANCORP, INC., *pg.* 782, *pg.* 1553
MIDDLEFIELD BANC CORP., *pg.* 783, *pg.* 1465
MIDSOUTH BANCORP, INC., *pg.* 783, *pg.* 745
MIDSOUTH BANK N.A., *pg.* 783, *pg.* 745
MORGAN STANLEY, *pg.* 783, *pg.* 1261
MORRIS COUPLING COMPANY, *pg.* 1057, *pg.* 1530
MUTUALFIRST FINANCIAL, INC., *pg.* 785, *pg.* 696
NATIONAL BANK OF CANADA, *pg.* 785, *pg.* 1956
NATIONAL BANK OF INDIANAPOLIS CORPORATION, *pg.* 785, *pg.* 688
NATIONAL BANK OF SOUTH CAROLINA, *pg.* 785, *pg.* 1614
NATIONAL BANKSHARES, INC., *pg.* 785, *pg.* 1776
NATIONAL PENN BANCSHARES, INC., *pg.* 786, *pg.* 1517
NEW ENGLAND BANCSHARES, INC., *pg.* 786, *pg.* 346
NEW HAMPSHIRE THRIFT BANCSHARES, INC., *pg.* 786, *pg.* 1038
NEW YORK COMMERCIAL BANK, *pg.* 787, *pg.* 1169
NEWBRIDGE BANCORP, *pg.* 787, *pg.* 1375
NORTHEAST BANCORP, *pg.* 787, *pg.* 751
THE NORTHERN TRUST COMPANY, *pg.* 787, *pg.* 585
NORTHERN TRUST CORPORATION, *pg.* 787, *pg.* 585
NORTHRIM BANCORP, INC., *pg.* 788, *pg.* 10
NORTHWAY FINANCIAL, INC., *pg.* 788, *pg.* 1033
NORTHWEST BANCSHARES, INC., *pg.* 788, *pg.* 1590
NORWOOD FINANCIAL CORP., *pg.* 788, *pg.* 1539
OAK RIDGE FINANCIAL SERVICES, INC., *pg.* 789, *pg.* 1386
OCEAN SHORE HOLDING CO., *pg.* 789, *pg.* 1100
OCEANFIRST BANK, *pg.* 789, *pg.* 1125
OCEANFIRST FINANCIAL CORP., *pg.* 789, *pg.* 1125
OHIO FARMERS INSURANCE COMPANY, *pg.* 1213, *pg.* 1480
OLD LINE BANCSHARES, INC., *pg.* 789, *pg.* 766
OLD NATIONAL BANCORP, *pg.* 789, *pg.* 679
OLD POINT FINANCIAL CORPORATION, *pg.* 789, *pg.* 1783
OLD SECOND BANCORP, INC., *pg.* 789, *pg.* 555
ONEIDA SAVINGS BANK, *pg.* 790, *pg.* 1319
ONEUNITED BANK, *pg.* 790, *pg.* 137
OPUS BANK, *pg.* 790, *pg.* 1819
ORIENTAL FINANCIAL GROUP INC, *pg.* 790, *pg.* 1599
ORRSTOWN FINANCIAL SERVICES, INC., *pg.* 791, *pg.* 1586
PACIFIC & WESTERN CREDIT CORP., *pg.* 791, *pg.* 1922
PACIFIC CONTINENTAL CORPORATION, *pg.* 791, *pg.* 1497
PACIFIC FINANCIAL CORPORATION, *pg.* 791, *pg.* 1813
PACIFIC PREMIER BANK, *pg.* 791, *pg.* 114
PALMETTO BANCSHARES, INC., *pg.* 791, *pg.* 1618
PARK NATIONAL CORPORATION, *pg.* 792, *pg.* 1468
PARK STERLING BANK, *pg.* 792, *pg.* 1373
PEAPACK-GLADSTONE BANK, *pg.* 792, *pg.* 1071
PEAPACK-GLADSTONE FINANCIAL CORPORATION, *pg.* 792, *pg.* 1044
PENNS WOODS BANCORP, INC., *pg.* 304, *pg.* 1595
PEOPLES BANCORP INC., *pg.* 793, *pg.* 1458
PEOPLES BANCORP OF NORTH CAROLINA, INC., *pg.* 793, *pg.* 1386
PEOPLES FINANCIAL CORPORATION, *pg.* 793, *pg.* 968
PEOPLE'S UNITED BANK, *pg.* 793, *pg.* 749
PEOPLE'S UNITED BANK, *pg.* 793, *pg.* 340
PIEDMONT FEDERAL SAVINGS BANK, *pg.* 794, *pg.* 1395
PINNACLE FINANCIAL PARTNERS, INC., *pg.* 794, *pg.* 1653
PLAINS CAPITAL CORPORATION, *pg.* 794, *pg.* 1685
PLATTE VALLEY FINANCIAL SERVICE COMPANIES INC., *pg.* 794, *pg.* 1019
PLUMAS BANCORP, *pg.* 794, *pg.* 186
THE PNC FINANCIAL SERVICES GROUP, INC., *pg.* 795, *pg.* 1579
PREMIER BANK, *pg.* 795, *pg.* 404
PRIVATEBANCORP INC., *pg.* 796, *pg.* 587
PROSPERITY BANCSHARES, INC., *pg.* 796, *pg.* 1713
PROVIDENT FINANCIAL HOLDINGS, INC., *pg.* 796, *pg.* 194
PSB HOLDINGS, INC., *pg.* 797, *pg.* 1898
QCR HOLDINGS, INC., *pg.* 797, *pg.* 633
READING COOPERATIVE BANK, *pg.* 798, *pg.* 842
REAL INDUSTRY, INC., *pg.* 1215, *pg.* 278
REGIONS FINANCIAL CORPORATION, *pg.* 798, *pg.* 4
RENASANT BANK, *pg.* 798, *pg.* 533
RENASANT CORPORATION, *pg.* 799, *pg.* 972
REPUBLIC BANCORP, INC., *pg.* 799, *pg.* 737
REPUBLIC BANK & TRUST COMPANY, *pg.* 799, *pg.* 737
REPUBLIC FIRST BANCORP, INC., *pg.* 799, *pg.* 1570
RIVERVIEW COMMUNITY BANK, *pg.* 799, *pg.* 1506
RIVERVIEW FINANCIAL CORPORATION, *pg.* 799, *pg.* 1535
ROYAL BANK OF CANADA, *pg.* 800, *pg.* 1942
SALEM FIVE CENTS SAVINGS BANK, *pg.* 800, *pg.* 843
SALISBURY BANCORP, INC., *pg.* 801, *pg.* 353
SALISBURY BANK & TRUST COMPANY, *pg.* 801, *pg.* 353
SANDY SPRING BANCORP, INC., *pg.* 801, *pg.* 774
SANDY SPRING BANK, *pg.* 801, *pg.* 774
SB FINANCIAL GROUP, *pg.* 801, *pg.* 1447
SCBT FINANCIAL CORPORATION, *pg.* 801, *pg.* 1614
SELECT BANK & TRUST, *pg.* 803, *pg.* 1370
SEVERN BANCORP, INC., *pg.* 803, *pg.* 754
SHORE BANCSHARES, INC., *pg.* 803, *pg.* 769
SIERRA BANCORP, *pg.* 803, *pg.* 185
SOUTHCOAST FINANCIAL CORPORATION, *pg.* 804, *pg.* 1620
SOUTHEASTERN BANK FINANCIAL CORPORATION, *pg.* 804, *pg.* 525
SOUTHEASTERN BANKING CORP., *pg.* 804, *pg.* 530
SOUTHERN MISSOURI BANCORP, INC., *pg.* 804, *pg.* 989
SOUTHSIDE BANCSHARES INC., *pg.* 804, *pg.* 1748
SOUTHWEST GEORGIA FINANCIAL CORPORATION, *pg.* 804, *pg.* 536
STATE STREET CORPORATION, *pg.* 805, *pg.* 801
STEWARDSHIP FINANCIAL CORPORATION, *pg.* 805, *pg.* 1084
SUN BANCORP, INC., *pg.* 806, *pg.* 1127
SUN TRUST BANK, ATLANTA, *pg.* 806, *pg.* 520
SUNTRUST BANK, NASHVILLE REGION, *pg.* 807, *pg.* 1654
SUNTRUST BANKS, INC., *pg.* 807, *pg.* 520
SUNWEST BANK, *pg.* 807, *pg.* 116
SUSQUEHANNA BANK, *pg.* 807, *pg.* 1548
SVB FINANCIAL GROUP, *pg.* 808, *pg.* 270
T BANCSHARES, INC., *pg.* 808, *pg.* 1688
TCF FINANCIAL CORPORATION, *pg.* 808, *pg.* 966
TEXAS CAPITAL BANCSHARES, INC., *pg.* 809, *pg.* 1737
THE TORONTO-DOMINION BANK, *pg.* 810, *pg.* 1945
TOTALBANK CORP., *pg.* 811, *pg.* 447
TOWNEBANK, *pg.* 811, *pg.* 1798
TRI-COUNTY FINANCIAL CORPORATION, *pg.* 811, *pg.* 780
TRICO BANCSHARES, *pg.* 811, *pg.* 65
TRUSTCO BANK CORP NY, *pg.* 811, *pg.* 1162
TRUSTMARK CORPORATION, *pg.* 812, *pg.* 7
TRUSTMARK NATIONAL BANK, *pg.* 812, *pg.* 969
UMB FINANCIAL CORPORATION, *pg.* 812, *pg.* 987
UMPQUA HOLDINGS CORPORATION, *pg.* 813, *pg.* 1507
THE UNION BANK CO., *pg.* 813, *pg.* 1445
UNION BANK, N.A., *pg.* 813, *pg.* 230
UNION BANKSHARES, INC., *pg.* 813, *pg.* 1767
UNION FIRST MARKET BANKSHARES CORPORATION, *pg.* 813, *pg.* 1804
UNIONBANCAL CORPORATION, *pg.* 813, *pg.* 230
UNITED BANCORP, INC., *pg.* 813, *pg.* 1459
UNITED BANKSHARES, INC., *pg.* 813, *pg.* 1849
UNITED COMMUNITY BANCORP, *pg.* 813, *pg.* 693
UNITED COMMUNITY BANKS, INC., *pg.* 814, *pg.* 526
UNITED SECURITY BANCSHARES, *pg.* 814, *pg.* 93
UNITED SECURITY BANCSHARES, INC., *pg.* 814, *pg.* 8
UNITED TENNESSEE BANKSHARES, INC., *pg.* 814, *pg.* 1655
UNITY BANCORP, INC., *pg.* 814, *pg.* 1052
UNITY BANK, *pg.* 814, *pg.* 1052
UNIVERSITY BANCORP, INC., *pg.* 814, *pg.* 867
UNIVEST CORPORATION OF PENNSYLVANIA, *pg.* 814, *pg.* 1586
U.S. BANCORP, *pg.* 815, *pg.* 945
VALLEY NATIONAL BANCORP, *pg.* 815, *pg.* 1130
VIST BANK, *pg.* 818, *pg.* 1596
VIST FINANCIAL CORP., *pg.* 818, *pg.* 1596
WASHINGTON FEDERAL INC., *pg.* 818, *pg.* 1842
WASHINGTON TRUST BANCORP, INC., *pg.* 818, *pg.* 1610
WAYNE BANK, *pg.* 819, *pg.* 1540
WEBSTER CITY FEDERAL BANCORP, *pg.* 819, *pg.* 712
WELLS FARGO & COMPANY, *pg.* 819, *pg.* 232
WESBANCO, INC., *pg.* 821, *pg.* 1851
WEST SUBURBAN BANCORP, INC., *pg.* 821, *pg.* 631
WESTAMERICA BANCORPORATION, *pg.* 821, *pg.* 258
WESTERN ALLIANCE BANCORPORATION, *pg.* 821, *pg.* 20
WHITNEY HOLDING CORPORATION, *pg.* 822, *pg.* 747
WILSHIRE BANCORP INC., *pg.* 823, *pg.* 141
WILSON BANK HOLDING COMPANY, *pg.* 823, *pg.* 1640
WSFS FINANCIAL CORPORATION, *pg.* 823, *pg.* 392
YADKIN VALLEY FINANCIAL CORPORATION, *pg.* 824, *pg.* 1372
YOUR COMMUNITY BANKSHARES, INC., *pg.* 824, *pg.* 696
ZIONS FIRST NATIONAL BANK, N.A., *pg.* 824, *pg.* 1762

6035 - Savings Institutions, Federally Chartered

AMB FINANCIAL CORP., *pg.* 711, *pg.* 696
ANDROSCOGGIN SAVINGS BANK, *pg.* 716, *pg.* 751
APPLE BANK FOR SAVINGS, *pg.* 716, *pg.* 1196
ASHEVILLE SAVINGS BANK SSB, *pg.* 716, *pg.* 1358
ASTORIA FEDERAL SAVINGS & LOAN, *pg.* 716, *pg.* 1171
ASTORIA FINANCIAL CORPORATION, *pg.* 717, *pg.* 1172
BANCORPSOUTH, INC., *pg.* 717, *pg.* 971
THE BANK OF NOVA SCOTIA, *pg.* 721, *pg.* 1935
BANKFINANCIAL CORPORATION, *pg.* 722, *pg.* 560
BANNER CORPORATION, *pg.* 722, *pg.* 1846
BAR HARBOR BANK & TRUST, *pg.* 722, *pg.* 749
BB&T, *pg.* 723, *pg.* 423
BB&T CORPORATION, *pg.* 723, *pg.* 1393
BBVA COMPASS BANK, *pg.* 723, *pg.* 2
BBX CAPITAL, *pg.* 723, *pg.* 423
BCB BANCORP, INC., *pg.* 723, *pg.* 1042
BLACKHAWK BANCORP INC., *pg.* 724, *pg.* 1854
BMO HARRIS BANK N.A., *pg.* 725, *pg.* 567
BOFI HOLDING, INC., *pg.* 726, *pg.* 200
BROADWAY FEDERAL BANK, F.S.B., *pg.* 727, *pg.* 127
BRUNSWICK BANCORP, *pg.* 727, *pg.* 1091
CAMBRIDGE SAVINGS BANK, *pg.* 728, *pg.* 807
CAPE BANCORP, INC., *pg.* 730, *pg.* 1049
CAPE COD FIVE CENTS SAVINGS BANK, *pg.* 730, *pg.* 840
CARVER FEDERAL SAVINGS BANK, *pg.* 732, *pg.* 1209
CENTRUE FINANCIAL CORPORATION, *pg.* 733, *pg.* 994
CFG COMMUNITY BANK, *pg.* 734, *pg.* 756
CHEVIOT FINANCIAL CORP., *pg.* 735, *pg.* 1409
CHICOPEE BANCORP, INC., *pg.* 735, *pg.* 815
CITIZENS BANK & TRUST, *pg.* 737, *pg.* 976
CITIZENS FIRST CORPORATION, *pg.* 737, *pg.* 725
CITY NATIONAL BANK, *pg.* 737, *pg.* 725
CITY NATIONAL CORPORATION, *pg.* 738, *pg.* 128
CLIFTON SAVINGS BANCORP, INC., *pg.* 738, *pg.* 1052
COLORADO FEDERAL SAVINGS BANK, *pg.* 739, *pg.* 330
COMERICA INCORPORATED, *pg.* 740, *pg.* 1677
COMMUNITY BANK, N.A., *pg.* 741, *pg.* 1155
CULLEN/FROST BANKERS, INC., *pg.* 742, *pg.* 1740
CULLMAN BANCORP, INC., *pg.* 743, *pg.* 5
DIME COMMUNITY BANCSHARES, INC., *pg.* 744, *pg.* 1146
EAGLE BANCORP, INC., *pg.* 745, *pg.* 762
EASTERN BANK CORPORATION-SOUTH REGION HEADQUARTERS, *pg.* 745, *pg.* 833
EMIGRANT SAVINGS BANK, *pg.* 747, *pg.* 1227
ESB FINANCIAL CORPORATION, *pg.* 749, *pg.* 1529
E*TRADE FINANCIAL CORPORATION, *pg.* 749, *pg.* 1230
EXCHANGE BANK, *pg.* 750, *pg.* 277
FARM BUREAU BANK FSB, *pg.* 750, *pg.* 1740
FIDELITY SOUTHERN CORPORATION, *pg.* 752, *pg.* 505
FIRST BANCORP OF INDIANA, INC., *pg.* 753, *pg.* 678
FIRST FINANCIAL BANKSHARES, INC., *pg.* 755, *pg.* 1657
FIRST FINANCIAL HOLDINGS, INC., *pg.* 755, *pg.* 1614
FIRST HARRISON BANK, *pg.* 755, *pg.* 676
FIRST INTERSTATE BANCSYSTEM, INC., *pg.* 755, *pg.* 1008
FIRST MIDWEST BANCORP INC., *pg.* 756, *pg.* 620
FIRST NATIONAL BANK, *pg.* 756, *pg.* 1553
FIRST NIAGARA BANK, *pg.* 757, *pg.* 358
FIRST NIAGARA BANK, *pg.* 756, *pg.* 1174
FIRST NIAGARA FINANCIAL GROUP, INC., *pg.* 757, *pg.* 1148
FIRST SOUTH BANCORP, INC., *pg.* 757, *pg.* 1392
FIRSTBANK HOLDING COMPANY OF COLORADO, INC., *pg.* 758, *pg.* 333
FIRSTMERIT CORPORATION, *pg.* 758, *pg.* 1400
FIRSTRUST SAVINGS BANK, *pg.* 758, *pg.* 1523
FLAGSTAR BANCORP, INC., *pg.* 758, *pg.* 910
FLUSHING FINANCIAL CORPORATION, *pg.* 759, *pg.* 1172
FLUSHING SAVINGS BANK INC., *pg.* 759, *pg.* 1172
FNBH BANCORP, INC., *pg.* 759, *pg.* 893
GATE CITY BANK, *pg.* 761, *pg.* 1397
GLACIER BANK, *pg.* 762, *pg.* 1009
GOUVERNEUR BANCORP, INC., *pg.* 763, *pg.* 1162
GOUVERNEUR SAVINGS & LOAN ASSOCIATION, *pg.* 763, *pg.* 1162
GRAYSON BANKSHARES, INC., *pg.* 763, *pg.* 1786
GREAT SOUTHERN BANCORP, INC., *pg.* 763, *pg.* 1006
GREAT WESTERN BANK, *pg.* 763, *pg.* 708
GUARANTY BANK, *pg.* 764, *pg.* 1006
HF FINANCIAL CORP., *pg.* 766, *pg.* 1625
HINGHAM INSTITUTION FOR SAVINGS, *pg.* 766, *pg.* 824
HMN FINANCIAL, INC., *pg.* 766, *pg.* 955

HOME BANCORP, INC., pg. 766, pg. 744
HOPFED BANCORP, INC., pg. 766, pg. 729
HORIZON BANCORP, pg. 767, pg. 694
HUNTINGTON BANCSHARES INCORPORATED, pg. 767, pg. 1440
THE HUNTINGTON NATIONAL BANK, pg. 767, pg. 1440
INDEPENDENT BANK CORP., pg. 768, pg. 843
INVESTORS BANCORP, INC., pg. 771, pg. 1121
JACKSONVILLE BANCORP, INC., pg. 771, pg. 433
KEARNY FINANCIAL CORP., pg. 773, pg. 1065
KENTUCKY BANCSHARES, INC., pg. 773, pg. 739
LAKE SHORE BANCORP, INC., pg. 775, pg. 1156
LAPORTE BANCORP, INC., pg. 775, pg. 692
LIBERTY BANK INC., pg. 776, pg. 356
LOUISIANA BANCORP, INC., pg. 777, pg. 745
M&T BANK CORPORATION, pg. 777, pg. 1149
MALVERN FEDERAL BANCORP, INC., pg. 778, pg. 1558
MERIDIAN INTERSTATE BANCORP, INC., pg. 782, pg. 817
MUTUALFIRST FINANCIAL, INC., pg. 785, pg. 696
NASB FINANCIAL, INC., pg. 785, pg. 978
NAUGATUCK VALLEY FINANCIAL CORPORATION, pg. 786, pg. 358
NEW HAMPSHIRE THRIFT BANCSHARES, INC., pg. 786, pg. 1038
NEWBURYPORT FIVE CENTS SAVINGS BANK, pg. 787, pg. 836
THE NORTHERN TRUST COMPANY, pg. 787, pg. 585
NORTHERN TRUST CORPORATION, pg. 787, pg. 585
NORTHRIM BANCORP, INC., pg. 788, pg. 10
NORTHWEST BANCSHARES, INC., pg. 788, pg. 1590
OCEAN SHORE HOLDING CO., pg. 789, pg. 1100
OCEANFIRST BANK, pg. 789, pg. 1125
OCEANFIRST FINANCIAL CORP., pg. 789, pg. 1125
OLD NATIONAL BANCORP, pg. 789, pg. 679
ONEIDA FINANCIAL CORP., pg. 790, pg. 1318
ONEIDA SAVINGS BANK, pg. 790, pg. 1319
ORIENTAL FINANCIAL GROUP INC, pg. 790, pg. 1599
PARK BANCORP, INC., pg. 792, pg. 587
PATAPSCO BANCORP, pg. 792, pg. 758
PATHFINDER BANCORP, INC., pg. 792, pg. 1320
PEOPLES BANCORP INC., pg. 793, pg. 1458
PEOPLE'S UNITED FINANCIAL, INC., pg. 793, pg. 340
PIEDMONT FEDERAL SAVINGS BANK, pg. 794, pg. 1395
PINNACLE FINANCIAL PARTNERS, INC., pg. 794, pg. 1653
THE PNC FINANCIAL SERVICES GROUP, INC., pg. 795, pg. 1579
PROVIDENT FINANCIAL SERVICES, INC., pg. 796, pg. 1075
PULASKI FINANCIAL CORP., pg. 797, pg. 1002
RENASANT CORPORATION, pg. 799, pg. 972
RIVER VALLEY BANCORP, pg. 799, pg. 694
RIVERVIEW BANCORP, INC., pg. 799, pg. 1846
ROYAL BANK OF CANADA, pg. 800, pg. 1942
SALEM FIVE CENTS SAVINGS BANK, pg. 800, pg. 843
SALISBURY BANCORP, INC., pg. 801, pg. 353
SANDY SPRING BANCORP, INC., pg. 801, pg. 774
SANDY SPRING BANK, pg. 801, pg. 774
SANTANDER HOLDINGS USA, INC., pg. 801, pg. 800
SECURITY FEDERAL CORPORATION, pg. 802, pg. 1612
SELECT BANK & TRUST, pg. 803, pg. 1370
SEVERN BANCORP, INC., pg. 803, pg. 754
SI FINANCIAL GROUP, INC., pg. 803, pg. 385
THE SOUTHERN BANC COMPANY, INC., pg. 804, pg. 5
SOUTHERN MISSOURI BANCORP, INC., pg. 804, pg. 989
STONEHAM BANK, pg. 806, pg. 846
SUNTRUST BANKS, INC., pg. 807, pg. 520
THIRD FEDERAL SAVINGS & LOAN ASSOCIATION, pg. 810, pg. 1436
TIMBERLAND BANCORP, INC., pg. 810, pg. 1820
TOTALBANK CORP., pg. 811, pg. 447
TRUSTMARK CORPORATION, pg. 812, pg. 969
TRUSTMARK NATIONAL BANK, pg. 812, pg. 969
UMB FINANCIAL CORPORATION, pg. 812, pg. 987
UNIONBANCAL CORPORATION, pg. 813, pg. 230
UNITED BANKSHARES, INC., pg. 813, pg. 1849
UNITED COMMUNITY BANKS, INC., pg. 814, pg. 526
UNITED COMMUNITY FINANCIAL CORP., pg. 814, pg. 1483
UNITED TENNESSEE BANKSHARES, INC., pg. 814, pg. 1655
UNITED WATER RESOURCES INC., pg. 1954, pg. 1073
U.S. BANCORP, pg. 815, pg. 945
VALLEY NATIONAL BANCORP, pg. 815, pg. 1130
WASHINGTON FEDERAL INC., pg. 818, pg. 1842
WATERSTONE FINANCIAL, INC., pg. 818, pg. 1899
WATERTOWN SAVINGS BANK INC., pg. 818, pg. 855
WAYNE SAVINGS BANCSHARES, INC., pg. 819, pg. 1482
WHITNEY HOLDING CORPORATION, pg. 822, pg. 747
WILMINGTON SAVINGS FUND SOCIETY, FEDERAL SAVINGS BANK, pg. 822, pg. 392
WSFS FINANCIAL CORPORATION, pg. 823, pg. 392

6061 - Credit Unions, Federally Chartered

ACE CASH EXPRESS, INC., pg. 710, pg. 1717

6082 - Foreign Trade & International Banking Institutions

ALLY FINANCIAL INC., pg. 711, pg. 878
AMERICAN STUDENT ASSISTANCE, pg. 714, pg. 789
BALCHEM CORPORATION, pg. 830, pg. 1183
BB&T CORPORATION, pg. 723, pg. 1393
CARDINAL BANK N.A., pg. 732, pg. 1790
CB RICHARD ELLIS GROUP, INC., pg. 1085, pg. 127
CIT GROUP INC., pg. 735, pg. 1212
CONSUMER PORTFOLIO SERVICES, INC., pg. 741, pg. 109
COUSINS PROPERTIES INCORPORATED, pg. 1088, pg. 501
CREDIT ACCEPTANCE CORPORATION, pg. 742, pg. 906
DFC GLOBAL CORPORATION, pg. 743, pg. 1515
DORAL FINANCIAL CORPORATION, pg. 744, pg. 1599
EARLYBIRDCAPITAL INC., pg. 745, pg. 1226
EZCORP, INC., pg. 750, pg. 1662
FAIRWAY INDEPENDENT MORTGAGE CORPORATION, pg. 750, pg. 1866
FEDERAL AGRICULTURAL MORTGAGE CORPORATION, pg. 751, pg. 399
FEDERAL HOME LOAN MORTGAGE CORPORATION, pg. 751, pg. 1790
FINOTEC GROUP, INC., pg. 753, pg. 1231
FIRST CASH FINANCIAL SERVICES, INC., pg. 754, pg. 1659
FIRST HORIZON NATIONAL CORPORATION, pg. 755, pg. 1644
FLORIDA HOUSING FINANCE CORPORATION, pg. 758, pg. 469
GENERAL ELECTRIC COMPANY, pg. 1297, pg. 347
GREATER NEW HAVEN ASSOCIATION OF REALTORS, pg. 142, pg. 360
GREENLIGHT FINANCIAL SERVICES, pg. 764, pg. 111
HOLMGREN & ASSOCIATES, pg. 766, pg. 171
HSBC BANK USA, pg. 767, pg. 1241
KILROY REALTY CORPORATION, pg. 1099, pg. 134
M.D.C. HOLDINGS, INC., pg. 1104, pg. 321
MICROFINANCIAL INCORPORATED, pg. 782, pg. 805
PEOPLES TRUST COMPANY, pg. 793, pg. 1912
PROSPECT MORTGAGE, LLC, pg. 796, pg. 278
RABO CAPITAL SERVICES, INC., pg. 797, pg. 1284
REAL INDUSTRY, INC., pg. 1215, pg. 278
ROTHSCHILD NORTH AMERICA INC., pg. 800, pg. 1287
SIMON PROPERTY GROUP, INC., pg. 1112, pg. 690
SLM CORPORATION, pg. 804, pg. 388
UNION BANK, N.A., pg. 813, pg. 230
WELLS FARGO FINANCIAL, INC., pg. 821, pg. 707

6099 - Functions Related to Depository Banking, NEC

ACE CASH EXPRESS, INC., pg. 710, pg. 1717
ACI WORLDWIDE, pg. 710, pg. 1777
ALLY FINANCIAL INC., pg. 711, pg. 878
AMERICAN EXPRESS COMPANY, pg. 712, pg. 1190
AUTHORIZE.NET HOLDINGS, INC., pg. 356, pg. 1751
BB&T CORPORATION, pg. 723, pg. 1393
BOTTOMLINE TECHNOLOGIES INC., pg. 363, pg. 483
BRIEFING.COM, pg. 727, pg. 568
BROADRIDGE FINANCIAL SOLUTIONS INC., pg. 727, pg. 1172
CAMBRIDGE CREDIT COUNSELING CORP., pg. 728, pg. 781
CARDTRONICS, INC., pg. 732, pg. 1703
CLAYTON HOLDINGS, INC., pg. 738, pg. 370
COMDATA CORPORATION, pg. 739, pg. 1627
CONSUMER CREDIT COUNSELING SERVICES, pg. 741, pg. 501
CORELOGIC, INC., pg. 1198, pg. 109
DFC GLOBAL CORPORATION, pg. 743, pg. 1515
DIRECT INSITE CORP., pg. 387, pg. 425
DISCOVER FINANCIAL SERVICES, pg. 744, pg. 653
DORAL FINANCIAL CORPORATION, pg. 744, pg. 1599
DOUGLAS-GUARDIAN SERVICES CORPORATION, pg. 388, pg. 1704
DST SYSTEMS, INC., pg. 388, pg. 982
EDGAR ONLINE, INC., pg. 746, pg. 776
ELECTRONIC TRANSFER, INC., pg. 746, pg. 1843
EMDEON, INC., pg. 747, pg. 1650
ENCORE CAPITAL GROUP, INC., pg. 747, pg. 202
EQUIFAX INC., pg. 748, pg. 504
E*TRADE FINANCIAL CORPORATION, pg. 749, pg. 1230
FAIR ISAAC CORPORATION, pg. 1247, pg. 955
FIDELITY INFORMATION SERVICES, INC., pg. 397, pg. 433
FIRST CASH FINANCIAL SERVICES, INC., pg. 754, pg. 1659
FIRST DATA CORPORATION, pg. 754, pg. 505
FIRST NATIONWIDE LENDING, INC., pg. 756, pg. 466
FISERV, INC., pg. 397, pg. 1855
FLEETCOR TECHNOLOGIES, INC., pg. 758, pg. 537
FRANKLIN RESOURCES, INC., pg. 760, pg. 254
FTI CONSULTING, INC., pg. 760, pg. 478
GENERAL ELECTRIC COMPANY, pg. 1297, pg. 347
GLOBAL PAYMENTS INC., pg. 762, pg. 508
GSC ENTERPRISES, INC., pg. 1021, pg. 1746
HEARTLAND PAYMENT SYSTEMS, INC., pg. 765, pg. 1111
HSBC FINANCE CORPORATION, pg. 767, pg. 632
IDEALAB, INC., pg. 1258, pg. 180
INTERCONTINENTALEXCHANGE, INC., pg. 769, pg. 512
INTERSECTIONS INC., pg. 769, pg. 1777
INVESTMENT SEMINARS, INC., pg. 420, pg. 466
IPAYMENT, INC., pg. 771, pg. 306
ISABELLA BANK CORPORATION, pg. 771, pg. 901
JEFFERIES GROUP, INC., pg. 772, pg. 1246
MARKETAXESS HOLDINGS INC., pg. 778, pg. 1256
MASTERCARD INCORPORATED, pg. 779, pg. 1325
MASTERCARD INTERNATIONAL, INC., pg. 780, pg. 1326
MEDASSETS INC., pg. 1561, pg. 484
MONEYGRAM INTERNATIONAL, INC., pg. 783, pg. 1684
ORBITZ WORLDWIDE, INC., pg. 1918, pg. 586
ORTHOSYNETICS, INC., pg. 791, pg. 1657
PACIFIC & WESTERN CREDIT CORP., pg. 791, pg. 1922
PAYPAL INC., pg. 1274, pg. 248
THE PNC FINANCIAL SERVICES GROUP, INC., pg. 795, pg. 1579
PRUDENTIAL FINANCIAL, INC., pg. 797, pg. 1097
RABO CAPITAL SERVICES, INC., pg. 797, pg. 1284
SEI INVESTMENTS COMPANY, pg. 802, pg. 1558
SENIOR MARKET SALES, INC., pg. 1217, pg. 1018
THE STREET, INC., pg. 1283, pg. 1296
THOMSON ELITE, pg. 484, pg. 72
THOMSON REUTERS - CORPORATE HEADQUARTERS, pg. 1693, pg. 1299
THOMSON REUTERS CORPORATION, pg. 1693, pg. 1944
TOTAL SYSTEM SERVICES, INC., pg. 484, pg. 528
USA FINANCIAL, pg. 815, pg. 864
USA TECHNOLOGIES, INC., pg. 815, pg. 1550
VISA INC., pg. 816, pg. 230
VISA U.S.A., INC., pg. 817, pg. 231
THE WESTERN UNION COMPANY, pg. 822, pg. 327
WRIGHT EXPRESS CORPORATION, pg. 493, pg. 753

6141 - Personal Credit Institutions

1ST FRANKLIN FINANCIAL CORPORATION, pg. 710, pg. 542
ACE CASH EXPRESS, INC., pg. 710, pg. 1717
ADVANCE AMERICA CASH ADVANCE CENTERS, INC., pg. 711, pg. 1622
AGSOUTH FARM CREDIT, pg. 711, pg. 540
ALLY FINANCIAL INC., pg. 711, pg. 878
AMERICAN EXPRESS COMPANY, pg. 712, pg. 1190
AMERICAN NATIONAL BANKSHARES INC., pg. 714, pg. 1779
AMERICAN STUDENT ASSISTANCE, pg. 714, pg. 789
AMEX BANK OF CANADA, pg. 715, pg. 1923
ASSET ACCEPTANCE CAPITAL CORP., pg. 716, pg. 912
ATLANTICUS CORPORATION, pg. 717, pg. 490
BALCHEM CORPORATION, pg. 839, pg. 1183
BANK OF AMERICA CORPORATION, pg. 718, pg. 1362
THE BANK OF NEW YORK MELLON CORPORATION, pg. 720, pg. 1200

First page reference indicates Business Class Edition
Second page reference indicates Geographic Edition

BANNER CORPORATION, pg. 722, pg. 1846
BB&T CORPORATION, pg. 723, pg. 1393
BOTETOURT BANKSHARES, INC., pg. 726, pg. 1777
BRYN MAWR BANK CORPORATION, pg. 728, pg. 1519
CADENCE FINANCIAL CORPORATION, pg. 728, pg. 971
CAPITAL CITY BANK GROUP, INC., pg. 730, pg. 469
CAPITAL ONE FINANCIAL CORPORATION, pg. 730, pg. 1789
CAPITALSOURCE INC., pg. 731, pg. 127
CARDINAL BANK N.A., pg. 732, pg. 1790
CARDINAL FINANCIAL CORP., pg. 732, pg. 1790
CASCADE BANCORP, pg. 732, pg. 1496
CATHAY GENERAL BANCORP, INC., pg. 732, pg. 127
CB RICHARD ELLIS GROUP, INC., pg. 1085, pg. 127
CHASE CARD SERVICES, INC., pg. 734, pg. 215
CHEMUNG FINANCIAL CORPORATION, pg. 734, pg. 1157
CHEVIOT FINANCIAL CORP., pg. 735, pg. 1409
CIT GROUP INC., pg. 735, pg. 1212
CITIGROUP INC., pg. 735, pg. 1212
CITIZENS FIRST CORPORATION, pg. 737, pg. 725
COASTAL BANKING COMPANY, INC., pg. 739, pg. 1612
COLUMBIA BANKING SYSTEM, INC., pg. 739, pg. 1844
COMMUNITY BANCORP, pg. 741, pg. 1766
CONSUMER PORTFOLIO SERVICES, INC., pg. 741, pg. 109
COUSINS PROPERTIES INCORPORATED, pg. 1088, pg. 501
CREDIT ACCEPTANCE CORPORATION, pg. 742, pg. 906
CREDITCARDS.COM, INC., pg. 1237, pg. 1661
CROGHAN BANCSHARES, INC., pg. 742, pg. 1454
CYBERSOURCE CORPORATION, pg. 381, pg. 216
DEERE & COMPANY, pg. 703, pg. 632
DFC GLOBAL CORPORATION, pg. 743, pg. 1515
DISCOVER FINANCIAL SERVICES, pg. 744, pg. 653
DISCOVER STUDENT LOANS, pg. 744, pg. 373
DORAL FINANCIAL CORPORATION, pg. 744, pg. 1599
DRIVETIME AUTOMOTIVE GROUP, INC., pg. 169, pg. 16
EARLYBIRDCAPITAL INC., pg. 745, pg. 1226
EASTERN BANK CORPORATION-SOUTH REGION HEADQUARTERS, pg. 745, pg. 833
EASTERN VIRGINIA BANKSHARES, INC., pg. 746, pg. 1808
EMKAY, INC., pg. 1906, pg. 619
EQUIFAX INC., pg. 748, pg. 504
EZCORP, INC., pg. 750, pg. 1662
FAIRWAY INDEPENDENT MORTGAGE CORPORATION, pg. 750, pg. 1866
FARMERS NATIONAL BANC CORP., pg. 750, pg. 1407
FEDERAL AGRICULTURAL MORTGAGE CORPORATION, pg. 751, pg. 399
FEDERAL HOME LOAN MORTGAGE CORPORATION, pg. 751, pg. 1790
FENTURA FINANCIAL, INC., pg. 752, pg. 886
FIRST CASH FINANCIAL SERVICES, INC., pg. 754, pg. 1659
FIRST COMMUNITY CORPORATION, pg. 754, pg. 1620
FIRST DATA CORPORATION, pg. 754, pg. 505
FIRST HORIZON NATIONAL CORPORATION, pg. 755, pg. 1644
FIRST INVESTORS FINANCIAL SERVICES GROUP, INC., pg. 756, pg. 1706
FLORIDA HOUSING FINANCE CORPORATION, pg. 758, pg. 469
GE CAPITAL, pg. 761, pg. 362
GENERAL ELECTRIC COMPANY, pg. 1297, pg. 347
GERMAN AMERICAN BANCORP, INC., pg. 762, pg. 691
GRAYSON BANKSHARES, INC., pg. 763, pg. 1786
GREATER NEW HAVEN ASSOCIATION OF REALTORS, pg. 142, pg. 360
GREEN DOT CORPORATION, pg. 763, pg. 180
GREENLIGHT FINANCIAL SERVICES, pg. 764, pg. 111
GROUP 1 AUTOMOTIVE, INC., pg. 177, pg. 1706
HEARTLAND PAYMENT SYSTEMS, INC., pg. 765, pg. 1111
HOLMGREN & ASSOCIATES, pg. 766, pg. 171
HSBC FINANCE CORPORATION, pg. 767, pg. 632
THE HUNTINGTON NATIONAL BANK, pg. 767, pg. 1440
JPMORGAN CHASE & CO., pg. 772, pg. 1246
JUNIATA VALLEY FINANCIAL CORP., pg. 773, pg. 1553
KAUFMAN FINANCIAL GROUP, INC., pg. 1205, pg. 886
KILROY REALTY CORPORATION, pg. 1099, pg. 134
KOMATSU AMERICA CORP., pg. 92, pg. 655
MASTERCARD INCORPORATED, pg. 779, pg. 1325
MASTERCARD WORLDWIDE INC., pg. 780, pg. 988
M.D.C. HOLDINGS, INC., pg. 1104, pg. 321
MEDALLION FINANCIAL CORP., pg. 781, pg. 1258
MERCHANTS BANCSHARES, INC., pg. 782, pg. 1768
MICROFINANCIAL INCORPORATED, pg. 782, pg. 805
MIDDLEBURG FINANCIAL CORPORATION, pg. 782, pg. 1795
NATIONAL BANKSHARES, INC., pg. 785, pg. 1776
NBS TECHNOLOGIES INC., pg. 786, pg. 1941
NELNET, INC., pg. 786, pg. 1012
NICHOLAS FINANCIAL, INC., pg. 787, pg. 416
NORTHERN TRUST CORPORATION, pg. 787, pg. 585
NORTHWEST BANCORPORATION INC., pg. 788, pg. 1844
NORWOOD FINANCIAL CORP., pg. 788, pg. 1539
OPUS BANK, pg. 790, pg. 1819
PEOPLES SECURITY BANK & TRUST, pg. 793, pg. 1535
PEOPLES TRUST COMPANY, pg. 793, pg. 1912
PHH CORPORATION, pg. 793, pg. 1090
PROSPECT MORTGAGE, LLC, pg. 796, pg. 278
PSB HOLDINGS, INC., pg. 797, pg. 1898
PULTEGROUP, INC., pg. 1109, pg. 873
QC HOLDINGS, INC., pg. 797, pg. 719
REAL INDUSTRY, INC., pg. 1215, pg. 278
REGIONS FINANCIAL CORPORATION, pg. 798, pg. 4
RENASANT CORPORATION, pg. 799, pg. 972
ROTHSCHILD NORTH AMERICA INC., pg. 800, pg. 1287
ROYAL BANCSHARES OF PENNSYLVANIA, INC., pg. 800, pg. 1555
ROYAL BANK OF CANADA, pg. 800, pg. 1942
SEVERN BANCORP, INC., pg. 803, pg. 754
SIMON PROPERTY GROUP, INC., pg. 1112, pg. 690
SLM CORPORATION, pg. 804, pg. 388
SOUTHERN COMPANY, pg. 1952, pg. 520
SOUTHSIDE BANCSHARES INC., pg. 804, pg. 1748
SUSSEX BANCORP, pg. 807, pg. 1068
TD AUTO FINANCE, pg. 809, pg. 886
TMX FINANCE LLC, pg. 810, pg. 540
UMB FINANCIAL CORPORATION, pg. 812, pg. 987
UNITED COMMUNITY BANKS, INC., pg. 814, pg. 526
UNITY BANCORP, INC., pg. 814, pg. 1052
VISA INC., pg. 816, pg. 230
VISA U.S.A., INC., pg. 817, pg. 231
VIST FINANCIAL CORP., pg. 818, pg. 1596
WEBBANK, pg. 819, pg. 1761
WELLS FARGO & COMPANY, pg. 819, pg. 232
WELLS FARGO FINANCIAL, INC., pg. 821, pg. 707
WORLD ACCEPTANCE CORPORATION, pg. 823, pg. 1619
WYNDHAM VACATION OWNERSHIP, pg. 1119, pg. 457

6159 - Miscellaneous Business Credit Institutions

1ST FRANKLIN FINANCIAL CORPORATION, pg. 710, pg. 542
ACE CASH EXPRESS, INC., pg. 710, pg. 1717
ADVANCE AMERICA CASH ADVANCE CENTERS, INC., pg. 711, pg. 1622
AGSOUTH FARM CREDIT, pg. 711, pg. 540
ALLY FINANCIAL INC., pg. 711, pg. 878
AMERICAN EXPRESS COMPANY, pg. 712, pg. 1190
AMERICAN NATIONAL BANKSHARES INC., pg. 714, pg. 1779
AMERICAN STUDENT ASSISTANCE, pg. 714, pg. 789
AMEX BANK OF CANADA, pg. 715, pg. 1923
ASSET ACCEPTANCE CAPITAL CORP., pg. 716, pg. 912
ATLANTICUS CORPORATION, pg. 717, pg. 490
BALCHEM CORPORATION, pg. 839, pg. 1183
BANK OF AMERICA CORPORATION, pg. 718, pg. 1362
THE BANK OF NEW YORK MELLON CORPORATION, pg. 720, pg. 1200
BANNER CORPORATION, pg. 722, pg. 1846
BB&T CORPORATION, pg. 723, pg. 1393
BOTETOURT BANKSHARES, INC., pg. 726, pg. 1777
BRYN MAWR BANK CORPORATION, pg. 728, pg. 1519
CADENCE FINANCIAL CORPORATION, pg. 728, pg. 971
CAPITAL CITY BANK GROUP, INC., pg. 730, pg. 469
CAPITAL ONE FINANCIAL CORPORATION, pg. 730, pg. 1789
CAPITALSOURCE INC., pg. 731, pg. 127
CARDINAL BANK N.A., pg. 732, pg. 1790
CARDINAL FINANCIAL CORP., pg. 732, pg. 1790
CASCADE BANCORP, pg. 732, pg. 1496
CB RICHARD ELLIS GROUP, INC., pg. 1085, pg. 127
CHASE CARD SERVICES, INC., pg. 734, pg. 215
CHEMUNG FINANCIAL CORPORATION, pg. 734, pg. 1157
CHEVIOT FINANCIAL CORP., pg. 735, pg. 1409
CIT GROUP INC., pg. 735, pg. 1212
CITIGROUP INC., pg. 735, pg. 1212
CITIZENS FIRST CORPORATION, pg. 737, pg. 725
COASTAL BANKING COMPANY, INC., pg. 739, pg. 1612
COLUMBIA BANKING SYSTEM, INC., pg. 739, pg. 1844
COMMUNITY BANCORP, pg. 741, pg. 1766
CONSUMER PORTFOLIO SERVICES, INC., pg. 741, pg. 109
COUSINS PROPERTIES INCORPORATED, pg. 1088, pg. 501
CREDIT ACCEPTANCE CORPORATION, pg. 742, pg. 906
CREDITCARDS.COM, INC., pg. 1237, pg. 1661
CROGHAN BANCSHARES, INC., pg. 742, pg. 1454
DEERE & COMPANY, pg. 703, pg. 632
DFC GLOBAL CORPORATION, pg. 743, pg. 1515
DISCOVER FINANCIAL SERVICES, pg. 744, pg. 653
DISCOVER STUDENT LOANS, pg. 744, pg. 373
DORAL FINANCIAL CORPORATION, pg. 744, pg. 1599
DRIVETIME AUTOMOTIVE GROUP, INC., pg. 169, pg. 16
EARLYBIRDCAPITAL INC., pg. 745, pg. 1226
EASTERN BANK CORPORATION-SOUTH REGION HEADQUARTERS, pg. 745, pg. 833
EASTERN VIRGINIA BANKSHARES, INC., pg. 746, pg. 1808
EMKAY, INC., pg. 1906, pg. 619
EZCORP, INC., pg. 750, pg. 1662
FAIRWAY INDEPENDENT MORTGAGE CORPORATION, pg. 750, pg. 1866
FEDERAL AGRICULTURAL MORTGAGE CORPORATION, pg. 751, pg. 399
FEDERAL HOME LOAN MORTGAGE CORPORATION, pg. 751, pg. 1790
FENTURA FINANCIAL, INC., pg. 752, pg. 886
FINOTEC GROUP, INC., pg. 753, pg. 1231
FIRST CASH FINANCIAL SERVICES, INC., pg. 754, pg. 1659
FIRST COMMUNITY CORPORATION, pg. 754, pg. 1620
FIRST DATA CORPORATION, pg. 754, pg. 505
FIRST HORIZON NATIONAL CORPORATION, pg. 755, pg. 1644
FIRST INVESTORS FINANCIAL SERVICES GROUP, INC., pg. 756, pg. 1706
FLORIDA HOUSING FINANCE CORPORATION, pg. 758, pg. 469
GE CAPITAL, pg. 761, pg. 362
GENERAL ELECTRIC COMPANY, pg. 1297, pg. 347
GRAYSON BANKSHARES, INC., pg. 763, pg. 1786
GREATER NEW HAVEN ASSOCIATION OF REALTORS, pg. 142, pg. 360
GREEN DOT CORPORATION, pg. 763, pg. 180
GREENLIGHT FINANCIAL SERVICES, pg. 764, pg. 111
GROUP 1 AUTOMOTIVE, INC., pg. 177, pg. 1706
HEARTLAND PAYMENT SYSTEMS, INC., pg. 765, pg. 1111
HOLMGREN & ASSOCIATES, pg. 766, pg. 171
HSBC BANK USA, pg. 767, pg. 1241
HSBC FINANCE CORPORATION, pg. 767, pg. 632
THE HUNTINGTON NATIONAL BANK, pg. 767, pg. 1440
JPMORGAN CHASE & CO., pg. 772, pg. 1246
JUNIATA VALLEY FINANCIAL CORP., pg. 773, pg. 1553
KAUFMAN FINANCIAL GROUP, INC., pg. 1205, pg. 886
KILROY REALTY CORPORATION, pg. 1099, pg. 134
KOMATSU AMERICA CORP., pg. 92, pg. 655
MASTERCARD INCORPORATED, pg. 779, pg. 1325
MASTERCARD WORLDWIDE INC., pg. 780, pg. 988
M.D.C. HOLDINGS, INC., pg. 1104, pg. 321
MEDALLION FINANCIAL CORP., pg. 781, pg. 1258
MICROFINANCIAL INCORPORATED, pg. 782, pg. 805
MIDDLEBURG FINANCIAL CORPORATION, pg. 782, pg. 1795
NATIONAL BANKSHARES, INC., pg. 785, pg. 1776
NBS TECHNOLOGIES INC., pg. 786, pg. 1941
NELNET, INC., pg. 786, pg. 1012
NICHOLAS FINANCIAL, INC., pg. 787, pg. 416
NORTHERN TRUST CORPORATION, pg. 787, pg. 585
NORTHWEST BANCORPORATION INC., pg. 788, pg. 1844
NORWOOD FINANCIAL CORP., pg. 788, pg. 1539
PEOPLES SECURITY BANK & TRUST, pg. 793, pg. 1535
PEOPLES TRUST COMPANY, pg. 793, pg. 1912
PHH CORPORATION, pg. 793, pg. 1090
PROSPECT MORTGAGE, LLC, pg. 796, pg. 278
PSB HOLDINGS, INC., pg. 797, pg. 1898
PULTEGROUP, INC., pg. 1109, pg. 873
QC HOLDINGS, INC., pg. 797, pg. 719
RABO CAPITAL SERVICES, INC., pg. 797, pg. 1284
REAL INDUSTRY, INC., pg. 1215, pg. 278
REGIONS FINANCIAL CORPORATION, pg. 798, pg. 4

6163 - Loan Brokers

6211 - Security Brokers, Dealers & Flotation Companies

First page reference indicates Business Class Edition
Second page reference indicates Geographic Edition

WHITNEY HOLDING CORPORATION, pg. 822, pg. 747
WILLIAM BLAIR & COMPANY LLC, pg. 822, pg. 596
THE ZIEGLER COMPANIES, INC., pg. 824, pg. 597

6221 - Commodity Contracts Brokers & Dealers

ACE CASH EXPRESS, INC., pg. 710, pg. 1717
ACI WORLDWIDE, pg. 710, pg. 1777
AKANA, pg. 346, pg. 125
ALLY FINANCIAL INC., pg. 711, pg. 878
AMERICAN EXPRESS COMPANY, pg. 712, pg. 1190
AUTHORIZE.NET HOLDINGS, INC., pg. 356, pg. 1751
BB&T CORPORATION, pg. 723, pg. 1393
BOTTOMLINE TECHNOLOGIES INC., pg. 363, pg. 483
BRIEFING.COM, pg. 727, pg. 568
CAMBRIDGE CREDIT COUNSELING CORP., pg. 728, pg. 781
CARDTRONICS, INC., pg. 732, pg. 1703
CLAYTON HOLDINGS, INC., pg. 738, pg. 370
CME GROUP, INC., pg. 738, pg. 571
COMDATA CORPORATION, pg. 739, pg. 1627
CONSUMER CREDIT COUNSELING SERVICES, pg. 741, pg. 501
CUNA MUTUAL INSURANCE SOCIETY, pg. 743, pg. 1865
DFC GLOBAL CORPORATION, pg. 743, pg. 1515
DIRECT INSITE CORP., pg. 387, pg. 425
DISCOVER FINANCIAL SERVICES, pg. 744, pg. 653
DOMINICK & DOMINICK, LLC, pg. 744, pg. 1225
DORAL FINANCIAL CORPORATION, pg. 744, pg. 1599
THE DREYFUS CORPORATION, pg. 745, pg. 1226
DST SYSTEMS, INC., pg. 388, pg. 982
ELECTRONIC TRANSFER, INC., pg. 746, pg. 1843
EMDEON, INC., pg. 747, pg. 1650
ENCORE CAPITAL GROUP, INC., pg. 747, pg. 202
E*TRADE FINANCIAL CORPORATION, pg. 749, pg. 1230
FAIR ISAAC CORPORATION, pg. 1247, pg. 955
FCSTONE GROUP, INC., pg. 751, pg. 982
FIDELITY INFORMATION SERVICES, INC., pg. 397, pg. 433
FINOTEC GROUP, INC., pg. 753, pg. 1231
FIRST CASH FINANCIAL SERVICES, INC., pg. 754, pg. 1659
FIRST DATA CORPORATION, pg. 754, pg. 505
FIRST NATIONWIDE LENDING, INC., pg. 756, pg. 466
FISERV, INC., pg. 397, pg. 1855
FLEETCOR TECHNOLOGIES, INC., pg. 758, pg. 537
FRANKLIN RESOURCES, INC., pg. 760, pg. 254
GENERAL ELECTRIC COMPANY, pg. 1297, pg. 347
GLOBAL PAYMENTS INC., pg. 762, pg. 508
GSC ENTERPRISES, INC., pg. 1021, pg. 1746
HEARTLAND PAYMENT SYSTEMS, INC., pg. 765, pg. 1111
HSBC BANK USA, pg. 767, pg. 1241
HSBC FINANCE CORPORATION, pg. 767, pg. 632
INTERACTIVE DATA CORPORATION, pg. 769, pg. 785
INTERCONTINENTALEXCHANGE, INC., pg. 769, pg. 512
INTERSECTIONS INC., pg. 769, pg. 1777
INVESTORS CAPITAL CORPORATION, pg. 771, pg. 830
IPAYMENT, INC., pg. 771, pg. 306
JAMS, THE RESOLUTION EXPERTS, pg. 423, pg. 111
JEFFERIES GROUP, INC., pg. 772, pg. 1246
JPMORGAN CHASE - MIDWEST REGIONAL OFFICE, pg. 773, pg. 579
KOCH INDUSTRIES, INC., pg. 1463, pg. 724
MARKETAXESS HOLDINGS INC., pg. 778, pg. 1256
MASTERCARD INCORPORATED, pg. 779, pg. 1325
MASTERCARD INTERNATIONAL, INC., pg. 780, pg. 1326
MEDASSETS INC., pg. 1561, pg. 484
MONEYGRAM INTERNATIONAL, INC., pg. 783, pg. 1684
NRG ENERGY, INC., pg. 1948, pg. 1712
OPTIONSXPRESS HOLDINGS, INC., pg. 790, pg. 586
ORBITZ WORLDWIDE, INC., pg. 1918, pg. 586
PACIFIC & WESTERN CREDIT CORP., pg. 791, pg. 1922
PAYPAL INC., pg. 1274, pg. 248
THE PNC FINANCIAL SERVICES GROUP, INC., pg. 795, pg. 1579
PRUDENTIAL FINANCIAL, INC., pg. 797, pg. 1097
RABO CAPITAL SERVICES, INC., pg. 797, pg. 1284
SEI INVESTMENTS COMPANY, pg. 802, pg. 1558
SENIOR MARKET SALES, INC., pg. 1217, pg. 1018
SIEBERT FINANCIAL CORP., pg. 803, pg. 1291
T. ROWE PRICE GROUP INC., pg. 808, pg. 759
TOTAL SYSTEM SERVICES, INC., pg. 484, pg. 528
UBS FINANCIAL SERVICES INC., pg. 812, pg. 1306
UNITED STATES COAST GUARD, pg. 1008, pg. 406
USA FINANCIAL, pg. 815, pg. 864
USA TECHNOLOGIES, INC., pg. 815, pg. 1550
VISA INC., pg. 816, pg. 230
VISA U.S.A., INC., pg. 817, pg. 231
WADDELL & REED FINANCIAL, INC., pg. 818, pg. 721
WESTERN FINANCIAL GROUP, INC., pg. 821, pg. 1906
THE WESTERN UNION COMPANY, pg. 822, pg. 327
WRIGHT EXPRESS CORPORATION, pg. 493, pg. 753

6231 - Security & Commodity Exchanges

CBOE HOLDINGS, INC., pg. 733, pg. 569
CME GROUP INC., pg. 738, pg. 571
CME GROUP, INC., pg. 738, pg. 571
GFI GROUP INC., pg. 762, pg. 1234
INTERACTIVE DATA PRICING & REFERENCE DATA, INC., pg. 769, pg. 785
INTERCONTINENTALEXCHANGE, INC., pg. 769, pg. 512
THE NASDAQ OMX GROUP, INC., pg. 785, pg. 1263
NYSE EURONEXT, pg. 789, pg. 1274
TMX GROUP, INC., pg. 810, pg. 1945
THE TORONTO STOCK EXCHANGE INC., pg. 811, pg. 1946

6282 - Investment Advice

AMERIPRISE FINANCIAL, INC., pg. 715, pg. 930
AMERITAS INVESTMENT CORP., pg. 1192, pg. 1410
AMERITAS LIFE INSURANCE CORP., pg. 1192, pg. 1011
ASSET MARKETING SYSTEMS INSURANCE SERVICES, LLC, pg. 1193, pg. 200
ATTO & ASSOCIATES INSURANCE BROKERS, INC., pg. 1194, pg. 1924
AXA EQUITABLE LIFE INSURANCE COMPANY, pg. 1194, pg. 1199
AZOY TAX, pg. 717, pg. 423
BANK OF AMERICA CORPORATION, pg. 718, pg. 1362
BANK OF AMERICA GLOBAL WEALTH & INVESTMENT MANAGEMENT, pg. 720, pg. 789
THE BANK OF NOVA SCOTIA, pg. 721, pg. 1935
BANKRATE, INC., pg. 1231, pg. 451
BAR HARBOR BANK & TRUST, pg. 722, pg. 749
BARTLETT & CO., pg. 722, pg. 1410
BB&T CORPORATION, pg. 723, pg. 1393
BLACKROCK, INC., pg. 724, pg. 1203
THE BOSTON COMPANY ASSET MANAGEMENT, LLC, pg. 726, pg. 790
CAISSE DE DEPOT ET PLACEMENT DU QUEBEC, pg. 728, pg. 1953
CALAMOS ASSET MANAGEMENT INC, pg. 728, pg. 635
CAPITAL FINANCIAL HOLDINGS, INC., pg. 730, pg. 1398
CAPITALONE INVESTING, pg. 731, pg. 1834
CIGNA CORPORATION, pg. 1197, pg. 338
CIT GROUP INC., pg. 735, pg. 1212
CONMED HEALTHCARE MANAGEMENT, INC., pg. 1518, pg. 772
COUNSEL CORPORATION, pg. 742, pg. 1937
CREDIT SUISSE SECURITIES (USA) LLC, pg. 742, pg. 1220
CREDITCARDS.COM, INC., pg. 1237, pg. 1661
CUNA MUTUAL INSURANCE SOCIETY, pg. 743, pg. 1865
DEALERTRACK HOLDINGS, INC., pg. 743, pg. 1172
DISCOVER FINANCIAL SERVICES, pg. 744, pg. 653
THE DREYFUS CORPORATION, pg. 745, pg. 1226
DUFF & PHELPS CORPORATION, pg. 745, pg. 1226
EATON VANCE CORP., pg. 746, pg. 794
EDELMAN FINANCIAL SERVICES LLC, pg. 746, pg. 1705
EDR TRUST, pg. 1090, pg. 1642
EMERGENT CAPITAL, INC., pg. 747, pg. 411
EVERI HOLDINGS INC., pg. 749, pg. 1023
FACTSET RESEARCH SYSTEMS INC., pg. 1247, pg. 381
FEDERAL FARM CREDIT BANKS FUNDING CORPORATION, pg. 751, pg. 1075
FEDERATED INVESTORS, INC., pg. 752, pg. 1575
FINANCIAL BROKERAGE INC., pg. 1200, pg. 1015
FINANCIAL ENGINES, INC., pg. 753, pg. 285
FINANCIAL INDEPENDENCE GROUP INC., pg. 1200, pg. 1370
FINOTEC GROUP, INC., pg. 753, pg. 1231
FIRST BUSEY CORPORATION, pg. 754, pg. 562
FIRST INVESTORS FINANCIAL SERVICES GROUP, INC., pg. 756, pg. 1706
FIRST NIAGARA BANK, pg. 756, pg. 1174
FIRST NIAGARA FINANCIAL GROUP, INC., pg. 757, pg. 1148
FLORIDA POWER & LIGHT COMPANY, pg. 1943, pg. 435
FMR LLC (FIDELITY INVESTMENTS), pg. 759, pg. 794
FORBES, INC., pg. 1641, pg. 1232
FRANKLIN RESOURCES, INC., pg. 760, pg. 254
FULTON FINANCIAL CORPORATION, pg. 760, pg. 1546
GAIN CAPITAL HOLDINGS, INC., pg. 760, pg. 1043
GAMCO INVESTORS, INC., pg. 761, pg. 1339
GENWORTH FINANCIAL, INC., pg. 761, pg. 1802
GILMAN CIOCIA, INC., pg. 762, pg. 1324
THE GLENMEDE TRUST COMPANY, pg. 762, pg. 1566
GLOBAL FRANCHISE MANAGEMENT LLC, pg. 1771, pg. 537
THE GOLDMAN SACHS GROUP, INC., pg. 762, pg. 1236
THE GUARDIAN LIFE INSURANCE COMPANY OF AMERICA, pg. 1202, pg. 1237
GUIDEONE INSURANCE COMPANY, pg. 1202, pg. 713
THE HACKETT GROUP, INC., pg. 1255, pg. 443
THE HARTFORD FINANCIAL SERVICES GROUP, INC., pg. 1202, pg. 352
H.D. VEST, INC., pg. 765, pg. 1720
HSB GROUP, INC., pg. 1204, pg. 352
IHS HEROLD, INC., pg. 768, pg. 362
INO.COM, pg. 1259, pg. 777
INVESCO LTD., pg. 771, pg. 513
INVESTORS BUSINESS DAILY, INC., pg. 1653, pg. 133
INVESTORS CAPITAL CORPORATION, pg. 771, pg. 830
JANUS CAPITAL GROUP, INC., pg. 772, pg. 320
JEFFERIES GROUP, INC., pg. 772, pg. 1246
J.H. BAXTER & COMPANY, pg. 89, pg. 255
JPMORGAN CHASE - MIDWEST REGIONAL OFFICE, pg. 773, pg. 579
KENNEDY-WILSON, INC., pg. 1099, pg. 46
KEYCORP, pg. 774, pg. 1432
KKR & CO. L.P., pg. 774, pg. 1249
LEGG MASON, INC., pg. 775, pg. 758
LINCOLN NATIONAL CORPORATION, pg. 776, pg. 1567
LOOMIS, SAYLES & COMPANY, L.P., pg. 777, pg. 798
M FINANCIAL HOLDINGS INC., pg. 1207, pg. 1504
MASSACHUSETTS MUTUAL LIFE INSURANCE COMPANY, pg. 1207, pg. 845
MATRIXX INITIATIVES, INC., pg. 1559, pg. 23
MCG CAPITAL CORPORATION, pg. 781, pg. 1774
MEDALLION FINANCIAL CORP., pg. 781, pg. 1258
MILLENNIUM MARKETING GROUP, LLC, pg. 1209, pg. 1016
THE MONEY TREE INC., pg. 783, pg. 526
MORGAN STANLEY, pg. 783, pg. 1261
MORGAN STANLEY SMITH BARNEY LLC, pg. 784, pg. 1262
MORLEY FINANCIAL SERVICES, pg. 784, pg. 1504
MORNINGSTAR, INC., pg. 784, pg. 583
THE MOTLEY FOOL, INC., pg. 784, pg. 1771
MUTUAL OF AMERICA LIFE INSURANCE COMPANY, pg. 1210, pg. 1263
NATIONWIDE MUTUAL INSURANCE COMPANY, pg. 1210, pg. 1442
NOMURA SECURITIES INTERNATIONAL, INC., pg. 787, pg. 1273
NORTHERN TRUST CORPORATION, pg. 787, pg. 585
OCEANFIRST BANK, pg. 789, pg. 1125
OPPENHEIMERFUNDS, INC., pg. 790, pg. 1274
PACIFIC INVESTMENT MANAGEMENT COMPANY LLC, pg. 791, pg. 165
PACIFIC LIFE INSURANCE COMPANY, pg. 1213, pg. 166
PARKLAND FUEL CORPORATION, pg. 983, pg. 1906
PRIMERICA FINANCIAL SERVICES, INC., pg. 795, pg. 531
PRINCETON FINANCIAL SYSTEMS, INC., pg. 795, pg. 1112
PRUDENTIAL FINANCIAL, INC., pg. 797, pg. 1097
PUTNAM INVESTMENTS, LLC, pg. 797, pg. 800
RABO CAPITAL SERVICES, INC., pg. 797, pg. 1284
RAYMOND JAMES FINANCIAL, INC., pg. 798, pg. 464
REPUBLIC FIRST BANCORP, INC., pg. 799, pg. 1570
ROTHSCHILD INC., pg. 799, pg. 1287
ROYAL BANK OF CANADA, pg. 800, pg. 1942
RUSSELL INVESTMENT GROUP, pg. 800, pg. 1845
SAFEGUARD SCIENTIFICS, INC., pg. 464, pg. 1592
SCOTTRADE, INC., pg. 802, pg. 1003
SECURITY NATIONAL FINANCIAL CORPORATION, pg. 802, pg. 1760
SENIOR MARKET SALES, INC., pg. 1217, pg. 1018
SOUTHWEST SECURITIES, INC., pg. 804, pg. 47
STANDARD & POOR'S RATINGS SERVICES, pg. 805, pg. 1296

STATE STREET CORPORATION, *pg.* 805, *pg.* 801
STEN CORPORATION, *pg.* 1597, *pg.* 950
SVB FINANCIAL GROUP, *pg.* 808, *pg.* 270
SWISS AMERICA TRADING CORPORATION, *pg.* 808, *pg.* 20
T. ROWE PRICE GROUP INC., *pg.* 808, *pg.* 759
TEACHERS INSURANCE & ANNUITY ASSOCIATION - COLLEGE RETIREMENT EQUITIES FUND, *pg.* 1219, *pg.* 1297
TITANIUM ASSET MANAGEMENT CORP., *pg.* 810, *pg.* 1881
TRACK DATA CORPORATION, *pg.* 1284, *pg.* 1147
TRAVELERS INSURANCE, *pg.* 1220, *pg.* 963
UMB FINANCIAL CORPORATION, *pg.* 812, *pg.* 987
UPROMISE, INC., *pg.* 815, *pg.* 837
U.S. BANCORP, *pg.* 815, *pg.* 945
U.S. GLOBAL INVESTORS, INC., *pg.* 815, *pg.* 1743
USI HOLDINGS CORPORATION, *pg.* 1222, *pg.* 1144
VALUE LINE, INC., *pg.* 1699, *pg.* 1308
VULCAN PRODUCTIONS INC., *pg.* 317, *pg.* 1842
WADDELL & REED FINANCIAL, INC., *pg.* 818, *pg.* 721
WEBBANK, *pg.* 819, *pg.* 1761
WEBMD HEALTH SERVICES GROUP, *pg.* 1609, *pg.* 1508
WEISS RESEARCH, *pg.* 819, *pg.* 436
WELLS FARGO ADVISORS, LLC, *pg.* 819, *pg.* 1005
W.P. CAREY & CO., LLC, *pg.* 823, *pg.* 1315
XOOM CORPORATION, *pg.* 1289, *pg.* 234
ZENITH MARKETING GROUP, INC., *pg.* 1224, *pg.* 1071
THE ZIEGLER COMPANIES, INC., *pg.* 824, *pg.* 597

6289 - Services Allied With Exchange of Securities or Commodities, NEC

ACACIA RESEARCH CORPORATION, *pg.* 1398, *pg.* 165
ACORN ENERGY, INC., *pg.* 341, *pg.* 389
AMERICAN CENTURY INVESTMENTS, *pg.* 711, *pg.* 980
AMERICAN SECURITIES LLC, *pg.* 714, *pg.* 1193
AMERIPRISE FINANCIAL, INC., *pg.* 715, *pg.* 930
ARES CAPITAL- WASHINGTON, DC OFFICE, *pg.* 716, *pg.* 395
ARLINGTON ASSET INVESTMENT CORP., *pg.* 716, *pg.* 1772
ATLAS HOLDINGS LLC, *pg.* 1452, *pg.* 349
AXA EQUITABLE LIFE INSURANCE COMPANY, *pg.* 1194, *pg.* 1199
AXEL JOHNSON INC., *pg.* 717, *pg.* 1199
BANCORPSOUTH, INC., *pg.* 717, *pg.* 971
BANK OF AMERICA CORPORATION, *pg.* 718, *pg.* 1362
BANK OF AMERICA GLOBAL WEALTH & INVESTMENT MANAGEMENT, *pg.* 720, *pg.* 789
BANK OF HAWAII CORPORATION, *pg.* 720, *pg.* 543
THE BANK OF NOVA SCOTIA, *pg.* 721, *pg.* 1935
BARTLETT & CO., *pg.* 722, *pg.* 1410
BB&T CORPORATION, *pg.* 723, *pg.* 1393
BBVA COMPASS BANK, *pg.* 723, *pg.* 2
BERKSHIRE HATHAWAY INC., *pg.* 1195, *pg.* 1013
BFC FINANCIAL CORPORATION, *pg.* 724, *pg.* 423
BLACKROCK, INC., *pg.* 724, *pg.* 1203
BUSINESS DEVELOPMENT BANK OF CANADA, *pg.* 72, *pg.* 1953
CAISSE DE DEPOT ET PLACEMENT DU QUEBEC, *pg.* 728, *pg.* 1953
CALAMOS ASSET MANAGEMENT INC, *pg.* 728, *pg.* 635
CALIFORNIA FIRST NATIONAL BANCORP, *pg.* 728, *pg.* 109
CAMBRIDGE INFORMATION GROUP, INC., *pg.* 1625, *pg.* 761
CANADIAN WESTERN BANK, *pg.* 729, *pg.* 1906
CAPITAL FINANCIAL HOLDINGS, INC., *pg.* 730, *pg.* 1398
CAPITAL Z, *pg.* 731, *pg.* 1209
CAPITALONE INVESTING, *pg.* 731, *pg.* 1834
CAPITALSOURCE INC., *pg.* 731, *pg.* 127
CARGILL, INC., *pg.* 845, *pg.* 965
CHARLES SCHWAB & COMPANY, INC., *pg.* 734, *pg.* 215
CIGNA CORPORATION, *pg.* 1197, *pg.* 338
CIT GROUP INC., *pg.* 735, *pg.* 1212
CITIZENS FIRST CORPORATION, *pg.* 737, *pg.* 725
CITIZENS INC., *pg.* 1197, *pg.* 1661
COMERICA INCORPORATED, *pg.* 740, *pg.* 1677
COMMUNITY BANCORP, *pg.* 741, *pg.* 1766
COMMUNITY BANK, N.A., *pg.* 741, *pg.* 1155
COMPASS GROUP DIVERSIFIED HOLDINGS LLC, *pg.* 741, *pg.* 383
CORE MEDIA GROUP, *pg.* 1765, *pg.* 1218
COWEN GROUP, INC., *pg.* 742, *pg.* 1219
CREDIT SUISSE SECURITIES (USA) LLC, *pg.* 742, *pg.* 1220
CULLEN/FROST BANKERS, INC., *pg.* 742, *pg.* 1740
CUNA MUTUAL INSURANCE SOCIETY, *pg.* 743, *pg.* 1865
DOLLAR FINANCIAL GROUP INC., *pg.* 744, *pg.* 1515
DOMINICK & DOMINICK, LLC, *pg.* 744, *pg.* 1225
DORAL FINANCIAL CORPORATION, *pg.* 744, *pg.* 1599
THE DREYFUS CORPORATION, *pg.* 745, *pg.* 1226
DUFF & PHELPS CORPORATION, *pg.* 745, *pg.* 1226
EDELMAN FINANCIAL SERVICES LLC, *pg.* 746, *pg.* 1705
EDWARD D. JONES & CO., LP, *pg.* 746, *pg.* 995
EGPI FIRECREEK, INC., *pg.* 976, *pg.* 21
ENVESTNET, INC., *pg.* 748, *pg.* 573
E*TRADE FINANCIAL CORPORATION, *pg.* 749, *pg.* 1230
FEDERATED INVESTORS, INC., *pg.* 752, *pg.* 1575
FINOTEC GROUP, INC., *pg.* 753, *pg.* 1231
FIRST BUSEY CORPORATION, *pg.* 754, *pg.* 562
FIRST CASH FINANCIAL SERVICES, INC., *pg.* 754, *pg.* 1659
FIRST FINANCIAL BANKSHARES, INC., *pg.* 755, *pg.* 1657
FIRST MIDWEST BANCORP INC., *pg.* 756, *pg.* 620
FIRST NIAGARA BANK, *pg.* 756, *pg.* 1174
FIRST NIAGARA FINANCIAL GROUP, INC., *pg.* 757, *pg.* 1148
FIRST SURGICAL PARTNERS INC., *pg.* 1531, *pg.* 1668
FMR LLC (FIDELITY INVESTMENTS), *pg.* 759, *pg.* 794
FNBH BANCORP, INC., *pg.* 759, *pg.* 893
FONDS DE SOLIDARITE FTQ, *pg.* 759, *pg.* 1955
FORSTMANN LITTLE & CO., *pg.* 759, *pg.* 1232
FORUM NATIONAL INVESTMENTS LTD., *pg.* 1200, *pg.* 1908
FRANKLIN RESOURCES, INC., *pg.* 760, *pg.* 254
GAIN CAPITAL HOLDINGS, INC., *pg.* 760, *pg.* 1043
GAMCO INVESTORS, INC., *pg.* 761, *pg.* 1339
GE CAPITAL AVIATION SERVICES, *pg.* 228, *pg.* 362
GENERAL FINANCE CORPORATION, *pg.* 761, *pg.* 180
GENWORTH FINANCIAL, INC., *pg.* 761, *pg.* 1802
GFI GROUP INC., *pg.* 762, *pg.* 1234
THE GOLDMAN SACHS GROUP, INC., *pg.* 762, *pg.* 1236
H.D. VEST, INC., *pg.* 765, *pg.* 1720
HFF, INC., *pg.* 766, *pg.* 1576
HUNTINGTON BANCSHARES INCORPORATED, *pg.* 767, *pg.* 1440
THE HUNTINGTON NATIONAL BANK, *pg.* 767, *pg.* 1440
ICAHN ENTERPRISES L.P., *pg.* 1097, *pg.* 1243
IDEALAB, INC., *pg.* 1258, *pg.* 180
INFINITY AUGMENTED REALITY, INC., *pg.* 768, *pg.* 1243
INTERACTIVE DATA CORPORATION, *pg.* 769, *pg.* 785
INTERCONTINENTALEXCHANGE, INC., *pg.* 769, *pg.* 512
INVESCO LTD., *pg.* 771, *pg.* 513
INVESTORS CAPITAL CORPORATION, *pg.* 771, *pg.* 830
JAGUAR FINANCIAL INC., *pg.* 1351, *pg.* 1939
JANNEY MONTGOMERY SCOTT LLC, *pg.* 772, *pg.* 1566
JANUS CAPITAL GROUP, INC., *pg.* 772, *pg.* 320
JEFFERIES GROUP, INC., *pg.* 772, *pg.* 1246
JMB REALTY CORPORATION, *pg.* 1099, *pg.* 579
JPMORGAN CHASE & CO., *pg.* 772, *pg.* 1246
JPMORGAN CHASE - MIDWEST REGIONAL OFFICE, *pg.* 773, *pg.* 579
KEYCORP, *pg.* 774, *pg.* 1432
KIRTLAND CAPITAL PARTNERS, *pg.* 774, *pg.* 1405
KKR & CO. L.P., *pg.* 774, *pg.* 1249
KKR FINANCIAL HOLDINGS LLC, *pg.* 774, *pg.* 220
KODIAK VENTURE PARTNERS, L.P., *pg.* 774, *pg.* 856
KOPPERS HOLDINGS INC., *pg.* 1170, *pg.* 1577
LAZARD FRERES & CO., LLC, *pg.* 775, *pg.* 1250
LEGG MASON, INC., *pg.* 775, *pg.* 758
LEUCADIA NATIONAL CORPORATION, *pg.* 775, *pg.* 1251
LINCOLN NATIONAL CORPORATION, *pg.* 776, *pg.* 1567
LIQUIDNET HOLDINGS, INC., *pg.* 776, *pg.* 1251
LONG POINT CAPITAL LLC, *pg.* 776, *pg.* 1252
LOOMIS, SAYLES & COMPANY, L.P., *pg.* 777, *pg.* 798
LPL FINANCIAL CORPORATION, *pg.* 777, *pg.* 798
M&T BANK CORPORATION, *pg.* 777, *pg.* 1149
MANULIFE FINANCIAL CORPORATION, *pg.* 778, *pg.* 1939
MARKETAXESS HOLDINGS INC., *pg.* 778, *pg.* 1256
MARSH & MCLENNAN COMPANIES INC., *pg.* 1207, *pg.* 1256
MCCOMBS ENTERPRISES, *pg.* 781, *pg.* 1741
MCG CAPITAL CORPORATION, *pg.* 781, *pg.* 1774
M.D.C. HOLDINGS, INC., *pg.* 1104, *pg.* 321
MEDALLION FINANCIAL CORP., *pg.* 781, *pg.* 1258
MERRIMAN HOLDINGS INC., *pg.* 782, *pg.* 223
MONARCH CASINO & RESORT, INC., *pg.* 564, *pg.* 1031
THE MONEY TREE INC., *pg.* 783, *pg.* 526
MONEY.NET, INC., *pg.* 1268, *pg.* 1261
MORGAN KEEGAN, INC., *pg.* 783, *pg.* 1645
MORGAN STANLEY, *pg.* 783, *pg.* 1261
MORGAN STANLEY SMITH BARNEY LLC, *pg.* 784, *pg.* 1262
MORNINGSTAR, INC., *pg.* 784, *pg.* 583
MSCI INC., *pg.* 785, *pg.* 1262
THE NASDAQ OMX GROUP, INC., *pg.* 785, *pg.* 1263
NATIONWIDE MUTUAL INSURANCE COMPANY, *pg.* 1210, *pg.* 1442
NETWORK 1 FINANCIAL GROUP, INC., *pg.* 1465, *pg.* 1114
NOMURA SECURITIES INTERNATIONAL, INC., *pg.* 787, *pg.* 1273
THE NORTHWESTERN MUTUAL LIFE INSURANCE COMPANY, *pg.* 1212, *pg.* 1879
NUVEEN INVESTMENTS, INC., *pg.* 788, *pg.* 586
OCEANFIRST BANK, *pg.* 789, *pg.* 1125
OHIO FARMERS INSURANCE COMPANY, *pg.* 1213, *pg.* 1480
OLD NATIONAL BANCORP, *pg.* 789, *pg.* 679
OPPENHEIMERFUNDS, INC., *pg.* 790, *pg.* 1274
OPTIONSXPRESS HOLDINGS, INC., *pg.* 790, *pg.* 586
OTC MARKETS GROUP INC., *pg.* 791, *pg.* 1275
PAULSON CAPITAL CORP., *pg.* 792, *pg.* 1505
PEOPLES BANCORP INC., *pg.* 793, *pg.* 1458
PEOPLE'S UNITED BANK, *pg.* 793, *pg.* 340
PHH CORPORATION, *pg.* 793, *pg.* 1090
PINNACLE FINANCIAL PARTNERS, INC., *pg.* 794, *pg.* 1653
PIPER JAFFRAY COMPANIES, *pg.* 794, *pg.* 941
THE PNC FINANCIAL SERVICES GROUP, INC., *pg.* 795, *pg.* 1579
PRIMERICA FINANCIAL SERVICES, INC., *pg.* 795, *pg.* 531
PRINCIPAL FINANCIAL GROUP, INC., *pg.* 796, *pg.* 706
PRUDENTIAL FINANCIAL, INC., *pg.* 797, *pg.* 1097
RABO CAPITAL SERVICES, INC., *pg.* 797, *pg.* 1284
RAYMOND JAMES FINANCIAL, INC., *pg.* 798, *pg.* 464
RBC CAPITAL MARKETS, *pg.* 798, *pg.* 225
THE RESERVE GROUP, *pg.* 799, *pg.* 1402
ROTHSCHILD INC., *pg.* 799, *pg.* 1287
ROTHSCHILD NORTH AMERICA INC., *pg.* 800, *pg.* 1287
ROYAL BANK OF CANADA, *pg.* 800, *pg.* 1942
ROYAL GOLD, INC., *pg.* 11, *pg.* 323
SANDY SPRING BANCORP, INC., *pg.* 801, *pg.* 774
SANDY SPRING BANK, *pg.* 801, *pg.* 774
SANTANDER HOLDINGS USA, INC., *pg.* 801, *pg.* 800
SCOTTRADE, INC., *pg.* 802, *pg.* 1003
SEAWAY VALLEY CAPITAL CORPORATION, *pg.* 802, *pg.* 1162
THE SHIDLER GROUP, *pg.* 1112, *pg.* 545
SIEBERT FINANCIAL CORP., *pg.* 803, *pg.* 1291
SOUTHWEST SECURITIES, INC., *pg.* 804, *pg.* 47
SPROTT RESOURCE LENDING CORP., *pg.* 805, *pg.* 1912
SUN LIFE ASSURANCE COMPANY OF CANADA, *pg.* 806, *pg.* 1944
SUNSTONE HOTEL INVESTORS, INC., *pg.* 1116, *pg.* 41
SWORDFISH FINANCIAL, INC., *pg.* 1430, *pg.* 1737
TD AMERITRADE HOLDING CORPORATION, *pg.* 808, *pg.* 1018
THOMAS WEISEL PARTNERS LLC, *pg.* 810, *pg.* 228
TIDELANDS BANCSHARES, INC., *pg.* 810, *pg.* 1620
TRACK DATA CORPORATION, *pg.* 1284, *pg.* 1147
TRADESTATION GROUP, INC., *pg.* 811, *pg.* 459
TRANSUNION CORP., *pg.* 811, *pg.* 591
TRUSTMARK CORPORATION, *pg.* 812, *pg.* 969
TRUSTMARK NATIONAL BANK, *pg.* 812, *pg.* 969
UBS FINANCIAL SERVICES INC., *pg.* 812, *pg.* 1306
UMB FINANCIAL CORPORATION, *pg.* 812, *pg.* 987
UNIONBANCAL CORPORATION, *pg.* 813, *pg.* 230
UNITED BANKSHARES, INC., *pg.* 813, *pg.* 1849
UNITED COMMUNITY BANKS, INC., *pg.* 814, *pg.* 526
UNITED DOMINION REALTY L.P., *pg.* 814, *pg.* 332
UNITED SERVICES AUTOMOBILE ASSOCIATION, *pg.* 1221, *pg.* 1743
UNITED STATES OIL & GAS CORPORATION, *pg.* 986, *pg.* 1147
UNIVEST CORPORATION OF PENNSYLVANIA, *pg.* 814, *pg.* 1586
UPROMISE, INC., *pg.* 815, *pg.* 837
U.S. BANCORP, *pg.* 815, *pg.* 945
VALLEY NATIONAL BANCORP, *pg.* 815, *pg.* 1130
WADDELL & REED FINANCIAL, INC., *pg.* 818, *pg.* 721
WELLS FARGO ADVISORS, LLC, *pg.* 819, *pg.* 1005
WESCO FINANCIAL CORPORATION, *pg.* 821, *pg.* 181

First page reference indicates Business Class Edition
Second page reference indicates Geographic Edition

WHITNEY HOLDING CORPORATION, pg. 822, pg. 747
WILLIAM BLAIR & COMPANY LLC, pg. 822, pg. 596
WIND POINT PARTNERS, pg. 823, pg. 596
WISDOMTREE INVESTMENTS, INC., pg. 823, pg. 1314
WSFS FINANCIAL CORPORATION, pg. 823, pg. 392
THE ZIEGLER COMPANIES, INC., pg. 824, pg. 597

6311 - Life Insurance

21ST CENTURY INSURANCE GROUP, pg. 1187, pg. 389
AEGON USA, INC., pg. 1187, pg. 755
AETNA INC., pg. 1187, pg. 351
AFLAC INCORPORATED, pg. 1188, pg. 527
AIG ANNUITIES, pg. 1188, pg. 125
ALLIANZ LIFE INSURANCE COMPANY OF NORTH AMERICA, pg. 1188, pg. 929
THE ALLSTATE CORPORATION, pg. 1189, pg. 639
AMERCO, pg. 1898, pg. 1031
AMERICAN EQUITY INVESTMENT LIFE HOLDING COMPANY, pg. 711, pg. 712
AMERICAN FAMILY MUTUAL INSURANCE COMPANY, pg. 1190, pg. 1864
AMERICAN FINANCIAL GROUP, INC., pg. 714, pg. 1410
AMERICAN INTERNATIONAL GROUP, pg. 1190, pg. 1648
AMERICAN INTERNATIONAL GROUP, INC., pg. 1190, pg. 1193
AMERICAN NATIONAL INSURANCE COMPANY, pg. 1191, pg. 1697
AMERICAN REPUBLIC INSURANCE COMPANY, pg. 1191, pg. 704
AMERITAS INVESTMENT CORP., pg. 1192, pg. 1410
AMERITAS LIFE INSURANCE CORP., pg. 1192, pg. 1011
AMICA MUTUAL INSURANCE CO., pg. 1192, pg. 1602
ANTHEM BLUE CROSS BLUE SHIELD, pg. 1192, pg. 1886
ANTHEM HEALTH PLANS OF VIRGINIA, pg. 1192, pg. 1800
ANTHEM, INC., pg. 1192, pg. 683
ARROWPOINT CAPITAL CORP., pg. 1193, pg. 1361
ASSET MARKETING SYSTEMS INSURANCE SERVICES, LLC, pg. 1193, pg. 200
ASSURANT HEALTH, pg. 1193, pg. 1873
ASSURANT, INC., pg. 1193, pg. 1198
ASSURITY LIFE INSURANCE COMPANY, pg. 1194, pg. 1011
ATHENE ANNUITY & LIFE ASSURANCE COMPANY OF NEW YORK, pg. 1194, pg. 1318
AVEMCO INSURANCE COMPANY, pg. 1194, pg. 769
AVERA HEALTH, pg. 1194, pg. 1625
AXA EQUITABLE LIFE INSURANCE COMPANY, pg. 1194, pg. 1199
BANKERS LIFE & CASUALTY COMPANY, pg. 1194, pg. 566
BERKSHIRE HATHAWAY INC., pg. 1195, pg. 1013
BLUE CROSS & BLUE SHIELD ASSOCIATION, pg. 1195, pg. 566
BLUE CROSS & BLUE SHIELD OF FLORIDA, INC., pg. 1507, pg. 432
BLUE CROSS & BLUE SHIELD OF KANSAS CITY, INC., pg. 1507, pg. 981
BLUE CROSS & BLUE SHIELD OF MICHIGAN, pg. 1195, pg. 879
BLUE CROSS & BLUE SHIELD OF RHODE ISLAND, pg. 1195, pg. 1606
BLUE SHIELD OF CALIFORNIA, pg. 1195, pg. 214
BOSTON MUTUAL LIFE INSURANCE COMPANY, pg. 1196, pg. 810
CATHOLIC ORDER OF FORESTERS, pg. 1196, pg. 635
CIGNA CORPORATION, pg. 1197, pg. 338
CIGNA-HEALTHSPRING, pg. 1515, pg. 1632
CITIZENS INC., pg. 1197, pg. 1661
CNO FINANCIAL GROUP, INC., pg. 1198, pg. 675
CORVEL CORPORATION, pg. 1198, pg. 109
COVENTRY HEALTH CARE, INC., pg. 1519, pg. 761
EHEALTH, INC., pg. 1242, pg. 153
EMIGRANT SAVINGS BANK, pg. 747, pg. 1227
FARMERS GROUP, INC., pg. 1199, pg. 130
FINANCIAL BROKERAGE INC., pg. 1200, pg. 1015
FIRST MIDWEST BANCORP INC., pg. 756, pg. 620
GALLAGHER BOLLINGER, pg. 1200, pg. 1121
GENWORTH FINANCIAL, INC., pg. 761, pg. 1802
GENWORTH LIFE AND ANNUITY INSURANCE COMPANY, pg. 1201, pg. 1802
GERBER LIFE INSURANCE COMPANY, pg. 1201, pg. 1352
GLOBE LIFE & ACCIDENT INSURANCE COMPANY, pg. 1201, pg. 1486
GOVERNMENT EMPLOYEES HOSPITAL ASSOCIATION, INC., pg. 142, pg. 979
THE GUARDIAN LIFE INSURANCE COMPANY OF AMERICA, pg. 1202, pg. 1237
THE HARTFORD FINANCIAL SERVICES GROUP, INC., pg. 1202, pg. 352
HARVARD PILGRIM HEALTH CARE, INC., pg. 1539, pg. 856
HEALTH CARE SERVICE CORPORATION, pg. 1203, pg. 576
HEALTH NET, INC., pg. 1540, pg. 308
HEALTHPARTNERS, INC., pg. 1203, pg. 918
HEALTHWAYS, INC., pg. 1540, pg. 1632
HIGHMARK BLUE CROSS BLUE SHIELD, pg. 1203, pg. 1576
HORACE MANN COMPANIES, pg. 1203, pg. 662
HORIZON BLUE CROSS BLUE SHIELD OF NEW JERSEY, pg. 1203, pg. 1096
HUMANA, INC., pg. 1204, pg. 734
INDIANA FARM BUREAU INSURANCE, pg. 1204, pg. 687
JOHN HANCOCK FINANCIAL SERVICES, pg. 1205, pg. 796
KAISER FOUNDATION HEALTH PLAN OF THE MID-ATLANTIC STATES, INC., pg. 1205, pg. 776
KAISER PERMANENTE, pg. 1552, pg. 171
KINGSTONE COMPANIES, INC., pg. 1205, pg. 1166
LIBERTY MUTUAL INSURANCE GROUP INC., pg. 1205, pg. 797
LIBERTY NATIONAL LIFE INSURANCE CO., pg. 1206, pg. 5
LINCOLN FINANCIAL GROUP, pg. 1206, pg. 1375
LINCOLN NATIONAL CORPORATION, pg. 776, pg. 1567
THE LINCOLN NATIONAL LIFE INSURANCE CO., pg. 1207, pg. 680
MANULIFE FINANCIAL CORPORATION, pg. 778, pg. 1939
MEDICA, INC., pg. 1208, pg. 949
METLIFE, INC., pg. 1208, pg. 1258
METROPOLITAN HEALTH NETWORKS, INC., pg. 1567, pg. 412
MILLENNIUM MARKETING GROUP, LLC, pg. 1209, pg. 1016
THE MINNESOTA LIFE INSURANCE COMPANY, pg. 1209, pg. 962
MODERN WOODMEN OF AMERICA, pg. 1209, pg. 654
MOLINA HEALTHCARE, INC., pg. 1569, pg. 123
MULTIPLAN, INC., pg. 1570, pg. 852
MUTUAL OF AMERICA LIFE INSURANCE COMPANY, pg. 1210, pg. 1263
MUTUAL OF OMAHA INSURANCE COMPANY, pg. 1210, pg. 1016
MYLAN, INC., pg. 1570, pg. 1520
NATIONAL LIFE INSURANCE COMPANY, pg. 1210, pg. 1766
THE NATIONAL SECURITY GROUP, INC., pg. 1210, pg. 5
NATIONAL WESTERN LIFE INSURANCE COMPANY, pg. 1210, pg. 1664
NATIONWIDE MUTUAL INSURANCE COMPANY, pg. 1211, pg. 706
NEIGHBORHOOD HEALTH PLAN INC., pg. 1211, pg. 798
NEW YORK LIFE INSURANCE COMPANY, pg. 1211, pg. 1268
NORTH CAROLINA MUTUAL LIFE INSURANCE COMPANY, pg. 1212, pg. 1372
THE NORTHWESTERN MUTUAL LIFE INSURANCE COMPANY, pg. 1212, pg. 1879
ODYSSEY RE HOLDINGS CORP., pg. 1212, pg. 376
OLD AMERICAN INSURANCE COMPANY, pg. 1213, pg. 985
OLD NATIONAL BANCORP, pg. 789, pg. 679
OXFORD LIFE INSURANCE COMPANY, pg. 1213, pg. 18
PACIFIC LIFE INSURANCE COMPANY, pg. 1213, pg. 166
PAN-AMERICAN LIFE INSURANCE COMPANY, pg. 1213, pg. 747
PBC HEALTH BENEFITS SOCIETY, pg. 1214, pg. 1911
PENN TREATY AMERICAN CORPORATION, pg. 793, pg. 1514
PENNSYLVANIA NATIONAL MUTUAL CASUALTY INSURANCE COMPANY, pg. 1214, pg. 1537
THE PHOENIX COMPANIES, INC., pg. 1214, pg. 352
PHYSICIANS MUTUAL INSURANCE CO., pg. 1214, pg. 1017
PREMERA BLUE CROSS, pg. 1214, pg. 1823
PRINCIPAL FINANCIAL GROUP, INC., pg. 796, pg. 706
PROTECTIVE LIFE CORPORATION, pg. 1215, pg. 4
PROTECTIVE LIFE INSURANCE COMPANY, pg. 1215, pg. 4
PRUDENTIAL FINANCIAL, INC., pg. 797, pg. 1097
QUALCARE, INC., pg. 1215, pg. 1109
REGENCE BLUECROSS BLUESHIELD OF OREGON, pg. 1215, pg. 1506
RELIANCE STANDARD LIFE INSURANCE COMPANY, pg. 1215, pg. 1570
RLI CORP., pg. 1216, pg. 652
SAMMONS ENTERPRISES, INC., pg. 1373, pg. 1686
SBLI USA LIFE INSURANCE COMPANY, INC., pg. 1216, pg. 1288
SECURITY MUTUAL LIFE INSURANCE COMPANY OF NEW YORK, pg. 1216, pg. 1142
SECURITY NATIONAL FINANCIAL CORPORATION, pg. 802, pg. 1760
THE SEIBELS BRUCE GROUP, INC., pg. 1216, pg. 1614
SENTARA HEALTHCARE, pg. 1593, pg. 1797
SIRIUS AMERICA REINSURANCE COMPANY, pg. 1217, pg. 1292
STANDARD INSURANCE COMPANY, pg. 1217, pg. 1506
STANDARD LIFE & ACCIDENT INSURANCE COMPANY, pg. 1217, pg. 1725
STATE FARM MUTUAL AUTOMOBILE INSURANCE CO., pg. 1218, pg. 557
SUN LIFE FINANCIAL INC., pg. 806, pg. 1944
TEACHERS INSURANCE & ANNUITY ASSOCIATION - COLLEGE RETIREMENT EQUITIES FUND, pg. 1219, pg. 1297
THRIVENT FINANCIAL FOR LUTHERANS, pg. 1219, pg. 944
THE TRAVELERS COMPANIES, INC., pg. 1220, pg. 352
UNITED FIRE GROUP, INC, pg. 1220, pg. 703
UNITED SERVICES AUTOMOBILE ASSOCIATION, pg. 1221, pg. 1743
UNITEDHEALTH GROUP INCORPORATED, pg. 1221, pg. 950
UNUM GROUP, pg. 1222, pg. 1629
U.S. PHYSICAL THERAPY, INC., pg. 1604, pg. 1716
UTG, INC., pg. 1222, pg. 662
UTICA MUTUAL INSURANCE COMPANY, pg. 1222, pg. 1183
WELCOME FUNDS, INC., pg. 1223, pg. 413
WELLCARE HEALTH PLANS INC., pg. 1223, pg. 476
WESCO FINANCIAL CORPORATION, pg. 821, pg. 181
WILLIS HRH, INC., pg. 1223, pg. 1314
W.R. BERKLEY CORPORATION, pg. 1223, pg. 350

6321 - Accident & Health Insurance

AETNA INC., pg. 1187, pg. 351
AIG ANNUITIES, pg. 1188, pg. 125
AMERICAN INTERNATIONAL GROUP, INC., pg. 1190, pg. 1193
AMERICAN REPUBLIC INSURANCE COMPANY, pg. 1191, pg. 704
ANTHEM BLUE CROSS BLUE SHIELD, pg. 1192, pg. 1886
ANTHEM HEALTH PLANS OF VIRGINIA, pg. 1192, pg. 1800
ANTHEM, INC., pg. 1192, pg. 683
ASSURANT HEALTH, pg. 1193, pg. 1873
ASSURANT, INC., pg. 1193, pg. 1198
ASSURITY LIFE INSURANCE COMPANY, pg. 1194, pg. 1011
AVEMCO INSURANCE COMPANY, pg. 1194, pg. 769
AVERA HEALTH, pg. 1194, pg. 1625
BANKERS LIFE & CASUALTY COMPANY, pg. 1194, pg. 566
BERKSHIRE HATHAWAY INC., pg. 1195, pg. 1013
BLUE CROSS & BLUE SHIELD ASSOCIATION, pg. 1195, pg. 566
BLUE CROSS & BLUE SHIELD OF FLORIDA, INC., pg. 1507, pg. 432
BLUE CROSS & BLUE SHIELD OF KANSAS CITY, INC., pg. 1507, pg. 981
BLUE CROSS & BLUE SHIELD OF MICHIGAN, pg. 1195, pg. 879
BLUE CROSS & BLUE SHIELD OF RHODE ISLAND, pg. 1195, pg. 1606
BLUE SHIELD OF CALIFORNIA, pg. 1195, pg. 214
CIGNA CORPORATION, pg. 1197, pg. 338
CIGNA-HEALTHSPRING, pg. 1515, pg. 1632
CITIZENS INC., pg. 1197, pg. 1661
CNO FINANCIAL GROUP, INC., pg. 1198, pg. 675
CORVEL CORPORATION, pg. 1198, pg. 109
COVENTRY HEALTH CARE, INC., pg. 1519, pg. 761
EHEALTH, INC., pg. 1242, pg. 153
FARMERS GROUP, INC., pg. 1199, pg. 130
FIRST MIDWEST BANCORP INC., pg. 756, pg. 620
GENWORTH FINANCIAL, INC., pg. 761, pg. 1802

6331 - Fire, Marine & Casualty Insurance

First page reference indicates Business Class Edition
Second page reference indicates Geographic Edition

PENN TREATY AMERICAN CORPORATION, pg. 793, pg. 1514
PENNSYLVANIA NATIONAL MUTUAL CASUALTY INSURANCE COMPANY, pg. 1214, pg. 1537
PHYSICIANS MUTUAL INSURANCE CO., pg. 1214, pg. 1017
PREMERA BLUE CROSS, pg. 1214, pg. 1823
PRINCIPAL FINANCIAL GROUP, INC., pg. 796, pg. 706
PROASSURANCE CORPORATION, pg. 1214, pg. 3
THE PROGRESSIVE CORPORATION, pg. 1214, pg. 1463
PROTECTIVE LIFE CORPORATION, pg. 1215, pg. 4
PROTECTIVE LIFE INSURANCE COMPANY, pg. 1215, pg. 4
QUALCARE, INC., pg. 1215, pg. 1109
QUINCY MUTUAL FIRE INSURANCE COMPANY, pg. 1215, pg. 842
REGENCE BLUECROSS BLUESHIELD OF OREGON, pg. 1215, pg. 1506
RLI CORP., pg. 1216, pg. 652
ROYAL BANK OF CANADA, pg. 800, pg. 1942
SAFEAUTO INSURANCE COMPANY, pg. 1216, pg. 1443
SAFEWAY INSURANCE COMPANY, pg. 1216, pg. 669
SECURITY MUTUAL LIFE INSURANCE COMPANY OF NEW YORK, pg. 1216, pg. 1142
SECURITY NATIONAL FINANCIAL CORPORATION, pg. 802, pg. 1760
THE SEIBELS BRUCE GROUP, INC., pg. 1216, pg. 1614
SELECTIVE INSURANCE GROUP, INC., pg. 1216, pg. 1045
SENTARA HEALTHCARE, pg. 1593, pg. 1797
SIRIUS AMERICA REINSURANCE COMPANY, pg. 1217, pg. 1292
STANDARD INSURANCE COMPANY, pg. 1217, pg. 1506
STANDARD LIFE & ACCIDENT INSURANCE COMPANY, pg. 1217, pg. 1725
STATE AUTOMOBILE MUTUAL INSURANCE COMPANY, pg. 1217, pg. 1444
STATE FARM MUTUAL AUTOMOBILE INSURANCE CO., pg. 1218, pg. 557
SWISS REINSURANCE AMERICA CORPORATION, pg. 1218, pg. 1140
THRIVENT FINANCIAL FOR LUTHERANS, pg. 1219, pg. 944
THE TRAVELERS COMPANIES, INC., pg. 1220, pg. 352
TRAVELERS INSURANCE, pg. 1220, pg. 963
UMB FINANCIAL CORPORATION, pg. 812, pg. 987
UNITED FIRE GROUP, INC, pg. 1220, pg. 703
UNITED INSURANCE HOLDINGS CORP., pg. 1220, pg. 465
UNITED SERVICES AUTOMOBILE ASSOCIATION, pg. 1221, pg. 1743
UNITED STATES AIRCRAFT INSURANCE GROUP, pg. 1221, pg. 1307
UNITEDHEALTH GROUP INCORPORATED, pg. 1221, pg. 950
UNUM GROUP, pg. 1222, pg. 1629
U.S. BANCORP, pg. 815, pg. 945
U.S. PHYSICAL THERAPY, INC., pg. 1604, pg. 1716
UTG, INC., pg. 1222, pg. 662
UTICA MUTUAL INSURANCE COMPANY, pg. 1222, pg. 1183
VISION FINANCIAL CORPORATION, pg. 1222, pg. 1035
WEBBANK, pg. 819, pg. 1761
WELLCARE HEALTH PLANS INC., pg. 1223, pg. 476
WELLS FARGO ADVISORS, LLC, pg. 819, pg. 1005
WELLS FARGO & COMPANY, pg. 819, pg. 232
WESCO FINANCIAL CORPORATION, pg. 821, pg. 181
WESTERN NATIONAL MUTUAL INSURANCE CO., pg. 1223, pg. 946
WILLIS HRH, INC., pg. 1223, pg. 1314
W.R. BERKLEY CORPORATION, pg. 1223, pg. 350
ZURICH HOLDING COMPANY OF AMERICA, INC., pg. 1224, pg. 660

6361 - Title Insurance

21ST CENTURY INSURANCE GROUP, pg. 1187, pg. 389
AUTO-OWNERS INSURANCE GROUP, pg. 1194, pg. 895
FARMERS GROUP, INC., pg. 1199, pg. 130
OLD NATIONAL BANCORP, pg. 789, pg. 679
WELLS FARGO & COMPANY, pg. 819, pg. 232

6371 - Pension, Health & Welfare Funds

AIG ANNUITIES, pg. 1188, pg. 125
AMERICAN FAMILY AGENCIES, pg. 1190, pg. 415
AMERICAN INTERNATIONAL GROUP, INC., pg. 1190, pg. 1193
AMERITAS INVESTMENT CORP., pg. 1192, pg. 1410
AMERITAS LIFE INSURANCE CORP., pg. 1192, pg. 1011
AON RISK SERVICES INC., pg. 1193, pg. 564
ARROWPOINT CAPITAL CORP., pg. 1193, pg. 1361
ASSET MARKETING SYSTEMS INSURANCE SERVICES, LLC, pg. 1193, pg. 200
ASSURANT, INC., pg. 1193, pg. 1198
ASSURITY LIFE INSURANCE COMPANY, pg. 1194, pg. 1011
ATTO & ASSOCIATES INSURANCE BROKERS, INC., pg. 1194, pg. 1924
AUTO-OWNERS INSURANCE GROUP, pg. 1194, pg. 895
AUTOMOBILE CLUB OF SOUTHERN CALIFORNIA, pg. 134, pg. 126
AZOY TAX, pg. 717, pg. 423
BANKRATE, INC., pg. 1231, pg. 451
BB&T - OSWALD TRIPPE & CO., pg. 1194, pg. 427
BEECH STREET CORPORATION, pg. 1503, pg. 121
BERKSHIRE HATHAWAY INC., pg. 1195, pg. 1013
BROWN & BROWN, INC., pg. 1196, pg. 419
CAPITAL FINANCIAL HOLDINGS, INC., pg. 730, pg. 1398
CAPITALONE INVESTING, pg. 731, pg. 1834
CIGI DIRECT INSURANCE SERVICES, INC., pg. 1197, pg. 335
CIGNA CORPORATION, pg. 1197, pg. 338
CIT GROUP INC., pg. 735, pg. 1212
THE CO-OPERATORS GROUP LIMITED, pg. 1198, pg. 1920
COLUMBIAN MUTUAL LIFE INSURANCE COMPANY, pg. 1198, pg. 1142
CONMED HEALTHCARE MANAGEMENT, INC., pg. 1518, pg. 772
COUNTRY FINANCIAL, pg. 1198, pg. 557
CRAWFORD & COMPANY, pg. 1199, pg. 502
CREDITCARDS.COM, INC., pg. 1237, pg. 1661
CUNA MUTUAL INSURANCE SOCIETY, pg. 743, pg. 1865
DEALERTRACK HOLDINGS, INC., pg. 743, pg. 1172
DISCOVER FINANCIAL SERVICES, pg. 744, pg. 653
THE DOCTORS COMPANY, pg. 1199, pg. 163
DUFF & PHELPS CORPORATION, pg. 745, pg. 1226
EHEALTH, INC., pg. 1242, pg. 153
EMERGENT CAPITAL, INC., pg. 747, pg. 411
EQUIINSURANCE, LLC, pg. 748, pg. 448
ESURANCE, INC., pg. 1243, pg. 217
EVERI HOLDINGS INC., pg. 749, pg. 1023
THE F. DOHMEN CO., pg. 1530, pg. 1858
FACTORY MUTUAL INSURANCE COMPANY, pg. 1199, pg. 1601
FACTSET RESEARCH SYSTEMS INC., pg. 1247, pg. 361
FARMERS GROUP, INC., pg. 1199, pg. 130
FEDERAL FARM CREDIT BANKS FUNDING CORPORATION, pg. 751, pg. 1075
FINANCIAL BROKERAGE INC., pg. 1200, pg. 1015
FINANCIAL ENGINES, INC., pg. 753, pg. 285
FINANCIAL INDEPENDENCE GROUP INC., pg. 1200, pg. 1370
FINOTEC GROUP, INC., pg. 753, pg. 1231
FIRST BUSEY CORPORATION, pg. 754, pg. 562
FIRST FINANCIAL HOLDINGS, INC., pg. 755, pg. 1614
FIRST FINANCIAL GROUP OF AMERICA, pg. 755, pg. 1705
FIRST INVESTORS FINANCIAL SERVICES GROUP, INC., pg. 756, pg. 1706
FIRST NIAGARA BANK, pg. 756, pg. 1174
FIRST NIAGARA FINANCIAL GROUP, INC., pg. 757, pg. 1148
FMR LLC (FIDELITY INVESTMENTS), pg. 759, pg. 794
FORUM NATIONAL INVESTMENTS LTD., pg. 1200, pg. 1908
FRENKEL & CO. INC., pg. 1200, pg. 1233
FULTON FINANCIAL CORPORATION, pg. 760, pg. 1546
GAIN CAPITAL HOLDINGS, INC., pg. 760, pg. 1043
GALLAGHER BOLLINGER, pg. 1200, pg. 1121
GEICO CORPORATION, pg. 1200, pg. 399
GEICO GENERAL INSURANCE COMPANY, pg. 1201, pg. 766
GENWORTH LIFE AND ANNUITY INSURANCE COMPANY, pg. 1201, pg. 1802
GEOVERA INSURANCE COMPANY INC., pg. 1201, pg. 86
GRINNELL MUTUAL REINSURANCE COMPANY INC., pg. 1201, pg. 708
THE GUARDIAN LIFE INSURANCE COMPANY OF AMERICA, pg. 1202, pg. 1237
GUIDEONE INSURANCE COMPANY, pg. 1202, pg. 713
HALLMARK FINANCIAL SERVICES, INC., pg. 1202, pg. 1695
THE HANOVER INSURANCE COMPANY, pg. 1202, pg. 862
THE HARTFORD FINANCIAL SERVICES GROUP, INC., pg. 1202, pg. 352
H.D. VEST, INC., pg. 765, pg. 1720
HEALTH CARE SERVICE CORPORATION, pg. 1203, pg. 576
HOOPER HOLMES, INC., pg. 1542, pg. 718
HORIZON BLUE CROSS BLUE SHIELD OF NEW JERSEY, pg. 1203, pg. 1096
HORTICA INSURANCE, pg. 1204, pg. 609
HSB GROUP, INC., pg. 1204, pg. 352
INDIANA FARM BUREAU INSURANCE, pg. 1204, pg. 687
INSURANCE BROKERS & AGENTS OF THE WEST, pg. 144, pg. 183
INSURANCE.COM, INC., pg. 1205, pg. 1473
INSWEB CORPORATION, pg. 1205, pg. 186
KINGSTONE COMPANIES, INC., pg. 1205, pg. 1166
LIFE QUOTES, INC., pg. 1206, pg. 598
LINCOLN FINANCIAL BENEFIT PARTNERS, pg. 1206, pg. 1016
MANULIFE FINANCIAL CORPORATION, pg. 778, pg. 1939
MARKEL CORPORATION, pg. 1207, pg. 1783
MARSH & MCLENNAN COMPANIES INC., pg. 1207, pg. 1256
MASSACHUSETTS MUTUAL LIFE INSURANCE COMPANY, pg. 1207, pg. 845
MEDALLION FINANCIAL CORP., pg. 781, pg. 1258
MERCHANTS GROUP, INC., pg. 1208, pg. 1149
METLIFE, INC., pg. 1208, pg. 1258
MILLENNIUM MARKETING GROUP, LLC, pg. 1209, pg. 1016
THE MONEY TREE INC., pg. 783, pg. 526
MORGAN STANLEY, pg. 783, pg. 1261
MUTUAL OF AMERICA LIFE INSURANCE COMPANY, pg. 1210, pg. 1263
MUTUAL OF OMAHA INSURANCE COMPANY, pg. 1210, pg. 1016
NATIONAL WESTERN LIFE INSURANCE COMPANY, pg. 1210, pg. 1664
NATIONWIDE MUTUAL INSURANCE COMPANY, pg. 1210, pg. 1442
NATIONWIDE MUTUAL INSURANCE COMPANY, pg. 1211, pg. 1536
OHIO FARMERS INSURANCE COMPANY, pg. 1213, pg. 1480
OLD NATIONAL BANCORP, pg. 789, pg. 679
PACIFIC LIFE INSURANCE COMPANY, pg. 1213, pg. 166
PATRIOT NATIONAL INSURANCE GROUP, pg. 1213, pg. 426
PENN TREATY AMERICAN CORPORATION, pg. 793, pg. 1514
PEOPLES BANCORP INC., pg. 793, pg. 1458
PLATTE VALLEY FINANCIAL SERVICE COMPANIES INC., pg. 794, pg. 1019
PRIMERICA FINANCIAL SERVICES, INC., pg. 795, pg. 531
PRINCIPAL FINANCIAL GROUP, INC., pg. 796, pg. 706
PROASSURANCE CORPORATION, pg. 1214, pg. 404
PROASSURANCE CORPORATION, pg. 1214, pg. 3
PRUDENTIAL FINANCIAL, INC., pg. 797, pg. 1097
QUALCARE, INC., pg. 1215, pg. 1109
QUINCY MUTUAL FIRE INSURANCE COMPANY, pg. 1215, pg. 842
REGENCE BLUECROSS BLUESHIELD OF OREGON, pg. 1215, pg. 1506
RENASANT CORPORATION, pg. 799, pg. 972
RICHARDS & SUMMERS INC., pg. 1216, pg. 1053
ROYAL BANK OF CANADA, pg. 800, pg. 1942
SAFELITE SOLUTIONS LLC, pg. 109, pg. 1443
SELECTIVE INSURANCE GROUP, INC., pg. 1216, pg. 1045
SENIOR MARKET SALES, INC., pg. 1217, pg. 1018
SENTRY INSURANCE GROUP, pg. 1217, pg. 1895
SOLERA HOLDINGS, INC., pg. 1217, pg. 1749
STAHL & ASSOCIATES INSURANCE, pg. 1217, pg. 464
STATE AUTOMOBILE MUTUAL INSURANCE COMPANY, pg. 1217, pg. 1444
STEN CORPORATION, pg. 1597, pg. 950
SVB FINANCIAL GROUP, pg. 808, pg. 270
TEACHERS INSURANCE & ANNUITY ASSOCIATION - COLLEGE RETIREMENT EQUITIES FUND, pg. 1219, pg. 1297
TECHNOLOGY EXECUTIVES CLUB, LTD., pg. 482, pg. 627
TRANSAMERICA INSURANCE & INVESTMENT GROUP,

pg. 1219, pg. 141
TRAVEL GUARD GROUP, INC., pg. 1925, pg. 1895
TRAVELERS INSURANCE, pg. 1220, pg. 963
UMB FINANCIAL CORPORATION, pg. 812, pg. 987
UNICO AMERICAN CORPORATION, pg. 1220, pg. 308
UNITED INSURANCE HOLDINGS CORP., pg. 1220, pg. 465
UNIVEST CORPORATION OF PENNSYLVANIA, pg. 814, pg. 1586
UPROMISE, INC., pg. 815, pg. 837
USI HOLDINGS CORPORATION, pg. 1222, pg. 1144
VERISK ANALYTICS, INC., pg. 1222, pg. 1076
VETERINARY PET INSURANCE CO., pg. 1222, pg. 49
VREELAND INSURANCE INC., pg. 1223, pg. 1116
VULCAN PRODUCTIONS INC., pg. 317, pg. 1842
WEBBANK, pg. 819, pg. 1761
WEBMD HEALTH SERVICES GROUP, pg. 1609, pg. 1508
WELLS FARGO & COMPANY, pg. 819, pg. 232
WESCO FINANCIAL CORPORATION, pg. 821, pg. 181
WEST SUBURBAN BANCORP, INC., pg. 821, pg. 631
WILLIS HRH, INC., pg. 1223, pg. 1314
XOOM CORPORATION, pg. 1289, pg. 234
ZECCO TRADING, pg. 824, pg. 181
ZENITH MARKETING GROUP, INC., pg. 1224, pg. 1071

6399 - Insurance Carriers, NEC

21ST CENTURY INSURANCE GROUP, pg. 1187, pg. 389
AEGON USA, INC., pg. 1187, pg. 755
AFLAC INCORPORATED, pg. 1188, pg. 527
AIG ANNUITIES, pg. 1188, pg. 125
ALLIANZ LIFE INSURANCE COMPANY OF NORTH AMERICA, pg. 1188, pg. 929
THE ALLSTATE CORPORATION, pg. 1189, pg. 639
AMERCO, pg. 1898, pg. 1031
AMERICAN AUTOMOBILE ASSOCIATION, pg. 1190, pg. 429
AMERICAN EQUITY INVESTMENT LIFE HOLDING COMPANY, pg. 711, pg. 712
AMERICAN FAMILY MUTUAL INSURANCE COMPANY, pg. 1190, pg. 1864
AMERICAN FINANCIAL GROUP, INC., pg. 714, pg. 1410
AMERICAN INTERNATIONAL GROUP, pg. 1190, pg. 1648
AMERICAN INTERNATIONAL GROUP, INC., pg. 1190, pg. 1193
AMERICAN NATIONAL INSURANCE COMPANY, pg. 1191, pg. 1697
AMERICAN REPUBLIC INSURANCE COMPANY, pg. 1191, pg. 704
AMERISAFE, INC., pg. 1191, pg. 743
AMERISURE MUTUAL INSURANCE COMPANY, pg. 1191, pg. 885
AMERITAS INVESTMENT CORP., pg. 1192, pg. 1410
AMERITAS LIFE INSURANCE CORP., pg. 1192, pg. 1011
AMICA MUTUAL INSURANCE CO., pg. 1192, pg. 1602
ARROWPOINT CAPITAL CORP., pg. 1193, pg. 1361
ASSET MARKETING SYSTEMS INSURANCE SERVICES, LLC, pg. 1193, pg. 200
ASSURANT, INC., pg. 1193, pg. 1198
ASSURITY LIFE INSURANCE COMPANY, pg. 1194, pg. 1011
ATHENE ANNUITY & LIFE ASSURANCE COMPANY OF NEW YORK, pg. 1194, pg. 1318
AUTO-OWNERS INSURANCE GROUP, pg. 1194, pg. 895
AVEMCO INSURANCE COMPANY, pg. 1194, pg. 769
AXA EQUITABLE LIFE INSURANCE COMPANY, pg. 1194, pg. 1199
BANKERS LIFE & CASUALTY COMPANY, pg. 1194, pg. 566
BERKSHIRE HATHAWAY INC., pg. 1195, pg. 1013
BITCO INSURANCE, pg. 1195, pg. 654
BOSTON MUTUAL LIFE INSURANCE COMPANY, pg. 1196, pg. 810
CAREFIRST BLUECROSS BLUESHIELD, pg. 1196, pg. 397
CATHOLIC ORDER OF FORESTERS, pg. 1196, pg. 635
CENTRAL MUTUAL INSURANCE COMPANY, pg. 1196, pg. 1478
THE CHUBB CORPORATION, pg. 1196, pg. 1128
CIGNA CORPORATION, pg. 1197, pg. 338
CITIZENS INC., pg. 1197, pg. 1661
CNA INSURANCE COMPANIES, pg. 1198, pg. 571
CNO FINANCIAL GROUP, INC., pg. 1198, pg. 675
COMPREHENSIVE CARE CORPORATION, pg. 1517, pg. 472
CSE INSURANCE GROUP, pg. 1199, pg. 304
THE DOCTORS COMPANY, pg. 1199, pg. 163
EMIGRANT SAVINGS BANK, pg. 747, pg. 1227
FACTORY MUTUAL INSURANCE COMPANY, pg. 1199, pg. 1601
FARMERS GROUP, INC., pg. 1199, pg. 130
FARMERS MUTUAL HAIL INSURANCE COMPANY OF IOWA, pg. 1199, pg. 713
FEDERAL DEPOSIT INSURANCE CORPORATION, pg. 751, pg. 399
FEDERATED MUTUAL INSURANCE COMPANY, pg. 1200, pg. 952
FINANCIAL BROKERAGE INC., pg. 1200, pg. 1015
FIREMAN'S FUND INSURANCE COMPANY, pg. 1200, pg. 168
FIRST ACCEPTANCE CORPORATION, pg. 1200, pg. 1650
FIRST NIAGARA BANK, pg. 756, pg. 1174
GALLAGHER BOLLINGER, pg. 1200, pg. 1121
GEICO CORPORATION, pg. 1200, pg. 399
GEICO GENERAL INSURANCE COMPANY, pg. 1201, pg. 766
GENWORTH FINANCIAL, INC., pg. 761, pg. 1802
GENWORTH LIFE AND ANNUITY INSURANCE COMPANY, pg. 1201, pg. 1802
GERBER LIFE INSURANCE COMPANY, pg. 1201, pg. 1352
GLOBE LIFE & ACCIDENT INSURANCE COMPANY, pg. 1201, pg. 1486
GREATER NEW YORK MUTUAL INSURANCE COMPANY, pg. 1201, pg. 1236
GRINNELL MUTUAL REINSURANCE COMPANY INC., pg. 1201, pg. 708
THE GUARDIAN LIFE INSURANCE COMPANY OF AMERICA, pg. 1202, pg. 1237
GUIDEONE INSURANCE COMPANY, pg. 1202, pg. 713
HALLMARK FINANCIAL SERVICES, INC., pg. 1202, pg. 1695
THE HANOVER INSURANCE COMPANY, pg. 1202, pg. 862
THE HARTFORD FINANCIAL SERVICES GROUP, INC., pg. 1202, pg. 352
HEALTH CARE SERVICE CORPORATION, pg. 1203, pg. 576
HORACE MANN COMPANIES, pg. 1203, pg. 662
HSB GROUP, INC., pg. 1204, pg. 352
HUMANA, INC., pg. 1204, pg. 734
INDIANA FARM BUREAU INSURANCE, pg. 1204, pg. 687
INFINITY PROPERTY & CASUALTY CORPORATION, pg. 1205, pg. 3
JOHN HANCOCK FINANCIAL SERVICES, pg. 1205, pg. 796
KEMPER CORPORATION, pg. 1205, pg. 579
KINGSTONE COMPANIES, INC., pg. 1205, pg. 1166
LIBERTY MUTUAL INSURANCE GROUP INC., pg. 1205, pg. 797
LIBERTY NATIONAL LIFE INSURANCE CO., pg. 1206, pg. 5
LIBERTY PROPERTY TRUST, pg. 1101, pg. 1550
LINCOLN FINANCIAL GROUP, pg. 1206, pg. 1375
LINCOLN NATIONAL CORPORATION, pg. 776, pg. 1567
THE LINCOLN NATIONAL LIFE INSURANCE CO., pg. 1207, pg. 680
MANULIFE FINANCIAL CORPORATION, pg. 778, pg. 1939
MAPFRE INSURANCE, pg. 1207, pg. 856
MARKEL CORPORATION, pg. 1207, pg. 1783
THE MEDICAL PROTECTIVE COMPANY, pg. 1208, pg. 680
MERCHANTS GROUP, INC., pg. 1208, pg. 1149
METLIFE, INC., pg. 1208, pg. 1258
MILLENNIUM MARKETING GROUP, LLC, pg. 1209, pg. 1016
THE MINNESOTA LIFE INSURANCE COMPANY, pg. 1209, pg. 962
MODERN WOODMEN OF AMERICA, pg. 1209, pg. 654
MOTORISTS MUTUAL INSURANCE CO., pg. 1210, pg. 1442
MUTUAL OF AMERICA LIFE INSURANCE COMPANY, pg. 1210, pg. 1263
MUTUAL OF OMAHA INSURANCE COMPANY, pg. 1210, pg. 1016
NATIONAL LIFE INSURANCE COMPANY, pg. 1210, pg. 1766
THE NATIONAL SECURITY GROUP, INC., pg. 1210, pg. 5
NATIONAL WESTERN LIFE INSURANCE COMPANY, pg. 1210, pg. 1664
NATIONWIDE MUTUAL INSURANCE COMPANY, pg. 1210, pg. 1442
NATIONWIDE MUTUAL INSURANCE COMPANY, pg. 1211, pg. 706
NEW JERSEY MANUFACTURERS INSURANCE COMPANY, pg. 1211, pg. 1132
NEW YORK LIFE INSURANCE COMPANY, pg. 1211, pg. 1268
NORTH CAROLINA MUTUAL LIFE INSURANCE COMPANY, pg. 1212, pg. 1372
THE NORTHWESTERN MUTUAL LIFE INSURANCE COMPANY, pg. 1212, pg. 1879
ODYSSEY RE HOLDINGS CORP., pg. 1212, pg. 376
OHIO FARMERS INSURANCE COMPANY, pg. 1213, pg. 1480
OLD AMERICAN INSURANCE COMPANY, pg. 1213, pg. 985
OLD NATIONAL BANCORP, pg. 789, pg. 679
PACIFIC LIFE INSURANCE COMPANY, pg. 1213, pg. 166
PAN-AMERICAN LIFE INSURANCE COMPANY, pg. 1213, pg. 747
PENN TREATY AMERICAN CORPORATION, pg. 793, pg. 1514
PENNSYLVANIA NATIONAL MUTUAL CASUALTY INSURANCE COMPANY, pg. 1214, pg. 1537
THE PHOENIX COMPANIES, INC., pg. 1214, pg. 352
PHYSICIANS MUTUAL INSURANCE CO., pg. 1214, pg. 1017
PRINCIPAL FINANCIAL GROUP, INC., pg. 796, pg. 706
PROASSURANCE CORPORATION, pg. 1214, pg. 3
THE PROGRESSIVE CORPORATION, pg. 1214, pg. 1463
PROTECTIVE LIFE CORPORATION, pg. 1215, pg. 4
PROTECTIVE LIFE INSURANCE COMPANY, pg. 1215, pg. 4
PRUDENTIAL FINANCIAL, INC., pg. 797, pg. 1097
QUINCY MUTUAL FIRE INSURANCE COMPANY, pg. 1215, pg. 842
REGENCE BLUECROSS BLUESHIELD OF OREGON, pg. 1215, pg. 1506
RELIANCE STANDARD LIFE INSURANCE COMPANY, pg. 1215, pg. 1570
SAFEAUTO INSURANCE COMPANY, pg. 1216, pg. 1443
SAFEWAY INSURANCE COMPANY, pg. 1216, pg. 669
SAMMONS ENTERPRISES, INC., pg. 1373, pg. 1686
SBLI USA LIFE INSURANCE COMPANY, INC., pg. 1216, pg. 1288
SECURITY MUTUAL LIFE INSURANCE COMPANY OF NEW YORK, pg. 1216, pg. 1142
SECURITY NATIONAL FINANCIAL CORPORATION, pg. 802, pg. 1760
THE SEIBELS BRUCE GROUP, INC., pg. 1216, pg. 1614
SELECTIVE INSURANCE GROUP, INC., pg. 1216, pg. 1045
STANDARD INSURANCE COMPANY, pg. 1217, pg. 1506
STANDARD LIFE & ACCIDENT INSURANCE COMPANY, pg. 1217, pg. 1725
STATE AUTOMOBILE MUTUAL INSURANCE COMPANY, pg. 1217, pg. 1444
STATE FARM MUTUAL AUTOMOBILE INSURANCE CO., pg. 1218, pg. 557
SUN LIFE FINANCIAL INC., pg. 806, pg. 1944
SWISS REINSURANCE AMERICA CORPORATION, pg. 1218, pg. 1140
TEACHERS INSURANCE & ANNUITY ASSOCIATION - COLLEGE RETIREMENT EQUITIES FUND, pg. 1219, pg. 1297
THRIVENT FINANCIAL FOR LUTHERANS, pg. 1219, pg. 944
THE TRAVELERS COMPANIES, INC., pg. 1220, pg. 352
TRAVELERS INSURANCE, pg. 1220, pg. 963
UNITED FIRE GROUP, INC, pg. 1220, pg. 703
UNITED INSURANCE HOLDINGS CORP., pg. 1220, pg. 465
UNITED SERVICES AUTOMOBILE ASSOCIATION, pg. 1221, pg. 1743
UNITED STATES AIRCRAFT INSURANCE GROUP, pg. 1221, pg. 1307
UNITEDHEALTH GROUP INCORPORATED, pg. 1221, pg. 950
UNUM GROUP, pg. 1222, pg. 1629
UTG, INC., pg. 1222, pg. 662
UTICA MUTUAL INSURANCE COMPANY, pg. 1222, pg. 1183
VISION FINANCIAL CORPORATION, pg. 1222, pg. 1035
WARRANTECH CORPORATION, pg. 491, pg. 1668
WELCOME FUNDS, INC., pg. 1223, pg. 413
WELLS FARGO & COMPANY, pg. 819, pg. 232
WESCO FINANCIAL CORPORATION, pg. 821, pg. 181
WESTERN NATIONAL MUTUAL INSURANCE CO., pg. 1223, pg. 946
WILLIS HRH, INC., pg. 1223, pg. 1314
W.R. BERKLEY CORPORATION, pg. 1223, pg. 350
ZURICH HOLDING COMPANY OF AMERICA, INC., pg. 1224, pg. 660

First page reference indicates Business Class Edition
Second page reference indicates Geographic Edition

6411 - Insurance Agents, Brokers & Service

AIG ANNUITIES, *pg.* 1188, *pg.* 125
AMERICAN FAMILY AGENCIES, *pg.* 1190, *pg.* 415
AMERICAN INTERNATIONAL GROUP, INC., *pg.* 1190, *pg.* 1193
AMERITAS INVESTMENT CORP., *pg.* 1192, *pg.* 1410
AMERITAS LIFE INSURANCE CORP., *pg.* 1192, *pg.* 1011
AON RISK SERVICES INC., *pg.* 1193, *pg.* 564
ARROWPOINT CAPITAL CORP., *pg.* 1193, *pg.* 1361
ASSET MARKETING SYSTEMS INSURANCE SERVICES, LLC, *pg.* 1193, *pg.* 200
ASSURANT, INC., *pg.* 1193, *pg.* 1198
ASSURITY LIFE INSURANCE COMPANY, *pg.* 1194, *pg.* 1011
ATTO & ASSOCIATES INSURANCE BROKERS, INC., *pg.* 1194, *pg.* 1924
AUTO-OWNERS INSURANCE GROUP, *pg.* 1194, *pg.* 895
AUTOMOBILE CLUB OF SOUTHERN CALIFORNIA, *pg.* 134, *pg.* 126
BB&T - OSWALD TRIPPE & CO., *pg.* 1194, *pg.* 427
BEECH STREET CORPORATION, *pg.* 1503, *pg.* 121
BERKSHIRE HATHAWAY INC., *pg.* 1195, *pg.* 1013
BROWN & BROWN, INC., *pg.* 1196, *pg.* 419
CIGI DIRECT INSURANCE SERVICES, INC., *pg.* 1197, *pg.* 335
THE CO-OPERATORS GROUP LIMITED, *pg.* 1198, *pg.* 1920
COLUMBIAN MUTUAL LIFE INSURANCE COMPANY, *pg.* 1198, *pg.* 1142
COUNTRY FINANCIAL, *pg.* 1198, *pg.* 557
CRAWFORD & COMPANY, *pg.* 1199, *pg.* 502
CUNA MUTUAL INSURANCE SOCIETY, *pg.* 743, *pg.* 1865
THE DOCTORS COMPANY, *pg.* 1199, *pg.* 163
EHEALTH, INC., *pg.* 1242, *pg.* 153
EMERGENT CAPITAL, INC., *pg.* 747, *pg.* 411
EQUIINSURANCE, LLC, *pg.* 748, *pg.* 448
ESURANCE, INC., *pg.* 1243, *pg.* 217
THE F. DOHMEN CO., *pg.* 1530, *pg.* 1858
FACTORY MUTUAL INSURANCE COMPANY, *pg.* 1199, *pg.* 1601
FARMERS GROUP, INC., *pg.* 1199, *pg.* 130
FINANCIAL BROKERAGE INC., *pg.* 1200, *pg.* 1015
FINANCIAL INDEPENDENCE GROUP INC., *pg.* 1200, *pg.* 1370
FIRST FINANCIAL HOLDINGS, INC., *pg.* 755, *pg.* 1614
FIRST FINANCIAL GROUP OF AMERICA, *pg.* 755, *pg.* 1705
FIRST NIAGARA BANK, *pg.* 756, *pg.* 1174
FIRST NIAGARA FINANCIAL GROUP, INC., *pg.* 757, *pg.* 1148
FORUM NATIONAL INVESTMENTS LTD., *pg.* 1200, *pg.* 1908
FRENKEL & CO. INC., *pg.* 1200, *pg.* 1233
GALLAGHER BOLLINGER, *pg.* 1200, *pg.* 1121
GEICO CORPORATION, *pg.* 1200, *pg.* 399
GEICO GENERAL INSURANCE COMPANY, *pg.* 1201, *pg.* 766
GENWORTH LIFE AND ANNUITY INSURANCE COMPANY, *pg.* 1201, *pg.* 1802
GEOVERA INSURANCE COMPANY INC., *pg.* 1201, *pg.* 86
GRINNELL MUTUAL REINSURANCE COMPANY INC., *pg.* 1201, *pg.* 708
THE GUARDIAN LIFE INSURANCE COMPANY OF AMERICA, *pg.* 1202, *pg.* 1237
GUIDEONE INSURANCE COMPANY, *pg.* 1202, *pg.* 713
HALLMARK FINANCIAL SERVICES, INC., *pg.* 1202, *pg.* 1695
THE HANOVER INSURANCE COMPANY, *pg.* 1202, *pg.* 862
THE HARTFORD FINANCIAL SERVICES GROUP, INC., *pg.* 1202, *pg.* 352
HEALTH CARE SERVICE CORPORATION, *pg.* 1203, *pg.* 576
HOOPER HOLMES, INC., *pg.* 1542, *pg.* 718
HORIZON BLUE CROSS BLUE SHIELD OF NEW JERSEY, *pg.* 1203, *pg.* 1096
HORTICA INSURANCE, *pg.* 1204, *pg.* 609
HSB GROUP, INC., *pg.* 1204, *pg.* 352
INDIANA FARM BUREAU INSURANCE, *pg.* 1204, *pg.* 687
INSURANCE BROKERS & AGENTS OF THE WEST, *pg.* 144, *pg.* 183
INSURANCE.COM, INC., *pg.* 1205, *pg.* 1473
INSWEB CORPORATION, *pg.* 1205, *pg.* 186
KINGSTONE COMPANIES, INC., *pg.* 1205, *pg.* 1166
LIFE QUOTES, INC., *pg.* 1206, *pg.* 598
LINCOLN FINANCIAL BENEFIT PARTNERS, *pg.* 1206, *pg.* 1016
MANULIFE FINANCIAL CORPORATION, *pg.* 778, *pg.* 1939
MARKEL CORPORATION, *pg.* 1207, *pg.* 1783
MARSH & MCLENNAN COMPANIES INC., *pg.* 1207, *pg.* 1256
MERCHANTS GROUP, INC., *pg.* 1208, *pg.* 1149
METLIFE, INC., *pg.* 1208, *pg.* 1258
MILLENNIUM MARKETING GROUP, LLC, *pg.* 1209, *pg.* 1016
MUTUAL OF AMERICA LIFE INSURANCE COMPANY, *pg.* 1210, *pg.* 1263
MUTUAL OF OMAHA INSURANCE COMPANY, *pg.* 1210, *pg.* 1016
NATIONAL WESTERN LIFE INSURANCE COMPANY, *pg.* 1210, *pg.* 1664
NATIONWIDE MUTUAL INSURANCE COMPANY, *pg.* 1211, *pg.* 1536
OHIO FARMERS INSURANCE COMPANY, *pg.* 1213, *pg.* 1480
OLD NATIONAL BANCORP, *pg.* 789, *pg.* 679
PATRIOT NATIONAL INSURANCE GROUP, *pg.* 1213, *pg.* 426
PENN TREATY AMERICAN CORPORATION, *pg.* 793, *pg.* 1514
PEOPLES BANCORP INC., *pg.* 793, *pg.* 1458
PLATTE VALLEY FINANCIAL SERVICE COMPANIES INC., *pg.* 794, *pg.* 1019
PRIMERICA FINANCIAL SERVICES, INC., *pg.* 795, *pg.* 531
PRINCIPAL FINANCIAL GROUP, INC., *pg.* 796, *pg.* 706
PROASSURANCE CORPORATION, *pg.* 1214, *pg.* 404
PROASSURANCE CORPORATION, *pg.* 1214, *pg.* 3
QUALCARE, INC., *pg.* 1215, *pg.* 1109
QUINCY MUTUAL FIRE INSURANCE COMPANY, *pg.* 1215, *pg.* 842
REGENCE BLUECROSS BLUESHIELD OF OREGON, *pg.* 1215, *pg.* 1506
RENASANT CORPORATION, *pg.* 799, *pg.* 972
RICHARDS & SUMMERS INC., *pg.* 1216, *pg.* 1053
ROYAL BANK OF CANADA, *pg.* 800, *pg.* 1942
SAFELITE SOLUTIONS LLC, *pg.* 109, *pg.* 1443
SELECTIVE INSURANCE GROUP, INC., *pg.* 1216, *pg.* 1045
SENIOR MARKET SALES, INC., *pg.* 1217, *pg.* 1018
SENTRY INSURANCE GROUP, *pg.* 1217, *pg.* 1895
SOLERA HOLDINGS, INC., *pg.* 1217, *pg.* 1749
STAHL & ASSOCIATES INSURANCE, *pg.* 1217, *pg.* 464
STATE AUTOMOBILE MUTUAL INSURANCE COMPANY, *pg.* 1217, *pg.* 1444
TECHNOLOGY EXECUTIVES CLUB, LTD., *pg.* 482, *pg.* 627
TRANSAMERICA INSURANCE & INVESTMENT GROUP, *pg.* 1219, *pg.* 141
TRAVEL GUARD GROUP, INC., *pg.* 1925, *pg.* 1895
TRAVELERS INSURANCE, *pg.* 1220, *pg.* 963
UMB FINANCIAL CORPORATION, *pg.* 812, *pg.* 987
UNICO AMERICAN CORPORATION, *pg.* 1220, *pg.* 308
UNITED INSURANCE HOLDINGS CORP., *pg.* 1220, *pg.* 465
UNIVEST CORPORATION OF PENNSYLVANIA, *pg.* 814, *pg.* 1586
USI HOLDINGS CORPORATION, *pg.* 1222, *pg.* 1144
VERISK ANALYTICS, INC., *pg.* 1222, *pg.* 1076
VETERINARY PET INSURANCE CO., *pg.* 1222, *pg.* 49
VREELAND INSURANCE INC., *pg.* 1223, *pg.* 1116
WELLS FARGO & COMPANY, *pg.* 819, *pg.* 232
WESCO FINANCIAL CORPORATION, *pg.* 821, *pg.* 181
WEST SUBURBAN BANCORP, INC., *pg.* 821, *pg.* 631
WILLIS HRH, INC., *pg.* 1223, *pg.* 1314
ZECCO TRADING, *pg.* 824, *pg.* 181
ZENITH MARKETING GROUP, INC., *pg.* 1224, *pg.* 1071

6512 - Operators of Nonresidential Buildings

AMALGAMATED LITHOGRAPHERS OF AMERICA, *pg.* 126, *pg.* 1189
AMC, INC., *pg.* 1759, *pg.* 487
AMERICAN CONSERVATORY THEATRE, *pg.* 528, *pg.* 212
ANCIRA ENTERPRISES INC., *pg.* 164, *pg.* 1739
ATLANTIC AVIATION, *pg.* 224, *pg.* 1772
BALTIMORE SYMPHONY ORCHESTRA, *pg.* 532, *pg.* 755
BROOKFIELD FINANCIAL PROPERTIES, INC., *pg.* 1083, *pg.* 1207
DALLAS MARKET CENTER COMPANY, *pg.* 78, *pg.* 1678
EDISON INTERNATIONAL, *pg.* 1941, *pg.* 194
EMPIRE STATE BUILDING COMPANY LLC, *pg.* 546, *pg.* 1227
FOREST CITY ENTERPRISES, INC., *pg.* 1092, *pg.* 1430
GARFF ENTERPRISES INC., *pg.* 174, *pg.* 1758
HELMSLEY ENTERPRISES, INC., *pg.* 1094, *pg.* 1240
ICAHN ENTERPRISES L.P., *pg.* 1097, *pg.* 1243
JOHN BUCK COMPANY, *pg.* 1099, *pg.* 579
JOURNAL INC., *pg.* 1655, *pg.* 972
KENNEDY-WILSON, INC., *pg.* 1099, *pg.* 46
KILROY REALTY CORPORATION, *pg.* 1099, *pg.* 134
LARKEN ASSOCIATES, *pg.* 93, *pg.* 1073
LEFRAK ORGANIZATION INC., *pg.* 1100, *pg.* 1251
LOFFLER BUSINESS SYSTEMS INC., *pg.* 428, *pg.* 918
MASSACHUSETTS CONVENTION CENTER AUTHORITY, *pg.* 561, *pg.* 798
MERROW MACHINE COMPANY, *pg.* 58, *pg.* 819
MILLER INDUSTRIES, INC., *pg.* 185, *pg.* 1655
MUSICAL ARTS ASSOCIATION, *pg.* 565, *pg.* 1433
NEWMARK GRUBB KNIGHT FRANK, *pg.* 1106, *pg.* 1271
NORTH SHORE PHILHARMONIC ORCHESTRA, *pg.* 571, *pg.* 816
PBI/GORDON CORPORATION, *pg.* 1176, *pg.* 985
THE PHILADELPHIA ORCHESTRA ASSOCIATION, *pg.* 575, *pg.* 1569
PROPPER MANUFACTURING COMPANY, INC., *pg.* 1586, *pg.* 1175
PS BUSINESS PARKS, INC., *pg.* 1108, *pg.* 98
SEATTLE THEATRE GROUP, *pg.* 582, *pg.* 1840
SIMON PROPERTY GROUP, INC., *pg.* 1112, *pg.* 690
SPELNA, INC., *pg.* 157, *pg.* 1782
SUNBEAM TELEVISION CORP., *pg.* 311, *pg.* 447
TCR CORPORATION, *pg.* 1380, *pg.* 944
TEJON RANCH COMPANY, *pg.* 1116, *pg.* 122
TRAMMELL CROW COMPANY, *pg.* 1116, *pg.* 1689
W.P. CAREY & CO., LLC, *pg.* 823, *pg.* 1315

6513 - Operators of Apartment Buildings

ABM INDUSTRIES, INC., *pg.* 64, *pg.* 1186
ADVANCE REALTY GROUP, LLC, *pg.* 1079, *pg.* 1045
AFFINIA HOSPITALITY, *pg.* 1487, *pg.* 1188
AIMCO PROPERTIES, L.P., *pg.* 1079, *pg.* 316
ALLETE, INC., *pg.* 1933, *pg.* 921
AMERICAN CAMPUS COMMUNITIES, INC., *pg.* 1079, *pg.* 1660
AV HOMES INC., *pg.* 1080, *pg.* 20
BB&T, *pg.* 723, *pg.* 423
BERKSHIRE HATHAWAY HOME SERVICES, *pg.* 1081, *pg.* 200
BERKSHIRE HATHAWAY HOME SERVICES, *pg.* 1081, *pg.* 469
BEVERLY-HANKS & ASSOCIATES INC., *pg.* 1082, *pg.* 1358
BINSWANGER CORPORATION, *pg.* 1082, *pg.* 1559
BLUEGREEN CORPORATION, *pg.* 1082, *pg.* 410
BRUTGER EQUITIES, INC., *pg.* 1083, *pg.* 956
CALDWELL WATSON REAL ESTATE GROUP, *pg.* 1084, *pg.* 1702
CANDY SWICK & COMPANY, *pg.* 1084, *pg.* 465
CARLSON REAL ESTATE COMPANY, *pg.* 1084, *pg.* 947
CB RICHARD ELLIS GROUP, INC., *pg.* 1085, *pg.* 127
CB RICHARD ELLIS, INC., *pg.* 1085, *pg.* 1210
CBSHOME REAL ESTATE, *pg.* 1085, *pg.* 1013
CENTURY 21 REAL ESTATE LLC, *pg.* 1085, *pg.* 1080
CHAMPION REALTY INC., *pg.* 1085, *pg.* 777
COLDWELL BANKER REAL ESTATE LLC, *pg.* 1087, *pg.* 1103
COLDWELL BANKER RESIDENTIAL BROKERAGE, *pg.* 1087, *pg.* 850
COLLIERS INTERNATIONAL, *pg.* 1087, *pg.* 1834
COMSTOCK HOLDING COMPANIES INC., *pg.* 1087, *pg.* 1798
CONCORD PACIFIC GROUP, *pg.* 1087, *pg.* 1910
CONSOLIDATED-TOMOKA LAND CO., *pg.* 1087, *pg.* 419
CORCORAN SUNSHINE MARKETING GROUP, *pg.* 1088, *pg.* 1218
CORELOGIC, INC., *pg.* 1198, *pg.* 109
COSTAR GROUP, INC., *pg.* 742, *pg.* 397
COUNTRY WIDE REALTY INC., *pg.* 1088, *pg.* 1144
COUSINS PROPERTIES INCORPORATED, *pg.* 1088, *pg.* 501
CRESA PARTNERS LLC, *pg.* 1088, *pg.* 1220
CRESCENT COMMUNITIES, LLC, *pg.* 702, *pg.* 1365

6531 - Real Estate Agents & Managers

First page reference indicates Business Class Edition
Second page reference indicates Geographic Edition

THE TRUMP ORGANIZATION, LLC, pg. 1117, pg. 1305
UNITED, INC., pg. 1117, pg. 1905
UNITED STATES REALTY & INVESTMENT COMPANY, pg. 1117, pg. 1307
VICEROY HOMES LIMITED, pg. 118, pg. 1932
WCI COMMUNITIES, INC., pg. 1118, pg. 414
WEICHERT REALTORS, pg. 1118, pg. 1087
WOODS BROS REALTY, INC., pg. 1119, pg. 1012
W.P. CAREY & CO., LLC, pg. 823, pg. 1315
WYNDHAM VACATION OWNERSHIP, pg. 1119, pg. 457
WYNN LAS VEGAS, LLC, pg. 1119, pg. 1030
WYNN RESORTS LIMITED, pg. 1119, pg. 1030
WYNNESTONE COMMUNITIES, pg. 1120, pg. 908
ZILLOW GROUP, INC., pg. 1292, pg. 1843
ZIPREALTY, INC., pg. 1120, pg. 85

6552 - Land Subdividers & Developers, Except Cemeteries

ADAM'S MARK HOTELS & RESORTS, pg. 1079, pg. 990
AMERICAN CAMPUS COMMUNITIES, INC., pg. 1079, pg. 1660
BLUEGREEN CORPORATION, pg. 1082, pg. 410
BROOKFIELD FINANCIAL PROPERTIES, INC., pg. 1083, pg. 1207
BURROUGHS & CHAPIN CO. INC., pg. 72, pg. 1621
CB RICHARD ELLIS GROUP, INC., pg. 1085, pg. 127
CENTRAL FLORIDA INVESTMENTS INC., pg. 1085, pg. 452
CONSOLIDATED-TOMOKA LAND CO., pg. 1087, pg. 419
CRESCENT COMMUNITIES, LLC, pg. 702, pg. 1365
THE DELTONA CORPORATION, pg. 1089, pg. 452
DOMINION HOMES, INC., pg. 79, pg. 1449
D.R. HORTON, INC./SCHULER HOMES LLC, pg. 1090, pg. 543
ERICKSON LIVING, pg. 1090, pg. 766
FLORIDA EAST COAST INDUSTRIES, INC., pg. 1909, pg. 433
HBE CORPORATION, pg. 86, pg. 998
THE IRVINE COMPANY INC., pg. 1098, pg. 165
JACKSON HOLE MOUNTAIN RESORT, pg. 1098, pg. 1901
JAY PEAK, INC., pg. 1098, pg. 1766
JIM WILSON & ASSOCIATES, INC., pg. 1098, pg. 7
JMB REALTY CORPORATION, pg. 1099, pg. 579
LENNAR CORPORATION, pg. 1100, pg. 443
MATRIX DEVELOPMENT GROUP INC., pg. 1104, pg. 1053
NEW VALLEY CORPORATION, pg. 786, pg. 444
NORTH SHORE PHILHARMONIC ORCHESTRA, pg. 571, pg. 816
NTS DEVELOPMENT COMPANY, pg. 1106, pg. 737
OPUS CORPORATION, pg. 101, pg. 949
PUBLIC STORAGE, pg. 1467, pg. 98
PULTEGROUP, INC., pg. 1109, pg. 873
RAMPART CAPITAL CORPORATION, pg. 798, pg. 1672
THE RESORT AT LONGBOAT KEY CLUB, pg. 1110, pg. 438
THE RITZ-CARLTON HOTEL COMPANY LLC, pg. 1110, pg. 766
STRATUS INVESTMENTS, LLC, pg. 1115, pg. 421
STRATUS PROPERTIES, INC., pg. 1115, pg. 1666
TEJON RANCH COMPANY, pg. 1116, pg. 122
TRAMMELL CROW COMPANY, pg. 1116, pg. 1689
WCI COMMUNITIES, INC., pg. 1118, pg. 414

6553 - Cemetery Subdividers & Developers

BATESVILLE CASKET COMPANY, INC., pg. 1393, pg. 673
HILLENBRAND, INC., pg. 1394, pg. 673
ROSE HILLS COMPANY, pg. 1395, pg. 307
SECURITY NATIONAL FINANCIAL CORPORATION, pg. 802, pg. 1760
SERVICE CORPORATION INTERNATIONAL, pg. 1395, pg. 1714
STONEMOR PARTNERS L.P., pg. 1396, pg. 1548

6712 - Offices of Bank Holding Companies

ACCESS NATIONAL CORPORATION, pg. 710, pg. 1798
ACNB CORPORATION, pg. 710, pg. 1534
AMB FINANCIAL CORP., pg. 711, pg. 696
AMBOY BANCORPORATION, pg. 711, pg. 1100
AMERICAN BANK INCORPORATED, pg. 711, pg. 1513
AMERICAN RIVER BANKSHARES, pg. 714, pg. 186
AMERICANWEST BANCORPORATION, pg. 715, pg. 1843
AMERIS BANCORP, pg. 715, pg. 536
ASSOCIATED BANC-CORP, pg. 716, pg. 1859
ASTORIA FINANCIAL CORPORATION, pg. 717, pg. 1172
ATHENS BANCSHARES CORPORATION, pg. 717, pg. 1627
ATLANTIC COAST FINANCIAL CORPORATION, pg. 717, pg. 432
BAKER BOYER BANCORP, pg. 717, pg. 1846
BANCFIRST CORPORATION, pg. 717, pg. 1484
BANCORPSOUTH, INC., pg. 717, pg. 971
BANK OF AMERICA CORPORATION, pg. 718, pg. 1362
BANK OF HAWAII CORPORATION, pg. 720, pg. 543
BANK OF MARIN BANCORP, pg. 720, pg. 168
THE BANK OF NEW YORK MELLON CORPORATION, pg. 720, pg. 1200
BANK OF SOUTH CAROLINA CORPORATION, pg. 721, pg. 1613
BANK OF THE OZARKS, INC., pg. 721, pg. 33
BANKFINANCIAL CORPORATION, pg. 722, pg. 560
BANNER CORPORATION, pg. 722, pg. 1846
BB&T CORPORATION, pg. 723, pg. 1393
BBCN BANCORP, INC., pg. 723, pg. 126
BBX CAPITAL, pg. 723, pg. 423
BCB BANCORP, INC., pg. 723, pg. 1042
BENEFICIAL MUTUAL BANCORP, INC., pg. 724, pg. 1559
BLACKHAWK BANCORP INC., pg. 724, pg. 1854
BLUE VALLEY BAN CORP, pg. 725, pg. 718
BNC BANCORP, pg. 726, pg. 1379
BOFI HOLDING, INC., pg. 726, pg. 200
BOK FINANCIAL CORPORATION, pg. 726, pg. 1489
BOTETOURT BANKSHARES, INC., pg. 726, pg. 1777
BRIDGE BANCORP, INC., pg. 727, pg. 1144
BROOKLINE BANCORP, INC., pg. 727, pg. 804
BRUNSWICK BANCORP, pg. 727, pg. 1091
BRYN MAWR BANK CORPORATION, pg. 728, pg. 1519
C&F FINANCIAL CORPORATION, pg. 728, pg. 1811
CALIFORNIA FIRST NATIONAL BANCORP, pg. 728, pg. 109
CAPE BANCORP, INC., pg. 730, pg. 1049
CAPITAL BANK, pg. 730, pg. 1393
CAPITAL BANK CORPORATION, pg. 730, pg. 1386
CAPITOL FEDERAL FINANCIAL, INC., pg. 731, pg. 721
CARDINAL FINANCIAL CORP., pg. 732, pg. 1790
CAROLINA BANK HOLDINGS, INC., pg. 732, pg. 1374
CASCADE BANCORP, pg. 732, pg. 1496
CCFNB BANCORP, INC., pg. 733, pg. 1517
CENTRAL FEDERAL CORPORATION, pg. 733, pg. 1453
CENTRAL PACIFIC FINANCIAL CORPORATION, pg. 733, pg. 543
CENTRAL VALLEY COMMUNITY BANCORP, pg. 733, pg. 93
CENTRUE FINANCIAL CORPORATION, pg. 733, pg. 994
CFG COMMUNITY BANK, pg. 734, pg. 756
CHARTER FINANCIAL CORPORATION, pg. 734, pg. 542
CHEMICAL FINANCIAL CORPORATION, pg. 734, pg. 898
CHESAPEAKE FINANCIAL SHARES, INC., pg. 735, pg. 1787
CHEVIOT FINANCIAL CORP., pg. 735, pg. 1409
CHICOPEE BANCORP, INC., pg. 735, pg. 815
CHOICEONE FINANCIAL SERVICES, INC., pg. 735, pg. 908
CIB MARINE BANCSHARES, INC., pg. 735, pg. 1897
CIT GROUP INC., pg. 735, pg. 1212
CITIGROUP INC., pg. 735, pg. 1212
CITIZENS BANK & TRUST, pg. 737, pg. 976
CITIZENS COMMUNITY BANCORP, INC., pg. 737, pg. 1857
CITIZENS FIRST CORPORATION, pg. 737, pg. 725
CITIZENS HOLDING COMPANY, pg. 737, pg. 971
CITY HOLDING COMPANY, pg. 737, pg. 1849
CITY NATIONAL CORPORATION, pg. 738, pg. 128
CIVISTA BANCSHARES, INC., pg. 738, pg. 1472
CLIFTON SAVINGS BANCORP, INC., pg. 738, pg. 1052
CMS ENERGY CORPORATION, pg. 1937, pg. 893
CNB FINANCIAL CORPORATION, pg. 739, pg. 1522
COASTAL BANKING COMPANY, INC., pg. 739, pg. 1612
CODORUS VALLEY BANCORP, INC., pg. 739, pg. 1596
COLONY BANKCORP, INC., pg. 739, pg. 532
COMERICA INCORPORATED, pg. 740, pg. 1677
COMMERCE BANCSHARES, INC., pg. 740, pg. 982
COMMERCIAL BANCSHARES, INC., pg. 740, pg. 1477
COMMERCIAL NATIONAL FINANCIAL CORPORATION, pg. 740, pg. 1547
COMMUNITY BANCORP, pg. 741, pg. 1766
COMMUNITY BANK SYSTEM, INC., pg. 741, pg. 1155
COMMUNITY PARTNERS BANCORP, pg. 741, pg. 1084
COMMUNITY SHORES BANK CORPORATION, pg. 741, pg. 901
COMMUNITYONE BANCORP, pg. 741, pg. 1358
CULLEN/FROST BANKERS, INC., pg. 742, pg. 1740
CULLMAN BANCORP, INC., pg. 743, pg. 5
DORAL FINANCIAL CORPORATION, pg. 744, pg. 1599
EAGLE BANCORP, INC., pg. 745, pg. 762
EAGLE FINANCIAL SERVICES, INC., pg. 745, pg. 1776
EASTERN BANK CORPORATION, pg. 745, pg. 793
EASTERN VIRGINIA BANKSHARES, INC., pg. 746, pg. 1808
EDELMAN FINANCIAL SERVICES LLC, pg. 746, pg. 1705
EMCLAIRE FINANCIAL CORP., pg. 747, pg. 1529
ENB FINANCIAL CORP., pg. 747, pg. 1530
ENTERPRISE BANCORP INC., pg. 747, pg. 829
ESB FINANCIAL CORPORATION, pg. 749, pg. 1529
ESSA BANCORP, INC., pg. 749, pg. 1587
EVANS BANCORP, INC., pg. 749, pg. 1138
EVERBANK FINANCIAL CORP., pg. 749, pg. 432
F&M BANK CORP., pg. 750, pg. 1808
FARMERS & MERCHANTS BANCORP, pg. 750, pg. 1403
FAUQUIER BANKSHARES INC, pg. 751, pg. 1810
FENTURA FINANCIAL, INC., pg. 752, pg. 886
FIDELITY D & D BANCORP INC., pg. 752, pg. 1527
FIDELITY SOUTHERN CORPORATION, pg. 752, pg. 505
FINANCIAL INSTITUTIONS, INC., pg. 753, pg. 1349
FIRST BANCORP OF INDIANA, INC., pg. 753, pg. 678
THE FIRST BANCSHARES, INC., pg. 753, pg. 969
FIRST BANKS, INC., pg. 754, pg. 976
FIRST BUSEY CORPORATION, pg. 754, pg. 562
FIRST CAPITAL BANCORP, INC., pg. 754, pg. 1782
FIRST CITIZENS BANCSHARES, INC., pg. 754, pg. 1387
FIRST COMMONWEALTH FINANCIAL CORPORATION, pg. 754, pg. 1541
FIRST COMMUNITY BANCSHARES, INC., pg. 754, pg. 1776
FIRST COMMUNITY CORPORATION, pg. 754, pg. 1620
FIRST FINANCIAL BANKSHARES, INC., pg. 755, pg. 1657
FIRST FINANCIAL HOLDINGS, INC., pg. 755, pg. 1614
FIRST HARRISON BANK, pg. 755, pg. 676
FIRST HORIZON NATIONAL CORPORATION, pg. 755, pg. 1644
FIRST INTERSTATE BANCSYSTEM, INC., pg. 755, pg. 1008
FIRST MARINER BANCORP, pg. 756, pg. 757
FIRST MERCHANTS CORPORATION, pg. 756, pg. 695
FIRST MIDWEST BANCORP INC., pg. 756, pg. 620
FIRST NATIONAL COMMUNITY BANCORP, INC., pg. 756, pg. 1527
FIRST NIAGARA BANK, pg. 757, pg. 358
FIRST NIAGARA FINANCIAL GROUP, INC., pg. 757, pg. 1148
FIRST ROBINSON FINANCIAL CORPORATION, pg. 757, pg. 654
FIRST SAVINGS FINANCIAL GROUP INC., pg. 757, pg. 675
FIRST SECURITY BANCORP INC., pg. 757, pg. 35
FIRST SECURITY GROUP, INC., pg. 757, pg. 1629
FIRSTMERIT CORPORATION, pg. 758, pg. 1400
FLAGSTAR BANCORP, INC., pg. 758, pg. 910
FLUSHING FINANCIAL CORPORATION, pg. 759, pg. 1172
F.N.B. CORPORATION, pg. 759, pg. 1575
FNBH BANCORP, INC., pg. 759, pg. 893
FRANKLIN FINANCIAL SERVICES CORPORATION, pg. 760, pg. 1521
FULTON FINANCIAL CORPORATION, pg. 760, pg. 1546
GERMAN AMERICAN BANCORP, INC., pg. 762, pg. 691
GLACIER BANCORP, INC., pg. 762, pg. 1009
GLEN BURNIE BANCORP, pg. 762, pg. 771
THE GOLDMAN SACHS GROUP, INC., pg. 762, pg. 1236
GOUVERNEUR BANCORP, INC., pg. 763, pg. 1162
GRAYSON BANKSHARES, INC., pg. 763, pg. 1786
GREAT AMERICAN BANCORP, INC., pg. 763, pg. 562
GREAT SOUTHERN BANCORP, INC., pg. 763, pg. 1006
GREAT WESTERN BANK, pg. 763, pg. 708
GREENE COUNTY BANCORP, INC., pg. 764, pg. 1152
GUARANTY BANCSHARES, INC., pg. 764, pg. 1728
GUARANTY BANK, pg. 764, pg. 1006
HAMPTON ROADS BANKSHARES, INC., pg. 765, pg. 1796
HANCOCK HOLDING COMPANY, pg. 765, pg. 968
THE HARTFORD FINANCIAL SERVICES GROUP, INC., pg. 1202, pg. 352
HAWTHORN BANCSHARES, INC., pg. 765, pg. 987
HEARTLAND FINANCIAL USA, INC., pg. 765, pg. 707
HERITAGE COMMERCE CORP., pg. 765, pg. 246
HERITAGE FINANCIAL CORPORATION, pg. 765, pg. 1823

HF FINANCIAL CORP., *pg.* 766, *pg.* 1625
HIBERNIA BANK, *pg.* 766, *pg.* 747
HMN FINANCIAL, INC., *pg.* 766, *pg.* 955
HOME BANCORP, INC., *pg.* 766, *pg.* 744
HOME BANCSHARES, INC., *pg.* 766, *pg.* 31
HOPFED BANCORP, INC., *pg.* 766, *pg.* 729
HORIZON BANCORP, *pg.* 767, *pg.* 694
HUNTINGTON BANCSHARES INCORPORATED, *pg.* 767, *pg.* 1440
IBERIABANK CORPORATION, *pg.* 768, *pg.* 744
IBW FINANCIAL CORP., *pg.* 768, *pg.* 401
INDEPENDENT BANK CORPORATION, *pg.* 768, *pg.* 893
INDEPENDENT BANK CORP., *pg.* 768, *pg.* 843
INTERNATIONAL BANCSHARES CORPORATION, *pg.* 769, *pg.* 1725
INVESTORS BANCORP, INC., *pg.* 771, *pg.* 1121
IOWA FIRST BANCSHARES CORP., *pg.* 771, *pg.* 710
ISABELLA BANK CORPORATION, *pg.* 771, *pg.* 901
JACKSONVILLE BANCORP, INC., *pg.* 771, *pg.* 433
JEFFERSONVILLE BANCORP, *pg.* 772, *pg.* 1170
JPMORGAN CHASE & CO., *pg.* 772, *pg.* 1246
JUNIATA VALLEY FINANCIAL CORP., *pg.* 773, *pg.* 1553
KEARNY FINANCIAL CORP., *pg.* 773, *pg.* 1065
KENTUCKY BANCSHARES, INC., *pg.* 773, *pg.* 739
KEYCORP, *pg.* 774, *pg.* 1432
LAKE SHORE BANCORP, INC., *pg.* 775, *pg.* 1156
LANDMARK BANCORP, INC., *pg.* 775, *pg.* 717
LAPORTE BANCORP, INC., *pg.* 775, *pg.* 692
LIBERTY BANCORP, INC., *pg.* 775, *pg.* 987
LOUISIANA BANCORP, INC., *pg.* 777, *pg.* 745
M&T BANK CORPORATION, *pg.* 777, *pg.* 1149
MACATAWA BANK CORPORATION, *pg.* 778, *pg.* 892
MACKINAC FINANCIAL CORPORATION, *pg.* 778, *pg.* 898
MALVERN FEDERAL BANCORP, INC., *pg.* 778, *pg.* 1558
MB FINANCIAL, INC., *pg.* 781, *pg.* 581
MERCANTILE BANK CORPORATION, *pg.* 782, *pg.* 888
MERCHANTS BANCSHARES, INC., *pg.* 782, *pg.* 1768
MERIDIAN INTERSTATE BANCORP, INC., *pg.* 782, *pg.* 817
METRO BANCORP, INC., *pg.* 782, *pg.* 1537
MID PENN BANCORP, INC., *pg.* 782, *pg.* 1553
MIDDLEBURG FINANCIAL CORPORATION, *pg.* 782, *pg.* 1795
MIDDLEFIELD BANC CORP., *pg.* 783, *pg.* 1465
MIDSOUTH BANCORP, INC., *pg.* 783, *pg.* 745
MINDEN BANCORP, INC., *pg.* 783, *pg.* 746
MONARCH FINANCIAL HOLDINGS, INC., *pg.* 783, *pg.* 1778
MORGAN STANLEY, *pg.* 783, *pg.* 1261
MUTUALFIRST FINANCIAL, INC., *pg.* 785, *pg.* 696
NASB FINANCIAL, INC., *pg.* 785, *pg.* 978
NATIONAL BANK OF INDIANAPOLIS CORPORATION, *pg.* 785, *pg.* 688
NATIONAL BANK OF SOUTH CAROLINA, *pg.* 785, *pg.* 1614
NATIONAL BANKSHARES, INC., *pg.* 785, *pg.* 1776
NATIONAL PENN BANCSHARES, INC., *pg.* 786, *pg.* 1517
NAUGATUCK VALLEY FINANCIAL CORPORATION, *pg.* 786, *pg.* 358
NEW ENGLAND BANCSHARES, INC., *pg.* 786, *pg.* 346
NEW HAMPSHIRE THRIFT BANCSHARES, INC., *pg.* 786, *pg.* 1038
NEWBRIDGE BANCORP, *pg.* 787, *pg.* 1375
NORTHEAST BANCORP, *pg.* 787, *pg.* 751
NORTHRIM BANCORP, INC., *pg.* 788, *pg.* 10
NORTHWAY FINANCIAL, INC., *pg.* 788, *pg.* 1033
NORTHWEST BANCSHARES, INC., *pg.* 788, *pg.* 1590
OAK RIDGE FINANCIAL SERVICES, INC., *pg.* 789, *pg.* 1386
OCEAN SHORE HOLDING CO., *pg.* 789, *pg.* 1100
OCEANFIRST FINANCIAL CORP., *pg.* 789, *pg.* 1125
OLD LINE BANCSHARES, INC., *pg.* 789, *pg.* 766
OLD NATIONAL BANCORP, *pg.* 789, *pg.* 679
OLD POINT FINANCIAL CORPORATION, *pg.* 789, *pg.* 1783
ONEIDA FINANCIAL CORP., *pg.* 790, *pg.* 1318
OPUS BANK, *pg.* 790, *pg.* 1819
ORITANI FINANCIAL CORP., *pg.* 790, *pg.* 1129
PACIFIC & WESTERN CREDIT CORP., *pg.* 791, *pg.* 1922
PACIFIC CONTINENTAL CORPORATION, *pg.* 791, *pg.* 1497
PACIFIC FINANCIAL CORPORATION, *pg.* 791, *pg.* 1813
PALMETTO BANCSHARES, INC., *pg.* 791, *pg.* 1618
PARK BANCORP, INC., *pg.* 792, *pg.* 587
PARK NATIONAL CORPORATION, *pg.* 792, *pg.* 1468
PARK STERLING BANK, *pg.* 792, *pg.* 1373
PATAPSCO BANCORP, *pg.* 792, *pg.* 758
PATHFINDER BANCORP, INC., *pg.* 792, *pg.* 1320
PEAPACK-GLADSTONE FINANCIAL CORPORATION, *pg.* 792, *pg.* 1044
PENNS WOODS BANCORP, INC., *pg.* 304, *pg.* 1595
PEOPLES BANCORP INC., *pg.* 793, *pg.* 1458
PEOPLES FINANCIAL CORPORATION, *pg.* 793, *pg.* 968
PEOPLES SECURITY BANK & TRUST, *pg.* 793, *pg.* 1535
PEOPLE'S UNITED FINANCIAL, INC., *pg.* 793, *pg.* 340
PINNACLE FINANCIAL PARTNERS, INC., *pg.* 794, *pg.* 1653
PLAINS CAPITAL CORPORATION, *pg.* 794, *pg.* 1685
PLATTE VALLEY FINANCIAL SERVICE COMPANIES INC., *pg.* 794, *pg.* 1019
PLUMAS BANCORP, *pg.* 794, *pg.* 186
THE PNC FINANCIAL SERVICES GROUP, INC., *pg.* 795, *pg.* 1579
PRIVATEBANCORP INC., *pg.* 796, *pg.* 587
PROSPERITY BANCSHARES, INC., *pg.* 796, *pg.* 1713
PROVIDENT FINANCIAL HOLDINGS, INC., *pg.* 796, *pg.* 194
PROVIDENT FINANCIAL SERVICES, INC., *pg.* 796, *pg.* 1075
PSB HOLDINGS, INC., *pg.* 797, *pg.* 1898
PULASKI FINANCIAL CORP., *pg.* 797, *pg.* 1002
QCR HOLDINGS, INC., *pg.* 797, *pg.* 633
REAL INDUSTRY, INC., *pg.* 1216, *pg.* 278
REGIONS FINANCIAL CORPORATION, *pg.* 798, *pg.* 4
RENASANT BANK, *pg.* 798, *pg.* 533
RENASANT CORPORATION, *pg.* 799, *pg.* 972
REPUBLIC BANCORP, INC., *pg.* 799, *pg.* 737
RIVER VALLEY BANCORP, *pg.* 799, *pg.* 694
RIVERVIEW FINANCIAL CORPORATION, *pg.* 799, *pg.* 1535
ROYAL BANK OF CANADA, *pg.* 800, *pg.* 1942
SALISBURY BANCORP, INC., *pg.* 801, *pg.* 353
SANDY SPRING BANCORP, INC., *pg.* 801, *pg.* 774
SANTANDER HOLDINGS USA, INC., *pg.* 801, *pg.* 800
SB FINANCIAL GROUP, *pg.* 801, *pg.* 1447
SCBT FINANCIAL CORPORATION, *pg.* 801, *pg.* 1614
SECURITY FEDERAL CORPORATION, *pg.* 802, *pg.* 1612
SELECT BANK & TRUST, *pg.* 803, *pg.* 1370
SHORE BANCSHARES, INC., *pg.* 803, *pg.* 769
SI FINANCIAL GROUP, INC., *pg.* 803, *pg.* 385
SIERRA BANCORP, *pg.* 803, *pg.* 185
SKAGIT STATE BANCORP, INC., *pg.* 804, *pg.* 1819
SOUTHCOAST FINANCIAL CORPORATION, *pg.* 804, *pg.* 1620
SOUTHEASTERN BANK FINANCIAL CORPORATION, *pg.* 804, *pg.* 525
THE SOUTHERN BANC COMPANY, INC., *pg.* 804, *pg.* 5
SOUTHERN MISSOURI BANCORP, INC., *pg.* 804, *pg.* 989
STANDARD FINANCIAL CORP., *pg.* 805, *pg.* 1553
STATE STREET CORPORATION, *pg.* 805, *pg.* 801
STERLING BANCORP, *pg.* 805, *pg.* 1183
STEWARDSHIP FINANCIAL CORPORATION, *pg.* 805, *pg.* 1084
SUNTRUST BANKS, INC., *pg.* 807, *pg.* 520
SUSQUEHANNA BANK, *pg.* 807, *pg.* 1548
SUSSEX BANCORP, *pg.* 807, *pg.* 1068
SVB FINANCIAL GROUP, *pg.* 808, *pg.* 270
T BANCSHARES, INC., *pg.* 808, *pg.* 1688
TCF FINANCIAL CORPORATION, *pg.* 808, *pg.* 966
TD BANK US HOLDING COMPANY, *pg.* 809, *pg.* 1051
TEXAS CAPITAL BANCSHARES, INC., *pg.* 809, *pg.* 1737
TIDELANDS BANCSHARES, INC., *pg.* 810, *pg.* 1620
TIMBERLAND BANCORP, INC., *pg.* 810, *pg.* 1820
TRI-COUNTY FINANCIAL CORPORATION, *pg.* 811, *pg.* 780
TRICO BANCSHARES, *pg.* 811, *pg.* 65
TRUSTCO BANK CORP NY, *pg.* 811, *pg.* 1162
TRUSTMARK CORPORATION, *pg.* 812, *pg.* 7
TRUSTMARK CORPORATION, *pg.* 812, *pg.* 969
UMB FINANCIAL CORPORATION, *pg.* 812, *pg.* 987
UMPQUA HOLDINGS CORPORATION, *pg.* 813, *pg.* 1507
THE UNION BANK CO., *pg.* 813, *pg.* 1445
UNION BANKSHARES, INC., *pg.* 813, *pg.* 1767
UNION FIRST MARKET BANKSHARES CORPORATION, *pg.* 813, *pg.* 1804
UNIONBANCAL CORPORATION, *pg.* 813, *pg.* 230
UNITED BANCORP, INC., *pg.* 813, *pg.* 1459
UNITED BANKSHARES, INC., *pg.* 813, *pg.* 1849
UNITED COMMUNITY BANCORP, *pg.* 813, *pg.* 693
UNITED COMMUNITY BANKS, INC., *pg.* 814, *pg.* 526
UNITED COMMUNITY FINANCIAL CORP., *pg.* 814, *pg.* 1483
UNITED SECURITY BANCSHARES, *pg.* 814, *pg.* 93
UNITED SECURITY BANCSHARES, INC., *pg.* 814, *pg.* 8
UNITED TENNESSEE BANKSHARES, INC., *pg.* 814, *pg.* 1655
UNITY BANCORP, INC., *pg.* 814, *pg.* 1052
UNIVERSITY BANCORP, INC., *pg.* 814, *pg.* 867
UNIVEST CORPORATION OF PENNSYLVANIA, *pg.* 814, *pg.* 1586
U.S. BANCORP, *pg.* 815, *pg.* 945
VALLEY NATIONAL BANCORP, *pg.* 815, *pg.* 1130
VILLAGE BANK & TRUST FINANCIAL CORP., *pg.* 816, *pg.* 1796
VIST FINANCIAL CORP., *pg.* 818, *pg.* 1596
WASHINGTON FEDERAL INC., *pg.* 818, *pg.* 1842
WASHINGTON TRUST BANCORP, INC., *pg.* 818, *pg.* 1610
WATERSTONE FINANCIAL, INC., *pg.* 818, *pg.* 1899
WAYNE SAVINGS BANCSHARES, INC., *pg.* 819, *pg.* 1482
WEBSTER CITY FEDERAL BANCORP, *pg.* 819, *pg.* 712
WELLS FARGO & COMPANY, *pg.* 819, *pg.* 232
WEST SUBURBAN BANCORP, INC., *pg.* 821, *pg.* 631
WESTAMERICA BANCORPORATION, *pg.* 821, *pg.* 258
WESTERN ALLIANCE BANCORPORATION, *pg.* 821, *pg.* 20
WHITNEY HOLDING CORPORATION, *pg.* 822, *pg.* 747
WILMINGTON TRUST CORPORATION, *pg.* 822, *pg.* 392
WILSON BANK HOLDING COMPANY, *pg.* 823, *pg.* 1640
WSFS FINANCIAL CORPORATION, *pg.* 823, *pg.* 392
YADKIN VALLEY FINANCIAL CORPORATION, *pg.* 824, *pg.* 1372
YOUR COMMUNITY BANKSHARES, INC., *pg.* 824, *pg.* 696
ZIONS BANCORPORATION, *pg.* 824, *pg.* 1762

6719 - Offices of Holding Companies, NEC

1859 HISTORIC HOTELS LTD., *pg.* 1079, *pg.* 1697
21ST CENTURY INSURANCE GROUP, *pg.* 1187, *pg.* 389
A&E TELEVISION NETWORKS, LLC, *pg.* 267, *pg.* 1185
ACORN ENERGY, INC., *pg.* 341, *pg.* 389
AFFILIATED FOODS, INC., *pg.* 1012, *pg.* 1658
AFFINIA GROUP INTERMEDIATE HOLDINGS INC., *pg.* 197, *pg.* 1373
AFFINION GROUP, INC., *pg.* 1225, *pg.* 372
AIG ANNUITIES, *pg.* 1188, *pg.* 125
ALASKA AIR GROUP, INC., *pg.* 1897, *pg.* 1830
ALLIANT ENERGY CORPORATION, *pg.* 1933, *pg.* 1864
ALLIED VAUGHN INC., *pg.* 269, *pg.* 929
ALLY FINANCIAL INC., *pg.* 711, *pg.* 878
ALTAIR CORPORATION, *pg.* 1312, *pg.* 910
ALTRA HOLDINGS, INC., *pg.* 198, *pg.* 802
ALTRIA GROUP, INC., *pg.* 1893, *pg.* 1800
AMERCO, *pg.* 1898, *pg.* 1031
AMERICAN AIRLINES GROUP INC., *pg.* 224, *pg.* 1693
AMERICAN AXLE & MANUFACTURING HOLDINGS, INC., *pg.* 198, *pg.* 879
AMERICAN BANKNOTE CORPORATION, *pg.* 1615, *pg.* 1067
AMERICAN EQUITY INVESTMENT LIFE HOLDING COMPANY, *pg.* 711, *pg.* 712
AMERICAN FINANCIAL GROUP, INC., *pg.* 714, *pg.* 1410
AMERICAN FOODS GROUP, LLC, *pg.* 837, *pg.* 1859
AMERICAN INTERNATIONAL GROUP, INC., *pg.* 1190, *pg.* 1193
AMERICAN SEAFOODS, LP, *pg.* 837, *pg.* 1833
AMERISAFE, INC., *pg.* 1191, *pg.* 743
AMSCAN HOLDINGS, INC., *pg.* 1760, *pg.* 1158
ANHEUSER-BUSCH COMPANIES, LLC, *pg.* 237, *pg.* 991
ANTENNA PRODUCTS CORPORATION, *pg.* 618, *pg.* 1727
ANTHEM, INC., *pg.* 1192, *pg.* 683
ASCENT CAPITAL GROUP, *pg.* 270, *pg.* 330
ASHLAND INC., *pg.* 972, *pg.* 726
ASTEC INDUSTRIES, INC., *pg.* 69, *pg.* 1628
AUTHENTIDATE HOLDING CORP., *pg.* 356, *pg.* 1044
AUTO-OWNERS INSURANCE GROUP, *pg.* 1194, *pg.* 895
AV HOMES INC., *pg.* 1080, *pg.* 20
AVON PRODUCTS, INC., *pg.* 500, *pg.* 1198
B&B CORPORATE HOLDINGS, INC., *pg.* 1015, *pg.* 471
BALL CORPORATION, *pg.* 1452, *pg.* 311
BASF CORPORATION, *pg.* 1149, *pg.* 1066
BEAM SUNTORY INC., *pg.* 1957, *pg.* 599
BEHRINGER HOLDINGS, LLC, *pg.* 1081, *pg.* 1657
BERKSHIRE HATHAWAY INC., *pg.* 1195, *pg.* 1013
BET HOLDINGS LLC, *pg.* 271, *pg.* 396
BFC FINANCIAL CORPORATION, *pg.* 724, *pg.* 423
BIOSCRIP, INC., *pg.* 1506, *pg.* 1158
BLUELINX HOLDINGS, INC., *pg.* 70, *pg.* 491
BMC SELECT, *pg.* 71, *pg.* 546
BOEHRINGER INGELHEIM PHARMACEUTICALS, INC., *pg.* 1507, *pg.* 368
BOISE CASCADE HOLDINGS, L.L.C., *pg.* 1453, *pg.* 546
BP AMERICA INC., *pg.* 972, *pg.* 1702
THE BRINK'S COMPANY, *pg.* 364, *pg.* 1800
BROWN-FORMAN CORPORATION, *pg.* 1958, *pg.* 732

BURLINGTON NORTHERN SANTA FE, LLC, *pg.* 1901, *pg.* 1694
BURNHAM HOLDINGS, INC., *pg.* 1069, *pg.* 1546
BWAY HOLDING COMPANY, *pg.* 1454, *pg.* 491
CABLEVISION SYSTEMS CORPORATION, *pg.* 272, *pg.* 1141
CAESARS ENTERTAINMENT CORPORATION, *pg.* 1083, *pg.* 1023
CAMBRIDGE INFORMATION GROUP, INC., *pg.* 1625, *pg.* 761
CANFOR CORPORATION, *pg.* 1454, *pg.* 1910
CANUCKS SPORTS & ENTERTAINMENT, *pg.* 536, *pg.* 1910
CAPITAL FINANCIAL HOLDINGS, INC., *pg.* 730, *pg.* 1398
CAPITAL ONE FINANCIAL CORPORATION, *pg.* 730, *pg.* 1789
CARLSON COMPANIES INC., *pg.* 1084, *pg.* 947
CARNIVAL CORPORATION, *pg.* 1902, *pg.* 441
CBOE HOLDINGS, INC., *pg.* 733, *pg.* 569
CCS MEDICAL HOLDINGS, INC., *pg.* 1514, *pg.* 415
CDI, *pg.* 1405, *pg.* 121
CELLCO PARTNERSHIP, *pg.* 1869, *pg.* 1042
CENTURYLINK, INC, *pg.* 1870, *pg.* 317
CH ENERGY GROUP, INC., *pg.* 973, *pg.* 1324
CHAMPION ENTERPRISES HOLDINGS, LLC, *pg.* 75, *pg.* 910
CHICAGO BRIDGE & IRON COMPANY, *pg.* 75, *pg.* 1747
THE CHUBB CORPORATION, *pg.* 1196, *pg.* 1128
CIGNA CORPORATION, *pg.* 1197, *pg.* 338
CINEMARK HOLDINGS, INC., *pg.* 540, *pg.* 1729
CITIZENS INC., *pg.* 1197, *pg.* 1661
CLUBCORP, INC., *pg.* 1086, *pg.* 1677
CME GROUP INC., *pg.* 738, *pg.* 571
CNO FINANCIAL GROUP, INC., *pg.* 1198, *pg.* 675
COMCAST SPECTACOR, L.P., *pg.* 278, *pg.* 1562
COMMUNITY HEALTH SYSTEMS, INC., *pg.* 1516, *pg.* 1632
COMPASS GROUP DIVERSIFIED HOLDINGS LLC, *pg.* 741, *pg.* 383
CONAGRA FOODS, *pg.* 826, *pg.* 994
CONNECTICUT WATER SERVICE, INC., *pg.* 1938, *pg.* 342
CONSOLIDATED COMMUNICATIONS HOLDINGS, INC., *pg.* 630, *pg.* 631
CONSOLIDATED EDISON, INC., *pg.* 1938, *pg.* 1218
CONVERGYS CORPORATION, *pg.* 379, *pg.* 1412
CROWN HOLDINGS, INC., *pg.* 1456, *pg.* 1562
CTV INC., *pg.* 280, *pg.* 1937
CUMULUS MEDIA INC., *pg.* 280, *pg.* 503
CUNA MUTUAL INSURANCE SOCIETY, *pg.* 743, *pg.* 1865
CYALUME TECHNOLOGIES HOLDINGS, INC., *pg.* 1295, *pg.* 856
DELEK US HOLDINGS, INC., *pg.* 975, *pg.* 1627
DFC GLOBAL CORPORATION, *pg.* 743, *pg.* 1515
DOCTOR'S ASSOCIATES INC., *pg.* 1726, *pg.* 356
THE DOLAN COMPANY, *pg.* 1636, *pg.* 932
DOLLAR TREE, INC., *pg.* 1767, *pg.* 1778
THE DOW CHEMICAL COMPANY, *pg.* 1157, *pg.* 898
DTE ENERGY COMPANY, *pg.* 1940, *pg.* 880
EGPI FIRECREEK, INC., *pg.* 976, *pg.* 21
EHEALTH, INC., *pg.* 1242, *pg.* 153
ELECSYS CORPORATION, *pg.* 635, *pg.* 717
EMCOR GROUP, INC., *pg.* 80, *pg.* 361
EMERGENT CAPITAL, INC., *pg.* 747, *pg.* 411
EMPIRE COMPANY LIMITED, *pg.* 1019, *pg.* 1917
EMRISE CORPORATION, *pg.* 637, *pg.* 1371
ENERFAB, INC., *pg.* 81, *pg.* 1412
ENERGIZER HOLDINGS, INC., *pg.* 637, *pg.* 996
ENERGY FUTURE HOLDINGS CORP., *pg.* 1941, *pg.* 1680
ENTERPRISE HOLDINGS, INC., *pg.* 1906, *pg.* 996
EQUITY GROUP INVESTMENTS, LLC, *pg.* 748, *pg.* 573
ESPN, INC., *pg.* 285, *pg.* 340
E*TRADE FINANCIAL CORPORATION, *pg.* 749, *pg.* 1230
EVERI HOLDINGS INC., *pg.* 749, *pg.* 1023
EVERSOURCE, *pg.* 977, *pg.* 794
EXAMWORKS GROUP, INC., *pg.* 1529, *pg.* 505
EXELON CORPORATION, *pg.* 1942, *pg.* 573
FEDEX CORPORATION, *pg.* 1907, *pg.* 1642
FGX INTERNATIONAL, INC., *pg.* 5, *pg.* 1608
FIRSTENERGY CORP., *pg.* 1942, *pg.* 1400
FJ MANAGEMENT, INC., *pg.* 978, *pg.* 1758
FLEXCON CORPORATION, *pg.* 1457, *pg.* 844
FLORIDA EAST COAST INDUSTRIES, INC., *pg.* 1909, *pg.* 433
FLUOR CORPORATION, *pg.* 82, *pg.* 1719
FMC CORPORATION, *pg.* 1163, *pg.* 1564
FORTUNE BRANDS HOME & SECURITY, INC., *pg.* 55, *pg.* 600
FORUM NATIONAL INVESTMENTS LTD., *pg.* 1200, *pg.* 1908
FOX ENTERTAINMENT GROUP, INC., *pg.* 288, *pg.* 131
FRANKLIN RESOURCES, INC., *pg.* 760, *pg.* 254
FREEDOM COMMUNICATIONS, INC., *pg.* 1643, *pg.* 110
FTD GROUP, INC., *pg.* 1795, *pg.* 608
FUJIFILM U.S.A., INC., *pg.* 1414, *pg.* 1348
GAMCO INVESTORS, INC., *pg.* 761, *pg.* 1339
GANNETT CO., INC., *pg.* 289, *pg.* 1681
GARTNER, INC., *pg.* 1248, *pg.* 374
GEICO CORPORATION, *pg.* 1200, *pg.* 399
GENERAC HOLDINGS INC., *pg.* 1340, *pg.* 1897
GENERAL ELECTRIC COMPANY, *pg.* 1297, *pg.* 347
GNC HOLDINGS INC., *pg.* 1537, *pg.* 1576
GOOD TECHNOLOGY, INC., *pg.* 1249, *pg.* 285
GRANITE CONSTRUCTION INCORPORATED, *pg.* 84, *pg.* 305
GRAPHIC PACKAGING HOLDING COMPANY, *pg.* 1459, *pg.* 509
GRAYCOR INC., *pg.* 84, *pg.* 619
GREAT AMERICAN GROUP, INC., *pg.* 1394, *pg.* 308
GREAT PLAINS ENERGY INCORPORATED, *pg.* 1944, *pg.* 983
GREATER NEW YORK MUTUAL INSURANCE COMPANY, *pg.* 1201, *pg.* 1236
GSC ENTERPRISES, INC., *pg.* 1021, *pg.* 1746
GUCKENHEIMER ENTERPRISES, INC., *pg.* 1730, *pg.* 190
H&R BLOCK, INC., *pg.* 764, *pg.* 983
HALLIBURTON COMPANY, *pg.* 978, *pg.* 1707
HARPO, INC., *pg.* 290, *pg.* 576
HARRIS CORPORATION, *pg.* 642, *pg.* 439
HAWAIIAN HOLDINGS, INC., *pg.* 1910, *pg.* 544
HAYWARD POOL PRODUCTS, *pg.* 1049, *pg.* 1057
HCA HOLDINGS, INC., *pg.* 1539, *pg.* 1651
HEALTH CARE SERVICE CORPORATION, *pg.* 1203, *pg.* 576
THE HEARST CORPORATION, *pg.* 1649, *pg.* 1239
HERTZ GLOBAL HOLDINGS, INC., *pg.* 179, *pg.* 450
HILL-ROM HOLDINGS, INC., *pg.* 1542, *pg.* 673
HILTON WORLDWIDE, INC., *pg.* 1094, *pg.* 1791
HOB-LOB LIMITED PARTNERSHIP, *pg.* 552, *pg.* 1486
THE HOME DEPOT, INC., *pg.* 1050, *pg.* 510
HOME MERIDIAN INTERNATIONAL, INC., *pg.* 928, *pg.* 1379
HOSTESS BRANDS LLC, *pg.* 1856, *pg.* 984
HOUCHENS INDUSTRIES INC., *pg.* 1023, *pg.* 726
HOVNANIAN ENTERPRISES, INC., *pg.* 1096, *pg.* 1114
HOWARD MILLER COMPANY, *pg.* 7, *pg.* 914
HULMAN & COMPANY, *pg.* 864, *pg.* 698
HUNTSMAN CORPORATION, *pg.* 1167, *pg.* 1758
HUSSMANN INTERNATIONAL, INC., *pg.* 1347, *pg.* 973
IBM, *pg.* 410, *pg.* 1449
ICAHN ENTERPRISES L.P., *pg.* 1097, *pg.* 1243
IDACORP, INC., *pg.* 1944, *pg.* 546
IHEARTMEDIA INC., *pg.* 292, *pg.* 1741
IMPRESO, INC., *pg.* 413, *pg.* 1671
INDEL, INC., *pg.* 1348, *pg.* 1113
INFOGROUP INC., *pg.* 1652, *pg.* 1016
INTEGRA LIFESCIENCES HOLDINGS CORPORATION, *pg.* 1545, *pg.* 1109
INTERNATIONAL MONETARY SYSTEMS, LTD., *pg.* 769, *pg.* 1884
INTERNATIONAL SPEEDWAY CORPORATION, *pg.* 553, *pg.* 420
THE INTERTECH GROUP, INC., *pg.* 1350, *pg.* 1613
INVENTIV HEALTH CLINICAL, *pg.* 1547, *pg.* 1111
INVESCO LTD., *pg.* 771, *pg.* 513
ION MEDIA NETWORKS, INC., *pg.* 293, *pg.* 479
ITC HOLDINGS CORP., *pg.* 1945, *pg.* 903
JBS USA HOLDING, INC., *pg.* 865, *pg.* 330
J.C. PENNEY COMPANY, INC., *pg.* 1774, *pg.* 1732
JEFFERIES GROUP, INC., *pg.* 772, *pg.* 1246
KEYSTONE AUTOMOTIVE OPERATIONS, INC., *pg.* 210, *pg.* 1531
KKR FINANCIAL HOLDINGS LLC, *pg.* 774, *pg.* 220
KONAMI CORPORATION OF AMERICA INC., *pg.* 960, *pg.* 80
L-3 COMMUNICATIONS HOLDINGS INC., *pg.* 650, *pg.* 1250
LA PETITE ACADEMY, INC., *pg.* 603, *pg.* 903
LANCASTER COLONY CORPORATION, *pg.* 873, *pg.* 1441
LARRY H. MILLER GROUP OF COMPANIES, *pg.* 182, *pg.* 1762
LEUCADIA NATIONAL CORPORATION, *pg.* 775, *pg.* 1251
THE LGL GROUP, INC., *pg.* 652, *pg.* 454
LIBERATOR MEDICAL HOLDINGS, INC., *pg.* 1555, *pg.* 468
LIBERTY MEDIA CORPORATION, *pg.* 652, *pg.* 326
LIQUIDNET HOLDINGS, INC., *pg.* 776, *pg.* 1251
LOEHMANN'S HOLDINGS INC., *pg.* 29, *pg.* 1144
M FINANCIAL HOLDINGS INC., *pg.* 1207, *pg.* 1504
MACANDREWS & FORBES HOLDINGS INC., *pg.* 777, *pg.* 1254
THE MAJESTIC STAR CASINO, LLC, *pg.* 560, *pg.* 1027
THE MANITOWOC COMPANY, INC., *pg.* 1358, *pg.* 1868
MARKETAXESS HOLDINGS INC., *pg.* 778, *pg.* 1256
MARY KAY INC., *pg.* 516, *pg.* 1657
MASTERCARD INCORPORATED, *pg.* 779, *pg.* 1325
MATEC INSTRUMENT COMPANIES, INC., *pg.* 1421, *pg.* 839
MATERION CORPORATION, *pg.* 1359, *pg.* 1463
MCG CAPITAL CORPORATION, *pg.* 781, *pg.* 1774
MDU RESOURCES GROUP, INC., *pg.* 981, *pg.* 1397
MESA AIR GROUP, INC., *pg.* 1915, *pg.* 18
MESQUITE GAMING, LLC, *pg.* 1104, *pg.* 1030
MESTEK, INC., *pg.* 1074, *pg.* 857
METLIFE, INC., *pg.* 1208, *pg.* 1258
METRO-GOLDWYN-MAYER INC., *pg.* 298, *pg.* 47
MGM RESORTS INTERNATIONAL, *pg.* 1105, *pg.* 1028
MICHIGAN.COM, *pg.* 1665, *pg.* 884
MICROS SYSTEMS, INC., *pg.* 435, *pg.* 768
MIDAMERICAN ENERGY HOLDINGS COMPANY, *pg.* 1946, *pg.* 706
MIMI'S CAFE, LLC, *pg.* 1741, *pg.* 297
MMODAL INC., *pg.* 441, *pg.* 1633
MOLSON COORS BREWING COMPANY, *pg.* 256, *pg.* 321
MONARCH CASINO & RESORT, INC., *pg.* 564, *pg.* 1031
MONDELEZ INTERNATIONAL, INC., *pg.* 878, *pg.* 601
MONSTER BEVERAGE CORPORATION, *pg.* 257, *pg.* 69
MORINDA HOLDINGS INC., *pg.* 1569, *pg.* 1754
MORRIS PUBLISHING GROUP, LLC, *pg.* 1666, *pg.* 525
MOVADO GROUP, INC., *pg.* 10, *pg.* 1101
MUTUAL OF OMAHA INSURANCE COMPANY, *pg.* 1210, *pg.* 1016
NASHVILLE PREDATORS, LLC, *pg.* 565, *pg.* 1652
NATIONAL AMUSEMENTS, INC., *pg.* 299, *pg.* 840
NATIONAL BEDDING CO., *pg.* 935, *pg.* 618
NATIONWIDE MUTUAL INSURANCE COMPANY, *pg.* 1211, *pg.* 1536
NBC UNIVERSAL, INC., *pg.* 300, *pg.* 1266
NCI BUILDING SYSTEMS, INC., *pg.* 1364, *pg.* 1712
NEENAH ENTERPRISES, INC., *pg.* 99, *pg.* 1883
NER HOLDINGS INC., *pg.* 444, *pg.* 1071
NETSPEND CORPORATION, *pg.* 786, *pg.* 1665
NEWMARK GRUBB KNIGHT FRANK, *pg.* 1106, *pg.* 1271
NEWSDAY MEDIA GROUP, *pg.* 1670, *pg.* 1181
NEXSTAR BROADCASTING GROUP, INC., *pg.* 303, *pg.* 1723
NICOR GAS AN AGL RESOURCES COMPANY, *pg.* 1947, *pg.* 636
NL INDUSTRIES, INC., *pg.* 1174, *pg.* 1684
NORTHROP GRUMMAN CORPORATION, *pg.* 231, *pg.* 1781
NV ENERGY, INC., *pg.* 1948, *pg.* 1028
NYSE EURONEXT, *pg.* 789, *pg.* 1274
OGE ENERGY CORP., *pg.* 1948, *pg.* 1486
OHIO FARMERS INSURANCE COMPANY, *pg.* 1213, *pg.* 1480
OPPENHEIMERFUNDS, INC., *pg.* 790, *pg.* 1274
OPUS CORPORATION, *pg.* 101, *pg.* 949
OWENS & MINOR, INC., *pg.* 1579, *pg.* 1795
PANDA RESTAURANT GROUP, INC., *pg.* 1743, *pg.* 194
PAPA GINOS-DEANGELO HOLDING CORPORATION, INC., *pg.* 1743, *pg.* 817
PARASOLE RESTAURANT HOLDINGS, INC., *pg.* 1744, *pg.* 925
PAULSON CAPITAL CORP., *pg.* 792, *pg.* 1505
PENN TREATY AMERICAN CORPORATION, *pg.* 793, *pg.* 1514
PENSKE AUTOMOTIVE GROUP, INC., *pg.* 188, *pg.* 873
PEOPLES EDUCATIONAL HOLDINGS INC., *pg.* 606, *pg.* 1118
PGT, INC., *pg.* 104, *pg.* 452
PINNACLE FOODS GROUP LLC, *pg.* 889, *pg.* 1104
PIPER JAFFRAY COMPANIES, *pg.* 794, *pg.* 941
PNM RESOURCES, INC., *pg.* 1949, *pg.* 1135
POTAMKIN AUTOMOTIVE, *pg.* 189, *pg.* 445
PREMIERE GLOBAL SERVICES, INC., *pg.* 1275, *pg.* 518
PRINCIPAL FINANCIAL GROUP, INC., *pg.* 796, *pg.* 706
PROASSURANCE CORPORATION, *pg.* 1214, *pg.* 3
THE PROGRESSIVE CORPORATION, *pg.* 1214, *pg.* 1463
PROGRESSIVE WASTE SOLUTIONS, *pg.* 796, *pg.* 1947
PROVISION HOLDING, INC., *pg.* 665, *pg.* 65
PUBCO CORPORATION, *pg.* 457, *pg.* 1434

PUBLIX SUPER MARKETS, INC., *pg.* 1031, *pg.* 437
PUGET ENERGY, INC., *pg.* 1950, *pg.* 1816
PULTEGROUP, INC., *pg.* 1109, *pg.* 873
QUESTAR CORPORATION, *pg.* 983, *pg.* 1760
RADIO ONE, INC., *pg.* 305, *pg.* 778
RAYMOND JAMES FINANCIAL, INC., *pg.* 798, *pg.* 464
R.B. PAMPLIN CORPORATION, *pg.* 707, *pg.* 1506
RBS GLOBAL, INC., *pg.* 1371, *pg.* 1879
READING INTERNATIONAL, INC., *pg.* 578, *pg.* 139
REGAL ENTERTAINMENT GROUP, *pg.* 579, *pg.* 1638
REPUBLIC AIRWAYS HOLDINGS INC., *pg.* 1894, *pg.* 689
RESEARCH SOLUTIONS, INC., *pg.* 1680, *pg.* 85
REVLON, INC., *pg.* 521, *pg.* 1286
RGC RESOURCES, INC., *pg.* 1951, *pg.* 1806
RICHLINE GROUP, INC., *pg.* 11, *pg.* 470
RLI CORP., *pg.* 1216, *pg.* 652
ROGERS COMMUNICATIONS INC., *pg.* 668, *pg.* 1942
RPM INTERNATIONAL INC., *pg.* 1447, *pg.* 1464
SABRE HOLDINGS CORPORATION, *pg.* 1922, *pg.* 1745
SAFEAUTO INSURANCE COMPANY, *pg.* 1216, *pg.* 1443
SAFEGUARD SCIENTIFICS, INC., *pg.* 464, *pg.* 1592
SAFETY-KLEEN HOLDCO, INC., *pg.* 1180, *pg.* 1734
SAGENT HOLDING CO., *pg.* 1591, *pg.* 659
SCHLUMBERGER LIMITED, *pg.* 801, *pg.* 1714
SELECTIVE INSURANCE GROUP, INC., *pg.* 1216, *pg.* 1045
SEMPRA ENERGY, *pg.* 1951, *pg.* 209
SGS NORTH AMERICA INC., *pg.* 1428, *pg.* 1118
SIMS METAL MANAGEMENT, *pg.* 1396, *pg.* 590
SINCLAIR BROADCAST GROUP, INC., *pg.* 308, *pg.* 773
SPECTRUM BRANDS HOLDINGS, INC., *pg.* 60, *pg.* 1867
SPEEDWAY MOTORSPORTS, INC., *pg.* 584, *pg.* 1370
SPRINT CORPORATION, *pg.* 1874, *pg.* 719
STAGE STORES, INC., *pg.* 33, *pg.* 1715
STATER BROTHERS HOLDINGS, *pg.* 1034, *pg.* 198
SUMMER INFANT, INC., *pg.* 1139, *pg.* 1610
SUPER SKY PRODUCTS, INC., *pg.* 113, *pg.* 1871
SUTTER HEALTH, *pg.* 1600, *pg.* 197
TARGET CORPORATION, *pg.* 1786, *pg.* 942
TAYLOR CORPORATION, *pg.* 1691, *pg.* 952
TEAM HEALTH HOLDINGS, INC., *pg.* 1601, *pg.* 1639
TECHNE CORPORATION, *pg.* 1601, *pg.* 944
TELLABS, INC., *pg.* 678, *pg.* 637
THOMSON REUTERS - CORPORATE HEADQUARTERS, *pg.* 1693, *pg.* 1299
THOMSON BROTHERS REUTERS CORPORATION, *pg.* 1693, *pg.* 1944
TIFFANY & CO. INTERNATIONAL, *pg.* 14, *pg.* 1300
THE TIFFEN COMPANY LLC, *pg.* 1432, *pg.* 1165
TITANIUM ASSET MANAGEMENT CORP., *pg.* 810, *pg.* 1881
TMX GROUP, INC., *pg.* 810, *pg.* 1945
TOPS HOLDING CORPORATION, *pg.* 1036, *pg.* 1355
TORSTAR CORPORATION, *pg.* 1695, *pg.* 1946
TOWN SPORTS INTERNATIONAL HOLDINGS, INC., *pg.* 589, *pg.* 1303
TOWNSQUARE MEDIA, INC., *pg.* 313, *pg.* 350
TOYOTA MOTOR NORTH AMERICA, INC., *pg.* 192, *pg.* 1303
TOYS "R" US, INC., *pg.* 968, *pg.* 1130
TRANE INC., *pg.* 116, *pg.* 1109
TRIBUNE MEDIA COMPANY, *pg.* 1696, *pg.* 592
TRUMP ENTERTAINMENT RESORTS, INC., *pg.* 1117, *pg.* 1041
THE TRUMP ORGANIZATION, LLC, *pg.* 1117, *pg.* 1305
TYCO INTERNATIONAL (US) INC., *pg.* 1891, *pg.* 1113
UGI CORPORATION, *pg.* 1953, *pg.* 1544
UNICO AMERICAN CORPORATION, *pg.* 1220, *pg.* 308
UNITED CONTINENTAL HOLDINGS, INC., *pg.* 1927, *pg.* 593
UNITED INSURANCE HOLDINGS CORP., *pg.* 1220, *pg.* 465
UNITEDHEALTH GROUP INCORPORATED, *pg.* 1221, *pg.* 950
UNIVAR INC., *pg.* 1184, *pg.* 1829
UNIVERSAL FOREST PRODUCTS, INC., *pg.* 117, *pg.* 890
UNIVEST CORPORATION OF PENNSYLVANIA, *pg.* 814, *pg.* 1586
UNIVISION COMMUNICATIONS INC., *pg.* 683, *pg.* 1307
UNUM GROUP, *pg.* 1222, *pg.* 1629
UTG, INC., *pg.* 1222, *pg.* 662
VALHI, INC., *pg.* 1185, *pg.* 1690
VELATEL GLOBAL COMMUNICATIONS, INC., *pg.* 685, *pg.* 210
VERIFONE SYSTEMS, INC., *pg.* 487, *pg.* 251
VERISK ANALYTICS, INC., *pg.* 1222, *pg.* 1076
VIAD CORP., *pg.* 816, *pg.* 20
VISANT HOLDING CORP., *pg.* 1396, *pg.* 1140
VITAMIN SHOPPE, INC., *pg.* 1608, *pg.* 1098
VITERRA INC., *pg.* 834, *pg.* 1962
VWR FUNDING, INC., *pg.* 1608, *pg.* 1583
WARNER BROS. ENTERTAINMENT INC., *pg.* 319, *pg.* 54
WEC ENERGY GROUP, INC., *pg.* 1954, *pg.* 1881
THE WENDY'S COMPANY, *pg.* 1755, *pg.* 1450
WERNER HOLDING CO., *pg.* 121, *pg.* 1534
WESCO FINANCIAL CORPORATION, *pg.* 821, *pg.* 181
THE WESTERN & SOUTHERN FINANCIAL GROUP, *pg.* 1223, *pg.* 1427
WORTHINGTON INDUSTRIES, INC., *pg.* 123, *pg.* 1444
XENONICS HOLDINGS, INC., *pg.* 1308, *pg.* 62
XO HOLDINGS, INC., *pg.* 689, *pg.* 1786
YASHENG GROUP, *pg.* 910, *pg.* 192
YRC WORLDWIDE INC., *pg.* 1931, *pg.* 720
YUM! BRANDS, INC., *pg.* 1756, *pg.* 738
ZEP INC., *pg.* 338, *pg.* 524
ZIMMER BIOMET HOLDINGS, INC., *pg.* 1611, *pg.* 699
ZURICH HOLDING COMPANY OF AMERICA, INC., *pg.* 1224, *pg.* 660

6722 - Management Investment Companies, Open-End

AMERITAS LIFE INSURANCE CORP., *pg.* 1192, *pg.* 1011
BLACKROCK, INC., *pg.* 724, *pg.* 1203
FEDERATED INVESTORS, INC., *pg.* 752, *pg.* 1575
THE HARTFORD FINANCIAL SERVICES GROUP, INC., *pg.* 1202, *pg.* 352
JANUS CAPITAL GROUP, INC., *pg.* 772, *pg.* 320
J.P. MORGAN ASSET MANAGEMENT HOLDINGS INC., *pg.* 772, *pg.* 1246
KKR FINANCIAL HOLDINGS LLC, *pg.* 774, *pg.* 220
MFS INVESTMENT MANAGEMENT, *pg.* 782, *pg.* 798
MONEX DEPOSIT COMPANY, *pg.* 10, *pg.* 165
MORLEY FINANCIAL SERVICES, *pg.* 784, *pg.* 1504
PARKLAND FUEL CORPORATION, *pg.* 983, *pg.* 1906
PIONEER INVESTMENTS, *pg.* 794, *pg.* 800
PUTNAM INVESTMENTS, LLC, *pg.* 797, *pg.* 800
SUN LIFE FINANCIAL INC., *pg.* 806, *pg.* 1944
SWISS WATER DECAFFEINATED COFFEE INCOME FUND, *pg.* 900, *pg.* 1907
UMB FINANCIAL CORPORATION, *pg.* 812, *pg.* 987
THE VANGUARD GROUP, INC., *pg.* 816, *pg.* 1550
WADDELL & REED FINANCIAL, INC., *pg.* 818, *pg.* 721
WISDOMTREE INVESTMENTS, INC., *pg.* 823, *pg.* 1314

6732 - Educational, Religious & Charitable Trusts

AVON FOUNDATION, *pg.* 134, *pg.* 1198
BENTON FOUNDATION, *pg.* 134, *pg.* 396
THE GLENMEDE TRUST COMPANY, *pg.* 762, *pg.* 1566

6733 - Trusts, Except Educational, Religious & Charitable

ACACIA RESEARCH CORPORATION, *pg.* 1398, *pg.* 165
ACE CASH EXPRESS, INC., *pg.* 710, *pg.* 1717
ACI WORLDWIDE, *pg.* 710, *pg.* 1777
ACORN ENERGY, INC., *pg.* 341, *pg.* 389
ALLY FINANCIAL INC., *pg.* 711, *pg.* 878
AMERICAN CENTURY INVESTMENTS, *pg.* 711, *pg.* 980
AMERICAN EXPRESS COMPANY, *pg.* 712, *pg.* 1190
AMERICAN SECURITIES LLC, *pg.* 714, *pg.* 1193
AMERIPRISE FINANCIAL, INC., *pg.* 715, *pg.* 930
ARES CAPITAL- WASHINGTON, DC OFFICE, *pg.* 716, *pg.* 395
ATLAS HOLDINGS LLC, *pg.* 1452, *pg.* 349
AUTHORIZE.NET HOLDINGS, INC., *pg.* 356, *pg.* 1751
AXEL JOHNSON INC., *pg.* 717, *pg.* 1199
BANK OF AMERICA CORPORATION, *pg.* 718, *pg.* 1362
BANK OF AMERICA GLOBAL WEALTH & INVESTMENT MANAGEMENT, *pg.* 720, *pg.* 789
BAR HARBOR BANK & TRUST, *pg.* 722, *pg.* 749
BB&T CORPORATION, *pg.* 723, *pg.* 1393
BERKSHIRE HATHAWAY INC., *pg.* 1195, *pg.* 1013
BFC FINANCIAL CORPORATION, *pg.* 724, *pg.* 423
BLACKROCK, INC., *pg.* 724, *pg.* 1203
BOTTOMLINE TECHNOLOGIES INC., *pg.* 363, *pg.* 483
BRIEFING.COM, *pg.* 727, *pg.* 568
CAISSE DE DEPOT ET PLACEMENT DU QUEBEC, *pg.* 728, *pg.* 1953
CALAMOS ASSET MANAGEMENT INC, *pg.* 728, *pg.* 635
CALIFORNIA FIRST NATIONAL BANCORP, *pg.* 728, *pg.* 109
CAMBRIDGE CREDIT COUNSELING CORP., *pg.* 728, *pg.* 781
CAMBRIDGE INFORMATION GROUP, INC., *pg.* 1625, *pg.* 761
CAPITAL Z, *pg.* 731, *pg.* 1209
CARDTRONICS, INC., *pg.* 732, *pg.* 1703
CARGILL, INC., *pg.* 845, *pg.* 965
CITIZENS FIRST CORPORATION, *pg.* 737, *pg.* 725
CLAYTON HOLDINGS, INC., *pg.* 738, *pg.* 370
COMDATA CORPORATION, *pg.* 739, *pg.* 1627
COMMUNITY BANCORP, *pg.* 741, *pg.* 1766
COMMUNITY BANK, N.A., *pg.* 741, *pg.* 1155
COMPASS GROUP DIVERSIFIED HOLDINGS LLC, *pg.* 741, *pg.* 383
CONSUMER CREDIT COUNSELING SERVICES, *pg.* 741, *pg.* 501
CORE MEDIA GROUP, *pg.* 1765, *pg.* 1218
COWEN GROUP, INC., *pg.* 742, *pg.* 1219
CUNA MUTUAL INSURANCE SOCIETY, *pg.* 743, *pg.* 1865
DFC GLOBAL CORPORATION, *pg.* 743, *pg.* 1515
DIRECT INSITE CORP., *pg.* 387, *pg.* 425
DISCOVER FINANCIAL SERVICES, *pg.* 744, *pg.* 653
DOLLAR FINANCIAL GROUP INC., *pg.* 744, *pg.* 1515
DORAL FINANCIAL CORPORATION, *pg.* 744, *pg.* 1599
THE DREYFUS CORPORATION, *pg.* 745, *pg.* 1226
DST SYSTEMS, INC., *pg.* 388, *pg.* 982
DUFF & PHELPS CORPORATION, *pg.* 745, *pg.* 1226
EDR TRUST, *pg.* 1090, *pg.* 1642
EGPI FIRECREEK, INC., *pg.* 976, *pg.* 21
ELECTRONIC TRANSFER, INC., *pg.* 746, *pg.* 1843
EMDEON, INC., *pg.* 747, *pg.* 1650
ENCORE CAPITAL GROUP, INC., *pg.* 747, *pg.* 202
E*TRADE FINANCIAL CORPORATION, *pg.* 749, *pg.* 1230
FAIR ISAAC CORPORATION, *pg.* 1247, *pg.* 955
FIDELITY INFORMATION SERVICES, INC., *pg.* 397, *pg.* 433
FIRST CASH FINANCIAL SERVICES, INC., *pg.* 754, *pg.* 1659
FIRST DATA CORPORATION, *pg.* 754, *pg.* 505
FIRST NATIONWIDE LENDING, INC., *pg.* 756, *pg.* 466
FIRST NIAGARA BANK, *pg.* 756, *pg.* 1174
FIRST NIAGARA FINANCIAL GROUP, INC., *pg.* 757, *pg.* 1148
FIRST SURGICAL PARTNERS INC., *pg.* 1531, *pg.* 1668
FISERV, INC., *pg.* 397, *pg.* 1855
FLEETCOR TECHNOLOGIES, INC., *pg.* 758, *pg.* 537
FMR LLC (FIDELITY INVESTMENTS), *pg.* 759, *pg.* 794
FONDS DE SOLIDARITE FTQ, *pg.* 759, *pg.* 1955
FORSTMANN LITTLE & CO., *pg.* 759, *pg.* 1232
FORUM NATIONAL INVESTMENTS LTD., *pg.* 1200, *pg.* 1908
FRANKLIN RESOURCES, INC., *pg.* 760, *pg.* 254
GAMCO INVESTORS, INC., *pg.* 761, *pg.* 1339
GE CAPITAL AVIATION SERVICES, *pg.* 228, *pg.* 362
GENERAL ELECTRIC COMPANY, *pg.* 1297, *pg.* 347
GENERAL FINANCE CORPORATION, *pg.* 761, *pg.* 180
GENWORTH FINANCIAL, INC., *pg.* 761, *pg.* 1802
GLOBAL PAYMENTS INC., *pg.* 762, *pg.* 508
THE GOLDMAN SACHS GROUP, INC., *pg.* 762, *pg.* 1236
GSC ENTERPRISES, INC., *pg.* 1021, *pg.* 1746
THE HARTFORD FINANCIAL SERVICES GROUP, INC., *pg.* 1202, *pg.* 352
HEARTLAND PAYMENT SYSTEMS, INC., *pg.* 765, *pg.* 1111
HFF, INC., *pg.* 766, *pg.* 1576
HSBC FINANCE CORPORATION, *pg.* 767, *pg.* 632
HUNTINGTON BANCSHARES INCORPORATED, *pg.* 767, *pg.* 1440
ICAHN ENTERPRISES L.P., *pg.* 1097, *pg.* 1243
IDEALAB, INC., *pg.* 1258, *pg.* 180
INFINITY AUGMENTED REALITY, INC., *pg.* 768, *pg.* 1243
INTERACTIVE DATA CORPORATION, *pg.* 769, *pg.* 785
INTERCONTINENTALEXCHANGE, INC., *pg.* 769, *pg.* 512
INTERSECTIONS INC., *pg.* 769, *pg.* 1777
INVESCO LTD., *pg.* 771, *pg.* 513
IPAYMENT, INC., *pg.* 771, *pg.* 306
JAGUAR FINANCIAL INC., *pg.* 1351, *pg.* 1939
JANUS CAPITAL GROUP, INC., *pg.* 772, *pg.* 320
JEFFERIES GROUP, INC., *pg.* 772, *pg.* 1246
JMB REALTY CORPORATION, *pg.* 1099, *pg.* 579
JPMORGAN CHASE & CO., *pg.* 772, *pg.* 1246
JPMORGAN CHASE - MIDWEST REGIONAL OFFICE, *pg.* 773, *pg.* 579
KEYCORP, *pg.* 774, *pg.* 1432

First page reference indicates Business Class Edition
Second page reference indicates Geographic Edition

KIRTLAND CAPITAL PARTNERS, pg. 774, pg. 1405
KKR & CO. L.P., pg. 774, pg. 1249
KKR FINANCIAL HOLDINGS LLC, pg. 774, pg. 220
KODIAK VENTURE PARTNERS, L.P., pg. 774, pg. 856
KOPPERS HOLDINGS INC., pg. 1170, pg. 1577
LEUCADIA NATIONAL CORPORATION, pg. 775, pg. 1251
LINCOLN NATIONAL CORPORATION, pg. 776, pg. 1567
MANULIFE FINANCIAL CORPORATION, pg. 778, pg. 1939
MARKETAXESS HOLDINGS INC., pg. 778, pg. 1256
MARSH & MCLENNAN COMPANIES INC., pg. 1207, pg. 1256
MASTERCARD INCORPORATED, pg. 779, pg. 1325
MASTERCARD INTERNATIONAL, INC., pg. 780, pg. 1326
MATRIXX INITIATIVES, INC., pg. 1559, pg. 23
MCCOMBS ENTERPRISES, pg. 781, pg. 1741
MCG CAPITAL CORPORATION, pg. 781, pg. 1774
M.D.C. HOLDINGS, INC., pg. 1104, pg. 321
MEDALLION FINANCIAL CORP., pg. 781, pg. 1258
MEDASSETS INC., pg. 1561, pg. 484
MONARCH CASINO & RESORT, INC., pg. 564, pg. 1031
THE MONEY TREE INC., pg. 783, pg. 526
MONEYGRAM INTERNATIONAL, INC., pg. 783, pg. 1684
MONEY.NET, INC., pg. 1268, pg. 1261
MORGAN STANLEY, pg. 783, pg. 1261
MORGAN STANLEY SMITH BARNEY LLC, pg. 784, pg. 1262
MORNINGSTAR, INC., pg. 784, pg. 583
MSCI INC., pg. 785, pg. 1262
NATIONWIDE MUTUAL INSURANCE COMPANY, pg. 1210, pg. 1442
NETWORK 1 FINANCIAL GROUP, INC., pg. 1465, pg. 1114
NORTHERN TRUST CORPORATION, pg. 787, pg. 585
NUVEEN INVESTMENTS, INC., pg. 788, pg. 586
OCEANFIRST BANK, pg. 789, pg. 1125
OLD NATIONAL BANCORP, pg. 789, pg. 679
OPPENHEIMERFUNDS, INC., pg. 790, pg. 1274
OPTIONSXPRESS HOLDINGS, INC., pg. 790, pg. 586
ORBITZ WORLDWIDE, INC., pg. 1918, pg. 586
OTC MARKETS GROUP INC., pg. 791, pg. 1275
PACIFIC & WESTERN CREDIT CORP., pg. 791, pg. 1922
PARKLAND FUEL CORPORATION, pg. 983, pg. 1906
PAULSON CAPITAL CORP., pg. 792, pg. 1505
PAYPAL INC., pg. 1274, pg. 248
PEOPLE'S UNITED BANK, pg. 793, pg. 340
PHH CORPORATION, pg. 793, pg. 1090
THE PNC FINANCIAL SERVICES GROUP, INC., pg. 795, pg. 1579
PRINCIPAL FINANCIAL GROUP, INC., pg. 796, pg. 706
PRUDENTIAL FINANCIAL, INC., pg. 797, pg. 1097
RABO CAPITAL SERVICES, INC., pg. 797, pg. 1284
THE RESERVE GROUP, pg. 799, pg. 1402
ROYAL BANK OF CANADA, pg. 800, pg. 1942
ROYAL GOLD, INC., pg. 11, pg. 323
SANDY SPRING BANCORP, INC., pg. 801, pg. 774
SEAWAY VALLEY CAPITAL CORPORATION, pg. 802, pg. 1162
SEI INVESTMENTS COMPANY, pg. 802, pg. 1558
SENIOR MARKET SALES, INC., pg. 1217, pg. 1018
THE SHIDLER GROUP, pg. 1112, pg. 545
SPROTT RESOURCE LENDING CORP., pg. 805, pg. 1912
SUNSTONE HOTEL INVESTORS, INC., pg. 1116, pg. 41
SWORDFISH FINANCIAL, INC., pg. 1430, pg. 1737
THOMAS WEISEL PARTNERS LLC, pg. 810, pg. 228
TOTAL SYSTEM SERVICES, INC., pg. 484, pg. 528
TRACK DATA CORPORATION, pg. 1284, pg. 1147
TRANSUNION CORP., pg. 811, pg. 591
TRUSTMARK CORPORATION, pg. 812, pg. 969
UMB FINANCIAL CORPORATION, pg. 812, pg. 987
UNITED DOMINION REALTY L.P., pg. 814, pg. 332
UNITED SERVICES AUTOMOBILE ASSOCIATION, pg. 1221, pg. 1743
UNITED STATES OIL & GAS CORPORATION, pg. 986, pg. 1147
UPROMISE, INC., pg. 815, pg. 837
U.S. BANCORP, pg. 815, pg. 945
USA FINANCIAL, pg. 815, pg. 864
USA TECHNOLOGIES, INC., pg. 815, pg. 1550
VISA INC., pg. 816, pg. 230
VISA U.S.A., INC., pg. 817, pg. 231
WEBBANK, pg. 819, pg. 1761
WELLS FARGO ADVISORS, LLC, pg. 819, pg. 1005
WESCO FINANCIAL CORPORATION, pg. 821, pg. 181
THE WESTERN UNION COMPANY, pg. 822, pg. 327
WHITNEY HOLDING CORPORATION, pg. 822, pg. 747
WIND POINT PARTNERS, pg. 823, pg. 596
WISDOMTREE INVESTMENTS, INC., pg. 823, pg. 1314
WRIGHT EXPRESS CORPORATION, pg. 493, pg. 753
WSFS FINANCIAL CORPORATION, pg. 823, pg. 392

6794 - Patent Owners & Lessors

ADOBE SYSTEMS INCORPORATED, pg. 342, pg. 235
ARTHUR MURRAY INTERNATIONAL, INC., pg. 530, pg. 417
ASHLEY FURNITURE INDUSTRIES, INC., pg. 914, pg. 1852
AUNTIE ANNE'S INC., pg. 1715, pg. 1546
AVIS BUDGET GROUP, INC., pg. 1900, pg. 1102
BACK YARD BURGERS, INC., pg. 1715, pg. 1648
BLUE CROSS & BLUE SHIELD ASSOCIATION, pg. 1195, pg. 566
BRUEGGER'S CORPORATION, pg. 1718, pg. 1764
CASEY'S GENERAL STORES, INC., pg. 1017, pg. 701
CEC ENTERTAINMENT, INC., pg. 1721, pg. 1717
CENTURY 21 REAL ESTATE LLC, pg. 1085, pg. 1080
CHEROKEE GLOBAL BRANDS, pg. 21, pg. 278
CONCORD MUSIC GROUP, INC., pg. 1765, pg. 46
COVERALL NORTH AMERICA, INC., pg. 329, pg. 421
DARDEN RESTAURANTS, INC., pg. 1724, pg. 453
DENNY'S CORPORATION, pg. 1725, pg. 1622
DENNY'S, INC., pg. 1725, pg. 1622
DINEEQUITY, INC., pg. 1725, pg. 95
DOLBY LABORATORIES, INC., pg. 284, pg. 217
DURACLEAN INTERNATIONAL, INC., pg. 329, pg. 553
EGGLAND'S BEST, INC., pg. 854, pg. 1542
EMERSON RADIO CORP., pg. 636, pg. 1087
GALARDI GROUP, INC., pg. 1729, pg. 110
GARAGETEK INC., pg. 1457, pg. 1179
GLOBAL FRANCHISE MANAGEMENT LLC, pg. 1771, pg. 537
GREASE MONKEY INTERNATIONAL, INC., pg. 84, pg. 331
H&R BLOCK, INC., pg. 764, pg. 983
HOME INSTEAD, INC., pg. 1542, pg. 1016
HOOTERS OF AMERICA LLC, pg. 1731, pg. 511
INFORMATION BUILDERS INC., pg. 415, pg. 1243
INTERCONTINENTAL HOTELS CORPORATION, pg. 1097, pg. 511
INTERNATIONAL HOUSE OF PANCAKES, INC., pg. 1732, pg. 96
JAZZERCISE, INC., pg. 554, pg. 59
JENNIFER CONVERTIBLES INC., pg. 931, pg. 1355
THE JOHNNY ROCKETS GROUP, INC., pg. 1733, pg. 41
KAHALA FRANCHISING LLC, pg. 1025, pg. 23
KAMPGROUNDS OF AMERICA, INC., pg. 555, pg. 1008
KFC CORPORATION, pg. 1733, pg. 735
LA ROSA'S, INC., pg. 1735, pg. 1416
LAMP POST FRANCHISE CORPORATION, pg. 1735, pg. 297
LAWN DOCTOR INC., pg. 1796, pg. 1074
LEARFIELD COMMUNICATIONS, INC., pg. 296, pg. 979
LEE MYLES ASSOCIATES CORPORATION, pg. 210, pg. 1584
LUCASFILM, LTD., pg. 297, pg. 222
MAIDS INTERNATIONAL INC., pg. 1395, pg. 1016
MARTIN FRANCHISES INC., pg. 332, pg. 1458
MARVEL ENTERTAINMENT, LLC, pg. 1662, pg. 1257
MASSAGE ENVY LIMITED, LLC, pg. 516, pg. 23
MAZZIO'S CORPORATION, pg. 1737, pg. 1490
MCCOLLA ENTERPRISES LTD., pg. 1737, pg. 722
MIGHTY DISTRIBUTING SYSTEM OF AMERICA, pg. 213, pg. 538
PAPA GINOS-DEANGELO HOLDING CORPORATION, INC., pg. 1743, pg. 817
PLANET BEACH FRANCHISING CORPORATION, pg. 520, pg. 745
PORT OF SUBS INC., pg. 1746, pg. 1032
RESTAURANT DEVELOPERS CORP., pg. 1747, pg. 1464
ROCKY ROCOCO CORPORATION, pg. 1748, pg. 1885
ROYAL GOLD, INC., pg. 11, pg. 323
SEALY CORPORATION, pg. 942, pg. 1391
SHAKEY'S USA, INC., pg. 1749, pg. 40
SHONEY'S NORTH AMERICA, LLC, pg. 1749, pg. 1654
SINCLAIR BROADCAST GROUP, INC., pg. 308, pg. 773
SIR SPEEDY, INC., pg. 1687, pg. 149
SPECTRUM BRANDS HOLDINGS, INC., pg. 60, pg. 1867
STEAMATIC INC., pg. 60, pg. 1696
TACO BELL CORP., pg. 1752, pg. 117
TACO JOHN'S INTERNATIONAL, INC., pg. 1753, pg. 1901
WAFFLE HOUSE, INCORPORATED, pg. 1754, pg. 538
WALLPAPERS-TO-GO, INC., pg. 1791, pg. 1744
THE WENDY'S COMPANY, pg. 1755, pg. 1450
WESTERN SIZZLIN CORPORATION, pg. 1755, pg. 1806
WETZEL'S PRETZELS LLC, pg. 910, pg. 181
WHATABURGER, INC., pg. 1755, pg. 1744
YUM! BRANDS, INC., pg. 1756, pg. 738

6798 - Real Estate Investment Trusts

AMERICAN CAMPUS COMMUNITIES, INC., pg. 1079, pg. 1660
APARTMENT INVESTMENT AND MANAGEMENT COMPANY, pg. 1079, pg. 316
ARDEN REALTY, INC., pg. 1080, pg. 126
ARLINGTON ASSET INVESTMENT CORP., pg. 716, pg. 1772
ASHFORD HOSPITALITY TRUST, INC., pg. 716, pg. 1674
ASSOCIATED ESTATES REALTY CORPORATION, pg. 1080, pg. 1471
COMINAR REAL ESTATE INVESTMENT TRUST, pg. 740, pg. 1958
COUSINS PROPERTIES INCORPORATED, pg. 1088, pg. 501
CRESCENT REAL ESTATE EQUITIES LP, pg. 1088, pg. 1694
CUBESMART, pg. 1088, pg. 1591
DDR CORP., pg. 1089, pg. 1405
EDR TRUST, pg. 1090, pg. 1642
EQUITY LIFESTYLE PROPERTIES, INC., pg. 1090, pg. 573
ESSEX PROPERTY TRUST, INC., pg. 1091, pg. 175
EXTRA SPACE STORAGE, INC., pg. 1091, pg. 1757
FELCOR LODGING TRUST INCORPORATED, pg. 1092, pg. 1719
GE CAPITAL REAL ESTATE, pg. 1093, pg. 362
GENERAL GROWTH PROPERTIES, INC., pg. 1093, pg. 574
HERSHA HOSPITALITY TRUST, pg. 1094, pg. 1536
HOME PROPERTIES INC., pg. 1096, pg. 1336
HOST HOTELS & RESORTS, INC., pg. 1096, pg. 762
INNSUITES HOSPITALITY TRUST, pg. 1097, pg. 17
INVESTORS REAL ESTATE TRUST, pg. 1098, pg. 1398
KILROY REALTY CORPORATION, pg. 1099, pg. 134
LIBERTY PROPERTY TRUST, pg. 1101, pg. 1550
THE MACERICH COMPANY, pg. 1101, pg. 275
MACK-CALI REALTY CORPORATION, pg. 1102, pg. 1056
MORGAN KEEGAN, INC., pg. 783, pg. 1645
POST PROPERTIES, INC., pg. 1108, pg. 518
POTLATCH CORPORATION, pg. 1467, pg. 1844
PROLOGIS, pg. 1108, pg. 322
PS BUSINESS PARKS, INC., pg. 1108, pg. 98
PUBLIC STORAGE, pg. 1467, pg. 98
RAYONIER INC., pg. 1179, pg. 434
REALTY INCOME CORPORATION, pg. 798, pg. 85
RIOCAN REAL ESTATE INVESTMENT TRUST, pg. 799, pg. 1941
SIMON PROPERTY GROUP, INC., pg. 1112, pg. 690
SOVRAN SELF STORAGE, INC., pg. 472, pg. 1355
SUN COMMUNITIES, INC., pg. 1115, pg. 907
SUNSTONE HOTEL INVESTORS, INC., pg. 1116, pg. 41
TANGER FACTORY OUTLET CENTERS, INC., pg. 1116, pg. 1376
TANGER PROPERTIES LIMITED PARTNERSHIP, pg. 1116, pg. 1376
UDR, INC., pg. 812, pg. 332
VORNADO REALTY TRUST, pg. 1118, pg. 1312
WASHINGTON PRIME GROUP INC., pg. 1118, pg. 1444
WELLS REAL ESTATE FUNDS, INC., pg. 1118, pg. 538
WYNDHAM WORLDWIDE CORPORATION, pg. 1119, pg. 1107

6799 - Investors, NEC

AKANA, pg. 346, pg. 125
ARLINGTON ASSET INVESTMENT CORP., pg. 716, pg. 1772
AXA EQUITABLE LIFE INSURANCE COMPANY, pg. 1194, pg. 1199
BANCORPSOUTH, INC., pg. 717, pg. 971
BANK OF AMERICA CORPORATION, pg. 718, pg. 1362
BANK OF AMERICA GLOBAL WEALTH & INVESTMENT MANAGEMENT, pg. 720, pg. 789
BANK OF HAWAII CORPORATION, pg. 720, pg. 543
THE BANK OF NOVA SCOTIA, pg. 721, pg. 1935
BARTLETT & CO., pg. 722, pg. 1410
BB&T CORPORATION, pg. 723, pg. 1393

BBVA COMPASS BANK, *pg.* 723, *pg.* 2
BLACKROCK, INC., *pg.* 724, *pg.* 1203
BUSINESS DEVELOPMENT BANK OF CANADA, *pg.* 72, *pg.* 1953
CALAMOS ASSET MANAGEMENT INC, *pg.* 728, *pg.* 635
CANADIAN WESTERN BANK, *pg.* 729, *pg.* 1906
CAPITAL FINANCIAL HOLDINGS, INC., *pg.* 730, *pg.* 1398
CAPITALONE INVESTING, *pg.* 731, *pg.* 1834
CAPITALSOURCE INC., *pg.* 731, *pg.* 127
CHARLES SCHWAB & COMPANY, INC., *pg.* 734, *pg.* 215
CIGNA CORPORATION, *pg.* 1197, *pg.* 338
CIT GROUP INC., *pg.* 735, *pg.* 1212
CITIZENS INC., *pg.* 1197, *pg.* 1661
COMERICA INCORPORATED, *pg.* 740, *pg.* 1677
COMMUNITY BANK, N.A., *pg.* 741, *pg.* 1155
COWEN GROUP, INC., *pg.* 742, *pg.* 1219
CREDIT SUISSE SECURITIES (USA) LLC, *pg.* 742, *pg.* 1220
CULLEN/FROST BANKERS, INC., *pg.* 742, *pg.* 1740
CUNA MUTUAL INSURANCE SOCIETY, *pg.* 743, *pg.* 1865
DOMINICK & DOMINICK, LLC, *pg.* 744, *pg.* 1225
THE DREYFUS CORPORATION, *pg.* 745, *pg.* 1226
DUFF & PHELPS CORPORATION, *pg.* 745, *pg.* 1226
EDELMAN FINANCIAL SERVICES LLC, *pg.* 746, *pg.* 1705
EDWARD D. JONES & CO., LP, *pg.* 746, *pg.* 995
ENVESTNET, INC., *pg.* 748, *pg.* 573
E*TRADE FINANCIAL CORPORATION, *pg.* 749, *pg.* 1230
FEDERATED INVESTORS, INC., *pg.* 752, *pg.* 1575
FINOTEC GROUP, INC., *pg.* 753, *pg.* 1231
FIRST BUSEY CORPORATION, *pg.* 754, *pg.* 562
FIRST FINANCIAL BANKSHARES, INC., *pg.* 755, *pg.* 1657
FIRST MIDWEST BANCORP INC., *pg.* 756, *pg.* 620
FIRST NIAGARA BANK, *pg.* 756, *pg.* 1174
FIRST NIAGARA FINANCIAL GROUP, INC., *pg.* 757, *pg.* 1148
FMR LLC (FIDELITY INVESTMENTS), *pg.* 759, *pg.* 794
FNBH BANCORP, INC., *pg.* 759, *pg.* 893
FRANKLIN RESOURCES, INC., *pg.* 760, *pg.* 254
GAIN CAPITAL HOLDINGS, INC., *pg.* 760, *pg.* 1043
GAMCO INVESTORS, INC., *pg.* 761, *pg.* 1339
GFI GROUP INC., *pg.* 762, *pg.* 1234
THE GOLDMAN SACHS GROUP, INC., *pg.* 762, *pg.* 1236
H.D. VEST, INC., *pg.* 765, *pg.* 1720
HSBC BANK USA, *pg.* 767, *pg.* 1241
HUNTINGTON BANCSHARES INCORPORATED, *pg.* 767, *pg.* 1440
THE HUNTINGTON NATIONAL BANK, *pg.* 767, *pg.* 1440
INTERCONTINENTALEXCHANGE, INC., *pg.* 769, *pg.* 512
INVESTORS CAPITAL CORPORATION, *pg.* 771, *pg.* 830
JAGUAR FINANCIAL INC., *pg.* 1351, *pg.* 1939
JAMS, THE RESOLUTION EXPERTS, *pg.* 423, *pg.* 111
JANNEY MONTGOMERY SCOTT LLC, *pg.* 772, *pg.* 1566
JEFFERIES GROUP, INC., *pg.* 772, *pg.* 1246
JPMORGAN CHASE & CO., *pg.* 772, *pg.* 1246
JPMORGAN CHASE - MIDWEST REGIONAL OFFICE, *pg.* 773, *pg.* 579
KEYCORP, *pg.* 774, *pg.* 1432
KKR FINANCIAL HOLDINGS LLC, *pg.* 774, *pg.* 220
LAZARD FRERES & CO., LLC, *pg.* 775, *pg.* 1250
LEGG MASON, INC., *pg.* 775, *pg.* 758
LIQUIDNET HOLDINGS, INC., *pg.* 776, *pg.* 1251
LONG POINT CAPITAL LLC, *pg.* 776, *pg.* 1252
LOOMIS, SAYLES & COMPANY, L.P., *pg.* 777, *pg.* 798
LPL FINANCIAL CORPORATION, *pg.* 777, *pg.* 798
M&T BANK CORPORATION, *pg.* 777, *pg.* 1149
MARKETAXESS HOLDINGS INC., *pg.* 778, *pg.* 1256
MERRIMAN HOLDINGS INC., *pg.* 782, *pg.* 223
MORGAN KEEGAN, INC., *pg.* 783, *pg.* 1645
MORGAN STANLEY, *pg.* 783, *pg.* 1261
MORNINGSTAR, INC., *pg.* 784, *pg.* 583
THE NASDAQ OMX GROUP, INC., *pg.* 785, *pg.* 1263
NOMURA SECURITIES INTERNATIONAL, INC., *pg.* 787, *pg.* 1273
THE NORTHWESTERN MUTUAL LIFE INSURANCE COMPANY, *pg.* 1212, *pg.* 1879
OCEANFIRST BANK, *pg.* 789, *pg.* 1125
OHIO FARMERS INSURANCE COMPANY, *pg.* 1213, *pg.* 1480
OLD NATIONAL BANCORP, *pg.* 789, *pg.* 679
OPPENHEIMERFUNDS, INC., *pg.* 790, *pg.* 1274
OPTIONSXPRESS HOLDINGS, INC., *pg.* 790, *pg.* 586
PEOPLES BANCORP INC., *pg.* 793, *pg.* 1458
PINNACLE FINANCIAL PARTNERS, INC., *pg.* 794, *pg.* 1653
PIPER JAFFRAY COMPANIES, *pg.* 794, *pg.* 941
THE PNC FINANCIAL SERVICES GROUP, INC., *pg.* 795, *pg.* 1579
PRIMERICA FINANCIAL SERVICES, INC., *pg.* 795, *pg.* 531
RABO CAPITAL SERVICES, INC., *pg.* 797, *pg.* 1284
RAYMOND JAMES FINANCIAL, INC., *pg.* 798, *pg.* 464
RBC CAPITAL MARKETS, *pg.* 798, *pg.* 225
ROTHSCHILD INC., *pg.* 799, *pg.* 1287
ROTHSCHILD NORTH AMERICA INC., *pg.* 800, *pg.* 1287
ROYAL BANK OF CANADA, *pg.* 800, *pg.* 1942
SANDY SPRING BANK, *pg.* 801, *pg.* 774
SANTANDER HOLDINGS USA, INC., *pg.* 801, *pg.* 800
SCOTTRADE, INC., *pg.* 802, *pg.* 1003
SIEBERT FINANCIAL CORP., *pg.* 803, *pg.* 1291
SOUTHWEST SECURITIES, INC., *pg.* 804, *pg.* 47
SPROTT RESOURCE LENDING CORP., *pg.* 805, *pg.* 1912
SUN LIFE ASSURANCE COMPANY OF CANADA, *pg.* 806, *pg.* 1944
TD AMERITRADE HOLDING CORPORATION, *pg.* 808, *pg.* 1018
THOMAS WEISEL PARTNERS LLC, *pg.* 810, *pg.* 228
TIDELANDS BANCSHARES, INC., *pg.* 810, *pg.* 1620
TRACK DATA CORPORATION, *pg.* 1284, *pg.* 1147
TRADESTATION GROUP, INC., *pg.* 811, *pg.* 459
TRUSTMARK CORPORATION, *pg.* 812, *pg.* 969
TRUSTMARK NATIONAL BANK, *pg.* 812, *pg.* 969
UBS FINANCIAL SERVICES INC., *pg.* 812, *pg.* 1306
UMB FINANCIAL CORPORATION, *pg.* 812, *pg.* 987
UNIONBANCAL CORPORATION, *pg.* 813, *pg.* 230
UNITED BANKSHARES, INC., *pg.* 813, *pg.* 1849
UNITED COMMUNITY BANKS, INC., *pg.* 814, *pg.* 526
UNITED STATES COAST GUARD, *pg.* 1008, *pg.* 406
UNIVEST CORPORATION OF PENNSYLVANIA, *pg.* 814, *pg.* 1586
U.S. BANCORP, *pg.* 815, *pg.* 945
VALLEY NATIONAL BANCORP, *pg.* 815, *pg.* 1130
WADDELL & REED FINANCIAL, INC., *pg.* 818, *pg.* 721
WELLS FARGO ADVISORS, LLC, *pg.* 819, *pg.* 1005
WHITNEY HOLDING CORPORATION, *pg.* 822, *pg.* 747
WILLIAM BLAIR & COMPANY LLC, *pg.* 822, *pg.* 596
THE ZIEGLER COMPANIES, INC., *pg.* 824, *pg.* 597

7011 - Hotels & Motels

1859 HISTORIC HOTELS LTD., *pg.* 1079, *pg.* 1697
ACCOR, *pg.* 1079, *pg.* 1657
ADAM'S MARK HOTELS & RESORTS, *pg.* 1079, *pg.* 990
ADVENTURE LANDS OF AMERICA, INC., *pg.* 526, *pg.* 701
AMERICAN CASINO & ENTERTAINMENT PROPERTIES LLC, *pg.* 527, *pg.* 1022
AMERISTAR CASINOS, INC., *pg.* 528, *pg.* 1022
ARCHON CORPORATION, *pg.* 1080, *pg.* 1030
ATLIFIC INC., *pg.* 1080, *pg.* 1953
AUBERGE RESORTS, LLC, *pg.* 1080, *pg.* 145
BALLY'S PARK PLACE, INC., *pg.* 1080, *pg.* 1041
BARONA RESORT & CASINO, *pg.* 1080, *pg.* 121
BENCHMARK HOSPITALITY INTERNATIONAL INC., *pg.* 1081, *pg.* 1747
BENSON'S, INC., *pg.* 1850, *pg.* 526
THE BEVERLY HILLS HOTEL, *pg.* 1082, *pg.* 46
BORGATA HOTEL CASINO & SPA, *pg.* 1082, *pg.* 1041
BOYD GAMING CORPORATION, *pg.* 1082, *pg.* 1022
BOYNE USA RESORTS INC., *pg.* 1082, *pg.* 874
BROADMOOR HOTEL, INC., *pg.* 1083, *pg.* 315
BRUTGER EQUITIES, INC., *pg.* 1083, *pg.* 956
CAESARS ENTERTAINMENT CORPORATION, *pg.* 1083, *pg.* 1023
CAESARS NEW JERSEY, INC., *pg.* 1084, *pg.* 1041
CANYON RANCH MANAGEMENT, LLC, *pg.* 1084, *pg.* 27
CARLSON COMPANIES INC., *pg.* 1084, *pg.* 947
CARLSON WAGONLIT TRAVEL, *pg.* 1902, *pg.* 948
CASINO QUEEN, INC., *pg.* 537, *pg.* 609
CEDAR FAIR, L.P., *pg.* 537, *pg.* 1471
CEDAR POINT, *pg.* 537, *pg.* 1472
CENTRAL FLORIDA INVESTMENTS INC., *pg.* 1085, *pg.* 452
CHATTANOOGA CHOO-CHOO HOLIDAY INN, *pg.* 1086, *pg.* 1628
CHOICE HOTELS INTERNATIONAL, INC., *pg.* 1086, *pg.* 775
CIRCUS CIRCUS CASINOS, INC., *pg.* 1086, *pg.* 1023
THE CLIFFS COMMUNITIES, INC., *pg.* 1086, *pg.* 1623
THE COEUR D'ALENE RESORT, *pg.* 1087, *pg.* 549
CONDE NAST TRAVELER, *pg.* 1630, *pg.* 1218
CRESTED BUTTE MOUNTAIN RESORT, INC., *pg.* 1088, *pg.* 316
CRESTLINE HOTELS & RESORTS, INC., *pg.* 1088, *pg.* 1779
DAYS INNS WORLDWIDE, INC., *pg.* 1089, *pg.* 1103
DELAWARE NORTH COMPANIES, INC., *pg.* 1089, *pg.* 1148
DENIHAN HOSPITALITY GROUP, LLC, *pg.* 1089, *pg.* 1223
DIVI HOTELS, INC., *pg.* 1090, *pg.* 1361
DOVER DOWNS GAMING & ENTERTAINMENT, INC., *pg.* 545, *pg.* 387
ELDORADO RESORTS, INC., *pg.* 546, *pg.* 1031
EMBASSY SUITES HOTELS, *pg.* 1090, *pg.* 1790
EMPIRE RESORTS, INC., *pg.* 1090, *pg.* 1183
EQUITY LIFESTYLE PROPERTIES, INC., *pg.* 1090, *pg.* 573
EXCLUSIVE RESORTS, LLC, *pg.* 1091, *pg.* 319
EXTENDED STAY HOTELS LLC, *pg.* 1091, *pg.* 1622
FAIRMONT HOTELS & RESORTS INC., *pg.* 1091, *pg.* 1938
FELCOR LODGING TRUST INCORPORATED, *pg.* 1092, *pg.* 1719
FOUR SEASONS HOTELS LIMITED, *pg.* 1092, *pg.* 1938
FOUR WINDS CASINO RESORT, *pg.* 1092, *pg.* 902
FOXWOODS RESORT CASINO, *pg.* 549, *pg.* 353
G6 HOSPITALITY LLC, *pg.* 1092, *pg.* 1669
GALAXY HOTEL SYSTEMS LLC, *pg.* 1092, *pg.* 297
GARDEN CITY HOTEL INC., *pg.* 1093, *pg.* 1161
GILA RIVER GAMING ENTERPRISES, INC., *pg.* 1093, *pg.* 12
GOLD COAST HOTEL & CASINO, *pg.* 1093, *pg.* 1024
GOLDEN NUGGET HOTEL, *pg.* 550, *pg.* 1024
GRAND OLE OPRY, *pg.* 289, *pg.* 1651
GREAT WOLF RESORTS, INC., *pg.* 1093, *pg.* 1866
THE GREENBRIER, *pg.* 1094, *pg.* 1851
GUNSTOCK RECREATION AREA, *pg.* 1094, *pg.* 1034
HARD ROCK CAFE INTERNATIONAL, INC., *pg.* 1730, *pg.* 454
HARRAH'S LOUISIANA DOWNS CASINO & RACETRACK, *pg.* 551, *pg.* 743
HBE CORPORATION, *pg.* 86, *pg.* 998
HERSHA HOSPITALITY TRUST, *pg.* 1094, *pg.* 1536
HERSHEY ENTERTAINMENT & RESORTS COMPANY, *pg.* 1094, *pg.* 1539
HILTON WORLDWIDE, INC., *pg.* 1094, *pg.* 1791
HOST HOTELS & RESORTS, INC., *pg.* 1096, *pg.* 762
HYATT HOTELS CORPORATION, *pg.* 1096, *pg.* 577
HYATT REGENCY LAKE TAHOE RESORT & CASINO, *pg.* 1097, *pg.* 1021
ICAHN ENTERPRISES L.P., *pg.* 1097, *pg.* 1243
INNSUITES HOSPITALITY TRUST, *pg.* 1097, *pg.* 17
INTERCONTINENTAL HOTELS CORPORATION, *pg.* 1097, *pg.* 511
INTOWN SUITES MANAGEMENT, INC., *pg.* 1098, *pg.* 513
INTRAWEST ULC, *pg.* 1098, *pg.* 320
ISLE OF CAPRI CASINOS, INC., *pg.* 553, *pg.* 998
JAY PEAK, INC., *pg.* 1098, *pg.* 1766
JOHN Q. HAMMONS HOTELS INC., *pg.* 1099, *pg.* 1006
KIAWAH RESORT ASSOCIATES LP, *pg.* 1099, *pg.* 1620
KIMPTON HOTEL & RESTAURANT GROUP, *pg.* 1099, *pg.* 220
KSL RESORTS, *pg.* 1099, *pg.* 120
LA QUINTA CORPORATION, *pg.* 1099, *pg.* 1722
LA QUINTA INNS, INC., *pg.* 1100, *pg.* 1722
LAGO MAR PROPERTIES, INC., *pg.* 1100, *pg.* 425
LAKE AUSTIN SPA RESORT, *pg.* 1100, *pg.* 1663
LANCASTER HOST RESORT & CONFERENCE CENTER, *pg.* 1100, *pg.* 1546
LAS VEGAS SANDS CORP., *pg.* 1100, *pg.* 1027
THE LEADING HOTELS OF THE WORLD, LTD., *pg.* 1100, *pg.* 1250
LODGIAN INC., *pg.* 1101, *pg.* 513
LOEWS HOTELS HOLDING CORPORATION, *pg.* 1101, *pg.* 1252
THE MAJESTIC STAR CASINO, LLC, *pg.* 560, *pg.* 1027
MAMMOTH MOUNTAIN SKI AREA, *pg.* 1102, *pg.* 142
THE MARCUS CORPORATION, *pg.* 1102, *pg.* 1877
MARRIOTT INTERNATIONAL, INC., *pg.* 1102, *pg.* 764
MESQUITE GAMING, LLC, *pg.* 1104, *pg.* 1030
MGM GRAND HOTEL, LLC, *pg.* 1104, *pg.* 1028
MGM RESORTS INTERNATIONAL, *pg.* 1105, *pg.* 1028
MIRAGE RESORTS INCORPORATED, *pg.* 1105, *pg.* 1028
MIRAVAL RESORT, *pg.* 1105, *pg.* 12
MISSION INN RESORTS INC., *pg.* 1105, *pg.* 431
MOHEGAN TRIBAL GAMING AUTHORITY, *pg.* 564, *pg.* 381
MONARCH CASINO & RESORT, INC., *pg.* 564, *pg.* 1031
MORGANS HOTEL GROUP CO., *pg.* 1105, *pg.* 1262
MOTEL 6, *pg.* 1106, *pg.* 1669
MOUNT SNOW LTD., *pg.* 564, *pg.* 1769
MYRTLE BEACH AREA CONVENTION AND VISITORS BUREAU, *pg.* 565, *pg.* 1621
NAPLES BEACH HOTEL & GOLF CLUB, *pg.* 1106, *pg.* 451

First page reference indicates Business Class Edition
Second page reference indicates Geographic Edition

NEVADA GOLD & CASINOS, INC., pg. 1106, pg. 1028
NORTHCOTT HOSPITALITY INTERNATIONAL, LLC, pg. 1742, pg. 920
OCEAN PROPERTIES, LTD., pg. 1106, pg. 422
OJAI VALLEY INN & SPA, pg. 1106, pg. 173
THE OMNI HOMESTEAD RESORT, pg. 1106, pg. 1786
OMNI HOTELS & RESORTS, pg. 1107, pg. 1685
ORBITZ WORLDWIDE, INC., pg. 1918, pg. 586
OUTRIGGER ENTERPRISES, INC., pg. 1107, pg. 544
PACIFICA HOTEL COMPANY, pg. 1107, pg. 114
PARK PLACE HOTEL, pg. 1107, pg. 909
PEABODY HOTEL GROUP, INC., pg. 1107, pg. 1645
PEAK RESORTS, INC., pg. 574, pg. 1007
PEDDLER'S VILLAGE, INC., pg. 1107, pg. 1545
PENN NATIONAL GAMING, INC., pg. 574, pg. 1595
PINNACLE ENTERTAINMENT, INC., pg. 576, pg. 1029
POCONO MANOR GOLF RESORT & SPA, pg. 1108, pg. 1582
PUEBLO BONITO HOTELS & RESORTS, pg. 1108, pg. 206
RAYNOR GARAGE DOORS, pg. 106, pg. 607
RED LION HOTELS CORP., pg. 1110, pg. 1844
RED ROOF INNS, INC., pg. 1110, pg. 1443
REYNOLDS PLANTATION, pg. 1110, pg. 533
THE RITZ-CARLTON CHICAGO, pg. 1110, pg. 589
THE RITZ-CARLTON HOTEL COMPANY LLC, pg. 1110, pg. 766
ROGER SMITH HOTELS CORP., pg. 1111, pg. 1286
ROSEWOOD HOTELS & RESORTS LLC, pg. 1111, pg. 1686
RYMAN HOSPITALITY PROPERTIES, INC, pg. 1111, pg. 1653
SADDLEBROOK RESORTS, INC., pg. 1111, pg. 478
SALAMANDER INNISBROOK, LLC, pg. 1111, pg. 457
SANDALS RESORTS INTERNATIONAL, pg. 1111, pg. 446
SANDESTIN GOLF & BEACH RESORT, pg. 1111, pg. 422
SEA ISLAND ACQUISITION LLC, pg. 1111, pg. 540
SEA PINES RESORT, LLC, pg. 1112, pg. 1620
SEMINOLE TRIBE OF FLORIDA, INC., pg. 156, pg. 431
THE SHERATON CORPORATION, pg. 1112, pg. 378
SILVERLEAF RESORTS, INC., pg. 1112, pg. 1686
SINCLAIR OIL CORPORATION, pg. 984, pg. 1760
SIRVA, INC., pg. 1923, pg. 669
SKI ROUNDTOP OPERATING CORP., pg. 1113, pg. 1548
SMSC ENTERPRISES, pg. 584, pg. 954
SNOW KING RESORT, INC., pg. 1113, pg. 1901
SONESTA INTERNATIONAL HOTELS CORPORATION, pg. 1113, pg. 836
SOVEREIGN CRUISES LLC, pg. 1924, pg. 461
STARWOOD HOTELS & RESORTS WORLDWIDE, INC., pg. 1114, pg. 378
STATION CASINOS, INC., pg. 585, pg. 1030
STRATOSPHERE CORPORATION, pg. 1115, pg. 1030
STRATTON MOUNTAIN RESORT, pg. 1115, pg. 1768
SUGARLOAF/USA, pg. 586, pg. 749
SUN VALLEY COMPANY, pg. 1115, pg. 550
SUNBURST HOSPITALITY CORPORATION, pg. 1115, pg. 778
SUNDAY RIVER SKIWAY CORP., pg. 586, pg. 749
SUNSTONE HOTEL INVESTORS, INC., pg. 1116, pg. 41
SUNSTREAM, INC., pg. 1116, pg. 428
TRADEWINDS ISLANDS RESORTS ON SAINT PETE BEACH, pg. 1116, pg. 461
TRAVELCENTERS OF AMERICA, LLC, pg. 1925, pg. 1481
TRAVELODGE HOTELS, INC., pg. 1117, pg. 1106
TRIPADVISOR, INC., pg. 1926, pg. 835
TRUMP ENTERTAINMENT RESORTS, INC., pg. 1117, pg. 1041
VAGABOND FRANCHISE SYSTEM, INC., pg. 1117, pg. 141
VAIL RESORTS, INC., pg. 1117, pg. 313
WALDORF ASTORIA NAPLES, pg. 1118, pg. 451
WESTIN HOTELS & RESORTS, pg. 1118, pg. 379
WYNDHAM WORLDWIDE CORPORATION, pg. 1119, pg. 1107
WYNN LAS VEGAS, LLC, pg. 1119, pg. 1030
WYNN RESORTS LIMITED, pg. 1119, pg. 1030

7021 - Rooming & Boarding Houses

EDR TRUST, pg. 1090, pg. 1642

7032 - Sporting & Recreational Camps

CAMPGROUP LLC, pg. 536, pg. 1351
KAMPGROUNDS OF AMERICA, INC., pg. 555, pg. 1008
MIA'S THERAPEUTIC MASSAGE, pg. 1395, pg. 451
RCI, LLC, pg. 1921, pg. 675
VARSITY BRANDS, INC., pg. 1847, pg. 1647

7033 - Recreational Vehicle Parks & Campsites

LAZY DAYS R.V. CENTER, INC., pg. 182, pg. 467

7212 - Garment Pressing & Agents for Laundries & Dry Cleaners

A&E STORES, INC., pg. 17, pg. 1124
ANGELICA CORPORATION, pg. 38, pg. 483
COVE CLEANERS, INC., pg. 329, pg. 465
SUNRISE BRANDS, LLC, pg. 33, pg. 140

7213 - Linen Supply Services

ANGELICA CORPORATION, pg. 38, pg. 483
ARAMARK CANADA LTD., pg. 1014, pg. 1935
G&K SERVICES INC., pg. 693, pg. 949
SYSCO GUEST SUPPLY, LLC, pg. 336, pg. 1085

7215 - Coin-Operated Laundries & Dry Cleaning

MAC-GRAY CORPORATION, pg. 58, pg. 852

7217 - Carpet & Upholstery Cleaning

ABM INDUSTRIES, INC., pg. 64, pg. 1186
MAXONS RESTORATIONS, pg. 332, pg. 1257
SERVPRO INDUSTRIES, INC., pg. 335, pg. 1635
STANLEY STEEMER INTERNATIONAL, INC., pg. 944, pg. 1450

7218 - Industrial Launderers

ANGELICA CORPORATION, pg. 38, pg. 483
CINTAS CORPORATION, pg. 372, pg. 1411
G&K SERVICES INC., pg. 693, pg. 949
UNIFIRST CORPORATION, pg. 50, pg. 860

7221 - Photographic Studios, Portrait

LIFETOUCH, INC., pg. 1420, pg. 922
PORTRAIT INNOVATIONS HOLDING COMPANY, pg. 1427, pg. 1368

7231 - Beauty Shops

AUBREY ORGANICS INC., pg. 499, pg. 470
AVEDA CORPORATION, pg. 499, pg. 917
BOBIT BUSINESS MEDIA, pg. 1622, pg. 293
THE CLIFFS COMMUNITIES, INC., pg. 1086, pg. 1623
THE COEUR D'ALENE RESORT, pg. 1087, pg. 549
DESSANGE INTERNATIONAL, INC., pg. 506, pg. 787
GREAT CLIPS, INC., pg. 510, pg. 937
GREEN ENDEAVORS, INC., pg. 511, pg. 1758
JAMES GRIFFITH SALON, pg. 512, pg. 477
MIRAVAL RESORT, pg. 1105, pg. 12
OJAI VALLEY INN & SPA, pg. 1106, pg. 173
PLANET BEACH FRANCHISING CORPORATION, pg. 520, pg. 745
THE RATNER COMPANIES, pg. 520, pg. 1809
REGIS CORPORATION, pg. 521, pg. 941
SPORT CLIPS, INC., pg. 523, pg. 1698
SUPERCUTS, INC., pg. 523, pg. 942
TONI & GUY USA, INC., pg. 523, pg. 1689
ULTA SALON, COSMETICS & FRAGRANCE, INC., pg. 524, pg. 559
VIDAL SASSOON CO., pg. 524, pg. 1426
WELLQUEST MEDICAL & WELLNESS CORPORATION, pg. 1610, pg. 31

7241 - Barber Shops

SPORT CLIPS, INC., pg. 523, pg. 1698

7261 - Funeral Service & Crematories

BATESVILLE CASKET COMPANY, INC., pg. 1393, pg. 673
HILLENBRAND, INC., pg. 1394, pg. 673
SERVICE CORPORATION INTERNATIONAL, pg. 1395, pg. 1714

7291 - Tax Return Preparation Services

AZOY TAX, pg. 717, pg. 423
CBIZ, INC., pg. 733, pg. 1429
ERNST & YOUNG GLOBAL LIMITED, pg. 748, pg. 1228
GILMAN CIOCIA, INC., pg. 762, pg. 1324
H&R BLOCK, INC., pg. 764, pg. 983
HABIF, AROGETI & WYNNE, LLP, pg. 764, pg. 509
INTUIT INC., pg. 769, pg. 158
JACKSON HEWITT TAX SERVICE INC., pg. 771, pg. 1103
KPMG LLP, pg. 774, pg. 1086
LIBERTY TAX SERVICE, pg. 776, pg. 1810
PRICEWATERHOUSECOOPERS LLP, pg. 795, pg. 1283

7299 - Miscellaneous Personal Services, NEC

AFFINION GROUP, INC., pg. 1225, pg. 372
AGILTRON, INC., pg. 1398, pg. 860
AIRIQ, INC., pg. 346, pg. 1932
ALCATEL-LUCENT, pg. 615, pg. 1094
ALMOST FAMILY, INC., pg. 1492, pg. 731
AMERCO, pg. 1898, pg. 1031
ANGELICA CORPORATION, pg. 38, pg. 483
AT&T ALASCOM, pg. 619, pg. 10
AUTOMOTIVE RESOURCES INTERNATIONAL (ARI), pg. 1900, pg. 1090
AVIS BUDGET GROUP, INC., pg. 1900, pg. 1102
BABYCENTER, LLC, pg. 1231, pg. 212
BCE INC., pg. 1936, pg. 1960
BEAUTICONTROL COSMETICS, INC., pg. 501, pg. 1669
BLACKBERRY, pg. 625, pg. 1717
BRIDGESTREET WORLDWIDE INC., pg. 1083, pg. 1772
BRIGHT HOUSE NETWORKS LLC, pg. 272, pg. 461
BROADVIEW NETWORKS, INC., pg. 365, pg. 1339
BUDGET RENT A CAR SYSTEM, INC., pg. 1901, pg. 1102
CAMBRIDGE CREDIT COUNSELING CORP., pg. 728, pg. 781
CENTURYLINK, INC., pg. 1870, pg. 746
CIQ, INC., pg. 1235, pg. 415
COMFORCE CORPORATION, pg. 377, pg. 1355
COMMUNICATIONS SYSTEMS, INC., pg. 630, pg. 948
CONSOLIDATED COMMUNICATIONS HOLDINGS, INC., pg. 630, pg. 631
CONSOLIDATED CREDIT COUNSELING SERVICES, INC., pg. 741, pg. 424
COX COMMUNICATIONS, INC., pg. 279, pg. 501
CURVES INTERNATIONAL INC., pg. 542, pg. 1748
DAVE SYVERSON INC., pg. 168, pg. 915
DIET CENTER WORLDWIDE, INC., pg. 1524, pg. 1400
DIGITALGLOBE, pg. 227, pg. 1785
DIGITALGLOBE, INC., pg. 1408, pg. 333
DIRECTV GROUP HOLDINGS, LLC, pg. 281, pg. 79
EASYLINK SERVICES CORPORATION, pg. 1240, pg. 1108
EASYLINK SERVICES INTERNATIONAL CORPORATION, pg. 389, pg. 536
EHARMONY.COM, INC., pg. 1242, pg. 180
EQUINIX, INC., pg. 394, pg. 190
EXECUTIVE CAR LEASING CO., pg. 1907, pg. 130
FORM YOU 3 INTERNATIONAL, INC., pg. 1531, pg. 1400
FREEREALTIME.COM INC., pg. 1248, pg. 121
GENBAND, INC., pg. 640, pg. 1731
GLOBECOMM SYSTEMS INC., pg. 640, pg. 1164
GRANDE COMMUNICATIONS NETWORKS LLC, pg. 1871, pg. 1744
H&R BLOCK, INC., pg. 764, pg. 983
HAIR CLUB FOR MEN, LTD., INC., pg. 511, pg. 411
HAWAIIAN TELCOM COMMUNICATIONS, INC., pg. 1872,

pg. 544
HEMISPHERE GPS INC., *pg.* 642, *pg.* 1903
HOLLYWOOD MEDIA CORP., *pg.* 1256, *pg.* 412
HUGHES NETWORK SYSTEMS LLC, *pg.* 643, *pg.* 770
IBIQUITY DIGITAL CORPORATION, *pg.* 409, *pg.* 767
INCONTACT, INC., *pg.* 413, *pg.* 1752
INTEGRA TELECOM, INC., *pg.* 644, *pg.* 938
INTELIUS, INC., *pg.* 416, *pg.* 1815
INTERMETRO COMMUNICATIONS, INC., *pg.* 417, *pg.* 278
INTERNAP NETWORK SERVICES CORPORATION, *pg.* 417, *pg.* 513
INTERNATIONAL DATACASTING CORPORATION, *pg.* 419, *pg.* 1921
INTRADO INC., *pg.* 420, *pg.* 334
INTRALINKS INC., *pg.* 420, *pg.* 1244
INVERNESS CORPORATION, *pg.* 512, *pg.* 783
IPC SYSTEMS, INC., *pg.* 648, *pg.* 1075
IRIDIUM COMMUNICATIONS INC., *pg.* 293, *pg.* 1792
IXIA, *pg.* 422, *pg.* 50
J2 GLOBAL COMMUNICATIONS, INC., *pg.* 1260, *pg.* 133
KINDRED HEALTHCARE, INC., *pg.* 1553, *pg.* 736
LORAL SPACE & COMMUNICATIONS INC., *pg.* 231, *pg.* 1252
MAC-GRAY CORPORATION, *pg.* 58, *pg.* 852
MARITIME BROADBAND, *pg.* 1265, *pg.* 1146
MASSAGE ENVY LIMITED, LLC, *pg.* 516, *pg.* 23
MATCH.COM, LLC, *pg.* 1265, *pg.* 1683
MDU COMMUNICATIONS INTERNATIONAL, INC., *pg.* 653, *pg.* 1126
MESSAGEBROADCAST INC., *pg.* 1266, *pg.* 165
METROPCS, INC., *pg.* 1872, *pg.* 1683
MIKE ALBERT LEASING, INC., *pg.* 185, *pg.* 1417
MITEL NETWORKS CORPORATION, *pg.* 654, *pg.* 1921
MOTOROLA SOLUTIONS, INC., *pg.* 657, *pg.* 659
MR. ROOTER CORPORATION, *pg.* 1057, *pg.* 1749
NATIONAL TRUCK LEASING SYSTEM, *pg.* 1916, *pg.* 649
NETWOLVES CORPORATION, *pg.* 1271, *pg.* 474
NEUSTAR, INC., *pg.* 1872, *pg.* 1807
NUTRISYSTEM, INC., *pg.* 1577, *pg.* 1533
ORANGE BUSINESS SERVICES, *pg.* 1273, *pg.* 1785
OUTERWALL INC., *pg.* 1367, *pg.* 1816
PACKETVIDEO CORPORATION, *pg.* 304, *pg.* 205
PALM BEACH TAN, INC., *pg.* 519, *pg.* 1671
PAREXEL INTERNATIONAL CORPORATION, *pg.* 1580, *pg.* 853
PENSKE CORPORATION, *pg.* 188, *pg.* 873
PENSKE LOGISTICS, LLC, *pg.* 188, *pg.* 1584
PENSKE TRUCK LEASING COMPANY, L.P., *pg.* 188, *pg.* 1585
PEPCO HOLDINGS, INC., *pg.* 1949, *pg.* 404
PHYSICIANS WEIGHT LOSS CENTERS, INC., *pg.* 1585, *pg.* 1402
PREMIERE GLOBAL SERVICES, INC., *pg.* 1275, *pg.* 518
QUALCOMM INCORPORATED, *pg.* 1873, *pg.* 207
RADIANCE TECHNOLOGIES, INC., *pg.* 1277, *pg.* 6
RAYTHEON COMPANY, *pg.* 233, *pg.* 854
RENT-A-WRECK OF AMERICA, INC., *pg.* 1921, *pg.* 773
ROCKEFELLER GROUP, INC., *pg.* 1110, *pg.* 1286
RUSH ENTERPRISES INC., *pg.* 189, *pg.* 1728
RYDER SYSTEM, INC., *pg.* 1922, *pg.* 446
SBA COMMUNICATIONS CORPORATION, *pg.* 671, *pg.* 413
SIRIUS CANADA INC., *pg.* 308, *pg.* 1943
SIRIUS XM HOLDINGS INC., *pg.* 308, *pg.* 1292
SNAP INTERACTIVE, INC., *pg.* 1281, *pg.* 1293
SPARK NETWORKS, INC., *pg.* 472, *pg.* 140
SPRINT CORPORATION, *pg.* 1874, *pg.* 719
STARTEC GLOBAL COMMUNICATIONS CORPORATION, *pg.* 1874, *pg.* 768
SYNIVERSE HOLDINGS, INC., *pg.* 479, *pg.* 475
T-SYSTEMS NORTH AMERICA INC., *pg.* 1875, *pg.* 630
TELECOMMUNICATION SYSTEMS INC., *pg.* 483, *pg.* 754
TELKONET, INC., *pg.* 678, *pg.* 1881
TELUS CORPORATION, *pg.* 1952, *pg.* 1912
TOWERSTREAM CORP., *pg.* 1284, *pg.* 1602
TRIMBLE NAVIGATION LIMITED, *pg.* 1384, *pg.* 288
U-HAUL INTERNATIONAL, INC., *pg.* 1926, *pg.* 20
UNIFIRST CORPORATION, *pg.* 50, *pg.* 860
UNITED RENTALS, *pg.* 1386, *pg.* 24
VERISIGN, INC., *pg.* 488, *pg.* 1799
VERIZON COMMUNICATIONS INC., *pg.* 1875, *pg.* 1309
VRINGO, INC., *pg.* 687, *pg.* 1312
WEGENER CORPORATION, *pg.* 687, *pg.* 533
WEIGHT WATCHERS INTERNATIONAL, INC., *pg.* 1609, *pg.* 1313
WEST CORPORATION, *pg.* 492, *pg.* 1019
WESTCON GROUP, INC., *pg.* 492, *pg.* 1345
WHEC-TV LLC, *pg.* 321, *pg.* 1338
WHEELS INC., *pg.* 1931, *pg.* 607
WINDSTREAM CORPORATION, *pg.* 321, *pg.* 34
XO COMMUNICATIONS, *pg.* 497, *pg.* 1786
XTRA LEASE LLC, *pg.* 195, *pg.* 1005
ZOOSK INC., *pg.* 1292, *pg.* 235

7311 - Advertising Agencies

THE ALDERMAN COMPANY, *pg.* 1614, *pg.* 1379
BAD BOY WORLDWIDE ENTERTAINMENT GROUP, *pg.* 270, *pg.* 1199
THE BERRY COMPANY LLC, *pg.* 1869, *pg.* 1445
BEST WESTERN INTERNATIONAL, INC., *pg.* 1081, *pg.* 15
CONVERSANT, INC., *pg.* 1393, *pg.* 306
THE DENVER NEWSPAPER AGENCY, *pg.* 1634, *pg.* 318
DOUBLECLICK, INC., *pg.* 1239, *pg.* 1225
THE ELTRON COMPANY, *pg.* 507, *pg.* 103
FAIRWAY OUTDOOR ADVERTISING, *pg.* 1640, *pg.* 525
FAIRWAY OUTDOOR ADVERTISING OF GEORGIA-ALABAMA, *pg.* 1640, *pg.* 486
FAIRWAY OUTDOOR ADVERTISING OF THE GSA, *pg.* 1640, *pg.* 1615
FAIRWAY OUTDOOR ADVERTISING OF THE PIEDMONT TRIAD, *pg.* 1640, *pg.* 1374
FAIRWAY OUTDOOR ADVERTISING OF THE TRIANGLE EAST, *pg.* 1640, *pg.* 1387
GAME SHOW PLACEMENTS LTD., *pg.* 550, *pg.* 132
HEARST BUSINESS MEDIA, *pg.* 1773, *pg.* 1346
JARCO/U.S. CASTINGS, *pg.* 1051, *pg.* 1127
MARCHEX, INC., *pg.* 1395, *pg.* 1837
MARKET LEADER, INC., *pg.* 1102, *pg.* 1822
MODE MEDIA, *pg.* 1267, *pg.* 50
MYPOINTS.COM, INC., *pg.* 1269, *pg.* 223
NIELSEN AUDIO, *pg.* 446, *pg.* 768
PALISADES MEDIA GROUP, INC., *pg.* 452, *pg.* 275
RETAILMENOT INC., *pg.* 1782, *pg.* 1665
STRUCTURAL GRAPHICS, LLC, *pg.* 1689, *pg.* 346
TREMOR VIDEO, *pg.* 682, *pg.* 1305

7313 - Radio, Television & Publishers' Advertising Representatives

ADVERTISING.COM, LLC, *pg.* 1225, *pg.* 755
BATANGA, INC., *pg.* 533, *pg.* 418
BZZAGENT, INC., *pg.* 1233, *pg.* 792
DESERT DISPATCH, *pg.* 1635, *pg.* 45
EVEO INC., *pg.* 1244, *pg.* 217
LIVE NATION ENTERTAINMENT, INC., *pg.* 558, *pg.* 47
METRO-PUCK COMICS NETWORK, *pg.* 1665, *pg.* 1259
THE MONITOR, *pg.* 1665, *pg.* 1726
PROFESSIONAL EDUCATION INSTITUTE, *pg.* 457, *pg.* 561
THE WASHINGTON TIMES, LLC, *pg.* 1701, *pg.* 408
WFAA-TV, *pg.* 320, *pg.* 1690

7319 - Advertising, NEC (except media buying, display advertising, except outdoor; and advertising material distributors)

180S, LLC, *pg.* 1824, *pg.* 754
A&E STORES, INC., *pg.* 17, *pg.* 1124
ACCURATE COMMUNICATIONS, INC., *pg.* 340, *pg.* 1013
ADSTRUC, INC., *pg.* 1393, *pg.* 1187
ADVERTISING CHECKING BUREAU INCORPORATED, *pg.* 345, *pg.* 1187
THE ADVERTISING COUNCIL, INC., *pg.* 125, *pg.* 1187
AFFINION GROUP, INC., *pg.* 1225, *pg.* 372
AIRIQ, INC., *pg.* 346, *pg.* 1932
ALABAMA BUREAU OF TOURISM & TRAVEL, *pg.* 988, *pg.* 7
ALACHUA COUNTY VISITORS & CONVENTION BUREAU, *pg.* 527, *pg.* 428
THE ALDERMAN COMPANY, *pg.* 1614, *pg.* 1379
ALLEGRA NETWORK LLC, *pg.* 1614, *pg.* 904
ALLEN COMMUNICATION LEARNING SERVICES, INC., *pg.* 346, *pg.* 1755
ALLEY THEATRE, *pg.* 527, *pg.* 1699
ALLIANCE OF CONFESSING EVANGELICALS, INC., *pg.* 126, *pg.* 1545
ALLSCRIPTS HEALTHCARE SOLUTIONS, INC., *pg.* 1492, *pg.* 563
ALSTATE PROCESS SERVICE INC., *pg.* 347, *pg.* 1155
ALTA RESOURCES CORPORATION, *pg.* 347, *pg.* 1882
ALVIMAR GENESIS, *pg.* 1825, *pg.* 886
AMALIE ARENA, *pg.* 527, *pg.* 470
AMCOR FLEXIBLES INC., *pg.* 1492, *pg.* 635
AMERICAN APPRAISAL ASSOCIATES, INC., *pg.* 349, *pg.* 1872
AMERICAN CRANE & EQUIPMENT CORPORATION, *pg.* 1312, *pg.* 1526
AMERICAN INCORPORATORS LTD., *pg.* 714, *pg.* 389
AMERICAN MOLD REMOVAL, INC., *pg.* 1393, *pg.* 436
AMERICAN REPROGRAPHICS COMPANY, *pg.* 1616, *pg.* 303
AMERICA'S CALL CENTER, INC., *pg.* 349, *pg.* 431
AMERIX CORPORATION, *pg.* 715, *pg.* 767
ANAHEIM/ORANGE COUNTY VISITOR & CONVENTION BUREAU, *pg.* 988, *pg.* 42
ANDERSON SYMPHONY ORCHESTRA, *pg.* 528, *pg.* 673
ANDRITZ INC., *pg.* 1451, *pg.* 539
ANGIE'S LIST INC, *pg.* 1228, *pg.* 682
ARAMARK CANADA LTD., *pg.* 1014, *pg.* 1935
ARCADIA ALL-FLORIDA CHAMPIONSHIP RODEO, *pg.* 529, *pg.* 409
ARCHIE COMICS ENTERTAINMENT, LLC, *pg.* 270, *pg.* 360
ARENA STAGE, *pg.* 529, *pg.* 395
ARIZONA OFFICE OF TOURISM, *pg.* 988, *pg.* 14
ASCENT CAPITAL GROUP, *pg.* 270, *pg.* 330
ASSET MARKETING SYSTEMS INSURANCE SERVICES, LLC, *pg.* 1193, *pg.* 200
ATHENAHEALTH, INC., *pg.* 1497, *pg.* 855
ATLANTA CONVENTION & VISITORS BUREAU, *pg.* 989, *pg.* 489
AUDIO VISUAL INNOVATIONS, INC., *pg.* 621, *pg.* 471
AUGUSTA METROPOLITAN CONVENTION & VISITORS BUREAU, INC., *pg.* 989, *pg.* 524
AUTO DRIVEAWAY CO., *pg.* 1900, *pg.* 566
AUTOMATIC DATA PROCESSING, INC., *pg.* 357, *pg.* 1117
AUTONOMY PLEASANTON, *pg.* 358, *pg.* 183
AVAGO TECHNOLOGIES, *pg.* 358, *pg.* 238
AVENTION, *pg.* 1230, *pg.* 815
AVERY DENNISON CORPORATION, *pg.* 1452, *pg.* 95
BAD BOY WORLDWIDE ENTERTAINMENT GROUP, *pg.* 270, *pg.* 1199
BANCTEC, INC., *pg.* 360, *pg.* 1717
BANNER DIRECT, *pg.* 1619, *pg.* 1200
BARBARA B. MANN PERFORMING ARTS HALL, *pg.* 532, *pg.* 427
BATON ROUGE AREA CONVENTION & VISITORS BUREAU, *pg.* 989, *pg.* 741
BEECH STREET CORPORATION, *pg.* 1503, *pg.* 121
BERKSHIRE VISITORS BUREAU, *pg.* 989, *pg.* 841
BERLITZ INTERNATIONAL, INC., *pg.* 598, *pg.* 1110
BET HOLDINGS LLC, *pg.* 271, *pg.* 396
BIG APPLE CIRCUS LTD., *pg.* 533, *pg.* 1145
BIOSCRIP, INC., *pg.* 1506, *pg.* 1158
BIZFILINGS, *pg.* 724, *pg.* 1865
BLANC INDUSTRIES SIGNAGE & DISPLAY GROUP, *pg.* 1621, *pg.* 1053
BLUE PHOENIX MEDIA, *pg.* 1232, *pg.* 1205
BLUE STAR JETS, INC., *pg.* 1901, *pg.* 1205
BOB EVANS FARMS, LLC, *pg.* 841, *pg.* 1467
BOGDANCO CONSULTING, *pg.* 918, *pg.* 174
BOULDER BRANDS, INC., *pg.* 1016, *pg.* 310
BRANDVIA ALLIANCE, INC., *pg.* 364, *pg.* 239
BROADRIDGE FINANCIAL SOLUTIONS INC., *pg.* 727, *pg.* 1172
BROWN & BIGELOW, INC., *pg.* 1624, *pg.* 959
BULLHORN, INC., *pg.* 1233, *pg.* 792
BUSINESS BROKERS NETWORK, *pg.* 135, *pg.* 1735
BUTLER AMERICA, *pg.* 366, *pg.* 370
BUYERZONE.COM, LLC, *pg.* 1233, *pg.* 850
CABLEVISION SYSTEMS CORPORATION, *pg.* 272, *pg.* 1141
CALIBRUS, INC., *pg.* 368, *pg.* 25
CALIFORNIA SPORTS, INC., *pg.* 536, *pg.* 78
CAMBRIDGE INFORMATION GROUP, INC., *pg.* 1625, *pg.* 761
CANADIAN COMMERCIAL CORPORATION, *pg.* 729, *pg.* 1931
CANEPA DESIGN GROUP, *pg.* 167, *pg.* 278
CANUCKS SPORTS & ENTERTAINMENT, *pg.* 536, *pg.* 1910
CAPELLA EDUCATION COMPANY, *pg.* 599, *pg.* 931
CARFAX INC., *pg.* 202, *pg.* 1777

First page reference indicates Business Class Edition
Second page reference indicates Geographic Edition

CARLSON JPM STORE FIXTURES, *pg.* 369, *pg.* 919
CAROLINA HURRICANES HOCKEY CLUB, *pg.* 537, *pg.* 1386
CARS.COM, *pg.* 1234, *pg.* 568
CATALINA MARKETING CORPORATION, *pg.* 369, *pg.* 462
CBIZ, INC., *pg.* 733, *pg.* 1429
CCH INC., *pg.* 1626, *pg.* 653
CDS GLOBAL, INC., *pg.* 370, *pg.* 704
CEDAR FAIR, L.P., *pg.* 537, *pg.* 1471
CHARITY NAVIGATOR, *pg.* 136, *pg.* 1071
CHICAGO CONVENTION & TOURISM BUREAU, *pg.* 990, *pg.* 569
CIBT EDUCATION GROUP INC., *pg.* 599, *pg.* 1910
CINCINNATI MUSEUM CENTER INC., *pg.* 540, *pg.* 1411
CINTAS CORPORATION, *pg.* 372, *pg.* 1411
CIRQUE DU SOLEIL INC., *pg.* 540, *pg.* 1954
CITIZENS FOR GLOBAL SOLUTIONS, *pg.* 137, *pg.* 397
CLASSIFIED VENTURES, LLC, *pg.* 1235, *pg.* 571
CLAYTON HOLDINGS, INC., *pg.* 738, *pg.* 370
CLEAN HARBORS, INC., *pg.* 376, *pg.* 839
COGNIZANT TECHNOLOGY SOLUTIONS CORPORATION, *pg.* 377, *pg.* 1124
THE COLAD GROUP, INC., *pg.* 377, *pg.* 1147
COLLECTORS UNIVERSE INC., *pg.* 377, *pg.* 260
COLORADO TOURISM OFFICE, *pg.* 991, *pg.* 318
COMCAST SPECTACOR, L.P., *pg.* 278, *pg.* 1562
COMTEX NEWS NETWORK, INC., *pg.* 1236, *pg.* 1770
CONCUR TECHNOLOGIES, *pg.* 1903, *pg.* 501
CONSTANT CONTACT, INC., *pg.* 379, *pg.* 850
CONVERGYS CORPORATION, *pg.* 379, *pg.* 1412
CORELOGIC, INC., *pg.* 1198, *pg.* 109
CORPORATION SERVICE COMPANY, *pg.* 380, *pg.* 390
COSTAR GROUP, INC., *pg.* 742, *pg.* 397
CREATIVE BRANCH, *pg.* 922, *pg.* 1704
CRITZAS INDUSTRIES, INC., *pg.* 329, *pg.* 995
DALLAS CONVENTION & VISITORS BUREAU, *pg.* 991, *pg.* 1678
DATA LISTING SERVICE LLC, *pg.* 382, *pg.* 919
DAYTONA BEACH RESORT AREA CONVENTION & VISITORS BUREAU, *pg.* 991, *pg.* 420
DEFYMEDIA, *pg.* 1237, *pg.* 1222
DELUXE CORPORATION, *pg.* 1634, *pg.* 964
DENVER CENTER FOR THE PERFORMING ARTS INC., *pg.* 544, *pg.* 318
DENVER METRO CONVENTION & VISITORS BUREAU, *pg.* 991, *pg.* 318
THE DENVER NEWSPAPER AGENCY, *pg.* 1634, *pg.* 318
DES MOINES SYMPHONY ASSOCIATION, *pg.* 544, *pg.* 705
DESIGN WITHIN REACH, INC., *pg.* 923, *pg.* 216
DESTINATION DC, *pg.* 991, *pg.* 398
DEX ONE CORPORATION, *pg.* 1635, *pg.* 1360
THE DIAN FOSSEY GORILLA FUND INTERNATIONAL, *pg.* 139, *pg.* 504
DICK CLARK PRODUCTIONS, INC., *pg.* 281, *pg.* 273
DIGG, INC., *pg.* 1238, *pg.* 1224
DIPCRAFT MANUFACTURING COMPANY, *pg.* 79, *pg.* 1518
DIRECT HOLDINGS AMERICAS INC., *pg.* 1636, *pg.* 1780
DIVING EQUIPMENT & MARKETING ASSOCIATION, *pg.* 139, *pg.* 202
THE DOLAN COMPANY, *pg.* 1636, *pg.* 932
DOMINION ENTERPRISES, *pg.* 1636, *pg.* 1796
DOUBLECLICK, INC., *pg.* 1239, *pg.* 1225
DOUGLAS-GUARDIAN SERVICES CORPORATION, *pg.* 388, *pg.* 1704
DOW JONES & COMPANY, INC., *pg.* 1637, *pg.* 1225
DRIVESAVERS DATA RECOVERY, INC., *pg.* 388, *pg.* 168
THE DUN & BRADSTREET CORP., *pg.* 1637, *pg.* 1120
DYNTEK, INC., *pg.* 389, *pg.* 165
EBSCO INDUSTRIES, INC., *pg.* 1638, *pg.* 2
EDGAR ONLINE, INC., *pg.* 746, *pg.* 776
ELECTION SERVICES CORPORATION, *pg.* 390, *pg.* 1161
EMDEON, INC., *pg.* 747, *pg.* 1650
EMERALD EXPOSITIONS, *pg.* 392, *pg.* 1352
EMUSIC.COM, INC., *pg.* 1243, *pg.* 1227
ENGLOBAL CORPORATION, *pg.* 81, *pg.* 1705
EPOCRATES, INC., *pg.* 1529, *pg.* 254
EQUIFAX INC., *pg.* 748, *pg.* 504
EXAMWORKS GROUP, INC., *pg.* 1529, *pg.* 505
EXTENDICARE HEALTH SERVICES INC., *pg.* 1530, *pg.* 1874
EXTERRAN HOLDINGS, INC., *pg.* 977, *pg.* 1705
FAIR ISAAC CORPORATION, *pg.* 1247, *pg.* 955
FAIRWAY OUTDOOR ADVERTISING, *pg.* 1640, *pg.* 525
FAIRWAY OUTDOOR ADVERTISING OF GEORGIA-ALABAMA, *pg.* 1640, *pg.* 486
FAIRWAY OUTDOOR ADVERTISING OF THE GSA, *pg.* 1640, *pg.* 1615
FAIRWAY OUTDOOR ADVERTISING OF THE PIEDMONT TRIAD, *pg.* 1640, *pg.* 1374
FAIRWAY OUTDOOR ADVERTISING OF THE TRIANGLE EAST, *pg.* 1640, *pg.* 1387
FEDEX EXPRESS CORPORATION, *pg.* 1908, *pg.* 1644
FELD ENTERTAINMENT, INC., *pg.* 547, *pg.* 458
FILECONTROL PARTNERS LTD, *pg.* 1247, *pg.* 1746
FINANCIAL PACIFIC LEASING, LLC, *pg.* 753, *pg.* 1820
FLEETCOR TECHNOLOGIES, INC., *pg.* 758, *pg.* 537
FLORIDA DEPARTMENT OF AGRICULTURE & CONSUMER SERVICES - DIVISION OF MARKETING & DEVELOPMENT, *pg.* 992, *pg.* 469
FOREST CITY ENTERPRISES, INC., *pg.* 1092, *pg.* 1430
FORT DEARBORN COMPANY, *pg.* 1457, *pg.* 610
FOX ASSOCIATES, LLC, *pg.* 549, *pg.* 997
FOX VALLEY SYMPHONY ASSOCIATION INC., *pg.* 549, *pg.* 1852
FRENCH GOVERNMENT TOURIST OFFICE, *pg.* 992, *pg.* 1233
FTI CONSULTING, INC., *pg.* 760, *pg.* 478
G&K SERVICES INC., *pg.* 693, *pg.* 949
G4S SECURE SOLUTIONS USA, *pg.* 399, *pg.* 436
GANNETT CO., INC., *pg.* 1643, *pg.* 1790
GE HEALTHCARE, *pg.* 399, *pg.* 1765
GETTY IMAGES, INC., *pg.* 1645, *pg.* 1836
GIBRALTAR PACKAGING GROUP, INC., *pg.* 1459, *pg.* 1011
GLOBAL RESPONSE CORPORATION, *pg.* 400, *pg.* 439
GOOGLE INC., *pg.* 1249, *pg.* 153
GOVDELIVERY, INC., *pg.* 1255, *pg.* 961
GREAT AMERICAN GROUP, INC., *pg.* 1394, *pg.* 308
GREATER BOSTON CONVENTION & VISITORS BUREAU INC., *pg.* 993, *pg.* 795
GREATER CINCINNATI CONVENTION & VISITORS BUREAU, *pg.* 993, *pg.* 1414
GREATER HOUSTON CONVENTION & VISITORS BUREAU, *pg.* 993, *pg.* 1706
GREATER MIAMI CONVENTION & VISITORS BUREAU, *pg.* 993, *pg.* 442
GREATER RALEIGH CONVENTION & VISITORS BUREAU, *pg.* 994, *pg.* 1387
THE GREATER VANCOUVER CONVENTION & VISITOR BUREAU, *pg.* 994, *pg.* 1910
GREEK NATIONAL TOURIST ORGANIZATION, *pg.* 994, *pg.* 1236
GREENSBORO CONVENTION & VISITORS BUREAU, *pg.* 994, *pg.* 1374
GUIDELINE, INC., *pg.* 402, *pg.* 1237
GUYETTE & DEETER, *pg.* 1772, *pg.* 776
HARMONIX MUSIC SYSTEMS, INC., *pg.* 1256, *pg.* 808
HARSCO CORPORATION, *pg.* 86, *pg.* 1519
HAWAII VISITORS & CONVENTION BUREAU, *pg.* 994, *pg.* 543
HEALTHPORT, INC., *pg.* 403, *pg.* 484
HEARTLAND EXPRESS, INC., *pg.* 1910, *pg.* 710
THE HIBBERT GROUP, *pg.* 407, *pg.* 1126
HOLLYWOOD MEDIA CORP., *pg.* 1256, *pg.* 412
HOMEGAIN.COM, INC., *pg.* 1256, *pg.* 83
HOT SPRINGS CONVENTION & VISITORS BUREAU, *pg.* 995, *pg.* 33
HUNTSVILLE SYMPHONY ORCHESTRA, *pg.* 553, *pg.* 6
I2SMS, *pg.* 1257, *pg.* 511
IDEALAB, INC., *pg.* 1258, *pg.* 180
IDEO, INC., *pg.* 411, *pg.* 178
IHS AUTOMOTIVE DRIVEN BY POLK, *pg.* 1652, *pg.* 907
ILLINOIS BUREAU OF TOURISM, *pg.* 995, *pg.* 578
ILLINOIS SYMPHONY ORCHESTRA, *pg.* 553, *pg.* 662
IMPREMEDIA LLC, *pg.* 1652, *pg.* 133
INDIANAPOLIS CONVENTION & VISITORS ASSOCIATION, *pg.* 995, *pg.* 687
INFOGROUP INC., *pg.* 1652, *pg.* 1016
INFORMATION TODAY INC., *pg.* 1653, *pg.* 1084
INTCOMEX, INC., *pg.* 416, *pg.* 443
INTEGRAMED AMERICA, INC., *pg.* 1546, *pg.* 1325
INTERACTIVE COMMUNICATIONS INC, *pg.* 1872, *pg.* 511
INTERACTIVE DATA PRICING & REFERENCE DATA, INC., *pg.* 769, *pg.* 785
INTERIORS BY STEVEN G INC., *pg.* 929, *pg.* 459
INTERNATIONAL DECISION SYSTEMS, *pg.* 419, *pg.* 938
INTERNATIONAL MONETARY SYSTEMS, LTD., *pg.* 769, *pg.* 1884
INTERNATIONAL ROAD DYNAMICS INC., *pg.* 1912, *pg.* 1962
INTERNATIONAL SPEEDWAY CORPORATION, *pg.* 553, *pg.* 420
INTERSECTIONS INC., *pg.* 769, *pg.* 1777
INTERSIL CORPORATION, *pg.* 647, *pg.* 146
INVENDA CORPORATION, *pg.* 1259, *pg.* 762
INVESTMENT SEMINARS, INC., *pg.* 420, *pg.* 466
IPAYMENT, INC., *pg.* 771, *pg.* 306
IRVING CONVENTION & VISITORS BUREAU, *pg.* 996, *pg.* 1720
ISABELLA BANK CORPORATION, *pg.* 771, *pg.* 901
ISRAEL MINISTRY OF TOURISM INFORMATION CENTER, *pg.* 996, *pg.* 1244
ITALIAN GOVERNMENT TOURIST BOARD-NORTH AMERICA, *pg.* 996, *pg.* 1244
ITW HI-CONE, *pg.* 1461, *pg.* 620
IXIA, *pg.* 422, *pg.* 56
JACKSON SYMPHONY ASSOCIATION INC., *pg.* 554, *pg.* 1635
JAMAICA TOURIST BOARD, *pg.* 996, *pg.* 443
JAMES ALEXANDER CORPORATION, *pg.* 1461, *pg.* 1044
JHANE BARNES, INC., *pg.* 42, *pg.* 1246
JOHN F. KENNEDY CENTER FOR THE PERFORMING ARTS, *pg.* 555, *pg.* 401
JONES DAY, *pg.* 423, *pg.* 1431
KAESER & BLAIR INCORPORATED, *pg.* 1656, *pg.* 1405
KANSAS CITY CONVENTION & VISITORS ASSOCIATION, *pg.* 996, *pg.* 984
KANSAS CITY SYMPHONY, *pg.* 555, *pg.* 985
THE KAUFMAN CENTER, *pg.* 556, *pg.* 1248
KENTUCKY DEPARTMENT OF TOURISM, *pg.* 996, *pg.* 728
KISSIMMEE-ST. CLOUD CONVENTION & VISITORS BUREAU, *pg.* 997, *pg.* 436
LANGUAGE LINE SERVICES HOLDINGS, INC., *pg.* 426, *pg.* 151
LARRY H. MILLER GROUP OF COMPANIES, *pg.* 182, *pg.* 1762
LAS VEGAS CONVENTION & VISITORS AUTHORITY, *pg.* 997, *pg.* 1027
LEDIC MANAGEMENT GROUP, *pg.* 1100, *pg.* 1645
LEGAL SHIELD, *pg.* 775, *pg.* 1484
LEGALZOOM.COM, INC., *pg.* 1261, *pg.* 96
LEXINGTON PHILHARMONIC SOCIETY, *pg.* 557, *pg.* 730
LEXISNEXIS GROUP, *pg.* 1658, *pg.* 1446
LEXISNEXIS LITIGATION SOLUTIONS, *pg.* 1659, *pg.* 1446
LIFELOCK INC., *pg.* 776, *pg.* 26
LIVE NATION ENTERTAINMENT, INC., *pg.* 558, *pg.* 47
LIVE NATION WORLDWIDE - TIMES SQUARE OFFICE, *pg.* 558, *pg.* 1252
LOCAL.COM CORPORATION, *pg.* 1264, *pg.* 113
LOS ANGELES CONVENTION & VISITORS BUREAU, *pg.* 997, *pg.* 135
LOS ANGELES PHILHARMONIC ASSOCIATION, *pg.* 559, *pg.* 135
LOUISIANA PHILHARMONIC ORCHESTRA, *pg.* 559, *pg.* 747
LOUISVILLE CONVENTION & VISITORS BUREAU, *pg.* 998, *pg.* 736
LUFKIN INDUSTRIES, INC., *pg.* 1357, *pg.* 1726
LYNCH TECHNOLOGIES, INC., *pg.* 1357, *pg.* 526
MADISON SQUARE GARDEN NETWORK, *pg.* 297, *pg.* 1255
MAPQUEST, INC., *pg.* 1265, *pg.* 321
MARC-MICHAELS INTERIOR DESIGN, INC., *pg.* 934, *pg.* 480
MARCHEX, INC., *pg.* 1395, *pg.* 1837
MARITZ INC., *pg.* 1914, *pg.* 977
MARTINDALE-HUBBELL, INC., *pg.* 1662, *pg.* 1095
MARUDAS PRINT SERVICES & PROMOTIONAL PRODUCTS, INC., *pg.* 430, *pg.* 962
MASSACHUSETTS OFFICE OF TRAVEL & TOURISM, *pg.* 998, *pg.* 798
MATRIX INTEGRATION LLC, *pg.* 430, *pg.* 692
MAXIMUS, INC., *pg.* 780, *pg.* 1799
MAYO PERFORMING ARTS CENTER, *pg.* 561, *pg.* 1089
MEDALLION FINANCIAL CORP., *pg.* 781, *pg.* 1258
MEDASSETS INC., *pg.* 1561, *pg.* 484
MEDIABISTRO, INC., *pg.* 1266, *pg.* 1258
MEGATRAX PRODUCTION MUSIC, INC., *pg.* 297, *pg.* 167
METROPOLITAN PIER & EXPOSITION AUTHORITY, *pg.* 562, *pg.* 581
METROPOLITAN TUCSON CONVENTION & VISITORS BUREAU, *pg.* 998, *pg.* 27
MEXICO TOURISM BOARD, *pg.* 998, *pg.* 136
MFV EXPOSITIONS, LLC, *pg.* 434, *pg.* 1101
MICROBILT CORPORATION, *pg.* 782, *pg.* 534
MOD-PAC CORP., *pg.* 1665, *pg.* 1150

MONAKER GROUP, INC., *pg.* 298, *pg.* 479
MOOD MEDIA, *pg.* 298, *pg.* 1616
MORNINGSTAR, INC., *pg.* 784, *pg.* 583
MORRIS COMMUNICATIONS COMPANY LLC, *pg.* 1666, *pg.* 525
MOTOR TREND AUTO SHOWS, LLC, *pg.* 564, *pg.* 1537
NATIONAL ARTS CENTRE CORPORATION, *pg.* 566, *pg.* 1932
NATIONAL CINEMEDIA, INC., *pg.* 567, *pg.* 314
NBA PROPERTIES, INC., *pg.* 569, *pg.* 1120
NETSMART TECHNOLOGIES, INC., *pg.* 445, *pg.* 1163
NETSUITE, INC., *pg.* 1270, *pg.* 255
NETWOLVES CORPORATION, *pg.* 1271, *pg.* 474
NEW MEXICO TOURISM DEPARTMENT, *pg.* 1001, *pg.* 1136
NEW SMYRNA BEACH AREA VISITORS BUREAU, *pg.* 1001, *pg.* 451
NEW YORK RANGERS HOCKEY CLUB, *pg.* 570, *pg.* 1269
NICE-PAK PRODUCTS, INC., *pg.* 1465, *pg.* 1319
NIELSEN BUSINESS MEDIA, *pg.* 1671, *pg.* 1272
THE NIELSEN COMPANY B.V., *pg.* 1671, *pg.* 1272
NIGHTINGALE-CONANT CORPORATION, *pg.* 152, *pg.* 670
NORTHBROOK SYMPHONY ORCHESTRA INC., *pg.* 571, *pg.* 641
NTT DATA, *pg.* 447, *pg.* 799
NUANCE COMMUNICATIONS, INC., *pg.* 447, *pg.* 806
NUANCE TRANSCRIPTION, *pg.* 1576, *pg.* 516
NYC & COMPANY, INC., *pg.* 1002, *pg.* 1274
OKLAHOMA CITY CONVENTION & VISITORS BUREAU, *pg.* 1002, *pg.* 1487
OKLAHOMA TOURISM & RECREATION DEPARTMENT, *pg.* 1003, *pg.* 1487
OLD FASHION FOODS, INC., *pg.* 1028, *pg.* 525
OMAHA COMMUNITY PLAYHOUSE, *pg.* 572, *pg.* 1017
OMTOOL, LTD., *pg.* 449, *pg.* 782
OPENTEXT, *pg.* 1272, *pg.* 1956
OPENX TECHNOLOGIES, INC., *pg.* 1272, *pg.* 180
OPERA AMERICA, *pg.* 572, *pg.* 1274
OPTIMIZERX CORPORATION, *pg.* 1673, *pg.* 905
ORLANDO/ORANGE COUNTY CONVENTION & VISITORS BUREAU, INC., *pg.* 1003, *pg.* 455
ORTHOSYNETICS, INC., *pg.* 791, *pg.* 1657
OTTAWA SENATORS HOCKEY CLUB, *pg.* 573, *pg.* 1921
OUTFRONT MEDIA, *pg.* 1465, *pg.* 1275
PALLADIUM THEATER, INC., *pg.* 573, *pg.* 463
PALM BEACH COUNTY CONVENTION & VISITORS BUREAU, *pg.* 1003, *pg.* 479
PALM SPRINGS DESERT RESORTS CONVENTION & VISITORS AUTHORITY, *pg.* 1003, *pg.* 187
PAREXEL INTERNATIONAL CORPORATION, *pg.* 1580, *pg.* 853
PDI, INC., *pg.* 1580, *pg.* 1104
PENSACOLA BAY AREA CONVENTION & VISITORS BUREAU, *pg.* 1004, *pg.* 458
PENTON MEDIA, INC., *pg.* 1676, *pg.* 719
PENTON MEDIA, INC., *pg.* 1676, *pg.* 1277
PEPSI-COLA NORTH AMERICA, *pg.* 259, *pg.* 1327
PERLA LICHI LLC, *pg.* 940, *pg.* 418
PFSWEB, INC., *pg.* 1275, *pg.* 1733
PHILADELPHIA CONVENTION & VISITORS BUREAU, *pg.* 1004, *pg.* 1568
PHILHARMONIC SOCIETY OF NORTHEASTERN PENNSYLVANIA, *pg.* 575, *pg.* 1594
PHILHARMONIC SYMPHONY SOCIETY OF NEW YORK INC., *pg.* 575, *pg.* 1282
PINELLAS SUNCOAST TRANSIT AUTHORITY, *pg.* 1919, *pg.* 463
PIVOTAL RESOURCES, INC., *pg.* 455, *pg.* 304
POLAR COVE, INC., *pg.* 1275, *pg.* 1607
PORT AUTHORITY OF NEW YORK & NEW JERSEY, *pg.* 1919, *pg.* 1283
POSITIVELY CLEVELAND, *pg.* 1004, *pg.* 1434
POWERSECURE INTERNATIONAL, INC., *pg.* 105, *pg.* 1392
PRATT & LAMBERT PAINTS, *pg.* 1446, *pg.* 1434
PRECISION ROLL GRINDERS, INC., *pg.* 1370, *pg.* 1514
PRICEWATERHOUSECOOPERS LLP, *pg.* 795, *pg.* 1283
PROVIDENCE PERFORMING ARTS CENTER, *pg.* 578, *pg.* 1607
PTA CORPORATION, *pg.* 1888, *pg.* 368
PUBLISHERS CIRCULATION FULFILLMENT INC., *pg.* 1679, *pg.* 780
Q INTERACTIVE INC., *pg.* 1276, *pg.* 588
QUINCY SYMPHONY ORCHESTRA ASSOCIATION, *pg.* 578, *pg.* 653
QUINSTREET, INC., *pg.* 1276, *pg.* 89
RAINMAKER SYSTEMS INC., *pg.* 458, *pg.* 58
RE/MAX INTERNATIONAL, INC., *pg.* 1109, *pg.* 322
REACHLOCAL, INC., *pg.* 1277, *pg.* 308
RECORDED BOOKS, LLC, *pg.* 1680, *pg.* 775
REED EXHIBITIONS USA, *pg.* 460, *pg.* 364
REGISTER.COM, INC., *pg.* 1277, *pg.* 434
REPLY! INC., *pg.* 1277, *pg.* 260
RESEARCH SOLUTIONS, INC., *pg.* 1680, *pg.* 85
RHODE ISLAND COALITION AGAINST DOMESTIC VIOLENCE, *pg.* 155, *pg.* 1609
ROCHESTER PHILHARMONIC ORCHESTRA INC., *pg.* 579, *pg.* 1337
ROSARIO SALAZAR DESIGN INC., *pg.* 941, *pg.* 418
ROUNDABOUT THEATRE COMPANY, *pg.* 579, *pg.* 1287
ROUNDER RECORDS CORPORATION, *pg.* 307, *pg.* 807
SACRAMENTO KINGS, *pg.* 579, *pg.* 197
SAFEGUARD SCIENTIFICS, INC., *pg.* 464, *pg.* 1592
SAFER PRINTS INC., *pg.* 32, *pg.* 1098
SAGE SOFTWARE, INC., *pg.* 404, *pg.* 116
SAN ANTONIO CONVENTION & VISITORS BUREAU, *pg.* 1004, *pg.* 1742
SAN DIEGO CONVENTION & VISITORS BUREAU, *pg.* 1004, *pg.* 208
SAN FRANCISCO TRAVEL ASSOCIATION, *pg.* 1005, *pg.* 227
SAN JOSE CONVENTION/VISITORS BUREAU, *pg.* 1005, *pg.* 250
SANTA FE LEATHER CORPORATION, *pg.* 12, *pg.* 1059
SARASOTA CONVENTION & VISITORS BUREAU, *pg.* 1005, *pg.* 467
SARATOGA PERFORMING ARTS CENTER, INC., *pg.* 581, *pg.* 1340
SCIQUEST, INC., *pg.* 468, *pg.* 1361
SCREENVISION CINEMA NETWORK LLC, *pg.* 581, *pg.* 1290
SEATTLE CONVENTION & VISITORS BUREAU, *pg.* 1005, *pg.* 1839
SENIOR MARKET SALES, INC., *pg.* 1217, *pg.* 1018
SGK, *pg.* 1686, *pg.* 590
SHERLOQ SOLUTIONS, *pg.* 156, *pg.* 475
SHOPLOCAL, LLC, *pg.* 1280, *pg.* 590
SHOPPING.COM, LTD., *pg.* 1280, *pg.* 50
SHORELINE IMAGE WORKS LLC, *pg.* 1785, *pg.* 477
SIGHTLINE SYSTEMS CORPORATION, *pg.* 469, *pg.* 1780
SITEL CORPORATION, *pg.* 470, *pg.* 1654
SMAATO INC., *pg.* 1281, *pg.* 228
SOLUTIONS OFFICE INTERIORS, INC., *pg.* 112, *pg.* 250
SONY MUSIC ENTERTAINMENT, *pg.* 309, *pg.* 1294
SOUTH AFRICAN TOURISM, *pg.* 1005, *pg.* 1294
SOUTH CENTRAL COMMUNICATIONS CORPORATION, *pg.* 310, *pg.* 679
SOUTH DAKOTA SYMPHONY ORCHESTRA, *pg.* 584, *pg.* 1625
SOUTHEAST TOURISM SOCIETY, *pg.* 1006, *pg.* 539
SPA FINDER, INC., *pg.* 1113, *pg.* 1295
SPECTRUM GROUP INTERNATIONAL, INC., *pg.* 472, *pg.* 116
SRDS, INC., *pg.* 1688, *pg.* 657
ST. AUGUSTINE, PONTE VEDRA & THE BEACHES VISITORS & CONVENTION BUREAU, *pg.* 1006, *pg.* 461
ST. LOUIS CONVENTION & VISITORS COMMISSION, *pg.* 1006, *pg.* 1003
STEFANINI TECHTEAM GLOBAL, INC., *pg.* 476, *pg.* 907
STRATUS TECHNOLOGIES, INC., *pg.* 477, *pg.* 832
THE STREET, INC., *pg.* 1283, *pg.* 1296
SUCCESSFACTORS, INC., *pg.* 477, *pg.* 228
SUMNER COMMUNICATIONS INC., *pg.* 1690, *pg.* 338
SUMTOTAL SYSTEMS, INC., *pg.* 477, *pg.* 429
SUNBELT BUSINESS ADVISORS NETWORK, LLC, *pg.* 806, *pg.* 1456
SUNRISE BRANDS, LLC, *pg.* 33, *pg.* 140
SUPPORTSAVE SOLUTIONS, INC., *pg.* 478, *pg.* 911
SURETY, INC., *pg.* 1283, *pg.* 1799
SWISS AMERICA TRADING CORPORATION, *pg.* 808, *pg.* 20
SWITZERLAND TOURISM, *pg.* 1006, *pg.* 1297
TAMPA BAY & CO., *pg.* 1007, *pg.* 476
TAPJOY, INC., *pg.* 1396, *pg.* 228
TASC, INC., *pg.* 1431, *pg.* 1777
TEAM HEALTH HOLDINGS, INC., *pg.* 1601, *pg.* 1639
TECHNOLOGY MARKETING CORP., *pg.* 1691, *pg.* 364
TENDER CORPORATION, *pg.* 1601, *pg.* 1035
THE TENNIS CHANNEL, INC., *pg.* 679, *pg.* 276
TESSCO TECHNOLOGIES, INC., *pg.* 679, *pg.* 773
TEXPAK INC., *pg.* 1470, *pg.* 1161
THEATER LEAGUE INC., *pg.* 587, *pg.* 986
THEO KALOMIRAKIS THEATERS, *pg.* 115, *pg.* 1298
THOMSON ELITE, *pg.* 484, *pg.* 72
THOMSON REUTERS - CORPORATE HEADQUARTERS, *pg.* 1693, *pg.* 1299
THOMSON REUTERS CORPORATION, *pg.* 1693, *pg.* 1944
TICKETMASTER ENTERTAINMENT LLC, *pg.* 1284, *pg.* 48
TIX CORPORATION, *pg.* 588, *pg.* 281
TM STUDIOS, INC., *pg.* 588, *pg.* 1689
TORONTO CONVENTION & VISITORS ASSOCIATION, *pg.* 1007, *pg.* 1945
TOUCHSTONE ENERGY COOPERATIVES, *pg.* 1953, *pg.* 1775
TRADE COMMISSION OF SPAIN, *pg.* 158, *pg.* 1304
TRANSLATIONS.COM, *pg.* 485, *pg.* 1304
TRAVEL PORTLAND, *pg.* 1008, *pg.* 1507
TRUVEN HEALTH ANALYTICS, *pg.* 1696, *pg.* 867
TTC AMERIDIAL, LLC, *pg.* 486, *pg.* 593
TUPPERWARE BRANDS CORPORATION, *pg.* 1139, *pg.* 456
ULTIMATE TECHNOLOGY CORPORATION, *pg.* 486, *pg.* 1349
UNIFIED SIGNAL, INC., *pg.* 682, *pg.* 1822
UNISYS CORPORATION, *pg.* 487, *pg.* 1517
UNITED ONLINE, INC., *pg.* 1286, *pg.* 308
USA FINANCIAL, *pg.* 815, *pg.* 864
USA TECHNOLOGIES, INC., *pg.* 815, *pg.* 1550
THE UTICA SYMPHONY ORCHESTRA, *pg.* 590, *pg.* 1347
VALASSIS COMMUNICATIONS, INC., *pg.* 1287, *pg.* 897
VARESE SARABANDE RECORDS, INC., *pg.* 1789, *pg.* 281
VERISK ANALYTICS, INC., *pg.* 1222, *pg.* 1076
THE VERNON COMPANY, *pg.* 488, *pg.* 710
VERTICALRESPONSE, INC., *pg.* 489, *pg.* 230
VIAD CORP., *pg.* 816, *pg.* 20
VICTORIA LESSER, INC., *pg.* 946, *pg.* 436
VIRGINIA TOURISM AUTHORITY, *pg.* 1010, *pg.* 1804
VISITING NURSE ASSOCIATION OF CENTRAL JERSEY, *pg.* 1607, *pg.* 1114
VISITING NURSE ASSOCIATION OF STATEN ISLAND, *pg.* 1607, *pg.* 1343
WARNER BROS. RECORDS, INC., *pg.* 1791, *pg.* 55
WARRANTECH CORPORATION, *pg.* 491, *pg.* 1668
WEB.COM GROUP, INC., *pg.* 1288, *pg.* 435
WELCOME FUNDS, INC., *pg.* 1223, *pg.* 413
WELOCALIZE, INC., *pg.* 1289, *pg.* 769
WESTERN NEWSPAPERS, INC., *pg.* 1702, *pg.* 28
WESTROCK COMPANY, *pg.* 1472, *pg.* 1805
WILLIAMSPORT SYMPHONY ORCHESTRA, *pg.* 592, *pg.* 1595
WINDOWS AND WALLS UNLIMITED, INC., *pg.* 946, *pg.* 1343
WIS INTERNATIONAL, *pg.* 493, *pg.* 211
WISCONSIN DELLS VISITOR & CONVENTION BUREAU, *pg.* 1011, *pg.* 1899
WMS INDUSTRIES INC., *pg.* 593, *pg.* 666
WOLFTRAP FOUNDATION FOR THE PERFORMING ARTS, *pg.* 594, *pg.* 1809
WOODRUFF ARTS CENTER, *pg.* 595, *pg.* 524
WORD OF LIFE FELLOWSHIP, INC., *pg.* 161, *pg.* 1341
WORLD WRESTLING ENTERTAINMENT, INC., *pg.* 595, *pg.* 380
WRIGHT EXPRESS CORPORATION, *pg.* 493, *pg.* 753
XEROX CORPORATION, *pg.* 494, *pg.* 365
XO GROUP INC., *pg.* 1289, *pg.* 1316
XPO LOGISTICS, INC., *pg.* 1931, *pg.* 350
YAHOO! CANADA CO., *pg.* 1289, *pg.* 1947
ZONES, INC., *pg.* 1292, *pg.* 1813

7322 - Adjustment & Collection Services

ASSET ACCEPTANCE CAPITAL CORP., *pg.* 716, *pg.* 912
EGS FINANCIAL CARE, INC., *pg.* 746, *pg.* 1540
ENCORE CAPITAL GROUP, INC., *pg.* 747, *pg.* 202
EQUIFAX INC., *pg.* 748, *pg.* 504

7323 - Credit Reporting Services

CONSUMER CREDIT COUNSELING SERVICES, *pg.* 741, *pg.* 501
EQUIFAX INC., *pg.* 748, *pg.* 504
EXPERIAN CONSUMER DIRECT, *pg.* 1245, *pg.* 71
INCHARGE INSTITUTE OF AMERICA, INC., *pg.* 768, *pg.* 454

OWENS ONLINE, INC., pg. 1273, pg. 475

7331 - Direct Mail Advertising Services

ACXIOM CORPORATION, pg. 342, pg. 607
ADVERTISING DISTRIBUTORS OF AMERICA INC., pg. 345, pg. 1338
AMERICAN LIST COUNSEL, INC., pg. 349, pg. 1110
AMERIMARK DIRECT, LLC, pg. 1759, pg. 1428
CONCLUSIVE ANALYTICS, pg. 1236, pg. 1380
CONCORDIA PUBLISHING HOUSE, pg. 1629, pg. 995
HAINES & COMPANY, INC., pg. 1646, pg. 1468
THE HIBBERT GROUP, pg. 407, pg. 1126
INFOGROUP, pg. 414, pg. 350
INFOGROUP, pg. 769, pg. 1038
JAPS-OLSON COMPANY, pg. 1654, pg. 956
Q INTERACTIVE INC., pg. 1276, pg. 588
STAT RESOURCE GROUP, INC., pg. 1689, pg. 345
TAYLOR CORPORATION, pg. 1691, pg. 952
VALASSIS, pg. 1698, pg. 386
VALPAK DIRECT MARKETING SYSTEMS, INC., pg. 1699, pg. 438
VERTICALRESPONSE, INC., pg. 489, pg. 230

7335 - Commercial Photography

THE ALDERMAN COMPANY, pg. 1614, pg. 1379
ASCENSION HEALTH ALLIANCE, pg. 1496, pg. 992
CARDIONET, INC., pg. 1513, pg. 1523
CENTRASTATE HEALTHCARE SYSTEM INC., pg. 1514, pg. 1071
CORBIS CORPORATION, pg. 380, pg. 1834
CORD BLOOD AMERICA, INC., pg. 1519, pg. 1023
CRYO-CELL INTERNATIONAL, INC., pg. 1520, pg. 452
CRYOLIFE, INC., pg. 1520, pg. 534
DAXOR CORPORATION, pg. 1522, pg. 1221
DIGITALGLOBE, INC., pg. 1408, pg. 333
GETTY IMAGES, INC., pg. 1645, pg. 1836
HEALTHWAYS, INC., pg. 1540, pg. 1632
HEMACARE CORPORATION, pg. 1541, pg. 300
HIGHMARK BLUE CROSS BLUE SHIELD, pg. 1203, pg. 1576
HOOPER HOLMES, INC., pg. 1542, pg. 718
INTEGRAMED AMERICA, INC., pg. 1546, pg. 1325
JOSTENS, INC., pg. 7, pg. 938
MORRISON MANAGEMENT SPECIALISTS, INC., pg. 1028, pg. 515
NATIONAL MARROW DONOR PROGRAM, INC., pg. 150, pg. 941
NEW YORK BLOOD CENTER, INC., pg. 1573, pg. 1268
ONEBLOOD, INC., pg. 1578, pg. 463
PORTRAIT INNOVATIONS HOLDING COMPANY, pg. 1427, pg. 1368
RURAL/METRO CORPORATION, pg. 1591, pg. 24
SHUTTERSTOCK, INC., pg. 1280, pg. 1291
TRACK GROUP, pg. 1603, pg. 1761
U.S. PHYSICAL THERAPY, INC., pg. 1604, pg. 1716
VIACORD, pg. 1606, pg. 810
WELLSTAR HEALTH SYSTEM, INC., pg. 161, pg. 536
ZUMA PRESS, INC., pg. 1704, pg. 199

7336 - Commercial Art & Graphic Design

AMERICAN REPROGRAPHICS COMPANY, pg. 1616, pg. 303
CHYRONHEGO, pg. 371, pg. 1179
CIBT EDUCATION GROUP INC., pg. 599, pg. 1910
FEDEX OFFICE & PRINT SERVICES, INC., pg. 396, pg. 1681
GETTY IMAGES, INC., pg. 1645, pg. 1836
MONDO MEDIA CORPORATION, pg. 1268, pg. 223
QUAD/GRAPHICS, INC., pg. 1468, pg. 1896
RALPH PUCCI INTERNATIONAL LTD., pg. 940, pg. 1285
SCHAWK CANADA INC., pg. 1683, pg. 1928
SGK, pg. 1686, pg. 590
STRUCTURAL GRAPHICS, LLC, pg. 1689, pg. 346
TAYLOR CORPORATION, pg. 1691, pg. 952
TUFCO TECHNOLOGIES, INC., pg. 1697, pg. 1860

7338 - Secretarial & Court Reporting Services

ACTUATE CANADA, pg. 1225, pg. 1933
AMERICAN REPROGRAPHICS COMPANY, pg. 1616, pg. 303
ANACOMP, INC., pg. 350, pg. 1777
EASYLINK SERVICES CORPORATION, pg. 1240, pg. 1108
EASYLINK SERVICES INTERNATIONAL CORPORATION, pg. 389, pg. 536
FREEDOM RINGS DOCUMENT PREPARATION SERVICES, pg. 1394, pg. 466
MERRILL CORPORATION, pg. 1664, pg. 962
NUANCE DICTAPHONE HEALTHCARE SOLUTIONS, pg. 447, pg. 806
OMTOOL, LTD., pg. 449, pg. 782
PROCESS ACADEMY, INC., pg. 456, pg. 1951

7342 - Disinfecting & Pest Control Services

CLEAN HARBORS, INC., pg. 376, pg. 839
ECOLAB INC., pg. 329, pg. 960
ECOLAB INC.-FOOD & BEVERAGE DIVISION, pg. 330, pg. 960
EVOQUA, pg. 1336, pg. 1590
HERMAN MILLER, INC., pg. 926, pg. 913
MIDDLESEX WATER COMPANY, pg. 1946, pg. 1075
ORKIN, INC., pg. 1798, pg. 517
PROGRESSIVE WASTE SOLUTIONS, pg. 796, pg. 1947
PURESAFE WATER SYSTEMS, INC., pg. 333, pg. 1322
ROLLINS, INC., pg. 1179, pg. 519
THE SERVICEMASTER COMPANY, LLC, pg. 335, pg. 1646
SMITHEREEN PEST MANAGEMENT SERVICES, pg. 1800, pg. 638
THE TERMINIX INTERNATIONAL COMPANY LIMITED PARTNERSHIP, pg. 337, pg. 1646
TRUGREEN-CHEMLAWN, pg. 1801, pg. 1647
WALTHAM SERVICES, INC., pg. 1801, pg. 855
WASTE MANAGEMENT, INC., pg. 1954, pg. 1716

7349 - Building Cleaning & Maintenance Services, NEC

ABM INDUSTRIES, INC., pg. 64, pg. 1186
ACCO ENGINEERED SYSTEMS, pg. 1068, pg. 95
AERO CONTROLS, INC., pg. 223, pg. 439
AEROGROW INTERNATIONAL, INC., pg. 1393, pg. 310
AHERN RENTALS, INC., pg. 345, pg. 1022
ALIMAK HEK INC, pg. 66, pg. 1749
ALSTATE PROCESS SERVICE INC., pg. 347, pg. 1155
AMERICAN MOLD REMOVAL, INC., pg. 1393, pg. 436
AMPCO-PITTSBURGH CORPORATION, pg. 1313, pg. 1573
ANTHONY & SYLVAN POOLS CORPORATION, pg. 1826, pg. 1428
APOGEE ENTERPRISES, INC., pg. 67, pg. 930
APSCO APPLIANCE CENTERS, pg. 51, pg. 415
ARAMARK CANADA LTD., pg. 1014, pg. 1935
ATIS GROUP INC., pg. 1042, pg. 1952
AVIALL, INC., pg. 224, pg. 1676
BAYLOFF STAMPED PRODUCTS, pg. 1317, pg. 1457
BRAND ENERGY, INC., pg. 71, pg. 533
BRAUNSCHWEIGER JEWELERS, pg. 2, pg. 1088
CENTURY FENCE COMPANY, pg. 74, pg. 1886
CHEMED CORPORATION, pg. 327, pg. 1410
CLEAN HARBORS, INC., pg. 376, pg. 839
CLESTRA HAUSERMAN, INC., pg. 76, pg. 1526
COMPLEMAR PARTNERS, pg. 1455, pg. 1333
COVERALL NORTH AMERICA, INC., pg. 329, pg. 421
DESIGN WITHIN REACH, INC., pg. 923, pg. 216
DUALITE SALES & SERVICE, INC., pg. 1296, pg. 1482
THE DWYER GROUP, INC., pg. 79, pg. 1748
ECOLAB INC., pg. 329, pg. 960
ECOLAB INC.-FOOD & BEVERAGE DIVISION, pg. 330, pg. 960
E.L. WAGNER CO., INC., pg. 80, pg. 339
ELCAR FENCE & SUPPLY CO., pg. 80, pg. 319
ENERFAB, INC., pg. 81, pg. 1412
EVOQUA, pg. 1336, pg. 1590
EXIDE TECHNOLOGIES, pg. 204, pg. 483
EXTERRAN HOLDINGS, INC., pg. 977, pg. 1705
FLUOR CORPORATION, pg. 82, pg. 1719
GE CONSUMER & INDUSTRIAL, pg. 55, pg. 733
GLOBAL EPOINT INC., pg. 400, pg. 67
THE GOLDFIELD CORPORATION, pg. 84, pg. 439
GROSSENBURG IMPLEMENT, INC., pg. 1344, pg. 1626
HENRY BONA POOLS & SPAS, pg. 1836, pg. 1078
HERMAN MILLER, INC., pg. 926, pg. 913
HOBART FOOD EQUIPMENT GROUP CANADA, pg. 56, pg. 1929
HUDSON TECHNOLOGIES, INC., pg. 1073, pg. 1320
JASPER ELECTRIC MOTORS, pg. 209, pg. 691
JVC AMERICAS CORP., pg. 648, pg. 1129
KIMMINS CORP., pg. 91, pg. 473
KONE INC., pg. 1353, pg. 633
MAXONS RESTORATIONS, pg. 332, pg. 1257
MIDDLESEX WATER COMPANY, pg. 1946, pg. 1075
THE MILLARD GROUP, pg. 440, pg. 628
MINAEAN INTERNATIONAL CORPORATION, pg. 97, pg. 1911
ORKIN, INC., pg. 1798, pg. 517
PARAGON TECHNOLOGIES, INC., pg. 1367, pg. 1528
PROGRESSIVE WASTE SOLUTIONS, pg. 796, pg. 1947
PURESAFE WATER SYSTEMS, INC., pg. 333, pg. 1322
REAL GOODS SOLAR, INC., pg. 1075, pg. 334
ROLLINS, INC., pg. 1179, pg. 519
THE SERVICEMASTER COMPANY, LLC, pg. 335, pg. 1646
SMITHEREEN PEST MANAGEMENT SERVICES, pg. 1800, pg. 638
STEBBINS ENGINEERING & MANUFACTURING COMPANY, pg. 113, pg. 1349
SWARTWOUT DIVISION, pg. 114, pg. 978
SWISHER HYGIENE INC., pg. 900, pg. 1369
SWISHER INTERNATIONAL, INC., pg. 1600, pg. 1369
TD INDUSTRIES, INC., pg. 1077, pg. 1688
THE TERMINIX INTERNATIONAL COMPANY LIMITED PARTNERSHIP, pg. 337, pg. 1646
TRUGREEN-CHEMLAWN, pg. 1801, pg. 1647
UGL SERVICES, pg. 486, pg. 784
WALTHAM SERVICES, INC., pg. 1801, pg. 855
WASTE MANAGEMENT, INC., pg. 1954, pg. 1716
THE W.W. WILLIAMS COMPANY, pg. 1390, pg. 1444

7352 - Medical Equipment Rental & Leasing

HEALTHTRONICS, INC., pg. 1540, pg. 1663
UNIVERSAL HOSPITAL SERVICES, INC., pg. 1604, pg. 945

7353 - Heavy Construction Equipment Rental & Leasing

AHERN RENTALS, INC., pg. 345, pg. 1022
BUTLER MACHINERY COMPANY, pg. 1321, pg. 1397
GREGORY POOLE EQUIPMENT COMPANY INC., pg. 85, pg. 1387
H&E EQUIPMENT SERVICES, INC., pg. 85, pg. 742
JLG INDUSTRIES, INC., pg. 1351, pg. 1551
KOMATSU CANADA LIMITED, pg. 1353, pg. 1927
NES RENTALS HOLDINGS, INC., pg. 186, pg. 584
NORDCO, INC., pg. 1365, pg. 1884
PARKER DRILLING COMPANY, pg. 982, pg. 1712
POWER EQUIPMENT COMPANY INC, pg. 1369, pg. 1637
RPC, INC., pg. 984, pg. 519
STEWART & STEVENSON, LLC, pg. 985, pg. 1715
TITAN MACHINERY INC., pg. 1383, pg. 1398
UNITED RENTALS, INC., pg. 1386, pg. 350

7359 - Equipment Rental & Leasing, NEC

AARON'S, INC., pg. 912, pg. 486
AHERN RENTALS, INC., pg. 345, pg. 1022
ALAN GORDON ENTERPRISES, INC., pg. 1399, pg. 125
ALGOMA CENTRAL CORPORATION, pg. 1898, pg. 1933
BESTWAY, INC., pg. 52, pg. 1676
CARNIVAL CORPORATION, pg. 1902, pg. 441
CINEQUIPT INC., pg. 629, pg. 932
CORT BUSINESS SERVICES CORPORATION, pg. 921, pg. 1777
CSX CORPORATION, pg. 1904, pg. 432
ELECTRO RENT CORPORATION, pg. 390, pg. 300
FLETCHER CHICAGO INC., pg. 1413, pg. 574
FLEXI-VAN LEASING, INC., pg. 1909, pg. 1077
GAMEFLY, INC., pg. 953, pg. 132
GE CAPITAL AVIATION SERVICES, pg. 228, pg. 362
GREAT LAKES DREDGE & DOCK CORPORATION, pg. 84,

pg. 645
H&E EQUIPMENT SERVICES, INC., pg. 85, pg. 742
HANSLER MANUTENTION, INC, pg. 178, pg. 1950
HEALTHTRONICS, INC., pg. 1540, pg. 1663
THE HERTZ CORPORATION, pg. 1911, pg. 450
LAWN DOCTOR INC., pg. 1796, pg. 1074
LG ELECTRONICS CANADA, INC., pg. 651, pg. 1927
MCGRATH RENTCORP, pg. 1104, pg. 122
MICROFINANCIAL INCORPORATED, pg. 782, pg. 805
NES RENTALS HOLDINGS, INC., pg. 186, pg. 584
NLB CORP., pg. 1365, pg. 913
ODYSSEY MARINE EXPLORATION, INC., pg. 1918, pg. 475
OFFICE DEPOT, INC., pg. 448, pg. 412
PITNEY BOWES INC., pg. 454, pg. 376
PORT AUTHORITY OF NEW YORK & NEW JERSEY, pg. 1919, pg. 1283
PRO-DEX, INC., pg. 1586, pg. 115
PROFESSIONAL SOUND SERVICES, INC., pg. 665, pg. 1283
Q A GROUP LLC., pg. 1427, pg. 89
RENT-A-CENTER, INC., pg. 940, pg. 1734
RPC, INC., pg. 984, pg. 519
SAFWAY SERVICES, LLC, pg. 109, pg. 1898
SANMINA-SCI CORPORATION, pg. 671, pg. 250
STEAMATIC INC., pg. 60, pg. 1696
SUNBELT RENTALS, pg. 1786, pg. 1616
SWISHER INTERNATIONAL, INC., pg. 1600, pg. 1369
TRINITY INDUSTRIES, INC., pg. 116, pg. 1690
UNITED RENTALS, pg. 1386, pg. 24
UNITED RENTALS, INC., pg. 1386, pg. 350
UNIVERSAL HOSPITAL SERVICES, INC., pg. 1604, pg. 945
WESCO FINANCIAL CORPORATION, pg. 821, pg. 181
YOUNG ELECTRIC SIGN COMPANY, pg. 1308, pg. 1762

7361 - Employment Agencies

20TH CENTURY FOX FILM CORP., pg. 267, pg. 124
ACADEMIC INNOVATIONS, pg. 1613, pg. 262
ACCENTURE, pg. 1392, pg. 1186
ACNIELSEN CORPORATION, pg. 341, pg. 1187
ADECCO USA, INC., pg. 342, pg. 1178
ADVERTISING DISTRIBUTORS OF AMERICA INC., pg. 345, pg. 1338
AFFINION GROUP, INC., pg. 1225, pg. 372
ALLEN & HOSHALL, INC., pg. 66, pg. 1641
ALLIN CORPORATION, pg. 347, pg. 1572
ALPHA CTP SYSTEM, pg. 347, pg. 848
ALTA RESOURCES CORPORATION, pg. 347, pg. 1882
AMBER ROAD, INC., pg. 348, pg. 1054
AMERICAN CONSERVATORY THEATRE, pg. 528, pg. 212
THE AMERICAN STAGE COMPANY INC., pg. 528, pg. 461
AMN HEALTHCARE SERVICES, INC., pg. 1494, pg. 200
ANC SPORTS ENTERPRISES, LLC, pg. 1825, pg. 1325
ANSELL, pg. 1495, pg. 1114
AON HEWITT, pg. 350, pg. 627
APPLEBEE'S INTERNATIONAL, INC., pg. 1715, pg. 980
ASSET ACCEPTANCE CAPITAL CORP., pg. 716, pg. 912
ASSOCIATION OF AMERICAN UNIVERSITY PRESSES, pg. 133, pg. 1197
AT&T GOVERNMENT SOLUTIONS, pg. 355, pg. 1809
ATC HEALTHCARE, INC., pg. 1497, pg. 1184
BAD BOY WORLDWIDE ENTERTAINMENT GROUP, pg. 270, pg. 1199
BALLET THEATRE FOUNDATION, INC., pg. 531, pg. 1200
BARRETT BUSINESS SERVICES, INC., pg. 360, pg. 1845
BENCHMARK HOSPITALITY INTERNATIONAL INC., pg. 1081, pg. 1747
BEYOND.COM, INC., pg. 1231, pg. 1543
BIRNER DENTAL MANAGEMENT SERVICES, INC., pg. 1506, pg. 317
BLUE MAN PRODUCTIONS, INC., pg. 533, pg. 1205
BOOZ ALLEN HAMILTON INC, pg. 363, pg. 1788
BOSTON BALLET INC., pg. 533, pg. 790
THE BOSTON CONSULTING GROUP, INC., pg. 363, pg. 790
BOULDER PHILHARMONIC ORCHESTRA, pg. 534, pg. 310
BRAINERD DAILY DISPATCH, pg. 1623, pg. 919
BRAINSTORM GROUP, INC., pg. 364, pg. 838
BRANDMUSCLE, INC., pg. 364, pg. 1660
BRIGHTSTAR CORPORATION, pg. 627, pg. 440
BROOKFIELD GLOBAL RELOCATION SERVICES, pg. 1083, pg. 560
BUFFALO PHILHARMONIC ORCHESTRA SOCIETY INC., pg. 535, pg. 1147
BULLDOG MEDIA GROUP, pg. 599, pg. 1624
BUTLER AMERICA, pg. 366, pg. 370
CACI INTERNATIONAL INC., pg. 367, pg. 1773
CALIFORNIA MUSICAL THEATRE CORPORATION, pg. 536, pg. 196
CALIPER CORPORATION, pg. 368, pg. 1111
CANCER TREATMENT CENTERS OF AMERICA, pg. 1511, pg. 410
CAREERBUILDER, LLC, pg. 1234, pg. 568
CARLSON WAGONLIT TRAVEL, pg. 1902, pg. 948
CARTESIAN, pg. 369, pg. 718
CASESTACK, INC., pg. 369, pg. 272
THE CASEY GROUP, pg. 369, pg. 1102
CBIZ, INC., pg. 733, pg. 1429
CEB INC., pg. 733, pg. 1773
CELERIT CORPORATION, pg. 371, pg. 33
CENTER THEATRE GROUP OF LOS ANGELES, INC., pg. 538, pg. 128
CERIDIAN CORPORATION, pg. 371, pg. 932
CGI GROUP INC., pg. 371, pg. 1954
CHG HEALTHCARE SERVICES, INC., pg. 1515, pg. 1756
CHICAGO THEATRE GROUP INC., pg. 539, pg. 570
CHOICE HOTELS INTERNATIONAL, INC., pg. 1086, pg. 775
CINCINNATI MUSEUM CENTER INC., pg. 540, pg. 1411
CIRQUE DU SOLEIL INC., pg. 540, pg. 1954
COLOMBIAN COFFEE FEDERATION, INC., pg. 137, pg. 1216
COMFORCE CORPORATION, pg. 377, pg. 1355
COMPUTER SCIENCES CORPORATION, pg. 378, pg. 1780
COMSCORE, INC, pg. 1236, pg. 1798
CONSTELLATION BRANDS, INC., pg. 1960, pg. 1348
CONVERGYS CORPORATION, pg. 379, pg. 1412
CONVERSANT, INC., pg. 1393, pg. 306
COTTON INCORPORATED CONSUMER MARKETING HEADQUARTERS, pg. 692, pg. 1218
CRESA PARTNERS LLC, pg. 1088, pg. 1220
CROSS COUNTRY HEALTHCARE, INC., pg. 1520, pg. 411
CROZER-KEYSTONE HEALTH SYSTEM INC., pg. 1520, pg. 1587
THE DALLAS OPERA, pg. 543, pg. 1679
DAVID A. STRAZ JR. CENTER, pg. 543, pg. 472
DEARBORN SYMPHONY ORCHESTRA, pg. 543, pg. 876
DELOITTE & TOUCHE USA LLP, pg. 743, pg. 1222
DELUXE LABORATORIES, INC., pg. 281, pg. 103
DETERMINE, INC., pg. 386, pg. 254
DEX ONE CORPORATION, pg. 1635, pg. 1360
DHI GROUP, INC., pg. 1238, pg. 1223
DICE.COM, pg. 1238, pg. 712
DIGITAL RIVER, INC., pg. 1238, pg. 948
DISNEY THEATRICAL PRODUCTIONS, pg. 545, pg. 1224
D.R. HORTON/CONTINENTAL SERIES, pg. 79, pg. 330
EAGLE POINT SOFTWARE CORPORATION, pg. 389, pg. 707
EAGLE:XM, pg. 1239, pg. 319
EDGEWATER TECHNOLOGY, INC., pg. 389, pg. 848
EGGLAND'S BEST, INC., pg. 854, pg. 1542
ENERGY & POWER SOLUTIONS, INC., pg. 392, pg. 71
ENHERENT CORP., pg. 393, pg. 1343
ENTERTAINMENT SOFTWARE RATING BOARD, pg. 992, pg. 1228
THE F. DOHMEN CO., pg. 1530, pg. 1858
FCSTONE GROUP, INC., pg. 751, pg. 982
FORD'S THEATRE SOCIETY INC., pg. 549, pg. 399
FORT WORTH SYMPHONY ASSOCIATION, pg. 549, pg. 1694
FOX ENTERTAINMENT GROUP, INC., pg. 288, pg. 131
FRANKLIN COVEY CO., pg. 1642, pg. 1758
FTI CONSULTING, INC., pg. 760, pg. 478
FUTUREDONTICS, INC., pg. 1532, pg. 131
FUTURESTEP, pg. 399, pg. 131
THE GALLUP ORGANIZATION, pg. 399, pg. 399
THE GALLUP ORGANIZATION-PRINCETON, pg. 1643, pg. 1111
GAME SHOW PLACEMENTS LTD., pg. 550, pg. 132
GEISINGER HEALTH SYSTEM, pg. 1533, pg. 1526
GENERAL EMPLOYMENT ENTERPRISES, INC., pg. 400, pg. 636
GILMAN CIOCIA, INC., pg. 762, pg. 1324
GLOBALOPTIONS GROUP, INC., pg. 1394, pg. 1235
GOODWILL INDUSTRIES-SUNCOAST, INC., pg. 142, pg. 462
GRANT THORNTON INTERNATIONAL LTD., pg. 763, pg. 575
GRILL CONCEPTS, INC., pg. 1730, pg. 308
GUIDELINE, INC., pg. 402, pg. 1237
THE HACKETT GROUP, INC., pg. 1255, pg. 443
HEALTH GRADES, INC., pg. 1256, pg. 319
HEALTHPORT, INC., pg. 403, pg. 484
HEALTHWAYS, INC., pg. 1540, pg. 1632
HEERY INTERNATIONAL, INC., pg. 86, pg. 510
HILL INTERNATIONAL INC., pg. 87, pg. 1083
HIRERIGHT, INC., pg. 1256, pg. 111
HOUSTON GRAND OPERA ASSOCIATION, pg. 552, pg. 1707
HUNTING COMPANY, US OFFICE, pg. 979, pg. 1708
HUNTINGTON SYMPHONY ORCHESTRA, pg. 553, pg. 1850
IHS HEROLD, INC., pg. 768, pg. 362
IKEA NORTH AMERICA SERVICES LLC, pg. 929, pg. 1523
IMAKENEWS, INC., pg. 413, pg. 851
IMS HEALTH, INC., pg. 1544, pg. 344
INDUSTRIAL SERVICES OF AMERICA, INC., pg. 1884, pg. 734
INFOGIX INC., pg. 414, pg. 636
INFOGROUP, pg. 769, pg. 1038
INO.COM, pg. 1259, pg. 777
INSPERITY, INC., pg. 416, pg. 1725
INSTITUTE OF REAL ESTATE MANAGEMENT, pg. 144, pg. 578
INTERSTATE WORLDWIDE RELOCATION, INC., pg. 1912, pg. 1807
IPC THE HOSPITALIST COMPANY, INC., pg. 1547, pg. 167
IRI GROUP, pg. 421, pg. 579
ITAGROUP, INC., pg. 422, pg. 713
ITRONICS INC., pg. 1169, pg. 1031
J.B. HUNT TRANSPORT SERVICES, INC., pg. 1913, pg. 34
J.J. KELLER & ASSOCIATES, INC., pg. 1654, pg. 1883
JOSTENS, INC., pg. 7, pg. 938
THE JUDGE GROUP, INC., pg. 424, pg. 1594
KAWASAKI HEAVY INDUSTRIES (U.S.A.), INC., pg. 1352, pg. 1248
KEPNER-TREGOE, INC., pg. 424, pg. 1112
KFORCE INC., pg. 1261, pg. 473
KONA GRILL INC., pg. 1734, pg. 23
KSL RESORTS, pg. 1099, pg. 120
THE LADDERS.COM, INC., pg. 1261, pg. 1250
LINCOLN CENTER FOR THE PERFORMING ARTS, INC., pg. 557, pg. 1251
LIQUIDITY SERVICES, INC., pg. 1263, pg. 401
LIVE NATION ENTERTAINMENT, INC., pg. 558, pg. 47
LYRIS, INC., pg. 429, pg. 84
MACANDREWS & FORBES HOLDINGS INC., pg. 777, pg. 1254
MACE SECURITY INTERNATIONAL, INC., pg. 1172, pg. 1541
MAGELLAN HEALTH SERVICES, INC., pg. 1557, pg. 337
MAGLINE, INC., pg. 1358, pg. 908
MALCO PRODUCTS, INC., pg. 1172, pg. 1404
MANAGEMENT RECRUITERS INTERNATIONAL, INC., pg. 429, pg. 1567
MARCHEX, INC., pg. 1395, pg. 1837
MARITZ INC., pg. 1914, pg. 977
MARKETING INNOVATORS INTERNATIONAL, INC., pg. 430, pg. 657
MARSH & MCLENNAN COMPANIES INC., pg. 1207, pg. 1256
MARTS & LUNDY, INC., pg. 146, pg. 1080
MAXIMUS, INC., pg. 780, pg. 1799
MAYO PERFORMING ARTS CENTER, pg. 561, pg. 1089
MC2, pg. 431, pg. 1153
MCG CAPITAL CORPORATION, pg. 781, pg. 1774
MCGLADREY, LLP, pg. 781, pg. 938
MECHANICAL PROTECTION PLAN, pg. 184, pg. 717
MEDIEVAL TIMES INC., pg. 561, pg. 51
MEDSTAFF, INC., pg. 431, pg. 1556
MEETING PROFESSIONALS INTERNATIONAL (MPI), pg. 146, pg. 1683
MERCER INC., pg. 1395, pg. 1258
MHI GLOBAL, pg. 434, pg. 474
MIAMI CITY BALLET, INC., pg. 562, pg. 448
MICROBILT CORPORATION, pg. 782, pg. 534
MILLER HEIMAN INC., pg. 440, pg. 1031
MILWAUKEE SYMPHONY ORCHESTRA INC., pg. 563, pg. 1878
MIQ LOGISTICS, LLC, pg. 1267, pg. 719
MONSTER WORLDWIDE, INC., pg. 1268, pg. 859
MSX INTERNATIONAL, INC., pg. 98, pg. 912
NATIONAL FOOTBALL LEAGUE PLAYERS INCORPORATED, pg. 149, pg. 401
THE NATIONAL THEATRE CORPORATION, pg. 569, pg.

First page reference indicates Business Class Edition
Second page reference indicates Geographic Edition

403
NAVIGANT CONSULTING, INC., pg. 786, pg. 584
NEGOTIATION INSTITUTE, INC., pg. 151, pg. 1268
NET-TEMPS, INC., pg. 1269, pg. 838
NEUSTAR, INC., pg. 1872, pg. 1807
NEW JERSEY HOSPITAL ASSOCIATION, pg. 152, pg. 1112
NEW YORK CITY BALLET, pg. 569, pg. 1268
NEW YORK CITY DEPARTMENT OF CITY WIDE ADMINISTRATIVE SERVICES, pg. 1001, pg. 1268
NEW YORK CITY OPERA INC., pg. 570, pg. 1268
NEWGROUND RESOURCES, pg. 99, pg. 975
NIC INC., pg. 445, pg. 718
NOOTER/ERIKSEN, INC., pg. 1075, pg. 977
NOVAPRO, pg. 1574, pg. 474
NOVATION LLC, pg. 446, pg. 1723
NUTRITION MANAGEMENT SERVICES COMPANY, pg. 1742, pg. 1543
OLIVER WYMAN, INC., pg. 790, pg. 1274
ON ASSIGNMENT, INC., pg. 449, pg. 56
OPENTEXT, pg. 450, pg. 1665
OPERA AMERICA, pg. 572, pg. 1274
OPERA OMAHA INC., pg. 572, pg. 1017
OPTIMIZERX CORPORATION, pg. 1673, pg. 905
OPUS INTERNATIONAL, INC., pg. 450, pg. 421
ORIEL STAT-A-MATRIX, INC., pg. 451, pg. 1057
PASADENA PLAYHOUSE, pg. 574, pg. 181
PDI, INC., pg. 1580, pg. 1104
PLAYHOUSE SQUARE FOUNDATION, pg. 577, pg. 1434
PREMIER HEALTHCARE ALLIANCE, pg. 1586, pg. 1368
PRESTIGE BRANDS HOLDINGS, INC., pg. 520, pg. 1345
PRICEWATERHOUSECOOPERS LLP, pg. 795, pg. 1283
PROVIDENCE HEALTH SYSTEM, pg. 1587, pg. 1829
THE PUBLIC THEATER, pg. 578, pg. 1283
PUTNAM INVESTMENTS, LLC, pg. 797, pg. 800
QUINSTREET, INC., pg. 1276, pg. 89
RAINMAKER SYSTEMS INC., pg. 458, pg. 58
REACHLOCAL, INC., pg. 1277, pg. 308
RESOURCES CONNECTION, INC., pg. 461, pg. 115
ROBERT HALF INTERNATIONAL INC., pg. 462, pg. 145
RUSSELL REYNOLDS ASSOCIATES INC., pg. 463, pg. 1287
RYDER SYSTEM, INC., pg. 1922, pg. 446
S. GRAHAM & ASSOCIATES, pg. 463, pg. 589
SALES PERFORMANCE INTERNATIONAL, INC., pg. 464, pg. 1368
THE SCHMIDT GROUP, INC., pg. 1374, pg. 1618
SCHNEIDER, pg. 1922, pg. 1859
SCHWARTZ & BENJAMIN, INC., pg. 1818, pg. 1290
SELECTREMEDY, pg. 468, pg. 263
THE SHAKESPEARE THEATRE, INC., pg. 583, pg. 404
SMILE BRANDS GROUP INC., pg. 1594, pg. 116
SOUTH CAROLINA MANUFACTURING EXTENSION PARTNERSHIP, pg. 1377, pg. 1614
SPA FINDER, INC., pg. 1113, pg. 1295
SPELNA, INC., pg. 157, pg. 1782
SPICY PICKLE FRANCHISING, INC., pg. 1751, pg. 323
SRDS, INC., pg. 1688, pg. 657
STAGES PRODUCTIONS, INC., pg. 585, pg. 468
STATE STREET CORPORATION, pg. 805, pg. 801
THE STATE THEATRE, pg. 585, pg. 1094
SUMTOTAL SYSTEMS, INC., pg. 477, pg. 429
SUNGARD FINANCIAL SYSTEMS-RELIUS-JACKSONVILLE, pg. 477, pg. 435
SUPPLEMENTAL HEALTH CARE SERVICES, INC., pg. 478, pg. 1754
SUPPLY TECHNOLOGIES LLC, pg. 1064, pg. 1436
SVM, LP, pg. 1786, pg. 606
SYNYGY, INC., pg. 481, pg. 1521
TEAM HEALTH, INC., pg. 482, pg. 1639
TEXAS ROADHOUSE, INC., pg. 1753, pg. 738
THEATER & ARTS FOUNDATION, pg. 587, pg. 120
THEATRE FOR A NEW AUDIENCE, pg. 587, pg. 1298
THEATREWORKSUSA, pg. 587, pg. 1298
TRUEBLUE, INC., pg. 485, pg. 1845
TSS, INC., pg. 117, pg. 768
TTC AMERIDIAL, LLC, pg. 486, pg. 593
THE ULTIMATE SOFTWARE GROUP, INC., pg. 486, pg. 479
UNITED SERVICES AUTOMOBILE ASSOCIATION, pg. 1221, pg. 1743
U.S. GLOBAL INVESTORS, INC., pg. 815, pg. 1743
UTAH SYMPHONY & OPERA, pg. 590, pg. 1761
VALASSIS COMMUNICATIONS, INC., pg. 1287, pg. 897
VENUE OF SCOTTSDALE, pg. 1754, pg. 25
VETJOBS, INC., pg. 1287, pg. 535
VIAD CORP., pg. 816, pg. 20
WEB.COM GROUP, INC., pg. 1288, pg. 435
WEICHERT RELOCATION RESOURCES INC., pg. 1118, pg. 1087
WESTON SOLUTIONS HOLDINGS, INC., pg. 1437, pg. 1593
WEXFORD HEALTH SOURCES INC., pg. 1610, pg. 1582
WHITMAN'S CANDIES, INC., pg. 1863, pg. 987
WORD OF LIFE FELLOWSHIP, INC., pg. 161, pg. 1341
YANKEES ENTERTAINMENT & SPORTS NETWORK, LLC, pg. 324, pg. 1316
YRC WORLDWIDE INC., pg. 1931, pg. 720
ZILLIANT, INC., pg. 497, pg. 1668
ZOGBY ANALYTICS, pg. 1292, pg. 1347
ZONES, INC., pg. 1292, pg. 1813

7363 - Help Supply Services

123 STAFFING, INC., pg. 339, pg. 1123
ADECCO USA, INC., pg. 342, pg. 1178
AMN HEALTHCARE SERVICES, INC., pg. 1494, pg. 200
ATC HEALTHCARE, INC., pg. 1497, pg. 1184
BARRETT BUSINESS SERVICES, INC., pg. 360, pg. 1845
BHI ENERGY, pg. 361, pg. 1489
BUTLER AMERICA, pg. 366, pg. 370
COMFORCE CORPORATION, pg. 377, pg. 1355
CROSS COUNTRY HEALTHCARE, INC., pg. 1520, pg. 411
EMPLOYMENT ENTERPRISES INC., pg. 392, pg. 1787
ENHERENT CORP., pg. 393, pg. 1343
GENERAL EMPLOYMENT ENTERPRISES, INC., pg. 400, pg. 636
H&R BLOCK, INC., pg. 764, pg. 983
INSPERITY, INC., pg. 416, pg. 1725
INTERIM HEALTHCARE INC., pg. 417, pg. 469
ISABELLA BANK CORPORATION, pg. 771, pg. 901
KELLY SERVICES, INC., pg. 424, pg. 911
KFORCE INC., pg. 1261, pg. 473
MANPOWER GROUP, pg. 430, pg. 1710
MANPOWER INC., pg. 430, pg. 1877
MAXIM HEALTHCARE SERVICES, pg. 1559, pg. 767
MAXIM HEALTHCARE SERVICES INC., pg. 1559, pg. 1537
ON ASSIGNMENT, INC., pg. 449, pg. 56
PAYCHEX, INC., pg. 792, pg. 1336
PROGRESSIVE NURSING STAFFERS INC., pg. 457, pg. 1807
RANDSTAD USA, pg. 459, pg. 941
ROBERT HALF INTERNATIONAL INC., pg. 462, pg. 145
SELECTREMEDY, pg. 468, pg. 263
SNELLING STAFFING SERVICES, pg. 471, pg. 1686
TRUEBLUE, INC., pg. 485, pg. 1845
VOLT INFORMATION SCIENCES, INC., pg. 490, pg. 1312
WORKPLACE OPTIONS, pg. 493, pg. 1389

7371 - Computer Programming Services

3M, pg. 339, pg. 179
3T SYSTEMS, INC., pg. 339, pg. 330
ACACIA RESEARCH CORPORATION, pg. 1398, pg. 165
ACD SYSTEMS INTERNATIONAL INC., pg. 340, pg. 1913
ACSIS, INC., pg. 341, pg. 1083
ACTIVISION BLIZZARD, INC., pg. 948, pg. 271
ADVENT SOFTWARE, INC., pg. 345, pg. 211
ALLEN SYSTEMS GROUP, INC., pg. 346, pg. 449
APPLIED SYSTEMS INC., pg. 352, pg. 663
ARCSOFT, INC., pg. 352, pg. 90
ARI NETWORK SERVICES, INC., pg. 353, pg. 1873
ART & LOGIC, INC., pg. 1229, pg. 179
ASA INTERNATIONAL LTD., pg. 353, pg. 1036
ASPECT SOFTWARE, INC., pg. 354, pg. 813
ASPEN TECHNOLOGY, INC., pg. 354, pg. 804
ATEX MEDIA COMMAND, INC., pg. 355, pg. 848
ATTACHMATE CORPORATION, pg. 356, pg. 1833
AUTOBYTEL INC., pg. 1230, pg. 107
AUTONOMY, INC., pg. 358, pg. 212
AVAGO TECHNOLOGIES, pg. 358, pg. 238
BARE BONES SOFTWARE, INC., pg. 360, pg. 838
BAYARD INC., pg. 1620, pg. 359
BMC SOFTWARE, INC., pg. 362, pg. 1701
BOTTOMLINE TECHNOLOGIES (DE), INC., pg. 727, pg. 1038
BOTTOMLINE TECHNOLOGIES INC., pg. 363, pg. 483
BRADY/TISCOR, INC., pg. 364, pg. 200
BRIDGELINE DIGITAL, INC., pg. 364, pg. 861
BRION TECHNOLOGIES INC., pg. 1319, pg. 265
BSQUARE CORPORATION, pg. 366, pg. 1813
BULLHORN, INC., pg. 1233, pg. 792
CACI INTERNATIONAL INC., pg. 367, pg. 1773
CALERO SOFTWARE, LLC, pg. 368, pg. 1333
CALLIDUS SOFTWARE INC., pg. 368, pg. 183
THE CASEY GROUP, pg. 369, pg. 1102
CATAMARAN, pg. 1514, pg. 628
CELERIT CORPORATION, pg. 371, pg. 33
CEVA, INC., pg. 628, pg. 153
CGI GROUP INC., pg. 371, pg. 1954
CHARLES SCHWAB, pg. 1235, pg. 1661
CIBER, INC., pg. 372, pg. 330
CICERO INC., pg. 372, pg. 1360
CISION, INC., pg. 375, pg. 761
CITRIX SYSTEMS, INC., pg. 375, pg. 424
COFFEECUP SOFTWARE INC., pg. 1236, pg. 501
COMBIMATRIX CORPORATION, pg. 1407, pg. 109
COMMENCE CORPORATION, pg. 377, pg. 1055
COMPUCOM SYSTEMS, INC., pg. 378, pg. 1678
COMPUTER PROGRAMS & SYSTEMS, INC., pg. 378, pg. 7
COMPUTER TASK GROUP, INC., pg. 378, pg. 1147
COMPUWARE CORPORATION, pg. 379, pg. 879
CONCUR TECHNOLOGIES, pg. 1903, pg. 501
CONCUR TECHNOLOGIES, INC., pg. 1236, pg. 1813
COPERNIC INC., pg. 1237, pg. 1958
CORBIS CORPORATION, pg. 380, pg. 1834
CRAWFORD & COMPANY, pg. 1199, pg. 502
CRAY INC., pg. 380, pg. 1834
CROIX CONNECT, pg. 1237, pg. 1809
CTI GROUP HOLDINGS INC., pg. 381, pg. 684
DAEGIS INC, pg. 381, pg. 195
DASSAULT SYSTEMS ENOVIA, pg. 382, pg. 851
DATAVIZ, INC., pg. 383, pg. 356
DELTEK, INC., pg. 386, pg. 1784
DEMAND MEDIA, INC., pg. 1238, pg. 273
DETERMINE, INC., pg. 386, pg. 254
DIGITAL RIVER, INC., pg. 1238, pg. 948
DST SYSTEMS, INC., pg. 388, pg. 982
DYNTEK, INC., pg. 389, pg. 165
EAGLE POINT SOFTWARE CORPORATION, pg. 389, pg. 707
EARTHLINK HOLDINGS CORP., pg. 1240, pg. 504
EASYLINK SERVICES CORPORATION, pg. 1240, pg. 1108
EASYLINK SERVICES INTERNATIONAL CORPORATION, pg. 389, pg. 536
ECHELON CORPORATION, pg. 389, pg. 245
ECORA SOFTWARE CORPORATION, pg. 389, pg. 1662
EDGEWATER TECHNOLOGY, INC., pg. 389, pg. 848
EGAIN COMMUNICATIONS CORPORATION, pg. 1242, pg. 284
EGENERA, INC., pg. 390, pg. 802
EMC CORPORATION, pg. 391, pg. 825
EMS CONSULTING, pg. 392, pg. 472
ENHERENT CORP., pg. 393, pg. 1343
ENVIRONMENTAL SYSTEMS RESEARCH INSTITUTE INC., pg. 393, pg. 188
ENVISION, pg. 393, pg. 1835
EQ WORKS, pg. 1243, pg. 1938
ERICSSON, pg. 395, pg. 1108
ESKER, INC., pg. 395, pg. 1865
ESSINTIAL ENTERPRISE SOLUTIONS, pg. 395, pg. 1552
EVOLVING SYSTEMS, INC., pg. 395, pg. 326
F5 NETWORKS, INC., pg. 396, pg. 1835
FACTSET RESEARCH SYSTEMS INC., pg. 1247, pg. 361
FALCONSTOR SOFTWARE, INC., pg. 396, pg. 1179
FIDELITY NATIONAL INFORMATION SERVICES, pg. 397, pg. 1549
FISERV, INC., pg. 397, pg. 1855
GLASSHOUSE TECHNOLOGIES, INC., pg. 400, pg. 844
GLOBALSCAPE INC., pg. 401, pg. 1740
GLU MOBILE INC., pg. 954, pg. 219
GOOGLE INC., pg. 1249, pg. 153
GREENVIEW DATA, INC., pg. 401, pg. 866
HERE, pg. 404, pg. 576
HP ENTERPRISE SERVICES, LLC, pg. 409, pg. 1731
HURCO COMPANIES, INC., pg. 409, pg. 686
HYLAND SOFTWARE, INC., pg. 409, pg. 1480
ID SOFTWARE, INC., pg. 956, pg. 1727
IGATE CORPORATION, pg. 411, pg. 91
IGATE CORPORATION, pg. 411, pg. 809
IHS INC., pg. 1652, pg. 326
IMAGINATION TECHNOLOGIES, pg. 412, pg. 285
INCENTIVE LOGIC, INC., pg. 1258, pg. 22
INFOR LAWSON, pg. 414, pg. 961

INFORMATICA CORPORATION, *pg.* 414, *pg.* 190
INSPIRATION SOFTWARE, INC., *pg.* 1653, *pg.* 1503
INTEGRAL SYSTEMS, INC., *pg.* 416, *pg.* 767
INTEGRATED SOFTWARE DESIGN, INC., *pg.* 416, *pg.* 830
INTELLICORP, INC., *pg.* 417, *pg.* 268
INTERACTIVE INTELLIGENCE, INC., *pg.* 417, *pg.* 687
INTERNAP NETWORK SERVICES CORPORATION, *pg.* 417, *pg.* 513
INTERNATIONAL BUSINESS MACHINES CORPORATION, *pg.* 418, *pg.* 1138
INTERNATIONAL GAME TECHNOLOGY, *pg.* 420, *pg.* 1606
INTERNATIONAL GAME TECHNOLOGY, *pg.* 957, *pg.* 1024
ISLAND PACIFIC, *pg.* 422, *pg.* 111
JDA SOFTWARE GROUP, INC., *pg.* 423, *pg.* 22
KENWOOD USA CORPORATION, *pg.* 649, *pg.* 123
KOFAX IMAGE PRODUCTS, INC., *pg.* 1419, *pg.* 112
LANDACORP, INC., *pg.* 426, *pg.* 65
LAPLINK SOFTWARE, INC., *pg.* 426, *pg.* 1815
LAVASTORM ANALYTICS, *pg.* 427, *pg.* 797
LIMELIGHT NETWORKS, INC., *pg.* 1262, *pg.* 26
LIVE365, INC., *pg.* 1264, *pg.* 89
LOGIKA CORPORATION, *pg.* 1264, *pg.* 581
LOGILITY, INC., *pg.* 428, *pg.* 513
MANPOWER GROUP, *pg.* 430, *pg.* 1710
MATRIX INTEGRATION LLC, *pg.* 430, *pg.* 692
MAXIMUS, INC., *pg.* 780, *pg.* 1799
MEDECISION, INC., *pg.* 431, *pg.* 1592
MEDICAL INFORMATION TECHNOLOGY, INC., *pg.* 431, *pg.* 859
MEGGITT TRAINING SYSTEMS, *pg.* 1839, *pg.* 541
MELISSA DATA CORP., *pg.* 432, *pg.* 188
MENTOR GRAPHICS CORPORATION, *pg.* 432, *pg.* 1510
MERGE ECLINICAL INC., *pg.* 1266, *pg.* 1385
METRIXLAB, *pg.* 1266, *pg.* 223
MICROSTRATEGY, INC., *pg.* 1266, *pg.* 1809
MITEK SYSTEMS, INC., *pg.* 440, *pg.* 204
MONOTYPE IMAGING HOLDINGS, INC., *pg.* 656, *pg.* 861
MTI SYSTEMS INC., *pg.* 442, *pg.* 857
NAGRA USA, *pg.* 443, *pg.* 223
NETSOL TECHNOLOGIES, INC., *pg.* 1270, *pg.* 56
NETWORK SYSTEMS INTERNATIONAL, INC., *pg.* 445, *pg.* 1375
NIC INC., *pg.* 445, *pg.* 718
NIGHTINGALE, *pg.* 446, *pg.* 186
NORTHROP GRUMMAN CORPORATION, *pg.* 231, *pg.* 1781
NTT DATA, *pg.* 447, *pg.* 799
NUANCE COMMUNICATIONS, INC., *pg.* 447, *pg.* 806
NUANCE DICTAPHONE HEALTHCARE SOLUTIONS, *pg.* 447, *pg.* 806
NUANCE DOCUMENT IMAGING SOLUTIONS, *pg.* 1271, *pg.* 1037
NVIDIA CORPORATION, *pg.* 447, *pg.* 268
OBSIDIAN ENTERTAINMENT, INC., *pg.* 448, *pg.* 114
OMTOOL, LTD., *pg.* 449, *pg.* 782
ONVIA, INC., *pg.* 1272, *pg.* 1838
OPENTEXT, *pg.* 1272, *pg.* 1956
OPENTEXT CORPORATION, *pg.* 450, *pg.* 1948
PANTHEON SOFTWARE, INC., *pg.* 1274, *pg.* 1774
PCTEL, INC., *pg.* 452, *pg.* 557
PEGASUS SOLUTIONS, INC., *pg.* 452, *pg.* 1685
PEGASYSTEMS INC., *pg.* 453, *pg.* 809
PERFICIENT, INC., *pg.* 1274, *pg.* 1002
PLANPRESCRIBER, INC., *pg.* 1275, *pg.* 832
POINTS INTERNATIONAL LTD., *pg.* 1275, *pg.* 1941
POLAR COVE, INC., *pg.* 1275, *pg.* 1607
PREMIER HEALTHCARE ALLIANCE, *pg.* 1586, *pg.* 1368
PROGRESS SOFTWARE CORPORATION, *pg.* 457, *pg.* 786
QUANTROS, INC., *pg.* 1587, *pg.* 147
QUARK, INC., *pg.* 458, *pg.* 322
QUORUM INFORMATION TECHNOLOGIES INC., *pg.* 458, *pg.* 1904
RAXCO SOFTWARE, INC., *pg.* 459, *pg.* 770
REALNETWORKS, INC., *pg.* 460, *pg.* 1839
REALPAGE, INC., *pg.* 1277, *pg.* 1669
RED HAT, INC., *pg.* 460, *pg.* 1388
RIVERBED PERFORMANCE MANAGEMENT, *pg.* 462, *pg.* 765
ROGUE WAVE SOFTWARE, INC., *pg.* 462, *pg.* 311
RSA SECURITY INC., *pg.* 463, *pg.* 786
SAIC, INC., *pg.* 464, *pg.* 1794
SALON MEDIA GROUP, INC., *pg.* 1278, *pg.* 226
SAP, *pg.* 465, *pg.* 78
SCIENTIFIC GAMES CORPORATION, *pg.* 468, *pg.* 1029
SEQUENOM, INC., *pg.* 1593, *pg.* 209
SIEMENS ENERGY, INC., *pg.* 469, *pg.* 1341
SIEMENS PLM SOFTWARE, *pg.* 469, *pg.* 1734
SILVON SOFTWARE INC., *pg.* 470, *pg.* 669
SIRSIDYNIX CORPORATION, *pg.* 470, *pg.* 1751
SOLIDWORKS CORPORATION, *pg.* 472, *pg.* 815
SONIC FOUNDRY, INC., *pg.* 472, *pg.* 1867
SONOS, INC., *pg.* 675, *pg.* 263
SPECTORSOFT CORPORATION, *pg.* 1281, *pg.* 478
SRA INTERNATIONAL, INC., *pg.* 473, *pg.* 1780
SS&C TECHNOLOGIES HOLDINGS, INC., *pg.* 473, *pg.* 386
THE SSI GROUP, INC., *pg.* 473, *pg.* 7
STEELCLOUD, INC., *pg.* 476, *pg.* 1776
STEFANINI TECHTEAM GLOBAL, INC., *pg.* 476, *pg.* 907
STRATUS TECHNOLOGIES, INC., *pg.* 477, *pg.* 832
STRUCTURED COMMUNICATION SYSTEMS, INC., *pg.* 477, *pg.* 1497
SUMTOTAL SYSTEMS, INC., *pg.* 477, *pg.* 429
SUNGARD FINANCIAL SYSTEMS-RELIUS-JACKSONVILLE, *pg.* 477, *pg.* 435
SUPPORT.COM, INC., *pg.* 1283, *pg.* 192
SUREQUEST SYSTEMS, INC., *pg.* 900, *pg.* 1669
SWISSLOG LOGISTICS, *pg.* 1380, *pg.* 1796
SYKES ENTERPRISES, INCORPORATED, *pg.* 478, *pg.* 475
SYMANTEC CORPORATION, *pg.* 478, *pg.* 161
SYMANTEC CORPORATION, *pg.* 479, *pg.* 1753
SYNOPSYS, INC., *pg.* 480, *pg.* 162
SYNTEL, INC., *pg.* 480, *pg.* 911
SYNYGY, INC., *pg.* 481, *pg.* 1521
TAKE-TWO INTERACTIVE SOFTWARE, INC., *pg.* 481, *pg.* 1297
TANGOE, INC., *pg.* 481, *pg.* 368
TAXWARE, *pg.* 808, *pg.* 860
TECHHEALTH, INC., *pg.* 1283, *pg.* 476
TIBCO SOFTWARE INC., *pg.* 484, *pg.* 178
TIGERLOGIC CORPORATION, *pg.* 484, *pg.* 117
TRADEPAQ CORPORATION, *pg.* 1284, *pg.* 1304
TRANSEND CORPORATION, *pg.* 485, *pg.* 178
TRIPWIRE, INC., *pg.* 485, *pg.* 1507
UBICS, INC., *pg.* 486, *pg.* 1520
UES, INC., *pg.* 1449, *pg.* 1447
US DATAWORKS, INC., *pg.* 1286, *pg.* 1746
VERISIGN, INC., *pg.* 488, *pg.* 1799
VERITEQ, *pg.* 488, *pg.* 422
VERTAFORE INC., *pg.* 1222, *pg.* 386
VERTICAL SEARCH WORKS INC., *pg.* 489, *pg.* 1809
VERTICALRESPONSE, INC., *pg.* 489, *pg.* 230
VOLT INFORMATION SCIENCES, INC., *pg.* 490, *pg.* 1312
WEBROOT SOFTWARE, INC., *pg.* 1289, *pg.* 313
WIND RIVER SYSTEMS, INC., *pg.* 493, *pg.* 38
WIPRO GALLAGHER SOLUTIONS, *pg.* 823, *pg.* 447
XAP CORPORATION, *pg.* 1289, *pg.* 73
XILINX, INC., *pg.* 496, *pg.* 252

7372 - Prepackaged Software

3D SYSTEMS CORPORATION, *pg.* 339, *pg.* 1621
505 GAMES (US), INC., *pg.* 948, *pg.* 38
8X8, INC., *pg.* 1865, *pg.* 282
ABB, *pg.* 340, *pg.* 486
ACCELRYS, INC., *pg.* 340, *pg.* 199
ACCUSOFT, *pg.* 1398, *pg.* 470
ACD SYSTEMS INTERNATIONAL INC., *pg.* 340, *pg.* 1913
ACI WORLDWIDE INC., *pg.* 341, *pg.* 1010
ACTIVISION BLIZZARD, INC., *pg.* 948, *pg.* 271
ACTUATE CORPORATION, *pg.* 342, *pg.* 253
A.D.A.M., INC., *pg.* 1225, *pg.* 487
ADOBE SYSTEMS INCORPORATED, *pg.* 342, *pg.* 235
ADVENT SOFTWARE, INC., *pg.* 345, *pg.* 211
ALLEN SYSTEMS GROUP, INC., *pg.* 346, *pg.* 449
ALLSCRIPTS HEALTHCARE SOLUTIONS, INC., *pg.* 1492, *pg.* 563
ALTERA CORPORATION, *pg.* 348, *pg.* 237
AMDOCS INC., *pg.* 348, *pg.* 974
AMERICAN REPROGRAPHICS COMPANY, *pg.* 1616, *pg.* 303
AMERICAN SOFTWARE, INC., *pg.* 349, *pg.* 488
ANSWERS CORPORATION, *pg.* 1229, *pg.* 1195
API HEALTHCARE CORP., *pg.* 350, *pg.* 1860
APPNETA, *pg.* 352, *pg.* 1909
APTIFY, *pg.* 352, *pg.* 395
ARIBA, INC., *pg.* 353, *pg.* 283
ARRHYTHMIA RESEARCH TECHNOLOGY, INC., *pg.* 1496, *pg.* 819
ASA INTERNATIONAL LTD., *pg.* 353, *pg.* 1036
ASPECT SOFTWARE, INC., *pg.* 354, *pg.* 238
ASTEA INTERNATIONAL INC., *pg.* 355, *pg.* 1540
ASTRO-MED, INC., *pg.* 619, *pg.* 1609
ATARI, INC., *pg.* 355, *pg.* 1198
ATTACHMATE CORPORATION, *pg.* 356, *pg.* 1833
AUTHENTIDATE HOLDING CORP., *pg.* 356, *pg.* 1044
AUTODESK INC., *pg.* 356, *pg.* 257
AUTONOMY, INC., *pg.* 358, *pg.* 212
AVAYA INC., *pg.* 621, *pg.* 264
AVF CONSULTING, INC., *pg.* 358, *pg.* 755
AVID TECHNOLOGY, INC., *pg.* 622, *pg.* 804
B-SCADA, INC., *pg.* 1231, *pg.* 419
BARE BONES SOFTWARE, INC., *pg.* 360, *pg.* 838
BENTLEY SYSTEMS, INC., *pg.* 361, *pg.* 1531
BLACKBAUD, INC., *pg.* 361, *pg.* 1613
BLACKBOARD INC., *pg.* 1232, *pg.* 396
BLIZZARD ENTERTAINMENT, *pg.* 950, *pg.* 107
BMC SOFTWARE, INC., *pg.* 362, *pg.* 1701
BOINGO WIRELESS, INC., *pg.* 625, *pg.* 127
BOTTOMLINE TECHNOLOGIES (DE), INC., *pg.* 727, *pg.* 1038
BRAVOSOLUTION US, *pg.* 1233, *pg.* 1549
BRIDGELINE DIGITAL, INC., *pg.* 364, *pg.* 861
BRILLIANT DIGITAL, *pg.* 1233, *pg.* 281
BROADCAST ELECTRONICS, INC., *pg.* 627, *pg.* 653
BROADSOFT, INC., *pg.* 1233, *pg.* 770
BROADVISION, INC., *pg.* 365, *pg.* 189
BSQUARE CORPORATION, *pg.* 366, *pg.* 1813
BUGOPOLIS, INC., *pg.* 366, *pg.* 278
BULLHORN, INC., *pg.* 1233, *pg.* 792
CA TECHNOLOGIES, *pg.* 366, *pg.* 1168
CADENCE DESIGN SYSTEMS, INC., *pg.* 367, *pg.* 239
CALERO SOFTWARE, LLC, *pg.* 368, *pg.* 1333
CALLIDUS SOFTWARE INC., *pg.* 368, *pg.* 183
CAPCOM USA, INC., *pg.* 950, *pg.* 254
CATAMARAN, *pg.* 1514, *pg.* 628
CBT DIRECT, LLC, *pg.* 1234, *pg.* 415
CERNER CORPORATION, *pg.* 1514, *pg.* 981
CERTICOM CORP., *pg.* 371, *pg.* 1925
CHYRONHEGO, *pg.* 371, *pg.* 1179
CIENA CORPORATION, *pg.* 628, *pg.* 771
CIMETRIX INCORPORATED, *pg.* 372, *pg.* 1756
CISION, INC., *pg.* 375, *pg.* 761
CITRIX SYSTEMS, INC., *pg.* 375, *pg.* 424
CLOUDMARK, INC., *pg.* 376, *pg.* 216
COFFEECUP SOFTWARE INC., *pg.* 1236, *pg.* 501
COMMENCE CORPORATION, *pg.* 377, *pg.* 1055
COMMVAULT SYSTEMS, INC., *pg.* 377, *pg.* 1125
COMPASSLEARNING, INC., *pg.* 1628, *pg.* 1661
COMPONENTSOURCE HOLDING CORPORATION, *pg.* 378, *pg.* 533
COMPUCOM SYSTEMS, INC., *pg.* 378, *pg.* 1678
COMPUWARE CORPORATION, *pg.* 379, *pg.* 879
CONCUR TECHNOLOGIES, INC., *pg.* 1236, *pg.* 1813
CONDUSIV TECHNOLOGIES, *pg.* 379, *pg.* 51
CONNECTUS SOFTWARE, *pg.* 379, *pg.* 772
COREL CORPORATION, *pg.* 380, *pg.* 1931
CSR, *pg.* 280, *pg.* 284
CTI GROUP HOLDINGS INC., *pg.* 381, *pg.* 684
CYBERSOURCE CORPORATION, *pg.* 381, *pg.* 216
D.A. KOPP & ASSOCIATES, INC., *pg.* 381, *pg.* 1126
DAEGIS INC, *pg.* 381, *pg.* 195
DASSAULT SYSTEMS ENOVIA, *pg.* 382, *pg.* 851
DATATRAK INTERNATIONAL, INC., *pg.* 383, *pg.* 1462
DATAWATCH CORPORATION, *pg.* 383, *pg.* 813
DEALERTRACK HOLDINGS, INC., *pg.* 743, *pg.* 1172
DELL SOFTWARE, *pg.* 385, *pg.* 40
DELL STORAGE, *pg.* 386, *pg.* 922
DELTEK, INC., *pg.* 386, *pg.* 1784
DEMAND MEDIA, INC., *pg.* 1238, *pg.* 273
DETERMINE, INC., *pg.* 386, *pg.* 254
DIGI INTERNATIONAL INC., *pg.* 387, *pg.* 948
DIGITAL INSIGHT, *pg.* 744, *pg.* 189
DIGITAL RIVER, INC., *pg.* 1238, *pg.* 948
DIMENSIONAL INSIGHT, INC., *pg.* 387, *pg.* 805
DIRECT INSITE CORP., *pg.* 387, *pg.* 425
DOUBLECLICK, INC., *pg.* 1239, *pg.* 1225
DST SYSTEMS, INC., *pg.* 388, *pg.* 982
EASYLINK SERVICES INTERNATIONAL CORPORATION, *pg.* 389, *pg.* 536
EBIX INC., *pg.* 1241, *pg.* 504
ECLINICALWORKS, LLC, *pg.* 389, *pg.* 857
ECORA SOFTWARE CORPORATION, *pg.* 389, *pg.* 1662
EDGEWAVE INC, *pg.* 390, *pg.* 202
EDMENTUM, INC., *pg.* 390, *pg.* 917
EGAIN COMMUNICATIONS CORPORATION, *pg.* 1242, *pg.*

284
EGENERA, INC., pg. 390, pg. 802
ELECTRONIC ARTS INC., pg. 951, pg. 189
ELECTRONICS FOR IMAGING, INC., pg. 390, pg. 88
ELEKTA, pg. 391, pg. 284
ELLIE MAE, INC., pg. 1243, pg. 183
EMC CORPORATION, pg. 391, pg. 825
ENERGY & POWER SOLUTIONS, INC., pg. 392, pg. 71
ENTRUST, INC., pg. 393, pg. 1680
EPICOR SOFTWARE CORPORATION, pg. 393, pg. 110
ERESEARCH TECHNOLOGY INC., pg. 1243, pg. 1564
EVOLVING SYSTEMS, INC., pg. 395, pg. 326
EXACTTARGET INC., pg. 1244, pg. 685
THE F. DOHMEN CO., pg. 1530, pg. 1858
F5 NETWORKS, INC., pg. 396, pg. 1835
FAIR ISAAC CORPORATION, pg. 1247, pg. 955
FALCONSTOR SOFTWARE, INC., pg. 396, pg. 1179
FILEMAKER, INC., pg. 639, pg. 265
FLEXERA SOFTWARE INC., pg. 398, pg. 658
FLIR SYSTEMS, INC., pg. 1413, pg. 1510
FUNMOBILITY, INC., pg. 640, pg. 183
GDT TEK, INC., pg. 399, pg. 453
GE INTELLIGENT PLATFORMS, pg. 1339, pg. 1777
GEEKNET, INC., pg. 1248, pg. 1780
GEMSTONE SYSTEMS, INC., pg. 400, pg. 1492
GLOBALLOGIC, INC., pg. 400, pg. 1791
GLOBALSCAPE INC., pg. 401, pg. 1740
GLU MOBILE INC., pg. 954, pg. 219
GOOD TECHNOLOGY, INC., pg. 1249, pg. 285
GOOGLE INC., pg. 1249, pg. 153
HAIGHTS CROSS COMMUNICATIONS, INC., pg. 1646, pg. 1237
HARLAND CLARKE HOLDINGS CORP., pg. 1647, pg. 1741
HEALTH MANAGEMENT SYSTEMS, INC., pg. 1540, pg. 1238
HEALTHPORT, INC., pg. 403, pg. 484
HEALTHSTREAM, INC., pg. 1649, pg. 1651
HEAT SOFTWARE, pg. 403, pg. 145
HEWLETT-PACKARD COMPANY, pg. 404, pg. 175
HP ENTERPRISE SERVICES, LLC, pg. 409, pg. 1731
HYLAND SOFTWARE, INC., pg. 409, pg. 1480
IBM, pg. 410, pg. 1449
ICAD, INC., pg. 643, pg. 1037
ICIMS, INC., pg. 411, pg. 1083
IENTERTAINMENT NETWORK, INC., pg. 1258, pg. 1360
IMAGEWARE SYSTEMS, INC., pg. 412, pg. 203
IMS HEALTH, INC., pg. 1544, pg. 344
INCONTACT, INC., pg. 413, pg. 1752
INFERX CORPORATION, pg. 414, pg. 1807
INFOACCESS.NET LLC, pg. 1258, pg. 1456
INFOGIX INC., pg. 414, pg. 636
INFOR LAWSON, pg. 414, pg. 961
INFORMATICA CORPORATION, pg. 414, pg. 190
INTEL CORPORATION, pg. 645, pg. 266
INTELLICHECK MOBILISA, INC., pg. 416, pg. 1823
INTERACTIVE INTELLIGENCE, INC., pg. 417, pg. 687
INTERNATIONAL BUSINESS MACHINES CORPORATION, pg. 418, pg. 1138
INTERNATIONAL DECISION SYSTEMS, pg. 419, pg. 938
INTERNATIONAL GAME TECHNOLOGY, pg. 420, pg. 1606
INTERPLAY ENTERTAINMENT CORP., pg. 420, pg. 133
INTERSECTIONS INC., pg. 769, pg. 1777
INTERVALZERO INC., pg. 420, pg. 851
INTRALINKS INC., pg. 420, pg. 1244
INTUIT INC., pg. 769, pg. 158
IPSWITCH, INC., pg. 421, pg. 828
IRON MOUNTAIN INCORPORATED, pg. 421, pg. 796
ISLAND PACIFIC, pg. 422, pg. 111
IVEDA SOLUTIONS, INC., pg. 88, pg. 13
JACK HENRY & ASSOCIATES, INC., pg. 422, pg. 988
JDA SOFTWARE GROUP, INC., pg. 423, pg. 22
JOHN WILEY & SONS, INC., pg. 1655, pg. 1073
JUNIPER NETWORKS, pg. 424, pg. 809
KAYAK, pg. 1260, pg. 363
KRONOS INCORPORATED, pg. 425, pg. 813
LANDACORP, INC., pg. 426, pg. 65
LIVEPERSON, INC., pg. 1264, pg. 1252
LOGILITY, INC., pg. 428, pg. 513
LYNX SOFTWARE TECHNOLOGIES, pg. 429, pg. 247
LYRIS, INC., pg. 429, pg. 84
MAJESCO, pg. 429, pg. 1089
MAJESCO ENTERTAINMENT COMPANY, pg. 429, pg. 1056
MANHATTAN ASSOCIATES, INC., pg. 430, pg. 513
MARKET VELOCITY, INC., pg. 1265, pg. 527
MARKETAXESS HOLDINGS INC., pg. 778, pg. 1256
MEDICAL INFORMATION TECHNOLOGY, INC., pg. 431, pg. 859
MEDIDATA SOLUTIONS, INC., pg. 431, pg. 1258
MEDIWARE INFORMATION SYSTEMS, INC., pg. 431, pg. 716
MEGGITT TRAINING SYSTEMS, pg. 1839, pg. 541
MENTOR GRAPHICS CORPORATION, pg. 432, pg. 1510
MERGE ECLINICAL INC., pg. 1266, pg. 1385
MICROS SYSTEMS, INC., pg. 435, pg. 768
MICROSOFT CORPORATION, pg. 435, pg. 1824
MICROSOFT CORP., pg. 440, pg. 321
MICROSOFT GAME STUDIOS, pg. 964, pg. 1828
MICROSTRATEGY, INC., pg. 1266, pg. 1809
MICROSYSTEMS, pg. 440, pg. 608
MMODAL INC., pg. 441, pg. 1633
MRI SOFTWARE, LLC, pg. 1106, pg. 1473
MSC SOFTWARE CORPORATION, pg. 441, pg. 262
MTI SYSTEMS INC., pg. 442, pg. 857
NAGRA USA, pg. 443, pg. 223
NATIONAL INSTRUMENTS CORPORATION, pg. 443, pg. 1664
NETMOTION WIRELESS, INC., pg. 445, pg. 1837
NETSMART TECHNOLOGIES, INC., pg. 445, pg. 1163
NETSOL TECHNOLOGIES, INC., pg. 1270, pg. 56
NETSUITE, INC., pg. 1270, pg. 255
NETWORK SYSTEMS INTERNATIONAL, INC., pg. 445, pg. 1375
NETWORKFLEET, INC., pg. 445, pg. 205
NIELSEN AUDIO, pg. 446, pg. 768
NIGHTINGALE, pg. 446, pg. 186
NOVELL INC., pg. 446, pg. 852
NUANCE COMMUNICATIONS, INC., pg. 447, pg. 806
NUANCE DICTAPHONE HEALTHCARE SOLUTIONS, pg. 447, pg. 806
NUANCE DOCUMENT IMAGING SOLUTIONS, pg. 1271, pg. 1037
NUVIEW WEST, pg. 447, pg. 1496
OMNICELL INC., pg. 1578, pg. 161
OMNICOMM SYSTEMS, INC., pg. 1272, pg. 426
OMNITRACS, LLC, pg. 449, pg. 1685
OMTOOL, LTD., pg. 449, pg. 782
OPENAIR, INC., pg. 1272, pg. 800
OPENLINK FINANCIAL, INC., pg. 449, pg. 1346
OPENTABLE, INC., pg. 450, pg. 224
OPENTEXT CORPORATION, pg. 450, pg. 1948
ORACLE CORPORATION, pg. 450, pg. 191
PACKETVIDEO CORPORATION, pg. 304, pg. 205
PARAMETRIC TECHNOLOGY CORPORATION, pg. 452, pg. 835
PARK CITY GROUP, INC., pg. 452, pg. 1760
PASSUR AEROSPACE, INC., pg. 233, pg. 376
PC MAGAZINE, pg. 1674, pg. 1276
PCTEL, INC., pg. 452, pg. 557
PEGASYSTEMS INC., pg. 453, pg. 74
PEGASYSTEMS INC., pg. 453, pg. 809
PERCEPTICS, LLC, pg. 1426, pg. 1637
PERCEPTRON, INC., pg. 215, pg. 904
PHOENIX TECHNOLOGIES LTD., pg. 454, pg. 147
PITNEY BOWES SOFTWARE INC., pg. 455, pg. 1346
PIXAR ANIMATION STUDIOS, pg. 304, pg. 85
THE PLANNING SHOP, pg. 1677, pg. 178
PREMIERE GLOBAL SERVICES, INC., pg. 1275, pg. 518
PRESIDIO, pg. 456, pg. 1725
PROGRESS SOFTWARE CORPORATION, pg. 457, pg. 786
QLIK TECHNOLOGIES INC., pg. 457, pg. 1583
QNX SOFTWARE SYSTEMS LTD, pg. 458, pg. 1932
QSOUND LABS, INC., pg. 666, pg. 1904
QUALITY SYSTEMS, INC., pg. 1587, pg. 115
QUARK, INC., pg. 458, pg. 322
QVIDIAN, pg. 458, pg. 829
RAINMAKER SYSTEMS INC., pg. 458, pg. 58
RALLY SOFTWARE DEVELOPMENT CORP., pg. 459, pg. 311
RAND WORLDWIDE, INC., pg. 459, pg. 821
RAXCO SOFTWARE, INC., pg. 459, pg. 770
RCM TECHNOLOGIES, INC., pg. 459, pg. 1108
REALNETWORKS, INC., pg. 460, pg. 1839
REALPAGE, INC., pg. 1277, pg. 1669
RED HAT, INC., pg. 460, pg. 1388
RENAISSANCE LEARNING, INC., pg. 607, pg. 1899
RENTRAK CORPORATION, pg. 306, pg. 1506
THE REYNOLDS & REYNOLDS COMPANY, pg. 461, pg. 1457
RIVERBED PERFORMANCE MANAGEMENT, pg. 462, pg. 765
RIVERBED TECHNOLOGY, INC., pg. 1277, pg. 225
ROCKET ALDON, pg. 462, pg. 85
ROGUE WAVE SOFTWARE, INC., pg. 462, pg. 311
ROSETTA STONE INC., pg. 462, pg. 1774
ROVI CORPORATION, pg. 463, pg. 269
RSA SECURITY INC., pg. 463, pg. 786
SABA SOFTWARE, INC., pg. 464, pg. 192
SAGE SOFTWARE, INC., pg. 464, pg. 116
SAJAN, INC., pg. 1278, pg. 1890
SALESFORCE.COM, INC., pg. 1278, pg. 226
SAND TECHNOLOGY, INC., pg. 465, pg. 1961
SAP, pg. 465, pg. 78
SAP AMERICA, INC., pg. 466, pg. 1557
SAS INSTITUTE (CANADA), INC., pg. 466, pg. 1943
SAS INSTITUTE INC., pg. 466, pg. 1361
SCANTRON CORPORATION, pg. 467, pg. 922
SCIQUEST, INC., pg. 468, pg. 1361
SERENA SOFTWARE, INC., pg. 468, pg. 192
SIMULATIONS PLUS, INC., pg. 470, pg. 121
SKILLSOFT PLC, pg. 470, pg. 1037
SMART SOFTWARE, INC., pg. 470, pg. 787
SMEAD MANUFACTURING COMPANY, pg. 470, pg. 926
SMITH MICRO SOFTWARE, INC., pg. 471, pg. 41
SOFTWARE AG, INC., pg. 471, pg. 1799
SOFTWARE HOUSE INTERNATIONAL, INC. (SHI), pg. 471, pg. 1122
SOLARWINDS, INC., pg. 471, pg. 1666
SOLERA HOLDINGS, INC., pg. 1217, pg. 1749
SPEED COMMERCE, INC., pg. 967, pg. 1737
SPS COMMERCE, INC., pg. 472, pg. 942
SS&C TECHNOLOGIES HOLDINGS, INC., pg. 473, pg. 386
THE SSI GROUP, INC., pg. 473, pg. 7
SUCCESSFACTORS, INC., pg. 477, pg. 228
SUMTOTAL SYSTEMS, INC., pg. 477, pg. 429
SUNGARD DATA SYSTEMS INC., pg. 477, pg. 1592
SUNGARD EMPLOYEE BENEFIT SYSTEMS, pg. 477, pg. 4
SUNGARD FINANCIAL SYSTEMS-RELIUS-JACKSONVILLE, pg. 477, pg. 435
SUPPORT.COM, INC., pg. 1283, pg. 192
SUREQUEST SYSTEMS, INC., pg. 900, pg. 1669
SYMANTEC CORPORATION, pg. 478, pg. 161
SYMANTEC CORPORATION, pg. 479, pg. 1753
SYNOPSYS, INC., pg. 480, pg. 162
TABLEAU SOFTWARE, INC., pg. 481, pg. 1841
TAKE-TWO INTERACTIVE SOFTWARE, INC., pg. 481, pg. 1297
TANDBERG DATA, pg. 481, pg. 311
TANGOE, INC., pg. 481, pg. 368
TECH DATA CORPORATION, pg. 482, pg. 416
TELECOMMUNICATION SYSTEMS INC., pg. 483, pg. 754
THOMSON REUTERS - CORPORATE HEADQUARTERS, pg. 1693, pg. 1299
THOMSON REUTERS CORPORATION, pg. 1693, pg. 1944
THOMSON REUTERS TAX & ACCOUNTING, pg. 484, pg. 905
TIBCO SOFTWARE INC., pg. 484, pg. 178
TIGERLOGIC CORPORATION, pg. 484, pg. 117
TPR EDUCATION, LLC, pg. 1695, pg. 822
TRADESTATION GROUP, INC., pg. 811, pg. 459
TRANSCORE HOLDINGS INC., pg. 485, pg. 1541
TRIMBLE NAVIGATION LIMITED, pg. 1384, pg. 288
TRIPWIRE, INC., pg. 485, pg. 1507
TRIZETTO CORPORATION, pg. 485, pg. 327
TRUSTWAVE HOLDINGS, INC., pg. 1285, pg. 593
TYLER TECHNOLOGIES, INC., pg. 486, pg. 1690
UBISOFT INC., pg. 589, pg. 229
THE ULTIMATE SOFTWARE GROUP, INC., pg. 486, pg. 479
UNICOM ENGINEERING, pg. 1286, pg. 812
US DATAWORKS, INC., pg. 1286, pg. 1746
VALVE CORPORATION, pg. 487, pg. 1817
VERIFONE SYSTEMS, INC., pg. 487, pg. 251
VERINT SYSTEMS INC., pg. 488, pg. 1182
VERINT WITNESS ACTIONABLE SOLUTIONS, pg. 488, pg. 539
VERISIGN, INC., pg. 488, pg. 1799
VERTICAL COMMUNICATIONS, INC., pg. 488, pg. 270
VERTICAL SEARCH WORKS INC., pg. 489, pg. 1809
VIEW SYSTEMS, INC., pg. 489, pg. 760
VIQ SOLUTIONS INC., pg. 490, pg. 1905
VITRIA TECHNOLOGY, INC., pg. 490, pg. 289
VMWARE, INC., pg. 490, pg. 179
WATCHGUARD TECHNOLOGIES, INC., pg. 491, pg. 1842
WEBEX COMMUNICATIONS, INC., pg. 491, pg. 270
WEBSENSE, INC., pg. 491, pg. 210

WIND RIVER SYSTEMS, INC., pg. 493, pg. 38
WIZZARD SPEECH LLC., pg. 493, pg. 1582
XILINX, INC., pg. 496, pg. 252
ZIX CORPORATION, pg. 497, pg. 1691

7373 - Computer Integrated Systems Design

3M, pg. 339, pg. 179
3T SYSTEMS, INC., pg. 339, pg. 330
ACORN ENERGY, INC., pg. 341, pg. 389
ACSIS, INC., pg. 341, pg. 1083
ACTUATE CANADA, pg. 1225, pg. 1933
A.D.A.M., INC., pg. 1225, pg. 487
ADEPT TECHNOLOGY, INC., pg. 1310, pg. 182
ADVENT SOFTWARE, INC., pg. 345, pg. 211
AGFA CORPORATION, pg. 1398, pg. 1114
AKAMAI TECHNOLOGIES, INC., pg. 1226, pg. 007
ALLIN CORPORATION, pg. 347, pg. 1572
ALLSCRIPTS HEALTHCARE SOLUTIONS, INC., pg. 1492, pg. 563
AMAZON.COM, INC., pg. 1226, pg. 1831
AMDOCS INC., pg. 348, pg. 974
APPLIED GLOBAL TECHNOLOGIES, pg. 352, pg. 460
APPLIED SOFTWARE TECHNOLOGY, INC., pg. 352, pg. 488
APPNETA, pg. 352, pg. 1909
ART & LOGIC, INC., pg. 1229, pg. 179
ARUBA NETWORKS, INC., pg. 353, pg. 284
ASA INTERNATIONAL LTD., pg. 353, pg. 1036
ASPECT SOFTWARE, INC., pg. 354, pg. 238
ASPECT SOFTWARE, INC., pg. 354, pg. 813
ASPIRE LIFESTYLES OF THE AMERICAS, pg. 1230, pg. 1770
ASPYRA, INC., pg. 355, pg. 306
ASURE SOFTWARE, INC., pg. 355, pg. 1660
ATHENAHEALTH, INC., pg. 1497, pg. 855
ATS AUTOMATION TOOLING SYSTEMS INC., pg. 355, pg. 1919
ATTACHMATE CORPORATION, pg. 356, pg. 1833
AUDIOCODES USA, pg. 356, pg. 1121
AUTHENTIDATE HOLDING CORP., pg. 356, pg. 1044
AUTOBYTEL INC., pg. 1230, pg. 107
AUTOMATIC DATA PROCESSING, INC., pg. 357, pg. 1117
AVF CONSULTING, INC., pg. 358, pg. 755
AXEDA SYSTEMS INC., pg. 359, pg. 819
BACKUPWORKS.COM INC., pg. 359, pg. 120
BANCTEC, INC., pg. 360, pg. 1717
BANDWIDTH.COM, INC., pg. 360, pg. 1386
BARRISTER GLOBAL SERVICES NETWORK, INC., pg. 360, pg. 744
BELL INDUSTRIES, INC., pg. 624, pg. 683
BLACK BOX CORPORATION, pg. 361, pg. 1547
BLOGHER INC., pg. 1232, pg. 45
BLUE COAT SYSTEMS, INC., pg. 362, pg. 284
BRADY/TISCOR, INC., pg. 364, pg. 200
CACI INTERNATIONAL INC., pg. 367, pg. 1773
CAE USA, INC., pg. 226, pg. 472
CALIBRUS, INC., pg. 368, pg. 25
CAMO SOFTWARE, INC., pg. 368, pg. 1133
CANADIAN ADVANCED TECHNOLOGY ALLIANCE, pg. 136, pg. 1931
CANADIAN ASSOCIATION OF INTERNET PROVIDERS, pg. 136, pg. 1931
CERNER CORPORATION, pg. 1514, pg. 981
CERTICOM CORP., pg. 371, pg. 1925
CGI GROUP INC., pg. 371, pg. 1954
CGI TECHNOLOGIES & SOLUTIONS INC., pg. 371, pg. 1779
CHERRYROAD TECHNOLOGIES INC., pg. 1235, pg. 1087
CHYRONHEGO, pg. 371, pg. 1179
CIBER, INC., pg. 372, pg. 330
CIENA CORPORATION, pg. 628, pg. 771
CINCOM SYSTEMS, INC., pg. 372, pg. 1411
CLOUDMARK, INC., pg. 376, pg. 216
COMMVAULT SYSTEMS, INC., pg. 377, pg. 1125
COMPASSLEARNING, INC., pg. 1628, pg. 1661
COMPUCOM SYSTEMS, INC., pg. 378, pg. 1678
COMPUMED, INC., pg. 378, pg. 128
COMPUTER PROGRAMS & SYSTEMS, INC., pg. 378, pg. 7
COMPUTER SCIENCES CORPORATION, pg. 378, pg. 1780
COMPUTER TASK GROUP, INC., pg. 378, pg. 1147
CONCUR TECHNOLOGIES, pg. 1903, pg. 501
CONCURRENT COMPUTER CORPORATION, pg. 379, pg. 531
CONVERGYS CORPORATION, pg. 379, pg. 1412
CSPI TECHNOLOGY SOLUTIONS, pg. 381, pg. 421
CUBIC CORPORATION, pg. 632, pg. 201
CUBIC TRANSPORTATION SYSTEMS, INC., pg. 1905, pg. 202
CYBERRESEARCH INC., pg. 381, pg. 339
DAEGIS INC, pg. 381, pg. 195
DATALINK CORPORATION, pg. 382, pg. 922
DEALERTRACK HOLDINGS, INC., pg. 743, pg. 1172
DELL, INC., pg. 385, pg. 1037
DELL SOFTWARE, pg. 385, pg. 40
DELOITTE & TOUCHE USA LLP, pg. 743, pg. 1222
DHI GROUP, INC., pg. 1238, pg. 1223
DIALOGIC INC., pg. 281, pg. 243
DIGITAL INSIGHT, pg. 744, pg. 189
DIGITALGLOBE, INC., pg. 1408, pg. 333
DIRECT INSITE CORP., pg. 387, pg. 425
DOCUMENT SECURITY SYSTEMS, INC., pg. 388, pg. 1333
DXSTORM.COM INC., pg. 1239, pg. 1930
EASYLINK SERVICES INTERNATIONAL CORPORATION, pg. 389, pg. 536
EBIX INC., pg. 1241, pg. 504
EDGEWATER TECHNOLOGY, INC., pg. 389, pg. 848
THE ELECTRIC MAIL COMPANY, pg. 1242, pg. 1907
ELECTRO STANDARDS LABORATORIES INC., pg. 390, pg. 1600
ELECTROSONIC SYSTEMS, INC., pg. 635, pg. 949
ELLIE MAE, INC., pg. 1243, pg. 183
EMC CORPORATION, pg. 391, pg. 825
EMTEC, INC., pg. 392, pg. 1123
EN POINTE TECHNOLOGIES, INC., pg. 1243, pg. 94
ENHERENT CORP., pg. 393, pg. 1343
EOLAS TECHNOLOGIES, INC., pg. 1243, pg. 573
EQUIFAX WORKFORCE SOLUTIONS, pg. 394, pg. 997
ERESEARCH TECHNOLOGY INC., pg. 1243, pg. 1564
ERICSSON, pg. 395, pg. 1108
ESPIAL GROUP INC., pg. 1243, pg. 1932
EVOLVING SYSTEMS, INC., pg. 395, pg. 326
EXCENTUS CORPORATION, pg. 977, pg. 1681
FEI SYSTEMS, pg. 397, pg. 772
FILECONTROL PARTNERS LTD, pg. 1247, pg. 1746
FILEMAKER, INC., pg. 639, pg. 265
FUJITSU COMPUTER SYSTEMS CORPORATION, pg. 398, pg. 285
FUJITSU CONSULTING, pg. 398, pg. 1955
GDT TEK, INC., pg. 399, pg. 453
GE INTELLIGENT PLATFORMS, pg. 1339, pg. 1777
GEEKNET, INC., pg. 1248, pg. 1780
GLASSHOUSE TECHNOLOGIES, INC., pg. 400, pg. 844
GO DADDY INC., pg. 1249, pg. 21
H&S BUSINESS EXPRESS INC., pg. 402, pg. 1320
HEALTHSTREAM, INC., pg. 1649, pg. 1651
HEALTHTRIO INC., pg. 403, pg. 320
HIRERIGHT, INC., pg. 1256, pg. 111
HP ENTERPRISE SERVICES, LLC, pg. 409, pg. 1731
HTC GLOBAL SERVICES INC., pg. 409, pg. 911
IGATE CORPORATION, pg. 411, pg. 809
IHS INC., pg. 1652, pg. 326
IMODULES SOFTWARE, INC., pg. 1258, pg. 716
INFORMATION BUILDERS (CANADA) INC., pg. 1259, pg. 1939
INFORMATION BUILDERS INC., pg. 415, pg. 1243
INSIGHT ENTERPRISES, INC., pg. 415, pg. 26
INTEGRACORE, INC., pg. 416, pg. 1763
INTEGRAL SYSTEMS, INC., pg. 416, pg. 767
INTEGRATED SYSTEMS ANALYSTS, INC., pg. 416, pg. 1771
INTELLICHECK MOBILISA, INC., pg. 416, pg. 1823
INTERDIGITAL, INC., pg. 1872, pg. 1543
INTERNAP NETWORK SERVICES CORPORATION, pg. 417, pg. 513
INTERNATIONAL BUSINESS MACHINES CORPORATION, pg. 418, pg. 1138
INTERNATIONAL DECISION SYSTEMS, pg. 419, pg. 938
INTERNATIONAL GAME TECHNOLOGY, pg. 420, pg. 1606
INTERNATIONAL ROAD DYNAMICS INC., pg. 1912, pg. 1962
INTRUSION INC., pg. 1259, pg. 1736
INTUIT INC., pg. 769, pg. 158
IPC SYSTEMS, INC., pg. 648, pg. 1075
IRI GROUP, pg. 421, pg. 579
IRON MOUNTAIN INCORPORATED, pg. 421, pg. 796
JACK HENRY & ASSOCIATES, INC., pg. 422, pg. 988
JUNIPER NETWORKS, pg. 424, pg. 809
KEYNOTE SYSTEMS INCORPORATED, pg. 425, pg. 255
KNOVATION, pg. 1261, pg. 1415
LAM RESEARCH CORPORATION, pg. 1354, pg. 246
LANDACORP, INC., pg. 426, pg. 65
LAWRENCE PAPER COMPANY, pg. 1463, pg. 715
LCG TECHNOLOGIES CORPORATION, pg. 1261, pg. 779
LEVEL 3 COMMUNICATIONS, INC., pg. 1262, pg. 312
LIONBRIDGE TECHNOLOGIES INC., pg. 428, pg. 851
LIVE CURRENT MEDIA INC., pg. 1263, pg. 1911
LOGIKA CORPORATION, pg. 1264, pg. 581
LOGMEIN, INC., pg. 428, pg. 861
LYCOS, INC., pg. 1265, pg. 852
LYRIS, INC., pg. 429, pg. 84
MAD CATZ INTERACTIVE INC., pg. 429, pg. 204
MANHATTAN ASSOCIATES, INC., pg. 430, pg. 513
MARKET AMERICA WORLDWIDE, INC., pg. 1265, pg. 1375
MARKETAXESS HOLDINGS INC., pg. 778, pg. 1256
MATRIX INTEGRATION LLC, pg. 430, pg. 692
MAXIMUS, INC., pg. 780, pg. 1799
MDI ENTERTAINMENT LLC, pg. 964, pg. 484
MEDASSETS INC., pg. 1561, pg. 484
MEDIDATA SOLUTIONS, INC., pg. 431, pg. 1258
MEDIWARE INFORMATION SYSTEMS, INC., pg. 431, pg. 716
MEGAPATH, INC., pg. 432, pg. 71
MEGGITT TRAINING SYSTEMS, pg. 1839, pg. 541
MICROAGE, INC., pg. 434, pg. 26
MIDWEST MICROSYSTEMS, LLC, pg. 1267, pg. 1012
MINDBLAZER, INC., pg. 1267, pg. 1367
MMODAL INC., pg. 441, pg. 1633
MONEXA TECHNOLOGIES CORPORATION, pg. 1268, pg. 1911
MOTOROLA SOLUTIONS, INC., pg. 657, pg. 659
MSC SOFTWARE CORPORATION, pg. 441, pg. 262
MTM TECHNOLOGIES, INC., pg. 442, pg. 375
MULTIMEDIA GAMES INC., pg. 442, pg. 1664
NAVISITE, INC., pg. 1269, pg. 782
NETAPP, INC., pg. 444, pg. 287
NETMOTION WIRELESS, INC., pg. 445, pg. 1837
NETSCOUT SYSTEMS, INC., pg. 1270, pg. 858
NETSUITE, INC., pg. 1270, pg. 255
NETWOLVES CORPORATION, pg. 1271, pg. 474
NIGHTINGALE, pg. 446, pg. 186
NL INDUSTRIES, INC., pg. 1174, pg. 1684
NORTHROP GRUMMAN CORPORATION, pg. 231, pg. 1781
NORTHROP GRUMMAN INFORMATION SYSTEMS, pg. 1424, pg. 1794
NTT DATA, pg. 447, pg. 799
OMNICELL INC., pg. 1578, pg. 161
OMNITRACS, LLC, pg. 449, pg. 1685
ONMOBILE LIVE, INC., pg. 449, pg. 829
ONSTREAM MEDIA CORPORATION, pg. 449, pg. 459
ONVIA, INC., pg. 1272, pg. 1838
OPENCONNECT SYSTEMS, INC., pg. 449, pg. 1685
OPTUM CLINICAL SOLUTIONS, pg. 450, pg. 848
ORACLE CORPORATION, pg. 450, pg. 191
PAR TECHNOLOGY CORPORATION, pg. 452, pg. 1183
PARAMETRIC TECHNOLOGY CORPORATION, pg. 452, pg. 835
PARK CITY GROUP, INC., pg. 452, pg. 1760
PASSUR AEROSPACE, INC., pg. 233, pg. 376
PCTEL, INC., pg. 452, pg. 557
PEAPOD, LLC, pg. 1029, pg. 661
PEGASYSTEMS INC., pg. 453, pg. 809
PERFICIENT, INC., pg. 1274, pg. 1002
PFSWEB, INC., pg. 1275, pg. 1733
POMEROY IT SOLUTIONS, INC., pg. 456, pg. 728
PRESIDIO, pg. 456, pg. 1725
PRESILIENT, LLC, pg. 456, pg. 313
PRIMA GAMES, pg. 965, pg. 693
QUALITY SYSTEMS, INC., pg. 1587, pg. 115
RACKSPACE HOSTING, INC., pg. 1277, pg. 1742
RADISYS CORPORATION, pg. 458, pg. 1498
RAND A TECHNOLOGY CORPORATION, pg. 459, pg. 774
RCM TECHNOLOGIES, INC., pg. 459, pg. 1108
REALNETWORKS, INC., pg. 460, pg. 1839
THE REYNOLDS & REYNOLDS COMPANY, pg. 461, pg. 1457
RICHARDSON ELECTRONICS, LTD., pg. 667, pg. 622
RSA SECURITY INC., pg. 463, pg. 786
SAFEGUARD SCIENTIFICS, INC., pg. 464, pg. 1592
SAIC, INC., pg. 464, pg. 1794
SAP, pg. 465, pg. 78
SCAN-OPTICS, LLC, pg. 467, pg. 354
SCANTRON CORPORATION, pg. 467, pg. 922

First page reference indicates Business Class Edition
Second page reference indicates Geographic Edition

SCIENTIFIC GAMES CORPORATION, *pg.* 468, *pg.* 1029
SCIQUEST, INC., *pg.* 468, *pg.* 1361
SIEMENS PLM SOFTWARE, *pg.* 469, *pg.* 1734
SILICON GRAPHICS INTERNATIONAL CORP, *pg.* 470, *pg.* 148
SIMULATIONS PLUS, INC., *pg.* 470, *pg.* 121
SIRSIDYNIX CORPORATION, *pg.* 470, *pg.* 1751
SNAP INTERACTIVE, INC., *pg.* 1281, *pg.* 1293
SOFTCHOICE CORPORATION, *pg.* 471, *pg.* 1943
SOLARWINDS, INC., *pg.* 471, *pg.* 1666
SPAR GROUP, INC., *pg.* 1687, *pg.* 1349
SPS COMMERCE, INC., *pg.* 472, *pg.* 942
STEELCLOUD, INC., *pg.* 476, *pg.* 1776
STEFANINI TECHTEAM GLOBAL, INC., *pg.* 476, *pg.* 907
STRATASYS, INC., *pg.* 476, *pg.* 923
STRATEGIC FOCUS, *pg.* 1283, *pg.* 92
STRATUS TECHNOLOGIES, INC., *pg.* 477, *pg.* 832
STRUCTURED COMMUNICATION SYSTEMS, INC., *pg.* 477, *pg.* 1497
SUCCESSFACTORS, INC., *pg.* 477, *pg.* 228
SUNGARD DATA SYSTEMS INC., *pg.* 477, *pg.* 1592
SYKES ENTERPRISES, INCORPORATED, *pg.* 478, *pg.* 475
SYNACOR, INC., *pg.* 1283, *pg.* 1151
SYNIVERSE HOLDINGS, INC., *pg.* 479, *pg.* 475
SYNNEX CORPORATION, *pg.* 480, *pg.* 92
SYNOPSYS, INC., *pg.* 480, *pg.* 162
TASC, INC., *pg.* 1431, *pg.* 1777
TAXWARE, *pg.* 808, *pg.* 860
TECHTARGET, INC., *pg.* 482, *pg.* 837
TELECOMMUNICATION SYSTEMS INC., *pg.* 483, *pg.* 754
TELKONET, INC., *pg.* 678, *pg.* 1881
TELOS CORPORATION, *pg.* 483, *pg.* 1776
TIBCO SOFTWARE INC., *pg.* 484, *pg.* 178
TRIMBLE NAVIGATION LIMITED, *pg.* 1384, *pg.* 288
TROY GROUP INC., *pg.* 485, *pg.* 71
TSS, INC., *pg.* 117, *pg.* 768
TYLER TECHNOLOGIES, INC., *pg.* 486, *pg.* 1690
UNICOM ENGINEERING, *pg.* 1286, *pg.* 812
UNISYS CORPORATION, *pg.* 487, *pg.* 1517
USA TECHNOLOGIES, INC., *pg.* 815, *pg.* 1550
VERINT SYSTEMS INC., *pg.* 488, *pg.* 1182
VERIZON TERREMARK, *pg.* 685, *pg.* 447
VERTICAL SEARCH WORKS INC., *pg.* 489, *pg.* 1809
VIRTUSA CORPORATION, *pg.* 490, *pg.* 857
VMWARE, INC., *pg.* 490, *pg.* 179
VOLT INFORMATION SCIENCES, INC., *pg.* 490, *pg.* 1312
WATCHGUARD TECHNOLOGIES, INC., *pg.* 491, *pg.* 1842
WAUSAU FINANCIAL SYSTEMS INC., *pg.* 819, *pg.* 1882
WEB.COM GROUP, INC., *pg.* 1288, *pg.* 435
WEBEX COMMUNICATIONS, INC., *pg.* 491, *pg.* 270
WEBSENSE, INC., *pg.* 491, *pg.* 210
WELOCALIZE, INC., *pg.* 1289, *pg.* 769
WHITE SKY, INC., *pg.* 492, *pg.* 256
WILLOUGHBY'S KONICA MINOLTA IMAGING CENTER, *pg.* 1437, *pg.* 1314
WIND RIVER SYSTEMS, INC., *pg.* 493, *pg.* 38
WIRELESS RONIN TECHNOLOGIES INC., *pg.* 689, *pg.* 951
WORDEN BROTHERS, INC., *pg.* 823, *pg.* 1372
XPLORE TECHNOLOGIES CORP., *pg.* 497, *pg.* 1667
XURA, INC., *pg.* 689, *pg.* 849
YAHOO! INC., *pg.* 1289, *pg.* 289

7374 - Computer Processing & Data Preparation & Processing Services

ACTUATE CANADA, *pg.* 1225, *pg.* 1933
ACXIOM CORPORATION, *pg.* 342, *pg.* 607
ACXIOM CORPORATION, *pg.* 342, *pg.* 33
ALLSCRIPTS HEALTHCARE SOLUTIONS, INC., *pg.* 1492, *pg.* 563
ATLANTIC TELE-NETWORK, INC., *pg.* 620, *pg.* 787
AUTOMATIC DATA PROCESSING, INC., *pg.* 357, *pg.* 1117
BANCTEC, INC., *pg.* 360, *pg.* 1717
BARCODING INC., *pg.* 360, *pg.* 755
BLUCORA, *pg.* 1232, *pg.* 1813
BOTTOMLINE TECHNOLOGIES INC., *pg.* 363, *pg.* 483
BROADRIDGE FINANCIAL SOLUTIONS INC., *pg.* 727, *pg.* 1172
BROADVIEW NETWORKS, INC., *pg.* 365, *pg.* 1339
CARBONITE, INC., *pg.* 368, *pg.* 792
CDS GLOBAL, INC., *pg.* 370, *pg.* 704
CENTURYLINK, INC, *pg.* 1870, *pg.* 317
COCC, *pg.* 376, *pg.* 337
COMDATA CORPORATION, *pg.* 739, *pg.* 1627
CONCUR TECHNOLOGIES, *pg.* 1903, *pg.* 501
CONVERGYS CORPORATION, *pg.* 379, *pg.* 1412
CYBERSOURCE CORPORATION, *pg.* 381, *pg.* 216
DRIVESAVERS DATA RECOVERY, INC., *pg.* 388, *pg.* 168
DST SYSTEMS, INC., *pg.* 388, *pg.* 982
EASYLINK SERVICES INTERNATIONAL CORPORATION, *pg.* 389, *pg.* 536
EMC CORPORATION, *pg.* 391, *pg.* 825
EVERI HOLDINGS INC., *pg.* 749, *pg.* 1023
FACTSET RESEARCH SYSTEMS INC., *pg.* 1247, *pg.* 361
FIRSTBANK DATA CORPORATION, *pg.* 397, *pg.* 333
FISERV, INC., *pg.* 397, *pg.* 1855
FISERV, INC., *pg.* 758, *pg.* 537
GE ENERGY, *pg.* 399, *pg.* 439
GLOBAL GEOPHYSICAL SERVICES, INC., *pg.* 1414, *pg.* 1727
GOOD TECHNOLOGY, INC., *pg.* 1249, *pg.* 285
GOOGLE INC., *pg.* 1249, *pg.* 153
GOVDELIVERY, INC., *pg.* 1255, *pg.* 961
HDI SOLUTIONS, INC., *pg.* 403, *pg.* 1
HEADSTRONG CORPORATION, *pg.* 403, *pg.* 1798
HEALTH GRADES, INC., *pg.* 1256, *pg.* 319
HEALTH MANAGEMENT SYSTEMS, INC., *pg.* 1540, *pg.* 1238
HEARTLAND PAYMENT SYSTEMS, INC., *pg.* 765, *pg.* 1111
HP ENTERPRISE SERVICES, LLC, *pg.* 409, *pg.* 1731
IGN ENTERTAINMENT, INC., *pg.* 1258, *pg.* 220
IMMERSION CORPORATION, *pg.* 413, *pg.* 246
IMS HEALTH, INC., *pg.* 1544, *pg.* 344
INFOCROSSING, INC., *pg.* 414, *pg.* 1079
INNODATA ISOGEN, INC., *pg.* 1259, *pg.* 1072
INTELIUS, INC., *pg.* 416, *pg.* 1815
INTERSECTIONS INC., *pg.* 769, *pg.* 1777
IPASS, INC., *pg.* 1259, *pg.* 193
KEYNOTE SYSTEMS INCORPORATED, *pg.* 425, *pg.* 255
LIVE CURRENT MEDIA INC., *pg.* 1263, *pg.* 1911
LOOKSMART, LTD., *pg.* 1265, *pg.* 221
MANPOWER GROUP, *pg.* 430, *pg.* 1710
MEDIABISTRO, INC., *pg.* 1266, *pg.* 1258
MERGENT, INC., *pg.* 1664, *pg.* 1616
MRI SOFTWARE, LLC, *pg.* 1106, *pg.* 1473
MULTI-AD, INC., *pg.* 1666, *pg.* 652
MYBIZOFFICE, INC, *pg.* 443, *pg.* 1785
NCR CORPORATION, *pg.* 443, *pg.* 531
NETSMART TECHNOLOGIES, INC., *pg.* 445, *pg.* 1163
NIELSEN AUDIO, *pg.* 446, *pg.* 768
OPENTEXT GXS, *pg.* 1272, *pg.* 770
PACKETVIDEO CORPORATION, *pg.* 304, *pg.* 205
PAYPAL INC., *pg.* 1274, *pg.* 248
PEGASUS SOLUTIONS, INC., *pg.* 452, *pg.* 1685
PEGASYSTEMS INC., *pg.* 453, *pg.* 809
PERCEPTIVE SOFTWARE, *pg.* 453, *pg.* 1775
PFSWEB, INC., *pg.* 1275, *pg.* 1733
PITNEY BOWES SOFTWARE INC., *pg.* 455, *pg.* 1346
RACKSPACE HOSTING, INC., *pg.* 1277, *pg.* 1742
SABRE HOLDINGS CORPORATION, *pg.* 1922, *pg.* 1745
SAFEGUARD BUSINESS SYSTEMS, INC., *pg.* 464, *pg.* 1686
SCANTRON CORPORATION, *pg.* 467, *pg.* 922
SCHAWK CANADA INC., *pg.* 1683, *pg.* 1928
SUNGARD DATA SYSTEMS INC., *pg.* 477, *pg.* 1592
TERADATA CORPORATION, *pg.* 483, *pg.* 1447
TRIMBLE NAVIGATION LIMITED, *pg.* 1384, *pg.* 288
TRIZETTO CORPORATION, *pg.* 485, *pg.* 327
TRUSTWAVE HOLDINGS, INC., *pg.* 1285, *pg.* 593
TUCOWS, INC., *pg.* 1285, *pg.* 1946
URSCHEL LABORATORIES INCORPORATED, *pg.* 1386, *pg.* 698
VERISIGN, INC., *pg.* 488, *pg.* 1799
VERITEQ, *pg.* 488, *pg.* 422
WEB RESULTS, INC., *pg.* 1288, *pg.* 460
WEB.COM, INC., *pg.* 1288, *pg.* 524
YOUTUBE, LLC, *pg.* 1291, *pg.* 198
ZIPREALTY, INC., *pg.* 1120, *pg.* 85
ZIX CORPORATION, *pg.* 497, *pg.* 1691

7375 - Information Retrieval Services

1&1 INTERNET, INC., *pg.* 1225, *pg.* 1521
10BEST, INC., *pg.* 1225, *pg.* 1617
ACXIOM CORPORATION, *pg.* 342, *pg.* 33
ADVANCED INTERNET TECHNOLOGIES INC., *pg.* 1225, *pg.* 1372
ALACRA, INC., *pg.* 346, *pg.* 1188
ALASKA COMMUNICATIONS SYSTEMS GROUP, INC., *pg.* 269, *pg.* 10
ANCESTRY.COM LLC, *pg.* 1228, *pg.* 1754
AOL INC., *pg.* 1229, *pg.* 1195
ARI NETWORK SERVICES, INC., *pg.* 353, *pg.* 1873
AT&T ALASCOM, *pg.* 619, *pg.* 10
AT&T INC., *pg.* 1867, *pg.* 1674
AT&T WEST, *pg.* 1869, *pg.* 212
AUTOBYTEL INC., *pg.* 1230, *pg.* 107
BABCOX MEDIA, *pg.* 1619, *pg.* 1400
BESTTRANSPORT, INC., *pg.* 1231, *pg.* 1482
BIZRATE.COM, *pg.* 1231, *pg.* 126
BLACKHAWK ENGAGEMENT SOLUTIONS, INC., *pg.* 1232, *pg.* 1725
BLUCORA, *pg.* 1232, *pg.* 1813
BRIGHT HOUSE NETWORKS LLC, *pg.* 272, *pg.* 461
BROADVIEW NETWORKS, INC., *pg.* 365, *pg.* 1339
BRS MEDIA INC., *pg.* 1233, *pg.* 214
CAFEPRESS.COM, INC., *pg.* 1234, *pg.* 254
CENTURYLINK, INC, *pg.* 1870, *pg.* 317
CHARTER COMMUNICATIONS, INC., *pg.* 274, *pg.* 372
CHEMINDUSTRY.COM, INC., *pg.* 1235, *pg.* 150
CITRIX ONLINE LLC, *pg.* 1235, *pg.* 99
COPERNIC INC., *pg.* 1237, *pg.* 1958
COX COMMUNICATIONS, INC., *pg.* 279, *pg.* 501
CROIX CONNECT, *pg.* 1237, *pg.* 1809
DELTATHREE, INC., *pg.* 1238, *pg.* 1068
DXSTORM.COM INC., *pg.* 1239, *pg.* 1930
E! ONLINE, INC., *pg.* 1239, *pg.* 129
EARTHLINK HOLDINGS CORP., *pg.* 1240, *pg.* 504
ELEMICA, INC., *pg.* 1242, *pg.* 1591
FRONTIER COMMUNICATIONS CORPORATION, *pg.* 1871, *pg.* 362
GRANDE COMMUNICATIONS NETWORKS LLC, *pg.* 1871, *pg.* 1744
GRASSROOTS ENTERPRISE, INC., *pg.* 1255, *pg.* 400
HAWAIIAN TELCOM COMMUNICATIONS, INC., *pg.* 1872, *pg.* 544
HOSTWAY CORPORATION, *pg.* 1256, *pg.* 577
IDT CORPORATION, *pg.* 643, *pg.* 1096
IMODULES SOFTWARE, INC., *pg.* 1258, *pg.* 716
INNODATA ISOGEN, INC., *pg.* 1259, *pg.* 1072
INTERNAP NETWORK SERVICES CORPORATION, *pg.* 417, *pg.* 513
INTRALINKS INC., *pg.* 420, *pg.* 1244
IPASS, INC., *pg.* 1259, *pg.* 193
IPOWERWEB INC., *pg.* 1259, *pg.* 274
J2 GLOBAL COMMUNICATIONS, INC., *pg.* 1260, *pg.* 133
LIVE365, INC., *pg.* 1264, *pg.* 89
LIVEWORLD, INC., *pg.* 1264, *pg.* 246
LOCAL.COM CORPORATION, *pg.* 1264, *pg.* 113
LOOKSMART, LTD., *pg.* 1265, *pg.* 221
MARCHEX, INC., *pg.* 1395, *pg.* 1837
MARITIME BROADBAND, *pg.* 1265, *pg.* 1146
MEDIACOM LLC, *pg.* 297, *pg.* 1182
MILITARY ADVANTAGE, INC., *pg.* 1267, *pg.* 223
MIRROR IMAGE INTERNET, INC., *pg.* 1267, *pg.* 848
MONDO MEDIA CORPORATION, *pg.* 1268, *pg.* 223
MONEY.NET, INC., *pg.* 1268, *pg.* 1261
MTONE WIRELESS CORPORATION, *pg.* 658, *pg.* 268
MYWEBGROCER.COM CORP., *pg.* 1269, *pg.* 1769
NET ACCESS CORPORATION, *pg.* 1269, *pg.* 1104
NEUSTAR, INC., *pg.* 1872, *pg.* 1807
OLM, LLC, *pg.* 1271, *pg.* 381
OOVOO LLC, *pg.* 1272, *pg.* 1274
ORACLE CORPORATION, *pg.* 1272, *pg.* 786
PINTEREST, *pg.* 1275, *pg.* 225
QUEBECOR MEDIA INC., *pg.* 1679, *pg.* 1956
QUESTIA MEDIA INC., *pg.* 1276, *pg.* 1713
REGISTER.COM, INC., *pg.* 1277, *pg.* 434
RIVERBED TECHNOLOGY, INC., *pg.* 1277, *pg.* 225
SALON MEDIA GROUP, INC., *pg.* 1278, *pg.* 226
SINA CORP., *pg.* 1280, *pg.* 161
SITESTAR CORPORATION, *pg.* 1280, *pg.* 1787
SOFTLAYER TECHNOLOGIES INC, *pg.* 471, *pg.* 1686
STREAMING MEDIA, INC., *pg.* 1689, *pg.* 385
SURETY, INC., *pg.* 1283, *pg.* 1799
TECHNICAL COMMUNITIES, INC., *pg.* 1283, *pg.* 198
TECHNOBRANDS, INC., *pg.* 1788, *pg.* 1778
TELUS CORPORATION, *pg.* 1952, *pg.* 1912
THOMSON COMPUMARK, *pg.* 484, *pg.* 838
TIME WARNER INC., *pg.* 312, *pg.* 1302
THE TOPEKA CAPITAL-JOURNAL, *pg.* 1695, *pg.* 722

TRUECAR INC., *pg.* 1284, *pg.* 276
TRUVEN HEALTH ANALYTICS, *pg.* 486, *pg.* 331
TUCOWS, INC., *pg.* 1285, *pg.* 1946
UNIVERSUM USA, *pg.* 1286, *pg.* 1307
US INTERNET CORPORATION, *pg.* 1287, *pg.* 950
USADATA, INC., *pg.* 1287, *pg.* 1308
VENDIO, INC., *pg.* 1287, *pg.* 256
VERIO INC., *pg.* 1287, *pg.* 332
VIDEOTRON LTD., *pg.* 317, *pg.* 1957
WARWICK VALLEY TELEPHONE CO., *pg.* 1877, *pg.* 1349
WEB.COM, INC., *pg.* 1288, *pg.* 524
WEBSENSE, INC., *pg.* 491, *pg.* 210
WORKING MOTHER MEDIA, INC., *pg.* 1702, *pg.* 1315
XAP CORPORATION, *pg.* 1289, *pg.* 73
XO GROUP INC., *pg.* 1289, *pg.* 1316
YAHOO! MOBILE, *pg.* 1291, *pg.* 290
YET2.COM, INC., *pg.* 1291, *pg.* 835
ZILLIANT, INC., *pg.* 497, *pg.* 1668

7376 - Computer Facilities Management Services

CGI GROUP INC., *pg.* 371, *pg.* 1954
COGNIZANT TECHNOLOGY SOLUTIONS CORPORATION, *pg.* 377, *pg.* 1124
COMPUCOM SYSTEMS, INC., *pg.* 378, *pg.* 1678
COMPUTER SCIENCES CORPORATION, *pg.* 378, *pg.* 1780
CONVERGYS CORPORATION, *pg.* 379, *pg.* 1412
DAEGIS INC, *pg.* 381, *pg.* 195
DELL, INC., *pg.* 385, *pg.* 1037
HEALTHSTREAM, INC., *pg.* 1649, *pg.* 1651
NAVISITE, INC., *pg.* 1269, *pg.* 782
POMEROY IT SOLUTIONS, INC., *pg.* 456, *pg.* 728
SEI INVESTMENTS COMPANY, *pg.* 802, *pg.* 1558
VOLT INFORMATION SCIENCES, INC., *pg.* 490, *pg.* 1312

7378 - Computer Maintenance & Repair

AHEARN & SOPER INC., *pg.* 345, *pg.* 1932
ASPYRA, INC., *pg.* 355, *pg.* 306
BLACK BOX CORPORATION, *pg.* 361, *pg.* 1547
CSPI TECHNOLOGY SOLUTIONS, *pg.* 381, *pg.* 421
EMERSON NETWORK POWER, *pg.* 1071, *pg.* 1479
HITACHI DATA SYSTEMS CORPORATION, *pg.* 407, *pg.* 265
IBM CANADA LIMITED, *pg.* 411, *pg.* 1923
INC.COM LLC, *pg.* 1258, *pg.* 1243
MATRIX INTEGRATION LLC, *pg.* 430, *pg.* 692
SCANTRON CORPORATION, *pg.* 467, *pg.* 922
SONY ELECTRONICS, INC., *pg.* 676, *pg.* 209

7379 - Computer Related Services, NEC

ACORN ENERGY, INC., *pg.* 341, *pg.* 389
ACTUATE CANADA, *pg.* 1225, *pg.* 1933
A.D.A.M., INC., *pg.* 1225, *pg.* 487
AGFA CORPORATION, *pg.* 1398, *pg.* 1114
ALLSCRIPTS HEALTHCARE SOLUTIONS, INC., *pg.* 1492, *pg.* 563
AMAZON.COM, INC., *pg.* 1226, *pg.* 1831
APPLIED SOFTWARE TECHNOLOGY, INC., *pg.* 352, *pg.* 488
APPNETA, *pg.* 352, *pg.* 1909
ARUBA NETWORKS, INC., *pg.* 353, *pg.* 284
ATHENAHEALTH, INC., *pg.* 1497, *pg.* 855
ATTACHMATE CORPORATION, *pg.* 356, *pg.* 1833
AUDIOCODES USA, *pg.* 356, *pg.* 1121
AUTHENTIDATE HOLDING CORP., *pg.* 356, *pg.* 1044
AUTOMATIC DATA PROCESSING, INC., *pg.* 357, *pg.* 1117
BANDWIDTH.COM, INC., *pg.* 360, *pg.* 1386
BARRISTER GLOBAL SERVICES NETWORK, INC., *pg.* 360, *pg.* 744
BLACK BOX CORPORATION, *pg.* 361, *pg.* 1547
CANADIAN ADVANCED TECHNOLOGY ALLIANCE, *pg.* 136, *pg.* 1931
CANADIAN ASSOCIATION OF INTERNET PROVIDERS, *pg.* 136, *pg.* 1931
CGI GROUP INC., *pg.* 371, *pg.* 1954
CHYRONHEGO, *pg.* 371, *pg.* 1179
COMPASSLEARNING, INC., *pg.* 1628, *pg.* 1661
COMPUCOM SYSTEMS, INC., *pg.* 378, *pg.* 1678
COMPUTER SCIENCES CORPORATION, *pg.* 378, *pg.* 1780
CONVERGYS CORPORATION, *pg.* 379, *pg.* 1412
CUBIC CORPORATION, *pg.* 632, *pg.* 201
DELL, INC., *pg.* 385, *pg.* 1037
DHI GROUP, INC., *pg.* 1238, *pg.* 1223
DIGITAL INSIGHT, *pg.* 744, *pg.* 189
DIGITALGLOBE, INC., *pg.* 1408, *pg.* 333
DXSTORM.COM INC., *pg.* 1239, *pg.* 1930
EASYLINK SERVICES INTERNATIONAL CORPORATION, *pg.* 389, *pg.* 536
EBIX INC., *pg.* 1241, *pg.* 504
THE ELECTRIC MAIL COMPANY, *pg.* 1242, *pg.* 1907
ELLIE MAE, INC., *pg.* 1243, *pg.* 183
EMC CORPORATION, *pg.* 391, *pg.* 825
EMTEC, INC., *pg.* 392, *pg.* 1123
EOLAS TECHNOLOGIES, INC., *pg.* 1243, *pg.* 573
ERESEARCH TECHNOLOGY INC., *pg.* 1243, *pg.* 1564
FILECONTROL PARTNERS LTD, *pg.* 1247, *pg.* 1746
FUJITSU COMPUTER SYSTEMS CORPORATION, *pg.* 398, *pg.* 285
GO DADDY INC., *pg.* 1249, *pg.* 21
HEALTHTRIO INC., *pg.* 403, *pg.* 320
HIRERIGHT, INC., *pg.* 1256, *pg.* 111
HP ENTERPRISE SERVICES, LLC, *pg.* 409, *pg.* 1731
INSIGHT ENTERPRISES, INC., *pg.* 415, *pg.* 26
INTEGRACORE, INC., *pg.* 416, *pg.* 1763
INTERNATIONAL BUSINESS MACHINES CORPORATION, *pg.* 418, *pg.* 1138
INTERNATIONAL DECISION SYSTEMS, *pg.* 419, *pg.* 938
INTUIT INC., *pg.* 769, *pg.* 158
IPC SYSTEMS, INC., *pg.* 648, *pg.* 1075
IRON MOUNTAIN INCORPORATED, *pg.* 421, *pg.* 796
KEYNOTE SYSTEMS INCORPORATED, *pg.* 425, *pg.* 255
LAM RESEARCH CORPORATION, *pg.* 1354, *pg.* 246
LIONBRIDGE TECHNOLOGIES INC., *pg.* 428, *pg.* 851
LIVE CURRENT MEDIA INC., *pg.* 1263, *pg.* 1911
LOGMEIN, INC., *pg.* 428, *pg.* 861
LYCOS, INC., *pg.* 1265, *pg.* 852
MAD CATZ INTERACTIVE INC., *pg.* 429, *pg.* 204
MARKET AMERICA WORLDWIDE, INC., *pg.* 1265, *pg.* 1375
MARKETAXESS HOLDINGS INC., *pg.* 778, *pg.* 1256
MAXIMUS, INC., *pg.* 780, *pg.* 1799
MEDASSETS INC., *pg.* 1561, *pg.* 484
MONEXA TECHNOLOGIES CORPORATION, *pg.* 1268, *pg.* 1911
MOTOROLA SOLUTIONS, INC., *pg.* 657, *pg.* 659
MULTIMEDIA GAMES INC., *pg.* 442, *pg.* 1664
NAVISITE, INC., *pg.* 1269, *pg.* 782
NETMOTION WIRELESS, INC., *pg.* 445, *pg.* 1837
NETSUITE, INC., *pg.* 1270, *pg.* 255
NIGHTINGALE, *pg.* 446, *pg.* 186
NORTHROP GRUMMAN CORPORATION, *pg.* 231, *pg.* 1781
PASSUR AEROSPACE, INC., *pg.* 233, *pg.* 376
PEAPOD, LLC, *pg.* 1029, *pg.* 661
PERFICIENT, INC., *pg.* 1274, *pg.* 1002
PFSWEB, INC., *pg.* 1275, *pg.* 1733
POMEROY IT SOLUTIONS, INC., *pg.* 456, *pg.* 728
RACKSPACE HOSTING, INC., *pg.* 1277, *pg.* 1742
RADISYS CORPORATION, *pg.* 458, *pg.* 1498
THE REYNOLDS & REYNOLDS COMPANY, *pg.* 461, *pg.* 1457
RSA SECURITY INC., *pg.* 463, *pg.* 786
SAFEGUARD SCIENTIFICS, INC., *pg.* 464, *pg.* 1592
SCANTRON CORPORATION, *pg.* 467, *pg.* 922
SIRSIDYNIX CORPORATION, *pg.* 470, *pg.* 1751
SNAP INTERACTIVE, INC., *pg.* 1281, *pg.* 1293
SOLARWINDS, INC., *pg.* 471, *pg.* 1666
SPS COMMERCE, INC., *pg.* 472, *pg.* 942
STEELCLOUD, INC., *pg.* 476, *pg.* 1776
STRATASYS, INC., *pg.* 476, *pg.* 923
SUNGARD DATA SYSTEMS INC., *pg.* 477, *pg.* 1592
SYNNEX CORPORATION, *pg.* 480, *pg.* 92
TECHTARGET, INC., *pg.* 482, *pg.* 837
TRIMBLE NAVIGATION LIMITED, *pg.* 1384, *pg.* 288
TSS, INC., *pg.* 117, *pg.* 768
UNISYS CORPORATION, *pg.* 487, *pg.* 1517
USA TECHNOLOGIES, INC., *pg.* 815, *pg.* 1550
VERIZON TERREMARK, *pg.* 685, *pg.* 447
VIRTUSA CORPORATION, *pg.* 490, *pg.* 857
VMWARE, INC., *pg.* 490, *pg.* 179
VOLT INFORMATION SCIENCES, INC., *pg.* 490, *pg.* 1312
WEB.COM GROUP, INC., *pg.* 1288, *pg.* 435
WELOCALIZE, INC., *pg.* 1289, *pg.* 769

7381 - Detective, Guard & Armored Car Services

ALLIEDBARTON SECURITY SERVICES, *pg.* 616, *pg.* 1523
BAE SYSTEMS MOBILITY & PROTECTION SYSTEMS, *pg.* 359, *pg.* 1452
THE BRINK'S COMPANY, *pg.* 364, *pg.* 1800
BRINK'S U.S., *pg.* 1901, *pg.* 1670
COMMAND SECURITY CORPORATION, *pg.* 377, *pg.* 1171
G4S SECURE SOLUTIONS USA, *pg.* 399, *pg.* 436
GUARDSMARK, LLC, *pg.* 401, *pg.* 1237
HIRERIGHT, INC., *pg.* 1256, *pg.* 111
THE INTELLIGENCE GROUP, *pg.* 417, *pg.* 1043
KROLL INC., *pg.* 425, *pg.* 1249

7382 - Security Systems Services

3M, *pg.* 339, *pg.* 179
THE ADT CORPORATION, *pg.* 612, *pg.* 409
ALLIED SECURITY INNOVATIONS, INC., *pg.* 1041, *pg.* 1066
ANIXTER INTERNATIONAL INC., *pg.* 1313, *pg.* 614
APPLIED DNA SCIENCES, INC., *pg.* 1393, *pg.* 1343
ASSA ABLOY DOOR SECURITY SOLUTIONS, *pg.* 1042, *pg.* 358
BAE SYSTEMS PRODUCTS GROUP, *pg.* 359, *pg.* 432
BARRACUDA NETWORKS, INC., *pg.* 360, *pg.* 58
BOSCH SECURITY SYSTEMS, INC., *pg.* 626, *pg.* 1158
BSM TECHNOLOGIES INC., *pg.* 627, *pg.* 1949
CERTICOM CORP., *pg.* 371, *pg.* 1925
CREATIVE VISTAS INC., *pg.* 1044, *pg.* 1948
DIEBOLD, INCORPORATED, *pg.* 387, *pg.* 1407
THE EASTERN COMPANY, *pg.* 1331, *pg.* 357
FEDERAL SIGNAL CORPORATION, *pg.* 638, *pg.* 645
FIRE KING SECURITY GROUP, *pg.* 1336, *pg.* 696
G4S SECURE SOLUTIONS USA, *pg.* 399, *pg.* 436
GUARDIAN ALARM COMPANY, *pg.* 641, *pg.* 907
INTELIUS, INC., *pg.* 416, *pg.* 1815
INTELLICHECK MOBILISA, INC., *pg.* 416, *pg.* 1823
INTERSECTIONS INC., *pg.* 769, *pg.* 1777
INTRUSION INC., *pg.* 1259, *pg.* 1736
IVEDA SOLUTIONS, INC., *pg.* 88, *pg.* 13
KASTLE SYSTEMS LLC, *pg.* 648, *pg.* 1773
LAW ENFORCEMENT ASSOCIATES CORPORATION, *pg.* 651, *pg.* 1387
MACE SECURITY INTERNATIONAL, INC., *pg.* 1172, *pg.* 1541
MONITRONICS INTERNATIONAL, INC., *pg.* 656, *pg.* 1684
NAPCO SECURITY SYSTEMS, INC., *pg.* 658, *pg.* 1138
ONSTAR CORPORATION, *pg.* 214, *pg.* 884
PROTECTION ONE, INC., *pg.* 665, *pg.* 715
ROPER TECHNOLOGIES, INC., *pg.* 1372, *pg.* 467
SENTRY TECHNOLOGY CORPORATION, *pg.* 672, *pg.* 1339
SLOMIN'S INC., *pg.* 1076, *pg.* 1167
SPRINT CORPORATION, *pg.* 1874, *pg.* 719
TRACK GROUP, *pg.* 1603, *pg.* 1761
TRUSTWAVE HOLDINGS, INC., *pg.* 1285, *pg.* 593
TSS, INC., *pg.* 117, *pg.* 768
TYCO INTERNATIONAL (US) INC., *pg.* 1891, *pg.* 1113
TYCO SIMPLEXGRINNELL LP, *pg.* 682, *pg.* 859
VERIZON TERREMARK, *pg.* 685, *pg.* 447
VIEW SYSTEMS, INC., *pg.* 489, *pg.* 760
YOTTAMARK, *pg.* 497, *pg.* 193
ZIX CORPORATION, *pg.* 497, *pg.* 1691

7384 - Photofinishing Laboratories

THE ALDERMAN COMPANY, *pg.* 1614, *pg.* 1379
CANDID COLOR SYSTEMS, INC., *pg.* 1404, *pg.* 1485
DISTRICT PHOTO INC., *pg.* 1408, *pg.* 761
FEDEX OFFICE & PRINT SERVICES, INC., *pg.* 396, *pg.* 1681
SHUTTERFLY, INC., *pg.* 1280, *pg.* 192

7389 - Business Services, NEC

180S, LLC, *pg.* 1824, *pg.* 754
3M COMPANY, *pg.* 1142, *pg.* 956
A&E STORES, INC., *pg.* 17, *pg.* 1124
A&K RAILROAD MATERIALS INC., *pg.* 1896, *pg.* 1755
A BRITE COMPANY, *pg.* 1144, *pg.* 1697
A. M. CASTLE & CO., *pg.* 64, *pg.* 644

ABATIX CORP., pg. 1309, pg. 1672
ACCURATE COMMUNICATIONS, INC., pg. 340, pg. 1013
ACCURATE FASTENERS INC., pg. 1309, pg. 789
AERO CONTROLS, INC., pg. 223, pg. 439
AFFILIATED FOODS MIDWEST INC., pg. 1012, pg. 1013
AFFINION GROUP, INC., pg. 1225, pg. 372
A.G. DAVIS/AA GAGE, pg. 1310, pg. 908
AHERN RENTALS, INC., pg. 345, pg. 1022
AIRBUS HELICOPTERS, INC., pg. 223, pg. 1698
AIRCRAFT SPRUCE & SPECIALTY CO., pg. 1759, pg. 69
AIRIQ, INC., pg. 346, pg. 1932
A.J. JERSEY INC., pg. 1310, pg. 1123
ALABAMA BUREAU OF TOURISM & TRAVEL, pg. 988, pg. 7
ALACHUA COUNTY VISITORS & CONVENTION BUREAU, pg. 527, pg. 428
ALAMO IRON WORKS, pg. 1311, pg. 1739
THE ALDERMAN COMPANY, pg. 1614, pg. 1379
ALIMAK HEK INC, pg. 66, pg. 1749
ALLEGRA NETWORK LLC, pg. 1614, pg. 904
ALLEN COMMUNICATION LEARNING SERVICES, INC., pg. 346, pg. 1755
ALLEY THEATRE, pg. 527, pg. 1699
ALLIANCE OF CONFESSING EVANGELICALS, INC., pg. 126, pg. 1545
ALLIED RUBBER & RIGGING SUPPLY, pg. 1878, pg. 1519
ALLSCRIPTS HEALTHCARE SOLUTIONS, INC., pg. 1492, pg. 563
ALSTATE PROCESS SERVICE INC., pg. 347, pg. 1155
ALTA RESOURCES CORPORATION, pg. 347, pg. 1882
ALTAIR CORPORATION, pg. 1312, pg. 910
AMALGAMATED LITHOGRAPHERS OF AMERICA, pg. 126, pg. 1189
AMALIE ARENA, pg. 527, pg. 470
AMC, INC., pg. 1759, pg. 487
AMCOR FLEXIBLES INC., pg. 1492, pg. 635
AMERICAN APPRAISAL ASSOCIATES, INC., pg. 349, pg. 1872
AMERICAN CONSERVATORY THEATRE, pg. 528, pg. 212
AMERICAN CRANE & EQUIPMENT CORPORATION, pg. 1312, pg. 1526
AMERICAN HONDA MOTOR CO., INC., pg. 163, pg. 292
AMERICAN INCORPORATORS LTD., pg. 714, pg. 389
AMERICAN MOLD REMOVAL, INC., pg. 1393, pg. 436
AMERICAN REPROGRAPHICS COMPANY, pg. 1616, pg. 303
AMERICAN TIRE DISTRIBUTORS HOLDINGS, INC., pg. 199, pg. 1379
AMERICA'S CALL CENTER, INC., pg. 349, pg. 431
AMERIX CORPORATION, pg. 715, pg. 767
AMPCO-PITTSBURGH CORPORATION, pg. 1313, pg. 1573
ANAHEIM/ORANGE COUNTY VISITOR & CONVENTION BUREAU, pg. 988, pg. 42
ANCIRA ENTERPRISES INC., pg. 164, pg. 1739
ANDERSON & VREELAND, INC., pg. 1616, pg. 1064
ANDERSON SYMPHONY ORCHESTRA, pg. 528, pg. 673
ANDRITZ INC., pg. 1451, pg. 539
ANGIE'S LIST INC, pg. 1228, pg. 682
ANIXTER PENTACON, INC., pg. 1313, pg. 64
APPLIED INDUSTRIAL TECHNOLOGIES, INC., pg. 199, pg. 1428
ARAMARK CANADA LTD., pg. 1014, pg. 1935
ARBURG, INC., pg. 1314, pg. 359
ARCADIA ALL-FLORIDA CHAMPIONSHIP RODEO, pg. 529, pg. 409
ARCHIE COMICS ENTERTAINMENT, LLC, pg. 270, pg. 360
ARENA STAGE, pg. 529, pg. 395
ARGO INTERNATIONAL CORPORATION, pg. 1314, pg. 1196
ARIZONA OFFICE OF TOURISM, pg. 988, pg. 14
ARNOLD MACHINERY COMPANY, pg. 1314, pg. 1755
AROTECH CORPORATION, pg. 1042, pg. 865
ASCENT CAPITAL GROUP, pg. 270, pg. 330
ASHLAND INC., pg. 972, pg. 726
ASSET MARKETING SYSTEMS INSURANCE SERVICES, LLC, pg. 1193, pg. 200
ASTEC INDUSTRIES, INC., pg. 69, pg. 1628
ATHENAHEALTH, INC., pg. 1497, pg. 855
ATLANTA CONVENTION & VISITORS BUREAU, pg. 989, pg. 489
ATLANTIC AVIATION, pg. 224, pg. 1772
ATLAS BOLT & SCREW COMPANY, pg. 1042, pg. 1403
ATMOS ENERGY CORPORATION, pg. 1935, pg. 1675
AUDI OF AMERICA, INC., pg. 164, pg. 1784
AUDIO VISUAL INNOVATIONS, INC., pg. 621, pg. 471
AUGUSTA METROPOLITAN CONVENTION & VISITORS BUREAU, INC., pg. 989, pg. 524
AUTO DRIVEAWAY CO., pg. 1900, pg. 566
AUTOMATIC DATA PROCESSING, INC., pg. 357, pg. 1117
AUTOMATION MAILING AND SHIPPING SOLUTIONS, INC., pg. 358, pg. 1428
AUTONOMY PLEASANTON, pg. 358, pg. 183
AVAGO TECHNOLOGIES, pg. 358, pg. 238
AVENTION, pg. 1230, pg. 815
AVERY DENNISON CORPORATION, pg. 1452, pg. 95
AVIALL, INC., pg. 224, pg. 1676
AWISCO NY CORPORATION, pg. 1315, pg. 1177
B&G FOODS, INC., pg. 838, pg. 1102
BAD BOY WORLDWIDE ENTERTAINMENT GROUP, pg. 270, pg. 1199
BALTIMORE SYMPHONY ORCHESTRA, pg. 532, pg. 755
BANCTEC, INC., pg. 360, pg. 1717
BANNER DIRECT, pg. 1619, pg. 1200
BARBARA B. MANN PERFORMING ARTS HALL, pg. 532, pg. 427
BATON ROUGE AREA CONVENTION & VISITORS BUREAU, pg. 989, pg. 741
BEECH STREET CORPORATION, pg. 1503, pg. 121
BEHLEN MFG. CO., pg. 701, pg. 1010
BELL-MARK CORPORATION, pg. 1620, pg. 1108
BELLA GROUP, pg. 166, pg. 1599
BENJAMIN OBDYKE, INC., pg. 70, pg. 1540
BERKSHIRE VISITORS BUREAU, pg. 989, pg. 841
BERLITZ INTERNATIONAL, INC., pg. 598, pg. 1110
BET HOLDINGS LLC, pg. 271, pg. 396
BIG APPLE CIRCUS LTD., pg. 533, pg. 1145
BIOSCRIP, INC., pg. 1506, pg. 1158
BIZFILINGS, pg. 724, pg. 1865
BLUE STAR JETS, INC., pg. 1901, pg. 1205
BMW OF NORTH AMERICA, LLC, pg. 166, pg. 1133
BOB EVANS FARMS, LLC, pg. 841, pg. 1467
BOGDANCO CONSULTING, pg. 918, pg. 174
BOLTON-EMERSON AMERICAS, INC., pg. 1318, pg. 827
BOSCH INSPECTION TECHNOLOGY INC., pg. 1319, pg. 1041
BOULDER BRANDS, INC., pg. 1016, pg. 310
BP CORPORATION NORTH AMERICA INC., pg. 973, pg. 665
BRENNAN INDUSTRIES INC., pg. 1319, pg. 1429
BROADRIDGE FINANCIAL SOLUTIONS INC., pg. 727, pg. 1172
BROCK-MCVEY COMPANY, pg. 1043, pg. 729
BROOKFIELD FINANCIAL PROPERTIES, INC., pg. 1083, pg. 1207
BROTHER INTERNATIONAL CORPORATION - USA, pg. 53, pg. 1046
BRUNSWICK CORPORATION, pg. 1828, pg. 623
BRYANT GRINDER, pg. 1320, pg. 1768
BTU INTERNATIONAL, INC., pg. 1320, pg. 838
BULLHORN, INC., pg. 1233, pg. 792
BURRIS LOGISTICS, pg. 843, pg. 387
BUSINESS BROKERS NETWORK, pg. 135, pg. 1735
BUTLER AMERICA, pg. 366, pg. 370
BUTLER MACHINERY COMPANY, pg. 1321, pg. 1397
BUYERZONE.COM, LLC, pg. 1233, pg. 850
C&D TECHNOLOGIES, INC., pg. 627, pg. 1517
C&H DISTRIBUTORS, LLC, pg. 1044, pg. 1873
C&S WHOLESALE GROCERS, INC., pg. 1016, pg. 1035
CABLEVISION SYSTEMS CORPORATION, pg. 272, pg. 1141
CALAVO GROWERS, INC., pg. 843, pg. 276
CALIBRUS, INC., pg. 368, pg. 25
CALIFORNIA SPORTS, INC., pg. 536, pg. 78
CAMBRIDGE CREDIT COUNSELING CORP., pg. 728, pg. 781
CAMBRIDGE INFORMATION GROUP, INC., pg. 1625, pg. 761
CAMERON VALVES & MEASUREMENT, pg. 1321, pg. 1703
CANADIAN COMMERCIAL CORPORATION, pg. 729, pg. 1931
CANEPA DESIGN GROUP, pg. 167, pg. 278
CANUCKS SPORTS & ENTERTAINMENT, pg. 536, pg. 1910
CAPELLA EDUCATION COMPANY, pg. 599, pg. 931
CARFAX INC., pg. 202, pg. 1777
CARLSON JPM STORE FIXTURES, pg. 369, pg. 919
CAROLINA HURRICANES HOCKEY CLUB, pg. 537, pg. 1386
CBIZ, INC., pg. 733, pg. 1429
CCH INC., pg. 1626, pg. 653
CDS GLOBAL, INC., pg. 370, pg. 704
CEDAR FAIR, L.P., pg. 537, pg. 1471
CENTRAL STEEL & WIRE COMPANY, pg. 74, pg. 569
C.H. HANSON COMPANY, pg. 1322, pg. 636
CHARITY NAVIGATOR, pg. 136, pg. 1071
CHERRY CENTRAL COOPERATIVE, INC., pg. 847, pg. 909
CHICAGO CONVENTION & TOURISM BUREAU, pg. 990, pg. 569
CHICAGO METAL FABRICATORS, INC., pg. 1323, pg. 569
CHICAGO TUBE & IRON CO., pg. 1323, pg. 656
CINCINNATI MUSEUM CENTER INC., pg. 540, pg. 1411
CINTAS CORPORATION, pg. 372, pg. 1411
CIRQUE DU SOLEIL INC., pg. 540, pg. 1954
CITATIONAIR, pg. 1903, pg. 350
CITIZENS FOR GLOBAL SOLUTIONS, pg. 137, pg. 397
CLARK MATERIAL HANDLING COMPANY, pg. 1323, pg. 729
CLAYTON HOLDINGS, INC., pg. 738, pg. 370
CLEAN HARBORS, INC., pg. 376, pg. 839
COGNIZANT TECHNOLOGY SOLUTIONS CORPORATION, pg. 377, pg. 1124
THE COLAD GROUP, INC., pg. 377, pg. 1147
COLLECTORS UNIVERSE INC., pg. 377, pg. 260
COLORADO TOURISM OFFICE, pg. 991, pg. 318
COMCAST SPECTACOR, L.P., pg. 278, pg. 1562
COMMERCIAL METALS COMPANY, pg. 76, pg. 1718
COMTEX NEWS NETWORK, INC., pg. 1236, pg. 1770
CONAGRA FOODS LAMB WESTON, INC., pg. 850, pg. 549
CONCUR TECHNOLOGIES, pg. 1903, pg. 501
CONSEW, pg. 53, pg. 1049
CONSOLIDATED CREDIT COUNSELING SERVICES, INC., pg. 741, pg. 424
CONSTANT CONTACT, INC., pg. 379, pg. 850
CONVERGYS CORPORATION, pg. 379, pg. 1412
CORELOGIC, INC., pg. 1198, pg. 109
CORPORATION SERVICE COMPANY, pg. 380, pg. 390
COSTAR GROUP, INC., pg. 742, pg. 397
CREATIVE BRANCH, pg. 922, pg. 1704
CRITZAS INDUSTRIES, INC., pg. 329, pg. 995
CRYOVAC, INC., pg. 1456, pg. 1615
CUTTER AVIATION, INC., pg. 227, pg. 16
D&S CAR WASH EQUIPMENT CO., pg. 1327, pg. 979
DALLAS CONVENTION & VISITORS BUREAU, pg. 991, pg. 1678
DALLAS MARKET CENTER COMPANY, pg. 78, pg. 1678
DANAHER MOTION, pg. 1327, pg. 1593
DASSAULT FALCON JET CORP., pg. 227, pg. 1122
DATA LISTING SERVICE LLC, pg. 382, pg. 919
DAYTONA BEACH RESORT AREA CONVENTION & VISITORS BUREAU, pg. 991, pg. 420
DEDERT CORPORATION, pg. 1408, pg. 649
DEL-TRON PRECISION, INC., pg. 1328, pg. 337
DE'LONGHI AMERICA INC., pg. 54, pg. 1118
DELUXE CORPORATION, pg. 1634, pg. 964
DENVER CENTER FOR THE PERFORMING ARTS INC., pg. 544, pg. 318
DENVER METRO CONVENTION & VISITORS BUREAU, pg. 991, pg. 318
DES MOINES SYMPHONY ASSOCIATION, pg. 544, pg. 705
DESIGN WITHIN REACH, INC., pg. 923, pg. 216
DESTINATION DC, pg. 991, pg. 398
DEUTZ CORPORATION, pg. 1328, pg. 536
DEVAR, INC., pg. 633, pg. 339
DEVON ENERGY CORPORATION, pg. 975, pg. 1485
THE DIAN FOSSEY GORILLA FUND INTERNATIONAL, pg. 139, pg. 504
DICK CLARK PRODUCTIONS, INC., pg. 281, pg. 273
DIEHL WOODWORKING MACHINERY, INC., pg. 1328, pg. 698
DIGG, INC., pg. 1238, pg. 1224
DIPCRAFT MANUFACTURING COMPANY, pg. 79, pg. 1518
DIRECT HOLDINGS AMERICAS INC., pg. 1636, pg. 1780
DIVING EQUIPMENT & MARKETING ASSOCIATION, pg. 139, pg. 202
DIXON VALVE & COUPLING COMPANY, pg. 1045, pg. 766
THE DOALL COMPANY, pg. 1329, pg. 670
THE DOLAN COMPANY, pg. 1636, pg. 932
DOMINION ENTERPRISES, pg. 1636, pg. 1796
DOUGLAS DYNAMICS, INC., pg. 204, pg. 1874
DOUGLAS-GUARDIAN SERVICES CORPORATION, pg. 388, pg. 1704
DOW JONES & COMPANY, INC., pg. 1637, pg. 1225
DOWNS CRANE & HOIST CO, INC., pg. 1330, pg. 129
DREMEL, pg. 1046, pg. 634
DRIVESAVERS DATA RECOVERY, INC., pg. 388, pg. 168
THE DUN & BRADSTREET CORP., pg. 1637, pg. 1120

First page reference indicates Business Class Edition
Second page reference indicates Geographic Edition

DYNISCO INSTRUMENTS LLC, pg. 1526, pg. 823
DYNTEK, INC., pg. 389, pg. 165
EARLE M. JORGENSEN COMPANY, pg. 80, pg. 142
EASTERN STATES EXPOSITION, pg. 992, pg. 857
EATON'S CROUSE-HINDS, pg. 1296, pg. 1344
EBSCO INDUSTRIES, INC., pg. 1638, pg. 2
EDGAR ONLINE, INC., pg. 746, pg. 776
EDISON INTERNATIONAL, pg. 1941, pg. 194
ELECTION SERVICES CORPORATION, pg. 390, pg. 1161
EMBRAER AIRCRAFT HOLDING INC., pg. 227, pg. 425
EMDEON, INC., pg. 747, pg. 1650
EMERALD EXPOSITIONS, pg. 392, pg. 1352
EMERY-WATERHOUSE COMPANY, pg. 1047, pg. 751
EMPIRE STATE BUILDING COMPANY LLC, pg. 546, pg. 1227
EMUSIC.COM, INC., pg. 1243, pg. 1227
ENCON SAFETY PRODUCTS, pg. 1334, pg. 1705
ENERFAB, INC., pg. 81, pg. 1412
ENGLOBAL CORPORATION, pg. 81, pg. 1705
ENTHONE INC., pg. 1161, pg. 381
EPOCRATES, INC., pg. 1529, pg. 254
EQUIFAX INC., pg. 748, pg. 504
EQUIPMENT DEPOT LTD., pg. 1335, pg. 1749
ESSENTRA COMPONENTS, pg. 1335, pg. 901
EXAMWORKS GROUP, INC., pg. 1529, pg. 505
EXTENDICARE HEALTH SERVICES INC., pg. 1530, pg. 1874
EXTERRAN HOLDINGS, INC., pg. 977, pg. 1705
EXXON MOBIL CORPORATION, pg. 977, pg. 1718
FABREEKA INTERNATIONAL, INC., pg. 1882, pg. 847
FAIR ISAAC CORPORATION, pg. 1247, pg. 955
FASTENAL COMPANY, pg. 396, pg. 966
FEDERAL HOSE MANUFACTURING INC., pg. 1047, pg. 1469
FEDEX EXPRESS CORPORATION, pg. 1908, pg. 1644
FELD ENTERTAINMENT, INC., pg. 547, pg. 458
FERRARI NORTH AMERICA, INC., pg. 171, pg. 1060
FILECONTROL PARTNERS LTD, pg. 1247, pg. 1746
FINANCIAL PACIFIC LEASING, LLC, pg. 753, pg. 1820
FLEETCOR TECHNOLOGIES, INC., pg. 758, pg. 537
FLORIDA DEPARTMENT OF AGRICULTURE & CONSUMER SERVICES - DIVISION OF MARKETING & DEVELOPMENT, pg. 992, pg. 469
FLOWERS FOODS, INC., pg. 855, pg. 541
FOOD SERVICES OF AMERICA, INC., pg. 856, pg. 21
FOREST CITY ENTERPRISES, INC., pg. 1092, pg. 1430
FORKLIFTS OF MINNESOTA, INC., pg. 174, pg. 918
FORT DEARBORN COMPANY, pg. 1457, pg. 610
FORTUNET, INC., pg. 953, pg. 1024
FOX ASSOCIATES, LLC, pg. 549, pg. 997
FOX VALLEY SYMPHONY ASSOCIATION INC., pg. 549, pg. 1852
FRENCH GOVERNMENT TOURIST OFFICE, pg. 992, pg. 1233
FROSTY ACRES BRANDS, INC., pg. 1020, pg. 484
FTI CONSULTING, INC., pg. 760, pg. 478
FURUNO USA, INC., pg. 640, pg. 1819
F.W. BRYCE, INC., pg. 857, pg. 823
G&K SERVICES INC., pg. 693, pg. 949
G4S SECURE SOLUTIONS USA, pg. 399, pg. 436
GARDNER DENVER NASH, pg. 1338, pg. 381
GARFF ENTERPRISES INC., pg. 174, pg. 1758
GE HEALTHCARE, pg. 399, pg. 1765
GEMA USA INC., pg. 1339, pg. 686
GENERAL BEARING CORPORATION, pg. 205, pg. 1350
GENERAL MILLS CANADA CORP., pg. 828, pg. 1926
GENERAL MOTORS COMPANY, pg. 175, pg. 881
GERBER SCIENTIFIC, INC., pg. 1414, pg. 380
GIBBS WIRE & STEEL COMPANY, INC., pg. 1048, pg. 371
GIBRALTAR PACKAGING GROUP, INC., pg. 1459, pg. 1011
GLEASON CORPORATION, pg. 1340, pg. 1335
GLOBAL RESPONSE CORPORATION, pg. 400, pg. 439
GORDON FOOD SERVICE INC., pg. 1021, pg. 913
GOULDS PUMPS, INCORPORATED, pg. 1342, pg. 1341
GOVDELIVERY, INC., pg. 1255, pg. 961
GREAT AMERICAN GROUP, INC., pg. 1394, pg. 308
GREATER BOSTON CONVENTION & VISITORS BUREAU INC., pg. 993, pg. 795
GREATER CINCINNATI CONVENTION & VISITORS BUREAU, pg. 993, pg. 1414
GREATER HOUSTON CONVENTION & VISITORS BUREAU, pg. 993, pg. 1706
GREATER MIAMI CONVENTION & VISITORS BUREAU, pg. 993, pg. 442
GREATER RALEIGH CONVENTION & VISITORS BUREAU, pg. 994, pg. 1387
THE GREATER VANCOUVER CONVENTION & VISITOR BUREAU, pg. 994, pg. 1910
GREEK NATIONAL TOURIST ORGANIZATION, pg. 994, pg. 1236
GREENSBORO CONVENTION & VISITORS BUREAU, pg. 994, pg. 1374
GREGORY POOLE EQUIPMENT COMPANY INC., pg. 85, pg. 1387
GUIDELINE, INC., pg. 402, pg. 1237
GULF OIL LIMITED PARTNERSHIP, pg. 978, pg. 814
GULF STATES TOYOTA, INC., pg. 177, pg. 1707
GUYETTE & DEETER, pg. 1772, pg. 776
H&E EQUIPMENT SERVICES, INC., pg. 85, pg. 742
HACO-ATLANTIC, INC., pg. 1344, pg. 1707
HAECO AMERICAS, pg. 228, pg. 1374
HARBORMASTER MARINE, INC., pg. 1707, pg. 896
HARLAND CLARKE HOLDINGS CORP., pg. 1647, pg. 1741
HARMONIX MUSIC SYSTEMS, INC., pg. 1256, pg. 808
HARSCO CORPORATION, pg. 86, pg. 1519
HAWAII VISITORS & CONVENTION BUREAU, pg. 994, pg. 543
HAWKINS, INC., pg. 1165, pg. 937
HEADWATERS INCORPORATED, pg. 978, pg. 1763
HEALTHPORT, INC., pg. 403, pg. 484
HEARTLAND EXPRESS, INC., pg. 1910, pg. 710
HELMSLEY ENTERPRISES, INC., pg. 1094, pg. 1240
HI-VAC CORPORATION, pg. 56, pg. 1458
THE HIBBERT GROUP, pg. 407, pg. 1126
HICKMAN, WILLIAMS & COMPANY, pg. 87, pg. 1414
HIGH LINER FOODS, pg. 862, pg. 1796
HILL & GRIFFITH COMPANY, pg. 1167, pg. 1414
HIRSCH INTERNATIONAL CORP., pg. 694, pg. 1164
HITACHI KOKI USA, LTD., pg. 1050, pg. 537
HKN, INC., pg. 979, pg. 1745
HOLLYWOOD MEDIA CORP., pg. 1256, pg. 412
HOLMATRO, INC., pg. 1346, pg. 771
HONDA CANADA INC., pg. 179, pg. 1938
HOT SPRINGS CONVENTION & VISITORS BUREAU, pg. 995, pg. 33
HOUGEN MANUFACTURING INC., pg. 1347, pg. 908
THE H.T. HACKNEY COMPANY, pg. 1023, pg. 1637
HUDSON TECHNOLOGIES, INC., pg. 1073, pg. 1320
HUNTSVILLE SYMPHONY ORCHESTRA, pg. 553, pg. 6
HYUNDAI MOTOR AMERICA, pg. 179, pg. 89
ICAHN ENTERPRISES L.P., pg. 1097, pg. 1243
IDEALAB, INC., pg. 1258, pg. 180
IDEO, INC., pg. 411, pg. 178
IFCO SYSTEMS NORTH AMERICA, pg. 411, pg. 1708
IHS AUTOMOTIVE DRIVEN BY POLK, pg. 1652, pg. 907
ILLINOIS BUREAU OF TOURISM, pg. 995, pg. 578
ILLINOIS SYMPHONY ORCHESTRA, pg. 553, pg. 662
IMPREMEDIA LLC, pg. 1652, pg. 133
INDIANAPOLIS CONVENTION & VISITORS ASSOCIATION, pg. 995, pg. 687
INDUSTRIAL DISTRIBUTION GROUP, INC., pg. 413, pg. 1358
INFOGROUP INC., pg. 1652, pg. 1016
INFORMATION TODAY INC., pg. 1653, pg. 1084
INSTITUTION FOOD HOUSE, INC., pg. 864, pg. 1378
INTCOMEX, INC., pg. 416, pg. 443
INTEGRAMED AMERICA, INC., pg. 1546, pg. 1325
INTELLIGRATED, INC., pg. 1349, pg. 1460
INTELLIGRATED SYSTEMS LLC, pg. 1350, pg. 998
INTERACTIVE COMMUNICATIONS INC, pg. 1872, pg. 511
INTERACTIVE DATA PRICING & REFERENCE DATA, INC., pg. 769, pg. 785
INTERIORS BY STEVEN G INC., pg. 929, pg. 459
INTERNATIONAL DECISION SYSTEMS, pg. 419, pg. 938
INTERNATIONAL MONETARY SYSTEMS, LTD., pg. 769, pg. 1884
INTERNATIONAL ROAD DYNAMICS INC., pg. 1912, pg. 1962
INTERNATIONAL SPEEDWAY CORPORATION, pg. 553, pg. 420
INTERSECTIONS INC., pg. 769, pg. 1777
INTERSIL CORPORATION, pg. 647, pg. 146
INVESTMENT SEMINARS, INC., pg. 420, pg. 466
IPAYMENT, INC., pg. 771, pg. 306
IRONPLANET, INC., pg. 1259, pg. 183
IRVING CONVENTION & VISITORS BUREAU, pg. 996, pg. 1720
IRVING OIL CORPORATION, pg. 980, pg. 1038
ISABELLA BANK CORPORATION, pg. 771, pg. 901
ISRAEL MINISTRY OF TOURISM INFORMATION CENTER, pg. 996, pg. 1244
ITALIAN GOVERNMENT TOURIST BOARD-NORTH AMERICA, pg. 996, pg. 1244
ITOCHU INTERNATIONAL INC., pg. 1351, pg. 1245
ITT CORPORATION, pg. 1351, pg. 1354
ITW HI-CONE, pg. 1461, pg. 620
IXIA, pg. 422, pg. 56
JACKSON SYMPHONY ASSOCIATION INC., pg. 554, pg. 1635
JAGUAR LAND ROVER NORTH AMERICA LLC, pg. 180, pg. 1081
JAMAICA TOURIST BOARD, pg. 996, pg. 443
JAMES ALEXANDER CORPORATION, pg. 1461, pg. 1044
JENKINS AUTO SALES OF FLORIDA, pg. 180, pg. 459
JHANE BARNES, INC., pg. 42, pg. 1246
JM FAMILY ENTERPRISES INC., pg. 180, pg. 421
JOHN BUCK COMPANY, pg. 1099, pg. 579
JOHN F. KENNEDY CENTER FOR THE PERFORMING ARTS, pg. 555, pg. 401
JOHNSON MANUFACTURING COMPANY, pg. 1169, pg. 712
JONES DAY, pg. 423, pg. 1431
JOURNAL INC., pg. 1655, pg. 972
JOY GLOBAL, INC., pg. 1351, pg. 1876
KAMAN CORPORATION, pg. 229, pg. 338
KANSAS CITY CONVENTION & VISITORS ASSOCIATION, pg. 996, pg. 984
KANSAS CITY SYMPHONY, pg. 555, pg. 985
THE KAUFMAN CENTER, pg. 556, pg. 1248
KAWASAKI MOTORS CORP., U.S.A., pg. 1708, pg. 111
KEENELAND ASSOCIATION INC., pg. 1477, pg. 730
KENNEDY-WILSON, INC., pg. 1099, pg. 46
KENTUCKY DEPARTMENT OF TOURISM, pg. 996, pg. 728
KIA MOTORS AMERICA INC., pg. 181, pg. 112
KILROY REALTY CORPORATION, pg. 1099, pg. 134
KISSIMMEE-ST. CLOUD CONVENTION & VISITORS BUREAU, pg. 997, pg. 436
KOCH ENTERPRISES, INC., pg. 91, pg. 679
KOMATSU AMERICA INDUSTRIES, LLC, pg. 1353, pg. 656
KOMORI AMERICA CORPORATION, pg. 1353, pg. 656
THE KRAFT HEINZ COMPANY, pg. 870, pg. 1577
KSB INC., pg. 1354, pg. 1802
LANGUAGE LINE SERVICES HOLDINGS, INC., pg. 426, pg. 151
LARKEN ASSOCIATES, pg. 93, pg. 1073
LARRY H. MILLER GROUP OF COMPANIES, pg. 182, pg. 1762
LAS VEGAS CONVENTION & VISITORS AUTHORITY, pg. 997, pg. 1027
LAWSON PRODUCTS, INC., pg. 1355, pg. 580
L.B. FOSTER COMPANY, pg. 1355, pg. 1578
LEDIC MANAGEMENT GROUP, pg. 1100, pg. 1645
LEFRAK ORGANIZATION INC., pg. 1100, pg. 1251
LEGAL SHIELD, pg. 775, pg. 1484
LEGALZOOM.COM, INC., pg. 1261, pg. 96
LEXINGTON PHILHARMONIC SOCIETY, pg. 557, pg. 730
LEXISNEXIS GROUP, pg. 1658, pg. 1446
LEXISNEXIS LITIGATION SOLUTIONS, pg. 1659, pg. 1446
LEXUS DIVISION, pg. 182, pg. 294
LIFELOCK INC., pg. 776, pg. 26
LITTLE GIANT PUMP COMPANY, pg. 1356, pg. 1486
LIVE NATION ENTERTAINMENT, INC., pg. 558, pg. 47
LIVE NATION WORLDWIDE - TIMES SQUARE OFFICE, pg. 558, pg. 1252
LOCAL & WESTERN OF TEXAS, INC., pg. 1026, pg. 1683
LOFFLER BUSINESS SYSTEMS INC., pg. 428, pg. 918
LOS ANGELES CONVENTION & VISITORS BUREAU, pg. 997, pg. 135
LOS ANGELES PHILHARMONIC ASSOCIATION, pg. 559, pg. 135
LOUISIANA PHILHARMONIC ORCHESTRA, pg. 559, pg. 747
LOUISVILLE CONVENTION & VISITORS BUREAU, pg. 998, pg. 736
LUFKIN INDUSTRIES, INC., pg. 1357, pg. 1726
LUSTER-ON PRODUCTS, INC., pg. 1171, pg. 845
LYNCH TECHNOLOGIES, INC., pg. 1357, pg. 526
MADISON SQUARE GARDEN NETWORK, pg. 297, pg. 1255
MAKINO INC., pg. 1358, pg. 1461
MANITEX INTERNATIONAL, INC., pg. 1358, pg. 559
THE MANITOWOC COMPANY, INC., pg. 1358, pg. 1868
MANITOWOC ICE, INC., pg. 58, pg. 1868
MAPQUEST, INC., pg. 1265, pg. 321
MARC-MICHAELS INTERIOR DESIGN, INC., pg. 934, pg.

480
MARCHEX, INC., *pg.* 1395, *pg.* 1837
MARITZ INC., *pg.* 1914, *pg.* 977
MARLEY ENGINEERED PRODUCTS, *pg.* 1074, *pg.* 1612
MARMON/KEYSTONE CORPORATION, *pg.* 1359, *pg.* 1519
MARTINDALE-HUBBELL, INC., *pg.* 1662, *pg.* 1095
MASERATI NORTH AMERICA, INC., *pg.* 183, *pg.* 1060
MASSACHUSETTS CONVENTION CENTER AUTHORITY, *pg.* 561, *pg.* 798
MASSACHUSETTS OFFICE OF TRAVEL & TOURISM, *pg.* 998, *pg.* 798
MATHESON VALLEY, *pg.* 981, *pg.* 1456
MATRIX INTEGRATION LLC, *pg.* 430, *pg.* 692
MAXIMUS, INC., *pg.* 780, *pg.* 1799
MAYFRAN INTERNATIONAL, INC., *pg.* 1359, *pg.* 1432
MAYO PERFORMING ARTS CENTER, *pg.* 561, *pg.* 1089
MAZDA NORTH AMERICAN OPERATIONS, *pg.* 183, *pg.* 113
MEDASSETS INC., *pg.* 1561, *pg.* 484
MEDIABISTRO, INC., *pg.* 1266, *pg.* 1258
MEGATRAX PRODUCTION MUSIC, INC., *pg.* 297, *pg.* 167
MERCEDES-BENZ USA, LLC, *pg.* 184, *pg.* 514
MERCHANT & EVANS, INC., *pg.* 97, *pg.* 1048
MERROW MACHINE COMPANY, *pg.* 58, *pg.* 819
MESTEK, INC., *pg.* 1074, *pg.* 857
METALS USA, INC., *pg.* 97, *pg.* 425
METROPOLITAN PIER & EXPOSITION AUTHORITY, *pg.* 562, *pg.* 581
METROPOLITAN TUCSON CONVENTION & VISITORS BUREAU, *pg.* 998, *pg.* 27
METZGAR CONVEYOR COMPANY, *pg.* 1360, *pg.* 875
MEXICO TOURISM BOARD, *pg.* 998, *pg.* 136
MFV EXPOSITIONS, LLC, *pg.* 434, *pg.* 1101
MHI INJECTION MOLDING MACHINERY, INC., *pg.* 1886, *pg.* 620
MICHIGAN BLUEBERRY GROWERS ASSOCIATION, *pg.* 147, *pg.* 886
MICROBILT CORPORATION, *pg.* 782, *pg.* 534
MIDAS, INC., *pg.* 212, *pg.* 620
MIDAS INTERNATIONAL, INC., *pg.* 212, *pg.* 620
MIKE KASHTAN'S SUPERIOR AUTO SALES, *pg.* 185, *pg.* 458
MILE MARKER INTERNATIONAL INC., *pg.* 213, *pg.* 459
MILLER INDUSTRIES, INC., *pg.* 185, *pg.* 1655
MITSUBISHI FUSO TRUCK OF AMERICA, INC., *pg.* 185, *pg.* 1045
MITSUBISHI INTERNATIONAL CORPORATION, *pg.* 185, *pg.* 1260
MITSUBISHI MOTORS NORTH AMERICA, INC., *pg.* 185, *pg.* 75
MOD-PAC CORP., *pg.* 1665, *pg.* 1150
MODERN TRACK MACHINERY, *pg.* 98, *pg.* 610
MODERN WELDING COMPANY, INC., *pg.* 1363, *pg.* 739
MOOD MEDIA, *pg.* 298, *pg.* 1616
MORNINGSTAR, INC., *pg.* 784, *pg.* 583
MOTION INDUSTRIES, INC., *pg.* 213, *pg.* 3
MOTOR TREND AUTO SHOWS, LLC, *pg.* 564, *pg.* 1537
MOTORCAR PARTS OF AMERICA, INC., *pg.* 213, *pg.* 295
MSC INDUSTRIAL DIRECT CO., INC., *pg.* 1057, *pg.* 1181
MURRY'S, INC., *pg.* 882, *pg.* 780
MUSICAL ARTS ASSOCIATION, *pg.* 565, *pg.* 1433
NACCO INDUSTRIES, INC., *pg.* 1174, *pg.* 1433
NATIONAL ARTS CENTRE CORPORATION, *pg.* 566, *pg.* 1932
NATIONAL BULK EQUIPMENT, INC., *pg.* 1479, *pg.* 892
NATIONAL OILWELL VARCO, INC., *pg.* 1364, *pg.* 1712
NBA PROPERTIES, INC., *pg.* 569, *pg.* 1120
NETJETS INC., *pg.* 1917, *pg.* 1442
NETSMART TECHNOLOGIES, INC., *pg.* 445, *pg.* 1163
NETSUITE, INC., *pg.* 1270, *pg.* 255
NETWOLVES CORPORATION, *pg.* 1271, *pg.* 474
NEW ENGLAND MACHINERY, INC., *pg.* 1364, *pg.* 415
NEW MEXICO TOURISM DEPARTMENT, *pg.* 1001, *pg.* 1136
NEW SMYRNA BEACH AREA VISITORS BUREAU, *pg.* 1001, *pg.* 451
NEW YORK RANGERS HOCKEY CLUB, *pg.* 570, *pg.* 1269
NEWMARK GRUBB KNIGHT FRANK, *pg.* 1106, *pg.* 1271
NICE-PAK PRODUCTS, INC., *pg.* 1465, *pg.* 1319
NIELSEN BUSINESS MEDIA, *pg.* 1671, *pg.* 1272
THE NIELSEN COMPANY B.V., *pg.* 1671, *pg.* 1272
NIGHTINGALE-CONANT CORPORATION, *pg.* 152, *pg.* 670
NORTH SHORE PHILHARMONIC ORCHESTRA, *pg.* 571, *pg.* 816
NORTHBROOK SYMPHONY ORCHESTRA INC., *pg.* 571, *pg.* 641
NOSHOK INC., *pg.* 1366, *pg.* 1406
NRG ENERGY, INC., *pg.* 1948, *pg.* 1712
NTT DATA, *pg.* 447, *pg.* 799
NUANCE COMMUNICATIONS, INC., *pg.* 447, *pg.* 806
NUANCE TRANSCRIPTION, *pg.* 1576, *pg.* 516
NUCOR CORPORATION, *pg.* 101, *pg.* 1368
NUTTING, *pg.* 1366, *pg.* 1626
NYC & COMPANY, INC., *pg.* 1002, *pg.* 1274
O.A. NEWTON & SON CO, *pg.* 1366, *pg.* 387
O'BRIEN AUTOMOTIVE TEAM, *pg.* 187, *pg.* 663
O'GARA COACH LA JOLLA, *pg.* 187, *pg.* 120
OIL-DRI CORPORATION OF AMERICA, *pg.* 1480, *pg.* 586
OKLAHOMA CITY CONVENTION & VISITORS BUREAU, *pg.* 1002, *pg.* 1487
OKLAHOMA TOURISM & RECREATION DEPARTMENT, *pg.* 1003, *pg.* 1487
OKUMA AMERICA CORPORATION, *pg.* 1366, *pg.* 1368
OLD FASHION FOODS, INC., *pg.* 1028, *pg.* 525
OLYMPIC STEEL INC., *pg.* 101, *pg.* 1433
OMAHA COMMUNITY PLAYHOUSE, *pg.* 572, *pg.* 1017
OMTOOL, LTD., *pg.* 449, *pg.* 782
OPENTEXT, *pg.* 1272, *pg.* 1956
OPERA AMERICA, *pg.* 572, *pg.* 1274
ORLANDO/ORANGE COUNTY CONVENTION & VISITORS BUREAU, INC., *pg.* 1003, *pg.* 455
ORTHOSYNETICS, INC., *pg.* 791, *pg.* 1657
OTTAWA SENATORS HOCKEY CLUB, *pg.* 573, *pg.* 1921
OWEN INDUSTRIES, INC., *pg.* 102, *pg.* 702
P. KAY METAL SUPPLY INC., *pg.* 1176, *pg.* 137
PALLADIUM THEATER, INC., *pg.* 573, *pg.* 463
PALM BEACH COUNTY CONVENTION & VISITORS BUREAU, *pg.* 1003, *pg.* 479
PALM SPRINGS DESERT RESORTS CONVENTION & VISITORS AUTHORITY, *pg.* 1003, *pg.* 187
PARAGON TECHNOLOGIES, INC., *pg.* 1367, *pg.* 1528
PAREXEL INTERNATIONAL CORPORATION, *pg.* 1580, *pg.* 853
PBI/GORDON CORPORATION, *pg.* 1176, *pg.* 985
PDI, INC., *pg.* 1580, *pg.* 1104
PEIRCE-PHELPS, INC., *pg.* 1075, *pg.* 1568
PENFLEX, INC., *pg.* 104, *pg.* 1534
PENSACOLA BAY AREA CONVENTION & VISITORS BUREAU, *pg.* 1004, *pg.* 458
PENTON MEDIA, INC., *pg.* 1676, *pg.* 719
PENTON MEDIA, INC., *pg.* 1676, *pg.* 1277
PEPSI-COLA NORTH AMERICA, *pg.* 259, *pg.* 1327
PERFORMANCE FOOD GROUP COMPANY, LLC, *pg.* 1030, *pg.* 1803
PERLA LICHI LLC, *pg.* 940, *pg.* 418
PERRY VIDEX LLC, *pg.* 1368, *pg.* 1072
PFSWEB, INC., *pg.* 1275, *pg.* 1733
PHILADELPHIA CONVENTION & VISITORS BUREAU, *pg.* 1004, *pg.* 1568
THE PHILADELPHIA ORCHESTRA ASSOCIATION, *pg.* 575, *pg.* 1569
PHILHARMONIC SOCIETY OF NORTHEASTERN PENNSYLVANIA, *pg.* 575, *pg.* 1594
PHILHARMONIC SYMPHONY SOCIETY OF NEW YORK INC., *pg.* 575, *pg.* 1282
PINELLAS SUNCOAST TRANSIT AUTHORITY, *pg.* 1919, *pg.* 463
PIVOTAL RESOURCES, INC., *pg.* 455, *pg.* 304
PLAINS ALL AMERICAN PIPELINE, L.P., *pg.* 983, *pg.* 1712
POLAR COVE, INC., *pg.* 1275, *pg.* 1607
PORSCHE CARS NORTH AMERICA, INC., *pg.* 189, *pg.* 518
PORT AUTHORITY OF NEW YORK & NEW JERSEY, *pg.* 1919, *pg.* 1283
POSITIVELY CLEVELAND, *pg.* 1004, *pg.* 1434
POWER EQUIPMENT COMPANY INC, *pg.* 1369, *pg.* 1637
POWERSECURE INTERNATIONAL, INC., *pg.* 105, *pg.* 1392
POWIN CORPORATION, *pg.* 1369, *pg.* 1509
PRAB, INC., *pg.* 1369, *pg.* 894
PRATT & LAMBERT PAINTS, *pg.* 1446, *pg.* 1434
PRECIPART, *pg.* 1370, *pg.* 1160
PRECISION ROLL GRINDERS, INC., *pg.* 1370, *pg.* 1514
PRECISION VALVE CORPORATION, *pg.* 1060, *pg.* 1357
PRICEWATERHOUSECOOPERS LLP, *pg.* 795, *pg.* 1283
PROPPER MANUFACTURING COMPANY, INC., *pg.* 1586, *pg.* 1175
PROVIDENCE PERFORMING ARTS CENTER, *pg.* 578, *pg.* 1607
PS BUSINESS PARKS, INC., *pg.* 1108, *pg.* 98
PTA CORPORATION, *pg.* 1888, *pg.* 368
PUBLISHERS CIRCULATION FULFILLMENT INC., *pg.* 1679, *pg.* 780
PURAFIL, INC., *pg.* 333, *pg.* 530
PURVIS BEARING SERVICE LTD., *pg.* 1371, *pg.* 1686
Q A GROUP LLC., *pg.* 1427, *pg.* 89
QUAKER VALLEY FOODS INC., *pg.* 1031, *pg.* 1570
QUEST SAFETY PRODUCTS, INC., *pg.* 1371, *pg.* 689
QUINCY SYMPHONY ORCHESTRA ASSOCIATION, *pg.* 578, *pg.* 653
RACETRAC PETROLEUM, INC., *pg.* 983, *pg.* 519
RAINMAKER SYSTEMS INC., *pg.* 458, *pg.* 58
R.D. BITZER CO. INC., *pg.* 106, *pg.* 1515
RE/MAX INTERNATIONAL, INC., *pg.* 1109, *pg.* 322
RECORDED BOOKS, LLC, *pg.* 1680, *pg.* 775
REED EXHIBITIONS USA, *pg.* 460, *pg.* 364
REGISTER.COM, INC., *pg.* 1277, *pg.* 434
RELIANCE STEEL & ALUMINUM CO., *pg.* 1371, *pg.* 139
REMA TIP TOP/NORTH AMERICA, INC., *pg.* 1889, *pg.* 1099
RENTZEL PUMP MANUFACTURING, LP, *pg.* 707, *pg.* 1726
RESCO PRODUCTS GREENSBORO, *pg.* 107, *pg.* 1375
RESEARCH SOLUTIONS, INC., *pg.* 1680, *pg.* 85
RHODE ISLAND COALITION AGAINST DOMESTIC VIOLENCE, *pg.* 155, *pg.* 1609
RICHMOND FORD, *pg.* 189, *pg.* 1803
RINNAI AMERICA CORP., *pg.* 1076, *pg.* 538
RITE-HITE HOLDING CORPORATION, *pg.* 1372, *pg.* 1880
ROCHESTER PHILHARMONIC ORCHESTRA INC., *pg.* 579, *pg.* 1337
ROFIN-SINAR TECHNOLOGIES, INC., *pg.* 668, *pg.* 904
ROLLEM CORPORATION OF AMERICA, *pg.* 1372, *pg.* 43
ROSARIO SALAZAR DESIGN INC., *pg.* 941, *pg.* 418
ROUNDABOUT THEATRE COMPANY, *pg.* 579, *pg.* 1287
ROUNDER RECORDS CORPORATION, *pg.* 307, *pg.* 807
RUSH ENTERPRISES INC., *pg.* 189, *pg.* 1728
RUSSEL METALS INC., *pg.* 1180, *pg.* 1928
RYERSON INC., *pg.* 1373, *pg.* 589
SACRAMENTO KINGS, *pg.* 579, *pg.* 197
SAFEGUARD SCIENTIFICS, INC., *pg.* 464, *pg.* 1592
SAFER PRINTS INC., *pg.* 32, *pg.* 1098
SAFWAY SERVICES, LLC, *pg.* 109, *pg.* 1898
SAGE SOFTWARE, INC., *pg.* 464, *pg.* 116
SAMMONS ENTERPRISES, INC., *pg.* 1373, *pg.* 1686
SAN ANTONIO CONVENTION & VISITORS BUREAU, *pg.* 1004, *pg.* 1742
SAN DIEGO CONVENTION & VISITORS BUREAU, *pg.* 1004, *pg.* 208
SAN FRANCISCO TRAVEL ASSOCIATION, *pg.* 1005, *pg.* 227
SAN JOSE CONVENTION/VISITORS BUREAU, *pg.* 1005, *pg.* 250
SARASOTA CONVENTION & VISITORS BUREAU, *pg.* 1005, *pg.* 467
SARATOGA PERFORMING ARTS CENTER, INC., *pg.* 581, *pg.* 1340
THE SCHMIDT GROUP, INC., *pg.* 1374, *pg.* 1618
SCIQUEST, INC., *pg.* 468, *pg.* 1361
SEALING DEVICES INC., *pg.* 1889, *pg.* 1173
SEATTLE CONVENTION & VISITORS BUREAU, *pg.* 1005, *pg.* 1839
SEATTLE THEATRE GROUP, *pg.* 582, *pg.* 1840
SECO/WARWICK CORPORATION, *pg.* 1076, *pg.* 1552
SEELEY INTERNATIONAL AMERICAS, *pg.* 1076, *pg.* 19
SENIOR MARKET SALES, INC., *pg.* 1217, *pg.* 1018
SEQUA CORPORATION, *pg.* 1180, *pg.* 1290
SETCO SALES COMPANY, *pg.* 1061, *pg.* 1426
SGK, *pg.* 1686, *pg.* 590
SHELL OIL COMPANY, *pg.* 984, *pg.* 1714
SHERLOQ SOLUTIONS, *pg.* 156, *pg.* 475
SIEMENS, *pg.* 1376, *pg.* 1466
SIGHTLINE SYSTEMS CORPORATION, *pg.* 469, *pg.* 1780
SIMON PROPERTY GROUP, INC., *pg.* 1112, *pg.* 690
SIMS METAL MANAGEMENT, *pg.* 1396, *pg.* 590
SINGER SEWING COMPANY, *pg.* 698, *pg.* 1639
SITEL CORPORATION, *pg.* 470, *pg.* 1654
SOLUTIONS OFFICE INTERIORS, INC., *pg.* 112, *pg.* 250
SONY MUSIC ENTERTAINMENT, *pg.* 309, *pg.* 1294
SOUTH AFRICAN TOURISM, *pg.* 1005, *pg.* 1294
SOUTH CENTRAL COMMUNICATIONS CORPORATION, *pg.* 310, *pg.* 679
SOUTH DAKOTA SYMPHONY ORCHESTRA, *pg.* 584, *pg.* 1625
SOUTHEAST TOURISM SOCIETY, *pg.* 1006, *pg.* 539
SOUTHEAST TOYOTA DISTRIBUTORS, LLC, *pg.* 190, *pg.* 421
SOUTHERN PIPE & SUPPLY CO., INC., *pg.* 112, *pg.* 970
SPA FINDER, INC., *pg.* 1113, *pg.* 1295

SPECTRUM GROUP INTERNATIONAL, INC., *pg.* 472, *pg.* 116
SPELNA, INC., *pg.* 157, *pg.* 1782
SPENCER FLUID POWER, *pg.* 1889, *pg.* 1822
SPRAYING SYSTEMS CO., *pg.* 1063, *pg.* 670
SRDS, INC., *pg.* 1688, *pg.* 657
ST. AUGUSTINE, PONTE VEDRA & THE BEACHES VISITORS & CONVENTION BUREAU, *pg.* 1006, *pg.* 461
ST. LOUIS CONVENTION & VISITORS COMMISSION, *pg.* 1006, *pg.* 1003
STAGES PRODUCTIONS, INC., *pg.* 585, *pg.* 468
STANDARD MOTOR PRODUCTS, INC., *pg.* 218, *pg.* 1176
STEFANINI TECHTEAM GLOBAL, INC., *pg.* 476, *pg.* 907
STRATUS TECHNOLOGIES, INC., *pg.* 477, *pg.* 832
THE STREET, INC., *pg.* 1283, *pg.* 1296
SUBARU OF AMERICA, INC., *pg.* 191, *pg.* 1050
SUBURBAN PROPANE PARTNERS, L.P., *pg.* 113, *pg.* 1132
SUCCESSFACTORS, INC., *pg.* 477, *pg.* 228
SUMNER COMMUNICATIONS INC., *pg.* 1690, *pg.* 338
SUMTOTAL SYSTEMS, INC., *pg.* 477, *pg.* 429
SUNBEAM TELEVISION CORP., *pg.* 311, *pg.* 447
SUNBELT BUSINESS ADVISORS NETWORK, LLC, *pg.* 806, *pg.* 1456
SUNCOR ENERGY INC., *pg.* 985, *pg.* 1905
SUNRISE BRANDS, LLC, *pg.* 33, *pg.* 140
SUPPLY TECHNOLOGIES LLC, *pg.* 1064, *pg.* 1436
SUPPORTSAVE SOLUTIONS, INC., *pg.* 478, *pg.* 911
SURETY, INC., *pg.* 1283, *pg.* 1799
SWISS AMERICA TRADING CORPORATION, *pg.* 808, *pg.* 20
SWITZERLAND TOURISM, *pg.* 1006, *pg.* 1297
TAMPA BAY & CO., *pg.* 1007, *pg.* 476
TASC, INC., *pg.* 1431, *pg.* 1777
TCI PRECISION METALS, INC., *pg.* 1380, *pg.* 95
TCR CORPORATION, *pg.* 1380, *pg.* 944
TEAM HEALTH HOLDINGS, INC., *pg.* 1601, *pg.* 1639
TECHNOLOGY MARKETING CORP., *pg.* 1691, *pg.* 364
TECK RESOURCES LIMITED, *pg.* 1183, *pg.* 1912
TEJON RANCH COMPANY, *pg.* 1116, *pg.* 122
TENDER CORPORATION, *pg.* 1601, *pg.* 1035
THE TENNIS CHANNEL, INC., *pg.* 679, *pg.* 276
TEREX CORPORATION, *pg.* 1381, *pg.* 384
TESLA MOTORS, INC., *pg.* 191, *pg.* 178
TESSCO TECHNOLOGIES, INC., *pg.* 679, *pg.* 773
TEXPAK INC., *pg.* 1470, *pg.* 1161
THEATER LEAGUE INC., *pg.* 587, *pg.* 986
THEO KALOMIRAKIS THEATERS, *pg.* 115, *pg.* 1298
THOMAS ENGINEERING INC., *pg.* 1382, *pg.* 619
THOMPSON INTERNATIONAL INC., *pg.* 1382, *pg.* 729
THOMSON ELITE, *pg.* 484, *pg.* 72
THOMSON REUTERS - CORPORATE HEADQUARTERS, *pg.* 1693, *pg.* 1299
THOMSON REUTERS CORPORATION, *pg.* 1693, *pg.* 1944
TITAN MACHINERY INC., *pg.* 1383, *pg.* 1398
TIX CORPORATION, *pg.* 588, *pg.* 281
TM STUDIOS, INC., *pg.* 588, *pg.* 1689
TORONTO CONVENTION & VISITORS ASSOCIATION, *pg.* 1007, *pg.* 1945
TOUCHSTONE ENERGY COOPERATIVES, *pg.* 1953, *pg.* 1775
TOYOTA MOTOR SALES, U.S.A., INC., *pg.* 193, *pg.* 296
TRADE COMMISSION OF SPAIN, *pg.* 158, *pg.* 1304
TRAMMELL CROW COMPANY, *pg.* 1116, *pg.* 1689
TRAMMO, *pg.* 986, *pg.* 1304
TRANSLATIONS.COM, *pg.* 485, *pg.* 1304
TRAVEL PORTLAND, *pg.* 1008, *pg.* 1507
TRI STAR ENERGY, LLC, *pg.* 986, *pg.* 1655
TRICORBRAUN, *pg.* 1471, *pg.* 1004
TRUVEN HEALTH ANALYTICS, *pg.* 1696, *pg.* 867
TTC AMERIDIAL, LLC, *pg.* 486, *pg.* 593
TUBULAR STEEL INC., *pg.* 117, *pg.* 1004
TUPPERWARE BRANDS CORPORATION, *pg.* 1139, *pg.* 456
TWIN DISC, INCORPORATED, *pg.* 220, *pg.* 1889
ULTIMATE TECHNOLOGY CORPORATION, *pg.* 486, *pg.* 1349
UNIFIED SIGNAL, INC., *pg.* 682, *pg.* 1822
UNISYS CORPORATION, *pg.* 487, *pg.* 1517
UNITED ONLINE, INC., *pg.* 1286, *pg.* 308
UNITED REFINING COMPANY, *pg.* 986, *pg.* 1590
UNITED RENTALS, INC., *pg.* 1386, *pg.* 350
U.S. TSUBAKI, INC., *pg.* 221, *pg.* 670
USA FINANCIAL, *pg.* 815, *pg.* 864
USA TECHNOLOGIES, INC., *pg.* 815, *pg.* 1550
THE UTICA SYMPHONY ORCHESTRA, *pg.* 590, *pg.* 1347
VALERO ENERGY CORPORATION, *pg.* 986, *pg.* 1743
VALMONT INDUSTRIES, INC., *pg.* 1387, *pg.* 1019
VAN SON HOLLAND INK CORPORATION OF AMERICA, *pg.* 487, *pg.* 1169
VARESE SARABANDE RECORDS, INC., *pg.* 1789, *pg.* 281
VERISK ANALYTICS, INC., *pg.* 1222, *pg.* 1076
VERTICALRESPONSE, INC., *pg.* 489, *pg.* 230
VIAD CORP., *pg.* 816, *pg.* 20
VIBRA SCREW INC., *pg.* 1387, *pg.* 1126
VICTORIA LESSER, INC., *pg.* 946, *pg.* 436
VINTAGE PARTS, *pg.* 119, *pg.* 1854
VIP FOODSERVICE, *pg.* 908, *pg.* 545
VIRGINIA TOURISM AUTHORITY, *pg.* 1010, *pg.* 1804
VISITING NURSE ASSOCIATION OF CENTRAL JERSEY, *pg.* 1607, *pg.* 1114
VISITING NURSE ASSOCIATION OF STATEN ISLAND, *pg.* 1607, *pg.* 1343
VOLKSWAGEN GROUP OF AMERICA, INC., *pg.* 194, *pg.* 1785
VOLVO CARS OF NORTH AMERICA LLC, *pg.* 195, *pg.* 1117
VOLVO PENTA OF THE AMERICAS, INC., *pg.* 1712, *pg.* 1778
WARNER BROS. RECORDS, INC., *pg.* 1791, *pg.* 55
WARRANTECH CORPORATION, *pg.* 491, *pg.* 1668
WATSCO INC., *pg.* 1078, *pg.* 417
WEATHERFORD PRODUCTION OPTIMIZATION, *pg.* 987, *pg.* 1725
WELCOME FUNDS, INC., *pg.* 1223, *pg.* 413
WELOCALIZE, INC., *pg.* 1289, *pg.* 769
WESCO FINANCIAL CORPORATION, *pg.* 821, *pg.* 181
WESCO INTERNATIONAL INC., *pg.* 687, *pg.* 1582
WESTERN FAMILY HOLDING CO., INC., *pg.* 1037, *pg.* 1509
WESTROCK COMPANY, *pg.* 1472, *pg.* 1805
WHITE CASTLE MANAGEMENT CO., *pg.* 1756, *pg.* 1444
THE WILLAMETTE VALLEY COMPANY, *pg.* 1186, *pg.* 1497
WILLIAMSPORT SYMPHONY ORCHESTRA, *pg.* 592, *pg.* 1595
WINDOWS AND WALLS UNLIMITED, INC., *pg.* 946, *pg.* 1343
WIS INTERNATIONAL, *pg.* 493, *pg.* 211
WISCONSIN DELLS VISITOR & CONVENTION BUREAU, *pg.* 1011, *pg.* 1899
WMS INDUSTRIES INC., *pg.* 593, *pg.* 666
THE WOLF MACHINE CO., *pg.* 1389, *pg.* 1427
WOLFTRAP FOUNDATION FOR THE PERFORMING ARTS, *pg.* 594, *pg.* 1809
WOODRUFF ARTS CENTER, *pg.* 595, *pg.* 524
WORD OF LIFE FELLOWSHIP, INC., *pg.* 161, *pg.* 1341
WORLD WRESTLING ENTERTAINMENT, INC., *pg.* 595, *pg.* 380
W.P. CAREY & CO., LLC, *pg.* 823, *pg.* 1315
WRIGHT EXPRESS CORPORATION, *pg.* 493, *pg.* 753
W.W. GRAINGER, INC., *pg.* 1390, *pg.* 625
W.W. WALLWORK, INC., *pg.* 195, *pg.* 1398
THE W.W. WILLIAMS COMPANY, *pg.* 1390, *pg.* 1444
XEROX CORPORATION, *pg.* 494, *pg.* 365
XO GROUP INC., *pg.* 1289, *pg.* 1316
XPO LOGISTICS, INC., *pg.* 1931, *pg.* 350
YAHOO! CANADA CO., *pg.* 1289, *pg.* 1947
YAMAHA MOTOR CORPORATION USA, *pg.* 1713, *pg.* 76
YANMAR AMERICA CORPORATION, *pg.* 196, *pg.* 482
YELP! INC., *pg.* 1291, *pg.* 235
ZIMMERMAN-MCDONALD MACHINERY, INC., *pg.* 1391, *pg.* 1005
ZONES, INC., *pg.* 1292, *pg.* 1813

7514 - Passenger Car Rental

ALAMO RENT-A-CAR, LLC, *pg.* 1897, *pg.* 1489
AUTO EUROPE, LLC, *pg.* 1900, *pg.* 751
AVIS BUDGET GROUP, INC., *pg.* 1900, *pg.* 1102
AVIS RENT A CAR SYSTEM, LLC, *pg.* 165, *pg.* 1102
BUDGET RENT A CAR SYSTEM, INC., *pg.* 1901, *pg.* 1102
DOLLAR THRIFTY AUTOMOTIVE GROUP, INC., *pg.* 169, *pg.* 1489
THE HERTZ CORPORATION, *pg.* 1911, *pg.* 450
HERTZ GLOBAL HOLDINGS, INC., *pg.* 179, *pg.* 450
NATIONAL CAR RENTAL, *pg.* 1916, *pg.* 1490
RENT-A-WRECK OF AMERICA, INC., *pg.* 1921, *pg.* 773
STEVE FOLEY CADILLAC, *pg.* 190, *pg.* 641
ZIPCAR, INC., *pg.* 1931, *pg.* 810

7515 - Passenger Car Leasing

ALLY FINANCIAL INC., *pg.* 711, *pg.* 878
AUTOMOTIVE RESOURCES INTERNATIONAL (ARI), *pg.* 1900, *pg.* 1090
BEUCKMAN FORD INC., *pg.* 166, *pg.* 973
ENTERPRISE HOLDINGS, INC., *pg.* 1906, *pg.* 996
EXECUTIVE CAR LEASING CO., *pg.* 1907, *pg.* 130
FCA US LLC, *pg.* 170, *pg.* 868
THE HERTZ CORPORATION, *pg.* 1911, *pg.* 450
MIKE ALBERT LEASING, INC., *pg.* 185, *pg.* 1417
THE MOTORLEASE CORPORATION, *pg.* 1916, *pg.* 349
WHEELS INC., *pg.* 1931, *pg.* 607

7519 - Utility Trailer & Recreational Vehicle Rental

AMERCO, *pg.* 1898, *pg.* 1031
AUTOMOTIVE RESOURCES INTERNATIONAL (ARI), *pg.* 1900, *pg.* 1090
AVIS BUDGET GROUP, INC., *pg.* 1900, *pg.* 1102
BUDGET RENT A CAR SYSTEM, INC., *pg.* 1901, *pg.* 1102
DAVE SYVERSON INC., *pg.* 168, *pg.* 915
EXECUTIVE CAR LEASING CO., *pg.* 1907, *pg.* 130
MIKE ALBERT LEASING, INC., *pg.* 185, *pg.* 1417
MR. ROOTER CORPORATION, *pg.* 1057, *pg.* 1749
NATIONAL TRUCK LEASING SYSTEM, *pg.* 1916, *pg.* 649
PENSKE CORPORATION, *pg.* 188, *pg.* 873
PENSKE LOGISTICS, LLC, *pg.* 188, *pg.* 1584
PENSKE TRUCK LEASING COMPANY, L.P., *pg.* 188, *pg.* 1585
RENT-A-WRECK OF AMERICA, INC., *pg.* 1921, *pg.* 773
RUSH ENTERPRISES INC., *pg.* 189, *pg.* 1728
RYDER SYSTEM, INC., *pg.* 1922, *pg.* 446
U-HAUL INTERNATIONAL, INC., *pg.* 1926, *pg.* 20
UNITED RENTALS, *pg.* 1386, *pg.* 24
WHEELS INC., *pg.* 1931, *pg.* 607
XTRA LEASE LLC, *pg.* 195, *pg.* 1005

7521 - Automobile Parking

EDISON PROPERTIES, LLC, *pg.* 1906, *pg.* 1096
MASSACHUSETTS CONVENTION CENTER AUTHORITY, *pg.* 561, *pg.* 798
SP PLUS CORPORATION, *pg.* 190, *pg.* 590

7532 - Top, Body, Upholstery Repair Shops & Paint Shops

ARMORED AUTOGROUP INC., *pg.* 199, *pg.* 342
CANEPA DESIGN GROUP, *pg.* 167, *pg.* 278
CARSTAR, *pg.* 168, *pg.* 718
DENT WIZARD INTERNATIONAL CORP., *pg.* 204, *pg.* 973
MAACO FRANCHISING, INC., *pg.* 211, *pg.* 1367
PRECISION AUTO CARE, INC., *pg.* 215, *pg.* 1787
RENNTECH, INC., *pg.* 216, *pg.* 436
TUFFY ASSOCIATES CORPORATION, *pg.* 220, *pg.* 1477

7533 - Automotive Exhaust System Repair Shops

CORSA PERFORMANCE, *pg.* 203, *pg.* 1406
MIDAS, INC., *pg.* 212, *pg.* 620
MIDAS INTERNATIONAL, INC., *pg.* 212, *pg.* 620
MONRO MUFFLER BRAKE, INC., *pg.* 213, *pg.* 1336
TUFFY ASSOCIATES CORPORATION, *pg.* 220, *pg.* 1477

7534 - Tire Retreading & Repair Shops

LES SCHWAB TIRE CENTERS OF OREGON, INC., *pg.* 210, *pg.* 1508

7536 - Automotive Glass Replacement Shops

AUTO DRIVEAWAY CO., *pg.* 1900, *pg.* 566
GREASE MONKEY INTERNATIONAL, INC., *pg.* 84, *pg.* 331
JIFFY LUBE INTERNATIONAL, INC., *pg.* 209, *pg.* 1709
STANDARD BENT GLASS CORPORATION, *pg.* 218, *pg.* 1519

First page reference indicates Business Class Edition
Second page reference indicates Geographic Edition

7537 - Automotive Transmission Repair Shops

AAMCO TRANSMISSIONS, INC., *pg.* 197, *pg.* 1540
LEE MYLES ASSOCIATES CORPORATION, *pg.* 210, *pg.* 1584
MORAN INDUSTRIES, INC., *pg.* 213, *pg.* 632

7538 - General Automotive Repair Shops

ADVANCE AUTO PARTS, INC., *pg.* 197, *pg.* 1805
CROWLEY AUTO GROUP, *pg.* 168, *pg.* 340
DIMMITT LUXURY MOTORS, *pg.* 169, *pg.* 416
FAIRWAY FORD LINCOLN, *pg.* 170, *pg.* 1617
FLEETPRIDE, INC., *pg.* 205, *pg.* 1747
THE GOODYEAR TIRE & RUBBER COMPANY, *pg.* 1883, *pg.* 1401
JOHN EAGLE HONDA OF HOUSTON, *pg.* 180, *pg.* 1709
KELLEY AUTOMOTIVE GROUP, *pg.* 181, *pg.* 680
LEE MYLES ASSOCIATES CORPORATION, *pg.* 210, *pg.* 1584
LITHIA MOTORS INC, *pg.* 183, *pg.* 1499
MAITA ENTERPRISES INC., *pg.* 183, *pg.* 196
MEINEKE CAR CARE CENTERS, INC., *pg.* 212, *pg.* 1367
MIDAS, INC., *pg.* 212, *pg.* 620
MIDAS INTERNATIONAL, INC., *pg.* 212, *pg.* 620
MONRO MUFFLER BRAKE, INC., *pg.* 213, *pg.* 1336
NAPLETON SCHAUMBURG MOTORS, INC., *pg.* 185, *pg.* 659
PACIFICO ENTERPRISES, INC., *pg.* 188, *pg.* 1568
PRECISION AUTO CARE, INC., *pg.* 215, *pg.* 1787
RELIABLE CHEVROLET, *pg.* 189, *pg.* 1736
SOMERSET TIRE SERVICE, INC., *pg.* 217, *pg.* 1047
TIRE KINGDOM, INC., *pg.* 219, *pg.* 436

7539 - Automobile Repair Shops, NEC

AHERN RENTALS, INC., *pg.* 345, *pg.* 1022
ARCTIC FREEZE DISCOUNT AUTO & TRUCK REPAIR, *pg.* 199, *pg.* 437
ARMORED AUTOGROUP INC., *pg.* 199, *pg.* 342
AUTO DRIVEAWAY CO., *pg.* 1900, *pg.* 566
AUTOMOTIVE SUPPLY ASSOCIATES, INC., *pg.* 200, *pg.* 1033
BEECHMONT AUTOMOTIVE GROUP, *pg.* 166, *pg.* 1410
FLEETPRIDE, INC., *pg.* 205, *pg.* 1747
FREE SERVICE TIRE COMPANY, INC., *pg.* 205, *pg.* 1635
GOLD EAGLE COMPANY, *pg.* 206, *pg.* 575
GREASE MONKEY INTERNATIONAL, INC., *pg.* 84, *pg.* 331
JIFFY LUBE INTERNATIONAL, INC., *pg.* 209, *pg* 1709
LES SCHWAB TIRE CENTERS OF OREGON, INC., *pg.* 210, *pg.* 1508
MEINEKE CAR CARE CENTERS, INC., *pg.* 212, *pg.* 1367
THE PEP BOYS - MANNY, MOE & JACK, *pg.* 215, *pg.* 1568
POPULAR MECHANICS, *pg.* 1677, *pg.* 1282
SEQUA CORPORATION, *pg.* 1180, *pg.* 1290
TBC CORPORATION, *pg.* 1889, *pg.* 457
THEXTON MANUFACTURING COMPANY, INC., *pg.* 218, *pg.* 925
ZIEBART INTERNATIONAL CORPORATION, *pg.* 222, *pg.* 912

7542 - Car Washes

MACE SECURITY INTERNATIONAL, INC., *pg.* 1172, *pg.* 1541

7549 - Automobile Services, Except Repair & Car Washes

AUTO DRIVEAWAY CO., *pg.* 1900, *pg.* 566
GREASE MONKEY INTERNATIONAL, INC., *pg.* 84, *pg.* 331
JIFFY LUBE INTERNATIONAL, INC., *pg.* 209, *pg.* 1709

7629 - Electrical & Electronic Repair Shops, NEC

ACCO ENGINEERED SYSTEMS, *pg.* 1068, *pg.* 95
AERO CONTROLS, INC., *pg.* 223, *pg.* 439
AEROGROW INTERNATIONAL, INC., *pg.* 1393, *pg.* 310
AESCULAP, INC., *pg.* 1487, *pg.* 1521
AHERN RENTALS, INC., *pg.* 345, *pg.* 1022
ALIMAK HEK INC, *pg.* 66, *pg.* 1749
AMPCO-PITTSBURGH CORPORATION, *pg.* 1313, *pg.* 1573
APSCO APPLIANCE CENTERS, *pg.* 51, *pg.* 415
AVIALL, INC., *pg.* 224, *pg.* 1676
BAYLOFF STAMPED PRODUCTS, *pg.* 1317, *pg.* 1457
BEST BUY CANADA LTD., *pg.* 1761, *pg.* 1907
BLACK BOX CORPORATION, *pg.* 361, *pg.* 1547
BRAUNSCHWEIGER JEWELERS, *pg.* 2, *pg.* 1088
CALGON CARBON CORPORATION, *pg.* 1151, *pg.* 1574
CHEMED CORPORATION, *pg.* 327, *pg.* 1410
DELPHAX TECHNOLOGIES INC., *pg.* 386, *pg.* 917
THE DWYER GROUP, INC., *pg.* 79, *pg.* 1748
EXIDE TECHNOLOGIES, *pg.* 204, *pg.* 483
EXTERRAN HOLDINGS, INC., *pg.* 977, *pg.* 1705
FEINTOOL EQUIPMENT CORP., *pg.* 1336, *pg.* 1413
FONAR CORPORATION, *pg.* 1413, *pg.* 1179
GE CONSUMER & INDUSTRIAL, *pg.* 55, *pg.* 733
GENERAL DATACOMM INDUSTRIES, INC., *pg.* 400, *pg.* 357
GLOBAL EPOINT INC., *pg.* 400, *pg.* 67
GRC ENTERPRISES, INC., *pg.* 1344, *pg.* 677
GROSSENBURG IMPLEMENT, INC., *pg.* 1344, *pg.* 1626
HOBART FOOD EQUIPMENT GROUP CANADA, *pg.* 56, *pg.* 1929
HONEYWELL AEROSPACE, *pg.* 228, *pg.* 16
HUDSON TECHNOLOGIES, INC., *pg.* 1073, *pg.* 1320
INSTRON CORPORATION, *pg.* 1349, *pg.* 839
JASPER ELECTRIC MOTORS, *pg.* 209, *pg.* 691
JVC AMERICAS CORP., *pg.* 648, *pg.* 1129
KOMATSU AMERICA INDUSTRIES, LLC, *pg.* 1353, *pg.* 656
KONE INC., *pg.* 1353, *pg.* 633
KSB INC., *pg.* 1354, *pg.* 1802
MAXONS RESTORATIONS, *pg.* 332, *pg.* 1257
MEGGER INC., *pg.* 1422, *pg.* 1557
METTLER-TOLEDO INTERNATIONAL INC., *pg.* 1423, *pg.* 1441
MINT TURBINES LLC, *pg.* 231, *pg.* 1488
MOVADO GROUP, INC., *pg.* 10, *pg.* 1101
MULTIBAND CORPORATION, *pg.* 442, *pg.* 940
NANOMETRICS INCORPORATED, *pg.* 1423, *pg.* 147
NORTHROP GRUMMAN CORPORATION, *pg.* 231, *pg.* 1781
ORBOTECH INC., *pg.* 1367, *pg.* 788
PARAGON TECHNOLOGIES, INC., *pg.* 1367, *pg.* 1528
PHILADELPHIA GEAR CORPORATION, *pg.* 1368, *pg.* 1544
STARKEY LABORATORIES, INC., *pg.* 1597, *pg.* 923
TD INDUSTRIES, INC., *pg.* 1077, *pg.* 1688
T.D. WILLIAMSON, INC., *pg.* 1380, *pg.* 1490
TELETOUCH COMMUNICATIONS, INC., *pg.* 483, *pg.* 1696
TOSHIBA AMERICA CONSUMER PRODUCTS, LLC, *pg.* 681, *pg.* 1130
TRANSCAT, INC., *pg.* 682, *pg.* 1307
VOITH HYDRO INC., *pg.* 1387, *pg.* 1598
WAUKESHA ELECTRIC SYSTEMS, *pg.* 687, *pg.* 1898
WOODWARD, INC., *pg.* 122, *pg.* 329
THE W.W. WILLIAMS COMPANY, *pg.* 1390, *pg.* 1444

7641 - Reupholstery & Furniture Repair

DREAM POLISHERS, INC., *pg.* 923, *pg.* 422
KINDEL FURNITURE COMPANY, *pg.* 931, *pg.* 887

7699 - Repair Shops & Related Services, NEC

ACCO ENGINEERED SYSTEMS, *pg.* 1068, *pg.* 95
AERO CONTROLS, INC., *pg.* 223, *pg.* 439
AEROGROW INTERNATIONAL, INC., *pg.* 1393, *pg.* 310
AHERN RENTALS, INC., *pg.* 345, *pg.* 1022
ALIMAK HEK INC, *pg.* 66, *pg.* 1749
ALUMACRAFT BOAT COMPANY, *pg.* 1705, *pg.* 964
AMPCO-PITTSBURGH CORPORATION, *pg.* 1313, *pg.* 1573
APSCO APPLIANCE CENTERS, *pg.* 51, *pg.* 415
AVIALL, INC., *pg.* 224, *pg.* 1676
BAYLOFF STAMPED PRODUCTS, *pg.* 1317, *pg.* 1457
BOMBARDIER RECREATIONAL PRODUCTS, INC., *pg.* 201, *pg.* 1960
BOSTON WHALER, INC., *pg.* 1705, *pg.* 422
BRAUNSCHWEIGER JEWELERS, *pg.* 2, *pg.* 1088
BRISTOL MARINE, *pg.* 1705, *pg.* 1600
BRUNSWICK CORPORATION, *pg.* 1828, *pg.* 623
CATALINA YACHTS, INC., *pg.* 1706, *pg.* 307
CHEMED CORPORATION, *pg.* 327, *pg.* 1410
CHRIS-CRAFT CORPORATION, *pg.* 1706, *pg.* 465
CONFLUENCE WATERSPORTS CO. INC., *pg.* 1706, *pg.* 1617
CORRECT CRAFT, INC., *pg.* 1706, *pg.* 452
DREAM POLISHERS, INC., *pg.* 923, *pg.* 422
THE DWYER GROUP, INC., *pg.* 79, *pg.* 1748
EXIDE TECHNOLOGIES, *pg.* 204, *pg.* 483
EXTERRAN HOLDINGS, INC., *pg.* 977, *pg.* 1705
GE CONSUMER & INDUSTRIAL, *pg.* 55, *pg.* 733
GLOBAL EPOINT INC., *pg.* 400, *pg.* 67
GRADY-WHITE BOATS, INC., *pg.* 1707, *pg.* 1377
GROSSENBURG IMPLEMENT, INC., *pg.* 1344, *pg.* 1626
HATTERAS YACHTS, *pg.* 1708, *pg.* 1386
HOBART FOOD EQUIPMENT GROUP CANADA, *pg.* 56, *pg.* 1929
HOBIE CAT COMPANY, *pg.* 1708, *pg.* 173
HUCKINS YACHT CORPORATION, *pg.* 1708, *pg.* 433
HUDSON TECHNOLOGIES, INC., *pg.* 1073, *pg.* 1320
JASPER ELECTRIC MOTORS, *pg.* 209, *pg.* 691
JOHNSON OUTDOORS INC., *pg.* 1837, *pg.* 1888
JVC AMERICAS CORP., *pg.* 648, *pg.* 1129
KCS INTERNATIONAL, INC., *pg.* 556, *pg.* 1885
KINDEL FURNITURE COMPANY, *pg.* 931, *pg.* 887
KONE INC., *pg.* 1353, *pg.* 633
MARLOW-HUNTER LLC, *pg.* 1709, *pg.* 409
MASTERCRAFT BOAT COMPANY LLC, *pg.* 1709, *pg.* 1656
MAXONS RESTORATIONS, *pg.* 332, *pg.* 1257
PALMER JOHNSON INCORPORATED, *pg.* 1709, *pg.* 1895
PARAGON TECHNOLOGIES, INC., *pg.* 1367, *pg.* 1528
POLARIS INDUSTRIES INC., *pg.* 1709, *pg.* 928
S2 YACHTS, INC., *pg.* 1710, *pg.* 892
SABRE CORPORATION, *pg.* 1710, *pg.* 752
SEA RAY BOATS, INC., *pg.* 1710, *pg.* 1638
SILVER SHIPS, INC., *pg.* 1923, *pg.* 8
SKIER'S CHOICE INC., *pg.* 1711, *pg.* 1640
TAYLOR MADE GROUP, *pg.* 1711, *pg.* 1162
TD INDUSTRIES, INC., *pg.* 1077, *pg.* 1688
TRINITY YACHTS, LLC, *pg.* 1712, *pg.* 968
VIKING YACHT COMPANY, *pg.* 1712, *pg.* 1094
THE W.W. WILLIAMS COMPANY, *pg.* 1390, *pg.* 1444

7812 - Motion Picture & Video Tape Production

20TH CENTURY FOX FILM CORP., *pg.* 267, *pg.* 124
3ALITY TECHNICA, *pg.* 526, *pg.* 51
4LICENSING CORPORATION, *pg.* 948, *pg.* 1185
ABC FAMILY CHANNEL, *pg.* 268, *pg.* 51
THE ACADEMY OF SCIENCE FICTION, FANTASY & HORROR FILMS, *pg.* 125, *pg.* 125
ACTIVE PARENTING PUBLISHERS, *pg.* 1613, *pg.* 535
AMC NETWORKS INC., *pg.* 269, *pg.* 1189
AMERICAN SOCIETY OF CINEMATOGRAPHERS, *pg.* 1616, *pg.* 103
ARCHIE COMICS ENTERTAINMENT, LLC, *pg.* 270, *pg.* 360
ASCENT CAPITAL GROUP, *pg.* 270, *pg.* 330
AVATAR STUDIOS, *pg.* 270, *pg.* 992
BBC WORLDWIDE AMERICA INC., *pg.* 271, *pg.* 1201
BEACHBODY, LLC, *pg.* 271, *pg.* 272
BET HOLDINGS LLC, *pg.* 271, *pg.* 396
BIG IDEA, INC., *pg.* 271, *pg.* 1632
CARMIKE CINEMAS, *pg.* 537, *pg.* 423
CORE MEDIA GROUP, *pg.* 1765, *pg.* 1218
DELUXE LABORATORIES, INC., *pg.* 281, *pg.* 103
DREAMWORKS ANIMATION SKG, INC., *pg.* 284, *pg.* 96
EPOCH FILMS INC., *pg.* 285, *pg.* 1228
EXODUS FILM GROUP, *pg.* 546, *pg.* 301
FOCUS FEATURES, *pg.* 287, *pg.* 273
FOX BROADCASTING COMPANY, *pg.* 287, *pg.* 130
FOX ENTERTAINMENT GROUP, INC., *pg.* 288, *pg.* 131
GUTHY-RENKER LLC, *pg.* 289, *pg.* 273
HARPO, INC., *pg.* 290, *pg.* 576
THE HEARST CORPORATION, *pg.* 1649, *pg.* 1239
IMAGINE ENTERTAINMENT, *pg.* 292, *pg.* 46
INTERNATIONAL BUSINESS EXCHANGE CORPORATION, *pg.* 647, *pg.* 1739
THE JIM HENSON COMPANY, *pg.* 293, *pg.* 103
LIONS GATE ENTERTAINMENT CORP., *pg.* 296, *pg.* 274
LIVE NATION ENTERTAINMENT, INC., *pg.* 558, *pg.* 47
LUCASFILM, LTD., *pg.* 297, *pg.* 222
MACNEIL/LEHRER PRODUCTIONS, *pg.* 297, *pg.* 1774

MARTHA STEWART LIVING OMNIMEDIA, INC., *pg.* 1661, *pg.* 1256
MARVEL ENTERTAINMENT, LLC, *pg.* 1662, *pg.* 1257
METRO-GOLDWYN-MAYER INC., *pg.* 298, *pg.* 47
MIRAMAX FILM CORP., *pg.* 298, *pg.* 275
NATIONAL FILM BOARD OF CANADA, *pg.* 299, *pg.* 1959
NBC UNIVERSAL, INC., *pg.* 300, *pg.* 1266
NEW HORIZONS PICTURE CORP., *pg.* 302, *pg.* 137
NEWS CORPORATION, *pg.* 1669, *pg.* 1271
NFL FILMS, INC., *pg.* 303, *pg.* 1090
NTN BUZZTIME, INC., *pg.* 659, *pg.* 60
OXYGEN MEDIA LLC, *pg.* 303, *pg.* 1275
PARAMOUNT PICTURES CORPORATION, *pg.* 304, *pg.* 138
PHOENIX PICTURES INC., *pg.* 304, *pg.* 138
PIXAR ANIMATION STUDIOS, *pg.* 304, *pg.* 85
RELATIVITY MEDIA, LLC, *pg.* 306, *pg.* 47
RENTPATH, INC., *pg.* 1680, *pg.* 538
RENTRAK CORPORATION, *pg.* 306, *pg.* 1506
SAMUEL GOLDWYN FILMS, *pg.* 307, *pg.* 140
SESAME WORKSHOP, *pg.* 307, *pg.* 1290
SHAW MEDIA INC., *pg.* 308, *pg.* 1943
SONAR ENTERTAINMENT, *pg.* 309, *pg.* 140
SONY CORPORATION OF AMERICA, *pg.* 675, *pg.* 1293
SONY PICTURES ENTERTAINMENT INC., *pg.* 309, *pg.* 72
SPEED COMMERCE, INC., *pg.* 967, *pg.* 1737
TAPESTRY FILMS, *pg.* 311, *pg.* 47
TIME WARNER INC., *pg.* 312, *pg.* 1302
TIMES-SHAMROCK, INC., *pg.* 313, *pg.* 1586
TWISTED SCHOLAR, INC., *pg.* 315, *pg.* 1842
TYNDALE HOUSE PUBLISHERS, INC., *pg.* 1697, *pg.* 561
UNIVERSAL STUDIOS, INC., *pg.* 315, *pg.* 298
VIACOM INC., *pg.* 316, *pg.* 1310
VULCAN PRODUCTIONS INC., *pg.* 317, *pg.* 1842
WALDEN MEDIA, LLC, *pg.* 317, *pg.* 141
THE WALT DISNEY COMPANY, *pg.* 317, *pg.* 52
WARNER BROS. ANIMATION INC., *pg.* 319, *pg.* 54
WARNER BROS. ENTERTAINMENT INC., *pg.* 319, *pg.* 54
WORLD WRESTLING ENTERTAINMENT, INC., *pg.* 595, *pg.* 380

7819 - Services Allied to Motion Picture Production

20TH CENTURY FOX FILM CORP., *pg.* 267, *pg.* 124
DELUXE LABORATORIES, INC., *pg.* 281, *pg.* 103
FOX ENTERTAINMENT GROUP, INC., *pg.* 288, *pg.* 131

7822 - Motion Picture & Video Tape Distribution

20TH CENTURY FOX FILM CORP., *pg.* 267, *pg.* 124
20TH CENTURY FOX HOME ENTERTAINMENT, INC., *pg.* 267, *pg.* 125
4LICENSING CORPORATION, *pg.* 948, *pg.* 1185
ACADEMY OF MOTION PICTURE ARTS & SCIENCES, *pg.* 526, *pg.* 46
ANCHOR BAY ENTERTAINMENT, INC., *pg.* 270, *pg.* 910
ASCENT CAPITAL GROUP, *pg.* 270, *pg.* 330
BAKER & TAYLOR, INC., *pg.* 1619, *pg.* 1362
BEACHBODY, LLC, *pg.* 271, *pg.* 272
BET HOLDINGS LLC, *pg.* 271, *pg.* 396
COLUMBIA TRISTAR MOTION PICTURE GROUP, *pg.* 275, *pg.* 72
CORUS ENTERTAINMENT INC., *pg.* 279, *pg.* 1937
DELUXE LABORATORIES, INC., *pg.* 281, *pg.* 103
EUE SCREEN GEMS LTD., *pg.* 286, *pg.* 1393
FOX ENTERTAINMENT GROUP, INC., *pg.* 288, *pg.* 131
FREMANTLEMEDIA NORTH AMERICA INC., *pg.* 288, *pg.* 1233
GAIAM, INC., *pg.* 1532, *pg.* 334
HARMONIC, INC., *pg.* 402, *pg.* 246
HARPO, INC., *pg.* 290, *pg.* 576
THE HEARST CORPORATION, *pg.* 1649, *pg.* 1239
INGRAM ENTERTAINMENT INC., *pg.* 292, *pg.* 1639
KINO INTERNATIONAL CORP., *pg.* 294, *pg.* 1249
LIONS GATE ENTERTAINMENT CORP., *pg.* 296, *pg.* 274
METRO-GOLDWYN-MAYER INC., *pg.* 298, *pg.* 47
MIRAMAX FILM CORP., *pg.* 298, *pg.* 275
MONAKER GROUP, INC., *pg.* 298, *pg.* 479
MTI HOME VIDEO, *pg.* 298, *pg.* 444
NATIONAL AMUSEMENTS, INC., *pg.* 299, *pg.* 840
NATIONAL FILM BOARD OF CANADA, *pg.* 299, *pg.* 1959
NBC UNIVERSAL, INC., *pg.* 300, *pg.* 1266
NEW FRONTIER MEDIA, INC., *pg.* 302, *pg.* 311
NTN BUZZTIME, INC., *pg.* 659, *pg.* 60
THE ORCHARD ENTERPRISES, INC., *pg.* 572, *pg.* 1274
POINT.360, INC., *pg.* 305, *pg.* 52
RELATIVITY MEDIA, LLC, *pg.* 306, *pg.* 47
RLJ ENTERTAINMENT, INC., *pg.* 306, *pg.* 778
SIMON & SCHUSTER, INC., *pg.* 1687, *pg.* 1292
SONAR ENTERTAINMENT, *pg.* 309, *pg.* 140
SONY PICTURES ENTERTAINMENT INC., *pg.* 309, *pg.* 72
SONY PICTURES HOME ENTERTAINMENT, *pg.* 310, *pg.* 72
SONY PICTURES RELEASING CORPORATION, *pg.* 310, *pg.* 72
SPEED COMMERCE, INC., *pg.* 967, *pg.* 1737
SUNDANCE INSTITUTE, *pg.* 311, *pg.* 1754
SWANK MOTION PICTURES INC., *pg.* 311, *pg.* 1004
VIRGIL FILMS & ENTERTAINMENT, *pg.* 317, *pg.* 1311
VRINGO, INC., *pg.* 687, *pg.* 1312
WARNER BROS. ENTERTAINMENT INC., *pg.* 319, *pg.* 54
WARNER HOME VIDEO INC., *pg.* 319, *pg.* 55
WXYZ-TV, *pg.* 323, *pg.* 908

7829 - Services Allied to Motion Picture Distribution

20TH CENTURY FOX FILM CORP., *pg.* 267, *pg.* 124
ACADEMY OF MOTION PICTURE ARTS & SCIENCES, *pg.* 526, *pg.* 46
ASCENT CAPITAL GROUP, *pg.* 270, *pg.* 330
BET HOLDINGS LLC, *pg.* 271, *pg.* 396
CORUS ENTERTAINMENT INC., *pg.* 279, *pg.* 1937
DELUXE LABORATORIES, INC., *pg.* 281, *pg.* 103
ENTERTAINMENT SOFTWARE RATING BOARD, *pg.* 992, *pg.* 1228
EUE SCREEN GEMS LTD., *pg.* 286, *pg.* 1393
FOX ENTERTAINMENT GROUP, INC., *pg.* 288, *pg.* 131
HARMONIC, INC., *pg.* 402, *pg.* 246
LIVE NATION ENTERTAINMENT, INC., *pg.* 558, *pg.* 47
MACANDREWS & FORBES HOLDINGS INC., *pg.* 777, *pg.* 1254
METRO-GOLDWYN-MAYER INC., *pg.* 298, *pg.* 47
MONAKER GROUP, INC., *pg.* 298, *pg.* 479
NEW FRONTIER MEDIA, INC., *pg.* 302, *pg.* 311
NTN BUZZTIME, INC., *pg.* 659, *pg.* 60
THE ORCHARD ENTERPRISES, INC., *pg.* 572, *pg.* 1274
POINT.360, INC., *pg.* 305, *pg.* 52
SONAR ENTERTAINMENT, *pg.* 309, *pg.* 140
SUNDANCE INSTITUTE, *pg.* 311, *pg.* 1754
SWANK MOTION PICTURES INC., *pg.* 311, *pg.* 1004
VRINGO, INC., *pg.* 687, *pg.* 1312
WARNER BROS. ENTERTAINMENT INC., *pg.* 319, *pg.* 54
WXYZ-TV, *pg.* 323, *pg.* 908
YANKEES ENTERTAINMENT & SPORTS NETWORK, LLC, *pg.* 324, *pg.* 1316

7832 - Motion Picture Theaters, Except Drive-In

AMC ENTERTAINMENT INC., *pg.* 527, *pg.* 716
CARMIKE CINEMAS, *pg.* 537, *pg.* 423
CARMIKE CINEMAS, INC., *pg.* 273, *pg.* 528
CINEMARK HOLDINGS, INC., *pg.* 540, *pg.* 1729
CINEPLEX ENTERTAINMENT LP, *pg.* 275, *pg.* 1936
GOODRICH QUALITY THEATERS, *pg.* 289, *pg.* 887
THE MARCUS CORPORATION, *pg.* 1102, *pg.* 1877
METROPOLITAN THEATRES CORPORATION, *pg.* 562, *pg.* 136
NATIONAL AMUSEMENTS, INC., *pg.* 299, *pg.* 840
READING INTERNATIONAL, INC., *pg.* 578, *pg.* 139
REGAL ENTERTAINMENT GROUP, *pg.* 579, *pg.* 1638
SONY CORPORATION OF AMERICA, *pg.* 675, *pg.* 1293
TRANS-LUX CORPORATION, *pg.* 681, *pg.* 365

7841 - Video Tape Rental

GAMEFLY, INC., *pg.* 953, *pg.* 132
MOVIES UNLIMITED INC., *pg.* 1779, *pg.* 1567
NETFLIX, INC., *pg.* 1269, *pg.* 141
REDBOX AUTOMATED RETAIL, LLC, *pg.* 306, *pg.* 649
TLA ENTERTAINMENT GROUP, INC., *pg.* 313, *pg.* 1571

7911 - Dance Halls, Studios & Schools

THE ART INSTITUTE OF CHICAGO, *pg.* 530, *pg.* 565
CEDAR RAPIDS SYMPHONY, *pg.* 538, *pg.* 702
EDUCATION MANAGEMENT CORPORATION, *pg.* 601, *pg.* 1575
THE JUILLIARD SCHOOL, *pg.* 603, *pg.* 1247
MIAMI CITY BALLET, INC., *pg.* 562, *pg.* 448
NEW YORK CITY BALLET, *pg.* 569, *pg.* 1268
NEWPORT ART MUSEUM, *pg.* 571, *pg.* 1603

7922 - Theatrical Producers, (Except Motion Picture) & Miscellaneous Theatrical Services

THE DALLAS OPERA, *pg.* 543, *pg.* 1679
HOUSTON GRAND OPERA ASSOCIATION, *pg.* 552, *pg.* 1707
KONA GRILL INC., *pg.* 1734, *pg.* 23
NEW YORK CITY OPERA INC., *pg.* 570, *pg.* 1268
OPERA OMAHA INC., *pg.* 572, *pg.* 1017
TEXAS ROADHOUSE, INC., *pg.* 1753, *pg.* 738
UTAH SYMPHONY & OPERA, *pg.* 590, *pg.* 1761

7929 - Bands, Orchestras, Actors & other Entertainers & Entertainment Groups

ABILENE PHILHARMONIC ASSOCIATION, *pg.* 526, *pg.* 1657
ACADIANA SYMPHONY ASSOCIATION, *pg.* 526, *pg.* 744
AKRON SYMPHONY ORCHESTRA, *pg.* 526, *pg.* 1400
ALABAMA SYMPHONY ORCHESTRA, *pg.* 526, *pg.* 1
ALBANY SYMPHONY ORCHESTRA, *pg.* 527, *pg.* 482
ALEXANDRIA SYMPHONY ORCHESTRA, *pg.* 527, *pg.* 1770
AMERICAN SYMPHONY ORCHESTRA LEAGUE, *pg.* 528, *pg.* 1194
ANCHORAGE SYMPHONY ORCHESTRA, *pg.* 528, *pg.* 10
ANN ARBOR SYMPHONY ORCHESTRA, *pg.* 529, *pg.* 865
ANNAPOLIS SYMPHONY ORCHESTRA ASSOCIATION INC., *pg.* 529, *pg.* 754
ASHEVILLE SYMPHONY SOCIETY INC., *pg.* 530, *pg.* 1358
ASHLAND SYMPHONY ORCHESTRA, *pg.* 530, *pg.* 1403
ATLANTA SYMPHONY ORCHESTRA, *pg.* 531, *pg.* 490
AUGUSTA SYMPHONY INC., *pg.* 531, *pg.* 524
AUSTIN SYMPHONY ORCHESTRA, *pg.* 531, *pg.* 1660
BAD BOY WORLDWIDE ENTERTAINMENT GROUP, *pg.* 270, *pg.* 1199
BAKERSFIELD SYMPHONY ORCHESTRA, *pg.* 531, *pg.* 44
BALTIMORE SYMPHONY ORCHESTRA, *pg.* 532, *pg.* 755
BANGOR SYMPHONY ORCHESTRA, *pg.* 532, *pg.* 749
BERKELEY SYMPHONY ORCHESTRA, *pg.* 533, *pg.* 45
BILLINGS SYMPHONY SOCIETY INC., *pg.* 533, *pg.* 1008
BLUE MAN PRODUCTIONS, INC., *pg.* 533, *pg.* 1205
BOISE PHILHARMONIC ASSOCIATION, INC., *pg.* 533, *pg.* 546
BOSTON SYMPHONY ORCHESTRA INC., *pg.* 534, *pg.* 791
BOULDER PHILHARMONIC ORCHESTRA, *pg.* 534, *pg.* 310
BUFFALO PHILHARMONIC ORCHESTRA SOCIETY INC., *pg.* 535, *pg.* 1147
CALGARY PHILHARMONIC ORCHESTRA, *pg.* 536, *pg.* 1902
CALIFORNIA MUSICAL THEATRE CORPORATION, *pg.* 536, *pg.* 196
CALIFORNIA PHILHARMONIC ORCHESTRA, *pg.* 536, *pg.* 253
CARMEL SYMPHONY ORCHESTRA, INC., *pg.* 536, *pg.* 675
CENTRAL WISCONSIN SYMPHONY ORCHESTRA INC., *pg.* 538, *pg.* 1895
CHAMBER ORCHESTRA OF PHILADELPHIA, *pg.* 538, *pg.* 1559
CHANCE RIDES MANUFACTURING CO., *pg.* 538, *pg.* 723
CHANEY ENTERTAINMENT, INC., *pg.* 538, *pg.* 174
CHARLOTTE SYMPHONY ORCHESTRA, *pg.* 538, *pg.* 1365
CHATTANOOGA SYMPHONY & OPERA ASSOCIATION, *pg.* 538, *pg.* 1628
CHEYENNE SYMPHONY SOCIETY, INC., *pg.* 538, *pg.* 1901
CHICAGO SYMPHONY ORCHESTRA, *pg.* 539, *pg.* 570
CINCINNATI SYMPHONY ORCHESTRA, *pg.* 540, *pg.* 1411
CIRQUE DU SOLEIL INC., *pg.* 540, *pg.* 1954
COLORADO SYMPHONY ASSOCIATION INC., *pg.* 542, *pg.* 318

THE COLUMBIA ORCHESTRA, *pg.* 542, *pg.* 769
COLUMBUS PRO MUSICA INC., *pg.* 542, *pg.* 676
DALLAS SYMPHONY ASSOCIATION INC., *pg.* 543, *pg.* 1679
DAYTON PHILHARMONIC ORCHESTRA ASSOCIATION, INC., *pg.* 543, *pg.* 1445
DELAWARE SYMPHONY ASSOCIATION, *pg.* 544, *pg.* 390
DES MOINES SYMPHONY ASSOCIATION, *pg.* 544, *pg.* 705
DETROIT SYMPHONY ORCHESTRA, INC., *pg.* 544, *pg.* 880
DULUTH SUPERIOR SYMPHONY ORCHESTRA, *pg.* 545, *pg.* 921
EAST TEXAS SYMPHONY ORCHESTRA, *pg.* 545, *pg.* 1748
EL PASO SYMPHONY ORCHESTRA, *pg.* 546, *pg.* 1691
ERIE PHILHARMONIC, *pg.* 546, *pg.* 1530
EVANSTON SYMPHONY ORCHESTRA ASSOCIATION, *pg.* 546, *pg.* 611
EVANSVILLE PHILHARMONIC ORCHESTRA CORP., *pg.* 546, *pg.* 678
FAIRBANKS SYMPHONY ASSOCIATION, *pg.* 547, *pg.* 10
FLAGSTAFF SYMPHONY ASSOCIATION, *pg.* 548, *pg.* 12
THE FLORIDA ORCHESTRA, *pg.* 548, *pg.* 462
FORT WAYNE PHILHARMONIC ORCHESTRA, *pg.* 549, *pg.* 680
FREMONT SYMPHONY ORCHESTRA, *pg.* 549, *pg.* 91
GARDEN STATE PHILHARMONIC, *pg.* 550, *pg.* 1125
GLENS FALLS SYMPHONY ORCHESTRA, INC., *pg.* 550, *pg.* 1162
GRAND RAPIDS SYMPHONY SOCIETY, *pg.* 551, *pg.* 887
GREENWICH SYMPHONY ORCHESTRA INC., *pg.* 551, *pg.* 350
HARTFORD SYMPHONY ORCHESTRA INC., *pg.* 551, *pg.* 352
HELENA SYMPHONY SOCIETY INC., *pg.* 552, *pg.* 1008
HOLLAND SYMPHONY ORCHESTRA, *pg.* 552, *pg.* 892
HOUSTON SYMPHONY SOCIETY, *pg.* 552, *pg.* 1708
ILLINOIS PHILHARMONIC ORCHESTRA, *pg.* 553, *pg.* 650
INDIANAPOLIS SYMPHONY ORCHESTRA, *pg.* 553, *pg.* 687
JACKSONVILLE SYMPHONY ASSOCIATION, *pg.* 554, *pg.* 434
JOHNSTOWN SYMPHONY ORCHESTRA, *pg.* 555, *pg.* 1542
JUNEAU SYMPHONY, *pg.* 555, *pg.* 11
KALAMAZOO SYMPHONY ORCHESTRA, *pg.* 555, *pg.* 894
KANSAS CITY SYMPHONY, *pg.* 555, *pg.* 985
LA CROSSE SYMPHONY ORCHESTRA, INC., *pg.* 556, *pg.* 1864
LAKE SHORE SYMPHONY ORCHESTRA, *pg.* 556, *pg.* 580
LANCASTER SYMPHONY ORCHESTRA, *pg.* 556, *pg.* 1546
LANSING SYMPHONY ORCHESTRA, *pg.* 557, *pg.* 895
LAS COLINAS SYMPHONY ORCHESTRA ASSOCIATION INC., *pg.* 557, *pg.* 1722
LINCOLN SYMPHONY ORCHESTRA, *pg.* 557, *pg.* 1012
LITTLETON SYMPHONY ORCHESTRA, *pg.* 558, *pg.* 333
LONG BEACH SYMPHONY ORCHESTRA, *pg.* 558, *pg.* 123
LONG ISLAND PHILHARMONIC, *pg.* 558, *pg.* 1180
LOUISVILLE ORCHESTRA, INC., *pg.* 559, *pg.* 736
LUBBOCK SYMPHONY ORCHESTRA, *pg.* 560, *pg.* 1726
LYNCHBURG SYMPHONY ORCHESTRA, *pg.* 560, *pg.* 1787
MARYLAND SYMPHONY ORCHESTRA, *pg.* 561, *pg.* 771
MEMPHIS SYMPHONY ORCHESTRA, *pg.* 561, *pg.* 1645
MICHIGAN PHILHARMONIC, *pg.* 562, *pg.* 904
THE MID-TEXAS SYMPHONY SOCIETY, *pg.* 562, *pg.* 1745
MINNESOTA ORCHESTRA, *pg.* 563, *pg.* 940
MISSISSIPPI SYMPHONY ORCHESTRA, *pg.* 564, *pg.* 969
MOBILE SYMPHONY, INC., *pg.* 564, *pg.* 7
MODESTO SYMPHONY ORCHESTRA, *pg.* 564, *pg.* 150
MUSICAL ARTS ASSOCIATION, *pg.* 565, *pg.* 1433
NASHVILLE SYMPHONY ASSOCIATION, *pg.* 565, *pg.* 1653
NATIONAL PHILHARMONIC, *pg.* 568, *pg.* 765
NATIONAL SYMPHONY ORCHESTRA, *pg.* 568, *pg.* 403
THE NEW HAMPSHIRE PHILHARMONIC, *pg.* 569, *pg.* 1036
NEW HAVEN SYMPHONY ORCHESTRA, *pg.* 569, *pg.* 359
NORTH CAROLINA SYMPHONY, *pg.* 571, *pg.* 1388
OKLAHOMA CITY PHILHARMONIC ORCHESTRA SOCIETY, INC., *pg.* 571, *pg.* 1487
OMAHA SYMPHONY ASSOCIATION, *pg.* 572, *pg.* 1017
ORCHESTRE SYMPHONIQUE DE MONTREAL, *pg.* 572, *pg.* 1956
ORLANDO PHILHARMONIC ORCHESTRA INC., *pg.* 573, *pg.* 455
PADUCAH SYMPHONY ORCHESTRA, *pg.* 573, *pg.* 739
PASADENA SYMPHONY ASSOCIATION, *pg.* 574, *pg.* 181
THE PHILADELPHIA ORCHESTRA ASSOCIATION, *pg.* 575, *pg.* 1569
PHILHARMONIA BAROQUE ORCHESTRA, *pg.* 575, *pg.* 225
PHOENIX SYMPHONY ASSOCIATION, *pg.* 576, *pg.* 19
PITTSBURGH SYMPHONY INC., *pg.* 577, *pg.* 1579
PLAINFIELD SYMPHONY SOCIETY INC., *pg.* 577, *pg.* 1109
PORTLAND SYMPHONY ORCHESTRA, *pg.* 577, *pg.* 752
PRINCETON SYMPHONY ORCHESTRA, *pg.* 577, *pg.* 1112
PROMUSICA CHAMBER ORCHESTRA, *pg.* 578, *pg.* 1443
QUEENS SYMPHONY ORCHESTRA, *pg.* 578, *pg.* 1160
RAINIER SYMPHONY, *pg.* 578, *pg.* 1839
READING SYMPHONY ORCHESTRA ASSOCIATION, *pg.* 578, *pg.* 1585
RHODE ISLAND PHILHARMONIC ORCHESTRA INC., *pg.* 579, *pg.* 1601
RICHMOND SYMPHONY, *pg.* 579, *pg.* 1803
ROANOKE SYMPHONY SOCIETY, *pg.* 579, *pg.* 1806
ROCKFORD SYMPHONY ORCHESTRA, *pg.* 579, *pg.* 655
SACRAMENTO PHILHARMONIC ORCHESTRA, *pg.* 579, *pg.* 197
THE SAINT PAUL CHAMBER ORCHESTRA, *pg.* 580, *pg.* 963
SAN DIEGO SYMPHONY ORCHESTRA ASSOCIATION, *pg.* 580, *pg.* 208
SAN FRANCISCO SYMPHONY, *pg.* 581, *pg.* 227
SARASOTA OPERA, *pg.* 581, *pg.* 467
SEATTLE PHILHARMONIC ORCHESTRA, *pg.* 582, *pg.* 1839
SEATTLE SYMPHONY ORCHESTRA, *pg.* 582, *pg.* 1840
SHREVEPORT SYMPHONY ORCHESTRA, *pg.* 583, *pg.* 748
SIOUX CITY SYMPHONY ORCHESTRA, *pg.* 583, *pg.* 712
SNOHOMISH COUNTY MUSIC PROJECT, *pg.* 584, *pg.* 1819
THE SOUND SYMPHONY, *pg.* 584, *pg.* 1168
SOUTH CAROLINA PHILHARMONIC ASSOCIATION INC., *pg.* 584, *pg.* 1615
SOUTHWEST FLORIDA SYMPHONY, *pg.* 584, *pg.* 428
SPOKANE SYMPHONY ORCHESTRA, *pg.* 584, *pg.* 1844
SPRINGFIELD SYMPHONY ORCHESTRA, *pg.* 585, *pg.* 1473
ST. LOUIS PHILHARMONIC ORCHESTRA, *pg.* 585, *pg.* 1003
ST. LOUIS SYMPHONY ORCHESTRA, *pg.* 585, *pg.* 1004
STAGES PRODUCTIONS, INC., *pg.* 585, *pg.* 468
THE STAMFORD SYMPHONY ORCHESTRA, *pg.* 585, *pg.* 378
SYMPHONY IN C, *pg.* 586, *pg.* 1049
SYMPHONY OF THE SOUTHWEST, *pg.* 586, *pg.* 13
TOLEDO SYMPHONY, *pg.* 588, *pg.* 1477
TORONTO SYMPHONY ORCHESTRA, *pg.* 589, *pg.* 1946
TUCSON SYMPHONY ORCHESTRA, *pg.* 589, *pg.* 27
UTAH SYMPHONY & OPERA, *pg.* 590, *pg.* 1761
VANCOUVER SYMPHONY ORCHESTRA, *pg.* 590, *pg.* 1913
VERMONT SYMPHONY ORCHESTRA, *pg.* 590, *pg.* 1765
VICTORIA SYMPHONY SOCIETY, *pg.* 590, *pg.* 1913
VIRGINIA SYMPHONY ORCHESTRA, *pg.* 590, *pg.* 1797
WALLA WALLA SYMPHONY SOCIETY, *pg.* 590, *pg.* 1847
WEST VIRGINIA SYMPHONY ORCHESTRA INC., *pg.* 592, *pg.* 1849
WESTCHESTER PHILHARMONIC, *pg.* 592, *pg.* 1354
WESTERN PIEDMONT SYMPHONY, *pg.* 592, *pg.* 1379
WESTERVILLE SYMPHONY ORCHESTRA, *pg.* 592, *pg.* 1480
WICHITA SYMPHONY SOCIETY INC., *pg.* 592, *pg.* 724
WILMINGTON SYMPHONY ORCHESTRA, *pg.* 592, *pg.* 1393
WINDSOR SYMPHONY SOCIETY, *pg.* 593, *pg.* 1949
WINSTON-SALEM SYMPHONY ASSOCIATION INC., *pg.* 593, *pg.* 1396
WISCONSIN CHAMBER ORCHESTRA, *pg.* 593, *pg.* 1867
YORK SYMPHONY ORCHESTRA, *pg.* 595, *pg.* 1598

7933 - Bowling Alleys

BOWL AMERICA INCORPORATED, *pg.* 534, *pg.* 1770
BOWLMOR AMF, *pg.* 1828, *pg.* 1206
BRUNSWICK CORPORATION, *pg.* 1828, *pg.* 623

7941 - Professional Sports Clubs & Promoters

ANAHEIM DUCKS HOCKEY CLUB, LLC, *pg.* 528, *pg.* 42
ANGELS BASEBALL, L.P., *pg.* 529, *pg.* 42
ARIZONA CARDINALS FOOTBALL CLUB, INC., *pg.* 529, *pg.* 25
ARIZONA DIAMONDBACKS, *pg.* 529, *pg.* 14
ATLANTA FALCONS FOOTBALL CLUB, LLC, *pg.* 530, *pg.* 532
ATLANTA NATIONAL LEAGUE BASEBALL CLUB, INC., *pg.* 530, *pg.* 490
BALTIMORE ORIOLES, L.P., *pg.* 532, *pg.* 755
BALTIMORE RAVENS LIMITED PARTNERSHIP, *pg.* 532, *pg.* 755
THE BASEBALL CLUB OF SEATTLE, L.P., *pg.* 532, *pg.* 1833
BOSTON CELTICS LIMITED PARTNERSHIP, *pg.* 533, *pg.* 790
BOSTON PROFESSIONAL HOCKEY ASSOCIATION, INC., *pg.* 534, *pg.* 791
BOSTON RED SOX BASEBALL CLUB LIMITED PARTNERSHIP, *pg.* 534, *pg.* 791
BROOKLYN NETS, *pg.* 534, *pg.* 1145
BUCCANEERS LIMITED PARTNERSHIP, *pg.* 534, *pg.* 471
BUFFALO BILLS, INC., *pg.* 535, *pg.* 1319
CALGARY FLAMES LIMITED PARTNERSHIP, *pg.* 535, *pg.* 1902
CANUCKS SPORTS & ENTERTAINMENT, *pg.* 536, *pg.* 1910
CAROLINA HURRICANES HOCKEY CLUB, *pg.* 537, *pg.* 1386
CHICAGO BEARS FOOTBALL CLUB, INC., *pg.* 538, *pg.* 623
CHICAGO BLACKHAWK HOCKEY TEAM, INC., *pg.* 538, *pg.* 569
CHICAGO NATIONAL LEAGUE BALL CLUB, LLC, *pg.* 539, *pg.* 569
CHICAGO PROFESSIONAL SPORTS LIMITED PARTNERSHIP, *pg.* 539, *pg.* 570
CHICAGO WHITE SOX LTD., *pg.* 539, *pg.* 570
CINCINNATI BENGALS, INC., *pg.* 540, *pg.* 1410
CLEVELAND BROWNS FOOTBALL COMPANY LLC, *pg.* 541, *pg.* 1406
CLEVELAND CAVALIERS/QUICKEN LOANS ARENA, *pg.* 541, *pg.* 1429
CLEVELAND INDIANS BASEBALL COMPANY, INC., *pg.* 541, *pg.* 1429
CLUB DE HOCKEY CANADIEN, INC., *pg.* 541, *pg.* 1954
COLORADO AVALANCHE, LLC, *pg.* 541, *pg.* 317
COLORADO ROCKIES BASEBALL CLUB, LTD., *pg.* 542, *pg.* 317
COMCAST SPECTACOR, L.P., *pg.* 278, *pg.* 1562
COYOTES HOCKEY, LLC, *pg.* 542, *pg.* 13
DALLAS COWBOYS FOOTBALL CLUB, LTD., *pg.* 543, *pg.* 1718
DALLAS MAVERICKS, *pg.* 543, *pg.* 1678
DALLAS STARS L.P., *pg.* 543, *pg.* 1697
DENVER BRONCOS FOOTBALL CLUB, *pg.* 544, *pg.* 325
THE DENVER NUGGETS LIMITED PARTNERSHIP, *pg.* 544, *pg.* 319
THE DETROIT LIONS, INC., *pg.* 544, *pg.* 864
DETROIT PISTONS BASKETBALL COMPANY, *pg.* 544, *pg.* 868
DETROIT TIGERS BASEBALL CLUB, INC., *pg.* 545, *pg.* 880
EDMONTON OILERS HOCKEY CLUB, *pg.* 546, *pg.* 1906
FLORIDA MARLINS, L.P., *pg.* 548, *pg.* 442
FLORIDA PANTHERS HOCKEY CLUB, LTD., *pg.* 548, *pg.* 469
GENERAL SPORTS & ENTERTAINMENT, LLC, *pg.* 550, *pg.* 905
GOLDEN STATE WARRIORS, LLC, *pg.* 550, *pg.* 171
GREEN BAY PACKERS, INC., *pg.* 551, *pg.* 1859
HAWKS BASKETBALL, INC., *pg.* 551, *pg.* 509
HOCKEY WESTERN NEW YORK, LLC, *pg.* 552, *pg.* 1149
HOUSTON ASTROS BASEBALL CLUB, *pg.* 552, *pg.* 1707
HOUSTON ROCKETS, *pg.* 552, *pg.* 1707
HOUSTON TEXANS, L.P., *pg.* 553, *pg.* 1708
INDIANAPOLIS COLTS, INC., *pg.* 553, *pg.* 687
JACKSONVILLE JAGUARS, LTD., *pg.* 554, *pg.* 433
JAZZ BASKETBALL INVESTORS, INC., *pg.* 554, *pg.* 1759
KANSAS CITY CHIEFS FOOTBALL CLUB, INC., *pg.* 555, *pg.* 984
KANSAS CITY ROYALS BASEBALL CORPORATION, *pg.* 555, *pg.* 985
LARRY H. MILLER GROUP OF COMPANIES, *pg.* 182, *pg.* 1762
LIGHTNING HOCKEY LP, *pg.* 557, *pg.* 474
LOS ANGELES CLIPPERS, *pg.* 558, *pg.* 135
LOS ANGELES DODGERS INC., *pg.* 559, *pg.* 135
LOS ANGELES KINGS HOCKEY CLUB L.P., *pg.* 559, *pg.* 135
MAPLE LEAF SPORTS & ENTERTAINMENT LTD., *pg.* 560, *pg.* 1940
MEMPHIS GRIZZLIES, *pg.* 561, *pg.* 1645
MIAMI DOLPHINS, LTD., *pg.* 562, *pg.* 419
MIAMI HEAT LIMITED PARTNERSHIP, *pg.* 562, *pg.* 444
MILWAUKEE BREWERS BASEBALL CLUB, INC., *pg.* 562,

pg. 1878
MILWAUKEE BUCKS, INC., pg. 563, pg. 1878
MINNESOTA TIMBERWOLVES BASKETBALL LIMITED PARTNERSHIP, pg. 563, pg. 940
MINNESOTA TWINS, LLC, pg. 563, pg. 940
MINNESOTA VIKINGS FOOTBALL CLUB, INC., pg. 563, pg. 923
MINNESOTA WILD HOCKEY CLUB, LP, pg. 563, pg. 962
NASHVILLE PREDATORS, LLC, pg. 565, pg. 1652
NATIONAL COLLEGIATE ATHLETIC ASSOCIATION, pg. 567, pg. 688
NEW ENGLAND PATRIOTS FOOTBALL CLUB, INC., pg. 569, pg. 819
NEW JERSEY DEVILS LLC, pg. 569, pg. 1097
NEW ORLEANS PELICANS NBA LIMITED PARTNERSHIP, pg. 569, pg. 747
NEW ORLEANS SAINTS L.P., pg. 569, pg. 745
THE NEW YORK GIANTS, pg. 570, pg. 1055
NEW YORK ISLANDERS HOCKEY CLUB, L.P., pg. 570, pg. 1346
NEW YORK JETS FOOTBALL CLUB, INC., pg. 570, pg. 1067
NEW YORK KNICKERBOCKERS, pg. 570, pg. 1268
NEW YORK RANGERS HOCKEY CLUB, pg. 570, pg. 1269
NEW YORK YANKEES, pg. 570, pg. 1144
OAKLAND ATHLETICS LIMITED PARTNERSHIP, pg. 571, pg. 172
THE OAKLAND RAIDERS, L.P., pg. 571, pg. 38
OKLAHOMA CITY THUNDER, pg. 571, pg. 1487
ORLANDO MAGIC, pg. 572, pg. 455
OTTAWA SENATORS HOCKEY CLUB, pg. 573, pg. 1921
PACERS BASKETBALL, LLC, pg. 573, pg. 689
PADRES L.P., pg. 573, pg. 206
PANTHERS FOOTBALL, LLC, pg. 573, pg. 1368
PHILADELPHIA 76ERS, L.P., pg. 575, pg. 1568
PHILADELPHIA EAGLES FOOTBALL CLUB, INC., pg. 575, pg. 1569
PHILADELPHIA FLYERS, L.P., pg. 575, pg. 1569
THE PHILLIES, L.P., pg. 575, pg. 1569
PHOENIX SUNS, pg. 576, pg. 19
PITTSBURGH BASEBALL, INC., pg. 576, pg. 1578
PITTSBURGH PENGUINS LLC, pg. 577, pg. 1578
PITTSBURGH STEELERS SPORTS INC., pg. 577, pg. 1578
PORTLAND TRAIL BLAZERS, pg. 577, pg. 1505
RANGERS BASEBALL LLC, pg. 578, pg. 1659
REDS BASEBALL PARTNERS, LLC, pg. 578, pg. 1425
SAINT LOUIS CARDINALS, L.P., pg. 580, pg. 1002
SAINT LOUIS RAMS FOOTBALL COMPANY, pg. 580, pg. 1002
SALT LAKE BEES, pg. 580, pg. 1760
SAN ANTONIO SPURS LLC, pg. 580, pg. 1742
SAN DIEGO CHARGERS FOOTBALL CO., pg. 580, pg. 208
SAN FRANCISCO FORTY NINERS, LTD., pg. 581, pg. 270
SAN FRANCISCO GIANTS BASEBALL CLUB, pg. 581, pg. 226
SAN JOSE SHARKS, LLC, pg. 581, pg. 250
SEATTLE SEAHAWKS, pg. 582, pg. 1830
SEATTLE STORM, pg. 582, pg. 1839
ST. LOUIS BLUES HOCKEY CLUB, LLC, pg. 585, pg. 1003
STERLING METS, L.P., pg. 586, pg. 1160
TAMPA BAY RAYS BASEBALL, LTD., pg. 586, pg. 464
TAMPA BAY STORM, pg. 587, pg. 476
TENNESSEE FOOTBALL, INC., pg. 587, pg. 1654
TORONTO BLUE JAYS BASEBALL CLUB, pg. 588, pg. 1945
TORONTO MAPLE LEAF HOCKEY CLUB, pg. 588, pg. 1945
TORONTO RAPTORS BASKETBALL CLUB INC., pg. 588, pg. 1945
WASHINGTON CAPITALS, pg. 591, pg. 1775
WASHINGTON FOOTBALL, INC., pg. 591, pg. 1776
WASHINGTON NATIONALS, L.P., pg. 591, pg. 407
WASHINGTON WIZARDS, pg. 591, pg. 408
WNBA ENTERPRISES, LLC, pg. 594, pg. 1314

7948 - Racing, Including Track Operation

ATLANTA MOTOR SPEEDWAY, INC., pg. 530, pg. 533
CANTERBURY PARK HOLDING CORPORATION, pg. 536, pg. 964
CHURCHILL DOWNS, INC., pg. 540, pg. 733
DOVER DOWNS GAMING & ENTERTAINMENT, INC., pg. 545, pg. 387
DOVER MOTORSPORTS, INC., pg. 545, pg. 387
ELDORADO RESORTS, INC., pg. 546, pg. 1031
FAIR GROUNDS CORPORATION, pg. 547, pg. 747
FINGER LAKES RACING ASSOCIATION INC., pg. 548, pg. 1160
HARRAH'S LOUISIANA DOWNS CASINO & RACETRACK, pg. 551, pg. 743
HULMAN & COMPANY, pg. 864, pg. 698
INTERNATIONAL SPEEDWAY CORPORATION, pg. 553, pg. 420
ISLE OF CAPRI CASINOS, INC., pg. 553, pg. 998
LOS ANGELES TURF CLUB, INCORPORATED, pg. 559, pg. 43
MAYWOOD PARK TROTTING ASSOCIATION, INC., pg. 561, pg. 631
NATIONAL HOT ROD ASSOCIATION, pg. 149, pg. 99
OAKLAWN JOCKEY CLUB, INC., pg. 571, pg. 32
PENN NATIONAL GAMING, INC., pg. 574, pg. 1595
SARATOGA CASINO & RACEWAY, pg. 581, pg. 1340
SPEEDWAY MOTORSPORTS, INC., pg. 584, pg. 1370

7991 - Physical Fitness Facilities

24 HOUR FITNESS WORLDWIDE INC., pg. 526, pg. 258
ALL-AMERICAN SPORTPARK, INC., pg. 527, pg. 1022
AMERICAN GOLF CORPORATION, pg. 528, pg. 272
ARCHON CORPORATION, pg. 1080, pg. 1030
ASHEVILLE SYMPHONY SOCIETY INC., pg. 530, pg. 1358
BALLY TOTAL FITNESS HOLDINGS CORPORATION, pg. 532, pg. 1200
B.A.S.S., L.L.C., pg. 270, pg. 1
BAYOU GOLF CLUB, pg. 1081, pg. 438
BENCHMARK HOSPITALITY INTERNATIONAL INC., pg. 1081, pg. 1747
CANLAN ICE SPORTS CORPORATION, pg. 536, pg. 1907
CEDAR FAIR, L.P., pg. 537, pg. 1471
CENTURY CASINOS INC., pg. 538, pg. 315
THE CLIFFS COMMUNITIES, INC., pg. 1086, pg. 1623
CLUBCORP, INC., pg. 1086, pg. 1677
THE COEUR D'ALENE RESORT, pg. 1087, pg. 549
COLUMBUS BLUE JACKETS, pg. 542, pg. 1439
CONSOLIDATED-TOMOKA LAND CO., pg. 1087, pg. 419
CURVES INTERNATIONAL INC., pg. 542, pg. 1748
THE DELTONA CORPORATION, pg. 1089, pg. 452
ECHO FARMS GOLF & COUNTRY CLUB, INC., pg. 1833, pg. 1392
EQUINOX FITNESS CLUBS, pg. 546, pg. 1228
FLORIDA PANTHERS HOCKEY CLUB, LTD., pg. 548, pg. 469
FORUM NATIONAL INVESTMENTS LTD., pg. 1200, pg. 1908
GOLD'S GYM, pg. 550, pg. 1681
THE GREENBRIER, pg. 1094, pg. 1851
HEALTH FITNESS CORPORATION, pg. 1539, pg. 937
HOBE SOUND GOLF CLUB, INC., pg. 1095, pg. 430
HONOURS GOLF COMPANY, LLC, pg. 1096, pg. 3
JACKSON HOLE MOUNTAIN RESORT, pg. 1098, pg. 1901
LA FITNESS INTERNATIONAL, LLC, pg. 1394, pg. 112
LIFE TIME FITNESS, INC., pg. 1556, pg. 920
LITTLEFIELD CORPORATION, pg. 558, pg. 1664
MGM RESORTS INTERNATIONAL, pg. 1105, pg. 1028
MINNESOTA GOLF ASSOCIATION, pg. 147, pg. 925
MISSION INN RESORTS INC., pg. 1105, pg. 431
NAPLES BEACH HOTEL & GOLF CLUB, pg. 1106, pg. 451
OJAI VALLEY INN & SPA, pg. 1106, pg. 173
THE OMNI HOMESTEAD RESORT, pg. 1106, pg. 1786
ORANGE COUNTY NATIONAL GOLF CENTER & LODGE, pg. 1107, pg. 480
PENN NATIONAL GAMING, INC., pg. 574, pg. 1595
PGA TOUR, INC., pg. 574, pg. 460
SADDLEBROOK RESORTS, INC., pg. 1111, pg. 478
SEA ISLAND ACQUISITION LLC, pg. 1111, pg. 540
SEA PINES RESORT, LLC, pg. 1112, pg. 1620
SOUTHWOOD GOLF CLUB, pg. 1113, pg. 470
STATION CASINOS, INC., pg. 585, pg. 1030
TARPON TOTAL FITNESS, pg. 1847, pg. 477
TELLURIDE SKI & GOLF COMPANY LLP, pg. 587, pg. 336
TOWN SPORTS INTERNATIONAL HOLDINGS, INC., pg. 589, pg. 1303
VAIL RESORTS, INC., pg. 1117, pg. 313
WYNN RESORTS LIMITED, pg. 1119, pg. 1030

7993 - Coin-Operated Amusement Devices

CAPCOM USA, INC., pg. 950, pg. 254
CEC ENTERTAINMENT, INC., pg. 1721, pg. 1717
MR. GATTI'S, LP, pg. 1741, pg. 1664
PENN NATIONAL GAMING, INC., pg. 574, pg. 1595
PETER PIPER, INC., pg. 1744, pg. 18

7996 - Amusement Parks

ADVENTURE LANDS OF AMERICA, INC., pg. 526, pg. 701
ALL-AMERICAN SPORTPARK, INC., pg. 527, pg. 1022
BUSCH GARDENS TAMPA BAY, pg. 535, pg. 472
CANADA'S WONDERLAND COMPANY, pg. 536, pg. 1947
CAROWINDS, pg. 537, pg. 1364
CBS CORPORATION, pg. 273, pg. 1210
CEDAR FAIR, L.P., pg. 537, pg. 1471
CEDAR POINT, pg. 537, pg. 1472
DISNEY INTERACTIVE MEDIA GROUP, pg. 1239, pg. 95
FIESTA TEXAS, INC., pg. 548, pg. 1740
FLORIDA STATE FAIR AUTHORITY, pg. 549, pg. 473
GODWIN'S GATORLAND, INC., pg. 550, pg. 453
GRAND OLE OPRY, pg. 289, pg. 1651
GREAT AMERICA, pg. 551, pg. 265
GREAT WOLF RESORTS, INC., pg. 1093, pg. 1866
HERSCHEND FAMILY ENTERTAINMENT CORP., pg. 552, pg. 973
HERSHEY ENTERTAINMENT & RESORTS COMPANY, pg. 1094, pg. 1539
KNOTT'S BERRY FARM, pg. 556, pg. 50
LEGOLAND CALIFORNIA LLC, pg. 557, pg. 59
ONTARIO PLACE CORPORATION, pg. 572, pg. 1941
SEAWORLD ORLANDO, pg. 582, pg. 455
SEAWORLD PARKS & ENTERTAINMENT LLC, pg. 582, pg. 456
SEAWORLD TEXAS, pg. 583, pg. 1742
SILVER SPRINGS, INC., pg. 583, pg. 468
SIX FLAGS ENTERTAINMENT CORPORATION, pg. 583, pg. 1698
SIX FLAGS OVER GEORGIA, INC., pg. 583, pg. 525
SIX FLAGS OVER TEXAS, INC., pg. 583, pg. 1660
SIX FLAGS SAINT LOUIS LLC, pg. 584, pg. 977
SIX FLAGS THEME PARKS INC., pg. 584, pg. 1699
UNIVERSAL ORLANDO, pg. 590, pg. 456
THE WALT DISNEY COMPANY, pg. 317, pg. 52
WEEKI WACHEE SPRINGS, LLC, pg. 591, pg. 478
WET 'N WILD, INC., pg. 592, pg. 457
WILD ADVENTURES, INC., pg. 592, pg. 542
WILDWATER KINGDOM, pg. 592, pg. 1404

7997 - Membership Sports & Recreation Clubs

AMERICAN GOLF CORPORATION, pg. 528, pg. 272
BAYOU GOLF CLUB, pg. 1081, pg. 438
BENCHMARK HOSPITALITY INTERNATIONAL INC., pg. 1081, pg. 1747
THE CLIFFS COMMUNITIES, INC., pg. 1086, pg. 1623
CLUBCORP, INC., pg. 1086, pg. 1677
THE COEUR D'ALENE RESORT, pg. 1087, pg. 549
CONSOLIDATED-TOMOKA LAND CO., pg. 1087, pg. 419
HOBE SOUND GOLF CLUB, INC., pg. 1095, pg. 430
HONOURS GOLF COMPANY, LLC, pg. 1096, pg. 3
MINNESOTA GOLF ASSOCIATION, pg. 147, pg. 925
MISSION INN RESORTS INC., pg. 1105, pg. 431
OJAI VALLEY INN & SPA, pg. 1106, pg. 173
ORANGE COUNTY NATIONAL GOLF CENTER & LODGE, pg. 1107, pg. 480
PGA TOUR, INC., pg. 574, pg. 460
SOUTHWOOD GOLF CLUB, pg. 1113, pg. 470

7999 - Amusement & Recreation Services, NEC

AFFINITY GAMING LLC, pg. 526, pg. 1022
ALL-AMERICAN SPORTPARK, INC., pg. 527, pg. 1022
AMERICAN GOLF CORPORATION, pg. 528, pg. 272
AMERISTAR CASINOS, INC., pg. 528, pg. 1022
AMF BOWLING CENTERS, INC., pg. 528, pg. 1795
ARCHON CORPORATION, pg. 1080, pg. 1030
ARKANSAS DEPARTMENT OF PARKS & TOURISM, pg. 988, pg. 33
THE ART INSTITUTE OF CHICAGO, pg. 530, pg. 565
ASCENT CAPITAL GROUP, pg. 270, pg. 330
ATLANTA MOTOR SPEEDWAY, INC., pg. 530, pg. 533
AUDUBON NATURE INSTITUTE, pg. 531, pg. 746

BALLY TECHNOLOGIES, INC., *pg.* 531, *pg.* 1022
BALLY'S PARK PLACE, INC., *pg.* 1080, *pg.* 1041
BATAVIA DOWNS GAMING, *pg.* 533, *pg.* 1140
BAYOU GOLF CLUB, *pg.* 1081, *pg.* 438
BELLINGRATH GARDENS & HOME, *pg.* 1794, *pg.* 8
BENCHMARK HOSPITALITY INTERNATIONAL INC., *pg.* 1081, *pg.* 1747
BOYD GAMING CORPORATION, *pg.* 1082, *pg.* 1022
BUSCH GARDENS TAMPA BAY, *pg.* 535, *pg.* 472
CAESARS ENTERTAINMENT CORPORATION, *pg.* 1083, *pg.* 1023
CAESARS NEW JERSEY, INC., *pg.* 1084, *pg.* 1041
CALGARY STAMPEDE, *pg.* 536, *pg.* 1902
CANTERBURY PARK HOLDING CORPORATION, *pg.* 536, *pg.* 964
CAPCOM USA, INC., *pg.* 950, *pg.* 254
CARMIKE CINEMAS, INC., *pg.* 273, *pg.* 528
CARNIVAL CORPORATION, *pg.* 1902, *pg.* 441
CASINO PLAYERS, INC., *pg.* 537, *pg.* 421
CEC ENTERTAINMENT, INC., *pg.* 1721, *pg.* 1717
CEDAR FAIR, L.P., *pg.* 537, *pg.* 1471
CEDAR RAPIDS SYMPHONY, *pg.* 538, *pg.* 702
CENTURY CASINOS INC., *pg.* 538, *pg.* 315
CHANCE RIDES MANUFACTURING CO., *pg.* 538, *pg.* 723
CHICAGO ZOOLOGICAL SOCIETY, INC., *pg.* 539, *pg.* 559
CHILDREN'S MUSEUM OF DENVER, INC., *pg.* 540, *pg.* 317
CHURCHILL DOWNS, INC., *pg.* 540, *pg.* 733
THE CLIFFS COMMUNITIES, INC., *pg.* 1086, *pg.* 1623
CLUBCORP, INC., *pg.* 1086, *pg.* 1677
THE COEUR D'ALENE RESORT, *pg.* 1087, *pg.* 549
COFFEE HOLDING CO., INC., *pg.* 849, *pg.* 1343
COMMONWEALTH ZOOLOGICAL CORP., *pg.* 542, *pg.* 793
CONSOLIDATED-TOMOKA LAND CO., *pg.* 1087, *pg.* 419
CORE MEDIA GROUP, *pg.* 1765, *pg.* 1218
DAVE & BUSTER'S ENTERTAINMENT, INC., *pg.* 1724, *pg.* 1679
DAYBREAK GAME COMPANY, LLC, *pg.* 1237, *pg.* 202
D.C. LOTTERY & CHARITABLE GAMES CONTROL BOARD, *pg.* 991, *pg.* 398
THE DELTONA CORPORATION, *pg.* 1089, *pg.* 452
DETROIT ENTERTAINMENT, LLC, *pg.* 1089, *pg.* 879
DIAMOND JO, LLC, *pg.* 1089, *pg.* 707
DIVI HOTELS, INC., *pg.* 1090, *pg.* 1361
DORAKU CORP., *pg.* 1727, *pg.* 448
DOVER DOWNS GAMING & ENTERTAINMENT, INC., *pg.* 545, *pg.* 387
DOVER MOTORSPORTS, INC., *pg.* 545, *pg.* 387
EASTERN STATES EXPOSITION, *pg.* 992, *pg.* 857
ECHO FARMS GOLF & COUNTRY CLUB, INC., *pg.* 1833, *pg.* 1392
EDUCATION MANAGEMENT CORPORATION, *pg.* 601, *pg.* 1575
ELDORADO RESORTS, INC., *pg.* 546, *pg.* 1031
EMPIRE RESORTS, INC., *pg.* 1090, *pg.* 1183
FAIR GROUNDS CORPORATION, *pg.* 547, *pg.* 747
FINGER LAKES RACING ASSOCIATION INC., *pg.* 548, *pg.* 1160
FLORIDA GAMING CORPORATION, *pg.* 548, *pg.* 442
THE FLORIDA LOTTERY, *pg.* 992, *pg.* 469
FORTUNET, INC., *pg.* 953, *pg.* 1024
FRIENDFINDER NETWORKS INC., *pg.* 1643, *pg.* 411
GAMING PARTNERS INTERNATIONAL CORPORATION, *pg.* 954, *pg.* 1024
GEORGIA LOTTERY CORPORATION, *pg.* 993, *pg.* 506
GODWIN'S GATORLAND, INC., *pg.* 550, *pg.* 453
GOLD STRIKE CASINO RESORT, *pg.* 1093, *pg.* 971
GREAT WOLF RESORTS, INC., *pg.* 1093, *pg.* 1866
HARD ROCK CAFE INTERNATIONAL, INC., *pg.* 1730, *pg.* 454
HARMONIX MUSIC SYSTEMS, INC., *pg.* 1256, *pg.* 808
HARRAH'S LOUISIANA DOWNS CASINO & RACETRACK, *pg.* 551, *pg.* 743
HOBE SOUND GOLF CLUB, INC., *pg.* 1095, *pg.* 430
HOLLYWOOD MEDIA CORP., *pg.* 1256, *pg.* 412
HONOURS GOLF COMPANY, LLC, *pg.* 1096, *pg.* 3
HUGGER MUGGER YOGA PRODUCTS LLC, *pg.* 1836, *pg.* 1758
HULMAN & COMPANY, *pg.* 864, *pg.* 698
IDAHO LOTTERY, *pg.* 995, *pg.* 547
ILLINOIS STATE LOTTERY, *pg.* 995, *pg.* 578
INTERNATIONAL GAME TECHNOLOGY, *pg.* 420, *pg.* 1606
INTERNATIONAL GAME TECHNOLOGY, *pg.* 957, *pg.* 1024
INTERNATIONAL SPEEDWAY CORPORATION, *pg.* 553, *pg.* 420
INTRAWEST ULC, *pg.* 1098, *pg.* 320
ISLE OF CAPRI CASINOS, INC., *pg.* 553, *pg.* 998
JOHN G. SHEDD AQUARIUM, *pg.* 555, *pg.* 579
THE JUILLIARD SCHOOL, *pg.* 603, *pg.* 1247
KEENELAND ASSOCIATION INC., *pg.* 1477, *pg.* 730
KENTUCKY LOTTERY CORPORATION, *pg.* 996, *pg.* 735
LAS VEGAS SANDS CORP., *pg.* 1100, *pg.* 1027
LIFE TIME FITNESS, INC., *pg.* 1556, *pg.* 920
LINCOLN PARK ZOO, *pg.* 557, *pg.* 580
LITTLEFIELD CORPORATION, *pg.* 558, *pg.* 1664
LIVE NATION ENTERTAINMENT, INC., *pg.* 558, *pg.* 47
LOS ANGELES COUNTY FAIR ASSOCIATION, *pg.* 559, *pg.* 185
LOS ANGELES TURF CLUB, INCORPORATED, *pg.* 559, *pg.* 43
LOUISIANA LOTTERY CORPORATION, *pg.* 997, *pg.* 742
LOWRY PARK ZOOLOGICAL SOCIETY OF TAMPA INC., *pg.* 559, *pg.* 474
MAJOR LEAGUE SOCCER LLC, *pg.* 560, *pg.* 1256
MAMMOTH MOUNTAIN SKI AREA, *pg.* 1102, *pg.* 142
MARINELAND OF FLORIDA, *pg.* 561, *pg.* 461
MARYLAND ZOOLOGICAL SOCIETY, INC., *pg.* 561, *pg.* 758
MAYWOOD PARK TROTTING ASSOCIATION, INC., *pg.* 561, *pg.* 631
METROPOLITAN PIER & EXPOSITION AUTHORITY, *pg.* 562, *pg.* 581
MGM RESORTS INTERNATIONAL, *pg.* 1105, *pg.* 1028
MIAMI CITY BALLET, INC., *pg.* 562, *pg.* 448
MICHIGAN STATE LOTTERY BUREAU, *pg.* 999, *pg.* 895
MINNESOTA GOLF ASSOCIATION, *pg.* 147, *pg.* 925
MISSION INN RESORTS INC., *pg.* 1105, *pg.* 431
MISSOURI LOTTERY, *pg.* 999, *pg.* 979
MOHEGAN TRIBAL GAMING AUTHORITY, *pg.* 564, *pg.* 381
MONTANA LOTTERY, *pg.* 1000, *pg.* 1008
MOUNT CRANMORE SKI RESORT, INC., *pg.* 564, *pg.* 1038
MR. GATTI'S, LP, *pg.* 1741, *pg.* 1664
MULTIMEDIA GAMES INC., *pg.* 442, *pg.* 1664
NAPLES BEACH HOTEL & GOLF CLUB, *pg.* 1106, *pg.* 451
NAPLES ZOO INC., *pg.* 565, *pg.* 451
NATIONAL AQUARIUM IN BALTIMORE INC., *pg.* 565, *pg.* 758
NATIONAL CINEMEDIA, INC., *pg.* 567, *pg.* 314
NATIONAL COLLEGIATE ATHLETIC ASSOCIATION, *pg.* 567, *pg.* 688
NATIONAL HOT ROD ASSOCIATION, *pg.* 149, *pg.* 99
NATIONAL MARINE MANUFACTURERS ASSOCIATION, *pg.* 149, *pg.* 584
NATIONAL PARK FOUNDATION, *pg.* 1000, *pg.* 402
NATIONAL THOROUGHBRED RACING ASSOCIATION, *pg.* 569, *pg.* 730
NEBRASKA LOTTERY, *pg.* 1000, *pg.* 1012
NEVADA GOLD & CASINOS, INC., *pg.* 1106, *pg.* 1028
NEW JERSEY STATE LOTTERY, *pg.* 1000, *pg.* 1126
NEW YORK CITY BALLET, *pg.* 569, *pg.* 1268
NEWPORT AQUARIUM, *pg.* 571, *pg.* 739
NEWPORT ART MUSEUM, *pg.* 571, *pg.* 1603
NTN BUZZTIME, INC., *pg.* 659, *pg.* 60
OAKLAWN JOCKEY CLUB, INC., *pg.* 571, *pg.* 32
ODYSSEY MARINE EXPLORATION, INC., *pg.* 1918, *pg.* 475
OHIO LOTTERY COMMISSION, *pg.* 1002, *pg.* 1433
OJAI VALLEY INN & SPA, *pg.* 1106, *pg.* 173
OKLAHOMA CITY ZOOLOGICAL PARK, *pg.* 572, *pg.* 1487
OMAHA ZOOLOGICAL SOCIETY, *pg.* 572, *pg.* 1017
THE OMNI HOMESTEAD RESORT, *pg.* 1106, *pg.* 1786
ORANGE COUNTY NATIONAL GOLF CENTER & LODGE, *pg.* 1107, *pg.* 480
THE PALEY CENTER FOR MEDIA, *pg.* 573, *pg.* 1275
PEAK RESORTS, INC., *pg.* 574, *pg.* 1007
PENN NATIONAL GAMING, INC., *pg.* 574, *pg.* 1595
PETER PIPER, INC., *pg.* 1744, *pg.* 18
PGA TOUR, INC., *pg.* 574, *pg.* 460
PHILADELPHIA 76ERS, L.P., *pg.* 575, *pg.* 1568
PINNACLE ENTERTAINMENT, INC., *pg.* 576, *pg.* 1029
POLYNESIAN CULTURAL CENTER, *pg.* 577, *pg.* 545
PREMIER EXHIBITIONS, INC., *pg.* 577, *pg.* 518
PRINCESS TOURS, *pg.* 1920, *pg.* 1838
RHODE ISLAND LOTTERY, *pg.* 1004, *pg.* 1600
ROOMLINX, INC., *pg.* 307, *pg.* 313
RYMAN HOSPITALITY PROPERTIES, INC, *pg.* 1111, *pg.* 1653
SADDLEBROOK RESORTS, INC., *pg.* 1111, *pg.* 478
SARATOGA CASINO & RACEWAY, *pg.* 581, *pg.* 1340
SCIENTIFIC GAMES CORPORATION, *pg.* 468, *pg.* 1029
SEA ISLAND ACQUISITION LLC, *pg.* 1111, *pg.* 540
SEA PINES RESORT, LLC, *pg.* 1112, *pg.* 1620
SEAWORLD ORLANDO, *pg.* 582, *pg.* 455
SEAWORLD TEXAS, *pg.* 583, *pg.* 1742
SENECA PARK ZOOLOGICAL SOCIETY, *pg.* 583, *pg.* 1337
SILVER SPRINGS, INC., *pg.* 583, *pg.* 468
SINCLAIR OIL CORPORATION, *pg.* 984, *pg.* 1760
SIX FLAGS OVER TEXAS, INC., *pg.* 583, *pg.* 1660
SIX FLAGS SAINT LOUIS LLC, *pg.* 584, *pg.* 977
SMSC ENTERPRISES, *pg.* 584, *pg.* 954
SOUTH FLORIDA MUSEUM, *pg.* 584, *pg.* 415
SOUTHWOOD GOLF CLUB, *pg.* 1113, *pg.* 470
SPEEDWAY MOTORSPORTS, INC., *pg.* 584, *pg.* 1370
SPOLETO FESTIVAL USA, *pg.* 584, *pg.* 1613
THE STATE LOTTERY COMMISSION OF INDIANA, *pg.* 1006, *pg.* 690
STATION CASINOS, INC., *pg.* 585, *pg.* 1030
STEAMBOAT SKI & RESORT CORPORATION, *pg.* 1115, *pg.* 336
STRATOSPHERE CORPORATION, *pg.* 1115, *pg.* 1030
STRATTON MOUNTAIN RESORT, *pg.* 1115, *pg.* 1768
SUGARLOAF/USA, *pg.* 586, *pg.* 749
SUNDAY RIVER SKIWAY CORP., *pg.* 586, *pg.* 749
TAOS SKI VALLEY, INC., *pg.* 1116, *pg.* 1136
TELLURIDE SKI & GOLF COMPANY LLP, *pg.* 587, *pg.* 336
TEXAS LOTTERY COMMISSION, *pg.* 1007, *pg.* 1666
THANKSGIVING POINT, *pg.* 587, *pg.* 1751
TICKETMASTER ENTERTAINMENT LLC, *pg.* 1284, *pg.* 48
TOMMY BARTLETT, INC., *pg.* 588, *pg.* 1899
TOURISM NEW ZEALAND, *pg.* 1008, *pg.* 276
TOWN SPORTS INTERNATIONAL HOLDINGS, INC., *pg.* 589, *pg.* 1303
VAIL RESORTS, INC., *pg.* 1117, *pg.* 313
VCG HOLDING CORP., *pg.* 590, *pg.* 333
VIA RAIL CANADA INC., *pg.* 1930, *pg.* 1957
VIRGINIA STATE LOTTERY DEPARTMENT, *pg.* 1010, *pg.* 1804
WARNER MUSIC GROUP CORP., *pg.* 590, *pg.* 1313
WEEKI WACHEE SPRINGS, LLC, *pg.* 591, *pg.* 478
WILDLIFE CONSERVATION SOCIETY, *pg.* 592, *pg.* 1145
WMS INDUSTRIES INC., *pg.* 593, *pg.* 666
WORLD WRESTLING ENTERTAINMENT, INC., *pg.* 595, *pg.* 380
WYNN LAS VEGAS, LLC, *pg.* 1119, *pg.* 1030
WYNN RESORTS LIMITED, *pg.* 1119, *pg.* 1030
ZOOLOGICAL SOCIETY OF SAN DIEGO, *pg.* 595, *pg.* 211

8011 - Offices & Clinics of Doctors of Medicine

21ST CENTURY ONCOLOGY, INC., *pg.* 1483, *pg.* 427
ANCILLA SYSTEMS INCORPORATED, *pg.* 1494, *pg.* 682
ASCENSION HEALTH ALLIANCE, *pg.* 1496, *pg.* 992
COHEN'S FASHION OPTICAL INC., *pg.* 1406, *pg.* 1161
COMMUNITY HEALTH SYSTEMS, INC., *pg.* 1516, *pg.* 1632
COMPREHENSIVE CARE CORPORATION, *pg.* 1517, *pg.* 472
CONTINUCARE CORPORATION, *pg.* 1518, *pg.* 442
COVENTRY HEALTH CARE, INC., *pg.* 1519, *pg.* 761
THE DETROIT MEDICAL CENTER, *pg.* 1524, *pg.* 880
ERLANGER HEALTH SYSTEM, *pg.* 1529, *pg.* 1629
FUJIREBIO DIAGNOSTICS INC., *pg.* 1531, *pg.* 1550
GLAUCOMA RESEARCH FOUNDATION, *pg.* 142, *pg.* 219
GRIFFIN HEALTH SERVICES CORPORATION, *pg.* 1538, *pg.* 345
HEALTH GRADES, INC., *pg.* 1256, *pg.* 319
HEALTHPARTNERS, INC., *pg.* 1203, *pg.* 918
HEALTHWAYS, INC., *pg.* 1540, *pg.* 1632
HUMANA, INC., *pg.* 1204, *pg.* 734
KAISER PERMANENTE, *pg.* 1552, *pg.* 171
LAHEY CLINIC, *pg.* 1554, *pg.* 805
LCA-VISION INC., *pg.* 1419, *pg.* 1416
MAGELLAN HEALTH SERVICES, INC., *pg.* 1557, *pg.* 337
MAINE COAST REGIONAL HEALTH FACILITIES INC., *pg.* 1557, *pg.* 749
MANATEE MEMORIAL HOSPITAL & HEALTH SYSTEM, *pg.* 1558, *pg.* 415
MARSHFIELD CLINIC, *pg.* 1558, *pg.* 1869
MEMORIAL HEALTH SERVICES INC., *pg.* 1565, *pg.* 90
MICHAEL DATTOLI MD, LLC, *pg.* 1568, *pg.* 466
MOLINA HEALTHCARE, INC., *pg.* 1569, *pg.* 123
NORTHSIDE HOSPITAL, *pg.* 1574, *pg.* 516
NORTHWESTERN MEMORIAL HEALTHCARE, *pg.* 1574, *pg.* 585
SAINT THOMAS MIDTOWN HOSPITAL, *pg.* 1591, *pg.* 1654
SECHRIST INDUSTRIES, INC., *pg.* 1593, *pg.* 43
SMITHS MEDICAL MD, INC., *pg.* 1594, *pg.* 963

SOUTH BEND CLINIC LLP, *pg.* 1113, *pg.* 697
SPARKS HEALTH SYSTEM, *pg.* 1595, *pg.* 32
UNITED SURGICAL PARTNERS INTERNATIONAL, INC., *pg.* 1604, *pg.* 1658
UNIVERSITY OF ARKANSAS FOR MEDICAL SCIENCES, *pg.* 608, *pg.* 34
WATAUGA MEDICAL CENTER, *pg.* 1609, *pg.* 1358
WELLCARE HEALTH PLANS INC., *pg.* 1223, *pg.* 476
WELLQUEST MEDICAL & WELLNESS CORPORATION, *pg.* 1610, *pg.* 31
WELLSTAR HEALTH SYSTEM, INC., *pg.* 161, *pg.* 536

8021 - Offices & Clinics of Dentists

BIRNER DENTAL MANAGEMENT SERVICES, INC., *pg.* 1506, *pg.* 317
DENTAL ONE, INC., *pg.* 1522, *pg.* 1462
LAS VEGAS INSTITUTE FOR ADVANCED DENTAL STUDIES, *pg.* 145, *pg.* 1027
ORTHOSYNETICS, INC., *pg.* 791, *pg.* 1657

8042 - Offices & Clinics of Optometrists

LCA-VISION INC., *pg.* 1419, *pg.* 1416

8049 - Offices & Clinics of Health Practitioners, NEC

ACADEMIC COMMUNICATION ASSOCIATES, INC., *pg.* 1613, *pg.* 173
ASCENSION HEALTH ALLIANCE, *pg.* 1496, *pg.* 992
CONTINUCARE CORPORATION, *pg.* 1518, *pg.* 442
EMERGENCY MEDICAL SERVICES CORPORATION, *pg.* 1528, *pg.* 331
GUS COMMUNICATIONS, INC., *pg.* 1538, *pg.* 1817
HANGER INC., *pg.* 1539, *pg.* 1663
HEALTHSOUTH CORPORATION, *pg.* 1540, *pg.* 3
HOOPER HOLMES, INC., *pg.* 1542, *pg.* 718
KAISER PERMANENTE, *pg.* 1552, *pg.* 171
LCA-VISION INC., *pg.* 1419, *pg.* 1416
MAGELLAN HEALTH SERVICES, INC., *pg.* 1557, *pg.* 337
MASSAGE ENVY LIMITED, LLC, *pg.* 516, *pg.* 23
SCHIFF NUTRITION INTERNATIONAL, INC., *pg.* 1592, *pg.* 1760
UNITYPOINT HEALTH, *pg.* 1604, *pg.* 706
US ONCOLOGY, INC., *pg.* 1604, *pg.* 1747
U.S. PHYSICAL THERAPY, INC., *pg.* 1604, *pg.* 1716
WELLSTAR HEALTH SYSTEM, INC., *pg.* 161, *pg.* 536

8051 - Skilled Nursing Care Facilities

ADCARE HEALTH SYSTEMS, INC., *pg.* 1486, *pg.* 539
ASCENSION HEALTH ALLIANCE, *pg.* 1496, *pg.* 992
BROOKDALE SENIOR LIVING INC., *pg.* 1511, *pg.* 1627
GENESIS HEALTHCARE CORP., *pg.* 1534, *pg.* 1543
GOLDEN LIVING, *pg.* 1538, *pg.* 32
JEWISH HOME LIFECARE, *pg.* 1548, *pg.* 1246
LIFE CARE CENTERS OF AMERICA, *pg.* 1555, *pg.* 1630
MAGELLAN HEALTH SERVICES, INC., *pg.* 1557, *pg.* 337
THE RENFREW CENTERS INC., *pg.* 1589, *pg.* 1570
RES-CARE, INC., *pg.* 1589, *pg.* 738
SUNRISE SENIOR LIVING, INC., *pg.* 1599, *pg.* 1795
UNIVERSITY GENERAL HEALTH SYSTEM INC, *pg.* 1396, *pg.* 1716

8059 - Nursing & Personal Care Facilities, NEC

ADCARE HEALTH SYSTEMS, INC., *pg.* 1486, *pg.* 539
BANNER HEALTH SYSTEM, *pg.* 1498, *pg.* 15
BROOKDALE SENIOR LIVING INC., *pg.* 1511, *pg.* 1627
CAPITAL SENIOR LIVING CORPORATION, *pg.* 1084, *pg.* 1677
CENTERLIGHT HEALTH SYSTEM, *pg.* 1514, *pg.* 1144
EXTENDICARE, *pg.* 1530, *pg.* 1923
EXTENDICARE HEALTH SERVICES INC., *pg.* 1530, *pg.* 1874
GENESIS HEALTHCARE CORP., *pg.* 1534, *pg.* 1543
GENTIVA HEALTH SERVICES, INC., *pg.* 1534, *pg.* 506
GOLDEN LIVING, *pg.* 1538, *pg.* 32
HCR MANORCARE, INC., *pg.* 1539, *pg.* 1476
HEALTHSOUTH CORPORATION, *pg.* 1540, *pg.* 3
KINDRED HEALTHCARE, INC., *pg.* 1553, *pg.* 736
LIFE CARE CENTERS OF AMERICA, *pg.* 1555, *pg.* 1630
PRESENCE HEALTH, *pg.* 1586, *pg.* 587
RES-CARE, INC., *pg.* 1589, *pg.* 738
REVERA INC., *pg.* 799, *pg.* 1928
SAVA SENIOR CARE LLC, *pg.* 1592, *pg.* 519
SUNRISE SENIOR LIVING, INC., *pg.* 1599, *pg.* 1795
TEMPLE UNIVERSITY HEALTH SYSTEM, *pg.* 1601, *pg.* 1571

8062 - General Medical and Surgical Hospitals

ADVOCATE HEALTH CARE, *pg.* 1487, *pg.* 607
ALEXIAN BROTHERS HEALTH SYSTEM FOUNDATION, *pg.* 1489, *pg.* 553
ALL CHILDREN'S HOSPITAL INC., *pg.* 1490, *pg.* 461
ALLINA HEALTH SYSTEM, INC., *pg.* 1491, *pg.* 929
ASCENSION HEALTH ALLIANCE, *pg.* 1496, *pg.* 992
ATLANTIC HEALTH SYSTEM INC., *pg.* 1498, *pg.* 1087
BANNER HEALTH SYSTEM, *pg.* 1498, *pg.* 15
BAYFRONT HEALTH SYSTEM, INC., *pg.* 1500, *pg.* 461
BAYLOR HEALTH CARE SYSTEM, *pg.* 1500, *pg.* 1676
BAYSTATE HEALTH SYSTEM, INC., *pg.* 1501, *pg.* 845
BON SECOURS HEALTH SYSTEM, INC., *pg.* 1508, *pg.* 774
CALIFORNIA PACIFIC MEDICAL CENTER, *pg.* 1511, *pg.* 214
CANCER TREATMENT CENTERS OF AMERICA, *pg.* 1511, *pg.* 410
CAREGROUP, INC., *pg.* 1513, *pg.* 792
CARILION HEALTH SYSTEM, *pg.* 1513, *pg.* 1806
CENTEGRA NORTHERN ILLINOIS MEDICAL CENTER, *pg.* 1196, *pg.* 632
CHRISTIANA CARE CORPORATION, *pg.* 1515, *pg.* 390
CITY OF HOPE NATIONAL MEDICAL CENTER, *pg.* 1516, *pg.* 77
CLEVELAND CLINIC, *pg.* 1516, *pg.* 1429
COMMUNITY HEALTH SYSTEMS, INC., *pg.* 1516, *pg.* 1632
CONMED HEALTHCARE MANAGEMENT, INC., *pg.* 1518, *pg.* 772
THE DEAN A. MCGEE EYE INSTITUTE, *pg.* 138, *pg.* 1485
THE DETROIT MEDICAL CENTER, *pg.* 1524, *pg.* 880
DUKE UNIVERSITY HEALTH SYSTEM, *pg.* 601, *pg.* 1371
DYNACQ HEALTHCARE, INC., *pg.* 1526, *pg.* 1728
EAST ALABAMA MEDICAL CENTER, *pg.* 1526, *pg.* 8
ERLANGER HEALTH SYSTEM, *pg.* 1529, *pg.* 1629
GREENVILLE HOSPITAL SYSTEM INC., *pg.* 1538, *pg.* 1617
GRIFFIN HEALTH SERVICES CORPORATION, *pg.* 1538, *pg.* 345
HALIFAX MEDICAL CENTER, *pg.* 1538, *pg.* 420
HCA HOLDINGS, INC., *pg.* 1539, *pg.* 1651
HCR MANORCARE, INC., *pg.* 1539, *pg.* 1476
INOVA HEALTH SYSTEM, *pg.* 1545, *pg.* 1781
INTERMOUNTAIN HEALTH CARE INC., *pg.* 1546, *pg.* 1759
IPC THE HOSPITALIST COMPANY, INC., *pg.* 1547, *pg.* 167
KENNEDY HEALTH SYSTEM, *pg.* 1553, *pg.* 1128
KINDRED HEALTHCARE, INC., *pg.* 1553, *pg.* 736
LAHEY CLINIC, *pg.* 1554, *pg.* 805
LEE MEMORIAL HEALTH SYSTEM, *pg.* 1555, *pg.* 428
LEGACY HEALTH SYSTEM, *pg.* 1555, *pg.* 1504
LENOX HILL HOSPITAL, *pg.* 1555, *pg.* 1251
MAGELLAN HEALTH SERVICES, INC., *pg.* 1557, *pg.* 337
MAINE COAST REGIONAL HEALTH FACILITIES INC., *pg.* 1557, *pg.* 749
MANATEE MEMORIAL HOSPITAL & HEALTH SYSTEM, *pg.* 1558, *pg.* 415
MARIANJOY REHABILITATION HOSPITAL, *pg.* 1558, *pg.* 669
MEMORIAL HEALTH SERVICES INC., *pg.* 1565, *pg.* 90
MEMORIAL HERMANN HEALTHCARE SYSTEM, *pg.* 1565, *pg.* 1711
MEMORIAL SLOAN-KETTERING CANCER CENTER INC., *pg.* 1565, *pg.* 1258
MONTEFIORE MEDICAL CENTER, *pg.* 1569, *pg.* 1144
MOUNT SINAI MEDICAL CENTER, *pg.* 1569, *pg.* 448
NEW YORK-PRESBYTERIAN HEALTHCARE SYSTEM, *pg.* 1573, *pg.* 1269
NICKLAUS CHILDREN'S HOSPITAL, *pg.* 1573, *pg.* 444
NORTHSIDE HOSPITAL, *pg.* 1574, *pg.* 516
NORTHWESTERN MEMORIAL HEALTHCARE, *pg.* 1574, *pg.* 585
OAKWOOD HEALTHCARE, INC., *pg.* 1577, *pg.* 878
O'CONNOR HOSPITAL, *pg.* 1577, *pg.* 248
OHIOHEALTH, *pg.* 1578, *pg.* 1443
OSF HEALTHCARE SYSTEM, *pg.* 1579, *pg.* 652
PARTNERS HEALTHCARE SYSTEM, INC., *pg.* 1580, *pg.* 800
PRESBYTERIAN HEALTHCARE SERVICES, *pg.* 1586, *pg.* 1135
PRESENCE HEALTH, *pg.* 1586, *pg.* 587
PROVIDENCE HEALTH SYSTEM, *pg.* 1587, *pg.* 1829
THE RENFREW CENTERS INC., *pg.* 1589, *pg.* 1570
SAINT PETERSBURG GENERAL HOSPITAL, *pg.* 1591, *pg.* 464
SAINT THOMAS MIDTOWN HOSPITAL, *pg.* 1591, *pg.* 1654
SCRIPPS, *pg.* 1593, *pg.* 209
SCRIPPS MERCY HOSPITAL, *pg.* 1593, *pg.* 209
SENTARA HEALTHCARE, *pg.* 1593, *pg.* 1797
SHRINERS HOSPITALS FOR CHILDREN, *pg.* 1594, *pg.* 475
SOUTH BROWARD HOSPITAL DISTRICT, *pg.* 1595, *pg.* 431
ST. ALPHONSUS REGIONAL MEDICAL CENTER, *pg.* 1596, *pg.* 548
ST. JOHN HEALTH, *pg.* 1596, *pg.* 912
ST. JUDE CHILDREN'S RESEARCH HOSPITAL, *pg.* 1596, *pg.* 1646
ST. VINCENT MEDICAL CENTER, *pg.* 1597, *pg.* 140
SUNLINK HEALTH SYSTEMS, INC., *pg.* 1430, *pg.* 520
SUTTER HEALTH, *pg.* 1600, *pg.* 197
TENET HEALTHCARE CORPORATION, *pg.* 1601, *pg.* 1688
UNITED SURGICAL PARTNERS INTERNATIONAL, INC., *pg.* 1604, *pg.* 1658
UNIVERSAL HEALTH SERVICES INC., *pg.* 1604, *pg.* 1544
UNIVERSITY HOSPITAL & MEDICAL CENTER, *pg.* 1604, *pg.* 470
VITAS HEALTHCARE CORPORATION, *pg.* 1608, *pg.* 447
WATAUGA MEDICAL CENTER, *pg.* 1609, *pg.* 1358
WELLSTAR HEALTH SYSTEM, INC., *pg.* 161, *pg.* 536

8063 - Psychiatric Hospitals

ASCENSION HEALTH ALLIANCE, *pg.* 1496, *pg.* 992
COMPREHENSIVE CARE CORPORATION, *pg.* 1517, *pg.* 472
CONMED HEALTHCARE MANAGEMENT, INC., *pg.* 1518, *pg.* 772
INTERMOUNTAIN HOSPITAL, *pg.* 1546, *pg.* 547
MAGELLAN HEALTH SERVICES, INC., *pg.* 1557, *pg.* 337
UNIVERSAL HEALTH SERVICES INC., *pg.* 1604, *pg.* 1544

8069 - Specialty Hospitals, Except Psychiatric (except childrenÆs and substance abuse hospitals)

ALL CHILDREN'S HOSPITAL INC., *pg.* 1490, *pg.* 461
ASCENSION HEALTH ALLIANCE, *pg.* 1496, *pg.* 992
CANCER TREATMENT CENTERS OF AMERICA, *pg.* 1511, *pg.* 410
CHILDREN'S HOSPITAL LOS ANGELES, *pg.* 275, *pg.* 128
CONMED HEALTHCARE MANAGEMENT, INC., *pg.* 1518, *pg.* 772
DYNACQ HEALTHCARE, INC., *pg.* 1526, *pg.* 1728
GREENVILLE HOSPITAL SYSTEM INC., *pg.* 1538, *pg.* 1617
KINDRED HEALTHCARE, INC., *pg.* 1553, *pg.* 736
MAGELLAN HEALTH SERVICES, INC., *pg.* 1557, *pg.* 337
MARIANJOY REHABILITATION HOSPITAL, *pg.* 1558, *pg.* 669
MEMORIAL SLOAN-KETTERING CANCER CENTER INC., *pg.* 1565, *pg.* 1258
NICKLAUS CHILDREN'S HOSPITAL, *pg.* 1573, *pg.* 444
OSF HEALTHCARE SYSTEM, *pg.* 1579, *pg.* 652
THE RENFREW CENTERS INC., *pg.* 1589, *pg.* 1570
SHRINERS HOSPITALS FOR CHILDREN, *pg.* 1594, *pg.* 475
TENET HEALTHCARE CORPORATION, *pg.* 1601, *pg.* 1688
VITAS HEALTHCARE CORPORATION, *pg.* 1608, *pg.* 447

8071 - Medical Laboratories (diagnostic imaging centers)

AMERICAN SHARED HOSPITAL SERVICES, *pg.* 1493, *pg.* 212
BIO-REFERENCE LABORATORIES, INC., *pg.* 1402, *pg.* 1058
BIOCLINICA, INC., *pg.* 1506, *pg.* 1556

BOSTWICK LABORATORIES, INC., *pg.* 1509, *pg.* 1782
BRAINSTORM CELL THERAPEUTICS INC., *pg.* 1509, *pg.* 1072
CALADRIUS BIOSCIENCES, INC., *pg.* 1511, *pg.* 1209
CDI, *pg.* 1405, *pg.* 121
CONMED HEALTHCARE MANAGEMENT, INC., *pg.* 1518, *pg.* 772
CONTINENTAL ANALYTICAL SERVICES INC., *pg.* 1518, *pg.* 721
DR. TATTOFF, INC., *pg.* 1525, *pg.* 46
ENZO BIOCHEM INC., *pg.* 1529, *pg.* 1228
ERESEARCH TECHNOLOGY INC., *pg.* 1243, *pg.* 1564
EXACT SCIENCES CORPORATION, *pg.* 1529, *pg.* 1865
GEISINGER HEALTH SYSTEM, *pg.* 1533, *pg.* 1526
GENELINK, INC., *pg.* 1533, *pg.* 438
GENOPTIX, INC., *pg.* 1534, *pg.* 59
HEMACARE CORPORATION, *pg.* 1541, *pg.* 300
IMAGING DIAGNOSTIC SYSTEMS, INC., *pg.* 1544, *pg.* 425
LABORATORY CORPORATION OF AMERICA HOLDINGS, *pg.* 1554, *pg.* 1359
LEGACY HEALTH SYSTEM, *pg.* 1555, *pg.* 1504
MEDTOX SCIENTIFIC, INC., *pg.* 1422, *pg.* 962
NATIONAL DENTEX CORPORATION, *pg.* 1570, *pg.* 834
OMNICELL INC., *pg.* 1578, *pg.* 161
PRAHEALTH SCIENCES, *pg.* 1585, *pg.* 1388
QUEST DIAGNOSTICS INCORPORATED, *pg.* 1587, *pg.* 1080
VIRTUAL RADIOLOGIC CORPORATION, *pg.* 1607, *pg.* 924
WELLSTAR HEALTH SYSTEM, INC., *pg.* 161, *pg.* 536

8072 - Dental Laboratories

CONMED HEALTHCARE MANAGEMENT, INC., *pg.* 1518, *pg.* 772
NATIONAL DENTEX CORPORATION, *pg.* 1570, *pg.* 834

8082 - Home Health Care Services

ADDUS HOMECARE CORPORATION, *pg.* 1487, *pg.* 650
ALERE HEALTH SYSTEMS, INC., *pg.* 1488, *pg.* 535
ALMOST FAMILY, INC., *pg.* 1492, *pg.* 731
AMEDISYS, INC., *pg.* 1493, *pg.* 741
APRIA HEALTHCARE GROUP INC., *pg.* 1495, *pg.* 120
BAYADA NURSES INC., *pg.* 1499, *pg.* 1087
BIOSCRIP, INC., *pg.* 1506, *pg.* 1158
CORAM SPECIALTY INFUSION SERVICES, *pg.* 1519, *pg.* 318
DYNACQ HEALTHCARE, INC., *pg.* 1526, *pg.* 1728
EXTENDICARE, *pg.* 1530, *pg.* 1923
GENTIVA HEALTH SERVICES, INC., *pg.* 1534, *pg.* 506
THE GURWIN JEWISH GERIATRIC CENTER, *pg.* 1538, *pg.* 1153
HEALTH WATCH INC., *pg.* 1540, *pg.* 411
HOME INSTEAD, INC., *pg.* 1542, *pg.* 1016
INTERIM HEALTHCARE INC., *pg.* 417, *pg.* 469
INVACARE CANADA LP, *pg.* 1546, *pg.* 1927
JEWISH HOME LIFECARE, *pg.* 1548, *pg.* 1246
LEGACY HEALTH SYSTEM, *pg.* 1555, *pg.* 1504
LIFE CARE CENTERS OF AMERICA, *pg.* 1555, *pg.* 1630
METROPOLITAN JEWISH HEALTH SYSTEM, *pg.* 1568, *pg.* 1146
NATIONAL HOME HEALTH CARE CORP., *pg.* 1570, *pg.* 1340
NORTHWESTERN MEMORIAL HEALTHCARE, *pg.* 1574, *pg.* 585
PS KIDS LLC, *pg.* 1587, *pg.* 538
RES-CARE, INC., *pg.* 1589, *pg.* 738
SCRIPPS, *pg.* 1593, *pg.* 209
U.S. PHYSICAL THERAPY, INC., *pg.* 1604, *pg.* 1716
VISITING NURSE ASSOCIATION OF FLORIDA, *pg.* 1607, *pg.* 468
VISITING NURSE ASSOCIATION OF SOMERSET HILLS INC., *pg.* 1607, *pg.* 1042
VISITING NURSE SERVICE OF NEW YORK, *pg.* 1607, *pg.* 1311
VISITING NURSE SERVICES IN WESTCHESTER, INC., *pg.* 1607, *pg.* 1354
WELLSTAR HEALTH SYSTEM, INC., *pg.* 161, *pg.* 536

8092 - Kidney Dialysis Centers

FRESENIUS MEDICAL CARE NORTH AMERICA, *pg.* 1531, *pg.* 851
HEALTHWAYS, INC., *pg.* 1540, *pg.* 1632

8093 - Specialty Outpatient Facilities, NEC

ASCENSION HEALTH ALLIANCE, *pg.* 1496, *pg.* 992
CARDIONET, INC., *pg.* 1513, *pg.* 1523
CATASYS, INC., *pg.* 1514, *pg.* 127
CENTRASTATE HEALTHCARE SYSTEM INC., *pg.* 1514, *pg.* 1071
CONTINUCARE CORPORATION, *pg.* 1518, *pg.* 442
CORAM SPECIALTY INFUSION SERVICES, *pg.* 1519, *pg.* 318
CORD BLOOD AMERICA, INC., *pg.* 1519, *pg.* 1023
CRYO-CELL INTERNATIONAL, INC., *pg.* 1520, *pg.* 452
CRYOLIFE, INC., *pg.* 1520, *pg.* 534
DAXOR CORPORATION, *pg.* 1522, *pg.* 1221
DR. TATTOFF, INC., *pg.* 1525, *pg.* 46
HANGER INC., *pg.* 1539, *pg.* 1663
HEALTHSOUTH CORPORATION, *pg.* 1540, *pg.* 3
HEALTHWAYS, INC., *pg.* 1540, *pg.* 1632
HEMACARE CORPORATION, *pg.* 1541, *pg.* 300
HIGHMARK BLUE CROSS BLUE SHIELD, *pg.* 1203, *pg.* 1576
HOOPER HOLMES, INC., *pg.* 1542, *pg.* 718
INTEGRAMED AMERICA, INC., *pg.* 1546, *pg.* 1325
KAISER PERMANENTE, *pg.* 1552, *pg.* 171
LCA-VISION INC., *pg.* 1419, *pg.* 1416
MAGELLAN HEALTH SERVICES, INC., *pg.* 1557, *pg.* 337
MARIANJOY REHABILITATION HOSPITAL, *pg.* 1558, *pg.* 669
MEDEXPRESS URGENT CARE, *pg.* 1561, *pg.* 1850
MORRISON MANAGEMENT SPECIALISTS, INC., *pg.* 1028, *pg.* 515
NATIONAL MARROW DONOR PROGRAM, INC., *pg.* 150, *pg.* 941
NEW JERSEY MANUFACTURERS INSURANCE COMPANY, *pg.* 1211, *pg.* 1132
NEW YORK BLOOD CENTER, INC., *pg.* 1573, *pg.* 1268
ONEBLOOD, INC., *pg.* 1578, *pg.* 463
PLANNED PARENTHOOD FEDERATION OF AMERICA, INC., *pg.* 154, *pg.* 1282
RURAL/METRO CORPORATION, *pg.* 1591, *pg.* 24
TRACK GROUP, *pg.* 1603, *pg.* 1761
US ONCOLOGY, INC., *pg.* 1604, *pg.* 1747
U.S. PHYSICAL THERAPY, INC., *pg.* 1604, *pg.* 1716
VIACORD, *pg.* 1606, *pg.* 810
WELLSTAR HEALTH SYSTEM, INC., *pg.* 161, *pg.* 536

8099 - Health and Allied Services, NEC (except blood and organ banks, medical artists, medical photography, and childbirth preparation classes)

ASCENSION HEALTH ALLIANCE, *pg.* 1496, *pg.* 992
CARDIONET, INC., *pg.* 1513, *pg.* 1523
CENTRASTATE HEALTHCARE SYSTEM INC., *pg.* 1514, *pg.* 1071
CORD BLOOD AMERICA, INC., *pg.* 1519, *pg.* 1023
CRYO-CELL INTERNATIONAL, INC., *pg.* 1520, *pg.* 452
CRYOLIFE, INC., *pg.* 1520, *pg.* 534
DAXOR CORPORATION, *pg.* 1522, *pg.* 1221
HEALTHWAYS, INC., *pg.* 1540, *pg.* 1632
HEMACARE CORPORATION, *pg.* 1541, *pg.* 300
HIGHMARK BLUE CROSS BLUE SHIELD, *pg.* 1203, *pg.* 1576
HOOPER HOLMES, INC., *pg.* 1542, *pg.* 718
INTEGRAMED AMERICA, INC., *pg.* 1546, *pg.* 1325
MORRISON MANAGEMENT SPECIALISTS, INC., *pg.* 1028, *pg.* 515
NATIONAL MARROW DONOR PROGRAM, INC., *pg.* 150, *pg.* 941
NEW YORK BLOOD CENTER, INC., *pg.* 1573, *pg.* 1268
ONEBLOOD, INC., *pg.* 1578, *pg.* 463
RURAL/METRO CORPORATION, *pg.* 1591, *pg.* 24
TRACK GROUP, *pg.* 1603, *pg.* 1761
U.S. PHYSICAL THERAPY, INC., *pg.* 1604, *pg.* 1716
VIACORD, *pg.* 1606, *pg.* 810
WELLSTAR HEALTH SYSTEM, INC., *pg.* 161, *pg.* 536

8111 - Legal Services

AMERICAN AUCTION COMPANY, *pg.* 349, *pg.* 14
AON RISK SERVICES INC., *pg.* 1193, *pg.* 564
FINDLAW, *pg.* 1641, *pg.* 285
FOLEY HOAG LLP, *pg.* 398, *pg.* 794
JACOBY & MEYERS LLP, *pg.* 423, *pg.* 1317
JONES DAY, *pg.* 423, *pg.* 1431
KEVLIN CORPORATION, *pg.* 649, *pg.* 1034
LEGAL SHIELD, *pg.* 775, *pg.* 1484
LRP PUBLICATIONS, *pg.* 1660, *pg.* 1540
MERCURY INSURANCE COMPANY, *pg.* 1208, *pg.* 136
MILLER, NASH, WIENER, HAGER & CARLSEN, *pg.* 440, *pg.* 1504
PAN-AMERICAN LIFE INSURANCE COMPANY, *pg.* 1213, *pg.* 747
THE SOUTHERN POVERTY LAW CENTER, *pg.* 157, *pg.* 7

8211 - Elementary & Secondary Schools

CINCINNATI HILLS CHRISTIAN ACADEMY, *pg.* 599, *pg.* 1411
EDISONLEARNING, INC., *pg.* 140, *pg.* 1636
THE JOHNS HOPKINS UNIVERSITY, *pg.* 603, *pg.* 757
PRIMROSE HOLDINGS INC., *pg.* 606, *pg.* 482

8221 - Colleges, Universities & Professional Schools

AMERICAN PUBLIC EDUCATION, INC., *pg.* 597, *pg.* 1849
AMERICAN UNIVERSITY, *pg.* 597, *pg.* 395
APOLLO EDUCATION GROUP INC., *pg.* 597, *pg.* 14
BRIDGEPOINT EDUCATION, INC., *pg.* 598, *pg.* 201
CAPELLA EDUCATION COMPANY, *pg.* 599, *pg.* 931
CIBT EDUCATION GROUP INC., *pg.* 599, *pg.* 1910
COLORADO TECHNICAL UNIVERSITY, *pg.* 599, *pg.* 315
DEVRY EDUCATION GROUP INC., *pg.* 600, *pg.* 607
DEVRY UNIVERSITY INC., *pg.* 600, *pg.* 649
DUKE UNIVERSITY, *pg.* 600, *pg.* 1371
EDUCATION MANAGEMENT CORPORATION, *pg.* 601, *pg.* 1575
EMBRY-RIDDLE AERONAUTICAL UNIVERSITY, *pg.* 601, *pg.* 420
GOLDEN GATE UNIVERSITY, *pg.* 602, *pg.* 219
GRAND CANYON EDUCATION, INC., *pg.* 602, *pg.* 16
ITT EDUCATIONAL SERVICES, INC., *pg.* 603, *pg.* 675
LAUREATE EDUCATION, INC., *pg.* 603, *pg.* 757
MILWAUKEE SCHOOL OF ENGINEERING, *pg.* 605, *pg.* 1878
MOODY BIBLE INSTITUTE, *pg.* 605, *pg.* 583
NEW YORK INSTITUTE OF TECHNOLOGY, *pg.* 605, *pg.* 1318
NORTHEASTERN UNIVERSITY, *pg.* 605, *pg.* 799
NORTHWESTERN UNIVERSITY, *pg.* 606, *pg.* 612
OSF HEALTHCARE SYSTEM, *pg.* 1579, *pg.* 652
PENN FOSTER EDUCATION GROUP, INC., *pg.* 606, *pg.* 1586
PRATT INSTITUTE, *pg.* 606, *pg.* 1146
SHENANDOAH UNIVERSITY, *pg.* 607, *pg.* 1812
STRAYER EDUCATION INC., *pg.* 607, *pg.* 1785
TRINITY COLLEGE OF FLORIDA, *pg.* 608, *pg.* 451
UNIVERSITY OF ARKANSAS, *pg.* 608, *pg.* 31
UNIVERSITY OF MINNESOTA, *pg.* 609, *pg.* 945
UNIVERSITY OF PENNSYLVANIA, *pg.* 609, *pg.* 1571
THE UNIVERSITY OF PHOENIX, INC., *pg.* 610, *pg.* 27
WEST COAST UNIVERSITY, *pg.* 610, *pg.* 118
YALE UNIVERSITY PRESS, *pg.* 1703, *pg.* 359

8222 - Junior Colleges & Technical Institutes

ITT EDUCATIONAL SERVICES, INC., *pg.* 603, *pg.* 675

8231 - Libraries & Information Centers

ACCUWEATHER, INC., *pg.* 268, *pg.* 1587
BLUCORA, *pg.* 1232, *pg.* 1813
THE NEW YORK PUBLIC LIBRARY, *pg.* 605, *pg.* 1269
QUESTIA MEDIA INC., *pg.* 1276, *pg.* 1713

8243 - Data Processing Schools

APPLIED SOFTWARE TECHNOLOGY, INC., pg. 352, pg. 488
ATTACHMATE CORPORATION, pg. 356, pg. 1833
EVANS & SUTHERLAND COMPUTER CORPORATION, pg. 638, pg. 1757
GLOBAL LEARNING SYSTEMS LLC, pg. 400, pg. 769
LEARNING TREE INTERNATIONAL, INC., pg. 604, pg. 1799
LINCOLN EDUCATIONAL SERVICES CORPORATION, pg. 604, pg. 1131
NEW HORIZONS WORLDWIDE, INC., pg. 445, pg. 43
SAS INSTITUTE INC., pg. 466, pg. 1361
SYS-CON MEDIA, INC., pg. 1690, pg. 1134

8244 - Business & Secretarial Schools

CAREER EDUCATION CORPORATION, pg. 599, pg. 658
LINCOLN EDUCATIONAL SERVICES CORPORATION, pg. 604, pg. 1131
SIEBEL INSTITUTE OF TECHNOLOGY, pg. 607, pg. 590

8249 - Vocational Schools, NEC

THE ACADEMY OF RADIO BROADCASTING, INC., pg. 597, pg. 104
AMERICAN SCHOOL OF CORRESPONDENCE, pg. 597, pg. 626
APPLIED SOFTWARE TECHNOLOGY, INC., pg. 352, pg. 488
ATTACHMATE CORPORATION, pg. 356, pg. 1833
BRODY COMMUNICATIONS, LTD., pg. 598, pg. 1542
CAPITAL SENIOR LIVING CORPORATION, pg. 1084, pg. 1677
CHARLES ATLAS, LTD., pg. 538, pg. 1211
CIE DIRECT, pg. 599, pg. 1429
CORTINA LEARNING INTERNATIONAL, INC., pg. 600, pg. 385
EVANS & SUTHERLAND COMPUTER CORPORATION, pg. 638, pg. 1757
GLOBAL LEARNING SYSTEMS LLC, pg. 400, pg. 769
LEARNING TREE INTERNATIONAL, INC., pg. 604, pg. 1799
LINCOLN EDUCATIONAL SERVICES CORPORATION, pg. 604, pg. 1131
NEW HORIZONS WORLDWIDE, INC., pg. 445, pg. 43
PENN FOSTER EDUCATION GROUP, INC., pg. 606, pg. 1586
SAS INSTITUTE INC., pg. 466, pg. 1361
SMART SOFTWARE, INC., pg. 470, pg. 787
SYS-CON MEDIA, INC., pg. 1690, pg. 1134
TIGRENT INC., pg. 608, pg. 415
UNIVERSAL TECHNICAL INSTITUTE, INC., pg. 608, pg. 24
VALE NATIONAL TRAINING CENTER INC., pg. 610, pg. 1660

8299 - Schools & Educational Services, NEC

3T SYSTEMS, INC., pg. 339, pg. 330
THE ACADEMY OF RADIO BROADCASTING, INC., pg. 597, pg. 104
ACORN ENERGY, INC., pg. 341, pg. 389
ACT INC., pg. 597, pg. 708
ACTUATE CANADA, pg. 1225, pg. 1933
ADVERTISING CHECKING BUREAU INCORPORATED, pg. 345, pg. 1187
AECOM, pg. 64, pg. 812
AECOM TECHNOLOGY CORPORATION, pg. 65, pg. 125
ALION SCIENCE AND TECHNOLOGY CORPORATION, pg. 615, pg. 1788
ALLEN COMMUNICATION LEARNING SERVICES, INC., pg. 346, pg. 1755
AMBASSADORS GROUP, INC., pg. 1898, pg. 1843
AMERICAN APPRAISAL ASSOCIATES, INC., pg. 349, pg. 1872
AMERICAN AUCTION COMPANY, pg. 349, pg. 14
AMERICAN FORESTS, pg. 128, pg. 394
AMERICAN PUBLIC EDUCATION, INC., pg. 597, pg. 1849
AMERICAN SCHOOL OF CORRESPONDENCE, pg. 597, pg. 626
ANALYSTS INTERNATIONAL CORPORATION, pg. 350, pg. 930
APOLLO EDUCATION GROUP INC., pg. 597, pg. 14
APTIFY, pg. 352, pg. 395
ARI NETWORK SERVICES, INC., pg. 353, pg. 1873
THE ARISTOTLE CORPORATION, pg. 1496, pg. 372
AT&T GOVERNMENT SOLUTIONS, pg. 355, pg. 1809
THE AUSTIN COMPANY, pg. 69, pg. 1428
AUTHORIZE.NET HOLDINGS, INC., pg. 356, pg. 1751
BERLITZ INTERNATIONAL, INC., pg. 598, pg. 1110
BIRNER DENTAL MANAGEMENT SERVICES, INC., pg. 1506, pg. 317
BRIDGEPOINT EDUCATION, INC., pg. 598, pg. 201
BRODY COMMUNICATIONS, LTD., pg. 598, pg. 1542
CAE INC., pg. 226, pg. 1959
CAMBIUM LEARNING GROUP, INC., pg. 599, pg. 1677
CAMBRIDGE CREDIT COUNSELING CORP., pg. 728, pg. 781
CAMBRIDGE INFORMATION GROUP, INC., pg. 1625, pg. 761
CAPGEMINI U.S., pg. 368, pg. 1209
CAPITAL SENIOR LIVING CORPORATION, pg. 1084, pg. 1677
CAREER EDUCATION CORPORATION, pg. 599, pg. 658
CARTESIAN, pg. 369, pg. 718
CATASYS, INC., pg. 1514, pg. 127
CDM SMITH, pg. 74, pg. 807
CENGAGE LEARNING, pg. 1626, pg. 215
CERC, pg. 990, pg. 369
CGI GROUP INC., pg. 371, pg. 1954
CGI TECHNOLOGIES & SOLUTIONS INC., pg. 371, pg. 1779
CHARLES ATLAS, LTD., pg. 538, pg. 1211
CIBER, INC., pg. 372, pg. 330
CIBT EDUCATION GROUP INC., pg. 599, pg. 1910
CIE DIRECT, pg. 599, pg. 1429
CLAYTON HOLDINGS, INC., pg. 738, pg. 370
CLUNE CONSTRUCTION CO., pg. 76, pg. 571
COGNIZANT TECHNOLOGY SOLUTIONS CORPORATION, pg. 377, pg. 1124
COMPUCOM SYSTEMS, INC., pg. 378, pg. 1678
CONVERGYS CORPORATION, pg. 379, pg. 1412
COOLEY GROUP, INC., pg. 691, pg. 1603
CORTINA LEARNING INTERNATIONAL, INC., pg. 600, pg. 385
CORVEL CORPORATION, pg. 1198, pg. 109
CROSS COUNTRY HEALTHCARE, INC., pg. 1520, pg. 411
CRYO-CELL INTERNATIONAL, INC., pg. 1520, pg. 452
CULINART, INC., pg. 1017, pg. 1321
CWK NETWORK, INC., pg. 281, pg. 503
DALE CARNEGIE TRAINING, pg. 600, pg. 1221
DEVRY EDUCATION GROUP INC., pg. 600, pg. 607
DICE.COM, pg. 1238, pg. 712
EA ENGINEERING, SCIENCE & TECHNOLOGY, INC., pg. 389, pg. 772
EAGLE POINT SOFTWARE CORPORATION, pg. 389, pg. 707
ECOLOGY AND ENVIRONMENT, INC., pg. 1410, pg. 1173
EDGEWATER TECHNOLOGY, INC., pg. 389, pg. 848
EDISONLEARNING, INC., pg. 140, pg. 1636
EDMENTUM, INC., pg. 390, pg. 917
EDUCATION MANAGEMENT CORPORATION, pg. 601, pg. 1575
EDUCATIONAL TESTING SERVICE INC., pg. 1394, pg. 1111
ELENCO ELECTRONICS, INC., pg. 953, pg. 670
ENERGY & POWER SOLUTIONS, INC., pg. 392, pg. 71
ENHERENT CORP., pg. 393, pg. 1343
ERESEARCH TECHNOLOGY INC., pg. 1243, pg. 1564
ERM GROUP, INC., pg. 1412, pg. 1531
ESSINTIAL ENTERPRISE SOLUTIONS, pg. 395, pg. 1552
EVAN-MOOR CORPORATION, pg. 1639, pg. 151
EVANS & SUTHERLAND COMPUTER CORPORATION, pg. 638, pg. 1757
EXCELLIGENCE LEARNING CORP., pg. 1768, pg. 151
THE F.A. BARTLETT TREE EXPERT COMPANY, pg. 1795, pg. 373
FLIGHTSAFETY INTERNATIONAL, INC., pg. 601, pg. 1160
THE FORUM CORPORATION, pg. 398, pg. 794
FRANKLIN COVEY CO., pg. 1642, pg. 1758
THE FRANKLIN INSTITUTE, pg. 549, pg. 1565
FTI CONSULTING, INC., pg. 760, pg. 478
GALE CENGAGE LEARNING, pg. 1643, pg. 885
THE GALLUP ORGANIZATION, pg. 399, pg. 399
GARTNER, INC., pg. 1248, pg. 374
GEOSPATIAL HOLDINGS, INC., pg. 84, pg. 1585
GLASSHOUSE TECHNOLOGIES, INC., pg. 400, pg. 844
GRAND CANYON EDUCATION, INC., pg. 602, pg. 16
GUIDELINE, INC., pg. 402, pg. 1237
HABIF, AROGETI & WYNNE, LLP, pg. 764, pg. 509
THE HACKETT GROUP, INC., pg. 1255, pg. 443
HEADSTRONG CORPORATION, pg. 403, pg. 1798
HEALTH FITNESS CORPORATION, pg. 1539, pg. 937
HEALTHSTREAM, INC., pg. 1649, pg. 1651
HILL INTERNATIONAL INC., pg. 87, pg. 1083
HOLSTEIN ASSOCIATION USA, INC., pg. 143, pg. 1764
HOME SCHOOL HOLDINGS, INC., pg. 1256, pg. 606
HP ENTERPRISE SERVICES, LLC, pg. 409, pg. 1731
HUGGER MUGGER YOGA PRODUCTS LLC, pg. 1836, pg. 1758
HURON CONSULTING GROUP INC., pg. 768, pg. 577
INFOR LAWSON, pg. 414, pg. 961
INTEGRITY SOLUTIONS, pg. 145, pg. 22
INTERACTIVE DATA CORPORATION, pg. 769, pg. 785
IRON MOUNTAIN INCORPORATED, pg. 421, pg. 796
ITRADE NETWORK, pg. 1259, pg. 77
ITT EDUCATIONAL SERVICES, INC., pg. 603, pg. 675
K12, INC., pg. 1260, pg. 1785
KAPLAN, INC., pg. 603, pg. 425
KEPNER-TREGOE, INC., pg. 424, pg. 1112
KROLL INC., pg. 425, pg. 1249
THE KULJIAN CORPORATION, pg. 92, pg. 1566
LAS VEGAS INSTITUTE FOR ADVANCED DENTAL STUDIES, pg. 145, pg. 1027
LAUREATE EDUCATION, INC., pg. 603, pg. 757
LCC INTERNATIONAL, INC., pg. 651, pg. 1792
LEARNING TREE INTERNATIONAL, INC., pg. 604, pg. 1799
LENOX HILL NEIGHBORHOOD HOUSE, pg. 146, pg. 1251
LEXICON MARKETING CORPORATION, pg. 604, pg. 134
LINCOLN EDUCATIONAL SERVICES CORPORATION, pg. 604, pg. 1131
LOCKHEED MARTIN SIMULATION, TRAINING & SUPPORT, pg. 231, pg. 454
MANAGEMENT & TRAINING CORPORATION, pg. 146, pg. 1751
MANPOWER GROUP, pg. 430, pg. 1710
MANPOWER INC., pg. 430, pg. 1877
MARITZ INC., pg. 1914, pg. 977
MARSH & MCLENNAN COMPANIES INC., pg. 1207, pg. 1256
MAXIMUS, INC., pg. 780, pg. 1799
MCG CAPITAL CORPORATION, pg. 781, pg. 1774
MHI GLOBAL, pg. 434, pg. 474
MICROS SYSTEMS, INC., pg. 435, pg. 768
MOCON, INC., pg. 1363, pg. 940
MSX INTERNATIONAL, INC., pg. 98, pg. 912
MTM TECHNOLOGIES, INC., pg. 442, pg. 375
MWH GLOBAL, INC., pg. 98, pg. 312
THE NATIONAL ASSOCIATION FOR PET CONTAINER RESOURCES, pg. 147, pg. 279
NAVIGANT CONSULTING, INC., pg. 786, pg. 584
NEW HORIZONS WORLDWIDE, INC., pg. 445, pg. 43
NEXAGE, INC., pg. 1271, pg. 799
NIGHTINGALE-CONANT CORPORATION, pg. 152, pg. 670
NOBEL LEARNING COMMUNITIES, INC., pg. 605, pg. 1593
NUTRITION MANAGEMENT SERVICES COMPANY, pg. 1742, pg. 1543
OFFSHORE SAILING SCHOOL, LTD., INC., pg. 606, pg. 428
OPENTEXT, pg. 1272, pg. 1956
ORIEL STAT-A-MATRIX, INC., pg. 451, pg. 1057
PADI AMERICAS, pg. 573, pg. 188
PANTHEON SOFTWARE, INC., pg. 1274, pg. 1774
PAREXEL INTERNATIONAL CORPORATION, pg. 1580, pg. 853
PEARSON ASSESSMENT & INFORMATION, pg. 1674, pg. 1742
PENN FOSTER EDUCATION GROUP, INC., pg. 606, pg. 1586
PENNSYLVANIA CHAMBER OF BUSINESS & INDUSTRY, pg. 153, pg. 1537
PEOPLES EDUCATIONAL HOLDINGS INC., pg. 606, pg. 1118
PERFICIENT, INC., pg. 1274, pg. 1002
P.J. DICK-TRUMBULL-LINDY, pg. 104, pg. 1579
PRICEWATERHOUSECOOPERS LLP, pg. 795, pg. 1283
QUESTAR ASSESSMENT, INC., pg. 1679, pg. 1143
REPUBLIC SERVICES, INC., pg. 107, pg. 19
THE REYNOLDS & REYNOLDS COMPANY, pg. 461, pg. 1457
RICHARDSON GROUP INC., pg. 461, pg. 1570
ROSETTA STONE INC., pg. 462, pg. 1774
SCIENTIFIC LEARNING CORPORATION, pg. 607, pg. 172
SHL, pg. 803, pg. 942

SKILLSOFT PLC, *pg.* 470, *pg.* 1037
SMART SOFTWARE, INC., *pg.* 470, *pg.* 787
SMARTPROS LTD., *pg.* 1281, *pg.* 1166
SOLARWINDS, INC., *pg.* 471, *pg.* 1666
SPECIALTY CATALOG CORPORATION, *pg.* 1786, *pg.* 856
SPHERIX INC., *pg.* 1596, *pg.* 1808
SRA INTERNATIONAL, INC., *pg.* 473, *pg.* 1780
STANDARD & POOR'S RATINGS SERVICES, *pg.* 805, *pg.* 1296
STATE STREET CORPORATION, *pg.* 805, *pg.* 801
STRAYER EDUCATION INC., *pg.* 607, *pg.* 1785
STRUCTURED COMMUNICATION SYSTEMS, INC., *pg.* 477, *pg.* 1497
SUREQUEST SYSTEMS, INC., *pg.* 900, *pg.* 1669
SYNCHRONOSS TECHNOLOGIES, INC., *pg.* 479, *pg.* 1047
TETRA TECH, INC., *pg.* 115, *pg.* 181
THOMSON REUTERS TAX & ACCOUNTING, *pg.* 1693, *pg.* 1299
TIGRENT INC., *pg.* 608, *pg.* 415
TORCON, INC., *pg.* 116, *pg.* 1114
TPR EDUCATION, LLC, *pg.* 1695, *pg.* 822
TRC COMPANIES, INC., *pg.* 1383, *pg.* 386
TRIMBLE NAVIGATION LIMITED, *pg.* 1384, *pg.* 288
UNISYS CORPORATION, *pg.* 487, *pg.* 1517
UNITED BUSINESS MEDIA LLC, *pg.* 1697, *pg.* 1177
UNITED SERVICES AUTOMOBILE ASSOCIATION, *pg.* 1221, *pg.* 1743
UNIVERSAL TECHNICAL INSTITUTE, INC., *pg.* 608, *pg.* 24
UNZ & COMPANY, INC., *pg.* 1698, *pg.* 1084
UPROMISE, INC., *pg.* 815, *pg.* 837
USA FINANCIAL, *pg.* 815, *pg.* 864
VALE NATIONAL TRAINING CENTER INC., *pg.* 610, *pg.* 1660
VERISIGN, INC., *pg.* 488, *pg.* 1799
VERSAR, INC., *pg.* 1435, *pg.* 1807
VHA INC., *pg.* 1606, *pg.* 1724
VIRTUSA CORPORATION, *pg.* 490, *pg.* 857
WEB.COM GROUP, INC., *pg.* 1288, *pg.* 435
WENTE VINEYARDS, *pg.* 1972, *pg.* 122
WESTON SOLUTIONS HOLDINGS, INC., *pg.* 1437, *pg.* 1593
THE WHITMAN COMPANIES, INC., *pg.* 121, *pg.* 1053
WILDLIFE CONSERVATION SOCIETY, *pg.* 592, *pg.* 1145
YELLOWBRIX, INC., *pg.* 1291, *pg.* 1775

8322 - Individual & Family Social Services

92ND STREET YOUNG MEN'S & YOUNG WOMEN'S HEBREW ASSOCIATION, *pg.* 124, *pg.* 1185
ALEXANDER GRAHAM BELL ASSOCIATION FOR THE DEAF AND HARD OF HEARING, *pg.* 126, *pg.* 393
ALMOST FAMILY, INC., *pg.* 1492, *pg.* 731
AMERICAN SOCIETY OF PLASTIC SURGEONS INC., *pg.* 131, *pg.* 553
AUTISM SPEAKS, INC., *pg.* 133, *pg.* 1198
BOY SCOUTS OF AMERICA, *pg.* 134, *pg.* 1717
CATHOLIC RELIEF SERVICES, *pg.* 136, *pg.* 756
COMSTOCK HOLDING COMPANIES INC., *pg.* 1087, *pg.* 1798
EMERGENCY MEDICAL SERVICES CORPORATION, *pg.* 1528, *pg.* 331
ENVISION, *pg.* 1394, *pg.* 1412
GIRL SCOUTS OF THE UNITED STATES OF AMERICA, *pg.* 142, *pg.* 1235
THE GLADNEY CENTER FOR ADOPTION, *pg.* 142, *pg.* 1695
LIFE CARE CENTERS OF AMERICA, *pg.* 1555, *pg.* 1630
LIGHTHOUSE INTERNATIONAL, *pg.* 1557, *pg.* 1251
MADAME WALKER THEATRE CENTER, *pg.* 560, *pg.* 688
METROPOLITAN MINISTRIES INC., *pg.* 146, *pg.* 474
NATIONAL HOME HEALTH CARE CORP., *pg.* 1570, *pg.* 1340
THE PARTNERSHIP AT DRUGFREE.ORG, *pg.* 153, *pg.* 1276
PINES INTERNATIONAL, INC., *pg.* 889, *pg.* 715
PLAN USA, INC., *pg.* 154, *pg.* 1609
RHODE ISLAND COALITION AGAINST DOMESTIC VIOLENCE, *pg.* 155, *pg.* 1609
RONALD MCDONALD HOUSE CHARITIES, INC., *pg.* 155, *pg.* 648
SAVE THE CHILDREN FEDERATION, INC., *pg.* 156, *pg.* 384
SERVPRO INDUSTRIES, INC., *pg.* 335, *pg.* 1635
SPECIAL OLYMPICS INTERNATIONAL, INC., *pg.* 157, *pg.* 405
VISITING NURSE ASSOCIATION OF SOMERSET HILLS INC., *pg.* 1607, *pg.* 1042

8331 - Job Training & Vocational Rehabilitation Services

GOODWILL INDUSTRIES INTERNATIONAL, INC., *pg.* 1771, *pg.* 776
KNOWLOGY CORPORATION, *pg.* 425, *pg.* 1809
LIGHTHOUSE INTERNATIONAL, *pg.* 1557, *pg.* 1251
MANAGEMENT & TRAINING CORPORATION, *pg.* 146, *pg.* 1751
STRAYER UNIVERSITY, *pg.* 607, *pg.* 405
SUNCOAST WORKFORCE BOARD, INC., *pg.* 158, *pg.* 467
U.S. PHYSICAL THERAPY, INC., *pg.* 1604, *pg.* 1716

8351 - Child Day Care Services

AFTERSCHOOL ALLIANCE, *pg.* 125, *pg.* 393
BRIGHT HORIZONS FAMILY SOLUTIONS INC., *pg.* 598, *pg.* 855
CENTERLIGHT HEALTH SYSTEM, *pg.* 1514, *pg.* 1144
GODDARD SYSTEMS, INC., *pg.* 142, *pg.* 1543
LA PETITE ACADEMY, INC., *pg.* 603, *pg.* 903
LEARNING CARE GROUP INC., *pg.* 604, *pg.* 903
LENOX HILL NEIGHBORHOOD HOUSE, *pg.* 146, *pg.* 1251
NOBEL LEARNING COMMUNITIES, INC., *pg.* 605, *pg.* 1593

8361 - Residential Care

ASCENSION HEALTH ALLIANCE, *pg.* 1496, *pg.* 992
BROOKDALE SENIOR LIVING INC., *pg.* 1511, *pg.* 1627
GENESIS HEALTHCARE CORP., *pg.* 1534, *pg.* 1543
GOLDEN LIVING, *pg.* 1538, *pg.* 32
JEWISH HOME LIFECARE, *pg.* 1548, *pg.* 1246
LIFE CARE CENTERS OF AMERICA, *pg.* 1555, *pg.* 1630
MAGELLAN HEALTH SERVICES, INC., *pg.* 1557, *pg.* 337
THE RENFREW CENTERS INC., *pg.* 1589, *pg.* 1570
RES-CARE, INC., *pg.* 1589, *pg.* 738
SUNRISE SENIOR LIVING, INC., *pg.* 1599, *pg.* 1795
UNIVERSITY GENERAL HEALTH SYSTEM INC, *pg.* 1396, *pg.* 1716

8399 - Social Services, NEC

AARP, *pg.* 124, *pg.* 393
AARP PUBLICATIONS, *pg.* 1613, *pg.* 1185
ALMOST FAMILY, INC., *pg.* 1492, *pg.* 731
AMERICAN FORESTS, *pg.* 128, *pg.* 394
THE AMERICAN GASTROENTEROLOGICAL ASSOCIATION, *pg.* 128, *pg.* 761
AMERICAN HEART ASSOCIATION INC., *pg.* 128, *pg.* 1673
AMERICAN KENNEL CLUB, INC., *pg.* 129, *pg.* 1193
AMERICAN LUNG ASSOCIATION, *pg.* 129, *pg.* 395
AMERICAN RED CROSS, *pg.* 130, *pg.* 395
AMERICAN SOCIETY FOR THE PREVENTION OF CRUELTY TO ANIMALS, *pg.* 131, *pg.* 1193
AMNESTY INTERNATIONAL USA, *pg.* 131, *pg.* 1194
ANIMAL CARE & CONTROL OF NEW YORK CITY, INC., *pg.* 132, *pg.* 1195
ASCENSION HEALTH ALLIANCE, *pg.* 1496, *pg.* 992
CANADIAN PARKS AND WILDERNESS SOCIETY, *pg.* 136, *pg.* 1931
CHILDFUND INTERNATIONAL, *pg.* 137, *pg.* 1801
THE CHILDREN'S HEALTH FUND, *pg.* 137, *pg.* 1211
COALITION FOR A DRUG-FREE GREATER CINCINNATI, *pg.* 137, *pg.* 1412
DARE 2 SHARE MINISTRIES INTERNATIONAL, INC., *pg.* 138, *pg.* 310
DOCTORS WITHOUT BORDERS USA, INC., *pg.* 139, *pg.* 1225
EARTH SHARE, *pg.* 140, *pg.* 762
EASTERN STATES EXPOSITION, *pg.* 992, *pg.* 857
EDUCATIONAL ASSISTANCE LTD., *pg.* 140, *pg.* 613
ENTERTAINMENT INDUSTRY FOUNDATION, *pg.* 140, *pg.* 130
ENVIRONMENTAL DEFENSE FUND, *pg.* 140, *pg.* 1228
FOCUS: HOPE, *pg.* 141, *pg.* 881
FRENCH INSTITUTE ALLIANCE FRANCAISE, *pg.* 141, *pg.* 1233
FRESH AIR FUND, *pg.* 141, *pg.* 1233
FRIENDS OF ANIMALS, INC., *pg.* 141, *pg.* 345
GAIAM, INC., *pg.* 1532, *pg.* 334
GOODWILL INDUSTRIES-SUNCOAST, INC., *pg.* 142, *pg.* 462
THE GREATER BOSTON FOOD BANK, *pg.* 993, *pg.* 795
GREENPEACE, *pg.* 142, *pg.* 400
HABITAT FOR HUMANITY INTERNATIONAL, INC., *pg.* 143, *pg.* 486
HEALTHWISE, INCORPORATED, *pg.* 143, *pg.* 546
THE HUMANE SOCIETY OF THE UNITED STATES, *pg.* 143, *pg.* 400
INSPIRE YOUTH PROJECT, *pg.* 144, *pg.* 1836
JUVENILE DIABETES RESEARCH FOUNDATION INTERNATIONAL, *pg.* 145, *pg.* 1247
KENTUCKY DERBY FESTIVAL, INC., *pg.* 556, *pg.* 735
MAKE-A-WISH FOUNDATION OF GREATER LOS ANGELES, *pg.* 146, *pg.* 136
MARCH OF DIMES BIRTH DEFECTS FOUNDATION, *pg.* 146, *pg.* 1354
MEMORIAL SLOAN-KETTERING CANCER CENTER INC., *pg.* 1565, *pg.* 1258
MERCY HEALTH, *pg.* 1479, *pg.* 888
THE METROPOLITAN OPERA, *pg.* 561, *pg.* 1260
NATIONAL AUDUBON SOCIETY, *pg.* 148, *pg.* 1263
NATIONAL BRAIN TUMOR SOCIETY, *pg.* 148, *pg.* 223
NATIONAL EATING DISORDERS ASSOCIATION, *pg.* 148, *pg.* 1264
NATIONAL FFA ORGANIZATION, *pg.* 149, *pg.* 688
NATIONAL PARKS CONSERVATION ASSOCIATION, *pg.* 150, *pg.* 403
NATIONAL RIFLE ASSOCIATION, *pg.* 151, *pg.* 1780
THE NATURE CONSERVANCY, *pg.* 151, *pg.* 1774
NORTH SHORE ANIMAL LEAGUE, INC., *pg.* 152, *pg.* 1323
PARENT PROJECT MUSCULAR DISTROPHY, *pg.* 153, *pg.* 1465
PARENTS TELEVISION COUNCIL, *pg.* 574, *pg.* 138
PASADENA SYMPHONY ASSOCIATION, *pg.* 574, *pg.* 181
QUALITY SERVICES FOR THE AUTISM COMMUNITY, *pg.* 154, *pg.* 1284
ROCHESTER PHILHARMONIC ORCHESTRA INC., *pg.* 579, *pg.* 1337
ROLLER SKATING ASSOCIATION INTERNATIONAL, *pg.* 155, *pg.* 689
ROTARY INTERNATIONAL, *pg.* 155, *pg.* 612
THE SALVATION ARMY, *pg.* 155, *pg.* 1771
SAVE THE MANATEE CLUB, INC., *pg.* 156, *pg.* 439
SEMINOLE TRIBE OF FLORIDA, INC., *pg.* 156, *pg.* 431
SIERRA CLUB, *pg.* 156, *pg.* 227
SOCIETY OF MANUFACTURING ENGINEERS, *pg.* 157, *pg.* 878
THE SOUTHERN POVERTY LAW CENTER, *pg.* 157, *pg.* 7
SPRINGFIELD SYMPHONY ASSOCIATION, INC., *pg.* 585, *pg.* 1007
SUPPLEMENTAL HEALTH CARE SERVICES, INC., *pg.* 478, *pg.* 1754
SURFRIDER FOUNDATION, *pg.* 158, *pg.* 199
SUSAN G. KOMEN FOR THE CURE, *pg.* 158, *pg.* 1688
SYMPHONY OF THE SOUTHWEST, *pg.* 586, *pg.* 13
TEMPLE UNIVERSITY HEALTH SYSTEM, *pg.* 1601, *pg.* 1571
THEATER & ARTS FOUNDATION, *pg.* 587, *pg.* 120
TRUTH INITIATIVE, *pg.* 158, *pg.* 405
UNITED NATIONS CHILDREN'S FUND, *pg.* 159, *pg.* 1306
UNITED NEGRO COLLEGE FUND, INC., *pg.* 159, *pg.* 405
UNTIL THERE'S A CURE FOUNDATION, *pg.* 160, *pg.* 192
WATERLOO-CEDAR FALLS SYMPHONY ORCHESTRA, *pg.* 591, *pg.* 702
WESTMORELAND SYMPHONY ORCHESTRA, *pg.* 592, *pg.* 1534
THE WHAT TO EXPECT FOUNDATION, *pg.* 161, *pg.* 1314
WILDAID, *pg.* 161, *pg.* 234
WILLIAMSPORT SYMPHONY ORCHESTRA, *pg.* 592, *pg.* 1595
W.K. KELLOGG FOUNDATION, *pg.* 161, *pg.* 872
WORLD WILDLIFE FUND CANADA, *pg.* 162, *pg.* 1947
WORLD WILDLIFE FUND, INC., *pg.* 162, *pg.* 408
ZERO - THE PROJECT TO END PROSTATE CANCER, *pg.* 162, *pg.* 1772

8412 - Museums & Art Galleries

THE ADLER PLANETARIUM & ASTRONOMY MUSEUM, *pg.* 526, *pg.* 563
ANDREAS ENTERPRISES, INC., *pg.* 529, *pg.* 1795

THE ANDY WARHOL MUSEUM, *pg.* 529, *pg.* 1573
THE ARMED FORCES MILITARY MUSEUM, *pg.* 530, *pg.* 438
THE ART INSTITUTE OF CHICAGO, *pg.* 530, *pg.* 565
THE CHILDREN'S MUSEUM AT SARATOGA, *pg.* 540, *pg.* 1340
CHILDREN'S MUSEUM OF DENVER, INC., *pg.* 540, *pg.* 317
CINCINNATI ART MUSEUM, *pg.* 540, *pg.* 1410
COLLEGE FOOTBALL HALL OF FAME, *pg.* 541, *pg.* 501
COLONIAL WILLIAMSBURG FOUNDATION, *pg.* 541, *pg.* 1811
DELAWARE ART MUSEUM, *pg.* 543, *pg.* 390
DELAWARE MUSEUM OF NATURAL HISTORY, *pg.* 543, *pg.* 390
DISCOVERY CENTER OF IDAHO, *pg.* 545, *pg.* 546
DISCOVERY GATEWAY CHILDREN'S MUSEUM, *pg.* 545, *pg.* 1757
ELVIS PRESLEY ENTERPRISES, INC., *pg.* 1090, *pg.* 1642
EXPLORA SCIENCE CENTER & CHILDREN'S MUSEUM OF ALBUQUERQUE, *pg.* 546, *pg.* 1135
THE FIELD MUSEUM, *pg.* 548, *pg.* 573
FLORIDA HOLOCAUST MUSEUM, INC., *pg.* 548, *pg.* 462
THE FRANKLIN INSTITUTE, *pg.* 549, *pg.* 1565
HENRY FORD MUSEUM AND GREENFIELD VILLAGE, *pg.* 552, *pg.* 878
LIBERTY SCIENCE CENTER, INC., *pg.* 557, *pg.* 1075
LONG ISLAND CHILDREN'S MUSEUM, *pg.* 558, *pg.* 1161
LOS ANGELES COUNTY FAIR ASSOCIATION, *pg.* 559, *pg.* 185
THE MENNELLO MUSEUM OF AMERICAN ART, *pg.* 561, *pg.* 454
THE METROPOLITAN MUSEUM OF ART, *pg.* 561, *pg.* 1259
MICHIGAN SCIENCE CENTER, *pg.* 562, *pg.* 884
MISSISSIPPI MUSEUM OF ART, *pg.* 563, *pg.* 969
THE MOB MUSEUM, *pg.* 564, *pg.* 1028
MORRIS MUSEUM INC., *pg.* 564, *pg.* 1089
MOSI (MUSEUM OF SCIENCE & INDUSTRY), *pg.* 564, *pg.* 474
MUSEUM OF DISCOVERY & SCIENCE, INC., *pg.* 565, *pg.* 425
MUSEUM OF FINE ARTS OF ST. PETERSBURG FLORIDA INC., *pg.* 565, *pg.* 463
THE MUSEUM OF MODERN ART, *pg.* 565, *pg.* 1263
MUSEUM OF SCIENCE AND INDUSTRY, *pg.* 565, *pg.* 583
NATIONAL BASEBALL HALL OF FAME & MUSEUM, INC., *pg.* 566, *pg.* 1154
NATIONAL FOOTBALL MUSEUM, INC., *pg.* 568, *pg.* 1408
NATIONAL TRUST FOR HISTORIC PRESERVATION, *pg.* 151, *pg.* 403
NEW YORK HALL OF SCIENCE, *pg.* 570, *pg.* 1155
NEWPORT ART MUSEUM, *pg.* 571, *pg.* 1603
THE PALEY CENTER FOR MEDIA, *pg.* 573, *pg.* 1275
PHILADELPHIA MUSEUM OF ART, *pg.* 575, *pg.* 1569
SALVADOR DALI MUSEUM, *pg.* 580, *pg.* 464
SAN DIEGO SOCIETY OF NATURAL HISTORY, *pg.* 580, *pg.* 208
THE SCIENCE CENTER, *pg.* 581, *pg.* 1570
SOUTH FLORIDA MUSEUM, *pg.* 584, *pg.* 415
ST. PETERSBURG MUSEUM OF HISTORY, *pg.* 585, *pg.* 464
WORLD GOLF HALL OF FAME, *pg.* 595, *pg.* 461
WOW! WORLD OF WONDER CHILDREN'S MUSEUM, *pg.* 595, *pg.* 332

8422 - Arboreta & Botanical or Zoological Gardens

AUDUBON NATURE INSTITUTE, *pg.* 531, *pg.* 746
BELLINGRATH GARDENS & HOME, *pg.* 1794, *pg.* 8
BUSCH GARDENS TAMPA BAY, *pg.* 535, *pg.* 472
CHICAGO ZOOLOGICAL SOCIETY, INC., *pg.* 539, *pg.* 559
COMMONWEALTH ZOOLOGICAL CORP., *pg.* 542, *pg.* 793
JOHN G. SHEDD AQUARIUM, *pg.* 555, *pg.* 579
LINCOLN PARK ZOO, *pg.* 557, *pg.* 580
LOWRY PARK ZOOLOGICAL SOCIETY OF TAMPA INC., *pg.* 559, *pg.* 474
MARYLAND ZOOLOGICAL SOCIETY, INC., *pg.* 561, *pg.* 758
NAPLES ZOO INC., *pg.* 565, *pg.* 451
NATIONAL AQUARIUM IN BALTIMORE INC., *pg.* 565, *pg.* 758
NEWPORT AQUARIUM, *pg.* 571, *pg.* 739
OKLAHOMA CITY ZOOLOGICAL PARK, *pg.* 572, *pg.* 1487
OMAHA ZOOLOGICAL SOCIETY, *pg.* 572, *pg.* 1017
SEAWORLD ORLANDO, *pg.* 582, *pg.* 455
SEAWORLD TEXAS, *pg.* 583, *pg.* 1742
SENECA PARK ZOOLOGICAL SOCIETY, *pg.* 583, *pg.* 1337
SOUTH FLORIDA MUSEUM, *pg.* 584, *pg.* 415
WILDLIFE CONSERVATION SOCIETY, *pg.* 592, *pg.* 1145
ZOOLOGICAL SOCIETY OF SAN DIEGO, *pg.* 595, *pg.* 211

8611 - Business Associations

THE ADHESIVE AND SEALANT COUNCIL, INC., *pg.* 125, *pg.* 761
AEROSPACE INDUSTRIES ASSOCIATION, *pg.* 125, *pg.* 1772
AIRLINE PASSENGER EXPERIENCE ASSOCIATION, *pg.* 125, *pg.* 1188
ALBUQUERQUE CONVENTION & VISITORS BUREAU, *pg.* 988, *pg.* 1135
AMERICAN ARCHITECTURAL MANUFACTURERS ASSOCIATION, *pg.* 126, *pg.* 658
THE AMERICAN BANKERS ASSOCIATION, *pg.* 126, *pg.* 394
AMERICAN BUSINESS MEDIA, *pg.* 126, *pg.* 1190
THE AMERICAN CLEANING INSTITUTE, *pg.* 127, *pg.* 394
AMERICAN COUNCIL OF LIFE INSURERS, *pg.* 127, *pg.* 394
AMERICAN EGG BOARD, *pg.* 128, *pg.* 650
AMERICAN FOREST & PAPER ASSOCIATION, *pg.* 128, *pg.* 394
AMERICAN HEREFORD ASSOCIATION, *pg.* 129, *pg.* 980
AMERICAN IRON AND STEEL INSTITUTE, *pg.* 129, *pg.* 394
AMERICAN PLASTICS COUNCIL, *pg.* 130, *pg.* 395
AMERICAN PUBLIC TRANSPORTATION ASSOCIATION, *pg.* 130, *pg.* 395
AMERICAN SHEEP INDUSTRY ASSOCIATION, INC., *pg.* 131, *pg.* 325
AMERICAN SHORTHORN ASSOCIATION, *pg.* 131, *pg.* 1013
APA-THE ENGINEERED WOOD ASSOCIATION, *pg.* 132, *pg.* 1844
ASM INTERNATIONAL, *pg.* 132, *pg.* 1461
ASPHALT INSTITUTE, *pg.* 133, *pg.* 729
ASSOCIATION OF AMERICAN PUBLISHERS, INC., *pg.* 133, *pg.* 1197
THE ASSOCIATION OF MAGAZINE MEDIA, *pg.* 133, *pg.* 1197
ASSOCIATION OF NATIONAL ADVERTISERS, INC., *pg.* 133, *pg.* 1197
AUTOMOTIVE SERVICE ASSOCIATION, *pg.* 134, *pg.* 1670
THE BETTER BUSINESS BUREAU OF METROPOLITAN NEW YORK, *pg.* 134, *pg.* 1202
BLUE DIAMOND GROWERS, *pg.* 840, *pg.* 195
BRICK INDUSTRY ASSOCIATION, *pg.* 135, *pg.* 1798
BUFFALO NIAGARA CONVENTION & VISITORS BUREAU, INC., *pg.* 1901, *pg.* 1147
CALIFORNIA AVOCADO COMMISSION, *pg.* 135, *pg.* 108
CALIFORNIA DRIED PLUM BOARD, *pg.* 135, *pg.* 195
CALIFORNIA FIG ADVISORY BOARD, *pg.* 135, *pg.* 92
CALIFORNIA MANUFACTURED HOUSING INSTITUTE, *pg.* 135, *pg.* 194
CALIFORNIA OLIVE COMMITTEE, *pg.* 135, *pg.* 92
CALIFORNIA RAISIN MARKETING BOARD, *pg.* 1017, *pg.* 93
CALIFORNIA REDWOOD ASSOCIATION, *pg.* 135, *pg.* 182
CALIFORNIA STRAWBERRY COMMISSION, *pg.* 135, *pg.* 305
CALIFORNIA TABLE GRAPE COMMISSION, *pg.* 135, *pg.* 93
CANADIAN ADVANCED TECHNOLOGY ALLIANCE, *pg.* 136, *pg.* 1931
CANADIAN ASSOCIATION OF INTERNET PROVIDERS, *pg.* 136, *pg.* 1931
CANADIAN MARKETING ASSOCIATION, *pg.* 136, *pg.* 1936
CANADIAN PLASTICS INDUSTRY ASSOCIATION, *pg.* 136, *pg.* 1925
CANADIAN TOURISM COMMISSION, *pg.* 136, *pg.* 1910
CHERRY MARKETING INSTITUTE, *pg.* 136, *pg.* 884
CHICAGO AUTOMOBILE TRADE ASSOCIATION, *pg.* 137, *pg.* 649
COIN LAUNDRY ASSOCIATION, *pg.* 137, *pg.* 649
COMMON GROUND ALLIANCE, *pg.* 137, *pg.* 1770
COPPER DEVELOPMENT ASSOCIATION INC., *pg.* 138, *pg.* 1218
CREDIT UNION NATIONAL ASSOCIATION, *pg.* 138, *pg.* 1865
CRUISE LINES INTERNATIONAL ASSOCIATION, INC., *pg.* 138, *pg.* 424
DAIRY MANAGEMENT, INC., *pg.* 138, *pg.* 656
DAKOTA ELECTRIC ASSOCIATION, *pg.* 1939, *pg.* 925
DALLAS CONVENTION & VISITORS BUREAU, *pg.* 991, *pg.* 1678
DETROIT METRO CONVENTION & VISITORS BUREAU, *pg.* 139, *pg.* 880
THE DIRECT MARKETING ASSOCIATION INC., *pg.* 139, *pg.* 1224
DIRECT SELLING ASSOCIATION, *pg.* 139, *pg.* 398
DISTILLED SPIRITS COUNCIL OF THE UNITED STATES, INC., *pg.* 139, *pg.* 398
EDISON ELECTRIC INSTITUTE, *pg.* 1941, *pg.* 398
ENTERPRISE FLORIDA, INC., *pg.* 992, *pg.* 453
ENTERTAINMENT INDUSTRY FOUNDATION, *pg.* 140, *pg.* 130
FLORIDA AVOCADO ADMINISTRATIVE COMMITTEES, *pg.* 140, *pg.* 431
FLORIDA FRUIT & VEGETABLE ASSOCIATION, *pg.* 140, *pg.* 438
FLORIDA HOSPITAL ASSOCIATION, *pg.* 140, *pg.* 469
FLORIDA TOMATO COMMITTEE, *pg.* 141, *pg.* 438
FOODSERVICE & PACKAGING INSTITUTE, INC., *pg.* 141, *pg.* 1781
FORGING INDUSTRY ASSOCIATION, *pg.* 141, *pg.* 1431
FRENCH-AMERICAN CHAMBER OF COMMERCE, *pg.* 141, *pg.* 1565
GREATER MILWAUKEE CONVENTION & VISITORS BUREAU, *pg.* 993, *pg.* 1874
GREENWICH SYMPHONY ORCHESTRA INC., *pg.* 551, *pg.* 350
GUTHRIE THEATER FOUNDATION, *pg.* 551, *pg.* 937
HARDWOOD PLYWOOD & VENEER ASSOCATION, *pg.* 143, *pg.* 1798
INDEPENDENT INSURANCE AGENTS & BROKERS OF AMERICA, INC., *pg.* 144, *pg.* 1770
THE INDEPENDENT LUBRICANT MANUFACTURERS ASSOCIATION, *pg.* 144, *pg.* 1770
INSTITUTE OF REAL ESTATE MANAGEMENT, *pg.* 144, *pg.* 578
INTERNATIONAL DAIRY-DELI-BAKERY-ASSOCIATION, *pg.* 145, *pg.* 1866
INTERNATIONAL SPA ASSOCIATION, *pg.* 145, *pg.* 730
IOWA BEEF INDUSTRY COUNCIL, *pg.* 145, *pg.* 701
ISSA, *pg.* 145, *pg.* 640
JAPAN AMERICA SOCIETY OF GREATER PHILADELPHIA, *pg.* 145, *pg.* 1566
KENTUCKY DERBY FESTIVAL, INC., *pg.* 556, *pg.* 735
THE LEADING HOTELS OF THE WORLD, LTD., *pg.* 1100, *pg.* 1250
LEAGUE OF SOUTHEASTERN CREDIT UNIONS, *pg.* 145, *pg.* 469
LINCOLN ELECTRIC HOLDINGS, INC., *pg.* 1355, *pg.* 1432
MAINE POTATO BOARD, *pg.* 146, *pg.* 752
MICHIGAN APPLE COMMITTEE, *pg.* 147, *pg.* 895
MICHIGAN ASSOCIATION OF INSURANCE AGENTS, *pg.* 147, *pg.* 895
THE NATIONAL ASSOCIATION FOR FEMALE EXECUTIVES, *pg.* 147, *pg.* 1263
NATIONAL ASSOCIATION OF CONVENIENCE STORES, *pg.* 148, *pg.* 1771
NATIONAL ASSOCIATION OF ORTHOPAEDIC NURSES, *pg.* 148, *pg.* 584
NATIONAL ASSOCIATION OF REALTORS, *pg.* 1666, *pg.* 584
NATIONAL CATTLEMEN'S BEEF ASSOCIATION, *pg.* 148, *pg.* 314
NATIONAL COFFEE ASSOCIATION OF USA, INC., *pg.* 148, *pg.* 1264
NATIONAL COMMUNITY PHARMACISTS ASSOCIATION, *pg.* 148, *pg.* 1771
NATIONAL CONCRETE MASONRY ASSOCIATION, *pg.* 148, *pg.* 1785
NATIONAL COTTON COUNCIL OF AMERICA, *pg.* 148, *pg.* 1631
NATIONAL ELECTRICAL MANUFACTURERS ASSOCIATION, *pg.* 149, *pg.* 1806
NATIONAL FOUNDATION FOR CREDIT COUNSELING, *pg.* 786, *pg.* 402
NATIONAL MARINE MANUFACTURERS ASSOCIATION, *pg.* 149, *pg.* 584
NATIONAL NOTARY ASSOCIATION, *pg.* 150, *pg.* 64
NATIONAL PEANUT BOARD, *pg.* 150, *pg.* 515
NATIONAL PORK BOARD, *pg.* 882, *pg.* 703
NATIONAL PORK PRODUCERS COUNCIL, *pg.* 150, *pg.* 712
NATIONAL POTATO PROMOTION BOARD, *pg.* 150, *pg.* 322

First page reference indicates Business Class Edition
Second page reference indicates Geographic Edition

NATIONAL RESTAURANT ASSOCIATION, *pg.* 150, *pg.* 403
NATIONAL SPORTING GOODS ASSOCIATION, *pg.* 151, *pg.* 634
NATIONAL VENTURE CAPITAL ASSOCIATION, *pg.* 151, *pg.* 1774
NATSO, INC., *pg.* 151, *pg.* 1771
NEW ENGLAND APPLE ASSOCIATION, *pg.* 151, *pg.* 824
NEW JERSEY HOSPITAL ASSOCIATION, *pg.* 152, *pg.* 1112
NEW YORK APPLE ASSOCIATION, INC., *pg.* 152, *pg.* 1160
OPTICIANS ASSOCIATION OF AMERICA, *pg.* 152, *pg.* 1639
OREGON BEEF COUNCIL, *pg.* 152, *pg.* 1504
OUTDOOR ADVERTISING ASSOCIATION OF AMERICA, *pg.* 152, *pg.* 403
PEAR BUREAU NORTHWEST, *pg.* 153, *pg.* 1500
PENNSYLVANIA CHAMBER OF BUSINESS & INDUSTRY, *pg.* 153, *pg.* 1537
PHARMACEUTICAL RESEARCH & MANUFACTURERS OF AMERICA, *pg.* 153, *pg.* 404
THE PLASTICS PIPE INSTITUTE, INC., *pg.* 154, *pg.* 1723
PORTLAND BUSINESS ALLIANCE, *pg.* 1004, *pg.* 1505
PRECAST/PRESTRESSED CONCRETE INSTITUTE, *pg.* 154, *pg.* 587
PREFERRED HOTEL GROUP, *pg.* 1108, *pg.* 587
PRODUCE MARKETING ASSOCIATION, *pg.* 154, *pg.* 388
QUALITY CHEKD DAIRIES, INC., *pg.* 154, *pg.* 630
RECREATION VEHICLE INDUSTRY ASSOCIATION, *pg.* 155, *pg.* 1799
SAE INTERNATIONAL, *pg.* 108, *pg.* 1591
SNOWMASS VILLAGE RESORT ASSOCIATION, *pg.* 1113, *pg.* 335
SOCIETY OF AMERICAN FLORISTS, *pg.* 156, *pg.* 1771
SOCIETY OF CHEMICAL MNAUFACTURERS & AFFILIATES, INC., *pg.* 156, *pg.* 404
THE SOCIETY OF THE PLASTICS INDUSTRY, INC., *pg.* 157, *pg.* 404
SOUTHERN FOREST PRODUCTS ASSOCIATION, *pg.* 157, *pg.* 744
SPECIALTY EQUIPMENT MARKET ASSOCIATION, *pg.* 157, *pg.* 77
ST. PETERSBURG AREA CHAMBER OF COMMERCE, *pg.* 157, *pg.* 464
STEVIE AWARDS, INC., *pg.* 157, *pg.* 1780
STOWE AREA ASSOCIATION, INC., *pg.* 1115, *pg.* 1768
THE SUGAR ASSOCIATION, INC., *pg.* 157, *pg.* 405
TOY INDUSTRY ASSOCIATION, INC., *pg.* 158, *pg.* 1303
TULSA METRO CHAMBER, *pg.* 1008, *pg.* 1491
UNITED EGG PRODUCERS, *pg.* 907, *pg.* 485
UNITED STATES BOWLING CONGRESS, *pg.* 159, *pg.* 1660
UNITED STATES TELECOM ASSOCIATION, *pg.* 159, *pg.* 407
USA RICE FEDERATION, *pg.* 160, *pg.* 1775
VERMONT SKI AREAS ASSOCIATION, INC., *pg.* 160, *pg.* 1767
VIDEO ADVERTISING BUREAU, *pg.* 160, *pg.* 1311
VIRGINIA TOURISM AUTHORITY, *pg.* 1010, *pg.* 1804
WASHINGTON STATE APPLE COMMISSION, *pg.* 160, *pg.* 1847
WASHINGTON STATE DAIRY PRODUCTS COMMISSION, *pg.* 161, *pg.* 1822
WASHINGTON STATE FRUIT COMMISSION, *pg.* 161, *pg.* 1847
WEST MICHIGAN TOURIST ASSOCIATION, *pg.* 1930, *pg.* 891
WESTERN WOOD PRODUCTS ASSOCIATION, *pg.* 161, *pg.* 1508
WISCONSIN BEEF COUNCIL, INC., *pg.* 161, *pg.* 1867
WISCONSIN MILK MARKETING BOARD, INC., *pg.* 161, *pg.* 1868
WORLD GOLD COUNCIL, *pg.* 162, *pg.* 1315

8621 - Professional Membership Organizations

ACADEMY OF MOTION PICTURE ARTS & SCIENCES, *pg.* 526, *pg.* 46
AIIM INTERNATIONAL, *pg.* 1614, *pg.* 777
AMERICAN ASSOCIATION FOR THE ADVANCEMENT OF SCIENCE, *pg.* 126, *pg.* 394
AMERICAN ASSOCIATION OF CRITICAL-CARE NURSES, *pg.* 126, *pg.* 40
AMERICAN COLLEGE OF NURSE-MIDWIVES, *pg.* 127, *pg.* 777
AMERICAN CONCRETE INSTITUTE, *pg.* 127, *pg.* 885
AMERICAN CONFERENCE OF GOVERNMENTAL INDUSTRIAL HYGIENISTS, *pg.* 127, *pg.* 1409
THE AMERICAN DENTAL ASSOCIATION, *pg.* 127, *pg.* 564
AMERICAN DIABETES ASSOCIATION, *pg.* 127, *pg.* 1770
AMERICAN HORT, *pg.* 129, *pg.* 1437
AMERICAN INSTITUTE OF CERTIFIED PUBLIC ACCOUNTANTS INC., *pg.* 129, *pg.* 1192
AMERICAN INSTITUTE OF CHEMICAL ENGINEERS, *pg.* 129, *pg.* 1193
AMERICAN LIBRARY ASSOCIATION, *pg.* 1615, *pg.* 564
AMERICAN MEDICAL ASSOCIATION, *pg.* 130, *pg.* 564
AMERICAN METEOROLOGICAL SOCIETY, *pg.* 1616, *pg.* 789
AMERICAN PODIATRIC MEDICAL ASSOCIATION, *pg.* 130, *pg.* 761
AMERICAN SOCIETY OF CINEMATOGRAPHERS, *pg.* 1616, *pg.* 103
AMERICAN SOCIETY OF HEALTH-SYSTEM PHARMACISTS, *pg.* 131, *pg.* 761
AMERICAN SOCIETY OF PLASTIC SURGEONS INC., *pg.* 131, *pg.* 553
AMERICAN WATER WORKS ASSOCIATION, *pg.* 131, *pg.* 316
ASSOCIATION OF AMERICAN UNIVERSITY PRESSES, *pg.* 133, *pg.* 1197
BUSINESS SOFTWARE ALLIANCE, INC., *pg.* 135, *pg.* 397
CMI MARKETING, INC., *pg.* 137, *pg.* 1214
COUNTRY MUSIC ASSOCIATION, *pg.* 138, *pg.* 1649
DUCTILE IRON PIPE RESEARCH ASSOCIATION, *pg.* 140, *pg.* 2
FOUNDATION FOR BIOMEDICAL RESEARCH, *pg.* 141, *pg.* 399
INDUSTRIAL DESIGNERS SOCIETY OF AMERICA, *pg.* 144, *pg.* 1785
INSTITUTE OF ELECTRICAL AND ELECTRONICS ENGINEERS, INC., *pg.* 144, *pg.* 1109
INSTITUTE OF MANAGEMENT ACCOUNTANTS, INC., *pg.* 144, *pg.* 1086
MASSACHUSETTS MEDICAL SOCIETY, *pg.* 1559, *pg.* 852
MEDSTAR HEALTH INC., *pg.* 1563, *pg.* 767
NATIONAL EDUCATION ASSOCIATION, *pg.* 148, *pg.* 401
NATIONAL ELECTRICAL MANUFACTURERS ASSOCIATION, *pg.* 149, *pg.* 1806
NATIONAL FIRE PROTECTION ASSOCIATION, *pg.* 149, *pg.* 842
NATIONAL NOTARY ASSOCIATION, *pg.* 150, *pg.* 64
THE NEW ENGLAND JOURNAL OF MEDICINE, *pg.* 1667, *pg.* 799
THE NORTH AMERICAN BLUEBERRY COUNCIL, *pg.* 152, *pg.* 86
PADI AMERICAS, *pg.* 573, *pg.* 188
PHILANTHROPEDIA, *pg.* 153, *pg.* 1811
THE PROFESSIONAL PUTTERS ASSOCIATION, *pg.* 154, *pg.* 1735
THE SOCIETY OF AMERICAN MILITARY ENGINEERS, *pg.* 156, *pg.* 1771
SOCIETY OF MANUFACTURING ENGINEERS, *pg.* 157, *pg.* 878
THEATRE COMMUNICATIONS GROUP, INC., *pg.* 587, *pg.* 1298
UNITE HERE, *pg.* 159, *pg.* 1306

8631 - Labor Unions & Similar Labor Organizations

AMALGAMATED LITHOGRAPHERS OF AMERICA, *pg.* 126, *pg.* 1189
AMERICAN FEDERATION OF LABOR - CONGRESS OF INDUSTRIAL ORGANIZATIONS, *pg.* 128, *pg.* 394
ASSOCIATION OF AMERICAN RAILROADS, *pg.* 133, *pg.* 396
COMMUNICATIONS WORKERS OF AMERICA, *pg.* 137, *pg.* 397
DIRECTORS GUILD OF AMERICA, INC., *pg.* 139, *pg.* 129
IOWA BEEF INDUSTRY COUNCIL, *pg.* 145, *pg.* 701
NATIONAL EDUCATION ASSOCIATION, *pg.* 148, *pg.* 401
PATROLMAN'S BENEVOLENT ASSOCIATION OF THE CITY OF NEW YORK, INC., *pg.* 153, *pg.* 1276
RECORDING MUSICIANS ASSOCIATION LOS ANGELES, *pg.* 154, *pg.* 139

8641 - Civic, Social & Fraternal Associations

THE ADVENTURE PROJECT, *pg.* 125, *pg.* 1145
AMERICAN FILM INSTITUTE, *pg.* 528, *pg.* 126
AMERICAN FORESTS, *pg.* 128, *pg.* 394
AMERICAN RADIO RELAY LEAGUE, INC., *pg.* 130, *pg.* 359
AMNESTY INTERNATIONAL USA, *pg.* 131, *pg.* 1194
ATLANTA SYMPHONY ORCHESTRA, *pg.* 531, *pg.* 490
BERKSHIRE HATHAWAY HOME SERVICES, *pg.* 1081, *pg.* 469
BLUEGREEN CORPORATION, *pg.* 1082, *pg.* 410
BOAT OWNERS ASSOCIATION OF THE UNITED STATES, *pg.* 134, *pg.* 1770
CANADIAN PARKS AND WILDERNESS SOCIETY, *pg.* 136, *pg.* 1931
COALITION FOR A DRUG-FREE GREATER CINCINNATI, *pg.* 137, *pg.* 1412
CONSUMER HEALTHCARE PRODUCTS ASSOCIATION, *pg.* 138, *pg.* 397
DARE 2 SHARE MINISTRIES INTERNATIONAL, INC., *pg.* 138, *pg.* 310
DOCTORS WITHOUT BORDERS USA, INC., *pg.* 139, *pg.* 1225
FOCUS: HOPE, *pg.* 141, *pg.* 881
FRENCH INSTITUTE ALLIANCE FRANCAISE, *pg.* 141, *pg.* 1233
FRESH AIR FUND, *pg.* 141, *pg.* 1233
GOODWILL INDUSTRIES-SUNCOAST, INC., *pg.* 142, *pg.* 462
THE GREATER BOSTON FOOD BANK, *pg.* 993, *pg.* 795
HEALTHWISE, INCORPORATED, *pg.* 143, *pg.* 546
HOLSTEIN ASSOCIATION USA, INC., *pg.* 143, *pg.* 1764
KENTUCKY DERBY FESTIVAL, INC., *pg.* 556, *pg.* 735
KNOXVILLE SYMPHONY SOCIETY INC., *pg.* 556, *pg.* 1637
LENOX HILL NEIGHBORHOOD HOUSE, *pg.* 146, *pg.* 1251
MAJOR LEAGUE BASEBALL, *pg.* 560, *pg.* 1255
MAKE-A-WISH FOUNDATION OF GREATER LOS ANGELES, *pg.* 146, *pg.* 136
MCO PROPERTIES INC., *pg.* 1104, *pg.* 13
THE METROPOLITAN OPERA, *pg.* 561, *pg.* 1260
MISSISSIPPI MUSEUM OF ART, *pg.* 563, *pg.* 969
MOTHERS AGAINST DRUNK DRIVING (MADD), *pg.* 147, *pg.* 1723
NATIONAL ASSOCIATION FOR STOCK CAR AUTO RACING, *pg.* 566, *pg.* 420
NATIONAL ASSOCIATION OF PROFESSIONAL BASEBALL LEAGUES, INC., *pg.* 566, *pg.* 463
NATIONAL AUDUBON SOCIETY, *pg.* 148, *pg.* 1263
NATIONAL BASKETBALL ASSOCIATION, *pg.* 566, *pg.* 1264
NATIONAL COUNCIL ON PROBLEM GAMBLING, *pg.* 148, *pg.* 401
NATIONAL FFA ORGANIZATION, *pg.* 149, *pg.* 688
NATIONAL FOOTBALL LEAGUE, *pg.* 567, *pg.* 1264
NATIONAL HOCKEY LEAGUE, *pg.* 568, *pg.* 1265
NATIONAL PARKS CONSERVATION ASSOCIATION, *pg.* 150, *pg.* 403
NATIONAL RIFLE ASSOCIATION, *pg.* 151, *pg.* 1780
THE NATURE CONSERVANCY, *pg.* 151, *pg.* 1774
NEW YORK ROAD RUNNERS CLUB, INC., *pg.* 152, *pg.* 1269
THE OPIUM GROUP, *pg.* 572, *pg.* 448
PASADENA SYMPHONY ASSOCIATION, *pg.* 574, *pg.* 181
PRUDENTIAL REAL ESTATE AFFILIATES, INC., *pg.* 1108, *pg.* 115
QSAC INC., *pg.* 154, *pg.* 1284
ROCHESTER PHILHARMONIC ORCHESTRA INC., *pg.* 579, *pg.* 1337
ROLLER SKATING ASSOCIATION INTERNATIONAL, *pg.* 155, *pg.* 689
THE SALVATION ARMY, *pg.* 155, *pg.* 1771
SAVE THE MANATEE CLUB, INC., *pg.* 156, *pg.* 439
SEMINOLE TRIBE OF FLORIDA, INC., *pg.* 156, *pg.* 431
SIERRA CLUB, *pg.* 156, *pg.* 227
SNOHOMISH COUNTY MUSIC PROJECT, *pg.* 584, *pg.* 1819
SOCIETY OF MANUFACTURING ENGINEERS, *pg.* 157, *pg.* 878
SUNDANCE INSTITUTE, *pg.* 311, *pg.* 1754
SURFRIDER FOUNDATION, *pg.* 158, *pg.* 199
SYMPHONY OF THE SOUTHWEST, *pg.* 586, *pg.* 13
THEATER & ARTS FOUNDATION, *pg.* 587, *pg.* 120
TRAVEL INDUSTRY ASSOCIATION OF AMERICA, *pg.* 158, *pg.* 405
UNITED STATES OLYMPIC COMMITTEE, *pg.* 589, *pg.* 315
UNITED THROUGH READING, *pg.* 160, *pg.* 210
UPSPRING, *pg.* 160, *pg.* 1426
WATERLOO-CEDAR FALLS SYMPHONY ORCHESTRA, *pg.*

591, *pg.* 702
WESTMORELAND SYMPHONY ORCHESTRA, *pg.* 592, *pg.* 1534
THE WHAT TO EXPECT FOUNDATION, *pg.* 161, *pg.* 1314
WILLIAMSPORT SYMPHONY ORCHESTRA, *pg.* 592, *pg.* 1595

8651 - Political Organizations

AMNESTY INTERNATIONAL USA, *pg.* 131, *pg.* 1194
DEMOCRATIC NATIONAL COMMITTEE, *pg.* 139, *pg.* 398

8661 - Religious Organizations

ANSWERS IN GENESIS, *pg.* 132, *pg.* 740
ASTARA, INC., *pg.* 1618, *pg.* 186
ATHLETES IN ACTION, *pg.* 133, *pg.* 1482
THE CHRISTIAN BROADCASTING NETWORK INC., *pg.* 275, *pg.* 1810
CHRISTIANITY TODAY INTERNATIONAL, *pg.* 1627, *pg.* 561
COMMENTARY, *pg.* 1628, *pg.* 1216
DAVID C. COOK, *pg.* 1633, *pg.* 315
FAMILY FIRST, *pg.* 140, *pg.* 472
FULL GOSPEL BUSINESS MEN'S FELLOWSHIP INTERNATIONAL, *pg.* 141, *pg.* 110
INTERNATIONAL FELLOWSHIP OF CHRISTIANS & JEWS, INC., *pg.* 145, *pg.* 579
INTERNATIONAL LUTHERAN LAYMEN'S LEAGUE, *pg.* 293, *pg.* 998
METROPOLITAN MINISTRIES INC., *pg.* 146, *pg.* 474
MOODY BIBLE INSTITUTE, *pg.* 605, *pg.* 583
MORRIS CERULLO WORLD EVANGELISM, *pg.* 147, *pg.* 205
THE TIMES-NEWS, *pg.* 1694, *pg.* 1359
THE UPPER ROOM, *pg.* 1698, *pg.* 1655
WORD OF LIFE FELLOWSHIP, INC., *pg.* 161, *pg.* 1341
THE ZONDERVAN CORPORATION, *pg.* 1703, *pg.* 891

8699 - Membership Organizations, NEC

ADVANCE REALTY GROUP, LLC, *pg.* 1079, *pg.* 1045
AFFINIA HOSPITALITY, *pg.* 1487, *pg.* 1188
AIMCO PROPERTIES, L.P., *pg.* 1079, *pg.* 316
ALLETE, INC., *pg.* 1933, *pg.* 921
AMERICAN CAMPUS COMMUNITIES, INC., *pg.* 1079, *pg.* 1660
AMERICAN FILM INSTITUTE, *pg.* 528, *pg.* 126
AMERICAN FORESTS, *pg.* 128, *pg.* 394
AMERICAN RADIO RELAY LEAGUE, INC., *pg.* 130, *pg.* 359
AMNESTY INTERNATIONAL USA, *pg.* 131, *pg.* 1194
ATLANTA SYMPHONY ORCHESTRA, *pg.* 531, *pg.* 490
AV HOMES INC., *pg.* 1080, *pg.* 20
BB&T, *pg.* 723, *pg.* 423
BERKSHIRE HATHAWAY HOME SERVICES, *pg.* 1081, *pg.* 200
BERKSHIRE HATHAWAY HOME SERVICES, *pg.* 1081, *pg.* 469
BEVERLY-HANKS & ASSOCIATES INC., *pg.* 1082, *pg.* 1358
BINSWANGER CORPORATION, *pg.* 1082, *pg.* 1559
BLUEGREEN CORPORATION, *pg.* 1082, *pg.* 410
BOAT OWNERS ASSOCIATION OF THE UNITED STATES, *pg.* 134, *pg.* 1770
CALDWELL WATSON REAL ESTATE GROUP, *pg.* 1084, *pg.* 1702
CANADIAN PARKS AND WILDERNESS SOCIETY, *pg.* 136, *pg.* 1931
CANDY SWICK & COMPANY, *pg.* 1084, *pg.* 465
CARLSON REAL ESTATE COMPANY, *pg.* 1084, *pg.* 947
CB RICHARD ELLIS GROUP, INC., *pg.* 1085, *pg.* 127
CB RICHARD ELLIS, INC., *pg.* 1085, *pg.* 1210
CBSHOME REAL ESTATE, *pg.* 1085, *pg.* 1013
CENTURY 21 REAL ESTATE LLC, *pg.* 1085, *pg.* 1080
CHAMPION REALTY INC., *pg.* 1085, *pg.* 777
COALITION FOR A DRUG-FREE GREATER CINCINNATI, *pg.* 137, *pg.* 1412
COLDWELL BANKER REAL ESTATE LLC, *pg.* 1087, *pg.* 1103
COLDWELL BANKER RESIDENTIAL BROKERAGE, *pg.* 1087, *pg.* 850
COLLIERS INTERNATIONAL, *pg.* 1087, *pg.* 1834
COMSTOCK HOLDING COMPANIES INC., *pg.* 1087, *pg.* 1798
CONCORD PACIFIC GROUP, *pg.* 1087, *pg.* 1910
CONSOLIDATED-TOMOKA LAND CO., *pg.* 1087, *pg.* 419
CONSUMER HEALTHCARE PRODUCTS ASSOCIATION, *pg.* 138, *pg.* 397
CORCORAN SUNSHINE MARKETING GROUP, *pg.* 1088, *pg.* 1218
CORELOGIC, INC., *pg.* 1198, *pg.* 109
COSTAR GROUP, INC., *pg.* 742, *pg.* 397
COUNTRY WIDE REALTY INC., *pg.* 1088, *pg.* 1144
COUSINS PROPERTIES INCORPORATED, *pg.* 1088, *pg.* 501
CRESA PARTNERS LLC, *pg.* 1088, *pg.* 1220
CRESCENT COMMUNITIES, LLC, *pg.* 702, *pg.* 1365
CUSHMAN & WAKEFIELD, INC., *pg.* 1088, *pg.* 1220
CUSHMAN & WAKEFIELD OF FLORIDA, INC., *pg.* 1089, *pg.* 442
DANIEL DECARO REAL ESTATE AUCTIONS, INC., *pg.* 1089, *pg.* 438
DARE 2 SHARE MINISTRIES INTERNATIONAL, INC., *pg.* 138, *pg.* 310
DOCTORS WITHOUT BORDERS USA, INC., *pg.* 139, *pg.* 1225
DOUGLAS-GUARDIAN SERVICES CORPORATION, *pg.* 388, *pg.* 1704
DRAPER & KRAMER RETIREMENT PROPERTY SERVICES, *pg.* 1090, *pg.* 572
ERGON, INC., *pg.* 976, *pg.* 969
ESSLINGER-WOOTEN-MAXWELL REALTORS, INC., *pg.* 1091, *pg.* 418
EXIT REALTY CENTRAL, *pg.* 1091, *pg.* 1796
FARMERS NATIONAL COMPANY, *pg.* 703, *pg.* 1015
THE FLATLEY COMPANY, *pg.* 1092, *pg.* 802
FLORIDA EAST COAST INDUSTRIES, INC., *pg.* 1909, *pg.* 433
FOCUS: HOPE, *pg.* 141, *pg.* 881
FRENCH INSTITUTE ALLIANCE FRANCAISE, *pg.* 141, *pg.* 1233
FRESH AIR FUND, *pg.* 141, *pg.* 1233
GH III MANAGEMENT LLC, *pg.* 1093, *pg.* 1706
GLORIA NILSON GMAC REAL ESTATE, *pg.* 1093, *pg.* 1084
GOODWILL INDUSTRIES-SUNCOAST, INC., *pg.* 142, *pg.* 462
THE GREATER BOSTON FOOD BANK, *pg.* 993, *pg.* 795
HARRY NORMAN REALTORS, *pg.* 1094, *pg.* 509
HEALTHWISE, INCORPORATED, *pg.* 143, *pg.* 546
HFF, INC., *pg.* 766, *pg.* 1576
HOLSTEIN ASSOCIATION USA, INC., *pg.* 143, *pg.* 1764
HOME REAL ESTATE INC., *pg.* 1096, *pg.* 1012
HOMEGAIN.COM, INC., *pg.* 1256, *pg.* 83
HOMES.COM, INC., *pg.* 1256, *pg.* 203
HOMESERVICES OF AMERICA, INC., *pg.* 1096, *pg.* 938
HOST HOTELS & RESORTS, INC., *pg.* 1096, *pg.* 762
HOULIHAN/LAWRENCE INC., *pg.* 1096, *pg.* 1145
HUNT BUILDING COMPANY LIMITED, *pg.* 87, *pg.* 1692
ICAHN ENTERPRISES L.P., *pg.* 1097, *pg.* 1243
THE IRVINE COMPANY INC., *pg.* 1098, *pg.* 165
JIM WILSON & ASSOCIATES, INC., *pg.* 1098, *pg.* 7
J.L. TODD AUCTION CO., *pg.* 1774, *pg.* 539
KENNEDY-WILSON, INC., *pg.* 1099, *pg.* 46
KENTUCKY DERBY FESTIVAL, INC., *pg.* 556, *pg.* 735
KNOXVILLE SYMPHONY SOCIETY INC., *pg.* 556, *pg.* 1637
LENOX HILL NEIGHBORHOOD HOUSE, *pg.* 146, *pg.* 1251
LIMONEIRA COMPANY, *pg.* 705, *pg.* 276
LONG REALTY COMPANY, *pg.* 1101, *pg.* 27
LOOPNET, INC., *pg.* 1265, *pg.* 222
THE MACERICH COMPANY, *pg.* 1101, *pg.* 275
MAJOR LEAGUE BASEBALL, *pg.* 560, *pg.* 1255
MAKE-A-WISH FOUNDATION OF GREATER LOS ANGELES, *pg.* 146, *pg.* 136
MARCUS & MILLICHAP REAL ESTATE INVESTMENT COMPANY, *pg.* 1102, *pg.* 56
MARI VESCI REALTORS, INC., *pg.* 1102, *pg.* 451
MARKET LEADER, INC., *pg.* 1102, *pg.* 1822
MARSHALL & SWIFT/BOECKH, LLC, *pg.* 1661, *pg.* 136
MCLEAN FAULCONER INC., *pg.* 1104, *pg.* 1778
MCO PROPERTIES INC., *pg.* 1104, *pg.* 13
THE METROPOLITAN OPERA, *pg.* 561, *pg.* 1260
MICHAEL SAUNDERS & COMPANY, *pg.* 1105, *pg.* 466
MISSISSIPPI MUSEUM OF ART, *pg.* 563, *pg.* 969
MOTHERS AGAINST DRUNK DRIVING (MADD), *pg.* 147, *pg.* 1723
MOVE, INC., *pg.* 1268, *pg.* 247
MRI SOFTWARE, LLC, *pg.* 1106, *pg.* 1473
NATIONAL ASSOCIATION FOR STOCK CAR AUTO RACING, *pg.* 566, *pg.* 420
NATIONAL ASSOCIATION OF PROFESSIONAL BASEBALL LEAGUES, INC., *pg.* 566, *pg.* 463
NATIONAL AUDUBON SOCIETY, *pg.* 148, *pg.* 1263
NATIONAL BASKETBALL ASSOCIATION, *pg.* 566, *pg.* 1264
NATIONAL COUNCIL ON PROBLEM GAMBLING, *pg.* 148, *pg.* 401
NATIONAL FFA ORGANIZATION, *pg.* 149, *pg.* 688
NATIONAL FOOTBALL LEAGUE, *pg.* 567, *pg.* 1264
NATIONAL HOCKEY LEAGUE, *pg.* 568, *pg.* 1265
NATIONAL PARKS CONSERVATION ASSOCIATION, *pg.* 150, *pg.* 403
NATIONAL RIFLE ASSOCIATION, *pg.* 151, *pg.* 1780
THE NATURE CONSERVANCY, *pg.* 151, *pg.* 1774
NETWORK COMMUNICATIONS INC., *pg.* 1271, *pg.* 534
NEW YORK ROAD RUNNERS CLUB, INC., *pg.* 152, *pg.* 1269
NEWMARK GRUBB KNIGHT FRANK, *pg.* 1106, *pg.* 1271
NTS DEVELOPMENT COMPANY, *pg.* 1106, *pg.* 737
THE OPIUM GROUP, *pg.* 572, *pg.* 448
OXFORD REALTY, INC., *pg.* 1107, *pg.* 455
PACIFICA HOTEL COMPANY, *pg.* 1107, *pg.* 114
PASADENA SYMPHONY ASSOCIATION, *pg.* 574, *pg.* 181
PHILLIPS DEVELOPMENT & REALTY, LLC, *pg.* 1108, *pg.* 475
PORTSMOUTH SQUARE, INC., *pg.* 1108, *pg.* 139
POST APARTMENT HOMES, L.P., *pg.* 1108, *pg.* 518
PRUDENTIAL FINANCIAL, INC., *pg.* 797, *pg.* 1097
PRUDENTIAL REAL ESTATE AFFILIATES, INC., *pg.* 1108, *pg.* 115
PS BUSINESS PARKS, INC., *pg.* 1108, *pg.* 98
PUBLIC STORAGE, *pg.* 1467, *pg.* 98
PULTEGROUP, INC., *pg.* 1109, *pg.* 873
QUICKEN LOANS, INC., *pg.* 797, *pg.* 884
READING INTERNATIONAL, INC., *pg.* 578, *pg.* 139
REALOGY CORPORATION, *pg.* 1109, *pg.* 1081
REALPAGE, INC., *pg.* 1277, *pg.* 1669
REALTYSOUTH, *pg.* 1109, *pg.* 4
REECE & NICHOLS REALTORS, *pg.* 1110, *pg.* 716
THE RESORT AT LONGBOAT KEY CLUB, *pg.* 1110, *pg.* 438
ROCHESTER PHILHARMONIC ORCHESTRA INC., *pg.* 579, *pg.* 1337
ROLLER SKATING ASSOCIATION INTERNATIONAL, *pg.* 155, *pg.* 689
ROYAL BANK OF CANADA, *pg.* 800, *pg.* 1942
THE SALVATION ARMY, *pg.* 155, *pg.* 1771
SAVE THE MANATEE CLUB, INC., *pg.* 156, *pg.* 439
THE SCHULTZ ORGANIZATION, *pg.* 1111, *pg.* 1133
SEASIDE PROPERTIES GROUP, INC., *pg.* 1112, *pg.* 426
SEMINOLE TRIBE OF FLORIDA, INC., *pg.* 156, *pg.* 431
SEMONIN REALTORS, *pg.* 1112, *pg.* 738
SIERRA CLUB, *pg.* 156, *pg.* 227
SILVERLEAF RESORTS, INC., *pg.* 1112, *pg.* 1686
SIMON PROPERTY GROUP, INC., *pg.* 1112, *pg.* 690
SKYLINE EQUITIES REALTY, LLC, *pg.* 1113, *pg.* 446
SNOHOMISH COUNTY MUSIC PROJECT, *pg.* 584, *pg.* 1819
SOCIETY OF MANUFACTURING ENGINEERS, *pg.* 157, *pg.* 878
SOTHEBY'S INTERNATIONAL REALTY, INC., *pg.* 1113, *pg.* 1294
SRS REAL ESTATE PARTNERS, *pg.* 1113, *pg.* 1687
ST. BARTH PROPERTIES, INC., *pg.* 1114, *pg.* 823
STONECUTTER MILLS CORP., *pg.* 113, *pg.* 1391
STRATUS PROPERTIES, INC., *pg.* 1115, *pg.* 1666
SUN COMMUNITIES, INC., *pg.* 1115, *pg.* 907
SUNDANCE INSTITUTE, *pg.* 311, *pg.* 1754
SURFRIDER FOUNDATION, *pg.* 158, *pg.* 199
SYMPHONY OF THE SOUTHWEST, *pg.* 586, *pg.* 13
TANGER FACTORY OUTLET CENTERS, INC., *pg.* 1116, *pg.* 1376
TANGER PROPERTIES LIMITED PARTNERSHIP, *pg.* 1116, *pg.* 1376
TAYLOR MORRISON, *pg.* 1116, *pg.* 24
THEATER & ARTS FOUNDATION, *pg.* 587, *pg.* 120
TOWNE PROPERTIES, *pg.* 1116, *pg.* 1426
TRAVEL INDUSTRY ASSOCIATION OF AMERICA, *pg.* 158, *pg.* 405
THE TRUMP ORGANIZATION, LLC, *pg.* 1117, *pg.* 1305
UNITED, INC., *pg.* 1117, *pg.* 1905
UNITED STATES OLYMPIC COMMITTEE, *pg.* 589, *pg.* 315
UNITED STATES REALTY & INVESTMENT COMPANY, *pg.* 1117, *pg.* 1307
UNITED WAY WORLDWIDE, *pg.* 160, *pg.* 1772
UPSPRING, *pg.* 160, *pg.* 1426

VICEROY HOMES LIMITED, *pg.* 118, *pg.* 1932
WATERLOO-CEDAR FALLS SYMPHONY ORCHESTRA, *pg.* 591, *pg.* 702
WCI COMMUNITIES, INC., *pg.* 1118, *pg.* 414
WEICHERT REALTORS, *pg.* 1118, *pg.* 1087
WESTMORELAND SYMPHONY ORCHESTRA, *pg.* 592, *pg.* 1534
THE WHAT TO EXPECT FOUNDATION, *pg.* 161, *pg.* 1314
WILLIAMSPORT SYMPHONY ORCHESTRA, *pg.* 592, *pg.* 1595
WOODS BROS REALTY, INC., *pg.* 1119, *pg.* 1012
W.P. CAREY & CO., LLC, *pg.* 823, *pg.* 1315
WYNDHAM VACATION OWNERSHIP, *pg.* 1119, *pg.* 457
WYNN LAS VEGAS, LLC, *pg.* 1119, *pg.* 1030
WYNN RESORTS LIMITED, *pg.* 1119, *pg.* 1030
WYNNESTONE COMMUNITIES, *pg.* 1120, *pg.* 908
ZILLOW GROUP, INC., *pg.* 1292, *pg.* 1843
ZIPREALTY, INC., *pg.* 1120, *pg.* 85

8711 - Engineering Services

AECOM, *pg.* 64, *pg.* 173
AECOM, *pg.* 64, *pg.* 1187
AECOM TECHNOLOGY CORPORATION, *pg.* 65, *pg.* 125
ALION SCIENCE AND TECHNOLOGY CORPORATION, *pg.* 615, *pg.* 1788
ALLEN & HOSHALL, INC., *pg.* 66, *pg.* 1641
THE ALLIED POWER GROUP, *pg.* 1312, *pg.* 1699
AMERICAN ELECTRIC POWER SERVICE CORPORATION, *pg.* 1934, *pg.* 1437
ANDRITZ INC., *pg.* 1451, *pg.* 539
THE AUSTIN COMPANY, *pg.* 69, *pg.* 1428
BARNES GROUP INC., *pg.* 1317, *pg.* 340
BROWN AND CALDWELL, *pg.* 72, *pg.* 303
BURGESS & NIPLE, INC., *pg.* 72, *pg.* 1438
BURGESS-NORTON MANUFACTURING COMPANY, *pg.* 202, *pg.* 613
CACI INTERNATIONAL INC., *pg.* 367, *pg.* 1773
CDM SMITH, *pg.* 74, *pg.* 807
CH2M HILL COMPANIES, LTD., *pg.* 75, *pg.* 325
CLEAN HARBORS, INC., *pg.* 376, *pg.* 839
CLUNE CONSTRUCTION CO., *pg.* 76, *pg.* 571
CORRPRO COMPANIES, INC., *pg.* 631, *pg.* 1464
EA ENGINEERING, SCIENCE & TECHNOLOGY, INC., *pg.* 389, *pg.* 772
ECOLOGY AND ENVIRONMENT, INC., *pg.* 1410, *pg.* 1173
ENGINE COMPONENTS, INC., *pg.* 227, *pg.* 1740
ENGLOBAL CORPORATION, *pg.* 81, *pg.* 1705
EPSILON SYSTEMS SOLUTIONS, *pg.* 1412, *pg.* 202
ERM GROUP, INC., *pg.* 1412, *pg.* 1531
EXTERRAN HOLDINGS, INC., *pg.* 977, *pg.* 1705
FEINTOOL EQUIPMENT CORP., *pg.* 1336, *pg.* 1413
FLUOR CORPORATION, *pg.* 82, *pg.* 1719
HALLIBURTON COMPANY, *pg.* 978, *pg.* 1707
HILL INTERNATIONAL INC., *pg.* 87, *pg.* 1083
IAV AUTOMOTIVE ENGINEERING INC., *pg.* 208, *pg.* 902
I.C. THOMASSON ASSOCIATES, INC., *pg.* 88, *pg.* 1651
IGATE CORPORATION, *pg.* 411, *pg.* 91
INTERMAP TECHNOLOGIES CORPORATION, *pg.* 417, *pg.* 1903
JACOBS ENGINEERING GROUP, INC., *pg.* 88, *pg.* 180
JARMEL KIZEL ARCHITECTS & ENGINEERS, INC., *pg.* 89, *pg.* 1079
KBR, INC., *pg.* 90, *pg.* 1709
THE KULJIAN CORPORATION, *pg.* 92, *pg.* 1566
MCCAULEY PROPELLER SYSTEMS, *pg.* 231, *pg.* 724
MTS SYSTEMS CORPORATION, *pg.* 442, *pg.* 923
MWH GLOBAL, INC., *pg.* 98, *pg.* 312
NORTHROP GRUMMAN INFORMATION SYSTEMS, *pg.* 1424, *pg.* 1794
PARSONS & WHITTEMORE, INC., *pg.* 103, *pg.* 1339
PARSONS BRINCKERHOFF INC., *pg.* 103, *pg.* 1276
RECARO NORTH AMERICA, INC., *pg.* 216, *pg.* 869
SAE INTERNATIONAL, *pg.* 108, *pg.* 1591
SBA COMMUNICATIONS CORPORATION, *pg.* 671, *pg.* 413
SCS ENGINEERS, *pg.* 109, *pg.* 124
SHANNON & WILSON, INC., *pg.* 110, *pg.* 1840
SIEMENS ENERGY, INC., *pg.* 469, *pg.* 1341
SILICON GRAPHICS INTERNATIONAL CORP, *pg.* 470, *pg.* 148
SNC-LAVALIN GROUP INC., *pg.* 111, *pg.* 1956
STEDMAN MACHINE COMPANY, *pg.* 1379, *pg.* 673
TANKNOLOGY INC, *pg.* 114, *pg.* 1666
TENSAR CORPORATION, *pg.* 114, *pg.* 485
TETRA TECH, INC., *pg.* 115, *pg.* 181
TIAX LLC, *pg.* 115, *pg.* 829
TRC COMPANIES, INC., *pg.* 1383, *pg.* 386
TRIMBLE NAVIGATION LIMITED, *pg.* 1384, *pg.* 288
TYCO INTERNATIONAL (US) INC., *pg.* 1891, *pg.* 1113
UOP LLC, *pg.* 1386, *pg.* 606
URS CORPORATION, *pg.* 1386, *pg.* 1667
VERSAR, INC., *pg.* 1435, *pg.* 1807
THE WHITMAN COMPANIES, INC., *pg.* 121, *pg.* 1053

8712 - Architectural Services

AECOM, *pg.* 64, *pg.* 173
AECOM, *pg.* 64, *pg.* 1187
AECOM TECHNOLOGY CORPORATION, *pg.* 65, *pg.* 125
THE AUSTIN COMPANY, *pg.* 69, *pg.* 1428
BURGESS & NIPLE, INC., *pg.* 72, *pg.* 1438
THE ENKEBOLL COMPANY, *pg.* 923, *pg.* 63
HEERY INTERNATIONAL, INC., *pg.* 86, *pg.* 510
JARMEL KIZEL ARCHITECTS & ENGINEERS, INC., *pg.* 89, *pg.* 1079

8713 - Surveying Services

BOLT TECHNOLOGY CORPORATION, *pg.* 1318, *pg.* 360
CGGVERITAS SERVICES (U.S.) INC., *pg.* 973, *pg.* 1703
CODA OCTOPUS GROUP, INC., *pg.* 629, *pg.* 437
DAWSON GEOPHYSICAL COMPANY, *pg.* 383, *pg.* 1727
DIGITALGLOBE, *pg.* 227, *pg.* 1785
GEOSPATIAL HOLDINGS, INC., *pg.* 84, *pg.* 1585
GLOBAL GEOPHYSICAL SERVICES, INC., *pg.* 1414, *pg.* 1727
HERE, *pg.* 404, *pg.* 576
INTERMAP TECHNOLOGIES CORPORATION, *pg.* 417, *pg.* 1903
ION GEOPHYSICAL CORPORATION, *pg.* 1350, *pg.* 1708
MAPQUEST, INC., *pg.* 1265, *pg.* 321
SHANNON & WILSON, INC., *pg.* 110, *pg.* 1840
TECK RESOURCES LIMITED, *pg.* 1183, *pg.* 1912
YAMANA GOLD INC., *pg.* 1396, *pg.* 1947

8721 - Accounting, Auditing & Bookkeeping Services

ACI WORLDWIDE, *pg.* 710, *pg.* 1777
ALLIANCE DATA SYSTEMS CORPORATION, *pg.* 347, *pg.* 1729
AUTOMATIC DATA PROCESSING, INC., *pg.* 357, *pg.* 1117
BDO SEIDMAN, LLP, *pg.* 724, *pg.* 1202
BEDERSON & COMPANY LLP, *pg.* 724, *pg.* 1064
BOSTON PRIVATE, *pg.* 726, *pg.* 254
CBIZ, INC., *pg.* 733, *pg.* 1429
CERIDIAN CORPORATION, *pg.* 371, *pg.* 932
COHNREZNICK LLP, *pg.* 739, *pg.* 1118
DELOITTE & TOUCHE USA LLP, *pg.* 743, *pg.* 1222
EMPLOYMENT ENTERPRISES INC., *pg.* 392, *pg.* 1787
ERNST & YOUNG GLOBAL LIMITED, *pg.* 748, *pg.* 1228
FROST COMPANY, *pg.* 760, *pg.* 1629
GILMAN CIOCIA, INC., *pg.* 762, *pg.* 1324
GRANT THORNTON INTERNATIONAL LTD., *pg.* 763, *pg.* 575
H&R BLOCK, INC., *pg.* 764, *pg.* 983
HABIF, AROGETI & WYNNE, LLP, *pg.* 764, *pg.* 509
HEARTLAND PAYMENT SYSTEMS, INC., *pg.* 765, *pg.* 1111
HILL BARTH & KING LLC, *pg.* 766, *pg.* 1483
INTUIT INC., *pg.* 769, *pg.* 158
KPMG LLP, *pg.* 774, *pg.* 1086
MCGLADREY, LLP, *pg.* 781, *pg.* 938
NORTECH SYSTEMS INCORPORATED, *pg.* 659, *pg.* 966
OLD MUTUAL ASSET MANAGEMENT, *pg.* 789, *pg.* 799
PAYCHEX, INC., *pg.* 792, *pg.* 1336
PRICEWATERHOUSECOOPERS LLP, *pg.* 795, *pg.* 1283
SAXBST, *pg.* 801, *pg.* 1137
SOUTHEAST TOYOTA DISTRIBUTORS, LLC, *pg.* 190, *pg.* 421
TRIZETTO CORPORATION, *pg.* 485, *pg.* 327
WISS & COMPANY LLP, *pg.* 823, *pg.* 1080

8732 - Commercial Economic, Sociological & Educational Research

ACNIELSEN CORPORATION, *pg.* 341, *pg.* 1187
ALEXA INTERNET, INC., *pg.* 1226, *pg.* 212
BIZRATE.COM, *pg.* 1231, *pg.* 126
BRANDMUSCLE, INC., *pg.* 364, *pg.* 1660
CEB INC., *pg.* 733, *pg.* 1773
CX ACT, INC., *pg.* 1394, *pg.* 1773
FORRESTER RESEARCH, INC., *pg.* 1642, *pg.* 807
THE GALLUP ORGANIZATION, *pg.* 399, *pg.* 399
THE GALLUP ORGANIZATION-PRINCETON, *pg.* 1643, *pg.* 1111
GARTNER, INC., *pg.* 1248, *pg.* 374
IHS AUTOMOTIVE DRIVEN BY POLK, *pg.* 1652, *pg.* 907
IMS HEALTH, INC., *pg.* 1544, *pg.* 344
INFOGROUP INC., *pg.* 1652, *pg.* 1016
INTERNATIONAL DATA GROUP, *pg.* 1653, *pg.* 796
IPSOS-ASI, INC., *pg.* 421, *pg.* 363
IRI GROUP, *pg.* 421, *pg.* 579
MARITZ INC., *pg.* 1914, *pg.* 977
MARKET DATA RETRIEVAL, *pg.* 1661, *pg.* 370
METRIXLAB, *pg.* 1266, *pg.* 223
NATIONAL RESEARCH CORPORATION, *pg.* 443, *pg.* 1012
NIELSEN AUDIO, *pg.* 446, *pg.* 768
THE NIELSEN COMPANY B.V., *pg.* 1671, *pg.* 1272
NIELSEN MEDIA RESEARCH, INC., *pg.* 303, *pg.* 1272
NOVUS INTERNATIONAL, INC., *pg.* 706, *pg.* 1001
THE NPD GROUP, INC., *pg.* 1672, *pg.* 1323
OPENAIR, INC., *pg.* 1272, *pg.* 800
QUODD FINANCIAL INFORMATION SERVICES, *pg.* 1276, *pg.* 1076
RADIANT RESEARCH INC., *pg.* 1588, *pg.* 1425
RENASANT BANK, *pg.* 798, *pg.* 533
SCOTTISH DEVELOPMENT INTERNATIONAL, *pg.* 1005, *pg.* 801
SMARTPROS LTD., *pg.* 1281, *pg.* 1166
SONIC FOUNDRY, INC., *pg.* 472, *pg.* 1867
SPAR GROUP, INC., *pg.* 1687, *pg.* 1349
SRDS, INC., *pg.* 1688, *pg.* 657
SURVEY SAMPLING INTERNATIONAL LLC, *pg.* 1690, *pg.* 371
THOMAS REGISTER OF AMERICAN MANUFACTURERS, *pg.* 1692, *pg.* 1299
USADATA, INC., *pg.* 1287, *pg.* 1308
WESTAT INC., *pg.* 161, *pg.* 776
ZOGBY ANALYTICS, *pg.* 1292, *pg.* 1347

8733 - Noncommercial Research Organizations

AAR CORP., *pg.* 223, *pg.* 671
ACNIELSEN CORPORATION, *pg.* 341, *pg.* 1187
AERO SYSTEMS ENGINEERING INC., *pg.* 223, *pg.* 959
AEROJET ROCKETDYNE, *pg.* 223, *pg.* 1782
AEROJET ROCKETDYNE HOLDINGS, INC., *pg.* 1145, *pg.* 186
AEROJET ROCKETDYNE INC, *pg.* 614, *pg.* 186
AEROVIRONMENT, INC., *pg.* 223, *pg.* 150
AFEXA LIFE SCIENCES INC., *pg.* 1487, *pg.* 1905
AFFYMETRIX, INC., *pg.* 1487, *pg.* 263
AGROPUR COOPERATIVE, *pg.* 836, *pg.* 1950
AIR INDUSTRIES GROUP, INC., *pg.* 223, *pg.* 1141
AIRBUS HELICOPTERS, INC., *pg.* 223, *pg.* 1698
AIRBUS NORTH AMERICA HOLDINGS, INC., *pg.* 1897, *pg.* 1784
AKZO NOBEL COATINGS INC., *pg.* 1439, *pg.* 1437
ALCOA WHEEL & FORGED PRODUCTS, *pg.* 66, *pg.* 1427
ALEXION PHARMACEUTICALS, INC., *pg.* 1489, *pg.* 341
ALIMERA SCIENCES, INC., *pg.* 1490, *pg.* 482
ALION SCIENCE AND TECHNOLOGY CORPORATION, *pg.* 615, *pg.* 1788
ALLEN AIRCRAFT PRODUCTS, INC., *pg.* 223, *pg.* 1471
ALLERGAN, *pg.* 1490, *pg.* 1101
AMBAC INTERNATIONAL CORPORATION, *pg.* 198, *pg.* 1615
AMERICAN CANCER SOCIETY, INC., *pg.* 126, *pg.* 487
AMERICAN ENTERPRISE INSTITUTE FOR PUBLIC POLICY RESEARCH, *pg.* 128, *pg.* 394
AMERICAN MATHEMATICAL SOCIETY, INC., *pg.* 129, *pg.* 1605
AMGEN INC., *pg.* 1493, *pg.* 291
APTOSE BIOSCIENCES, *pg.* 1495, *pg.* 1934
ARDEA BIOSCIENCES, INC., *pg.* 1495, *pg.* 200
ARENA PHARMACEUTICALS, INC., *pg.* 1495, *pg.* 200
AROTECH CORPORATION, *pg.* 1042, *pg.* 865
ASPHALT INSTITUTE, *pg.* 133, *pg.* 729

ASTROTECH CORPORATION, pg. 1400, pg. 1660
ATI LADISH FORGING, pg. 69, pg. 1856
AVANIR PHARMACEUTICALS, pg. 1498, pg. 40
AVIALL, INC., pg. 224, pg. 1676
BABYCENTER, LLC, pg. 1231, pg. 212
BALL CORPORATION, pg. 1452, pg. 311
BARBOUR STOCKWELL INCORPORATED, pg. 1316, pg. 861
BATTELLE MEMORIAL INSTITUTE, pg. 1401, pg. 1437
BAYER CORPORATION, pg. 1499, pg. 1573
BE AEROSPACE, INC., pg. 224, pg. 478
BELL HELICOPTER TEXTRON, INC., pg. 224, pg. 1693
BIOANALYTICAL SYSTEMS, INC., pg. 1402, pg. 700
THE BOEING COMPANY, pg. 225, pg. 567
THE BOEING COMPANY - HELICOPTER DIVISION, pg. 226, pg. 13
BOMBARDIER INC., pg. 1318, pg. 1953
BOSTON GEAR, pg. 201, pg. 802
BOSTON SCIENTIFIC CORPORATION, pg. 1508, pg. 831
BRAINSTORM CELL THERAPEUTICS INC., pg. 1509, pg. 1072
BREAST CANCER RESEARCH FOUNDATION, pg. 134, pg. 1206
BREEZE-EASTERN CORPORATION, pg. 1319, pg. 1132
BREWER SCIENCE, INC., pg. 1150, pg. 989
BRIMROSE CORPORATION, pg. 1403, pg. 756
BRUKER CORPORATION, pg. 1511, pg. 788
CALADRIUS BIOSCIENCES, INC., pg. 1511, pg. 1209
CAMERON BALLOONS U.S., pg. 1829, pg. 884
CELL THERAPEUTICS, INC., pg. 1514, pg. 1834
CESSNA AIRCRAFT COMPANY, pg. 226, pg. 723
CHIESI USA, INC., pg. 1515, pg. 1359
CIRRUS DESIGN CORPORATION, pg. 226, pg. 921
CLEARFIELD, INC., pg. 1406, pg. 953
CMC ELECTRONICS INC., pg. 376, pg. 1959
CODEXIS, INC., pg. 1154, pg. 189
CONTINENTAL ANALYTICAL SERVICES INC., pg. 1518, pg. 721
CONTINENTAL MOTORS, pg. 227, pg. 7
COUNCIL ON FOREIGN RELATIONS, pg. 138, pg. 1219
CRANE CO., pg. 227, pg. 373
CYCLACEL PHARMACEUTICALS, INC., pg. 1521, pg. 1044
DASSAULT FALCON JET CORP., pg. 227, pg. 1122
DATATRAK INTERNATIONAL, INC., pg. 383, pg. 1462
DENDREON CORPORATION, pg. 1522, pg. 1835
DEPOMED, INC., pg. 1523, pg. 143
DIGITALGLOBE, pg. 227, pg. 1785
DUCOMMUN TECHNOLOGIES, INC., pg. 634, pg. 63
DYAX CORP., pg. 1525, pg. 805
DYNATEX INTERNATIONAL, pg. 635, pg. 277
EDAC TECHNOLOGIES CORPORATION, pg. 1332, pg. 342
EDUCATIONAL TESTING SERVICE INC., pg. 1394, pg. 1111
ELECTRIC POWER RESEARCH INSTITUTE INC, pg. 140, pg. 175
EMISPHERE TECHNOLOGIES, INC., pg. 1528, pg. 1118
ENCORIUM GROUP, INC., pg. 1528, pg. 1591
ENDO PHARMACEUTICALS HOLDINGS, INC., pg. 1528, pg. 1549
ENGINE COMPONENTS, INC., pg. 227, pg. 1740
ENZO BIOCHEM INC., pg. 1529, pg. 1228
EXACT SCIENCES CORPORATION, pg. 1529, pg. 1865
FAIR ISAAC CORPORATION, pg. 1247, pg. 955
FAMILY FIRST, pg. 140, pg. 472
FIBROCELL SCIENCE, INC., pg. 1530, pg. 1531
FIRST AVIATION SERVICES INC., pg. 227, pg. 384
FLUIDIGM CORPORATION, pg. 1413, pg. 279
FORRESTER RESEARCH, INC., pg. 1642, pg. 807
FREESCALE SEMICONDUCTOR, INC., pg. 398, pg. 1662
GE AVIATION, pg. 227, pg. 1413
GENELINK, INC., pg. 1533, pg. 438
GENENTECH, INC., pg. 1533, pg. 279
GENERAL DYNAMICS CORPORATION, pg. 228, pg. 1781
GENERAL ELECTRIC COMPANY, pg. 1297, pg. 347
GENOPTIX, INC., pg. 1534, pg. 59
GILEAD SCIENCES, INC., pg. 1535, pg. 88
GLAUCOMA RESEARCH FOUNDATION, pg. 142, pg. 219
GLAXOSMITHKLINE, pg. 1536, pg. 1389
THE GLEASON WORKS, pg. 1341, pg. 1336
GULFSTREAM AEROSPACE CORPORATION, pg. 228, pg. 540
HEICO CORPORATION, pg. 228, pg. 431
HELWIG CARBON PRODUCTS, INC., pg. 1346, pg. 1875
HEXCEL CORPORATION, pg. 1884, pg. 375
HONEYWELL INTERNATIONAL INC., pg. 407, pg. 1088
IDERA PHARMACEUTICALS, INC., pg. 1543, pg. 808
IHS AUTOMOTIVE DRIVEN BY POLK, pg. 1652, pg. 907
ILLUMINA, INC., pg. 412, pg. 203
IMMUNOGEN, INC., pg. 1544, pg. 851
IMMUNOMEDICS, INC., pg. 1544, pg. 1087
IMPAX LABORATORIES, INC., pg. 1544, pg. 101
INCYTE CORPORATION, pg. 1545, pg. 392
THE INTELLIGENCE GROUP, pg. 417, pg. 1043
INTERNATIONAL AIDS VACCINE INITIATIVE, pg. 145, pg. 1244
ISIS PHARMACEUTICALS, INC., pg. 1548, pg. 59
ITRONICS INC., pg. 1169, pg. 1031
ITUS CORPORATION, pg. 422, pg. 1180
JUVENILE DIABETES RESEARCH FOUNDATION INTERNATIONAL, pg. 145, pg. 1247
KAMAN CORPORATION, pg. 229, pg. 338
KERYX BIOPHARMACEUTICALS, INC., pg. 1553, pg. 1248
KILGORE FLARES, pg. 1170, pg. 1656
L-3 COMMUNICATIONS HOLDINGS INC., pg. 650, pg. 1250
LEXICON PHARMACEUTICALS, INC., pg. 1555, pg. 1747
LIGAND PHARMACEUTICALS INC., pg. 1556, pg. 119
LIVANOVA, pg. 1557, pg. 1710
LOCKHART COMPANY, pg. 1171, pg. 1534
LOCKHEED MARTIN CORPORATION, pg. 229, pg. 762
LORD CORPORATION, pg. 1357, pg. 1360
LUMINEX CORPORATION, pg. 1421, pg. 1664
LUNA INNOVATIONS INC., pg. 1557, pg. 1806
MANNKIND CORPORATION, pg. 1558, pg. 299
MECHANICAL TECHNOLOGY, INCORPORATED, pg. 1422, pg. 1137
MEDIMMUNE LLC, pg. 1562, pg. 770
MEGGITT SAFETY SYSTEMS, INC., pg. 653, pg. 279
MERA PHARMACEUTICALS, INC., pg. 1566, pg. 545
MICHAEL J. FOX FOUNDATION FOR PARKINSON'S RESEARCH, pg. 147, pg. 1260
MICROVISION, INC., pg. 654, pg. 1828
MILLENNIUM: THE TAKEDA ONCOLOGY COMPANY, pg. 1568, pg. 809
THE MISTRAL INC., pg. 1173, pg. 765
MOCON, INC., pg. 1363, pg. 940
MONOGRAM BIOSCIENCES, INC., pg. 1569, pg. 280
MOOG INC., pg. 231, pg. 1156
MOTE MARINE LABORATORY, INC., pg. 564, pg. 466
MPI RESEARCH, INC., pg. 1569, pg. 898
MTI INSTRUMENTS INC., pg. 658, pg. 1137
NATIONAL KIDNEY FOUNDATION, INC., pg. 149, pg. 1265
NATIONAL RESEARCH CORPORATION, pg. 443, pg. 1012
NEKTAR THERAPEUTICS, pg. 1572, pg. 224
NEUROMETRIX, INC., pg. 1572, pg. 852
NOBLES MANUFACTURING, INC., pg. 59, pg. 1890
NORDION INC., pg. 1573, pg. 1932
NORTHROP GRUMMAN CORPORATION, pg. 231, pg. 1781
NORTHSTAR AEROSPACE, INC., pg. 232, pg. 1941
NOVARTIS PHARMACEUTICALS CORP., pg. 1575, pg. 1054
NOVARTIS VACCINES & DIAGNOSTICS, INC., pg. 1575, pg. 809
NOVEN PHARMACEUTICALS, INC., pg. 1576, pg. 445
NUVASIVE, INC., pg. 1577, pg. 205
OCULUS INNOVATIVE SCIENCES, pg. 1577, pg. 182
ONCOGENEX PHARMACEUTICALS, INC., pg. 1578, pg. 1818
ONCOTHYREON INC., pg. 1578, pg. 1838
ONE AVIATION CORPORATION, pg. 232, pg. 1135
ORAGENICS, INC., pg. 1578, pg. 475
ORASURE TECHNOLOGIES INC, pg. 1578, pg. 1516
ORBITAL ATK, pg. 1425, pg. 1779
THE OVARIAN CANCER RESEARCH FUND, INC., pg. 153, pg. 1275
PAREXEL INTERNATIONAL CORPORATION, pg. 1580, pg. 853
PHARMACEUTICAL PRODUCT DEVELOPMENT, INC., pg. 1584, pg. 1393
PHILANTHROPEDIA, pg. 153, pg. 1811
PIPER AIRCRAFT, INC., pg. 233, pg. 477
PPG AEROSPACE, pg. 1178, pg. 290
PPG INDUSTRIES, INC., pg. 1445, pg. 1579
PRAHEALTH SCIENCES, pg. 1585, pg. 1388
PRATT & WHITNEY, pg. 233, pg. 345
PRATT & WHITNEY CANADA CORP., pg. 1370, pg. 1952
PRECISION CASTPARTS CORP., pg. 105, pg. 1506
RAYTHEON COMPANY, pg. 233, pg. 854
RBC LIFE SCIENCES, INC., pg. 1588, pg. 1723
REGENERON PHARMACEUTICALS, INC., pg. 1588, pg. 1345
REPLIGEN CORPORATION, pg. 1589, pg. 854
ROBINSON HELICOPTER COMPANY, pg. 234, pg. 295
ROCHE NIMBLEGEN, INC., pg. 667, pg. 1867
ROGERSON AIRCRAFT CORPORATION, pg. 234, pg. 115
ROLLS-ROYCE CORPORATION, pg. 216, pg. 689
SAIC, INC., pg. 464, pg. 1794
SANDISK CORPORATION, pg. 465, pg. 147
SCALABLE SOFTWARE, INC., pg. 467, pg. 1665
SEQUA CORPORATION, pg. 1180, pg. 1290
SEQUENOM, INC., pg. 1593, pg. 209
SGS U.S. TESTING COMPANY INC., pg. 1181, pg. 1065
SIEMENS HEALTHCARE DIAGNOSTICS, pg. 673, pg. 604
SION POWER CORPORATION, pg. 674, pg. 27
SPACEDEV INC., pg. 234, pg. 186
SPECTRAL DIAGNOSTICS INC., pg. 1430, pg. 1943
SPIRE CORPORATION, pg. 1378, pg. 786
ST. JUDE CHILDREN'S RESEARCH HOSPITAL, pg. 1596, pg. 1646
SUCAMPO PHARMACEUTICALS, INC., pg. 1599, pg. 765
SURFACE COMBUSTION, INC., pg. 1077, pg. 1462
TAKEDA PHARMACEUTICALS USA, INC., pg. 1600, pg. 605
TECH SPRAY, L.P., pg. 1183, pg. 1659
TECHNE CORPORATION, pg. 1601, pg. 944
TELEDYNE BROWN ENGINEERING, INC., pg. 235, pg. 6
TELEFLEX INCORPORATED, pg. 48, pg. 1548
TEXTRON INC., pg. 235, pg. 1607
TEXTRON SYSTEMS CORPORATION, pg. 235, pg. 860
TOTAL NUTRACEUTICAL SOLUTIONS, INC., pg. 1603, pg. 1509
TRIUMPH THERMAL SYSTEMS, INC., pg. 235, pg. 1454
TRUVEN HEALTH ANALYTICS, pg. 1696, pg. 867
UES, INC., pg. 1449, pg. 1447
ULTRALIFE CORPORATION, pg. 1385, pg. 1317
UNISON INDUSTRIES, LLC, pg. 235, pg. 435
UNITED TECHNOLOGIES CORPORATION, pg. 235, pg. 353
URS CORPORATION, pg. 1386, pg. 1667
UTC AEROSPACE SYSTEMS, pg. 236, pg. 1369
VERTEX PHARMACEUTICALS INCORPORATED, pg. 1606, pg. 801
VIACORD, pg. 1606, pg. 810
VIVUS, INC., pg. 1608, pg. 163
WISCONSIN MILK MARKETING BOARD, INC., pg. 161, pg. 1868
WOODWARD, INC., pg. 122, pg. 329
XOMA CORPORATION, pg. 1611, pg. 46
ZODIAC WATER & WASTE SYSTEMS, pg. 236, pg. 64

8734 - Testing Laboratories

BIO-REFERENCE LABORATORIES, INC., pg. 1402, pg. 1058
BIOANALYTICAL SYSTEMS, INC., pg. 1402, pg. 700
CORRPRO COMPANIES, INC., pg. 631, pg. 1464
ECOLOGY AND ENVIRONMENT, INC., pg. 1410, pg. 1173
ERESEARCH TECHNOLOGY INC., pg. 1243, pg. 1564
FINISAR CORPORATION, pg. 639, pg. 285
INDIANA CROP IMPROVEMENT ASSOCIATION, INC., pg. 144, pg. 693
LABORATORY CORPORATION OF AMERICA HOLDINGS, pg. 1554, pg. 1359
LANDAUER, INC., pg. 1554, pg. 615
MEDTOX SCIENTIFIC, INC., pg. 1422, pg. 962
MISTRAS GROUP, INC., pg. 1362, pg. 1113
NATIONAL TECHNICAL SYSTEMS INC., pg. 99, pg. 56
PERKINELMER, INC., pg. 1426, pg. 853
RESPONSE GENETICS, INC., pg. 1590, pg. 139
SGS U.S. TESTING COMPANY INC., pg. 1181, pg. 1065
TERADYNE INC., pg. 679, pg. 838
UNDERWRITERS LABORATORIES INC., pg. 1396, pg. 641
VCA INC., pg. 1606, pg. 141

8741 - Management Services

ALLINA HEALTH SYSTEM, INC., pg. 1491, pg. 929
ALOETTE COSMETICS, INC., pg. 498, pg. 487
ASIANA AIRLINES, pg. 1899, pg. 126
BAYFRONT HEALTH SYSTEM, INC., pg. 1500, pg. 461
BAYSTATE HEALTH SYSTEM, INC., pg. 1501, pg. 845
BJC HEALTHCARE, pg. 1506, pg. 993
CENTRASTATE HEALTHCARE SYSTEM INC., pg. 1514, pg. 1071
CEOEXPRESS COMPANY, pg. 1235, pg. 807

First page reference indicates Business Class Edition
Second page reference indicates Geographic Edition

COUNTRY KITCHEN INTERNATIONAL, INC., *pg.* 1723, *pg.* 1865
DAUGHTERS OF CHARITY HEALTH SYSTEM, *pg.* 1522, *pg.* 124
FIDUCIAL, INC., *pg.* 752, *pg.* 767
GILMAN CIOCIA, INC., *pg.* 762, *pg.* 1324
HALLMARK BUSINESS CONNECTIONS, *pg.* 402, *pg.* 937
INTEGRAMED AMERICA, INC., *pg.* 1546, *pg.* 1325
KENNEDY HEALTH SYSTEM, *pg.* 1553, *pg.* 1128
KIMPTON HOTEL & RESTAURANT GROUP, *pg.* 1099, *pg.* 220
LA QUINTA CORPORATION, *pg.* 1099, *pg.* 1722
LA QUINTA INNS, INC., *pg.* 1100, *pg.* 1722
LODGIAN INC., *pg.* 1101, *pg.* 513
M-B COMPANIES, INC., *pg.* 1357, *pg.* 1884
MAYS CHEMICAL COMPANY, *pg.* 1172, *pg.* 688
MEDSTAR HEALTH INC., *pg.* 1563, *pg.* 767
MOODY PUBLISHERS, *pg.* 1665, *pg.* 583
NEW COUNTRY MOTOR CAR GROUP INC., *pg.* 186, *pg.* 1340
NISSAN NORTH AMERICA, INC., *pg.* 186, *pg.* 1633
NOVANT HEALTH, INC., *pg.* 1574, *pg.* 1394
OSF HEALTHCARE SYSTEM, *pg.* 1579, *pg.* 652
RAINMAKER SYSTEMS INC., *pg.* 458, *pg.* 58
SANDALS RESORTS INTERNATIONAL, *pg.* 1111, *pg.* 446
THE SHERATON CORPORATION, *pg.* 1112, *pg.* 378
SHERWIN WILLIAMS, *pg.* 1448, *pg.* 1436
STRAW HAT COOPERATIVE CORPORATION, *pg.* 1751, *pg.* 260
SUNBURST HOSPITALITY CORPORATION, *pg.* 1115, *pg.* 778
SYMONS CAPITAL MANAGEMENT, *pg.* 1600, *pg.* 1582
TEAM HEALTH HOLDINGS, INC., *pg.* 1601, *pg.* 1639

8742 - Management Consulting Services

ACADEMIC INNOVATIONS, *pg.* 1613, *pg.* 262
ACCENTURE, *pg.* 1392, *pg.* 1186
ACNIELSEN CORPORATION, *pg.* 341, *pg.* 1187
ADVERTISING DISTRIBUTORS OF AMERICA INC., *pg.* 345, *pg.* 1338
AFFINION GROUP, INC., *pg.* 1225, *pg.* 372
ALBA WHEELS UP INTERNATIONAL, INC., *pg.* 1898, *pg.* 1170
ALEXANDER & BALDWIN, INC., *pg.* 1079, *pg.* 543
ALLEN & HOSHALL, INC., *pg.* 66, *pg.* 1641
ALLIN CORPORATION, *pg.* 347, *pg.* 1572
ALLSTATES WORLDCARGO, INC., *pg.* 1898, *pg.* 1042
ALPHA CTP SYSTEM, *pg.* 347, *pg.* 848
AMBER ROAD, INC., *pg.* 348, *pg.* 1054
AMERICAN RED BALL TRANSIT CO. INC., *pg.* 1899, *pg.* 682
ANC SPORTS ENTERPRISES, LLC, *pg.* 1825, *pg.* 1325
ANSELL, *pg.* 1495, *pg.* 1114
AON HEWITT, *pg.* 350, *pg.* 627
APPLEBEE'S INTERNATIONAL, INC., *pg.* 1715, *pg.* 980
ARKANSAS BEST CORPORATION, *pg.* 1899, *pg.* 32
ASSET ACCEPTANCE CAPITAL CORP., *pg.* 716, *pg.* 912
ASSOCIATED GLOBAL SYSTEMS, INC., *pg.* 1899, *pg.* 1184
ASSOCIATION OF AMERICAN UNIVERSITY PRESSES, *pg.* 133, *pg.* 1197
AT&T GOVERNMENT SOLUTIONS, *pg.* 355, *pg.* 1809
ATLAS VAN LINES, INC., *pg.* 1900, *pg.* 678
BAD BOY WORLDWIDE ENTERTAINMENT GROUP, *pg.* 270, *pg.* 1199
BDP INTERNATIONAL INC., *pg.* 1900, *pg.* 1559
BENCHMARK HOSPITALITY INTERNATIONAL INC., *pg.* 1081, *pg.* 1747
BIRNER DENTAL MANAGEMENT SERVICES, INC., *pg.* 1506, *pg.* 317
BOOZ ALLEN HAMILTON INC, *pg.* 363, *pg.* 1788
THE BOSTON CONSULTING GROUP, INC., *pg.* 363, *pg.* 790
BRAINERD DAILY DISPATCH, *pg.* 1623, *pg.* 919
BRAINSTORM GROUP, INC., *pg.* 364, *pg.* 838
BRANDMUSCLE, INC., *pg.* 364, *pg.* 1660
BRIGHTSTAR CORPORATION, *pg.* 627, *pg.* 440
BUFFALO PHILHARMONIC ORCHESTRA SOCIETY INC., *pg.* 535, *pg.* 1147
BULLDOG MEDIA GROUP, *pg.* 599, *pg.* 1624
CACI INTERNATIONAL INC., *pg.* 367, *pg.* 1773
CANADIAN NATIONAL RAILWAY COMPANY, *pg.* 1902, *pg.* 1953
CANCER TREATMENT CENTERS OF AMERICA, *pg.* 1511, *pg.* 410
CARLSON WAGONLIT TRAVEL, *pg.* 1902, *pg.* 948
CARTESIAN, *pg.* 369, *pg.* 718
CASESTACK, INC., *pg.* 369, *pg.* 272
THE CASEY GROUP, *pg.* 369, *pg.* 1102
CBIZ, INC., *pg.* 733, *pg.* 1429
CEB INC., *pg.* 733, *pg.* 1773
CELERIT CORPORATION, *pg.* 371, *pg.* 33
CERIDIAN CORPORATION, *pg.* 371, *pg.* 932
CGI GROUP INC., *pg.* 371, *pg.* 1954
CHOICE HOTELS INTERNATIONAL, INC., *pg.* 1086, *pg.* 775
CINCINNATI MUSEUM CENTER INC., *pg.* 540, *pg.* 1411
COLOMBIAN COFFEE FEDERATION, INC., *pg.* 137, *pg.* 1216
COMPUTER SCIENCES CORPORATION, *pg.* 378, *pg.* 1780
COMSCORE, INC, *pg.* 1236, *pg.* 1798
CONSTELLATION BRANDS, INC., *pg.* 1960, *pg.* 1348
CONVERSANT, INC., *pg.* 1393, *pg.* 306
COTTON INCORPORATED CONSUMER MARKETING HEADQUARTERS, *pg.* 692, *pg.* 1218
CRESA PARTNERS LLC, *pg.* 1088, *pg.* 1220
CROZER-KEYSTONE HEALTH SYSTEM INC., *pg.* 1520, *pg.* 1587
CSX CORPORATION, *pg.* 1904, *pg.* 432
DELOITTE & TOUCHE USA LLP, *pg.* 743, *pg.* 1222
DETERMINE, INC., *pg.* 386, *pg.* 254
DEX ONE CORPORATION, *pg.* 1635, *pg.* 1360
DIGITAL RIVER, INC., *pg.* 1238, *pg.* 948
D.R. HORTON/CONTINENTAL SERIES, *pg.* 79, *pg.* 330
EAGLE POINT SOFTWARE CORPORATION, *pg.* 389, *pg.* 707
EAGLE:XM, *pg.* 1239, *pg.* 319
EDGEWATER TECHNOLOGY, INC., *pg.* 389, *pg.* 848
EGGLAND'S BEST, INC., *pg.* 854, *pg.* 1542
ENERGY & POWER SOLUTIONS, INC., *pg.* 392, *pg.* 71
THE F. DOHMEN CO., *pg.* 1530, *pg.* 1858
FCSTONE GROUP, INC., *pg.* 751, *pg.* 982
FEDEX CORPORATION, *pg.* 1907, *pg.* 1642
FRANKLIN COVEY CO., *pg.* 1642, *pg.* 1758
FTI CONSULTING, INC., *pg.* 760, *pg.* 478
FUTUREDONTICS, INC., *pg.* 1532, *pg.* 131
GAINES MOTOR LINES INCORPORATED, *pg.* 1338, *pg.* 1378
THE GALLUP ORGANIZATION, *pg.* 399, *pg.* 399
THE GALLUP ORGANIZATION-PRINCETON, *pg.* 1643, *pg.* 1111
GAME SHOW PLACEMENTS LTD., *pg.* 550, *pg.* 132
GEISINGER HEALTH SYSTEM, *pg.* 1533, *pg.* 1526
GILMAN CIOCIA, INC., *pg.* 762, *pg.* 1324
GLOBALOPTIONS GROUP, INC., *pg.* 1394, *pg.* 1235
GRANT THORNTON INTERNATIONAL LTD., *pg.* 763, *pg.* 575
GUIDELINE, INC., *pg.* 402, *pg.* 1237
THE HACKETT GROUP, INC., *pg.* 1255, *pg.* 443
HEALTH GRADES, INC., *pg.* 1256, *pg.* 319
HEALTHPORT, INC., *pg.* 403, *pg.* 484
HEALTHWAYS, INC., *pg.* 1540, *pg.* 1632
HEERY INTERNATIONAL, INC., *pg.* 86, *pg.* 510
HILL INTERNATIONAL INC., *pg.* 87, *pg.* 1083
HUNTING COMPANY, US OFFICE, *pg.* 979, *pg.* 1708
IHS HEROLD, INC., *pg.* 768, *pg.* 362
IKEA NORTH AMERICA SERVICES LLC, *pg.* 929, *pg.* 1523
IMAKENEWS, INC., *pg.* 413, *pg.* 851
IMS HEALTH, INC., *pg.* 1544, *pg.* 344
INDUSTRIAL SERVICES OF AMERICA, INC., *pg.* 1884, *pg.* 734
INFOGIX INC., *pg.* 414, *pg.* 636
INFOGROUP, *pg.* 769, *pg.* 1038
INO.COM, *pg.* 1259, *pg.* 777
INSPERITY, INC., *pg.* 416, *pg.* 1725
INSTITUTE OF REAL ESTATE MANAGEMENT, *pg.* 144, *pg.* 578
INTERSTATE WORLDWIDE RELOCATION, INC., *pg.* 1912, *pg.* 1807
IPC THE HOSPITALIST COMPANY, INC., *pg.* 1547, *pg.* 167
IRI GROUP, *pg.* 421, *pg.* 579
ITRONICS INC., *pg.* 1169, *pg.* 1031
J.B. HUNT TRANSPORT SERVICES, INC., *pg.* 1913, *pg.* 34
J.J. KELLER & ASSOCIATES, INC., *pg.* 1654, *pg.* 1883
JOSTENS, INC., *pg.* 7, *pg.* 938
KAWASAKI HEAVY INDUSTRIES (U.S.A.), INC., *pg.* 1352, *pg.* 1248
KEPNER-TREGOE, INC., *pg.* 424, *pg.* 1112
KSL RESORTS, *pg.* 1099, *pg.* 120
LIQUIDITY SERVICES, INC., *pg.* 1263, *pg.* 401
LYRIS, INC., *pg.* 429, *pg.* 84
MACE SECURITY INTERNATIONAL, INC., *pg.* 1172, *pg.* 1541
MAERSK INC., *pg.* 1914, *pg.* 1080
MAGELLAN HEALTH SERVICES, INC., *pg.* 1557, *pg.* 337
MAGLINE, INC., *pg.* 1358, *pg.* 908
MALCO PRODUCTS, INC., *pg.* 1172, *pg.* 1404
MARCHEX, INC., *pg.* 1395, *pg.* 1837
MARITZ INC., *pg.* 1914, *pg.* 977
MARSH & MCLENNAN COMPANIES INC., *pg.* 1207, *pg.* 1256
MARTS & LUNDY, INC., *pg.* 146, *pg.* 1080
MAXIMUS, INC., *pg.* 780, *pg.* 1799
MC2, *pg.* 431, *pg.* 1153
MCG CAPITAL CORPORATION, *pg.* 781, *pg.* 1774
MCGLADREY, LLP, *pg.* 781, *pg.* 938
MECHANICAL PROTECTION PLAN, *pg.* 184, *pg.* 717
MEETING PROFESSIONALS INTERNATIONAL (MPI), *pg.* 146, *pg.* 1683
MENLO WORLDWIDE, LLC, *pg.* 1915, *pg.* 255
MERCER INC., *pg.* 1395, *pg.* 1258
MHI GLOBAL, *pg.* 434, *pg.* 474
MICROBILT CORPORATION, *pg.* 782, *pg.* 534
MILLER HEIMAN INC., *pg.* 440, *pg.* 1031
MIQ LOGISTICS, LLC, *pg.* 1267, *pg.* 719
MONSTER WORLDWIDE, INC., *pg.* 1268, *pg.* 859
NATIONAL FOOTBALL LEAGUE PLAYERS INCORPORATED, *pg.* 149, *pg.* 401
NATIONAL VAN LINES, INC., *pg.* 1916, *pg.* 559
NAVIGANT CONSULTING, INC., *pg.* 786, *pg.* 584
NEGOTIATION INSTITUTE, INC., *pg.* 151, *pg.* 1268
NEUSTAR, INC., *pg.* 1872, *pg.* 1807
NEW JERSEY HOSPITAL ASSOCIATION, *pg.* 152, *pg.* 1112
NEW YORK CITY DEPARTMENT OF CITY WIDE ADMINISTRATIVE SERVICES, *pg.* 1001, *pg.* 1268
NEWGROUND RESOURCES, *pg.* 99, *pg.* 975
NIC INC., *pg.* 445, *pg.* 718
NOOTER/ERIKSEN, INC., *pg.* 1075, *pg.* 977
NOVATION LLC, *pg.* 446, *pg.* 1723
OLD DOMINION FREIGHT LINE, INC., *pg.* 1918, *pg.* 1391
OLIVER WYMAN, INC., *pg.* 790, *pg.* 1274
OPENTEXT, *pg.* 450, *pg.* 1665
OPERA AMERICA, *pg.* 572, *pg.* 1274
OPTIMIZERX CORPORATION, *pg.* 1673, *pg.* 905
ORIEL STAT-A-MATRIX, INC., *pg.* 451, *pg.* 1057
PDI, INC., *pg.* 1580, *pg.* 1104
PREMIER HEALTHCARE ALLIANCE, *pg.* 1586, *pg.* 1368
PRESTIGE BRANDS HOLDINGS, INC., *pg.* 520, *pg.* 1345
PRICEWATERHOUSECOOPERS LLP, *pg.* 795, *pg.* 1283
PROVIDENCE HEALTH SYSTEM, *pg.* 1587, *pg.* 1829
PUTNAM INVESTMENTS, LLC, *pg.* 797, *pg.* 800
QUINSTREET, INC., *pg.* 1276, *pg.* 89
RAINMAKER SYSTEMS INC., *pg.* 458, *pg.* 58
REACHLOCAL, INC., *pg.* 1277, *pg.* 308
RESOURCES CONNECTION, INC., *pg.* 461, *pg.* 115
RYDER SYSTEM, INC., *pg.* 1922, *pg.* 446
S. GRAHAM & ASSOCIATES, *pg.* 463, *pg.* 589
THE SCHMIDT GROUP, INC., *pg.* 1374, *pg.* 1618
SCHNEIDER, *pg.* 1922, *pg.* 1859
SCHWARTZ & BENJAMIN, INC., *pg.* 1818, *pg.* 1290
SMILE BRANDS GROUP INC., *pg.* 1594, *pg.* 116
SOUTH CAROLINA MANUFACTURING EXTENSION PARTNERSHIP, *pg.* 1377, *pg.* 1614
SPA FINDER, INC., *pg.* 1113, *pg.* 1295
SPELNA, INC., *pg.* 157, *pg.* 1782
SRDS, INC., *pg.* 1688, *pg.* 657
STATE STREET CORPORATION, *pg.* 805, *pg.* 801
STEVENS GROUP, INC., *pg.* 1924, *pg.* 906
THE SUDDATH COMPANIES INC., *pg.* 1924, *pg.* 435
SUMTOTAL SYSTEMS, INC., *pg.* 477, *pg.* 429
SUPPLY TECHNOLOGIES LLC, *pg.* 1064, *pg.* 1436
SVM, LP, *pg.* 1706, *pg.* 606
SYNYGY, INC., *pg.* 481, *pg.* 1521
TEAM HEALTH, INC., *pg.* 482, *pg.* 1639
TRI-STATE MOTOR TRANSIT CO., *pg.* 1926, *pg.* 980
TSS, INC., *pg.* 117, *pg.* 768
TTC AMERIDIAL, LLC, *pg.* 486, *pg.* 593
THE ULTIMATE SOFTWARE GROUP, INC., *pg.* 486, *pg.* 479
UNITED CONTINENTAL HOLDINGS, INC., *pg.* 1927, *pg.* 593
UNITED SERVICES AUTOMOBILE ASSOCIATION, *pg.* 1221, *pg.* 1743
US 1 INDUSTRIES, INC., *pg.* 1929, *pg.* 698

U.S. GLOBAL INVESTORS, INC., *pg.* 815, *pg.* 1743
U.S. XPRESS ENTERPRISES, INC., *pg.* 1929, *pg.* 1630
VALASSIS COMMUNICATIONS, INC., *pg.* 1287, *pg.* 897
VIAD CORP., *pg.* 816, *pg.* 20
VITRAN CORPORATION, INC., *pg.* 1930, *pg.* 1946
WEB.COM GROUP, INC., *pg.* 1288, *pg.* 435
WEICHERT RELOCATION RESOURCES INC., *pg.* 1118, *pg.* 1087
WERNER ENTERPRISES, INC., *pg.* 1930, *pg.* 1019
WESTON SOLUTIONS HOLDINGS, INC., *pg.* 1437, *pg.* 1593
WEXFORD HEALTH SOURCES INC., *pg.* 1610, *pg.* 1582
WHEATON VAN LINES, INC., *pg.* 1930, *pg.* 691
WHITMAN'S CANDIES, INC., *pg.* 1863, *pg.* 987
YRC WORLDWIDE INC., *pg.* 1931, *pg.* 720
ZILLIANT, INC., *pg.* 497, *pg.* 1668
ZIM-AMERICAN ISRAELI SHIPPING CO., *pg.* 1931, *pg.* 1798
ZOGBY ANALYTICS, *pg.* 1292, *pg.* 1347
ZONES, INC., *pg.* 1292, *pg.* 1813

8743 - Public Relations Services

AMERICAN DAIRY ASSOCIATION, *pg.* 127, *pg.* 656
BIOSPACE, INC., *pg.* 1231, *pg.* 1082
CALIFORNIA DRIED PLUM BOARD, *pg.* 135, *pg.* 195
CATTLEMEN'S BEEF PROMOTION & RESEARCH BOARD, *pg.* 136, *pg.* 314
EARTHCAM, INC., *pg.* 1239, *pg.* 1072
EDUCATIONAL COIN COMPANY, *pg.* 746, *pg.* 1167
INDUSTRIAL DESIGNERS SOCIETY OF AMERICA, *pg.* 144, *pg.* 1785
NATIONAL HONEY BOARD, *pg.* 149, *pg.* 328
NATIONAL WATERMELON PROMOTION BOARD, *pg.* 151, *pg.* 454
PACIFIC NORTHWEST CANNED PEAR SERVICE, INC., *pg.* 153, *pg.* 1847
PEAR BUREAU NORTHWEST, *pg.* 153, *pg.* 1500
QANTAS AIRWAYS - USA, *pg.* 1920, *pg.* 139
STARTSAMPLING, INC., *pg.* 1283, *pg.* 561
TOURISM AUSTRALIA, *pg.* 1007, *pg.* 140
UNITED STATES BOWLING CONGRESS, *pg.* 159, *pg.* 1660
VISIT FLORIDA INC., *pg.* 1010, *pg.* 470

8744 - Facilities Support Management Services

ABM INDUSTRIES, INC., *pg.* 64, *pg.* 1186
ARAMARK, *pg.* 1013, *pg.* 1558
ARAMARK CANADA LTD., *pg.* 1014, *pg.* 1935
BUTLER AMERICA, *pg.* 366, *pg.* 370
CHEMED CORPORATION, *pg.* 327, *pg.* 1410
THE DAVEY TREE EXPERT COMPANY, *pg.* 1794, *pg.* 1456
EMCOR GROUP, INC., *pg.* 80, *pg.* 361

8748 - Business Consulting Services, NEC

3T SYSTEMS, INC., *pg.* 339, *pg.* 330
ACORN ENERGY, INC., *pg.* 341, *pg.* 389
ACTUATE CANADA, *pg.* 1225, *pg.* 1933
ADVERTISING CHECKING BUREAU INCORPORATED, *pg.* 345, *pg.* 1187
AECOM, *pg.* 64, *pg.* 812
AECOM TECHNOLOGY CORPORATION, *pg.* 65, *pg.* 125
AMERICAN APPRAISAL ASSOCIATES, INC., *pg.* 349, *pg.* 1872
AMERICAN AUCTION COMPANY, *pg.* 349, *pg.* 14
AMERICAN FORESTS, *pg.* 128, *pg.* 394
ANALYSTS INTERNATIONAL CORPORATION, *pg.* 350, *pg.* 930
APTIFY, *pg.* 352, *pg.* 395
ARI NETWORK SERVICES, INC., *pg.* 353, *pg.* 1873
AT&T GOVERNMENT SOLUTIONS, *pg.* 355, *pg.* 1809
THE AUSTIN COMPANY, *pg.* 69, *pg.* 1428
AUTHORIZE.NET HOLDINGS, INC., *pg.* 356, *pg.* 1751
BIRNER DENTAL MANAGEMENT SERVICES, INC., *pg.* 1506, *pg.* 317
CAPGEMINI U.S., *pg.* 368, *pg.* 1209
CARTESIAN, *pg.* 369, *pg.* 718
CATASYS, INC., *pg.* 1514, *pg.* 127
CDM SMITH, *pg.* 74, *pg.* 807
CERC, *pg.* 990, *pg.* 369
CGI GROUP INC., *pg.* 371, *pg.* 1954
CGI TECHNOLOGIES & SOLUTIONS INC., *pg.* 371, *pg.* 1779
CIBER, INC., *pg.* 372, *pg.* 330
CLAYTON HOLDINGS, INC., *pg.* 738, *pg.* 370
CLUNE CONSTRUCTION CO., *pg.* 76, *pg.* 571
COGNIZANT TECHNOLOGY SOLUTIONS CORPORATION, *pg.* 377, *pg.* 1124
COMPUCOM SYSTEMS, INC., *pg.* 378, *pg.* 1678
CONVERGYS CORPORATION, *pg.* 379, *pg.* 1412
COOLEY GROUP, INC., *pg.* 691, *pg.* 1603
CORVEL CORPORATION, *pg.* 1198, *pg.* 109
CROSS COUNTRY HEALTHCARE, INC., *pg.* 1520, *pg.* 411
CRYO-CELL INTERNATIONAL, INC., *pg.* 1520, *pg.* 452
CULINART, INC., *pg.* 1017, *pg.* 1321
EA ENGINEERING, SCIENCE & TECHNOLOGY, INC., *pg.* 389, *pg.* 772
EAGLE POINT SOFTWARE CORPORATION, *pg.* 389, *pg.* 707
ECOLOGY AND ENVIRONMENT, INC., *pg.* 1410, *pg.* 1173
EDGEWATER TECHNOLOGY, INC., *pg.* 389, *pg.* 848
EDISONLEARNING, INC., *pg.* 140, *pg.* 1636
ENERGY & POWER SOLUTIONS, INC., *pg.* 392, *pg.* 71
ENHERENT CORP., *pg.* 393, *pg.* 1343
ERESEARCH TECHNOLOGY INC., *pg.* 1243, *pg.* 1564
ERM GROUP, INC., *pg.* 1412, *pg.* 1531
ESSINTIAL ENTERPRISE SOLUTIONS, *pg.* 395, *pg.* 1552
THE F.A. BARTLETT TREE EXPERT COMPANY, *pg.* 1795, *pg.* 373
FRANKLIN COVEY CO., *pg.* 1642, *pg.* 1758
FTI CONSULTING, INC., *pg.* 760, *pg.* 478
THE GALLUP ORGANIZATION, *pg.* 399, *pg.* 399
GARTNER, INC., *pg.* 1248, *pg.* 374
GEOSPATIAL HOLDINGS, INC., *pg.* 84, *pg.* 1585
GLASSHOUSE TECHNOLOGIES, INC., *pg.* 400, *pg.* 844
GUIDELINE, INC., *pg.* 402, *pg.* 1237
HABIF, AROGETI & WYNNE, LLP, *pg.* 764, *pg.* 509
THE HACKETT GROUP, INC., *pg.* 1255, *pg.* 443
HEADSTRONG CORPORATION, *pg.* 403, *pg.* 1798
HEALTH FITNESS CORPORATION, *pg.* 1539, *pg.* 937
HILL INTERNATIONAL INC., *pg.* 87, *pg.* 1083
HOLSTEIN ASSOCIATION USA, INC., *pg.* 143, *pg.* 1764
HP ENTERPRISE SERVICES, LLC, *pg.* 409, *pg.* 1731
HURON CONSULTING GROUP INC., *pg.* 768, *pg.* 577
INFOR LAWSON, *pg.* 414, *pg.* 961
INTERACTIVE DATA CORPORATION, *pg.* 769, *pg.* 785
IRON MOUNTAIN INCORPORATED, *pg.* 421, *pg.* 796
ITRADE NETWORK, *pg.* 1259, *pg.* 77
KROLL INC., *pg.* 425, *pg.* 1249
THE KULJIAN CORPORATION, *pg.* 92, *pg.* 1566
LCC INTERNATIONAL, INC., *pg.* 651, *pg.* 1792
MANPOWER GROUP, *pg.* 430, *pg.* 1710
MARITZ INC., *pg.* 1914, *pg.* 977
MARSH & MCLENNAN COMPANIES INC., *pg.* 1207, *pg.* 1256
MAXIMUS, INC., *pg.* 780, *pg.* 1799
MCG CAPITAL CORPORATION, *pg.* 781, *pg.* 1774
MHI GLOBAL, *pg.* 434, *pg.* 474
MICROS SYSTEMS, INC., *pg.* 435, *pg.* 768
MOCON, INC., *pg.* 1363, *pg.* 940
MSX INTERNATIONAL, INC., *pg.* 98, *pg.* 912
MTM TECHNOLOGIES, INC., *pg.* 442, *pg.* 375
MWH GLOBAL, INC., *pg.* 98, *pg.* 312
THE NATIONAL ASSOCIATION FOR PET CONTAINER RESOURCES, *pg.* 147, *pg.* 279
NAVIGANT CONSULTING, INC., *pg.* 786, *pg.* 584
NEXAGE, INC., *pg.* 1271, *pg.* 799
NUTRITION MANAGEMENT SERVICES COMPANY, *pg.* 1742, *pg.* 1543
OPENTEXT, *pg.* 1272, *pg.* 1956
PANTHEON SOFTWARE, INC., *pg.* 1274, *pg.* 1774
PAREXEL INTERNATIONAL CORPORATION, *pg.* 1580, *pg.* 853
PENNSYLVANIA CHAMBER OF BUSINESS & INDUSTRY, *pg.* 153, *pg.* 1537
PERFICIENT, INC., *pg.* 1274, *pg.* 1002
P.J. DICK-TRUMBULL-LINDY, *pg.* 104, *pg.* 1579
PRICEWATERHOUSECOOPERS LLP, *pg.* 795, *pg.* 1283
REPUBLIC SERVICES, INC., *pg.* 107, *pg.* 19
THE REYNOLDS & REYNOLDS COMPANY, *pg.* 461, *pg.* 1457
RICHARDSON GROUP INC., *pg.* 461, *pg.* 1570
SOLARWINDS, INC., *pg.* 471, *pg.* 1666
SPHERIX INC., *pg.* 1596, *pg.* 1808
SRA INTERNATIONAL, INC., *pg.* 473, *pg.* 1780
STANDARD & POOR'S RATINGS SERVICES, *pg.* 805, *pg.* 1296
STATE STREET CORPORATION, *pg.* 805, *pg.* 801
STRUCTURED COMMUNICATION SYSTEMS, INC., *pg.* 477, *pg.* 1497
SUREQUEST SYSTEMS, INC., *pg.* 900, *pg.* 1669
SYNCHRONOSS TECHNOLOGIES, INC., *pg.* 479, *pg.* 1047
TETRA TECH, INC., *pg.* 115, *pg.* 181
THOMSON REUTERS TAX & ACCOUNTING, *pg.* 1693, *pg.* 1299
TORCON, INC., *pg.* 116, *pg.* 1114
TRC COMPANIES, INC., *pg.* 1383, *pg.* 386
TRIMBLE NAVIGATION LIMITED, *pg.* 1384, *pg.* 288
UNISYS CORPORATION, *pg.* 487, *pg.* 1517
UNITED BUSINESS MEDIA LLC, *pg.* 1697, *pg.* 1177
UNITED SERVICES AUTOMOBILE ASSOCIATION, *pg.* 1221, *pg.* 1743
USA FINANCIAL, *pg.* 815, *pg.* 864
VERISIGN, INC., *pg.* 488, *pg.* 1799
VERSAR, INC., *pg.* 1435, *pg.* 1807
VHA INC., *pg.* 1606, *pg.* 1724
VIRTUSA CORPORATION, *pg.* 490, *pg.* 857
WEB.COM GROUP, INC., *pg.* 1288, *pg.* 435
WENTE VINEYARDS, *pg.* 1972, *pg.* 122
WESTON SOLUTIONS HOLDINGS, INC., *pg.* 1437, *pg.* 1593
THE WHITMAN COMPANIES, INC., *pg.* 121, *pg.* 1053
YELLOWBRIX, INC., *pg.* 1291, *pg.* 1775

8999 - Services, NEC

20TH CENTURY FOX FILM CORP., *pg.* 267, *pg.* 124
ACCURACY IN MEDIA, INC., *pg.* 125, *pg.* 761
ACCUWEATHER, INC., *pg.* 268, *pg.* 1587
THE ASSOCIATED PRESS, INC., *pg.* 270, *pg.* 1197
BAD BOY WORLDWIDE ENTERTAINMENT GROUP, *pg.* 270, *pg.* 1199
BIRDSALL INTERACTIVE, INC., *pg.* 1231, *pg.* 120
BLOOMBERG L.P., *pg.* 725, *pg.* 1204
BOSTON HERALD INC., *pg.* 1623, *pg.* 791
BROWN AND CALDWELL, *pg.* 72, *pg.* 303
CHICAGO TRIBUNE COMPANY, *pg.* 1627, *pg.* 570
COMTEX NEWS NETWORK, INC., *pg.* 1236, *pg.* 1770
DELUXE LABORATORIES, INC., *pg.* 281, *pg.* 103
DOW JONES & COMPANY, INC., *pg.* 1637, *pg.* 1225
ENTERTAINMENT SOFTWARE RATING BOARD, *pg.* 992, *pg.* 1228
EWS, *pg.* 395, *pg.* 466
FILM SCORE MONTHLY, *pg.* 1641, *pg.* 103
FOX ENTERTAINMENT GROUP, INC., *pg.* 288, *pg.* 131
IAC SEARCH & MEDIA, INC., *pg.* 1257, *pg.* 171
K-TEL INTERNATIONAL, INC., *pg.* 1052, *pg.* 953
LEARFIELD COMMUNICATIONS, INC., *pg.* 296, *pg.* 979
LIVE NATION ENTERTAINMENT, INC., *pg.* 558, *pg.* 47
LOS ANGELES TIMES COMMUNICATIONS, LLC, *pg.* 1660, *pg.* 135
MACANDREWS & FORBES HOLDINGS INC., *pg.* 777, *pg.* 1254
PR NEWSWIRE ASSOCIATION LLC, *pg.* 1678, *pg.* 1283
ROCHESTER BROADWAY THEATRE LEAGUE, *pg.* 579, *pg.* 1337
RUSH COMMUNICATIONS, INC., *pg.* 307, *pg.* 1287
SONY MUSIC ENTERTAINMENT, *pg.* 309, *pg.* 1294
THOMSON REUTERS - CORPORATE HEADQUARTERS, *pg.* 1693, *pg.* 1299
THOMSON REUTERS CORPORATION, *pg.* 1693, *pg.* 1944
TIHATI PRODUCTIONS LTD., INC., *pg.* 587, *pg.* 545
TRC COMPANIES, INC., *pg.* 1383, *pg.* 386
TYBIT UNIFIED SEARCH, *pg.* 1286, *pg.* 1372
UNITED PRESS INTERNATIONAL, INC., *pg.* 1698, *pg.* 405
VARESE SARABANDE RECORDS, INC., *pg.* 1789, *pg.* 281
WORLD WRESTLING ENTERTAINMENT, INC., *pg.* 595, *pg.* 380
YANKEES ENTERTAINMENT & SPORTS NETWORK, LLC, *pg.* 324, *pg.* 1316

9111 - Executive Offices

BMW OF NORTH AMERICA, LLC, *pg.* 166, *pg.* 1133
OREGON TOURISM COMMISSION, *pg.* 1003, *pg.* 1508
TOURISM NEW ZEALAND, *pg.* 1008, *pg.* 276
UNITED STATES DEPARTMENT OF ENERGY, *pg.* 1008, *pg.* 406

9121 - Legislative Bodies

CITY HOLDING COMPANY, *pg.* 737, *pg.* 1849

9131 - Executive & Legislative Offices Combined

CHICAGO BRIDGE & IRON COMPANY, *pg.* 75, *pg.* 1747
DIODES INCORPORATED, *pg.* 634, *pg.* 1729
SIMS METAL MANAGEMENT, *pg.* 1396, *pg.* 590

9199 - General Government, NEC

BUFFALO NIAGARA CONVENTION & VISITORS BUREAU, INC., *pg.* 1901, *pg.* 1147
FLORIDA DEPARTMENT OF AGRICULTURE & CONSUMER SERVICES - DIVISION OF MARKETING & DEVELOPMENT, *pg.* 992, *pg.* 469
GREATER MILWAUKEE CONVENTION & VISITORS BUREAU, *pg.* 993, *pg.* 1874
ILLINOIS BUREAU OF TOURISM, *pg.* 995, *pg.* 578
MARYLAND OFFICE OF TOURISM DEVELOPMENT, *pg.* 998, *pg.* 758
MAXIMUS, INC., *pg.* 780, *pg.* 1799
NEVADA COMMISSION ON TOURISM, *pg.* 1000, *pg.* 1021
NEW YORK POWER AUTHORITY, INC., *pg.* 1947, *pg.* 1137
NORTH CAROLINA SYMPHONY, *pg.* 571, *pg.* 1388
ONVIA, INC., *pg.* 1272, *pg.* 1838
SOUTH CAROLINA PARKS RECREATION & TOURISM, *pg.* 1005, *pg.* 1614
TOURISM IRELAND, *pg.* 1007, *pg.* 1303
U.S. DEPARTMENT OF HOUSING & URBAN DEVELOPMENT, *pg.* 1009, *pg.* 407
WISCONSIN DEPARTMENT OF AGRICULTURE, TRADE & CONSUMER PROTECTION, *pg.* 1011, *pg.* 1867

9222 - Legal Counsel & Prosecution

FINDLAW, *pg.* 1641, *pg.* 285

9224 - Fire Protection

ANSUL, INCORPORATED, *pg.* 1147, *pg.* 1869
COOPER WHEELOCK, *pg.* 630, *pg.* 1080
E.D. BULLARD COMPANY, *pg.* 1332, *pg.* 727
EMCOR SERVICES NORTHEAST COMMAIR/BALCO, *pg.* 1071, *pg.* 847
IDEX CORPORATION, *pg.* 1347, *pg.* 623
JOHNSON CONTROLS, INC., *pg.* 209, *pg.* 1876
KIDDE FIRE FIGHTING, *pg.* 1170, *pg.* 1531
THE PROTECTOSEAL COMPANY, *pg.* 1370, *pg.* 556
RURAL/METRO CORPORATION, *pg.* 1591, *pg.* 24
TREMCO INCORPORATED, *pg.* 116, *pg.* 1405
TYCO INTERNATIONAL (US) INC., *pg.* 1891, *pg.* 1113
TYCO SIMPLEXGRINNELL LP, *pg.* 682, *pg.* 859

9311 - Public Finance, Taxation & Monetary Policy

ARIZONA LOTTERY, *pg.* 988, *pg.* 14
AVIS BUDGET GROUP, INC., *pg.* 1900, *pg.* 1102
CALIFORNIA LOTTERY, *pg.* 990, *pg.* 196
EMBRACE HOME LOANS, INC., *pg.* 747, *pg.* 1603
FEDERAL DEPOSIT INSURANCE CORPORATION, *pg.* 751, *pg.* 399
THE FLORIDA LOTTERY, *pg.* 992, *pg.* 469
GEORGIA LOTTERY CORPORATION, *pg.* 993, *pg.* 506
IDAHO LOTTERY, *pg.* 995, *pg.* 547
ILLINOIS STATE LOTTERY, *pg.* 995, *pg.* 578
IOWA LOTTERY, *pg.* 996, *pg.* 705
KENTUCKY LOTTERY CORPORATION, *pg.* 996, *pg.* 735
LOUISIANA LOTTERY CORPORATION, *pg.* 997, *pg.* 742
MASSACHUSETTS STATE LOTTERY, *pg.* 998, *pg.* 802
MEDALLION FINANCIAL CORP., *pg.* 781, *pg.* 1258
MICHIGAN STATE LOTTERY BUREAU, *pg.* 999, *pg.* 895
MINNESOTA STATE LOTTERY, *pg.* 999, *pg.* 956
MISSOURI LOTTERY, *pg.* 999, *pg.* 979
MONTANA LOTTERY, *pg.* 1000, *pg.* 1008
NEBRASKA LOTTERY, *pg.* 1000, *pg.* 1012
NELNET, INC., *pg.* 786, *pg.* 1012
NEW JERSEY STATE LOTTERY, *pg.* 1000, *pg.* 1126
NEW YORK STATE LOTTERY, *pg.* 1001, *pg.* 1340
OHIO LOTTERY COMMISSION, *pg.* 1002, *pg.* 1433
OREGON STATE LOTTERY, *pg.* 1003, *pg.* 1508
PENNSYLVANIA STATE LOTTERY, *pg.* 1003, *pg.* 1552
RHODE ISLAND LOTTERY, *pg.* 1004, *pg.* 1600
THE SOUTH CAROLINA EDUCATION LOTTERY, *pg.* 1005, *pg.* 1614
SOUTH DAKOTA LOTTERY, *pg.* 1006, *pg.* 1624
TEXAS LOTTERY COMMISSION, *pg.* 1007, *pg.* 1666
UNITED STATES MINT, *pg.* 814, *pg.* 406
VERMONT LOTTERY COMMISSION, *pg.* 1010, *pg.* 1764
VIRGINIA STATE LOTTERY DEPARTMENT, *pg.* 1010, *pg.* 1804
WASHINGTON STATE LOTTERY, *pg.* 1011, *pg.* 1823
WEST VIRGINIA LOTTERY, *pg.* 1011, *pg.* 1849

9411 - Administration of Educational Programs

AMBASSADORS GROUP, INC., *pg.* 1898, *pg.* 1843
AMERICAN UNIVERSITY, *pg.* 597, *pg.* 395
THE ARISTOTLE CORPORATION, *pg.* 1496, *pg.* 372
BRIDGEPOINT EDUCATION, INC., *pg.* 598, *pg.* 201
CAPELLA EDUCATION COMPANY, *pg.* 599, *pg.* 931
CIBT EDUCATION GROUP INC., *pg.* 599, *pg.* 1910
GURNICK ACADEMY OF MEDICAL ARTS, *pg.* 602, *pg.* 255
REGIS CORPORATION, *pg.* 521, *pg.* 941
SMITHSONIAN MAGAZINE, *pg.* 1687, *pg.* 404
STRAYER EDUCATION INC., *pg.* 607, *pg.* 1785
TIGRENT INC., *pg.* 608, *pg.* 415

9431 - Administration of Public Health Programs

CAREFIRST, INC., *pg.* 1513, *pg.* 756
THE CENTER FOR DISEASE CONTROL & PREVENTION, *pg.* 990, *pg.* 492
CENTERS FOR MEDICARE & MEDICAID SERVICES, *pg.* 990, *pg.* 756
CIGNA-HEALTHSPRING, *pg.* 1515, *pg.* 1632
HEALTH FITNESS CORPORATION, *pg.* 1539, *pg.* 937
NEW YORK STATE DEPARTMENT OF HEALTH, *pg.* 1001, *pg.* 1137
WEBMD HEALTH SERVICES GROUP, *pg.* 1609, *pg.* 1508
WELLCARE HEALTH PLANS INC., *pg.* 1223, *pg.* 476

9441 - Administration of Social, Human Resource and Income Maintenance Programs

CANADIAN TOURISM COMMISSION, *pg.* 136, *pg.* 1910
CERIDIAN CORPORATION, *pg.* 371, *pg.* 932
MOLINA HEALTHCARE, INC., *pg.* 1569, *pg.* 123
OHIO DEPARTMENT OF DEVELOPMENT, *pg.* 1002, *pg.* 1442

9451 - Administration of VeteransÆ Affairs, Except Health and Insurance

HIRE HEROES USA, *pg.* 143, *pg.* 484

9511 - Air and Water Resource and Solid Waste Management

BLUE EARTH, INC., *pg.* 70, *pg.* 1021
ENTECH SOLAR, INC., *pg.* 1335, *pg.* 1694
LIMONEIRA COMPANY, *pg.* 705, *pg.* 276
MWH GLOBAL, INC., *pg.* 98, *pg.* 312
TERRABIOGEN TECHNOLOGIES INC., *pg.* 1890, *pg.* 1908
UNITED STATES ENVIRONMENTAL PROTECTION AGENCY, *pg.* 1009, *pg.* 406

9512 - Land, Mineral, Wildlife, and Forest Conservation

CALIFORNIA DEPARTMENT OF CONSERVATION, *pg.* 989, *pg.* 195
NATIONAL PARK FOUNDATION, *pg.* 1000, *pg.* 402
UNITED STATES DEPARTMENT OF THE INTERIOR, *pg.* 1009, *pg.* 406

9531 - Administration of Housing Programs

EMPIRE STATE DEVELOPMENT CORPORATION, *pg.* 747, *pg.* 1227
GOODWILL INDUSTRIES-SUNCOAST, INC., *pg.* 142, *pg.* 462

9532 - Administration of Urban Planning and Community and Rural Development

CITY OF CHICAGO-DEPARTMENT OF PLANNING & DEVELOPMENT, *pg.* 991, *pg.* 570
CRESCENT COMMUNITIES, LLC, *pg.* 702, *pg.* 1365
EMPIRE STATE DEVELOPMENT CORPORATION, *pg.* 747, *pg.* 1227
EMPIRE STATE DEVELOPMENT-DIVISION OF TOURISM, *pg.* 992, *pg.* 1227
HAMPTON ROADS ECONOMIC DEVELOPMENT ALLIANCE, *pg.* 994, *pg.* 1797
MAUI LAND & PINEAPPLE COMPANY, INC., *pg.* 876, *pg.* 545
MISSISSIPPI DEVELOPMENT AUTHORITY, *pg.* 999, *pg.* 969
NEW YORK CITY ECONOMIC DEVELOPMENT CORPORATION, *pg.* 1001, *pg.* 1268
SAN ANTONIO ECONOMIC DEVELOPMENT FOUNDATION, *pg.* 1004, *pg.* 1742
TULSA METRO CHAMBER, *pg.* 1008, *pg.* 1491
WASHINGTON STATE DEPARTMENT OF COMMUNITY, TRADE & ECONOMIC DEVELOPMENT, *pg.* 1010, *pg.* 1823
WEST VIRGINIA DEPARTMENT OF COMMERCE, *pg.* 1011, *pg.* 1849
WYOMING BUSINESS COUNCIL, *pg.* 1011, *pg.* 1901

9611 - Administration of General Economic Programs

ALASKA DEPARTMENT OF COMMERCE, COMMUNITY & ECONOMIC DEVELOPMENT, *pg.* 988, *pg.* 10
ARIZONA OFFICE OF TOURISM, *pg.* 988, *pg.* 14
ARKANSAS DEPARTMENT OF ECONOMIC DEVELOPMENT, *pg.* 988, *pg.* 33
AUSTRALIAN TRADE COMMISSION, *pg.* 989, *pg.* 1198
CALIFORNIA DEPARTMENT OF CONSUMER AFFAIRS, *pg.* 990, *pg.* 195
CANADIAN COMMERCIAL CORPORATION, *pg.* 729, *pg.* 1931
CITY OF CHICAGO-DEPARTMENT OF PLANNING & DEVELOPMENT, *pg.* 991, *pg.* 570
DELAWARE TOURISM OFFICE, *pg.* 991, *pg.* 387
EXPLORE MINNESOTA TOURISM, *pg.* 992, *pg.* 960
FONDS DE SOLIDARITE FTQ, *pg.* 759, *pg.* 1955
GEORGIA DEPARTMENT OF ECONOMIC DEVELOPMENT, *pg.* 992, *pg.* 506
GOVERNOR'S OFFICE OF ECONOMIC DEVELOPMENT & TOURISM, *pg.* 993, *pg.* 1662
HAMPTON ROADS ECONOMIC DEVELOPMENT ALLIANCE, *pg.* 994, *pg.* 1797
HONG KONG TOURISM BOARD - NEW YORK, *pg.* 1911, *pg.* 1241
IDAHO DEPARTMENT OF COMMERCE, *pg.* 995, *pg.* 547
IOWA DEPARTMENT OF ECONOMIC DEVELOPMENT, *pg.* 995, *pg.* 705
LOUISIANA DEPARTMENT OF ECONOMIC DEVELOPMENT, *pg.* 997, *pg.* 742
LOUISIANA OFFICE OF TOURISM, *pg.* 997, *pg.* 742
MARYLAND OFFICE OF TOURISM DEVELOPMENT, *pg.* 998, *pg.* 758
THE MICHIGAN ECONOMIC DEVELOPMENT CORPORATION, TOURISM & MARKETING, *pg.* 999, *pg.* 895
MISSISSIPPI DEVELOPMENT AUTHORITY, *pg.* 999, *pg.* 969
NEBRASKA DEPARTMENT OF ECONOMIC DEVELOPMENT, *pg.* 1000, *pg.* 1012
NEW MEXICO ECONOMIC DEVELOPMENT DEPARTMENT,

pg. 1001, *pg.* 1136
NEW MEXICO TOURISM DEPARTMENT, *pg.* 1001, *pg.* 1136
NEW ORLEANS TOURISM MARKETING CORPORATION, *pg.* 1001, *pg.* 747
NEW YORK CITY ECONOMIC DEVELOPMENT CORPORATION, *pg.* 1001, *pg.* 1268
NORTH CAROLINA DEPARTMENT OF COMMERCE DIVISION OF TOURISM, FILM & SPORTS DEVELOPMENT, *pg.* 1001, *pg.* 1388
NORTH DAKOTA DEPARTMENT OF COMMERCE TOURISM DIVISION, *pg.* 1002, *pg.* 1397
PENINSULA COUNCIL FOR WORKFORCE DEVELOPMENT, *pg.* 1003, *pg.* 1796
PINELLAS COUNTY ECONOMIC DEVELOPMENT, *pg.* 1004, *pg.* 416
RHODE ISLAND COMMERCE CORPORATION, *pg.* 1004, *pg.* 1607
SAN ANTONIO ECONOMIC DEVELOPMENT FOUNDATION, *pg.* 1004, *pg.* 1742
SOUTH DAKOTA'S DEPARTMENT OF TOURISM, *pg.* 1006, *pg.* 1624
TENNESSEE DEPARTMENT OF TOURIST DEVELOPMENT, *pg.* 1007, *pg.* 1654
VERMONT DEPARTMENT OF TOURISM & MARKETING, *pg.* 1010, *pg.* 1767
VIRGINIA ECONOMIC DEVELOPMENT PARTNERSHIP, *pg.* 1010, *pg.* 1804
WASHINGTON STATE DEPARTMENT OF COMMUNITY, TRADE & ECONOMIC DEVELOPMENT, *pg.* 1010, *pg.* 1823

9621 - Regulation and Administration of Transportation Programs (except air traffic control)

ARKANSAS DEPARTMENT OF PARKS & TOURISM, *pg.* 988, *pg.* 33
DELAWARE RIVER PORT AUTHORITY OF PENNSYLVANIA & NEW JERSEY, *pg.* 1905, *pg.* 1049
HAECO AMERICAS, *pg.* 228, *pg.* 1374
LOUISIANA OFFICE OF TOURISM, *pg.* 997, *pg.* 742
NATIONAL RAILROAD PASSENGER CORPORATION, *pg.* 1916, *pg.* 403
NIAGARA FRONTIER TRANSPORTATION AUTHORITY, *pg.* 1917, *pg.* 1150
NJ TRANSIT CORPORATION, *pg.* 1917, *pg.* 1097
PORT OF GALVESTON, *pg.* 1919, *pg.* 1697
PORT OF HOUSTON AUTHORITY, *pg.* 1920, *pg.* 1713
PORT OF OAKLAND, *pg.* 1920, *pg.* 172
PORT OF PORTLAND, *pg.* 1920, *pg.* 1505
REGIONAL TRANSPORTATION AUTHORITY, *pg.* 1921, *pg.* 588
SAINT PAUL PORT AUTHORITY, *pg.* 1922, *pg.* 963
TAMPA PORT AUTHORITY INC., *pg.* 1925, *pg.* 476
VIRGINIA PORT AUTHORITY, *pg.* 1930, *pg.* 1797

9631 - Regulation and Administration of Communications, Electric, Gas, and Other Utilities

B.C. HYDRO, *pg.* 1936, *pg.* 1909
MOMENTUM TELECOM, INC., *pg.* 1872, *pg.* 3
MUNICIPAL ELECTRIC AUTHORITY OF GEORGIA, *pg.* 1946, *pg.* 515

9641 - Regulation of Agricultural Marketing and Commodities

ALASKA SEAFOOD MARKETING INSTITUTE, *pg.* 125, *pg.* 10
THE ALMOND BOARD OF CALIFORNIA, *pg.* 1013, *pg.* 149
CAL-MAINE FOODS, INC., *pg.* 843, *pg.* 969
CALAVO GROWERS, INC., *pg.* 843, *pg.* 276
DAIRY FARMERS OF AMERICA, INC., *pg.* 851, *pg.* 982
FARMS.COM LTD., *pg.* 1247, *pg.* 1922
FLORIDA DEPARTMENT OF AGRICULTURE & CONSUMER SERVICES - DIVISION OF MARKETING & DEVELOPMENT, *pg.* 992, *pg.* 469
IDAHO POTATO COMMISSION, *pg.* 144, *pg.* 549
NORTH DAKOTA STATE SEED DEPARTMENT, *pg.* 1002, *pg.* 1397
STATE OF FLORIDA DEPARTMENT OF CITRUS, *pg.* 1006, *pg.* 437
U.S. PREMIUM BEEF, LLC, *pg.* 907, *pg.* 987

9651 - Regulation, Licensing, and Inspection of Miscellaneous Commercial Sectors

ASK THE SEAL, LLC, *pg.* 1393, *pg.* 470
BLACKBERRY, *pg.* 625, *pg.* 1717
ESTES PARK CONVENTION & VISITORS BUREAU, *pg.* 992, *pg.* 328
GREATER AUSTIN CHAMBER OF COMMERCE, *pg.* 993, *pg.* 1663
GREATER NAPLES CHAMBER OF COMMERCE, *pg.* 994, *pg.* 450
GREATER PHOENIX CHAMBER OF COMMERCE, *pg.* 994, *pg.* 16
GREATER TAMPA CHAMBER OF COMMERCE, *pg.* 994, *pg.* 473
IDAHO DEPARTMENT OF COMMERCE, *pg.* 995, *pg.* 547
IPC THE HOSPITALIST COMPANY, INC., *pg.* 1547, *pg.* 167
KANSAS DEPARTMENT OF COMMERCE, *pg.* 996, *pg.* 722
MANATEE CHAMBER OF COMMERCE, *pg.* 998, *pg.* 414
METRO ATLANTA CHAMBER OF COMMERCE, *pg.* 998, *pg.* 514
NATIONAL FOOTBALL LEAGUE PLAYERS INCORPORATED, *pg.* 149, *pg.* 401
YBOR CITY CHAMBER OF COMMERCE, *pg.* 1011, *pg.* 477

9661 - Space Research and Technology

THE BOEING COMPANY, *pg.* 225, *pg.* 567
HONEYWELL AEROSPACE ELECTRONIC SYSTEMS, *pg.* 228, *pg.* 17
NATIONAL AERONAUTICS & SPACE ADMINISTRATION (NASA), *pg.* 1000, *pg.* 401
NORTHROP GRUMMAN CORPORATION, *pg.* 231, *pg.* 1781
SEQUA CORPORATION, *pg.* 1180, *pg.* 1290
SPACEDEV INC., *pg.* 234, *pg.* 186

9711 - National Security

ALION SCIENCE AND TECHNOLOGY CORPORATION, *pg.* 615, *pg.* 1788
CACI INTERNATIONAL INC., *pg.* 367, *pg.* 1773
DOCUMENT SECURITY SYSTEMS, INC., *pg.* 388, *pg.* 1333
GLOBALOPTIONS GROUP, INC., *pg.* 1394, *pg.* 1235
THE UNITED STATES AIR FORCE, *pg.* 1008, *pg.* 748
UNITED STATES AIR FORCE RECRUITING SERVICE, *pg.* 1008, *pg.* 1735
UNITED STATES ARMY, *pg.* 1008, *pg.* 405
UNITED STATES NAVY, *pg.* 1009, *pg.* 1647
UNITED STATES NAVY RECRUITING COMMAND, *pg.* 1009, *pg.* 1648

9721 - International Affairs

BROADCASTING BOARD OF GOVERNORS, *pg.* 989, *pg.* 396
UNITED STATES DEPARTMENT OF STATE, *pg.* 1008, *pg.* 406
VOICE OF AMERICA, *pg.* 1010, *pg.* 407

PERSONNEL INDEX

A

Aafaqi, Bushra, Specialist-Digital Mktg - Revera Inc.; pg. 799, pg. 1928
Aakre, Scott, VP-Mktg - Hormel Foods Corporation; pg. 863, pg. 915
Aamodt, Lauren, Brand Mgr - Zoes Kitchen, Inc.; pg. 1757, pg. 1735
Aamoth, Erica, Specialist-Customer Mktg Segmentation - DSW, Inc.; pg. 1807, pg. 1439
Aaron, Charlotte, Sr Dir-Classified Adv - San Antonio Express News; pg. 1682, pg. 1742
Aaron, Christopher, Mgr-Integrated Mktg - The Scotts Miracle-Gro Company; pg. 1799, pg. 1459
Aaron, David, Dir-Digital Adv Sls - BET Holdings LLC; pg. 271, pg. 396
Aaron, Donna, Mgr-Mktg - FCA US LLC; pg. 170, pg. 868
Aaron, Stacey, Dir-Natl Mktg Ops - Cellco Partnership; pg. 1869, pg. 1042
Aaron, Wayne, VP-Mktg Programs & Distr Strategy - Delta Air Lines, Inc.; pg. 1905, pg. 503
Aaronian, Jenna, Assoc Media Planner-Retail - New Balance Athletic Shoe, Inc.; pg. 1811, pg. 798
Aarons, Natasha, Mgr-Mktg & Music Industry - YouTube, LLC; pg. 1291, pg. 198
Aaserud, Brooke, Mktg Comm - Siemens Process Industries and Drives; pg. 673, pg. 485
Abaci, Ahmet, VP-Brand Mktg & Mgmt - Mizuno USA, Inc.; pg. 1839, pg. 538
Abad, Rita, Dir-Promos & Partner Mktg - Redbox Automated Retail, LLC; pg. 306, pg. 649
Abascal, Jorge, Dir-Creative & Art - JPMorgan Chase & Co.; pg. 772, pg. 1246
Abato, Theresa, Sr Dir-Corp Sls & Suites Admin - Baltimore Ravens Limited Partnership; pg. 532, pg. 755
Abaunza, Elizabeth, Asst Dir-Advising Svcs - Golden Gate University; pg. 602, pg. 219
Abbadie, Gigi, Dir-Mktg-Global - Aveda Corporation; pg. 499, pg. 917
Abbas, Jeanna, Specialist-Customer Mktg - Meijer, Inc.; pg. 1779, pg. 888
Abbate, Jeremy A., VP-Global Media Alliances - Scientific American, Inc.; pg. 1685, pg. 1290
Abbate, Salvatore, CMO & Chief Sls Officer - Andersen Corporation; pg. 67, pg. 916
Abbazia, Melissa, Supvr-Creative - Conair Corporation; pg. 505, pg. 1055
Abbene, Matthew, VP-Sls & Svc-Indus Grp - FEI Company; pg. 1413, pg. 1498
Abbey, Joel, Mgr-Ambassador Program & Specialist-Social Media - Medtronic, Inc.; pg. 1564, pg. 939
Abbey, Michael, Specialist-Mktg - United Rentals, Inc.; pg. 1386, pg. 350
Abbey, Mitch, Sr Mgr-Enterprise Product Line - Western Digital Corporation; pg. 492, pg. 118
Abbey, Richard E., VP-Contract Sls - Sysco Corporation; pg. 1035, pg. 1716
Abbinante, Johanna, Head-Brand Mktg-Gen Mgmt Expertise - E&J Gallo Winery; pg. 1962, pg. 149
Abbondante, Liberta, Sr VP-Consumer Mktg - The Hearst Corporation; pg. 1649, pg. 1239
Abbot, Suzanne, Dir-Creative-Global - WestRock Company; pg. 1472, pg. 1805
Abbott, Bill, Pres & CEO-Crown Media Holdings - Hallmark Cards, Inc.; pg. 1646, pg. 983
Abbott, Cate Smith, Sr Mgr-InHouse - Target Corporation; pg. 1786, pg. 942
Abbott, Darren, Grp VP-Creative - Hallmark Cards, Inc.; pg. 1646, pg. 983
Abbott, Dave, VP-Online Mktg - The Home Depot, Inc.; pg. 1050, pg. 510
Abbott, David, Mgr-Aftermarket Sls - SPX Process Equipment; pg. 1378, pg. 1551
Abbott, Kelly, Asst VP-Mktg-Atlanta - CBIZ, INC.; pg. 733, pg. 1429
Abbott, Nate, VP-Product - MapQuest, Inc.; pg. 1265, pg. 321
Abcarian, Kelly, Sr VP-Product Mgmt - Nielsen Business Media; pg. 1671, pg. 1272
Abcarian, Kelly, Sr VP-Watch Product Architecture - The Nielsen Company B.V.; pg. 1671, pg. 1272
Abdalla, Noha, Sr Dir-Digital Brand Strategy & Brand Social Media - Capital One Financial Corporation; pg. 730, pg. 1789
Abdallah, Angela, Assoc Mgr-Mktg-Loyalty - Dunkin' Brands Group, Inc.; pg. 1727, pg. 810
Abdallah, Sandra, VP-Field Sls - L'Oreal USA; pg. 514, pg. 1252
Abdel-Rahman, Mohamed, VP-Exploration & Production - Royale Energy, Inc.; pg. 984, pg. 208
Abdelmalek, Bola, Coord-Mktg - VITAMIN SHOPPE, INC.; pg. 1608, pg. 1098
Abdelmaseh, Aaron, Mgr-Digital Mktg-Global - Cigna Corporation; pg. 1197, pg. 338
Abdelrahman, Mohamed, Brand Mgr-Mens Private Brands - Saks Fifth Avenue, Inc.; pg. 1783, pg. 1287
Abdi, Fuad, Specialist-Bus Dev & Sls Advisory - IBM Canada Limited; pg. 411, pg. 1923
Abdulrahman, Marzuq, Dir-Sls Ops - Boehringer Ingelheim Pharmaceuticals, Inc.; pg. 1507, pg. 368
Abegg, Joe, Dir-Channel Mktg - MillerCoors LLC; pg. 255, pg. 582
Abel Lucci, Deborah, Sr Dir-New Bus & Corp Partnerships - National Geographic Society; pg. 1667, pg. 402
Abel, John, Sr Dir-Comm & Brand Integration-Global - Mazda North American Operations; pg. 183, pg. 113
Abel, Mandi L., Mgr-Mktg Comm - Sunoco Inc.; pg. 985, pg. 1571
Abel, Simon, Rep-Sls-US - Interpoint Corporation; pg. 647, pg. 1824
Abell, Teri, Dir-Local Mktg-Colorado - Anthem, Inc.; pg. 1192, pg. 683
Abello, Casie, Sr Dir-Online Mktg & Creative Svcs - Good Technology, Inc.; pg. 1249, pg. 285
Abello, Jean-Pierre, Dir-Product Engrg - The Nielsen Company B.V.; pg. 1671, pg. 1272
Abelman, David, Exec VP-Mktg - Rite Aid Corporation; pg. 1590, pg. 1519
Abels, Kathy, Specialist-Technical Mktg - Sigma-Aldrich Corporation; pg. 1181, pg. 1003
Aber, John N., Mgr-Mktg - Day-Glo Color Corp.; pg. 1441, pg. 1429
Abercrombie, Erica, Principal-Mktg - FedEx Corporation; pg. 1907, pg. 1642
Abercrombie, Fowler, Mgr-Product Dev & Mgmt - Verizon Communications Inc.; pg. 1875, pg. 1309
Abercrombie, Karen, VP-Corp Mktg & Comm - ION Geophysical Corporation; pg. 1350, pg. 1708
Abergel, David, Mgr-Digital Mktg-Global - Alcon; pg. 1399, pg. 530
Aberle, Chris, VP-Investments & Dir-Sls - FCStone Group, Inc.; pg. 751, pg. 982
Abernathy, Jennifer, Dir-Mktg - Anthem, Inc.; pg. 1192, pg. 683
Abernethy, Michael, Dir-Creative, Corp Comm & Mktg - Gannett Co., Inc.; pg. 1643, pg. 1790
Ablassmeir, Michael, Dir-Products & Markets - The McGraw-Hill Companies Inc.; pg. 1663, pg. 1257
Abler, Stacey, Dir-Digital Mktg - National Vision, Inc.; pg. 1423, pg. 534
Abney, Ashley, Planner-Mktg & Event - Visit Florida Inc.; pg. 1010, pg. 470
AbouAmmo, Ahmad, Head-Media Partnerships-MENA - Twitter, Inc.; pg. 1285, pg. 228
Aboudi, Omar, Brand Mgr-ISAIA - Saks Fifth Avenue, Inc.; pg. 1783, pg. 1287
Abouezzi, Michael, Sr Dir-Global LSS - PepsiCo, Inc.; pg. 259, pg. 1327
Abouzeid, Nehme, Exec Dir-Brand Mktg & Adv - Wynn Las Vegas, LLC; pg. 1119, pg. 1030
Abraczinskas, Jennifer, Dir-Mktg Comm - Genworth Financial, Inc.; pg. 761, pg. 1802
Abraham, Amy, VP-Mktg & Comm - BP America Inc.; pg. 972, pg. 1702
Abraham, Bob, Dir-Digital Audio Products - Shure Incorporated; pg. 672, pg. 638
Abraham, Nick, Sr Dir-Underwriting & Production - Markel Corporation; pg. 1207, pg. 1783
Abraham, Scott, Sr VP-Mktg - NBC Universal, Inc.; pg. 300, pg. 1266
Abraham, Scott, Sr VP-Creative Svcs - Universal Studios, Inc.; pg. 315, pg. 298
Abrahamson, Jennifer, Dir-Legal Dynamic Documents-Global Mktg Svcs - FRANKLIN RESOURCES, INC.; pg. 760, pg. 254
Abrahamson, Siri, Sr Mgr-Bus Dev - The Associated Press, Inc.; pg. 270, pg. 1197
Abrahim, Adib, Sr Mgr-Digital Comm - American Airlines Inc.; pg. 1898, pg. 1693
Abramkin, Vladimir, Mgr-Sls-Russia, CIS & Baltic States - The Ripley Company; pg. 1305, pg. 342
Abramo, David, Head-Media-Global - Reebok International Ltd.; pg. 1817, pg. 811
Abramova, Svetlana, Dir-Sls Ops & Retirement Svcs - Automatic Data Processing, Inc.; pg. 357, pg. 1117
Abramowitz, Elissa, Assoc Mgr-Sls Plng - In Style Magazine; pg. 1652, pg. 1243
Abramowitz, Randi, VP-Sls & Ops-New York - BioScrip, Inc.; pg. 1506, pg. 1158
Abrams, Ed, VP-Mktg-Enterprise Bus - Samsung Electronics America, Inc.; pg. 669, pg. 1115
Abrams, Ellen, Coord-Mktg-Viking Books - Penguin Random House; pg. 1675, pg. 1276
Abrams, Ethan, Dir-Product Mgmt - BroadSoft, Inc.; pg. 1233, pg. 770
Abrams, Jennifer, Mgr-Mktg Comm - Brady Corporation; pg. 363, pg. 1873
Abrams, Martin, Dir-Mktg - Land O'Lakes, Inc.; pg. 873, pg. 915
Abrams, Michael, Sr Dir-Leadership Dev & Talent Optimization - Banner Health System; pg. 1498, pg. 15
Abrams, Paul, Dir-PR - Roto-Rooter, Inc.; pg. 108, pg. 1425
Abramski, Adam, Mgr-Strategic Product-Transportation Solutions Div - Intel Corporation; pg. 645, pg. 266
Abramson, Eric, VP-Dermatology & Immunology Mktg - Valeant Pharmaceuticals International; pg. 1605, pg. 1047
Abramson, Nicole, Mgr-Shopper Mktg - S.C. Johnson & Son, Inc.; pg. 334, pg. 1889
Abrego, Alyson, Mgr-Product Mktg - Adobe Systems Incorporated; pg. 342, pg. 235
Abreu, Michelle, VP-Digital Mktg - Bank of America Corporation; pg. 718, pg. 1362
Abrishamchian, Hadi, Mgr-Global Comml Sls Activation & Digital Mktg - Mattel Games/Puzzles; pg. 962, pg. 80
Abrishamchian, Hadi, Mgr-Global Comml Sls Activation & Digital Mktg - MATTEL, INC.; pg. 962, pg. 81
Abruzzese, Joseph, Pres-Adv Sls - Discovery Communications, Inc.; pg. 282, pg. 777
Abruzzi, Corinne, Brand Mgr-Giorgio Armani Eyewear - Luxottica Retail; pg. 8, pg. 1460
Abzug, Rachel, Sr Mgr-Digital Customer Experience - American Express Company; pg. 712, pg. 1190
Acas, Christine, VP-Product Mgmt-North America Mobile & Tablet-GCMIO - Citigroup Inc.; pg. 735, pg. 1212
Acatrinei, Gabriela, Sr Mgr-Digital Mktg - Scholastic Inc.; pg. 1683, pg. 1288
Accardo, Paul, Mgr-Mktg Comm - The Chamberlain Group, Inc.; pg. 75, pg. 611
Acebal, Alejandro, Dir-Digital Sls & Integration - Telemundo Network Inc.; pg. 311, pg. 430
Aceto, Alexandra, Sr Specialist-Social Media Content Dev - Liberty Mutual Insurance Group Inc.; pg. 1205, pg. 797
Acevedo Murillo, Carmen, Dir-Mktg - The Melting Pot Restaurants Inc.; pg. 1741, pg. 474
Acham, Sandra, Mgr-Mktg - Cisco Systems, Inc.; pg. 372, pg. 240
Achanta, Sharada, VP-Product Mgmt-Oracle Fusion Middleware North America - Oracle Corporation; pg. 1272, pg. 786
Achar, David, Mgr-Mdse - Baker & Taylor, Inc.; pg. 1619, pg.

1362
Achara, Chidi, Sr VP & Dir-Global Creative - Simon Property Group, Inc.; *pg.* 1112, *pg.* 690
Achatz, Anthony W., Dir-OEM & Intl Sls - BrassCraft Manufacturing Company; *pg.* 1043, *pg.* 902
Achtor, Dan, Sr Mgr-Mktg-Molecular Imaging-PET & SPECT - Philips Electronics North America; *pg.* 662, *pg.* 782
Acierno, Ann, Exec VP-Mdsg, Design & Product Dev - David's Bridal, Inc.; *pg.* 23, *pg.* 1523
Acker, Kristin, VP-Product Dev - Zillow Group, Inc.; *pg.* 1292, *pg.* 1843
Acker, Lori, VP-Mktg & Customer Experience - National Grid USA; *pg.* 1946, *pg.* 852
Acker, Sheila, Dir-Mktg & CRM - Henry Ford Health System; *pg.* 1541, *pg.* 883
Acker, Todd, Dir-Mktg - Peterbilt Motors Co.; *pg.* 188, *pg.* 1691
Ackerman, Allison, Exec Dir-Digital Mktg - Dow Jones & Company, Inc.; *pg.* 1037, *pg.* 1226
Ackerman, Billie, Dir-Mktg - National Vision, Inc.; *pg.* 1423, *pg.* 534
Ackerman, Jane, Head-Brand & Mktg Comm-Global - Broadridge Financial Solutions Inc.; *pg.* 727, *pg.* 1172
Ackerman, John, Mgr-Mktg-Global Specialty Chemical Catalysts - Clariant Corporation; *pg.* 1153, *pg.* 1365
Ackerman, Rebecca, Dir-Mktg - Haband Company, Inc.; *pg.* 1772, *pg.* 1099
Ackerman, Scott, Sr VP-Product Dev - Vacation.com, Inc.; *pg.* 1287, *pg.* 1772
Ackermann, Jeff, VP-Mktg - Universal Studios, Inc.; *pg.* 315, *pg.* 298
Ackermann, Lisa, Exec VP-Sls & Mktg - Urologix, Inc.; *pg.* 1604, *pg.* 945
Ackerson, Amy J., Sr Mgr-Corp Comm - Avis Budget Group, Inc.; *pg.* 1900, *pg.* 1102
Ackerson, Eric, Sr Mgr-Product Mktg & Brand - Acer America Corporation; *pg.* 341, *pg.* 235
Ackley, Robert E., VP-Custom Products - Span-America Medical Systems, Inc.; *pg.* 1595, *pg.* 1618
Acklin, Larry, Mgr-Applications Product Mktg - Hewlett-Packard Company; *pg.* 404, *pg.* 175
Ackroyd, Carson J., VP-Mktg & Comm - ATCO Ltd.; *pg.* 1935, *pg.* 1902
Acks, Ashley, Dir-Mktg & Mgr-Promos - GameStop Corp.; *pg.* 399, *pg.* 1699
Acomb, James, Sr Dir-Product Mktg-Worldwide - Apple Inc.; *pg.* 350, *pg.* 73
Acos, Julianna, Mgr-Mktg Programs & Pub Sector - Adobe Systems Incorporated; *pg.* 342, *pg.* 235
Acosta, Armando, Product Mgr-Hadoop - Dell Inc.; *pg.* 383, *pg.* 1737
Acosta, John, Dir-Mktg-Customer Acq - Bass Pro Shops, Inc.; *pg.* 1826, *pg.* 1006
Acosta, Larissa, Sr Dir-Hispanic Mktg - The University of Phoenix, Inc.; *pg.* 610, *pg.* 27
Acosta, Ron, Mgr-Multicultural Mktg-Chicago - MillerCoors LLC; *pg.* 255, *pg.* 582
Acosta, Sandra, Mgr-Mktg Strategy & Natl Promos - PetSmart, Inc.; *pg.* 1481, *pg.* 18
Acosta-Franco, Luisa, VP & Head-Recruitment Mktg & Field Support - Farmers Group, Inc.; *pg.* 1199, *pg.* 130
Acquafredda, Dan, VP-Global Bus Dev-Media Collaboration - ClearOne Communications, Inc.; *pg.* 629, *pg.* 1756
Acree, Todd, Dir-Product Mgmt - Extreme Networks Inc; *pg.* 287, *pg.* 245
Acton, Kipp, Sr VP-Sls - Victorinox Swiss Army Inc.; *pg.* 1139, *pg.* 357
Acton, Leigh, Dir-Digital & Social Media - Avon Products, Inc.; *pg.* 500, *pg.* 1198
Acuff, Courtney Jane, VP-Insights & Design-Product - Catalina Marketing Corporation; *pg.* 369, *pg.* 462
Acunto, John, VP-Mktg Comm - National Basketball Association; *pg.* 566, *pg.* 1264
Adabi, Fazel, Mgr-PR-Automotive - NVIDIA Corporation; *pg.* 447, *pg.* 268
Adair, Marian, Mgr-Pur & Distributor Sls - Active Parenting Publishers; *pg.* 1613, *pg.* 535
Adam, Bob, Sr Dir-Bus Rels & Trng - Mannatech, Incorporated; *pg.* 1558, *pg.* 1671
Adam, Brian, Dir-Mktg Ops - Saba Software, Inc.; *pg.* 464, *pg.* 192
Adam, Gary, Pres-Sls-Intl - Rocky Brands, Inc.; *pg.* 1818, *pg.* 1466
Adam, Lenore, Sr Product Mgr - Cisco Systems, Inc.; *pg.* 372, *pg.* 240
Adam, Marc, Sr Dir-CLT-Mktg & Audience-Worldwide - Microsoft Corporation; *pg.* 435, *pg.* 1824
Adam, Randi, Dir-Mktg - Greater Cincinnati Convention & Visitors Bureau; *pg.* 993, *pg.* 1414
Adam, Susan, Dir-Mktg-NOTIFIER - Honeywell International Inc.; *pg.* 407, *pg.* 1088
Adam, Tim, VP-Sls - Avitae USA LLC; *pg.* 838, *pg.* 1471
Adamakis, Nicolas, Dir-Mktg-College of Liberal Arts & Sciences - Arizona State University; *pg.* 597, *pg.* 25
Adamcik, Mark, VP-Sls & Mdsg - Giant of Maryland LLC; *pg.* 1021, *pg.* 773
Adamec, Colleen, Mgr-Mktg - PepsiCo, Inc.; *pg.* 259, *pg.* 1327
Adami, Zeno, Brand Mgr-Global - Gillette; *pg.* 1536, *pg.* 795
Adamiak, Adam, Sr Assoc Brand Mgr-Duracell Central Europe - The Procter & Gamble Company; *pg.* 1129, *pg.* 1418
Adamian, Carrie Ellen, Dir-Mktg & Ticket Sls - The Dallas Opera; *pg.* 543, *pg.* 1679
Adamo, Alba, Grp Dir-Hispanic Mktg - The Coca-Cola Company; *pg.* 240, *pg.* 493
Adamo, Glenn, VP-Brdcst & Media Ops - National Football League; *pg.* 567, *pg.* 1264
Adamo, Jo, VP-Mktg-Wines & Champagnes - Pernod Ricard USA, Inc.; *pg.* 1968, *pg.* 1332
Adamoli-Kalbli, Ginevra, Analyst-Digital Mktg - Visit Florida Inc.; *pg.* 1010, *pg.* 470
Adamopoulos, Danny, Product Mgr - Motorola Solutions, Inc.; *pg.* 657, *pg.* 659
Adamoski, Rob, Dir-Mktg-OLP - Gilead Sciences, Inc.; *pg.* 1535, *pg.* 88
Adamowicz, Kerry, Dir-Mktg - AXA Equitable Life Insurance Company; *pg.* 1194, *pg.* 1199
Adams, Andy, Sr Mgr-ECommerce & Brand Websites - La Quinta Corporation; *pg.* 1099, *pg.* 1722
Adams, Andy, Sr Mgr-ECommerce & Brand Websites - La Quinta Inns, Inc.; *pg.* 1100, *pg.* 1722
Adams, Ann, Dir-ACI Worldwide Customer Mgmt-Americas Sls Ops & Customer Mgmt - ACI Worldwide Inc.; *pg.* 341, *pg.* 1010
Adams, Belinda, Sr Mgr-Mktg Campaign - PayPal Inc.; *pg.* 1274, *pg.* 248
Adams, Bill, VP-Sls-US - New Era Cap Company Inc.; *pg.* 1840, *pg.* 1155
Adams, Bryan, Mgr-Social Media Channel - The Vanguard Group, Inc.; *pg.* 816, *pg.* 1550
Adams, Carolyn, Brand Mgr - Manna Pro Corporation; *pg.* 1478, *pg.* 975
Adams, Chuck, Sr VP & Gen Mgr-Sls - Intelligrated Systems Inc.; *pg.* 1349, *pg.* 1414
Adams, Cody, Mgr-PR - The J.M. Smucker Company; *pg.* 865, *pg.* 1468
Adams, Colby, VP-Sls & Mktg - ASD Healthcare; *pg.* 1496, *pg.* 1697
Adams, Craig, Dir-Gas Supply & Mktg - Calpine Corporation; *pg.* 1936, *pg.* 1702
Adams, David, Mgr-Mktg-Fin Svcs - The Toro Company; *pg.* 1065, *pg.* 918
Adams, Diane, CMO & Sr VP-Consumer Products Div - FXI; *pg.* 1163, *pg.* 1552
Adams, Eric A, Engr-Technical Mktg - Intel Corporation; *pg.* 645, *pg.* 266
Adams, Gregg T., Exec VP-Mktg & Sls - BankFinancial Corporation; *pg.* 722, *pg.* 560
Adams, Heidi, Sr Dir-Mktg - Pacific Sunwear of California, Inc.; *pg.* 1781, *pg.* 43
Adams, Jeffery, Exec Dir-Mktg & Comm-Global - AM General, LLC; *pg.* 163, *pg.* 697
Adams, Jen, Sr Mgr-Adv - National Instruments Corporation; *pg.* 443, *pg.* 1664
Adams, Jennifer, Mng Dir-Integrated Mktg - American Airlines Inc.; *pg.* 1898, *pg.* 1693
Adams, Jennifer, Dir-Production - Harper's Magazine Foundation; *pg.* 1648, *pg.* 1238
Adams, Jennifer, Dir-Enterprise Solutions Mktg - Plantronics, Inc.; *pg.* 663, *pg.* 270
Adams, John, Dir-Sls & Mktg-LATAM - Echo Incorporated; *pg.* 1046, *pg.* 626
Adams, Jonathan, Sr Mgr-Electrical Engrg & Personal Audio - Beats Electronics LLC; *pg.* 624, *pg.* 272
Adams, Karen, Sr Dir-Mktg Capabilities-Global - Mondelez International, Inc.; *pg.* 878, *pg.* 601
Adams, Karen, Acting Dir-Social Mktg - QVC Inc; *pg.* 305, *pg.* 1593
Adams, Keith, VP-Sls - JDA Software Group, Inc.; *pg.* 423, *pg.* 22
Adams, Ken, Sr VP & Head-Sls-US - LeapFrog Enterprises, Inc.; *pg.* 961, *pg.* 84
Adams, Kristi, Dir-Vertical Svcs Mktg - Dell Inc.; *pg.* 383, *pg.* 1737
Adams, Kymberlie, Sr Mgr-Social Media - American Society for the Prevention of Cruelty to Animals; *pg.* 131, *pg.* 1193
Adams, Leigh, VP-Private Wealth Mktg - UMB Financial Corporation; *pg.* 812, *pg.* 987
Adams, Maggie, Sr Mgr-Mktg Comm - Microsoft Corporation; *pg.* 435, *pg.* 1824
Adams, Melanne, VP-Mktg Plng & Fin - Stage Stores, Inc.; *pg.* 33, *pg.* 1715
Adams, Michael, VP-Intl Carrier Sls - FUSION TELECOMMUNICATIONS INTERNATIONAL, INC.; *pg.* 1248, *pg.* 1233
Adams, Moira, Dir-Sls-Control East - Diageo North America Inc.; *pg.* 248, *pg.* 1223
Adams, Molly, Exec VP-Product Dev-Global - The Walt Disney Company; *pg.* 317, *pg.* 52
Adams, Myra, VP-Mktg - Southeast Toyota Distributors, LLC; *pg.* 190, *pg.* 421
Adams, Nicole, Dir-Affiliate Mktg - AMC Networks Inc.; *pg.* 269, *pg.* 1189
Adams, Patricia, Sr VP-Mdsg, Apparel & Accessories - Target Corporation; *pg.* 1786, *pg.* 942
Adams, Paul M., Mgr-Media Rels - Exelon Corporation; *pg.* 1942, *pg.* 573
Adams, Richard, Dir-Sls - United Bankshares, Inc.; *pg.* 813, *pg.* 1849
Adams, Rob, Dir-Mktg - Chiquita Brands International, Inc.; *pg.* 847, *pg.* 1365
Adams, Robert, CIO & Chief Strategy Officer - 99 Cents Only Stores LLC; *pg.* 1759, *pg.* 66
Adams, Ronda, Mgr-Mktg - Wells Fargo & Company; *pg.* 819, *pg.* 232
Adams, Sara, Sr Mgr-Channel Mktg - Polycom, Inc.; *pg.* 664, *pg.* 249
Adams, Shane, Dir-Guest Loyalty & Social Mktg - AMC Entertainment Inc.; *pg.* 527, *pg.* 716
Adams, Stacey, Sr Mgr-CRM - Crate & Barrel, Inc.; *pg.* 922, *pg.* 640
Adams, Stacy, VP-Mktg - mBlox Inc.; *pg.* 1266, *pg.* 286
Adams, Stephanie, Sr Mgr-Media & Interactive - The Coca-Cola Company; *pg.* 240, *pg.* 493
Adams, Steve, Sr Dir-Product Design & Delivery-Customer Mktg - Hilton Worldwide, Inc.; *pg.* 1094, *pg.* 1791
Adams, Tina, Mgr-Global Mktg Comm & Program Dev - Henkel Corporation; *pg.* 1165, *pg.* 1535
Adams, Wendell, Mgr-Creative Svcs & Catalog Production - Cardinal Health, Inc.; *pg.* 1512, *pg.* 1448
Adams, Will, Dir-Sls - LendingTree, LLC; *pg.* 775, *pg.* 1367
Adams, Yvonne, Sr Mgr-ECommerce - Hilton Worldwide, Inc.; *pg.* 1094, *pg.* 1791
Adamski, Jason, Area Mgr-Media - Ferrero U.S.A., Inc.; *pg.* 1852, *pg.* 1121
Adamson, David, Sr VP-Mktg - Oakley, Inc.; *pg.* 1840, *pg.* 86
Adamson, Guy N., Rep-Investment Advisor - Bank of McKenney; *pg.* 720, *pg.* 1788
Adamson, Jennifer, Sr Dir-Integrated Media & Promos - Universal Orlando; *pg.* 590, *pg.* 456
Adamson, Mark, VP-Sls & Mktg - DOUGLAS DYNAMICS, INC.; *pg.* 204, *pg.* 1874
Adamson, Michael, VP-Sports New Products-Turner Sports Interactive - Turner Broadcasting System, Inc.; *pg.* 314, *pg.* 521
Adamson, Shelli, Mgr-Mktg-SunGard Wealth Mgmt - SunGard Employee Benefit Systems; *pg.* 477, *pg.* 4
Adamson, Terry, Chief Legal Officer & Head-Media-Intl - National Geographic Society; *pg.* 1667, *pg.* 402
Adamy, Earl, Exec Dir-Mktg - Olympus America Inc.; *pg.* 1425, *pg.* 1521
Adamy, Mark, VP-Mktg Ops - Comcast Corporation; *pg.* 276, *pg.* 1560
Adan, Marilyn, Sr Mgr-Strategy & Corp Dev - Synopsys, Inc.; *pg.* 480, *pg.* 162
Adavi, Vinay, Product Mgr - Juniper Networks, Inc.; *pg.* 1260, *pg.* 286
Adcock, Celiena, Client Partner-Entertainment-Global Mktg Solutions - Facebook, Inc.; *pg.* 1245, *pg.* 143
Adcock, Elizabeth, Sr Specialist-Mktg - Cigna-HealthSpring; *pg.* 1515, *pg.* 1632
Adcock, Tom, Mgr-Mktg-Global - Henkel Corporation; *pg.* 1049, *pg.* 369
Addante, Frank, Founder, CEO & Chief Architect-Product - Rubicon Project; *pg.* 1278, *pg.* 182

First page reference indicates Business Class Edition
Second page reference indicates Geographic Edition

Addenbrooke, Erin, Dir-Adv - Colorado Community Newspapers; *pg.* 1628, *pg.* 332
Addesso, Anna Maria, Sr Mgr-Integrated Mktg - Apple Vacations Inc.; *pg.* 1899, *pg.* 1556
Addington, Dewayne D., Mgr-Applications Sls-Strategic Accounts & Customer Experience - Oracle Corporation; *pg.* 450, *pg.* 191
Addison, Afiya, Assoc Acct Mgr-Mktg Solutions - LinkedIn Corporation; *pg.* 1262, *pg.* 160
Addo, Denise, Sr Mgr-Brand Center - Georgia-Pacific LLC; *pg.* 1458, *pg.* 507
Adelberg, Ellen, Dir-Comm & Mktg - Canadian Parks and Wilderness Society; *pg.* 136, *pg.* 1931
Adelsberger, Adrienne, Dir-Partnership Mktg - World Wrestling Entertainment, Inc.; *pg.* 595, *pg.* 380
Adelson, Susie, Dir-Earned Media & Experiential - Spin Master Ltd.; *pg.* 967, *pg.* 1943
Ader, Barry, VP-Mktg - EMC Corporation; *pg.* 391, *pg.* 825
Ader, Seth, Sr Dir-Mktg - ESPN, Inc.; *pg.* 285, *pg.* 340
Adger, Doreen, VP-Mktg Strategy - The Street, Inc.; *pg.* 1283, *pg.* 1296
Adjunta, Jimmy, Product Mgr-Global - Molex Incorporated; *pg.* 655, *pg.* 628
Adkins, Heather, VP-Digital Mktg & Tech - Transamerica Insurance & Investment Group; *pg.* 1219, *pg.* 141
Adkins, Katherine, Product Mgr-Bon Ton - Bon Ton Stores, Inc.; *pg.* 1763, *pg.* 1596
Adkins-Green, Sheryl, CMO - Mary Kay Inc.; *pg.* 516, *pg.* 1657
Adkinson, Christy, Dir-Mktg - Cray Inc.; *pg.* 380, *pg.* 1834
Adler, Bob, Product Mgr-Print Sleeves-North America - Flint Group, Inc.; *pg.* 1163, *pg.* 904
Adler, Emily, Assoc Dir-Media & Consumer Engagement - The Kraft Heinz Company; *pg.* 871, *pg.* 641
Adler, Jonathan, Head-Corp & NA-Sls & Mktg Indirect Sourcing - Avon Products, Inc.; *pg.* 500, *pg.* 1198
Adler, Laina, VP-Mktg-HarperOne - HarperCollins Publishers Inc.; *pg.* 1647, *pg.* 1237
Adler, Laura, Specialist-Product Content - La-Z-Boy Incorporated; *pg.* 932, *pg.* 901
Adney, Joe, VP-Mktg Comm - Bob Evans Restaurants, Inc.; *pg.* 1717, *pg.* 1438
Adomaitis, Matthew, Mgr-Mktg-Indus Process & Food Bus Unit - Calgon Carbon Corporation; *pg.* 1151, *pg.* 1574
Adraneda, Marilen, Sr Mgr-HR - Wolverine World Wide, Inc.; *pg.* 1822, *pg.* 905
Adrian, Lynn, VP & Brand Mgr - Wells Fargo & Company; *pg.* 819, *pg.* 232
Adriance, Glenn E., CMO, Chief Sls Officer & VP - Mesa Laboratories, Inc.; *pg.* 1567, *pg.* 333
Adriance, Nicole, Sr Mgr-Brand Comm - Reebok International Ltd.; *pg.* 1817, *pg.* 811
Adusumilli, Ravi, Head-Enterprise Partnerships-Facebook Mktg Partner Program - Facebook, Inc.; *pg.* 1245, *pg.* 143
Aebischer, Marta, Dir-Global Mktg-Irwin Tools - Newell Rubbermaid Inc.; *pg.* 1128, *pg.* 515
Aed, Suzanne, Mgr-Natl Sls-Specialty Markets - Palm Springs Desert Resorts Convention & Visitors Authority; *pg.* 1003, *pg.* 187
Aedo, Rolando, CMO & Exec VP - Greater Miami Convention & Visitors Bureau; *pg.* 993, *pg.* 442
Aerts, Mike, Dir-Mktg & Membership Div - Florida Fruit & Vegetable Association; *pg.* 140, *pg.* 438
Aevermann, Mark, Product Mgr-GeForce products - NVIDIA Corporation; *pg.* 447, *pg.* 268
Afanador, Monica, Sr Mgr-Integrated Mktg - Hooters of America LLC; *pg.* 1731, *pg.* 511
Afarian, JoAnne, Dir-Global New Product Plng - CUBIST PHARMACEUTICALS, INC.; *pg.* 1521, *pg.* 828
Afergan, Michael M., Sr VP-Products-Asia Pacific & Japan - Akamai Technologies, Inc.; *pg.* 1226, *pg.* 807
Affel, John H., Dir-Mktg - World Finer Foods, Inc.; *pg.* 910, *pg.* 1044
Affeld, Jon, VP-Mktg & Bus Dev - Emulex Corporation; *pg.* 392, *pg.* 70
Afifi, Emad, Sr Dir-CMOS Engrg-Datacom & Consumer Product Lines - GigOptix, Inc.; *pg.* 400, *pg.* 245
Afshar, Mohamad, VP-Products-Weblogic, Glassfish, Java Cloud Svc & Exalogic - Oracle Corporation; *pg.* 450, *pg.* 191
Agabob, Keith, VP-Video Product Mgmt - Cablevision Systems Corporation; *pg.* 272, *pg.* 1141
Agadi, Harsha V., Interim CEO - Crawford & Company; *pg.* 1199, *pg.* 502
Agar-Studelska, Sandy, Mgr-Color Mktg & Decorating Product's - Diamond Vogel Paint, Inc.; *pg.* 1441, *pg.* 710
Agarwal, Amit, Product Mgr - Google Inc.; *pg.* 1249, *pg.* 153
Agarwal, Atul, Sr Mgr-Strategy Consulting - Accenture; *pg.* 1392, *pg.* 1186
Agarwal, Jyoti, Sr Dir-NBA Mktg & Media Plng - National Basketball Association; *pg.* 566, *pg.* 1264
Agarwal, Noopur, Designer-Bus Mktg - Snapchat, Inc.; *pg.* 1281, *pg.* 301
Agarwal, Richa, Dir-Product Dev - Eileen Fisher, Inc.; *pg.* 24, *pg.* 1168
Agarwal, Sachin, Product Mgr-Direct Messages - Twitter, Inc.; *pg.* 1285, *pg.* 228
Agarwal, Sameer, Dir-Mktg-Clean & Clear Global Franchise - Johnson & Johnson; *pg.* 1549, *pg.* 1091
Agarwal, Shalini, Sr Product Mgr - Google Inc.; *pg.* 1249, *pg.* 153
Agarwal, Sunil, VP & Head-Product Dev-Inflammation - Genentech, Inc.; *pg.* 1533, *pg.* 279
Agee, Angela, Principal & Assoc-Mktg Comm - Capital One Financial Corporation; *pg.* 730, *pg.* 1789
Agee, Carl, Product Mgr - Deere & Company; *pg.* 703, *pg.* 632
Agee, Kevin, Specialist-New Media - Missouri State University; *pg.* 605, *pg.* 1006
Agee, Mike, VP-Restaurant Mktg - Bob Evans Farms, LLC; *pg.* 841, *pg.* 1467
Agee, Mike, VP-Restaurant Mktg - Bob Evans Restaurants, Inc.; *pg.* 1717, *pg.* 1438
Aggarwal, Nibha, Sr Dir-Product Mktg - Amdocs Inc.; *pg.* 348, *pg.* 974
Aggus, Kerri, Sr Mgr-Mktg - Bonnier Corporation; *pg.* 1622, *pg.* 480
Agishtein, Anna, Mgr-Enterprise Mktg - Google Inc.; *pg.* 1249, *pg.* 153
Agius, Jim, Exec VP-Adv Sls - A&E Television Networks, LLC; *pg.* 267, *pg.* 1185
Agiwal, Ashish, Sr Mgr-Global Sourcing & Procurement - Amazon.com, Inc.; *pg.* 1226, *pg.* 1831
Aglione, Bob, Dir-Event Mktg & Comm - March of Dimes Birth Defects Foundation; *pg.* 146, *pg.* 1354
Agne, Jon, Sr Mgr-Sponsorships & Promos - Monster Worldwide, Inc.; *pg.* 1268, *pg.* 859
Agnello, Nicole, Sr Mgr-Global Brand Publicity - Hasbro, Inc.; *pg.* 954, *pg.* 1603
Agnew, John, Dir-Global Digital Strategy & Mktg - Apple Inc.; *pg.* 350, *pg.* 73
Agostini, Adrian, VP-Sls - Amazon.com, Inc.; *pg.* 1226, *pg.* 1831
Agostini, Marcos, Sr VP-Sls & Bus Dev-Latin America - Interval Leisure Group, Inc.; *pg.* 1912, *pg.* 443
Agostino, Michael, VP-Product-Platforms - FINANCIAL ENGINES, INC.; *pg.* 753, *pg.* 285
Agrait, Ada, Gen Mgr-Mktg, Cloud & Enterprise - Microsoft Corporation; *pg.* 435, *pg.* 1824
Agrawal, Puja, Sr Product Mgr - eBay Inc.; *pg.* 1240, *pg.* 243
Agresta, Anthony, Dir-Mktg - Stein Mart, Inc.; *pg.* 1786, *pg.* 435
Agrimanakis Sherman, Stephanie, Dir-Mktg - DraftKings, Inc.; *pg.* 545, *pg.* 793
Agro, Natalie, Dir-Mktg Svcs - Toronto Blue Jays Baseball Club; *pg.* 588, *pg.* 1945
Agronin, Matthew, Assoc Dir-Integrated Mktg - Cellco Partnership; *pg.* 1869, *pg.* 1042
Agrwal, Shubham, Sr Grp Mgr-Product Mgmt - The Home Depot, Inc.; *pg.* 1050, *pg.* 510
Agualimpia, Juan, CMO & Exec VP - MoneyGram International, Inc.; *pg.* 783, *pg.* 1684
Aguayo, Michelle, Rep-Media Rels - Xcel Energy Inc.; *pg.* 1955, *pg.* 946
Aguerrevere, Ignacio, VP-Product Mgmt & Mktg-Global - CTP Transportation Products; *pg.* 203, *pg.* 1006
Aguiar, Alison, Sr Mgr-Email Ops - Barnes & Noble, Inc.; *pg.* 1619, *pg.* 1201
Aguiar, Elizabeth, VP-Bus Dev & Product Mktg - Bridgepoint Education, Inc.; *pg.* 598, *pg.* 201
Aguila, Ernesto, Sr Assoc Brand Mgr - Toyota Motor Sales, U.S.A., Inc.; *pg.* 193, *pg.* 296
Aguilar, Candida, Dir-Mktg-Travel Retail-Skincare - The Estee Lauder Companies Inc.; *pg.* 508, *pg.* 1229
Aguilar, Cesar, Exec VP-Sls & Mktg - Lion Brothers Company, Inc.; *pg.* 696, *pg.* 774
Aguilar, Marc, VP-Sls-Latin America & Caribbean - Putzmeister America; *pg.* 1371, *pg.* 1896
Aguilar, Marcela, Dir-Mktg Comm-Global - Apple Inc.; *pg.* 350, *pg.* 73
Aguirre, Ana M., Mgr-Mktg Programs-Avnet Embedded-Latin America & Caribbean - Avnet, Inc.; *pg.* 622, *pg.* 15
Aguirre, Christine, Sr Mgr-Partners in Learning - Microsoft Corporation; *pg.* 435, *pg.* 1824
Aguirre, Jess, Sr VP-Res & Media Plng - Crown Media Holdings Inc.; *pg.* 280, *pg.* 281
Agustin, Walden, Sr Dir-Natl Accts - Philadelphia Convention & Visitors Bureau; *pg.* 1004, *pg.* 1568
Ahari, Sanaz, Grp Product Mgr - Google Inc.; *pg.* 1249, *pg.* 153
Aharonoff, Adam, Head-Digital Tech & Sr Dir - AutoNation, Inc.; *pg.* 165, *pg.* 423
Ahart, Curt, VP-Cellular Products - Digi International Inc.; *pg.* 387, *pg.* 948
Ahearn, Greg, CMO - LeapFrog Enterprises, Inc.; *pg.* 961, *pg.* 84
Ahern, Richard, VP-Mktg - Sterilite Corporation; *pg.* 1138, *pg.* 848
Ahlberg, Steve, VP-New Product Dev - Gannett Co., Inc.; *pg.* 1643, *pg.* 1790
Ahlert, Patty, Dir-Sls Plng Cat - Mars Petcare; *pg.* 1478, *pg.* 1633
Ahlman, Alissa, VP & Gen Mgr-Mdse - At Home Stores LLC; *pg.* 1760, *pg.* 1729
Ahmad, Hamzah, Sr Coord-Event Mktg & Travel Advance - Atlanta Falcons Football Club, LLC; *pg.* 530, *pg.* 532
Ahmad, Mariam, Coord-Global Mktg-Coty Prestige - Coty, Inc.; *pg.* 506, *pg.* 1219
Ahmad, Samir, Mgr-Mktg-Global Sys Integrators - Dell Inc.; *pg.* 383, *pg.* 1737
Ahmad, Waseem, Sr Dir-Insight & Indus Strategy - Oracle Corporation; *pg.* 450, *pg.* 191
Ahmadi, Ellie, Head-Global Emerging Channels & Mobile Mktg - Accenture; *pg.* 1392, *pg.* 1186
Ahmed, Arsalan, Product Mgr -Direct Mktg - Zappos.com, Inc.; *pg.* 1291, *pg.* 1030
Ahmed, Ishita, Sr Mgr-Mktg-CRM Loyalty & Email Mktg - The Home Depot, Inc.; *pg.* 1050, *pg.* 510
Ahmed, Rizwan, Dir-Product Mktg-SSD Bus Unit - SanDisk Corporation; *pg.* 465, *pg.* 147
Ahmed, Sabina, Exec Dir-Media Svcs - AT&T Communications Corp.; *pg.* 1866, *pg.* 1043
Ahmed, Sabina, Exec Dir-Media Svcs - AT&T Inc.; *pg.* 1867, *pg.* 1674
Ahmed, Taufique, Sr Mgr-Segment Mktg - Micron Technology, Inc.; *pg.* 435, *pg.* 547
Ahmed, Zia R., Sr VP & Head-Global Markets Comm & Media Rels - Bank of America Corporation; *pg.* 718, *pg.* 1362
Ahmer, Alan, VP-Sls & Production - Calavo Growers, Inc.; *pg.* 843, *pg.* 276
Ahn, Henry, Pres-Content Distr & Mktg - Scripps Networks Interactive, Inc.; *pg.* 1279, *pg.* 1638
Ahn, Ricky, Sr Mgr-Corp Dev - Skyworks Solutions, Inc.; *pg.* 674, *pg.* 862
Ahn, Sophia, Mgr-Digital Media - AIGA, the professional association for design; *pg.* 125, *pg.* 1188
Ahn, Thomas, Sr Mgr-Digital Mktg - L'Oreal USA; *pg.* 514, *pg.* 1252
Ahneman, Spence, VP-Sls - National Presto Industries, Inc; *pg.* 1128, *pg.* 1857
Ahner, David, Corp Sec & VP-Sls - Louis Maull Company; *pg.* 875, *pg.* 999
Aho, Lisa R., Dir-Sls - Mile Marker International Inc.; *pg.* 213, *pg.* 459
Ahrberg, Joseph, VP-Sls - Barton Mines Company LLC; *pg.* 1148, *pg.* 1171
Ahrendts, Angela, Sr VP-Sls & Online Retail - Apple Inc.; *pg.* 350, *pg.* 73
Ahrensdorf, Rob, Dir-Brand Mgmt, Customer Insights & Broadline Mktg - Shamrock Foods Company; *pg.* 895, *pg.* 20
Ahrioui, Aziz, Specialist-Offer Mktg-Electric Vehicle Bus - Schneider Canada, Inc.; *pg.* 1374, *pg.* 1928
Ahsmuhs, Jean A., Mgr-Mktg - General Growth Properties, Inc.; *pg.* 1093, *pg.* 574
Ahuja, Amit, Sr Dir-Product Mgmt - Adobe Systems Incorporated; *pg.* 342, *pg.* 235
Ahuja, Masuma, Producer-Social Apps - Cable News Network LP; *pg.* 1624, *pg.* 1208
Ahuja, Salil, Sr Product Mgr - IBM; *pg.* 410, *pg.* 1449
Aidan, Alexander, Brand Mgr-Global Digital - NIKE, Inc.; *pg.* 1812, *pg.* 1492
Aiello, Tania, Sr Mgr-Mktg-MILLENNIAL Brand Strategy - Hudson's Bay Company; *pg.* 1773, *pg.* 1938
Aiello, Thomas, Sr VP-Sls-Worldwide - Cicero Inc.; *pg.* 372,

pg. 1360
Aiese, Jessica, Sr Mgr-Creative & Adv - Barnes & Noble, Inc.; *pg.* 1619, *pg.* 1201
Aievoli, Rich, Sr VP-Sls & Customer Svc-Aurora Products Grp, LLC - Aurora Casket Company, Inc.; *pg.* 1393, *pg.* 673
Aigner, Rosemary, Coord-Media Rels - Cablevision Systems Corporation; *pg.* 272, *pg.* 1141
Aikawa, Stewart, VP & Sr Mgr-Relationship - Mechanics Bank; *pg.* 781, *pg.* 193
Aiken, Melissa J., Dir-Applications Software Grp Mktg - Alcatel-Lucent; *pg.* 615, *pg.* 38
Aikens, Regina A., Mgr-Mktg & Ops - United States Postal Service; *pg.* 1009, *pg.* 406
Aikman, Mark, Mgr-Digital Mktg & CRM Dept - Mercedes-Benz USA, LLC; *pg.* 184, *pg.* 514
Aikman, Russ, Dir-Mktg & PR - ABF Freight System, Inc.; *pg.* 1896, *pg.* 31
Ailsworth, Brady, Mgr-Mktg Comm - PolyOne Corporation; *pg.* 1177, *pg.* 1404
Aime, Ugo, Product Mgr-FASTON Terminal-EMEA - TE Connectivity Ltd.; *pg.* 677, *pg.* 1515
Ainbinder, Rorie, Sr Mgr-Mktg - Piper Aircraft, Inc.; *pg.* 233, *pg.* 477
Ainley, Karen, Head-Comml & Product Mktg SMB Europe - Sage Software, Inc.; *pg.* 464, *pg.* 116
Ainsworth, Alan, VP-Sls & Distr - Monticello Drug Co.; *pg.* 1569, *pg.* 434
Airel, Doug, Sr Mgr-Player Svcs - National Football League Players Incorporated; *pg.* 149, *pg.* 401
Aitken, Mark A., VP-Advanced Tech - Sinclair Broadcast Group, Inc.; *pg.* 308, *pg.* 773
Aittola, Maija, Sr Mgr-Mktg - General Mills, Inc.; *pg.* 828, *pg.* 933
Aivazian, Suzy, Mgr-Media & Adv - Nestle USA, Inc.; *pg.* 883, *pg.* 96
Ajami, Armin, VP & Mgr-Mobile Banking Product Mgmt - Wells Fargo & Company; *pg.* 819, *pg.* 232
Akana, Julie, Product Mgr-Lab Water-Global - Thermo Fisher Scientific Inc.; *pg.* 1431, *pg.* 854
Akana, Stephen, Assoc Mgr-Mktg - Sega of America Inc.; *pg.* 966, *pg.* 227
Akbar, Mehrdad, VP & Div Mgr-Mdse-Electronic Svcs & Digital Imaging - Wal-Mart.com; *pg.* 1287, *pg.* 50
Akbarin, Alex, Mgr-Sls-Ferrari - The Collection, Inc.; *pg.* 168, *pg.* 418
Akehurst, Ian, VP-Mktg Analytics - Kayak; *pg.* 1260, *pg.* 363
Akemann, Jamie, VP-Electronics, Media & School & Home Office - Meijer, Inc.; *pg.* 1779, *pg.* 888
Aken, Ben, Sr Dir-Community Rels - Kansas City Royals Baseball Corporation; *pg.* 555, *pg.* 985
Aker, Kevin, Dir-Product Integration & Sr Mgr-Market Strategy - Windstream Corporation; *pg.* 321, *pg.* 34
Akers, Ann, Dir-Adv - Empire Diamond Corporation; *pg.* 4, *pg.* 1227
Akers, Denise, Dir-Mktg - Louisiana Television Broadcasting Corporation; *pg.* 296, *pg.* 742
Akers, Gregory Neal, Sr VP-Advanced Security Initiatives Global Govt Solutions Grp - Cisco Systems, Inc.; *pg.* 372, *pg.* 240
Akgul, Lina, Dir-Adv & Brand Mgmt-Global - American Express Company; *pg.* 712, *pg.* 1190
Akhavan, Dadi, Co-Founder, Pres & CMO - ConsumerREVIEW, Inc.; *pg.* 1237, *pg.* 193
Akhtar, Manaaz, Reg Dir-Mktg-Europe - Subway Restaurants; *pg.* 1751, *pg.* 356
Aki, Michael, Dir-Digital Mktg - Aeropostale, Inc.; *pg.* 17, *pg.* 1188
Akiha, Nobby, Sr VP-Mktg - Actuate Corporation; *pg.* 342, *pg.* 253
Akin, Lyda, VP-Mktg - David Weekley Homes, LP; *pg.* 78, *pg.* 1704
Akkad, Jay, Product Mgr-Emerging Markets - Google Inc.; *pg.* 1249, *pg.* 153
Aklilu, Addis, Specialist-Corp PR - Charles Schwab & Company, Inc.; *pg.* 734, *pg.* 215
Akman, Kate, Mgr-CA Mktg - Sun Life Financial Inc.; *pg.* 806, *pg.* 1944
Akpaeti, Odudu, Specialist-Affiliate Mktg & CSE - Silver Star Brands; *pg.* 1785, *pg.* 1886
Akpata, Henrietta, Head-IBM Tealeaf Product Mktg - IBM; *pg.* 410, *pg.* 1449
Akre, Ron, Dir-Media Svcs - Central Garden & Pet Company; *pg.* 1475, *pg.* 303
Akuya, Alero, Brand Mgr-Nike Sportswear & NikeFuel - NIKE, Inc.; *pg.* 1812, *pg.* 1492
Al Omari, Waleed, Mgr-EG Country Sls - Hewlett-Packard Company; *pg.* 404, *pg.* 175
Al-Hasan, Shariq, Sr Mgr-Mktg - Expedia, Inc.; *pg.* 1244, *pg.* 1814
Al-Jehani, Hesham, Product Mgr-Mobile - comScore, Inc; *pg.* 1236, *pg.* 1798
Al-Sinjari, Omar, Mgr-Digital Mktg - McKesson Corporation; *pg.* 1560, *pg.* 222
Alaimo, Rosy, Mgr-Natl Sls & Mktg-OnStar & Satellite Radio - General Motors of Canada Ltd.; *pg.* 177, *pg.* 1931
Alam, Zaki, Sr Dir-IT Strategy - Ahold USA, Inc.; *pg.* 1013, *pg.* 1520
Alamad, Denise, Dir-Category Procurement-Mktg - United States Cellular Corporation; *pg.* 1875, *pg.* 594
Alamdari, Fariba E., VP-Mktg & Value Analysis-Boeing Comml Airplanes - The Boeing Company; *pg.* 225, *pg.* 567
Alan, Mark, Product Dir - NIKE, Inc.; *pg.* 1812, *pg.* 1492
Alaniz, Vicki, Sr Dir-Product & Distributor Mktg-North America - Herbalife International of America, Inc.; *pg.* 1541, *pg.* 132
Alarcon, Natasha, Sr Specialist-Mktg - FedEx Express Corporation; *pg.* 1908, *pg.* 1644
Alavi, Taj, Gen Mdsg Mgr-Brand, Adv & Customer Strategy - Intuit Inc.; *pg.* 769, *pg.* 158
Alba, Lauren, Dir-PR & Media Partnerships - The Leading Hotels of the World, Ltd.; *pg.* 1100, *pg.* 1250
Albanese, John, Sr Mgr-Product Intelligence-Xbox - Microsoft Corporation; *pg.* 435, *pg.* 1824
Albanese, Johne, Mng Dir-Homeware & VP-Corp Mktg - Hooker Furniture Corporation; *pg.* 928, *pg.* 1788
Albanese, Valerie, Sr VP-Brand Creative - Lifetime Entertainment Services LLC; *pg.* 296, *pg.* 1251
Albano, Jennifer, Sr Mgr-Reputation Comm - Pfizer Inc.; *pg.* 1581, *pg.* 1278
Albano, Lauren, Brand Mgr-KO Energy - The Coca-Cola Company; *pg.* 240, *pg.* 493
Albano, Patrick, VP-Sls-Mobile, Social & Innovation & Head-Adv Solutions-EMEA - Yahoo! Inc.; *pg.* 1289, *pg.* 289
Albano, Paul, Sr Mgr-Market & Competitive Intelligence - Canon U.S.A., Inc.; *pg.* 1404, *pg.* 1178
Albaugh, Caitlin, Mgr-PR - adidas America Inc.; *pg.* 1803, *pg.* 1500
Albaugh, Kelli, Assoc Mgr-Mktg - PepsiCo, Inc.; *pg.* 259, *pg.* 1327
Albelo, Juan, Sr VP-Sls - PeopleFluent; *pg.* 453, *pg.* 853
Alberding, Chris, VP-Product Mgmt - FairPoint Communications, Inc.; *pg.* 1871, *pg.* 1366
Alberico, Thomas, Sr VP-Sls & Mktg - Laird & Company, Inc.; *pg.* 1966, *pg.* 1119
Albers, Mandy, Sr Mgr-Comm - Tremor Video; *pg.* 682, *pg.* 1305
Albert, Alana, Sr Mgr-ECommerce-Direct Response - NBTY, Inc.; *pg.* 1572, *pg.* 1338
Albert, Gabrielle, Dir-Adv & Promos Procurement - Bacardi USA, Inc.; *pg.* 1956, *pg.* 417
Albert-Nelson, Ilene, Dir-Mktg - Pentel of America, Ltd.; *pg.* 453, *pg.* 295
Alberti, Peter, Head-Mktg-Global - Merck & Co., Inc.; *pg.* 1566, *pg.* 1077
Alberti, Sue, Sr VP-Mktg - Devon Energy Corporation; *pg.* 976, *pg.* 1704
Alberti, Sue, Sr VP-Mktg - Devon Energy Corporation; *pg.* 975, *pg.* 1485
Alberto, Eduardo L., Sr Dir-Global Mktg & Strategy - Eli Lilly and Company; *pg.* 1527, *pg.* 684
Alberts, Brad, Chief Revenue Officer & Exec VP - Dallas Stars L.P.; *pg.* 543, *pg.* 1697
Alberts, Caroline, Mgr-Leisure Sls - Air New Zealand Ltd. (U.S.A.); *pg.* 1897, *pg.* 78
Alberts, Mark, Product Mgr & Specialist-Market Dev - Dow AgroSciences LLC; *pg.* 1156, *pg.* 684
Albertson, Dave, Dir-Field Mktg - General Growth Properties, Inc.; *pg.* 1093, *pg.* 574
Alberty, Scott, Product Mgr - Steelcase Inc.; *pg.* 475, *pg.* 889
Albiero, Michael, Dir-Creative Svcs & Brand Mgmt-Natl - American Lung Association; *pg.* 129, *pg.* 395
Albin-Najera, Susie, Mgr-Destination Mktg-Mexico, Global Accounts & Airlines - Pleasant Holidays LLC; *pg.* 1919, *pg.* 307
Albracht, Meredith, Mgr-Adv - John Deere Consumer & Commercial Equipment, Inc.; *pg.* 705, *pg.* 1360
Albrecht, Amy, Mgr-Content Mktg - McKesson Corporation; *pg.* 1560, *pg.* 222
Albrecht, Beth, VP-Mktg-Western Reg - Anthem, Inc.; *pg.* 1192, *pg.* 683
Albrecht, Joanne, Strategist-Mktg Comm - CCA Industries, Inc.; *pg.* 503, *pg.* 1114
Albrecht, Mark, Sr Dir-Mktg Comm - Canadian Imperial Bank of Commerce; *pg.* 729, *pg.* 1935
Albright, Paul, VP-Sls - The Euclid Chemical Company; *pg.* 81, *pg.* 1430
Albright, Paul, Sr Mgr-Social Media Mktg - Safeway Inc.; *pg.* 1032, *pg.* 184
Albritten, Joy, Mgr-Visual Mktg - Big 5 Sporting Goods Corporation; *pg.* 1827, *pg.* 78
Albritton, Kevin, Exec VP-Sls & Mktg - Brookshire Grocery Company; *pg.* 1016, *pg.* 1748
Alcaine, Jose, Dir-Category Mgmt & Mktg - Safeway Inc.; *pg.* 1032, *pg.* 184
Alcantara, Adriana, Dir-Production & Mktg - Scripps Networks Interactive, Inc.; *pg.* 1279, *pg.* 1638
Alcantara, Glory, Reg Mgr-Mktg - General Mills, Inc.; *pg.* 828, *pg.* 933
Alcazar, Karla, Head-Reg Mktg-Bio Medicines LACAM - Eli Lilly and Company; *pg.* 1527, *pg.* 684
Alcocer, Rick, Sr VP-Fresh Sls - A. Duda & Sons Inc.; *pg.* 835, *pg.* 457
Alcorn, Dawn, Sr Mgr-Mktg - PetSmart, Inc.; *pg.* 1481, *pg.* 18
Alcuri, Matt, VP & Product Mgr-US Small Bus - MasterCard Worldwide Inc.; *pg.* 780, *pg.* 988
Alda, Donna, VP-Telemarketing Sls - Cablevision Systems Corporation; *pg.* 272, *pg.* 1141
Aldanese, Christina, Reg Dir-Travel Trade Mktg-Western Reg - Hawaii Visitors & Convention Bureau; *pg.* 994, *pg.* 543
Aldaz, Gina Petrelli, Dir-Mktg - Naples Daily News; *pg.* 1666, *pg.* 451
Alderson, Kris, Sr Mgr-Mktg - Bradley Corporation; *pg.* 71, *pg.* 1870
Alderson, Rikke, Sr Dir-Digital Mktg-Omni-Commerce - Big 5 Sporting Goods Corporation; *pg.* 1827, *pg.* 78
Alderson, Valerie, Sr Mgr-Mktg - Provide Commerce, Inc.; *pg.* 1276, *pg.* 206
Aldous, Ian, Dir-Creative - Apple Inc.; *pg.* 350, *pg.* 73
Aldous, Stephen, Product Mgr - Hewlett-Packard Company; *pg.* 404, *pg.* 175
Aldred, Duncan, VP-Sls & Mktg-GMC - General Motors Company; *pg.* 175, *pg.* 881
Aldrich, Alison, Dir-Brand Mktg - Carbonite, Inc.; *pg.* 368, *pg.* 792
Aldrich, Jason, Mgr-Product & Bus Dev - SOR, Inc.; *pg.* 1306, *pg.* 716
Aldrich, Joanne, Mgr-Mktg - United States Postal Service; *pg.* 1009, *pg.* 406
Aldrich, Matt, Dir-Mktg - Videojet Technologies Inc.; *pg.* 489, *pg.* 671
Aldrich, Steven, Mgr-Email Mktg - Birchbox; *pg.* 1762, *pg.* 1203
Aldridge, Kate, VP-Corp Comm - Travelport Limited; *pg.* 1925, *pg.* 521
Aleardi, Cindi, Sls Mgr-Private Brands - Acme Markets, Inc.; *pg.* 1012, *pg.* 1549
Alegnani, Mandy, Sr Mgr-Mktg Media - Hotels.com, L.P.; *pg.* 1257, *pg.* 1682
Aleksey, Amanda, Coord-Mktg & Media Buyer - Penguin Random House; *pg.* 1675, *pg.* 1276
Aleksich, Steve, Sr Mgr-Shopper Mktg - Del Monte Foods, Inc.; *pg.* 852, *pg.* 304
Aleman, Tricia, Exec Dir-Mktg Comm - University Health System; *pg.* 1604, *pg.* 1743
Aleo, Lindsay, Dir-Sls-Global - CBS Interactive, Inc.; *pg.* 369, *pg.* 215
Alepin, Suzanne, Reg Dir-Mktg - Manulife Financial Corporation; *pg.* 778, *pg.* 1939
Alesia, Daniel, Mgr-Shopper Mktg Process - The Kraft Heinz Company; *pg.* 871, *pg.* 641
Alessandrini, Steven M., Sr Dir-PR - Wyndham Worldwide Corporation; *pg.* 1119, *pg.* 1107
Alex, Fiz, Reg VP-Sls & Mktg-Caribbean & Latin America - Marriott International, Inc.; *pg.* 1102, *pg.* 764
Alex, Robin, Sr Mgr-Shopper Insights-Target, Safeway & Albertson - The Hershey Co.; *pg.* 1855, *pg.* 1538
Alexaitis, Wendy, Mgr-Mktg - Adecco USA, Inc.; *pg.* 342, *pg.* 1178
Alexakos, Lee, Corp VP-Mktg & Adv - Cedar Point; *pg.* 537, *pg.* 1472
Alexander, Adriana S., Analyst-Mktg - FedEx Express Corporation; *pg.* 1908, *pg.* 1644
Alexander, Alisa, Mgr-Mktg-Social Media Channel - Intuit Inc.; *pg.* 769, *pg.* 158
Alexander, Bill, VP-Production & Bus Dev - Atlus USA, Inc.; *pg.* 949, *pg.* 107

First page reference indicates Business Class Edition
Second page reference indicates Geographic Edition

Alexander, Brian, Exec VP-Sls - Swift Transportation; pg. 1924, pg. 20
Alexander, David, Mgr-Sls - Detex Corporation; pg. 633, pg. 1728
Alexander, Felicia, Sr Dir-Bus Dev - Demand Media, Inc.; pg. 1238, pg. 273
Alexander, Heather, Mgr-Pub & Media Rels - FedEx Corporation; pg. 1907, pg. 1642
Alexander, Jannine, Mgr-Recruiting-Worldwide Adv - Amazon.com, Inc.; pg. 1226, pg. 1831
Alexander, Jerome, Mgr-Field Mktg - NetApp, Inc.; pg. 444, pg. 287
Alexander, Jill Haynes, Sr Dir-Corp Comm - Isle of Capri Casinos, Inc.; pg. 553, pg. 998
Alexander, John, Product Mgr - Eaton Corporation; pg. 1331, pg. 1429
Alexander, Kara, Product Mgr-Mktg-Global - Belkin International, Inc.; pg. 361, pg. 182
Alexander, Kelly, Mgr-Mktg - United Parcel Service, Inc.; pg. 1928, pg. 522
Alexander, Kim, Mgr-Feline Mktg - IDEXX Laboratories, Inc.; pg. 1543, pg. 753
Alexander, Margaret, Dir-Respiratory Mktg - Boehringer Ingelheim Pharmaceuticals, Inc.; pg. 1507, pg. 368
Alexander, Marin, Mgr-Solutions Mktg - CDW Corporation; pg. 370, pg. 663
Alexander, Paul, Chief Mktg & Comm Officer - Eastern Bank Corporation; pg. 745, pg. 793
Alexander, Paula, Sr Mgr-Market - Honeywell International Inc.; pg. 407, pg. 1088
Alexander, Renee, Dir-Mdsg - Sabre Holdings Corporation; pg. 1922, pg. 1745
Alexander, Tara, Analyst-Mktg Comm - CA Technologies; pg. 366, pg. 1168
Alexander, Vahn, Assoc-Sls-REALTORS - Berkshire Hathaway Home Services; pg. 1081, pg. 200
Alexander, Whit, VP-Guest Plng & Loyalty Mktg - Target Corporation; pg. 1786, pg. 942
Alexander-Iverson, Crystal, Mgr-Retail Channel Mktg - ASICS America Corporation; pg. 1826, pg. 106
Alexeeva, Alexandra, Specialist-Comm & Social Media-Brand & Corp Comm Grp - Hitachi America, Ltd.; pg. 642, pg. 1344
Alexion-Tiernan, Karri, Dir-Product Mktg - Microsoft Corporation; pg. 435, pg. 1824
Alferness, Jon, Head-Mobile Ads & Dir-Product Mgmt - Google Inc.; pg. 1249, pg. 153
Alfieri, Amy, Mgr-Mktg Res - FedEx Corporation; pg. 1907, pg. 1642
Alfieri, John, VP-Sls & Mktg - Lista International Corporation; pg. 934, pg. 825
Alfieri, John, VP-Sls-SWS - Stanley Black & Decker, Inc.; pg. 1063, pg. 358
Alfishawi, Thabet, Product Mgr - Google Inc.; pg. 1249, pg. 153
Alfonsi, Richard, VP-Online Sls-Global - Twitter, Inc.; pg. 1285, pg. 228
Alford, Blair, VP-Sls & Mktg - Unified Brands Inc.; pg. 1385, pg. 970
Alford, Jordin, Sr Mgr-Global Strategic Insights Global Strategic Mktg - Johnson & Johnson Vision Care, Inc.; pg. 1552, pg. 434
Alford, Naomi, Asst Mgr-Media Content Plng & Distr - General Mills, Inc.; pg. 828, pg. 933
Alford, Nile, Mgr-Mktg - Comcast Corporation; pg. 276, pg. 1560
Alfred, Jason, Sr Specialist-Online Media - Nordstrom, Inc.; pg. 1779, pg. 1837
Algar, Liza, Exec Dir-Mktg - Chronicle Books; pg. 1627, pg. 216
Algeo, Misha, Mgr-Mktg-Fisher-Price-North American Mktg Team - MATTEL, INC.; pg. 962, pg. 81
Algie, Jenna, Brand Mgr-Miracle-Gro Plant Food - The Scotts Miracle-Gro Company; pg. 1799, pg. 1459
Algieri, Lori, Coord-Mktg - Simon Property Group, Inc.; pg. 1112, pg. 690
Algranati, David, Sr VP-Product Innovation & Custom Res - Rentrak Corporation; pg. 306, pg. 1506
Algstam, Joakim, Mgr-Product Mktg-Quad Core H Processors & Intel Iris - Intel Corporation; pg. 645, pg. 266
Alguire, John, Mgr-Advanced Product Mktg-Global - Ford Motor Company; pg. 172, pg. 876
Alharbi, Alaa, Product Mgr-Interior Paints Category - Jotun Paints, Inc.; pg. 1443, pg. 742
Ali, Afzal, Dir-Mktg - Deublin Company; pg. 78, pg. 666
Ali, Arshed, Mgr-Mktg-Web Mktg - Cisco Systems, Inc.; pg. 372, pg. 240
Ali, Ismail, Engr-Technical Mktg - Cisco Systems, Inc.; pg. 372, pg. 240
Ali, Sultana, Dir-PR - Liquidity Services, Inc.; pg. 1263, pg. 401
Ali-Hassan, Nader, Dir-Digital Mktg - The Progressive Corporation; pg. 1214, pg. 1463
Alicea, David, Mgr-Product Delivery - Pennsylvania State Lottery; pg. 1003, pg. 1552
Alix, Lindsay, Specialist-Adv - The TJX Companies, Inc.; pg. 1788, pg. 822
Alkaff, Najihah, Specialist-Brand Mktg - Chevron Corporation; pg. 974, pg. 259
Alkalay, Dani, Product Mgr - Azonix Corporation; pg. 1400, pg. 788
Alkire, Sinclaire, Dir-Mktg & Enrollment Res - Pratt Institute; pg. 606, pg. 1146
Allan, Laura, Coord-Creative Studio - TD Ameritrade Holding Corporation; pg. 808, pg. 1018
Allan, Robert, Head-Product Mktg - Maserati North America, Inc.; pg. 183, pg. 1060
Allan, Scott, VP-Sls-Western Reg - RealPage, Inc.; pg. 1277, pg. 1669
Allara, Nina, Sr Dir-Field Mktg - salesforce.com, inc.; pg. 1278, pg. 226
Allard, Steve, Product Mgr - FLEXcon Corporation; pg. 1457, pg. 844
Allbritton, Leigh, Dir-Mktg Events & Strategy - The Home Depot, Inc.; pg. 1050, pg. 510
Allcott, Truitt, Dir-Investor & Media Rels - Owens & Minor, Inc.; pg. 1579, pg. 1795
Alldred, Kathleen, Mgr-Mktg - Teachers Insurance & Annuity Association - College Retirement Equities Fund; pg. 1219, pg. 1297
Allee, Bethany, Sr Mgr-Americas OEM & GSI Mktg - Brocade Communications Systems, Inc.; pg. 365, pg. 239
AlLee, Guy, Product Mgr-Internet of Things Security - Intel Corporation; pg. 645, pg. 266
Allen, Amy, Dir-Restaurant Mktg - Chick-fil-A, Inc.; pg. 1721, pg. 492
Allen, Amy, Sr Mgr-Mktg-Hospitality - Vail Resorts, Inc.; pg. 1117, pg. 313
Allen, Ashley, Dir-Audience Ad Product Solutions - Time Inc.; pg. 1693, pg. 1300
Allen, Bill, Mgr-Software Product-Mobile Apps Grp - Bose Corporation; pg. 626, pg. 820
Allen, Blythe, Specialist-Mktg - Aflac Incorporated; pg. 1188, pg. 527
Allen, Carl, Mgr-Digital Mktg - The Walt Disney Company; pg. 317, pg. 52
Allen, Chelsea, Head-PR & Events - Restoration Hardware Holdings, Inc.; pg. 1060, pg. 70
Allen, Christi, Coord-Proposal & Mktg - Fluor Corporation; pg. 82, pg. 1719
Allen, Christina, Dir-Product Mgmt - LinkedIn Corporation; pg. 1262, pg. 160
Allen, Christine, Dir-Mktg, Comm & Membership Sls - Toll Brothers, Inc.; pg. 115, pg. 1541
Allen, Christine, Brand Mgr - United Parcel Service, Inc.; pg. 1928, pg. 522
Allen, Christopher, District Mgr-Sls - T-Mobile US, Inc.; pg. 676, pg. 1816
Allen, Daphnee, Mgr-Mktg-Calvin Klein Men's Fragrances-Coty Prestige - Coty, Inc.; pg. 506, pg. 1219
Allen, David, Sr VP-Sls & Mktg - Eight O'Clock Coffee; pg. 250, pg. 1086
Allen, David, Mgr-Sls - House of Raeford Farms, Inc.; pg. 864, pg. 1386
Allen, Denise, Sr Mgr-Comm Svc - The Hain Celestial Group, Inc.; pg. 860, pg. 1172
Allen, Don, Sr Dir-Technical Ops - Zulily; pg. 1792, pg. 1843
Allen, Drew, Sr Mgr-Mktg - The Coca-Cola Company; pg. 240, pg. 493
Allen, Drew, Sr Mgr-Mktg - Coca-Cola Refreshments USA, Inc.; pg. 247, pg. 500
Allen, Duane, Dir-Trade Mktg - Reckitt Benckiser Inc.; pg. 1136, pg. 1105
Allen, Gavin, VP-Mktg - Mercedes-Benz Canada Inc.; pg. 184, pg. 1940
Allen, Graham, Sr Dir-Product Mgmt - INCONTACT, INC.; pg. 413, pg. 1752
Allen, Jasmin, Sr Mgr-Digital Mktg - Ann Inc.; pg. 18, pg. 1195
Allen, Jason, Dir-Mktg - ConAgra Foods, Inc.; pg. 826, pg. 1014
Allen, Jayson, Sr Mgr-UX Design-Traffic, Ads & Monetization - eBay Inc.; pg. 1240, pg. 243
Allen, Jeff, Dir-Product Mktg - Adobe Systems Incorporated; pg. 342, pg. 235
Allen, Jeff, Project Mgr-Talent Acq & Mgr-Social Media - DISH Network Corporation; pg. 283, pg. 325
Allen, Jessica, Coord-Premium Seat Sls - Live Nation Entertainment, Inc.; pg. 558, pg. 47
Allen, Joanna, Dir-US Mktg-Burger King Customer Team - The Coca-Cola Company; pg. 240, pg. 493
Allen, Joshua, Mgr-Mktg - Staples; pg. 474, pg. 313
Allen, Katie, Mgr-Digital Mktg - Brown-Forman Corporation; pg. 1958, pg. 732
Allen, Katie, Head-Google Brand Mktg Comm - Google Inc.; pg. 1249, pg. 153
Allen, Kelly, Project Mgr-Mktg - Stryker Corporation; pg. 1598, pg. 894
Allen, Kimberly, Dir-Media Rels - Massachusetts Institute of Technology; pg. 604, pg. 809
Allen, Mark, VP-Sls, Mktg & Svcs - Quorum Information Technologies Inc.; pg. 458, pg. 1904
Allen, Matt, VP-Sls - Elizabeth Arden, Inc.; pg. 507, pg. 448
Allen, Matt, Mgr-Mktg-Food Svcs Beverage & Natural Foods - The J.M. Smucker Company; pg. 865, pg. 1468
Allen, Michael, Sr VP-Digital Products & Emerging Tech - National Basketball Association; pg. 566, pg. 1264
Allen, Mike, Mgr-Sls-Malt-O-Meal Company - Post Consumer Brands; pg. 833, pg. 927
Allen, Nicole, Dir-Mktg & Promos - Ticketmaster Entertainment LLC; pg. 1284, pg. 48
Allen, Quincy, CMO, Chief Strategy Officer & Sr VP - Unisys Corporation; pg. 487, pg. 1517
Allen, Robert, Sr Dir-Digital Innovations Grp - AstraZeneca Pharmaceuticals LP; pg. 1497, pg. 389
Allen, Robert, Mgr-Digital Mktg - Conde Nast Publications, Inc.; pg. 1629, pg. 1217
Allen, Sharon, Sr VP-Mktg Strategy-NBC Entertainment - NBC Universal, Inc.; pg. 300, pg. 1266
Allen, Tony, Mgr-Product & Process - Glen Raven, Inc.; pg. 693, pg. 1373
Allen, Tricia, Mgr-Mktg Plng - The Toronto-Dominion Bank; pg. 810, pg. 1945
Allen, Tui, Sr Product Mgr - Blackbaud, Inc.; pg. 361, pg. 1613
Allen, Vince, Sr Dir-Mktg Creative Svcs - West Marine, Inc.; pg. 1712, pg. 305
Allenbaugh, Martin, Sr Mgr-Mktg - T. Rowe Price Group Inc.; pg. 808, pg. 759
Allensworth, Kylie, Mgr-Mktg - Nordstrom, Inc.; pg. 1779, pg. 1837
Aller, Kateland, Strategist-eMarketing Media - Williams-Sonoma, Inc.; pg. 1140, pg. 234
Allessio, Carol, Asst VP-Adv - Toll Brothers, Inc.; pg. 115, pg. 1541
Alleva, John, VP-Digital Sls Plng - NBC Universal, Inc.; pg. 300, pg. 1266
Allexandre, Chris, Sr VP-Sls, Mktg & Supply Chain-Global - Fairchild Semiconductor Corporation; pg. 638, pg. 245
Allexant, Laetitia, Dir-Mktg-Nestle Pure Life, Resource & Splash - Nestle Waters North America Inc.; pg. 257, pg. 375
Alleyne, Ayanna, Mgr-Social Media Specialist & Community - Marriott International, Inc.; pg. 1102, pg. 764
Allgaier, Gina, Dir-Mktg-Walmart Team - The Kraft Heinz Company; pg. 871, pg. 641
Allgeier, Joanie, Mgr-Adv Sls - Louisville Convention & Visitors Bureau; pg. 998, pg. 736
Alli, Bibi N., Sr Mgr-Consumer Insights-Whirlpool, Maytag, Amana & Gladiator - Whirlpool Corporation; pg. 62, pg. 872
Allibhai, Mohamed, Product Mgr-Search & Analytics - DealerTrack Holdings, Inc.; pg. 743, pg. 1172
Allison, Beth, Dir-ECommerce Sls & Mktg - Moen Incorporated; pg. 1056, pg. 1468
Allison, Bob, Dir-Mktg Support - Safeway Inc.; pg. 1032, pg. 184
Allison, Kent, Dir-Product Dev - Dell Inc.; pg. 383, pg. 1737
Allison, Lane, Program Mgr-Adv - Sprint Corporation; pg. 1874, pg. 719
Allison, Lezlie, Sr Mgr-Mktg, Program & Pro Svcs - NetApp, Inc.; pg. 444, pg. 287
Allison, Lindsey, Brand Mgr-Denim & Supply-Wholesale - Ralph Lauren Corporation; pg. 46, pg. 1284
Allison, Marc, Sr VP-Mortgage & ABS Sls Europe - Jefferies

Group, Inc.; *pg.* 772, *pg.* 1246
Allison, Mike, Mgr-Creative-Mdsg - Raley's Inc.; *pg.* 1031, *pg.* 305
Allison, Renata Franco, Mgr-Multicultural Mktg - Cox Communications, Inc.; *pg.* 279, *pg.* 501
Allison, Richard, Bus Mgr - Educational Media Foundation; *pg.* 284, *pg.* 194
Allison, Todd, Dir-Mktg - Fruit of the Loom, Inc.; *pg.* 41, *pg.* 725
Allman, Tyler, Product Mgr-Compuware Mainframe - Compuware Corporation; *pg.* 379, *pg.* 879
Allmann, Andy, Dir-Customer Engagement & Partnership Mktg - Southwest Airlines Co.; *pg.* 1923, *pg.* 1687
Allmann, Ed, VP-Sls & Mktg - Turning Stone Resort Casino LLC; *pg.* 1117, *pg.* 1348
Allocco, Mark, Assoc Dir-Mktg Comm & Brand - Verizon Communications Inc.; *pg.* 1875, *pg.* 1309
Alloway, Debbie, Dir-Mktg Capabilities - Wendy's International, Inc.; *pg.* 1755, *pg.* 1451
Allred, Kathryn, Sr Mgr-Integrated Mktg - ABC, Inc.; *pg.* 268, *pg.* 1185
Allsop, Bob, Mgr-Global Mktg-Powder - Nordson Corporation; *pg.* 1365, *pg.* 1480
Allumbaugh, Ginny, Mgr-Franchise Mktg - Godfather's Pizza, Inc.; *pg.* 1729, *pg.* 1015
Allwood, Amanda, Mgr-Promos & Event Mktg - Sirius XM Holdings Inc.; *pg.* 308, *pg.* 1292
Allwood, Claudia, Dir-Digital Mktg-US - Benefit Cosmetics LLC; *pg.* 501, *pg.* 213
Alm, Christina, Mgr-Digital Mktg - General Mills, Inc.; *pg.* 828, *pg.* 933
Almario-Tanlapco, Trina, Mgr-Mktg - Johnson & Johnson; *pg.* 1549, *pg.* 1091
Almasri, Mazen, Dir-Mktg-Africa - PepsiCo, Inc.; *pg.* 259, *pg.* 1327
Almazan, Denise, Dir-PR - Children's Hospital Los Angeles; *pg.* 275, *pg.* 128
Almeida, Alicia, Sr Mgr-Mktg Promos - The Walt Disney Company; *pg.* 317, *pg.* 52
Almeida, Angelica, Sr Mgr-Mktg - Bulova Corporation; *pg.* 2, *pg.* 1356
Almeida, Chris, VP-Shopper Mktg-Core Bus & Loyalty - Safeway Inc.; *pg.* 1032, *pg.* 184
Almeraz, Laurie E., Mgr-Mktg - Honeywell International Inc.; *pg.* 407, *pg.* 1088
Almond, Amanda, Sr Product Mgr - E.T. Browne Drug Company, Inc.; *pg.* 509, *pg.* 1060
Almond, Jud, Dir-Local, Classified & Legal Sls - The Washington Times, LLC; *pg.* 1701, *pg.* 408
Almquist, Magnus, VP-Sls-Worldwide - ISC8; *pg.* 1350, *pg.* 71
Almquist, Sharon, Supvr-Global Mktg - 3M Company; *pg.* 1142, *pg.* 956
Alo-Mendosa, Shannon, Mgr-Reg Sls-Design Engrg & Sourcing - Penton Media, Inc.; *pg.* 1676, *pg.* 719
Alonso Viola, Ana Maria, Asst VP-Mktg-Global - L'Oreal USA; *pg.* 514, *pg.* 1252
Alonso, Alex, VP-Mktg - Telemundo Network Inc.; *pg.* 311, *pg.* 430
Alonso, Gabe, Head-Social & Digital Communities-Nike Running-Global - NIKE, Inc.; *pg.* 1812, *pg.* 1492
Alonso, George, Sr Dir-Mktg - Hewlett-Packard Company; *pg.* 404, *pg.* 175
Alonso, Nora, Sr Mgr-Comm - Tupperware Brands Corporation; *pg.* 1139, *pg.* 456
Alonso, Rodrigo, Mgr-US Country Mktg - Michelin North America Inc.; *pg.* 1886, *pg.* 1618
Alonso, Staci Columbo, CMO & Sr VP-Mktg - Station Casinos, Inc.; *pg.* 585, *pg.* 1030
Alosso, Jackie, Brand Mgr-Innovation - Welch Foods Inc.; *pg.* 909, *pg.* 815
Aloula, Gedioen, VP & Head-US Consumer Mktg - Visa U.S.A., Inc.; *pg.* 817, *pg.* 231
Alpanian, Alan, Chief Creative Officer - TEN: The Enthusiast Network; *pg.* 1691, *pg.* 1298
Alper-Leroux, Cecile, VP-Product Strategy - The Ultimate Software Group, Inc.; *pg.* 486, *pg.* 479
Alperin, Bruce, Sr Dir-Mktg-Facility Svcs-Education Sector - Aramark; *pg.* 1013, *pg.* 1558
Alpers, Tim, Dir-Lenovo Enterprise Bus Grp Solutions Mgmt & Mktg - Lenovo Group Ltd; *pg.* 427, *pg.* 1384
Alpert, Celina, Mgr-Mktg-Cultural Branding - PepsiCo, Inc.; *pg.* 259, *pg.* 1327
Alpert, Kathy, Specialist-Mktg Comm - W.R. Grace & Co.; *pg.* 123, *pg.* 810
Alpert, Michael, VP-Leather & Sls Ops - Buckman; *pg.* 1150, *pg.* 1641
Alrawi, Ahmad, Head-Global Transplant Franchise & Sr Dir-New Products - Alexion Pharmaceuticals, Inc.; *pg.* 1489, *pg.* 341
Alsdorf, Lisa, Specialist-Mktg Comm-Fall Protection - Honeywell International Inc.; *pg.* 407, *pg.* 1088
Alsikafi, Saboora, Brand Mgr-Candy - Mondelez International; *pg.* 877, *pg.* 1344
Alston, Ashley, Mgr-Mdsg & Mktg - Birchbox; *pg.* 1762, *pg.* 1203
Alstromer, Gustaf, Product Mgr-Growth - Airbnb, Inc.; *pg.* 1226, *pg.* 211
Alsup, Matt, Mgr-Digital Mktg - Hubbell Power Systems, Inc.; *pg.* 643, *pg.* 1614
Altan, Dagzen, Assoc Dir-Digital Mktg & Optimization - AT&T Inc.; *pg.* 1868, *pg.* 358
Altaras, Marian, Sr Mgr-Mktg-Camera, Photo & Video - Amazon.com, Inc.; *pg.* 1226, *pg.* 1831
Altenberger, Brian P., Dir-Global Product Line-Fuel Handling - Delphi Automotive LLP; *pg.* 204, *pg.* 910
Altenburg, Lauren, Coord-eMail Mktg - Ann Inc.; *pg.* 18, *pg.* 1195
Alter, Heather, Sr Mgr-Digital & Social Mktg - Cisco Systems, Inc.; *pg.* 372, *pg.* 240
Alter, Stephen, Dir-Adv, Sponsorship & Meetings - American Symphony Orchestra League; *pg.* 528, *pg.* 1194
Altergott, David, Designer-Supervising Adv - The Bradford Group; *pg.* 1763, *pg.* 637
Altergott, Missy, VP-Corp Mktg - Level 3 Communications, Inc.; *pg.* 1262, *pg.* 312
Alterman, Randi, Sr Mgr-Mktg & Comm - GE Capital; *pg.* 761, *pg.* 362
Althoff, Todd, VP-Mktg & Product Dev - Royal Consumer Information Products Inc.; *pg.* 463, *pg.* 1122
Altizer, Lance, VP-Mktg-Worldwide Flat Glass - Guardian Industries Corp.; *pg.* 85, *pg.* 869
Altman, Lori, VP-Adv - Gannett Co., Inc.; *pg.* 1643, *pg.* 1790
Altman, Pat, Assoc Dir-Mktg - Breast Cancer Research Foundation; *pg.* 134, *pg.* 1206
Altman, Sam, Exec VP-Mobile Products & Strategy & Dir - GREEN DOT CORPORATION; *pg.* 763, *pg.* 180
Altschuler, Jay, Head-Global Media - Samsung Electronics America, Inc.; *pg.* 669, *pg.* 1115
Altshuler, Janis, VP-Direct Mktg - Rooms To Go.com, Inc.; *pg.* 941, *pg.* 468
Altuch, Meryl, VP-Mktg & Brand Strategy - Juvenile Diabetes Research Foundation International; *pg.* 145, *pg.* 1247
Aluia, Mace, Mgr-Sponsorship Sls - Atlanta Falcons Football Club, LLC; *pg.* 530, *pg.* 532
Aluigi, Franco, Product Mgr - Santinelli International Inc.; *pg.* 1395, *pg.* 1165
Alutto, Kerrie, VP & Mgr-Digital Mktg - JPMorgan Chase & Co.; *pg.* 772, *pg.* 1246
Alva, Heath, Sr Dir-Product Mgmt - Smarter Travel Media LLC; *pg.* 1687, *pg.* 801
Alvarado, Azucena, Coord-Mktg - Health Net, Inc.; *pg.* 1540, *pg.* 308
Alvarado, Delia C., Mgr-Adv-Tablet Media & App Lab - Hearst Magazines; *pg.* 1649, *pg.* 1239
Alvarado, Gustavo, Sr Mgr-Mktg - Microsoft Corporation; *pg.* 435, *pg.* 1824
Alvarado, Gustavo, Sr Mgr-Marcom-Global - Xbox; *pg.* 970, *pg.* 1829
Alvarado, John, VP-Brand Mktg - Crown Imports LLC; *pg.* 248, *pg.* 572
Alvarez, Christine, VP-Integrated Mktg-Ad Sls - Discovery Communications, Inc.; *pg.* 282, *pg.* 777
Alvarez, Diane, Dir-Media Sls - Madison Square Garden Network; *pg.* 297, *pg.* 1255
Alvarez, Kerry, Sr Mgr-Client Mktg & Design - Infogroup; *pg.* 769, *pg.* 1038
Alvarez, Maria, Mgr-Sls Admin - Chicago Convention & Tourism Bureau; *pg.* 990, *pg.* 569
Alvarez, Mercedes, Sr VP & Dir-Mktg - EagleBank; *pg.* 745, *pg.* 762
Alvarez, Michael, Sr VP-Natl Sls - Telemundo Network Inc.; *pg.* 311, *pg.* 430
Alvarez, Nathalie, Dir-Mktg - A&E Television Networks, LLC; *pg.* 267, *pg.* 1185
Alvarez, Priscilla, Sr Mgr-Adv - Nintendo of America, Inc.; *pg.* 965, *pg.* 1829
Alvarez, Rosa M., Mgr-Mktg - The Boeing Company; *pg.* 225, *pg.* 567
Alvarez, Ryan, VP-Mktg - VelaTel Global Communications, Inc.; *pg.* 685, *pg.* 210
Alvarez, Santiago, Mgr-Technical Mktg Engrg Grp - Cisco Systems, Inc.; *pg.* 372, *pg.* 240
Alvarez, Sarah, Mgr-Pub Sector, Labor Mktg & Event - Aetna Inc.; *pg.* 1187, *pg.* 351
Alves, Jessica, Mgr-eMail Mktg - CVS Health Corporation; *pg.* 1765, *pg.* 1610
Alves, Kim, Dir-Intl Mktg & PR - J. Crew Group, Inc.; *pg.* 1773, *pg.* 1245
Alves, Rachel, Assoc Mgr-Digital Mktg - Ubisoft Inc.; *pg.* 589, *pg.* 229
Alvey, Ed, Dir-Mktg Strategy & Plng - Humana, Inc.; *pg.* 1204, *pg.* 734
Alviano, Danielle, Dir-Integrated Mktg - Toys "R" Us, Inc.; *pg.* 968, *pg.* 1130
Alvino, Katie, Dir-Product & Brand Mktg-Blizzard, Treats & Cakes - Dairy Queen Corporate Store; *pg.* 1724, *pg.* 932
Alvino, Katie, Dir-Product & Brand Mktg-Blizzard, Treats & Cakes - International Dairy Queen, Inc.; *pg.* 1732, *pg.* 938
Alward, Mark, Mgr-Aftersales & Brand Mgr Quality - General Motors Company; *pg.* 175, *pg.* 881
Alwran, Tim, Gen Mgr-Sls - WTVD-TV Inc.; *pg.* 323, *pg.* 1372
Alzamora, Mike, Sr Mgr-Comm-Global - Tenneco, Inc.; *pg.* 985, *pg.* 625
Alzayyat, Abdulilah, Engr-Sls - Bosch Rexroth Corporation; *pg.* 1319, *pg.* 1516
Alzola, Lauren, Brand Mktg Mgr - Arby's Restaurant Group, Inc.; *pg.* 1014, *pg.* 488
Alzona, Katherine, VP-Creative Svcs - Enesco, LLC; *pg.* 1124, *pg.* 620
Amacher, Gale, Mgr-Sls - Englefield Oil Company; *pg.* 976, *pg.* 1455
Amadio, Allan, Specialist-Global Email & Mktg Automation - Brady Corporation; *pg.* 363, *pg.* 1873
Amaditz, Michael, Dir-Creative - Save the Children Federation, Inc.; *pg.* 156, *pg.* 384
Amado, Alex, Sr Dir-Creative & Media - Adobe Systems Incorporated; *pg.* 342, *pg.* 235
Amado, Gerardo, Mgr-Indirect Sectors Mktg-Americas - Shell Oil Company; *pg.* 984, *pg.* 1714
Amador, Christy, Sr Mgr-Comm-Coca-Cola Ambassador Program - The Coca-Cola Company; *pg.* 240, *pg.* 493
Amador, Rey, Mgr-Mktg - Selective Insurance Group, Inc.; *pg.* 1216, *pg.* 1045
Amand, Gorm, Sr Mgr & Head-Global Discipline-UI - Nuance Communications, Inc.; *pg.* 447, *pg.* 806
Amante, Greg, Mgr-Mktg - Hologic, Inc.; *pg.* 1416, *pg.* 784
Amar, Jason, Brand Mgr - Bimbo Bakeries USA; *pg.* 840, *pg.* 151
Amaral, Jenna, Mgr-Search Engine Mktg - Hilton Worldwide, Inc.; *pg.* 1094, *pg.* 1791
Amat, Ed, Exec VP-Sls & Mktg - MPI Research, Inc.; *pg.* 1569, *pg.* 898
Amati, Ray, Dir-Media Plng-Mars Snackfood - Mars, Incorporated; *pg.* 1858, *pg.* 1792
Amato, Antonio, Dir-Digital Sls-East - Live Nation Entertainment, Inc.; *pg.* 558, *pg.* 47
Amato, Danielle, Mgr-Mktg Comm - PerkinElmer, Inc.; *pg.* 1426, *pg.* 853
Amato, Donna, Coord-Mktg - Glaxo Smith Kline Inc.; *pg.* 1536, *pg.* 1926
Amato, Lisa, Sr Mgr-Mktg - The Dress Barn, Inc.; *pg.* 1767, *pg.* 1343
Amato, Tarrah, Sr Mgr-Digital Mktg - PVH Corp.; *pg.* 46, *pg.* 1283
Ambachew, Ambi, Specialist-Inside Sls - LivingSocial, Inc.; *pg.* 1264, *pg.* 401
Ambeault, Joseph, Exec Dir-Consumer Video Product Mgmt - Verizon Communications Inc.; *pg.* 1875, *pg.* 1309
Amberg, Lucie, Specialist-New Media - Missouri State University; *pg.* 605, *pg.* 1006
Amberkar, Sanket, Sr Dir-Product Mktg-Innovation & New Ventures - Flextronics International Ltd.; *pg.* 81, *pg.* 245
Ambler, Isabelle, Coord-Global Strategic Mktg-Vodkas - Campari America; *pg.* 1960, *pg.* 214
Ambra, Jennifer, Sr Specialist-Mktg Comm-Ion Chromatography - Thermo Fisher Scientific Inc.; *pg.* 1431, *pg.* 854
Ambrose, Allison, Coord-Mktg & Graphics - Control Chief Holdings, Inc.; *pg.* 630, *pg.* 1518
Ambrose, Casey, Dir-Mktg & Comm-ASU Online - Arizona State University; *pg.* 597, *pg.* 25
Ambrose, Ed, Dir-Neighborhood Mktg & Mdsg - Fiesta Mart LLC; *pg.* 1019, *pg.* 1705
Ambrose, Ernie, Brand Mgr-Iced Coffee - The WhiteWave

Foods Company; *pg.* 1037, *pg.* 324
Ambrose, Gina, Specialist-Digital Commerce Mktg-US - NIKE, Inc.; *pg.* 1812, *pg.* 1492
Ambrosio, Christian, Dir-Digital Mktg - Bob's Discount Furniture Inc.; *pg.* 1763, *pg.* 354
Ambroza, Tony, Sr VP-Mktg - Carhartt, Inc.; *pg.* 39, *pg.* 875
Amburg, Chris Van, Sr VP-Mktg - Sony Pictures Entertainment Inc.; *pg.* 309, *pg.* 72
Amburgey, Tricia, Sr Dir-Sponsorship Sls - Churchill Downs, Inc.; *pg.* 540, *pg.* 733
Amby, Bob, Mgr-Mktg Automation - ABB Inc.; *pg.* 1309, *pg.* 1359
Amend, Elizabeth, Mgr-Sls - Pepperidge Farm, Inc.; *pg.* 888, *pg.* 363
Amendola, Pat, Reg Mgr-Comm & PR - Frontier Communications Corporation; *pg.* 1871, *pg.* 362
Amerongen, Lisa A., Mgr-Mktg-Pro Alliances - Ameriprise Financial, Inc.; *pg.* 715, *pg.* 930
Ames, Joan P., Dir-Mktg - United States Aircraft Insurance Group; *pg.* 1221, *pg.* 1307
Ames, Justin, Dir-Intl Sls & Mktg - Heaven Hill Distilleries, Inc.; *pg.* 1964, *pg.* 725
Ames, Tom, VP-Mktg & Bus Dev - Blauer Manufacturing Company, Inc.; *pg.* 20, *pg.* 789
Ames, Tracy, VP-Mktg - Lions Gate Entertainment Corp.; *pg.* 296, *pg.* 274
Amick, Gray, Mgr-Adv - Carolina Biological Supply Company; *pg.* 1513, *pg.* 1359
Amidon, Jason, Mgr-Sls & Mktg-Global - 3M Company; *pg.* 1142, *pg.* 956
Amigo, Alberto, Mgr-Product Dev - Acer America Corporation; *pg.* 341, *pg.* 235
Amihud, Jon, Strategist-Social Media-Global - Starwood Hotels & Resorts Worldwide, Inc.; *pg.* 1114, *pg.* 378
Amill, Andrew, VP-Weight Watchers Media - Weight Watchers International, Inc.; *pg.* 1609, *pg.* 1313
Amin, Dharini, Dir-Mktg & Corp Accounts - Johnson & Johnson; *pg.* 1549, *pg.* 1091
Amin, Dhiren, Brand Mgr-Dev-Global - Unilever United States, Inc.; *pg.* 904, *pg.* 1061
Amin, Manish, Brand Mgr - Mars North America; *pg.* 1859, *pg.* 1072
Amin, Reema, Mgr-Social Media - Weight Watchers International, Inc.; *pg.* 1609, *pg.* 1313
Amin, Shama, Program Mgr-Mktg - Bloomberg L.P.; *pg.* 725, *pg.* 1204
Aming, Anthony, Dir-Product Mgmt-Drilling & Micro Seismic - Baker Hughes Incorporated; *pg.* 1315, *pg.* 1700
Amir, Maggie, Brand Mgr - CaesarStone; *pg.* 919, *pg.* 299
Amirani, Shahrzad, VP-New Products, Launch Excellence & Alliance Mgmt - Sanofi US; *pg.* 1592, *pg.* 1046
Amirault, Ryan, Sr Mgr-Social Media Mktg-Global - Whole Foods Market, Inc.; *pg.* 1038, *pg.* 1667
Amirian, Christine, VP-Corp Mktg & Brand Mktg - Samsung Electronics America, Inc.; *pg.* 669, *pg.* 1115
Amirshahi, Bobby, VP-PR - Time Warner Cable Inc.; *pg.* 312, *pg.* 1301
Amiry, Saied, Head-Education Vertical Mktg - LinkedIn Corporation; *pg.* 1262, *pg.* 160
Amjadi, Layla, Product Mgr - Facebook, Inc.; *pg.* 1245, *pg.* 143
Amkreutz, Michael, Exec VP-Mdsg, Mktg & ECommerce - Guitar Center, Inc.; *pg.* 1771, *pg.* 306
Amladi, Pradeep, VP-Mktg & Head-High Tech, Mfg, Energy & Resources - SAP; *pg.* 465, *pg.* 78
Amling, Alan P., Dir-Contract Logistics Mktg-Global - United Parcel Service, Inc.; *pg.* 1928, *pg.* 522
Amlinger, Jerome J., VP-Sls & Mktg - High Liner Foods Incorporated; *pg.* 862, *pg.* 1917
Ammari, Ramzi S., Sr VP-Product Plng & Strategy-Global - Universal Electronics, Inc.; *pg.* 683, *pg.* 262
Ammazzalorso, Nick, Mgr-Mktg Comm - Toyota Motor Sales, U.S.A., Inc.; *pg.* 193, *pg.* 296
Ammer, Michael, Sr Dir Environmental Projects - NRG Energy, Inc.; *pg.* 1948, *pg.* 1712
Amo, Bob, Sr Dir-Mktg-Global Portfolio Strategy & Innovation - Johnson & Johnson; *pg.* 1549, *pg.* 1091
Amorese, Frank, Dir-Media - Heineken USA Inc.; *pg.* 252, *pg.* 1352
Amoroso, Betsy, Sr Dir-Mktg & Corp Comm - Mannington Mills, Inc.; *pg.* 934, *pg.* 1119
Amoroso, Marilyn, Dir-Media - Cellino & Barnes; *pg.* 1293, *pg.* 1147
Amoruso, Joe, Sr Dir-Portfolio Mgmt - Siemens Healthcare Diagnostics; *pg.* 673, *pg.* 604
Amos, Paul, Mgr-Mktg - 3M Company; *pg.* 1142, *pg.* 956
Amos, Peter, Mgr-PR - Advanced Micro Devices, Inc.; *pg.* 613, *pg.* 282
Amram, Ron, Sr Dir-Media - Heineken USA Inc.; *pg.* 252, *pg.* 1352
Amsbaugh, Kim, Sr Mgr-Corp Comm - Intuit Inc.; *pg.* 769, *pg.* 158
Amschler, Carla, Dir-Direct Mktg - Build-A-Bear Workshop, Inc.; *pg.* 950, *pg.* 993
Amundson, Erika, Brand Mgr-Youth - Under Armour, Inc.; *pg.* 49, *pg.* 759
Amundson, Lindsay, Assoc Mgr-Mktg-Saute Express - Land O'Lakes, Inc.; *pg.* 873, *pg.* 915
Amundson, Scott, Product Mgr - Snap-on Incorporated; *pg.* 1062, *pg.* 1862
Amurao, Cristina, Mgr-Mktg - Logan's Roadhouse, Inc.; *pg.* 1736, *pg.* 1652
An, Katherine, Mgr-Mktg-AppExchange - salesforce.com, inc.; *pg.* 1278, *pg.* 226
An, Mark, Sr Program Mgr & Product Mgr - Smith Micro Software, Inc.; *pg.* 471, *pg.* 41
Ana Giossi, Betty, Mgr-Social Media & Email Mktg - Canon U.S.A., Inc.; *pg.* 1404, *pg.* 1178
Anadale, Katy, Dir-Digital Mktg - National Geographic Channel; *pg.* 299, *pg.* 402
Anand, Manu, Product Mgr-Digital Mktg - Adobe Systems Incorporated; *pg.* 342, *pg.* 235
Anassori, Sarah, Brand Mgr-Suncare - Neutrogena Corporation; *pg.* 517, *pg.* 137
Anastas, Jonathan, VP & Head-Digital & Social Mktg-Global - Activision Blizzard, Inc.; *pg.* 948, *pg.* 271
Anastasio, Kathryn, Sr VP & Dir-Mktg - UMB Financial Corporation; *pg.* 812, *pg.* 987
Anastaskis, Tiffany, Sr VP-Mktg & Comm - St. John Knits International, Inc.; *pg.* 33, *pg.* 116
Anathan, Karen, VP-Digital Mktg & ECommerce - Movado Group, Inc.; *pg.* 10, *pg.* 1101
Anauate, Fabiana, Sr Dir-Global Brand Mgmt - Burger King Corporation; *pg.* 1719, *pg.* 440
Anaya, Jennifer, VP-Mktg-North America - Ingram Micro Inc.; *pg.* 415, *pg.* 261
Ancrile, Joel, Brand Mgr-Cracker Innovation - Kellogg Company; *pg.* 831, *pg.* 870
Anda, Jeremy, Reg Mgr-Mktg - Heineken USA Inc.; *pg.* 252, *pg.* 1352
Andaluz, Elizabeth, Dir-Licensing & Creative - Discovery Communications, Inc.; *pg.* 282, *pg.* 777
Andberg, Julie, Dir-Mktg & Member Experience - UnitedHealth Group Incorporated; *pg.* 1221, *pg.* 950
Andeer, Mark, VP-Creative - Kmart Corporation; *pg.* 1775, *pg.* 617
Anderla, Julie, Sr Mgr-Mktg Comm, Cheerios & Cascadian Farm - General Mills, Inc.; *pg.* 828, *pg.* 933
Anderle, Judith, Product Dir-Global Mktg-Allergy Franchise - Alcon; *pg.* 1399, *pg.* 530
Andersen, Brandon, Dir-Mktg - Cision, Inc.; *pg.* 375, *pg.* 761
Andersen, Heidi Lautrup, Sr Dir-Core & Emerging Mktg Solutions - LinkedIn Corporation; *pg.* 1262, *pg.* 160
Andersen, Julie, Dir-Mktg-Global - Johnson Outdoors Inc.; *pg.* 1837, *pg.* 1888
Andersen, Katie, Coord-Engagement Mktg - Red Robin Gourmet Burgers, Inc.; *pg.* 1747, *pg.* 331
Andersen, Kerry, Dir-PR - Pinnacle Entertainment, Inc.; *pg.* 576, *pg.* 1029
Andersen, Kirby, Supvr-Media Mgmt - AMC Networks Inc.; *pg.* 269, *pg.* 1189
Andersen, Kris, Brand Mgr-Mktg - Zale Corporation; *pg.* 16, *pg.* 1724
Andersen, Stacia, Sr VP-Mdsg & Home - Target Corporation; *pg.* 1786, *pg.* 942
Andersen, Stephanie, Mgr-Integrated Mktg-FORTUNE & Money - Fortune; *pg.* 1642, *pg.* 1232
Anderson, Ami Miesner, Sr Dir-Adv & Media - CEC Entertainment, Inc.; *pg.* 1721, *pg.* 1717
Anderson, Amy, Dir-Channel Mktg - Graco, Inc.; *pg.* 1342, *pg.* 935
Anderson, Andy, VP-Sls-Eastern Reg - American Urban Radio Networks; *pg.* 269, *pg.* 1573
Anderson, Angela, Specialist-Mktg - ChoiceOne Financial Services, Inc.; *pg.* 735, *pg.* 908
Anderson, Anna, Sr Mgr-Branding & Mktg Comm - ENTEGRIS, INC.; *pg.* 1882, *pg.* 788
Anderson, April, Dir-Indus & Retail Sls - Google Inc.; *pg.* 1249, *pg.* 153
Anderson, Barbara, Sr Specialist-Mktg - Ameriprise Financial, Inc.; *pg.* 715, *pg.* 930
Anderson, Barkley, Sr Mgr-Online Creative - The Home Depot, Inc.; *pg.* 1050, *pg.* 510
Anderson, Bill, Sr Counsel-Trademark, Mktg & Adv - Motorola Mobility LLC; *pg.* 657, *pg.* 627
Anderson, Bob, Product Mgr-Global - TSI Incorporated; *pg.* 1432, *pg.* 965
Anderson, Brad, Sr VP-Global Sls, Mktg & Customer Svc - Sea Ray Boats, Inc.; *pg.* 1710, *pg.* 1638
Anderson, Brendan, VP-Mktg & Product Mgmt-Char-Broil - W.C. Bradley Co.; *pg.* 62, *pg.* 528
Anderson, Brent, Rep-Sls - Saia, Inc.; *pg.* 1922, *pg.* 533
Anderson, Brenton, Asst Mgr-Direct Mktg - Southwest Airlines Co.; *pg.* 1923, *pg.* 1687
Anderson, Brian, Brand Mgr-Digital Orthodontics-Global - 3M Company; *pg.* 1142, *pg.* 956
Anderson, Brian, Brand Mgr-Digital Orthodontics-Global - 3M Unitek Corporation; *pg.* 1483, *pg.* 150
Anderson, Brian, VP-Product Mktg-Enterprise Solutions - Sierra Wireless Incorporated; *pg.* 673, *pg.* 1909
Anderson, Bruce E., Dir-External Comm & Social Media - Honeywell International Inc.; *pg.* 407, *pg.* 1088
Anderson, Caroline, VP-Mktg-Global - Revlon Consumer Products Corporation; *pg.* 521, *pg.* 1286
Anderson, Chad, Sr Mgr-Equipment & Channel Dev - Starbucks Corporation; *pg.* 897, *pg.* 1840
Anderson, Chris, VP-Product Mgmt - GameFly, Inc.; *pg.* 953, *pg.* 132
Anderson, Chris, Dir-Mktg - Verizon Communications Inc.; *pg.* 1875, *pg.* 1309
Anderson, Christine, Sr Assoc Mgr-Mktg-Yoplait Greek - General Mills, Inc.; *pg.* 828, *pg.* 933
Anderson, Christine Carly, Sr Assoc Mgr-Mktg - Yoplait USA, Inc.; *pg.* 910, *pg.* 947
Anderson, Christopher, Dir-Mktg - Sewell Automotive Companies; *pg.* 190, *pg.* 1686
Anderson, Cindy, Mgr-Mktg Production - Diamond Comic Distributors, Inc.; *pg.* 1635, *pg.* 772
Anderson, Claire, Creative Dir-Creative Services - Bentley University; *pg.* 598, *pg.* 850
Anderson, Colby, Strategist-Social & Digital - Bojangles' Restaurants, Inc.; *pg.* 1717, *pg.* 1364
Anderson, Craig, Sr VP-Ops & Mktg Svcs - Publishers Clearing House; *pg.* 1782, *pg.* 1324
Anderson, Darby, Chief Strategy Officer & Chief Bus Dev Officer - ADDUS HOMECARE CORPORATION; *pg.* 1487, *pg.* 650
Anderson, David, Dir-Sls & Mktg - Anheuser-Busch Companies, LLC; *pg.* 237, *pg.* 991
Anderson, David S., Interim CFO - Huntington Bancshares Incorporated; *pg.* 767, *pg.* 1440
Anderson, Dawn, VP-Client & Corp Mktg - AMN Healthcare Services, Inc.; *pg.* 1494, *pg.* 200
Anderson, Debbie, Sr Dir-Lifestyle Mktg - Microsoft Corporation; *pg.* 435, *pg.* 1824
Anderson, Deborah A., Dir-Mktg-Automation, Informatics & Consulting Svcs - Abbott Laboratories; *pg.* 1484, *pg.* 551
Anderson, Donnie, VP-Sls - Gibraltar Industries, Inc.; *pg.* 1340, *pg.* 1148
Anderson, Elaine, Sr Dir-OTC Global Franchise Org - Johnson & Johnson; *pg.* 1549, *pg.* 1091
Anderson, Eric J., Mgr-Mktg - Weyerhaeuser Company; *pg.* 121, *pg.* 1820
Anderson, Erica, Sr Mgr-Mktg-Enterprise Div - SHUTTERFLY, INC.; *pg.* 1280, *pg.* 192
Anderson, Erin, Mgr-Media Acceleration & Innovation - General Mills, Inc.; *pg.* 828, *pg.* 933
Anderson, Erin, Sr Mgr-Field Mktg - Juniper Networks, Inc.; *pg.* 1260, *pg.* 286
Anderson, Erin, Asst Mgr-Media Pur - Menard, Inc.; *pg.* 1055, *pg.* 1857
Anderson, Erin, Mgr-Shopper Mktg - The WhiteWave Foods Company; *pg.* 1037, *pg.* 324
Anderson, Ethan, VP-Mktg-Sanuk-Global - Deckers Outdoor Corporation; *pg.* 1807, *pg.* 100
Anderson, Eva, Dir-Creative-Center for Health Literacy - MAXIMUS, Inc.; *pg.* 780, *pg.* 1799
Anderson, Gary, Sr VP-Grain Mktg & Processing & Food Ingredients-North America - CHS INC.; *pg.* 702, *pg.* 926
Anderson, Gina, Dir-Media Rels-North America Beverages - PepsiCo, Inc.; *pg.* 259, *pg.* 1327
Anderson, Greg, Mgr-Comml Mktg - Atmos Energy Corporation; *pg.* 1935, *pg.* 1675
Anderson, Heather F., Sr Mgr-Product Mktg - FairPoint Communications, Inc.; *pg.* 1871, *pg.* 1366

Anderson, Heidi, VP-Sls - WebMD Health Services Group; *pg.* 1609, *pg.* 1508
Anderson, Henry, Dir-Social Media-Novartis Intl - Novartis Corporation; *pg.* 1574, *pg.* 1273
Anderson, Henry, Dir-Social Media - Novartis Pharmaceuticals Corp.; *pg.* 1575, *pg.* 1054
Anderson, Holly, Specialist-Media Rels - State Farm Mutual Automobile Insurance Co.; *pg.* 1218, *pg.* 557
Anderson, Ian, Dir-Mktg - Nice-Pak Products, Inc.; *pg.* 1465, *pg.* 1319
Anderson, Ivy, Acct Exec-Partnership Mktg - National Hockey League; *pg.* 568, *pg.* 1265
Anderson, Jackie, Mgr-Media Rels-Global - Archer-Daniels-Midland Company; *pg.* 825, *pg.* 565
Anderson, Jane M., Mgr-Mktg & Comm - American Express Company; *pg.* 712, *pg.* 1190
Anderson, Janelle, VP-Shopper Mktg-Pepsico - Frito-Lay North America, Inc.; *pg.* 1853, *pg.* 1730
Anderson, Jared, Dir-Jarden Media Ventures - Jarden Consumer Solutions; *pg.* 57, *pg.* 412
Anderson, Jared, Dir-Jarden Media Ventures - Jarden Corporation; *pg.* 1885, *pg.* 412
Anderson, Jeff, Gen Mgr-Digital Programming Ops & Product - DISH Network Corporation; *pg.* 283, *pg.* 325
Anderson, Jenna, Specialist-Mktg Comm - Allina Health System, Inc.; *pg.* 1491, *pg.* 929
Anderson, Jennifer, VP-Mktg - Raising Cane's USA; *pg.* 1746, *pg.* 742
Anderson, Jesse, Assoc Analyst-Mktg-Naked Juice - PepsiCo, Inc.; *pg.* 259, *pg.* 1327
Anderson, Jessica, Editor-Social Strategy - The New York Times; *pg.* 1668, *pg.* 1270
Anderson, Jessie, Brand Mgr-Teavana Ecommerce - Starbucks Corporation; *pg.* 897, *pg.* 1840
Anderson, Jim, Dir-Reg Mktg - Papa John's International, Inc.; *pg.* 1743, *pg.* 737
Anderson, Jimmy, Gen Mgr-Sls - Bush Hog, Inc.; *pg.* 702, *pg.* 8
Anderson, John, Product Mgr-Flexo Plates Americas - Eastman Kodak Company; *pg.* 1408, *pg.* 1333
Anderson, John G., VP-Corp Sls & Moving Svcs - SIRVA, Inc.; *pg.* 1923, *pg.* 669
Anderson, Judy L., Mgr-Collaborative Mktg - The Kraft Heinz Company; *pg.* 871, *pg.* 641
Anderson, Karen, Dir-Mktg - Hovnanian Enterprises, Inc.; *pg.* 1096, *pg.* 1114
Anderson, Karen, Brand Mgr-Easter - Lindt & Sprungli (USA) Inc.; *pg.* 1857, *pg.* 1039
Anderson, Karen, Mgr-Natl Sls-Residential Satellite - Winegard Company; *pg.* 688, *pg.* 702
Anderson, Kari, Asst Dir-Corp Sls - Colorado Rockies Baseball Club, Ltd.; *pg.* 542, *pg.* 317
Anderson, Katie, Mgr-Mktg-National - Orange Leaf Frozen Yogurt; *pg.* 1742, *pg.* 1487
Anderson, Keith, Dir-Mktg, Comm & Tech - Cicero Inc.; *pg.* 372, *pg.* 1360
Anderson, Kenny, Sr VP-Mdsg-Americas - Hugo Boss Fashions Inc.; *pg.* 42, *pg.* 1242
Anderson, Kim, Mgr-Digital Mktg - Briggs & Stratton Corporation; *pg.* 201, *pg.* 1899
Anderson, Kim, Acct Exec-Grp Adv - Gannett Co., Inc.; *pg.* 1643, *pg.* 1790
Anderson, Kim, Product Mgr - Jennie-O Turkey Store, LLC; *pg.* 865, *pg.* 966
Anderson, Kris, Strategist-Social Mktg-Global - Hewlett-Packard Company; *pg.* 404, *pg.* 175
Anderson, Kristen, Brand Dir-Product - Eli Lilly and Company; *pg.* 1527, *pg.* 684
Anderson, Kristin, Deputy Dir-Mktg & Comm - West Virginia Department of Commerce; *pg.* 1011, *pg.* 1849
Anderson, Kristine, VP-Mktg-Courier Corporation - RR Donnelley; *pg.* 1682, *pg.* 838
Anderson, Larry, Mgr-Sls - CASCADE MICROTECH, INC.; *pg.* 1405, *pg.* 1492
Anderson, Lary J., VP-Mktg & Comm-XS - Xerox Corporation; *pg.* 494, *pg.* 365
Anderson, Laura, Grp Dir-Corp PR & Exec Comm - Intel Corporation; *pg.* 645, *pg.* 266
Anderson, Leigh Anne, Dir-Mktg & Promos - Creative Loafing, Inc.; *pg.* 1631, *pg.* 472
Anderson, Lisa, Dir-Social Bus - Southwest Airlines Co.; *pg.* 1923, *pg.* 1687
Anderson, Liz, Mgr-PR - Firehouse Subs; *pg.* 1728, *pg.* 433
Anderson, Lori, Mgr-Social Mktg - The WhiteWave Foods Company; *pg.* 1037, *pg.* 324
Anderson, Margee, VP-Video Sls Central - AOL Inc.; *pg.* 1229, *pg.* 1195
Anderson, Mark, Dir-Mktg-Keyboard Div - Yamaha Corporation of America; *pg.* 595, *pg.* 51
Anderson, Michael, Mgr-Media - Kao Brands Co. Inc.; *pg.* 513, *pg.* 1415
Anderson, Myles, Specialist-Online Mktg - TaxSlayer LLC; *pg.* 808, *pg.* 532
Anderson, Natanya, Dir-Social Media, CRM & Customer Svc-Global - Whole Foods Market, Inc.; *pg.* 1038, *pg.* 1667
Anderson, Natasha, Mgr-Integrated Mktg-Dog Snacks - Del Monte Foods, Inc.; *pg.* 852, *pg.* 304
Anderson, Nicholas, Controller-Engineered To Order Products North America - Schneider Electric; *pg.* 467, *pg.* 1609
Anderson, Nicole, Sr Dir-Corp Comm - CIENA Corporation; *pg.* 628, *pg.* 771
Anderson, Paige, Head-Social Media Team - Deluxe Corporation; *pg.* 1634, *pg.* 964
Anderson, Pamela, Coord-Mktg-Latin America - Zebra Technologies Corporation; *pg.* 690, *pg.* 628
Anderson, Patricia, Specialist-Digital & Print Media - The Berry Company LLC; *pg.* 1869, *pg.* 1445
Anderson, Rachel K., Specialist-Mktg Comm - Ceridian Corporation; *pg.* 371, *pg.* 932
Anderson, Rebecca, Program Mgr-Mktg - FedEx Corporation; *pg.* 1907, *pg.* 1642
Anderson, Rebecca M., Mgr-US Mktg - McDonald's Corporation; *pg.* 1737, *pg.* 645
Anderson, Rhonda, Assoc Dir-Mktg - American Diabetes Association; *pg.* 127, *pg.* 1770
Anderson, Roger, Mgr-Mktg Svcs Grp - Ipsen International, Inc.; *pg.* 1073, *pg.* 562
Anderson, Ronald, Mgr-Procurement & Brand Mgr - ABERCROMBIE & FITCH CO.; *pg.* 37, *pg.* 1466
Anderson, Ryan, Sr Mgr-Integrated Mktg Content - The Coca-Cola Company; *pg.* 240, *pg.* 493
Anderson, Ryan, Brand Mgr-Casa Noble Tequila - Crown Imports LLC; *pg.* 248, *pg.* 572
Anderson, Ryan, Dir-Mktg - ESPN, Inc.; *pg.* 285, *pg.* 340
Anderson, Sarah, Assoc Product Mgr - Hormel Foods Corporation; *pg.* 863, *pg.* 915
Anderson, Sarah E., Assoc Mgr-Mktg Program - Blackbaud, Inc.; *pg.* 361, *pg.* 1613
Anderson, Scott, Mgr-Mktg - General Growth Properties, Inc.; *pg.* 1093, *pg.* 574
Anderson, Shannon, Mgr-Field Mktg - PETCO Animal Supplies, Inc.; *pg.* 1480, *pg.* 206
Anderson, Simon, Mgr-Product Mktg - Tandberg Data; *pg.* 481, *pg.* 311
Anderson, Tevin, Sr Mgr-SEO-Expedia Americas - Expedia, Inc.; *pg.* 1244, *pg.* 1814
Anderson, Tim, VP-Sls-Natl - AMC Entertainment Inc.; *pg.* 527, *pg.* 716
Anderson, Tim, Sr Mgr-Plng - Illumina, Inc.; *pg.* 412, *pg.* 203
Anderson, Tim, Dir-Digital & Direct Mktg - ViaSat, Inc.; *pg.* 489, *pg.* 62
Anderson, Tom, Product Mgr - AVX Corporation; *pg.* 623, *pg.* 1616
Anderson, Trevor, Dir-Product Dev - Easton Sports, Inc.; *pg.* 1833, *pg.* 299
Anderson, Virginia, Sr Mgr-Americas Channel Mktg - Plantronics, Inc.; *pg.* 663, *pg.* 270
Anderson, Walt, Sr Product Mgr-Cisco WebEx - Cisco Systems, Inc.; *pg.* 372, *pg.* 240
Anderson, Zachery, VP-Mktg Science & Analytics - Electronic Arts Inc.; *pg.* 951, *pg.* 189
Anderson-Rhodes, Heidi, Sr Dir-Facility Mgmt Solutions - UGL Services; *pg.* 486, *pg.* 784
Anderson-Wall, Lisa, Pres & Designer - Ujena Swimwear and Fashions; *pg.* 34, *pg.* 163
Andersson, Bjorn, Dir-Indus & Vertical Solutions Mktg - Hitachi Data Systems Corporation; *pg.* 407, *pg.* 265
Andersson, Jan, Sr Mgr-Global Product-Turning - Kennametal Inc.; *pg.* 1052, *pg.* 1547
Andes, Jannelle, Reg Mgr-Mktg-Northeast, Moet Hennessy USA-LVMH - Moet Hennessy; *pg.* 1966, *pg.* 1260
Andes, Richard, Dir-Multiple Sclerosis & Neuroscience Brand Managed Markets Mktg - Novartis Pharmaceuticals Corp.; *pg.* 1575, *pg.* 1054
Andino, Katie, Dir-Mktg - Takeda Pharmaceuticals USA, Inc.; *pg.* 1600, *pg.* 605
Andrade, Gabriel, Assoc Mgr-Mktg - ABB Inc.; *pg.* 64, *pg.* 1959
Andrade, Joe, Sr Dir-Ticket Sls - Orlando Magic; *pg.* 572, *pg.* 455
Andrade, Jorge, VP-Sls & Mktg-North & South America-Marine Acq - CGGVeritas Services (U.S.) Inc.; *pg.* 973, *pg.* 1703
Andrade, Russell, Sr Product Mgr-Native SDK - BlackBerry Limited; *pg.* 625, *pg.* 1947
Andraos, Dory, Dir-Mktg & New Client Acq - VCA Inc.; *pg.* 1606, *pg.* 141
Andraskova, Eva, Sr Mgr-Sls Ops - Blackboard Inc.; *pg.* 1232, *pg.* 396
Andrea, Bill, Mgr-Interactive Mktg & Acq Mktg - The Goodyear Tire & Rubber Company; *pg.* 1883, *pg.* 1401
Andree, Gloria, Mgr-Media Svcs & Specialist-Media - Comcast Corporation; *pg.* 276, *pg.* 1560
Andree, Jason, Brand Mgr-Respiratory Health-Flonase - GlaxoSmithKline; *pg.* 1536, *pg.* 1389
Andreica, Dana, Dir-Shopper Mktg-Global - GlaxoSmithKline; *pg.* 1536, *pg.* 1389
Andreoni-Pomierski, Diane, Sr Dir-Creative - McDonald's Corporation; *pg.* 1737, *pg.* 645
Andres, Heather, Sr Mgr-Adv & Creative Svcs Ops - Thermo Fisher Scientific Inc.; *pg.* 1431, *pg.* 854
Andres, Michelle, VP-Digital Media - Baltimore Ravens Limited Partnership; *pg.* 532, *pg.* 755
Andreski, David, VP-Integrated Mktg - Charter Communications, Inc.; *pg.* 274, *pg.* 372
Andretta, Melissa Tytko, Mgr-Mktg & Comm-Americas - IceLandAir North America; *pg.* 1912, *pg.* 841
Andrew, Eric, Mgr-Dodge Charger & Challenger Mktg - FCA US LLC; *pg.* 170, *pg.* 868
Andrew, Paul, Sr Product Mgr-Technical - Microsoft Corporation; *pg.* 435, *pg.* 1824
Andrews, Amy, Assoc Dir-Shopper Mktg - Ubisoft Inc.; *pg.* 589, *pg.* 229
Andrews, Ashley, Dir-Mktg Svcs - Carbonite, Inc.; *pg.* 368, *pg.* 792
Andrews, Azania, Sr Dir-Consumer Connections - Anheuser-Busch Companies, LLC; *pg.* 237, *pg.* 991
Andrews, Chris, Sr Mgr-Mktg - Ameriprise Financial, Inc.; *pg.* 715, *pg.* 930
Andrews, Danielle, Sr Mgr-Global Licensing - General Mills, Inc.; *pg.* 828, *pg.* 933
Andrews, Deborah, VP-Foodservice Bakery Mktg - Rich Products Corporation; *pg.* 892, *pg.* 1150
Andrews, Eileen, VP-PR - John F. Kennedy Center for the Performing Arts; *pg.* 555, *pg.* 401
Andrews, Eric, VP-Mktg Ops - Juniper Networks, Inc.; *pg.* 1260, *pg.* 286
Andrews, Gerard, Sr Product Mgr-Audio & Voice IP - Cadence Design Systems, Inc.; *pg.* 367, *pg.* 239
Andrews, Jayne, Dir-Mktg - Carnival Cruise Lines; *pg.* 1902, *pg.* 441
Andrews, Jon, Mgr-Mktg-US Dairy Foods - Land O'Lakes, Inc.; *pg.* 873, *pg.* 915
Andrews, Julie, Dir-Sls & PR - Kerstin Florian, Inc.; *pg.* 513, *pg.* 121
Andrews, Kelly, Mgr-Mktg Campaign-Global - Red Hat, Inc.; *pg.* 460, *pg.* 1388
Andrews, Kevin, Head-Brand Comm-PR & Sponsorship - LG Electronics Canada, Inc.; *pg.* 651, *pg.* 1927
Andrews, Lara, Product Mgr-Fixed Income-Platform Svcs - Charles Schwab; *pg.* 1235, *pg.* 1661
Andrews, Larry, Dir-Retail Mktg - Alaska Seafood Marketing Institute; *pg.* 125, *pg.* 10
Andrews, Lynn, Assoc Dir-Mktg - THE DOW CHEMICAL COMPANY; *pg.* 1157, *pg.* 898
Andrews, Mallory, Sr VP-Sls Promo, Mktg & PR - Bergdorf Goodman, Inc.; *pg.* 1761, *pg.* 1202
Andrews, Mariah, Mgr-Digital Mktg - Frontier Natural Products Co-op; *pg.* 509, *pg.* 710
Andrews, Sally, VP-PR - Holland America Line Inc.; *pg.* 1911, *pg.* 1836
Andrews, Sarah, Mgr-Mktg Comm - ABB Inc.; *pg.* 1309, *pg.* 1359
Andrews, Tom, Mgr-Customer Mktg - International Paper Company; *pg.* 1460, *pg.* 1644
Andriani, Patrick, Mgr-Mktg - Verizon Communications Inc.; *pg.* 1875, *pg.* 1309
Andriesen, Timothy J., Mng Dir-Agricultural Products - CME Group Inc.; *pg.* 738, *pg.* 571
Andronico Trageser, Christine, Sr Product Designer - Funrise Toy Corp.; *pg.* 549, *pg.* 300
Andros, Gerry, VP-Sls & Mktg-Global - TECHNE Corporation; *pg.* 1601, *pg.* 944
Andrus, Sarah, Sr Mgr-Mktg Comm - Athleta; *pg.* 19, *pg.* 181
Andrushko, Wendy, Dir-Sls-North America - Liqui-Box Corporation; *pg.* 1464, *pg.* 1802

First page reference indicates Business Class Edition
Second page reference indicates Geographic Edition

Andruszka, Ken, Sr Engr-Tech Svc & Product Dev - ConocoPhillips; pg. 975, pg. 1703
Andrysick, Guy, Exec VP-Global Sls & Mktg - Armored AutoGroup Inc.; pg. 199, pg. 342
Andujar, Alex, Exec Dir-Media & Promos - Sony Pictures Entertainment Inc.; pg. 309, pg. 72
Anello, Pat, Dir-Mktg - Wahl Clipper Corporation; pg. 524, pg. 662
Anello, Tony, Sr VP-Sls - SHL; pg. 803, pg. 942
Anes, Tiago, Dir-Sls - Setra Systems, Inc.; pg. 1428, pg. 802
ANFang, Heather, VP-Mktg-US Dairy Foods - Land O'Lakes, Inc.; pg. 873, pg. 915
Ang, Eric, Sr Mgr-Developer Program - Dolby Laboratories, Inc.; pg. 284, pg. 217
Ang, Maia, Product Mgr - Maybelline LLC; pg. 516, pg. 1257
Angarita, Maria, Dir-Mktg-La Roche-Posay - L'Oreal USA; pg. 514, pg. 1252
Angarsky, Anna, Acct Coord-TV Ad Sls - BBC Worldwide America Inc.; pg. 271, pg. 1201
Angeledes, Alex, Dir-Indus-Media & Entertainment - Google Inc.; pg. 1249, pg. 153
Angeles, Charlito, Project Mgr-Mktg Dev - Comcast Corporation; pg. 276, pg. 1560
Angeli, Stefanie, Dir-Sls-Natl - Newsday Media Group; pg. 1670, pg. 1181
Angelides, Katie, Dir-Product & Solutions Mktg Ops - NetApp, Inc.; pg. 444, pg. 287
Angelillo, Gianna, Creative Dir - Concierge Choice Physicians; pg. 1517, pg. 1338
Angelini, Marisol, VP-Mktg-Global Waters & Teas Portfolio - The Coca-Cola Company; pg. 240, pg. 493
Angelinovich, Marc, Mgr-Product Mktg-Data Center SAN - Brocade Communications Systems, Inc.; pg. 365, pg. 239
Angelo, Andrea, Dir-Mktg - Kayser-Roth Corporation; pg. 28, pg. 1374
Angelo, Carole, VP-NBC Digital Creative & Dev - NBC Universal, Inc.; pg. 300, pg. 1266
Angelo, Gary, Sr Dir-Strategy & Plng - Hewlett-Packard Company; pg. 404, pg. 175
Angelo, Loren, Mktg Dir - Audi of America, Inc.; pg. 164, pg. 1784
Angelo, Sara, Mgr-Digital Mktg - Coty, Inc.; pg. 506, pg. 1219
Angelo, Ted, Product Dir-Engine Aftermarket-Global - Donaldson Company, Inc.; pg. 1329, pg. 917
Angeloni, Ben, VP-Mktg - Stonyfield Farm, Inc.; pg. 899, pg. 1035
Anggono, Rudi, Head-Creative Team-The ZOO - Google Inc.; pg. 1249, pg. 153
Anginoli, Karen, Coord-Mktg - Pepperidge Farm, Inc.; pg. 888, pg. 363
Angiolet, Brian, Sr VP-Consumer Product & Mktg - Verizon Communications Inc.; pg. 1875, pg. 1309
Angone, Robert, Sr Dir-Creative - Sears Holdings Corporation; pg. 1784, pg. 618
Angorn, Matt, VP-Creative & Mktg Comm - Audible, Inc.; pg. 1230, pg. 1095
Angradi, Jenna, Mgr-Creative - Ouidad; pg. 519, pg. 1275
Angstadt, Edward, VP & Head-Customer Mktg - Web.com Group, Inc.; pg. 1288, pg. 435
Angstadt, Edward, VP-Mktg - Web.com, Inc.; pg. 1288, pg. 524
Anguizola, Carlos, Brand Mgr-Bottled Frappuccino - Starbucks Corporation; pg. 897, pg. 1840
Angulo, Carlos, Mgr-Product Mktg-HDTV - VIZIO, Inc.; pg. 686, pg. 118
Angulo, Yolanda, Dir-Multicultural Mktg - The Kraft Heinz Company; pg. 871, pg. 641
Anhalt, David, VP & Gen Mgr-Iridium PRIME - Iridium Communications Inc.; pg. 293, pg. 1792
Aniano, Jon, Sr Dir-Product Mgmt - salesforce.com, inc.; pg. 1278, pg. 226
Aniceto, Victor, VP-Sls - Meade Instruments Corporation; pg. 1422, pg. 113
Anido-Lopez, Melissa, Dir-Media Plng & Analytics - Carnival Corporation; pg. 1902, pg. 441
Anido-Lopez, Melissa, Dir-Media Plng & Analytics - Carnival Cruise Lines; pg. 1902, pg. 441
Anima, Mario, Product Mgr - Google Inc.; pg. 1249, pg. 153
Anisman, Shari E., VP-Mktg - Nobel Learning Communities, Inc.; pg. 605, pg. 1593
Ankeny, Vana, Sr Mgr-Mktg Comm - The Toro Company; pg. 1065, pg. 918
Ankrom, Brian, Mgr-Sls-Natl - Webster Industries Inc.; pg. 1388, pg. 1475
Ann To, Linda, Reg Mgr-Mktg - Charter Communications, Inc.; pg. 274, pg. 372
Annecharico, David, Mgr-Direct Consumer Mktg-Web-Usability, Analytics & Design - Aetna Inc.; pg. 1187, pg. 351
Annen, Steve, Mgr-Mktg - Warner Bros. Entertainment Inc.; pg. 319, pg. 54
Annerino, Matt, Sr VP-Mktg, Social & Mobile - Live Nation Entertainment, Inc.; pg. 558, pg. 47
Annese, Joseph, Asst Mgr-Mdse - adidas America Inc.; pg. 1803, pg. 1500
Annis, Adrienne, Head-Team & Product Mgr - ScanSource, Inc.; pg. 671, pg. 1618
Annis, Kelly, Dir-Consumer Promos & Shopper Mktg - Post Holdings, Inc.; pg. 833, pg. 1002
Anop, Jeff, Sr Dir-Product Mgmt-Personal Solutions - Equifax Inc.; pg. 748, pg. 504
Ansel, Barry, Sr VP-Sls & Mktg - Tabatchnick Fine Foods, Inc.; pg. 900, pg. 1122
Ansell, Kayce, Dir-Mktg - NewGround Resources; pg. 99, pg. 975
Anshutz, Juli, Dir-Mktg - Sioux Steel Company; pg. 707, pg. 1625
Anslinger, April, Assoc Dir-Mktg-Global Herbal Essences - The Procter & Gamble Company; pg. 1129, pg. 1418
Anstine, Autumn, Product Mgr-Global - Dentsply International Inc.; pg. 1522, pg. 1596
Ansusinha, Ted, VP-Product Mgmt - Fair Isaac Corporation; pg. 1247, pg. 955
Antaya, Sherry, Dir-Convention Sls - Greater Miami Convention & Visitors Bureau; pg. 993, pg. 442
Antczak, David, Reg Dir-Adv & PR - MetroPCS, Inc.; pg. 1872, pg. 1683
Anthes, Sheryn, Dir-Merchant Mktg - LivingSocial, Inc.; pg. 1264, pg. 401
Anthony, Barry, Dir-Mktg - McKee Foods Corporation; pg. 1860, pg. 1630
Anthony, Jim, Sr Dir-PR - NorthShore University HealthSystem; pg. 606, pg. 612
Anthony, Julie, Sr Mgr-Product Mktg - Cynosure, Inc.; pg. 1521, pg. 858
Anthony, Terri-Lisa, VP & Div Mgr-Mktg-Consumer Banking - BOK Financial Corporation; pg. 726, pg. 1489
Anthony, Theresa, VP-Sls & Mktg - ROCKFORD CORPORATION; pg. 667, pg. 26
Anthony, Todd, Dir-Sls Trng & Dev - Cumberland Pharmaceuticals, Inc.; pg. 1521, pg. 1650
Anthony, Tye, VP-Sls & Mktg-Fort Worth - Associated Wholesale Grocers, Inc.; pg. 1015, pg. 715
Antill, Micah, Sr Mgr-Mktg-North America - Dell Inc.; pg. 383, pg. 1737
Antippas, Lydia, Head-Mktg-North America & Sr Dir-CyberSource - Visa Inc.; pg. 816, pg. 230
Antippas, Lydia, Sr Dir & Head-North America Mktg-CyberSource - Visa U.S.A., Inc.; pg. 817, pg. 231
Antol, John, Sr Dir-Clinical Mktg - Analogic Corporation; pg. 1399, pg. 840
Antolik, Heather L., Specialist-Web Mktg - Armstrong World Industries, Inc.; pg. 914, pg. 1545
Anton, Bryan, VP-Sls - Philadelphia Flyers, L.P.; pg. 575, pg. 1569
Anton, Dismary, Brand Mgr-D:FI-Global - Revlon Consumer Products Corporation; pg. 521, pg. 1286
Anton, Dismary, Brand Mgr-D:FI-Global - Revlon, Inc.; pg. 521, pg. 1286
Anton, John, Reg Mgr-Sls-Metro NY, NJ, PA & DE - Freixenet U.S.A.; pg. 1963, pg. 279
Antonacci, Laura, Sr Mgr-School & Library Mktg - Penguin Random House; pg. 1675, pg. 1276
Antonczyk, Mike, Reg Mgr-Mktg - MillerCoors LLC; pg. 255, pg. 582
Antonelli, Robert, VP-Sls - Fancort Industries, Inc.; pg. 1336, pg. 1131
Antonelli, Steve, Sr Dir-Sls - Sears Holdings Corporation; pg. 1784, pg. 618
Antonelli, Todd, VP-Sls & Mktg - PGT, Inc.; pg. 104, pg. 452
Antonetti, Santos, VP-After Sls-Bella Intl - Bella Group; pg. 166, pg. 1599
Antoni, Kimberli, Dir-Brand Mktg-Ringling Bros, Barnum & Bailey - Feld Entertainment, Inc.; pg. 547, pg. 458
Antoniades, Corey, Product Mgr-Technical-SCBG-Ceramics - KEMET Corporation; pg. 649, pg. 1621
Antonian, Anie, Asst Dir-Mktg - City of Hope National Medical Center; pg. 1516, pg. 77
Antonides, Becki, Coord-Sls & Mktg - Atlas Bolt & Screw Company; pg. 1042, pg. 1403
Antonietta, Diane, Mgr-Mktg Comm - Cornell Dubilier Electronics; pg. 630, pg. 1620
Antonini, Joel, VP-Mktg - Cardtronics, Inc.; pg. 732, pg. 1703
Antonopoulos, Christina, VP & Dir-Creative - Jet.com, Inc.; pg. 1260, pg. 1073
Antonucci, Chris, Sr Mgr-Mktg - STERIS Corporation; pg. 1597, pg. 1464
Antonucci, Donna A., Sls Mgr - Weichert Realtors; pg. 1118, pg. 1087
Antos, Kerry, Head-Global Media - PayPal Inc.; pg. 1274, pg. 248
Antos, Laura, Sr Mgr-360 Mktg Ops - New Jersey State Lottery; pg. 1000, pg. 1126
Anuskiewicz, John, Mgr-Diesel Products - Bacharach Inc.; pg. 1400, pg. 1556
Anvari, Ahmad, Product Mgr-Google Display Network - Google Inc.; pg. 1249, pg. 153
Anvary, Goly, Sr Dir-Mktg & Creative-Gap Online-Global - The Gap, Inc.; pg. 1770, pg. 218
Anzelone, Jenna, Mgr-Partnership Mktg - Macy's, Inc.; pg. 1778, pg. 1417
Aown, Josh, Coord-Mktg - Boyne USA Resorts Inc.; pg. 1082, pg. 874
Apanay, Sherry, Mng Dir-Sls - Urban Financial of America, LLC.; pg. 815, pg. 1491
Aparicio, Steve, Mgr-Production - The Caxton Printers Ltd.; pg. 1626, pg. 548
Aparo, Judy, VP-Corp Sls - EBSCO Information Services Walpole; pg. 1638, pg. 849
Apelbaum, Suzana, Dir-Creative - Google Inc.; pg. 1249, pg. 153
Apfel, Brian, Dir-Social Media & Online Mktg - Marist College; pg. 604, pg. 1325
Apgar, Rich, Sr Acct Mgr-Strategic Bus Sls - T-Mobile US, Inc.; pg. 676, pg. 1816
Apicella-Luning, Michele, Sr Dir-Adv - Loehmann's Holdings Inc.; pg. 29, pg. 1144
Aplin, Lauren, Brand Mgr-Innovation-Global - Burt's Bees Inc.; pg. 502, pg. 1370
Aplin, Mike, Product Dir-Toy Haulers - Jayco Inc.; pg. 1708, pg. 695
Apmann, Todd, Dir-Program Mktg & Adv - Showtime Networks Inc.; pg. 308, pg. 1291
Apodaca, Paul, Dir-Product Mgmt - Microsoft Corporation; pg. 435, pg. 1824
Apolito, Angela, Coord-PR - New York & Company, Inc.; pg. 1779, pg. 1268
Aponte, Phil, Mgr-Mktg-OEM & PC Based Automation - Siemens Process Industries and Drives; pg. 673, pg. 485
Apostolico, David, Sr VP-Affiliate Sls & Mktg - QVC Inc; pg. 305, pg. 1593
Apostolidis, Nikos, Brand Mgr-Equity-Finish Dishwashing - Reckitt Benckiser Inc.; pg. 1136, pg. 1105
Appa, Yohini, Sr Dir-R&D - Johnson & Johnson; pg. 1549, pg. 1091
Appapogu, Karun, Mgr-Digital Adv Ops - The Vanguard Group, Inc.; pg. 816, pg. 1550
Appel, Jason, Dir-Multichannel Mktg - Amgen Inc.; pg. 1493, pg. 291
Appel, Lori, Mgr-Mktg Comm - Custom Sensors & Technologies; pg. 1407, pg. 152
Appel, Stephen, Pres-Sls & Mktg - ION Media Networks, Inc.; pg. 293, pg. 479
Appel, Suzanne, Sr Mgr-Digital Acq & Web - Medtronic, Inc.; pg. 1564, pg. 939
Appelbaum, Daniel, Dir-Sls & Mktg - Peabody Energy Corporation; pg. 1176, pg. 1001
Appiah, Rich, Grp Product Dir - Janssen Biotech, Inc.; pg. 1548, pg. 1540
Apple, Aisha, Sr Analyst-Social Media Customer Rels - CarMax, Inc.; pg. 167, pg. 1800
Apple, Amanda, Dir-Mktg - Perry Ellis International, Inc.; pg. 45, pg. 445
Apple, Andrew R., Dir-Product Dev - AT&T Mobility LLC; pg. 619, pg. 488
Apple, Hal, Sr Dir-Worldwide Mktg & Creative - Herbalife International of America, Inc.; pg. 1541, pg. 132
Apple, Travis, VP-Ticket Sls & Svc - Phoenix Suns; pg. 576, pg. 19
Applebaugh, Colleen, Mgr-Comm & Mktg Svcs - Osram Sylvania, Inc.; pg. 1302, pg. 816
Applebee, Jennifer, Sr Mgr-Experiential Mktg - FCA US LLC; pg. 170, pg. 868
Applebee, Scott, VP-Mktg - Travelpro International, Inc.; pg. 14, pg. 413

Appleby, Celinda, Head-Global Employer Branding & Recruitment Mktg - Oracle Corporation; *pg.* 1272, *pg.* 786
Appleby, Nancy, Sr Dir-Adv & Mktg - Giant Food Stores, LLC; *pg.* 1021, *pg.* 1520
Applegate, Diane L., VP-Supply Chain & Mdse Ops - The Buckle, Inc.; *pg.* 1764, *pg.* 1011
Applewhite, Hunter, Dir-Adv & PR - Dominion Resources, Inc.; *pg.* 1939, *pg.* 1802
Apricio, Michelle, Dir-Sls-Embassy Suites Colorado Springs - Embassy Suites Hotels; *pg.* 1090, *pg.* 1790
April-Fritz, Elizabeth, Product Mgr - R.C. Bigelow, Inc.; *pg.* 891, *pg.* 348
Aprile, Allison, Asst Brand Dir-Web & Digital Media - Wynn Resorts Limited; *pg.* 1119, *pg.* 1030
Aquilino, Pete, Dir-Eastern Adv - People Magazine; *pg.* 1676, *pg.* 1278
Aquino, Cristina, Mgr-Consumer Mktg - Ford Motor Company; *pg.* 172, *pg.* 876
Aquino, Marc, Dir-Hepatitis Mktg - Gilead Sciences, Inc.; *pg.* 1535, *pg.* 88
Aquino, Shawn, Sr Mgr-Product Mktg - Symantec Corporation; *pg.* 478, *pg.* 161
Araamudhu, Sunitha, VP-Digital Mktg - Career Education Corporation; *pg.* 599, *pg.* 658
Arabitg, Melissa, Specialist-Strategic Partners & Key Accts Mktg - Carnival Corporation; *pg.* 1902, *pg.* 441
Arac, Ardan, Sr Product Mgr - Google Inc.; *pg.* 1249, *pg.* 153
Aradhya, Prakash, Product Dir-Mgmt - Red Hat, Inc.; *pg.* 460, *pg.* 1388
Aragaki, Phyllis, VP-Creative - Crate & Barrel, Inc.; *pg.* 922, *pg.* 640
Aragon, Karen, Coord-Sls & Mktg - General Motors of Canada Ltd.; *pg.* 177, *pg.* 1931
Araiza, Adan, Sr Specialist-Mktg-Refining Catalysts - BASF Corporation; *pg.* 1149, *pg.* 1066
Arak, Dana, Counsel-Mktg & Promos - Live Nation Entertainment, Inc.; *pg.* 558, *pg.* 47
Arakaki, Ryan, Dir-Mktg - Kelly-Moore Paint Company, Inc.; *pg.* 1443, *pg.* 198
Arakawa, Curt, Mgr-Mktg - Daiwa Corporation; *pg.* 1832, *pg.* 75
Araki, Eiji, VP-Social Games - GREE International, Inc.; *pg.* 1255, *pg.* 219
Araldi, Alessandro, VP-Mktg-Global - Honeywell International Inc.; *pg.* 407, *pg.* 1088
Aramini, Michela, Sr Mgr-Integrated Mktg-SELF - Conde Nast Publications, Inc.; *pg.* 1629, *pg.* 1217
Aranador, Andrea, Mgr-Mktg Comm - BMW of North America, LLC; *pg.* 166, *pg.* 1133
Arancio, Jori, VP-Media Rels - ABC Family Channel; *pg.* 268, *pg.* 51
Aranda, Greg, Mgr-Internet Mktg - Graybar Electric Company, Inc.; *pg.* 1299, *pg.* 997
Arant, David, Gen Mgr & Dir-Mktg & Bus Dev - Interline Brands, Inc.; *pg.* 1051, *pg.* 433
Araps, Cristina, Mgr-Digital Mktg & Assoc Mgr - ESPN, Inc.; *pg.* 285, *pg.* 340
Arasu, Ananda, Mgr-Product Mktg - Autodesk Inc.; *pg.* 356, *pg.* 257
Arasu, Raji, CTO & VP-Product & Tech - StubHub, Inc.; *pg.* 586, *pg.* 228
Arata, Todd, VP-Brand Mktg & Comm - Comcast Cable Communications, Inc.; *pg.* 276, *pg.* 1560
Arata, Tom, VP-Global Tech Platforms & Anchor Mktg - Ecolab Inc.; *pg.* 329, *pg.* 960
Araten-Castillo, Luis, Brand Mgr - Campbell Soup Company; *pg.* 844, *pg.* 1048
Araujo, Claudia, Dir-Content Mktg-Latin America - Netflix, Inc.; *pg.* 1269, *pg.* 141
Araujo, Jennifer, Dir-Creative - Health Magazine; *pg.* 1648, *pg.* 1238
Araujo, Vicki, Sr Mgr-Partner Mktg-Global - Cisco Systems, Inc.; *pg.* 372, *pg.* 240
Araujo-Salazar, Cindy, Mgr-North America Mktg Fulfillment - Shell Lubricants; *pg.* 217, *pg.* 1714
Arazi, Guy, Dir-Product Mgmt - Vicon Industries, Inc.; *pg.* 685, *pg.* 1166
Arball, John, Gen Mgr-Sls - Riverside Ford; *pg.* 189, *pg.* 885
Arbetter, Lou, Sr Dir-Mktg-Pepsi - PepsiCo, Inc.; *pg.* 259, *pg.* 1327
Arbogast, Maureen, Dir-Mktg - University of Minnesota; *pg.* 609, *pg.* 945
Arboleda, Jessica, Mgr-Mktg-West Div - Comcast Corporation; *pg.* 276, *pg.* 1560
Arbour, Emily, Brand Mgr-Consumer Insights & Innovation - Community Coffee Company LLC; *pg.* 849, *pg.* 741
Arbuckle, Cynthia, Coord-Mktg - Corpus Christi Caller-Times; *pg.* 1630, *pg.* 1671
Arbusto, Maria, Exec Dir-Global Digital Mktg & Online Commerce Practice - International Business Machines Corporation; *pg.* 418, *pg.* 1138
Archambault, Derek, Sr Mgr-Mktg - Keurig Green Mountain, Inc.; *pg.* 868, *pg.* 1768
Archambault, Lisa, Head-Demand Generation Mktg - Zappos.com, Inc.; *pg.* 1291, *pg.* 1030
Archbald, Kevin, VP-Sls - FiberMark Inc.; *pg.* 1457, *pg.* 1764
Archdeacon, Peg, Dir-Mktg & Comm - Philadelphia Convention & Visitors Bureau; *pg.* 1004, *pg.* 1568
Archer, Alan, VP-Strategic Sls Svcs - Discovery Communications, Inc.; *pg.* 282, *pg.* 777
Archer, Candace Hirleman, VP-Creative Svcs-KGO-TV - KGO Television, Inc.; *pg.* 294, *pg.* 220
Archer, Cynthia, VP-Mktg & Dev - Sunoco Inc.; *pg.* 985, *pg.* 1571
Archer, Darin, Dir-IoT Indus Solutions Retail, CPG & Consumer Products - Intel Corporation; *pg.* 645, *pg.* 266
Archer, Jena, Asst Mgr-Mktg - Briggs & Stratton Corporation; *pg.* 201, *pg.* 1899
Archer, Regina, Mgr-Mktg Comm - UnitedHealth Group Incorporated; *pg.* 1221, *pg.* 950
Archer, Roshny M., Sr Dir-Global Talent & Team Member Experience - W.W. Grainger, Inc.; *pg.* 1390, *pg.* 625
Archibong, Tony, Head-Vertical Bus Dev & Distr Mktg - Hulu LLC; *pg.* 1257, *pg.* 274
Archival, Nestor, Specialist-Technical Product-Google Analytics Premium - Google Inc.; *pg.* 1249, *pg.* 153
Archuleta, Joyce, Gen Mgr-Sls - Outfront Media; *pg.* 1465, *pg.* 1275
Archuleta, Kellan, Specialist-Social Experience - Kohl's Corporation; *pg.* 1775, *pg.* 1870
Arciszewski, Julie C., VP-Channel Mktg - Magellan Health Services, Inc.; *pg.* 1557, *pg.* 337
Arcuri, Dean, VP-Mktg & Creative Svcs - Sean John Clothing, Inc.; *pg.* 48, *pg.* 1290
Ard, Jay, VP-Sls-Natl - Coca-Cola Refreshments USA, Inc.; *pg.* 247, *pg.* 500
Ardelan, Mike, VP-OEM Sls - Sierra Wireless Incorporated; *pg.* 673, *pg.* 1909
Ardell, Kristy, Dir-Mktg - Munchkin, Inc.; *pg.* 964, *pg.* 300
Arden, Allison, VP & Publr-Adv Age - Crain Communications, Inc.; *pg.* 1631, *pg.* 879
Arden, Jodi, Dir-Brand Mktg & Promos - USA Networks; *pg.* 315, *pg.* 1308
Arden, Matt, VP & Dir-Creative - Screenvision Cinema Network LLC; *pg.* 581, *pg.* 1290
Ardiff, Bill, Mgr-Retail Mktg Support - Bridgestone Americas, Inc.; *pg.* 201, *pg.* 1649
Ardis, John, Sr VP-Sls-CRM Solutions Grp - Conversant, Inc.; *pg.* 1393, *pg.* 306
Arecchi, Mike, VP-Mdsg Consumer Products Div - L'Oreal USA; *pg.* 514, *pg.* 1252
Arehart, Christopher, Global Product Mgr-Crime Insurance-Grp Of Insurance Companies - The Chubb Corporation; *pg.* 1196, *pg.* 1128
Arellano, Belen, Brand Mgr - The Clorox Company; *pg.* 327, *pg.* 169
Arena, Frank, Sr VP-Established Relationship Sls & Comml Ops - PDI, Inc.; *pg.* 1580, *pg.* 1104
Arena, Joe, Mgr-Interactive & Digital Mktg - Bayer Corporation; *pg.* 1499, *pg.* 1573
Arencibia, Gabrielle, Mgr-Field Mktg - VeriSign, Inc.; *pg.* 488, *pg.* 1799
Arends, Larry, Mgr-Mktg - G&W Electric Company; *pg.* 1338, *pg.* 558
Arends, Mitch, Sr Dir-Indirect, Logistics & BPO Procurement - The Kraft Heinz Company; *pg.* 871, *pg.* 641
Arends, Robert, Mgr-PR - San Diego Convention & Visitors Bureau; *pg.* 1004, *pg.* 208
Arens, Tom, Dir-Mktg-Contact Lens Care & Dry Eye - Abbott Laboratories; *pg.* 1484, *pg.* 551
Arenson, Raymond, Exec VP-Mdsg & Design - Euromarket Designs, Inc.; *pg.* 1124, *pg.* 640
Arevalo, David, Dir-Mktg-Pro Sound & Visual Div - Pioneer Electronics (USA) Inc.; *pg.* 663, *pg.* 124
Arevalo, Denise, Sr Mgr-IP & Mktg Category - Office Depot, Inc.; *pg.* 448, *pg.* 412
Arevalo, Leidy, Coord-PR - Knott's Berry Farm; *pg.* 556, *pg.* 50
Arevian, Garin, Mng Dir-Tech, Media & Telecom Investment Banking Grp-Boston - Piper Jaffray Companies; *pg.* 794, *pg.* 941
Arfa, Atoosa, Assoc Mgr-PR & Consumer Engagement-Goody & Levolor - Newell Rubbermaid Inc.; *pg.* 1128, *pg.* 515
Arfalk, Erik, VP-Mktg, Comm & Branding-Atlas Copco Compressor Technique US - Atlas Copco Comptec LLC; *pg.* 1314, *pg.* 1349
Arganbright, Maggie, Dir-Emerging Media - Philadelphia Eagles Football Club, Inc.; *pg.* 575, *pg.* 1569
Argentino, Bo, Sr VP-Adv & Media Sls-NBCUniversal Domestic Television Distr - NBC Universal, Inc.; *pg.* 300, *pg.* 1266
Argeris, Meredith, Product Mktg Mgr-Google Play & Mgr-SMB Sls & Global Ad Ops - Google Inc.; *pg.* 1249, *pg.* 153
Arguello, Jennifer, VP-Brand Mktg - Darden Restaurants, Inc.; *pg.* 1724, *pg.* 453
Arguello, Jennifer, VP-Brand Mktg - Olive Garden Italian Restaurant; *pg.* 1742, *pg.* 454
Argueta, Alex, Mgr-Mdse - SKECHERS U.S.A., INC.; *pg.* 1819, *pg.* 143
Argyilan, Kristi, Sr VP-Media & Guest Engagement - Target Corporation; *pg.* 1786, *pg.* 942
Arias, CarrieAnn, VP-Mktg & Dir-Mktg & Innovation - DOLE FOOD COMPANY, INC.; *pg.* 853, *pg.* 306
Arias, Dasha, Acct Mgr-Adv - Google Inc.; *pg.* 1249, *pg.* 153
Arias, Katherine, Asst Project Mgr-Creative Svcs - Coach, Inc.; *pg.* 3, *pg.* 1214
Arias, Kristen, Dir-Consumer & Digital Mktg - GE Capital; *pg.* 761, *pg.* 362
Arias, Noa, Sr Mgr-Retail Indus Dev - American Express Company; *pg.* 712, *pg.* 1190
Arida, Chuck, VP-Content Mktg & Social Media - Nationwide Mutual Insurance Company; *pg.* 1210, *pg.* 1442
Arima, Lonnie, VP-Channel Sls Dev-Americas - Here; *pg.* 404, *pg.* 576
Aristizabal, Johanna, Mgr-Mktg-US - Mattel Games/Puzzles; *pg.* 962, *pg.* 80
Aristizabal, Johanna, Mgr-Mktg-US - MATTEL, INC.; *pg.* 962, *pg.* 81
Ariyoshi, Eric, Brand Mgr-Wild Turkey - Campari America; *pg.* 1960, *pg.* 214
Ariyoshi, Koji, Exec VP & Dir-Mktg & Sls - Aflac Incorporated; *pg.* 1188, *pg.* 527
Arjomand, Marty, Sr Mgr-Medical Comm - Amgen Inc.; *pg.* 1493, *pg.* 291
Arkan, Erhun, Sr Dir-Wearables & IoT SW Mktg & Tech Scaling - Intel Corporation; *pg.* 645, *pg.* 266
Arkin, Eran, Product Mgr - Google Inc.; *pg.* 1249, *pg.* 153
Arman, Mark, VP-Worldwide Channel Sls - Polycom, Inc.; *pg.* 664, *pg.* 249
Armand, Kelesha, Mng Dir & Sr Counsel-Mktg-Chase Consumer & Community Banking - JPMorgan Chase & Co.; *pg.* 772, *pg.* 1246
Armando, Robyn, Strategist-Reg Mktg-Northeast - MetLife, Inc.; *pg.* 1208, *pg.* 1258
Armantrout, Jeff, Principal & Product Mgr - Amazon.com, Inc.; *pg.* 1226, *pg.* 1831
Armata, Raegan, Dir-Product Mgmt & US Comml Product Dev & Product Mgr - Cigna Corporation; *pg.* 1197, *pg.* 338
Armato, Anthony, Brand Mgr-Pabst Blue Ribbon - Pabst Brewing Company; *pg.* 258, *pg.* 137
Armbrester, Kyle, Acting Chief Product Officer - athenahealth, Inc.; *pg.* 1497, *pg.* 855
Armbrust, Danielle, Sr Dir-Global Brand Strategy & Mktg - Hasbro, Inc.; *pg.* 954, *pg.* 1603
Armendariz, Arlene, Mgr-Comm-Digital Mktg - MetLife, Inc.; *pg.* 1208, *pg.* 1258
Armenteros, Arlene, Dir-Mktg - Visa Inc.; *pg.* 816, *pg.* 230
Armenteros, Arlene, Dir-Mktg - Visa U.S.A., Inc.; *pg.* 817, *pg.* 231
Armfield, Jeff, Exec Dir-Global Product Strategy & Dev - Columbus McKinnon Corporation; *pg.* 1325, *pg.* 1138
Armington, Colleen K., VP-Connected Vehicle, Partner Mktg & Customer Experience - Sirius XM Holdings Inc.; *pg.* 308, *pg.* 1292
Armistead, Michael, Sr Mgr-Comml, Plng & Activation - Diageo Canada, Inc.; *pg.* 1961, *pg.* 1937
Armitage, Chris K., Mgr-Natl Sls & Mktg-Consumer Health Care Div - 3M Company; *pg.* 1142, *pg.* 956
Armitage, Jon, VP-Mktg - Trunk Club; *pg.* 49, *pg.* 593
Armon, Susan, Analyst-Media-US CENTCOM - CACI International Inc.; *pg.* 367, *pg.* 1773
Armour, Julie, Sr Dir-Comm-Global-GEP - Pfizer Inc.; *pg.* 1581, *pg.* 1278
Armour, Katie, Head-Leisure Sector Mktg & Sr Mgr-US Travel & Hospitality - Deloitte & Touche USA LLP; *pg.* 743, *pg.*

First page reference indicates Business Class Edition
Second page reference indicates Geographic Edition

1222
Armour, Ladonna, Mgr-Strategic Mktg - WestRock Company; *pg.* 1472, *pg.* 1805
Armour, Richard, Sr Dir-Multi-Channel - GameStop Corp.; *pg.* 399, *pg.* 1699
Arms, Robert, VP-Sls Mid Enterprise - TRIPWIRE, INC.; *pg.* 485, *pg.* 1507
Armstrong, Amber, Program Dir-Social, Mobile, Commerce Amplification & Digital - International Business Machines Corporation; *pg.* 418, *pg.* 1138
Armstrong, Ana, Sr Mgr-Mktg & Digital - American Express Company; *pg.* 712, *pg.* 1190
Armstrong, Angela Grove, Mgr-Mktg Comm - Zimmer Biomet Holdings, Inc.; *pg.* 1611, *pg.* 699
Armstrong, Bonnie, Sr Dir-Digital Sls & Bus Dev - Community Coffee Company LLC; *pg.* 849, *pg.* 741
Armstrong, Brian, Sr Mgr-Enterprise Program Mgmt - United States Cellular Corporation; *pg.* 1875, *pg.* 594
Armstrong, Charles, Product Mgr-Street View & Trusted Program - Google Inc.; *pg.* 1249, *pg.* 153
Armstrong, Chris, Sr Dir-Bus Applications - LinkedIn Corporation; *pg.* 1262, *pg.* 160
Armstrong, Crystal, Mgr-Creative Svcs - The Gaston Gazette; *pg.* 1644, *pg.* 1373
Armstrong, David, Sr Dir-Creative - Dillard's, Inc.; *pg.* 1766, *pg.* 34
Armstrong, David L, Mgr-Mktg & Digital Channels Fin - American Airlines Inc.; *pg.* 1898, *pg.* 1693
Armstrong, Janet, Acct Exec-Charter Media - Charter Communications, Inc.; *pg.* 274, *pg.* 372
Armstrong, Jean, Dir-Brand Mktg - Williams-Sonoma, Inc.; *pg.* 1140, *pg.* 234
Armstrong, Jeff, Mgr-Digital Mktg - Herman Miller, Inc.; *pg.* 926, *pg.* 913
Armstrong, John A., Dir-Mktg Tech - Legg Mason, Inc.; *pg.* 775, *pg.* 758
Armstrong, Juliet, Sr Mgr-Transformation - PepsiCo, Inc.; *pg.* 259, *pg.* 1327
Armstrong, Kathryn, Strategist-Mktg Content - Penske Corporation; *pg.* 188, *pg.* 873
Armstrong, Kelly, Product Mgr-Turbo Tax - Intuit Inc.; *pg.* 769, *pg.* 158
Armstrong, Kevin, Sr Mgr-Adv, Social Media & Brand - Club Med Sales, Inc.; *pg.* 1903, *pg.* 441
Armstrong, Kim, Mgr-Mktg Comm - The Sherwin-Williams Company; *pg.* 1447, *pg.* 1435
Armstrong, Kim, Mgr-Mktg Comm - Sherwin Williams; *pg.* 1448, *pg.* 1436
Armstrong, Laurie, Dir-Media Rels-US & Canada - San Francisco Travel Association; *pg.* 1005, *pg.* 227
Armstrong, Lea, Mgr-PR - Philips Electronics North America; *pg.* 662, *pg.* 782
Armstrong, Lisa, Program Mgr-Mktg Event - Intel Corporation; *pg.* 645, *pg.* 266
Armstrong, Lydia, Sr Dir-New Products-Global - Novartis Pharmaceuticals Corp.; *pg.* 1575, *pg.* 1054
Armstrong, Marca, VP-Mktg - Panasonic Corporation of North America; *pg.* 661, *pg.* 1120
Armstrong, Marty, Sr VP-Sls & Mktg - Conair Corporation; *pg.* 505, *pg.* 1055
Armstrong, Melani Schuss, Mgr-Mktg - Intuit Inc.; *pg.* 769, *pg.* 158
Armstrong, Melanie, Dir-Retail Mktg - Colgate-Palmolive Company; *pg.* 504, *pg.* 1215
Armstrong, Pam, Mgr-Creative Svcs & Production - Frontier Airlines, Inc.; *pg.* 1909, *pg.* 319
Armstrong, Philip, Sr VP-Mktg - Bank of America Corporation; *pg.* 718, *pg.* 1362
Armstrong, Sarah, Bus Mgr - The Coca-Cola Company; *pg.* 240, *pg.* 493
Armstrong, Sterling, Specialist-Relationship Mktg - Audi of America, Inc.; *pg.* 164, *pg.* 1784
Armstrong, Tony, Dir-Product Mktg-Power Products - Linear Technology Corp.; *pg.* 652, *pg.* 147
Armstrong-Grandison, Clasonda V., Brand Mgr-Partners - United Airlines, Inc.; *pg.* 1927, *pg.* 593
Armus, Steve, VP-Consumer Products - Major League Baseball; *pg.* 560, *pg.* 1255
Arnaudon, Marianne, Dir-Corp Mktg - Sun Life Financial Inc.; *pg.* 806, *pg.* 1944
Arneodo, Severine, Mgr-Client Mktg - Valassis; *pg.* 1698, *pg.* 386
Arnesen, Erna, VP-Global Channel & Field Mktg - Plantronics, Inc.; *pg.* 663, *pg.* 270
Arneson, Latham, VP-Digital Mktg - Paramount Pictures Corporation; *pg.* 304, *pg.* 138
Arnett, Chris, Sr Dir-Franchise Mgmt - Choice Hotels International, Inc.; *pg.* 1086, *pg.* 775
Arnett, Harry, Sr VP-Mktg - Callaway Golf Company; *pg.* 1829, *pg.* 58
Arnette, Sandra, Mgr-PR - Verizon Communications Inc.; *pg.* 1875, *pg.* 1309
Arnholt, Christine, VP-Onboard Mktg - Carnival Corporation; *pg.* 1902, *pg.* 441
Arnholt, Christine, VP-Onboard Mktg - Carnival Cruise Lines; *pg.* 1902, *pg.* 441
Arnold, Bob, Head-NA Digital Media & Strategy - Google Inc.; *pg.* 1249, *pg.* 153
Arnold, Bruce, Dir-Sls - St. Louis Convention & Visitors Commission; *pg.* 1006, *pg.* 1003
Arnold, Chris, Dir-PR - Chipotle Mexican Grill, Inc.; *pg.* 1722, *pg.* 317
Arnold, Chuck, VP-Sls & Mktg - Seattle Seahawks; *pg.* 582, *pg.* 1830
Arnold, David P., Mgr-Field Mktg - Atmel Corporation; *pg.* 621, *pg.* 238
Arnold, Dirk, VP-Product, Tech & Sports Comm-Press & PR Events - BMW of North America, LLC; *pg.* 166, *pg.* 1133
Arnold, James, VP-Sls & Ops-AgWeb.com - Farm Journal Media; *pg.* 1640, *pg.* 1564
Arnold, Jamie, Mgr-PR & Internal Comm - Welch Allyn Inc.; *pg.* 1436, *pg.* 1342
Arnold, Jeffrey M., Sr VP-Sls - Elizabeth Arden, Inc.; *pg.* 507, *pg.* 448
Arnold, Jennifer, Sr Mgr-Mktg Comm-Channel Mktg - Tennant Company; *pg.* 1381, *pg.* 944
Arnold, Jonathan, Head-Next-Generation Diagnostics Mktg - Siemens Healthcare Diagnostics; *pg.* 673, *pg.* 604
Arnold, Ken, Sr Mgr-Mktg - Sierra Wireless Incorporated; *pg.* 673, *pg.* 1909
Arnold, Kristin, Mgr-Mktg Comm - Hewlett-Packard Company; *pg.* 404, *pg.* 175
Arnold, Latoya, Sr Assoc Brand Mgr - Georgia-Pacific LLC; *pg.* 1458, *pg.* 507
Arnold, Michael, Reg Mgr-Sls - William H. Sadlier, Inc.; *pg.* 1702, *pg.* 1314
Arnold, Mike, Assoc Dir-Mktg - Leprino Foods Company; *pg.* 874, *pg.* 320
Arnold, Steve, Exec VP-Mktg - Associated Wholesale Grocers, Inc.; *pg.* 1015, *pg.* 715
Arnold, Steve, VP-Sls & Mktg - Corpus Christi Caller-Times; *pg.* 1630, *pg.* 1671
Arnold, Zena, Head-North America Mktg-Google Play - Google Inc.; *pg.* 1249, *pg.* 153
Arnoldt, Jennifer, Dir-Mktg-Brand Experience - Taco Bell Corp.; *pg.* 1752, *pg.* 117
Arnone, James, Specialist-Mktg - Canon U.S.A., Inc.; *pg.* 1404, *pg.* 1178
Arnone, John R., Mgr-PR - Mitsubishi Motors North America, Inc.; *pg.* 185, *pg.* 75
Arnot, Nada, VP-Mktg & Growth-Hearst Digital Studios - The Hearst Corporation; *pg.* 1649, *pg.* 1239
Arnott, Nina, Head-PR-UK - Domino's Pizza, Inc.; *pg.* 1726, *pg.* 865
Arnow, Don, Dir-Sls - Bridge Publications Inc.; *pg.* 1623, *pg.* 127
Arnowitz, Glenn J., Dir-Creative Solutions - Pfizer Inc.; *pg.* 1581, *pg.* 1278
Arntson, Heather, Sr Planner-Digital Mktg - General Mills, Inc.; *pg.* 828, *pg.* 933
Arntz, Mike, Sr VP-Sls-Americas - NetSuite, Inc.; *pg.* 1270, *pg.* 255
Arocho, Lourdes, VP-Intl Consumer Products - Nickelodeon Direct Inc.; *pg.* 303, *pg.* 1271
Aroff, Debbie, Asst Dir-Brand Mktg - Penguin Random House; *pg.* 1675, *pg.* 1276
Arole, Maria O., Dir-Clinical Product Strategy - Catamaran; *pg.* 1514, *pg.* 628
Aron, David, Mgr-Mktg - Hewlett-Packard Company; *pg.* 404, *pg.* 175
Aron, Tammie, Mgr-SMB Segment Outbound Mktg - Hewlett-Packard Company; *pg.* 404, *pg.* 175
Arone, Geoffrey, Exec VP-Products - WhitePages.com Inc.; *pg.* 1289, *pg.* 1842
Aronoff, Jill, Sr Dir-Mdse Branding - Milwaukee Brewers Baseball Club, Inc.; *pg.* 562, *pg.* 1878
Aronoff, Joel R., VP-Product Dev & Deployment - Authentidate Holding Corp.; *pg.* 356, *pg.* 1044
Aronoff, Laura, Coord-Mktg - New Orleans Tourism Marketing Corporation; *pg.* 1001, *pg.* 747
Arons, David, Chief Pub Policy & Advocacy Officer - National Brain Tumor Society; *pg.* 148, *pg.* 223
Arons, Russell, Sr VP-Mktg - Warner Bros. Entertainment Inc.; *pg.* 319, *pg.* 54
Aronson, Chris, VP-Sls-North America - Cynosure, Inc.; *pg.* 1521, *pg.* 858
Aronson, Doron, Mgr-PR-Security - Cisco Systems, Inc.; *pg.* 372, *pg.* 240
Aronson, Tom, VP-Digital Mktg-Walt Disney Parks & Resorts - The Walt Disney Company; *pg.* 317, *pg.* 52
Arora, Abhisht, Gen Mgr-Product Mgmt & Bing - Microsoft Corporation; *pg.* 435, *pg.* 1824
Arora, Ashi, Rep-Digital Sls - Anixter International Inc.; *pg.* 1313, *pg.* 614
Arora, Meenakshi, Mgr-Mktg Analytics & Program Measurement - The Allstate Corporation; *pg.* 1189, *pg.* 639
Arora, Navin, Sr Mgr-Strategy & Corp Dev - TE Connectivity Ltd.; *pg.* 677, *pg.* 1515
Arora, Puneet, Sr VP-Sls-Global - 8x8, Inc.; *pg.* 1865, *pg.* 282
Arovaara, Jussi, VP-Sls-Global - Corel Corporation; *pg.* 380, *pg.* 1931
Arrabal, Diego, Reg VP-Sls-Southern Europe & Middle East - F5 Networks, Inc.; *pg.* 396, *pg.* 1835
Arredondo, Dolores L., VP & Mgr-Mktg - Wells Fargo & Company; *pg.* 819, *pg.* 232
Arredondo, Manny, Dir-Product Mgmt - Lam Research Corporation; *pg.* 1354, *pg.* 91
Arreola, Federico, VP-Consumer Products Brand Bus Unit - The Kraft Heinz Company; *pg.* 870, *pg.* 1577
Arriagada, Margarita, Sr VP-Mdsg - Sephora USA Inc; *pg.* 522, *pg.* 227
Arrigoni, Marco, Dir-Mktg - Coherent, Inc.; *pg.* 1406, *pg.* 265
Arriola, Fernando, VP-Media & Integration - ConAgra Foods, Inc.; *pg.* 826, *pg.* 1014
Arrowsmith, Matthew, VP-Sls - Cal-Maine Foods, Inc.; *pg.* 843, *pg.* 969
Arroyo, Gladys, VP-Sls & City Reg - Chicago Sun Times; *pg.* 1627, *pg.* 570
Arroyo, Lisa, Sr Mgr-Digital Social Media Mktg - Plantronics, Inc.; *pg.* 663, *pg.* 270
Arroyo, Mina, Mgr-Customer Mktg-Walmart, Target & Costco - Solo Cup Company; *pg.* 1469, *pg.* 625
Arroyo, Sara, Brand Mgr - Revlon, Inc.; *pg.* 521, *pg.* 1286
Arruda, Daniel, Reg Mgr-Sls-Coatings & Construction - THE DOW CHEMICAL COMPANY; *pg.* 1157, *pg.* 898
Arsenault, Christopher, Product Mgr-Strategic Response Team - New Balance Athletic Shoe, Inc.; *pg.* 1811, *pg.* 798
Arsenault, Joseph, Sr Mgr-Analysis & Metrics - Time Warner Cable Inc.; *pg.* 312, *pg.* 1301
Arsenault, Julie, VP-Mktg - Randall-Reilly Publishing Company LLC; *pg.* 1679, *pg.* 8
Arshad, Iqbal, Sr VP-Engrg-Global Product Dev - Motorola Mobility LLC; *pg.* 657, *pg.* 627
Arsonneau, Philippe, Sr VP-Global Sls-IT Bus - Schneider Electric; *pg.* 467, *pg.* 1609
Arsuaga, Beatriz, Dir-Field Mktg - MillerCoors LLC; *pg.* 255, *pg.* 582
Artale, Tina J., Mgr-Sls - Merck & Co., Inc.; *pg.* 1566, *pg.* 1077
Artemenko, Andrew, Sr Dir-PlatformOne Solutions - NeuStar, Inc.; *pg.* 1872, *pg.* 1807
Arter, Joshua, Coord-Digital Mktg - Briggs & Stratton Corporation; *pg.* 201, *pg.* 1899
Arterburn, Susan, Mgr-Mktg - Fastline Publications Inc.; *pg.* 1641, *pg.* 726
Arthur, Brian, VP-Product Dev - KVH Industries Inc; *pg.* 650, *pg.* 1602
Arthur, Gary, Jr., Corp Sr VP-Wholesale Mktg & Product Supply - Valero Energy Corporation; *pg.* 986, *pg.* 1743
Arthur, Jen, Head-Mktg - Interactive Intelligence, Inc.; *pg.* 417, *pg.* 687
Arthur, Mike, Mgr-Channel-Bus Mktg & Strategy - AT&T; *pg.* 1865, *pg.* 258
Arthur, Richard, VP-Brand Mktg & Creative - QVC Inc; *pg.* 305, *pg.* 1593
Arthur, Shawn, Mgr-Creative Svcs - Republic National Distributing Company; *pg.* 264, *pg.* 1713
Arthurs, Dave, Product Mgr-Specialty Connectors - API Technologies Corp.; *pg.* 618, *pg.* 452
Artiaga, Louis, Mgr-Premier Sls & Svcs - Chicago National League Ball Club, LLC; *pg.* 539, *pg.* 569
Artigliere, Maryann, Category Head-Global Shopper Mktg - GlaxoSmithKline; *pg.* 1536, *pg.* 1389
Artim, Jean M., Specialist-Sls & Mktg-Data Integration - The

Dun & Bradstreet Corp.; *pg.* 1637, *pg.* 1120
Artin, Matt, Dir-Partnership Creative - Golden State Warriors, LLC; *pg.* 550, *pg.* 171
Artin, Michelle, Mgr-Media - CKE Restaurants Inc.; *pg.* 1723, *pg.* 63
Arts, Sander, VP-Corp Mktg - Atmel Corporation; *pg.* 621, *pg.* 238
Artz, David, Sr Dir-Tech-AOL Media Platform - AOL Inc.; *pg.* 1229, *pg.* 1195
Artz, Mabelle, Sr Mgr-Mktg & Digital Customer Experience - Adobe Systems Incorporated; *pg.* 342, *pg.* 235
Arum, Rebecca, VP-Mktg & Mdse Presentation - Big Lots, Inc.; *pg.* 1762, *pg.* 1438
Arusell, Hannah, Mgr-Mktg Comm-Global Adv - Microsoft Corporation; *pg.* 435, *pg.* 1824
Arvedon, Robyn, Asst VP-Mktg - HomeGoods, Inc.; *pg.* 1125, *pg.* 821
Arvedon, Robyn, Asst VP-Mktg - Marshalls of MA, Inc.; *pg.* 1778, *pg.* 821
Arvedon, Robyn, Asst VP-Mktg - T.J. Maxx; *pg.* 1788, *pg.* 822
Arvedon, Robyn, Asst VP-Mktg - The TJX Companies, Inc.; *pg.* 1788, *pg.* 822
Arvidson, Wayne, VP-Mktg-ATTO Tech - BackupWorks.com Inc.; *pg.* 359, *pg.* 120
Arvin, Jennifer, Dir-Comm & Mktg - Barnes-Jewish Hospital; *pg.* 1498, *pg.* 992
Asamoah, Akosua, Brand Mgr-Robitussin - Pfizer Inc.; *pg.* 1581, *pg.* 1278
Asaro, Beth, Reg Mgr-Sls Ops - AT&T Inc.; *pg.* 1867, *pg.* 1674
Asbell, Steve, Sr VP-Production - 20th Century Fox Film Corp.; *pg.* 267, *pg.* 124
Asbill, Kim E., Head-Social Media & Specialist-Pub Affairs - SCANA Corporation; *pg.* 1951, *pg.* 1612
Asbury, Barbara, Mgr-Adv-Global - Agilent Technologies, Inc.; *pg.* 614, *pg.* 264
Asbury, Lori D., Sr VP-Mktg, Creative & Brand Strategy-Scripps Networks-HGTV - Home & Garden Television; *pg.* 290, *pg.* 1637
Asbury, Mike, Grp VP & Mgr-Mdsg - SunTrust Banks, Inc.; *pg.* 807, *pg.* 520
Ascione, Lorraine, Dir-Direct Mktg Svcs - American Express Company; *pg.* 712, *pg.* 1190
Ascolese, Anthony B., Dir-Sls & Mktg - KB Home; *pg.* 90, *pg.* 134
Asencio, Anthony, Mgr-Integrated Mktg - Complex Media, Inc.; *pg.* 1628, *pg.* 1217
Asencio, Araseli, Mgr-Adv & Partnership Mktg - Crystal Cruises LLC; *pg.* 1904, *pg.* 128
Asencio, Paul, Sr VP-Corp Sls & Svcs - Sterling Mets, L.P.; *pg.* 586, *pg.* 1160
Asermely, Taylor, Asst Mgr-Mktg - Sephora USA Inc; *pg.* 522, *pg.* 227
Asevedo, Teresa, Coord-Mktg - American Greetings Corporation; *pg.* 1615, *pg.* 1428
Asgari, Reza, Product Mgr - Rudolph Technologies, Inc.; *pg.* 669, *pg.* 918
Ash, Helen S., Asst VP-Sls Merchant Svcs - TD Bank US Holding Company; *pg.* 809, *pg.* 1051
Ash, Richard, Sr Mgr-Media Plng & Strategy - Nissan North America, Inc.; *pg.* 186, *pg.* 1633
Ashare, Shaina, Assoc Mgr-Mktg - General Mills, Inc.; *pg.* 828, *pg.* 933
Ashburn, Kara, Brand Mgr - Bush Brothers & Company; *pg.* 843, *pg.* 1636
Ashburner, Charlotte, Area Mgr-Mktg - Brown-Forman Corporation; *pg.* 1958, *pg.* 732
Ashby, Carol, Dir-Customer Mktg-Sls Enablement - AutoTrader, Inc.; *pg.* 1230, *pg.* 490
Ashby, Joel, Dir-Creative - Landry's, Inc.; *pg.* 1735, *pg.* 1709
Ashcraft, Pete, Sr VP-Global Sls & Bus Dev - TurboChef Technologies, Inc.; *pg.* 902, *pg.* 1670
Ashe, Amanda, Sr Mgr-PR - Revlon, Inc.; *pg.* 521, *pg.* 1286
Ashe, Jason, Mgr-GC Product - Agilent Technologies, Inc.; *pg.* 614, *pg.* 264
Ashe, Valerie, Sr Mgr-Global Named Accts Mktg - Autodesk Inc.; *pg.* 356, *pg.* 257
Ashekian, Peter, Sr Mgr-Client Dev - R.R. Bowker LLC; *pg.* 1682, *pg.* 1095
Asher, Carl, Assoc Dir-Mktg - Kimberly-Clark Corporation; *pg.* 1461, *pg.* 1720
Asher, Katy, Dir-PR-Windows Phone - Microsoft Corporation; *pg.* 435, *pg.* 1824
Asher-Rabun, Leigh, Sr VP-Corp Mktg - Fiserv, Inc.; *pg.* 397, *pg.* 1855
Ashford, Elizabeth, Sr Dir-Global Comm - Activision Blizzard, Inc.; *pg.* 948, *pg.* 271
Ashford, Jocelyn, Mgr-Oncology Mktg & New Bus Insights - AbbVie Inc.; *pg.* 1486, *pg.* 638
Ashley, Bruce, Dir-Creative - Anthem, Inc.; *pg.* 1192, *pg.* 683
Ashley, Kate, Brand Mgr-Direct Mail Comm - Capital One Bank (USA), N.A.; *pg.* 730, *pg.* 1789
Ashley, Kate, Brand Mgr-Direct Mail Comm - Capital One Financial Corporation; *pg.* 730, *pg.* 1789
Ashley, Lisa, Dir-Media Rels - Port of Houston Authority; *pg.* 1920, *pg.* 1713
Ashley, Muriel C., Mgr-Mktg - Magellan Health Services, Inc.; *pg.* 1557, *pg.* 337
Ashley, Tyler, Planner-Sls - BBC Worldwide America Inc.; *pg.* 271, *pg.* 1201
Ashley-Rogness, Paula, VP-Media & Field Mktg - Long John Silver's, LLC; *pg.* 1736, *pg.* 736
Ashlock, Christian, Mgr-Product Mktg-Google+ - Google Inc.; *pg.* 1249, *pg.* 153
Ashman, Andrew, Mgr-Lincoln Sls Ops & Client Experience - Ford Motor Company; *pg.* 172, *pg.* 876
Ashman, Ron, Dir-Sls & Sourcing - Hanesbrands Inc.; *pg.* 26, *pg.* 1394
Ashmore, Amy, Dir-Mktg - Live Nation Entertainment, Inc.; *pg.* 558, *pg.* 47
Ashmus, Janis, Dir-Retail Mktg & Store Design - Jockey International, Inc.; *pg.* 27, *pg.* 1861
Ashok, Gopal, Mgr-Product Line Grp - VMware, Inc.; *pg.* 490, *pg.* 179
Ashton, Alexandra, Acct Exec-Corp Partnership Mktg - Maple Leaf Sports & Entertainment Ltd.; *pg.* 560, *pg.* 1940
Ashton, Andrew, Analyst-Social Media - YUM! Brands, Inc.; *pg.* 1756, *pg.* 738
Ashurst, James, VP-PR & Adv - Recreation Vehicle Industry Association; *pg.* 155, *pg.* 1799
Ashworth, Chris, Dir-Creative-Brand Design Studio & Windows Phone - Microsoft Corporation; *pg.* 435, *pg.* 1824
Ashworth, Lindsay, Specialist-Mktg & Comm - Hewlett-Packard Company; *pg.* 404, *pg.* 175
Asirvatham, Edward, Specialist-Technical Mktg - Honeywell International Inc.; *pg.* 407, *pg.* 1088
Aske, Dan, Mgr-Mktg Comm - Medline Industries, Inc.; *pg.* 1562, *pg.* 635
Askenazi, Elise, Sr Mgr-Small Bus Comm - The ADT Corporation; *pg.* 612, *pg.* 409
Askew, Angela, Interim Dir-Product Mgmt - CCH; *pg.* 1626, *pg.* 569
Askew, Cynthia, Specialist-Mktg - SYNNEX Corporation; *pg.* 480, *pg.* 92
Askew, Sophie, Dir-PR Art - Tiffany & Co.; *pg.* 13, *pg.* 1299
Aslani, Amir, Sr Mgr-Product Mgmt-Amazon Speech Platform - Amazon.com, Inc.; *pg.* 1226, *pg.* 1831
Aslesen, Brooke, Mgr-Mktg-Integrated Mktg Comm - The Allstate Corporation; *pg.* 1189, *pg.* 639
Asmar, Tina, Sr Mgr-PR - QUALCOMM Incorporated; *pg.* 1873, *pg.* 207
Asmara, Deborah, Dir-Mktg, Strategy & Capabilities-Global - Amway Corporation; *pg.* 326, *pg.* 864
Asner, Mike, Dir-Team Mktg & Bus Ops - National Basketball Association; *pg.* 566, *pg.* 1264
Asnip, Whitney, Dir-Mktg - Equifax Workforce Solutions; *pg.* 394, *pg.* 997
Aspaas, Anthony, Sr Dir-Season Ticket Sls - Washington Capitals; *pg.* 591, *pg.* 1775
Aspinall, David, VP-Sls-AT&T Global Client Grp & Exec Dir - AT&T Inc.; *pg.* 1867, *pg.* 1674
Aspinwall, Kerry, Head-Mktg-Global Sourcing - Google Inc.; *pg.* 1249, *pg.* 153
Asposto, Stephen, Sr Dir-Brdcst Ops - Buffalo Bills, Inc.; *pg.* 535, *pg.* 1319
Asprelli, Phil, Dir-Shopper Mktg & Insights - Novartis Pharmaceuticals Corp.; *pg.* 1575, *pg.* 1054
Assadi, Amanda, Dir-Creative - DIRECTV Group Holdings, LLC; *pg.* 281, *pg.* 79
Assalone, Rita, Sr Dir-Comm - Siemens Healthcare Diagnostics; *pg.* 673, *pg.* 604
Assimakopoulos, George, VP-Mktg Svcs - Penton Media, Inc.; *pg.* 1676, *pg.* 1277
Asthana, Abhinav, Product Mgr - Wipro Gallagher Solutions; *pg.* 823, *pg.* 447
Asthana, Sanjiv, Sr VP-Sls & Mktg-Worldwide - Integrated Silicon Solution, Inc.; *pg.* 645, *pg.* 145
Astorga, Jorge, Sr Product Mgr-Mobile - salesforce.com, inc.; *pg.* 1278, *pg.* 226
Astra-Liss, Mona, Dir-Corp PR-USA - Ikea North America Services LLC; *pg.* 929, *pg.* 1523
Astramecki, Ross, Sr VP-Sls - Insperity, Inc.; *pg.* 416, *pg.* 1725
Astrom, Paul, Dir-Mktg Analytics & Strategy - Hawaiian Airlines, Inc.; *pg.* 1910, *pg.* 543
Atakhanov, Sharaf, Mgr-Digital Mktg - Boiron USA Inc.; *pg.* 1507, *pg.* 1556
Atcheson, Denice, Sr Dir-Reg Fin - Ventura County Star; *pg.* 1699, *pg.* 57
Atchicon, Case, Mgr-Sls-West Reg - Harris Waste Management Group, Inc.; *pg.* 1345, *pg.* 526
Atchison, Dave, Sr VP-Mktg - Zulily; *pg.* 1792, *pg.* 1843
Atchison, Jena, Dir-Adv - AT&T; *pg.* 1865, *pg.* 258
Atencio, Jeffrey, Sr Mgr-Digital Sls Ops - ABC Family Channel; *pg.* 268, *pg.* 51
Atendido, Sean, Reg Dir-Sls - Takeda Pharmaceuticals USA, Inc.; *pg.* 1600, *pg.* 605
Athanas, Evan, VP-Sls - Anheuser-Busch Companies, LLC; *pg.* 237, *pg.* 991
Athanason, John, Mgr-PR - Weeki Wachee Springs, LLC; *pg.* 591, *pg.* 478
Atherholt, Sue, Dir-Sls - QVC Inc; *pg.* 305, *pg.* 1593
Atherley, Rebecca, Dir-PR-EMEA - AT&T Inc.; *pg.* 1868, *pg.* 358
Atherton, Alynn, Mgr-Mktg Comm - ACI Worldwide Inc.; *pg.* 341, *pg.* 1010
Athey, Patricia R., Mgr-Intl Mktg, Comm & Svcs-Energy Saving Glass Products - PPG Industries, Inc.; *pg.* 1445, *pg.* 1579
Athman, Laura, Brand Mgr-Cosmetics Global Design - The Procter & Gamble Company; *pg.* 1129, *pg.* 1418
Athreya, Rupa, Sr VP-Product Dev - OppenheimerFunds, Inc.; *pg.* 790, *pg.* 1274
Atienza, Ryan, VP-Sls-Denville Scientific Inc - Harvard Bioscience, Inc.; *pg.* 1539, *pg.* 824
Atilano, Ryan, Specialist-App Mktg - Electronic Arts Inc.; *pg.* 951, *pg.* 189
Atkins, Bryan, Specialist-Sls & Mktg - The Dun & Bradstreet Corp.; *pg.* 1637, *pg.* 1120
Atkins, Cory, Sr Dir-Sls - Cineplex Entertainment LP; *pg.* 275, *pg.* 1936
Atkins, Elizabeth, Sr Specialist-Brand Mktg-Portable Deep Cleaning - Bissell Homecare, Inc.; *pg.* 52, *pg.* 887
Atkins, Robert, Sr Specialist-Product Mktg-Global - FRANKLIN RESOURCES, INC.; *pg.* 760, *pg.* 254
Atkins, Sylvie, Mgr-Mktg Comm - Microsoft Corporation; *pg.* 435, *pg.* 1824
Atkins, Terry, Sr Dir-Mktg Comm - Extended Stay Hotels LLC; *pg.* 1091, *pg.* 1622
Atkinson, Aaron, Sr Mgr-Product Mktg - Quest Diagnostics Incorporated; *pg.* 1587, *pg.* 1080
Atkinson, Carl, Dir-Sls & Mktg - Voith Hydro Inc.; *pg.* 1387, *pg.* 1598
Atkinson, Christopher, Engr-Technical Mktg - Cisco Systems, Inc.; *pg.* 372, *pg.* 240
Atkinson, Don, Mng Dir-Sls & VP-Mktg - Weyerhaeuser Company; *pg.* 121, *pg.* 1820
Atkinson, Fran G., VP-Mktg - Kennedy Health System; *pg.* 1553, *pg.* 1128
Atkinson, Gail, Sr Specialist-Mktg Ops - The Procter & Gamble Company; *pg.* 1129, *pg.* 1418
Atkinson, Jarem, Mgr-Social Mktg - ZAGG INCORPORATED; *pg.* 690, *pg.* 1762
Atkinson, Jen, Sr Mgr-Social Media Strategy - Adobe Systems Incorporated; *pg.* 342, *pg.* 235
Atkinson, Michelle, Dir-Mktg-Global - Energizer Holdings, Inc.; *pg.* 637, *pg.* 996
Atkinson, Troy, Reg VP-Sls-MidAtlantic - The Standard Register Company; *pg.* 473, *pg.* 1446
Ator, Cameron, Head-Mktg - Monsanto Company; *pg.* 1173, *pg.* 999
Atreya, Mohan, VP-Product Mgmt Security Svcs - NeuStar, Inc.; *pg.* 1872, *pg.* 1807
Atta, AJ, VP-Comml Plng, Activation & Div Mktg - Diageo North America Inc.; *pg.* 248, *pg.* 1223
Attard, Amy, Mgr-Integrated Mktg - Xilinx, Inc.; *pg.* 496, *pg.* 252
Attarian, Leon, Dir-Mktg - PennEngineering Fastening Technologies; *pg.* 1059, *pg.* 1526
Attenberger, Amy, Sr Mgr-Channel-Adult Feminine Care Drug Channel - Kimberly-Clark Corporation; *pg.* 1461, *pg.* 1720
Attenborough, Charlie, Mng Dir-Intl Adv - National Geographic Society; *pg.* 1667, *pg.* 402
Attila, Jeff, Mgr-Digital Mktg-Global Basketball - adidas America Inc.; *pg.* 1803, *pg.* 1500
Atwater, Christine, Coord-Partnership Mktg - LifeLock Inc.; *pg.*

First page reference indicates Business Class Edition
Second page reference indicates Geographic Edition

776, *pg.* 26
Atwell, Kathleen, Program Mgr-Competitive Solutions Mktg - Polycom, Inc.; *pg.* 664, *pg.* 249
Atwell, Laura M., VP-Mktg - Tanger Factory Outlet Centers, Inc.; *pg.* 1116, *pg.* 1376
Atwell, Michael, Sr Dir-Mktg-Media Execution & Optimization-Small Comml - The Hartford Financial Services Group, Inc.; *pg.* 1202, *pg.* 352
Atwood, Anthony, Sr Designer-Mktg - Yahoo! Inc.; *pg.* 1289, *pg.* 289
Atwood, Brandon, Sr Dir-Digital Creative - American Eagle Outfitters, Inc.; *pg.* 37, *pg.* 1572
Atwood, Brian, Dir-Field Mktg - Del Taco Restaurants, Inc.; *pg.* 1725, *pg.* 121
Atwood, Cathy, Sr Mgr-Sourcing - J.C. Penney Company, Inc.; *pg.* 1774, *pg.* 1732
Atwood, Christopher, VP-Product Mgmt US Verticals & Head-Decision360 - Equifax Inc.; *pg.* 748, *pg.* 504
Atwood, Damon G., Mgr-Technical Sls - Wenger Corporation; *pg.* 1307, *pg.* 952
Atwood, Faith, Mgr-Mktg-Cape Cod Potato Chips - Cape Cod Potato Chip Company; *pg.* 845, *pg.* 826
Au, Mandy, Mgr-Shopper Mktg - Unilever Canada Inc.; *pg.* 903, *pg.* 1946
Au, Tom, Dir-Creative-Brand - Toys "R" Us, Inc.; *pg.* 968, *pg.* 1130
Aube, Wanda, Coord-Mktg - Toyota Canada, Inc.; *pg.* 192, *pg.* 1934
Aubert, Brian, VP-Digital Mktg Strategy - JPMorgan Chase & Co.; *pg.* 772, *pg.* 1246
Aubry, Michael, Mgr-Technical Mktg - Autodesk Inc.; *pg.* 356, *pg.* 257
Aubry, Sylvain, Corp Sec & Sr Dir-Legal Affairs - Alimentation Couche-Tard Inc.; *pg.* 1013, *pg.* 1951
Auclair, Christopher, Brand Mgr - Xerox Corporation; *pg.* 494, *pg.* 365
Aucoin, Amanda L., Specialist-Client Mktg - Aetna Inc.; *pg.* 1187, *pg.* 351
Audette, Brian, Sr VP-Independent Sls, Mdsg & Mktg - SUPERVALU, Inc.; *pg.* 1035, *pg.* 924
Audette, Megan, Mgr-Mktg-Social Media Strategy - Ally Financial Inc.; *pg.* 711, *pg.* 878
Audino, Paul, Sr Mgr-Shopper Mktg - Ubisoft Inc.; *pg.* 589, *pg.* 229
Auen, Tim, Product Dir-Mobility - Intrado Inc.; *pg.* 420, *pg.* 334
Auerbach, Adam, Sr Dir - Capital One Bank (USA), N.A.; *pg.* 730, *pg.* 1789
Auerbach, Alexa, Dir-Media Rels & Investment Mgmt Div - MORNINGSTAR, INC.; *pg.* 784, *pg.* 583
Auerbach, Bryan, Sr Mgr-Customer Capability Dev - American Express Company; *pg.* 712, *pg.* 1190
Auerbach, Jonathan, Chief Strategy Officer, Chief Growth Officer & Sr VP - PayPal Inc.; *pg.* 1274, *pg.* 248
Aug, Dan, Sr Mgr-Social Media Dept & Internet Mktg - Canon U.S.A., Inc.; *pg.* 1404, *pg.* 1178
Auger, Michael P., VP-Trade Mktg Dev - R.J. Reynolds Tobacco Co.; *pg.* 1895, *pg.* 1395
August, Doug, Sr Product Mgr-Software & Solutions - Oki Data Americas, Inc.; *pg.* 449, *pg.* 1090
August, Hannah, Dir-Mktg-Natl Geographic Kids - National Geographic Society; *pg.* 1667, *pg.* 402
Augustine, Michael, Dir-Global Retail & Mktg - Sonos, Inc.; *pg.* 675, *pg.* 263
Augustine, Zach, Dir-Creative - NIKE, Inc.; *pg.* 1812, *pg.* 1492
Aulenbach, Carol, Sr Specialist-Mktg Comm - Carpenter Technology Corporation; *pg.* 73, *pg.* 1584
Ault, Chris, Sr Product Mgr - QNX Software Systems Ltd; *pg.* 458, *pg.* 1932
Ault, Lisa, Specialist-Mktg - SONOSITE, INC.; *pg.* 1429, *pg.* 1818
Auman, Debbie, Sr Dir-Product Mktg - Jockey International, Inc.; *pg.* 27, *pg.* 1861
Aumer, Michael, VP-Product Mgmt - Valencell, Inc.; *pg.* 684, *pg.* 1389
Aurand, Gary, Supvr-Brdcst Media - GEICO Corporation; *pg.* 1200, *pg.* 399
Auriemma, Jerry, CMO & Chief Sls Officer - The Casey Group; *pg.* 369, *pg.* 1102
Aurora, Sandeep, Dir-Mktg & Market Dev - Intel Corporation; *pg.* 645, *pg.* 266
Aust, Jared, Specialist-Email Mktg - AutoNation, Inc.; *pg.* 165, *pg.* 423
Aust, Lindsay, Sr Mgr-Mktg - Crocs, Inc.; *pg.* 1806, *pg.* 335
Austerberry, John, Sr Specialist-Media Rels - DTE Energy Company; *pg.* 1940, *pg.* 880
Austin, Annalisa, Mgr-Channel Mktg - Pacific Life Insurance Company; *pg.* 1213, *pg.* 166
Austin, Bill, Mgr-Adv - Makita U.S.A., Inc.; *pg.* 1358, *pg.* 120
Austin, Carol, VP-Mktg - Dunkin' Brands Group, Inc.; *pg.* 1727, *pg.* 810
Austin, David, Bus Mgr-Subscription - Hewlett-Packard Company; *pg.* 404, *pg.* 175
Austin, Ethan, Dir-Mktg - Sugarloaf/USA; *pg.* 586, *pg.* 749
Austin, Greg, Mgr-Global Product-Below-Grade Waterproofing - W.R. Grace & Co.; *pg.* 123, *pg.* 810
Austin, Heather, Brand Mgr-Premium Wines - E&J Gallo Winery; *pg.* 1962, *pg.* 149
Austin, Jocelyn, Sr VP-Corp Comm & PR - Al Jazeera America, LLC; *pg.* 269, *pg.* 1188
Austin, Joyce, Mgr-Inside Sls & Customer Svc - IAC Industries, Inc.; *pg.* 929, *pg.* 48
Austin, Kerianne, Coord-Mktg - Eaton Vance Corp.; *pg.* 746, *pg.* 794
Austin, Kim, Mgr-Mktg-Collaboration Tech Grp - Cisco Systems, Inc.; *pg.* 372, *pg.* 240
Austin, Meredith, Mgr-Sls Dev - Tyson Foods, Inc.; *pg.* 902, *pg.* 35
Austin, Rick, Dir-Sls & Mktg - B.C. Tree Fruits Ltd.; *pg.* 1015, *pg.* 1908
Austin, Steve, VP-Corp Media Rels - FMR LLC (Fidelity Investments); *pg.* 759, *pg.* 794
Auston, Brooke, Mgr-Mktg - Versace USA; *pg.* 34, *pg.* 1310
Auyeung, Derrick, Brand Mgr-Lipton Iced Tea - PepsiCo, Inc.; *pg.* 259, *pg.* 1327
Avalos, Dario, Sr Mgr-Channel Mktg - SanDisk Corporation; *pg.* 465, *pg.* 147
Avantini, Craig, Dir-Sls - Marriott International, Inc.; *pg.* 1102, *pg.* 764
Avat, Xavier, Dir-HCV Mktg-Launch Team & US Comml - Gilead Sciences, Inc.; *pg.* 1535, *pg.* 88
Avelar, Tracy, Dir-Global Mktg Sourcing - Visa Inc.; *pg.* 816, *pg.* 230
Avello, Miguel, Dir-Product Org-Global - Whirlpool Corporation; *pg.* 62, *pg.* 872
Avendano, Pauline, Dir-Mktg & Comm - Herbalife International of America, Inc.; *pg.* 1541, *pg.* 132
Avent, Casey, VP-Sls & Mktg - Smead Manufacturing Company; *pg.* 470, *pg.* 926
Avera, Greg, VP-Global OEM Sls & Bus Dev - Kensington Technology Group; *pg.* 424, *pg.* 191
Averbook, Amy, Dir-Mktg Svcs - United Business Media LLC; *pg.* 1697, *pg.* 1177
Averbuck, Julia, Mgr-Mktg - Justworks, Inc.; *pg.* 424, *pg.* 1247
Averill, Bill, Dir-Field Mktg - MillerCoors LLC; *pg.* 255, *pg.* 582
Avery Cittadine, Alexis, Dir-PR & Mktg - bebe stores, inc.; *pg.* 19, *pg.* 49
Avery, Amanda, Sr Mgr-Mktg - Coty, Inc.; *pg.* 506, *pg.* 1219
Avery, Annika, Dir-Mktg - Vascular Solutions, Inc.; *pg.* 1434, *pg.* 946
Avery, Ed, VP-Upholstery Product Dev - Bassett Furniture Industries, Incorporated; *pg.* 916, *pg.* 1776
Avery, James C, Sr Mgr-New Franchise Bus Dev - Pizza Hut, Inc.; *pg.* 1744, *pg.* 1733
Avery, Judy, Dir-Sls & Mktg - Sun Journal; *pg.* 1690, *pg.* 1386
Avery, Kathleen, Sr Dir-HR - US Oncology, Inc.; *pg.* 1604, *pg.* 1747
Avery, Martha, Mgr-Mktg - Remy International, Inc.; *pg.* 216, *pg.* 696
Avery, Melissa, Creative Dir - Combe Incorporated; *pg.* 1516, *pg.* 1351
Avery, Tracy, Dir-Strategic Mktg - Travelers Insurance; *pg.* 1220, *pg.* 963
Avetta, Peterson, Dir-Ticket Sls - Carolina Hurricanes Hockey Club; *pg.* 537, *pg.* 1386
Avidan, Yael, Dir-Product Mgmt-Adv & Data - Yahoo! Inc.; *pg.* 1289, *pg.* 289
Avila, Cuca, Analyst-Mktg - State Farm Mutual Automobile Insurance Co.; *pg.* 1218, *pg.* 557
Avila, Daphne C., Dir-Media Rels & Corp Affairs - J.C. Penney Company, Inc.; *pg.* 1774, *pg.* 1732
Avila, Oriana, Sr Mgr-Mktg - Bonnier Corporation; *pg.* 1622, *pg.* 480
Avila, Orlando, Sr Mgr-Mktg & Brdcst Svcs - Arizona Cardinals Football Club, Inc.; *pg.* 529, *pg.* 25
Aviles, Clarilu, Brand Mgr-Oncology - Bristol-Myers Squibb Company; *pg.* 1509, *pg.* 1206
Aviles, Nick, Analyst-Social Media Mktg - State Farm Mutual Automobile Insurance Co.; *pg.* 1218, *pg.* 557
Aviles-Osorio, Gracie, Assoc Mgr-Integrated Mktg Comm - The Allstate Corporation; *pg.* 1189, *pg.* 639
Avitabile, Amy, VP-Integrated Mktg - Toys "R" Us, Inc.; *pg.* 968, *pg.* 1130
Avivi, Samantha, Dir-Mktg-Global - Kimberly-Clark Corporation; *pg.* 1461, *pg.* 1720
Avril, Beau, Head-Product Commercialization-Google Preferred-Global - Google Inc.; *pg.* 1249, *pg.* 153
Awan, Faisal, Sr Dir-ECommerce-Global - Staples, Inc.; *pg.* 474, *pg.* 821
Awana, Renee, Sr Dir-Product Dev - Hawaiian Holdings, Inc.; *pg.* 1910, *pg.* 544
Awdish, Michael, Gen Mgr-Digital Mktg - Volkswagen Group of America, Inc.; *pg.* 194, *pg.* 1785
Awe, Jenny, Mgr-Mktg - Uber USA, LLC; *pg.* 1286, *pg.* 229
Awwa, Sacha, Mgr-Mktg - The New York Times Company; *pg.* 1668, *pg.* 1270
Axberg, Kari, VP-Branding & Adv - New York Life Insurance Company; *pg.* 1211, *pg.* 1268
Axe, Lauren, Dir-Brand Mktg - Checkers Drive-In Restaurants, Inc.; *pg.* 1017, *pg.* 472
Axline, Cindy J., Mgr-Sls & Mktg-BP Solar - BP America Inc.; *pg.* 972, *pg.* 1702
Axt, Katherine, Sr Mgr-Mktg-Outdoors & Outdoor Apparel - Amazon.com, Inc.; *pg.* 1226, *pg.* 1831
Ay, Marisa Edmund, Exec VP-Mktg & Comm - Edmund Industrial Optics Inc.; *pg.* 1411, *pg.* 1041
Ayala, Adrian, Mgr-Digital Mktg - Warner Bros. Records, Inc.; *pg.* 1791, *pg.* 55
Ayass, Basil, Dir-Mktg - Dell Inc.; *pg.* 383, *pg.* 1737
Ayaz, Asad, Exec VP-Mktg - The Walt Disney Company; *pg.* 317, *pg.* 52
Aybaz, Diana, Assoc Store Mgr-Sls - Williams-Sonoma, Inc.; *pg.* 1140, *pg.* 234
Aycock, Carrol, Mgr-Sls - Texas Refinery Corp.; *pg.* 986, *pg.* 1696
Aye, Semone, VP-Mktg - Stearns Lending, LLC.; *pg.* 805, *pg.* 262
Ayele, Daniel, Product Mgr - LinkedIn Corporation; *pg.* 1262, *pg.* 160
Ayer, Mark, VP-Sls-Canada - Kraft Canada Inc.; *pg.* 869, *pg.* 1939
Ayers, Angela, Dir-Mktg & Comm-Bioengineering & Biosciences - Georgia Institute Of Technology; *pg.* 602, *pg.* 506
Ayers, Darryl, Dir-Production - The Times-News; *pg.* 1694, *pg.* 1359
Aykan, Cem, Sr Product Mgr-Delve & Office Graph - Microsoft Corporation; *pg.* 435, *pg.* 1824
Ayling, Tim, Dir-Sls & Mktg - Kinder Morgan; *pg.* 1945, *pg.* 1709
Aylsworth, Lauren, Brand Mgr - Amway Corporation; *pg.* 326, *pg.* 864
Aylward, John, Sr VP-Mktg - CNBC; *pg.* 275, *pg.* 1059
Ayoub, Misaa, Dir-Digital Mktg - Shiseido Cosmetics America of SAC; *pg.* 522, *pg.* 1291
Ayre, Kim, Mgr-Mktg Comm - IDEXX Laboratories, Inc.; *pg.* 1543, *pg.* 753
Ayres, Nick, Dir-Social Mktg - InterContinental Hotels Corporation; *pg.* 1097, *pg.* 511
Aytek, Melissa, Specialist-Americas Field Mktg - Autodesk Inc.; *pg.* 356, *pg.* 257
Ayvazian, Vahe, Dir-Mktg-US Diagnostics Bus - Abbott Laboratories; *pg.* 1484, *pg.* 551
Ayyappan, Anish, Mgr-Mktg-North America - Netflix, Inc.; *pg.* 1269, *pg.* 141
Azali, Elicia, Assoc VP-NI Brand Mktg-Affinity Mktg & Consumer Innovation - Nationwide Mutual Insurance Company; *pg.* 1210, *pg.* 1442
Azam, Barie, Mgr-Mktg - Canon U.S.A., Inc.; *pg.* 1404, *pg.* 1178
Azar, Larry, Sr VP & Div Mgr-Mdsg - Kohl's Corporation; *pg.* 1775, *pg.* 1870
Azcuy, Mariela, Sr Dir-Adv Sls Mktg - Univision Communications Inc.; *pg.* 683, *pg.* 1307
Azer, Christian, Head-Mktg - Shutterstock, Inc.; *pg.* 1280, *pg.* 1291
Azerrad, Jessica, Specialist-Local Mktg - Ikea North America Services LLC; *pg.* 929, *pg.* 1523
Aziz, Dave, Mgr-Social Media - LG Electronics U.S.A., Inc.; *pg.* 651, *pg.* 1060
Aziz, Pam, Mgr-Demand Programs Mktg - IBM Canada Limited; *pg.* 411, *pg.* 1923
Aznavour, Tina, Sr Mgr-Licensing-Lucasfilm - The Walt Disney

Company; pg. 317, pg. 52
Azotam, Dozie, Sr Mgr-Mktg-CBS Corporation - CBS Broadcasting Inc.; pg. 273, pg. 1210
Azotam, Dozie, Sr Mgr-Mktg - CBS Corporation; pg. 273, pg. 1210
Azria, Lubov, Chief Creative Officer - BCBG Max Azria Group LLC; pg. 19, pg. 301
Azuma, Naomi, Dir-Art-US & Intl Mktg - J. Crew Group, Inc.; pg. 1773, pg. 1245
Azzahimi, Mostapha, Product Mgr-Medium Voltage Switchgear - Eaton Corporation; pg. 1331, pg. 1429
Azzara, Adam, Sr Product Mgr - NuVasive, Inc.; pg. 1577, pg. 205
Azzarello, James, Dir-Sls - Rochling Glastic Composites; pg. 1889, pg. 1435
Azzaretti, Marco, Mgr-AIS Product Mgmt - Key Technology, Inc.; pg. 868, pg. 1847
Azzarito, Dawn, Dir-Digital Mktg & ECommerce - Wyndham Vacation Ownership; pg. 1119, pg. 457
Azzi, Anne-Marie, Mgr-Mktg-Sls Enablement - Cisco Systems, Inc.; pg. 372, pg. 240
Azzola, Stefania, Dir-Mktg - Safilo USA Inc.; pg. 11, pg. 1106

B

Baack, Sara, CMO - Equinix, Inc.; pg. 394, pg. 190
Baad, Cathy, Sr VP & Mgr-Mktg Program Dev - Bank of America Corporation; pg. 718, pg. 1362
Baauw, Kathelijne, Dir-Mktg & Global Duty Free-White Spirits - Diageo North America, Inc.; pg. 1961, pg. 361
Baba, Ann Marie, Sr Mgr-Mktg Campaigns - Adobe Systems Incorporated; pg. 342, pg. 235
Babb, Kristen, Sr VP & Sr Mgr-Comm - Bank of America Corporation; pg. 718, pg. 1362
Babbington, Danielle, Mgr-Consumer PR - Boost Mobile; pg. 1869, pg. 107
Babbits, Christina, VP-Multi-Media Sls - The Wall Street Journal; pg. 1700, pg. 1312
Babcock, Aimee, Dir-Creative-Integrated Retail & Special Projects - Sears Holdings Corporation; pg. 1784, pg. 618
Babcock, Ken, Sr Dir-Conservation Programs - Ducks Unlimited, Inc.; pg. 139, pg. 1642
Babcock, Kristina, Mgr-Mktg - Compass Group Diversified Holdings LLC; pg. 741, pg. 383
Babcock-Brown, Melanie, Sr Dir-Social Media - The Home Depot, Inc.; pg. 1050, pg. 510
Baber, Courtney, Sr VP-Mktg, Mdsg & PR-Urban Decay - L'Oreal USA; pg. 514, pg. 1252
Babiar, Lorraine, Mgr-Product & Mktg - General Motors Company; pg. 175, pg. 881
Babiarz, Paul, Reg Sls Dir-Sls-NE - Honeywell International Inc.; pg. 407, pg. 1088
Babiarz, Sara, Mgr-Social Media - Travel Channel LLC; pg. 313, pg. 766
Babich, Stefan, Dir-Adv - The Roanoke Times; pg. 1680, pg. 1806
Babics, David, Product Mgr-Section Doors - Raynor Garage Doors; pg. 106, pg. 607
Babin, Ira, Dir-Mktg - Louisiana Office of Tourism; pg. 997, pg. 742
Babine, Jayne, VP-Media & Adv Sls-Neustar Mktg Svcs - NeuStar, Inc.; pg. 1872, pg. 1807
Babineau, Brian, VP-Product & Channel Mktg - Barracuda Networks, Inc.; pg. 360, pg. 58
Babineau, Katherine, Mgr-Social Mktg & Sports Mktg - GoPro; pg. 1414, pg. 255
Babitts, Gerard, Sr Dir-Digital Mktg - Rite Aid Corporation; pg. 1590, pg. 1519
Babl, Nic, Specialist-Mobile Mktg - Foot Locker, Inc.; pg. 1808, pg. 1231
Babson, Kristen, Asst Mgr-Production-Madewell - J. Crew Group, Inc.; pg. 1773, pg. 1245
Babusci, Tina, Sr Product Dir-Direct Import - Ross Stores, Inc.; pg. 1783, pg. 78
Baby, Emily, Acct Mgr-Adv Sls - Meredith Corporation; pg. 1663, pg. 705
Babylon, Hank, Head-Global Sourcing Product - National Oilwell Varco, Inc.; pg. 1364, pg. 1712
Baca, Carl, Dir-Strategic Mktg, Roofing & Asphalt - Owens Corning; pg. 102, pg. 1476
Baca, Joel, Sr Mgr-Oncology Consumer Mktg - Amgen Inc.; pg. 1493, pg. 291
Bacal, Amanda McCormick, VP-Mktg - Ralph Lauren Corporation; pg. 46, pg. 1284
Baccam, Phoukham, Asst Dir-eBusiness Mktg - Principal Financial Group, Inc.; pg. 796, pg. 706
Bacco, Scott, Sr Dir-Brand Mktg - Chobani LLC; pg. 847, pg. 1318
Bach, Amanda, Sr Mgr-Package Design - Nestle USA, Inc.; pg. 883, pg. 96
Bach, Karen, Dir-Budget, Products & Comm - Arizona Lottery; pg. 988, pg. 14
Bach, Lisa, Assoc Dir-Special Sls - Chronicle Books; pg. 1627, pg. 216
Bach, Melissa, Dir-PR & Corp Comm - XO Group Inc.; pg. 1289, pg. 1316
Bach, Susan, Sr Mgr-Gift Cards - J.C. Penney Company, Inc.; pg. 1774, pg. 1732
Bacharach, Jim, VP-Brand, Mktg & Creative Svcs - John Hancock Financial Services; pg. 1205, pg. 796
Bacharidis, Nico, Head-Global Tender & Contracting-Established Products - Pfizer Inc.; pg. 1581, pg. 1278
Bachicha, Louis R., Exec VP-Sls - Sealy Corporation; pg. 942, pg. 1391
Bachman, Jim, Mgr-Sls & Mktg-Natl - E.I. du Pont de Nemours & Company; pg. 1159, pg. 390
Bachman, Theresa, VP-Mktg - Fulton Financial Corporation; pg. 760, pg. 1546
Bachmann, Ashley, Brand Mgr-Miracle-Gro - The Scotts Miracle-Gro Company; pg. 1799, pg. 1459
Bachmann, Jeff, Analyst-Digital Media Mktg - Anheuser-Busch Companies, LLC; pg. 237, pg. 991
Bachmann, Tilly M., Dir-Sls & Svcs - SkyAuction.com, Inc.; pg. 1281, pg. 1293
Bachmann, Urs, Mgr-Field Mktg Grp-North America - F5 Networks, Inc.; pg. 396, pg. 1835
Bachrach, Beth, Sr VP-Local Sls & Strategy Res - Univision Communications Inc.; pg. 683, pg. 1307
Bachrach, Brian, Sr Mgr-Mktg & Innovation - Just Born, Inc.; pg. 1857, pg. 1516
Bachta, Robert, Dir-Mktg - Vaughan & Bushnell Manufacturing Company, Inc.; pg. 1066, pg. 616
Bacik, Lori, Sr Mgr-Adv - The J.M. Smucker Company; pg. 865, pg. 1468
Back, Blaine, Dir-Sls - Silver Springs, Inc.; pg. 583, pg. 468
Back, Darren, Sr Dir-WRD Comm - Pfizer Inc.; pg. 1581, pg. 1278
Backer, Lindsay Maxwell, Mgr-Mktg-Snacks-Walmart - General Mills, Inc.; pg. 828, pg. 933
Backer-Herzog, Kristin, Dir-Mktg - Diamond Foods, Inc.; pg. 1851, pg. 216
Backhaus, Steve, Dir-Email Mktg-Personal Insurance - Liberty Mutual Insurance Group Inc.; pg. 1205, pg. 797
Backlund, Diana M., Mgr-Adv-Intl - Graham Holdings Company; pg. 1645, pg. 1773
Backstrom, Jack, Dir-Mktg-Intl - In-Sink-Erator; pg. 57, pg. 1888
Bacon, Lindsay, Mgr-Adv & Collateral - Porsche Cars North America, Inc.; pg. 189, pg. 518
Bacon, Melinda, Dir-Mktg - Bright House Networks LLC; pg. 272, pg. 461
Bacon, Seth, Sr VP-Media - Major League Soccer LLC; pg. 560, pg. 1256
Bacon, Terrill, Product Mgr - Hormel Foods Corporation; pg. 863, pg. 915
Bacus, John, Dir-Product Mgmt-SketchUp - Trimble Navigation Limited; pg. 1384, pg. 288
Baczek, Greg, Dir-Channel Mktg - Stanley Black & Decker, Inc.; pg. 1063, pg. 358
Badavas, Keri, Product Mgr-Women's Running-Global - Reebok International Ltd.; pg. 1817, pg. 811
Badawiyeh, Basil, Sr Dir-Video Products-Media - Charter Communications, Inc.; pg. 274, pg. 372
Baddeley, Curtis, Sr Dir-Rental Suites - Chicago Professional Sports Limited Partnership; pg. 539, pg. 570
Bader, Gregory, VP-Comm & Mktg - Baltimore Orioles, L.P.; pg. 532, pg. 755
Bader, James, Sr Mgr-SEO - CVS Health Corporation; pg. 1765, pg. 1610
Bader, Jeffrey M., VP-Embedded Solutions Grp Mktg - Micron Technology, Inc.; pg. 435, pg. 547
Bader, Lisa, Dir-Shopper Mktg - Intel Corporation; pg. 645, pg. 266
Bader, Ron, Dir-Sls-North America & Europe - Rogers Corporation; pg. 1305, pg. 369
Badescu-Bodoff, Juliana, Sr Mgr - Pfizer Inc.; pg. 1581, pg. 1278
Badger, Brandon, Grp Product Mgr-Niantic Labs - Google Inc.; pg. 1249, pg. 153
Badger, Sydney, Sr Mgr-Direct Mktg-Amazon Fashion - Amazon.com, Inc.; pg. 1226, pg. 1831
Badia, Carmelita, Mgr-Mktg-Comml Vans - General Motors Company; pg. 175, pg. 881
Badichi, Ronen, Pres-Battery & Energy Products Div - Arotech Corporation; pg. 1042, pg. 865
Bado, Geoff, Sr Mgr-Content Production - Campbell Soup Company; pg. 844, pg. 1048
Badolato, Vincent, Sr Mgr-Sls - ESPN, Inc.; pg. 285, pg. 340
Badosa, Monica, Mgr-Digital Adv - Yurman Design, Inc.; pg. 15, pg. 1316
Baebler, Christine, Mgr-Mktg - Coty, Inc.; pg. 506, pg. 1219
Baechler, Evan, Brand Mgr-Global Digital-Nike Football - NIKE, Inc.; pg. 1812, pg. 1492
Baeckler, Tracy, Sr Mgr-Paid Social Media - eBay Inc.; pg. 1240, pg. 243
Baehman, Schuyler, Sr Mgr-Comm - National Hockey League; pg. 568, pg. 1265
Baehman, Tiffany, Exec Dir-Mktg - AT&T Mobility LLC; pg. 620, pg. 1152
Baek, Sam M., Sr Mgr-Entertainment & Digital Experience Analytics - DIRECTV Group Holdings, LLC; pg. 281, pg. 79
Baekgaard, Barbara Bradley, Co-Founder, Chief Creative Officer & Dir - VERA BRADLEY, INC.; pg. 15, pg. 697
Baen, Thomas, Sr Analyst-Digital Mktg - Academy Sports & Outdoors, Ltd.; pg. 1824, pg. 1724
Baer, Bill, Sr Product Mgr-SharePoint - Microsoft Corporation; pg. 435, pg. 1824
Baer, Dave, VP-Strategy & Mktg - Tyco SimplexGrinnell LP; pg. 682, pg. 859
Baer, Earl D., VP-Sls - The Providence Journal; pg. 1678, pg. 1607
Baer, Eldree, Sr Mgr-Segment Comm - Wellmark, Inc; pg. 1223, pg. 707
Baer, Jason, VP-Sls & Mktg - The Vermont Teddy Bear Company; pg. 969, pg. 1767
Baer, Jim, Sr Dir-Data Science - LinkedIn Corporation; pg. 1262, pg. 160
Baerlocher, Shawn, VP-Products & Sys - HARRIS CORPORATION; pg. 642, pg. 439
Baetz, John, Dir-Mktg Svcs, Natl Print & Paper Procurement - Sears Holdings Corporation; pg. 1784, pg. 618
Baez, Cara, Mgr-Personal Sys Attach Svcs Category Mktg - Hewlett-Packard Company; pg. 404, pg. 175
Baez, Christina, specialist-PR - Norwegian Cruise Line; pg. 1917, pg. 444
Baez, Eduardo, Sr Mgr-Mktg & Strategy-Private Brand - Office Depot, Inc.; pg. 448, pg. 412
Baez, John, VP-Integrated Mktg Ops - MTV Networks Company; pg. 298, pg. 1262
Baez, Sandra, VP-Digital Strategy, Ops & Product & Gen Mgr-NYPost Verticals - News Corporation; pg. 1669, pg. 1271
Baeza, Hector, Assoc Dir-Mktg-Global - Alexion Pharmaceuticals, Inc.; pg. 1489, pg. 341
Baeza, Orlando, Sr Mgr-Consumer Mktg - Activision Blizzard, Inc.; pg. 948, pg. 271
Baffoe-Bonnie, Marcus, Dir-Retail Mktg - Tempur Sealy International, Inc.; pg. 944, pg. 731
Bagan, Dan, Sr VP-Agriculture, Food & Mktg Grp - Penton Media, Inc.; pg. 1676, pg. 719
Bagby, Bob, VP-Mktg - Zebco; pg. 1848, pg. 1491
Bagg, Jonathan, Engr-Pr Supplier Quality - Medtronic, Inc.; pg. 1564, pg. 939
Bagger, Kevin, Sr Dir-Strategic Res & Analytics - Las Vegas Convention & Visitors Authority; pg. 997, pg. 1027
Baggett, Dana, Dir-Mktg - Valassis; pg. 1698, pg. 386
Bagierek, Joe, Dir-Mktg - TBC Corporation; pg. 1889, pg. 457
Baginski, Tom, Sr Mgr-Mktg Strategy - W.W. Grainger, Inc.; pg. 1390, pg. 625
Bagley, Daniel, VP-Global Product Safety - Colgate-Palmolive Company; pg. 504, pg. 1215
Bagley, Jason, Sr Mgr-Beef Quality & Export - Texas Beef Council; pg. 158, pg. 1666
Bagley, Karen, Project Mgr-Brand Mktg-Global - Staples, Inc.; pg. 474, pg. 821
Bagley, Natalie, VP & Dir-Creative Svcs & Brand Identity - Citizens Financial Group, Inc.; pg. 737, pg. 1606
Bagli, Deris, Dir-Sls - McKee Foods Corporation; pg. 1860, pg. 1630
Baglione, Joeanna, Sr Mgr-Mktg, Display & Social-Australia - eBay Inc.; pg. 1240, pg. 243
Baglivo, Mary, CMO & VP-Mktg-Global - Northwestern University; pg. 606, pg. 612
Bagshaw, Jim, VP-Adv, Sponsorship & Mktg - Calgary Flames

First page reference indicates Business Class Edition
Second page reference indicates Geographic Edition

Limited Partnership; *pg.* 535, *pg.* 1902
Bagshaw, Troy, Dir-Mktg - AT&T Mobility LLC; *pg.* 619, *pg.* 488
Bah, Sekou, Specialist-Mktg - LivingSocial, Inc.; *pg.* 1264, *pg.* 401
Bahm, Ernie, Sr Dir - Broadcom Corporation; *pg.* 364, *pg.* 108
Bahr, Ira, CMO & Sr VP - TiVo Inc.; *pg.* 313, *pg.* 251
Bahr, Ola Von, Founder & Dir-Creative - Fortune; *pg.* 1642, *pg.* 1232
Bai, Meg, Sr Product Mgr - Pfizer Inc.; *pg.* 1581, *pg.* 1278
Baicy, Elizabeth, Head-Product Mktg-Amazon Digital Devices - Amazon.com, Inc.; *pg.* 1226, *pg.* 1831
Baiden, Edward, Dir-Mktg & Product Strategy-Africa-DuPont Pioneer - E.I. du Pont de Nemours & Company; *pg.* 1159, *pg.* 390
Baik, Joshua, Sr Product Mgr-Mktg - Sharp Electronics Corporation; *pg.* 672, *pg.* 1082
Bailey, Aaron R., COO & VP-Fin, Ops & Mktg Svcs Div-RBI - BuyerZone.com, LLC; *pg.* 1233, *pg.* 850
Bailey, Andrew, Principal-Mktg - FedEx Corporation; *pg.* 1907, *pg.* 1642
Bailey, Andy, Sr Mgr - Apple Inc.; *pg.* 350, *pg.* 73
Bailey, Debbie, Sr Specialist-Mktg - Kawasaki Motors Corp., U.S.A.; *pg.* 1708, *pg.* 111
Bailey, Douglas G., VP-Mktg - Power Integrations, Inc.; *pg.* 1369, *pg.* 249
Bailey, Edward, Mgr-Mktg - General Motors Company; *pg.* 175, *pg.* 881
Bailey, George, Dir-Technical Mktg - Synopsys, Inc.; *pg.* 480, *pg.* 162
Bailey, Heidi, Sr Mgr-Mktg-Growth Markets - LEGO Systems, Inc.; *pg.* 961, *pg.* 346
Bailey, James, Product Mgr-Red Hat Customer Portal - Red Hat, Inc.; *pg.* 460, *pg.* 1388
Bailey, Jan, Mgr-Sls-Worldwide - Mechanical Products Inc.; *pg.* 1302, *pg.* 894
Bailey, Jay, Mgr-Mktg - Valero Energy Corporation; *pg.* 986, *pg.* 1743
Bailey, Jon, Sr Asst Brand Mgr - DISH Network Corporation; *pg.* 283, *pg.* 325
Bailey, Joseph, Sr Mgr - Ernst & Young Global Limited; *pg.* 748, *pg.* 1228
Bailey, Julia, Mgr-Mktg Events - Protective Life Insurance Company; *pg.* 1215, *pg.* 4
Bailey, Justin, Mgr-Sports & Entertainment Mktg - MillerCoors LLC; *pg.* 255, *pg.* 582
Bailey, Kerri M., Dir-Sls - Yahoo! Inc.; *pg.* 1289, *pg.* 289
Bailey, Kimberly, Mgr-Mktg-Grocery - Wal-Mart.com; *pg.* 1287, *pg.* 50
Bailey, Lalita, Dir-Media - Hair Club for Men, Ltd., Inc.; *pg.* 511, *pg.* 411
Bailey, Lance, Mgr-Mktg & Programs - Dupont Pioneer; *pg.* 1795, *pg.* 708
Bailey, Laura, Sr Mgr-Mdsg Strategy - Dr Pepper Snapple Group, Inc.; *pg.* 250, *pg.* 1729
Bailey, Lesley, VP-Channel Mktg & Brand Mgmt-EMEA - Turner Broadcasting System, Inc.; *pg.* 314, *pg.* 521
Bailey, Levena, Sr Dir-Enterprise Security - Hilton Worldwide, Inc.; *pg.* 1094, *pg.* 1791
Bailey, Lisa, Sr Dir-Media Strategy & Activation - Select Comfort Corporation; *pg.* 942, *pg.* 942
Bailey, Marybeth, Mgr-Search Mktg - Bonnier Corporation; *pg.* 1622, *pg.* 480
Bailey, Michael, Sr Mgr-Mktg-Google Digital Media - Google Inc.; *pg.* 1249, *pg.* 153
Bailey, Perrin, Mgr-Social Media Mktg - The New York Times Company; *pg.* 1668, *pg.* 1270
Bailey, Robyn, VP-Field Mktg - Church's Chicken, Inc.; *pg.* 1722, *pg.* 493
Bailey, Roger, Pres-North America Power Products - ABB Inc.; *pg.* 1309, *pg.* 1359
Bailey, Rosa, Mgr-Experiential Mktg - FCA US LLC; *pg.* 170, *pg.* 868
Bailey, Sarah, Mgr-Social Media Mktg - Dow Jones & Company, Inc.; *pg.* 1637, *pg.* 1225
Bailey, Seymour, Mgr-Bus Dev-Barbados Tourism Mktg Inc. - Barbados Tourism Authority; *pg.* 1900, *pg.* 1200
Bailey, Sheri, Assoc Dir-Mktg - AT&T; *pg.* 1865, *pg.* 258
Bailey, Steven, Sr Dir-Fin - Match.Com, LLC; *pg.* 1265, *pg.* 1683
Bailey, Sue, Dir-Major Appliance Product Mgmt - Viking Range Corporation; *pg.* 61, *pg.* 968
Bailey, Trisha, Sr Mgr-Mktg - Frito-Lay North America, Inc.; *pg.* 1853, *pg.* 1730
Bailey, Trisha, Sr Mgr-Mktg - PepsiCo, Inc.; *pg.* 259, *pg.* 1327
Bailis, Bevin, Sr VP-Comm & PR - Kohl's Corporation; *pg.* 1775, *pg.* 1870
Baillie, Pamela E., Mgr-Beauty & Grooming PR - Procter & Gamble Inc.; *pg.* 333, *pg.* 1929
Bain, Alison, Head-Intl Adv, Brand & 360 Comms - American Express Company; *pg.* 712, *pg.* 1190
Bain, Lara, Sr Specialist-Social Media - Nordstrom, Inc.; *pg.* 1779, *pg.* 1837
Bain, Mary Catherine, Dir-Mktg-Natl Events - U.S. News & World Report, L.P.; *pg.* 1698, *pg.* 1308
Bain, Renee, Head-Social Media-Global - IBM; *pg.* 410, *pg.* 1449
Bain, Sheri, Reg Dir-Media - Coca-Cola Refreshments USA, Inc.; *pg.* 247, *pg.* 500
Bainbridge, Morgan, Mgr-Mktg - Huron Consulting Group Inc.; *pg.* 768, *pg.* 577
Bainbridge, Stacey, Media Planner-Online - QVC Inc; *pg.* 305, *pg.* 1593
Baines, Susan, Dir-Mktg - Komori America Corporation; *pg.* 1353, *pg.* 656
Bainter, John, Product Mgr - Gilead Sciences, Inc.; *pg.* 1535, *pg.* 88
Bair, Neil, Exec Dir-Mktg, Pricing & Access - Amgen Inc.; *pg.* 1493, *pg.* 291
Baird, Ann, Dir-Mktg - Meredith Corporation; *pg.* 1663, *pg.* 705
Baird, Donna, VP-Mktg - Revlon Consumer Products Corporation; *pg.* 521, *pg.* 1286
Baird, Donna, VP-Mktg - Revlon, Inc.; *pg.* 521, *pg.* 1286
Baird, Lisa, CMO - United States Olympic Committee; *pg.* 589, *pg.* 315
Baird, Sarah, VP-Mktg & Comm - Dairy Management, Inc.; *pg.* 138, *pg.* 656
Bairos, John, Sr Mgr-Govt & Regulatory Affairs - Comcast Corporation; *pg.* 276, *pg.* 1560
Bajaj, Binay, Sr Dir-Mobile Product Mktg - Atmel Corporation; *pg.* 621, *pg.* 238
Bajaj, Parul, Sr Mgr-Comm - Bridgestone Americas, Inc.; *pg.* 1879, *pg.* 1648
Bajaj, Sangeeta, Partner-Strategic Mktg & Sr Dir - JDA Software Group, Inc.; *pg.* 423, *pg.* 22
Bajrech, Kim, Sr VP & Gen Mgr-Mdse - The Wet Seal, LLC; *pg.* 35, *pg.* 88
Bajtos, Scott, Sr VP-Svcs & Customer Advocacy-Global - VMware, Inc.; *pg.* 490, *pg.* 179
Bajwa, Bik, Assoc Dir-Mktg - Genentech, Inc.; *pg.* 1533, *pg.* 279
Bakas, Ana, Dir-Product Mgmt - PCTEL, Inc.; *pg.* 452, *pg.* 557
Baker, Abby, Mgr-Customer Mktg - Tractor Supply Company; *pg.* 708, *pg.* 1627
Baker, Ali, Mgr-ECommerce Mktg - Verizon Communications Inc.; *pg.* 1875, *pg.* 1309
Baker, Alysia, Mgr-Worldwide Product Mktg-ThinkPad - Lenovo Group Ltd; *pg.* 427, *pg.* 1384
Baker, Amy, Exec VP-Natl Ad Sls - A&E Television Networks, LLC; *pg.* 267, *pg.* 1185
Baker, Amy, Mgr-Product Mktg - Epicor Software Corporation; *pg.* 393, *pg.* 110
Baker, Amy, Sr VP-Sls - The History Channel; *pg.* 290, *pg.* 1240
Baker, Andy, Sr VP & Grp Dir-Creative - National Geographic Channel; *pg.* 299, *pg.* 402
Baker, Anita, Sr Dir-Worldwide Consumer & Small Bus Mktg - Symantec Corporation; *pg.* 478, *pg.* 161
Baker, Anna, Mgr-Reg Field & Channel Mktg - Quantum Corporation; *pg.* 458, *pg.* 250
Baker, Antonia, Dir-Mktg-Trade Comm & Events - Food Network; *pg.* 287, *pg.* 1231
Baker, Barb, Dir-Adv & Community Rels - Grinnell Mutual Reinsurance Company Inc.; *pg.* 1201, *pg.* 708
Baker, Brad, Dir-Digital Mktg-Disney Parks & Resorts - The Walt Disney Company; *pg.* 317, *pg.* 52
Baker, Brandon, Engr-Adobe Social-Social Media Product Support - Adobe Systems Incorporated; *pg.* 342, *pg.* 235
Baker, Brian, Mng Dir-Health Program Sls - Accenture; *pg.* 1392, *pg.* 1186
Baker, Brian, Dir-Sls - Thomson CompuMark; *pg.* 484, *pg.* 838
Baker, Celessa, Sr Mgr-Integrated Mktg-Color - Sephora USA Inc; *pg.* 522, *pg.* 227
Baker, Chris, Head-Global Mktg Procurement - Heineken USA Inc.; *pg.* 252, *pg.* 1352
Baker, Cindy, VP-Brand Mktg & Ops - Hilton Worldwide, Inc.; *pg.* 1094, *pg.* 1791
Baker, Darrell, Sr Dir-Sls - Amkor Technology, Inc.; *pg.* 67, *pg.* 25
Baker, Darren, Product Mgr - Google Inc.; *pg.* 1249, *pg.* 153
Baker, David, Dir-Digital Mktg Quality & Svc Delivery - Adobe Systems Incorporated; *pg.* 342, *pg.* 235
Baker, Deann, Sr Dir-Bus Dev - Telecommunication Systems Inc.; *pg.* 483, *pg.* 754
Baker, Deonn, Mgr-Mktg - Electrolux Home Products North America; *pg.* 54, *pg.* 1366
Baker, Donna, Reg VP-Midwest & Mgr-Market-Cumulus Media Kansas City - Cumulus Media Inc.; *pg.* 280, *pg.* 503
Baker, Dustin, Mgr-Production Issues - National Pork Producers Council; *pg.* 150, *pg.* 712
Baker, Elisa, Sr Mgr-Brand Comm & Mgr - PepsiCo, Inc.; *pg.* 259, *pg.* 1327
Baker, Elizabeth, Specialist-PR & Comm - Pima Medical Institute; *pg.* 1585, *pg.* 27
Baker, Elizabeth, Mgr-Mktg-W Hotels of New York - Starwood Hotels & Resorts Worldwide, Inc.; *pg.* 1114, *pg.* 378
Baker, Glenn D., Acct Mgr-Sls Bus-EPC, IPP & Dev Bus Dev Americas - Siemens Process Industries and Drive; *pg.* 1376, *pg.* 1587
Baker, Greg, Sr Dir-Upstream Chemicals - Baker Petrolite Corporation; *pg.* 1148, *pg.* 1745
Baker, Howard, Sr Dir-Grand Openings - Chick-fil-A, Inc.; *pg.* 1721, *pg.* 492
Baker, Jaime, Mgr-Mktg - 1-800-Flowers.com, Inc.; *pg.* 1758, *pg.* 1151
Baker, Jared, Sr Dir-Mktg-Oscar Mayer Cold Cuts - The Kraft Heinz Company; *pg.* 871, *pg.* 641
Baker, Jason, Dir-Respiratory Payer Mktg - GlaxoSmithKline; *pg.* 1536, *pg.* 1565
Baker, Jeff, Sr Dir-Brand Experience - Arby's Restaurant Group, Inc.; *pg.* 1014, *pg.* 488
Baker, Jody, Mgr-Product Mktg Team - Matco Tools Corporation; *pg.* 1055, *pg.* 1474
Baker, John, Dir-Sls CPG Indus W/Expertise-Mktg, Plng, Strategy & Leadership - MATTEL, INC.; *pg.* 962, *pg.* 81
Baker, Judson, Product Mgr-Derivatives & Collateral Mgmt - Northern Trust Corporation; *pg.* 787, *pg.* 585
Baker, Karen, Sr Mgr-Mktg, Global Pkg & Mdsg - Intuit Inc.; *pg.* 769, *pg.* 158
Baker, Karla, Mgr-Sls-Natl - Snowmass Village Resort Association; *pg.* 1113, *pg.* 335
Baker, Kathy, Sr VP-Digital Mktg - Sony Music Entertainment; *pg.* 309, *pg.* 1294
Baker, Kelly, VP-HR, US Retail Org & Mktg Function - General Mills, Inc.; *pg.* 828, *pg.* 933
Baker, Ken, Head-Tech Implementation-Sls & Mktg - Aon Risk Services Inc.; *pg.* 1193, *pg.* 564
Baker, Laura, Dir-Mktg - Helzberg's Diamond Shops, Inc.; *pg.* 6, *pg.* 984
Baker, Lauri, VP-Brand Strategy & Sls - TheHuffingtonPost.com, Inc.; *pg.* 1692, *pg.* 1298
Baker, Lisa, Dir-Worldwide Mktg-Bus Mobility Solutions - Hewlett-Packard Company; *pg.* 404, *pg.* 175
Baker, Martin, Sr Mgr-Global Digital Content - The Hershey Co.; *pg.* 1855, *pg.* 1538
Baker, Megan, Specialist-Social Media - The Boston Beer Company, Inc.; *pg.* 239, *pg.* 790
Baker, Meredith, Mgr-Adv-Natl - Domino's Pizza, Inc.; *pg.* 1726, *pg.* 865
Baker, Michael, Mgr-Digital Mktg - Raymour & Flanigan Furniture Co.; *pg.* 940, *pg.* 1174
Baker, Michelle, Mgr-Mktg - Intuit Inc.; *pg.* 769, *pg.* 158
Baker, Mike, Principal & Product Mgr - Office Depot, Inc.; *pg.* 448, *pg.* 412
Baker, Patricia, Mgr-Shopper Mktg Plng - Safeway Inc.; *pg.* 1032, *pg.* 184
Baker, Rick, Sr Mgr - Apple Inc.; *pg.* 350, *pg.* 73
Baker, Rick, Sr VP-Corp Mktg - Herschend Family Entertainment Corp.; *pg.* 552, *pg.* 973
Baker, Rodney, Sr Mgr-Applications Dev - Fifth Third Bancorp; *pg.* 752, *pg.* 1413
Baker, Ron, Sr Dir-IT-Solutions Delivery - Payless Shoesource, Inc.; *pg.* 31, *pg.* 722
Baker, Russell, VP-Shopper Mktg - The Coca-Cola Company; *pg.* 240, *pg.* 493
Baker, Sahar, Sr Specialist-Digital Media - Food Lion, LLC; *pg.* 1019, *pg.* 1390
Baker, Scott, Mgr-Mktg Comm - Porsche Cars North America, Inc.; *pg.* 189, *pg.* 518
Baker, Stephen, VP-Product Mgmt - MRI Software, LLC; *pg.* 1106, *pg.* 1473
Baker, Suzanne, Gen Mgr-Sls - Randall Reed's Prestige

Lincoln Mercury; *pg.* 189, *pg.* 1698
Baker, Therese A., Sr Mgr-Events Mktg - The Reynolds & Reynolds Company; *pg.* 461, *pg.* 1457
Baker, Tina, VP-Sls - Boyer Candy Company Inc.; *pg.* 1851, *pg.* 1514
Baker, Todd, Head-IOx Product Mgmt - Cisco Systems, Inc.; *pg.* 372, *pg.* 240
Baker, Tony, Mgr-Mktg - Military Advantage, Inc.; *pg.* 1267, *pg.* 223
Baker, Wayne, Div Mgr-Sls - The Boston Globe; *pg.* 1623, *pg.* 790
Baker, Wendy, Mgr-Events Mktg Comm - Cisco Systems, Inc.; *pg.* 372, *pg.* 240
Baker, Yolanda, Asst Mgr-Mktg - Unilever United States, Inc.; *pg.* 904, *pg.* 1061
Baker, Yvonne, Assoc Product Mgr-Consumer Healthcare - Pfizer Inc.; *pg.* 1581, *pg.* 1278
Bakish, Bob, Pres/CEO-Viacom Intl Media Networks - Viacom Inc.; *pg.* 316, *pg.* 1310
Bakken, Laura, Dir-Americas Comm & Sls Exec Comm - Symantec Corporation; *pg.* 478, *pg.* 161
Bakker, Dorothy, Brand Mgr - Moet Hennessy; *pg.* 1966, *pg.* 1260
Bakker-Arkema, Haley, Specialist-Media - NIKE, Inc.; *pg.* 1812, *pg.* 1492
Bakshi, Aseem, Gen Mgr-Adv - SeaChange International, Inc.; *pg.* 1279, *pg.* 781
Bakst, Mitchell, Sr Project Mgr-Digital Mktg - Bare Escentuals, Inc.; *pg.* 500, *pg.* 213
Bakunas, Leighann, Dir-Mktg Svcs - Texas Monthly; *pg.* 1692, *pg.* 1666
Bala, Erin, Brand Mgr - WD-40 Company; *pg.* 337, *pg.* 210
Bala, Ganesh, Sr Dir-Customer Insights & Analytics - Sam's Club; *pg.* 1783, *pg.* 29
Bala, Lavinia, Analyst-Mktg - Level 3 Communications, Inc.; *pg.* 1262, *pg.* 312
Balach, Christopher, Head-Shopper Mktg & Consumer Promos - Wm. Wrigley Jr. Company; *pg.* 1863, *pg.* 596
Balagam, Anisa, Specialist-Mktg - Ben & Jerry's Homemade, Inc.; *pg.* 1850, *pg.* 1767
Balaguer, Rafael, Sr Mgr-Mktg - Charles Schwab & Company, Inc.; *pg.* 734, *pg.* 215
Balaj, Steve, Dir-IT-Global Mktg, Sls & Svc - Ford Motor Company; *pg.* 172, *pg.* 876
Balas, Christina, Mgr-Integrated Mktg Comm - Toys "R" Us, Inc.; *pg.* 968, *pg.* 1130
Balazs, Ricardo, Mgr-Sports Mktg Experience - Clif Bar Inc.; *pg.* 848, *pg.* 83
Balbale, Sumaiya, VP-Mktg - Jet.com, Inc.; *pg.* 1260, *pg.* 1073
Balcauski, Dan, Grp Product Mgr - SOLARWINDS, INC.; *pg.* 471, *pg.* 1666
Balch, Christopher H., Mgr-Middle Market Sls & Underwriting - The Hartford Financial Services Group, Inc.; *pg.* 1202, *pg.* 352
Balch, Jonathan M., Head-US Pharmaceutical Mktg - Alcon; *pg.* 1399, *pg.* 530
Balchak, Jim, VP-Comml Mktg - FirstMerit Corporation; *pg.* 758, *pg.* 1400
Balchun, Jason, Mgr-eMail Mktg - Carnival Cruise Lines; *pg.* 1902, *pg.* 441
Balcy, Anna, Dir-Production - Scintrex Ltd.; *pg.* 1374, *pg.* 1920
Bald, Jill M., Mgr-Mktg Upstream - CareFusion Corporation; *pg.* 1513, *pg.* 201
Baldan, Carlo, Sr VP-Mdsg - Roundy's Supermarkets Inc.; *pg.* 1032, *pg.* 1880
Baldari, Brian, Dir-Pipeline Mktg, Cardiovascular & Metabolism - Boehringer Ingelheim Pharmaceuticals, Inc.; *pg.* 1507, *pg.* 368
Baldasare, Vince, Mgr-Sls-Engineered Sys - The Gorman-Rupp Company; *pg.* 1341, *pg.* 1458
Baldassarri, Karina, Sr Mgr-Media & Digital - Van Cleef & Arpels, Inc.; *pg.* 15, *pg.* 1308
Baldasty, Anna, Sr Copywriter-Penguin Academic & Library Mktg - Penguin Random House; *pg.* 1675, *pg.* 1276
Baldasty, Anna, Sr Copywriter-Penguin Academic & Library Mktg - Penguin Random House; *pg.* 1675, *pg.* 1276
Balderas, Nicole, Assoc Dir-Mktg-Cracker Portfolio - Kellogg Company; *pg.* 831, *pg.* 870
Balderrama, Rick, Dir-Partner Mktg - Brocade Corporation; *pg.* 365, *pg.* 312
Balderree, Judy, VP-Retail Sls - Aromatique Inc.; *pg.* 499, *pg.* 32
Baldini, Elliot, Dir-Strategic Mktg Initiatives - Guitar Center, Inc.; *pg.* 1771, *pg.* 306
Baldner, Jodi, Dir-Mktg - Principal Financial Group, Inc.; *pg.* 796, *pg.* 706
Baldock, Donald, Coord-Adv - J. Strickland & Company; *pg.* 512, *pg.* 970
Baldon, Aretta, Dir-Digital Analytics, Media Currency & Ops - Turner Broadcasting System, Inc.; *pg.* 314, *pg.* 521
Baldwin, Barbara, Dir-Brand & Adv - VMware, Inc.; *pg.* 490, *pg.* 179
Baldwin, Brent, Mgr-Mktg & Brand Dev - The Cartoon Network; *pg.* 273, *pg.* 492
Baldwin, James S., Mgr-Segment & Brand Mktg-Lubrizol Additives - The Lubrizol Corporation; *pg.* 1171, *pg.* 1481
Baldwin, Jennifer, Sr Mgr-Channel Mktg-Global - Philips Electronics North America; *pg.* 662, *pg.* 782
Baldwin, Judy, Dir-CRM Mktg & Brand Ops - ACT Inc.; *pg.* 597, *pg.* 708
Baldwin, Kerry Cullen, VP-Adv Solutions - Web.com Group, Inc.; *pg.* 1288, *pg.* 435
Baldwin, Marie, Sr Product Mgr-eMarketing & Patient Mktg Ischemic Heart Disease - Gilead Sciences, Inc.; *pg.* 1535, *pg.* 88
Baldwin, Matt, Dir-Mktg - Nationwide Mutual Insurance Company; *pg.* 1210, *pg.* 1442
Baldwin, Melissa, Sr Mgr-Monetization - Kohl's Corporation; *pg.* 1775, *pg.* 1870
Baldwin, Michael, VP-Mktg Comm - Intralinks Inc.; *pg.* 420, *pg.* 1244
Baldwin, Paula, Dir-PR - Best Buy Co., Inc.; *pg.* 1761, *pg.* 954
Baldwin, Rikki, Sr Mgr-Strategic Solutions - Yahoo! Inc.; *pg.* 1289, *pg.* 289
Baldwin, Suzanne, Head-Global Creative-SB Catalog, Seasonal, Promo & Photography - Dell Inc.; *pg.* 383, *pg.* 1737
Baldwin, William, Mgr-Sls-Natl - Hall Communications Inc.; *pg.* 290, *pg.* 367
Balentine, Gary, Sr VP-Inside Sls & Sls Ops - EBSCO Information Services Walpole; *pg.* 1638, *pg.* 849
Bales, David, Product Mgr - Pioneer Electronics (USA) Inc.; *pg.* 663, *pg.* 124
Balestrieri, Gina, Mgr-Mktg - Uber USA, LLC; *pg.* 1286, *pg.* 229
Balfour, Nicki, Brand Mgr - Glaxo Smith Kline Inc.; *pg.* 1536, *pg.* 1926
Balian, Libra, Sr Dir-Mktg Ops - Ann Inc.; *pg.* 18, *pg.* 1195
Balik, Paula, Dir-Mktg Comm-Worldwide - Eastman Kodak Company; *pg.* 1408, *pg.* 1333
Balistreri, Nicole, Sr Mgr-Digital Programs - Office Depot, Inc.; *pg.* 448, *pg.* 412
Balkam, Alyssa, Sr Assoc-Mktg Strategies & Programs - KPMG LLP; *pg.* 774, *pg.* 1086
Balkcom, Carter, Head-Product Launch Mgmt - Audi of America, Inc.; *pg.* 164, *pg.* 1784
Balken, Veronica, VP & Product Mgr-Insurance & Annuity - Citigroup Inc.; *pg.* 735, *pg.* 1212
Balkovich, Laura, Head-Social-APAC - Google Inc.; *pg.* 1249, *pg.* 153
Ball, Amy, Sr Mgr-Accountant Customer Conversations - Intuit Inc.; *pg.* 769, *pg.* 158
Ball, Amy, Program Mgr-Advertising - Recreational Equipment, Inc.; *pg.* 1843, *pg.* 1821
Ball, Brenda, Dir-Digital Experience & Email Mktg - Barneys New York, Inc.; *pg.* 38, *pg.* 1201
Ball, Genevieve, Dir-Mktg-Oncology Brands & Emerging Markets - Eli Lilly and Company; *pg.* 1527, *pg.* 684
Ball, Haley, Product Mgr - Similasan Corporation; *pg.* 1594, *pg.* 332
Ball, Janet, Head-Strategic Mktg-Specialty Retail & Canada - PayPal Inc.; *pg.* 1274, *pg.* 248
Ball, Jennifer, Exec VP-Content Distr Mktg & Partnerships - Univision Communications Inc.; *pg.* 683, *pg.* 1307
Ball, Kenneth F., Mgr-Mktg-Fine Chemicals - Pfizer Inc.; *pg.* 1581, *pg.* 1278
Ball, Louis, VP-Sls Mgmt - Green Earth Technologies, Inc.; *pg.* 704, *pg.* 1352
Ball, Rachel, Mgr-Mktg-Garnier Fructis - L'Oreal USA; *pg.* 514, *pg.* 1252
Ball, Sabrina, Project Mgr-Small Ag Tactical Mktg - Deere & Company; *pg.* 703, *pg.* 632
Ball, Senikha J., Mgr-Mktg-Enterprise Events & Sponsorships - Teachers Insurance & Annuity Association - College Retirement Equities Fund; *pg.* 1219, *pg.* 1297
Balla, John, Principal-Digital Mktg - SAS Institute Inc.; *pg.* 466, *pg.* 1361
Ballanco, Jeremy, VP-iWay Software Sls - Information Builders Inc.; *pg.* 415, *pg.* 1243
Ballantyne, Shannon, Product Mgr - OXO; *pg.* 1058, *pg.* 1275
Ballard, Cynthia, Sr Mgr-Digital Media-Mktg - T-Mobile US, Inc.; *pg.* 676, *pg.* 1816
Ballard, Gabrielle, Mgr-Mktg-FX Networks - FX Networks, LLC; *pg.* 288, *pg.* 131
Ballard, Gisela, Exec Dir-Mktg - Shiseido Cosmetics America of SAC; *pg.* 522, *pg.* 1291
Ballard, Mike, Sr Mgr-Digital Mktg - Lenovo Group Ltd; *pg.* 427, *pg.* 1384
Ballard, Nigel, Dir-Federal Mktg - Intel Corporation; *pg.* 645, *pg.* 266
Ballard, Tiffanni, Sr Mgr-Integrated Mktg & Comm - Alliance Data Systems Corporation; *pg.* 347, *pg.* 1729
Ballas, Alexandra, Dir-PR-Mile High Reg - Comcast Cable Communications, Inc.; *pg.* 276, *pg.* 1560
Ballem, John, Mgr-Comm-Canadian Banking Sls - Royal Bank of Canada; *pg.* 800, *pg.* 1942
Ballon Brownstein, Meredith, Sr Mgr-Creative & Mgr-Production - The Metropolitan Museum of Art; *pg.* 561, *pg.* 1259
Ballentine, Jane, Dir-PR - Maryland Zoological Society, Inc.; *pg.* 561, *pg.* 758
Ballentine, Jarod, Brand Mgr-Digital - The WhiteWave Foods Company; *pg.* 1037, *pg.* 324
Ballereau, Laura, Dir-Creative Svcs - Briggs & Riley Travelware; *pg.* 2, *pg.* 1164
Ballew, June A., VP-Sls-Cooper Notification - Cooper Wheelock; *pg.* 630, *pg.* 1080
Balliet, Heather, Mgr-Acq Mktg - DIRECTV Group Holdings, LLC; *pg.* 281, *pg.* 79
Ballou, Joyce, Sr Dir-HR - Griffith Laboratories Ltd.; *pg.* 860, *pg.* 1934
Ballou, Kelly, Dir-Consumer Mktg - Wolverine World Wide, Inc.; *pg.* 1822, *pg.* 905
Ballou, Mary, Coord-Production - IDEXX Laboratories, Inc.; *pg.* 1543, *pg.* 753
Ballou, Mike, Product Mgr - Deere & Company; *pg.* 703, *pg.* 632
Balluck, Terry, Assoc Dir-Mktg Comm & Branding - Kimberly-Clark Corporation; *pg.* 1461, *pg.* 1720
Balman, Lloyd, VP & Sr Mgr-Events Mgmt - TD Bank US Holding Company; *pg.* 809, *pg.* 1051
Balmer, James H., Mgr-Adv Svcs - Barron's; *pg.* 1620, *pg.* 1201
Balmer, Steve, Product Mgr-Crime - Travelers Insurance; *pg.* 1220, *pg.* 963
Balmoris, Michael, Exec Dir-Federal Media Rels - AT&T Inc.; *pg.* 1867, *pg.* 1674
Balnis, Sheila, Dir-Client & Partner Svcs-Shopper Mktg - ShopLocal, LLC; *pg.* 1280, *pg.* 590
Baloh, Diane L., Dir-Sls & Membership - American Concrete Institute; *pg.* 127, *pg.* 885
Balois, Stephanie C., Program Mgr-Credit Payment Products - Citigroup Inc.; *pg.* 735, *pg.* 1212
Balosky, Ann, Mgr-Integrated Mktg - Ace Hardware Corporation; *pg.* 1040, *pg.* 644
Balotro, Irene, Mgr-Content Mktg - Hulu LLC; *pg.* 1257, *pg.* 274
Balow, Michael, Exec VP-Sls & Applications - Cypress Semiconductor Corporation; *pg.* 1326, *pg.* 243
Bals, Jeffrey W., Sr Mgr-Customer & Market Engagement - The Boeing Company; *pg.* 225, *pg.* 567
Balsam, Joe, Sr Mgr-Mktg - Sony Electronics, Inc.; *pg.* 676, *pg.* 209
Balsam, Kareen, Sr Mgr-ECommerce & Online Mktg - Godiva Chocolatier, Inc.; *pg.* 1854, *pg.* 1235
Balsara, Angela, Sr Mgr-Customer Insights-Shopper Res - The Kraft Heinz Company; *pg.* 871, *pg.* 641
Balsavich, Jeff, Program Mgr-Mktg - BP Corporation North America Inc.; *pg.* 973, *pg.* 665
Baltakov, Andon, VP-Product Mgmt-News-ProQuest - Thermo Fisher Scientific Inc.; *pg.* 1602, *pg.* 61
Baltazar, Maricar, Coord-Adv - R.R. Donnelley & Sons Company; *pg.* 1682, *pg.* 589
Baltronis, Joe, Sr VP-Mktg-Worldwide - Pelican Products; *pg.* 1467, *pg.* 843
Baltronis, Joe, Sr VP-Mktg-Worldwide - Pelican Products, Inc.; *pg.* 1842, *pg.* 295
Baltzell, Brienne, Sr Mgr-Mktg-Sutter Home Family Vineyards - Trinchero Family Estates; *pg.* 1971, *pg.* 197
Balzan, Susan, VP-Sls & Mdsg - Calvin Klein, Inc.; *pg.* 20, *pg.* 1209
Balzano, Casandra, Coord-Mktg-Active Cosmetics Div -

L'Oreal USA; *pg.* 514, *pg.* 1252
Balzer, Julie, Brand Mgr-Archway & Stella D'oro - Snyder's-Lance, Inc.; *pg.* 896, *pg.* 1368
Balzer, Sandy, Mgr-Campaign Mktg-Adobe MAX - Adobe Systems Incorporated; *pg.* 342, *pg.* 235
Bamberger, Bettina, Dir-Mktg-Acqua Di Parma, Fendi & Kenzo - LVMH Inc.; *pg.* 9, *pg.* 1254
Bambrick, Hannah, Specialist-Mktg - SIRVA, Inc.; *pg.* 1923, *pg.* 669
Bamford, Gail, Mgr-Indus Mktg-Defense, Aerospace & Intelligence - SAS Institute Inc.; *pg.* 466, *pg.* 1361
Bamrick, Bethany, Brand Mgr-Mktg-Global - Hasbro, Inc.; *pg.* 954, *pg.* 1603
Bamrick, Tom, VP-Sls, VAR & SMB Markets - Ingram Micro Inc.; *pg.* 415, *pg.* 261
Bamundo, Paul, Dir-Sports Mktg & Strategic Partnerships-Global - Doctor's Associates Inc.; *pg.* 1726, *pg.* 356
Banahasky, Krystina, Sr Mgr-eCommerce - Caleres, Inc.; *pg.* 1805, *pg.* 993
Banavali, Rajiv, CTO-Fluorine Products at Honeywell Intl - Honeywell International Inc.; *pg.* 407, *pg.* 1088
Bancroft, Lisa, Bus Mgr - Gerber Life Insurance Company; *pg.* 1201, *pg.* 1352
Bancroft, Tricia, Dir-Brand Strategy, Integrated Mktg & Events Strategy-Global - Pitney Bowes Inc.; *pg.* 454, *pg.* 376
Banda, Melyssa, Head-Mktg & Comm - Western Digital Corporation; *pg.* 492, *pg.* 118
Banda, Sara, Mgr-PR & Comm - Pratt & Whitney; *pg.* 233, *pg.* 345
Banda, Scott, Dir-Mktg-Consumer & Construction Bus Unit - Bostik Inc.; *pg.* 1150, *pg.* 833
Bandi, Aditya, Product Mgr - Yahoo! Inc.; *pg.* 1289, *pg.* 289
Bandith, Linda, Mgr-Digital Adv - Xerox Corporation; *pg.* 494, *pg.* 365
Bandlow, Kyle, Mgr-Media Rels - THE DOW CHEMICAL COMPANY; *pg.* 1157, *pg.* 898
Bandur, Vienna, Sr Mgr-Mktg - Design Within Reach, Inc.; *pg.* 923, *pg.* 216
Bandy, Eric, Mgr-Mktg-Americas - The Associated Press, Inc.; *pg.* 270, *pg.* 1197
Bandy, Meredith, Rep-PR - Universal Orlando; *pg.* 590, *pg.* 456
Bane, Judy, Asst VP-Global New Products - Pfizer Inc.; *pg.* 1581, *pg.* 1278
Bane, Regis, Sr Dir-Ticket Ops - Milwaukee Brewers Baseball Club, Inc.; *pg.* 562, *pg.* 1878
Banerjee, Aahona, Mgr-Mktg & Confectionery - Nestle Canada Inc.; *pg.* 883, *pg.* 1929
Banerjee, Neil, Product Mgr-Digital - Wells Fargo & Company; *pg.* 819, *pg.* 232
Banfield, Hannah, Head-Mktg - The ServiceMaster Company, LLC; *pg.* 335, *pg.* 1646
Bang, Andres, Sr Dir-Sls & Ops Sys-Global - LinkedIn Corporation; *pg.* 1262, *pg.* 160
Bang, Chong, Sr VP-Mdsg & Mktg - Shoppers Drug Mart Corporation; *pg.* 1594, *pg.* 1943
Bangs, James C., VP-Sls Ops & Enablement - LexisNexis Litigation Solutions; *pg.* 1659, *pg.* 1446
Bangs, Jessica, Dir-Media - Parfums Christian Dior, Inc; *pg.* 519, *pg.* 1276
Banister, Brad, Mgr-Western Adv - TEN: The Enthusiast Network; *pg.* 1691, *pg.* 1298
Banker, Betsey, Mgr-Mktg Comm - Ergotron, Inc.; *pg.* 395, *pg.* 960
Banker, Jay, Brand Mgr-Intel - CDW Corporation; *pg.* 370, *pg.* 663
Banker, Jean, Dir-Maritime & Deputy Exec Dir - Port of Oakland; *pg.* 1920, *pg.* 172
Banker, Jessica, Mgr-Interactive Mktg -GFGB - 1-800-Flowers.com, Inc.; *pg.* 1758, *pg.* 1151
Banker, Melanie, Mgr-Mustang Mktg - Ford Motor Company; *pg.* 172, *pg.* 876
Banket, Shavon, Specialist-Social Media - Tribune Media Company; *pg.* 1696, *pg.* 592
Bankhead, Paul, Grp Product Mgr - Google Inc.; *pg.* 1249, *pg.* 153
Bankoski, James, Product Mgr-Chrome Media - Google Inc.; *pg.* 1249, *pg.* 153
Banks, Alison, Mgr-Email Mktg - L.L. Bean, Inc.; *pg.* 1777, *pg.* 750
Banks, Allison, Mgr-Channel Mktg - Bacardi USA, Inc.; *pg.* 1956, *pg.* 417
Banks, Christine, VP-US Mktg-Redken - L'Oreal USA; *pg.* 514, *pg.* 1252
Banks, David V., Exec Dir-Consumer Mktg - AT&T Inc.; *pg.* 1867, *pg.* 1674
Banks, Hunter, VP-Specialty Sls - Medline Industries, Inc.; *pg.* 1562, *pg.* 635
Banks, Jim, Sr Dir-Bus Dev - Stryker Orthopaedics; *pg.* 1599, *pg.* 1082
Banks, Kevin, Mgr-B2B Mktg - Assurant, Inc.; *pg.* 1193, *pg.* 1198
Banks, Kirk, Sr Product Mgr - LegalZoom.com, Inc.; *pg.* 1261, *pg.* 96
Banks, Mark, Dir-Mktg & Comm - Atkins Nutritionals, Inc.; *pg.* 1498, *pg.* 316
Banks, Simon, Dir-Global Mktg-Aquafresh Family - GlaxoSmithKline Consumer Healthcare; *pg.* 510, *pg.* 1554
Bannell, Scott, VP-Brand Mktg - Stanley Black & Decker, Inc.; *pg.* 1063, *pg.* 358
Banner, Patrick, Sr Mgr-Quality, M&P, Process - AT&T Communications Corp.; *pg.* 1866, *pg.* 1043
Banner, Patrick, Sr Mgr-Quality, M&P & Process - AT&T Inc.; *pg.* 1867, *pg.* 1674
Banning, Gregory S., VP-SMB Sls & Gen Mgr-Costa Rica Ops - Tech Data Corporation; *pg.* 482, *pg.* 416
Bannister, Bruce, VP-Product Dev & Engrg - Airstream, Inc.; *pg.* 163, *pg.* 1456
Bannon, Deirdre, VP-Product-Nielsen Social - The Nielsen Company B.V.; *pg.* 1671, *pg.* 1272
Bannon, Dennis, Sr Dir-Adv - ConAgra Foods, Inc.; *pg.* 826, *pg.* 1014
Bannon, Melissa, Sr Dir-Digital Experiences & Content Strategy - Samsung Electronics America, Inc.; *pg.* 669, *pg.* 1115
Bannon, Michael, Dir-Adv - Bob's Discount Furniture Inc.; *pg.* 1763, *pg.* 354
Bannon, Robert, Sr Dir-IR - Reynolds American Inc.; *pg.* 1894, *pg.* 1395
Bansal, Nimit, Dir-Mktg - Church & Dwight Co., Inc.; *pg.* 1153, *pg.* 1063
Bansal, Tanuj, Sr Dir-Office Bus Grp - Microsoft Corporation; *pg.* 435, *pg.* 1824
Banton, Sheena, Sr Mgr-Email Mktg - AutoNation, Inc.; *pg.* 165, *pg.* 423
Banzon Drymalski, Kristina, Assoc Dir-Mktg Svcs Procurement-North America - Mondelez International; *pg.* 877, *pg.* 1344
Baptista, Andres, Dir-Mktg-Global Brand Mgmt Shoe Care - S.C. Johnson & Son, Inc.; *pg.* 334, *pg.* 1889
Baptiste, Kristine, Mgr-Retail Mktg - Bose Corporation; *pg.* 626, *pg.* 820
Bar, Debra, Sr VP & Head-Mktg - Bank Leumi USA; *pg.* 718, *pg.* 1200
Barabasova, Linda, Sr Mgr-Consumer Mktg-R.J. Reynolds Vapor Company - R.J. Reynolds Tobacco Co.; *pg.* 1895, *pg.* 1395
Barabino, Vernon, Sr Dir-Fin Svcs - Southern Forest Products Association; *pg.* 157, *pg* 744
Baracz, Robert, Dir-Mktg - SeaWorld Texas; *pg.* 583, *pg.* 1742
Barad, Eric, Specialist-Mktg Comm - Anthem, Inc.; *pg.* 1192, *pg.* 683
Barag, Nancy, Dir-Sls & Mktg - Hilton Worldwide, Inc.; *pg.* 1094, *pg.* 1791
Barajas, Melisenda, Brand Mgr - Bimbo Bakeries USA Inc.; *pg.* 840, *pg.* 1540
Barajas, Richard, VP-Sls - RentPath, Inc.; *pg.* 1680, *pg.* 538
Barajas-Trevizo, Rosa, Mgr-Sls-Intl - OPI Products Inc.; *pg.* 518, *pg.* 167
Barak, Dan, Product Mgr - Facebook, Inc.; *pg.* 1245, *pg.* 143
Barak, Nora, Mgr-Social Media - The New York Post; *pg.* 1668, *pg.* 1269
Baral, Jim, Sr VP-Integrated Sls - Liberman Broadcasting Corporation; *pg.* 296, *pg.* 52
Baram, Tyler, Head-Asset Mgmt & Banking Portfolio Mktg - KPMG LLP; *pg.* 774, *pg.* 1086
Baran, Jeff, Sr Mgr-Corp Mktg - Synopsys, Inc.; *pg.* 480, *pg.* 162
Baran, Michelle, Mgr-Mktg & Global Partner Mktg - Cisco Systems, Inc.; *pg.* 372, *pg.* 240
Baranek, Stefanie, Mgr-Mktg-Global Programs - Arrow Electronics, Inc.; *pg.* 619, *pg.* 325
Baranko, Kelly, Dir-Managed Brands Mktg & Dev - Walgreen Co.; *pg.* 1608, *pg.* 605
Barash, Lauren, Sr Dir-Mktg - Moe's Southwest Grill, LLC; *pg.* 1027, *pg.* 514
Baratte, Gregory, Head-ECommerce & Digital Mktg & Exec Dir - Chanel, Inc.; *pg.* 503, *pg.* 1211
Barausky, Sasha, Dir-Product Mgmt - Staples, Inc.; *pg.* 474, *pg.* 821
Barba, Rebecca, Mgr-Mktg-Global Tour Ops - Royal Caribbean Cruises Ltd; *pg.* 1921, *pg.* 446
Barbach, Erin, Mgr-Social Media - Volvo Cars of North America LLC; *pg.* 195, *pg.* 1117
Barbagallo, Joseph, Mgr-Mktg Comm - Maserati North America, Inc.; *pg.* 183, *pg.* 1060
Barbano, Sharon, VP-PR & Events - Saucony, Inc.; *pg.* 1818, *pg.* 828
Barbari, Massimo, Exec VP-Sls & Mktg - Florida Tile Industries, Inc.; *pg.* 82, *pg.* 730
Barbati, John C., Sr Dir-Installed Base, Analyst Rels & Natl Accts-CT BU - Siemens Healthcare Diagnostics; *pg.* 673, *pg.* 604
Barbato, Christian, Mgr-Digital Content Mktg - Unisys Corporation; *pg.* 487, *pg.* 1517
Barbeau, Jean-Loup, Dir-Sls-Canada - Jig-A-World; *pg.* 980, *pg.* 1951
Barbeau, Michelle, Sr Mgr-Mktg-Pillsbury - General Mills, Inc.; *pg.* 828, *pg.* 933
Barbeau, Tony, VP-Document Imaging-Products & Svcs - Eastman Kodak Company; *pg.* 1408, *pg.* 1333
Barbee, Jeff A., Supvr-Mktg Svcs-Caterpillar Forest Products - Caterpillar, Inc.; *pg.* 1321, *pg.* 650
Barber, Georgia, Mgr-Mktg - Frosty Acres Brands, Inc.; *pg.* 1020, *pg.* 484
Barber, Mindy, Mgr-Online Mktg - Chico's FAS, Inc.; *pg.* 21, *pg.* 427
Barber, Sara, Dir-Digital Mktg-Websites - General Growth Properties, Inc.; *pg.* 1093, *pg.* 574
Barber, Zachry, Sr Dir-Corp Comm - Vertex Pharmaceuticals Incorporated; *pg.* 1606, *pg.* 801
Barberio, Marcy, Mgr-Mktg Comm - ITT Corporation; *pg.* 1351, *pg.* 1354
Barbes, Ted, VP-Mktg Data & Analytics - Bank of America Corporation; *pg.* 718, *pg.* 1362
Barbian, Amanda, Sr Specialist-Mktg - 24 Hour Fitness Worldwide Inc.; *pg.* 526, *pg.* 258
Barbier, Jody, Sr Mgr-Network & Sys - New Orleans Saints L.P.; *pg.* 569, *pg.* 745
Barbieri, Rene, Assoc Brand Mgr-Retail Mktg Support - Bridgestone Americas, Inc.; *pg.* 201, *pg.* 1649
Barbitta, Tom, Sr VP-Mktg & Sls - Carolina Beverage Corporation; *pg.* 239, *pg.* 1390
Barbo, John, Head-AI Sls & Mktg - Morgan Stanley; *pg.* 783, *pg.* 1261
Barbosa, Elena, Assoc Brand Mgr-Global Mktg - Ocean Spray Cranberries, Inc.; *pg.* 887, *pg.* 827
Barbosa, Lisa, VP-Sls & Mktg-Men's Underwear & Loungewear - PVH Corp.; *pg.* 46, *pg.* 1283
Barbosa, Meghan, Brand Mgr-Lighter Mktg - BIC Corporation; *pg.* 501, *pg.* 369
Barbour, Jamie, Mgr-Site & Social Adv-Chevrolet Digital - General Motors Company; *pg.* 175, *pg.* 881
Barca, Heather, VP & Head-Creative Center of Excellence - Citigroup Inc.; *pg.* 735, *pg.* 1212
Barcia, Julie, Assoc Mgr-Digital Sls Dev-Cooking Light & MyRecipes - Time Inc.; *pg.* 1693, *pg.* 1300
Barclay, Dennis, Sr Mgr-Adv - AT&T; *pg.* 1865, *pg.* 258
Barclay, Kristin, VP-Mktg - Speakman Company; *pg.* 112, *pg.* 388
Barcus, Bill, Sr Product Mgr - Emerson Network Power Liebert; *pg.* 1071, *pg.* 1439
Barcus, Dan, Exec Dir-Acq & Direct Mktg - Comcast Corporation; *pg.* 276, *pg.* 1560
Barczyk, Natalie, Sr Specialist-Sls Support & Mktg Comm - Comcast Cable Communications, Inc.; *pg.* 276, *pg.* 1560
Bardacke, Brynn, Grp Dir-Creative-Global - The Coca-Cola Company; *pg.* 240, *pg.* 493
Barden, Elaine, VP-Mktg & Sls - Comcast Corporation; *pg.* 276, *pg.* 1560
Barden, Rob, Dir-Product Mktg - Aeroflex Incorporated; *pg.* 614, *pg.* 1321
Bardin, Mike, Sr Dir-Pub & Govt Affairs - Scripps; *pg.* 1593, *pg.* 209
Bardon, Maxwell, VP-Global Payments Products - Amazon.com, Inc.; *pg.* 1226, *pg.* 1831
Bardwaj, Seema, Mgr-Mktg Comm-Global - Ford Motor Company; *pg.* 172, *pg.* 876
Bardy, Sophie, Sr Dir-Mktg Comm-Global - Kinetic Concepts, Inc.; *pg.* 1553, *pg.* 1741
Bardzik, Bobbie, Mgr-Community Mktg-Baltimore & Central PA - Dick's Sporting Goods, Inc.; *pg.* 1832, *pg.* 1524
Bare, James K., Exec Dir & Sr Dir-Ticket Ops - Chicago Blackhawk Hockey Team, Inc.; *pg.* 538, *pg.* 569

Bareis, Janet, VP & Gen Mgr-Brand, Product & Bus Dev - Wal-Mart Stores, Inc.; *pg.* 1790, *pg.* 29
Barendt, Fred, Dir-Interactive Mktg - Delta Faucet Company; *pg.* 78, *pg.* 684
Baretz, Marnie, VP-Mktg - NYC & Company, Inc.; *pg.* 1002, *pg.* 1274
Barfoot, Frances, VP-Mktg Comm - The Chubb Corporation; *pg.* 1196, *pg.* 1128
Bargamian, CJ, Dir-Digital & Social Media Mktg - Turner Broadcasting System, Inc.; *pg.* 314, *pg.* 521
Barger, Austin, Mgr-Enhancement Mktg - Alliance Data Systems Corporation; *pg.* 347, *pg.* 1729
Barger, David, Mgr-Sls - Cherry Central Cooperative, Inc.; *pg.* 847, *pg.* 909
Barger, Donald, Sr Dir - National Parks Conservation Association; *pg.* 150, *pg.* 403
Barger, Laura, Mng Dir & Head-Corp Mktg Initiatives-Global - The Bank of New York Mellon Corporation; *pg.* 720, *pg.* 1200
Barger, Mike, Sr Mgr-Corp Comm - Kinetic Concepts, Inc.; *pg.* 1553, *pg.* 1741
Bargerhuff, Rita, CMO & Sr VP-Mktg - Rent-A-Center, Inc.; *pg.* 940, *pg.* 1734
Barhoover, Bret, Sr Mgr-Mktg - General Mills, Inc.; *pg.* 828, *pg.* 933
Baribault, Paul, VP-Animation Mktg & Disneynature - The Walt Disney Company; *pg.* 317, *pg.* 52
Barichivich, Melanie, Brand Mgr-Beverage & Digital Media - Popeye's Chicken & Biscuits; *pg.* 1745, *pg.* 517
Barichivich, Melanie, Brand Mgr-Beverage & Digital Media - Popeyes Louisiana Kitchen, Inc.; *pg.* 1745, *pg.* 517
Baril, Amy, Strategist-Mktg Comm - Blue Cross & Blue Shield Association; *pg.* 1195, *pg.* 566
Baril, Angela, Sr Dir-Art & Designer - Crain Communications, Inc.; *pg.* 1631, *pg.* 879
Barile, Antonette, Dir-Mktg - Ameriprise Financial, Inc.; *pg.* 715, *pg.* 930
Barillas, Alex, Dir-Digital & Interactive Sls - ImpreMedia LLC; *pg.* 1652, *pg.* 133
Barilleaux, Charlotte, Mgr-Mktg Project-Media - Recreational Equipment, Inc.; *pg.* 1843, *pg.* 1821
Baringer, Michael, Mgr-Experiential Mktg - Blue Cross & Blue Shield of Florida, Inc.; *pg.* 1507, *pg.* 432
Baris, Hilary, Dir-Digital Media & Mktg - The Partnership at Drugfree.org; *pg.* 153, *pg.* 1276
Barisa, Loris, Mng Dir-Europe Sls - Thomson Reuters Markets; *pg.* 810, *pg.* 1299
Barish, Amy, Mgr-Mktg Comm - Cost Plus World Market; *pg.* 921, *pg.* 170
Barish, Jeff, Head-Digital Sales & Strategy-Glamour - Conde Nast Digital; *pg.* 1237, *pg.* 1217
Barkan, Angela, VP-Media & Artist Dev-Sony Masterworks - Sony Music Entertainment; *pg.* 309, *pg.* 1294
Barker, Andrew, Dir-Media Investment Strategy & Content Plng - Dr Pepper Snapple Group, Inc.; *pg.* 250, *pg.* 1729
Barker, Beth, Dir-Retail Mktg - Cigna Corporation; *pg.* 1197, *pg.* 338
Barker, Bradford, Brand Mgr-Digital & Loyalty - Starbucks Corporation; *pg.* 897, *pg.* 1840
Barker, Brandon, Brand Mgr-Justin Original Workboots - Justin Brands, Inc.; *pg.* 1810, *pg.* 1695
Barker, Courtney, Mgr-Mktg & Brand - Northwestern Memorial HealthCare; *pg.* 1574, *pg.* 585
Barker, Greg, Sr VP-Mktg & Economic Dev - Alabama Power Company; *pg.* 1933, *pg.* 1
Barker, Jeff, Dir-Mktg - Kansas City Symphony; *pg.* 555, *pg.* 985
Barker, Judy, Sr Product Mgr-Global - Kensington Technology Group; *pg.* 424, *pg.* 191
Barker, Lisa, Dir-Creative - PulteGroup, Inc.; *pg.* 1109, *pg.* 873
Barksdale, Stephanie, Mgr-Adv - Verizon Communications Inc.; *pg.* 1875, *pg.* 1309
Barlage, Jean, Mgr-Worldwide Mktg, Sls Education & Enablement - IBM; *pg.* 410, *pg.* 1449
Barlik, Len, Exec VP-Product Mgmt & Dev - Cox Communications, Inc.; *pg.* 279, *pg.* 501
Barlin, Marissa, Dir-Consumer Mktg - Cotton Incorporated Consumer Marketing Headquarters; *pg.* 692, *pg.* 1218
Barlow, Arnold, Sr Mgr-Mktg - United Parcel Service, Inc.; *pg.* 1928, *pg.* 522
Barlow, Jeanette, Dir-Product Line Mgmt - International Business Machines Corporation; *pg.* 418, *pg.* 1138
Barlow, Lucinda, Head-Mktg-Australia & New Zealand - Google Inc.; *pg.* 1249, *pg.* 153
Barlow, Michele A., Exec VP-Enterprise Mktg - Bank of America Corporation; *pg.* 718, *pg.* 1362
Barlow, Monica, Dir-PR - Baltimore Orioles, L.P.; *pg.* 532, *pg.* 755
Barnard, Barb, VP-Sls-North America - Carlson Wagonlit Travel; *pg.* 1902, *pg.* 948
Barnard, Gregg, Mgr-Mktg & Online Comm - In-N-Out Burgers, Inc.; *pg.* 1732, *pg.* 111
Barnard, Steve, Dir-Enterprise & Pub Sector Mktg - Lenovo Group Ltd; *pg.* 427, *pg.* 1384
Barnard, Windy, Mgr-Special Events & Sls Center - Dave & Buster's Entertainment, Inc.; *pg.* 1724, *pg.* 1679
Barnas, Don, VP-Worldwide Sls - API Technologies Corp.; *pg.* 618, *pg.* 452
Barnes, Angella, Specialist-Mktg - Arris Group, Inc.; *pg.* 353, *pg.* 541
Barnes, Bianca, Sr Dir-Mktg - Ralph Lauren Corporation; *pg.* 46, *pg.* 1284
Barnes, Brandon, Dir-Sls & Mktg-Intl - Atlanta Convention & Visitors Bureau; *pg.* 989, *pg.* 489
Barnes, Carla, Dir-Mktg - Kennesaw State University; *pg.* 603, *pg.* 534
Barnes, Cory, Mgr-Digital Mktg - Exxel Outdoors LLC; *pg.* 1833, *pg.* 311
Barnes, Dale, Div Mgr-Mktg - Yamaha Motor Corporation USA; *pg.* 1713, *pg.* 76
Barnes, Dan, Mgr-Southeastern Sls - Heat Seal LLC; *pg.* 1345, *pg.* 1431
Barnes, Daniel, Brand Mgr-Payer Mktg - Eli Lilly and Company; *pg.* 1527, *pg.* 684
Barnes, Dave, Mgr-Technical Mktg - Emulex Corporation; *pg.* 392, *pg.* 70
Barnes, Heather, Mgr-SE Reg Mktg - Meritage Homes Corporation; *pg.* 97, *pg.* 23
Barnes, Jeremy, Dir-PR & Brand Experience - Mazda North American Operations; *pg.* 183, *pg.* 113
Barnes, John, Sr Mgr-Natl Accounts - Southwest Airlines Co.; *pg.* 1923, *pg.* 1687
Barnes, Mark, VP-Sls - Volkswagen Group of America, Inc.; *pg.* 194, *pg.* 1785
Barnes, Michaela, Dir-Product Mgmt - VeriSign, Inc.; *pg.* 488, *pg.* 1799
Barnes, Natalie, Mgr-Trade Mktg-Global Travel & Middle East - Diageo North America, Inc.; *pg.* 1961, *pg.* 361
Barnes, Paul, Head-Practice-Comm & Media-North America - Pegasystems Inc.; *pg.* 453, *pg.* 809
Barnes, Paula, Dir-Mdsg - Jockey International, Inc.; *pg.* 27, *pg.* 1861
Barnes, Red, Brand Mgr-Licensed - Imperial International; *pg.* 1837, *pg.* 1050
Barnes, Shad, Mgr-Online Mktg - Oregon State Lottery; *pg.* 1003, *pg.* 1508
Barnes, Valerie, Mgr-Adv & Comm - LEGOLAND California LLC; *pg.* 557, *pg.* 59
Barnet, Andrew, VP-Adv Sls-Western Reg - DIRECTV Group Holdings, LLC; *pg.* 281, *pg.* 79
Barnett, Bob, Mgr-Trade Mktg - Boehringer Ingelheim Pharmaceuticals, Inc.; *pg.* 1507, *pg.* 368
Barnett, Deisha, Sr Dir-Corp Comm - Wal-Mart Stores, Inc.; *pg.* 1790, *pg.* 29
Barnett, Karen, Dir-Mktg Analytics - AT&T Communications Corp.; *pg.* 1866, *pg.* 1043
Barnett, Patricia CMP, Exec Mgr-Meetings Sls - St. Louis Convention & Visitors Commission; *pg.* 1006, *pg.* 1003
Barnett, Shawna, Dir-Mktg-Creative & Media - Grand Canyon Education, Inc.; *pg.* 602, *pg.* 16
Barnett, Tessa, Coord-Mktg - Bon Secours Health System, Inc.; *pg.* 1508, *pg.* 774
Barnett, Tracy D., Dir-Sls-Broadband Utility - Graybar Electric Company, Inc.; *pg.* 1299, *pg.* 997
Barnett, Willie, Sr Dir-Reg Mktg - Putnam Investments, LLC; *pg.* 797, *pg.* 800
Barneveld, Evert, Mgr-Sls-Hospital - Welch Allyn Inc.; *pg.* 1436, *pg.* 1342
Barney, Dave, Product Mgr - Google Inc.; *pg.* 1249, *pg.* 153
Barnhart, Amy, Coord-Comm & Social Media - United States Tennis Association; *pg.* 160, *pg.* 1354
Barnhart, Christine P., Dir-Mktg - Magellan Health Services, Inc.; *pg.* 1557, *pg.* 337
Barnhart, Gena, Dir-Mktg Digital Distr - NBC Universal, Inc.; *pg.* 300, *pg.* 1266
Barnhart, Matt, Dir-Media Rels - The Detroit Lions, Inc.; *pg.* 544, *pg.* 864
Barnhill, Robin, Mgr-Mktg - GlaxoSmithKline; *pg.* 1536, *pg.* 1565
Barnhill, Sue, Dir-Portfolio Mktg - BancTec, Inc.; *pg.* 360, *pg.* 1717
Barnhill, Teresa, Dir-Multicultural Mktg & Bus Dev - St. Jude Children's Research Hospital; *pg.* 1596, *pg.* 1646
Barninger, Stacy, Sr Mgr-Licensing-Disney Baby-Disney Consumer Products - The Walt Disney Company; *pg.* 317, *pg.* 52
Barno, Terrence J., Sr Dir-Natl Accounts - Pfizer Inc.; *pg.* 1581, *pg.* 1278
Barocco, David, Mgr-Sls - Cargill Meat Solutions; *pg.* 846, *pg.* 722
Baron, Justin, Dir-Mktg - Cummins Inc.; *pg.* 1326, *pg.* 676
Baron, Kim, Mgr-Mktg Data & Assoc Mgr-Mktg Product - Moen Incorporated; *pg.* 1056, *pg.* 1468
Baron, Paul, Mgr-Adv & Promos-Sports Programming - Home Box Office, Inc.; *pg.* 290, *pg.* 1240
Baron, Richard, Exec Dir-Mktg - Boehringer Ingelheim Pharmaceuticals, Inc.; *pg.* 1507, *pg.* 368
Barone, Allison, VP & Analyst-Mktg - Citigroup Inc.; *pg.* 735, *pg.* 1212
Barone, Beth, Dir-Distr Sls & Ops - Sony Electronics, Inc.; *pg.* 676, *pg.* 209
Barone, Jason, Dir-Direct Mktg-Strategic Initiatives - Time Warner Cable Inc.; *pg.* 312, *pg.* 1301
Barone, Louis, Mng Dir & Mgr-Comml Sls-Northeast Reg - CIT GROUP INC.; *pg.* 735, *pg.* 1212
Barone, Salvatore, Team Head-Hematology Mktg-US Oncology & Dir - Pfizer Inc.; *pg.* 1581, *pg.* 1278
Barone, Sarah, Sr Mgr-Acq Mktg - Constant Contact, Inc.; *pg.* 379, *pg.* 850
Barousse, Clark, Chief Sls Officer & Sr VP-Worldwide Sls - BioLase Technology, Inc.; *pg.* 1506, *pg.* 107
Baroutas, Nancy, VP-Mktg - Citigroup Inc.; *pg.* 735, *pg.* 1212
Barow, Sarah, Sr Mgr-Comm - HP Hood LLC; *pg.* 864, *pg.* 829
Barr, Aileen, Sr Mgr-Mktg - Halliburton Company; *pg.* 978, *pg.* 1707
Barr, Amanda, Sr Mgr-HR - The Coca-Cola Company; *pg.* 240, *pg.* 493
Barr, Brandon, Brand Mgr-Lunchables Innovation - The Kraft Heinz Company; *pg.* 871, *pg.* 641
Barr, Cara, Mgr-Channel Sls - Concur Technologies; *pg.* 1903, *pg.* 501
Barr, Jennifer, Sr Mgr-Mktg-Recipe Mixes, Hispanic & Billy Bee - McCormick & Company, Incorporated; *pg.* 1027, *pg.* 779
Barr, Jessica, Specialist-Mktg - Siemens Medical Solutions USA, Inc.; *pg.* 469, *pg.* 1550
Barr, Patrick, Mgr-Channel Mktg-Analytics-North America - IBM; *pg.* 410, *pg.* 1449
Barrack, Melissa, Sr Mgr-Mktg-Pub Sector - Adobe Systems Incorporated; *pg.* 342, *pg.* 235
Barraco, Gary, Sr Dir-Supply Chain Solutions - Amber Road, Inc.; *pg.* 348, *pg.* 1054
Barragan, Carolyn, Dir-Interactive Mktg & Client Svcs Mgr - eBay Inc.; *pg.* 1240, *pg.* 243
Barragan, Karen, Head-PR-Original Series - Netflix, Inc.; *pg.* 1269, *pg.* 141
Barran, Danielle, VP-Mktg-Coffee - Smucker Foods Of Canada Co.; *pg.* 896, *pg.* 1924
Barrard, Pierre, VP-Mktg Passenger Car & Light Truck Bus - Michelin North America Inc.; *pg.* 1886, *pg.* 1618
Barrasso, Nick, Coord-E-Mail Mktg - Wayfair LLC; *pg.* 1288, *pg.* 801
Barratt, Cherry Park, Sr Mgr-Digital Mktg - Ubisoft Inc.; *pg.* 589, *pg.* 229
Barredo, Jackie, Mgr-Adv Production - ESPN, Inc.; *pg.* 285, *pg.* 340
Barresi, Matt, Dir-Mktg-North America Family Care - The Procter & Gamble Company; *pg.* 1129, *pg.* 1418
Barress, Gretchen, VP-Sls-Retirement Svcs - Principal Financial Group, Inc.; *pg.* 796, *pg.* 706
Barreto, Carlos, VP-Mktg-Global - Revlon Consumer Products Corporation; *pg.* 521, *pg.* 1286
Barreto, Carlos, VP-Mktg-Global - Revlon, Inc.; *pg.* 521, *pg.* 1286
Barreto, Eric, Coord-Mktg - Jacksonville Symphony Association; *pg.* 554, *pg.* 434
Barreto, Yolanda, Sr Dir-HR - Miami Dolphins, Ltd.; *pg.* 562, *pg.* 419
Barrett, Aaron, Rep-Soccer Specialty Sls - adidas America Inc.; *pg.* 1803, *pg.* 1500
Barrett, Chip, VP-Sls & Ops Plng-Europe - General Cable Corporation; *pg.* 83, *pg.* 729
Barrett, Chris, Sr VP-US Sls - Boehringer Ingelheim Pharmaceuticals, Inc.; *pg.* 1507, *pg.* 368

First page reference indicates Business Class Edition
Second page reference indicates Geographic Edition

Barrett, Cub, Dir-PR - Architectural Digest; pg. 1617, pg. 1196
Barrett, Cub, Dir-PR-Architectural Digest - Conde Nast Publications, Inc.; pg. 1629, pg. 1217
Barrett, Jack, Sr Dir-Strategic Field Engagement - Juniper Networks, Inc.; pg. 1260, pg. 286
Barrett, Jacqueline, Sr Mgr-Mktg-US Thomas & Friends - Mattel Games/Puzzles; pg. 962, pg. 80
Barrett, Jacqueline, Sr Mgr-Mktg-US Thomas & Friends - MATTEL, INC.; pg. 962, pg. 81
Barrett, Jessica, Project Mgr-Creative Adv - J.C. Penney Company, Inc.; pg. 1774, pg. 1732
Barrett, Kathleen, Mgr-PPS-A Mktg Comm - Hewlett-Packard Company; pg. 404, pg. 175
Barrett, Kristy, Editor & Mgr-Comm & Corp Mktg - AmerisourceBergen Corporation; pg. 1493, pg. 1522
Barrett, Mark S., Grp VP-Engrg, Product Dev & Procurement - American Axle & Manufacturing Holdings, Inc.; pg. 198, pg. 879
Barrett, Mike, Principal & Product Mgr - Red Hat, Inc.; pg. 460, pg. 1388
Barrett, Paul, Sr Mgr-Production Stage - Atlanta Symphony Orchestra; pg. 531, pg. 490
Barrett, Robertson, VP-Media Initiatives - Yahoo! Inc.; pg. 1289, pg. 289
Barrett, Stephen, Dir-Product Mgmt & Mktg-Conveyance Products & Drainage - Watts Water Technologies, Inc.; pg. 1078, pg. 837
Barrett, Todd, VP-Strategic Mktg-Global - Pall Corporation; pg. 232, pg. 1323
Barrett, Tyeesha, Project Mgr-Creative Svcs, Mktg & Adv - Sterling Jewelers Inc.; pg. 13, pg. 1402
Barrette, Melissa, Coord-Mktg - Rousseau Metal, Inc.; pg. 463, pg. 1960
Barrette, Michael, VP-Sls, Mktg & Franchising - Dippin' Dots LLC; pg. 853, pg. 739
Barretto, Mike, Reg Mgr-Sls - HD SUPPLY, INC.; pg. 86, pg. 509
Barriault, Stephanie, Mgr-Mktg Comm - Plantronics, Inc.; pg. 663, pg. 270
Barrick, Angie Senner, Head-Indus, Media & Entertainment - Google Inc.; pg. 1249, pg. 153
Barrick, Chessney, Dir-Comm & Cause Mktg - Stop Hunger Now; pg. 1396, pg. 1389
Barrientos, Felipe, Reg Mgr-Sls - Thermon Americas Inc.; pg. 1077, pg. 1744
Barrientos, Joe, Sr Assoc Brand Mgr - Campbell Soup Company; pg. 844, pg. 1048
Barringer, Wayne, Dir-Creative Svcs - The Boeing Company; pg. 225, pg. 567
Barrington, Amy, Mgr-Integrated Mktg - Zebra Technologies Corporation; pg. 690, pg. 628
Barrington, Matt, Sr Mgr-Sponsorship Mktg - Royal Bank of Canada; pg. 800, pg. 1942
Barrios, George, CFO & Chief Strategy Officer - World Wrestling Entertainment, Inc.; pg. 595, pg. 380
Barrios, Janette, Mgr-PR - Apple Inc.; pg. 350, pg. 73
Barron, Alejandra, Sr Mgr-Brand Mktg-North America - Newell Rubbermaid Inc.; pg. 1128, pg. 515
Barron, Anne, Asst-Mktg - Capital City Bank Group, Inc.; pg. 730, pg. 469
Barron, Kristi Rose, Sr Mgr-Sample - MetrixLab; pg. 1266, pg. 223
Barron, Meg, Dir-New Product Dev & Portfolio Mgmt - American Medical Association; pg. 130, pg. 564
Barron, Rusty, VP-North America Mktg, Brands & Ops - Shell Lubricants; pg. 217, pg. 1714
Barros, Maria, VP-Mktg & Community Rels-Telemundo 51 & WSCV - Telemundo Network Inc.; pg. 311, pg. 430
Barrott, Jason, Rep-Sls - Aurora Casket Company, Inc.; pg. 1393, pg. 673
Barrow, Andrew, Dir-Worldwide Consumer Product Mktg - Lenovo Group Ltd; pg. 427, pg. 1384
Barrowman, Andrew, Bus Mgr-Customer Support - Nicor Gas an AGL Resources Company; pg. 1947, pg. 636
Barry, Catherine, Dir-Mktg - National Honey Board; pg. 149, pg. 328
Barry, Christopher, Sr VP-Intl Strategy & Digital Media - A&E Television Networks, LLC; pg. 267, pg. 1185
Barry, Doug, Producer-Mktg Comm & Writer - FLIR Systems, Inc.; pg. 1413, pg. 1510
Barry, Jaimie, Coord-Reg Mktg - RBC Capital Markets; pg. 798, pg. 225
Barry, Joe, Mgr-Performance Mktg - InterContinental Hotels Corporation; pg. 1097, pg. 511
Barry, John, Sr VP-Adv Sls-Eastern Reg - Travel Channel LLC; pg. 313, pg. 766
Barry, Kelly, Sr Mgr-Mktg & Bus Resources-ARAMARK Healthcare - Aramark; pg. 1013, pg. 1558
Barry, Kevin, Acct Exec-Charter Media - Charter Communications, Inc.; pg. 274, pg. 372
Barry, Kevin, Sr Mgr-IR - Staples, Inc.; pg. 474, pg. 821
Barry, Krista, Sr Specialist-Mktg - Federated Investors, Inc.; pg. 752, pg. 1575
Barry, Lauren, Mgr-Product Mktg - LOGMEIN, INC.; pg. 428, pg. 861
Barry, Lisa, Sr Mgr-Mktg Effectiveness & Intelligence Home Monitoring - Philips Healthcare; pg. 1585, pg. 783
Barry, Mark, Sr VP-Sls - Rawlings Sporting Goods Co., Inc.; pg. 1843, pg. 1002
Barry, Mindy, Dir-Mktg-Iams - Mars, Incorporated; pg. 1858, pg. 1792
Barry, Sean, Program Mgr-Mktg - Staples, Inc.; pg. 474, pg. 821
Barry, William D., Sr VP-Enterprise Sls - CompuCom Systems, Inc.; pg. 378, pg. 1678
Barsa, Carolina, Mgr-Mktg, Sls Strategy & Plng - The Dannon Company, Inc.; pg. 851, pg. 1351
Barsch, Rebekah, VP-Plng & Sls - The Northwestern Mutual Life Insurance Company; pg. 1212, pg. 1879
Barsegyan, Artur, Specialist-Comm-Email Mktg - Kohler Co.; pg. 91, pg. 1862
Barsky, Jeannette, VP-Mktg - PC Mall, Inc.; pg. 452, pg. 295
Barstow, Megan, Sr Mgr-Adv-Global - Accenture; pg. 1392, pg. 1186
Barstow, R. Lee, VP-Digital Adv Ops & Solutions - A&E Television Networks, LLC; pg. 267, pg. 1185
Bartee, Alanna, Product Dir - Johnson & Johnson; pg. 1549, pg. 1091
Bartel, Beth, Dir-HP Global Alliances Mktg - Hewlett-Packard Company; pg. 404, pg. 175
Bartell, Jessica, Dir-Mktg - Lifetouch, Inc.; pg. 1420, pg. 922
Bartelt, Tara, Sr Mgr-Strategic Partnerships - The Coca-Cola Company; pg. 240, pg. 493
Barth, Alex, Sr Mgr-Mktg-Amazon Kindle - Amazon.com, Inc.; pg. 1226, pg. 1831
Barth, Annette, Sr Dir-Art-In-Store Visual - Beall's, Inc.; pg. 1760, pg. 414
Barth, Bob, Dir-Print & Digital Adv - The Topeka Capital-Journal; pg. 1695, pg. 722
Barth, Dave, Sr Product Mgr-Google Maps Mobile - Google Inc.; pg. 1249, pg. 153
Barth, Michelle, Dir-Mktg - Ross Stores, Inc.; pg. 1783, pg. 78
Barth, Wendy, Sr VP-Mktg-Global - Rich Products Corporation; pg. 892, pg. 1150
Barth-Huff, Jan, VP-Mktg - Blackhawk Bancorp Inc.; pg. 724, pg. 1854
Barthel, Joanne, Mgr-Mktg - Standard Functional Foods Group(SFFG); pg. 1862, pg. 1654
Barthel, John, Sr Dir-Ops - Wal-Mart Stores, Inc.; pg. 1790, pg. 29
Barthelemy, Paul, Asst Dir-Brand & Adv - The Northwestern Mutual Life Insurance Company; pg. 1212, pg. 1879
Barthels, Jennifer, Asst Product Mgr-Motorcycle - Sentry Insurance Group; pg. 1217, pg. 1895
Bartholf, Patty, Project Mgr-Mktg - Wells Fargo & Company; pg. 819, pg. 232
Bartholomew, Katie, Sr Dir-Consumer Insights - ConAgra Foods, Inc.; pg. 826, pg. 1014
Bartholomew, Sue, Dir-Global Mktg Comm & Mktg Ops - ESAB Welding & Cutting Products; pg. 1335, pg. 1615
Bartholomew, Tony, Sr VP-Pro Sls - O'Reilly Automotive, Inc.; pg. 214, pg. 1006
Bartiromo, Angela, Sr Mgr-Product Data Mgmt - The J.M. Smucker Company; pg. 865, pg. 1468
Bartkiewicz, Vicki, Dir-Mall Mktg-South Shore Plaza - Simon Property Group, Inc.; pg. 1112, pg. 690
Bartle, Amy, Dir-Media & Digital Mktg - La Quinta Inns, Inc.; pg. 1100, pg. 1722
Bartle, Nick, Sr Dir-Mktg Comm - Apple Inc.; pg. 350, pg. 73
Bartle, Samantha, Sr Mgr-Mktg - Rue La La; pg. 1278, pg. 800
Bartlett, Chad, Sr Specialist-Mktg Comm - Ecolab Inc.; pg. 329, pg. 960
Bartlett, Christine, Sr Mgr-Security Strategy & Integrated Mktg - Cisco Systems, Inc.; pg. 372, pg. 240
Bartlett, Jason, VP-Digital Mktg & ECommerce - Pitney Bowes Inc.; pg. 454, pg. 376
Bartlett, Jeff, VP-Mktg & Adv - Total Wine & More; pg. 1971, pg. 775
Bartlett, Julia, Assoc Mgr-Mktg-Activation & Partnerships - Meredith Corporation; pg. 1663, pg. 705
Bartlett, Matthew, Dir-Mktg & Strategic Plng - Amgen Inc.; pg. 1493, pg. 291
Bartlett, Rohan, Dir-AMS Demand Mgmt Svcs-Global Mktg - Hewlett-Packard Company; pg. 404, pg. 175
Bartlett, Sean, Dir-Digital Experience, Product & Omni-Channel Integration - Lowe's Companies, Inc.; pg. 1053, pg. 1383
Bartlett, Stephanie, Sr Mgr-Customer Mktg-Natl Accounts-US Vision Care - Alcon; pg. 1399, pg. 530
Barto, Mary Ellen, VP-Media Svcs - Arby's Restaurant Group, Inc.; pg. 1014, pg. 488
Bartoli, Stephen, VP-Product Mktg-Global - FCA US LLC; pg. 170, pg. 868
Bartolomeo, Catherine, Coord-Mktg & Event - Zoetis Inc.; pg. 1611, pg. 1067
Bartolucci, Bruce, Mgr-Sls-Natl - BIC Corporation; pg. 501, pg. 369
Barton, Amy, Mgr-Mktg & Developer Programs - Intel Corporation; pg. 645, pg. 266
Barton, Dan, Project Mgr-Pkg & Mktg Acct - International Paper Company; pg. 1460, pg. 1644
Barton, Gerald D., VP-Global Product & Platform Dev - LexisNexis Group; pg. 1658, pg. 1446
Barton, Kathy, Mgr-Field Mktg - MillerCoors; pg. 254, pg. 1877
Barton, Kris, Chief Product Officer - ReachLocal, Inc.; pg. 1277, pg. 308
Barton, Nina, Sr VP-Mktg Innovation & R&D - The Kraft Heinz Company; pg. 870, pg. 1577
Barton, Nina, VP-Mktg - The Kraft Heinz Company; pg. 871, pg. 641
Barton, Rachel, Product Mgr - Google Inc.; pg. 1249, pg. 153
Barton, Rieman, Mgr-Inside Sls - 180s, LLC; pg. 1824, pg. 754
Barton, Scott, Sr VP-Branded Digital Content & Products - Starz Entertainment, LLC; pg. 310, pg. 327
Bartos, Hank M., Interim Pres-Truckload - XPO Logistics, Inc.; pg. 1931, pg. 350
Bartosevich, Catherine, Sr Dir-Press - Buzzfeed; pg. 1233, pg. 1208
Bartow, Katy, Coord-Mktg - TAB Products Co. LLC; pg. 481, pg. 1869
Bartron, Lynne, VP-Brand Mktg - J.C. Penney Company, Inc.; pg. 1774, pg. 1732
Bartulovic, Tanja, Head-Adv & PR - Rockwell Automation, Inc.; pg. 668, pg. 1880
Baruch, Shelly, Dir-Mktg-Global Fragrance - Avon Products, Inc.; pg. 500, pg. 1198
Baruch, Steve, VP-Digital, Strategy & Mktg - MSC Industrial Direct Co., Inc.; pg. 1057, pg. 1181
Baruk, Peter, Sr Dir-Field Sls - General Mills, Inc.; pg. 828, pg. 933
Baruth, Seana, VP-Product Mgmt-Showtime Anytime - Showtime Networks Inc.; pg. 308, pg. 1291
Barwell, Jackie, Product Mgr-Fraud - ACI Worldwide Inc.; pg. 341, pg. 1010
Barys, Julie, Dir-Mktg Plng-North America - The Western Union Company; pg. 822, pg. 327
Basa, Tim, VP-Sls - BullsEye Telecom Inc.; pg. 366, pg. 906
Basalone, Jon, Sr VP-Mktg - Trader Joe's Co.; pg. 1789, pg. 151
Basch, Rebecca, Mgr-Sls & Mktg Acctg-Fleet, Comml & Intl Ops - General Motors Company; pg. 175, pg. 881
Basche, Malia, Dir-Product Line-GoToWebinar - Citrix Systems, Inc.; pg. 375, pg. 424
Baschnagel, Heidi, Dir-Mktg Talent Dev - National Instruments Corporation; pg. 443, pg. 1664
Bascones, Pedro, Sr Dir-Mktg-Intl Markets Shoe Care Category - S.C. Johnson & Son, Inc.; pg. 334, pg. 1889
Bascus-Leslie, Marvalee, Dir-Mktg - American Express Company; pg. 712, pg. 1190
Baselice, Charles, Product Mgr-Fuels & Industrial Gases - Airgas, Inc.; pg. 1146, pg. 1583
Baselici, Tony, Mgr-Creative Design - Acuity Brands, Inc.; pg. 1294, pg. 487
Basen, Rich, Sr VP-Mktg - Palm Beach County Convention & Visitors Bureau; pg. 1003, pg. 479
Baser, David, Mgr-Product Mgmt - Facebook, Inc.; pg. 1245, pg. 143
Baseri, Sean, Mgr-Registry Security & Product Mgmt - NeuStar, Inc.; pg. 1872, pg. 1807
Basford, Doug, Reg Mgr-Sls - Babcox Media; pg. 1619, pg. 1400

Bash, Darrin, Project Mgr-Product Dev - K12, Inc.; *pg.* 1260, *pg.* 1785
Basha, Ike, Project Mgr-Mktg - Bashas' Supermarkets; *pg.* 1015, *pg.* 12
Bashani, Surendra, Sr Product Mgr - Amazon.com, Inc.; *pg.* 1226, *pg.* 1831
Bashaw, Paul, Corp Dir-Sls-Global - Benchmark Hospitality International Inc.; *pg.* 1081, *pg.* 1747
Bashirrad, Avideh, VP & Dir-Mktg - Penguin Random House; *pg.* 1675, *pg.* 1276
Bashor, Michelle, Sr Specialist-Integrated Brand Mktg - Mary Kay Inc.; *pg.* 516, *pg.* 1657
Bashor, Michelle, Sr Specialist-Integrated Brand Mktg - Mary Kay Inc.; *pg.* 516, *pg.* 1657
Basil, Benjamin, Sr Dir-US Alzheimer's, Neuroscience & Puerto Rico Mktg - Eli Lilly and Company; *pg.* 1527, *pg.* 684
Basil, Keith, Principal & Product Mgr-OpenStack - Red Hat, Inc.; *pg.* 460, *pg.* 1388
Basile, Leo, VP-Sls - Abita Brewing Company; *pg.* 237, *pg.* 741
Basini, Denise, Dir-Mktg-Better Homes & Gardens Magazine - Meredith Corporation; *pg.* 1663, *pg.* 705
Baskel, Elise, VP-Mktg & Alliances - Career Education Corporation; *pg.* 599, *pg.* 658
Baskin, Jason, Product Mgr - Hormel Foods Corporation; *pg.* 863, *pg.* 915
Baskin, Sarah, Dir-Mktg-Wedding Paper Divas - SHUTTERFLY, INC.; *pg.* 1280, *pg.* 192
Basler, Matthew, Brand Mgr - Nestle Purina PetCare Company; *pg.* 1479, *pg.* 1000
Basloe, Brian, Chief Strategy Officer-Suite & Ticket Sls & Exec VP - Brooklyn Nets; *pg.* 534, *pg.* 1145
Basney, Barbara, VP-Global Adv, Brand Content & Media - Xerox Corporation; *pg.* 494, *pg.* 365
Basquez, Melinda, Dir-Customer Svc & Mktg - Elgin-Butler Brick Company; *pg.* 80, *pg.* 1662
Bass, Jon, Dir-Retail Mktg Strategy - BB&T Corporation; *pg.* 723, *pg.* 1393
Bass, Lauren, Specialist-Mktg-Digital User Experience Team - FedEx Corporation; *pg.* 1907, *pg.* 1642
Bass, Lindsay, Mgr-Mktg-Digital Mktg Delivery Solutions - American Express Company; *pg.* 712, *pg.* 1190
Bass, Natalie, Dir-Mktg - Houlihan's Restaurants, Inc.; *pg.* 1731, *pg.* 716
Bass, Scott, Dir-Mktg & Comm - Management Recruiters International, Inc.; *pg.* 429, *pg.* 1567
Bass, Shauna, Sr Mgr-Digital & Social Media - Sean John Clothing, Inc.; *pg.* 48, *pg.* 1290
Bassail, Miguel, Mgr-Multicultural Mktg - Verizon Communications Inc.; *pg.* 1875, *pg.* 1309
Bassel, Darren, Dir-Sls & Mktg-Valvoline - Ashland Inc.; *pg.* 972, *pg.* 726
Bassett, Charles, Sr Mgr-PR - AT&T Inc.; *pg.* 1867, *pg.* 1674
Bassett, Robert W., VP-Sls & Mktg - Menlo Worldwide, LLC; *pg.* 1915, *pg.* 255
Bassett, Thomas, Analyst-Sls Info - Bose Corporation; *pg.* 626, *pg.* 820
Basso, Kaitlyn, Mgr-Direct Mktg - Ralph Lauren Corporation; *pg.* 46, *pg.* 1284
Basso, Robyn, Sr Dir-Travel Indus Partnerships - Hawaii Visitors & Convention Bureau; *pg.* 994, *pg.* 543
Basson, Alf, Dir-Sls & Mktg - The Frog, Switch & Manufacturing Company; *pg.* 1338, *pg.* 1520
Bastholm, Lars, Chief Creative Officer-Global - Google Inc.; *pg.* 1249, *pg.* 153
Bastiaanse, Gerard, VP-Mktg - Farmer Brothers Company; *pg.* 855, *pg.* 293
Bastian, Hanna, Coord-Mktg - Pandora Media Inc.; *pg.* 1273, *pg.* 172
Bastian, Steven, Dir-Product Dev - National Notary Association; *pg.* 150, *pg.* 64
Bastin, Andrew J., Mgr-Digital Mktg - Crozer-Keystone Health System Inc.; *pg.* 1520, *pg.* 1587
Bastone, Mike, VP-Sls - Walker & Zanger, Inc.; *pg.* 119, *pg.* 281
Bastos, Jessie, Head-Sls-Small Bus Accts - T-Mobile US, Inc.; *pg.* 676, *pg.* 1816
Bastos, Vivian, Brand Mgr - Kao Brands Co. Inc.; *pg.* 513, *pg.* 1415
Basu, Santanu, Sr Product Mgr-Cortana & Bing - Microsoft Corporation; *pg.* 435, *pg.* 1824
Baszto, Mark, Dir-Corp Mktg - Arrow Electronics, Inc.; *pg.* 619, *pg.* 325
Bataille, Marissa, Sr Mgr-Mktg - Yahoo! Inc.; *pg.* 1289, *pg.* 289
Batcheller, Courtney, Mgr-Product Dev-Popeyes Louisiana Kitchen - Popeye's Chicken & Biscuits; *pg.* 1745, *pg.* 517
Batcheller, Courtney, Mgr-Product Dev - Popeyes Louisiana Kitchen, Inc.; *pg.* 1745, *pg.* 517
Batcheller, Meredith, Analyst-Global Sponsorship & Corp Mktg - American International Group, Inc.; *pg.* 1190, *pg.* 1193
Batchelor, Abby, Sr Analyst-Mktg, Sustainability & Comm - INTERCONTINENTALEXCHANGE, INC.; *pg.* 769, *pg.* 512
Batchelor, Heather, Sr Specialist-Product Complaint - GlaxoSmithKline; *pg.* 1536, *pg.* 1565
Batchelor, Scarlet, Gen Mgr-Mdse-NA Footwear - New Balance Athletic Shoe, Inc.; *pg.* 1811, *pg.* 798
Bateman, Angela, Sr Mgr-Mktg - Mattel Games/Puzzles; *pg.* 962, *pg.* 80
Bateman, Angela, Sr Mgr-Mktg - MATTEL, INC.; *pg.* 962, *pg.* 81
Bateman, Danielle, Sr Dir-Mktg & Adv - Save-A-Lot, Ltd.; *pg.* 894, *pg.* 977
Bateman, J.R., VP-Sls & Mktg - Dril-Quip, Inc.; *pg.* 1330, *pg.* 1704
Bateman, Marge, Coord-Media - Kentucky Department of Tourism; *pg.* 996, *pg.* 728
Bates, Brianne, Mgr-PR-North America - Oakley, Inc.; *pg.* 1840, *pg.* 86
Bates, Chris, Mgr-Product Portfolio & Pro Svcs - Daktronics, Inc.; *pg.* 633, *pg.* 1624
Bates, Damon, VP-Field Mktg & Promo - Massachusetts Mutual Life Insurance Company; *pg.* 1207, *pg.* 845
Bates, David R., VP-Mktg - Xerox Corporation; *pg.* 494, *pg.* 365
Bates, Duane, Sr Dir-Digital Comm Strategy & New Media - Habitat for Humanity International, Inc.; *pg.* 143, *pg.* 486
Bates, Eowyn, Sr Dir-Dev & Membership - San Diego Society of Natural History; *pg.* 580, *pg.* 208
Bates, Ernest R., VP-Sls & Bus Dev - American Shared Hospital Services; *pg.* 1493, *pg.* 212
Bates, Gina Chiasson, Mgr-Shopper Mktg-Multi-Channel & ECommerce - Kimberly-Clark Corporation; *pg.* 1461, *pg.* 1720
Bates, Janie, Sr Dir-Global Mktg - Medtronic, Inc.; *pg.* 1564, *pg.* 939
Bates, Joan, Sr Dir-Investor & Media Rels - DeVry Education Group Inc.; *pg.* 600, *pg.* 607
Bates, Kathy, Rep-Adv - Palm Springs Desert Resorts Convention & Visitors Authority; *pg.* 1003, *pg.* 187
Bates, Katie, Specialist-Interactive Mktg - Marshalls of MA, Inc.; *pg.* 1778, *pg.* 821
Bates, Katie, Specialist-Interactive Mktg - T.J. Maxx; *pg.* 1788, *pg.* 822
Bates, Katie, Specialist-Interactive Mktg - The TJX Companies, Inc.; *pg.* 1788, *pg.* 822
Bates, Kevin, Sr VP-Mktg - Precision Auto Care, Inc.; *pg.* 215, *pg.* 1787
Bates, Kristy, Mgr-Mktg - Uber USA, LLC; *pg.* 1286, *pg.* 229
Bates, Matt, Product Mgr-Mktg-Consumer Products - Garmin International, Inc.; *pg.* 1414, *pg.* 717
Bates, Paul R., Exec VP-Sls Mktg & Transportation - Golden Flake Snack Foods, Inc.; *pg.* 1854, *pg.* 3
Bates, Ryan, Analyst-Mktg - Hobby Lobby Stores Inc.; *pg.* 927, *pg.* 1486
Bateson, Anna, Dir-Global Mktg Comm - YouTube, LLC; *pg.* 1291, *pg.* 198
Bateson, Charlie, Dir-Product & Comml - Abercrombie & Kent USA, LLC; *pg.* 1896, *pg.* 607
Bathel, Charles, Coord-Gaming Community & Mktg - Logitech Inc.; *pg.* 1264, *pg.* 164
Bathey, Jim, VP-Consumer Mktg - Milwaukee Brewers Baseball Club, Inc.; *pg.* 562, *pg.* 1878
Bathrick, Sarah, Second VP-Risk Control Res & Product Dev - Travelers Insurance; *pg.* 1220, *pg.* 963
Batina, Susan, VP-Closed-End Funds Mktg - Nuveen Investments, Inc.; *pg.* 788, *pg.* 586
Batista, Rosa, Sr Dir-New Bus Dev - Automatic Data Processing, Inc.; *pg.* 357, *pg.* 1117
Batiste, Melanie, Mgr-Natl Mktg Fin - Toyota Motor Sales, U.S.A., Inc.; *pg.* 193, *pg.* 296
Batkoff, Blake, Dir-Mktg & Sls - Petersen Aluminum Corporation; *pg.* 104, *pg.* 611
Bator, Alice, Coord-Social Media - JAND, Inc.; *pg.* 1418, *pg.* 1245
Bator, John, Product Mgr - Vision-Ease Lens Corporation; *pg.* 1436, *pg.* 954
Batra, Nitin, Dir-Mktg-Intl - ConAgra Foods, Inc.; *pg.* 826, *pg.* 1014
Batra, Vikrant, VP-Worldwide Mktg - Hewlett-Packard Company; *pg.* 404, *pg.* 175
Batraski, Ethan, VP-Product Design - Box Inc.; *pg.* 1232, *pg.* 124
Batt, Kevin, VP-Ops, Product & Dev - Club Med Sales, Inc.; *pg.* 1903, *pg.* 441
Batta, Reema, Sr Mgr-Database Mktg - Hotwire, Inc.; *pg.* 1912, *pg.* 219
Battaglia, Greg, Sr Mgr - Ernst & Young Global Limited; *pg.* 748, *pg.* 1228
Battaglia, Tammy, Sr Specialist-Media Rels - Henry Ford Health System; *pg.* 1541, *pg.* 883
Batten, John, VP-Mktg & Bus Dev - Harbor Freight Tools; *pg.* 1772, *pg.* 55
Battenberg, Alysha, Mgr-Mktg - Mattel Games/Puzzles; *pg.* 962, *pg.* 80
Battenberg, Alysha, Assoc Mgr-Mktg - MATTEL, INC.; *pg.* 962, *pg.* 81
Battin, Matt, VP-Oncology Mktg - GlaxoSmithKline; *pg.* 1536, *pg.* 1565
Battin, Molly, Chief Media Officer - Turner Broadcasting System, Inc.; *pg.* 314, *pg.* 521
Battista, Anthony J., Sr Engr-Sls - Verizon Communications Inc.; *pg.* 1875, *pg.* 1309
Battista, Steve, Sr VP-Global Brand Creative - Under Armour, Inc.; *pg.* 49, *pg.* 759
Battle, Caroline, Mgr-Event Sls & Mktg - Porsche Cars North America, Inc.; *pg.* 189, *pg.* 518
Battle, Colleen, Mgr-Digital Mktg-Global - Alcon; *pg.* 1399, *pg.* 530
Battles, Kenya, Asst VP & Brand Mgr - Capital One Financial Corporation; *pg.* 730, *pg.* 1789
Battles, Molly, Mgr-PR - Bonnier Corporation; *pg.* 1622, *pg.* 480
Battles, Rob, Sr VP-Creative Svcs - AMC Networks Inc.; *pg.* 269, *pg.* 1189
Battu, Sheela, Dir-Web Mktg - Calvin Klein, Inc.; *pg.* 20, *pg.* 1209
Batty, Erin, Sr Mgr-Sls Comm-Global - LinkedIn Corporation; *pg.* 1262, *pg.* 160
Batty, Ryan, Dir-Mktg-Global Content & Channels, Talent Solutions - LinkedIn Corporation; *pg.* 1262, *pg.* 160
Batzli, Jeff, Dir-Creative & Trade Books - Rodale, Inc.; *pg.* 1681, *pg.* 1530
Baubonis, Rich, Sr VP & Mgr-Mktg Resources Allocation - Bank of America Corporation; *pg.* 718, *pg.* 1362
Baudon, Veronique, Sr Mgr-Partner Bus - Hewlett-Packard Company; *pg.* 404, *pg.* 175
Baudrand, Caroline, Mgr-Assoc Trade Mktg - Kind LLC; *pg.* 868, *pg.* 1249
Bauer, Amanda, Mgr-Retail Mktg - Dick Blick Company; *pg.* 1766, *pg.* 617
Bauer, Christina, Mgr-Mktg Comm - Siemens Corporation; *pg.* 803, *pg.* 1291
Bauer, Christopher, Mgr-Aviation OEM Sls & Mktg - Garmin International, Inc.; *pg.* 1414, *pg.* 717
Bauer, Jaymi, CMO & Head-Sls & Mktg - Gaiam, Inc.; *pg.* 1532, *pg.* 334
Bauer, Jeffrey, Assoc Mgr-Trade Mktg - LeapFrog Enterprises, Inc.; *pg.* 961, *pg.* 84
Bauer, Jennifer, VP-Mktg - Diamond Foods, Inc.; *pg.* 1851, *pg.* 216
Bauer, Lauren, Mgr-Mktg, Media & Entertainment - Deloitte & Touche USA LLP; *pg.* 743, *pg.* 1222
Bauer, Nancy, VP-Sls & Corp Sponsorships - Connecticut Public Broadcasting Corp.; *pg.* 279, *pg.* 351
Bauer, Richard, VP-Global Sls-Honeywell Fire Sys - Notifier Co.; *pg.* 659, *pg.* 360
Bauer, Rick, Brand Mgr-SKIL Power Tools - Robert Bosch Tool Corp; *pg.* 1060, *pg.* 634
Bauerlein, Marty, Sr VP-Sls-US - Tech Data Corporation; *pg.* 482, *pg.* 416
Baugh, Ted, Sr Dir-Corp Partnerships - Cleveland Indians Baseball Company, Inc.; *pg.* 541, *pg.* 1429
Baughman, James H., Dir-Sls & Mktg - Planes Moving & Storage, Inc.; *pg.* 1919, *pg.* 1479
Baughman, Michael J., VP-Fin-Medical Products - Baxter International Inc.; *pg.* 1499, *pg.* 599
Baulier, Jamie, Brand Mgr-Innovation-M&M'S Brand - Mars North America; *pg.* 1859, *pg.* 1072
Baum, Chris, Sr VP-Brdcst & Corp Sls - Jazz Basketball Investors, Inc.; *pg.* 554, *pg.* 1759
Baum, Debra, Exec Dir-Mktg-Clinique - The Estee Lauder Companies Inc.; *pg.* 508, *pg.* 1229
Baum, Mark, VP & Mgr-Sls - The Ford Meter Box Company,

First page reference indicates Business Class Edition
Second page reference indicates Geographic Edition

Inc.; *pg.* 1047, *pg.* 698
Baum, Ryan, Sr Mgr-Prime Engagement & Retention - Amazon.com, Inc.; *pg.* 1226, *pg.* 1831
Bauman, Amanda, Sr Mgr-Community Affairs - Campbell Soup Company; *pg.* 844, *pg.* 1048
Bauman, Bill, Sr Mgr-Technical Mktg-Global Partners - Red Hat, Inc.; *pg.* 460, *pg.* 1388
Bauman, Kevin, Sr Dir-Product Mgmt - Penn Foster Education Group, Inc.; *pg.* 606, *pg.* 1586
Bauman, Mark, Dir-Creative Svcs - McKesson Corporation; *pg.* 1560, *pg.* 222
Bauman, Tina, Supvr-Mktg - 3M Company; *pg.* 1142, *pg.* 956
Baumann, Amy, Assoc Dir-Mktg, US HCC Strategy & Odanacatib - Merck & Co., Inc.; *pg.* 1566, *pg.* 1077
Baumann, Andrew, Dir-Mktg - Jones Soda Co.; *pg.* 253, *pg.* 1836
Baumann, Jared, Product Mgr-B2B Solutions - C Spire Wireless; *pg.* 628, *pg.* 971
Baumann, Steph, Brand Mgr-Global - Medtronic, Inc.; *pg.* 1564, *pg.* 939
Baumer, Jillian, Coord-Loyalty Mktg - The Sports Authority, Inc.; *pg.* 1846, *pg.* 326
Baumgarten, Rachel, VP-Integrated Mktg - MTV Networks Company; *pg.* 298, *pg.* 1262
Baumgarthuber, Sabine, Mgr-Digital Mktg-Global - Autodesk Inc.; *pg.* 356, *pg.* 257
Baumgartner, Adam, VP-Mktg - Wells Enterprises, Inc.; *pg.* 909, *pg.* 709
Baumgartner, Brad, Exec VP-Sls & Mktg - Questar Assessment, Inc.; *pg.* 1679, *pg.* 1143
Baumgartner, Jeanie, VP-Mktg & Programming - New York Rangers Hockey Club; *pg.* 570, *pg.* 1269
Baumgartner, Jen, Mgr-PR - Broadcom Corporation; *pg.* 364, *pg.* 108
Baumgartner, John, VP-Operational Support & Sls Dev-Western Div Field Ops - Aamco Transmissions, Inc.; *pg.* 197, *pg.* 1540
Baumgartner, Richard, Mgr-Sls-Ontario & Quebec - Plasti-Fab Ltd.; *pg.* 1888, *pg.* 1904
Baumhover, Michelle, Dir-Consumer Mktg - Iowa Beef Industry Council; *pg.* 145, *pg.* 701
Baumuller, Ted, Sr Dir-IT - Cisco Systems, Inc.; *pg.* 372, *pg.* 240
Bausano, Maggie, VP & Dir-Media - U.S. Bancorp; *pg.* 815, *pg.* 945
Bausch, Caryn, Mgr-Product Mktg - Paychex, Inc.; *pg.* 792, *pg.* 1336
Bausch, Ken, VP-Interactive Mktg - World Kitchen LLC; *pg.* 1141, *pg.* 657
Bauzon, Holly B., VP-Sls & Managed Markets - Vermillion, Inc.; *pg.* 1435, *pg.* 1667
Baver, Michael P., Mgr-Product Mktg-Data Center Software Div - Intel Corporation; *pg.* 645, *pg.* 266
Bavlnka, Dave, VP-Adv - Wisconsin Milk Marketing Board, Inc.; *pg.* 161, *pg.* 1868
Bavor, Clay, VP-Product Mgmt - Google Inc.; *pg.* 1249, *pg.* 153
Bawany, Aziz, Mgr-Social Mktg-Social Sensei - Zappos.com, Inc.; *pg.* 1291, *pg.* 1030
Bawduniak, Michael, Reg Dir-Sls - Genzyme Corporation; *pg.* 1534, *pg.* 808
Bawinkel, Vicki, Mgr-Svcs Field Mktg - Cisco Systems, Inc.; *pg.* 372, *pg.* 240
Baxendale, Nikki, VP-Global & Dir-Creative-Mktg - Claire's Stores, Inc.; *pg.* 1764, *pg.* 617
Baxter, Ashley, Sr Mgr-Social & PR - Cricket Wireless LLC; *pg.* 381, *pg.* 483
Baxter, Jeff, Sr Product Mgr - Thermo Fisher Scientific Inc.; *pg.* 1602, *pg.* 61
Baxter, Jeff, Sr Product Mgr-Global - Thermo Fisher Scientific Inc.; *pg.* 1431, *pg.* 854
Baxter, Julia, Assoc Dir-Mktg-Wag.com - Quidsi, Inc.; *pg.* 1276, *pg.* 1076
Baxter, Mary, Sr Mgr-Mktg & ECommerce - Marriott International, Inc.; *pg.* 1102, *pg.* 764
Baxter, Mike, Sr VP-Product Dev - DataCard Corporation; *pg.* 382, *pg.* 948
Baxter, Molly, Acct Exec-Natl-Outfront Media - Outfront Media; *pg.* 1465, *pg.* 1275
Baxter, Rick, Reg Dir-Mktg-Florida - The E.W. Scripps Company; *pg.* 1639, *pg.* 1412
Baxter, Wayne, Dir-Product Mgmt - Herman Miller, Inc.; *pg.* 926, *pg.* 913
Bay, Carey, Sr Dir-Acct Dev - Bandai America Incorporated; *pg.* 950, *pg.* 75
Bayard, Jennifer, Dir-Digital Adv - Time Inc.; *pg.* 1693, *pg.* 1300
Bayer, Ed, Dir-Media Plng - The Kraft Heinz Company; *pg.* 871, *pg.* 641
Bayer, Kellie M., Mgr-Event Mktg - Intel Corporation; *pg.* 645, *pg.* 266
Bayer, Kim, Sr Dir-Mktg-West Div - McDonald's Corporation; *pg.* 1737, *pg.* 645
Bayer, Sally, VP-Mktg - Roto-Rooter, Inc.; *pg.* 108, *pg.* 1425
Baylerian, Tom, VP-Adv & Sls - Journal Media Group, Inc.; *pg.* 1655, *pg.* 1876
Bayless Blanton, Robin, Sr Dir-Mktg - McAlister's Deli; *pg.* 1737, *pg.* 484
Bayless, Django, Sr VP-New Media Tech, Artist Rels & Digital Svcs - Live Nation Entertainment, Inc.; *pg.* 558, *pg.* 47
Bayley, Jacqueline, Sr Specialist-Mktg Comm - CB Richard Ellis, Inc.; *pg.* 1085, *pg.* 1210
Baylis, Paula, VP-Production - Structural Graphics, LLC; *pg.* 1689, *pg.* 346
Baylock, Karen, Reg Dir-Sls - Novartis Corporation; *pg.* 1574, *pg.* 1273
Baylor, Scott, Mgr-Digital Mktg - RACKSPACE HOSTING, INC.; *pg.* 1277, *pg.* 1742
Bayne, Shelly, Dir-Ad Sls Mktg - The Hallmark Channel; *pg.* 290, *pg.* 281
Bayne, Tamara, Mgr-Mktg-Consumer Mktg - Abbott Laboratories; *pg.* 1484, *pg.* 551
Baynes, Emily, Sr Assoc Brand Mgr-Trident - Mondelez International, Inc.; *pg.* 878, *pg.* 601
Baysinger, Steve, Sr Product Mgr - The Gates Corporation; *pg.* 205, *pg.* 319
Bayton, Lauren, Mgr-Creative Presentation & Training - Ralph Lauren Corporation; *pg.* 46, *pg.* 1284
Baytosh, David, Sr VP-Mktg - Discount Drug Mart Inc.; *pg.* 1524, *pg.* 1464
Bazanos, Elena, Mgr-Sls - Comcast Sportsnet; *pg.* 278, *pg.* 1562
Bazant, David, Dir-Online Mktg - Sears Holdings Corporation; *pg.* 1784, *pg.* 618
Bazante, Jennifer, Exec VP-Mktg - Humana, Inc.; *pg.* 1204, *pg.* 734
Bazik, Yvonne, Mgr-Small Bus Mktg - United Parcel Service, Inc.; *pg.* 1928, *pg.* 522
Bazille, Ken, Rep-Sls - Adco, Inc.; *pg.* 325, *pg.* 482
Bazini, Francois, VP-Mktg-Europe Middle East Africa - Beam Suntory Inc.; *pg.* 1957, *pg.* 599
Bazzell, Meredith, Mgr-Mktg Comm-Global - Cummins Inc.; *pg.* 1326, *pg.* 676
Bazzi, Suzan, Sr Analyst-Mktg - Canadian Imperial Bank of Commerce; *pg.* 729, *pg.* 1935
Beach, Alan, VP-Mdsg - 7-Eleven, Inc.; *pg.* 1012, *pg.* 1672
Beach, Arren, Brand Mgr-SHEBA - Mars Petcare; *pg.* 1478, *pg.* 1633
Beach, Brad, Sr Dir-Product Dev-Home Mgmt Portfolio - Wal-Mart Stores, Inc.; *pg.* 1790, *pg.* 29
Beach, Wendy, Dir-Brand Mktg - Choice Hotels International, Inc.; *pg.* 1086, *pg.* 775
Beachnau, Lori, Dir-Mktg - ProAssurance Corporation; *pg.* 1214, *pg.* 3
Beadle, Ed, Sr Mgr-Digital Strategy - American Honda Motor Co., Inc.; *pg.* 163, *pg.* 292
Beadle, Susan, Dir-Bus Travel & Worldwide Sls - InterContinental Hotels Corporation; *pg.* 1097, *pg.* 511
Beadleson, Brett, VP-Sls - Baker Knapp & Tubbs Inc.; *pg.* 916, *pg.* 566
Beadon, Christopher, Coord-Sports Mktg - Everlast Worldwide Inc.; *pg.* 1833, *pg.* 1230
Beahm, Max, Exec Dir-Digital Media - Comcast Corporation; *pg.* 276, *pg.* 1560
Beahm, Michael, Mgr-Channel Mktg-Emerging Market - Blackbaud, Inc.; *pg.* 361, *pg.* 1613
Beahm, Steven, VP-Sls Ops - FCA US LLC; *pg.* 170, *pg.* 868
Beal, Jamie M., Sr Mgr-Internal Comm - Toys "R" Us, Inc.; *pg.* 968, *pg.* 1130
Beal, John, Dir-Comml Mktg-Western Div - Heineken USA Inc.; *pg.* 252, *pg.* 1352
Beale, Kevin, Dir-Suite Sls & Client Svcs - The Phillies, L.P.; *pg.* 575, *pg.* 1569
Beale, Les, Sr VP & Product Mgr-Global IOO - Northern Trust Corporation; *pg.* 787, *pg.* 585
Beale, Polly, Dir-Creative - Transamerica Insurance & Investment Group; *pg.* 1219, *pg.* 141
Beale, Robert, Media Planner-On-Air - BET Holdings LLC; *pg.* 271, *pg.* 396
Beale, Samantha, S Mgr-Mktg-Digital Media - Doctor's Associates Inc.; *pg.* 1726, *pg.* 356
Beale, Samantha, Sr Mgr-Mktg & Digital Media - Subway Restaurants; *pg.* 1751, *pg.* 356
Beall, Kevin, VP-Sls - KB Home; *pg.* 90, *pg.* 134
Beals, Hannah, Mgr-Mktg-Intl - BCBG Max Azria Group LLC; *pg.* 19, *pg.* 301
Beals, Kylie, Mgr-ECommerce Mktg - Clarks Companies; *pg.* 1806, *pg.* 836
Beam, Todd, Mgr-Media Rels - Detroit Red Wings, Inc.; *pg.* 544, *pg.* 880
Beaman, Bruce, Sr Dir-Adabas & Natural Product Mktg - Software AG, Inc.; *pg.* 471, *pg.* 1799
Beaman, Denise, Mgr-Mktg & Corp Mktg - AmerisourceBergen Corporation; *pg.* 1493, *pg.* 1522
Bean, Jason, Dir-Field Mktg - Red Lion Hotels Corp.; *pg.* 1110, *pg.* 1844
Bean, Michael, Gen Mgr-Sls - Finch Paper LLC; *pg.* 1457, *pg.* 1161
Bean, Michael, Product Mgr-Global - Molex Incorporated; *pg.* 655, *pg.* 628
Bean, Reginald, Dir-Multicultural Mktg - Coca-Cola Bottling Co. Consolidated; *pg.* 240, *pg.* 1365
Bean, Tricia, Head-Mktg Mgr-Hispanic Sponsorships & TV Content - AT&T; *pg.* 1865, *pg.* 258
Beane, Scott, VP & Mgr-Sls - Coldwell Banker Residential Brokerage; *pg.* 1087, *pg.* 850
Beaney, Sara, VP-Creative & Adv-Global - The Estee Lauder Companies Inc.; *pg.* 508, *pg.* 1229
Bear, Debbie, VP & Sr Product Mgr - U.S. Bancorp; *pg.* 815, *pg.* 945
Bear, Meg, Grp VP-Cloud Social Platform - Oracle Corporation; *pg.* 450, *pg.* 191
Bearcroft, Andrea, VP-Mktg Small Bus - The ADT Corporation; *pg.* 612, *pg.* 409
Beard, Chris, Mgr-Media-Olive Garden - Darden Restaurants, Inc.; *pg.* 1724, *pg.* 453
Beard, John M., Pres-Northwest Advisors, Inc. - Northwest Bancshares, Inc.; *pg.* 788, *pg.* 1590
Beard, Kenneth S., Dir-Mktg - Business Brokers Network; *pg.* 135, *pg.* 1735
Beard, Nick, Specialist-PR - Mazda North American Operations; *pg.* 183, *pg.* 113
Beardall, Chris, Exec VP-Sls-Global - Spin Master Ltd.; *pg.* 967, *pg.* 1943
Beardall, Larry K., Exec VP-Sls & Mktg - Dynatronics Corporation; *pg.* 1526, *pg.* 1757
Bearden, Ken, Corp Dir-Integrated Mktg - The Detroit Medical Center; *pg.* 1524, *pg.* 880
Beardslee, Tim, Mgr-Technical Mktg - Xerox Corporation; *pg.* 494, *pg.* 365
Beardsley, Corie, Mgr-Mktg Creative Ops - Ann Inc.; *pg.* 18, *pg.* 1195
Bearer, Basil, Dir-Creative - Kohl's Corporation; *pg.* 1775, *pg.* 1870
Bearfield, Lori, Dir-Creative-Photography - Wayfair LLC; *pg.* 1288, *pg.* 801
Beasley, Chelsea, Mgr-Social Mktg - Marriott International, Inc.; *pg.* 1102, *pg.* 764
Beasley, John, VP-Mktg-EMEA - Monster Beverage Corporation; *pg.* 257, *pg.* 69
Beasley, Steven, Dir-Digital Media - Museum of Science and Industry; *pg.* 565, *pg.* 583
Beato, Chris, Coord-Internet Mktg - Wegmans Food Markets, Inc.; *pg.* 1037, *pg.* 1337
Beaton, Matt, VP-Olympic Digital Sls - NBC Sports Network; *pg.* 300, *pg.* 375
Beaton, Matt, Mgr-Franchise Sls - NBC Universal, Inc.; *pg.* 300, *pg.* 1266
Beatty, Davora Davidson, Sr Mgr-Shopper Insights & Category Dev - Abbott Laboratories; *pg.* 1484, *pg.* 551
Beatty, Kjerstin, Sr VP-Media - NBC Universal, Inc.; *pg.* 300, *pg.* 1266
Beatty, Mark S., VP Sls & Natl Accts - Pabst Brewing Company; *pg.* 258, *pg.* 137
Beatty, Sally, Dir-Media Rels, Vaccines, Oncology & Consumer Products - Pfizer Inc.; *pg.* 1581, *pg.* 1278
Beatty, Sally, Brand Mgr-Acct Svc - Raymond James Financial, Inc.; *pg.* 798, *pg.* 464
Beaubien Ball, Michelle, Dir-Mktg & Comm - Interstate Worldwide Relocation, Inc.; *pg.* 1912, *pg.* 1807
Beauchamp, Erik, Sr Product Mgr - CCH Inc.; *pg.* 1626, *pg.* 653
Beauchamp, Gary, Sr VP & Gen Mgr-Gennum Product Grp - Semtech Corporation; *pg.* 671, *pg.* 57
Beauchamp, Gary M., Sr VP & Gen Mgr-Gennum Product Grp

- Semtech Corporation Gennum Products; *pg.* 671, *pg.* 1919

Beaudet, Alexis, Mgr-Strategic Sls Comm-ABC Family - ABC Family Channel; *pg.* 268, *pg.* 51

Beaudet, Mark, VP-Mktg & Sls - Paladin Labs, Inc.; *pg.* 1579, *pg.* 1956

Beaudette, Rory, COO-Cleaning Products - ACS Industries, Inc.; *pg.* 1040, *pg.* 1602

Beaudin, Chris, Mgr-Mktg-Strategic Initiatives - American Woodmark Corporation; *pg.* 913, *pg.* 1811

Beaudo, Daren J., Dir-Media Rels - ConocoPhillips; *pg.* 975, *pg.* 1703

Beaudry, Jenny, Brand Mgr-Global Mktg - Eli Lilly and Company; *pg.* 1527, *pg.* 684

Beaufils, Ludovic, VP-Product Mktg - Whirlpool Corporation; *pg.* 62, *pg.* 872

Beaufort, Marie De, Dir-EMEA B2B Mktg - Lenovo Group Ltd; *pg.* 427, *pg.* 1384

Beaulieu, Lauren, Dir-Comml Mktg-Customer Promos & Retention - Advance Auto Parts, Inc.; *pg.* 197, *pg.* 1805

Beaulieu, Michael, Assoc Dir-Digital Media Sls - Wayfair LLC; *pg.* 1288, *pg.* 801

Beaumont, Danielle, Grp Product Mgr-Adobe Muse - Adobe Systems Incorporated; *pg.* 342, *pg.* 235

Beauparlant, David, Head-Adv, media & brand partnerships-Microsoft Office - Microsoft Corporation; *pg.* 435, *pg.* 1824

Beauregard, Mark, VP-Mktg - Matthews International Corporation; *pg.* 1662, *pg.* 1578

Beaven, John, Exec Dir-Ticket Sls - Golden State Warriors, LLC; *pg.* 550, *pg.* 171

Beaver, Kris, Product Mgr-Global Aerospace, Defense & Marine - TE Connectivity Ltd.; *pg.* 677, *pg.* 1515

Beaver, Nancy, VP & Mktg Mgr-Customer Loyalty-Wells Fargo Bank - Wells Fargo & Company; *pg.* 819, *pg.* 232

Beaver, Troy, VP-Mktg-American Century Investments - American Century Investments; *pg.* 711, *pg.* 980

Beaverson, Mike, Mgr-Mktg & Digital - Cargill, Inc.; *pg.* 845, *pg.* 965

Bebart, Karen, VP-Mktg, Digital Mktg & Mktg Res - National Association of Realtors; *pg.* 1666, *pg.* 584

Bebee, Linda, VP-Domestic Mktg - Texas Beef Council; *pg.* 158, *pg.* 1666

Beber, Kevin M., VP-Bus Dev & Mktg - ENERGY FOCUS, INC.; *pg.* 1411, *pg.* 1472

Becchetti, Lisa, Dir-Digital Mktg - Best Buy Co., Inc.; *pg.* 1761, *pg.* 954

Bechamps, Diane, VP-Strategy & Mktg - Virginia Tourism Authority; *pg.* 1010, *pg.* 1804

Becht, Bart, Chm & Interim CEO - Coty, Inc.; *pg.* 506, *pg.* 1219

Becht, Heidi, Dir-Mktg - The Pep Boys - Manny, Moe & Jack; *pg.* 215, *pg.* 1568

Becht, Kathryn, Brand Mgr - Chobani LLC; *pg.* 847, *pg.* 1318

Bechtel, Brad, Sr Dir-Sls - MTD Products, Inc.; *pg.* 1057, *pg.* 1478

Bechtel, Jessica, Asst Mgr-Mktg - PepsiCo, Inc.; *pg.* 259, *pg.* 1327

Bechtel, Matt, Sr Mgr-Digital Mktg - Lockheed Martin Corporation; *pg.* 229, *pg.* 762

Beck, Andrea, Dir-Retail Mktg Comm - The Sherwin-Williams Company; *pg.* 1447, *pg.* 1435

Beck, Andrea, Dir-Retail Mktg Comm - Sherwin Williams; *pg.* 1448, *pg.* 1436

Beck, Angela, Mgr-Digital Customer Mktg - Mattel Games/Puzzles; *pg.* 962, *pg.* 80

Beck, Angela, Mgr-Digital Customer Mktg - MATTEL, INC.; *pg.* 962, *pg.* 81

Beck, Bill, Sr Dir-Whirlpool, Maytag, Value Brands & Channel Mktg - Whirlpool Corporation; *pg.* 62, *pg.* 872

Beck, Chris, Brand Mgr-Srixon - Roger Cleveland Golf Company, Inc.; *pg.* 1844, *pg.* 105

Beck, Donald, Sr VP-Sls & Bus Dev - LifeLock Inc.; *pg.* 776, *pg.* 26

Beck, Doug, Mgr-Corp Partnership Sls - Minnesota Twins, LLC; *pg.* 563, *pg.* 940

Beck, Douglas A., VP-Sls & Mktg - Clark Grave Vault Company; *pg.* 76, *pg.* 1438

Beck, George, Specialist-Mktg - J.C. Penney Company, Inc.; *pg.* 1774, *pg.* 1732

Beck, James, VP-Shopper Mktg-Walmart & Sam's Team - The Coca-Cola Company; *pg.* 240, *pg.* 493

Beck, Jon, Dir-Comml Mktg - AutoZone, Inc.; *pg.* 200, *pg.* 1641

Beck, Leanna, Dir-Membership Rewards Earn Product Strategy - American Express Company; *pg.* 712, *pg.* 1190

Beck, Mary, Sr VP-Mktg & Promos - MLB Network; *pg.* 298, *pg.* 1120

Beck, Mary Abrams, Sr VP-Mktg & Promos - Major League Baseball; *pg.* 560, *pg.* 1255

Beck, Mike, Sr Exec Producer-Dev & Production - Time Inc.; *pg.* 1693, *pg.* 1300

Beck, Scott, Gen Mgr-Mktg Ops-North America - Harley-Davidson, Inc.; *pg.* 178, *pg.* 1874

Beck, Stacey, Head-Mktg-North America Consumer Goods & Svcs - Accenture; *pg.* 1392, *pg.* 1186

Beck, Steve, Mgr-Display Adv - The Lima News; *pg.* 1659, *pg.* 1457

Beck, Tom, VP-Sls - Broadcast Electronics, Inc.; *pg.* 627, *pg.* 653

Beck, Tyler, Sr Asst Brand Mgr-Swiffer - The Procter & Gamble Company; *pg.* 1129, *pg.* 1418

Becker, Amanda, Analyst-Digital Mktg Delivery Solutions - American Express Company; *pg.* 712, *pg.* 1190

Becker, Amy, Sr Mgr-Activation - Mizkan Americas, Inc.; *pg.* 877, *pg.* 634

Becker, Dave, VP-Consumer Sls - Pelican Products, Inc.; *pg.* 1842, *pg.* 295

Becker, Erin D., Brand Mgr-Shopper Mktg - Starbucks Corporation; *pg.* 897, *pg.* 1840

Becker, Jared, VP-Design & Mktg - Walker & Zanger, Inc.; *pg.* 119, *pg.* 281

Becker, Jessica, Sr Mgr-PR, Social Media & Internal Comm - The Rockport Group; *pg.* 1818, *pg.* 812

Becker, Joe, Mgr-Intl Mktg-Cat Footwear - Wolverine World Wide, Inc.; *pg.* 1822, *pg.* 905

Becker, Kathryn, Dir-Mktg - Automatic Data Processing, Inc.; *pg.* 357, *pg.* 1117

Becker, Kathryn B., Dir-Global Mktg & Companion Diagnostics - Abbott Laboratories; *pg.* 1484, *pg.* 551

Becker, Michelle, Sr Mgr-Exec Comm-Worldwide SMS&P - Microsoft Corporation; *pg.* 435, *pg.* 1824

Becker, Pam, Sr Mgr-PR - General Mills, Inc.; *pg.* 828, *pg.* 933

Becker, Rachel, Dir-Events & Mktg & Assoc Planner-Fin - The Northwestern Mutual Life Insurance Company; *pg.* 1212, *pg.* 1879

Becker, Richard E., VP-Sls - VF Imagewear; *pg.* 50, *pg.* 476

Becker, Sandy, Dir-Distr Mktg - FX Networks, LLC; *pg.* 288, *pg.* 131

Becker, Ted, Sr VP-Sls & Mktg-Americas - Exide Technologies; *pg.* 204, *pg.* 483

Becker, Tom, Mgr-Sls-Natl - Daktronics, Inc.; *pg.* 633, *pg.* 1624

Becker, Yin, VP-Comm, Pub Affairs & Strategic Mktg - Stryker Orthopaedics; *pg.* 1599, *pg.* 1082

Becker-Matthews, Keri Ann, Sr Mgr-Mktg & Licensing - American Society for the Prevention of Cruelty to Animals; *pg.* 131, *pg.* 1193

Beckert, Jessica, Assoc Mgr-Email Mktg - American Eagle Outfitters, Inc.; *pg.* 37, *pg.* 1572

Beckes, Tim, Mgr-Mdsg-Intl - GNC Holdings Inc.; *pg.* 1537, *pg.* 1576

Beckett, Barry, Sr Mgr-Mktg - The Toro Company; *pg.* 1065, *pg.* 918

Beckett, Carolyn, Sr Mgr-Brand Payer Mktg - GlaxoSmithKline; *pg.* 1536, *pg.* 1565

Beckett, Wendy, Dir-Creative-HomeGoods - HomeGoods, Inc.; *pg.* 1125, *pg.* 821

Beckham, Ben, VP-Sls-North America - Perseon Corporation; *pg.* 1581, *pg.* 1760

Beckham, Mike, VP & Mgr-Sls - Turner Broadcasting System, Inc.; *pg.* 314, *pg.* 521

Beckler, Amanda, Mgr-Local Sls - Sinclair Broadcast Group, Inc.; *pg.* 308, *pg.* 773

Beckler, Ryan, Mgr-Social Media - Daily News, L.P.; *pg.* 1632, *pg.* 1221

Beckley, Natasha, Dir-Mktg Comm - Quantum Corporation; *pg.* 458, *pg.* 250

Beckman, Carl, Sr VP & Dir-Strategic Dev & Central Product - Northern Trust Corporation; *pg.* 787, *pg.* 585

Beckman, Dana, Sr Mgr-Corp Affairs - Alliance Data Systems Corporation; *pg.* 347, *pg.* 1729

Beckman, Jill Dearing, VP-Mktg & Adv - Moran Foods, Inc.; *pg.* 1028, *pg.* 976

Beckman, Robert, Mgr-Email Mktg - CenturyLink, Inc.; *pg.* 1870, *pg.* 746

Beckmann, Chris, Product Mgr - Google Inc.; *pg.* 1249, *pg.* 153

Becsey, Jenna, Mgr-Online Mktg - Spanx Inc.; *pg.* 32, *pg.* 520

Becvar, John, Sr Dir-HR - Groupon, Inc.; *pg.* 1255, *pg.* 575

Bedair, Cheri G., Head-Collaboration Solutions Sls - International Business Machines Corporation; *pg.* 418, *pg.* 1138

Bedard, Brett, Mgr-Mktg Comm, Events & Promos - Deere & Company; *pg.* 703, *pg.* 632

Bedard, Kristin O., Mgr-Global Council-The CMO Grp - Forrester Research, Inc.; *pg.* 1642, *pg.* 807

Bedard, Madison, Sr Brand Mgr-Mktg & Innovation-FUZE - The Coca-Cola Company; *pg.* 240, *pg.* 493

Bedard, Michele, VP-Mktg - Sub Zero Wolf; *pg.* 60, *pg.* 1867

Beddingfield, JoAnna, VP-Mktg - Fruit of the Loom, Inc.; *pg.* 41, *pg.* 725

Beddoe, Sarah, VP-Natl Mktg - SONIC Corp.; *pg.* 1750, *pg.* 1487

Beddor, Robin, Sr Dir-Brand & Mktg Comm - Regis Corporation; *pg.* 521, *pg.* 941

Beddow, Josh, Mgr-Mktg-Sitework Sys - The Toro Company; *pg.* 1065, *pg.* 918

Bedell, Lynne, Mgr-Mktg Comm - Boston Scientific Corporation; *pg.* 1508, *pg.* 831

Bedell, Rebecca, Mgr-Mktg - McGladrey, LLP; *pg.* 781, *pg.* 938

Bedford, Bruce, VP-Mktg - Oberweis Dairy, Inc.; *pg.* 887, *pg.* 638

Bedi, Pro, Head-Product Mktg - AT&T Inc.; *pg.* 1868, *pg.* 358

Bedilion, Margaret, Sr Mgr-Sls - Newport Aquarium; *pg.* 571, *pg.* 739

Bednar, Courtney, Dir-Mktg-Global Corelle Bus Unit - World Kitchen LLC; *pg.* 1141, *pg.* 657

Bednar, Tammy, Dir-Product Mgmt-Oracle Database Appliance - Oracle Corporation; *pg.* 450, *pg.* 191

Bednarczyk, Michal, Specialist-Social Media - Tootsie Roll Industries, Inc.; *pg.* 1863, *pg.* 591

Bednash, Graham, Dir-Consumer Mktg - Google Inc.; *pg.* 1249, *pg.* 153

Bedon, Valerie, Sr Mgr-CRM Strategy - StubHub, Inc.; *pg.* 586, *pg.* 228

Bedore, Dan, Dir-Product Comm - Nissan North America, Inc.; *pg.* 186, *pg.* 1633

Bedore, Fred, Sr Dir-Sustainability - Wal-Mart Stores, Inc.; *pg.* 1790, *pg.* 29

Bedrosian, Peter, Sr Mgr-Product Plng - Nissan North America, Inc.; *pg.* 186, *pg.* 1633

Beebe, David, VP-Creative & Content Mktg - Marriott International, Inc.; *pg.* 1102, *pg.* 764

Beebe, Janet, Sr Mgr-Mktg Programs-Security & Demand Generation - Akamai Technologies, Inc.; *pg.* 1226, *pg.* 807

Beebe, Jon, Dir-Digital Adv & Analytics-Global - General Motors Company; *pg.* 175, *pg.* 881

Beecher, Mark, Exec VP-Sls & Mktg - Bank of the West; *pg.* 721, *pg.* 213

Beede, Katherine, VP & Dir-Mktg-TJ Maxx - Marshalls of MA, Inc.; *pg.* 1778, *pg.* 821

Beede, Katherine, VP & Dir-Mktg-TJ Maxx - The TJX Companies, Inc.; *pg.* 1788, *pg.* 822

Beegle, Jennifer, Supvr-Digital Mktg-Programmatic - GEICO Corporation; *pg.* 1200, *pg.* 399

Beem, Carol, Mgr-Mktg Comm - The Protectoseal Company; *pg.* 1370, *pg.* 556

Beenders, Antoinette, Sr VP-Creative & Dir-Creative-Global - Aveda Corporation; *pg.* 499, *pg.* 917

Beepath, Mark, Brand Mgr-Fin - Unilever United States, Inc.; *pg.* 904, *pg.* 1061

Beering, Mike, Product Mgr - X-Rite, Incorporated; *pg.* 1437, *pg.* 891

Beers, Samantha, Dir-Interactive Ad Sls Mktg - Scripps Networks Interactive, Inc.; *pg.* 1279, *pg.* 1638

Beers, Tanya, Brand Mgr - Constellation Brands, Inc.; *pg.* 1960, *pg.* 1348

Beeson, Holly, Mgr-Mktg - Lowe's Companies, Inc.; *pg.* 1053, *pg.* 1383

Beetsch, Carly, Specialist-Digital Mktg - General Mills, Inc.; *pg.* 828, *pg.* 933

Begalle, Mary, Sr Dir-Natl Accounts - The Schwan Food Company; *pg.* 894, *pg.* 928

Begandy, Katie, Mgr-Performance Mktg - Dick's Sporting Goods, Inc.; *pg.* 1832, *pg.* 1524

Begeman, Kim, Sr Mgr-CRM & Loyalty - Kellogg Company; *pg.* 831, *pg.* 870

Begg, Eileen, VP-Mktg - Credit Suisse Securities (USA) LLC; *pg.* 742, *pg.* 1220

Beghtol, Bob, Dir-Media Rels - Chicago White Sox Ltd.; *pg.* 539, *pg.* 570

Begin, Gene, Sr Dir-Integrated Mktg - Babson College; *pg.* 598, *pg.* 784

Begley, Carol, Asst VP-Adv - Toll Brothers, Inc.; pg. 115, pg. 1541
Begley, Melissa A., Dir-Creative - The Hanover Insurance Company; pg. 1202, pg. 862
Behar, Michelle, Coord-PR - Kelley Blue Book Co., Inc.; pg. 1656, pg. 112
Behar, Orly, Mgr-Mktg - Amdocs Inc.; pg. 348, pg. 974
Behl, Nikhil, Head-Mktg - Fair Isaac Corporation; pg. 1247, pg. 955
Behlke, Dixie, Dir-Mathematics Sls - Nasco International, Inc.; pg. 1779, pg. 1858
Behm, Rachel, Brand Mgr - Johnson & Johnson; pg. 1549, pg. 1091
Behne, Nicole L., Dir-Mktg-Grocery Products Div - Hormel Foods Corporation; pg. 863, pg. 915
Behrendt, Kimberly, Assoc Mgr-Mktg-Channel Solutions - MillerCoors LLC; pg. 255, pg. 582
Behrens, Courtney, Sr Mgr-Mktg-Web Solutions & Svcs - Brother International Corporation - USA; pg. 53, pg. 1046
Behrens, Doug, Chief Customer Officer & Pres-Sls - The WhiteWave Foods Company; pg. 1037, pg. 324
Behrens, Jeffrey, Dir-Digital Mktg-Global - The Nielsen Company B.V.; pg. 1671, pg. 1272
Behrman, Rory, Sr Mgr-Media-Kindle Mktg - Amazon.com, Inc.; pg. 1226, pg. 1831
Behun, Bobbi Jo, Sr Dir-Customer Analytics & Intelligence-WHBM - Chico's FAS, Inc.; pg. 21, pg. 427
Beierly, Sean, Mgr-Mktg - Cisco Systems, Inc.; pg. 372, pg. 240
Beightler, Kimberly, Mgr-Mktg Comm - Parker Hannifin Corporation; pg. 1368, pg. 1434
Beightler, Leslie, Planner-Digital Media - Palisades Media Group, Inc.; pg. 452, pg. 275
Beijar, Christopher, Sr Mgr-Adv - Dunkin' Brands Group, Inc.; pg. 1727, pg. 810
Beilenson, Andrew, Sr Mgr-Bus Dev - Major League Soccer LLC; pg. 560, pg. 1256
Beilfuss, Dan, Dir-Sls-Magnetek-Matl Handling - Magnetek, Inc.; pg. 1301, pg. 1870
Beinner, Steve, Dir-Mktg-Global - Xbox; pg. 970, pg. 1829
Beirne, Kristen, Dir-Product Dev - Johnson & Johnson; pg. 1549, pg. 1091
Beirne, Nazli, VP & Sr Strategist-Product-Corp & Investment Bank - JPMorgan Chase & Co.; pg. 772, pg. 1246
Beisen, Liz, Rep-North America Sls-CMS - Linear Technology Corp.; pg. 652, pg. 147
Beisler-Krukowski, Liz, Sr Dir-Global Corp Affairs-Comm & Engagement - The Gap, Inc.; pg. 1770, pg. 218
Beisswanger, Debbie, Sr Dir-Enterprise Mktg, Media & Plng - PetSmart, Inc.; pg. 1481, pg. 18
Beitzel, Brett, Dir-Product Dev - Republic Services, Inc.; pg. 107, pg. 19
Bejan, Bob, Sr VP & Exec Dir-Creative-Worldwide - AOL Inc.; pg. 1229, pg. 1195
Bejan, Bob, VP-Sls & Mktg-North America - Microsoft Corporation; pg. 435, pg. 1824
Bekas, Danielle, VP-Interactive Mktg - Warner Bros. Entertainment Inc.; pg. 319, pg. 54
Beker, Hannah, Sr Mgr-Media Analytics - Rosetta Stone Inc.; pg. 462, pg. 1774
Bekke, Nathan, VP-Consumer Sls & Mktg - Lee Enterprises, Incorporated; pg. 1658, pg. 704
Bekker, Igor, VP-ECommerce & Digital Mktg - Alex and Ani; pg. 1, pg. 1600
Bel Bruno, Robert, VP-AMC Ad Sls - AMC Networks Inc.; pg. 269, pg. 1189
Beladi, Donna L., Chief Strategy Officer - The Standard Register Company; pg. 473, pg. 1446
Belak, Cynthia, First VP-Mktg - People's United Bank; pg. 793, pg. 340
Belakovskaia, Katya, Assoc Mgr-Mktg Promos Global - Elizabeth Arden, Inc.; pg. 507, pg. 448
Belalcazar, Mari, Sr Dir-Mktg Partnerships - National Geographic Channel; pg. 299, pg. 402
Belalcazar, Mari, Sr Dir-Mktg Partnerships - National Geographic Society; pg. 1667, pg. 402
Belanger, Kristen, Head-Brand & Sr Mgr-Mktg Comm - Blackbaud, Inc.; pg. 361, pg. 1613
Belanger, Ron, Gen Mgr-Americas-Social.com - salesforce.com, inc.; pg. 1278, pg. 226
Belatti, Steve, VP-Product - LaCrosse Footwear, Inc.; pg. 1811, pg. 1503
Belazi, Ahmed, Sr Mgr-CMTS Ops - Charter Communications, Inc.; pg. 274, pg. 372
Belbin, Charles, Dir-PR - Novelis Inc.; pg. 100, pg. 516
Belcher, Dan, Product Mgr - Google Inc.; pg. 1249, pg. 153
Belcher, Mike, VP-Media & Consumer Engagement - T-Mobile US, Inc.; pg. 676, pg. 1816
Belcher, Monique, Mgr-Events & Mktg-Global - Atmel Corporation; pg. 621, pg. 238
Belciano, Robert, Acct Exec-Multimedia Sls - ESPN, Inc.; pg. 285, pg. 340
Belec, Melissa, Specialist-Mktg Comm Program - Tyler Technologies, Inc.; pg. 486, pg. 1690
Belenkiy, Ilya, Dir-Mktg-Oncology Portfolio & Global Established Pharma BU - Pfizer Inc.; pg. 1581, pg. 1278
Beley, Lauren, Sr Mgr-eMail Mktg - David's Bridal, Inc.; pg. 23, pg. 1523
Belgaonkar, Sunil, Dir-Product Strategy - Progress Software Corporation; pg. 457, pg. 786
Beliard, Annemarie, Sr Product Mgr-Mktg - Adobe Systems Incorporated; pg. 342, pg. 235
Belikoff, Cyril, Dir-Surface Mktg - Microsoft Corporation; pg. 435, pg. 1824
Belin, Herb, Mgr-Product Innovation - Smith & Wesson Holding Corporation; pg. 1845, pg. 846
Belisle, Sarah, VP & Sr Div Mgr-Mktg - Bank of the West; pg. 721, pg. 213
Beljin, Alen, Mgr-PR - Penske Truck Leasing Company, L.P.; pg. 188, pg. 1585
Belknap, Lynne, Dir-Creative-Lowe's-Meredith Xcelerated Mktg - Meredith Corporation; pg. 1663, pg. 705
Belknap, Michael, Dir-Creative-Better Homes & Gardens Brand - Meredith Corporation; pg. 1663, pg. 705
Belknap, Robert, Exec Dir-Trade, Specialty Sls & Ops - Boehringer Ingelheim Pharmaceuticals, Inc.; pg. 1507, pg. 368
Bell Braid, Joy, Sr Mgr-Contract Mfg-Frozen Bakery & Meat - Hillshire Brands; pg. 862, pg. 576
Bell, Amy, Sr VP-Brand Strategy & Mktg Comm - Starz Entertainment, LLC; pg. 310, pg. 327
Bell, Andrew J., District Sls Mgr-Merchant Svcs - BB&T Corporation; pg. 723, pg. 1393
Bell, Anne Marie, Sr Dir-Global Employee Comm - eBay Inc.; pg. 1240, pg. 243
Bell, Brad, Dir-Mktg - ZAGG INCORPORATED; pg. 690, pg. 1762
Bell, Brian, Mgr-PR - Dr Pepper Snapple Group, Inc.; pg. 250, pg. 1729
Bell, Brian, Dir-Product & Svc Innovation - T-Mobile US, Inc.; pg. 676, pg. 1816
Bell, Corey, Acct Exec-Fundraising Program Liaison-Ticket Sls - Detroit Tigers Baseball Club, Inc.; pg. 545, pg. 880
Bell, Daniel, Dir-Retail Product Mktg-US - MetLife, Inc.; pg. 1208, pg. 1258
Bell, David, Sr Dir - The Medicines Company; pg. 1561, pg. 1104
Bell, Elliot, Sr Dir-Strategic Sls & Dev-Yahoo Media Network - Yahoo! Inc.; pg. 1289, pg. 289
Bell, Garry, VP-Corp Mktg - Gildan Activewear Inc.; pg. 1835, pg. 1955
Bell, James, Analyst-Digital Mktg - American Automobile Association; pg. 1190, pg. 429
Bell, Jeff, Dir-Mktg Strategy - Gordmans Stores Inc.; pg. 1771, pg. 1016
Bell, Jeffrey, Sr Mgr-Media Rels - Siemens Healthcare Diagnostics; pg. 673, pg. 604
Bell, Joe, Dir-Corp Mktg - The Kroger Co.; pg. 1025, pg. 1416
Bell, John, VP-Enterprise Digital Mktg - The Travelers Companies, Inc.; pg. 1220, pg. 352
Bell, John, VP-Enterprise Digital Mktg - Travelers Insurance; pg. 1220, pg. 963
Bell, Jori, Product Mgr - Wenner Media LLC; pg. 1701, pg. 1314
Bell, Julie, Exec VP-Mktg-Global - Benefit Cosmetics LLC; pg. 501, pg. 213
Bell, Kathleen, Dir-Natl Mktg - Subway Restaurants; pg. 1751, pg. 356
Bell, Kristine, Mgr-Creative Svcs - Manulife Financial Corporation; pg. 778, pg. 1939
Bell, Lindsey, Mgr-Online Mktg - Quantum Corporation; pg. 458, pg. 250
Bell, Lisa A., VP-Strategic Field Mktg - General Growth Properties, Inc.; pg. 1093, pg. 574
Bell, Maurice, Sr Dir-Sls Strategy & Brand Dev-Gatorade - PepsiCo, Inc.; pg. 259, pg. 1327
Bell, Michele, Sr VP-Creative Svcs - Paramount Pictures Corporation; pg. 304, pg. 138
Bell, Michelle, Mgr-Sls-Natl Channel - Cytosport, Inc.; pg. 1018, pg. 45
Bell, Noelle, Sr Mgr-Comm - Bank of America Global Wealth & Investment Management; pg. 720, pg. 789
Bell, Pat, Coord-Sls & Project - The Grand Island Daily Independent; pg. 1646, pg. 1010
Bell, Pete, Sr VP-Sls-Global - Internap Network Services Corporation; pg. 417, pg. 513
Bell, Robin, Mgr-Mktg - The J.M. Smucker Company; pg. 865, pg. 1468
Bell, Sheretha, Dir-Creative & Content - Atlanta Convention & Visitors Bureau; pg. 989, pg. 489
Bell, Sichia, Mgr-Mktg Ops-Global - LinkedIn Corporation; pg. 1262, pg. 160
Bell, Tom, Sr VP-Sls & Mktg-Global - The Boeing Company; pg. 225, pg. 567
Bell, Whitney, Sr Asst Brand Mgr-Building-Dove - Unilever Canada Inc.; pg. 903, pg. 1946
Bella, Mark, VP-Sls - Purple Communications, Inc.; pg. 457, pg. 194
Bella, Michelle, VP-Sls & Consumer Mktg - ESPN, Inc.; pg. 285, pg. 340
Bellack, Jonathan B., Dir-Product Mgmt & Publr Adv Platforms - Google Inc.; pg. 1249, pg. 153
Bellamy, Anna, Mgr-US Brand Adv-Fuels - Shell Lubricants; pg. 217, pg. 1714
Bellamy, Anna, Mgr-US Brand Adv-Fuels - Shell Oil Company; pg. 984, pg. 1714
Bellamy, Debbie, Dir-Mktg - LexisNexis Group; pg. 1658, pg. 1446
Bellamy, Janeita, Coord-Production - BET Holdings LLC; pg. 271, pg. 396
Bellanti, Beth, Mgr-Relationship Mktg & Social Media - Fifth Generation, Inc.; pg. 1963, pg. 1662
Bellar, Cleve, VP-Mktg-Revenue Performance Center - Sage Software, Inc.; pg. 464, pg. 116
Bellar, Lisa, Sr Dir-Consumer Insight-Global - Pfizer Inc.; pg. 1581, pg. 1278
Belle, Roxann, Mgr-Global Product Mktg - Activision Blizzard, Inc.; pg. 948, pg. 271
Belledin, Amy, Dir-Beauty Creative - Nordstrom, Inc.; pg. 1779, pg. 1837
Bellej, Michelle, VP-Portfolio-Mktg Central Reg - Simon Property Group, Inc.; pg. 1112, pg. 690
Bellerose, Jim, Mgr-Mktg - Dexter-Russell Inc.; pg. 1123, pg. 844
Belleville, Jennifer, Mgr-Mktg-Neuromodulation - Boston Scientific Corporation; pg. 1508, pg. 831
Bellew, Brooke, Assoc Mgr-Mktg-Brand Design Retail Activation - PepsiCo, Inc.; pg. 259, pg. 1327
Belleza, Lara, Mgr-Retail Channel Mktg - Sony Computer Entertainment America LLC; pg. 966, pg. 256
Bellina, Brandy, Dir-Mktg - American International Group, Inc.; pg. 1190, pg. 1193
Bellinaso, Marcelo, Dir-Product Mgmt-Cloud Support Offerings - Microsoft Corp.; pg. 440, pg. 321
Belliotti, Joe, Dir-Entertainment Mktg - The Coca-Cola Company; pg. 240, pg. 493
Bellitt, Linda, Dir-Mktg Tech & Res - Hunter Douglas, Inc.; pg. 928, pg. 1320
Bellmore, Katherine, Sr Mgr-Loyalty Mktg - Recreational Equipment, Inc.; pg. 1843, pg. 1821
Bello, Dana, Sr Coord-Adv - Toll Brothers, Inc.; pg. 115, pg. 1541
Bello, Eric, VP-Sls - Las Vegas Sands Corp.; pg. 1100, pg. 1027
Belloni, Greg, Sr Mgr-Corp Comm - Sony Corporation of America; pg. 675, pg. 1293
Bellows, Melina, Publr, Exec VP & Chief Creative Officer-Books, Kids & Family - National Geographic Society; pg. 1667, pg. 402
Belmear, Tracy, Dir-Corp Mktg & Bus Dev - New York Jets Football Club, Inc.; pg. 570, pg. 1067
Belohlavek, Caleb, Dir-Product Mgmt-Suites - Adobe Systems Incorporated; pg. 342, pg. 235
Belschner, Faye, Asst Dir-Sls Promo & Integration - The Northwestern Mutual Life Insurance Company; pg. 1212, pg. 1879
Belsky, Scott, VP-Products-Community & Head-Behance - Adobe Systems Incorporated; pg. 342, pg. 235
Belt, Jennifer, Mgr-Catalog Mktg & eContent - Applied Industrial Technologies, Inc.; pg. 199, pg. 1428
Belt, Karen, Dir-Search Mktg - Teachers Insurance & Annuity Association - College Retirement Equities Fund; pg. 1219, pg. 1297
Belter, Stacy, Brand Mgr-Prestige Brands - Bacardi USA, Inc.; pg. 1956, pg. 417

Belthoff, Christopher, Dir-Indus Mktg - Pegasystems Inc.; *pg.* 453, *pg.* 809
Belton, Marc, Exec VP-Strategy, Growth & Mktg Innovation-Global - General Mills, Inc.; *pg.* 828, *pg.* 933
Belton, Maria, Dir-Bus Line Mktg - AXA Equitable Life Insurance Company; *pg.* 1194, *pg.* 1199
Beltramo, Dan, Exec VP-Product Leadership-Mktg Effectiveness - The Nielsen Company B.V.; *pg.* 1671, *pg.* 1272
Beltramo, Ron, VP-Trade Mktg - Aidells Sausage Company; *pg.* 836, *pg.* 253
Beltzner, Mike, Head-Product, Mobile & Web Apps - Pinterest; *pg.* 1275, *pg.* 225
Belur, Shirin, Brand Mgr - Clif Bar Inc.; *pg.* 848, *pg.* 83
Bemoras, David, VP-Sls & Mktg-WESCO Distr-Global - WESCO International Inc.; *pg.* 687, *pg.* 1582
Ben-Canaan, Ari, Sr Mgr-Adv Svcs-Global - The Hershey Co.; *pg.* 1855, *pg.* 1538
Ben-Levi, Sharone, VP-Mktg & Bus Dev-North America AudioCodes USA; *pg.* 356, *pg.* 1121
Ben-Shmuel, Bonnie, Sr Product Mgr-US Hemophilia Mktg - Pfizer Inc.; *pg.* 1581, *pg.* 1278
Ben-Simon, Samantha, Mgr-Creative Svcs - Saucony, Inc.; *pg.* 1818, *pg.* 828
Ben-Yair, Shimrit, Product Mgr-Kids - YouTube, LLC; *pg.* 1291, *pg.* 198
Ben-Yishai, Ori, Mng Dir & Head-Bus Line Mktg - AXA Equitable Life Insurance Company; *pg.* 1194, *pg.* 1199
Benander, Kelley, Dir-Media Rels-Global - Levi Strauss & Co.; *pg.* 43, *pg.* 220
Benarouche, Jeremie, Project Mgr-Mktg - Guess?, Inc.; *pg.* 25, *pg.* 132
Benatar, Suzann, Brand Mgr-Private-Jewelry - Michaels Stores, Inc.; *pg.* 1127, *pg.* 1722
Bencsics, John, Dir-Mktg-Geocel Products Grp - The Sherwin-Williams Company; *pg.* 1447, *pg.* 1435
Bendele, Lisa, Project Mgr-IT-Corp Comm, PR & Govt Affairs - United Airlines, Inc.; *pg.* 1927, *pg.* 593
Bender, Bob, VP-Sls - Oatey Supply Chain Services; *pg.* 30, *pg.* 1433
Bender, Brad, VP-Product Mgmt - Google Inc.; *pg.* 1249, *pg.* 153
Bender, Bryan, Dir-Brdcst & Production - The Detroit Lions, Inc.; *pg.* 544, *pg.* 864
Bender, Cheryl, Sr Dir-Creative & Mktg-Global - Mylan, Inc.; *pg.* 1570, *pg.* 1520
Bender, Ivy Simon, Mgr-Retail Mktg-Consumables - Walgreen Co.; *pg.* 1608, *pg.* 605
Bender, Robert, Dir-Comm & Data Sls - Graybar Electric Company, Inc.; *pg.* 1299, *pg.* 997
Bender, Shawn, Sr Specialist-Mktg - FedEx Corporation; *pg.* 1907, *pg.* 1642
Bender, Ursula, Mgr-Off-Site Channel Mktg - Chicago Zoological Society, Inc.; *pg.* 539, *pg.* 559
Bendesky, Yonathan, Mgr-Multicultural Mktg - Pernod Ricard USA, Inc.; *pg.* 1968, *pg.* 1332
Bendetson, Alyssa, Mgr-Media Rels - Macy's East; *pg.* 1777, *pg.* 1254
Bendetson, Alyssa, Mgr-Media Rels - Macy's, Inc.; *pg.* 1778, *pg.* 1417
Bendfeldt, Jan, Mgr-Mktg - Emerson Process Management; *pg.* 1334, *pg.* 1636
Bendix, Keith, Territory Sls Mgr & Mgr-Customer Svc - ABB Inc.; *pg.* 1309, *pg.* 1359
Bene, David Di, Dir-Retail Mktg - Google Inc.; *pg.* 1249, *pg.* 153
Bene, Michele, Brand Mgr-Shopper Mktg - Henkel Consumer Adhesives, Inc.; *pg.* 403, *pg.* 1480
Bene, Michele, Brand Mgr-Shopper Mktg - Henkel Corporation; *pg.* 1049, *pg.* 369
Bene, Niki del, Acct Dir-Creative Svcs - Coach, Inc.; *pg.* 3, *pg.* 1214
Benedetti, Analia, Sr Mgr-Multicultural Mktg - Kellogg Company; *pg.* 831, *pg.* 870
Benedetto, Frank, Head-Market-Sls - Aetna Inc.; *pg.* 1187, *pg.* 351
Benedetto, Lori, Product Mgr-Laboratory Supplies & Consumables - PerkinElmer, Inc.; *pg.* 1426, *pg.* 853
Benedick, Julianna, Dir-Mktg - Panasonic Corporation of North America; *pg.* 661, *pg.* 1120
Benedick, Rachel, VP-Sls & Svcs - Denver Metro Convention & Visitors Bureau; *pg.* 991, *pg.* 318
Benedict, Brian, Mgr-Mktg & Media - Google Inc.; *pg.* 1249, *pg.* 153
Benedict, Joe, Dir-Medical Mktg - Span-America Medical Systems, Inc.; *pg.* 1595, *pg.* 1618
Benedict, Lauren, Dir-Adv Sls - Hulu LLC; *pg.* 1257, *pg.* 274
Benedict, Michael, Chief Product Officer - Progress Software Corporation; *pg.* 457, *pg.* 786
Benedict, Michael, Asst Mgr-Zone Mktg - State Farm Mutual Automobile Insurance Co.; *pg.* 1218, *pg.* 557
Benedict, Stacy Gross, VP-ECommerce & Mktg - Berkshire Hathaway Home Services; *pg.* 1081, *pg.* 469
Benedict, Zac, Mgr-Online Mktg - California Avocado Commission; *pg.* 135, *pg.* 108
Benedicto, Brandon, Mgr-Database Mktg - Winn Dixie Stores, Inc.; *pg.* 1038, *pg.* 435
Benedik, Brian, Head-Adv Sls-Global - Spotify; *pg.* 1282, *pg.* 1295
Benediktsson, Johann, Mgr-Mktg - IceLandAir North America; *pg.* 1912, *pg.* 841
Benedum, Mary, VP-Mktg Strategy - Kohl's Corporation; *pg.* 1775, *pg.* 1870
Beneko, Jim, VP-Technical Mktg-Global - Avnet Electronics Marketing; *pg.* 622, *pg.* 15
Benerofe, Jory, VP-Brand Creative - Vineyard Vines LLC; *pg.* 50, *pg.* 379
Benesh, David, VP-Mktg & Comm - Insurance Brokers & Agents of the West; *pg.* 144, *pg.* 183
Benetka, Adam, Brand Mgr-EAS - Abbott Nutrition; *pg.* 1485, *pg.* 1437
Benevento, Kelli, Mgr-Mktg Comm - Harmonic, Inc.; *pg.* 402, *pg.* 246
BenEzra, Natali, Head-Entertainment, Media & Comm Mktg - PricewaterhouseCoopers LLP; *pg.* 795, *pg.* 1283
Benfield, Dana, VP-Engagement Mktg - Red Robin Gourmet Burgers, Inc.; *pg.* 1747, *pg.* 331
Benfield, Steve, Sr Dir-Creative - SAS Institute Inc.; *pg.* 466, *pg.* 1361
Benfield, Vanessa, Sr VP-Sls - AMC Networks Inc.; *pg.* 269, *pg.* 1189
Benford, Michael, Mgr-Creative Svcs - Atlanta Falcons Football Club, LLC; *pg.* 530, *pg.* 532
Bengtson, Jared, Mgr-Global Mktg-IBM Digital Experience Software Solutions - International Business Machines Corporation; *pg.* 418, *pg.* 1138
Bengtson, Ove, Product Mgr - Hasselblad USA, Inc.; *pg.* 1416, *pg.* 1065
Benike, Kimberley, Mgr-Multichannel Strategy & Digital Vendor Mktg-Canada - Target Corporation; *pg.* 1786, *pg.* 942
Benincasa, Jennifer, Mgr-Mktg, Fin Svcs & Insurance Indus - LinkedIn Corporation; *pg.* 1262, *pg.* 160
Benincasa, Patsy, Dir-Foodservice Mktg - T. Marzetti Company; *pg.* 900, *pg.* 1444
Benintende, J. William, VP-PR & Mktg Comm - Wilmington Trust Corporation; *pg.* 822, *pg.* 392
Benisi, Mona, Sr Dir-Sustainability - Simon Property Group, Inc.; *pg.* 1112, *pg.* 690
Benito, Nacho, Dir-Sls-Spain & Portugal - X-Rite, Incorporated; *pg.* 1437, *pg.* 891
Benjamin, Mike, Head-USERLabs Richmond-Product Innovation, Res & UX - Capital One Financial Corporation; *pg.* 730, *pg.* 1789
Benjamin, Mike, Sr VP-Mktg & Tech - T.D. Williamson, Inc.; *pg.* 1380, *pg.* 1490
Benjamin, Sade, Brand Mgr-Employment - Wal-Mart Stores, Inc.; *pg.* 1790, *pg.* 29
Benjamin, Stevie, Sr Dir-Mktg Connections - MillerCoors; *pg.* 254, *pg.* 1877
Benjamin, Stevie, VP-Media Strategy - Target Corporation; *pg.* 1786, *pg.* 942
Benjamin, Yann, Mgr-Mktg-Beaver Creek - Vail Resorts, Inc.; *pg.* 1117, *pg.* 313
Benjamins, J.P., Mgr-Mktg-NA Consumer Engines - Briggs & Stratton Corporation; *pg.* 201, *pg.* 1899
Benkard, Elise, Dir-Mdsg-Ann Taylor - Ann Inc.; *pg.* 18, *pg.* 1195
Benkendorfer, Gregg, Brand Mgr-Camry & Avalon-Natl - Toyota Motor Sales, U.S.A., Inc.; *pg.* 193, *pg.* 296
Benko, Michelle, Sr Dir-Corp Comm - CDK Global, Inc.; *pg.* 370, *pg.* 617
Benkonvich, Adrian, Dir-Field Mktg - MillerCoors LLC; *pg.* 255, *pg.* 582
Benmesbah, Sarah, Mgr-Dealer Sls - Ford Motor Company of Canada, Limited; *pg.* 174, *pg.* 1930
Benmour, Eric, Sr Dir-External Comm - Kindred Healthcare, Inc.; *pg.* 1553, *pg.* 736
Bennedsen, Thomas, Sr Dir-Creative-Skagen Denmark - Fossil Group, Inc.; *pg.* 5, *pg.* 1735
Benner, Jeff, Sr Dir-Season Tickets, Renewals & Bus Strategy - Colorado Rockies Baseball Club, Ltd.; *pg.* 542, *pg.* 317
Benner, Pete, Mgr-Sls-Natl - McKeon Products, Inc.; *pg.* 1559, *pg.* 912
Bennett, Adrian, Strategist-Performance Mktg Digital - International Business Machines Corporation; *pg.* 418, *pg.* 1138
Bennett, Bill, Assoc Dir-Brand & Product Mktg - Ansell; *pg.* 1495, *pg.* 1114
Bennett, Brad, VP-Sls - Universal Instruments Corporation; *pg.* 683, *pg.* 1154
Bennett, Carolyn, Dir-Mktg-Global - Pfizer Inc.; *pg.* 1581, *pg.* 1278
Bennett, Caty, Mgr-PR - XO Group Inc.; *pg.* 1289, *pg.* 1316
Bennett, Cheryl, Mgr-Pepsi Mktg - PepsiCo, Inc.; *pg.* 259, *pg.* 1327
Bennett, Christina, Sr Dir-PR-Global - Elizabeth Arden, Inc.; *pg.* 507, *pg.* 448
Bennett, Colette C., Mgr-Sports Mktg-Natl - Rolex Watch U.S.A., Inc.; *pg.* 11, *pg.* 1286
Bennett, Craig, Sr VP-Sls & Mktg - Utility Trailer Manufacturing Company; *pg.* 1712, *pg.* 68
Bennett, David, VP-Worldwide SMB, Consumer & Online Sls - Webroot Software, Inc.; *pg.* 1289, *pg.* 313
Bennett, Devin A., Sr Mgr-Comm - Electronic Arts Inc.; *pg.* 951, *pg.* 189
Bennett, Eryn, Mgr-Culinary & Product Innovation - The Wendy's Company; *pg.* 1755, *pg.* 1450
Bennett, Gayle, Dir-Mktg - Philips Electronics North America; *pg.* 662, *pg.* 782
Bennett, Harold Craig, Sr VP-Sls & Mktg - Utility Trailer Manufacturing Company; *pg.* 1712, *pg.* 68
Bennett, Ira, Dir-Mktg - The Harris Products Group; *pg.* 1345, *pg.* 533
Bennett, James, Sr Dir-Integrated Mktg & Partnerships - Turner Broadcasting System, Inc.; *pg.* 314, *pg.* 521
Bennett, Jeremy, Sr Mgr-Production-AYR - Bonobos; *pg.* 39, *pg.* 1205
Bennett, Jessica, Assoc Mgr-Mktg-Consumer Comm - Transitions Optical, Inc.; *pg.* 1432, *pg.* 458
Bennett, Jodie, Mgr-Sls-Indus Products - Industrial Electronic Engineers, Inc.; *pg.* 644, *pg.* 300
Bennett, Kathy, Dir-Mktg - Mount Cranmore Ski Resort, Inc.; *pg.* 564, *pg.* 1038
Bennett, Kelly, CMO - Netflix, Inc.; *pg.* 1269, *pg.* 141
Bennett, Kim, Sr Mgr-Mktg-Shoes - Nordstrom, Inc.; *pg.* 1779, *pg.* 1837
Bennett, Leslie, Mgr-Comml Mktg Programs - Advance Auto Parts, Inc.; *pg.* 197, *pg.* 1805
Bennett, Liane, Brand Mgr - Starbucks Corporation; *pg.* 897, *pg.* 1840
Bennett, Lindsay, Mgr-Mktg Ops - Randstad USA; *pg.* 459, *pg.* 941
Bennett, Lizzie, Mgr-PR - Autodesk Inc.; *pg.* 356, *pg.* 257
Bennett, Mike, Sr Mgr-Bus Dev & Emerging Bus Markets - AT&T Southeast; *pg.* 1868, *pg.* 489
Bennett, Mike, VP-Display Sls-Americas - TripAdvisor, Inc.; *pg.* 1926, *pg.* 835
Bennett, Nina, Sr Mgr-Direct Mktg-EMEA - Eaton Corporation; *pg.* 1331, *pg.* 1429
Bennett, Pam, Sr Mgr-Comm - The North Face, Inc.; *pg.* 1840, *pg.* 252
Bennett, Patricia, Dir-Adv-CNHI - The Daily Item; *pg.* 1632, *pg.* 1588
Bennett, Patty, Dir-Adv-CNHI - The Daily Item; *pg.* 1632, *pg.* 829
Bennett, Paul, Chief Creative Officer - IDEO, Inc.; *pg.* 411, *pg.* 178
Bennett, Paul, Head-Mktg & Client Experience - MetLife, Inc.; *pg.* 1208, *pg.* 1258
Bennett, Richard, Dir-Customer Dev-Natl Accts, Trade Mktg & Sls Ops - The J.M. Smucker Company; *pg.* 865, *pg.* 1468
Bennett, Ross, Asst Mgr-Mktg - Edible Arrangements International, Inc.; *pg.* 1768, *pg.* 382
Bennett, Sam, Dir-Brand Adv - Best Buy Co., Inc.; *pg.* 1761, *pg.* 954
Bennett, Sara, Assoc Specialist-Mktg Comm - Medtronic, Inc.; *pg.* 1564, *pg.* 939
Bennett, Shanna, Coord-Tour & Mktg Grp - Bellingrath Gardens & Home; *pg.* 1794, *pg.* 8
Bennett, Stephanie, Specialist-Mktg & Adv - Family Dollar Stores, Inc.; *pg.* 1768, *pg.* 1382
Bennett, Steve, Mgr-Sprint Bus Dev-Machine-to-Machine Sls - Sprint Corporation; *pg.* 1874, *pg.* 719
Bennett, Susan, Dir-Consumer Field Mktg - CenturyLink, Inc.; *pg.* 1870, *pg.* 746

Bennett, Tracy, Product Mgr - Welch Allyn Inc.; *pg.* 1436, *pg.* 1342
Bennette, Amanda, Mgr-Mktg Strategy Enhancements-Macys.com - Macy's East; *pg.* 1777, *pg.* 1254
Bennette, Dan, Dir-Product Dev - Crocs, Inc.; *pg.* 1806, *pg.* 335
Bennetts, Marylou, Dir-Mktg & Sls - Calgary Philharmonic Orchestra; *pg.* 536, *pg.* 1902
Bennie, Braden, Brand Mgr - Kellogg Company; *pg.* 831, *pg.* 870
Benning, Connie, Sr Dir-Mktg - McGladrey, LLP; *pg.* 781, *pg.* 938
Benning, De, Area Mgr-Mktg-North Coast Select Operation - Cisco Systems, Inc.; *pg.* 372, *pg.* 240
Benning, Kathleen M., Exec VP & Chief Strategy Officer-Brand & Bus Dev - BUFFALO WILD WINGS, INC.; *pg.* 1718, *pg.* 931
Bennink, Julie, Mgr-Media Rels-Global - Accenture; *pg.* 1392, *pg.* 1186
Beno, Steven, Dir-Design-New Product Dev - ACCO Brands Corporation; *pg.* 340, *pg.* 626
Benoit, Craig, Brand Mgr - Dunkin' Brands Group, Inc.; *pg.* 1727, *pg.* 810
Benoit, Marie, Brand Mgr - Macy's East; *pg.* 1777, *pg.* 1254
Benoit, Nathaniel, Mgr-Web Mktg & Design - Baldor Electric Company; *pg.* 1316, *pg.* 32
Benosman, Perrine, Strategist-Digital Mktg - Discover Financial Services; *pg.* 744, *pg.* 653
Bensen, Jessica, Mgr-Mktg-Chili's - Brinker International, Inc.; *pg.* 1718, *pg.* 1676
Benshoof, Lori, Coord-Mktg - American Architectural Manufacturers Association; *pg.* 126, *pg.* 658
Bensinger, Zac, Product Mgr-Dev-Private Brands - Walgreen Co.; *pg.* 1608, *pg.* 605
Bensley, Jessica, Product Mgr-Global-Women & Kids-Muck Boot Company - Honeywell International Inc.; *pg.* 407, *pg.* 1088
Benson, Ashley, Specialist-Social Media - PETCO Animal Supplies, Inc.; *pg.* 1480, *pg.* 206
Benson, Buster, Product Mgr - Twitter, Inc.; *pg.* 1285, *pg.* 228
Benson, Cindy, Mgr-Field Mktg - Dickey's Barbecue Restaurants, Inc.; *pg.* 1725, *pg.* 1680
Benson, Felicia Walker, Dir-Social Media & Beauty - Bergdorf Goodman, Inc.; *pg.* 1761, *pg.* 1202
Benson, James, Gen Mgr-Global Mktg-Pro Lighting - General Electric Company; *pg.* 1297, *pg.* 347
Benson, Jeff, Dir-Digital Mktg - UnitedHealth Group Incorporated; *pg.* 1221, *pg.* 950
Benson, Joe, Head-Ram Product Plng-Comml Vehicles - FCA US LLC; *pg.* 170, *pg.* 868
Benson, John, Chief Strategy Officer - DHI Group, Inc.; *pg.* 1238, *pg.* 1223
Benson, Kyle, Dir-Global Channel Mktg & Dev - Citrix Systems, Inc.; *pg.* 375, *pg.* 424
Benson, Lorien, Coord-Reg Mktg & Promos - Regal Entertainment Group; *pg.* 579, *pg.* 1638
Benson, Matt, Mgr-Mktg-UK & APAC - 505 Games (US), Inc.; *pg.* 948, *pg.* 38
Benson, Mike, Head-Brand Mktg & Creative Dev-Amazon Digital Video - Amazon.com, Inc.; *pg.* 1226, *pg.* 1831
Benson, Rich, Mgr-New Product Dev-High Power Products - Molex Incorporated; *pg.* 655, *pg.* 628
Benson, Sig G., VP-Mktg - Lindal Cedar Homes, Inc.; *pg.* 94, *pg.* 1837
Bensoussan, Jenna, Mgr-Digital Mktg - CELSIUS HOLDINGS, INC.; *pg.* 239, *pg.* 411
Benstock, Peter, Exec VP-Sls - Superior Uniform Group, Inc.; *pg.* 33, *pg.* 468
Bentall, Tristan, Mgr-Media & Ents - Google Inc.; *pg.* 1249, *pg.* 153
Bentel, Matias, Dir-Reg Mktg-LAR - Brown-Forman Corporation; *pg.* 1958, *pg.* 732
Bentley, Cristy, Specialist-Product Mktg - Honeywell International Inc.; *pg.* 407, *pg.* 1088
Bentley, Ian, VP-Product Dev - Autobytel Inc.; *pg.* 1230, *pg.* 107
Benton, Julie, Sr Specialist-Mktg - Polaris Industries Inc.; *pg.* 1709, *pg.* 928
Benton, Tom, VP-Mktg - Cooper Wiring Devices; *pg.* 1295, *pg.* 538
Benton, Tom, Vice Chm-Mktg EDGE & CEO-Direct Mktg Association - The Direct Marketing Association Inc.; *pg.* 139, *pg.* 1224
Bentow, Amy, Assoc Dir-Mktg - WebMD Health Corporation; *pg.* 1288, *pg.* 1313
Bentson, Sara, Asst Mgr-Sports Sls & Mktg - Tiffany & Co.; *pg.* 13, *pg.* 1299
Bentubo, Jim, Mgr-Social Media - Sonic Automotive, Inc.; *pg.* 190, *pg.* 1369
Bentz, Doug, Dir-Mktg & Digital Media - San Jose Sharks, LLC; *pg.* 581, *pg.* 250
Bentz, Nelly, Assoc Dir-Insights, Consumer Products & Food Svc - The Kraft Heinz Company; *pg.* 870, *pg.* 1577
Benveniste, Graciela, Asst VP-Media - L'Oreal USA; *pg.* 514, *pg.* 1252
Benvenuto, Nicole, Mgr-Social Media Channel - Florida Power & Light Company; *pg.* 1943, *pg.* 435
Benyam, Yared, Sr Mgr-Mktg-Individual & Small Grp Segments - Kaiser Permanente; *pg.* 1552, *pg.* 171
Benz, Christian, Product Mgr - X-Rite, Incorporated; *pg.* 1437, *pg.* 891
Benz, William, VP-Digital Mktg - Morgan Stanley; *pg.* 783, *pg.* 1261
Benzel, Craig, VP-Sls & Bus Dev - Green Bay Packers, Inc.; *pg.* 551, *pg.* 1859
Benzimra, Edith, Mgr-Mktg Comm-Pfizer Animal Health - Pfizer Inc.; *pg.* 1581, *pg.* 1278
Bequette, Roger, Dir-Regional Mktg & Catering-Houston - Dickey's Barbecue Restaurants, Inc.; *pg.* 1725, *pg.* 1680
Beran, Nichole, Mgr-Sls-Natl - Omaha Convention and Visitors Bureau; *pg.* 152, *pg.* 1017
Beranek, Andrew F., Rep-Fusion Middleware Sls - Oracle Corporation; *pg.* 1272, *pg.* 786
Beranek, Corrine S., Mgr-Mktg & Res Svcs-Pharma-Biotech Solutions - McKesson Corporation; *pg.* 1560, *pg.* 222
Berard, Leah, Project Coord-Creative Comm - Medtronic, Inc.; *pg.* 1564, *pg.* 939
Berard, Pierre, Sr VP-Spirits Mktg - Pernod Ricard USA, Inc.; *pg.* 1968, *pg.* 1332
Berardinelli, Michelle, Coord-Mktg - Eaton Vance Corp.; *pg.* 746, *pg.* 794
Berardo, Kathy, Sr Mgr-Customer Relationship - Swiss Water Decaffeinated Coffee Income Fund; *pg.* 900, *pg.* 1907
Berberich, Chad, VP-RLI Exec Products Grp - RLI Corp.; *pg.* 1216, *pg.* 652
Berdat, Daniel A., VP-Sls & Mktg-Intl - Exactech, Inc.; *pg.* 1529, *pg.* 428
Berdela, Jim, Dir-Mktg - Becton, Dickinson & Company; *pg.* 1501, *pg.* 1068
Berdine, Anna, Sr Dir-Genetic Analysis Market Dev - Life Technologies; *pg.* 1420, *pg.* 1497
Berelson, Edith, Mgr-Mktg - The New York Times; *pg.* 1668, *pg.* 1270
Berendzen, Jay, Brand Mgr - Anheuser-Busch Companies, LLC; *pg.* 237, *pg.* 991
Berentson, Rochelle, Specialist-Product Mktg - Lifetouch, Inc.; *pg.* 1420, *pg.* 922
Beres, Suzanne, Sr Mgr-Mktg - General Growth Properties, Inc.; *pg.* 1093, *pg.* 574
Beresford, Sara, Asst VP-Digital Media - L'Oreal USA; *pg.* 514, *pg.* 1252
Berey, Christina, Specialist-Mktg - Marshalls of MA, Inc.; *pg.* 1778, *pg.* 821
Berey, Christina, Specialist-Mktg - T.J. Maxx; *pg.* 1788, *pg.* 822
Berey, Christina, Specialist-Mktg - The TJX Companies, Inc.; *pg.* 1788, *pg.* 822
Berezina, Anna, Sr Specialist-Mktg & Comm - Liberty Mutual Insurance Group Inc.; *pg.* 1205, *pg.* 797
Berg, Brendan, Sr Dir-Global Learning - Burger King Corporation; *pg.* 1719, *pg.* 440
Berg, Bret, Sr Mgr & Specialist-Mobile & Desktop Computing Products - Samsung Electronics America, Inc.; *pg.* 669, *pg.* 1115
Berg, Brian, Gen Mgr-Mktg - The Timken Company; *pg.* 218, *pg.* 1408
Berg, E. Darren, VP-Sls - Liftomatic Material Handling Inc.; *pg.* 94, *pg.* 560
Berg, Fredrik, VP-Sls - Wilmington Trust Corporation; *pg.* 822, *pg.* 392
Berg, Inger, Mgr-Mktg-Paul Mitchell - John Paul Mitchell Systems; *pg.* 512, *pg.* 133
Berg, Jaime, Rep-Sls - Designtex Group Inc.; *pg.* 692, *pg.* 1223
Berg, Jen, Sr Mgr-Category Solutions - AOL Inc.; *pg.* 1229, *pg.* 1195
Berg, Jen, Coord-Media Strategy - Best Buy Co., Inc.; *pg.* 1761, *pg.* 954
Berg, John J., Exec VP-Mktg & Sls - Heartland Financial USA, Inc.; *pg.* 765, *pg.* 707
Berg, Liz, VP-Trade Mktg - Elizabeth Arden, Inc.; *pg.* 507, *pg.* 448
Berg, Marlene, Mgr-i-Mktg - Hewlett-Packard Company; *pg.* 404, *pg.* 175
Berg, Mike, Mgr-Mktg - Land O'Lakes, Inc.; *pg.* 873, *pg.* 915
Berg, Steve, VP-Sls & Mktg - Thwing-Albert Instrument Company; *pg.* 1432, *pg.* 1131
Berg, Susan, VP-Mktg & Adv - Concur Technologies, Inc.; *pg.* 1236, *pg.* 1813
Berganza, Olivia, Mgr-Adv-Designer Fragrances - The Estee Lauder Companies Inc.; *pg.* 508, *pg.* 1229
Bergeman, David, Dir-Consumer Mktg - The Atlantic Monthly Group; *pg.* 1618, *pg.* 396
Bergen, Brian, VP-Product Mktg - CBS Interactive, Inc.; *pg.* 369, *pg.* 215
Bergen, Jamie, Product Mgr-Mktg-Intl Grounds - The Toro Company; *pg.* 1065, *pg.* 918
Bergenholtz, Tom, VP-Global Sales - ViaTech Publishing Solutions; *pg.* 489, *pg.* 1141
Bergeot, Helene, Dir-Organized Play & Trade Mktg - Wizards of the Coast, Inc.; *pg.* 970, *pg.* 1830
Berger, Adam, Head-Creative Insights & Distr - Facebook, Inc.; *pg.* 1245, *pg.* 143
Berger, James, Sr Product Mgr-IBD Mktg - Takeda Pharmaceuticals USA, Inc.; *pg.* 1600, *pg.* 605
Berger, Jed, VP-Brand Mktg - Foot Locker, Inc.; *pg.* 1808, *pg.* 1231
Berger, Jennifer, VP-Global Creative Studios - Starbucks Corporation; *pg.* 897, *pg.* 1840
Berger, Jessica, Mgr-Customer Mktg - Kimberly-Clark Corporation; *pg.* 1461, *pg.* 1720
Berger, Joshua, Sr VP-AMC Networks-Media Mgmt - AMC Networks Inc.; *pg.* 269, *pg.* 1189
Berger, Krista, Dir-Mktg-Preschool & Kids Brands - MATTEL, INC.; *pg.* 962, *pg.* 81
Berger, Mary, VP-Sls-West Coast - TV Guide Magazine Group, Inc.; *pg.* 1697, *pg.* 1305
Berger, Nancy L., Sr Specialist-Sls & Promos - SUPERVALU, Inc.; *pg.* 1035, *pg.* 924
Berger, Scott, Gen Mgr-Adv Sls - DISH Network Corporation; *pg.* 283, *pg.* 325
Berger, Steve, Sr VP & Dir-Media Plng - Combe Incorporated; *pg.* 1516, *pg.* 1351
Berger, Valarie, Sr Mgr-Online Customer Experience - Wyndham Worldwide Corporation; *pg.* 1119, *pg.* 1107
Bergerac, Michele, Sr VP & Gen Mgr-Mdsg - Payless Shoesource, Inc.; *pg.* 31, *pg.* 722
Bergeron, Claude, Global Product Mgr-Nordson EFD - Nordson Corporation; *pg.* 1365, *pg.* 1480
Bergeron, Lora, Mgr-Mktg Channel - Constellation Energy Resources, LLC; *pg.* 1938, *pg.* 756
Bergeron, Marc, Exec VP-Sls-Global - BravoSolution US; *pg.* 1233, *pg.* 1549
Bergeron, Matt, VP-Mktg - Exxon Mobil Corporation; *pg.* 977, *pg.* 1718
Bergerson, Kevin, Sr Dir-New Customer Mktg - The Sportsman's Guide, Inc.; *pg.* 1846, *pg.* 965
Bergeth, Bob, Gen Mgr-Contract Builder Sls & Mktg - Whirlpool Corporation; *pg.* 62, *pg.* 872
Bergevine, Cory, Mgr-Mktg - Comcast Corporation; *pg.* 276, *pg.* 1560
Bergin, Conor, Mgr-Mktg - AGCO Corporation; *pg.* 700, *pg.* 530
Bergin, Jeff, Sr VP-Adv - San Francisco Chronicle; *pg.* 1683, *pg.* 226
Bergman, Betsy, VP-Mktg - Sony Pictures Entertainment Inc.; *pg.* 309, *pg.* 72
Bergman, Elizabeth, Head-PR & Dir-Brand Comm-Global - Avon Products, Inc.; *pg.* 500, *pg.* 1198
Bergman, John, Mgr-Procurement-Mktg & Sls - Apple Inc.; *pg.* 350, *pg.* 73
Bergman, John, Sr Mgr-Online Mktg - Time Warner Cable Inc.; *pg.* 312, *pg.* 1301
Bergman, Tobias, Product Mgr-Distr-Refuse Trucks & Alternative Drivelines - Volvo Trucks North America, Inc.; *pg.* 195, *pg.* 1377
Bergman-Nicolini, Alessandra, Dir-National & Hispanic Sls - Tropicana Products, Inc.; *pg.* 902, *pg.* 592
Bergmann, Bethany, Dir-Mktg - Global Payments Inc.; *pg.* 762, *pg.* 508
Bergmann, Charlie, Product Mgr-Global - Bayer CropScience; *pg.* 1149, *pg.* 981
Bergmann, Hugo, Product Mgr-RDX-Germany - Tandberg Data; *pg.* 481, *pg.* 311
Bergmann, Leon, Exec VP-Sls & Procurement - Unified

Grocers, Inc.; pg. 1036, pg. 66
Bergofin, Bill, Sr VP-Mktg - NBC Sports Network; pg. 300, pg. 375
Bergofin, Bill, Sr VP-Mktg & Promo-NBC Sports - NBC Universal, Inc.; pg. 300, pg. 1266
Bergquist, Betty A., VP-Sls & Svc Ops - American Family Mutual Insurance Company; pg. 1190, pg. 1864
Bergren, Jenna, Sr Mgr-Mktg-Hardgoods - PetSmart, Inc.; pg. 1481, pg. 18
Bergstedt, Randy, Grp Product Mgr-Epson Active - Epson America Inc.; pg. 394, pg. 122
Bergstrom, Lukas, Product Mgr - Google Inc.; pg. 1249, pg. 153
Bergstrom, Peter, Sr Mgr-iOS Engrg - Groupon, Inc.; pg. 1255, pg. 575
Bergstrom, Rochelle, Mgr-Adv - Alaska Airlines, Inc.; pg. 1897, pg. 1830
Beriont, Mary, Dir-Mktg - Pacira Pharmaceuticals, Inc.; pg. 1579, pg. 1104
Berisford, John, Acting Pres - Standard & Poor's Ratings Services; pg. 805, pg. 1296
Berish, Daniel, VP-Mktg - DJO Incorporated; pg. 1524, pg. 302
Beristain, Jorge Azpiazu, Dir-Creative - Lexicon Marketing Corporation; pg. 604, pg. 134
Berk, Caryn, Dir-Media-Natl Brdcst & Branded Entertainment - Macy's, Inc.; pg. 1778, pg. 1417
Berk, Jane, Dir-PR - ABC Carpet & Home Inc.; pg. 912, pg. 1185
Berke, Christopher, Specialist-Product Support & Rep - Caterpillar, Inc.; pg. 1321, pg. 650
Berke, Leslie, Sr Dir-Events Mktg - The Ultimate Software Group, Inc.; pg. 486, pg. 479
Berkeley, Cara, Specialist-Mktg Comm - Schneider Electric USA, Inc.; pg. 1306, pg. 650
Berkenstock, Dan, Head-Product & Partner Dev, Skybox - Google Inc.; pg. 1249, pg. 153
Berkman, Cindy, Mgr-Mktg-Olympic Partnership Team-US - BP America Inc.; pg. 972, pg. 1702
Berkowitz, Irene, Dir-Mktg - Time Inc.; pg. 1693, pg. 1300
Berkowitz, Susan, Mgr-Mktg - Long Motor Corporation; pg. 211, pg. 716
Berkshire, Leslie, VP & Reg Mgr-Mktg & Sponsorship - U.S. Bancorp; pg. 815, pg. 945
Berl, Ken, Grp Dir-Creative - Bank of America Corporation; pg. 718, pg. 1362
Berliant, Stefanie, Sr Mgr-Campaign Mktg-Origin - Electronic Arts Inc.; pg. 951, pg. 189
Berlier, Noreen, Supvr-Co-op Adv - Fry's Electronics, Inc.; pg. 640, pg. 245
Berlin, Arielle, Mgr-PR & Mktg - The Detroit Medical Center; pg. 1524, pg. 880
Berlin, Dave, Dir-Mktg-America's Reg-OEM, HD & BP - BP America Inc.; pg. 972, pg. 1702
Berline, Erin, Dir-Events & Gen Mgr-Mktg - Forbes, Inc.; pg. 1641, pg. 1232
Berlingo, Craig, VP-Product-Programmatic - Tremor Video; pg. 682, pg. 1305
Berlinsky-Schine, Laura, Copywriter-Academic Mktg - Penguin Random House; pg. 1675, pg. 1276
Berlinsky-Schine, Laura, Copywriter-Academic Mktg-Penguin Grp USA - Penguin Random House; pg. 1675, pg. 1276
Berman, Brian, Dir-Retail & Svcs Mktg - Guitar Center, Inc.; pg. 1771, pg. 306
Berman, Debra, Sr VP-Consumer Mktg - Yahoo! Inc.; pg. 1289, pg. 289
Berman, Frank, Exec VP-Mktg - Bloomingdale's, Inc.; pg. 1763, pg. 1204
Berman, Keith, Sr Mgr-Mktg - The Coca-Cola Company; pg. 240, pg. 493
Berman, Kevin, Dir-North America Adv & Mktg Svcs - Lenovo Group Ltd; pg. 427, pg. 1384
Berman, Liz, VP-Integration, Innovation & Mktg-Safeway & Albertsons - Safeway Inc.; pg. 1032, pg. 184
Berman, Melinda, Coord-PR - Four Seasons Hotels Limited; pg. 1092, pg. 1938
Berman, Shelley, VP-Mktg - Mary Brown's, Inc.; pg. 1737, pg. 1924
Bermudez, Martha, Dir-Mktg - Pepsi-Cola North America; pg. 259, pg. 1327
Bernabe, Jose, Sr Mgr-Comm - Computer Sciences Corporation; pg. 378, pg. 1780
Bernabe, Randy, Mgr-Traffic & Coord-Media Svc - Anaheim Ducks Hockey Club, LLC; pg. 528, pg. 42
Bernacchi, Dino, Dir-US Mktg - Harley-Davidson, Inc.; pg. 178, pg. 1874
Bernahl, Bill, VP-Digital Mktg - Herman Miller, Inc.; pg. 926, pg. 913
Bernal, Alex, Mgr-Adv - GSC Enterprises, Inc.; pg. 1021, pg. 1746
Bernal, Angela, Mgr-Mktg - Medtronic, Inc.; pg. 1564, pg. 939
Bernal, Cecelia, Mgr-Sls-Natl - UVP, Inc.; pg. 1434, pg. 298
Bernal, Diana, Assoc Dir-Integrated Mktg - Entertainment Weekly Inc.; pg. 1639, pg. 1228
Bernales, Monica, Sr Mgr-Brand Dev-Global - Unilever United States, Inc.; pg. 904, pg. 1061
Bernard, Andrea, VP & Assoc Gen Counsel-Mktg & Trademark - Colgate-Palmolive Company; pg. 504, pg. 1215
Bernard, Catherine, Mgr-Global Platform Mktg - FMC Corporation; pg. 1163, pg. 1564
Bernard, Cheri, Mgr-Creative Svcs - Payless Shoesource, Inc.; pg. 31, pg. 722
Bernard, Daniel, Head-Product - Time Inc.; pg. 1693, pg. 1300
Bernard, David, Sr Dir-Global R&D Bus, Info Solutions - PepsiCo, Inc.; pg. 259, pg. 1327
Bernard, Francis X., Rep-Sls - William H. Sadlier, Inc.; pg. 1702, pg. 1314
Bernard, Greg, Supvr-Adv - Wakefern Food Corporation; pg. 1037, pg. 1058
Bernard, Julie, Sr VP-Customer Strategy, Loyalty & Credit Mktg - Macy's, Inc.; pg. 1778, pg. 1417
Bernard, Laura, Dir-New Bus & Integrated Mktg - Food Network; pg. 287, pg. 1231
Bernard, Laurel, Sr VP-Mktg - Fox Broadcasting Company; pg. 287, pg. 130
Bernard, Solange, Sr Mgr-Adv & Media - McDonald's Restaurants of Canada Ltd.; pg. 1740, pg. 1940
Bernard, Tenique, Dir-PR - Ralph Lauren Corporation; pg. 46, pg. 1284
Bernardi, Alli, Specialist-Mktg Comm - Schneider Electric USA, Inc.; pg. 1306, pg. 650
Bernardino, David, Dir-Mktg-Frozen Meals - Pinnacle Foods Group LLC; pg. 889, pg. 1104
Bernardo, Sandra A., Mgr-PR - Experian Consumer Direct; pg. 1245, pg. 71
Berndt, Andy, Mng Dir-Creative Lab - Google Inc.; pg. 1249, pg. 153
Berndt, Greg, Dir-Media & Mktg Fins - Regis Corporation; pg. 521, pg. 941
Berne, Nadine, Sr Mgr-Mktg Innovation-Lay's - Frito-Lay North America, Inc.; pg. 1853, pg. 1730
Berne, Nadine, Sr Mgr-Mktg Innovation-Lay's - PepsiCo, Inc.; pg. 259, pg. 1327
Berner, Bill, Sr Dir-Global Brand Protection - NIKE, Inc.; pg. 1812, pg. 1492
Berner, Kathleen A., Dir-Bus Svcs Mktg - Staples, Inc.; pg. 474, pg. 821
Bernhard, Sharon, Coord-Adv & Promos - Daytona Beach Resort Area Convention & Visitors Bureau; pg. 991, pg. 420
Bernhardt, Andrea, Head-Digital & Media - Reckitt Benckiser Inc.; pg. 1136, pg. 1105
Bernhardt, Karen, Sr VP-Mass Adv - Bank of America Corporation; pg. 718, pg. 1362
Berni, Robyn, Mgr-Downstream Mktg - The Timken Company; pg. 218, pg. 1408
Bernick, Craig A., District Mgr-Sls - INCONTACT, INC.; pg. 413, pg. 1752
Bernier, Mark A., Sr Mgr-Mktg-Machine-to-Machine Tech - AT&T; pg. 1865, pg. 258
Bernier, Sydney, Owner & VP-Mktg - Fisher Development Inc.; pg. 81, pg. 218
Berning, Jacob, Dir-Mktg - The WhiteWave Foods Company; pg. 1037, pg. 324
Berning, Mel, Pres-Ad Sls - A&E Television Networks, LLC; pg. 267, pg. 1185
Bernkopf, Karin, Sr Dir-Mktg-Northstar New Jersey - New Jersey State Lottery; pg. 1000, pg. 1126
Bernosky, Richard E., VP-Product Mgmt - Electro Rent Corporation; pg. 390, pg. 300
Berns, Francie, VP-Adv - Los Angeles Times Communications, LLC; pg. 1660, pg. 135
Berns, Scott, Dir-Mktg Ops-Bus Markets - CenturyLink, Inc.; pg. 1870, pg. 746
Bernsen, Eric, Coord-Comml Sls - LoJack Corporation; pg. 210, pg. 811
Bernstein, AJ, Dir-Mktg-CPG - Bolthouse Farms; pg. 841, pg. 44
Bernstein, Alison, VP-Product Dev & Natl Ad Sls - XO Group Inc.; pg. 1289, pg. 1316
Bernstein, Bob, Exec Dir-Federal Govt Mktg & Channel Mgmt - AT&T Government Solutions; pg. 355, pg. 1809
Bernstein, Eduardo, Dir-Mktg - JBS USA Holding, Inc.; pg. 865, pg. 330
Bernstein, Fran, Dir-Mktg & Brand Mgmt - Standard & Poor's Ratings Services; pg. 805, pg. 1296
Bernstein, Jeff, Sr VP-Mktg - eHealth, Inc.; pg. 1242, pg. 153
Bernstein, Jon, Mgr-Social Media - Hyperion Books; pg. 1651, pg. 1242
Bernstein, Lauren, Dir-Programmatic Sls - Meredith Corporation; pg. 1663, pg. 705
Bernstein, Louis, VP-Sls - Case Paper Company Inc.; pg. 1455, pg. 1163
Bernstein, Marc, Sr VP-Consumer Sls - GF Health Products, Inc.; pg. 1535, pg. 508
Bernstein, MaryAnn, Sr Mgr-Product Mktg - AT&T Mobility LLC; pg. 619, pg. 488
Bernstein, Paul, Sr Product Mgr-Health & Fitness - Timex Corporation; pg. 14, pg. 355
Bernstein, Paul, Dir-Mktg-Strategic Accounts - Valassis; pg. 1698, pg. 386
Bernstein, Paul, Dir-Mktg-Strategic Accounts - Valassis Communications, Inc.; pg. 1287, pg. 897
Bernstein, Rob, VP-Digital Media - World Wrestling Entertainment, Inc.; pg. 595, pg. 380
Bernstein, Ron, VP-Mdsg - Motorcar Parts of America, Inc.; pg. 213, pg. 295
Bernstein, Ron, Sr VP-Adv Sls & Ops - Synacor, Inc.; pg. 1283, pg. 1151
Beroth, Seth, Program Mgr-Mktg-US Enterprise & Comml Field Mktg - Cisco Systems, Inc.; pg. 372, pg. 240
Berowski, Becky, Mgr-Social Media-Radius Fitness - NBC Universal, Inc.; pg. 300, pg. 1266
Berquist, Julie, VP-Product Lines & Mktg - Assurant Health; pg. 1193, pg. 1873
Berretta, Antonino, Specialist-Mktg Support - Canon U.S.A., Inc.; pg. 1404, pg. 1178
Berrettini, Katie, Dir-Mktg & Dev - College Football Hall of Fame; pg. 541, pg. 501
Berrey, Ab, Head-Sls Bus Excellence - Nestle Canada Inc.; pg. 883, pg. 1929
Berrey, Sheila, Mgr-PR-The Swiss Colony, Inc. - Colony Brands Inc.; pg. 849, pg. 1881
Berrien, Lacey, Specialist-Keds Social Media - Wolverine World Wide, Inc.; pg. 1822, pg. 905
Berru, Alexandra, Mgr-Mktg - Save the Queen, LLC.; pg. 1111, pg. 124
Berry, Alex, Coord-Mktg - Dickey's Barbecue Restaurants, Inc.; pg. 1725, pg. 1680
Berry, Becky, Acct Mgr-Intl & Supvr-Intl Sls - Leupold & Stevens, Inc.; pg. 1420, pg. 1492
Berry, Brian, Dir-Sls & Mktg - Air Lift Company; pg. 198, pg. 895
Berry, Kim, Sr Mgr-Events & Promos-BRIDES Magazine - Conde Nast Publications, Inc.; pg. 1629, pg. 1217
Berry, Lesley, VP-Mktg & Comm - Dallas Mavericks; pg. 543, pg. 1678
Berry, Maggie, Mgr-Digital Mktg - J. Crew Group, Inc.; pg. 1773, pg. 1245
Berry, Mark, VP-Test Sls & Mgr-Bus Dev-IDM Accounts-US - Amkor Technology, Inc.; pg. 67, pg. 25
Berry, Mauri, Dir-Mktg & ECommerce - Marriott International, Inc.; pg. 1102, pg. 764
Berry, Paul, Dir-PR, Adv & Brand - Spirit Airlines, Inc.; pg. 234, pg. 449
Berry, Ray, Product Mgr - ITW Magnaflux; pg. 1418, pg. 615
Berry, Russ, Mgr-Sls - Joe Machens Ford Inc.; pg. 180, pg. 976
Berry, Tac, Sr Mgr-Product Mktg - Avaya Inc.; pg. 621, pg. 264
Berry, Tricia, Dir-Creative Svcs - Horace Mann Companies; pg. 1203, pg. 662
Berryman, Anita, Sr Mgr-Corp Comm - Parametric Technology Corporation; pg. 452, pg. 835
Berryman, William, Dir-Central Reg Sls - MicroStrategy, Inc.; pg. 1266, pg. 1809
Bersin, Adam, Dir-Mktg - FX Networks, LLC; pg. 288, pg. 131
Bert, Camila, Coord-Digital Mktg - Sony Pictures Entertainment Inc.; pg. 309, pg. 72
Berthiaume, Joanne, Mgr-PR - Bose Corporation; pg. 626, pg. 820
Bertholdt, Joerg, Dir-Embedded Software Mktg & Plng - Altera Corporation; pg. 348, pg. 237
Bertholon, Gerard J., Chief Strategy Officer - Cuisine

First page reference indicates Business Class Edition
Second page reference indicates Geographic Edition

Solutions, Inc.; *pg.* 850, *pg.* 1770

Bertinetti, Dyana, Team Head & Sr Specialist-Mktg - LivingSocial, Inc.; *pg.* 1264, *pg.* 401

Bertolani, Michael, Mgr-Sls-Rental &Retail Div - New Age Electronics, Inc.; *pg.* 659, *pg.* 63

Bertolini, Lauren, Product Mgr - Gawker Media LLC; *pg.* 1248, *pg.* 1234

Bertollini, Vanessa, Mgr-Mktg - McCarthy Building Companies, Inc.; *pg.* 96, *pg.* 999

Bertolotti, Larissa, Mgr-PR & Social Media - Voxx International; *pg.* 686, *pg.* 1166

Bertolucci, Helen, Dir-Cross Channel Mktg & Plng - W.W. Grainger, Inc.; *pg.* 1390, *pg.* 625

Bertolucci, Lewis, Head-Social Media & Mgr-Integrated Digital Mktg - Humana, Inc.; *pg.* 1204, *pg.* 734

Bertone, Andrea, Exec VP & Gen Mgr-Sls-Europe & North America - Monster Worldwide, Inc.; *pg.* 1268, *pg.* 859

Bertram, Laretta, Sr Mgr-Mktg Comm-Global - Texas Instruments Incorporated; *pg.* 679, *pg.* 1688

Bertram, Naming Nick, Sr VP-Mdsg Strategy & Support - Ahold USA, Inc.; *pg.* 1013, *pg.* 1520

Bertrams, Kristyn, Mgr-Mktg - ACCO Brands Corporation; *pg.* 340, *pg.* 626

Bertrams, Tessie, Brand Mgr-Internet Mktg - A Book Company, LLC; *pg.* 1225, *pg.* 729

Bertrand, Cheryl, Sr Mgr-Mktg-Hershey's & Kisses - Hershey Canada, Inc.; *pg.* 1855, *pg.* 1926

Bertrand, Eric, Product Mgr - Mettler-Toledo International Inc.; *pg.* 1423, *pg.* 1441

Bertrand, Ian, Sr Mgr-Retail Brand Presentation - NIKE, Inc.; *pg.* 1812, *pg.* 1492

Bertrandt, Ben, Dir-Online Mktg - Meritage Homes Corporation; *pg.* 97, *pg.* 23

Bertsch, Erica, Sr Mgr-Mktg-Productions - Carnival Corporation; *pg.* 1902, *pg.* 441

Bertsch, Erica, Sr Mgr-Mktg-Productions - Carnival Cruise Lines; *pg.* 1902, *pg.* 441

Bertsch, Jace, Mgr-Mktg-Intl - The Toro Company; *pg.* 1065, *pg.* 918

Berwick, Frances, Pres-Bravo & Oxygen Media - NBC Universal, Inc.; *pg.* 300, *pg.* 1266

Bes, Michel, VP-Retail Sls - Inter Parfums, Inc.; *pg.* 512, *pg.* 1244

Besa, Maricar, Acct Mgr-Mktg - Ingram Micro Inc.; *pg.* 415, *pg.* 261

Bescherer, Lisa, VP-Mktg - ConAgra Foods, Inc.; *pg.* 826, *pg.* 1014

Bescherer, Lisa, VP-Mktg - ConAgra Foods Lamb Weston, Inc.; *pg.* 850, *pg.* 549

Beschta-Newborn, Amy, Mgr-Digital Media, Comm & Analytics - The American Dental Association; *pg.* 127, *pg.* 564

Beser, James, Grp Product Mgr - Google Inc.; *pg.* 1249, *pg.* 153

Beshar, Michael, Sr Dir-Strategic Sls & Dev - Yahoo! Inc.; *pg.* 1289, *pg.* 289

Beshke, Thomas, Mgr-Global Technical Mktg - Methode Electronics, Inc.; *pg.* 654, *pg.* 581

Besonen, Gary, Mgr-Natl Woodworking Equipment Sls - Timesavers Inc.; *pg.* 1382, *pg.* 928

Bessant, Catherine P., Pres-Product Solutions-Global - Bank of America Corporation; *pg.* 718, *pg.* 1362

Besserer, Marla, Head-Client Rels & Branding & Bus Mgr - Sun Life Financial Inc.; *pg.* 806, *pg.* 1944

Bessette, Amy B., Sr Dir-Corp PR - Apple Inc.; *pg.* 350, *pg.* 73

Bessette, Rebecca, VP-Mktg - Intrado Inc.; *pg.* 420, *pg.* 334

Best, Brian, Assoc VP-Digital Strategy & Mktg - Arizona State University; *pg.* 597, *pg.* 25

Best, Cliff, VP-Distributor Sls - J&J Snack Foods Corporation; *pg.* 865, *pg.* 1107

Best, Donna, Mgr-Worldwide Mktg Budget - Xilinx, Inc.; *pg.* 496, *pg.* 252

Best, Karen, Dir-Adv Resources - Bristol-Myers Squibb Company; *pg.* 1509, *pg.* 1206

Best, Mike, VP-Sls - Bissell Homecare, Inc.; *pg.* 52, *pg.* 887

Best, Sarah, Exec Dir-Sls-Global - MGM Resorts International; *pg.* 1105, *pg.* 1028

Best, Sheri, Dir-Targeted Shopper Mktg & Offer Mgmt - H-E-B; *pg.* 1022, *pg.* 1740

Beste, Laura, Sr Mgr-Mktg - Frito-Lay North America, Inc.; *pg.* 1853, *pg.* 1730

Beswick, Vicki, Mgr-Image & Mdsg - The Wendy's Company; *pg.* 1755, *pg.* 1450

Betancur, Judy, Mgr-Strategic Mktg-Global - THE DOW CHEMICAL COMPANY; *pg.* 1157, *pg.* 898

Betaneli, Christine, Sr Dir-PR - Educational Testing Service Inc.; *pg.* 1394, *pg.* 1111

Betasso, Angela, VP-Sls Media Ops - Gannett Co., Inc.; *pg.* 289, *pg.* 1681

Beth, Mary Cowardin, Dir-Mktg-Produce - T. Marzetti Company; *pg.* 900, *pg.* 1444

Bethke, Alan, VP-Mktg - Subaru of America, Inc.; *pg.* 191, *pg.* 1050

Betron, Patricia, Sr VP-Multimedia Sls - ESPN, Inc.; *pg.* 285, *pg.* 340

Bettcher, Brian, Dir-Product Mktg - The Sports Authority, Inc.; *pg.* 1846, *pg.* 326

Bettinger, Nicole, Mgr-Content & Mktg - Amazon.com, Inc.; *pg.* 1226, *pg.* 1831

Bettinson, Mary, Mgr-Search Mktg - Guthy-Renker LLC; *pg.* 289, *pg.* 273

Bettis, Mary, Dir-Sls & Operational Plng - Sigma-Aldrich Corporation; *pg.* 1181, *pg.* 1003

Bettison, Mike, Mgr-Digital Mktg-Intl Div - General Mills, Inc.; *pg.* 828, *pg.* 933

Bettman, Kathy, Specialist-Mktg Product - Varian Medical Systems, Inc.; *pg.* 1434, *pg.* 178

Bettner, John, Mgr-Sls-Global - Intel Corporation; *pg.* 645, *pg.* 266

Betts, Michael, Dir-Mktg - Bright House Networks LLC; *pg.* 272, *pg.* 461

Betts, Rick, Dir-Mktg Medical Diagnostics - Abaxis, Inc.; *pg.* 1483, *pg.* 298

Betts, Susan, Sr Dir-Consumer Brand Strategy - Microsoft Corporation; *pg.* 435, *pg.* 1824

Betz, Debby, Dir-Mktg - Reckitt Benckiser Inc.; *pg.* 1136, *pg.* 1105

Betzold, Sarah, Sr Mgr-Mktg - Dupont Pioneer; *pg.* 1795, *pg.* 708

Beukema, Shaun, Product Mgr-Canadian Chequing - The Toronto-Dominion Bank; *pg.* 810, *pg.* 1945

Beup, Lee, Dir-Mktg - Airgas, Inc.; *pg.* 1146, *pg.* 1583

Beurman, Todd, Sr VP-Mktg - Shoe Carnival, Inc.; *pg.* 1819, *pg.* 679

Beuzelin-Mayer, Sabine, Sr Brand Mgr-Special K Brand Mktg-USA - Kellogg Company; *pg.* 831, *pg.* 870

Bevacqua, Elizabeth, VP-Mktg - General Electric Company; *pg.* 1297, *pg.* 347

Bevan, Maureen, Dir-Library Svcs & Sr Product Mgr-Premium Memberships - MORNINGSTAR, INC.; *pg.* 784, *pg.* 583

Bevan, Mike, Dir-Dealer Mktg Svcs - The Chamberlain Group, Inc.; *pg.* 75, *pg.* 611

Bevard, Robby, Coord-Production - Antarctic Press; *pg.* 1617, *pg.* 1739

Bevel, Christopher, Strategist-Digital Mktg - FedEx Express Corporation; *pg.* 1908, *pg.* 1644

Bever, Laurie, Dir-Consumer Adv - National Pork Board; *pg.* 882, *pg.* 703

Beveridge, Jill, Dir-Mktg Innovation - Hostess Brands LLC; *pg.* 1856, *pg.* 984

Beveridge, Laura, Dir-Retention Mktg & Sr Mgr - drugstore.com, inc.; *pg.* 1239, *pg.* 1814

Beverly, Gilbert, Sr Dir-Sports Mgmt-College Sports - ESPN, Inc.; *pg.* 285, *pg.* 340

Beverstock, John, Specialist-Digital & Direct Mktg-Global Brand Mktg - Moen Incorporated; *pg.* 1056, *pg.* 1468

Bevilacqua, Gabe, VP-Product Mgmt-Viacom Vantage - Viacom Inc.; *pg.* 316, *pg.* 1310

Beville, Bob, Gen Mgr-Sls - WZVN TV ABC 7; *pg.* 323, *pg.* 428

Bevington, Graham, Chief Sls Officer - Mitel Networks Corporation; *pg.* 654, *pg.* 1921

Bevis, Rino, Rep-Sls-West Carolinas - Stryker Corporation; *pg.* 1598, *pg.* 894

Bewkes, Chandler, Sr Mgr-Brand Mgmt - American Express Company; *pg.* 712, *pg.* 1190

Beyer, Chris, Sr Dir-Sponsorship Sls - Los Angeles Clippers; *pg.* 558, *pg.* 135

Beyer, Curt, Mgr-Protimax Technical & Product - Trouw Nutrition USA; *pg.* 1482, *pg.* 616

Beyer, Krista, Media Buyer - Jo-Ann Stores LLC; *pg.* 696, *pg.* 1455

Beyer, Marianne, Assoc Dir-Audit Mktg - KPMG LLP; *pg.* 774, *pg.* 1086

Beyhaut, Graciano, Sr Mgr-Product Line-Transactional Power Products Bus - Eaton Corporation - Industrial Controls; *pg.* 1296, *pg.* 1874

Beyroutey, Barbara A., VP-Property & Casualty Mktg - USI Holdings Corporation; *pg.* 1222, *pg.* 1144

Bezner, Farrah, Dir-Mktg-Halls & Candy-Mondelez International - Kraft Canada Inc.; *pg.* 869, *pg.* 1939

Bezner, Farrah, Dir-Mktg-Halls & Candy-North America - Mondelez International; *pg.* 877, *pg.* 1344

Bezold, M. Todd, Dir-Mktg-Subscriptions - Cincinnati Symphony Orchestra; *pg.* 540, *pg.* 1411

Bhadarka, Rajesh J., Bus Mgr-Asia - NN, Inc.; *pg.* 1365, *pg.* 1635

Bhadra, Simon, Sr Mgr-Mktg & Pro Svcs - United Parcel Service, Inc.; *pg.* 1928, *pg.* 522

Bhadsavle, Ash, Product Mgr - GEA Refrigeration North America, Inc.; *pg.* 1072, *pg.* 1597

Bhaijee, Yousuf, Sr Dir-Growth - Zynga Inc.; *pg.* 1292, *pg.* 235

Bhalla, Atul, Sr Mgr-Mktg-Customer & Channel Mktg - Pfizer Inc.; *pg.* 1581, *pg.* 1278

Bhalla, Pankaj, Assoc Dir-Mktg-Global Oral Care - The Procter & Gamble Company; *pg.* 1129, *pg.* 1418

Bhandaraar, Mangesh, Dir-Product Mgmt - Adobe Systems Incorporated; *pg.* 342, *pg.* 235

Bhandari, Harish, VP-Creative-Global - Aveda Corporation; *pg.* 499, *pg.* 917

Bhandari, Vivek, Sr Mgr-Product Mgmt & Mktg - Cisco Systems, Inc.; *pg.* 372, *pg.* 240

Bhanote, Monica, Brand Mgr-Hair Care-Global - Unilever United States, Inc.; *pg.* 904, *pg.* 1061

Bharadwaj, Divya, Sr Assoc Brand Mgr - Post Holdings, Inc.; *pg.* 833, *pg.* 1002

Bharadwaj, Ravi, Head-Sls Strategy & Insights-Global - The Western Union Company; *pg.* 822, *pg.* 327

Bhardwaj, Amit, Sr Dir-Customer Loyalty - Marsh Supermarkets, Inc.; *pg.* 1027, *pg.* 688

Bhardwaj, Manish, Sr Mgr-Mktg-Middle East & Turkey - Aruba Networks, Inc.; *pg.* 353, *pg.* 284

Bhargava, Ashish, Dir-Product Mktg-Cloud Mgmt BU - VMware, Inc.; *pg.* 490, *pg.* 179

Bhargava, Monica, Exec VP-Product Dev - Williams-Sonoma, Inc.; *pg.* 1140, *pg.* 234

Bhargava, Vikas, Sr Mgr-Digital Mktg - Publishers Clearing House; *pg.* 1782, *pg.* 1324

Bhashyam, Sanjay, Sr Mgr-Comml CRM Applications - PepsiCo, Inc.; *pg.* 259, *pg.* 1327

Bhaskar, Sidd, Product Mgr-Mobile - Bed Bath & Beyond Inc.; *pg.* 1121, *pg.* 1127

Bhat, Pali, Dir-Product Mgmt - Google Inc.; *pg.* 1249, *pg.* 153

Bhat, Tapan, Chief Product Officer - Lithium Technologies; *pg.* 1263, *pg.* 221

Bhat, Tapan, Chief Product Officer - Move, Inc.; *pg.* 1268, *pg.* 247

Bhatia, Krishan, Exec VP-Bus Ops & Strategy-Adv Sls - NBC Universal, Inc.; *pg.* 300, *pg.* 1266

Bhatia, Qamar, Pres-Specialty Products - Honeywell International Inc.; *pg.* 407, *pg.* 1088

Bhattacharya, Ritesh, Sr Mgr-Loyalty Feature Dev - American Express Company; *pg.* 712, *pg.* 1190

Bhattacharyya, Amit, Sr Mgr-Mobile Shopping - Amazon.com, Inc.; *pg.* 1226, *pg.* 1831

Bhattacharyya, Megan, Mgr-Mktg & Assoc Program - Amazon.com, Inc.; *pg.* 1226, *pg.* 1831

Bhavnani, Vin, Mgr-Advance Scouting - Oklahoma City Thunder; *pg.* 571, *pg.* 1487

Bhirud, Kathryn, Mgr-School & Library Mktg - Penguin Random House; *pg.* 1675, *pg.* 1276

Bhirud, Kathryn, Mgr-School & Library Mktg-Penguin Grp USA - Penguin Random House; *pg.* 1675, *pg.* 1276

Bhola, Arun, Dir-Engrg, Retail & Sls Application Dev - Apple Inc.; *pg.* 350, *pg.* 73

Bhola, Ramya, Mgr-Mktg - CNA Insurance Companies; *pg.* 1198, *pg.* 571

Bi, Cathay, Product Mgr - YouTube, LLC; *pg.* 1291, *pg.* 198

Biagi, Giulia, Product Mgr - Canson Inc.; *pg.* 1625, *pg.* 844

Biagini, Kate, Mgr-Client Insights & Mktg Svcs-Global - FRANKLIN RESOURCES, INC.; *pg.* 760, *pg.* 254

Biagioli, Alana, Acct Exec-Retail Adv - The New York Post; *pg.* 1668, *pg.* 1269

Bialecki, Lisa, Sr Dir-Integrated Comm - Rust-Oleum Corporation; *pg.* 1447, *pg.* 664

Bialko, Lauren, Mgr-Mktg - Party City Corporation; *pg.* 1781, *pg.* 1116

Biancamano, Kate, Sr Mgr-Mktg - Sephora USA Inc; *pg.* 522, *pg.* 227

Bianchi, Kara, VP-Brand Mktg - The Talbots, Inc.; *pg.* 34, *pg.* 824

Bianchine, Robert, Dir-Olympics & Sports Sls - NBC Universal Television Networks Group; *pg.* 302, *pg.* 1267

Bianchini, Denise, Sr Mgr-Global Mktg Org - Abbott

Laboratories; *pg.* 1484, *pg.* 551
Bianco, Donato, Mgr-Segment Mktg - Micron Technology, Inc.; *pg.* 435, *pg.* 547
Biasotti, Lisa, Sr Product Mgr-Youth - The North Face, Inc.; *pg.* 1840, *pg.* 252
Bibas, Marcos, Dir-Sls-Global Travel Retail Americas - Diageo North America, Inc.; *pg.* 1961, *pg.* 361
Bibbings, James P., Dir-Mktg & Mdsg - Whirlpool Corporation; *pg.* 62, *pg.* 872
Bibby, Geoff R., VP-Corp Mktg - Zix Corporation; *pg.* 497, *pg.* 1691
Bibby, Roslyn, VP-Media Rels-FX Networks & FX Productions - FX Networks, LLC; *pg.* 288, *pg.* 131
Biblarz, Dina, Dir-Creative Solutions - Conde Nast Publications, Inc.; *pg.* 1629, *pg.* 1217
Biblarz, Dina, Dir-Integrated Mktg & Creative Solutions-Bon Appetit & Epicurious - Vogue Magazine; *pg.* 1700, *pg.* 1311
Bibliowicz, Gideon, Sr Product Mgr-SharePoint Product Grp - Microsoft Corporation; *pg.* 435, *pg.* 1824
Bice, Jenifer, Sr Dir-Assoc Comm-Global - Wal-Mart Stores, Inc.; *pg.* 1790, *pg.* 29
Bice, Mark, Sr Mgr-Real Estate & Acq - Potlatch Corporation; *pg.* 1467, *pg.* 1844
Bicher, Renee H., Mgr-Mktg-Enterprise Field Mktg-North America - Level 3 Communications, Inc.; *pg.* 1262, *pg.* 312
Bicicchi, Diana, Assoc Mgr-Mktg & Assoc Brand Mgr - PetSmart, Inc.; *pg.* 1481, *pg.* 18
Bick, Tom, Sr Dir-Integrated Mktg & Adv - The Kraft Heinz Company; *pg.* 871, *pg.* 641
Bickel, Andrew, Sr Dir-Facility Ops - The Hallmark Channel; *pg.* 290, *pg.* 281
Bickel, Peter, Dir-Mktg - Villanova University; *pg.* 610, *pg.* 1589
Bickerstaff, Robert, VP-Data Product Mgmt - AT&T Southeast; *pg.* 1868, *pg.* 489
Bickford, Cady Zildjian, Assoc Product Mgr-Apparel & Novelty Items - Avedis Zildjian Company; *pg.* 531, *pg.* 839
Bickford, Jennifer, Mgr-Digital Mktg-PBM Mktg - CVS Health Corporation; *pg.* 1765, *pg.* 1610
Bickford, Lori, Specialist-Clinical Mktg - Philips Electronics North America; *pg.* 662, *pg.* 782
Bickley, John, VP-Sustainable Utility Sls - Hydrotex Partners Ltd.; *pg.* 979, *pg.* 1692
Biddle, Susan, Dir-Vertical Solutions Mktg-Healthcare - Citrix Systems, Inc.; *pg.* 375, *pg.* 424
Biddlecombe, Bob, Sr VP-Sls - ConAgra Foods, Inc.; *pg.* 826, *pg.* 1014
Bidegary, Tamra, VP & Mgr-Mktg - Bank of the West; *pg.* 721, *pg.* 213
Biden, Bobby, Mgr-Mktg - T. Rowe Price Group Inc.; *pg.* 808, *pg.* 759
Bidgoli, Mike, VP-Product - LivingSocial, Inc.; *pg.* 1264, *pg.* 401
Bidgood, David A., Pres-Sls & Mktg-Natl - Bluegreen Corporation; *pg.* 1082, *pg.* 410
Bidinger, Rory, Brand Mgr-Advocacy & Mktg - Gold'n Plump Poultry, Inc.; *pg.* 858, *pg.* 956
Bidmead, Warren, III, Dir-Mktg - Brown-Forman Corporation; *pg.* 1958, *pg.* 732
Bidwell, Eric, Product Mgr-Amphenol Aerospace-Class L - Amphenol Corporation; *pg.* 616, *pg.* 381
Bieber, Roy, Product Mgr-Roofing & Cladding - SFS intec, Inc.; *pg.* 1061, *pg.* 1596
Biebl, Liz, Sr Mgr-Comm-Vail Mountain - Vail Resorts, Inc.; *pg.* 1117, *pg.* 313
Biedenbach, Adelyn, Coord-Digital Media & Comm - Florida Panthers Hockey Club, Ltd.; *pg.* 548, *pg.* 469
Biederman, Rob, Sr Mgr-Midwest Pub Affairs & Govt Rels - Google Inc.; *pg.* 1249, *pg.* 153
Biedermann, Kevin, Sr VP-Residential Flooring Products - Armstrong World Industries, Inc.; *pg.* 914, *pg.* 1545
Biegacki, Steven R., Sr VP-Sls & Mktg - Belden, Inc.; *pg.* 624, *pg.* 993
Biehl, Adam, VP-Global Brand Strategy & Mktg - Hasbro, Inc.; *pg.* 954, *pg.* 1603
Biehl, Douglas, Brand Mgr-New Products - Dairy Farmers of America, Inc.; *pg.* 851, *pg.* 982
Bielfeldt, Jon, VP-Sls & Mktg - Lisle Corporation; *pg.* 1356, *pg.* 703
Bieli, Patrick, Sr Mgr-Design - American Express Company; *pg.* 712, *pg.* 1190
Bielinski, Angelea, Strategist-Social Media - Williams-Sonoma, Inc.; *pg.* 1140, *pg.* 234
Bielowicz, Theo, Dir-Sls-Channel Partners-North America - Datamax Corporation; *pg.* 1633, *pg.* 453
Biemer, James, Bus Dir-Consumer Mktg - Conde Nast Publications, Inc.; *pg.* 1629, *pg.* 1217
Bien, Kevin, Product Mgr-Mktg - AGCO Corporation; *pg.* 700, *pg.* 530
Bien, Rachel, Sr Mgr-Global Media - American Express Company; *pg.* 712, *pg.* 1190
Bienema, Christie, Sr Specialist-Mktg Comm - W.W. Grainger, Inc.; *pg.* 1390, *pg.* 625
Bienenfeld, Robert, Sr Mgr-Environment & Energy Strategy - American Honda Motor Co., Inc.; *pg.* 163, *pg.* 292
Bierbaum, Tom, Dir-Mktg-Exclusive Brands - SpartanNash Co.; *pg.* 1034, *pg.* 925
Bierbrauer, Laura, Sr Dir-Sls Enablement & Leadership Dev - Equinix, Inc.; *pg.* 394, *pg.* 190
Bierle, Todd, Dir-Consumer Mktg - Meredith Corporation; *pg.* 1663, *pg.* 705
Bierline, Stephen, Sr Dir-Mktg Insights - Alliance Data Systems Corporation; *pg.* 347, *pg.* 1729
Biermann, Lloyd, Mgr-Mktg - General Motors Company; *pg.* 175, *pg.* 881
Biernat, Brent, First VP-Sls - COCC; *pg.* 376, *pg.* 337
Bieseman, Tom, Mgr-Sys & Software-EMEA Product Mktg - Brady Corporation; *pg.* 363, *pg.* 1873
Biespiel, Matt, Sr Dir-Global Brand Dev - McDonald's Corporation; *pg.* 1737, *pg.* 645
Bifulco, Frank P., Jr., Exec VP-Mktg-Global - Staples, Inc.; *pg.* 474, *pg.* 821
Bigalow, Jamia, Sr VP-Distr Mktg - Fox Television Stations Inc.; *pg.* 288, *pg.* 131
Bigalow, Jamia, Sr VP-Distr Mktg - FX Networks, LLC; *pg.* 288, *pg.* 131
Bigelow, Angela, Sr Acct Mgr-Pub Sector Sls - Plantronics, Inc.; *pg.* 663, *pg.* 270
Bigelow, Chandler, Interim CFO & Chief Strategies & Ops Officer - Tribune Media Company; *pg.* 1696, *pg.* 592
Bigelow, Coleman, Dir-Global Mktg-Johnson's & Aveeno Baby - Johnson & Johnson Baby Products, Inc.; *pg.* 1552, *pg.* 1094
Bigelow, Shirley, Head-Mktg Plng & Sls Support - The Northwestern Mutual Life Insurance Company; *pg.* 1212, *pg.* 1879
Biggar, Lynne, Exec VP-Consumer Mktg & Revenue - Time Inc.; *pg.* 1693, *pg.* 1300
Bigger, Lauren, Brand Mgr-Maytag Brand Laundry - Whirlpool Corporation; *pg.* 62, *pg.* 872
Bigger, Todd, Dir-Worldwide Product Mgmt-Graphics Bus - Eastman Kodak Company; *pg.* 1408, *pg.* 1333
Biggers, Alison, Sr VP-Mktg-Worldwide - Sony Pictures Home Entertainment; *pg.* 310, *pg.* 72
Biggers, Landin, Sr Assoc Brand Mgr-Greenies - Mars Petcare; *pg.* 1478, *pg.* 1633
Biggers, Sarah, Coord-Social & Digital Media - California Pizza Kitchen Inc.; *pg.* 1720, *pg.* 127
Bigham, Rick, Product Mgr-Magnetic Separation - Bunting Magnetics Co.; *pg.* 1320, *pg.* 717
Bigland, Reid, Pres/CEO-Ram Truck Brand & Head-Sls-US - FCA US LLC; *pg.* 170, *pg.* 868
Bigler, Jason, Dir-Product Mgmt - Google Inc.; *pg.* 1249, *pg.* 153
Bigman, Dan, Mgr-Mng Editor & Editorial Product - Forbes.com LLC; *pg.* 1247, *pg.* 1232
Bihary, Keith, Dir-Corp Sls - Molded Fiber Glass Companies; *pg.* 1886, *pg.* 1403
Bihlmier, Joseph, VP-Media-Global - American Express Company; *pg.* 712, *pg.* 1190
Bihm, Kristine Wimmerstedt, Dir-Adv Svcs - The Reader's Digest Association, Inc.; *pg.* 1679, *pg.* 1322
Bijlani, Nikhil, Product Mgr - CAPITAL BANK CORPORATION; *pg.* 730, *pg.* 1386
Bikman, Joel, Sr VP-Sls & Mktg - Mannatech, Incorporated; *pg.* 1558, *pg.* 1671
Bikoff, Rebecca, Brand Mgr - Solo Cup Company; *pg.* 1469, *pg.* 625
Bildstein, Emily, Mgr-Citywide Sls-West Reg - Denver Metro Convention & Visitors Bureau; *pg.* 991, *pg.* 318
Bilello, Patrice N., Specialist-Mktg Comm-Global - Chevron Corporation; *pg.* 974, *pg.* 259
Bilger, Beth, Bus Mgr-Initiative - Wells Fargo & Company; *pg.* 819, *pg.* 232
Bilinski, Brandon, Sr Product Mgr - Google Inc.; *pg.* 1249, *pg.* 153
Bilkey, Susan J., Mgr-Mktg Comm - Xerox Corporation; *pg.* 494, *pg.* 365
Bill, Amber, Mgr-Sls-Natl - Hormel Foods Corporation; *pg.* 863, *pg.* 915
Bille, Chris, Sr Mgr-Offline Mktg - Bose Corporation; *pg.* 626, *pg.* 820
Billger, Aaron, Dir-PR - Highmark Blue Cross Blue Shield; *pg.* 1203, *pg.* 1576
Billgren, Henrik, VP-Product Mgmt & Dev - Infor; *pg.* 414, *pg.* 484
Billie, Dan, Exec VP-Sls & Mktg - AP Exhaust Products, Inc.; *pg.* 199, *pg.* 1373
Billig, Nicholaus, Product Mgr - AVX Corporation; *pg.* 623, *pg.* 1616
Billik, Holly, Sr Mgr-Mktg Comm-Global - Avery Dennison Corporation; *pg.* 1452, *pg.* 95
Billinghurst, Becky, Sr Mgr-Customer Insight & Presence Mktg - Herman Miller, Inc.; *pg.* 926, *pg.* 913
Billings, Brittany, Sr Dir-Bus Dev - Gilt Groupe Inc.; *pg.* 24, *pg.* 1234
Billings, Carol, Dir-Mktg Comm - Stonyfield Farm, Inc.; *pg.* 899, *pg.* 1035
Billings, Jay, VP-Global Innovation & North America Mktg - Ball Corporation; *pg.* 1452, *pg.* 311
Billings, Joy, Sr Product Mgr - Amazon.com, Inc.; *pg.* 1226, *pg.* 1831
Billingsley, Ben, Sr VP-Global Watch Mktg & Comm - The Nielsen Company B.V.; *pg.* 1671, *pg.* 1272
Billingsley, Jeff, Dir-Mktg - Deschutes Brewery Inc.; *pg.* 248, *pg.* 1496
Billingsley, Laura, Dir-Mktg - The New York Times; *pg.* 1668, *pg.* 1270
Billingsley, Roger D., Sr VP-Tech & Product Dev - Dole Fresh Vegetables; *pg.* 854, *pg.* 198
Billingsley, Scott, Dir-Generics Program Mktg - McKesson Corporation; *pg.* 1560, *pg.* 222
Bills, Amy, Dir-Mktg - Blackbaud, Inc.; *pg.* 361, *pg.* 1613
Billy, Jeremy, Sr Dir-Bus Dev - Gannett Co., Inc.; *pg.* 1643, *pg.* 1790
Bilodeau, Eric, CIO-Setco Sls - Setco Sales Company; *pg.* 1061, *pg.* 1426
Bilodeau, Ron, Mgr-Product & Mktg - Hussey Seating Co.; *pg.* 929, *pg.* 751
Biloon, David E., Dir-Mktg-New Product Plng-Emerging Market Bus Unit - Eli Lilly and Company; *pg.* 1527, *pg.* 684
Bilte, Greg, Dir-Sls - Cox Media Group; *pg.* 280, *pg.* 502
Bilus, Kate, Dir-Mktg - L'Oreal USA; *pg.* 514, *pg.* 1252
Bilyeu, Paul B., Dir-PR - David A. Straz Jr. Center; *pg.* 543, *pg.* 472
Bimont, Jose, Head-CRM, Digital Mktg & ECommerce - Allergan, Inc.; *pg.* 1491, *pg.* 106
Binder, Abby, Mgr-US Mktg-Truvia Consumer Products - Cargill, Inc.; *pg.* 845, *pg.* 965
Binder, John, Mgr-Mktg-Global - Nordson Corporation; *pg.* 1365, *pg.* 1480
Binder, Oren, Sr Mgr-Mktg-SP Mobility - Cisco Systems, Inc.; *pg.* 372, *pg.* 240
Binder, Peter, Mgr-Product Mktg-Digital Solutions - Pitney Bowes Inc.; *pg.* 454, *pg.* 376
Binder, Stacy, Mgr-Field Mktg - Starwood Hotels & Resorts Worldwide, Inc.; *pg.* 1114, *pg.* 378
Binderman, Warren, Acting CFO - VYSTAR CORPORATION; *pg.* 1891, *pg.* 532
Bindman, Jessica, Brand Mgr-Global Dev-Dove Bar - Unilever United States, Inc.; *pg.* 904, *pg.* 1061
Bindra, Kimberly, Head-Mktg & Corp Fin & Dir-Digital Strategy & Content - Duff & Phelps Corporation; *pg.* 745, *pg.* 1226
Bing, Rich, Dir-New Product Dev Facility Svcs - Cintas Corporation; *pg.* 372, *pg.* 1411
Bingham, Dan, Sr Mgr-Mktg-PC Client Grp - Intel Corporation; *pg.* 645, *pg.* 266
Bingham, Leigh, Dir-Consumer Mktg-Active Interest Network - Bonnier Corporation; *pg.* 1622, *pg.* 480
Bingham, Rick, Dir-Mktg - Del Monte Foods, Inc.; *pg.* 852, *pg.* 304
Bingham, Tom, Sr Dir-Mktg & Product Engrg - Gold Eagle Company; *pg.* 206, *pg.* 575
Biniwale, Samir N., Reg Mgr-Mktg-Canada-Transformer Insulation & Components - ABB Inc.; *pg.* 64, *pg.* 1959
Binkerd, Julia, Sr Mgr-Mktg & Small Bus - Verizon Communications Inc.; *pg.* 1875, *pg.* 1309
Binks, Livia, VP-Integrated Mktg - FMR LLC (Fidelity Investments); *pg.* 759, *pg.* 794
Binner, James, Mgr-Natl Foodservice Channel Mktg - Lactalis American Group; *pg.* 873, *pg.* 1149
Binns, Dick, Mgr-Mktg - Intel Corporation; *pg.* 645, *pg.* 266
Binns, Kristin E., VP-PR - Anthem, Inc.; *pg.* 1192, *pg.* 683
Binns, Simon, Product Mgr-Global - Applied Materials, Inc.;

pg. 618, *pg.* 264
Binns-Brown, Ava, Analyst-Mktg Expense Mgmt - The Coca-Cola Company; *pg.* 240, *pg.* 493
Bintz, Bill, Exec VP-Product Dev, Engrg & Mktg - Axcelis Technologies, Inc.; *pg.* 1400, *pg.* 787
Bio, Frank, Dir-Sls Dev, Specialty Vehicle & Alternate Fuels - Volvo Trucks North America, Inc.; *pg.* 195, *pg.* 1377
Biondi, Rose, Exec Dir-Creative - The Estee Lauder Companies Inc.; *pg.* 508, *pg.* 1229
Biondo, John, Brand Mgr-Brand Analytics - Johnson & Johnson; *pg.* 1549, *pg.* 1091
Birch, Bernie, Mgr-Sls-Asia Pacific - Reliv International, Inc.; *pg.* 1589, *pg.* 975
Birch, Mike, Product Mgr - Tubular Steel Inc.; *pg.* 117, *pg.* 1004
Birch, Peter, Product Mgr - Google Inc.; *pg.* 1249, *pg.* 153
Birch, Steve, Dir-Mktg - CareFusion Corporation; *pg.* 1513, *pg.* 201
Birchall, Angus, Head-Vertical & Publr-Sls - Facebook, Inc.; *pg.* 1245, *pg.* 143
Birchby, Jennifer, Mgr-Creative - Merck & Co., Inc.; *pg.* 1566, *pg.* 1077
Birchell, Christy L., Asst VP-Mktg - Washington Trust Bancorp, Inc.; *pg.* 818, *pg.* 1610
Bircher, Steve, Dir-Sls & Mktg-GeoConsulting NALA - CGGVeritas Services (U.S.) Inc.; *pg.* 973, *pg.* 1703
Bird, Bonnie J., Analyst-Rels, Thought Leadership & Social Bus - CIBER, Inc.; *pg.* 372, *pg.* 330
Bird, Cameron, Mgr-Trade Mktg - Keurig Green Mountain, Inc.; *pg.* 868, *pg.* 1768
Bird, Esteban, Mgr-Sls & Trade Mktg for Latin America - Nintendo of America, Inc.; *pg.* 965, *pg.* 1829
Bird, Jim, Partner & Sr Mgr-Fin-Global - Ocean Spray Cranberries, Inc.; *pg.* 887, *pg.* 827
Bird, Jon, Mgr-Creative Svcs - American Airlines Inc.; *pg.* 1898, *pg.* 1693
Bird, Kristin, VP-Convenience Store Sls & Mktg - Tyson Foods, Inc.; *pg.* 902, *pg.* 35
Bird, Robert, VP-Mktg - ZYNEX, INC.; *pg.* 690, *pg.* 333
Birdsall, Maureen, Owner & Strategist-Creative Force & Social - Birdsall Interactive, Inc.; *pg.* 1231, *pg.* 120
Birenbaum, Liz, VP-Employer Brand Mktg - MasterCard Worldwide Inc.; *pg.* 780, *pg.* 988
Birk, Nick, Specialist-Mktg-Brdcst & AV Solutions - Belden, Inc.; *pg.* 624, *pg.* 993
Birkel, Marty, Pres-Sls - Constellation Brands, Inc.; *pg.* 1960, *pg.* 1348
Birkeland, Jacque, Specialist-Social Media - Dominion Enterprises; *pg.* 1636, *pg.* 1796
Birko, Laurie, Sr Product Mgr - Moen Incorporated; *pg.* 1056, *pg.* 1468
Birmingham, Courtney, Dir-Media Svcs & Creative - Foxwoods Resort Casino; *pg.* 549, *pg.* 353
Birnbaum, Scott K, Sr VP-Mktg & ECommerce - Aeropostale, Inc.; *pg.* 17, *pg.* 1188
Biroscak, Vincent, Dir-Mktg - Nestle Purina PetCare Company; *pg.* 1479, *pg.* 1000
Bischel, Laurie, Exec Dir-Corp Mktg & Comm - CME Group Inc.; *pg.* 738, *pg.* 571
Bischel, Laurie, Exec Dir-Corp Mktg & Comm - CME Group, Inc.; *pg.* 738, *pg.* 571
Bischof, Haley, Dir-Grp Mktg - Bonnier Corporation; *pg.* 1622, *pg.* 480
Bischoff, Donna, VP-Adv - St. Louis Post-Dispatch LLC; *pg.* 1688, *pg.* 1004
Bischoff, Maureen, Analyst-Mktg - Xerox Corporation; *pg.* 494, *pg.* 365
Biser, Krystyne, Dir-Global Product Dev - Revlon Consumer Products Corporation; *pg.* 521, *pg.* 1286
Bish, Brian, Product Mgr-Global - Milacron LLC; *pg.* 1361, *pg.* 1405
Bisha, Raymond, Dir-Media Rels-North America Radio & Press - Naxos of America Inc.; *pg.* 1779, *pg.* 1633
Bishara, Mike, Sr VP-Products & Gen Mgr-TV Everywhere - Synacor, Inc.; *pg.* 1283, *pg.* 1151
Bishop, Amanda, Product Mgr-Chrome - Google Inc.; *pg.* 1249, *pg.* 153
Bishop, Ann, Sr Mgr-Media Rels - J.C. Penney Company, Inc.; *pg.* 1774, *pg.* 1732
Bishop, Austin, Dir-Scrum Master-Digital Search Products - Marriott International, Inc.; *pg.* 1102, *pg.* 764
Bishop, Brett, Product Mgr - Hitachi Koki USA, Ltd.; *pg.* 1050, *pg.* 537
Bishop, Chris, Product Mgr-Converged Infrastructure - CDW Corporation; *pg.* 370, *pg.* 663
Bishop, Deana, VP-Retail Sls-Natl - Coca-Cola Refreshments USA, Inc.; *pg.* 247, *pg.* 500
Bishop, Graham, Mgr-Digital Mktg - ACNielsen Corporation; *pg.* 341, *pg.* 1187
Bishop, Jackie, Dir-Sls - Kao Brands Co. Inc.; *pg.* 513, *pg.* 1415
Bishop, Karen K., Sr Mgr-HR-Global Benefits - Cabot Corporation; *pg.* 1151, *pg.* 792
Bishop, Lisa, VP-Product Strategy - Gray Television, Inc.; *pg.* 289, *pg.* 509
Bishop, Rachel R., Chief Strategy Officer & Sr VP - TreeHouse Foods, Inc.; *pg.* 901, *pg.* 649
Bishop, Stephen, Mng Dir-Media Strategy & Plng - American Cancer Society, Inc.; *pg.* 126, *pg.* 487
Bishop, Wendy, Grp Product Mgr-Women's Health & Personal Care - Church & Dwight Co., Inc.; *pg.* 1153, *pg.* 1063
Bishop-Schoenheit, Ellen, Sr Dir-Mdsg - Office Depot, Inc.; *pg.* 448, *pg.* 412
Bisikirski, Pam, Dir-Mktg - National Vision, Inc.; *pg.* 1423, *pg.* 534
Bisio, Lauren, Mgr-Digital Mktg-Intl - Dunkin' Brands Group, Inc.; *pg.* 1727, *pg.* 810
Bisnette, Bridget, Sr Dir-Partner Mktg-Cisco Portfolio - Cisco Systems, Inc.; *pg.* 372, *pg.* 240
Bisogno, Keith, VP-Corp Mktg & Social Media - Thermo Fisher Scientific Inc.; *pg.* 1431, *pg.* 854
Bisoni, Chris, Sr Mgr-Loyalty Mktg - Sirius XM Holdings Inc.; *pg.* 308, *pg.* 1292
Bissani, Karen D., Sr Dir-Global Integrated Mktg & Comm - Cisco Systems, Inc.; *pg.* 372, *pg.* 240
Bisson, Thomas E., VP-Sls - General Cable Corporation; *pg.* 83, *pg.* 729
Bissu, Meredith, Dir-Consumer Mktg - Sesame Workshop; *pg.* 307, *pg.* 1290
Biswas, Tania, Sr Mgr-Branding & Product Mktg-Global - SanDisk Corporation; *pg.* 465, *pg.* 147
Bitel, Vince, VP-Creative Svcs - TechTarget, Inc.; *pg.* 482, *pg.* 837
Bitner, Livia, VP-Product Mgmt & Technical Svcs-Baker & Taylor - Baker & Taylor, Inc.; *pg.* 1619, *pg.* 1362
Bitonti, Stephanie, Brand Mgr-AXE - Unilever United States, Inc.; *pg.* 904, *pg.* 1061
Bittencourt, JP, Dir-Mktg Innovation - PepsiCo, Inc.; *pg.* 259, *pg.* 1327
Bitterman, Rhonda, Dir-Sls - Pandora Media Inc.; *pg.* 1273, *pg.* 172
Bittner, Brian, Brand Mgr-New Product - Zippo Manufacturing Company, Inc.; *pg.* 1895, *pg.* 1518
Bittner, Jane, Dir-Global Mktg Svcs Procurement - Merck & Co., Inc.; *pg.* 1566, *pg.* 1077
Biundo, Rosie, Sr Dir-Product Mktg - Equifax Inc.; *pg.* 748, *pg.* 504
Bixby, Chad, Mgr-Americas Sls - Caterpillar, Inc.; *pg.* 1321, *pg.* 650
Bixby, Christopher, Assoc Mgr-Mktg - General Mills, Inc.; *pg.* 828, *pg.* 933
Bixby, Dustin, Dir-Mktg & Promo - Atlanta Motor Speedway, Inc.; *pg.* 530, *pg.* 533
Bixby, Jill A., VP-Sls Western Area-Con-way Freight - XPO Logistics, Inc.; *pg.* 1931, *pg.* 350
Bixler, Jeff, Mgr-Digital Mktg - Georgia-Pacific LLC; *pg.* 1458, *pg.* 507
Bixler, Jordan, Mgr-Media-Global - Activision Blizzard, Inc.; *pg.* 948, *pg.* 271
Bizik, Lee, Sr Dir-Brand & Mktg Comm - Regis Corporation; *pg.* 521, *pg.* 941
Bizzack, Maryellen, Dir-Mktg & Comm-Global - Philips Respironics; *pg.* 1585, *pg.* 1555
Bjarnason, Joanne, VP-Mktg - Lafarge Canada Inc.; *pg.* 92, *pg.* 1958
Bjerke, Jennifer, Sr Mgr-ECommerce Production - Cost Plus World Market; *pg.* 921, *pg.* 170
Bjork, Ross, Mgr-Sls & Mktg-Hospitality - Sonifi Solutions; *pg.* 1281, *pg.* 1625
Bjorklund, Roger, VP-Mktg - Leatherman Tool Group, Inc.; *pg.* 1053, *pg.* 1504
Bjorklund, Travis, Mgr-Solutions Mktg - RACKSPACE HOSTING, INC.; *pg.* 1277, *pg.* 1742
Blaakman, Timothy, Program Mgr-Technical Product Support-LOB - Xerox Corporation; *pg.* 494, *pg.* 365
Blache, Patrick, Sr Dir-IT - John Q. Hammons Hotels Inc.; *pg.* 1099, *pg.* 1006
Black, Alissa M., Mgr-Mktg Comm - Diebold, Incorporated; *pg.* 387, *pg.* 1407
Black, Brett, Dir-Mktg-Diabetes Bus Unit - Eli Lilly and Company; *pg.* 1527, *pg.* 684
Black, Camille, Dir-Mktg - Les Trois Petits Cochons, Inc.; *pg.* 874, *pg.* 1146
Black, Chris, Div VP-Media Svcs - Sears Holdings Corporation; *pg.* 1784, *pg.* 618
Black, Donald, VP-Mktg-Barron's - Dow Jones & Company, Inc.; *pg.* 1637, *pg.* 1225
Black, Drew, Mgr-Product Line-Batting Gloves & Protective - Wilson Sporting Goods Co.; *pg.* 1848, *pg.* 596
Black, Eddie, Sr Mgr-Bus Dev - Amazon.com, Inc.; *pg.* 1226, *pg.* 1831
Black, Hang, Mgr-Sls Enablement - Cisco Systems, Inc.; *pg.* 372, *pg.* 240
Black, Jay, VP-Brand Mktg-Global - Maui Jim, Inc.; *pg.* 9, *pg.* 651
Black, Jennifer, Jr Brand Mgr - Tweezerman International; *pg.* 524, *pg.* 1324
Black, Jessica, Dir-Partnerships Mktg - NBC Universal, Inc.; *pg.* 300, *pg.* 1266
Black, Kaitlyn, Sr Coord-Digital Mktg - rue21, inc.; *pg.* 32, *pg.* 1591
Black, Keith, Product Mgr-Managed Care Mktg - Abbott Diabetes Care, Inc.; *pg.* 1483, *pg.* 38
Black, Ken, Sr Dir-Category & Creative - NIKE, Inc.; *pg.* 1812, *pg.* 1492
Black, Kimberly, Dir-Mktg - Manulife Financial Corporation; *pg.* 778, *pg.* 1939
Black, Lisa, Assoc Client Svcs Mgr-Mktg - Ingram Micro Inc.; *pg.* 415, *pg.* 261
Black, Lucas, Sr Dir-Adv Sys Product Mgmt - AOL Inc.; *pg.* 1229, *pg.* 1195
Black, Marian, Sr Mgr-Procurement Ops - The Boeing Company; *pg.* 225, *pg.* 567
Black, Marnie, Exec VP-PR - AMC Networks Inc.; *pg.* 269, *pg.* 1189
Black, Reid, Dir-Mktg-Toronto Maple Leafs & Toronto Marlies - Maple Leaf Sports & Entertainment Ltd.; *pg.* 560, *pg.* 1940
Black, Richard, Dir-Mktg - Acer America Corporation; *pg.* 341, *pg.* 235
Black, Richard, Exec Dir-Health Sys Mktg - Astellas Pharma US, Inc.; *pg.* 1496, *pg.* 640
Black, Robin Spinelli, Sr Dir-HR - The BLUE Buffalo Co.; *pg.* 1474, *pg.* 385
Black, Sean, Specialist-Digital Mktg - W.F. Young, Inc.; *pg.* 1610, *pg.* 817
Black, Steve, Dir-Mktg - Smead Manufacturing Company; *pg.* 470, *pg.* 926
Black, Tasha, Sr Mgr-Mktg - The Andersons Incorporated; *pg.* 1793, *pg.* 1461
Blackburn, Hilary J., Sr VP-Product Dev & ECommerce - Cardinal Bank N.A.; *pg.* 732, *pg.* 1790
Blackburn, Mitchell, Engr-Technical Mktg - NetApp, Inc.; *pg.* 444, *pg.* 287
Blackburn, Robert, VP-Sls-US Cloud & Content Verticals - Equinix, Inc.; *pg.* 394, *pg.* 190
Blacker, Courtney, Dir-Brand Mktg - The North Face, Inc.; *pg.* 1840, *pg.* 252
Blacker, Kevin, Asst Dir-Mktg - Knouse Foods Cooperative Inc.; *pg.* 869, *pg.* 1558
Blacker, Peter, Exec VP-Digital Media & Emerging Businesses - NBC Universal, Inc.; *pg.* 300, *pg.* 1266
Blacker, Peter, Exec VP-Digital Media & Emerging Businesses - Telemundo Network Inc.; *pg.* 311, *pg.* 430
Blackett, David M., VP-Mktg - PerkinElmer, Inc.; *pg.* 1426, *pg.* 853
Blackett, Jason, Sr Product Mgr - Novell Inc.; *pg.* 446, *pg.* 852
Blackey, Jeff, Sr VP-Mktg - Broadview Networks, Inc.; *pg.* 365, *pg.* 1339
Blackford, Scott, Sr VP-Sls & Mktg - TODCO, Inc.; *pg.* 115, *pg.* 1459
Blackledge, John, Sr Analyst-Equity Res Internet & New Media - Cowen Group, Inc.; *pg.* 742, *pg.* 1219
Blackman, Don, VP-Mktg & Domestic Sls-ASCO Power Technologies - Emerson Network Power; *pg.* 1071, *pg.* 1479
Blackmar, Angie, Sr Producer-Content Mktg - Aflac Incorporated; *pg.* 1188, *pg.* 527
Blackmon, Ashley, Sr Analyst-Mktg-Lipton Iced Tea - PepsiCo, Inc.; *pg.* 259, *pg.* 1327
Blackmon, Ashley, Sr Dir-Mktg, Online & Mobile Mktg - Zillow Group, Inc.; *pg.* 1292, *pg.* 1843
Blackmur, Branden, Dir-Mktg - Caesars Entertainment Corporation; *pg.* 1083, *pg.* 1023
Blackstock, Hayley, Specialist-Mktg-Global - Crocs, Inc.; *pg.*

1806, pg. 335
Blackwelder, Kimry, Sr Dir-PR - Cole-Haan LLC; pg. 1806, pg. 1034
Blackwell, Aaron, Specialist-Adv Ops - Media General, Inc.; pg. 297, pg. 1803
Blackwell, Al, Sr Mgr-New Hire Training Customer Support - Match.Com, LLC; pg. 1265, pg. 1683
Blackwell, Carl, CMO & Sr VP-Mktg & Comm - National Marine Manufacturers Association; pg. 149, pg. 584
Blackwell, Kathryn, VP-Comm & Mktg-NAFTA Reg - Continental Tire North America, Inc.; pg. 1880, pg. 1615
Blackwell, Morrice, Mgr-New Product Sls & Market Dev - Badger Meter, Inc.; pg. 1401, pg. 1873
Blackwell, Peter, Dir-Mktg - Volkswagen Canada, Inc.; pg. 194, pg. 1918
Blackwood, Cheryl, Plant Mgr-Specialty Products-NAFTA - Osram Sylvania, Inc.; pg. 1302, pg. 816
Blackwood, Eric, Dir-Mktg - Dr Pepper Snapple Group, Inc.; pg. 250, pg. 1729
Blackwood-Wicker, Gina, Dir-Design & Creative - Glen Raven, Inc.; pg. 693, pg. 1373
Blades, Joseph, Specialist-Digital Mktg - Boyd Gaming Corporation; pg. 1082, pg. 1022
Blagg, Larry, Sr VP-Mktg - California Raisin Marketing Board; pg. 1017, pg. 93
Blaha, Diane J., Sr VP-Sls & Acct Mgmt - CorVel Corporation; pg. 1198, pg. 109
Blaicher, Jon, Product Mgr - Yamaha Motor Canada Ltd.; pg. 1712, pg. 1947
Blaido, Jeremy, Sr Dir-Mktg Comm - CEC Entertainment, Inc.; pg. 1721, pg. 1717
Blaine, Melissa, Program Mgr-Acct-Based Mktg-Americas - Texas Instruments Incorporated; pg. 679, pg. 1688
Blaine, Scott, Reg Mgr-Sls-West - Cooper Interconnect; pg. 630, pg. 1118
Blair, Alyssa, VP-Regions Corp Mktg - Regions Financial Corporation; pg. 798, pg. 4
Blair, Brittany, Product Mgr-Respiratory Consumer Mktg - GlaxoSmithKline; pg. 1536, pg. 1389
Blair, Brooke, Sr Mgr-Medical Education - LifeCell Corporation; pg. 1556, pg. 1045
Blair, Catherine B., VP-Mdsg & Design - Sport Haley, Inc.; pg. 33, pg. 333
Blair, Kirsten, Mgr-Global Brand Mktg Ops-Nike Women - NIKE, Inc.; pg. 1812, pg. 1492
Blair, Laurie, Sr Mgr-Strategy & Program Dev - Walgreen Co.; pg. 1608, pg. 605
Blair, Melanie, Reg Mgr-Mktg-West Coast-Restaurant - Kimpton Hotel & Restaurant Group; pg. 1099, pg. 220
Blair, Misty, Mgr-Sls & Mktg - D.R. Horton, Inc.; pg. 1090, pg. 1694
Blair, Nathan, Mgr-Search Mktg - 1-800 CONTACTS, INC.; pg. 1758, pg. 1753
Blair, Timothy, Corp VP-Mktg & Comm - Huron Consulting Group Inc.; pg. 768, pg. 577
Blair, Wayne, Mgr-Parts Sls - Harsco Rail; pg. 1345, pg. 1623
Blair-Smith, Bob, Sr Mgr-Sls Engrg - T-Mobile US, Inc.; pg. 676, pg. 1816
Blais, Michael, Head-Global Display Mktg - eBay Inc.; pg. 1240, pg. 243
Blais, Richard, VP & Mgr-Sls-Natl - Waters Corporation; pg. 1436, pg. 834
Blaisdell, Andrew, Product Mktg Mgr-Cisco Tidal Enterprise Scheduler - Cisco Systems, Inc.; pg. 372, pg. 240
Blaisdell, Emily, Brand Mgr - Ameriprise Financial, Inc.; pg. 715, pg. 930
Blaise, Kristy, Sr Dir-Channel Mktg - Comcast Cable Communications, Inc.; pg. 276, pg. 1560
Blaize, Madeline, Brand Mgr - Parfums De Coeur Ltd.; pg. 519, pg. 376
Blake, Abby, Mgr-Mktg-Subscriber Retention - Birchbox; pg. 1762, pg. 1203
Blake, Abigail, Specialist-Social Media Mktg - Live Nation Entertainment, Inc.; pg. 558, pg. 47
Blake, Brady R., Sr Mgr-Customer Mktg & Head-Acct-Walmart.com - Electronic Arts Inc.; pg. 951, pg. 189
Blake, Derek, VP-Partnership Mktg & Military Programs - La Quinta Corporation; pg. 1099, pg. 1722
Blake, Derek, VP-Partnership Mktg & Military Programs - La Quinta Inns, Inc.; pg. 1100, pg. 1722
Blake, Jason, Sr Assoc Mgr-Mktg - HP Hood LLC; pg. 864, pg. 829
Blake, Jeff, Chm-Mktg & Distr-Worldwide & Vice Chm-Sony Pictures Entertainment - Sony Pictures Entertainment Inc.; pg. 309, pg. 72
Blake, Judy, Dir-PR & Mktg Comm - Hughes Network Systems LLC; pg. 643, pg. 770
Blake, Michael, Exec VP-Secondary Mktg - Fairway Independent Mortgage Corporation; pg. 750, pg. 1866
Blake, Monica, Mgr-Digital Brand Mktg-Luxury & Lifestyle Brands - Hilton Worldwide, Inc.; pg. 1094, pg. 1791
Blake, Natalie, Gen Mgr-Mktg-Global - Nalco Co.; pg. 1174, pg. 636
Blake, Ron, Dir-Mktg Programs - The Scotts Miracle-Gro Company; pg. 1799, pg. 1459
Blake, Terri L., Mgr-Indus Mktg - Intel Corporation; pg. 645, pg. 266
Blakely, Eric, Dir-Adv - Edelbrock Corporation; pg. 204, pg. 293
Blakely, Reginald, Sr Mgr-Product Dev - Monitronics International, Inc.; pg. 656, pg. 1684
Blakely, Shannon, Brand Mgr-Whirlpool Brand - Whirlpool Corporation; pg. 62, pg. 872
Blakeman, Molly, Sr Mgr-Media Rel-Natl - Wal-Mart.com; pg. 1287, pg. 50
Blakeman, Richard, Mng Dir-Channel Sls Center of Excellence - Miller Heiman Inc.; pg. 440, pg. 1031
Blakemore, Mark, Sr Dir-Product Dev - Coventry Health Care, Inc.; pg. 1519, pg. 761
Blaker, Spencer, Dir-Retail Mktg-Global - Burt's Bees Inc.; pg. 502, pg. 1370
Blakesley, Ben, Sr Mgr-Social Media-Global - Reebok International Ltd.; pg. 1817, pg. 811
Blakley, Amy, Sr Mgr-Comm-Guaranteed Cost Ops - The Travelers Companies, Inc.; pg. 1220, pg. 352
Blakley, Suzi, Mgr-Social Media - Sterling Jewelers Inc.; pg. 13, pg. 1402
Blalock, Amy, Specialist-Customer Rels & Social Media - Bloomin' Brands, Inc.; pg. 1716, pg. 471
Blalock, Kevin, Sr Mgr-Mktg - Medtronic, Inc.; pg. 1564, pg. 939
Blalock, Paul, VP-Sls - IRONPLANET, INC.; pg. 1259, pg. 183
Blanc, Eric L., VP-Mktg-Deli & Convenience Store - Tyson Foods, Inc.; pg. 902, pg. 35
Blanc, Rob, Mng Dir-US Mktg - Pfizer Inc.; pg. 1581, pg. 1278
Blancarte, Denisse Gomez, Sr Analyst-Digital Mktg - Rooms To Go.com, Inc.; pg. 941, pg. 468
Blanchard, Amy, Mgr-Mktg - Cisco Systems, Inc.; pg. 372, pg. 240
Blanchard, Becky, Dir-Ram Brand Mktg - FCA US LLC; pg. 170, pg. 868
Blanchard, Brent, Sr Dir-Worldwide Channel Sls - Link Snacks, Inc.; pg. 874, pg. 1881
Blanchard, Lawrence E., Grp VP-Sls & Mktg-Secure Benefits Solution Div - Security Mutual Life Insurance Company of New York; pg. 1216, pg. 1142
Blanchard, Tammy, Mgr-Online Mktg - The Tire Rack Inc.; pg. 1890, pg. 697
Blanchette, Kevin, Dir-Consumer Mktg - Home Box Office, Inc.; pg. 290, pg. 1240
Blanchfield, Leann, VP-Product Dev - Truven Health Analytics; pg. 486, pg. 331
Blanck, Kasey, Sr Mgr-Content Mktg & New Product Dev - Kelly Services, Inc.; pg. 424, pg. 911
Blanco, Allister, Dir-Interactive Mktg - Orkin, Inc.; pg. 1798, pg. 517
Blanco, Amanda Lechner, VP-Mktg - Sidney Frank Importing Co., Inc.; pg. 1970, pg. 1184
Blanco, Jessica, Mgr-Mktg - Gartner, Inc.; pg. 1248, pg. 374
Blanco, Susan, Sr Mgr-Events - Kansas City Convention & Visitors Association; pg. 996, pg. 984
Bland, Shawnda, Sr Mgr-Mktg Campaign - Intuit Inc.; pg. 769, pg. 158
Blandford, Jameson, Mgr-Technical Mktg - Cisco Systems, Inc.; pg. 372, pg. 240
Blandford, Jayne, Brand Mgr-Partnership - Amazon.com, Inc.; pg. 1226, pg. 1831
Blandina, Gerard, Dir-Sls-Eastern Zone - Lightolier; pg. 1301, pg. 819
Blando, Holly, Coord-Online Mktg - Vail Resorts, Inc.; pg. 1117, pg. 313
Blandon, Josecarlos, Dir-Media-Intl - Paramount Pictures Corporation; pg. 304, pg. 138
Blaney, Lori A., VP-Natl Acct Sls-Con-way Freight - XPO Logistics, Inc.; pg. 1931, pg. 350
Blanford, Whitney, Analyst-Mktg - A&W All-American Food Restaurants, Inc.; pg. 1714, pg. 731
Blangiardi, Barbara, Sr VP-Strategies & Creative Partnerships - Fox Sports Net; pg. 288, pg. 131
Blank, Diana, Mgr-Web Mktg - Autodesk Inc.; pg. 356, pg. 257
Blank, Jason, Reg Sls Mgr-West Software Practice - CDW Corporation; pg. 370, pg. 663
Blank, Joel, Dir-Brdcst & Production - Houston Rockets; pg. 552, pg. 1707
Blank, Jonathan, Dir-Relationship Mktg - Dice.com; pg. 1238, pg. 712
Blank, Karen, Brand Mgr-Specialty Select - Starwood Hotels & Resorts Worldwide, Inc.; pg. 1114, pg. 378
Blank, Thomas, VP-Sls & Mktg - Wahl Clipper Corporation; pg. 524, pg. 662
Blanke, Ranae, Dir-Social Media - Hobby Lobby Stores Inc.; pg. 927, pg. 1486
Blankenship, Mark, Chief Strategy Officer, Chief People Officer & Exec VP - Jack in the Box Inc.; pg. 1732, pg. 204
Blankenship, Mike, Mgr-Local Mktg - Universal Technical Institute, Inc.; pg. 608, pg. 24
Blankman, Alan, Mgr-Technical Product Mktg-Signal Integrity - Teledyne LeCroy; pg. 1431, pg. 1153
Blanks, Belinda, VP-Mktg & Partner Dev - MasterCard Worldwide Inc.; pg. 780, pg. 988
Blanks, Marcus, Brand Mgr-Global Digital Bus Strategy - The Procter & Gamble Company; pg. 1129, pg. 1418
Blanksma, Katie, Copywriter-Product - Nordstrom, Inc.; pg. 1779, pg. 1837
Blanton, J. Scott, VP-Brand Creative - PETCO Animal Supplies, Inc.; pg. 1480, pg. 206
Blanton, Rocky J., VP-Sls & Svcs - Teradata Corporation; pg. 483, pg. 1447
Blas, Alexander, Exec-Inside Sls - Ingram Micro Mobility; pg. 415, pg. 697
Blaser, Brian J., Exec VP-Diagnostics Products - Abbott Laboratories; pg. 1484, pg. 551
Blaser, David, Dir-Digital Mktg - Activision Blizzard, Inc.; pg. 948, pg. 271
Blaser, Mary, Dir-Mktg & Bus Dev-Frommelt & Zoneworks Products - Rite-Hite Holding Corporation; pg. 1372, pg. 1880
Blashford, Lynn, Dir-Mktg - White Castle Management Co.; pg. 1756, pg. 1444
Blasi, Sarah, Dir-Mktg - A&W All-American Food Restaurants, Inc.; pg. 1714, pg. 731
Blaszkowski, Dave, Dir-Grp Sls & Mktg - Tribune Media Company; pg. 1696, pg. 592
Blatcher, Richard, Sr Mgr-Global Indus Mktg & Mfg - Autodesk Inc.; pg. 356, pg. 257
Blatchford, Nick, Dir-Sports Mktg - Under Armour, Inc.; pg. 49, pg. 759
Blattner, Randy, Sr VP-Digital Banking & Enterprise Architecture & Sr Dir - BOK Financial Corporation; pg. 726, pg. 1489
Blau, Andy, Sr VP-Fin & Adv - Time Inc.; pg. 1693, pg. 1300
Blaug, Suzanne, Sr VP-Mktg & Comml Dev-Global - Amgen Inc.; pg. 1493, pg. 291
Blauner, Earl, Sr Dir-Gift Plng & Endowment - KQED Inc.; pg. 294, pg. 220
Blauvelt, Katrina, Sr Dir-Assoc Comm - The Home Depot, Inc.; pg. 1050, pg. 510
Blecherman, Neil, Dir-IoT Solutions Product Mgmt-Global - Intel Corporation; pg. 645, pg. 266
Blechle, Kristin, Specialist-Digital Mktg-O'Reilly Auto Parts - O'Reilly Automotive, Inc.; pg. 214, pg. 1006
Blechman, Charlotte, Exec VP-Mktg & Comm - Barneys New York, Inc.; pg. 38, pg. 1201
Blechman, Joe, Sr Mgr-Res-Consumer Analytics & Res - AOL Inc.; pg. 1229, pg. 1195
Blechman, Michelle, Assoc Dir-Mktg Sciences - Astellas Pharma US, Inc.; pg. 1496, pg. 640
Blechman, Nicholas, Creative Dir - The New Yorker Magazine, Inc.; pg. 1669, pg. 1271
Bleecher, Grant, Mgr-Mktg-Global Beverage Innovation - PepsiCo, Inc.; pg. 259, pg. 1327
Bleedorn, Gina, Exec Brand Dir - NewGround Resources; pg. 99, pg. 975
Bleile, Carolyn T.B., VP-Mdse & Home Furnishings - Flexsteel Industries, Inc.; pg. 925, pg. 707
Blevens, Chuck, Sr Mgr-Global Product Mktg-Xbox-Interactive Entertainment Bus - Microsoft Corporation; pg. 435, pg. 1824
Blewett, Troy, Dir-Dealer Channel Mktg - Briggs & Stratton Corporation; pg. 201, pg. 1899
Blichasz, Lori, Analyst-Digital Mktg & Content - Subaru of America, Inc.; pg. 191, pg. 1050
Blichfeld, Anne, Assoc Mgr-Mktg - Banana Republic; pg.

1760, *pg.* 212
Blick-White, Katie, Brand Mgr - Cargill, Inc.; *pg.* 845, *pg.* 965
Blick-White, Katie, Brand Mgr - Cargill Meat Solutions; *pg.* 846, *pg.* 722
Blicker, Stacey, Sr Dir-Inventory Mgmt, Plng & Production - VITACOST.COM, INC.; *pg.* 1607, *pg.* 414
Bliese, Faye, Head-Integrated Mktg Comm-Winfield Solutions - Land O'Lakes, Inc.; *pg.* 873, *pg.* 915
Bliss, Jason, Dir-Sls - Kind LLC; *pg.* 868, *pg.* 1249
Bliss, Jude, Mgr-Mktg Svcs - Winegard Company; *pg.* 688, *pg.* 702
Blissenbach, Nick, Sr Mgr-Mktg-Integrated Media - American Dairy Queen Corporation; *pg.* 1714, *pg.* 930
Blissenbach, Nick, Sr Mgr-Mktg-Integrated Media - Dairy Queen Corporate Store; *pg.* 1724, *pg.* 932
Blissenbach, Nick, Sr Mgr-Mktg-Integrated Media - International Dairy Queen, Inc.; *pg.* 1732, *pg.* 938
Blitz, Erica, Mgr-Mktg Project-Sundance TV - AMC Networks Inc.; *pg.* 269, *pg.* 1189
Blizzard, Jerry, Dir-Classified & Online Sls - Carroll County Times; *pg.* 1626, *pg.* 780
Bloch, Carrie, Mgr-Product Mktg-Economic Graph - LinkedIn Corporation; *pg.* 1262, *pg.* 160
Bloch, Heather, Mgr-Creative-Photography - Toys "R" Us, Inc.; *pg.* 968, *pg.* 1130
Bloch, Laurel, Mgr-Mktg Comm - Milton Roy Company; *pg.* 1361, *pg.* 1542
Bloch, Stephanie, Brand Mgr - Hormel Foods Corporation; *pg.* 863, *pg.* 915
Bloch, Stephanie, Brand Mgr - Hormel Foods Corporation - Foodservice Division; *pg.* 864, *pg.* 916
Block, Andrew, Dir-Strategic Mktg & Product Mktg - Flextronics International Ltd.; *pg.* 81, *pg.* 245
Block, Avery, Mgr-HR Social Mktg & Engagement - Taco Bell Corp.; *pg.* 1752, *pg.* 117
Block, Diana, VP-New Build Projects - Royal Caribbean Cruises Ltd; *pg.* 1921, *pg.* 446
Block, Linda, Dir-Mktg-Animal Health - Merck Animal Health; *pg.* 1478, *pg.* 1124
Block, Linda, Dir-Mktg - Zoetis Inc.; *pg.* 1611, *pg.* 1067
Block, Randolph, VP-Sls & Mktg - Screw Conveyor Industries; *pg.* 1374, *pg.* 682
Block, Suzanne, Mgr-Production - Famous Dave's of America, Inc.; *pg.* 1728, *pg.* 926
Blocker, Adrian, Sr VP-Wood Products - Weyerhaeuser Company; *pg.* 121, *pg.* 1820
Blocker, Larry, Sr Dir-Game Presentation & Events - Florida Marlins, L.P.; *pg.* 548, *pg.* 442
Blockey, Clea, Dir-Solution Mktg-SMB - Concur Technologies, Inc.; *pg.* 1236, *pg.* 1813
Blodgett, Carolyn, Brand Mgr - PepsiCo, Inc.; *pg.* 259, *pg.* 1327
Blodgett, Katherine, VP-Comm & PR - The Philadelphia Orchestra Association; *pg.* 575, *pg.* 1569
Blodgett, Lindsey, Sr Assoc Brand Mgr - Mars, Incorporated; *pg.* 1858, *pg.* 1792
Bloedel, Theresa, Mgr-Interactive Mktg - Ameriprise Financial, Inc.; *pg.* 715, *pg.* 930
Bloemendaal, Bevan, VP-Global Environments & Creative Svcs - The Timberland Company; *pg.* 1821, *pg.* 1039
Bloemendaal, Marco, Sr VP-Sls - Greater Milwaukee Convention & Visitors Bureau; *pg.* 993, *pg.* 1874
Blofield, Julie, Mgr-Mktg Svcs - Marvin Windows & Doors; *pg.* 934, *pg.* 965
Blokzijl, Berend, Dir-Sls-Video & Data EMEA - International Datacasting Corporation; *pg.* 419, *pg.* 1921
Blom, Sandy, Assoc Mgr-Product Mktg - Pella Corporation; *pg.* 104, *pg.* 711
Blomberg, Jeffrey, Sr Dir-Global Labs & Product Svcs - Hitachi Data Systems Corporation; *pg.* 407, *pg.* 265
Blomquist, Jeff, Product Mgr - 3M Company; *pg.* 1142, *pg.* 956
Blomquist, Rick, Pres-Consumer Branded Products - Central Garden & Pet Company; *pg.* 1475, *pg.* 303
Blomseth, Rich, Product Dir-Mgmt - Echelon Corporation; *pg.* 389, *pg.* 245
Blomstrom, Marissa, Brand Category Mktg Mgr-Owned Brands - Target Corporation; *pg.* 1786, *pg.* 942
Blondin, Laurie, Sr Mgr-Mktg - Avid Technology, Inc.; *pg.* 622, *pg.* 804
Blood, Christina, Mgr-Mktg - Anna's Linen Company Inc.; *pg.* 1760, *pg.* 70
Bloodsaw, Daryl G., Dir-Adv - The New York Times; *pg.* 1668, *pg.* 1270
Bloodworth, Russell, Mgr-Mktg-Walmart Radio - Wal-Mart Stores, Inc.; *pg.* 1790, *pg.* 29
Bloom, Allison Miles, Sr Copywriter & Sr Specialist-Mktg Comm - Cigna Corporation; *pg.* 1197, *pg.* 338
Bloom, Amanda, Sr Product Mgr - NuVasive, Inc.; *pg.* 1577, *pg.* 205
Bloom, Joan, Exec VP-Mktg & Product Mgmt - FMR LLC (Fidelity Investments); *pg.* 759, *pg.* 794
Bloom, Joe, Product Mgr - GovDelivery, Inc.; *pg.* 1255, *pg.* 961
Bloom, Steve, Pres-Enterprise Fleet Mgmt & Sr VP-Car Sls - Enterprise Holdings, Inc.; *pg.* 1906, *pg.* 996
Bloomfield, Nathalie, Dir-Mktg & Comm-Global - Raytheon Company; *pg.* 233, *pg.* 854
Bloomquist, Annie, Chief Product Officer & Sr VP - Select Comfort Corporation; *pg.* 942, *pg.* 942
Bloomquist, Leilani, Mgr-Mktg & Digital Experience - Capella Education Company; *pg.* 599, *pg.* 931
Bloor, Joanna, VP-Sls Ops - Pandora Media Inc.; *pg.* 1273, *pg.* 172
Blosil, Jason, Sr Mgr-Product Mktg & Core Software - NetApp, Inc.; *pg.* 444, *pg.* 287
Blough, Gary R., Exec VP-Sls-Worldwide - Interactive Intelligence, Inc.; *pg.* 417, *pg.* 687
Blough, Matthew, Coord-Digital Mktg-Digital Center of Excellence - Johnson & Johnson; *pg.* 1549, *pg.* 1091
Blount, Jerry, Product Mgr-Consumer Platforms - Gannett Co., Inc.; *pg.* 1643, *pg.* 1790
Blount, Jesse, Div VP-Mktg - Beall's, Inc.; *pg.* 1760, *pg.* 414
Blount, Karen, Mgr-Creative Svcs - Kaba Ilco Corp.; *pg.* 1052, *pg.* 1390
Blount, Katie, Mgr-Sls Ops & Plng - Beckman Coulter, Inc.; *pg.* 1402, *pg.* 48
Blount, Terry, VP-PR & Comm - National Hot Rod Association; *pg.* 149, *pg.* 99
Blouse, Gretchen, Media Buyer-Print - Beall's, Inc.; *pg.* 1760, *pg.* 414
Blozis, Steve, Mgr-Product Mktg-Intl - NXP Semiconductors; *pg.* 660, *pg.* 248
Blue, Allen, VP-Product Mgmt - LinkedIn Corporation; *pg.* 1262, *pg.* 160
Blue, Bruce, Mgr-Mktg - The Procter & Gamble Company; *pg.* 1129, *pg.* 1418
Blue, Dave, VP-Sls & Mktg-Americas - Cubic Transportation Systems, Inc.; *pg.* 1905, *pg.* 202
Blue, Vicky, Mgr-Integrated Mktg - Del Monte Foods, Inc.; *pg.* 852, *pg.* 304
Bluemer Gearhart, Kristie, Mgr-Mktg - Maui Jim, Inc.; *pg.* 9, *pg.* 651
Bluestone, Derek, Sr Dir-Product Mgmt-Sungard Availability Svcs - SunGard Data Systems Inc.; *pg.* 477, *pg.* 1592
Blum, Phil, Sr Mgr-Social Media Customer Care - Time Warner Cable Inc.; *pg.* 312, *pg.* 1301
Blum, Steve, Sr VP-Sls & Svcs-Worldwide - Autodesk Inc.; *pg.* 356, *pg.* 257
Blum, Wayne G., Dir-Digital Mktg & ECommerce - Nestle USA, Inc.; *pg.* 883, *pg.* 96
Blumberg, Andy, Mgr-Adv & Strategic Mktg - The Johns Hopkins University; *pg.* 603, *pg.* 757
Blumberg, David, Dir-PR - TransUnion Corp.; *pg.* 811, *pg.* 591
Blumberg, Jim, Dir-Integrated Mktg - The WhiteWave Foods Company; *pg.* 1037, *pg.* 324
Blumberg, Roger, VP-Sourcing Product Mgmt & Ops - Elemica, Inc.; *pg.* 1242, *pg.* 1591
Blumenstein, Howard, Product Mktg Mgr-Strategy & Insights, YouTube - Google Inc.; *pg.* 1249, *pg.* 153
Blumenthal, David, Sr Dir-Corp Comm - The Weather Channel LLC; *pg.* 320, *pg.* 523
Blumenthal, Philip, Dir-Mktg Strategy & Analysis - Blackboard Inc.; *pg.* 1232, *pg.* 396
Blumenthal, Toby, Mgr-Facility Sls - Baltimore Symphony Orchestra; *pg.* 532, *pg.* 755
Blumer, Mallory, Specialist-Integrated Mktg - Ennis, Inc.; *pg.* 393, *pg.* 1727
Blumer, Stefan, Sr Dir-Tech - Thomson Reuters Corporation; *pg.* 1693, *pg.* 1944
Blumer, Stefan, Sr Dir-Tech - Truven Health Analytics; *pg.* 486, *pg.* 331
Blundell, Angus, Dir-Mktg-EMEA - Sun Chemical Ink; *pg.* 1182, *pg.* 643
Blundell, Bethany, Sr Mgr-Domestic Channel Mktg - Nautica Apparel, Inc.; *pg.* 45, *pg.* 1265
Blunt, Michael, Mgr-Retail Mktg-Global - Diageo North America, Inc.; *pg.* 1961, *pg.* 361
Blunt, Robin, Sr VP-Retailer Mktg - Simon Property Group, Inc.; *pg.* 1112, *pg.* 690
Bluth, Justin, Dir-Mktg - Newell Rubbermaid Inc.; *pg.* 1128, *pg.* 515
Bluth, Meg, Dir-Knowledge & Insights-Media Insights - The Coca-Cola Company; *pg.* 240, *pg.* 493
Bluth, Thomas J., VP-Mining Products Div - Caterpillar, Inc.; *pg.* 1321, *pg.* 650
Bluvstein, Jake, Specialist-Partnership Mktg - DSW, Inc.; *pg.* 1807, *pg.* 1439
Blythe, Shayne, Dir-Sls & Mktg Logistics - Retractable Technologies Inc.; *pg.* 1590, *pg.* 1725
Boags, Erica, Mgr-Interactive Mktg Strategy - Raymond James Financial, Inc.; *pg.* 798, *pg.* 464
Boan, John C., VP-Mktg - KEMET Corporation; *pg.* 649, *pg.* 1621
Boardman, David, Dean-School of Media & Comm - Temple University Health System; *pg.* 1601, *pg.* 1571
Boardman, Melody, Rep-Mktg - Pacific Life Insurance Company; *pg.* 1213, *pg.* 166
Boas, Wesley, Dir-Mktg-Knorr North America - Unilever United States, Inc.; *pg.* 904, *pg.* 1061
Boath, Kimberley, Dir-Adv - The Record-Journal Publishing Company; *pg.* 1680, *pg.* 354
Boatner, Bryan, Dir-Product Mktg - Cognex Corporation; *pg.* 1406, *pg.* 834
Boatright, Rex, Dir-Creative Svcs - Valassis Communications, Inc.; *pg.* 1287, *pg.* 897
Boaz, Amy, Mgr-ECommerce Mktg-North America - Lenovo Group Ltd; *pg.* 427, *pg.* 1384
Boban, Viola, Mgr-Sls-Eastern Europe-Perfecseal - Bemis Healthcare Packaging; *pg.* 1453, *pg.* 1885
Bobb, Jason, VP-Global Sls-East - CenturyLink, Inc.; *pg.* 1870, *pg.* 746
Bobb-Semple, Lisa, Mgr-Mktg Svcs - United States Postal Service; *pg.* 1009, *pg.* 406
Bobba, Durga P., Head-Global Mktg-Cardiovascular & Metabolic Franchises - Amgen Inc.; *pg.* 1493, *pg.* 291
Bobbett, Dena, Product Mgr-Neurology & Emergency Dept & CT Mktg - Siemens Healthcare Diagnostics; *pg.* 673, *pg.* 604
Bober, Andrew, Dir-Customer Intelligence Product Mgmt - SAS Institute Inc.; *pg.* 466, *pg.* 1361
Bobkowski, Peter, Sr Dir-Internal Audit - Esterline Technologies Corporation; *pg.* 1412, *pg.* 1814
Bobowski, Sharon, Dir-Mktg-Print Production - Office Depot, Inc.; *pg.* 448, *pg.* 412
Bobrik, Laura, Sr Mgr-Risk Assurance Mktg - PricewaterhouseCoopers LLP; *pg.* 795, *pg.* 1283
Bobroff, Stacy, Sr Mgr-Mktg - American Express Company; *pg.* 712, *pg.* 1190
Bobst, Al, Sr Rep-Sls, Technical & Specialty Papers - Monadnock Paper Mills, Inc.; *pg.* 1464, *pg.* 1033
Bocchi, Mark, Mng Dir-Sls & Community Mktg - Alaska Airlines, Inc.; *pg.* 1897, *pg.* 1830
Bocciarelli, Lorenzo, Mgr-Sls - Kitchen-Quip, Inc.; *pg.* 1885, *pg.* 699
Bochand, Benjamin, Product Mgr-Global - Molex Incorporated; *pg.* 655, *pg.* 628
Bochanski, George V., Jr., Dir-PR - Children's Hospital of Philadelphia; *pg.* 1515, *pg.* 1560
Boches, Edward, Professor-Adv - Boston University; *pg.* 598, *pg.* 791
Bochner, Danielle, Planner-Sls - Turner Broadcasting System, Inc.; *pg.* 314, *pg.* 521
Bochynska, Margaret, Brand Mgr-Jewelry - Macy's East; *pg.* 1777, *pg.* 1254
Bochynska, Margaret, Brand Mgr-Jewelry - Macy's, Inc.; *pg.* 1778, *pg.* 1417
Bock, Bruce, Mgr-Mktg Comm - Andis Company; *pg.* 498, *pg.* 1895
Bock, Daniel, Sr Mgr-Product Mktg - Dell Storage; *pg.* 386, *pg.* 922
Bock, Marcia, Mgr-Mktg Comm - Affymetrix, Inc.; *pg.* 1487, *pg.* 263
Bockhorn, Phil, Head-Fleet Mktg - FCA US LLC; *pg.* 170, *pg.* 868
Bocking, Andrew, Product Mgr-Internet org - Facebook, Inc.; *pg.* 1245, *pg.* 143
Bocquet, Carine, Brand Mgr & Product Mgr - Hunter Douglas, Inc.; *pg.* 928, *pg.* 1320
Bodapati, Narsi, VP-Mktg - Sherwin Williams; *pg.* 1448, *pg.* 1436
Bodard, Alexis, Sr Dir-Mktg - Ubisoft Inc.; *pg.* 589, *pg.* 229
Bodbyl, Libby, Mgr-Mktg - Universal Forest Products, Inc.; *pg.* 117, *pg.* 890

Bodden, Linda, Project Mgr-Brand & Creative Svcs & Specialist-Mktg - Associated Banc-Corp; *pg.* 716, *pg.* 1859
Bodell, Anita, Mgr-Global Fin Svcs Mktg - Cisco Systems, Inc.; *pg.* 372, *pg.* 240
Bodell, Karstin, VP-Gen Bus Mktg - IBM; *pg.* 410, *pg.* 1449
Bodenhamer, Greg, VP-Sls-US Indus & Global Strategic Accounts - Eaton Corporation; *pg.* 1331, *pg.* 1429
Bodenhamer, Jim, Supvr-Mktg-Super 1 Foods - Brookshire Grocery Company; *pg.* 1016, *pg.* 1748
Bodensteiner, Beth, Sr VP-Revenue Mgmt & Product Mktg - Holland America Line Inc.; *pg.* 1911, *pg.* 1836
Bodin, Christophe, Sr VP-Worldwide Field Ops, Strategy, Sls & Mktg - BMC Software, Inc.; *pg.* 362, *pg.* 1701
Bodnar, Anne, Mgr-Database Mktg - GEICO Corporation; *pg.* 1200, *pg.* 399
Bodnar, Barbara, Mgr-Integrated Mktg - Unilever United States, Inc.; *pg.* 904, *pg.* 1061
Bodnar, Gina F., Copywriter-Internet Creative - J.C. Penney Company, Inc.; *pg.* 1774, *pg.* 1732
Bodurka, Derek, Mgr-Mktg - Best Buy Co., Inc.; *pg.* 1761, *pg.* 954
Bodwell, Ray, Mgr-Mktg-North America - E.I. du Pont de Nemours & Company; *pg.* 1159, *pg.* 390
Boebel, Bruce, Sr Mgr-Product-Tracked Products - Komatsu America Corp.; *pg.* 92, *pg.* 655
Boeckman, Brian, Dir-Product Mgmt-Telehandlers-Global - JLG Industries, Inc.; *pg.* 1351, *pg.* 1551
Boedeker, Beth, Mgr-Sls & Mktg - Avnet, Inc.; *pg.* 622, *pg.* 15
Boegel, Connor, Sr Mgr-Comm - Canadian Imperial Bank of Commerce; *pg.* 729, *pg.* 1935
Boehm, Alexandra, Mgr-Mktg & Partnerships - American Express Company; *pg.* 712, *pg.* 1190
Boehm, Amy, Mgr-Mktg Brand - BUFFALO WILD WINGS, INC.; *pg.* 1718, *pg.* 931
Boehm, Brittney, Mgr-PR & Social Media - The Children's Place, Inc.; *pg.* 22, *pg.* 1119
Boehm, Ivy, Sr Dir-Consumer Insights & Analytics - Chico's FAS, Inc.; *pg.* 21, *pg.* 427
Boehm, Julie, Assoc Mgr-Mktg - American Eagle Outfitters, Inc.; *pg.* 37, *pg.* 1572
Boeker, Orlantha, Sr Product Mgr-Private Label - Safeway Inc.; *pg.* 1032, *pg.* 184
Boenisch, Danielle, Mgr-Cross-Channel Mktg - Overstock.com, Inc.; *pg.* 1273, *pg.* 1760
Boer, TJ, Sr Dir-Strategic Dev - Synopsys, Inc.; *pg.* 480, *pg.* 162
Boerger, Claas, Product Mgr-Moisture Analyzer - Mettler-Toledo International Inc.; *pg.* 1423, *pg.* 1441
Boerger, Patti, Dir-PR - Federal Home Loan Mortgage Corporation; *pg.* 751, *pg.* 1790
Boero, Ashley, Mgr-Mktg - Nordstrom, Inc.; *pg.* 1779, *pg.* 1837
Boertje, Jason, Dir-Mktg - MasterCraft Boat Company LLC; *pg.* 1709, *pg.* 1656
Boes, Katie, Exec Dir-Integrated Mktg & Strategy, Travel & Leisure - Time Inc.; *pg.* 1693, *pg.* 1300
Boettcher, Jeff, Dir-Creative - Microsoft Corporation; *pg.* 435, *pg.* 1824
Boettcher, Ken, Specialist-Mktg - FedEx Corporation; *pg.* 1907, *pg.* 1642
Boettcher, Shanen, Gen Mgr-Product Mgmt - Microsoft Corporation; *pg.* 435, *pg.* 1824
Boettinger, David, Sr Mgr-Sls - Washington Capitals; *pg.* 591, *pg.* 1775
Boever, Tracy, Dir-PR & Mktg Comm - American Pop Corn Company; *pg.* 825, *pg.* 712
Boffa, Jeannine, Sr Mktg Mgr-Enterprise Rels - Office Depot, Inc.; *pg.* 448, *pg.* 412
Bofinger, Jack, District Mgr-Mktg-Special Markets California - Graybar Electric Company, Inc.; *pg.* 1299, *pg.* 997
Bogaards, Paul, Exec VP & Exec Dir-Publicity, Promo & Media Rels - Alfred A. Knopf, Inc.; *pg.* 1614, *pg.* 1189
Bogaards, Paul, Exec VP & Exec Dir-Publicity, Promo & Media Rels-Knopf - Penguin Random House; *pg.* 1675, *pg.* 1276
Bogach, Lewis, VP-Production - Country Music Television, Inc.; *pg.* 279, *pg.* 1649
Bogard, Travis, VP-Product Mktg & Strategy - AliphCom, Inc.; *pg.* 616, *pg.* 212
Bogaty, Nick, Head-Digital Publ & Sr Dir - Adobe Systems Incorporated; *pg.* 342, *pg.* 235
Bogdan, Mario, CEO & Engr-Product Design - BogdanCo Consulting; *pg.* 918, *pg.* 174
Bogdan, Michele, VP-Corp Mktg & Branding-Global - Cisco Systems, Inc.; *pg.* 372, *pg.* 240
Bogdanov, Mary, Mgr-Product Mktg - Go Daddy Inc.; *pg.* 1249, *pg.* 21
Boggs, Heather, Dir-Mktg - FSC Franchise Co., LLC; *pg.* 1729, *pg.* 473
Boggs, Janet, Sr Writer-Mktg & Comm - The Boeing Company; *pg.* 225, *pg.* 567
Boggs, Tim T, Sr Dir-Admin - Chick-fil-A, Inc.; *pg.* 1721, *pg.* 492
Boggs-Rowe, Jean, Dir-Creative - K-VA-T Food Stores, Inc.; *pg.* 1025, *pg.* 1770
Boglarsky, Kevin, Dir-Global Products - Discover Financial Services; *pg.* 744, *pg.* 653
Boglio, Chris, Sr Specialist-Mktg - PetSmart, Inc.; *pg.* 1481, *pg.* 18
Bogner, Dean, VP-Sls & Mktg - Webster Industries Inc.; *pg.* 1388, *pg.* 1475
Bohac, Megan, Brand Mgr - The Coca-Cola Company; *pg.* 240, *pg.* 493
Bohde, Bill, Sr VP-Sls & Mktg - Detroit Metro Convention & Visitors Bureau; *pg.* 139, *pg.* 880
Bohl, Erika, Sr Mgr-Bus Analysis & Info - Amgen Inc.; *pg.* 1493, *pg.* 291
Bohlander, Brian, Dir-Sports & Event Mktg - Old World Industries, Inc.; *pg.* 1175, *pg.* 641
Bohlin, Robert, VP & Gen Mgr-Mdse - Hammacher Schlemmer & Co., Inc.; *pg.* 1124, *pg.* 637
Bohling, Keith, Sr Mgr-Natl Media - J.C. Penney Company, Inc.; *pg.* 1774, *pg.* 1732
Bohm, Kerry, Dir-Mktg - Living Proof, Inc.; *pg.* 514, *pg.* 809
Bohm, Pauline, Sr VP-Mktg-Intl - NBC Universal Television Networks Group; *pg.* 302, *pg.* 1267
Bohman, Steve, VP-Production-Global - VERA BRADLEY, INC.; *pg.* 15, *pg.* 697
Bohn, Karina Forbes, VP-Mktg - Arizona Diamondbacks; *pg.* 529, *pg.* 14
Bohn, Magali, Sr Mgr-Mktg-Global 2000 Accounts - Cisco Systems, Inc.; *pg.* 372, *pg.* 240
Bohn, Mary Lou, VP-Mktg - Acushnet Company; *pg.* 1824, *pg.* 818
Bohn, Michael, Head-Global Mktg-Bosch - BSH Home Appliances Corporation; *pg.* 53, *pg.* 108
Bohne, Kristin, Mgr-Mktg & Events - AT&T Alascom; *pg.* 619, *pg.* 10
Bohne, Sara, Mgr-Mktg Production - Hilton Worldwide, Inc.; *pg.* 1094, *pg.* 1791
Bohnert, Brad, Dir-PR & Events - HSN, Inc.; *pg.* 291, *pg.* 462
Bohorad, Nicole, Sr Mgr-Content Distr & Analytics - Under Armour, Inc.; *pg.* 49, *pg.* 759
Bohorquez, Laura, Sr Mgr-Mktg-Weight Watchers Health Solutions - Weight Watchers International, Inc.; *pg.* 1609, *pg.* 1313
Bohorquez, Natasha, Mgr-Sls-Global - Dell Inc.; *pg.* 383, *pg.* 1737
Bohren, Robbie, Dir-Media Rels - Tennessee Football, Inc.; *pg.* 587, *pg.* 1654
Bohrer, Angie, Product Mgr-Licensed Stores - Starbucks Corporation; *pg.* 897, *pg.* 1840
Bohrer, Chris, Dir-EMEA Consumer Mktg - Hewlett-Packard Company; *pg.* 404, *pg.* 175
Boice, Cindy, Sr Mgr-Mktg-Global Strategy - Johnson & Johnson; *pg.* 1549, *pg.* 1091
Boido, Federica, VP-Mktg-Global - Harry Winston, Inc.; *pg.* 6, *pg.* 1238
Boidy, Katherine, Assoc Dir-Mktg-SEC Network - ESPN, Inc.; *pg.* 285, *pg.* 340
Boisson, Catrina, Specialist-Mktg & Customer Experience-ExperienceOne Worldwide - IBM; *pg.* 410, *pg.* 1449
Boissy, Alan, Product Mgr-vCloud Gov Svc Offering - VMware, Inc.; *pg.* 490, *pg.* 179
Boisvert, Guy, Specialist-Chemistry Sls - Waters Corporation; *pg.* 1436, *pg.* 834
Boisvert, Travis, Sr Mgr-Mktg-Best Buy Everywhere - Best Buy Co., Inc.; *pg.* 1761, *pg.* 954
Boitano, Greg P., Mgr-Mktg - Intel Corporation; *pg.* 645, *pg.* 266
Boitano, Joseph, Chief Mdsg & Design Officer & Exec VP - Lands' End, Inc.; *pg.* 1776, *pg.* 1857
Bojanic, Dee D., Sr Mgr-Medical Comm Cardiovascular - Amgen Inc.; *pg.* 1493, *pg.* 291
Bokariza, Kyle, Product Mgr-PR - TIBCO Software Inc.; *pg.* 484, *pg.* 178
Bokern, Julie Von, Dir-Mktg - ScanSource, Inc.; *pg.* 671, *pg.* 1618
Boklund, Sandy, Sr Mgr-Channel Mktg - Plantronics, Inc.; *pg.* 663, *pg.* 270
Bokor, Michael, Asst Dir-XTANDI Mktg - Astellas Pharma US, Inc.; *pg.* 1496, *pg.* 640
Bolain, Brian, Mgr-Product Mktg & Mktg Comm-Lexus Corp - Toyota Motor Sales, U.S.A., Inc.; *pg.* 193, *pg.* 296
Boland, Allison, Brand Mgr - Nestle Purina PetCare Company; *pg.* 1479, *pg.* 1000
Boland, Bill, Dir-Creative - Patagonia; *pg.* 31, *pg.* 301
Boland, Brian, VP-Ads Product Mktg & Atlas - Facebook, Inc.; *pg.* 1245, *pg.* 143
Boland, John, Sr VP-Media & Comm Solutions Grp - Arris Group, Inc.; *pg.* 353, *pg.* 541
Bolander, Jim, Dir-Creative-Pkg - General Nutrition Centers, Inc.; *pg.* 1534, *pg.* 1575
Bolander, Larry A., VP-Sls & Mktg - Fluor Corporation; *pg.* 82, *pg.* 1719
Bolanos, Hector, Producer-Mktg Svcs - Blizzard Entertainment; *pg.* 950, *pg.* 107
Bold, Jesse, Dir-Media - MGA Entertainment, Inc.; *pg.* 964, *pg.* 300
Bolden, Craig, Mgr-Sls & Sr Engr-Applications - Clary Corporation; *pg.* 226, *pg.* 150
Bolden, Ross, VP-Sls-APAC - SumTotal Systems, Inc.; *pg.* 477, *pg.* 429
Bolding, Barry C., VP-Storage & Data Mgmt & Corp Mktg - Cray Inc.; *pg.* 380, *pg.* 1834
Bolding, Deborah G., Sr Mgr-External Comm-North America - GlaxoSmithKline Consumer Healthcare; *pg.* 510, *pg.* 1554
Boldman, Carrie, Corp VP-Mdse & Games - Cedar Fair, L.P.; *pg.* 537, *pg.* 1471
Bolduc, David J., VP-Sls - EMCOR Services Northeast CommAir/BALCO; *pg.* 1071, *pg.* 847
Bolek, Gayle, Sr Specialist-Diabetes Sls - Abbott Diabetes Care, Inc.; *pg.* 1483, *pg.* 38
Bolen, Alison, Editor-Blogs & Social Content - SAS Institute Inc.; *pg.* 466, *pg.* 1361
Boles, Karen, Sr Mgr-Field Mktg Programs - Pegasystems Inc.; *pg.* 453, *pg.* 809
Boles, Margaret, Dir-Federal Media Rels - AT&T Inc.; *pg.* 1867, *pg.* 1674
Bolger, Jessica, Sr Mgr-Consumer Insights - Keurig Green Mountain, Inc.; *pg.* 868, *pg.* 1768
Bolger, Mark, Sr Dir-Mktg-Xbox LIVE Studios - Microsoft Corporation; *pg.* 435, *pg.* 1824
Bolin, Melodie, Brand Mgr - Mars Petcare; *pg.* 1478, *pg.* 1633
Bolino, Mike, Mng Dir-Digital Mktg & Strategy - American Diabetes Association; *pg.* 127, *pg.* 1770
Bolivar, Rafael, Partner-Mktg Bus-Americas Reg - Aetna Inc.; *pg.* 1187, *pg.* 351
Bollero, Alessandra, Specialist-Mktg - Wilson Sporting Goods Co.; *pg.* 1848, *pg.* 596
Bollig, Diane, Mgr-Mktg - Tractor Supply Company; *pg.* 708, *pg.* 1627
Bollig, Todd, VP-Sls Ops-Constellation Brands-Beer Div - Crown Imports LLC; *pg.* 248, *pg.* 572
Bolling, Michael, Mgr-Growth Product Mktg - WhitePages.com Inc.; *pg.* 1289, *pg.* 1842
Bollinger, Aviva, Mgr-Digital Mktg-Pharmacy, Health & Wellness - Walgreen Co.; *pg.* 1608, *pg.* 605
Bollinger, Jenifer, VP-Retail Mktg & Mktg Ops - Perry Ellis International, Inc.; *pg.* 45, *pg.* 445
Bollinger, Katie, Coord-Adv & Mktg - Baltimore Ravens Limited Partnership; *pg.* 532, *pg.* 755
Bollinger, Steve, Dir-Creative - Georgia Institute Of Technology; *pg.* 602, *pg.* 506
Bolls, Lindsey, Mgr-Shopper Mktg Plng - Safeway Inc.; *pg.* 1032, *pg.* 184
Bolonda, Joanne, Dir-Sls - Kind LLC; *pg.* 868, *pg.* 1249
Bolt, Lyndsey, Dir-Mktg & Client Rels - The Northwestern Mutual Life Insurance Company; *pg.* 1212, *pg.* 1879
Boltik, Lou, Dir-Mktg Comm - Joy Mining Machinery; *pg.* 1352, *pg.* 1591
Bolton, Carrie, Sr Mgr-Digital Intelligence Strategy - The Vanguard Group, Inc.; *pg.* 816, *pg.* 1550
Bolton, Gary, VP-Mktg-Global - ADTRAN, Inc.; *pg.* 344, *pg.* 6
Bolton, John, Dir-Mktg - Tensar Corporation; *pg.* 114, *pg.* 485
Bolton, Margaret-Ann, Sr Dir-Field Mktg-Global - Red Hat, Inc.; *pg.* 460, *pg.* 1388
Bolz, Tara, Head-Natl Retail & Reg Carrier Mktg - Motorola Mobility LLC; *pg.* 657, *pg.* 627
Bomar, Steve, Sr Dir-Ticketing - Arizona Cardinals Football Club, Inc.; *pg.* 529, *pg.* 25
Bombier, Denise, Dir-Mktg Comm-Toronto - TELUS CORPORATION; *pg.* 1952, *pg.* 1912
Bomstein, Howard, Category Mgr-Adv-Real Estate & Property Mgmt - The Washington Post; *pg.* 1701, *pg.* 407
Bon, Christine, Mgr-Digital Mktg & Comm - Advocate Health

First page reference indicates Business Class Edition
Second page reference indicates Geographic Edition

Care; *pg.* 1487, *pg.* 607
Bona, Jackie, Sr Mgr-Product Mktg - Twitter, Inc.; *pg.* 1285, *pg.* 228
Bonacasa, Natalie, Mgr-Direct Mktg-Customer Mktg - Barnes & Noble, Inc.; *pg.* 1619, *pg.* 1201
Bonacci, Michael, Dir-Mktg - Hahn Automotive Warehouse, Inc.; *pg.* 206, *pg.* 1336
Bonacum, Gene, Reg Mgr-Sls - TRUMPF Inc.; *pg.* 1385, *pg.* 349
Bonadio, Dominic, Mgr-Mktg Ops - Payless Shoesource, Inc.; *pg.* 31, *pg.* 722
Bonadonna, Alexa, Dir-PR & Comm - Destination Maternity Corporation; *pg.* 23, *pg.* 1563
Bonafede, Gina F., Specialist-Mktg Comm - Armstrong World Industries, Inc.; *pg.* 914, *pg.* 1545
Bonafede, Margaret, Sr Sls Exec-Commodities & Energy - Interactive Data Corporation; *pg.* 769, *pg.* 785
Bonanni, Jon, Sr Dir-Bus Dev-Emerging Technologies - National Association for Stock Car Auto Racing; *pg.* 566, *pg.* 420
Bonar, Karl, Sr Mgr-Mktg-Innovation-Coors TM - Molson Coors Canada Inc.; *pg.* 256, *pg.* 1955
Bonbrest, Max, Sr Mgr-PR & Brand Mktg - Bonobos; *pg.* 39, *pg.* 1205
Bond, Aaron, Coord-Category Adv - The Home Depot, Inc.; *pg.* 1050, *pg.* 510
Bond, Adam, Acct Exec-External Comm & PR - Grant Thornton International Ltd.; *pg.* 763, *pg.* 575
Bond, Blair, Head-Product Asset-Comml & Small Bus - Dell Inc.; *pg.* 383, *pg.* 1737
Bond, Brenda, Coord-Mktg & Comm - Dallas Convention & Visitors Bureau; *pg.* 991, *pg.* 1678
Bond, Casey, Product Mgr-Collection - Herman Miller, Inc.; *pg.* 926, *pg.* 913
Bond, Derek, Sr VP-Production Strategy - Univision Communications Inc.; *pg.* 683, *pg.* 1307
Bond, Emily, VP-Global Mktg & Fragrance Bus Dev - Coty, Inc.; *pg.* 506, *pg.* 1219
Bond, Jan, Assoc VP-Mktg & Comm - Georgia Southern University; *pg.* 602, *pg.* 541
Bond, LaDonna, Reg Mgr-Mktg & Plng Center - GEICO Corporation; *pg.* 1200, *pg.* 399
Bond, Ralph, Mgr-PR - Autodesk Inc.; *pg.* 356, *pg.* 257
Bond, Rick, Sr Mgr-Mktg-Men's - J.C. Penney Company, Inc.; *pg.* 1774, *pg.* 1732
Bond, Stephanie, Dir-Product Mdsg & Ops-BURBERRY WATCHES - Fossil Group, Inc.; *pg.* 5, *pg.* 1735
Bonde, Allen, VP-Product Mktg & Innovation - Actuate Corporation; *pg.* 342, *pg.* 253
Bonde, Karen, Sr Dir-Product Dev - MGA Entertainment, Inc.; *pg.* 964, *pg.* 300
Bonder, Jacqui, Sr Product Mgr-ENT Video - Olympus America Inc.; *pg.* 1425, *pg.* 1521
Bonder, Karyn, Reg Dir-Mktg - Lennar Corporation; *pg.* 1100, *pg.* 443
Bondoc, Edmund, Sr Mgr-Product Mktg - Intuit Inc.; *pg.* 769, *pg.* 158
Bondoc, Nicole, Dir-Strategic Mktg - Overstock.com, Inc.; *pg.* 1273, *pg.* 1760
Bondolowski, Cristina, VP-Mktg-Southeast Asia - The Coca-Cola Company; *pg.* 240, *pg.* 493
Bone, Bridget, Brand Mgr - Starbucks Corporation; *pg.* 897, *pg.* 1840
Bonelli, Charles E., VP-Mktg - Southeast Tourism Society; *pg.* 1006, *pg.* 539
Bonenberger, John, VP & Mgr-Sls-Natl - William H. Sadlier, Inc.; *pg.* 1702, *pg.* 1314
Bonetti, Tony, Assoc Mgr-Sports Mktg & Partnerships - Subway Restaurants; *pg.* 1751, *pg.* 356
Bonfig, Steve, Mgr-Mktg Ops-Global - 3M Company; *pg.* 1142, *pg.* 956
Bonforte, Jeff, Sr VP-Comm Products - Yahoo! Inc.; *pg.* 1289, *pg.* 289
Bongiovanni, Juan, Dir-Digital Mktg-Latin America - Netflix, Inc.; *pg.* 1269, *pg.* 141
Bongiovanni, Kaila, Sr Mgr-Digital Mktg - Microsoft Corporation; *pg.* 435, *pg.* 1824
Bongiovanni, Mia, Asst Gen Mgr-Media & Presentations - The Metropolitan Opera; *pg.* 561, *pg.* 1260
Bongiovanni, Mia, Mgr-Mktg-Werther's Original - Storck USA, L.P.; *pg.* 1862, *pg.* 591
Bongo, Jason, Sr Mgr-ECommerce - Universal Orlando; *pg.* 590, *pg.* 456
Bongo-Box, Christina, VP-Global QA & Product Engrg - Popeye's Chicken & Biscuits; *pg.* 1745, *pg.* 517
Bonick, Teresa, Sr Mgr-Mktg-Customer Retention & Engagement - Autodesk Inc.; *pg.* 356, *pg.* 257
Bonifacio, Luciana, Deputy Asst VP & Sr Dir-Global Corp Partnerships - Save the Children Federation, Inc.; *pg.* 156, *pg.* 384
Bonifer, Nikki, Dir-Mktg-Individual Products-Medicare & HumanaOne - Humana, Inc.; *pg.* 1204, *pg.* 734
Bonilla, Reina, Sr Mgr-HR - Bandai America Incorporated; *pg.* 950, *pg.* 75
Bonistalli, Jeffery J., Div Dir-Adv & Mktg - American Medical Association; *pg.* 130, *pg.* 564
Bonitatibus, Anthony, Assoc Brand Mktg Mgr - Dunkin' Brands Group, Inc.; *pg.* 1727, *pg.* 810
Bonitto, Lizette, Dir-Mktg - NBTY, Inc.; *pg.* 1572, *pg.* 1338
Bonk, Cheryl, VP-Sls & Mktg-Chicago Div - M/I Homes, Inc.; *pg.* 95, *pg.* 1441
Bonkowski, Janet, Mgr-Pub Rels - Schneider; *pg.* 1922, *pg.* 1859
Bonn, Richelle, Sr Mgr-Digital Mktg - The Chamberlain Group, Inc.; *pg.* 75, *pg.* 611
Bonneau, Mark, Sr VP-Corp Sls - Ottawa Senators Hockey Club; *pg.* 573, *pg.* 1921
Bonnel, Heidi, Sr Mgr-eMarketing - Coldwell Banker Residential Brokerage; *pg.* 1087, *pg.* 850
Bonner, Brian, Product Mgr-Hydrogen Energy Sys-Global - Air Products and Chemicals, Inc.; *pg.* 1145, *pg.* 1513
Bonner, Kaitlin, Mgr-Mktg Comm-Global - iRobot Corp.; *pg.* 1418, *pg.* 785
Bonner, Kristi, Sr Dir-IR - Keurig Green Mountain, Inc.; *pg.* 868, *pg.* 1768
Bonner, Monique S., VP-Mktg-Global - Dell Inc.; *pg.* 383, *pg.* 1737
Bonner, Sheila, VP-Shopper Mktg - Dr Pepper Snapple Group, Inc.; *pg.* 250, *pg.* 1729
Bonnett, Bernice Clark, Sr VP-Mktg - Macy's East; *pg.* 1777, *pg.* 1254
Bonnett, Bernice Clark, Sr VP-Mktg - Macy's, Inc.; *pg.* 1778, *pg.* 1417
Bonnett, Fan, Sr Brand Mgr-Digital Mktg-North America - The Procter & Gamble Company; *pg.* 1129, *pg.* 1418
Bonneville, Audrey, Mgr-Experiential Mktg - Facebook, Inc.; *pg.* 1245, *pg.* 143
Bonney, Ginny, Bus Mgr-Medical Dept - Westlake Plastics Company; *pg.* 1892, *pg.* 1548
Bonney, Leslie, Chief Strategy Officer - Qlik Technologies Inc.; *pg.* 457, *pg.* 1583
Bonnichsen, Jennifer, Sr Dir-Ops-Meredith Print Advantage - Meredith Corporation; *pg.* 1663, *pg.* 705
Bonsall, Kelley, VP-PR & Corp Social Responsibility - LifeLock Inc.; *pg.* 776, *pg.* 26
Bonsang, Erin, Dir-Digital Mktg - Hasbro, Inc.; *pg.* 954, *pg.* 1603
Bontomasi, Jennifer, Product Mgr-Lighting, Federal-Mogul Vehicle Components Segment - Federal-Mogul Holdings Corporation; *pg.* 205, *pg.* 907
Bonura, Marge, Dir-Sls & Mktg - New England Machinery, Inc.; *pg.* 1364, *pg.* 415
Bonzagni, Maria, Sr Dir-Mktg - Acushnet Company; *pg.* 1824, *pg.* 818
Bonzer, Clarice, VP-Creative - The Boppy Company, LLC; *pg.* 20, *pg.* 329
Boo, Michael, Chief Strategy Officer - National Marrow Donor Program, Inc.; *pg.* 150, *pg.* 941
Boocock, Brooke, Sr Mgr-Mktg - Jamba, Inc.; *pg.* 1024, *pg.* 84
Boocock, Richard, VP-Products, Tech & Operational Excellence - Air Products and Chemicals, Inc.; *pg.* 1145, *pg.* 1513
Book, Joel, Principal-Mktg Insights - ExactTarget Inc.; *pg.* 1244, *pg.* 685
Bookbinder, Judith, VP-Creative Comm - The Hearst Corporation; *pg.* 1649, *pg.* 1239
Booker, Jason, Sr Dir-Corp Sponsorships & Brdcst Sls - Kansas City Royals Baseball Corporation; *pg.* 555, *pg.* 985
Booker, John, Mgr-Mktg - Levi Strauss & Co.; *pg.* 43, *pg.* 220
Booker, Marcus V., Asst Product Mgr-Orajel Adult Oral Care - Church & Dwight Co., Inc.; *pg.* 1153, *pg.* 1063
Booker, Wendy, Dir-Mktg, Product Mgmt & NPD - Fenner Drives; *pg.* 1336, *pg.* 1551
Booles, Sherry, VP-Mktg - Acxiom Corporation; *pg.* 342, *pg.* 607
Boon, Laura, Mgr-Mktg Sys Enablement - IBM; *pg.* 410, *pg.* 1449
Boone, Chrystal, Dir-Mktg & Bus Dev - Restoration Hardware Holdings, Inc.; *pg.* 1060, *pg.* 70
Boone, Jicara M., Specialist-Mktg - FedEx Corporation; *pg.* 1907, *pg.* 1642
Boone, Patrice C., Sr Mgr-Mktg-LTC - McKesson Corporation; *pg.* 1560, *pg.* 222
Boonman, Nellie, Mgr-Digital Mktg - Annie's Inc.; *pg.* 1760, *pg.* 45
Boor, Anthony W., Interim Pres - Blackbaud, Inc.; *pg.* 361, *pg.* 1613
Boord, Michael, Dir-Mobile Products-Global - The Associated Press, Inc.; *pg.* 270, *pg.* 1197
Boorjian, Jeffrey, Reg VP-Mktg-Eastern Div - Caesars Entertainment Corporation; *pg.* 1083, *pg.* 1023
Boorstin, Ariel, Brand Mgr-Wines - Pernod Ricard USA, Inc.; *pg.* 1968, *pg.* 1332
Boose, Shelley, VP-PR & Social Media - TRIPWIRE, INC.; *pg.* 485, *pg.* 1507
Boosin, Greg, Sr VP & Grp Head-Product Mktg-Global - MasterCard Worldwide Inc.; *pg.* 780, *pg.* 988
Boote, Courtney, Acct Coord-Koch Creative Grp - Koch Industries, Inc.; *pg.* 1463, *pg.* 724
Booth, Andrew, Sr Mgr-PR - Daytona Beach Resort Area Convention & Visitors Bureau; *pg.* 991, *pg.* 420
Booth, Brad, Dir-Global Adv & Brand Mgmt - The Boeing Company - Helicopter Division; *pg.* 226, *pg.* 13
Booth, Brad, Dir-Consumer Dealer Sls-Tire Ops - Bridgestone Americas, Inc.; *pg.* 1879, *pg.* 1648
Booth, Eric, Sr Mgr-PR - Mazda North American Operations; *pg.* 183, *pg.* 113
Booth, James, Dir-Sls-Central US - Kind LLC; *pg.* 868, *pg.* 1249
Booth, Randy, Head-Direct Mktg & Comm - Aetna Inc.; *pg.* 1187, *pg.* 351
Booth, Shawn, Dir-US XELJANZ Mktg - Pfizer Inc.; *pg.* 1581, *pg.* 1278
Boothman, Cortney, Sr Mgr-Mktg Comm, Messaging & Mdsg - Comcast Corporation; *pg.* 276, *pg.* 1560
Booton, Samantha, Mgr-Mktg & Demand Generation-Indus Standard Server Solutions - Hewlett-Packard Company; *pg.* 404, *pg.* 175
Boots, Sally, Mgr-Digital Mktg-Media - Constellation Brands, Inc.; *pg.* 1960, *pg.* 1348
Booy, Michelle, Mgr-Sls Enablement Events - Adobe Systems Incorporated; *pg.* 342, *pg.* 235
Boraczek, Bill, Sr VP-Mktg, R&D, Product Dev - Coty, Inc.; *pg.* 506, *pg.* 1219
Boragine, Ellie, VP & Sr Counsel-Adv - American Express Company; *pg.* 712, *pg.* 1190
Borak, Andrew, VP-Content Distr & Mktg - MTV Networks Company; *pg.* 298, *pg.* 1262
Borak, Lisa, Dir-Global New Product Innovation - Church & Dwight Co., Inc.; *pg.* 1153, *pg.* 1063
Borawski, Kathryn, Mgr-Product Mktg - Google Inc.; *pg.* 1249, *pg.* 153
Borba, Janet Graham, VP-Production - Home Box Office, Inc.; *pg.* 290, *pg.* 1240
Borberg, David, VP & Dir-Product Mgmt & Dev - Ivy Funds Distributor Inc.; *pg.* 771, *pg.* 719
Borchardt, Lori, Brand Mgr - Kimberly-Clark Corporation; *pg.* 1461, *pg.* 1720
Borda, Catherine, Dir-Youth Strategy & Mktg - AT&T Mobility LLC; *pg.* 619, *pg.* 488
Bordainick, Michael, Dir-Global Mktg-Kleenex, Viva & Scott - Kimberly-Clark Corporation; *pg.* 1461, *pg.* 1720
Bordelon, Geraldine, Dir-Destination Sls - Baton Rouge Area Convention & Visitors Bureau; *pg.* 989, *pg.* 741
Bordelon, Scott, Sr Product Mgr - Sears Holdings Corporation; *pg.* 1784, *pg.* 618
Borden, Gathan D., Dir-Brand Mktg & Adv - Louisville Convention & Visitors Bureau; *pg.* 998, *pg.* 736
Borden, Rob, VP-Customer Mktg-Carnival Cruise Lines - Carnival Corporation; *pg.* 1902, *pg.* 441
Borden, Rob, VP-Customer Mktg - Carnival Cruise Lines; *pg.* 1902, *pg.* 441
Border, Brian, Sr Dir-CRM Mktg - SHUTTERFLY, INC.; *pg.* 1280, *pg.* 192
Borders, Colby, Mgr-Mktg - CME Group Inc.; *pg.* 738, *pg.* 571
Borders, Colby, Mgr-Mktg - CME Group, Inc.; *pg.* 738, *pg.* 571
Borders, Terry, Mgr-Mktg Production - Chico's FAS, Inc.; *pg.* 21, *pg.* 427
Bordes, Nathalie, Sr Dir-Emerging Platforms Res - ESPN, Inc.; *pg.* 285, *pg.* 340
Bordley, Raymond, Specialist-Mktg - LivingSocial, Inc.; *pg.* 1264, *pg.* 401

Bordner, Jennifer, Head-Mobile Mktg-CRM - The Gap, Inc.; *pg.* 1770, *pg.* 218
Bordonaro, Matt, Second VP & Head-Media Rels - The Travelers Companies, Inc.; *pg.* 1220, *pg.* 352
Bordson, Juliet, Sr Mgr-Mktg-Home Depot Div - Andersen Corporation; *pg.* 67, *pg.* 916
Bordwell, David, Global Product Mgr - Graco, Inc.; *pg.* 1342, *pg.* 935
Boreham, Nicole, Analyst- Email Mktg & CRM - Guess?, Inc.; *pg.* 25, *pg.* 132
Borek, Chris, Dir-Enterprise Digital Mktg - Olive Garden Italian Restaurant; *pg.* 1742, *pg.* 454
Borella, Robert, Sr Dir-Mktg - Giant Eagle, Inc.; *pg.* 1020, *pg.* 1575
Borelli, Dina, Dir-Wholesale Field Sls & Mdsg - Kate Spade LLC; *pg.* 28, *pg.* 1248
Boren, Jeffrey, VP-Sls & Mktg - Impreso, Inc.; *pg.* 413, *pg.* 1671
Borenstein, Neil B., Sr Mgr-Mktg - The Toro Company; *pg.* 1065, *pg.* 918
Borg, Steven, Sr VP & Dir-Corp Mktg - California Bank & Trust; *pg.* 728, *pg.* 201
Borgersen, Ran, Sr Dir-Multifamily Mktg & Customer Mgmt - Federal Home Loan Mortgage Corporation; *pg.* 751, *pg.* 1790
Borgerson, Todd, Sr Dir-Mktg-Sunglass Hut North America - Luxottica Retail; *pg.* 8, *pg.* 1460
Borges, Erika, Corp Mgr-Shopper Mktg-Channel Dev - Starbucks Corporation; *pg.* 897, *pg.* 1840
Borges, Licia, Asst Mgr-Paid Media - General Mills, Inc.; *pg.* 828, *pg.* 933
Borges, Patricia, Brand Mgr-Assurance - Factory Mutual Insurance Company; *pg.* 1199, *pg.* 1601
Borgia, Kristi, Mgr-Consumer Mktg-Americas - NVIDIA Corporation; *pg.* 447, *pg.* 268
Borgmann, Jennifer, Head-Consumer & Assoc Dir-Global Mktg - Merck & Co., Inc.; *pg.* 1566, *pg.* 1077
Borgna, Brandon, Mgr-Media Rels - Volvo Trucks North America, Inc.; *pg.* 195, *pg.* 1377
Borgstedt, Eric, Mgr-Indus Products Mktg - Honeywell International Inc.; *pg.* 407, *pg.* 1088
Borgwing, Kristina, Mgr-Digital Media - Ralph Lauren Corporation; *pg.* 46, *pg.* 1284
Bori, Carlos, VP-Product Mktg - Skyworks Solutions, Inc.; *pg.* 674, *pg.* 862
Boring, Brian, VP-Creative & Design - Under Armour, Inc.; *pg.* 49, *pg.* 759
Boris, John, CMO & Sr VP - SHUTTERFLY, INC.; *pg.* 1280, *pg.* 192
Borkar, Ratan, VP-Bus Dev, Strategic Plng, Intl Sls & Mktg - Quidel Corporation; *pg.* 1588, *pg.* 207
Borman, Taylor, Coord-Social Media Mktg - Gaiam, Inc.; *pg.* 1532, *pg.* 334
Bormann, Jessica, Assoc Mgr-Mktg - ACH Food Companies, Inc.; *pg.* 835, *pg.* 1631
Bormann, Lisa, Sr Mgr-HR Strategic Comm - General Mills, Inc.; *pg.* 828, *pg.* 933
Born, David A., VP-Database Mktg & Analytics - Eagle:XM; *pg.* 1239, *pg.* 319
Born, Kelley, Sr Mgr-Digital Mktg - DeWALT Industrial Tool Company; *pg.* 1328, *pg.* 757
Born, Kelley, Sr Mgr-Digital Mktg-DEWALT & BOSTITCH - Stanley Black & Decker, Inc.; *pg.* 1063, *pg.* 358
Born, Steve, VP-Mktg - Group Voyagers, Inc.; *pg.* 1910, *pg.* 333
Bornemann, Sean, Dir-Creative Svcs - Toll Brothers, Inc.; *pg.* 115, *pg.* 1541
Bornholdt, Thorsten, Product Mgr-Fluid Lecithin - Cargill, Inc.; *pg.* 845, *pg.* 965
Bornling, Niclas, VP-Mktg - Black Diamond, Inc.; *pg.* 1827, *pg.* 1756
Bornstein, Arnie F., Dir-Mktg & Corp Comm - BDP International Inc.; *pg.* 1900, *pg.* 1559
Bornstein, Jason, Sr Mgr-Mktg - Bonobos; *pg.* 39, *pg.* 1205
Borofsky, Gary, VP & Gen Mgr-Mdse-Cosmetics - Dillard's, Inc.; *pg.* 1766, *pg.* 34
Borosky, Karen, Sr Mgr-Field Mktg-SLED East - NetApp, Inc.; *pg.* 444, *pg.* 287
Borovich, Scott, VP-Sls & Program Mgmt - Shiloh Industries, Inc.; *pg.* 1375, *pg.* 1478
Borovoy, Rick, Product Mgr - Google Inc.; *pg.* 1249, *pg.* 153
Borow, Rich, Sr Mgr-Strategic Insights - Mars Petcare; *pg.* 1478, *pg.* 1633
Borowski, Sara, Sr Product Mgr - Amazon.com, Inc.; *pg.* 1226, *pg.* 1831
Borrego, Gaby, Dir-Retail Sls - Cellco Partnership; *pg.* 1869, *pg.* 1042
Borrell, Tim, Sr Dir-Mktg - United Parcel Service, Inc.; *pg.* 1928, *pg.* 522
Borrelle, Bill, Sr VP-Brand Strategy & Integrated Mktg Comm - Pitney Bowes Inc.; *pg.* 454, *pg.* 376
Borrelli, Anthony, Grp Product Mgr - Boston Scientific Corporation; *pg.* 1508, *pg.* 831
Borris, Sonia, Sr VP-Worldwide TV Mktg - Warner Bros. Entertainment Inc.; *pg.* 319, *pg.* 54
Borrmann, Lars, Dir-Mktg - Eppendorf North America; *pg.* 1412, *pg.* 1164
Borromeo, Lisa, Dir-Adv & Brand - JetBlue Airways Corporation; *pg.* 1913, *pg.* 1174
Borsari, Kristen, VP-Mktg-North American - Ocean Spray Cranberries, Inc.; *pg.* 887, *pg.* 827
Borsecnik, Mary, Specialist-Corp Mktg Comm - J.J. Keller & Associates, Inc.; *pg.* 1654, *pg.* 1883
Borst, Bill, Interim Pres-Ivantage Select Agency - The Allstate Corporation; *pg.* 1189, *pg.* 639
Bortells, John P., VP-Sls & Mktg - Clover Stornetta Farms Inc.; *pg.* 848, *pg.* 182
Bortinger, Michael, Assoc Mgr-Mktg - General Mills, Inc.; *pg.* 828, *pg.* 933
Borton, Andrea, Assoc Dir-Global Mktg Snacks-Design to Value - Kellogg Company; *pg.* 831, *pg.* 870
Bortz, Jason, Brand Mgr-Lysol, Dettol & Sagrotan - Reckitt Benckiser Inc.; *pg.* 1136, *pg.* 1105
Bortz, Will, Sr Mgr-Brand Partnerships & Sponsorships - Taco Bell Corp.; *pg.* 1752, *pg.* 117
Borunda, Elizabeth, VP-Mktg Partnerships-Worldwide - Paramount Pictures Corporation; *pg.* 304, *pg.* 138
Bosamia, Kamal, Mgr-Media Rels-Fashion, Center Core & Branding - Macy's, Inc.; *pg.* 1778, *pg.* 1417
Boscacci, Jenifer, Sr Mgr-Corp Comm - CBS Interactive, Inc.; *pg.* 369, *pg.* 215
Bosch, Anita, Sr VP-Consumer Wealth Mgmt & Sls Dir - Citigroup Inc.; *pg.* 735, *pg.* 1212
Bosch, Talya, VP-Social Ventures, Internal Comm & Transformation Comm - The Western Union Company; *pg.* 822, *pg.* 327
Boschert, Stephen, Dir-Comm Data Sls - Graybar Electric Company, Inc.; *pg.* 1299, *pg.* 997
Boschi, Steve, Exec Dir-Mktg Plng & Res - Comcast Cable Communications, Inc.; *pg.* 276, *pg.* 1560
Bosco, Ariel, Mgr-Mktg & Online Strategy - Affinion Group, Inc.; *pg.* 1225, *pg.* 372
Bosco, Kathy, Sr Mgr-Event - McKesson Corporation; *pg.* 1560, *pg.* 222
Bosco, Michael, Sr Mgr-Digital Mktg - TD Ameritrade Holding Corporation; *pg.* 808, *pg.* 1018
Bose, Ahin, Dir-Mktg-Diversified Brands - Sherwin Williams; *pg.* 1448, *pg.* 1436
Bose, Partha, CMO - Oliver Wyman, Inc.; *pg.* 790, *pg.* 1274
Bosio, Lisa, Mgr-Mktg - Wells Manufacturing, L.P.; *pg.* 222, *pg.* 1858
Bosle, Traycee, Mgr-Mktg Production - Eat'n Park Hospitality Group; *pg.* 1728, *pg.* 1539
Bosley, Ken, Mgr-Software Product Mktg - Hewlett-Packard Company; *pg.* 404, *pg.* 175
Bosman, Andy, Principal & Head-Mktg & Sls-Natl - McGladrey, LLP; *pg.* 781, *pg.* 938
Bosnjak, Lindsay, Media Buyer-Print - Kohl's Corporation; *pg.* 1775, *pg.* 1870
Boss, Randi, Assoc Product Mgr-Purdy Brand - The Sherwin-Williams Company; *pg.* 1447, *pg.* 1435
Boss, Randi, Assoc Product Mgr-Purdy Brand - Sherwin Williams; *pg.* 1448, *pg.* 1436
Bossardet, Mark, VP-Sports Mktg-Global - Saucony, Inc.; *pg.* 1818, *pg.* 828
Bosse, Jennifer, Mgr-Mktg-Gaylord Palms Resort & Convention Center - Ryman Hospitality Properties, Inc; *pg.* 1111, *pg.* 1653
Bossier, Jennifer, Bus Mgr - Sinclair Broadcast Group, Inc.; *pg.* 308, *pg.* 773
Bossingham, Ken, Sr VP-Casino Core Product - International Game Technology; *pg.* 957, *pg.* 1024
Bossolo, Paula, Brand Mgr - Gucci America Inc.; *pg.* 6, *pg.* 1237
Bost, Wendy H., Dir-Media Rels - Quest Diagnostics Incorporated; *pg.* 1587, *pg.* 1080
Bostedor, Barry, Mgr-Production & Mktg - Scripps Networks Interactive, Inc.; *pg.* 1279, *pg.* 1638
Bostelman, Patricia, VP-Mktg - Barnes & Noble, Inc.; *pg.* 1619, *pg.* 1201
Bostick, Jim, Sr VP-Mountain Reg Sls - NetJets Inc.; *pg.* 1917, *pg.* 1442
Bostick, Suzanne, Mgr-Product Mktg - Canon U.S.A., Inc.; *pg.* 1404, *pg.* 1178
Bostocky, Jerry, VP-Sls - B.J. Alan Company; *pg.* 1150, *pg.* 1483
Boston, Sean T., Sr Dir-Strategic Sourcing & Mdsg - Interline Brands, Inc.; *pg.* 1051, *pg.* 433
Boston, Stirling, Reg Mgr-Sls-South Central - A.O. Smith Corporation; *pg.* 1313, *pg.* 1872
Bostwick, Mary, Dir-Mktg & Customer Svc - Delta Apparel, Inc.; *pg.* 39, *pg.* 1617
Bosveld, Tim, VP-Mktg - Dunn-Edwards Corporation; *pg.* 1442, *pg.* 129
Boswell, Bill, Sr Dir-Cloud Svcs Mktg & Bus Strategy - Siemens PLM Software; *pg.* 469, *pg.* 1734
Boswell, John, Sr VP-Mktg, Insights & ECommerce - Sam's Club; *pg.* 1783, *pg.* 29
Bosworth, Brain, Sr Mgr-Sls Dev - Pandora Media Inc.; *pg.* 1273, *pg.* 172
Bosworth, Brian, Dir-Center Store Sls & Mdsg - Weis Markets, Inc.; *pg.* 1037, *pg.* 1588
Bosworth, Kara, Mgr-Mktg - Adecco USA, Inc.; *pg.* 342, *pg.* 1178
Bosworth, Tom, Mgr-North America Reg & Mktg - Philips Lighting; *pg.* 1303, *pg.* 806
Botcheller, Christine, Planner-Creative Resource - Bose Corporation; *pg.* 626, *pg.* 820
Botelho, Dwain, Dir-Sls & Mktg - NRG Energy, Inc.; *pg.* 1948, *pg.* 1712
Botelho, Laura, Dir-PR-Caribbean & Latin America - Marriott International, Inc.; *pg.* 1102, *pg.* 764
Botella, Eneida, Specialist-Mktg - TracFone Wireless, Inc.; *pg.* 681, *pg.* 447
Both, Scott, Engr-Programmatic Sls-Hearst Digital - Hearst Magazines; *pg.* 1649, *pg.* 1239
Botham, Lydia, Exec Dir-Land O'Lakes Foundation & Dir-PR - Land O'Lakes, Inc.; *pg.* 873, *pg.* 915
Bothun, Deborah, Head-US Entertainment, Media & Comm - PricewaterhouseCoopers LLP; *pg.* 795, *pg.* 1283
Bothwell, Yatisha, Dir-Network Sls Mktg Res - Telemundo Network Inc.; *pg.* 311, *pg.* 430
Botka, Andy, Sr Mgr-R&D - Agilent Technologies, Inc.; *pg.* 614, *pg.* 264
Botkins, David, Dir-Media Rels - Dominion Resources, Inc.; *pg.* 1939, *pg.* 1802
Botsford, Holly, Mgr-PR - BUYSEASONS, Inc.; *pg.* 20, *pg.* 1883
Botsford, Holly, Mgr-PR-BuySeasons, Inc. - Celebrate Express, Inc.; *pg.* 1764, *pg.* 1883
Bott, Brent R., Exec Dir-Consumer Mktg - National Beverage Corp.; *pg.* 257, *pg.* 425
Bott, Courtney, VP-Mktg & Digital - The E.W. Scripps Company; *pg.* 1639, *pg.* 1412
Bott, Katrina, Sr Mgr-Mktg Procurement - L'Oreal USA; *pg.* 514, *pg.* 1252
Bott, Ken, Dir-Enterprise Mktg-Commerce Programs & Partnerships - Olive Garden Italian Restaurant; *pg.* 1742, *pg.* 454
Bott, Kendall, Sr Mgr-Brand Mgmt - Pfizer Inc.; *pg.* 1581, *pg.* 1278
Bottallo, Fabio, Sr Mgr-Mktg-Latin America - Kingston Technology Company, Inc.; *pg.* 425, *pg.* 90
Bottcher, Dale, Sr VP-Sls & Ops - Audio Visual Innovations, Inc.; *pg.* 621, *pg.* 471
Botti, Nicole, Mgr-Internal Media Plng - Cablevision Systems Corporation; *pg.* 272, *pg.* 1141
Botting, Chris, Gen Mgr & Sr Dir - Cisco Systems, Inc.; *pg.* 372, *pg.* 240
Bottini, Mark A., Sr VP-Sls - Paychex, Inc.; *pg.* 792, *pg.* 1336
Bottinick, William, Sr VP-Social Insights & Servicing - Citigroup Inc.; *pg.* 735, *pg.* 1212
Bottjer, Greg, Mng Dir & Head-Product Strategy - Nuveen Investments, Inc.; *pg.* 788, *pg.* 586
Bottke, Luke, Mgr-Digital Mktg-Global - StubHub, Inc.; *pg.* 586, *pg.* 228
Botto, Allyson, Sr Mgr-Mktg, Sponsorship & Adv - Avis Budget Group, Inc.; *pg.* 1900, *pg.* 1102
Bottomley, Debbi, Assoc VP-Mktg Strategy - McKesson Corporation; *pg.* 1560, *pg.* 222
Bottomley, John, Sr Dir-Retail Mdsg - Sargento Foods Inc.; *pg.* 894, *pg.* 1886
Bottomley, Michelle, CMO & Chief Sls Officer - Mercer Inc.; *pg.* 1395, *pg.* 1258
Bottomly, Glenn, Sr VP-Online Mktg & Innovation - Taylor

Corporation; pg. 1691, pg. 952
Bottone, Mary Ellen, VP-Sls - Showtime Networks Inc.; pg. 308, pg. 1291
Bottorff, Brett, Mgr-Mktg - CD Baby, Inc.; pg. 1764, pg. 1501
Botu, Oneeka, Dir-Mktg & Trng-Bvlgari - LVMH Inc.; pg. 9, pg. 1254
Botwick, Debbie, Dir-Mktg Excellence Team - Pfizer Inc.; pg. 1581, pg. 1278
Bouchard, Leslie, Sr Dir-HR - Ethan Allen Interiors Inc.; pg. 924, pg. 343
Bouchard, Phil, Mgr-Sls-US - Lincoln Electric Holdings, Inc.; pg. 1355, pg. 1432
Boucher, Ashley, Mgr-PR - Produce Marketing Association; pg. 154, pg. 388
Boucher, Claude, VP-Direct Sls - Atis Group Inc.; pg. 1042, pg. 1952
Boucher, Meg, Sr Mgr-Recruiting Ops & Sourcing Teams - SRA International, Inc.; pg. 473, pg. 1780
Boucher, Steve, Dir-Mktg & Comm - Southern New Hampshire University; pg. 607, pg. 1036
Boucher, Theresa, Sr Mgr-Mktg - Verizon Communications Inc.; pg. 1875, pg. 1309
Bouchie, Kristen, Brand Mgr - High Liner Foods (USA) Incorporated; pg. 862, pg. 816
Bouda, Ali, Dir-Mktg - MGA Entertainment, Inc.; pg. 964, pg. 300
Boudary, Chakib, Chief Strategy Officer - SAP America, Inc.; pg. 466, pg. 1557
Boudewyns, Rhonda, Assoc Specialist-Integrated Mktg Program - Deluxe Corporation; pg. 1634, pg. 964
Boudreau, Daniel, VP-IT-Grp Media, TVA Productions, Ops & Technologies - TVA Group, Inc.; pg. 315, pg. 1957
Boudreau, Nicole, Mgr-PR - Comcast Corporation; pg. 276, pg. 1560
Boudreaux, Mark, Sr Dir-Federal Rels - Exxon Mobil Corporation; pg. 977, pg. 1718
Bouffard, Mark, Sr Mgr-Comm - Avery Dennison Corporation; pg. 1452, pg. 95
Bough, B. Bonin, VP-Media & Consumer Engagement-Global - Mondelez International; pg. 877, pg. 1344
Bough, B. Bonin, VP-Media & Consumer Engagement-Global - Mondelez International, Inc.; pg. 878, pg. 601
Bougher, Jerry, Mgr-Mktg-Toilet Seats - Kohler Co.; pg. 91, pg. 1862
Boughey, Kathy, Sr Product Mgr - AT&T Southeast; pg. 1868, pg. 489
Bouhadana, Karen, Mgr-Global Mktg-NiQuitin - GlaxoSmithKline; pg. 1536, pg. 1565
Boulben, Frank, Chief Strategy Officer - Rogers Communications Inc.; pg. 668, pg. 1942
Bould, Eve, Dir-Mktg - City Sports; pg. 1830, pg. 860
Bould, Paul, VP-Global Mktg Intelligence - Abbott Laboratories; pg. 1484, pg. 551
Bouleau, Cedric, Mgr-Global Bus-Cloud & Software Products - Schlumberger Limited; pg. 801, pg. 1714
Boulukos, Samantha, VP-Mktg & Professional Oral Care Sls-Canada - Colgate-Palmolive Company; pg. 504, pg. 1215
Bouma, Elizabeth, Analyst-Bus & Mktg - Exelon Corporation; pg. 1942, pg. 573
Boundey, Megan, Product Mgr - Google Inc.; pg. 1249, pg. 153
Bounds, Holly, Mgr-Digital Mktg - General Electric Company; pg. 1297, pg. 347
Bourdage, Valerie, Mgr-Retail Mktg - St. John Knits International, Inc.; pg. 33, pg. 116
Bourdeau, Michelle, Specialist-Mktg - The Procter & Gamble Company; pg. 1129, pg. 1418
Bourdganis, Jim, Area Mgr-Sls - Audi of America, Inc.; pg. 164, pg. 1784
Bourgeois, John, Mgr-Ready-to-Wear & Designer - Saks Fifth Avenue, Inc.; pg. 1783, pg. 1287
Bourgoin, Laurent, VP-Sls-Europe & Middle East - WestRock Company; pg. 1472, pg. 1805
Bourie, April, Mgr-Tourism Sls - Metropolitan Tucson Convention & Visitors Bureau; pg. 998, pg. 27
Bourke, Ryan, Dir-Mktg & Membership Comm - AARP; pg. 124, pg. 393
Bourn, Margaret, Mgr-PR - adidas America Inc.; pg. 1803, pg. 1500
Bourne, Matt, VP-Bus PR - Major League Baseball; pg. 560, pg. 1255
Bourne-Marth, Mary, VP-Key Acct Mktg - Showtime Networks Inc.; pg. 308, pg. 1291
Bournes, Sharon S., Dir-Adv, PR & Mktg Comm-Global - Zimmer Biomet Holdings, Inc.; pg. 1611, pg. 699
Boush, Charlie, Reg Mgr-Sls-Natl - WSAZ-TV; pg. 323, pg. 1850
Boushy, Eli, Dir-Sls Ops-Central - Xerox Canada Inc.; pg. 494, pg. 1930
Bousquet, Karla, VP-Client Exec Mktg & Global Recognition Programs - IBM; pg. 410, pg. 1449
Boutcher, Ann, CMO & VP - Voxx International; pg. 686, pg. 1166
Bouteiller, Kate, Mgr-Brand Mktg-North America Soccer - NIKE, Inc.; pg. 1812, pg. 1492
Boutin, Roger, Exec Dir-Mktg - PRAHealth Sciences; pg. 1585, pg. 1388
Bouton, Greg, Specialist-Mktg - LOGMEIN, INC.; pg. 428, pg. 861
Boutot, Holly, Mgr-Mktg Comm - Atlas Copco Comptec LLC; pg. 1314, pg. 1349
Bouts, Amber, Mgr-eMail Mktg Channel - Bank of America Corporation; pg. 718, pg. 1362
Boutwell, Todd, Assoc Dir-CF Mktg - Vertex Pharmaceuticals Incorporated; pg. 1606, pg. 801
Bouve, Dave, Dir-Mktg & Adv - United States Navy Recruiting Command; pg. 1009, pg. 1648
Bouve, David, Dir-Navy Mktg & Adv-Natl - United States Navy; pg. 1009, pg. 1647
Bouw, Matthew, Chief Strategy Officer & Chief HR Officer - Cushman & Wakefield, Inc.; pg. 1088, pg. 1220
Bouwman, Katrien, Sr Dir-Mktg-NIKE+ Western Europe - NIKE, Inc.; pg. 1812, pg. 1492
Bouza, Jacki, Sr VP-Adv & Mktg-Global - The Donna Karan Company LLC; pg. 23, pg. 1225
Bouza, Kevin, VP-Product Dev & Sourcing - 180s, LLC; pg. 1824, pg. 754
Bova, Anthony J., Engr-Project Sls - EMCOR Services Northeast CommAir/BALCO; pg. 1071, pg. 847
Bovara, Gina M., Mgr-Event Mktg - Intel Corporation; pg. 645, pg. 266
Bove, Kerry M., Interim CFO - Mine Safety Appliances Company; pg. 1361, pg. 1525
Bove, Monica, Brand Mgr-Global - Tiffany & Co. International; pg. 14, pg. 1300
Bovee, Jeff, Sr Product Mgr-Mktg - Wahl Clipper Corporation; pg. 524, pg. 662
Bovencamp, Brian, Sr Dir-Ops - 7-Eleven Canada, Inc.; pg. 237, pg. 1909
Bovensiep, Corie, Dir-Mktg - Jazzercise, Inc.; pg. 554, pg. 59
Bovian, Michelle, Mgr-Convention Sls - Augusta Metropolitan Convention & Visitors Bureau, Inc.; pg. 989, pg. 524
Bow, Andy, Engr-Technical Mktg - Cisco Systems, Inc.; pg. 372, pg. 240
Bowden, Marilyn, Dir-Global Product Dev-Accessories - Weber-Stephen Products LLC; pg. 62, pg. 650
Bowden, Mark, Sr Product Mgr - ChyronHego; pg. 371, pg. 1179
Bowden, Tricia, Sr Mgr-Mktg - Verengo, Inc.; pg. 1954, pg. 297
Bowe, Paula, VP-Sls & Mktg - Josam Company; pg. 89, pg. 695
Bowen, Carmen, Assoc Dir-Ophthalmology Mktg - Regeneron Pharmaceuticals, Inc.; pg. 1588, pg. 1345
Bowen, David, Exec Dir-Brand & Mktg Comm - Verizon Communications Inc.; pg. 1875, pg. 1309
Bowen, Don, Product Dir-Respiratory Mktg - GlaxoSmithKline; pg. 1536, pg. 1389
Bowen, Doug, Reg Sls Dir-Southeast - Herman Miller, Inc.; pg. 926, pg. 913
Bowen, Edward, Sr Dir-Translational & Bioinformatics - Pfizer Inc.; pg. 1581, pg. 1278
Bowen, Greg, Mgr-Mktg Comm-Well Intervention - Schlumberger Limited; pg. 801, pg. 1714
Bowen, Holly, Dir-Mktg - Hughes Network Systems LLC; pg. 643, pg. 770
Bowen, Jennifer, VP-Product Dev - Augusta Metropolitan Convention & Visitors Bureau, Inc.; pg. 989, pg. 524
Bowen, Joan, Mgr-BMW EV & i Brand Mktg - BMW of North America, LLC; pg. 166, pg. 1133
Bowen, Karen Singer, Mgr-Digital Project, Content & Global Mktg - Alcon; pg. 1399, pg. 530
Bowen, Keith, Chief Revenue Officer - Tribune Media Company; pg. 1696, pg. 592
Bowen, Megan, Sr Counsel-Compliance, Insurance & Mktg-Harley Davidson Fin Svcs - Harley-Davidson, Inc.; pg. 178, pg. 1874
Bowen, Nicola Katharina, Dir-Mktg Europe - Electra Bicycle Company; pg. 1706, pg. 303
Bowen, Peter, Sr VP-Sls - CBS Corporation; pg. 273, pg. 1210
Bowen, Preston, Sr VP-Sls & Customer Care - Overhead Door Corporation; pg. 102, pg. 1725
Bowen, Rob, Exec VP-Sls & Mktg - Cumberland Packing Corp.; pg. 851, pg. 1146
Bowen, Sarah, Dir-Mktg - Magellan Health Services, Inc.; pg. 1557, pg. 337
Bowens, Cynthia, Mgr-Channel Mktg - Logitech Inc.; pg. 1264, pg. 164
Bowens, Trenton, Specialist-Product - Whirlpool Corporation; pg. 62, pg. 872
Bower, David, Product Mgr - Klein Tools Inc.; pg. 1052, pg. 627
Bower, Jessica, Dir-Mktg Comm - Gartner, Inc.; pg. 1248, pg. 374
Bower, Matt, Mgr-Natl Mktg & Sls Support - Xerox Canada Inc.; pg. 494, pg. 1930
Bowering, Drew, Sr Dir-Distr Accounts - Expedia, Inc.; pg. 1244, pg. 1814
Bowers, Andrew, Product Mgr - Google Inc.; pg. 1249, pg. 153
Bowers, Christa, Dir-Comm-Engineered Products & Solutions - Alcoa Inc.; pg. 65, pg. 1188
Bowers, David, Sr VP-Digital Sls, Bus Dev & Strategy - HBG Books, Inc.; pg. 1648, pg. 1238
Bowers, Eric, Brand Mgr-Smart Ones - The Kraft Heinz Company; pg. 870, pg. 1577
Bowers, Kailee, Sr Specialist-Category Mktg, Apparel & Accessories - Target Corporation; pg. 1786, pg. 942
Bowers, Kristin, VP-Internet Sls - HarperCollins Publishers Inc.; pg. 1647, pg. 1237
Bowers, Natalie Y., Sr Rep-Mktg-Brand Identity - United Airlines, Inc.; pg. 1927, pg. 593
Bowers, Terri, Sr Mgr-Procurement - Microsoft Corporation; pg. 435, pg. 1824
Bowersock, Paul R., Sr VP-Sls & Distr - Alltel Wireless Communications Corporation; pg. 1865, pg. 33
Bowes, Julian, VP-Sls & Engrg - Cameron International; pg. 1151, pg. 1702
Bowie, Kelly, Sr Mgr-Market Intelligence & Insights - Aflac Incorporated; pg. 1188, pg. 527
Bowis, Lynne M., Reg Dir-Sls - Palm Springs Desert Resorts Convention & Visitors Authority; pg. 1003, pg. 187
Bowlby, Jeffrey L., CMO-Pro Liability Grp & Sr VP - ProAssurance Corporation; pg. 1214, pg. 3
Bowler, Brian, Dir-Mktg - LEGO Systems, Inc.; pg. 961, pg. 346
Bowler, Tracy, Dir-Promos & Adv Bus-Global - Schnuck Markets, Inc.; pg. 1033, pg. 1002
Bowles, Amber, Coord-Mktg - First Option Mortgage, LLC; pg. 757, pg. 505
Bowles, Brenda, Brand Mgr-Global - SPX Corporation; pg. 218, pg. 1369
Bowles, Pete, Reg Mgr-Sls-Southern - GSC Enterprises, Inc.; pg. 1021, pg. 1746
Bowley, Jim, VP-Product Mgmt - PeopleFluent; pg. 453, pg. 853
Bowley, Stewart, VP-Product Mgmt Content - Atex Media Command, Inc.; pg. 355, pg. 848
Bowling, Karen E., VP-Mktg - LRAD Corporation; pg. 652, pg. 204
Bowling, Nicolle, Sr Mgr-Demand Generation Mktg - Blackbaud, Inc.; pg. 361, pg. 1613
Bowling, Ryan, Dir-Press Office & Digital Media-Global - Mars, Incorporated; pg. 1858, pg. 1792
Bowling, Stuart, Dir-Content & Creative Rels - Dolby Laboratories, Inc.; pg. 284, pg. 217
Bowman, Andy, Sr Mgr-Comm-iPad - Apple Inc.; pg. 350, pg. 73
Bowman, Cathi, Sr Mgr-Compliance - Amgen Inc.; pg. 1493, pg. 291
Bowman, David, Dir-Bus Dev & Strategic Sls - Sabre Holdings Corporation; pg. 1922, pg. 1745
Bowman, Eddie, Sr Product Mgr-Channel Mktg - AT&T; pg. 1865, pg. 258
Bowman, Giles, Sr VP-Mdsg-Building Matls - The Home Depot, Inc.; pg. 1050, pg. 510
Bowman, Jason, VP-Ad Sls - Blogher Inc.; pg. 1232, pg. 45
Bowman, Jennifer, Sr Mgr-Mktg & Plng - Molina Healthcare, Inc.; pg. 1569, pg. 123
Bowman, Joel, Dir-Adv Sls - Bright House Networks LLC; pg. 272, pg. 461
Bowman, Kenneth, Sr Product Mgr-Progressive Insurance - The Progressive Corporation; pg. 1214, pg. 1463
Bowman, Meghan, Mgr-Mktg-Strategic Programs - eBay Inc.;

pg. 1240, pg. 243
Bowman, Michelle, Dir-Mktg Promos - FedEx Corporation; pg. 1907, pg. 1642
Bowman, Natalie, VP-Media - Neiman Marcus, Inc.; pg. 30, pg. 1684
Bowman, Paul, Sr VP-Sls-Dedicated Svcs - U.S. Xpress Enterprises, Inc.; pg. 1929, pg. 1630
Bowman, Petra, Sr Dir-Digital Mktg - Bankrate, Inc.; pg. 1231, pg. 451
Bowman, Vicki, Mgr-Sls Enablement Program & Digital Strategy - Baker Hughes Incorporated; pg. 1315, pg. 1700
Bown, Brenda, Sr Dir-Microsoft Adv - Microsoft Corporation; pg. 435, pg. 1824
Bowron, Mark, Sr VP-Mktg, Mgr & Mgr-P&C Carrier - Wells Fargo & Company; pg. 819, pg. 232
Bowser, Doug, VP-Sls - Nintendo of America, Inc.; pg. 965, pg. 1829
Bowser, Jennifer, Product Mgr-Mobile-eBusiness Mktg - The Allstate Corporation; pg. 1189, pg. 639
Bowser, Kelly, Coord-Mktg-New Balance & Drydock Footwear Grp - New Balance Athletic Shoe, Inc.; pg. 1811, pg. 798
Bowsher, Jay, VP-Sls & Specialty Biologics - Pfizer Inc.; pg. 1581, pg. 1278
Boxall, Ron, Project Mgr-Product Dev - Sun Life Financial Inc.; pg. 806, pg. 1944
Boxer, Melissa, VP-CRM Product Mgmt & Strategy - Oracle Corporation; pg. 450, pg. 191
Boyars, Lisa, Exec Dir-Grp Mktg-Hearst Men's Group - The Hearst Corporation; pg. 1649, pg. 1239
Boyce, Ashley, Brand Mgr-Building-Personal Care Strategy & Innovation - Unilever United States, Inc.; pg. 904, pg. 1061
Boyce, Dianna, Sr Dir-Corp Comm - The Finish Line, Inc.; pg. 1769, pg. 686
Boyce, Onnolee, Gen Mgr-Mktg Comm - Xerox Canada Inc.; pg. 494, pg. 1930
Boyce, Robin, Sr Mgr-Affiliate Mktg - Classified Ventures, LLC; pg. 1235, pg. 571
Boyce, Satrina, Dir-Mktg Procurement-Global - Mondelez International, Inc.; pg. 878, pg. 601
Boychuk, Michael, Exec Dir-Creative - Amazon.com, Inc.; pg. 1226, pg. 1831
Boyd, Alison, Mgr-Brand & Interactive Adv - FedEx Corporation; pg. 1907, pg. 1642
Boyd, Andrew, CMO & Chief Strategy Officer - Dimensional Insight, Inc.; pg. 387, pg. 805
Boyd, April, Sr Dir-Federal Govt Affairs - Yahoo! Inc.; pg. 1289, pg. 289
Boyd, Barbara, Brand Mgr-Private Label - The Mentholatum Company; pg. 1565, pg. 1320
Boyd, Carol, Exec Dir-Adv-Global - Yurman Design, Inc.; pg. 15, pg. 1316
Boyd, Carolyn, Mgr-Multimedia Sls - Transport Topics Publishing Group; pg. 1696, pg. 1772
Boyd, Dennis W., Mgr-Digital Media & Corp Comm - Brown-Forman Corporation; pg. 1958, pg. 732
Boyd, James, VP-PR - Singapore Airlines; pg. 1923, pg. 82
Boyd, Jennifer, Mgr-Mktg & PR - Arkansas Best Corporation; pg. 1899, pg. 32
Boyd, John, Dir-Sls & Bus Accts - Charter Communications, Inc.; pg. 274, pg. 372
Boyd, Kendall, Dir-Portfolio Mktg-Global - Microsoft Corporation; pg. 435, pg. 1824
Boyd, Kimberly, Sr Dir-Mktg-Global - Hasbro, Inc.; pg. 954, pg. 1603
Boyd, Martin, Sr Mgr-Corp Mktg - Cascade Corporation; pg. 1321, pg. 1497
Boyd, Matthew, Sr VP-Western Sls - Conversant, Inc.; pg. 1393, pg. 306
Boyd, MIke, VP-Mktg - 21st Century Insurance Group; pg. 1187, pg. 389
Boyd, Rachel, Mgr-Mktg - Magellan Health Services, Inc.; pg. 1557, pg. 337
Boyd, Rhasheda, Mng Dir-Mktg - Susan G. Komen for the Cure; pg. 158, pg. 1688
Boyd, Wesley, Dir-Mktg & Applications Engrg - Skyworks Solutions, Inc.; pg. 674, pg. 862
Boyden, Gail D., Dir-Mktg - Merck & Co., Inc.; pg. 1566, pg. 1077
Boydston, Brent, Sr Mgr-Mktg - H&R Block, Inc.; pg. 764, pg. 983
Boyer, Alain, VP-Creative - Boston Proper, Inc.; pg. 20, pg. 410
Boyer, Andy, Sr VP-Sls & Mktg - Allergan; pg. 1490, pg. 1101
Boyer, Bradley S., Sr VP-Remodel Sls & Mktg - American Woodmark Corporation; pg. 913, pg. 1811
Boyer, Brooks, Sr VP-Sls & Mktg - Chicago White Sox Ltd.; pg. 539, pg. 570
Boyer, Greg, Mgr-Mktg - Hosokawa Micron Powder Systems; pg. 1347, pg. 1124
Boyer, Jan, Mgr-Mktg - Badger Meter, Inc.; pg. 1401, pg. 1873
Boyer, Lauren, Editor-Social Media - U.S. News & World Report, L.P.; pg. 1698, pg. 1308
Boyer-White, Sally, Sr brand Mgr-Americas Retail Mktg - Starbucks Corporation; pg. 897, pg. 1840
Boyes, Jeanne, Sr Mgr-Brand Strategy & Comm - Medtronic, Inc.; pg. 1564, pg. 939
Boyette, Richard, VP-Mfg-Polyvinyl Chloride Products - AEP Industries Inc.; pg. 1878, pg. 1085
Boyette, Roland, Sr VP-Sls - AMERICAN TIRE DISTRIBUTORS HOLDINGS, INC.; pg. 199, pg. 1379
Boykan, Kim, Mgr-Mktg-Caribbean & Latin America - Marriott International, Inc.; pg. 1102, pg. 764
Boykin, Ivan, Mgr-Retail Mktg - Ford Motor Company; pg. 172, pg. 876
Boykin, Linda, VP-Mdsg - Office Depot, Inc.; pg. 448, pg. 412
Boykin, William, VP-Sls SE Reg & Natl Accts - Castle Brands Inc.; pg. 239, pg. 1209
Boyko, Derek, Dir-Football Media Svcs - Philadelphia Eagles Football Club, Inc.; pg. 575, pg. 1569
Boyko, Vika, Sr Mgr-Multi Channel Mktg - Genentech, Inc.; pg. 1533, pg. 279
Boylan, Katie, Dir-PR - Target Corporation; pg. 1786, pg. 942
Boylan, Perry, Mgr-Digital Mktg - The Scotts Miracle-Gro Company; pg. 1799, pg. 1459
Boyland, Michael, Rep-Sls - Republic Services, Inc.; pg. 107, pg. 19
Boyle, Alison, Dir-Product Dev-Anthem Comml Bus - Anthem, Inc.; pg. 1192, pg. 683
Boyle, Bob, Dir-Power Transmission Products - Applied Industrial Technologies, Inc.; pg. 199, pg. 1428
Boyle, Donna, Mgr-Mktg - CIBER, Inc.; pg. 372, pg. 330
Boyle, Ed, Mgr-Interactive Mktg - Urban Outfitters, Inc.; pg. 1789, pg. 1571
Boyle, Glenda, Coord-Mktg Comm - Nordson Corporation; pg. 1365, pg. 1480
Boyle, Jennifer, Dir-Creative-Retail Decor & Brand - CVS Health Corporation; pg. 1765, pg. 1610
Boyle, Joe, Sr VP-Brand Mdsg & Design - Columbia Sportswear Company; pg. 1830, pg. 1501
Boyle, Katharine, Mgr-Mktg Comm - BASF Corporation; pg. 1149, pg. 1066
Boyle, Kevin, Head-Global Segment Mktg-Strategic Programs - General Electric Company; pg. 1297, pg. 347
Boyle, Mark, Dir-Steering & Suspension Products - Federal-Mogul Holdings Corporation; pg. 205, pg. 907
Boyle, Mick, VP-Sls - Broadridge Financial Solutions Inc.; pg. 727, pg. 1172
Boyle, Nancy, Head-Global Dog Portfolio Mktg & Innovation - Nestle Purina PetCare Company; pg. 1479, pg. 1000
Boyle, Richard, VP-Sls & Mktg - Melnor, Inc.; pg. 1055, pg. 1811
Boyle, Rob, Product Mgr - Facebook, Inc.; pg. 1245, pg. 143
Boyle, Steve, Dir-Adv - The Morning Call, Inc.; pg. 1665, pg. 1513
Boyle, Thomas, Sr Mgr-Innovation-Consumer Lighting - General Electric Company; pg. 1297, pg. 347
Boyle-Ciccone, Christine, VP-Global ECommerce & Online Mktg - Wyndham Worldwide Corporation; pg. 1119, pg. 1107
Boyles, Eric, Specialist-Mktg - Medtronic, Inc.; pg. 1564, pg. 939
Boyles, Shane, Mgr-Mktg - United Parcel Service, Inc.; pg. 1928, pg. 522
Boyles, Trudy, Sr VP-Mktg & Comm - Advance America Cash Advance Centers, Inc.; pg. 711, pg. 1622
Boyll, David, Dir-Media Tech Solutions-Oracle Mktg Brand Creative - Oracle Corporation; pg. 450, pg. 191
Boyman, Lauren, COO-Mktg & Head-Mktg Strategy - Morgan Stanley; pg. 783, pg. 1261
Boynton, John, VP-Sls - Icicle Seafoods, Inc.; pg. 864, pg. 1836
Boynton, Kimberly, Mgr-Mktg-Intl - TASER International, Inc.; pg. 677, pg. 24
Boynton, Kimberly, Dir-Mktg - Uno Restaurant Holdings Corporation; pg. 1754, pg. 856
Boynton-Trigg, Anne, VP-Export Sls & Mktg - Scholastic Corporation; pg. 1683, pg. 1288
Boyschau, Jorgen, Brand Mgr-Jose Cuervo - Proximo Spirits, Inc.; pg. 1969, pg. 1076
Boyum, Brett, VP-Mktg-Marvin & Integrity - Marvin Windows & Doors; pg. 934, pg. 965
Bozak, Cathy, Specialist-Mktg Promo & Event - Comcast Cable Communications, Inc.; pg. 276, pg. 1560
Bozarth, Stephanie, Sr Mgr-Digital Mktg - NetSpend Corporation; pg. 786, pg. 1665
Bozenhard, Alexandra, Sr Mgr-Mktg - Pfizer Inc.; pg. 1581, pg. 1278
Bozich, Eric, VP-Product & Mktg - CenturyLink, Inc; pg. 1870, pg. 317
Bozkurt-Ozan, Esra Gul, Dir-Mktg - Pfizer Inc.; pg. 1581, pg. 1278
Bozman, Larry, Mgr-Media Rels - Intel Corporation; pg. 645, pg. 266
Bozzelli, Tracey, Dir-Sls - Blackbaud, Inc.; pg. 361, pg. 1613
Braakman, Don, Sr Dir-Pub Affairs - Abbott Laboratories; pg. 1484, pg. 551
Braaten, Jake, VP-New Product Dev & Engrg - ROCKFORD CORPORATION; pg. 667, pg. 26
Braaten, Jamie, Head-Mktg Comm & Brand - GE Capital; pg. 761, pg. 362
Braatz, Barb, Product Mgr-Mktg - Enzymatic Therapy Inc.; pg. 1529, pg. 1859
Brabants, Matthew, Sr VP-Intl Media Distr & Bus Ops - National Basketball Association; pg. 566, pg. 1264
Brabec, Filip, Dir-Product Mgmt - Audi of America, Inc.; pg. 164, pg. 1784
Brabender, Nicole, Mgr-Strategic Mktg - Schneider Electric USA, Inc.; pg. 1306, pg. 650
Bracken, Chris, Dir-Mktg - Loews Hotels Holding Corporation; pg. 1101, pg. 1252
Bracken, Dan, Dir-Digital Strategy & Shopper Mktg - Church & Dwight Co., Inc.; pg. 1153, pg. 1063
Brackett, Mark L., Sr Dir-Enterprise Applications - Chick-fil-A, Inc.; pg. 1721, pg. 492
Bracy, Carl, VP-Mktg - Essilor of America, Inc.; pg. 1412, pg. 1680
Bracy, Patrick, Sr Mgr-Mktg - Dupont Pioneer; pg. 1795, pg. 708
Bradburne, Mary W., Sr Mgr-Social Media Comm - Cisco Systems, Inc.; pg. 372, pg. 240
Bradbury, Anthony, Dir-Global Mktg Comm - Jaguar Land Rover North America LLC; pg. 180, pg. 1081
Bradbury, Heath, Mgr-eBusiness Mktg - Advance Auto Parts, Inc.; pg. 197, pg. 1805
Bradbury, Marla, Dir-Mktg - Henkel Corporation; pg. 1166, pg. 897
Bradbury-Hills, Alyssa, Dir-Mktg - New England Confectionery Company Inc.; pg. 1860, pg. 842
Braddix, Dionne, Brand Mgr-Intl Center for Mktg Expertise - 3M Company; pg. 1142, pg. 956
Braden, Laura, Sr Dir-Comm - Sacramento Kings; pg. 579, pg. 197
Bradfish, Andrew, Specialist-Mktg - CARIBOU COFFEE COMPANY, INC.; pg. 1764, pg. 932
Bradford, Abby, Sr Mgr-Mktg & Comm - Hitachi Koki USA, Ltd.; pg. 1050, pg. 537
Bradford, Chuck, Sr Mgr-Integrated Media - Chick-fil-A, Inc.; pg. 1721, pg. 492
Bradford, Jamie, Dir-Mktg - NutriSystem, Inc.; pg. 1577, pg. 1533
Bradford, Matthew, Sls Information - Harbormaster Marine, Inc.; pg. 1707, pg. 896
Bradford, Mike, VP-Sls & Mktg - Penetone Corporation; pg. 333, pg. 1050
Bradford, Paige, Coord-Mktg - Noosa Yoghurt; pg. 886, pg. 310
Bradford, Peter, Head-Product Mgmt Pro-IBM Design - International Business Machines Corporation; pg. 418, pg. 1138
Bradford, Reggie, Sr VP-Product Dev - Oracle Corporation; pg. 1272, pg. 786
Bradford, Roger, Mgr-Product Mktg - Intel Corporation; pg. 645, pg. 266
Bradford, Stephen, Dir-Sls - Unilever United States, Inc.; pg. 904, pg. 1061
Brading, Neil, Sr Mgr-Global Brand Dev-Dove Men & Care - Unilever United States, Inc.; pg. 904, pg. 1061
Bradley, Bill, Sr Dir-Corp Social Responsibility Adv & Outreach - Anheuser-Busch Companies, LLC; pg. 237, pg. 991
Bradley, David, Mgr-Field Mktg-Natl - True Value Company; pg. 1065, pg. 592
Bradley, Glen, VP-Mktg Analytics - Price Chopper Operating Co., Inc.; pg. 1030, pg. 1341
Bradley, Kelly, Sr Mgr-Social Media - The Home Depot, Inc.;

pg. 1050, pg. 510
Bradley, Nisa, VP-Mktg, Energy & Sustainability Svcs - Schneider Electric USA, Inc.; pg. 1306, pg. 650
Bradley, Steve, Dir-Product Mktg-Global Support Svcs - KLA-Tencor Corporation; pg. 1353, pg. 146
Bradley, Tod, Sr Dir-Sls & Mktg - Elster American Meter Company; pg. 1411, pg. 1387
Bradner, Jennifer, Interim Pres & Interim CEO - Memphis Symphony Orchestra; pg. 561, pg. 1645
Bradshaw, Addie, Sr Mgr-DELL Bus Unit - SYNNEX Corporation; pg. 480, pg. 92
Bradshaw, Brad, VP-Product Mgmt - Mighty Distributing System of America; pg. 213, pg. 538
Bradshaw, Brent, VP-Mktg - Flowers Foods, Inc.; pg. 855, pg. 541
Bradshaw, Bruce, VP-Mktg-North America - Stratasys, Inc.; pg. 476, pg. 923
Bradshaw, Chris, CMO & Sr VP-Media, Entertainment & Reputation - Autodesk Inc.; pg. 356, pg. 257
Bradshaw, Sondra, Analyst-Mktg Procurement - SYNNEX Corporation; pg. 480, pg. 92
Bradstock, Drew, Sr Product Mgr - Google Inc.; pg. 1249, pg. 153
Brady Gill, Lisa, Exec Dir-North America Mktg - Texas Instruments Incorporated; pg. 679, pg. 1688
Brady, Aaron, Dir-Product Mgmt - RealPage, Inc.; pg. 1277, pg. 1669
Brady, Adam, Dir-Publ & New Media - Anaheim Ducks Hockey Club, LLC; pg. 528, pg. 42
Brady, Caitlyn, Assoc Mgr-Direct Mktg-North America - Coach, Inc.; pg. 3, pg. 1214
Brady, Christa, Dir-Creative Strategy-Global - Kao Brands Co. Inc.; pg. 513, pg. 1415
Brady, Deanna T., Pres-Consumer Product Sls & Grp VP - Hormel Foods Corporation; pg. 863, pg. 915
Brady, George, VP-Sls-TV, Cable & Digital Out of Home - Nielsen Audio; pg. 446, pg. 768
Brady, Gwen, Dir-Product Mktg - Staples, Inc.; pg. 474, pg. 821
Brady, Jason, Dir-Sls & Bus Dev - Lonza Inc.; pg. 1171, pg. 1041
Brady, Jennifer, VP-Mktg & Student Recruitment - Southern New Hampshire University; pg. 607, pg. 1036
Brady, Jim, Sr Mgr-PR - Cisco Systems, Inc.; pg. 372, pg. 240
Brady, Karen, VP-Sls-East Coast - National CineMedia, Inc.; pg. 567, pg. 314
Brady, Kate, Dir-Consumer Engagement, Media Strategy & Investment - PepsiCo, Inc.; pg. 259, pg. 1327
Brady, Kris Ann, Brand Mgr-Citracal - Bayer Healthcare Consumer Care Division; pg. 1500, pg. 1087
Brady, Lindsay, Dir-Mktg - Hillshire Brands; pg. 862, pg. 576
Brady, Marsha, Dir-Creative - American Apparel, Inc.; pg. 18, pg. 126
Brady, Martin, Dir-Consumer Mktg - Hamilton Beach Brands, Inc.; pg. 56, pg. 1783
Brady, Paula, Mgr-PR - Neiman Marcus, Inc.; pg. 30, pg. 1684
Brady, Ryan, Sr Mgr-Sls & Mktg IT Dev - General Motors Company; pg. 175, pg. 881
Brady, Sean, Sr Dir-Retail Brand Presentation-Nike Stores-Global - NIKE, Inc.; pg. 1812, pg. 1492
Brady, Stacy, Specialist-Adv Ops Product - Kelley Blue Book Co., Inc.; pg. 1656, pg. 112
Brady, Stephanie, Sr Dir-Institutional Mktg - Janus Capital Group, Inc.; pg. 772, pg. 320
Brady-Harris, Brigitte, VP-Brand Mktg & Licensing - Williams-Sonoma, Inc.; pg. 1140, pg. 234
Braelow, Christine, VP-Sls-Americas - iPass, Inc.; pg. 1259, pg. 193
Braet, Kathryn, Assoc Dir-Tablet Mktg - Meredith Corporation; pg. 1663, pg. 705
Braford, Coleen, Supvr-Co-op Adv - Best Buy Co., Inc.; pg. 1761, pg. 954
Bragaglia, Robert, Dir-Mktg - @Xi Computer Corporation; pg. 355, pg. 199
Bragan, Christine, VP-Mktg & Comm - AMC Networks Inc.; pg. 269, pg. 1189
Bragg, Braxton, Product Mgr - Zynga Inc.; pg. 1292, pg. 235
Bragg, Edwin, VP-Mktg & Comm - Shake Shack Inc.; pg. 1749, pg. 1291
Bragg, Melanie, Sr Dir-Strategic Comm-Worldwide Svcs & Functional Programs - Cisco Systems, Inc.; pg. 372, pg. 240
Brague, Michelle, Mgr-Trade Mktg - Constellation Brands, Inc.; pg. 1960, pg. 1348
Brain, Shawn, Sr Mgr-Brand Mktg-Global - The Ritz-Carlton Hotel Company LLC; pg. 1110, pg. 766
Brain-Mennes, Jennifer, Dir-Media & PR-Post Foods - Post Holdings, Inc.; pg. 833, pg. 1002
Brait, Robert, Product Mgr-PET & CT-Natl - Siemens Medical Solutions USA, Inc.; pg. 469, pg. 1550
Braithwait, Ross E., VP-Sls & Mktg - Varco Pruden Buildings, Inc.; pg. 118, pg. 1647
Braithwaite, Michael, Chief Strategy Officer - ClearOne Communications, Inc.; pg. 629, pg. 1756
Brajer, Stan, Mgr-Natl Sls - Garmin International, Inc.; pg. 1414, pg. 717
Braker, Emily, Assoc Dir-Relationship Mktg - Kellogg Company; pg. 831, pg. 870
Brakken, Erika, Dir-Mktg-Global-Teva - Deckers Outdoor Corporation; pg. 1807, pg. 100
Braman, Alison, Dir-On-Air Branding & Design-ABC Family Creative - The Walt Disney Company; pg. 317, pg. 52
Bramante, Christina, Dir-Product Support & Toxicology - Cabot Corporation; pg. 1151, pg. 792
Bramble, Kathleen A., Mgr-Mktg Dev - 3M Company; pg. 1142, pg. 956
Bramble, Natasha, Sr Mgr-Mktg-US Retail - MFS Investment Management; pg. 782, pg. 798
Bramer, Jerry, Brand Mgr-Mktg-Accessories - Smith & Wesson Holding Corporation; pg. 1845, pg. 846
Bramwell, Dick, VP-Sls - Daubert Industries, Inc.; pg. 1155, pg. 561
Brancato, Linda, VP-Adv - Daily News, L.P.; pg. 1632, pg. 1221
Brancazio, Candice, Sr Dir-Revenue & Controller - Viacom Inc.; pg. 316, pg. 1310
Branch, Andre, CMO-Consumer Products Grp - NBTY, Inc.; pg. 1572, pg. 1338
Branch, Bill, Project Dir-Mktg - Northern Arizona University; pg. 606, pg. 12
Branch, Elizabeth, Brand Mgr-Mktg-Farm Rich Snacks & Appetizers - Rich Products Corporation; pg. 892, pg. 1150
Branch, Rachel, VP-Mktg & PR-Thomas Pink - LVMH Inc.; pg. 9, pg. 1254
Branch, Richard, Dir-Media - The Sports Authority, Inc.; pg. 1846, pg. 326
Branch, Sarah, Dir-Mktg - CustomInk, LLC; pg. 22, pg. 1780
Branco, Leonardo, Brand Mgr-Fruit, Plastic Fruit Cups & Squeezers Pouches - Del Monte Foods, Inc.; pg. 852, pg. 304
Branco, Margaret, Dir-Digital Mktg-Retail Annuities - New York Life Insurance Company; pg. 1211, pg. 1268
Brand, Christiaan, Product Mgr-Security & Identity - Google Inc.; pg. 1249, pg. 153
Brand, Dalana N., Sr Dir-Benefits-Global - Whirlpool Corporation; pg. 62, pg. 872
Brand, Eric, Head-Mktg - Morgan Stanley; pg. 783, pg. 1261
Brand, Harriet, Dir-PR - TPR Education, LLC; pg. 1695, pg. 822
Brand, Robert, Dir-EY Brand, Comm & Mktg - Ernst & Young Global Limited; pg. 748, pg. 1228
Brandeburg, Rebecca, Mgr-Channel Mktg - Intuit Inc.; pg. 769, pg. 158
Brandeisky, Howard, Sr VP-Global Mktg & Customer Solutions - John B. Sanfilippo & Son, Inc.; pg. 1024, pg. 610
Brandenburg, Kathleen, Coord-Mktg - ProLogis; pg. 1108, pg. 322
Brandes, Robert P., Exec VP-Global Products Strategy - FLEETCOR TECHNOLOGIES, INC.; pg. 758, pg. 537
Brandner, Kim, Sr Dir-Sourcing-Dry & Frozen Grocery - Wal-Mart Stores, Inc.; pg. 1790, pg. 29
Brandon, Crystal, Sr Mgr-Adv & Digital Innovation - AT&T Mobility LLC; pg. 619, pg. 488
Brandow, Glen, Mng Dir-Media Rels & Events-Global - FedEx Corporation; pg. 1907, pg. 1642
Brandow, Paul, Acting Chief Risk Officer - E*TRADE Financial Corporation; pg. 749, pg. 1230
Brandreth, Scott, Dir-Mdsg - The Phillies, L.P.; pg. 575, pg. 1569
Brandt, Chris, Mgr-Natl Mktg & Brand Mgr - General Motors Company; pg. 175, pg. 881
Brandt, Craig, Strategist-Retail Mktg - Dell Inc.; pg. 383, pg. 1737
Brandt, Jim, Mgr-Mktg - Simpson Door Company; pg. 110, pg. 1823
Brandt, Melissa, Mgr-Mktg - Lincoln Financial Group; pg. 1206, pg. 1375
Brandt, Susie, Mgr-Channel Mktg - Anheuser-Busch Companies, LLC; pg. 237, pg. 991
Brandwein, Mark, VP-Sls - D.A. Kopp & Associates, Inc.; pg. 381, pg. 1126
Braney, Debbie, VP-Integrated Mktg Programs - Hitachi Data Systems Corporation; pg. 407, pg. 265
Branham, Allen, Dir-Sls-East - Harsco Rail; pg. 1345, pg. 1623
Brann, Gentry, VP-Comm & Mktg-Global - Chicago Bridge & Iron Company; pg. 75, pg. 1747
Brannan, Scott, VP-Digital Mktg - Bank of America Corporation; pg. 718, pg. 1362
Brannvall, Jonas, Grp Mgr-Product-Global - ABB Inc.; pg. 1309, pg. 1359
Branscomb, Brittany, Analyst-Digital Media-User Acq - National Football League; pg. 567, pg. 1264
Branscum, Stephen G., Sr Mgr-Mktg Bus Unit Ops - Burlington Northern Santa Fe, LLC; pg. 1901, pg. 1694
Brant, Steve, Mgr-Channel Mktg - Armstrong World Industries, Inc.; pg. 914, pg. 1545
Brant, Tim, Mgr-Reg Mktg-US Trust - Bank of America Corporation; pg. 718, pg. 1362
Brantley, Pam, Sr Area Mgr-Mktg-Americas West - Riverbed Technology, Inc.; pg. 1277, pg. 225
Brao, Jose, Sr Mgr-Event - Waldorf Astoria Naples; pg. 1118, pg. 451
Brar, Hardeep Singh, VP-Sls-India - General Motors Company; pg. 175, pg. 881
Brar, Steve, Dir-Product Mktg - Riverbed Technology, Inc.; pg. 1277, pg. 225
Brar, Surinder, Chief Strategy Officer - Cisco Systems, Inc.; pg. 372, pg. 240
Brashear, Denise, Head-PR-Global & Exec Dir - Novartis Corporation; pg. 1574, pg. 1273
Brashear, Karen, Mgr-Mktg - The Florida Times-Union; pg. 1641, pg. 433
Brashears, Ken, Product Mgr-Software - Melissa Data Corp.; pg. 432, pg. 188
Brasic, Cindy, Brand Mgr-Global Private Label - Ace Hardware Corporation; pg. 1040, pg. 644
Brasington Clark, Becky, Dir-Mktg & Online Book Publ - The Johns Hopkins University Press; pg. 1655, pg. 757
Braskamp, Ana, Specialist-PR, Mobile & Emerging Products - Yahoo! Inc.; pg. 1289, pg. 289
Brassard, Julie, Dir-Mktg - Liberty Mutual Insurance Group Inc.; pg. 1205, pg. 797
Braswell, Christy, Rep-Adv Sls - News-Leader; pg. 1670, pg. 422
Braswell, Joel, Assoc Dir-Media - AT&T Mobility LLC; pg. 619, pg. 488
Brathwaite, Jerome, Reg Mgr-Mktg-Skincare - Avon Products, Inc.; pg. 500, pg. 1198
Bratkovich, Lisa, Sr VP-Mktg - Guthy-Renker LLC; pg. 289, pg. 273
Bratt, Dan, Mgr-Sls-Natl-Great Plains Ag Div - Great Plains Manufacturing, Incorporated; pg. 704, pg. 721
Bratthauar, Chris, Dir-Mktg-Global - Manitowoc Crane Shady Grove; pg. 1359, pg. 1586
Bratton, Richard, VP-Sls-North America - Kayak; pg. 1260, pg. 363
Brau, Susan, Brand Mgr - Michael Foods, Inc.; pg. 877, pg. 949
Braude, Sasha, Sr Dir-Campaign Mktg - Adobe Systems Incorporated; pg. 342, pg. 235
Brauer, Amy, Sr Mgr-Brand Connections - Foot Locker, Inc.; pg. 1808, pg. 1231
Brauer, Karl, Sr Dir-Insights - Kelley Blue Book Co., Inc.; pg. 1656, pg. 112
Braulick, Tim, Sr Mgr-Creative Svcs - Vital Images, Inc.; pg. 1607, pg. 950
Brault, Julie, VP-Brand & Interactive Media - Videotron Ltd.; pg. 317, pg. 1957
Brault, Mary Beth, Sr Mgr-Corp Comm - Hamilton Beach Brands, Inc.; pg. 56, pg. 1783
Braun, Dakota, Coord-Media Production - National CineMedia, Inc.; pg. 567, pg. 314
Braun, David, Dir-Western Sls & Svc - The Penn Companies; pg. 10, pg. 1568
Braun, Jane, Sr Project Mgr-Comm-Comml Mktg - Schneider Electric USA, Inc.; pg. 1306, pg. 650
Braun, John, Mgr-TV Sls - Comcast Spectacor, L.P.; pg. 278, pg. 1562
Braun, Liz, Mgr-Mktg-Swingline - ACCO Brands Corporation; pg. 340, pg. 626
Braun, Raymond, Mgr-Social Mktg-YouTube - Google Inc.; pg. 1249, pg. 153

Braun, Sara, Sr Dir-Mktg-Kraft Macaroni & Cheese - The Kraft Heinz Company; *pg.* 871, *pg.* 641
Braun, Tammy, Brand Mgr-Mktg - Taylor Corporation; *pg.* 1691, *pg.* 952
Braun, Wayne, Corp Dir-Mktg & Bus Dev - Bradken; *pg.* 1150, *pg.* 714
Brauner, Ron, VP-Mktg Comm - Assurant, Inc.; *pg.* 1193, *pg.* 1198
Braunshausen, Andy, Dir-Mktg-US Dairy Foods - Land O'Lakes, Inc.; *pg.* 873, *pg.* 915
Braunstein, Daniel, Specialist-Mktg Automation - Avid Technology, Inc.; *pg.* 622, *pg.* 804
Braunstein, Shawna, Reg Mgr-Mktg - Beazer Homes USA, Inc.; *pg.* 1081, *pg.* 491
Braut, Scott, Head-Content-Creative Cloud - Adobe Systems Incorporated; *pg.* 342, *pg.* 235
Braverman, Erik, Sr Dir-Mktg & Brdcst - Los Angeles Dodgers Inc.; *pg.* 559, *pg.* 135
Braverman, Julie, Sr Specialist-Search Engine Mktg - Laureate Education, Inc.; *pg.* 603, *pg.* 757
Braverman, Marnie, VP-Mktg-Health - Health Magazine; *pg.* 1648, *pg.* 1238
Braverman, Marnie, VP-Mktg-Health - Time Inc.; *pg.* 1693, *pg.* 1300
Bravo, Bibiana, Corp Mgr-Mktg - Calavo Growers, Inc.; *pg.* 843, *pg.* 276
Bravo, Correy, Bus Mgr-Walmart.com Marketplace - Wal-Mart.com; *pg.* 1287, *pg.* 50
Bravo, Yina, Dir-Mktg - MasterCard Worldwide Inc.; *pg.* 780, *pg.* 988
Brawley, Andrew, Mgr-eMail & Mobile Mktg - Papa Murphy's International, LLC; *pg.* 1743, *pg.* 1846
Brawley, Nick, Sr Mgr-Web Comm - Panera Bread Company; *pg.* 1029, *pg.* 1001
Brawn, Karen, Dir-Mktg - KraftMaid Cabinetry, Inc.; *pg.* 1053, *pg.* 1465
Brawner, Trish, Dir-Adv & Brand Comm - Cancer Treatment Centers of America; *pg.* 1511, *pg.* 410
Bray, Bethany, Brand Mgr - Lindt & Sprungli (USA) Inc.; *pg.* 1857, *pg.* 1039
Bray, David, Gen Mgr-Fuel Sls & Mktg - Shell Oil Company; *pg.* 984, *pg.* 1714
Bray, Frances, Sr Mgr-Creative Svcs - Blackboard Inc.; *pg.* 1232, *pg.* 396
Bray, Glenn, Sr Dir-Product Mgmt & Cloud Collaboration - Cisco Systems, Inc.; *pg.* 372, *pg.* 240
Bray, Jo, Exec Dir-Mktg-Cosmopolitan Magazine - The Hearst Corporation; *pg.* 1649, *pg.* 1239
Bray-Sweet, Ariana, Coord-Mktg Svcs-Global - Oregon Tourism Commission; *pg.* 1003, *pg.* 1508
Brayer, Doug, Dir-Mktg & Brand Mgmt - CooperVision, Inc.; *pg.* 1407, *pg.* 1159
Braz, Hugo, Rep-Mktg - Caterpillar, Inc.; *pg.* 1321, *pg.* 650
Brazil, Joel, Mgr-Strategic Partner-Programmatic Adv Sls - Microsoft Corporation; *pg.* 435, *pg.* 1824
Brazle, Joel, Dir-Product Dev - Zappos.com, Inc.; *pg.* 1291, *pg.* 1030
Brazytis, Jim, Mgr-Mktg Comm-Label & Pkg Matls - Avery Dennison Corporation; *pg.* 1452, *pg.* 95
Brazzini, Francisco, Mgr-Mktg - Italian Government Tourist Board-North America; *pg.* 996, *pg.* 1244
Brearey, Paul, Mgr-Mktg-Enthusiast Events - Ford Motor Company of Canada, Limited; *pg.* 174, *pg.* 1930
Breault, Donna, Dir-Mktg Comm - iCad, Inc.; *pg.* 643, *pg.* 1037
Breault, Scott, Dir-Mktg - Ultimate Fitness Group, LLC; *pg.* 589, *pg.* 427
Breaux, Annie, Sr Mgr-Integrated Mktg Branded Solutions - Time Inc.; *pg.* 1693, *pg.* 1300
Breaux, Randy, Sr VP-Mktg & Strategic Plng - Motion Industries, Inc.; *pg.* 213, *pg.* 3
Breaux, Tim, VP-Sls - duPont Registry; *pg.* 1637, *pg.* 462
Breaux, Warren, Corp Dir-Sls-Global - Benchmark Hospitality International Inc.; *pg.* 1081, *pg.* 1747
Brecher, Sari, Dir-PR & Entertainment Mktg - Diageo North America Inc.; *pg.* 248, *pg.* 1223
Breckenfeld, Del, Dir-Entertainment Mktg - Fender Musical Instruments Corporation; *pg.* 547, *pg.* 21
Breckenfelder, Julie, Mgr-Mktg - Huron Consulting Group Inc.; *pg.* 768, *pg.* 577
Breckenridge, Sean, Sr Dir-Mktg - Bass Pro Shops, Inc.; *pg.* 1826, *pg.* 1006
Breda, Carina, Sr VP-Mktg - Orly International, Inc.; *pg.* 518, *pg.* 137
Bredemann, Betty, Bus Mgr-Intl - Clif Bar Inc.; *pg.* 848, *pg.* 83
Bredeson, Liz, Dir-Consumer Mktg - Meredith Corporation; *pg.* 1663, *pg.* 705
Breed, Alan M, VP-Deepwater Mktg - Rowan Companies, Inc.; *pg.* 984, *pg.* 1713
Breed, Carl, Dir-Mktg - Blue Bell Creameries, L.P.; *pg.* 1851, *pg.* 1668
Breen, Doak, Dir-Creative Svcs-CBS RADIO & WWJ DETROIT - CBS Broadcasting Inc.; *pg.* 273, *pg.* 1210
Breen, Doak, Dir-Creative Svcs - CBS Corporation; *pg.* 273, *pg.* 1210
Breen, Edward, Interim Chm & Interim CEO - E.I. du Pont de Nemours & Company; *pg.* 1159, *pg.* 390
Breen, Ken, VP-Product Mgmt - EBSCO Information Services Walpole; *pg.* 1638, *pg.* 849
Breezer, Harlon, Mgr-Automotive Sls - TriEnda, LLC; *pg.* 1890, *pg.* 1887
Bregder, Michael, Mgr-Adv - Mercury Insurance Company; *pg.* 1208, *pg.* 136
Bregel, Wendy, Dir-Mktg - Ecolab Inc.; *pg.* 329, *pg.* 960
Breger, David, Head-Mobile Product - LinkedIn Corporation; *pg.* 1262, *pg.* 160
Brehler, Fletcher, Sr Mgr-Mktg - Hospira, Inc.; *pg.* 1542, *pg.* 623
Brehm, Katie, Mgr-Digital Mktg - New York & Company, Inc.; *pg.* 1779, *pg.* 1268
Brehm, Matt, Mgr-Digital Media - Capital Brands, LLC; *pg.* 53, *pg.* 127
Brehm, Sarah, Head-Mktg-Brand Adv & Comm - Best Buy Co., Inc.; *pg.* 1761, *pg.* 954
Brehmer, Jeff, Product Mgr-FiberMax & Stoneville Cotton-US - Bayer CropScience; *pg.* 1149, *pg.* 981
Breit, Charlie, Dir-Digital Mktg - The Northwestern Mutual Life Insurance Company; *pg.* 1212, *pg.* 1879
Breithaupt, Art, VP-Sls & Mktg - AAR Corp.; *pg.* 223, *pg.* 671
Breithaupt, Jennifer, Sr VP-Entertainment Mktg - Citigroup Inc.; *pg.* 735, *pg.* 1212
Brekka, Maureen, Sr VP & Dir-Mktg-North America Reg - Brown-Forman Corporation; *pg.* 1958, *pg.* 732
Breland, Michael, Sr Mgr-Sls - Baker Hughes Incorporated; *pg.* 1315, *pg.* 1700
Brelus, John J., Gen Mgr-Global Product-Discharge & LED Retrofit Lighting Sys - General Electric Company; *pg.* 1297, *pg.* 347
Bremmer, Geoff, VP-Mktg - Monster Beverage Corporation; *pg.* 257, *pg.* 69
Bremmer, Geoff, VP-Mktg - Rockstar, Inc.; *pg.* 265, *pg.* 1029
Breneiser, Todd, Head-Product Plng-NAFTA - FCA US LLC; *pg.* 170, *pg.* 868
Breneman, Andrea, Coord-Social Mktg - Kohl's Corporation; *pg.* 1775, *pg.* 1870
Breningmeyer, Gregg, Dir-Mktg & Sls - Deere & Company; *pg.* 703, *pg.* 632
Brenkert, Steve, Product Dir - The Dun & Bradstreet Corp.; *pg.* 1637, *pg.* 1120
Brenman, Bobby, Mgr-Product Mktg - Google Inc.; *pg.* 1249, *pg.* 153
Brennan, Beth, Dir-Client Mktg-Enterprise Americas - Concur Technologies, Inc.; *pg.* 1236, *pg.* 1813
Brennan, Billy, Sr Mgr-Sustainability & Intl Comm - Monsanto Company; *pg.* 1173, *pg.* 999
Brennan, Chris, Mgr-US Bus Comm-Supply Chain & Media - W.W. Grainger, Inc.; *pg.* 1390, *pg.* 625
Brennan, Christopher, Mng Dir & Reg Dir-Sls - Avid Technology, Inc.; *pg.* 622, *pg.* 804
Brennan, Colleen, Dir-Global Content & Creative Svcs - Hyatt Hotels Corporation; *pg.* 1096, *pg.* 577
Brennan, Jack, Dir-PR - Cincinnati Bengals, Inc.; *pg.* 540, *pg.* 1410
Brennan, Jenna, Assoc Dir-Mktg Comm-Siemens Healthcare - Siemens Medical Solutions USA, Inc.; *pg.* 469, *pg.* 1550
Brennan, John, Sr VP-Sls - Weiman Products, LLC; *pg.* 337, *pg.* 616
Brennan, Joseph, Sr Mgr-Mktg-Demand Generation Programs & Analysis - Advent Software, Inc.; *pg.* 345, *pg.* 211
Brennan, Joseph, Sr VP-Sls & Mktg - ProPhase Labs, Inc.; *pg.* 1586, *pg.* 1526
Brennan, Katy, Brand Mgr-Delivery-DDF Skincare - The Procter & Gamble Company; *pg.* 1129, *pg.* 1418
Brennan, Kelly, Assistant-Mktg & Comm - Missouri State University; *pg.* 605, *pg.* 1006
Brennan, Mary Ann, Sr Dir-Procurement-Global - Mattel Games/Puzzles; *pg.* 962, *pg.* 80
Brennan, Mary Ann, Sr Dir-Procurement-Global - MATTEL, INC.; *pg.* 962, *pg.* 81
Brennan, Megan, Sr Mgr-MileagePlus Partnerships - United Airlines, Inc.; *pg.* 1927, *pg.* 593
Brennan, Michael, VP-Mktg - Southeast Toyota Distributors, LLC; *pg.* 190, *pg.* 421
Brennan, Nancy, Mng Dir & Head-Mktg, Global Banking & Markets - Bank of America Corporation; *pg.* 718, *pg.* 1362
Brennan, Niall, Dir-Office of Info Products & Data Analytics - Centers for Medicare & Medicaid Services; *pg.* 990, *pg.* 756
Brennan, Patricia, Sr Mgr - Sanofi US; *pg.* 1592, *pg.* 1046
Brennan, Pete, Sr Mgr-Mktg-Fresh Chicken - Foster Farms; *pg.* 856, *pg.* 122
Brennan, Rick, Mgr-Dealer Mktg-Brand Programs - Carfax Inc.; *pg.* 202, *pg.* 1777
Brennan, Susan, Mgr-Mktg - Philips Lighting; *pg.* 1303, *pg.* 806
Brennen, Fran, Sr Dir-Mktg Comm - VEECO INSTRUMENTS INC.; *pg.* 1434, *pg.* 1322
Brenner, Andrew, Product Mgr-Android Auto - Google Inc.; *pg.* 1249, *pg.* 153
Brenner, Andrew, Sr Mgr-Global Comm-100 Resilient Cities - The Rockefeller Foundation; *pg.* 155, *pg.* 1286
Brenner, Beth, Chief Revenue Officer-Domino Media Group - Domino's Pizza, Inc.; *pg.* 1726, *pg.* 865
Brenner, Candace, Dir-Brand Mktg-Global - Daybreak Game Company, LLC; *pg.* 1237, *pg.* 202
Brenner, Dave, Bus Mgr-CPG-Global - Google Inc.; *pg.* 1249, *pg.* 153
Brenner, Jason, Sr Mgr - Jet.com, Inc.; *pg.* 1260, *pg.* 1073
Brenner, Jason, Brand Mgr-Entertainment - The Upper Deck Company, LLC; *pg.* 969, *pg.* 62
Brenner, Kiersa, Mgr-Bus Dev Sls-Kerastase & Shu Uemura Art of Hair - L'Oreal USA; *pg.* 514, *pg.* 1252
Brenner, Kim N., Sr Mgr-Consumer Healthcare & Global Comm - Pfizer Inc.; *pg.* 1581, *pg.* 1278
Brenner, Matt, Brand Mgr-NIKEiD-Global - NIKE, Inc.; *pg.* 1812, *pg.* 1492
Brenner, Melissa Rosenthal, Sr VP-Mktg - National Basketball Association; *pg.* 566, *pg.* 1264
Brenner, Richard, Sr Dir-Digital Mktg-SEO, SEM & Social Media - Automatic Data Processing, Inc.; *pg.* 357, *pg.* 1117
Brenner, Sam, Mgr-Brand Mktg - Captain D's, LLC; *pg.* 1720, *pg.* 1649
Brenner, Tyler, Dir-Mktg & PR - Better Homes & Gardens Books; *pg.* 1620, *pg.* 704
Brennion, Travis, Sr Assoc Brand Mgr - Del Monte Foods, Inc.; *pg.* 852, *pg.* 304
Brent, Kimberly, Asst VP-Mktg & Program Mgr - Wells Fargo & Company; *pg.* 819, *pg.* 232
Brentani, Maristella, VP-Product Strategy & Line Plng-North America - Luxottica Group; *pg.* 8, *pg.* 1323
Brentham, Shane, VP-Mktg - GlobalLogic, Inc.; *pg.* 400, *pg.* 1791
Brentlinger, Ann, Dir-Mktg - National American University; *pg.* 605, *pg.* 1624
Brentlinger, Nina, Specialist-Mktg & Creative Cloud Product Mktg - Adobe Systems Incorporated; *pg.* 342, *pg.* 235
Brenton, Melissa, Sr Dir-Mktg Comm - Constant Contact, Inc.; *pg.* 379, *pg.* 850
Brescia, Colleen, Mgr-Product Dev - Unum Group; *pg.* 1222, *pg.* 1629
Breseman, Brian, Dir-PR - Tampa Bay Storm; *pg.* 587, *pg.* 476
Bresemann, David, Chief Product Officer & Sr VP - Silicon Laboratories Inc.; *pg.* 674, *pg.* 1666
Breskin, Madeline, Mgr-PR - adidas America Inc.; *pg.* 1803, *pg.* 1500
Breskin, Nicole, Dir-Product Mgmt - The New York Times Company; *pg.* 1668, *pg.* 1270
Bresler, Justin, VP-Mktg - Denver Metro Convention & Visitors Bureau; *pg.* 991, *pg.* 318
Breslin, Genny, Acct Mgr-Natl Adv - TEN: The Enthusiast Network; *pg.* 1691, *pg.* 1298
Breslin, Michelle, Brand Mgr-Digital Mktg - Toys "R" Us, Inc.; *pg.* 968, *pg.* 1130
Breslin, Mike, Sr Dir-Global Brand Strategy & Mktg-Marvel - Hasbro, Inc.; *pg.* 954, *pg.* 1603
Breslin, Tim, Sr VP-Product & Tech - Onion, Inc.; *pg.* 1673, *pg.* 586
Bresn, Nolan, Dir-Creative Svcs - Abercrombie & Kent USA, LLC; *pg.* 1896, *pg.* 607
Bresnahan, Heather, Sr Mgr-Global Media & Agency Mgmt - Microsoft Corporation; *pg.* 435, *pg.* 1824
Bresnahan, J. Todd, Mgr-Northeastern Reg Sls - Reliable Automatic Sprinkler Co., Inc.; *pg.* 1137, *pg.* 1158

First page reference indicates Business Class Edition
Second page reference indicates Geographic Edition

Bresnahan, Steve, Gen Mgr-Sls & Mktg - Armstrong World Industries, Inc.; *pg.* 914, *pg.* 1545
Bressan, Nick, Mgr-Multimedia Sls - The State Journal-Register; *pg.* 1689, *pg.* 662
Bressers, Josh, Product Mgr-Security - Red Hat, Inc.; *pg.* 460, *pg.* 1388
Bressner, Karen, Head-Digital Adv - AccuWeather, Inc.; *pg.* 268, *pg.* 1587
Bretillon, Mathieu, Head-Mktg Intelligence-North America - Air France, USA; *pg.* 1897, *pg.* 1188
Brett, Harris, Product Mgr - Hormel Foods Corporation; *pg.* 863, *pg.* 915
Brett, Michelle, VP-Retail Sls - Living Proof, Inc.; *pg.* 514, *pg.* 809
Brett, Steve, Sr Mgr-Pub Affairs - Abbott Laboratories; *pg.* 1484, *pg.* 551
Bretthorst, Ty, Dir-Mktg-Toothbrushes-Asia Div - Colgate-Palmolive Company; *pg.* 504, *pg.* 1215
Brettingen, Timothy, Mgr-Media - Showtime Networks Inc.; *pg.* 308, *pg.* 1291
Bretzman, Whitney Grones, Dir-Digital & Events Mktg - Baker & Taylor, Inc.; *pg.* 1619, *pg.* 1362
Breuner, Kevin, VP-Mktg - CD Baby, Inc.; *pg.* 1764, *pg.* 1501
Breunig, Mark, Reg Product Mgr-CIJ-NA - Videojet Technologies Inc.; *pg.* 489, *pg.* 671
Breunle, Jean, Sr Mgr-Retention - Bonnier Corporation; *pg.* 1622, *pg.* 480
Brevard, Mike, Dir-Infrastructure Platform & Private Cloud Sls-Worldwide - Microsoft Corporation; *pg.* 435, *pg.* 1824
Brewer, Ali, Dir-Mktg-Baseball & Softball Div - Wilson Sporting Goods Co.; *pg.* 1848, *pg.* 596
Brewer, Anna, Sr Mgr-Relationship-Tech Solutions - EarthLink Holdings Corp.; *pg.* 1240, *pg.* 504
Brewer, Ashley, Mgr-Franchise & Local Store Mktg - Einstein Noah Restaurant Group, Inc.; *pg.* 1019, *pg.* 332
Brewer, Ashley, Brand Mgr - Eli Lilly and Company; *pg.* 1527, *pg.* 684
Brewer, Bob, Sr Dir-Sls-Dell - SanDisk Corporation; *pg.* 465, *pg.* 147
Brewer, Brady, Sr VP-Mktg, Category & Store Design-China & Asia-Pacific Reg - Starbucks Corporation; *pg.* 897, *pg.* 1840
Brewer, Brian, Brand Mgr-Intl Brands - Safilo USA Inc.; *pg.* 11, *pg.* 1106
Brewer, Catherine, Mgr-Natl Media - Dr Pepper Snapple Group, Inc.; *pg.* 250, *pg.* 1729
Brewer, Eric, Sr Dir-Pub Affairs & Govt Rels - Wal-Mart Stores, Inc.; *pg.* 1790, *pg.* 29
Brewer, Jack, Dir-Mktg & Bus Dev - AAR Corp.; *pg.* 223, *pg.* 671
Brewer, Julian, Analyst-Sls & Mktg - Crane Carrier Company; *pg.* 168, *pg.* 1489
Brewer, Seth, Sr Dir-Social Media Mktg - The Travelers Companies, Inc.; *pg.* 1220, *pg.* 352
Brewer, Seth, Sr Dir-Social Media Mktg - Travelers Insurance; *pg.* 1220, *pg.* 963
Brewer, Shannon, Producer-Global Creative-Channel - Apple Inc.; *pg.* 350, *pg.* 73
Brewer, Ty, Sr VP-Strategic Mktg - RealPage, Inc.; *pg.* 1277, *pg.* 1669
Brewer, Whitney, Dir-Digital Media-Intl - Sony Pictures Entertainment Inc.; *pg.* 309, *pg.* 72
Brewin, Fred, Product Mgr - Google Inc.; *pg.* 1249, *pg.* 153
Brewster, Lemuel, Sr Dir-PR - Thomson Reuters - Corporate Headquarters; *pg.* 1693, *pg.* 1299
Brey, Greg, Mgr-Sls - Heresite Protective Coatings, Inc.; *pg.* 1442, *pg.* 1868
Breyer, Lizzie, Mgr-Mktg - General Mills, Inc.; *pg.* 828, *pg.* 933
Brian, Dan, Exec VP-Media - Demand Media, Inc.; *pg.* 1238, *pg.* 273
Briar, John, Reg Mgr-Sls - FUJIFILM U.S.A., Inc.; *pg.* 1414, *pg.* 1348
Bricca, Dave, Sr Mgr-Web Design & Dev - Dell Inc.; *pg.* 383, *pg.* 1737
Briccola, Barbara, Reg Mgr-Sls - Atlantic Aviation Corporation; *pg.* 224, *pg.* 1729
Brichetto, Nena P., Mgr-Channel Mktg - Zebra Technologies Corporation; *pg.* 690, *pg.* 628
Brick, Hillary, Sr VP-Mktg - Giumarra Vineyards Corporation; *pg.* 1964, *pg.* 45
Bricker, Tammy, Sr Mgr-Mktg - Apartment Investment and Management Company; *pg.* 1079, *pg.* 316
Brickl, McKenzie, Mgr-Social Media Mktg-Victoria's Secret - L Brands, Inc.; *pg.* 1776, *pg.* 1441
Brickley, Colin, Mgr-Sls & Mktg-Onitsuka Tiger & ASICS Tiger - ASICS America Corporation; *pg.* 1826, *pg.* 106
Brickmeier, James, Sr VP-Strategic Mktg - Concurrent Computer Corporation; *pg.* 379, *pg.* 531
Briden, Pat, Head-Creative Svcs - Honeywell International Inc.; *pg.* 407, *pg.* 1088
Bridger, Christine, Sr VP-Creative & Content Strategy - Current USA, Inc.; *pg.* 1765, *pg.* 315
Bridges, Andrew, Dir-Global Expert Mktg-Smokers' Health - GlaxoSmithKline; *pg.* 1536, *pg.* 1389
Bridges, Elaine, Dir-Adv Art - J.C. Penney Company, Inc.; *pg.* 1774, *pg.* 1732
Bridges, James, Dir-New Media - Shawnee News-Star; *pg.* 1686, *pg.* 1488
Bridges, Janet, Sr Dir-Fin Svcs Treasury - Chick-fil-A, Inc.; *pg.* 1721, *pg.* 492
Bridges, Karen, Mgr-Customer Mktg - International Paper Company; *pg.* 1460, *pg.* 1644
Bridges, Kimberly McIntosh, Sr VP-Sls & Mktg-Vascular Intervention Div - The Spectranetics Corporation; *pg.* 1595, *pg.* 315
Bridges, May, Dir-Mktg - Sun Life Financial Inc.; *pg.* 806, *pg.* 1944
Bridges, Mike, VP-Mktg & Comm - League of Southeastern Credit unions; *pg.* 145, *pg.* 469
Bridges, Mikelyn, Mgr-Mktg Svcs - Bourns, Inc.; *pg.* 627, *pg.* 193
Bridgford, Michael, Reg Mgr-Sls - Bridgford Foods Corporation; *pg.* 842, *pg.* 42
Bridgham, Walter, Product Dir - Macy's East; *pg.* 1777, *pg.* 1254
Bridoux, Kathleen, Dir-Mktg - Audemars Piguet (North America); *pg.* 1, *pg.* 1198
Brien, Nick, Pres-Mktg Svcs - Hearst Magazines; *pg.* 1649, *pg.* 1239
Briere, Sidney, Specialist-Media & Trng - Auto-Owners Insurance Group; *pg.* 1194, *pg.* 895
Briese, Yvonne, VP-Brand Mktg-Whisky - Diageo North America, Inc.; *pg.* 1961, *pg.* 361
Brieve, Tiffany, Sr Mgr-Mktg-Healthcare - Herman Miller, Inc.; *pg.* 926, *pg.* 913
Brigger, Mike, Dir-Mktg-eBusiness - Cintas Corporation; *pg.* 372, *pg.* 1411
Briggs, Amy, Brand Mgr-Dev - WD-40 Company; *pg.* 337, *pg.* 210
Briggs, Andrew, Sr Dir-Mktg, Product Plng & Technical Svcs - Yokohama Tire Corporation; *pg.* 1892, *pg.* 94
Briggs, Chris C., Gen Mgr-Gas Mktg - Anadarko Petroleum Corporation; *pg.* 971, *pg.* 1746
Briggs, Jason, Sr Dir-Bus Dev - Comcast Corporation; *pg.* 276, *pg.* 1560
Briggs, Jon, VP-Issuer Mktg - MasterCard Worldwide Inc.; *pg.* 780, *pg.* 988
Briggs, Scott, VP-Mktg & Sls - Noven Pharmaceuticals, Inc.; *pg.* 1576, *pg.* 445
Briggs, Tony, VP-Sls & Distr - Vermeer Manufacturing Company; *pg.* 708, *pg.* 711
Bright, Daniel, Sr Analyst-Fin & Mktg - Jack Henry & Associates, Inc.; *pg.* 422, *pg.* 988
Bright, David, VP-Mktg - DOLE FOOD COMPANY, INC.; *pg.* 853, *pg.* 306
Bright, Mark J., VP-Oil & Gas Mktg & Midstream-North America - Apache Corporation; *pg.* 1934, *pg.* 1700
Bright, Morgan, Asst Mgr-Digital Commerce Mktg Chico's - Chico's FAS, Inc.; *pg.* 21, *pg.* 427
Bright, Stacie, Dir-Mktg Comm-Global - Unilever United States, Inc.; *pg.* 904, *pg.* 1061
Brightbill, Kelly, Portfolio Mgr-Mktg-BRILINTA - AstraZeneca Pharmaceuticals LP; *pg.* 1497, *pg.* 389
Briley, John, Dir-Sls - InfoGroup; *pg.* 414, *pg.* 350
Briley, Russ, Sr Dir-Circulation Sls West Reg - Ventura County Star; *pg.* 1699, *pg.* 57
Brill, Ira, Dir-Mktg Svcs - Foster Farms; *pg.* 856, *pg.* 122
Brill, Jake, Product Mgr-Mgmt - Facebook, Inc.; *pg.* 1245, *pg.* 143
Brill, Jim, Mgr-Mktg-Product Mktg Grp - United Parcel Service, Inc.; *pg.* 1928, *pg.* 522
Brill, LaSandra, Sr Dir-Paid & Earned Media - Symantec Corporation; *pg.* 478, *pg.* 161
Brill, Molly, Dir-Brand Adv - SONIC Corp.; *pg.* 1750, *pg.* 1487
Brillhart, Randy, Brand Mgr-Global - Chevron Corporation; *pg.* 974, *pg.* 259
Brilliant, Philip A., VP-Licensing & Mktg - A&A Global Industries Inc.; *pg.* 948, *pg.* 767
Brim, Charlie, Mgr-Adv & Sponsorships - Interstate Battery System of America Inc.; *pg.* 208, *pg.* 1682
Brim-Edwards, Julia, Sr Dir-Global Strategy & Ops-Govt & Pub Affairs - NIKE, Inc.; *pg.* 1812, *pg.* 1492
Briman, Eran, VP-Mktg - CEVA, Inc.; *pg.* 628, *pg.* 153
Brindel, Jason, Mgr-Interactive Mktg & New Channel Dev - SeaWorld Parks & Entertainment LLC; *pg.* 582, *pg.* 456
Brindle, Shelley, Exec VP-Domestic Network Distr & Mktg - Home Box Office, Inc.; *pg.* 290, *pg.* 1240
Brindley, Lauren, Grp VP & Gen Mgr-Mdse-Beauty & Personal Care - Walgreen Co.; *pg.* 1608, *pg.* 605
Brine, John, VP-PR - Ameriprise Financial, Inc.; *pg.* 715, *pg.* 930
Bringger, Ryan, Sr Dir-New Bus Dev - Lightning Hockey LP; *pg.* 557, *pg.* 474
Bringgold, Terese, Sr Mgr-Mktg Comm - Ecolab Inc.; *pg.* 329, *pg.* 960
Brink, Diane, VP-Mktg-Global Tech Svcs - International Business Machines Corporation; *pg.* 418, *pg.* 1138
Brinker, Stephanie, Grp Product Mgr-Oral Care Innovation - Church & Dwight Co., Inc.; *pg.* 1153, *pg.* 1063
Brinkerhoff, Darcy, Mgr-Wholesale Mktg-UGG Australia - Deckers Outdoor Corporation; *pg.* 1807, *pg.* 100
Brinkley, Emily, Dir-Online Mktg Analytics & Email - Nordstrom, Inc.; *pg.* 1779, *pg.* 1837
Brinkman, Rich, VP-Sls & Mktg-Fiesta Brand & Wholesale - The Homer Laughlin China Company; *pg.* 1125, *pg.* 1850
Brinkman, Sara, Assoc Mgr-Mktg - Great Clips, Inc.; *pg.* 510, *pg.* 937
Brinkworth, Douglas T., VP-Product Supply - Suburban Propane Partners, L.P.; *pg.* 113, *pg.* 1132
Brinn, Robyn, Asst VP-Mktg - Voxx International; *pg.* 686, *pg.* 1166
Brintnall, Jim, Sr Dir-Mktg - DeVry Education Group Inc.; *pg.* 600, *pg.* 607
Brioche, Rudy, Counsel-Policy & Sr Dir - Comcast Corporation; *pg.* 276, *pg.* 1560
Briody, Jo, Dir-Mktg & PR-Royal Caribbean International - Royal Caribbean Cruises Ltd; *pg.* 1921, *pg.* 446
Briody, Kathy, Sr Dir-Intl Media - Microsoft Corporation; *pg.* 435, *pg.* 1824
Briscoe, Catie, Mgr-Retail Mktg-America's Mktg - Bose Corporation; *pg.* 626, *pg.* 820
Briscoe, Clint, Product Mgr - Acuity Brands, Inc.; *pg.* 1294, *pg.* 487
Brisebois, Paul, VP-Sls-Die Sets North America - Anchor Danly; *pg.* 67, *pg.* 1948
Briseno, Alberto, Dir-Mktg - Dell Inc.; *pg.* 383, *pg.* 1737
Briskie, Douglas, Chief Strategy Officer & Sr VP - National Technical Systems Inc.; *pg.* 99, *pg.* 56
Brisky, Kerri, Specialist-Mktg Comm - Lincoln Electric Holdings, Inc.; *pg.* 1355, *pg.* 1432
Brissette, Ron, Sr Dir-Digital Design - Fossil Group, Inc.; *pg.* 5, *pg.* 1735
Brisson, Cyrille, VP-Mktg-EMEA - Eaton Corporation; *pg.* 1331, *pg.* 1429
Brisson, John E., Sr Dir-Fin - DeVry Education Group Inc.; *pg.* 600, *pg.* 607
Brisson, Kevin, Product Mgr-QuickLabel Systems Product Grp - Astro-Med, Inc.; *pg.* 619, *pg.* 1609
Brist, Jason, Exec VP-Adv Sls - The Outdoor Channel; *pg.* 303, *pg.* 291
Brist, Travis, Sr Product Mgr-Mktg - Synopsys, Inc.; *pg.* 480, *pg.* 162
Bristol, Ashley, Mgr-Mktg-Capabilities - Dr Pepper Snapple Group, Inc.; *pg.* 250, *pg.* 1729
Bristol, Diane, Dir-Mktg & Product Mdsg - Simms Fishing Products Corp.; *pg.* 1845, *pg.* 1008
Bristol, Jeffrey, VP-Sls-OEM & Distr - Universal Lighting Technologies; *pg.* 1307, *pg.* 1655
Bristol, Johnice, Dir-Trade Mktg - Reebok International Ltd.; *pg.* 1817, *pg.* 811
Bristol, Kim Reinhard, Partner-Digital Innovation Bus-Mobile Mktg Path - Diageo North America Inc.; *pg.* 248, *pg.* 1223
Bristol, Mike, Dir-Sls-CRM - Infor; *pg.* 414, *pg.* 484
Bristow, Lauren, VP-Brand Mktg - Foot Locker, Inc.; *pg.* 1808, *pg.* 1231
Britain, David, Sr Dir-Media-Global - Microsoft Corporation; *pg.* 435, *pg.* 1824
Britchfield, Michael, VP-Sls-EMEA - Analog Devices, Inc.; *pg.* 617, *pg.* 839
Brito, Cristina, Dir-Mktg-Promos & Direct Mail - Sephora USA Inc; *pg.* 522, *pg.* 227
Brittain, Alan, VP-Sls, Political & Issue Advocacy - Univision Communications Inc.; *pg.* 683, *pg.* 1307
Brittain, Rob, Dir-Franchise Mktg - Golden Corral Corporation;

pg. 1730, *pg.* 1387
Brittain, Robert, Mgr-Consumer Brands PR - 3M Company; *pg.* 1142, *pg.* 956
Brittan, Larry, Dir-Sponsor & Mktg Partnerships - Life Time Fitness, Inc.; *pg.* 1556, *pg.* 920
Britten, Dan, VP & Gen Mgr-Fasteners & Special Products - A&K Railroad Materials Inc.; *pg.* 1896, *pg.* 1755
Brittin, Denise, Mgr-Mktg-Collaboration User Grp - Cisco Systems, Inc.; *pg.* 372, *pg.* 240
Brittingham, Andrew, Asst VP & Mgr-Sls & Svc - TD Bank US Holding Company; *pg.* 809, *pg.* 1051
Britton, Bill, VP-Sls & Mktg - American Gilsonite Co.; *pg.* 1313, *pg.* 1700
Britton, Sharonda, Dir-Media Integrations & Strategic Partnerships - Wal-Mart Stores, Inc.; *pg.* 1790, *pg.* 29
Britton, Shelby, Sr Product Mgr-Mktg - Adobe Systems Incorporated; *pg.* 342, *pg.* 235
Britton-Parris, Sheraun, Grp VP-Mktg - SunTrust Banks, Inc.; *pg.* 807, *pg.* 520
Brizendine, Chad, Brand Mgr-North America Baby Care Delivery - The Procter & Gamble Company; *pg.* 1129, *pg.* 1418
Brizendine, Tim, Product Mgr-Cooling - Lennox International Inc.; *pg.* 1073, *pg.* 1736
Brletich, Danyel, Specialist-Intl Mktg - Polaris Industries Inc.; *pg.* 1709, *pg.* 928
Broach, Candace, Sr Mgr-Leadership Comm & Strategic Initiatives - Pfizer Inc.; *pg.* 1581, *pg.* 1278
Broadbear, Ed, VP-Mktg-Canada - FCA US LLC; *pg.* 170, *pg.* 868
Broadnax, Lewis, Exec Dir-Web Sls & Mktg - Lenovo Group Ltd; *pg.* 427, *pg.* 1384
Broadus, Brian, Sr Dir-Asset & Profit Protection - Sears Holdings Corporation; *pg.* 1784, *pg.* 618
Broadwater, April, Asst Mgr-Mktg - FRESH DEL MONTE PRODUCE INC.; *pg.* 856, *pg.* 418
Broadway, Andy, Sr VP-Sls & Mktg - CardioNet, Inc.; *pg.* 1513, *pg.* 1523
Brocato, Justin, Sr Mgr-Mktg Ops - Cisco Systems, Inc.; *pg.* 372, *pg.* 240
Brochstein, Michael, Sr VP-Sls - Fox Entertainment Group, Inc.; *pg.* 288, *pg.* 131
Brochstein, Michael, Sr VP-FX & FXM Adv Sls - FX Networks, LLC; *pg.* 288, *pg.* 131
Brock, Abby, Brand Mgr-Innovation - MillerCoors; *pg.* 254, *pg.* 1877
Brock, Abby, Brand Mgr-Innovation - MillerCoors LLC; *pg.* 255, *pg.* 582
Brock, Bryant, Reg Mgr-Channel Mktg-Americas Distr & LATAM Channel - Brocade Communications Systems, Inc.; *pg.* 365, *pg.* 239
Brock, Corrie, Mgr-Comml Mktg - Lennox International Inc.; *pg.* 1073, *pg.* 1736
Brock, Dan, VP-Sls - Bozzuto's Inc.; *pg.* 1016, *pg.* 342
Brock, Darrell, Rep-Adv & Creative Svcs - Northrop Grumman Corporation; *pg.* 231, *pg.* 1781
Brock, Evan S., Dir-Mktg - Spangler Candy Company; *pg.* 1862, *pg.* 1407
Brock, Graham C., Pres-Sls & Mktg-Global, Reg Pres-Europe & Exec VP - Molex Incorporated; *pg.* 655, *pg.* 628
Brock, Kelly, Sr Mgr-Mktg - United Parcel Service, Inc.; *pg.* 1928, *pg.* 522
Brock, Ken, Mgr-Natl Sls-Mass & Emerging Markets - Perfetti Van Melle USA, Inc.; *pg.* 1860, *pg.* 727
Brock, Russell, Sr Mgr-Mktg, Web & ECommerce, Licensed Brands & Contact Lens - Luxottica Retail; *pg.* 8, *pg.* 1460
Brockelmeyer, Scott, VP-Corp Comm & Mktg - Ferrellgas Partners, L.P.; *pg.* 977, *pg.* 718
Brockie, Peter, Dir-Global Strategic Mktg-BRILINTA - AstraZeneca Pharmaceuticals LP; *pg.* 1497, *pg.* 389
Brockington, Stuart, Sr Dir-Integrated Adv - Here Media Inc.; *pg.* 290, *pg.* 132
Brockman, Brian, Sr Mgr-Corp Comm - Nissan North America, Inc.; *pg.* 186, *pg.* 1633
Brockman, Craig, Mgr-Mktg-Presence Sensing - Rockwell Automation, Inc.; *pg.* 668, *pg.* 1880
Brod, Jason, Sr Mgr-Creative - Academy Sports & Outdoors, Ltd.; *pg.* 1824, *pg.* 1724
Broderick, Krista, Mgr-Worldwide Product Mktg-Enterprise Svcs - Hewlett-Packard Company; *pg.* 404, *pg.* 175
Broderick, Lanette, Mgr-Mktg Comm Medium, Large, Small Bus, Healthcare, Legal & Fin - CDW Corporation; *pg.* 370, *pg.* 663
Broderick, Matt, Mgr-Mktg-MassMutual Fin Grp - Massachusetts Mutual Life Insurance Company; *pg.* 1207, *pg.* 845
Broderick, Sean, Mgr-DDGS Mktg - CHS INC.; *pg.* 702, *pg.* 926
Broderson, Richard, Mgr-Sls-Natl - Stanley Furniture Co., Inc.; *pg.* 943, *pg.* 1379
Brodeur, Jean, VP-Comm & PR - Agropur Cooperative; *pg.* 836, *pg.* 1950
Brodeur, Mark, Head-Digital Innovation-Mktg-Global - Nestle USA, Inc.; *pg.* 883, *pg.* 96
Brodie, Bill, Sr VP-Sls & Bus Dev - Vital Connect; *pg.* 686, *pg.* 58
Brodie, Erin, Dir-Mktg - Advent Software, Inc.; *pg.* 345, *pg.* 211
Brodo, James A., Sr VP-Mktg - Richardson Group Inc.; *pg.* 461, *pg.* 1570
Brodowsky, Jenny, Dir-Programmatic Sls - Live Nation Entertainment, Inc.; *pg.* 558, *pg.* 47
Brodrick, Scott, Product Mgr - Apple Inc.; *pg.* 350, *pg.* 73
Brody, Andrea, Sr VP-Mktg-Global - BravoSolution US; *pg.* 1233, *pg.* 1549
Brody, Chris, Mgr-Mktg-Hot Pockets - Nestle USA, Inc.; *pg.* 883, *pg.* 96
Brody, Jeb, Pres-Production - Focus Features; *pg.* 287, *pg.* 273
Brody, Lisa, Dir-Retail Mktg - Perry Ellis International, Inc.; *pg.* 45, *pg.* 445
Brody, Michael, VP-Sls - M.S. Walker, Inc.; *pg.* 1967, *pg.* 843
Brody, Sara Sinclair, Product Mgr - Google Inc.; *pg.* 1249, *pg.* 153
Broe, Kevin, VP-Center Store Sls & Mdsg - Weis Markets, Inc.; *pg.* 1037, *pg.* 1588
Broehm, Ben, Sr Dir-Mktg-Global Pro Markets - S.C. Johnson & Son, Inc.; *pg.* 334, *pg.* 1889
Brogan, Brad, VP-Sls - Fiserv, Inc.; *pg.* 397, *pg.* 1855
Brogan, Monica, Mgr-Sls Support & Corp Mktg - CertainTeed Corporation; *pg.* 74, *pg.* 1589
Brogna, Sal, Exec VP-Product Ops - Intuitive Surgical, Inc.; *pg.* 1546, *pg.* 286
Brogowicz, Michael, Sr Dir-Mktg-Global - Electronic Arts Inc.; *pg.* 951, *pg.* 189
Brogunier, Claude R., Head-Revenue Mktg Svcs - General Electric Company; *pg.* 1297, *pg.* 347
Broili, Kelly, Mgr-Social Media-Global Digital Mktg - Starbucks Corporation; *pg.* 897, *pg.* 1840
Broitman, Adam, VP & Sr Head-Bus-Global Digital Mktg - MasterCard Worldwide Inc.; *pg.* 780, *pg.* 988
Broitman, Richard, Interim CFO - The Street, Inc.; *pg.* 1283, *pg.* 1296
Brojan, Phil, Sr VP-Mktg - RCI, LLC; *pg.* 1921, *pg.* 675
Brojan, Phil, Sr VP-Mktg - Wyndham Worldwide Corporation; *pg.* 1119, *pg.* 1107
Brokamp, Linda C., Specialist-Mktg Comm - IDEXX Laboratories, Inc.; *pg.* 1543, *pg.* 753
Broll, Janet, Dir-Mktg-Natl - Hallmark Cards, Inc.; *pg.* 1646, *pg.* 983
Bromage, Kathy, Sr VP-Strategy & Mktg - The Hartford Financial Services Group, Inc.; *pg.* 1202, *pg.* 352
Bromberg, David, Reg Mgr-Sls - Middle Atlantic Products Inc.; *pg.* 1360, *pg.* 1065
Bromberg, Jenna, Sr Assoc Brand Mgr-Digital Engagement - Pizza Hut, Inc.; *pg.* 1744, *pg.* 1733
Bromberg, Jesse, Mng Dir-Wealth Mgmt & Sr Dir-Portfolio Mgmt - Morgan Stanley Smith Barney LLC; *pg.* 784, *pg.* 1262
Bromley, Katie, Mgr-PR & AR - Brocade Corporation; *pg.* 365, *pg.* 312
Brommers, Craig, Sr VP-Mktg - ABERCROMBIE & FITCH CO.; *pg.* 37, *pg.* 1466
Bronaugh, Tim, Dir-Amateur Hockey Sls - Washington Capitals; *pg.* 591, *pg.* 1775
Bronson, Emilie, Specialist-Mktg - Johnson Outdoors Inc.; *pg.* 1837, *pg.* 1888
Bronson, Jeremy, Community Mgr-Global Digital Media - Starbucks Corporation; *pg.* 897, *pg.* 1840
Bronstein, Francine, Mgr-Mktg-Prepaid Solutions - First Data Corporation; *pg.* 754, *pg.* 505
Bronstein, Jacob, Mgr-Mktg-iBooks - Apple Inc.; *pg.* 350, *pg.* 73
Bronte, Vanessa, Brand Mgr-Global - Mattel Games/Puzzles; *pg.* 962, *pg.* 80
Bronte, Vanessa, Brand Mgr-Global - MATTEL, INC.; *pg.* 962, *pg.* 81
Brook, Lori, Mgr-Shopper Mktg - Smucker Foods Of Canada Co.; *pg.* 896, *pg.* 1924
Brooke, Courtney P., Sr Mgr-Comm - Comcast Corporation; *pg.* 276, *pg.* 1560
Brooke, Natalie, Mgr-Mktg-BioLab, Inc - Chemtura Corporation; *pg.* 1152, *pg.* 355
Brooker, Brian, Exec Creative Dir - Garmin International, Inc.; *pg.* 1414, *pg.* 717
Brooker, Eileen, VP-Sls Alliances-OEM & Strategic Partners-Worldwide - Extreme Networks Inc; *pg.* 287, *pg.* 245
Brooker, Michael, Sr Mgr-Market - Battelle Memorial Institute; *pg.* 1401, *pg.* 1437
Brookhart, Michael, Dir-Mktg - StarKist Foods Inc.; *pg.* 898, *pg.* 1581
Brookhouse, Nat, Dir-Sls Support & Mktg - Sunbelt Rentals; *pg.* 1786, *pg.* 1616
Brookmeyer, Derek, Mgr-Mktg - Dolby Laboratories, Inc.; *pg.* 284, *pg.* 217
Brooks, Alan, Sr Assoc Brand Mgr - The Hershey Co.; *pg.* 1855, *pg.* 1538
Brooks, Amy, Sr VP-Team Mktg & Bus Ops - National Basketball Association; *pg.* 566, *pg.* 1264
Brooks, Anne, Mktg Mgr-Creative, Adv & Brand - Halliburton Company; *pg.* 978, *pg.* 1707
Brooks, Barry, Sr Mgr-Procurement - Snyder's-Lance, Inc.; *pg.* 896, *pg.* 1368
Brooks, Brian, Dir-Wireless Sls - Shenandoah Telecommunications Co.; *pg.* 672, *pg.* 1779
Brooks, Chris, Sr Mgr-Digital Engagement & Corp Comm-Global - Hilton Worldwide, Inc.; *pg.* 1094, *pg.* 1791
Brooks, Chris, Dir-Mktg - Setra Systems, Inc.; *pg.* 1428, *pg.* 802
Brooks, Daniel, Brand Mgr - International Paper Company; *pg.* 1460, *pg.* 1644
Brooks, David, Sr Dir-Tech Strategy - Dolby Laboratories, Inc.; *pg.* 284, *pg.* 217
Brooks, Debbie, Mgr-Mdse - Tampa Bay Rays Baseball, Ltd.; *pg.* 586, *pg.* 464
Brooks, Jake, Sr Mgr-Product Dev - ESPN, Inc.; *pg.* 285, *pg.* 340
Brooks, Jason, Dir-Creative - Electronic Arts Inc.; *pg.* 951, *pg.* 189
Brooks, Jeanine, Supvr-Mktg Comm - 3M Company; *pg.* 1142, *pg.* 956
Brooks, Joanie, Sr Dir-Mktg & Acq - Comcast Cable Communications, Inc.; *pg.* 276, *pg.* 1560
Brooks, Katherine V., Mgr-Search Engine Optimization-Integrated Channels Mktg - Bank of America Corporation; *pg.* 718, *pg.* 1362
Brooks, Kelly, Dir-Media - Burlington Coat Factory; *pg.* 1764, *pg.* 1047
Brooks, Kristan, Product Mgr - Newell Rubbermaid Inc.; *pg.* 1128, *pg.* 515
Brooks, Kristy, Mgr-Mktg - Brasfield & Gorrie, LLC; *pg.* 71, *pg.* 2
Brooks, Laura, Assoc Dir-Shopper Mktg & Omnichannel Strategy - The Clorox Company; *pg.* 327, *pg.* 169
Brooks, Marion, Dir-Mktg-TOBI Brands-Cystic Fibrosis - Novartis Pharmaceuticals Corp.; *pg.* 1575, *pg.* 1054
Brooks, McKenna, Dir-Mktg-O'Keeffe's - Gorilla Glue Co.; *pg.* 1048, *pg.* 1414
Brooks, Michael, Sr Analyst-Website Search & Mdsg - Tractor Supply Company; *pg.* 708, *pg.* 1627
Brooks, Shannon, Mgr-In-store Mktg - LG Electronics U.S.A., Inc.; *pg.* 651, *pg.* 1060
Brooks, Stacey, Dir-Global Mktg Comm & Pro Svcs - Philips Electronics North America; *pg.* 662, *pg.* 782
Brooks, Todd, Sr Dir-Global Brand Mktg-Identity & Design - Visa Inc.; *pg.* 816, *pg.* 230
Brooks, Todd, Sr Dir-Global Brand Mktg-Identity & Design - Visa U.S.A., Inc.; *pg.* 817, *pg.* 231
Brooks, William, VP-Sls-Technical Svcs - Tech Data Corporation; *pg.* 482, *pg.* 416
Broom, Andrew, Div Dir-Corp Comm & Mktg-Honda Aircraft Company - American Honda Motor Co., Inc.; *pg.* 163, *pg.* 292
Broom, Kevin, Dir-PR - Recreation Vehicle Industry Association; *pg.* 155, *pg.* 1799
Broomham, Rob, VP-Sls - Occidental Petroleum Corporation; *pg.* 1175, *pg.* 137
Brophy, Michael, Partner-US & Mgr-Product Mktg-Surface - Microsoft Corp.; *pg.* 440, *pg.* 321
Brophy, Robin, VP-Mktg - Pearson Assessment & Information; *pg.* 1674, *pg.* 1742
Brophy, Robin, VP-Mktg - Pearson Assessments; *pg.* 1674, *pg.* 918
Brophy, Staci, Brand Mgr-Cross Channel Strategy - Capital One Financial Corporation; *pg.* 730, *pg.* 1789

First page reference indicates Business Class Edition
Second page reference indicates Geographic Edition

Broski, Gerry, Sr Dir-Mktg-Food Safety - Neogen Corporation; *pg.* 883, *pg.* 896
Brosnan, Drew, Mgr-Acq-Search Mktg - Macy's, Inc.; *pg.* 1778, *pg.* 1417
Brossard, Shane, Dir-Mktg - Wisconsin Department of Tourism; *pg.* 1011, *pg.* 1868
Brosseit, Nancy, Mgr-Sls & Mktg - Lawry's Restaurants, Inc.; *pg.* 1735, *pg.* 180
Brostrom, Gregory, Mgr-Mktg-Brand Strategy-Diabetes - GlaxoSmithKline; *pg.* 1536, *pg.* 1389
Brosz, John, VP-Sls & Mktg - Hour Publishing Company; *pg.* 1651, *pg.* 362
Brothers, Autumn, Specialist-Digital Mktg - Silver Star Brands; *pg.* 1785, *pg.* 1886
Brothers, Carl W., Sr VP-Mktg - Riceland Foods, Inc.; *pg.* 892, *pg.* 36
Brothers, Jim, Dir-Mktg - Six Flags Over Texas, Inc.; *pg.* 583, *pg.* 1660
Brothers, John, Sr Dir-Learning & Org Dev - Wal-Mart Stores, Inc.; *pg.* 1790, *pg.* 29
Brotherton, Aaron, Dir-Mktg - Nautilus, Inc.; *pg.* 1840, *pg.* 1846
Brott, John R., Dir-Sls - Master Appliance Corp.; *pg.* 1055, *pg.* 1888
Brott, Tiffany, Sr Mgr-Mktg & Comm - Accenture; *pg.* 1392, *pg.* 1186
Brough, Cathy, Dir-Sls Strategy-LA - AOL Inc.; *pg.* 1229, *pg.* 1195
Brough, Rob, Exec VP-Mktg & Comm - Zions First National Bank, N.A.; *pg.* 824, *pg.* 1762
Broughton, Kyle, Sr Specialist-Online Display Adv - Cabela's Incorporated; *pg.* 535, *pg.* 1019
Brouillard, Cynthia, Brand Mgr - Guthy-Renker LLC; *pg.* 289, *pg.* 273
Brous, Maria, Dir-Media & Community Rels - Publix Super Markets, Inc.; *pg.* 1031, *pg.* 437
Broussard, Lisa, Mgr-IR & Revenue Mgmt - Cedar Fair, L.P.; *pg.* 537, *pg.* 1471
Broussard, Susan, Sr Product Mgr - Jarden Consumer Solutions; *pg.* 57, *pg.* 412
Brousseau, Martin, Product Mgr - OpenText; *pg.* 1272, *pg.* 1956
Brousseau, Monique M., Dir-Mktg - The Travelers Companies, Inc.; *pg.* 1220, *pg.* 352
Brovont, Stan, VP-Mktg - Arris Group, Inc.; *pg.* 353, *pg.* 541
Brow, Rick, Dir-Mktg - CENTRIA Architectural Systems; *pg.* 74, *pg.* 1554
Broward, Douglas, Exec VP-Mktg - AMC, Inc.; *pg.* 1759, *pg.* 487
Browder, Emily, Sr Mgr-Corp Affairs & Innovative Pharma Comm-Global - Pfizer Inc.; *pg.* 1581, *pg.* 1278
Browder, Lindsay, Dir-Women's Design & Mdsg - Peter Millar; *pg.* 46, *pg.* 1372
Browdy, Annette, Exec Dir-Mktg Comm - Thomas Publishing Company LLC; *pg.* 1692, *pg.* 1299
Brower, Dave, VP-Mktg - EIS, Inc.; *pg.* 80, *pg.* 504
Brower, Gary, Mgr-Mktg Comm - Anthem, Inc.; *pg.* 1192, *pg.* 683
Brower, Laura, Dir-Rels, Global Adv & Brand Mgmt Grp - American Express Company; *pg.* 712, *pg.* 1190
Brown, Aaron, Grp Product Mgr - Google Inc.; *pg.* 1249, *pg.* 153
Brown, Adam, Asst VP-Actuarial Product Dev - Allianz Life Insurance Company of North America; *pg.* 1188, *pg.* 929
Brown, Adele, Sr Dir-Global Mktg & Comm - Kroll Inc.; *pg.* 425, *pg.* 1249
Brown, Adrienne, Dir-Mktg & HCP Promo Diabetes - Eli Lilly and Company; *pg.* 1527, *pg.* 684
Brown, Alastair, Sr Product Mgr - TripAdvisor, Inc.; *pg.* 1926, *pg.* 835
Brown, Alison, Dir-Sports Mktg & Events - Rodale, Inc.; *pg.* 1681, *pg.* 1530
Brown, Allison, Sr Mgr-Social Media Mktg - United Continental Holdings, Inc.; *pg.* 1927, *pg.* 593
Brown, AlLysha, Analyst-Mktg - Windstream Corporation; *pg.* 321, *pg.* 34
Brown, Allyson, Creative Dir-Mktg - Essence Magazine; *pg.* 1639, *pg.* 1229
Brown, Amanda, Sr Mgr-Creative Ops - The E.W. Scripps Company; *pg.* 1639, *pg.* 1412
Brown, Amanda, Mgr-National Mktg & Media - Golden Corral Corporation; *pg.* 1730, *pg.* 1387
Brown, Amanda, Dir-Mktg - Hotwire, Inc.; *pg.* 1912, *pg.* 219
Brown, Amanda, Specialist-Social Media - NIKE, Inc.; *pg.* 1812, *pg.* 1492
Brown, Amani, Brand Mgr - Kellogg Company; *pg.* 831, *pg.* 870
Brown, Amber, Sr Product Mgr - Allergan, Inc.; *pg.* 1491, *pg.* 106
Brown, Amy, Specialist-Social Media - Wendy's International, Inc.; *pg.* 1755, *pg.* 1451
Brown, Amy H., Mgr-Mktg Comm - ViaSat, Inc.; *pg.* 489, *pg.* 62
Brown, Andrew, Mgr-Ticket Sls - Cincinnati Bengals, Inc.; *pg.* 540, *pg.* 1410
Brown, Angela, Assoc Mgr-Mktg - General Motors Company; *pg.* 175, *pg.* 881
Brown, Anita, Chief Strategy Officer - Truven Health Analytics; *pg.* 1696, *pg.* 867
Brown, Ashley, Grp Dir-Digital Comm & Social Media - The Coca-Cola Company; *pg.* 240, *pg.* 493
Brown, Barbara, VP-Multimedia Sls - ESPN, Inc.; *pg.* 285, *pg.* 340
Brown, Barry, Dir-Adv - Boys' Life Magazine; *pg.* 1623, *pg.* 1206
Brown, Barry, VP-Sls & Mktg - Broadmoor Hotel, Inc.; *pg.* 1083, *pg.* 315
Brown, Becky, Dir-Media - Intel Corporation; *pg.* 645, *pg.* 266
Brown, Becky, Mgr-PR - PFIP, LLC; *pg.* 1842, *pg.* 1037
Brown, Bob, VP-Mktg & Sls-North America - Branson Ultrasonics Corporation-Precision Cleaning Div; *pg.* 1319, *pg.* 343
Brown, Bob, Dir-Adv - Gander Mountain Company; *pg.* 1834, *pg.* 960
Brown, Candace, Project Mgr-Digital Interactive Mktg - FCA US LLC; *pg.* 170, *pg.* 868
Brown, Candia L., Dir-Product Mktg-Single Cell Genomics Bus - Fluidigm Corporation; *pg.* 1413, *pg.* 279
Brown, Carrie, Grp Product Mgr - Epson America Inc.; *pg.* 394, *pg.* 122
Brown, Casey, Assoc Mgr-Mktg - Dunkin' Brands Group, Inc.; *pg.* 1727, *pg.* 810
Brown, Chanda, Mgr-Mktg & Promos - Georgia Lottery Corporation; *pg.* 993, *pg.* 506
Brown, Chris, Sr VP & Product Mgr-Mobile - Citi Trends Inc.; *pg.* 22, *pg.* 539
Brown, Chris, Chief Product Officer - Orbitz Worldwide, Inc.; *pg.* 1918, *pg.* 586
Brown, Christine, Head-Corp Mktg & Comm-EMEA - Advanced Micro Devices, Inc.; *pg.* 613, *pg.* 282
Brown, Christopher, Sr VP-Independent Sls - C&S Wholesale Grocers, Inc.; *pg.* 1016, *pg.* 1035
Brown, Christopher, Sr Dir-Mktg Brand Mgmt-Intl Markets Home Cleaning & Innovation - S.C. Johnson & Son, Inc.; *pg.* 334, *pg.* 1889
Brown, Chuck, Mgr-Sls - The Andersons Incorporated; *pg.* 1793, *pg.* 1461
Brown, Clare, Dir-IT, Global Mktg Technologies, Strategy & Analytics - The Coca-Cola Company; *pg.* 240, *pg.* 493
Brown, Colony, VP-Mktg & Comm - ZERO - The Project to End Prostate Cancer; *pg.* 162, *pg.* 1772
Brown, Connie, Sr Dir-HR - The E.W. Scripps Company; *pg.* 1639, *pg.* 1412
Brown, Courtney, VP & Dir-Creative - Madison Square Garden Network; *pg.* 297, *pg.* 1255
Brown, Cynthia, Sr Mgr-Mktg - MATTEL, INC.; *pg.* 962, *pg.* 81
Brown, Dan, Sr Dir-Production - Cable News Network LP; *pg.* 1624, *pg.* 1208
Brown, Danielle, Assoc Mgr-Product Mktg - Google Inc.; *pg.* 1249, *pg.* 153
Brown, Darrell, Dir-Product Mgmt - ADTRAN, Inc.; *pg.* 344, *pg.* 6
Brown, Debbie, Mgr-Global Solutions-IBM Digital Sls - IBM; *pg.* 410, *pg.* 1449
Brown, Derrick, VP-Corp Mktg & Strategic Bus Dev - Materion Microelectronics & Services; *pg.* 1559, *pg.* 1149
Brown, Don, Dir-Consumer Products - National Football League; *pg.* 567, *pg.* 1264
Brown, Donna, Coord-Mktg & Sls Admin - New World Pasta Company; *pg.* 885, *pg.* 1537
Brown, Drew, Sr VP-Production - AMC Networks Inc.; *pg.* 269, *pg.* 1189
Brown, Emily, Mgr-Mktg Projects & Comm - Pier 1 Imports, Inc.; *pg.* 940, *pg.* 1695
Brown, Emma, Brand Mgr-Comml Australian Wines - Treasury Wine Estates; *pg.* 1971, *pg.* 164
Brown, Erin M., Specialist-Mktg-ECommerce - Whirlpool Corporation; *pg.* 62, *pg.* 872
Brown, Frank, Grp VP-Media Rels - National Hockey League; *pg.* 568, *pg.* 1265
Brown, Glen, Mgr-Graphics-PC Products Grp - Dell Inc.; *pg.* 383, *pg.* 1737
Brown, Glenette, Mgr-Local Mktg Specialist - Toys "R" Us, Inc.; *pg.* 968, *pg.* 1130
Brown, Heather, Brand Mgr-Logitech - CDW Corporation; *pg.* 370, *pg.* 663
Brown, Heidi Leliefeld, Assoc Producer-Global Creative Studios - Starbucks Corporation; *pg.* 897, *pg.* 1840
Brown, Hilary, Sr Product Mgr-Impressions, Restoratives & Whitening - Den-Mat Corporation; *pg.* 1522, *pg.* 271
Brown, Ivy, Sr Dir-Mktg-Global Brand Mgmt-ACUVUE Brand - Johnson & Johnson; *pg.* 1549, *pg.* 1091
Brown, Jake, Specialist-Trader Mktg, Plng & Strategy Team - TD Ameritrade Holding Corporation; *pg.* 808, *pg.* 1018
Brown, James, Dir-Social Media Mktg - Perry Ellis International, Inc.; *pg.* 45, *pg.* 445
Brown, Jamie, VP-Mktg - Caesars Entertainment Corporation; *pg.* 1083, *pg.* 1023
Brown, Janet, Mgr-Bus Ops-Sys-Care Mktg - Johnson & Johnson; *pg.* 1549, *pg.* 1091
Brown, Jason, VP & Head-Sls-Natl - DIRECTV Group Holdings, LLC; *pg.* 281, *pg.* 79
Brown, Jay, VP-Sls & Bus Dev - Do It Best Corp.; *pg.* 1045, *pg.* 680
Brown, Jayme, Mgr-Digital Content & Relationship Mktg - William Grant & Sons, Inc.; *pg.* 1972, *pg.* 1057
Brown, Jeff, Sr Dir-Fin & Northern Div - The Home Depot, Inc.; *pg.* 1050, *pg.* 510
Brown, Jeff S., Dir-Sls & Mktg - Citizens Energy Group; *pg.* 1937, *pg.* 683
Brown, Jeffrey, Brand Mgr-Whirlpool Brand - Whirlpool Corporation; *pg.* 62, *pg.* 872
Brown, Jen, Sr Mgr-Comm-Beaver Creek - Vail Resorts, Inc.; *pg.* 1117, *pg.* 313
Brown, Jennifer, Sr Mgr-Mktg & Customer Tech Mktg - United Parcel Service, Inc.; *pg.* 1928, *pg.* 522
Brown, Jennifer S., Dir-Mktg - Incyte Corporation; *pg.* 1545, *pg.* 392
Brown, Jim, Sr VP-Digital Sls & Mktg - Bank of America Global Wealth & Investment Management; *pg.* 720, *pg.* 789
Brown, Jody, Exec VP-PR, Corp Comm & Congressional Rels - CACI International Inc.; *pg.* 367, *pg.* 1773
Brown, Josh, Brand Mgr - The Scotts Miracle-Gro Company; *pg.* 1799, *pg.* 1459
Brown, Justin, Assoc Mgr-Social Media-Basketball - Under Armour, Inc.; *pg.* 49, *pg.* 759
Brown, Kamari, Mgr-Cable Mktg - Home Box Office, Inc.; *pg.* 290, *pg.* 1240
Brown, Karen, Sr Dir-HR - Nathan's Famous Inc.; *pg.* 1741, *pg.* 1171
Brown, Karen, Brand Mgr - Neutrogena Corporation; *pg.* 517, *pg.* 137
Brown, Karin, Principal & Product Mgr - ACI Worldwide Inc.; *pg.* 341, *pg.* 1010
Brown, Karina, Brand Mgr-Multicultural Mktg - BJ's Wholesale Club, Inc.; *pg.* 1762, *pg.* 857
Brown, Katie, VP-Sls & Mktg - Steamboat Ski & Resort Corporation; *pg.* 1115, *pg.* 336
Brown, Kay, Sr Mgr-Mktg Comm - AT&T Inc.; *pg.* 1867, *pg.* 1674
Brown, Kazy, Sr Dir-Interactive Mktg - Warner Bros. Records, Inc.; *pg.* 1791, *pg.* 55
Brown, Kelley, Dir-Social Media - BP America Inc.; *pg.* 972, *pg.* 1702
Brown, Kelly Hollis, VP-Natl Sls-Automotive - Tremor Video; *pg.* 682, *pg.* 1305
Brown, Kennedy, Dir-Mktg-Data Center Solutions - Intel Corporation; *pg.* 645, *pg.* 266
Brown, Kent, Sr Product Mgr-Agriculture Tractors - Kubota Tractor Corporation; *pg.* 705, *pg.* 294
Brown, Kevin, Asst VP-Mktg - Servpro Industries, Inc.; *pg.* 335, *pg.* 1635
Brown, Kim, Mgr-Sls-Multi-Market Adv - Mlive Media Group; *pg.* 1665, *pg.* 888
Brown, Kim L., Dir-Mktg-Higher Education & Pro Div - Human Kinetics Publishers Inc.; *pg.* 1651, *pg.* 562
Brown, Krysta, Program Mgr-Digital Mktg - Oakley, Inc.; *pg.* 1840, *pg.* 86
Brown, Lana, Coord-Mktg Automation - CommScope, Inc.; *pg.* 278, *pg.* 1378
Brown, Marie, Dir-Mktg-US Cardiovascular Bus Unit - Amgen Inc.; *pg.* 1493, *pg.* 291
Brown, Martin, Mgr-Bus Dev & Technical Mktg - Daktronics, Inc.; *pg.* 633, *pg.* 1624

Brown, Mary, VP-Product & Mktg Strategy-Schwan's Home Delivery - The Schwan Food Company; pg. 894, pg. 928
Brown, Matt, Product Mgr - Skier's Choice Inc.; pg. 1711, pg. 1640
Brown, Maureen, Sr VP & Dir-PR - The Huntington National Bank; pg. 767, pg. 1440
Brown, Melissa, Dir-Mktg-Europe - Mary Kay Inc.; pg. 516, pg. 1657
Brown, Michael, Exec VP-Worldwide Mktg - Metro-Goldwyn-Mayer Inc.; pg. 298, pg. 47
Brown, Michael K, VP-Security Product Mgmt & Res - BlackBerry Limited; pg. 625, pg. 1947
Brown, Michele, Project Mgr-Supply Chain Ops-Retail Mktg - Sunoco Inc.; pg. 985, pg. 1571
Brown, Misty, Mgr-Affiliate Mktg - eBags, Inc.; pg. 1240, pg. 331
Brown, Molly, District Mgr-Sls-Houston - CDW Corporation; pg. 370, pg. 663
Brown, Molly, Dir-Mktg Ops - Comcast Corporation; pg. 270, pg. 1560
Brown, Monica, VP-Product Mktg - LeapFrog Enterprises, Inc.; pg. 961, pg. 84
Brown, Moya, VP-Mktg - Campbell Company of Canada Ltd; pg. 844, pg. 1935
Brown, Nancy, Mgr-PR - Dynamic Resource Group; pg. 1637, pg. 674
Brown, Nick, Mng Dir & Head-Fin Product Brokerage-North America - GFI Group Inc.; pg. 762, pg. 1234
Brown, Orion, Brand Mgr-A1 & Grey Poupon - The Kraft Heinz Company; pg. 871, pg. 641
Brown, Pam, Dir-Sls Ops - Del Monte Foods, Inc.; pg. 852, pg. 304
Brown, Pamela, Brand Mgr - Johnson & Johnson; pg. 1549, pg. 1091
Brown, Patti, Dir-Adv - Stater Brothers Holdings; pg. 1034, pg. 198
Brown, Perry, Sr Dir-Bus Intelligence & Ops - The Terlato Wine Group; pg. 1971, pg. 555
Brown, Rachel, Coord-Digital Mktg - Ann Inc.; pg. 18, pg. 1195
Brown, Randy, Sr VP-Sls & Mktg-Global - Dayton Superior Corporation; pg. 1328, pg. 1464
Brown, Rebecca, VP-Mktg - E.T. Browne Drug Company, Inc.; pg. 509, pg. 1060
Brown, Renee, Sr VP & Dir-Social Media - Wells Fargo & Company; pg. 819, pg. 232
Brown, Richard, Head-Social Media-Global - Discover Financial Services; pg. 744, pg. 653
Brown, Richard, VP-Sls-EMEA - Interactive Intelligence, Inc.; pg. 417, pg. 687
Brown, Richard A., Sr VP-Mdsg & Mktg - Sears Canada Inc.; pg. 1784, pg. 1943
Brown, Rick, Reg Dir-Sls-West Reg - FUJIFILM U.S.A., Inc.; pg. 1414, pg. 1348
Brown, Rob, Dir-Corp Sls & Distr - Southwest Airlines Co.; pg. 1923, pg. 1687
Brown, Robert, VP-Cineplex Media - Cineplex Entertainment LP; pg. 275, pg. 1936
Brown, Robert, Dir-Database Mktg - Go Daddy Inc.; pg. 1249, pg. 21
Brown, Robert, Sr Mgr-Interactive Mktg - Nissan North America, Inc.; pg. 186, pg. 1633
Brown, Robert M., VP-Mktg & Sls-North America - Branson Ultrasonics Corporation; pg. 1319, pg. 342
Brown, Robert M., VP-Mktg & Sls-North America - Branson Ultrasonics Corporation - Plastics Joining Division; pg. 1403, pg. 343
Brown, Robin D., Dir-HR & Mktg - First Community Corporation; pg. 754, pg. 1620
Brown, Ryan, Exec Dir-Creative Svcs-Conde Nast Traveler - Conde Nast Publications, Inc.; pg. 1629, pg. 1217
Brown, Ryan, Sr Brand Mktg Dir - Loblaw Companies Limited; pg. 1026, pg. 1918
Brown, Sally Ann, Sr Specialist-PR - Henry Ford Health System; pg. 1541, pg. 883
Brown, Samuel A., VP-Adv - The Miami Herald; pg. 1665, pg. 444
Brown, Sara, Mgr-Social Media & Loyalty Mktg - Peapod, LLC; pg. 1029, pg. 661
Brown, Sarah, Product Mgr - Invacare Corporation; pg. 1546, pg. 1451
Brown, Sarah M., Sr Mgr-Comm - Capital One Financial Corporation; pg. 730, pg. 1789
Brown, Simon E., Head-Consumer Products & Member - KKR & CO. L.P.; pg. 774, pg. 1249
Brown, Stacy, Mgr-Mktg Program-Institutional Retirement & Trust - Wells Fargo & Company; pg. 819, pg. 232
Brown, Stephanie, VP-Corp Mktg-Dow Jones & The Wall Street Journal - Dow Jones & Company, Inc.; pg. 1637, pg. 1225
Brown, Stephanie, Sr Dir-Mktg & PR - The San Diego Union-Tribune, LLC; pg. 1682, pg. 208
Brown, Stephanie Dobbs, VP-Corp Mktg - The Wall Street Journal; pg. 1700, pg. 1312
Brown, Steve, Mgr-Mktg Database - Bestop, Inc.; pg. 200, pg. 312
Brown, Steve, Sr Product Mgr-Managed Svcs-Cox Bus Svcs - Cox Communications, Inc.; pg. 279, pg. 501
Brown, Steve, Dir-Creative - The Fechheimer Brothers Company; pg. 41, pg. 1412
Brown, Sue Harvey, Mgr-Patagonia Footwear Mktg - Wolverine World Wide, Inc.; pg. 1822, pg. 905
Brown, Susan, VP-OEM Adv & Bus Dev - Kelley Blue Book Co., Inc.; pg. 1656, pg. 112
Brown, Taryn, Analyst-Mktg Ops - Autodesk Inc.; pg. 356, pg. 257
Brown, Teryl, VP-Adv Sls-AETN & Lifetime Networks - Lifetime Entertainment Services LLC; pg. 296, pg. 1251
Brown, Tiffany, VP-Corp Mktg & Sponsorships - Union Bank, N.A.; pg. 813, pg. 230
Brown, Tim, Sr Specialist-Internet Mktg & eMail - Canon U.S.A., Inc.; pg. 1404, pg. 1178
Brown, Tonya R., Project Coord-Mktg & Adv - Medtronic, Inc.; pg. 1564, pg. 939
Brown, Tor, Mgr-Global Product Line-Men's Running Apparel - NIKE, Inc.; pg. 1812, pg. 1492
Brown, Vanessa, Mgr-Mktg Comm - Canadian Imperial Bank of Commerce; pg. 729, pg. 1935
Brown, Virginia, Brand Mgr - Bruce Foods Corporation; pg. 842, pg. 743
Brown, Wade, VP-Field Svcs & Svcs Mktg - Roche Diagnostics Corporation; pg. 1590, pg. 689
Brown, Will W., Dir-Mktg & Acct Svcs - Kinder Morgan; pg. 1945, pg. 1709
Brown, William, Assoc VP-Product Dev - D-Link Systems, Inc.; pg. 381, pg. 89
Brown, William A., Dir-Sls - O.F. Mossberg & Sons, Inc.; pg. 1842, pg. 360
Brown, William M., Jr., Gen Mgr-Sls & Mktg-Long Products - Steel Dynamics, Inc.; pg. 113, pg. 681
Browne, Jeffrey, Sr Mgr-Design - Newell Rubbermaid Inc.; pg. 1128, pg. 515
Browne, Michael, Dir-Bontrager Mktg - Trek Bicycle Corporation; pg. 1847, pg. 1896
Browne, Mike, VP-Sls & Mktg - Bluegreen Corporation; pg. 1082, pg. 410
Browne, Mike, VP-Customer Mktg-Morning Foods Div - Kellogg Company; pg. 831, pg. 870
Brownell, Pete, Mgr-Sls - Milton Roy Company; pg. 1361, pg. 1542
Brownfield, Kip, Sr Dir-Ticket Sls - Indianapolis Colts, Inc.; pg. 553, pg. 687
Brownie, Brian, Dir-Adv Ops - eBay Inc.; pg. 1240, pg. 243
Browning, Abigail, Dir-Mktg, ECommerce & Brand Licensing - Asimov's Science Fiction Magazine; pg. 1618, pg. 1197
Browning, Colin, Dir-Social Media Mktg Svcs - IDG Enterprise; pg. 1258, pg. 821
Browning, Janeen, Dir-Svc Line Mktg - Baylor Health Care System; pg. 1500, pg. 1676
Browning, Jeannette, Head-Digital Sls Strategy-North Americas - IBM; pg. 410, pg. 1449
Browning, Kathy, Mgr-Mktg - Intel Corporation; pg. 645, pg. 266
Browning, Mardi, Dir-Circulation & Mktg - Santa Cruz Sentinel; pg. 1683, pg. 278
Browning, Meike, Dir-Global Mktg-Lifestyle Fabrics - Make it Coats; pg. 696, pg. 1367
Browning, Stephen E., Chief Strategy Officer & Chief Dev Officer - Weston Solutions Holdings, Inc.; pg. 1437, pg. 1593
Brownstein, Alec, Dir-Creative - Dollar Shave Club, Inc.; pg. 507, pg. 273
Brownstein, Evan, Sr Dir-Mktg - Checkers Drive-In Restaurants, Inc.; pg. 1017, pg. 472
Brownstein, Karin, VP-Media & Adv - Citigroup Inc.; pg. 735, pg. 1212
Brownstein, Michael, Exec VP & Chief Revenue Officer-Corp Sls - Meredith Corporation; pg. 1663, pg. 705
Brubaker, Anita, Mgr-Global Event Mktg - First Data Corporation; pg. 754, pg. 505
Brubeck, Anita S., Specialist-Mktg Comm - Trane Inc.; pg. 116, pg. 1109
Bruce, Alison, Brand Mgr-Woodcare - PPG Industries, Inc.; pg. 1445, pg. 1579
Bruce, Andre, Sr Mgr-Sports Field - Kansas City Chiefs Football Club, Inc.; pg. 555, pg. 984
Bruce, David, Sr Dir-Brand & Integrated Mktg - Major League Soccer LLC; pg. 560, pg. 1256
Bruce, Katy, Analyst-Mktg - JBS USA Holding, Inc.; pg. 865, pg. 330
Bruce, Michael, Dir-Sls & North American Retail - Acuity Brands, Inc.; pg. 1294, pg. 487
Bruchey, Ryan, Asst VP & Brand Mgr-Comm - T. Rowe Price Group Inc.; pg. 808, pg. 759
Bruck, Larry, VP-Mktg-Global - Kellogg Company; pg. 831, pg. 870
Bruckner, Jamie, Brand Mgr-Vitaminwater - The Coca-Cola Company; pg. 240, pg. 493
Bruder, Meredith, Mgr-Mktg Comm - The Lubrizol Corporation; pg. 1171, pg. 1481
Bruder, Rob, Grp Head-Mktg Comm-Emerging Media - Lincoln Electric Holdings, Inc.; pg. 1355, pg. 1432
Brudzinski, Randy, VP-Global Sls-Frequency & Time Div - Microsemi Corporation; pg. 435, pg. 41
Brueckner, Robert, Dir-Mktg - Principal Financial Group, Inc.; pg. 796, pg. 706
Bruegging, Bob, VP-Sls - Mr. Gasket Inc.; pg. 213, pg. 1406
Bruening, Lisa, Sr Mgr-Tourism Sls - Denver Metro Convention & Visitors Bureau; pg. 991, pg. 318
Bruennig, Robert, Sr VP & Gen Mgr-Mdse - Payless Shoesource, Inc.; pg. 31, pg. 722
Brugaletta, Vincenzo, Head-Integrated Mktg - Luxottica Retail; pg. 8, pg. 1460
Bruggeman, Meghan, Acct Exec-Strategic-Digital Vendor Mktg - Target Corporation; pg. 1786, pg. 942
Bruggeman, Ronald, Dir-Global Product Mgmt - Alliance Laundry Holdings LLC; pg. 51, pg. 1890
Brugiere-Garde, Francois, Brand Mgr-Danone Core-Brazil - The Dannon Company, Inc.; pg. 851, pg. 1351
Brugnoli, Cara, Sr Mgr-Publicity - DIRECTV Group Holdings, LLC; pg. 281, pg. 79
Bruinsma, Troy A., Dir-Field Sls - Valassis; pg. 1698, pg. 386
Brujis, Nicole, Product Mgr - J. Crew Group, Inc.; pg. 1773, pg. 1245
Bruley, Jared M., Supvr-Mktg - Constellation Energy Resources, LLC; pg. 1938, pg. 756
Brull, Chris, VP-Mktg - Kawasaki Motors Corp., U.S.A.; pg. 1708, pg. 111
Brumbaugh, Chris, Dir-Social Media - Kissimmee-St. Cloud Convention & Visitors Bureau; pg. 997, pg. 436
Brumbaugh, Merry L., VP-Tubular Products - L.B. Foster Company; pg. 1355, pg. 1578
Brumfield, Chad, Brand Mgr & Mgr-Adv - Entergy Corporation; pg. 1941, pg. 746
Brumfield, Chad, Brand Mgr & Mgr-Adv - Entergy New Orleans, Inc.; pg. 1942, pg. 746
Brumfield, Tammy, VP-Shopper Mktg - Conagra Foods; pg. 826, pg. 994
Brumfield, Tammy, VP-Shopper Mktg - ConAgra Foods, Inc.; pg. 826, pg. 1014
Brumley, Larry D., Sr VP Mktg Comm & Chief of Staff - Mercer University; pg. 604, pg. 535
Brummer, Amy, Mgr-Customer Mktg - Brown-Forman Corporation; pg. 1958, pg. 732
Brundridge, Randy, Dir-Product Sls-North America - Alstom Signaling, Inc.; pg. 1312, pg. 1350
Brune, Carrie, Brand Mgr - The Coca-Cola Company; pg. 240, pg. 493
Brune, Liz, Mgr-Mktg-Allstate Insurance Company - The Allstate Corporation; pg. 1189, pg. 639
Brunell, Sarah, Mgr-Customer Mktg-Bose Automotive - Bose Corporation; pg. 626, pg. 820
Brunelle, Fletch, Sr VP-Mktg Guest Strategy - MGM Resorts International; pg. 1105, pg. 1028
Bruner, Frank, Sr Dir-Hilton Brand Performance-Americas - Hilton Worldwide, Inc.; pg. 1094, pg. 1791
Brunet, Paul, VP-Mktg, Cloud & ECommerce - International Business Machines Corporation; pg. 418, pg. 1138
Brunette, Dave, Dir-Sports Mktg - Anheuser-Busch Companies, LLC; pg. 237, pg. 991
Brunette, Paul, Dir-Sls - Concordia Publishing House; pg. 1629, pg. 995
Brungardt, Amy, Specialist-Email Mktg - Helzberg's Diamond Shops, Inc.; pg. 6, pg. 984
Brungardt, Susan, Mgr-Bus Direct Mktg - Windstream

First page reference indicates Business Class Edition
Second page reference indicates Geographic Edition

Corporation; *pg.* 321, *pg.* 34
Bruni, Josh, Dir-Digital Mktg & Ecommerce - Pacific Sunwear of California, Inc.; *pg.* 1781, *pg.* 43
Bruni, Lynn, VP-Mktg Comm - San Francisco Travel Association; *pg.* 1005, *pg.* 227
Bruning, Christa, Mgr-Mktg Programs - University Of Denver; *pg.* 609, *pg.* 323
Brunke, Karen, Dir-Mktg & Events - The Coca-Cola Company; *pg.* 240, *pg.* 493
Brunmark, Jeane, Dir-Sls-Latin America - OraSure Technologies Inc; *pg.* 1578, *pg.* 1516
Brunner, Becky, Brand Mgr-Purina Cat Chow - Nestle Purina PetCare Company; *pg.* 1479, *pg.* 1000
Brunner, Mark, Dir-PR - Shure Incorporated; *pg.* 672, *pg.* 638
Brunner, Maureen, VP-Mktg - Cutera, Inc.; *pg.* 1521, *pg.* 49
Brunnett, Dennis, Product Mgr - FLEXcon Corporation; *pg.* 1457, *pg.* 844
Brunnick, Gregg, Dir-Product Mgmt, Mktg & Technical Svcs - Epson America Inc.; *pg.* 394, *pg.* 122
Bruno, C. J., VP & Gen Mgr-Americas Sls & Mktg - Intel Corporation; *pg.* 645, *pg.* 266
Bruno, Dianne, Principal-Svcs Provider & Cloud Partner Mktg-US Theatre - Cisco Systems, Inc.; *pg.* 372, *pg.* 240
Bruno, Eric, VP-Video Product Mgmt - Rogers Communications Inc.; *pg.* 668, *pg.* 1942
Bruno, Jamie, Sr Mgr-Mktg - Conde Nast Publications, Inc.; *pg.* 1629, *pg.* 1217
Bruno, Joe, Mgr-Digital Mktg-Global - Cigna Corporation; *pg.* 1197, *pg.* 338
Bruno, Mike, Analyst-Mktg - Canadian Imperial Bank of Commerce; *pg.* 729, *pg.* 1935
Bruno, Pier-Luca, VP & Sr Mgr-Relationship - TD Bank US Holding Company; *pg.* 809, *pg.* 1051
Bruno, Ramon, Reg Mgr-Sls - TDK-Lambda High Power Division; *pg.* 1380, *pg.* 1090
Bruno, Stephen, VP-Originals Mktg - Netflix, Inc.; *pg.* 1269, *pg.* 141
Bruno, Teresa, Acct Mgr-Media-Talent Brand - LinkedIn Corporation; *pg.* 1262, *pg.* 160
Bruno, Tony, Specialist-Vertical Mktg - Ricoh Americas Corporation; *pg.* 461, *pg.* 1131
Bruno, Vincent, Dir-Mktg - Crestron Electronics Inc.; *pg.* 631, *pg.* 1116
Brunone, Christian, Sr Mgr-CRM & Loyalty & Res - Foot Locker, Inc.; *pg.* 1808, *pg.* 1231
Brunory, Kevin, VP-Sls-US & Canada - Blistex, Inc.; *pg.* 502, *pg.* 644
Bruns, Jesse, Dir-Digital Mktg - Career Education Corporation; *pg.* 599, *pg.* 658
Bruns, Julia K., Sr Mgr-Vendor Bus-IBM PureSystems - Ingram Micro Inc.; *pg.* 415, *pg.* 261
Brunswick, Sara M., Dir-Mktg Ops - Alcatel-Lucent; *pg.* 615, *pg.* 38
Brunt, Will, Sr VP-Mktg & R&D - Smithfield Foods, Inc.; *pg.* 896, *pg.* 1806
Bruntil, Bennett, Reg Mgr-Sls - Sono-Tek Corporation; *pg.* 112, *pg.* 1182
Bruntse, Lars, Mgr-Mktg & Bus Dev - Howe Furniture Corporation; *pg.* 928, *pg.* 998
Brunzell, Linda, VP-Global Mktg-Wolverine Brand - Wolverine World Wide, Inc.; *pg.* 1822, *pg.* 905
Brusaschetti, Marilee, Mgr-Mktg & Client Solutions - Cox Communications, Inc.; *pg.* 279, *pg.* 501
Bruscato, Andrea, Mgr-Mktg-Shop Your Way - Sears Holdings Corporation; *pg.* 1784, *pg.* 618
Brush, Chris, Sr VP-Affiliate Mktg - ESPN, Inc.; *pg.* 285, *pg.* 340
Brusnighan, Diane, Dir-Mktg - Liberty Mutual Insurance Group Inc.; *pg.* 1205, *pg.* 797
Brust, Danielle, Designer-Adv - The Bradford Group; *pg.* 1763, *pg.* 637
Brutocao, Giancarlo, Dir-Mktg Programs - McKesson Corporation; *pg.* 1560, *pg.* 222
Bruton, Christine, Brand Mgr-Rubbermaid Food & Beverage - Newell Rubbermaid Inc.; *pg.* 1128, *pg.* 515
Brutten, Mark, Dir-Brand Mktg - Zenni Optical, Inc.; *pg.* 1438, *pg.* 168
Bruyere, Chris, Dir-Brand Adv-Global - Reebok International Ltd.; *pg.* 1817, *pg.* 811
Bryan, Beth, Dir-Adv - Ducks Unlimited, Inc.; *pg.* 139, *pg.* 1642
Bryan, Jennifer, Mgr-Social & Digital Media - Gordmans Stores Inc.; *pg.* 1771, *pg.* 1016
Bryan, Judy, Mgr-Mktg Comm-Global - Nordson Corporation; *pg.* 1365, *pg.* 1480
Bryan, Keith, VP-Media & Media Network - Best Buy Co., Inc.; *pg.* 1761, *pg.* 954
Bryan, Matthew W., Head-Retirement Mktg & Dir - The Guardian Life Insurance Company of America; *pg.* 1202, *pg.* 1237
Bryan, Michele, Sr Acct Mgr-New Media - PGA Tour, Inc.; *pg.* 574, *pg.* 460
Bryans, Darryl, Mgr-Product Line-DSP - Bose Corporation; *pg.* 626, *pg.* 820
Bryant, Anna, Specialist-Pub Affairs-Media Rels - State Farm Mutual Automobile Insurance Co.; *pg.* 1218, *pg.* 557
Bryant, Christa, Dir-Channel & Customer Mktg - Brown-Forman Corporation; *pg.* 1958, *pg.* 732
Bryant, Connie, Dir-PR - Lowe's Companies, Inc.; *pg.* 1053, *pg.* 1383
Bryant, Harold, VP-Production & Exec Producer-CBS Sports - CBS Broadcasting Inc.; *pg.* 273, *pg.* 1210
Bryant, Harold D, VP-Production & Exec Producer - CBS Sports Division; *pg.* 274, *pg.* 1211
Bryant, Jay, VP-Sls - LiveWorld, Inc.; *pg.* 1264, *pg.* 246
Bryant, Jim, Mgr-Experiential Mktg-Natl - Xerox Canada Inc.; *pg.* 494, *pg.* 1930
Bryant, Jonathan, VP-Strategic Mktg Herbicides-Global - BASF Corporation; *pg.* 1149, *pg.* 1066
Bryant, Kate, Asst Mgr-Social Media - Nintendo of America, Inc.; *pg.* 965, *pg.* 1829
Bryant, Kevin, Dir-Natl Mktg - Tractor Supply Company; *pg.* 708, *pg.* 1627
Bryant, Kiara, Coord-PR - St. Louis Convention & Visitors Commission; *pg.* 1006, *pg.* 1003
Bryant, Lisa, Dir-PR - Hickory Farms, Inc.; *pg.* 862, *pg.* 1462
Bryant, Malisa, Sr VP-North America Sls & Focused Mark - Herman Miller, Inc.; *pg.* 926, *pg.* 913
Bryant, Mark, Rep-Inside Sls - CPP, Inc.; *pg.* 1631, *pg.* 153
Bryant, Mat, Product Mgr-New Digital Platform - The Travelers Companies, Inc.; *pg.* 1220, *pg.* 352
Bryant, Misty, Sr Mgr-Pur - Sensient Flavors Inc.; *pg.* 895, *pg.* 690
Bryant, Natarsha, Dir-Mktg - K12, Inc.; *pg.* 1260, *pg.* 1785
Bryant, Nicole, Coord-Sls - Americo Manufacturing Co., Inc.; *pg.* 325, *pg.* 482
Bryant, Pat, Sr Product Mgr-Software - Bloomberg BNA; *pg.* 1621, *pg.* 1772
Bryant, R. Jeep, Exec VP-Mktg & Corp Affairs - The Bank of New York Mellon Corporation; *pg.* 720, *pg.* 1200
Bryant, Richard, Reg Mgr-Mktg Comm-Americas - Tourism New Zealand; *pg.* 1008, *pg.* 276
Bryant, Rick, Exec VP-Sls Ops - Volvo Cars of North America LLC; *pg.* 195, *pg.* 1117
Bryant, Shayne, Grp Mgr-Mktg Comm - Dex Media Inc; *pg.* 1635, *pg.* 1680
Bryant, Vicki, VP-Event Svcs & Mdsg - Saint Louis Cardinals, L.P.; *pg.* 580, *pg.* 1002
Brydon, Neil, Dir-Product Line Mgmt, Compression & Stream Processing - Harmonic, Inc.; *pg.* 402, *pg.* 246
Brye, Marcy, Head-Media - CarMax, Inc.; *pg.* 167, *pg.* 1800
Brytowski, Mary, Mgr-Multi-Media Self Svc Sls - Worcester Telegram & Gazette Corp.; *pg.* 1702, *pg.* 863
Brzeski, Maciek, VP-Product Mktg & Dev-Branded Storage Products - Toshiba America, Inc.; *pg.* 681, *pg.* 1302
Brzezinski, Carrie, VP-Mktg Solutions - ESPN, Inc.; *pg.* 285, *pg.* 340
Brzozowski, Alicia, Specialist-Mktg Comm - Lincoln Electric Holdings, Inc.; *pg.* 1355, *pg.* 1432
Brzygot, Jennifer, Mgr-Mktg - Applied Industrial Technologies, Inc.; *pg.* 199, *pg.* 1428
Bubar, Benay R., Assoc Dir-Production - Good Housekeeping; *pg.* 1645, *pg.* 1236
Bubel, Marc, Specialist-Mktg Comm-Global - Schlumberger Limited; *pg.* 801, *pg.* 1714
Bubenhofer, Rick, Dir-PR - Brown-Forman Corporation; *pg.* 1958, *pg.* 732
Buberel, Jason, Product Mgr - Google Inc.; *pg.* 1249, *pg.* 153
Bubniak, Cindy Crossley, Dir-Mktg-Health & Wellness - Weight Watchers International, Inc.; *pg.* 1609, *pg.* 1313
Bubulka, Tom, Mgr-Mktg Comm - Anixter International Inc.; *pg.* 1313, *pg.* 614
Bucaille, Alice, VP-Madewell Brand Creative - J. Crew Group, Inc.; *pg.* 1773, *pg.* 1245
Buccafurri, Cole, Mgr-Digital Mktg-Apps - Ford Motor Company; *pg.* 172, *pg.* 876
Buccella, Brian, VP-Bus Dev & VP-Mktg - Segway Inc.; *pg.* 1923, *pg.* 1033
Buccellato, Scott, VP-Trade Mktg & ECommerce - The Hain Celestial Group, Inc.; *pg.* 860, *pg.* 1172
Bucci, Ester, Mgr-Adv, Comm & Svc Mktg-Natl - General Motors of Canada Ltd.; *pg.* 177, *pg.* 1931
Bucci, Marie, Dir-Mktg - John Hancock Financial Services; *pg.* 1205, *pg.* 796
Bucciarelli, Paul, VP, Sr Mgr-Ops & Mgr-Strategic Sourcing - The PNC Financial Services Group, Inc.; *pg.* 795, *pg.* 1579
Bucek, Matthew, Mgr-Mktg Comm - Littelfuse, Inc.; *pg.* 1301, *pg.* 580
Bucek, Mike, VP-Mktg & Bus Dev - Kansas City Royals Baseball Corporation; *pg.* 555, *pg.* 985
Bucey, Katie J., Sr Mgr-Mktg - Fresenius Kabi USA; *pg.* 1531, *pg.* 626
Buch, Vineet, Dir-Product Mgmt - Google Inc.; *pg.* 1249, *pg.* 153
Buchanan, Alan, Assoc Dir-Creative - Apple Inc.; *pg.* 350, *pg.* 73
Buchanan, Allison, Dir-Mktg Comm-Alcoa Global Pkg - Alcoa Inc.; *pg.* 65, *pg.* 1188
Buchanan, Brooke, Sr Dir-Corp Comm - Wal-Mart.com; *pg.* 1287, *pg.* 50
Buchanan, Gary, Mng Editor-Social Media-Disney Parks PR - The Walt Disney Company; *pg.* 317, *pg.* 52
Buchanan, Patricia, Mgr-Local Sls-Telemundo - NBC Universal, Inc.; *pg.* 300, *pg.* 1266
Buchanan, Stephen G., Exec VP-OPRY Entertainment Grp - Ryman Hospitality Properties, Inc; *pg.* 1111, *pg.* 1653
Buchanan, Taria, Sr Assoc Brand Mgr-Starburst - Wm. Wrigley Jr. Company; *pg.* 1863, *pg.* 596
Bucher, Doreen, VP-Mktg - Symrise, Inc.; *pg.* 1183, *pg.* 1125
Bucher, Fred, Grp VP-Mktg - Time Warner Cable Inc.; *pg.* 312, *pg.* 1301
Bucher, Susan, Dir-Sls & Mktg - Morinaga Nutritional Foods, Inc.; *pg.* 1028, *pg.* 295
Buchert, Richard, Sr VP-Production - Bauer Publishing USA; *pg.* 1620, *pg.* 1059
Buchheim, Denis, VP-Product Mgmt-Display Adv - Yahoo! Inc.; *pg.* 1289, *pg.* 289
Buchholz, Valerie, Sr Mgr-Mktg - ConAgra Foods, Inc.; *pg.* 826, *pg.* 1014
Buchi, Bob, Sr VP-Mktg - Paramount Pictures Corporation; *pg.* 304, *pg.* 138
Buchko, Bill, Product Mgr - Sentry Group, Inc.; *pg.* 468, *pg.* 1337
Buchman, Laura, VP-Publr Sls - Tremor Video; *pg.* 682, *pg.* 1305
Buchner, Pete, Reg Dir-Mktg - Cox Communications, Inc.; *pg.* 279, *pg.* 501
Bucich, Richard, Sr Mgr-Product Mktg-SEO - Move, Inc.; *pg.* 1268, *pg.* 247
Buck, David, Sr VP-Mktg - The Phillies, L.P.; *pg.* 575, *pg.* 1569
Buck, Gene, Bus Mgr - Joe Machens Ford Inc.; *pg.* 180, *pg* 976
Buck, Greg, Mgr-Shopper Mktg - Hillshire Brands; *pg.* 862, *pg.* 576
Buck, James, Dir-Natl Sls-BTA & MPS - Oki Data Americas, Inc.; *pg.* 449, *pg.* 1090
Buck, Kelly, Analyst-Mktg - Hammacher Schlemmer & Co., Inc.; *pg.* 1124, *pg.* 637
Buck, Melinda, Sr Analyst-Mktg - FedEx Corporation; *pg.* 1907, *pg.* 1642
Buckalew, Michelle, Dir-Media Rels - MoneyGram International, Inc.; *pg.* 783, *pg.* 1684
Buckalew, Mindy, Dir-Sls Strategy & Product Plng - The Atlanta Journal-Constitution; *pg.* 1618, *pg.* 490
Buckbee, Alana, Sr Mgr-Community Dev - Penguin Random House; *pg.* 1675, *pg.* 1276
Buckham, Brian H., Gen Mgr-Comml Mktg - The Goodyear Tire & Rubber Company; *pg.* 1883, *pg.* 1401
Buckingham, Blane, Dir-Sls-Natl - Whirlpool Corporation; *pg.* 62, *pg.* 872
Buckingham, Chuck, Sr Mgr-Channel Mktg - MillerCoors LLC; *pg.* 255, *pg.* 582
Buckingham, Thomas S., Exec VP-Product & Ops - The Phoenix Companies, Inc.; *pg.* 1214, *pg.* 352
Buckingham, Valerie, Head-Mktg-North America-Microsoft Mobile Devices - Microsoft Corporation; *pg.* 435, *pg.* 1824
Buckle, Kevin, Assoc VP-Cardiovascular Portfolio US Mktg - Sanofi US; *pg.* 1592, *pg.* 1046
Buckler, Ozzie, Mgr-Adv & Promos - Lennox International Inc.; *pg.* 1073, *pg.* 1736
Bucklew, Aaron, Sr Dir-Enterprise Sys & DBA - The Home Depot, Inc.; *pg.* 1050, *pg.* 510
Buckley, Alyssa, Coord-Production - Sun Life Financial Inc.;

pg. 806, pg. 1944
Buckley, Amy, Dir-Global Loyalty Mktg-SPG - Starwood Hotels & Resorts Worldwide, Inc.; pg. 1114, pg. 378
Buckley, Brianna, Analyst-Customer Mktg-Orbit, Eclipse, Extra, Lifesavers & Altoids - Wm. Wrigley Jr. Company; pg. 1863, pg. 596
Buckley, Chris, Sr Dir-Amateur Scouting - Reds Baseball Partners, LLC; pg. 578, pg. 1425
Buckley, Courtney, Assoc Mgr-Mktg - The Allstate Corporation; pg. 1189, pg. 639
Buckley, David, Mgr-Mktg & Bus Analysis - SCANA Corporation; pg. 1951, pg. 1612
Buckley, Ethan, Dir-Oncology Global Mktg Strategy - Astellas Pharma US, Inc.; pg. 1496, pg. 640
Buckley, Jamie, Assoc Mgr-Mktg-Digital - Toys "R" Us, Inc.; pg. 968, pg. 1130
Buckley, Kristin, Sr Mgr-Community Affairs - Capital One Bank (USA), N.A.; pg. 730, pg. 1789
Buckley, Leigh, Mgr-Mktg - Boulder Brands, Inc.; pg. 1016, pg. 310
Buckley, Matthew, Sr Mgr-Bus Dev - Micron Technology, Inc.; pg. 435, pg. 547
Buckley, Michael, Sr Dir-Digital Mktg - VistaPrint USA, Incorporated; pg. 1700, pg. 829
Buckley, Michael J., Sr VP-Sls & Distr - Bankers Life & Casualty Company; pg. 1194, pg. 566
Buckley, Nicole, Mgr-Mktg-BCBGeneration - BCBG Max Azria Group LLC; pg. 19, pg. 301
Buckley, Peter, Reg Mgr-Sls - Vapor Bus International; pg. 221, pg. 560
Buckley, Rachel, Sr Specialist-Mktg - Comcast Corporation; pg. 276, pg. 1560
Buckley, Thomas, Analyst-Database Mktg - The Talbots, Inc.; pg. 34, pg. 824
Buckley, Timothy D., VP-Global Mktg & North American Sls - IRIDEX Corporation; pg. 648, pg. 160
Buckley, Tom, Dir-Sls - Lantronix, Inc.; pg. 426, pg. 112
Bucklin, Tammy, Assoc Dir-Sls - Palm Springs Desert Resorts Convention & Visitors Authority; pg. 1003, pg. 187
Buckman, Jad, Dir-Sls - Penn Station, Inc.; pg. 1744, pg. 1465
Buckman, Kathleen, Mgr-Mktg Svcs - UVP, Inc.; pg. 1434, pg. 298
Buckman, Kevin, VP-One-To-One Mktg & Field Trng - Market America Worldwide, Inc.; pg. 1265, pg. 1375
Buckmiller, Robin, Sr Mgr-PR - Microsoft Corporation; pg. 435, pg. 1824
Buckner, Eric, Sr Product Mgr-Mobile - Sears Holdings Corporation; pg. 1784, pg. 618
Bucks, Laura, Brand Mgr-Personal Care Innovation - Colgate-Palmolive Company; pg. 504, pg. 1215
Buckwalter, Randy, Mgr-PR - PHARMACEUTICAL PRODUCT DEVELOPMENT, INC.; pg. 1584, pg. 1393
Budaraju, Hema, Product Mgr-Facebook Events - Facebook, Inc.; pg. 1245, pg. 143
Buday, Andrew, Sr Specialist-Mktg & Comm - Sun Life Financial Inc.; pg. 806, pg. 1944
Budd, Ashley, Asst Dir-Social Media Strategy - Cornell University Press; pg. 1630, pg. 1169
Budd, John, Chief Dev Officer & Chief Strategy Officer - SONIC Corp.; pg. 1750, pg. 1487
Budd, Jon C., Sr Grp Mgr-New Media - Hyundai Motor America; pg. 179, pg. 89
Budd, Mike, Dir-Sls-Intl - Triad Speakers, Inc.; pg. 682, pg. 1507
Buddenbaum, Don, Head-Social Bus Community Grp Standards - International Business Machines Corporation; pg. 418, pg. 1138
Budinick, Kathy, Sr Dir-Comm - Plum Creek Timber Company, Inc.; pg. 105, pg. 1838
Budinsky, Molly, Specialist-Direct to Consumer Online Mktg - Black Diamond, Inc.; pg. 1827, pg. 1756
Budke, Brooke, Dir-Mktg - TITLE Boxing Club; pg. 588, pg. 717
Budnik, Robert, Dir-Creative-Print, Digital & Brdcst Mktg - Academy Sports & Outdoors, Ltd.; pg. 1824, pg. 1724
Budry, Dallas, Mgr-Digital Mktg - La-Z-Boy Incorporated; pg. 932, pg. 901
Budzinski, Christine, Dir-Reg Mktg - The Boeing Company; pg. 225, pg. 567
Budzynski, Rebecca, Assoc Dir-HIV Mktg - Gilead Sciences, Inc.; pg. 1535, pg. 88
Buell, Melissa, Brand Mgr-End User Computing-Healthcare & Life Sciences - Dell Inc.; pg. 383, pg. 1737
Bueltel, Margaret, Sr Mgr-Mktg Res - Land O'Lakes, Inc.; pg. 873, pg. 915
Bueno, Ignacio, Dir-Mktg Florida Reg - AutoNation, Inc.; pg. 165, pg. 423
Buergi, Simona, Mktg Dir - HemCon Medical Technologies, Inc.; pg. 1541, pg. 1503
Buerry, Cammie, Mgr-Media - Station Casinos, Inc.; pg. 585, pg. 1030
Buetikofer, Alyssa, Mgr-Digital Mktg-Global - McDonald's Corporation; pg. 1737, pg. 645
Buettner, Heather, Sr Dir-New Product Dev - The Kraft Heinz Company; pg. 871, pg. 641
Buettner, Sandy, Program Mgr-Mktg Comm - Johnson Controls, Inc.; pg. 209, pg. 1876
Buffington, Scott, Mgr-Natl Sls-MassMutual Retirement Svcs - Massachusetts Mutual Life Insurance Company; pg. 1207, pg. 845
Buford, Katharine, Mgr-Mktg-Barbie Global Brand Team - Mattel Games/Puzzles; pg. 962, pg. 80
Buford, Katharine, Mgr-Mktg-Barbie Global Brand Team - MATTEL, INC.; pg. 962, pg. 81
Buford, Pamela, Dir-US Urology Franchise & Head-US Consumer Mktg - Astellas Pharma US, Inc.; pg. 1496, pg. 640
Bugg, Chris, Dir-Digital Mktg - Calvin Klein, Inc.; pg. 20, pg. 1209
Bugg, Jay C., Sr VP-IMO Mktg - National Life Insurance Company; pg. 1210, pg. 1766
Bugg, Jeannette, Sr Product Mgr & Dir - Bank of America Corporation; pg. 718, pg. 1362
Bugos, Joanne, Dir-Product Mgmt & Comml PCs - Hewlett-Packard Company; pg. 404, pg. 175
Buhl, Jay, Sr VP-Sls-The Americas - QubicaAMF; pg. 1843, pg. 1795
Buhler, Laura, Sr Mgr-Bus Dev - Gilt Groupe Inc.; pg. 24, pg. 1234
Buhling, Armin, Mgr-Mktg - SACHEM Inc.; pg. 1180, pg. 1665
Buhowski, Bob, Mgr-Digital Mktg-Influencer Mktg - LG Electronics U.S.A., Inc.; pg. 651, pg. 1060
Buhr, Ellen J., Sr Mgr-Comm - The Boeing Company; pg. 225, pg. 567
Buhr, Martin, Product Mgr-Kubernetes - Google Inc.; pg. 1249, pg. 153
Buhr, Phil, Product Mgr-Coil & Building Products - PPG Industries, Inc.; pg. 1445, pg. 1579
Buhs, Lori, Bus Mgr-Banking Relationship - IBERIABANK Corporation; pg. 768, pg. 744
Bui, Jennifer, Mgr-Mktg-Prime Now - Amazon.com, Inc.; pg. 1226, pg. 1831
Buijs, Thomas, Product Mgr - ABB Inc.; pg. 1309, pg. 1359
Buijs, Thomas, Product Mgr - ABB Inc.; pg. 64, pg. 1959
Buisson, Blake, Sr Mgr-Mktg - LinkedIn Corporation; pg. 1262, pg. 160
Buisson, Lise, Sr Mgr-Brand Mgmt-Global - Royal Bank of Canada; pg. 800, pg. 1942
Buist, Robyn, Dir-Comm-Secure Supply Chain & Portfolio Mgr-Corp Mktg - AmerisourceBergen Corporation; pg. 1493, pg. 1522
Buiten, Fred Van, Mgr-Sls Comm - Hewlett-Packard Company; pg. 404, pg. 175
Bujeker, Ryan, Sr Mgr-Global Digital Mktg Comm - United Continental Holdings, Inc.; pg. 1927, pg. 593
Bukaty, Peter, Grp Brand Mgr-Global Brands - Illinois Tool Works Inc.; pg. 1348, pg. 614
Bukit, Aldo, Sr Mgr-Online Mktg-Affiliates, CPC Networks & APIs - Wal-Mart.com; pg. 1287, pg. 50
Bukosky, Debbie, Sr Mgr-Unified Comm - Plantronics, Inc.; pg. 663, pg. 270
Bukvic, David, Dir-Mktg & Comm - Dayton Philharmonic Orchestra Association, Inc.; pg. 543, pg. 1445
Bulan, Jamy, Grp Head-Comml Products - Lincoln Electric Holdings, Inc.; pg. 1355, pg. 1432
Bulan, Michelle, Exec Dir-Mktg & Corp Comm - Perry's Ice Cream Co., Inc.; pg. 1861, pg. 1137
Bulandr, Laura, Mgr-Adv Acctg - CDW Corporation; pg. 370, pg. 663
Bulaon, Christopher M., Engr-Technical Mktg - Intel Corporation; pg. 645, pg. 266
Bulbul, Cenk, Head-Strategy & Insights-YouTube Google Brand Ads Mktg - YouTube, LLC; pg. 1291, pg. 198
Buleza, John, VP-Digital Mktg - Performance Direct, Inc.; pg. 1781, pg. 1361
Bulf, Joe, Mgr-Sls-Southern Reg-Wal Mart - Crown Prince, Inc.; pg. 850, pg. 67
Bulgatz, Sarah, Dir-Corp PR - Charles Schwab; pg. 1235, pg. 1661
Bulger, Michael, Sr Dir-Corp Comm - Capital One Bank (USA), N.A.; pg. 730, pg. 1789
Bulkowski, Emily, Coord-Product Category-Outdoor - Philips Electronics North America; pg. 662, pg. 782
Bull, David, Brand Mgr - Sony Computer Entertainment America LLC; pg. 966, pg. 256
Bull, Molly, Sr Mgr-Comm-Microsoft Disaster Response - Microsoft Corporation; pg. 435, pg. 1824
Bullard, Erica, Sr VP-Mdsg - Healthy Directions; pg. 1649, pg. 775
Bullington, Patty, Corp Dir-Mktg - Charter Communications, Inc.; pg. 274, pg. 372
Bullitt, David, Sr Dir-Mktg-Americas - NVIDIA Corporation; pg. 447, pg. 268
Bullock, Bill, Dir-New Media - WCPO-TV; pg. 320, pg. 1427
Bullock, Fred, VP-Corp & Brand Mktg - Citrix Systems, Inc.; pg. 375, pg. 424
Bullock, John, Brand Mgr - Church & Dwight Co., Inc.; pg. 1153, pg. 1063
Bullock, Josh, Sr Dir-Corp Partnerships - Tampa Bay Rays Baseball, Ltd.; pg. 586, pg. 464
Bullock, Kristi, Sr Dir-Product Mktg - Arby's Restaurant Group, Inc.; pg. 1014, pg. 488
Bullock, Nathan, Sr Mgr-Direct Mktg - Intuit Inc.; pg. 769, pg. 158
Bullock, Ryan, VP-Mktg - Keg Restaurants, Ltd.; pg. 1733, pg. 1908
Bullock, Todd, Sr Mgr-Customer Mktg - Del Monte Foods, Inc.; pg. 852, pg. 304
Bullock-McGrail, Beth, Sr Dir-Strategy & Innovation - Friendly Ice Cream, LLC; pg. 1853, pg. 859
Bullwinkel, George J., Jr., Pres/COO-SCANA Energy Mktg-Inc. & Sr VP - SCANA Corporation; pg. 1951, pg. 1612
Bulman, Paul, Sr Category Mgr-Mktg - Ventura Foods, LLC; pg. 908, pg. 49
Bulmer, Kevin, Dir-Consumer Mktg - National Geographic Channel; pg. 299, pg. 402
Bulmer, Mj, Mgr-Natl Mktg-Managed Print Svcs - Xerox Canada Inc.; pg. 494, pg. 1930
Buls, Karen, Dir-Mktg, Production, Creative Svcs & E-Mail Mktg - American Airlines Inc.; pg. 1898, pg. 1693
Bultman, Niels, Dir-Trade Mktg - Reckitt Benckiser Inc.; pg. 1136, pg. 1105
Bulycz, Glenn, Head-CRM & Email Mktg - Apple Inc.; pg. 350, pg. 73
Buma, Jason, VP-Sls-Enterprise Accts - Miller Heiman Inc.; pg. 440, pg. 1031
Bumann, Kelly, Sr VP-Digital Mktg - Starz Entertainment, LLC; pg. 310, pg. 327
Bumbaca, Christina, Sr Mgr-Strategic Mktg - Electronic Arts Inc.; pg. 951, pg. 189
Bumrarb, Pattra, Dir-Digital Promos Mktg - Turner Broadcasting System, Inc.; pg. 314, pg. 521
Bunch, John, Sr Dir-R&D - American Snuff Company; pg. 1893, pg. 1641
Bunch, Mark, Mgr-Product Strategy-Branded Automotive Fuels - BP America Inc.; pg. 972, pg. 1702
Bundenthal, Cori, Head-Digital Studio & Designer-UX - Benjamin Moore & Co.; pg. 1440, pg. 1085
Bundschuh, Elisabeth, Assoc Mgr-Mktg-GQ Magazine - Conde Nast Publications, Inc.; pg. 1629, pg. 1217
Bundschuh, Elisabeth, Mgr-Mktg-GQ - Vogue Magazine; pg. 1700, pg. 1311
Bunker, Frank C., Jr., VP-Pre-Sls, Strategic Customers & IT - Silvon Software Inc.; pg. 470, pg. 669
Bunks, Lauren, Mgr-ECommerce Mktg - United Airlines, Inc.; pg. 1927, pg. 593
Bunnell, Jim, VP-Sls - General Motors Company; pg. 175, pg. 881
Bunner, Bruce, VP-Sls-Global - Author Solutions, Inc.; pg. 1618, pg. 674
Bunner, Kristin, Sr Mgr-Worldwide Events - SunPower Corporation; pg. 1952, pg. 250
Bunner, Laura, Reg Specialist-Mktg - Stanley Steemer International, Inc.; pg. 944, pg. 1450
Bunsen, Samantha, Mgr-Partnership Mktg - FTD Group, Inc.; pg. 1795, pg. 608
Bunszel, Amy, VP-AutoCAD Products - Autodesk Inc.; pg. 356, pg. 257
Bunting, Robert , Jr., Product Mgr-Metal Detection - Bunting Magnetics Co.; pg. 1320, pg. 717
Bunting, Sinead, Dir-Mktg-UK & Ireland - Monster Worldwide, Inc.; pg. 1268, pg. 859
Bunton, Diane, Dir-Mktg-Global Online ECommerce-SEO, Video, BtoB & Content Mgmt - Dell Inc.; pg. 383, pg. 1737

First page reference indicates Business Class Edition
Second page reference indicates Geographic Edition

Buntz, Marissa, Mgr-PR - Jenny Craig Operations, Inc.; pg. 1548, pg. 59
Bunyan, Moshe, Dir-Sls - Amkor Technology, Inc.; pg. 67, pg. 25
Bunzel, Bree, Mgr-Brand & Adv Mktg-Small Bus Mktg - Intuit Inc.; pg. 769, pg. 158
Buonadonna, Michael, Assoc Mgr-Mktg-Intl Pub Safety - Zoll Medical Corporation; pg. 1612, pg. 814
Buonanno, Alicia, Mgr-PR - QVC Inc; pg. 305, pg. 1593
Buonanno, Julia, Coord-Guerlain Skincare Mktg - LVMH Inc.; pg. 9, pg. 1254
Buonocore, Anthony, Mgr-Mktg Controlling - Beiersdorf North America Inc.; pg. 501, pg. 385
Buonomo, Jacqueline, Sr Mgr-Mktg - The Coca-Cola Company; pg. 240, pg. 493
Burbach, Matt, Sr Mgr-Global Retail Mktg & Brand Experience - Black Diamond, Inc.; pg. 1827, pg. 1756
Burbach, Mindy, Asst VP & Dir-Mktg - Platte Valley Financial Service Companies Inc.; pg. 794, pg. 1019
Burbary, Jill, Dir-Mktg & Comm - Wells Fargo & Company; pg. 819, pg. 232
Burbidge, Lori, Specialist-Mktg - Commerce Bancshares, Inc.; pg. 740, pg. 982
Burby, Lisa, VP-Brand Mktg Plng & Integration - Wyndham Vacation Ownership; pg. 1119, pg. 457
Burch, Bill, VP-Sls-Global - Thomson Elite; pg. 484, pg. 72
Burch, Brian, VP-Global Consumer & Small Bus Segment Mktg - Symantec Corporation; pg. 478, pg. 161
Burch, Jeffrey, VP-Adv - Daily Racing Form, LLC; pg. 1632, pg. 1221
Burch, Jennifer, Mgr-Sponsorship Digital Mktg - Save the Children Federation, Inc.; pg. 156, pg. 384
Burch, Michael, Sr VP-Sls & Mktg-Natl - Speedway Motorsports, Inc.; pg. 584, pg. 1370
Burch, Sandra, VP & Dir-Creative - Sotheby's Inc.; pg. 472, pg. 1294
Burch, Sarena D., Sr VP-Fuel Procurement, Asset Mgmt & Power Mktg - SCANA Corporation; pg. 1951, pg. 1612
Burchard, Greg, Sr Mgr-Rights, Reproductions & Photographic Svcs - The Andy Warhol Museum; pg. 529, pg. 1573
Burchell, Edward, VP-Strategic Partnerships & Sls - Baltimore Ravens Limited Partnership; pg. 532, pg. 755
Burchett, Katheryn, Sr VP-Mdse & Mktg Integration - J.C. Penney Company, Inc.; pg. 1774, pg. 1732
Burchett, Mark J., Program Mgr-Mktg - Xerox Corporation; pg. 494, pg. 365
Burchfield, Elaine, Sr Mgr-Innovation & Commercialization - T. Marzetti Company; pg. 900, pg. 1444
Burchman, Suzanne, VP & Project Mgr-Mktg - City National Bank; pg. 737, pg. 725
Burchman, Suzanne, VP & Project Mgr-Mktg - City National Corporation; pg. 738, pg. 128
Burckhardt, Alison, Brand Mgr-Kidswear - Nordstrom, Inc.; pg. 1779, pg. 1837
Burckhardt, Carl, Dir-Digital Mktg & Analytics - Virgin America Inc.; pg. 1930, pg. 55
Burd, Elizabeth, Specialist-Mktg Comm - Philips Lighting; pg. 1303, pg. 806
Burd, Laura, Dir-Mktg - Nationwide Mutual Insurance Company; pg. 1210, pg. 1442
Burd, Randy, Mgr-Product Dev - Multi-Ad, Inc.; pg. 1666, pg. 652
Burd, Sam, VP & Gen Mgr-Personal Computer Product Grp - Dell Inc.; pg. 383, pg. 1737
Burde, Rich, Mgr-Product & Market Dev-Endoscopic Ultrasound - Olympus America Inc.; pg. 1425, pg. 1521
Burden, Mike, Mgr-Sls - Surplus Center; pg. 1380, pg. 1012
Burdett, Christopher, Sr Mgr-Digital Media - Jacksonville Jaguars, Ltd.; pg. 554, pg. 433
Burdette, Blair, Sr Mgr-Mktg - Carter's, Inc.; pg. 21, pg. 491
Burdette, Julie, Mgr-Mktg - Big Lots, Inc.; pg. 1762, pg. 1438
Burdette, Justen, Product Mgr - Amazon.com, Inc.; pg. 1226, pg. 1831
Burdette, Matt, Mgr-B2B Sls & Mktg - Omaha Steaks International, Inc.; pg. 1780, pg. 1017
Burdette, Melinda, Brand Mgr-Own Brands - Giant Eagle, Inc.; pg. 1020, pg. 1575
Burdick, Brenda D., Sr Mgr-Mktg & PR - General Dynamics Corporation; pg. 228, pg. 1781
Burdick, Christopher, Sr Specialist-Web Content-Integrated Mktg Comm - Moody Bible Institute; pg. 605, pg. 583
Burdick, Paula, Specialist-Mktg - FedEx Corporation; pg. 1907, pg. 1642
Burditt, Elise, Sr Assoc Brand Mgr-OREO - Mondelez International; pg. 877, pg. 1344
Burdon, David, Sr Dir-Art - Apple Inc.; pg. 350, pg. 73
Burdsall, Scott, Sr Mgr-Email Mktg - CareerBuilder, LLC; pg. 1234, pg. 568
Burdulis, Nate, Dir-Strategic Sls Plng & Admin - Holland America Line Inc.; pg. 1911, pg. 1836
Bureau, Duncan, VP-Sls-Global - Air Canada; pg. 1896, pg. 1902
Buresh, Pete, Reg VP-Africa Intl Sls - Gulfstream Aerospace Corporation; pg. 228, pg. 540
Burg, Suzanne, Sr Mgr-Mktg & Comm - American Express Company; pg. 712, pg. 1190
Burg-Levi, Janice, Exec Dir-Audit Mktg - KPMG LLP; pg. 774, pg. 1086
Burgar, Ian, Sr Dir-CPE Ops-Supply Chain - Cox Communications, Inc.; pg. 279, pg. 501
Burgart, Jonathan, Mgr-Mktg - Abbott Laboratories; pg. 1484, pg. 551
Burge, Ian, VP-Sls - Revera Inc.; pg. 799, pg. 1928
Burge, Sara, Sr Mgr-Web Mktg - Intuit Inc.; pg. 769, pg. 158
Burger, Kate, Sr Mgr-Sls - Louisville Convention & Visitors Bureau; pg. 998, pg. 736
Burger, Kellen, Analyst/Specialist-Consumer Mktg-US - MasterCard Incorporated; pg. 779, pg. 1325
Burgess, Adam, Sr VP-Mktg Strategies - Bank of America Corporation; pg. 718, pg. 1362
Burgess, Barbara, Mgr-Global Media & Analyst Rels - Accenture; pg. 1392, pg. 1186
Burgess, Caty, VP-Media Strategies - The CW Television Network; pg. 632, pg. 52
Burgess, Jan, Mgr-Mktg - Ingram Micro Inc.; pg. 415, pg. 261
Burgess, Kim, Reg Mgr-Mktg-Kansas Missouri Market Unit - PepsiCo, Inc.; pg. 259, pg. 1327
Burgess, Leah, Mgr-Field Mktg - Bloomin' Brands, Inc.; pg. 1716, pg. 471
Burgess, Lena M., Mgr-Adv Production - Burlington Coat Factory; pg. 1764, pg. 1047
Burgess, Lynn, VP & Div Mgr-Mdse-Men's Clothing & Designer - Nordstrom, Inc.; pg. 1779, pg. 1837
Burgess, Michelle, Mgr-Direct Sls Customer Svc - The Penn Companies; pg. 10, pg. 1568
Burgess, Peter, Sr VP-Mktg - Lionel LLC; pg. 961, pg. 875
Burgess-Smith, Rebekah, Sr Mgr-Intl Mktg-Digital - World Wrestling Entertainment, Inc.; pg. 595, pg. 380
Burgfechtel, John, Sr VP-Sls - totes Isotoner Corporation; pg. 14, pg. 1426
Burggraf, Karen, Sr Mgr-Mktg-Integrated Mktg Comm - The Allstate Corporation; pg. 1189, pg. 639
Burghardt, Christopher, VP-Bus Dev & Sls-Europe - First Solar, Inc.; pg. 639, pg. 26
Burgos, Patricia, Mgr-Distr Partnership Mktg Grp - Univision Communications Inc.; pg. 683, pg. 1307
Burgos, Ray, Dir-Creative Svcs - Kennesaw State University; pg. 603, pg. 534
Burhans, William, Assoc Dir-Mktg & Sls Sourcing - Pfizer Inc.; pg. 1581, pg. 1278
Buring, Michele, Principal-Mktg - FedEx Corporation; pg. 1907, pg. 1642
Burk, Don, Corp Dir-Sls - The McClatchy Company; pg. 1662, pg. 196
Burk, Megan, Specialist-Search Mktg - Arrow Electronics, Inc.; pg. 619, pg. 325
Burka, Jacquelyn, Mgr-Strategic Program & Interactive Mktg - Konica Minolta Business Solutions USA, Inc.; pg. 1419, pg. 1113
Burkart, Marian, Dir-Sls Reporting & Mgmt Info - Nationwide Mutual Insurance Company; pg. 1210, pg. 1442
Burke, Bill, VP-Mktg-CBS Consumer Products - CBS Broadcasting Inc.; pg. 273, pg. 1210
Burke, Bill, VP-Mktg-CBS Consumer Products - CBS Corporation; pg. 273, pg. 1210
Burke, Bill, Sr VP-P&C Ops Mktg - Nationwide Mutual Insurance Company; pg. 1210, pg. 1442
Burke, Brendan, VP-Mktg - Jazz Basketball Investors, Inc.; pg. 554, pg. 1759
Burke, Brian, VP-Sls - The Dun & Bradstreet Corp.; pg. 1637, pg. 1120
Burke, Brian, Sr Mgr-PR - NVIDIA Corporation; pg. 447, pg. 268
Burke, Caitlin, Sr Mgr-Mktg, Media & Branded Entertainment - Subway Restaurants; pg. 1751, pg. 356
Burke, Claire, Partner & Mgr-Mktg - Hulu LLC; pg. 1257, pg. 274
Burke, Connie, Sr Mgr-Corp Diversity - General Motors Company; pg. 175, pg. 881
Burke, Damian, Dir-Mktg-Health & Wellness Digital Solutions - Sears Holdings Corporation; pg. 1784, pg. 618
Burke, Glenn, VP-Mktg & Bus Dev - Avis Budget Group, Inc.; pg. 1900, pg. 1102
Burke, Glenn, VP-Mktg & Bus Dev - Avis Rent A Car System, LLC; pg. 165, pg. 1102
Burke, Jenny, Sr VP-Sls Strategy & Plng - NBC Universal, Inc.; pg. 300, pg. 1266
Burke, Jeremy, Mgr-Mktg Brand - BUFFALO WILD WINGS, INC.; pg. 1718, pg. 931
Burke, Jerry, Sr Mgr-Mobile Svcs - VITACOST.COM, INC.; pg. 1607, pg. 414
Burke, Jim, Dir-PR - HARRIS CORPORATION; pg. 642, pg. 439
Burke, John, VP-Sls - Snyder's of Hanover, Inc.; pg. 1862, pg. 1536
Burke, Joseph, Sr Dir-Facilities Mgmt & Corp Real Estate - Endo Pharmaceuticals Holdings, Inc.; pg. 1528, pg. 1549
Burke, Joseph, Sr Mgr-Ops - Oracle Corporation; pg. 1272, pg. 786
Burke, Karen, Mgr-Sls Resource - Texas Monthly; pg. 1692, pg. 1666
Burke, Kayse, Asst Mgr-Mktg - Playtex Apparel, Inc.; pg. 31, pg. 1395
Burke, Kim, Sr Dir-Membership Mktg - Sam's Club; pg. 1783, pg. 29
Burke, Lori, Mgr-PR - Ameristar Casinos, Inc.; pg. 528, pg. 1022
Burke, Maggie, Sr Dir-Corp Mktg - EMC Corporation; pg. 391, pg. 825
Burke, Mike, Mgr-Ticket Sls & Hospitality - Baltimore Ravens Limited Partnership; pg. 532, pg. 755
Burke, Mike, Dir-Product Sustainability - Colgate-Palmolive Company; pg. 504, pg. 1215
Burke, Mike, Mgr-Sls & Mktg-Natl - Duncan Toys Company; pg. 951, pg. 1465
Burke, Mike, VP-Sls & Mktg - Sea Ray Boats, Inc.; pg. 1710, pg. 1638
Burke, Patrick, Reg Mgr-Sls-North Atlantic - F.W. Bryce, Inc.; pg. 857, pg. 823
Burke, Patti, Dir-Mktg & Customer Technologies - Cardinal Health, Inc.; pg. 1512, pg. 1448
Burke, Rebecca, Assoc Mgr-Mktg - The Quaker Oats Company; pg. 834, pg. 588
Burke, Rick, Dir-Customer Relationship Mktg - Abbott Diabetes Care, Inc.; pg. 1483, pg. 38
Burke, Robert, Dir-Global Brand Mktg Events & Sports Moments - NIKE, Inc.; pg. 1812, pg. 1492
Burke, Ryan, Product Mgr-Digital Product - VistaPrint USA, Incorporated; pg. 1700, pg. 829
Burke, Scott, Sr VP-Adv Tech & Data Platforms - Yahoo! Inc.; pg. 1289, pg. 289
Burke, Sean, Sr Mgr-Media Bus Dev - United Airlines, Inc.; pg. 1927, pg. 593
Burke, Steven, Sr Dir-Guest Svcs - Colorado Rockies Baseball Club, Ltd.; pg. 542, pg. 317
Burke, Sue, Sr Dir-Digital Mktg & PR - ConAgra Foods, Inc.; pg. 826, pg. 1014
Burke, Todd, VP-Comm & PR - Popeyes Louisiana Kitchen, Inc.; pg. 1745, pg. 517
Burke, Tom, Dir-Mktg Comm-New Brunswick Products - Eppendorf North America; pg. 1412, pg. 1164
Burke, Tracy, Brand Mgr-Hammermill - International Paper Company; pg. 1460, pg. 1644
Burke, Tricia, Brand Mgr - Trek Bicycle Corporation; pg. 1847, pg. 1896
Burke, William, Rep-Sls - Acushnet Company; pg. 1824, pg. 818
Burkett, Jeff, Sr Dir-Adv Innovations & Client Svcs - Graham Holdings Company; pg. 1645, pg. 1773
Burkett, Kara, Sr Mgr-Product Mktg - AT&T; pg. 1865, pg. 258
Burkhalter, Billy, Sr Mgr-Community Mktg - Dick's Sporting Goods, Inc.; pg. 1832, pg. 1524
Burkhardt, David, Area VP-Mktg Cloud - salesforce.com, inc.; pg. 1278, pg. 226
Burkhart, Jay, Sr VP-Mktg-Global - Federal-Mogul Holdings Corporation; pg. 205, pg. 907
Burkhart, Lisa, Dir-Mktg - Belkin International, Inc.; pg. 361, pg. 182
Burkhart, Liz, Sr Specialist-Media Rels-Global - Whole Foods Market, Inc.; pg. 1038, pg. 1667
Burkhoff, Stuart, VP-Mktg Programs - Ameriprise Financial, Inc.; pg. 715, pg. 930
Burkholder, Helen, Dir-Media - Dick's Sporting Goods, Inc.; pg. 1832, pg. 1524

Burkitt, Brian, Product Dir-Aerospace Matls - NuSil Technology LLC; *pg.* 1887, *pg.* 63
Burkland, Melissa, Sr Mgr-Strategic Procurement - Liberty Mutual Insurance Group Inc.; *pg.* 1205, *pg.* 797
Burks, Dale, VP-Sls & Mktg-Global - Standard Motor Products, Inc.; *pg.* 218, *pg.* 1176
Burkum, Kevin, Sr VP-Mktg - American Egg Board; *pg.* 128, *pg.* 650
Burleson, Mimi, Head-Mktg Comm Reg Ops - Dell Inc.; *pg.* 383, *pg.* 1737
Burleson, Timory, Specialist-Mktg Comm - Avid Technology, Inc.; *pg.* 622, *pg.* 804
Burley, Becky, Sr Mgr-Mktg-Relationship Mktg - Capella Education Company; *pg.* 599, *pg.* 931
Burley, Margaret, Specialist-Mktg - Hewlett-Packard Company; *pg.* 404, *pg.* 175
Burley, Shannon, Sr VP-Mktg & Bus Ops - Seattle Storm; *pg.* 582, *pg.* 1839
Burlison, Amanda, Assoc Mgr-Mktg - General Mills, Inc.; *pg.* 828, *pg.* 933
Burlison, Sandy, Specialist-Media - Kissimmee-St. Cloud Convention & Visitors Bureau; *pg.* 997, *pg.* 436
Burnell, Darin Kaye, Mgr-Mktg - Benefit Cosmetics LLC; *pg.* 501, *pg.* 213
Burnell, David, Coord-Mktg - Vermont Department of Tourism & Marketing; *pg.* 1010, *pg.* 1767
Burnell, Elissa, Brand Mgr-Portfolio Digital Strategy - Diageo North America Inc.; *pg.* 248, *pg.* 1223
Burnell-Fraser, Jane, VP-Sls-The Americas - Four Seasons Hotels Limited; *pg.* 1092, *pg.* 1938
Burness, Michael J., Sr Dir-Quality & Regulatory Affairs - Godiva Chocolatier, Inc.; *pg.* 1854, *pg.* 1235
Burnett, Christopher, Product Mgr-Technical - Thermo Fisher Scientific Inc.; *pg.* 1431, *pg.* 854
Burnett, Diane, Dir-ECommerce Mktg - Cost Plus World Market; *pg.* 921, *pg.* 170
Burnett, Jason, Sr Dir-Content-Lifestyle Digital Grp - Time Inc.; *pg.* 1693, *pg.* 1300
Burnett, Kelly, Mgr-Social Media - Hobby Lobby Stores Inc.; *pg.* 927, *pg.* 1486
Burnett, Kevin, Dir-Creative - Pleasant Holidays LLC; *pg.* 1919, *pg.* 307
Burnett, Kimberly, Specialist-Sls Comm & Support - United States Postal Service; *pg.* 1009, *pg.* 406
Burnett, Kristin, Designer-Digital - NIKE, Inc.; *pg.* 1812, *pg.* 1492
Burnette, James, Dir-Sls Dev-Global - LinkedIn Corporation; *pg.* 1262, *pg.* 160
Burnham, Carolyn, Category Mgr-Mdse - Recreational Equipment, Inc.; *pg.* 1843, *pg.* 1821
Burnham, Heather, VP-Mktg - CorVel Corporation; *pg.* 1198, *pg.* 109
Burnham, Hugh, Mgr-Interactive Web Mktg - Snapfish; *pg.* 1687, *pg.* 228
Burnham, John N., VP-Corp Mktg - IBM; *pg.* 410, *pg.* 1449
Burnham, Philippe, Dir-Product Mktg - Valeant Pharmaceuticals International; *pg.* 1605, *pg.* 1047
Burns, Brad, Sr VP-Media Rels-Global - AT&T Inc.; *pg.* 1867, *pg.* 1674
Burns, Cindy, Dir-Mktg Ops & Brand - CareFusion Corporation; *pg.* 1513, *pg.* 201
Burns, Colin, Mgr-Adv Content & Compliance - COUNTRY Financial; *pg.* 1198, *pg.* 557
Burns, Craig, Sr Mgr-University Accounts - ZIPCAR, INC.; *pg.* 1931, *pg.* 810
Burns, Dan, VP-Sls - LeapFrog Enterprises, Inc.; *pg.* 961, *pg.* 84
Burns, Dean, Mgr-Mktg - Alcon; *pg.* 1399, *pg.* 530
Burns, Deb, VP-Mktg - School Specialty, Inc.; *pg.* 467, *pg.* 1860
Burns, Elyse, Assoc Mgr-Mktg - ACCO Brands Corporation; *pg.* 340, *pg.* 626
Burns, Emmet, Dir-Brand & Integrated Mktg - SunTrust Banks, Inc.; *pg.* 807, *pg.* 520
Burns, Emmy, Dir-Digital Creative & Strategist-Global Digital & Social Media - Elizabeth Arden, Inc.; *pg.* 507, *pg.* 448
Burns, Jennifer, Brand Mgr-Retail-Women's-DTC North America - NIKE, Inc.; *pg.* 1812, *pg.* 1492
Burns, Jennifer, Head-Trader Mktg Strategy - TD Ameritrade Holding Corporation; *pg.* 808, *pg.* 1018
Burns, Jenny, Dir-Mission & Natural Channel Brand Mktg - Honest Tea; *pg.* 253, *pg.* 762
Burns, Jessica, Dir-Adv, Integrated Mktg & Comm - Jockey International, Inc.; *pg.* 27, *pg.* 1861
Burns, Joanne, Chief Strategy Officer & Sr VP - Cerner Corporation; *pg.* 1514, *pg.* 981
Burns, Kate, Dir-Mktg-Global Consumer Campaign Creative - Dell, Inc.; *pg.* 385, *pg.* 1037
Burns, Katie, Assoc Dir-Nivolumab-Oncology Mktg - Bristol-Myers Squibb Company; *pg.* 1509, *pg.* 1206
Burns, Kevin, Interim Pres & COO - Chobani LLC; *pg.* 847, *pg.* 1318
Burns, Kevin, Project Mgr-Mktg - Rockwell Automation, Inc.; *pg.* 668, *pg.* 1880
Burns, Kristie, VP-Solutions Mktg - ResMed Inc.; *pg.* 1589, *pg.* 207
Burns, Laura, Exec Dir-Mktg - ABC Cable Networks Group; *pg.* 268, *pg.* 51
Burns, Lauren, Dir-PR - The Gatorade Company; *pg.* 251, *pg.* 574
Burns, Lisa, Dir-Corp Mktg & Branding - Corning Incorporated; *pg.* 1122, *pg.* 1154
Burns, Mary A., Specialist-Brand Sls - Arrow Electronics, Inc.; *pg.* 619, *pg.* 325
Burns, Mary A., Sr Acct Mgr-Mktg-Vmware Comml & Cloud - Ingram Micro Inc.; *pg.* 415, *pg.* 261
Burns, Meghan, Mgr-Social Media - Vineyard Vines LLC; *pg.* 50, *pg.* 379
Burns, Michele, Sr Mgr-Mktg, Media & Digital - Nestle Waters North America Inc.; *pg.* 257, *pg.* 375
Burns, Mieka, Brand Mgr-Premium Coffee - Kraft Canada Inc.; *pg.* 869, *pg.* 1939
Burns, Neil, Mgr-Canadian Natl Sls-Utility - Sherman & Reilly, Inc.; *pg.* 1062, *pg.* 1629
Burns, Nisha, Dir-Mktg - Abbott Laboratories; *pg.* 1484, *pg.* 551
Burns, Patrick, Sr Dir-Global Acquirer Processing - Visa Inc.; *pg.* 816, *pg.* 230
Burns, Peter, Sr Mgr-Mktg - QUALCOMM Incorporated; *pg.* 1873, *pg.* 207
Burns, Sabina, Sr Dir-Corp Mktg - Synopsys, Inc.; *pg.* 480, *pg.* 162
Burns, Stephen, VP-Sls - Medline Industries, Inc.; *pg.* 1562, *pg.* 635
Burns, Terri, Sr Mgr-Mktg Strategic Sourcing & Procurement - Aflac Incorporated; *pg.* 1188, *pg.* 527
Burns, Tim, Product Mgr-Drivetrain & Aftermarket - Meritor, Inc.; *pg.* 212, *pg.* 911
Burns, Veda, Dir-Mktg Procurement - InterContinental Hotels Corporation; *pg.* 1097, *pg.* 511
Burns-Fernandes, Kathy, Dir-Sls-OEM - Polar Electro Inc.; *pg.* 664, *pg.* 1173
Burnside, Megan, Sr Mgr-Capabilities Mktg - Alliance Data Systems Corporation; *pg.* 347, *pg.* 1729
Burque, Lisa, Sr Dir-Mktg - Natus Medical Incorporated; *pg.* 1572, *pg.* 199
Burr, James M., VP-Energy Products - FCStone Group, Inc.; *pg.* 751, *pg.* 982
Burr, Jenny, Sr Mgr-Speech Science - Convergys Corporation; *pg.* 379, *pg.* 1412
Burrage, Ronald, Head-Global Design & Sr Dir - The Hershey Co.; *pg.* 1855, *pg.* 1538
Burrell, Damon, Sr VP-Consumer & Digital Mktg - MTV Networks Company; *pg.* 298, *pg.* 1262
Burrill, Jeffrey, Mgr-Field Mktg - MillerCoors; *pg.* 254, *pg.* 1877
Burrill, Jessica, Dir-Mktg, Bond & Fin Products - The Travelers Companies, Inc.; *pg.* 1220, *pg.* 352
Burrill, Jessica, Dir-Mktg, Bond & Fin Products - Travelers Insurance; *pg.* 1220, *pg.* 963
Burris, Michael, Mgr-Channel Mktg & Customer Mktg - General Mills, Inc.; *pg.* 828, *pg.* 933
Burroughs, Alicia, Mgr-Global Segment Mktg - Concur Technologies; *pg.* 1903, *pg.* 501
Burroughs, Allyson, VP-Mktg - Xerox Corporation; *pg.* 494, *pg.* 365
Burroughs, Hilary, Dir-Mktg - Sanderson Farms, Inc.; *pg.* 893, *pg.* 970
Burrows, Angela, Mgr-Comm & Mktg - CB Richard Ellis Group, Inc.; *pg.* 1085, *pg.* 127
Burrows, Kathy M., Mgr-PR - The Hershey Co.; *pg.* 1855, *pg.* 1538
Burrows, Kathy McCleaf, Mgr-PR - Hershey Entertainment & Resorts Company; *pg.* 1094, *pg.* 1539
Burrows, Rachel F., Sr Mgr-Customer Mktg - Coca-Cola Refreshments USA, Inc.; *pg.* 247, *pg.* 500
Burrows, Ryan, Head-Creative - Sussex Bancorp; *pg.* 807, *pg.* 1068
Burruto, Lauren, Dir-Sls - WHEC-TV LLC; *pg.* 321, *pg.* 1338
Bursa, Karin L., VP-Mktg - Logility, Inc.; *pg.* 428, *pg.* 513
Burstin, Matt, Dir-Partnership Mktg - World Wrestling Entertainment, Inc.; *pg.* 595, *pg.* 380
Burstin, Michaelle, Head-Index Mktg Strategy-Global - MSCI Inc.; *pg.* 785, *pg.* 1262
Burt, David, VP-Sls Special Markets Div - Bumble Bee Foods LLC; *pg.* 842, *pg.* 201
Burt, David, Sr Product Mgr-Mktg & Cloud & Enterprise - Microsoft Corporation; *pg.* 435, *pg.* 1824
Burt, Judy, Specialist-Media-Charter Media - Charter Communications, Inc.; *pg.* 274, *pg.* 372
Burt, Lucas, Brand Mgr-Nike Technology - NIKE, Inc.; *pg.* 1812, *pg.* 1492
Burt, Marc, Sr Mgr-Office-Inclusion & Diversity - American Honda Motor Co., Inc.; *pg.* 163, *pg.* 292
Burt, Molly, Assoc Mgr-Field Mktg-Northeast Reg - Dunkin' Brands Group, Inc.; *pg.* 1727, *pg.* 810
Burtchell, Susan E., Dir-Adv - Worcester Telegram & Gazette Corp.; *pg.* 1702, *pg.* 863
Burtin, Anna, Coord-Studio Mktg - Sun Life Financial Inc.; *pg.* 806, *pg.* 1944
Burtnick, Ken, Sr Product Mgr - Paychex, Inc.; *pg.* 792, *pg.* 1336
Burton, Alfonzo, Dir-Creative & User Experience - Glu Mobile Inc.; *pg.* 954, *pg.* 219
Burton, Brad, Acct Mgr-Marine Market Sls-OEM - Thetford Corporation; *pg.* 337, *pg.* 867
Burton, Bridget, Brand Mgr - StubHub, Inc.; *pg.* 586, *pg.* 228
Burton, Clive, VP-Sls - PODS Enterprises, Inc.; *pg.* 1919, *pg.* 416
Burton, Heddie, Sr Mgr-Global Alliance Mktg Campaigns - VMware, Inc.; *pg.* 490, *pg.* 179
Burton, Jeremy, Pres-Products & Mktg-Info Infrastructure - EMC Corporation; *pg.* 391, *pg.* 825
Burton, Jody, Mgr-Loyalty Mktg - GameStop Corp.; *pg.* 399, *pg.* 1699
Burton, LeAnn W., Mgr-Mktg Comm - NuVasive, Inc.; *pg.* 1577, *pg.* 205
Burton, Marion, Mgr-Mktg-Global Foods & Ingredients - Ocean Spray Cranberries, Inc.; *pg.* 887, *pg.* 827
Burton, Matthew, Dir-Digital Strategy & Mktg - Equinox Fitness Clubs; *pg.* 546, *pg.* 1228
Burton, Nigel B., CMO - Colgate Oral Pharmaceutical; *pg.* 1516, *pg.* 1214
Burton, Scott, Dir-Mktg-Champs Sports-Foot Locker - Champs Sports; *pg.* 1806, *pg.* 414
Burton, Scott, Gen Mgr-Sls - Cox Media Group; *pg.* 280, *pg.* 502
Burton, Scott, VP-Sls & Mktg - Gilead Sciences, Inc.; *pg.* 1535, *pg.* 88
Bury, Greg, Sr Mgr-PR & Corp Comm - Medica, Inc.; *pg.* 1208, *pg.* 949
Bury, Stephen, Sr Mgr-Marcom - Microsoft Corporation; *pg.* 435, *pg.* 1824
Buryta, Nichole, Brand Mgr - Perry's Ice Cream Co., Inc.; *pg.* 1861, *pg.* 1137
Burzynski, Brennar, Coord-Mktg - Rubio's Restaurants, Inc.; *pg.* 1748, *pg.* 60
Burzynski, Kimberly, Mgr-Retail Mktg - New Era Cap Company Inc.; *pg.* 1840, *pg.* 1155
Busby, John, Sr VP-Mktg & Consumer Insights - Marchex, Inc.; *pg.* 1395, *pg.* 1837
Busby, Ricky, Sr Assoc Brand Mgr - Georgia-Pacific LLC; *pg.* 1458, *pg.* 507
Buscani, Pete, Exec VP-Mktg - La Rosa's, Inc.; *pg.* 1735, *pg.* 1416
Buscarino, Christine, VP-ECommerce Mktg - Office Depot, Inc.; *pg.* 448, *pg.* 412
Busch, Adam, Product Mgr-CEREC - Sirona Dental Systems, Inc.; *pg.* 1429, *pg.* 1175
Busch, Joe, VP-Sls - Associated Wholesale Grocers, Inc.; *pg.* 1015, *pg.* 715
Busch, Tom, Sr Mgr-Comm Infrastructure - FRANKLIN RESOURCES, INC.; *pg.* 760, *pg.* 254
Busche, Paul, Dir-Mktg - Nalco Co.; *pg.* 1174, *pg.* 636
Buscher, Bruce, VP-Sls - Daifuku Webb; *pg.* 1327, *pg.* 885
Buser, Eileen, Sr Dir-Special Events - Major League Baseball; *pg.* 560, *pg.* 1255
Bush, Ben, Mgr-Social & Digital Media - Anytime Fitness; *pg.* 529, *pg.* 926
Bush, Celeste T, Sr Mgr-Mktg Comm - AT&T Inc.; *pg.* 1867, *pg.* 1674
Bush, Erin, Mgr-Online Mktg & Social Media - CustomInk, LLC; *pg.* 22, *pg.* 1780
Bush, Greg, Sr Dir-Ops - Churchill Downs, Inc.; *pg.* 540, *pg.* 733

First page reference indicates Business Class Edition
Second page reference indicates Geographic Edition

Bush, James, Mgr-Mktg - Lafarge Canada Inc.; *pg.* 92, *pg.* 1958
Bush, Lisa, Mgr-Events Mktg - General Electric Company; *pg.* 1297, *pg.* 347
Bush, Neal, Mgr-Customer Mktg - Citrix Online LLC; *pg.* 1235, *pg.* 99
Bush, Stephanie, Assoc Specialist-Social Media - DSW, Inc.; *pg.* 1807, *pg.* 1439
Bushbaker, Peter, Brand Mgr-Glucerna - Abbott Laboratories; *pg.* 1484, *pg.* 551
Bushell, Dan, Assoc Dir-Mktg Ops - Gilead Sciences, Inc.; *pg.* 1535, *pg.* 88
Bushey, Elizabeth, Assoc Dir-Mktg-Good Housekeeping - The Hearst Corporation; *pg.* 1649, *pg.* 1239
Bushkin, Nancy, VP-PR & Corp Comm - Care.com; *pg.* 1960, *pg.* 850
Bushman, Scott, Product Mgr-Global - Applied Materials, Inc; *pg.* 618, *pg.* 1009
Bushnell, Caroline, Product Mgr-Innovation-Celestial Seasonings - The Hain Celestial Group, Inc.; *pg.* 860, *pg.* 1172
Bushnell, Scott, Dir-Adv Creative - John F. Kennedy Center for the Performing Arts; *pg.* 555, *pg.* 401
Bushong, Cassie, Planner-Digital Sls - Scripps Networks Interactive, Inc.; *pg.* 1279, *pg.* 1638
Bushong, Steven, Sr VP-Mktg Ops - The Walt Disney Company; *pg.* 317, *pg.* 52
Bushoven, Glenn, Mgr-Sls - Wayne Tile Co.; *pg.* 946, *pg.* 1130
Bushway, Kathy, Sr VP & Dir-Segment Mktg - FirstMerit Corporation; *pg.* 758, *pg.* 1400
Busi, John, Exec VP & Head-V&A Valuation & Advisory-Global - Cushman & Wakefield, Inc.; *pg.* 1088, *pg.* 1220
Busk, Douglas, Grp Dir-Digital Comm & Social Media-Global - The Coca-Cola Company; *pg.* 240, *pg.* 493
Buskirk, Heide Van, Dir-Strategy, Plng, Mktg & Ops - Hewlett-Packard Company; *pg.* 404, *pg.* 175
Busse, Yolande, Sr Mgr-Mktg & Product Brand Mgr - BeautiControl Cosmetics, Inc.; *pg.* 501, *pg.* 1669
Bussen, Scott, Dir-Mktg Comm & Meetings & Events - MillerCoors LLC; *pg.* 255, *pg.* 582
Bussler, Bill, Assoc Mgr-PR-Power Grp - Kohler Co.; *pg.* 91, *pg.* 1862
Busso, Chris, Sr Mgr-Product Mktg - Teledyne LeCroy; *pg.* 1431, *pg.* 1153
Busson, Chantal, Grp Brand Dir - GlaxoSmithKline Consumer Healthcare; *pg.* 510, *pg.* 1554
Bustamante, Maria, Mgr-Sls-Intl - Vicon Industries, Inc.; *pg.* 685, *pg.* 1166
Bustillos, Carrie, Dir-Mktg Programs & Ops - Autodesk Inc.; *pg.* 356, *pg.* 257
Bustillos, Hassam, Mgr-Mktg-Fossil + Skagen-Americas Reg - Fossil Group, Inc.; *pg.* 5, *pg.* 1735
Butcher, Aisha, Sr Mgr-Bus Analysis - WellCare Health Plans Inc.; *pg.* 1223, *pg.* 476
Butcher, Art, VP-Global Mktg-Endoscopy Div - Boston Scientific Corporation; *pg.* 1508, *pg.* 831
Butcher, Rob, Dir-Media Rels - Reds Baseball Partners, LLC; *pg.* 578, *pg.* 1425
Butel, Renaud, Dir-Mktg & Innovation-Belvedere - LVMH Inc.; *pg.* 9, *pg.* 1254
Buten, John, Sr Dir-Global Mktg Campaigns & Enablement - Akamai Technologies, Inc.; *pg.* 1226, *pg.* 807
Buter, Alicia, Sr Product Mgr-Canada - Elmer's Products, Inc.; *pg.* 1442, *pg.* 1479
Butera, Marilyn S., Mgr-Corp Mktg Ops - Hewlett-Packard Company; *pg.* 404, *pg.* 175
Buterbaugh, Charlie, Specialist-Mktg Comm - VWR Funding, Inc.; *pg.* 1608, *pg.* 1583
Butler, Adam, Dir-Mktg-McCafe Beverages - The Kraft Heinz Company; *pg.* 871, *pg.* 641
Butler, Ariana Hellebuyck, VP-Brand Mktg-Natl - The University of Phoenix, Inc.; *pg.* 610, *pg.* 27
Butler, Ashley, Strategist-Social Media - Chobani LLC; *pg.* 847, *pg.* 1318
Butler, Butch, Mgr-Sls-Southeast Reg - Crane Carrier Company; *pg.* 168, *pg.* 1489
Butler, Cheryl, Mgr-Mktg-Engineered Films Division - Raven Industries, Inc.; *pg.* 1888, *pg.* 1625
Butler, Cindy, Sr Mgr-Scale Digital Mktg - Georgia-Pacific LLC; *pg.* 1458, *pg.* 507
Butler, Dan, Dir-Mktg Comm - Kyocera Document Solutions America; *pg.* 426, *pg.* 1065
Butler, Debra, VP-Creative Mktg - Firmenich Incorporated; *pg.* 509, *pg.* 1109
Butler, Duke, Sr Dir-Technical Dev - Brocade Communications Systems, Inc.; *pg.* 365, *pg.* 239
Butler, Eric L., Exec VP-Mktg & Sls - Union Pacific Corporation; *pg.* 1927, *pg.* 1018
Butler, Erin, Media Buyer - Anheuser-Busch Companies, LLC; *pg.* 237, *pg.* 991
Butler, Everett, Mgr-Global Email Mktg - Tesla Motors, Inc.; *pg.* 191, *pg.* 178
Butler, Fabia, VP & Mgr-Community & PR - Bank of Marin Bancorp; *pg.* 720, *pg.* 168
Butler, Grace, Brand Mgr - United Continental Holdings, Inc.; *pg.* 1927, *pg.* 593
Butler, Jim , Sr., Treas & Sr Dir-Fin - Pulse Electronics Corporation; *pg.* 666, *pg.* 206
Butler, Jimmy, Sr Mgr-Quality - The Boeing Company; *pg.* 225, *pg.* 567
Butler, Joe, Sr Dir-Server Sys Validation - Intel Corporation; *pg.* 645, *pg.* 266
Butler, Josh, Product Mgr - Facebook, Inc.; *pg.* 1245, *pg.* 143
Butler, Kari, Analyst-Mktg - State Farm Mutual Automobile Insurance Co.; *pg.* 1218, *pg.* 557
Butler, Kevin, VP-Ground Beef Sls - American Foods Group, LLC; *pg.* 837, *pg.* 1859
Butler, Kevin, Dir-Social Media - ESPN, Inc.; *pg.* 285, *pg.* 340
Butler, Lori J., Sr Mgr-Mktg Comm - Fujitsu Computer Systems Corporation; *pg.* 398, *pg.* 285
Butler, Marc, Sr VP-Mktg & Product Dev - Hooters of America LLC; *pg.* 1731, *pg.* 511
Butler, Nicholas, Grp Mgr-Embedded Sys Product Mktg - National Instruments Corporation; *pg.* 443, *pg.* 1664
Butler, Nikki, Sr Reg Mgr-Mktg - BUFFALO WILD WINGS, INC.; *pg.* 1718, *pg.* 931
Butler, Paul, Mgr-Mktg - Nissan North America, Inc.; *pg.* 186, *pg.* 1633
Butler, Roberta M., Sr VP-Mktg - Factory Mutual Insurance Company; *pg.* 1199, *pg.* 1601
Butler, Russell, VP-Product Dev - Oracle Corporation; *pg.* 1272, *pg.* 786
Butler, Theresa, Reg Dir-Mktg - Aramark; *pg.* 1013, *pg.* 1558
Butler, William, Sr VP-Promo & Corp Mktg - Sinclair Broadcast Group, Inc.; *pg.* 308, *pg.* 773
Butt, Naaz F., Mgr-Mktg & Program Mgr - Intuit Inc.; *pg.* 769, *pg.* 158
Butt, Nayyar, Head-Mktg Metrics & Analysis-Global - Bloomberg L.P.; *pg.* 725, *pg.* 1204
Buttars, Fiona, Dir-Mktg Ops - Toronto Symphony Orchestra; *pg.* 589, *pg.* 1946
Butterfield, Tristan, Dir-Creative-Global - Kohler Co.; *pg.* 91, *pg.* 1862
Butters, Amy, Assoc Dir-Site Comm & PR - Pfizer Inc.; *pg.* 1581, *pg.* 1278
Butterworth, Nicholas, Head-Product & Digital Entertainment-People com & EW com - Time Inc.; *pg.* 1693, *pg.* 1300
Buttimer, Jessica, Head-Mktg-AMPAC - Sonos, Inc.; *pg.* 675, *pg.* 263
Butts, Colin, Dir-Mktg - Wolverine World Wide, Inc.; *pg.* 1822, *pg.* 905
Butts, Paul, VP-Beverage, Food & Chemical Sls - Owens-Illinois, Inc.; *pg.* 1466, *pg.* 1470
Butts, Ray, VP & Dir-Creative-North America & Brand Design - NIKE, Inc.; *pg.* 1812, *pg.* 1492
Buttshaw, Michael, VP-Sls & Mktg - MGP Ingredients, Inc.; *pg.* 877, *pg.* 714
Butz, Greg, Exec VP-Sls & Mktg Ops-Comcast Cable - Comcast Cable Communications, Inc.; *pg.* 276, *pg.* 1560
Butz, Michelle, Sr Mgr-Digital Media - The Allstate Corporation; *pg.* 1189, *pg.* 639
Buxton, Claire, Dir-Integrated Mktg Comm-Redken & Pureology - L'Oreal USA; *pg.* 514, *pg.* 1252
Buxton, Janelle, Mgr-Mktg Comm-Global - Dupont Pioneer; *pg.* 1795, *pg.* 708
Buzzard, Natalie, Mgr-Adv - The Lima News; *pg.* 1659, *pg.* 1457
Byall, Lisa, Product Mgr - Lincoln Electric Holdings, Inc.; *pg.* 1355, *pg.* 1432
Byar, Christian, Mgr-Mktg - American Grease Stick Co.; *pg.* 971, *pg.* 902
Bycel, Liat, Dir-Sls - Twitter, Inc.; *pg.* 1285, *pg.* 228
Byczek, Justin, VP-Strategic Partnerships & Mktg - NBC Sports Network; *pg.* 300, *pg.* 375
Byczek, Justin, VP-Strategic Partnerships & Mktg - NBC Universal, Inc.; *pg.* 300, *pg.* 1266
Bye, Erik, Sr Web Developer-Mktg - 24 Hour Fitness Worldwide Inc.; *pg.* 526, *pg.* 258
Bye, Jake, VP-Ticket Sls & Premium Seating - Saint Louis Rams Football Company; *pg.* 580, *pg.* 1002
Byerly, Daron, Brand Mgr-Innovation - Seventh Generation, Inc.; *pg.* 335, *pg.* 1765
Byerly, Don, VP-Sls - RefrigiWear, Inc.; *pg.* 47, *pg.* 529
Byerly, Jonathan, Dir-Global SAP Sls Alliances - Dell Inc.; *pg.* 383, *pg.* 1737
Byers, Deb, Specialist-Mktg - Quantum Corporation; *pg.* 458, *pg.* 250
Byers, Seth, Exec VP-Creative Strategy & Res-Universal Pictures Mktg - NBC Universal, Inc.; *pg.* 300, *pg.* 1266
Byers, Sharon, Sr VP-Sports & Entertainment Mktg Partnerships - The Coca-Cola Company; *pg.* 240, *pg.* 493
Byers, Shelly, Mgr-Digital Mktg - UnitedHealth Group Incorporated; *pg.* 1221, *pg.* 950
Byers, Steve, Sr Dir - Harsco Rail; *pg.* 1345, *pg.* 1623
Bygrave, Donna, Mgr-Mktg - United, Inc.; *pg.* 1117, *pg.* 1905
Byk, Bradley C., Sr VP-Worldwide Sls - Skyworks Solutions, Inc.; *pg.* 674, *pg.* 862
Bylos, Stephanie, Assoc Product Mgr - Newell Rubbermaid Inc.; *pg.* 1128, *pg.* 515
Bylsma, Alyssa, Product Mgr - Universal Forest Products, Inc.; *pg.* 117, *pg.* 890
Bynoe, Kenyatta, Sr Dir-Mktg - Spalding; *pg.* 1845, *pg.* 846
Bynoe-Reed, Pamela A., Strategist-Mktg & Promos - SCANA Corporation; *pg.* 1951, *pg.* 1612
Byrd, Eric, Assoc Dir-Mktg - Purdue Pharma LP; *pg.* 1587, *pg.* 377
Byrd, James E., Sr Dir & Assoc Gen Counsel - LexisNexis Group; *pg.* 1658, *pg.* 1446
Byrd, Jason, Analyst-Mktg - DTE Energy Company; *pg.* 1940, *pg.* 880
Byrd, Matt, Mgr-Email Mktg - Uber USA, LLC; *pg.* 1286, *pg.* 229
Byrd, Michele, Mgr-Product Mktg - CBS Interactive, Inc.; *pg.* 369, *pg.* 215
Byrd, Richard, Dir-Creative - Schlumberger Limited; *pg.* 801, *pg.* 1714
Byrne, Christine, Sr Mgr-Media Rels-Bentley Sys - Bentley Systems, Inc.; *pg.* 361, *pg.* 1531
Byrne, David, Dir-Mktg Programs - Hyatt Hotels Corporation; *pg.* 1096, *pg.* 577
Byrne, Ila, Sr Mgr-Innovation & Ideation - Diageo North America Inc.; *pg.* 248, *pg.* 1223
Byrne, Julie, Dir-On Premise Trade Mktg - Sidney Frank Importing Co., Inc.; *pg.* 1970, *pg.* 1184
Byrne, Karina, Head-Media Rels-Americas - UBS Financial Services Inc.; *pg.* 812, *pg.* 1306
Byrne, Pat, Mgr-Mktg-Natl - Maxell Corporation of America; *pg.* 652, *pg.* 1079
Byrne, Patrick, Mgr-Publicity & Digital Media - Home Box Office, Inc.; *pg.* 290, *pg.* 1240
Byrne, Robert W., Sr Mgr-Dev-Mens UGG & Tsubo - Deckers Outdoor Corporation; *pg.* 1807, *pg.* 100
Byrne, Shivonne, Sr Dir-Enterprise Mktg - Microsoft Corporation; *pg.* 435, *pg.* 1824
Byrne, Taylor, Asst Mgr-Customer Mktg-Global Travel Retail - Bacardi USA, Inc.; *pg.* 1956, *pg.* 417
Byrne, Toby, Pres-Adv Sls - Fox Broadcasting Company; *pg.* 287, *pg.* 130
Byrnes, Brian M., Sr VP-Sls & Mktg - Oklahoma City Thunder; *pg.* 571, *pg.* 1487
Byrnes, James, Mgr-Sls & Mktg - Potdevin Machine Company; *pg.* 1369, *pg.* 1131
Byrnes, Kevin, VP-Television Adv Sls - NewsMax Media, Inc.; *pg.* 1271, *pg.* 479
Byrnes, Shannon, Asst Mktg Mgr-Res - BIC Corporation; *pg.* 501, *pg.* 369
Byron, Jeff, Sr Dir-Mktg - Alliance Data Systems Corporation; *pg.* 347, *pg.* 1729
Byron, Jill, Sr VP-Mktg - Mode Media; *pg.* 1267, *pg.* 50
Byrum, Erica Campbell, Dir-Social Media - Homes.com, Inc.; *pg.* 1256, *pg.* 203
Byrum, Warren, Dir-Category Mgmt, Mktg, Adv & Media Svcs - American Express Company; *pg.* 712, *pg.* 1190
Bytell, Amy, S Mgr-Media Mktg - Doctor's Associates Inc.; *pg.* 1726, *pg.* 356
Bythewood, Michelle, VP-Brand Mktg - CiCi Enterprises LP; *pg.* 1723, *pg.* 1670

C

Cabaco, Jose, VP & Creative Dir-Brand - Eddie Bauer, Inc.; *pg.* 40, *pg.* 1814
Caballero, Luis, Exec Dir-Mktg Segmentation - Cox

Communications, Inc.; pg. 279, pg. 501
Caballero, Maite, Mgr-NPD Mktg - American Express Company; pg. 712, pg. 1190
Caballero, Mariel, Mgr-Mktg & Multicultural Markets - American Heart Association Inc.; pg. 128, pg. 1673
Cabalquinto, Joseph, Dir-Creative-Global - Claire's Stores, Inc.; pg. 1764, pg. 617
Caban, Cynthia, Asst Mgr-Digital Media - Lord & Taylor LLC; pg. 1777, pg. 1252
Cabanday, Phil, Mgr-Mktg Events - Ixia; pg. 422, pg. 56
Cable, Jeff, Dir-Mktg - Lexar Media, Inc.; pg. 1262, pg. 146
Cabot, Samantha, Dir-Field Mktg-US - Robert Half International Inc.; pg. 462, pg. 145
Cabral, Julio, VP-On-Air Creative-Film, TV & Sports - Fox Broadcasting Company; pg. 287, pg. 130
Cabrera, Jano, Sr VP-US Comm, Global Media & PR - McDonald's Corporation; pg. 1737, pg. 645
Cabrera, Mario, Dir-US Retail & Shopper Mktg-Pet Nutrition - Colgate-Palmolive Company; pg. 504, pg. 1215
Cabrero-Frey, Veronica, Sr Mgr-Customer Mktg - The Coca-Cola Company; pg. 240, pg. 493
Cabrero-Frey, Veronica, Brand Mgr-Yard House - Olive Garden Italian Restaurant; pg. 1742, pg. 454
Cabus, Pere, Dir-Worldwide Product Mktg - Hewlett-Packard Company; pg. 404, pg. 175
Cacace, Kathy, Mgr-Web Creative - Ethan Allen Interiors Inc.; pg. 924, pg. 343
Cacatian, Juvie, Assoc Mgr-Mktg - Home Box Office, Inc.; pg. 290, pg. 1240
Caccia, Robert M., Mgr-Mktg - Wells Fargo & Company; pg. 819, pg. 232
Cacciamani, Carlos, Head-ECommerce Mktg - Royal Caribbean Cruises Ltd; pg. 1921, pg. 446
Cacciatori, Lauran, Sr Dir-Corp Mktg & Comm - Deltek, Inc.; pg. 386, pg. 1784
Caceres, Ricardo, Dir-Sustainability-Global Mktg - The Coca-Cola Company; pg. 240, pg. 493
Caceres, Sergio, Sr Engr-Product Dev - Intel Corporation; pg. 645, pg. 266
Cachua, Luis, Dir-Multicultural Mktg Strategy - The Northwestern Mutual Life Insurance Company; pg. 1212, pg. 1879
Caciolo, Candy, Dir-Portfolio & Pro Engagement Mktg - Nestle Purina PetCare Company; pg. 1479, pg. 1000
Cacioppo, Erin, Mgr-Channel Mktg - Blackbaud, Inc.; pg. 361, pg. 1613
Cacopardo, Joe, Dir-Mktg - Hatteras Yachts; pg. 1708, pg. 1386
Cacy, Jeff, Reg Dir-Mktg-Americas - The Boeing Company; pg. 225, pg. 567
Cadd, Malcolm, Dir-Product Mktg Mobile Svcs - NeuStar, Inc.; pg. 1872, pg. 1807
Cadden, Rachel, Exec VP-Mktg - Relativity Media, LLC; pg. 306, pg. 47
Cadden, Ricky, Mgr-Social & Digital Content-TripCase - Sabre Corporation; pg. 1710, pg. 752
Cade, Yolanda Clark, Mng Dir-PR-Natl - American Automobile Association; pg. 1190, pg. 429
Cadelli, Andrea, Sr Mgr-Digital Mktg & MRM - Sam's Club; pg. 1783, pg. 29
Cadena, Chuck, CEO-Comm & Sr Dir-Internal - The Boeing Company; pg. 225, pg. 567
Cadet, Ronald, Assoc Dir-Mktg - Purdue Pharma LP; pg. 1587, pg. 377
Cadicamo, Jennifer, VP-Mktg-Partnership Activation - The Detroit Lions, Inc.; pg. 544, pg. 864
Cadigan, John R., Exec VP & Head-Natl Sls - Behringer Holdings, LLC; pg. 1081, pg. 1657
Cadiz, Treena, Mgr-Integrated Digital Mktg - Glaxo Smith Kline Inc.; pg. 1536, pg. 1926
Cadle, Brian, District Mgr-Sls - FedEx Corporation; pg. 1907, pg. 1642
Cadle, Joe, Dir-Shopper Mktg - GlaxoSmithKline; pg. 1536, pg. 1389
Cadoret-Manier, Jilani, VP-Sls, Mktg & Respiratory - Genentech, Inc.; pg. 1533, pg. 279
Cady, Joseph, VP-Digital Strategy & Adv Sls - NBC Universal, Inc.; pg. 300, pg. 1266
Caesar, Ted, Mgr-Internet Mktg - MacNeil Automotive Products, Ltd.; pg. 211, pg. 559
Caetano, Tomas, VP-Brand Mktg-Global - Volvo Cars of North America LLC; pg. 195, pg. 1117
Cafaro, Kevin, Product Mgr-Technical - The McGraw-Hill Companies Inc.; pg. 1663, pg. 1257
Cafferty, Alicia, Dir-Product Mktg-Cooking & Laundry - BSH Home Appliances Corporation; pg. 53, pg. 108
Cafferty, Linda, Mgr-Mktg-Red Hat Enterprise Linux solutions - Red Hat, Inc.; pg. 460, pg. 1388
Cafferty, Suzanne, Dir-Product Mktg-Global - Motorola Solutions, Inc.; pg. 657, pg. 659
Caffrey, Kelly, Dir-Institutional Acq Mktg - TD Ameritrade Holding Corporation; pg. 808, pg. 1018
Caffrey, Matt, Sr Dir-Consumer Mktg - Eli Lilly and Company; pg. 1527, pg. 684
Cafiero, Stacey, Mgr-Mktg - Aetna Inc.; pg. 1187, pg. 351
Caggiano, Donatella, Dir-PR - Oakley, Inc.; pg. 1840, pg. 86
Cagle, Alison, Mgr-Customer Mktg-Pyrex - World Kitchen LLC; pg. 1141, pg. 657
Cagle, John R., Sr VP-Sls - EF Johnson Technologies, Inc.; pg. 390, pg. 1718
Cagnazzi, Michael, Sr VP-Digital Product Dev - AMC Networks Inc.; pg. 269, pg. 1189
Cahalane, Shanna, Dir-Mktg & VP - Reading Cooperative Bank; pg. 798, pg. 842
Cahayag, Tess, Program Mgr-PR - Synopsys, Inc.; pg. 480, pg. 162
Cahill, Claudia, Dir-PR - MicroStrategy, Inc.; pg. 1266, pg. 1809
Cahill, John, Mgr-Mktg Comm - Eastman Chemical Company; pg. 1159, pg. 1636
Cahill, Liz, VP-Mktg - Lee Jeans; pg. 43, pg. 721
Cahill, Rebecca, Mgr-Mktg Res - United Parcel Service, Inc.; pg. 1928, pg. 522
Cahn, Chas, Sr Mgr-Mktg - Frito-Lay North America, Inc.; pg. 1853, pg. 1730
Cahn, Chas C., Sr Mgr-Mktg - PepsiCo, Inc.; pg. 259, pg. 1327
Cahn, Mitch, Dir-Mktg & Bus Dev - Reeds Jewelers, Inc.; pg. 11, pg. 1393
Cai, Charlie, Product Mgr-Automotive TVS Diodes-Global - Littelfuse, Inc.; pg. 1301, pg. 580
Cai, Cynthia, Sr Dir-Workflow Solutions-Mass Spectrometry Div - Agilent Technologies, Inc.; pg. 614, pg. 264
Cai, William, Sr Mgr-ROW Smart Phone Product Operation & Bus Dev - Lenovo Group Ltd; pg. 427, pg. 1384
Cain, Dave, Dir-Mktg - Sonny's Real Pit Bar-B-Que; pg. 1751, pg. 461
Cain, Jim, Sr Mgr-Sls & Exec Comm - General Motors Company; pg. 175, pg. 881
Cain, Katherine, Mgr-PR - The Gap, Inc.; pg. 1770, pg. 218
Cain, Kerri, Mgr-Mktg-North America - The Timberland Company; pg. 1821, pg. 1039
Cain, Linda, VP-Mktg & Sls - Valley Fig Growers, Inc.; pg. 908, pg. 93
Cain, Wally, Dir-Sls Support - Middle Atlantic Products Inc.; pg. 1360, pg. 1065
Caine, John, Chief Product Officer - The Priceline Group Inc.; pg. 1276, pg. 364
Caines, Dwight, Pres-Theatrical Mktg - Sony Pictures Entertainment Inc.; pg. 309, pg. 72
Caisley, Charles A., VP-Mktg & Pub Affairs - Great Plains Energy Incorporated; pg. 1944, pg. 983
Cajka, Connie, Dir-Sls - Godfather's Pizza, Inc.; pg. 1729, pg. 1015
Calabrese, Nick, Dir-Consumerism Product Mgmt - Cigna Corporation; pg. 1197, pg. 338
Calabria, Jennifer, Dir-Digital, Adv & Emerging Media - Viacom Inc.; pg. 316, pg. 1310
Calabro, Coley, Product Mgr-US Mktg Rare Genetic Disease - Genzyme Corporation; pg. 1534, pg. 808
Calabro, Thom, Dir-Mktg & Product Dev - Fujinon Inc.; pg. 1414, pg. 1129
Calacci, Rick, Sr VP-Home Entertainment Sls - LG Electronics U.S.A., Inc.; pg. 651, pg. 1060
Calandra, Heather, Specialist-Mktg Comm - Schneider Electric USA, Inc.; pg. 1306, pg. 650
Calandro, Nicole, Specialist-Product - First Data Corporation; pg. 754, pg. 505
Calandruccio, Bob, VP-Sls - Scripps Networks Interactive, Inc.; pg. 1279, pg. 1638
Calarie Widdowson, Natalie, VP & Sr Mgr-Content Mktg - T. Rowe Price Group Inc.; pg. 808, pg. 759
Caldarelli, O. Joe, Pres/CEO-Comm & Medical Products Div - CPI International, Inc.; pg. 631, pg. 175
Caldarola, Catherine, Mgr-Specialty & Enrichment Mktg - FlightSafety International, Inc.; pg. 601, pg. 1160
Caldas, Max, VP-Mktg Strategy - American Woodmark Corporation; pg. 913, pg. 1811
Calderaro, Joia, Sr Media Planner & Buyer - Conair Corporation; pg. 505, pg. 1055
Calderon, Aileen, Mgr-Channel Mktg - Belkin International, Inc.; pg. 361, pg. 182
Calderon, Jeffrey S., Reg Sls Mgr-Specialty Product Lines - The Allstate Corporation; pg. 1189, pg. 639
Calderon, Karla, VP-Mdsg - Kirkland's Inc.; pg. 1126, pg. 1652
Calderon, Monica, Sr Mgr-Promos - Live Nation Entertainment, Inc.; pg. 558, pg. 47
Calderon, Ricardo A., Dir-Latin America Mktg - Dell Inc.; pg. 383, pg. 1737
Calderoni, Bob, Interim CEO - Citrix Systems, Inc.; pg. 375, pg. 424
Calderwood, Daniel, VP-Mktg-SEALY Portfolio - Tempur Sealy International, Inc.; pg. 944, pg. 731
Caldwell, Amy, Dir-Mktg - Vermont Symphony Orchestra; pg. 590, pg. 1765
Caldwell, Chris, Sr Dir-Mktg Ops - RACKSPACE HOSTING, INC.; pg. 1277, pg. 1742
Caldwell, Deanna, Mgr-Media Svcs - The Detroit Lions, Inc.; pg. 544, pg. 864
Caldwell, Michelle, Mgr-Mktg - Carrier Corporation; pg. 1070, pg. 349
Caldwell, Phillip, Product Mgr-Asset Pooling - Northern Trust Corporation; pg. 787, pg. 585
Caldwell, Richard, Sr Mgr-Mktg-Intl - Omnicell Inc.; pg. 1578, pg. 161
Caldwell-Wenman, Alexzandra, Mgr-Product Mktg-QuickBooks Payroll - Intuit Inc.; pg. 769, pg. 158
Caleca, Lisa, Mgr-Mktg - RECARO North America, Inc.; pg. 216, pg. 869
Calero, Maria, Mgr-Mktg Program - PayPal Inc.; pg. 1274, pg. 248
Caley, Lindsey, Assoc Mgr-Mktg - Burt's Bees Inc.; pg. 502, pg. 1370
Calhoun, Jake, Mgr-Mktg-Gourmet Coffee - The J.M. Smucker Company; pg. 865, pg. 1468
Calhoun, Kathy, Mgr-Mktg Comm - Wilsonart International, Inc.; pg. 1450, pg. 1746
Calhoun, Michelle A., Dir-Sls & Mktg - AbbVie Inc.; pg. 1486, pg. 638
Cali, Elaine, VP-Attendee Mktg & Community Rels - Anaheim/Orange County Visitor & Convention Bureau; pg. 988, pg. 42
Califano, Matt, Sr Dir-Program Scheduling & Acq - Spike TV; pg. 310, pg. 1295
Calizaire, Carla, Brand Dir-Metabolics Mktg-INVOKANA - Johnson & Johnson; pg. 1549, pg. 1091
Calka, Bryan, Exec Dir-Corp Sls & Sponsorship - New York Yankees; pg. 570, pg. 1144
Calkin, Courtney, Mgr-Mktg - Microsoft Corporation; pg. 435, pg. 1824
Call, Adam, Mgr-Natl Sls-Herman Miller Collection - Herman Miller, Inc.; pg. 926, pg. 913
Call, Jared L., Mgr-OEM Mktg - Brocade Communications Systems, Inc.; pg. 365, pg. 239
Call, Tim, Exec VP-Sls - Miller Heiman Inc.; pg. 440, pg. 1031
Callaghan, Caitlin, Brand Mgr - Nestle Waters North America Inc.; pg. 257, pg. 375
Callaghan, Lisa, Asst VP-Grp Benefits Product - Manulife Financial Corporation; pg. 778, pg. 1939
Callahan, Amy, Brand Mgr-Jewellery - Macy's East; pg. 1777, pg. 1254
Callahan, Anastasia, Sr Dir-Franchise Ops - Marriott International, Inc.; pg. 1102, pg. 764
Callahan, Angie, Dir-Adv - Daily Press; pg. 1632, pg. 302
Callahan, Ashley, Mgr-Content Strategy & PR - Chick-fil-A, Inc.; pg. 1721, pg. 492
Callahan, Brendan, Assoc Mgr-Mktg, Meals & Sauce - Campbell Soup Company; pg. 844, pg. 1048
Callahan, Brian C., Sr Dir-Global Comm - EMC Corporation; pg. 391, pg. 825
Callahan, Brianne, Mgr-Mktg - Extended Stay Hotels LLC; pg. 1091, pg. 1622
Callahan, Dan, VP-Programmatic Sls-Fox Networks Grp - Fox Broadcasting Company; pg. 287, pg. 130
Callahan, Dawn, Sr VP-Sls & Mktg-Global - Boingo Wireless, Inc.; pg. 625, pg. 127
Callahan, Emily, CMO - St. Jude Children's Research Hospital; pg. 1596, pg. 1646
Callahan, Jack, Exec Dir-OTC Products - CME Group Inc.; pg. 738, pg. 571
Callahan, Jason, Mgr-Internet Mktg - Voxx International; pg. 686, pg. 1166
Callahan, Jessica, Brand Mgr-Beaulieu Vineyards & Chalone Vineyards - Diageo North America, Inc.; pg. 1961, pg. 361

First page reference indicates Business Class Edition
Second page reference indicates Geographic Edition

Callahan, Jim, Mgr-Mktg Comm - BMW of North America, LLC; *pg.* 166, *pg.* 1133

Callahan, John, VP-Mktg - Zep Inc.; *pg.* 338, *pg.* 524

Callahan, Kari, Sr Mgr-Media - Amazon.com, Inc.; *pg.* 1226, *pg.* 1831

Callahan, Lindsay, Engr-Technical Mktg - Cisco Systems, Inc.; *pg.* 372, *pg.* 240

Callahan, Lucile, VP-Adv - Pfizer Inc.; *pg.* 1581, *pg.* 1278

Callahan, Mark, VP-Fresh Sls - Icicle Seafoods, Inc.; *pg.* 864, *pg.* 1836

Callahan, Michael, VP-Global Brand, Campaign & Event Mktg - Juniper Networks, Inc.; *pg.* 1260, *pg.* 286

Callahan, Nikole, VP-Strategic Mktg - Citigroup Inc.; *pg.* 735, *pg.* 1212

Callahan, Susannah, Mgr-Mktg-Strategic Partnerships-Home Solar - NRG Energy, Inc.; *pg.* 1948, *pg.* 1712

Callan, Jill, Sr Dir-Mktg - SHUTTERFLY, INC.; *pg.* 1280, *pg.* 192

Callanan, Meredith, VP-Corp Mktg & Comm - T. Rowe Price Group Inc.; *pg.* 808, *pg.* 759

Callaway, Jessica L., Project Specialist-Cloud Mktg-Consulting Svcs - Cisco Systems, Inc.; *pg.* 372, *pg.* 240

Callaway, Stephanie, Sr Dir-Mktg - United Parcel Service, Inc.; *pg.* 1928, *pg.* 522

Calle, Alex, Dir-Product Mgmt - AT&T Inc.; *pg.* 1867, *pg.* 1674

Calle, Craig, Chief Strategy Officer & Head-Partner Mgmt & TAO - Software House International, Inc. (SHI); *pg.* 471, *pg.* 1122

Callegaro, Jennifer, Sr Mgr-Mktg-Canada - Expedia, Inc.; *pg.* 1244, *pg.* 1814

Callen, Daniel, Product Mgr - Coherent, Inc.; *pg.* 1406, *pg.* 265

Callen, Jack, Dir-Comm & Data Sls - Graybar Electric Company, Inc.; *pg.* 1299, *pg.* 997

Callendar, Mike, Mgr-Digital Mktg - Ford Motor Company; *pg.* 172, *pg.* 876

Callender, Rachel, Sr Project Specialist-Mktg Comm - St. Jude Medical, Inc.; *pg.* 1596, *pg.* 963

Callery, Anton, Product Mgr - Xylem Inc.; *pg.* 1078, *pg.* 1339

Callison-Burch, Vanessa, Product Mgr - Facebook, Inc.; *pg.* 1245, *pg.* 143

Callister, Jeff, Specialist-Mktg - Associated Food Stores, Inc.; *pg.* 1014, *pg.* 1756

Callistus De Almeida, Danister, Sr Dir-Worldwide & North America Channel Partner Mktg - Polycom, Inc.; *pg.* 664, *pg.* 249

Calo, Amber, Sr Mgr-Creative Intelligence - Corbis Corporation; *pg.* 380, *pg.* 1834

Calosso, Mary-Grace, Specialist-Mktg Automation - Bio-Rad Laboratories, Inc.; *pg.* 1504, *pg.* 101

Calouette, Therese, Sr Mgr-Adv & Circulation - Our Sunday Visitor, Inc.; *pg.* 1673, *pg.* 682

Caltagirone, Angela, VP-eMarketing & eMail Mktg - Williams-Sonoma, Inc.; *pg.* 1140, *pg.* 234

Caltagirone, Beth, Mgr-Product Mktg-Software Storage Solutions - SanDisk Corporation; *pg.* 465, *pg.* 147

Caltagirone, Joseph, First Asst VP & Sr Mgr-Programming & Internet Svcs - Astoria Financial Corporation; *pg.* 717, *pg.* 1172

Caluori, Rai, Exec VP-Guest Experience & Product Dev - Princess Cruise Lines Ltd.; *pg.* 1920, *pg.* 270

Caluori, Sabrina, VP-Digital & Social Media - Home Box Office, Inc.; *pg.* 290, *pg.* 1240

Calva, Luis, Dir-Mktg - Nationwide Mutual Insurance Company; *pg.* 1210, *pg.* 1442

Calve, Joanne, Sr Dir-Mktg Comm - Agilent Technologies, Inc.; *pg.* 614, *pg.* 264

Calvert, John, Dir-Product Mgmt & Production - Albertson's LLC; *pg.* 1013, *pg.* 546

Calvert, Luanne, CMO & VP - Virgin America Inc.; *pg.* 1930, *pg.* 55

Calvert, McQueen, Brand Mgr-Home Cleaning Category - Georgia-Pacific LLC; *pg.* 1458, *pg.* 507

Calvesbert, Neil, VP-Mktg-Creative, Digital Mktg, Social Media & Brand Lifestyle - Monster Beverage Corporation; *pg.* 257, *pg.* 69

Calvin, Louie, Product Mgr-Acctg CS - Thomson Reuters Tax & Accounting; *pg.* 1693, *pg.* 1299

Calvin, Suzanne, Dir-Media & PR - The Dallas Opera; *pg.* 543, *pg.* 1679

Calvo, Krista, Dir-Mktg Ops - Adobe Systems Incorporated; *pg.* 342, *pg.* 235

Calvo, Raul, VP-DOS National Sls - IHeartMedia Inc.; *pg.* 292, *pg.* 1741

Calvosa, Gregory, Dir-Mktg - Madison Square Garden Network; *pg.* 297, *pg.* 1255

Calwell, Curtis, Product Mgr - Mercedes-Benz Canada Inc.; *pg.* 184, *pg.* 1940

Camacho, Marissa, Brand Mgr-Retail Dev - Ralph Lauren Corporation; *pg.* 46, *pg.* 1284

Camangian, Rory, Dir-Digital Sls-East Coast - Live Nation Entertainment, Inc.; *pg.* 558, *pg.* 47

Camara, George, Dir-Mdsg-Nike Africa - NIKE, Inc.; *pg.* 1812, *pg.* 1492

Camarata, Mary, Dir-PR-Global - Amazon.com, Inc.; *pg.* 1226, *pg.* 1831

Camargo, Mary Lou, Sr Mgr-Global Events - AT&T; *pg.* 1865, *pg.* 258

Camarillo, Nathan, Product Mgr-Cast - Google Inc.; *pg.* 1249, *pg.* 153

Camba, Casey, Sr Mgr-Technical Mktg - Dolby Laboratories, Inc.; *pg.* 284, *pg.* 217

Cambria, Anne Montgomery, Dir-Adv & Sponsorships - Athleta; *pg.* 19, *pg.* 181

Cambria, Tony, Dir-Integrated Mktg - Stryker Orthopaedics; *pg.* 1599, *pg.* 1082

Cambron, Steve, VP-Mktg-Corp Adv Products & Solutions - Time Inc.; *pg.* 1693, *pg.* 1300

Camenzind, Betty, Mgr-Mktg-Natl - Ennis, Inc.; *pg.* 393, *pg.* 1727

Camerlengo, Justin, Dir-Mktg - EarthCam, Inc.; *pg.* 1239, *pg.* 1072

Cameron, Amy, Mgr-Mktg - Wine.com, Inc.; *pg.* 1972, *pg.* 234

Cameron, Coogan, Mgr-Global Product Line - Milton Roy Company; *pg.* 1361, *pg.* 1542

Cameron, Don, Reg Mgr-Sls - Eberhard Manufacturing Division; *pg.* 1046, *pg.* 1475

Cameron, Evins, Sr Assoc Brand Mgr-Intl Delight Innovation - The WhiteWave Foods Company; *pg.* 1037, *pg.* 324

Cameron, Jaime, Sr Specialist-Mktg - SYNNEX Corporation; *pg.* 480, *pg.* 92

Cameron, Jannice, Sr VP-Mktg - Hollander Sleep Products; *pg.* 927, *pg.* 411

Cameron, Jason, Sr Dir-Mktg Sys & Analytics - Regis Corporation; *pg.* 521, *pg.* 941

Cameron, Jeff, Asst Mgr-Mktg - E&J Gallo Winery; *pg.* 1962, *pg.* 149

Cameron, Mitchell, Mgr-Mktg - MATTEL, INC.; *pg.* 962, *pg.* 81

Cameron, Rick, Sr Asst VP-Mktg Comm - Mercer University; *pg.* 604, *pg.* 535

Cameron, Robert, Sr VP-Mktg-Global - Moet Hennessy; *pg.* 1966, *pg.* 1260

Cameron, Tiffany, Mgr-Mktg & Media - Georgia-Pacific LLC; *pg.* 1458, *pg.* 507

Camfferman, Chris, Sr Product Mgr - Universal Forest Products, Inc.; *pg.* 117, *pg.* 890

Camilletti, Chris, Dir Mktg - Dell Inc.; *pg.* 383, *pg.* 1737

Camiolo, Stephen, Dir-Oncology Mktg - Gilead Sciences, Inc.; *pg.* 1535, *pg.* 88

Camlek, Dennis, Sr VP-Turner Media Grp - Turner Broadcasting System, Inc.; *pg.* 314, *pg.* 521

Cammack, Chris, Product Mgr-Interior & Forward Lighting - Grote Industries, Inc.; *pg.* 206, *pg.* 693

Cammack, Kevin, Sr Dir-Diabetes Mktg - Eli Lilly and Company; *pg.* 1527, *pg.* 684

Cammarata, Paul, Mgr-CSG Creative Studio - Ernst & Young Global Limited; *pg.* 748, *pg.* 1228

Cammarota, Laura, Sr Mgr-Shopper Mktg - Beiersdorf North America Inc.; *pg.* 501, *pg.* 385

Cammell, Allyson, Mgr-Mktg Client Svcs - Ingram Micro Inc.; *pg.* 415, *pg.* 261

Cammilleri, Katie, Mgr-Mktg Program-Comparison Shopping Engines - Recreational Equipment, Inc.; *pg.* 1843, *pg.* 1821

Camou, Jenai, Mgr-Mktg - Academy of Art University; *pg.* 597, *pg.* 211

Camozzi, Kimi, Mgr-Interactive Multi-Channel Mktg - Genentech, Inc.; *pg.* 1533, *pg.* 279

Camp, Arianne, Mgr-Private Brand Product - Michaels Stores, Inc.; *pg.* 1127, *pg.* 1722

Camp, Brandon, Dir-Global Mktg Programs - Ancestry.com LLC; *pg.* 1228, *pg.* 1754

Camp, Gary, Dir-PR - Dover Motorsports, Inc.; *pg.* 545, *pg.* 387

Camp, W. Brad, VP-Mktg - Intermountain Farmers Association; *pg.* 705, *pg.* 1759

Campagna, Dennis F., Sr Dir-Fin, Ops & Sls - Pandora Media Inc.; *pg.* 1273, *pg.* 172

Campagna, Karen R., Sr Mgr-Field Mktg Programs - Cisco Systems, Inc.; *pg.* 372, *pg.* 240

Campagne, Tommy, Sr Mgr-Mktg Comm-Global-Sanuk - Deckers Outdoor Corporation; *pg.* 1807, *pg.* 100

Campagnolo, Angela, Sr Mgr-Market - Expedia, Inc.; *pg.* 1244, *pg.* 1814

Campagnuolo, Bonnie, Sr Dir-Brand Mktg-Global - Hilton Worldwide, Inc.; *pg.* 1094, *pg.* 1791

Campana, Julia, Strategist-Mktg-Thrivent Federal Credit Union - Thrivent Financial for Lutherans; *pg.* 1219, *pg.* 944

Campana, Michael E., Sr Mgr-Healthcare Mktg & Mgr-Mktg, Bus & Tech - Ricoh Americas Corporation; *pg.* 461, *pg.* 1131

Campanella, Donna M., Exec Dir-Media-Global - Avon Products, Inc.; *pg.* 500, *pg.* 1198

Campanella, Molly, Sr Asst Brand Mgr - The Procter & Gamble Company; *pg.* 1129, *pg.* 1418

Campanile, Gina, Mgr-Mktg Comm - Stryker Corporation; *pg.* 1598, *pg.* 894

Campari, Daniela, Sr VP-Mktg - American Cancer Society, Inc.; *pg.* 126, *pg.* 487

Campbell, Andrea, Dir-Field Mktg - AARON'S, INC.; *pg.* 912, *pg.* 486

Campbell, Anne, Mgr-Suite Sls Svc - The Detroit Lions, Inc.; *pg.* 544, *pg.* 864

Campbell, Ashley, Mgr-Mktg Comm - Butler Manufacturing Company; *pg.* 72, *pg.* 981

Campbell, Belinda, Specialist-Mktg Dev - Atmos Energy Corporation; *pg.* 1935, *pg.* 1675

Campbell, Ben L., Reg Mgr-Mktg-Phoenix, Tucson & Las Vegas - Meritage Homes Corporation; *pg.* 97, *pg.* 23

Campbell, Bill, Sr Product Mgr-UPS Power Sys - Emerson Network Power Liebert; *pg.* 1071, *pg.* 1439

Campbell, Brean, Mgr-Technical Mktg-UCS Performance Team - Cisco Systems, Inc.; *pg.* 372, *pg.* 240

Campbell, Bruce, Dir-Sls Enablement - Keynote Systems Incorporated; *pg.* 425, *pg.* 255

campbell, bruce, Chief Creative Officer - salesforce.com, inc.; *pg.* 1278, *pg.* 226

Campbell, Cam, Mgr-Wholesale Product Sls - Wellmaster Carts; *pg.* 1388, *pg.* 1934

Campbell, Carmen, Sr Mgr-Mktg - T. Rowe Price Group Inc.; *pg.* 808, *pg.* 759

Campbell, Carol, Exec Dir-Sls Dev - Hearst Magazines; *pg.* 1649, *pg.* 1239

Campbell, Cheryl, Mgr-Trade & Product Mktg-MAKE UP FOR EVER - LVMH Inc.; *pg.* 9, *pg.* 1254

Campbell, Chris, Mgr-Digital Mktg Tech - Boston Scientific Corporation; *pg.* 1508, *pg.* 831

Campbell, Chris, Sr Mgr-Product Mktg - Citrix Systems, Inc.; *pg.* 375, *pg.* 424

Campbell, Chris, Sr VP-Mktg & Comm - CNO Financial Group, Inc.; *pg.* 1198, *pg.* 675

Campbell, Chris, Sr Mgr-Insights & Analytics - Post Holdings, Inc.; *pg.* 833, *pg.* 1002

Campbell, Clark, Gen Mgr-Experiential Mktg - Volkswagen Group of America, Inc.; *pg.* 194, *pg.* 1785

Campbell, Crystal, Head-Digital Mktg-Encompass Brand - The Allstate Corporation; *pg.* 1189, *pg.* 639

Campbell, Curtis W., VP-Sls - SigmaTron International, Inc.; *pg.* 674, *pg.* 611

Campbell, Daniele, VP-CRM & Digital Media Grp - Marvel Entertainment, LLC; *pg.* 1662, *pg.* 1257

Campbell, David, Dir-Mktg-Venture & Emerging Brands - The Coca-Cola Company; *pg.* 240, *pg.* 493

Campbell, David, Sr Dir-Products-LogMeIn Rescue - LOGMEIN, INC.; *pg.* 428, *pg.* 861

Campbell, David, Dir-Sls & Mktg - Rosewood Hotels & Resorts LLC; *pg.* 1111, *pg.* 1686

Campbell, Dee Dee, Mgr-Dealer Sls Ops - Thomas Built Buses, Inc.; *pg.* 191, *pg.* 1379

Campbell, Denise, Sr Dir-Consumer Mktg Immunology - AbbVie Inc.; *pg.* 1486, *pg.* 638

Campbell, Doug, Dir-Mktg-Beer - Diageo North America Inc.; *pg.* 248, *pg.* 1223

Campbell, Eileen, CMO - Imax Corporation; *pg.* 1417, *pg.* 1926

Campbell, Elizabeth, Brand Mgr - Chattanooga Bakery Inc.; *pg.* 847, *pg.* 1628

Campbell, Elizabeth, Sr Dir-Mktg-US - McDonald's Corporation; *pg.* 1737, *pg.* 645

Campbell, Erica, Brand Mgr - Cargill, Inc.; *pg.* 845, *pg.* 965

Campbell, Ewan, Product Mgr - Morgan Advanced Materials; *pg.* 1363, *pg.* 835

Campbell, Gary, Mgr-Product Ops - Avaya Inc.; *pg.* 621, *pg.*

264
Campbell, Heather, Dir-Art-Wholesale Mktg - Rocky Brands, Inc.; *pg.* 1818, *pg.* 1466
Campbell, James, Assoc Mgr-Mktg - AdvancePierre Foods, Inc.; *pg.* 1714, *pg.* 1409
Campbell, Jared, Mgr-Email Mktg - Angie's List Inc; *pg.* 1228, *pg.* 682
Campbell, Jarrett, Sr Mgr-Mktg-Global Alliances - Schneider Electric USA, Inc.; *pg.* 1306, *pg.* 650
Campbell, Jeff, Sr Dir-Product Mgmt - LIGHTING SCIENCE GROUP CORPORATION; *pg.* 1301, *pg.* 467
Campbell, Jenna, Mgr-Retail Mktg - Toms Shoe's Inc; *pg.* 1821, *pg.* 276
Campbell, Jennifer, Mgr-Mktg - Castrol North America Inc.; *pg.* 973, *pg.* 1129
Campbell, Jill, Sr Dir-Adv & Mktg - Colorado Rockies Baseball Club, Ltd.; *pg.* 542, *pg.* 317
Campbell, John, Dir-Ops & Product Mgmt-MSC - ASPEN TECHNOLOGY, INC.; *pg.* 354, *pg.* 804
Campbell, John, VP-Sls - Chattanooga Bakery Inc.; *pg.* 847, *pg.* 1628
Campbell, John, Mgr-Sls - Diagraph; *pg.* 387, *pg.* 989
Campbell, John, Dir-Mktg - Maverick Brands LLC; *pg.* 876, *pg.* 161
Campbell, John, Dir-Mktg & Comm - The University of Virginia; *pg.* 610, *pg.* 1778
Campbell, Katrina, Brand Mgr - Bayer CropScience; *pg.* 1149, *pg.* 981
Campbell, Kevin, VP-Sls-US Wholesale - Moen Incorporated; *pg.* 1056, *pg.* 1468
Campbell, Kristen, VP-Mktg-Global - Michael Kors (USA), Inc.; *pg.* 29, *pg.* 1260
Campbell, Kristen, Analyst-Mktg & Social Media-Natl - Orange Leaf Frozen Yogurt; *pg.* 1742, *pg.* 1487
Campbell, Laura, Sr Mgr-Mktg Svcs - Fluor Corporation; *pg.* 82, *pg.* 1719
Campbell, Lauren, Specialist-Mktg - UnitedHealth Group Incorporated; *pg.* 1221, *pg.* 950
Campbell, Lisa, Dir-PR & Mktg Comm - Mars Petcare; *pg.* 1478, *pg.* 1633
Campbell, Lisa, Sr Dir-Corp Comm & Community Rels - St. Jude Medical, Inc.; *pg.* 1596, *pg.* 963
Campbell, Lisa, Brand Mgr - The Yankee Candle Company, Inc.; *pg.* 1792, *pg.* 843
Campbell, Lorenzo, District Supvr & Rep-Mktg - Hess Corporation; *pg.* 979, *pg.* 1240
Campbell, Lori, Sr Mgr-Mktg - United Services Automobile Association; *pg.* 1221, *pg.* 1743
Campbell, Mark, VP-Sls & Mktg - DS Waters of America, Inc.; *pg.* 250, *pg.* 504
Campbell, Mark, Exec Dir-Consumer Mktg-Intl - The New York Times Company; *pg.* 1668, *pg.* 1270
Campbell, Mary, Dir-Mktg - D&H Distributing Co., Inc.; *pg.* 381, *pg.* 1536
Campbell, Mary, Sr VP-Mdsg - QVC Inc; *pg.* 305, *pg.* 1593
Campbell, Matt, Sr Mgr-Mktg - Southwest Airlines Co.; *pg.* 1923, *pg.* 1687
Campbell, Neal J., CMO & Sr VP - CDW Corporation; *pg.* 370, *pg.* 663
Campbell, Noni, Coord-Brand Mktg - The Wendy's Company; *pg.* 1755, *pg.* 1450
Campbell, Pat, Exec Dir-Sls - Amgen Inc.; *pg.* 1493, *pg.* 291
Campbell, Pat, Mgr-Sls & Mdsg-Bakery - Farm Fresh Inc.; *pg.* 1019, *pg.* 1810
Campbell, Patrice, Specialist-Mktg-HSES - McKesson Corporation; *pg.* 1560, *pg.* 222
Campbell, Richard, Dir-Product Dev - Quadrant Engineering Plastic Products; *pg.* 1178, *pg.* 1585
Campbell, Rick, Product Mgr - Hensley Industries, Inc.; *pg.* 1166, *pg.* 1682
Campbell, Robert, VP-Innovation & Product Res - Insulet Corporation; *pg.* 644, *pg.* 785
Campbell, Ronnie, Sr Specialist-Mktg - FedEx Corporation; *pg.* 1907, *pg.* 1642
Campbell, Saundra, Mgr-Operational Mktg - Dupont Pioneer; *pg.* 1795, *pg.* 708
Campbell, Stephanie, Coord-Mktg & Social Media - American Eagle Outfitters, Inc.; *pg.* 37, *pg.* 1572
Campbell, Stewart, Sr Dir-Mktg - Microsystems; *pg.* 440, *pg.* 608
Campbell, Susan, Grp Mgr-Vertical Mktg - Panasonic Corporation of North America; *pg.* 661, *pg.* 1120
Campbell, Tim, Mgr-Mktg - Anthem, Inc.; *pg.* 1192, *pg.* 683
Campbell, Toby, Sr Dir-Global Mktg-US & Canada - Libbey, Inc.; *pg.* 1126, *pg.* 1476
Campbell, Tommy, Rep-Sls-Black Box Telecommunications - Black Box Corporation; *pg.* 361, *pg.* 1547
Campbell, Wes, Sr Mgr-Retail Mktg - Tempur Sealy International, Inc.; *pg.* 944, *pg.* 731
Campbell-Robinson, Lisann, Sr Project Mgr-Mktg - The Hartford Financial Services Group, Inc.; *pg.* 1202, *pg.* 352
Campi, Michael, Brand Mgr - The Kraft Heinz Company; *pg.* 871, *pg.* 641
Campinell, Joseph, Pres-Consumer Products Div - L'Oreal USA; *pg.* 514, *pg.* 1252
Campion, Dan, Sr Mgr-Mobile OEM Sls - Liquid Controls, Inc.; *pg.* 1356, *pg.* 622
Campion, Joan, Sr Dir - Pfizer Inc.; *pg.* 1581, *pg.* 1278
Campisi, Christina, Dir-Mktg-Global - Elizabeth Arden, Inc.; *pg.* 507, *pg.* 448
Campos, Lenora, Sr Mgr-PR - Toto USA, Inc.; *pg.* 1065, *pg.* 536
Campos, Manuel, Dir-Hispanic Mktg - Sprint Corporation; *pg.* 1874, *pg.* 719
Campos, Petra, Dir-Retirement Products - Charles Schwab; *pg.* 1235, *pg.* 1661
Campos, Rodrigo, Dir-Media & Digital Strategy - New York University; *pg.* 605, *pg.* 1271
Camuti, Ned, VP-Sls & Mktg - ABB Inc. - Automation Technologies Instrumentation Products; *pg.* 1398, *pg.* 1590
Can, Ilkay, Sr Dir-Mktg - Zynga Inc.; *pg.* 1292, *pg.* 235
Can, Susan, Dir-Corp Equity-Global Mktg Grp - Johnson & Johnson; *pg.* 1549, *pg.* 1091
Canabal, Andrea, Sr Dir-Media Rels-Global - PepsiCo, Inc.; *pg.* 259, *pg.* 1327
Canaday, Amy, Sr Mgr-PR - Match.Com, LLC; *pg.* 1265, *pg.* 1683
Canaday, John, Dir-Natl Mktg-Clubs & Theaters - Live Nation Entertainment, Inc.; *pg.* 558, *pg.* 47
Canady, Sara, Specialist-Mktg - Hy-Vee, Inc.; *pg.* 1023, *pg.* 713
Canales, Robert, Dir-Sls - Sinclair Broadcast Group, Inc.; *pg.* 308, *pg.* 773
Canan, Jim, Mgr-Mktg - Xerox Corporation; *pg.* 494, *pg.* 365
Canary, Kate, Assoc Editor-Mktg Content - Birchbox; *pg.* 1762, *pg.* 1203
Canavan, Corinne, Coord-Ad Sls Mktg - Scripps Networks Interactive, Inc.; *pg.* 1279, *pg.* 1638
Canavan, Kevin, VP-ECommerce Sls & Admin - Keystone Automotive Operations, Inc.; *pg.* 210, *pg.* 1531
Canavera, John, Mgr-Mktg - Live Nation Entertainment, Inc.; *pg.* 558, *pg.* 47
Candee, Cody, Product Mgr-Global Payments - Intuit Inc.; *pg.* 769, *pg.* 158
Candela, Anthony, Sr Mgr-Integrated Mktg-W - Conde Nast Publications, Inc.; *pg.* 1629, *pg.* 1217
Candela, Anthony, Assoc Dir-Integrated Mktg-W - Vogue Magazine; *pg.* 1700, *pg.* 1311
Candido, Lisa M., Dir-Conference & Events-Firmwide Mktg - Morgan Stanley; *pg.* 783, *pg.* 1261
Candler, Brett, Dir-Zone Sls-Automotive Refinish - PPG Industries, Inc.; *pg.* 1445, *pg.* 1579
Candor, Jim, Chief Strategy Officer - AccuWeather, Inc.; *pg.* 268, *pg.* 1587
Canelake, John, Dir-Sls - Folkmanis, Inc.; *pg.* 953, *pg.* 83
Canepa, Steve, Gen Mgr-Global Media & Entertainment Indus - IBM; *pg.* 410, *pg.* 1449
Canessa, Luis J., Reg Dir-Sls-Developers Programs, Alliances & Strategic Partners - Motorola Mobility LLC; *pg.* 657, *pg.* 627
Canez, Victor, VP-Funds Network & Product Analytics - FMR LLC (Fidelity Investments); *pg.* 759, *pg.* 794
Canfield, Caryn, Product Mgr-Digital - Scripps Networks Interactive, Inc.; *pg.* 1279, *pg.* 1638
Canfield, Kim, Dir-Media-US - Colgate-Palmolive Company; *pg.* 504, *pg.* 1215
Canfield, Stephen, Mgr-Natl Culture Mktg - Red Bull North America, Inc.; *pg.* 264, *pg.* 275
Canino, Jill, Sr Dir-Federal Govt Rels - Cigna Corporation; *pg.* 1197, *pg.* 338
Canino, Suzanne, Dir-Corp Mktg - Seattle Times Company; *pg.* 1685, *pg.* 1840
Canitano, Dee, Sr Mgr-Mktg - Deloitte & Touche USA LLP; *pg.* 743, *pg.* 1222
Cann, Ben, Sr Product Mgr-Video Ads - Google Inc.; *pg.* 1249, *pg.* 153
Cann, Galit, Dir-Mktg-Portfolio Activation - PepsiCo, Inc.; *pg.* 259, *pg.* 1327
Cannataro, Julie, Reg Coord-Sls & Mktg - Susquehanna Bank; *pg.* 807, *pg.* 1548
Cannella, Matt, Rep-Media Sls-Charter Media - Charter Communications, Inc.; *pg.* 274, *pg.* 372
Cannida, Chinette, Sr Mgr-Field Mktg-New Bus - Digital Insight; *pg.* 744, *pg.* 189
Canning, Ann, Sr VP-Adv Mgmt - Bank of America Corporation; *pg.* 718, *pg.* 1362
Cannizzo, Janice, Sr Dir-Mktg - CSL Behring LLC; *pg.* 1520, *pg.* 1543
Cannon, Chris, Dir-Digital Mktg - Spa Finder, Inc.; *pg.* 1113, *pg.* 1295
Cannon, Greg, Corp VP-Content Mktg - Caesars Entertainment Corporation; *pg.* 1083, *pg.* 1023
Cannon, Heather, Mgr-Mktg Comm-Emerson Process Mgmt - Emerson Process Management; *pg.* 1334, *pg.* 1636
Cannon, John, Sr Sls Dir-Energy & Fin Accounts - IHS Herold, Inc.; *pg.* 768, *pg.* 362
Cannone, Santo, Chief Product Officer-Open Solutions - Fiserv, Inc.; *pg.* 758, *pg.* 537
Cannuscio, Thomas, Head-Tech & Consumer Electronics-Google Media Sls - Google Inc.; *pg.* 1249, *pg.* 153
Cano, Aaron, VP-Mktg Plng, Analysis & Ops - FreshDirect, LLC; *pg.* 857, *pg.* 1174
Cano, Amanda, Coord-Mktg - Helen of Troy L.P.; *pg.* 511, *pg.* 1692
Cano, Jose, Supvr-PR - United Parcel Service, Inc.; *pg.* 1928, *pg.* 522
Cano, Nathalie, Specialist-Social Media - Kforce Inc.; *pg.* 1261, *pg.* 473
Canova, Katie, Brand Mgr-Digital - Anheuser-Busch Companies, LLC; *pg.* 237, *pg.* 991
Cantabene, Deborah, VP-Mktg - Xerox Corporation; *pg.* 494, *pg.* 365
Cantara, Virginia, Mgr-Mktg Comm - Unifrax Corporation; *pg.* 220, *pg.* 1317
Cantello, Diane, VP-Mktg & Comm - The Hartford Financial Services Group, Inc.; *pg.* 1202, *pg.* 352
Canter, Chip, Sr VP-Product & Bus Dev-Digital Distr - NBC Universal, Inc.; *pg.* 300, *pg.* 1266
Cantiello, Adam, Mgr-Mktg-Partnerships - Urban Outfitters, Inc.; *pg.* 1789, *pg.* 1571
Cantin, Jeannette, Dir-Digital Mktg & Comm - Sun Life Financial Inc.; *pg.* 806, *pg.* 1944
Canton, Craig, Mgr-Relationship-Sls Solutions Team - LinkedIn Corporation; *pg.* 1262, *pg.* 160
Canton, Odette, Mgr-Digital-Integrated Mktg Solutions - Bayer HealthCare Pharmaceutical Division; *pg.* 1500, *pg.* 1132
Cantor, Allyson, Dir-Partnership Mktg - Time Warner Cable Inc.; *pg.* 312, *pg.* 1301
Cantor, Chad, Dir-Sls-US - ITW - Evercoat; *pg.* 1443, *pg.* 1415
Cantrell, DeeDee, Dir-Info Mgmt-Trade Mktg - R.J. Reynolds Tobacco Co.; *pg.* 1895, *pg.* 1395
Cantu, Ana, Campaign Mgr-Social Media - Google Inc.; *pg.* 1249, *pg.* 153
Cantu, James, Assoc Mgr-Mktg - Land O'Lakes, Inc.; *pg.* 873, *pg.* 915
Cantu, Stephanie, Product Mgr-Digital - Best Buy Co., Inc.; *pg.* 1761, *pg.* 954
Cantun, Tritia, Mgr-Online Mktg - Air New Zealand Ltd. (U.S.A.); *pg.* 1897, *pg.* 78
Cantwell, Ken, Dir-Mktg - CRC Industries, Inc.; *pg.* 329, *pg.* 1590
Canty, David, Dir-Loyalty & Partnership Mktg - JetBlue Airways Corporation; *pg.* 1913, *pg.* 1174
Cao, Simon, Specialist-Digital Mktg - NBC Universal, Inc.; *pg.* 300, *pg.* 1266
Cao, Stephanie, Product Mktg Mgr-AdWords Search - Google Inc.; *pg.* 1249, *pg.* 153
Cao, Thanh, Mgr-Content Mktg - Netflix, Inc.; *pg.* 1269, *pg.* 141
Cao, Tina, Assoc Mgr-Mktg-Intl Retail - Blue Diamond Growers; *pg.* 840, *pg.* 195
Caouette, David, Head-Media Rels-Global & Exec Dir - Amgen Inc.; *pg.* 1493, *pg.* 291
Capalbo, Brittany, Asst Mgr-Digital Mktg & Media - Ann Inc.; *pg.* 18, *pg.* 1195
Capaldi, Michael, Assoc VP-Civic Action & Social Networking - Sanofi US; *pg.* 1592, *pg.* 1046
Capaldo, Paula, Head-BI Mktg & Mgr-IT - Sunoco Inc.; *pg.* 985, *pg.* 1571
Caparelli, Jason, Rep-Mktg - ConocoPhillips; *pg.* 975, *pg.* 1703
Capart, Philippe, Gen Mgr-Global Mktg Rheumatology - AbbVie Inc.; *pg.* 1486, *pg.* 638

First page reference indicates Business Class Edition
Second page reference indicates Geographic Edition

Capasso, Jerry, Product Mgr-Bath Team - Moen Incorporated; *pg.* 1056, *pg.* 1468
Capasso, Kimberly, Sr Dir-Mktg - World Wrestling Entertainment, Inc.; *pg.* 595, *pg.* 380
Capece, Ginevra, Strategist-Creative - Facebook, Inc.; *pg.* 1245, *pg.* 143
Capel, Deanna, Dir-Creative & Comm - First Busey Corporation; *pg.* 754, *pg.* 562
Capeloto, Kim J., Exec VP-Mktg & Ops - RIVERVIEW BANCORP, INC.; *pg.* 799, *pg.* 1846
Capener, Andy, Dir-Mktg - Cisco Systems, Inc.; *pg.* 372, *pg.* 240
Capener, Erin, Assoc Dir-Mktg - Gilead Sciences, Inc.; *pg.* 1535, *pg.* 88
Capers, Averil, Dir-Mktg & Res - Worcester Telegram & Gazette Corp.; *pg.* 1702, *pg.* 863
Capers, Garry, Gen Mgr-NACS Mktg Data Svcs - Equifax Inc.; *pg.* 748, *pg.* 504
Capitani, Liz, Mgr-Mktg-HOKA ONE ONE - Deckers Outdoor Corporation; *pg.* 1807, *pg.* 100
Capitani, Walter, VP-Mktg - International Datacasting Corporation; *pg.* 419, *pg.* 1921
Caplan, Amy, Sr VP-Sls Strategy & Comm - Univision Communications Inc.; *pg.* 683, *pg.* 1307
Caplan, Jonathan, Mgr-Mktg - Intel Corporation; *pg.* 645, *pg.* 266
Caplan, Mike, Sr Acct Exec-Mktg Solutions - LinkedIn Corporation; *pg.* 1262, *pg.* 160
Caplinger, Linda, Head-Global Search & Digital Mktg Organization - NVIDIA Corporation; *pg.* 447, *pg.* 268
Caplinger, Nathan, VP-Sls-Pharma, Biotech & Indus - VWR Funding, Inc.; *pg.* 1608, *pg.* 1583
Capon, Ellen, VP-Mdse, Licensing & Venue Tours - Madison Square Garden Network; *pg.* 297, *pg.* 1255
Capone, Deirdre, Mgr-Sls Admin & Trade Show - White Rose Foods; *pg.* 910, *pg.* 1050
Capone, Mike, Dir-Regulatory Adv & Promo Policy - GlaxoSmithKline; *pg.* 1536, *pg.* 1565
Caponetti, Stacy, Mgr-Mktg - Equifax Workforce Solutions; *pg.* 394, *pg.* 997
Caponetto, Shannon, Key Acct Mgr-Mktg - Columbia Sportswear Company; *pg.* 1830, *pg.* 1501
Caponi, Colleen, Dir-Corp Mktg - Apple Vacations Inc.; *pg.* 1899, *pg.* 1556
Capossela, Chris, CMO & Exec VP - Microsoft Corporation; *pg.* 435, *pg.* 1824
Capozzi, Vincent, Sr VP-Sls & Customer Svc - Harvard Pilgrim Health Care, Inc.; *pg.* 1539, *pg.* 856
Capp, Brian, VP-Mktg - Les Schwab Tire Centers of Oregon, Inc.; *pg.* 210, *pg.* 1508
Cappel, Robert, Sr Dir-Mktg - KLA-Tencor Corporation; *pg.* 1353, *pg.* 146
Cappella, Melanie, Sr Mgr-Mktg - PepsiCo, Inc.; *pg.* 259, *pg.* 1327
Cappellanti, Robert, Asst Dir-Mktg - Georgia Institute Of Technology; *pg.* 602, *pg.* 506
Cappelletti, Alberto, Dir-Global Mktg Capability - The Coca-Cola Company; *pg.* 240, *pg.* 493
Cappelletti, Kate, Assoc Mgr-Customer Mktg - PepsiCo, Inc.; *pg.* 259, *pg.* 1327
Cappellini, Marnie, Dir-Mktg - Movado Group, Inc.; *pg.* 10, *pg.* 1101
Cappelossa, Cassio L., Brand Mgr-Customer Experience-Global - Hewlett-Packard Company; *pg.* 404, *pg.* 175
Capperella, Jay, Dir-Sls & Franchise-Natl - Dessange International, Inc.; *pg.* 506, *pg.* 787
Capps, Karen, Sr Mgr-Tradeshow & Event Plng - Hologic, Inc.; *pg.* 1416, *pg.* 784
Capra, Rose, Mgr-Mktg - Sprint Corporation; *pg.* 1874, *pg.* 719
Capriotti, Roger, Sr Dir-Product Mktg-Microsoft Edge Browser - Microsoft Corporation; *pg.* 435, *pg.* 1824
Capron, Ben, Dir-Category Mktg - Specialized Bicycle Components, Inc.; *pg.* 1711, *pg.* 152
Capron, Lauren, Brand Mgr-CLEAN & CLEAR - Johnson & Johnson Inc.; *pg.* 1552, *pg.* 1923
Capsambelis, Mike, Product Mgr - Google Inc.; *pg.* 1249, *pg.* 153
Capucille, Tony, Chief Sls Officer - Heartland Payment Systems, Inc.; *pg.* 765, *pg.* 1111
Caputo, Dave, Dir-Product & Programs - Owens Corning; *pg.* 102, *pg.* 1476
Caputo, Gabrielle, Dir-Comml Products Americas - Kelly Services, Inc.; *pg.* 424, *pg.* 911
Caputo, Sarah, Sr Dir-Mktg Comm - Comcast Corporation; *pg.* 276, *pg.* 1560
Caputo, Steven, VP-Mktg Svcs - Chanel, Inc.; *pg.* 503, *pg.* 1211
Caputo, Vince, Product Mgr-Base Station Antennas-North America - CommScope; *pg.* 630, *pg.* 668
Capuzzo, Maurizio, VP-Mktg-Americas - Polycom, Inc.; *pg.* 664, *pg.* 249
Cara, Phil, Sr VP-Digital Media Sls - NBC Universal, Inc.; *pg.* 300, *pg.* 1266
Caraballo, Migdalia, Analyst-Mktg & Comm - American International Group, Inc.; *pg.* 1190, *pg.* 1193
Caracci, Maria, Exec Dir-Corp Mktg Solutions - Meredith Corporation; *pg.* 1663, *pg.* 705
Caracciolo, Toni, VP-Mktg & Sls - SeaWorld Parks & Entertainment LLC; *pg.* 582, *pg.* 456
Caraher, Kelly, Sr Mgr-Corp Comm & PR - CDW Corporation; *pg.* 370, *pg.* 663
Carangelo, Catherine, Mgr-Mktg Programs - Bullhorn, Inc.; *pg.* 1233, *pg.* 792
Carano, Emily, Mgr-Global Product Line-Athletic & Racing - Saucony, Inc.; *pg.* 1818, *pg.* 828
Caras, Corey, Brand Mgr - Dunkin' Brands Group, Inc.; *pg.* 1727, *pg.* 810
Caravaggio, Dante V., Exec VP-Sls-Global - Parsons Corporation; *pg.* 103, *pg.* 180
Carawan, Leland, VP-Adv - W.S. Badcock Corporation; *pg.* 947, *pg.* 449
Caraway, Katie McBride, Sr Mgr-Digital Media - J.C. Penney Company, Inc.; *pg.* 1774, *pg.* 1732
Carbary, Cory, Dir-Ticket Sls - The Baseball Club of Seattle, L.P.; *pg.* 532, *pg.* 1833
Carbine, Gene, Sr Mgr-Database Mktg Ops & Strategy - Express Scripts, Inc.; *pg.* 1530, *pg.* 997
Carbone, Maia, Mgr-Mktg & Comm Sourcing - Ingersoll-Rand Company; *pg.* 1349, *pg.* 1370
Carbone, Peter, VP-Mktg - Renesas Electronics America Inc.; *pg.* 667, *pg.* 269
Card, Beth, Mgr-Mktg-Intl - Blissworld LLC; *pg.* 501, *pg.* 1204
Card, Matthew, Sr VP-Comm & Media Rels - Bank of America Corporation; *pg.* 718, *pg.* 1362
Card, Samantha, Mgr-Mktg-Honeywell Performance Materials & Tech - Honeywell International Inc.; *pg.* 407, *pg.* 1088
Cardarelli, Annalisa, Mgr-Mktg-Color Cosmetics - Avon Products, Inc.; *pg.* 500, *pg.* 1198
Cardazone, Ron, Sr Designer-Print Mktg & Supvr-Package Design - VITAMIN SHOPPE, INC.; *pg.* 1608, *pg.* 1098
Cardec, Lesly, Sr Dir-PR & Content Mktg - Randstad USA; *pg.* 459, *pg.* 941
Cardellicchio, Maura C., Mgr-Mktg Comm - Verizon Communications Inc.; *pg.* 1875, *pg.* 1309
Cardello, Louis, Sr Specialist-Social Media Mktg - New York Life Insurance Company; *pg.* 1211, *pg.* 1268
Cardenas, Andrea, Dir-Post Acute Mktg - Kinetic Concepts, Inc.; *pg.* 1553, *pg.* 1741
Cardenas, Kenneth J., Mgr-Corp Comm, Web & Multi-Media - Toys "R" Us, Inc.; *pg.* 968, *pg.* 1130
Cardenas, Scott, Mgr-Mktg-Licensing - Nintendo of America, Inc.; *pg.* 965, *pg.* 1829
Cardenas, Ted, VP-Mktg-Car Electronics Div - Pioneer Electronics (USA) Inc.; *pg.* 663, *pg.* 124
Carder, Brittney, Mgr-Mktg-Intl - Go Daddy Inc.; *pg.* 1249, *pg.* 21
Cardiello, Jay, Reg Dir-Sls - Takeda Pharmaceuticals USA, Inc.; *pg.* 1600, *pg.* 605
Cardillo, Nicole, Exec Dir-Comm & Social Media - Shiseido Cosmetics America of SAC; *pg.* 522, *pg.* 1291
Cardin, Rocky, Reg Assoc Mgr-Mktg - The Allstate Corporation; *pg.* 1189, *pg.* 639
Cardin, Trisha, Dir-Client Mktg - Valassis; *pg.* 1698, *pg.* 386
Cardinal, Michele, VP & Head-Global Brand & Product Mktg - Visa Inc.; *pg.* 816, *pg.* 230
Cardinal, Michele, VP & Head-Global Brand & Product Mktg - Visa U.S.A., Inc.; *pg.* 817, *pg.* 231
Cardinal, Ryan, Coord-Digital Mktg - Minnesota Vikings Football Club, Inc.; *pg.* 563, *pg.* 923
Cardon, Alexandre, Sr Dir-Global Distr - Brightstar Corporation; *pg.* 627, *pg.* 440
Cardon, Matthew, Mgr-Innovation & Product Mgmt-Retail Brands - ConAgra Foods, Inc.; *pg.* 826, *pg.* 1014
Cardona, David, Dir-Shopper Mktg, Advisory Svcs & Multi Cultural - The Clorox Company; *pg.* 327, *pg.* 169
Cardone, Deanna, Dir-Mktg - MORNINGSTAR, INC.; *pg.* 784, *pg.* 583
Cardoso, Catherine Diaz, Mgr-Mktg-US & CA - Philips Healthcare; *pg.* 1585, *pg.* 783
Cardoso, Marcio, VP-Sls & Aftermarket-South America - JLG Industries, Inc.; *pg.* 1351, *pg.* 1551
Cardot, Susan L., Dir-Integrated Mktg Comm-Worldwide - Eastman Kodak Company; *pg.* 1408, *pg.* 1333
Cardoza, Julie, Mgr-Mktg Activation - Jamba, Inc.; *pg.* 1024, *pg.* 84
Cardwell, Aaron, Mgr-Social Media-Global - Quiksilver, Inc.; *pg.* 31, *pg.* 104
Cardwell, Ben, Sr VP-Global Wireless Sls - CommScope, Inc.; *pg.* 278, *pg.* 1378
Cardwell, Matt, Dir-Social Media - Quicken Loans, Inc.; *pg.* 797, *pg.* 884
Care, Margaret, Mgr-Adv - Universal Health Services Inc.; *pg.* 1604, *pg.* 1544
Careaga, Selman, VP-Mktg-Mexico Bus Unit - The Coca-Cola Company; *pg.* 240, *pg.* 493
Carelli, Anne, Sr Mgr-Sports & Entertainment - The Coca-Cola Company; *pg.* 240, *pg.* 493
Carelli, Julianne, Sr Mgr-PR - Office Depot, Inc.; *pg.* 448, *pg.* 412
Carey, Alane R., Exec VP & Dir-Mktg-Global - Odyssey Re Holdings Corp.; *pg.* 1212, *pg.* 376
Carey, Casey, Dir-Google Analytics Mktg - Google Inc.; *pg.* 1249, *pg.* 153
Carey, Heather, Specialist-Mktg - Alaska Seafood Marketing Institute; *pg.* 125, *pg.* 10
Carey, Jason, VP-Production - Animal Planet, LLC; *pg.* 270, *pg.* 777
Carey, Jason, Program Mgr-Brand & Adv-In Store Digital Signage - Wells Fargo & Company; *pg.* 819, *pg.* 232
Carey, Orla, Mgr-Adv, Direct Mktg & eMarketing - Tourism Ireland; *pg.* 1007, *pg.* 1303
Carey, Sherry, Mgr-Worldwide Mktg - Hewlett-Packard Company; *pg.* 404, *pg.* 175
Carey, Steven, Mgr-Product Line - PC Connection, Inc.; *pg.* 452, *pg.* 1036
Carey, Tim, Mgr-Product Line - Aeroflex Incorporated; *pg.* 614, *pg.* 1321
Carey, Tom, VP-Sls - BrassCraft Manufacturing Company; *pg.* 1043, *pg.* 902
Carey-Hargrave, Jill, Sr Mgr-Corp Comm-Global - Baxter International Inc.; *pg.* 1499, *pg.* 599
Carfagno, Russell, Sr Product Mgr-Airside Comml Sys - Johnson Controls, Inc.; *pg.* 209, *pg.* 1876
Carfagno, Tony, Sr VP-Sls-Global - Igloo Products Corporation; *pg.* 1126, *pg.* 1724
Carfrae, Malcolm, Head-Comm, PR & Media-Global - Ralph Lauren Corporation; *pg.* 46, *pg.* 1284
Cargill, Stephanie, Mgr-Mktg Comm - Transtar Industries, Inc.; *pg.* 219, *pg.* 1478
Cariddi, Barbara, Producer-New Media News & Content - Maine Public Broadcasting Network; *pg.* 297, *pg.* 751
Cariddi, Tony, Dir-Mktg-Audio - Avid Technology, Inc.; *pg.* 622, *pg.* 804
Carignan, Dean, Sr Dir-Xbox Strategy & Insights-EMEA - Microsoft Corporation; *pg.* 435, *pg.* 1824
Carini, Courtney, Dir-Digital Mktg - Scripps Networks Interactive, Inc.; *pg.* 1279, *pg.* 1638
Carion, Jenny, Project Mgr-Sls Mktg - Pandora Media Inc.; *pg.* 1273, *pg.* 172
Carioti, Michael, Mgr-Field Mktg-Advanced Computing Div - Ingram Micro Inc.; *pg.* 415, *pg.* 261
Cariou, Andre, VP-Sls-Global - Harris Moran Seed Co.; *pg.* 1796, *pg.* 150
Carl, Casey, Pres-Multichannel & Sr VP-Mdsg - Target Corporation; *pg.* 1786, *pg.* 942
Carl, Jeff, Mgr-ECommerce Mktg - Angie's List Inc; *pg.* 1228, *pg.* 682
Carl, Kristine, Sr Mgr-Corp PR - Charles Schwab; *pg.* 1235, *pg.* 1661
Carla, Torres, Brand Mgr-Oncology - Bristol-Myers Squibb Company; *pg.* 1509, *pg.* 1206
Carlat, Jeff, Dir-Converged Sys Product Mgmt - Hewlett-Packard Company; *pg.* 404, *pg.* 175
Carlberg, Robert M., Sr VP-Men's Mdsg - The Buckle, Inc.; *pg.* 1764, *pg.* 1011
Carle, Bob, Bus Mgr-East - Pecora Corporation; *pg.* 1444, *pg.* 1536
Carleton, Cindy, Mgr-Creative Svcs - Valassis; *pg.* 1698, *pg.* 386
Carley, Allison, VP-Sls-B2B - Alex and Ani; *pg.* 1, *pg.* 1600
Carley, Vera, Dir-Media Rels & Fin Comm - Assurant, Inc.; *pg.* 1193, *pg.* 1198
Carlier, Joe, Sr VP-Sls - Penske Logistics, LLC; *pg.* 188, *pg.* 1584

Carlin, Alexandra, VP & Exec Dir-PR - The Hearst Corporation; pg. 1649, pg. 1239
Carlin, Andy, Chief Sls Officer & Sr VP - Select Comfort Corporation; pg. 942, pg. 942
Carlin, Chris, Sr Mgr-Mktg & Social Media - The Upper Deck Company, LLC; pg. 969, pg. 62
Carlin, Jason, Sr Designer-Product - YouTube, LLC; pg. 1291, pg. 198
Carlin, Jeff, Brand Mktg Mgr - Sony Electronics, Inc.; pg. 676, pg. 209
Carlin, Samantha, Mgr-Mktg - The New York Times Company; pg. 1668, pg. 1270
Carling, Jeff, Coord-Recruiting, Digital Assoc & Social Media - 1-800 CONTACTS, INC.; pg. 1758, pg. 1753
Carlini, Diane, Dir-PR - Intuit Inc.; pg. 769, pg. 158
Carlini, Kevin, Dir-Creative - Woolrich, Inc.; pg. 699, pg. 1595
Carlino, Jodi, Brand Mgr-Retail Dev - Ralph Lauren Corporation; pg. 46, pg. 1284
Carlioz, Remi, Head-Consumer Mktg-Global - Puma North America, Inc.; pg. 1816, pg. 858
Carlisle, Candy, Dir-Mall Mktg & Bus Dev - Simon Property Group, Inc.; pg. 1112, pg. 690
Carlisle, Phil, Product Mgr-New Malibu & Impala - General Motors Company; pg. 175, pg. 881
Carll, Thomas W., VP & Dir-Sls-Worldwide - Astro-Med, Inc.; pg. 619, pg. 1609
Carlomusto, Iris, VP-Mktg - Alex and Ani; pg. 1, pg. 1600
Carlon, Jackie, Dir-Mktg - Piper Aircraft, Inc.; pg. 233, pg. 477
Carlos, Allister, Sr Dir-Email Mktg - Live Nation Entertainment, Inc.; pg. 558, pg. 47
Carlos, Sergio, Mgr-Adv & Brand - Salt River Project; pg. 707, pg. 26
Carlos, Zenon, Dir-Product Mgmt - Vonage Holdings Corp.; pg. 686, pg. 1074
Carlotti, Steve, Exec VP-Mktg - Michaels Stores, Inc.; pg. 1127, pg. 1722
Carls, Jenna, Sr Assoc Brand Mgr-Global Sweets Innovation - The Hershey Co.; pg. 1855, pg. 1538
Carlsen, Brett, Mgr-Mktg-Rohto - The Mentholatum Company; pg. 1565, pg. 1320
Carlson, Allyson, Mgr-Sls & Mktg - Arrow Electronics, Inc.; pg. 619, pg. 325
Carlson, Alyssa, Asst Mgr-Product Dev - American Greetings Corporation; pg. 1615, pg. 1428
Carlson, Amber, Mgr-Digital Adv Sls & Solutions - The American Dental Association; pg. 127, pg. 564
Carlson, Amie, Mgr-Product & Mktg - Tyndale House Publishers, Inc.; pg. 1697, pg. 561
Carlson, Annie, Mgr-Field Mktg - Taco John's International, Inc.; pg. 1753, pg. 1901
Carlson, Brennan, Sr VP-Bus Dev & Product Strategy - Lyris, Inc.; pg. 429, pg. 84
Carlson, Brent, Sr Mgr-Client Solutions-Global Gaming Sls - Facebook, Inc.; pg. 1245, pg. 143
Carlson, Carrie, Dir-PR - Hearst Magazines; pg. 1649, pg. 1239
Carlson, Chris, Sr VP-Creative-Velocity M&E, Spike - Viacom Inc.; pg. 316, pg. 1310
Carlson, Doug, Sr Dir-Global Benefits & HR Shared Svcs - NCR Corporation; pg. 443, pg. 531
Carlson, Erik, Brand Mgr-Coffee Creamers & Beverages Innovation - The WhiteWave Foods Company; pg. 1037, pg. 324
Carlson, Evan, Sr Mgr-Mktg-Pizza - The Schwan Food Company; pg. 894, pg. 928
Carlson, Fred, VP-Sls - U.S. Pumice Company; pg. 1185, pg. 65
Carlson, Gary, Dir-Production - Moore Fans LLC; pg. 1363, pg. 987
Carlson, Ian, Dir-Product Mktg-HP Helion - Hewlett-Packard Company; pg. 404, pg. 175
Carlson, Jamee, Mgr-Mktg-Customer Brands - Wells Enterprises, Inc.; pg. 909, pg. 709
Carlson, Jessica, Sr Producer-Meetings & Media Production - Target Corporation; pg. 1786, pg. 942
Carlson, Karen C., Dir-Menu Strategy & Mktg - International House of Pancakes, Inc.; pg. 1732, pg. 96
Carlson, Karen Chella, Dir-Menu Strategy & Mktg - DineEquity, Inc.; pg. 1725, pg. 95
Carlson, Kevin, Mgr-Mktg & Promos - Samsung Electronics America, Inc.; pg. 669, pg. 1115
Carlson, Liz R., Sr Mgr-Pub Affairs-West Central Market Area - State Farm Mutual Automobile Insurance Co.; pg. 1218, pg. 557
Carlson, Lynn, Specialist-Mktg Comm - Tommy Bahama; pg. 48, pg. 1842
Carlson, Mark, Sr Dir-Creative - McDonald's Corporation; pg. 1737, pg. 645
Carlson, Rolf, VP-Sourcing & Product Dev - Stonyfield Farm, Inc.; pg. 899, pg. 1035
Carlson, Shauna, Brand Mgr - The University of Phoenix, Inc.; pg. 610, pg. 27
Carlson, Steve, Acct Exec-Ticket Sls - Arizona Cardinals Football Club, Inc.; pg. 529, pg. 25
Carlson, Vanessa, Dir-Mktg-Mountain Reg - Pepsi Beverages Company; pg. 258, pg. 1342
Carlson, Vic, Sr VP-Mktg - Hunter Douglas, Inc.; pg. 928, pg. 1320
Carlson, Victoria, Mgr-Mktg-AWS Game Svcs - Amazon.com, Inc.; pg. 1226, pg. 1831
Carlstrom, Courtney, Mgr-Mktg - Medline Industries, Inc.; pg. 1562, pg. 635
Carlton, Angela, Mgr-Mktg - CB Richard Ellis Group, Inc.; pg. 1085, pg. 127
Carlton, Michelle, Mgr-Content Mktg - OpenText; pg. 450, pg. 1665
Carlucci, Michelle, Supvr-PR - The Boston Beer Company, Inc.; pg. 239, pg. 790
Carman, Kevin, Dir-Education Segment Mktg - AT&T Mobility LLC; pg. 619, pg. 488
Carman, Scott, Dir-PR - Choice Hotels International, Inc.; pg. 1086, pg. 775
Carmedelle, Paul, VP & Dir-Mktg & Customer Integration - CIT GROUP INC.; pg. 735, pg. 1212
Carmen, Liane, Mgr-Mktg Property Activation - The Coca-Cola Company; pg. 240, pg. 493
Carmichael, Craig, Dir-Digital Mktg & Comm - Webster University; pg. 610, pg. 1004
Carmichael, James, Brand Mgr - National Football League; pg. 567, pg. 1264
Carmichael, Kara, Dir-PR - Chicago Convention & Tourism Bureau; pg. 990, pg. 569
Carmichael, Kirk, VP-Sls - American Freightways; pg. 1899, pg. 200
Carmody Corry, Kerri, Grp VP-Product Strategy - Affinion Group, Inc.; pg. 1225, pg. 372
Carmona, Elizabeth, Mgr-ECommerce & Digital Media - Citi Trends Inc.; pg. 22, pg. 539
Carn, Chuck, Product Dir-North America Elastomers - THE DOW CHEMICAL COMPANY; pg. 1157, pg. 898
Carnaggio, Michaelle, Sr VP & Dir-Mktg - IBERIABANK Corporation; pg. 768, pg. 744
Carnahan, Ginya, Dir-Adv, Mktg, Comm & Event Mgmt - Michael Dattoli MD, LLC; pg. 1568, pg. 466
Carneiro, Yolanda, VP-Travel Indus Partnerships & Inside Sls - Carey International, Inc.; pg. 1902, pg. 397
Carnes, Kevin, Acct Exec-Charter Media - Charter Communications, Inc.; pg. 274, pg. 372
Carnevale, Melissa, Mgr-Digital Mktg-Healthcare Transformation Svcs - Philips Electronics North America; pg. 662, pg. 782
Carney, Beth, Dir-Mktg Comm - 8x8, Inc.; pg. 1865, pg. 282
Carney, Bryan, Sr Mgr-Employee Experience - Beachbody, LLC; pg. 271, pg. 272
Carney, Caitlin, Project Mgr-Mktg-Staples Rewards - Staples, Inc.; pg. 474, pg. 821
Carney, Chad, Bus Mgr-Performance Label Matls-Global - 3M Company; pg. 1142, pg. 956
Carney, Courtney, Dir-Mktg-Parasiticides - Virbac Corporation; pg. 1606, pg. 1696
Carney, Kevin J., Exec Dir-Brand Mktg - Anchor Bay Entertainment, Inc.; pg. 270, pg. 910
Carney, Kristin, Reg Sls Mgr-Neuroscience Parkinson's - AbbVie Inc.; pg. 1486, pg. 638
Carney, Michael, VP-Mktg - 24 Hour Fitness Worldwide Inc.; pg. 526, pg. 258
Carney, Ryan, Specialist-PR - Bose Corporation; pg. 626, pg. 820
Carney, Ryndee, Mgr-Bus Media Strategy - General Motors Company; pg. 175, pg. 881
Caro, Teresa, Sr VP-Mktg - Atlanticus Corporation; pg. 717, pg. 490
Carol, Chas, Brand Mgr-Solutions - Mead Johnson Nutrition Company; pg. 1561, pg. 615
Carola, Angela, Mgr-Integrated Sls Dev - Advertising Age; pg. 1613, pg. 1187
Carolan, F. Patrick, Rep-Mktg Comm - Port Authority of New York & New Jersey; pg. 1919, pg. 1283
Carolus, Kyndal, Mgr-Digital Mktg - The Finish Line, Inc.; pg. 1769, pg. 686
Caron, Gerry, VP-Innovation & Product Mgmt-OtterBox & LifeProof Brands - OtterBox Products LLC; pg. 451, pg. 329
Caron, Michael, VP-Product & Program Dev - Avis Budget Group, Inc.; pg. 1900, pg. 1102
Caron, Michael, VP-Product & Program Dev - Avis Rent A Car System, LLC; pg. 165, pg. 1102
Caron, Monica, Sr Mgr-Mdsg - Travelzoo Inc; pg. 1926, pg. 1304
Carothers, Kevin, Mgr-Mktg - Seattle Coffee Company; pg. 265, pg. 1839
Carpen, Jamie, Sr Mgr-District PR - Robert Half International Inc.; pg. 462, pg. 145
Carpenter, Amy, Dir-Media & Partnerships-Global - Whole Foods Market, Inc.; pg. 1038, pg. 1667
Carpenter, Carolyn, Brand Mgr-Proactiv-Intl - Guthy-Renker LLC; pg. 289, pg. 273
Carpenter, Charles, VP-Sls-Mid-Central Region - Food Network; pg. 287, pg. 1231
Carpenter, Charlie, VP-Adv Sls-Mid-Central Reg - Scripps Networks Interactive, Inc.; pg. 1279, pg. 1638
Carpenter, Christopher T., Mgr-Direct Mktg - AT&T; pg. 1865, pg. 258
Carpenter, Daniel, Sr Mgr-Mktg Comm - Gartner, Inc.; pg. 1248, pg. 374
Carpenter, Debbie, Sr Mgr-Sls & Mktg-Natl - Kikkoman International Inc.; pg. 868, pg. 220
Carpenter, Ellen, Sr Mgr-Comm - Microsoft Corporation; pg. 435, pg. 1824
Carpenter, Frank, Sr Analyst-Mktg Comm - CA Technologies; pg. 366, pg. 1168
Carpenter, Heather, Mgr-PR & Head-Special Projects-Reuters - Truven Health Analytics; pg. 486, pg. 331
Carpenter, Jane, Dir-PR - Wayfair LLC; pg. 1288, pg. 801
Carpenter, Joe, VP & Gen Mgr-Mdse - The Orvis Company, Inc.; pg. 1781, pg. 1764
Carpenter, John, Product Mgr - Multimedia Games Inc.; pg. 442, pg. 1664
Carpenter, Katie, Product Mgr-Global - Medtronic, Inc.; pg. 1564, pg. 939
Carpenter, Kim, Dir-Sls - Pinnacle Entertainment, Inc.; pg. 576, pg. 1029
Carpenter, Kurt, Product Mgr - Trane Inc.; pg. 116, pg. 1109
Carpenter, Larry, Mgr-Sls - Forklifts of Minnesota, Inc.; pg. 174, pg. 918
Carpenter, Lindsay, Project Mgr-Mktg - Adecco USA, Inc.; pg. 342, pg. 1178
Carpenter, Lisa, Sr Dir-Strategy & Performance-Global Responsibility - The Gap, Inc.; pg. 1770, pg. 218
Carpenter, Lynn, VP-Mktg - California Travel & Tourism Commission; pg. 990, pg. 196
Carpenter, Marissa, Dir-Mdsg & Sr Buyer-Enterprise - J.C. Penney Company, Inc.; pg. 1774, pg. 1732
Carpenter, Matt, Brand Mgr-Heritage - The Kraft Heinz Company; pg. 870, pg. 1577
Carpenter, Megan, Sr Mgr-Mktg Comm - Microsoft Corporation; pg. 435, pg. 1824
Carpenter, Molly, Mgr-Channel Mktg - Brocade Communications Systems, Inc.; pg. 365, pg. 239
Carpenter, Randall, VP-Corp Mktg - Briggs & Stratton Corporation; pg. 201, pg. 1899
Carpenter, Randel, VP-Sls & Mktg - KB Home; pg. 90, pg. 134
Carpenter, Sara, Sr Product Mgr-Emergen-C - Pfizer Inc.; pg. 1581, pg. 1278
Carpenter, Scott, Dir-Sls Flatroof - SFS intec, Inc.; pg. 1061, pg. 1596
Carpenter, Tami, Sr Mgr-Trade & Sls Plng - Ocean Spray Cranberries, Inc.; pg. 887, pg. 827
Carpenter, Teresa R., Dir-Mktg - Apollo Education Group Inc.; pg. 597, pg. 14
Carpenter, Todd, Sr Dir-IR - Medtronic; pg. 1563, pg. 830
Carper, Beth, Brand Mgr-Corp Mktg - Blue Cross & Blue Shield of Florida, Inc.; pg. 1507, pg. 432
Carpio, Aliza, Mgr-Social Media Mktg - Intuit Inc.; pg. 769, pg. 158
Carpio, Fabiana, Mgr-High Impact Mktg-Americas Mktg - Citrix Systems, Inc.; pg. 375, pg. 424
Carr Balzer, Julie, Brand Mgr-Emerging Brands - Snyder's-Lance, Inc.; pg. 896, pg. 1368
Carr, Ann, CMO - Jostens, Inc.; pg. 7, pg. 938
Carr, Brandon, Brand Mgr-Pabst Blue Ribbon - Pabst Brewing Company; pg. 258, pg. 137
Carr, Emily, Assoc Mgr-Consumer Mktg & Program Adv - Home Box Office, Inc.; pg. 290, pg. 1240

Carr, Fergal, Dir-Dev T Brand Studio & Platform Innovation - The New York Times Company; pg. 1668, pg. 1270
Carr, Garett, Mgr-Electrification Mktg - Ford Motor Company; pg. 172, pg. 876
Carr, Jason, Asst Dir-Media Rels - Chicago National League Ball Club, LLC; pg. 539, pg. 569
Carr, Laura, Coord-Mktg - Simon Property Group, Inc.; pg. 1112, pg. 690
Carr, Laura W., Sr Rep-Crude Oil Mktg - Apache Corporation; pg. 1934, pg. 1700
Carr, Lauren, Mgr-Mktg Comm - True Temper Sports, Inc.; pg. 1847, pg. 1647
Carr, Matthew, Dir-Display & Mobile Adv - Amazon.com, Inc.; pg. 1226, pg. 1831
Carr, Matthew, Sr VP-Area Mktg & Ops, Midwest Area - Verizon Communications Inc.; pg. 1875, pg. 1309
Carr, Micah, Brand Mgr - Kimberly-Clark Corporation; pg. 1461, pg. 1720
Carr, Nick, Dir-Mktg - Red Hat, Inc.; pg. 460, pg. 1388
Carr, Tim, Dir-Social Media & Content Mktg-US Concerts - Live Nation Entertainment, Inc.; pg. 558, pg. 47
Carragher, Kaitlin, Sls Rep-Salesforce1 Platform Specialist - salesforce.com, inc.; pg. 1278, pg. 226
Carraher, Robert, Sr Exec VP-Mktg - CCA Industries, Inc.; pg. 503, pg. 1114
Carrales, Angela, Sr Dir-Mktg - 7-Eleven, Inc.; pg. 1012, pg. 1672
Carrara, Tony, Product Mgr - Rockwell Automation, Inc.; pg. 668, pg. 1880
Carraro, Johnny, Mgr-Natl-Sls - Fastline Publications Inc.; pg. 1641, pg. 726
Carrasco, Yvonne, Asst Dir-PR - Los Angeles Dodgers Inc.; pg. 559, pg. 135
Carrasquillo, Mari, Sr Dir-Mktg-Latin America - Jarden Consumer Solutions; pg. 57, pg. 412
Carreiro-Battaglia, Liz, Sr Mgr-Strategic Learning Initiatives - Royal Bank of Canada; pg. 800, pg. 1942
Carreker, Lynsi, Dir-Mktg & Bus Dev - First Option Mortgage, LLC; pg. 757, pg. 505
Carrel, David, Dir-Prime Mktg Worldwide - Amazon.com, Inc.; pg. 1226, pg. 1831
Carrella, Chris, Dir-Tech, Mktg & Sls - Leviton Manufacturing Company, Inc.; pg. 1301, pg. 1180
Carrelli, Bill, VP-Strategic Mktg - Siemens Corporation; pg. 803, pg. 1291
Carreno, Pablo, Category Mgr-Mktg Procurement-Global - Bloomberg L.P.; pg. 725, pg. 1204
Carrera, Jacquelynn, Dir-Creative Mktg - Entravision Communications Corporation; pg. 285, pg. 273
Carrera, Mario M., Chief Revenue Officer - Entravision Communications Corporation; pg. 285, pg. 273
Carrero, Miguel, Head-Products & Solutions-ArcSight. Enterprise Security Products - Hewlett-Packard Company; pg. 404, pg. 175
Carretero, Cristina, Sr Mgr-Demand Programs-Worldwide AIM & Websphere - International Business Machines Corporation; pg. 418, pg. 1138
Carrico, Lucy, Head-Mktg-Wealth - Wells Fargo & Company; pg. 819, pg. 232
Carriedo, Ruben, VP-Sls - Campbell Soup Company; pg. 844, pg. 1048
Carrier, Joyce, Dir-Adv - United States Postal Service; pg. 1009, pg. 406
Carrier, Matt, Sr Dir-Mobile Product Mgmt - SAP America, Inc.; pg. 466, pg. 1557
Carriere, Nicole, Mgr-PR - AutoTrader, Inc.; pg. 1230, pg. 490
Carrigan, Kevin, Dir-Creative-Global - Calvin Klein, Inc.; pg. 20, pg. 1209
Carriger, Doug, Sr Dir-Mktg - Airbus Helicopters, Inc.; pg. 223, pg. 1698
Carrillos, Marissa, Mgr-Mktg & Bus Svcs - Comcast Corporation; pg. 276, pg. 1560
Carrington, Caroline, Reg Head-Mktg - Nationwide Mutual Insurance Company; pg. 1210, pg. 1442
Carrington, Ian, Mng Dir-Performance Media Solutions-EMEA - Google Inc.; pg. 1249, pg. 153
Carrion, Omar, Dir-Integrated Mktg Comm-Latam - Kellogg Company; pg. 831, pg. 870
Carro, Kevin, Assoc Mgr-Mktg-Werther's Original - Storck USA, L.P.; pg. 1862, pg. 591
Carroll Cox, Heather, Chief Mktg Officer & Chief Digital Officer - Citigroup Inc.; pg. 735, pg. 1212
Carroll, Anja, Sr Dir-Media & Digital Mktg-Global - McDonald's Corporation; pg. 1737, pg. 645
Carroll, Bob, Reg Mgr-Sls - David Clark Company Incorporated; pg. 633, pg. 862
Carroll, Chris, Chief Adv Officer - Subway Restaurants; pg. 1751, pg. 356
Carroll, Frank, Gen Mgr-Mdse - Ace Hardware Corporation; pg. 1040, pg. 644
Carroll, Jan, Brand Mgr-Retail - McIlhenny Company; pg. 876, pg. 741
Carroll, Jennifer, Dir-Mktg-Bus Dev-South Hills Village - Simon Property Group, Inc.; pg. 1112, pg. 690
Carroll, Jonathan, Sr Dir-R&D - OpenText; pg. 1272, pg. 1956
Carroll, Kimberli, Sr VP-Sls-Foodservice Div - Ruiz Food Products, Inc.; pg. 893, pg. 77
Carroll, Kirta, VP-Brand Mktg-Lady Foot Locker & SIX:02 - Foot Locker, Inc.; pg. 1808, pg. 1231
Carroll, Lynn, Sr Dir-Pipeline & Brand Mktg - Acorda Therapeutics, Inc.; pg. 1486, pg. 1138
Carroll, Michael, Mgr-Digital Mktg - Regal Entertainment Group; pg. 579, pg. 1638
Carroll, Michael, Assoc Publr-Adv - Town & Country; pg. 1695, pg. 1303
Carroll, Michael J., Dir-Travel, Spirits & CPG Adv - The New York Times; pg. 1668, pg. 1270
Carroll, Mike, VP-Sls Support-Worldwide - Datawatch Corporation; pg. 383, pg. 813
Carroll, Mike, Dir-Electrical Sls - Graybar Electric Company, Inc.; pg. 1299, pg. 997
Carroll, Mike, Dir-Global Sls Capabilities - Mars, Incorporated; pg. 1858, pg. 1792
Carroll, Paul, VP-Digital & ECommerce Creative - New York & Company, Inc.; pg. 1779, pg. 1268
Carroll, Ryan, Mgr-SEO & Content Mktg - UniGroup, Inc.; pg. 1927, pg. 977
Carroll, Shawn, Acct Mgr-Sls - Antec Incorporated; pg. 350, pg. 90
Carroll, Steven, Specialist-Brand Mktg - Plantronics, Inc.; pg. 663, pg. 270
Carroll, Tara, Strategist-Search & Media Planner-Digital - GEICO Corporation; pg. 1200, pg. 399
Carroll, Tim, VP-Small Bus Mktg - Deluxe Corporation; pg. 1634, pg. 964
Carroll, Tom, Dir-Product Dev, Sweets & Refreshment - The Hershey Co.; pg. 1855, pg. 1538
Carroll, Trish, Sr VP-Targeted Media - The Baltimore Sun Company; pg. 1619, pg. 755
Carrothers, Troy, Sr VP & Gen Mgr-Retail Payment Solutions, Digital Sls & Svc - Kohl's Corporation; pg. 1775, pg. 1870
Carrozza, Carol, VP-Mktg - Ansell; pg. 1495, pg. 1114
Carruth, Cheryl, Mgr-Corp & Enterprise Mktg-PPS Americas - Hewlett-Packard Company; pg. 404, pg. 175
Carruth, Patty, Mgr-Enterprise Field Mktg-USA East - Dell Inc.; pg. 383, pg. 1737
Carruthers, Heather, Brand Mgr-Clairol North America - The Procter & Gamble Company; pg. 1129, pg. 1418
Carsey, Madison, Coord-Email Mktg - Overstock.com, Inc.; pg. 1273, pg. 1760
Carskadden, Rush, Dir-Product Mgmt - Juniper Networks, Inc.; pg. 1260, pg. 286
Carsky-Wilson, Meg, Sr Mgr-Mktg Res - Church & Dwight Co., Inc.; pg. 1153, pg. 1063
Carson, Audra, Mgr-Mktg-BettyCrocker.com - General Mills, Inc.; pg. 828, pg. 933
Carson, Chandra, Mgr-Social Media - Lindt & Sprungli (USA) Inc.; pg. 1857, pg. 1039
Carson, Dana, Mgr-Media Svcs - MGA Entertainment, Inc.; pg. 964, pg. 300
Carson, Dorian, VP & Analyst-Mktg - Citigroup Inc.; pg. 735, pg. 1212
Carson, Jeff, Dir-Specialty Care Mktg-Rare Diseases - Pfizer Inc.; pg. 1581, pg. 1278
Carson, Mary, Dir-Adv - Fisher-Price, Inc.; pg. 953, pg. 1156
Carson, Molly, Dir-Creative - Dillard's, Inc.; pg. 1766, pg. 34
Cartagena, Chiqui, VP-Corp Mktg - Univision Communications Inc.; pg. 683, pg. 1307
Carter, Chris, Sr Mgr - Del Monte Foods, Inc.; pg. 852, pg. 304
Carter, CJ, Dir-Mktg - Winmark Corporation; pg. 1792, pg. 946
Carter, Damien, Sr Mgr-Global Strategic Mktg-Emerging Brands - MedImmune LLC; pg. 1562, pg. 770
Carter, David, VP-Mktg & Comm - Old Dominion Freight Line, Inc.; pg. 1918, pg. 1391
Carter, Fiona, Sr VP & Head-Brand Mktg, Adv & Sponsorships - AT&T Inc.; pg. 1867, pg. 1674
Carter, Gord, District Mgr-Sls - Acklands-Grainger Inc.; pg. 197, pg. 1933
Carter, Hannah, Brand Mgr-Crowne Plaza Hotels & Resorts-Global - InterContinental Hotels Corporation; pg. 1097, pg. 511
Carter, Jeanette, VP-Integrated Consumer Mktg - Hallmark Cards, Inc.; pg. 1646, pg. 983
Carter, Joan, Exec Dir-TIME Live Media - Time Inc.; pg. 1693, pg. 1300
Carter, John, Dir-Sls-Global - Limoneira Company; pg. 705, pg. 276
Carter, Joshua, Mgr-PR - Target Corporation; pg. 1786, pg. 942
Carter, Kara, Project Mgr-Creative Adv - J.C. Penney Company, Inc.; pg. 1774, pg. 1732
Carter, Kathy, Pres-Soccer United Mktg - Major League Soccer LLC; pg. 560, pg. 1256
Carter, Kelly, Dir-Sls Plng-Bone-Cardio Div - Amgen Inc.; pg. 1493, pg. 291
Carter, Kevin, Sr Mgr-PR - TripAdvisor, Inc.; pg. 1926, pg. 835
Carter, Leigh, Supvr-Distr Sls - Quality Bicycle Products; pg. 1710, pg. 918
Carter, Molly, Sr Dir-Comm - The Gatorade Company; pg. 251, pg. 574
Carter, Nicholas, Rep-Field Sls - LG Electronics Canada, Inc.; pg. 651, pg. 1927
Carter, Pete, Specialist-Harley Procter Mktg & Adv - The Procter & Gamble Company; pg. 1129, pg. 1418
Carter, Sandy, Gen Mgr-IBM Ecosystems & Social Bus Evangelism - International Business Machines Corporation; pg. 418, pg. 1138
Carter, Savannah, Coord-Mktg - Lennar Corporation; pg. 1100, pg. 443
Carter, Scott, Analyst-Social Media - Adobe Systems Incorporated; pg. 342, pg. 235
Carter, Sonia, Head-Digital & Social Media-Europe - Mondelez International, Inc.; pg. 878, pg. 601
Carter, Styletta, Dir-Mktg Comm - Equifax Inc.; pg. 748, pg. 504
Carter, Tim, Dir-Field Mktg - Bacardi USA, Inc.; pg. 1956, pg. 417
Carter, Tom, Sr Mgr-Ops-New Product Introductions-TELUS Health - TELUS CORPORATION; pg. 1952, pg. 1912
Carter, Verona, Global Dir-PR-Luxury & Lifestyle Brands - Marriott International, Inc.; pg. 1102, pg. 764
Cartledge, Ron, Dir-Production - Fayetteville Publishing Co.; pg. 1641, pg. 1372
Cartmell, Craig, Asst Dir-Promos, Event Production & Brdcst Mktg - New York Yankees; pg. 570, pg. 1144
Cartner, Jackie, Mgr-Mktg-Electrical & Electronics-Emerging Markets - PolyOne Corporation; pg. 1177, pg. 1404
Cartwright, Christina, Brand Mgr-Pedialyte - Abbott Laboratories; pg. 1484, pg. 551
Cartwright, Ethan, VP-Adv - Station Casinos, Inc.; pg. 585, pg. 1030
Cartwright, Jeff, VP, Dir-Sls & Mgr-Market - Cumulus Media Inc.; pg. 280, pg. 503
Carty, Devin C., Chief Strategy Officer - Cancer Treatment Centers of America; pg. 1511, pg. 410
Carty, Tracy, Sr Territory Mgr-Sls - Valero Energy Corporation; pg. 986, pg. 1743
Caruana, Ken, Exec VP-Strategy, Mktg & HR - Ross Stores, Inc.; pg. 1783, pg. 78
Carucci, Michael, Sr Dir - SRA International, Inc.; pg. 473, pg. 1780
Caruso, Brooke, Assoc Dir-Shopper Mktg Food & Alternate Channel - GlaxoSmithKline; pg. 1536, pg. 1565
Caruso, Catherine, Dir-Mktg & Innovation - ConAgra Foods, Inc.; pg. 826, pg. 1014
Caruso, Christina, Brand Mgr-Intl Brands - Safilo USA Inc.; pg. 11, pg. 1106
Caruso, Deborah, Dir-Mktg Ops - Highmark Blue Cross Blue Shield; pg. 1203, pg. 1576
Caruso, Jay, Sr Mgr-Comm-Internal Comm - Cablevision Systems Corporation; pg. 272, pg. 1141
Caruso, John, Sr VP-TV Network Sls - ABC, Inc.; pg. 268, pg. 1185
Caruso, John, Dir-Mktg - Toys "R" Us, Inc.; pg. 968, pg. 1130
Caruso, Mike, VP-PR - St. Louis Blues Hockey Club, LLC; pg. 585, pg. 1003
Caruso, Phil, Specialist-Media Rels - Walgreen Co.; pg. 1608, pg. 605
Caruso, Rachel, Sr Project Mgr-Mktg, Customer & Product Experience - National Grid USA; pg. 1946, pg. 852
Caruth, J.J., Dir-Mktg & Distr-Focus World - Focus Features; pg. 287, pg. 273

Caruthers, Michelle, Mgr-Email Mktg - TaxSlayer LLC; pg. 808, pg. 532
Carvajal, Pete, Sr Dir-IT - Real Mex Restaurants, Inc.; pg. 1746, pg. 75
Carvajal, Roberto, Brand Mgr - Jarden Home Brands; pg. 1126, pg. 920
Carvalheira, Lou, Sr Mgr-Advanced Analytics - Cisco Systems, Inc.; pg. 372, pg. 240
Carvalho, Lisa, VP-PR - L'Oreal USA; pg. 514, pg. 1252
Carvalho, Mariana, Head-Customer Mktg Westlac Caribbean & Central America - Diageo North America, Inc.; pg. 1961, pg. 361
Carvalho, Matheus, Principal & Product Mgr-Localization Latin America - NetSuite, Inc.; pg. 1270, pg. 255
Carvallo, Alejandra, Mgr-Shopping Mktg & Audience - Intel Corporation; pg. 645, pg. 266
Carvelho, Christian, VP-Sls & Mktg-Intl - Munchkin, Inc.; pg. 964, pg. 300
Carver, Caroline, Dir-Audience Dev & Digital Mktg - Univision Communications Inc.; pg. 683, pg. 1307
Carver, Dave, Exec Dir-Mktg Ops-Global - Merck & Co., Inc.; pg. 1566, pg. 1077
Carver, Jeffrey M., Dir-XELJANZ Global Mktg & Comml Dev - Pfizer Inc.; pg. 1581, pg. 1278
Carver, Kelli, Mgr-Mktg - Country Music Television, Inc.; pg. 279, pg. 1649
Carvill, Jon, Sr Dir-PR - QUALCOMM Incorporated; pg. 1873, pg. 207
Carville, Emily, Dir-Adv & Online Mktg - L.L. Bean, Inc.; pg. 1777, pg. 750
Cary, Britt, Dir-Sls - The Challenge Machinery Company; pg. 1322, pg. 902
Cary, Jay, VP-Mktg Strategy & Customer Loyalty - AT&T; pg. 1865, pg. 258
Cary, Julie, CMO - La Quinta Inns, Inc.; pg. 1100, pg. 1722
Cary, Lindsay Diamond, Partner & Mgr-Mktg - Intuit Inc.; pg. 769, pg. 158
Casabona, Bart, Dir-Social Media - Pitney Bowes Inc.; pg. 454, pg. 376
Casabona, Olga, Sr Dir-Advertiser Analytics & Insights - Turner Broadcasting System, Inc.; pg. 314, pg. 521
Casado, Lisa M., Reg Mgr-Mktg - H&R Block, Inc.; pg. 764, pg. 983
Casagrande, Noelle, Dir-Social Mktg - Chico's FAS, Inc.; pg. 21, pg. 427
Casaleggio, Mike, Reg Mgr-Sls - AEP Industries Inc.; pg. 1878, pg. 1085
Casamento, Louise, Sr Dir-Hospitality Mktg - Oracle Corporation; pg. 1272, pg. 786
Casanova, Frank, Sr Dir-iPhone Partner Mktg - Apple Inc.; pg. 350, pg. 73
Casanova, Stephanie, Dir-PR-Loews Chicago Hotel - Loews Hotels Holding Corporation; pg. 1101, pg. 1252
Casanova, Vanessa, Asst Dir-Mktg - NorthWestern Corporation; pg. 1947, pg. 1625
Casanta, Jane, Dir-Mktg-Titleist Accessories Worldwide - Acushnet Company; pg. 1824, pg. 818
Casart, Bree, Dir-Digital Mktg-West Elm - Williams-Sonoma, Inc.; pg. 1140, pg. 234
Casas, Anna, Mgr-Mktg - Yahoo! Inc.; pg. 1289, pg. 289
Casas, Sasha, Mgr-Mktg Comm - Accuray Incorporated; pg. 1486, pg. 282
Casavant, Mark, Sr VP-Product Dev-Global - Klipsch Group, Inc.; pg. 649, pg. 688
Casbon, Hartley, Mgr-Mktg - New Orleans Tourism Marketing Corporation; pg. 1001, pg. 747
Cascadden, Janet, Mgr-Dealer Mktg Tools, Dev & Deployment - General Motors Company; pg. 175, pg. 881
Cascarano, Ceili, Brand Mgr - Johnson & Johnson; pg. 1549, pg. 1091
Cascio, Michael, VP-Natl Adv - The New York Post; pg. 1668, pg. 1269
Case, Dennis, Sr Product Mgr-Insurance - Northern Trust Corporation; pg. 787, pg. 585
Case, John, Pres-Consumer Products Grp - Leggett & Platt, Incorporated; pg. 933, pg. 974
Case, John, Corp VP-Mktg - Microsoft Corporation; pg. 435, pg. 1824
Case, Joseph, Dir-Digital Media - Northeastern University; pg. 605, pg. 799
Case, Linda, Dir-Creative Svcs - San Antonio Express News; pg. 1682, pg. 1742
Case, Lisa, Mgr-Mktg-Natl - Dave & Buster's Entertainment, Inc.; pg. 1724, pg. 1679
Case, Mark, Chief Sls Officer - RealPage, Inc.; pg. 1277, pg. 1669
Case, Matt, Sr Analyst-Corp Mktg-Innovation - FedEx Corporation; pg. 1907, pg. 1642
Casebeer, Steve, Sr VP-Mktg & Sls - Kentucky Lottery Corporation; pg. 996, pg. 735
Casebolt, Elizabeth, Coord-Mktg - Briggs & Stratton Corporation; pg. 201, pg. 1899
Casebolt, Kathy, Sr Coord-Adv - The Kroger Co.; pg. 1025, pg. 1416
Casement, Mary Beth, Project Mgr-Mktg - Goodwill Industries International, Inc.; pg. 1771, pg. 776
Casenave, Blandon, VP-Digital Media Res - NBC Universal, Inc.; pg. 300, pg. 1266
Caseras, Teresa, Asst VP-Mktg & Retail Banking Strategy - Comerica Incorporated; pg. 740, pg. 1677
Casey, Chad, Dir-Sls - Zimmer Biomet Holdings, Inc.; pg. 1611, pg. 699
Casey, Dan, Sr Dir-Sls-Northeast Reg - Sanofi Pasteur, Inc; pg. 1501, pg. 1688
Casey, Dana, Assoc Dir-Integrated Mktg-Vanity Fair - Conde Nast Publications, Inc.; pg. 1629, pg. 1217
Casey, Dana, Assoc Dir-Integrated Mktg - Vanity Fair; pg. 1699, pg. 1308
Casey, Dylan, VP-Product Mgmt - Yahoo! Inc.; pg. 1289, pg. 289
Casey, Geoff, Mgr-Product Design - Santa Cruz Bicycles; pg. 1710, pg. 271
Casey, Glen, Sr VP & Head-Global Products - American Century Investments; pg. 711, pg. 980
Casey, James, Dir-Mktg - Milton Roy Company; pg. 1361, pg. 1542
Casey, Jennifer L., Sr Specialist-Exec Sls-Oncology - Eli Lilly and Company; pg. 1527, pg. 684
Casey, Josh, Head-Creative Team & Sr Copywriter - IDEXX Laboratories, Inc.; pg. 1543, pg. 753
Casey, Kevin, Dir-Sls & Reg Chains - Emery-Waterhouse Company; pg. 1047, pg. 751
Casey, Kim, Head-Retail Sls - Abbott Nutrition; pg. 1485, pg. 1437
Casey, Kimberly, Sr Mgr-Brand Comm - Raytheon Company; pg. 233, pg. 854
Casey, Kristen, Asst VP & Product Mgr-ECommerce - Bank of America Corporation; pg. 718, pg. 1362
Casey, Linda, Mgr-Sls - Long Realty Company; pg. 1101, pg. 27
Casey, Margaret, Coord-PR - Greater Milwaukee Convention & Visitors Bureau; pg. 993, pg. 1874
Casey, Mary, Sr VP-Sls-North America - Starwood Hotels & Resorts Worldwide, Inc.; pg. 1114, pg. 378
Casey, Peggy, VP-Retail Sls - Promotion In Motion, Inc.; pg. 1861, pg. 1052
Casey, RC, Mgr-Sls-Amazon Media Grp LLC - Amazon.com, Inc.; pg. 1226, pg. 1831
Casey, Sean, VP-Sls-Turf & Ornamental - Nufarm Americas Inc; pg. 1798, pg. 552
Casey, Tami, Sr Mgr-PR - BMC Software, Inc.; pg. 362, pg. 1701
Casey, William J., Sr Dir-Global Corp Comm, Brand & Customer Experience - Ingram Micro Inc.; pg. 415, pg. 261
Cash, Ann, Sr Specialist-Mktg - FedEx Corporation; pg. 1907, pg. 1642
Cash, Don, VP-Worldwide Inside Sls - BMC Software, Inc.; pg. 362, pg. 1701
Cash, Greg, VP-Sls - Ecodyne Heat Exchangers, Inc.; pg. 1071, pg. 1705
Cash, John, Reg Dir-Sls - BlackBerry; pg. 625, pg. 1717
Cash, Melissa, Brand Mgr - DavCo Restaurants Inc.; pg. 1724, pg. 768
Cash, Melissa, Brand Mgr - The Wendy's Company; pg. 1755, pg. 1450
Cash, Trey, Mgr-District Sls-MS - Terral Seed, Inc.; pg. 1801, pg. 748
Cashen, Joseph, Sr Mgr-Mktg Analytics - Nissan North America, Inc.; pg. 186, pg. 1633
Cashiola, Stacy, Mgr-Media - The Mattress Firm, Inc.; pg. 934, pg. 1711
Cashman, Molly, Dir-Mktg - Pure Barre; pg. 578, pg. 1623
Casino, Bruce, Exec VP-Television & New Media Distr - NBC Universal, Inc.; pg. 300, pg. 1266
Caskey, James, Mgr-Digital Mktg-Sports - Red Bull North America, Inc.; pg. 264, pg. 275
Caskey, Richard V., Pres-Mdse - Snap-on Incorporated; pg. 1062, pg. 1862
Caso, Christine, Dir-Mktg - Bluegreen Corporation; pg. 1082, pg. 410
Caso, Jeanne, Dir-Digital Brand Mktg, Partnerships & Digital Media Program Mgmt - Toys "R" Us, Inc.; pg. 968, pg. 1130
Cason, Arika, Mgr-Mktg - American Heart Association Inc.; pg. 128, pg. 1673
Cason, Brandon, VP-Mktg - Deep Eddy Vodka; pg. 1961, pg. 1691
Caspar, Abigail, VP-Mktg Strategy - Comcast Corporation; pg. 276, pg. 1560
Casparian, Robert, Product Mgr - General Motors Company; pg. 175, pg. 881
Casper, Michele, Sr Dir-PR - Lands' End, Inc.; pg. 1776, pg. 1857
Casper, Tom, Mgr-Natl Product & Sls Trng - Kohler Co.; pg. 91, pg. 1862
Caspersen, Julie, Assoc-Mktg - Riviana Foods Inc.; pg. 892, pg. 1713
Cass, Cody, Sr Mgr-Pharma Contract Strategy - Express Scripts, Inc.; pg. 1530, pg. 997
Cass, Tara, Sr Mgr - Pfizer Inc.; pg. 1581, pg. 1278
Cassady, Ryan, Mgr-Product Mktg & Creative - LOUD Technologies Inc.; pg. 652, pg. 1847
Cassara, Melissa, Dir-Mdsg & Category Mgr - VITACOST.COM, INC.; pg. 1607, pg. 414
Cassel, Megan, Mgr-Email Mktg - Hershey Entertainment & Resorts Company; pg. 1094, pg. 1539
Casselano, Jerry, VP-Sls & Mktg - Flowtron Outdoor Products; pg. 639, pg. 830
Cassell, Kim, Analyst-Mktg - Brown & Brown, Inc.; pg. 1196, pg. 419
Cassese, Lisa, Assoc Mgr-Digital Media - Macy's East; pg. 1777, pg. 1254
Cassidy, Joey, Mgr-Direct & Database Mktg - Excelligence Learning Corp.; pg. 1768, pg. 151
Cassidy, Kevin, Dir-Visual Design & Sr Mgr-Creative Svcs - E*TRADE Financial Corporation; pg. 749, pg. 1230
Cassidy, Patrick, Sr Dir-Digital Brand Mktg-Global - New Balance Athletic Shoe, Inc.; pg. 1811, pg. 798
Cassidy, Sean, VP-Sls-Comml - Newell Rubbermaid Inc.; pg. 1128, pg. 515
Cassidy, Tom, Dir-Mktg - Deb Shops, Inc.; pg. 23, pg. 1563
Cassiere, Dave, Sr Mgr-Mktg - AT&T; pg. 1865, pg. 258
Cassis, Eugene G., Interim CFO - Waters Corporation; pg. 1436, pg. 834
Cassleman, Pat, Mgr-Platform Mktg - Intel Corporation; pg. 645, pg. 266
Cast, Erin, VP-Mktg-Garnier Hair Care - L'Oreal USA; pg. 514, pg. 1252
Castagnola, Dennis A., Exec VP-Mfg & New Product Dev - The Coast Distribution System, Inc.; pg. 1706, pg. 152
Castainca, Caitlin, Mgr-Partnership Mktg Special Projects - Virginia Tourism Authority; pg. 1010, pg. 1804
Castaneda, Brittany, Brand Mgr-CND Vinylux - Revlon, Inc.; pg. 521, pg. 1286
Castaneda, Carmen, Sr Coord-Mktg - MetroPCS, Inc.; pg. 1872, pg. 1683
Castanon, Peter, Program Mgr-NA iPhone & iPad Carrier Sls - Apple Inc.; pg. 350, pg. 73
Castanon, Roxanne, Accountant-Gas Mktg - Enterprise Products Partners L.P.; pg. 976, pg. 1705
Castelein, Craig, VP-Sls Fin Svcs - TransUnion Corp.; pg. 811, pg. 591
Castelino, John, VP-Product Mgmt & Comml Excellence - Stanley Black & Decker, Inc.; pg. 1063, pg. 358
Castellani, Adam, Sr Mgr-Internal & External Comm-Oncology - Pfizer Inc.; pg. 1581, pg. 1278
Castellanos, Erwin, Head-Sls - LiveRail; pg. 1264, pg. 145
Castelli, Tim, Sr Mgr-BPO Portfolio Mktg - Hewlett-Packard Company; pg. 404, pg. 175
Castelli, Tim, Pres-Natl Sls, Mktg & Partnerships - IHeartMedia Inc.; pg. 292, pg. 1741
Castellini, Kathy, VP-Sls - Consolidated Metal Products, Inc.; pg. 1325, pg. 1412
Castello, Daniel, Dir-Data Adv Solutions - TechTarget, Inc.; pg. 482, pg. 837
Castello, Wolfgang, Sr Dir-Visual Mdsg - Lucky Brand Dungarees, Inc.; pg. 29, pg. 301
Castillejos, Sergio, VP-Mktg & Product Mgmt - Lennox International Inc.; pg. 1073, pg. 1736
Castillo, Alejandro, Brand Mgr-Client Solutions - Dell Inc.; pg. 383, pg. 1737
Castillo, Barbara, Program Mgr-Mktg - MetroPCS, Inc.; pg. 1872, pg. 1683
Castillo, Carla, Sr Mgr-Internal Comm - LinkedIn Corporation; pg. 1262, pg. 160

First page reference indicates Business Class Edition
Second page reference indicates Geographic Edition

Castillo, Donna, Sr Mgr-Global Event Mktg - Atmel Corporation; *pg.* 621, *pg.* 238
Castillo, James, Sr Dir-Acq Mktg - Teachers Insurance & Annuity Association - College Retirement Equities Fund; *pg.* 1219, *pg.* 1297
Castillo, Joni Bree, Specialist-Mktg-RAC Family Brands - Rent-A-Center, Inc.; *pg.* 940, *pg.* 1734
Castillo, Luis, Brand Mgr - Campbell Soup Company; *pg.* 844, *pg.* 1048
Castillo, Mahil, Mgr-Channel Mktg-Americas - Hewlett-Packard Company; *pg.* 404, *pg.* 175
Castillo, Rafael, VP-Sls-Latin America - SeaChange International, Inc.; *pg.* 1279, *pg.* 781
Castillo, Sharon, Dir-Media Rels-Latin America & USGR - Pfizer Inc.; *pg.* 1581, *pg.* 1278
Castle, Christine, Sr Dir-GTM Seller Enablement - Cisco Systems, Inc.; *pg.* 372, *pg.* 240
Castle, Cory, Sr Mgr-Event & Production Svcs - Charles Schwab; *pg.* 1235, *pg.* 1661
Castle, Irena, Dir-Mktg - T. Marzetti Company; *pg.* 900, *pg.* 1444
Castle, Michael, Dir-Global Mktg & Strategy-Software & Informatics - Agilent Technologies, Inc.; *pg.* 614, *pg.* 264
Castle, Scott, Grp Product Mgr-Digital Media - Adobe Systems Incorporated; *pg.* 342, *pg.* 235
Castleberry, Chris, VP-Global Product Mgmt & Engrg - Thomas & Betts Corporation; *pg.* 680, *pg.* 1646
Castor, Sidra, Sr Mgr-HR - Rag & Bone; *pg.* 46, *pg.* 1284
Castor, Todd, Sr Dir-Vacation Package Product Strategy & Sls - Marriott International, Inc.; *pg.* 1102, *pg.* 764
Castrejon, Juan Enrique, Dir-New Product Strategy-Urology-Global Mktg - Astellas Pharma US, Inc.; *pg.* 1496, *pg.* 640
Castri, Jennifer, Product Mgr-Digital - OppenheimerFunds, Inc.; *pg.* 790, *pg.* 1274
Castrilli, Linda, Sr Dir-Programs & Ops - Pfizer Inc.; *pg.* 1581, *pg.* 1278
Castrillo, Alexandra, Brand Mgr - Novus International, Inc.; *pg.* 706, *pg.* 1001
Castro, Carmen, Mgr-Product Dev & Mktg - MAPA Professional; *pg.* 1885, *pg.* 555
Castro, Dee Dee, Mgr-Classified Ad Sls - Dance Magazine; *pg.* 1633, *pg.* 1221
Castro, Fabian, Sr VP-Multicultural Mktg - Universal Studios, Inc.; *pg.* 315, *pg.* 298
Castro, Greg, Brand Mgr-Digital-Running - The Finish Line, Inc.; *pg.* 1769, *pg.* 686
Castro, Lori, Dir-Mktg, Plng & Admin - Red Lion Hotels Corp.; *pg.* 1110, *pg.* 1844
Castro, Michelle, Mgr-Member Mktg AT&T U-Verse - AT&T; *pg.* 1865, *pg.* 258
Castro, Piero, Brand Mgr-Fungicides & Insecticides-Canada - BASF Corporation; *pg.* 1149, *pg.* 1066
Castronovo, Russell, Dir-PR - Broadcom Corporation; *pg.* 364, *pg.* 108
Caswell, Racheal, Sr Mgr-PR - Nexon America Inc.; *pg.* 1271, *pg.* 82
Catala, Lois, Mgr-Mktg Comm - Agfa Corporation; *pg.* 1398, *pg.* 1114
Catalan, Rodrigo, Sr Product Mgr - Epson America Inc.; *pg.* 394, *pg.* 122
Catalana, Anna, Sr Dir-Mktg - Autonomy, Inc.; *pg.* 358, *pg.* 212
Catalano, Brian, Sr Brand Mgr-Global ecommerce & Digital Mktg - Pepperidge Farm, Inc.; *pg.* 888, *pg.* 363
Catalano, Mark J., VP-Enterprise, Comml & Svc Provider Sls - World Wide Technology Holding Co., Inc.; *pg.* 493, *pg.* 988
Catalano, Michael T., Sr Mgr-Interactive Mktg-Global - Kelly Services, Inc.; *pg.* 424, *pg.* 911
Catalano, Molly, VP-Mktg & Comm - Five Guys Enterprises LLC; *pg.* 1728, *pg.* 1787
Cataldi, Donald, Mgr-Sls - Rhode Island Lottery; *pg.* 1004, *pg.* 1600
Cataldo, Leonardo, Head-Customer Mktg Capability-Global - Diageo North America, Inc.; *pg.* 1961, *pg.* 361
Catalina, Erin, Dir-Digital Comm & Creative Svcs - Alcoa Inc.; *pg.* 65, *pg.* 1188
Catallo, Dennis, Reg VP-Sls-Intl - Anixter Pentacon, Inc.; *pg.* 1313, *pg.* 64
Catanach, Claire, Dir-Mktg Strategy - BROOKDALE SENIOR LIVING INC.; *pg.* 1511, *pg.* 1627
Catani, Thomas P., VP-Sls - United States Cellular Corporation; *pg.* 1875, *pg.* 594
Catania, Chris, Mgr-Internal Social Media - Walgreen Co.; *pg.* 1608, *pg.* 605
Catano, Geo, Dir-Customer Adoption Mktg - SAP America, Inc.; *pg.* 466, *pg.* 1557
Catanzariti, Bob, VP-Sls - Swepco Tube Corporation; *pg.* 114, *pg.* 1052
Catanzaro, Amy, Dir-Sls - Cincinnati Symphony Orchestra; *pg.* 540, *pg.* 1411
Catardi, Anthony, Product Mgr - Culligan International Company; *pg.* 54, *pg.* 656
Catarelli, Sherrie, Assoc Mgr-Adv - SeaWorld Parks & Entertainment LLC; *pg.* 582, *pg.* 456
Catarino, Christine, Assoc Mgr-Digital Mktg - Hasbro, Inc.; *pg.* 954, *pg.* 1603
Catarozoli, Lance, Mgr-Subscription Sls - Autodesk Inc.; *pg.* 356, *pg.* 257
Catcho, Catherine, Assoc Mgr-Social Media Mktg - Mead Johnson Nutrition Company; *pg.* 1561, *pg.* 615
Cater, Jason, VP-Mdsg & Design - Peter Millar; *pg.* 46, *pg.* 1372
Cater, Jenny, Sr Mgr-Customer Mktg - The Coca-Cola Company; *pg.* 240, *pg.* 493
Cater, Michelle, Sr Dir-Activation - Beam Suntory Inc.; *pg.* 1957, *pg.* 599
Cates, Coco, Mgr-Adv Dept - Altex Electronics, Ltd.; *pg.* 348, *pg.* 1739
Cates, Julian, Sr Engr-Technical Mktg - NetApp, Inc.; *pg.* 444, *pg.* 287
Cates, Kelly S., Mgr-Online Mktg, Brand Relationships & Direct Sls - Hanesbrands Inc.; *pg.* 26, *pg.* 1394
Cathcart, Amy, Mgr-GMC CRM & Social - General Motors Company; *pg.* 175, *pg.* 881
Cathcart, Will, Dir-Product Mgmt - Facebook, Inc.; *pg.* 1245, *pg.* 143
Cathers, Lindsay, Mgr-Retail Mktg - La-Z-Boy Incorporated; *pg.* 932, *pg.* 901
Cathey, Miles, Dir-Sls - KHOU-TV, Inc.; *pg.* 294, *pg.* 1709
Cathrow, Andrew, Sr Mgr-Product Mgmt - Red Hat, Inc.; *pg.* 460, *pg.* 1388
Catino, Isabelle, Dir-Mktg - Kobrand Corporation; *pg.* 1965, *pg.* 1325
Catlett, Anna, Dir-Mktg - UnitedHealth Group Incorporated; *pg.* 1221, *pg.* 950
Cato, Maria, Dir-Mktg - Pacific Life Insurance Company; *pg.* 1213, *pg.* 166
Cato, Rob, Dir-Channel Sls - Lenovo Group Ltd; *pg.* 427, *pg.* 1384
Catrair, Jordan, Coord-Mktg - Miami Dolphins, Ltd.; *pg.* 562, *pg.* 419
Cattanach, Curtis, Brand Mgr-Dev-LongHorn Steakhouse - Darden Restaurants, Inc.; *pg.* 1724, *pg.* 453
Cattanach, Curtis, Brand Mgr-Dev & LongHorn Steakhouse - Olive Garden Italian Restaurant; *pg.* 1742, *pg.* 454
Cattapan, David, VP-Sls & Mktg - Mitek Systems, Inc.; *pg.* 440, *pg.* 204
Cattapan, Shannon, Sr Mgr-Digital Innovation & Global ECommerce - New Balance Athletic Shoe, Inc.; *pg.* 1811, *pg.* 798
Cattell, Aubrey, Sr Dir-Bus Dev & Ops - Autodesk Inc.; *pg.* 356, *pg.* 257
Caty, Patrick, Mgr-Global Product-Automatic Pool Cleaners - Hayward Pool Products; *pg.* 1049, *pg.* 1057
Caudel, Lacy, Strategist-Mktg - Chipotle Mexican Grill, Inc.; *pg.* 1722, *pg.* 317
Caudill, Bill, Product Mgr - The Progressive Corporation; *pg.* 1214, *pg.* 1463
Caudill, Cheryl, Dir-Mktg & Comm - Multi-Plastics, Inc.; *pg.* 1886, *pg.* 1457
Caughel, Nathan, Product Mgr-Global - Molex Incorporated; *pg.* 655, *pg.* 628
Cauli, Justin, Sr Mgr-Sls - Pandora Media Inc.; *pg.* 1273, *pg.* 172
Caulkins, Carrie, Dir-Strategic Mktg-Global - Allergan, Inc.; *pg.* 1491, *pg.* 106
Causse, Jessica, Assoc Mgr-Mktg - Taco Bell Corp.; *pg.* 1752, *pg.* 117
Cautela, Mark, Sr Mgr-PR - Staples, Inc.; *pg.* 474, *pg.* 821
Cauterman, Sean, Mgr-Mktg-Pepsi - PepsiCo, Inc.; *pg.* 259, *pg.* 1327
Cauthen, Erin, Sr Mgr-Mktg-Global - Brooklyn Nets; *pg.* 534, *pg.* 1145
Cauvel, Kiley, Dir-Adv & Creative Svcs - Pittsburgh Baseball, Inc.; *pg.* 576, *pg.* 1578
Cavaliere, John, Dir-Mktg - Eggland's Best, Inc.; *pg.* 854, *pg.* 1542
Cavaliere, Phyllis, Chm/CEO-Metro Newspaper Advertising Services, Inc - Metro-Puck Comics Network; *pg.* 1665, *pg.* 1259
Cavalieri, Judy, VP-Voice Svcs & Prepaid Products - AT&T Mobility LLC; *pg.* 620, *pg.* 1152
Cavallaro, Christa, Planner-Digital Sls - Conde Nast Publications, Inc.; *pg.* 1629, *pg.* 1217
Cavallaro, Christa, Planner-Digital Sls - Vogue Magazine; *pg.* 1700, *pg.* 1311
Cavallucci, Brian, Mgr-Adv-Natl - Subaru of America, Inc.; *pg.* 191, *pg.* 1050
Cavalo, Tony, VP-Sls - Dynatect Manufacturing Inc.; *pg.* 1330, *pg.* 1883
Cavaluzzi, Todd, Reg Mgr-Mktg - Maserati North America, Inc.; *pg.* 183, *pg.* 1060
Cavanagh, Colby, Dir-Adv-Canada Safeway Limited - Safeway Inc.; *pg.* 1032, *pg.* 184
Cavanagh, Deborah, Sr VP-Mktg - The Talbots, Inc.; *pg.* 34, *pg.* 824
Cavanagh, Mark, Sr VP-Mortgage Banking Sls - Oneida Savings Bank; *pg.* 790, *pg.* 1319
Cavanagh, Seana, Mgr-Product Mktg - Major League Baseball; *pg.* 560, *pg.* 1255
Cavanaugh, Cheryl, Brand Mgr-North American Whiskey - Pernod Ricard USA, Inc.; *pg.* 1968, *pg.* 1332
Cavanaugh, Colleen, Dir-Creative Svcs - Cost Plus World Market; *pg.* 921, *pg.* 170
Cavanaugh, Jim, Sr Dir-Product Strategy & Global Sls Ops - Analogic Corporation; *pg.* 1399, *pg.* 840
Cavanaugh, Mark, Gen Mgr-Sports Mktg & Team Sports - New Balance Athletic Shoe, Inc.; *pg.* 1811, *pg.* 798
Cavanaugh, Mary, Dir-Integrated Mktg Comm - General Mills, Inc.; *pg.* 828, *pg.* 933
Cavanaugh, Susan, Brand Mgr-Media Innovation & Ethnic Comm Plng - The Procter & Gamble Company; *pg.* 1129, *pg.* 1418
Cavanaugh, Tim, Sr Mgr - The Vanguard Group, Inc.; *pg.* 816, *pg.* 1550
Cave, Ann, Mgr-PR - Fiserv, Inc.; *pg.* 397, *pg.* 1855
Cave, Ann S., Sr Mgr-PR - Fiserv, Inc.; *pg.* 758, *pg.* 537
Cave, Doy, Mgr-Mktg Content - Georgia Southern University; *pg.* 602, *pg.* 541
Cavella, Frank, Dir-Sls & Mktg - Waldorf Astoria Naples; *pg.* 1118, *pg.* 451
Caveney, Andy, Sr VP-Mktg-Global - Panduit Corp.; *pg.* 661, *pg.* 663
Cavicchioli, Milena, VP-Mktg - Luxottica Group; *pg.* 8, *pg.* 1323
Cavin, Nicole, Sr Dir-Mktg-Stacy's Pita Chips & Lay's Kettle Cooked - Frito-Lay North America, Inc.; *pg.* 1853, *pg.* 1730
Cavin, Nicole, Sr Dir-Mktg - PepsiCo, Inc.; *pg.* 259, *pg.* 1327
Cavnor, Thomas, Mgr-Sls Promo - Pernod Ricard USA, Inc.; *pg.* 1968, *pg.* 1332
Cawley, Christopher R., VP-Sls & Mktg - Loews Hotels Holding Corporation; *pg.* 1101, *pg.* 1252
Cawley, Eileen, Mgr-Interactive Mktg & Consumer Engagement - Dunkin' Brands Group, Inc.; *pg.* 1727, *pg.* 810
Cawley, Jay, Dir-Fin-Indus Strategy & Mktg - Autodesk Inc.; *pg.* 356, *pg.* 257
Cawley, Nicholas J., Analyst-Adv Sys - Travelport Limited; *pg.* 1925, *pg.* 521
Cawood, Mike, Mgr-Product Line - Thomas & Betts Corporation; *pg.* 680, *pg.* 1646
Cayer, John, VP-Mktg-Global - Kimberly-Clark Corporation; *pg.* 1461, *pg.* 1720
Cayer, Keith, Dir-Mktg Strategy - Safeway Inc.; *pg.* 1032, *pg.* 184
Cayer, Natalie, Mgr-Mktg - Cisco Systems, Inc.; *pg.* 372, *pg.* 240
Cayia, Mark, Mgr-Mktg & Sls - Vermont Lottery Commission; *pg.* 1010, *pg.* 1764
Caylor, Mark A, Pres-Enterprise Svcs, Chief Strategy Officer & Corp VP - Northrop Grumman Corporation; *pg.* 231, *pg.* 1781
Cayne, Janis, Mgr-Mktg - The Spencer Turbine Co.; *pg.* 1378, *pg.* 386
Caywood, Clarke L., Professor-Integrated Mktg Comm & PR - Northwestern University; *pg.* 606, *pg.* 612
Cazel, Marcea, Mgr-Mktg - OttLite; *pg.* 1303, *pg.* 475
Cebron, Liz, VP-Mktg-Madewell - J. Crew Group, Inc.; *pg.* 1773, *pg.* 1245
Cecchi, Mark, Reg Dir-Mktg - Zimmer Biomet Holdings, Inc.; *pg.* 1611, *pg.* 699
Cecco, Janelle, Planner-Digital Sls - Discovery Communications, Inc.; *pg.* 282, *pg.* 777
Cecil, Mike, Dir-Mktg-Laundry Specialties - Henkel Consumer

Goods; pg. 511, pg. 22
Cederholm, Annie, Mgr-Mktg-ITCG Prof Marcomm & Education Div - Canon U.S.A., Inc.; pg. 1404, pg. 1178
Cedo, Alex, Rep-MDU Mktg - Comcast Cable Communications, Inc.; pg. 276, pg. 1560
Cedo, Eric, Dir-Mktg Comm - Crain Communications, Inc.; pg. 1631, pg. 879
Cedrone, Rebecca, Sr Mgr-Mktg-Burger King Acct Team - Coca-Cola Refreshments USA, Inc.; pg. 247, pg. 500
Ceesay, Abraham, VP-Mktg & Ops - Keryx Biopharmaceuticals, Inc.; pg. 1553, pg. 1248
Ceipek, Clemens, Officer-Global Product - LexisNexis Litigation Solutions; pg. 1659, pg. 1446
Cejka, Dan, Product Mgr-Tightening & Welding Sys - Bosch Rexroth Corporation; pg. 1319, pg. 1516
Celada, Maria, Mgr-Consumer Mktg-OPTIFAST - Nestle USA, Inc.; pg. 883, pg. 96
Celata, Edward, Dir-Adv - The New York Times Company; pg. 1668, pg. 1270
Celemin, Teresa, Mgr-Adv Studio - Coach, Inc.; pg. 3, pg. 1214
Celeski, Sarah, Specialist-Adv - Domino's Pizza, Inc.; pg. 1726, pg. 865
Celestino, Vianey, Mgr-Hispanic Mktg - Phoenix Suns; pg. 576, pg. 19
Celi, Tasha, Mgr-Mktg - 24 Hour Fitness Worldwide Inc.; pg. 526, pg. 258
Cella, Josh, Sr VP-Digital Media Sls - Univision Communications Inc.; pg. 683, pg. 1307
Celley, Christine, Mgr-Convention Sls - Greater Milwaukee Convention & Visitors Bureau; pg. 993, pg. 1874
Cembali, Tiziano, Sr Dir-Customer Analytics - Luxottica Group; pg. 8, pg. 1323
Cen, Christopher, Coord-Sls & Mktg - NBC Universal, Inc.; pg. 300, pg. 1266
Cendejas, Kandy, Product Mgr - Bio-Rad Laboratories, Inc.; pg. 1504, pg. 101
Cenname, Anthony, VP-Adv & Publr-WSJ Magazine - The Wall Street Journal; pg. 1700, pg. 1312
Centeno, Diane, VP-Mktg - SeaWorld Parks & Entertainment LLC; pg. 582, pg. 456
Centeno, Diane, VP-Mktg - SeaWorld Texas; pg. 583, pg. 1742
Centeno, Natalie, Sr Mgr-New Product Dev - American Express Company; pg. 712, pg. 1190
Centner, Karen, VP & Gen Mgr-Mdsg - eBags, Inc.; pg. 1240, pg. 331
Cento, Daniel, Brand Mgr-White Spirits - Diageo North America, Inc.; pg. 1961, pg. 361
Centola, Pat, Mgr-Mktg & Comm - Bose Corporation; pg. 626, pg. 820
Ceo, Marco, Dir-Creative - Hershey Entertainment & Resorts Company; pg. 1094, pg. 1539
Cepa, Dan, Sr Dir-Sls - Thermos L.L.C.; pg. 61, pg. 660
Cepeda, Claudia M., Product Mgr - BOK Financial Corporation; pg. 726, pg. 1489
Ceppos, Abby, Assoc Dir-Mktg - Klein Tools Inc.; pg. 1052, pg. 627
Cerami, Annette, Mgr-Mktg Procurement-US - Beam Suntory Inc.; pg. 1957, pg. 599
Ceraolo, Ashley, VP-Mktg - California Pizza Kitchen Inc.; pg. 1720, pg. 127
Cerasoli, Thomas, VP-Mktg Partnerships - Madison Square Garden Network; pg. 297, pg. 1255
Cerato, Kimberly, Sr Assoc Brand Mgr-Gevalia Coffee - The Kraft Heinz Company; pg. 871, pg. 641
Cerda, Maria, Dir-Mktg-Innovation - Diamond Foods, Inc.; pg. 1851, pg. 216
Cereno, Gilbert, Sr Specialist-eMail Mktg - Toshiba America, Inc.; pg. 681, pg. 1302
Cerise, Nick, VP & Head-Global Consumer Payments & Social Media - The Western Union Company; pg. 822, pg. 327
Cerna, Paula, Brand Mgr & Product Mgr - Hunter Douglas, Inc.; pg. 928, pg. 1320
Cerna, Yvonne, Dir-Mktg & Comm - Univision Communications Inc.; pg. 683, pg. 1307
Cerne, Brandy, Mgr-Mktg & Comm - Shake Shack Inc.; pg. 1749, pg. 1291
Cernik-Price, Linda, Brand Mgr - WD-40 Company; pg. 337, pg. 210
Cerra, Allison, VP-Mktg, Comm & Pub Affairs-Americas - Alcatel-Lucent; pg. 615, pg. 38
Cerritelli, Justin, Sr Mgr-Customer Dev-Innovation - Campbell Soup Company; pg. 844, pg. 1048
Cerruti, Deseri, Office Mgr-Legal Adv - Pamplin Media Group; pg. 1674, pg. 1504
Cervini, Andrea, Analyst-Mktg - United Parcel Service, Inc.; pg. 1928, pg. 522
Cesare, Bethany, Mgr-Mktg Activation - PepsiCo, Inc.; pg. 259, pg. 1327
Cesario, Leila, Mgr-Natl Adv-Acura - American Honda Motor Co., Inc.; pg. 163, pg. 292
Cesario, Tracy Bergfeld, Dir-Corp Mktg & Comm - FONA International Inc.; pg. 855, pg. 613
Cesaro, Angela, Sr Product Mgr-Digital - Scientific American, Inc.; pg. 1685, pg. 1290
Cesaro, David, Dir-Client Mktg - Valassis; pg. 1698, pg. 386
Cesaro, Meghan, Mgr-Brand Mktg - TripAdvisor, Inc.; pg. 1926, pg. 835
Cespedes, Priscilla, Sr Mgr-Intl Mktg & Visual - Ann Inc.; pg. 18, pg. 1195
Cetin, Kemal, VP-Comml, Mktg, Analytics-GDBS - Diageo North America, Inc.; pg. 1961, pg. 361
Cevallos, Bolivar, Sr Mgr-Juice Dev Food Svc - The Coca-Cola Company; pg. 240, pg. 493
Cha, Grace, Sr VP-Global Mktg & Commun - D.V.F. Studios; pg. 24, pg. 1226
Cha, Karen, Dir-Bus to Bus Mktg - Burlington Coat Factory; pg. 1764, pg. 1047
Cha, UJ Emily, Program Mgr-Internet Mktg-Affiliate Program - Recreational Equipment, Inc.; pg. 1843, pg. 1821
Chabot, Paul, Dir-Natl Sls & Mktg - ABB Inc.; pg. 64, pg. 1959
Chabot, Sharon, Dir-Mktg Deliveries - Bai Brands; pg. 238, pg. 1073
Chack, Dennis M., Sr VP-Mktg & Branding - FirstEnergy Corp.; pg. 1942, pg. 1400
Chacko, Roger, Chief Branding & Mktg Officer/Exec VP-Carlson Rezidor Hotel Grp - Carlson Companies Inc.; pg. 1084, pg. 947
Chacon, Agustin, VP-Latin Subsidiary Sls & Ops - Epson America Inc.; pg. 394, pg. 122
Chacon, Alice, Sr Mgr-Mktg-Credit Card Loyalty - Canadian Imperial Bank of Commerce; pg. 729, pg. 1935
Chacon, Andres, Mgr-Mktg-FOX Deportes - Fox Broadcasting Company; pg. 287, pg. 130
Chacon, Andres, Mgr-Mktg-FOX Deportes - FX Networks, LLC; pg. 288, pg. 131
Chacon, Cara, Dir-Social & Environmental Responsibility - Patagonia; pg. 31, pg. 301
Chacon, Jose, Sr Dir-Brand & Mktg - Florida Power & Light Company; pg. 1943, pg. 435
Chadha, Chanchal, Mng Dir-India & VP-Intl Sls & Mktg - NBTY, Inc.; pg. 1572, pg. 1338
Chadha, Jasmeet, Mgr-Mktg - Quidsi, Inc.; pg. 1276, pg. 1076
Chadha, Kamal, Sr Dir-Ad Tech - CBS Interactive, Inc.; pg. 369, pg. 215
Chadwick, David, Mgr-Product Mktg - Siemens PLM Software; pg. 469, pg. 1734
Chadwick, Laura, Sr Mgr-Mktg - Tech Data Corporation; pg. 482, pg. 416
Chadwick, Madeline, Sr Dir-Global Comm-eBay Marketplaces - eBay Inc.; pg. 1240, pg. 243
Chadwick, Quick, Dir-Mktg - AMERICAN TIRE DISTRIBUTORS HOLDINGS, INC.; pg. 199, pg. 1379
Chae, Mina, Brand Mgr - Revlon Consumer Products Corporation; pg. 521, pg. 1286
Chae, Mina, Brand Mgr - Revlon, Inc.; pg. 521, pg. 1286
Chafe, Adam, VP-Mktg - Sherwin Williams; pg. 1448, pg. 1436
Chafe, Justin, Mgr-Mktg - Nestle USA, Inc.; pg. 883, pg. 96
Chafer, Sarah, Sr Dir-Strategic Accts & Plng - Tapjoy, Inc.; pg. 1396, pg. 228
Chaffee, E.L., Mgr-Adv & Promo - Harley-Davidson, Inc.; pg. 178, pg. 1874
Chaffee, Mark, VP-Brand Mktg - Taco Incorporated; pg. 1077, pg. 1601
Chagas, Rodrigo Arquer, Mgr-Sls-Natl - Luxottica Group; pg. 8, pg. 1323
Chahine, Andrei, VP & Dir-Creative - MTV Networks Company; pg. 298, pg. 1262
Chahrour, Chaker, VP & Gen Mgr-Global Sls & Mktg - GE Aviation; pg. 227, pg. 1413
Chai, Jennifer, Sr VP-Worldwide Mktg & Strategy - 20th Century Fox Home Entertainment, Inc.; pg. 267, pg. 125
Chain, Rowland, Dir-Sls Dev - The Walt Disney Company; pg. 317, pg. 52
Chaine, Clark, VP-Sls Mktg-Global - CNBC; pg. 275, pg. 1059
Chakravarthy, Anil, Acting CEO - Informatica Corporation; pg. 414, pg. 190
Chalifoux, Julie, Mgr-Brand & Adv - Aetna Inc.; pg. 1187, pg. 351
Challa, Sai, Asst Brand Mgr-Retail Mktg - SanDisk Corporation; pg. 465, pg. 147
Challen, Nate, Assoc Dir-Mktg-Internals - Chattem, Inc.; pg. 1515, pg. 1628
Challifour, Jacqueline, Mgr-Direct Mktg - Toyota Motor Sales, U.S.A., Inc.; pg. 193, pg. 296
Challman, Alison, VP-Mktg & Brand Solutions-HP Solutions Grp - Avnet Technology Solutions; pg. 359, pg. 25
Challman, Robert, Sr Dir-Engrg - Jarden Corporation; pg. 1885, pg. 412
Chalmers, Kristian, Product Mgr - Pilkington North America, Inc.; pg. 215, pg. 1477
Chalmers, Patricia M., Mgr-Sls Comm-Customer Experience - Pitney Bowes Inc.; pg. 454, pg. 376
Chalonec, Andre, Sr Mgr-Adv & Mktg - PepsiCo, Inc.; pg. 259, pg. 1327
Chaloupka, Tracy, Assoc Mgr-Mktg - General Mills, Inc.; pg. 828, pg. 933
Chambard, Kathleen, Sr Dir-Digital Mktg - Scholastic Corporation; pg. 1683, pg. 1288
Chamberlain, Kristie, Dir-Mktg - Kao Brands Co. Inc.; pg. 513, pg. 1415
Chamberlain, Lisa, Mgr-Natl Sls-Florida & Georgia - Tampa Bay & Co.; pg. 1007, pg. 476
Chamberlin, Kelly, Brand Mgr - Bertucci's Corp.; pg. 1716, pg. 838
Chamberlin, Mark R., Mgr-Sls & Mktg - Sasol North America Inc.; pg. 984, pg. 1713
Chamberlin, Tamara, VP-Sls - Networkfleet, Inc.; pg. 445, pg. 205
Chambers, Anna, Specialist-Mktg - Zimmer Biomet Holdings, Inc.; pg. 1611, pg. 699
Chambers, Dwayne, CMO & Sr VP - Krispy Kreme Doughnuts, Inc.; pg. 1734, pg. 1394
Chambers, Eva, Mgr-Outbound Mktg - Veeder-Root Company; pg. 61, pg. 371
Chambers, Eve, Dir-Mktg-Western Div-US - CB Richard Ellis, Inc.; pg. 1085, pg. 1210
Chambers, Jocelyn, Dir-Media - Citrix Online LLC; pg. 1235, pg. 99
Chambers, John, Sr Mgr-Programmatic Mktg-Global - Netflix, Inc.; pg. 1269, pg. 141
Chambers, Lynn, VP-Client Mktg - Corus Entertainment Inc.; pg. 279, pg. 1937
Chambers, Paul, Sr Mgr-Ops-Global External Supply - Pfizer Inc.; pg. 1581, pg. 1278
Chambers, Phillip, Product Line Dir-Comm Products - Citrix Systems, Inc.; pg. 375, pg. 424
Chambers, Rachel, Sr Dir-Shopper Mktg & Shopper Insights-CPG Channels - Starbucks Corporation; pg. 897, pg. 1840
Chambers, Robert C., Dir-Sls-Walmart Canada Health & Grooming - Procter & Gamble Inc.; pg. 333, pg. 1929
Chambers, Scott, Sr VP & Gen Mgr-Media & Licensing-North America - Sesame Workshop; pg. 307, pg. 1290
Chambers, ShaDonna, Head-Daily Ops-Creative Svcs Dept - Sony Corporation of America; pg. 675, pg. 1293
Chambers, Shane, Dir-Mktg - Hershey Canada, Inc.; pg. 1855, pg. 1926
Chambers, Tim, Mgr-Mktg - Pennwell Publishing Company Inc.; pg. 1676, pg. 1490
Chambless, Robert, Sr VP-Sls & Mktg - Coca-Cola Bottling Co. Consolidated; pg. 240, pg. 1365
Chamblin, Keith, Sr VP-Mktg & Indus Rels - National Thoroughbred Racing Association; pg. 569, pg. 730
Chambliss, Betty, Dir-Adv & Community Rels - Manatee Memorial Hospital & Health System; pg. 1558, pg. 415
Chamorro, Ana, Coord-ECommerce Mktg - Hugo Boss Fashions Inc.; pg. 42, pg. 1242
Chamoun, George, Co-Founder & Exec VP-Sls & Mktg - Synacor, Inc.; pg. 1283, pg. 1151
Champ, Lauren, Project Mgr-Mktg - Nuveen Investments, Inc.; pg. 788, pg. 586
Champ, Mark, Sr Product Mgr-Prescription Diet - Hill's Pet Nutrition, Inc.; pg. 1476, pg. 721
Champi, Steve, Dir-Mktg Ops - Imperva, Inc.; pg. 413, pg. 193
Champlin, David, Sr VP-Sls - Harvest Hill Beverage Company; pg. 251, pg. 375
Chan, Andy, Mgr-Product Engrg - The Home Depot, Inc.; pg. 1050, pg. 510
Chan, Arthur, Exec VP-Digital Mktg - Palisades Media Group, Inc.; pg. 452, pg. 275

First page reference indicates Business Class Edition
Second page reference indicates Geographic Edition

Chan, Christopher, Assistant-Mktg - Indochino; *pg.* 42, *pg.* 1911
Chan, Eddy, Head-Mktg Tech - Kimberly-Clark Corporation; *pg.* 1461, *pg.* 1720
Chan, Elaine, Sr Dir-Compensation Governance - Canadian Imperial Bank of Commerce; *pg.* 729, *pg.* 1935
Chan, Hansen, Mgr-Video Mktg-Brand Comm - Juniper Networks, Inc.; *pg.* 1260, *pg.* 286
Chan, Jacqueline, Dir-Mktg - Shiseido Cosmetics America of SAC; *pg.* 522, *pg.* 1291
Chan, James, Dir-Mktg & Bus Plng-Mitsubishi Electric Visual Imaging Systems - Mitsubishi Digital Electronics America, Inc.; *pg.* 655, *pg.* 113
Chan, Jane, Mgr-Mktg - Merck & Co., Inc.; *pg.* 1566, *pg.* 1077
Chan, Janet, Mgr-Corp Digital Mktg & Innovation - Mary Kay Inc.; *pg.* 516, *pg.* 1657
Chan, Janet, Mgr-Corp Digital Mktg & Innovation - Mary Kay Inc.; *pg.* 516, *pg.* 1657
Chan, Jason, Product Mgr - BMW of North America, LLC; *pg.* 166, *pg.* 1133
Chan, Jessie, Mgr-Integrated Media & Res - Chevron Corporation; *pg.* 974, *pg.* 259
Chan, Jonathan, Dir-Sls - MORNINGSTAR, INC.; *pg.* 784, *pg.* 583
Chan, Julie, Sr Dir-Global Franchise Media & Rels - Pfizer Inc.; *pg.* 1581, *pg.* 1278
Chan, Kenneth, Mgr-Brand Mktg - Sony Computer Entertainment America LLC; *pg.* 966, *pg.* 256
Chan, Lilly, Brand Mgr-AXE & Innovation - Unilever United States, Inc.; *pg.* 904, *pg.* 1061
Chan, Matt, VP-Mktg-Global Enterprise & Education - Rosetta Stone Inc.; *pg.* 462, *pg.* 1774
Chan, Megan, Dir-Digital Media - NBC Universal, Inc.; *pg.* 300, *pg.* 1266
Chan, Melissa Ann, Mgr-Product & Mktg - Google Inc.; *pg.* 1249, *pg.* 153
Chan, Mimi, Mgr-Asian Mktg - AT&T Mobility LLC; *pg.* 619, *pg.* 488
Chan, Nelson, Sr Engr-Technical Mktg - Intel Corporation; *pg.* 645, *pg.* 266
Chan, Nicholas, Sr Dir-Mid-Market Sls & Bus Dev - Yahoo! Inc.; *pg.* 1289, *pg.* 289
Chan, Nina, Dir-Mktg Analytics - Liberty Mutual Insurance Group Inc.; *pg.* 1205, *pg* 797
Chan, Rachel, Dir-Worldwide Media Strategy-PPS - Hewlett-Packard Company; *pg.* 404, *pg.* 175
Chan, Serene, Dir-Mktg - GameFly, Inc.; *pg.* 953, *pg.* 132
Chan, Stephanie, Assoc Mgr-Mktg & Shopper Mktg-Subway Restaurants Customer Team - PepsiCo, Inc.; *pg.* 259, *pg.* 1327
Chan, Sue, Mgr-PR & Special Events - Bergdorf Goodman, Inc.; *pg.* 1761, *pg.* 1202
Chan, Susan, Designer-Production - Home Box Office, Inc.; *pg.* 290, *pg.* 1240
Chan, Viola, Creative Dir-Design-Oleg Cassini - David's Bridal, Inc.; *pg.* 23, *pg.* 1523
Chan, YK, VP-Sls-Asia - The Associated Press, Inc.; *pg.* 270, *pg.* 1197
Chanavat, Andre, Sr Product Mgr - Thomson Reuters Markets; *pg.* 810, *pg.* 1299
Chance, Ralph, Reg Mgr-Sls-South Central - David Clark Company Incorporated; *pg.* 633, *pg.* 862
Chancellor, Codi, Coord-Adv - Burlington Coat Factory; *pg.* 1764, *pg.* 1047
Chancellor, Rocky, Specialist-Social Media - United Parcel Service, Inc.; *pg.* 1928, *pg.* 522
Chancey, Rebecca, Mgr-Trade Mktg-Global - Oakley, Inc.; *pg.* 1840, *pg.* 86
Chanco, Rachel, Sr Mgr-Product Mktg - Electronic Arts Inc.; *pg.* 951, *pg.* 189
Chancy, Sukiana, Mgr-Mktg-Global - The Estee Lauder Companies Inc.; *pg.* 508, *pg.* 1229
Chand, Gaurav, Exec Dir-Datacenter Solutions Mktg & Bus Dev - Dell Inc.; *pg.* 383, *pg.* 1737
Chander, Hareesh, Mgr-Mktg-Snacks Div - General Mills, Inc.; *pg.* 828, *pg.* 933
Chandilya, Sharanya, Bus Mgr - AOL Inc.; *pg.* 1229, *pg.* 1195
Chandler, Andy, Sr VP & Div Mgr-Mdse - Shoe Carnival, Inc.; *pg.* 1819, *pg.* 679
Chandler, Ernie, Acct Exec-Outside Sls - Cox Communications, Inc.; *pg.* 279, *pg.* 501
Chandler, Phillip, Head-Field Territory Sls-Technical Support Svcs - IBM; *pg.* 410, *pg.* 1449
Chandler, Scott, Sr Dir-Bus Dev - Yahoo! Inc.; *pg.* 1289, *pg.* 289
Chandler, Scott, Sr Dir-Bus Dev - Yahoo! Mobile; *pg.* 1291, *pg.* 290
Chandler, Scott A., Sr VP-Strategic Sls - Infinera Corporation; *pg.* 644, *pg.* 286
Chandok, Simran, Mgr-Digital Mktg & Nautica - Nautica Apparel, Inc.; *pg.* 45, *pg.* 1265
Chandra, Claudia, VP-Product Mgmt - Informatica Corporation; *pg.* 414, *pg.* 190
Chandra, Jim, Product Mgr & Mgr-Pricing - General Motors Company; *pg.* 175, *pg.* 881
Chandra, Rishi, Dir-Product Mgmt-Chromecast - Google Inc.; *pg.* 1249, *pg.* 153
Chandramouli, Ashwin, Mgr-Mktg-US Diagnostics Bus - Abbott Laboratories; *pg.* 1484, *pg.* 551
Chandran, Jay, Mgr-Sls - Special Metals Corporation; *pg.* 1377, *pg.* 1850
Chandrani, Mitul, Mgr-Mktg-Xantrex Brand - Schneider Canada, Inc.; *pg.* 1374, *pg.* 1928
Chandrasekaran, Balaji, Dir-Strategy & Mktg - Applied Materials, Inc.; *pg.* 618, *pg.* 264
Chandy, Grischa, Sr Mgr-Product & Cellular Imaging - Molecular Devices Corporation; *pg.* 1568, *pg.* 287
Chaney, Rachel, Sr Analyst-Social Media & Online Mktg - CORT Business Services Corporation; *pg.* 921, *pg.* 1777
Chaney, Tim, Dir-Mktg - Kia Motors America Inc.; *pg.* 181, *pg.* 112
Chang, Alex, Exec VP-Mktg Solutions - RealPage, Inc.; *pg.* 1277, *pg.* 1669
Chang, Amber, Mgr-Multicultural Mktg - Cellco Partnership; *pg.* 1869, *pg.* 1042
Chang, Brandon, Sr Mgr-Software Dev - Amazon.com, Inc.; *pg.* 1226, *pg.* 1831
Chang, Brian, Asst VP-Media-Lancome - L'Oreal USA; *pg.* 514, *pg.* 1252
Chang, Charles, Gen Mgr-Bus Partner Alliance & Solutions Mktg - Xerox Canada Inc.; *pg.* 494, *pg.* 1930
Chang, Christina Ranhee, Sr Dir-Art - Capital One Financial Corporation; *pg.* 730, *pg.* 1789
Chang, Christopher, Sr VP-Tech Strategy, Dev & Digital Mktg - Darden Restaurants, Inc.; *pg.* 1724, *pg.* 453
Chang, Christopher, Sr VP-Tech Strategy, Dev & Digital Mktg - Olive Garden Italian Restaurant; *pg.* 1742, *pg.* 454
Chang, Cindy, Head-Global Digital Channel Mktg - General Electric Company; *pg.* 1297, *pg.* 347
Chang, Colin, Coord-Mktg-Payment Svcs - Blackbaud, Inc.; *pg.* 361, *pg.* 1613
Chang, Daniel, Asst VP-Mktg Strategy - Farmers Group, Inc.; *pg.* 1199, *pg.* 130
Chang, Daniel Wei-Chin, Dir-Mktg - Newegg Inc.; *pg.* 1271, *pg.* 67
Chang, David, VP-Digital Mktg Svcs-Global - Cognizant Technology Solutions Corporation; *pg.* 377, *pg.* 1124
Chang, David, Sr Mgr-Sls-Solar Bus - LG Electronics U.S.A., Inc.; *pg.* 651, *pg.* 1060
Chang, David, Sr Dir-Product Innovation - Visa Inc.; *pg.* 816, *pg.* 230
Chang, Dorothy Jean, Dir-PR - FourSquare Labs, Inc; *pg.* 1248, *pg.* 1232
Chang, Ella, Brand Mktg Mgr-West Elm - Williams-Sonoma, Inc.; *pg.* 1140, *pg.* 234
Chang, Ethan, Mgr-Product Mktg - Skyworks Solutions, Inc.; *pg.* 674, *pg.* 862
Chang, Feng, Sr Mgr-Digital Mktg Strategy - Rue La La; *pg.* 1278, *pg.* 800
Chang, Flora, Product Mgr-Virtualization & Cloud - Barracuda Networks, Inc.; *pg.* 360, *pg.* 58
Chang, Frank, Dir-Product Mgmt-Pan America Desktop - Acer America Corporation; *pg.* 341, *pg.* 235
Chang, Grace, Product Mgr & Mgr-Community & Customer Success - Hewlett-Packard Company; *pg.* 404, *pg.* 175
Chang, Harvey, Sr Mgr-Sponsorships & Sports Mktg - United Services Automobile Association; *pg.* 1221, *pg.* 1743
Chang, James, Sr Mgr-Search Engine Mktg - Local.com Corporation; *pg.* 1264, *pg.* 113
Chang, Jeff, Product Mgr-Android Wear - Google Inc.; *pg.* 1249, *pg.* 153
Chang, Johnny, Product Mgr-LV UltraMOV TM Series Varistor - Littelfuse, Inc.; *pg.* 1301, *pg.* 580
Chang, Joseph Y., Chief Scientific Officer & Exec VP-Product Dev - Nu Skin Enterprises, Inc.; *pg.* 518, *pg.* 1755
Chang, Lawrence, Product Mgr-Mobile - Google Inc.; *pg.* 1249, *pg.* 153
Chang, Leslie, Mgr-Mktg - Nestle USA, Inc.; *pg.* 883, *pg.* 96
Chang, Linda, VP-Mdsg - Forever 21, Inc.; *pg.* 24, *pg.* 130
Chang, Marcus, Sr Mgr-Mktg - SanDisk Corporation; *pg.* 465, *pg.* 147
Chang, Michael, Sr Mgr-Product & Inventory Plng-Global - Amazon.com, Inc.; *pg.* 1226, *pg.* 1831
Chang, Paul, Brand Mgr-NSW & Fuelband - NIKE, Inc.; *pg.* 1812, *pg.* 1492
Chang, Ronald, VP & Sr Mgr-Private Banking - Bank of Hawaii Corporation; *pg.* 720, *pg.* 543
Chang, Stephanie, Mgr-Ethnic Mktg - Kia Motors America Inc.; *pg.* 181, *pg.* 112
Chang, Tony, VP-US Product & Client Mktg - Visa Inc.; *pg.* 816, *pg.* 230
Chang, Wei, Dir-Mktg-Mobile & Wireless - Broadcom Corporation; *pg.* 364, *pg.* 108
Chanliau, Marc, Dir-Product Mgmt - Oracle Corporation; *pg.* 450, *pg.* 191
Channell, Adam, Product Mgr-EMEA - PR Newswire Association LLC; *pg.* 1678, *pg.* 1283
Chao, Andrea, Dir-Adv-The GUESS Foundation - Guess?, Inc.; *pg.* 25, *pg.* 132
Chao, Bernice, Product Mgr-Gerber - Nestle USA, Inc.; *pg.* 883, *pg.* 96
Chao, Evan, Sr Mgr-Strategic Programs & Ops-Sls Sys - LinkedIn Corporation; *pg.* 1262, *pg.* 160
Chao, Florence, Sr Mgr-Field Mktg-Microcontroller Bus Unit - Atmel Corporation; *pg.* 621, *pg.* 238
Chao, Kevin, Mgr-Product Growth-Mktg Partnerships - Facebook, Inc.; *pg.* 1245, *pg.* 143
Chao, Michael, Sr Mgr-Platform Engrg-Memory - NVIDIA Corporation; *pg.* 447, *pg.* 268
Chao, Verna G., Dir-Global Security Solutions Mktg - Dell Inc.; *pg.* 383, *pg.* 1737
Chao-Rivera, Eveline, Brand Mgr-AM Food - Starbucks Corporation; *pg.* 897, *pg.* 1840
Chapa, Paulina, Sr Coord-Mktg - National Basketball Association; *pg.* 566, *pg.* 1264
Chapa, Paulina, Sr Coord-Mktg Innovation & Growth Platforms - NBA Properties, Inc.; *pg.* 569, *pg.* 1120
Chaparro, Gaby, Specialist-Multicultural & Adv - Macy's, Inc.; *pg.* 1778, *pg.* 1417
Chapdelaine, Karen, Mgr-Mktg , Adv & Brand Mktg - Starbucks Corporation; *pg.* 897, *pg.* 1840
Chapin, Drew, VP-Mktg - Hyland Software, Inc.; *pg.* 409, *pg.* 1480
Chapin, Jennifer, Mgr-Mktg - Cisco Systems, Inc.; *pg.* 372, *pg.* 240
Chapin, Martha, Sr Mgr-Education & Web Svcs - The American Cleaning Institute; *pg.* 127, *pg.* 394
Chapin, Maureen, Mgr-Global Mktg Comm-Infection Prevention Div - 3M Company; *pg.* 1142, *pg.* 956
Chapin, Susan, Sr Mgr-Brand Dev - Luxottica Retail; *pg.* 8, *pg.* 1460
Chaplin, Monica, Mgr-Creative Adv - Tribune Media Company; *pg.* 1696, *pg.* 592
Chapline, Joe, VP-Retail Mktg - Fifth Third Bancorp; *pg.* 752, *pg.* 1413
Chapman, Andrew, Sr Analyst-Media & Entertainment - Caesars Entertainment Corporation; *pg.* 1083, *pg.* 1023
Chapman, Aoife, Product Mgr-Technical - ProPhotonix Limited; *pg.* 1427, *pg.* 1039
Chapman, Ashley, Assoc Dir-Global PR, Aloft, Element & Four Points by Sheraton - Starwood Hotels & Resorts Worldwide, Inc.; *pg.* 1114, *pg.* 378
Chapman, Benjamin, Div Mgr-Mdse - Amazon.com, Inc.; *pg.* 1226, *pg.* 1831
Chapman, Bill, Sr Dir-IR - W.W. Grainger, Inc.; *pg.* 1390, *pg.* 625
Chapman, Brian, Supvr-Creative & Brand Strategist - C.R. Bard, Inc.; *pg.* 1519, *pg.* 1094
Chapman, Christine, Mgr-Channel Mktg - Makita U.S.A., Inc.; *pg.* 1358, *pg.* 120
Chapman, Craig, Mgr-Channel Sls - Cars.com; *pg.* 1234, *pg.* 568
Chapman, Craig, Dir-Shop Your Way Mktg - Sears Holdings Corporation; *pg.* 1784, *pg.* 618
Chapman, Jeanne, Exec VP-Corp Mktg Solutions - Entertainment Publications, Inc.; *pg.* 1639, *pg.* 910
Chapman, Jeremy, Brand Mgr - Spin Master Ltd.; *pg.* 967, *pg.* 1943
Chapman, Jessie, Sr Dir-Brand & Mktg Comm - Broadridge Financial Solutions Inc.; *pg.* 727, *pg.* 1172
Chapman, Juliana, Sr Dir-Events Mktg - Gartner, Inc.; *pg.* 1248, *pg.* 374
Chapman, Kristen, Coord-Mktg - Collectors Universe Inc.; *pg.* 377, *pg.* 260
Chapman, Kristin, Mgr-Mktg-Brand Strategy - Nordstrom, Inc.;

pg. 1779, pg. 1837
Chapman, Lance, Mgr-Mktg Comm - Honeywell International Inc.; pg. 407, pg. 1088
Chapman, Mary, Specialist-Mktg - Constellation Brands, Inc.; pg. 1960, pg. 1348
Chapman, Melissa, Supvr-Mktg Comm - 3M Company; pg. 1142, pg. 956
Chapman, Michele, Head-Sls Ops-Kindle Education & Enterprise - Amazon.com, Inc.; pg. 1226, pg. 1831
Chapman, Randy, Chief Strategy Officer - Snyder's-Lance, Inc.; pg. 896, pg. 1368
Chapman, Richard, Sr VP-Sls - Makita U.S.A., Inc.; pg. 1358, pg. 120
Chapman, Rob, VP-Technical Advisory Svcs - Electric Power Research Institute Inc; pg. 140, pg. 175
Chapman, Tyler, VP-Mktg - Frito-Lay North America, Inc.; pg. 1853, pg. 1730
Chapman, Wink, VP-Sls & Mktg - Friedrich Air Conditioning Co.; pg. 1072, pg. 1740
Chapman, Zachary, VP-Global Digital & Publ Sls Strategy - ESPN, Inc.; pg. 285, pg. 340
Chappell, Becky, Mgr-Product Mktg - Google Inc.; pg. 1249, pg. 153
Chappell, Charles, Head-Media & Adv-Global & Sr Dir-Mktg - The Hershey Co.; pg. 1855, pg. 1538
Chappell, Deb, Sr Mgr-Real Estate - Qdoba Mexican Grill Inc.; pg. 1031, pg. 336
Chappell, Lisa, VP-Sls Ops-Global - Pegasystems Inc.; pg. 453, pg. 74
Chappell, Stephanie, Mgr-Ad Sls Comm-The TBS & TNT Sponsor Shop - Turner Broadcasting System, Inc.; pg. 314, pg. 521
Chapper, Jon, Mgr-PR - Los Angeles Dodgers Inc.; pg. 559, pg. 135
Chaput, Erin, Specialist-Product Mdsg - 1-800 CONTACTS, INC.; pg. 1758, pg. 1753
Chaput, Jessica W., Sr Mgr-Mktg-Customer Acq - CBS Interactive, Inc.; pg. 369, pg. 215
Charach, Michael, Dir-Mktg & Affiliate Rels-CBS Television Distribution - CBS Corporation; pg. 273, pg. 1210
Charay, Jason, Sr Dir-Mktg - Nolet Spirits USA Inc.; pg. 1967, pg. 41
Charbonneau, Marie, Dir-Mktg - IBM Canada Limited; pg. 411, pg. 1923
Charbonneau, Mark, Mgr-Product Dev-J-Plasma - Bovie Medical Corporation; pg. 1402, pg. 1178
Chard, Bill, VP-Product Mgmt - Evolving Systems, Inc.; pg. 395, pg. 326
Charest, Larry, Dir-Production - The Denver Newspaper Agency; pg. 1634, pg. 318
Chari, Salil, Mng Dir-Mktg - FedEx Corporation; pg. 1907, pg. 1642
Chariag, Belgacem, Pres-Global Products & Svcs - Baker Hughes Incorporated; pg. 1315, pg. 1700
Charif, Mona, VP-Mktg & Comm - Dell Inc.; pg. 383, pg. 1737
Charkiewicz, Nancy, Mgr-Adv - MTI Systems Inc.; pg. 442, pg. 857
Charlebois, Owen, Sr Mgr-Cross Media Res - Google Inc.; pg. 1249, pg. 153
Charles Cowan, Gwynet, Head-Entertainment Mktg & Event Sponsorships - Emmis Communications Corporation; pg. 285, pg. 685
Charles Stump, Cassandre, Assoc Dir-Recruitment & Mktg - New York University; pg. 605, pg. 1271
Charles, Aminah, Mgr-Sports Mktg - The Gatorade Company; pg. 251, pg. 574
Charles, Brad, Sr Dir-Plng, Logistics & Contract Mfg - Pepperidge Farm, Inc.; pg. 888, pg. 363
Charles, Harlan, Mgr-Chevrolet Corvette Product Mktg - General Motors Company; pg. 175, pg. 881
Charles, Kimberly, Brand Mgr-Adv - Choice Hotels International, Inc.; pg. 1086, pg. 775
Charles, Maura, Sr Product Mgr-Real Simple Digital - Time Inc.; pg. 1693, pg. 1300
Charles, Maureen, Specialist-Mktg - The Guardian Life Insurance Company of America; pg. 1202, pg. 1237
Charles, Melissa, Brand Mgr-Beauty & Personal Care Mktg - Amway Corporation; pg. 326, pg. 864
Charles, Randi, Sr Mgr-Intl Digital Acq - American Express Company; pg. 712, pg. 1190
Charles, Sherry, VP-Federal Sls - AT&T Government Solutions; pg. 355, pg. 1809
Charles-Pierre, Anupa, Mgr-Digital Mktg - Ferrari North America, Inc.; pg. 171, pg. 1060
Charlesworth, Bret, Sr VP-Sls - Professional Education Institute; pg. 457, pg. 561
Charlston, Scott, Mgr-PR - Verizon Communications Inc.; pg. 1875, pg. 1309
Charlton, Angela, Sr Mgr-Adv, Digital & Social Mktg Comm - Sprint Corporation; pg. 1874, pg. 719
Charlton, Christy J., Mgr-Adv & Creative Dev - Humana, Inc.; pg. 1204, pg. 734
Charlton, Joline, Product Mgr-ECommerce - Delta Air Lines, Inc.; pg. 1905, pg. 503
Charlton, Linda, VP-Mktg & Audience Dev - North Carolina Symphony; pg. 571, pg. 1388
Charnas, Leanne, Dir-Product & Mktg Mgmt - Cardinal Health, Inc.; pg. 1512, pg. 1448
Charriez, Laston, Sr VP-Mktg-Americas - The Western Union Company; pg. 822, pg. 327
Charron, Marc Andre, Brand Mktg Dir-Reebok-CCM Hockey Div-Global - Reebok-CCM Hockey, Inc.; pg. 1844, pg. 1960
Chartier, Doug, Sr VP-Mktg - T-Mobile US, Inc.; pg. 676, pg. 1816
Chartier, Lisa R., Sr Mgr-Employer Brand & Recruitment Mktg Comm - Philips Electronics North America; pg. 662, pg. 782
Charvat, Julie, VP-Mktg - Real Mex Restaurants, Inc.; pg. 1746, pg. 75
Chasan, Noam, Dir-Mktg - Dorman Products, Inc.; pg. 204, pg. 1522
Chase, Aleta, Dir-Mktg-Pop-Tarts - Kellogg Company; pg. 831, pg. 870
Chase, Allison, Sr Mgr-Digital Analytics - DIRECTV Group Holdings, LLC; pg. 281, pg. 79
Chase, Elaine, Sr Dir-Brand Strategy & Mktg-Global - Wizards of the Coast, Inc.; pg. 970, pg. 1830
Chase, Kathleen, Mgr-Mktg - The J.M. Smucker Company; pg. 865, pg. 1468
Chase, Kierin, Sr Mgr-Organized Play Programs & Ops - Wizards of the Coast, Inc.; pg. 970, pg. 1830
Chase, Linda, Mgr-Mktg Comm - Jeld-Wen, Inc.; pg. 1051, pg. 1499
Chase, Lori J., Sr VP & Dir-PR - IBERIABANK Corporation; pg. 768, pg. 744
Chase, Melanie, Sr Mgr-Product Mktg - Fitbit Inc.; pg. 639, pg. 218
Chase, Mike, Dir-Mktg Tech - Mount Snow Ltd.; pg. 564, pg. 1769
Chase, Peter, Dir-Media Rels - Chicago National League Ball Club, LLC; pg. 539, pg. 569
Chase, Randy, Sr Dir-North America Mktg-EA SPORTS - Electronic Arts Inc.; pg. 951, pg. 189
Chasse, Michelle, Dir-Integrated Mktg Movies & Video Games - Viacom Inc.; pg. 316, pg. 1310
Chastain, Lindsay, Dir-Digital Mktg - Sephora USA Inc; pg. 522, pg. 227
Chastain, Lisanne, Sr Mgr-Partner Mktg-Travel Portals & Global Mktg - Expedia, Inc.; pg. 1244, pg. 1814
Chastain, Stephenie, Sr Mgr-Solutions Engrg - Cisco Systems, Inc.; pg. 372, pg. 240
Chasteen, Jennifer, Sr Dir-Brand & Product Strategy - Church's Chicken, Inc.; pg. 1722, pg. 493
Chatchaikarn, Aroonchat, Mgr-Mktg - Skyworks Solutions, Inc.; pg. 674, pg. 862
Chatfield, Jesse, Mgr-Corp Partnerships & Mktg - Anaheim Ducks Hockey Club, LLC; pg. 528, pg. 42
Chatfield, Joann, VP-Mktg - MoneyGram International, Inc.; pg. 783, pg. 1684
Chatila, Sultan, Dir-Strategic Mktg - UOP LLC; pg. 1386, pg. 606
Chatterjee, Sanjay, VP-CRM & Online Mktg - Time Warner Cable Inc.; pg. 312, pg. 1301
Chatwin, Alistair, Dir-Product Mgmt - DISH Network Corporation; pg. 283, pg. 325
Chau, Brian, Sr Dir-Product Innovation - Wheels Inc.; pg. 1931, pg. 607
Chau, Shirley, Dir-Mktg - General Mills, Inc.; pg. 828, pg. 933
Chaudhari, Jimshade, Dir-Product Mktg & Mgmt - DISH Network Corporation; pg. 283, pg. 325
Chaudhri, Omer, Dir-Segmentation & Adv Measurement-Global Merchant Svcs - American Express Company; pg. 712, pg. 1190
Chaudhri, Prabal, Sr Asst Brand Mgr-Gillette North America - The Procter & Gamble Company; pg. 1129, pg. 1418
Chaudry, Javed, Head-Emerging Payments, Product Mgmt & Partnerships - Citigroup Inc.; pg. 735, pg. 1212
Chauvin, Ralph, VP-Sls-North America - Perfetti Van Melle USA, Inc.; pg. 1860, pg. 727
Chavaria, Elvira, Specialist-eBusiness Mktg - 3M Company; pg. 1142, pg. 956
Chaveco, Kimberly, Brand Mgr-Safilo Group - Safilo USA Inc.; pg. 11, pg. 1106
Chavera, Steve, Mgr-Social Media - Dallas Mavericks; pg. 543, pg. 1678
Chaves, Mark, Dir-Media Intelligence Solutions - SAS Institute Inc.; pg. 466, pg. 1361
Chavez, Erika, Grp Mgr-Mktg & Digital Media Strategy - Starbucks Corporation; pg. 897, pg. 1840
Chavez, Nick, Sr Dir-Consumer Mktg - Nintendo of America, Inc.; pg. 965, pg. 1829
Chavez, Patti, Sr Mgr-Ops Analysis-DISH Media Sls - DISH Network Corporation; pg. 283, pg. 325
Chavez, Rick, Gen Mgr-Adv & Consumer Monetization - Microsoft Corp.; pg. 440, pg. 321
Chavez, Theresa, Mgr-Product Mktg - Advanced Micro Devices, Inc.; pg. 613, pg. 282
Chavez, Tracy, Dir-Natl Media - J.C. Penney Company, Inc.; pg. 1774, pg. 1732
Chawla, Jagjit, Product Mgr - Google Inc.; pg. 1249, pg. 153
Che, Bryan, Gen Mgr-Cloud Product Strategy - Red Hat, Inc.; pg. 460, pg. 1388
Cheaney, Kevin, Specialist-Product Plng - Nissan North America, Inc.; pg. 186, pg. 1633
Cheatham, Erin, Mgr-Vendor Mktg - Academy Sports & Outdoors, Ltd.; pg. 1824, pg. 1724
Cheatham, Lisa, Dir-Mktg - Global Franchise Management LLC; pg. 1771, pg. 537
Checco, Marc, Rep-Mktg - Auto-Owners Insurance Group; pg. 1194, pg. 895
Check, Timothy, Product Mgr-Pro Imaging - Epson America Inc.; pg. 394, pg. 122
Chee, Emily, Area Mgr-Sls - Novartis Pharmaceuticals Corp.; pg. 1575, pg. 1054
Cheek, Scott, Sr Mgr-Product Mktg - Honeywell International Inc.; pg. 407, pg. 1088
Cheemalapati, Prabha, Dir-Mktg-Brand Dannon & Kids - The Dannon Company, Inc.; pg. 851, pg. 1351
Cheeseman, Kelly, Sr Mgr-Comm - Amazon.com, Inc.; pg. 1226, pg. 1831
Cheever, Marshall, Sr Mgr-Facilities Engrg - Arizona Diamondbacks; pg. 529, pg. 14
Cheevers, Devin, Mgr-Product Mktg - Facebook, Inc.; pg. 1245, pg. 143
Chehade, Salim, Territory Mgr-Western Reg Sls - Blonder Tongue Laboratories, Inc.; pg. 625, pg. 1100
Cheifetz, Nicole, Mgr-Natl Accts & Trade Mktg - National Beverage Corp.; pg. 257, pg. 425
Chekowsky, Lu, Sr VP-Brand Creative & Comedy Central - Comedy Partners; pg. 278, pg. 1216
Chelala, Pete, VP-Mobile & Cross-Platform Video Adv Sls - Viacom Inc.; pg. 316, pg. 1310
Chelf, Pat, Sr VP-Sls & Bus Dev - The ROHO Group; pg. 1591, pg. 556
Chellani, Anju, VP-Digital Mktg - Century 21 Real Estate LLC; pg. 1085, pg. 1080
Chelwick, Jennifer, VP-Retail Sls-Houston Chronicle Media Group - Houston Chronicle; pg. 1651, pg. 1707
Chemij, Morgan, Sr Dir-SEO, PPC, Social & Affiliates - Provide Commerce, Inc.; pg. 1276, pg. 206
Chen, Alice, Mgr-Mktg-Sally Hansen - Coty, Inc.; pg. 506, pg. 1219
Chen, Amy, Gen Mgr & Sr Dir-Sls-CVS Customer Team - PepsiCo, Inc.; pg. 259, pg. 1327
Chen, Andrew, Sr Mgr-Mktg-Intl - L'Oreal USA; pg. 514, pg. 1252
Chen, Andrew, Sr Mgr-Mktg-Intl - Maybelline LLC; pg. 516, pg. 1257
Chen, Angel, Sr Mgr-Comm - Van Cleef & Arpels, Inc.; pg. 15, pg. 1308
Chen, Bo, Mgr-Product Mktg - Philips Electronics North America; pg. 662, pg. 782
Chen, Bo, Product Mgr-Mktg-Point Source - Philips Lighting; pg. 1303, pg. 806
Chen, Channing, Dir-Brand Mktg - Fazoli's Management Inc.; pg. 1728, pg. 729
Chen, Charlotte, Product Mgr - Acer America Corporation; pg. 341, pg. 235
Chen, Christine, Assoc Mgr-Mktg-CRM - Banana Republic; pg. 1760, pg. 212
Chen, Cliff, Mgr-Mktg Ops - LPL Financial Corporation; pg. 777, pg. 798
Chen, Connie, Mgr-Mktg Strategy & Plng-Global - The Walt Disney Company; pg. 317, pg. 52

Chen, Deng-Kai, Dir-Product Mgmt - Yahoo! Inc.; *pg.* 1289, *pg.* 289
Chen, Desiree, Brand Mgr-Brita Innovation - The Clorox Company; *pg.* 327, *pg.* 169
Chen, Edwin, Dir-Mktg - Boulder Brands, Inc.; *pg.* 1016, *pg.* 310
Chen, Emily, Mgr-Digital Mktg - Logitech Inc.; *pg.* 1264, *pg.* 164
Chen, Emily, Mgr-Mktg-Innovation & Strategy-Digital, eMail & CRM - Time Inc.; *pg.* 1693, *pg.* 1300
Chen, Jackie, Dir-Social Media - Macy's East; *pg.* 1777, *pg.* 1254
Chen, Jackie, Dir-Social Media - Macy's, Inc.; *pg.* 1778, *pg.* 1417
Chen, James, Mgr-Mktg-Pet Nutrition - Central Garden & Pet Company; *pg.* 1475, *pg.* 303
Chen, James, VP-Product Dev & Engrg - Hewlett-Packard Company; *pg.* 404, *pg.* 175
Chen, Jason, Dir-Sls-China - Harsco Rail; *pg.* 1345, *pg.* 1623
Chen, Jay, Sr Mgr-Product Line - PNY Technologies, Inc.; *pg.* 455, *pg.* 1105
Chen, Jennifer, Sr Mgr-Digital Mktg - Mattel Games/Puzzles; *pg.* 962, *pg.* 80
Chen, Jennifer, Sr Mgr-Digital Mktg - MATTEL, INC.; *pg.* 962, *pg.* 81
Chen, Kyle, Mgr-Mktg - Bridgestone Americas, Inc.; *pg.* 201, *pg.* 1649
Chen, Liliana, Mgr-PR - Swatch Group USA; *pg.* 13, *pg.* 1131
Chen, Linda, Pres-Wynn Intl Mktg, Ltd - Wynn Las Vegas, LLC; *pg.* 1119, *pg.* 1030
Chen, Linda, Pres-Wynn Intl Mktg, Ltd - Wynn Resorts Limited; *pg.* 1119, *pg.* 1030
Chen, Lisa, Dir-Global Mktg-BedandBreakfast.com - HomeAway, Inc.; *pg.* 1911, *pg.* 1663
Chen, Martin, VP-Sls & Bus Dev - Clougherty Packing Company; *pg.* 848, *pg.* 128
Chen, Maureen, Dir-Mktg - Museum of Science and Industry; *pg.* 565, *pg.* 583
Chen, Mimi, Sr Mgr & Mgr-Premium Svcs Product Strategy - American Airlines Inc.; *pg.* 1898, *pg.* 1693
Chen, Patrick, Product Mgr-Mobile Connectivity - Epson America Inc.; *pg.* 394, *pg.* 122
Chen, Patrick, Sr Product Mgr - NVIDIA Corporation; *pg.* 447, *pg.* 268
Chen, Peter, Dir-Product Mktg-Intel - ASI Corporation; *pg.* 354, *pg.* 90
Chen, Q., Sr Assoc Brand Mgr-Meow Mix - Big Heart Pet Brands; *pg.* 1474, *pg.* 213
Chen, Robert, Dir-Global Solutions Mktg - VMware, Inc.; *pg.* 490, *pg.* 179
Chen, Roxanne, Dir-Product Mgmt-Fodor's Travel - Penguin Random House; *pg.* 1675, *pg.* 1276
Chen, Sandra, Asst Mgr-Online Mktg - Toys "R" Us, Inc.; *pg.* 968, *pg.* 1130
Chen, Stephanie, Strategist-Product Quality Ops - Google Inc.; *pg.* 1249, *pg.* 153
Chen, Tianwen, Product Mgr-Data Capabilities - MORNINGSTAR, INC.; *pg.* 784, *pg.* 583
Chen, Tina, Sr Asst Brand Mgr-Duracell - Procter & Gamble Inc.; *pg.* 333, *pg.* 1929
Chen, Vivian, Dir-Mktg - McDonald's Corporation; *pg.* 1737, *pg.* 645
Chen, Wendy, Dir-Ortho Channel Mktg - Align Technology, Inc.; *pg.* 1489, *pg.* 237
Chen, Yong, Reg Mgr-Sls-Asia & Australia - Anaren, Inc.; *pg.* 617, *pg.* 1157
Chen-Wong, Pachi, Sr Mgr-Product Mktg & Elements - Adobe Systems Incorporated; *pg.* 342, *pg.* 235
Cheney, Chris, Sr Dir-Medical Mktg-Global - Alexion Pharmaceuticals, Inc.; *pg.* 1489, *pg.* 341
Cheng, Albert, Head-Product Mktg-Global - Google Inc.; *pg.* 1249, *pg.* 153
Cheng, Carolyn Wellsfry, Sr Mgr-Demand Generation - ShoreTel, Inc.; *pg.* 469, *pg.* 288
Cheng, Christina, Sr Dir-IR - DSW, Inc.; *pg.* 1807, *pg.* 1439
Cheng, Deanna, Coord-Mktg - Microsoft Corporation; *pg.* 435, *pg.* 1824
Cheng, Frank, Sr VP-Mktg, Bus Dev & Ops - Stereotaxis, Inc.; *pg.* 1597, *pg.* 1004
Cheng, Howard, VP-Asia Pacific Sls - Analog Devices, Inc.; *pg.* 617, *pg.* 839
Cheng, Jing, Mgr-Innovation Mktg - PepsiCo, Inc.; *pg.* 259, *pg.* 1327
Cheng, Katie, VP-Mktg & Demand Generation - Samsung Electronics America, Inc.; *pg.* 669, *pg.* 1115
Cheng, Rebecca, Brand Mktg Mgr - Sephora USA Inc; *pg.* 522, *pg.* 227
Cheng, Wendy, Head-Product Design Grp-Global Olay Total Effects - The Procter & Gamble Company; *pg.* 1129, *pg.* 1418
Cheng, Wilson, Mgr-Product Mktg - Sony Computer Entertainment America LLC; *pg.* 966, *pg.* 256
Chengary, Lisa, Product Mgr-Obesity Mktg - Takeda Pharmaceuticals USA, Inc.; *pg.* 1600, *pg.* 605
Chenier, James P., VP-Aftermarket Sls & Mktg - Volvo Trucks North America, Inc.; *pg.* 195, *pg.* 1377
Chenier, Shirley, Sr Dir-IR - Bombardier Inc.; *pg.* 1318, *pg.* 1953
Chennapragada, Aparna, Product Mgr-Google Search - Google Inc.; *pg.* 1249, *pg.* 153
Chennavasin, Don, Sr Dir-Product Mgmt & Mobile - Groupon, Inc.; *pg.* 1255, *pg.* 575
Chenoweth, Susan, Sr VP-Mktg - ELLIE MAE, INC.; *pg.* 1243, *pg.* 183
Cheong, Joseph, Assoc Dir-Creative - Apple Inc.; *pg.* 350, *pg.* 73
Chepelsky, Robert, Mng Dir & Product Mgr-Canadian Fixed Income - Manulife Financial Corporation; *pg.* 778, *pg.* 1939
Chereck, Emily, Product Mgr - BioSpace, Inc.; *pg.* 1231, *pg.* 1082
Cheretes, Ashley, Mgr-Recruitment Mktg - Automatic Data Processing, Inc.; *pg.* 357, *pg.* 1117
Cheretes, Ashley, Mgr-Talent Brand & Media - Avis Rent A Car System, LLC; *pg.* 165, *pg.* 1102
Cherfoli, Josh, Mgr-Mktg Comm - Porsche Cars North America, Inc.; *pg.* 189, *pg.* 518
Cherian, Anoop, Dir-Database Mktg - Anthropologie, Inc.; *pg.* 18, *pg.* 1558
Cheris, Shawn, Brand Mgr-Design-Icons - Adobe Systems Incorporated; *pg.* 342, *pg.* 235
Cherkezian, Christina, Mgr-Digital Product Mgmt-Americanexpress.com - American Express Company; *pg.* 712, *pg.* 1190
Cherkin, Scott, Exec VP-Product & Bus Dev - Complex Media, Inc.; *pg.* 1628, *pg.* 1217
Chermak, Natalie, Mgr-Creative Svcs & Mktg - Tommy Hilfiger USA; *pg.* 48, *pg.* 1302
Cherniak, Walt, Reg Mgr-PR - Aetna Inc.; *pg.* 1187, *pg.* 351
Cherny, Ginger, Brand Mgr - The Coca-Cola Company; *pg.* 240, *pg.* 493
Cherry, Daniel, Sr VP-Mktg-North America - Diageo North America Inc.; *pg.* 248, *pg.* 1223
Cherry, Daniel , III, Chief Mktg & Innovation Officer - New Jersey Devils LLC; *pg.* 569, *pg.* 1097
Cherry, Felicia, Product Mgr-Physical & Earth Sciences - Carolina Biological Supply Company; *pg.* 1513, *pg.* 1359
Cherry, Jason, Brand Mgr-Visual-Construction & Forestry Div - Deere & Company; *pg.* 703, *pg.* 632
Cherry, Jason, Brand Mgr-Visual-Construction & Forestry Div - John Deere Consumer & Commercial Equipment, Inc.; *pg.* 705, *pg.* 1360
Cherry, Kevin M., Dir-Project Online Sls - Microsoft Corporation; *pg.* 435, *pg.* 1824
Cherry, Lisel, Dir-Mktg & Brand Mgmt - Molina Healthcare, Inc.; *pg.* 1569, *pg.* 123
Cherry, Liz, Dir-Mktg-Intl - The Motley Fool, Inc.; *pg.* 784, *pg.* 1771
Cherry, Marisa, Sr Program Mgr-Mktg - Adobe Systems Incorporated; *pg.* 342, *pg.* 235
Cherry, Marquitta, Sr Assoc Mgr-Mktg - Capital One Financial Corporation; *pg.* 730, *pg.* 1789
Cherry, Quincy, Dir-Creative - Capital One Bank (USA), N.A.; *pg.* 730, *pg.* 1789
Chertok, Brian, Dir-Mktg - Kronos Incorporated; *pg.* 425, *pg.* 813
Chertok, Phillip, Specialist-Mktg - GE Canada Company; *pg.* 1296, *pg.* 1926
Chertudi, Mikel, Sr Dir-Global Media & Demand Mktg - Adobe Systems Incorporated; *pg.* 342, *pg.* 235
Chesbro, Cindy, Mgr-Mktg & Showroom - BiNW; *pg.* 918, *pg.* 1833
Chesebro, Chris, Asst VP-Digital Mktg - L'Oreal USA; *pg.* 514, *pg.* 1252
Chesley, Nancy, Gen Mgr-Relationship Mktg-CRM - Audi of America, Inc.; *pg.* 164, *pg.* 1784
Chesley, Philip, Sr VP & Gen Mgr-Precision Products - Intersil Corporation; *pg.* 647, *pg.* 146
Chesney, Steve, Sr Dir-Corp HR - Rite Aid Corporation; *pg.* 1590, *pg.* 1519
Chesnut, Laura, Strategist-Mktg - 3M Company; *pg.* 1142, *pg.* 956
Chesnut, Todd, VP-Sls - Case Paper Company Inc.; *pg.* 1455, *pg.* 1163
Chessen, Chad, Application Sls Mgr-Healthcare - Oracle Corporation; *pg.* 1272, *pg.* 786
Chesser-Garcia, Melanie, Sr Mgr-Comm - BMC Software, Inc.; *pg.* 362, *pg.* 1701
Chessin, Dayna, Dir-Brand Mktg - Express, Inc.; *pg.* 24, *pg.* 1440
Chessman, Ryan, Sr Mgr-T-Mobile Work Direct-Southwest Reg - T-Mobile US, Inc.; *pg.* 676, *pg.* 1816
Chester, Barry, Sr Mgr - Pfizer Inc.; *pg.* 1581, *pg.* 1278
Chester, Dan, VP-Sls-Answer Cloud Svcs - Answers Corporation; *pg.* 1229, *pg.* 1195
Chester, Karen, VP-Media Svcs - Bloomin' Brands, Inc.; *pg.* 1716, *pg.* 471
Chesterman, Bob, Sr VP-Programming & Production - National Hockey League; *pg.* 568, *pg.* 1265
Chesterman, John, Mgr-Product Mktg-Four Wheel Drive Loaders - John Deere Consumer & Commercial Equipment, Inc.; *pg.* 705, *pg.* 1360
Chesters, Sophie, Head-Mktg-Google Canada - Google Inc.; *pg.* 1249, *pg.* 153
Chestnut, Lottie, Dir-Interim Mktg-North Asia - Brown-Forman Corporation; *pg.* 1958, *pg.* 732
Chestnutt, Jennifer, Sr Mgr-Creative Mktg - Apartment Investment and Management Company; *pg.* 1079, *pg.* 316
Chettayar, Krishna, Sr VP & Gen Mgr-Digital Mktg Solutions - TransUnion Corp.; *pg.* 811, *pg.* 591
Chettiar, Christina, Mgr-Mktg-Batiste Dry Shampoo & RUB A535 - Church & Dwight Canada Corp.; *pg.* 503, *pg.* 1925
Cheung, Alan, Dir-Mktg - Reckitt Benckiser Inc.; *pg.* 1136, *pg.* 1105
Cheung, Candice, Head-Creative Brand - Intuit Inc.; *pg.* 769, *pg.* 158
Cheung, Cindy, Assoc VP-Global Mktg & Product Dev - L'Oreal USA; *pg.* 514, *pg.* 1252
Cheung, Darren, Product Mgr-Desktop Discrete Graphics - Advanced Micro Devices, Inc.-Markham; *pg.* 345, *pg.* 1922
Cheung, Jacqueline, Specialist-Mktg & eCommerce-Global - VistaPrint USA, Incorporated; *pg.* 1700, *pg.* 829
Cheung, Jeffery, Sr Mgr-Global Product Mktg - Logitech Inc.; *pg.* 1264, *pg.* 164
Cheung, Kristie, Sr Mgr-Promos-Global - The Walt Disney Company; *pg.* 317, *pg.* 52
Cheung, Stephen, Sr Mgr-Consumer Mktg - Philips Electronics North America; *pg.* 662, *pg.* 782
Chevalier, Tom, Dir-Product Mgmt - Monster Worldwide, Inc.; *pg.* 1268, *pg.* 859
Chevallier, Frank, VP-Products & Software Engrg - LiveWorld, Inc.; *pg.* 1264, *pg.* 246
Chevlen, Kate Tansey, Sr Mgr-Mktg - Amgen Inc.; *pg.* 1493, *pg.* 291
Chew, Angela, Sr VP-Sourcing & Product Dev-Global - Destination XL Group, Inc.; *pg.* 40, *pg.* 810
Chew, Lindsay, Dir-Mktg-Global - Hewlett-Packard Company; *pg.* 404, *pg.* 175
Chewning, Dolly, Mgr-Sls-Intl - South Carolina Parks Recreation & Tourism; *pg.* 1005, *pg.* 1614
Cheyrou, Matthieu, Dir-Mktg-Europe & North America-Veet & Calgon - Reckitt Benckiser Inc.; *pg.* 1136, *pg.* 1105
Chhangani, Naveen, Dir-Product Mktg & Mgmt-Worldwide - NETGEAR, Inc.; *pg.* 444, *pg.* 247
Chhatwal, Sanjiv, VP-Trade Mktg - Anheuser-Busch Companies, LLC; *pg.* 237, *pg.* 991
Chhibber, Suparna, Sr Mgr-Intl Mktg-Fulfillment by Amazon - Amazon.com, Inc.; *pg.* 1226, *pg.* 1831
Chi, Gene, Brand Mgr-Brand Mktg, Product Mktg & PR-IOGEAR - IOGEAR, Inc.; *pg.* 421, *pg.* 86
Chi, Rosalie, Asst Mgr-Mktg - El Pollo Loco, Inc.; *pg.* 1728, *pg.* 70
Chi, Ted, Head-Mktg, Media & Brand Partnerships - Yahoo! Inc.; *pg.* 1289, *pg.* 289
Chia, Clarence, VP-Mktg - FIJI Water; *pg.* 251, *pg.* 130
Chianese, John, Dir-Sls-Discovery Solutions - Discovery Communications, Inc.; *pg.* 282, *pg.* 777
Chiang, Catherine, Brand Mgr - Hasbro, Inc.; *pg.* 954, *pg.* 1603
Chiang, Catherine, Grp Product Mgr-Unified Login - PayPal Inc.; *pg.* 1274, *pg.* 248
Chiang, Jennifer, Brand Mgr-Light & Fit Innovation - The Dannon Company, Inc.; *pg.* 851, *pg.* 1351
Chiantera, Michelle, Sr Dir-Americas Partner & US Comml Mktg - Cisco Systems, Inc.; *pg.* 372, *pg.* 240

Chiaramida, Tory, Dir-Sls Ops - WebMD Health Corporation; *pg.* 1288, *pg.* 1313
Chiarella, Janet, VP-Mktg - Towne Properties; *pg.* 1116, *pg.* 1426
Chiarella, Lisa, Dir-Mktg-Direct to Consumer - LEGO Systems, Inc.; *pg.* 961, *pg.* 346
Chiarello, Amandine, Product Mgr-North America & Europe - BD Medical; *pg.* 1501, *pg.* 1762
Chibber, Seema, VP-Mktg Plng & Strategy - MasterCard Incorporated; *pg.* 779, *pg.* 1325
Chibber, Seema, VP-Mktg Plng, Strategy, Media Investment & Strategic Partnerships - MasterCard Worldwide Inc.; *pg.* 780, *pg.* 988
Chichester, David N., Acting CFO - Central Garden & Pet Company; *pg.* 1475, *pg.* 303
Chichester, Jennifer, Sr Mgr-Digital Mktg & Shared Svcs-Global - SITEL Corporation; *pg.* 470, *pg.* 1654
Chick, Jim, Dir-Sls & Mktg - Bestop, Inc.; *pg.* 200, *pg.* 312
Chick, Russell T., Corp Dir-Mktg - Spartan Motors, Inc.; *pg.* 217, *pg.* 874
Chickering, Marcy, Dir-Client Mktg-Natl Sls-West - Valassis; *pg.* 1698, *pg.* 386
Chico, Jennifer, Dir-Digital Mktg - Deloitte & Touche USA LLP; *pg.* 743, *pg.* 1222
Chico, Mike, Sr VP-Telemundo Sls & Brdcst Ops - NBC Universal, Inc.; *pg.* 300, *pg.* 1266
Chicoine, Dan, Mgr-Mobile & Trader Mktg - TD Ameritrade Holding Corporation; *pg.* 808, *pg.* 1018
Chiddick, Gerald K., VP-Mktg - Amerisure Mutual Insurance Company; *pg.* 1191, *pg.* 885
Chidiac, Claude, VP-Products, Strategy & Customer Support - CMC Electronics Inc.; *pg.* 376, *pg.* 1959
Chidsey, Bruce E., VP-Technical Svcs & New Product Dev - Aamco Transmissions, Inc.; *pg.* 197, *pg.* 1540
Chien, Susan, Sr Mgr-Programmatic Video & Mobile Video - Yahoo! Inc.; *pg.* 1289, *pg.* 289
Chien, Tony, Sr Dir-Mktg - Atari, Inc.; *pg.* 355, *pg.* 1198
Chieng, Connie, Sr Mgr-Online Mktg - Williams-Sonoma, Inc.; *pg.* 1140, *pg.* 234
Chieng, Jeff, Dir-Sports Mktg - The Gatorade Company; *pg.* 251, *pg.* 574
Chiera, Brian, Sr Dir-Mktg & Special Events - Pittsburgh Baseball, Inc.; *pg.* 576, *pg.* 1578
Chiera, Gabriella, Specialist-Mktg Comm-Wyndham Hotel Grp - Wyndham Worldwide Corporation; *pg.* 1119, *pg.* 1107
Chikelu, Michael, Sr Mgr-Corp FP&A & IR - Intuit Inc.; *pg.* 769, *pg.* 158
Childers, Elizabeth, Sr Mgr-Mktg-Ohio, Kentucky & Indiana - PricewaterhouseCoopers LLP; *pg.* 795, *pg.* 1283
Childers, Elizabeth, Assoc Mgr-Mktg - W.W. Grainger, Inc.; *pg.* 1390, *pg.* 625
Childers, Keith, VP-Western Store Ops & Sls - O'Reilly Automotive, Inc.; *pg.* 214, *pg.* 1006
Childress, Alice, VP-Adv & Creative Svcs - Vera Wang Bridal House Ltd.; *pg.* 34, *pg.* 1309
Childress, Gary, Mgr-Natl Sls-Honda Marine - American Honda Motor Co., Inc.; *pg.* 163, *pg.* 292
Childress, Sarah, Brand Mktg Mgr - Colonial Williamsburg Foundation; *pg.* 541, *pg.* 1811
Childs, Andrew, VP-Mktg - Paychex, Inc.; *pg.* 792, *pg.* 1336
Childs, Brad, Mgr-Interactive Mktg - L'Oreal USA; *pg.* 514, *pg.* 1252
Childs, Don, Sr Mgr-Mktg-Indus Vertical Solutions - Lenovo Group Ltd; *pg.* 427, *pg.* 1384
Childs, Theresa, Mgr-Mktg Comm - Rollins, Inc.; *pg.* 1179, *pg.* 519
Childs, Tracey, Dir-Product Mktg - Samsonite Corporation; *pg.* 11, *pg.* 830
Childs, William, Dir-Creative - The Morning Call, Inc.; *pg.* 1665, *pg.* 1513
Chillingworth, Noah, VP-Mktg - Del Taco Restaurants, Inc.; *pg.* 1725, *pg.* 121
Chilton, Don, VP-Product Mgmt - Affinia Group Intermediate Holdings Inc.; *pg.* 197, *pg.* 1373
Chin, Caroline, Dir-Digital Brand Mktg - Ralph Lauren Corporation; *pg.* 46, *pg.* 1284
Chin, Erin, Dir-Mktg - Proximo Spirits, Inc.; *pg.* 1969, *pg.* 1076
Chin, Jason, Sr Mgr-Mktg - Reser's Fine Foods Inc.; *pg.* 1032, *pg.* 1496
Chin, Jeff, Dir-Product Mktg-BU Semiconductor - Littelfuse, Inc.; *pg.* 1301, *pg.* 580
Chin, Jim, VP-Sls - Newly Weds Foods, Inc.; *pg.* 886, *pg.* 585
Chin, John, Reg Mgr-Sls - Magnetic Metals Corp.; *pg.* 1358, *pg.* 1049
Chin, Karen, Counsel-Mktg & Consumer Law - Cellco Partnership; *pg.* 1869, *pg.* 1042
Chin, Michelle, VP-Integrated Mktg, Comm & Loyalty-North America - Godiva Chocolatier, Inc.; *pg.* 1854, *pg.* 1235
Chin, Robert, VP-Mktg Svcs - E&J Gallo Winery; *pg.* 1962, *pg.* 149
Chin-You, Lisa, Planner-Digital Media - The Atlanta Journal-Constitution; *pg.* 1618, *pg.* 490
China, Ernesto, Dir-Global Midsize Bus Mktg - NetApp, Inc.; *pg.* 444, *pg.* 287
Ching, Albert, VP-Sls & Mktg-Asia-Pacific & China Regions - Printronix, Inc.; *pg.* 456, *pg.* 115
Ching, Andrea, Sr VP-CNN & Turner Digital Mktg & Promos - Turner Broadcasting System, Inc.; *pg.* 314, *pg.* 521
Ching, Connie, Dir-New Member Direct Mail Mktg - American Express Company; *pg.* 712, *pg.* 1190
Ching, Daisy, Campaign Planner-Mktg Solutions - LinkedIn Corporation; *pg.* 1262, *pg.* 160
Ching, Francis, Dir-Sls-Westbound, MCI & Military - Polynesian Cultural Center; *pg.* 577, *pg.* 545
Chiniaeff, Teresa, VP-Adv Sls - The Outdoor Channel; *pg.* 303, *pg.* 291
Chiovaro, Lisa, Sr Mgr-Segment Mktg - T-Mobile US, Inc.; *pg.* 676, *pg.* 1816
Chipman, Jack, VP-Sls - Amy's Kitchen, Inc.; *pg.* 837, *pg.* 276
Chipman, Paul S., VP-Sls & Strategy - Toppan Photomasks, Inc.; *pg.* 1432, *pg.* 1739
Chirico, Tom, VP-Digital, Social Mktg & Engagement - MTVN Video Hits Inc.; *pg.* 299, *pg.* 1263
Chirillo, Sarah, Sr Mgr-Trade Mktg - Newell Rubbermaid Inc.; *pg.* 1128, *pg.* 515
Chirsty, Lena, Mgr-PR - Motorola Mobility LLC; *pg.* 657, *pg.* 627
Chisholm, Gordon, Dir-Field Mktg - Bacardi USA, Inc.; *pg.* 1956, *pg.* 417
Chisholm, Karen, Dir-BRM, Customer Mktg, Mktg & Innovation - Diageo North America Inc.; *pg.* 248, *pg.* 1223
Chisholm, Matt, Mgr-Media Rels - San Francisco Giants Baseball Club; *pg.* 581, *pg.* 226
Chislett, Melanie, Asst Mgr-Mktg - Nestle Canada Inc.; *pg.* 883, *pg.* 1929
Chism, Brent, Dir-Mktg-Dr Pepper, Crush & Schweppes - Dr Pepper Snapple Group, Inc.; *pg.* 250, *pg.* 1729
Chism, Eric, Sr Mgr-Direct to Consumer Mktg & CRM - Spanx Inc.; *pg.* 32, *pg.* 520
Chism, Michelle, Dir-Corp Comm & PR - CEC Entertainment, Inc.; *pg.* 1721, *pg.* 1717
Chisolm, David, VP-Mktg - A.O. Smith Corporation; *pg.* 1313, *pg.* 1872
Chisum, Steve, Sr Mgr-Bus Dev - United Parcel Service, Inc.; *pg.* 1928, *pg.* 522
Chitkara, Vinod, Sr VP-Sls & Mktg - L-3 Communications Narda Microwave-East; *pg.* 650, *pg.* 1165
Chittaro, Gary, Mgr-Mktg Svcs - EIS, Inc.; *pg.* 80, *pg.* 504
Chitwood, Ami, Sr Mgr-Social Media Team - Deloitte & Touche USA LLP; *pg.* 743, *pg.* 1222
Chitwood, Natalie, Mgr-Global Brand Procurement & Production - Columbia Sportswear Company; *pg.* 1830, *pg.* 1501
Chiu, Adrian, Sr Mgr-Bus Strategy & Product & Planner - Microsoft Corporation; *pg.* 435, *pg.* 1824
Chiu, Arthur, Dir-Strategic Mktg - Chemtura Corporation; *pg.* 1152, *pg.* 355
Chiu, Carlie, Dir-Mktg - Google Inc.; *pg.* 1249, *pg.* 153
Chiu, Dennis, Dir-Mktg - Focus Features; *pg.* 287, *pg.* 273
Chiu, Jack, Acct Mgr-Sls - Antec Incorporated; *pg.* 350, *pg.* 90
Chiu, Lawrence, Sr Product Mgr-Office 365 - Microsoft Corporation; *pg.* 435, *pg.* 1824
Chivington, Brad, VP-Mktg-Turkey Hill Minit Markets & Div of Kroger - Turkey Hill Dairy, Inc.; *pg.* 902, *pg.* 1522
Chizmadia, Tom, Sr VP-Govt Affairs, PR & Sustainability - Lehigh Hanson, Inc.; *pg.* 93, *pg.* 1513
Chlopecki, Melissa, Product Mgr - MORNINGSTAR, INC.; *pg.* 784, *pg.* 583
Chmura, Michael, Dir-PR - Babson College; *pg.* 598, *pg.* 784
Cho, Andy, Sr Dir-ECommerce & Digital Analytics - Yurman Design, Inc.; *pg.* 15, *pg.* 1316
Cho, Daniel, Mgr-Digital Mktg - Turner Broadcasting System, Inc.; *pg.* 314, *pg.* 521
Cho, Elizabeth, Dir-Media & PR - Siemens Corporation; *pg.* 803, *pg.* 1291
Cho, Francis, Mgr-Image Events & Media - Giorgio Armani Corporation; *pg.* 25, *pg.* 1234
Cho, Hannah, Mgr-Mktg-Global-Scuderia Ferrari Orologi Watches - Movado Group, Inc.; *pg.* 10, *pg.* 1101
Cho, Jane, Product Mgr-Macy's Mdsg Grp - Macy's East; *pg.* 1777, *pg.* 1254
Cho, Jeannie, Sr Dir-Mktg-Doritos & Cheetos - Frito-Lay North America, Inc.; *pg.* 1853, *pg.* 1730
Cho, Jeannie, Sr Dir-Mktg-Doritos & Cheetos - PepsiCo, Inc.; *pg.* 259, *pg.* 1327
Cho, Jennifer, Sr Mgr-Brand Plng - The Gap, Inc.; *pg.* 1770, *pg.* 218
Cho, Pyounguk, Sr Principal & Product Mgr - Oracle Corporation; *pg.* 450, *pg.* 191
Cho, Stephen, Asst Product Mgr - Church & Dwight Co., Inc.; *pg.* 1153, *pg.* 1063
Cho, Stephen P., Dir-Bus Dev, Channels & Product Mgmt - Google Inc.; *pg.* 1249, *pg.* 153
Cho, Steve, Mgr-Mktg & Project Mgr - Samsung Electronics America, Inc.; *pg.* 669, *pg.* 1115
Cho, Winnie, Dir-Global Mktg-Skincare - Elizabeth Arden, Inc.; *pg.* 507, *pg.* 448
Chodera, Sarah, Mng Dir & Dir-Corp Mktg - Nuveen Investments, Inc.; *pg.* 788, *pg.* 586
Choe, Judy, VP-Integrated Adv Sls Mktg - Discovery Communications, Inc.; *pg.* 282, *pg.* 777
Choe, Robin, Dir-Customer Mktg-Asia Pacific Reg - MATTEL, INC.; *pg.* 962, *pg.* 81
Choi, Brian, Sr Product Mgr-Mktg - NVIDIA Corporation; *pg.* 447, *pg.* 268
Choi, Cathy, Dir-Social Media - Sephora USA Inc; *pg.* 522, *pg.* 227
Choi, Criswell, Mgr-Product Mktg - SanDisk Corporation; *pg.* 465, *pg.* 147
Choi, Dario, VP-Sls-Asia Pacific Reg - Harmonic, Inc.; *pg.* 402, *pg.* 246
Choi, Everlyn, Dir-Mktg - CB Richard Ellis Group, Inc.; *pg.* 1085, *pg.* 127
Choi, Henry, Sr Mgr-Adv Budget - Ross Stores, Inc.; *pg.* 1783, *pg.* 78
Choi, Irene, Sr Mgr-Email Mktg - The Children's Place, Inc.; *pg.* 22, *pg.* 1119
Choi, Jennifer, Dir-Digital Mktg-Global - Tiffany & Co.; *pg.* 13, *pg.* 1299
Choi, Jinu, Mgr-Product Mktg - Lantronix, Inc.; *pg.* 426, *pg.* 112
Choi, John D., Sr Mgr-PR - Cisco Systems, Inc.; *pg.* 372, *pg.* 240
Choi, Min, Dir-Sls & Mktg Ops - Mercury Insurance Company; *pg.* 1208, *pg.* 136
Choi, Sharon, Sr Mgr-CRM & Email Mktg - Guess?, Inc.; *pg.* 25, *pg.* 132
Choi, Stephanie, Brand Mgr-Innovation - Starbucks Corporation; *pg.* 897, *pg.* 1840
Choi, Tanya, Sr Mgr-Mktg - Sephora USA Inc; *pg.* 522, *pg.* 227
Chokachi, Susan, Sr VP-Mktg & Comm - Gucci America Inc.; *pg.* 6, *pg.* 1237
Chomiak, Carrie, Head-US Mktg Franchise & Sr Dir - Pfizer Inc.; *pg.* 1581, *pg.* 1278
Chong, Alyssa, Mgr-Digital Mktg & Online Retail - Keurig Green Mountain, Inc.; *pg.* 868, *pg.* 1768
Chong, Joseph, Mgr-Product Mktg - Twitter, Inc.; *pg.* 1285, *pg.* 228
Chong, Leanne, Sr Mgr-Mktg Enablement & Ops - Royal Bank of Canada; *pg.* 800, *pg.* 1942
Chope, Ric, Dir-Mktg - Cadence Design Systems, Inc.; *pg.* 367, *pg.* 239
Chopey, Chris, Sr Dir-Suites & Premium Sls & Svc - Sacramento Kings; *pg.* 579, *pg.* 197
Chopra, Rajat, Sr Mgr-Mobile - Bell Canada; *pg.* 1936, *pg.* 1960
Choroco, Katherine Kim, Exec Dir-Mktg-Men's Fragrances - Chanel, Inc.; *pg.* 503, *pg.* 1211
Choromanski, David, Sr Dir-Consumer Mktg-ICL Product Line - STAAR Surgical Company; *pg.* 1597, *pg.* 151
Chose, David, Mgr-Sls-Identification Technologies-North America - HID Global Corporation; *pg.* 1416, *pg.* 111
Chou, Jack, Head-Product - Pinterest; *pg.* 1275, *pg.* 225
Chou, Jonathan H., Interim CEO - Kulicke & Soffa Industries, Inc.; *pg.* 650, *pg.* 1533
Chou, Phidias, VP-Sls-Worldwide - Super Micro Computer, Inc.; *pg.* 478, *pg.* 251
Chou, Rachel, Sr Mgr-Consumer Comm - Texas Beef Council; *pg.* 158, *pg.* 1666
Chou, William, Exec Dir-CV Mktg, Brand Max & Established Medicines - Novartis Pharmaceuticals Corp.; *pg.* 1575, *pg.*

1054
Choudhary, Salahuddin, Product Mgr-Google Mobile Maps & Local Search - Google Inc.; *pg.* 1249, *pg.* 153
Choudhuri, Bhaskar, Dir-Mktg - Lenovo Group Ltd; *pg.* 427, *pg.* 1384
Choudhuri, Roy, Sr Product Mgr - VMware, Inc.; *pg.* 490, *pg.* 179
Chouinard, Raymond, Dir-Media & PR - Royal Bank of Canada; *pg.* 800, *pg.* 1942
Chow, Amandine, Sr Mgr-Digital Mktg - Bloomingdale's, Inc.; *pg.* 1763, *pg.* 1204
Chow, Anne, Sr VP-Solutions & Sls Ops-Global - AT&T Inc.; *pg.* 1867, *pg.* 1674
Chow, Jeanette, Dir-Creative-The Parents Network - Meredith Corporation; *pg.* 1663, *pg.* 705
Chow, Jeanne, Sr Dir-On-Air Mktg - NBC Universal, Inc.; *pg.* 300, *pg.* 1266
Chow, Jeanne, Sr Dir-On-Air Mktg - USA Networks; *pg.* 315, *pg.* 1308
Chow, Katherine, Sr Mgr-R&D - Athleta; *pg.* 19, *pg.* 181
Chow, Kristie, Product Mgr - Facebook, Inc.; *pg.* 1245, *pg.* 143
Chow, Maria, Dir-Event Mktg - athenahealth, Inc.; *pg.* 1497, *pg.* 855
Chow, Marvin, Sr Dir-Global Mktg-Google+ - Google Inc.; *pg.* 1249, *pg.* 153
Chow, Pauline, Sr Dir-Global Sourcing & Product Dev-Loft, LOS & Corp Accessories - Ann Inc.; *pg.* 18, *pg.* 1195
Chow, Terri, Sr Mgr-Mktg-Program Dev - Molson Coors Canada Inc.; *pg.* 256, *pg.* 1955
Chowdhury, Tariq, Chief Architect-Comm Products - Comcast Corporation; *pg.* 276, *pg.* 1560
Chown, Amy, VP-Mktg - The Atlanta Journal-Constitution; *pg.* 1618, *pg.* 490
Choy, May, Bus Mgr - Penguin Random House; *pg.* 1675, *pg.* 1276
Choy, Nathalie, Mgr-Web Mktg Ops - Kia Motors America Inc.; *pg.* 181, *pg.* 112
Choy, Patrick, Dir-Product Mgmt - Newegg Inc.; *pg.* 1271, *pg.* 67
Chrapaty, Alicia, Sr Mgr-Mktg - AOL Inc.; *pg.* 1229, *pg.* 1195
Chretien, Jean-Luc, Exec VP-Distr Sls & Loyalty - Accor; *pg.* 1079, *pg.* 1657
Chrietzberg, Emily, Dir-TLC Integrated Mktg - Discovery Communications, Inc.; *pg.* 282, *pg.* 777
Chris, Roux, Mgr-Mktg Programs-Pub Sector - PC Connection, Inc.; *pg.* 452, *pg.* 1036
Chrislip, Mark, Dir-Sls & Mktg - White's Electronics; *pg.* 688, *pg.* 1509
Chrisman, Kelly, Brand Mgr - eBay Inc.; *pg.* 1240, *pg.* 243
Chrisman, Kenneth P., Pres-Product Care Div - Sealed Air Corporation; *pg.* 1468, *pg.* 1058
Chriss, Stephen, Sr Dir-Consumer Engagement & Mktg Svcs-North America - Mondelez International; *pg.* 877, *pg.* 1344
Christa-Cathey, Judy, VP-Global Brand Mktg-Hampton Hotels & Hilton Garden Inn - Hilton Worldwide, Inc.; *pg.* 1094, *pg.* 1791
Christaldi, Mark, Dir-Global Products, Partnerships & Emerging Tech - AstraZeneca Pharmaceuticals LP; *pg.* 1497, *pg.* 389
Christanell, Corey, Dir-Sports & Entertainment Mktg - Anheuser-Busch Companies, LLC; *pg.* 237, *pg.* 991
Christen, Kimberlie, Sr Mgr-Mobile Mktg - Redbox Automated Retail, LLC; *pg.* 306, *pg.* 649
Christensen Araujo, Karen, Dir-Product Mktg - American Medical Association; *pg.* 130, *pg.* 564
Christensen, Adam, Sr Dir-Comm, Integrated Mktg & Social Media-PayPal - PayPal Inc.; *pg.* 1274, *pg.* 248
Christensen, Cole, Strategist-Mktg - 3M Company; *pg.* 1142, *pg.* 956
Christensen, Dawn, Sr Dir-Comm - Las Vegas Convention & Visitors Authority; *pg.* 997, *pg.* 1027
Christensen, Eric D., Reg VP-Mktg - Embraer Aircraft Holding Inc.; *pg.* 227, *pg.* 425
Christensen, John, Dir-Sls & Adv-Natl - Our Sunday Visitor, Inc.; *pg.* 1673, *pg.* 682
Christensen, Melissa, Dir-Mktg-Media & Entertainment Mktg Programs - Autodesk Inc.; *pg.* 356, *pg.* 257
Christensen, Michael, Dir-Creative - Big Apple Circus Ltd.; *pg.* 533, *pg.* 1145
Christensen, Monica, Brand Mgr - Robert Bosch Tool Corp; *pg.* 1060, *pg.* 634
Christensen, Nicole, Sr Mgr-Product Mktg-Origin - Electronic Arts Inc.; *pg.* 951, *pg.* 189
Christensen, Robert, Dir-Product Mgmt - Samsung Electronics America, Inc.; *pg.* 669, *pg.* 1115
Christensen, Susan, Sr Dir-Corp Comm - ConAgra Foods, Inc.; *pg.* 826, *pg.* 1014
Christensen, Susan, VP-Sls - Crown Crafts Infant Products, Inc.; *pg.* 922, *pg.* 68
Christensen, Susan, VP-Mktg - Farmers National Company; *pg.* 703, *pg.* 1015
Christensen, Thomas, Mgr-Mktg-Global - Chr. Hansen; *pg.* 847, *pg.* 1873
Christensen, Tiffany, Planner-Mktg - Humana, Inc.; *pg.* 1204, *pg.* 734
Christenson, Mark, Assoc Dir-Mktg-Global Fabric Care Innovation - The Procter & Gamble Company; *pg.* 1129, *pg.* 1418
Christenson, Phil, Sr Product Mgr-Tech - Expedia, Inc.; *pg.* 1244, *pg.* 1814
Christian, Bryan, Sr Mgr-Category Mktg - Time Inc.; *pg.* 1693, *pg.* 1300
Christian, Cameron, VP-Mktg - Frontier Communications Corporation; *pg.* 1871, *pg.* 362
Christian, Chris, VP-Mktg - California Strawberry Commission; *pg.* 135, *pg.* 305
Christian, Dana, Mgr-Adv - Foxworth-Galbraith Lumber Company; *pg.* 1047, *pg.* 1730
Christian, Danial, Dir-Product Mgmt & Bus Dev - Overhead Door Corporation; *pg.* 102, *pg.* 1725
Christian, Daniel, Sr Product Mgr-Bus Dev, Mergers & Acq - Wayne-Dalton Corp.; *pg.* 120, *pg.* 1465
Christian, Kerri, Dir-Mktg - The Home Depot, Inc.; *pg.* 1050, *pg.* 510
Christian, Mark, Sr Dir-Online Mktg - Google Inc.; *pg.* 1249, *pg.* 153
Christian, Susan, VP-Sls Ops - Vascular Solutions, Inc.; *pg.* 1434, *pg.* 946
Christian, Victoria, Sr Mgr-Mktg-Global - Amgen Inc.; *pg.* 1493, *pg.* 291
Christiano, Rob, Exec VP-Mktg-Global - Bulova Corporation; *pg.* 2, *pg.* 1356
Christiansen, Anna, Mgr-Mktg Comm - SanDisk Corporation; *pg.* 465, *pg.* 147
Christiansen, Dale, Mgr-Sls & Convenience Channel - American Foods Group, LLC; *pg.* 837, *pg.* 1859
Christiansen, Kristina, Dir-Digital Sls-Martha Stewart Digital - Meredith Corporation; *pg.* 1663, *pg.* 705
Christiansen, Mark, Assoc Product Mgr - Tennant Company; *pg.* 1381, *pg.* 944
Christiansen, Maureen, Sr Dir-Customer Mktg - Bolthouse Farms; *pg.* 841, *pg.* 44
Christiansen, Rachel, Head-Mycogen Seeds Portfolio Mktg-Soybeans - Dow AgroSciences LLC; *pg.* 1156, *pg.* 684
Christianson, Eric, VP-Mktg - Perdue Farms Incorporated; *pg.* 889, *pg.* 777
Christie, Andrew, Assoc Mgr-Media Rels - American Airlines Group Inc.; *pg.* 224, *pg.* 1693
Christie, Anthony, CMO - Level 3 Communications, Inc.; *pg.* 1262, *pg.* 312
Christie, Holly, Second VP-Strategic Mktg & Comm - Travelers Insurance; *pg.* 1220, *pg.* 963
Christie, Julie, Mgr-Worldwide Campaign-IBM Global Alliances & Acct Focused Mktg - IBM; *pg.* 410, *pg.* 1449
Christie, Nick, Brand Mgr-Creative - Tilted Kilt Franchise Operating LLC; *pg.* 1754, *pg.* 27
Christie, Tom, Exec VP-Affiliate Sls - Showtime Networks Inc.; *pg.* 308, *pg.* 1291
Christley, Jason, Sr Mgr-Comm-Reg & Touring Series - National Association for Stock Car Auto Racing; *pg.* 566, *pg.* 420
Christman, Diane, Sr VP-Mktg & Dev - The Cable Center; *pg.* 535, *pg.* 317
Christman, Gregg, Sr Product Mgr-Database Performance - Oracle Corporation; *pg.* 450, *pg.* 191
Christman, Suzanne, Sr Mgr-Bus Dev - Pinellas County Economic Development; *pg.* 1004, *pg.* 416
Christnacht, Robert, Dir-Wholesale Sls-Worldwide - Pendleton Woolen Mills, Inc.; *pg.* 697, *pg.* 1505
Christoffersen, Adam, District Mgr-Sls - Winnebago Industries, Inc.; *pg.* 1712, *pg.* 707
Christon, Alexa, Head-Media Innovation - General Electric Company; *pg.* 1297, *pg.* 347
Christoph, Kathleen, Sr Specialist-Mktg Automation - Thermo Fisher Scientific Inc.; *pg.* 1431, *pg.* 854
Christopher, Allison, Specialist-Mktg - Cousins Properties Incorporated; *pg.* 1088, *pg.* 501
Christopher, Clay, Sr Dir-Corp Sponsorships - Dallas Mavericks; *pg.* 543, *pg.* 1678
Christopher, Debbie, Dir-Integrated Mktg - FMR LLC (Fidelity Investments); *pg.* 759, *pg.* 794
Christopher, Gilbert, VP-Mktg - Insulet Corporation; *pg.* 644, *pg.* 785
Christopher, Keri, Reg Mgr-Mktg - PepsiCo, Inc.; *pg.* 259, *pg.* 1327
Christopher, Leonard, Mgr-Future Products - Eastman Kodak Company; *pg.* 1408, *pg.* 1333
Christopher, Nathan, Exec Dir-PR - The Hearst Corporation; *pg.* 1649, *pg.* 1239
Christopher, Ryan, Producer-Trade Mktg - Tumblr, Inc.; *pg.* 1285, *pg.* 1305
Christopher, Scott, Assoc Mgr-Product Mktg-Google Partners - Google Inc.; *pg.* 1249, *pg.* 153
Christopherson, Mark, Mgr-CDJ Sls - Dave Syverson Inc.; *pg.* 168, *pg.* 915
Christopherson, Roger, Product Dev Mgr - Medtronic, Inc.; *pg.* 1564, *pg.* 939
Christopoulos, Christine, Coord-Sls & Mktg - Chicago Bears Football Club, Inc.; *pg.* 538, *pg.* 623
Christopoulos, Thomas, Engr-Technical Mktg - Cisco Systems, Inc.; *pg.* 372, *pg.* 240
Christou, Lorri, Sr VP-Strategic Mktg & Comm - Cruise Lines International Association, Inc.; *pg.* 138, *pg.* 424
Christus, Matthew, VP-Product Ops-Global - Epicor Software Corporation; *pg.* 393, *pg.* 110
Christy, Betsy Reuther, Sr Dir-Fin - Miami Dolphins, Ltd.; *pg.* 562, *pg.* 419
Christy, Kevin D., Sr Mgr-Customer Support & OEM Liaison - BE Aerospace, Inc.; *pg.* 224, *pg.* 478
Chronic, Jan, Div Dir-Mktg, Comm, Brand & Sls Div - National FFA Organization; *pg.* 149, *pg.* 688
Chrudimsky, Brad, Specialist-Product-Gen Purpose & Severe Duty Motors - Baldor Electric Company; *pg.* 1316, *pg.* 32
Chrysafidis, Jordan, VP-US Sls & Mktg-OEM - Microsoft Corporation; *pg.* 435, *pg.* 1824
Chu, Alan, Sr VP-Media Grp - Smithsonian Magazine; *pg.* 1687, *pg.* 404
Chu, Andy, Head-Product Mktg-Energy Storage Solutions - Applied Materials, Inc.; *pg.* 618, *pg.* 264
Chu, April, Mgr-Field Mktg-Corp & Inside Sls - Equinix, Inc.; *pg.* 394, *pg.* 190
Chu, Carmen, Dir-CRM, Retention Mktg & Experimentation - Macy's East; *pg.* 1777, *pg.* 1254
Chu, Charissa, VP-Intl Mktg & Creative Svcs - NBC Universal, Inc.; *pg.* 300, *pg.* 1266
Chu, Daniel, Grp Product Mgr-Google Self-Driving Car - Google Inc.; *pg.* 1249, *pg.* 153
Chu, Helen, Sr Mgr-Mktg - Fisher-Price, Inc.; *pg.* 953, *pg.* 1156
Chu, Humby, Analyst-Search & Auction Media - The Walt Disney Company; *pg.* 317, *pg.* 52
Chu, Jeannie, Dir-Brand, Mktg & Comm - American Express Company; *pg.* 712, *pg.* 1190
Chu, Jennifer, Mgr-Product Innovation - Plum Organics; *pg.* 890, *pg.* 85
Chu, Joanne, Sr Product Mgr-Global Mktg-Pfizer Consumer Healthcare - Pfizer Inc.; *pg.* 1581, *pg.* 1278
Chu, Peter, VP-Strategy & Product Mgmt - BroadVision, Inc.; *pg.* 365, *pg.* 189
Chu, Serena, Brand Mgr - Neutrogena Corporation; *pg.* 517, *pg.* 137
Chu, Yiatin, Sr VP-Mktg - WebMD Health Corporation; *pg.* 1288, *pg.* 1313
Chuang, James, Mgr-Technical Mktg - Synopsys, Inc.; *pg.* 480, *pg.* 162
Chuckarbutty, Abhishek, Dir-Mktg-Korea - Reckitt Benckiser Inc.; *pg.* 1136, *pg.* 1105
Chufo, Christine, Mgr-Customer Mktg-Intl - Clif Bar Inc.; *pg.* 848, *pg.* 83
Chughtai, Sam, Sr Mgr-Mktg-Content & Project Mgmt - 1-800-Flowers.com, Inc.; *pg.* 1758, *pg.* 1151
Chuh, Jeff, Dir-Retail Product Mktg & Visual Mdsg - Skullcandy, Inc.; *pg.* 674, *pg.* 1754
Chulick, Caroline, Dir-Mktg-Softsoap - Colgate-Palmolive Company; *pg.* 504, *pg.* 1215
Chumbley, Nicole, Sr Dir-Strategic Partnerships & Bus Dev - General Growth Properties, Inc.; *pg.* 1093, *pg.* 574
Chumley, Amy, Dir-Digital Ad Sls Mktg Activation - Scripps Networks Interactive, Inc.; *pg.* 1279, *pg.* 1638
Chun, Amy, Sr Brand Mgr-Shopper Mktg CVS - Colgate-Palmolive Company; *pg.* 504, *pg.* 1215
Chun, Betty, Brand Mgr - Solo Cup Company; *pg.* 1469, *pg.* 625
Chun, Brad, Sr Dir-Engrg - Hawaiian Airlines, Inc.; *pg.* 1910,

pg. 543
Chun, Gina, Dir-Consumer Mktg - Hawaii Visitors & Convention Bureau; *pg.* 994, *pg.* 543
Chun, Hena, Coord-Mktg & Comm - Ralph Lauren Corporation; *pg.* 46, *pg.* 1284
Chun, Jennifer, Sr VP-Media Distr-Global - National Basketball Association; *pg.* 566, *pg.* 1264
Chun, Ted, Analyst-Online Mktg - Manulife Financial Corporation; *pg.* 778, *pg.* 1939
Chung, Bsa, Sr Mgr-Product Mktg & Bus Mgmt - SanDisk Corporation; *pg.* 465, *pg.* 147
Chung, Connie, Sr Product Mgr-Payments - Expedia, Inc.; *pg.* 1244, *pg.* 1814
Chung, Danny, Mgr-Digital Mktg & Social Media - D.V.F. Studios; *pg.* 24, *pg.* 1226
Chung, David, Mgr-Mktg Partnership Strategy & Integration-Natl - Toyota Motor North America, Inc.; *pg.* 192, *pg.* 1303
Chung, David, Mgr-Mktg Partnership Strategy & Integration-Natl - Toyota Motor Sales, U.S.A., Inc.; *pg.* 193, *pg.* 296
Chung, Elena, Brand Mgr-Canned Fruit - Del Monte Foods, Inc.; *pg.* 852, *pg.* 304
Chung, Grace, Specialist-PR - Amazon.com, Inc.; *pg.* 1226, *pg.* 1831
Chung, Janet, Mgr-Partner Svcs Mktg Comm - Cisco Systems, Inc.; *pg.* 372, *pg.* 240
Chung, Jennifer, Brand Mgr - GlaxoSmithKline Consumer Healthcare; *pg.* 510, *pg.* 1554
Chung, Richard, Dir-Worldwide Technical Mktg - Fairchild Semiconductor Corporation; *pg.* 638, *pg.* 245
Chung, Will, Dir-Bus Dev & Mdsg - Sephora USA Inc; *pg.* 522, *pg.* 227
Chungu, Charlie, Sr Mgr-Mktg - Charles River Laboratories, Inc.; *pg.* 1475, *pg.* 360
Chupick, Jason, Dir-PR-Hearst Magazines Digital Media - The Hearst Corporation; *pg.* 1649, *pg.* 1239
Chupin, Fred, VP-Mktg-North America - Henkel Corporation; *pg.* 1165, *pg.* 1535
Chupin, Frederic, VP-Mktg & Trade Mktg-North America - Henkel Corporation; *pg.* 1049, *pg.* 369
Chupp, Bryan, Dir-Digital Mktg - Pfizer Inc.; *pg.* 1581, *pg.* 1278
Church, Doug, VP-Mktg & Sls - Pacific Press Publishing Association; *pg.* 1674, *pg.* 550
Church, Heather, Mgr-Online Mktg-Consumer Digital Experience - AT&T; *pg.* 1865, *pg.* 258
Church, Justin, Sr Mgr-Insights - LinkedIn Corporation; *pg.* 1262, *pg.* 160
Church, Lisa, Head-Channel Mktg - The Dun & Bradstreet Corp.; *pg.* 1637, *pg.* 1120
Church, Steve, Sr Dir-Bus Unit Comm - Georgia-Pacific LLC; *pg.* 1458, *pg.* 507
Church, Susanna, Principal-Campaign Mktg - Adobe Systems Incorporated; *pg.* 342, *pg.* 235
Church, Whitney, Mgr-Seasonal Mktg-Mars Chocolate North America - Mars, Incorporated; *pg.* 1858, *pg.* 1792
Churchill, Angela, Sr Mgr-Mktg-Northeast Div - Comcast Corporation; *pg.* 276, *pg.* 1560
Churchill, Gabriella, Mgr-Mktg Comm - Federal Signal Corporation; *pg.* 638, *pg.* 645
Churchill, Liz, VP-Sls & Mktg - Matthews International Corporation; *pg.* 1662, *pg.* 1578
Churchill, Marcella, Sr Dir-Mktg - Sega of America Inc.; *pg.* 966, *pg.* 227
Churchill, Randy, Sr Mgr-Bus Dev & Mktg - D&H Distributing Co., Inc.; *pg.* 381, *pg.* 1536
Churchill, Ron, Dir-Creative Svcs - Schawk Canada Inc.; *pg.* 1683, *pg.* 1928
Chwan, Jamie, Product Mgr-ECommerce - Dick's Sporting Goods, Inc.; *pg.* 1832, *pg.* 1524
Chyu, Erika, Mgr-Mktg-Small & Medium Bus - Facebook, Inc.; *pg.* 1245, *pg.* 143
Ciaccia, Grace, Dir-Integrated Adv - Coach, Inc.; *pg.* 3, *pg.* 1214
Cianfrocca, Mike, Dir-PR - Charles Schwab; *pg.* 1235, *pg.* 1661
Ciangiulli, Lisa, Dir-Mktg-Optism Mobile Commerce & Payment Solutions - Alcatel-Lucent USA, Inc.; *pg.* 615, *pg.* 1728
Ciantra, Nicholas, VP-Brand & Creative Svcs - Liberty Mutual Insurance Group Inc.; *pg.* 1205, *pg.* 797
Ciappina, Nino, Dir-Acq Mktg - Gilt Groupe Inc.; *pg.* 24, *pg.* 1234
Ciarallo, Joe, Sr Dir-PR - salesforce.com, inc.; *pg.* 1278, *pg.* 226
Ciaramita, Jeff M., Sr Dir-Special Events & Stewardship - Chicago Theatre Group Inc.; *pg.* 539, *pg.* 570
Ciaramitaro, Charlie, Dir-Digital Access Mktg-FedEx Svcs - FedEx Corporation; *pg.* 1907, *pg.* 1642
Ciarcia, Michael, Dir-Digital Creative - Time Inc.; *pg.* 1693, *pg.* 1300
Ciardi, Marisa, Brand Mgr - Mondelez International, Inc.; *pg.* 878, *pg.* 601
Ciarkowski, Laura, Dir-Value Add Mktg - New York Life Insurance Company; *pg.* 1211, *pg.* 1268
Ciavarra, Christopher A., Sr VP-Mktg - Cracker Barrel Old Country Store, Inc.; *pg.* 1723, *pg.* 1639
Ciaverelli, Eric, Sr Mgr-Decision Analytics - Sanofi US; *pg.* 1592, *pg.* 1046
Cibik, Kaylee, Mgr-Corp Mktg Programs - Jeld-Wen, Inc.; *pg.* 1051, *pg.* 1499
Cibor, Frank, Mgr-Eccentric Retail Adv - HomeTown Communications Network, Inc.; *pg.* 1650, *pg.* 904
Cicale, Ed, VP-Media - AutoNation, Inc.; *pg.* 165, *pg.* 423
Cicarone, Stella, Sr Dir-Mktg - Party City Corporation; *pg.* 1781, *pg.* 1116
Ciccarelli, Jan, Dir-Mktg & Community Rels - Presence Health; *pg.* 1586, *pg.* 587
Ciccarello, Chris, Sr Dir-Pricing & Customer Analytics - ConAgra Foods, Inc.; *pg.* 826, *pg.* 1014
Ciccarone, Steve, Dir-Mid-Mktg Sls - Constellation Energy Resources, LLC; *pg.* 1938, *pg.* 756
Ciccolini, Jon, Sr Mgr-Mktg - Blue Shield of California; *pg.* 1195, *pg.* 214
Ciccone, Jessica, Sr Dir-Content - New York Jets Football Club, Inc.; *pg.* 570, *pg.* 1067
Ciccone, Rob, CMO/Chief Product Officer-American Express Centurion - American Express Company; *pg.* 712, *pg.* 1190
Ciccone, Terri, Editor-Social Media-Decider.com - The New York Post; *pg.* 1668, *pg.* 1269
Cicero, Sara, Mgr-PR - Cisco Systems, Inc.; *pg.* 372, *pg.* 240
Cicero, Stacey, Mgr-Mktg Strategies & Programs - KPMG LLP; *pg.* 774, *pg.* 1086
Ciciliano, Claudia, Sr Mgr-Digital & CRM - Novartis Corporation; *pg.* 1574, *pg.* 1273
Cicogna, Frances, Mgr-Product Mktg - Canon U.S.A., Inc.; *pg.* 1404, *pg.* 1178
Cicola, Amanda, Brand Mgr - The Scotts Miracle-Gro Company; *pg.* 1799, *pg.* 1459
Cielocha, Gina, Sr Dir-Mktg - Empire Today, LLC; *pg.* 923, *pg.* 643
Ciernia, Paul C., VP-Sls Ops - Cray Inc.; *pg.* 380, *pg.* 1834
Ciervo, Chris, Sr Mgr-Product & Mktg-Lifestyle & Awareness Solutions - Honeywell International Inc.; *pg.* 407, *pg.* 1088
Cieslak, Kimberly L., VP-Mktg - LeMaitre Vascular, Inc.; *pg.* 1555, *pg.* 805
Cieslik, David, Mgr-Creative Svcs Power Tools & Accessories - Robert Bosch Tool Corp; *pg.* 1060, *pg.* 634
Cieszynski, Andrew, Sr Planner-Mdse-Men's Outlet Div - Pacific Sunwear of California, Inc.; *pg.* 1781, *pg.* 43
Cifelli, Claire, Analyst-Digital Mktg & Adv - Sony Pictures Entertainment Inc.; *pg.* 309, *pg.* 72
Cifrese, Alison, Mgr-Mktg-Kerastase - L'Oreal USA; *pg.* 514, *pg.* 1252
Cifu, Amanda, Coord-Comm & Digital Media - Florida Panthers Hockey Club, Ltd.; *pg.* 548, *pg.* 469
Cigarran, Jason, VP-Corp Mktg & Comm - Comverge, Inc.; *pg.* 1325, *pg.* 536
Cihock, Steve, Mgr-Adv, Promos & Events - Komatsu America Corp.; *pg.* 92, *pg.* 655
Cima, Kathryn, Mgr-Adv-Natl - Kia Motors America Inc.; *pg.* 181, *pg.* 112
Cimato, Fernando A., Mgr-Channel Partner Sls & Mktg - Hewlett-Packard Company; *pg.* 404, *pg.* 175
Cimilluca, Greg, Dir-Product Mgmt - National Geographic Society; *pg.* 1667, *pg.* 402
Cincu, Sally, Sr Dir-News, Info & Employee Comm-Global - Hewlett-Packard Company; *pg.* 404, *pg.* 175
Cindric, Lucy, Sr VP & Gen Mgr-Mdse - Big Lots, Inc.; *pg.* 1762, *pg.* 1438
Cinelli, Joshua, Chief Media Rels Officer - The Ford Foundation; *pg.* 141, *pg.* 1232
Cinelli, Melissa, Assoc Product Mgr - Leviton Manufacturing Company, Inc.; *pg.* 1301, *pg.* 1180
Cinotti, Carolyn, Dir-PR-Global - Bose Corporation; *pg.* 626, *pg.* 820
Cio, Michelle, Sr Specialist-Mktg - Hitachi America, Ltd.; *pg.* 642, *pg.* 1344
Cioffi, Alana, Mgr-Product Line-Global Performance Apparel - Puma North America, Inc.; *pg.* 1816, *pg.* 858
Ciolek, David, Product Mgr-Retail Network - Mettler-Toledo International Inc.; *pg.* 1423, *pg.* 1441
Ciolek, Tina, Sr VP-Home Lending Portfolio Mktg - Wells Fargo & Company; *pg.* 819, *pg.* 232
Cipperman, David, Dir-Creative - Croscill, Inc.; *pg.* 1122, *pg.* 1220
Cippola, Becky, Coord-Mktg - W.W. Grainger, Inc.; *pg.* 1390, *pg.* 625
Cipra, Andrew R., VP-Mktg - DISH Network Corporation; *pg.* 283, *pg.* 325
Cipriano, Janelle, Acct Mgr-Global Creative Team - Electronic Arts Inc.; *pg.* 951, *pg.* 189
Cipriano, John, Mgr-Product Line-IOTG Internet of Things Grp - Intel Corporation; *pg.* 645, *pg.* 266
Ciraulo, John, VP-Mktg Meat Div - Stater Bros. Markets; *pg.* 1034, *pg.* 198
Cirella, Ed, Dir-Sls - Highfield Manufacturing Co.; *pg.* 1346, *pg.* 339
Ciriaco, Leslie, Sr Analyst-Process-Sls & Mktg Ops - Pacific Life Insurance Company; *pg.* 1213, *pg.* 166
Cirillo, Frank, Mgr-PR - Sterling Jewelers Inc.; *pg.* 13, *pg.* 1402
Cirino, Joe, Mgr-Mktg - Federal-Mogul Holdings Corporation; *pg.* 205, *pg.* 907
Cirulis, Suzy, VP-Mktg - Crate & Barrel, Inc.; *pg.* 922, *pg.* 640
Cisek, Kerry, Sr Head-Sourcing Processing-Mktg & Adv - Verizon Communications Inc.; *pg.* 1875, *pg.* 1309
Cissel, Kimberly, Sr Mgr-Customer Engagement & Integrated Strategy - Universal Orlando; *pg.* 590, *pg.* 456
Cistaro, Anthony, VP & Producer-Digital Mktg Audiovisual Production - BlackRock, Inc.; *pg.* 724, *pg.* 1203
Cisterna, Pedro, Mgr-Bus Sls - D-Link Systems, Inc.; *pg.* 381, *pg.* 89
Citrin, Steve, Sr Producer-Reg Adv-North America - Unilever United States, Inc.; *pg.* 904, *pg.* 1061
Citro, James, Sr Dir-Customer & Bus Insights - GlaxoSmithKline; *pg.* 1536, *pg.* 1565
Citro, James, Sr Dir-Customer & Bus Insights - GlaxoSmithKline Consumer Healthcare; *pg.* 510, *pg.* 1554
City, Terry, VP-Sls-West Coast - Buzzfeed; *pg.* 1233, *pg.* 1208
Ciuba, Mark, Mgr-Sls - Groov-Pin Corporation; *pg.* 1049, *pg.* 1608
Civa, Jack, Dir-Mktg - Taco Cabana, Inc.; *pg.* 1753, *pg.* 1743
Civello, Joe, Product Mgr-ADS-Eesof EDA - Agilent Technologies, Inc.; *pg.* 614, *pg.* 264
Civiello, Michael, Sr Dir-Mktg - Broadcom Corporation; *pg.* 364, *pg.* 108
Civik, Thomas, VP-Sls & Mktg-Avastin - Genentech, Inc.; *pg.* 1533, *pg.* 279
Civiletto, Marianne, Assoc Publr-Mktg - Redbook; *pg.* 1680, *pg.* 1285
Clabots, Amy, Mgr-PR - Ulta Salon, Cosmetics & Fragrance, Inc.; *pg.* 524, *pg.* 559
Clachko, Jeff, VP-Universal Sports Sls & Mktg - NBC Universal, Inc.; *pg.* 300, *pg.* 1266
Clack, Grace, Grp Mgr-Media - Nordstrom, Inc.; *pg.* 1779, *pg.* 1837
Claflin, Elizabeth, Mgr-Sls & Mktg - Vacuum Technology Associates, Inc.; *pg.* 1386, *pg.* 824
Claiborne, Trevor, Mgr-Product Mktg - Google Inc.; *pg.* 1249, *pg.* 153
Clair, Katy, Coord-Mktg-Global - Oregon Tourism Commission; *pg.* 1003, *pg.* 1508
Clairmont, Alan, Reg VP-Mktg & Sls - Comcast Corporation; *pg.* 276, *pg.* 1560
Clamme, Sandy, Dir-Adv - Marsh Supermarkets, Inc.; *pg.* 1027, *pg.* 688
Clancey, David, CTO, Chief Strategy Officer & Exec VP - Edgewater Technology, Inc.; *pg.* 389, *pg.* 848
Clancy, Suzanne, Sr Mgr-PR-Regulated Markets - Thermo Fisher Scientific Inc.; *pg.* 1602, *pg.* 61
Clancy-Gesell, Susan, Assoc Dir-Sls & Mktg Ops - ESPN, Inc.; *pg.* 285, *pg.* 340
Clanton, Steve, VP-Sls & Svcs - San Antonio Convention & Visitors Bureau; *pg.* 1004, *pg.* 1742
Clapham, Holly, VP-Mktg - Greater Houston Convention & Visitors Bureau; *pg.* 993, *pg.* 1706
Clapp, Tracey, Dir-Mktg-Vodka & Gin - Sazerac Company, Inc.; *pg.* 1969, *pg.* 745
Clar, Carmen, Specialist-Mktg Comm - SPX Process Equipment; *pg.* 1378, *pg.* 1337
Clardy, Vallory, Sr Analyst-Field Mktg - State Farm Mutual Automobile Insurance Co.; *pg.* 1218, *pg.* 557
Clarity, Jimmy, Coord-PR - Universal Orlando; *pg.* 590, *pg.* 456

First page reference indicates Business Class Edition
Second page reference indicates Geographic Edition

Clarizio, Lynda, Pres-Media-US - The Nielsen Company B.V.; *pg.* 1671, *pg.* 1272
Clark, Abby, VP-Sls - The Dispatch Printing Company; *pg.* 1636, *pg.* 1439
Clark, Alex, Head-Corp Comm & Sr Dir - Mattel Games/Puzzles; *pg.* 962, *pg.* 80
Clark, Alison, Sr Dir-Global Brand Mgmt-Marriott Hotels & Resorts - Marriott International, Inc.; *pg.* 1102, *pg.* 764
Clark, Alison, Sr Dir-Mktg & Comm - Teachers Insurance & Annuity Association - College Retirement Equities Fund; *pg.* 1219, *pg.* 1297
Clark, Amy, Mgr-Digital Mktg - BIC Corporation; *pg.* 501, *pg.* 369
Clark, Angie L., Partner & Mgr-Mktg - World Wide Technology Holding Co., Inc.; *pg.* 493, *pg.* 988
Clark, Anne, VP-Media & Adv - Sterling Jewelers Inc.; *pg.* 13, *pg.* 1402
Clark, Billy, VP-Sls, Retail Analytics & Client Svcs - HBG Books, Inc.; *pg.* 1648, *pg.* 1238
Clark, Bob, VP-Mktg - Herr Foods Inc.; *pg.* 861, *pg.* 1557
Clark, Bob, Mgr-Sls-East - Setra Systems, Inc.; *pg.* 1428, *pg.* 802
Clark, Bryce, Product Mgr-Technical-OEM & Special Markets - David Clark Company Incorporated; *pg.* 633, *pg.* 862
Clark, Camila, Dir-Mktg Comm - Brand USA; *pg.* 1901, *pg.* 396
Clark, Carla, Bus Mgr - WNYT-TV; *pg.* 322, *pg.* 1137
Clark, Carolyn, Sr Mgr-Mktg-Global - PureCircle USA Inc.; *pg.* 1861, *pg.* 648
Clark, Carolyn, Sr Mgr-Internal & Media - Yahoo! Inc.; *pg.* 1289, *pg.* 289
Clark, Cassandra, Mgr-Social Media - Discover Financial Services; *pg.* 744, *pg.* 653
Clark, Cassandra, Mgr-Mktg-LinkedIn Mktg Solutions - LinkedIn Corporation; *pg.* 1262, *pg.* 160
Clark, Christina R., Mgr-Trade Mktg-Grilling Solutions - Bush Brothers & Company; *pg.* 843, *pg.* 1636
Clark, Christopher, Sr Dir-Security - Buffalo Bills, Inc.; *pg.* 535, *pg.* 1319
Clark, Darcy, Mgr-Mktg - The Walt Disney Company; *pg.* 317, *pg.* 52
Clark, David, Dir-Mktg - Coherent, Inc.; *pg.* 1406, *pg.* 265
Clark, David, VP-Brand & Product Dev - Meijer, Inc.; *pg.* 1779, *pg.* 888
Clark, Deborah, Sr Dir-Global Product Mktg-Norton Bus Unit - Symantec Corporation; *pg.* 478, *pg.* 161
Clark, Dennis, Sr Mgr-Solutions Mktg - NetApp, Inc.; *pg.* 444, *pg.* 287
Clark, Dina, VP-Mktg-McCormick Canada - La Cie McCormick Canada Co.; *pg.* 872, *pg.* 1922
Clark, Dwight, VP-Sls & Mktg - Jamison Door Company; *pg.* 89, *pg.* 771
Clark, Emily, Mgr-PR - Lettuce Entertain You Enterprises, Inc.; *pg.* 1735, *pg.* 580
Clark, Emily, Sr Mgr-Benefits - Q.E.P. CO., INC.; *pg.* 1371, *pg.* 413
Clark, Garry R., Exec Dir-Mktg Svcs - Quest Diagnostics Incorporated; *pg.* 1587, *pg.* 1080
Clark, Gary, Brand Mgr-Ben Meadows - Ariens Company Inc.; *pg.* 700, *pg.* 1855
Clark, Gary L., Sr VP-Mktg - Goodman Group, Inc.; *pg.* 1072, *pg.* 1706
Clark, Gina, CMO & Sr VP - AmerisourceBergen Corporation; *pg.* 1493, *pg.* 1522
Clark, Gregory, Sr Mgr-OEM Mktg - iBiquity Digital Corporation; *pg.* 409, *pg.* 767
Clark, Ian, Dir-Product Line-FloTHERM Products - Mentor Graphics Corporation; *pg.* 432, *pg.* 1510
Clark, Jay, Sr Dir-Carrier Sls & Ops - Cox Communications, Inc.; *pg.* 279, *pg.* 501
Clark, Jeff, VP-Product Dev - CareerBuilder, LLC; *pg.* 1234, *pg.* 568
Clark, Jennifer, Brand Mgr-SCOTT Brand Strategy & Innovation - Kimberly-Clark Corporation; *pg.* 1461, *pg.* 1720
Clark, Jimmy, Dir-Sls-Natl - Whirlpool Corporation; *pg.* 62, *pg.* 872
Clark, Joe, VP-Svc & Sls - San Antonio Spurs LLC; *pg.* 580, *pg.* 1742
Clark, Jonathan, Sr Mgr-Digital Mktg - Ingram Micro Inc.; *pg.* 415, *pg.* 261
Clark, Jp, Sr Mgr-Corp Comm - Broadcom Corporation; *pg.* 364, *pg.* 108
Clark, Julie, VP-Programmatic Sls & Strategy - The Hearst Corporation; *pg.* 1649, *pg.* 1239
Clark, Kari, Sr Product Mgr-Accessories - Google Inc.; *pg.* 1249, *pg.* 153
Clark, Katie, Sr Dir-Design-Women's Knits & Sweaters - American Eagle Outfitters, Inc.; *pg.* 37, *pg.* 1572
Clark, Krista, Exec Mgr-Mktg - Pearson Education; *pg.* 1675, *pg.* 800
Clark, Kristen, Brand Mgr - Stanley Black & Decker, Inc.; *pg.* 1063, *pg.* 358
Clark, Kristen, Mgr-PR - Universal Orlando; *pg.* 590, *pg.* 456
Clark, Kyle, VP & Bus Head-Product Dev - MasterCard Incorporated; *pg.* 779, *pg.* 1325
Clark, Laura, Sr Dir-Global Mktg-Fast Moving Consumer Goods - Avery Dennison Corporation; *pg.* 1452, *pg.* 95
Clark, Laura, Dir-Political & Govt Sls-Natl - Radio One, Inc.; *pg.* 305, *pg.* 778
Clark, Leslie, Dir-Mktg - Butler Manufacturing Company; *pg.* 72, *pg.* 981
Clark, Lucy, Mgr-European Mktg-Heinz Tomato Ketchup - The Kraft Heinz Company; *pg.* 870, *pg.* 1577
Clark, Maggie, Mgr-Mktg - NeuStar, Inc.; *pg.* 1872, *pg.* 1807
Clark, Meryl F., Sr Mgr-Mktg & Events - AT&T; *pg.* 1865, *pg.* 258
Clark, Napoleon D., Exec Dir-Mktg-US GENERICS - Allergan; *pg.* 1490, *pg.* 1101
Clark, Nick, Dir-Mktg & Comm - Rose Hills Company; *pg.* 1395, *pg.* 307
Clark, Paul, Head-Institutional Strategy & Product Mgmt - Broadridge Financial Solutions Inc.; *pg.* 727, *pg.* 1172
Clark, Raymond, Mgr-Production & Librarian - Toledo Symphony; *pg.* 588, *pg.* 1477
Clark, Robin, Dir-Brand Image-Nat'l Adv - Pizza Hut, Inc.; *pg.* 1744, *pg.* 1733
Clark, Sara, Dir-Web & New Media - Missouri State University; *pg.* 605, *pg.* 1006
Clark, Sean, Head-Surgical Mktg-US - Alcon; *pg.* 1399, *pg.* 530
Clark, Stacy, Mgr-Mktg - Verizon Terremark; *pg.* 685, *pg.* 447
Clark, Stephanie, Coord-Mktg - CDI; *pg.* 1405, *pg.* 121
Clark, Sue, VP-Product Mgmt-Search - Scripps Networks Interactive, Inc.; *pg.* 1279, *pg.* 1638
Clark, Tim, Sr Dir-Digital Platform - National Association for Stock Car Auto Racing; *pg.* 566, *pg.* 420
Clark, Tory, Mgr-Market Sls - Cintas Corporation; *pg.* 372, *pg.* 1411
Clark, Wayne L., VP-Community Rels & Mktg - Legacy Health System; *pg.* 1555, *pg.* 1504
Clark, Wendy, Pres-Sparkling Brands & Strategic Mktg - Coca-Cola North America; *pg.* 848, *pg.* 500
Clark-Leyda, Rhonda, Sr Mgr-Mktg & Comm - The Weitz Company; *pg.* 121, *pg.* 707
Clarke, Allison, Sr VP-Ad Sls-AMC Networks & WE tv - AMC Networks Inc.; *pg.* 269, *pg.* 1189
Clarke, Antoinette, VP-Branded Entertainment & Media Innovation - CBS Corporation; *pg.* 273, *pg.* 1210
Clarke, Chris, Sr VP-Mktg & Comm - Habitat for Humanity International, Inc.; *pg.* 143, *pg.* 486
Clarke, Christina, Sr Dir-Mktg & Portfolio - Frito-Lay North America, Inc.; *pg.* 1853, *pg.* 1730
Clarke, Forrest, Product Mgr-Electronic Payments - Capital One Financial Corporation; *pg.* 730, *pg.* 1789
Clarke, Garrett, Sr Mgr-Bus Dev & Strategy - Microsoft Corporation; *pg.* 435, *pg.* 1824
Clarke, Itir, Sr Product Mgr-UCS - Cisco Systems, Inc.; *pg.* 372, *pg.* 240
Clarke, Julie, Sr Mgr-Integrated Mktg - Xilinx, Inc.; *pg.* 496, *pg.* 252
Clarke, K.C., Product Mgr-Sportswear - adidas America Inc.; *pg.* 1803, *pg.* 1500
Clarke, Karen, Dir-Mktg Comm-Customer Experience Org - Cigna Corporation; *pg.* 1197, *pg.* 338
Clarke, Karen B., VP-Strategic Mktg - Temple University; *pg.* 608, *pg.* 1571
Clarke, Marie, Strategist-Digital Media - NBC Universal, Inc.; *pg.* 300, *pg.* 1266
Clarke, Matthew, Dir-Digital Mktg - Kayak; *pg.* 1260, *pg.* 363
Clarkin, Gina, Mgr-Solutions Mktg - Interactive Intelligence, Inc.; *pg.* 417, *pg.* 687
Clarot, Timothy L., Sr VP-R&D & Product Quality - Matrixx Initiatives, Inc.; *pg.* 1559, *pg.* 23
Clary, Laura, Dir & Product Mgr - Fiserv, Inc.; *pg.* 397, *pg.* 1855
Claster, Bari, Mgr-Digital Mktg - Remy Cointreau USA Inc.; *pg.* 1969, *pg.* 1285
Claudio, Anne, VP-Res, Data Products & Yield - CBS Interactive, Inc.; *pg.* 369, *pg.* 215
Clausen, Holly, Dir-Mktg-Popular Presentations - Atlanta Symphony Orchestra; *pg.* 531, *pg.* 490
Clausen, Nancy A, Sr Dir-Mktg-Tyndale Momentum - Tyndale House Publishers, Inc.; *pg.* 1697, *pg.* 561
Clauson, Alissa, Mgr-Social Mktg-Upscale Brands - InterContinental Hotels Corporation; *pg.* 1097, *pg.* 511
Clauson, Laurie, Sr Mgr-Global Consumer Insights - General Mills, Inc.; *pg.* 828, *pg.* 933
Clauss, Ed, Planner-Production - North Jersey Media Group Inc.; *pg.* 1672, *pg.* 1072
Clauss, Wendi, Mgr-Product Dev - Wawa, Inc.; *pg.* 1037, *pg.* 1552
Clavelli, Victor, VP-Sls & Mktg - Pfizer Inc.; *pg.* 1581, *pg.* 1278
Clavijo, Lina, Sr Mgr-Mktg-Health Care - Univision Communications Inc.; *pg.* 683, *pg.* 1307
Clawson, Brooke, Sr Mgr-Mktg - Ancestry.com LLC; *pg.* 1228, *pg.* 1754
Clawson, Kevin, Sr Dir-Art & Mgr-Loyalty Mktg - AutoZone, Inc.; *pg.* 200, *pg.* 1641
Clawson, Marcena H., VP-Corp Sls - UTAH MEDICAL PRODUCTS, INC.; *pg.* 1605, *pg.* 1752
Clawson, Mark, Mgr-Chevrolet Mktg-Tahoe, Suburban, City Express & Express - General Motors Company; *pg.* 175, *pg.* 881
Clawson, Scott L., VP-Global Adv & Online - Oracle Corporation; *pg.* 450, *pg.* 191
Claxton, Susan, Sr Dir-Brand Engagement-Scratch - Viacom Inc.; *pg.* 316, *pg.* 1310
Clay, Ashlie, Assoc Mgr-Integrated Mktg Content - Dr Pepper Snapple Group, Inc.; *pg.* 250, *pg.* 1729
Clay, Herb, Mgr-Publ & Product - ImageWorks; *pg.* 1544, *pg.* 1158
Clay, Jennifer, VP-Corp Comm & Mktg - SKECHERS U.S.A., INC.; *pg.* 1819, *pg.* 143
Clay, John, Sr Mgr-Mktg-Consumer Insights - H&R Block, Inc.; *pg.* 764, *pg.* 983
Clay, Julie, Sr Mgr-Category Insights-Sam's Club - The Hershey Co.; *pg.* 1855, *pg.* 1538
Claybaugh, Dan, VP-Mktg & Bus Dev - Kelly-Moore Paint Company, Inc.; *pg.* 1443, *pg.* 198
Claybaugh, Jennifer, Mgr-Media & Digital Mktg - T.G.I. Friday's Inc.; *pg.* 1754, *pg.* 1669
Clayborne, Kira, Mgr-Digital Media - Church's Chicken, Inc.; *pg.* 1722, *pg.* 493
Clayborne, Ronda, Sr Mgr-Digital Mktg & Demand Generation - SAP America, Inc.; *pg.* 466, *pg.* 1557
Claybrooks, John, Dir-Brand, Digital Media & Mktg Comm-Global - CSX Corporation; *pg.* 1904, *pg.* 432
Clayton, Beth, Asst Dir & Dir-Mktg - Ameriprise Financial, Inc.; *pg.* 715, *pg.* 930
Clayton, Cameron, Pres-Product & Tech - The Weather Channel LLC; *pg.* 320, *pg.* 523
Clayton, Corey, Dir-Social Media - World Wrestling Entertainment, Inc.; *pg.* 595, *pg.* 380
Clayton, Debra, Sr VP & Product Mgr-Global - Northern Trust Corporation; *pg.* 787, *pg.* 585
Clayton, Drew, Sr Product Mgr - Los Angeles Times Communications, LLC; *pg.* 1660, *pg.* 135
Clayton-Hine, Toni A., VP-Global Mktg & Value Proposition - Xerox Corporation; *pg.* 494, *pg.* 365
Claywell, Chris, Sr Mgr-Comm Technologies - Panera Bread Company; *pg.* 1029, *pg.* 1001
Clear Nowell, Briana, Mgr-Brand Mktg - Dick's Sporting Goods, Inc.; *pg.* 1832, *pg.* 1524
Cleary, Jennifer, Dir-Membership & Mktg - Theatre Communications Group, Inc.; *pg.* 587, *pg.* 1298
Cleary, Kevin, Mgr-Mktg-Sponsorships & Promotions - Nestle Waters North America Inc.; *pg.* 257, *pg.* 375
Cleary, Kristine, Sr Product Mgr-Eaton's Bussmann Bus - Eaton Corporation; *pg.* 1331, *pg.* 1429
Cleary, Laura, Program Mgr-Social Advocacy - Travelocity, Inc.; *pg.* 1284, *pg.* 1745
Cleary, Matt, Dir-Mktg-Tea - Nestle Waters North America Inc.; *pg.* 257, *pg.* 375
Cleary, Megan, Program Mgr-Mktg - Brocade Corporation; *pg.* 365, *pg.* 312
Cleary, Stuart, Dir-Bus Dev-Media Products - Akamai Technologies, Inc.; *pg.* 1226, *pg.* 807
Cleary, Sue, Sr Strategist-Direct Mktg - CDW Corporation; *pg.* 370, *pg.* 663
Cleave, Jim Van, Dir-Mktg-Metals - CSX Transportation, Inc.; *pg.* 1904, *pg.* 432
Cleaver, Alan, Dir-Sls & Mktg - Comcast Corporation; *pg.* 276, *pg.* 1560

Cleek, Gabe, Sr Dir-Mktg & Brand Mgmt-Home Cleaning - S.C. Johnson & Son, Inc.; *pg.* 334, *pg.* 1889
Clegg, Ed, VP-In-Theatre Mktg - Focus Features; *pg.* 287, *pg.* 273
Clegg, Haley, Mgr-North America Digital & Social Mktg - Visa Inc.; *pg.* 816, *pg.* 230
Clegg, Haley, Mgr-North America Digital & Social Mktg - Visa U.S.A., Inc.; *pg.* 817, *pg.* 231
Clegg, Jennifer, Dir-Mktg Automation & Analytics - CA Technologies; *pg.* 366, *pg.* 1168
Clegg, Kevin, Reg Dir-Sls - GlaxoSmithKline; *pg.* 1536, *pg.* 1565
Clem, John, Chief Strategy Officer & Chief Product Officer - Stamps.com Inc.; *pg.* 1282, *pg.* 82
Clem, Kerry, Sr VP-Sls - Acorda Therapeutics, Inc.; *pg.* 1486, *pg.* 1138
Clemens, Ben, Mgr-Creative Svcs - The Finish Line, Inc.; *pg.* 1769, *pg.* 686
Clemens, Jon, Mgr-Production-L-3 Comm - L-3 Communications Holdings Inc.; *pg.* 650, *pg.* 1250
Clemens, Sara, Chief Strategy Officer - Pandora Media Inc.; *pg.* 1273, *pg.* 172
Clement, Andrew, VP-Sls - Kimberly-Clark Corporation; *pg.* 1461, *pg.* 1720
Clement, Dale, Mgr-Sls - Napco Security Systems, Inc.; *pg.* 658, *pg.* 1138
Clement, Jeanne, Dir-Shopper Mktg-Sam's Club - The Kraft Heinz Company; *pg.* 871, *pg.* 641
Clement, Kristyn, VP-Ad Sls Res & Strategy Analytics - NBC Universal, Inc.; *pg.* 300, *pg.* 1266
Clement, Megan, Specialist-Social Media - The Weather Channel LLC; *pg.* 320, *pg.* 523
Clemente, Rick, Exec VP-Sls & Svc - Santinelli International Inc.; *pg.* 1395, *pg.* 1165
Clements, Clint, VP-Sls Ops-Global - Rocket Aldon; *pg.* 462, *pg.* 85
Clements, Erin, Asst Mgr-Shopper Marketing - General Mills, Inc.; *pg.* 828, *pg.* 933
Clements, Kathy, Sr VP-Media Ops - Gannett Co., Inc.; *pg.* 289, *pg.* 1681
Clements, Ryan, Specialist-Social Media - Sony Computer Entertainment America LLC; *pg.* 966, *pg.* 256
Clemmer, Kristin, Dir-Mktg - Fresh Mark, Inc.; *pg.* 856, *pg.* 1461
Clendenin, Michael, Dir-Media Rels - Consolidated Edison, Inc.; *pg.* 1938, *pg.* 1218
Clendenin, Thomas, Sr VP-Mktg - CNBC; *pg.* 275, *pg.* 1059
Clerico, Ron, VP-Mktg Strategies & Solutions - Cardinal Health, Inc.; *pg.* 1512, *pg.* 1448
Clerico, Vincent, VP-Sls & Mktg - Heat-Timer Corporation; *pg.* 1072, *pg.* 1065
Clerico-Parham, Patty, Sr Mgr-Creative Program Mgmt - NVIDIA Corporation; *pg.* 447, *pg.* 268
Clermont, Jan, Mgr-Mktg - Anthem, Inc.; *pg.* 1192, *pg.* 683
Cleveland, Ann, Sr Dir-Global Media-Banana Republic - The Gap, Inc.; *pg.* 1770, *pg.* 218
Cleveland, Diane, Mgr-Direct Mktg - Royal Caribbean Cruises Ltd; *pg.* 1921, *pg.* 446
Cleveland, Laura, VP & Reg Dir-Mktg - Wilmington Trust Corporation; *pg.* 822, *pg.* 392
Cleveland, Mike, Sls Mgr-Natl - Great Plains Manufacturing, Incorporated; *pg.* 704, *pg.* 721
Cleveland, Sean, Sr Mgr-Technical Mktg - NVIDIA Corporation; *pg.* 447, *pg.* 268
Cleveland, Susan, Mgr-Digital & Social Media - WestRock Company; *pg.* 1472, *pg.* 1805
Clevenger, Agata, Sr Dir-Strategic Sls & Mktg Partnerships - David's Bridal, Inc.; *pg.* 23, *pg.* 1523
Clevenger, Chuck, Product Mgr - McKee Foods Corporation; *pg.* 1860, *pg.* 1630
Clevenger, Yumi, Dir-Mktg - DPR Construction, Inc.; *pg.* 79, *pg.* 189
Clewley, Michael, Dir-Software Product Mgmt - BlackBerry Limited; *pg.* 625, *pg.* 1947
Clifford, Aaron, Dir-Web & Social Media Svcs - HCA HOLDINGS, INC.; *pg.* 1539, *pg.* 1651
Clifford, Dan, Sr VP-Mktg - Express, Inc.; *pg.* 24, *pg.* 1440
Clifford, Dan, Mgr-Mktg - Victoria's Secret Stores, LLC; *pg.* 1789, *pg.* 1471
Clifford, Katie, Mgr-Brand Mktg - The North Face, Inc.; *pg.* 1840, *pg.* 252
Clifford, Patrick, Mgr-Mktg-Global - Honeywell International Inc.; *pg.* 407, *pg.* 1088
Clifford, Scott, VP-Mktg & Sls Ops - Amkor Technology, Inc.; *pg.* 67, *pg.* 25
Clift, Erin, VP-Mktg & Partnerships-Global - Spotify; *pg.* 1282, *pg.* 1295
Clifton, David, CMO - Huntington Bancshares Incorporated; *pg.* 767, *pg.* 1440
Clifton, Heather, Sr VP-Global Res & Mktg Analytics - Visa U.S.A., Inc.; *pg.* 817, *pg.* 231
Clifton, Jackie, Dir-Shopper Mktg Quaker Foods & Snacks - PepsiCo, Inc.; *pg.* 259, *pg.* 1327
Clifton, Josh, Mgr-Nissan Brand Comm & New Product Launch - Nissan North America, Inc.; *pg.* 186, *pg.* 1633
Clifton, Laura, Gen Mgr-Builder Sls - Purcell Murray Company Inc.; *pg.* 59, *pg.* 50
Clifton, Loren, Mgr-Sls - Sanderson Ford Inc.; *pg.* 190, *pg.* 13
Clifton, Matt, Sr Mgr-Mktg & Brand Mgmt - Naterra International Inc.; *pg.* 59, *pg.* 1684
Clifton, Tammi, Dir-Sls - Q Interactive Inc.; *pg.* 1276, *pg.* 588
Clifton-Welker, Sebastian, Dir-PR-Intl - Elizabeth Arden, Inc.; *pg.* 507, *pg.* 448
Climer, Thomas, Dir-Product Mktg-Data Storage Products - Samsung Electronics America, Inc.; *pg.* 669, *pg.* 1115
Clinard, David, Rep-Sls-Intl - Beutlich Pharmaceuticals LP; *pg.* 1503, *pg.* 665
Cline, John, Sr Mgr-Event & Guest Svcs - Baltimore Ravens Limited Partnership; *pg.* 532, *pg.* 755
Cline, Josie, Sr Mgr-Mktg - Universal Orlando; *pg.* 590, *pg.* 456
Cline, Katie, Mgr-Global PR- W Hotels & Le Meridien - Starwood Hotels & Resorts Worldwide, Inc.; *pg.* 1114, *pg.* 378
Cline, Keith, Interim Pres & CEO - La Quinta Corporation; *pg.* 1099, *pg.* 1722
Cline, Marianne, Brand Mgr-Environments - American Airlines Inc.; *pg.* 1898, *pg.* 1693
Cline, Sara, Specialist-Mktg Comm Grp - Blue Cross & Blue Shield Association; *pg.* 1195, *pg.* 566
Cline, Tom, Mgr-Sls-Natl - Competition Specialties Inc.; *pg.* 203, *pg.* 1813
Clinesmith, Jennifer, Rep-Mktg - State Farm Mutual Automobile Insurance Co.; *pg.* 1218, *pg.* 557
Clingan, Jamie L., Sr VP-Mktg - Q.E.P. CO., INC.; *pg.* 1371, *pg.* 413
Clinger, Bill, Dir-Mktg - The Lima News; *pg.* 1659, *pg.* 1457
Clinton, Michael, Pres-Mktg & Dir-Publ - Hearst Magazines; *pg.* 1649, *pg.* 1239
Clinton, Michael A., Pres-Mktg & Dir-Publ - The Association of Magazine Media; *pg.* 133, *pg.* 1197
Clinton, Renee, Sr Mgr-Mktg - Banana Republic; *pg.* 1760, *pg.* 212
Clinton, Scott, Sr Dir-Product Mgmt & Mktg - Red Hat, Inc.; *pg.* 460, *pg.* 1388
Clive, Spencer, Sr Dir-Mdse Fin-Food, Bev, Consumables, H&W - Sam's Club; *pg.* 1783, *pg.* 29
Clock, Martin, Bus Mgr - American Association for the Advancement of Science; *pg.* 126, *pg.* 394
Clock, Michael, Specialist-Store Mktg - Golfsmith International Holdings, Inc.; *pg.* 1835, *pg.* 1662
Clokey, Robin, Head-Mktg-EMEA - Crayola LLC; *pg.* 951, *pg.* 1528
Clonan, Kristen, Mgr-PR & Comm - Avon Products, Inc.; *pg.* 500, *pg.* 1198
Clooney, Cara, Brand Mgr - AstraZeneca Pharmaceuticals LP; *pg.* 1497, *pg.* 389
Close, Tim, Sr Dir-Mktg & Trade - David C. Cook; *pg.* 1633, *pg.* 315
Clothier, Gerry J., VP-Sls - A&A Global Industries Inc.; *pg.* 948, *pg.* 767
Cloud, Cindy, Sr Mgr-Global Talent Attraction & Recruitment Mktg - Informatica Corporation; *pg.* 414, *pg.* 190
Cloud, Lori, VP-Mktg-W Publishing Group - HarperCollins Publishers Inc.; *pg.* 1647, *pg.* 1237
Cloud, Pamela H., Sr VP-Mdsg - Tiffany & Co.; *pg.* 13, *pg.* 1299
Clough, Alison, Dir-Product Mgmt - K12, Inc.; *pg.* 1260, *pg.* 1785
Clough, Don, Mgr-Sls-Regional - Antec Incorporated; *pg.* 350, *pg.* 90
Clougherty, Dennis, Grp Product Mgr - Clougherty Packing Company; *pg.* 848, *pg.* 128
Clouse, Laura, Mgr-Mktg Comm-Global - Zimmer Biomet Holdings, Inc.; *pg.* 1611, *pg.* 699
Clouse, Phil, Pres-Post Sls Support - MTD Products, Inc.; *pg.* 1057, *pg.* 1478
Clouser, Frank, Sr Mgr-Corp Rels - The Allstate Corporation; *pg.* 1189, *pg.* 639
Cloutier, Dawn, Dir-Field & Channel Mktg - PepsiCo, Inc.; *pg.* 259, *pg.* 1327
Cloutman, Kim, Mgr-Corp Media Center - Norfolk Southern Corporation; *pg.* 1917, *pg.* 1797
Clowes, Mark, Head-Adv-Global - American International Group, Inc.; *pg.* 1190, *pg.* 1193
Cluck, Betsy, Mgr-Consumer PC Mktg Comm - Hewlett-Packard Company; *pg.* 404, *pg.* 175
Cluff, Jared, VP-Mktg - Blue Apron, Inc.; *pg.* 1016, *pg.* 1205
Clunie, Kevin, Dir-Mktg-Americas - Avery Dennison Corporation; *pg.* 1452, *pg.* 95
Clute, Harold, Dir-Sls & Mktg - Air-Lec Industries LLC; *pg.* 1041, *pg.* 1864
Clynes, Terri, VP-Power Mktg-Comml Gas & Power - ConocoPhillips; *pg.* 975, *pg.* 1703
Coache, Sheila, Mgr-Mktg - Autodesk Inc.; *pg.* 356, *pg.* 257
Coacher, Adam, Div VP-Mktg - The Hartz Mountain Corp.; *pg.* 1476, *pg.* 1120
Coad, Jeff, VP-Mktg-Power Products - Briggs & Stratton Corporation; *pg.* 201, *pg.* 1899
Coakley, Renee, Sr Mgr-Email Mktg - The Talbots, Inc.; *pg.* 34, *pg.* 824
Coalson, Tony, Sr VP-Sls-Americas - Murata Electronics North America, Inc.; *pg.* 658, *pg.* 540
Coari, Jason, Dir-Intl Mktg-EMEA/APAC - Silicon Graphics International Corp; *pg.* 470, *pg.* 148
Coates, Corinne, Specialist-ECommerce Mktg - Church & Dwight Co., Inc.; *pg.* 1153, *pg.* 1063
Coates, Desiree, Specialist-Mktg-Integrated Global Comm - NetApp, Inc.; *pg.* 444, *pg.* 287
Cobar, Sal, VP-Sls & Mktg-Worldwide - Sigma Designs, Inc.; *pg.* 469, *pg.* 148
Cobb Earnest, Jenny, Dir-Mdse Mktg-Decor - The Home Depot, Inc.; *pg.* 1050, *pg.* 510
Cobb, Ben, Mgr-Social Media - The Boston Consulting Group, Inc.; *pg.* 363, *pg.* 790
Cobb, Jon, Exec VP-Mktg-Global - Stratasys, Inc.; *pg.* 476, *pg.* 923
Cobb, Karen, Mgr-Corp PR - Lowe's Companies, Inc.; *pg.* 1053, *pg.* 1383
Cobb, Keith, VP-Enterprise Portals, eDelivery & Mktg Technologies - Anthem, Inc.; *pg.* 1192, *pg.* 683
Cobb, Lucas, Designer-Interactive - Blackbaud, Inc.; *pg.* 361, *pg.* 1613
Cobb, Michael, CMO - Gold's Gym; *pg.* 550, *pg.* 1681
Cobb, Michael, VP-Sls & Mktg - Stratton Mountain Resort; *pg.* 1115, *pg.* 1768
Cobb, Peter, Co-Founder & Exec VP-Mktg & IR - eBags, Inc.; *pg.* 1240, *pg.* 331
Coberley, Kati, Mgr-Retail Mktg-Key Accts - Columbia Sportswear Company; *pg.* 1830, *pg.* 1501
Cobin, Sandy, Sr Dir-Comm Svcs - The Hain Celestial Group, Inc.; *pg.* 860, *pg.* 1172
Coble, Margo, VP-Mktg & Local Digital Strategy - Advance Publications, Inc.; *pg.* 1613, *pg.* 1343
Coble-Penning, EJ, Head-Mktg Comm - Bayer CropScience; *pg.* 1149, *pg.* 981
Cobleigh, Geoffrey W., Sr VP-Sls-Americas - Logility, Inc.; *pg.* 428, *pg.* 513
Coblentz, Julia, Sr Mgr-Mktg - Barnes & Noble, Inc.; *pg.* 1619, *pg.* 1201
Coburn, Allison, Dir-Consumer Mktg - American Student Assistance; *pg.* 714, *pg.* 789
Coburn, Caitlin, Mgr-Mktg - NBC Sports Network; *pg.* 300, *pg.* 375
Coburn, Caitlin, Mgr-Mktg - NBC Universal, Inc.; *pg.* 300, *pg.* 1266
Coburn, Rob, Product Mgr-Indus & Process Air Heating-Global - Chromalox, Inc.; *pg.* 1070, *pg.* 1574
Coccari, Andrew , Jr., Sr VP-Sls & Mktg - Smith & Wesson Holding Corporation; *pg.* 1845, *pg.* 846
Cocchiola, Jessica, Sr Mgr-Category - LIFETIME BRANDS, INC.; *pg.* 1127, *pg.* 1161
Cochran, Bill, Dir-Adv & Promo Compliance - Allergan, Inc.; *pg.* 1491, *pg.* 106
Cochran, Lauren, Sr Mgr-Mktg - H&R Block, Inc.; *pg.* 764, *pg.* 983
Cochran, Lauren, Dir-Interactive Mktg & New Media - Miami Heat Limited Partnership; *pg.* 562, *pg.* 444
Cochran, Linda, Coord-Adv Sls-Midwest - Essence Magazine; *pg.* 1639, *pg.* 1229
Cochran, Megan, Brand Mgr-Givenchy - Saks Fifth Avenue, Inc.; *pg.* 1783, *pg.* 1287
Cochran, Ronald, Mgr-Sls & Mktg - American Marking Systems, Inc.; *pg.* 349, *pg.* 1051
Cochran, Steve, Co-Dir-Mktg - TheatreworksUSA; *pg.* 587,

pg. 1298
Cochran, Terry, Mgr-Mktg Comm - Quantum Corporation; *pg.* 458, *pg.* 250
Cochran, Thomas, Dir-Adv - Austin Powder Company; *pg.* 1148, *pg.* 1428
Cochrane, Courtney, Grp VP-Tech, Games & Media - CBS Interactive, Inc.; *pg.* 369, *pg.* 215
Cochrane, Jessica, Asst VP & Dir-Internal Comm & Brand Mktg - T.J. Maxx; *pg.* 1788, *pg.* 822
Cochrane, Jessica, Asst VP & Dir-Internal Comm & Brand Mktg - The TJX Companies, Inc.; *pg.* 1788, *pg.* 822
Cochs, Christian, Mgr-Sls - Twitter, Inc.; *pg.* 1285, *pg.* 228
Cockley, Bridget, Mgr-Integrated Media - KeyCorp; *pg.* 774, *pg.* 1432
Cockram, Michael, Dir-Mktg-Travel Retail Global - Beam Suntory Inc.; *pg.* 1957, *pg.* 599
Cockrell, Jeremy, VP & Dir-Creative - Scottrade, Inc.; *pg.* 802, *pg.* 1003
Cockrum, Carey, Mgr-Creative - Humana, Inc.; *pg.* 1204, *pg.* 734
Cocks, Aaron, Mgr-Online Mktg Optimization - Toll Brothers, Inc.; *pg.* 115, *pg.* 1541
Cocuzzo, Rich, VP-Sls - FedEx Corporation; *pg.* 1907, *pg.* 1642
Coda, Jeff, Mgr-Sls-Natl - Elenco Electronics, Inc.; *pg.* 953, *pg.* 670
Codd, Tom, VP-Sls Enablement & Ops - Hewlett-Packard Company; *pg.* 404, *pg.* 175
Codding, David, VP & Exec Dir-Creative - AMC Entertainment Inc.; *pg.* 527, *pg.* 716
Codella, Steve, Sr VP-Sls - Couristan Inc.; *pg.* 921, *pg.* 1067
Codianni, Ashley, Dir-Social Publ - Cable News Network LP; *pg.* 1624, *pg.* 1208
Cody, Lori, Dir-Mktg - The Buckle, Inc.; *pg.* 1764, *pg.* 1011
Coe, Barry, Mgr-Sls - Waterous Company; *pg.* 1387, *pg.* 965
Coe, Phillip, Dir-Digital & Creative Svcs - Manulife Financial Corporation; *pg.* 778, *pg.* 1939
Coelho, Marty, Mng Dir-Natl Mktg & Comm - American Cancer Society, Inc.; *pg.* 126, *pg.* 487
Coffee, Rick, Dir-Category Mktg & Hardlines - Lowe's Companies, Inc.; *pg.* 1053, *pg.* 1383
Coffelt, Donna, Creative Dir - The University of Texas System; *pg.* 610, *pg.* 1667
Coffelt, Lindsay, Mgr-Media Strategy - Choice Hotels International, Inc.; *pg.* 1086, *pg.* 775
Coffer, Charlotte, Mgr-Event Mktg - Scripps Networks Interactive, Inc.; *pg.* 1279, *pg.* 1638
Coffey, Brad, VP-Product - HubSpot, Inc.; *pg.* 409, *pg.* 808
Coffey, Chelsea, Mgr-Mktg-Music - Rockstar, Inc.; *pg.* 265, *pg.* 1029
Coffey, Craig, Mgr-Mktg Comm-US - Lincoln Electric Holdings, Inc.; *pg.* 1355, *pg.* 1432
Coffey, Craig, Exec VP & Head-Mktg & eBusiness - Wells Fargo & Company; *pg.* 819, *pg.* 232
Coffey, Kelly, Sr Mgr-PR & Mktg - Michael Stars, Inc.; *pg.* 29, *pg.* 100
Coffey, Kevin, Mgr-Global Brand Strategy & Creative Svcs - United Parcel Service, Inc.; *pg.* 1928, *pg.* 522
Coffey, Kurt, Dir-Sls & Mktg-CNH Industrial Reman - CNH America LLC; *pg.* 702, *pg.* 560
Coffey, Lela, Brand Mgr-Olay-North America - The Procter & Gamble Company; *pg.* 1129, *pg.* 1418
Coffey, Marjani, Brand Mgr - The Kraft Heinz Company; *pg.* 871, *pg.* 641
Coffey, Maurice, Assoc Dir-Mktg & Brand Mgr - The Procter & Gamble Company; *pg.* 1129, *pg.* 1418
Coffey, Mike, VP-Sls - American Equity Mortgage Inc.; *pg.* 712, *pg.* 991
Coffey, Peter, Specialist-Culinary Sls-Natl Chain Accounts - Cuisine Solutions, Inc.; *pg.* 850, *pg.* 1770
Coffey, Terence, VP-Media Plng & Strategy - Nickelodeon Direct Inc.; *pg.* 303, *pg.* 1271
Coffman, Stefanie, Sr Mgr-Mktg-Digital & Consumer Svcs - T. Marzetti Company; *pg.* 900, *pg.* 1444
Coffman, Tobias, Mgr-Product Mktg - AliphCom, Inc.; *pg.* 616, *pg.* 212
Coflin, Mark, Sr Dir-Global BD&L Alliance Mgmt - Baxter International Inc.; *pg.* 1499, *pg.* 599
Cofran, Jame, CMO & Sr VP - CGI Technologies & Solutions Inc.; *pg.* 371, *pg.* 1779
Cofsky, Steve, Product Mgr - Home Box Office, Inc.; *pg.* 290, *pg.* 1240
Cogan, Chris, Mgr-Mdsg - Campbell Soup Company; *pg.* 844, *pg.* 1048
Cogan, Nicole, Mgr-Mktg Ops - ViaSat, Inc.; *pg.* 489, *pg.* 62
Cogan, Oana, Sr Mgr-Brand Pkg - Williams-Sonoma, Inc.; *pg.* 1140, *pg.* 234
Coger, Holly, Mgr-Sls-Natl - Tampa Bay & Co.; *pg.* 1007, *pg.* 476
Coggin, Mark, Sr Dir-Product Mktg - Red Hat, Inc.; *pg.* 460, *pg.* 1388
Coggins, J. Matthew, Sr VP-CFMP & Dir-Mktg - Enterprise Bancorp Inc.; *pg.* 747, *pg.* 829
Cogley, Lisa, VP-Sls & Mktg - M/I Homes, Inc.; *pg.* 95, *pg.* 1441
Cognata, Lora, Mgr-Product Mktg - Siemens Medical Solutions USA, Inc.; *pg.* 469, *pg.* 1550
Cogswell, Dana, Exec Dir-Mktg & CRM - AT&T; *pg.* 1865, *pg.* 258
Cogswell, Josh, Chief Product Officer - Tribune Media Company; *pg.* 1696, *pg.* 592
Cohan, Pablo, VP-Product & Sr Head-Bus-MasterPass US - MasterCard Incorporated; *pg.* 779, *pg.* 1325
Cohane, Neal, Sr VP-Sls & Mktg - Reed's, Inc.; *pg.* 264, *pg.* 139
Cohen, Adam, Mgr-Social Media - Thomson Reuters Markets; *pg.* 810, *pg.* 1299
Cohen, Alana, Brand Mgr - Penguin Random House; *pg.* 1675, *pg.* 1276
Cohen, Ali, Assoc Mgr-Mktg & Promo - Meredith Corporation; *pg.* 1663, *pg.* 705
Cohen, Andrea, Mgr-HPS Mktg - Xerox Corporation; *pg.* 494, *pg.* 365
Cohen, Ashley, Specialist-Mktg-Global Partnerships - ZIPCAR, INC.; *pg.* 1931, *pg.* 810
Cohen, Barry Lee, Dir-Mktg & Comm-Global - Enthone Inc.; *pg.* 1161, *pg.* 381
Cohen, Blair, Mgr-Social Media - Ralph Lauren Corporation; *pg.* 46, *pg.* 1284
Cohen, Boaz, VP-Product Mgmt - TiVo Inc.; *pg.* 313, *pg.* 251
Cohen, Bruce, Sr VP-Sls & Mktg - Irwin Seating Company Inc.; *pg.* 929, *pg.* 887
Cohen, Cherie R., Sr VP-Portfolio Sls - NBC Universal, Inc.; *pg.* 300, *pg.* 1266
Cohen, Dan, Dir-PR - Beam Suntory Inc.; *pg.* 1957, *pg.* 599
Cohen, Dan, Exec VP-Sls - California Products Corporation; *pg.* 1441, *pg.* 781
Cohen, Dan, Dir-PR - Jim Beam Brands Co.; *pg.* 1965, *pg.* 601
Cohen, David, Dir-Digital Creative - Automatic Data Processing, Inc.; *pg.* 357, *pg.* 1117
Cohen, Douglas, Mgr-Digital Mktg & SEO - The ADT Corporation; *pg.* 612, *pg.* 409
Cohen, Evan, Reg Dir-Sls - MillerCoors LLC; *pg.* 255, *pg.* 582
Cohen, Harvey, CMO, Chief Creative Officer & Sr VP - Empire State Development Corporation; *pg.* 747, *pg.* 1227
Cohen, Harvey, VP-Sls & Consumer Div - GF Health Products, Inc.; *pg.* 1535, *pg.* 508
Cohen, Heather, Dir-Mktg-SEM - Ticketmaster Entertainment LLC; *pg.* 1284, *pg.* 48
Cohen, Hilary, Specialist-Brand Mktg-Hair Cuttery - The Ratner Companies; *pg.* 520, *pg.* 1809
Cohen, Jarrod, Coord-Social Media Mktg - Kayem Foods, Inc.; *pg.* 867, *pg.* 814
Cohen, Jason, Sr Dir-Digital Mktg - Sony Music Entertainment; *pg.* 309, *pg.* 1294
Cohen, Jed, Exec VP & Gen Mgr-Sls - The Walt Disney Company; *pg.* 317, *pg.* 52
Cohen, Jodie, Sr Mgr-Mktg - Penguin Random House; *pg.* 1675, *pg.* 1276
Cohen, Josh, Product Mgr-Bus - Google Inc.; *pg.* 1249, *pg.* 153
Cohen, Josh, Acct Exec-Partnership Mktg - National Hockey League; *pg.* 568, *pg.* 1265
Cohen, Josh, Product Mgr-Programmatic - The New York Times; *pg.* 1668, *pg.* 1270
Cohen, Kate, Assoc Mgr-Mktg-Self-Treat - Godiva Chocolatier, Inc.; *pg.* 1854, *pg.* 1235
Cohen, Kate, Assoc Mgr-Mktg - Home Box Office, Inc.; *pg.* 290, *pg.* 1240
Cohen, Kirby, Asst Mgr-Co-Op Adv & Brand Partnerships - Neiman Marcus, Inc.; *pg.* 30, *pg.* 1684
Cohen, Lauren, Dir-Mktg, Global Comm, Exhibits & Events - Boston Scientific Corporation; *pg.* 1508, *pg.* 831
Cohen, Lauren, Designer-Visual Interactive - Match.Com, LLC; *pg.* 1265, *pg.* 1683
Cohen, Linda B., VP-Mktg - Toll Brothers, Inc.; *pg.* 115, *pg.* 1541
Cohen, Lindsay, Assoc Dir-Digital Mktg - Ubisoft Inc.; *pg.* 589, *pg.* 229
Cohen, Liz, Dir-Mktg-Global Video Surveillance Solutions - Anixter International Inc.; *pg.* 1313, *pg.* 614
Cohen, Marc, Sr Product Mgr - Gilead Sciences, Inc.; *pg.* 1535, *pg.* 88
Cohen, Mitch, Dir-Sls-Central Reg - Unified Brands Inc.; *pg.* 1385, *pg.* 970
Cohen, Nimrod, Dir-Product Mktg - Stratasys, Inc.; *pg.* 476, *pg.* 923
Cohen, Peter, Dir-Mktg Comm - MicroStrategy, Inc.; *pg.* 1266, *pg.* 1809
Cohen, Ramsey, Mgr-Retail Mktg - Clayton Homes, Inc.; *pg.* 1086, *pg.* 1640
Cohen, Randy B., Sr Mgr-Audit - Wiss & Company LLP; *pg.* 823, *pg.* 1080
Cohen, Robert, Brand Mgr-Insights & Analytics - Panera Bread Company; *pg.* 1029, *pg.* 1001
Cohen, Samantha, Mgr-Media Plng - The Weather Channel LLC; *pg.* 320, *pg.* 523
Cohen, Sarah, Coord-Mktg - Jimlar Corporation; *pg.* 1810, *pg.* 1246
Cohen, Scott, Mgr-Mktg & Mdse - The Home Depot, Inc.; *pg.* 1050, *pg.* 510
Cohen, Scott, Mgr-Natl Product Trng - Samsung Electronics America, Inc.; *pg.* 669, *pg.* 1115
Cohen, Sharon, Exec VP-Partnership Mktg - Nickelodeon Direct Inc.; *pg.* 303, *pg.* 1271
Cohen, Stefani, Exec Dir-Corp Media North America - The Estee Lauder Companies Inc.; *pg.* 508, *pg.* 1229
Cohen, Stephen E., Corp VP-Sls & Mktg - The Commercial Furniture Group; *pg.* 920, *pg.* 994
Cohen, Tomer, Dir-Product Mgmt-Mobile - LinkedIn Corporation; *pg.* 1262, *pg.* 160
Cohen, Trace, Head-Digital Mktg - BlackBerry; *pg.* 625, *pg.* 1717
Cohen, Warren, Sr Mgr-IT Contracts & Procurement Mgmt - Staples, Inc.; *pg.* 474, *pg.* 821
Cohen, Zachary, Dir-Brand Mktg-Radisson - Carlson Companies Inc.; *pg.* 1084, *pg.* 947
Cohen-Lichtenstein, Susan, Sr Mgr-Mktg-Customer Experience - Office Depot, Inc.; *pg.* 448, *pg.* 412
Cohen-Nathan, Melanie, Mgr-PR - Chico's FAS, Inc.; *pg.* 21, *pg.* 427
Cohig, Susan, Sr VP-Integrated Mktg - National Hockey League; *pg.* 568, *pg.* 1265
Cohl, Stacey, Specialist-Mktg Comm - The Seibels Bruce Group, Inc.; *pg.* 1216, *pg.* 1614
Cohn, Abby, VP-Mktg & Adv - CIT GROUP INC.; *pg.* 735, *pg.* 1212
Cohn, Danielle, Sr Dir-Entrepreneurial Engagement - Comcast Corporation; *pg.* 276, *pg.* 1560
Cohn, Deborah Y., Assoc Professor-Mktg - New York Institute of Technology; *pg.* 605, *pg.* 1318
Cohn, Doug, Sr VP-Music Mktg & Talent-Nickelodeon & Viacom Media Networks - MTV Networks Company; *pg.* 298, *pg.* 1262
Cohn, Dustin, Mng Dir & Head-Brand Mgmt & Mktg Comm-Direct to Consumer - The Goldman Sachs Group, Inc.; *pg.* 762, *pg.* 1236
Cohn, Jason, Dir-Mktg-Western Reg - NIKE, Inc.; *pg.* 1812, *pg.* 1492
Cohn, Jim, Sr Mgr-Media Rels - Walgreen Co.; *pg.* 1608, *pg.* 605
Cohn, Melanie, Mgr-Social Media Mktg - Dunkin' Brands Group, Inc.; *pg.* 1727, *pg.* 810
Cohn, Melody, Dir-Product Monetization - IGN Entertainment, Inc.; *pg.* 1258, *pg.* 220
Cohn, Robert, Sr Dir-Consumer Mktg - Bonnier Corporation; *pg.* 1622, *pg.* 480
Cohn, Stu, Dir-Creative Svcs - Wilson Sporting Goods Co.; *pg.* 1848, *pg.* 596
Coia, John L., VP-Sls - Perry Products Corporation; *pg.* 1368, *pg.* 1072
Coimbra, Louise, Assoc Dir-Acq & Digital Products-Consumer Reports - Consumers Union of the United States, Inc.; *pg.* 1630, *pg.* 1356
Coker, Glenn, Dir-Creative - Fairway Outdoor Advertising of the GSA; *pg.* 1640, *pg.* 1615
Coker, Terry C., VP-Mktg - Old Fashion Foods, Inc.; *pg.* 1028, *pg.* 525
Colabatistto, Gene, Grp Pres-Defense & Security - CAE INC.; *pg.* 226, *pg.* 1959
Colacchio, Phillip, Dir-Mktg & New Bus Dev - ACCO Brands Corporation; *pg.* 340, *pg.* 626
Colacino, Don, Sr Mgr-Customer Mktg - Avago Technologies; *pg.* 358, *pg.* 238

Colaco, Joseph, Dir-Mktg & Insights - Samsung Electronics America, Inc.; *pg.* 669, *pg.* 1115
Colafrancesco, Stephen, Corp VP-Mktg & Sls - Bright House Networks LLC; *pg.* 272, *pg.* 461
Colandrea, Rich, Dir-Adv - North Jersey Media Group Inc.; *pg.* 1672, *pg.* 1072
Colanero, Stephen, CMO & Exec VP-AMC Theatres - AMC Entertainment Inc.; *pg.* 527, *pg.* 716
Colantoni, Lauren, Mgr-Online Mktg - Chico's FAS, Inc.; *pg.* 21, *pg.* 427
Colantonio, Donald, Sr Dir-Production Enhancements & Exec Producer-ITV - ESPN, Inc.; *pg.* 285, *pg.* 340
Colaprico, Christie, Mgr-Social Media Mktg - Showtime Networks Inc.; *pg.* 308, *pg.* 1291
Colarik, Jean C., Sr Dir-HR & Retail Ops - Giant Eagle American Seaway Foods; *pg.* 1020, *pg.* 1405
Colarte, Susana, Analyst-Travel Retail-Fin & Mktg - Bacardi USA, Inc.; *pg.* 1956, *pg.* 417
Colasuonno, Lenny, VP-Sls & Mktg - Powers Fasteners Inc.; *pg.* 1059, *pg.* 1143
Colbert, Kelly, VP-Mktg - U.S. Bancorp; *pg.* 815, *pg.* 945
Colborn, James, Dir-Targeting & Programmatic Team-Microsoft Adv - Microsoft Corporation; *pg.* 435, *pg.* 1824
Colcord, Austin, Sr Dir-Enterprise Mktg - LifeLock Inc.; *pg.* 776, *pg.* 26
Coldwell, Ryan, Dir-Digital Mktg - Cabela's Incorporated; *pg.* 535, *pg.* 1019
Cole, Alexander, Coord-Sports Mktg - Iconix Brand Group, Inc.; *pg.* 26, *pg.* 1243
Cole, Andrea Jean, Assoc Mgr-Brand Mktg-Global - Wizards of the Coast, Inc.; *pg.* 970, *pg.* 1830
Cole, Brandi, Specialist-Social Media - Zulily; *pg.* 1792, *pg.* 1843
Cole, Brandon, Mgr-Media & Bus Dev - Iconix Brand Group, Inc.; *pg.* 26, *pg.* 1243
Cole, Carrington, VP-US Mktg-Pureology - L'Oreal USA; *pg.* 514, *pg.* 1252
Cole, Chris, VP-Sls - Burden Sales Company; *pg.* 702, *pg.* 1011
Cole, Chris, VP-Sls - Surplus Center; *pg.* 1380, *pg.* 1012
Cole, Christy, Head-DaaS Sls - AOL Inc.; *pg.* 1229, *pg.* 1195
Cole, Cory, Dir-Social Media - Iconix Brand Group, Inc.; *pg.* 26, *pg.* 1243
Cole, David, VP-Mktg-Sally Hansen Cosmetics-Total Beauty Brand - Coty, Inc.; *pg.* 506, *pg.* 1219
Cole, Don, Rep-Inside Sls-Global 500 - Dell Inc.; *pg.* 383, *pg.* 1737
Cole, Erin, Head-Mktg Team - Whole Foods Market, Inc.; *pg.* 1038, *pg.* 1667
Cole, Graham, Dir-New Media & Affiliate Strategy - Scripps Networks Interactive, Inc.; *pg.* 1279, *pg.* 1638
Cole, Jason, Product Mgr-GC & MS - Thermo Fisher Scientific Inc.; *pg.* 1431, *pg.* 854
Cole, Jean, Mgr-Mktg - Public Utilities Reports, Inc.; *pg.* 1678, *pg.* 1809
Cole, Jeff, Dir-Global Digital Mktg-Jack Daniel's - Brown-Forman Corporation; *pg.* 1958, *pg.* 732
Cole, Jennifer, Dir-Online & Mobile Mktg - Chico's FAS, Inc.; *pg.* 21, *pg.* 427
Cole, Julie, Mgr-Mktg Comm - Hologic, Inc.; *pg.* 1416, *pg.* 784
Cole, Julie, VP-Mktg-North America - MANPOWER INC.; *pg.* 430, *pg.* 1877
Cole, Karen, Sr Mgr-Comm - Georgia-Pacific LLC; *pg.* 1458, *pg.* 507
Cole, Katherine, Reg Dir-Mktg - Hotels.com, L.P.; *pg.* 1257, *pg.* 1682
Cole, Kenneth D., Chm & Chief Creative Officer - Kenneth Cole Productions, Inc.; *pg.* 1810, *pg.* 1248
Cole, Kevin, VP-Global Product Mgmt - Elo Touch Solutions; *pg.* 635, *pg.* 145
Cole, Nikki, Mgr-Mktg - Cargill, Inc.; *pg.* 845, *pg.* 965
Cole, Noah, Sr Mgr-Corp Comm & Social Media - Autodesk Inc.; *pg.* 356, *pg.* 257
Cole, Peter, Sr Mgr-Engrg - Apple Inc.; *pg.* 350, *pg.* 73
Cole, Remyi, Mgr-Sls-Houston - Clestra Hauserman, Inc.; *pg.* 76, *pg.* 1526
Cole, Seth, VP-Sports Sponsorship Sls & Mktg - Turner Broadcasting System, Inc.; *pg.* 314, *pg.* 521
Cole, Sue, Sr VP-Mktg - Fidelity Bank; *pg.* 752, *pg.* 505
Cole, Taylor L., Dir-PR & Social Media-Hotels.com - Hotels.com, L.P.; *pg.* 1257, *pg.* 1682
Cole, Ted, VP-Channel Sls - ADTRAN, Inc.; *pg.* 344, *pg.* 6
Cole, Titi, Sr VP-Retail Products & Underwriting - Bank of America Global Wealth & Investment Management; *pg.* 720, *pg.* 789
Cole, Veronica, Mgr-PR - Ojai Valley Inn & Spa; *pg.* 1106, *pg.* 173
Cole, Wendy, Sr Mgr-Adobe Employee Experience Team - Adobe Systems Incorporated; *pg.* 342, *pg.* 235
Colehower, Jonathan, CMO & Sr VP - Manhattan Associates, Inc.; *pg.* 430, *pg.* 513
Colella, Denise, Sr VP-Advanced Adv Products & Strategy-Adv Sls - NBC Universal, Inc.; *pg.* 300, *pg.* 1266
Coleman Collins, Sherry, Sr Mgr-Peanut Bd Mktg & Comm-Natl - National Peanut Board; *pg.* 150, *pg.* 515
Coleman, Adrienne, VP-Deposits & Credit Cards Mktg - SunTrust Banks, Inc.; *pg.* 807, *pg.* 520
Coleman, Amy, Sr Dir-Mktg - Toyo Tire (U.S.A.) Corporation; *pg.* 1890, *pg.* 76
Coleman, Bob, Dir-Mktg - Jones-Blair Company; *pg.* 1443, *pg.* 1682
Coleman, Branden, Specialist-Natl Mktg - Meritage Homes Corporation; *pg.* 97, *pg.* 23
Coleman, Brian, VP-Mktg-US - Hasbro, Inc.; *pg.* 954, *pg.* 1603
Coleman, Chad, Mgr-Social Media - Callaway Golf Company; *pg.* 1829, *pg.* 58
Coleman, Christie, Sr Mgr-Mktg - Ingram Micro Inc.; *pg.* 415, *pg.* 261
Coleman, Colin, Sr Dir-Analytics Products Strategy & Data Governance - Turner Broadcasting System, Inc.; *pg.* 314, *pg.* 521
Coleman, David, Head-Global Product-Display Ads & Content Recommendations - Google Inc.; *pg.* 1249, *pg.* 153
Coleman, Doug, Mgr-Natl Vehicle Mktg-Prius Family, Electric & Fuel Cell Vehicles - Toyota Motor Sales, U.S.A., Inc.; *pg.* 193, *pg.* 296
Coleman, Greg, Grp Head-Mktg Comm - Lincoln Electric Holdings, Inc.; *pg.* 1355, *pg.* 1432
Coleman, Henry, Head-Mktg - Hammacher Schlemmer & Co., Inc.; *pg.* 1124, *pg.* 637
Coleman, Jacqi, Sr Mgr-Mktg - PepsiCo, Inc.; *pg.* 259, *pg.* 1327
Coleman, Jer'rel, Acct Mgr & Media Planner-Digital - Move, Inc.; *pg.* 1268, *pg.* 247
Coleman, Joanne, Dir-Media - Crown Imports LLC; *pg.* 248, *pg.* 572
Coleman, Jon, Pres-Sls, Mktg & Clinical Res-Worldwide - Masimo Corporation; *pg.* 1558, *pg.* 113
Coleman, Jonathan, Dir-Mktg - Juniper Networks, Inc.; *pg.* 1260, *pg.* 286
Coleman, Kelley, Sr Dir-Ecommerce Product Mgmt - Ann Inc.; *pg.* 18, *pg.* 1195
Coleman, Kelly, VP-Mktg - Goodwill Industries International, Inc.; *pg.* 1771, *pg.* 776
Coleman, Kendall, Mgr-PR - Williams-Sonoma, Inc.; *pg.* 1140, *pg.* 234
Coleman, Kenneth E., Sr VP-Mktg - Georgia Power Company; *pg.* 1943, *pg.* 508
Coleman, Mamie, VP-Music & Production - Fox Broadcasting Company; *pg.* 287, *pg.* 130
Coleman, Matt, Mng Dir-Cause Mktg - American Cancer Society, Inc.; *pg.* 126, *pg.* 487
Coleman, Michael, Mgr-Mktg Automation - W.W. Grainger, Inc.; *pg.* 1390, *pg.* 625
Coleman, Patrick, Mgr-Social Media-Americas - Carlson Companies Inc.; *pg.* 1084, *pg.* 947
Coleman, Rick, Dir-Adv Tech & Content - CVS Health Corporation; *pg.* 1765, *pg.* 1610
Coleman, Roxanne, Sr Mgr-Field Mktg - Pure Fishing, Inc.; *pg.* 1843, *pg.* 1614
Coleman, Tanya, Mgr-Mktg Adv - Publix Super Markets, Inc.; *pg.* 1031, *pg.* 437
Coleman, Tina, Specialist-Mktg - American Library Association; *pg.* 1615, *pg.* 564
Coleman, Wade, Dir-PR - Fiserv, Inc.; *pg.* 758, *pg.* 537
Coleman-Hagler, Verna, Brand Mgr-Natura Pet - Mars Petcare; *pg.* 1478, *pg.* 1633
Colen, Jeffrey, Product Mgr-Mktg-Display Adv - Google Inc.; *pg.* 1249, *pg.* 153
Coleridge, Christina, Mgr-Global Mktg-Consumer Brands - Chevron Corporation; *pg.* 974, *pg.* 259
Colestock, Regan, Asst Mgr-Online Mktg - Oxford University Press, Inc.; *pg.* 1673, *pg.* 1275
Coletta, Tonia, Sr Mgr-PR & Social Media Mktg - Molson Coors Canada Inc.; *pg.* 256, *pg.* 1955
Coletti, David, VP-Digital Media Res & Analytics - ESPN, Inc.; *pg.* 285, *pg.* 340
Colford, Paul, Dir-Media Rels - The Associated Press, Inc.; *pg.* 270, *pg.* 1197
Colgan, Cathy, Mgr-Internal Mktg Comm - Brocade Communications Systems, Inc.; *pg.* 365, *pg.* 239
Colgan, Diane, Sr VP-Mktg & Bus Analysis - Tops Markets, LLC; *pg.* 1036, *pg.* 1355
Colgan, Sarah, Coord-Mktg Events - Insight Enterprises, Inc.; *pg.* 415, *pg.* 26
Coli, Steve, Sr Mgr-IR - Brocade Communications Systems, Inc.; *pg.* 365, *pg.* 239
Coli, Vincent, Product Mgr - Socket Mobile, Inc.; *pg.* 471, *pg.* 164
Colip, Randy, Exec VP-Motor Products Grp - Baldor Electric Company; *pg.* 1316, *pg.* 32
Coll, John, VP-Mktg-Global - Eaton Corporation; *pg.* 1331, *pg.* 1429
Collado-Aleman, Margarita, Mgr-Mktg-Latin America - Converse Inc.; *pg.* 1831, *pg.* 793
Collard, Adrian, Head-Brand Strategy & Mktg-Global - PayPal Inc.; *pg.* 1274, *pg.* 248
Collard, Susan, Dir-Career Dev-Global Mktg Talent & Capabilities - Dell Inc.; *pg.* 383, *pg.* 1737
Colle, Claire, Mgr-Channels Mktg & Comm - IBM Canada Limited; *pg.* 411, *pg.* 1923
Colleary, Chris, Exec Dir-Ticket Sls & Svc - Buffalo Bills, Inc.; *pg.* 535, *pg.* 1319
Colleran, Matt, Dir-US Mktg-Girls Toys - Hasbro, Inc.; *pg.* 954, *pg.* 1603
Collett, Robert, Assoc Mgr-OLP Ops & Mktg Ops - Gilead Sciences, Inc.; *pg.* 1535, *pg.* 88
Colley, Phil, Gen Mgr & Strategist-Social Media - General Motors Company; *pg.* 175, *pg.* 881
Colliard, Mary, Mgr-Corp Mktg - Epicor Software Corporation; *pg.* 393, *pg.* 110
Collier, Ben, Sr Dir-Brand Mktg - The Leading Hotels of the World, Ltd.; *pg.* 1100, *pg.* 1250
Collier, Beth L., Mgr-Mktg Strategy - Charter Communications, Inc.; *pg.* 274, *pg.* 372
Collier, Carlton, VP-Sls & Mktg - Aromatique Inc.; *pg.* 499, *pg.* 32
Collier, Mika, Mgr-Mktg Product Line - Aviall, Inc.; *pg.* 224, *pg.* 1676
Collier, Terence, Dir-Mktg - Fasig-Tipton Co. Inc.; *pg.* 750, *pg.* 729
Colligan, Megan, Pres-Worldwide Mktg & Distr - Paramount Pictures Corporation; *pg.* 304, *pg.* 138
Collin, Dave, Sr VP-Sls & Mktg-Global - Crescent Cardboard Company, L.L.C.; *pg.* 1456, *pg.* 670
Collin, Myrianne, Sr VP-Strategy & Mktg - Videotron Ltd.; *pg.* 317, *pg.* 1957
Collings, Andrew, VP-Mdsg - Bookazine Company, Inc.; *pg.* 1622, *pg.* 1042
Collings, Hannah, Sr Mgr-Mktg - Turner Broadcasting System, Inc.; *pg.* 314, *pg.* 521
Collingwood, Patricia, Dir-Retail Mktg - Jos. A. Bank Clothiers, Inc.; *pg.* 42, *pg.* 771
Collins, Alex, Product Mgr - Google Inc.; *pg.* 1249, *pg.* 153
Collins, Alexandra, Assoc Mgr-Mktg-Food Svc - PepsiCo, Inc.; *pg.* 259, *pg.* 1327
Collins, Amee, Media Buyer-Brdcst - Dr Pepper Snapple Group, Inc.; *pg.* 250, *pg.* 1729
Collins, Amy, Brand Mgr-Post-it - 3M; *pg.* 339, *pg.* 179
Collins, Anne, Mgr-Sls - Marquis Who's Who, LLC; *pg.* 1661, *pg.* 1044
Collins, Ashley, Exec Dir-PR, Comm & Social Media - USANA Health Sciences, Inc.; *pg.* 1605, *pg.* 1761
Collins, Bentley, VP-Sls & Mktg - Sabre Corporation; *pg.* 1710, *pg.* 752
Collins, Beth, VP-Mktg - Lone Star Steakhouse & Saloon, Inc.; *pg.* 1736, *pg.* 1733
Collins, Bill, Coord-Sls & Mktg - Standard Motor Products, Inc.; *pg.* 218, *pg.* 1176
Collins, Billy, Sr Mgr-Mktg & Strategic Alliances-Oral Care - Johnson & Johnson; *pg.* 1549, *pg.* 1091
Collins, Brenda, Reg Mgr-Sls - ITW Magnaflux; *pg.* 1418, *pg.* 615
Collins, Brett, Brand Mgr & Experienced Relationship - St. Jude Children's Research Hospital; *pg.* 1596, *pg.* 1646
Collins, Casey, Exec VP-Consumer Products - World Wrestling Entertainment, Inc.; *pg.* 595, *pg.* 380
Collins, Cassie, Mgr-Mktg-Homeowners Insurance - The Allstate Corporation; *pg.* 1189, *pg.* 639
Collins, Catherine, Mgr-PR-Customer Spotlight Program - Microsoft Corporation; *pg.* 435, *pg.* 1824
Collins, Chris, VP-Multi Media Sls - Dow Jones & Company, Inc.; *pg.* 1637, *pg.* 1225

First page reference indicates Business Class Edition
Second page reference indicates Geographic Edition

Collins, Claire, Specialist-PR - Autodesk Inc.; pg. 356, pg. 257
Collins, Cynthia, Dir-Mktg - The New York Times Company; pg. 1668, pg. 1270
Collins, David, Dir-Corp Mktg - PUBLIC STORAGE; pg. 1467, pg. 98
Collins, Dennis, Dir-Mktg-Conferencing & Collaboration - InterCall, Inc.; pg. 417, pg. 578
Collins, Emilio, Sr VP-Mktg Partnerships-Global - National Basketball Association; pg. 566, pg. 1264
Collins, Gina, CMO - Build-A-Bear Workshop, Inc.; pg. 950, pg. 993
Collins, Jamie, Dir-Case IH Parts Sls & Mktg - CNH America LLC; pg. 702, pg. 560
Collins, Janice, Sr Dir-PR - Scripps; pg. 1593, pg. 209
Collins, Jeanne, VP-Global Mktg-Intimate Health & Denture Care - Combe Incorporated; pg. 1516, pg. 1351
Collins, Jeff, VP-Retail Sls - Nautilus, Inc.; pg. 1840, pg. 1846
Collins, Jennifer, Sr Mgr-Insights - United States Cellular Corporation; pg. 1875, pg. 594
Collins, John, VP-Sls-Global - Patagonia; pg. 31, pg. 301
Collins, John, Project Mgr-Mktg Comm - Texas Instruments Incorporated; pg. 679, pg. 1688
Collins, Julie, Dir-Digital Mktg-Global - Alcon; pg. 1399, pg. 530
Collins, Justin, Sr Mgr-Mktg - Kelley Blue Book Co., Inc.; pg. 1656, pg. 112
Collins, Karen, Mgr-Mktg Comm - Broan-NuTone LLC; pg. 1069, pg. 1860
Collins, Katie, Analyst-Product - Cars.com; pg. 1234, pg. 568
Collins, Kevin, Head-Sales, Retirement Plan Svcs - T. Rowe Price Group Inc.; pg. 808, pg. 759
Collins, Kevin B., Sr Dir-Global Mktg-Point-of-Care Bus Unit - Siemens Healthcare Diagnostics; pg. 673, pg. 604
Collins, Kim, Dir-Mktg & Bus Dev - Anritsu Company; pg. 618, pg. 152
Collins, Lauren, Sr Mgr-Mktg - Cheesecake Factory Incorporated; pg. 1017, pg. 56
Collins, Lisa, Area Dir-Sls & Mktg Kindred Rehabilitation - Kindred Healthcare, Inc.; pg. 1553, pg. 736
Collins, Megan, Mgr-Mktg Comm - Crested Butte Mountain Resort, Inc.; pg. 1088, pg. 316
Collins, Mei, Project Dir-Brand Mktg - Choice Hotels International, Inc.; pg. 1086, pg. 775
Collins, Michael, Dir-Product Dev - CEM Corporation; pg. 1405, pg. 1382
Collins, Natasha, Dir-Media Rels - Kentucky Utilities Company; pg. 1945, pg. 730
Collins, Nina, VP-Sls & Mktg-Retail & Custom Product Dev - Warner Music Group Corp.; pg. 590, pg. 1313
Collins, Nora, Brand Mgr - Promotion In Motion, Inc.; pg. 1861, pg. 1052
Collins, Peter, Sr Dir-PR - Papa John's International, Inc.; pg. 1743, pg. 737
Collins, Ramona, Mgr-Social Media - Wal-Mart Stores, Inc.; pg. 1790, pg. 29
Collins, Ryan, Dir-Sports Mktg-Bus & Strategy - Under Armour, Inc.; pg. 49, pg. 759
Collins, Scott, Exec VP-AMC & Wetv Adv Sls - AMC Networks Inc.; pg. 269, pg. 1189
Collins, Shauna, Sr Dir-Brand Strategy - Aetna Inc.; pg. 1187, pg. 351
Collins, Simon, Product Mgr - GE Intelligent Platforms; pg. 1339, pg. 1777
Collins, Steve, VP-Sls-Global - RadiSys Corporation; pg. 458, pg. 1498
Collins, Stormey, Sr Mgr-Mktg-Food & Beverage - Sam's Club; pg. 1783, pg. 29
Collins, Susan, Mgr-Mktg - IBM Canada Limited; pg. 411, pg. 1923
Collins, Tanja, Dir-Mktg - Performance Food Group Company, LLC; pg. 1030, pg. 1803
Collins, Tim, Sr VP-Experiential Mktg - Wells Fargo & Company; pg. 819, pg. 232
Collins, Wayne, Mgr-Indus Mktg-Worldwide - Agilent Technologies, Inc.; pg. 614, pg. 264
Collom, Chris, Sr Dir-Corp Comm - Aramark; pg. 1013, pg. 1558
Collura, Sam, VP-Comml Sls-North America - Telecommunication Systems Inc.; pg. 483, pg. 754
Colman, Evan, Head-Market Access Mktg-US Managed Markets - Novartis Pharmaceuticals Corp.; pg. 1575, pg. 1054
Colombana, Chris, Dir-Mktg Sys & Processes - Safeway Inc.; pg. 1032, pg. 184
Colombo, Marcelo, Dir-Mktg-Giorgio Armani & Designer Fragrances - L'Oreal USA; pg. 514, pg. 1252
Colombo, Pete, Product Dir-DuPont Tate & Lyle Bio Products - E.I. du Pont de Nemours & Company; pg. 1159, pg. 390
Colon, Florentino, Dir-Multicultural Mktg - Aetna Inc.; pg. 1187, pg. 351
Colon, Gene, Asst VP-Medical & Media Rels - L'Oreal USA; pg. 514, pg. 1252
Colon, Geoffrey, Mgr-Grp Product Mktg & Emerging Media - Microsoft Corp.; pg. 440, pg. 321
Colon, Jim, VP-Sls - Toyota Motor Sales, U.S.A., Inc.; pg. 193, pg. 296
Colon, Maria, Dir-Mktg - De'Longhi America Inc.; pg. 54, pg. 1118
Colon, William, Dir-Mktg - Medtronic, Inc.; pg. 1564, pg. 939
Colon, Wilma, Mgr-Media Rels - The Walt Disney Company; pg. 317, pg. 52
Colonna, Chip, Dir-Mktg - The Terminix International Company Limited Partnership; pg. 337, pg. 1646
Colonna, CJ, Brand Mktg Mgr - NIKE, Inc.; pg. 1812, pg. 1492
Colorado, Audrey Palacios, Mgr-PR & Mktg-Global - Fossil Group, Inc.; pg. 5, pg. 1735
Colorado, Rafael, Dir-Mktg-Desktop Virtualization Solutions - Dell Inc.; pg. 383, pg. 1737
Colorito, Alan, Mgr-Channel Mktg-North America - Eaton Corporation; pg. 1331, pg. 1429
Colosi, Heather, Dir-Mktg & Special Events - Lancaster Symphony Orchestra; pg. 556, pg. 1546
Colosino, Robert, VP-Mktg & Bus Dev - TECSYS, Inc.; pg. 482, pg. 1956
Colston, Will, VP-Mktg & Ops - The Atlantic Monthly Group; pg. 1618, pg. 396
Colston, Will, VP-Mktg & Ops - National Journal Group; pg. 1667, pg. 402
Colter, Kim, Program Mgr-Global Digital Mktg - InterContinental Hotels Corporation; pg. 1097, pg. 511
Coltrin, David, Sr Dir-Product Mktg & Strategy - Denny's Corporation; pg. 1725, pg. 1622
Colucci, Jennifer, Mgr-PR, Social Media & Sponsorships - Olympus America Inc.; pg. 1425, pg. 1521
Colucci, Sofia, Mktg Dir-Quaker - PepsiCo, Inc.; pg. 259, pg. 1327
Columbia, Peter, Exec VP-Sls - Parfums De Coeur Ltd.; pg. 519, pg. 376
Columbo, Jeanine, Dir-Direct Mktg & Sr Mgr-Mktg - American International Group, Inc.; pg. 1190, pg. 1193
Columbus, Brian, Sr Mgr-Dev Ops - Toronto Symphony Orchestra; pg. 589, pg. 1946
Columbus, Jamie, Sr Dir & Divisional Mdse Mgr-Peripherals & New Products - Office Depot, Inc.; pg. 448, pg. 412
Columbus, John D., Mgr-PR - Verizon Communications Inc.; pg. 1875, pg. 1309
Colvard, Kaylee, Reg Assoc Mgr-Mktg - The Allstate Corporation; pg. 1189, pg. 639
Colvin, Dionne, Dir-Natl Media, Traditional & Emerging - Toyota Motor North America, Inc.; pg. 192, pg. 1303
Colvin, Dionne, Dir-Traditional & New Media - Toyota Motor Sales, U.S.A., Inc.; pg. 193, pg. 296
Colvin, Peggy, Sr Mgr-Design - LensCrafters, Inc.; pg. 1420, pg. 1460
Colwell, Chris, Pres-Carlson Paving Products, Inc - Astec Industries, Inc.; pg. 69, pg. 1628
Colwell, Chris, Assoc Mgr-Creative Svcs - Meredith Corporation; pg. 1663, pg. 705
Colwell, Justin, VP-Wireless Product - Charter Communications, Inc.; pg. 274, pg. 372
Colwell, Nicole, Sr Assoc Brand Mgr-Kool-Aid - The Kraft Heinz Company; pg. 871, pg. 641
Colyer, John, Sr VP-Global Indus Products & Protective Solution - Sonoco Products Company; pg. 1469, pg. 1619
Comacchio, Brenna, Analyst-Search Mktg - Autodesk Inc.; pg. 356, pg. 257
Comak, Amanda, Dir-Baseball Media Rels Comm & New Media - Washington Nationals, L.P.; pg. 591, pg. 407
Combs, Bob, Engr-Sls & Application - Post Glover Resistors Inc.; pg. 1585, pg. 727
Combs, Brad, Mgr-Brand & Product Ops-Disney Interactive - Disney Interactive Media Group; pg. 1239, pg. 95
Combs, Cathleen, Dir-Svc Mktg - Canon U.S.A., Inc.; pg. 1404, pg. 1178
Combs, Cathy, Acct Mgr-Mktg Comm - Eastman Chemical Company; pg. 1159, pg. 1636
Combs, Dave, VP-Sls & Mktg - DEUTZ Corporation; pg. 1328, pg. 536
Combs, Dustin, VP-Sls, BOGS & Rafters Brands - Weyco Group, Inc.; pg. 1822, pg. 1858
Combs, Kiersten, Exec Bus Dir-Primary Care Sls - AstraZeneca Pharmaceuticals LP; pg. 1497, pg. 389
Combs, P. J., Asst Dir-PR - Cincinnati Bengals, Inc.; pg. 540, pg. 1410
Combs, Riley, VP-Sls, BOGS & Rafters Brands - Weyco Group, Inc.; pg. 1822, pg. 1858
Comer, Donald, Dir-Digital Access Mktg - FedEx Corporation; pg. 1907, pg. 1642
Comer, Kevin, Exec Dir-Customer Mktg - CME Group, Inc.; pg. 738, pg. 571
Comerford, Frank, Chief Revenue Officer & Pres-Comml Ops-NBCU Local Media - NBC Universal, Inc.; pg. 300, pg. 1266
Comiskey, Paul B., Pres-Residential Sls - The Dixie Group, Inc.; pg. 692, pg. 1629
Comissiong, John, Dir-Outreach Mktg - Harley-Davidson, Inc.; pg. 178, pg. 1874
Comley, Ellen, VP-Integrated Media - Staples, Inc.; pg. 474, pg. 821
Commandeur, Denise, Mgr-Adv Fin Ops - Apple Inc.; pg. 350, pg. 73
Como, Matt, VP-Sls - LIFETIME BRANDS, INC.; pg. 1127, pg. 1161
Companey, Julie, Sr Mgr-Client Mktg - Valassis; pg. 1698, pg. 386
Compres, Fabiola, Sr Mgr-HR & Org Dev - The Leading Hotels of the World, Ltd.; pg. 1100, pg. 1250
Compston-Wells, Toni, Head-Digital Mktg-O&G, Measurement & Control - General Electric Company; pg. 1297, pg. 347
Compton, Chris, Dir-Sponsorship Sls, Digital Adv & Partnership Mktg - Major League Baseball; pg. 560, pg. 1255
Compton, James E., Vice Chm & Chief Revenue Officer - United Continental Holdings, Inc.; pg. 1927, pg. 593
Compton, Jim, Vice Chm & Chief Revenue Officer - United Airlines, Inc.; pg. 1927, pg. 593
Compton, Leonora, Mgr-Product Mktg - National Oilwell Varco, Inc.; pg. 1364, pg. 1712
Compton, Marc, Mgr-Nurture Mktg - Adobe Systems Incorporated; pg. 342, pg. 235
Conangla, Lauren, Product Mgr-Dominican Republic & Cartagena, Colombia - Apple Vacations Inc.; pg. 1899, pg. 1556
Conaway, Gaines, Head-Major Mktg Initiatives - C Spire Wireless; pg. 628, pg. 971
Conaway, Mari Prieto, Product Mgr-Ion Sources - Thermo Fisher Scientific Inc.; pg. 1431, pg. 854
Conboy, Tricia, Dir-Adv - Sun Life Financial Inc.; pg. 806, pg. 1944
Concepcion, Danielle, Mgr-Mktg-Brands - Pacific Sunwear of California, Inc.; pg. 1781, pg. 43
Concepcion, Roel, Dir-Creative-Content - Under Armour, Inc.; pg. 49, pg. 759
Condiff, Helene, Bus Mgr-Plasma Proteins - Siemens Healthcare Diagnostics; pg. 673, pg. 604
Condon, Billy, VP-Mktg - Tourism Ireland; pg. 1007, pg. 1303
Condon, Emmett, Brand Mgr - LEGO Systems, Inc.; pg. 961, pg. 346
Condon, Erin, VP-Upromise by Sallie Mae Mktg - SLM Corporation; pg. 804, pg. 388
Condon, Jeff, Sr VP-Mktg Solutions - Live Nation Entertainment, Inc.; pg. 558, pg. 47
Condon, John, VP-Sls-North America - Vapor Bus International; pg. 221, pg. 560
Condon, Kathryn, Sr VP-Media, Digital Mktg & CRM - FMR LLC (Fidelity Investments); pg. 759, pg. 794
Condon, Kristin, Sr Mgr-Mktg Programs-Global - Pegasystems Inc.; pg. 453, pg. 809
Condon, Lori, Sr Mgr-Mktg Program-Global - Pegasystems Inc.; pg. 453, pg. 809
Condon, Marie R., Sr Mgr-Events - Juniper Networks, Inc.; pg. 1260, pg. 286
Condon, Tara Flynn, VP-Corp Dev & Mktg - API Technologies Corp.; pg. 618, pg. 452
Condos, James, Dir-IT, Sls & Mktg - Motorola Solutions, Inc.; pg. 657, pg. 659
Condyles, Cady, Mgr-Mktg-Paid Search - Amazon.com, Inc.; pg. 1226, pg. 1831
Cone, Jim, Sr VP-Mktg - Loews Hotels Holding Corporation; pg. 1101, pg. 1252
Conell, Nick, Sr Mgr-US Nephrology Comml Strategy - Amgen Inc.; pg. 1493, pg. 291
Coney, Kathleen, Dir-Brand Mktg - Marriott International, Inc.;

pg. 1102, *pg.* 764
Confort, Susan, VP-Mktg - International Business Machines Corporation; *pg.* 418, *pg.* 1138
Conforti, Cathleen, Product Mgr-PayPass Solutions-Global - MasterCard Incorporated; *pg.* 779, *pg.* 1325
Confrey, John, VP-Mktg - Aerco International Inc.; *pg.* 1068, *pg.* 1142
Conger, Beth, Sr Mgr-Brand Experience-LensCrafters - LensCrafters, Inc.; *pg.* 1420, *pg.* 1460
Conguta, Orlando, Sr Dir-Team Admin - Major League Soccer LLC; *pg.* 560, *pg.* 1256
Coniglio, Charlie, VP-Mktg & Distr & Head-DTG Integration - The Hertz Corporation; *pg.* 1911, *pg.* 450
Coniglio, Lisa, Product Mgr - Brother International Corporation - USA; *pg.* 53, *pg.* 1046
Conklin, David, Head-Product & Support - Unison Industries, LLC; *pg.* 235, *pg.* 435
Conklin, Rex, Dir-Media & Partnership Mktg - The Home Depot, Inc.; *pg.* 1050, *pg.* 510
Conklin, Sarah, Dir-Mktg-Tea - Starbucks Corporation; *pg.* 897, *pg.* 1840
Conklin, Tami, Sr Mgr-Ops Mgmt - NIKE, Inc.; *pg.* 1812, *pg.* 1492
Conkrite, Matt, Mgr-Mktg Comm - General Electric Company; *pg.* 1297, *pg.* 347
Conley, Clare, Sr Mgr - QUALCOMM Incorporated; *pg.* 1873, *pg.* 207
Conley, Kelly, Dir-Mktg - Avista Corporation; *pg.* 1935, *pg.* 1843
Conley, Lenna, Sr Mgr-Brand Dev-Global - Jarden Consumer Solutions; *pg.* 57, *pg.* 412
Conley, Lori, Dir-Mktg - MeadWestvaco Consumer & Office Products; *pg.* 431, *pg.* 1456
Conley, Marcia, Dir-Mktg Comm - Highmark Blue Cross Blue Shield; *pg.* 1203, *pg.* 1576
Conley, Paul, Mgr-Mktg - 3M Company; *pg.* 1142, *pg.* 956
Conlin, Ryan, Specialist-Mktg - Culver Franchising System, Inc.; *pg.* 1724, *pg.* 1887
Conly, Shawn, VP-Global Adv & Branding - Electronic Arts Inc.; *pg.* 951, *pg.* 189
Conn, Grad, Head-Microsoft US Central Mktg Org - Microsoft Corporation; *pg.* 435, *pg.* 1824
Conn, Scott, Mgr-Production - Chicago Theatre Group Inc.; *pg.* 539, *pg.* 570
Connally, Carlisle, Sr Dir-Search & Affiliate Mktg - Choice Hotels International, Inc.; *pg.* 1086, *pg.* 775
Connally, Patrick, Product Mgr-High Performance Oscilloscopes - Teledyne LeCroy; *pg.* 1431, *pg.* 1153
Connaughton, Steve, Mgr-Product Line - Sloan Valve Company; *pg.* 1062, *pg.* 613
Connell, Jeff, Dir-Mktg - Intel Corporation; *pg.* 645, *pg.* 266
Connell, Terry, VP-Sls - Barnes International Inc.; *pg.* 1317, *pg.* 654
Connell, Wendy, VP-Mktg - CustomInk, LLC; *pg.* 22, *pg.* 1780
Connelly, Bill, Bus Mgr - Cincinnati Bengals, Inc.; *pg.* 540, *pg.* 1410
Connelly, Chris, Mgr-Product Mktg - Google Inc.; *pg.* 1249, *pg.* 153
Connelly, David, Dir-PR - Museum of Fine Arts of St. Petersburg Florida Inc.; *pg.* 565, *pg.* 463
Connelly, Julie Brennan, Mgr-Digital Mktg - MetLife, Inc.; *pg.* 1208, *pg.* 1258
Connelly, Kelly, Sr Specialist-PR - Lowe's Companies, Inc.; *pg.* 1053, *pg.* 1383
Connelly, Kevin, Mgr-Programmatic Sls - Fox Television Stations Inc.; *pg.* 288, *pg.* 131
Connelly, Kristin, Dir-Mktg & Comm - New York Jets Football Club, Inc.; *pg.* 570, *pg.* 1067
Connelly, Robyn, Dir-Customer Experience & Mktg Integration - Wyndham Worldwide Corporation; *pg.* 1119, *pg.* 1107
Connelly, Saunya, Specialist-Mktg - National Railroad Passenger Corporation; *pg.* 1916, *pg.* 403
Conner, David, Sr Mgr-Mktg & Reg Product Mgr - AT&T; *pg.* 1865, *pg.* 258
Conner, Erika, Community Mgr-Social Media - Chevron Corporation; *pg.* 974, *pg.* 259
Conner, Holly, Dir-Mktg & Bus Dev - Simon Property Group, Inc.; *pg.* 1112, *pg.* 690
Conner, Laura, Mgr-Mktg - Eli Lilly and Company; *pg.* 1527, *pg.* 684
Conner, Mark, Asst VP-Mktg - Lithia Motors Inc; *pg.* 183, *pg.* 1499
Conner, Nancy, Sr Dir-Product Mktg - Equifax Inc.; *pg.* 748, *pg.* 504
Conner, Rebecca, Brand Mktg Mgr - Luby's, Inc.; *pg.* 1736, *pg.* 1710
Connery, Colleen, Sr Dir-Employee Comm & Community Rels - Lam Research Corporation; *pg.* 1354, *pg.* 246
Connley, Lauren, Dir-Creative - Gorilla Glue Co.; *pg.* 1048, *pg.* 1414
Connly, Linda, Sr VP-Global Inside Sls - EMC Corporation; *pg.* 391, *pg.* 825
Connolly, Chris, Dir-Mktg-Northeast - PepsiCo, Inc.; *pg.* 259, *pg.* 1327
Connolly, Colleen, Planner-Integrated Sls - The New York Times; *pg.* 1668, *pg.* 1270
Connolly, Dana Cameron, Media Planner - Northwestern University; *pg.* 606, *pg.* 612
Connolly, Jerry, Sr VP-Mktg - Al Jazeera America, LLC; *pg.* 269, *pg.* 1188
Connolly, Keith, Mgr-Adv - The Telegram; *pg.* 1691, *pg.* 1916
Connolly, Mike, Dir-Snacks & Foodservice New Product Dev - Pepperidge Farm, Inc.; *pg.* 888, *pg.* 363
Connolly, Pat, VP-Mktg Solutions - Conde Nast Publications, Inc.; *pg.* 1629, *pg.* 1217
Connolly, Rick, Sr VP-Sls & Mktg-G4S Secure Solutions - G4S Secure Solutions USA; *pg.* 399, *pg.* 436
Connolly, Scott C., Sr VP-Sls & Mktg - The Providence Journal; *pg.* 1678, *pg.* 1607
Connor, Amy, VP-Mktg - Luxottica Retail; *pg.* 8, *pg.* 1460
Connor, Catherine, Mgr-Solutions Mktg - Rally Software Development Corp.; *pg.* 459, *pg.* 311
Connor, Dana, Dir-Mktg - IMS Health, Inc.; *pg.* 1544, *pg.* 344
Connor, Danielle, Sr VP-Brand Mktg - Red Lobster; *pg.* 1747, *pg.* 455
Connor, Ian, Dir-Mktg-ColdPruf - Indera Mills Company; *pg.* 26, *pg.* 1396
Connor, Jennifer, Brand Mgr - Destination XL Group, Inc.; *pg.* 40, *pg.* 810
Connor, Jerry, Dir-Product Mgmt - CCH; *pg.* 1626, *pg.* 569
Connor, Kathleen, Sr Dir-Field & Channel Mktg - Concur Technologies, Inc.; *pg.* 1236, *pg.* 1813
Connor, Kevin, Sr VP-Affiliate Sls & Mktg - Tribune Media Company; *pg.* 1696, *pg.* 592
Connor, Margaret M., Sr Dir-HR & Retirement Programs - Metropolitan Transportation Authority; *pg.* 1915, *pg.* 1260
Connor, Mark A., Dir-Sls-Territory 3 - Reliable Automatic Sprinkler Co., Inc.; *pg.* 1137, *pg.* 1158
Connor, Patrick J., Sr VP-Sls-Consumer Products - Hormel Foods Corporation; *pg.* 863, *pg.* 915
Connor, Rich, VP-Sls Focus Channels - Nestle Professional Beverages; *pg.* 257, *pg.* 474
Connor, Sacha, Assoc Dir-Mktg-Pine Sol, Green Works & Fraganzia - The Clorox Company; *pg.* 327, *pg.* 169
Connor, Sean, Mgr-Media Svcs & Pur - Sanofi US; *pg.* 1592, *pg.* 1046
Connor-Ingram, Maria, Asst Mgr-Mktg-Female Mass Underwear - Hanesbrands Inc.; *pg.* 26, *pg.* 1394
Connors, Betsy, Mgr-Mktg-Taste of Home Media - The Reader's Digest Association, Inc.; *pg.* 1679, *pg.* 1322
Connors, Bill, VP-Consumer Mktg - MasterCard International, Inc.; *pg.* 780, *pg.* 1326
Connors, Bill, Head-Brand Mktg - Red Bull North America, Inc.; *pg.* 264, *pg.* 275
Connors, Brittany, Specialist-Mktg - E&J Gallo Winery; *pg.* 1962, *pg.* 149
Connors, Courtney, VP-Integrated Mktg - Major League Baseball; *pg.* 560, *pg.* 1255
Connors, Don, Dir-Builder Sls - Purcell Murray Company Inc.; *pg.* 59, *pg.* 50
Connors, Jill, Mgr-Media & Comm - KVH Industries Inc; *pg.* 650, *pg.* 1602
Connors, Keri, Head-Digital & Social Media & Sr Mgr-Global Comm & Branding - Raytheon Company; *pg.* 233, *pg.* 854
Connors, Lindsay, Coord-Mktg - Colorado State University; *pg.* 599, *pg.* 328
Connors, Matthew, Dir-Operational Mktg - E*TRADE Financial Corporation; *pg.* 749, *pg.* 1230
Connors, Rob, Asst VP-Brand Mktg-Natl Car Rental - Enterprise Holdings, Inc.; *pg.* 1906, *pg.* 996
Connors, Stephen, Assoc Mgr-Digital Adv-Global - Accenture; *pg.* 1392, *pg.* 1186
Connors, Tim, Exec VP-Sls & Mktg - Prestige Brands Holdings, Inc.; *pg.* 520, *pg.* 1345
Conolly, Marie, Project Mgr-Email Mktg - Brooks Brothers Group, Inc.; *pg.* 39, *pg.* 1208
Conover, Charles E, Product Mgr - The Progressive Corporation; *pg.* 1214, *pg.* 1463
Conquest, Geraldine D., Acct Exec-New Bus Agency Sls - Google Inc.; *pg.* 1249, *pg.* 153
Conrad, Ginger M., Mgr-Mktg - DIRECTV Group Holdings, LLC; *pg.* 281, *pg.* 79
Conrad, Jeff, VP-Sls-Acura - American Honda Motor Co., Inc.; *pg.* 163, *pg.* 292
Conrad, Jeff, VP-Sls & Market Dev - Dr Pepper Snapple Group, Inc.; *pg.* 250, *pg.* 1729
Conrad, Kari, Mgr-Private Brand Sls - SUPERVALU, Inc.; *pg.* 1035, *pg.* 924
Conrad, Laura, Sr Specialist-PR - Mitsubishi Motors North America, Inc.; *pg.* 185, *pg.* 75
Conrad, Rick, VP-Foodservice Sls - Country Pure Foods, Inc.; *pg.* 247, *pg.* 1400
Conrad, Rick, Mgr-Mktg - Frisch's Restaurants, Inc.; *pg.* 1729, *pg.* 1413
Conrad, Robyn, Dir-Mktg - Michelin North America Inc.; *pg.* 1886, *pg.* 1618
Conrad, Stacy, VP-Channel Sls - FUSION TELECOMMUNICATIONS INTERNATIONAL, INC.; *pg.* 1248, *pg.* 1233
Conrad, Stacy, Brand Mgr - Pfizer Inc.; *pg.* 1581, *pg.* 1278
Conrad, Stefanie, Brand Mgr - Dr Pepper Snapple Group, Inc.; *pg.* 250, *pg.* 1729
Conrado, Eduardo, Chief Strategy Officer, Chief Innovation Officer & Exec VP - Motorola Solutions, Inc.; *pg.* 657, *pg.* 659
Conran, Melanie, Dir-Creative - Air Lift Company; *pg.* 198, *pg.* 895
Conroy, Catherine Ann, Mgr-Global Corp Mktg & Brand - Cabot Microelectronics Corporation; *pg.* 1151, *pg.* 554
Conroy, Charles, COO & Exec Dir-Sls & Mktg - Positron Corp.; *pg.* 665, *pg.* 680
Conroy, David, Dir-Intermodal Sls - CR England, Inc.; *pg.* 1904, *pg.* 1756
Conroy, Fred, VP-Sls - Vulcan Electric Company; *pg.* 1078, *pg.* 751
Conroy, Jamie, Sr Product Dir - TripAdvisor, Inc.; *pg.* 1926, *pg.* 835
Conroy, John, Dir-Creative Svcs - Chicago Bears Football Club, Inc.; *pg.* 538, *pg.* 623
Conroy, Kelly, Mgr-Mktg Strategy & Comm - Liberty Mutual Insurance Group Inc.; *pg.* 1205, *pg.* 797
Conroy, Trip, Specialist-Sls & Mktg - The Dun & Bradstreet Corp.; *pg.* 1637, *pg.* 1120
Conroy, Troy, Sr Mgr-Bus Integration-Enterprise Sys - W.W. Grainger, Inc.; *pg.* 1390, *pg.* 625
Conry, Bart, VP-Chassis Pool Sls - Omaha Standard Palfinger; *pg.* 706, *pg.* 704
Considine, Brad, VP-Sls & Mktg-Global - Baltimore Aircoil Company; *pg.* 1069, *pg.* 773
Console, Sara, Dir-Mktg Comm - Comcast Cable Communications, Inc.; *pg.* 276, *pg.* 1560
Consson, Fredrik, Dir-Digital Mktg - Tektronix, Inc.; *pg.* 1431, *pg.* 1496
Constable, Jen, Dir-Mktg & Creative Svcs-Boulder - University Of Colorado; *pg.* 608, *pg.* 323
Constance, Shannon, Dir-Creative-White Barn - Bath & Body Works, LLC; *pg.* 500, *pg.* 1471
Constantine, Alexandra, Specialist-PR - Autodesk Inc.; *pg.* 356, *pg.* 257
Constantine, Hank, Dir-Mktg-aeDs - Zoll Medical Corporation; *pg.* 1612, *pg.* 814
Constantine, Rob, Dir-MetLife Retail & Diverse Markets Mktg - MetLife, Inc.; *pg.* 1208, *pg.* 1258
Constantino, Jeff, Asst VP-Mktg - Truth Initiative; *pg.* 158, *pg.* 405
Constantino, Tor, Dir-PR & External Affairs-Global - MedImmune LLC; *pg.* 1562, *pg.* 770
Consuegra, Corey, Dir-Mktg-Golf Balls - Bridgestone Golf, Inc.; *pg.* 1828, *pg.* 528
Conte, Camila, Mgr-Media Rels - PR Newswire Association LLC; *pg.* 1678, *pg.* 1283
Conte, Christopher, Mgr-Mktg - Transamerica Insurance & Investment Group; *pg.* 1219, *pg.* 141
Conte, John, Specialist-Product Dev - Wal-Mart.com; *pg.* 1287, *pg.* 50
Conte, Lou, Mgr-Mktg - Dunkin' Brands Group, Inc.; *pg.* 1727, *pg.* 810
Conte, Max, Coord-Adv Sls - The Wall Street Journal; *pg.* 1700, *pg.* 1312
Conte, Peter B., Sr Mgr-Boeing Comml Airplanes & Engrg Comm - The Boeing Company; *pg.* 225, *pg.* 567
Conte, Tara, VP-Worldwide Mktg Partnerships & Consumer Products - Paramount Pictures Corporation; *pg.* 304, *pg.* 138
Contenti, Cecilia, Sr Product Mgr-Mktg - International Rectifier

First page reference indicates Business Class Edition
Second page reference indicates Geographic Edition

Corporation; *pg.* 647, *pg.* 80
Conti, Doris, Dir-STG Product Dev - International Business Machines Corporation; *pg.* 418, *pg.* 1138
Conti, Nadia, Mgr-Mktg Campaigns & Customer Analytics - Chico's FAS, Inc.; *pg.* 21, *pg.* 427
Contino, James, Mgr-North American Office Product Mktg - Xerox Corporation; *pg.* 494, *pg.* 365
Contis, Denise, Exec VP-Dev & Production - Discovery Communications, Inc.; *pg.* 282, *pg.* 777
Contoravdis, George, Mgr-Mktg - CNA Insurance Companies; *pg.* 1198, *pg.* 571
Contos, Adam, Sr VP-Mktg-RE/MAX, LLC - RE/MAX International, Inc.; *pg.* 1109, *pg.* 322
Contreras, Alex, Product Mgr-Acne - Galderma Laboratories, L.P.; *pg.* 1532, *pg.* 1695
Contreras, Beatrice, Coord-Mktg - American Leather LP; *pg.* 912, *pg.* 1673
Contreras, Christian, Sr Mgr-Global Accounts - Hotwire, Inc.; *pg.* 1912, *pg.* 219
Contreras, Craig, Sls Plng Mgr-Beauty Care - Henkel Consumer Goods; *pg.* 511, *pg.* 22
Contreras, Javier, Sr Mgr-Innovation & Sourcing - The Clorox Company; *pg.* 327, *pg.* 169
Contreras, Juan, Mgr-Customer Mktg - MillerCoors; *pg.* 254, *pg.* 1877
Contreras, Maurice, Reg Dir-Sls Ops-Indirect - AT&T Communications Corp.; *pg.* 1866, *pg.* 1043
Contreras, Maurice, Reg Dir-Sls Ops-Indirect - AT&T Inc.; *pg.* 1867, *pg.* 1674
Contreras, Michael, Mgr-Digital Mktg - DOLE FOOD COMPANY, INC.; *pg.* 853, *pg.* 306
Contreras, Somerlea, Specialist-Digital Channel, Social Media & Branded Communities - lululemon athletica inc.; *pg.* 44, *pg.* 1911
Converse, Tim, Head-Search Science Engrg & Sr Dir - eBay Inc.; *pg.* 1240, *pg.* 243
Conville, Brian, Mgr-Market Sls - FedEx Corporation; *pg.* 1907, *pg.* 1642
Conway, Andrew, Sr Dir-Product Mktg-Enterprise Mobility Suite - Microsoft Corporation; *pg.* 435, *pg.* 1824
Conway, Betsy, Mgr-Charlotte Community Affairs & Sports Mktg - Duke Energy Corporation; *pg.* 1940, *pg.* 1366
Conway, Bill, Sr VP-Sls - athenahealth, Inc.; *pg.* 1497, *pg.* 855
Conway, John, VP-eMarketing & Corp Mktg - EMC Corporation; *pg.* 391, *pg.* 825
Conway, Katherine, Sr Dir-Digital - Parfums Christian Dior, Inc; *pg.* 519, *pg.* 1276
Conway, Kimberly, Product Mgr - Summer Infant, Inc.; *pg.* 1139, *pg.* 1610
Conway, Maggie, Sr Mgr-Special projects - Coach, Inc.; *pg.* 3, *pg.* 1214
Conway, Mark, Dir-Trade Mktg - Pinnacle Foods Group LLC; *pg.* 889, *pg.* 1104
Conway, Meghan, Coord-Mktg-Consumer & Social Media - A&E Television Networks, LLC; *pg.* 267, *pg.* 1185
Conway, Michael, Mgr-Product Mktg - AVX Corporation; *pg.* 623, *pg.* 1616
Conway, Paul, Sr Dir-Design - National Hockey League; *pg.* 568, *pg.* 1265
Conway, Scott, Mgr-Adv - Nintendo of America, Inc.; *pg.* 965, *pg.* 1829
Conway, Sean, Dir-Global Media & Analyst Rels-Fin Svcs Grp - Accenture; *pg.* 1392, *pg.* 1186
Conway, Susan, Sr Dir-IR - Cognex Corporation; *pg.* 1406, *pg.* 834
Conyard, Scott, Dir-Imaging & Mktg Svcs - Eastman Kodak Company; *pg.* 1408, *pg.* 1333
Conzemius, Justin, Dir-Mktg-Snacks Category Expansion - General Mills, Inc.; *pg.* 828, *pg.* 933
Coogan, Craig, Dir-Product Mgmt - Arris Group, Inc.; *pg.* 353, *pg.* 541
Cook, Adrian, Product Mgr-Infrastructure Protection Div-Global - 3M Company; *pg.* 1142, *pg.* 956
Cook, Alicia, Mgr-Film Mktg-AMC Theatres - AMC Entertainment Inc.; *pg.* 527, *pg.* 716
Cook, Alistair L.W., Sr VP-Wood Products Ops-Canada - Canfor Corporation; *pg.* 1454, *pg.* 1910
Cook, Amy, Coord-ECommerce Mktg - Carter's, Inc.; *pg.* 21, *pg.* 491
Cook, Amy, Dir-Global Creative Ops - Oakley, Inc.; *pg.* 1840, *pg.* 86
Cook, Audra, Mgr-Acq Sls - Corpus Christi Caller-Times; *pg.* 1630, *pg.* 1671
Cook, Connie, Product Mgr - Crescent Cardboard Company, L.L.C.; *pg.* 1456, *pg.* 670
Cook, Connie G., Sr Specialist-Mktg Comm - Acuity Brands, Inc.; *pg.* 1294, *pg.* 487
Cook, Dan, Brand Mktg Mgr-Jeep - FCA US LLC; *pg.* 170, *pg.* 868
Cook, Dennine, Dir-Community & Media Rels - The Gurwin Jewish Geriatric Center; *pg.* 1538, *pg.* 1153
Cook, Greg, VP-Sls & Mktg - Braun North America; *pg.* 52, *pg.* 792
Cook, Holly, Dir-Mktg - US Career Institute; *pg.* 610, *pg.* 329
Cook, Jay, Mgr-Strategic Sourcing-Worldwide Mktg, Comm & Policy - Facebook, Inc.; *pg.* 1245, *pg.* 143
Cook, Jeff, Mgr-Mktg - GEA Refrigeration North America, Inc.; *pg.* 1072, *pg.* 1597
Cook, Jenell, VP-Adv Ops - United Online, Inc.; *pg.* 1286, *pg.* 308
Cook, Jim, Dir-Sls - Emery-Waterhouse Company; *pg.* 1047, *pg.* 751
Cook, John, Reg Mgr-Sls - Hyundai Motor America; *pg.* 179, *pg.* 89
Cook, Katie, Sr Mgr-Brand & Channel-Architectural Coatings - PPG Industries, Inc.; *pg.* 1445, *pg.* 1579
Cook, Kelly, Dir-Mktg-Werther's Original Caramels - Storck USA, L.P.; *pg.* 1862, *pg.* 591
Cook, Khristina, Mgr-Mktg-Los Angeles - The Reserve Group; *pg.* 799, *pg.* 1402
Cook, Langdon, Dir-PR-Natl - Deloitte & Touche USA LLP; *pg.* 743, *pg.* 1222
Cook, Lisa, Dir-Mktg - Anthem, Inc.; *pg.* 1192, *pg.* 683
Cook, Matt, VP-Sls-Natl Grocery Channel - Hillshire Brands; *pg.* 862, *pg.* 576
Cook, Matthew, Mgr-Mktg - Newfield Exploration Company; *pg.* 45, *pg.* 1747
Cook, Melanie, Sr Dir-Labor & Employment - Dollar General Corporation; *pg.* 1767, *pg.* 1635
Cook, Nathan, Sr Mgr-Govt & Community Rels - US Oncology, Inc.; *pg.* 1604, *pg.* 1747
Cook, Patty, Dir-System-Consumer Relationship Mktg - Baylor Health Care System; *pg.* 1500, *pg.* 1676
Cook, Rachael J., Dir-Mktg & Sls Channel Enablement-West Div - Comcast Corporation; *pg.* 276, *pg.* 1560
Cook, Ron, VP & Dir-Mktg - Niemann Foods Inc.; *pg.* 1028, *pg.* 653
Cook, Rynell, Assoc Product Line Mgr-Teva - Deckers Outdoor Corporation; *pg.* 1807, *pg.* 100
Cook, Sari, Asst VP-Mktg & Distr - The Hanover Insurance Company; *pg.* 1202, *pg.* 862
Cook, Sean, Product Mgr-Mobile Platform - Twitter, Inc.; *pg.* 1285, *pg.* 228
Cook, Steve, Dir-Product Tech - Tech Spray, L.P.; *pg.* 1183, *pg.* 1659
Cook, Thomas H., Sr VP-Global Sls & Customer Experience - Dow Corning Corporation; *pg.* 1159, *pg.* 900
Cook, Todd, Dir-Mktg - G.H. Bass & Co.; *pg.* 1809, *pg.* 1234
Cook, Todd, Sr VP-Retail Mktg-Heritage Brands - PVH Corp.; *pg.* 46, *pg.* 1283
Cook, Tracy, Dir-Mktg Innovation - INVISTA B.V.; *pg.* 1168, *pg.* 723
Cook, Tyler, Coord-Adv Ops Traffic - Kelley Blue Book Co., Inc.; *pg.* 1656, *pg.* 112
Cook-Manely, Rosemary, VP-Mktg - Home Properties Inc.; *pg.* 1096, *pg.* 1336
Cooke, Brent, VP-Guest & Digital Mktg - AMC Entertainment Inc.; *pg.* 527, *pg.* 716
Cooke, Dan, Dir-eBusiness & Digital Shopper Mktg - Kellogg Company; *pg.* 831, *pg.* 870
Cooke, John, Reg Mgr-Sls-East Reg - Triangle Package Machinery Co.; *pg.* 1383, *pg.* 592
Cooke, Randi, Mgr-Mktg Comm - Extended Stay Hotels LLC; *pg.* 1091, *pg.* 1622
Cooke, Shelly, Dir-Creative-Natl - PulteGroup, Inc.; *pg.* 1109, *pg.* 873
Cooksley, Mark, Product Mgr - Belden, Inc.; *pg.* 624, *pg.* 993
Cool, Marc, Dir-Mktg & Strategy-China - Dupont Pioneer; *pg.* 1795, *pg.* 708
Cool, Renee, Product Mgr-Retail - Jennie-O Turkey Store, LLC; *pg.* 865, *pg.* 966
Cooley, Hillary, Asst VP-Brand & Mktg-Global - MetLife, Inc.; *pg.* 1208, *pg.* 1258
Cooley, Tiffany, VP-Mktg - Bon Ton Stores, Inc.; *pg.* 1763, *pg.* 1596
Coombe, John, VP-Global Mktg, Branding & Sponsorship - Liberty Mutual Insurance Group Inc.; *pg.* 1205, *pg.* 797
Coomber, Jamie, Dir-Digital Brand Mktg & Comm-Global - Converse Inc.; *pg.* 1831, *pg.* 793
Coombes, Jim, Sr Mgr-Real Estate Dev - Fred Meyer Stores, Inc.; *pg.* 1769, *pg.* 1502
Coombs, Patrick J., VP-Revenue Mgmt - Saia, Inc.; *pg.* 1922, *pg.* 533
Coombs, Shawn, Dir-Product Mgmt-Search & Personalization - The Home Depot, Inc.; *pg.* 1050, *pg.* 510
Coomer, Tim, VP-Product Dev - Escort, Inc.; *pg.* 1412, *pg.* 1479
Coon, Robert, Mgr-Natl Sls-Mobile & Kindle - Amazon.com, Inc.; *pg.* 1226, *pg.* 1831
Cooney, Christie, Dir-Mdsg & Online Mktg - Carl Karcher Enterprises, Inc.; *pg.* 1720, *pg.* 63
Cooney, Dan, Jr., Sr VP-Sls TRU - JAKKS Pacific, Inc.; *pg.* 960, *pg.* 142
Cooney, Jay, Mgr-Content Mktg & Social Media - Omni Hotels & Resorts; *pg.* 1107, *pg.* 1685
Coons, Brad, Sr Mgr-Market - Unum Group; *pg.* 1222, *pg.* 1629
Coons, Nellena Anna, Dir-Sports & Sls Mktg - Emmis Communications Corporation; *pg.* 285, *pg.* 685
Coontz, Thad W., Dir-Sls & Mktg - Tribune Media Company; *pg.* 1696, *pg.* 592
Coop, Teresa, Specialist-Mktg - FedEx Corporation; *pg.* 1907, *pg.* 1642
Cooper Houston, Aubrecia, Brand Mgr-Arnold, Brownberry & Oroweat Breads - Bimbo Bakeries USA Inc.; *pg.* 840, *pg.* 1540
Cooper, Angela, Mgr-Mktg-Autodesk Education - Autodesk Inc.; *pg.* 356, *pg.* 257
Cooper, Brittany, Head-Creative Talent - International Business Machines Corporation; *pg.* 418, *pg.* 1138
Cooper, Cathy, Sr Dir-Community Partnerships & Giving-Sponsorships & Promos - Meijer, Inc.; *pg.* 1779, *pg.* 888
Cooper, Cathy E., Sr VP-Mktg & Comm - Washington Federal Inc.; *pg.* 818, *pg.* 1842
Cooper, Cecilia, Dir-Mktg Strategy-Alumni Affairs & Dev - Harvard University; *pg.* 602, *pg.* 808
Cooper, Cody, Specialist-Mktg Comm - Trimble Navigation Limited; *pg.* 1384, *pg.* 288
Cooper, David, Mgr-Sls-Natl - Thomson CompuMark; *pg.* 484, *pg.* 838
Cooper, David M., VP-Sls & Mktg-Europe - Mercer Inc.; *pg.* 1395, *pg.* 1258
Cooper, Donna, Exec VP-Sls - La Quinta Corporation; *pg.* 1099, *pg.* 1722
Cooper, Donna, Exec VP-Sls - La Quinta Inns, Inc.; *pg.* 1100, *pg.* 1722
Cooper, Emily, Dir-Adv Sls Mktg & Product Integration - National Geographic Channel; *pg.* 299, *pg.* 402
Cooper, Emily R., Brand Mgr-Global - Computer Sciences Corporation; *pg.* 378, *pg.* 1780
Cooper, Erica Lapidus, Sr Dir-Brand & Internal Comm - Godiva Chocolatier, Inc.; *pg.* 1854, *pg.* 1235
Cooper, Frank , III, CMO & Chief Creative Officer - Buzzfeed; *pg.* 1233, *pg.* 1208
Cooper, James, Mgr-Global Mktg-Head, Eye & Face Protection - 3M Company; *pg.* 1142, *pg.* 956
Cooper, Jane, Dir-Mktg-Design Engrg & Sourcing - Penton Media, Inc.; *pg.* 1676, *pg.* 1277
Cooper, Jennifer, Head-Media, Entertainment, Social & Gaming Indus Strategy-Global - Adobe Systems Incorporated; *pg.* 342, *pg.* 235
Cooper, Jennifer, Sr Mgr - Chattem, Inc.; *pg.* 1515, *pg.* 1628
Cooper, Jim, CMO - Financial Independence Group Inc.; *pg.* 1200, *pg.* 1370
Cooper, Kevin, Sr Dir-Comm - Houston Texans, L.P.; *pg.* 553, *pg.* 1708
Cooper, Kevin, Mgr-Mktg-Digital Comm - The Scotts Miracle-Gro Company; *pg.* 1799, *pg.* 1459
Cooper, Kevin C., Mgr-Comm & PR-Kirkwood Mountain Resort - Vail Resorts, Inc.; *pg.* 1117, *pg.* 313
Cooper, Lance, Product Mgr - SOR, Inc.; *pg.* 1306, *pg.* 716
Cooper, Margo, Product Mgr-Gastroenterology - Janssen Pharmaceutica Products, L.P.; *pg.* 1548, *pg.* 1125
Cooper, Michael, VP-Distr Mktg - FX Networks, LLC; *pg.* 288, *pg.* 131
Cooper, Mitch, Sr Dir-Sls - MATTEL, INC.; *pg.* 962, *pg.* 81
Cooper, Mitchell, Mgr-Brand Mktg-Patrick Cudahy, La Abuelita, Higueral - Patrick Cudahy Inc.; *pg.* 888, *pg.* 1856
Cooper, Natalie, Sr Assoc-Firm Mktg & Strategy - New York Life Insurance Company; *pg.* 1211, *pg.* 1268
Cooper, Pat, Gen Mgr-Sls - Gator Ford Truck Sales Inc.; *pg.* 174, *pg.* 467
Cooper, Patrick, Sr Mgr-Customer Strategy & Dev - Del Monte Foods, Inc.; *pg.* 852, *pg.* 304

Cooper, Robbyn, Mgr-IR & PR - Cleco Corporation; pg. 1937, pg. 748
Cooper, Sarah, Mgr-Media & Digital Mktg-Global - Coty, Inc.; pg. 506, pg. 1219
Cooper, Terry, Dir-Mktg - Cavender's Stores Limited; pg. 39, pg. 1748
Cooper, Wyatt, Sr Assoc Brand Mgr-Capri Sun & Crystal Light - The Kraft Heinz Company; pg. 871, pg. 641
Cooper, Zachary, Brand Mgr - KFC Corporation; pg. 1733, pg. 735
Cooper, Zachary, Brand Mgr-KFC - YUM! Brands, Inc.; pg. 1756, pg. 738
Coopersmith, Marvin, Mgr-Sls - Ranir LLC; pg. 520, pg. 888
Cooperstein, Sam, VP-Sls & Mktg - Allfast Fastening Systems, Inc.; pg. 1041, pg. 66
Cooreman, John, Reg Sls Mgr-Avionics - Gulfstream Aerospace Corporation; pg. 228, pg. 540
Coots, Jason, VP-Mktg-TIAA Direct - Teachers Insurance & Annuity Association - College Retirement Equities Fund; pg. 1219, pg. 1297
Copa, Vincent, Sr Product Mgr - Boston Scientific Corporation; pg. 1508, pg. 831
Copacino, Steven, Specialist-Product Mktg - Penn Foster Education Group, Inc.; pg. 606, pg. 1586
Cope, Liz, VP-Mktg-Global - TTI Floor Care North America; pg. 61, pg. 1473
Cope, Rich, Dir-Mktg - Lawry's Restaurants, Inc.; pg. 1735, pg. 180
Cope, Traci, Coord-Mktg - Tetra Tech, Inc.; pg. 115, pg. 181
Copeland, Jeff, Sr Product Mgr-Content - Dex One Corporation; pg. 1635, pg. 1360
Copeland, Jennifer, VP & Mgr-Experiential Mktg - Wells Fargo & Company; pg. 819, pg. 232
Copeland, Michael, Sr Mgr-Mktg - QUALCOMM Incorporated; pg. 1873, pg. 207
Copelovitch, Julie, Brand Mktg Mgr - Sephora USA Inc; pg. 522, pg. 227
Copeman, Alisa, VP-Mktg & Global Network Partnerships-Europe - American Express Company; pg. 712, pg. 1190
Copernik, Perla, Assoc Dir-Science Media Rels - MedImmune LLC; pg. 1562, pg. 770
Coplin, Lennard, Dir-Leasing & Sr Mgr-Property - Kennedy-Wilson, Inc.; pg. 1099, pg. 46
Copp, Richard W., VP-Sls & Mktg - Resco Products, Inc.; pg. 107, pg. 1581
Copp, Vernon L., Mgr-Local Sls - KLOS-FM Radio, LLC; pg. 294, pg. 134
Coppelman, Adam, Mgr-Mktg Strategy & Plng - United States Cellular Corporation; pg. 1875, pg. 594
Coppels, Lori, Mgr-CTIS, TMP & Grp Tour Sls - Pensacola Bay Area Convention & Visitors Bureau; pg. 1004, pg. 458
Coppernoll, Julie, VP-Mktg-Mobile & Security Platforms - Intel Corporation; pg. 645, pg. 266
Coppes, Michael, Sr Mgr-Mktg-Consumer Comm - Transitions Optical, Inc.; pg. 1432, pg. 458
Coppess, Emily, Coord-Mktg-The Grand Ole Opry - Ryman Hospitality Properties, Inc; pg. 1111, pg. 1653
Coppock, Ronald M., Pres-Sls & Mktg-Worldwide - Arris Group, Inc.; pg. 353, pg. 541
Coppola, Karen, Sr VP-Mktg - Marshalls of MA, Inc.; pg. 1778, pg. 821
Coppola, Kelli, Sr Dir-Brand Comm-Global - New Era Cap Company Inc.; pg. 1840, pg. 1155
Coppola, Matt, Sr Specialist-PR - Becton, Dickinson & Company; pg. 1501, pg. 1068
Coppola, Renee, Asst-Outlet Mktg - Brooks Brothers Group, Inc.; pg. 39, pg. 1208
Coradini, David, VP-Sls & Sponsorships - Spalding; pg. 1845, pg. 846
Corbacho, Marc, VP-Sls-America - Mentor Graphics Corporation; pg. 432, pg. 1510
Corbeil, Chuck, Grp VP-Mktg - Harris Teeter, Inc.; pg. 1022, pg. 1383
Corbera, Carlos, Mgr-Digital Mktg-Global - Alere San Diego; pg. 1489, pg. 199
Corbett, Denise A., Assoc Dir-Growth Mktg-Sls Enablement - Verizon Communications Inc.; pg. 1875, pg. 1309
Corbett, Elizabeth, Dir-Sls & New Bus Dev - Neenah Paper, Inc.; pg. 1465, pg. 484
Corbett, Frederique Covington, Dir-Mktg-Intl - Twitter, Inc.; pg. 1285, pg. 228
Corbin, Bill, Exec VP-Global Sls & Partner Mgmt - Westcon Group, Inc.; pg. 492, pg. 1345
Corbin, Casey C., Coord-Mktg - MedImmune LLC; pg. 1562, pg. 770
Corbin, Chuck, Sr VP-Sls & Mktg - BancTec, Inc.; pg. 360, pg. 1717
Corbin, Daron, Mgr-Adv - United Supermarkets, L.L.C.; pg. 1036, pg. 1726
Corbin, Larry, Dir-Mktg-CCF Div - Blount International, Inc.; pg. 1043, pg. 1501
Corbitt, Candy S., Head-Mktg Category-Enterprise Sourcing - McKesson Corporation; pg. 1560, pg. 222
Corbitt, Kristin Mays, Dir-Sls, Distr & Logistics - Mays Chemical Company; pg. 1172, pg. 688
Corby, Karen, Sr Product Mgr - Google Inc.; pg. 1249, pg. 153
Corces, Lalania, Sr Specialist-Mktg Comm - ABB Inc.; pg. 1309, pg. 1359
Corcillo, Isabella, Planner-Digital Sls - BBC Worldwide America Inc.; pg. 271, pg. 1201
Corcoran, Alex, Sr Dir-Seasons - The Hershey Co.; pg. 1855, pg. 1538
Corcoran, Kevin, Mgr-Mktg Comm - Volvo Cars of North America LLC; pg. 195, pg. 1117
Corcoran, Maria, Mgr-Search Mktg Media-Worldwide - Adobe Systems Incorporated; pg. 342, pg. 235
Corcos, Claude, Mgr-Mktg-Americas - The Toro Company; pg. 1065, pg. 918
Cordeiro, Roy, Dir-Sls & Mktg - Outrigger Enterprises, Inc.; pg. 1107, pg. 544
Cordeiro, Sigal, Gen Dir-Chevrolet Global Mktg - General Motors Company; pg. 175, pg. 881
Cordell, Bob, Mgr-Digital Mktg - Lenovo Group Ltd; pg. 427, pg. 1384
Cordell, Roy G., Sr Dir-Creative Svcs - University of Arkansas; pg. 608, pg. 31
Cordella, Rick, Sr VP & Gen Mgr-Digital Media-NBC Sports Grp - NBC Sports Network; pg. 300, pg. 375
Cordella, Rick, Sr VP & Gen Mgr-Digital Media-NBC Sports Grp - NBC Universal, Inc.; pg. 300, pg. 1266
Cordero, James, Sr Dir-Sourcing-Private Label - Wal-Mart Stores, Inc.; pg. 1790, pg. 29
Cordero, Juan Carlos, Sr Dir-Car Sls Mktg & ECommerce - The Hertz Corporation; pg. 1911, pg. 450
Cordero, Natalie, Mgr-Mktg-Color - Parfums Christian Dior, Inc; pg. 519, pg. 1276
Cordero, Nelda L., Reg Mgr-Mktg - H&R Block, Inc.; pg. 764, pg. 983
Cordero, Sandy, Brand Mgr-Fine Fragrance & Artistry Men's Skincare - Amway Corporation; pg. 326, pg. 864
Cordes, Christoph J., Sr Dir-Global Commercialization - Luminex Corporation; pg. 1421, pg. 1664
Cordes, Mark, Sr Mgr-Creative - Applebee's International, Inc.; pg. 1715, pg. 980
Cordes, Mark, Sr Dir-Mktg Plng & Ops - Walgreen Co.; pg. 1608, pg. 605
Cordes, Mo, VP-Mktg & Tech - Schlumberger Limited; pg. 801, pg. 1714
Cordes, Shawn, Dir-Customer Product Experience - The Priceline Group Inc.; pg. 1276, pg. 364
Cordier, Dan, VP-Sls-USA - Hutchens Industries Inc.; pg. 208, pg. 1006
Cordiner, Tom, VP-Sls-Intl - Avid Technology, Inc.; pg. 622, pg. 804
Cordingley, Sheri, Mgr-Digital Mktg - Royal Bank of Canada; pg. 800, pg. 1942
Cordle, Pat, VP-Field Sls - BIC Corporation; pg. 501, pg. 369
Cordom, Christopher, Sr VP-Sls - NaviSite, Inc.; pg. 1269, pg. 782
Cordova, Jacqueline, Coord-Reg Sls Mktg - Cigna Corporation; pg. 1197, pg. 338
Cordova, Janet, Sr Mgr-Mktg - Epicor Software Corporation; pg. 393, pg. 110
Cordry Shaffer, Elizabeth, Assoc Dir-Product - Jet.com, Inc.; pg. 1260, pg. 1073
Corella, Jose, Brand Mgr - Kimberly-Clark Corporation; pg. 1461, pg. 1720
Coriale, Matt, Sr Mgr-Experience Design - Lexmark International, Inc.; pg. 427, pg. 730
Corica, Craig, Mgr-PR & Social Media - Adobe Systems Incorporated; pg. 342, pg. 235
Corigliano, Valerie, Coord-Mktg - General Magnaplate Corporation; pg. 1164, pg. 1079
Corin, Clive, Mgr-Mktg-Intl - Hologic, Inc.; pg. 1416, pg. 784
Corio, Kirsten, VP-Team Mktg & Bus Ops - National Basketball Association; pg. 566, pg. 1264
Corkhill, Tim, Reg Mgr-Mktg - Academy Sports & Outdoors, Ltd.; pg. 1824, pg. 1724
Corkins, Calleen, Program Mgr-Mktg - Red Hat, Inc.; pg. 460, pg. 1388
Corley, Christina M., Sr VP-Corp Sls - CDW Corporation; pg. 370, pg. 663
Corley, Steve, Chief Sls Officer-Americas - DEUTZ Corporation; pg. 1328, pg. 536
Corley, Tom, Pres-Sls & Exec VP - The Kraft Heinz Company; pg. 871, pg. 641
Corliss, Dave, Sr Dir-Mktg - Pacific Life Insurance Company; pg. 1213, pg. 166
Corman, Kendra, Dir-Mktg - Kaufman Financial Group, Inc.; pg. 1205, pg. 886
Cormier, Christopher, Assoc Publr-Integrated Sls - Details Magazine; pg. 1635, pg. 1223
Cormier, Danielle, Dir-PR - Oracle Corporation; pg. 450, pg. 191
Cormier, Julie, Dir-Mktg Comm & Brand Mgmt - Mitel Networks Corporation; pg. 654, pg. 1921
Cormier, Paul J., Pres-Products & Tech - Red Hat, Inc.; pg. 460, pg. 1388
Corn, Amy W., Sr VP-Corp Comm & Mktg - Global Payments Inc.; pg. 762, pg. 508
Cornell, Harper, Mgr-PR - Mizuno USA, Inc.; pg. 1839, pg. 538
Cornell, Kurt, Sr Mgr-Pre-Owned & Fleet Sls - Mercedes-Benz USA, LLC; pg. 184, pg. 514
Cornet, Thierry, VP-Home Mortgage Digital Mktg - Wells Fargo & Company; pg. 819, pg. 232
Corning, Jessie, Sr Mgr-Mktg - Culver Franchising System, Inc.; pg. 1724, pg. 1887
Cornish, Blair, Dir-Headquarter Customer Mktg - Del Monte Foods, Inc.; pg. 852, pg. 304
Cornish, Katie, Sr Mgr-Entertainment & Trend Mktg - Nintendo of America, Inc.; pg. 965, pg. 1829
Cornwell, Christine, Mgr-Content Mktg & Social Media - LexisNexis Group; pg. 1658, pg. 1446
Cornwell, Katie, Mgr-Shopper Mktg, Target & Mass Electronics Channel - Energizer Holdings, Inc.; pg. 637, pg. 996
Cornwell, Todd, VP-Sls - United States Bakery; pg. 907, pg. 1507
Coroalles, Stefanie, Mgr-Social & Consumer Engagement - Jarden Consumer Solutions; pg. 57, pg. 412
Corominas, Berta Cruz, Mgr-Mktg-NESCAFE - Nestle USA, Inc.; pg. 883, pg. 96
Corona, Carley, Asst Mgr-Mktg Comm - Jeld-Wen, Inc.; pg. 1051, pg. 1499
Corona, Michelle, Specialist-PR - Vans, Inc.; pg. 1821, pg. 76
Corona, Robert, Mgr-Mktg-Trade Show - Epicor Software Corporation; pg. 393, pg. 110
Coronel, Paulette, Specialist-Mktg-Clinique - The Estee Lauder Companies Inc.; pg. 508, pg. 1229
Corr, Paul J., Reg VP-Comml Sls - Armstrong World Industries, Inc.; pg. 914, pg. 1545
Corral, Rodrigo, Dir-Creative - Farrar, Straus & Giroux, Inc.; pg. 1640, pg. 1231
Corrales, Eugenia, Sr VP-Product - ShoreTel, Inc.; pg. 469, pg. 288
Correa, Caio, Mgr-Mktg-Yoplait Innovation - General Mills, Inc.; pg. 828, pg. 933
Correa, Cecilia, Mgr-Adv-Global - International Business Machines Corporation; pg. 418, pg. 1138
Correa, Eladio, Sr Product Mgr-Mktg-Global - Vans, Inc.; pg. 1821, pg. 76
Correa, Jeff, Dir-Mktg-Intl - Pear Bureau Northwest; pg. 153, pg. 1500
Correa, Jessica, Sr VP-Mktg - PFIP, LLC; pg. 1842, pg. 1037
Correa, Steven, Specialist-Mktg & Sls - State Farm Mutual Automobile Insurance Co.; pg. 1218, pg. 557
Correale, Alfonso, Area VP-Sls-South Europe - Verizon Communications Inc.; pg. 1875, pg. 1309
Correia, Filipe, Engr-Solutions & Mktg IP - Alcatel-Lucent USA, Inc.; pg. 615, pg. 1728
Correia, Linda Tse, Assoc Dir-Creative Svcs - AARP; pg. 124, pg. 393
Correia, Stephanie, Dir-Mktg - Hasbro, Inc.; pg. 954, pg. 1603
Correnti, Corey, Sr VP-Mktg Sls & Supply - BP America Inc.; pg. 972, pg. 1702
Corrick, Thomas, Exec VP-Wood Products - Boise Cascade Holdings, L.L.C.; pg. 1453, pg. 546
Corriero, Joseph, Head-Digital Mktg-Bank of America Merrill Lynch & Dir - Bank of America Corporation; pg. 718, pg. 1362
Corrigan, Anna, Sr Dir-Design-Women's Accessories - American Eagle Outfitters, Inc.; pg. 37, pg. 1572
Corrigan, Dennis, VP-Sls & Revenue Mgmt - JetBlue Airways Corporation; pg. 1913, pg. 1174

First page reference indicates Business Class Edition
Second page reference indicates Geographic Edition

Corrigan, Grittiya, Sr Dir-Reg Mktg - Pacific Life Insurance Company; *pg.* 1213, *pg.* 166
Corrigan, Kean, VP-Mktg - Leslie's Poolmart, Inc.; *pg.* 1838, *pg.* 17
Corrigan, Todd, VP-Sls-North America - Electrolux Home Products North America; *pg.* 54, *pg.* 1366
Corrigan, Tom, Dir-Sls-UK - Avnet Technology Solutions; *pg.* 359, *pg.* 25
Corrigan-Bastuk, Therese, Dir-Worldwide Mktg-Paper & Output Sys - Eastman Kodak Company; *pg.* 1408, *pg.* 1333
Corrigen, Michael, VP-Mktg - Airlite Plastics Company; *pg.* 1451, *pg.* 1013
Corsaro, Sandro, Chief Creative Officer - Fandango Media, LLC; *pg.* 1247, *pg.* 130
Corsi, Jay, Dir-Adv & Sls - Chicago Theatre Group Inc.; *pg.* 539, *pg.* 570
Corsi, John, VP-Media & PR - CH2M HILL Companies, Ltd.; *pg.* 75, *pg.* 325
Corsinita, Julie, VP-Media & Brand Partnerships - Taco Bell Corp.; *pg.* 1752, *pg.* 117
Corson, Debbie, Mgr-Integrated Mktg Comm - Assurant, Inc.; *pg.* 1193, *pg.* 1198
Corson, Kristel, VP-Mktg Comm - LeapFrog Enterprises, Inc.; *pg.* 961, *pg.* 84
Cortellesi, Matthew, Sr Specialist-Mktg-Global - United Nations Children's Fund; *pg.* 159, *pg.* 1306
Cortese, Anthony, Specialist-Online Mktg - Eggland's Best, Inc.; *pg.* 854, *pg.* 1542
Cortese, Ed, Sr VP-Mktg - Lefrak Organization Inc.; *pg.* 1100, *pg.* 1251
Cortese, Karen, VP-Mktg - Transamerica Insurance & Investment Group; *pg.* 1219, *pg.* 141
Cortese, Rina, Head-Media Rels-Corp Com-Global - Royal Bank of Canada; *pg.* 800, *pg.* 1942
Corteville, Rick, VP-Product Mktg-Tech - CBS Interactive, Inc.; *pg.* 369, *pg.* 215
Cortez, Noemi, Mgr-Mktg - General Growth Properties, Inc.; *pg.* 1093, *pg.* 574
Cortez, Salvador, Asst Gen Mgr-Mdsg - The Gap, Inc.; *pg.* 1770, *pg.* 218
Cortez, Tony, Sr Mgr-Partner Adv - Ticketmaster Entertainment LLC; *pg.* 1284, *pg.* 48
Corti, Stephan, Sr VP-Sls-Worldwide - Pelican Products, Inc.; *pg.* 1842, *pg.* 295
Cortina, Luis, Sr Mgr-Creative Svcs-Entertainment & News - Univision Communications Inc.; *pg.* 683, *pg.* 1307
Cortina, Shannon Gotthelf, Dir-Mktg-Global - TANGOE, INC.; *pg.* 481, *pg.* 368
Corwin, Amanda, Specialist-Mktg-FedEx Svcs - FedEx Corporation; *pg.* 1907, *pg.* 1642
Corwin, Daniel, VP-Bus Dev & Mktg - Young & Franklin, Inc.; *pg.* 1391, *pg.* 1174
Corwin, Jeff, Gen Mgr-Digital Media Grp Support - ABC, Inc.; *pg.* 268, *pg.* 1185
Corwin, Larry, Dir-Creative - Facebook, Inc.; *pg.* 1245, *pg.* 143
Cosand, Serena, Mgr-Digital Mktg - T.J. Maxx; *pg.* 1788, *pg.* 822
Cosand, Serena, Mgr-Digital Mktg - The TJX Companies, Inc.; *pg.* 1788, *pg.* 822
Coscia, Carmel, VP-Global Field Mktg - BlackBerry; *pg.* 625, *pg.* 1717
Coscia, Rick, Asst VP & Sr Mgr-Institutional Mktg - Eaton Vance Corp.; *pg.* 746, *pg.* 794
Cosentini, Sonya, Mgr-Mktg-Marshalls - The TJX Companies, Inc.; *pg.* 1788, *pg.* 822
Cosentino, Andrew, Brand Mgr - Giant Eagle, Inc.; *pg.* 1020, *pg.* 1575
Cosenza, Alex, Reg Mgr-Sls-Southern & Western US, Mexico - Newage Testing Instruments, Inc.; *pg.* 1058, *pg.* 1532
Cosenza, Robyn, Mgr-Mktg Comm-Silent Knight & Gamewell-FCI - Honeywell International Inc.; *pg.* 407, *pg.* 1088
Cosfol, Ann, Dir-Interactive Mktg - Penske Truck Leasing Company, L.P.; *pg.* 188, *pg.* 1585
Cosgrove, Colleen, Sr Mgr-Global Events - Reebok International Ltd.; *pg.* 1817, *pg.* 811
Cosgrove, Colleen, Brand Mgr-Global - Toys "R" Us, Inc.; *pg.* 968, *pg.* 1130
Cosgrove, Kali, Assoc Mgr-Mktg - BCBG Max Azria Group LLC; *pg.* 19, *pg.* 301
Cosgrove, Kristin, Dir-Mktg & PR - Anchorage Symphony Orchestra; *pg.* 528, *pg.* 10
Cosgrove, Mike, Dir-Sls - Gorman-Rupp of Canada Ltd.; *pg.* 1341, *pg.* 1933
Cosio, Henry, VP-Sls-US & Mexico - Vans, Inc.; *pg.* 1821, *pg.* 76
Cosler, Amy, VP-Sls-Global - Landauer, Inc.; *pg.* 1554, *pg.* 615
Cosma, Sandra Mariscal, Assoc Brand Mgr-Product Innovation-Global - Avon Products, Inc.; *pg.* 500, *pg.* 1198
Cosoroaba, Adrian, Mgr-Mktg - Xilinx, Inc.; *pg.* 496, *pg.* 252
Cossette, Jason, Mgr-Mktg & Customer Svc-Siemens Infrastructure & Cities - Siemens Process Industries and Drives; *pg.* 673, *pg.* 485
Cossette, Triston, Sr Mgr-Customer Analytics - Esurance, Inc.; *pg.* 1243, *pg.* 217
Cost, Dean, Sr Mgr-Mktg-Bayer HealthCare Animal Health - Bayer Corporation; *pg.* 1499, *pg.* 1573
Costa, Alexis, Mgr-Media Mktg-Global - Fossil Group, Inc.; *pg.* 5, *pg.* 1735
Costa, Angela, Sr Mgr-Corp PR - Autodesk Inc.; *pg.* 356, *pg.* 257
Costa, Cindy, Sr Mgr-Mktg, Consumer Insights & Bus Intelligence - YUM! Brands, Inc.; *pg.* 1756, *pg.* 738
Costa, Darren, Asst Dir-Athletics Mktg & Promos - Northeastern University; *pg.* 605, *pg.* 799
Costa, Greg, Sr Dir-Mdsg - Dollar General Corporation; *pg.* 1767, *pg.* 1635
Costa, Jason, Product Mgr - Pinterest; *pg.* 1275, *pg.* 225
Costa, Joseph, Dir-Mktg - Omnicell Inc.; *pg.* 1578, *pg.* 161
Costa, Kellie, Sr Mgr-Mktg-Titleist & Pinnacle Golf Balls - Acushnet Company; *pg.* 1824, *pg.* 818
Costa, Melissa, Head-Luxury Brand Mktg & PR-ZapposCouture.com - Zappos.com, Inc.; *pg.* 1291, *pg.* 1030
Costa, Ron, Reg VP-Mdsg - CarMax, Inc.; *pg.* 167, *pg.* 1800
Costa, Tara, Sr Mgr-Digital-Global - Jarden Corporation; *pg.* 1885, *pg.* 412
Costa-White, Donna, Dir-Inside Sls - Team Health, Inc.; *pg.* 482, *pg.* 1639
Costabile, Jennifer, Gen Dir-Used Vehicle Activities, Fleet, Comml Adv & Mktg - General Motors Company; *pg.* 175, *pg.* 881
Costabilo, Carrie, Sr Mgr-Product Mktg & Mobile Products - Zebra Technologies Corporation; *pg.* 690, *pg.* 628
Costantino, Amber, Coord-Digital Mktg - Anna's Linen Company Inc.; *pg.* 1760, *pg.* 70
Costantino, Cristina, Dir-Mktg - The New York Times; *pg.* 1668, *pg.* 1270
Costanza, Valerie, Specialist-Mktg - Epicor Software Corporation; *pg.* 393, *pg.* 110
CostaPozza, Patricia, Sr Asst Brand Mgr-Fabric Care - The Procter & Gamble Company; *pg.* 1129, *pg.* 1418
Costello, Aida, Sr Mgr-HR - PepsiCo, Inc.; *pg.* 259, *pg.* 1327
Costello, Becky, VP-Advertising - Browning; *pg.* 1828, *pg.* 1752
Costello, Colin, Brand Mgr-Skoal - Altria Group, Inc.; *pg.* 1893, *pg.* 1800
Costello, Dawn Hollowell, Dir-Digital Sls-Northeast - Scripps Networks Interactive, Inc.; *pg.* 1279, *pg.* 1638
Costello, Jennifer, Sr Dir-Internal & External Comm - Equifax Inc.; *pg.* 748, *pg.* 504
Costello, John, Pres-Global Mktg Innovation - Dunkin' Brands Group, Inc.; *pg.* 1727, *pg.* 810
Costello, John, Dir-Global Mktg & Comm - Webster University; *pg.* 610, *pg.* 1004
Costello, Kerry, Dir-Global Mktg-Cystic Fibrosis - Vertex Pharmaceuticals Incorporated; *pg.* 1606, *pg.* 801
Costello, Laura, VP-Reg Sls-Patient Monitoring - Philips Electronics North America; *pg.* 662, *pg.* 782
Costello, Michael, Reg Specialist-Mktg - Academy Sports & Outdoors, Ltd.; *pg.* 1824, *pg.* 1724
Costello, Steve, VP-Mktg & Adv - Lewiston Daily Sun; *pg.* 1658, *pg.* 751
Costigan, Michael, VP-Mktg & Bus Innovation-Avnet Asia Pacific - Avnet, Inc.; *pg.* 622, *pg.* 15
Costley, Kevin, Sr Mgr-Digital Creative - ABC, Inc.; *pg.* 268, *pg.* 1185
Coston, Shenique, Mgr-Mktg - Samsung Electronics America, Inc.; *pg.* 669, *pg.* 1115
Costopoulos, Constantine, Dir-Digital Mktg - Sony Pictures Entertainment Inc.; *pg.* 309, *pg.* 72
Cotch, Carrie, Mgr-Mktg Comm - Graco, Inc.; *pg.* 1342, *pg.* 935
Cote, Caroline, Asst VP-Mktg Integration - Wells Fargo & Company; *pg.* 819, *pg.* 232
Cote, Stephane, VP-Sls - Corby Distilleries Ltd.; *pg.* 1961, *pg.* 1937
Cotey, Stan, VP-R&D-Electronics & Product Innovation - Fender Musical Instruments Corporation; *pg.* 547, *pg.* 21
Cotignola, Frank, Assoc Dir-Media Insights & Analytics - Mondelez International; *pg.* 877, *pg.* 1344
Cotler, Valerie, Dir-Adv & Head-Promo Review-Regulatory Affairs - Novartis Corporation; *pg.* 1574, *pg.* 1273
Cotner, Angela, Reg VP-Music Sls - Live Nation Entertainment, Inc.; *pg.* 558, *pg.* 47
Cotney-Bethea, Katie, Dir-Mktg - AOL Inc.; *pg.* 1229, *pg.* 1195
Cottam, James, Product Mgr-Infections & Gastro Intestinal Diseases - ALERE INC.; *pg.* 1488, *pg.* 849
Cotter, Dave, Dir-Sls Ops-FIG - Fiserv, Inc.; *pg.* 397, *pg.* 1855
Cotter, Ellen M., Interim Pres & Interim CEO - READING INTERNATIONAL, INC.; *pg.* 578, *pg.* 139
Cotter, Lisa, VP-Mktg - Orlando Magic; *pg.* 572, *pg.* 455
Cotterill, Louise, Assoc Dir-Digital, Social & Content - Kashi Company; *pg.* 830, *pg.* 119
Cottick, Scot, Sr Mgr-Social Media Mktg - Nissan North America, Inc.; *pg.* 186, *pg.* 1633
Cotton, Alanna, VP-Mobile Computing Mktg - Samsung Electronics America, Inc.; *pg.* 669, *pg.* 1115
Cotton, Chris, Dir-Mktg - Nationwide Mutual Insurance Company; *pg.* 1210, *pg.* 1442
Cotton, Geoff, VP-Sls & Mktg-HIV Bus Unit - Gilead Sciences, Inc.; *pg.* 1535, *pg.* 88
Cotton, Mark, Mgr-Mktg - 3M Company; *pg.* 1142, *pg.* 956
Cotton, Noah, Product Mgr - Cummins Power Generation; *pg.* 1326, *pg.* 932
Cottonaro, Joseph A., Sr Dir-Taxes - The Hershey Co.; *pg.* 1855, *pg.* 1538
Cottrell, Kimberly Whinna, Sr Mgr-Mktg Programs - Autodesk Inc.; *pg.* 356, *pg.* 257
Cottrell, Marie, Sr Mgr-Event Experiences - Hewlett-Packard Company; *pg.* 404, *pg.* 175
Cottrell, Marie, Reg Supvr-Mktg - White Castle Management Co.; *pg.* 1756, *pg.* 1444
Cottrell, Matthew, VP-Intl Sls-EMEA - Alto-Shaam Inc.; *pg.* 836, *pg.* 1869
Cottrell, Rebecca, Sr Mgr-Mktg-Boys Brands-Asia Pacific Reg - MATTEL, INC.; *pg.* 962, *pg.* 81
Coubrie, John Mc, Mgr-Mktg - Hewlett-Packard Company; *pg.* 404, *pg.* 175
Couch, Troy, Sr Dir-CMC Regulatory-Global - Pfizer Inc.; *pg.* 1581, *pg.* 1278
Couch, William, Mgr-Inside Sls & Coord-Central & South America Distr Sls - Felt Racing LLC; *pg.* 1707, *pg.* 110
Coudray, Christophe, CMO-New Product Dev & Asia Pacific-Global - Kaz, Inc.; *pg.* 58, *pg.* 844
Coughlin, Catherine, Sr Exec VP & Global Mktg Officer - AT&T Mobility LLC; *pg.* 619, *pg.* 488
Coughlin, Cindy, Mgr-Mktg - Pelican Products; *pg.* 1467, *pg.* 843
Coughlin, Margaret, Chief Mktg & Comm Officer & Sr VP - Boston Children's Hospital; *pg.* 1508, *pg.* 790
Coughlin, Stephanie, Specialist-Mktg - TD Ameritrade Holding Corporation; *pg.* 808, *pg.* 1018
Coughlin, Tim, VP-Sls - Translations.com; *pg.* 485, *pg.* 1304
Coughlon, Mike, VP-Pre-Media - Multi-Ad, Inc.; *pg.* 1666, *pg.* 652
Coulston, Lauren, VP-Brand Mktg, Content & Social Team - JPMorgan Chase & Co.; *pg.* 772, *pg.* 1246
Coultas, Kate, Sr Mgr-Corp Comm - J.C. Penney Company, Inc.; *pg.* 1774, *pg.* 1732
Coulter, Derek, VP-Product Dev Svcs - VF Jeanswear Limited Partnership; *pg.* 50, *pg.* 1377
Coulter, Jesse, Chief Creative Officer - Samsung Electronics America, Inc.; *pg.* 669, *pg.* 1115
Coulter, Jesse, Chief Creative Officer - Samsung Semiconductor, Inc.; *pg.* 670, *pg.* 250
Coulter, John, Supvr-Mktg Equipment - Pepsi Beverages Company; *pg.* 258, *pg.* 1342
Coulter, Jorja, VP-Mktg - National Van Lines, Inc.; *pg.* 1916, *pg.* 559
Coulter, Keegan, Dir-Mktg - Seura, Inc.; *pg.* 672, *pg.* 1860
Council, Marian, Dir-Creative - Benelli USA Corporation; *pg.* 1827, *pg.* 754
Councill, Moore, Sr VP-Sls - Kindel Furniture Company; *pg.* 931, *pg.* 887
Counter, Erik, Exec VP-Creative Mktg - Paramount Pictures Corporation; *pg.* 304, *pg.* 138
Counter, Joel, Mgr-Corp Mktg Comm - EMCORE Corporation; *pg.* 636, *pg.* 39
Coupe, Suzanne, Head-Sector Mktg-US - PricewaterhouseCoopers LLP; *pg.* 795, *pg.* 1283

Couples, Keri, Dir-Mktg - Virtual Radiologic Corporation; pg. 1607, pg. 924
Coureau, Laurent, Mgr-Worldwide Sls & & Mktg-Oil & Gas Market - Mercury Computer Systems, Inc.; pg. 434, pg. 813
Courier, Deb, Specialist-Field Mktg - Papa Ginos-Deangelo Holding Corporation, Inc.; pg. 1743, pg. 817
Cournoyer, Bill, VP & Div Mgr-Mdse - Bergdorf Goodman, Inc.; pg. 1761, pg. 1202
Coursey, Cameron, VP-Product Dev, Ops & Internet - AT&T Southeast; pg. 1868, pg. 489
Courtain, Rocky, Mgr-Sls - Morehouse-COWLES; pg. 1363, pg. 66
Courtemanche, Marcel, Mgr-Sls & Indus Products - AirBoss of America Corp.; pg. 1878, pg. 1929
Courtien, Kristin, Brand Mgr - Coty, Inc.; pg. 506, pg. 1219
Courtney, Brendan, Sr Dir-Innovation - Diageo North America, Inc.; pg. 1961, pg. 361
Courtney, Erin, Coord-PR - Varco Pruden Buildings, Inc.; pg. 118, pg. 1647
Courtney, H. Mark, Sr VP-Sls - Flowers Foods, Inc.; pg. 855, pg. 541
Courtney, John, Sr Mgr-Mktg - Paslode; pg. 1059, pg. 664
Courtney, Joyce, Sr Specialist-Display & Mdsg - Nestle Purina PetCare Company; pg. 1479, pg. 1000
Courtney, Kim, Dir-Mktg Bus Affairs - MillerCoors LLC; pg. 255, pg. 582
Courtney, Madonna, VP-Corp Mktg - Roberts-Gordon Inc.; pg. 1076, pg. 1151
Courtney, Pat, Sr VP-PR - Major League Baseball; pg. 560, pg. 1255
Courtney, Sherry, Mgr-Digital Mktg - MillerCoors LLC; pg. 255, pg. 582
Courtney, Thomas P., Dir-New Product Dev-Global - The Gleason Works; pg. 1341, pg. 1336
Courtoy, Matt, Specialist-Social & Digital Media - Whole Foods Market, Inc.; pg. 1038, pg. 1667
Courville, Clay, Sr VP-Mktg-McKesson Medical Surgical - McKesson Corporation; pg. 1560, pg. 222
Courville, Grant, Dir-Product Mgmt - QNX Software Systems Ltd; pg. 458, pg. 1932
Cousins, Dean, VP-Strategy, Mktg & Innovation - Mersen; pg. 1302, pg. 836
Cousins, Kye, Sr Dir-Mktg-Latin America Events - Gartner, Inc.; pg. 1248, pg. 374
Couture, Michael, Sr VP-Sls & Mktg Grp - QuickPlay Media Inc.; pg. 666, pg. 1941
Covell, Kevin, VP-Mktg-Customer Retention - DISH Network Corporation; pg. 283, pg. 325
Cover, Brian, Sr Product Mgr-Streaming Solutions - DTS, Inc.; pg. 634, pg. 55
Covert, Ian, VP-Sls-Natl Accts - Stanfield's Limited; pg. 48, pg. 1917
Covey, George, Asst VP-Digital Mktg - Massachusetts Mutual Life Insurance Company; pg. 1207, pg. 845
Covington, Frederique, Dir-Intl Mktg-Singapore - Twitter, Inc.; pg. 1285, pg. 228
Covington, Marielle, Mgr-Mktg - Autodesk Inc.; pg. 356, pg. 257
Covitz, Jason, Sr VP-Fin & Sls - First Data Corporation; pg. 754, pg. 505
Cowan, Adri, Mgr-Social Media - Marvel Entertainment, LLC; pg. 1662, pg. 1257
Cowan, Anita, Dir-Mktg, Promotions & Events - Cumulus Media Inc.; pg. 280, pg. 503
Cowan, Diana, Sr Specialist-Social Media - Sun Life Financial Inc.; pg. 806, pg. 1944
Cowan, Katie, Sr Mgr-Brand Comm - Motorola Solutions, Inc.; pg. 657, pg. 659
Cowan, Laura, Dir-Global Mktg & Comml Dev-Viagra & Toviaz - Pfizer Inc.; pg. 1581, pg. 1278
Cowan, Maura, Mgr-Mktg-Ice Cream, Tea & Home Care Categories - Unilever Canada Inc.; pg. 903, pg. 1946
Cowan, Neil, Sr Mgr-Design - Kellogg Company; pg. 831, pg. 870
Cowell, Andrew, Sr VP-Power Mgmt Products Grp - Intersil Corporation; pg. 647, pg. 146
Cowell, Dean, Sr VP-Mktg Strategy - Citigroup Inc.; pg. 735, pg. 1212
Cowen, Veronica, Asst Mgr-Interactive Mktg - General Mills, Inc.; pg. 828, pg. 933
Cowgill, Lisa, Project Mgr-Interactive Mktg - Zebra Technologies Corporation; pg. 690, pg. 628
Cowie, Robert, Bus Mgr-Customer Satisfaction - Intel Corporation; pg. 645, pg. 266
Cowing, Theresa, Product Mgr-Mobile - Toys "R" Us, Inc.; pg. 968, pg. 1130
Cowles, Eric, Sr VP-Strategic Mktg - L'Oreal USA; pg. 514, pg. 1252
Cowles, Lisa, Sr Dir-Corp Events - A&E Television Networks, LLC; pg. 267, pg. 1185
Cowman, Chad R., Dir-Mktg - JPMorgan Chase & Co.; pg. 772, pg. 1246
Cox, Barron, VP-HR, Go-To-Market Ops-Customer Success, Mktg & Sls - NetApp, Inc.; pg. 444, pg. 287
Cox, Bill, Sr Dir-Strategy - Microsoft Corporation; pg. 435, pg. 1824
Cox, Bob, Sr Mgr-Comm & Media Rels - Airbus Helicopters, Inc.; pg. 223, pg. 1698
Cox, Chris, Chief Product Officer - Facebook, Inc.; pg. 1245, pg. 143
Cox, Chris, Sr Mgr-Global Digital Mktg - The Hershey Co.; pg. 1855, pg. 1538
Cox, David, VP-Sls & Distr-Americas - Take-Two Interactive Software, Inc.; pg. 481, pg. 1297
Cox, David, Mgr-Live Events Mktg - World Wrestling Entertainment, Inc.; pg. 595, pg. 380
Cox, David E., VP-Equipment Sls - Snap-on Incorporated; pg. 1062, pg. 1862
Cox, Denielle, Coord-PR & Social Media - Universal Orlando; pg. 590, pg. 456
Cox, Elliott, Sr Mgr-Mktg-Enterprise Mktg Strategy & Activation - Bank of America Corporation; pg. 718, pg. 1362
Cox, Erin, Dir-Media-Fragrance + Beaute - Chanel, Inc.; pg. 503, pg. 1211
Cox, Gabriel, Program Mgr-Online Mktg & Loyalty - VITACOST.COM, INC.; pg. 1607, pg. 414
Cox, Gwen, Sr Mgr-ECommerce Mktg - Best Buy Co., Inc.; pg. 1761, pg. 954
Cox, Hovey, Sr VP-Mktg & Strategy - CGGVeritas Services (U.S.) Inc.; pg. 973, pg. 1703
Cox, Isabella C., Reg Mgr-Commodity-Mktg & Comm Svcs - Siemens Corporation; pg. 803, pg. 1291
Cox, Jessica, Dir-Digital & Direct Mktg - AMC Entertainment Inc.; pg. 527, pg. 716
Cox, John, Product Dir-Automotive Adhesives - Dow Chemical; pg. 1156, pg. 1563
Cox, Julie, Rep-Mktg - Auto-Owners Insurance Group; pg. 1194, pg. 895
Cox, Karen, Mgr-Convention Sls & Svcs - Buffalo Niagara Convention & Visitors Bureau, Inc.; pg. 1901, pg. 1147
Cox, Kristin, Mgr-Mktg Ops Plng - Mannington Mills, Inc.; pg. 934, pg. 1119
Cox, Laura J., VP-Mktg - Peoples Bancorp Inc.; pg. 793, pg. 1458
Cox, Matt, VP-Mktg - Bob's Red Mill Natural Foods, Inc.; pg. 841, pg. 1500
Cox, Matt, VP-Sls & Customer Svcs - OttLite; pg. 1303, pg. 475
Cox, Matthew, Dir-Product Mgmt-Call of Duty - Activision Blizzard, Inc.; pg. 948, pg. 271
Cox, Melissa, Sr Mgr-Trade Mktg - Pabst Brewing Company; pg. 258, pg. 137
Cox, Michael, Product Mgr - Carlisle Tire & Wheel Company; pg. 1880, pg. 1612
Cox, Perrin, Rep-PR - Broadcom Corporation; pg. 364, pg. 108
Cox, Rita, Sr VP-Mktg & External Affairs - Saratoga Casino & Raceway; pg. 581, pg. 1340
Cox, Rob, Reg Mgr-Bus Indirect Sls - Sprint Corporation; pg. 1874, pg. 719
Cox, Ron, Dir-Consumer Mktg & Plng - SpartanNash Co; pg. 1034, pg. 889
Cox, Roshni, Head-Email & Mobile Mktg - DIRECTV Group Holdings, LLC; pg. 281, pg. 79
Cox, Ryan, Mgr-Web Mktg - SIRVA, Inc.; pg. 1923, pg. 669
Cox, Sean, Mgr-Mktg Ops-North America - NIKE, Inc.; pg. 1812, pg. 1492
Cox, Stephanie, Specialist-Digital Mktg - Susan G. Komen for the Cure; pg. 158, pg. 1688
Cox, Sumter, Sr Dir-Mktg & Comm - Mood Media; pg. 298, pg. 1616
Cox, Tara K., Sr Dir-Mktg - Toll Brothers, Inc.; pg. 115, pg. 1541
Cox, Thomas, VP-Digital Ops-Local Media Grp - Meredith Corporation; pg. 1663, pg. 705
Cox, Thomas, Exec VP-Sls - MSC Industrial Direct Co., Inc.; pg. 1057, pg. 1181
Cox, Tim, Dir-Creative Svcs - Publix Super Markets, Inc.; pg. 1031, pg. 437
Cox, Wendy, VP-Mktg - Da-Lite Screen Company; pg. 632, pg. 698
Coxon, Nick, Mgr-Online Mktg - GNC Holdings Inc.; pg. 1537, pg. 1576
Coy, Ben, Mgr-Field Sls Ops - Mazda North American Operations; pg. 183, pg. 113
Coy, Linda J., Mgr-Strategic Mktg-Customer Excellence - Siemens Process Industries and Drives; pg. 673, pg. 485
Coyle, Angela, Mgr-Mktg - Carfax Inc.; pg. 202, pg. 1777
Coyle, Ed, Rep-Digital Media - Cars.com; pg. 1234, pg. 568
Coyle, Sean, VP-Design & Mdsg - Perry Ellis International, Inc.; pg. 45, pg. 445
Coyle, Shawn, VP-Retail Network Solutions Sls-North America - MSX International, Inc.; pg. 98, pg. 912
Coyle, Tim, Mgr-Mktg - Blue Diamond Growers; pg. 840, pg. 195
Coyne, Doreen, Mgr-Mktg - IBM Canada Limited; pg. 411, pg. 1923
Cozens, Robert, Sr VP-Mdsg - 7-Eleven, Inc.; pg. 1012, pg. 1672
Cozzi, Kathleen, Mgr-Mktg-Online Programs - Boston University; pg. 598, pg. 791
Crabtree, Rich, Dir-RF Products Bus Dev - Ducommun Technologies, Inc.; pg. 634, pg. 63
Crace, David, VP-Mktg-Imagewear - V.F. Corporation; pg. 34, pg. 1376
Cradle, Shaunese, Specialist-Mktg-Customer Acq - Comcast Corporation; pg. 276, pg. 1560
Craft, Gerald, Brand Dir-Mktg - McNett Corporation; pg. 1839, pg. 1817
Craft, Jay, VP-Product Dev Svcs - V.F. Corporation; pg. 34, pg. 1376
Craft, Jay, VP-Product Dev Svcs - VF Jeanswear Limited Partnership; pg. 50, pg. 1377
Craft, Jennifer, Gen Mgr-Digital Mktg - DISH Network Corporation; pg. 283, pg. 325
Craft, Martha, VP-PR & Corp Comm - Rollins, Inc.; pg. 1179, pg. 519
Craft, Tracey, Sr Product Mgr - Getty Images, Inc.; pg. 1645, pg. 1836
Crafton, Colleen, Head-Comml-Collaboration Field Mktg - Cisco Systems, Inc.; pg. 372, pg. 240
Crager, Julie, Sr Mgr-Mktg - Pepperidge Farm, Inc.; pg. 888, pg. 363
Craig, Allison, Mgr-Mktg - Vail Resorts, Inc.; pg. 1117, pg. 313
Craig, Colleen, Mgr-Tradeshow Mktg - IDEXX Laboratories, Inc.; pg. 1543, pg. 753
Craig, Cyndi, Mgr-Mktg-Mid-West Steel - NCI BUILDING SYSTEMS, INC.; pg. 1364, pg. 1712
Craig, David, Dir-Sls & Mktg-Intl - Cooper Tire & Rubber Company; pg. 1881, pg. 1453
Craig, Jonathan, CMO & Exec VP - Charles Schwab; pg. 1235, pg. 1661
Craig, Jonathan, CMO & Exec VP - Charles Schwab & Company, Inc.; pg. 734, pg. 215
Craig, Julie, Mgr-Retail Mktg - Cracker Barrel Old Country Store, Inc.; pg. 1723, pg. 1639
Craig, Julie, Sr Mgr-Shopper & Category Insights-COE - Pfizer Inc.; pg. 1581, pg. 1278
Craig, Lisa, Dir-Comm & Mktg - American Heart Association Inc.; pg. 128, pg. 1673
Craig, Michael, Mgr-Mktg-Pepsi - PepsiCo, Inc.; pg. 259, pg. 1327
Craig, Phil, Exec VP & Chief Creative Officer-Discovery Networks Intl - Discovery Communications, Inc.; pg. 282, pg. 777
Craig, Stephen, Assoc Mgr-Creative Ops-Digital Commerce - Chico's FAS, Inc.; pg. 21, pg. 427
Crain, Natalie, Sr Dir-Customer Acq - Lands' End, Inc.; pg. 1776, pg. 1857
Crain, Rance, Head-Internet Mktg & Conversions - Crain Communications, Inc.; pg. 1631, pg. 879
Craine, Catherine, Mgr-Digital Retail Mktg - Alliance Data Systems Corporation; pg. 347, pg. 1729
Cralley, Todd M., Corp Dir-Sls-Long Form Adv - Sinclair Broadcast Group, Inc.; pg. 308, pg. 773
Cram, Janis, Specialist-Mktg - MetroPCS, Inc.; pg. 1872, pg. 1683
Cramb, Patrick, Sr Mgr-Innovation - Ocean Spray Cranberries, Inc.; pg. 887, pg. 827
Cramer, Amanda, Coord-Mktg Partnerships-Global - National Basketball Association; pg. 566, pg. 1264
Cramer, Bernice, Head-Mktg, Product Mgmt & Sls-Noise Reduction Tech Grp - Bose Corporation; pg. 626, pg. 820

First page reference indicates Business Class Edition
Second page reference indicates Geographic Edition

Cramer, Bob, VP-Sports Mktg, Field & Experiential Mktg - The Coca-Cola Company; pg. 240, pg. 493
Cramer, Christine, Dir-PR - CVS Health Corporation; pg. 1765, pg. 1610
Cramer, Rebecca, Corp Mgr-Mktg - Dell Inc.; pg. 383, pg. 1737
Cramer, Tommy, Product Mgr - Exactech, Inc.; pg. 1529, pg. 428
Cramlett, Nicole, Dir-Creative, Mktg & Brand Mgmt - The American Dental Association; pg. 127, pg. 564
Crampshee, Marti, VP-Mktg - Versace USA; pg. 34, pg. 1310
Crandall, Catherine, Sr Mgr-Mktg - NetApp, Inc.; pg. 444, pg. 287
Crandall, Steven J., VP-Mktg - Ashaway Line & Twine Mfg. Co.; pg. 1826, pg. 1600
Crandell, Nicol, Brand Mgr - DISH Network Corporation; pg. 283, pg. 325
Crandell, Paul, Sr VP-Mktg - GoPro; pg. 1414, pg. 255
Crane, Dana, Sr Product Mgr - CA Technologies; pg. 366, pg. 1168
Crane, Greg, Dir-Distributor Mktg & Pricing - Wiremold/LeGrand; pg. 689, pg. 383
Crane, Martin, Sr VP-Sls - Pernod Ricard USA, Inc.; pg. 1968, pg. 1332
Crane, Neil, Dir-Product Strategy - Cicero Inc.; pg. 372, pg. 1360
Crane, Nicky, Product Mgr-Monetization - YouTube, LLC; pg. 1291, pg. 198
Crane, Russell, Mgr-Audio Product Mktg - Texas Instruments Incorporated; pg. 679, pg. 1688
Craney, Jeff, VP-Mktg Div - Miami Heat Limited Partnership; pg. 562, pg. 444
Craney, Mike, Mgr-Digital Media Sls - Cox Media Group; pg. 280, pg. 502
Cranford, Nathan, Mgr-Mktg - Duke Energy Corporation; pg. 1940, pg. 1366
Crann, Paul, Sr VP-Product Mgmt & Solutions Architecture - SeaChange International, Inc.; pg. 1279, pg. 781
Cranner, Chris, VP & Dir-Creative - CBS Broadcasting Inc.; pg. 273, pg. 1210
Cranner, Chris, VP & Dir-Creative - CBS Corporation; pg. 273, pg. 1210
Cransberg, Alan J., Pres-Global Primary Products-Australia & VP - Alcoa Inc.; pg. 65, pg. 1188
Cranston, Cassandra, Mgr-Mktg - PRAHealth Sciences; pg. 1585, pg. 1388
Crape, Wesley, Mgr-Direct Mktg - Helzberg's Diamond Shops, Inc.; pg. 6, pg. 984
Crary, Ian, Sr Mgr-Athlete Svc - adidas America Inc.; pg. 1803, pg. 1500
Cratty, Thomas, Dir-International Adv, Mktg & Procurement-Global - PepsiCo, Inc.; pg. 259, pg. 1327
Cravaritis, Robert D., Exec VP-Sls - Houston Chronicle; pg. 1651, pg. 1707
Craven, Kimberly, Sr Principal Mgr-Product Mktg - Red Hat, Inc.; pg. 460, pg. 1388
Craven, Tom, Product Mgr-Operator Interface - GE Intelligent Platforms; pg. 1339, pg. 1777
Craviso, Ralph, Interim Pres & Interim CEO - Rochester Philharmonic Orchestra Inc.; pg. 579, pg. 1337
Cravotta, Frank, VP-Creative Svcs - Hockey Western New York, LLC; pg. 552, pg. 1149
Crawford, Alex, Mgr-Production-EMEIA 3D Fixtures & Display - Apple Inc.; pg. 350, pg. 73
Crawford, Chad, Dir-Mktg Impact - Popeyes Louisiana Kitchen, Inc.; pg. 1745, pg. 517
Crawford, Charlie, Sr Dir-Customer Engagement Products - Papa Murphy's International, LLC; pg. 1743, pg. 1846
Crawford, Chris, Coord-Social Media - Taco Bell Corp.; pg. 1752, pg. 117
Crawford, Dwayne, Mgr-Product Line - Belden, Inc.; pg. 624, pg. 993
Crawford, Emily, Dir-Sls Ops - Cisco Systems, Inc.; pg. 372, pg. 240
Crawford, Gary, Dir-Sls - United States Pipe & Foundry Company, Inc.; pg. 117, pg. 5
Crawford, Greg, Sr Dir-Creative-Mktg - Pacific Sunwear of California, Inc.; pg. 1781, pg. 43
Crawford, Jeff, Dir-IT-Harris Product Group-Lincoln Electric - The Harris Products Group; pg. 1345, pg. 533
Crawford, Karen, Dir-Media Adv & Mktg - Nestle USA, Inc.; pg. 883, pg. 96
Crawford, Karna, Sr VP & Head-Mktg Strategy & Digital Dev - JPMorgan Chase & Co.; pg. 772, pg. 1246
Crawford, Kristie T., Mgr-Brand Mktg-Global - The Walt Disney Company; pg. 317, pg. 52
Crawford, Lily, Mgr-Mktg-US - Mattel Games/Puzzles; pg. 962, pg. 80
Crawford, Lily, Mgr-Mktg-US - MATTEL, INC.; pg. 962, pg. 81
Crawford, Matt, Dir-Solutions Mktg - Citrix Systems, Inc.; pg. 375, pg. 424
Crawford, Melissa, Sr VP-Markets, Product & Tech - Physicians Mutual Insurance Co.; pg. 1214, pg. 1017
Crawford, Michele, Sr Rep-Mktg - Auto-Owners Insurance Group; pg. 1194, pg. 895
Crawford, Steve, VP-Mktg - Alpine Electronics of America, Inc.; pg. 616, pg. 292
Crawford, Tara, Sr Mgr-Mktg - SoulCycle Holdings LLC; pg. 1845, pg. 1294
Crawford, Tena, Mgr-Mktg Event - McKesson Corporation; pg. 1560, pg. 222
Crawford-Duner, Joanne, Dir-Mktg Comm - Nestle USA, Inc.; pg. 883, pg. 96
Crawley, Ben, Mgr-Global & ENA Mktg-Woolite - Reckitt Benckiser Inc.; pg. 1136, pg. 1105
Crawley, Dawn, Strategist-Media - Seattle Times Company; pg. 1685, pg. 1840
Crawley, Eric, Sr Dir-Engrg - Akamai Technologies, Inc.; pg. 1226, pg. 807
Crawley, Nic, Pres-Intl Mktg & Distr - Paramount Pictures Corporation; pg. 304, pg. 138
Crawley, Pierre, VP-Mktg - Strohmeyer & Arpe Company; pg. 899, pg. 1042
Cray, Will C., Dir-Mktg - Triangle Package Machinery Co.; pg. 1383, pg. 592
Crayner, Chris, Sr VP-Integrated Media & Digital - NBC Universal, Inc.; pg. 300, pg. 1266
Crays, Tammy, Writer-Social Media Technical - AT&T Mobility LLC; pg. 619, pg. 488
Creager, Kristen, Planner-Vehicle Mktg & Comm-Camry - Toyota Motor Sales, U.S.A., Inc.; pg. 193, pg. 296
Creagh, Erin, Sr Mgr-Exec Comm - Adobe Systems Incorporated; pg. 342, pg. 235
Crean, Bill, Dir-Product Mgmt - InterDigital, Inc.; pg. 1872, pg. 1543
Crean, Michelle, Assoc Designer-Social Media - Staples, Inc.; pg. 474, pg. 821
Creech, Laurie, Dir-Sls & Mktg - Simpson Lumber Company, LLC; pg. 110, pg. 1845
Creech, Timothy J., Acting CFO & Sr VP-Fin & Admin Svcs - Salix Pharmaceuticals, Inc.; pg. 1591, pg. 1388
Creeden, Catherine, Mgr-Social Media Mktg - Relativity Media, LLC; pg. 306, pg. 47
Creegan, Jennifer, Gen Mgr-Creative Products - Microsoft Corporation; pg. 435, pg. 1824
Creekmore, Krista, Mgr-Adv Creative - W.S. Badcock Corporation; pg. 947, pg. 449
Creekmore, Rob, Mgr-Adv Res & Mktg Science - Facebook, Inc.; pg. 1245, pg. 143
Creely, Maureen, Dir-Sls Ink Jet Printing Solutions & Comml Print - Eastman Kodak Company; pg. 1408, pg. 1333
Cregeur, Lucie, Category Mgr-Mktg-Digital Imaging - Best Buy Co., Inc.; pg. 1761, pg. 954
Creighton, Christine, Specialist-Mktg - Aetna Inc.; pg. 1187, pg. 351
Creighton, Laird, VP-Fin & Admin-US Consumer Products Div - McCormick & Company, Incorporated; pg. 1027, pg. 779
Creighton, Scott, VP-Mktg Excellence-Global - Johnson & Johnson; pg. 1549, pg. 1091
Cremen, Michael, Exec VP-Sls-Global - Hitachi Data Systems Corporation; pg. 407, pg. 265
Crenshaw, Ambrose, Dir-eMedia Strategy & Dev - North American Publishing Company; pg. 1671, pg. 1567
Crenshaw, Belinda, Mgr-Mktg - Cisco Systems, Inc.; pg. 372, pg. 240
Crenshaw, Scott, Sr VP-Strategy & Product - RACKSPACE HOSTING, INC.; pg. 1277, pg. 1742
Crepeau, Michelle, Assoc Dir-Mktg - Cognizant Technology Solutions Corporation; pg. 377, pg. 1124
Crescimanno, Greg, Product Mgr - PayPal Inc.; pg. 1274, pg. 248
Crespo, Patricia, Mgr-Mktg-Global Licensing - Aeropostale, Inc.; pg. 17, pg. 1188
Cress, James, Assoc Publr-Integrated Mktg-Fitness Enthusiast Grp - American Media, Inc.; pg. 1615, pg. 410
Cress, Jill, Sr VP-Global Consumer Mktg - MasterCard Worldwide Inc.; pg. 780, pg. 988
Cress, Keith, Mgr-Mktg - Power & Telephone Supply Company; pg. 665, pg. 1646
Cress, Scott, Sr Dir-Mktg - Hughes Network Systems LLC; pg. 643, pg. 770
Crevello, Drew, Sr VP-Production - Warner Bros. Entertainment Inc.; pg. 319, pg. 54
Creviston, Steven E., Pres-Cellular Products Grp & Corp VP - RF Micro Devices, Inc.; pg. 667, pg. 1376
Crew, Alissa, Specialist-Mktg Comm - MetroPCS, Inc.; pg. 1872, pg. 1683
Crews, Robert, Sr VP-Mktg - Ovation Brands; pg. 1743, pg. 921
Crews, Ted, Sr Dir-Comm - Saint Louis Rams Football Company; pg. 580, pg. 1002
Crickenberger, Stacy, Program Mgr-Bus Banking Mktg - Wells Fargo & Company; pg. 819, pg. 232
Crider, Tricia, Brand Mgr - DISH Network Corporation; pg. 283, pg. 325
Crilly, Holly, Dir-Mktg - Cisco Systems, Inc.; pg. 372, pg. 240
Crilly, Megan, Specialist-eMail Mktg - TransUnion Corp.; pg. 811, pg. 591
Crimmins, Art, Sr Mgr-Solutions Mktg - Brocade Communications Systems, Inc.; pg. 365, pg. 239
Cring, Tiffany, Sr Dir-SBV Mktg Ops - Simon Property Group, Inc.; pg. 1112, pg. 690
Criniti, Dale Rudberg, VP-Institutional Mktg - Teachers Insurance & Annuity Association - College Retirement Equities Fund; pg. 1219, pg. 1297
Cripps, Denise, Specialist-Mktg - Universal Forest Products, Inc.; pg. 117, pg. 890
Crisanti, Cliff, Sr Mgr-Corp Comm - Ingram Micro Inc.; pg. 415, pg. 261
Criscione, Angelika, Dir-Mktg - Universal Photonics, Inc.; pg. 1433, pg. 1167
Criscuolo, Santo, Sr VP-Media Grp - United Online, Inc.; pg. 1286, pg. 308
Crisman, Jennifer, Mgr-Technical Mktg - The Euclid Chemical Company; pg. 81, pg. 1430
Crisman, Roger, Dir-Data & Video Product Mgmt - Cox Communications, Inc.; pg. 279, pg. 501
Crisp, John, VP-New Media - The Blade Co.; pg. 1621, pg. 1476
Crispen, Mark, Dir-Mktg & Intl Sls - Inclinator Company of America; pg. 88, pg. 1536
Crispo, Anthony, Sr Product Mgr-Ad Products - Amazon.com, Inc.; pg. 1226, pg. 1831
Crissman, Scott, Sr Mgr-Mktg - Electronic Arts Inc.; pg. 951, pg. 189
Cristman, Heather, Head-Global Product - Google Inc.; pg. 1249, pg. 153
Crithary, Peter, Mgr-Mktg-Large Sensor Acq - Sony Electronics, Inc.; pg. 676, pg. 209
Critz, Brian, Dir-Mktg - Unilever United States, Inc.; pg. 904, pg. 1061
Croce, Cara, VP-Adv Standards, Digital & Emerging Media - Viacom Inc.; pg. 316, pg. 1310
Croce, Roberto, VP-Mdsg & Plng-ae & aerie Direct - American Eagle Outfitters, Inc.; pg. 37, pg. 1572
Crochet, Jeff, Mgr-Mktg & Comm - Tahiti Tourisme North America, Inc.; pg. 1007, pg. 83
Croci, Patrice, VP-Media & Events - Express, Inc.; pg. 24, pg. 1440
Crociata, Kevin, Dir-North America Hair Care Mktg - The Procter & Gamble Company; pg. 1129, pg. 1418
Crock, Tena, VP-eComm & Digital Mktg - The Step2 Company LLC; pg. 1889, pg. 1474
Crocker, Don, Sr Dir-Real Estate - Chick-fil-A, Inc.; pg. 1721, pg. 492
Crocker, Elizabeth, Assoc Mgr-Mktg - General Mills, Inc.; pg. 828, pg. 933
Crocker, Janet, Coord-Mktg Comm - Mercer University; pg. 604, pg. 535
Crocker, Penelope, Dir-Restaurant Mktg Strategy - Kimpton Hotel & Restaurant Group; pg. 1099, pg. 220
Crocker-Pierce, Brenda E., Head-Event Mgmt-Mktg & Comm - General Electric Company; pg. 1297, pg. 347
Crockett, Alissa, Dir-Sls - Kind LLC; pg. 868, pg. 1249
Crockett, Sarah, VP-Global Consumer Mktg - Vans, Inc.; pg. 1821, pg. 76
Crockett, Shelley, Program Mgr-Social Media - Choice Hotels International, Inc.; pg. 1086, pg. 775
Croda, Jack, Assoc-Sls - Semonin Realtors; pg. 1112, pg. 738
Crofoot, Art, Dir-Natl, Retail & Fin Sls - The Washington Times, LLC; pg. 1701, pg. 408
Croft, Kristen, Product Mgr - Hallmark Cards, Inc.; pg. 1646, pg. 983
Croft, Lisa, Sr Mgr-Product Mktg - Adobe Systems

Incorporated; *pg.* 342, *pg.* 235
Croft, Mark, Dir-Mktg - Microsoft Corporation; *pg.* 435, *pg.* 1824
Crofut, Peter, Head-Creative Platform Solutions - Google Inc.; *pg.* 1249, *pg.* 153
Croissant, TJ, Asst VP & Dir-Mktg - Sierra Trading Post Inc.; *pg.* 1819, *pg.* 1901
Croke, Lisa Lamb, Dir-Mktg & Sls Comm-Corp Accounts & Healthcare Solutions - Boston Scientific Corporation; *pg.* 1508, *pg.* 831
Croker, Ginia Hairston, VP-Mktg - David C. Cook; *pg.* 1633, *pg.* 315
Croll, Bob, Product Mgr-Harleysville Insurance - Nationwide Mutual Insurance Company; *pg.* 1211, *pg.* 1536
Cromp, Claudine, Product Mgr-Cable Duct & Metal Structure - Thomas & Betts Corporation; *pg.* 680, *pg.* 1646
Cromwell, Brett, Mgr-Mktg Comm - Medtronic, Inc.; *pg.* 1564, *pg.* 939
Cromwell, Christopher, Mgr-Sls-Intl - Blue Diamond Growers; *pg.* 840, *pg.* 195
Cromwell, Glen, VP-Event Mktg-Natl - National Hot Rod Association; *pg.* 149, *pg.* 99
Cromwell, Jarvis, Head-Consumer Mktg & Content Strategy - Bloomberg L.P.; *pg.* 725, *pg.* 1204
Crone, Laura G., VP-Sls & Mktg & Dir-Accts-Global - Intel Corporation; *pg.* 645, *pg.* 266
Crone, Mai, Sr Planner-Integrated Shopper Mktg - General Mills, Inc.; *pg.* 828, *pg.* 933
Crone, Mark, Sr Dir-Email & Database Mktg - Bonnier Corporation; *pg.* 1622, *pg.* 480
Cronin, Beau, Sr Product Mgr - salesforce.com, inc.; *pg.* 1278, *pg.* 226
Cronin, Brian, Brand Mgr - National Grid USA; *pg.* 1946, *pg.* 852
Cronin, Chris, Sr Dir-Global Pain Therapies Mktg - Medtronic, Inc.; *pg.* 1564, *pg.* 939
Cronin, Colleen, Mgr-Mktg Programs-Core Markets - Analog Devices, Inc.; *pg.* 617, *pg.* 839
Cronin, Madeline, Assoc Mgr-Social Media & Mktg-Ann Taylor - Ann Inc.; *pg.* 18, *pg.* 1195
Cronin, Matt, VP-Mktg - Perry Ellis International, Inc.; *pg.* 45, *pg.* 445
Cronin, Timothy C., Sr VP-Product Dev - Allen-Edmonds Shoe Corp.; *pg.* 1804, *pg.* 1887
Cronk, Jennifer, Mgr-HiEd Mktg Programs-Education & Field Mktg - Apple Inc.; *pg.* 350, *pg.* 73
Cronk, Mike, Sr VP-Strategic Mktg - Grass Valley, Inc.; *pg.* 641, *pg.* 164
Cronk, Shantel, Sr Mgr-Mdsg-Teva - Deckers Outdoor Corporation; *pg.* 1807, *pg.* 100
Cronkhite, Judy, Dir-Sls & Mktg - Hyatt Hotels Corporation; *pg.* 1096, *pg.* 577
Cronkright, Sally, Mgr-Sls - Mlive Media Group; *pg.* 1665, *pg.* 888
Crook, Benjamin, Dir-Mktg - Unilever United States, Inc.; *pg.* 904, *pg.* 1061
Crook, Elizabeth A., Dir-Mktg - Travelers Insurance; *pg.* 1220, *pg.* 963
Crook, Kaysie, Assoc Mgr-Mdsg - Dr Pepper Snapple Group, Inc.; *pg.* 250, *pg.* 1729
Crook, Martyn, Sr Dir-Global Capabilities - Kimberly-Clark Corporation; *pg.* 1461, *pg.* 1720
Crook, Todd, Sr Dir-Bakery Ops - Hostess Brands LLC; *pg.* 1856, *pg.* 984
Crooks, Amy, Sr Mgr-Consumer Insights-Jenn-Air & KitchenAid Brands-Licensing - Whirlpool Corporation; *pg.* 62, *pg.* 872
Crooks, Darhil, Dir-Creative - The Atlantic Monthly Group; *pg.* 1618, *pg.* 396
Crooks, David, Sr VP-Product & Ops - World Travel Holdings; *pg.* 1931, *pg.* 860
Cropp, Katie, Head-Mktg Comm & Canadian Mktg - Mettler-Toledo International Inc.; *pg.* 1423, *pg.* 1441
Crosby, Frederick, VP-Mktg & Bus Dev-WU Digital-Global - The Western Union Company; *pg.* 822, *pg.* 327
Crosby, Jamie, Rep-Inside Sls - Electro Rent Corporation; *pg.* 390, *pg.* 300
Crosby, Jenny, Sr Mgr-Mktg-Mobile & Affiliates-TurboTax & Quicken - Intuit Inc.; *pg.* 769, *pg.* 158
Crosby, Justine, Sr Mgr-Strategic Comm - Autodesk Inc.; *pg.* 356, *pg.* 257
Crosby, Peter, Product Mgr-FlashSoft - SanDisk Corporation; *pg.* 465, *pg.* 147
Crosby, Ralph , III, Exec Dir-Corp & VIP Sls - Airbus Helicopters, Inc.; *pg.* 223, *pg.* 1698
Crosby, Ryan, VP-Consumer Mktg - Activision Blizzard, Inc.; *pg.* 948, *pg.* 271
Crosby, Steve, Sr VP-Regulatory, Legislative & PR - Frontier Communications Corporation; *pg.* 1871, *pg.* 362
Crosby, Steve, Dir-Digital Media - Hess Corporation; *pg.* 979, *pg.* 1240
Crose, Daniel J., VP-Water Product Supply-Global - Franklin Electric Co., Inc.; *pg.* 1337, *pg.* 680
Crose, Daniel J., VP-Global Water Products Supply - Little Giant Pump Company; *pg.* 1356, *pg.* 1486
Crosier, Marc, Mgr-Mktg Events - McKesson Corporation; *pg.* 1560, *pg.* 222
Cross, Alexander Layton, Mgr-Mktg-ARPU P&L - DISH Network Corporation; *pg.* 283, *pg.* 325
Cross, Bailey, Mgr-Field Mktg - Concur Technologies, Inc.; *pg.* 1236, *pg.* 1813
Cross, Brenda, Sr Mgr-Mktg-Americas - Kelly Services, Inc.; *pg.* 424, *pg.* 911
Cross, Chet H., Pres-Indus Products Grp & Exec VP - Chemtura Corporation; *pg.* 1152, *pg.* 355
Cross, Christine Nath, Sr Dir-Domains - Go Daddy Inc.; *pg.* 1249, *pg.* 21
Cross, Jim, Mgr-Comml Mktg - Briggs & Stratton Corporation; *pg.* 201, *pg.* 1899
Cross, Justin, Brand Mgr-Seasons 52 - Darden Restaurants, Inc.; *pg.* 1724, *pg.* 453
Cross, Kiki, Sr Assoc Brand Mgr - Pepperidge Farm, Inc.; *pg.* 888, *pg.* 363
Cross, Larry, Mgr-Mktg Comm - Gentex Corporation; *pg.* 206, *pg.* 913
Cross, Linda, Dir-PR & Media Rels - Harvard University Press; *pg.* 1648, *pg.* 808
Cross, Lori, Sr Dir-Corp Comm - Riverbed Technology, Inc.; *pg.* 1277, *pg.* 225
Cross, Melissa, Asst Mgr-Mktg-Ahnu - Deckers Outdoor Corporation; *pg.* 1807, *pg.* 100
Cross, Paulette, Exec VP & Dir-Mktg - Cardinal Bank N.A.; *pg.* 732, *pg.* 1790
Cross, Rebecca, Mgr-Health Mart Mktg - McKesson Corporation; *pg.* 1560, *pg.* 222
Cross, Simon, Product Mgr - Facebook, Inc.; *pg.* 1245, *pg.* 143
Cross, Tara, Dir-Mktg - Allegro Coffee Co.; *pg.* 836, *pg.* 336
Crossen, Alison, Media Planner-Integrated - Gucci America Inc.; *pg.* 6, *pg.* 1237
Crossland, McKinzey, Sr Analyst-PR - Whole Foods Market, Inc.; *pg.* 1038, *pg.* 1667
Crossman, Bruce, Rep-Mktg - State Farm Mutual Automobile Insurance Co.; *pg.* 1218, *pg.* 557
Crossman, Doug, VP-Sls - Anachemia Canada, Inc.; *pg.* 1147, *pg.* 1951
Crossman, Michelle, Planner-Sls - Hulu LLC; *pg.* 1257, *pg.* 274
Crost, Sharon, Sr Head-Social Bus - Hitachi Data Systems Corporation; *pg.* 407, *pg.* 265
Crosthwait, Kristin, Sr Mgr-Mktg - Justin Brands, Inc.; *pg.* 1810, *pg.* 1695
Croston, Lorie, Product Mgr - Thermo Fisher Scientific Inc.; *pg.* 1431, *pg.* 854
Croston, Nancy, Sr VP-Integrated Sls & Mktg - Fox Broadcasting Company; *pg.* 287, *pg.* 130
Croteau, Lise, Acting Pres & CEO - Hydro-Quebec; *pg.* 1944, *pg.* 1955
Crotty, Sasha, Product Mgr-Revit Core - Autodesk Inc.; *pg.* 356, *pg.* 257
Crouch, Brian, Dir-Sls & Mktg - Art's-Way Manufacturing Co., Inc.; *pg.* 701, *pg.* 701
Crouch, Calvin, Head-Digital Mktg & Ecommerce - Timex Corporation; *pg.* 14, *pg.* 355
Crouch, Eddie, Mgr-Adv - The Sedalia Democrat; *pg.* 1685, *pg.* 1005
Crouch, Greg, Reg Dir-Sls - Takeda Pharmaceuticals USA, Inc.; *pg.* 1600, *pg.* 605
Crouch, James, Mgr-Farm Segment Mktg - Michelin North America Inc.; *pg.* 1886, *pg.* 1618
Crouch, Shannon, Mgr-Database Mktg - Fandango Media, LLC; *pg.* 1247, *pg.* 130
Crouse, Angela, Sr Mgr-Sls & Mktg Support - The Woodstream Corporation; *pg.* 1801, *pg.* 1549
Crouse, Kelly, VP-Sls-Foodservice - The J.M. Smucker Company; *pg.* 865, *pg.* 1468
Crow, Jeffrey, VP-Mktg - Central Garden & Pet Company; *pg.* 1475, *pg.* 303
Crowder, Alice, VP-Mktg - The Krystal Company; *pg.* 1734, *pg.* 1629
Crowder, Brian, Sr Mgr-Design - Yahoo! Inc.; *pg.* 1289, *pg.* 289
Crowder, Linda, Sr Dir-Peapod Interactive - Peapod, LLC; *pg.* 1029, *pg.* 661
Crowder, Ron, Sr Dir-Sls - ACR Electronics, Inc.; *pg.* 612, *pg.* 422
Crowder, Zora, Brand Dir-Mktg - Energizer Holdings, Inc.; *pg.* 637, *pg.* 996
Crowe, Glenn, Mgr-Product Mgmt - Expedia, Inc.; *pg.* 1244, *pg.* 1814
Crowe, Jan, Mgr-Americas Mktg - Exxon Mobil Corporation; *pg.* 977, *pg.* 1718
Crowe, Phillip, Dir-Social Media - Global Response Corporation; *pg.* 400, *pg.* 439
Crowe-Grande, Trish, Mgr-Instore Mktg - Procter & Gamble Inc.; *pg.* 333, *pg.* 1929
Crowell, Chris, Rep-Technical Sls - Wellmaster Carts; *pg.* 1388, *pg.* 1934
Crowell, Marisa, Sr Product Mgr-HCV Mktg - Gilead Sciences, Inc.; *pg.* 1535, *pg.* 88
Crowley, Gitti, Dir-Mktg-Consumer & Retail - Novartis Vaccines & Diagnostics, Inc.; *pg.* 1575, *pg.* 809
Crowley, James, Pres, CEO & VP-Mktg - Safe-Hit Corporation; *pg.* 1889, *pg.* 589
Crowley, Jean, Dir-Sls-Natl - Meredith Corporation; *pg.* 1663, *pg.* 705
Crowley, Jennifer, Specialist-Mktg Comm - Cerner Corporation; *pg.* 1514, *pg.* 981
Crowley, Mark, Sr Mgr-Internal Com-Global - Staples, Inc.; *pg.* 474, *pg.* 821
Crowley, Michael, Sr Dir-Bus Dev - Genentech, Inc.; *pg.* 1533, *pg.* 279
Crowley, Ryan, Mng Dir-Digital Products - JPMorgan Chase & Co.; *pg.* 772, *pg.* 1246
Crowner, Stacy, Brand Mgr-Blended & Smoothies - Starbucks Corporation; *pg.* 897, *pg.* 1840
Crownover, Jessica, Specialist-Mktg - FedEx Corporation; *pg.* 1907, *pg.* 1642
Crowson, Frank, Sr VP-Mktg - Guitar Center, Inc.; *pg.* 1771, *pg.* 306
Crozier, Ryan, Assoc Product Mgr - Tyson Foods, Inc.; *pg.* 902, *pg.* 35
Crozier, Ryan, Sr Mgr-Mktg - Wal-Mart Stores, Inc.; *pg.* 1790, *pg.* 29
Cruciani, Alan, Reg Mgr-Mktg - Audi of America, Inc.; *pg.* 164, *pg.* 1784
Crucius, Matthew, Sr Mgr-Online Mktg - Design Within Reach, Inc.; *pg.* 923, *pg.* 216
Crudup, Robert F., Exec VP-IT, Ops & Product Mgmt - SEI Investments Company; *pg.* 802, *pg.* 1558
Cruice, Bonnie, Strategist-Creative - The Vanguard Group, Inc.; *pg.* 816, *pg.* 1550
Cruickshank, Jacqueline, Bus Mgr - Hologic, Inc.; *pg.* 1416, *pg.* 784
Cruickshank, John, Pres-Star Media Grp & Publr-Toronto Star - Torstar Corporation; *pg.* 1695, *pg.* 1946
Cruikshank, Terry, Sr Mgr-Indus Mktg - Oki Data Americas, Inc.; *pg.* 449, *pg.* 1090
Cruise, Connie, Mgr-Local Mktg Svcs - Texas Monthly; *pg.* 1692, *pg.* 1666
Cruise, Jennifer, Mgr-Mktg - Medifast, Inc.; *pg.* 1562, *pg.* 774
Cruise, Todd, Sr Mgr-Mdse Strategy & Supplier Dev - Sam's Club; *pg.* 1783, *pg.* 29
Crum, Jen, Dir-Mktg & Comm - Microsoft Corp.; *pg.* 440, *pg.* 321
Crumb, Keith, Sr Dir-Mktg - The Travelers Companies, Inc.; *pg.* 1220, *pg.* 352
Crumbley, Stephon, Sr Dir-Ops - BET Holdings LLC; *pg.* 271, *pg.* 396
Crummey, Christopher, Dir-Sls-Social Bus & Exceptional Web Experience-Worldwide - IBM; *pg.* 410, *pg.* 1449
Crump, Amanda, Mgr-Mdse Mktg-Outdoor Garden - The Home Depot, Inc.; *pg.* 1050, *pg.* 510
Crump, Edward, Sr Specialist-Mktg-Private Brands & Category Mktg - Lowe's Companies, Inc.; *pg.* 1053, *pg.* 1383
Crump, Tiffany B., Asst VP-GIB & GM Mktg - Bank of America Corporation; *pg.* 718, *pg.* 1362
Crumpacker, Mark, Chief Dev Officer & Chief Creative Officer - Chipotle Mexican Grill, Inc.; *pg.* 1722, *pg.* 317
Crupi, Dennis, Dir-Creative Svcs - Ingram Micro Inc.; *pg.* 415, *pg.* 261
Cruse, Thor, Mgr-Mktg & Strategic Plng-North America - E.I. du Pont de Nemours & Company; *pg.* 1159, *pg.* 390
Crutchfield, Kim, Analyst-Mktg & Bus - Xerox Corporation; *pg.* 494, *pg.* 365

First page reference indicates Business Class Edition
Second page reference indicates Geographic Edition

Crutchfield, Serena, Dir-Mktg - Restaurant Associates Corporation; pg. 1747, pg. 1285
Cruz, Astrid, VP-Social Media Analysis - Wells Fargo & Company; pg. 819, pg. 232
Cruz, Caroline, Principal Product Mgr-AOL On Consumer Products - AOL Inc.; pg. 1229, pg. 1195
Cruz, Ciro, Sr Product Mgr-Global - Johnson Controls, Inc.; pg. 1073, pg. 1597
Cruz, Courtney, Sr Mgr-Media - Pfizer Inc.; pg. 1581, pg. 1278
Cruz, Dave, Mgr-Mktg Dev - California Avocado Commission; pg. 135, pg. 108
Cruz, Debra, VP-Global eBusiness & Digital Mktg - MetLife, Inc.; pg. 1208, pg. 1258
Cruz, Esther, Mgr-Insights & Content Mktg - LinkedIn Corporation; pg. 1262, pg. 160
Cruz, Gustavo, Dir-Sls-Automotive-North America - Eaton Corporation; pg. 1331, pg. 1429
Cruz, Joe, VP-Brand & Retail Mktg - Univision Communications Inc.; pg. 683, pg. 1307
Cruz, Maggy, Specialist-Mktg - FedEx Corporation; pg. 1907, pg. 1642
Cruz, Marilyn, Assoc Mgr-Production-Vogue - Conde Nast Publications, Inc.; pg. 1629, pg. 1217
Cruz, Marilyn, Assoc Mgr-Production-Vogue - Vogue Magazine; pg. 1700, pg. 1311
Cruz, Richie, Specialist-Lifestyle Mktg - PepsiCo, Inc.; pg. 259, pg. 1327
Cruz, Tami, Sr Dir-Mktg-North America - Level 3 Communications, Inc.; pg. 1262, pg. 312
Cruz, Veronica, Mgr-Mktg Ops - Sirius XM Holdings Inc.; pg. 308, pg. 1292
Crye, Claire H., Mgr-PR - McKesson Corporation; pg. 1560, pg. 222
Cryer, Mike, Mgr-New Markets Mktg - Graco, Inc.; pg. 1342, pg. 935
Csellar, Maralee, Dir-Media Rels - The George Washington University; pg. 602, pg. 400
Csupo, Jenny, Specialist-Client Svc-Media & Adv Partnerships - NeuStar, Inc.; pg. 1872, pg. 1807
Cuadrado, Jaimi, Sr Dir-Mktg Ops - Wal-Mart Stores, Inc.; pg. 1790, pg. 29
Cuberos, Ainoa, Mgr-Mktg - Yahoo! Inc.; pg. 1289, pg. 289
Cuchra, Craig, Mgr-Mktg-Intl - Perfetti Van Melle USA, Inc.; pg. 1860, pg. 727
Cudahy, Mandy, Mgr-Integrated Mktg - Emerald Expositions; pg. 392, pg. 1352
Cuddeback, Cory, Dir-Sls - Beasley Broadcast Group, Inc.; pg. 271, pg. 450
Cuddy, David, Sr Mgr-PR, Legal & Corp Affairs - Microsoft Corporation; pg. 435, pg. 1824
Cuddy, Tom, Sr Mgr-Nuclear Comm - PG&E Corporation; pg. 1949, pg. 224
Cudley, Lisa, Mgr-Trader Mktg Analytics - TD Ameritrade Holding Corporation; pg. 808, pg. 1018
Cudmore, Vanessa, Mgr-Mktg - The Men's Wearhouse, Inc.; pg. 44, pg. 1711
Cuebas, Jessica, Sr Dir-Brand & Product Mktg-Global - Visa Inc.; pg. 816, pg. 230
Cuene, Stefanie, Specialist-Global Mktg Comm-Channel Partner Engagement - Honeywell Aerospace Electronic Systems; pg. 228, pg. 17
Cuevas, Christie, Mgr-Content Mktg Strategy - Direct Energy; pg. 1939, pg. 1704
Cuevas, Katherine, Sr Mgr-Digital Content Mgmt Strategy & Capabilities - American Express Company; pg. 712, pg. 1190
Cuevas, Ximena, Sr Dir-Brand & Acq Metro PCS - T-Mobile US, Inc.; pg. 676, pg. 1816
Cuffe, Molly, Dir-Brand Mktg-Global - SmartWool; pg. 32, pg. 335
Cuffy, Gilbertson, Sr Mgr-Mktg-Beverage Innovation - PepsiCo, Inc.; pg. 259, pg. 1327
Cugino, Steve, Pres-Intl Consumer Products & Exec VP - Church & Dwight Co., Inc.; pg. 1153, pg. 1063
Cugley, Suzanne, Sr Mgr-Ad Policy - Yahoo! Inc.; pg. 1289, pg. 289
Cui, Sunny, Brand Mgr - Essilor of America, Inc.; pg. 1412, pg. 1680
Cukaj, Katrina, Exec VP-Sls & Mktg - Turner Broadcasting System, Inc.; pg. 314, pg. 521
Cukar, Mike, Sr Dir-Design - JAKKS Pacific, Inc.; pg. 960, pg. 142
Culberson, Abbie, Specialist-Mktg - Chevron Corporation; pg. 974, pg. 259
Culberson, Lynne, Mgr-Mktg - Zurich Holding Company of America, Inc.; pg. 1224, pg. 660
Culbert, Kurt, Sr Dir-Racing Comm - National Association for Stock Car Auto Racing; pg. 566, pg. 420
Culbertson, Cathi, VP-Event Mktg & Conferences & Exec Dir-Event Mktg & Protocol - Forbes, Inc.; pg. 1641, pg. 1232
Culbertson, Katie, Project Mgr-Creative Mktg - Kao Brands Co. Inc.; pg. 513, pg. 1415
Culbertson, Lauren, Mgr-Product Mktg - Blackbaud, Inc.; pg. 361, pg. 1613
Culbertson, Lisa, Mgr-Mktg & Player Dev - Ameristar Casinos, Inc.; pg. 528, pg. 1022
Culbreath, Mitch, Bus Unit Mgr-Global - 3M Company; pg. 1142, pg. 956
Culella, Joe, Sr Dir - Samsung Telecommunications America, LLC; pg. 670, pg. 1736
Culhane, Barbara, Corp Mgr-Mktg - Brooks Automation, Inc.; pg. 1320, pg. 813
Culhane, Jeff, Sr VP-Mdsg - Tops Markets, LLC; pg. 1036, pg. 1355
Cull, Brendon, Sr Dir-Govt Rels & Regulatory Affairs - The Kroger Co.; pg. 1025, pg. 1416
Cull, Brian, Grp VP-Integrated Mktg - National Hockey League; pg. 568, pg. 1265
Cullen, Andrew, Mgr-Digital Mktg & Comm-WaterCraft Grp - Yamaha Motor Corporation USA; pg. 1713, pg. 76
Cullen, Carrie, Assoc Publr-Adv HGTV Magazine - Hearst Magazines; pg. 1649, pg. 1239
Cullen, Doug, Sr VP & Head-Solution Sls - Merrill Corporation; pg. 1664, pg. 962
Cullen, Heidi Bronner, Sr Dir-Mktg - Sephora USA Inc; pg. 522, pg. 227
Cullen, Jaye, Coord-CRM Mktg - Ticketmaster Entertainment LLC; pg. 1284, pg. 48
Cullen, Kelsey, Coord-District Mktg - H&R Block, Inc.; pg. 764, pg. 983
Cullen, Tracy, VP-Comm & Mktg - The Society of the Plastics Industry, Inc.; pg. 157, pg. 404
Cullen, Wayne, Sr Mgr-Mktg - Cisco Systems, Inc.; pg. 372, pg. 240
Cullerton, John, Sr VP-Product Innovation & Mgmt - Equifax Inc.; pg. 748, pg. 504
Culleton, Kathie, Sr VP-Mktg Ops - CBS Broadcasting Inc.; pg. 273, pg. 1210
Culleton, Kathie, Sr VP-Mktg Ops - CBS Corporation; pg. 273, pg. 1210
Culley, Jim, Sr Dir-Mktg - Hologic, Inc.; pg. 1416, pg. 784
Culley, Kevin, Sr Dir-Bus Dev & Innovation - Under Armour, Inc.; pg. 49, pg. 759
Culligan, Pat, Asst VP-Agency & Mktg - State Farm Mutual Automobile Insurance Co.; pg. 1218, pg. 557
Cullinan, Chris, Mgr-Mktg-Global Rubber Blacks - Cabot Corporation; pg. 1151, pg. 792
Cullinan, Diarmuid, Sr Product Mgr-Global - Molex Incorporated; pg. 655, pg. 628
Cullinane, Jeff, Brand Mgr-North America Vicks Design - The Procter & Gamble Company; pg. 1129, pg. 1418
Cully, David, Pres-Retail Markets & Exec VP-Mdsg & Digital Media Svcs - Baker & Taylor, Inc.; pg. 1619, pg. 1362
Culotta, Catherine, VP-Retail Sls - Aveda Corporation; pg. 499, pg. 917
Culp, Joel, VP-Mktg - Wilsonart International, Inc.; pg. 1450, pg. 1746
Culp, John, Mgr-Product Mgmt - Emerson Process Management; pg. 1334, pg. 1636
Culpepper, Chandra, Head-Social Strategy Consulting - Oracle Corporation; pg. 450, pg. 191
Culver, Angela, VP-Brand & Corp Mktg - NeuStar, Inc.; pg. 1872, pg. 1807
Cumbaa, Charles T., Sr VP-Corp & Product Strategy - Blackbaud, Inc.; pg. 361, pg. 1613
Cumberbatch, Michael, Product Mgr-YouTube for Artists - YouTube, LLC; pg. 1291, pg. 198
Cumbers, Angela, Bus Mgr-Canada - Rosco Laboratories, Inc.; pg. 1782, pg. 378
Cumins, Nicholas, Sr VP-Products - OpenX Technologies, Inc.; pg. 1272, pg. 180
Cummings, Buddy, VP-Product Dev - Globe Composite Solutions, Ltd.; pg. 1883, pg. 842
Cummings, Courtney, Sr Media Buyer & Planner - Empire Today, LLC; pg. 923, pg. 643
Cummings, John, Mng Dir-Mktg, Bus Dev, Components & Sys Grp - Applied Materials, Inc; pg. 618, pg. 1009
Cummings, Karen, Exec VP-Sls & Mktg - Omtool, Ltd.; pg. 449, pg. 782
Cummings, Mike, Asst Dir-Media Rels - Kansas City Royals Baseball Corporation; pg. 555, pg. 985
Cummings, Sandy, VP-Comm & Content Mktg - Healthways, Inc.; pg. 1540, pg. 1632
Cummings, Shannon, Brand Mgr - United Services Automobile Association; pg. 1221, pg. 1743
Cummings, Tanya, Sr Mgr-Digital Mktg - Stanley Black & Decker, Inc.; pg. 1063, pg. 358
Cummings, Tom, Dir-Natural Channel Sls - Coca-Cola North America; pg. 848, pg. 500
Cummins, Andrew, Mgr-Mktg - Intel Corporation; pg. 645, pg. 266
Cummins, Brian, Product Mgr-Foreign Exchange Trading Sys - GFI Group Inc.; pg. 762, pg. 1234
Cummins, Cheryl, Sr Product Mgr - Essentra Components; pg. 1047, pg. 612
Cummins, Don, Sr VP-Mktg - Brother International Corporation - USA; pg. 53, pg. 1046
Cummins, John, VP-Product Tech - Hydrotex Partners Ltd.; pg. 979, pg. 1692
Cummins, Sarah, Dir-Strategic Mktg & Comm - Discovery Communications, Inc.; pg. 282, pg. 777
Cummins, Tim, Dir-PR - Ubisoft Inc.; pg. 589, pg. 229
Cummins, Valerie, Dir-Category Sls Dev-Ice Cream - Nestle Canada Inc.; pg. 883, pg. 1929
Cummiskey, Tom, Sr VP-Sls-Global - Nortek Security & Control LLC; pg. 659, pg. 59
Cummo, Jennifer, Sr Mgr-Mktg - Conde Nast Publications, Inc.; pg. 1629, pg. 1217
Cummo, Jennifer, Sr Mgr-Mktg - Vogue Magazine; pg. 1700, pg. 1311
Cundey, Carol Lee, Mgr-Mktg Comm - Johnson Outdoors Inc.; pg. 1837, pg. 1888
Cune, Adriana, Brand Mgr-No Yolks - New World Pasta Company; pg. 885, pg. 1537
Cuneo, F. Peter, Chm & Interim CEO - Iconix Brand Group, Inc.; pg. 26, pg. 1243
Cunha, Bob, Mng Dir-Mktg & Distr Strategy - Eaton Vance Corp.; pg. 746, pg. 794
Cunha, Carly, Planner-Digital Media - Palisades Media Group, Inc.; pg. 452, pg. 275
Cunha, Paulo, Sr Dir-North America Mktg & Strategy - Hotels.com, L.P.; pg. 1257, pg. 1682
Cunha, Stephanie, Mgr-PR - CVS Health Corporation; pg. 1765, pg. 1610
Cunningham, Alan, Sr Mgr-Mktg-Cereal Innovation - General Mills, Inc.; pg. 828, pg. 933
Cunningham, Angela, Product Mgr - Arrow Fastener Company, Inc.; pg. 1042, pg. 1118
Cunningham, Ann, Dir-Americas Mktg - ACI Worldwide Inc.; pg. 341, pg. 1010
Cunningham, Brendan, Sr VP-Sls - Florida Marlins, L.P.; pg. 548, pg. 442
Cunningham, Derrick, Specialist-Mktg & Comm-Loyalty Mktg - Alaska Air Group, Inc.; pg. 1897, pg. 1830
Cunningham, Jennifer, Brand Mgr-Nike Basketball-NA - NIKE, Inc.; pg. 1812, pg. 1492
Cunningham, John, VP-Mktg - DC Comics, Inc.; pg. 1633, pg. 1221
Cunningham, John, Pres-Consumer Products Grp - Stanley Black & Decker, Inc.; pg. 1063, pg. 358
Cunningham, Julie, Dir-Mktg - Hilton Worldwide, Inc.; pg. 1094, pg. 1791
Cunningham, Kevin, Sr Mgr-Mktg - Applied Materials, Inc.; pg. 618, pg. 264
Cunningham, Liz, Brand Mgr-Mktg - AMN Healthcare Services, Inc.; pg. 1494, pg. 200
Cunningham, Mike, Dir-Sponsorship & Global Accounts Mktg-WW - Lenovo Group Ltd; pg. 427, pg. 1384
Cunningham, Robert F., Chief Strategy Officer - DynaVox Inc.; pg. 635, pg. 1574
Cunningham, Stacey, Brand Mgr-Smirnoff - Diageo North America Inc.; pg. 248, pg. 1223
Cunningham, Stacy, Exec VP-Mktg - Foot Locker, Inc.; pg. 1808, pg. 1231
Cunningham, Tom, VP-Sls Enablement-Global - SkillSoft plc; pg. 470, pg. 1037
Cunningham, Vicki, Supvr-Mktg Comm & Creative - Ritchie Bros. Auctioneers Incorporated; pg. 1372, pg. 1907
Cunningham, William, Sr Head-Specialist Mktg & Mktg Res Grp - Total System Services, Inc.; pg. 484, pg. 528
Cupo, Michael, Sr Dir-Tech - ESPN, Inc.; pg. 285, pg. 340
Cupp, Colin, Product Mktg Mgr-Maya - Autodesk Inc.; pg. 356, pg. 257
Cupp, Krista, Specialist-PR - Tyson Foods, Inc.; pg. 902, pg.

35
Cupp, Tim, Area Mgr-Sls & Product - Ferrari North America, Inc.; *pg.* 171, *pg.* 1060
Cuppari, Scott, Dir-Mktg-Coca-Cola Freestyle-Global - The Coca-Cola Company; *pg.* 240, *pg.* 493
Cupples, Courtney, Head-aHUS Global Mktg & Sr Dir - Alexion Pharmaceuticals, Inc.; *pg.* 1489, *pg.* 341
Curella, Michael, Dir-Customer Mktg - Coty, Inc.; *pg.* 506, *pg.* 1219
Curich, James, Dir-PR - William Grant & Sons, Inc.; *pg.* 1972, *pg.* 1057
Curin, Matthew, Asst Dir-Ops & Mktg Strategy-Global - Astellas Pharma US, Inc.; *pg.* 1496, *pg.* 640
Curl, John, Sr Mgr-Cross Carline Product Plng - Nissan North America, Inc.; *pg.* 186, *pg.* 1633
Curler, Amy, Head-Mktg-Retail Environment Grp - Harley-Davidson, Inc.; *pg.* 178, *pg.* 1874
Curley, Emily, Sr Mgr-Mktg-Global - Red Hat, Inc.; *pg.* 460, *pg.* 1388
Curley, Jay, Sr Mgr-Mktg-Global - Ben & Jerry's Homemade, Inc.; *pg.* 1850, *pg.* 1767
Curley, Joe, Dir-Mktg-Technical Computing Grp - Intel Corporation; *pg.* 645, *pg.* 266
Curley, Nancy, Sr Strategist-Mktg Comm - Principal Financial Group, Inc.; *pg.* 796, *pg.* 706
Curley, Sue, VP & Div Mgr-Mdse-Intimate Apparel - Belk, Inc.; *pg.* 1760, *pg.* 1364
Curmi, Michael, Head-Experiential Mktg-Chrysler, Jeep, Dodge & Ram Brands - FCA US LLC; *pg.* 170, *pg.* 868
Curran, Allison, Mgr-Mktg - General Mills, Inc.; *pg.* 828, *pg.* 933
Curran, Brynne, Brand Mgr-Little Tikes-Global - MGA Entertainment, Inc.; *pg.* 964, *pg.* 300
Curran, Denise, Sr Mgr-Change Comm - Royal Bank of Canada; *pg.* 800, *pg.* 1942
Curran, Eileen, Dir-Mktg Comm - Sealed Air Corporation; *pg.* 1468, *pg.* 1058
Curran, Jim, Mgr-Mktg - Agilent Technologies, Inc.; *pg.* 614, *pg.* 264
Curran, Kevin, VP-Fin-Global Sls & Mktg - CommScope; *pg.* 630, *pg.* 668
Curran, Kristin, Brand Mgr-Quality - General Motors Company; *pg.* 175, *pg.* 881
Curran, Laurie, Sr Mgr-Mktg-Global Enterprise Mktg - Dell Inc.; *pg.* 383, *pg.* 1737
Curran, Meghan, Sr VP-Mktg, Guest Experience & Sls - John G. Shedd Aquarium; *pg.* 555, *pg.* 579
Curran, Mike, Asst Mgr-Mktg - Ocean Spray Cranberries, Inc.; *pg.* 887, *pg.* 827
Curren, Lauren, Sr Mgr-Portfolio Comm - Pfizer Inc.; *pg.* 1581, *pg.* 1278
Curren, William, Dir-Product Dev - Bed Bath & Beyond Inc.; *pg.* 1121, *pg.* 1127
Currer, Amy, Mgr-Solutions Mktg-Security - CDW Corporation; *pg.* 370, *pg.* 663
Currie, Kirsten, Dir-Mktg-Appliances & Home Essentials - Best Buy Co., Inc.; *pg.* 1761, *pg.* 954
Currie, Mark, Product Mgr-Global - Henkel Corporation; *pg.* 1049, *pg.* 369
Currie, Mark, Product Mgr-Global - Henkel Corporation; *pg.* 1165, *pg.* 1535
Currie, Mike, Brand Mgr-Frank's RedHot - Reckitt Benckiser Inc.; *pg.* 1136, *pg.* 1105
Currie, Sue, Sr Mgr-Mdsg Info Mgmt - Harry & David Holdings, Inc.; *pg.* 1022, *pg.* 1499
Currie, Travis, Coord-PR - Atlanta Convention & Visitors Bureau; *pg.* 989, *pg.* 489
Currier, Chuck, Sr Engr-Product Support - Unison Industries, LLC; *pg.* 235, *pg.* 435
Currier, Suzanne Berg, Dir-Media - GNC Holdings Inc.; *pg.* 1537, *pg.* 1576
Curry, Daren, Mgr-Mktg - The Procter & Gamble Company; *pg.* 1129, *pg.* 1418
Curry, Gregory, Mgr-Mktg - Lowe's Companies, Inc.; *pg.* 1053, *pg.* 1383
Curry, Heidi, Sr Mgr-Bakery R&D - Dunkin' Brands Group, Inc.; *pg.* 1727, *pg.* 810
Curry, Joe, Mgr-Social Ops-Social Media - Target Corporation; *pg.* 1786, *pg.* 942
Curry, Jolene, Dir-Recruiting & Mktg-MassMutual Fin Grp - Massachusetts Mutual Life Insurance Company; *pg.* 1207, *pg.* 845
Curry, Josh, VP-Mktg - MetroPCS, Inc.; *pg.* 1872, *pg.* 1683
Curry, Joy M., Program Mgr-Mktg-Wells Fargo Bank-Northeast Reg - Wells Fargo & Company; *pg.* 819, *pg.* 232
Curry, Kelly, Dir-Event Mktg - Office Depot, Inc.; *pg.* 448, *pg.* 412
Curry, Kyle, Sr Mgr-Intl Mktg - Hologic, Inc.; *pg.* 1416, *pg.* 784
Curry, Leah, Mgr-Mobile Mktg - American Eagle Outfitters, Inc.; *pg.* 37, *pg.* 1572
Curry, Melissa, Partner-Mktg Comm & Channel Mktg - Cardinal Health, Inc.; *pg.* 1512, *pg.* 1448
Curry, Whitney, Dir-Mktg-Social & Promotions - Zillow Group, Inc.; *pg.* 1292, *pg.* 1843
Curtin, Chad, Specialist-Sls Ops - Ford Motor Company of Canada, Limited; *pg.* 174, *pg.* 1930
Curtin, Chris, Chief Digital Officer & Head-New Platform Mktg - Visa Inc.; *pg.* 816, *pg.* 230
Curtin, Chris, Chief Digital Officer & Head-New Platform Mktg - Visa U.S.A., Inc.; *pg.* 817, *pg.* 231
Curtin, Heather, Dir-New Product Dev - Range Kleen Manufacturing Inc.; *pg.* 60, *pg.* 1458
Curtin, Samantha, Assoc Acct Exec-Creative Shared Svcs - Staples, Inc.; *pg.* 474, *pg.* 821
Curtin, Yolonda Salts, Dir-Mktg-Specialty Retail Div - Caleres, Inc.; *pg.* 1805, *pg.* 993
Curtis, Cari, Brand Mgr-Global - Energizer Holdings, Inc.; *pg.* 637, *pg.* 996
Curtis, Christopher, Analyst-Mktg - BizRate.com; *pg.* 1231, *pg.* 126
Curtis, Christopher, Mgr-Channel Mktg - The Genie Company; *pg.* 55, *pg.* 1403
Curtis, David, Specialist-Mktg - MetroPCS, Inc.; *pg.* 1872, *pg.* 1683
Curtis, Deborah, VP-Entertainment Mktg & Sponsorships - American Express Company; *pg.* 712, *pg.* 1190
Curtis, Deborah, Asst VP-Mktg-Maybelline New York - Maybelline LLC; *pg.* 516, *pg.* 1257
Curtis, Duncan, Product Mgr-Google Play Games - Google Inc.; *pg.* 1249, *pg.* 153
Curtis, Elise Zielsdorf, Mgr-Comm-Mktg - Marvin Windows & Doors; *pg.* 934, *pg.* 965
Curtis, Erica, Dir-Mktg Analytics - Penguin Random House; *pg.* 1675, *pg.* 1276
Curtis, Gretchen, Dir-Media - Panera Bread Company; *pg.* 1029, *pg.* 1001
Curtis, Jeanette, Sr Mgr-Deposit Svcs - Peoples Trust Company; *pg.* 793, *pg.* 1912
Curtis, Jim, Chief Revenue Officer - HealthCentral; *pg.* 1256, *pg.* 1773
Curtis, John D., Mgr-Lease Mktg & Xerox Fin Svcs-US Customer Financing Solutions - Xerox Corporation; *pg.* 494, *pg.* 365
Curtis, Jordyn, Brand Mgr-Home Grown IP's-The LEGO Movie & Ninjago - LEGO Systems, Inc.; *pg.* 961, *pg.* 346
Curtis, Kathy, Area Mgr-Sls - Taylor Morrison; *pg.* 1116, *pg.* 24
Curtis, Kenny, Sr Dir-Kids & Family Programming - Sirius XM Holdings Inc.; *pg.* 308, *pg.* 1292
Curtis, Lanny, Dir-Customer Mktg - Meijer, Inc.; *pg.* 1779, *pg.* 888
Curtis, Megan, Brand Mgr - Stryker Corporation; *pg.* 1598, *pg.* 894
Curtis, Melissa, Mgr-Comm & PR - Deloitte & Touche USA LLP; *pg.* 743, *pg.* 1222
Curtis, Tom, Assoc Mgr-Digital Mktg - Ubisoft Inc.; *pg.* 589, *pg.* 229
Curtis-Magley, Debbie, Dir-SAP Cross-Cloud Social & Community - Ariba, Inc.; *pg.* 353, *pg.* 283
Curtiss, Peter, Dir-Digital Mktg - United Services Automobile Association; *pg.* 1221, *pg.* 1743
Curts, Steve, Chief Strategy Officer-American Express Global Bus Travel - American Express Company; *pg.* 712, *pg.* 1190
Cusack, Deidre E., Grp Mgr-Global Product-Distr Transformers - ABB Inc.; *pg.* 1309, *pg.* 1359
Cusack, Joe, Sr Mgr-Market - Unum Group; *pg.* 1222, *pg.* 1629
Cusano, Ron, Mgr-Section-Energy Efficiency Mktg - Consolidated Edison, Inc.; *pg.* 1938, *pg.* 1218
Cushing, Kate, Product Mgr - YouTube, LLC; *pg.* 1291, *pg.* 198
Cushing, Meghan, Specialist-PR - Target Corporation; *pg.* 1786, *pg.* 942
Cushma, Angel, Head-Svc Provider Channel Mktg - ShoreTel, Inc.; *pg.* 469, *pg.* 288
Cushman, Candice, Mgr-Mktg-Aetna Natl Accounts - Aetna Inc.; *pg.* 1187, *pg.* 351
Cushman, Janine, Mgr-Promos Mktg - General Mills, Inc.; *pg.* 828, *pg.* 933
Cushman, Karin, Dir-Meetings & Education Mktg - American Society of Health-System Pharmacists; *pg.* 131, *pg.* 761
Cushman, Timothy, Sr Mgr-Mktg - Emerson Process Management; *pg.* 1334, *pg.* 1636
Cushman, Venera, Program Mgr-Americas Mktg Comm - Tektronix, Inc.; *pg.* 1431, *pg.* 1496
Cushway, Dawn, Mgr-Mktg Tech & Automation - Anthem, Inc.; *pg.* 1192, *pg.* 683
Cusic, Kristin, Dir-Brand Mktg - Converse Inc.; *pg.* 1831, *pg.* 793
Cusick, Abigail, Sr Mgr-Social Media - Bravo Media LLC; *pg.* 271, *pg.* 1206
Cusick, Ken, Mgr-Adv - The Kroger Co.; *pg.* 1025, *pg.* 1416
Cusick, Randy, Mgr-Technical Mktg - Xerox Corporation; *pg.* 494, *pg.* 365
Cusick, Wayne, Asst Dir-Tourism Sls & Svcs - Kentucky Department of Tourism; *pg.* 996, *pg.* 728
Cuson, Matt, Sr Dir-Cinema Emerging Bus - Dolby Laboratories, Inc.; *pg.* 284, *pg.* 217
Custer, Kevin, Product Mgr-Media Production - GoPro; *pg.* 1414, *pg.* 255
Custodio, Jessica, Mgr-Mktg - Western Digital Corporation; *pg.* 492, *pg.* 118
Cutaia, Marina, Coord-Online Mktg - The Mattress Firm, Inc.; *pg.* 934, *pg.* 1711
Cutbirth, Jason, Sr VP-Mktg - Insperity, Inc.; *pg.* 416, *pg.* 1725
Cutburth, Jamie, Sr VP-Mktg-Bravo & Oxygen & VP-Ad Sls Mktg - NBC Universal, Inc.; *pg.* 300, *pg.* 1266
Cuthbert, Brad, Dir-Mktg - Kemps LLC; *pg.* 867, *pg.* 961
Cuthbert, James, Brand Mgr - The Coca-Cola Company; *pg.* 240, *pg.* 493
Cutler, Jeanette K., Sr Dir-Integrated Mktg Comm - The Kraft Heinz Company; *pg.* 871, *pg.* 641
Cutler, Justine, Mgr-Database Mktg - Esurance, Inc.; *pg.* 1243, *pg.* 217
Cutler, Rob, Mgr-Sls Ops - Caleres, Inc.; *pg.* 1805, *pg.* 993
Cutler, Seth, Sr Product Mgr-Growth Initiatives - General Electric Company; *pg.* 1297, *pg.* 347
Cutlip, Lauren, Sr Mgr-Bus Dev - Kayak; *pg.* 1260, *pg.* 363
Cutright, Keisha, Asst Professor-Mktg - University of Pennsylvania; *pg.* 609, *pg.* 1571
Cutter, Dana, Sr Mgr-Mktg - Aetna Inc.; *pg.* 1187, *pg.* 351
Cutter, Michelle, VP-ECommerce & Mktg - Tumi, Inc.; *pg.* 15, *pg.* 1123
Cuttic, Evan, Assoc Mgr-Consumer Mktg - Home Box Office, Inc.; *pg.* 290, *pg.* 1240
Cutting, Tracy, Assoc-Sls - Semonin Realtors; *pg.* 1112, *pg.* 738
Cutting, Wade, Product Mgr - Preformed Line Products Company; *pg.* 1370, *pg.* 1434
Cutts, Suzanne, Sr VP-Brand & Adv - Wells Fargo & Company; *pg.* 819, *pg.* 232
Cuzman, Cristina E., Sr Specialist-Product Comm - FRANKLIN RESOURCES, INC.; *pg.* 760, *pg.* 254
Cybert, Candace, Sr Mgr-Pur-A&P - Moet Hennessy; *pg.* 1966, *pg.* 1260
Cybulak, Lynne, Sr Mgr-Mktg - General Electric Company; *pg.* 1297, *pg.* 347
Cydylo, Courtney, Sr Specialist-Mktg - ACI Worldwide Inc.; *pg.* 341, *pg.* 1010
Cye, Beverly, Rep-Mktg - Mercury Insurance Company; *pg.* 1208, *pg.* 136
Cygan, David, Sr VP-Direct Mktg - BROOKDALE SENIOR LIVING INC.; *pg.* 1511, *pg.* 1627
Cynaumon, Megan, Sr Analyst-Search Mktg - Dell Inc.; *pg.* 383, *pg.* 1737
Cyphers, Bill, Sr VP-Sls - Subaru of America, Inc.; *pg.* 191, *pg.* 1050
Cyr, Brian D., Dir-USA Product & Design - Hi-Tec Sports USA, Inc.; *pg.* 1809, *pg.* 150
Cyr, Rollie, VP-Sls - Calgary Flames Limited Partnership; *pg.* 535, *pg.* 1902
Cyree, Christine, VP-Creative Svcs - Scripps Networks Interactive, Inc.; *pg.* 1279, *pg.* 1638
Cytroen, Andrew, Sr Mgr-Corp Equity-Corp Equity Grp & Global Corp Affairs - Johnson & Johnson; *pg.* 1549, *pg.* 1091
Czapko, Ray H., Dir-Mktg - Surco Products, Inc.; *pg.* 336, *pg.* 1581
Czarkowski, Chris, Sr VP-Hispanic Grp Adv Sls-NBC Universo - NBC Universal, Inc.; *pg.* 300, *pg.* 1266
Czarkowski, Joe, VP & Mgr-Sls-Natl - Discovery Communications, Inc.; *pg.* 282, *pg.* 777
Czarnik, Ross, Mgr-Mktg - Greater Cincinnati Convention &

First page reference indicates Business Class Edition
Second page reference indicates Geographic Edition

Visitors Bureau; *pg.* 993, *pg.* 1414
Czarnowski, Ashley, Sr Mgr-Brand Comm & Digital Mktg - adidas America Inc.; *pg.* 1803, *pg.* 1500
Czerniak, Chad, Sr Mgr-Mktg-NetApp - Arrow Electronics, Inc.; *pg.* 619, *pg.* 325
Czerniuk, Mark, Mgr-Search Engine Mktg - CareerBuilder, LLC; *pg.* 1234, *pg.* 568
Czik, Alexander, Analyst-Data Mktg - Penguin Random House; *pg.* 1675, *pg.* 1276
Czuchan, Frank, Grp VP-Brand Strategy & Mktg - Newsday Media Group; *pg.* 1670, *pg.* 1181
Czyzewski, Ken, Mgr-Sls - Dynatect Manufacturing Inc.; *pg.* 1330, *pg.* 1883

D

D'Addario, Nikki, Mgr-PR - Kronos Incorporated; *pg.* 425, *pg.* 813
D'Agostino, Chris, Partner-IT Bus-Global Mktg - Kimberly-Clark Corporation; *pg.* 1461, *pg.* 1720
D'Agostino, Gerry, Dir-Mktg-Comml - Travelers Insurance; *pg.* 1220, *pg.* 963
D'Agostino, Linda, Dir-Sls & Govt Rels - Buffalo Niagara Convention & Visitors Bureau, Inc.; *pg.* 1901, *pg.* 1147
D'agostino, Michele, Product Mgr-Mktg - Boston Scientific Corporation; *pg.* 1508, *pg.* 831
D'Agostino, Sharon, Sr Dir - Johnson & Johnson; *pg.* 1549, *pg.* 1091
D'Alessandro, Dan, VP-Mktg - Kraft Canada Inc.; *pg.* 869, *pg.* 1939
D'Alessandro, Greg, Brand Mgr - Kellogg Company; *pg.* 831, *pg.* 870
D'Alessio, Jim, VP-Mktg - Trimac Corporation; *pg.* 1926, *pg.* 1905
D'Aloise, Kim, Mgr-Digital Mktg-Global - Colgate-Palmolive Company; *pg.* 504, *pg.* 1215
D'Aloise, Robin, VP-Sls-Retail PCA - Helen of Troy L.P.; *pg.* 511, *pg.* 1692
D'Alonzo, Thomas W., Chm & Acting CEO - Salix Pharmaceuticals, Inc.; *pg.* 1591, *pg.* 1388
D'Amato, Keith, Dir-Sls-Intl - The Ripley Company; *pg.* 1305, *pg.* 342
D'Ambrogi, Kate, Assoc Mgr-Mktg-Ruffino & Assoc Export Mgr UK & Europe - Constellation Brands, Inc.; *pg.* 1960, *pg.* 1348
D'Amico, Heather, Mgr-Local Guides Social Media & Content Mktg-Google - Adecco USA, Inc.; *pg.* 342, *pg.* 1178
D'Amico, Jennifer, Mgr-Mktg - General Electric Company; *pg.* 1297, *pg.* 347
D'Amico, Judi, Mgr-Direct Mktg - Watts Water Technologies, Inc.; *pg.* 1078, *pg.* 837
D'Amico, Kimberly, Mgr-Creative Svcs - McKesson Corporation; *pg.* 1560, *pg.* 222
D'Amico, Rich, Deputy Dir-Mktg - Ikea North America Services LLC; *pg.* 929, *pg.* 1523
D'Amico, Skip, Mgr-Cadillac Global Mktg-Creative Content - General Motors Company; *pg.* 175, *pg.* 881
D'Andrea, Jill, Brand Mgr-Vince - Saks Fifth Avenue, Inc.; *pg.* 1783, *pg.* 1287
D'Angelo, Ann, Mgr-Field Mktg-Pepsi Cola North America - Pepsi Beverages Company; *pg.* 258, *pg.* 1342
D'Angelo, Gerry, Dir-Media-Europe - Mondelez International; *pg.* 877, *pg.* 1344
D'Angelo, Joseph, Sr VP-Brdcst Programs & Advanced Svcs - iBiquity Digital Corporation; *pg.* 409, *pg.* 767
D'Angelo, Michael, VP-Sls-Intl - Goodway Technologies Corporation; *pg.* 1341, *pg.* 374
D'Angelo, Rhiannon, Sr Specialist-Media - Eversource; *pg.* 977, *pg.* 794
D'Anjou, Liana, Assoc Mgr-Mktg - Wal-Mart Stores, Inc.; *pg.* 1790, *pg.* 29
D'Anna, Vanessa, Mgr-Relationship Mktg - Orbitz Worldwide, Inc.; *pg.* 1918, *pg.* 586
D'Antonio, Barbara, Brand Mgr-Guardsman Svcs-Global - The Valspar Corporation; *pg.* 1449, *pg.* 945
D'Antonio, Jackie, Dir-Digital Bus Dev & Reg Dir-Sls - Bonnier Corporation; *pg.* 1622, *pg.* 480
D'Aoust, Cindy, Acting CEO & Exec VP-Membership & Ops - Cruise Lines International Association, Inc.; *pg.* 138, *pg.* 424
D'Aragon, Catherine, Asst VP-Mktg-Vichy Laboratories - L'Oreal USA; *pg.* 514, *pg.* 1252
D'Arcy, Mark, Chief Creative Officer & VP-Facebook Creative Shop - Facebook, Inc.; *pg.* 1245, *pg.* 143
D'Arcy, Raymond L., Pres-Sls & Mktg - Interactive Data Pricing & Reference Data, Inc.; *pg.* 769, *pg.* 785
D'Armond, Jackson, Mgr-Mktg Comm - Stihl, Inc.; *pg.* 1064, *pg.* 1810
D'Arrigo-Martin, Margaret, Exec VP-Sls & Mktg - D'Arrigo Bros. Company; *pg.* 852, *pg.* 197
D'Ascenzo, Kyle, Mgr-Brand Adv, Graphics & Identity-DoubleTree - Hilton Worldwide, Inc.; *pg.* 1094, *pg.* 1791
D'Avolio, John, Mgr-Worldwide PR-HP Storage & Networking - Hewlett-Packard Company; *pg.* 404, *pg.* 175
D'Elia, Art, VP-Mktg-Oikos, Brand Dannon & Kids - The Dannon Company, Inc.; *pg.* 851, *pg.* 1351
D'Entremont, Rebecca, Dir-Digital Mktg - FMR LLC (Fidelity Investments); *pg.* 759, *pg.* 794
D'Ermilio, Lou, Sr VP-Media Rels - Fox Sports Net; *pg.* 288, *pg.* 131
D'Olimpio, Dienna, Mgr-Partnership Mktg - Teleflora LLC; *pg.* 1801, *pg.* 140
D'Onofrio, Ralph, VP-Adv-Community Newspaper Grp - The New York Post; *pg.* 1668, *pg.* 1269
D'Orso, Chris, VP-Sls & Ticket Ops - Orlando Magic; *pg.* 572, *pg.* 455
D'Ortenzio, Amanda, Sr Asst Brand Mgr-Degree Deodorants - Unilever Canada Inc.; *pg.* 903, *pg.* 1946
D'sa, Justin, Sr Mgr-Brand Comm & Strategy - Bristol-Myers Squibb Company; *pg.* 1509, *pg.* 1206
D'Silva, David, Mgr-Global Support Brand Products - Google Inc.; *pg.* 1249, *pg.* 153
D'Silva, Kyle, Mgr-Pharma & Biopharma Mktg - Thermo Fisher Scientific Inc.; *pg.* 1431, *pg.* 854
D'Souza, Amy, Mgr-Media-Constellation Brands - Crown Imports LLC; *pg.* 248, *pg.* 572
D'Souza, Shaman, Sr Product Mgr-Amazon Appstore for Android - Amazon.com, Inc.; *pg.* 1226, *pg.* 1831
D'souza, Vincent, Brand Mgr-Refreshment Drinks - Diageo Canada, Inc.; *pg.* 1961, *pg.* 1937
D'Sylva, Blaise, VP-Media & Content Plng - Dr Pepper Snapple Group, Inc.; *pg.* 250, *pg.* 1729
D'Vorkin, Lewis, Chief Product Officer - Forbes, Inc.; *pg.* 1641, *pg.* 1232
Dabby, Jordan, VP-Partnership Mktg - Macy's East; *pg.* 1777, *pg.* 1254
Dabe, Erin, Sr Mgr-Member Mktg - Blink Fitness; *pg.* 533, *pg.* 1204
Dabir, Catherine, Specialist-OEM Mktg - NVIDIA Corporation; *pg.* 447, *pg.* 268
Dabney, Melinda, Dir-Mktg - Principal Financial Group, Inc.; *pg.* 796, *pg.* 706
Dabrowski, Derek, Dir-Mktg-Snapple - Dr Pepper Snapple Group, Inc.; *pg.* 250, *pg.* 1729
Dabrowski, Jack, Dir-Mktg & Comm - BJC HealthCare; *pg.* 1506, *pg.* 993
Dacay, Marissa, Mgr-Integrated Mktg-Strategic Accounts & Verticals - Adobe Systems Incorporated; *pg.* 342, *pg.* 235
Dachowski, Stephen, Sr Dir-Adult Vaccines - Merck & Co., Inc.; *pg.* 1566, *pg.* 1077
Dachroeden, Ana, Assoc Dir-Digital Customer Mktg - Fox Broadcasting Company; *pg.* 287, *pg.* 130
DaCosta, Jennifer, Principal-Global Mktg Comm-Urology & Women's Health - Boston Scientific Corporation; *pg.* 1508, *pg.* 831
DaCosta, Soraya, Sr Mgr-Direct Mktg - Lenovo Group Ltd; *pg.* 427, *pg.* 1384
DaCunha, Imar, Specialist-Database & Production - Red Lobster; *pg.* 1747, *pg.* 455
Dacyshyn, Anne-Marie, VP-Mktg - Burton Snowboard Company; *pg.* 1829, *pg.* 1765
Dadas, Andrea, VP & Head-HR Mktg & Comm-Global - The Goldman Sachs Group, Inc.; *pg.* 762, *pg.* 1236
Dadgar, Nina, Sr Dir-Bus Dev - National Community Pharmacists Association; *pg.* 148, *pg.* 1771
Daehnert, Christy, Sr Dir & Program Mgr-M2016 - Meritor, Inc.; *pg.* 212, *pg.* 911
Daele, Petra Van, Sr Dir-Wealth Mgmt Comm - Canadian Imperial Bank of Commerce; *pg.* 729, *pg.* 1935
Daems, Randy, Dir-Mktg - LensCrafters, Inc.; *pg.* 1420, *pg.* 1460
Daems, Randy, Dir-Mktg - Luxottica Retail; *pg.* 8, *pg.* 1460
Dagan, Tiran, Partner-Strategy & Analytics & Head-Media & Entertainment - IBM; *pg.* 410, *pg.* 1449
Daggett, Patricia, Sr Mgr-Mktg-Hospital Market - Zoll Medical Corporation; *pg.* 1612, *pg.* 814
Dagiantis, Chris, Product Mgr - Cornelius Inc.; *pg.* 54, *pg.* 614
Dagistino, Lauren, Sr Mgr-Acct Mgmt Ops - Disney Interactive Media Group; *pg.* 1239, *pg.* 95
Daglian, Lusine, Mgr-Product Dev - Health Net, Inc.; *pg.* 1540, *pg.* 308
Dagostino, Robin, Dir-Social Media & Digital Comm - Comcast Corporation; *pg.* 276, *pg.* 1560
Dahan, Guetty, Dir-Loyalty Mktg - American Express Company; *pg.* 712, *pg.* 1190
Dahdaly, Mitri, Dir-Product Mgmt & Strategy - Infor; *pg.* 414, *pg.* 484
Daher, Mona A., Rep-Inside Sls & Analyst-Mktg - ABB Inc.; *pg.* 64, *pg.* 1959
Dahill, Heather, Dir-North America Mktg, Digital Partnerships & Branded Content - Citi Trends Inc.; *pg.* 22, *pg.* 539
Dahl, Bev, Mgr-Natl Accounts Sls - Hubbell Lighting - Progress Lighting Division; *pg.* 1300, *pg.* 1617
Dahl, John, Mgr-Outbound Mktg - Expedia, Inc.; *pg.* 1244, *pg.* 1814
Dahl, Keith, Corp Mgr-Motorsports & Engagement Mktg - Toyota Motor Sales, U.S.A., Inc.; *pg.* 193, *pg.* 296
Dahl, William, VP-Mktg & Comm - Solidscape, Inc.; *pg.* 1063, *pg.* 1037
Dahlen, Carly, Dir-Mktg - JustFab, Inc.; *pg.* 27, *pg.* 80
Dahlgren, Dana L., VP-Sls & Mktg - Kewaunee Scientific Corporation; *pg.* 931, *pg.* 1391
Dahlgren, Matt, Sr Product Mgr-Mktg Strategy - Capcom USA, Inc.; *pg.* 950, *pg.* 254
Dahlquist, Ann, Dir-Mktg Ops-Client Solutions Mktg - Dell Inc.; *pg.* 383, *pg.* 1737
Dahlquist, Cheryl, Exec Dir-Database Mktg Svcs - Meredith Corporation; *pg.* 1663, *pg.* 705
Dahlquist, Christiane, Sr Product Mgr-Enbrel Consumer Mktg - Pfizer Inc.; *pg.* 1581, *pg.* 1278
Dahm, Betsy, Sr Dir-IR - Marriott International, Inc.; *pg.* 1102, *pg.* 764
Dahm, Christine, VP-Mktg - Noosa Yoghurt; *pg.* 886, *pg.* 310
Dahm, Kati, Mgr-Corp Social Media - Cisco Systems, Inc.; *pg.* 372, *pg.* 240
Dahmen, Carol, Mgr-Political Mktg - Comcast Cable Communications, Inc.; *pg.* 276, *pg.* 1560
Dahmer, Eric, Dir-Mktg - The Kraft Heinz Company; *pg.* 871, *pg.* 641
Dahms, Lindsay, Mgr-Brand Mktg - Motorola Mobility LLC; *pg.* 657, *pg.* 627
Dahncke, Mark, Sr Mgr-Product & Motorsports Comm - Audi of America, Inc.; *pg.* 164, *pg.* 1784
Dahnert, Mike, Product Mgr-Global - Best Buy Co., Inc.; *pg.* 1761, *pg.* 954
Daigle, Bob, Product Mgr - David Clark Company Incorporated; *pg.* 633, *pg.* 862
Daigle, Emily, Assoc Mgr-Mktg - General Mills, Inc.; *pg.* 828, *pg.* 933
Dail, Michael, VP-Global Brand Mktg-Marriott Hotels & Resorts - Marriott International, Inc.; *pg.* 1102, *pg.* 764
Dail, Nathan, Sr Mgr-Brand Mktg & Menu - California Pizza Kitchen Inc.; *pg.* 1720, *pg.* 127
Dailey, Beth, Dir-Mktg - AARP; *pg.* 124, *pg.* 393
Dailey, John, Sr VP-Corp Adv Sls - Scripps Networks Interactive, Inc.; *pg.* 1279, *pg.* 1638
Dailey, Kimberly, Specialist-Sls & Mktg Solutions - The Dun & Bradstreet Corp.; *pg.* 1637, *pg.* 1120
Dailey, Ted, Dir-Sls Mid-Atlantic - Eppendorf North America; *pg.* 1412, *pg.* 1164
Daily, Collier, VP-Sls & Mktg - Intown Suites Management, Inc.; *pg.* 1098, *pg.* 513
Daily, Pete, COO-Mktg & Supply - Delek US Holdings, Inc.; *pg.* 975, *pg.* 1627
Daily, Robert, VP-Mktg - Virbac Corporation; *pg.* 1606, *pg.* 1696
Dainello, Gina, Planner-Sls - HomeAway, Inc.; *pg.* 1911, *pg.* 1663
Dakshin, Venk, Sr Dir-IT-Global Sls, Mktg & CRM Applications - Pitney Bowes Inc.; *pg.* 454, *pg.* 376
Dalati, Roy, Mgr-Trader & Sls-Distillates - LyondellBasell Industries; *pg.* 980, *pg.* 1710
Dalby, Kimberly, Dir-Mktg & Adv Ops - Cablevision Systems Corporation; *pg.* 272, *pg.* 1141
Dale, Bob, Sr VP-Sls - Protection One, Inc.; *pg.* 665, *pg.* 715
Dale, Chris, Sr Mgr-Corp Comm & Pub Affairs - Google Inc.; *pg.* 1249, *pg.* 153
Dale, Christopher, Dir-PR-Global - ADTRAN, Inc.; *pg.* 344, *pg.* 6
Dale, Damian, Sr Mgr-Partnership & Mobile & Social - Ubisoft Inc.; *pg.* 589, *pg.* 229
Dale, Emily C., Dir-Div Mktg-Global - Bio-Rad Laboratories, Inc.; *pg.* 1504, *pg.* 101
Dale, John, Dir-Mktg & Sls - Bunge Limited; *pg.* 842, *pg.* 1351

Dale, Lauren, Mgr-Product Mktg - Google Inc.; *pg.* 1249, *pg.* 153
Dale, Taylor, Specialist-Mktg & Comm - Special Olympics International, Inc.; *pg.* 157, *pg.* 405
Dale, Thomas, Dir-Mktg-FedEx Svcs - FedEx Corporation; *pg.* 1907, *pg.* 1642
Dalessio, Ian, Specialist-Mktg-MassMutual Fin Grp - Massachusetts Mutual Life Insurance Company; *pg.* 1207, *pg.* 845
Daley, Bob, Mgr-Production - TheatreworksUSA; *pg.* 587, *pg.* 1298
Daley, Cecilia C., Sr Mgr-Mktg - Pfizer Inc.; *pg.* 1581, *pg.* 1278
Daley, Christie, Assoc Mgr-Digital Mktg Analytics - CNBC; *pg.* 275, *pg.* 1059
Daley, Donna, Mgr-Mktg Div - The Allstate Corporation; *pg.* 1189, *pg.* 639
Daley, Jack, VP-Digital Content Strategy & Production - MTV Networks Company; *pg.* 298, *pg.* 1262
Daley, Jim, Mgr-Mktg Comm - Microsoft Corporation; *pg.* 435, *pg.* 1824
Daley, Kerri, Mgr-Sls & Mktg - Safeway Inc.; *pg.* 1032, *pg.* 184
Daley, Sandra, Sr Dir & Head-Global Comml-Oncology - Halozyme Therapeutics, Inc.; *pg.* 1539, *pg.* 203
Daley, Stephen, Mgr-Creative - CarMax, Inc.; *pg.* 167, *pg.* 1800
Daley, Tom, Mgr-Mktg-HOKA ONE ONE - Deckers Outdoor Corporation; *pg.* 1807, *pg.* 100
Daley-Francois, Sandra, Dir-Sls - Greater Miami Convention & Visitors Bureau; *pg.* 993, *pg.* 442
Dalhausser, Todd, Sr VP-North American Sls - Saucony, Inc.; *pg.* 1818, *pg.* 828
Dalian, Lara, Sr Mgr-Brand Mktg-Global - Mattel Games/Puzzles; *pg.* 962, *pg.* 80
Dalian, Lara, Sr Mgr-Brand Mktg-Global - MATTEL, INC.; *pg.* 962, *pg.* 81
Dalipi, Jennifer, Sr Dir-Digital Mktg-COTY Beauty - Coty, Inc.; *pg.* 506, *pg.* 1219
Dallaire, Seth, VP-Adv Sls-Global - Amazon.com, Inc.; *pg.* 1226, *pg.* 1831
Dallas-Feeney, Juliette, Mgr-Social Media - Birchbox; *pg.* 1762, *pg.* 1203
Dalley, Tami, Sr Dir-Res - Buzzfeed; *pg.* 1233, *pg.* 1208
Dalley, Travis, Mgr-Creative Svcs - Henry Schein, Inc.; *pg.* 1541, *pg.* 1180
Dallman, Jodi, Specialist-Mktg - Cargill Animal Nutrition; *pg.* 1475, *pg.* 965
Dally, Jennifer, Sr Mgr-Mktg Strategy & Capability Dev - Abbott Nutrition; *pg.* 1485, *pg.* 1437
Dally, Robin, VP-Mktg Solutions - National Basketball Association; *pg.* 566, *pg.* 1264
Dally, Troy J., Sr VP & Mgr-Gen Mdsg, Hardlines & Building Products - Lowe's Companies, Inc.; *pg.* 1053, *pg.* 1383
Dalmas, Robin, Editor-in-Chief-Bus Circle & Copywriter-Mktg - AT&T; *pg.* 1865, *pg.* 258
Dalmia, Atul, VP-Data Platforms & Mktg Capabilities - American Express Company; *pg.* 712, *pg.* 1190
Dalrymple, Michelle, Product Mgr-Oncology Mktg-XGEVA - Amgen Inc.; *pg.* 1493, *pg.* 291
Dalrymple, Rich R., VP-PR & Comm - Dallas Cowboys Football Club, Ltd.; *pg.* 543, *pg.* 1718
DalSanto, Kaitlyn E., Coord-Mktg - CNA Insurance Companies; *pg.* 1198, *pg.* 571
Dalton, Daniel, Sr VP-Mktg & Small Bus Lending - Citigroup Inc.; *pg.* 735, *pg.* 1212
Dalton, Elaine, VP-Sls - Keds LLC; *pg.* 1810, *pg.* 828
Dalton, Elisabeth, Assoc Dir-Oncology Mktg - Astellas Pharma US, Inc.; *pg.* 1496, *pg.* 640
Dalton, Faith, Specialist-Digital Sls - Putman Media, Inc.; *pg.* 1679, *pg.* 621
Dalton, Joe, Sr Mgr-Mktg - Wayfair LLC; *pg.* 1288, *pg.* 801
Dalton, Kelly, Mgr-Mktg - The Timberland Company; *pg.* 1821, *pg.* 1039
Dalton, Mark, VP-Media Rels - Arizona Cardinals Football Club, Inc.; *pg.* 529, *pg.* 25
Dalton, Mark, VP-Software Sls - CompuCom Systems, Inc.; *pg.* 378, *pg.* 1678
Dalton, Mika, VP-Creative - David's Bridal, Inc.; *pg.* 23, *pg.* 1523
Dalton, Olivia Alair, Sr VP-Comm & Mktg - Human Rights Campaign; *pg.* 143, *pg.* 400
Dalton, Rex, VP-Real Estate Mktg - Bank of America Corporation; *pg.* 718, *pg.* 1362
Dalton, Sarah M., Sr Strategist-Mktg - Edward D. Jones & Co., LP; *pg.* 746, *pg.* 995
Dalton, Wayne, Dir-Creative - Associated Food Stores, Inc.; *pg.* 1014, *pg.* 1756
Dalvi, Sonia, Brand Mgr-Shopper Mktg - Chobani LLC; *pg.* 847, *pg.* 1318
Daly, Catherine, Mgr-Product Mktg - Absolute Software Corporation; *pg.* 340, *pg.* 1909
Daly, Christopher, VP-Media - Macy's East; *pg.* 1777, *pg.* 1254
Daly, Daniel D., Exec VP-Sls - Utica Mutual Insurance Company; *pg.* 1222, *pg.* 1183
Daly, Debbie, Specialist-Integrated Mktg Events - Cisco Systems, Inc.; *pg.* 372, *pg.* 240
Daly, Ed, Sr Dir-Delivery Ops & Advanced Tech Sls - Cisco Systems, Inc.; *pg.* 372, *pg.* 240
Daly, Eileen, VP-Global Mktg Aramis & Designer-Fragrances - The Estee Lauder Companies Inc.; *pg.* 508, *pg.* 1229
Daly, Jim, Dir-Reg Customer Mktg-PCBU Mktg - Pfizer Inc.; *pg.* 1581, *pg.* 1278
Daly, Karin, VP-Integrated Media - Cancer Treatment Centers of America; *pg.* 1511, *pg.* 410
Daly, Katherine, Sr VP-Mktg & Corp Affairs-Global - Bank of America Corporation; *pg.* 718, *pg.* 1362
Daly, Katie, Coord-Category & Brand Mktg - Kohl's Corporation; *pg.* 1775, *pg.* 1870
Daly, Lydia, VP-Social Media Activation & Earned Media - Viacom Inc.; *pg.* 316, *pg.* 1310
Daly, Maggie, Supvr-Mktg & Promos - Pace; *pg.* 1918, *pg.* 553
Daly, Maia, Mgr-Mktg - The J.M. Smucker Company; *pg.* 865, *pg.* 1468
Daly, Marty, Sr VP & Dir-News & Late Night Sls-CBS Television Network - CBS Broadcasting Inc.; *pg.* 273, *pg.* 1210
Daly, Marty, Sr VP & Dir-News & Late Night Sls-CBS Television Network - CBS Corporation; *pg.* 273, *pg.* 1210
Daly, Meg, Sr Mgr-Bus Dev-New York City Metro Area & New Jersey - Norwegian Cruise Line; *pg.* 1917, *pg.* 444
Daly-Jennings, Kathleen, Sr VP-Mktg - Haverty Furniture Companies, Inc.; *pg.* 926, *pg.* 509
Dalzell, Greg, Dir-Mktg - Cisco Systems, Inc.; *pg.* 372, *pg.* 240
Dalziel, Keith, Mgr-Mktg - General Mills, Inc.; *pg.* 828, *pg.* 933
Dambach, Joe, Product Mgr - Molex Incorporated; *pg.* 655, *pg.* 628
Dambrauskas, Daiva, Sr Mgr-Global Benefits - Expedia, Inc.; *pg.* 1244, *pg.* 1814
Damdar, Sherwin, Product Mgr-Expansion Joints - Garlock Sealing Technologies; *pg.* 205, *pg.* 1320
Dament, Anne, Sr VP-Mdsg - Target Corporation; *pg.* 1786, *pg.* 942
Dames, Laura, Sr VP-Network, Ad Sls Bus Integration & Marketplace Image - Turner Broadcasting System, Inc.; *pg.* 314, *pg.* 521
Damiani, Joseph A., Exec VP-Sls & Mktg - Universal Lighting Technologies; *pg.* 1307, *pg.* 1655
Damiano, Laura, Owner, CEO & Designer - Laura Damiano Designs; *pg.* 1658, *pg.* 1354
Damiano, Paul, VP-Mktg Sls - Kaman Music Corporation; *pg.* 555, *pg.* 339
Damiba, Bertrand, Product Mgr - Google Inc.; *pg.* 1249, *pg.* 153
Damico, Meghan, Coord-Mktg - Black Box Corporation; *pg.* 361, *pg.* 1547
Damit, Carol, Strategist-Mktg - Verizon Communications Inc.; *pg.* 1875, *pg.* 1309
Damkoehler, Laura, Sr Mgr & Product Mgr-ECommerce - Esurance, Inc.; *pg.* 1243, *pg.* 217
Damman, Drew, Assoc Dir-Mktg - Chanel, Inc.; *pg.* 503, *pg.* 1211
Damman, Zak, Specialist-Social Media Community - Big Lots, Inc.; *pg.* 1762, *pg.* 1438
Damon, Christopher, Supvr-Media Adv - GEICO Corporation; *pg.* 1200, *pg.* 399
Damon, Thomas, Sls Mgr-Central Zone-X-ray & Women's Healthcare - General Electric Company; *pg.* 1297, *pg.* 347
Damore, Greg, Rep-Personal Lines Sls - State Automobile Mutual Insurance Company; *pg.* 1217, *pg.* 1444
Damra, Diane, Brand Mktg Mgr - Vail Resorts, Inc.; *pg.* 1117, *pg.* 313
Damron, Russ, Sr Dir-Procurement-Global - PepsiCo, Inc.; *pg.* 259, *pg.* 1327
Damsgaard, Jesper, Dir-Creative - Bergdorf Goodman, Inc.; *pg.* 1761, *pg.* 1202
Dan, Ana, Dir-Digital & Mobile Mktg - The Scotts Miracle-Gro Company; *pg.* 1799, *pg.* 1459
Dana, Amanda Dyson, Sr Mgr-Sls - Atlanta Convention & Visitors Bureau; *pg.* 989, *pg.* 489
Dana, Charlie, Sr Mgr-Naming Strategy - Cisco Systems, Inc.; *pg.* 372, *pg.* 240
Dana, Chris, Bus Mgr-Process Improvement - Vermeer Manufacturing Company; *pg.* 708, *pg.* 711
Dana, Kevin, Dir-Mktg & Product Dev - CORT Business Services Corporation; *pg.* 921, *pg.* 1777
Dana, Martin, Exec VP-Sls & Mktg - Northwest Pipe Company; *pg.* 100, *pg.* 1846
Dancer, David, Exec VP & Head-Mktg - Teleflora LLC; *pg.* 1801, *pg.* 140
Dancer, Sue, Sr Mgr-Americas Mktg Comm - Tektronix, Inc.; *pg.* 1431, *pg.* 1496
Dancy, Allison, VP-Mktg - CDS Global, Inc.; *pg.* 370, *pg.* 704
Dancy, Desiree, Sr Dir-Diversity & Inclusion - Teachers Insurance & Annuity Association - College Retirement Equities Fund; *pg.* 1219, *pg.* 1297
Dandawate, Milan, Mgr-Enterprise Mktg-East Reg - IBM; *pg.* 410, *pg.* 1449
Dandekar, Shree, Sr Dir-Data Analytics & Gen Mgr - Dell Inc.; *pg.* 383, *pg.* 1737
Dando, Kevin, Sr Dir-Social Media Strategy & Digital Comm - Public Broadcasting Service; *pg.* 305, *pg.* 1774
Dandrea, Amanda, Brand Mgr-Aerie Mktg - American Eagle Outfitters, Inc.; *pg.* 37, *pg.* 1572
Dandrea, Robert, Exec VP-Sls & Mktg - TracFone Wireless, Inc.; *pg.* 681, *pg.* 447
Dandurand, Amy, Mgr-Enhancement Mktg & Sr Client Acct Exec-Alliance Data - Alliance Data Systems Corporation; *pg.* 347, *pg.* 1729
Danehy, Steve, Dir-Media Rels-Global Innovative Pharmaceuticals - Pfizer Inc.; *pg.* 1581, *pg.* 1278
Daneke, Bob, Coord-Field Mktg - Publix Super Markets, Inc.; *pg.* 1031, *pg.* 437
Danes, Allison, Mgr-Events Mktg - Blackboard Inc.; *pg.* 1232, *pg.* 396
Danes, Johanna, Sr Mgr-Mktg - Apple Inc.; *pg.* 350, *pg.* 73
Danes, Robin, Dir-Sls - Bermuda Department of Tourism; *pg.* 989, *pg.* 1202
Danforth, Blake, VP-Creative - Fox Sports Net; *pg.* 288, *pg.* 131
Danforth, Leroy, Sr Mgr-Architectural Programs - Brick Industry Association; *pg.* 135, *pg.* 1798
Dang, Anne, Dir-Mktg - USANA Health Sciences, Inc.; *pg.* 1605, *pg.* 1761
Dang, Ashmi, Dir-Social Mktg - Showtime Networks Inc.; *pg.* 308, *pg.* 1291
Dang, Chandan Deep Singh, Dir-Mktg - Tupperware Brands Corporation; *pg.* 1139, *pg.* 456
Dang, Duc, Sr Mgr-Mktg & Product Dev - Toshiba America, Inc.; *pg.* 681, *pg.* 1302
Dang, Jason, Assoc Analyst-Mktg & Targeting - Valassis; *pg.* 1698, *pg.* 386
Dang, Quynh, Dir-Mktg - Ann Inc.; *pg.* 18, *pg.* 1195
Dangel, Misty D., Specialist-PR - USANA Health Sciences, Inc.; *pg.* 1605, *pg.* 1761
Daniel, Ashley, Mgr-Integrated Mktg Comm - SONIC Corp.; *pg.* 1750, *pg.* 1487
Daniel, Chris, Sr Product Mgr - NVIDIA Corporation; *pg.* 447, *pg.* 268
Daniel, Deedre, Dir-Mktg-Partnership, Affinity & Membership Discounts - GEICO Corporation; *pg.* 1200, *pg.* 399
Daniel, Jason, Sr Dir-Global Mktg-Whiskey - Campari America; *pg.* 1960, *pg.* 214
Daniel, Jill, Dir-Mktg - Simon Property Group, Inc.; *pg.* 1112, *pg.* 690
Daniel, Mark, Writer-Mktg - IBM; *pg.* 410, *pg.* 1449
Daniel, Michael, VP-Comml Sls - Frontier Communications Corporation; *pg.* 1871, *pg.* 362
Daniel, Nicole, Sr Mgr-Assoc Comm - The Home Depot, Inc.; *pg.* 1050, *pg.* 510
Daniel, Rob, Product Mgr - Facebook, Inc.; *pg.* 1245, *pg.* 143
Daniel, Sahsha, Specialist-Social Media Community - Ulta Salon, Cosmetics & Fragrance, Inc.; *pg.* 524, *pg.* 559
Daniel, Sara, VP-Ticket Sls & Svc - Carolina Hurricanes Hockey Club; *pg.* 537, *pg.* 1386
Daniel, Scott, Dir-New Products - Bush Brothers & Company; *pg.* 843, *pg.* 1636
Daniel, Valerie, Specialist-Health Comm-Social Media - Northrop Grumman Information Systems; *pg.* 1424, *pg.* 1794
Danieli, Jill, Sr Mgr-Shopper Mktg - The Coca-Cola Company; *pg.* 240, *pg.* 493

Daniello, Jerry J., Sr VP-Integrated Mktg - ABC, Inc.; *pg.* 268, *pg.* 1185
Daniels, Adrienne, Dir-Mktg - E&J Gallo Winery; *pg.* 1962, *pg.* 149
Daniels, Calvin, Dir-Mktg - Eli Lilly and Company; *pg.* 1527, *pg.* 684
Daniels, Chris, VP-Product-Internet.org - Facebook, Inc.; *pg.* 1245, *pg.* 143
Daniels, Dan, VP-Sls & Mktg-Orchids Paper Products - Orchids Paper Products Company; *pg.* 1465, *pg.* 1488
Daniels, David, Dir-Mktg-Bud Light Brands - Anheuser-Busch Companies, LLC; *pg.* 237, *pg.* 991
Daniels, Emily, Analyst-Mktg - Humana, Inc.; *pg.* 1204, *pg.* 734
Daniels, Jennifer, Dir-Product Mktg & Customer Acq - RealNetworks, Inc.; *pg.* 460, *pg.* 1839
Daniels, Jerilynn, Sr Mgr-Community Investments & Mktg-AB & Territories - Royal Bank of Canada; *pg.* 800, *pg.* 1942
Daniels, Karen, Sr Mgr-Mktg Matls - Coca-Cola Refreshments USA, Inc.; *pg.* 247, *pg.* 500
Daniels, Kate, Dir-Event Mktg - UBS Financial Services Inc.; *pg.* 812, *pg.* 1306
Daniels, Kim, Media Buyer - Les Schwab Tire Centers of Oregon, Inc.; *pg.* 210, *pg.* 1508
Daniels, Lia, Asst VP-Mktg-Private Banking USA - Credit Suisse Securities (USA) LLC; *pg.* 742, *pg.* 1220
Daniels, Nancy, Dir-PR - Outrigger Enterprises, Inc.; *pg.* 1107, *pg.* 544
Daniels, Ross, Dir-Solutions Mktg - Cisco Systems, Inc.; *pg.* 372, *pg.* 240
Daniels-Sutton, Vicky L., VP & Mgr-Direct Mktg - Wells Fargo & Company; *pg.* 819, *pg.* 232
Danielski, Sandy, Mgr-Shopper Mktg - General Mills, Inc.; *pg.* 828, *pg.* 933
Danielson, Jeffrey J., VP-Sls - MWI Veterinary Supply, Inc.; *pg.* 1570, *pg.* 548
Danielson, Kurt, Pres-Comml Tire Sls-US & Canada - Bridgestone Americas, Inc.; *pg.* 1879, *pg.* 1648
Danielson, Morgen, Head-Digital Mktg Analytics-ECommerce & Digital Acq - Shaw Communications Inc.; *pg.* 307, *pg.* 1904
Danielson, Paul, Mgr-Fin Mktg - The Toro Company; *pg.* 1065, *pg.* 918
Danihel, Andy, Dir-Mktg - Tekra Corporation; *pg.* 1184, *pg.* 1884
Danino, Ravit, Sr Dir-Product Mgmt-HP Software - Hewlett-Packard Company; *pg.* 404, *pg.* 175
Danis, Stephen, Sr Mgr-Acctg - National Molding, LLC; *pg.* 1887, *pg.* 430
Dankenbring, Sharon, Dir-Mktg - The Examiner; *pg.* 1640, *pg.* 979
Danley, Megan, Mgr-Mktg - Chico's FAS, Inc.; *pg.* 21, *pg.* 427
Dann, Erica, Brand Mgr-Mktg-Dearfoams Footwear - R.G. Barry Corporation; *pg.* 1818, *pg.* 1470
Dann, Lisa, Acct Mgr-Mktg Comm - Aetna Inc.; *pg.* 1187, *pg.* 351
Dannemiller, Beth, Mgr-Mktg - Cisco Systems, Inc.; *pg.* 372, *pg.* 240
Dannenfelser, Peter, Dir-Pharmaceutical Digital Mktg-North America - Janssen Pharmaceutica Products, L.P.; *pg.* 1548, *pg.* 1125
Dannenfelser, Peter, Dir-Pharmaceutical Digital Mktg-North America - Johnson & Johnson; *pg.* 1549, *pg.* 1091
Danoff, Keith, Dir-Mktg-NUTRO - Mars Petcare; *pg.* 1478, *pg.* 1633
Danon, Bill, Sr Mgr - Autodesk Inc.; *pg.* 356, *pg.* 257
Dansbury, Laura, Sr Dir-Product Mgmt - Ancestry.com LLC; *pg.* 1228, *pg.* 1754
Dant, Shirish, Head-Strategic Mktg Res - Aetna Inc.; *pg.* 1187, *pg.* 351
Dantas, Beto, VP-Mktg, Strategy & Innovation - Consolidated Metco Inc.; *pg.* 1325, *pg.* 1846
Dantzler, Troy, Mgr-Mktg-Campaign Strategy & Execution - Teachers Insurance & Annuity Association - College Retirement Equities Fund; *pg.* 1219, *pg.* 1297
Danziger, Robin, Dir-Mktg - Educational Coin Company; *pg.* 746, *pg.* 1167
Danzo, Claudio, Sr Mgr-Customer Bus-Dr. Scholl's Custom Fit Orthotics Walmart - Bayer Corporation; *pg.* 1499, *pg.* 1573
Dao, Hugh, Strategist-Creative-Brand & Mktg Comm - Medtronic, Inc.; *pg.* 1564, *pg.* 939
Dao, Kim, Brand Mgr-Healthy Snacks - Clif Bar Inc.; *pg.* 848, *pg.* 83
Dao, Phuong L., Coord-Mktg - Health Net, Inc.; *pg.* 1540, *pg.* 308
Dapkiewicz, Stephen, Mgr-Creative Svcs - W.R. Grace & Co.; *pg.* 123, *pg.* 810
Darafeev, George, Analyst-Mktg-Global - 3M Company; *pg.* 1142, *pg.* 956
Darby, Ken, Dir-Global Adv & Brand Mgmt - Lockheed Martin Corporation; *pg.* 229, *pg.* 762
Darby, Stephanie, Dir-Mktg - QubicaAMF; *pg.* 1843, *pg.* 1795
Darcy, Gary, Sr VP-Sls & Mktg - National Hot Rod Association; *pg.* 149, *pg.* 99
Darden, Elizabeth, Reg Mgr-Sls - Smithfield Foods, Inc.; *pg.* 896, *pg.* 1806
Dardinski, Charleen, Bus Mgr-Federal Partner - CommVault Systems, Inc.; *pg.* 377, *pg.* 1125
Dardis, Kylie, Project Mgr-Loyalty Mktg - Nordstrom, Inc.; *pg.* 1779, *pg.* 1837
Darezzo, Greg, Mgr-Mktg Commodity - Intel Corporation; *pg.* 645, *pg.* 266
Dargis, Robert, Sr Mgr-Global Digital Mktg & Sls Support - General Motors Company; *pg.* 175, *pg.* 881
Dario, Jim, Mng Dir-Product Mgmt & Strategy - TD Ameritrade Holding Corporation; *pg.* 808, *pg.* 1018
Dark, Alan, Sr VP-Sls-RMI - Rogers Communications Inc.; *pg.* 668, *pg.* 1942
Dark, Alan, Sr VP-Sls & RMI-Rogers Communications - Rogers Media Inc.; *pg.* 1681, *pg.* 1942
Dark, Jay, Dir-Search & Mobile Mktg - Hewlett-Packard Company; *pg.* 404, *pg.* 175
Dark, Shane, Mgr-Digital Adv & Revenue Generation - Sprint Corporation; *pg.* 1874, *pg.* 719
Darling, Armundo, Sr Mgr-Technical Mktg - Autodesk Inc.; *pg.* 356, *pg.* 257
Darling, Patrick, Mgr-Online Media Rels - Intel Corporation; *pg.* 645, *pg.* 266
Darlington, Greg, VP-Mktg & Ops-Americas - Nu Skin Enterprises, Inc.; *pg.* 518, *pg.* 1755
Darlington, Meagan, Dir-Global Sls Strategy, Audience & Programmatic-Adv & Online - Microsoft Corp.; *pg.* 440, *pg.* 321
Darlow, Jeremy, Sr Mgr-Brand & Digital Mktg - adidas America Inc.; *pg.* 1803, *pg.* 1500
Darlow, Margaret, Strategist-Mktg-Global Equity Derivatives - UBS Financial Services Inc.; *pg.* 812, *pg.* 1306
Darne, Mike, Sr Dir-Loyalty & Rewards Strategy - Capital One Financial Corporation; *pg.* 730, *pg.* 1789
Darnell, Alison, Mgr-Mktg Ops-Bus Analytics - International Business Machines Corporation; *pg.* 418, *pg.* 1138
Darnell, Liza, Sr Mgr-Digital-Frito Lay Portfolio - Frito-Lay North America, Inc.; *pg.* 1853, *pg.* 1730
Darnell, Liza, Sr Mgr-Digital-Frito Lay Portfolio - PepsiCo, Inc.; *pg.* 259, *pg.* 1327
Darnell, Phil, VP-Mktg Ops - Hewlett-Packard Company; *pg.* 404, *pg.* 175
Darnell, Tommy, Chief Sls Officer & Exec VP - BancorpSouth, Inc.; *pg.* 717, *pg.* 971
Darner, Nickie, Coord-Mktg, School Product & Brand - ACCO Brands Corporation; *pg.* 340, *pg.* 626
Darrell, Devin, Product Mgr-Process - CEM Corporation; *pg.* 1405, *pg.* 1382
Darrohn, Jaclyn, Sr Mgr-Corp Rels-NY Reg - The Allstate Corporation; *pg.* 1189, *pg.* 639
Darrough, Steve, VP-Mktg - Zilog Inc.; *pg.* 497, *pg.* 252
Darson, Lauren, Specialist-Media Rels - SAIC, Inc.; *pg.* 464, *pg.* 1794
Dart, Kevin, VP-Ticket Sls, Svc & Ops - New York Yankees; *pg.* 570, *pg.* 1144
Darts, Dana, Sr Mgr-Reg Mktg - Panera Bread Company; *pg.* 1029, *pg.* 1001
Dartt, Jon, VP-Sls - Delta Faucet Company; *pg.* 78, *pg.* 684
Darvas, Jaclyn, Sr Mgr-Media - Sanofi US; *pg.* 1592, *pg.* 1046
Darver, Allen, VP-Sls & Mktg - Local & Western of Texas, Inc.; *pg.* 1026, *pg.* 1683
Darville, Chuck, VP-Mktg & Program Mgmt - Southern Company; *pg.* 1952, *pg.* 520
Darwin, Chad, Mgr-PR - J.C. Penney Company, Inc.; *pg.* 1774, *pg.* 1732
Darwin, Dean, CMO & Sr VP-Mktg-Worldwide - F5 Networks, Inc.; *pg.* 396, *pg.* 1835
Darwish, Shereen, Mgr-Global Mktg Programs-Molecular Cytogenetics - Agilent Technologies, Inc.; *pg.* 614, *pg.* 264
Dasal, Jason, VP-Mktg - Genesco Inc.; *pg.* 1809, *pg.* 1650
Dasal, Jason, VP-Mktg-Genesco - Johnston & Murphy Co.; *pg.* 1810, *pg.* 1651
Dase, Caroline Courtney, Dir-Mktg - MORNINGSTAR, INC.; *pg.* 784, *pg.* 583
Dasgupta, Rajat, Dir-Mktg - Colgate-Palmolive Company; *pg.* 504, *pg.* 1215
Dasher, Morgan, Mgr-Mktg-Global - PolyOne Corporation; *pg.* 1177, *pg.* 1404
DaSilva, Marissa, Sr Program Mgr-Adv Solutions-Global - TripAdvisor, Inc.; *pg.* 1926, *pg.* 835
Dasque, Erik, Sr Dir-Engrg - Constant Contact, Inc.; *pg.* 379, *pg.* 850
Dassanaike, Nuvan, VP-Integrated Mktg-Global - Mylan, Inc.; *pg.* 1570, *pg.* 1520
Daswani, Pia, Dir-Mktg - E*TRADE Financial Corporation; *pg.* 749, *pg.* 1230
Daswani, Pia, Dir-Strategic Mktg-Thomson Reuters - Truven Health Analytics; *pg.* 486, *pg.* 331
Daszkiewicz, Rosemary, Sr Dir-Law - Plum Creek Timber Company, Inc.; *pg.* 105, *pg.* 1838
Datcher, Terence, VP-Sls & Sports Mktg - The Clorox Company; *pg.* 327, *pg.* 169
Date, Scott, Sr Product Mgr - Adobe Systems Incorporated; *pg.* 342, *pg.* 235
Datt, Ashwin, Sr Dir-HR PTB & PTNA - Genentech, Inc.; *pg.* 1533, *pg.* 279
Datt, Sarah, Brand Mgr - The Kraft Heinz Company; *pg.* 870, *pg.* 1577
Datta, Debasis, Sr Mgr-EDW Architecture Strategy & Plng - General Motors Company; *pg.* 175, *pg.* 881
Datta, Monish, Reg Partner-Product Mktg-Global Mktg Solutions - Facebook, Inc.; *pg.* 1245, *pg.* 143
Dau, Chad, Assoc Dir-Mktg Analytics - Astellas Pharma US, Inc.; *pg.* 1496, *pg.* 640
Dau, James, Dir-Media Rels - AARP; *pg.* 124, *pg.* 393
Dau, Sarah, Program Mgr-Direct Mktg - American Century Investments; *pg.* 711, *pg.* 980
Dauberman, Mike, Sr Dir-Mktg & Interactive - The Goodyear Tire & Rubber Company; *pg.* 1883, *pg.* 1401
Dauble, Jennifer, Dir-PR - CNBC; *pg.* 275, *pg.* 1059
Daudet, Mike, Dir-Sls & Guest Analytics - Jack in the Box Inc.; *pg.* 1732, *pg.* 204
Dauer, Marty, CMO - Duff & Phelps Corporation; *pg.* 745, *pg.* 1226
Daugherty, Cole, Sr VP-Mktg Comm - Dallas Market Center Company; *pg.* 78, *pg.* 1678
Daugherty, Michael, Mgr-Mktg Comm - Flowserve Corporation; *pg.* 82, *pg.* 1719
Daugherty, Mike, VP-Sls & Mktg - Cookie Tree Bakeries; *pg.* 1851, *pg.* 1756
Daugherty, Rebecca, VP-Entertainment Mktg - ABC, Inc.; *pg.* 268, *pg.* 1185
Daughtrey, William T., Exec VP-Mktg - W.S. Badcock Corporation; *pg.* 947, *pg.* 449
Daum, Avelina, Sr Mgr-Global Brand Comm - Reebok International Ltd.; *pg.* 1817, *pg.* 811
Dausy, Elaine, Strategist-Digital Mktg - FedEx Corporation; *pg.* 1907, *pg.* 1642
Davar, Usheen, Dir-Digital Adv Sls - Meredith Corporation; *pg.* 1663, *pg.* 705
Davda, Pritesh, Asst VP-Digital Mktg IT - L'Oreal USA; *pg.* 514, *pg.* 1252
Dave, Chhaya, Sr Dir-Product Mgmt - Cars.com; *pg.* 1234, *pg.* 568
Dave, Kriti, Mgr-Mktg-Food & Wine, Travel & Leisure, Real Simple - Time Inc.; *pg.* 1693, *pg.* 1300
Dave, Pankaj, Head-Global Mktg-Allergic Rhinitis & Allergy Immunotherapy - Merck & Co., Inc.; *pg.* 1566, *pg.* 1077
Dave, Smita, Mgr-Mktg & Global Mktg - Cisco Systems, Inc.; *pg.* 372, *pg.* 240
Davenport, Beth, Coord-Mktg - I.C. Thomasson Associates, Inc.; *pg.* 88, *pg.* 1651
Davenport, Candice, Dir-Digital Mktg - AARP; *pg.* 124, *pg.* 393
Davenport, Gwen, Mgr-Sls-State Park Svc - South Carolina Parks Recreation & Tourism; *pg.* 1005, *pg.* 1614
Davenport, Jeff, Sr Dir-Team Travel & Clubhouse Ops - Kansas City Royals Baseball Corporation; *pg.* 555, *pg.* 985
Davenport, Jennifer, VP-Mktg & Community Dev - Houston Texans, L.P.; *pg.* 553, *pg.* 1708
Davenport, Laura, Sr Mgr-Comm - Intuit Inc.; *pg.* 769, *pg.* 158
Davenport, Lindsay, Mgr-Adv - NBC Sports Network; *pg.* 300, *pg.* 375
Davenport, Lisa, Assoc Mgr-Mktg - ACCO Brands Corporation; *pg.* 340, *pg.* 626
Davenport, Rob, Mgr-Sls - The C.F. Sauer Company; *pg.* 847, *pg.* 1801
Davenport, Suya, Corp Dir-Leisure Sls-Personal Luxury

Resorts & Hotels - Benchmark Hospitality International Inc.; pg. 1081, pg. 1747
Davenport, Terry, Sr VP-Mktg - Starbucks Corporation; pg. 897, pg. 1840
Daverio, Paul, Mgr-Mktg Strategy & Analytics-Natl - Toyota Motor Sales, U.S.A., Inc.; pg. 193, pg. 296
Davey, Andrea, VP-Mktg-Global - Tiffany & Co.; pg. 13, pg. 1299
Davey, Jim, VP-Global Mktg - The Timberland Company; pg. 1821, pg. 1039
Davi, Deirdre, Dir-Bus Mktg-North America - Facebook, Inc.; pg. 1245, pg. 143
Davia, Paul, Sr Acct Exec-Comml Sls - salesforce.com, inc.; pg. 1278, pg. 226
David, Angelito, Sr Mgr-Customer Mktg-Travel Retail Americas - Bacardi USA, Inc.; pg. 1956, pg. 417
David, Cathy, Exec VP-Mdsg - Pier 1 Imports, Inc.; pg. 940, pg. 1695
David, Evans, Dir-Creative-Natl - Toni & Guy USA, Inc.; pg. 523, pg. 1689
David, Irina, Dir-Digital Mktg - Wenner Media LLC; pg. 1701, pg. 1314
David, Linda, Mgr-Sls Meeting & Event - New Balance Athletic Shoe, Inc.; pg. 1811, pg. 798
David, Michelle, Grp Dir-Mktg - MacFadden Communications Group, LLC; pg. 1660, pg. 1254
David, Paulita, Head-Media & Entertainment - Google Inc.; pg. 1249, pg. 153
Davidoff, Simon, Sr Dir & Bus Mgr-Plant Data Svcs - Siemens Process Industries and Drives; pg. 673, pg. 485
Davidson, Adam, Sr Mgr-Hyundai Capital Insurance - Hyundai Motor America; pg. 179, pg. 89
Davidson, Adam, Brand Mgr-Furniture Care Products & Pro Svcs-Global - The Valspar Corporation; pg. 1449, pg. 945
Davidson, Andrew, Head-Mktg, Hosting, Network & Security Solutions - Fujitsu Computer Systems Corporation; pg. 398, pg. 285
Davidson, Ann M., Mgr-Offering Mktg - Xerox Corporation; pg. 494, pg. 365
Davidson, Blake, VP-Licensing & Consumer Products - National Association for Stock Car Auto Racing; pg. 566, pg. 420
Davidson, Carol, VP-Brand Mktg-Global - SmartWool; pg. 32, pg. 335
Davidson, Christine, Sr VP-Sls - Park City Group, Inc.; pg. 452, pg. 1760
Davidson, Damara L., Sr Mgr-Visual Mdsg, Health & Wellness - Wal-Mart.com; pg. 1287, pg. 50
Davidson, Fletcher G., Grp VP-Product Support Div - Toyota Motor Sales, U.S.A., Inc.; pg. 193, pg. 296
Davidson, Gary, VP-CBA Sls - HBG Books, Inc.; pg. 1648, pg. 1238
Davidson, Harley, Reg Dir-Sls - AutoTrader, Inc.; pg. 1230, pg. 490
Davidson, Ian, Sr Dir-Platform Demand - OpenX Technologies, Inc.; pg. 1272, pg. 180
Davidson, Ian T., Mgr-Indus Mktg-Global - Exxon Mobil Corporation; pg. 977, pg. 1718
Davidson, Jennifer, Sr Mgr-Shopper Mktg - GlaxoSmithKline Consumer Healthcare; pg. 510, pg. 1554
Davidson, John, Dir-Market Access, Reg Sls Mgr & Mgr-Engagement - The Medicines Company; pg. 1561, pg. 1104
Davidson, Kellie, Assoc Mgr-Mktg-Client Svc - Ingram Micro Inc.; pg. 415, pg. 261
Davidson, Melissa, Dir-Consumer Mktg - Crown Media Holdings Inc.; pg. 280, pg. 281
Davidson, Melissa, Dir-Consumer Mktg - The Hallmark Channel; pg. 290, pg. 281
Davidson, Mende, Sr Mgr-Mktg - AT&T Mobility LLC; pg. 619, pg. 488
Davidson, P.J., Acct Exec-Grp Sls - New York Yankees; pg. 570, pg. 1144
Davidson, Peggy, VP-Sls Force Comm & Education - Mary Kay Inc.; pg. 516, pg. 1657
Davidson, Peggy, VP-Sls-US - Mary Kay Inc.; pg. 516, pg. 1657
Davidson, Vanessa, Brand Mgr-CiCi's Pizza - CiCi Enterprises LP; pg. 1723, pg. 1670
Davidson, Whitney, Mgr-Comm & Media - CB Richard Ellis, Inc.; pg. 1085, pg. 1210
Davies, Al, Dir-Product Mktg - Perle Systems Limited; pg. 454, pg. 1924
Davies, Anne, Mgr-Social Media Mktg - General Growth Properties, Inc.; pg. 1093, pg. 574
Davies, Candace, Head-Bus & Product Dev-Enterprise Security Solutions - MasterCard Worldwide Inc.; pg. 780, pg. 988
Davies, Cheri, Dir-Mktg - Comcast Corporation; pg. 276, pg. 1560
Davies, Chuck, VP-Sls - Stahl & Associates Insurance; pg. 1217, pg. 464
Davies, Dave, Sr Dir-Strategy, Product Mgmt & Connected Devices Bus Unit - Cisco Systems, Inc.; pg. 372, pg. 240
Davies, David, Product Mgr - FMC Corporation; pg. 1163, pg. 1564
Davies, Jerry, Asst VP-Media & PR-North America - Farmers Group, Inc.; pg. 1199, pg. 130
Davies, John, VP-Mktg - Benchmark Hospitality International Inc.; pg. 1081, pg. 1747
Davies, Kevin, Product Mgr - Zebra Technologies Corporation; pg. 690, pg. 628
Davies, Mike, Head-Market, Credit, Product & Investment Risk - Morgan Stanley; pg. 783, pg. 1261
Davies, Mike, Sr Mgr-Tax - PricewaterhouseCoopers LLP; pg. 795, pg. 1283
Davies, Neil, Dir-Mktg - Hornady Manufacturing Company; pg. 1836, pg. 1010
Davies, Paul, Dir-Mktg Comm - Microsoft Corporation; pg. 435, pg. 1824
Davies, Philip, VP-Sls & Mktg-Global - Vicor Corporation; pg. 1435, pg. 783
Davies, Richard, CMO - Newell Rubbermaid Inc.; pg. 1128, pg. 515
Davila, Santiago, Mgr-Worldwide Mktg - Hewlett-Packard Company; pg. 404, pg. 175
Davila, Ursula, Reg Brand Mgr-LAM - Hasbro, Inc.; pg. 954, pg. 1603
Davila-Gibson, Evelyn, Program Mgr-Mktg Comm - Hess Corporation; pg. 979, pg. 1240
Daviner, Heather, Project Mgr-Mktg - Apartment Investment and Management Company; pg. 1079, pg. 316
Davion, Rozenna, Exec Coord-Strategic Sls & Solutions - Tribune Media Company; pg. 1696, pg. 592
Davis, Adriana, Reg Mgr-Sls - Dr Pepper Snapple Group, Inc.; pg. 250, pg. 1729
Davis, Adrienne, Dir-Mktg - Tiffany & Co.; pg. 13, pg. 1299
Davis, Aimee L., Dir-Mktg Comm-Global - Eastman Chemical Company; pg. 1159, pg. 1636
Davis, Alissa, Dir-Mktg - J&J Snack Foods Corporation; pg. 865, pg. 1107
Davis, Alyssa, Brand Mgr-Agriculture - BioSafe Systems, LLC; pg. 1149, pg. 345
Davis, Amy, VP-Brand Mktg & Ops - General Nutrition Centers, Inc.; pg. 1534, pg. 1575
Davis, Andrew, Sr Mgr-External, Internal Comm & Diabetes - AstraZeneca Pharmaceuticals LP; pg. 1497, pg. 389
Davis, Andrew, Dir-Mktg-New Ventures - General Mills Canada Corp.; pg. 828, pg. 1926
Davis, Andrew, Mgr-Digital Mktg Campaign - The Kroger Co.; pg. 1025, pg. 1416
Davis, Ann, Specialist-Mktg Comm - Teleflex Incorporated; pg. 48, pg. 1548
Davis, Arnell, Mgr-Original Series Mktg - Netflix, Inc.; pg. 1269, pg. 141
Davis, Arthell, VP-Grp Mktg Ops - North Carolina Mutual Life Insurance Company; pg. 1212, pg. 1372
Davis, Aubrey, Media Buyer - Blue Bell Creameries, L.P.; pg. 1851, pg. 1668
Davis, Beky, Dir-Creative - Tribune Media Company; pg. 1696, pg. 592
Davis, Bill, Sr Mgr - Capital One Financial Corporation; pg. 730, pg. 1789
Davis, Bill, Dir-Indus, Intl Channel Sls & Mktg - Sears Holdings Corporation; pg. 1784, pg. 618
Davis, Blake, Mgr-PR & Buzz Mktg - Safeway Inc.; pg. 1032, pg. 184
Davis, Brad, Mgr-Bus Dev-Indus Products Grp - Grain Processing Corporation; pg. 859, pg. 709
Davis, Brian, VP-Mktg - Allegiant Travel Company; pg. 346, pg. 1022
Davis, Brian, Sr VP-Mktg & Pur-US - Tech Data Corporation; pg. 482, pg. 416
Davis, Brian, Dir-Mktg-Customer Acq - Time Warner Cable Inc.; pg. 312, pg. 1301
Davis, Brittany, Sr Mgr-Integrated Mktg-O-The Oprah Magazine - The Hearst Corporation; pg. 1649, pg. 1239
Davis, Bryant, VP-Sls - Bridgestone Americas, Inc.; pg. 1879, pg. 1648
Davis, Cameron, Coord-Mktg - Chick-fil-A, Inc.; pg. 1721, pg. 492
Davis, Carlee, Reg Specialist-Mktg - Comcast Cable Communications, Inc.; pg. 276, pg. 1560
Davis, Clinton T., Sr VP & Mgr-Gen Mdsg-Kitchen & Bath - Lowe's Companies, Inc.; pg. 1053, pg. 1383
Davis, Dana, Assoc Planner-Mktg - TD Bank US Holding Company; pg. 809, pg. 1051
Davis, Danielle, Brand Mgr-Acute Care Mktg - Abbott Nutrition; pg. 1485, pg. 1437
Davis, Darren, Pres-iHeart Radio & iHeart Media Networks - IHeartMedia Inc.; pg. 292, pg. 1741
Davis, Dax C., Dir-Mktg & Social Media - Entrust, Inc.; pg. 393, pg. 1680
Davis, Dean, Mgr-Mktg Ops - Cisco Systems, Inc.; pg. 372, pg. 240
Davis, Deena J., Mgr-Mktg Svcs - Herculite Products, Inc.; pg. 694, pg. 1529
Davis, Denise, Sr Specialist-Mktg - Comcast Corporation; pg. 276, pg. 1560
Davis, Desta, Sr Mgr-PR - Kohl's Corporation; pg. 1775, pg. 1870
Davis, Donna, Sr Mgr-Mktg-Global Bus Dev - PayPal Inc.; pg. 1274, pg. 248
Davis, Ellie, Program Mgr-Mktg Comm - Molex Incorporated; pg. 655, pg. 628
Davis, Emily, Mgr-Digital Mktg - Penguin Random House; pg. 1675, pg. 1276
Davis, Emily, Mgr-Mktg-Clarkson Potter & Harmony - Penguin Random House Children's Books; pg. 1676, pg. 1277
Davis, Emily, Analyst-Mktg - Windstream Corporation; pg. 321, pg. 34
Davis, Erich, Mgr-Retirement Mktg - FRANKLIN RESOURCES, INC.; pg. 760, pg. 254
Davis, Florita, Mgr-Sls - Long Beach Symphony Orchestra; pg. 558, pg. 123
Davis, Gina, VP-Branding & Creative - The Mattress Firm, Inc.; pg. 934, pg. 1711
Davis, Gina, VP-Branding & Creative - Sleep Country USA, Inc.; pg. 943, pg. 1822
Davis, Glenn, Dir-Sls-East Reg - PPG Industries, Inc.; pg. 1445, pg. 1579
Davis, Gwynedd, Sr Asst Brand Mgr-Old Spice - The Procter & Gamble Company; pg. 1129, pg. 1418
Davis, Horace, VP-Sls-North America - Megger Inc.; pg. 1422, pg. 1557
Davis, Jason, Product Mgr-Power Transmission - The Gates Corporation; pg. 205, pg. 319
Davis, Jason, Mgr-Adv-Natl - Yamaha Motor Corporation USA; pg. 1713, pg. 76
Davis, Jeff, Sr VP-Sls - D&H Distributing Co., Inc.; pg. 381, pg. 1536
Davis, Jeff, Sr Mgr-Mktg-Global SEO & Content Mktg - Intuit Inc.; pg. 769, pg. 158
Davis, Jeffrey, Sr VP-Media Rels - AARP; pg. 124, pg. 393
Davis, Jennifer, Mgr-PR - Charles Schwab; pg. 1235, pg. 1661
Davis, Jennifer, VP-Mktg - Planar Systems, Inc.; pg. 455, pg. 1495
Davis, Jennifer, Acct Exec-Sls-Natl - Univision Communications Inc.; pg. 683, pg. 1307
Davis, Jennifer Jd, Dir-Social Media Ops - AT&T Inc.; pg. 1867, pg. 1674
Davis, Jerry, Category Mgr-Sls - Winn Dixie Stores, Inc.; pg. 1038, pg. 435
Davis, Jesse, Dir-PR & Comm - Denver Metro Convention & Visitors Bureau; pg. 991, pg. 318
Davis, Jesse, Sr Dir-DataDirect R&D - Progress DataDirect; pg. 457, pg. 1385
Davis, Jim, Mgr-Goodyear PR - The Goodyear Tire & Rubber Company; pg. 1883, pg. 1401
Davis, Jim, CMO & Sr VP - SAS Institute Inc.; pg. 466, pg. 1361
Davis, John, Sr VP-Global Sls & Mktg - CryoLife, Inc.; pg. 1520, pg. 534
Davis, John, VP-Mktg & Product Mgmt - Unified Brands Inc.; pg. 1385, pg. 970
Davis, John P, Dir-Live Event Mktg - World Wrestling Entertainment, Inc.; pg. 595, pg. 380
Davis, Jonathan, Sr Mgr-Channel Mktg - Jacuzzi Brands Corporation; pg. 554, pg. 65
Davis, Julie, Sr Dir-IR - Liquidity Services, Inc.; pg. 1263, pg. 401
Davis, Kaia, Brand Mgr-Nike Better World Innovation-Global - NIKE, Inc.; pg. 1812, pg. 1492
Davis, Kaitlyn, Specialist-Comm & Analyst-Mktg - Conmed

First page reference indicates Business Class Edition
Second page reference indicates Geographic Edition

Corporation; *pg.* 1517, *pg.* 1347
Davis, Karen, Sr VP-Global Philanthropy & Social Impact - Hasbro, Inc.; *pg.* 954, *pg.* 1603
Davis, Kate, Mgr-Software & Defined Storage Mktg - Hewlett-Packard Company; *pg.* 404, *pg.* 175
Davis, Katherine, Brand Mgr - Unilever United States, Inc.; *pg.* 904, *pg.* 1061
Davis, Katie, Assoc Mgr-Mktg - Igloo Products Corporation; *pg.* 1126, *pg.* 1724
Davis, Katrina, Sr Project Specialist-Digital Creative - J.C. Penney Company, Inc.; *pg.* 1774, *pg.* 1732
Davis, Kelly, VP-Product Mktg - Sony Electronics, Inc.; *pg.* 676, *pg.* 209
Davis, Kendall B., Sr VP-Bus, IT Products & Svcs - Gartner, Inc.; *pg.* 1248, *pg.* 374
Davis, Kimberly, Mgr-Social Media - The Home Depot, Inc.; *pg.* 1050, *pg.* 510
Davis, Kristen, Dir-Media Rels-Global - Amgen Inc.; *pg.* 1493, *pg.* 291
Davis, Larry, VP-Mktg - Ross-Simons Inc.; *pg.* 1783, *pg.* 1600
Davis, Lauren, Coord-Mktg - Keds LLC; *pg.* 1810, *pg.* 828
Davis, Lee, Sr Mgr-PR - Cisco Systems, Inc.; *pg.* 372, *pg.* 240
Davis, Lee, VP-Integrated Mktg Comm - Johnson & Johnson; *pg.* 1549, *pg.* 1091
Davis, Lindsay, Mgr-Integrated Mktg - People Magazine; *pg.* 1676, *pg.* 1278
Davis, Lisa, Strategist-Creative - Target Corporation; *pg.* 1786, *pg.* 942
Davis, Lisa M., VP-Virginia Market Unit Sls Ops - The Coca-Cola Company; *pg.* 240, *pg.* 493
Davis, Loretta, Mgr-Mktg - CH2M HILL Companies, Ltd.; *pg.* 75, *pg.* 325
Davis, Lori, Sr Dir-Customer Engagement - Charter Communications, Inc.; *pg.* 274, *pg.* 372
Davis, Lynne, VP-Natl Brdcst Media & Talent Rels - Home & Garden Television; *pg.* 290, *pg.* 1637
Davis, Maria, Dir-Sls & Svc - The Popcorn Factory; *pg.* 1861, *pg.* 625
Davis, Mark, Sr VP-Sls & Mktg - HAECO Americas; *pg.* 228, *pg.* 1374
Davis, Mark, Dir-Enterprise Accounts-Healthcare Sls - United Parcel Service, Inc.; *pg.* 1928, *pg.* 522
Davis, Mark Z., Dir-Mktg Svcs - Computer Sciences Corporation; *pg.* 378, *pg.* 1780
Davis, Marquita, Mgr-Market Product - Capella Education Company; *pg.* 599, *pg.* 931
Davis, Marshall, Mgr-Global Mktg-Cushe Footwear - Wolverine World Wide, Inc.; *pg.* 1822, *pg.* 905
Davis, Mary Jo, VP-Product Mgmt - Ceridian Corporation; *pg.* 371, *pg.* 932
Davis, Matt, Mgr-Mktg, Promos, ECommerce & Comm - CARQUEST Corporation; *pg.* 168, *pg.* 1386
Davis, Matt, Head-FIAT Product Mktg North America - FCA US LLC; *pg.* 170, *pg.* 868
Davis, Matthew, Brand Mgr - Reckitt Benckiser Inc.; *pg.* 1136, *pg.* 1105
Davis, Megan, Planner-Mktg - Williams-Sonoma, Inc.; *pg.* 1140, *pg.* 234
Davis, Melissa, Mgr-Partnership Mktg - Bose Corporation; *pg.* 626, *pg.* 820
Davis, Michael, Dir-Creative Svcs - Michaels Stores, Inc.; *pg.* 1127, *pg.* 1722
Davis, Michael, Sr Product Mgr - Staples; *pg.* 474, *pg.* 313
Davis, Mickey, VP-Sls & Mktg-Worldwide - The DoALL Company; *pg.* 1329, *pg.* 670
Davis, Mike, Gen Mgr-Product - The Trade Desk, Inc.; *pg.* 1284, *pg.* 301
Davis, Mindy, Dir-Mktg - Zoes Kitchen, Inc.; *pg.* 1757, *pg.* 1735
Davis, Moira, VP-Mktg - ESPN, Inc.; *pg.* 285, *pg.* 340
Davis, Molly, Sr Dir-Mktg - E&J Gallo Winery; *pg.* 1962, *pg.* 149
Davis, Moses, Rep Sls & Mktg - Warner Music Group Corp.; *pg.* 590, *pg.* 1313
Davis, Nick, Mgr-PR - Cray Inc.; *pg.* 380, *pg.* 1834
Davis, Nicole, Sr Analyst-Mktg Fin - CDW Corporation; *pg.* 370, *pg.* 663
Davis, Nora, Coord-Mktg & Comm - CH2M HILL Companies, Ltd.; *pg.* 75, *pg.* 325
Davis, Paul, Sr Dir-Product Grp - Dell, Inc.; *pg.* 385, *pg.* 1037
Davis, Paul, Sr Category Mgr-Agency & Media - Johnson & Johnson; *pg.* 1549, *pg.* 1091
Davis, Penny, Assoc Dir-Global CMC Biologics New Products - Pfizer Inc.; *pg.* 1581, *pg.* 1278
Davis, Philip E., Assoc Dir-Mktg Comm - Praxair, Inc.; *pg.* 1178, *pg.* 344
Davis, Rachel, Specialist-Mktg-Global - Crocs, Inc.; *pg.* 1806, *pg.* 335
Davis, Rachel, Dir-Content Mktg - Office Depot, Inc.; *pg.* 448, *pg.* 412
Davis, Ralph, Brand Mgr-Emerging Brands - Scripps Networks Interactive, Inc.; *pg.* 1279, *pg.* 1638
Davis, Randy, Analyst-Mktg & Bus - General Motors of Canada Ltd.; *pg.* 177, *pg.* 1931
Davis, Reginald, Exec VP & Head-Consumer Deposit Products - SunTrust Banks, Inc.; *pg.* 807, *pg.* 520
Davis, Ron, Sr Dir-Brand Protection - QUALCOMM Incorporated; *pg.* 1873, *pg.* 207
Davis, Rosie L., Coord-Mktg - FedEx Corporation; *pg.* 1907, *pg.* 1642
Davis, Scott, VP-Product Dev & Mktg - ClosetMaid Corporation; *pg.* 920, *pg.* 452
Davis, Scott, VP-Worldwide Sls & Enterprise Solutions - Sierra Wireless Incorporated; *pg.* 673, *pg.* 1909
Davis, Scott, Sr VP-Sls-Worldwide - Western Digital Corporation; *pg.* 492, *pg.* 118
Davis, Sean, Mgr-Ops Mktg-North America - Converse Inc.; *pg.* 1831, *pg.* 793
Davis, Sherri, Sr Dir-Brand Experience - Comcast Corporation; *pg.* 276, *pg.* 1560
Davis, Stephen, Dir-Mktg-Intl - American Airlines Inc.; *pg.* 1898, *pg.* 1693
Davis, Stephen, Grp Rep-Sls - The Guardian Life Insurance Company of America; *pg.* 1202, *pg.* 1237
Davis, Stuart, Head-Aesthetics Mktg - Sanofi US; *pg.* 1592, *pg.* 1046
Davis, Susan C., Mgr-Category Mktg Analytics - Cardinal Health, Inc.; *pg.* 1512, *pg.* 1448
Davis, Tamara, Dir-Mktg - Bio-Rad Laboratories, Inc.; *pg.* 1504, *pg.* 101
Davis, Ted, CMO & Chief Sls Officer - Benchmark Hospitality International Inc.; *pg.* 1081, *pg.* 1747
Davis, Terry, Dir-Digital Mktg - Jeld-Wen, Inc.; *pg.* 1051, *pg.* 1499
Davis, Tiana, Mgr-Global Mktg, Media Strategy, & Brand Partnerships - The Gap, Inc.; *pg.* 1770, *pg.* 218
Davis, Tina, Sr VP-Corp Sponsorships & Mktg - Citigroup Inc.; *pg.* 735, *pg.* 1212
Davis, Todd, Dir-Channel Mktg - CenturyLink, Inc.; *pg.* 1870, *pg.* 746
Davis, Tom, CMO-Forbes Media - Forbes, Inc.; *pg.* 1641, *pg.* 1232
Davis, Tracie, Brand Mgr - Miele Inc.; *pg.* 59, *pg.* 1112
Davis, Tracy, Specialist-Mktg - Digi International Inc.; *pg.* 387, *pg.* 948
Davis, Tracy, Mgr-Mktg - M/I Homes, Inc.; *pg.* 95, *pg.* 1441
Davis, Trevor, Head-Products - CTI Group Holdings Inc.; *pg.* 381, *pg.* 684
Davis, Valerie, Mgr-Mktg-Boeing Comml Airplanes - The Boeing Company; *pg.* 225, *pg.* 567
Davis, Walt, Sr Dir-Product Mgmt & Technical Svcs - Blonder Tongue Laboratories, Inc.; *pg.* 625, *pg.* 1100
Davis, Wendi, Dir-Creative-Mktg-Hearst Design Grp - The Hearst Corporation; *pg.* 1649, *pg.* 1239
Davis, Yvette, Supvr-Media - The Home Depot, Inc.; *pg.* 1050, *pg.* 510
Davis, Zack, Dir-Mktg - Louisville Convention & Visitors Bureau; *pg.* 998, *pg.* 736
Davis-Brayman, JoAnn, VP-Comml Mktg - Armstrong World Industries, Inc.; *pg.* 914, *pg.* 1545
Davison, Susan, Sr Dir-External Comm - Kellogg Company; *pg.* 831, *pg.* 870
Davison, Timothy R., Rep-Crude Oil Mktg - ConocoPhillips; *pg.* 975, *pg.* 1703
Davisson, Brandie, Acct Mgr-Sls - Gannett Co., Inc.; *pg.* 1643, *pg.* 1790
Davitt, Mike, Dir-Mktg - The Scotts Miracle-Gro Company; *pg.* 1799, *pg.* 1459
Davoren, Doug, Mgr-Mktg - The Guardian Life Insurance Company of America; *pg.* 1202, *pg.* 1237
Daw, Ann, VP-Mktg - JanSport; *pg.* 1837, *pg.* 38
Dawe, Jacqueline, Rep-Sls - TD Bank US Holding Company; *pg.* 809, *pg.* 1051
Dawe, Michael, VP-Sls-Intl - TII Network Technologies, Inc.; *pg.* 680, *pg.* 1157
Dawes, Adam, Product Mgr - Google Inc.; *pg.* 1249, *pg.* 153
Dawes, Gail, Project Mgr-Adv - Deere & Company; *pg.* 703, *pg.* 632
Dawes, Jessie, Dir-Digital Mktg-Global - Clinique Laboratories LLC; *pg.* 503, *pg.* 1214
Daws, Sally, Exec VP-Mktg & Digital Media - FX Networks, LLC; *pg.* 288, *pg.* 131
Dawson, Allison, Mgr-Mktg-Pub Sector Dynamics-US - Microsoft Corporation; *pg.* 435, *pg.* 1824
Dawson, Deanna, Mgr-Mktg Comm - AT&T Mobility LLC; *pg.* 619, *pg.* 488
Dawson, Drew, Product Mgr-Travel - Concur Technologies; *pg.* 1903, *pg.* 501
Dawson, Drew, Mgr-Channel Mktg - RetailMeNot Inc.; *pg.* 1782, *pg.* 1665
Dawson, Frank, Dir-Database Mktg - Citigroup Inc.; *pg.* 735, *pg.* 1212
Dawson, Gail, Coord-Sls - Scintrex Ltd.; *pg.* 1374, *pg.* 1920
Dawson, Garry, Mgr-Mktg Comm & Americas Adv - Hewlett-Packard Company; *pg.* 404, *pg.* 175
Dawson, Jessica, District Mgr-Sls & Aftersales-Chevrolet - General Motors Company; *pg.* 175, *pg.* 881
Dawson, Karen, VP-Global Digital & Social Strategy - Hyatt Hotels Corporation; *pg.* 1096, *pg.* 577
Dawson, Kass, Head-Automotive-Global Vertical Mktg - Facebook, Inc.; *pg.* 1245, *pg.* 143
Dawson, LeAnn, Mgr-Digital Media - Atkins Nutritionals, Inc.; *pg.* 1498, *pg.* 316
Dawson, Lisa, Sr Dir-Creative Svcs - Bloomin' Brands, Inc.; *pg.* 1716, *pg.* 471
Dawson, Matthew, Sr Mgr-Strategic Mktg - LifeCell Corporation; *pg.* 1556, *pg.* 1045
Dawson, Scott, Sr Dir-Treasury - Illumina, Inc.; *pg.* 412, *pg.* 203
Dawson, Stephanie, COO-Acting - Port Authority of New York & New Jersey; *pg.* 1919, *pg.* 1283
Dawson, Susan, Dir-Integrated Mktg & Brand Strategy - PETCO Animal Supplies, Inc.; *pg.* 1480, *pg.* 206
Dawson, Suzanne, VP & Div Mgr-Mdse-Intimate Apparel & Active - Kohl's Corporation; *pg.* 1775, *pg.* 1870
Dax, Chris, Sr VP-Mktg - Masimo Corporation; *pg.* 1558, *pg.* 113
Day, Amy, Brand Mktg Mgr - Papa Murphy's International, LLC; *pg.* 1743, *pg.* 1846
Day, Cathy, Sr Analyst-Customer Engagement Mktg - American Express Company; *pg.* 712, *pg.* 1190
Day, Gail, VP-Global Adv & Publr-HBR - Harvard Business Review; *pg.* 1648, *pg.* 1238
Day, Jennifer, Mgr-Mktg - Schneider Electric; *pg.* 467, *pg.* 1609
Day, Kelly, Sr Specialist-Mktg - Edward D. Jones & Co., LP; *pg.* 746, *pg.* 995
Day, Kenny, Sr VP-Political Sls & Strategy - IHeartMedia Inc.; *pg.* 292, *pg.* 1741
Day, Kyle, VP-Territory Sls-Automation Grp - Datalogic; *pg.* 382, *pg.* 1588
Day, Patti, VP-Creative Svcs - Coach, Inc.; *pg.* 3, *pg.* 1214
Day, Rebecca, Sr Mgr-Mktg Comm - Captain D's, LLC; *pg.* 1720, *pg.* 1649
Day, Richard, Grp Product Mgr - Epson America Inc.; *pg.* 394, *pg.* 122
Day, Robert, VP-Mktg - Lynx Software Technologies; *pg.* 429, *pg.* 247
Day, Sarah, Sr VP-Consumer & Small Bus Mktg & Customer Care - Windstream Corporation; *pg.* 321, *pg.* 34
Day, Sharon, VP-Sls - Catalina Yachts, Inc.; *pg.* 1706, *pg.* 307
Day, Sherrie, Dir-Product Dev & Brand-Women's Modern & Contemporary Apparel - J.C. Penney Company, Inc.; *pg.* 1774, *pg.* 1732
Day, Tom, Sr VP-Natl Sls-DGUSA - Diageo North America, Inc.; *pg.* 1961, *pg.* 361
Day, William B., Exec VP-Mdsg & Supply Chain - Sysco Corporation; *pg.* 1035, *pg.* 1716
Day, Zane, VP-Sls & Mdsg - Smith's Food & Drug Centers, Inc.; *pg.* 1034, *pg.* 1761
Dayan, John, VP-Sls Programs Tech Svcs - Hewlett-Packard Company; *pg.* 404, *pg.* 175
Dayan, Paula, Mgr-Media Mktg - The Procter & Gamble Company; *pg.* 1129, *pg.* 1418
Dayley, Todd, Dir-Sls - Old Dominion Freight Line, Inc.; *pg.* 1918, *pg.* 1391
Dayton, Pamela, Dir-Digital & Mobile Mktg - Safeway Inc.; *pg.* 1032, *pg.* 184
Dazhan, Anthony, Asst Mgr-Mktg-SEO - Macy's East; *pg.* 1777, *pg.* 1254
De Bonis, Daniel, Sr Mgr-Digital Mktg - Sharp Electronics Corporation; *pg.* 672, *pg.* 1082
de Boursetty, Benoit, Product Mgr - Google Inc.; *pg.* 1249,

pg. 153
de Dongo, Fabrice, Sr Mgr-Media Rels - HSBC Bank Canada; pg. 767, pg. 1911
de Dreuille, Martin, VP-Prestige Mktg - Pernod Ricard USA, Inc.; pg. 1968, pg. 1332
De Feo, Michael, Mng Dir-DCIO & Strategic Platform Sls - Nuveen Investments, Inc.; pg. 788, pg. 586
de Graaf, Eline, Dir-Mktg & New Bus Dev - Philips Healthcare; pg. 1585, pg. 783
De Graaff, Audrey, Brand Mgr-French's Mustard - Reckitt Benckiser Inc.; pg. 1136, pg. 1105
de Guzman, Wilfred, Brand Mgr - Mondelez International, Inc.; pg. 878, pg. 601
De Hertogh, Michelle, Sr Dir-Global Alliance & Service Provider Mktg - EMC Corporation; pg. 391, pg. 825
De Jesus, Verna, Head-CPG Adv - Amazon.com, Inc.; pg. 1226, pg. 1831
De La Cruz, Jennifer, Sr Dir-PR - Carnival Corporation; pg. 1902, pg. 441
de la Cruz, Roger, Sr Mgr-Mktg Comm - Cisco Systems, Inc.; pg. 372, pg. 240
de la Hoz, Cristina, Sr Head-Bus & Head-Brand Mgmt, Sponsorships & Mktg Svcs - Visa Inc.; pg. 816, pg. 230
De La Mater, Derek, Pres-Sls & Exec VP - ConAgra Foods, Inc.; pg. 826, pg. 1014
De La Rosa, Tony, Mgr-Mktg Programs - Cisco Systems, Inc.; pg. 372, pg. 240
de la Torre, Liza, VP-Mktg-APAC - Toms Shoe's Inc; pg. 1821, pg. 276
De Leon, Tomas Ponce, Sr Bus Mgr-Display Adv - eBay Inc.; pg. 1240, pg. 243
De Los Santos, Gorki, Sr Mgr-Pub Affairs & Comm - Coca-Cola Refreshments USA, Inc.; pg. 247, pg. 500
de los Santos, Jessica, Specialist-Display Adv - Google Inc.; pg. 1249, pg. 153
de Lourdes Flores, Maria, Assoc Mgr-Customer Mktg-Personal Care - Unilever United States, Inc.; pg. 904, pg. 1061
de Maria, Michele, Mgr-Mktg & Promos - Univision Communications Inc.; pg. 683, pg. 1307
De Martini, Christine, Dir-Global Media & Mktg - Electronic Arts Inc.; pg. 951, pg. 189
De Mello, Gustavo, Sr VP-Mktg, Strategy, Plng & Integration - National Basketball Association; pg. 566, pg. 1264
de Montes, Martha G., Sr Mgr-Media Rels-Southwest - Macy's, Inc.; pg. 1778, pg. 1417
De Nardi, Denise, Dir-NA Sls & Retail Ops - Aveda Corporation; pg. 499, pg. 917
De Pablos- Barbier, Berta, VP-Mktg - Mars North America; pg. 1859, pg. 1072
De Palm, Matt, Specialist-Email Mktg - Tesla Motors, Inc.; pg. 191, pg. 178
De Palma, Francesca, Sr Mgr-Integrated Mktg-CBS Local - CBS Broadcasting Inc.; pg. 273, pg. 1210
De Palma, Francesca, Sr Mgr-Integrated Mktg-CBS Local - CBS Corporation; pg. 273, pg. 1210
de Place, Astrid, Asst VP-Mktg - Van Cleef & Arpels, Inc.; pg. 15, pg. 1308
De Souza, Veronica, Editor-Social Media - Digg, Inc.; pg. 1238, pg. 1224
De Villegas, Marcia Diaz, Dir-Admin, Mktg, Outreach & PR - Nicklaus Children's Hospital; pg. 1573, pg. 444
De Vos, Dirk, Sr VP-Comml Mktg - Heineken USA Inc.; pg. 252, pg. 1352
De Vries, Roel, Gen Mgr-Product Plng & strategy - Nissan North America, Inc.; pg. 186, pg. 1633
de Zayas, Bryan, Dir-Mktg-Alienware Life Cycle Mgmt - Dell, Inc.; pg. 385, pg. 1037
De, Roma, Dir-Product Mgmt - Netflix, Inc.; pg. 1269, pg. 141
DeAbreu, Pedro, Specialist-Mktg - Gartner, Inc.; pg. 1248, pg. 374
Deacon, Archie, Sr Analyst-Mktg - Transamerica Insurance & Investment Group; pg. 1219, pg. 141
Deakes, Lisa, Sr Mgr-Mktg-Education - Adobe Systems Incorporated; pg. 342, pg. 235
Deal, Cyndi, Coord-Mktg - State Farm Mutual Automobile Insurance Co.; pg. 1218, pg. 557
Deal, Dawn, Sr Dir-Mktg - Wal-Mart Stores, Inc.; pg. 1790, pg. 29
Deam, Jim, Sr Mgr-Mktg - AT&T; pg. 1865, pg. 258
DeAmicis, Karen, VP-Retail Sls & Svc Support-The Home Savings & Loan Company - United Community Financial Corp.; pg. 814, pg. 1483
Dean, Amy, Brand Mgr-Sleeman & Sapporo-Natl - Sleeman Breweries, Ltd.; pg. 265, pg. 1920
Dean, Christopher, Dir-Adv Sls - BBC Worldwide America Inc.; pg. 271, pg. 1201
Dean, Claire, Sr Dir-Global Strategy - Symantec Corporation; pg. 478, pg. 161
Dean, Dustin, Exec VP-Global Sls & Customer Success - LivePerson, Inc.; pg. 1264, pg. 1252
Dean, Ed, Mgr-Sls-Natl - Reeves International, Inc.; pg. 966, pg. 1108
Dean, Emily, Analyst-Digital Media - Kia Motors America Inc.; pg. 181, pg. 112
Dean, Gaye, Sr Mgr-Mktg - Target Corporation; pg. 1786, pg. 942
Dean, Heather, Sr Dir-Area Sls - Takeda Pharmaceuticals USA, Inc.; pg. 1600, pg. 605
Dean, Julie, Sr Dir-Comm - GlaxoSmithKline; pg. 1536, pg. 1565
Dean, Kristen, Mgr-Mktg Creative Svcs - CVS Health Corporation; pg. 1765, pg. 1610
Dean, Mary, Specialist-Mktg Comm - Teradyne Inc.; pg. 679, pg. 838
Dean, Michael, Product Mgr - Highway Equipment Company; pg. 704, pg. 702
Dean, Mike, VP-Programmatic & Data-Driven Sls - ABC, Inc.; pg. 268, pg. 1185
Dean, Misty, Mgr-Mktg - Comcast Corporation; pg. 276, pg. 1560
Dean, Simon, Sr Dir-Advanced Engrg & Electronics - Meritor, Inc.; pg. 212, pg. 911
Dean, Thomas, Dir-Reg Sls - CNH America LLC; pg. 702, pg. 560
Dean-Woepple, Sarah, Assoc Mgr-Mktg Comm - Olympus America Inc.; pg. 1425, pg. 1521
Deang, Carmela, Sr Mgr-Mktg-L'Oreal Paris Cosmetics - L'Oreal USA; pg. 514, pg. 1252
DeAngelis, Anne, Sr Mgr-Global Brand Mgmt & Adv - The Boeing Company; pg. 225, pg. 567
DeAngelis, Christopher, VP-Sls - Survey Sampling International LLC; pg. 1690, pg. 371
DeAngelis, Kelly, Analyst-PR - Highmark Blue Cross Blue Shield; pg. 1203, pg. 1576
DeAngelis, Lauren, Writer-Mktg & Comm - CACI International Inc.; pg. 367, pg. 1773
DeAngelis, Margaret, Mgr-Mktg Comm-Global - Eaton Corporation - Industrial Controls; pg. 1296, pg. 1874
DeAngelis, Mike, Dir-PR - CVS Health Corporation; pg. 1765, pg. 1610
DeAngelis, Susan, Mgr-Portfolio Mktg-Global Solutions - Schneider Electric; pg. 467, pg. 1609
Dear, Andy, Sr Mgr-PR - Pegasystems Inc.; pg. 453, pg. 809
Dear, Frances, Sr Analyst-Mktg-Corp Intl Bus Dev - Raytheon Company; pg. 233, pg. 854
DeArment, Ryan, VP-Sls & Mktg - Channellock, Inc.; pg. 1044, pg. 1551
Dearth, Ginger, Dir-Mktg Ops - HealthSouth Corporation; pg. 1540, pg. 3
Dearwester, Michael, Assoc-Mktg - Diageo North America Inc.; pg. 248, pg. 1223
Deas, Michael, Sr Mgr-Comm - ProLogis; pg. 1108, pg. 322
Deason, Jeffrey, Sr Mgr-Workplace Technologies - Chick-fil-A, Inc.; pg. 1721, pg. 492
Deatherage, John, Dir-Product Mktg - Intel Corporation; pg. 645, pg. 266
Deaton, John, Sr VP-Brand & Product Dev - The Home Depot, Inc.; pg. 1050, pg. 510
Deaver, Scott, Chief Strategy Officer & Exec VP-Global Mktg - Avis Budget Group, Inc.; pg. 1900, pg. 1102
DeBaene, Ken, Sr VP-Sls - Matrixx Initiatives, Inc.; pg. 1559, pg. 23
DeBarr, Amber, Dir-Mktg - OhioHealth; pg. 1578, pg. 1443
Debebe, Eden, Sr Principal-Adv Review - E*TRADE Financial Corporation; pg. 749, pg. 1230
Debelis, Cheryl, Dir-Mktg - Implant Sciences Corporation; pg. 1348, pg. 860
DeBell, Mike, Chief Sls Officer - Crocs, Inc.; pg. 1806, pg. 335
DeBenedette, Sue, Dir-Mktg & PR - Tucson Symphony Orchestra; pg. 589, pg. 27
DeBenedictis, Liz, VP-M Mktg & Products - Teachers Insurance & Annuity Association - College Retirement Equities Fund; pg. 1219, pg. 1297
DeBerio, Meg, Product Mgr-Mobile - Panera Bread Company; pg. 1029, pg. 1001
DeBiasio, Alice, Dir-Product Mktg - Honeywell International Inc.; pg. 407, pg. 1088
DeBie, Tod, Sr Mgr-Web Product Mgmt - Ingram Micro Inc.; pg. 415, pg. 261
DeBisschop, Kevin J., Dir-Claim Mktg & Comm - The Travelers Companies, Inc.; pg. 1220, pg. 352
DeBlieck, Amber, Dir-Mktg Plng & Strategy - Valpak Direct Marketing Systems, Inc.; pg. 1699, pg. 438
DeBoer, Alicia, Coord-Enterprise Social Media - Royal Bank of Canada; pg. 800, pg. 1942
DeBoer, Jase, Mgr-Mktg & Mdsg - Universal Forest Products, Inc.; pg. 117, pg. 890
DeBoer, Jerry, Sr VP-Mktg - Jos. A. Bank Clothiers, Inc.; pg. 42, pg. 771
deBoer, Margaret, Sr VP-Corp Mktg - Houghton Mifflin Harcourt Publishing Company; pg. 1651, pg. 454
DeBoer, Tom, Sr Mgr-Product Line - Haworth, Inc.; pg. 402, pg. 891
Debold, Joseph, Sr VP-Sls & Mktg-Global - Wireless Telecom Group, Inc.; pg. 689, pg. 1106
DeBolt, George, Sr VP-Media & Promos - Showtime Networks Inc.; pg. 308, pg. 1291
Debono, Rebecca, Mgr-Social Media - Provide Commerce, Inc.; pg. 1276, pg. 206
DeBonville, Christian, Dir-Adv Sls Res - ESPN, Inc.; pg. 285, pg. 340
Debrincat, Frank, Sr Mgr-Package Dev - Mars, Incorporated; pg. 1858, pg. 1792
Debuono, Laureen, CFO-Interim - Rodan + Fields, LLC; pg. 522, pg. 225
Dec, Jeff, Sr Dir-Mktg-Trademark Pepsi - PepsiCo, Inc.; pg. 259, pg. 1327
Decaire, Rick, Dir-Sls North American Natl Accts - Meritor, Inc.; pg. 212, pg. 911
Decalmbre, Barry, Sr Mgr-Digital Mktg & ECommerce-FLAG - Blount International, Inc.; pg. 1043, pg. 1501
DeCamp, David, Product Mgr-Pro Svcs - Vertafore Inc.; pg. 1222, pg. 386
DeCamp, Mike, Sr Mgr-Mktg Comm - Eaton Corporation; pg. 1331, pg. 1429
DeCandia, Erica, Dir-Offline Media & Sponsorships - E*TRADE Financial Corporation; pg. 749, pg. 1230
Decaria, Dan, Mgr-Store Mktg Strategies - DSW, Inc.; pg. 1807, pg. 1439
DeCarlo, Frank, VP-Production & Res - Hair Club for Men, Ltd., Inc.; pg. 511, pg. 411
Decato, Vern, Mgr-On-line Mktg - Royal Caribbean Cruises Ltd; pg. 1921, pg. 446
Decca, Daniela, Dir-Creative Svcs Production & Ops - BBC Worldwide America Inc.; pg. 271, pg. 1201
Decelian, Steven, Acct Mgr-Inside Sls - AT&T; pg. 1865, pg. 258
December, Dave, Dir-Channel Mktg - CNH America LLC; pg. 702, pg. 560
Dechenne, Jill, Mgr-Digital Mktg - Intel Corporation; pg. 645, pg. 266
Decina, David, Dir-Team Sls - Madison Square Garden Network; pg. 297, pg. 1255
Decio, Terrence M., VP-Sls & Mktg - Skyline Corporation; pg. 1711, pg. 677
Deck, Nancy, VP-Portfolio & Full Svc Brand Mktg - Hilton Worldwide, Inc.; pg. 1094, pg. 1791
Decker, Jamie, Dir-Sls-Team Target - Jarden Consumer Solutions; pg. 57, pg. 412
Decker, Jordan, Mgr-Demand Media Studios Community - Demand Media, Inc.; pg. 1238, pg. 273
Decker, Kate, Sr Specialist-PR - Target Corporation; pg. 1786, pg. 942
Decker, Kathleen, Mgr-Sls Ops & Events - Neiman Marcus, Inc.; pg. 30, pg. 1684
Decker, Katie, Sr Dir-Global Oral Care - Johnson & Johnson; pg. 1549, pg. 1091
Decker, Kelly, Category Mgr-Mktg - Lowe's Companies, Inc.; pg. 1053, pg. 1383
Decker, Melinda, Sr Dir-Intelligent Pharmaceuticals-Global Medicines Dev - MedImmune LLC; pg. 1562, pg. 770
Decker, Nicole, Assoc Specialist-Social Media - DSW, Inc.; pg. 1807, pg. 1439
Decker, Patty, Coord-Mktg & Comm - The Valspar Corporation; pg. 1449, pg. 945
Decker, Steven B., Pres-Consumer Products - Milestone AV Technologies, Inc.; pg. 654, pg. 964
Decker, Zachary, Sr Assoc Brand Mgr - The Kraft Heinz Company; pg. 871, pg. 641
Deckinger, Jessica, VP-Mktg - Wolverine World Wide, Inc.; pg. 1822, pg. 905
DeClouette, Dwight, VP-Comm Media & Entertainment - Hitachi Data Systems Corporation; pg. 407, pg. 265
Declues, Jessica, Mgr-Mktg - Ingram Micro Inc.; pg. 415, pg.

First page reference indicates Business Class Edition
Second page reference indicates Geographic Edition

261
DeCosta-Smith, Melissa, Mgr-Brand Mktg - Lowe's Companies, Inc.; pg. 1053, pg. 1383
DeCoste, Kendra H., Sr Mgr-Mktg-Global Alliances - VMware, Inc.; pg. 490, pg. 179
DeCovich, Sherry, Asst VP-Mktg - The Macerich Company; pg. 1101, pg. 275
Decross, Derek L., VP-Sls-Global - American Airlines Group Inc.; pg. 224, pg. 1693
Dederian, Chena, Sr VP & Head-Event Mktg - Bank of America Corporation; pg. 718, pg. 1362
Dedes, Tracy, Specialist-Mktg & Comm - PricewaterhouseCoopers LLP; pg. 795, pg. 1283
DeDie, Gayle, Head-Media Solutions - Google Inc.; pg. 1249, pg. 153
Dee, Matt, Dir-Adv Production - The Wendy's Company; pg. 1755, pg. 1450
Dee, Matthew, Dir-Adv Production - Wendy's International, Inc.; pg. 1755, pg. 1451
Deeder, Ashley, Mgr-Mktg - Advance America Cash Advance Centers, Inc.; pg. 711, pg. 1622
Deegan, Bryan, District Mgr-Sls - AstraZeneca Pharmaceuticals LP; pg. 1497, pg. 389
Deegan, Stephanie, Brand Mgr-KitchenAid - Whirlpool Corporation; pg. 62, pg. 872
Deeken, Laura, Assoc Mgr-Mktg - Mattel Games/Puzzles; pg. 962, pg. 80
Deeken, Laura, Assoc Mgr-Mktg - MATTEL, INC.; pg. 962, pg. 81
Deel, Stacy M., Analyst-PR - Highmark Blue Cross Blue Shield; pg. 1203, pg. 1576
Deemer, Angela, Mgr-Mktg-Strategic Plng - CSX Transportation, Inc.; pg. 1904, pg. 432
Deep, Hannan, Dir-Mktg & PR-Henry Ford Wyandotte Hospital - Henry Ford Health System; pg. 1541, pg. 883
Deering, Teresa A., Specialist-Mktg Comm - CHS INC.; pg. 702, pg. 926
Dees, Monika, Sr Mgr-Product Mktg-Bus Inkjets - Epson America Inc.; pg. 394, pg. 122
Deese, Jennifer, Sr Mgr-Consulting - Convergys Corporation; pg. 379, pg. 1412
Defalco, Jeff, Bus Mgr - ESAB Welding & Cutting Products; pg. 1335, pg. 1615
DeFauw, Nancy, Sr Mgr-Ticket Ops - Chicago Professional Sports Limited Partnership; pg. 539, pg. 570
DeFazio, Frank, Dir-Customer Experience & Digital Mktg - Highmark Blue Cross Blue Shield; pg. 1203, pg. 1576
DeFeo, Jessica, Specialist-Cause Mktg & Brand Dev - The Boston Beer Company, Inc.; pg. 239, pg. 790
Deffenbaugh, Dan, Dir-Mktg - Chicago Tube & Iron Co.; pg. 1323, pg. 656
Defoe, Nadine, Dir-Global Creative Acct Svcs - Avon Products, Inc.; pg. 500, pg. 1198
DeFoe, Scott, Dir-Global Mktg, R & D, Strategy & Portfolio Mgmt - Medtronic, Inc.; pg. 1564, pg. 939
Defosse, Matthew, Mgr-Mktg Comm-Europe - PolyOne Corporation; pg. 1177, pg. 1404
DeFosset, Barbara, Specialist-Personal Mktg Svc - Liberty Mutual Insurance Group Inc.; pg. 1205, pg. 797
Defoy, Jean-Sebastien, Dir-Mktg-Accessibility & Digital Enterprise - National Film Board of Canada; pg. 299, pg. 1959
DeFranco, Frannie, Mgr-Digital Media - GlaxoSmithKline; pg. 1536, pg. 1389
DeFranco, Frannie, Mgr-Digital Media - GlaxoSmithKline; pg. 1536, pg. 1565
DeFranco, Frannie, Mgr-Digital Media - GlaxoSmithKline Consumer Healthcare; pg. 510, pg. 1554
DeFranco, Linda, Mgr-Mktg - Honeywell International Inc.; pg. 407, pg. 1088
Defratus, Kellie, VP-Sls, Warehouse Direct West & Retail Execution - Dr Pepper Snapple Group, Inc.; pg. 250, pg. 1729
DeFrino, Steven, Brand Mgr - Pinnacle Foods Group LLC; pg. 889, pg. 1104
Defruscio, Suzanne, Sr Mgr-Strategic Client Rels - Aramark; pg. 1013, pg. 1558
Defuria, Joseph, Brand Mgr-BioLab, Inc - Chemtura Corporation; pg. 1152, pg. 355
Defurio, Lori, Sr Strategist-Social Media - Adobe Systems Incorporated; pg. 342, pg. 235
DeGance, Tonya, Mng Editor & Program Mgr-Intel Visual Computing Mktg - Intel Corporation; pg. 645, pg. 266
Degelman, Jack, Mgr-Mktg - Degelman Industries Ltd.; pg. 703, pg. 1962
Degen, Dale, Sr Mgr-Mktg-Worldwide - Hewlett-Packard Company; pg. 404, pg. 175
Degens, Mary Jo, Dir-Mktg - Amgen Inc.; pg. 1493, pg. 291
DeGeorge, Glenn, VP & Mgr-Mktg - Wells Fargo & Company; pg. 819, pg. 232
DeGeorge, Jason, Sr Mgr-Brand Mktg, Email & Web - Euromarket Designs, Inc.; pg. 1124, pg. 640
Degerlia, Janice, Supvr-Wholesale Sls - Forrest Keeling Nursery, Inc.; pg. 1795, pg. 977
deGeus, Stuart, VP-Mktg Svcs - Little Caesars Enterprises, Inc.; pg. 1736, pg. 883
Degnan, Annette, Dir-Mktg Comm - CHS INC.; pg. 702, pg. 926
Degnan, Scott, VP-Sls, Mktg & Product Mgmt - Winnebago Industries, Inc.; pg. 1712, pg. 707
Degnan, Thomas, Mgr-Mktg - Leviton Manufacturing Company, Inc.; pg. 1301, pg. 1180
Degner, Chris, Sr Dir-IR - Occidental Petroleum Corporation; pg. 1175, pg. 137
DeGobbi, Christian, Mgr-Mktg Strategies & Programs - KPMG LLP; pg. 774, pg. 1086
DeGrace, Chip, Exec Dir-Creative - Interface, Inc.; pg. 695, pg. 512
DeGrasse, Cheryl, Sr Dir-Digital Media - American Eagle Outfitters, Inc.; pg. 37, pg. 1572
DeGraw, Lauren, Planner-Digital Sls - Turner Broadcasting System, Inc.; pg. 314, pg. 521
DeGraw, Robin, Sr Mgr-Promos - Disney Interactive Media Group; pg. 1239, pg. 95
Deguine, Etienne, Product Mgr - Google Inc.; pg. 1249, pg. 153
DeGuzman, Dan, Sr Dir-Strategic Adv - Sony Music Entertainment; pg. 309, pg. 1294
Deh, Dai, Brand Mgr-Builder's - Clif Bar Inc.; pg. 848, pg. 83
DeHahn, Katie E., Specialist-Mktg Comm - CNA Insurance Companies; pg. 1198, pg. 571
DeHamer, Matthew, Sr Mgr-Mktg-Wearables - QUALCOMM Incorporated; pg. 1873, pg. 207
Dehamilton, Deborah, Sr Mgr-Media & Web Comm - Benjamin Moore & Co.; pg. 1440, pg. 1085
Deharo, Andy, Sr Mgr-Demand Partnerships-Americas - Smaato Inc.; pg. 1281, pg. 228
DeHart, Dina, Mgr-Mktg - Coty, Inc.; pg. 506, pg. 1219
Dehner, Joseph, Head-Ram & Dodge Design-Product Design - FCA US LLC; pg. 170, pg. 868
Dehnert, Nick, Sr Mgr-Mktg-Intl Retail - Blue Diamond Growers; pg. 840, pg. 195
Deian, Helen, Mgr-Social Media - Shell Oil Company; pg. 984, pg. 1714
Deighton, Anthony, CTO & Sr VP-Products - Qlik Technologies Inc.; pg. 457, pg. 1583
Deighton, Matthew, Mgr-PR - Ancestry.com LLC; pg. 1228, pg. 1754
Deiss, Jonathan, Exec Dir-Creative & Digital - Beachbody, LLC; pg. 271, pg. 272
Deiss, Molly, Sr Mgr-Mktg-Plavix - Sanofi US; pg. 1592, pg. 1046
Deiters, Barry, Product Mgr-Mdse - Deere & Company; pg. 703, pg. 632
Deitert, Eric J., Sr Dir-Insurance Indus Mktg - Pegasystems Inc.; pg. 453, pg. 74
Dejan, Daniel, Mgr-North American ETC Print & Creative - Sappi Fine Paper North America; pg. 1468, pg. 801
DeJesus, Karen, Dir-Sls-Ahold & C&S - Hillshire Brands; pg. 862, pg. 576
deJesus, Maureen, Mgr-Mktg - LPL Financial Corporation; pg. 777, pg. 798
Dejohn, Joseph A., VP-Sls - Endologix, Inc.; pg. 1528, pg. 109
DeJong, Eric, Sr Mgr-Product Dev-Innovation Pipeline, Product Roadmap, P&L Mgmt - Whirlpool Corporation; pg. 62, pg. 872
DeJong, Jessica, Mgr-Mktg & PR - Health Grades, Inc.; pg. 1256, pg. 319
Dejoux, Gaby, Specialist-Mktg - Fossil Group, Inc.; pg. 5, pg. 1735
DeJulio, Denise, Exec Dir-Convention Sls - Kansas City Convention & Visitors Association; pg. 996, pg. 984
Dekle, Thomas, CMO-Digital Sls Globally - International Business Machines Corporation; pg. 418, pg. 1138
Dekle, William, Sr Dir-Worldwide Bus Dev-First Party - Microsoft Game Studios; pg. 964, pg. 1828
Dekorte, Jeffrey, VP-Digital Mktg-Global - Royal Caribbean Cruises Ltd; pg. 1921, pg. 446
DeKruif, Anna, Mgr-Mktg, Advocacy, Influencer Mktg & Social Media - Go Daddy Inc.; pg. 1249, pg. 21
Del Arco, Ignacio, Dir-Global Mktg-Smirnoff - Diageo North America Inc.; pg. 248, pg. 1223
Del Castillo, Ixchel, Mgr-Hispanic Mktg - Cox Communications, Inc.; pg. 279, pg. 501
Del Chiaro, Tarra, Dir-Digital Mktg Strategy-Global - Guess?, Inc.; pg. 25, pg. 132
Del Mar Rosa, Coral, Mgr-Latin America Mktg - Quiksilver, Inc.; pg. 31, pg. 104
Del Percio, Daniela, Dir-Creative-Apparel - Fila USA; pg. 1808, pg. 779
del Pilar Casal, Maria, Mgr-Social Media - Univision Communications Inc.; pg. 683, pg. 1307
Del Ponte, Erin, Dir-Mktg-Acq - BUYSEASONS, Inc.; pg. 20, pg. 1883
Del Prete, Chloe, Acct Exec-Global Integration & Global Mktg Partnerships - National Basketball Association; pg. 566, pg. 1264
Del Prince, Barbara, Mgr-Global Mktg-Women's Health - GE Healthcare; pg. 399, pg. 1765
del Rio, Fabiola, Mgr-Mktg-Butterfinger - Nestle USA, Inc.; pg. 883, pg. 96
Del Santo, Melissa, Dir-Mktg-CRM - The Gap, Inc.; pg. 1770, pg. 218
del Sol, Adrianne C., Sr Mgr-Watches - Amazon.com, Inc.; pg. 1226, pg. 1831
Del Tatto, John, Dir-Adv - The Mattress Firm, Inc.; pg. 934, pg. 1711
Del Valle, Marimar Velasco, Coord-Mktg - 3M Company; pg. 1142, pg. 956
Del Vecchio, Anthony, Dir-Brand & Retail Mktg - AutoNation, Inc.; pg. 165, pg. 423
Del Vigna, Yvonne, Mgr-Procurement, Sls & Mktg - FCA US LLC; pg. 170, pg. 868
Del-Cid, Vincent, VP-Sls - Oneida Ltd; pg. 1129, pg. 1318
Delabriere, Thomas, VP-Mktg - Mars, Incorporated; pg. 1858, pg. 1792
Delach, Sara, Brand Mgr - Mizkan Americas, Inc.; pg. 877, pg. 634
DeLacoste, Eric, Project Mgr-Mktg - Eversource; pg. 977, pg. 794
DeLaCruz, Jen, VP-PR - Carnival Cruise Lines; pg. 1902, pg. 441
DeLancey, Toni, Sr Mgr-PR - United States Postal Service; pg. 1009, pg. 406
DeLanders, Jennifer, Mgr-US Brand Mktg-Girls Toys - Hasbro, Inc.; pg. 954, pg. 1603
DeLanders, Kate, Mgr-Digital Mktg & CRM - Reebok International Ltd.; pg. 1817, pg. 811
DeLaney, Aniko, Mng Dir & Head-Corp Mktg-Global - The Bank of New York Mellon Corporation; pg. 720, pg. 1200
Delaney, Crissy, Sr Mgr-Email & Mobile Mktg - HSN, Inc.; pg. 291, pg. 462
Delaney, Douglas J., Exec VP-Worldwide Sls - Cynosure, Inc.; pg. 1521, pg. 858
DeLaney, Jennifer, Dir-Mktg-Nivea Body Wash & Men's Care - Beiersdorf North America Inc.; pg. 501, pg. 385
Delaney, John, Mgr-Multi-Asset Strategies Mktg - FRANKLIN RESOURCES, INC.; pg. 760, pg. 254
Delaney, Joy, Sr VP & Creative Dir - Nine West Holdings, Inc.; pg. 1815, pg. 1272
Delaney, Katie, Planner-Mktg & Events-Global Media Solutions - Electronic Arts Inc.; pg. 951, pg. 189
Delaney, Kristen, VP-Mktg & Comm - Atlanta Symphony Orchestra; pg. 531, pg. 490
Delaney, Mary, Mgr-Mktg - CUNA Mutual Insurance Society; pg. 743, pg. 1865
Delaney, Norma, Head-Global Women's Mktg - New Balance Athletic Shoe, Inc.; pg. 1811, pg. 798
Delaney, Tom, Mgr-Sector Media Rels - Northrop Grumman Corporation; pg. 231, pg. 1781
DeLanghe, Jaime, Sr Product Mgr - Etsy, Inc.; pg. 1768, pg. 1230
Delanty, Karen, Coord-Mktg Comm - QUALCOMM Incorporated; pg. 1873, pg. 207
Delanty, Lisa, Brand Mgr-Global - MATTEL, INC.; pg. 962, pg. 81
DelaRaba, Adrianne, Dir-Digital Mktg-Global - NBTY, Inc.; pg. 1572, pg. 1338
Delarge, Steve, Acting CEO - AS America, Inc.; pg. 68, pg. 1108
DeLaurentis, Chris, Sr Mgr-ECommerce Self Svc & Bus Ops - Comcast Corporation; pg. 276, pg. 1560
DeLay-Helser, Mickey, Sr VP & Dir-Reg Mktg - Wells Fargo & Company; pg. 819, pg. 232

Delcheccolo, Marc, Dir-Outbound Mktg - Brookstone, Inc.; *pg.* 1764, *pg.* 1036

DelDuco, Chris, Specialist-Mktg Ops - The Procter & Gamble Company; *pg.* 1129, *pg.* 1418

DeLellis, Michael, VP-Adv - Calvin Klein, Inc.; *pg.* 20, *pg.* 1209

DeLeo, Marc, Dir-Mktg - Ameristar Casinos, Inc.; *pg.* 528, *pg.* 1022

Deleo, Monica, Dir-Mktg-Center - HCA HOLDINGS, INC.; *pg.* 1539, *pg.* 1651

DeLeo, Patty, Assoc Dir-Adv - Verizon Communications Inc.; *pg.* 1875, *pg.* 1309

deLeon, Jeff, Dir-Mktg - Kraco Enterprises, LLC; *pg.* 210, *pg.* 68

DeLeon, Leilani, Mgr-Product Mktg - QUALCOMM Incorporated; *pg.* 1873, *pg.* 207

Deleray, John T., VP & Dir-Pacific Region Corp Trust Sls - Wilmington Trust Corporation; *pg.* 822, *pg.* 392

Delery, Michelle J., Sr Mgr-Employee Comm - Entergy Corporation; *pg.* 1941, *pg.* 746

Delfinis, Brittany, Acct Exec-Digital Sls-Us Weekly - Wenner Media LLC; *pg.* 1701, *pg.* 1314

Delfino, Jimena, VP-Issuer Mktg-Latin America & Caribbean Reg - MasterCard Incorporated; *pg.* 779, *pg.* 1325

Delgadillo, Penny, Sr VP-Global Audience Mktg & Line of Bus - SAP; *pg.* 465, *pg.* 78

Delgado, Celi, Coord-Branded Product Program - Nathan's Famous Inc.; *pg.* 1741, *pg.* 1171

Delgado, Chris, VP-Sls - Briggs & Riley Travelware; *pg.* 2, *pg.* 1164

Delgado, Javier M., Dir-Mktg - Wal-Mart.com; *pg.* 1287, *pg.* 50

Delgado-Granados, Javier, Dir-Mktg - Wal-Mart Stores, Inc.; *pg.* 1790, *pg.* 29

Delgado-Jenkins, Jesus, Exec VP-Mdsg, Mktg, Logistics & Innovation - 7-Eleven, Inc.; *pg.* 1012, *pg.* 1672

Delgatti, Mike, Exec VP-Sls & Mktg-Hooker Upholstery - Hooker Furniture Corporation; *pg.* 928, *pg.* 1788

DelGiorno, Joseph, Sr Analyst-Strategic Sourcing & Mktg - The Gap, Inc.; *pg.* 1770, *pg.* 218

DelGiudice, Brian, Mgr-Biomedical Media Svcs - Genzyme Corporation; *pg.* 1534, *pg.* 808

DelGreco, Gary, VP-Traditional Sls - Motorcar Parts of America, Inc.; *pg.* 213, *pg.* 295

Delialis, Konstantinos, Mgr-Mktg-Global - The Coca-Cola Company; *pg.* 240, *pg.* 493

DeLilli, Dedra, Dir-Social Media Mktg & Corp Sponsorships - TD Ameritrade Holding Corporation; *pg.* 808, *pg.* 1018

DeLillio, Anthony, Specialist-Sls & Mktg - FedEx Corporation; *pg.* 1907, *pg.* 1642

DeLima, Sharon, Mgr-Intl Comm & Mktg - National Basketball Association; *pg.* 566, *pg.* 1264

Delimata, Victor, Sr Dir-New Products Commercialization - Novartis Pharmaceuticals Corp.; *pg.* 1575, *pg.* 1054

Delimon, Laurie, Program Mgr-Mktg - IDT Corporation; *pg.* 643, *pg.* 1096

DeLine, Rob, Dir-Mktg-Ultrabooks - Intel Corporation; *pg.* 645, *pg.* 266

DeLisio, Adrienne, Mgr-Media - Lord & Taylor LLC; *pg.* 1777, *pg.* 1252

Dell'Aquilo, Bobbie, Sr Dir-Strategic Messaging - New York Institute of Technology; *pg.* 605, *pg.* 1318

Dell, Cary J., Mgr-Employee & Mktg Comm - Alcoa Inc.; *pg.* 65, *pg.* 1188

Dell, Dave, Dir-Global Mktg & Sls - CTB International Corp.; *pg.* 850, *pg.* 695

DellaCamera, Robert, Sr Dir-Mktg Comm-Global - Medtronic; *pg.* 1563, *pg.* 830

DellaFave, Joe, Brand Mgr - Benjamin Moore & Co.; *pg.* 1440, *pg.* 1085

Dellemonico, Michael, VP-Sls - Uno Restaurant Holdings Corporation; *pg.* 1754, *pg.* 856

Dellicicchi, Kathy, Dir-Payer Mktg-Oncology - Millennium: The Takeda Oncology Company; *pg.* 1568, *pg.* 809

Dellinger, Meghan, Strategist-Mktg - United States Tennis Association; *pg.* 160, *pg.* 1354

Delloca, Janina, Mgr-Multicultural Mktg - Dunkin' Brands Group, Inc.; *pg.* 1727, *pg.* 810

Delman, Sharon L., Dir-Mktg & Product-Small Bus Grp-QuickBooks Checks & Supplies - Intuit Inc.; *pg.* 769, *pg.* 158

Delmont, Kim, Sr Mgr-Mktg - Pfizer Inc.; *pg.* 1581, *pg.* 1278

DelMonte, Lisa, Dir-Art-Print & Digital Adv - 20th Century Fox Film Corp.; *pg.* 267, *pg.* 124

Deloach, Harris E., Jr., Territory Mgr-Sls & Procurement - Sonoco Products Company; *pg.* 1469, *pg.* 1619

DeLoach, Kristin, Assoc Dir-Mktg-ECommerce & Small Bus - Kimberly-Clark Corporation; *pg.* 1461, *pg.* 1720

deLong, Benjamin, Coord-Mktg Spend-Oscar Mayer - The Kraft Heinz Company; *pg.* 871, *pg.* 641

Delong, Brian, Dir-Mktg & PR - Goddard Systems, Inc.; *pg.* 142, *pg.* 1543

DeLong, Scott, Sr Analyst-Case Design & Mktg - Pacific Life Insurance Company; *pg.* 1213, *pg.* 166

Delos Reyes, Elaine, Dir-Fan Mktg & Res - Chicago Bears Football Club, Inc.; *pg.* 538, *pg.* 623

DeLozier, Kenneth, Analyst-Sls-Sam's Club - Georgia-Pacific LLC; *pg.* 1458, *pg.* 507

DelPorto, Jerome, Sr Dir-Global Expansion Team - 7-Eleven, Inc.; *pg.* 1012, *pg.* 1672

DelRizzo, Bryan, Mgr-PR - NVIDIA Corporation; *pg.* 447, *pg.* 268

DelRosario, Bobby, Sr Mgr-Americas Field Mktg - Autodesk Inc.; *pg.* 356, *pg.* 257

Deluca, Bryan, Sr Dir-Content & Online Strategies - The Hearst Corporation; *pg.* 1649, *pg.* 1239

Deluca, Chris, Dir-Bus Practices & Media Monitoring-Social Media - Education Management Corporation; *pg.* 601, *pg.* 1575

DeLuca, Christine, Sr Mgr - KPMG LLP; *pg.* 774, *pg.* 1086

Deluca, Don, Engr-PR Sys - Axcelis Technologies, Inc.; *pg.* 1400, *pg.* 787

DeLuca, Maria Laino, Sr VP-Consumer & Trade Mktg - Bravo Media LLC; *pg.* 271, *pg.* 1206

DeLuca, Peter, Sr VP-Brand Adv & Comm - T-Mobile US, Inc.; *pg.* 676, *pg.* 1816

DeLuca, Steven, Interim Publr - In Style Magazine; *pg.* 1652, *pg.* 1243

DeLuca-Imral, Regina T., Sr Specialist-Media - Edward D. Jones & Co., LP; *pg.* 746, *pg.* 995

DeLucia, Jerry, Dir-Mktg - Fresh Enterprises, LLC; *pg.* 1729, *pg.* 110

DeLucia, Tracy, Mgr-Integrated Mktg - Education Management Corporation; *pg.* 601, *pg.* 1575

Deluise, Tom, Mgr-Natl Toyota Certified & Rent A Car Sls & Ops - Toyota Motor Sales, U.S.A., Inc.; *pg.* 193, *pg.* 296

DelValle, Rachel, Sr Asst Mgr-Shopper Mktg - Unilever United States, Inc.; *pg.* 904, *pg.* 1061

Delyser, Jan, VP-Mktg - California Avocado Commission; *pg.* 135, *pg.* 108

Delz, Heather, Mgr-Mktg & Broadband Utility - Graybar Electric Company, Inc.; *pg.* 1299, *pg.* 997

Demal-Felix, Sandrine, Sr Mgr-Field Events & Programs - Charles Schwab; *pg.* 1235, *pg.* 1661

DeMara, Paul, Mgr-Corp Mktg Comm & Res - Henkels & McCoy, Inc.; *pg.* 86, *pg.* 1517

DeMarco, Charlie, Dir-Creative & User Experience - National Football League; *pg.* 567, *pg.* 1264

DeMarco, Chris, Sr Mgr-Mktg - Pepsi-Cola North America; *pg.* 259, *pg.* 1327

DeMarco, Christopher, Sr Mgr-Mktg - PepsiCo, Inc.; *pg.* 259, *pg.* 1327

DeMarco, Danielle, Dir-Digital Mktg - Chanel, Inc.; *pg.* 503, *pg.* 1211

Demarco, Kristy, Sr Mgr-Mktg Programs-Kapow Software - Kofax Image Products, Inc.; *pg.* 1419, *pg.* 112

DeMarcy, Denny, Sr Dir-Loss Prevention - Dick's Sporting Goods, Inc.; *pg.* 1832, *pg.* 1524

Demarest, Craig, Sr Dir-Procurement - R.J. Reynolds Tobacco Co.; *pg.* 1895, *pg.* 1395

DeMaria, David, VP-Mktg-Verification Grp - Synopsys, Inc.; *pg.* 480, *pg.* 162

DeMaria, Tom, Sr Dir-IOT Strategy & Tech - Intel Corporation; *pg.* 645, *pg.* 266

DeMaria, Tricia, Mgr-PR - Reedman Toll Auto World; *pg.* 189, *pg.* 1547

DeMarino, Jared, Dir-Natl Audience Sls - Meredith Corporation; *pg.* 1663, *pg.* 705

Demaris, Peter, VP-Mktg & Digital-Medicare Segment - UnitedHealth Group Incorporated; *pg.* 1221, *pg.* 950

Demarta, Jean-Christophe, Sr VP-Adv-Global - The New York Times Company; *pg.* 1668, *pg.* 1270

DeMartino, Alison, Dir-Mktg Comm - Wilsonart International, Inc.; *pg.* 1450, *pg.* 1746

DeMartino, Elizabeth, Mgr-Mktg Partnerships & Promos - Relativity Media, LLC; *pg.* 306, *pg.* 47

Demartino, Johnny, Dir-Brand Identity & Product Mktg - Levi Strauss & Co.; *pg.* 43, *pg.* 220

Demas, Bethanne, Dir-PR, Outreach & Mktg - Shriners Hospitals For Children; *pg.* 1594, *pg.* 475

DeMatteis, Drue, Dir-eChannels & Interactive Mktg - FirstMerit Corporation; *pg.* 758, *pg.* 1400

DeMatteis, Jennifer, Product Mgr-Mktg-Hospital Sls & Svcs - Cardinal Health, Inc.; *pg.* 1512, *pg.* 1448

DeMay, Stephen, VP-Gypsum Sls-North America - Lafarge North America Inc.; *pg.* 93, *pg.* 779

Demboski, Jennifer, Specialist-Digital Mktg - Nationwide Mutual Insurance Company; *pg.* 1210, *pg.* 1442

Demchuk, Brett, VP-Product Quality - Vascular Solutions, Inc.; *pg.* 1434, *pg.* 946

Demcsak, Elizabeth, Product Mgr - IAC/InterActiveCorp; *pg.* 292, *pg.* 1242

DeMent, Anna, Mgr-Digital Commerce Mktg - Nautilus, Inc.; *pg.* 1840, *pg.* 1846

DeMerlier, David, VP-Mktg-Intl - Princess Cruise Lines Ltd.; *pg.* 1920, *pg.* 270

Demers, Joseph, Sr Mgr-Regulatory Affairs-Adv & Promo - Amgen Inc.; *pg.* 1493, *pg.* 291

Demers, Joseph R., Dir-Product Line-Photonic Sys - EMCORE Corporation; *pg.* 638, *pg.* 39

Demetrio, Anne, Sr Product Mgr-US Afinitor Mktg - Novartis Pharmaceuticals Corp.; *pg.* 1575, *pg.* 1054

DeMets, Jim A., VP-Retail Products Sls & Mktg - Honeywell International Inc.; *pg.* 407, *pg.* 1088

DeMichele, Kara D., Sr Specialist-Mktg - CB Richard Ellis, Inc.; *pg.* 1085, *pg.* 1210

Demichele, Peter, Sr Head-Trade Mktg Process-Mobile Technologies - GOJO Industries, Inc.; *pg.* 330, *pg.* 1401

DeMichillie, Greg, Dir-Product Mgmt-Google Cloud Platform - Google Inc.; *pg.* 1249, *pg.* 153

DeMike, Joe, Head-Mktg Consultants - Google Inc.; *pg.* 1249, *pg.* 153

DeMille, Laurie, Dir-Product Info & Patient Svc - GlaxoSmithKline; *pg.* 1536, *pg.* 1565

Deming, John, Mgr-Mktg, Mktg Database, SEM & Loyalty - Seventh Generation, Inc.; *pg.* 335, *pg.* 1765

Demirjian, Elizabeth, Dir-Digital Mktg - Hewlett-Packard Company; *pg.* 404, *pg.* 175

Demise, Mesfin, Sr Dir-Fin - Primus Telecommunications Group, Incorporated; *pg.* 665, *pg.* 1794

Deml, Brandon, Specialist-Equipment Mktg - Land O'Lakes, Inc.; *pg.* 873, *pg.* 915

Demma, Ken, VP-Mktg - SAP; *pg.* 465, *pg.* 78

Demmer, Cole, Brand Mgr - Keurig Green Mountain, Inc.; *pg.* 868, *pg.* 1768

Demont, Diana, Mgr-Shopper Mktg-HQ & East Div - The Dannon Company, Inc.; *pg.* 851, *pg.* 1351

Demorest, Faith, Mgr-Personnel & Production & Librarian-Music - Michigan Philharmonic; *pg.* 562, *pg.* 904

Demos, Mary, Mgr-Customer Mktg - The Coca-Cola Company; *pg.* 240, *pg.* 493

Demouthe, Amanda, Mgr-Mktg-East Market Area - Ford Motor Company; *pg.* 172, *pg.* 876

Dempsey, Alison Kiczek, Sr Mgr-Social Media & PR - Quidsi, Inc.; *pg.* 1276, *pg.* 1076

Dempsey, Dave, VP-Field Mktg-North America - Pepsi Beverages Company; *pg.* 258, *pg.* 1342

Dempsey, Jillian, Dir-Global Creative Color - Avon Products, Inc.; *pg.* 500, *pg.* 1198

Dempsey, Kaylah, Coord-Mktg - Big Lots, Inc.; *pg.* 1762, *pg.* 1438

Dempsey, Matthew, Sr Assoc-Mktg - VistaPrint USA, Incorporated; *pg.* 1700, *pg.* 829

Dempsey, Nancy L., Program Mgr-PR - Xerox Corporation; *pg.* 494, *pg.* 365

Dempsey, Robert, Sr Media Buyer & Planner - Shire; *pg.* 1593, *pg.* 1532

Dempsey, Sean, VP & Sls Dir - Saddlebrook Resorts, Inc.; *pg.* 1111, *pg.* 478

Dempster, David, Mgr-Mktg Analytics - MetroPCS, Inc.; *pg.* 1872, *pg.* 1683

Demshki, Mike, Sr Mgr-Mktg - Intel Corporation; *pg.* 645, *pg.* 266

Demski, Lawrence P., Dept Head-Aftersls Bus Dev & Mktg - BMW of North America, LLC; *pg.* 166, *pg.* 1133

Demski, Yvonne, Brand Mgr-Design-Store Brands & Food Svc - ConAgra Foods, Inc.; *pg.* 826, *pg.* 1014

Demuth, Bob, Mgr-Sls-Europe, Middle East & Africa - Broadcast Electronics, Inc.; *pg.* 627, *pg.* 653

DeMuth, Jennifer, Mgr-Adv - BP America Inc.; *pg.* 972, *pg.* 1702

Denas, Karen S., Sr VP & Reg Mgr-Sls & Svc - Cardinal Financial Corp.; *pg.* 732, *pg.* 1790

Denat, Laurence, Dir-Mktg-Global - The Coca-Cola Company; *pg.* 240, *pg.* 493

Denda, Alejandra, Dir-Shopper Mktg - Pinnacle Foods Group LLC; pg. 889, pg. 1104
Deneau, Inid, Dir-Mktg - Landauer, Inc.; pg. 1554, pg. 615
Deneffe, Mike, Dir-Mktg - NVIDIA Corporation; pg. 447, pg. 268
Denega, Kristen, Sr Asst Brand Mgr-Building-Becel - Unilever Canada Inc.; pg. 903, pg. 1946
Denekas, Heather, Dir-Sls-Sears - Whirlpool Corporation; pg. 62, pg. 872
Denenberg, David, Sr VP-Global Media Distr & Bus Affairs - National Basketball Association; pg. 566, pg. 1264
Denfeld, Peggy, Product Mgr-Menswear - Pendleton Woolen Mills, Inc.; pg. 697, pg. 1505
Denfeld, Vicki, Exec VP-Sls & Mktg - Crestline Hotels & Resorts, Inc.; pg. 1088, pg. 1779
Deng, Fei, Sr Analyst-Global Insights & Mktg Intelligence - Avon Products, Inc.; pg. 500, pg. 1198
Dengler, M. Heide, VP-Graphics & Production - Information Today Inc.; pg. 1653, pg. 1084
DeNike, Jim, Sr Dir-Comm & IR - OncoGenex Pharmaceuticals, Inc.; pg. 1578, pg. 1818
Denio, Thomas F., Mgr-Sls & Mktg-Reference Products - General Electric Company; pg. 1297, pg. 347
Denishenko, Vadim, Brand Mgr-Global - Hasbro, Inc.; pg. 954, pg. 1603
Denison, Jill, VP-Mktg - Pinnacle Foods Group LLC; pg. 889, pg. 1104
Denissova, Jenya, Head-Channel Sls, Traditional Media & Emerging Bus-North America - Google Inc.; pg. 1249, pg. 153
Denisyuk, Yulia, Brand Mgr-Strategy-Shock Top - Anheuser-Busch Companies, LLC; pg. 237, pg. 991
Denke, John, VP-Intl Sls Grp - Reed Exhibitions USA; pg. 460, pg. 364
Denman, Kelly, Supvr-Interactive Mktg & Head-Mktg Automation - 3M Company; pg. 1142, pg. 956
Denman, Kurt, Sr VP-Mktg - Congoleum Corporation; pg. 921, pg. 1084
Dennard, Jill, Mgr-North American Mktg Events - Philips Lighting; pg. 1303, pg. 806
Dennebaum, Liz, Sr Mgr-Social Media-Tiny Prints - SHUTTERFLY, INC.; pg. 1280, pg. 192
Dennebaum, Matt, Sr Product Mgr - Twitter, Inc.; pg. 1285, pg. 228
Dennehy, Brian K., CMO & Exec VP - Nordstrom, Inc.; pg. 1779, pg. 1837
Denney, Ashley, Sr Mgr-Mktg-Promos & Gap Online - The Gap, Inc.; pg. 1770, pg. 218
Denney, Jim, VP-Product Mktg - TiVo Inc.; pg. 313, pg. 251
Denney, T. Baxter, VP-Online Mktg & Ops - New Relic, Inc.; pg. 445, pg. 224
Denning, Beth, Exec Dir-Home Security Sls - Cox Communications, Inc.; pg. 279, pg. 501
Denning, Brian, Dir-Mktg - Hubbell Power Systems, Inc.; pg. 643, pg. 1614
Denning, Robert, Dir-Adv & Creative Svcs - Banner Health System; pg. 1498, pg. 15
Dennis, Ashley, Sr Mgr-Mktg - Samsung Telecommunications America, LLC; pg. 670, pg. 1736
Dennis, Brandon, Sr Dir-ECommerce - MTD Products, Inc.; pg. 1057, pg. 1478
Dennis, Chris, Head-Fixed Income Sls-US - Liquidnet Holdings, Inc.; pg. 776, pg. 1251
Dennis, David, Grp Mgr-Corp PR - Microsoft Corporation; pg. 435, pg. 1824
Dennis, David, Sr VP-Product Mktg - SYNNEX Corporation; pg. 480, pg. 92
Dennis, George, Exec Dir-Ad Sls-Natl - AccuWeather, Inc.; pg. 268, pg. 1587
Dennis, Gregory, VP & Head-Gen Medicine & Global Product Dev - PHARMACEUTICAL PRODUCT DEVELOPMENT, INC.; pg. 1584, pg. 1393
Dennis, Jackie, Dir-Brand-PR - Las Vegas Convention & Visitors Authority; pg. 997, pg. 1027
Dennis, Jennifer, Dir-Global Events-Oracle Mktg Cloud - Oracle Corporation; pg. 1272, pg. 786
Dennis, Katy, Mgr-Media - The Walt Disney Company; pg. 317, pg. 52
Dennis, Kenisha, Analyst-Mktg - Time Warner Cable Inc.; pg. 312, pg. 1301
Dennis, Marie, VP-Mktg & Comm - Wells Fargo & Company; pg. 819, pg. 232
Dennis, Martha, Dir-Mktg & Comm - University of Georgia; pg. 609, pg. 486
Dennis, Pat, Dir-Customer Svc, Consumer & Specialty Sls - AutoTrader, Inc.; pg. 1230, pg. 490
Dennis, Patrick, VP & Gen Mgr-HBC Sls & Mdse - Albertson's LLC; pg. 1013, pg. 546
Dennis, Shawna, Asst VP-Mktg & Comm - Manulife Financial Corporation; pg. 778, pg. 1939
Dennis, Todd, Dir-Mktg - Symantec Corporation; pg. 478, pg. 161
Dennison, David C., Mgr-Mktg-Isobutylene & Oxyfuels - LyondellBasell Industries; pg. 980, pg. 1710
Dennison, Jim, Sr Mgr-Market - H.B. Fuller Company; pg. 1165, pg. 961
Dennison, Kristen, Coord-US CAI Mktg - Siemens Healthcare Diagnostics; pg. 673, pg. 604
Dennison, Sean, Sr Mgr-Social Media - National Hockey League; pg. 568, pg. 1265
Denniston, John, Sr Mgr-Mktg - QUALCOMM Incorporated; pg. 1873, pg. 207
Denny, John, Sr Mgr-Mktg - Philips Electronics North America; pg. 662, pg. 782
Denny, Randy, VP-Sls-Americas - Xplore Technologies Corp.; pg. 497, pg. 1667
Denomme, Peggy, VP-Mktg-ColdPruf - Indera Mills Company; pg. 26, pg. 1396
Denor, David, Dir-Custom Media - Automotive News; pg. 1618, pg. 879
DeNoyior, Stacy, VP-Sls - Broadridge Financial Solutions Inc.; pg. 727, pg. 1172
Denslaw, Sara, Specialist-Adv Signing - Target Corporation; pg. 1786, pg. 942
Dent, Gail, Assoc Dir-Pub & Media Rels-NCAA Comm Div - National Collegiate Athletic Association; pg. 567, pg. 688
Dent, Phyllis, Coord-Social Media & Brand Intelligence - Aflac Incorporated; pg. 1188, pg. 527
Dente, Lori, Grp VP-Fin-Adv Sls & Mktg Svcs - Time Inc.; pg. 1693, pg. 1300
Denton, Hayley, Mgr-Media Strategies - Scripps Networks Interactive, Inc.; pg. 1279, pg. 1638
Denton, Jordan, Sr Mgr-Consumer Strategy & Insights - The Procter & Gamble Company; pg. 1129, pg. 1418
Denton, Melissa, Sr Mgr-Mktg-Global - Baxter International Inc.; pg. 1499, pg. 599
Dentz, Sharon, Dir-Mktg - The Wooster Brush Company; pg. 1450, pg. 1482
Denys, Ryan, Dir-Mktg-Confectionery - Nestle Canada Inc.; pg. 883, pg. 1929
Denz, Lauren M., Sr Mgr-Comm - Catamaran; pg. 1514, pg. 628
Deo, Anne, Sr VP-Media Measurement & Analysis - The Advertising Council, Inc.; pg. 125, pg. 1187
Deoudes, Meri-Margaret, VP-Strategic Alliances, Corp Rels & Cause Mktg - March of Dimes Birth Defects Foundation; pg. 146, pg. 1354
Depace, Dan, Sr Dir - Office Depot, Inc.; pg. 448, pg. 412
DePaepe, Karen, VP-Product Sls Mgmt, Online Sls & Mktg - Wells Fargo & Company; pg. 819, pg. 232
DePalma McCartney, Casey, Sr Mgr-Mktg Comm - Unilever United States, Inc.; pg. 904, pg. 1061
DePalma, Rachel, Category Brand Mgr - True Value Company; pg. 1065, pg. 592
Depanfilis, Michael, VP-Shopper Mktg - The Hershey Co.; pg. 1855, pg. 1538
DePaoli, Piero, Sr Dir-Global Product Mktg-Enterprise Security - Symantec Corporation; pg. 478, pg. 161
DePaul, Bobby, Sr Dir-Pro Personnel - Chicago Bears Football Club, Inc.; pg. 538, pg. 623
Depelteau, Adam, Sr Specialist-Product Mktg - VistaPrint USA, Incorporated; pg. 1700, pg. 829
DePena, Patricia, Head-Mktg-Land Discoveries & Cruise Tours - Royal Caribbean Cruises Ltd; pg. 1921, pg. 446
Depencier, Alan, VP-Mktg - Royal Bank of Canada; pg. 800, pg. 1942
Depenhart, Courtney, Mgr-Firm Mktg - FRANKLIN RESOURCES, INC.; pg. 760, pg. 254
DePeppo, Jamie, Asst VP-Direct Bus & Digital Mktg - MetLife, Inc.; pg. 1208, pg. 1258
DePerez, Fred, Dir & Sr Mgr-Mktg - Nissan North America, Inc.; pg. 186, pg. 1633
Deperio, Lisa, Sr Dir - Fossil Group, Inc.; pg. 5, pg. 1735
DePetro, Mike, Product Mgr-Panamera & Macan - Porsche Cars North America, Inc.; pg. 189, pg. 518
DePew, Alan, Mgr-Strategic Mktg - Big Lots, Inc.; pg. 1762, pg. 1438
Depietro, Katie, Product Mgr - Newell Rubbermaid Inc.; pg. 1128, pg. 515
DePoy, Andrew, Mgr-Brand & Market Comm-Corp Mktg Team - ENTEGRIS, INC.; pg. 1882, pg. 788
DePrizio, Suzy, Grp Brand Dir - Neutrogena Corporation; pg. 517, pg. 137
DeProssino, Stacey, Specialist-Mktg - Ethan Allen Interiors Inc.; pg. 924, pg. 343
Deptula, Larry, Sr Rep-Sls - Southwestern Industries, Inc.; pg. 1429, pg. 69
DePuy, Kezia, Sr Product Mgr - AbbVie Inc.; pg. 1486, pg. 638
Der, Michelle Karam, Sr VP-Sls - Randa Accessories, LLC; pg. 47, pg. 657
Deras, Mariela, Assoc Dir-Integrated Sls & Mktg-Fox Hispanic Media - Fox Broadcasting Company; pg. 287, pg. 130
Derbick, John, Dir-Adv-Global - Principal Financial Group, Inc.; pg. 796, pg. 706
Derby, Dave, Sr VP-Mktg - Trinchero Family Estates; pg. 1971, pg. 197
Derby, John, Dir-Adv - Wegmans Food Markets, Inc.; pg. 1037, pg. 1337
Derby, Mark, VP-Distr Sls & Ops - GN Netcom Inc.; pg. 640, pg. 1037
Derbyshire, Jim, Mgr-Sls-Natl - BASF; pg. 1793, pg. 992
Derderian, Rob, Head-Shopper Mktg - Google Inc.; pg. 1249, pg. 153
Derella, Matt, VP-US DSO Sls - Twitter, Inc.; pg. 1285, pg. 228
Dereniak, Andreana, Dir-Mktg, Brand & Commercialization - Abbott Diabetes Care, Inc.; pg. 1483, pg. 38
Derezin, Mike, VP-Sls Solutions - LinkedIn Corporation; pg. 1262, pg. 160
DeRidder, Jim, Dir-OEM Mktg, Comm & Bus Dev - iBiquity Digital Corporation; pg. 409, pg. 767
Derin, Robin M., Sr Mgr-HR & Comm - Continental Grain Company; pg. 1475, pg. 1218
Derks, Melanie, Mktg Coord-Sports Sponsorships-Electronic Media - Sport Clips, Inc.; pg. 523, pg. 1698
Derman, Josh, Mgr-Bus Dev Sls & Mktg - United States Olympic Committee; pg. 589, pg. 315
Dermo, Mike, VP-Retail Sls - NutriSystem, Inc.; pg. 1577, pg. 1533
Dermott, Ross, Dir-Wireless Product Mgmt - Micron Technology, Inc.; pg. 435, pg. 547
Dern, Chad, Dir-Brand & Adv - The Northwestern Mutual Life Insurance Company; pg. 1212, pg. 1879
Dern, John, VP-PR - The Boeing Company; pg. 225, pg. 567
Dern, John, VP-PR - The Boeing Company - Helicopter Division; pg. 226, pg. 13
Dernedde, Mary, Mgr-Online Digital Mktg-AT&T Bus - AT&T Mobility LLC; pg. 619, pg. 488
DerOhannessian, Lena, VP & Dir-Mktg-Global - Brown-Forman Corporation; pg. 1958, pg. 732
Deroos, Dirk, Head-Technical Sls-InfoSphere BigInsights-Worldwide - International Business Machines Corporation; pg. 418, pg. 1138
Deroos, Elice, Asst VP-Mktg - Zurich Holding Company of America, Inc.; pg. 1224, pg. 660
DeRosa, Ed, Dir-Mktg-Bloodstock Res Info Svcs - Churchill Downs, Inc.; pg. 540, pg. 733
DeRosa, Frank, Sr Dir-Mktg - IBM; pg. 410, pg. 1449
Derose, Dena, Dir-Adv - Ashland Daily Tidings; pg. 1617, pg. 1499
DeRose, Linda, Coord-Mktg Comm - Meridian Bioscience Inc.; pg. 1422, pg. 1417
Derouin, David, Producer-Digital Brand Mktg - Hasbro, Inc.; pg. 954, pg. 1603
DeRousse, Sara Allison, Dir-Global Strategic Mktg-World Wide Pro Education - Johnson & Johnson; pg. 1549, pg. 1091
Derov, Carol, Mgr-Color & Mktg Svcs - Sherwin Williams; pg. 1448, pg. 1436
Derrick, Brian, VP-Mktg - Mentor Graphics Corporation; pg. 432, pg. 1510
Derrick, Laurel, Sr Analyst-Mktg - The J.M. Smucker Company; pg. 865, pg. 1468
Derrick, Sally, Dir-Sls & Mktg - Newport Aquarium; pg. 571, pg. 739
Derrickson, Joe, Bus Mgr-Indus Products - Westlake Plastics Company; pg. 1892, pg. 1548
Derrico, Joe, Sr Dir-Corp Pricing Strategy-Pricing Center of Excellence - Automatic Data Processing, Inc.; pg. 357, pg. 1117
Derrig, Deanna, Head-Central Reg Mktg - Accenture; pg. 1392, pg. 1186
Derrig, Diana M., Dir-Database Mktg - Gartner, Inc.; pg. 1248, pg. 374
Derrow, Mandi, Sr Specialist-Social Mktg - Chico's FAS, Inc.;

pg. 21, *pg.* 427

Derry, Lynn C., Sr VP & Gen Mgr-Mdse - Christopher & Banks Corporation; *pg.* 22, *pg.* 953

Dertadian, Jack, Specialist-Mktg - Diageo North America Inc.; *pg.* 248, *pg.* 1223

Derussy, Gabrielle, VP-Sls Ops - TechTarget, Inc.; *pg.* 482, *pg.* 837

Deruyter, Mark, Dir-Digital Mktg-North America & Europe - Columbia Sportswear Company; *pg.* 1830, *pg.* 1501

Dery, Rick, CMO, Chief Sls Officer & Sr VP - Gulf Oil Limited Partnership; *pg.* 978, *pg.* 814

Derynoski, Dave, Mgr-Sls & Mktg - EDAC Technologies Corporation; *pg.* 1332, *pg.* 342

Desai, Amit, Sr VP-Mktg & Global Franchise Mgmt - Warner Bros. Entertainment Inc.; *pg.* 319, *pg.* 54

Desai, Chinar, Mgr-Global Digital Media - McDonald's Corporation; *pg.* 1737, *pg.* 645

Desai, Chirantan, Pres-Emerging Tech Products Div - EMC Corporation; *pg.* 391, *pg.* 825

Desai, Jignesh, Sr Mgr-Brand Solutions Grp - NCR Corporation; *pg.* 443, *pg.* 531

Desai, Kimberly, Assoc Dir-Brita & Mgr-Mktg-Brita Bus - The Clorox Company; *pg.* 327, *pg.* 169

Desai, Lopa, Exec Dir-US Mktg & Oncology - Amgen Inc.; *pg.* 1493, *pg.* 291

Desai, Milin, Sr Dir-Product Mgmt-NSX - VMware, Inc.; *pg.* 490, *pg.* 179

Desai, Nima, Mgr-Sls Enablement Mktg - Cisco Systems, Inc.; *pg.* 372, *pg.* 240

Desai, Pavan P., Sr Mgr-Web & New Media Comm - Lockheed Martin Corporation; *pg.* 229, *pg.* 762

Desai, Sameer, Sr Analyst-Mktg-Cheetos - PepsiCo, Inc.; *pg.* 259, *pg.* 1327

Desai, Shreya, Mgr-Ad Product - Electronic Arts Inc.; *pg.* 951, *pg.* 189

Desai, Subina, Sr Mgr-Digital Mktg-SEO & Content - Intuit Inc.; *pg.* 769, *pg.* 158

Desai, Tim, Sr Mgr-Product Mktg - Hitachi Data Systems Corporation; *pg.* 407, *pg.* 265

DeSanctis, Adam, Mgr-Economic Issues Media - National Association of Realtors; *pg.* 1666, *pg.* 584

DeSanctis, Alex, Dir-Adv - Time Inc.; *pg.* 1693, *pg.* 1300

DeSantis, Stephanie, Dir-Mktg - Quidsi, Inc.; *pg.* 1276, *pg.* 1076

DeSantis, Vincent, CMO, Sr VP & Gen Mgr-ECommerce - Payless Shoesource, Inc.; *pg.* 31, *pg.* 722

Desberg, Kerry, Dir-Mktg Comm, PR & Social Media-Global - WatchGuard Technologies, Inc.; *pg.* 491, *pg.* 1842

Deschapelles, Carlos, Exec VP-Network & Digital Sls - Univision Communications Inc.; *pg.* 683, *pg.* 1307

DesForges, Jacqueline, Mgr-Social Media & Community - Rail Europe Inc.; *pg.* 1920, *pg.* 1354

Deshotel, Kathy, Mgr-Product Line Mktg - Aviall, Inc.; *pg.* 224, *pg.* 1676

Deshpande, Vyenkatesh, Mgr-Product Line - VMware, Inc.; *pg.* 490, *pg.* 179

Desiderio, Rick, Mgr-Mktg-Consumer Engagement-Mobile Channel - The Allstate Corporation; *pg.* 1189, *pg.* 639

Desilets, Dave, Sr Mgr-Corp PR - Raytheon Company; *pg.* 233, *pg.* 854

Desilva, Shelley, VP-Mktg - The HON Company; *pg.* 928, *pg.* 709

DeSimone, Eric, Engr-Natl Sls-Comm - MicroStrategy, Inc.; *pg.* 1266, *pg.* 1809

Desjardins, D.P., Dir-Product Comm Svcs - Xerox Canada Inc.; *pg.* 494, *pg.* 1930

Desjardins, Jesse, Mgr-Social Media & Advocacy - Tourism Australia; *pg.* 1007, *pg.* 140

Desjardins, Renee, Sr Mgr-Social Media Mktg - The Weather Channel LLC; *pg.* 320, *pg.* 523

Desmarais, Aurelie, Sr Dir-Artistic Plng - Houston Symphony Society; *pg.* 552, *pg.* 1708

Desmarais, John H., Mgr-Mktg-Appliance Parts Div - General Electric Company; *pg.* 1297, *pg.* 347

Desmond, Courtney, Sr Mgr-Bus Conduct - Gilead Sciences, Inc.; *pg.* 1535, *pg.* 88

Desmond, David, Dir-Sls, New Media & Entertainment-Natl - PGA Tour, Inc.; *pg.* 574, *pg.* 460

Desmond, Jerry, Div VP-US Sls & Field Svc & Ops-Nestle Professional Beverages - Nestle Professional Beverages; *pg.* 257, *pg.* 474

Desmond, Michelle, Sr Dir-Global Innovation Platforms - Starbucks Corporation; *pg.* 897, *pg.* 1840

Desmond, Ned, COO-TechCrunch & Gen Mgr-AOL Tech Media - AOL Inc.; *pg.* 1229, *pg.* 1195

Desmond, Shaun, Dir-Analytics & Digital Mktg-Free People - Urban Outfitters, Inc.; *pg.* 1789, *pg.* 1571

Desnos, Philippe, Pres-Products & Service Solutions - Delphi Automotive LLP; *pg.* 204, *pg.* 910

DeSocio, David, Sr VP-Ad Sls Partnerships & Mktg - A&E Television Networks, LLC; *pg.* 267, *pg.* 1185

DeSocio, Jim, Exec VP-Field Ops, Sls, Pro Svcs & Bus Dev - Omnitracs, LLC; *pg.* 449, *pg.* 1685

DeSonier, David M., Chief Strategy Officer & Sr VP-Corp Strategy, IR, FPA & Comm - Leggett & Platt, Incorporated; *pg.* 933, *pg.* 974

Desouza, Adam, Sr Mgr-Quality Engrg - Boston Scientific Corporation; *pg.* 1508, *pg.* 831

DeSpain, Patrick M., Sr VP & Dir-Treasury Mgmt Sls - Florida Community Banks, Inc.; *pg.* 758, *pg.* 431

Despins, Abby, Mgr-PR - Wisconsin Milk Marketing Board, Inc.; *pg.* 161, *pg.* 1868

DeSplinter, Jennifer Ann, Product Mgr-Wild Roots & Kretschmer Wheat Germ - Continental Mills, Inc.; *pg.* 827, *pg.* 1845

Despot, Dan, Product Mgr-StoryTeller Interactive Touchscreen System - AccuWeather, Inc.; *pg.* 268, *pg.* 1587

Despotes, Mike, Reg Mgr-Sls - Avnet, Inc.; *pg.* 622, *pg.* 15

Dessau, Nigel, CMO - Stratus Technologies, Inc.; *pg.* 477, *pg.* 832

DeStafney, Dani, Mgr-Mktg-Natl Adv - AT&T Mobility LLC; *pg.* 619, *pg.* 488

DeStefanis, Carl, Dir-Mktg - Johnson & Johnson; *pg.* 1549, *pg.* 1091

DeStefano-Orebaugh, Lisa, VP-Mktg - The Home Depot, Inc.; *pg.* 1050, *pg.* 510

Destross, Scott, Asst Mgr-Digital Mktg - General Motors Company; *pg.* 175, *pg.* 881

Desuyo, Marissa, VP-Brand & Adv - BlackRock, Inc.; *pg.* 724, *pg.* 1203

Detenber, Derek, Sr VP-Mktg - Massage Envy Limited, LLC; *pg.* 516, *pg.* 23

Deter, Jaclyn, Sr Mgr-Mktg Comm - Sealed Air Corporation; *pg.* 1468, *pg.* 1058

Deters, John, Chief Strategy Officer & Head-Corp Initiatives - CBOE Holdings, Inc.; *pg.* 733, *pg.* 569

Detlet, Ken, VP-Digital Adv Strategy & Sls - The Associated Press, Inc.; *pg.* 270, *pg.* 1197

Detloff, Joan, Mgr-Mktg - 3M Company; *pg.* 1142, *pg.* 956

Detraglia, Julie, Sr VP-Strategic Digital & Brdcst Mktg Res - NBC Universal, Inc.; *pg.* 300, *pg.* 1266

Detrinidad, Javier, Strategist-Multicultural Mktg - Edward D. Jones & Co., LP; *pg.* 746, *pg.* 995

DeTrude, Jim, Dir-Sls-Nissan Motor Acceptance Corporation - Nissan North America, Inc.; *pg.* 186, *pg.* 1633

Dettman, Adam, Dir-Sports & Entertainment Mktg - MillerCoors LLC; *pg.* 255, *pg.* 582

Detweiler, Deborah, Mgr-Mktg - General Growth Properties, Inc.; *pg.* 1093, *pg.* 574

Detweiler, Karena, Mgr-Global Mktg & Comm - Bose Corporation; *pg.* 626, *pg.* 820

Detwiler, Robert, Mgr-Product Mktg - InFocus Corporation; *pg.* 644, *pg.* 1503

Detwiller, Bryant, Mgr-Product Mktg - Google Inc.; *pg.* 1249, *pg.* 153

Deutch, Ken, Sr Acct Exec-Adv-Charter Media - Charter Communications, Inc.; *pg.* 274, *pg.* 372

Deuth, Brent, Dir-NARS Product Mktg - Xerox Corporation; *pg.* 494, *pg.* 365

Deutsch, Adam, Sr Dir-Product Dev-Global X Games - ESPN, Inc.; *pg.* 285, *pg.* 340

Deutsch, Bernhard, VP-Product Line Mgmt-Optical Connectivity Solutions - Corning Cable Systems LLC; *pg.* 1407, *pg.* 1378

Deutsch, Ryan, Div VP-Digital Addressable Mktg - Sears Holdings Corporation; *pg.* 1784, *pg.* 618

Deutsch, Samantha, Dir-Adv - American Media, Inc.; *pg.* 1615, *pg.* 410

Devanathan, Sriram, Sr Mgr-Software Dev-Kindle BookStore - Amazon.com, Inc.; *pg.* 1226, *pg.* 1831

Devane, Christine, Mgr-Product Mktg - Rand McNally & Company; *pg.* 1679, *pg.* 661

Devane, Maureen, Sr Mgr-Procurement-Global Insights - PepsiCo, Inc.; *pg.* 259, *pg.* 1327

Devaney, Tom, Dir-Sls - Dexter Magnetic Technologies, Inc.; *pg.* 634, *pg.* 610

Devarasetty, Muralidhar, Dir-Product Line Mgmt - Juniper Networks, Inc.; *pg.* 1260, *pg.* 286

DeVard, Jerri, CMO & Sr VP - The ADT Corporation; *pg.* 612, *pg.* 409

Devault, Adam, Mgr-Mktg Entertainment - Nashville Predators, LLC; *pg.* 565, *pg.* 1652

DeVault, Scott, Specialist-Adv & Collateral - Porsche Cars North America, Inc.; *pg.* 189, *pg.* 518

Devencenzi, Michele, Sr Mgr-Mktg - AT&T; *pg.* 1865, *pg.* 258

Devenecia, Dorothy, Brand Mgr-Baileys & Liqueurs - Diageo North America, Inc.; *pg.* 1961, *pg.* 361

Devenecia, Dorothy, Brand Mgr-Baileys & Liqueurs - Diageo North America Inc.; *pg.* 248, *pg.* 1223

Deveney, Mark, VP-Customer Mktg - Diageo North America Inc.; *pg.* 248, *pg.* 1223

Devenzio, Terry B., Mgr-Medicaid Customer Mktg - Merck & Co., Inc.; *pg.* 1566, *pg.* 1077

Dever, Brianne, Asst Specialist-Mktg Comm - Armstrong World Industries, Inc.; *pg.* 914, *pg.* 1545

Dever, Hugh, Dir-Retail Products & Licensing - Weight Watchers International, Inc.; *pg.* 1609, *pg.* 1313

Devereux, Anne, Chief Strategy Officer - Lantern Lane Entertainment Ltd.; *pg.* 296, *pg.* 56

Devereux, Bob, Mgr-Western States Media Rels - State Farm Mutual Automobile Insurance Co.; *pg.* 1218, *pg.* 557

Devic, Michael, VP-Sls & Mktg - KADANT INC.; *pg.* 1352, *pg.* 858

DeVilla, Richard, Sr VP-Wholesale & Mktg-North America - Ben Sherman USA; *pg.* 19, *pg.* 1202

Devine, Alison, Exec Dir-Mktg, Chanel Fashion, Watches & Fine Jewelry - Chanel, Inc.; *pg.* 503, *pg.* 1211

Devine, Bess, Mgr-Integrated Sls - Forbes.com LLC; *pg.* 1247, *pg.* 1232

Devine, Daniel, Strategist-Digital Mktg - Burton Snowboard Company; *pg.* 1829, *pg.* 1765

Devine, David, Gen Mgr-Fence & Galvanized Mechanical Products - Wheatland Tube Company; *pg.* 121, *pg.* 1594

Devine, Jim, Product Mgr - Walgreen Co.; *pg.* 1608, *pg.* 605

Devine, John, Sr Mgr-Mdsg - Bose Corporation; *pg.* 626, *pg.* 820

Devine, Karen, Dir-Mktg-Intuit QuickBase - Intuit Inc.; *pg.* 769, *pg.* 158

Devine, Kelly, Sr Specialist-Mktg - Comcast Corporation; *pg.* 276, *pg.* 1560

Devine, Michael L., VP-Grocery Products Ops - Hormel Foods Corporation; *pg.* 863, *pg.* 915

Devine, Tracy, Mgr-Mktg - Royal Bank of Canada; *pg.* 800, *pg.* 1942

DeVita, Annette, VP-Mktg-Sally Hansen - Coty, Inc.; *pg.* 506, *pg.* 1219

Devito, Brian, Dir-Creative Svcs - Vineyard Vines LLC; *pg.* 50, *pg.* 379

Devlin, Danny, Mgr-Comml Mktg - Sony Music Entertainment; *pg.* 309, *pg.* 1294

Devlin, Margaret, Recruiter-Sls - The Boston Beer Company, Inc.; *pg.* 239, *pg.* 790

Devlin, Marie, Sr VP-Global Adv, Media, Sponsorships & Insights - American Express Company; *pg.* 712, *pg.* 1190

DeVoe, Stacey, Dir-Shopper Mktg - Safeway Inc.; *pg.* 1032, *pg.* 184

Devonshire, Mark, Product Mgr - Rockwell Automation, Inc.; *pg.* 668, *pg.* 1880

Devore, Alyssa, Dir-Mktg - Calico Corners; *pg.* 691, *pg.* 1543

Devore, Ken, Sr Dir-Customer Svc-Bus Customer Div-Southern California Edison - Edison International; *pg.* 1941, *pg.* 194

Devoto, Kristin, Project Mgr-Mktg - AARON'S, INC.; *pg.* 912, *pg.* 486

DeVries, Cristin, VP-Branded Entertainment & Media Innovation - CBS Corporation; *pg.* 273, *pg.* 1210

DeVries, Denise, Mgr-Mktg-North America - Armstrong International, Inc.; *pg.* 1069, *pg.* 909

DeVries, Natalie, Rep-Field Mktg - Whirlpool Corporation; *pg.* 62, *pg.* 872

deVries, Reynolds, Sr Mgr-Vendor Mktg - Ingram Micro Inc.; *pg.* 415, *pg.* 261

Dew, Allison, VP-Global Mktg-End User Computing - Dell Inc.; *pg.* 383, *pg.* 1737

DeWalt, Teri, Dir-HPC Mktg - Lenovo Group Ltd; *pg.* 427, *pg.* 1384

Dewar, Ian, Sr Mgr-CRM & Loyalty - The North Face, Inc.; *pg.* 1840, *pg.* 252

Dewar, Sharon, Dir-PR - Lincoln Park Zoo; *pg.* 557, *pg.* 580

Dewberry, Jason, VP-Mktg - Garden of Life, Inc.; *pg.* 1532, *pg.* 478

deWees, Ann Marie, Asst Dir-Mktg - Northern Arizona University; *pg.* 606, *pg.* 12

Dewell, Heidi, VP-Creative Svcs-Williams-Sonoma & Williams-Sonoma Home Brands - Williams-Sonoma, Inc.; *pg.* 1140,

First page reference indicates Business Class Edition
Second page reference indicates Geographic Edition

pg. 234
DeWert, Ron, VP-Market Res & Media Strategy - Empire Today, LLC; *pg.* 923, *pg.* 643
DeWerth, Doug, Dir-Digital Mktg - Sterling Jewelers Inc.; *pg.* 13, *pg.* 1402
Dewester, Phil, Dir-Brand Mktg - Olive Garden Italian Restaurant; *pg.* 1742, *pg.* 454
Dewester, Phil, Dir-Brand Mktg - Red Lobster; *pg.* 1747, *pg.* 455
Dewet, Madeleine, Mgr-Catering & Sls - Aramark; *pg.* 1013, *pg.* 1558
Dewey, Tom, Mgr-Mktg-Global - 3M Company; *pg.* 1142, *pg.* 956
Dewhirst, Susan, Mgr-PR & Goodness Programs - Tom's of Maine, Inc.; *pg.* 523, *pg.* 750
Dewitt, Jordan, Head-Brand Mktg & Adv-Canada - Capital One Financial Corporation; *pg.* 730, *pg.* 1789
DeWitte, Matt, Dir-Global Mktg-Merrell - Wolverine World Wide, Inc.; *pg.* 1822, *pg.* 905
DeWolf, Julie, Dir-Retail Mktg - Sunkist Growers, Inc.; *pg.* 899, *pg.* 299
DeWolfe, Kimberly, Dir-Channel Mktg-Global - Avaya Inc.; *pg.* 621, *pg.* 264
DeWolfe, Scott, Dir-Sls & Mktg Support - Siemens; *pg.* 1376, *pg.* 1466
Dewsnap, Hal, Sr VP & Gen Mgr-Sls-US - LoJack Corporation; *pg.* 210, *pg.* 811
Dexter, Stephanie, Jr Brand Mgr-Dos Equis - Heineken USA Inc.; *pg.* 252, *pg.* 1352
Dey, Jenn, Dir-Creative Svcs - Guess?, Inc.; *pg.* 25, *pg.* 132
Deyo, Dan, Product Mgr-Global - Applied Materials, Inc; *pg.* 618, *pg.* 1009
Dezen, Todd, Assoc Dir-Media Rels - March of Dimes Birth Defects Foundation; *pg.* 146, *pg.* 1354
Deziel, Melanie, Strategist-Creative - Time Inc.; *pg.* 1693, *pg.* 1300
Dhall, Meghan, Brand Mgr-Crizal - Essilor of America, Inc.; *pg.* 1412, *pg.* 1680
Dhallan, Namita, Exec VP-Product Strategy & Engrg - Deltek, Inc.; *pg.* 386, *pg.* 1784
Dhamdhere, Neel, Sr Mgr-Competitive Mktg & Mobile - Intel Corporation; *pg.* 645, *pg.* 266
Dhaniwal, Piyush, Product Mgr - Electronic Arts Inc.; *pg.* 951, *pg.* 189
Dhavale, Shantanu, Dir-Mktg-Global - Atmel Corporation; *pg.* 621, *pg.* 238
Dhawan, Puneet, Sr Mgr-Product Plng-Dell Storage - Dell Inc.; *pg.* 383, *pg.* 1737
Dhawan, Rohit, Dir-Product Mgmt - Google Inc.; *pg.* 1249, *pg.* 153
Dhawan, Sonali, Dir-Mktg-India - The Procter & Gamble Company; *pg.* 1129, *pg.* 1418
Dhayagude, Tushar, Dir-Mktg - Atmel Corporation; *pg.* 621, *pg.* 238
Dhoot, Kanupriya, Mgr-Online Mktg - Getty Images, Inc.; *pg.* 1645, *pg.* 1836
Dhyne, Christian, Mgr-Mktg Analytics & Insights - The Walt Disney Company; *pg.* 317, *pg.* 52
Di Como, Luis, Sr VP-Media-Global - Unilever United States, Inc.; *pg.* 904, *pg.* 1061
Di Dia, Dominique, Coord-Mktg & Promos - Los Angeles Kings Hockey Club L.P.; *pg.* 559, *pg.* 135
Di John, Elizabeth, Brand Mgr - John Morrell & Co.; *pg.* 866, *pg.* 1415
Di Leo, Bruno, Sr VP-Sls & Distr - International Business Machines Corporation; *pg.* 418, *pg.* 1138
Di Leo, John, Sr VP-Sls & Svc-Global - DataCard Corporation; *pg.* 382, *pg.* 948
Di Nome, Tom, Sr Mgr-PR - Sony Electronics, Inc.; *pg.* 676, *pg.* 209
Di Pietro, Larry, VP-Sls - Wente Vineyards; *pg.* 1972, *pg.* 122
Di Sano, Stephanie, Acct Mgr-Direct Sls - Twitter, Inc.; *pg.* 1285, *pg.* 228
Di Stadio, Christine, Dir-Digital, Mobile & Social Media - KHOU-TV, Inc.; *pg.* 294, *pg.* 1709
Di Ubaldi, Darren, Specialist-Mktg-Online Storefronts - VITAMIN SHOPPE, INC.; *pg.* 1608, *pg.* 1098
Di Vito, Paul, VP-Mktg-Irish & North American Whiskey - Pernod Ricard USA, Inc.; *pg.* 1968, *pg.* 1332
Dia, Alia, Brand Mgr-Grey Goose - Bacardi USA, Inc.; *pg.* 1956, *pg.* 417
Dia, Lana, Asst Mgr-Mktg - Aldo Group; *pg.* 1804, *pg.* 1959
Diamant, Doug, Product Mktg-Non-Traditional Products & Svcs - LifeLock Inc.; *pg.* 776, *pg.* 26
Diamantidis, Stelios, Sr Mgr-Product Mgmt & Mktg - Synopsys, Inc.; *pg.* 480, *pg.* 162
Diamantis, Angela, Mgr-Strategic Mktg - ScanSource, Inc.; *pg.* 671, *pg.* 1618
Diamond, Adam, Sr VP-Mktg - Eddie Bauer, Inc.; *pg.* 40, *pg.* 1814
Diamond, Alex, Assoc Mgr-Consumer Mktg - Home Box Office, Inc.; *pg.* 290, *pg.* 1240
Diamond, Gordon, Head-Comm & Sls Ops - Hewlett-Packard Company; *pg.* 404, *pg.* 175
Diamond, James, Mgr-Traffic-Creative Svcs - AutoTrader, Inc.; *pg.* 1230, *pg.* 490
Diamond, Jenny, Mgr-Mktg - Meredith Corporation; *pg.* 1663, *pg.* 705
Diamond, Kim, Sr Dir-Corp Comm - Alexion Pharmaceuticals, Inc.; *pg.* 1489, *pg.* 341
Diamond, Laura, Rep-Media Rels - Georgia Institute Of Technology; *pg.* 602, *pg.* 506
Diamond, Michael, Sr VP-Sls & New Bus Dev - Mitek Systems, Inc.; *pg.* 440, *pg.* 204
Diamond, Nicolas, Brand Mgr - Amazon.com, Inc.; *pg.* 1226, *pg.* 1831
Diamond, Steve, Sr Dir-Product Mktg & Sls Cloud - salesforce.com, inc.; *pg.* 1278, *pg.* 226
Diamond-Khoury, Kim, Mgr-Tech Sls-Natl - Henry Schein, Inc.; *pg.* 1541, *pg.* 1180
Diamonon, John, Brand Mktg Mgr - Capcom USA, Inc.; *pg.* 950, *pg.* 254
Dias, Maria, Sr Mgr-Corp Comm - Getty Images, Inc.; *pg.* 1645, *pg.* 1836
Dias, Megan, Mgr-Mktg-Enterprise Mktg & Comm - American Medical Association; *pg.* 130, *pg.* 564
Dias, Pedro Ribeiro, Brand Mgr-TAP Maintenance & Engrg - TAP Portugal; *pg.* 1925, *pg.* 1098
Diaz, Alma, Mgr-Shopper Mktg - Safeway Inc.; *pg.* 1032, *pg.* 184
Diaz, Aubrey, Category Mgr-Mktg - Publix Super Markets, Inc.; *pg.* 1031, *pg.* 437
Diaz, Cara Forte, Sr Mgr-PR - Dolce & Gabbana USA, Inc.; *pg.* 23, *pg.* 1225
Diaz, Carlos Andres, Mgr-Mktg-Colombia - Nestle Purina PetCare Company; *pg.* 1479, *pg.* 1000
Diaz, David, Engr-Deep Water Sls-Gulf of Mexico - Schlumberger Limited; *pg.* 801, *pg.* 1714
Diaz, Diana C., Sr Dir-Corp & Community Rels - Univision Communications Inc.; *pg.* 683, *pg.* 1307
Diaz, Fred M., Sr VP-Sls, Mktg & Ops - Nissan North America, Inc.; *pg.* 186, *pg.* 1633
Diaz, Genaro Perez, VP-Mktg-Global - P.F. Chang's China Bistro, Inc.; *pg.* 1030, *pg.* 24
Diaz, Jennifer, Sr Mgr-Creative Svcs - Hologic, Inc.; *pg.* 1416, *pg.* 784
Diaz, Jennifer, Mgr-Global Mktg Comm, Life Sciences & Medical - Pall Corporation; *pg.* 232, *pg.* 1323
Diaz, Jesus, Mgr-Multicultural Field Mktg - PepsiCo, Inc.; *pg.* 259, *pg.* 1327
Diaz, Kenia, Product Mgr - Goya Foods, Inc.; *pg.* 859, *pg.* 1075
Diaz, Marta, Sr Mgr-Customer Loyalty & Customer Insights - Ryder System, Inc.; *pg.* 1922, *pg.* 446
Diaz, Marusia, Brand Mgr-Downy Mexico - The Procter & Gamble Company; *pg.* 1129, *pg.* 1418
Diaz, Natalia, Asst Mgr-Customer Mktg - Revlon Consumer Products Corporation; *pg.* 521, *pg.* 1286
Diaz, Natalia, Asst Mgr-Customer Mktg - Revlon, Inc.; *pg.* 521, *pg.* 1286
Diaz, Peter L., Pres-Media Ops - Gannett Co., Inc.; *pg.* 289, *pg.* 1681
Diaz, Sandra, Sr VP-Mktg - JustFab, Inc.; *pg.* 27, *pg.* 80
Diaz, Sarah, Sr Mgr-Global Product Trng-Go-To-Market - Oakley, Inc.; *pg.* 1840, *pg.* 86
Diaz, Vanessa, Mgr-Mktg-Northern California - Meritage Homes Corporation; *pg.* 97, *pg.* 23
Diaz, Xochitl, Sr Mgr - Delphi Automotive LLP; *pg.* 204, *pg.* 910
Dibble, Joel, Dir-PR - Robert Half International Inc.; *pg.* 462, *pg.* 145
DiBease, Michael L., VP-Mktg - Batesville Casket Company, Inc.; *pg.* 1393, *pg.* 673
DiBella, John, VP-Mktg & Sls - Simulations Plus, Inc.; *pg.* 470, *pg.* 121
DiBianca, Nicole, Specialist-Digital Mktg-Non Paint Products - The Sherwin-Williams Company; *pg.* 1447, *pg.* 1435
Dibiase, Greg, VP-Ethanol Sls & Mktg - Pacific Ethanol, Inc.; *pg.* 982, *pg.* 197
Dibiase, Sonya, Product Mgr - Reebok-CCM Hockey, Inc.; *pg.* 1844, *pg.* 1960
DiBlasi, Nicole, Reg Mgr-Sls & Mktg - Wells Fargo & Company; *pg.* 819, *pg.* 232
Dibs, Todd, Sls Mgr-Natl - San Jose Convention/Visitors Bureau; *pg.* 1005, *pg.* 250
DiCanio, Theresa, Sr Specialist-Mktg Comm - Videojet Technologies Inc.; *pg.* 489, *pg.* 671
DiCapua, Lawrence, Head-Revenue Mktg Center of Excellence-Global - General Electric Company; *pg.* 1297, *pg.* 347
Dicarlo, Janine, VP-Mktg - WABC-TV Inc.; *pg.* 317, *pg.* 1312
DiCarlo, Kate, Sr Mgr-Comm-Global Old Spice, Gillette, Safeguard, Secret & Olay - The Procter & Gamble Company; *pg.* 1129, *pg.* 1418
DiCarlo, Kirsten, Dir-Mktg - Fisher-Price, Inc.; *pg.* 953, *pg.* 1156
Dicarlo, Nicholas, VP & Gen Mgr-Immersive Products & Virtual Reality - Samsung Telecommunications America, LLC; *pg.* 670, *pg.* 1736
DiCarlo, Rachel, VP-PR - American Eagle Outfitters, Inc.; *pg.* 37, *pg.* 1572
Dice, Justin, Sr Mgr-Mktg-Analytics, Insights & Targeted Mktg - AT&T Mobility LLC; *pg.* 619, *pg.* 488
Dichiro, Kayla, Mgr-Internet Mktg - Ross-Simons Inc.; *pg.* 1783, *pg.* 1600
DiCianni, Denise, Mgr-Adv & Mktg - Tribune Media Company; *pg.* 1696, *pg.* 592
Dicicco, Aimee, Sr VP-Sls - FedEx Corporation; *pg.* 1907, *pg.* 1642
Dick, George, Sr VP & Dir-Affiliate Mktg - Fifth Third Bancorp; *pg.* 752, *pg.* 1413
Dick, Joelle, Brand Mgr - Pfizer Inc.; *pg.* 1581, *pg.* 1278
Dick, Jon, Dir-Mktg - Trunk Club; *pg.* 49, *pg.* 593
Dicken, Allie, Asst Mgr-Mktg - Phoenix Suns; *pg.* 576, *pg.* 19
Dickens, Erick, VP-Mktg - King's Hawaiian Bakery West, Inc.; *pg.* 869, *pg.* 293
Dickens, Mark, Mgr-Adv & Promos - Bridgestone Americas, Inc.; *pg.* 1879, *pg.* 1648
Dickens, Mark, Dir-PR-Global - United Parcel Service, Inc.; *pg.* 1928, *pg.* 522
Dickens-Hunter, Deb, Asst VP-Product Mgmt - Selective Insurance Group, Inc.; *pg.* 1216, *pg.* 1045
Dicker, Joy E., Sr Dir-Mktg & Alliance Mgmt - MannKind Corporation; *pg.* 1558, *pg.* 299
Dickerhoof, Linda, Dir-Mktg - Aspire Lifestyles of the Americas; *pg.* 1230, *pg.* 1770
Dickerson, Alice, Corp Mgr-Mktg Comm - AGC Glass North America, Inc.; *pg.* 65, *pg.* 482
Dickerson, Ashley, Sr Specialist-PR - Canon U.S.A., Inc.; *pg.* 1404, *pg.* 1178
Dickerson, Eric, Dir-PR - Allison Transmission, Inc.; *pg.* 198, *pg.* 682
Dickerson, Eva, Sr Mgr-Ops & Community Affairs - Microsoft Corporation; *pg.* 435, *pg.* 1824
Dickerson, Ryan, Product Mgr-Social Tech - Cox Media Group; *pg.* 280, *pg.* 502
Dickert, Corey, Dir-Product Mgmt - Milwaukee Electric Tool Corp.; *pg.* 1056, *pg.* 1855
Dickert, Linda H., Mgr-Mktg - M/I Homes, Inc.; *pg.* 95, *pg.* 1441
Dickey, Ashley, Mgr-Mktg - Sam's Club; *pg.* 1783, *pg.* 29
Dickey, Chuck, Dir-Mktg - Mercury Insurance Company; *pg.* 1208, *pg.* 136
Dickey, Corinne, Specialist-Project-Digital, Social & Global Partner Mktg - Cisco Systems, Inc.; *pg.* 372, *pg.* 240
Dickey, Georgianne, Mgr-Mktg - Affinia Group Intermediate Holdings Inc.; *pg.* 197, *pg.* 1373
Dickey, Jody, Asst VP-Mktg - Caliber Home Loans, Inc.; *pg.* 728, *pg.* 1717
Dickey, Stephanie, VP-Sls & Creative Dev - Horizon Designs, Inc.; *pg.* 695, *pg.* 1011
Dickinson, Doug, Mgr-Media Rels - Linear Technology Corp.; *pg.* 652, *pg.* 147
Dickinson, Phillip, VP-Sls - Hubbell Power Systems, Inc.; *pg.* 643, *pg.* 1614
Dickinson, Rob, Sr Mgr-Software Engrg - Dell Inc.; *pg.* 383, *pg.* 1737
Dickinson, Rose, Mgr-Mktg & Adv - National Hot Rod Association; *pg.* 149, *pg.* 99
Dickinson, Tyler, VP-Sls-Regional - Coverall North America, Inc.; *pg.* 329, *pg.* 421
Dickinson, Whitney, Mgr-Mktg - Lions Gate Entertainment Corp.; *pg.* 296, *pg.* 274
Dickman, Kate, Head-Brand Mktg-Global - Airbnb, Inc.; *pg.* 1226, *pg.* 211

Dickson, Angela, Mgr-Mktg - American Architectural Manufacturers Association; pg. 126, pg. 658
Dickson, Dave, Sr Product Mktg Mgr-Digital Publ - Adobe Systems Incorporated; pg. 342, pg. 235
Dickson, Hal, Dir-Product Remarketing - Mack Trucks, Inc.; pg. 183, pg. 1375
Dickson, Kelly, Mgr-Revenue Mktg Ops - CommScope, Inc.; pg. 278, pg. 1378
Dickson, Kerry, Planner-Product Mktg & Strategy - Volkswagen Group of America, Inc.; pg. 194, pg. 1785
Dickson, Rex, Dir-Creative - Electronic Arts Inc.; pg. 951, pg. 189
Dickson, Richard, Sr VP-Strategy, Mktg, Price & Promos - Loblaw Companies Limited; pg. 1026, pg. 1918
Dickson, Ricky, VP-Sls & Mktg - Blue Bell Creameries, L.P.; pg. 1851, pg. 1668
Dickson, Sherry, Specialist-Mktg-Home Appliance Div - Brother International Corporation - USA; pg. 53, pg. 1046
Dickstein, Andrea, Dir eBusiness & Mktg Comm - Eppendorf North America; pg. 1412, pg. 1164
Dickstein, Jeffrey, Dir-Ad Sales - Ubisoft Inc.; pg. 589, pg. 229
DiCorleto, Kristen, Dir-Affinity Mktg Programs - Liberty Mutual Insurance Group Inc.; pg. 1205, pg. 797
DiCristina, Mark, Dir-Mktg - The Rocket Science Group, LLC; pg. 1278, pg. 519
Didier, Kristen, Corp Mgr-Adv, Media & Brand - SeaWorld Parks & Entertainment LLC; pg. 582, pg. 456
DiDonato, Sarah, Mgr-PR - Microsoft Corporation; pg. 435, pg. 1824
DiDuca, Elizabeth, Area Dir-Mktg & Bus Dev - Simon Property Group, Inc.; pg. 1112, pg. 690
Diebel, Craig, VP-Adv & Digital Media - Fort Worth Star-Telegram; pg. 1642, pg. 1694
Diederich, Ann, Dir-Mktg - Intuit Inc.; pg. 769, pg. 158
Diedrich, Linda, Project Mgr-Mktg & Comm - The Vollrath Company LLC; pg. 1139, pg. 1894
Diedrichsen, Jan, Sr VP-Mktg - AMC Networks Inc.; pg. 269, pg. 1189
Diefenbach, John, Dir-Retail Sls-New England - T-Mobile US, Inc.; pg. 676, pg. 1816
Diegnan, Dan, Dir-Mktg-Electrical & Electronic - EIS, Inc.; pg. 80, pg. 504
Diego, Dee, Mgr-Mktg & Relationship-UnitedHealthcare Alliance - Ameriprise Financial, Inc.; pg. 715, pg. 930
Diehl, Kevin, Mgr-Mktg-US - Dr. Martens AirWair USA LLC; pg. 1807, pg. 1502
Diehl, Mark, Sr VP-Sls - Dansko Inc.; pg. 1807, pg. 1594
Diehl, Meghan, Mgr-Mktg - Humana, Inc.; pg. 1204, pg. 734
Diehl, Mike, Product Mgr-Personal Workstations - Hewlett-Packard Company; pg. 404, pg. 175
Dieker, Barbara, Dir-Mktg Effectiveness - Adobe Systems Incorporated; pg. 342, pg. 235
Diekmann, Ashley, Product Mgr - adidas America Inc.; pg. 1803, pg. 1500
Diel, Jordan, Media Buyer - Cabela's Incorporated; pg. 535, pg. 1019
Diemer, Pat, Mgr-Sls - Valero Energy Corporation; pg. 986, pg. 1743
Diep, Lynn, VP & Sr Mgr-Mktg - Union Bank, N.A.; pg. 813, pg. 230
Dierberg, Keith, Gen Mgr-Grocery Mktg - Community Coffee Company LLC; pg. 849, pg. 741
Dierig, Jeff, Specialist-Mktg & Internet-Global - Sweco; pg. 1380, pg. 728
Dierke, Laura A., Dir-Thrivent Choice, Mktg & Products - Thrivent Financial for Lutherans; pg. 1219, pg. 944
Dierkes, Kaitlyn, Mgr-Worldwide PR-Consumer Personal Sys - Hewlett-Packard Company; pg. 404, pg. 175
Dierking, Elizabeth, Brand Mgr - NBTY, Inc.; pg. 1572, pg. 1338
Dierks, Jeffrey, Dir-Pain Care Mktg - Janssen Pharmaceutica Products, L.P.; pg. 1548, pg. 1125
Dieruf, Adam, Mgr-Mktg-Programmatic Media - Target Corporation; pg. 1786, pg. 942
Dieruf, Keith, Sr Dir-Mktg & Media Strategy - Life Time Fitness, Inc.; pg. 1556, pg. 920
Diesel, Scott, Dir-Mktg Comm - Thermo Fisher Scientific Inc.; pg. 1431, pg. 854
Dieterle, Mark, Dir-Bus & Product Dev - Quest Safety Products, Inc.; pg. 1371, pg. 689
Dieterle, Michael M., VP-Field Mktg & Underwriting - Amerisure Mutual Insurance Company; pg. 1191, pg. 885
Dietrich, Hattie, Mgr-Client Svcs & ECommerce Digital Mktg - Cardinal Health, Inc.; pg. 1512, pg. 1448
Dietsch, Alicia, VP-Mktg Comm - AT&T Inc.; pg. 1867, pg. 1674
Dietsch, Nicholas, Sr Mgr-Mktg Analytics - Red Hat, Inc.; pg. 460, pg. 1388
Dietz, Alex, Product Mgr-Hospitality & Travel - SAS Institute Inc.; pg. 466, pg. 1361
Dietz, Diane M., CMO & Exec VP - Safeway Inc.; pg. 1032, pg. 184
Dietz, Diane M., CMO & Exec VP - Vons A Safeway Company; pg. 1036, pg. 43
Dietz, Jennifer, Planner-Mdse - Carter's, Inc.; pg. 21, pg. 491
Dietz, Mark, VP-Mktg - John Morrell & Co.; pg. 866, pg. 1415
Dietz, Patrick C., VP-Mktg - DOUGLAS DYNAMICS, INC.; pg. 204, pg. 1874
Dietz, Rich, Sr Product Mgr-Digital Fundraising - Abila, Inc.; pg. 340, pg. 1660
Dietz, Stacey, Grp Dir & Dir-Creative-Adv & PR - Tiffany & Co.; pg. 13, pg. 1299
Dietz, Steven, Mgr-Segment Mktg - INVISTA B.V.; pg. 1168, pg. 723
Diffenbach, Julie, VP & Grp Dir-Media - DIRECTV Group Holdings, LLC; pg. 281, pg. 79
Diffley, Tina, Product Mgr - PNY Technologies, Inc.; pg. 455, pg. 1105
DiFilippo, Louise, Mgr-Dev & Production - The Vanguard Group, Inc.; pg. 816, pg. 1550
Diforio, Steve, Dir-Global Digital Media-Redken, Phrenology & Mizani - L'Oreal USA; pg. 514, pg. 1252
DiFranco, Concetta, Sr Specialist-PR - Allscripts Healthcare Solutions, Inc.; pg. 1492, pg. 563
DiFuccia, Jason, Dir-Mktg, Polaris Off-Road Vehicles - Polaris Industries Inc.; pg. 1709, pg. 928
DiGangi, Diane, Sr Dir-Managed Markets Reg Accts - Takeda Pharmaceuticals USA, Inc.; pg. 1600, pg. 605
DiGangi, Kim, Mgr-Mktg - National Association of Realtors; pg. 1666, pg. 584
DiGeronimo, Lauren, VP-Media Rels - Citizens Financial Group, Inc.; pg. 737, pg. 1606
DiGeronimo, Richard, Exec VP-Product & Strategy - Charter Communications, Inc.; pg. 274, pg. 372
Diggs, Kip, Mgr-Media Rels - State Farm Mutual Automobile Insurance Co.; pg. 1218, pg. 557
DiGiacomo, Laura, Mgr-Bus Dev Mktg - UnitedHealth Group Incorporated; pg. 1221, pg. 950
Digioia, Dan, Mgr-Mktg - EAO Switch Corporation; pg. 1046, pg. 356
Dignan, Andy, Sr Dir-Collaboration Market & Solutions Dev - Cisco Systems, Inc.; pg. 372, pg. 240
Dignan, Ben, Mgr-Digital & Social Media Mktg - Showtime Networks Inc.; pg. 308, pg. 1291
Dignan, Patrick, VP-Adv Sls - The Street, Inc.; pg. 1283, pg. 1296
Diiorio, Matt, Asst VP-Brand & Mktg-Global - MetLife, Inc.; pg. 1208, pg. 1258
Dijk, Arjan, VP-Mktg - Google Inc.; pg. 1249, pg. 153
Dikowitz, Jerry, Sr VP-Mktg & Adv - Armitron Watch Division; pg. 1, pg. 1174
Dilando, Rich, Mgr-Global Product Mktg-Classics & Basketball Footwear - Reebok International Ltd.; pg. 1817, pg. 811
Dilandro, Christine, Sr VP & Head-Media & Integrated Mktg - Citigroup Inc.; pg. 735, pg. 1212
Dilday, Chris, Dir-Sls-Natl - Intown Suites Management, Inc.; pg. 1098, pg. 513
DiLenardi, Steve, Sr Mgr-Grp Tickets & Special Projects - Chicago Blackhawk Hockey Team, Inc.; pg. 538, pg. 569
DiLeonardo, Albert T., Pres-Vector East & CEO-Vector Sls - Vector Marketing Corporation; pg. 1139, pg. 1318
Dilger, Carol, Mgr-Corp Media - Ariens Company Inc.; pg. 700, pg. 1855
Dilger, Maureen, Dir-Global Brand Strategy & Mktg-FurReal Friends - Hasbro, Inc.; pg. 954, pg. 1603
Diliberto, Lisa, Sr Dir-Brand Mktg-Global - The Hertz Corporation; pg. 1911, pg. 450
Dill, Adam, VP-Field Sls-Walmart - General Mills, Inc.; pg. 828, pg. 933
Dill, Jaimie, Dir-Programmatic Sls - BBC Worldwide America Inc.; pg. 271, pg. 1201
Dill, Jennifer, Assoc Dir-Media-Turner Media Grp - Turner Broadcasting System, Inc.; pg. 314, pg. 521
Dill, Michael, Dir-Mktg Tech - Fluor Corporation; pg. 82, pg. 1719
Dillard, Jeff, Mgr-Sls - Lazy Days R.V. Center, Inc.; pg. 182, pg. 467
Dillard, Kristen, Head-QuickBooks Payments Product-Intuit - Intuit Inc.; pg. 769, pg. 158
Dillard, Melanie, Corp Mgr-Mktg - Popeye's Chicken & Biscuits; pg. 1745, pg. 517
Dillard, Melanie, Corp Mgr-Mktg - Popeyes Louisiana Kitchen, Inc.; pg. 1745, pg. 517
Dillavou, Gaylon, Engr-Mktg - Intel Corporation; pg. 645, pg. 266
Dille, Pete, CMO - Tapjoy, Inc.; pg. 1396, pg. 228
Dillen, Jeffery C., Reg Mgr-Sls-Midwest - Noshok Inc.; pg. 1366, pg. 1406
Diller, Heather, Product Mgr-Partner Digital - Starbucks Corporation; pg. 897, pg. 1840
Dilley, Justin, Sr Product Mgr-Kindle Fire - Amazon.com, Inc.; pg. 1226, pg. 1831
Dillner, Scott, Dir-Mktg Svcs - SPX Corporation; pg. 218, pg. 1369
Dillon, Bob, Dir-Global Display Sls & Strategy - Google Inc.; pg. 1249, pg. 153
Dillon, Brendan, Product Mgr-Matls - Stratasys, Inc.; pg. 476, pg. 923
Dillon, Daniel W., Dir-Retail Sls - Herff Jones, Inc.; pg. 7, pg. 686
Dillon, Jackie, Mgr-Technical Mktg - Xerox Corporation; pg. 494, pg. 365
Dillon, Jarrod, Exec VP-Sls & Mktg - Lightning Hockey LP; pg. 557, pg. 474
Dillon, Jim, Mgr-Product Mktg - Brooks Instrument, LLC; pg. 1403, pg. 1537
Dillon, Kevin, Sr Dir-Corp Dev - Pfizer Inc.; pg. 1581, pg. 1278
Dillon, Meryl, Assoc Brand Mgr & Head-Mktg-Air Care, Glade Candles - S.C. Johnson & Son, Inc.; pg. 334, pg. 1889
Dillon, Paul, VP-Sls, Mktg & Svc - Canlan Ice Sports Corporation; pg. 536, pg. 1907
Dillon, Sanyu, Sr VP & Dir-Mktg-Random House Publ Grp - Penguin Random House; pg. 1675, pg. 1276
Dillree, Jessica, Coord-Mktg Comm - Louisville Convention & Visitors Bureau; pg. 998, pg. 736
Dills, Mark, Dir-Production - The Hamilton Spectator; pg. 1647, pg. 1921
Dilnik, Rebecca, Head-Mktg Res Technical - Kimberly-Clark Corporation; pg. 1461, pg. 1720
Dilts, Jessica, Specialist-Sls - Rockwell Medical Technologies, Inc.; pg. 1590, pg. 913
DiLullo, John, Exec VP-Worldwide Sls - F5 Networks, Inc.; pg. 396, pg. 1835
Dilworth, Becki, Sr VP-Mktg - Bridgeline Digital, Inc.; pg. 364, pg. 861
Dimaano, Kim, Mgr-Strategic Pursuit Mktg - Hewlett-Packard Company; pg. 404, pg. 175
DiMaggio, Anthony, Mgr-Sls & Bus Dev - FMC Lithium Division; pg. 1163, pg. 1366
Dimakis, Dina, Mgr-Mktg - Avis Budget Group, Inc.; pg. 1900, pg. 1102
DiMarco, Laura, Dir-Media - Showtime Networks Inc.; pg. 308, pg. 1291
DiMarco, Peter, VP-VAR Sls-Computer Products Div - D&H Distributing Co., Inc.; pg. 381, pg. 1536
Dimaria, John, VP-Sls - Townecraft, Inc.; pg. 1139, pg. 1071
DiMartino, Cheryl, VP-Mktg - Time Inc.; pg. 1693, pg. 1300
Dimartino, Linda, Brand Mgr-Info Center - AstraZeneca Pharmaceuticals LP; pg. 1497, pg. 389
DiMarzio, Mark, VP-Mktg & Bus Dev - Garnet Hill; pg. 1771, pg. 1034
DiMarzo, Robert, VP-Comml Dev & Product Category Mgmt-Animal Health Grp - Henry Schein, Inc.; pg. 1541, pg. 1180
Dimascio, Meg, Mgr-Field Mktg - Dunkin' Brands Group, Inc.; pg. 1727, pg. 810
Dimatos, Annette, Exec Dir-Mktg & Adv - Sony Pictures Entertainment Inc.; pg. 309, pg. 72
DiMatteo, Tosca, Brand Mgr - Pernod Ricard USA, Inc.; pg. 1968, pg. 1332
DiMattesa, Christiana, Sr Mgr-Retail Mktg - Under Armour, Inc.; pg. 49, pg. 759
Dimeo, Dave, Sr Dir - Hewlett-Packard Company; pg. 404, pg. 175
DiMicco, Holly, Dir-Comml Aviation Svcs-Reg Mktg - The Boeing Company; pg. 225, pg. 567
DiMichele, Patricia, Mgr-Adv Dev - The Procter & Gamble Company; pg. 1129, pg. 1418
DiMiero, Mandy, Product Mgr - SKECHERS U.S.A., INC.; pg. 1819, pg. 143
Dimisko, Brian N., Div Mgr-Energy Efficiency Svcs & Natural Gas Mktg - Central Hudson Gas & Electric Corporation; pg. 1937, pg. 1324

First page reference indicates Business Class Edition
Second page reference indicates Geographic Edition

Dimitri, Janai, Dir-Digital & Email Mktg - Guthy-Renker LLC; pg. 289, pg. 273
Dimitrievski, Elizabeth, Sr Product Mgr-Mktg & Comm-Bus Products & Svcs - Canadian Imperial Bank of Commerce; pg. 729, pg. 1935
Dimitriou, Jaclyn, Sr Mgr-Mktg - Standard & Poor's Ratings Services; pg. 805, pg. 1296
Dimitroff, Mike, VP-Sls & Mktg - Chicago White Metal Casting, Inc.; pg. 1153, pg. 556
Dimitry, Irene, VP-Mktg & Renewables-DTE Electric - DTE Energy Company; pg. 1940, pg. 880
Dimmick, Sean, VP-Retail Chain Sls - Ste. Michelle Wine Estates Ltd.; pg. 1970, pg. 1847
Dimmitt, Craig, Bus Mgr - Porterville Recorder; pg. 1677, pg. 185
Dimodica, Alexandra, Head-Natl Mktg & Specialist - Deloitte & Touche USA LLP; pg. 743, pg. 1222
Dimond-Kase, Lisa, Specialist-Mktg Comm - Xerox Corporation; pg. 494, pg. 365
Dimonte, Annalisa, Dir-Relational Mktg-Worldwide - Gucci America Inc.; pg. 6, pg. 1237
Dimou, Victoria, Dir-Creative Grp-Timberland - V.F. Corporation; pg. 34, pg. 1376
Dimperio, Giovanna, Mgr-Digital Mktg & Social Media - Lands' End, Inc.; pg. 1776, pg. 1857
Dimson, Robert, Sr Dir-Natl Field Mktg - Church's Chicken, Inc.; pg. 1722, pg. 493
Dimuccio, Kristen, Sr Brand Mgr-Mktg - Hasbro, Inc.; pg. 954, pg. 1603
DiMuzio, Joe, Mgr-Mktg - Wells Fargo & Company; pg. 819, pg. 232
Din, Norman, VP-Strategic Sls - Wheels Inc.; pg. 1931, pg. 607
Dinallo, Bob, Reg Mgr-Sls - Eberhard Manufacturing Division; pg. 1046, pg. 1475
Dinardo, Chris, Head-Mktg - AstraZeneca Pharmaceuticals LP; pg. 1497, pg. 389
Dince, Adam, Dir-Earned Media-SB - Deluxe Corporation; pg. 1634, pg. 964
Dincer, Umut, Dir-Online Mktg - The Home Depot, Inc.; pg. 1050, pg. 510
Dincin, Bruce, Sr Dir-Media Strategy & Analytics - Choice Hotels International, Inc.; pg. 1086, pg. 775
Dineen, Hugh, VP & Head-Global Marketing-Skincare & Personal Care - Avon Products, Inc.; pg. 500, pg. 1198
Dineen, Michael, VP-Sls & Mktg - Streamlight Inc.; pg. 1306, pg. 1527
Dinello, Nicole, Dir-Mktg - Bristol-Myers Squibb Company; pg. 1509, pg. 1206
Ding, Bonnie, Program Mgr-Digital Mktg - MasterCard Incorporated; pg. 779, pg. 1325
Ding, Helly, Brand Mgr-Zone Perfect - Abbott Nutrition; pg. 1485, pg. 1437
Ding, Jason, Sr Dir-Performance Engrg-SaaS - salesforce.com, inc.; pg. 1278, pg. 226
Ding, Lester, Brand Mgr - The Hartz Mountain Corp.; pg. 1476, pg. 1120
Dinges, Valerie F., Mgr-Respiratory Brand Payer Mktg - GlaxoSmithKline; pg. 1536, pg. 1565
Dingle, Don, Assoc Specialist-Natl Mktg - Xerox Corporation; pg. 494, pg. 365
Dinh, Quyen, Mgr-Integrated Mktg & Promotions - American Diabetes Association; pg. 127, pg. 1770
Dinh, Rosie, Acct Exec-Mktg Comm - Varian Medical Systems, Inc.; pg. 1434, pg. 178
Dinh, Tonia, Sr Mgr-Mktg - salesforce.com, inc.; pg. 1278, pg. 226
Dinino, Anthony, Sr VP-Insert Media - InfoGroup; pg. 414, pg. 350
Dinka, Tsega, Sr Dir-Digital Product - Dollar Shave Club, Inc.; pg. 507, pg. 273
Dinkeldein, Jonathan, Dir-Mktg Comm EMEA - Eaton Corporation; pg. 1331, pg. 1429
Dinman, Joshua, Sr Dir-Mktg Comm - Orbital ATK; pg. 1425, pg. 1779
Dinndorf, Mark, Brand Mgr - Red Wing Shoe Company, Inc.; pg. 1817, pg. 954
Dinneen, Leslie Hernandez, Mgr-Product Mktg-Employment Brand - Google Inc.; pg. 1249, pg. 153
Dinneen, Mike, Sr VP & Dir-Mktg, Product Mgmt & PR - Sun Bancorp, Inc.; pg. 806, pg. 1127
Dinnsen, Liz, Exec Dir-Media - AT&T Inc.; pg. 1867, pg. 1674
Dinon, Jessica, Mgr-PR & Comm-Olive Garden - Darden Restaurants, Inc.; pg. 1724, pg. 453
Dinsdale, Richard, Dir-Mktg-Employer Sponsored Retiree Health - UnitedHealth Group Incorporated; pg. 1221, pg. 950
Dinsdale, Scott, Head-Media & Entertainment-ANZ & APAC - Accenture; pg. 1392, pg. 1186
Dinsmore, Bob, Specialist-Outside Sls - Southern Lumber & Millwork Corp.; pg. 112, pg. 1613
Dinu, Raluca, Sr VP-Sls & Mktg-Global - GigOptix, Inc.; pg. 400, pg. 245
Dinucci, Sarah, Mgr-Product Dev-Michael Kors Jewelry - Fossil Group, Inc.; pg. 5, pg. 1735
DiNunzio, Ryan, Sr Mgr-Mktg-Football/CORE Sports - New Era Cap Company Inc.; pg. 1840, pg. 1155
Dionelli, Maria, Mgr-Mktg-Global Personal Care - Colgate-Palmolive Company; pg. 504, pg. 1215
Dionisi, Rob, VP-Sls & Mktg - Essar Steel Algoma Inc.; pg. 81, pg. 1933
Dionisio, John, Sr Dir-Performance Mktg - Zynga Inc.; pg. 1292, pg. 235
Dionisio, Lori, Office Mgr-Adv - East Valley Tribune; pg. 1638, pg. 25
Dionne, David, Sr Dir-Syco Brand Dev - Sysco Corporation; pg. 1035, pg. 1716
Dionne, Jim, Dir-Global Procurement-Strategy, Ops & Mktg - Beam Suntory Inc.; pg. 1957, pg. 599
Dionne, John, Sr Dir-Global Alliances & Partners - Kronos Incorporated; pg. 425, pg. 813
Dioury, Ali, Mgr-Mktg Dev-MDM - Intel Corporation; pg. 645, pg. 266
Dipaola, Charlene Iniguez, Sr Dir-Bus Intelligence - SpinMedia; pg. 1282, pg. 104
DiPaola, Matthew, Rep Mgr-Bus Dev-Direct Sls, Online Mktg, Social Media & SaaS - Deluxe Corporation; pg. 1634, pg. 964
Dipasquale, Andrea, Sr Dir-Digital Strategy - International Business Machines Corporation; pg. 418, pg. 1138
DiPasquale, Patricia, Sr Mgr-Internet Mktg - Canon U.S.A., Inc.; pg. 1404, pg. 1178
DiPietro, Robert, Grp VP-Bus Dev & Product Strategy - Affinion Group, Inc.; pg. 1225, pg. 372
Diplock, Jason, VP-Ticket Sls & Svc - Toronto Blue Jays Baseball Club; pg. 588, pg. 1945
Diplock, Mike, Mgr-Technical Sls-Client Architects - IBM Canada Limited; pg. 411, pg. 1923
DiPrima, Sandi, Project Mgr-Mktg Comm - Fresenius Medical Care North America; pg. 1531, pg. 851
DiPrimio, Edward M., Mgr-Mktg-Event Sponsorship-NA & LA - Gartner, Inc.; pg. 1248, pg. 374
DiProsa, David, Dir-Sls - WHAM-TV; pg. 321, pg. 1338
Dircks, Robert, Sr Dir-Category Mktg - The Schwan Food Company; pg. 894, pg. 928
Director, Jennifer, Sr Mgr-Digital Paid Media Mktg - American Express Company; pg. 712, pg. 1190
Dirga, Carol, Sr Assoc Dir-Creative Svcs - Bentley University; pg. 598, pg. 850
Dirienzo, Amanda, Mgr-Sls - CareerBuilder, LLC; pg. 1234, pg. 568
Dirks, Kyle, Supvr-Adv Production - Meredith Corporation; pg. 1663, pg. 705
DiSalle, Tony, VP-Buick & GMC Mktg-US - General Motors Company; pg. 175, pg. 881
Disalvo, Kathleen, Coord-Mktg - Ameristar Casinos, Inc.; pg. 528, pg. 1022
DiSalvo, Lino, Dir-Creative - Paramount Pictures Corporation; pg. 304, pg. 138
DiSalvo, Tony, VP-Sls - Creative Loafing, Inc.; pg. 1631, pg. 472
DiSante, Cathy, VP-Adv - Art Van Furniture, Inc.; pg. 914, pg. 912
DiSanto, Bethany, Dir-Mktg - Constellation Brands, Inc.; pg. 1960, pg. 1348
Disbro, John, Reg Assoc Product Mgr - Mallinckrodt Pharmaceuticals; pg. 1557, pg. 978
Disbrow, Jeff, Product Mgr - Emerson Network Power; pg. 1071, pg. 1479
Disch, Meghan, Brand Mgr-Silk Innovation - The WhiteWave Foods Company; pg. 1037, pg. 324
Discher, Brenda, VP-Strategy & Mktg - Autodesk Inc.; pg. 356, pg. 257
Dischert, Libby, Mgr-Natl Convention Sls - St. Louis Convention & Visitors Commission; pg. 1006, pg. 1003
Dischler, Jerry, VP-Product Mgmt - Google Inc.; pg. 1249, pg. 153
DiSciascio, Denise, Sr Mgr-Promo Ops - Pfizer Inc.; pg. 1581, pg. 1278
Discioscia, Phyllis, Sr Mgr-Brand Activation - PepsiCo, Inc.; pg. 259, pg. 1327
Dise, Janet, Sr Mgr-Sls - Hershey Entertainment & Resorts Company; pg. 1094, pg. 1539
Dishman, Sean, Dir-Sls & Mktg - Bonnier Corporation; pg. 1622, pg. 480
Disimile, Mary A., Dir-Mktg - Cardinal Health, Inc.; pg. 1512, pg. 1448
Diskin, Chris, VP & Mgr-Digital Mktg - Wells Fargo Advisors, LLC; pg. 819, pg. 1005
Dismuke, D'Lana, Specialist-Adv Solutions - Microsoft Corporation; pg. 435, pg. 1824
Dismuke, Lauren, Sr Mgr-Mktg-Grp Markets - Atlanta Convention & Visitors Bureau; pg. 989, pg. 489
Disotto, Susanna, Dir-Mktg - Conair Corporation; pg. 505, pg. 1055
Disselhorst, Steve, Sr Product Mgr-Managed Care Mktg - Genentech, Inc.; pg. 1533, pg. 279
Distad, Pete, VP-Product Mktg - Apple Inc.; pg. 350, pg. 73
Distasi, Nick, Dir-Sls & Mktg-Media & Procurement - Sanofi US; pg. 1592, pg. 1046
Distaulo, Carol, Dir-Media - Panasonic Corporation of North America; pg. 661, pg. 1120
Distefano, Brian, Grp Dir-Creative - Staples, Inc.; pg. 474, pg. 821
Distefano, Gregory, Exec Dir-University Mktg - Johnson & Wales University; pg. 603, pg. 1606
DiStefano, Mike, Exec VP, Mgr & Client Advisory Grp-Knoxville - Pinnacle Financial Partners, Inc.; pg. 794, pg. 1653
Distel, Beth, Head-Interactive Media - W.W. Grainger, Inc.; pg. 1390, pg. 625
Ditka, Ashton L., Sr VP-Mktg - United Refining Company; pg. 986, pg. 1590
Ditloff, Heidi, Dir-Mktg - Gloria Nilson GMAC Real Estate; pg. 1093, pg. 1084
Ditria, Dayna, Sr Dir-Mktg Comm - Herbalife International of America, Inc.; pg. 1541, pg. 132
Ditsch, Terry, VP-Product Svc - Echo Incorporated; pg. 1046, pg. 626
Dittenber, Jamie, Brand Mgr-Consumer Brands - Dawn Food Products, Inc.; pg. 1018, pg. 893
Dittmar, Anika, Brand Mgr-Dev - Unilever United States, Inc.; pg. 904, pg. 1061
Dittmeier, Alison, Mgr-Media Rels & Comm-Parker Aerospace - Parker Hannifin Corporation; pg. 1368, pg. 1434
Dittmer, Chris, Sr Dir-Bus Dev - SAP America, Inc.; pg. 466, pg. 1557
Ditto, Kathy, Sr Dir-US Pub Sector Mktg - Cisco Systems, Inc.; pg. 372, pg. 240
Ditto, Laura, Mgr-Mktg Comm - Central Mutual Insurance Company; pg. 1196, pg. 1478
Ditzel, Markus, Mgr-Mktg-Cloud Solutions - Hewlett-Packard Company; pg. 404, pg. 175
Divaris, Mathew, VP-Mktg - Dermalogica, Inc.; pg. 1523, pg. 63
DiVeglio, Amanda, Sr Specialist-Mktg - Ally Financial Inc.; pg. 711, pg. 878
DiVincent, Greg, Dir-Mktg - Hard Rock Cafe International, Inc.; pg. 1730, pg. 454
DiVincenzo, Kim, Assoc Dir-Creative - VistaPrint USA, Incorporated; pg. 1700, pg. 829
Divine, Brian, Dir-Mktg-JBL Professional - Harman Consumer, Inc.; pg. 641, pg. 1355
Diwby, Carl, Mgr-Adv Sls - ISSA; pg. 145, pg. 640
Dix, Ian, VP-Bus Mktg - CenturyLink, Inc; pg. 1870, pg. 317
Dix, Scott M., Sr VP & Sr Mgr-Tech-Card Issuance Technology - Bank of America Corporation; pg. 718, pg. 1362
Dixen, Heather, Head-Practice iQ Mktg - Aetna Inc.; pg. 1187, pg. 351
Dixit, Iva, Deputy Editor-Social Media & Engagement - Newsweek Daily Beast Co.; pg. 1670, pg. 1271
Dixon, Amy, Mgr-Channel Mktg - ACCO Brands Corporation; pg. 340, pg. 626
Dixon, Archie, Dir-Sponsorship Sls & Strategy - BET Holdings LLC; pg. 271, pg. 396
Dixon, Cheryl, Specialist-Mktg - Humana, Inc.; pg. 1204, pg. 734
Dixon, Christopher Bryce, Mgr-Mktg-Foster Farms Deli Meats - Foster Farms; pg. 856, pg. 122
Dixon, Doug, Dir-Mktg-Global - Henkel Corporation; pg. 1166, pg. 897
Dixon, Doug, Brand Mgr-Holiday Inn - InterContinental Hotels Corporation; pg. 1097, pg. 511
Dixon, Drew, Mgr-Mktg - Ford Motor Company; pg. 172, pg. 876
Dixon, EF, Partner & Head-Growth Markets Comm & PR -

Mercer Inc.; *pg.* 1395, *pg.* 1258
Dixon, Frank, Mgr-Production - The Denver Newspaper Agency; *pg.* 1634, *pg.* 318
Dixon, Fred, Mgr-Sls-Natl - Gill Athletics, Inc.; *pg.* 1835, *pg.* 562
Dixon, Graham, Sr Product Mgr - MORNINGSTAR, INC.; *pg.* 784, *pg.* 583
Dixon, Joe, Sr VP-Sourcing, Technical Design, Product Dev & Production Mgmt - Brooks Brothers Group, Inc.; *pg.* 39, *pg.* 1208
Dixon, John, Mgr-Product Mktg - Planar Systems, Inc.; *pg.* 455, *pg.* 1495
Dixon, Kathy, Sr Planner-Mktg & Comm - General Mills, Inc.; *pg.* 828, *pg.* 933
Dixon, Margaret, Coord-Sls Mktg - Eby-Brown Co.; *pg.* 1767, *pg.* 636
Dixon, Michael, Dir-Retail Brand Mktg-Finish Line - NIKE, Inc.; *pg.* 1812, *pg.* 1492
Dixon, Mike, Dir-Adv - The Spokesman-Review; *pg.* 1687, *pg.* 1844
Dixon, Nicole, Mgr-Digital Mktg & Ops-Global Pub Sector - Amazon.com, Inc.; *pg.* 1226, *pg.* 1831
Dixon, Scott, VP-Mktg & Strategy - eResearch Technology Inc.; *pg.* 1243, *pg.* 1564
Dixon, Sheena, Product Mgr-SPAN - NovAtel Inc.; *pg.* 1424, *pg.* 1904
Dixon, Terry, Exec VP-Sls & Mktg - Global Imaging Systems, Inc.; *pg.* 400, *pg.* 473
Dixon, Tommy, Specialist-Mktg & Comm-Fin Svcs Grp - Xerox Corporation; *pg.* 494, *pg.* 365
Dixon, Tripp, VP & Dir-Creative - NBC Sports Network; *pg.* 300, *pg.* 375
Dizon, Rom, Sr Product Mgr - eBay Inc.; *pg.* 1240, *pg.* 243
Dizon, Sylvia, Mgr-Mktg - Intuit Inc.; *pg.* 769, *pg.* 158
Dizzine, Jason, VP-Tech Mktg - Ricoh Americas Corp.; *pg.* 462, *pg.* 538
Djabbarah, Ryan, VP-Corp Sponsorships & Mktg - Citigroup Inc.; *pg.* 735, *pg.* 1212
Djandji, Patrick, Mgr-Mktg - Maple Leaf Foods Inc.; *pg.* 875, *pg.* 1927
DJangi, Taraneh, Mgr-Mktg - Penguin Random House; *pg.* 1675, *pg.* 1276
DJangi, Taraneh, Mgr-Mktg - Penguin Random House; *pg.* 1675, *pg.* 1276
Djiguerian, Leon, Sr Dir-ECommerce - MGA Entertainment, Inc.; *pg.* 964, *pg.* 300
Dlugopolski, Stephanie, Mgr-PR & Social Media - Johnsonville Sausage, LLC; *pg.* 867, *pg.* 1894
Do Lago Leite, Alexandre T., Dir-Global Apps Product Mktg-Microsoft Adv & Media - Microsoft Corporation; *pg.* 435, *pg.* 1824
Doak, Donald, Sr VP-Sls - EBSCO Information Services Walpole; *pg.* 1638, *pg.* 849
Doan, Brooke, Mgr-Mktg - Lavoi Corporation; *pg.* 874, *pg.* 513
Doan, Chris, Mgr-Respiratory Brand Payer Access Mktg - GlaxoSmithKline; *pg.* 1536, *pg.* 1565
Doan, Jonathan, Dir-Mktg - Nordson Corporation; *pg.* 1365, *pg.* 1480
Doan, Karen, Sr Mgr-Customer Mktg - Tyson Foods, Inc.; *pg.* 902, *pg.* 35
Doan, Steve, Brand Mgr-Jose Cuervo - Proximo Spirits, Inc.; *pg.* 1969, *pg.* 1076
Doane, Jeff, VP-Sls & Mktg-Americas - Fairmont Hotels & Resorts Inc.; *pg.* 1091, *pg.* 1938
Doar, Burke, VP-Sls & Mktg - TRUMPF Inc.; *pg.* 1385, *pg.* 349
Dobbins, David, Dir-Global Media-Sourcing - Boehringer Ingelheim Pharmaceuticals, Inc.; *pg.* 1507, *pg.* 368
Dobbins, Janelle, Mgr-Bear Mktg Programs - Build-A-Bear Workshop, Inc.; *pg.* 950, *pg.* 993
Dobecka, Johnny, Supvr-Crude Oil Mktg - Apache Corporation; *pg.* 1934, *pg.* 1700
Dobies, Josh, Sr Dir-Product Mktg & Strategy - Riverbed Technology, Inc.; *pg.* 1277, *pg.* 225
Dobkowski, Keith, Sr Dir-Audience Dev - Fox Sports Net; *pg.* 288, *pg.* 131
Doble, Douglas, Sr Mgr-Mktg-Experience Mgmt & Site Optimization - E*TRADE Financial Corporation; *pg.* 749, *pg.* 1230
Dobrev, Dobri, Assoc Product Mgr - Yahoo! Inc.; *pg.* 1289, *pg.* 289
Dobreva, Iskra, Strategist-Social Media - Verizon Communications Inc.; *pg.* 1875, *pg.* 1309
Dobrik, Renata, Mgr-Sls Programs - Fairmont Hotels & Resorts Inc.; *pg.* 1091, *pg.* 1938
Dobrow, Alice, Dir-System Implementations, Adv & CRM Sys - Time Inc.; *pg.* 1693, *pg.* 1300
Dobrozdravic, Nancy, VP-Mktg - Aspect Software, Inc.; *pg.* 354, *pg.* 238
Dobrzynski, Nicole, Brand Mgr-Global Football - NIKE, Inc.; *pg.* 1812, *pg.* 1492
Dobson, Bryan, Sr Dir-Bus Dev-Snack Factory, LLC - Snyder's-Lance, Inc.; *pg.* 896, *pg.* 1368
Dobson, Bryan, Sr Dir-Bus Dev-Snack Factory, LLC - Snyder's of Hanover, Inc.; *pg.* 1862, *pg.* 1536
Dobson, Darlene M., Mgr-Product Mktg - The Boeing Company; *pg.* 225, *pg.* 567
Dobson, Kimberly, VP-Digital Media & Partnerships - The History Channel; *pg.* 290, *pg.* 1240
Dochelli, Harry, Sr VP-Sls & Customer Care - Essendant Inc.; *pg.* 1907, *pg.* 600
Docherty, Robert, Dir-Global Media & Sponsorships - FRANKLIN RESOURCES, INC.; *pg.* 760, *pg.* 254
Docking, Jeffrey, Acct Supvr-Adv - Staples, Inc.; *pg.* 474, *pg.* 821
Docktor, David, Mgr-Motorcycle Mktg - Yamaha Motor Corporation USA; *pg.* 1713, *pg.* 76
Doctorow, David, CMO-Global Mktg & Sr VP - Expedia, Inc.; *pg.* 1244, *pg.* 1814
Doda, Robert, VP-Product Dev - Q.E.P. CO., INC.; *pg.* 1371, *pg.* 413
Dodd, Cathy K., VP-Mktg - PolyOne Corporation; *pg.* 1177, *pg.* 1404
Dodd, Elisa, Sr Mgr-Strategic Mktg & Global Outbound Programs-LSI - Avago Technologies; *pg.* 358, *pg.* 238
Dodd, Greg, VP-Natural Gas Mktg & Supply - Devon Energy Corporation; *pg.* 975, *pg.* 1485
Dodd, Katie, Brand Mgr-Digital-Stella Artois & Shock Top - Anheuser-Busch Companies, LLC; *pg.* 237, *pg.* 991
Dodd, Ken, Sr VP-Sls & Mktg - Xerox Corporation; *pg.* 494, *pg.* 365
Dodd, Laura, Sr Mgr-Comm - Microsoft Corporation; *pg.* 435, *pg.* 1824
Dodd, Paul, Head-Sls - Google Inc.; *pg.* 1249, *pg.* 153
Dodd, Penny, Mgr-Integrated Mktg Comm - Cisco Systems, Inc.; *pg.* 372, *pg.* 240
Dodd, Rick, Sr VP-Mktg - CIENA Corporation; *pg.* 628, *pg.* 771
Dodd, Tracy, Dir-Performance Mktg - RentPath, Inc.; *pg.* 1680, *pg.* 538
Dodds, Douglas W., Chief Strategy Officer - Maple Leaf Foods Inc.; *pg.* 875, *pg.* 1927
Dodds, John R., Dir-Brand & Mktg Comm-Global - Air Products and Chemicals, Inc.; *pg.* 1145, *pg.* 1513
Dodds, Keith, Sr VP-Mktg & Ops - Apartment Investment and Management Company; *pg.* 1079, *pg.* 316
Dodero, Mary Kay, Sr Mgr-Comm & PR - Johnson Controls, Inc.; *pg.* 209, *pg.* 1876
Dodge, Larry, Dir-Sls & Mktg - Mlive Media Group; *pg.* 1665, *pg.* 888
Dodge, Mary, Mgr-Mktg Comm - Parker Hannifin Corporation; *pg.* 1368, *pg.* 1434
Dodge, Melanie Cepeda, Sr Mgr-Wholesale Mktg - Cole-Haan LLC; *pg.* 1806, *pg.* 1034
Dodge, Morgan, Brand Mgr-Graphic - Golden Gate University; *pg.* 602, *pg.* 219
Dodge, Stacey, Dir-Adv Sls - National Association of Convenience Stores; *pg.* 148, *pg.* 1771
Dodos, Suzanne, Sr Mgr-Mktg - GN Netcom Inc.; *pg.* 640, *pg.* 1037
Dodson, Alma, Head-Global Brand Campaign Creative - Dell Inc.; *pg.* 383, *pg.* 1737
Dodson, Bryan, Analyst-Display Adv - Scottrade, Inc.; *pg.* 802, *pg.* 1003
Dodson, Greg, VP-Tech & Product Mgmt-Process Sys - Cameron International; *pg.* 1151, *pg.* 1702
Dodson, Jennifer, Dir-Adv - Cricket Wireless LLC; *pg.* 381, *pg.* 483
Dodson, Michael, Sr VP-Sls - OpenTable, Inc.; *pg.* 450, *pg.* 224
Dodson, Richard, Specialist-Digital Adv & Mktg - Google Inc.; *pg.* 1249, *pg.* 153
Dodson, Tammie, Mgr-Mktg Campaign - ADTRAN, Inc.; *pg.* 344, *pg.* 6
Doebler, Alyssa J., Specialist-Earned Media - Deluxe Corporation; *pg.* 1634, *pg.* 964
Doege, Jennifer, Sr Mgr-Adv Sys & Support - The Arizona Republic; *pg.* 1617, *pg.* 14
Doench, Debra, Mgr-Mktg Comm - Hobart Brothers Company; *pg.* 1346, *pg.* 1477
Doenecke, Scott, Sr Mgr-IoT Frameworks & Wireless UX Mktg - Intel Corporation; *pg.* 645, *pg.* 266
Doepp, Ashley, Dir-Mktg & SBV - Simon Property Group, Inc.; *pg.* 1112, *pg.* 690
Doerfler, Cody, Product Mgr-CommCAD - Zoll Medical Corporation; *pg.* 1612, *pg.* 814
Doering, Mark, Engr-Technical Mktg - Cisco Systems, Inc.; *pg.* 372, *pg.* 240
Doerr, Kelly, Mgr-Natl Sls - Hunter Boot USA; *pg.* 1810, *pg.* 1242
Doerr, Ray, Engr-Technical Mktg - Cisco Systems, Inc.; *pg.* 372, *pg.* 240
Doerr, Tom, Dir-Transportation Mktg & Comm - CH2M HILL Companies, Ltd.; *pg.* 75, *pg.* 325
Doft, Nili, Sr Dir-Direct & Digital Mktg - National Hockey League; *pg.* 568, *pg.* 1265
Doggendorf, Katie, Sr Mgr-Media - United Services Automobile Association; *pg.* 1221, *pg.* 1743
Doggett, Richard, VP-Field Mktg - Sysco Corporation; *pg.* 1035, *pg.* 1716
Doherty, Bethany, Dir-Media - NBC Universal, Inc.; *pg.* 300, *pg.* 1266
Doherty, Brian, Designer-Web & Print Media - Aer Lingus; *pg.* 1896, *pg.* 1171
Doherty, Brian, Sr VP-Sls-Natl - The CW Television Network; *pg.* 632, *pg.* 52
Doherty, Ian, VP-Asian Sls & Mktg - Koppers Holdings Inc.; *pg.* 1170, *pg.* 1577
Doherty, Kerryn, Supvr-Adv - The TJX Companies, Inc.; *pg.* 1788, *pg.* 822
Doherty, Laura, Sr Mgr-PR-Global - Vans, Inc.; *pg.* 1821, *pg.* 76
Doherty, Michael, Dir-Creative-Brand Presentation - NIKE, Inc.; *pg.* 1812, *pg.* 1492
Doherty, Sean, Dir-Digital & Social Media Engagement - National Association for Stock Car Auto Racing; *pg.* 566, *pg.* 420
Doherty, Sean, Chief Sls Officer-Application Dev & Deployment - Progress Software Corporation; *pg.* 457, *pg.* 786
Doherty, Sean, Sr Dir-Global New Product Plng - Vertex Pharmaceuticals Incorporated; *pg.* 1606, *pg.* 801
Doherty, Shannon, Sr Specialist-Mktg & Comm - Sun Life Financial Inc.; *pg.* 806, *pg.* 1944
Doherty, Tracy Scott, Sr Dir-Strategic Global Design - WestRock Company; *pg.* 1472, *pg.* 1805
Doi, Derrick K., VP-Quick & Franchise Print Segment Mktg - Xerox Corporation; *pg.* 494, *pg.* 365
Doise, David, Area Mgr-Sls - Terral Seed, Inc.; *pg.* 1801, *pg.* 748
Dolan, Alex, Dir-Mktg & Comm - Energy Recovery, Inc.; *pg.* 1334, *pg.* 252
Dolan, Ann M., Sr Rep-Mktg Comm - Air Products and Chemicals, Inc.; *pg.* 1145, *pg.* 1513
Dolan, Brian, Brand Mgr-Men's Hair Brands - Unilever United States, Inc.; *pg.* 904, *pg.* 1061
Dolan, Chris, Dir-Mktg-North America Flat Glass - Guardian Industries Corp.; *pg.* 85, *pg.* 869
Dolan, Chris, Sr Mgr-Category Sls-Office, Indus & Healthcare - Philips Lighting; *pg.* 1303, *pg.* 806
Dolan, Claire, Dir-Creative - Apple Inc.; *pg.* 350, *pg.* 73
Dolan, Fab, Head-Large Advertiser & Agency Mktg - Google Inc.; *pg.* 1249, *pg.* 153
Dolan, Grace, Head-Global Mobile Brand Strategy, Sls & Bus Dev - Google Inc.; *pg.* 1249, *pg.* 153
Dolan, Jack, VP-Media Rels - American Council of Life Insurers; *pg.* 127, *pg.* 394
Dolan, Kim, Dir-Sls-Natl - Tremor Video; *pg.* 682, *pg.* 1305
Dolan, Melissa, Mgr-PR - Epson America Inc.; *pg.* 394, *pg.* 122
Dolan, Siobhan, Assoc Mgr-Mktg - Accenture; *pg.* 1392, *pg.* 1186
Dolbier, George, CTO-Interactive & Social Media - IBM; *pg.* 410, *pg.* 1449
Dolcemaschio, Steven, Mgr-Music Mktg-Global - Converse Inc.; *pg.* 1831, *pg.* 793
Dold, Ben, Dir-Mktg Analytics & Insights - Midcontinent Communications Co.; *pg.* 298, *pg.* 1625
Dole, Elizabeth, VP-Ops & Production - NewsMax Media, Inc.; *pg.* 1271, *pg.* 479
Dole, Leah, Dir-Creative Svcs - Woolrich, Inc.; *pg.* 699, *pg.* 1595
Dolechek, Melanie, Dir-Publ & Mktg - Allen Press Inc.; *pg.* 1614, *pg.* 715

Dolen, Derya, Sr Mgr-Mktg-Global - LivaNova; *pg.* 1557, *pg.* 1710
Dolensek, Veronica, VP-Sls-Latin America - Buffalo Wire Works Co., Inc.; *pg.* 72, *pg.* 1147
Doleys, Mary Lynne, Coord-Mktg - ISSA; *pg.* 145, *pg.* 640
Dolgetta, Maria, Sr VP-PR & Corp Comm - Iconix Brand Group, Inc.; *pg.* 26, *pg.* 1243
Dolginoff, Lori, Head-Brand PR-Skincare & Consumer Health Care & Sr Dir - Johnson & Johnson; *pg.* 1549, *pg.* 1091
Dolipschi, Wendy, Dir-Mktg-Central US Div - The Nature Conservancy; *pg.* 151, *pg.* 1774
Dolkart, Courtney, Mgr-Shopper Mktg - Reckitt Benckiser Inc.; *pg.* 1136, *pg.* 1105
Doll, Kristin, Sr Mgr-Mktg-Amazon Appstore - Amazon.com, Inc.; *pg.* 1226, *pg.* 1831
Doll, Ron, Dir-Product Health-Electric Rope Shovels - Caterpillar, Inc.; *pg.* 1321, *pg.* 650
Dollenmayer, Brian, Exec VP-Mktg & Promos - Tribune Media Company; *pg.* 1696, *pg.* 592
Dolynchuk, Paul, Sr Product Mgr-Infrastructure - Middle Atlantic Products Inc.; *pg.* 1360, *pg.* 1065
Dolzine, Amy, Analyst-Bus, Social Media, Content Mgmt & Knowledge Mgmt - The Lubrizol Corporation; *pg.* 1171, *pg.* 1481
Doman, Courtney, Mgr-Content Mktg - Spredfast; *pg.* 1282, *pg.* 1666
Domans, Kate, Supvr-Media - Conair Corporation; *pg.* 505, *pg.* 1055
Dombek, Paula W., Mgr-Product Line Mktg - Armstrong World Industries, Inc.; *pg.* 914, *pg.* 1545
Dombroski, Pepper, Dir-Sls - Broadmoor Hotel, Inc.; *pg.* 1083, *pg.* 315
Dombrowa, Beth, Mgr-PR - THE DOW CHEMICAL COMPANY; *pg.* 1157, *pg.* 898
Dome, Matthew, Sr Mgr-Content Ops - Hulu LLC; *pg.* 1257, *pg.* 274
Domenick, Joe, VP-Mdsg - The TJX Companies, Inc.; *pg.* 1788, *pg.* 822
Domenico, Joanna Di, Brand Mgr-Nivea Body - Beiersdorf North America Inc.; *pg.* 501, *pg.* 385
Domenico, Katherine, Acct Mgr-Comml Insulation Sls-Natl - Johns Manville Corporation; *pg.* 89, *pg.* 320
Domer, Melanie, VP-Mktg-North America Air Care - S.C. Johnson & Son, Inc.; *pg.* 334, *pg.* 1889
Domier, Steve, VP-Distr Mktg-The CW Television Network - Warner Bros. Entertainment Inc.; *pg.* 319, *pg.* 54
Dominguez, Alex, Sr Dir-Real Estate - Chick-fil-A, Inc.; *pg.* 1721, *pg.* 492
Dominguez, Eddie, Sr VP-Mktg, Comm & Community Rels - City National Bank; *pg.* 737, *pg.* 725
Dominguez, Eddie, Sr VP-Mktg, Comm & Community Rels - City National Corporation; *pg.* 738, *pg.* 128
Dominguez, Hugo, Designer-Creative - Huron Consulting Group Inc.; *pg.* 768, *pg.* 577
Dominguez, Jennifer, Sr Mgr-Brand Strategy-Global - Symantec Corporation; *pg.* 478, *pg.* 161
Dominguez, Kimberley, Div Mgr-Mdse-Furniture & Lighting - Cost Plus World Market; *pg.* 921, *pg.* 170
Dominguez, Leilani, Sr Dir-Customer Plng - Coca-Cola Bottling Co. Consolidated; *pg.* 240, *pg.* 1365
Dominguez, Maria, Mgr-Creative Svcs - Assurant, Inc.; *pg.* 1193, *pg.* 1198
Dominguez, Mark, Project Mgr-Tech-Sls & Mktg Events - Intel Corporation; *pg.* 645, *pg.* 266
Dominic, Kirk, Producer-Mktg - Los Angeles Dodgers Inc.; *pg.* 559, *pg.* 135
Dominici, Kathleen, Coord-Digital Adv & Mktg Interactive Traffic - Cablevision Systems Corporation; *pg.* 272, *pg.* 1141
Dominie, Taryn, Mgr-Mdse Mktg - The Home Depot, Inc.; *pg.* 1050, *pg.* 510
Dominus, Ellen, Sr VP-Entertainment Grp Ad Sls - Viacom Inc.; *pg.* 316, *pg.* 1310
Domke, Gary, Dir-Mktg at American Home Shield - The ServiceMaster Company, LLC; *pg.* 335, *pg.* 1646
Domke, Todd, Product Mgr - Solidworks Corporation; *pg.* 472, *pg.* 815
Dommisse, Jon, Dir-Mktg & Strategic Dev-Global - Bradley Corporation; *pg.* 71, *pg.* 1870
Doms, Scott, Acct Exec-x86 & Specialist-Pure sys Sls - Lenovo Group Ltd; *pg.* 427, *pg.* 1384
Don, David, Sr Dir-Multimedia Svcs - Oakland Athletics Limited Partnership; *pg.* 571, *pg.* 172
Donaghy, Daniel J., Sr VP-Sls - Gannett Co., Inc.; *pg.* 1643, *pg.* 1790
Donahue, Bob, Mgr-Adv-Special Projects - Bon Ton Stores, Inc.; *pg.* 1763, *pg.* 1596
Donahue, Caroline, CMO & Chief Sls Officer - Intuit Inc.; *pg.* 769, *pg.* 158
Donahue, Kathlene, Dir-Consumer Mktg - Worcester Telegram & Gazette Corp.; *pg.* 1702, *pg.* 863
Donahue, Kelly, Sr Mgr-Database Mktg - Expedia, Inc.; *pg.* 1244, *pg.* 1814
Donahue, Kieran, VP-Mktg-Americas - Hilton Worldwide, Inc.; *pg.* 1094, *pg.* 1791
Donahue, Laura, VP-Mktg Svcs - CarMax, Inc.; *pg.* 167, *pg.* 1800
Donahue, Pat, Mgr-Digital Media - Los Angeles Kings Hockey Club L.P.; *pg.* 559, *pg.* 135
Donahue, Sue, Dir-Mktg - Walpole Woodworkers, Inc.; *pg.* 120, *pg.* 849
Donahue, Tess, Mgr-Mktg Comm-Global - St. Jude Medical, Inc.; *pg.* 1596, *pg.* 963
Donahue-Dalton, Ellen, CMO & Exec VP - MEDecision, Inc.; *pg.* 431, *pg.* 1592
Donald Rogers, Ashley, Sr Mgr-Demand Generation Mktg - Blackbaud, Inc.; *pg.* 361, *pg.* 1613
Donald, Clare, Head-Ops & Creative Lab - Google Inc.; *pg.* 1249, *pg.* 153
Donald, Joesph, Dir-Worldwide Unified Comm Sls-Americas - Microsoft Corporation; *pg.* 435, *pg.* 1824
Donaldson, Bryan, Exec Dir-Twins Community Fund & Sr Dir-Community Rels - Minnesota Twins, LLC; *pg.* 563, *pg.* 940
Donaldson, Hunter, VP-Sls & Customer Svc - TechnoBrands, Inc.; *pg.* 1788, *pg.* 1778
Donaldson, Margaret, Mgr-PR - Neiman Marcus, Inc.; *pg.* 30, *pg.* 1684
Donaldson, Marybeth, Sr Mgr-Mktg-Solutions - Siemens Process Industries and Drives; *pg.* 673, *pg.* 485
Donaldson, Veronica A., Mgr-Adv & Mktg - Gannett Co., Inc.; *pg.* 1643, *pg.* 1790
Donat, Lindsey, Sr Product Mgr-Checkout & Post Order - Sears Holdings Corporation; *pg.* 1784, *pg.* 618
Donatacci, Tom, Exec VP-Sls & Mktg - Clayton Holdings, Inc.; *pg.* 738, *pg.* 370
Donathy, Phil, Sr Product Dir - Travelport Limited; *pg.* 1925, *pg.* 521
Donati, Nancy, VP-Creative Svcs - San Francisco Giants Baseball Club; *pg.* 581, *pg.* 226
Donato, Christine, Sr Specialist-Integrated Mktg - SAP; *pg.* 465, *pg.* 78
Donato, Christy Coleman, Sr Dir-Global Brand Mgmt-JW Marriott Hotels & Resorts - Marriott International, Inc.; *pg.* 1102, *pg.* 764
Donatoni, Angie, Mgr-Brand Mktg - LinkedIn Corporation; *pg.* 1262, *pg.* 160
Donelan, David, VP-Mktg - Pegasystems Inc.; *pg.* 453, *pg.* 74
Donerson, Erica D., Sr Specialist-Media Rels - DTE Energy Company; *pg.* 1940, *pg.* 880
Dong, Esther, Sr VP-Sls & Mktg - AmorePacific US, Inc.; *pg.* 498, *pg.* 1195
Dong, Kathy, Dir-HCV Mktg - Gilead Sciences, Inc.; *pg.* 1535, *pg.* 88
Dongo, Mireya, VP-Distr Sls & Mktg-Western Reg - Univision Communications Inc.; *pg.* 683, *pg.* 1307
Donics, Alexander, Mgr-Mktg-Beverage Innovation - PepsiCo, Inc.; *pg.* 259, *pg.* 1327
Donikian, Lindsay Jacobson, Sr Mgr-Mktg Program-Gift Cards - Amazon.com, Inc.; *pg.* 1226, *pg.* 1831
Doninger, Eric, VP & Dir-Global Mktg Creative-Jack Daniel's Family of Brands - Brown-Forman Corporation; *pg.* 1958, *pg.* 732
Donkin, Andrew, Head-Worldwide Brand & Mass Mktg - Amazon.com, Inc.; *pg.* 1226, *pg.* 1831
Donlan, Catherine, VP-Sls - Converse Inc.; *pg.* 1831, *pg.* 793
Donlan, Jayar, VP-Social Media - World Wrestling Entertainment, Inc.; *pg.* 595, *pg.* 380
Donlevy, Cynthia, Dir-Web Mktg - Polycom, Inc.; *pg.* 664, *pg.* 249
Donley, JoAnn, Supvr-Mktg Programs Fin - The Toro Company; *pg.* 1065, *pg.* 918
Donlin, Lou, Specialist-Unified Comm Product Sls - Cisco Systems, Inc.; *pg.* 372, *pg.* 240
Donlon, John P., Exec VP-Intl Sls & Svc - Hurco Companies, Inc.; *pg.* 409, *pg.* 686
Donlon, Ken, VP-Corp Sls - Medtronic; *pg.* 1563, *pg.* 183
Donn, Alex, Sr Mgr-Mktg - AT&T Inc.; *pg.* 1867, *pg.* 1674
Donnarumma, Lenny, Mgr-Creative Svcs & Interactive - BJ's Wholesale Club, Inc.; *pg.* 1762, *pg.* 857
Donnarummo, Taryn, Dir-Mktg & Promos - Cumulus Media Inc.; *pg.* 280, *pg.* 503
Donnell, Kimberly, Dir-Mktg & Comm - The Northwestern Mutual Life Insurance Company; *pg.* 1212, *pg.* 1879
Donnellan, Peter, Dir-After Sls - Audi of America, Inc.; *pg.* 164, *pg.* 1784
Donnellon, Mary P., VP-Mktg - Blackbaud, Inc.; *pg.* 361, *pg.* 1613
Donnelly, Amanda, Mgr-Digital Media - Nissan North America, Inc.; *pg.* 186, *pg.* 1633
Donnelly, Brian, Dir-Retina Mktg - Allergan, Inc.; *pg.* 1491, *pg.* 106
Donnelly, David, Sr Mgr-Strategic Sourcing & Comml - The Hershey Co.; *pg.* 1855, *pg.* 1538
Donnelly, John, Publr-Inc. Media - Mansueto Ventures LLC; *pg.* 1661, *pg.* 1256
Donnelly, Kathryn, Project Mgr-Mktg - Arrow Electronics, Inc.; *pg.* 619, *pg.* 325
Donnelly, Maureen, Sr Mgr-Facility Plng & Construction - Ryder System, Inc.; *pg.* 1922, *pg.* 446
Donnelly, Michael, Sr VP & Grp Head-Global Digital Mktg - MasterCard Incorporated; *pg.* 779, *pg.* 1325
Donnelly, Michael J., Exec VP-Mdsg - The Kroger Co.; *pg.* 1025, *pg.* 1416
Donnelly, Michael J., Dir-Sls & Mktg Ops - Novartis Corporation; *pg.* 1574, *pg.* 1273
Donnelly, Mike, Sr VP-Mdsg - Ralphs Grocery Company; *pg.* 1031, *pg.* 69
Donnelly, Shaun, Sr VP-Sls & Bus Dev - support.com, inc.; *pg.* 1283, *pg.* 192
Donnelly, Steve, VP & Bus Mgr-Global-Petroleum Products - R.T. Vanderbilt Company, Inc.; *pg.* 1180, *pg.* 364
Donnelly, Tanya, Dir-Social Media-Global - Schneider Electric USA, Inc.; *pg.* 1306, *pg.* 650
Donnelly, Vinny, Mgr-Mktg-Market Analysis and Customer Profitability Mgmt - United Parcel Service, Inc.; *pg.* 1928, *pg.* 522
Donnelson, Nicki, Specialist-PR - Missouri State University; *pg.* 605, *pg.* 1006
Donner, Jean-Michel, Sr Dir-European Bus - Monster Inc.; *pg.* 656, *pg.* 50
Donnici, Gina, Product Mgr - Sprint Corporation; *pg.* 1874, *pg.* 719
Donnon, Michael, VP-Acq Mktg - Demand Media, Inc.; *pg.* 1238, *pg.* 273
Donofrio, Keri, VP-Linear & Digital Adv Sls-Music Grp - Viacom Inc.; *pg.* 316, *pg.* 1310
Donofrio, Nikki, Sr VP-Strategic Brand Mktg - Great Wolf Resorts, Inc.; *pg.* 1093, *pg.* 1866
Donoghue, Jessica, VP-Mktg & Design - Parfums De Coeur Ltd.; *pg.* 519, *pg.* 376
Donoghue, Tom, Sr Mgr-Key Accounts Program - Cars.com; *pg.* 1234, *pg.* 568
Donoghue, Tom, Dir-Global Mktg-Residential Brands - INVISTA B.V.; *pg.* 1168, *pg.* 723
Donohoe, Lauren, Coord-Women's Fashion PR - Ralph Lauren Corporation; *pg.* 46, *pg.* 1284
Donohoe, Michelle Dukeman, Brand Mktg Mgr-Comml Tires - The Goodyear Tire & Rubber Company; *pg.* 1883, *pg.* 1401
Donohue, Angela, Mgr-Global Product Mktg-Xbox 360 & Kinect - Microsoft Corporation; *pg.* 435, *pg.* 1824
Donohue, Brendan, Sr VP-Team Mktg & Bus Ops - NBA Properties, Inc.; *pg.* 569, *pg.* 1120
Donohue, Brian, Reg Dir-Sls - Diageo North America Inc.; *pg.* 248, *pg.* 1223
Donohue, Colleen, Sr Coord-PR - American Eagle Outfitters, Inc.; *pg.* 37, *pg.* 1572
Donohue, Jim, Chief Product Officer & Exec VP - Cengage Learning; *pg.* 1626, *pg.* 215
Donohue, Jim, Dir-Media - Pfizer Inc.; *pg.* 1581, *pg.* 1278
Donohue, Michael, Sr Dir-Fortify Product R&D - Hewlett-Packard Company; *pg.* 404, *pg.* 175
Donohue, Ryann, Dir-Mktg Ops, Strategy & Dev - Constellation Energy Resources, LLC; *pg.* 1938, *pg.* 756
Donohue, Shannon, Dir-Global Mktg Plng - Starbucks Corporation; *pg.* 897, *pg.* 1840
Donohue, Tom, Sr VP-Tech - Cablevision Systems Corporation; *pg.* 272, *pg.* 1141
Donovan, Allie, Mgr-Email Mktg - Total Wine & More; *pg.* 1971, *pg.* 775
Donovan, Anne M., Product Mgr - Paychex, Inc.; *pg.* 792, *pg.* 1336
Donovan, Cynthia, Mgr-Classified Adv - Lee Enterprises, Incorporated; *pg.* 1658, *pg.* 704
Donovan, Dan, VP-Sls-Natl - WABC-TV Inc.; *pg.* 317, *pg.*

1312
Donovan, Jeanne, Brand Mgr-Employee Experience - Sprint Corporation; *pg.* 1874, *pg.* 719
Donovan, Karen, Sr Mgr-Global Digital Analytics - FCA US LLC; *pg.* 170, *pg.* 868
Donovan, Kathleen, Sr Coord-PR - CUTCO Corporation; *pg.* 1123, *pg.* 1318
Donovan, Mandy, Assoc Dir-Creative & Copy - ZIPCAR, INC.; *pg.* 1931, *pg.* 810
Donovan, Rae, Mgr-Social Media Programs - United Airlines, Inc.; *pg.* 1927, *pg.* 593
Donovan, Shawn, Chief Sls Officer - Fiserv, Inc.; *pg.* 397, *pg.* 1855
Donovan, Verna, Assoc VP-Strategic Mktg & Branding - DePaul University; *pg.* 600, *pg.* 572
Doo, Johnny, Sr VP-Mktg, Sls & Customer Svc - Continental Motors; *pg.* 227, *pg.* 7
Doody, Mary, Sr Specialist-Mktg Comm - Charles Schwab; *pg.* 1235, *pg.* 1661
Doolan, Peter, Sr VP-Global Enterprise Sls Engrg - salesforce.com, inc.; *pg.* 1278, *pg.* 226
Dooley, Amy, Media Buyer - Blue Bell Creameries, L.P.; *pg.* 1851, *pg.* 1668
Dooley, Amy, Mgr-Mktg - Lennar Corporation; *pg.* 1100, *pg.* 443
Dooley, Annamaria, Sr VP-Product Dev - Summer Infant, Inc.; *pg.* 1139, *pg.* 1610
Dooley, Raymond, VP-Mktg - TruTV; *pg.* 314, *pg.* 1305
Dopp, Liza, Sr Mgr-Mktg - General Mills, Inc.; *pg.* 828, *pg.* 933
Doppelt, Cory, Product Mgr - Weber-Stephen Products LLC; *pg.* 62, *pg.* 650
Dorado, Jason, Coord-PR - QUALCOMM Incorporated; *pg.* 1873, *pg.* 207
Doran, Brian, Dir-Mktg - Nationwide Mutual Insurance Company; *pg.* 1210, *pg.* 1442
Doran, Cathy, Sr VP-Admin Membership & Mktg Programs - Greater Boston Convention & Visitors Bureau Inc.; *pg.* 993, *pg.* 795
Doran, Kara, Analyst-Data & Social Media - National Geographic Society; *pg.* 1667, *pg.* 402
Doran, Mary E., Sr Acct Exec-Sls - Unum Group; *pg.* 1222, *pg.* 1629
Doran, Zion, Assoc Dir-Integrated Promotions & Shopper Mktg - Kellogg Company; *pg.* 831, *pg.* 870
Dorazio, Gregg, Mgr-Multicultural Mktg - General Mills, Inc.; *pg.* 828, *pg.* 933
Dorbrandt, Christian, VP & Mng Dir-Consumer Mktg - Scientific American, Inc.; *pg.* 1685, *pg.* 1290
Dorcak, Kevin, Mgr-Mktg-US - Philips Respironics; *pg.* 1585, *pg.* 1555
Dorcely, Melissa, Analyst-Mktg - Morgan Stanley; *pg.* 783, *pg.* 1261
Dorcus, Diana, Mgr-Mktg & Pro Products - OPI Products Inc.; *pg.* 518, *pg.* 167
Dordevic, George, VP-Adv - Safeway Inc.; *pg.* 1032, *pg.* 184
Dore, Bridget, Dir-Adv & Digital Mktg - DePaul University; *pg.* 600, *pg.* 572
Dore, Dave, Sr VP & Dir-Creative-Entertainment Mktg - NBC Universal, Inc.; *pg.* 300, *pg.* 1266
Doren, Greg, Product Mgr - Plasti-Fab Ltd.; *pg.* 1888, *pg.* 1904
Doren, Stacy, VP-Mktg-Levi's America - Levi Strauss & Co.; *pg.* 43, *pg.* 220
Dorf, Barron J., Sr Mgr-Market-San Diego & Orange County - Unum Group; *pg.* 1222, *pg.* 1629
Dorf, David, Sr Dir-Tech Strategy - Oracle Corporation; *pg.* 450, *pg.* 191
Dorffi, Christine, Program Mgr & Editor-Web Mktg - Cisco Systems, Inc.; *pg.* 372, *pg.* 240
Dorfman, Barbara, Dir-Product Dev & Sourcing - Croscill, Inc.; *pg.* 1122, *pg.* 1220
Dorfman, Doug, VP-Refined Fuels Mktg - CHS INC.; *pg.* 702, *pg.* 926
Dorfner, Brittany, Asst Mgr-Digital Mktg - Briggs & Stratton Corporation; *pg.* 201, *pg.* 1899
Doria, Joe, Dir-Enterprise Sys Mktg, Sys & Tech Grp - IBM; *pg.* 410, *pg.* 1449
Doria, Kelly, VP-Brand Mktg - Scottrade, Inc.; *pg.* 802, *pg.* 1003
Doria, Loretta, Sr Mgr-Mktg-Subscriptions - Birchbox; *pg.* 1762, *pg.* 1203
Doria, Scott, Mgr-Sls - Edd Helms Group, Inc.; *pg.* 1071, *pg.* 442
Dorion, Jeff, Specialist-Media Solutions-Xbox Adv - Microsoft Corporation; *pg.* 435, *pg.* 1824
Dority, Peter, VP-Sls & Mktg - Coral Chemical Company; *pg.* 1154, *pg.* 666
Doriza, Andriana M., Sr Specialist-Mktg - Canon U.S.A., Inc.; *pg.* 1404, *pg.* 1178
Dorman, Jay, Dir-Sls-Global - Gerber Scientific, Inc.; *pg.* 1414, *pg.* 380
Dorman, Jodi, Asst VP-PR - The Chubb Corporation; *pg.* 1196, *pg.* 1128
Dorman, Rachel, Mgr-Digital Mktg-Global - General Electric Company; *pg.* 1297, *pg.* 347
Dorman, Scott, Sr Mgr-Mktg - General Mills, Inc.; *pg.* 828, *pg.* 933
Dorn, Timothy A., Owner & VP Sls & Engrg - Amerequip Corporation; *pg.* 700, *pg.* 1862
Dornacher, Tony, Dir-Mktg Comm & Special Projects - General Growth Properties, Inc.; *pg.* 1093, *pg.* 574
Dornan, Beth, Mgr-PR & Bus Model-Global - Amway Corporation; *pg.* 326, *pg.* 864
Dornburg, Kim, Strategist-Product - Thrivent Financial for Lutherans; *pg.* 1219, *pg.* 944
Dorneman, Michael, Sr VP & Mgr-Consumer Product Strategy - Bank of America Corporation; *pg.* 718, *pg.* 1362
Dorobiala, Candice, Mgr-Comm-Worldwide Sls Compensation - Hewlett-Packard Company; *pg.* 404, *pg.* 175
Dorochina, Tatiana, Project Mgr-Digital Media & Tech - Copper Development Association Inc.; *pg.* 138, *pg.* 1218
Doronichev, Andre, Head-Product-YouTube Mobile - Google Inc.; *pg.* 1249, *pg.* 153
Dorosin, Heidi, VP-Mktg - The Clorox Company; *pg.* 327, *pg.* 169
Dorotheo, Terry, Asst VP-Creative Svcs - LPL Financial Corporation; *pg.* 777, *pg.* 798
Dorr, Chris, Sr Dir-HR - NIKE, Inc.; *pg.* 1812, *pg.* 1492
Dorr, Greg, Sr VP & Dir-Consumer Bank Mktg - U.S. Bancorp; *pg.* 815, *pg.* 945
Dorr, Gregg, Sr Mgr-Mktg-PepsiCo Foodservice - PepsiCo, Inc.; *pg.* 259, *pg.* 1327
Dorrance, Elizabeth, Dir-Media & Analytics - Expedia, Inc.; *pg.* 1244, *pg.* 1814
Dorrell, Nicole M., Sr Mgr-Mktg - American Express Company; *pg.* 712, *pg.* 1190
Dorrill, Mark, Sr Mgr-Media & Integration - The Home Depot, Inc.; *pg.* 1050, *pg.* 510
Dorrler, Nicole, VP-Mktg - Truth Initiative; *pg.* 158, *pg.* 405
Dorrough, Jamie, Strategist-Social Media Brand - Capital One Financial Corporation; *pg.* 730, *pg.* 1789
Dorsch, Michael D., Sr Mgr-Acctg - Chicago Blackhawk Hockey Team, Inc.; *pg.* 538, *pg.* 569
Dorset, Lish, Mgr-Social Media - Henry Ford Museum and Greenfield Village; *pg.* 552, *pg.* 878
Dorsey, Casey, Sr VP-Digital Sls & Mktg - Wells Fargo & Company; *pg.* 819, *pg.* 232
Dorsey, Lori, Sr VP & Dir-Mktg - Ivy Funds Distributor Inc.; *pg.* 771, *pg.* 719
Dorsey, Lori A., Sr VP & Dir-Mktg - Waddell & Reed Financial, Inc.; *pg.* 818, *pg.* 721
Dorsey, Meghan, Mgr-Event Mktg - AppNexus; *pg.* 352, *pg.* 1196
Dorsman, Jeff, Mgr-Mktg-Global - The Donna Karan Company LLC; *pg.* 23, *pg.* 1225
Dortheimer, Jill, Dir-PR - AMC Networks Inc.; *pg.* 269, *pg.* 1189
Dos Reis Nunes, Lana, VP-PR - Coach, Inc.; *pg.* 3, *pg.* 1214
Dos Santos, Ariel, Sr Mgr-Product Mgmt - Amazon.com, Inc.; *pg.* 1226, *pg.* 1831
Dose, Lana, Head-Consumer Mktg - Schreiber Foods, Inc.; *pg.* 894, *pg.* 1859
Doshi, Deepta, Sr Dir-Global Mktg-Banana Republic Online - Banana Republic; *pg.* 1760, *pg.* 212
Doshier, Michael, Head-Retirement & College Savings-Global Mktg Svcs - FRANKLIN RESOURCES, INC.; *pg.* 760, *pg.* 254
Doss, Amy, Brand Mgr - Hunter Fan Company; *pg.* 57, *pg.* 1631
Doss, Kelly, VP-North American Mktg - Beam Suntory Inc.; *pg.* 1957, *pg.* 599
Doss, Robin, Dir-Mktg - McDonald's Corporation; *pg.* 1737, *pg.* 645
Dossett, Jeff, Chief Revenue Officer - Demand Media, Inc.; *pg.* 1238, *pg.* 273
Dossett, Marvin Quinn, VP-Mktg - Louisiana Lottery Corporation; *pg.* 997, *pg.* 742
Dostal, Brett, Mgr-Mktg - The Allstate Corporation; *pg.* 1189, *pg.* 639
Doster, Travis, Sr Dir-Comm & Pub Affairs - Texas Roadhouse, Inc.; *pg.* 1753, *pg.* 738
Dotson, Candace G., Sr Mgr-Acq Mktg-North America - American Express Company; *pg.* 712, *pg.* 1190
Dotson, Chris W., VP-Mktg & Comm-RBC Global Asset Mgmt - Royal Bank of Canada; *pg.* 800, *pg.* 1942
Dotson, Rebecca, Analyst-Mktg Sys & Data - NCI BUILDING SYSTEMS, INC.; *pg.* 1364, *pg.* 1712
Dotson, Reggie, Reg Mgr-PR - Ameristar Casinos, Inc.; *pg.* 528, *pg.* 1022
Dotts-Wright, Nicole, Sr Mgr-Mktg-Food Svc - General Mills, Inc.; *pg.* 828, *pg.* 933
Doty, Brian, Planner-Strategic Mktg - Dell Inc.; *pg.* 383, *pg.* 1737
Doty, Chuck, Reg Mgr-Sls - Unex Manufacturing, Inc.; *pg.* 1385, *pg.* 1075
Doty, Dave, Sr Mgr-Network Plng & Performance - Southwest Airlines Co.; *pg.* 1923, *pg.* 1687
Doty, Jessica, Sr Specialist-Mktg - Schneider Electric; *pg.* 467, *pg.* 1609
Doty, Russell, Product Mgr-Tech - Red Hat, Inc.; *pg.* 460, *pg.* 1388
Douce, Casey, Mgr-Mktg - University of Georgia; *pg.* 609, *pg.* 486
Doucette, Alisha, Mgr-Mktg Comm-Global - Honeywell International Inc.; *pg.* 407, *pg.* 1088
Doucette, Craig, Mgr-Media Clearance - ESPN, Inc.; *pg.* 285, *pg.* 340
Doucette, Lauren, Assoc Mgr-Brand Mktg-Global - MATTEL, INC.; *pg.* 962, *pg.* 81
Doucette, Todd, VP-Sls & Mktg Ops-Americas - Philips Electronics North America; *pg.* 662, *pg.* 782
Dougan, Barry, VP-US-Microsoft Adv - Microsoft Corporation; *pg.* 435, *pg.* 1824
Dougan-Howard, Christy, Mgr-Mktg Ops-West Div - Comcast Corporation; *pg.* 276, *pg.* 1560
Dougherty, Erin, Dir-Mktg - Canyon Ranch Management, LLC; *pg.* 1084, *pg.* 27
Dougherty, Jared, Sr VP-Mktg - Real Mex Restaurants, Inc.; *pg.* 1746, *pg.* 75
Dougherty, Joanie, VP-Integrated Mktg - ABC Family Channel; *pg.* 268, *pg.* 51
Dougherty, John, Sr Dir-Mktg - Microsoft Corporation; *pg.* 435, *pg.* 1824
Dougherty, Katie, Reg Dir-PR & Adv - Caesars Entertainment Corporation; *pg.* 1083, *pg.* 1023
Dougherty, Rita, Coord-Mktg - Milton Roy Company; *pg.* 1361, *pg.* 1542
Dougherty, Wendy, Dir-PR - Medtronic, Inc.; *pg.* 1564, *pg.* 939
Doughney, John, Client Partner-Global Mktg Solutions - Facebook, Inc.; *pg.* 1245, *pg.* 143
Doughty, Kristin, Mgr-Brand Mktg - Capella Education Company; *pg.* 599, *pg.* 931
Doughty, Lisa K., Mgr-PR - Waste Management, Inc.; *pg.* 1954, *pg.* 1716
Douglas, Beth, Assoc Mgr-Mktg - Russell Brands LLC; *pg.* 698, *pg.* 726
Douglas, David, Sr Dir-Primary Care Mktg - McKesson Corporation; *pg.* 1560, *pg.* 222
Douglas, Donna, Sr Mgr-Bus Dev - Bermuda Department of Tourism; *pg.* 989, *pg.* 1202
Douglas, Georgia, Mgr-Creative Adv-Worldwide - Sony Pictures Home Entertainment; *pg.* 310, *pg.* 72
Douglas, Greg, Sr Mng Dir-Comm, Media & Tech - Accenture; *pg.* 1392, *pg.* 1186
Douglas, Jamari, Mgr-Digital Mktg - Bermuda Department of Tourism; *pg.* 989, *pg.* 1202
Douglas, Linda, Sr Dir-Mktg & Annual Giving - University of Michigan; *pg.* 609, *pg.* 867
Douglas, Mindy, Mgr-Mktg-Enterprise Bus Grp - Lenovo Group Ltd; *pg.* 427, *pg.* 1384
Douglas, Nasha-Monique, Brand Mgr-Spirits & Wines - Diageo Canada, Inc.; *pg.* 1961, *pg.* 1937
Douglas, Rosa, Specialist-Mktg - SYNNEX Corporation; *pg.* 480, *pg.* 92
Douglas, Tammy, Mgr-New Products - 3M Company; *pg.* 1142, *pg.* 956
Douglas, Tracy, Sr Mgr-Indus Mktg - Autodesk Inc.; *pg.* 356, *pg.* 257
Douglass, Chris, Mgr-Mktg - FedEx Corporation; *pg.* 1907, *pg.* 1642
Douglass, Jeffrey, Dir-Mktg - Weyco Group, Inc.; *pg.* 1822, *pg.* 1858
Douglass, Linda, Global Head-Comm-Bloomberg Media -

First page reference indicates Business Class Edition
Second page reference indicates Geographic Edition

Bloomberg L.P.; pg. 725, pg. 1204
Douglass, Mike, VP & Global Head-Strategic Sls - Sabre Corporation; pg. 1710, pg. 752
Douglass, Pat, Product Mgr - Mohawk Home; pg. 935, pg. 541
Douglass, Sarah, Sr VP & Mgr-Mktg-Wells Fargo Wealth Mgmt - Wells Fargo & Company; pg. 819, pg. 232
Douglass, Stephanie, Sr Dir-People & Culture - OpenTable, Inc.; pg. 450, pg. 224
Douglass, Tom, VP-Sls & Mktg-Global - SeaStar Solutions; pg. 1374, pg. 1548
Dove, Kevin, Head-External Comm & Media Rels - Canadian Imperial Bank of Commerce; pg. 729, pg. 1935
Dovel, Steve, Acct Mgr-Mktg & Strategy - Forrester Research, Inc.; pg. 1642, pg. 807
Dow, Amy, Sr Mgr-Corp Comm-Global - New Balance Athletic Shoe, Inc.; pg. 1811, pg. 798
Dow, Gabrielle Valdez, VP-Mktg & Fan Engagement - Green Bay Packers, Inc.; pg. 551, pg. 1859
Dow, Lauren, Assoc Product Mgr - Olympus America Inc.; pg. 1425, pg. 1521
Dow, Leslie, Mgr-Loyalty Mktg - Safeway Inc.; pg. 1032, pg. 184
Dow, Steve, Sr Dir-Adv Media - CVS Health Corporation; pg. 1765, pg. 1610
Dowd, David, Sr Dir-Ticket Sls - Chicago Professional Sports Limited Partnership; pg. 539, pg. 570
Dowd, Jennifer, Head-Social Media - MFS Investment Management; pg. 782, pg. 798
Dowd, Kathleen, Sr VP-Mktg - Boehringer Ingelheim Pharmaceuticals, Inc.; pg. 1507, pg. 368
Dowd, Sheila, Sr Mgr-Global Ad Production-GP - PepsiCo, Inc.; pg. 259, pg. 1327
Dowd, Thomas, Mgr-Mktg - Grossmans Bargain Outlet; pg. 85, pg. 847
Dowd, Tracy, Dir-Sls - HBG Books, Inc.; pg. 1648, pg. 1238
Dowdle, Jim, Sr VP-Adv Sls-Midwest & Mid-Central Reg - Time Inc.; pg. 1693, pg. 1300
Dowdle, Keith, Asst Mgr-After Sale Mktg Grp & Motorcycle Division - American Honda Motor Co., Inc.; pg. 163, pg. 292
Dowdy, L. Craig, Sr VP-External Affairs, Corp Comm & Mktg - The Laclede Group, Inc.; pg. 980, pg. 999
Dowe, Desiree, Brand Mgr-Innovation-Global - Neutrogena Corporation; pg. 517, pg. 137
Dower, Michelle, Dir-Creative - SGK; pg. 1686, pg. 590
Dowhan, Michael, Sr VP-Global Bus Dev & Sls - MORNINGSTAR, INC.; pg. 784, pg. 583
Dowlen, Ryan, Analyst-Mktg Compliance - FRANKLIN RESOURCES, INC.; pg. 760, pg. 254
Dowley, Cindy, Head-New Bus Sls-West-Google Analytics Premium - Google Inc.; pg. 1249, pg. 153
Dowley, Craig, Sr Dir-Mktg Comm - Cognex Corporation; pg. 1406, pg. 834
Dowling, Dorothy, Sr VP-Mktg & Sls - Best Western International, Inc.; pg. 1081, pg. 15
Dowling, Greg, Sr Mgr - Ernst & Young Global Limited; pg. 748, pg. 1228
Dowling, Jennifer, Mgr-Product Mgmt - TriZetto Corporation; pg. 485, pg. 327
Dowling, Joan, Mgr-Mktg Comm - AT&T; pg. 1865, pg. 258
Dowling, Laura, Dir-Mktg-US - Harry Winston, Inc.; pg. 6, pg. 1238
Dowling, Mike, Mgr-Mktg - Diamond Power International, Inc.; pg. 1070, pg. 1457
Dowling, Patrick J., Jr., Dir-US Sls-Document Solutions - Cincom Systems, Inc.; pg. 372, pg. 1411
Dowling, Stephanie, Deputy Dir-Mktg - Arizona Office of Tourism; pg. 988, pg. 14
Dowling, Steve, Sr Dir-Corp PR - Apple Inc.; pg. 350, pg. 73
Downard, Dan, Sr Dir-HR - ConAgra Foods Lamb Weston, Inc.; pg. 850, pg. 549
Downes, Jennifer, Dir-Direct Response Mktg - Lenovo Group Ltd; pg. 427, pg. 1384
Downes, Nancy, Specialist-Mktg - Enterprise Bancorp Inc.; pg. 747, pg. 829
Downes, Raymond, VP-Sls - Hill Phoenix Inc.; pg. 1072, pg. 528
Downes, Susan, Supvr-Adv Billing - The Reader's Digest Association, Inc.; pg. 1679, pg. 1322
Downey, Ashley, Mgr-Mktg-Gift Cards & Specialty Mdsg - Giant Eagle, Inc.; pg. 1020, pg. 1575
Downey, Karrie, Head-Comml-Oncology & Sr Dir-Comml Strategy - Sanofi US; pg. 1592, pg. 1046
Downey, Kerrie K., VP-Multi-Cultural & Retention Mktg - DIRECTV Group Holdings, LLC; pg. 281, pg. 79
Downey, Sean, Sr Product Mgr-Mktg - Comcast Cable Communications, Inc.; pg. 276, pg. 1560
Downie, Stacy, Mgr-Mktg-Initiative Strategy - Lowe's Companies, Inc.; pg. 1053, pg. 1383
Downing, John, Sr VP-Sls Ops-Worldwide - Netscout Systems, Inc.; pg. 1270, pg. 858
Downing, Kelsey, Asst VP & Mgr-Mktg - Fifth Third Bancorp; pg. 752, pg. 1413
Downs, Liz, VP-Acq Mktg - eHarmony.com, Inc.; pg. 1242, pg. 180
Doxey, Jack, VP-Worldwide Field & Channel Mktg - Autodesk Inc.; pg. 356, pg. 257
Doyal, Monika, Community Mgr-Social Engagement - The Procter & Gamble Company; pg. 1129, pg. 1418
Doyl, Herbert, VP-Sls & Mktg - Belmont Metals, Inc.; pg. 1317, pg. 1145
Doyle, Ben, VP-Sls Enablement - Extreme Networks Inc; pg. 287, pg. 245
Doyle, Bob, VP-Product Dev & Quality Assurance - Cracker Barrel Old Country Store, Inc.; pg. 1723, pg. 1639
Doyle, Brian, Sr Dir-ESPN Mobile & Digital Strategy - ESPN, Inc.; pg. 285, pg. 340
Doyle, Chris, VP-Corp PR - American Century Investments; pg. 711, pg. 980
Doyle, Chris, Brand Mgr-Finlandia Vodka - Brown-Forman Corporation; pg. 1958, pg. 732
Doyle, Courtney, Dir-Customer Dev & Mktg - Sentara Healthcare; pg. 1593, pg. 1797
Doyle, Daniel, Sr Mgr-Mktg - E*TRADE Financial Corporation; pg. 749, pg. 1230
Doyle, Jessica, Dir-Media Rels - Starwood Hotels & Resorts Worldwide, Inc.; pg. 1114, pg. 378
Doyle, Katie, Reg Specialist-Mktg - Grant Thornton International Ltd.; pg. 763, pg. 575
Doyle, Kerri, Mgr-Product Mktg - Siemens PLM Software; pg. 469, pg. 1734
Doyle, Kevin, Pres-Sls & Distr Ops - MillerCoors LLC; pg. 255, pg. 582
Doyle, Lauren, Mgr-Mktg-Dine-In Theatres - AMC Entertainment Inc.; pg. 527, pg. 716
Doyle, Leilani, VP-Product Mgmt & Mktg - US Dataworks, Inc.; pg. 1286, pg. 1746
Doyle, Luke, Dir-Digital Commerce Mktg - NIKE, Inc.; pg. 1812, pg. 1492
Doyle, Magz, Dir-Shopper Mktg & Category-Europe - Coca-Cola Refreshments USA, Inc.; pg. 247, pg. 500
Doyle, Mary, Mgr-Mktg - Sea Pines Resort, LLC; pg. 1112, pg. 1620
Doyle, Matt, Mgr-Digital Mktg - Apple Inc.; pg. 350, pg. 73
Doyle, Matthew, VP-Mktg - AMC, Inc.; pg. 1759, pg. 487
Doyle, Philip, Dir-Mktg-Gastroenterology - Olympus America Inc.; pg. 1425, pg. 1521
Doyle, Phyllis, Mgr-Sls-Natl - ITW Magnaflux; pg. 1418, pg. 615
Doyle, Rachel, Specialist-Mktg - WJBF-TV; pg. 321, pg. 525
Doyle, Robert F., VP-Product Dev & Quality Assurance - CBOCS, Inc.; pg. 1721, pg. 1639
Doyle, Sean F., VP-Sls - CQ Roll Call; pg. 1631, pg. 397
Doyle, Stacy, Mgr-PR & AR - Autodesk Inc.; pg. 356, pg. 257
Doyle, T. C., Sr Dir-Content-Editorial - Penton Media, Inc.; pg. 1676, pg. 1277
Doyne, Olivia, Sr Dir-Global Mktg-Gap - The Gap, Inc.; pg. 1770, pg. 218
Drabowicz, Barbara, Principal-Mktg-FedEx Svcs - FedEx Corporation; pg. 1907, pg. 1642
Draca, Nicolas, Sr Dir-Mktg Ops-Global - LinkedIn Corporation; pg. 1262, pg. 160
Dracolakis, Lisa, Sr Mgr-Brand Strategy & Mktg Res - ABC Cable Networks Group; pg. 268, pg. 51
Draer, Zeev, VP-Strategic Mktg - MRV Communications, Inc.; pg. 441, pg. 64
Draffen, Molly, Mgr-Adv & Promos - Simon & Schuster, Inc.; pg. 1687, pg. 1292
Dragan, Greg, VP-Mktg-Ralcorp Holdings - Conagra Foods; pg. 826, pg. 994
Drago, Christopher, Dir-Enterprise Media - Hewlett-Packard Company; pg. 404, pg. 175
Dragon, Christopher M., Dir-Brand Mktg - Harman Consumer, Inc.; pg. 641, pg. 1355
Dragoo, Darrell, Sr Mgr-Brand Design - ConAgra Foods, Inc.; pg. 826, pg. 1014
Dragoon, John K., CMO & Exec VP - Houghton Mifflin Harcourt Publishing Company; pg. 1651, pg. 796
Drahl, Barbara, VP-Mktg & Sls-SeaWorld San Diego - SeaWorld Parks & Entertainment LLC; pg. 582, pg. 456
Drain, Julia, Mgr-Mktg Data - The E.W. Scripps Company; pg. 1639, pg. 1412
Drake, Alec, Gen Mgr-Sls-Sportsradio - Cumulus Media Inc.; pg. 280, pg. 503
Drake, Andrew, Mgr-Consumer Mktg-Call of Duty - Activision Blizzard, Inc.; pg. 948, pg. 271
Drake, Benjamin, VP-Product Dev - Pita Pit Usa, Inc.; pg. 1744, pg. 549
Drake, Caleb, Analyst-Mktg Strategy - Highmark Blue Cross Blue Shield; pg. 1203, pg. 1576
Drake, Christopher, Head-Mktg-Global - Eli Lilly and Company; pg. 1527, pg. 684
Drake, Hunter, Planner-Sls - PGA Tour, Inc.; pg. 574, pg. 460
Drake, Jed, Sr VP & Exec Producer-Production - ESPN, Inc.; pg. 285, pg. 340
Drake, Justin, Mgr-PR - Dunkin' Brands Group, Inc.; pg. 1727, pg. 810
Drake, Kelley, Dir-Mktg-Intl - AOL Inc.; pg. 1229, pg. 1195
Drake, Kerlin, VP-Mktg - Anthony Forest Products Co., Inc.; pg. 67, pg. 31
Drake, Larisa Semmel, Sr VP-Mktg - Equity LifeStyle Properties, Inc.; pg. 1090, pg. 573
Drake, Peter, VP-Sls & Mktg - Blommer Chocolate Company; pg. 1851, pg. 566
Drake, Roger J., Sr VP-Mktg - Smokey Bones Barbeque & Grill; pg. 1750, pg. 456
Drake, Ryan, Product Mgr-Talent-Global - Apple Inc.; pg. 350, pg. 73
Drake, Sarah, Specialist-Creative Svc & Graphic Designer - Brady Corporation; pg. 363, pg. 1873
Drake, Susan, Mgr-Classified Adv - Daily Press; pg. 1632, pg. 302
Drake, Yvette, VP & Dir-Mktg - World Acceptance Corporation; pg. 823, pg. 1619
Drakton, Florence, Mgr-Social Media Mktg - Toyota Motor Sales, U.S.A., Inc.; pg. 193, pg. 296
Dralla, Lisa, Product Mgr - Banana Republic; pg. 1760, pg. 212
Dramis, George, Sr Mgr-Lipids Brand Fin - AstraZeneca Pharmaceuticals LP; pg. 1497, pg. 389
Draper, Brooke, Dir-Mktg-Global Brand Team - DeVry University Inc.; pg. 600, pg. 649
Draper, James, Mgr-US Mktg-CWZ & PM - 3M Company; pg. 1142, pg. 956
Draper, Julia, Mgr-Mktg Strategy - Victoria's Secret Stores, LLC; pg. 1789, pg. 1471
Draper, Marina, Sr Mgr-Regulatory CMC - CUBIST PHARMACEUTICALS, INC.; pg. 1521, pg. 828
Draper, Michelle, CMO - SVB Financial Group; pg. 808, pg. 270
Draper, Tom, Mgr-Product Mktg - AGCO Corporation; pg. 700, pg. 530
Drapisch, Jennifer, Mgr-Global Mktg-Ruffino - Constellation Brands, Inc.; pg. 1960, pg. 1348
Drapkin, Leah, Specialist-Product Support - Google Inc.; pg. 1249, pg. 153
Drapkin, Lisa, Dir-Mktg & Brand Mgmt - American Express Company; pg. 712, pg. 1190
Drasher, Glenn, Sr Dir-Mktg - Perkins & Marie Callender's Inc.; pg. 1744, pg. 1645
Drate, Leslie, Head-Social Media-Global - NVIDIA Corporation; pg. 447, pg. 268
Draude, Ryan, Sr Dir-Loyalty Mktg - Choice Hotels International, Inc.; pg. 1086, pg. 775
Draveling, Monica, Mgr-Mktg Comm - 3M Company; pg. 1142, pg. 956
Dravillas, Jim, Head-Adv Res - Google Inc.; pg. 1249, pg. 153
Drayton, Lachelle, Head-College Recruiting Diversity Sourcing & Mktg - UnitedHealth Group Incorporated; pg. 1221, pg. 950
Dreaden, Mike, VP-News & Mktg - Cox Media Group; pg. 280, pg. 502
Drebin, Greg, Sr VP-Mktg-Worldwide - 20th Century Fox Film Corp.; pg. 267, pg. 124
Dreibelbis, Leslie, Sr Dir - Johnson & Johnson; pg. 1549, pg. 1091
Dreke, Katie, Sr Brand Dir-Nike Global Media - NIKE, Inc.; pg. 1812, pg. 1492
Drennan, Holly, Dir-Mktg - Hormel Foods Corporation; pg. 863, pg. 915
Drennen, Colleen, Mgr-Retail Mktg-US - Dr. Martens AirWair USA LLC; pg. 1807, pg. 1502
Drennen, Dan C., Dir-Mktg-Travel Insurance & Intl Benefits - Senior Market Sales, Inc.; pg. 1217, pg. 1018

Drenning, Stephanie, District Head-Sls - Eli Lilly and Company; *pg.* 1527, *pg.* 684
Drenocky, Jamie, Dir-Respiratory Mktg - GlaxoSmithKline; *pg.* 1536, *pg.* 1565
Drenocky, Jamie, Dir-Respiratory Mktg - GlaxoSmithKline Consumer Healthcare; *pg.* 510, *pg.* 1554
Dres-Hajeski, Caren, Dir-Mktg - Lipo Chemicals Inc.; *pg.* 1171, *pg.* 1107
Dresen, Terri, Mgr-Mktg & Comm - Allina Health System, Inc.; *pg.* 1491, *pg.* 929
Dressel, Lori Ann, Mgr-Social Media - Mizuno USA, Inc.; *pg.* 1839, *pg.* 538
Dresser, Kelly, Mgr-Direct Mktg & Metrics Construction & Forestry Div - Deere & Company; *pg.* 703, *pg.* 632
Dressing, Monica, Dir-Mktg Comm - Cintas Corporation; *pg.* 372, *pg.* 1411
Dressler, Dana, Mgr-Corp Sls - Chicago Bears Football Club, Inc.; *pg.* 538, *pg.* 623
Dresti, Donovan, Mgr-Mktg - Red Bull North America, Inc.; *pg.* 264, *pg.* 275
Drevna, Nathan, Dir-Mktg Comm, Defense & Space-Honeywell Aerospace - Honeywell International Inc.; *pg.* 407, *pg.* 1088
Drew, Belinda, Assoc Dir-Global Hemophilia Mktg Excellence & Comm - Bayer HealthCare Pharmaceutical Division; *pg.* 1500, *pg.* 1132
Drew, Colleen, Mgr-Adv - Draper's & Damon's, Inc.; *pg.* 24, *pg.* 109
Drew, Krista, Dir-PR & Digital - Pernod Ricard USA, Inc.; *pg.* 1968, *pg.* 1332
Drew, Matt, Dir-Strategic Mktg - Archer-Daniels-Midland Company; *pg.* 825, *pg.* 565
Drew, Patrice, Analyst-Mktg - The New York Times Company; *pg.* 1668, *pg.* 1270
Drew, Susan, Mgr-PR & Media Rels - Siemens Healthcare Diagnostics; *pg.* 673, *pg.* 604
Drewsen, Astrid, Product Mgr-Powertrain - Volvo Trucks North America, Inc.; *pg.* 195, *pg.* 1377
Drey, Scott, Dir-Creative - Yelp! Inc.; *pg.* 1291, *pg.* 235
Dreyer, Adam, Brand Mgr-Kotex - Kimberly-Clark Corporation; *pg.* 1461, *pg.* 1720
Dreyer, Jodi L., Sr Coord-Mktg - Omnicare, Inc; *pg.* 1578, *pg.* 1418
Dreyer, Jonathon, Dir-Cloud & Mobile Solutions Mktg-Healthcare Div - Nuance Communications, Inc.; *pg.* 447, *pg.* 806
Dreyer, Maria, Sr VP-Advertiser Sls & Branded Entertainment - Sony Pictures Entertainment Inc.; *pg.* 309, *pg.* 72
Dreyer, Matt, Mgr-Product Line Grp - VMware, Inc.; *pg.* 490, *pg.* 179
Dreyer, Tim, Dir-PR & Analyst Rels - Aspect Software, Inc.; *pg.* 354, *pg.* 238
Drgon, Karla, Sr Specialist-Mktg & Comm - Accenture; *pg.* 1392, *pg.* 1186
Dribben, Colette, Brand Mgr-Global - Blissworld LLC; *pg.* 501, *pg.* 1204
Driehorst, Mike, Dir-Editorial-Online Media - FCA US LLC; *pg.* 170, *pg.* 868
Driggs, Ben, VP-Mktg - Honeywell International Inc.; *pg.* 407, *pg.* 1088
Driggs, Jeff, Assoc Brand Dir-Mktg-Strategy Design & Promo Plng - Salix Pharmaceuticals, Inc.; *pg.* 1591, *pg.* 1388
Driman, Idan, Dir-Digital Mktg & Production - Sears Canada Inc.; *pg.* 1784, *pg.* 1943
Drinkwater, Jared, VP-Mktg-Natl - Pizza Hut, Inc.; *pg.* 1744, *pg.* 1733
Driscoll, Erica, VP-Adv Sls-Natl - A&E Television Networks, LLC; *pg.* 267, *pg.* 1185
Driscoll, Sharon, VP-Mktg - International Business Machines Corporation; *pg.* 418, *pg.* 1138
Drislane, Tom, Mgr-Auto Sls - The Boston Globe; *pg.* 1623, *pg.* 790
Dristilaris, Megan, Brand Mgr-Mktg - Kaz, Inc.; *pg.* 58, *pg.* 844
Driver, John, CMO - PacketVideo Corporation; *pg.* 304, *pg.* 205
Driver, Michael, Dir-Intl Mktg & PR-Colorado Tourism Office - Colorado Tourism Office; *pg.* 991, *pg.* 318
Driver, Shannon Jamieson, Sr VP-Network Mktg & Creative Svcs - Scripps Networks Interactive, Inc.; *pg.* 1279, *pg.* 1638
Driver, Stephanie, Product Mgr-Ancillary - American Airlines Inc.; *pg.* 1898, *pg.* 1693
Drmanic, Lali, Sr Product Mgr-Food Preservation - Jarden Consumer Solutions; *pg.* 57, *pg.* 412
Drnec, Tim, Mgr-US Channel Mktg-Performance Sports - Oakley, Inc.; *pg.* 1840, *pg.* 86
Drobbin, Jay, Dir-Institutional Client Experience & Product Mktg - Teachers Insurance & Annuity Association - College Retirement Equities Fund; *pg.* 1219, *pg.* 1297
Drobick, Jeff, Chief Product Officer - Tapjoy, Inc.; *pg.* 1396, *pg.* 228
Drobney, Kristin Reineck, Sr Mgr-Mktg - Doctor's Associates Inc.; *pg.* 1726, *pg.* 356
Drobney, Kristin Reineck, Sr Mgr-Mktg - Subway Restaurants; *pg.* 1751, *pg.* 356
Drobny, Jerry, VP-Strategic Revenue Svcs - San Francisco Giants Baseball Club; *pg.* 581, *pg.* 226
Droessler, Michael, Brand Mgr-Gain Design - The Procter & Gamble Company; *pg.* 1129, *pg.* 1418
Droms, Justin, Sr Mgr-Mktg & Engagement - National Geographic Society; *pg.* 1667, *pg.* 402
Drongowski, Mike, Sr Specialist-Product-Nissan Motor Co., Ltd - Nissan North America, Inc.; *pg.* 186, *pg.* 1633
Dronitsky, Mary, Dir-Regulatory Affairs-Adv & Promo - Genzyme Corporation; *pg.* 1534, *pg.* 808
Dross, Heidi, Sr Dir-Grp insurance - Aetna Inc.; *pg.* 1187, *pg.* 351
Drossel, Corinna, Sr Dir-Art - Apple Inc.; *pg.* 350, *pg.* 73
Drouin, Jennifer, Sr Web Designer-Creative - L.L. Bean, Inc.; *pg.* 1777, *pg.* 750
Drover, Jim, Asst Mgr-Store-Sls - Best Buy Co., Inc.; *pg.* 1761, *pg.* 954
Drozdowski, William, Interim CFO - Hampshire Group Limited; *pg.* 25, *pg.* 1237
Drozdz, Chris, VP-Mktg & Sls - The Bonne Bell Company; *pg.* 502, *pg.* 1480
Druart, Tad, VP-Mktg - Abila, Inc.; *pg.* 340, *pg.* 1660
Drubetsky, Abby J., Brand Mgr-Gerber - Nestle USA, Inc.; *pg.* 883, *pg.* 96
Druian, Scott D., Mgr-Field Mktg-Southern Reg - Volvo Cars of North America LLC; *pg.* 195, *pg.* 1117
Druk, Julia, Dir-Product Mgmt - Marvel Entertainment, LLC; *pg.* 1662, *pg.* 1257
Drummond, April, Brand Mgr - Philip Morris USA Inc.; *pg.* 1894, *pg.* 1803
Drummond, Helena, Specialist-Mktg Procurement - SYNNEX Corporation; *pg.* 480, *pg.* 92
Drumond, Marcos, Mgr-Mktg-Room & Pillar - Caterpillar, Inc.; *pg.* 1321, *pg.* 650
Drury, Michael, Sr Dir-Mktg, Plng & Analysis - Vonage Holdings Corp.; *pg.* 686, *pg.* 1074
Drutz, David, VP-Sls-KNBR 680 & KTCT 1050 - Cumulus Broadcasting Inc; *pg.* 280, *pg.* 502
Druzga, Paula, Mgr-Mktg & Comm-Grp Benefits - Sun Life Financial Inc.; *pg.* 806, *pg.* 1944
Dry, Randy, VP-Brand Mgmt & Partner Mktg-Music - Sirius XM Holdings Inc.; *pg.* 308, *pg.* 1292
Dryden, Lee, Deputy Editor-Michigan Publ Hub-Digital First Media - The Daily Oakland Press; *pg.* 1632, *pg.* 905
Dryden, Will, Mgr-Natl Sls & Market-Imaging - Jones-Blair Company; *pg.* 1443, *pg.* 1682
Drye, Eddie, VP-Domestic Sls - Roger Cleveland Golf Company, Inc.; *pg.* 1844, *pg.* 105
Dryer, Matt P, Mgr-Suite Sls - Baltimore Orioles, L.P.; *pg.* 532, *pg.* 755
Dryg, Jennifer, Dir-Creative Solutions-Sephora University - Sephora USA Inc; *pg.* 522, *pg.* 227
Drymalski, Kristina, Assoc Dir-Mktg Svcs Procurement-North America - Mondelez International, Inc.; *pg.* 878, *pg.* 601
Drysdale, Bethany, Dir-PR - Nevada Commission on Tourism; *pg.* 1000, *pg.* 1021
Du Bois, Chris, VP-Interactive Mktg & Strategy - Allianz Life Insurance Company of North America; *pg.* 1188, *pg.* 929
Dua, Paul, Sr Mgr-Digital Mktg & Strategy - Cablevision Systems Corporation; *pg.* 272, *pg.* 1141
Dua, Robin, Head-Product Mgmt - Google Inc.; *pg.* 1249, *pg.* 153
Duan, Coco, Brand Mgr-Cepacol - Reckitt Benckiser Inc.; *pg.* 1136, *pg.* 1105
Duarte, Andres, Dir-Mktg - Diageo North America, Inc.; *pg.* 1961, *pg.* 361
Duarte, Juan, Brand Mgr-Global - Ingersoll-Rand Company; *pg.* 1349, *pg.* 1370
Duarte, Victor, Chief Product Officer-Global - International Game Technology; *pg.* 957, *pg.* 1024
Duartes, Rolo, Exec VP-Sls - Entravision Communications Corporation; *pg.* 285, *pg.* 273
Duban, Robert M., Exec VP-Contract Sls - Kravet Fabrics Inc.; *pg.* 932, *pg.* 1142
Dube, Jason, Sr Mgr-Brand - Specialty Foods Group-Field Packing Div.; *pg.* 897, *pg.* 739
Dube, Liza, Dir-PR & Digital Mktg - Stonyfield Farm, Inc.; *pg.* 899, *pg.* 1035
Dubejsky, Elizabeth, Brand Mgr-Global Male Shave Care - The Procter & Gamble Company; *pg.* 1129, *pg.* 1418
Dubin, Jennifer, Asst Mgr-Mktg-Aquafina - PepsiCo, Inc.; *pg.* 259, *pg.* 1327
Dubinsky, Amy, VP-Event Mktg & Sls-East Central Reg - Feld Entertainment, Inc.; *pg.* 547, *pg.* 458
Dublish, Pratul, Product Mgr - Google Inc.; *pg.* 1249, *pg.* 153
Dubner, Marc, Sr Mgr-Product Dev-Global - Toys "R" Us, Inc.; *pg.* 968, *pg.* 1130
DuBois, Chris, Mgr-Digital Mktg - The Procter & Gamble Company; *pg.* 1129, *pg.* 1418
DuBois, Connie, Brand Mgr-QC - Publix Super Markets, Inc.; *pg.* 1031, *pg.* 437
Dubois, Danielle, Sr Mgr-Brand & Bus Comm - The Coca-Cola Company; *pg.* 240, *pg.* 493
DuBois, Tim, Sr Mgr-Bus Dev - Twitter, Inc.; *pg.* 1285, *pg.* 228
DuBois, Todd R., Coord-PR - Charter Communications, Inc.; *pg.* 274, *pg.* 372
DuBose, Billy, Mgr-Mktg - International Paper Company; *pg.* 1460, *pg.* 1644
Dubow, Jennifer, Head-Global Inside Sls Social Bus Transformation - International Business Machines Corporation; *pg.* 418, *pg.* 1138
Dubreil, Pierrick, Dir-Sls-West - International Foods and Ingredients Inc.; *pg.* 865, *pg.* 616
Dubreuil, Bruno, VP-Product Mktg-WMS Solutions - TECSYS, Inc.; *pg.* 482, *pg.* 1956
Dubus, Tim, Dir-Creative & Mktg - The Denver Newspaper Agency; *pg.* 1634, *pg.* 318
Ducey, Bob, Mgr-Worldwide Mktg-Comml All-in-One PCs - Hewlett-Packard Company; *pg.* 404, *pg.* 175
Duchak, Donovan, Dir-Own Brand Product Dev - Staples, Inc.; *pg.* 474, *pg.* 821
Duchak, Sue, Sr Mgr - The Allstate Corporation; *pg.* 1189, *pg.* 639
Duchamp, Sebastien, Dir-Digital Comm & Media Rels - General Electric Company; *pg.* 1297, *pg.* 347
Ducharme, Jackie, Mgr-Product Portfolio - Xcel Energy Inc.; *pg.* 1955, *pg.* 946
DuCharme, Marc, Dir-Comml Sls - GOJO Industries, Inc.; *pg.* 330, *pg.* 1401
Ducharme, Ron, Product Mgr-Product Identification - FLEXcon Corporation; *pg.* 1457, *pg.* 844
Duchateau, Sylvia, Dir-Mktg - Alexian Brothers Health System Foundation; *pg.* 1489, *pg.* 553
Duchene, Nicole, Mgr-Trade Mktg - Michael Foods, Inc.; *pg.* 877, *pg.* 949
Duchi, Rebecca, Coord-Mktg - The Hain Celestial Group, Inc.; *pg.* 860, *pg.* 1172
Duck, Fred, Head-Internal Ops & Media Plng - Bloomberg L.P.; *pg.* 725, *pg.* 1204
Ducker, Michael, Sr Product Mgr - Twitter, Inc.; *pg.* 1285, *pg.* 228
Duckett, Joe, VP-Mktg & Sls - Windstar Cruises; *pg.* 1931, *pg.* 1843
Duckett, Michelle, Assoc Mgr-Mktg Ops - Blackbaud, Inc.; *pg.* 361, *pg.* 1613
Duckett, Raeven, Media Planner-Display - Adobe Systems Incorporated; *pg.* 342, *pg.* 235
Duckworth, Pam, Sr Dir-Adv Production & Events - DIRECTV Group Holdings, LLC; *pg.* 281, *pg.* 79
Ducre, Renee, Dir-Digital Mktg, IBM Commerce, Mobile & Social - International Business Machines Corporation; *pg.* 418, *pg.* 1138
Ducre, Renee E., Dir-Global Mktg-IBM Social Bus - IBM; *pg.* 410, *pg.* 1449
Duda, Ed, Dir-Comm Data Sls - Graybar Electric Company, Inc.; *pg.* 1299, *pg.* 997
Dudas, Sean, VP-Publicity-Field Mktg - The Walt Disney Company; *pg.* 317, *pg.* 52
Dudash, Erica, Sr Dir-CRM Strategies & Execution - American Eagle Outfitters, Inc.; *pg.* 37, *pg.* 1572
Dudash, Jeff, Sr Mgr-PR-North America, Asia, Middle East & Africa - NCR Corporation; *pg.* 443, *pg.* 531
Dudding, Chris, Dir-Mktg - Ski Roundtop Operating Corp.; *pg.* 1113, *pg.* 1548
Dudeck, Diane, Sr Dir-Go to Market Strategy, Plng & Ops - Cisco Systems, Inc.; *pg.* 372, *pg.* 240
Dudek, Jodie, Mgr-Creative Svcs - The Travelers Companies, Inc.; *pg.* 1220, *pg.* 352

Dudek, Stacey, Specialist-Mktg Comm & Channels - Merck & Co., Inc.; *pg.* 1566, *pg.* 1077
Dudenhoeffer, Tammy L., Acct Exec-Charter Media - Charter Communications, Inc.; *pg.* 274, *pg.* 372
Duderstadt, Will, Mgr-Mktg & Dev-Web Platforms - M/I Homes, Inc.; *pg.* 95, *pg.* 1441
Dudley, Brian, VP-Institutional Sls - TD Ameritrade Holding Corporation; *pg.* 808, *pg.* 1018
Dudley, Christopher, Dir-Mktg & Bus Dev - Simon Property Group, Inc.; *pg.* 1112, *pg.* 690
Dudley, Edward L., Sr VP-Sls & Mktg - Rocky Mountain Chocolate Factory, Inc.; *pg.* 1032, *pg.* 324
Dudley, Elizabeth, Planner-Event-US Investment Svcs Integrated Mktg - T. Rowe Price Group Inc.; *pg.* 808, *pg.* 759
Dudouit, Julien, Brand Mgr-Global IP-Legal Intellectual Property - eBay Inc.; *pg.* 1240, *pg.* 243
Dudrey, Donald, Mgr-Online & Video Products-Content Discovery & Product Comm - DISH Network Corporation; *pg.* 283, *pg.* 325
Dudukovich, Jim, Sr Counsel-Mktg, Digital & Social Media - The Coca-Cola Company; *pg.* 240, *pg.* 493
Dudum, Connie, Head-Internal Comm & Sr Mgr - Cisco Systems, Inc.; *pg.* 372, *pg.* 240
Dudziak, Connie, Mgr-Adv Ops - Vance Publishing Corporation; *pg.* 1699, *pg.* 627
Duell, Pamela, Mgr-Worldwide Creative Adv-Theatrical New Release - Warner Home Video Inc.; *pg.* 319, *pg.* 55
Duenas, Jose, Exec VP-Mktg - Olive Garden Italian Restaurant; *pg.* 1742, *pg.* 454
Duenas, Jose A., CMO & Exec VP-Olive Garden - Darden Restaurants, Inc.; *pg.* 1724, *pg.* 453
Duensing, Jessica, Head-Creative & Design-Corp Mktg - Red Hat, Inc.; *pg.* 460, *pg.* 1388
Duerr, Jeremy, Mgr-Product Mktg-U-verse TV - AT&T Communications Corp.; *pg.* 1866, *pg.* 1043
Duerr, Jeremy, Mgr-Product Mktg-U-verse TV - AT&T Inc.; *pg.* 1867, *pg.* 1674
Duerr, Tim, Mgr-Motorsports Mktg - Ford Motor Company; *pg.* 172, *pg.* 876
Duez, Guillaume, Asst VP-Mktg Global-Redken - L'Oreal USA; *pg.* 514, *pg.* 1252
Dufek, Alex C., Sr Mgr-PR - AT&T Inc.; *pg.* 1867, *pg.* 1674
Dufek, Ashlee, Product Mktg Mgr-Cisco - ScanSource, Inc.; *pg.* 671, *pg.* 1618
Dufek, Marjorie, Dir-Integrated Comm-North America - Brown-Forman Corporation; *pg.* 1958, *pg.* 732
Duff, Eleanor, Sr Mgr-Programmatic Media-eBay Enterprise - eBay Inc.; *pg.* 1240, *pg.* 243
Duff, Jason, Assoc Dir-Mktg-Global eBusiness - The Procter & Gamble Company; *pg.* 1129, *pg.* 1418
Duffett, Michael, VP & Gen Mgr-ITCG Printer Mktg, Internet Mktg & Mktg Svcs - Canon U.S.A., Inc.; *pg.* 1404, *pg.* 1178
Duffey, Amy, VP-Bus Dev & Sls-North America - Cartesian; *pg.* 369, *pg.* 718
Duffie, Deary Paul, Sr Dir-Learning & Org Dev - Genentech, Inc.; *pg.* 1533, *pg.* 279
Duffin, Peter, VP-Brand & Mktg - Lincoln Center for the Performing Arts, Inc.; *pg.* 557, *pg.* 1251
Duffin, Tim, Head-Mktg Comm - Ball Horticultural Company; *pg.* 1793, *pg.* 668
Duffner, Karla, Dir-Mktg-Cosmetics L'Oreal Paris-USA - L'Oreal USA; *pg.* 514, *pg.* 1252
Duffner, Steven, Grp Dir-Creative & Sr Mgr - Discover Financial Services; *pg.* 744, *pg.* 653
Duffy, Andrew, Mgr-Mktg - United Parcel Service, Inc.; *pg.* 1928, *pg.* 522
Duffy, Beth, Sr Mgr-Mktg Traffic - David's Bridal, Inc.; *pg.* 23, *pg.* 1523
Duffy, Brendan, VP-Mktg - Caravan Tours, Inc.; *pg.* 1902, *pg.* 568
Duffy, Brian, Sr Dir-Mktg - KLA-Tencor Corporation; *pg.* 1353, *pg.* 146
Duffy, Brian, Dir-Sls - TiVo Inc.; *pg.* 313, *pg.* 251
Duffy, Caitlin, Sr Mgr-Mktg Comm - Microsoft Corporation; *pg.* 435, *pg.* 1824
Duffy, Colleen, VP-Sls - ANC Sports Enterprises, LLC; *pg.* 1825, *pg.* 1325
Duffy, Danna, Mgr-Mktg - Rowenta (USA), Inc.; *pg.* 60, *pg.* 1084
Duffy, Gary, Sr Dir-Mktg - AT&T; *pg.* 1865, *pg.* 258
Duffy, Jennifer L., Dir-Food & Beverage Mktg - MGM Resorts International; *pg.* 1105, *pg.* 1028
Duffy, Jim, Sr Dir-Corp Comm - Automatic Data Processing, Inc.; *pg.* 357, *pg.* 1117
Duffy, Katie Ferguson, Brand Mgr-Coffee - The Kraft Heinz Company; *pg.* 871, *pg.* 641
Duffy, Leigh, Mgr-Mktg Comm - Ansell; *pg.* 1495, *pg.* 1114
Duffy, Mark A., Dir-Mktg - Nonni's Food Company Inc.; *pg.* 886, *pg.* 1490
Duffy, Mike, Pres-Medical Products - Cardinal Health, Inc.; *pg.* 1512, *pg.* 1448
Duffy, Patrick, VP-Strategic Mktg - Associated Estates Realty Corporation; *pg.* 1080, *pg.* 1471
Duffy, Shannon, VP-Mktg-Pardot - salesforce.com, inc.; *pg.* 1278, *pg.* 226
Duffy, Tom, VP-Sls-Vending Svcs Div - FreshBrew Coffee, LLC; *pg.* 857, *pg.* 1706
Dufour, Jennifer, Product Mgr - Zep Inc.; *pg.* 338, *pg.* 524
Dugal, Tiffany, Mgr-Global CT Product - Vital Images, Inc.; *pg.* 1607, *pg.* 950
Dugan, Darin, Sr VP-Mktg & Culinary-Applebee's, Dine Equity - Applebee's International, Inc.; *pg.* 1715, *pg.* 980
Dugan, Joe, Sr VP-Turner Digital Sls - Turner Broadcasting System, Inc.; *pg.* 314, *pg.* 521
Duggan, Colin, Dir-Product Line - Analog Devices, Inc.; *pg.* 617, *pg.* 839
Duggan, Daniel J., Pres-Intl Sls Div & VP - HMI Industries Inc.; *pg.* 56, *pg.* 1475
Duggan, George T., Grp VP-Coal Mktg - Burlington Northern Santa Fe, LLC; *pg.* 1901, *pg.* 1694
Duggan, Kate, Dir-Digital Mktg - Safeway Inc.; *pg.* 1032, *pg.* 184
Dugger, Jamie, VP-Creative - Animal Planet, LLC; *pg.* 270, *pg.* 777
Dugger, Jillian, Mgr-Shopper Mktg - GlaxoSmithKline; *pg.* 1536, *pg.* 1565
Duhaime, Melissa, Sr Mgr-Mktg-Pepsi Sports - PepsiCo, Inc.; *pg.* 259, *pg.* 1327
Duhaime, Patrick, Dir-Mktg Strategy - NACCO Industries, Inc.; *pg.* 1174, *pg.* 1433
Duhl, Dan, Dir-Sports Mktg & Sponsorships - Nationwide Mutual Insurance Company; *pg.* 1210, *pg.* 1442
Duhn, Brian S., VP & Specialist-Index Sls - MSCI Inc.; *pg.* 785, *pg.* 1262
Duhon, Ann, Sr Mgr-Comm-Global - BMC Software, Inc.; *pg.* 362, *pg.* 1701
Duhon, Bryant, Specialist-Inbound Mktg - AIIM International; *pg.* 1614, *pg.* 777
Dujan, Alexis, Sr Mgr-Innovation-Beauty New Bus Creation - The Procter & Gamble Company; *pg.* 1129, *pg.* 1418
Dujmovich, Lynne, Dir-Mktg - The Clorox Company; *pg.* 327, *pg.* 169
Dukalskis, Renada, Mgr-Mktg Programs-Datacom & Security - WESCO International Inc.; *pg.* 687, *pg.* 1582
Duke, Ben, VP-Mktg & Sls - Briggs & Stratton Corporation; *pg.* 201, *pg.* 1899
Duke, Brittney, Sr Dir-Partnership & Tech - Wal-Mart Stores, Inc.; *pg.* 1790, *pg.* 29
Duke, Eugene, Sr Mgr-Corp Comm - Canadian Imperial Bank of Commerce; *pg.* 729, *pg.* 1935
Duke, John, Dir-Sls Ops-Strategic Accounts - Level 3 Communications, Inc.; *pg.* 1262, *pg.* 312
Duke, Rebecca, Brand Mgr-Milky Way & 3 Musketeers - Mars North America; *pg.* 1859, *pg.* 1072
Duke, Sharon, Sr VP-Mktg - National Bank of South Carolina; *pg.* 785, *pg.* 1614
Dukeshire, Wendy J., Mgr-Mktg Comm - Dana Holding Corporation; *pg.* 203, *pg.* 1461
Dukhi, Sandy, Mgr-Mktg - Nestle Canada Inc.; *pg.* 883, *pg.* 1929
Dukowitz, Nikki Greer, Specialist-Mktg Project - Dallas Convention & Visitors Bureau; *pg.* 991, *pg.* 1678
Dula, Brian S., Mgr-Mktg - Siemens Corporation; *pg.* 803, *pg.* 1291
Dula, Christy, Dir-IT Bus Svcs-Mdsg, Mktg & Pricing - Family Dollar Stores, Inc.; *pg.* 1768, *pg.* 1382
Dulay, Carrie, Mgr-Recruitment Mktg-North America - Accenture; *pg.* 1392, *pg.* 1186
Duldulao, Richie, Sr Mgr-Online Consumer Mktg - Bonnier Corporation; *pg.* 1622, *pg.* 480
Dull, Dawn, Mgr-Field Mktg-Central US - F5 Networks, Inc.; *pg.* 396, *pg.* 1835
Dullinger, Roger, Mgr-Mktg Comm - Despatch Industries; *pg.* 1070, *pg.* 927
Dumaresq, Todd, Mgr-Mktg-Toll Brothers City Living - Toll Brothers, Inc.; *pg.* 115, *pg.* 1541
Dumars, Bert, VP-Digital Mktg - BI-LO, LLC; *pg.* 1015, *pg.* 1617
Dumas, Clark, Mgr-Strategy-CMT-Sls & Customer Svcs - Accenture; *pg.* 1392, *pg.* 1186
Dumesnil, Marie, Dir-Interactive Mktg-Leisure - Aramark; *pg.* 1013, *pg.* 1558
Dumford, Heather, Dir-Global Mktg-Media - ConAgra Foods, Inc.; *pg.* 826, *pg.* 1014
Dumler, Michelle, Sr Dir-Mktg - Tommy Bahama; *pg.* 48, *pg.* 1842
Dummett, Steve, VP-Product Dev - Winnebago Industries, Inc.; *pg.* 1712, *pg.* 707
Dumond, Susan, VP-Employee Digital Media Products - The Walt Disney Company; *pg.* 317, *pg.* 52
Dumont, Alex, Asst VP-Product Mgmt & Dev - Sun Life Financial Inc.; *pg.* 806, *pg.* 1944
Dumont, Jessica, Bus Head-Mass Market Consumer Mktg - MasterCard Incorporated; *pg.* 779, *pg.* 1325
Dumont, Kristen, Sr Mgr-Sls Plng & Ops-Intl - The Timberland Company; *pg.* 1821, *pg.* 1039
Dumont, Theo, Dir-PR - Metro-Goldwyn-Mayer Inc.; *pg.* 298, *pg.* 47
DuMoulin, Hillary, Mgr-Mktg Comm - Berry Plastics; *pg.* 1879, *pg.* 678
Dunagan, Brian, Dir-Retail Mktg - FedEx Corporation; *pg.* 1907, *pg.* 1642
Dunagan, Christine, Mgr-Digital Mktg - First Data Corporation; *pg.* 754, *pg.* 505
Dunagan, Tim, Grp Dir-Mktg - Forging Industry Association; *pg.* 141, *pg.* 1431
Dunaj, Michelle, Project Mgr-Mktg & Publr - Bluegreen Corporation; *pg.* 1082, *pg.* 410
Dunaj, Sara, Mgr-Social Media - Princess Cruise Lines Ltd.; *pg.* 1920, *pg.* 270
Dunayevich, Rama, Sr Mgr-PR, Film, TV & Bio/Nano/Programmable Matter - Autodesk Inc.; *pg.* 356, *pg.* 257
Dunbar, Cynthia, VP-Physician Mktg - Concierge Choice Physicians; *pg.* 1517, *pg.* 1338
Dunbar, Whitlock, Sr Mgr-Online Mktg - AT&T; *pg.* 1865, *pg.* 258
Duncan, Brian, Sr VP-Sls - EBSCO Information Services Walpole; *pg.* 1638, *pg.* 849
Duncan, Cameron, Mgr-Product Mktg-Alienware - Dell Inc.; *pg.* 383, *pg.* 1737
Duncan, Chris, VP-Strategic Mktg - Kohl's Corporation; *pg.* 1775, *pg.* 1870
Duncan, David, Mgr-Product Line - InFocus Corporation; *pg.* 644, *pg.* 1503
Duncan, David, Sr VP-Mktg-Mohawk Flooring Div - Mohawk Industries, Inc.; *pg.* 935, *pg.* 527
Duncan, Doug S., Sr Mgr-Strategic Mktg - Siemens Process Industries and Drives; *pg.* 673, *pg.* 485
Duncan, Ellen, Sr Mgr-Digital Mktg - The Coca-Cola Company; *pg.* 240, *pg.* 493
Duncan, Eric, Brand Mgr-Daybreak Games - Daybreak Game Company, LLC; *pg.* 1237, *pg.* 202
Duncan, Galen, Sr Dir-Player Dev - The Detroit Lions, Inc.; *pg.* 544, *pg.* 864
Duncan, Heather, Dir-Corp Mktg & Branding - Dollar Tree, Inc.; *pg.* 1767, *pg.* 1778
Duncan, Josie, Sr Dir-Art - Macy's East; *pg.* 1777, *pg.* 1254
Duncan, Josie, Sr Dir-Art - Macy's Florida; *pg.* 1777, *pg.* 444
Duncan, Keith, VP-Sls - RetailMeNot Inc.; *pg.* 1782, *pg.* 1665
Duncan, Kristina, VP-Mktg Comm-Barbie - MATTEL, INC.; *pg.* 962, *pg.* 81
Duncan, Lacey, Specialist-Mktg - The Finish Line, Inc.; *pg.* 1769, *pg.* 686
Duncan, Pat, Sr VP-Mktg, eCommerce & Distr - Helzberg's Diamond Shops, Inc.; *pg.* 6, *pg.* 984
Duncan, Patrick, Sr Mgr-Mktg Science - The Coca-Cola Company; *pg.* 240, *pg.* 493
Duncan, Suzanne, VP-Mktg - Sesame Workshop; *pg.* 307, *pg.* 1290
Duncan, Todd, Brand Mgr-Kobalt - Lowe's Companies, Inc.; *pg.* 1053, *pg.* 1383
Duncan, Tom, Mgr-Mktg Project & Process - Standard Motor Products, Inc.; *pg.* 218, *pg.* 1176
Duncan, Whit, Pres-Land Sls - Crescent Communities, LLC; *pg.* 702, *pg.* 1365
Duncan, Zack, Dir-Mktg Plng-Team Sports, Apparel, Footwear & Outerwear - Dick's Sporting Goods, Inc.; *pg.* 1832, *pg.* 1524
Duncombe, Linda, Mng Dir-Mktg, Digital & Customer Experience - Citigroup Inc.; *pg.* 735, *pg.* 1212
Dundas, Gail, Sr Mgr-Comm - Intel Corporation; *pg.* 645, *pg.* 266

Dundov, Missy, Specialist-Media - State Farm Mutual Automobile Insurance Co.; *pg.* 1218, *pg.* 557
Dungey, Rebecca, Sr Mgr-Trade Show - Intrado Inc.; *pg.* 420, *pg.* 334
Dungo, Aimee, Sr Mgr-Shopper Mktg - Pfizer Inc.; *pg.* 1581, *pg.* 1278
Dunham, Andrea, Dir-Creative - People Magazine; *pg.* 1676, *pg.* 1278
Dunham, Jon, Dir-Asset Servicing Sls-North America - Northern Trust Corporation; *pg.* 787, *pg.* 585
Dunham, Lisa, Dir-Consumer Mktg - Smithsonian Magazine; *pg.* 1687, *pg.* 404
Dunham, Nick, Dir-Media - Dunkin' Brands Group, Inc.; *pg.* 1727, *pg.* 810
Dunham, Rachel, Mgr-Digital Mktg - T.J. Maxx; *pg.* 1788, *pg.* 822
Duniam, Jeremy, Product Mgr-Advanced Tech Solutions & Challenger HHP Tractors - AGCO Corporation; *pg.* 700, *pg.* 530
Dunigan, Fran, Mgr-Mktg - Holmatro, Inc.; *pg.* 1346, *pg.* 771
Dunivan, Larry, CIO-Core Products & Tech - Ceridian Corporation; *pg.* 371, *pg.* 932
Dunivan, Luke, Program Mgr-Direct Mktg-eMail - Recreational Equipment, Inc.; *pg.* 1843, *pg.* 1821
Dunkak, David, VP-Comml Sls-US - Xplore Technologies Corp.; *pg.* 497, *pg.* 1667
Dunkin, Amy, VP-Mktg - Scholastic Corporation; *pg.* 1683, *pg.* 1288
Dunkley, Tammy, Mgr-Corp Adv - Sheetz, Inc.; *pg.* 1033, *pg.* 1514
Dunkley-Graves, Angel, Reg VP & VP-MarketPOINT Mktg - Humana, Inc.; *pg.* 1204, *pg.* 734
Dunlap, David, Gen Mgr-Retail Mktg - Volkswagen Group of America, Inc.; *pg.* 194, *pg.* 1785
Dunlap, Jonathan, Product Portfolio Mgr-Automotive LED Sys - Osram Sylvania, Inc.; *pg.* 1302, *pg.* 816
Dunlap, Julie, Specialist-Mktg - State Farm Mutual Automobile Insurance Co.; *pg.* 1218, *pg.* 557
Dunlap, Norm, Mgr-Sls - Atlantic Corporation; *pg.* 1452, *pg.* 1392
Dunlap, Steve, VP-Sls - Sub Zero Wolf; *pg.* 60, *pg.* 1867
Dunlavy, Joray, VP-Sls & Engrg - Metro Machine & Engineering Corp.; *pg.* 1360, *pg.* 923
Dunleavy, Annette, Dir-Retention & Dev Mktg - QVC Inc; *pg.* 305, *pg.* 1593
Dunleavy, Kathleen, Sr Mgr-Corp Comm - Sprint Corporation; *pg.* 1874, *pg.* 719
Dunleavy, Matt, Dir-Mktg & Customer Experience - Thermo Fisher Scientific Inc.; *pg.* 1431, *pg.* 854
Dunleavy, Michele, Sr Mgr-Comml Ops-US Compliance - AstraZeneca Pharmaceuticals LP; *pg.* 1497, *pg.* 389
Dunleavy, Rebecca B., Sr Mgr-Mktg Ops - Abbott Laboratories; *pg.* 1484, *pg.* 551
Dunlop, Christine, Mgr-Mktg-Creative & Production - Manulife Financial Corporation; *pg.* 778, *pg.* 1939
Dunn, Allison, Sr Mgr-Digital Mktg - Boyd Gaming Corporation; *pg.* 1082, *pg.* 1022
Dunn, Annie, Sr Analyst-Mktg - Republic Services, Inc.; *pg.* 107, *pg.* 19
Dunn, Ashlee, Brand Mgr - Reily Foods Company; *pg.* 891, *pg.* 747
Dunn, Brian, Brand Mgr - Sony Computer Entertainment America LLC; *pg.* 966, *pg.* 256
Dunn, Brodie, Sr Mgr-Insights - PepsiCo, Inc.; *pg.* 259, *pg.* 1327
Dunn, Carole, Sr Mgr-Tech Comm - Mentor Graphics Corporation; *pg.* 432, *pg.* 1510
Dunn, Carrie, Mgr-eMail Campaign - Big Lots, Inc.; *pg.* 1762, *pg.* 1438
Dunn, Chris, Dir-Vendor Mgmt Org & Consumer Card Mktg - American Express Company; *pg.* 712, *pg.* 1190
Dunn, Doris Patterson, Mgr-Sls Dept - J.C. Whitney & Co.; *pg.* 209, *pg.* 621
Dunn, James, Dir-Bus Dev, LifeShield Sls & Ops - DIRECTV Group Holdings, LLC; *pg.* 281, *pg.* 79
Dunn, Jean, VP-Strategic Mktg - T. Rowe Price Group Inc.; *pg.* 808, *pg.* 759
Dunn, Justin C., VP & Dir-Mktg Strategies & Product Dev - WSFS Financial Corporation; *pg.* 823, *pg.* 392
Dunn, Larry, Sr VP-Adv - Newsday Media Group; *pg.* 1670, *pg.* 1181
Dunn, Lindsay, Mgr-Mktg - Hershey Entertainment & Resorts Company; *pg.* 1094, *pg.* 1539
Dunn, Megan, Brand Mgr-Card Partnerships - Capital One Bank (USA), N.A.; *pg.* 730, *pg.* 1789
Dunn, Megan, Mgr-Mktg - MATTEL, INC.; *pg.* 962, *pg.* 81
Dunn, Michael, Assoc Dir-Global Product Supply Strategy & Plng - The Procter & Gamble Company; *pg.* 1129, *pg.* 1418
Dunn, Mindy, Specialist-Mktg - FedEx Corporation; *pg.* 1907, *pg.* 1642
Dunn, Montey, Sr Reg Mgr-Mktg - Jack in the Box Inc.; *pg.* 1732, *pg.* 204
Dunn, Nancy, Coord-Sls & Mktg - Johnson & Johnson Inc.; *pg.* 1552, *pg.* 1923
Dunn, Norm, Mgr-Technical Mktg - Cisco Systems, Inc.; *pg.* 372, *pg.* 240
Dunn, Peggy, VP-Mktg Analytics - Huntington Bancshares Incorporated; *pg.* 767, *pg.* 1440
Dunn, Rachel, Mgr-Mktg - American Medical Association; *pg.* 130, *pg.* 564
Dunn, Sandy, Specialist-Sls Comm - Boston Scientific Corporation; *pg.* 1508, *pg.* 831
Dunn, Shannon, Specialist-PR & Comm - Medtronic, Inc.; *pg.* 1564, *pg.* 939
Dunn, Stacie, Brand Mgr-Activation - Beam Suntory Inc.; *pg.* 1957, *pg.* 599
Dunn, Stephen, Sr Dir-Creative-Fossil Brand - Fossil Group, Inc.; *pg.* 5, *pg.* 1735
Dunn, Tara N., Supvr-Mktg - Quality Systems, Inc.; *pg.* 1587, *pg.* 115
Dunn, Thomas, VP-Indus Sls - Alimak Hek Inc; *pg.* 66, *pg.* 1749
Dunn, Tony, Chief Architect-Social Media - VMware, Inc.; *pg.* 490, *pg.* 179
Dunn, Tracy, Dir-Mktg-Consumables Div - PetSmart, Inc.; *pg.* 1481, *pg.* 18
Dunn-Rankin, Paige, Product Mgr - Google Inc.; *pg.* 1249, *pg.* 153
Dunnam, Tami, Mgr-Mktg-Corp Branding - QUALCOMM Incorporated; *pg.* 1873, *pg.* 207
Dunne, Carol, VP-Brand Mktg - La Quinta Corporation; *pg.* 1099, *pg.* 1722
Dunne, Jessica, Sr VP & Gen Mgr-Consumer Products - MATTEL, INC.; *pg.* 962, *pg.* 81
Dunne, Jim, VP-Sls - Heritage Sportswear, LLC; *pg.* 26, *pg.* 1455
Dunne, Kelly, Sr Mgr-Brand Adv - Zoosk Inc.; *pg.* 1292, *pg.* 235
Dunne, Marty, Exec VP-Sls - InterCall, Inc.; *pg.* 417, *pg.* 578
Dunne, Pat, Sr Dir-Channel Sls-EMEA - Blue Coat Systems, Inc.; *pg.* 362, *pg.* 284
Dunnigan, Virginie, Dir-Cancer Immunotherapeutics & Product & Portfolio Strategy - MedImmune LLC; *pg.* 1562, *pg.* 770
Dunnigan, Walter, Dir-IT & Designer-Home Theater - Gallery Model Homes, Inc.; *pg.* 926, *pg.* 1706
Dunning, Gina, Coord-Channel Mktg - Xerox Corporation; *pg.* 494, *pg.* 365
Dunning, Leila, Brand Mgr-Programs - Autodesk Inc.; *pg.* 356, *pg.* 257
Dunning, Vernon, Exec Dir-Creative - IBM; *pg.* 410, *pg.* 1449
Dunnington, Katie, VP-Grp Product Solutions - Lincoln Financial Group; *pg.* 1206, *pg.* 1375
Dunphy, William J., Jr., Sr Dir-Piedmont Reg - Chick-fil-A, Inc.; *pg.* 1721, *pg.* 492
Dunsche, Maria Mandel, VP & Head-Mktg - AT&T; *pg.* 1865, *pg.* 258
Dunsky, Ron, Sr VP-Mktg & Comm - PASSUR Aerospace, Inc.; *pg.* 233, *pg.* 376
Dunsmoor, Matt, Assoc Product Mgr-Employee Innovations - Zappos.com, Inc.; *pg.* 1291, *pg.* 1030
Dunwody, Cathy, Dir-Regal Mktg-RBU West - Pfizer Inc.; *pg.* 1581, *pg.* 1278
Dunwoody, Charles, Sr Dir-Acct Sls-Natl - Holland America Line Inc.; *pg.* 1911, *pg.* 1836
Dunworth-Miller, Kim, Mgr-Mktg - The Allstate Corporation; *pg.* 1189, *pg.* 639
Duong, David, Assoc Product Mgr-Skylanders - Activision Blizzard, Inc.; *pg.* 948, *pg.* 271
Duplessis, Arem, Dir-Creative - Apple Inc.; *pg.* 350, *pg.* 73
DuPont, Cedric, Product Mgr - Google Inc.; *pg.* 1249, *pg.* 153
Duprat, Enrique, VP-Spanish Language Production & Mktg - Eternal World Television Network, Inc.; *pg.* 286, *pg.* 6
Dupre, Danielle, Assoc Mgr-Digital Mktg Content - Reebok International Ltd.; *pg.* 1817, *pg.* 811
Dupre, Nancy, Mgr-Mktg - J.C. Penney Company, Inc.; *pg.* 1774, *pg.* 1732
Dupree, Tracy, Mgr-Media Rels - Alcatel-Lucent; *pg.* 615, *pg.* 1094
Duprey, Ashlee, Specialist-Product Mktg-Tech - McKesson Corporation; *pg.* 1560, *pg.* 222
Duprey, Keith, Dir-Segment Mktg - Interface, Inc.; *pg.* 695, *pg.* 512
Dupriest, Joseph, CMO & Sr VP - Washington Capitals; *pg.* 591, *pg.* 1775
Dupuis, Margie, VP-Online Strategy & Mktg - U.S. Bancorp; *pg.* 815, *pg.* 945
Duque, Connie, Sr Mgr-New Bus Dev - Jarden Consumer Solutions; *pg.* 57, *pg.* 412
Duquette, Ray, VP-Mktg & Bus Dev - CAE USA, Inc.; *pg.* 226, *pg.* 472
Durach, Stephan, Head-Product Line Grand Series-Process E/E & Driving Experience - BMW of North America, LLC; *pg.* 166, *pg.* 1133
Duran, Claudio, Dir-Digital Media Mktg - The ADT Corporation; *pg.* 612, *pg.* 409
Duran, Julie, Sr Mgr-Applications - Pier 1 Imports, Inc.; *pg.* 940, *pg.* 1695
Durand, Michael, Mgr-Media Rels-Massachusetts - Eversource; *pg.* 1942, *pg.* 845
Durange, Michael, VP-New Media & Intl Res - Home Box Office, Inc.; *pg.* 290, *pg.* 1240
Durazzano, David, Program Dir-IBM Social Bus Cloud - International Business Machines Corporation; *pg.* 418, *pg.* 1138
Durbha, Madhav, VP-Product Strategy - JDA Software Group, Inc.; *pg.* 423, *pg.* 22
Durbin, Amy, Mgr-Mktg - Gate City Bank; *pg.* 761, *pg.* 1397
Durbin, Eric, Mgr-Mktg Svc - Intuit Inc.; *pg.* 769, *pg.* 158
Durbin, Josephine, Mgr-Online Mktg & Social Media - HCA HOLDINGS, INC.; *pg.* 1539, *pg.* 1651
Durbin, Mark, Sr Rep-PR - FirstEnergy Corp.; *pg.* 1942, *pg.* 1400
Durbin, Matthew, VP-Mktg, Beverage, Bar Innovation & Revenue Activation - T.G.I. Friday's Inc.; *pg.* 1754, *pg.* 1669
Durden, Pamela, Coord-Adv & Show - Gammex RMI Inc.; *pg.* 1532, *pg.* 1872
Dureau, Amber, Brand Mgr-Smirnoff Vodka & Tanqueray Gin - Diageo Canada, Inc.; *pg.* 1961, *pg.* 1937
Dureau, Jennine, Mgr-Integrated Mktg Comm-Svc Provider - Cisco Systems, Inc.; *pg.* 372, *pg.* 240
Durgee, Julia, Analyst-Digital Mktg - L.L. Bean, Inc.; *pg.* 1777, *pg.* 750
Durham, Katherine, VP-Mktg & Comm - Standard Insurance Company; *pg.* 1217, *pg.* 1506
Durham, Lindsey, Sr Mgr-Digital Mktg - AT&T; *pg.* 1865, *pg.* 258
Durham, Tiara, Sr Mgr-Respiratory DTC Mktg - GlaxoSmithKline; *pg.* 1536, *pg.* 1565
Durham, Tyler, Mgr-Digital Mktg & Gift Card - Texas Roadhouse, Inc.; *pg.* 1753, *pg.* 738
Durkee, Steven E., Pres-Comml Products - Milestone AV Technologies, Inc.; *pg.* 654, *pg.* 964
Durkin, Greg, Sr VP-Mktg Analytics - Warner Bros. Entertainment Inc.; *pg.* 319, *pg.* 54
Durkin, Jodi, Sr Mgr-Digital Media - Wal-Mart Stores, Inc.; *pg.* 1790, *pg.* 29
Durliat, Tori, Dir-Mktg - Advanced Drainage Systems, Inc.; *pg.* 1878, *pg.* 1455
Durmashkin, Yelena, Mgr-PR - QUALCOMM Incorporated; *pg.* 1873, *pg.* 207
Durmaskin, Brian, Sr Assoc Mgr-Mktg - General Mills, Inc.; *pg.* 828, *pg.* 933
Durnford, Eva, Dir-Mktg Ops-Retail Markets - Manulife Financial Corporation; *pg.* 778, *pg.* 1939
Durniak, Anthony, Chm & Dir-Adv - Institute of Electrical and Electronics Engineers, Inc.; *pg.* 144, *pg.* 1109
Duron-Yu, Christina, Mgr-Interactive & Digital Mktg - Toyota Motor Sales, U.S.A., Inc.; *pg.* 193, *pg.* 296
Durr, Sonia, Mgr-Field Mktg & Media Buyer - AARON'S, INC.; *pg.* 912, *pg.* 486
Durrant, Ian, Product Mgr-Global Product Mgmt - Zoll Medical Corporation; *pg.* 1612, *pg.* 814
Durrant, Morgan, Sr Mgr-Corp Comm - Delta Air Lines, Inc.; *pg.* 1905, *pg.* 503
Durrett, Andrew, Strategist-Quality Engrg Social Media - Dell Inc.; *pg.* 383, *pg.* 1737
Dursema, Annie, Analyst-Product Mktg - Tyler Technologies, Inc.; *pg.* 486, *pg.* 1690
Durso, Danielle, Coord-Mktg - David Michael & Co. Inc.; *pg.* 852, *pg.* 1563
Durso, Mike, Sr Mgr-Trade Mktg-Vitamins Minerals Supplements - Church & Dwight Co., Inc.; *pg.* 1153, *pg.* 1063

First page reference indicates Business Class Edition
Second page reference indicates Geographic Edition

Durston, Garry, Dir-Mktg Comm-EMEA - PR Newswire Association LLC; pg. 1678, pg. 1283
Duschack, Julie, Coord-Mktg Comm - Manitowoc Ice, Inc.; pg. 58, pg. 1868
Duschinsky, Rhea, Analyst-Natl Customer Mktg - Wm. Wrigley Jr. Company; pg. 1863, pg. 596
Dusek, Katherine, Mgr-Integrated Mktg Comm - The Allstate Corporation; pg. 1189, pg. 639
Dushane, Mike, VP-Product Dev - Hearst Magazines; pg. 1649, pg. 1239
Dussault, Richard, VP-Mktg - Pratt & Whitney Canada Corp.; pg. 1370, pg. 1952
Dussi, Joe, Sr Mgr-Mktg Comm - Analog Devices, Inc.; pg. 617, pg. 839
Dustman, Tom, Dir-Sls-Intl - Sunnen Products Company; pg. 1379, pg. 1004
Duszynski, Kathryn, Sr Mgr-Retail Mktg - Outerwall Inc.; pg. 1367, pg. 1816
Duthie, Janelle, Brand Mgr - MATTEL, INC.; pg. 962, pg. 81
Dutko, Lauren, Mgr-PR - SKECHERS U.S.A., INC.; pg. 1819, pg. 143
Dutta, Anir, Dir-Worldwide & Bus Mgr-Mktg - Eastman Kodak Company; pg. 1408, pg. 1333
Dutta, Joanna, Gen Mgr & Sr Dir - PepsiCo, Inc.; pg. 259, pg. 1327
Dutton, Chaumanix, Brand Mgr-Mott's - Dr Pepper Snapple Group, Inc.; pg. 250, pg. 1729
Dutton, Elaine, Rep-Wholesale Mktg Sls-NE Reg - Valero Energy Corporation; pg. 986, pg. 1743
Dutton, Erin, Sr Copywriter-Mktg - Travelers Insurance; pg. 1220, pg. 963
Dutton, Jed, Sr Brand Mgr-Global Creative - WestRock Company; pg. 1472, pg. 1805
Dutton, Martha M., Specialist-Mktg - Schlumberger Limited; pg. 801, pg. 1714
Duty, Amy, Principal & Designer-Visual - The Gap, Inc.; pg. 1770, pg. 218
Duval, Olivier, Dir-Mktg-L'Oreal Paris - L'Oreal USA; pg. 514, pg. 1252
Duval, Robyn R., Sr Dir-Mktg - Aetna Inc.; pg. 1187, pg. 351
Duval, Stephane, VP-Mktg - Sleeman Breweries, Ltd.; pg. 265, pg. 1920
Duvall, David, Sr VP-Mktg & Comm - Novant Health, Inc.; pg. 1574, pg. 1394
DuVall, Desiree B., Mgr-Mktg - Hewlett-Packard Company; pg. 404, pg. 175
DuVall, Eric G., Exec Dir-Big Data Mktg Sys & Database Mktg - AT&T; pg. 1865, pg. 258
Duvall, Julia, Coord-Mktg Comm - QUALCOMM Incorporated; pg. 1873, pg. 207
Duvernet, Val, Sr Program Mgr-Content & Social Media Strategy-eBusiness - Advance Auto Parts, Inc.; pg. 197, pg. 1805
Dvi-vardhana, Sonja, Mgr-Digital Mktg - InterContinental Hotels Corporation; pg. 1097, pg. 511
Dvorak, Lisa A., Specialist-Sls Comm - Valmont Industries, Inc.; pg. 1387, pg. 1019
Dvorkin, Roy, Sr VP-Bus Dev, Digital Media & Branding - SDI Technologies, Inc.; pg. 671, pg. 1113
Dvornik, Janka, Mgr-Comm & PR - CMC Electronics Inc.; pg. 376, pg. 1959
Dwarakanath, Deepa, Sr Mgr-Mktg Database & Analytics - Gartner, Inc.; pg. 1248, pg. 374
Dwinell, Eric, Sr Mgr-Digital Mktg - General Mills, Inc.; pg. 828, pg. 933
Dwivedi, Vab, Dir-Mktg & Digital Customer Experience Optimization - Dell Inc.; pg. 383, pg. 1737
Dworakowski, Heather, Mgr-Mktg - Charter Communications, Inc.; pg. 274, pg. 372
Dworsky, Phil, Sr Dir-Mktg Analog & Mixed Signal IP - Synopsys, Inc.; pg. 480, pg. 162
Dwulet, Robert, Sr Dir-Indirect Procurement - Rite Aid Corporation; pg. 1590, pg. 1519
Dwyer, Bill, VP-Sls & Mktg - Putzmeister America; pg. 1371, pg. 1896
Dwyer, Christian, Sr VP-Revenue Products & Distr - Health Grades, Inc.; pg. 1256, pg. 319
Dwyer, Christopher, Reg Dir-Mktg-Europe & Comml Aviation Svcs-Boeing Comml Airplanes - The Boeing Company; pg. 225, pg. 567
Dwyer, Erin, Rels Mgr-Media-North America - Netflix, Inc.; pg. 1269, pg. 141
Dwyer, James, Specialist-Product-Natl - Windstream Corporation; pg. 321, pg. 34
Dwyer, Jen, Mgr-Market Res & Product Dev - Factory Mutual Insurance Company; pg. 1199, pg. 1601
Dwyer, Michael E., Dir-Sls & Mktg - NRG Energy, Inc.; pg. 1948, pg. 1712
Dwyer, Rick, VP-Sls & Mktg & Gen Mgr-Embedded Sls Grp - Intel Corporation; pg. 645, pg. 266
Dwyer, Sue, Coord-Mktg - The Talbots, Inc.; pg. 34, pg. 824
Dybeck, Heidi, Reg Acct Exec-Mktg - CACI International Inc.; pg. 367, pg. 1773
Dybedahl, Jacob, Analyst-Social Media - The Sportsman's Guide, Inc.; pg. 1846, pg. 965
Dybvig, Andy, Sr Mgr-Consumer Insights-Meals Div - General Mills, Inc.; pg. 828, pg. 933
Dybwad, Emily, Mgr-Digital Mktg - Benefit Cosmetics LLC; pg. 501, pg. 213
Dyck, Paul, Sr Dir-Govt Rels-Intl - Wal-Mart Stores, Inc.; pg. 1790, pg. 29
Dyck, Susan, Mgr-Mktg Comm & Individual Insurance - Manulife Financial Corporation; pg. 778, pg. 1939
Dyckes, James D., Sr Dir-Product Mgmt - DIRECTV Group Holdings, LLC; pg. 281, pg. 79
Dye, Alex, Bus Mgr-Food Grains - Union Pacific Corporation; pg. 1927, pg. 1018
Dye, Alex, Bus Mgr-Grain Products - Union Pacific Railroad Company; pg. 1927, pg. 1019
Dye, Janet, Dir-Consumer Mktg Comm - American Greetings Corporation; pg. 1615, pg. 1428
Dye, Justin, Sr Mgr-Cabin Mgmt & In-Flight Entertainment - Honeywell Aerospace; pg. 228, pg. 16
Dye, Kelly, Analyst-Mktg-Global Bus Ops - QUALCOMM Incorporated; pg. 1873, pg. 207
Dye, Melissa, Product Mgr - Dart Transit Company; pg. 1905, pg. 921
Dye, Troy, VP-Brand Mktg - Capital One Financial Corporation; pg. 730, pg. 1789
Dyer, Alex, Dir-Mktg-Crestor - AstraZeneca Pharmaceuticals LP; pg. 1497, pg. 389
Dyer, Bailey, Sr Asst Brand Mgr-Salon Pro Hair Care - The Procter & Gamble Company; pg. 1129, pg. 1418
Dyer, Chantal, Media Planner - T.J. Maxx; pg. 1788, pg. 822
Dyer, Chantal, Media Planner - The TJX Companies, Inc.; pg. 1788, pg. 822
Dyer, Christina, Sr Mgr-Online Mktg - David's Bridal, Inc.; pg. 23, pg. 1523
Dyer, Cindy, Dir-Brand Mktg - Sbarro, Inc.; pg. 1749, pg. 1182
Dyer, Colby, Assoc Mgr-Mktg - Ingram Micro Inc.; pg. 415, pg. 261
Dyer, Connie, VP-Field Mktg - General Growth Properties, Inc.; pg. 1093, pg. 574
Dyer, Darcie, Coord-Digital Mktg - Belk, Inc.; pg. 1760, pg. 1364
Dyer, Erin, Mgr-Mktg Comm - Newell Rubbermaid Inc.; pg. 1128, pg. 515
Dyer, Gina, Sr Mgr-Mktg Comm - Microsoft Corporation; pg. 435, pg. 1824
Dyer, Kerry, Publr-Adv - U.S. News & World Report, L.P.; pg. 1698, pg. 1308
Dyer, Mike, Mng Dir, Chief Strategy Officer & Chief Product Officer - Newsweek Daily Beast Co.; pg. 1670, pg. 1271
Dyer, Paul, Analyst-Market-Sls - Zoltek Companies, Inc.; pg. 123, pg. 974
Dyer, Peggy, CMO - American Red Cross; pg. 130, pg. 395
Dyer, Steve, Sr Dir-Mktg - Ridge Tool Company; pg. 1372, pg. 1452
Dyer, Toddy, Sr Mgr-Event - Zillow Group, Inc.; pg. 1292, pg. 1843
Dyer, Traci, Sr Dir-Brand Strategic Plng & Mktg Ops - Luxottica Retail; pg. 8, pg. 1460
Dykas, Dan, VP-Sls-Global - G&W Electric Company; pg. 1338, pg. 558
Dyke, Jason, Sr Dir-Mktg - Hood River Distillers Inc.; pg. 1964, pg. 1498
Dykeman, Rachel, Specialist-Mktg Automation - The Hanover Insurance Company; pg. 1202, pg. 862
Dykhoff, Cheryl, Mgr-Sls Support - Frontier Airlines, Inc.; pg. 1909, pg. 319
Dykhouse, Jans, Second VP-Sls Ops - Standard Insurance Company; pg. 1217, pg. 1506
Dykmann, Roger, VP-Mktg & Product Mgmt - Honeywell International Inc.; pg. 407, pg. 1088
Dykstra, David, VP-Distillery Sls & Mktg - MGP Ingredients, Inc.; pg. 877, pg. 714
Dykstra, Gary, VP-Gen Market Sls-Manitowoc Foodservice - Lincoln Foodservice Products, LLC; pg. 1127, pg. 1432
Dyrek, Gerri, Grp VP-Corp Comm & Mktg - Digital River, Inc.; pg. 1238, pg. 948
Dyson, Allen, Rep-Sls - Ingram Micro Inc.; pg. 415, pg. 261
Dyson-Handowski, Lisa, Sr Dir-Mktg - American Girl LLC; pg. 949, pg. 1871
Dyster, Mark, Product Mgr-Engrg - Clark Material Handling Company; pg. 1323, pg. 729
Dzadzic, Roman, Sr Product Mgr - CareerBuilder, LLC; pg. 1234, pg. 568
Dzambazova, Tatjana, Product Mgr-Reality Capture & Digital Fabrication - Autodesk Inc.; pg. 356, pg. 257
Dzanis, Marie, Sr VP & Head-Funds, Intermediary Sls & Servicing - The Northern Trust Company; pg. 787, pg. 585
Dzaran, John, VP-Adv - The News Tribune; pg. 1670, pg. 1845
Dzielak, Heather C., Head-Mktg-US Investment Svcs - T. Rowe Price Group Inc.; pg. 808, pg. 759
Dzierzanowski, Pam, VP-Event Mktg - The Patron Spirits Company; pg. 1967, pg. 1029
Dzik, Melissa, Coord-Seasonal Mktg - H&R Block, Inc.; pg. 764, pg. 983
Dzvonik, Frank, Sr Dir-Canada & Latin America - Abbott Diabetes Care, Inc.; pg. 1483, pg. 38

E

Ea, Monica, Mgr-Mktg-Snacks Portfolio for Convenience & Foodservice - General Mills, Inc.; pg. 828, pg. 933
Eaddy, Stephanie, Dir-Mktg-Global - The Coca-Cola Company; pg. 240, pg. 493
Eader, Sara, Sr Mgr-Digital Mktg - Spa Finder, Inc.; pg. 1113, pg. 1295
Eadie, Bonnie, Acct Dir-Integrated Mktg & Comm - FMR LLC (Fidelity Investments); pg. 759, pg. 794
Eadie, Michael T., VP-Wealth Mgmt Sls & Mktg Support - Washington Trust Bancorp, Inc.; pg. 818, pg. 1610
Eagle, Bob, Dir-Sls-Territory 2 - Reliable Automatic Sprinkler Co., Inc.; pg. 1137, pg. 1158
Eagle, Bobby, Sr Mgr-PR - Syniverse Holdings, Inc.; pg. 479, pg. 475
Eagle, Kathy, VP-Mktg & Mgr-Channel - Bank of America Corporation; pg. 718, pg. 1362
Eagle, Parnell, VP & Gen Mgr-ECommerce & Mktg - The Gymboree Corporation; pg. 25, pg. 77
Eagle, Wendy, Sr VP-Comml & Digital Media Ad Ops - Discovery Communications, Inc.; pg. 282, pg. 777
Eagles, Robyn Eckard, Dir-Natl PR - American Honda Motor Co., Inc.; pg. 163, pg. 292
Eaglin, Natalie, Sr Mgr-Mktg - California Pizza Kitchen Inc.; pg. 1720, pg. 127
Eakambaram, Mahadev, Dir-Product Mktg & ISV Enablement - Intel Corporation; pg. 645, pg. 266
Eames, Charlie, Mgr-Sls Admin - Greer Steel Company; pg. 85, pg. 1447
Eames, Kathleen, Specialist-Affiliate Mktg & Intl - Lord & Taylor LLC; pg. 1777, pg. 1252
Eamigh, Suzanne, Sr Mgr-Comm - Tupperware Brands Corporation; pg. 1139, pg. 456
Earl, Darrin, Mgr-Strategic Mktg-Intl Dev & Competitive Strategy - FedEx Corporation; pg. 1907, pg. 1642
Earley, Amanda, Brand Mgr - Darden Restaurants, Inc.; pg. 1724, pg. 453
Earley, Amanda, Brand Mgr - Olive Garden Italian Restaurant; pg. 1742, pg. 454
Earley, Todd, Mgr-Sls - JLG Industries, Inc.; pg. 1351, pg. 1551
Earls, David, Mgr-Adv - SGK; pg. 1686, pg. 590
Early, Lindsay, Mgr-Media Strategy - Best Buy Co., Inc.; pg. 1761, pg. 954
Earnhart, Allison W., Mgr-Sls & Corp Rels - Portland Symphony Orchestra; pg. 577, pg. 752
Earp, Leslie, Media Buyer - Casey's General Stores, Inc.; pg. 1017, pg. 701
Easley, John, VP-Sls & Mktg - Fischer Spindle Group; pg. 1047, pg. 1888
Easley, Reita, Dir-Adv - Shawnee News-Star; pg. 1686, pg. 1488
Easley, Todd, VP-Mktg - MannKind Corporation; pg. 1558, pg. 299
Eason, Jamal, Product Mgr-Android - Google Inc.; pg. 1249, pg. 153
Eason, Shawn, Assoc Mgr-Brand Activation-Rubbermaid Comml Products - Newell Rubbermaid Inc.; pg. 1128, pg. 515
Eason, Stephanie, Mgr-Consumer Mktg - Home Box Office,

Inc.; pg. 290, pg. 1240
East, Greg, Mgr-Svcs Mktg-Global - Brocade Communications Systems, Inc.; pg. 365, pg. 239
East, Mike, Mgr-Sls & Mktg - Brooks Sports Inc.; pg. 1805, pg. 1818
Eastepp, Kaylan, Dir-Interactive & Social Media - Rangers Baseball LLC; pg. 578, pg. 1659
Easter, Alison, Mgr-Mktg - AstraZeneca Pharmaceuticals LP; pg. 1497, pg. 389
Easter, Kevin, Product Mgr - Sysco Corporation; pg. 1035, pg. 1716
Easter, Temeka, Dir-Social Media - SLM Corporation; pg. 804, pg. 388
Easterday, Mary, Dir-Payer Mktg - Bayer Corporation; pg. 1499, pg. 1573
Easterling, Chad, Brand Mgr-East Basketball - NIKE, Inc.; pg. 1812, pg. 1492
Easterly, Richard, VP-Gas Mktg - Chesapeake Energy Corporation; pg. 1937, pg. 1485
Eastin, Meggin, Mgr-Digital Sls Div - Community Coffee Company LLC; pg. 849, pg. 741
Eastman, Danielle, Brand Mgr-Western Herbicides & Clearfield-Canada - BASF Corporation; pg. 1149, pg. 1066
Eastman, Jeff, Sr VP-Global Supplier Mktg & Asset Mgmt - Arrow Electronics, Inc.; pg. 619, pg. 325
Eaton, Dana J., Sr Analyst-Mktg - Pegasystems Inc.; pg. 453, pg. 809
Eaton, Esther, VP-Mktg & Adv - Lumber Liquidators Holdings, Inc.; pg. 94, pg. 1808
Eaton, Gary, Dir-Mktg - IDEXX Laboratories, Inc.; pg. 1543, pg. 753
Eaton, Sara, Mgr-Brand Mktg & Promos - NBC Universal, Inc.; pg. 300, pg. 1266
Ebacher, Katherine, VP & Sr Product Mgr - Fifth Third Bancorp; pg. 752, pg. 1413
Ebanks, Leroy, Brand Mktg Dir-Global Basketball - NIKE, Inc.; pg. 1812, pg. 1492
Ebanks, Mark L., Dir-Mktg-Americas-CIT Aerospace - CIT GROUP INC.; pg. 735, pg. 1212
Ebben, Karen, Dir-Global Analytics & Mktg Effectiveness - General Motors Company; pg. 175, pg. 881
Ebbers, Liz, Sr Mgr-Comm-Global - Medtronic, Inc.; pg. 1564, pg. 939
Ebel, Duffy-Marie, Mgr-Creative-Branding & Brdcst-Belk Stores Svcs - Belk, Inc.; pg. 1760, pg. 1364
Ebenezer, Victor, Engr-Technical Mktg - Cisco Systems, Inc.; pg. 372, pg. 240
Eberhard Pereira, Emily, Product Mktg Mgr-Shopping, Wildfire & Google Display Network - Google Inc.; pg. 1249, pg. 153
Eberhard, Douglas D., Sr Dir-Infrastructure Project Dev - Autodesk Inc.; pg. 356, pg. 257
Eberhardt, Doug, Mgr-Mktg - Sealing Devices Inc.; pg. 1889, pg. 1173
Eberhardt, Toni, Dir-PR & Mktg-Banner Medical Grp - Banner Health System; pg. 1498, pg. 15
Eberhart, Julia, Mgr-Mktg Comm-Live Events - Daktronics, Inc.; pg. 633, pg. 1624
Eberle, Peter, Exec VP-Sls & Mktg - Reliant Asset Management LLC; pg. 1921, pg. 1774
Ebersole, Chad, Product Mgr-Big Data Capabilities - American Express Company; pg. 712, pg. 1190
Ebert, Brian, Mgr-Brand & Retail Mktg - Under Armour, Inc.; pg. 49, pg. 759
Ebert, Ray, Sr Dir-Bus Sys - Miami Dolphins, Ltd.; pg. 562, pg. 419
Ebert, Regan, Sr VP-Mktg - Dr Pepper Snapple Group, Inc.; pg. 250, pg. 1729
Ebmeyer, Meagan, Sr Specialist-Digital Media - Jarden Consumer Solutions; pg. 57, pg. 412
Ebner, George, VP-Wholesale Sls - Broan-NuTone LLC; pg. 1069, pg. 1860
Ebner, Lauren, Mgr-Social Media - Scottrade, Inc.; pg. 802, pg. 1003
Ebright, Denise, Sr Mgr-Mktg - AT&T Mobility LLC; pg. 620, pg. 1152
Ebron, James, Sr Dir-Multicultural Dev & Sls - ESPN, Inc.; pg. 285, pg. 340
Eby, Celeste, Sr Mgr-Digital Media - Kohl's Corporation; pg. 1775, pg. 1870
Eby, Matthew, Sr VP-Consumer & Brand Mktg - The Weather Channel LLC; pg. 320, pg. 523
Eccher, Andy, VP-Vehicle Distr & Accessory Sls - Southeast Toyota Distributors, LLC; pg. 190, pg. 421
Ecclefield, Shawna, Coord-Sls & Mktg - KB Home; pg. 90, pg. 134
Eccles, Lesley Tyrie, Co-Founder & Exec VP-Mktg - FanDuel, Inc.; pg. 547, pg. 1231
Eccles, Michelle, Acct Mgr-PR - Horace Mann Companies; pg. 1203, pg. 662
Eccles, Simon M., Mgr-Customer Mktg-PC Client Grp - Intel Corporation; pg. 645, pg. 266
Echeverry, Natalia, Bus Mgr-Audi - The Collection, Inc.; pg. 168, pg. 418
Echikson, Jim, Sr Dir-Corp Partnerships - American Society for the Prevention of Cruelty to Animals; pg. 131, pg. 1193
Echlin, Lew, Dir-Mktg-Ford of Australia - Ford Motor Company; pg. 172, pg. 876
Echols, Lee, VP-Mktg & Comm - Northside Hospital; pg. 1574, pg. 516
Echols, Terumi, Sr VP-Adv & Circulation - Christianity Today International; pg. 1627, pg. 561
Echon, Annette, Mgr-Grp HR-CurtCo Robb Media - Robb Report; pg. 1681, pg. 142
Eck, Dave, Mgr-Partnership Mktg - Chicago Bears Football Club, Inc.; pg. 538, pg. 623
Eck, John W., Chief Local Media Officer - Univision Communications Inc.; pg. 683, pg. 1307
Eckel, Jeff, Product Mgr-Global - OpenText GXS; pg. 1272, pg. 770
Eckel, Richard, Sr Dir-Comm - Microsoft Corporation; pg. 435, pg. 1824
Ecker, Amy, VP-Mktg - Southwest Airlines Co.; pg. 1923, pg. 1687
Eckert, Antonette, Mgr-Adv & Co-op Mktg - California Travel & Tourism Commission; pg. 990, pg. 196
Eckert, Brian, CMO & Exec VP - Kastle Systems LLC; pg. 648, pg. 1773
Eckert, Lindsay, Dir-Media - Onion, Inc.; pg. 1673, pg. 586
Eckert, Regina, Dir-Digital Media Strategy - Univision Communications Inc.; pg. 683, pg. 1307
Eckert, Scott, VP-Mktg - Community Coffee Company LLC; pg. 849, pg. 741
Eckes-Borys, Stacy, Mgr-Social Media Relationship - Thrivent Financial for Lutherans; pg. 1219, pg. 944
Eckhardt, John, Dir-Mktg Analytics & CRM - Sally Beauty Holdings, Inc.; pg. 522, pg. 1691
Eckhardt, Mariah, Dir-Mktg-Global - Burt's Bees Inc.; pg. 502, pg. 1370
Eckhoff, Bob, VP-Sls - Pompeian, Inc.; pg. 890, pg. 759
Eckman, Kristy, Mgr-Channel Sls-Broad Market - New Balance Athletic Shoe, Inc.; pg. 1811, pg. 798
Eckstein, David, Mgr-Creative Svcs - DIRECTV Group Holdings, LLC; pg. 281, pg. 79
Eckstein, Greg, Dir-Global Segment Mktg-Critical Care - Philips Electronics North America; pg. 662, pg. 782
Eckstein, Jay, Dir-Mktg Svcs - Standard Motor Products, Inc.; pg. 218, pg. 1176
Eclavea, Melody E., Dir-Mktg - AT&T Mobility LLC; pg. 619, pg. 488
Eclevia, Racquel, Mgr-Channel Mktg - NVIDIA Corporation; pg. 447, pg. 268
Economou, Greg, Chief Revenue Officer & Exec VP - dick clark productions, inc.; pg. 281, pg. 273
Economou, Irene, Grp Mgr-Mktg Comm - Synopsys, Inc.; pg. 480, pg. 162
Eddie, Ryan P., Brand Mgr-Valmont - Valmont Industries, Inc.; pg. 1387, pg. 1019
Eddy, Fred, VP-Sls-Retail/E-Tail/DMR-Computer Products Div - D&H Distributing Co., Inc.; pg. 381, pg. 1536
Eddy, Kurt, Mgr-New Bus Mktg & Brand Mgr - DirectBuy, Inc.; pg. 1766, pg. 694
Eddy, Liz, Brand Mgr - Tom's of Maine, Inc.; pg. 523, pg. 750
Edel, Gerald, VP & Gen Mgr-Sls - Boulder Brands, Inc.; pg. 1016, pg. 310
Edelbach, Jamie, Rep-Special Events & Promos Sls - Six Flags Entertainment Corporation; pg. 583, pg. 1698
Edelboim, Jason, Sr VP-Global Product - PR Newswire Association LLC; pg. 1678, pg. 1283
Edell, Uri, Product Mgr-Eliquis Mktg - Bristol-Myers Squibb Company; pg. 1509, pg. 1206
Edelman, Barry, Sr Dir-Digital Mktg - Gartner, Inc.; pg. 1248, pg. 374
Edelman, Carol, Sr Mgr-Consumer Insights & Mobile - LG Electronics U.S.A., Inc.; pg. 651, pg. 1060
Edelman, Lauren, Exec Dir-Color Mktg - Chanel, Inc.; pg. 503, pg. 1211
Edelman-Goldberg, Lisa, Dir-Product & Program Innovation - Medifast, Inc.; pg. 1562, pg. 774
Edelson, Andrew, Dir-Mktg Dev-Digital Media - National Football League; pg. 567, pg. 1264
Edelson, Anne, Sr Writer & Project Mgr-Mktg Comm - AECOM Technology Corporation; pg. 65, pg. 125
Edelstein, Heidi, Assoc Publr-Mktg- Redbook - Hearst Magazines; pg. 1649, pg. 1239
Edelstein, Lauren, Mgr-Consumer Mktg - AutoTrader, Inc.; pg. 1230, pg. 490
Edelstein, Leslie, Dir-Brand & Creative Strategy - Choice Hotels International, Inc.; pg. 1086, pg. 775
Edens, Amanda, Brand Mgr-Pur-Store Design & Construction - L Brands, Inc.; pg. 1776, pg. 1441
Eder, David, Reg Mgr-Sls - Texas Refinery Corp.; pg. 986, pg. 1696
Ederra, Daniel, Reg Mgr-Mktg-DIRECTV Latin America - DIRECTV Group Holdings, LLC; pg. 281, pg. 79
Edgar, Derek, Dir-Mktg-Joint Reconstruction, Sports & Power Tools - DePuy Synthes; pg. 1523, pg. 1593
Edgar, Keisha, Brand Mgr - World Kitchen LLC; pg. 1141, pg. 657
Edgemon, Elliot, Strategist-Display Media - Adobe Systems Incorporated; pg. 342, pg. 235
Edgerton, Brendan, VP-Mktg - Harbor Freight Tools; pg. 1772, pg. 55
Edgin, Meg Way, Dir-Integrated Media IQ & Platforms-Global - Kimberly-Clark Corporation; pg. 1461, pg. 1720
Edgmon, Kevin, Specialist-Technical Field Sls-South Central - Cooper-Atkins Corporation; pg. 1407, pg. 355
Edinger, Stacey, Dir-Sls & Mktg - Hyatt Hotels Corporation; pg. 1096, pg. 577
Edison, Colie, VP-Mktg - Bowlmor AMF; pg. 1828, pg. 1206
Edison, Sonja, Specialist-Product Publicity - United States Postal Service; pg. 1009, pg. 406
Edling, Laura, Mgr-PR-Institutional Grp - SEI Investments Company; pg. 802, pg. 1558
Edlund, Alex, Sr Dir-Global Search Mktg - Marriott International, Inc.; pg. 1102, pg. 764
Edlund, Monte, Pres-Performance Products Div - Huntsman Corporation; pg. 1167, pg. 1758
Edmiston, Elizabeth L., Mgr-Solution Mktg-North America - IBM Canada Limited; pg. 411, pg. 1923
Edmond, Suzanne H., Mgr-Worldwide Network Svcs Mktg - Hewlett-Packard Company; pg. 404, pg. 175
Edmonds, Mike, VP-Svcs, Mktg & Program Mgmt - Honeywell Aerospace Electronic Systems; pg. 228, pg. 17
Edmonds, Paul, Product Mgr-Linear Sys - Bosch Rexroth Corporation; pg. 1319, pg. 1516
Edmondson, Anne, Sr Specialist-Mktg-Product Mktg - Comcast Cable Communications, Inc.; pg. 276, pg. 1560
Edmunds, Lee, Mgr-Natl Adv-Motorcycle Div - American Honda Motor Co., Inc.; pg. 163, pg. 292
Edson, Edward, Mgr-Mktg-Precision & Occasion Platforms - The Hershey Co.; pg. 1855, pg. 1538
Edstrom, Erin, Reg Mgr-Mktg - AGCO Corporation; pg. 700, pg. 530
Edstrom, Kristina, Mgr-Intl Mktg & Global Events - Digi International Inc.; pg. 387, pg. 948
Edwards, Alison, Sr Mgr-Mktg - Accenture; pg. 1392, pg. 1186
Edwards, Anthony, Sr Dir-Player Dev - Arizona Cardinals Football Club, Inc.; pg. 529, pg. 25
Edwards, Antoinette, Specialist-Mktg - MetroPCS, Inc.; pg. 1872, pg. 1683
Edwards, Ashley, Mgr-Social Media - Loews Hotels Holding Corporation; pg. 1101, pg. 1252
Edwards, Bill, VP-Mdsg-Customer Satisfaction - AutoZone, Inc.; pg. 200, pg. 1641
Edwards, Brad S., Jr., Dir-Product Line Mgmt - CommScope, Inc.; pg. 278, pg. 1378
Edwards, Bryan, Mgr-PR-Cedar Point Amusement Park & Resort - Cedar Fair, L.P.; pg. 537, pg. 1471
Edwards, Bryan, Mgr-PR - Cedar Point; pg. 537, pg. 1472
Edwards, Carol, Sr VP-Media Analytics - Nielsen Audio; pg. 446, pg. 768
Edwards, Coral, Head-Mktg - Justworks, Inc.; pg. 424, pg. 1247
Edwards, Cory, Head-Social Media Center of Excellence - Adobe Systems Incorporated; pg. 342, pg. 235
Edwards, Courtney, Mgr-Creative - DriveTime Automotive Group, Inc.; pg. 169, pg. 16
Edwards, David, Head-Product Enhancement Team - Pfizer Inc.; pg. 1581, pg. 1278
Edwards, David, Product Mgr-Vials & Closures - Thermo Fisher Scientific Inc.; pg. 1431, pg. 854
Edwards, Debbie M., Analyst-Mktg - Brown & Brown, Inc.; pg. 1196, pg. 419
Edwards, Don, VP-Sls Ops - Natrol, Inc.; pg. 1570, pg. 64

First page reference indicates Business Class Edition
Second page reference indicates Geographic Edition

Edwards, Ellen, Mgr-Mktg Comm - 3M Company; *pg.* 1142, *pg.* 956
Edwards, Freddie, Mgr-Mktg - IBM; *pg.* 410, *pg.* 1449
Edwards, Gwen, Supvr-Sls - Grady-White Boats, Inc.; *pg.* 1707, *pg.* 1377
Edwards, Jay, Sr Mgr-Comm-Pharma Global Technical - Genentech, Inc.; *pg.* 1533, *pg.* 279
Edwards, Jeanene, Sr Dir-Activewear Mktg - Fruit of the Loom, Inc.; *pg.* 41, *pg.* 725
Edwards, John, Specialist-Advanced Product Dev - 3M Company; *pg.* 1142, *pg.* 956
Edwards, John, Dir-Digital CRM & Direct Mktg - Cellco Partnership; *pg.* 1869, *pg.* 1042
Edwards, Kathy B., Mgr-Exec Briefing Center-North America Mktg - Lexmark International, Inc.; *pg.* 427, *pg.* 730
Edwards, Kenneth, Sr Mgr-Retail Brand - NIKE, Inc.; *pg.* 1812, *pg.* 1492
Edwards, Kurt, Mgr-Sls & Mktg - The Lubrizol Corporation; *pg.* 1171, *pg.* 1481
Edwards, Kurt, Dir-Adv Ops - MORNINGSTAR, INC.; *pg.* 784, *pg.* 583
Edwards, Larry, Sr Dir-Mktg - CUBIST PHARMACEUTICALS, INC.; *pg.* 1521, *pg.* 828
Edwards, Lisa, Mgr-Mktg-Pillsbury Baking - The J.M. Smucker Company; *pg.* 865, *pg.* 1468
Edwards, Mark, Sr VP-Sls & Mktg-Global - Printronix, Inc.; *pg.* 456, *pg.* 115
Edwards, Nataki, VP-Mktg, Digital Strategy & Ops - AARP; *pg.* 124, *pg.* 393
Edwards, Natalya, Mgr-Advanced Product Strategy - Hyundai Motor America; *pg.* 179, *pg.* 89
Edwards, Paul, VP-Chevrolet Mktg - General Motors Company; *pg.* 175, *pg.* 881
Edwards, Paul S., Analyst-Digital Mktg-Global - Imation Corp.; *pg.* 413, *pg.* 952
Edwards, Randy, Sr Mgr-Media Rels - The Nature Conservancy; *pg.* 151, *pg.* 1774
Edwards, Renee, Mgr-Mktg-Social Media - Samsung Electronics America, Inc.; *pg.* 669, *pg.* 1115
Edwards, Robert, Sr Dir-Circulation - Sun-Times Media Group, Inc.; *pg.* 1690, *pg.* 591
Edwards, Stephen, VP-Sls - ZONARE Medical Systems, Inc.; *pg.* 1612, *pg.* 163
Edwards, Thomas, VP-Sls - Keryx Biopharmaceuticals, Inc.; *pg.* 1553, *pg.* 1248
Edwards, Yolanda, Dir-Creative - Conde Nast Publications, Inc.; *pg.* 1629, *pg.* 1217
Edwards, Yolanda, Dir-Creative - Vogue Magazine; *pg.* 1700, *pg.* 1311
Edwardson, Kip, Head-Digital Mktg-Global Consumer - The Scotts Miracle-Gro Company; *pg.* 1799, *pg.* 1459
Edwardson, Kirk, Dir-Mktg - Espial Group Inc.; *pg.* 1243, *pg.* 1932
Edy, Josiane, Mgr-Alliances Mktg - Quantum Corporation; *pg.* 458, *pg.* 250
Eells, Chris, Sr Rep-Mktg - Utica Mutual Insurance Company; *pg.* 1222, *pg.* 1183
Efstratis, Lisa, Mgr-Mktg Comm - Cisco Systems, Inc.; *pg.* 372, *pg.* 240
Egan, Blake, Mgr-Sls & Bus Dev-ECommerce Channel-Sports Optics - Carl Zeiss, Inc.; *pg.* 1405, *pg.* 1345
Egan, Bob, Sr VP-North American Sls & Strategy - Federal-Mogul Holdings Corporation; *pg.* 205, *pg.* 907
Egan, Bobbie, Mgr-Media Rels - Alaska Airlines, Inc.; *pg.* 1897, *pg.* 1830
Egan, Diane, Corp Mgr-PR - Zoll Medical Corporation; *pg.* 1612, *pg.* 814
Egan, Elizabeth, Dir-Shopper Mktg-Strategy & Capability - The Coca-Cola Company; *pg.* 240, *pg.* 493
Egan, Greg, VP-Product Mgmt - NCR Corporation; *pg.* 443, *pg.* 531
Egan, James, Mgr-Partnership Mktg - The Hertz Corporation; *pg.* 1911, *pg.* 450
Egan, Joe, Mgr-Media Resources - The History Channel; *pg.* 290, *pg.* 1240
Egan, Kevin A., Sr Mgr-Competitive Intelligence - Cisco Systems, Inc.; *pg.* 372, *pg.* 240
Egan, Sarah, VP-Global Strategic Mktg-Kogenate - Bayer Corporation; *pg.* 1499, *pg.* 1573
Egan, Sarah, VP-Global Strategic Mktg-Kogenate - Bayer HealthCare Pharmaceutical Division; *pg.* 1500, *pg.* 1132
Egeland, David S., VP-Mktg - General Growth Properties, Inc.; *pg.* 1093, *pg.* 574
Egelhoff, Chad, Mgr-Vertical Mktg - Level 3 Communications, Inc.; *pg.* 1262, *pg.* 1664
Egemo, Dave, Mgr-Mktg - 3M Company; *pg.* 1142, *pg.* 956
Egen, Donna, Brand Mgr - TXU Energy Retail Company LLC; *pg.* 1953, *pg.* 1690
Eger, Elizabeth, Mgr-Global Mktg & Comm - The Donna Karan Company LLC; *pg.* 23, *pg.* 1225
Egge, Steven R., Exec Dir-Global Mktg-Women's Health - Merck & Co., Inc.; *pg.* 1566, *pg.* 1077
Egger, David, Mgr-Mktg - AT&T Mobility LLC; *pg.* 620, *pg.* 1824
Egger, Robert, Dir-Creative - Specialized Bicycle Components, Inc.; *pg.* 1711, *pg.* 152
Eggers, Jana, Sr VP-Products & Mktg - Blackbaud, Inc.; *pg.* 361, *pg.* 1613
Eggers, Michele, Dir-Customer Intelligence Product Line - SAS Institute Inc.; *pg.* 466, *pg.* 1361
Eggers, Scott, Dir-Product Mgmt-Broadband Devices - Motorola Solutions, Inc.; *pg.* 657, *pg.* 659
Eggert, Heidi, Dir-Global Sls ECommerce - NIKE, Inc.; *pg.* 1812, *pg.* 1492
Eggert, Laura, Assoc Dir-Shopper Mktg - GlaxoSmithKline Consumer Healthcare; *pg.* 510, *pg.* 1554
Eggert, Sean, Head-Sports Mktg - Red Bull North America, Inc.; *pg.* 264, *pg.* 275
Eggleston, Charles, VP-Adv Ops - AccuWeather, Inc.; *pg.* 268, *pg.* 1587
Eggleston, Kevin, Sr VP-Social Innovation & Global Industries - Hitachi Data Systems Corporation; *pg.* 407, *pg.* 265
Eggleston, Lenore, Dir-Mktg & Dev - Westchester Philharmonic; *pg.* 592, *pg.* 1354
Eglinton, Ken, Sr Product Mgr - Waters Corporation; *pg.* 1436, *pg.* 834
Egloff, David, Sr Dir-Sls Incentive Compensation - TransUnion Corp.; *pg.* 811, *pg.* 591
Egolf, Adrienne, Specialist-Mktg - The Nature Conservancy; *pg.* 151, *pg.* 1774
Eguchi, Lynda, Mgr-Lexus Product Mktg - Lexus Division; *pg.* 182, *pg.* 294
Ehase, Chris, Gen Mgr-Sls - Joe Machens Ford Inc.; *pg.* 180, *pg.* 976
Eheler, David, Engr-Product - Precision Castparts Corp.; *pg.* 105, *pg.* 1506
Ehle, Chad, Sr Mgr-Online Mktg - AT&T Inc.; *pg.* 1867, *pg.* 1674
Ehlers, Bobbie Joe, Dir-Global Mktg & Personal Care - The Procter & Gamble Company; *pg.* 1129, *pg.* 1418
Ehlers, Eric, Dir-Corp Mktg & Global Mktg Info Sys - Belden, Inc.; *pg.* 624, *pg.* 993
Ehlers, Jennifer, Mgr-Mktg-Perioperative Products - 3M Company; *pg.* 1142, *pg.* 956
Ehmann, Ashley, Brand Mktg Mgr - Groupon, Inc.; *pg.* 1255, *pg.* 575
Ehn, Erin, Mgr-Mktg - Assurant Health; *pg.* 1193, *pg.* 1873
Ehnert, Rebecca, Mgr-Mktg - Verizon Communications Inc.; *pg.* 1875, *pg.* 1309
Ehoodin, Jeffrey, Mgr-PR - Maserati North America, Inc.; *pg.* 183, *pg.* 1060
Ehrbar, Tad, Sr VP-Entertainment & Sports Mktg - Citigroup Inc.; *pg.* 735, *pg.* 1212
Ehrenfreund, Brittany, Assoc Mgr-Media - PetSmart, Inc.; *pg.* 1481, *pg.* 18
Ehrensing, Adrienne, Mgr-Mktg-Innovation - Reily Foods Company; *pg.* 891, *pg.* 747
Ehrensing, Charles, Sr Planner-Production - Pellerin Milnor Corporation; *pg.* 1368, *pg.* 744
Ehresman, Andrea L., Sr Mgr-Natl Foodservice Strategy & Dev - The Coca-Cola Company; *pg.* 240, *pg.* 493
Ehresmann, Jen, Dir-Mktg-Retail & Deli - Jennie-O Turkey Store, LLC; *pg.* 865, *pg.* 966
Ehret, John, Dir-Mktg - Bristol-Myers Squibb Company; *pg.* 1509, *pg.* 1206
Ehrhardt, Marc, Dir-Strategic Mktg Insecticides-Global - BASF Corporation; *pg.* 1149, *pg.* 1066
Ehrlich, Brent, VP-Mktg Plng - Office Depot, Inc.; *pg.* 448, *pg.* 412
Ehrlich, Gregor, Head-Social Media & Creative - The Clorox Company; *pg.* 327, *pg.* 169
Ehrlich, Michael, Mgr-PR - adidas America Inc.; *pg.* 1803, *pg.* 1500
Ehrmann, Alison, VP-Consumer Mktg - FreshDirect, LLC; *pg.* 857, *pg.* 1174
Ehrmann, Rich, Mgr-Media-Bayer HealthCare - Bayer Corporation; *pg.* 1499, *pg.* 1573
Ehsanipour, Bita, Sr Mgr-Social Media - The Men's Wearhouse, Inc.; *pg.* 44, *pg.* 1711
Eibeler, Paul, Brand Mgr-Desktop - Dell, Inc.; *pg.* 385, *pg.* 1037
Eibeler, Paul, Brand Mgr-Desktop - Dell Inc.; *pg.* 383, *pg.* 1737
Eibert, Joe, VP-Digital Mktg - Universal Studios, Inc.; *pg.* 315, *pg.* 298
Eich, Hans-Werner, Mgr-Mktg - Belden, Inc.; *pg.* 624, *pg.* 993
Eichele, Kevin, Dir-Sls-Western Reg - Monterey Mushrooms, Inc.; *pg.* 881, *pg.* 305
Eichenbaum, Charles, Sr Product Mgr - Microsoft Corporation; *pg.* 435, *pg.* 1824
Eichenseer, Jeff, Dir-Mktg - Conestoga Wood Specialties Corp.; *pg.* 921, *pg.* 1527
Eichenstein, Erin Jones, Sr Mgr-Digital, Media & Integrated Mktg-Maybelline, Garnier - L'Oreal USA; *pg.* 514, *pg.* 1252
Eicher, Robert, Mgr-Mktg Equipment - PepsiCo, Inc.; *pg.* 259, *pg.* 1327
Eichhorn, Mary, VP-Enterprise Mktg & Mgr-Mktg - Wells Fargo & Company; *pg.* 819, *pg.* 232
Eichler, Ed, Bus Mgr - The Lima News; *pg.* 1659, *pg.* 1457
Eichner, Jessica, Brand Mktg Mgr - Expedia, Inc.; *pg.* 1244, *pg.* 1814
Eick, Ryan, Assoc Mgr-Mktg-Snacks New Product Lab - General Mills, Inc.; *pg.* 828, *pg.* 933
Eickberg, Al, Mgr-Creative Production - Kohl's Corporation; *pg.* 1775, *pg.* 1870
Eickenhorst, Glenn, Mgr-Legacy Asset Servicing Mktg - Bank of America Corporation; *pg.* 718, *pg.* 1362
Eide, Andy, VP-Product Dev & Mfg - Aerus LLC; *pg.* 51, *pg.* 1673
Eide, Kristi A., Sr Product Mgr-Mktg & Network Coverage - AT&T Mobility LLC; *pg.* 619, *pg.* 488
Eidshaug Harding, Amanda, Asst VP-Mktg & Creative Svcs - The George Washington University; *pg.* 602, *pg.* 400
Eifel, Barbara, Product Mgr - American Greetings Corporation; *pg.* 1615, *pg.* 1428
Eigen, Tony, Mgr-Product, Market & Ops Mgmt-Mobile Internet & Convergence - Tellabs, Inc.; *pg.* 678, *pg.* 637
Eigendorff, Rich, COO-Media Networks - Viacom Inc.; *pg.* 316, *pg.* 1310
Eijdenberg, Adam, Product Mgr-Certificate Transparency - Google Inc.; *pg.* 1249, *pg.* 153
Eiland, Lee, Dir-Global Field Mktg-Glaceau - The Coca-Cola Company; *pg.* 240, *pg.* 493
Eilender, Deborah Kogan, Mng Dir-Mktg-US - Pfizer Inc.; *pg.* 1581, *pg.* 1278
Eilers, Stephanie, Specialist-North America Digital Media-Field Mktg - Starwood Hotels & Resorts Worldwide, Inc.; *pg.* 1114, *pg.* 378
Eilers, Valarie, Head-Dev-Mobile Applications & Product Dev - Caesars Entertainment Corporation; *pg.* 1083, *pg.* 1023
Einck, Brad, Sr Mgr-Customer - General Mills, Inc.; *pg.* 828, *pg.* 933
Einck, Stacy, Brand Mgr-PR & Social Media - Andersen Corporation; *pg.* 67, *pg.* 916
Einhauser, James G., VP-Sls - Wigwam Mills, Inc.; *pg.* 15, *pg.* 1894
Einkauf, Jon, Sr Product Mgr-Amazon Web Svcs - Amazon.com, Inc.; *pg.* 1226, *pg.* 1831
Eisbrener, Allen, Sr VP & Mgr-Creative Svcs-First Midwest Bank - First Midwest Bancorp Inc.; *pg.* 756, *pg.* 620
Eisdorfer, Danit, Sr Mgr-Mktg-Global Innovation - PepsiCo, Inc.; *pg.* 259, *pg.* 1327
Eisele, Carolyn, Mgr-NA Social Quality & Risk - Kimberly-Clark Corporation; *pg.* 1461, *pg.* 1720
Eisele, Marc, Sr VP-Mktg - West Corporation; *pg.* 492, *pg.* 1019
Eiselein, Jennifer, Dir-Mktg - VTech Electronics North America, LLC; *pg.* 969, *pg.* 554
Eisen, Eileen, Sr Mgr-Mktg-Billing Programs - Arizona Public Service Company; *pg.* 1935, *pg.* 14
Eisen, Julie, VP-Global Plng & Mktg - Starbucks Corporation; *pg.* 897, *pg.* 1840
Eisenbaum, Michael, VP-On Air Creative & Branded Entertainment - Animal Planet, LLC; *pg.* 270, *pg.* 777
Eisenberg, Alan, VP-Advisor Mktg - LPL Financial Corporation; *pg.* 777, *pg.* 798
Eisenberg, Betsey, Dir-Product Mgmt & Data Ops - EDGAR Online, Inc.; *pg.* 746, *pg.* 776
Eisenberg, Christina, Dir-Mktg-Pepsi & Starbucks North American Coffee Partnership - PepsiCo, Inc.; *pg.* 259, *pg.* 1327
Eisenberg, Jeffrey, Recruiter-Mktg - Google Inc.; *pg.* 1249, *pg.* 153
Eisenberg, Kelly, Brand Mgr-Content - LeapFrog Enterprises, Inc.; *pg.* 961, *pg.* 84

Eisenberg, Richard, Mng Dir & Head-Media Investment Banking - Nomura Securities International, Inc.; *pg.* 787, *pg.* 1273
Eisenberger, Larry, Sr Engr-Technical Mktg - AVX Corporation; *pg.* 623, *pg.* 1616
Eisenbrey, Lisa, Specialist-PR - Emerson Process Management; *pg.* 1334, *pg.* 1636
Eisenhart, Melissa, Dir-Corp Mktg Comm - Applied Materials, Inc; *pg.* 618, *pg.* 1009
Eisenhart, Melissa, Dir-Corp Mktg Comm - Applied Materials, Inc.; *pg.* 618, *pg.* 264
Eisenman, Josh, Sr Producer-Creative - Amazon.com, Inc.; *pg.* 1226, *pg.* 1831
Eisenstein, Heidi, Sr Mgr-Global Partner Mktg - Adobe Systems Incorporated; *pg.* 342, *pg.* 235
Eisinger, Jamie, Sr Coord-Mktg Comm-Qualcomm Life - QUALCOMM Incorporated; *pg.* 1873, *pg.* 207
Eisman, Amy, Dir-Media Entrepreneurship & Interactive Journalism - American University; *pg.* 597, *pg.* 395
Eisner, Craig, Dir-Mktg - AT&T Inc.; *pg.* 1867, *pg.* 1674
Eissing, Ken, Pres-In Store Media - Mood Media; *pg.* 298, *pg.* 1616
Eitel, Sandra, Dir-Mktg & Brand Mgmt - The American Dental Association; *pg.* 127, *pg.* 564
Eitelbach, Andrew, Sr Mgr-Mktg & Comm - Association of National Advertisers, Inc.; *pg.* 133, *pg.* 1197
Eitenbichler, Patrick, Dir-Mktg-PartnerOne Strategy - Hewlett-Packard Company; *pg.* 404, *pg.* 175
Ejantkar, Sanjay, Sr Mgr-Product Mktg - Epicor Software Corporation; *pg.* 393, *pg.* 110
Ek, Cindy, Corp Mgr-Mktg Comm - Publix Super Markets, Inc.; *pg.* 1031, *pg.* 437
Ekas, Colleen, Dir-Retail Mktg - AT&T Inc.; *pg.* 1867, *pg.* 1674
Ekdahl, Steve, Dir-Brand Mktg-Holiday Inn-Americas - InterContinental Hotels Corporation; *pg.* 1097, *pg.* 511
Ekizian, Claire L., Sr Mgr-Digital Mktg - Philips Lighting; *pg.* 1303, *pg.* 806
Eklund, Cecilia, Mgr-Global Retail Creative Mktg - Dell Inc.; *pg.* 383, *pg.* 1737
Ekmahachai, Sunny, Sr Mgr-Promos - Post Holdings, Inc.; *pg.* 833, *pg.* 1002
Ekstedt, Jade, Sr Mgr-PR - DIRECTV Group Holdings, LLC; *pg.* 281, *pg.* 79
Ekundayo, Bukola, Brand Mgr - Post Holdings, Inc.; *pg.* 833, *pg.* 1002
El Khalil, Samer, Mgr-Chevrolet Mktg & Sls Ops - General Motors Company; *pg.* 175, *pg.* 881
El Ters, Shaun, Coord-Mktg-Donor Comm - Northern Arizona University; *pg.* 606, *pg.* 12
El-Ashmawi, Amr, VP-Corp & Vertical Mktg-Worldwide - Microsemi Corporation; *pg.* 435, *pg.* 41
El-Assi, Omar, Dir-Oncology Sls-Southeast - Cardinal Health, Inc.; *pg.* 1512, *pg.* 1448
El-Gawly, Sherry, Dir-Mktg-Yves Saint Laurent Fragrances - L'Oreal USA; *pg.* 514, *pg.* 1252
El-Haj, Tiffany, Coord-Mktg-Advisor Mktg Team - Sun Life Financial Inc.; *pg.* 806, *pg.* 1944
Elavsky, Christy, Dir-Field Mktg Support - New York Life Insurance Company; *pg.* 1211, *pg.* 1268
Elawar, Manny, Sr Mgr-Enterprise Solutions - BlackBerry Limited; *pg.* 625, *pg.* 1947
Elbaum, Joshua, VP-Mktg - Astrotech Corporation; *pg.* 1400, *pg.* 1660
Elbert, Alec M., Chief Dev Officer & Chief Strategy Officer - Autism Speaks, Inc.; *pg.* 133, *pg.* 1198
Elbert, Craig, VP-Mktg - Bonobos; *pg.* 39, *pg.* 1205
Elbouchikhi, Ibrahim, Sr Product Mgr-App Discovery on Google Play - Google Inc.; *pg.* 1249, *pg.* 153
Elbourn, David, Sr Dir-Pre-Production - Michael Stars, Inc.; *pg.* 29, *pg.* 100
Elbow, Sherry, Sr Dir-Mktg-Regional & New Store Opening - Dickey's Barbecue Restaurants, Inc.; *pg.* 1725, *pg.* 1680
Elder, Jess, Sr Product Mgr - National Geographic Society; *pg.* 1667, *pg.* 402
Elder, Peggy, Mgr-Adv Ops - Valley Morning Star; *pg.* 1699, *pg.* 1699
Elders, Brad, Sr VP-Sls-East Reg - AOL Inc.; *pg.* 1229, *pg.* 1195
Eldin, Jennifer, Head-Social Media-Global & Dir - BlackRock, Inc.; *pg.* 724, *pg.* 1203
Eldred, Eric, VP-Digital Mktg-Online Acq - Wells Fargo & Company; *pg.* 819, *pg.* 232
Eldridge, Bryce, Analyst-Sls & Corp Partnerships - Maple Leaf Sports & Entertainment Ltd.; *pg.* 560, *pg.* 1940
Eldridge, Mary, Mgr-Digital Mktg & Media - GlaxoSmithKline; *pg.* 1536, *pg.* 1565
Eldridge, Rebecca, VP-Entertainment Mktg - National CineMedia, Inc.; *pg.* 567, *pg.* 314
Eldridge, Rob, VP-Product Mgmt-Fulfillment by Amazon - Amazon.com, Inc.; *pg.* 1226, *pg.* 1831
Eleftheriou, Nick, Head-Global Mktg Strategy & Plng - 3M Company; *pg.* 1142, *pg.* 956
Elenez, Jerome, Sr Dir-Natl Field Mktg - McDonald's Corporation; *pg.* 1737, *pg.* 645
Eleveld, Rob, VP-PRO Sls - WhitePages.com Inc.; *pg.* 1289, *pg.* 1842
Eley, Candice, Dir-PR - San Diego Convention & Visitors Bureau; *pg.* 1004, *pg.* 208
Elfers, Megan, VP-Mktg & Comm - Kum & Go; *pg.* 1775, *pg.* 713
Elfinger, Robert, Sr Mgr-Media Rels - Blue Cross & Blue Shield Association; *pg.* 1195, *pg.* 566
Elgas, David, Dir-Product Mgmt for Online & Mobile Products - DIRECTV Group Holdings, LLC; *pg.* 281, *pg.* 79
Elgindy, Waleed, Sr Dir-Global Olympics Sponsorship Mktg - Visa Inc.; *pg.* 816, *pg.* 230
Elgorriaga, Jose, Reg VP-Ad Sls-No California - Univision Communications Inc.; *pg.* 683, *pg.* 1307
Eliades, Jeanne, VP-Mktg - Pernod Ricard USA, Inc.; *pg.* 1968, *pg.* 1332
Elias, Augusto, Dir-Mktg-Portfolio Strategy & Innovation - The Coca-Cola Company; *pg.* 240, *pg.* 493
Elias, Lori, VP-Product Mktg & Distr - The Walt Disney Company; *pg.* 317, *pg.* 52
Elias, Nelia, Specialist-Mktg - Analog Devices, Inc.; *pg.* 617, *pg.* 839
Elias, Robert, Corp VP-Digital Mktg - New York Life Insurance Company; *pg.* 1211, *pg.* 1268
Elias, Yamile, Dir-Innovation & Customer Mktg - PepsiCo, Inc.; *pg.* 259, *pg.* 1327
Eliason, Christopher, VP-Product Dev - Belk, Inc.; *pg.* 1760, *pg.* 1364
Eliason, Keri, Brand Mktg Mgr - Hood River Distillers Inc.; *pg.* 1964, *pg.* 1498
Eliassen, Shekinah, Assoc Dir-Mktg - The Clorox Company; *pg.* 327, *pg.* 169
Eliasson, Fredrik J., Chief Sls & Mktg Officer & Exec VP - CSX Corporation; *pg.* 1904, *pg.* 432
Eliat, Sylvia, Dir-Mktg-Events - The Western Union Company; *pg.* 822, *pg.* 327
Eliav, Michael, Sr Dir-Mktg-North American Retention & Loyalty - Wyndham Worldwide Corporation; *pg.* 1119, *pg.* 1107
Elieson, Rick, VP-Global Partner Mktg - American Airlines Inc.; *pg.* 1898, *pg.* 1693
Eliopulos, Ellie, Mgr-Mktg-Reynolds Document Svcs - The Reynolds & Reynolds Company; *pg.* 461, *pg.* 1457
Elisha, Paige, Mgr-Mktg - American Express Company; *pg.* 712, *pg.* 1190
Elisson, Frida, Mgr-Mktg-Consumer Brand - Google Inc.; *pg.* 1249, *pg.* 153
Elizondo, Juan, Sr Mgr-Corp Comm - TXU Energy Retail Company LLC; *pg.* 1953, *pg.* 1690
Elkes, Amy, Sr Mgr-Mktg & Insights - Stonyfield Farm, Inc.; *pg.* 899, *pg.* 1035
Elkin, Beth, Grp VP-Mktg - JDA Software Group, Inc.; *pg.* 423, *pg.* 22
Elkin, Zach, Dir-Brand Mktg - BSH Home Appliances Corporation; *pg.* 53, *pg.* 108
Elkins, David, Sr Dir-Adv - TripAdvisor, Inc.; *pg.* 1926, *pg.* 835
Elkins, Debra, Dir-Relationship Mktg - Pfizer Inc.; *pg.* 1581, *pg.* 1278
Elkins, Diana, Mgr-Mktg - General Growth Properties, Inc.; *pg.* 1093, *pg.* 574
Elkins, Emily, Mgr-Mktg & Creative Pro - Monotype Imaging Holdings, Inc.; *pg.* 656, *pg.* 861
Elkins, Laura, Sr VP-Mktg-Global - The Estee Lauder Companies Inc.; *pg.* 508, *pg.* 1229
Elkins, Lorren, Head-Digital Media - Granite Broadcasting Corporation; *pg.* 289, *pg.* 1236
Elkins, Shannon, Dir-Sls & Mktg - Milne Food Products, Inc.; *pg.* 877, *pg.* 1824
Ellard, Beth Collins, Exec VP-Media - The Advertising Council, Inc.; *pg.* 125, *pg.* 1187
Elledge, Anna, Brand Mgr-Plng & Execution-KLEENEX - Kimberly-Clark Corporation; *pg.* 1461, *pg.* 1720
Ellen, Bas, Dir-Social & Content Mktg - eBay Inc.; *pg.* 1240, *pg.* 243
Eller, Brian, Mgr-Graphic Design & Mktg - LABORATORY CORPORATION OF AMERICA HOLDINGS; *pg.* 1554, *pg.* 1359
Eller, Carrie, Sr Mgr-Search Mktg - Blue Nile, Inc.; *pg.* 2, *pg.* 1834
Eller, Zachery, Sr VP-Mktg, Partnerships & Promos - 20th Century Fox Film Corp.; *pg.* 267, *pg.* 124
Ellermann, Ralf, Sr Mgr-Mktg-Siemens Hearing Instruments Inc. - Siemens Corporation; *pg.* 803, *pg.* 1291
Ellers, Debbie D., Mgr-Global Product Mktg - Tyco International (US) Inc.; *pg.* 1891, *pg.* 1113
Ellescas, Saun, Sr Mgr-Strategic Mktg - Benefit Cosmetics LLC; *pg.* 501, *pg.* 213
Ellett, Judy Z., Sr Mgr-Client Comm - Cerner Corporation; *pg.* 1514, *pg.* 981
Ellgass, Michael, VP-Mktg - Wal-Mart Stores, Inc.; *pg.* 1790, *pg.* 29
Ellicott, Steve, Mgr-Corp Sls-Long Form Adv - Sinclair Broadcast Group, Inc.; *pg.* 308, *pg.* 773
Ellin, Meredith, VP & Sr Mgr-Digital Mktg-Citi Cards - Citigroup Inc.; *pg.* 735, *pg.* 1212
Ellinger, Christy Chapin, Assoc Publr-Mktg - Entertainment Weekly Inc.; *pg.* 1639, *pg.* 1228
Ellinger, Doug, VP-Mktg - Bullhorn, Inc.; *pg.* 1233, *pg.* 792
Ellingson, Molly, Dir-Mktg & PR - Saks Fifth Avenue, Inc.; *pg.* 1783, *pg.* 1287
Ellingson, Patti, Dir-HVAC & R Sls-North America - Cooper-Atkins Corporation; *pg.* 1407, *pg.* 355
Ellington, Doug, Sr VP-Digital Mktg - Bank of America Corporation; *pg.* 718, *pg.* 1362
Ellingwood, Jennifer, Sr Specialist-Mktg Comm - Cigna Corporation; *pg.* 1197, *pg.* 338
Elliot, Diane, Sr Mgr-Community Investments - Canadian Imperial Bank of Commerce; *pg.* 729, *pg.* 1935
Elliot, Jon, Dir-Strategic Mktg - Mohegan Tribal Gaming Authority; *pg.* 564, *pg.* 381
Elliot, Peter, Product Mgr-Bloomberg Pro Svc-Lifestyle Functionality-Global - Bloomberg L.P.; *pg.* 725, *pg.* 1204
Elliott, Abigail, Mgr-Social Media Program - Puget Energy, Inc.; *pg.* 1950, *pg.* 1816
Elliott, Brian, Sr Mgr-Client Relationship - United Services Automobile Association; *pg.* 1221, *pg.* 1743
Elliott, Bryan, Sr Mgr-Integrated Mktg - Lucky Brand Dungarees, Inc.; *pg.* 29, *pg.* 301
Elliott, Bryant, Mgr-Sls-Texas Piper South-San Antonio - Cutter Aviation, Inc.; *pg.* 227, *pg.* 16
Elliott, Carrie Olin, Mgr-Mktg & Comm - The Florida Orchestra; *pg.* 548, *pg.* 462
Elliott, Chris, Sr Mgr-Integrated Mktg Comm-Internet of Things - Microsoft Corporation; *pg.* 435, *pg.* 1824
Elliott, Courtney, Brand Mgr-Entertainment Mktg-Global - NIKE, Inc.; *pg.* 1812, *pg.* 1492
Elliott, Delaney, Brand Mgr-Global Digital-Nike Women - NIKE, Inc.; *pg.* 1812, *pg.* 1492
Elliott, Frances, Mgr-Mktg - CB Richard Ellis Group, Inc.; *pg.* 1085, *pg.* 127
Elliott, Frances, Mgr-Mktg - CB Richard Ellis, Inc.; *pg.* 1085, *pg.* 1210
Elliott, Gregg, Mgr-Global CP Product Mktg - AVX Corporation; *pg.* 623, *pg.* 1616
Elliott, Heidi, Sr Dir-Mktg Programs - Avnet Electronics Marketing; *pg.* 622, *pg.* 15
Elliott, Heidi, Dir-Mktg Comm - Avnet, Inc.; *pg.* 622, *pg.* 15
Elliott, Jeff, Mgr-Mktg-aerospace & Defense - Xilinx, Inc.; *pg.* 496, *pg.* 252
Elliott, Jennifer, VP & Mgr-Digital Mktg - JPMorgan Chase & Co.; *pg.* 772, *pg.* 1246
Elliott, Jim, Corp VP-Memory Mktg - Samsung Semiconductor, Inc.; *pg.* 670, *pg.* 250
Elliott, Joe A., Dir-Mktg-Infertility & New Product Dev - Allergan; *pg.* 1490, *pg.* 1101
Elliott, Jon, Sr Dir-Sls & Mktg-Global - Sonesta International Hotels Corporation; *pg.* 1113, *pg.* 836
Elliott, Kendra, Sr VP-Media - Guthy-Renker LLC; *pg.* 289, *pg.* 273
Elliott, Lucas, Mgr-Digital Mktg-Latin America - Brown-Forman Corporation; *pg.* 1958, *pg.* 732
Elliott, Madison, Dir-Donor Mktg - The Salvation Army; *pg.* 155, *pg.* 1771
Elliott, Mark, Mgr-Sls-Latin America, Caribbean & Asia - The Protectoseal Company; *pg.* 1370, *pg.* 556
Elliott, Megan, Mgr-Mktg-Subscriptions - Birchbox; *pg.* 1762, *pg.* 1203
Elliott, Michael, Mgr-Relationship Mktg-Disney Cruise Line - The Walt Disney Company; *pg.* 317, *pg.* 52

Elliott, Molly, Dir-Mktg - Doctors Without Borders USA, Inc.; *pg.* 139, *pg.* 1225
Elliott, Nicole, Reg Specialist-Mktg - Comcast Cable Communications, Inc.; *pg.* 276, *pg.* 1560
Elliott, Rob, VP-Strategic Mktg - Hungry Howie's Pizza & Subs Inc.; *pg.* 1023, *pg.* 897
Elliott, Ruth, Mgr-European Mktg - Popchips; *pg.* 890, *pg.* 182
Elliott, Stacy, Sr Dir-Mktg & Brand Strategy - Microsoft Corporation; *pg.* 435, *pg.* 1824
Elliott, Teresa, Mgr-Indus Mktg - Autodesk Inc.; *pg.* 356, *pg.* 257
Elliott, Wade, VP-Mktg & Bus Dev - Tampa Port Authority Inc.; *pg.* 1925, *pg.* 476
Ellis, Andrew, Sr Mgr-Mktg - Battelle Memorial Institute; *pg.* 1401, *pg.* 1437
Ellis, Arica, Sr Specialist-Mktg-Mile High Reg - Comcast Cable Communications, Inc.; *pg.* 276, *pg.* 1560
Ellis, Brandi, Sr VP-VIP Mktg - Caesars Entertainment Corporation; *pg.* 1083, *pg.* 1023
Ellis, Brooke, Mgr-Adv-Chevrolet - General Motors Company; *pg.* 175, *pg.* 881
Ellis, Cathy, Sr Mgr-Shopper Mktg Digital & Online - Ubisoft Inc.; *pg.* 589, *pg.* 229
Ellis, Chris, Sr Dir-Bus Dev - FactSet Research Systems Inc.; *pg.* 1247, *pg.* 361
Ellis, Chris, Head-Intl Sls & Bus Dev-Mopar - FCA US LLC; *pg.* 170, *pg.* 868
Ellis, Dale M., Mgr-Sls - Humana, Inc.; *pg.* 1204, *pg.* 734
Ellis, David, VP-Mktg-O'Charley's - American Blue Ribbon Holdings; *pg.* 1714, *pg.* 1648
Ellis, David, VP-Mktg - O'Charley's Inc.; *pg.* 1742, *pg.* 1653
Ellis, Geoffrey, VP-Partner Mktg & Bus Dev - FTD Group, Inc.; *pg.* 1795, *pg.* 608
Ellis, Geoffrey, VP-Partner Mktg & Bus Dev - FTD.com Inc.; *pg.* 1770, *pg.* 608
Ellis, Jeff, VP-Sls & Mktg - Chris-Craft Corporation; *pg.* 1706, *pg.* 465
Ellis, Jim, Mgr-Website Mktg - Toyota Canada, Inc.; *pg.* 192, *pg.* 1934
Ellis, John, Sr Mgr-Bus Dev - Amazon.com, Inc.; *pg.* 1226, *pg.* 1831
Ellis, Katie, Mgr-Launch Product Mktg - Box Inc.; *pg.* 1232, *pg.* 124
Ellis, Kelly, Dir-Integrated Mktg - National Bedding Co.; *pg.* 935, *pg.* 618
Ellis, Kit, Sr Mgr-PR - Nintendo of America, Inc.; *pg.* 965, *pg.* 1829
Ellis, Maggie, Analyst-Email Mktg - Academy Sports & Outdoors, Ltd.; *pg.* 1824, *pg.* 1724
Ellis, Mark, Sr VP-Corp Sls - Time Inc.; *pg.* 1693, *pg.* 1300
Ellis, Maryanne, Reg Dir-Sls - AOL Inc.; *pg.* 1229, *pg.* 1195
Ellis, Megan, Dir-Digital Product Design-UX & UI - DIRECTV Group Holdings, LLC; *pg.* 281, *pg.* 79
Ellis, Mike, Mgr-Mktg Comm-SUV & CUV - Ford Motor Company of Canada, Limited; *pg.* 174, *pg.* 1930
Ellis, Rick, Sr VP-Mktg - Brookshire Grocery Company; *pg.* 1016, *pg.* 1748
Ellis, Sabrina, Dir-Product Mgmt - Google Inc.; *pg.* 1249, *pg.* 153
Ellis, Scott, VP-Mktg-North America & Gen Mgr-Canada - Storck USA, L.P.; *pg.* 1862, *pg.* 591
Ellis, Stacey, Sr Dir-Comm - Kimpton Hotel & Restaurant Group; *pg.* 1099, *pg.* 220
Ellis, Stephen, Mgr-Fuel Cell Vehicle Mktg - American Honda Motor Co., Inc.; *pg.* 163, *pg.* 292
Ellis, Vernon, Dir-Creative - Grossman Marketing Group; *pg.* 401, *pg.* 843
Ellison, David, Dir-Mktg - United Parcel Service, Inc.; *pg.* 1928, *pg.* 522
Ellison, Gail, Mgr-Mktg - IBM; *pg.* 410, *pg.* 1449
Ellison, Katherine, Sr Product Mgr-Companion Diagnostics - Thermo Fisher Scientific Inc.; *pg.* 1431, *pg.* 854
Ellison, Whitney, Mgr-Mktg & Promos, Consumer Segment & Global Markets - CenturyLink, Inc.; *pg.* 1870, *pg.* 746
Ellsworth, Angela, VP-Retail & Adv - Whitman's Candies, Inc.; *pg.* 1863, *pg.* 987
Ellsworth, Tim, Specialist-MobileFirst Sls - IBM; *pg.* 410, *pg.* 1449
Elmastian, Cynthia, Mgr-Digital Mktg - Nestle Waters North America Inc.; *pg.* 257, *pg.* 375
Elmore, Greg, Sr Dir-HR - Harbor Freight Tools; *pg.* 1772, *pg.* 55
Elmore, Rich, Mgr-Digital Mktg - Activision Blizzard, Inc.; *pg.* 948, *pg.* 271
Elms, Alison, Coord-Sls & Mktg - American Library Association; *pg.* 1615, *pg.* 564
Elms, Kristin, Specialist-Integrated Mktg - Lucky Brand Dungarees, Inc.; *pg.* 29, *pg.* 301
Elmurib, Raed O., VP-Corp Dev & Gen Mgr-Microprocessor Products Div - PMC-Sierra, Inc.; *pg.* 664, *pg.* 287
Elo, Mark, Exec VP-Mktg - Giga-tronics Incorporated; *pg.* 640, *pg.* 260
Elrod, Michele, Exec VP & Head-Mktg - Regions Financial Corporation; *pg.* 798, *pg.* 4
Elrod, Seth, Sr Mgr-Workers' Compensation Mktg - Express Scripts, Inc.; *pg.* 1530, *pg.* 997
Elsaesser, Amanda, VP-Investments Direct Mktg - Bank of America Corporation; *pg.* 718, *pg.* 1362
Elsass, Mark, Rep-Mktg - Auto-Owners Insurance Group; *pg.* 1194, *pg.* 895
Elsberg, Paul, Sr Mgr-Media Rels & Corp Comm - Exelon Corporation; *pg.* 1942, *pg.* 573
Elsbernd, Mark, Reg Mgr-Sls-North America - Epson America Inc.; *pg.* 394, *pg.* 122
Elscott, Sharla, Mgr-Natl Sls - The Vernon Company; *pg.* 488, *pg.* 710
Elsen, Tom, VP-Mktg - American Pop Corn Company; *pg.* 825, *pg.* 712
Elser, Liz, Mgr-Sls Zone-NY - Ford Motor Company; *pg.* 172, *pg.* 876
Elsharif, Desiree Sylvester, Sr Mgr-Global Employee Comm - Cisco Systems, Inc.; *pg.* 372, *pg.* 240
Elsie, Dean, Sr Mgr-Strategic Comm - Cisco Systems, Inc.; *pg.* 372, *pg.* 240
Elston, Brett, Sr Mgr-Online & Community - Capcom USA, Inc.; *pg.* 950, *pg.* 254
Eltherington, Laura, Sr Designer-Brand-Citrix Online - Citrix Systems, Inc.; *pg.* 375, *pg.* 424
Eltringham, Jeff, Dir-Interactive Mktg - Digi International Inc.; *pg.* 387, *pg.* 948
Elward, Bill, Sr Dir-SEO - Bankrate, Inc.; *pg.* 1231, *pg.* 451
Elwell, Carole, Dir-Mktg Solutions - Southwest Airlines Co.; *pg.* 1923, *pg.* 1687
Elwell, Jacquelyn, Mgr-Mktg Comm - Arrow Electronics, Inc.; *pg.* 619, *pg.* 325
Elwell, Tom, VP-Sls - New Balance Athletic Shoe, Inc.; *pg.* 1811, *pg.* 798
Elwood, Jennifer, VP-Consumer Mktg & Fundraising - American Red Cross; *pg.* 130, *pg.* 395
Elwood, Wynter, Sr Mgr-Mktg-B2B - T-Mobile US, Inc.; *pg.* 676, *pg.* 1816
Ely, Chelsea, Coord-Global Sls Comm - Google Inc.; *pg.* 1249, *pg.* 153
Ely, Rick, Sr Dir-Mktg-Oral Care & Compromised Skin-Asia Pacific - Johnson & Johnson; *pg.* 1549, *pg.* 1091
Ely, Tracy C., Dir-Strategic Mktg-Asia Pacific - Johnson & Johnson; *pg.* 1549, *pg.* 1091
Elzeftawi, Ahmed, Sr Product Mgr-Mktg - Cadence Design Systems, Inc.; *pg.* 367, *pg.* 239
Elzer, Steve, Sr VP-Media Rels - Columbia TriStar Motion Picture Group; *pg.* 275, *pg.* 72
Elzner, Robert, Dir-ECommerce Mktg - Dell Inc.; *pg.* 383, *pg.* 1737
Emami, Leah, Specialist-Digital Mktg - VIZIO, Inc.; *pg.* 686, *pg.* 118
Emamian, Shabnam, Product Mgr-ECommerce - Bloomingdale's, Inc.; *pg.* 1763, *pg.* 1204
Emans, Jedd, VP-Brand Mktg - The Hercules Tire & Rubber Company; *pg.* 1884, *pg.* 1454
Emanuelli, Gabriel, Dir-Sls-Global - Puerto Rico Tourism Company; *pg.* 1004, *pg.* 1599
Emany, Betsy, Sr Product Mgr - Bristol-Myers Squibb Company; *pg.* 1509, *pg.* 1206
Embree, Karen, Asst VP-Bank Mktg - United Services Automobile Association; *pg.* 1221, *pg.* 1743
Embree, Kari, Community Mgr-Social Media - Provide Commerce, Inc.; *pg.* 1276, *pg.* 206
Embretson, Cindy, Head-Reg Mktg-Honeywell Building Solutions - Honeywell International Inc.; *pg.* 407, *pg.* 1088
Embretson, Timothy, Sr Mgr-User Experience & Retail UX - Best Buy Co., Inc.; *pg.* 1761, *pg.* 954
Embry, Ellen, Mgr-Mktg - Lockheed Martin Corporation; *pg.* 229, *pg.* 762
Embry, Mike, Sr VP & Sr Mgr-Mktg - BOK Financial Corporation; *pg.* 726, *pg.* 1489
Embry, Scott, Dir-Adv - Fayetteville Publishing Co.; *pg.* 1641, *pg.* 1372
Emerick, Pamela, Sr Dir-Intl Div - The Clorox Company; *pg.* 327, *pg.* 169
Emerick, Susan, Dir-Mktg - The Timberland Company; *pg.* 1821, *pg.* 1039
Emerson, Danielle, Mgr-Media Rels-Natl - Virginia Tourism Authority; *pg.* 1010, *pg.* 1804
Emerson, David S., VP-Sls-Growth Markets - Jabil Circuit, Inc.; *pg.* 422, *pg.* 463
Emerson, LeRoy, Dir-Field Sls - Valassis; *pg.* 1698, *pg.* 386
Emerson, Marie, Mgr-Adv Ops - AT&T; *pg.* 1865, *pg.* 258
Emerson, Phil, Sr Dir-Acctg - Colorado Rockies Baseball Club, Ltd.; *pg.* 542, *pg.* 317
Emery, Angela E., Sr Dir-Global Brand Comm - MATTEL, INC.; *pg.* 962, *pg.* 81
Emery, Dennis, VP-Sls - Dualite Sales & Service, Inc.; *pg.* 1296, *pg.* 1482
Emery, Lauren, Specialist-Product Mktg - Deluxe Corporation; *pg.* 1634, *pg.* 964
Emery, Tim, VP-Sls & Mktg - Aeroflex Incorporated; *pg.* 614, *pg.* 1321
Emge, Heather, Brand Dir-Product-HCP Mktg - Eli Lilly and Company; *pg.* 1527, *pg.* 684
Emge, Ryan O., Sr Mgr-Social Media & Digital Mktg - Samsung Electronics America, Inc.; *pg.* 669, *pg.* 1115
Emig, Katy, Dir-Merchant Mktg & Bus Insights - American Express Company; *pg.* 712, *pg.* 1190
Emig, Terry, Dir-Motorsports & Event Mktg - Universal Technical Institute, Inc.; *pg.* 608, *pg.* 24
Emley, Roy, Rep-Sls-Comm, Data & Security - Graybar Electric Company, Inc.; *pg.* 1299, *pg.* 997
Emmel, Katie, VP-Product Mgmt - International Decision Systems; *pg.* 419, *pg.* 938
Emmenegger, Christi, Sr Mgr-Indus-Healthcare - PolyOne Corporation; *pg.* 1177, *pg.* 1404
Emmer, Gregg, CMO & VP - Kaeser & Blair Incorporated; *pg.* 1656, *pg.* 1405
Emmer, Jenna, Mgr-Mktg Ops - Kohl's Corporation; *pg.* 1775, *pg.* 1870
Emmert, Scott, Dir-Media Rels - San Jose Sharks, LLC; *pg.* 581, *pg.* 250
Emmett, Ashley, Sr Mgr-Shopper Mktg - Nestle Purina PetCare Canada; *pg.* 1479, *pg.* 1928
Emmett, Becky, Mgr-Ultrabook, PC & Consumer Media Rels Team - Intel Corporation; *pg.* 645, *pg.* 266
Emmi, Mark, VP-Sls - Ocean Bio Chem, Inc.; *pg.* 1444, *pg.* 426
Emo, Diane, VP-Mktg - Coverall North America, Inc.; *pg.* 329, *pg.* 421
Emrick, Tony, Sr VP-Sls-North America - CDS Global, Inc.; *pg.* 370, *pg.* 704
Enabnit, Nathan, Sr Analyst-Mktg Sys - Devon Energy Corporation; *pg.* 975, *pg.* 1485
Encizo, David, VP & Analyst-Social Media - Wells Fargo & Company; *pg.* 819, *pg.* 232
Endara, Homero, Head-Product Line - GE Water & Process Technologies; *pg.* 1339, *pg.* 1588
Endicott, Doug, Dir-Mktg - International Paper Company; *pg.* 1460, *pg.* 1644
Endicott, Eric, Dir-PR-Global - Illumina, Inc.; *pg.* 412, *pg.* 203
Endo, Koichi, Dir-Product Dev - Alpine Electronics of America, Inc.; *pg.* 616, *pg.* 292
Endo, Kurt, Sr Mgr-Convention Sls - Marriott International, Inc.; *pg.* 1102, *pg.* 764
Endres, Jeff, Mgr-Natl Sls-Soccer Care - Mueller Sports Medicine, Inc.; *pg.* 1570, *pg.* 1887
Enes, Kristine M., Mgr-Worldwide Channel Mktg-Bus Analytics - IBM; *pg.* 410, *pg.* 1449
Eng, Jessica, VP-Mktg - Allegra Network LLC; *pg.* 1614, *pg.* 904
Eng, June, Dir-Mktg - Larson Manufacturing Company; *pg.* 93, *pg.* 1624
Eng, Melissa, Mgr-Sls Support - Neiman Marcus, Inc.; *pg.* 30, *pg.* 1684
Eng, Ron, Mgr-Merchant Mktg-Global - Discover Financial Services; *pg.* 744, *pg.* 653
Engberg, Aaron, Mgr-Product Line Mobile Satellite - Winegard Company; *pg.* 688, *pg.* 702
Engberg, Eric, Dir-Suite Sls - Seattle Seahawks; *pg.* 582, *pg.* 1830
Engberg, John, Dir-Comm-Res & Media - Kohler Co.; *pg.* 91, *pg.* 1862
Engel, Bob, Dir-Mktg - Blount International, Inc.; *pg.* 1043, *pg.* 1501
Engel, Jamie, VP & Publr-Scholastic P&C Media - Scholastic Corporation; *pg.* 1683, *pg.* 1288
Engel, Lisa, VP-Product Dev & Mktg - ClosetMaid Corporation; *pg.* 920, *pg.* 452
Engel, Lisa, Mgr-Field Mktg Comm - Ecolab Inc.; *pg.* 329, *pg.*

960
Engel, Terry Kubarsky, Mgr-Natl Sls-Retail Sls - Chelsea Clock Co., Inc.; pg. 3, pg. 814
Engel, Vincent, Co-Dir-School of Adv - Academy of Art University; pg. 597, pg. 211
Engelbert, Chris, VP-Sls - TD Ameritrade Holding Corporation; pg. 808, pg. 1018
Engelhardt, Brian, Brand Mgr - Kellogg Company; pg. 831, pg. 870
Engelhart, Melissa, Dir-Corp Mktg & Global Brand - Medtronic, Inc.; pg. 1564, pg. 939
Engelman, Dave, Mgr-Media Rels - Porsche Cars North America, Inc.; pg. 189, pg. 518
Engelman, Lauren, Mgr-Digital Mktg - Chico's FAS, Inc.; pg. 21, pg. 427
Engelman, Rob, Sr VP-Mktg Strategy-Citi Retail Svcs - Citigroup Inc.; pg. 735, pg. 1212
Engelman, Scott, Sr Dir-Consumer Mktg - LinkedIn Corporation; pg. 1262, pg. 160
Engemann, Jenny, Sr Dir-Product Innovation-Global - Nu Skin Enterprises, Inc.; pg. 518, pg. 1755
Engen, Joanne, Rep-Liquids Mktg - EnCana Corp.; pg. 976, pg. 1903
Engerman, Fraser, Dir-Media Rels-Global - Johnson Controls, Inc.; pg. 209, pg. 1876
Engerman, Matthew J., VP-Sls - Weyco Group, Inc.; pg. 1822, pg. 1858
Engh, Lara, Mgr-Field Media & Mktg - Anheuser-Busch Companies, LLC; pg. 237, pg. 991
Engin, Reha, Brand Mgr-Bulgari - Saks Fifth Avenue, Inc.; pg. 1783, pg. 1287
England, Gale, VP-Customer Advocacy & Operational Effectiveness - Brocade Communications Systems, Inc.; pg. 365, pg. 239
England, Jason, Rep-Outside Sls - Callaway Golf Company; pg. 1829, pg. 58
England, Martha, VP-Mktg - Sport Clips, Inc.; pg. 523, pg. 1698
England, Tess, Rep-Social Care - Southwest Airlines Co.; pg. 1923, pg. 1687
Engle, Brian M., Mgr-Comm & Mktg Svcs Presales & Implementation Team-Global - Xerox Corporation; pg. 494, pg. 365
Engle, Chuck, Sr VP-Sls - Kind LLC; pg. 868, pg. 1249
Engle, Jill, VP-Mktg - Gannett Co., Inc.; pg. 1643, pg. 1790
Engle, Todd, VP-Sls & Mktg - IMPAX Laboratories, Inc.; pg. 1544, pg. 101
Englehart, Laurel, Mgr-Product Mktg-Intl - GOJO Industries, Inc.; pg. 330, pg. 1401
Engleman, Michael, Exec VP-Mktg, Digital & Global Brand Strategy-Syfy & Chiller - NBC Universal, Inc.; pg. 300, pg. 1266
Engleman, Michael, Exec VP-Mktg, Creative & Global Branding - Syfy; pg. 311, pg. 1297
Engler, Amy, Sr Mgr-Comm - Intuit Inc.; pg. 769, pg. 158
Englert, Aimee, Dir-CPG Client Mktg - Valassis Communications, Inc.; pg. 1287, pg. 897
Englert, Kimberly R., Mgr-Product Dev - Target Corporation; pg. 1786, pg. 942
English, Flaurel, VP-Mktg - Toyota Motor Sales, U.S.A., Inc.; pg. 193, pg. 296
English, Holly M., Mgr-Channel Mktg - Acuity Brands, Inc.; pg. 1294, pg. 487
English, Jennifer, Sr Dir-Partnerships & Station Rels-PBS KIDS - Public Broadcasting Service; pg. 305, pg. 1774
English, Jessica, Sr Mgr-Global Creative - Electronic Arts Inc.; pg. 951, pg. 189
English, Kathy, Sr Dir-Industry & Svcs Mktg - Cisco Systems, Inc.; pg. 372, pg. 240
English, Rob, Dir-Creative - Atom Factory; pg. 531, pg. 71
Englund, Christine, Dir-Software Mktg Comm - General Electric Company; pg. 1297, pg. 347
Englund, Stephen, Rep-Sls - State Farm Mutual Automobile Insurance Co.; pg. 1218, pg. 557
Engman, Erin, Mgr-Sls Strategy - Whirlpool Corporation; pg. 62, pg. 872
Engman, Mary C., Specialist-Contract & Mktg - Xerox Corporation; pg. 494, pg. 365
Engstrand, Jennifer L., Mgr-PR - Pier 1 Imports, Inc.; pg. 940, pg. 1695
Engstrom, Bruce, Mgr-Mktg Comm - ClosetMaid Corporation; pg. 920, pg. 452
Engstrom, Marie, Assoc Product Mgr - Terex Corporation; pg. 1381, pg. 384
Engstrom, Matt, Category Dir-Monitoring Products - Shure Incorporated; pg. 672, pg. 638
Engstrom, Sandra, Dir-Media Plng-NBC News & Msnbc - NBC Universal, Inc.; pg. 300, pg. 1266
Engwall, Heather Porter, Dir-Natl Product Comm - Wisconsin Milk Marketing Board, Inc.; pg. 161, pg. 1868
Ennis, Harry R., Sr Engr-Product - Siemens Corporation; pg. 803, pg. 1291
Ennis, Tara, Sr Dir-Consumer Comml Procurement - Johnson & Johnson; pg. 1549, pg. 1091
Enns, Neil, Principal & Product Mgr-Adobe Publish - Adobe Systems Incorporated; pg. 342, pg. 235
Enoch, Laura, Sr Mgr-Mktg - Shake Shack Inc.; pg. 1749, pg. 1291
Enokian, Serge, VP-Sls & Mktg - Pfizer Inc.; pg. 1581, pg. 1278
Enos, Randy, Sr Mgr-Product Mktg-Norton Mobile Products - Symantec Corporation; pg. 478, pg. 161
Enright, Anne, Dir-Media & Measurement - Starbucks Corporation; pg. 897, pg. 1840
Enright, Jeanne, Head-Brand Mktg & Comm - William Blair & Company LLC; pg. 822, pg. 596
Enright, Tom, Sr VP-Intl Sls - Mohawk Industries, Inc.; pg. 935, pg. 527
Enriquez, Antoinette, Mgr-Digital Mktg - Wenner Media LLC; pg. 1701, pg. 1314
Enriquez, David, Sr Dir-IT - Florida Marlins, L.P.; pg. 548, pg. 442
Enriquez, Karla, Mgr-Intl PR-Americas - Yahoo! Inc.; pg. 1289, pg. 289
Enriquez, Rob, VP-Convention Sls, Svcs & Sports - Albuquerque Convention & Visitors Bureau; pg. 988, pg. 1135
Ensley, Doug, Dir-Mktg Ops - Mohawk Industries, Inc.; pg. 935, pg. 527
Enterrios, Adam, Mgr-Brand Mktg-Dodge & Ram-Midwest Business Center - FCA US LLC; pg. 170, pg. 868
Entin, Dan, Dir-Digital Product Mgmt - ZAGAT; pg. 1703, pg. 1316
Entler, Jenny, Mgr-Design & Mktg - M/I Homes, Inc.; pg. 95, pg. 1441
Entwisle, Paige, Mgr-Mktg - PLANET BEACH FRANCHISING CORPORATION; pg. 520, pg. 745
Entz, John, Pres-Production - Fox Sports Net; pg. 288, pg. 131
Enyart, Lauren, Mgr-Mktg Svcs - Williamson-Dickie Manufacturing Company; pg. 50, pg. 1696
Enzor-DeMeo, Anthony, Sr Mgr-Ops Process Improvement, Sls, Products & Ops - Wayfair LLC; pg. 1288, pg. 801
Epidendio, Terri, Sr Mgr-Mktg - Brocade Communications Systems, Inc.; pg. 365, pg. 239
Epley, Cynthia, Dir-Media - Capital One Financial Corporation; pg. 730, pg. 1789
Epperson, Emory, Mgr-PR & AR - Brocade Communications Systems, Inc.; pg. 365, pg. 239
Epperson, Eric T., Sr Dir-PR & Comm - Medtronic, Inc.; pg. 1564, pg. 939
Eppich, John, Engr-Technical Mktg - Cisco Systems, Inc.; pg. 372, pg. 240
Eppink, Richard, VP-Mktg - New York Life Insurance Company; pg. 1211, pg. 1268
Eppner, Bethany, VP-Integrated Sls & Mktg-CBS Brand Studio - CBS Broadcasting Inc.; pg. 273, pg. 1210
Eppner, Bethany, VP-Integrated Sls & Mktg-CBS Brand Studio - CBS Corporation; pg. 273, pg. 1210
Epps, Camara, Mgr-Mktg - Home Box Office, Inc.; pg. 290, pg. 1240
Epps, Sarah, Product Mgr-Mktg - Facebook, Inc.; pg. 1245, pg. 143
Epshteyn, Lauren, Specialist-Sls Activation - Google Inc.; pg. 1249, pg. 153
Epstein, Dave, VP-Retail Sls - HBG Books, Inc.; pg. 1648, pg. 1238
Epstein, Jaclyn, Program Mgr-Direct Mktg - Liberty Mutual Insurance Group Inc.; pg. 1205, pg. 797
Epstein, Ken, Sr Dir-Brand Mgmt - Electronic Arts Inc.; pg. 951, pg. 189
Epstein, Lauren, VP-Mktg Strategy - MTV Networks Company; pg. 298, pg. 1262
Epstein, Lauren, Brand Mgr - Pepperidge Farm, Inc.; pg. 888, pg. 363
Epstein, Marc, VP-New Bus Integrated Mktg - Viacom Inc.; pg. 316, pg. 1310
Epstein, Michael, VP-Mktg - Artistic Tile Inc.; pg. 914, pg. 1119
Epstein, Robert, Head-Windows Consumer Mktg & Sr Product Mgr - Microsoft Corporation; pg. 435, pg. 1824
Epstein, Ron, Mgr-PR & Social Media - Sharp Electronics Corporation; pg. 672, pg. 1082
Epstein, Ronald M., Dir-Sls - Halocarbon Products Corporation; pg. 978, pg. 1116
Epting, Ann, Sr VP-Product Dev - Abercrombie & Kent USA, LLC; pg. 1896, pg. 607
Erba, Alisa, Mgr-Channel Mktg - VeriSign, Inc.; pg. 488, pg. 1799
Erbach, Chris, Mgr-Mktg Comm - Weber Packaging Solutions, Inc.; pg. 491, pg. 554
Erben, Drew, Mgr-Direct Mail Mktg - AutoNation, Inc.; pg. 165, pg. 423
Erbs, Michelle, Sr Mgr-Mktg-Ahnu Footwear - Deckers Outdoor Corporation; pg. 1807, pg. 100
Erceg, Luka, Mgr-Category Mgmt & Mktg - Accenture; pg. 1392, pg. 1186
Erceyes, Yilmaz, Brand Mgr-Fabric Care-UK & Ireland - The Procter & Gamble Company; pg. 1129, pg. 1418
Erck, Dan, Reg VP-Americas Sls-Adobe Primetime - Adobe Systems Incorporated; pg. 342, pg. 235
Erdem, Serab, Dir-Mktg Innovation-Africa & Eurasia Div - Colgate-Palmolive Company; pg. 504, pg. 1215
Erdos, Lori, Publr-Media & Bus Dev - Smithsonian Magazine; pg. 1687, pg. 404
Erhardt, Edward, Pres-Global Customer Mktg & Sls - ESPN, Inc.; pg. 285, pg. 340
Erhardt, Mark, Sr VP-Retail Product Mgmt - Fifth Third Bancorp; pg. 752, pg. 1413
Erhart, Jeff, Dir-Corp Mktg-Worldwide - Atmel Corporation; pg. 621, pg. 238
Erhartic, Jesse, Sr Mgr-Social & Digital Mktg - Papa Ginos-Deangelo Holding Corporation, Inc.; pg. 1743, pg. 817
Ericksen, Cooper, VP-Vehicle Mktg & Comm - Toyota Motor Sales, U.S.A., Inc.; pg. 193, pg. 296
Erickson, Adam, Dir-Product Mgmt - Catalina Marketing Corporation; pg. 369, pg. 462
Erickson, Alyssa, Mgr-Mktg - UnitedHealth Group Incorporated; pg. 1221, pg. 950
Erickson, Anne, Mgr-Mdsg - Denny's, Inc.; pg. 1725, pg. 1622
Erickson, Dennis, VP-Insert Media-Minneapolis - InfoGroup; pg. 414, pg. 350
Erickson, Derek, Sr Mgr-Channel - Milwaukee Electric Tool Corp.; pg. 1056, pg. 1855
Erickson, Eileen L., Assoc Publr & Dir-Comm & Mktg - The Society of American Military Engineers; pg. 156, pg. 1771
Erickson, Giulia, VP-Digital Mktg - Warner Bros. Entertainment Inc.; pg. 319, pg. 54
Erickson, Janet, Sr Dir-Supply Chain Ops - Brinker International, Inc.; pg. 1718, pg. 1676
Erickson, Joe, Asst Brand Mgr-Direct Mktg - DISH Network Corporation; pg. 283, pg. 325
Erickson, John, Mgr-Product Dev - Ergotron, Inc.; pg. 395, pg. 960
Erickson, Kathy M., Analyst-Mktg Database - Wells Fargo & Company; pg. 819, pg. 232
Erickson, Kirsten, Mgr-PR - Disney Interactive Media Group; pg. 1239, pg. 95
Erickson, Kristen, Mgr-Mktg Comm - ViaSat, Inc.; pg. 489, pg. 62
Erickson, Lucas, Dir-Mktg - Wm. Wrigley Jr. Company; pg. 1863, pg. 596
Erickson, Mark, Brand Mgr - Zimmer Biomet Holdings, Inc.; pg. 1611, pg. 699
Erickson, Michael E., VP-Sls - KSL Resorts; pg. 1099, pg. 120
Erickson, Michelle, Dir-Sls & Bus Dev - American Express Company; pg. 712, pg. 1190
Erickson, Michelle, Dir-PR - Travelzoo Inc; pg. 1926, pg. 1304
Erickson, Nick, Sr Mgr-Comm - UnitedHealth Group Incorporated; pg. 1221, pg. 950
Erickson, Pamela, Mgr-Co-Op Adv - Rolex Watch U.S.A., Inc.; pg. 11, pg. 1286
Erickson, Patrick, Planner-Digital Media - Valassis; pg. 1698, pg. 386
Erickson, Roxanne, Mgr-Sls-Natl - Metropolitan Tucson Convention & Visitors Bureau; pg. 998, pg. 27
Erickson, Scott, Brand Mgr - 3M Company; pg. 1142, pg. 956
Erickson, Scott, Sr Dir-HoloLens - Microsoft Corporation; pg. 435, pg. 1824
Ericson, Erin, Sr Mgr-Bus Dev - Samsung Electronics America, Inc.; pg. 669, pg. 1115
Ericson, Gary, Dir-Sls-Concrete Pipe - Besser Company; pg. 1317, pg. 865

First page reference indicates Business Class Edition
Second page reference indicates Geographic Edition

Ericson, Katrin E., Sr Mgr-Medical Comm - Amgen Inc.; pg. 1493, pg. 291
Ericson, Steve, VP-Product Mgmt - Digi International Inc.; pg. 387, pg. 948
Eriksen, Karen, Mgr-Mktg - The Vanguard Group, Inc.; pg. 816, pg. 1550
Eriksson, Bodil, Exec VP-Product, Brand, Mktg & Comm - Volvo Cars of North America LLC; pg. 195, pg. 1117
Eriksson, Emma, Dir-Mktg-Cereal - General Mills Canada Corp.; pg. 828, pg. 1926
Eriquez, Marta, Sr Dir-Style & Interior Design - Ethan Allen Interiors Inc.; pg. 924, pg. 343
Erixon, Lori, Sr Mgr-Mktg-AmazonFresh - Amazon.com, Inc.; pg. 1226, pg. 1831
Erjavec, Tim, VP-FPGA Product Mktg - Xilinx, Inc.; pg. 496, pg. 252
Erker, Barrett, Mgr-Mktg - Enterprise Holdings, Inc.; pg. 1906, pg. 996
Erland, Cynthia, Sr VP-Mktg - American Apparel, Inc.; pg. 18, pg. 126
Erlich, Rebecca K., Assoc Dir-Media & Consumer Engagement - The Kraft Heinz Company; pg. 871, pg. 641
Erlicht, Paul, Sr Mgr-Mktg - Intuit Inc.; pg. 769, pg. 158
Erlick, Tony, Dir-Sls - The North Face, Inc.; pg. 1840, pg. 252
Ermeti, Scott, VP-Sls & Mktg-Pelican Products - Pelican Products, Inc.; pg. 1842, pg. 295
Ernest, Steve, VP-Mktg & Bus Dev - Jacobs Vehicle Systems; pg. 1351, pg. 338
Ernst, Chris, Sr Mgr-Strategic Alliances - Boost Mobile; pg. 1869, pg. 107
Ernst, David, VP-Cross-Platform Media & Market Resources - Discovery Communications, Inc.; pg. 282, pg. 777
Ernst, Jeff, VP-Mktg - Forrester Research, Inc.; pg. 1642, pg. 807
Ernsting, Kristi D., Mgr-Media Rels - Hallmark Cards, Inc.; pg. 1646, pg. 983
Ernzen, Brandy, Brand Mgr - Ogden Publications, Inc.; pg. 1672, pg. 722
Errington, Craig, VP-Mktg Comm - V.F. Corporation; pg. 34, pg. 1376
Errington, Craig, VP-Mktg Comm - VF Jeanswear Limited Partnership; pg. 50, pg. 1377
Erry, Raashee Gupta, Head-Media - NeuStar, Inc.; pg. 1872, pg. 1807
Erskine, Dave, Sr Mgr-PR-GPG Products - Advanced Micro Devices, Inc.-Markham; pg. 345, pg. 1922
Erskine, Jessica, Sr Mgr-Media & Indus Rels - StubHub, Inc.; pg. 586, pg. 228
Erskine, Wendy, Coord-Mktg - Tervis Tumbler Company; pg. 1890, pg. 477
Erstad, Dean E., Sr VP-Sls - Seneca Foods Corporation; pg. 895, pg. 1177
Erston, Eric, VP-Global Sls - EnerNOC, Inc.; pg. 976, pg. 794
Ersun, Kaan, Dir-Mktg-Demand Generation-Svcs Cloud & Community Cloud - salesforce.com, inc.; pg. 1278, pg. 226
Ertel, Steve, Head-Media & External Affairs - World Wildlife Fund, Inc.; pg. 162, pg. 408
Erter, Aaron, VP & Gen Mgr-North America Consumer Products - The Valspar Corporation; pg. 1449, pg. 945
Ervin, Chad, Area Mgr-Sls - Terral Seed, Inc.; pg. 1801, pg. 748
Ervin, David, VP-Mktg Svcs - Tyson Foods, Inc.; pg. 902, pg. 35
Ervin, Mike, VP-Sls & Mktg - MKT Fastening, LLC; pg. 1056, pg. 34
Ervin, Rick, VP-Sls - Arizona Instrument LLC; pg. 1400, pg. 12
Ervin, Theartris O., Mgr-Mktg - Intel Corporation; pg. 645, pg. 266
Erwin, Maya, Mgr-Mktg - Blue Diamond Growers; pg. 840, pg. 195
Erwin, Michael, Dir-PR & Social Media-Intl - CareerBuilder, LLC; pg. 1234, pg. 568
Erwin, Walter, VP-Mktg - ABP Corporation; pg. 1714, pg. 789
Esarte, Marty, VP-Mktg - Wal-Mart Stores, Inc.; pg. 1790, pg. 29
Escalante, Jennifer, Coord-Sls & Mktg - Abaxis, Inc.; pg. 1483, pg. 298
Escartin, Erika M., Dir-Mktg-LATAM - Alexion Pharmaceuticals, Inc.; pg. 1489, pg. 341
Eschbacher, Joe, Sr Dir-Strategic Relationship Svcs - Express Scripts, Inc.; pg. 1530, pg. 997
Eschen, Doug, Dir-Sls & Mktg - The Guardian Life Insurance Company of America; pg. 1202, pg. 1237
Eschenbaum, Matt, Sr Digital Designer-Mktg & Comm - University Of Denver; pg. 609, pg. 323
Escher, Deb, Sr Mgr-Web Strategy, Digital Mktg & Ecommerce - T-Mobile US, Inc.; pg. 676, pg. 1816
Escher, Peter, Brand Mgr - Starbucks Corporation; pg. 897, pg. 1840
Eschette, Jamie, Mgr-Teva PR - Deckers Outdoor Corporation; pg. 1807, pg. 100
Esco, Joni, VP-Wireless POS Mktg-Global - Assurant, Inc.; pg. 1193, pg. 1198
Escobar, Claudia, Sr Mgr-Mktg-Corp Tax Tech - Truven Health Analytics; pg. 486, pg. 331
Escobar, Maren, Sr Specialist-Mktg - Cullen/Frost Bankers, Inc.; pg. 742, pg. 1740
Escobedo, Alberto, Head-Mktg Comm-Latin America & Caribbean - Apple Inc.; pg. 350, pg. 73
Escobedo, Johnna, Dir-PR - The Hearst Corporation; pg. 1649, pg. 1239
Escobedo, Johnna, Dir-PR - Hearst Magazines; pg. 1649, pg. 1239
Escobosa, Marc, VP-Product Mgmt-Consumer Products - Mode Media; pg. 1267, pg. 50
Escudero, Laura, Specialist-Online Mktg-Latin America - Epson America Inc.; pg. 394, pg. 122
Esecson, Scott, Grp Product Mgr-KADCYLA Mktg - Genentech, Inc.; pg. 1533, pg. 279
Esemplare, Gregory, VP-Natl Accounts-Sls & Svc - Reliance Standard Life Insurance Company; pg. 1215, pg. 1570
Eshleman, Mary, Specialist-Mktg Comm - McKesson Corporation; pg. 1560, pg. 222
Eskes, Berry, Reg Dir-Sls-Europe & Russia - International Datacasting Corporation; pg. 419, pg. 1921
Eskin, Barbara, Dir-Direct Mktg - Time Warner Cable Inc.; pg. 312, pg. 1301
Eskins, Stacy, Dir-Mktg - The Greenbrier; pg. 1094, pg. 1851
Eskridge, Joe, Mgr-Sls-Natl - WIKA Instrument Corporation; pg. 1437, pg. 534
Esmail, Alysse, Mgr-Digital & Social Media Community - Brocade Communications Systems, Inc.; pg. 365, pg. 239
Esmail, Muzammil, Product Mgr - Google Inc.; pg. 1249, pg. 153
Esneault, Lisa A., VP-Comm & PR-Global - Praxair, Inc.; pg. 1178, pg. 344
Espana, Emily, Coord-Digital Mktg - Jewel-Osco; pg. 1024, pg. 620
Esparo, Lynne, Sr Dir-Face to face Experiences - Nuance Communications, Inc.; pg. 447, pg. 806
Esparza, Anthony, Chief Creative Officer - SeaWorld Parks & Entertainment LLC; pg. 582, pg. 456
Esparza, Nic, Sr Dir-Brand Mktg-Running-W Europe - NIKE, Inc.; pg. 1812, pg. 1492
Esparza, Trey, Corp Mgr-Mktg Comm - Publix Super Markets, Inc.; pg. 1031, pg. 437
Espin-Christina, Maggie, Sr Mgr-Internal Comm - Spirit Airlines, Inc.; pg. 234, pg. 449
Espinal, Jennifer, Coord-Mktg & Comm - Trane Inc.; pg. 116, pg. 1109
Espino, Lawrence, Mgr-Sls - PNY Technologies, Inc.; pg. 455, pg. 1105
Espinosa, David, Sr Dir-Corp Mktg - Printronix, Inc.; pg. 456, pg. 115
Espinosa, Kevin, Mgr-Digital Mktg - Caterpillar, Inc.; pg. 1321, pg. 650
Espinosa, Michelle, Brand Mgr-Philippines - Dremel; pg. 1046, pg. 634
Espinoza, Andrea, Mgr-Mktg - John Paul Mitchell Systems; pg. 512, pg. 133
Espinoza, Carolina, Assoc Dir-Multicultural Mktg-West Area - Verizon Communications Inc.; pg. 1875, pg. 1309
Espinoza, Christine, Assoc Dir-Global & Brand Social Strategy - Starwood Hotels & Resorts Worldwide, Inc.; pg. 1114, pg. 378
Espinoza, Glenda, Dir-Production & Online - Emmis Communications Corporation; pg. 285, pg. 685
Espinoza, Jessica, Dir-Mktg Comm - SRA International, Inc.; pg. 473, pg. 1780
Espinoza, Patrick, Dir-Sls - Caesars Entertainment Corporation; pg. 1083, pg. 1023
Espinoza, Tricia, Dir-Digital Mktg - Starz Entertainment, LLC; pg. 310, pg. 327
Espiritu, Anne, VP-PR-Global - Yahoo! Inc.; pg. 1289, pg. 289
Espitia, Jose, Specialist-Mktg Delivery - Citigroup Inc.; pg. 735, pg. 1212
Espley, Alison, Mng Dir-Sls-Japan & Pacific - United Airlines, Inc.; pg. 1927, pg. 593
Esposito, Andrea, Sr Mgr-Mktg-Portfolio Strategy & Activation-PepsiCo - Pepsi Beverages Company; pg. 258, pg. 1342
Esposito, Carl, VP-Mktg & Product Mgmt - Honeywell Aerospace; pg. 228, pg. 16
Esposito, Carolyn, VP-Merchant Mktg-Retail & ECommerce & Head-Bus - MasterCard Worldwide Inc.; pg. 780, pg. 988
Esposito, Elisa, Sr Mgr-Mktg & Cloud Mktg - Ricoh Americas Corp.; pg. 462, pg. 538
Esposito, Greg, Sr Mgr-Digital - Phoenix Suns; pg. 576, pg. 19
Esposito, Kristen, Mgr-Mktg - Aldi Food Inc.; pg. 1013, pg. 556
Esposito, Neil, Dir-Art-Creative Svcs - Cablevision Systems Corporation; pg. 272, pg. 1141
Esposito, Nora, Dir-Online Mktg - Bath & Body Works, LLC; pg. 500, pg. 1471
Esposito, Russell, Sr Mgr-Publ - LEGO Systems, Inc.; pg. 961, pg. 346
Esposito, Susan, Head-Pur North America-Sls & Mktg - Sanofi US; pg. 1592, pg. 1046
Espy, Mignon, Sr VP-Mktg & Strategic Plng - Warner Music Group Corp.; pg. 590, pg. 1313
Esquivel, Anthony, Mgr-Mobile AFIS Product & Biometrics Mktg Comm - Motorola Mobility LLC; pg. 657, pg. 627
Esquivel, Eugenia M., VP & Project Mgr-Mktg-Direct Mktg - Citigroup Inc.; pg. 735, pg. 1212
Essen, Maud, Sr Mgr-Online Mktg - AT&T; pg. 1865, pg. 258
Esser, Mike, Mgr-Creative Strategy, Digital Media & Design - Red Hat, Inc.; pg. 460, pg. 1388
Esser, Richard, VP-Sls - Knouse Foods Cooperative Inc.; pg. 869, pg. 1558
Essex, Lauren, Sr Mgr-Adv & Sponsorship-AT&T Mobility - AT&T Mobility LLC; pg. 619, pg. 488
Essex-SantaMaria, Lauren, Sr Mgr-Adv & Sponsorship-AT&T Mobility - AT&T Communications Corp.; pg. 1866, pg. 1043
Essig, Jack, Chief Revenue Officer-Hearst Men's Grp - The Hearst Corporation; pg. 1649, pg. 1239
Estep, James, Mgr-Fin-Foodservice Sls & Mktg - Solo Cup Company; pg. 1469, pg. 625
Estep, Seth, VP & Div Mgr-Mdse - Tractor Supply Company; pg. 708, pg. 1627
Esterly, David, Principal & Mgr-Digital Mktg - Boston Scientific Corporation; pg. 1508, pg. 831
Estes, Ben, Mgr-Product Mktg - Apple Inc.; pg. 350, pg. 73
Estes, Ivy, Analyst-Mktg - Comcast Cable Communications, Inc.; pg. 276, pg. 1560
Estes, Mark, Sr Dir-Product Mktg - United Parcel Service, Inc.; pg. 1928, pg. 522
Estes, Thomas, Sr Mgr-Mktg - Johnson & Johnson; pg. 1549, pg. 1091
Esteves, Eduardo, VP-Product Mgmt - QUALCOMM Incorporated; pg. 1873, pg. 207
Esteves, Kristen, Mgr-Mktg - AXA Equitable Life Insurance Company; pg. 1194, pg. 1199
Esthus, Sara, Jr Brand Mgr - W.F. Young, Inc.; pg. 1610, pg. 817
Estrada, Claudia, Mgr-Integrated Mktg Comm-Latam - Cisco Systems, Inc.; pg. 372, pg. 240
Estrada, Erick, Dir-Mktg Eye & Acne Skin Care-USA - The Mentholatum Company; pg. 1565, pg. 1320
Estrin, Brad, Exec VP-Sls & Mktg - The Suddath Companies Inc.; pg. 1924, pg. 435
Ethe, Daniel, Dir-Mktg, Product & Solution Roadmap - Level 3 Communications, Inc.; pg. 1262, pg. 1664
Etherington, John, Mgr-Surfaces Mktg Comm - E.I. du Pont de Nemours & Company; pg. 1159, pg. 390
Etienne, Kristi, Coord-Mktg - La-Z-Boy Incorporated; pg. 932, pg. 901
Etlinger, Monica, Coord-Mktg Incentive - Ford Motor Company; pg. 172, pg. 876
Etrog Cohen, Gabrielle, VP-PR & Brand Strategy - SoulCycle Holdings LLC; pg. 1845, pg. 1294
Etten, Jessica, Sr Dir-Dev & External Affairs - The Saint Paul Chamber Orchestra; pg. 580, pg. 963
Ettenger, Katelyn, Assoc Mgr-Mktg & Global Sls Mktg - BabyCenter, LLC; pg. 1231, pg. 212
Etter, Jacqueline, Analyst-Mktg - American Express Company; pg. 712, pg. 1190
Etter, Kelly, Brand Mgr-Lenovo-CDW - CDW Corporation; pg. 370, pg. 663
Etter, Rebecca, Brand Mgr-Innovation - Diageo North America, Inc.; pg. 1961, pg. 361
Etter, Rebecca, Brand Mgr-Innovation - Diageo North America Inc.; pg. 248, pg. 1223
Etter, Susan, Sr Mgr-4-Walls & Digital Content - Panera Bread

Company; *pg.* 1029, *pg.* 1001
Ettingere, Michal, Mgr-ECommerce Mktg - StubHub, Inc.; *pg.* 586, *pg.* 228
Ettore, Nikki, Assoc Dir-Integrated Mktg & Partnerships - Bauer Publishing USA; *pg.* 1620, *pg.* 1059
Ettridge, Darren, Sr VP-Resort Sls & Bus Dev-EMEAA - Interval Leisure Group, Inc.; *pg.* 1912, *pg.* 443
Etzel, Brooke, Project Coord-Email Mktg-Digital Email Strategy - Kohl's Corporation; *pg.* 1775, *pg.* 1870
Etzel, Pamela, Mgr-Contracts & Mktg - Intuit Inc.; *pg.* 769, *pg.* 158
Eubank, Bob, Sr VP-Merrill Edge Direct Response & Analytic Mktg - Bank of America Corporation; *pg.* 718, *pg.* 1362
Eufrasio, Laura, Mgr-Mktg - The Vanguard Group, Inc.; *pg.* 816, *pg.* 1550
Eulenstein, Max, Product Mgr-News Feed - Facebook, Inc.; *pg.* 1245, *pg.* 143
Eull, Jessica, Mgr-Mktg-Dell Enterprise - Dell Inc.; *pg.* 383, *pg.* 1737
Euson, Dave, VP-Mktg & Sls - G&K Services Inc.; *pg.* 693, *pg.* 949
Eva, Ben, VP-Digital Mktg - Broadridge Financial Solutions Inc.; *pg.* 727, *pg.* 1172
Evangelist, Gittel, Editor-Copy & Designer-Page - Times Herald-Record; *pg.* 1694, *pg.* 1182
Evangelista, Brian, Brand Mgr-Peter Pan & Libby's - ConAgra Foods, Inc.; *pg.* 826, *pg.* 1014
Evangelista, Lauren, Sr Mgr-Mktg Oncology Bus Unit - Pfizer Inc.; *pg.* 1581, *pg.* 1278
Evangelisto, Shirl, Asst VP-North American Direct Mktg - TD Bank US Holding Company; *pg.* 809, *pg.* 1051
Evanko, Jennifer, Mgr-Napa Estates Mktg - Treasury Wine Estates; *pg.* 1971, *pg.* 164
Evanoff, Mike, Mgr-Product Strategy - Mitsubishi Motors North America, Inc.; *pg.* 185, *pg.* 75
Evanovich, Kelly, Mgr-Center Mktg - rue21, inc.; *pg.* 32, *pg.* 1591
Evans, Bill, Sr Dir-Market Info - Choice Hotels International, Inc.; *pg.* 1086, *pg.* 775
Evans, Bryan, Brand Mgr-Operation - The Coca-Cola Company; *pg.* 240, *pg.* 493
Evans, Carol, Pres-Working Mother Media - The National Association for Female Executives; *pg.* 147, *pg.* 1263
Evans, Carolyn, Dir-Mktg - Saladmaster; *pg.* 60, *pg.* 1659
Evans, Chad E., VP & Dir-Production - Aromatique Inc.; *pg.* 499, *pg.* 32
Evans, Chuck, Dir-Mktg & Sls Support - Bell Helicopter Textron, Inc.; *pg.* 224, *pg.* 1693
Evans, Claire, Dir-Mktg - Comcast Corporation; *pg.* 276, *pg.* 1560
Evans, Dave, VP-Social Strategy - Lithium Technologies; *pg.* 1263, *pg.* 221
Evans, Dean, CMO & VP - Hyundai Motor America; *pg.* 179, *pg.* 89
Evans, Douglas, Dir-Utility Coal Mktg - Norfolk Southern Corporation; *pg.* 1917, *pg.* 1797
Evans, Gordon, VP-Product Mktg - salesforce.com, inc.; *pg.* 1278, *pg.* 226
Evans, Helen, Exec VP-Laboratory Products - Avantor Performance Materials, Inc.; *pg.* 1148, *pg.* 1521
Evans, Ivey, Mgr-Digital Mktg - Aflac Incorporated; *pg.* 1188, *pg.* 527
Evans, Jami, Dir-Digital Mktg - Anthropologie, Inc.; *pg.* 18, *pg.* 1558
Evans, Jason, VP-Sls & Product Dev - Weatherby, Inc.; *pg.* 1848, *pg.* 181
Evans, Jeannene, Bus Mgr - WWMT-TV; *pg.* 323, *pg.* 895
Evans, Jennifer, Dir-Mktg-Print - Bed Bath & Beyond Inc.; *pg.* 1121, *pg.* 1127
Evans, Jennifer, Dir-Mktg - Benihana Inc.; *pg.* 1716, *pg.* 409
Evans, Jessica, Mgr-Reg Sls-Bay Area - Cars.com; *pg.* 1234, *pg.* 568
Evans, Jodie, Sr Mgr-Promos - Trans World Entertainment Corporation; *pg.* 313, *pg.* 1137
Evans, Justin, Sr Product Mgr-Residential - Clopay Building Products Company; *pg.* 76, *pg.* 1459
Evans, Karen, Sr Mgr-Technical Comm - Newell Rubbermaid Inc.; *pg.* 1128, *pg.* 515
Evans, Katy, Mgr-Sustainable Design Education Mktg - Autodesk Inc.; *pg.* 356, *pg.* 257
Evans, Kenny, Dir-Field Mktg - Panera Bread Company; *pg.* 1029, *pg.* 1001
Evans, Kent, Dir-StruxureWare Offer Mktg - Schneider Electric; *pg.* 467, *pg.* 1609
Evans, Kevin R., Dir-Strategic Mktg - Zoetis Inc.; *pg.* 1611, *pg.* 1067
Evans, Kim, Mgr-Info Mgmt Mktg - International Business Machines Corporation; *pg.* 418, *pg.* 1138
Evans, Kirsten, VP & Div Mgr-Mdse-Dry Grocery Mdsg - Wal-Mart Stores, Inc.; *pg.* 1790, *pg.* 29
Evans, Laura, Coord-Mktg Comm - Opex Corporation; *pg.* 450, *pg.* 1087
Evans, Lauren, Dir-Mktg & Campaign Production - Complex Media, Inc.; *pg.* 1628, *pg.* 1217
Evans, Lauren, Sr Brand Mktg Mgr-Home Appliance - Samsung Electronics America, Inc.; *pg.* 669, *pg.* 1115
Evans, Mark, Dir-Creative Strategy - Electronic Arts Inc.; *pg.* 951, *pg.* 189
Evans, Matt, Dir-Reg Sls - Samsung Electronics America, Inc.; *pg.* 669, *pg.* 1115
Evans, Melissa, Brand Mgr-Alexander McQueen - Saks Fifth Avenue, Inc.; *pg.* 1783, *pg.* 1287
Evans, Michael, Head-Mktg & Digital - Fresh & Easy Neighborhood Market Inc; *pg.* 1020, *pg.* 80
Evans, Niki, Mgr-PR - Express, Inc.; *pg.* 24, *pg.* 1440
Evans, Pamela, VP-Interactive Mktg - Premium Franchise Brands LLC; *pg.* 333, *pg.* 485
Evans, Pepper, VP-Branding & Mktg-Plenti - American Express Company; *pg.* 712, *pg.* 1190
Evans, Peter, VP-Mktg-Global - Hewlett-Packard Company; *pg.* 404, *pg.* 175
Evans, Sabrina, Grp Exec Dir-Brand Mktg - Meredith Corporation; *pg.* 1663, *pg.* 705
Evans, Sakina, Dir-HR, Global Product Divisions & Mktg Comm - Bose Corporation; *pg.* 626, *pg.* 820
Evans, Sarah, Specialist-Social Media Comm - Esurance, Inc.; *pg.* 1243, *pg.* 217
Evans, Shane, Product Mgr - Hewlett-Packard Company; *pg.* 404, *pg.* 175
Evans, Stuart, VP & Dir-Sls KTTV, KCOP & MyFoxLA - Fox Television Stations Inc.; *pg.* 288, *pg.* 131
Evans, Thomas, Dir-Display Mktg-Enterprise Bus Div - Samsung Electronics America, Inc.; *pg.* 669, *pg.* 1115
Evans, Tom, VP-Mktg & Bus Intelligence - Urban Financial of America, LLC.; *pg.* 815, *pg.* 1491
Evans, Zachary, Assoc Sls Mgr-Aviation OEM - Garmin International, Inc.; *pg.* 1414, *pg.* 717
Even, Michael, VP-Sls & Svcs - Buffalo Niagara Convention & Visitors Bureau, Inc.; *pg.* 1901, *pg.* 1147
Evenson, Jeffrey W., Chief Strategy Officer & Sr VP - Corning Incorporated; *pg.* 1122, *pg.* 1154
Evenson, Lori, Mgr-Wireless Programs & Mktg - American Automobile Association; *pg.* 1190, *pg.* 429
Everard, Amy, Brand Mgr - Unilever United States, Inc.; *pg.* 904, *pg.* 1061
Everett, Al, Sr Mgr-Mktg - Herman Miller, Inc.; *pg.* 926, *pg.* 913
Everett, Dianne, Grp Mgr-Mktg - The Coca-Cola Company; *pg.* 240, *pg.* 493
Everett, Heather, Assoc Mgr-Mktg - Wente Vineyards; *pg.* 1972, *pg.* 122
Everett, Marcie, Sr Mgr-Mktg, Social & Digital Media - Red Robin Gourmet Burgers, Inc.; *pg.* 1747, *pg.* 331
Everett, Michael A., CTO & VP - Maxwell Technologies, Inc.; *pg.* 653, *pg.* 204
Everett, Michele, Mgr-Adv Sls - Kelley Blue Book Co., Inc.; *pg.* 1656, *pg.* 112
Everett, Mollie, Sr Mgr-Healthcare Mktg - Herman Miller, Inc.; *pg.* 926, *pg.* 913
Everett, Patty, Assoc Dir-Media-Digital - Turner Broadcasting System, Inc.; *pg.* 314, *pg.* 521
Everett, Sean, Product Mgr-Digital Enterprise Video Platform - Piksel; *pg.* 1275, *pg.* 1282
Everett, Todd, Dir-Creative - The Terlato Wine Group; *pg.* 1971, *pg.* 555
Everett-Vaughan, Carrie, Mgr-US State & Local Govt Mktg - Cisco Systems, Inc.; *pg.* 372, *pg.* 240
Everhart, Brandy, Head-Media Strategy & Investment - Hanesbrands Inc.; *pg.* 26, *pg.* 1394
Everhart, Brian J., Assoc Dir-Global Mktg Comm-Insomnia Franchise - Merck & Co., Inc.; *pg.* 1566, *pg.* 1077
Everidge, Douglas, Dir-Global Mktg-Alzheimer's Disease - Eli Lilly and Company; *pg.* 1527, *pg.* 684
Everroad, Nicole, Media Buyer - Harbor Freight Tools; *pg.* 1772, *pg.* 55
Evers, Ed, Assoc-Sls - Semonin Realtors; *pg.* 1112, *pg.* 738
Everson, Carolyn, VP-Mktg Solutions-Global - Facebook, Inc.; *pg.* 1245, *pg.* 143
Everson, Henry, Mgr-Adv - Fry's Electronics, Inc.; *pg.* 640, *pg.* 245
Everton, Jason, Mgr-Sls-Enterprise Bus Solutions - CenturyLink, Inc.; *pg.* 1870, *pg.* 746
Everts, Sandra, Dir-Mktg & Pub Affairs - Milwaukee School of Engineering; *pg.* 605, *pg.* 1878
Every, Deanna, Mgr-PR - NutriSystem, Inc.; *pg.* 1577, *pg.* 1533
Evjen, Jason, Mgr-Digital Mktg - Best Western International, Inc.; *pg.* 1081, *pg.* 15
Evraire, Kirsten, Sr Dir-Corp Affairs & Specialty Care - AstraZeneca Pharmaceuticals LP; *pg.* 1497, *pg.* 389
Ewalt, Sally, Dir-Mktg - Equifax Inc.; *pg.* 748, *pg.* 504
Ewalt, Scott, VP-Consumer Mktg - Boingo Wireless, Inc.; *pg.* 625, *pg.* 127
Ewell, Amber, Planner-Parts & Svc Adv - Toyota Motor Sales, U.S.A., Inc.; *pg.* 193, *pg.* 296
Ewell, Joe, Brand Mgr-Innovation-Big Heart Pet Brands - Del Monte Foods, Inc.; *pg.* 852, *pg.* 304
Ewell, Kelly, Dir-Mktg Svcs - Brick Industry Association; *pg.* 135, *pg.* 1798
Ewen, Peter, Dir-Sls - Olympus America Inc.; *pg.* 1425, *pg.* 1521
Ewens, Peter A, Chief Strategy Officer - T-Mobile US, Inc.; *pg.* 676, *pg.* 1816
Ewers, Randy, Head-Uconnect Customer Product Mktg & Lifecycle Mgmt - FCA US LLC; *pg.* 170, *pg.* 868
Ewert, Becky, Strategist-Content Mktg - Capella Education Company; *pg.* 599, *pg.* 931
Ewert, Gregory C., Exec VP-Sls, Mktg & Bus Dev - Iridium Communications Inc.; *pg.* 293, *pg.* 1792
Ewert, Roxann, Specialist-Media - Golden Heritage Foods, LLC; *pg.* 858, *pg.* 715
Ewig, Andrew, Coord-Mktg - Briggs & Stratton Corporation; *pg.* 201, *pg.* 1899
Ewing, Brittany, Dir-Intl Mktg & Creative Svcs - NBC Universal Television Networks Group; *pg.* 302, *pg.* 1267
Ewing, Caroline, Sr Mgr-Mktg-Adv Creative - Wal-Mart.com; *pg.* 1287, *pg.* 50
Ewing, Lorraine, Sr Mgr-ECommerce Mktg - Stein Mart, Inc.; *pg.* 1786, *pg.* 435
Ewing, Nicole, Mgr-Brand Partnerships Mktg - Zappos.com, Inc.; *pg.* 1291, *pg.* 1030
Exarhos, Tina, Exec VP-Mktg & Brand Creative - MTV Networks Company; *pg.* 298, *pg.* 1262
Exberger, Meredith, Sr Mgr-Online Mktg - Hotwire, Inc.; *pg.* 1912, *pg.* 219
Exon, Wesley, Sr Mgr-Content Mktg - Ancestry.com LLC; *pg.* 1228, *pg.* 1754
Exum, Carly, Sr Analyst-OPEN Prospect Site Mktg - American Express Company; *pg.* 712, *pg.* 1190
Exume, Myriam, Dir-Eliquis Global Mktg - Bristol-Myers Squibb Company; *pg.* 1509, *pg.* 1206
Eyer, Devon, Dir-Corp Comm & Social Media - Johnson & Johnson; *pg.* 1549, *pg.* 1091
Eyers, Dean, Sr Dir-Strategic Mktg - Cisco Systems, Inc.; *pg.* 372, *pg.* 240
Eyl, Dave, VP-Sls - Johnson & Johnson; *pg.* 1549, *pg.* 1091
Eyler, Ben, VP-Comm & Mktg - Citigroup Inc.; *pg.* 735, *pg.* 1212
Eyler, Lee, Sr Mgr-Client Success - Oracle Corporation; *pg.* 450, *pg.* 191
Eyre, Bill, Dir-Branding & Corp Mktg - The Orvis Company, Inc.; *pg.* 1781, *pg.* 1764
Eyre, Kate, Sr Asst Brand Mgr-Global Olay - The Procter & Gamble Company; *pg.* 1129, *pg.* 1418
Eyring, Erica, Dir-Adv Sls & Acct Mgmt-North America & MediaSolutions - Expedia, Inc.; *pg.* 1244, *pg.* 1814
Eyssette, Pascal, Brand Mgr-Terrazas de los Andes, Cheval des Andes & Icon Wines - Moet Hennessy; *pg.* 1966, *pg.* 1260
Eyunni, Jay, Dir-Digital Media-Global - Ancestry.com LLC; *pg.* 1228, *pg.* 1754
Ezekiel, Rochelle, Div VP-Digital Mktg - Hudson's Bay Company; *pg.* 1773, *pg.* 1938
Ezell, Samantha, Coord-Mktg - West Coast University; *pg.* 610, *pg.* 118
Ezrick, Ben, Head-Mktg-Zagat - Google Inc.; *pg.* 1249, *pg.* 153
Ezrow, Ken, Head-Education Svcs Mktg - General Electric Company; *pg.* 1297, *pg.* 347
Ezzezew, Sam, Mgr-Production - Stefan Sydor Optics, Inc.; *pg.* 1430, *pg.* 1337

F

Faas, George, Sr Dir-Adv Ops - Microsoft Corporation; *pg.* 435, *pg.* 1824
Fabbri, Chris, Mgr-Global Mktg-Radiation Oncology Sys - Philips Electronics North America; *pg.* 662, *pg.* 782
Fabbri, Denise, Sr Mgr-Mktg Acct Mgmt - Ingram Micro Inc.; *pg.* 415, *pg.* 261
Fabbri, Kimberly, Brand Mgr - The Wine Group, Inc.; *pg.* 1972, *pg.* 234
Fabbri, Neil, Sr Coord-Mktg - MetroPCS, Inc.; *pg.* 1872, *pg.* 1683
Faber, Brandon, Sr Dir-Comm & Community Rels - Chicago Blackhawk Hockey Team, Inc.; *pg.* 538, *pg.* 569
Faber, Ida, VP-Mktg - Legal Sea Foods Inc.; *pg.* 1735, *pg.* 797
Faber, Richard, Mgr-Innovation Mktg - International Paper Company; *pg.* 1460, *pg.* 1644
Fabi, Christine, Dir-Mktg - Wine.com, Inc.; *pg.* 1972, *pg.* 234
Fabian, Richard, VP-Imaging Sys Mktg-The Americas - Philips Healthcare; *pg.* 1585, *pg.* 783
Fabish, Thad, Mgr-Sls-Natl - Marin Bikes; *pg.* 1708, *pg.* 168
Fabiszewski, Bill, Product Mgr-Line-Sportswear - Bemis Company, Inc.; *pg.* 1453, *pg.* 1882
Fabretti, Paul, Dir-Social Media-Global - Microsoft Corporation; *pg.* 435, *pg.* 1824
Fabrizio, Dominick, Mgr-Product Mktg - Brother International Corporation - USA; *pg.* 53, *pg.* 1046
Fabrizio, Dominick, Mgr-US Mktg Activation - New Balance Athletic Shoe, Inc.; *pg.* 1811, *pg.* 798
Fabrizio, Vince, Head-Midwest Strategic-Integrated Mktg - The Wall Street Journal; *pg.* 1700, *pg.* 1312
Fabry, Melinda, Asst Product Mgr - Carhartt, Inc.; *pg.* 39, *pg.* 875
Faccas, Alexandra, Mgr-Creative Svcs - New York Knickerbockers; *pg.* 570, *pg.* 1268
Facchiano, Cathy, Coord-PR - Rodale, Inc.; *pg.* 1681, *pg.* 1530
Facchini, Kleber, Product Mgr-Solar Inverter Products - Eaton Corporation - Industrial Controls; *pg.* 1296, *pg.* 1874
Facey, Todd, Sr VP-Sls & Mktg - Taco Incorporated; *pg.* 1077, *pg.* 1601
Faciane, Mario, Dir-Sls-Buyer Cloud - Rubicon Project; *pg.* 1278, *pg.* 182
Fackler, Jeff G., Mgr-Mktg-Global - E.I. du Pont de Nemours & Company; *pg.* 1159, *pg.* 390
Fackler, Tim, Mgr-Key Accounts Sls - 3M Company; *pg.* 1142, *pg.* 956
Factor, Joseph, Mgr-Mktg-Exclusive Brands - Best Buy Co., Inc.; *pg.* 1761, *pg.* 954
Faddie, Michelle, Mgr-Media Plng - Ford Motor Company; *pg.* 172, *pg.* 876
Fadool, John, Exec VP-Mktg-LongHorn - Darden Restaurants, Inc.; *pg.* 1724, *pg.* 453
Fadool, John, Exec VP-Mktg-LongHorn - Olive Garden Italian Restaurant; *pg.* 1742, *pg.* 454
Fadrhonc, Keely, Mgr-Mktg Comm - Annie's Inc.; *pg.* 1760, *pg.* 45
Faerber, George, VP-Creative Svcs - Guess?, Inc.; *pg.* 25, *pg.* 132
Faeth, AnNicole, Mgr-Mktg - Pennwell Publishing Company Inc.; *pg.* 1676, *pg.* 1490
Fagan, B.J., Mgr-Entertainment Mktg - Puma North America, Inc.; *pg.* 1816, *pg.* 858
Fagan, Catherine, Media Planner-Global - Calvin Klein, Inc.; *pg.* 20, *pg.* 1209
Fagan, Daniel, Brand Mgr-Jefferson's Bourbon & Irish Portfolio - Castle Brands Inc.; *pg.* 239, *pg.* 1209
Fagan, Donald Lee, VP-Sls-North America - STAAR Surgical Company; *pg.* 1597, *pg.* 151
Fagan, John, VP & Dir-Mktg - Penguin Random House; *pg.* 1675, *pg.* 1276
Fagan, John, VP & Dir-Mktg-Penguin Grp USA - Penguin Random House; *pg.* 1675, *pg.* 1276
Fagan, Michelle, Dir-Digital Mktg - Universal Studios, Inc.; *pg.* 315, *pg.* 298
Fagan, Stephanie, Brand Mgr - Ralph Lauren Corporation; *pg.* 46, *pg.* 1284
Fagan, Teresa, Mgr-Mktg Distr - University of Chicago Press; *pg.* 1698, *pg.* 594
Fagerquist, Patrick, Mgr-Indus Sls-North America - The Harris Products Group; *pg.* 1345, *pg.* 533
Fagg, Jenny, Exec VP-Products & Payments - Canadian Imperial Bank of Commerce; *pg.* 729, *pg.* 1935
Fagnani, Dario, Mgr-Editorial & Production-Product & Brand Mgmt - Guitar Center, Inc.; *pg.* 1771, *pg.* 306
Fahey, Andy, Mgr-Digital Mktg - Golden State Warriors, LLC; *pg.* 550, *pg.* 171
Fahey, Katie, Mgr-Wholesale Mktg & Media - The Timberland Company; *pg.* 1821, *pg.* 1039
Fahey, Lisa, Product Dir-Surgical Cell Salvage-Global - Haemonetics Corporation; *pg.* 1538, *pg.* 802
Fahey, Melanie, Asst VP-Creative & Education - Ouidad; *pg.* 519, *pg.* 1275
Fahey, Richard, Sr Product Mgr-Mktg - T&S Brass & Bronze Works, Inc.; *pg.* 114, *pg.* 1623
Fahey, Susie, Mgr-Creative Svcs - Philips Electronics North America; *pg.* 662, *pg.* 782
Fahey, Tara, Dir-Product Mktg & Comm - Ameriprise Financial, Inc.; *pg.* 715, *pg.* 930
Fahl, Leeann, Sr Mgr-Mktg-Global - TE Connectivity Ltd.; *pg.* 677, *pg.* 1515
Fahy, Cathy, Sr Mgr-Acctg - Boston Red Sox Baseball Club Limited Partnership; *pg.* 534, *pg.* 791
Faikish, Jennifer M., Dir-Mktg - Merck & Co., Inc.; *pg.* 1566, *pg.* 1077
Faile, Jim, 2nd VP-Enrollment, Sls & Mktg - Aflac Incorporated; *pg.* 1188, *pg.* 527
Faillace, Richard, Assoc Dir-Mktg - Gilead Sciences, Inc.; *pg.* 1535, *pg.* 88
Fain, Amber, Brand Mgr-Seasonal Platform Activation - Del Monte Foods, Inc.; *pg.* 852, *pg.* 304
Faiola, Cheriss, Mgr-Mktg - McNett Corporation; *pg.* 1839, *pg.* 1817
Fair, David, Mgr-Unified Networking Mktg - Intel Corporation; *pg.* 645, *pg.* 266
Fair, Deb, Sr Dir-Global Internal Comm & Community Engagement - Mars, Incorporated; *pg.* 1858, *pg.* 1792
Fair, Kristy, Mgr-Product Launch PR - Lenovo Group Ltd; *pg.* 427, *pg.* 1384
Fair, Tina, VP-Dev & Mktg - L'Oreal USA; *pg.* 514, *pg.* 1252
Fair, Tina, VP-Dev & Mktg-Global - Maybelline LLC; *pg.* 516, *pg.* 1257
Fairbairn, Nick, Sr Dir-Acq Mktg - FTD Group, Inc.; *pg.* 1795, *pg.* 608
Fairbairn, Nick, Sr Dir-Acq Mktg - Provide Commerce, Inc.; *pg.* 1276, *pg.* 206
Fairbairn, Scott, Bus Dev Mgr-Post-it & Scotch Brands New Product Mktg - 3M Company; *pg.* 1142, *pg.* 956
Fairbanks, Mary Ellen, Specialist-Product - The TJX Companies, Inc.; *pg.* 1788, *pg.* 822
Fairborne, Luisa, Dir-Ad Sls - MTV Networks Company; *pg.* 298, *pg.* 1262
Fairbourn, Zoe, Exec VP-Promos & Integrated Mktg - The Weinstein Company; *pg.* 591, *pg.* 1314
Fairchild, Andrea, VP-Brand Mktg - The Gatorade Company; *pg.* 251, *pg.* 574
Fairchild, Jason, Chief Revenue Officer - OpenX Technologies, Inc.; *pg.* 1272, *pg.* 180
Fairchild, Katherine, Dir-Corp Mktg - CareerBuilder, LLC; *pg.* 1234, *pg.* 568
Fairchild, Kristen, Mgr-Mktg & Americas West Area Field Mktg - NetApp, Inc.; *pg.* 444, *pg.* 287
Fairchild, Suzan, Mgr-Powersports Interactive & Experiential Mktg - American Honda Motor Co., Inc.; *pg.* 163, *pg.* 292
Faircloth, Jennifer, Mgr-Mktg Comm & Enterprise Mobility - Cisco Systems, Inc.; *pg.* 372, *pg.* 240
Fairleigh, Erik, Mgr-PR - Amazon.com, Inc.; *pg.* 1226, *pg.* 1831
Fairleigh, Joe, VP-Sls - Stratus Investments, LLC; *pg.* 1115, *pg.* 421
Faist, Michelle Ford, Sr Mgr-Corp Affairs - StarKist Foods Inc.; *pg.* 898, *pg.* 1581
Faistenhammer, Max, Brand Mgr-Protection - Federal-Mogul Holdings Corporation; *pg.* 205, *pg.* 907
Faith, Joe, Product Mgr-Cloud Platform - Google Inc.; *pg.* 1249, *pg.* 153
Fajardo, Melvin, Sr Analyst-Mktg - eHarmony.com, Inc.; *pg.* 1242, *pg.* 180
Fajolle, Lionel, Sr Dir-Global U300 Mktg Team & Global Diabetes Div - Sanofi US; *pg.* 1592, *pg.* 1046
Fakhouri, Dale, Brand Mgr-EFFEN Vodka - Beam Suntory Inc.; *pg.* 1957, *pg.* 599
Fakler, Ken, Head-Media & Adv Assurance Svcs - PricewaterhouseCoopers LLP; *pg.* 795, *pg.* 1283
Falaki, Akinjide, Asst Treas & Sr Dir-Fin - Best Buy Co., Inc.; *pg.* 1761, *pg.* 954
Falasca, Fernando, Dir-Mktg - The Procter & Gamble Company; *pg.* 1129, *pg.* 1418
Falco, Frank, Mgr-Sls-Natl - Conair Corporation; *pg.* 505, *pg.* 1055
Falcon, Martha, Exec Dir-Mktg & Comm - Philadelphia Convention & Visitors Bureau; *pg.* 1004, *pg.* 1568
Falcone, Brian, Sr VP-US Sls - Coty, Inc.; *pg.* 506, *pg.* 1219
Falcone, Joe, Mgr-Global New Product Dev-Hi-Speed Backplane Cables - Molex Incorporated; *pg.* 655, *pg.* 628
Falconeiri, Leah, Sr Brand Mktg Mgr-Global - Hasbro, Inc.; *pg.* 954, *pg.* 1603
Falconer, Andrea, Product Mgr - IDEXX Laboratories, Inc.; *pg.* 1543, *pg.* 753
Falconer, Laurie B., Sr Mgr-Corp Comm - QUALCOMM Incorporated; *pg.* 1873, *pg.* 207
Falerni, Jeff, Dir-Product Dev & Design - Toys "R" Us, Inc.; *pg.* 968, *pg.* 1130
Fales, Amber, Coord-Mktg Comm - QUALCOMM Incorporated; *pg.* 1873, *pg.* 207
Falk, Dave, VP-Mktg-CSD's & Snapple - Dr Pepper Snapple Group, Inc.; *pg.* 250, *pg.* 1729
Falk, Kirstin, Mng Dir-Mktg Innovation - Charles Schwab & Company, Inc.; *pg.* 734, *pg.* 215
Falkenstein, Kelly, Sr Mgr-Mktg - totes Isotoner Corporation; *pg.* 14, *pg.* 1426
Falkson, Cyd, Sr Mgr-Media Connections - The Dannon Company, Inc.; *pg.* 851, *pg.* 1351
Fallah, Zoya, Sr Mgr-Global Social Media - NetApp, Inc.; *pg.* 444, *pg.* 287
Fallin, Jennifer, Dir-Mktg & Promos - Cumulus Media Inc.; *pg.* 280, *pg.* 503
Fallin, Steve, Sr Product Mgr - NetMotion Wireless, Inc.; *pg.* 445, *pg.* 1837
Fallon, Christen, Coord-Mktg - Sonos, Inc.; *pg.* 675, *pg.* 263
Fallon, Dale, Dir-Product Mgmt-Sportsnet & NHL Digital - Rogers Media Inc.; *pg.* 1681, *pg.* 1942
Fallon, Joseph W., Sr., VP-Sls - American Van Equipment Inc.; *pg.* 199, *pg.* 1078
Fallon, Kathleen, VP-Mktg Comm - Reeves International, Inc.; *pg.* 966, *pg.* 1108
Fallon, Tim, Product Mgr-Mktg - Henry Pratt Company; *pg.* 1049, *pg.* 555
Fallon-Kolodka, Emily, Dir-Mktg - DraftKings, Inc.; *pg.* 545, *pg.* 793
Fallows, Tom, Dir-Global Expansion Products - Uber USA, LLC; *pg.* 1286, *pg.* 229
Faloon, Jonathan, Assoc Mgr-Mktg - General Mills, Inc.; *pg.* 828, *pg.* 933
Falor, Ryan, Product Mgr - Google Inc.; *pg.* 1249, *pg.* 153
Falta, Ken, Sr Dir-Mktg - Finisar Corporation; *pg.* 639, *pg.* 285
Falvo, Elisa, Planner-Sls - Turner Broadcasting System, Inc.; *pg.* 314, *pg.* 521
Fama, Roseanne, VP-Product Dev-Luxury Products Div - L'Oreal USA; *pg.* 514, *pg.* 1252
Famiglietti, Lyn, Mgr-PR - CustomInk, LLC; *pg.* 22, *pg.* 1780
Family, Cheryl, Sr VP-Brand Strategy & Creative - Viacom Inc.; *pg.* 316, *pg.* 1310
Famulari, Sara, Mgr-Mktg - Lindt & Sprungli (USA) Inc.; *pg.* 1857, *pg.* 1039
Fan, Cindy, Asst Mgr-Credit & Gift Card Mktg - Ann Inc.; *pg.* 18, *pg.* 1195
Fan, Jenna, Sr Dir-Global Brand Medical-Glivec & Tasigna-Novartis Oncology - Novartis Corporation; *pg.* 1574, *pg.* 1273
Fanelli, Michael, Brand Mgr-Ball Park Innovation - Hillshire Brands; *pg.* 862, *pg.* 576
Fanelli, Steve, Exec Dir-Ticket Sls & Ops - Oakland Athletics Limited Partnership; *pg.* 571, *pg.* 172
Fanelli, Steve, VP-Mktg Svcs & Ops - Unisys Corporation; *pg.* 487, *pg.* 1517
Fanelli, Tracey, Sr VP-Mktg & Sls Support - Wells Fargo & Company; *pg.* 819, *pg.* 232
Fang, Belinda, Sr Mgr-PR & Promos - Mikimoto (America) Co. Ltd.; *pg.* 10, *pg.* 1260
Fang, Claire, Principal & Product Mgr-Cloud Platform - Microsoft Corporation; *pg.* 435, *pg.* 1824
Fangman, Scott, VP-Institutional Sls - TD Ameritrade Holding Corporation; *pg.* 808, *pg.* 1018
Fangueiro, Bridget, Asst VP & Sr Mgr-Mktg - Eaton Vance Corp.; *pg.* 746, *pg.* 794
Fanjul Bilyeu, Aileen, Dir-Mktg - Jarden Consumer Solutions; *pg.* 57, *pg.* 412
Fannin, Kate, Exec Dir-Mktg - The Estee Lauder Companies Inc.; *pg.* 508, *pg.* 1229
Fanning, Sean, Sr VP-Mktg & Comm-Worldwide - Avnet Electronics Marketing; *pg.* 622, *pg.* 15
Fannon, Mike, Associate-Mktg-Partnerships - DraftKings, Inc.; *pg.* 545, *pg.* 793
Fannon, Paul, Grp Dir-Sls-Europe - Bottomline Technologies Inc.; *pg.* 363, *pg.* 483

Fannon, Paul J., Grp Dir-Sls-Europe - Bottomline Technologies (de), Inc.; *pg.* 727, *pg.* 1038
Fant, Erin, Mgr-Mktg-Social Media - Sephora USA Inc; *pg.* 522, *pg.* 227
Fantauzzo, Jessica, Coord-Social Media - Roots Canada Ltd.; *pg.* 47, *pg.* 1942
Fanto, Sharon, VP-Media - Cox Media Group; *pg.* 280, *pg.* 502
Fantuzzi, Chris, Grp Mgr-Creative - Discover Financial Services; *pg.* 744, *pg.* 653
Fanucci, Helen, Gen Mgr-Americas Reg-Windows Embedded Sls - Microsoft Corporation; *pg.* 435, *pg.* 1824
Fanuele, Michael, Chief Creative Officer - General Mills, Inc.; *pg.* 828, *pg.* 933
Faracci, Laurent, Sr VP-Global Mktg & Digital Excellence - Reckitt Benckiser Inc.; *pg.* 1136, *pg.* 1105
Faraci, John, Product Mgr - Flexbar Machine Corp.; *pg.* 1337, *pg.* 1169
Farahmandpour, David, Sr Mgr-ECommerce Infrastructure & Applications - Luxottica Group; *pg.* 8, *pg.* 1323
Faraj, Sammar, Dir-Digital Relationship Mktg - Cleveland Cavaliers/Quicken Loans Arena; *pg.* 541, *pg.* 1429
Faraj, Sammar, Sr Dir-Relationship Mktg - Quicken Loans, Inc.; *pg.* 797, *pg.* 884
Farber, Ellise, Sr Mgr-Mktg - Colorado Technical University; *pg.* 599, *pg.* 315
Farbrot, Tove, Assoc Dir-Digital Mktg - Bristol-Myers Squibb U.S. Pharmaceutical Group; *pg.* 1511, *pg.* 1110
Fard, Keyvan C., Sr VP-Sls & Mktg - CAE INC.; *pg.* 226, *pg.* 1959
Fardoost, Moe, Sr Dir-Product Mktg - Oracle Corporation; *pg.* 450, *pg.* 191
Farebrother, Sarah, Sr Mgr-Search Mktg-Domestic - Go Daddy Inc.; *pg.* 1249, *pg.* 21
Faren, Jennifer, Dir-Mktg - Brinker International, Inc.; *pg.* 1718, *pg.* 1676
Faresich, Bill, Sr Mgr-Product Mktg - AT&T Inc.; *pg.* 1868, *pg.* 358
Farfan, Javier, Head-Music, Entertainment & Culture Mktg - Pepsi Beverages Company; *pg.* 258, *pg.* 1342
Farfan, Javier, VP-Mktg - Verizon Communications Inc.; *pg.* 1875, *pg.* 1309
Fargo, Bernadette, Dir-Mktg - Wells Fargo & Company; *pg.* 819, *pg.* 232
Faria, Elizabeth De, Asst Mgr-PR - Neiman Marcus, Inc.; *pg.* 30, *pg.* 1684
Faria, Sarah B., Specialist-PR - MetLife, Inc.; *pg.* 1208, *pg.* 1258
Farias, Analisa, Community Mgr-Social Media - United Services Automobile Association; *pg.* 1221, *pg.* 1743
Faribault, Helene, Mgr-Mktg Comm - Sun Life Financial Inc.; *pg.* 806, *pg.* 1944
Faries, Johanna, Dir-Mktg & Fan Strategy - National Football League; *pg.* 567, *pg.* 1264
Farin, Julie, Sr Specialist-PR & Comm - Time Inc.; *pg.* 1693, *pg.* 1300
Farina, Adrian, Sr VP-Mktg-Latin America & Caribbean - Visa Inc.; *pg.* 816, *pg.* 230
Farina, Adrian, Sr VP-Mktg-Latin America & Caribbean - Visa U.S.A., Inc.; *pg.* 817, *pg.* 231
Farina, F. William, Sr VP-Cox Media - Cox Communications, Inc.; *pg.* 279, *pg.* 501
Farina, Jayme, VP-Sls-Traditional Markets - AP Exhaust Products, Inc.; *pg.* 199, *pg.* 1373
Farina, Sheila, Sr Mgr-Strategic Insight & Analytics - National CineMedia, Inc.; *pg.* 567, *pg.* 314
Farinacci, Melissa, Project Mgr-Mktg & Comm - Birks & Mayors Inc.; *pg.* 1, *pg.* 1953
Farinelli, Cristina, Asst Mgr-ECommerce Mktg - Aldo Group; *pg.* 1804, *pg.* 1959
Farinelli, Eduardo, VP-Sls-Latin America - AT&T Inc.; *pg.* 1867, *pg.* 1674
Faris, Steve, VP-Sls & Mktg - Bluegreen Corporation; *pg.* 1082, *pg.* 410
Farjami, Sharb, Dir-Natl Sls-Australia - News Corporation; *pg.* 1669, *pg.* 1271
Farjo, Melissa, Mgr-Mktg-Comm - MATTEL, INC.; *pg.* 962, *pg.* 81
Fark, Jevon, Sr Mgr-PR - Microsoft Corporation; *pg.* 435, *pg.* 1824
Farkas, Ashley, Dir-PR - MGM Resorts International; *pg.* 1105, *pg.* 1028
Farley, Christopher, Sr Dir-Editorial & Digital Features - The Wall Street Journal; *pg.* 1700, *pg.* 1312
Farley, Don, Dir-Mktg - Forging Industry Association; *pg.* 141, *pg.* 1431
Farley, Ed, Head-Corp Brand Strategy, Adv, Sports & Entertainment Sponsorship - Humana, Inc.; *pg.* 1204, *pg.* 734
Farley, Ruth, Interim Dir-Online Interactive Svcs & Sr Mgr - Verizon Communications Inc.; *pg.* 1875, *pg.* 1309
Farlow, Jessica, Sr Mgr-Corp Philanthropy, Community Affairs & Events - The WhiteWave Foods Company; *pg.* 1037, *pg.* 324
Farmer, Dave, Sr Dir-EMC PR - EMC Corporation; *pg.* 391, *pg.* 825
Farmer, David, Dir-Global Direct Mktg - iRobot Corp.; *pg.* 1418, *pg.* 785
Farmer, David B., VP-Product Strategy & Dev - Chick-fil-A, Inc.; *pg.* 1721, *pg.* 492
Farmer, Ginny, Specialist-Digital Media - The Kroger Co.; *pg.* 1025, *pg.* 1416
Farmer, Jody, VP-Strategic Mktg - CreditCards.com, Inc.; *pg.* 1237, *pg.* 1661
Farmer, Lisa, Dir-Brand & Mktg Automation Mgmt - ABM Industries, Inc.; *pg.* 64, *pg.* 1186
Farmer, Lynne, Brand Mgr - Bush Brothers & Company; *pg.* 843, *pg.* 1636
Farmer, Matt, Mgr-Sls Strategy - Whirlpool Corporation; *pg.* 62, *pg.* 872
Farmer, Robert, Sr Dir-Channels & Alliances-EMEA - Ipswitch, Inc.; *pg.* 421, *pg.* 828
Farmer, Terry, Sr Asst Brand Mgr - Mars Petcare; *pg.* 1478, *pg.* 1633
Farner, Jay, Pres & CMO - Quicken Loans, Inc.; *pg.* 797, *pg.* 884
Farnham, Kathy, Sr Product Mgr-Casablanca - Hunter Fan Company; *pg.* 57, *pg.* 1631
Farno, Peter, Bus Mgr-US Lawn & Landscape - Bayer CropScience; *pg.* 1149, *pg.* 981
Farnos, Alberto, Mgr-Sls - Sasol North America Inc.; *pg.* 984, *pg.* 1713
Farnum, Dane, Acct Exec-Mktg Solutions-Global - LinkedIn Corporation; *pg.* 1262, *pg.* 160
Farooq, Rizwan, Sr Product Mgr - Ticketmaster Entertainment LLC; *pg.* 1284, *pg.* 48
Farooqi, Seema, Sr Assoc Brand Mgr - The Hershey Co.; *pg.* 1855, *pg.* 1538
Farr, Elizabeth, Analyst-Mktg-Snacks - PepsiCo, Inc.; *pg.* 259, *pg.* 1327
Farr, John E., Mgr-Sls-Natl - David Clark Company Incorporated; *pg.* 633, *pg.* 862
Farrace, Angie, Mgr-Mktg - Destination Maternity Corporation; *pg.* 23, *pg.* 1563
Farragut, Paige Jackson, VP-Ticket Sls & Svc - Rangers Baseball LLC; *pg.* 578, *pg.* 1659
Farrant, Andrew, VP-Mktg & Corp Comm - Sequa Corporation; *pg.* 1180, *pg.* 1290
Farrar, Britt, Mgr-Social Media Strategy - Capital One Financial Corporation; *pg.* 730, *pg.* 1789
Farrar, Ryan, Category Mgr-Fall Product - Rawlings Sporting Goods Co., Inc.; *pg.* 1843, *pg.* 1002
Farrar, Shaun, Sr VP-Media Solutions - MyWebGrocer.com Corp.; *pg.* 1269, *pg.* 1769
Farrara, Kathryn, Sr Counsel-Mktg - Unilever United States, Inc.; *pg.* 904, *pg.* 1061
Farrel, Mary, Sr Mgr-Global Enterprise Learning & Dev - The Hershey Co.; *pg.* 1855, *pg.* 1538
Farrell, Amanda, Sr Mgr-Sls - Twitter, Inc.; *pg.* 1285, *pg.* 228
Farrell, Amie, Mgr-Sls Enablement & Comm-Worldwide - Hewlett-Packard Company; *pg.* 404, *pg.* 175
Farrell, Brian, Sr Dir-Member Rels - Edison Electric Institute; *pg.* 1941, *pg.* 398
Farrell, Dan, Sr VP-Sls & Mktg - Saint Louis Cardinals, L.P.; *pg.* 580, *pg.* 1002
Farrell, James, Sr VP-Mktg & Comm - OSF HealthCare System; *pg.* 1579, *pg.* 652
Farrell, Jason, Mgr-PR - Fender Musical Instruments Corporation; *pg.* 547, *pg.* 21
Farrell, Joe, Dir-Mktg - United Parcel Service, Inc.; *pg.* 1928, *pg.* 522
Farrell, Liam, VP-Mktg-Center Store Retail Brands - Del Monte Foods, Inc.; *pg.* 852, *pg.* 304
Farrell, Liam, Acct Mgr-Mktg Solutions - LinkedIn Corporation; *pg.* 1262, *pg.* 160
Farrell, Lisa, Dir-Sls Strategy & Fin & Mgr-Sls Fin - PepsiCo, Inc.; *pg.* 259, *pg.* 1327
Farrell, Patrick, Sr Mgr-Mktg - Siemens PLM Software; *pg.* 469, *pg.* 1734
Farrell, Paul M., VP-Digital Sls - Lee Enterprises, Incorporated; *pg.* 1658, *pg.* 704
Farrell, Stephen, Dir-Mdsg - Hammacher Schlemmer & Co., Inc.; *pg.* 1124, *pg.* 637
Farrell, Terry, Sr Mgr-Product & Mktg-Microsoft HoloLens-Microsoft - Xbox; *pg.* 970, *pg.* 1829
Farrell, Tom, Sr Dir-Design - The Coca-Cola Company; *pg.* 240, *pg.* 493
Farrelly, Sean, Dir-Mktg - Samsonite Corporation; *pg.* 11, *pg.* 830
Farrey, Kevin, Dir-Internet Sls - Farrey's Wholesale Hardware Co., Inc.; *pg.* 1047, *pg.* 442
Farrey, Paige, Dir-Mktg - Farrey's Wholesale Hardware Co., Inc.; *pg.* 1047, *pg.* 442
Farrimond, Alan, VP-Sls-EMEA - Anixter International Inc.; *pg.* 1313, *pg.* 614
Farrington, Ana, Brand Mgr-Nike Running-Global - NIKE, Inc.; *pg.* 1812, *pg.* 1492
Farrington, Michael, Dir-Mktg, Dispensing & Preparation Technologies - Becton, Dickinson & Company; *pg.* 1501, *pg.* 1068
Farrington, Robert, Mgr-Video & Online Mktg - Quantum Corporation; *pg.* 458, *pg.* 250
Farris, Brian, VP-Catering & Off-Premise Sls - Schlotzsky's, Ltd.; *pg.* 1749, *pg.* 1665
Farris, Glenn, VP-Mktg - Universal Instruments Corporation; *pg.* 683, *pg.* 1154
Farris, Libby, VP-Creative Svcs - Texas Monthly; *pg.* 1692, *pg.* 1666
Farris, Sienna, Exec Dir-Global Corp Social Mktg - The Estee Lauder Companies Inc.; *pg.* 508, *pg.* 1229
Farron, Jessica, Dir-Mktg-Piperlime - Banana Republic; *pg.* 1760, *pg.* 212
Farronato, Alberto, Dir-Product Mktg-Storage & Availability - VMware, Inc.; *pg.* 490, *pg.* 179
Farstveet, Lea, Mgr-Mktg - Pfizer Inc.; *pg.* 1581, *pg.* 1278
Faruqui, Saba, Sr Mgr-Online Mktg - Williams-Sonoma, Inc.; *pg.* 1140, *pg.* 234
Farver, Adam, Chm, Interim Pres & Interim CEO - Pella Corporation; *pg.* 104, *pg.* 711
Farver, Matthew, Brand Mgr-New Bus Dev - E&J Gallo Winery; *pg.* 1962, *pg.* 149
Farwell, Randy, Sr Mgr-Bus Dev - Northrop Grumman Corporation; *pg.* 231, *pg.* 1781
Farzad, Eddie, Engr-Technical Mktg - Cisco Systems, Inc.; *pg.* 372, *pg.* 240
Fasanella, Tony, VP-Digital Media Svcs - The News-Times; *pg.* 1670, *pg.* 344
Fasano, Erin, Bus Mgr-Dole Packaged Foods - DOLE FOOD COMPANY, INC.; *pg.* 853, *pg.* 306
Fasano, Steve, Dir-Strategy & Mktg - FMC Corporation; *pg.* 1163, *pg.* 1564
Fasbender, David J., Sr VP-Sls & Mktg - Smead Manufacturing Company; *pg.* 470, *pg.* 926
Fash, Lindsey, Mgr-Mktg & Global Nutrition Grp - PepsiCo, Inc.; *pg.* 259, *pg.* 1327
Faskow, Stephanie, Mgr-Mktg Strategy - PricewaterhouseCoopers LLP; *pg.* 795, *pg.* 1283
Faso, Gina, VP-Mktg, Category Mgmt & Mdsg - ACCO Brands Corporation; *pg.* 340, *pg.* 626
Fasoli, Luca, Sr Dir-Design Engrg - SanDisk Corporation; *pg.* 465, *pg.* 147
Fass, Sarah, Dir-Sls & Reg Key Accounts-Natl - Diageo North America, Inc.; *pg.* 1961, *pg.* 361
Fassino, Brandon, Mgr-Insights-Shopper Mktg - MillerCoors LLC; *pg.* 255, *pg.* 582
Fassler, Kristin, VP & Dir-Mktg - Penguin Random House; *pg.* 1675, *pg.* 1276
Fassnacht, John, Sr Dir - VHA Inc.; *pg.* 1606, *pg.* 1724
Fastrich, Sherri, VP-Natl Mktg - Meritage Homes Corporation; *pg.* 97, *pg.* 23
Fater, Michael, Sr Mgr-Franchise Strategy & Dev-My Little Pony - Hasbro, Inc.; *pg.* 954, *pg.* 1603
Fatt, William R., Specialist-Sls & Mktg, Americas-FRHI Hotels & Resorts - Fairmont Hotels & Resorts Inc.; *pg.* 1091, *pg.* 1938
Fattori, Amy, Mgr-Channel Mktg - Nestle Professional Beverages; *pg.* 257, *pg.* 474
Fatum, Tim, Sr Mgr-HR - Gordon Food Service Inc.; *pg.* 1021, *pg.* 913
Faucett, Shane, Sr VP-Sls & Customer Dev-US - New World Pasta Company; *pg.* 885, *pg.* 1537
Faucett, Shane R., VP-Sls & Customer Dev - Riviana Foods Inc.; *pg.* 892, *pg.* 1713
Faude, Marc, Product Mgr - Specialized Bicycle Components, Inc.; *pg.* 1711, *pg.* 152

First page reference indicates Business Class Edition
Second page reference indicates Geographic Edition

Faulds, Malcolm, Sr VP-Mktg - Bzzagent, Inc.; *pg.* 1233, *pg.* 792
Faulk, Kimberly, VP-Domestic Sls - Visit Florida Inc.; *pg.* 1010, *pg.* 470
Faulk, Stephanie, Mgr-PR & Outreach - Dallas Convention & Visitors Bureau; *pg.* 991, *pg.* 1678
Faulkner, Amy, Mgr-Mktg Alliance - Bluegreen Corporation; *pg.* 1082, *pg.* 410
Faulkner, Colin, VP-Sls & Partnerships - Chicago National League Ball Club, LLC; *pg.* 539, *pg.* 569
Faulkner, Colin, Product Mgr - NXP Semiconductors; *pg.* 660, *pg.* 248
Faulkner, Daryl, Dir-Mktg & Individual Insurance Sls - Manulife Financial Corporation; *pg.* 778, *pg.* 1939
Faulkner, David P., Exec VP-Sls & Mktg - CIMETRIX INCORPORATED; *pg.* 372, *pg.* 1756
Faulkner, Ian, Brand Mgr - High Liner Foods (USA) Incorporated; *pg.* 862, *pg.* 816
Faulkner, Jessica, Specialist-Mktg Comm - Teradyne Inc.; *pg.* 679, *pg.* 838
Faulkner, Lincoln, Analyst-Social Media - Pizza Hut, Inc.; *pg.* 1744, *pg.* 1733
Faulkner, Nancy, Mgr-Mktg Comm - Sprint Corporation; *pg.* 1874, *pg.* 719
Faulkner, Rebecca, Assoc Dir-Creative - StubHub, Inc.; *pg.* 586, *pg.* 228
Faura, Sara, Sr Specialist-Interactive Media - Scripps Networks Interactive, Inc.; *pg.* 1279, *pg.* 1638
Fauser, Christian, Mgr-Natl Foodservice Sls - Oregon Cherry Growers, Inc.; *pg.* 1028, *pg.* 1508
Fausett, Jessi, VP-Mktg - Forest City Enterprises, Inc.; *pg.* 1092, *pg.* 1430
Faust, Chris, VP-Distr Products - MacLean Power Systems; *pg.* 1054, *pg.* 1615
Faust, Dana, Dir-Adv-Seattle Natl Sls Office - The New York Times; *pg.* 1668, *pg.* 1270
Faust, Esther, Sr Assoc Mgr-Mktg-Global Innovation - The Hershey Co.; *pg.* 1855, *pg.* 1538
Faust, Janet, Sr Mgr-Mktg - Kinetic Concepts, Inc.; *pg.* 1553, *pg.* 1741
Faust, Judy, Head-Product Support-Lending Products - CUNA Mutual Insurance Society; *pg.* 743, *pg.* 1865
Faust, Matt, Sr Mgr-Integrated Comm - Electronic Arts Inc.; *pg.* 951, *pg.* 189
Faust, Ray, Chief Sls Officer - Heineken USA Inc.; *pg.* 252, *pg.* 1352
Faust, Ray, VP-Natl & Emerging Media Sls - The Star Tribune Company; *pg.* 1689, *pg.* 942
Faust, Sarah, Brand Mgr & Mgr-Adv - SeaWorld Parks & Entertainment LLC; *pg.* 582, *pg.* 456
Faust, Tom, VP-Sls - Omni Hotels & Resorts; *pg.* 1107, *pg.* 1685
Faustgen, John, Mgr-Mktg Res - Michelin North America Inc.; *pg.* 1886, *pg.* 1618
Faustman, Dean, Sr Mgr-Product Mktg - CBS Interactive, Inc.; *pg.* 369, *pg.* 215
Fauth, Cindy, Mgr-Mktg-Global - National Association of Realtors; *pg.* 1666, *pg.* 584
Faux, Ryan, Sr Mgr-Trade Mktg - The Boston Beer Company, Inc.; *pg.* 239, *pg.* 790
Favaloro, Michelle, Sr Dir-US Mktg - Hasbro, Inc.; *pg.* 954, *pg.* 1603
Favazza, Amelia, Mgr-Creative & Visual Mdsg - Caleres, Inc.; *pg.* 1805, *pg.* 993
Favreau, Andrew D., Specialist-Comm, Global Brand Mgmt & Adv - The Boeing Company; *pg.* 225, *pg.* 567
Fawaz, Ali, Dir-Social Media-FordDirect - Ford Motor Company; *pg.* 172, *pg.* 876
Fawcett, Chris, Rep-Mktg & Sls - ABB Inc.; *pg.* 64, *pg.* 1959
Fawcett, Jean, Mgr-Media Rels - Abercrombie & Kent USA, LLC; *pg.* 1896, *pg.* 607
Fawcett, Linda, Dir-Natl Accts Mktg - Sun Life Financial Inc.; *pg.* 806, *pg.* 1944
Fawcett, Robin, Dir-Mktg Comm - Tetra Tech, Inc.; *pg.* 115, *pg.* 181
Fawcette, Nicole, Head-Global Product Mktg-Crackdown - Microsoft Corporation; *pg.* 435, *pg.* 1824
Fay, Bill, Grp VP-Mktg-Toyota - Toyota Motor Sales, U.S.A., Inc.; *pg.* 193, *pg.* 296
Fay, Francis, Sr Dir-Digital Mktg - DirectBuy, Inc.; *pg.* 1766, *pg.* 694
Fay, Laura, VP-Mktg-Global - Cisco Systems, Inc.; *pg.* 372, *pg.* 240
Fay, Megan, Mgr-Mktg-Intl - Blissworld LLC; *pg.* 501, *pg.* 1204
Fay, Valerie, Assoc Dir-Mktg - KPMG LLP; *pg.* 774, *pg.* 1086
Fay, Walter, Dir-Product Mgmt - TII Network Technologies, Inc.; *pg.* 680, *pg.* 1157
Fayehun, Benson, Mgr-Brand Strategy-Oncology & Hematology Mktg - GlaxoSmithKline; *pg.* 1536, *pg.* 1565
Fazekas, Jim, Mgr-Sls-USA & Canada - Waterous Company; *pg.* 1387, *pg.* 965
Fazio, Mara, VP-Mktg - JPMorgan Chase & Co.; *pg.* 772, *pg.* 1246
Fazzini, Christopher A., Exec VP-Sls & Mktg - Reliance Standard Life Insurance Company; *pg.* 1215, *pg.* 1570
Fazzolari, Gulio, Exec Dir-Sls-Cineplex Media - Cineplex Entertainment LP; *pg.* 275, *pg.* 1936
Fear, Andrew, Sr Product Mgr-NVIDIA GRID - NVIDIA Corporation; *pg.* 447, *pg.* 268
Fearing, Robert, VP-ECommerce Mktg - McKesson Corporation; *pg.* 1560, *pg.* 222
Fearnley, Elaine, Dir-Indus Mktg - Pegasystems Inc.; *pg.* 453, *pg.* 74
Fearon, Marta K., Dir-Mktg - McDonald's Corporation; *pg.* 1737, *pg.* 645
Fearon, Rosie, Mgr-Product Mktg - AT&T; *pg.* 1865, *pg.* 258
Feather, Chris, Brand Mgr-Scotch Specialty Tapes - 3M Company; *pg.* 1142, *pg.* 956
Feathers, Chris, Sr VP & Mgr-Direct Mktg - Wells Fargo & Company; *pg.* 819, *pg.* 232
Featherston, John E., Jr., Sr Dir-Real Estate - Chick-fil-A, Inc.; *pg.* 1721, *pg.* 492
Featherston, Karen, Mgr-Mass Media - Charter Communications, Inc.; *pg.* 274, *pg.* 372
Featherston, Megan, Sr VP-Mdsg - Jo-Ann Stores LLC; *pg.* 696, *pg.* 1455
Fecher, Christina, Mgr-PR - Meijer, Inc.; *pg.* 1779, *pg.* 888
Fedak, Heidi, Sr Mgr-Social Media & External Comm - Gulfstream Aerospace Corporation; *pg.* 228, *pg.* 540
Fedak, Justine, Sr VP & Head-Brand, Adv & Sponsorships - BMO Harris Bank N.A.; *pg.* 725, *pg.* 567
Fedele, Bob, Dir-Product Mgmt - Fiserv, Inc.; *pg.* 397, *pg.* 1855
Fedele, Francesca, Coord-Mktg - Steven Madden, Ltd.; *pg.* 1819, *pg.* 1176
Fedelem, William, Dir-Mktg - Reynolds Plantation; *pg.* 1110, *pg.* 533
Feder, Alon, Dir-Mktg - Tiger Schulmann's Mixed Martial Arts; *pg.* 587, *pg.* 1059
Federanko, Debi, Specialist-Mktg - Tetra Tech, Inc.; *pg.* 115, *pg.* 181
Federman, Jessica, Brand Mgr - Kohl's Corporation; *pg.* 1775, *pg.* 1870
Federowicz, Suse, Rep-Mdsg - FGX International, Inc.; *pg.* 5, *pg.* 1608
Fedewa, Peter, Sr Coord-Digital Mktg - The North Face, Inc.; *pg.* 1840, *pg.* 252
Fedkenheuer, Paul, Sr Rep Technical Sls - Monadnock Paper Mills, Inc.; *pg.* 1464, *pg.* 1033
Fedonchik, Scott, VP-Mktg - Rolling Stone Magazine; *pg.* 1681, *pg.* 1287
Fedorak, Alex, Mgr-PR - Mitsubishi Motors North America, Inc.; *pg.* 185, *pg.* 75
Fee, Michael R., VP-Mktg & Sls Ops - Reliable Automatic Sprinkler Co., Inc.; *pg.* 1137, *pg.* 1158
Fee, Pate, Reg Mgr-Mktg - Hardees Food Systems, Inc.; *pg.* 1731, *pg.* 998
Fee, Robyn, Sr Mgr-Mktg - Teachers Insurance & Annuity Association - College Retirement Equities Fund; *pg.* 1219, *pg.* 1297
Feeley, Glen, VP-Sls-North America - Datalogic; *pg.* 382, *pg.* 1588
Feeley, Nora, Dir-PR - Trinchero Family Estates; *pg.* 1971, *pg.* 197
Feeney, Ben, Brand Mgr-Future Innovations - MillerCoors LLC; *pg.* 255, *pg.* 582
Feeney, Christopher, Dir-PR & Organizational Comm - Hill-Rom Holdings, Inc.; *pg.* 1542, *pg.* 673
Feeney, Darren, Dir-Adv - Acushnet Company; *pg.* 1824, *pg.* 818
Feeney, John, Assoc Mgr-Mktg - Burt's Bees Inc.; *pg.* 502, *pg.* 1370
Feeney, Susan, Sr Dir-Comm & Pub Policy - Kindred Healthcare, Inc.; *pg.* 1553, *pg.* 736
Feeney, Thomas, Dir-Production & Circulation - Citrus County Chronicle; *pg.* 1628, *pg.* 419
Fegan, Justin, Dir-Bus Dev-Mktg Solutions - The Standard Register Company; *pg.* 473, *pg.* 1446
Feggoudakis, Christina, Assoc Mgr-Mktg - Elizabeth Arden, Inc.; *pg.* 507, *pg.* 448
Fegley, Mike, VP-Sls - InterContinental Hotels Corporation; *pg.* 1097, *pg.* 511
Fego, Michael, Mgr-Product Mktg-Production Print - Konica Minolta Business Solutions USA, Inc.; *pg.* 1419, *pg.* 1113
Feher, Andrea, Specialist-Mktg - PerkinElmer, Inc.; *pg.* 1426, *pg.* 853
Fehl, Andrea, Coord-Digital Mktg - Starz Entertainment, LLC; *pg.* 310, *pg.* 327
Fehl, Patrice, Sr Mgr-Consumer Rels & Inside Sls-Global - The Hershey Co.; *pg.* 1855, *pg.* 1538
Fehrman, Jeff, Category Mgr-Adv & Promos - Speedway LLC; *pg.* 985, *pg.* 1452
Fehrman, Jim, Mgr-Mktg - The Gorman-Rupp Company; *pg.* 1341, *pg.* 1458
Fei, Jason, Sr Dir-Architecture & Digital Engrg - Walgreen Co.; *pg.* 1608, *pg.* 605
Feierabend, Cherylyn, Specialist-Social Advocacy - Go Daddy Inc.; *pg.* 1249, *pg.* 21
Feiereisel, Ines, Sr Mgr-Mktg-Young Customer & Kids/Baby - Nordstrom, Inc.; *pg.* 1779, *pg.* 1837
Feigel Bischke, Carrie, Dir-Brand Integrations & Brand Mktg - Ubisoft Inc.; *pg.* 589, *pg.* 229
Feigenbaum, Jared, Dir-Mktg Solutions - NBC Sports Network; *pg.* 300, *pg.* 375
Feigenbaum, Jared, Dir-Mktg Solutions - NBC Universal, Inc.; *pg.* 300, *pg.* 1266
Feil, Geoff, Dir-Mktg - The Kraft Heinz Company; *pg.* 871, *pg.* 641
Feil, Geoff, Dir-Mktg - Mondelez International, Inc.; *pg.* 878, *pg.* 601
Feilmeier, Jon, Coord-Mktg-Workplace Solutions - TD Ameritrade Holding Corporation; *pg.* 808, *pg.* 1018
Fein, Avi, Product Mgr-Adv - YouTube, LLC; *pg.* 1291, *pg.* 198
Fein, Michael, Sr Product Mgr-RFID - Zebra Technologies Corporation; *pg.* 690, *pg.* 628
Fein, Nicole, Dir-Mktg, Adv, PR, Social Media & Events - Bergdorf Goodman, Inc.; *pg.* 1761, *pg.* 1202
Feinbaum, Ron, Sr VP & Gen Mgr-Consumer Product-HGTV + DIY Network - Scripps Networks Interactive, Inc.; *pg.* 1279, *pg.* 1638
Feinberg, Brad, Dir-Media - MillerCoors LLC; *pg.* 255, *pg.* 582
Feinberg, Jenny, Dir-Product Mktg & Mobile - Zillow Group, Inc.; *pg.* 1292, *pg.* 1843
Feinberg, Larry, Sr VP-Product Mgmt-Global - Wells Fargo & Company; *pg.* 819, *pg.* 232
Feinberg, Marcee, VP-Mktg - Lazare Kaplan International, Inc.; *pg.* 8, *pg.* 1250
Feingold, Katie, Mgr-Community Mktg - The Sports Authority, Inc.; *pg.* 1846, *pg.* 326
Feinstein, Roger, Dir-Mktg & Market Res - Partners HealthCare System, Inc.; *pg.* 1580, *pg.* 800
Feintisch, Jessica, Mgr-Digital Mktg - Forbes, Inc.; *pg.* 1641, *pg.* 1232
Feist, Tom, Sr Dir-Mktg - Xilinx, Inc.; *pg.* 496, *pg.* 252
Feitl, David, VP-Sls - LaPolla Industries, Inc.; *pg.* 1444, *pg.* 1710
Fejervary, Christin, Brand Mgr-Calphalon - Newell Rubbermaid Inc.; *pg.* 1128, *pg.* 515
Felch, Laurie, Mgr-Online & Creative Svcs - Montana Lottery; *pg.* 1000, *pg.* 1008
Feldeisen, Ron, Sr VP-Global Sls, Mktg & Program Mgmt - Key Safety Systems, Inc.; *pg.* 210, *pg.* 908
Felder, Ian, Specialist-Mktg - Hologic, Inc.; *pg.* 1416, *pg.* 784
Felder, Max, Dir-Natl Events & Mktg Partnerships - Macy's East; *pg.* 1777, *pg.* 1254
Felder, Max, Dir-Natl Events & Mktg Partnerships - Macy's, Inc.; *pg.* 1778, *pg.* 1417
Feldhaus, Rich, Product Mgr - Trippe Manufacturing Company; *pg.* 220, *pg.* 592
Feldkamp, Sue, Dir-Digital Mktg - Miller Electric Manufacturing Co.; *pg.* 1361, *pg.* 1852
Feldman, Andrew, Brand Mgr-ECommerce & Digital Mktg - Reckitt Benckiser Inc.; *pg.* 1136, *pg.* 1105
Feldman, Bradley, Sr VP-Video Product Mgmt - Cablevision Systems Corporation; *pg.* 272, *pg.* 1141
Feldman, Brian, Sr Dir-eCommerce Retail Ops - AutoNation; *pg.* 165, *pg.* 773
Feldman, Carrie, Dir-Mktg-Online Wholesale Strategy & Mktg - Ralph Lauren Corporation; *pg.* 46, *pg.* 1284
Feldman, Darren, VP-Creative Svcs - Guitar Center, Inc.; *pg.* 1771, *pg.* 306
Feldman, Dave, Head-Field Sls-Kindle Offline Retail - Amazon.com, Inc.; *pg.* 1226, *pg.* 1831

Feldman, Denise, Sr Mgr-Employer Brand & Mktg-Global - Marriott International, Inc.; *pg.* 1102, *pg.* 764
Feldman, Erica, Sr Product Mgr - MetroPCS, Inc.; *pg.* 1872, *pg.* 1683
Feldman, Jill, Specialist-Email Mktg - Timex Corporation; *pg.* 14, *pg.* 355
Feldman, Joe, VP-Sls & Mktg - Ocean Mist Farms Corp.; *pg.* 887, *pg.* 64
Feldman, Joey, Dir-OE Key Acct Sls - Donaldson Company, Inc.; *pg.* 1329, *pg.* 917
Feldman, Joshua, Product Mgr-Sanitaryware - Delta Faucet Company; *pg.* 78, *pg.* 684
Feldman, Katie, Assoc Mgr-Mktg-Channel Solutions - MillerCoors LLC; *pg.* 255, *pg.* 582
Feldman, Lori, Exec VP-Brand Partnerships & Creative Synch Licensing - Warner Bros. Records, Inc.; *pg.* 1791, *pg.* 55
Feldman, Melissa, Head-Mktg Ops - Samsung Telecommunications America, LLC; *pg.* 670, *pg.* 1736
Feldman, Missy, Mgr Procurement & Mktg Svcs - SAP America, Inc.; *pg.* 466, *pg.* 1557
Feldman, Vikoriya, Product Mgr - Oracle Corporation; *pg.* 1272, *pg.* 786
Feldman, Vita, Sr Product Mgr-Matl Girl - Macy's East; *pg.* 1777, *pg.* 1254
Feldmann, Klaus, Head-Mktg-Oncology-EUCan - Merck & Co., Inc.; *pg.* 1566, *pg.* 1077
Feldstein, Eric, Mgr-Bus Banking Sls - M&T Bank Corporation; *pg.* 777, *pg.* 1149
Felenstein, Scott, Exec VP-Adv Sls - Discovery Communications, Inc.; *pg.* 282, *pg.* 777
Felenstein, Scott, Sr VP-Adv Sls-Eastern Reg - Travel Channel LLC; *pg.* 313, *pg.* 766
Felger, Brian G., VP-Sls Mktg & Dir-Gulf Coast - Atmos Energy Corporation; *pg.* 1935, *pg.* 1675
Felice, Jenny, Coord-Mktg Data - Sun Life Financial Inc.; *pg.* 806, *pg.* 1944
Felice, John, Program Mgr-Field Mktg - Avid Technology, Inc.; *pg.* 622, *pg.* 804
Felice, Nicole, Mgr-Mktg - McKesson Corporation; *pg.* 1560, *pg.* 222
Feliciano, Luis A., Sr Mgr-CM Program Mgmt - Alcatel-Lucent USA, Inc.; *pg.* 615, *pg.* 1728
Feliciano-Johnson, Synthia, Dir-Mktg - Medieval Times Inc.; *pg.* 561, *pg.* 51
Felish, Cara, Dir-Sls Ops-Clinical Diagnostics Div - Thermo Fisher Scientific Inc.; *pg.* 1431, *pg.* 854
Felix, Ariel, Sr Mgr-Programmatic Sls-Corp - Conde Nast Publications, Inc.; *pg.* 1629, *pg.* 1217
Felix, Carissa, Mgr-Client Mktg - Allscripts Healthcare Solutions, Inc.; *pg.* 1492, *pg.* 563
Felix, George, Brand Mgr-P&G Mobile Mktg Strategy & Innovation-Global - Procter & Gamble Inc.; *pg.* 333, *pg.* 1929
Felix, Lauren, Mgr-Integrated Digital Mktg - Glaxo Smith Kline Inc.; *pg.* 1536, *pg.* 1926
Felix, Lilian Sellaro, Product Mgr - Herman Miller, Inc.; *pg.* 926, *pg.* 913
Felix, Liz, Mgr-Online Mktg - Snapfish; *pg.* 1687, *pg.* 228
Feliz, Josie, Dir-Comm & Media Rels - The Partnership at Drugfree.org; *pg.* 153, *pg.* 1276
Felke, Magnus, Sr Dir-Global Partner Mktg - QUALCOMM Incorporated; *pg.* 1873, *pg.* 207
Felke, Susan, Sr Mgr-ECommerce & Web Mktg - Sony Electronics, Inc.; *pg.* 676, *pg.* 209
Felker, Mike, Mgr-Mktg - Mannington Mills, Inc.; *pg.* 934, *pg.* 1119
Felker, Todd, Exec VP-Mktg & Product Dev - I.D. Systems, Inc.; *pg.* 643, *pg.* 1134
Fell, Laura, Strategist-Search & Digital Mktg - Caterpillar, Inc.; *pg.* 1321, *pg.* 650
Fell, Lorne, Product Mgr-Separation Science - LECO Corporation; *pg.* 1355, *pg.* 906
Feller, Meg, Mgr-Mktg Comm - 3M Company; *pg.* 1142, *pg.* 956
Feller, Steve, VP-Sls-North America - Heaven Hill Distilleries, Inc.; *pg.* 1964, *pg.* 725
Feller, Tom, Dir-Event Mktg & Justin Brands - Justin Brands, Inc.; *pg.* 1810, *pg.* 1695
Fellis, Joel, Sr Mgr-Product Mktg, Sys & Genomic Svcs - Illumina, Inc.; *pg.* 412, *pg.* 203
Fellman, Brett, Sr VP-Mktg & Studio Rels - Deluxe Corporation; *pg.* 1634, *pg.* 964
Fellman, Ingrid, Specialist-Mktg Comm - Polaris Industries Inc.; *pg.* 1709, *pg.* 928
Fellner, Rosemary, VP & Dir-Mktg - Unity Bank; *pg.* 814, *pg.* 1052
Fellows, Becky, Analyst-Digital Mktg - Briggs & Stratton Corporation; *pg.* 201, *pg.* 1899
Fellows, Frank, Sr Mgr-Analyst & Press Rels - Microsoft Corporation; *pg.* 435, *pg.* 1824
Fellows, Trevor, Global Head-Media Sls - The Wall Street Journal; *pg.* 1700, *pg.* 1312
Fells-rashad, Cheryl, Asst Mgr-Adv - The Coca-Cola Company; *pg.* 240, *pg.* 493
Felsher, Jon, Dir-Mktg - Merck & Co., Inc.; *pg.* 1566, *pg.* 1077
Felsher, Louise, Sr Mgr-Event - Oracle Corporation; *pg.* 450, *pg.* 191
Felt, Matt, Mgr-Navy, Nuclear & Specialty Motor Mktg - Baldor Electric Company; *pg.* 1316, *pg.* 32
Felten, Jessica, Mgr-Mktg - Comcast Sportsnet; *pg.* 278, *pg.* 1562
Feltes, James, Sr Mgr - Siemens Energy, Inc.; *pg.* 469, *pg.* 1341
Feltman, Margo, Mgr-Sls Comm - Revlon, Inc.; *pg.* 521, *pg.* 1286
Feltner, Stephen, VP-Sls-North America - HomeAway, Inc.; *pg.* 1911, *pg.* 1663
Felton, Keith, Grp Dir-Product Mgmt & Mktg - Cadence Design Systems, Inc.; *pg.* 367, *pg.* 239
Felton, Randi, Sr Dir-Adv Sls Res - MTV Networks Company; *pg.* 298, *pg.* 1262
Felts, Joe, Mgr-Mktg Brand - Makita U.S.A., Inc.; *pg.* 1358, *pg.* 120
Fendrich, Denise, Program Mgr & Analyst-Mktg-Shopper Mktg - PepsiCo, Inc.; *pg.* 259, *pg.* 1327
Fendrock, Cecilia, Mgr-Mktg - MyWebGrocer.com Corp.; *pg.* 1269, *pg.* 1769
Fenech, David, VP-Digital Mktg & Creative Svcs - Kelly Services, Inc.; *pg.* 424, *pg.* 911
Fenelon, James, Product Mgr-eCommerce & Principal - HomeAway, Inc.; *pg.* 1911, *pg.* 1663
Feng, Jeff, Product Mgr - Tableau Software, Inc.; *pg.* 481, *pg.* 1841
Feng, Paul, Product Dir-Mgmt - Google Inc.; *pg.* 1249, *pg.* 153
Feng, Peiti, Dir-Brand Strategy & Mktg Comm-Sprint Prepaid - Sprint Corporation; *pg.* 1874, *pg.* 719
Fenichell, Stephen, Sr VP-Corp Comm & Corp Social - Bank of America Corporation; *pg.* 718, *pg.* 1362
Fening, Jennifer, Sr Coord-Mktg - Worthington Industries, Inc.; *pg.* 123, *pg.* 1444
Fenn, Noah, Dir-Sls & Strategy-Video - AOL Inc.; *pg.* 1229, *pg.* 1195
Fennelly, Julia, Asst Mgr-Corp PR & Consumer Brands PR - Kohl's Corporation; *pg.* 1775, *pg.* 1870
Fennessy, Krista L., Mgr-Mktg Comm-Worldwide - Eastman Kodak Company; *pg.* 1408, *pg.* 1333
Fenning, Amy, Sr Brand Mgr-Mktg - LexisNexis Group; *pg.* 1658, *pg.* 1446
Fenno, John, Dir-Mktg - Electronic Arts Inc.; *pg.* 951, *pg.* 189
Fenocketti, Nancy, Sr Mgr-Category Dev - General Mills, Inc.; *pg.* 828, *pg.* 933
Fenoglio, Alyssa, Dir-Consumer Mktg - NeuroMetrix, Inc.; *pg.* 1572, *pg.* 852
Fenske, Jake, Sr Dir-Channel Partnerships & Online Mktg - Redbox Automated Retail, LLC; *pg.* 306, *pg.* 649
Fenton, Jeff, Bus Mgr - Sasol North America Inc.; *pg.* 984, *pg.* 1713
Fenton, Paula, Mgr-Mktg - 7-Eleven, Inc.; *pg.* 1012, *pg.* 1672
Fenton, Suzanne, Dir-Mktg - TricorBraun; *pg.* 1471, *pg.* 1004
Fenwick, Alicia, Sr Mgr-Brand Activation - Newell Rubbermaid Inc.; *pg.* 1128, *pg.* 515
Feore, Dani, Dir-Digital & Mobile Sls-Eastern Reg - The Weather Channel LLC; *pg.* 320, *pg.* 523
Fera, Joe, Coord-Mktg - McKesson Corporation; *pg.* 1560, *pg.* 222
Fera, Scott, Sr VP-Sls & Mktg - FlightSafety International, Inc.; *pg.* 601, *pg.* 1160
Feracco, Christine, Sr Mgr-Consumer Comm - R.J. Reynolds Tobacco Co.; *pg.* 1895, *pg.* 1395
Feramisco, Celia, Sr Mgr-Mktg - Amgen Inc.; *pg.* 1493, *pg.* 291
Ferdinand, Alex, Dir-Worldwide Sls-North American Leisure & Canadian Corp - Best Western International, Inc.; *pg.* 1081, *pg.* 15
Ferdinandi, Mike, Sr Mgr-Mktg - Overstock.com, Inc.; *pg.* 1273, *pg.* 1760
Ferdman, Mark, VP-Global ECommerce & Digital Mktg-Origins - The Estee Lauder Companies Inc.; *pg.* 508, *pg.* 1229
Ference, Adam, Dir-Mktg - MTD Products, Inc.; *pg.* 1057, *pg.* 1478
Ferencz, Amanda, Mgr-Mktg - American Egg Board; *pg.* 128, *pg.* 650
Ferenczy, Bill, Sr Dir-Mktg - Quidel Corporation; *pg.* 1588, *pg.* 207
Ferengul, Corey, Exec VP-Product Mgmt & Mktg - Rovi Corporation; *pg.* 463, *pg.* 269
Ferenz, Nicola, Coord-Experience Mktg - Clif Bar Inc.; *pg.* 848, *pg.* 83
Feresten, Nancy, Sr VP-Education & Children's Media - National Geographic Society; *pg.* 1667, *pg.* 402
Feresten, Paul, Sr Product Mgr-Mktg-Intelligent Caching Products - NetApp, Inc.; *pg.* 444, *pg.* 287
Fergerstrom, Bobby, Sr Mgr-Philanthropic Svcs - Entertainment Industry Foundation; *pg.* 140, *pg.* 130
Ferguson, Amy, Mgr-Mdse - The History Channel; *pg.* 290, *pg.* 1240
Ferguson, Amy, Asst VP-Integrated Mktg & Corp Comm - NorthShore University HealthSystem; *pg.* 606, *pg.* 612
Ferguson, Brian, Sr VP & Gen Mgr-Mdse - The Children's Place, Inc.; *pg.* 22, *pg.* 1119
Ferguson, Dan, Sr Dir-Mktg - DIRECTV Group Holdings, LLC; *pg.* 281, *pg.* 79
Ferguson, Jayne, Dir-Americas Channel Mktg - SanDisk Corporation; *pg.* 465, *pg.* 147
Ferguson, Jeff, Dir-Sponsorship Sls - Live Nation Entertainment, Inc.; *pg.* 558, *pg.* 47
Ferguson, Jennifer, Program Mgr-Creative Svcs - Brocade Communications Systems, Inc.; *pg.* 365, *pg.* 239
Ferguson, Julie, Sr Mgr-Global Pub Affairs - Hospira, Inc.; *pg.* 1542, *pg.* 623
Ferguson, Kaitlin Callahan, VP & Mgr-Mktg Info - Bank of America Corporation; *pg.* 718, *pg.* 1362
Ferguson, Kim, Mgr-Mktg & Partnership Activation - Baltimore Ravens Limited Partnership; *pg.* 532, *pg.* 755
Ferguson, Laura, Brand Mgr-Colgate Total - Colgate-Palmolive Company; *pg.* 504, *pg.* 1215
Ferguson, Lisa, Mgr-Product Dev - Payless Shoesource, Inc.; *pg.* 31, *pg.* 722
Ferguson, Matt, Mgr-Mktg-YRC Freight - YRC Worldwide Inc.; *pg.* 1931, *pg.* 720
Ferguson, Michael, Dir-Technical Mktg & Bus Dev - Arris Group, Inc.; *pg.* 353, *pg.* 541
Ferguson, Roger, VP-Brand Adv & Sponsorships - Capital One Financial Corporation; *pg.* 730, *pg.* 1789
Ferguson, Teresa, Dir-Comm & PR - La Quinta Corporation; *pg.* 1099, *pg.* 1722
Ferguson, Tom, Sr VP-Sls-Grocery, Drug & Club - Keurig Green Mountain, Inc.; *pg.* 868, *pg.* 1768
Ferguson, Virginia, Dir-PR - YUM! Brands, Inc.; *pg.* 1756, *pg.* 738
Ferguson, Wayne, Brand Mgr-Assassins Creed - Ubisoft Inc.; *pg.* 589, *pg.* 229
Feringa, Dave, Exec VP-Sls-Worldwide - F5 Networks, Inc.; *pg.* 396, *pg.* 1835
Ferla, Marcello La, Dir-Creative - NBC Universal, Inc.; *pg.* 300, *pg.* 1266
Ferlauto, Tony, VP-Sls-Natl - Coca-Cola North America; *pg.* 848, *pg.* 500
Fern, Charle A., Dir-East Reg Field Mktg - Level 3 Communications, Inc.; *pg.* 1262, *pg.* 1664
Fern, Jonathan, Sr Product Mgr-Comml Innovation - Abbott Diabetes Care, Inc.; *pg.* 1483, *pg.* 38
Fernald, Karen, Sr VP-Mdsg-Food Lion - Food Lion, LLC; *pg.* 1019, *pg.* 1390
Fernander, Bob, Interim CEO - Imation Corp.; *pg.* 413, *pg.* 952
Fernandes, Andrea, Sr Mgr-Mktg & Brand - Peet's Coffee & Tea, Inc.; *pg.* 1029, *pg.* 85
Fernandes, Bernard, Mgr-PR - Advanced Micro Devices, Inc.-Markham; *pg.* 345, *pg.* 1922
Fernandes, Daniel, Brand Mgr - Lenox; *pg.* 1053, *pg.* 817
Fernandes, Joe, Dir-Product Mgmt-OpenShift PaaS - Red Hat, Inc.; *pg.* 460, *pg.* 1388
Fernandez, Cristina, Reg Mgr-Mktg - H&R Block, Inc.; *pg.* 764, *pg.* 983
Fernandez, Ellen M., Program Mgr-Enterprise Mktg - Lexmark International, Inc.; *pg.* 427, *pg.* 730
Fernandez, Frank, Dir-Sls & Mktg - Lennar Corporation; *pg.* 1100, *pg.* 443
Fernandez, Gary, VP-Sls & Mktg-Natl - Capital Senior Living Corporation; *pg.* 1084, *pg.* 1677
Fernandez, Isabel, Mgr-Mktg, Comm & Community Rels - City National Corporation; *pg.* 738, *pg.* 128
Fernandez, Ivette, Assoc Mgr-Adv - Xerox Corporation; *pg.*

494, pg. 365
Fernandez, Joe, Dir-Mobile Internet Growth & Revenue-Mktg - T-Mobile US, Inc.; pg. 676, pg. 1816
Fernandez, Joseph, Brand Mgr-Whiskies - Bacardi USA, Inc.; pg. 1956, pg. 417
Fernandez, Kathryn Holl, Sr Mgr-Mktg Comm - Unilever United States, Inc.; pg. 904, pg. 1061
Fernandez, Kelvin, Product Mgr-EFD - Nordson Corporation; pg. 1365, pg. 1480
Fernandez, Lauren, Mgr-Social Media - Academy Sports & Outdoors, Ltd.; pg. 1824, pg. 1724
Fernandez, Marissa, Dir-Fan Strategy & Mktg - National Football League; pg. 567, pg. 1264
Fernandez, Michelle, Dir-Mktg - Canon U.S.A., Inc.; pg. 1404, pg. 1178
Fernandez, Pablo, Sr Mgr-SEO, Analytics & Affiliates - TracFone Wireless, Inc.; pg. 681, pg. 447
Fernandez, Paul, Mgr-Circulation Retail Sls - The Morning Call, Inc.; pg. 1665, pg. 1513
Fernandez, Rafael, Sls Mgr Latin America & the Caribbean - Clearfield, Inc.; pg. 1406, pg. 953
Fernandez, Ricardo, VP-Mktg - General Mills, Inc.; pg. 828, pg. 933
Fernandez, Rudy, Program Dir-Radio Abilene-Townsquare Media - Townsquare Media, Inc.; pg. 313, pg. 350
Fernandez-Lamela, Damian, Sr Dir-Mktg Analytics - Fossil Group, Inc.; pg. 5, pg. 1735
Fernando, Dilini, Mgr-Digital Innovation & Mktg - MillerCoors LLC; pg. 255, pg. 582
Fernando, Lynn, Dir-Synergy & Partnership Mktg - Disney Interactive Media Group; pg. 1239, pg. 95
Fernando, Nate, Assoc Mgr-Mktg - General Mills, Inc.; pg. 828, pg. 933
Fernando, Roman, Exec Dir-Digital Adv Ops - Allrecipes.com; pg. 1226, pg. 1831
Fernands, Katie, Mgr-Online Mktg-Wealth Mgmt - U.S. Bancorp; pg. 815, pg. 945
Fernelius, Gretchen, Dir-Comm & Mktg Svcs - CARIBOU COFFEE COMPANY, INC.; pg. 1764, pg. 932
Ferney, Brian, Dir-Mktg Comm - Comcast Cable Communications, Inc.; pg. 276, pg. 1560
Ferradas, Matias, Mgr-Media - AutoNation, Inc.; pg. 165, pg. 423
Ferrali, Paul J., Dir-Adv Svcs & Quality Assurance - The New York Times Company; pg. 1668, pg. 1270
Ferrall, Nathaniel, Mgr-Mktg - Cleveland Cavaliers/Quicken Loans Arena; pg. 541, pg. 1429
Ferran, Dave, Head-Sls - Classic Vacations, LLC; pg. 1903, pg. 242
Ferrand, Paul-Henri, VP-US Sls & Ops - Google Inc.; pg. 1249, pg. 153
Ferrando, Jackie, Sr Mgr-Event Mktg - Boyd Gaming Corporation; pg. 1082, pg. 1022
Ferranti, Stephen, Sr Dir-IR - Skyworks Solutions, Inc.; pg. 674, pg. 862
Ferrantino, Trina, Sr Mgr-Mktg-TurboTax - Intuit Inc.; pg. 769, pg. 158
Ferrara, Jacquelyn, Dir-Mktg-Minwax & Formby's Brands - Sherwin Williams; pg. 1448, pg. 1436
Ferrara, Jerry, Exec VP-Adv Sls - Investors Business Daily, Inc.; pg. 1653, pg. 133
Ferrara, Patricio, Brand Mgr - Anheuser-Busch Companies, LLC; pg. 237, pg. 991
Ferrara, Patrick, Sr Dir-Procurement - Hughes Network Systems LLC; pg. 643, pg. 770
Ferrara, Russ, Sr Mgr-Shopper Mktg - Georgia-Pacific LLC; pg. 1458, pg. 507
Ferrara, Susan, Mgr-Field Mktg-Eastern United States - Benihana Inc.; pg. 1716, pg. 409
Ferrari, Bernie, Sr Dir-Product Mgmt & Mktg - Huttig Building Products, Inc.; pg. 88, pg. 998
Ferrari, Kathy A., Sr Specialist-Mktg - Canon U.S.A., Inc.; pg. 1404, pg. 1178
Ferrari, Kristen, Coord-Mktg - Steven Madden, Ltd.; pg. 1819, pg. 1176
Ferrari, Nicole, Sr Mgr-Mfg - Bausch & Lomb Incorporated; pg. 1401, pg. 1045
Ferrari, Nicole, Dir-Partner Mktg - NBC Universal, Inc.; pg. 300, pg. 1266
Ferraro, Alexis, VP-Brand Mktg & Creative - TPR Education, LLC; pg. 1695, pg. 822
Ferraro, James, VP-Mktg-Global - ProLogis; pg. 1108, pg. 322
Ferraro, John, Dir-Adv Sls - The Street, Inc.; pg. 1283, pg. 1296
Ferraro, John, VP-Ad Sls-West Reg - WhitePages.com Inc.; pg. 1289, pg. 1842
Ferraro, Kathy, Coord-Mktg - Samsung Electronics America, Inc.; pg. 669, pg. 1115
Ferraro, Leslie, Pres-Disney Consumer Products - The Walt Disney Company; pg. 317, pg. 52
Ferraro, Tomas, Coord-Mktg - ESPN, Inc.; pg. 285, pg. 340
Ferrato, Kelsea, Mgr-Mktg - Rocky Mountain Chocolate Factory, Inc.; pg. 1032, pg. 324
Ferrazzano, Laura, Sr Planner-Mdse - J. Crew Group, Inc.; pg. 1773, pg. 1245
Ferree, Gerry, Mgr-Mktg - D.R. Horton, Inc.; pg. 1090, pg. 1694
Ferreira, Victoria, Mgr-PR & Media Rels-Latin America - Netflix, Inc.; pg. 1269, pg. 141
Ferrell, Chad, Sr VP-Mktg - American National Insurance Company; pg. 1191, pg. 1697
Ferrentino, Brian, Engr-Sls - T-Mobile US, Inc.; pg. 676, pg. 1816
Ferrer, Barbara, Chief Strategy Officer - W.K. Kellogg Foundation; pg. 161, pg. 872
Ferrer, Jackie, Mgr-Mktg - The New York Times Company; pg. 1668, pg. 1270
Ferrer, Marianne, Mgr-Email Mktg - Bare Necessities, Inc.; pg. 19, pg. 1056
Ferreras-Meulen, Dortiz, Sr Dir-Mktg Strategy & Consumer Markets - Comcast Cable Communications, Inc.; pg. 276, pg. 1560
Ferretti, Richard, Sr VP & Dir-Global Creative - The Estee Lauder Companies Inc.; pg. 508, pg. 1229
Ferri, Jill, Mgr-Key Acct & Natl Sls - Cumulus Media Inc.; pg. 280, pg. 503
Ferrie, Jennifer, Mgr-Digital Mktg-Home Appliances - LG Electronics U.S.A., Inc.; pg. 651, pg. 1060
Ferrill, Wendy, VP-Sls-Worldwide - Best Western International, Inc.; pg. 1081, pg. 15
Ferris, Christine, Mgr-PR & Mktg - Smashburger Master LLC; pg. 1750, pg. 323
Ferris, Danielle, Sr Mgr-Comm - Intuit Inc.; pg. 769, pg. 158
Ferris, Gerald, VP-Sls-Global - Altra Holdings, Inc.; pg. 198, pg. 802
Ferris, Gerald, VP-Sls-Global - Altria Industrial Motion Corp.; pg. 1312, pg. 802
Ferris, Gerald P., VP-Sls-Global - Boston Gear; pg. 201, pg. 802
Ferris, Henry, VP-Sls & Mktg - Winn Dixie Stores, Inc.; pg. 1038, pg. 435
Ferris, James, Dir-Mktg - Electronic Arts Inc.; pg. 951, pg. 189
Ferris, Peter, Chief Sls Officer - Equinix, Inc.; pg. 394, pg. 190
Ferris, Richard T., Reg Dir-Sls - Calero Software, LLC; pg. 368, pg. 1333
Ferris, Scott, Sr Mgr-Tech Ops & Aircraft Maintenance Plng - United Airlines, Inc.; pg. 1927, pg. 593
Ferriso, Carissa, Sr Product Mgr-Epic Threads - Macy's East; pg. 1777, pg. 1254
Ferriss, Tracey, Sr Mgr-Mktg Comm, Info Security & Risk Mgmt Grp - Microsoft Corporation; pg. 435, pg. 1824
Ferro, Frank, Sr Mgr-Intl Trade - The Michigan Economic Development Corporation, Tourism & Marketing; pg. 999, pg. 895
Ferro, Frank, Sr Dir-Product Mktg - Rambus Inc.; pg. 459, pg. 288
Ferro, Rita, Exec VP-Disney Media Sls & Mktg - Disney Interactive Media Group; pg. 1239, pg. 95
Ferro, Rita, Exec VP-Disney Media Sls & Mktg - The Walt Disney Company; pg. 317, pg. 52
Ferrone, Jaime, Dir-Channel Mktg - Avis Budget Group, Inc.; pg. 1900, pg. 1102
Ferrone, Jaime, Dir-Channel Mktg - Avis Rent A Car System, LLC; pg. 165, pg. 1102
Ferrone, Morgan, Asst Mgr-Digital Commerce Mktg Chico's - Chico's FAS, Inc.; pg. 21, pg. 427
Ferschinger, Bryan, Dir-Mktg-Innovation & Design - MillerCoors; pg. 254, pg. 1877
Fertig, Heidi, Sr Mgr-HP Worldwide Exec Sponsor Program - Hewlett-Packard Company; pg. 404, pg. 175
Fertman, Don, Dir-Dev & Dir-Franchise Sls - Doctor's Associates Inc.; pg. 1726, pg. 356
Ferullo, Steve, VP-Sls & Mktg - ALERE INC.; pg. 1488, pg. 849
Fesperman, Jennifer, Project Mgr-Mktg Ops - Ceridian Corporation; pg. 371, pg. 932
Fess, Emily, Product Mgr-Online - The Home Depot, Inc.; pg. 1050, pg. 510
Fessatidis, Nancy, VP-Mktg Ops - SAP America, Inc.; pg. 466, pg. 1557
Festa, Jill, Dir-Digital Media - Novartis Corporation; pg. 1574, pg. 1273
Festa, Nick, Dir-Mktg-CRM for Global Connected Customer Experience - General Motors Company; pg. 175, pg. 881
Feste, Amy, Dir-Mktg Svcs - Genuine Parts Company; pg. 206, pg. 506
Feste, Amy, Dir-Mktg Svcs - National Automotive Parts Association; pg. 213, pg. 515
Festre, Carl, Area Mgr-Sls-France BeNeLux - E.I. du Pont de Nemours & Company; pg. 1159, pg. 390
Fetcher, Adam, Dir-PR & Comm-Global - Patagonia; pg. 31, pg. 301
Fetner, Chris, Dir-Global Media Engrg & Partnerships - Netflix, Inc.; pg. 1269, pg. 141
Fetterolf, Peter, Mgr-Bus & Tech Architecture Mktg - Cisco Systems, Inc.; pg. 372, pg. 240
Fetters, Aaron, Sr VP-Mktg Solutions - comScore, Inc; pg. 1236, pg. 1798
Fetters, Christoipher, Mgr-Upstream Mktg-Global - Abbott Point of Care, Inc.; pg. 1486, pg. 1110
Feuchtwanger, Jason, Dir-Corp Media Rels - The McGraw-Hill Companies Inc.; pg. 1663, pg. 1257
Feudner, Anne, Product Mgr - Kohler Co.; pg. 91, pg. 1862
Feuell, Christine, VP-Strategic Mktg & Building Efficiency - Johnson Controls, Inc.; pg. 1073, pg. 1597
Feuer, Jeri, Project Mgr-Brand Mktg-Global - Levi Strauss & Co.; pg. 43, pg. 220
Feuerabend, Michael F., Mgr-Midwest Sls - Finch Paper LLC; pg. 1457, pg. 1161
Feuerberg, Bryan, Reg Dir-Sls - TD Bank US Holding Company; pg. 809, pg. 1051
Feuerstein, Christine, Mgr-Mktg - Herman Miller, Inc.; pg. 926, pg. 913
Feuerstein, Jeff, VP & Gen Mgr-North America Prepaid Products - MasterCard Incorporated; pg. 779, pg. 1325
Feurle, Robert A., VP-Mktg & Program Mgmt, Compute & Networking Bus - Micron Technology, Inc.; pg. 435, pg. 547
Feury, Matt, Dir-Pro Video, Product & Segment Mktg - Avid Technology, Inc.; pg. 622, pg. 804
Few, Melanie, VP-Mktg, Consumer Insights & Retail Experience - ACE Cash Express, Inc.; pg. 710, pg. 1717
Fey, Angela, Mgr-Mktg-Client Mgmt & Cisco - Ingram Micro Inc.; pg. 415, pg. 261
Feyen, Devon, Mgr-Mktg Comm - TELUS CORPORATION; pg. 1952, pg. 1912
Ffrench, Celia, VP-Mktg - West Coast University; pg. 610, pg. 118
Fiaccone, Chris, Sr Specialist-Mktg - FedEx Express Corporation; pg. 1908, pg. 1644
Fiala, Jerry, Dir-Mktg - Capital One Financial Corporation; pg. 730, pg. 1789
Fialkowski, Jerry, Mgr-Sls-Eastern Reg - Morris Coupling Company; pg. 1057, pg. 1530
Fiamingo, Katie, Brand Mgr-Nestle Purina North America - Nestle Purina PetCare Company; pg. 1479, pg. 1000
Fibiger, Daniel, Sr Mgr-Vendor Engagement & Monitoring - The Gap, Inc.; pg. 1770, pg. 218
Fibison, Michael, Sr Dir-Strategic Sls - Angie's List Inc; pg. 1228, pg. 682
Ficarra, Chris, Sr VP-Mktg MTV Music Grp - MTV Networks Company; pg. 298, pg. 1262
Fichman, Jonathan, Mgr-Digital Mktg - Kayak; pg. 1260, pg. 363
Fick, Martin, Sr Product Mgr-South Africa - BlackBerry Limited; pg. 625, pg. 1947
Fiddelke, Deb, Sr Dir-External Affairs-Latin America - S.C. Johnson & Son, Inc.; pg. 334, pg. 1889
Fiedler, Scott A., Specialist-Media Rels - FedEx Corporation; pg. 1907, pg. 1642
Fiege, Robert, Dir-Production - News-Leader; pg. 1670, pg. 422
Fiel, Matthew, Mgr-Digital Mktg & Email Mktg - Kenneth Cole Productions, Inc.; pg. 1810, pg. 1248
Field, John T., Dir-Digital Mktg - Samsung Telecommunications America, LLC; pg. 670, pg. 1736
Field, Manning, Head-Mktg, Innovation, Sls Strategy & Corp Dev - Chase Card Services, Inc.; pg. 734, pg. 215
Field, Nupur, Brand Mgr - Novartis Corporation; pg. 1574, pg. 1273
Field, Rachel, Product Mgr-DotCom & Online Banking - Bank of America Corporation; pg. 718, pg. 1362

Fielding, Derek, Dir-Consumer Mktg - Libbey, Inc.; *pg.* 1126, *pg.* 1476
Fielding, Jim, Head-Global Consumer Products - DreamWorks Animation SKG, Inc.; *pg.* 284, *pg.* 96
Fielding, Paul, Dir-Sls & Mktg - Special Metals Corporation; *pg.* 1377, *pg.* 1850
Fielding, Steven, Sr Mgr-AR & PR - Microsoft Corporation; *pg.* 435, *pg.* 1824
Fields, Calvinia, Specialist-Mktg-CPVC Plumbing North America - The Lubrizol Corporation; *pg.* 1171, *pg.* 1481
Fields, Chelsey E., Product Mgr-Vegetable - W. Atlee Burpee & Co.; *pg.* 1801, *pg.* 1590
Fields, David, Asst VP-Mktg - CIT GROUP INC.; *pg.* 735, *pg.* 1212
Fields, Jeff, Sr Dir-Underwriting & Production - Markel Corporation; *pg.* 1207, *pg.* 1783
Fields, Laura, Sr Dir-Market Res-Diabetes - Sanofi US; *pg.* 1592, *pg.* 1046
Fields, Mark, Dir-Sls & Mktg - TreeHouse Foods, Inc.; *pg.* 901, *pg.* 649
Fields, Michelle, Dir-Global Digital & Web Mktg - Ashley Furniture Industries, Inc.; *pg.* 914, *pg.* 1852
Fields, Richard K., Dir-Mktg - Snap-on Incorporated; *pg.* 1062, *pg.* 1862
Fields, Robert, Sr Dir-Meat, Seafood & Gourmet - Sam's Club; *pg.* 1783, *pg.* 29
Fiely, Rachel, Sr Dir-Tropicana Pure Premium & Tropicana Innovation - PepsiCo, Inc.; *pg.* 259, *pg.* 1327
Fierle, Pete, Mgr-Digital Media & Comm - National Football Museum, Inc.; *pg.* 568, *pg.* 1408
Fierro, Trent, Sr Mgr-Mktg - Aruba Networks, Inc.; *pg.* 353, *pg.* 284
Fiessinger, Christophe, Product Mktg Mgr-Enterprise Social Grp - Microsoft Corporation; *pg.* 435, *pg.* 1824
Fieth, David, Product Mgr - Recreational Equipment, Inc.; *pg.* 1843, *pg.* 1821
Fifadra, Dina C., Dir-Channel Sls - Samsung Telecommunications America, LLC; *pg.* 670, *pg.* 1736
Fife, Stewart, Product Mgr-Cloud Platform - Google Inc.; *pg.* 1249, *pg.* 153
Fifield, Lauren, Mgr-Mktg-Running Events - ASICS America Corporation; *pg.* 1826, *pg.* 106
Figa, Barry, Specialist-Mktg Product - AGCO Corporation; *pg.* 700, *pg.* 530
Figdor, Suzanne, Dir-Mktg & Corp Brand Mgmt - The Walt Disney Company; *pg.* 317, *pg.* 52
Figel, Lisa, Dir-Media Investment Leverage - Johnson & Johnson; *pg.* 1549, *pg.* 1091
Figel, Melissa, Brand Mgr-Strategy Mktg - Nordstrom, Inc.; *pg.* 1779, *pg.* 1837
Figgins, Troy, Dir-Mktg - Frito-Lay North America, Inc.; *pg.* 1853, *pg.* 1730
Figgins, Troy C., Dir-Mktg - PepsiCo, Inc.; *pg.* 259, *pg.* 1327
Figroid, Kate, Analyst-Digital Mktg - Taco Bell Corp.; *pg.* 1752, *pg.* 117
Figuccio, Nicole, Sr Specialist-Mktg - Panasonic Corporation of North America; *pg.* 661, *pg.* 1120
Figueredo, Christine B., VP & Product Mgr-Corp Deposits - BB&T Corporation; *pg.* 723, *pg.* 1393
Figueroa, Maria Isabel, VP-Mktg - Telemundo Network Inc.; *pg.* 311, *pg.* 430
Figueroa, Wendy, Dir-Sls-Discovery En Espanol & Family - Discovery Communications, Inc.; *pg.* 282, *pg.* 777
Figurito, Louis, Specialist-Direct Mktg-Major Accounts - United States Postal Service; *pg.* 1009, *pg.* 406
Fike, Doug, Mgr-Mktg Comm - SKF Sealing Solutions; *pg.* 217, *pg.* 610
Fikes, Lorena, Reg Mgr-Mktg - Essex Property Trust, Inc.; *pg.* 1091, *pg.* 175
Filan, Kevin, VP-Customer Mktg & Indus Rels - AutoTrader, Inc.; *pg.* 1230, *pg.* 490
Filanowicz, Joseph, Dir-Digital Mktg - Sonic Automotive, Inc.; *pg.* 190, *pg.* 1369
Filar, Tom, Dir-Mktg-HUMIRA Patient Svcs - AbbVie Inc.; *pg.* 1486, *pg.* 638
Filardi, Chris, VP-Mktg - Werner Holding Co.; *pg.* 121, *pg.* 1534
Filek, Karyn, Exec Dir-Licensing & Special Market Sls - Sony Pictures Home Entertainment; *pg.* 310, *pg.* 72
Filer, Jim, Sr Mgr-Mktg - Honeywell International Inc.; *pg.* 407, *pg.* 1088
Files, Morgan, VP-Corp Mktg - BancorpSouth, Inc.; *pg.* 717, *pg.* 971
Filia, Stacy, Dir-Sls & Mktg - Hyatt Hotels Corporation; *pg.* 1096, *pg.* 577
Filipas, Ioana, Mgr-Product Engineering - LiveRail; *pg.* 1264, *pg.* 145
Filipovic, Robert, Gen Mgr-Jaguar Product Plng - Jaguar Land Rover North America LLC; *pg.* 180, *pg.* 1081
Filipovits, Kristin, Sr Mgr-Mktg - Comcast Corporation; *pg.* 276, *pg.* 1560
Filippelli, John, Pres-Production & Programming - Yankees Entertainment & Sports Network, LLC; *pg.* 324, *pg.* 1316
Filippelli, Pete, Sr VP-Sls & Mktg - Eli's Cheesecake Company; *pg.* 1852, *pg.* 572
Filips, Karen, Dir-Mktg Ops & Media - Beall's, Inc.; *pg.* 1760, *pg.* 414
Filla, Amanda, Mgr-Creative Dev - 20th Century Fox Home Entertainment, Inc.; *pg.* 267, *pg.* 125
Filla, Amanda, Mgr-Creative Dev - Fox Entertainment Group, Inc.; *pg.* 288, *pg.* 131
Filla, Michael, Sr VP-Sls & Bus Dev - Nooter/Eriksen, Inc.; *pg.* 1075, *pg.* 977
Filleau, Jonathan, Sr Mgr-Mktg-EMEA-Consumer Products - PNY Technologies, Inc.; *pg.* 455, *pg.* 1105
Filler, Linda, Chief Mdsg Officer & Pres-Retail Products - Walgreen Co.; *pg.* 1608, *pg.* 605
Filliat, Annette, Dir-PR - Boys and Girls Club of America; *pg.* 134, *pg.* 491
Fillinger, John, Dir-Utility Mktg - Badger Meter, Inc.; *pg.* 1401, *pg.* 1873
Fillingham, Gysela, Mgr-Citywide Sls - Denver Metro Convention & Visitors Bureau; *pg.* 991, *pg.* 318
Fillmore, Allison, Exec Dir-Sls - Atlanta Motor Speedway, Inc.; *pg.* 530, *pg.* 533
Filmer, Rebecca, Head-PR - Parfums Christian Dior, Inc; *pg.* 519, *pg.* 1276
Filon, Peter, Sr Dir-Federal Govt Affairs - Comcast Corporation; *pg.* 276, *pg.* 1560
Filosa, Kathy, VP-Mktg & Adv - Cablevision Systems Corporation; *pg.* 272, *pg.* 1141
Filso, Carol, Mgr-Mdsg & Promos - Building Products of Canada Corp.; *pg.* 72, *pg.* 1951
Filyk, Susan K., Dir-Mktg - U.S. Global Investors, Inc.; *pg.* 815, *pg.* 1743
Fimbres, Vanessa, Mgr-Mktg-The Parenting Grp - Bonnier Corporation; *pg.* 1622, *pg.* 480
Finan, Darrick, VP-Sls-Americas - Eaton Corporation - Industrial Controls; *pg.* 1296, *pg.* 1874
Finberg, Shannon C., VP-Content Strategy, Creation & Digital Mktg - K12, Inc.; *pg.* 1260, *pg.* 1785
Finch, Eileen, Head-eSupport & Social Media - Schneider Electric USA, Inc.; *pg.* 1306, *pg.* 650
Finch, Jay, Sr Mgr-Digital Mktg & Sls - Cox Communications, Inc.; *pg.* 279, *pg.* 501
Finch, Luanne, Mgr-Web Mktg - Affinia Wix Filtration Products; *pg.* 198, *pg.* 1373
Finch, Matt, Dir-Product Mktg - Nature's Sunshine Products, Inc.; *pg.* 1571, *pg.* 1754
Finch, Michelle, VP-Digital Mktg - MB Financial, Inc.; *pg.* 781, *pg.* 581
Finch, Paul, Mgr-Global Mktg-Oral Care - Colgate-Palmolive Company; *pg.* 504, *pg.* 1215
Finch, Richard, Dir-Mktg & Sls - Comcast Corporation; *pg.* 276, *pg.* 1560
Finch, Wendy, Coord-Mktg - Dover Chemical Corporation; *pg.* 1156, *pg.* 1447
Fincher, Andrew, Project Mgr-Digital Mktg - Staples, Inc.; *pg.* 474, *pg.* 821
Findell, Jessica, Community Mgr-Social Media - United Services Automobile Association; *pg.* 1221, *pg.* 1743
Findlay, Deirdre, Dir-Hardware Mktg-Global - Google Inc.; *pg.* 1249, *pg.* 153
Findlay, Marion, Sr Mgr-Consumer Mktg - The Kraft Heinz Company; *pg.* 870, *pg.* 1577
Findlay, Shelley, VP-Mktg-Women's & Family Specialty Television - Corus Entertainment Inc.; *pg.* 279, *pg.* 1937
Fine, Bob, Dir-Product Mktg - Dell Storage; *pg.* 386, *pg.* 922
Fine, Drew, Head-Mktg-Dermal Fillers - Galderma Laboratories, L.P.; *pg.* 1532, *pg.* 1695
Fine, Greg, Dir-Mktg - Nevada Commission on Tourism; *pg.* 1000, *pg.* 1021
Fine, James, VP-Trade Mktg-DSFG - Elizabeth Arden, Inc.; *pg.* 507, *pg.* 448
Fine, Jillian, Asst Mgr-Mktg-LEGO Brand Retail - LEGO Systems, Inc.; *pg.* 961, *pg.* 346
Fine, Rebecca, Sr Dir-Mktg - Trinchero Family Estates; *pg.* 1971, *pg.* 197
Fine, Russell, Product Mgr - Recreational Equipment, Inc.; *pg.* 1843, *pg.* 1821
Fine, Steve, Dir-Kenmore & Sears Mktg - Electrolux Home Products North America; *pg.* 54, *pg.* 1366
Fine, Steve, Sr Dir-Exec Comm & Internal Comm - Hitachi Data Systems Corporation; *pg.* 407, *pg.* 265
Finegan, Alan R., Dir-Mktg - Gleason - M&M Precision Systems Corporation; *pg.* 1341, *pg.* 1479
Finegan, Tim, Dir-Environmental Monitoring Products - Xylem Inc.; *pg.* 1078, *pg.* 1339
Finelli, James, VP-Sls - Promotion In Motion, Inc.; *pg.* 1861, *pg.* 1052
Finestone, Mark, Exec VP-Mdsg, Supply Chain & Mktg - AutoZone, Inc.; *pg.* 200, *pg.* 1641
Finger, Ben, Sr Mgr-IR - The Home Depot, Inc.; *pg.* 1050, *pg.* 510
Finger, Michael, Sr VP-Sls-Global - Maxwell Technologies, Inc.; *pg.* 653, *pg.* 204
Fingerhut, Steve, Sr VP-Storage Product Bus Unit - Toshiba America, Inc.; *pg.* 681, *pg.* 1302
Fingerman, Sara Anne, Mgr-Mktg & PR - Garden City Hotel Inc.; *pg.* 1093, *pg.* 1161
Fini, Jessica, Mgr-Natl PR-Acura - American Honda Motor Co., Inc.; *pg.* 163, *pg.* 292
Fink, Emily, VP-Digital & Social Mktg - Liberty Mutual Insurance Group Inc.; *pg.* 1205, *pg.* 797
Fink, Heather, Dir-Mktg - Inter Parfums, Inc.; *pg.* 512, *pg.* 1244
Fink, Josh, Sr Coord-Client Sls - Alliance Data Systems Corporation; *pg.* 347, *pg.* 1729
Fink, Larry, Product Mgr - Halliburton Company; *pg.* 978, *pg.* 1707
Fink, Laura, VP-Mktg-American Express Travel - American Express Company; *pg.* 712, *pg.* 1190
Fink, Lauren, Mgr-Mktg - Hunter Boot USA; *pg.* 1810, *pg.* 1242
Fink, Libby, Sr Mgr-Corp Comm - Parametric Technology Corporation; *pg.* 452, *pg.* 835
Fink, Marc J., Dir-Mktg - Chase Card Services, Inc.; *pg.* 734, *pg.* 215
Fink, Maryellen, Sr Mgr-PR - Movado Group, Inc.; *pg.* 10, *pg.* 1101
Fink, Michael, Product Mgr-Search Console - Google Inc.; *pg.* 1249, *pg.* 153
Finkbiner, Maggie, Brand Mgr - AstraZeneca Pharmaceuticals LP; *pg.* 1497, *pg.* 389
Finke, Don, Mgr-Digital Creative - Caleres, Inc.; *pg.* 1805, *pg.* 993
Finkel, Nathan, Dir-NBC Sports Group, Portfolio Sls Mktg - NBC Sports Network; *pg.* 300, *pg.* 375
Finkelstein, Kristin, Sr Mgr-Mktg - Tesla Motors, Inc.; *pg.* 191, *pg.* 178
Finkelstein, Stacie, Mgr-Digital Mktg - American Express Company; *pg.* 712, *pg.* 1190
Finken, John C., Div VP-Sls-Central Div - Knoll, Inc.; *pg.* 425, *pg.* 1527
Finkle, Ned, VP-Strategic Mktg - NVIDIA Corporation; *pg.* 447, *pg.* 268
Finkowski, Danielle, Mgr-Mktg - Ingram Micro Inc.; *pg.* 415, *pg.* 261
Finlaw, Jim, Mgr-Media Rels-Global - Accenture; *pg.* 1392, *pg.* 1186
Finlay, Julie, Strategist-Comm & Mktg - United Services Automobile Association; *pg.* 1221, *pg.* 1743
Finlayson, Paul, Sr VP-Product Mgr Strategic Initiatives - Northern Trust Corporation; *pg.* 787, *pg.* 585
Finley, Chasity LaToi, Bus Mgr - Teachers Insurance & Annuity Association - College Retirement Equities Fund; *pg.* 1219, *pg.* 1297
Finley, Jason, Dir-Mktg, Woods & Irons - Callaway Golf Company; *pg.* 1829, *pg.* 58
Finley, Kris, Mgr-Mktg Comm - Zimmer Biomet Holdings, Inc.; *pg.* 1611, *pg.* 699
Finley, Lewis, Coord-Mktg - ScanSource, Inc.; *pg.* 671, *pg.* 1618
Finley, Teresa, Sr VP-Global Mktg - United Parcel Service, Inc.; *pg.* 1928, *pg.* 522
Finlinson, Justin, Brand Mgr-North America - Nestle Purina PetCare Company; *pg.* 1479, *pg.* 1000
Finn, Andrew, VP-Grp Sls - Benchmark Hospitality International Inc.; *pg.* 1081, *pg.* 1747
Finn, Charla, Asst Mgr-Media - Nestle Purina PetCare Company; *pg.* 1479, *pg.* 1000
Finn, James, Exec VP-Corp & Mktg Comm-20th Century Fox Home Entertainment - 20th Century Fox Film Corp.; *pg.* 267, *pg.* 124
Finn, James, Exec VP-Corp & Mktg Comm - 20th Century Fox

First page reference indicates Business Class Edition
Second page reference indicates Geographic Edition

Home Entertainment, Inc.; pg. 267, pg. 125
Finn, James, Exec VP-Mktg Comm-Twentieth Century Fox Home Entertainment - Fox Entertainment Group, Inc.; pg. 288, pg. 131
Finn, Justin, Head-Event Mktg - StubHub, Inc.; pg. 586, pg. 228
Finn, Kate, Sr Dir-Corp Comm - Comcast Corporation; pg. 276, pg. 1560
Finn, Matthew, Sr Mgr-Portfolio - Thrivent Financial for Lutherans; pg. 1219, pg. 944
Finn, Stephanie, Mgr-Digital Mktg & Social Media - adidas America Inc.; pg. 1803, pg. 1500
Finn, Victoria, Dir-Global Creative Dev - The Walt Disney Company; pg. 317, pg. 52
Finnecy, Cindy, VP-Indus Mktg-North America - International Business Machines Corporation; pg. 418, pg. 1138
Finnegan, Keira, Mgr-Adv & Promos-Hollywood Casino Toledo - Penn National Gaming, Inc.; pg. 574, pg. 1595
Finnegan, Mike, VP-Programmatic & Product Innovation - Live Nation Entertainment, Inc.; pg. 558, pg. 47
Finnegan, Patrick, District Mgr-Sls-Buick & GMC - General Motors Company; pg. 175, pg. 881
Finnegan, Peter, Sr Mgr-Product Mktg - Teachers Insurance & Annuity Association - College Retirement Equities Fund; pg. 1219, pg. 1297
Finnerty, Caitlin, Sr Planner-Sls - The Washington Post; pg. 1701, pg. 407
Finnerty, Steven, VP-Sls - Zayo Group, LLC; pg. 1877, pg. 334
Finnie, Ann C., Mgr-PR-Worldwide - Hewlett-Packard Company; pg. 404, pg. 175
Finnie, Sarita, Sr Dir-Compromised Skin Global Franchise - Johnson & Johnson; pg. 1549, pg. 1091
Finnie, Steve, Dir-Customer Mktg - Mars, Incorporated; pg. 1858, pg. 1792
Finnis, Abby, Sr Dir-US Strategy & Insights-Mountain Dew, Energy & Aquafina - PepsiCo, Inc.; pg. 259, pg. 1327
Finsky, Rita, Mgr-Mktg Comm - Ecolab Inc.; pg. 329, pg. 960
Finucane, Anne, CMO & Chief Strategy Officer-Global - Bank of America Corporation; pg. 718, pg. 1362
Finucane, Eileen, Dir-Direct Mktg - Home Box Office, Inc.; pg. 290, pg. 1240
Fiore, Teresa, Assoc Dir-Sourcing Mktg & Sls-Global - Boehringer Ingelheim Pharmaceuticals, Inc.; pg. 1507, pg. 368
Fiorella, Rhonda, Sr Program Mgr-Worldwide Retention Mktg - Adobe Systems Incorporated; pg. 342, pg. 235
Fiorille, Frank, Sr Dir-Risk Mgmt - Paychex, Inc.; pg. 792, pg. 1336
Fiorino, Maria, Mgr-Mktg-ID - Siemens Healthcare Diagnostics; pg. 673, pg. 604
Firenza, Shawn D., Sr Dir-Product Technical Support Grp - National Oilwell Varco, Inc.; pg. 1364, pg. 1712
Firenze, Katrina, Mgr-Pkg Design-Global Creative - Bare Escentuals, Inc.; pg. 500, pg. 213
Firestone, Eric, Dir-Sls Comm-US - Boston Scientific Corporation; pg. 1508, pg. 831
Firestone, Matthew D., Product Mgr-Mktg-Android - Google Inc.; pg. 1249, pg. 153
Firth, James D., Sr VP-Comm, Pub Advocacy & Corp Rels - Exelon Corporation; pg. 1942, pg. 573
Firth, Quincey, Mgr-Mktg - Saks Fifth Avenue, Inc.; pg. 1783, pg. 1287
Fischenich, Ray, Country Mgr-Ops Mktg-Uniroyal & Private Brands - Michelin North America Inc.; pg. 1886, pg. 1618
Fischer, Amy, Dir-Social Ventures & Corp Archives - The Western Union Company; pg. 822, pg. 327
Fischer, Anne Cecil, Sr Dir-Digital Mktg - Papa John's International, Inc.; pg. 1743, pg. 737
Fischer, Carl, Head-Consumer Mktg-Media, Philanthropy & Brand-Global - Bloomberg L.P.; pg. 725, pg. 1204
Fischer, Carl R., IV, Head-Consumer Mktg-Media, Philanthropy & Brand-Global - Bloomberg BusinessWeek; pg. 1621, pg. 1204
Fischer, Cathy, Sr VP-Mktg - Sterling Jewelers Inc.; pg. 13, pg. 1402
Fischer, Colleen, Dir-Mktg Comm - Fiserv, Inc.; pg. 758, pg. 537
Fischer, Corey, VP-Sls & Mktg - iPass, Inc.; pg. 1259, pg. 193
Fischer, Cory, Mgr-Product Dev, R&D-Progressive Insurance - The Progressive Corporation; pg. 1214, pg. 1463
Fischer, David, VP-Bus & Mktg Partnerships - Facebook, Inc.; pg. 1245, pg. 143
Fischer, Gary, VP-Domestic Mktg - NATIONAL WESTERN LIFE INSURANCE COMPANY; pg. 1210, pg. 1664
Fischer, Glenn, Sr VP-Mktg - Allflex USA, Inc.; pg. 1878, pg. 1717
Fischer, Janell, Dir-Retail Mktg - Sony Corporation of America; pg. 675, pg. 1293
Fischer, June, Sr Mgr-Logistics & Supply Chain Sustainability - Kohl's Corporation; pg. 1775, pg. 1870
Fischer, Katie, Sr Mgr-Mktg Strategic Sourcing - United States Cellular Corporation; pg. 1875, pg. 594
Fischer, Linda, Bus Mgr - El Paso Symphony Orchestra; pg. 546, pg. 1691
Fischer, Matt, Sr Dir-App Store - Apple Inc.; pg. 350, pg. 73
Fischer, Mike, VP-Bus Ops, Product Dev & Distr-Corp Legal Dept - Allianz Life Insurance Company of North America; pg. 1188, pg. 929
Fischer, Nicole, Brand Mgr-Dev - Unilever United States, Inc.; pg. 904, pg. 1061
Fischer, Rich, Analyst-Rockies Crude Mktg - ConocoPhillips; pg. 975, pg. 1703
Fischer, Timothy, Assoc Analyst-Mktg Fin - PepsiCo, Inc.; pg. 259, pg. 1327
Fischer, Tom, VP-Mktg Comm - Equifax Workforce Solutions; pg. 394, pg. 997
Fischman, Leah, VP-Mktg & Comm-Global Media - Time Warner Cable Inc.; pg. 312, pg. 1301
Fischthal, Brent, Sr Mgr-Mktg, Products & Solutions - Panasonic Corporation of North America; pg. 661, pg. 1120
Fisco, Alan, Exec VP-Revenue & New Products - Seattle Times Company; pg. 1685, pg. 1840
Fish, Adam, Mgr-Mktg-Gatorade Brand Team - PepsiCo, Inc.; pg. 259, pg. 1327
Fish, Andrew J, Sr Mgr-Mktg-Automotive - AT&T Mobility LLC; pg. 619, pg. 488
Fish, Brian M., Mgr-Global Mktg-Oncology Global Franchise - GlaxoSmithKline; pg. 1536, pg. 1565
Fish, Crystal, Dir-Wholesale Fuel Sls - The Pantry, Inc.; pg. 1029, pg. 1360
Fish, Erin, Dir-Sls-Girl's Brands Walmart - Mattel Games/Puzzles; pg. 962, pg. 80
Fish, Erin, Dir-Sls-Girl's Brands-Walmart - MATTEL, INC.; pg. 962, pg. 81
Fish, Jamey, Sr Grp Dir-Mktg-Earthmover Div-North America - Michelin North America Inc.; pg. 1886, pg. 1618
Fish, Joyce, Head-Creative Svcs-Loft - Ann Inc.; pg. 18, pg. 1195
Fish, Matthew, Specialist-Mktg Program - Quicken Loans, Inc.; pg. 797, pg. 884
Fishback, Paul, Dir-Production & Mgr-Adv - Entrepreneur Media, Inc.; pg. 1639, pg. 110
Fishback, Robert, Sr Product Mgr - The North Face, Inc.; pg. 1840, pg. 252
Fishburne, E.G., Dir-Mktg-Gatorade - PepsiCo, Inc.; pg. 259, pg. 1327
Fishel, Jennifer A., Mgr-Mktg-Brand - Michaels Stores, Inc.; pg. 1127, pg. 1722
Fisher, Amy, Dir-Strategic Partnerships & Mktg - Wenner Media LLC; pg. 1701, pg. 1314
Fisher, Angela, Dir-Mktg - Lactalis American Group; pg. 873, pg. 1149
Fisher, Ashley, Mgr-Event Mktg - McKesson Corporation; pg. 1560, pg. 222
Fisher, Bear, Sr VP-Mktg & Brand Strategy-Domestic Television Distr - NBC Universal, Inc.; pg. 300, pg. 1266
Fisher, Bear, Sr VP-Mktg & Brand Strategy - NBC Universal Television Networks Group; pg. 302, pg. 1267
Fisher, Ben, Acct Exec-Charter Media - Charter Communications, Inc.; pg. 274, pg. 372
Fisher, Brad, Sr Dir-HR Ops-Global - Wal-Mart Stores, Inc.; pg. 1790, pg. 29
Fisher, Brent, VP-Distr-Affiliate Sls & Mktg - MLB Network; pg. 298, pg. 1120
Fisher, Brian, Brand Mgr-Caltex - Chevron Corporation; pg. 974, pg. 259
Fisher, Candace, Brand Mgr-Private & Global Sourcing - Michaels Stores, Inc.; pg. 1127, pg. 1722
Fisher, Charles, Product Mgr - Ashland Inc.; pg. 972, pg. 726
Fisher, Clay, Sr VP-Consumer Mktg - The New York Times Company; pg. 1668, pg. 1270
Fisher, Curt, VP-Sls - DirectBuy, Inc.; pg. 1766, pg. 694
Fisher, David, Exec VP & Gen Mgr-Mdse - Bloomingdale's, Inc.; pg. 1763, pg. 1204
Fisher, David, Product Mgr-Global - Pacific Investment Management Company LLC; pg. 791, pg. 165
Fisher, David, Sr Dir-Mktg - Valeant Pharmaceuticals International; pg. 1605, pg. 1047
Fisher, David A., Sr Mgr-Mktg Comm - Pall Corporation; pg. 232, pg. 1323
Fisher, Ellyn, VP-PR & Social Media - The Advertising Council, Inc.; pg. 125, pg. 1187
Fisher, Greg, Sr VP-Comml Sls - Bunn-O-Matic Corporation; pg. 53, pg. 661
Fisher, Jamie, Community Mgr-Social Media - Volt Information Sciences, Inc.; pg. 490, pg. 1312
Fisher, Jason, Mgr-Digital Mktg-Culture - Red Bull North America, Inc.; pg. 264, pg. 275
Fisher, Jesse, Dir-PR - Constellation Brands, Inc.; pg. 1960, pg. 1348
Fisher, Jody, Sr Mgr-PR - Canon U.S.A., Inc.; pg. 1404, pg. 1178
Fisher, Jody, Dir-Product Mgmt - IMS Health, Inc.; pg. 1544, pg. 344
Fisher, Joel, Dir-Display Sls - TripAdvisor, Inc.; pg. 1926, pg. 835
Fisher, John, Sr VP-Ticket Sls & Mktg - Arizona Diamondbacks; pg. 529, pg. 14
Fisher, John B., Pres/CEO-Federated Advisory Companies - Federated Investors, Inc.; pg. 752, pg. 1575
Fisher, Katherine, VP-Sls - Beaulieu Group, LLC; pg. 917, pg. 529
Fisher, Kelly D., Mgr-Creative Mktg - The Travelers Companies, Inc.; pg. 1220, pg. 352
Fisher, Kevin, Dir-Creative - National Audubon Society; pg. 148, pg. 1263
Fisher, Laura, Dir-Mktg & Product Dev - The Bradford Group; pg. 1763, pg. 637
Fisher, Leigh Ann, Controller-Global Primary Products Grp - Alcoa Inc.; pg. 65, pg. 1188
Fisher, Lindsay, Product Mgr-Shopping Experience - Overstock.com, Inc.; pg. 1273, pg. 1760
Fisher, Liz, Mgr-Creative Svcs - Sun Life Financial Inc.; pg. 806, pg. 1944
Fisher, Marie, Sr Mgr-HIV Market Access & Reimbursement - Gilead Sciences, Inc.; pg. 1535, pg. 88
Fisher, Mark, VP-Sls, Mktg & Engrg - Dwyer Instruments Inc.; pg. 1330, pg. 694
Fisher, Nichole, Mgr-Channel Mktg - Nestle USA, Inc.; pg. 883, pg. 96
Fisher, Patty, Rep-Sls - Brooks Brothers Group, Inc.; pg. 39, pg. 1208
Fisher, Ray, Community Mgr-Social Media - Shell Lubricants; pg. 217, pg. 1714
Fisher, Robert, VP-Mktg - Knouse Foods Cooperative Inc.; pg. 869, pg. 1558
Fisher, Rosann, Mgr-Mktg-EPANOVA - AstraZeneca Pharmaceuticals LP; pg. 1497, pg. 389
Fisher, Samuel K., VP-Rail Products - L.B. Foster Company; pg. 1355, pg. 1578
Fisher, Steve, Mgr-Inside Sls - Post Glover Resistors Inc.; pg. 1585, pg. 727
Fisher, Susan, VP-Mktg - Delta Faucet Company; pg. 78, pg. 684
Fisher, Yan, Sr Principal Mgr-Product Mktg - Red Hat, Inc.; pg. 460, pg. 1388
Fishman, Joshua, Sr Asst Brand Mgr-Building-AXE Deo & Masterbrand Brand Building - Unilever United States, Inc.; pg. 904, pg. 1061
Fishman, Lesley, Sr Dir-IR - Johnson & Johnson; pg. 1549, pg. 1091
Fishman, Meryl, Coord-Mktg - Saks Fifth Avenue, Inc.; pg. 1783, pg. 1287
Fishman, Ryan, Mgr-Interactive Mktg - 1-800-Flowers.com, Inc.; pg. 1758, pg. 1151
Fishman, Sigal, Sr Mgr-Mktg - Staples, Inc.; pg. 474, pg. 821
Fishman, Stephen, Sr Dir-Platform Svcs - AutoTrader, Inc.; pg. 1230, pg. 490
Fisk, Jonathan, Dir-ShilohCore Products - Shiloh Industries, Inc.; pg. 1375, pg. 1478
Fisk, Michael, Sr VP-Mktg-Intl - Sony Pictures Entertainment Inc.; pg. 309, pg. 72
Fisk, Richard, Acct Mgr-Shopper Mktg - Hewlett-Packard Company; pg. 404, pg. 175
Fiske, Jim, Sr VP-Mktg - The Chubb Corporation; pg. 1196, pg. 1128
Fiske, Mark, VP-Channel Mktg - Ancestry.com LLC; pg. 1228, pg. 1754
Fister, Matt, Mgr-Sports Mktg - Anheuser-Busch Companies, LLC; pg. 237, pg. 991
Fitch, Deb, Mgr-Sls Dev - Sears Holdings Corporation; pg. 1784, pg. 618
Fitch, Emilie, Brand Mgr - The Kraft Heinz Company; pg. 871,

pg. 641
Fitch, Michael, Specialist-Mktg Comm - Avnet Technology Solutions; pg. 359, pg. 25
Fitch, Samantha, Product Mgr-Consumer Products - Friedrich Air Conditioning Co.; pg. 1072, pg. 1740
Fitch-Markham, Allison, Dir-Mktg - National Association of Realtors; pg. 1666, pg. 584
Fitter, Robyn, Sr Mgr-Mktg-Promos & Plng - Nestle USA, Inc.; pg. 883, pg. 96
Fitts, Angie, Dir-Fin-Consumer Broadband Mktg - AT&T Inc.; pg. 1867, pg. 1674
Fitts, John, VP-Mktg - Baker & Taylor, Inc.; pg. 1619, pg. 1362
Fitts, Robert, Sr Dir-HR - Broadcom Corporation; pg. 364, pg. 108
Fitzek, Linda, Mgr-Mktg Automation - Google Inc.; pg. 1249, pg. 153
Fitzgerald, Andrew, Dir-Mktg & Comm - International Lutheran Laymen's League; pg. 200, pg. 908
Fitzgerald, Barb, Dir-Mktg Svcs - McDonald's Corporation; pg. 1737, pg. 645
Fitzgerald, Bernadette, Dir-Customer Mktg - GlaxoSmithKline; pg. 1536, pg. 1565
Fitzgerald, Bob, Sr Mgr-Bus Dev-Intl - Johnsonville Sausage, LLC; pg. 867, pg. 1894
Fitzgerald, Bret, Sr Mgr-PR - Attachmate Corporation; pg. 356, pg. 1833
Fitzgerald, Brian, VP-Mktg - EMC Corporation; pg. 391, pg. 825
Fitzgerald, Brian, Dir-Partnership Mktg & Digital Media - National Football League; pg. 567, pg. 1264
Fitzgerald, Cathy, Dir-Mktg Comm - The Vollrath Company LLC; pg. 1139, pg. 1894
Fitzgerald, Christine, Dir-Creative Svcs-User Experience - Anthem, Inc.; pg. 1192, pg. 683
Fitzgerald, Colt, VP-Sls & Mktg - A.L. Hansen Manufacturing Co.; pg. 1041, pg. 665
Fitzgerald, Courtney, Mgr-PR - Las Vegas Convention & Visitors Authority; pg. 997, pg. 1027
Fitzgerald, Eric S., VP-Direct Sls - Capstone Press, Inc.; pg. 1625, pg. 951
Fitzgerald, Erin, Dir-Mktg - Pima Medical Institute; pg. 1585, pg. 27
Fitzgerald, Holly, Mgr-Mktg-Lubrizol K2M - The Lubrizol Corporation; pg. 1171, pg. 1481
Fitzgerald, Jean D., Mng Dir & Head-US Trust Mktg - Bank of America Corporation; pg. 718, pg. 1362
FitzGerald, Joan, Sr VP-Television & Cross-Media Svcs - comScore, Inc; pg. 1236, pg. 1798
Fitzgerald, John, VP-Sls - ESPN, Inc.; pg. 285, pg. 340
Fitzgerald, Julie, Dir-Mktg - Abbott Laboratories; pg. 1484, pg. 551
Fitzgerald, Julie, Mgr-Channel Mktg - Siemens Process Industries and Drive; pg. 1376, pg. 1587
Fitzgerald, Kelly, Specialist-Collaboration Sls-Comml Select East - Cisco Systems, Inc.; pg. 372, pg. 240
Fitzgerald, Michelle, Dir-Ad Product Strategy - Pandora Media Inc.; pg. 1273, pg. 172
Fitzgerald, Patrick, Sr VP-Integrated Mktg & Comm - FedEx Corporation; pg. 1907, pg. 1642
Fitzgerald, Ray, Sr VP-Sls-Americas - SeaChange International, Inc.; pg. 1279, pg. 781
Fitzgerald, Richard, VP-Sls - King's Hawaiian Bakery West, Inc.; pg. 869, pg. 293
Fitzgerald, Rick M., Sr VP-Product Mgmt - TriZetto Corporation; pg. 485, pg. 327
Fitzgerald, Rita, Mgr-Production - Putman Media, Inc.; pg. 1679, pg. 621
Fitzgerald, Sarah, Assoc Program Mgr-Interactive Mktg - Liberty Mutual Insurance Group Inc.; pg. 1205, pg. 797
Fitzgerald, Scott, VP & Mgr-Product Line-Electronic Bill Presentment & Payment - ACI Worldwide Inc.; pg. 341, pg. 1010
Fitzgerald, Stephanie, Sr Mgr-Mktg - Conde Nast Publications, Inc.; pg. 1629, pg. 1217
Fitzgerald, Tom, Sr Dir-Corp Comm - Federal Home Loan Mortgage Corporation; pg. 751, pg. 1790
Fitzgibbon, Natasha, Sr Dir-Partnership Dev - Golden State Warriors, LLC; pg. 550, pg. 171
Fitzgibbon, Thomas, Mgr-Retail Banking Sls Support - M&T Bank Corporation; pg. 777, pg. 1149
Fitzgibbons, Kimberly, Mgr-Mktg - European Wax Center; pg. 1529, pg. 409
Fitzgibbons, Paige, Dir-Media Network Online, Mobile Adv Sls & Bus Dev - Best Buy Co., Inc.; pg. 1761, pg. 954
Fitzpatrick, Andrew, Sr Dir-Comm & Sports Programming - Sirius XM Holdings Inc.; pg. 308, pg. 1292
Fitzpatrick, Denise, Mgr-Athletics Mktg - Temple University Health System; pg. 1601, pg. 1571
Fitzpatrick, Gerald, Sr Mgr-Bus Dev - Haworth, Inc.; pg. 402, pg. 891
Fitzpatrick, Jennifer, Mgr-Creative Svcs - Meredith Corporation; pg. 1663, pg. 705
Fitzpatrick, Kevin, Sr Product Mgr-Running - New Balance Athletic Shoe, Inc.; pg. 1811, pg. 798
Fitzpatrick, Lisa A., CMO & VP - Bloomberg BNA; pg. 1621, pg. 1772
Fitzpatrick, Reese, VP-Mktg-Foot Care - Bayer Corporation; pg. 1499, pg. 1573
Fitzpatrick, Reese, VP-Mktg-Foot Care - Bayer Healthcare Consumer Care Division; pg. 1500, pg. 1087
Fitzpatrick, Ruth, Brand Mgr-Store Brands - CVS Health Corporation; pg. 1765, pg. 1610
Fitzpatrick, Shawn, Brand Mgr & Mgr-Special Projects - Crystal Geyser Water Company; pg. 248, pg. 57
Fitzpatrick, Steve, Mgr-Supplier-Mktg Svcs - Altria Group, Inc.; pg. 1893, pg. 1800
Fitzpatrick, Sybil, Mgr-Mktg & Comm - AT&T Mobility LLC; pg. 619, pg. 488
Fitzpatrick, Ted, Dir-Product Mktg, Running & Trng - Reebok International Ltd.; pg. 1817, pg. 811
FitzRoy, John L., Specialist-Sls & Mktg - The Dun & Bradstreet Corp.; pg. 1637, pg. 1120
Fitzsimmons, Patrick, Sr Rep-CNC Sls - Southwestern Industries, Inc.; pg. 1429, pg. 69
Fitzsimmons, Sarah, Sr Product Mgr-Retail Faucets - Kohler Co.; pg. 91, pg. 1862
Fitzsimons, Carolyn, Dir-Mktg - Genentech, Inc.; pg. 1533, pg. 279
Fitzsimons, Christina, Dir-Mktg & PR - Florida Hospital Association; pg. 140, pg. 469
Fitzsimons, Matt, VP-Media Delivery - Conversant, Inc.; pg. 1393, pg. 306
Fitzsimons, Morgan, Dir-Digital Mktg - CBS Broadcasting Inc.; pg. 273, pg. 1210
Fives, Michael, Product Head-Samsung Accelerator - Samsung Electronics America, Inc.; pg. 669, pg. 1115
Fix, Lewis, VP-Pulp Sls - Domtar Corporation; pg. 1456, pg. 1954
Fix, Nathan, Mgr-Mktg Partnerships - Minnesota Vikings Football Club, Inc.; pg. 563, pg. 923
Flaccavento, Anthony, VP-Natl CPG Sls - Tremor Video; pg. 682, pg. 1305
Flack, Alison, Sr Dir-Mktg - Saks Fifth Avenue, Inc.; pg. 1783, pg. 1287
Flack, Andrew, VP-Product Mktg Solutions - Hilton Worldwide, Inc.; pg. 1094, pg. 1791
Flack, Justin, Dir-Creative - 1-800 CONTACTS, INC.; pg. 1758, pg. 1753
Fladung, Bob, Dir-Adv - INO.Com; pg. 1259, pg. 777
Flagg, Alan, Gen Mgr-Light Oils Mktg - Citgo Petroleum Corporation; pg. 974, pg. 1703
Flagg, Jessica B., Mgr-Corp Mktg & Creative Svcs - Eastman Chemical Company; pg. 1159, pg. 1636
Flagg, Lauren, Brand Mgr & Copywriter - Quality Bicycle Products; pg. 1710, pg. 918
Flahavin, Ardene, Dir-Sls & Mktg - Er'go Candles Inc.; pg. 508, pg. 1680
Flaherty, Andrew P., Mgr-Global Perioperative Mktg Ops-3M Perioperative Bus - 3M Company; pg. 1142, pg. 956
Flaherty, Christine, Brand Mgr-Shopper Innovation - The Procter & Gamble Company; pg. 1129, pg. 1418
Flaherty, Edward, Mgr-Sls - Fairmont Hotels & Resorts Inc.; pg. 1091, pg. 1938
Flaherty, Erin, Mgr-Mktg - Citizens Financial Group, Inc.; pg. 737, pg. 1606
Flaherty, Janet, Sr Head-Exec Comm & Mktg Comm - General Electric Company; pg. 1297, pg. 347
Flaherty, Jeff, Sr Dir-Corp Rels-Global - Marriott International, Inc.; pg. 1102, pg. 764
Flaherty, Jim, Mgr-Product Mktg - Honeywell International Inc.; pg. 407, pg. 1088
Flaherty, John, Mgr-Adv-Natl - Rolex Watch U.S.A., Inc.; pg. 11, pg. 1286
Flaherty, Kristi, Program Mgr-Mktg-Schools Div - Tyler Technologies, Inc.; pg. 486, pg. 1690
Flaherty, Nora, Dir-Entertainment PR - Dolce & Gabbana USA, Inc.; pg. 23, pg. 1225
Flaig, Alison, Head-Mktg Comm & Events - Genworth Financial, Inc.; pg. 761, pg. 1802
Flaig, Patty, Mgr-Mktg - Land O'Lakes, Inc.; pg. 873, pg. 915
Flaks, Jason, Dir-Product & Engrg-Call Svcs - Marchex, Inc.; pg. 1395, pg. 1837
Flammer, EJ, Sr Mgr-Mktg-Basketball & Golf - New Era Cap Company Inc.; pg. 1840, pg. 1155
Flanagan, Andrew, Exec Dir-Digital Mktg, Social Media & Analytics - Lenovo Group Ltd; pg. 427, pg. 1384
Flanagan, David, Mgr-Mktg - Gravograph-New Hermes; pg. 1344, pg. 531
Flanagan, Heather, Dir-Mktg - Intellicheck Mobilisa, Inc.; pg. 416, pg. 1823
Flanagan, Helen, Sr Dir-Client Dev & Sls - CME Group Inc.; pg. 738, pg. 571
Flanagan, Jim, Sr Dir-Treasury - Catalina Marketing Corporation; pg. 369, pg. 462
Flanagan, Julie, Principal & Sr Mgr - Teachers Insurance & Annuity Association - College Retirement Equities Fund; pg. 1219, pg. 1297
Flanagan, Laurie M., Asst Dir-Mktg - The Hartford Financial Services Group, Inc.; pg. 1202, pg. 352
Flanagan, Michael, Dir-Strategic Mktg - Siemens Healthcare Diagnostics; pg. 673, pg. 604
Flanagan, Patrick, VP-Digital Mktg & Strategy - Simon Property Group, Inc.; pg. 1112, pg. 690
Flanagan, Rob, District Mgr-Sls - Vulcan Materials Company; pg. 119, pg. 4
Flanagan, Sheila O., Sr Writer-Creative-Global Mktg - Schneider Electric; pg. 467, pg. 1609
Flanagan, Tom, Sr Dir-Baseball Ops - Milwaukee Brewers Baseball Club, Inc.; pg. 562, pg. 1878
Flanders, Mimi, Mgr-Global Campaigns & Svcs Mktg - F5 Networks, Inc.; pg. 396, pg. 1835
Flandreau, Tyson, Dir-Adv - Hotwire, Inc.; pg. 1912, pg. 219
Flanigin, Kimberly, Sr Buyer-Strategic Sourcing, Purchasing-Mktg Svcs - Volkswagen Group of America, Inc.; pg. 194, pg. 1785
Flannery, Danielle, Product Mgr - Gilead Sciences, Inc.; pg. 1535, pg. 88
Flannery, Tim, Dir-Creative & Adv - Neiman Marcus, Inc.; pg. 30, pg. 1684
Flaris, Sam, Mgr-Global Sourcing-Worldwide Adv - Apple Inc.; pg. 350, pg. 73
Flaten, Thomas, Dir-Epilepsy Franchise Mktg - Eisai Inc.; pg. 1526, pg. 1133
Flatley, Matthew, Product Mgr - Evoqua Water Technologies; pg. 1162, pg. 541
Flatley, Tighe, Mgr-Digital Mktg - The Gap, Inc.; pg. 1770, pg. 218
Flatow, Kelly, Sr VP-Mktg Partnerships-Global - National Basketball Association; pg. 566, pg. 1264
Flatow, Kelly, Sr VP-Mktg Partnerships-Global - NBA Properties, Inc.; pg. 569, pg. 1120
Flatt, Andrew, Sr VP-Mktg-Disney Theatrical Grp - Disney Theatrical Productions; pg. 545, pg. 1224
Flatt, Steve, Dir-Sls Learning & Dev - MillerCoors LLC; pg. 255, pg. 582
Flatz, Sheila, Mgr-Mktg - University of Minnesota; pg. 609, pg. 945
Flaugher, Chris, Rep-Sls - Republic Services, Inc.; pg. 107, pg. 19
Flaviani, Joe, Mgr-Mktg-Natl - Schneider Electric; pg. 467, pg. 1609
Flavin, Jennifer, Acct Exec-Platform Sls - AppNexus; pg. 352, pg. 1196
Flavin, Nicole, Sr Dir-Mktg - PepsiCo, Inc.; pg. 259, pg. 1327
Flavin, Sean, Sr Dir-ECommerce Mktg Tech - Office Depot, Inc.; pg. 448, pg. 412
Fleagle, Mike, Brand Mgr - Cargill, Inc.; pg. 845, pg. 965
Fleck, Frances K., Sr Mgr-Mktg-Consumer Data Analytics - AT&T; pg. 1865, pg. 258
Fleck, Robert, Gen Mgr & Publr-Chicago Tribune Media Grp - Chicago Tribune Company; pg. 1627, pg. 570
Fleckenstein, Matt, VP-Mktg Automation - salesforce.com, inc.; pg. 1278, pg. 226
Flee, Katherine, Mgr-Sponsorship Mktg - FedEx Corporation; pg. 1907, pg. 1642
Flee, Travis, Dir-Digital Brand Mktg - Hilton Worldwide, Inc.; pg. 1094, pg. 1791
Fleeman, JJ, Chief Strategy Officer & Chief Dev Officer-Delhaize America - Food Lion, LLC; pg. 1019, pg. 1390
Fleener, Brenna, Brand Mgr-Intl - Clif Bar Inc.; pg. 848, pg. 83
Fleer, Zach, Asst Product Mgr-Trail Cameras - Bushnell Outdoor Products, Inc.; pg. 1403, pg. 718
Fleet, Peter, VP-Mktg, Sls & Svcs-Asia Pacific - Ford Motor Company; pg. 172, pg. 876

Fleisch, Brian, Sr Dir-Ops - Q Interactive Inc.; *pg.* 1276, *pg.* 588
Fleisch, Mark, Reg Dir-Sls - Microsoft Corporation; *pg.* 435, *pg.* 1824
Fleischer, Lauren, Sr Assoc Brand Mgr - Mondelez International; *pg.* 877, *pg.* 1344
Fleischer, Lauren, Sr Assoc Brand Mgr - Mondelez International, Inc.; *pg.* 878, *pg.* 601
Fleischman, Michael, Head-Media Science - Twitter, Inc.; *pg.* 1285, *pg.* 228
Fleischmann, Britney, Brand Mgr-Maxwell House - Kraft Canada Inc.; *pg.* 869, *pg.* 1939
Fleischmann, Emily, Sr Mgr-Mktg-Prepared Foods - Foster Farms; *pg.* 856, *pg.* 122
Fleischmann, Michael, Sr Mgr-Customer Mktg-Consumer Mktg - Solo Cup Company; *pg.* 1469, *pg.* 625
Fleisher, Jennifer H., Grp Mgr-Field Mktg-Pub Sector - Adobe Systems Incorporated; *pg.* 342, *pg.* 235
Fleming, Beth, Brand Mgr-Nordstrom Product Grp & Active - Nordstrom, Inc.; *pg.* 1779, *pg.* 1837
Fleming, Bill, VP-Mdsg - Sysco Food Services of Albany, LLC; *pg.* 1035, *pg.* 1163
Fleming, Christina, Sr Dir-Mktg & Enrollment Svcs - Blackbaud, Inc.; *pg.* 361, *pg.* 1613
Fleming, Christopher, Dir-Mktg - Ann Inc.; *pg.* 18, *pg.* 1195
Fleming, Colin, Head-Indus Mktg & Sr Dir - salesforce.com, inc.; *pg.* 1278, *pg.* 226
Fleming, Hillary, Sr Mgr-Shopper Mktg Club & Mass - Nestle Waters North America Inc.; *pg.* 257, *pg.* 375
Fleming, Krissy, Strategist-Mktg-Digital & Direct Mktg - Cellco Partnership; *pg.* 1869, *pg.* 1042
Fleming, Lisa, Mgr-PR - Paychex, Inc.; *pg.* 792, *pg.* 1336
Fleming, Maureen, Sr Mgr-Conference Ops - AXA Equitable Life Insurance Company; *pg.* 1194, *pg.* 1199
Fleming, Mitch, VP-Sls - ADTRAN, Inc.; *pg.* 344, *pg.* 6
Fleming, Molly, Coord-Mktg - Cameron International; *pg.* 1151, *pg.* 1702
Fleming, Russ, VP-Strategy, Innovation & Product Dev - FedEx Corporation; *pg.* 1907, *pg.* 1642
Fleming, Ruth, Sr Dir-Mktg-Neurosurgery - Integra LifeSciences Holdings Corporation; *pg.* 1545, *pg.* 1109
Fleming, Scott, Mgr-Mktg - FedEx Corporation; *pg.* 1907, *pg.* 1642
Flemming, Kevin, Sr Dir-IT - Edmonton Oilers Hockey Club; *pg.* 546, *pg.* 1906
Flener, Monique, Coord-Sls & Mktg - English Color & Supply Inc.; *pg.* 1442, *pg.* 1735
Fleschert, Stacey, Rep-Sls - Republic Services, Inc.; *pg.* 107, *pg.* 19
Flesh, Randall, District Mgr-Brand Mktg - Marathon Petroleum Company LLC; *pg.* 981, *pg.* 1454
Flessner, Laura, Sr Mgr-R&D Products Res - Pfizer Inc.; *pg.* 1581, *pg.* 1278
Fletcher, Bill, Dir-Mktg & Sls - Holland America Line Inc.; *pg.* 1911, *pg.* 1836
Fletcher, Chad C., Sr VP-Sls & Svc-Global - T.D. Williamson, Inc.; *pg.* 1380, *pg.* 1490
Fletcher, Cheryl, Mgr-Mktg - Antelope Valley Newspaper Inc.; *pg.* 1617, *pg.* 174
Fletcher, Cheryl, Sr Mgr-Internal Comm - Royal Bank of Canada; *pg.* 800, *pg.* 1942
Fletcher, Chuck, VP-Sls & Mktg - Dover Chemical Corporation; *pg.* 1156, *pg.* 1447
Fletcher, Eric, VP-Mktg - Ricoh Americas Corp.; *pg.* 462, *pg.* 538
Fletcher, Jason, Mgr-Search Mktg - Rakuten.com Shopping; *pg.* 1277, *pg.* 41
Fletcher, Kevin, Dir-Sls & Mktg - Attwood Corporation; *pg.* 1705, *pg.* 897
Fletcher, Lisa, Project Mgr-Mktg & Promos - Pixar Animation Studios; *pg.* 304, *pg.* 85
Fletcher, Mark, Mgr-Social Media Content & Strategy - The Allstate Corporation; *pg.* 1189, *pg.* 639
Fletcher, Matt, VP-Sls - Zebco; *pg.* 1848, *pg.* 1491
Fletcher, Mike, Dir-Global Promos & Mktg Partnerships - Hasbro, Inc.; *pg.* 954, *pg.* 1603
Fletcher, Nicholas, VP-Mktg Comm - Jack in the Box Inc.; *pg.* 1732, *pg.* 204
Fletcher, Rob, Sr Dir-Mktg-Global - Mallinckrodt Pharmaceuticals; *pg.* 1557, *pg.* 978
Fletcher, Stephen, Dir-Global Product Partnerships - Yahoo! Inc.; *pg.* 1289, *pg.* 289
Fletcher, Susan, Sr Dir-Comm-Intl - United Parcel Service, Inc.; *pg.* 1928, *pg.* 522
Fleuranges, Leslie, Dir-Upstream Innovation & New Products - Hill's Pet Nutrition, Inc.; *pg.* 1476, *pg.* 721
Fleury, Andrew, Principal & Mgr-Interactive Mktg - Medtronic, Inc.; *pg.* 1564, *pg.* 939
Fliegler, Russ, Sr Mgr-Mktg - PepsiCo, Inc.; *pg.* 259, *pg.* 1327
Flieller, Ana, Asst Mktg Mgr-Jewelry Team - The Bradford Group; *pg.* 1763, *pg.* 637
Flinn, Brian, Exec VP-Mktg & Comm - World Wrestling Entertainment, Inc.; *pg.* 595, *pg.* 380
Flinn, Pat, Mgr-Global Mktg-Cold Adhesives - Nordson Corporation; *pg.* 1365, *pg.* 1480
Flinn, Wendy, Mgr-Media - Blue Bell Creameries, L.P.; *pg.* 1851, *pg.* 1668
Flint, Courtney, Dir-Adv & Mktg - Gucci America Inc.; *pg.* 6, *pg.* 1237
Flint, Mason, Principal & Designer-User Experience-Azure - Microsoft Corporation; *pg.* 435, *pg.* 1824
Flinton, Robert P., VP-Mktg & Product Mgmt - Surety, Inc.; *pg.* 1283, *pg.* 1799
Flodell, Henrik, Sr Mgr-Product Mktg-Dev Tools - Atmel Corporation; *pg.* 621, *pg.* 238
Flohr, Jay, Product Mgr - Cabela's Incorporated; *pg.* 535, *pg.* 1019
Flood, Gary J, Pres-Products & Solutions-Global - MasterCard Incorporated; *pg.* 779, *pg.* 1325
Flood, Gary J., Pres-Global Products & Solutions - MasterCard International, Inc.; *pg.* 780, *pg.* 1326
Flood, Mary, VP-Sls - D.R. Horton, Inc./Schuler Homes LLC; *pg.* 1090, *pg.* 543
Flood, Nina, VP-Mktg & Strategy - Nautica Apparel, Inc.; *pg.* 45, *pg.* 1265
Flood, Steve, Dir-Sls Plng & Retail Ops - Hyundai Motor America; *pg.* 179, *pg.* 89
Flood, Syl, Product Mgr-Asset Gatherer Segment - MORNINGSTAR, INC.; *pg.* 784, *pg.* 583
Flood, T. J., Sr VP-Mktg-Canadian Tire Retail - Canadian Tire Corporation Limited; *pg.* 202, *pg.* 1936
Floor, Andrew, VP-Mktg - Campari America; *pg.* 1960, *pg.* 214
Flora, Chris, Brand Mgr-Lean Cuisine - Nestle USA, Inc.; *pg.* 883, *pg.* 96
Flora, Douglas, Mgr-Content Mktg - IBM; *pg.* 410, *pg.* 1449
Flora, Steven K., Sr VP-Sls - Zoll Medical Corporation; *pg.* 1612, *pg.* 814
Flore, Ruth Anne, Mgr-Mktg - Norseland, Inc.; *pg.* 886, *pg.* 376
Florentine, Mary Beth, Sr Mgr-Employee Comm - Comcast Cable Communications, Inc.; *pg.* 276, *pg.* 1560
Florentine, Mary Beth, Sr Mgr-Employee Comm - Comcast Corporation; *pg.* 276, *pg.* 1560
Florentino, Pedro, Sr Product Mgr-Licensing - Citrix Systems, Inc.; *pg.* 375, *pg.* 424
Flores, Alejandro, Mgr-Partner Integration & Video Adv Tech - Comcast Corporation; *pg.* 276, *pg.* 1560
Flores, Ana C., Mgr-Govt & Transportation Svcs Mktg - Xerox Corporation; *pg.* 494, *pg.* 365
Flores, Bob, Dir-Technical Sls - Allfast Fastening Systems, Inc.; *pg.* 1041, *pg.* 66
Flores, Bryan, Mgr-Consumer Mktg Strategy - Verizon Communications Inc.; *pg.* 1875, *pg.* 1309
Flores, Erick, Brand Mgr-Hair Care & Beauty Care - The Procter & Gamble Company; *pg.* 1129, *pg.* 1418
Flores, Everth, Sr Dir-Global Accts Bus Dev - Harmonic, Inc.; *pg.* 402, *pg.* 246
Flores, Georgina, VP-Integrated Mktg Comm - The Allstate Corporation; *pg.* 1189, *pg.* 639
Flores, Jorge, Dir-Brand Mktg-Global - Hasbro, Inc.; *pg.* 954, *pg.* 1603
Flores, Kristi Z., Mgr-Mktg Comm - Tektronix, Inc.; *pg.* 1431, *pg.* 1496
Flores, Marlon, Reg Mgr-Comml Sls-Texas - salesforce.com, inc.; *pg.* 1278, *pg.* 226
Flores, Omar, Mgr-Bus & Mktg-Global - 3M Company; *pg.* 1142, *pg.* 956
Flores, Sandra, VP & Mgr-Mktg Database Decision Strategy - Wells Fargo & Company; *pg.* 819, *pg.* 232
Florez-Estrada, Jaime, Brand Mgr-Intl & Duty Free - Altria Group, Inc.; *pg.* 1893, *pg.* 1800
Florie, Kenna, Sr VP-Mktg - bebe stores, inc.; *pg.* 19, *pg.* 49
Florin, Thobias, VP & Program Mgr-Global Mktg - Citi Trends Inc.; *pg.* 22, *pg.* 539
Florio, Jenna, Head-Social Recruiting Program - Ingersoll-Rand Company; *pg.* 1349, *pg.* 1370
Flot, Shehaam, Sr Product Mgr-Mobile, Stores & Gift Registry - Crate & Barrel, Inc.; *pg.* 922, *pg.* 640
Flournoy, Diane, Specialist-Mktg - Hewlett-Packard Company; *pg.* 404, *pg.* 175
Flournoy, Ray, Grp Product Mgr - Etsy, Inc.; *pg.* 1768, *pg.* 1230
Flower, Ashley, Sr Mgr-PR - Rite Aid Corporation; *pg.* 1590, *pg.* 1519
Flowers, Bryan, VP-Sls & Mktg - Morgan Foods, Inc.; *pg.* 881, *pg.* 673
Flowers, William, Dir-Sls-North America-Global Airports - Rockwell Collins, Inc.; *pg.* 234, *pg.* 702
Floyd, Amanda, Mgr-Consumer Mktg - AutoTrader, Inc.; *pg.* 1230, *pg.* 490
Floyd, Amanda, Mgr-Creative - Toys "R" Us, Inc.; *pg.* 968, *pg.* 1130
Floyd, Ericka, Mgr-PR - American University; *pg.* 597, *pg.* 395
Floyd, Hali, Mgr-Shopper Mktg - Dr Pepper Snapple Group, Inc.; *pg.* 250, *pg.* 1729
Floyd, Jennifer, Mgr-Mktg - Fresh Enterprises, LLC; *pg.* 1729, *pg.* 110
Floyd, Kathy, Dir-Sls - William Lyon Homes; *pg.* 122, *pg.* 166
Floyd, Kris, Sr Dir-Digital Mktg - Aetna Inc.; *pg.* 1187, *pg.* 351
Floyd, Mary, VP-Individual Sls - Anthem, Inc.; *pg.* 1192, *pg.* 683
Floyd, Mikela, Strategist-Internal Digital Media & Sr Writer - Whole Foods Market, Inc.; *pg.* 1038, *pg.* 1667
Floyd, R. Dale, Sr VP & Mgr-Client Advisory Grp-Rutherford County - Pinnacle Financial Partners, Inc.; *pg.* 794, *pg.* 1653
Floyd, Suzanne, Mgr-Mktg Ops - Advanced Micro Devices, Inc.; *pg.* 613, *pg.* 282
Floyd, Tom, Head-Sls Dev-Global - Facebook, Inc.; *pg.* 1245, *pg.* 143
Fluck, Adam, Sr Mgr-Interactive Mktg - Chicago Professional Sports Limited Partnership; *pg.* 539, *pg.* 570
Fluck, Michael, Dir-Digital Mktg - Bridgestone Americas, Inc.; *pg.* 201, *pg.* 1649
Fluet, Abby, Specialist-CRM Mktg - Bradley Corporation; *pg.* 71, *pg.* 1870
Flygare, Carl, Mgr-NVIDIA Quadro & NVS Product Mktg - PNY Technologies, Inc.; *pg.* 455, *pg.* 1105
Flynn, Edward B., III, Exec VP-Sls & Mktg-Worldwide - Automatic Data Processing, Inc.; *pg.* 357, *pg.* 1117
Flynn, Gavin, Sr VP-Strategic & Portfolio Mktg - InterContinental Hotels Corporation; *pg.* 1097, *pg.* 511
Flynn, Joey, Designer-Product - Facebook, Inc.; *pg.* 1245, *pg.* 143
Flynn, John, Grp VP-Gartner for Mktg Offerings - Gartner, Inc.; *pg.* 1248, *pg.* 374
Flynn, John, VP-Sls & Mktg - JBS; *pg.* 865, *pg.* 1751
Flynn, Joseph, Sr VP-Sls-Lightpath - Cablevision Systems Corporation; *pg.* 272, *pg.* 1141
Flynn, Kenneth, Sr Dir-Customer Retention & Upgrade Mktg - Comcast Cable Communications, Inc.; *pg.* 276, *pg.* 1560
Flynn, Kim, Sr VP & Head-Product Dev - Nuveen Investments, Inc.; *pg.* 788, *pg.* 586
Flynn, Lori, Dir-Midwest Adv - Entrepreneur Media, Inc.; *pg.* 1639, *pg.* 110
Flynn, Matthew, Specialist-eChannel Mktg & North American Sls Div - Bio-Rad Laboratories, Inc.; *pg.* 1504, *pg.* 101
Flynn, Mike, Sr Mgr-Product & Technical - Amazon.com, Inc.; *pg.* 1226, *pg.* 1831
Flynn, Nick, Sr VP-Enterprise Sls & Acct Mgmt - Shutterstock, Inc.; *pg.* 1280, *pg.* 1291
Flynn, Sean, VP-Mktg - Florida Marlins, L.P.; *pg.* 548, *pg.* 442
Flynn, Sean T., VP-ExperienceOne Sls-WW - IBM; *pg.* 410, *pg.* 1449
Flynn, Stephen, Mgr-Digital Media, Brand & Channel Mgmt - Siemens Healthcare Diagnostics; *pg.* 673, *pg.* 604
Flynn, Wayne, Dir-Agricultural Sls - CSX Transportation, Inc.; *pg.* 1904, *pg.* 432
Fobes, Andy, Dir-PR - Tampa Port Authority Inc.; *pg.* 1925, *pg.* 476
Fobes, Sherry, Mgr-Sls & Market - Philips Electronics North America; *pg.* 662, *pg.* 782
Fochs, Jill, Sr Mgr-Mktg - Ameriprise Financial, Inc.; *pg.* 715, *pg.* 930
Fodor, Sherry, Mgr-Mktg - Church & Dwight Canada Corp.; *pg.* 503, *pg.* 1925
Foerster, Kendra, Specialist-Product & Mktg - Manulife Financial Corporation; *pg.* 778, *pg.* 1939
Fogarty, Alison, Reg VP-Mktg - Caesars Entertainment Corporation; *pg.* 1083, *pg.* 1023
Fogarty, Kelley, Mgr-Mktg - Go Daddy Inc.; *pg.* 1249, *pg.* 21
Fogarty, Kelly, Mgr-Field Mktg - MillerCoors LLC; *pg.* 255, *pg.* 582
Fogarty, Michael, Exec VP-Consumer Sls & Mktg - WebMD

Health Corporation; *pg.* 1288, *pg.* 1313
Fogarty, Peter, Dir-Sls - Vintage Parts; *pg.* 119, *pg.* 1854
Fogarty, Phyllis, Sr Dir-Long Term Innovation - PepsiCo, Inc.; *pg.* 259, *pg.* 1327
Fogarty, Renae, Dir-Internet Mktg - FASTSIGNS International, Inc.; *pg.* 81, *pg.* 1669
Fogarty, Ryan, VP-Sls & Mktg - WellCare Health Plans Inc.; *pg.* 1223, *pg.* 476
Fogarty, Tom, Dir-Production - Vance Publishing Corporation; *pg.* 1699, *pg.* 627
Fogel, Lindsay, Sr Mgr-Mktg-Youth Partnerships - PepsiCo, Inc.; *pg.* 259, *pg.* 1327
Fogelson, Susie, Sr VP-Mktg & Brand Strategy-Food Network & Cooking Channel - Scripps Networks Interactive, Inc.; *pg.* 1279, *pg.* 1638
Fogg, Richard, Mng Dir-Media & Comm Grp - SunTrust Banks, Inc.; *pg.* 807, *pg.* 520
Fogge, Len, Pres-Mktg-NBC Entertainment - NBC Universal, Inc.; *pg.* 300, *pg.* 1266
Fogle, Ken, VP-Mktg - Atmos Energy Corporation; *pg.* 1935, *pg.* 1675
Fogle, Sandy, Sr Mgr-Internal Comm - Intuit Inc.; *pg.* 769, *pg.* 158
Fogleman, Dan, Sr Mgr-PR - Tyson Foods, Inc.; *pg.* 902, *pg.* 35
Foglesong, William, Sr VP-Mktg - Carter's, Inc.; *pg.* 21, *pg.* 491
Fohl, Blake, Chief Customer Officer & Sr VP-Mktg - True Value Company; *pg.* 1065, *pg.* 592
Fohr, Elizabeth, Asst Mgr-Mktg & Brand-Farm Rich, Farm Rich Smokehouse & Byron's - Rich Products Corporation; *pg.* 892, *pg.* 1150
Fohr, Tim, Mgr-Mktg - Lennar Corporation; *pg.* 1100, *pg.* 443
Foisset, Tim, Dir-Digital Sls & Mktg - Warner Music Group Corp.; *pg.* 590, *pg.* 1313
Foister, Sally, Dir-Mktg Svcs - Greenville Hospital System Inc.; *pg.* 1538, *pg.* 1617
Foisy, Claude, VP-Quebecor Media Display - Quebecor Media Inc.; *pg.* 1679, *pg.* 1956
Fok, Kay, Brand Mgr - Ocean Spray Cranberries, Inc.; *pg.* 887, *pg.* 827
Foland, George, VP-Sls - Broadview Networks, Inc.; *pg.* 365, *pg.* 1339
Foland, Jeffrey, Exec VP-Mktg, Tech & Strategy - United Airlines, Inc.; *pg.* 1927, *pg.* 593
Folckemer, Jeff, Pres-Media Svcs & Affiliates & Sr VP-Hearst Newspapers - The Hearst Corporation; *pg.* 1649, *pg.* 1239
Foldes, Dave, Mgr-Mktg-Cap'n Crunch - The Quaker Oats Company; *pg.* 834, *pg.* 588
Foldes, David, Mgr-Mktg-RTEs-Cap'n Crunch - PepsiCo, Inc.; *pg.* 259, *pg.* 1327
Folds, Becky, Dir-Mktg Capability & Dev-Global - Beam Suntory Inc.; *pg.* 1957, *pg.* 599
Foldvik, Kristin Mahaffey, Sr Mgr-Events-Global - Blackbaud, Inc.; *pg.* 361, *pg.* 1613
Foley, Bill, VP-Fabricated Products - WireCo WorldGroup; *pg.* 1389, *pg.* 987
Foley, Daniel P., VP-Mktg & Tech - Security Mutual Life Insurance Company of New York; *pg.* 1216, *pg.* 1142
Foley, Janice, Mgr-ExpertOne Program Mktg-Worldwide - Hewlett-Packard Company; *pg.* 404, *pg.* 175
Foley, Jim, VP-After-Market Sls - PneumaticScaleAngelus; *pg.* 1369, *pg.* 1445
Foley, Joan Doyle, Head-Enterprise Sls West & Sls Solutions - LinkedIn Corporation; *pg.* 1262, *pg.* 160
Foley, John P., Sr Mgr-Digital, CRM & Social Media-Chevrolet - General Motors Company; *pg.* 175, *pg.* 881
Foley, John P., VP-Domestic Ops & Product Dev - Pan-American Life Insurance Company; *pg.* 1213, *pg.* 747
Foley, Lisa, Dir-Brand Mktg - Crate & Barrel, Inc.; *pg.* 922, *pg.* 640
Foley, Paul, Sr Dir-Brand Protection - Converse Inc.; *pg.* 1831, *pg.* 793
Foley, Real, VP-Coal Mktg - Teck Resources Limited; *pg.* 1183, *pg.* 1912
Foley, Sean, VP-Integrated Mktg - SHUTTERFLY, INC.; *pg.* 1280, *pg.* 192
Foley, Tracy, Sr Mgr-Comm - Pfizer Inc.; *pg.* 1581, *pg.* 1278
Folk, Kimberly, Brand Mktg Dir-Running Div-Footwear & Apparel - Mizuno USA, Inc.; *pg.* 1839, *pg.* 538
Folkes, Amelia T., Specialist-Spanish Language Media - State Farm Mutual Automobile Insurance Co.; *pg.* 1218, *pg.* 557
Folkmanis, Elaine, Dir-Mktg - Folkmanis, Inc.; *pg.* 953, *pg.* 83
Follen, Ginny, Mgr-Channel Mktg - Good Technology, Inc.; *pg.* 1249, *pg.* 285
Follett, Lauren, Mgr-Mktg - WebEx Communications, Inc.; *pg.* 491, *pg.* 270
Follett, Norm, Dir-BTO Technical Mktg-HP Software - Hewlett-Packard Company; *pg.* 404, *pg.* 175
Folliot, Eric, Sr Mgr-Product Mgmt - Activision Blizzard, Inc.; *pg.* 948, *pg.* 271
Folmar, Christopher, Dir-CRM & SAAS Products - Dex Media Inc; *pg.* 1635, *pg.* 1680
Folsom, Heather, Product Mgr - Google Inc.; *pg.* 1249, *pg.* 153
Folts, Jacque, Mgr-Mktg - Atalanta Corporation; *pg.* 838, *pg.* 1057
Folts, Lori, Head-Mktg Comm-The Americas - DHL Holdings (USA), Inc.; *pg.* 1906, *pg.* 459
Foltynska, Ewa, Dir-Product Mktg Dishwashing Whirlpool & Indesit-EMEA - Whirlpool Corporation; *pg.* 62, *pg.* 872
Fondiller, David, Dir-PR & Comm - The Boston Consulting Group, Inc.; *pg.* 363, *pg.* 790
Fones, Hugh, Specialist-Adv - Gulf Power Company; *pg.* 1944, *pg.* 458
Fong Belliard, Lissette, Coord-Community Mktg - A&E Television Networks, LLC; *pg.* 267, *pg.* 1185
Fong, Ed, Head-Product Dev - California Lottery; *pg.* 990, *pg.* 196
Fong, Marcus, Brand Mgr-Digital Comm - Nestle Purina PetCare Company; *pg.* 1479, *pg.* 1000
Fong, Pamela, VP & Mgr-Digital Mktg-Consumer Deposit Products - Bank of America Corporation; *pg.* 718, *pg.* 1362
Fong, Terence, Sr Dir-Mdsg Ops - Williamson-Dickie Manufacturing Company; *pg.* 50, *pg.* 1696
Fongaro, Anthony, Mgr-Social Media - ACCO Brands Corporation; *pg.* 340, *pg.* 626
Fonseca, Murray, Dir-Sls-North LA - Shell Oil Company; *pg.* 984, *pg.* 1714
Fonseca, Noel C., Brand Mgr - The Wendy's Company; *pg.* 1755, *pg.* 1450
Font, Robert, Dir-Digital Mktg Comm - Subaru of America, Inc.; *pg.* 191, *pg.* 1050
Fontaine, Brigitte, Sr Mgr-Internal Comm - Progress Software Corporation; *pg.* 457, *pg.* 786
Fontaine, Connie, Dir-Mktg Comm-Ford Motor Co-Canada, Ltd - Ford Motor Company of Canada, Limited; *pg.* 174, *pg.* 1930
Fontaine, Kevin, Dir-Sls-Cloud Platform - MicroStrategy, Inc.; *pg.* 1266, *pg.* 1809
Fontana, Augusto, Dir-Sls - Daklen Inc.; *pg.* 851, *pg.* 129
Fontana, Jenni, Coord-Dev & Production-Original Programming - Esquire Network; *pg.* 286, *pg.* 1229
Fontana, Joelle, Sr Mgr-Strategic Sourcing - Amgen Inc.; *pg.* 1493, *pg.* 291
Fontana, Lauren Plateroti, Sr Mgr-Integrated Mktg - Time Inc.; *pg.* 1693, *pg.* 1300
Fontana, Zoie, Asst Product Mgr - La Cie McCormick Canada Co.; *pg.* 872, *pg.* 1922
Fontanez, David, Head-Digital Media & Assoc Dir - Verizon Communications Inc.; *pg.* 1875, *pg.* 1309
Fontenote, Troy, Dir-Institutional Sls - Lincoln Financial Group; *pg.* 1206, *pg.* 1375
Fontes, Kimberly, Sr Mgr-Comm - Mondelez International, Inc.; *pg.* 878, *pg.* 601
Fonzetti, Marc S., Dir-Media Strategy & Investment - Verizon Communications Inc.; *pg.* 1875, *pg.* 1309
Foo, Catherine, Sr Mgr-Mktg Plng-Global - Cisco Systems, Inc.; *pg.* 372, *pg.* 240
Foo, Katherine, Dir-Mktg - First Home Mortgage Corporation; *pg.* 755, *pg.* 757
Foodim, Gary, VP-Consumer Mktg - Conde Nast Publications, Inc.; *pg.* 1629, *pg.* 1217
Foodim, Gary, VP-Consumer Mktg - Vogue Magazine; *pg.* 1700, *pg.* 1311
Foor, Heather, Dir-Adv - The Blade Co.; *pg.* 1621, *pg.* 1476
Foor, Julie, Specialist-US Adv - Ikea North America Services LLC; *pg.* 929, *pg.* 1523
Foote, Andrea, Sr Dir-Brand Comm - PepsiCo, Inc.; *pg.* 259, *pg.* 1327
Foote, Todd Fooe, VP-Govt Sls & Mktg - Konica Minolta Business Solutions USA, Inc.; *pg.* 1419, *pg.* 1113
Foran, Tom, VP-Underwriting & Product Dev - Standard Insurance Company; *pg.* 1217, *pg.* 1506
Foray, Marissa, Assoc Mgr-Mktg - Godiva Chocolatier, Inc.; *pg.* 1854, *pg.* 1235
Forbeck, Sheryl, Specialist & Analyst-Forecast & Mktg - Olin Corporation; *pg.* 1176, *pg.* 976
Forbes, Alex, Mgr-Mktg - Intuit Inc.; *pg.* 769, *pg.* 158
Forbes, Harry, Dir-PR - WNET.org; *pg.* 322, *pg.* 1315
Forbes, Jessica, Specialist-Reg & LATAM Mktg - Blue Coat Systems, Inc.; *pg.* 362, *pg.* 284
Forbes, Judy, Sr Dir-Adv Art - J.C. Penney Company, Inc.; *pg.* 1774, *pg.* 1732
Forbes, Raymond, Dir-Design, Brand Dev & Corp Mktg - Univision Communications Inc.; *pg.* 683, *pg.* 1307
Forbes, Steve, Jr., Chm & Editor-in-Chief-Forbes Media - Forbes, Inc.; *pg.* 1641, *pg.* 1232
Forbidussi, Joe, Sr VP & Gen Mgr-Mdsg - The Cato Corporation; *pg.* 21, *pg.* 1364
Force, Wendie, Mgr-Media Svcs - Conair Corporation; *pg.* 505, *pg.* 1055
Ford, Alfred J., Jr., Sr VP-Sls-Global & Gen Mgr - Cardiac Science Corporation; *pg.* 1512, *pg.* 1897
Ford, Brian G., Acct Mgr-Digital Adv - ESPN, Inc.; *pg.* 285, *pg.* 340
Ford, Britt, Mgr-Dealer Mktg - Carfax Inc.; *pg.* 202, *pg.* 1777
Ford, Carolyn, Dir-Mktg - Raytheon; *pg.* 459, *pg.* 115
Ford, Chris, Mgr-Domestic Sls - Plains Cotton Cooperative Association; *pg.* 697, *pg.* 1726
Ford, Christina, Mgr-Mktg Svcs - Aviall, Inc.; *pg.* 224, *pg.* 1676
Ford, Christy, Sr Mgr-Media Strategy - Walgreen Co.; *pg.* 1608, *pg.* 605
Ford, Dee, Sr Acct Mgr-Mktg & Comm-Global - Georgia Department of Economic Development; *pg.* 992, *pg.* 506
Ford, Eric, VP-Sls & Mktg - Graphite Metallizing Corporation; *pg.* 1343, *pg.* 1356
Ford, Euan, Strategist-Product Mktg - American Family Mutual Insurance Company; *pg.* 1190, *pg.* 1864
Ford, Heather, Mgr-Mktg - Level 3 Communications, Inc.; *pg.* 1262, *pg.* 312
Ford, Jennifer, Brand Mgr-Customer Love & Digital Adoption Strategy - Capital One Bank (USA), N.A.; *pg.* 730, *pg.* 1789
Ford, Jennifer, Brand Mgr-Customer Love & Digital Adoption Strategy - Capital One Financial Corporation; *pg.* 730, *pg.* 1789
Ford, Jim, Mgr-Corp Product Mgmt - SouthCo, Inc.; *pg.* 1063, *pg.* 1522
Ford, Jody, VP-Mktg - eBay Inc.; *pg.* 1240, *pg.* 243
Ford, John, Mgr-Field Mktg-Michigan - MillerCoors LLC; *pg.* 255, *pg.* 582
Ford, Jonathan, Dir-Natl Sls-Non-Comml Channels - American Foods Group, LLC; *pg.* 837, *pg.* 1859
Ford, Karie, VP-Media - Subway Restaurants; *pg.* 1751, *pg.* 356
Ford, Kerry, VP-Americas Mktg - Blue Coat Systems, Inc.; *pg.* 362, *pg.* 284
Ford, Mark, Exec VP-Global Adv - Time Inc.; *pg.* 1693, *pg.* 1300
Ford, Nicole, Specialist-Products Mktg - Accenture; *pg.* 1392, *pg.* 1186
Ford, Sheree, Dir-Global Mktg & Campaign Mgmt - Philips Electronics North America; *pg.* 662, *pg.* 782
Ford, Steven, Sr Dir-BioScience Device Dev & BioSurgery Innovation - Baxter International Inc.; *pg.* 1499, *pg.* 599
Ford, Tim, Product Mgr-Global - General Electric Company; *pg.* 1297, *pg.* 347
Ford, Todd, Dir-Mktg - Stratosphere Corporation; *pg.* 1115, *pg.* 1030
Ford, Tracey, Sr Dir-IR - PayPal Inc.; *pg.* 1274, *pg.* 248
Ford, Wayne, Sr VP-Comml Sls-Worldwide - Kofax Image Products, Inc.; *pg.* 1419, *pg.* 112
Ford-Smith, Jennifer, Dir-Mktg & Single Ply Product Mgmt - Johns Manville Corporation; *pg.* 89, *pg.* 320
Forde, Matt, Exec VP-Content Production, Sls & Distr-North America - BBC Worldwide America Inc.; *pg.* 271, *pg.* 1201
Forde, Michael, Sr VP-Corp Partnerships & Premium Sls - Orlando Magic; *pg.* 572, *pg.* 455
Forde, Mike, Sr Mgr-Content Comm - National Association for Stock Car Auto Racing; *pg.* 566, *pg.* 420
Fordyce, Russ, Mng Dir-Mktg - Broadview Networks, Inc.; *pg.* 365, *pg.* 1339
Fore, Adam, Dir-Virtualization Solution Mktg - NetApp, Inc.; *pg.* 444, *pg.* 287
Fore, Peggy, Media Buyer - CarMax, Inc.; *pg.* 167, *pg.* 1800
Forell, Kerry, Product Mgr - Intel Corporation; *pg.* 645, *pg.* 266
Foreman, Aaron, Sr Dir-Digital Mktg - Sonos, Inc.; *pg.* 675, *pg.* 263
Foreman, Chris, Sr Producer-Mktg - The E.W. Scripps Company; *pg.* 1639, *pg.* 1412
Foreman, Don, Reg VP-Sls & Mktg - Loews Hotels Holding Corporation; *pg.* 1101, *pg.* 1252

First page reference indicates Business Class Edition
Second page reference indicates Geographic Edition

Foreman, Jim, Product Mgr - W.L. Gore & Associates, Inc.; *pg.* 122, *pg.* 388
Foreman, Ken, VP-Film Mktg - Regal Entertainment Group; *pg.* 579, *pg.* 1638
Foreman, Michael, Exec VP-Intl Bus, Govt Sls & Product Line Mgmt - Point Blank Solutions, Inc.; *pg.* 1467, *pg.* 460
Foreman, Sara, Mgr-Mktg & Sls - McCormick & Company, Incorporated; *pg.* 1027, *pg.* 779
Forero, Laura, Dir-Mktg - The Kraft Heinz Company; *pg.* 871, *pg.* 641
Forest, Lauren, Mgr-Online Sls - Lionbridge Technologies Inc.; *pg.* 428, *pg.* 851
Forestal, Alison, Dir-Media UK - Amazon.com, Inc.; *pg.* 1226, *pg.* 1831
Forestell, Jack, Head-Product-Global - Visa Inc.; *pg.* 816, *pg.* 230
Forgacs, Martha, Head-Mktg Svcs Program - Domino's Pizza, Inc.; *pg.* 1726, *pg.* 865
Forger, Jim, Dir-Product Line Mgmt-Connected Products - Eastman Kodak Company; *pg.* 1408, *pg.* 1333
Forger, Sarah, Sr Mgr-Brand Strategy & Mktg - American Express Company; *pg.* 712, *pg.* 1190
Forget, Leo, Product Mgr - QNX Software Systems Ltd; *pg.* 458, *pg.* 1932
Foristall, Missy, Head-Digital Mktg - JPMorgan Chase & Co.; *pg.* 772, *pg.* 1246
Forman, Christine, Acq Mktg - Discover Financial Services; *pg.* 744, *pg.* 653
Forman, Dan, Dir-PR & Digital Media - Honest Tea; *pg.* 253, *pg.* 762
Forman, Geoffrey, Mgr-Content Mktg & Analyst-Mktg - Edmund Industrial Optics Inc.; *pg.* 1411, *pg.* 1041
Forman, Gwen, VP-Mktg - Cumberland Farms, Inc.; *pg.* 1018, *pg.* 820
Forman, Jocelyn, Dir-Consumer Mktg - The Hearst Corporation; *pg.* 1649, *pg.* 1239
Forman, Lawrence H., Sr Dir-Corp Mergers & Acq - Teradata Corporation; *pg.* 483, *pg.* 1447
Forman, Lewis, Mgr-Digital Mktg - Penn Foster Education Group, Inc.; *pg.* 606, *pg.* 1586
Forman, Susan, VP-Corp PR - Charles Schwab; *pg.* 1235, *pg.* 1661
Formanek, Brian, Mgr-Mktg & Sls - The Kansas City Southern Railway Company; *pg.* 1913, *pg.* 985
Formanek, Jim, Dir-Product Dev - The Jim Henson Company; *pg.* 293, *pg.* 103
Formico, Karen, VP-Mktg - Andis Company; *pg.* 498, *pg.* 1895
Formidoni, Richard, Product Mgr-Trng - Korg USA, Inc.; *pg.* 556, *pg.* 1180
Forness, Nathan, Dir-Digital Group Creative & Sr Mgr-Creative Experience - New Balance Athletic Shoe, Inc.; *pg.* 1811, *pg.* 798
Forney, David, Sr Dir-Consumer Comm-Global - The Hershey Co.; *pg.* 1855, *pg.* 1538
Fornwall, Michael, Head-US Mktg-VORAPAXAR - Merck & Co., Inc.; *pg.* 1566, *pg.* 1077
Forrest, Darci, Sr Dir-Menu Innovation Team - McDonald's Corporation; *pg.* 1737, *pg.* 645
Forrest, Greg, Dir-Mktg Ops & Demand Central - Concur Technologies, Inc.; *pg.* 1236, *pg.* 1813
Forrest, Gretchen, VP-Product Dev-Girls' Properties - Hasbro, Inc.; *pg.* 954, *pg.* 1603
Forrest, Ian, Gen Mgr-Comml Sls & Mktg - GE Capital; *pg.* 761, *pg.* 362
Forrest, Jessica, Specialist-PR & Govt Rels - Comcast Corporation; *pg.* 276, *pg.* 1560
Forrest, Kelly, Coord-Mktg - Brennan Industries Inc.; *pg.* 1319, *pg.* 1429
Forrest, Kyra, Mgr-Mktg - General Electric Company; *pg.* 1297, *pg.* 347
Forrester, Joanne, VP-Mktg - Boston Pizza International, Inc.; *pg.* 1016, *pg.* 1908
Forrester, Ron, Sr Dir Digital Brand Engineering & Core Dev - NIKE, Inc.; *pg.* 1812, *pg.* 1492
Forrister, Kelly, Analyst-Customer Mktg - The Gorton Group; *pg.* 859, *pg.* 823
Fors, Charlotte, VP-Sls - mBlox Inc.; *pg.* 1266, *pg.* 286
Forsberg, Bob, VP-Sls & Bus Dev - Sappi Fine Paper North America; *pg.* 1468, *pg.* 801
Forsline, Joel, Mgr-Sls Ops - Ford Motor Company; *pg.* 172, *pg.* 876
Forslund, Jodi, Reg VP-Sls & Mktg - Benchmark Hospitality International Inc.; *pg.* 1081, *pg.* 1747
Forsner, Brian, Sr Dir-Ops - ShopLocal, LLC; *pg.* 1280, *pg.* 590
Forster, Frank, VP-Sls-EMEA - Altera Corporation; *pg.* 348, *pg.* 237
Forsthuber, Shelby, Sr Mgr-Field & Experiential Mktg - Coca-Cola Refreshments USA, Inc.; *pg.* 247, *pg.* 500
Forsyth, Erin, Dir-Global Product Mktg, Support & Deployment Svcs - Dell Inc.; *pg.* 383, *pg.* 1737
Forsyth, Kelly, Reg Dir-Sls-Enterprise Solutions & VP-Sls-Colorado - Integra Telecom, Inc.; *pg.* 644, *pg.* 938
Forsyth, Nancy, Sr VP-Sls Learning & Dev-North American Higher Education - Pearson Education; *pg.* 1675, *pg.* 800
Forsythe, Ken, Sr Product Mgr-CertainTeed Insulation - CertainTeed Corporation; *pg.* 74, *pg.* 1589
Forsythe, Ken, Mgr-Comm & Mktg - The Salvation Army; *pg.* 155, *pg.* 1771
Fort, Ricardo, Sr VP-Global Brand, Product & Sponsorship Mktg - Visa U.S.A., Inc.; *pg.* 817, *pg.* 231
Fort, Tim, Mgr-Mktg & Print Adv - Trans World Entertainment Corporation; *pg.* 313, *pg.* 1137
Forte, Caroline E., Sr Dir-HR Comm - Pfizer Inc.; *pg.* 1581, *pg.* 1278
Forte, Jennifer, Supvr-Outbound Mktg - Tech Data Corporation; *pg.* 482, *pg.* 416
Forte, Jill, Media Planner-Digital - The Atlanta Journal-Constitution; *pg.* 1618, *pg.* 490
Forte, Michael, Sr Mgr-Insurance Product Mgmt - American Express Company; *pg.* 712, *pg.* 1190
Fortenberry, Doug, Mgr-Mktg - SYNNEX Corporation; *pg.* 480, *pg.* 92
Fortgang, Adam, Dir-Mktg & Asst Dir-Press - Princeton University Press; *pg.* 1678, *pg.* 1112
Forth, Marc, VP-Sls & Mktg-Neurosciences - Allergan, Inc.; *pg.* 1491, *pg.* 106
Fortier, Erin, Brand Mgr - LEGO Systems, Inc.; *pg.* 961, *pg.* 346
Fortin, Cam, Sr Dir-Product Dev - Wine.com, Inc.; *pg.* 1972, *pg.* 234
Fortin, Dave, Sr VP-Mktg - Live Nation Entertainment, Inc.; *pg.* 558, *pg.* 47
Fortmueller, Chris, Brand Mgr-Design - Darden Restaurants, Inc.; *pg.* 1724, *pg.* 453
Fortner, Jeff, Sr Mgr-Market - Holcim (U.S.) Inc.; *pg.* 1346, *pg.* 885
Fortner, Kris, Head-Mktg Strategy, Corp Comm & PR - McKesson Corporation; *pg.* 1560, *pg.* 222
Fortney, Jeffrey, Acct Mgr-Digital Mktg Cloud - Adobe Systems Incorporated; *pg.* 342, *pg.* 235
Fortoloczki, Kalman, Asst VP & Head-Mktg Review Center-Core Compliance Svcs - Nuveen Investments, Inc.; *pg.* 788, *pg.* 586
Fortunato, Steve, VP-Sls - B&G Foods, Inc.; *pg.* 838, *pg.* 1102
Foschino, Paul, Sr Mgr-New Bus Dev - Ricoh Americas Corp.; *pg.* 462, *pg.* 538
Foss, Cheri, Mgr-Sls-Natl - WTVD-TV Inc.; *pg.* 323, *pg.* 1372
Foss, Emily, Mgr-Comm & Sls - The Allstate Corporation; *pg.* 1189, *pg.* 639
Foss, John, Mgr-Mktg - Hewlett-Packard Company; *pg.* 404, *pg.* 175
Foss, Kerrie L., Sr Mgr-Mktg-Global Consumer Pkg & Mdsg - Intuit Inc.; *pg.* 769, *pg.* 158
Foster, Andrew, Sr Product Mgr - Google Inc.; *pg.* 1249, *pg.* 153
Foster, Bill, Mgr-Mktg & Interactive Svcs - Universal Forest Products, Inc.; *pg.* 117, *pg.* 890
Foster, Bill, Specialist-Product - W.L. Gore & Associates, Inc.; *pg.* 122, *pg.* 388
Foster, Brett, Analyst-Mktg - Humana, Inc.; *pg.* 1204, *pg.* 734
Foster, Cedric, Sr VP-Brand Mktg, Digital & Fan Engagement Strategy - Spike TV; *pg.* 310, *pg.* 1295
Foster, Christian, Dir-OpenStack Private Cloud Mktg - RACKSPACE HOSTING, INC.; *pg.* 1277, *pg.* 1742
Foster, Dana, Bus Mgr-Alliances - United States Postal Service; *pg.* 1009, *pg.* 406
Foster, Dave, Mgr-Strategic Mktg & Comm - The Western & Southern Financial Group; *pg.* 1223, *pg.* 1427
Foster, David, Mgr-Field Mktg - True Value Company; *pg.* 1065, *pg.* 592
Foster, Dawn, Sr Dir-Brand Mktg - Captain D's, LLC; *pg.* 1720, *pg.* 1649
Foster, Doryan, VP-Sls-West Coast - The CW Television Network; *pg.* 632, *pg.* 52
Foster, Eric, Dir-Mktg-Global - GlaxoSmithKline; *pg.* 1536, *pg.* 1565
Foster, Erika, Reg Mgr-Sls - Dr Pepper Snapple Group, Inc.; *pg.* 250, *pg.* 1729
Foster, Frances, Coord-Natl Adv - The Home Depot, Inc.; *pg.* 1050, *pg.* 510
Foster, James A., Exec VP-Sls - Rug Doctor, LP; *pg.* 1373, *pg.* 1734
Foster, Julie, Global Product Mgr-Water Purification - Thermo Fisher Scientific Inc.; *pg.* 1431, *pg.* 854
Foster, Kate, VP-Mktg & ECommerce - NYDJ Apparel, LLC; *pg.* 30, *pg.* 302
Foster, Kelley, Assoc Product Mgr-Orajel, Baby Orajel Naturals - Church & Dwight Co., Inc.; *pg.* 1153, *pg.* 1063
Foster, Kelly, Brand Mgr & Product Mgr - Hunter Douglas, Inc.; *pg.* 928, *pg.* 1320
Foster, Kelly, Dir-Media Comm - Rolex Watch U.S.A., Inc.; *pg.* 11, *pg.* 1286
Foster, Kristina, Dir-Water Wastewater Segment Mktg-Global Solutions - Schneider Electric; *pg.* 467, *pg.* 1609
Foster, Laura, Head-Retail Mktg - John Hancock Financial Services; *pg.* 1205, *pg.* 796
Foster, Leticia, Brand Mgr-Private Brands - Lowe's Companies, Inc.; *pg.* 1053, *pg.* 1383
Foster, Lorrie, Product Mgr - Paychex, Inc.; *pg.* 792, *pg.* 1336
Foster, Marcie Davidson, VP-Mktg - Movado Group, Inc.; *pg.* 10, *pg.* 1101
Foster, Melissa, Mgr-Media & Film Rels - Henry Ford Museum and Greenfield Village; *pg.* 552, *pg.* 878
Foster, Michelle, Mgr-Mktg Comm - Belden, Inc.; *pg.* 624, *pg.* 993
Foster, Morgan, Mgr-Strategic Mktg - McKesson Corporation; *pg.* 1560, *pg.* 222
Foster, Myra, Sr Mgr-Mktg & Comm - Stratton Mountain Resort; *pg.* 1115, *pg.* 1768
Foster, Nicole, Dir-Mktg - Scholastic Inc.; *pg.* 1683, *pg.* 1288
Foster, Patrick, Sr Dir-Technical-Audience & Multi-Platform Technologies - Turner Broadcasting System, Inc.; *pg.* 314, *pg.* 521
Foster, Peter, VP-Solutions Dev & MMD Sls - Yahoo! Inc.; *pg.* 1289, *pg.* 289
Foster, Robert H., Owner & Mgr-Sls - George J. Foster Co. Inc.; *pg.* 1644, *pg.* 1033
Foster, Sharon, Sr Mgr-Engagement Mktg-Global - Electronic Arts Inc.; *pg.* 951, *pg.* 189
Foster, Stacie, Specialist-Mktg-Finger Lakes Gaming & Racetrack - Delaware North Companies, Inc.; *pg.* 1089, *pg.* 1148
Foster, Stuart, VP-Global Mktg, Luxury & Lifestyle Brand - Hilton Worldwide, Inc.; *pg.* 1094, *pg.* 1791
Foster, Tammy D., Rep-Dev-IBM Inside Sls-North America - IBM Canada Limited; *pg.* 411, *pg.* 1923
Foucher, Jeff, VP-Product Mktg - CA Technologies; *pg.* 366, *pg.* 1168
Fouladpour, Tony, Dir-Corp PR - Michelin North America Inc.; *pg.* 1886, *pg.* 1618
Foulk, Anthony, Product Mgr-A6, A7 & A8 - Audi of America, Inc.; *pg.* 164, *pg.* 1784
Foulkes, David, VP-Product Dev, Engrg & Racing - Mercury Marine; *pg.* 1709, *pg.* 1857
Foulkes, David M., CTO & VP-Product Dev, Eng & Racing-Mercury Marine - Brunswick Corporation; *pg.* 1828, *pg.* 623
Fountain, Robert, Dir-Shopper Mktg, Comml Plng & Activation - Diageo North America Inc.; *pg.* 248, *pg.* 1223
Fournais, Anne, Mgr-Creative Strategy - Electronic Arts Inc.; *pg.* 951, *pg.* 189
Fournier, Christopher, Sr Mgr-Digital Mktg - Panera Bread Company; *pg.* 1029, *pg.* 1001
Fournier, Dawn, Head-US Field Mktg - International Game Technology; *pg.* 957, *pg.* 1024
Fournier, Linda, Dir-Mktg Analytics - Cancer Treatment Centers of America; *pg.* 1511, *pg.* 410
Fournier, Marie, VP-Product Mgmt - TECSYS, Inc.; *pg.* 482, *pg.* 1956
Fournier, Paul, Sr Mgr-Info Security - Comcast Cable Communications, Inc.; *pg.* 276, *pg.* 1560
Fournier, Randy, Sr VP-Specialty Cellulose & Chemical Products-Temiscaming Ops - Tembec Inc.; *pg.* 114, *pg.* 1957
Fournier, Todd, Sr Mgr-Mktg - Major League Baseball; *pg.* 560, *pg.* 1255
Foushee, Jennifer, Mgr-Mktg - Brasfield & Gorrie, LLC; *pg.* 71, *pg.* 2
Foutch, Randy, Mgr-HUMMER Mktg - General Motors Company; *pg.* 175, *pg.* 881
Foutres, Dimitri, Sr Dir-Wall Strategy & Logistics Group - Coty, Inc.; *pg.* 506, *pg.* 1219

Fouts, Michael, VP-Worldwide Sls & Svcs Enablement - Citrix Systems, Inc.; *pg.* 375, *pg.* 424
Fouts, Sally, Dir-PR-Music & Video - Amazon.com, Inc.; *pg.* 1226, *pg.* 1831
Foutz, Christopher, Mgr-Mktg-Heat Transfer - Honeywell International Inc.; *pg.* 407, *pg.* 1088
Fowler, Carl, VP-Field Sls & Solutions-North America-Menlo Logistics - Menlo Worldwide, LLC; *pg.* 1915, *pg.* 255
Fowler, Chris, Dir-Consumer Mktg - Bellacor Inc.; *pg.* 917, *pg.* 929
Fowler, Craig, Sr Dir-Brand Mktg-Courtyard Hotels - Marriott International, Inc.; *pg.* 1102, *pg.* 764
Fowler, DeeDee, VP & Brand Mgr-Strategy - Wells Fargo & Company; *pg.* 819, *pg.* 232
Fowler, Janice, Dir-Media Mktg - Brady Corporation; *pg.* 363, *pg.* 1873
Fowler, Jennifer, Sr VP-Mktg & Revenue Generation - Sony Music Entertainment; *pg.* 309, *pg.* 1294
Fowler, John, VP-Product Dev, Engrg & Design - Huffy Corporation; *pg.* 1836, *pg.* 1409
Fowler, Kaci, Reg Supvr-Mktg - McDonald's Corporation; *pg.* 1737, *pg.* 645
Fowler, Ken, Mgr-Comm, Media & Tech Practice - Accenture; *pg.* 1392, *pg.* 1186
Fowler, Kevin, Coord-Mktg - GEICO Corporation; *pg.* 1200, *pg.* 399
Fowler, Lynne, Brand Mgr - Michelin North America Inc.; *pg.* 1886, *pg.* 1618
Fowler, Megan, Mgr-Mktg Comm - Fujitsu Computer Systems Corporation; *pg.* 398, *pg.* 285
Fowler, Ryan, Sr Specialist-Mktg - California Lottery; *pg.* 990, *pg.* 196
Fowler, Stacey, Sr VP-Product Innovation & New Venture Dev - The Schwan Food Company; *pg.* 894, *pg.* 928
Fowles, Matthew, Brand Mgr - The Scotts Miracle-Gro Company; *pg.* 1799, *pg.* 1459
Fowlkes, Kathy, Bus Mgr-Bath Div - Bacova Guild, Ltd.; *pg.* 916, *pg.* 1779
Fox, Amaryllis, Product Mgr - Twitter, Inc.; *pg.* 1285, *pg.* 228
Fox, Andrew, Sr Mgr-Corp Comm - Advanced Micro Devices, Inc.; *pg.* 613, *pg.* 282
Fox, Anita C., Mng Dir-Corp PR - Charles Schwab & Company, Inc.; *pg.* 734, *pg.* 215
Fox, Brian, VP & Gen Mgr-Private Label Cereal & Condiments Products - ConAgra Foods, Inc.; *pg.* 826, *pg.* 1014
Fox, Catherine, Brand Mgr-Mktg & Pkg - CHF Industries, Inc.; *pg.* 920, *pg.* 1211
Fox, Catherine Einig, Dir-Mktg-Foodservice - Land O'Lakes, Inc.; *pg.* 873, *pg.* 915
Fox, Chad, Sr Dir-Mktg-Food - Wal-Mart Stores, Inc.; *pg.* 1790, *pg.* 29
Fox, Chris, Product Mgr - Jacobsen Textron; *pg.* 1708, *pg.* 1367
Fox, Chris, Product Mgr & Brand Mgr - Universal Forest Products, Inc.; *pg.* 117, *pg.* 890
Fox, Christine, Mgr-Mktg - Ameriprise Financial, Inc.; *pg.* 715, *pg.* 930
Fox, Christopher, Dir-Comml Sls - Orkin, Inc.; *pg.* 1798, *pg.* 517
Fox, Corinna, Dir-Targeted Mktg - The Great Atlantic & Pacific Tea Company, Inc.; *pg.* 1021, *pg.* 1086
Fox, Eric B., Product Mgr - Roche Diagnostics Corporation; *pg.* 1590, *pg.* 689
Fox, Eva-Marie, VP-Mktg - T&S Brass & Bronze Works, Inc.; *pg.* 114, *pg.* 1623
Fox, Fred, Mgr-Product Requirements - BMW of North America, LLC; *pg.* 166, *pg.* 1133
Fox, Hugh, Specialist-Digital Media - Alcoa Inc.; *pg.* 65, *pg.* 1188
Fox, Jeanne, Dir-Ops & Mktg Comm - Apple Inc.; *pg.* 350, *pg.* 73
Fox, John, Sr Mgr-Product-Cloud Bus Unit - CommVault Systems, Inc.; *pg.* 377, *pg.* 1125
Fox, Josephine, Sr Mgr-Mktg - National Geographic Society; *pg.* 1667, *pg.* 402
Fox, Justen, Dir-Digital Product - The New Republic Inc.; *pg.* 1667, *pg.* 403
Fox, Karrie, Sr Mgr-ECommerce - Hilton Worldwide, Inc.; *pg.* 1094, *pg.* 1791
Fox, Kelly, Bus Mgr-Fine Watches, Fashion Watches & Fashion Jewelry - Macy's, Inc.; *pg.* 1778, *pg.* 1417
Fox, Kiernan, Sr Mgr-Brand Solutions Mktg & Global Media Solutions - Electronic Arts Inc.; *pg.* 951, *pg.* 189
Fox, Kimbra, VP-Mktg-Health Care Reform - Automatic Data Processing, Inc.; *pg.* 357, *pg.* 1117
Fox, Leslie, Coord-Sls - EMCOR Services Northeast CommAir/BALCO; *pg.* 1071, *pg.* 847
Fox, Megan, Sr Mgr-Corp Affairs - Amgen Inc.; *pg.* 1493, *pg.* 291
Fox, Michael, Sr Dir-Exec Comm - IMS Health, Inc.; *pg.* 1544, *pg.* 344
Fox, Michael, Mgr-Digital Mktg - The TJX Companies, Inc.; *pg.* 1788, *pg.* 822
Fox, Michelle, Mgr-Digital Mktg Channel - Bank of America Corporation; *pg.* 718, *pg.* 1362
Fox, Nick, VP-Product Mgmt - Google Inc.; *pg.* 1249, *pg.* 153
Fox, Sarah, Dir-Mktg & Product Strategy - The Walt Disney Company; *pg.* 317, *pg.* 52
Fox, Shaina, Mgr-Customer Mktg - Mars North America; *pg.* 1859, *pg.* 1072
Fox, Shannon, Dir-Team Sls - Madison Square Garden Network; *pg.* 297, *pg.* 1255
Fox, Steve, Product Mgr - Dell Inc.; *pg.* 383, *pg.* 1737
Fox, Steve, Dir-Ticket Sls - Detroit Tigers Baseball Club, Inc.; *pg.* 545, *pg.* 880
Fox, Steve, Assoc Dir-Media & Sponsorships - Verizon Communications Inc.; *pg.* 1875, *pg.* 1309
Fox, Steven, Dir-Product Dev - Thomson Reuters - Corporate Headquarters; *pg.* 1693, *pg.* 1299
Fox, Tiffany, Sr Dir-Corp Comm - OpenTable, Inc.; *pg.* 450, *pg.* 224
Fox, Travis, Mgr-Adv Production - Time Warner Cable Inc.; *pg.* 312, *pg.* 1301
Fox, Valerie, Exec Dir-Mktg & Comm - Bentley University; *pg.* 598, *pg.* 850
Fox, Victoria, Dir-New Media-AAMCO Transmissions & Total Car Care - Aamco Transmissions, Inc.; *pg.* 197, *pg.* 1540
Foxen, Casey, Assoc Mgr-Mktg-Retail Media - American Girl LLC; *pg.* 949, *pg.* 1871
Foxhoven, Mark, Mgr-Product Line - Applied Materials, Inc; *pg.* 618, *pg.* 1009
Foxley, Christina, Sr Mgr-Mktg-Harmony Books - Penguin Random House; *pg.* 1675, *pg.* 1276
Foxley, Lindsay, Mgr-Digital Mktg & Media Analytics - FCA US LLC; *pg.* 170, *pg.* 868
Foxworth, Fontaine, Product Mgr - Google Inc.; *pg.* 1249, *pg.* 153
Foxx, Chloe, Product Mgr-Men's Factory - Coach, Inc.; *pg.* 3, *pg.* 1214
Foy, Kelsey, Mgr-Mktg-Wag.com - Quidsi, Inc.; *pg.* 1276, *pg.* 1076
Frable, Anna, Exec Dir-PR - Novartis Corporation; *pg.* 1574, *pg.* 1273
Frable, Anna, Exec Dir-PR - Novartis Pharmaceuticals Corp.; *pg.* 1575, *pg.* 1054
Frabotta, Michael, VP-Sls - ZYNEX, INC.; *pg.* 690, *pg.* 333
Fraccalvieri, Tom, Mgr-Mktg - Rockstar, Inc.; *pg.* 265, *pg.* 1029
Fradin, Jackie, Sr Dir-Consumer Insights-Global - Hasbro, Inc.; *pg.* 954, *pg.* 1603
Fragnito, Joe, VP-Mktg, Lunchables, Boca & Claussen Brands - The Kraft Heinz Company; *pg.* 871, *pg.* 641
Frail, Meaghan, Asst VP-UHNW Mktg-Brand Delivery & Strategy - Bank of America Corporation; *pg.* 718, *pg.* 1362
Fraim, Jill, Dir-Sls Mktg Res & Programming - KFOR-TV; *pg.* 294, *pg.* 1486
Fralish, Allyson, Assoc Dir & Sr Mgr-Mktg Comm - AT&T Mobility LLC; *pg.* 620, *pg.* 1824
Frame, Don, Product Mgr-Lenovo Enterprise Products-North America - Lenovo Group Ltd; *pg.* 427, *pg.* 1384
Frana, Julia, Mgr-Mktg Comm - Marvin Windows & Doors; *pg.* 934, *pg.* 965
Franca, Marcus, Dir-Mktg-Global - L'Oreal USA; *pg.* 514, *pg.* 1252
France, Jeff, Dir-Creative - Rawlings Sporting Goods Co., Inc.; *pg.* 1843, *pg.* 1002
France, Lon, Sr VP-Sls & Mktg - Bandwidth.com, Inc.; *pg.* 360, *pg.* 1386
Franchi, Jim, Pres-Media - AutoTrader, Inc.; *pg.* 1230, *pg.* 490
Francione, Brian, Div VP & Mgr-Mdse - HomeGoods, Inc.; *pg.* 1125, *pg.* 821
Francis, Bob, Sr Mgr-Bus Dev - Cisco Systems, Inc.; *pg.* 372, *pg.* 240
Francis, Carolyn A., Mgr-Nonstop Mktg-Worldwide - Hewlett-Packard Company; *pg.* 404, *pg.* 175
Francis, Chris, Mgr-Digital Mktg - Roche Diagnostics Corporation; *pg.* 1590, *pg.* 689
Francis, Daryl, Bus Mgr & Mgr-Exports - Interplastic Corporation; *pg.* 1168, *pg.* 961
Francis, Dave, Sr Mgr-Res & Strategy - The Toro Company; *pg.* 1065, *pg.* 918
Francis, Jennifer, Exec Dir-Mktg & Comm - Philadelphia Museum of Art; *pg.* 575, *pg.* 1569
Francis, Kim, Bus Mgr-Woolworths-Natl - General Mills, Inc.; *pg.* 828, *pg.* 933
Francis, Lauren M., VP-Media Rels-Consumer & Community Banking - Chase Card Services, Inc.; *pg.* 734, *pg.* 215
Francis, Lori, Dir-Experiential Mktg-Global - Xerox Corporation; *pg.* 494, *pg.* 365
Francis, Mara F., Sr Mgr-Mktg-Natl Accts - PepsiCo, Inc.; *pg.* 259, *pg.* 1327
Francis, Mark, Mgr-Mktg - The Kroger Co.; *pg.* 1025, *pg.* 1416
Francis, Sarah, Sr Mgr-Mktg - FMR LLC (Fidelity Investments); *pg.* 759, *pg.* 794
Francisco, Daniel, Dir-Media Rels-Global - Micron Technology, Inc.; *pg.* 435, *pg.* 547
Francisco, Phil, VP-Data Mgmt Products & Strategy - International Business Machines Corporation; *pg.* 418, *pg.* 1138
Franco, Maricela, Mgr-Strategic Sls & Customer Mktg - MATTEL, INC.; *pg.* 962, *pg.* 81
Franco, Natalia, Chief Brand Officer, Chief Strategy Officer & Exec VP - California Pizza Kitchen Inc.; *pg.* 1720, *pg.* 127
Franco, Rosie, Mgr-Mktg - Custom Sensors & Technologies; *pg.* 1407, *pg.* 152
Franco, Valerie, VP-Mktg-Disputes, Investigations & Legal Mgmt Consulting - Duff & Phelps Corporation; *pg.* 745, *pg.* 1226
Francois, Olivier, CMO - FCA US LLC; *pg.* 170, *pg.* 868
Frangella, Louis, Acct Coord-Partnership Mktg - Brooklyn Nets; *pg.* 534, *pg.* 1145
Frank, Aimee, Dir-Mktg - Rochester Broadway Theatre League; *pg.* 579, *pg.* 1337
Frank, Amanda, Mgr-Mktg-Mass Media - Provide Commerce, Inc.; *pg.* 1276, *pg.* 206
Frank, Amanda, Sr Mgr-Mktg - Truven Health Analytics; *pg.* 1696, *pg.* 867
Frank, Annemarie, VP-Digital Mktg & Lifecycle Mktg - HSN, Inc.; *pg.* 291, *pg.* 462
Frank, Catalina, Product Mgr - Epson America Inc.; *pg.* 394, *pg.* 122
Frank, Holly, VP-Partnership Mktg - Universal Studios, Inc.; *pg.* 315, *pg.* 298
Frank, Janet, Mgr-Media-USR - Intermountain Health Care Inc.; *pg.* 1546, *pg.* 1759
Frank, Jason, Sr Designer-Web & New Media Comm - Lockheed Martin Corporation; *pg.* 229, *pg.* 762
Frank, Karen, VP-Skin Care Mktg & Mass-US - Kao Brands Co. Inc.; *pg.* 513, *pg.* 1415
Frank, Kathryn, Mgr-Creative Bus - Carhartt, Inc.; *pg.* 39, *pg.* 875
Frank, Lauren, Assoc Mgr-Mktg-New Pet - PetSmart, Inc.; *pg.* 1481, *pg.* 18
Frank, Lucas, Sr Mgr-Ram LD & HD Truck Product Plng - FCA US LLC; *pg.* 170, *pg.* 868
Frank, Lynne, Exec VP-Mktg-Intl - Warner Bros. Entertainment Inc.; *pg.* 319, *pg.* 54
Frank, Malcolm, CMO, Chief Strategy Officer & Exec VP - Cognizant Technology Solutions Corporation; *pg.* 377, *pg.* 1124
Frank, Melanie, Sr Dir-Tech - Capital One Bank (USA), N.A.; *pg.* 730, *pg.* 1789
Frank, Mike, Product Dir-Mgmt - Oracle Corporation; *pg.* 450, *pg.* 191
Frank, Richard, Dir-Creative Svcs & Brand Mktg - AccuWeather, Inc.; *pg.* 268, *pg.* 1587
Frank, Ryan, Dir-Mktg-PediaSure & Pedialyte - Abbott Nutrition; *pg.* 1485, *pg.* 1437
Frank, Sarah, Dir-Brand Mktg - Red Lion Hotels Corp.; *pg.* 1110, *pg.* 1844
Frank, Tracy, Dir-Social - Time Inc.; *pg.* 1693, *pg.* 1300
Frank, Wendy, Mgr-Sls-Natl - San Jose Convention/Visitors Bureau; *pg.* 1005, *pg.* 250
Frank-Finney, Leah, Brand Mgr - The Kroger Co.; *pg.* 1025, *pg.* 1416
Frankart, Ashley, Mgr-Global Integrated Mktg-Ink - Hewlett-Packard Company; *pg.* 404, *pg.* 175
Franke, Paul, Reg Mgr-Sls - Software AG, Inc.; *pg.* 471, *pg.* 1799
Frankel, Aaron, Dir-Mktg - Siemens PLM Software; *pg.* 469, *pg.* 1734
Frankel, Jessica, Brand Mgr-DASANI - The Coca-Cola Company; *pg.* 240, *pg.* 493

Frankel, Jessica, Brand Mgr-DASANI - Coca-Cola North America; *pg.* 848, *pg.* 500
Frankel, Lisa, Dir-Product Strategy & Insights - Luby's Fuddruckers Restaurants, LLC; *pg.* 1736, *pg.* 1710
Frankel, Malcolm, Dir-Sls & Mktg - A-1 Limousine Inc.; *pg.* 163, *pg.* 1110
Frankel, Paul, VP-Ad Sls Mktg - Screenvision Cinema Network LLC; *pg.* 581, *pg.* 1290
Frankel, Richard, Dir-Creative & Mktg Solutions Grp - Spotify; *pg.* 1282, *pg.* 1295
Frankenburg, Karina, Program Mgr-Direct Digital Mktg - Wells Fargo & Company; *pg.* 819, *pg.* 232
Frankenfield, Laura, Sr Mgr-Customer Mktg - The Coca-Cola Company; *pg.* 240, *pg.* 493
Frankle, Brenda, Product Mgr - The Nielsen Company B.V.; *pg.* 1671, *pg.* 1272
Franklin, Aaron, Product Mgr-Ops - Pinterest; *pg.* 1275, *pg.* 225
Franklin, Carolyn, Mgr-Mktg Svcs & Events-EW Scripps - The Evansville Courier & Press; *pg.* 1639, *pg.* 678
Franklin, Cary, Sr Acct Exec-Social.com - salesforce.com, inc.; *pg.* 1278, *pg.* 226
Franklin, Cynthia, VP-Sls & Mktg - Wyndham Vacation Ownership; *pg.* 1119, *pg.* 457
Franklin, Don, Dir-Internet Mktg - Group 1 Automotive, Inc.; *pg.* 177, *pg.* 1706
Franklin, Lexi, Product Mgr - Facebook, Inc.; *pg.* 1245, *pg.* 143
Franklin, Lisa, Dir-Product Strategy & Portfolio Mgmt-Global - Johnson Controls, Inc.; *pg.* 209, *pg.* 1876
Franklin, Myra, Coord-Adv - The Home Depot, Inc.; *pg.* 1050, *pg.* 510
Franklin, TD, Dir-Mktg Ops - American National Insurance Company; *pg.* 1191, *pg.* 1697
Franklin, Tim, Sr Mgr-Mktg-Nissan North America - Nissan Canada Inc.; *pg.* 214, *pg.* 1928
Frankos, Vasilios, Sr VP-Global Product Science, Safety & Compliance - Herbalife International of America, Inc.; *pg.* 1541, *pg.* 132
Franks, Adrian, Dir-UX Design & Strategist-Creative - IBM; *pg.* 410, *pg.* 1449
Franks, Adrian, Dir-Design/Strategist-Creative-Interactive Experience - International Business Machines Corporation; *pg.* 418, *pg.* 1138
Franks, Brian, VP-Creative Mktg - American Eagle Outfitters, Inc.; *pg.* 37, *pg.* 1572
Franks, Eric, VP-Mktg Comm-Electrical Sector - Eaton Corporation; *pg.* 1331, *pg.* 1429
Frantz, Collin, Assoc Mgr-Mktg-Snacks Div - General Mills, Inc.; *pg.* 828, *pg.* 933
Frantz, Jacob, Product Mgr - Facebook, Inc.; *pg.* 1245, *pg.* 143
Frantz, Steve, VP-Sls - Community Coffee Company LLC; *pg.* 849, *pg.* 741
Frantzich, Shira, Sr Mgr-PR - Informatica Corporation; *pg.* 414, *pg.* 190
Franz, Daniel, Mgr-Tech Product-UPS Developer Kit & UPS Billing Center - United Parcel Service, Inc.; *pg.* 1928, *pg.* 522
Franzino, Joe, Sr Mgr-New Categories - Sabra Dipping Company LLC; *pg.* 893, *pg.* 1686
Franzoso, Anthony, Dir-Mktg, Calcium Acetate Franchise & Renal Specialties - Fresenius Medical Care North America; *pg.* 1531, *pg.* 851
Frary, Adam, Dir-Creative Svcs & Local Programming - WTVD-TV Inc.; *pg.* 323, *pg.* 1372
Frascarelli, Debra, Mgr-Media-Home Entertainment - Sony Pictures Entertainment Inc.; *pg.* 309, *pg.* 72
Frascatore, Vincent A., Assoc Dir-Managed Care Brand Mktg - Merck & Co., Inc.; *pg.* 1566, *pg.* 1077
Fraser, Alison, VP-Mktg - Savaria Corporation; *pg.* 1592, *pg.* 1951
Fraser, Andrea, Team Head-Worldwide Comml Dev Lung Portfolio & Sr Dir - Pfizer Inc.; *pg.* 1581, *pg.* 1278
Fraser, Angela, Mgr-Mktg - California Avocado Commission; *pg.* 135, *pg.* 108
Fraser, Blaire, Brand Mgr-Buchanan's Whisky - Diageo North America Inc.; *pg.* 248, *pg.* 1223
Fraser, Mark, Sr VP-Direct Mktg - American International Group, Inc.; *pg.* 1190, *pg.* 1193
Frasetto, Bob, VP-Sls - Shingle Belting Company; *pg.* 1375, *pg.* 1544
Frash, Mary, Specialist-Mktg-Food & Household Div - Ball Corporation; *pg.* 1452, *pg.* 311
Frate, Daniel, Exec VP-Global Markets & Product - ACI Worldwide; *pg.* 341, *pg.* 449
Frate, Daniel, Exec VP-Global Markets & Product - ACI Worldwide Inc.; *pg.* 341, *pg.* 1010
Frater, Steve, Exec Chm-Global Draw, Games Media & Barcrest - Scientific Games Corporation; *pg.* 468, *pg.* 1029
Frati, Filippo, Bus Mgr - Luxottica Retail; *pg.* 8, *pg.* 1460
Frattali, Tom, Sr VP-Grocery Pur, Mdsg & Distr - Gelson's Markets; *pg.* 1020, *pg.* 85
Frattarola, Katherine, Head-US PWM Mktg & Bus Dev & Exec Dir - Morgan Stanley; *pg.* 783, *pg.* 1261
FrauNFelder, Ryan, Sr VP & Sr Mgr-Bus Banking Relationship - KeyBank; *pg.* 773, *pg.* 1319
Frausing, Trine, Dir-Mktg-North American Div - Mattel Games/Puzzles; *pg.* 962, *pg.* 80
Frausing, Trine, Dir-Mktg-North American Div - MATTEL, INC.; *pg.* 962, *pg.* 81
Frausto, Daniel, Sr Dir-Oncology Global Mktg & Customer Solutions - Eli Lilly and Company; *pg.* 1527, *pg.* 684
Frausto, Diana L., Rep-PR - Cigna Corporation; *pg.* 1197, *pg.* 338
Frausto, Susie, VP-Mktg - The Jel Sert Company; *pg.* 865, *pg.* 668
Frautschi, Whitney, Sr Assoc-Acq Mktg - RetailMeNot Inc.; *pg.* 1782, *pg.* 1665
Fravel, Brian, VP-Mktg-North America - Intel Corporation; *pg.* 645, *pg.* 266
Fravel, Gary, Dir-Mktg - VeriFone Systems, Inc.; *pg.* 487, *pg.* 251
Frayne, Lidia, Strategist-Mktg - Dell Inc.; *pg.* 383, *pg.* 1737
Frazer, Mary Lou, Sr Dir-Investor & Fin Comm - Canadian Imperial Bank of Commerce; *pg.* 729, *pg.* 1935
Frazer, Meghan, Sr Specialist-Mktg-New Concepts - Lowe's Companies, Inc.; *pg.* 1053, *pg.* 1383
Frazer, Toine, Mgr-Distributor Sls-Europe - Firestone Industrial Products Division; *pg.* 1882, *pg.* 686
Frazier, Bernard, Specialist-Internet Mktg - NewsMax Media, Inc.; *pg.* 1271, *pg.* 479
Frazier, Brad, Corp Dir-Global Bus Travel Sls - Omni Hotels & Resorts; *pg.* 1107, *pg.* 1685
Frazier, Caitlin, Editor-Social Media - The Atlantic Monthly Group; *pg.* 1618, *pg.* 396
Frazier, Gary, Dir-Media & Analyst Rels - ABB; *pg.* 340, *pg.* 486
Frazier, John, Brand Mgr-Brand Mktg-Global - Hasbro, Inc.; *pg.* 954, *pg.* 1603
Frazier, Mackenzie B., Specialist-Mktg - FedEx Corporation; *pg.* 1907, *pg.* 1642
Frazier, Mara, Sr Dir-Community Affairs & Westgate Foundation - Central Florida Investments Inc.; *pg.* 1085, *pg.* 452
Frazier, Michael, Sr VP-Comm & Digital Media - 9/11 Memorial; *pg.* 124, *pg.* 1185
Frazier, Tony, Sr VP-Mktg - DigitalGlobe; *pg.* 227, *pg.* 1785
Frazier-Moore, Christy, Dir-Mktg - Southern Missouri Bancorp, Inc.; *pg.* 804, *pg.* 989
Frazzette, John, Assoc Dir-Mktg - Merck & Co., Inc.; *pg.* 1566, *pg.* 1077
Frazzette, Mike, Pres-Advanced Surgical Devices - Smith & Nephew, Inc., Endoscopy Division; *pg.* 1594, *pg.* 783
Frease, Gina, Asst VP-Mktg Comm Concierge - Associated Banc-Corp; *pg.* 716, *pg.* 1859
Frechette, Allen, VP-Mktg-Comml Sys - FLIR Systems, Inc.; *pg.* 1413, *pg.* 1510
Frechette, Rebecca, Sr VP-Mdsg - 7-Eleven, Inc.; *pg.* 1012, *pg.* 1672
Frechette, Susan, Sr Mgr-PR - Wayfair LLC; *pg.* 1288, *pg.* 801
Fredell, Thomas, Chief Product Officer - Merrill Corporation; *pg.* 1664, *pg.* 962
Frederes, Kevin, Mgr-Sls-Kiln Furniture, Clays & Minerals - Resco Products Greensboro; *pg.* 107, *pg.* 1375
Frederick, Amanda, Brand Mgr-Kleenex Brand - Kimberly-Clark Corporation; *pg.* 1461, *pg.* 1720
Frederick, Brian, VP-Interactive Mktg - M&T Bank Corporation; *pg.* 777, *pg.* 1149
Frederick, Candice, Mgr-Mktg - Educational Testing Service Inc.; *pg.* 1394, *pg.* 1111
Frederick, Kat, Sr VP-Product Strategy - Ticketmaster Entertainment LLC; *pg.* 1284, *pg.* 48
Frederick, Scott, Mgr-Mktg Bus Dev - Schneider Electric; *pg.* 467, *pg.* 1609
Frederick, Stacey A., Area Mgr-Mktg - Sunoco Inc.; *pg.* 985, *pg.* 1571
Fredericks, Darlene M., Mgr-Mktg - Hewlett-Packard Company; *pg.* 404, *pg.* 175
Fredericks, Leslie, Assoc Mgr-Digital Mktg - Bridgestone Americas, Inc.; *pg.* 201, *pg.* 1649
Frederickson, George, Dir-Software Mktg-Global - Dell Inc.; *pg.* 383, *pg.* 1737
Frederiksen, John, VP-Product Mgmt - NetApp, Inc.; *pg.* 444, *pg.* 287
Frederking, Chuck, Reg Mgr-Sls - Cooper Interconnect; *pg.* 630, *pg.* 1118
Fredette, John, Mgr-Media & Sponsorship Mktg-Worldwide - International Business Machines Corporation; *pg.* 418, *pg.* 1138
Fredman, Ken, Head-Digital Mktg-Global - The Bank of New York Mellon Corporation; *pg.* 720, *pg.* 1200
Fredo, Mark, Dir-Creative - The Weather Channel LLC; *pg.* 320, *pg.* 523
Fredrickson, Cathy Lee, Mgr-Social Media - Casey's General Stores, Inc.; *pg.* 1017, *pg.* 701
Fredrickson, Gary, Mgr-Sls - Diehl Woodworking Machinery, Inc.; *pg.* 1328, *pg.* 698
Fredrickson, Karen, Mgr-Mktg - United States Postal Service; *pg.* 1009, *pg.* 406
Fredrickson, Mike, Mgr-Sls-Wire Div - Loos & Company, Inc.; *pg.* 1356, *pg.* 368
Fredrickson, Robert A., VP-Carrier Networks Sls - ADTRAN, Inc.; *pg.* 344, *pg.* 6
Free, Elene L., Art Buyer-Adv - J.C. Penney Company, Inc.; *pg.* 1774, *pg.* 1732
Free, Melissa, VP-Mktg-Las Vegas Reg - Caesars Entertainment Corporation; *pg.* 1083, *pg.* 1023
Free, Vicky, CMO & Exec VP-Mktg & Brand Strategy - BET Holdings LLC; *pg.* 271, *pg.* 396
Freeborn, Aubrey, Sr VP-Mktg & Product Mgmt-Digital Distr - 20th Century Fox Film Corp.; *pg.* 267, *pg.* 124
Freed, Andrew, Dir-Product Mktg & Talent Solutions - LinkedIn Corporation; *pg.* 1262, *pg.* 160
Freed, Jen, Assoc Dir-Sourcing, Consulting, Comml Analytics & Sls - Boehringer Ingelheim Pharmaceuticals, Inc.; *pg.* 1507, *pg.* 368
Freed, Sharon, Sr VP-Mktg - Interval Leisure Group, Inc.; *pg.* 1912, *pg.* 443
Freed, Vicki, Sr VP-Sls, Trade Support & Svc - Royal Caribbean Cruises Ltd; *pg.* 1921, *pg.* 446
Freedland, Jeanne, Specialist-Digital Sls - Putman Media, Inc.; *pg.* 1679, *pg.* 621
Freedman, Andrew, Acct Dir-Programmatic Sls-East - Demand Media, Inc.; *pg.* 1238, *pg.* 273
Freedman, Dennis, Exec VP & Dir-Creative - Barneys New York, Inc.; *pg.* 38, *pg.* 1201
Freedman, Jennie, Mgr-Mktg Comm - Dorel Juvenile Group, Inc.; *pg.* 923, *pg.* 676
Freedman, Tj, Brand Mgr-CVS Shopper Mktg - Colgate-Palmolive Company; *pg.* 504, *pg.* 1215
Freeland, Heather Hopkins, Head-Mktg Comm-Global - Facebook, Inc.; *pg.* 1245, *pg.* 143
Freeland, Jonathan, VP-Product Mktg-Natl - Cox Communications, Inc.; *pg.* 279, *pg.* 501
Freeland, Marney, Dir-Engagement Mktg - Allrecipes.com; *pg.* 1226, *pg.* 1831
Freeland, Scott, Sr Mgr-Consumer Mktg & ECommerce - AutoTrader, Inc.; *pg.* 1230, *pg.* 490
Freeley, Katherine, Sr Mgr-Source - Colgate-Palmolive Company; *pg.* 504, *pg.* 1215
Freeman, Amber, Mgr-PR - Manhattan Associates, Inc.; *pg.* 430, *pg.* 513
Freeman, Andrea, VP-Mktg - AARON'S, INC.; *pg.* 912, *pg.* 486
Freeman, Andrew, Mgr-Comml Mktg-Natl Accounts - Heineken USA Inc.; *pg.* 252, *pg.* 1352
Freeman, Brady, VP-Sls-Natl Accts - Eby-Brown Co.; *pg.* 1767, *pg.* 636
Freeman, Brenda, Head-TV Mktg-Global - DreamWorks Animation SKG, Inc.; *pg.* 284, *pg.* 96
Freeman, Chris G., Dir-Oncology Mktg - Gilead Sciences, Inc.; *pg.* 1535, *pg.* 88
Freeman, Christopher, Sr Mgr-Platform Innovation & Global Ops - Burger King Corporation; *pg.* 1719, *pg.* 440
Freeman, Dina, Strategist-Social & Blog - BabyCenter, LLC; *pg.* 1231, *pg.* 212
Freeman, Erin, VP-PR - Janus Capital Group, Inc.; *pg.* 772, *pg.* 320
Freeman, Jonathan S., Sr VP-Global Product Supply - World Kitchen LLC; *pg.* 1141, *pg.* 657
Freeman, Kim, Mgr-Global PR - General Electric Company; *pg.* 1297, *pg.* 347
Freeman, Mark, Mgr-Mktg Info - Caterpillar, Inc.; *pg.* 1321,

pg. 650
Freeman, Michael, VP-Adv - California Milk Advisory Board; *pg.* 843, *pg.* 149
Freeman, Rachel L., Dir-Mktg - Cigna Corporation; *pg.* 1197, *pg.* 338
Freeman, Rick, Global Product Mgr-Intelligent Devices - GE Intelligent Platforms; *pg.* 1339, *pg.* 1777
Freeman, Robert, Analyst-Customer Mktg - American Express Company; *pg.* 712, *pg.* 1190
Freeman, Seth, Dir-Mktg-Holiday Inn Express Americas - InterContinental Hotels Corporation; *pg.* 1097, *pg.* 511
Freeman, Shawn, Dir-Interactive Mktg - GNC Holdings Inc.; *pg.* 1537, *pg.* 1576
Freeman, Ted, Designer-Pkg & Graphics-Global Product & Branding - The Home Depot, Inc.; *pg.* 1050, *pg.* 510
Freeman, Terrence, Head-Americas Digital Mktg & Dir - BlackRock, Inc.; *pg.* 724, *pg.* 1203
Freemond, Kathryn, Sr Mgr-Consumer Activation - The Kraft Heinz Company; *pg.* 871, *pg.* 641
Freer, Steve, Mgr-Creative Svcs - Tribune Media Company; *pg.* 1696, *pg.* 592
Freese, Shauna, Dir-Global Brand Mktg-Roxy - Quiksilver, Inc.; *pg.* 31, *pg.* 104
Freestone, David, Exec Dir-Sys Mktg - Cepheid; *pg.* 1514, *pg.* 284
Freet, Brad, Sr Dir-Product Quality & Innovation - Hilton Worldwide, Inc.; *pg.* 1094, *pg.* 1791
Freeze, David, Mgr-Sls - Lufkin Industries, Inc.; *pg.* 1357, *pg.* 1726
Freeze, Jim, CMO & Sr VP - Aspect Software, Inc.; *pg.* 354, *pg.* 813
Frego, Jake, Sr VP-Affinity Products - Bank of America Global Wealth & Investment Management; *pg.* 720, *pg.* 789
Freher, Paul, Dir-Media - BUFFALO WILD WINGS, INC.; *pg.* 1718, *pg.* 931
Frehn, Carla, Dir-Corp Mktg - AmerisourceBergen Corporation; *pg.* 1493, *pg.* 1522
Freidenberg, Jake, Program Dir-Mktg - The Hartford Financial Services Group, Inc.; *pg.* 1202, *pg.* 352
Freiheit, Ronald R., Dir-Product Dev & Acoustics - Wenger Corporation; *pg.* 1307, *pg.* 952
Freij, Maha, VP-Sls & Mktg - Les Trois Petits Cochons, Inc.; *pg.* 874, *pg.* 1146
Freiland, Brian, Mgr-Portfolio Mktg - Lippincott Williams & Wilkins, Inc.; *pg.* 1659, *pg.* 1567
Freiman, James R., Sr VP-Strategy, Media Sls & Bus Dev - The Street, Inc.; *pg.* 1283, *pg.* 1296
Freire, Lissette, Dir-Diversity Mktg & Comm - UnitedHealth Group Incorporated; *pg.* 1221, *pg.* 950
Freitas, Kate, Sr Analyst-Sls Ops - Intuit Inc.; *pg.* 769, *pg.* 158
Freitas, Nathan, Dir-Mktg - salesforce.com, inc.; *pg.* 1278, *pg.* 226
Frelinghuysen, John, Exec VP-Digital Media, Strategy & Bus Dev - The Walt Disney Company; *pg.* 317, *pg.* 52
Fremar, Leanne, Sr VP & Dir-Creative-Women's - Under Armour, Inc.; *pg.* 49, *pg.* 759
Fremaux, Ellen, Mgr-Sls & Mktg - Lawry's Restaurants, Inc.; *pg.* 1735, *pg.* 180
Fremder, Michael, Mgr-Global Corp Mktg - Red Hat, Inc.; *pg.* 460, *pg.* 1388
Fremin, Traci, Reg Mgr-Sls - Atlantic Aviation Corporation; *pg.* 224, *pg.* 1729
French, Alison, Head-Product Portfolio-Rewards & Recognition - International Business Machines Corporation; *pg.* 418, *pg.* 1138
French, Christine, Specialist-Mktg - Varian Medical Systems, Inc.; *pg.* 1434, *pg.* 178
French, David, Sr VP-Mktg, Comm & Corp Partnerships - National Park Foundation; *pg.* 1000, *pg.* 402
French, Edward, CMO & Chief Sls Officer - The Ritz-Carlton Hotel Company LLC; *pg.* 1110, *pg.* 766
French, Janie, Sr Mgr-Bus Dev - SRS Real Estate Partners; *pg.* 1113, *pg.* 1687
French, Jenni, Product Mgr - Microsoft Corporation; *pg.* 435, *pg.* 1824
French, Laura, Specialist-CEMS Product - O'Brien Corporation; *pg.* 1366, *pg.* 1001
French, Mel, Coord-Mktg Comm - Parker Chomerics; *pg.* 662, *pg.* 862
French, Nick, Mgr-Website & Mobile Product Mgmt - Zappos.com, Inc.; *pg.* 1291, *pg.* 1030
French, Ryan, Sr Mgr-Corn Mktg - Dupont Pioneer; *pg.* 1795, *pg.* 708
French, Terry, Dir-Sls Admin, Book & Directory - RR Donnelley; *pg.* 1682, *pg.* 838
French, Tricia G., Sr VP-Database Mktg - Bank of America Corporation; *pg.* 718, *pg.* 1362
French, Whitney, Sr Mgr-ECommerce - CafePress.com, Inc.; *pg.* 1234, *pg.* 254
Frendo, Jenny, Sr Mgr-Mktg - Verizon Communications Inc.; *pg.* 1875, *pg.* 1309
Frenkel, Anna, Head-NY Partnerships & Mktg - Airbnb, Inc.; *pg.* 1226, *pg.* 211
Frennea, Robert, Exec VP & Gen Mgr-Mdse - Academy Sports & Outdoors, Ltd.; *pg.* 1824, *pg.* 1724
Frericks, Anson, Sr Dir-Brand Activation - Anheuser-Busch Companies, LLC; *pg.* 237, *pg.* 991
Frericks, Chris, Brand Mgr - The Procter & Gamble Company; *pg.* 1129, *pg.* 1418
Freshman, Amy, Sr Dir-Talent Acq - Automatic Data Processing, Inc.; *pg.* 357, *pg.* 1117
Fretz, Courtney, Dir-European Sls-Adhesives & Functional Matls - THE DOW CHEMICAL COMPANY; *pg.* 1157, *pg.* 898
Freund, Heather, Mgr-Adv - American Century Investments; *pg.* 711, *pg.* 980
Freund, Julie, Acct Mgr-Sls - Anaheim/Orange County Visitor & Convention Bureau; *pg.* 988, *pg.* 42
Freundlich, Hayley, Dir-Diverse Markets & Mktg Support - MetLife, Inc.; *pg.* 1208, *pg.* 1258
Frew, Christopher, VP-Sls - ATT Holding Co.; *pg.* 1043, *pg.* 1519
Frew, Courtenay, Sr Mgr-CRM - Newell Rubbermaid Inc.; *pg.* 1128, *pg.* 515
Frey, Beth, Dir-Integrated Mktg - HSN, Inc.; *pg.* 291, *pg.* 462
Frey, Debbie, Sr Mgr-Corp Comm - Comcast Corporation; *pg.* 276, *pg.* 1560
Frey, Debra, VP-Integrated Mktg - FMR LLC (Fidelity Investments); *pg.* 759, *pg.* 794
Frey, Doug, Interim Pres-Allstate Dealer Svcs - The Allstate Corporation; *pg.* 1189, *pg.* 639
Frey, Kelly, Dir-PR-Womenswear - Hugo Boss Fashions Inc.; *pg.* 42, *pg.* 1242
Frey, Nancy, Dir-Mktg Svcs - Kendall-Jackson Wine Estates, Ltd.; *pg.* 1965, *pg.* 277
Frey, Pete, Sr Officer-Mktg - SeaWorld Parks & Entertainment LLC; *pg.* 582, *pg.* 456
Frey, Rick, Sr VP-Print & Creative Svcs - The CW Television Network; *pg.* 632, *pg.* 52
Frey, Scott J., Mgr-Mktg Comm - Victaulic Company; *pg.* 1066, *pg.* 1529
Freyder, Sofia, Dir-Product Mgmt & Head-Bus - MasterCard Incorporated; *pg.* 779, *pg.* 1325
Freyermuth, Erin, Dir-Digital Mktg - Fox Sports Net; *pg.* 288, *pg.* 131
Freyre, Fabio, Dir-Adv - Facebook, Inc.; *pg.* 1245, *pg.* 143
Freyre, Pedro, Strategist-Mktg - 3M Company; *pg.* 1142, *pg.* 956
Freytes Dever, Janet, Mgr-Relationship Mktg & Brdcst Integrations - The Walt Disney Company; *pg.* 317, *pg.* 52
Frias, Tim, Engr-Technical Mktg - Cisco Systems, Inc.; *pg.* 372, *pg.* 240
Friberg, John, Dir-Customer Mktg - Mattel Games/Puzzles; *pg.* 962, *pg.* 80
Friberg, John, Dir-Customer Mktg - MATTEL, INC.; *pg.* 962, *pg.* 81
Fricano, John, Reg Mgr-Sls-Tenax Filament - Toho Tenax America, Inc.; *pg.* 1184, *pg.* 1655
Frick, Andrew, Dir-Sls - Ford Motor Company; *pg.* 172, *pg.* 876
Frick, David, Brand Mgr - Vail Resorts, Inc.; *pg.* 1117, *pg.* 313
Fricke, Doug, Dir-Trade Show Mktg - National Pork Producers Council; *pg.* 150, *pg.* 712
Fricke, Melissa, Brand Mgr - Activision Blizzard, Inc.; *pg.* 948, *pg.* 271
Fricke, Pierre, Dir-Product Line Mgmt & Mktg - Red Hat, Inc.; *pg.* 460, *pg.* 1388
Friday, Celena, Mgr-Brand & Mktg Comm-North America - Shell Oil Company; *pg.* 984, *pg.* 1714
Friday, Jennifer, Mgr-Natl Sls-Northeast, Southeast & Canada - Tampa Bay & Co.; *pg.* 1007, *pg.* 476
Friday, Susan, Dir-Mobile Product Mgmt - American Express Company; *pg.* 712, *pg.* 1190
Friddle, Jassy, Mgr-Mktg - Lennar Homes, Inc.; *pg.* 1101, *pg.* 443
Fridell, Brian, Sr VP-East Coast, Midwest & Canadian Sls - DefyMedia; *pg.* 1237, *pg.* 1222
Fried, Alex P., Mgr-Mehoopany PR, HSE & Energy Affairs - The Procter & Gamble Company; *pg.* 1129, *pg.* 1418
Fried, Alison, Sr VP-Fin & Ops-Digital & Print Media - Time Inc.; *pg.* 1693, *pg.* 1300
Fried, William, Sr Dir-Medical - Aetna Inc.; *pg.* 1187, *pg.* 351
Friedeman, Thad, Mgr-Creative Strategies - South Dakota's Department of Tourism; *pg.* 1006, *pg.* 1624
Frieden, James, Sr Mgr-Mktg Res-Bioscience - Baxter International Inc.; *pg.* 1499, *pg.* 599
Friedensohn, Caitlin, Mgr-Mktg - Scripps Networks Interactive, Inc.; *pg.* 1279, *pg.* 1638
Frieder, Stephen, Head-Americas Sls, Ops & Digital Mktg Bus - Adobe Systems Incorporated; *pg.* 342, *pg.* 235
Friedland, Andy, Mgr-CPG Media - Amazon.com, Inc.; *pg.* 1226, *pg.* 1831
Friedland, Paul, Dir-Mktg - Levi Strauss & Co.; *pg.* 43, *pg.* 220
Friedland-Howard, Kathy, VP-Adv - ShopKo; *pg.* 1785, *pg.* 1860
Friedlander, Alana, Mgr-Digital Brand Mktg-DoubleTree by Hilton - Hilton Worldwide, Inc.; *pg.* 1094, *pg.* 1791
Friedler, Mark, Sr Dir - Oracle Corporation; *pg.* 450, *pg.* 191
Friedler, Teri, Mgr-Mktg-Strategic Growth Initiatives & Consulting - Hewlett-Packard Company; *pg.* 404, *pg.* 175
Friedly, Gabrielle, Sr Mgr-Global Customer Mktg - ABB; *pg.* 340, *pg.* 486
Friedman, Abraham, Dir-Online Mktg - Adorama Camera Inc.; *pg.* 1398, *pg.* 1187
Friedman, Alison, Dir-Integrated Promo & Mktg-Redbook - The Hearst Corporation; *pg.* 1649, *pg.* 1239
Friedman, Brandon, Dir-Creative - Moe's Southwest Grill, LLC; *pg.* 1027, *pg.* 514
Friedman, Casie, Sr Dir-Global Distr & Sls - The Jim Henson Company; *pg.* 293, *pg.* 103
Friedman, Claire, Reg Mgr-Sls - Tremor Video; *pg.* 682, *pg.* 1305
Friedman, Deb, Sr Dir-Nike Women's NA - NIKE, Inc.; *pg.* 1812, *pg.* 1492
Friedman, Debra, Coord-Product-Comm - Lennox International Inc.; *pg.* 1073, *pg.* 1736
Friedman, Eric, Dir-Sls & Revenue Ops - FourSquare Labs, Inc; *pg.* 1248, *pg.* 1232
Friedman, Erica, Mgr-Healthcare Pro Mktg - Abbott Diabetes Care, Inc.; *pg.* 1483, *pg.* 38
Friedman, Ginny, Grp Brand Dir - Neutrogena Corporation; *pg.* 517, *pg.* 137
Friedman, Greg, Head-Product & Strategy-SelectCo - FMR LLC (Fidelity Investments); *pg.* 759, *pg.* 794
Friedman, Gregg, VP-Creative - Chico's FAS, Inc.; *pg.* 21, *pg.* 427
Friedman, Heather, Sr Mgr-Mktg-The Home Decorators Collection - The Home Depot, Inc.; *pg.* 1050, *pg.* 510
Friedman, Jordan, Sr Mgr-Mktg - Intuit Inc.; *pg.* 769, *pg.* 158
Friedman, Josh, Head-Creative, Sponsorships & Media - Google Inc.; *pg.* 1249, *pg.* 153
Friedman, Lauren, Mgr-Mktg - Cisco Systems, Inc.; *pg.* 372, *pg.* 240
Friedman, Lindsay, Sr Mgr-Licensing & Partnerships - Activision Blizzard, Inc.; *pg.* 948, *pg.* 271
Friedman, Lisa, Head-QuickBooks Online Customer Mktg & ARPC - Intuit Inc.; *pg.* 769, *pg.* 158
Friedman, Matthew, Sr product Mgr-PXI platform - National Instruments Corporation; *pg.* 443, *pg.* 1664
Friedman, Paul, VP & Dir Creative-On-Air Promo - CBS Corporation; *pg.* 273, *pg.* 1210
Friedman, Pete, VP-Product Dev & Quality Mgmt & Facilities - ACH Food Companies, Inc.; *pg.* 835, *pg.* 1631
Friedman, Randi, Exec Dir-PR - ELLE.com; *pg.* 1242, *pg.* 1227
Friedman, Samantha, Sr Coord-Online Mktg - QVC Inc; *pg.* 305, *pg.* 1593
Friedman, Sean, Brand Mgr - Weiman Products, LLC; *pg.* 337, *pg.* 616
Friedman, Shoshana, Mgr-Mktg Integration - United States Cellular Corporation; *pg.* 1875, *pg.* 594
Friedman-Perez, Jennifer, Sr Dir-Mktg Intelligence-Allure - Vogue Magazine; *pg.* 1700, *pg.* 1311
Friedmann, Jennifer, Mgr-Mktg Comm - Jiffy Lube International, Inc.; *pg.* 209, *pg.* 1709
Friedson, Jill, Assoc Publr-Mktg - Conde Nast Publications, Inc.; *pg.* 1629, *pg.* 1217
Friedson, Jill, Assoc Publr-Mktg & Bus Dev - Vogue Magazine; *pg.* 1700, *pg.* 1311
Friend, David, Editor-Creative Dev-Vanity Fair - Conde Nast Publications, Inc.; *pg.* 1629, *pg.* 1217
Friend, David, Editor-Creative Dev-Vanity Fair - Vanity Fair; *pg.* 1699, *pg.* 1308
Friend, Kent, Sr VP-Sls & Mktg - Kraco Enterprises, LLC; *pg.*

210, pg. 68
Friend, Kristine, Sr Dir-Segment Mktg - Marriott International, Inc.; pg. 1102, pg. 764
Friend, Tommy, Mgr-Consumer Mktg - AutoTrader, Inc.; pg. 1230, pg. 490
Fries, Laura, Mgr-Social Content Strategy-Pinterest, YouTube & Apron Blog - The Home Depot, Inc.; pg. 1050, pg. 510
Fries, Patti, Gen Mgr-Mktg Res & Consumer Insights - DISH Network Corporation; pg. 283, pg. 325
Friese, Whit, VP-Creative-Mktg - Cable News Network LP; pg. 1624, pg. 1208
Friesen, Kelvin, VP-Sls & Mktg - Sauder Manufacturing Company; pg. 941, pg. 1403
Friesen, Larissa, Brand Mgr-Platforms & Innovation - Plum Organics; pg. 890, pg. 85
Friesen, Shea, Mgr-Mktg & Innovation-Own Brands - Safeway Inc.; pg. 1032, pg. 184
Friesen, Tim, Product Mgr - Acklands-Grainger Inc.; pg. 197, pg. 1933
Friesinger, Jim, VP-Sls - Atlantic Corporation; pg. 1452, pg. 1392
Friesner, Donna, Mgr-Customer Svc & Inside Sls - KLW Plastics, Inc.; pg. 1463, pg. 1465
Friess, Joanne, Assoc VP-Creative & Brand - L Brands, Inc.; pg. 1776, pg. 1441
Frieswyk, Mike, Dir-IOT Innovation Sls-Global - Intel Corporation; pg. 645, pg. 266
Frigo, Cara M., Assoc Product Mgr-Reporting Solutions - MORNINGSTAR, INC.; pg. 784, pg. 583
Frimere, Ira, Sr Dir-Events Tech - Gartner, Inc.; pg. 1248, pg. 374
Frink, Randy, Sr Dir-Corp Mktg - CME Group Inc.; pg. 738, pg. 571
Frisch, Adam, VP-Digital Sls & Mktg - Bank of America Corporation; pg. 718, pg. 1362
Frish, Richard, Gen Mgr-Sls-99.5 The WOLF - Cumulus Media Inc.; pg. 280, pg. 503
Frisher, Beth, Mgr-Bus Dev & Intl Mktg - Port of Oakland; pg. 1920, pg. 172
Frisina, Paul, Dir-Retail Sls - Clougherty Packing Company; pg. 848, pg. 128
Fristik, Joseph A., Corp VP-Accts & Mktg-Natl - Rheem Manufacturing Company; pg. 1075, pg. 519
Fritch, Jennifer, Dir-Immuno-Oncology Melanoma Mktg Bristol-Myers Squibb Company; pg. 1509, pg. 1206
Fritchen, Robert, Brand Mgr-Sls-Modine Unitary Products - Modine Manufacturing Company; pg. 1074, pg. 1888
Fritsche, Anne, Sr Dir-Consumer & Marketplace Insights - Beam Suntory Inc.; pg. 1957, pg. 599
Fritsche, Tony, Mgr-Brand Mktg - Target Corporation; pg. 1786, pg. 942
Fritts, Erin, Mgr-Local Mktg - Panera Bread Company; pg. 1029, pg. 1001
Fritts, Lauren, Dir-Mktg-Global - PepsiCo, Inc.; pg. 259, pg. 1327
Fritts, Sidney, Sr Mgr-Design-Global DownyLenor & Unstopables - The Procter & Gamble Company; pg. 1129, pg. 1418
Fritz, Charles, Mgr-Direct Export Sls-Europe - Magnetic Metals Corp.; pg. 1358, pg. 1049
Fritz, Eric, Sr Mgr-Sys Bus Ops - ADTRAN, Inc.; pg. 344, pg. 6
Fritz, Greg, Sr VP-Home Entertainment & Consumer Products - Big Idea, Inc.; pg. 271, pg. 1632
Fritz, Kristin, Sr Dir-Content Mktg & Digital Marketplace Dev - Penguin Random House; pg. 1675, pg. 1276
Fritz, Pascal, Designer-Global Brand-Nike SB - NIKE, Inc.; pg. 1812, pg. 1492
Fritzges, Mariah, Mgr-Mktg - Knott's Berry Farm; pg. 556, pg. 50
Frizalone, Cathie, Sr Dir-Sls & Market Support & Imaging Sys - Philips Electronics North America; pg. 662, pg. 782
Frizzell, Alexandra, Mgr-Relationship Care Strategy-New Product Dev - American Express Company; pg. 712, pg. 1190
Froatz, Denise, Sr Product Mgr-Respiratory Mktg - Boehringer Ingelheim Pharmaceuticals, Inc.; pg. 1507, pg. 368
Frodsham, James, Chief Strategy Officer & Sr VP - CIENA Corporation; pg. 628, pg. 771
Froehlich, Rick C., Exec VP-Products & Consumer - EarthLink Holdings Corp.; pg. 1240, pg. 504
Froehlingsdorf, Tanja, Mgr-Channel Mktg - Brocade Communications Systems, Inc.; pg. 365, pg. 239
Froemming, Hagan, Mgr-Digital Mktg - The Home Depot, Inc.; pg. 1050, pg. 510
Froeschner, Kimberly, Mgr-Web Mktg-GTS, Cloud & TSS - IBM; pg. 410, pg. 1449
Froggatt, Vickie, Specialist-Comm-Integrated Mktg - Cisco Systems, Inc.; pg. 372, pg. 240
Frogge, Doug, Sr Mgr-Mktg - H&R Block, Inc.; pg. 764, pg. 983
Frogge, Robert, Dir-Digital Mktg - Service Corporation International; pg. 1395, pg. 1714
Frohman, Trish, Exec VP-Sports Sls Strategy & Partnerships - NBC Universal, Inc.; pg. 300, pg. 1266
Frolov, Ilia, Bus Mgr-Protection Technologies-Canada - Liqui-Box Corporation; pg. 1464, pg. 1802
Frolova, Maryna, Mgr-Social Media & PR - Digital River, Inc.; pg. 1238, pg. 948
Frome, Chris, Sr Dir-Event Presentation - St. Louis Blues Hockey Club, LLC; pg. 585, pg. 1003
Fromm, Justin, Head-Ad Sls Res & Dir - Hulu LLC; pg. 1257, pg. 274
Frommer, Ellen, Product Mgr-Multi-Device Protection Pack - AT&T Mobility LLC; pg. 619, pg. 488
Frommer, Jennifer, Head-Talent & Production - Conde Nast Publications, Inc.; pg. 1629, pg. 1217
Frommer, Tim, Sr Mgr-Loyalty Partnerships - Expedia, Inc.; pg. 1244, pg. 1814
Fromson, Sarah, Dir-Integrated Mktg-Kmart Apparel - Sears Holdings Corporation; pg. 1784, pg. 618
Froning, David, Principal & Product Mgr - SAS Institute Inc.; pg. 466, pg. 1361
Fronk, Shawna, Mgr-Health Solutions Mktg - HealthPartners, Inc.; pg. 1203, pg. 918
Fronti, Luca, Mgr-Mktg - Maserati North America, Inc.; pg. 183, pg. 1060
Frost, Andy, VP-Product Strategy - ACT Inc.; pg. 597, pg. 708
Frost, Betsy, Assoc Mgr-Mktg - General Mills, Inc.; pg. 828, pg. 933
Frost, Garrison, Dir-Mktg & Comm - National Audubon Society; pg. 148, pg. 1263
Frost, Gatorade, Supvr-Production - The Gatorade Company; pg. 251, pg. 574
Frost, Laura, Specialist-Mktg - IBM; pg. 410, pg. 1449
Frost, Leslie, Mgr-Mktg Comm - Stratasys, Inc.; pg. 476, pg. 923
Frost, Lizzy, Brand Mgr-Girls Licensed Entertainment Brands-Global - MATTEL, INC.; pg. 962, pg. 81
Frost, Matt, Head-Strategy & Partnerships-Chrome Media - Google Inc.; pg. 1249, pg. 153
Frost, Shirra, Dir-Mobile Mktg - Fiserv, Inc.; pg. 397, pg. 1855
Frost, Woody, VP-Global Sls & Svc - Stratasys, Inc.; pg. 476, pg. 923
Froyen, Scott, VP-Sls - Wellmark, Inc; pg. 1223, pg. 707
Frucci, Coley, VP-Sls-Americas & Asia Pac - Turtle Wax, Inc.; pg. 220, pg. 671
Fruechtnicht, Mark, Mgr-Product Mgmt & Plng - Porsche Cars North America, Inc.; pg. 189, pg. 518
Fruehstorfer, Amy, VP-Digital Mktg - JPMorgan Chase & Co.; pg. 772, pg. 1246
Frugoli, Heather, Dir-Mktg-New England - Comcast Sportsnet; pg. 278, pg. 1562
Frusci, Nicole, VP-Brand & Digital Mktg-US - Benefit Cosmetics LLC; pg. 501, pg. 213
Frushour, Krenda, Assoc Dir-Mktg-US Solutions - Mead Johnson Nutrition Company; pg. 1561, pg. 615
Frutchey, Julie, Program Mktg Mgr-Pub Sector - Red Hat, Inc.; pg. 460, pg. 1388
Frutiger, Donna, Mgr-Distr Mktg - Intel Corporation; pg. 645, pg. 266
Frutos-Smith, Deborah, Sr Dir-State Advocacy & Alliance Dev - GlaxoSmithKline; pg. 1536, pg. 1565
Fry, David, Mgr-Corp Mktg Fin - The Procter & Gamble Company; pg. 1129, pg. 1418
Fry, DeAnna, Sr Mgr-Strategic Sourcing Svcs & Utilities - Cracker Barrel Old Country Store, Inc.; pg. 1723, pg. 1639
Fry, Diana, Sr Specialist-Social Media - Universal Technical Institute, Inc.; pg. 608, pg. 24
Fry, Greg, Sr Mgr-Product Dev - Naked Juice Company, Inc.; pg. 882, pg. 150
Fry, Jason, Sr Dir-Product Mgmt - Equifax Inc.; pg. 748, pg. 504
Fry, Jay, Sr VP-Mktg - New Relic, Inc.; pg. 445, pg. 224
Fry, Jen, Coord-Mktg & Events - Insight Enterprises, Inc.; pg. 415, pg. 26
Fry, Jordan, Asst Mgr-Mktg-Grocery - Wal-Mart Stores, Inc.; pg. 1790, pg. 29
Fry, Karen, VP-Mktg - SunPower Corporation; pg. 1952, pg. 250
Fry, Robert, Dir-Product Mdsg & Design-Global - Mountain Hardwear, Inc.; pg. 1839, pg. 193
Frydenlund, Al, Mgr-Sls & Mktg-Bids & Estimating - Deco Products Co.; pg. 1045, pg. 704
Frye, Ellen, Media Planner - Buckman; pg. 1150, pg. 1641
Frye, Jeffery R., Assoc Mgr-Adv Production - Abbott Laboratories; pg. 1484, pg. 551
Frye, Jennifer, Office Mgr-Sls & Mktg Svcs - American Woodmark Corporation; pg. 913, pg. 1811
Frye, Joseph, Mgr-Coal Mktg-Indus Coal - Norfolk Southern Corporation; pg. 1917, pg. 1797
Frye, Steven, Mgr-Mktg-California Pizza Kitchen - Nestle USA, Inc.; pg. 883, pg. 96
Frye, Tracy, Sr Mgr-Sls - Whirlpool Corporation; pg. 62, pg. 872
Fryer, Carolina, Dir-Mktg Innovation - The WhiteWave Foods Company; pg. 1037, pg. 324
Fryer, Emma, Head-EMEA Mktg Comm - Tomy; pg. 968, pg. 648
Fryer, Laura, Dir-NA Wholesale Mktg - SmartWool; pg. 32, pg. 335
Fryer, Todd, Dir-Private Label Mktg - Smart & Final, Inc.; pg. 1034, pg. 66
Fryling, Michelle, Exec Dir-Comm & Media Rels - University of Pennsylvania; pg. 609, pg. 1571
Frysinger, Krista, Mgr-Olympic Sponsorship Mktg - Deloitte & Touche USA LLP; pg. 743, pg. 1222
Frystak, Dan, Mgr-Mktg - CDW Corporation; pg. 370, pg. 663
Fu, Bo, Sr Product Mgr - VMware, Inc.; pg. 490, pg. 179
Fu, Dennis, Sr Mgr-Mktg-New Product Commercialization - Amgen Inc.; pg. 1493, pg. 291
Fu, Mark, Sr Dir-Mktg - Cypress Semiconductor Corporation; pg. 1326, pg. 243
Fu, Shana, Client Svcs Mgr-Mktg-Tech Solutions - Ingram Micro Inc.; pg. 415, pg. 261
Fuchs, Jennifer, Project Mgr-IT, Social Media & Knowledge Mgmt - Honeywell International Inc.; pg. 407, pg. 1088
Fuchs, Ken, VP & Grp Head-Yahoo Sports, Yahoo Fin & Product Partnerships - Yahoo! Inc.; pg. 1289, pg. 289
Fuelling, John, Mgr-Production - Art's-Way Manufacturing Co., Inc.; pg. 701, pg. 701
Fuentes, Johanna, Sr VP-Corp PR - Showtime Networks Inc.; pg. 308, pg. 1291
Fuentes, Kylie, VP-Digital Product Mgmt - Rodan + Fields, LLC; pg. 522, pg. 225
Fuentes, Patricia, Sr Mgr-Comm - Capital One Financial Corporation; pg. 730, pg. 1789
Fuerstenau, Tabby, Planner-Production - J.R. Simplot Company; pg. 867, pg. 547
Fugett, Rob, Dir-Inside Sls - Choice Hotels International, Inc.; pg. 1086, pg. 775
Fuggetta, Cara, Mgr-Mktg - SHUTTERFLY, INC.; pg. 1280, pg. 192
Fuhr, Sam, Mgr-Sls Promo - Shiseido Cosmetics America of SAC; pg. 522, pg. 1291
Fuhrer, Kyle, Dir-Mobile Products - Alaska Air Group, Inc.; pg. 1897, pg. 1830
Fuhrman, Victor, CIO & VP-Mktg - Awisco NY Corporation; pg. 1315, pg. 1177
Fuhrmann, Kathryn, Mgr-Mktg & Loyalty - Barnes & Noble, Inc.; pg. 1619, pg. 1201
Fuhrmann, Katie, Mgr-Integrated Shopper Mktg-Box Tops for Education - General Mills, Inc.; pg. 828, pg. 933
Fuji, Liane, VP & Dir-Creative - Wells Fargo & Company; pg. 819, pg. 232
Fujitsuka, Mikio, Grp Brand Dir - Johnson & Johnson; pg. 1549, pg. 1091
Fukawa, Jun, Head-The Creative Shop-Japan - Facebook, Inc.; pg. 1245, pg. 143
Fukaye, Jo, Mgr-Mktg Comm - Xcel Energy Inc.; pg. 1955, pg. 946
Fukuda, Diane, Mgr-Mktg Programs - Hewlett-Packard Company; pg. 404, pg. 175
Fukuhara, Renato, Dir-Mktg-New Categories - Coca-Cola North America; pg. 848, pg. 500
Fukumoto, Joel, Mgr-Product Education-University of Toyota - Toyota Motor Sales, U.S.A., Inc.; pg. 193, pg. 296
Fulay, Amit, Product Mgr - Google Inc.; pg. 1249, pg. 153
Fulbright, Terry D., Sr Mgr-Multifamily Dev - RealPage, Inc.; pg. 1277, pg. 1669
Fulcher, Megann A., Dir-Customer Mktg & Sls Support-Practice iQ - Aetna Inc.; pg. 1187, pg. 351
Fulco, Tony, Mgr-Mktg - 3M Company; pg. 1142, pg. 956
Fuld, Steven, Sr VP-Mktg - Sony Corporation of America; pg. 675, pg. 1293

Fulgham, Dale, Mgr-Sls & Product - Harodite Industries, Inc.; pg. 693, pg. 847
Fulginiti, Michael, Dir-Reg Mktg & Customer Excellence - Merck & Co., Inc.; pg. 1566, pg. 1077
Fulkerson, Rick, VP-Mktg - Garff Enterprises Inc.; pg. 174, pg. 1758
Fulks, Rick, Sr Dir-Aftermarket Ops - Meritor, Inc.; pg. 212, pg. 911
Fuller, Alexandra, Coord-Mktg CRM - Groupon, Inc.; pg. 1255, pg. 575
Fuller, Brandie, VP-Mktg - Great Dane Trailers; pg. 1707, pg. 539
Fuller, Eric, Dir-Pepsi Mktg-Music - PepsiCo, Inc.; pg. 259, pg. 1327
Fuller, George, Mgr-Mktg Partnership Activation - The Coca-Cola Company; pg. 240, pg. 493
Fuller, Jacqueline, Mgr-Mktg - MORNINGSTAR, INC.; pg. 784, pg. 583
Fuller, Jamie, Mgr-Paid Search-Digital Mktg - J.C. Penney Company, Inc.; pg. 1774, pg. 1732
Fuller, Kevin, VP-Product Mktg-Global - Nu Skin Enterprises, Inc.; pg. 518, pg. 1755
Fuller, Melony, Dir-Mktg & Formulations - National Enzyme Company; pg. 882, pg. 978
Fuller, Nicola B., Sr Mgr-Mktg - Accenture; pg. 1392, pg. 1186
Fuller, Rachel, Mgr-Shopper Mktg - Newell Rubbermaid Inc.; pg. 1128, pg. 515
Fuller, Ricky, Rep-Mktg - Hewlett-Packard Company; pg. 404, pg. 175
Fuller, Robyn, Mgr-Direct Response - World Wildlife Fund, Inc.; pg. 162, pg. 408
Fuller, Scott, Sr VP & Dir-Corp Mktg - Amegy Bank, N.A.; pg. 711, pg. 1700
Fuller, Scott, VP-Sls & Mktg - Post Glover Resistors Inc.; pg. 1585, pg. 727
Fuller, Stacy, Brand Mgr-No nonsense - Kayser-Roth Corporation; pg. 28, pg. 1374
Fuller, Tom, Dir-Global Product Dev-Charcoal Platform - Weber-Stephen Products LLC; pg. 62, pg. 650
Fullerton, Adam, Specialist-Retail Mktg - Carhartt, Inc.; pg. 39, pg. 875
Fullerton, Cody, VP-Sls & Education - Ouidad; pg. 519, pg. 1275
Fullerton, Julie, Sr Mgr-Mktg - Amgen Inc.; pg. 1493, pg. 291
Fullerton, Tricia, Exec Dir-Digital Mktg - People Magazine; pg. 1676, pg. 1278
Fullmer, Teresa, Coord-Mktg Fin - Sony Pictures Entertainment Inc.; pg. 309, pg. 72
Fulmer, Jane, Sr Analyst-EC Mktg - FedEx Corporation; pg. 1907, pg. 1642
Fulmer, Tracey, Sr Mgr-Mktg - American Express Company; pg. 712, pg. 1190
Fuloria, Prashant, Sr VP-Adv Products - Yahoo! Inc.; pg. 1289, pg. 289
Fulton, Dana, Mgr-Social Media Content & Education Financing - Wells Fargo & Company; pg. 819, pg. 232
Fulton, David, Dir-CRM Product Mgmt - Oracle Corporation; pg. 1272, pg. 786
Fulton, Doug, Dir-Mktg - Andersen Corporation; pg. 67, pg. 916
Fulton, Ellen M., Territory Mgr-Sls - Armstrong World Industries, Inc.; pg. 914, pg. 1545
Fulton, Heather, Coord-Mktg - Times Record News; pg. 1695, pg. 1749
Fulton, John, Product Mgr-Zebra Enterprise Solutions - Zebra Technologies Corporation; pg. 690, pg. 628
Fulton, Rob, Mgr-Mktg Events - Ford Motor Company; pg. 172, pg. 876
Fulton, Stacy, Team Head-SMB Sls - Google Inc.; pg. 1249, pg. 153
Fults, Christine, Dir-Sponsorships & Strategic Mktg Initiatives - Dell, Inc.; pg. 385, pg. 1037
Fultz, Linda, Mgr-Corp Comm & Mktg - Archer-Daniels-Midland Company; pg. 825, pg. 565
Funaski, Kyle, Dir-Mktg - KHON-TV; pg. 294, pg. 544
Funderburk, Mark, Mgr-Trade Mktg - BIC Corporation; pg. 501, pg. 369
Fundis, Christie L., Sr Reg Mgr-Mktg Sponsorships & Promos - AT&T; pg. 1865, pg. 258
Fung, Joseph, VP-HCM Products - NetSuite, Inc.; pg. 1270, pg. 255
Funk, Chris, Product Mgr-Mktg - Zippo Manufacturing Company, Inc.; pg. 1895, pg. 1518
Funk, Edric, Dir-Worldwide Product Mktg - The Toro Company; pg. 1065, pg. 918
Funk, Katie, Brand Mgr-Glade - S.C. Johnson & Son, Inc.; pg. 334, pg. 1889
Funk, Kurt, Dir-Mktg Programs & Events - The Phillies, L.P.; pg. 575, pg. 1569
Funk, Tom, Sr Mgr-Digital Product & Web Content - Keurig Green Mountain, Inc.; pg. 868, pg. 1768
Funk, Wes, Head-Integrated Mktg Plng - Adobe Systems Incorporated; pg. 342, pg. 235
Funk, Will, Sr VP-Sponsorship Sls, Integration & Branded Programming - Turner Broadcasting System, Inc.; pg. 314, pg. 521
Funkhouser, Dan, Dir-Comml Dealer Sls - Yokohama Tire Corporation; pg. 1892, pg. 94
Fuoti, Julie, VP-Mktg-Natl - Kaplan, Inc.; pg. 603, pg. 425
Fuqua, Chris, VP-Brand Mktg-Dunkin' Donuts & Global Consumer Insights - Dunkin' Brands Group, Inc.; pg. 1727, pg. 810
Fuqua, Kate, Sr Dir-Design - Coach, Inc.; pg. 3, pg. 1214
Furey, Joe, Sr Mgr-Tax - BDO Seidman, LLP; pg. 724, pg. 1202
Furgason, Bill, Mgr-Digital Mktg - Ford Motor Company; pg. 172, pg. 876
Furia, Evelyn, Brand Mgr - GlaxoSmithKline; pg. 1536, pg. 1565
Furia, Evelyn, Brand Mgr - GlaxoSmithKline Consumer Healthcare; pg. 510, pg. 1554
Furman, Amy, Sr Dir - GEICO Corporation; pg. 1200, pg. 399
Furman, David M., Pres-Sls & Mktg - NACCO Industries, Inc.; pg. 1174, pg. 1433
Furnari, Bruno, VP-Product Leadership - The Nielsen Company B.V.; pg. 1671, pg. 1272
Furnari, Leo, Mgr-Mktg Intelligence - Valassis Communications, Inc.; pg. 1287, pg. 897
Furnas, Thomas P., Sr Dir-Tech - ideastream; pg. 292, pg. 1431
Furnish, Peter, VP-Mktg - Cineplex Entertainment LP; pg. 275, pg. 1936
Furniss, Jon, Mgr-Comml Mktg-North America - Rockwell Automation, Inc.; pg. 668, pg. 1880
Furno, John, Gen Mgr-Sls - Press Communications, LLC; pg. 305, pg. 1090
Furr, Cherette, Brand Mgr-Olive Garden - Darden Restaurants, Inc.; pg. 1724, pg. 453
Furr, Mary-Price, VP-Mktg - Home Meridian International, Inc.; pg. 928, pg. 1379
Furrier, Tracy, Grp VP-Mktg - Affinion Group, Inc.; pg. 1225, pg. 372
Furrow, Brittni, Sr Dir-Sustainability-Global Food Buses - Wal-Mart.com; pg. 1287, pg. 50
Furst, Antoinette, Sr Analyst-Mktg - QUALCOMM Incorporated; pg. 1873, pg. 207
Furstenberg, Michael, Mgr-Mktg Comm - Aetna Inc.; pg. 1187, pg. 351
Furtkamp, Paul, Mgr-Sls-Natl - Yamaha Corporation of America; pg. 595, pg. 51
Furtkevic, Bill, VP-Mktg - Party City Corporation; pg. 1781, pg. 1116
Furtney, Brad, Sls Mgr-Agency Grp - Twitter, Inc.; pg. 1285, pg. 228
Furuta, Wesley, Product Mgr - Google Inc.; pg. 1249, pg. 153
Fusa, Lilia, Brand Mgr - Colgate-Palmolive Company; pg. 504, pg. 1215
Fusco, Antonia, Dir-Digital Consumer Mktg - American Media, Inc.; pg. 1615, pg. 410
Fusco, Kaitlyn, Mgr-PR - Mote Marine Laboratory, Inc.; pg. 564, pg. 466
Fusco, Timothy, VP-Academic Sls - Cengage Learning; pg. 1626, pg. 215
Fusco-Kemp, Elena, Dir-Customer Mktg & Managed Care - Merck & Co., Inc.; pg. 1566, pg. 1077
Fussell, Craig, Sr Mgr-Media & Adv - Medtronic, Inc.; pg. 1564, pg. 939
Fussell, Gayla, Reg Dir-Sls - Dallas Convention & Visitors Bureau; pg. 991, pg. 1678
Fussell, Jennifer P., Asst VP-Sls & Mktg - The Kansas City Southern Railway Company; pg. 1913, pg. 985
Fussell, Matt, Supvr-Mktg - SYNNEX Corporation; pg. 480, pg. 92
Fussenegger, Bernie, Dir-Digital Mktg - Papa John's International, Inc.; pg. 1743, pg. 737
Fuster, Ileana, Brand Mgr - The Procter & Gamble Company; pg. 1129, pg. 1418
Futrell, J. R, Product Mgr-Adv - YouTube, LLC; pg. 1291, pg. 198
Fylonenko, Jordan, Mgr-PR - Quicken Loans, Inc.; pg. 797, pg. 884
Fylypowycz, Robert, VP-Sls - G-III Apparel Group, Ltd.; pg. 41, pg. 1233
Fynan, Tamara, VP-Mktg Svcs - The J.M. Smucker Company; pg. 865, pg. 1468
Fynboh, Joselynne, Mgr-Mktg - General Mills, Inc.; pg. 828, pg. 933

G

Gabe, Jon, VP-Sls - Fred Usinger, Inc.; pg. 856, pg. 1874
Gabel, DeAnne, Sr Dir-IR - Spirit Airlines, Inc.; pg. 234, pg. 449
Gaber, Mohammad, Sr Mgr-Mktg-Indus Strategy & Mktg-Travel & Hospitality - Adobe Systems Incorporated; pg. 342, pg. 235
Gable, Greg, Sr VP-Corp PR - Charles Schwab & Company, Inc.; pg. 734, pg. 215
Gabriel, David, Sr VP-Print, Sls & Mktg-Marvel Publ Worldwide - Marvel Entertainment, LLC; pg. 1662, pg. 1257
Gabriel, Howard, Exec VP-Mktg - Warner Bros. Records, Inc.; pg. 1791, pg. 55
Gabrielson, Liza, Sr Mgr-Indus Campaign & Product Mktg-Enterprise Solutions - NVIDIA Corporation; pg. 447, pg. 268
Gabron, Katherine, Sr Mgr-Shopper Mktg-Natl Accounts - The Coca-Cola Company; pg. 240, pg. 493
Gabrys, David, Brand Mgr-45NRTH - Quality Bicycle Products; pg. 1710, pg. 918
Gacesa, Chris, Sr Product Mgr-Tech Champion - Novell Inc.; pg. 446, pg. 852
Gach, Lawrence, Mgr-Sls - Ford Motor Company; pg. 172, pg. 876
Gacioch, Michael, Engr-Product Safety - John Deere Consumer & Commercial Equipment, Inc.; pg. 705, pg. 1360
Gad-el-hak, Kamal, Product Dir-Emerging Technologies - Kroll Inc.; pg. 425, pg. 1249
Gadd, Brandy, Mgr-Product Mktg - The Goodyear Tire & Rubber Company; pg. 1883, pg. 1401
Gaddy, Donald, Sr VP-Market Dev & Sls - VITAS Healthcare Corporation; pg. 1608, pg. 447
Gaddy, Kathie, Sr Mgr-Corp Comm - Cisco Systems, Inc.; pg. 372, pg. 240
Gadecki, Steven, Dir-Digital Mktg - Sony Pictures Entertainment Inc.; pg. 309, pg. 72
Gadhvi, Sachin, VP-Mktg - Ticketmaster Entertainment LLC; pg. 1284, pg. 48
Gadowski, Aaron, Product Mgr-ECommerce - XO Group Inc.; pg. 1289, pg. 1316
Gadowski, Denise, Program Mgr-Mktg Comm - Johnson Controls, Inc.; pg. 209, pg. 1876
Gadsby, Amber, Dir-Digital Mktg - Domino's Pizza, Inc.; pg. 1726, pg. 865
Gaebler, Frank, Sr Product Mgr-Mktg - Coherent, Inc.; pg. 1406, pg. 265
Gaedy, Benjamin, Dir-Integrated Sls - National Football League; pg. 567, pg. 1264
Gaeta, Sandy N., Dir-Mktg-GIP Women's Health - Pfizer Inc.; pg. 1581, pg. 1278
Gaeta, Tommy, Mgr-Brand Mktg - E&J Gallo Winery; pg. 1962, pg. 149
Gaffar, James, Principal Mgr-Technical Product Mktg-Video Platforms - AOL Inc.; pg. 1229, pg. 1195
Gaffney, C.J., Dir-Brand & Media Strategy - The History Channel; pg. 290, pg. 1240
Gaffney, Caroline, Head-SlideShare Product - LinkedIn Corporation; pg. 1262, pg. 160
Gaffney, John, Sr Dir-Quality & Release Mgmt - Limelight Networks, Inc.; pg. 1262, pg. 26
Gaffney, Luke B., VP-Corp Sls - LexisNexis Litigation Solutions; pg. 1659, pg. 1446
Gaffney, Valerie K., Mgr-Mailroom Quality Assurance & Adv Matls - Graham Holdings Company; pg. 1645, pg. 1773
Gaffney, Whitley, Coord-Online Mktg - HCA HOLDINGS, INC.; pg. 1539, pg. 1651
Gafni, Nili, Sr Mgr-Online Mktg-LinkedIn Mktg Solutions - LinkedIn Corporation; pg. 1262, pg. 160
Gafrick, Gretchen, Specialist-Mktg Comm - Sprint Corporation; pg. 1874, pg. 719
Gafsi-Oblisk, Sonya, VP-Mktg-Sam's Club - Wal-Mart Stores, Inc.; pg. 1790, pg. 29
Gage, Holly, Mgr-Global Comm-Comml Sls Ops - Dell Inc.;

pg. 383, pg. 1737
Gage, Stephanie, Mgr-Sls Ops - Ferrero U.S.A., Inc.; pg. 1852, pg. 1121
Gage, Stephen, Dir-Mktg & Comm-UnitedHealth Intl - UnitedHealth Group Incorporated; pg. 1221, pg. 950
Gagen, Dan, Dir-Mktg-Estate Brands - Kendall-Jackson Wine Estates, Ltd.; pg. 1965, pg. 277
Gager, Bob, Grp Product Mgr - Adobe Systems Incorporated; pg. 342, pg. 235
Gagliano, Amy, Product Dir & Brand Dir - Hunter Douglas, Inc.; pg. 928, pg. 1320
Gagliardi, Gerry, Mgr-Direct Sls - San Diego Symphony Orchestra Association; pg. 580, pg. 208
Gagliardi, James, VP-Product Strategy - Digital River, Inc.; pg. 1238, pg. 948
Gagliardi, John, Sr Mgr-Creative - Hammacher Schlemmer & Co., Inc.; pg. 1124, pg. 637
Gagliardi, Victoria, Specialist-Media Rels - Volkswagen Group of America, Inc.; pg. 194, pg. 1785
Gagliardo, Adam, Dir-Digital Mktg & Social Media - Burger King Corporation; pg. 1719, pg. 440
Gagne, Al, Product Mgr-Global - General Motors Company; pg. 175, pg. 881
Gagne, Barb, Sr Mgr-Acq Mktg - Carbonite, Inc.; pg. 368, pg. 792
Gagne, Dawn, Mgr-Customer Mktg & Activation - Exide Technologies; pg. 204, pg. 483
Gagnon, Jennifer, Sr Mgr-Mktg - IDEXX Laboratories, Inc.; pg. 1543, pg. 753
Gagnon, Megan, Sr Mgr-Customer Mktg - PepsiCo, Inc.; pg. 259, pg. 1327
Gagnon, Peter, VP-Programming & Production - Eternal World Television Network, Inc.; pg. 286, pg. 6
Gagnon, Ron, VP-Mktg & Design - Wilsonart International, Inc.; pg. 1450, pg. 1746
Gagos, Maria, Dir-Digital Acq, Experience & Product Mgmt - American Express Company; pg. 712, pg. 1190
Gagrani, Kishore, Product Dir-Software-Global - Dell Inc.; pg. 383, pg. 1737
Gahde, Jan, Mgr-Product Mgmt-BI - Infor; pg. 414, pg. 484
Gai, Eric, Sr Dir-Demand Generation - Robert Half International Inc.; pg. 462, pg. 145
Gaier, David, Sr Dir-Comm - NRG Energy, Inc.; pg. 1366, pg. 1112
Gail, Bonnie R., Dir-Integrated Mktg Comm - Xerox Corporation; pg. 494, pg. 365
Gaillard, Shelly, Specialist-Mktg Comm - Medtronic, Inc.; pg. 1564, pg. 939
Gainer, Nancy, Mgr-Mktg - Ricoh Americas Corporation; pg. 461, pg. 1131
Gaines, Alyssa, Coord-Electric Distr Underground Mktg & Comm - Dominion Resources, Inc.; pg. 1939, pg. 1802
Gaines, Kim, Asst VP-Mktg - Citizens Bank & Trust; pg. 737, pg. 976
Gainor, Tim, Mgr-Field Sls - CDW Corporation; pg. 370, pg. 663
Gaither, Chad, Sr Dir-CRM & Consumer Insight - 7-Eleven, Inc.; pg. 1012, pg. 1672
Gaither, Eric, Dir-Creative - Brocade Communications Systems, Inc.; pg. 365, pg. 239
Gaither, Stacy, Mgr-Mktg - The Upper Room; pg. 1698, pg. 1655
Gajadhar, Saudia, Sr Dir-Brand Mktg - Choice Hotels International, Inc.; pg. 1086, pg. 775
Gajendra, Sanjay, Dir-Product Line - Texas Instruments Incorporated; pg. 679, pg. 1688
Gajjar, Purvi, Mgr-Mktg Comm - Applied Materials, Inc.; pg. 618, pg. 264
Gala, Ed, VP-Global Mktg & Comm-Philips Healthcare - Philips Electronics North America; pg. 662, pg. 782
Gala, Vaishali, Mgr-NA Mktg Innovation - Burger King Corporation; pg. 1719, pg. 440
Galaise, Celine, Head-Enterprise Mktg - IBM Canada Limited; pg. 411, pg. 1923
Galal, Sejal, Mgr-Digital Media Mktg - Yahoo! Inc.; pg. 1289, pg. 289
Galambos, Andrea, Mgr-Mktg-Google Express - Google Inc.; pg. 1249, pg. 153
Galando, Jennifer, Mgr-Sls Trng - Hologic, Inc.; pg. 1416, pg. 784
Galante, David, Dir-Product Mgmt-Mobile - ExactTarget Inc.; pg. 1244, pg. 685
Galarza, Daniel, Rep-Hospital & Surgical Products - Pfizer Inc.; pg. 1581, pg. 1278
Galas, Patricia, Mgr-Mktg - MGM Resorts International; pg. 1105, pg. 1028
Galasso, Jennifer, Deputy Dir-Consumer Mktg - Sanofi Pasteur, Inc; pg. 1591, pg. 1588
Galatsky, Anna, Supvr-Digital Media - Palisades Media Group, Inc.; pg. 452, pg. 275
Galberth, Deisha, Sr Dir-Corp Comm - Wal-Mart Stores, Inc.; pg. 1790, pg. 29
Galbraith, Beckie, Product Mgr - O'Reilly Automotive, Inc.; pg. 214, pg. 1006
Galbraith, Ben, VP-Products-Global - Wal-Mart.com; pg. 1287, pg. 50
Galbraith, Greg, Dir-Mktg-All Star-Global - Converse Inc.; pg. 1831, pg. 793
Gale, Chip, Sr Mgr-Corp Dev - Synopsys, Inc.; pg. 480, pg. 162
Gale, Janet, Dir-Thought Leadership & Producer-Programs Mktg - Genworth Financial, Inc.; pg. 761, pg. 1802
Gale, Jim, Sr VP-Sls - CQ Roll Call; pg. 1631, pg. 397
Gale, Robert, Sr VP-Product Dev - Medical Information Technology, Inc.; pg. 431, pg. 859
Galea, Adam, Mgr-Mktg-Global Innovation - The Hershey Co.; pg. 1855, pg. 1538
Galea, Julie, Reg Sls Mgr - Hulu LLC; pg. 1257, pg. 274
Galeana, Frank, Analyst-Mktg Database - Wells Fargo & Company; pg. 819, pg. 232
Galeaz, Kerry, Mgr-Sls-Darling's Auto Mall - Darling's Inc.; pg. 168, pg. 749
Galego, Cristina, Mgr-PR - Port of Galveston; pg. 1919, pg. 1697
Galentine, Chrystin, Mgr-Social Media - Bridgford Foods Corporation; pg. 842, pg. 42
Gales, Charles C., Mgr-Automation Sls - Weldon Solutions; pg. 1388, pg. 1598
Galewski, Matthew, Mgr-Media-Catalog, Collateral & Direct Mail - Bon Ton Stores, Inc.; pg. 1763, pg. 1596
Galfi, Rudy, Product Mgr - Google Inc.; pg. 1249, pg. 153
Galgan, Priscilla, VP-Sls & Mktg - Trippe Manufacturing Company; pg. 220, pg. 592
Galiano, Greg, Dir-Sls Strategy & Execution - Boehringer Ingelheim Pharmaceuticals, Inc.; pg. 1507, pg. 368
Galiano, Greg, Dir-Mktg-ARZERRA Brand Strategy - GlaxoSmithKline Consumer Healthcare; pg. 510, pg. 1554
Galichon, Jennifer, Dir-Mktg Ops - Unilever United States, Inc.; pg. 904, pg. 1061
Galicia, Barbara, Mgr-Mktg - AT&T Inc.; pg. 1867, pg. 1674
Galietta, Laura, Sr VP-Adv Sls Mktg - Scripps Networks Interactive, Inc.; pg. 1279, pg. 1638
Galik, Fred, Dir-Creative - Adecco USA, Inc.; pg. 342, pg. 1178
Galik, Simona, Brand Mgr-Lowe's Home Improvement - Lowe's Companies, Inc.; pg. 1053, pg. 1383
Galin, Tomi, Sr VP-Comm, Mktg & Pub Affairs - Community Health Systems, Inc.; pg. 1516, pg. 1632
Galing, Christine, Mgr-Digital-Mobile Mktg - J.C. Penney Company, Inc.; pg. 1774, pg. 1732
Galinski, Andrea, Sr Mgr-Prod Dev - One Step Ahead; pg. 1780, pg. 1881
Galinsky, George, Sr VP-Mktg Comm - Mohegan Tribal Gaming Authority; pg. 564, pg. 381
Galipeau, Bryan, Dir-Social Media & Display - Nordstrom, Inc.; pg. 1779, pg. 1837
Galis, Sandra, Coord-Sls & Mktg & Planner-Event - Johnson Outdoors Inc.; pg. 1837, pg. 1888
Gall, Kristen, Sr Dir & Gen Mgr-Global E-Commerce - LeapFrog Enterprises, Inc.; pg. 961, pg. 84
Gall, Tom, Dir-Channel Mktg - Xerox Corporation; pg. 494, pg. 365
Gallacher, Sharon, Sr Dir-Global Multichannel Strategy & Effectiveness - GlaxoSmithKline; pg. 1536, pg. 1389
Gallaer, Jodi, Sr Mgr-Brand Partnership - Amazon.com, Inc.; pg. 1226, pg. 1831
Gallagher, Aaron, Sr VP-Digital Sls - Scripps Networks Interactive, Inc.; pg. 1279, pg. 1638
Gallagher, Ben, Mgr-Mktg-TV - Sony Electronics, Inc.; pg. 676, pg. 209
Gallagher, Cathryn, Dir-Diabetes Mktg - Sanofi US; pg. 1592, pg. 1046
Gallagher, Dennis, Assoc Mgr-Trade Mktg - Ocean Spray Cranberries, Inc.; pg. 887, pg. 827
Gallagher, Greg, Dir-Mktg - The Kraft Heinz Company; pg. 871, pg. 641
Gallagher, Greg, Dir-Mktg-Velveeta & Kraft Parmesan Cheese - Mondelez International, Inc.; pg. 878, pg. 601
Gallagher, Ian, Sr Mgr-Mktg - Comcast Corporation; pg. 276, pg. 1560
Gallagher, Jeanine, Sr Product Mgr - Astellas Pharma US, Inc.; pg. 1496, pg. 640
Gallagher, Jennifer, Dir-Sls - Godwin's Gatorland, Inc.; pg. 550, pg. 453
Gallagher, Jim, Head-Theatrical Mktg - DreamWorks Animation SKG, Inc.; pg. 284, pg. 96
Gallagher, John, VP-Adv Sls - MTV Networks Company; pg. 298, pg. 1262
Gallagher, John J., Dir-Adv - People Magazine; pg. 1676, pg. 1278
Gallagher, Julie, Head-Mktg & Dir - Pfizer Inc.; pg. 1581, pg. 1278
Gallagher, Kerry, Asst VP & Mgr-Social Media - Citizens Bank & Trust; pg. 737, pg. 976
Gallagher, Kerry, Mgr-Social Media - Citizens Financial Group, Inc.; pg. 737, pg. 1606
Gallagher, Kevin, Product Mgr - Exxel Outdoors LLC; pg. 1833, pg. 311
Gallagher, Lisa, Assoc Mgr-Product Comm - Hospira, Inc.; pg. 1542, pg. 623
Gallagher, Mary, Sr VP-Mdsg - Books-A-Million, Inc.; pg. 1623, pg. 2
Gallagher, Matt, Dir-Media Rels, Corp, Comml & Consumer - American International Group, Inc.; pg. 1190, pg. 1193
Gallagher, Mikella, Brand Mgr - Darden Restaurants, Inc.; pg. 1724, pg. 453
Gallagher, Neil, VP & Head-Mktg Svcs & Social Media - Bristol-Myers Squibb Company; pg. 1509, pg. 1206
Gallagher, Patrick, Exec VP-Sls & Mktg-NetJets US & Europe - NetJets Inc.; pg. 1917, pg. 1442
Gallagher, Peggy, Product Mgr-Trade Kitchen - Delta Faucet Company; pg. 78, pg. 684
Gallagher, Richard, VP-Digital Product Tech - Dex Media Inc; pg. 1635, pg. 1680
Gallagher, Richard D., Sr VP-Mdsg - Haverty Furniture Companies, Inc.; pg. 926, pg. 509
Gallagher, Scott, Mgr-Mktg - Atlas Minerals & Chemicals, Inc.; pg. 69, pg. 1552
Gallagher, Sean, Mgr-Natl Sls-Wireless Structures - Valmont Industries, Inc.; pg. 1387, pg. 1019
Gallagher, Shelly J., Product Mgr-Auto - Selective Insurance Group, Inc.; pg. 1216, pg. 1045
Gallagher, Suzanne, Mgr-Adv & Special Products - The News-Times; pg. 1670, pg. 344
Gallagher, Tara, VP-Ad Sls Mktg - Scripps Networks Interactive, Inc.; pg. 1279, pg. 1638
Gallant, Lauren, Specialist-Mktg - Comcast Corporation; pg. 276, pg. 1560
Gallant, Matthew, Sr Mgr-Production Svcs - Staples, Inc.; pg. 474, pg. 821
Gallant, Melissa, Mgr-Mktg-Betty Crocker & Bisquick - General Mills, Inc.; pg. 828, pg. 933
Gallant, Michael, Sr Dir-PR - EMC Corporation; pg. 391, pg. 825
Gallard, Van Rex, VP-Sls-Africa, Latin America & Caribbean - The Boeing Company; pg. 225, pg. 567
Gallardo, Antonio, Sr Dir-WW Ops IEI & New Customer Engagements - Flextronics International Ltd.; pg. 81, pg. 245
Gallardo, April, Sr Mgr-Trng & Dev - Pizza Hut, Inc.; pg. 1744, pg. 1733
Gallardo, Jeannie, Dir-Consumer Mktg - Carfax Inc.; pg. 202, pg. 1777
Gallardo, Lupe M., Sr Mgr-Claims - The Allstate Corporation; pg. 1189, pg. 639
Gallardo, Rob, Dir-Mktg Analytics & Targeting - Universal Orlando; pg. 590, pg. 456
Gallas, Debbie, Mgr-Media Svcs & Credentials - Oakland Athletics Limited Partnership; pg. 571, pg. 172
Gallaway, Wallace A., Specialist-Cloud Productivity Sls - Microsoft Corporation; pg. 435, pg. 1824
Gallegos, Anthony, Product Mgr-Solar & Semiconductor Technologies-Global - Technic Incorporated; pg. 1183, pg. 1601
Gallegos, Judy L., Mgr-Mktg Comm - Fujitsu Computer Systems Corporation; pg. 398, pg. 285
Gallegos, Maria, Principal & Product Mgr-Mktg - Red Hat, Inc.; pg. 460, pg. 1388
Gallegos, Maria Francisca, Exec Dir-Mktg - Save Mart Supermarkets; pg. 1033, pg. 150
Gallegos, Max, Dir-Mktg-Greater Southwest Reg - McDonald's Corporation; pg. 1737, pg. 645
Gallegos, Tami, Mgr-Federal Mktg - Symantec Corporation; pg. 478, pg. 161
Gallett, Scott, VP-Mktg & PR - BorgWarner Inc.; pg. 167, pg.

867
Galli, Bryan A., CMO - Peabody Energy Corporation; pg. 1176, pg. 1001
Gallic, Mike, Dir-Mktg & Assoc Publr - Bonnier Corporation; pg. 1622, pg. 480
Gallice, Stacie, Sr Dir-Governance & Plng - The American Gastroenterological Association; pg. 128, pg. 761
Galliera, Enrico, Sr VP-Comml & Mktg - Ferrari North America, Inc.; pg. 171, pg. 1060
Galliher, Mark A., Sr Dir-Member Rels - Association of National Advertisers, Inc.; pg. 133, pg. 1197
Gallimore, Sean, VP-Global Ultrasound Mktg - Philips Electronics North America; pg. 662, pg. 782
Gallinat, Dennis, Sr Mgr-Sls Compensation - Waste Management, Inc.; pg. 1954, pg. 1716
Gallivan, JungHwa, VP-Global Sls & Plng - Rag & Bone; pg. 46, pg. 1284
Gallo, Allison, Assoc Dir-Mktg Comm - Novartis Corporation; pg. 1574, pg. 1273
Gallo, Jennifer, Sr Assoc Brand Mgr - Pinnacle Foods Group LLC; pg. 889, pg. 1104
Gallo, Jessica A., Reg Mgr-Mktg - H&R Block, Inc.; pg. 764, pg. 983
Gallo, Natalie, Dir-Global Mktg & Branding - NYSE Euronext; pg. 789, pg. 1274
Gallo, Salena, Dir-Mktg, Consumer Goods & Svcs - Accenture; pg. 1392, pg. 1186
Gallo, Santiago, Dir-Brand Mktg - Crown Imports LLC; pg. 248, pg. 572
Gallo, Stephanie, Dir-Mktg - E&J Gallo Winery; pg. 1962, pg. 149
Gallone, Larry, Mgr-Comm & Mgr-Mktg Comm - Siemens Medical Solutions USA, Inc.; pg. 469, pg. 1550
Galloway, Brian, Sr Mgr-Digital & ECommerce - Keurig Green Mountain, Inc.; pg. 868, pg. 1768
Galloway, Christine, Dir-Digital Mktg - Sony Pictures Home Entertainment; pg. 310, pg. 72
Galloway, Erin, Assoc Dir-Publicity & Mktg - Penguin Random House; pg. 1675, pg. 1276
Galloway, James R., Sr VP & Mgr-Sls-Global - Factory Mutual Insurance Company; pg. 1199, pg. 1601
Galloway, John, CMO & VP - Hard Rock Cafe International, Inc.; pg. 1730, pg. 454
Galloway, Melissa, Sr Mgr-Mktg-Integrated Brand Campaign - PetSmart, Inc.; pg. 1481, pg. 18
Galloway, Michael, VP-Adv & New Media - Star Furniture Company; pg. 944, pg. 1715
Gallucci, Anne, Sr Dir-Adv & Brand Dev - Microsoft Corporation; pg. 435, pg. 1824
Galman, Donald P., Specialist-PR - Honeywell International Inc.; pg. 407, pg. 1088
Galo, Brad, Project Mgr-North America Mktg-Future State - Ford Motor Company; pg. 172, pg. 876
Galo, Daniel, Brand Mgr-Private Brand Pasta - Conagra Foods; pg. 826, pg. 994
Galovich, Ronald, VP-Global Mktg - STERIS Corporation; pg. 1597, pg. 1464
Galperin, Irene, Mgr-Global Mktg-Bloomberg for Enterprise - Bloomberg L.P.; pg. 725, pg. 1204
Galterio, Erin, Dir-Mktg - Iconix Brand Group, Inc.; pg. 26, pg. 1243
Galus, David, Engr-Technical Mktg - Intel Corporation; pg. 645, pg. 266
Galush, Bob, VP-Product Mktg - Lenovo Group Ltd; pg. 427, pg. 1384
Galuskin, Pete, Sr VP & Mgr-Sls-Natl - Turner Broadcasting System, Inc.; pg. 314, pg. 521
Galvani, Paul, VP-Mktg - Riviana Foods Inc.; pg. 892, pg. 1713
Galvanin, Donald, Dir-Sls-Boeing Comml Airplanes - The Boeing Company; pg. 225, pg. 567
Galvanin, Donald, Dir-Sls - The Boeing Company - Helicopter Division; pg. 226, pg. 13
Galvao, Flavia, Dir-Mktg-Activia, Light&Fit, Danactive - The Dannon Company, Inc.; pg. 851, pg. 1351
Galvin, Elizabeth B., Mgr-Social Media - Gartner, Inc.; pg. 1248, pg. 374
Galvin, Grainne, Brand Mgr-Ireland - Betty Crocker Products; pg. 840, pg. 931
Galvin, John, VP-Sls & Mktg Grp - Intel Corporation; pg. 645, pg. 266
Galvin, Kevin, VP-Media Rels & Strategic Comm - Arizona State University; pg. 597, pg. 25
Galvin, Meghan, Assoc Mgr-Mktg-Keds - Wolverine World Wide, Inc.; pg. 1822, pg. 905
Galvin, Molly, Mgr-Mktg Comm - USG Corporation; pg. 118, pg. 594
Galvin, Sandra, Brand Mgr - Diageo North America Inc.; pg. 248, pg. 1223
Galvin, Tiffany, VP-Media Rels - The Goldman Sachs Group, Inc.; pg. 762, pg. 1236
Galvin, Tim, Sr Mgr-Bus Dev - Amazon.com, Inc.; pg. 1226, pg. 1831
Gamache, Corinne, Assoc Mgr-Strategic Mktg-Global Brand Execution - Hasbro, Inc.; pg. 954, pg. 1603
Gamache, Ron, Mgr-Comml & Sls-US - The Carlyle Johnson Machine Company, L.L.C.; pg. 1321, pg. 339
Gamba, Therese, Sr VP-Mktg & Acquired Programming - NBC Universal, Inc.; pg. 300, pg. 1266
Gambardella, Ray, Dir-Casino Mktg - Station Casinos, Inc.; pg. 585, pg. 1030
Gambelli, Marianne, Pres-Adv Sls - NBC News; pg. 300, pg. 1265
Gambill, Amanda, Mgr-Mktg Comm - Emerson Network Power; pg. 1071, pg. 1479
Gambill, Anita, Specialist-PR - Stihl, Inc.; pg. 1064, pg. 1810
Gambill, Jim, Brand Mgr-Comml - Chevron Corporation; pg. 974, pg. 259
Gambill, Kristen, Specialist-Mktg-FedEx Svcs - FedEx Corporation; pg. 1907, pg. 1642
Gambin, Suzy, Dir-Digital Mktg - Esurance, Inc.; pg. 1243, pg. 217
Gambino, Frank, Product Mgr - Siemens PLM Software; pg. 469, pg. 1734
Gambke, Fred, COO & Dir-Sls-Natl - United States Beverage LLC; pg. 266, pg. 379
Gamble, Derek, Dir-Media Sales & Partnerships - Major League Soccer LLC; pg. 560, pg. 1256
Gamble, James, Specialist-Product Mktg - Polycom, Inc.; pg. 664, pg. 249
Gamble, Jeff, Sr Dir-Mktg - Brooklyn Nets; pg. 534, pg. 1145
Gamble, Wanda, Sr Dir-Health & Analytics Bus Unit - Battelle Memorial Institute; pg. 1401, pg. 1437
Gamboa, Meghan, Dir-Mktg-Girls Toys - Hasbro, Inc.; pg. 954, pg. 1603
Gamino, Sarah, Dir-Mktg Programs - Hewlett-Packard Company; pg. 404, pg. 175
Gan, Bai, Head-Mdsg & Comm - Zenni Optical, Inc.; pg. 1438, pg. 168
Ganahl, Jen, Brand Mgr-Solutions - Mead Johnson Nutrition Company; pg. 1561, pg. 615
Gananian, Justine, Specialist-Corp Comm & Media Rels - Hewlett-Packard Company; pg. 404, pg. 175
Gandara, Enrique, VP-Sls & Mktg - Pueblo Bonito Hotels & Resorts; pg. 1108, pg. 206
Gandara, Sarah P, Analyst-Mktg - 3M Company; pg. 1142, pg. 956
Ganderson, Amy, Dir-Digital Mktg - The Nature Conservancy; pg. 151, pg. 1774
Gandert, Bob, VP-Sls - Atkins Nutritionals, Inc.; pg. 1498, pg. 316
Gandert, Cheryl, Mgr-Media - The Scotts Miracle-Gro Company; pg. 1799, pg. 1459
Gandhi, Ashish, Mgr-Sls-North America - Owens Corning; pg. 102, pg. 1476
Gandhi, Nilay, Mgr-Mktg Content - MORNINGSTAR, INC.; pg. 784, pg. 583
Gandhi, Sanjay, Dir-Mktg & Sls-Alkali Chemicals - FMC Corporation; pg. 1163, pg. 1564
Gandhi, Sumi, Mgr-Export Sls Corp - Nupla Corporation; pg. 101, pg. 281
Gandhi, Taruna, Mgr-Product Line Mktg - VMware, Inc.; pg. 490, pg. 179
Gandsman, Dana E., Sr Dir-Reputation Comm - Pfizer Inc.; pg. 1581, pg. 1278
Ganeriwala, Vishal, Sr Dir-Technical Mktg-XenDesktop & XenApp - Citrix Systems, Inc.; pg. 375, pg. 424
Ganesan, Ashok, Sr Dir-Product Mgmt - Cisco Systems, Inc.; pg. 372, pg. 240
Ganesh, Bala, Dir-Mktg - United Parcel Service, Inc.; pg. 1928, pg. 522
Gangel, Rachel, Dir-Mktg Program Mgmt - Bank of America Corporation; pg. 718, pg. 1362
Gangeri, Linda, Mgr-Mktg Platforms & Technologies - Volvo Cars of North America LLC; pg. 195, pg. 1117
Gani, Heikal, Co-Founder, Pres & Chief Creative Officer - Indochino; pg. 42, pg. 1911
Ganley, Bob, Sr Mgr-Mktg-Enterprise Solutions - Dell Inc.; pg. 383, pg. 1737
Gann, Don, Dir-Mktg Produce Div - Stater Brothers Holdings; pg. 1034, pg. 198
Gann, Keith, Sr Mgr-IT Program - CenturyLink, Inc.; pg. 1870, pg. 746
Gannon, Cara, Sr Reg Mgr-Sls - CareerBuilder, LLC; pg. 1234, pg. 568
Gannon, Christy, Dir-Mktg - AIMCO Properties, L.P.; pg. 1079, pg. 316
Gannon, Chuck, Mgr-Corp Adv - L.L. Bean, Inc.; pg. 1777, pg. 750
Gannon, Stephanie, Mgr-Digital Mktg & ECommerce - Mikimoto (America) Co. Ltd.; pg. 10, pg. 1260
Gannon, Ted, Dir-Mktg-Veterinary Bus Solutions - Zoetis Inc.; pg. 1611, pg. 1067
Gannon, Tom, VP-Integrated Mktg Comm - T. Rowe Price Group Inc.; pg. 808, pg. 759
Gannon, Tom P., VP-Mktg - Kaiser Aluminum Corporation; pg. 90, pg. 86
Ganoe, Terry L., Product Mgr - First Data Corporation; pg. 754, pg. 505
Ganot, Ethan, Mgr-Mktg - Callaway Golf Company; pg. 1829, pg. 58
Ganotra, Shivesh, Engr-Technical Mktg-Enterprise Networking Grp - Cisco Systems, Inc.; pg. 372, pg. 240
Ganpule, Gauri, Assoc Dir-Product Mgmt-Ion Torrent Bus - Thermo Fisher Scientific Inc.; pg. 1431, pg. 854
Gans, Randy, Dir-Mktg Programs - Automatic Data Processing, Inc.; pg. 357, pg. 1117
Ganson, Douglas, Mgr-Mktg-Channel Mgmt - Verizon Communications Inc.; pg. 1875, pg. 1309
Gant, Chanel, Mgr-Interactive Media - Wm. Wrigley Jr. Company; pg. 1863, pg. 596
Gant, Charissa, Sr Mgr & Mgr-HR Program Comm - Cisco Systems, Inc.; pg. 372, pg. 240
Gant, Cheryl, Mgr-Sls - Daedalus Books, Inc.; pg. 1632, pg. 767
Gant, Chris, Mng Dir-Sls Americas-FedEx Supply Chain - FedEx Corporation; pg. 1907, pg. 1642
Gant, Garry, Mgr-Mktg - Oakley, Inc.; pg. 1840, pg. 86
Gant, Ron, Dir-Indus Mktg-Roads - Bentley Systems, Inc.; pg. 361, pg. 1531
Gantenbein, Mike, Dir-Creative Svcs - KTVL-TV; pg. 295, pg. 1499
Gantner, Keith, Sr VP-Grp Sls & Mktg-Diagnostics - Hologic, Inc.; pg. 1416, pg. 784
Gantz, Mary C., Brand Mktg Mgr-Private Brand - Walgreen Co.; pg. 1608, pg. 605
Ganzow, Dale, Mgr-Sls - San Diego Business Journal; pg. 1682, pg. 208
Gao, Jane, Sr Mgr-Channel & Partner Mktg - Microsoft Corporation; pg. 435, pg. 1824
Gao, Shenglong, Assoc Product Mgr-Mobile Weather Apps - Yahoo! Inc.; pg. 1289, pg. 289
Gao, Zheng, Mgr-Product Design - Apple Inc.; pg. 350, pg. 73
Gaona, Janet, Mgr-Retail Mktg - SKECHERS U.S.A., INC.; pg. 1819, pg. 143
Gaonach, Stephen, Brand Mgr - Mondelez International, Inc.; pg. 878, pg. 601
Gaonkar, Priti, Planner-Product - Emerson Climate Technologies, Inc.; pg. 1333, pg. 1472
Gapinski, Jane, Dir-Mktg Svcs - Sargento Foods Inc.; pg. 894, pg. 1886
Garabedian, Eddie, Dir-Creative Strategy - Electronic Arts Inc.; pg. 951, pg. 189
Garaitonandia, Monica, VP & Dir-Mktg & Strategy-Multicultural - Brown-Forman Corporation; pg. 1958, pg. 732
Garakanidze, Avtandil, Product Mgr-Cloud Platform - Google Inc.; pg. 1249, pg. 153
Garamella, Jennifer, Mgr-Mktg Events - Citigroup Inc.; pg. 735, pg. 1212
Garant, Michael, Mgr-Digital Mktg - Mazda North American Operations; pg. 183, pg. 113
Garate, Lou, Mng Dir-Partnership Mktg - National Association for Stock Car Auto Racing; pg. 566, pg. 420
Garaventa, John, Sr Mgr-Mktg - Trinchero Family Estates; pg. 1971, pg. 197
Garbarino, Andrew, Dir-Ad Sls Mktg - Screenvision Cinema Network LLC; pg. 581, pg. 1290
Garbato, Emily, Coord-Mktg - Proximo Spirits, Inc.; pg. 1969, pg. 1076
Garbeck, Mike, Second VP-Sls & Mktg Support - The Travelers Companies, Inc.; pg. 1220, pg. 352
Garber, Chris, Mng Counsel-Mktg & Intellectual Property - Nationwide Mutual Insurance Company; pg. 1210, pg. 1442
Garber, Deb, Brand Mgr-Global - Hewlett-Packard Company;

First page reference indicates Business Class Edition
Second page reference indicates Geographic Edition

pg. 404, *pg.* 175
Garber, Jeff, Dir-Bus Design-Sls & Distr - InterContinental Hotels Corporation; *pg.* 1097, *pg.* 511
Garber, Van L., VP-Mktg - Norandex/Reynolds Distribution, Inc.; *pg.* 99, *pg.* 1455
Garbin, Camila, Brand Mgr-Dove Global - Unilever United States, Inc.; *pg.* 904, *pg.* 1061
Garbow, Ann M., Sr Mgr-Product Portfolio - Xcel Energy Inc.; *pg.* 1955, *pg.* 946
Garces, Maria, Product Mgr - Cardinal Health, Inc.; *pg.* 1512, *pg.* 1448
Garchar, Steve, Dir-Creative & Coord-PR - Ford Motor Company; *pg.* 172, *pg.* 876
Garcia, Alex, Community Mgr & Analyst-Social Media - Barnes & Noble, Inc.; *pg.* 1619, *pg.* 1201
Garcia, Alex, Dir-Sls - Catallia Mexican Foods LLC; *pg.* 846, *pg.* 921
Garcia, Ana, VP-Mktg-US div - Jarden Consumer Solutions; *pg.* 57, *pg.* 412
Garcia, Anayda, Mgr-Sls-Corp Groups & BTS - Hilton Worldwide, Inc.; *pg.* 1094, *pg.* 1791
Garcia, Ariana, Mgr-Digital Mktg-Latin America - Netflix, Inc.; *pg.* 1269, *pg.* 141
Garcia, Art, Acct Mgr-Comml Sls - Hewlett-Packard Company; *pg.* 404, *pg.* 175
Garcia, Carlos, VP-Analog Products - Intersil Corporation; *pg.* 647, *pg.* 146
Garcia, Carlos, Mgr-Product Mktg - Luminex Corporation; *pg.* 1421, *pg.* 1664
Garcia, Carlos, Mgr-Export Sls - Plains Cotton Cooperative Association; *pg.* 697, *pg.* 1726
Garcia, Clara, Specialist-Mktg Comm - Schneider Electric; *pg.* 467, *pg.* 1609
Garcia, David, Mgr-Media & Brand Partnerships - Taco Bell Corp.; *pg.* 1752, *pg.* 117
Garcia, Eddie, Sr Graphic Designer-Mktg - Pacific Sunwear of California, Inc.; *pg.* 1781, *pg.* 43
Garcia, Edwin, Dir-Mktg-Remy Cointreau Travel Retail Americas - Remy Cointreau USA Inc.; *pg.* 1969, *pg.* 1285
Garcia, Elizabeth, Specialist-Social Media Engagement - PETA; *pg.* 153, *pg.* 1797
Garcia, Eloy, Head-Mutual Funds Mktg Strategy - State Farm Mutual Automobile Insurance Co.; *pg.* 1218, *pg.* 557
Garcia, Erica, Brand Mgr-Minute Maid - The Coca-Cola Company; *pg.* 240, *pg.* 493
Garcia, Eunice, Brand Mktg Mgr - Landry's, Inc.; *pg.* 1735, *pg.* 1709
Garcia, Fely, Coord-Natl Sls - Univision Communications Inc.; *pg.* 683, *pg.* 1307
Garcia, Gabriel, Brand Mgr-Authenticated - The Upper Deck Company, LLC; *pg.* 969, *pg.* 62
Garcia, Gerardo, Dir-Mktg Tech Platforms, Global Mktg & Comml Leadership-Global - The Coca-Cola Company; *pg.* 240, *pg.* 493
Garcia, Jeffrica, Analyst-Mktg - United Parcel Service, Inc.; *pg.* 1928, *pg.* 522
Garcia, Jennifer R., VP-Mktg Svcs - Texas Monthly; *pg.* 1692, *pg.* 1666
Garcia, Jesus, Mgr-Sls & Intl Tourism - Atlanta Convention & Visitors Bureau; *pg.* 989, *pg.* 489
Garcia, Jesus L., Mgr-Alliance Mktg - Intel Corporation; *pg.* 645, *pg.* 266
Garcia, Jody, VP-Consumer Sls & Svc - AT&T Communications Corp.; *pg.* 1866, *pg.* 1043
Garcia, Joe, Sr Dir-Talent Mgmt & Organizational Effectiveness - The Home Depot, Inc.; *pg.* 1050, *pg.* 510
Garcia, Justin, Sr Mgr-Mktg-Digital Acq - JPMorgan Chase & Co.; *pg.* 772, *pg.* 1246
Garcia, Kat, Mgr-Mktg - Taco Bell Corp.; *pg.* 1752, *pg.* 117
Garcia, Kim, Project Mgr-Content-Creative - GoPro; *pg.* 1414, *pg.* 255
Garcia, Krista M., Dir-Creative Svcs - Travelers Insurance; *pg.* 1220, *pg.* 963
Garcia, Kristina, Assoc-Bus Adv Sls - Pinellas Suncoast Transit Authority; *pg.* 1919, *pg.* 463
Garcia, Lainey, Mgr-Brand PR & Engagement - McDonald's Corporation; *pg.* 1737, *pg.* 645
Garcia, Lisa, Dir-Mktg Comm - KLA-Tencor Corporation; *pg.* 1353, *pg.* 146
Garcia, Lourdes, Product Mgr - PACCAR Inc.; *pg.* 187, *pg.* 1816
Garcia, Marci, Mgr-Product Mktg-FCB & Machine Vision Cameras - Sony Corporation of America; *pg.* 675, *pg.* 1293
Garcia, Marirosa, Asst Mgr-Mktg & Adv - Penguin Random House; *pg.* 1675, *pg.* 1276
Garcia, Marirosa, Asst Mgr-Mktg & Adv-Penguin Grp USA - Penguin Random House; *pg.* 1675, *pg.* 1276
Garcia, Melissa, Sr Mgr-Brand Comm-US Specialty Care - AstraZeneca Pharmaceuticals LP; *pg.* 1497, *pg.* 389
Garcia, Michelle, Sr Mgr-Mobile Channel - United Services Automobile Association; *pg.* 1221, *pg.* 1743
Garcia, Miguel, CTO & Sr VP-Product Dev - OpenText GXS; *pg.* 1272, *pg.* 770
Garcia, Paul, Dir-PR - Crystal Cruises LLC; *pg.* 1904, *pg.* 128
Garcia, R. L., Dir-Creative - PricewaterhouseCoopers LLP; *pg.* 795, *pg.* 1283
Garcia, Rachel, VP-Mktg & Social Media Strategy - BBC Worldwide America Inc.; *pg.* 271, *pg.* 1201
Garcia, Ragan, Sr Mgr-Sourcing-Hard Home - J.C. Penney Company, Inc.; *pg.* 1774, *pg.* 1732
Garcia, Sandra, Mgr-Digital Mktg & Product Mktg - Time Warner Cable Inc.; *pg.* 312, *pg.* 1301
Garcia, Silvia, VP-Media Plng & Multiplatform Strategy - Univision Communications Inc.; *pg.* 683, *pg.* 1307
Garcia, Tony, Product Mgr - Health Net, Inc.; *pg.* 1540, *pg.* 308
Garcia, Walter, Sr Mgr-HR - AbbVie Inc.; *pg.* 1486, *pg.* 638
Garcia-Todd, Paula, Mgr-Global Mktg-Pharma-POLYOXTM & ETHOCELTM - THE DOW CHEMICAL COMPANY; *pg.* 1157, *pg.* 898
Garcia-Vinyard, Sebastian, Brand Mgr - Neutrogena Corporation; *pg.* 517, *pg.* 137
Garcin, Jane, Dir-Mktg - EDGAR Online, Inc.; *pg.* 746, *pg.* 776
Gard, Catalina, Mgr-Comm, Media & Tech - Accenture; *pg.* 1392, *pg.* 1186
Garde, Vaibhav, Principal-Interactive Mktg Analytics & Global Brand Engagement - FedEx Corporation; *pg.* 1907, *pg.* 1642
Garden, Noah, Exec VP-Bus - Major League Baseball; *pg.* 560, *pg.* 1255
Gardenhire, Carrie, Dir-Online Mktg - Pennwell Publishing Company Inc.; *pg.* 1676, *pg.* 1490
Gardier, Christopher, Sr VP-Consumer Sls - John B. Sanfilippo & Son, Inc.; *pg.* 1024, *pg.* 610
Gardiner, Bob, VP-Mktg - CertainTeed Corporation; *pg.* 74, *pg.* 1589
Gardiner, Eric, Dir-Corp Mktg - Softchoice Corporation; *pg.* 471, *pg.* 1943
Gardiner, Katie, Brand Mgr - Taco Bell Corp.; *pg.* 1752, *pg.* 117
Gardiner, Matt, Reg Mgr-Mktg - Academy Sports & Outdoors, Ltd.; *pg.* 1824, *pg.* 1724
Gardiner, Monte, Dir-Mktg Programs - Best Western International, Inc.; *pg.* 1081, *pg.* 15
Gardiner, Richard, Mgr-Mktg Comm - GE Capital; *pg.* 761, *pg.* 362
Gardinier, Brian, Product Mgr-Accessories - Harris Corp. RF Communications Division; *pg.* 642, *pg.* 1336
Gardner, Alison, Dir-Customer Insights-Client Solutions Product Grp - Dell Inc.; *pg.* 383, *pg.* 1737
Gardner, Anthony, Sr Dir-Creative Svcs - Banana Republic; *pg.* 1760, *pg.* 212
Gardner, Bianca, Dir-Global Digital Mktg-Belvedere - LVMH Inc.; *pg.* 9, *pg.* 1254
Gardner, Bud, VP-Sls & Mktg - Standard Wire & Cable Co.; *pg.* 1306, *pg.* 187
Gardner, Chelsea, Planner-Mktg - Humana, Inc.; *pg.* 1204, *pg.* 734
Gardner, Colleen G., Sr Mgr-HR - Northrop Grumman Corporation; *pg.* 231, *pg.* 1781
Gardner, Connie, Sr Dir-Community Rels - Marsh Supermarkets, Inc.; *pg.* 1027, *pg.* 688
Gardner, Daren, Dir-Product Mgmt - EMC Corporation; *pg.* 391, *pg.* 825
Gardner, Derrick, Reg Acct Mgr-Indus & Contractor Sls - Anixter International Inc.; *pg.* 1313, *pg.* 614
Gardner, Don, Mgr-Technical Mktg, Launch & Support - Xerox Corporation; *pg.* 494, *pg.* 365
Gardner, Emma, Mgr-Adv - Dunkin' Brands Group, Inc.; *pg.* 1727, *pg.* 810
Gardner, Eric, Sr Product Mgr - Intel Corporation; *pg.* 645, *pg.* 266
Gardner, Gina, Dir-Mktg Ops - HealthSouth Corporation; *pg.* 1540, *pg.* 3
Gardner, Jack, VP-Mktg-Casey's Pubs - Prime Restaurants Inc.; *pg.* 1746, *pg.* 1947
Gardner, James, VP-Sls-Western Area - CooperVision, Inc.; *pg.* 1407, *pg.* 1159
Gardner, Jeff, VP-Mktg - Cryovac, Inc.; *pg.* 1456, *pg.* 1615
Gardner, Jennifer, Dir-Media Investment & Partnerships - Unilever United States, Inc.; *pg.* 904, *pg.* 1061
Gardner, Joseph, Product Mgr-Patient Experience Mktg - AbbVie Inc.; *pg.* 1486, *pg.* 638
Gardner, Karmen, Mgr-Retail Centralized Mktg - Pella Corporation; *pg.* 104, *pg.* 711
Gardner, Kevin, Sr Dir-Corp Affairs-Intl - Wal-Mart Stores, Inc.; *pg.* 1790, *pg.* 29
Gardner, Kirsten, Mgr-Product Mktg - Fiserv, Inc.; *pg.* 758, *pg.* 537
Gardner, Laura, Mgr-Retail Mktg Comm - Publix Super Markets, Inc.; *pg.* 1031, *pg.* 437
Gardner, Linda, Dir-Mktg - Cedar Fair, L.P.; *pg.* 537, *pg.* 1471
Gardner, Matt, Sr Dir-Promos & Digital Strategy - St. Louis Blues Hockey Club, LLC; *pg.* 585, *pg.* 1003
Gardner, Matthew, Sr Mgr-Corp Mktg Comm-Retail Markets - Publix Super Markets, Inc.; *pg.* 1031, *pg.* 437
Gardner, Michael, Planner-Finished Product - The Procter & Gamble Company; *pg.* 1129, *pg.* 1418
Gardner, Philip, VP-Mktg - Alfred Nickles Bakery, Inc.; *pg.* 836, *pg.* 1466
Gardner, Randy, Sr VP-Sls - Mohawk Home; *pg.* 935, *pg.* 541
Gardner, Rich M., Program Mgr-Defense & Federal Products - Caterpillar, Inc.; *pg.* 1321, *pg.* 650
Gardner, Rob, Mgr-Application Sls - Oracle Corporation; *pg.* 450, *pg.* 191
Gardner, Scott, Dir-Product Mgmt - Penton Media, Inc.; *pg.* 1676, *pg.* 1277
Gardocki, Vicki, Mgr-Creative Svcs - Southern Company; *pg.* 1952, *pg.* 520
Garfield, Alicia, Sr Mgr-Mktg - Hologic, Inc.; *pg.* 1416, *pg.* 784
Garfield, Lauren, Mgr-Ralph Lauren Home Mktg & Comm - Ralph Lauren Corporation; *pg.* 46, *pg.* 1284
Garfield, Malea, Dir-Mktg - Station Casinos, Inc.; *pg.* 585, *pg.* 1030
Garfin, Russ, Product Mgr - Winnebago Industries, Inc.; *pg.* 1712, *pg.* 707
Garfinkel, Debbie, Product Mgr-Rheumatology & Consumer Mktg - AbbVie Inc.; *pg.* 1486, *pg.* 638
Garfinkel, Megan, Sr Mgr-Owner & Franchise Comm & Dev Mktg - Marriott International, Inc.; *pg.* 1102, *pg.* 764
Garg, Manish, Sr Mgr-Product Mktg - Altera Corporation; *pg.* 348, *pg.* 237
Garg, Sachit, Engr-RF Product - Skyworks Solutions, Inc.; *pg.* 674, *pg.* 862
Gargano, Chris, Sr Dir-SFG Productions & Entertainment - San Francisco Giants Baseball Club; *pg.* 581, *pg.* 226
Gargano, Jennifer Pesonen, Brand Mgr-Dog Treats - The Hartz Mountain Corp.; *pg.* 1476, *pg.* 1120
Gargano, Tony, Dir-Sls & Mktg - Graco, Inc.; *pg.* 1342, *pg.* 935
Gargano, Trey, VP-Sls & Turner Digital-Turner Broadcasting Sales, Inc. - Turner Broadcasting System, Inc.; *pg.* 314, *pg.* 521
Gargas, Dave, Sr Mgr-Shopper Mktg-Quaker Foods & Snacks - PepsiCo, Inc.; *pg.* 259, *pg.* 1327
Gargione, David, Sr Mgr-Internal & External Comm - Pfizer Inc.; *pg.* 1581, *pg.* 1278
Gargotta, Tommy, Sr Exec VP-Mktg-Worldwide - Sony Pictures Entertainment Inc.; *pg.* 309, *pg.* 72
Garick, Lauren, Sr Mgr-Mktg Comm - Bose Corporation; *pg.* 626, *pg.* 820
Garimella, Ravi, Sr Analyst-Strategic Mktg - FedEx Corporation; *pg.* 1907, *pg.* 1642
Garin, David L., Grp VP-Indus Products - Burlington Northern Santa Fe, LLC; *pg.* 1901, *pg.* 1694
Garinois-Melenikiotou, Georgia, Exec VP-Corp Mktg - The Estee Lauder Companies Inc.; *pg.* 508, *pg.* 1229
Garland, James, Sr Dir-Creative - Amazon.com, Inc.; *pg.* 1226, *pg.* 1831
Garland, Travis, Sr Engr-Product Dev-Body Exterior Engrg - Ford Motor Company; *pg.* 172, *pg.* 876
Garlick, Melissa, Sr VP-Brand Creative Mktg - Verizon Communications Inc.; *pg.* 1875, *pg.* 1309
Garlick, Michael, Specialist-Local Area Mktg - Kmart Corporation; *pg.* 1775, *pg.* 617
Garlinger, Kay, Specialist-Sls Installment Plans - The Scotts Miracle-Gro Company; *pg.* 1799, *pg.* 1459
Garlington, Monique, Product Mgr-Mobility - Calero Software, LLC; *pg.* 368, *pg.* 1333
Garlow, Jim, Dir-Mktg Ops - CDW Corporation; *pg.* 370, *pg.* 663
Garmoe, Candice, Sr Mgr-PR - Symantec Corporation; *pg.* 478, *pg.* 161

Garneau, Pascal, Rep-Field Sls - LG Electronics Canada, Inc.; pg. 651, pg. 1927
Garner, Amanda, Dir-Mktg - Magellan Health Services, Inc.; pg. 1557, pg. 337
Garner, Charles O., Chief Strategy & Transformation Officer & Exec VP - MedAssets Inc.; pg. 1561, pg. 484
Garner, Debbie, Sr Dir-Global Strategic Mktg-Aesthetics & Dermatology - Allergan, Inc.; pg. 1491, pg. 106
Garner, Kate, VP-Mktg-Wal-Mart Customer Mgmt-PepsiCo - Frito-Lay North America, Inc.; pg. 1853, pg. 1730
Garner, Mark, Sr VP-Bus Dev, Analytics & Distr Mktg - A&E Television Networks, LLC; pg. 267, pg. 1185
Garner, Megan, Sr Mgr-Event Comm & Mktg - Special Olympics International, Inc.; pg. 157, pg. 405
Garner, Sara, Assoc Mgr-Mktg - PepsiCo, Inc.; pg. 259, pg. 1327
Garnero, Ben, Dir-Mktg - Kind LLC; pg. 868, pg. 1249
Garnett, Brad, Mgr-Solutions Mktg - Honeywell International Inc.; pg. 407, pg. 1000
Garnett, Kimberly, Mgr-Regulatory-Adv & Promo - Pfizer Inc.; pg. 1581, pg. 1278
Garney, Cara, VP-Retention Mktg - FairPoint Communications, Inc.; pg. 1871, pg. 1366
Garofola, Mike, Sr Mgr-Mktg - Oki Data Americas, Inc.; pg. 449, pg. 1090
Garofoli, Paul, VP-Mktg - NATIONAL WESTERN LIFE INSURANCE COMPANY; pg. 1210, pg. 1664
Garon, Tina, Dir-Mktg - Jewel-Osco; pg. 1024, pg. 620
Garratt, John, Interim CFO - Dollar General Corporation; pg. 1767, pg. 1635
Garratt, Michael A., Pres-Performance Products & Solutions - PolyOne Corporation; pg. 1177, pg. 1404
Garreffa, Nick, Brand Mgr-Consumer - Abbott Nutrition; pg. 1485, pg. 1437
Garretson, David, Mgr-Sls-Intl - Gold Medal Products Co.; pg. 55, pg. 1414
Garretson, Jim, Sr Product Mgr-Mobile - Constant Contact, Inc.; pg. 379, pg. 850
Garrett, Ember, Mgr-PR & Corp Comm-US - Allergan, Inc.; pg. 1491, pg. 106
Garrett, Gloria, VP-Mktg-Global - Dayton Superior Corporation; pg. 1328, pg. 1464
Garrett, Jennifer, Sr VP-Sls Channels & Strategy - Cox Communications, Inc.; pg. 279, pg. 501
Garrett, Jennifer, Designer-Product & Pkg - SDI Technologies, Inc.; pg. 671, pg. 1113
Garrett, Jennifer, Exec VP-Natl Enterprise Sls - XO Group Inc.; pg. 1289, pg. 1316
Garrett, Jim, Dir-Mktg & Product Mgmt-Luxury Audio & Loudspeakers - Harman International Industries, Incorporated; pg. 641, pg. 374
Garrett, Julie, Dir-Product Mgmt-Outside In Tech - Oracle Corporation; pg. 1272, pg. 786
Garrett, Justin, VP-Digital Sls & Publr - Here Media Inc.; pg. 290, pg. 132
Garrett, Justin, VP-Digital & Social Mktg - JPMorgan Chase & Co.; pg. 772, pg. 1246
Garrett, Justin, Sr Mgr-Product Mktg-Bing Mktg - Microsoft Corporation; pg. 435, pg. 1824
Garrett, Mary, VP-Mktg & Comm-Global Sls & Distr - International Business Machines Corporation; pg. 418, pg. 1138
Garrett, Patrick J., Sr Dir-Revenue Strategy & Plng - DIRECTV Group Holdings, LLC; pg. 281, pg. 79
Garrett, Paula, Sr Dir-Alzheimer's Global Mktg - Eli Lilly and Company; pg. 1527, pg. 684
Garrett, Stanley E., Sr Dir-Membership Svcs - The Cliffs Communities, Inc.; pg. 1086, pg. 1623
Garrett, Tracy, Jr., VP-Sls - PPG Aerospace Deft Facility; pg. 1445, pg. 115
Garrett, Trish, Dir-Mktg - Miramax Film Corp.; pg. 298, pg. 275
Garriga, Jose Maria, VP-Sports Sls - Univision Communications Inc.; pg. 683, pg. 1307
Garrigus, Jaime, Assoc Dir-Media & Consumer Engagement - The Kraft Heinz Company; pg. 871, pg. 641
Garringer, Kelly, Mgr-Mktg-Presource Products & Svcs - Cardinal Health, Inc.; pg. 1512, pg. 1448
Garris, Kimberlee, Dir-Entertainment Mktg - Brooklyn Nets; pg. 534, pg. 1145
Garrison, Cassandra, Editor-Social media & Live News - Thomson Reuters - Corporate Headquarters; pg. 1693, pg. 1299
Garrison, Debbie, VP & Sr Mgr-Talent Acq - Fifth Third Bancorp; pg. 752, pg. 1413
Garrison, Michael S., Sr Dir-Environmental Stewardship & Pkg - Chick-fil-A, Inc.; pg. 1721, pg. 492
Garrison, Peggy, Sr Mgr-Customer Mktg - PepsiCo, Inc.; pg. 259, pg. 1327
Garrity, Chris, Dir-Adv - The New York Times Company; pg. 1668, pg. 1270
Garrity, Tamsin, Analyst-Media - UBS Financial Services Inc.; pg. 812, pg. 1306
Garro, Kristin, Brand Mgr-Salsa & Guacamole - Sabra Dipping Company LLC; pg. 893, pg. 1686
Garroutte, Tracy, Mgr-Sls & Mktg Ops-Worldwide - Cisco Systems, Inc.; pg. 372, pg. 240
Garry, Aaron, VP-Sls & Mktg - Evans Adhesive Corporation, LTD.; pg. 1161, pg. 1440
Garry, Brian N., Sr Dir-Sls & Mktg-Global Hospitality Grp - Cintas Corporation; pg. 372, pg. 1411
Garry, Glenn, Dir-Mktg - Amgen Inc.; pg. 1493, pg. 291
Garry, Michelle, Sr VP-Multi-Platform & Affiliate Mktg - Fox Broadcasting Company; pg. 287, pg. 130
Garry, Michelle, Sr VP-Multi-Platform & Affiliate Mktg - Fox Entertainment Group, Inc.; pg. 288, pg. 131
Garry, Samantha, VP-Mktg Strategy - The Walt Disney Company; pg. 317, pg. 52
Garry, Tim, Mgr-Sls & Mktg - Hormel Foods Corporation; pg. 863, pg. 915
Garsh, Dave, Mgr-Interactive Mktg - Marshalls of MA, Inc.; pg. 1778, pg. 821
Garsh, Dave, Mgr-Interactive Mktg - T.J. Maxx; pg. 1788, pg. 822
Garsh, Dave, Mgr-Interactive Mktg - The TJX Companies, Inc.; pg. 1788, pg. 822
Garsha, Michelle, Sr Dir-Women's Health Mktg - Hologic, Inc.; pg. 1416, pg. 784
Garsten, Ed, Head-FCA Digital Media-Fiat Chrysler Automobiles - FCA US LLC; pg. 170, pg. 868
Garten, Yael, Mgr-Data Science-Mobile Products - LinkedIn Corporation; pg. 1262, pg. 160
Garter, Russ, Sr Dir-Mktg-Americas - HomeAway, Inc.; pg. 1911, pg. 1663
Garth, Denise, Sr VP-Strategic Mktg - Majesco; pg. 429, pg. 1089
Gartin, Ed, Mgr-Product Dev-Global - Toys "R" Us, Inc.; pg. 968, pg. 1130
Gartner, Ted, Sr Specialist-Media Rels - Garmin International, Inc.; pg. 1414, pg. 717
Gartside, Brian, Dir-Mktg-Integrated Customer Experience - GlaxoSmithKline; pg. 1536, pg. 1389
Gartside, Brian, Dir-Mktg-Integrated Customer Experience - GlaxoSmithKline Consumer Healthcare; pg. 510, pg. 1554
Garvelli, Kevin, Sr Mgr-Mktg - Verizon Communications Inc.; pg. 1875, pg. 1309
Garvens, Minda, Sr Mgr-Brand Comm & Digital Mktg - adidas America Inc.; pg. 1803, pg. 1500
Garvey, Emily, Dir-Digital Mktg-Global - Starwood Hotels & Resorts Worldwide, Inc.; pg. 1114, pg. 378
Garvin, Lou, Sr Product Mgr - ChyronHego; pg. 371, pg. 1179
Garvin, Tracey, Sr VP-Mktg - Sony Pictures Home Entertainment; pg. 310, pg. 72
Gary, George, Mgr-Product Mgmt-Cloud Collaboration Tech Grp - Cisco Systems, Inc.; pg. 372, pg. 240
Gary, Jason, CTO-Enterprise Social Solutions - International Business Machines Corporation; pg. 418, pg. 1138
Gary, Jennifer S., Mgr-Mktg - Entergy Corporation; pg. 1941, pg. 746
Garza, Brian, Dir-Ticket Sls & Svcs - Chicago National League Ball Club, LLC; pg. 539, pg. 569
Garza, Christina, Brand Mgr-Mktg Comm - Western Digital Corporation; pg. 492, pg. 118
Garza, Cristina, Sr Mgr-Plng-Intl Retail - SKECHERS U.S.A., INC.; pg. 1819, pg. 143
Garza, Eric, Mgr-Digital Mktg - MoneyGram International, Inc.; pg. 783, pg. 1684
Garza, Esperanza E., Sr Specialist-PR - Paychex, Inc.; pg. 792, pg. 1336
Garza, Tari, VP-Partnership Mktg & Promos - Universal Studios, Inc.; pg. 315, pg. 298
Garzarella, Domenica, Sr Mgr-Email Mktg & Strategy-Retention & Dev - QVC Inc; pg. 305, pg. 1593
Garzilli, Tom, Sr VP-Global Partner Mktg - Brand USA; pg. 1901, pg. 396
Garzon, Mariana, Engr-Product Application - Conexant Systems, Inc.; pg. 379, pg. 165
Garzon, Rich, Sr Mgr-Mktg - Coty, Inc.; pg. 506, pg. 1219
Garzon, Stefania, Specialist-Multicultural Mktg - Lowe's Companies, Inc.; pg. 1053, pg. 1383
Gasaway, Daniella, Dir-Adv - Oakley, Inc.; pg. 1840, pg. 86
Gascoigne, Doreen, Sr Mgr-Bus HR-US Comml - AbbVie Inc.; pg. 1486, pg. 638
Gascon, Bobby, Dir-Global Action Sports Mktg - Vans, Inc.; pg. 1821, pg. 76
Gashti, Sara, Brand Mgr-Partnership-Jewelry & Watches - Amazon.com, Inc.; pg. 1226, pg. 1831
Gaskey, Bart, VP-Sls - ABB Inc. - Automation Technologies Instrumentation Products; pg. 1398, pg. 1590
Gaskill, Brad, Sr Designer-Mktg Comm-Global - Eastman Chemical Company; pg. 1159, pg. 1636
Gaskin, Chris, Sr Dir-Trade Mktg - R.J. Reynolds Tobacco Co.; pg. 1895, pg. 1395
Gaskins, Mitzi, VP & Brand Mgr-Global-JW Marriott Hotels & Resorts - Marriott International, Inc.; pg. 1102, pg. 764
Gaskins, William, Territory Mgr-Sls - Herman Miller, Inc.; pg. 926, pg. 913
Gaspar, Heather, Brand Mgr-Sustainability - MillerCoors LLC; pg. 255, pg. 582
Gaspard, Brent, Mgr-Mktg Packaged & Indus Solutions - Tyco International (US) Inc.; pg. 1891, pg. 1113
Gasparini, T. Shawn, Mgr-Digital & Media Investment - Reckitt Benckiser Inc.; pg. 1136, pg. 1105
Gaspers, Cheryl, Sr Specialist-HR, PR & Disability - Ceridian Corporation; pg. 371, pg. 932
Gass, Judith, Dir-Veterinary Mktg - Veterinary Pet Insurance Co.; pg. 1222, pg. 49
Gass, Michelle, Chief Mdsg & Customer Officer - Kohl's Corporation; pg. 1775, pg. 1870
Gass, Ryan, Brand Mgr - Nestle Purina PetCare Company; pg. 1479, pg. 1000
Gasser, Eric, Sr Mgr-PR & Comm - Medtronic, Inc.; pg. 1564, pg. 939
Gassler, Lena, Specialist-Mktg Comm - Honeywell International Inc.; pg. 407, pg. 1088
Gassmere, Tim, Product Mgr-ECommerce-Photo - Walgreen Co.; pg. 1608, pg. 605
Gaston, Lisa, Mgr-Mktg Event & Emerging Companies - PricewaterhouseCoopers LLP; pg. 795, pg. 1283
Gastwirth, Jason, Sr VP-Mktg & Entertainment - Caesars Entertainment Corporation; pg. 1083, pg. 1023
Gastwirth, Lauren, VP & Mgr-Natl Sls - Discovery Communications, Inc.; pg. 282, pg. 777
Gasuad, Kimberly, Sr Dir-Brand Rx Strategy - McKesson Corporation; pg. 1560, pg. 222
Gatcomb, Steven, Dir-Sls & Mktg-Nuclear - Valcor Engineering Corporation; pg. 1386, pg. 1123
Gates, Cristie, Mgr-Media - Benelli USA Corporation; pg. 1827, pg. 754
Gates, Grok, Product Mgr - Bridgestone Americas, Inc.; pg. 201, pg. 1649
Gates, Jessica, Mgr-Mktg-Carnation Breakfast Essentials - Nestle USA, Inc.; pg. 883, pg. 96
Gates, Linda, VP-Creative & Brand Synergy - J.C. Penney Company, Inc.; pg. 1774, pg. 1732
Gates, Sandra, Mgr-Sls-Southeast Reg - Petroferm Inc.; pg. 1177, pg. 616
Gatewood, Annette, Sr Specialist-Mktg Budget - Adobe Systems Incorporated; pg. 342, pg. 235
Gatewood, Erik, Dir-New Product Dev-Metal Pkg - Ball Corporation; pg. 1452, pg. 311
Gattanella, Steve, Mgr-Mktg Svcs - Prestige Brands Holdings, Inc.; pg. 520, pg. 1345
Gatti, Greg, Sr Dir-IT - Atlanta National League Baseball Club, Inc.; pg. 530, pg. 490
Gatti, Guilherme, Mng Dir-Strategic Mktg & Pricing - FedEx Corporation; pg. 1907, pg. 1642
Gatto, Craig, Dir-Product Safety & Regulatory Compliance - Motorola Mobility LLC; pg. 657, pg. 627
Gatto, Denise, First VP & Dir-Product Mgmt & Mktg Info - Astoria Federal Savings & Loan; pg. 716, pg. 1171
Gatto, Jim, Dir-Global Sports Mktg-Basketball - adidas America Inc.; pg. 1803, pg. 1500
Gatto, Rob, Sr VP-Sls - NeuStar, Inc.; pg. 1872, pg. 1807
Gattshall, Timothy, Dir-Adv & Sponsorships - Living Essentials, LLC; pg. 1026, pg. 886
Gatz, Mike, Mgr-Mktg - Caterpillar, Inc.; pg. 1321, pg. 650
Gauba, Raheel, Head-Brand & Dir-Creative-Corp Mktg - Blackbaud, Inc.; pg. 361, pg. 1613
Gaudet, Glen, VP-Sls-Ops - Stanfield's Limited; pg. 48, pg. 1917
Gaudio, Nick, Dir-Adv Ops - The Reader's Digest Association, Inc.; pg. 1679, pg. 1322
Gaudry, Clint, VP-Mktg - Sears Canada Inc.; pg. 1784, pg. 1943

First page reference indicates Business Class Edition
Second page reference indicates Geographic Edition

Gaughan, Jay, Sr Mgr-Customer Acq - Highlights for Children, Inc.; *pg.* 1650, *pg.* 1440
Gaul, David L., VP-Sls & Mktg - Denver Wholesale Florists Company; *pg.* 1794, *pg.* 319
Gaulke, Paul, Dir-Creative Svcs-KSTP-TV & KSTC - Hubbard Broadcasting, Inc.; *pg.* 291, *pg.* 961
Gaulke, Paul, Dir-Creative Svcs-KSTP-TV & KSTC - KSTP-TV, LLC; *pg.* 295, *pg.* 962
Gault, Bob, Exec VP-Worldwide Sls, Channel & Svcs Org - Extreme Networks Inc; *pg.* 287, *pg.* 245
Gault, Carlee, Coord-Adv - The J.M. Smucker Company; *pg.* 865, *pg.* 1468
Gault, Rachel, Specialist-Mktg Comm - Syniverse Holdings, Inc.; *pg.* 479, *pg.* 475
Gaunt, Jeff, Dir-Mktg - Bar-S Foods Co.; *pg.* 839, *pg.* 15
Gaunt, Jerry, Head-Mktg - Genworth Financial, Inc.; *pg.* 761, *pg.* 1802
Gaunt, Peter, Head-Social Creative - Zappos.com, Inc.; *pg.* 1291, *pg.* 1030
Gause, Bill, Mgr-Sls-Natl Contractor - Makita U.S.A., Inc.; *pg.* 1358, *pg.* 120
Gause, Julia, Dir-Search Mktg - Scripps Networks Interactive, Inc.; *pg.* 1279, *pg.* 1638
Gaut, Steve, VP-PR - United Parcel Service, Inc.; *pg.* 1928, *pg.* 522
Gauthier, Aneta, Mgr-Production - Putman Media, Inc.; *pg.* 1679, *pg.* 621
Gauthier, Jana, Dir-Digital Media - New England Patriots Football Club, Inc.; *pg.* 569, *pg.* 819
Gauthier, Jay, VP-ECommerce & Mktg-Personal Insurance - The Travelers Companies, Inc.; *pg.* 1220, *pg.* 352
Gauthreaux, Rhonda, VP-Mktg - Southwire Company; *pg.* 1063, *pg.* 527
Gautier, Arnaud, Sr VP-Mktg & Product Mgmt - MegaPath, Inc.; *pg.* 432, *pg.* 71
Gauvain, Tucker, Product Mgr-Waring Products - Conair Corporation; *pg.* 505, *pg.* 1055
Gavan, Peggy, Sr Mgr-Comm - Express Scripts, Inc.; *pg.* 1530, *pg.* 997
Gavilan, Marisol, Mgr-Trade Mktg - Bacardi USA, Inc.; *pg.* 1956, *pg.* 417
Gavin, Anthony, Mgr-Unbranded Sls - Valero Energy Corporation; *pg.* 986, *pg.* 1743
Gavin, Dolores, Exec VP-Dev & Production - Discovery Communications, Inc.; *pg.* 282, *pg.* 777
Gavin, Ryan, Gen Mgr-Search, Cloud & Content Mktg - Microsoft Corporation; *pg.* 435, *pg.* 1824
Gavin, Sarah, Sr Dir-Integrated Mktg, Mdsg & Comm - Expedia, Inc.; *pg.* 1244, *pg.* 1814
Gaviria, Ruth, Exec VP-Corp Mktg - Univision Communications Inc.; *pg.* 683, *pg.* 1307
Gavriluk, Tom, Dir-Digital Brand Mktg-Boys Category-Hasbro Digital Media - Hasbro, Inc.; *pg.* 954, *pg.* 1603
Gawel, Rachel, Specialist-Paid Search Mktg - Quicken Loans, Inc.; *pg.* 797, *pg.* 884
Gawley, Alex, Dir-Product Mgmt - Google Inc.; *pg.* 1249, *pg.* 153
Gay, Jacqueline, Mgr-Mktg Svcs - Quincy Compressor Inc.; *pg.* 1371, *pg.* 653
Gay, Will, Dir-Creative - The Walt Disney Company; *pg.* 317, *pg.* 52
Gaydos, Jeff, Sr Mgr-Comm - Hess Corporation; *pg.* 979, *pg.* 1240
Gayed, Nancy, Head-Product Experience - Cisco Systems, Inc.; *pg.* 372, *pg.* 240
Gaylord, Peter, Dir-Product Mktg - salesforce.com, inc.; *pg.* 1278, *pg.* 226
Gaymont, Stephen, Dir-Creative Svcs & Distr Mktg - Univision Communications Inc.; *pg.* 683, *pg.* 1307
Gaynes, David, VP-Product Dev & Design - Sterling Jewelers Inc.; *pg.* 13, *pg.* 1402
Gaynor, Adam, VP-Media Sls & Analytics - DISH Network Corporation; *pg.* 283, *pg.* 325
Gaynor, Darby, Sr Mgr-PR - Gucci America Inc.; *pg.* 6, *pg.* 1237
Gaynor, Denis, Dir-Mktg Strategy-Microsoft Online Svcs - Microsoft Corporation; *pg.* 435, *pg.* 1824
Gaynor, Elisse, Sr Mgr-Brand Insights & Res - Panera Bread Company; *pg.* 1029, *pg.* 1001
Gayton, Chris, VP-Brand Mktg - The J. Jill Group, Inc.; *pg.* 1774, *pg.* 842
Gazale, Alex, Dir-Production - National Arts Centre Corporation; *pg.* 566, *pg.* 1932
Gazarian-Semerjian, Eliz, Dir-Natl Sls-Los Angeles - Telemundo Network Inc.; *pg.* 311, *pg.* 430
Gazay, Steve, Sr Acct Mgr-Corp Inside Sls - Informatica Corporation; *pg.* 414, *pg.* 190
Gazdick, Stephen, Mgr-Customer Mktg - Pure Fishing, Inc.; *pg.* 1843, *pg.* 1614
Gazley, David, VP-Meeting & Convention Sls - The Greater Vancouver Convention & Visitor Bureau; *pg.* 994, *pg.* 1910
Gazzola, Ron, VP-Mktg - Samsung Electronics America, Inc.; *pg.* 669, *pg.* 1115
Gdowik, Tom, VP-Federal Sls - Attachmate Corporation; *pg.* 356, *pg.* 1833
Ge, Vicky, Mgr-Mktg-Platinum Publr Programs-US Trade Books - Amazon.com, Inc.; *pg.* 1226, *pg.* 1831
Geadelmann, Levi, Sr Product Mgr - Honeywell International Inc.; *pg.* 407, *pg.* 1088
Gearhart, Mike, Sr Mgr-Mktg-VIP & Strategic Programs - NetApp, Inc.; *pg.* 444, *pg.* 287
Gearhart, Stacey, Dir-Product & Channel Mktg - Rheem Manufacturing Company; *pg.* 1075, *pg.* 519
Geary, Brandon, Sr Mgr - Accenture; *pg.* 1392, *pg.* 1186
Geary, Jeanette Fuller, Sr Mgr-Global Mktg-Alliances - F5 Networks, Inc.; *pg.* 396, *pg.* 1835
Geater, Kim, Mgr-North America Field Mktg-Transportation & Logistics - Motorola Solutions, Inc.; *pg.* 657, *pg.* 659
Gebauer, Francisco, Dir-Global External Comm-Pfizer Established Products Bus Unit - Pfizer Inc.; *pg.* 1581, *pg.* 1278
Gebbia, Joe, Co-Founder & Chief Product Officer - Airbnb, Inc.; *pg.* 1226, *pg.* 211
Gebbie, Michelle, Mgr-Global Employment Branding & Mktg - 3M Company; *pg.* 1142, *pg.* 956
Gebele, Mike, VP-Server Sys & Mktg - Lenovo Group Ltd; *pg.* 427, *pg.* 1384
Gebhard, Katie, Mgr-Mktg - Sony Pictures Entertainment Inc.; *pg.* 309, *pg.* 72
Gebhardt, Becky, Chief Creative Officer & Sr VP - Lands' End, Inc.; *pg.* 1776, *pg.* 1857
Gebhardt, Gina, Coord-Mktg & Promos - The Wall Street Journal; *pg.* 1700, *pg.* 1312
Gebhardt, Laura, Coord-PR - Neiman Marcus, Inc.; *pg.* 30, *pg.* 1684
Gebhart Nicholson, Devon, Brand Mgr - StubHub, Inc.; *pg.* 586, *pg.* 228
Gebhart, Candy, VP-Mktg-Global - L'Oreal USA; *pg.* 514, *pg.* 1252
Gebhart, Carrie, Grp VP-Sls - CORT Business Services Corporation; *pg.* 921, *pg.* 1777
Gebken, Juliette, Mgr-PR-Latin America - Universal Orlando; *pg.* 590, *pg.* 456
Gecmen, Serkan, Corp Dir-Digital Mktg - Pinnacle Entertainment, Inc.; *pg.* 576, *pg.* 1029
Geddes, Dean, Mgr-Retail Mktg Strategy - Ford Motor Company of Canada, Limited; *pg.* 174, *pg.* 1930
Geddes, Tom, Mgr-Sls-Natl - MHI Injection Molding Machinery, Inc.; *pg.* 1886, *pg.* 620
Gedid, Edwin, Mgr-Adv - General Nutrition Centers, Inc.; *pg.* 1534, *pg.* 1575
Gedney, Michelle, Mgr-Integrated Mktg Comm - Land O'Lakes, Inc.; *pg.* 873, *pg.* 915
Gee, Bryan, Dir-Mktg - Tensar Corporation; *pg.* 114, *pg.* 485
Gee, Douglas, Head-Sls-Asset Servicing Bus-EMEA - Northern Trust Corporation; *pg.* 787, *pg.* 585
Gee, Robyn J., Mgr-Mktg - General Growth Properties, Inc.; *pg.* 1093, *pg.* 574
Gee, Zorana, Sr Product Mgr-Photoshop - Adobe Systems Incorporated; *pg.* 342, *pg.* 235
Geehern, Chris, Exec VP-Mktg - Massachusetts Convention Center Authority; *pg.* 561, *pg.* 798
Geen, Kc, Head-Social Media-Global - Groupon, Inc.; *pg.* 1255, *pg.* 575
Geerlings, Evan, Dir-Mobile Products - Spark Networks, Inc.; *pg.* 472, *pg.* 140
Geffen, Zvee, Brand Mgr - The Topps Company, Inc.; *pg.* 588, *pg.* 1302
Geffke, Jacqueline, Asst Mgr-Sls Promo - L'Oreal USA; *pg.* 514, *pg.* 1252
Geffner, Julia Strongwater, VP-Mktg-North America - Wyndham Worldwide Corporation; *pg.* 1119, *pg.* 1107
Gegg, Rebecca, Coord-PR - Cerner Corporation; *pg.* 1514, *pg.* 981
Gegwich, Grant, VP-PR & Mktg - Crozer-Keystone Health System Inc.; *pg.* 1520, *pg.* 1587
Geherin, Jenna, Sr Planner-Digital Sls - The Sporting News; *pg.* 1688, *pg.* 1295
Gehlbach, Glenn R., VP & Mgr-Sls - Copland Fabrics, Inc.; *pg.* 692, *pg.* 1359
Gehling, Maren, Assoc Mgr-Product & Brand-Motorization - Hunter Douglas, Inc.; *pg.* 928, *pg.* 1320
Gehrett, Mark, Sr Mgr-Product Mktg - NCH Corporation; *pg.* 1174, *pg.* 1723
Gehrig, Richard, Assoc Dir-Opdivo US Mktg - Bristol-Myers Squibb Company; *pg.* 1509, *pg.* 1206
Gehring, Kay, Mgr-Mktg-High Capacity Conductors - 3M Company; *pg.* 1142, *pg.* 956
Geib, Kyle, Specialist-Mktg & Social Media - skinnyCorp L.L.C.; *pg.* 1280, *pg.* 590
Geib, Lindsay, Coord-Sls Res - Louisville Convention & Visitors Bureau; *pg.* 998, *pg.* 736
Geibel, Kent, Grp Controller-Worldwide Construction Products - Illinois Tool Works Inc.; *pg.* 1348, *pg.* 614
Geiger, Anna, Mgr-Field Mktg - Red Bull North America, Inc.; *pg.* 264, *pg.* 275
Geiger, Craig, Sr Mgr-Shopper Insights & Category Solutions-Walmart & Sam's - Campbell Soup Company; *pg.* 844, *pg.* 1048
Geiger, Daniel, Dir-Adv & Bus Dev-East-KBB - Kelley Blue Book Co., Inc.; *pg.* 1656, *pg.* 112
Geiger, Debbie, VP-Mktg-Global - ASTEA INTERNATIONAL INC.; *pg.* 355, *pg.* 1540
Geiger, Doug, VP & Head-New Therapeutic-Mktg Strategy - Astellas Pharma US, Inc.; *pg.* 1496, *pg.* 640
Geiger, John, Dir-Customer Relationship Mktg - Victoria's Secret Stores, LLC; *pg.* 1789, *pg.* 1471
Geiling, Christy, Dir-Mktg - Rubio's Restaurants, Inc.; *pg.* 1748, *pg.* 60
Geiman, Ray, VP-Product Design & Dev - Playmates Toys Inc.; *pg.* 965, *pg.* 82
Geis, David, Product Mgr-Parts & Accessories - ITW Magnaflux; *pg.* 1418, *pg.* 615
Geis, Judith, Sr Mgr-Mktg - American Express Company; *pg.* 712, *pg.* 1190
Geise, Ian, Sr VP-Mktg & Product Dev - Voxx International; *pg.* 686, *pg.* 1166
Geisel, Aaron, Reg Dir-Mktg - Charter Communications, Inc.; *pg.* 274, *pg.* 372
Geisel, Ross, Sr Dir-Partnerships - Hearst Magazines; *pg.* 1649, *pg.* 1239
Geiser, James, VP-Sls & Mktg - Six Flags Theme Parks Inc.; *pg.* 584, *pg.* 1699
Geiser, Jeff, Mgr-PR - Newport Aquarium; *pg.* 571, *pg.* 739
Geisler, Jamie, Analyst-Chemical Product Safety - The Timberland Company; *pg.* 1821, *pg.* 1039
Geismar, Meghan, Analyst-Mktg - Jefferies Group, Inc.; *pg.* 772, *pg.* 1246
Geissler, Rebecca, Product Mgr - Bradley Corporation; *pg.* 71, *pg.* 1870
Geist, John, VP-Sls - The Boston Beer Company, Inc.; *pg.* 239, *pg.* 790
Geist, Kent, Sr Dir-Dev & Comm - ideastream; *pg.* 292, *pg.* 1431
Geistman, Morgan, Mgr-Social Media & Digital - L'Oreal USA; *pg.* 514, *pg.* 1252
Geistman, Robert A., Exec VP-Sls & Mktg - Ingram Entertainment Inc.; *pg.* 292, *pg.* 1639
Geivett, Kathryn, Dir-Social Media - Holland America Line Inc.; *pg.* 1911, *pg.* 1836
Gelb, Brian, Brand Mgr - The Kraft Heinz Company; *pg.* 871, *pg.* 641
Gelb, Jenna, Dir-Sls - Buzzfeed; *pg.* 1233, *pg.* 1208
Gelb, Lisa, VP-Mktg & Sls - Motor Trend Auto Shows, LLC; *pg.* 564, *pg.* 1537
Gelbman, Ronald G., Interim CEO - Haemonetics Corporation; *pg.* 1538, *pg.* 802
Geldner, Carrie, CMO & Sr VP - Tanger Factory Outlet Centers, Inc.; *pg.* 1116, *pg.* 1376
GELDNER, Carrie A., CMO & Sr VP-Mktg - Tanger Properties Limited Partnership; *pg.* 1116, *pg.* 1376
Gelestathis, Teresa, Brand Mgr-Men's Tailored, Shoes & Accessories - Macy's, Inc.; *pg.* 1778, *pg.* 1417
Gelfand, Jeff, Dir-Natl Sls & Mktg-Printing Sys-USA - ABB Inc. - Automation Technologies Instrumentation Products; *pg.* 1398, *pg.* 1590
Gelfand, Lorin, Dir-Integrated Mktg - Craft Brewers Alliance, Inc; *pg.* 247, *pg.* 1502
Gelfond, Larry, VP-Mktg - KB Home; *pg.* 90, *pg.* 134
Gelfusa, Liz, Team Head-Product Design - Quicken Loans, Inc.; *pg.* 797, *pg.* 884
Geling, H.J.K., Sr Dir-Sls-Europe, Middle East, India & Africa - Key Technology, Inc.; *pg.* 868, *pg.* 1847
Geller, Lisa, Sr Product Mgr - First DataBank, Inc.; *pg.* 397, *pg.* 217

Geller, Penni, Sr Dir-Digital Content Mktg - CA Technologies; *pg.* 366, *pg.* 1168
Gellerman, Doug, Sr VP-Sls-West Coast - National CineMedia, Inc.; *pg.* 567, *pg.* 314
Gellman, Rachel, Mgr-Mktg-Publ - American Society of Health-System Pharmacists; *pg.* 131, *pg.* 761
Gellman, Richard, VP-Adv & Mktg - Tourneau Inc.; *pg.* 14, *pg.* 1303
Gelman, Eve, Sr Mgr-Comm - Peddler's Village, Inc.; *pg.* 1107, *pg.* 1545
Gelman, Jackie, Strategist-Creative-Prospect Mktg - The Vanguard Group, Inc.; *pg.* 816, *pg.* 1550
Gelman, Mitch, VP-Product - Gannett Co., Inc.; *pg.* 1643, *pg.* 1790
Gelman, Oren, Sr Dir-Global Strategic Mktg-Stryker IMT - Stryker Corporation; *pg.* 1598, *pg.* 894
Gelman, Sarah, Dir-PR - Amazon.com, Inc.; *pg.* 1226, *pg.* 1831
Gelt, Tim, Dir-Media Rels - The Denver Nuggets Limited Partnership; *pg.* 544, *pg.* 319
Gemborys, Lisa, Asst Brand Mgr & Asst Product Mgr - Toys "R" Us, Inc.; *pg.* 968, *pg.* 1130
Gemelli, Nick, Dir-Reg & Strategic Accounts Mktg - Diageo North America, Inc.; *pg.* 1961, *pg.* 361
Geml, Angela, Mgr-Mktg & PR - Columbia Restaurant Group; *pg.* 1723, *pg.* 472
Gemmell, Brian D., Dir-Sls & Mktg-Transmission Solutions - Siemens Corporation; *pg.* 803, *pg.* 1291
Gemmellaro, Kate, Sr Mgr-Media - Philips Healthcare; *pg.* 1585, *pg.* 783
Gemmill, Karen, Head-Product Innovation, Fixed & Life Products - Allianz Life Insurance Company of North America; *pg.* 1188, *pg.* 929
Gendron, Greg, Mgr-Mktg - Black Box Corporation; *pg.* 361, *pg.* 1547
Gendron, J.P., Sr Mgr-Exec & Strategic Comm - AECOM; *pg.* 64, *pg.* 1187
Gendron, Robert, VP-Mktg & Bus Dev - Vicor Corporation; *pg.* 1435, *pg.* 783
Genel, Dave, VP-Digital Brand Mktg-Global - NIKE, Inc.; *pg.* 1812, *pg.* 1492
Generaux, Janet R., Analyst-Mdsg - Toyota Motor North America, Inc.; *pg.* 192, *pg.* 1303
Genesio, Sebastian, Sr Dir-Strategy-Latin America - Mondelez International; *pg.* 877, *pg.* 1344
Genest, John, Brand Mgr - Pabst Brewing Company; *pg.* 258, *pg.* 137
Genet, Nadine, Mng Dir & Head-Adv-Global - UBS Financial Services Inc.; *pg.* 812, *pg.* 1306
Genevish, Nick, Product Mgr-Mktg-Preparedness, Health & Safety Svcs - American Red Cross; *pg.* 130, *pg.* 395
Geng, Carol, Mgr-Web Mktg - Cisco Systems, Inc.; *pg.* 372, *pg.* 240
Geng, Dan, Mgr-Mktg & Distr - Hulu LLC; *pg.* 1257, *pg.* 274
Geniviva, John L., Dir-Mktg & Display Technologies - Corning Incorporated; *pg.* 1122, *pg.* 1154
Genna, Jake, Mgr-Inside Sls - Lenovo Group Ltd; *pg.* 427, *pg.* 1384
Genna, Vicki, Dir-Adv & Promo - Farrar, Straus & Giroux, Inc.; *pg.* 1640, *pg.* 1231
Geno, Shannon, Mgr-Sls-Water Conservation Team - Rain Bird Corporation; *pg.* 707, *pg.* 44
Genova, Sue, Engr-Product - Cadence Design Systems, Inc.; *pg.* 367, *pg.* 239
Genovese, Chris, Dir-Global Mktg & Head-Respiratory - Merck & Co., Inc.; *pg.* 1566, *pg.* 1077
Genovese, Frank, Exec VP-Sls - Ste. Michelle Wine Estates Ltd.; *pg.* 1970, *pg.* 1847
Genovese, Laurie, Dir-Acq Strategy & Brand Mktg - Liberty Mutual Insurance Group Inc.; *pg.* 1205, *pg.* 797
Genovese, Yvonne, Mng VP-Gartner for Mktg Leaders - Gartner, Inc.; *pg.* 1248, *pg.* 374
Genshaft, Jodi, Brand Mgr-Shopper Mktg - Chobani LLC; *pg.* 847, *pg.* 1318
Gensley, Katie, Asst Mgr-Social Media - Charlotte Russe, Inc.; *pg.* 21, *pg.* 201
Gent, Allen, Head-Strategy & Product Mgr-US Soybean - Bayer CropScience; *pg.* 1149, *pg.* 981
Gentile, Lauren, Dir-Mktg - Allstar Products Group LLC; *pg.* 17, *pg.* 1166
Gentile, Matt, Dir-Social Media-Global - Century 21 Real Estate LLC; *pg.* 1085, *pg.* 1080
Gentile, Matt, Product Mgr-Datacom Products - General Cable Corporation; *pg.* 83, *pg.* 729
Gentili, Christina, Sr Mgr-Brand Mktg-Frozen Beverages - Dunkin' Brands Group, Inc.; *pg.* 1727, *pg.* 810
Gentin, Olivia, Dir-Mdsg - bebe stores, inc.; *pg.* 19, *pg.* 49
Gentry, Angela, Sr Dir-Strategic Mktg-Occupier Svcs - CB Richard Ellis Group, Inc.; *pg.* 1085, *pg.* 127
Gentry, Ron, Dir-Mktg - Boiron USA Inc.; *pg.* 1507, *pg.* 1556
Genuardi, Michael, Mgr-Maestro Products - Fiserv, Inc.; *pg.* 758, *pg.* 537
Geoffroy, Noel, Sr VP-Morning Foods Mktg & Innovation - Kellogg Company; *pg.* 831, *pg.* 870
Geoghegan, JP, Mgr-Adv - Breitling USA; *pg.* 2, *pg.* 385
Geon, Dave, VP-Sls-Enterprise Connectivity - Belden, Inc.; *pg.* 624, *pg.* 993
Geonnotti, Julie E., Specialist-Mktg - The Hanover Insurance Company; *pg.* 1202, *pg.* 862
Georg, David, Mgr-Strategic Mktg - ABB Inc.; *pg.* 1309, *pg.* 1359
George, Adam, Planner-Integrated Mktg Comm - General Mills, Inc.; *pg.* 828, *pg.* 933
George, Amy, Sr VP-Mktg & Comm - Mothers Against Drunk Driving (MADD); *pg.* 147, *pg.* 1723
George, Andrew, Planner-Adv - Nordstrom, Inc.; *pg.* 1779, *pg.* 1837
George, Bob, Dir-Sls & Mktg - Buck Knives, Inc.; *pg.* 1828, *pg.* 550
George, Cherie, Brand Mgr-Olive Garden - Darden Restaurants, Inc.; *pg.* 1724, *pg.* 453
George, Cherie, Brand Mgr-Olive Garden - Olive Garden Italian Restaurant; *pg.* 1742, *pg.* 454
George, Chris, Dir-Mktg - Comcast Corporation; *pg.* 276, *pg.* 1560
George, Diane, Sr Assoc Brand Mgr-Swanson Broth & Stock - Campbell Soup Company; *pg.* 844, *pg.* 1048
George, Duane v., Sr Dir-Proactive Support-Sys - Oracle Corporation; *pg.* 450, *pg.* 191
George, Jackson, Sr VP-Creative Adv - The Walt Disney Company; *pg.* 317, *pg.* 52
George, James, Mgr-Vehicle Mktg & Comm-Tacoma, 4Runner & FJ Cruiser - Toyota Motor Sales, U.S.A., Inc.; *pg.* 193, *pg.* 296
George, Jessica, Dir-Mktg Comm - TTI Floor Care North America; *pg.* 61, *pg.* 1473
George, K. Travis, VP-Fin-Comml Products Div - Molex Incorporated; *pg.* 655, *pg.* 628
George, Kara, Sr Mgr-Client Mktg Comm, Trader & Events - TD Ameritrade Holding Corporation; *pg.* 808, *pg.* 1018
George, Kedric, Dir-Mktg-Coors Light Brand - MillerCoors; *pg.* 254, *pg.* 1877
George, Kevin, Dir-Mktg-Snacks Portfolio - Nestle USA, Inc.; *pg.* 883, *pg.* 96
George, Kimberly, Dir-Mktg & Dev - The Salvation Army; *pg.* 155, *pg.* 1771
George, Matt, Coord-Mktg - The Hershey Co.; *pg.* 1855, *pg.* 1538
George, Michelle, VP-Mktg-Customer Experience & Comm - Wells Fargo & Company; *pg.* 819, *pg.* 232
George, Nick, Mgr-ECommerce Mktg - Levi Strauss & Co.; *pg.* 43, *pg.* 220
Georgenson, Katie, Sr Mgr-Product & Mktg - Cardinal Health, Inc.; *pg.* 1512, *pg.* 1448
Georger, Edward, Exec VP-Adv Sls & Gen Mgr-Hallmark Movie Channel - Crown Media Holdings Inc.; *pg.* 280, *pg.* 281
Georgeson, Kendal, Mgr-Mktg-Jackson Family Fine Wines - Kendall-Jackson Wine Estates, Ltd.; *pg.* 1965, *pg.* 277
Georghiou, Christos, Exec Dir-US Nephrology Mktg - Amgen Inc.; *pg.* 1493, *pg.* 291
Georgii, Peter, Mgr-New Product - Joseph Enterprises, Inc.; *pg.* 960, *pg.* 220
Georgiou, Anastasia, Product Mgr-UK Adviser Products - MORNINGSTAR, INC.; *pg.* 784, *pg.* 583
Georgiou, Andrew, VP-Mktg - Alfred Angelo, Inc.; *pg.* 17, *pg.* 1532
Georgousis, Fay, Dir-PR & Mktg - Greek National Tourist Organization; *pg.* 994, *pg.* 1236
Gephart, Gene G., Mgr-Mktg Comm - Smith & Nephew, Inc., Endoscopy Division; *pg.* 1594, *pg.* 783
Geppert, Brent, Product Mgr - Educational Insights, Inc.; *pg.* 951, *pg.* 187
Geraghty, Liz, VP-Brand Mktg - The Wendy's Company; *pg.* 1755, *pg.* 1450
Geraghty, Liz, VP-Brand Mktg - Wendy's International, Inc.; *pg.* 1755, *pg.* 1451
Geraghty, Rebecca, Specialist-Product Mktg-Mixed Reality - Canon U.S.A., Inc.; *pg.* 1404, *pg.* 1178
Geraghty, Simon, Brand Mgr-Neutrogena Naturals & Men's - Neutrogena Corporation; *pg.* 517, *pg.* 137
Geraghty, Theresa, Sr Dir-Product Mktg-Domains - Go Daddy Inc.; *pg.* 1249, *pg.* 21
Gerald, Lela, VP-Mktg-Global - Buckman; *pg.* 1150, *pg.* 1641
Geralde, Rhonda, Rep-Sls - Child Craft Industries, Inc.; *pg.* 920, *pg.* 1463
Gerard, Ashley, Specialist-Media Buying Support - The Tire Rack Inc.; *pg.* 1890, *pg.* 697
Gerard, Lesley, Coord-Mktg Project & Specialist-Graphic Design - Trouw Nutrition USA; *pg.* 1482, *pg.* 616
Gerbec, Jill, Mgr-Mktg - The Allstate Corporation; *pg.* 1189, *pg.* 639
Gerber, Adam, VP-Sls Dev & Mktg - ABC, Inc.; *pg.* 268, *pg.* 1185
Gerber, Audrey, VP-Brand Mktg-Pottery Barn Brands - Williams-Sonoma, Inc.; *pg.* 1140, *pg.* 234
Gerber, Lori, Sr VP-Sls-North America - The NPD Group, Inc.; *pg.* 1672, *pg.* 1323
Gerber, Manuela, Mgr-Global Mktg-Lab Div - Mettler-Toledo International Inc.; *pg.* 1423, *pg.* 1441
Gerber, Nathan B., Mgr-Global Energy Sls-TimkenSteel - The Timken Company; *pg.* 218, *pg.* 1408
Gerber, Shelley, Dir-Mktg-Campuses - Kaplan, Inc.; *pg.* 603, *pg.* 425
Gerchick, Keith, Dir-Creative-Essie - L'Oreal USA; *pg.* 514, *pg.* 1252
Gerdes, Hans J., Brand Mgr-Global B2B-Lubricants - Shell Lubricants; *pg.* 217, *pg.* 1714
Gerecitano, Talia, Dir-Originals Mktg - Netflix, Inc.; *pg.* 1269, *pg.* 141
Geremia, Jessica, Planner-Camry Mktg & Comm - Toyota Motor Sales, U.S.A., Inc.; *pg.* 193, *pg.* 296
Gerentine, Mike, VP-Channels & Midmarket Mktg-Global - IBM; *pg.* 410, *pg.* 1449
Gergeni, Matt, Sr Specialist-PR & Digital Mktg Comm - Magnetek, Inc.; *pg.* 1301, *pg.* 1870
Gerhart, Morgan, Sr Dir-Products - Citrix Systems, Inc.; *pg.* 375, *pg.* 424
Gerick, Brad, Dir-Social Media-New York - Daily News, L.P.; *pg.* 1632, *pg.* 1221
Gerike, Stephen, Dir-Foodservice Mktg - National Pork Board; *pg.* 882, *pg.* 703
Gerke, Jill, Coord-Mktg - Kao Brands Co. Inc.; *pg.* 513, *pg.* 1415
Gerken, Mary F., Dir-Sls - WTVG 13abc; *pg.* 323, *pg.* 1477
Gerkhardt, Sarah, Mgr-Email Mktg - BUYSEASONS, Inc.; *pg.* 20, *pg.* 1883
Gerlach, Rob, Div VP-Loyalty Mktg - Sears Holdings Corporation; *pg.* 1784, *pg.* 618
Gerlt, Andy, Dir-Global Mktg, Comm & Core Products - Visa Inc.; *pg.* 816, *pg.* 230
Gerlt, Andy, Dir-Global Mktg, Comm & Core Products - Visa U.S.A., Inc.; *pg.* 817, *pg.* 231
Germadnig, Dina, Mgr-Mktg - Audible, Inc.; *pg.* 1230, *pg.* 1095
Germain, Mark, Dir-Customer & Product Support - John Deere Consumer & Commercial Equipment, Inc.; *pg.* 705, *pg.* 1360
Germain, Steve, VP-Mktg - BJ's Wholesale Club, Inc.; *pg.* 1762, *pg.* 857
Germani, Susanna, Mgr-Procurement & Mktg Svcs - Diageo North America Inc.; *pg.* 248, *pg.* 1223
Germano, Elaine, Sr Education Policy Advisor - American College of Nurse-Midwives; *pg.* 127, *pg.* 777
Germany, Jasmine, Specialist-Media - Regions Financial Corporation; *pg.* 798, *pg.* 4
Germany, Rhonda, CMO, Chief Strategy Officer & Corp VP - Honeywell International Inc.; *pg.* 407, *pg.* 1088
Germer, Jennifer, VP-Mktg - Houston Astros Baseball Club; *pg.* 552, *pg.* 1707
Germer, Susie, Sr Mgr-Mktg Comm - Children's Hospital Los Angeles; *pg.* 275, *pg.* 128
Gerner, Janet, Sr Dir - Merck & Co., Inc.; *pg.* 1566, *pg.* 1077
Geroff, Megan, Sr Specialist-Mktg-Finish Line Macy's - The Finish Line, Inc.; *pg.* 1769, *pg.* 686
Geronimo, Catherine, Sr Mgr-Integrated Mktg Comm - Rust-Oleum Corporation; *pg.* 1447, *pg.* 664
Gerow, Suzy, Mgr-Mktg - Herman Miller, Inc.; *pg.* 926, *pg.* 913
Gerrells, Kalie, Dir-Restaurant Mktg - Chick-fil-A, Inc.; *pg.* 1721, *pg.* 492
Gerrish, Michael, VP-Mktg - Wellmark, Inc; *pg.* 1223, *pg.* 707
Gerrity, Carly, Sr Dir-Product Dev, Silver & Silver Ice Div - Yurman Design, Inc.; *pg.* 15, *pg.* 1316
Gerrity, Monika, Analyst-Mdsg - Spencer Gifts LLC; *pg.* 1786,

First page reference indicates Business Class Edition
Second page reference indicates Geographic Edition

pg. 1057

Gerrity, Tom, Sr Product Dir - 7-Eleven, Inc.; *pg.* 1012, *pg.* 1672

Gerron, Christian, Gen Mgr-Microsoft Adv - Microsoft Corporation; *pg.* 435, *pg.* 1824

Gersabeck, David, Product Mgr-SYNC Svcs & Global Svc Delivery Network - Ford Motor Company; *pg.* 172, *pg.* 876

Gersch, Jamie, VP-Mktg - The Gap, Inc.; *pg.* 1770, *pg.* 218

Gerschke, Colleen, Media Buyer-Digital - Kohl's Corporation; *pg.* 1775, *pg.* 1870

Gerscovich, Melissa, Sr Media Planner - AARP; *pg.* 124, *pg.* 393

Gersey, Daniel, Media Buyer-Online - The Tire Rack Inc.; *pg.* 1890, *pg.* 697

Gersh, Carl, Mgr-Americas Segment Mktg - Citrix Systems, Inc.; *pg.* 375, *pg.* 424

Gersh, Jodi, Dir-Social Media & Engagement - Gannett Co., Inc.; *pg.* 1643, *pg.* 1790

Gershenhorn, Alan, CMO, Chief Sls Officer & Chief Strategy Officer - United Parcel Service, Inc.; *pg.* 1928, *pg.* 522

Gershman, Mitch, CMO - Washington Football, Inc.; *pg.* 591, *pg.* 1776

Gerson, Jeremy, VP-Sports Mktg - Perry Ellis International, Inc.; *pg.* 45, *pg.* 445

Gerstein, Mel, Treas & Dir-Mktg, Adv & PR - Thermwell Products Co., Inc.; *pg.* 1065, *pg.* 1082

Gerstein, Tamar, Sr Mgr-Shopper Mktg - The Hershey Co.; *pg.* 1855, *pg.* 1538

Gerstenblatt, Brett, Dir-Enterprise Creative - CVS Health Corporation; *pg.* 1765, *pg.* 1610

Gerstenblatt, Randy, Sr VP-Adv Sls - Captivate; *pg.* 272, *pg.* 1209

Gerstenkorn, Liane, Specialist-Sls Enablement - PerkinElmer, Inc.; *pg.* 1426, *pg.* 853

Gerstl, Dan, Analyst-Social Media - Steven Madden, Ltd.; *pg.* 1819, *pg.* 1176

Gerten, Allen, Sr Dir-Mktg Growth Initiatives - Best Buy Co., Inc.; *pg.* 1761, *pg.* 954

Gertenbach, Mark, Sr Mgr-Mobility Mktg - AT&T; *pg.* 1865, *pg.* 258

Gerth, Jeffrey, Sr Mgr-Technical Svcs - The J.M. Smucker Company; *pg.* 865, *pg.* 1468

Gerth, Peto, Sr Graphic Designer-Creative Svcs - Warner Music Group Corp.; *pg.* 590, *pg.* 1313

Gertz-Casper, Karen, Dir-Mktg - Hoveround Corp.; *pg.* 1543, *pg.* 466

Gervais, Nicole, Sr Coord-Mktg - Forever 21, Inc.; *pg.* 24, *pg.* 130

Gery, Laurie, Sr Dir-Comml Ops-Global - Sanofi Pasteur, Inc; *pg.* 1591, *pg.* 1588

Geschel, Scott, Sr Mgr-IT Technical Infrastructure-IT Ops & Change Mgmt - QVC Inc; *pg.* 305, *pg.* 1593

Geser, Juerg, Sr Dir-Product Ops-Deckers Brands - Deckers Outdoor Corporation; *pg.* 1807, *pg.* 100

Gesheva, Violina, Mgr-Mktg Comm-EMEA - HID Global Corporation; *pg.* 1416, *pg.* 111

Geske, Gregg, Mgr-CAFS & Foam Sys Sls - Waterous Company; *pg.* 1387, *pg.* 965

Gesler, Shelley, Mgr-Social Media - The Sherwin-Williams Company; *pg.* 1447, *pg.* 1435

Gess, Bob, Territory Mgr-Sls - Sirona Dental Systems, Inc.; *pg.* 1429, *pg.* 1175

Gess, Joe, VP-Adv - The Tampa Tribune; *pg.* 1691, *pg.* 476

Gessel, Chris, Chief Strategy Officer & Exec Editor - Investors Business Daily, Inc.; *pg.* 1653, *pg.* 133

Gessin, Erika, Mgr-Digital Mktg - Constellation Brands, Inc.; *pg.* 1960, *pg.* 1348

Gessley, Travis, Sr Mgr-Product Line-Baseball Hardgoods - Under Armour, Inc.; *pg.* 49, *pg.* 759

Gessner, Brooke, Specialist-Digital Mktg - Select Comfort Corporation; *pg.* 942, *pg.* 942

Getman, Lawrence, VP-Corp Strategy & Mktg - Xilinx, Inc.; *pg.* 496, *pg.* 252

Getson, Eli, Exec VP & Gen Mgr-Mdse - Golfsmith International Holdings, Inc.; *pg.* 1835, *pg.* 1662

Gettel-Gilmartin, Marie, Mgr-Sustainability Mktg & Comm - CH2M HILL Companies, Ltd.; *pg.* 75, *pg.* 325

Gettig, Andrew, VP-Sls-Intl - Sport Court International Inc.; *pg.* 1846, *pg.* 1761

Getty, Tim, Dir-Sls-Natl - Goodman Group, Inc.; *pg.* 1072, *pg.* 1706

Getz, Hannah, Specialist-Adv - Marshalls of MA, Inc.; *pg.* 1778, *pg.* 821

Getz, Hannah, Specialist-Adv - T.J. Maxx; *pg.* 1788, *pg.* 822

Getz, Hannah, Specialist-Adv - The TJX Companies, Inc.; *pg.* 1788, *pg.* 822

Geurts, John Paul, Sr VP-Creative - Nickelodeon Direct Inc.; *pg.* 303, *pg.* 1271

Gevelber, Lisa, VP-Mktg - Google Inc.; *pg.* 1249, *pg.* 153

Gevry, Mylene, Mgr-Mktg-Sico, Polyprep & Corrostop Brands - PPG Canada Inc.; *pg.* 1178, *pg.* 1928

Geyvandova, Bella, Specialist-Mktg CRM - Pier 1 Imports, Inc.; *pg.* 940, *pg.* 1695

Gezik, Rudy, Sr Mgr-Customer Experience - The Allstate Corporation; *pg.* 1189, *pg.* 639

Gezon, Bruce, Mgr-Mktg - Helmick Corporation; *pg.* 1346, *pg.* 1849

Ghaffari, Rasa, Brand Mgr - Robert Bosch Tool Corp; *pg.* 1060, *pg.* 634

Ghaharian, Kasra, Product Mgr-Corp ECommerce - Las Vegas Sands Corp.; *pg.* 1100, *pg.* 1027

Ghahramani, Behnaz, Dir-Relational Mktg - Gucci America Inc.; *pg.* 6, *pg.* 1237

Ghai, Nidhi, Head-Fashion Sls-Amazon Media Grp - Amazon.com, Inc.; *pg.* 1226, *pg.* 1831

Ghangas, Roop, Brand Mgr-Frappuccino - Starbucks Corporation; *pg.* 897, *pg.* 1840

Gharapetian, Allen H., VP-Mktg & Product Plng - Clarion Corporation of America; *pg.* 629, *pg.* 75

Gharib, Linda, Sr VP-Global Digital Mktg & Head-Reg Partnerships - Citigroup Inc.; *pg.* 735, *pg.* 1212

Ghassemi, Crystal W., Mgr-PR - Dollar General Corporation; *pg.* 1767, *pg.* 1635

Ghatak, Subhra, Mgr-Mktg - Amazon.com, Inc.; *pg.* 1226, *pg.* 1831

Ghauri, Naeem, Pres-Sls-Global - NetSol Technologies, Inc.; *pg.* 1270, *pg.* 56

Ghazal, Gabriel, Product Mgr-Sterling Silver Jewelry - Macy's East; *pg.* 1777, *pg.* 1254

Ghazarian, Deena, VP-Sls & Strategy - Monster Inc.; *pg.* 656, *pg.* 50

Ghazarian, Vana, Program Mgr-Retail Mktg-Global - Intel Corporation; *pg.* 645, *pg.* 266

Gheewala, Hiral, Dir-Mktg - Intel Corporation; *pg.* 645, *pg.* 266

Gheller, Jonathan, Product Mgr - Facebook, Inc.; *pg.* 1245, *pg.* 143

Ghilardi, Emilio, Exec VP-Global Sls & Mktg-Silicon Valley - KEMET Corporation; *pg.* 649, *pg.* 1621

Ghiold, Eve, Dir-Mktg Comm - McKesson Corporation; *pg.* 1560, *pg.* 222

Ghiurau, Cosmin, Dir-Social Mktg - United Services Automobile Association; *pg.* 1221, *pg.* 1743

Gholston, Teneya, Dir-Mktg - Revlon, Inc.; *pg.* 521, *pg.* 1286

Ghori, Sonya, Mgr-Social Media & Digital Mktg - The Quizno's Master LLC; *pg.* 1746, *pg.* 322

Ghosh, Angana, Product Mgr-Android Location & Context-Google Fit - Google Inc.; *pg.* 1249, *pg.* 153

Ghosh, Jane, Dir-Mktg - Kellogg Company; *pg.* 831, *pg.* 870

Ghosh, Jay, Mgr-Global Strategic Mktg, Fuels & Lubricants Solutions - BASF Corporation; *pg.* 1149, *pg.* 1066

Ghosh, Mousumi, VP & Sr Mgr-Decision Tech - JPMorgan Chase & Co.; *pg.* 772, *pg.* 1246

Ghosh, Subhendu, Sr Product Mgr-Tech - Red Hat, Inc.; *pg.* 460, *pg.* 1388

Ghosh, Sumita, Mgr-Mktg-Swingline - ACCO Brands Corporation; *pg.* 340, *pg.* 626

Ghosh, Vikram, Head-Channel Strategy-Breadth Channels, Cloud & Enterprise Mktg - Microsoft Corporation; *pg.* 435, *pg.* 1824

Ghrayeb, Nadim, Reg Brand Mgr-Cadillac VSSM - General Motors Company; *pg.* 175, *pg.* 881

Giacalone, Laura, VP-Mktg - Discovery Communications, Inc.; *pg.* 282, *pg.* 777

Giacobello, Michael J., Sr VP-Retail Delivery Sls & Support - Peapack-Gladstone Financial Corporation; *pg.* 792, *pg.* 1044

Giacoia, Denise, Dir-Mktg Tech Product Mktg Ops - TriZetto Corporation; *pg.* 485, *pg.* 327

Giacomini, Davide, Dir-Automotive IC Product Mgmt & Application - International Rectifier Corporation; *pg.* 647, *pg.* 80

Giaconelli, Carol, Dir-Sls Promo - Pernod Ricard USA, Inc.; *pg.* 1968, *pg.* 1332

Giaimo, Beth, Specialist-Mktg-Meetings, Events & Tradeshow - Siemens Corporation; *pg.* 803, *pg.* 1291

Giallanella, Joe, Brand Mgr-Heinz Ketchup - The Kraft Heinz Company; *pg.* 870, *pg.* 1577

Giallanza, Chris, Sr Specialist-PR - The Home Depot, Inc.; *pg.* 1050, *pg.* 510

Giallombardo, Leslie, VP-Adv - Gannett Co., Inc.; *pg.* 1643, *pg.* 1790

Giampa, Diane M., Sr VP-HR & Mktg - Bay State Savings Bank; *pg.* 722, *pg.* 862

Giampietro, Vince, Sr Mgr-Mktg - GEICO Corporation; *pg.* 1200, *pg.* 399

Gianakaris, Niki, Dir-Media Rels - Drexel University; *pg.* 600, *pg.* 1564

Gianelli, Silvia, Dir-Integrated Mktg - Xilinx, Inc.; *pg.* 496, *pg.* 252

Gianesini, Pete, Sr Dir-Radio Programming & Digital Audio Content - ESPN, Inc.; *pg.* 285, *pg.* 340

Giani, Nading, Dir-Mktg Svcs - LIFETIME BRANDS, INC.; *pg.* 1127, *pg.* 1161

Giannascoli, Peter, Sr VP-Mktg-Home Media - Paramount Pictures Corporation; *pg.* 304, *pg.* 138

Giannelli, Marco, Dir-Quality, Product Mgmt, R&D - The Harris Products Group; *pg.* 1345, *pg.* 533

Giannetti, Terri, VP-Mktg - Wells Fargo & Company; *pg.* 819, *pg.* 232

Gianni, Christian, Sr VP-Product Dev - Whirlpool Corporation; *pg.* 62, *pg.* 872

Giannini, Sandro, Mgr-Sls-Small Bus - Royal Bank of Canada; *pg.* 800, *pg.* 1942

Giannini, Tony, Sr VP-Media & Mktg - Macy's East; *pg.* 1777, *pg.* 1254

Giannobile, Maria, Mgr-Mktg Comm-Global - BASF Corporation; *pg.* 1149, *pg.* 1066

Giannone, Frank, Dir-Mktg Comm - General DataComm Industries, Inc.; *pg.* 400, *pg.* 357

Gianutsos, Chris, Exec Dir-Media & Entertainment Practice - Ernst & Young Global Limited; *pg.* 748, *pg.* 1228

Giard, Jill, Assoc Mgr-Product Dev - The Yankee Candle Company, Inc.; *pg.* 1792, *pg.* 843

Giard, Kathy, Sr Dir-Revenue - Peter Pan Bus Lines, Inc.; *pg.* 1919, *pg.* 846

Giardina, Tarah, Coord-Product Release - LifeCell Corporation; *pg.* 1556, *pg.* 1045

Giardini, Victoria, Mgr-Mktg Programs - Netsmart Technologies, Inc.; *pg.* 445, *pg.* 1163

Giardino, Brad, Product Mgr-Portfolio Products - FactSet Research Systems Inc.; *pg.* 1247, *pg.* 361

Giarrusso, Joseph, Acct Exec-Mktg Solutions - LinkedIn Corporation; *pg.* 1262, *pg.* 160

Giassopoulos, George, Sr Dir-Procurement-Global Media & Mktg Agencies - Pfizer Inc.; *pg.* 1581, *pg.* 1278

Giattino, Chris, Pres-Sls Div - Fownes Brothers & Co., Inc.; *pg.* 5, *pg.* 1233

Giazzon, Al, VP-Mktg - ViewSonic Corporation; *pg.* 489, *pg.* 303

Giazzon, Guido, Sr Dir-Global Pro Strategies & Mktg - Takeda Pharmaceuticals USA, Inc.; *pg.* 1600, *pg.* 605

Gibb, Adrian, Mgr-PR - Nu Skin Enterprises, Inc.; *pg.* 518, *pg.* 1755

Gibbard, Leia, Specialist-Affiliate Mktg - Cleveland Cavaliers/Quicken Loans Arena; *pg.* 541, *pg.* 1429

Gibbard, Leia, Specialist-Affiliate Mktg - Quicken Loans, Inc.; *pg.* 797, *pg.* 884

Gibboney, Mary, Coord-Mktg - H&R Block, Inc.; *pg.* 764, *pg.* 983

Gibbons, Adrienne, Dir-Mktg Comm - Jelmar Company; *pg.* 331, *pg.* 660

Gibbons, David, Dir-Mktg - Wells Fargo & Company; *pg.* 819, *pg.* 232

Gibbons, Dina A., Sr Mgr-Strategic Comm Programs-Autodesk Education - Autodesk Inc.; *pg.* 356, *pg.* 257

Gibbons, Kim, Dir-Mktg - Cisco Systems, Inc.; *pg.* 372, *pg.* 240

Gibbons, Laura, Sr Dir-Digital Mktg - The Hertz Corporation; *pg.* 1911, *pg.* 450

Gibbons, Lisa, Sr Dir-Leadership & Corp Internal Comm - Mondelez International, Inc.; *pg.* 878, *pg.* 601

Gibbons, Myles, Sr VP-Small Comml-Field, Product Mgmt & Distr - The Travelers Companies, Inc.; *pg.* 1220, *pg.* 352

Gibbons, Myles P., Sr VP-Small Comml-Field, Product Mgmt & Distr - Travelers Insurance; *pg.* 1220, *pg.* 963

Gibbons, Peter, VP-Mdsg & Mktg - Cooking.com; *pg.* 1237, *pg.* 143

Gibbons, Stephanie, Pres-Mktg, Digital Media & On-Air Promos - FX Networks, LLC; *pg.* 288, *pg.* 131

Gibbons, Susan, Brand Mgr-Refreshment Beverages - The Kraft Heinz Company; *pg.* 871, *pg.* 641

Gibbs, Annette, Mgr-PR - The Walt Disney Company; *pg.* 317, *pg.* 52

Gibbs, Ashley, Dir-Mktg-Food - Wal-Mart.com; *pg.* 1287, *pg.*

50
Gibbs, Chris, Dir-Mktg - Prab, Inc.; pg. 1369, pg. 894
Gibbs, Debbie, Dir-Adv - Delta Farm Press; pg. 1634, pg. 968
Gibbs, Donald, VP & Reg Mgr-Sls - Gibbs Wire & Steel Company, Inc.; pg. 1048, pg. 371
Gibbs, Gabrielle, Mgr-Mktg Comm-Market Insights - Facebook, Inc.; pg. 1245, pg. 143
Gibbs, Jason, Dir-Field Mktg - CiCi Enterprises LP; pg. 1723, pg. 1670
Gibbs, Jessica, Principal-Mktg - FedEx Corporation; pg. 1907, pg. 1642
Gibbs, Jodi, Dir-Girls Apparel Product Dev - J.C. Penney Company, Inc.; pg. 1774, pg. 1732
Gibbs, Kristine, Brand Mgr-Experience - The Gap, Inc.; pg. 1770, pg. 218
Gibbs, Michael, Specialist-Motorsports Mktg - Red Bull North America, Inc.; pg. 264, pg. 275
Gibbs, Mike, Reg Mgr-Sls - Summit Plastic Co.; pg. 1470, pg. 1403
Gibbs, Steve, Dir-Product Portfolio Mgmt - Fiserv, Inc.; pg. 758, pg. 537
Giberovitch, Rhonda, Sr Mgr-Consumer Mktg - Pfizer Inc.; pg. 1581, pg. 1278
Gibis, Robin, Dir-Mktg Info - Lifetouch, Inc.; pg. 1420, pg. 922
Giblin, Patrick, Dir-PR - Webster University; pg. 610, pg. 1004
Gibney, Denis, Dir-Mdsg - Frito-Lay North America, Inc.; pg. 1853, pg. 1730
Gibney, Scott, VP-Product Mgmt Emerging Payments - MasterCard Incorporated; pg. 779, pg. 1325
Gibson, Barbara, Dir-Local Adv - The Boston Globe; pg. 1623, pg. 790
Gibson, Camille, VP-Mktg & Bus Dir-Cheerios, Wheaties, Fiber One & Total - General Mills, Inc.; pg. 828, pg. 933
Gibson, Candice, Mgr-Consumer Mktg-Tourism Vancouver - The Greater Vancouver Convention & Visitor Bureau; pg. 994, pg. 1910
Gibson, Christine, Sr Dir-Integrated Mktg - Entertainment Weekly Inc.; pg. 1639, pg. 1228
Gibson, Delta, Dir-Mktg-Strategic Markets - Aramark; pg. 1013, pg. 1558
Gibson, Emily, Assoc Mgr-Mktg-Betty Crocker Cake, Cookies & Gluten Free Desserts - General Mills, Inc.; pg. 828, pg. 933
Gibson, Eric, Brand Mgr-Eckrich - John Morrell Food Group; pg. 866, pg. 628
Gibson, Jennifer, Brand Mgr - Affinia Group Intermediate Holdings Inc.; pg. 197, pg. 1373
Gibson, John, Dir-Digital Media Sls-KJRH Tulsa Channel 2 - KJRH; pg. 294, pg. 1490
Gibson, John, Dir-Govt Mktg - Landstar System, Inc.; pg. 1914, pg. 434
Gibson, Kristin, Sr Mgr-Mktg - Swatch Group USA; pg. 13, pg. 1131
Gibson, Leann, Sr Mgr-Mktg - Amgen Inc.; pg. 1493, pg. 291
Gibson, Lori, Mgr-Mktg - Honeywell International Inc.; pg. 407, pg. 1088
Gibson, Mark, Asst VP-Mktg - State Farm Mutual Automobile Insurance Co.; pg. 1218, pg. 557
Gibson, Naima, Head-Global Strategic Mktg - W.L. Gore & Associates, Inc.; pg. 122, pg. 388
Gibson, Richard, Sr VP-Sls & Support-Global - Iveda Solutions, Inc.; pg. 88, pg. 13
Gibson, Robin, Acct Mgr-Adv - SUPERVALU, Inc.; pg. 1035, pg. 924
Gibson, Roger, Mgr-Media Mktg - 1-800 CONTACTS, INC.; pg. 1758, pg. 1753
Gibson, Ryan, Sr Brand Mgr-Foodservice & Mgr-Mktg - The J.M. Smucker Company; pg. 865, pg. 1468
Gibson, Terry, Asst Mgr-Mktg - Wilson Sporting Goods Co.; pg. 1848, pg. 596
Gibson, William, Dir-Product Support Global Distr - Gulfstream Aerospace Corporation; pg. 228, pg. 540
Gibson, Yvonne, Dir-Mktg & Digital Comm - GE Canada Company; pg. 1296, pg. 1926
Gibula, Darren, Sr Dir-Ops-Air Conditioning Sys - LG Electronics U.S.A., Inc.; pg. 651, pg. 1060
Gicker, William J., Dir-Creative - United States Postal Service; pg. 1009, pg. 406
Giddens, Maggie, Dir-PR - Hilton Worldwide, Inc.; pg. 1094, pg. 1791
Giddings, Kathy L., VP-Bus Sls - Assurity Life Insurance Company; pg. 1194, pg. 1011
Giddings, Lora, Mgr-Enhancement Mktg - Alliance Data Systems Corporation; pg. 347, pg. 1729
Gideoni, Michal, Dir-Product Mgmt - Microsoft Corporation; pg. 435, pg. 1824
Giderman, Mark, Mgr-Mktg - Intuit Inc.; pg. 769, pg. 158
Gidez, Chris, Dir-Global Enterprise Reputation & Media Affairs - Cargill, Inc.; pg. 845, pg. 965
Gidskehaug, Lars, Product Mgr - CAMO Software, Inc.; pg. 368, pg. 1133
Gidwani, Gita, Global Brand Mgr-Quaker State - Shell Lubricants; pg. 217, pg. 1714
Gielczyk, Amanda, Mgr-Mktg - General Growth Properties, Inc.; pg. 1093, pg. 574
Gierczynski, Lee, Mgr-PR - Verizon Communications Inc.; pg. 1875, pg. 1309
Giese, Ferdinand, Sr Mgr-Mktg Info-Global - Allergan, Inc.; pg. 1491, pg. 106
Gieselman, Jon, Sr VP-Mktg - DIRECTV Group Holdings, LLC; pg. 281, pg. 79
Gietzen, Melissa, Sr Mgr-Strategic Mktg - Stryker Corporation; pg. 1598, pg. 894
Giezentanner, Troy, Dir-Mktg & Sls - Comcast Cable Communications, Inc.; pg. 276, pg. 1560
Gifas, Jim, Sr VP-Treasury Mgmt & Head-Product, Strategy & Innovation - Capital One Financial Corporation; pg. 730, pg. 1789
Giffhorn, Monica, Dir-Mktg & Comm - Xerox Corporation; pg. 494, pg. 365
Giffney, Karin, VP-Mktg - T-Mobile US, Inc.; pg. 676, pg. 1816
Gifford, Keith, Dir-Mktg-Global - Tecumseh Products Company; pg. 1381, pg. 866
Gifkins, Colin, VP-Product Dev - The Goldman Sachs Group, Inc.; pg. 762, pg. 1236
Gigandet, David, Mgr-Mktg-GATOR Utility Vehicles - John Deere Consumer & Commercial Equipment, Inc.; pg. 705, pg. 1360
Giggy, Maria, Dir-Membership & Mktg - Michigan State Lottery Bureau; pg. 999, pg. 895
Giglia, Charles, Dir-Sport Sls - Buffalo Niagara Convention & Visitors Bureau, Inc.; pg. 1901, pg. 1147
Giglio, Caroline, Coord-Sports Team Ops & Integrated Mktg - New York Rangers Hockey Club; pg. 570, pg. 1269
Giglio, Dennis, VP-Mktg - Nationwide Mutual Insurance Company; pg. 1210, pg. 1442
Giglio, Rob, VP-Consumer & SMB Sls-Worldwide - Adobe Systems Incorporated; pg. 342, pg. 235
Gigliotti, Allison, Sr Mgr-Retail Mktg - The North Face, Inc.; pg. 1840, pg. 252
Gil, Carlos, Sr Mgr-Social Mktg - LinkedIn Corporation; pg. 1262, pg. 160
Gil, Eduardo, Acct Exec-Creative Svcs - Royal Caribbean Cruises Ltd; pg. 1921, pg. 446
Gil, Ingrid, Coord-Sls Event - Trex Company, Inc.; pg. 116, pg. 1812
Gil, Peter, Sr Dir-Sls-Intl - Natrol, Inc.; pg. 1570, pg. 64
Gilad, Itamar, Product Mgr - Google Inc.; pg. 1249, pg. 153
Gilb, Carolyn S., VP-Sls-West Reg - American Family Mutual Insurance Company; pg. 1190, pg. 1864
Gilbeck, Jon, Div Mgr-Mktg - Deere & Company; pg. 703, pg. 632
Gilberg, Cheryl L., Head-Mktg & Comm-Securities Div-Global - The Goldman Sachs Group, Inc.; pg. 762, pg. 1236
Gilberg, Pam, Assoc Mgr-Mktg & Strategic Partnerships - Wenner Media LLC; pg. 1701, pg. 1314
Gilbert Leonard, Sara, Dir-Shopper Mktg-Walmart Inc - Kimberly-Clark Corporation; pg. 1461, pg. 1720
Gilbert, Alfred, Sr Specialist-Media Mktg - United States Postal Service; pg. 1009, pg. 406
Gilbert, Anna, Dir-Mktg-Americas - Barracuda Networks, Inc.; pg. 360, pg. 58
Gilbert, Brant, Dir-Mktg - Land O'Lakes, Inc.; pg. 873, pg. 915
Gilbert, Carol S., Exec VP-Mktg & Programs - American Public Education, Inc.; pg. 597, pg. 1849
Gilbert, David, Sr Mgr-Advanced Analytics-Mars Petcare - Mars Petcare; pg. 1478, pg. 1633
Gilbert, Geoff W., Mgr-Power Sys Channel Mktg - IBM; pg. 410, pg. 1449
Gilbert, Guy, Sr Product Mgr-Microsoft Office Mobile - Microsoft Corporation; pg. 435, pg. 1824
Gilbert, JaKenna, Sr Mgr-Global Digital - Coty, Inc.; pg. 506, pg. 1219
Gilbert, James, Dir-Global Adv-US Retail & Breakthrough Innovation Bus Units - Campbell Soup Company; pg. 844, pg. 1048
Gilbert, Jeff, VP-Sls & Mktg - CTS Valpey Corporation; pg. 632, pg. 825
Gilbert, Jonathan, Mgr-Reg Sls Enterprise Tech - Oracle Corporation; pg. 1272, pg. 786
Gilbert, K.C., Bus Mgr - United Parcel Service, Inc.; pg. 1928, pg. 522
Gilbert, Kyra, Sr Mgr-Mktg - PepsiCo, Inc.; pg. 259, pg. 1327
Gilbert, Lindsay, Assoc-Mktg-Global - NYSE Euronext; pg. 789, pg. 1274
Gilbert, Lindsay, Sr Asst Brand Mgr-Global Swiffer - The Procter & Gamble Company; pg. 1129, pg. 1418
Gilbert, Lou, Dir-North American Mktg & Global Brand Dev - Allison Transmission, Inc.; pg. 198, pg. 682
Gilbert, Merritt, Brand Mgr - Mars Petcare; pg. 1478, pg. 1633
Gilbert, Michael, Exec VP-Product Dev - Kohl's Corporation; pg. 1775, pg. 1870
Gilbert, Michelle, VP-PR-Heartland Reg - Comcast Corporation; pg. 276, pg. 1560
Gilbert, Rich, Mgr-Travel Trade Sls - Maryland Office of Tourism Development; pg. 998, pg. 758
Gilbert, Steve, Dir-Mktg - Dell Inc.; pg. 383, pg. 1737
Gilbertson, Jessica, Brand Mgr-Macaroni & Cheese - The Kraft Heinz Company; pg. 871, pg. 641
Gilbertson, Krista, Specialist-PR - MGM Resorts International; pg. 1105, pg. 1028
Gilbertson, Scott, Sr Mgr-Local Mktg Strategy - Best Buy Co., Inc.; pg. 1761, pg. 954
Gilbronson, Dave R., VP-Intl Oil & Gas Mktg - Apache Corporation; pg. 1934, pg. 1700
Gilchrist, Alex, Dir-Media & Comm - Anaheim Ducks Hockey Club, LLC; pg. 528, pg. 42
Gilchrist, Chad, Mgr-Extended Service Plan Area Sls - Ford Motor Company; pg. 172, pg. 876
Gilchrist, Chakirra, Mgr-Sls Adv Support Ops - Sinclair Broadcast Group, Inc.; pg. 308, pg. 773
Gilchrist, Scott K., Specialist-PeerVue Product - McKesson Corporation; pg. 1560, pg. 222
Gilchrist, Sheri, Mng Dir & Head-Database Mktg-Global - The Bank of New York Mellon Corporation; pg. 720, pg. 1200
Gildea, Stephanie, Mgr-Consumer Mktg - Gannett Co., Inc.; pg. 1643, pg. 1790
Gildea, Tracie, Dir-Global Mktg-Hand Tools-CDIY Div - Stanley Black & Decker, Inc.; pg. 1063, pg. 358
Gilder, John R., Mgr-Strategic Mktg Comm - L-3 Communications Holdings Inc.; pg. 650, pg. 1250
Gildersleeve, Michelle, Dir-ACS Mktg Comm - Oracle Corporation; pg. 450, pg. 191
Giles, Jennifer, Sr Mgr-Shopper Mktg - Pfizer Inc.; pg. 1581, pg. 1278
Giles, Jennifer, Coord-Mktg - The Wine Group, Inc.; pg. 1972, pg. 234
Giles, Peter, Product Mgr-Underwater ISR - General Dynamics Corporation; pg. 228, pg. 1781
Gilfoil, Jenna, Mgr-Sls Mktg - Pandora Media Inc.; pg. 1273, pg. 172
Gilford, Courtney, Mgr-Social Media - Kingston Technology Company, Inc.; pg. 425, pg. 90
Gilham, Natalie, Mgr-Mktg Strategy Implementation - BB&T Corporation; pg. 723, pg. 1393
Giliberto, Patti, Sr Dir-Brand Mktg-North America - World Kitchen LLC; pg. 1141, pg. 657
Gill, Brandon, Sr Mgr-Property Solutions-Yahoo Entertainment - Yahoo! Inc.; pg. 1289, pg. 289
Gill, Jeff, Sr Dir-Engrg - Yahoo! Inc.; pg. 1289, pg. 289
Gill, Mike, Coord-Music & Media Licensing - MTV Networks Company; pg. 298, pg. 1262
Gill, Pam, Sr Mgr-Segment Mktg-Brdcst & Media - Avid Technology, Inc.; pg. 622, pg. 804
Gill, Ranjan, Mgr-Mktg Comm-Experiential & Events - TELUS CORPORATION; pg. 1952, pg. 1912
Gill, Tim, Mgr-Search Mktg - Amazon.com, Inc.; pg. 1226, pg. 1831
Gill, Tim J., Sr Rep-Mktg - Plains All American Pipeline, L.P.; pg. 983, pg. 1712
Gillan, Elizabeth, VP-Mktg-Global - Hewlett-Packard Company; pg. 404, pg. 175
Gillard, Tom, Mgr-Field Mktg - Harley-Davidson, Inc.; pg. 178, pg. 1874
Gillen, Brendan, Mgr-Consumer Mktg - ESPN, Inc.; pg. 285, pg. 340
Gillen, Nancy, VP-Mktg & Bus Dev - Toshiba America, Inc.; pg. 681, pg. 1302
Gilles, Carie, Dir-Brand Mktg - Learning Care Group Inc.; pg. 604, pg. 903
Gilles, Karin, Sr Dir-Bus Unit & Tech PR - Citrix Systems, Inc.; pg. 375, pg. 424
Gillespie, April, Reg Mgr-Sls - ViewSonic Corporation; pg. 489, pg. 303

First page reference indicates Business Class Edition
Second page reference indicates Geographic Edition

Gillespie, Barry N., VP-Aerospace Products - PPG Industries, Inc.; *pg.* 1445, *pg.* 1579
Gillespie, Evernolia, Dir-Media & Mktg - Iconix Brand Group, Inc.; *pg.* 26, *pg.* 1243
Gillespie, Gary, VP-Sls & Mktg-Compressor & Blower Products-Americas - Gardner Denver, Inc.; *pg.* 1338, *pg.* 1592
Gillespie, Heather, Program Mgr-New Product - Cisco Systems, Inc.; *pg.* 372, *pg.* 240
Gillespie, Jackie, Mgr-Social Media - Dell Inc.; *pg.* 383, *pg.* 1737
Gillespie, Jay, VP-Mktg & Brand - Fiskars Brands, Inc.; *pg.* 1124, *pg.* 1866
Gillespie, John, VP-Mktg - AS America, Inc.; *pg.* 68, *pg.* 1108
Gillespie, Lorrie, Supvr-Inside Sls & Customer Svc - Philips Emergency Lighting; *pg.* 1303, *pg.* 1631
Gillespie, Lynne, Mgr-SMB Segment Mktg-North America-Dell SecureWorks - Dell Inc.; *pg.* 383, *pg.* 1737
Gillespie, Marcie, Coord-Parts Adv - Deere & Company; *pg.* 703, *pg.* 632
Gillett, Andrew, Specialist-Digital Mktg - Meijer, Inc.; *pg.* 1779, *pg.* 888
Gillette, Brent, Dir-Sls - Sun Valley Company; *pg.* 1115, *pg.* 550
Gillette, Eben, VP-Mktg - The Wine Group, Inc.; *pg.* 1972, *pg.* 234
Gillette, Joanna, Mgr-Product Mktg - Allen Press Inc.; *pg.* 1614, *pg.* 715
Gillette, Kirk, Mgr-Mktg-Strategic Programs & Events - Hewlett-Packard Company; *pg.* 404, *pg.* 175
Gilley, Mark, Sr VP-Mktg - Red Lobster; *pg.* 1747, *pg.* 455
Gilliam, Elizabeth, Program Mgr-Mktg - Red Hat, Inc.; *pg.* 460, *pg.* 1388
Gilliam, Jacqueline, Specialist-Online Mktg - Bonnier Corporation; *pg.* 1622, *pg.* 480
Gilliam, Sabine, Reg Head-Mktg-Global Innovative Products-Asia Pacific & China - Pfizer Inc.; *pg.* 1581, *pg.* 1278
Gilliam, Sarah, Sr Program Mgr-Global Takeback Mktg - Dell Inc.; *pg.* 383, *pg.* 1737
Gillies, Karen, Assoc VP & Mgr-Bus Support & Social Media - Bank of America Corporation; *pg.* 718, *pg.* 1362
Gillies, Mark, Mgr-Product & Tech Comm - Volkswagen Group of America, Inc.; *pg.* 194, *pg.* 1785
Gilligan, Ann, Dir-Mktg - Eileen Fisher, Inc.; *pg.* 24, *pg.* 1168
Gilligan, David, Sr Specialist-Mktg Comm - Battelle Memorial Institute; *pg.* 1401, *pg.* 1437
Gilligan, Kevin, VP-Sls - Structural Graphics, LLC; *pg.* 1689, *pg.* 346
Gilligan, Peter M., VP-Sls - New Zealand Lamb Cooperative, Inc.; *pg.* 886, *pg.* 385
Gilligan, Sherri, Sr VP-Card Mktg - Capital One Financial Corporation; *pg.* 730, *pg.* 1789
Gillikin, Pam A, Dir-Interactive Sls & Mktg - Sherwin Williams; *pg.* 1448, *pg.* 1436
Gillilan, Mark, Mgr-Frozen Product Mktg - Atkins Nutritionals, Inc.; *pg.* 1498, *pg.* 316
Gilliland, Michael, Mgr-Product Mktg - SAS Institute Inc.; *pg.* 466, *pg.* 1361
Gillin, Michael, Dir-Wi-Fi Deployment & Product Mgmt - Cox Communications, Inc.; *pg.* 279, *pg.* 501
Gillingham, Maurice, Analyst-Bus-Mktg Transformation - IBM Canada Limited; *pg.* 411, *pg.* 1923
Gillis, Dan, Dir-Loyalty Mktg Tech - Starwood Hotels & Resorts Worldwide, Inc.; *pg.* 1114, *pg.* 378
Gillis, Kerrie, VP-Adv - The New York Times Company; *pg.* 1668, *pg.* 1270
Gillis, Shekeira, Coord-Mktg - H&R Block, Inc.; *pg.* 764, *pg.* 983
Gillispie, Shane, VP-Mktg & ECommerce - SmartPros Ltd.; *pg.* 1281, *pg.* 1166
Gillman, Deborah, Mgr-Field Mktg-Southwest Area - Symantec Corporation; *pg.* 479, *pg.* 1753
Gillooly, Patrick, Dir-Digital Comm & Social Media - Monster Worldwide, Inc.; *pg.* 1268, *pg.* 859
Gilman, Tina, Dir-Mktg Comm - Jimmy Johns Franchise, LLC; *pg.* 1024, *pg.* 562
Gilmore, Brigid, Dir-Frozen Scale & Shopper Mktg - Nestle USA, Inc.; *pg.* 883, *pg.* 96
Gilmore, Kathy, Sr Specialist-Mktg Comm - The Toro Company; *pg.* 1065, *pg.* 918
Gilmore-McPherson, Denise, Mgr-Mktg - Redbox Automated Retail, LLC; *pg.* 306, *pg.* 649
Gilmour, Scott, Dir-Product Mgmt - First Data Corporation; *pg.* 754, *pg.* 505
Gilpatric, Martin, Mgr-Technical Mktg - Xilinx, Inc.; *pg.* 496, *pg.* 252
Gilpin, Sean, Sr Mgr-Retail Mktg - Hyundai Motor America; *pg.* 179, *pg.* 89
Gilreath, Melissa, Sr Mgr-Mktg - HP Hood LLC; *pg.* 864, *pg.* 829
Gilreath, Shannon, Mgr-Mktg - Rich Products Corporation; *pg.* 892, *pg.* 1150
Gilroy, Anthony, Dir-Mktg & Comm - Steinway & Sons; *pg.* 586, *pg.* 1176
Gilroy, Sabrina, Sr VP-Digital Sls & Mktg - Bank of America Corporation; *pg.* 718, *pg.* 1362
Gilseth, Karen, Sr Specialist-Mktg Comm - Boston Scientific Corporation; *pg.* 1508, *pg.* 831
Gilson, Marcia, Rep-Sls - Cruisin' USA/BowlingShirt.com.; *pg.* 1765, *pg.* 995
Gilster, Timothy J., Sr Mgr-Acq Mktg Global Corp Payments - American Express Company; *pg.* 712, *pg.* 1190
Gim, Tura, Sr Product Mgr-New Zealand - Samsung Electronics America, Inc.; *pg.* 669, *pg.* 1115
Gimbl, Chris, Brand Mgr-Global - Starbucks Corporation; *pg.* 897, *pg.* 1840
Gimbl, Marissa, Mgr-Mktg-Corp Mktg Solutions - Meredith Corporation; *pg.* 1663, *pg.* 705
Gimlett, Michael, Sr VP-Mdse & Logistics - GameFly, Inc.; *pg.* 953, *pg.* 132
Gin, Garrett S., Sr VP-Mktg & Corp Affairs-Global - Bank of America Corporation; *pg.* 718, *pg.* 1362
Ginda, Courtney, Sr Mgr-Client Grp-Global - American Express Company; *pg.* 712, *pg.* 1190
Gindin, Jillian, VP-Global Direct To Consumer Brand Mktg - NIKE, Inc.; *pg.* 1812, *pg.* 1492
Ginestro, Suzanne, CMO & Sr VP-Mktg - Bolthouse Farms; *pg.* 841, *pg.* 44
Gingerich, Brent, Exec VP-Sls & Mktg - Sauder Woodworking Co.; *pg.* 941, *pg.* 1403
Gingiss, Dan, Head-Digital Customer Experience & Social Media - Discover Financial Services; *pg.* 744, *pg.* 653
Gingras, Carissa, Dir-Mktg-Consumer Engine & Svc - Briggs & Stratton Corporation; *pg.* 201, *pg.* 1899
Gingras, France, Acting Exec VP-HR - Standard & Poor's Ratings Services; *pg.* 805, *pg.* 1296
Gingras, Richard, Sr Dir-News & Social Products - Google Inc.; *pg.* 1249, *pg.* 153
Gingrich Odenthal, Shelley, Mgr-Digital Mktg Strategy-US Skincare - Johnson & Johnson; *pg.* 1549, *pg.* 1091
Gingrich, Drew, Coord-PR & Corp Comm - Hersha Hospitality Trust; *pg.* 1094, *pg.* 1536
Gingrich, Jon, Sr VP-Sls - Ameriprise Financial, Inc.; *pg.* 715, *pg.* 930
Gingrich, Kerry L., Mgr-Creative - J.C. Whitney & Co.; *pg.* 209, *pg.* 621
Ginieres, Alexandra, Mgr-Retirement Mktg - The Guardian Life Insurance Company of America; *pg.* 1202, *pg.* 1237
Ginley, John, Branch Mgr-Retail Sls - EverBank Financial Corp.; *pg.* 749, *pg.* 432
Ginn, Quantas L., Specialist-Mktg - Accenture; *pg.* 1392, *pg.* 1186
Ginsberg, Gary, Exec VP-Corp Mktg & Comm - Time Warner Inc.; *pg.* 312, *pg.* 1302
Ginsberg, Lori T., Sr Specialist-Mktg - Direct Energy; *pg.* 1939, *pg.* 1704
Ginsberg, Mark, Sr VP-Brand, Design & Product Dev - Marchon Eyewear, Inc.; *pg.* 1421, *pg.* 1180
Ginsberg, Meryl, Dir-PR - Varian Medical Systems, Inc.; *pg.* 1434, *pg.* 178
Ginsburg, Betsy, Sr Mgr-Payment Svcs - Discover Financial Services; *pg.* 744, *pg.* 653
Ginsburg, David, Sr Dir-Market & Consumer Res - Choice Hotels International, Inc.; *pg.* 1086, *pg.* 775
Ginsburg, Scott, Sr Dir-Independent Store Mktg - CARQUEST Corporation; *pg.* 168, *pg.* 1386
Ginsburg, Wendy, Mgr-Field Mktg - Philips Lighting; *pg.* 1303, *pg.* 806
Gintoft, Amanda, Mgr-PR - GE Healthcare; *pg.* 399, *pg.* 1765
Ginzl, Emily, Sr Mgr-Mktg - The Macerich Company; *pg.* 1101, *pg.* 275
Gioia, Anthony, Sr Dir-Game Presentation - Philadelphia Flyers, L.P.; *pg.* 575, *pg.* 1569
Gioia, Justin, VP-Mktg-Investor & Bank - Scottrade, Inc.; *pg.* 802, *pg.* 1003
Gioiella, Joan, Mgr-Mktg - Conair Corporation; *pg.* 505, *pg.* 1055
Gioja, Michael E., CIO & Sr VP-IT, Product Mgmt & Dev - Paychex, Inc.; *pg.* 792, *pg.* 1336
Giombolini, Michael, Brand Mgr-Dial for Men, Hand Soap & Lotions - Henkel Consumer Adhesives, Inc.; *pg.* 403, *pg.* 1480
Giombolini, Michael, Brand Mgr-Dial for Men, Hand Soap & Lotions - Henkel Consumer Goods; *pg.* 511, *pg.* 22
Gionta, Lynn, Sr Mgr-Patient & Customer Excellence - Shire; *pg.* 1593, *pg.* 1532
Giordano, Alison, VP-Consumer Mktg & Sponsorship-US - MasterCard Worldwide Inc.; *pg.* 780, *pg.* 988
Giordano, Kevin, Mgr-Corp Digital & Social Media Strategy - Bristol-Myers Squibb Company; *pg.* 1509, *pg.* 1206
Giordano, Michael, Head-Brand Measurement Mktg - Google Inc.; *pg.* 1249, *pg.* 153
Giordano, Steve, Mgr-Mktg Bus Analytics - DIRECTV Group Holdings, LLC; *pg.* 281, *pg.* 79
Giordano, Trish, VP-Sls & Mktg - Buca, Inc.; *pg.* 1718, *pg.* 931
Giorgi, Brittany, Project Mgr-Product Mktg - Harley-Davidson, Inc.; *pg.* 178, *pg.* 1874
Giorgi, Peter, Head-Adv & Content-Global - Airbnb, Inc.; *pg.* 1226, *pg.* 211
Giori, Kathy, Sr Product Mgr-Wireless Chipset Maker - QUALCOMM Incorporated; *pg.* 1873, *pg.* 207
Gioulis, Helen, Dir-Mdsg - Harriet Carter Gifts, Inc.; *pg.* 1773, *pg.* 1553
Giovine, Michelle, VP-Mktg-Ninety Nine Restaurants & Max & Emma's - American Blue Ribbon Holdings; *pg.* 1714, *pg.* 1648
Giovingo, Tom, Dir-Sls-Audience - Yahoo! Inc.; *pg.* 1289, *pg.* 289
Gipe, Melanie, Sr Mgr-Product Mgmt - Wells Fargo & Company; *pg.* 819, *pg.* 232
Gipson, Camille, Mgr-Global Mktg Excellence & Pro Brand Comm - Bayer CropScience; *pg.* 1149, *pg.* 981
Gipson, RaGann T., Specialist-Mktg - The Procter & Gamble Company; *pg.* 1129, *pg.* 1418
Giraldo, Carlos, Sr Dir-Mktg - Boar's Head Provisions Co., Inc.; *pg.* 841, *pg.* 465
Girao, Ana, Mgr-Retail Mktg - Hugo Boss Fashions Inc.; *pg.* 42, *pg.* 1242
Girard, Greg, Sr Product Mgr - Hill's Pet Nutrition, Inc.; *pg.* 1476, *pg.* 721
Girard, Maureen, VP-Mktg & Product Mgmt - Cardinal Health, Inc.; *pg.* 1512, *pg.* 1448
Girardo, Pam, Sr Dir-External Comm - Capital One Financial Corporation; *pg.* 730, *pg.* 1789
Girardot, Michael, Dir-Database Mktg - TD Ameritrade Holding Corporation; *pg.* 808, *pg.* 1018
Girdhar, Anupam, Sr Dir-Mktg-Global - Baxter International Inc.; *pg.* 1499, *pg.* 599
Girnau, Kristen, Specialist-Mktg - Patterson Dental Supply, Inc.; *pg.* 1580, *pg.* 963
Giron, Gotmar, Mgr-PR - Neiman Marcus, Inc.; *pg.* 30, *pg.* 1684
Girondo, Rita, Specialist-Mktg - Church's Chicken, Inc.; *pg.* 1722, *pg.* 493
Girotto, Lynn, VP-Global Product & Digital Mktg-Getty Images - Getty Images, Inc.; *pg.* 1645, *pg.* 1836
Giroux, Denise, VP-Mktg & Comm-Healthcare Sector - Aramark; *pg.* 1013, *pg.* 1558
Giroux, Emily, Sr Supvr-Mktg Call Center - Charles River Laboratories, Inc.; *pg.* 1475, *pg.* 360
Giroux, Jessica, Product Mgr-Accessories - United States Cellular Corporation; *pg.* 1875, *pg.* 594
Giroux, Steve, VP-Sls & Mktg - American Foods Group, LLC; *pg.* 837, *pg.* 1859
Girsky, Leslie, VP-Sls & Mktg - Jaco Electronics, Inc.; *pg.* 648, *pg.* 1165
Girty, Karen, Dir-Mktg - New York City Ballet; *pg.* 569, *pg.* 1268
Girvan, Christine, Mng Dir-Sls-Canada - MFS Investment Management; *pg.* 782, *pg.* 798
Gisclair, Jean-Paul, Dir-Online Mktg - New Orleans Tourism Marketing Corporation; *pg.* 1001, *pg.* 747
Gish, Lara, Brand Mgr - PETCO Animal Supplies, Inc.; *pg.* 1480, *pg.* 206
Gish, Rebecca, Assoc Dir-Global Talent Mktg - UnitedHealth Group Incorporated; *pg.* 1221, *pg.* 950
Giske, Nathalie, Sr Mgr-Mktg - American Express Company; *pg.* 712, *pg.* 1190
Gisondi, Steve, Brand Mgr - Campbell Soup Company; *pg.* 844, *pg.* 1048
Gispanski, Lauren, Specialist-PR - Syniverse Holdings, Inc.; *pg.* 479, *pg.* 475
Giss, R., Mgr-Product Mktg - Adobe Systems Incorporated; *pg.* 342, *pg.* 235

Gissy, Jim, Exec VP-Sls & Mktg - Central Florida Investments Inc.; pg. 1085, pg. 452
Gitahi, Kingori, Mgr-Operative Product & Devices - Microsoft Corporation; pg. 435, pg. 1824
Githens, Michael, Program Mgr-Mktg Lab - Ixia; pg. 422, pg. 56
Gitkin, Chuck, VP-Mktg, Innovation, R&D - John Morrell & Co.; pg. 866, pg. 1415
Gitlin, Lance, Dir-Brand Adv & Mktg - Major League Baseball; pg. 560, pg. 1255
Gitlin, Steven A., VP-Mktg Strategy & Comm - AeroVironment, Inc.; pg. 223, pg. 150
Gittens, Anthony, Sr Mgr-Mktg - Tellabs, Inc.; pg. 678, pg. 637
Gitter, Joe, Product Mgr - Miller Electric Manufacturing Co.; pg. 1361, pg. 1852
Gittings, Brian, Mgr-Sls & Central Bus Unit - Hubbard Feeds Inc.; pg. 1477, pg. 928
Gittings, Rob, Vice Chm & Head-Sls & Mktg - PricewaterhouseCoopers LLP; pg. 795, pg. 1283
Giuffrida, Caroline, Dir-Mktg - Cains Foods, L.P.; pg. 843, pg. 784
Giuffrida, Mary, Dir-Mktg - Siemens Process Industries and Drives; pg. 673, pg. 485
Giugliano, Rick, Coord-Mktg - Pittsburgh Steelers Sports Inc.; pg. 577, pg. 1578
Giuliani, Laura, Specialist-Email Mktg - Destination Maternity Corporation; pg. 23, pg. 1563
Giuliani, Richard, Mgr-Sourcing & Mktg Comm - Regeneron Pharmaceuticals, Inc.; pg. 1588, pg. 1345
Giuliani, Rosella, Chief Product Officer - True Religion Brand Jeans; pg. 49, pg. 143
Giunco, Massimo, Sr Dir-Mktg-Nike Russia - NIKE, Inc.; pg. 1812, pg. 1492
Giusti, Mike, Coord-Mktg - Lithia Motors Inc; pg. 183, pg. 1499
Gividen, Ron, Dir-PR & Media - Escort, Inc.; pg. 1412, pg. 1479
Gjergji, Silvana, Asst VP-Mktg & PR - Alma Bank; pg. 711, pg. 1140
Glackin, Mark, Sr Dir-Mktg - Allergan, Inc.; pg. 1491, pg. 106
Gladden, Faith, Planner-Mktg Events - Megger Inc.; pg. 1422, pg. 1557
Glade, Zoe, Mng Dir-Digital & Social Mktg - American Cancer Society, Inc.; pg. 126, pg. 487
Gladstone, Elwyn, Head-Mktg - Proximo Spirits, Inc.; pg. 1969, pg. 1076
Gladstone, Gini, VP-Courtyard Brand Mktg - Marriott International, Inc.; pg. 1102, pg. 764
Gladstone, Peter, Sr Dir-Adv & Innovation - The Boston Beer Company, Inc.; pg. 239, pg. 790
Gladstone, Peter, VP-Mktg - Jacksonville Symphony Association; pg. 554, pg. 434
Gladstone, Vicki, Head-Mktg-Online Adv - Quicken Loans, Inc.; pg. 797, pg. 884
Gladys, Lori A., Rep-Adv - Air Products and Chemicals, Inc.; pg. 1145, pg. 1513
Glaeser, Matthew, Assoc Dir-Media - Palisades Media Group, Inc.; pg. 452, pg. 275
Glakpe, Esinam, Sr Asst Brand Mgr - The Procter & Gamble Company; pg. 1129, pg. 1418
Glander, Michelle, Sr Dir-Mktg - Boston Market Corporation; pg. 1717, pg. 329
Glansberg, Meredith, Brand Mgr-Colgate Total - Colgate-Palmolive Company; pg. 504, pg. 1215
Glasberg, Jeffrey S., Sr Attorney-Advanced Mktg - Genworth Financial, Inc.; pg. 761, pg. 1802
Glaser, K.C., Mgr-Intl Product & Brand Mktg-South America & Caribbean - American Dairy Queen Corporation; pg. 1714, pg. 930
Glaser, K.C., Mgr-Intl Mktg-South America, Central America & The Caribbean - Dairy Queen Corporate Store; pg. 1724, pg. 932
Glaser, KC, Mgr-Intl Mktg-South America, Central America & The Caribbean - International Dairy Queen, Inc.; pg. 1732, pg. 938
Glaser, Mike, Sr Mgr-Product Mktg - Google Inc.; pg. 1249, pg. 153
Glaser, Steven L., Sr VP-Corp Strategy & Mktg - Xilinx, Inc.; pg. 496, pg. 252
Glasgow, Krissa, Sr Mgr-Environmental Innovation - The Home Depot, Inc.; pg. 1050, pg. 510
Glasgow, Shelly, Dir-Product Dev - Birkenstock Distribution USA Inc.; pg. 1805, pg. 168
Glass, Bret, Assoc Dir-Oncology Payer Mktg-Melanoma-Yervoy & Nivolumab - Bristol-Myers Squibb Company; pg. 1509, pg. 1206
Glass, Erin, Brand Mgr-Dixie Plates - Georgia-Pacific LLC; pg. 1458, pg. 507
Glass, Jennifer, Asst VP-Digital Mktg - M&T Bank Corporation; pg. 777, pg. 1149
Glass, Lori, VP-Mktg - Sterling Jewelers Inc.; pg. 13, pg. 1402
Glass, Monica, Mgr-Natl Culture Mktg - Red Bull North America, Inc.; pg. 264, pg. 275
Glass, Robin, Sr VP-Strategy & Mktg - Evolent Health LLC; pg. 1394, pg. 1773
Glass, Russ, Head-Products-Mktg Solutions - LinkedIn Corporation; pg. 1262, pg. 160
Glass, Stacy, Sr Mgr-Customer Mktg - Electronic Arts Inc.; pg. 951, pg. 189
Glasscoe, Jessica, Assoc Mgr-Shopper Mktg - Seventh Generation, Inc.; pg. 335, pg. 1765
Glassman, David, CMO & Sr VP - Onstream Media Corporation; pg. 449, pg. 459
Glassman, Edward, Head-Global Comml Products - MasterCard Incorporated; pg. 779, pg. 1325
Glassman, Judy, Dir-Mktg - Smithsonian Magazine; pg. 1687, pg. 404
Glassman, Michael E., Mgr-Franchise B-B Mktg-Intl - BP America Inc.; pg. 972, pg. 1702
Glatch, Lisa, Exec VP-Client Solutions & Sls - CH2M HILL Companies, Ltd.; pg. 75, pg. 325
Glatfelter, Dave, Sr Mgr-Product Mktg - NetApp, Inc.; pg. 444, pg. 287
Glatt, David L., Head-New Products-Infectious Diseases & Exec Dir - Merck & Co., Inc.; pg. 1566, pg. 1077
Glatt, Jennifer, Dir-Assurance & Tax-Natl Mktg - BDO Seidman, LLP; pg. 724, pg. 1202
Glaubitz, Kurt, Mgr-Media Rels-Global - Chevron Corporation; pg. 974, pg. 259
Glave, Geoff, Sr Product Mgr-Endpoint Security - Absolute Software Corporation; pg. 340, pg. 1909
Glavin, Bob, VP-Product Mgmt, Retail Branding & Info Solutions - Avery Dennison Corporation; pg. 1452, pg. 95
Glavin, Karen, Mgr-Mktg - United Parcel Service, Inc.; pg. 1928, pg. 522
Glazar, Christian, Sr Mgr-Comm & HR - C.R. Bard, Inc.; pg. 1519, pg. 1094
Glazer, Jamie S., VP-Fin Analysis & Revenue Controls - IPC The Hospitalist Company, Inc.; pg. 1547, pg. 167
Gleason, Heather, Sr Mgr-Comm - PepsiCo, Inc.; pg. 259, pg. 1327
Gleason, John, Chief Sls Officer & Exec VP - Ryder System, Inc.; pg. 1922, pg. 446
Gleason, K. Reed, VP-Adv Dev - CASCADE MICROTECH, INC.; pg. 1405, pg. 1492
Gleason, Mike, Dir-Adv - The Cincinnati Enquirer, Inc.; pg. 1628, pg. 1411
Gleason, Patrick, Asst Dir-Pub & Media Rels - Baltimore Ravens Limited Partnership; pg. 532, pg. 755
Gleason, Taylor, Project Mgr-Digital Mktg - Cigna Corporation; pg. 1197, pg. 338
Gleaves, Dwight, VP-Sls-Pupil Transportation - Hydrotex Partners Ltd.; pg. 979, pg. 1692
Gleeson, Alison, Sr VP-Comml Sls-US - Cisco Systems, Inc.; pg. 372, pg. 240
Gleespen, Gayle, Dir-Mall Mktg & Bus Dev - Simon Property Group, Inc.; pg. 1112, pg. 690
Gleich, Edward, Sr VP-Mktg-Global - Little Caesars Enterprises, Inc.; pg. 1736, pg. 883
Gleim, Matt, Sr Mgr-Mktg-Cloud Campaigns - ExactTarget Inc.; pg. 1244, pg. 685
Gleisner, Jerry, VP-Sls-US - ESAB Welding & Cutting Products; pg. 1335, pg. 1615
Gleiter, John H., VP-Worldwide Mktg-Digital Cable & Terrestrial Set Top Platforms - Broadcom Corporation; pg. 364, pg. 108
Glen, Robert, Sr Dir-Brand Mktg-Global - BlackBerry; pg. 625, pg. 1717
Glencross, Kara, Sr Exec Dir-Mktg Strategy & Portfolio - SAP America, Inc.; pg. 466, pg. 1557
Glendinning, Heather, Mgr-Mktg-Mfg - Autodesk Inc.; pg. 356, pg. 257
Glenn, Barbara, Dir-Mktg Ops - Mercury Insurance Company; pg. 1208, pg. 136
Glenn, Bill, Supvr-Creative-California Reg - Comcast Corporation; pg. 276, pg. 1560
Glenn, Chris, VP-Svc Sls & Customer Care - AutoNation; pg. 165, pg. 773
Glenn, Doug, VP-Sls - Consew; pg. 53, pg. 1049
Glenn, Martha, Dir-Mktg - L'Oreal USA; pg. 514, pg. 1252
Glenn, Scott, Brand Mgr-Enhancers New Product Dev - The Kraft Heinz Company; pg. 871, pg. 641
Glenn, Scott, Brand Mgr-Enhancers New Product Dev - Mondelez International, Inc.; pg. 878, pg. 601
Glenn-Gunnarson, Heather, Assoc Mgr-Mktg-Fabric Care Instore - The Procter & Gamble Company; pg. 1129, pg. 1418
Glenning, Bettina, Dir-Cross-Indus Mktg - Autodesk Inc.; pg. 356, pg. 257
Glessner, Gordon, Mgr-Online Mktg - Costco Wholesale Corporation; pg. 1765, pg. 1820
Glett, Braden L., VP-Roll Products - Spinnaker Coating, LLC; pg. 1470, pg. 1477
Glick, Mike, Sr Dir-Global Pediatric Nutrition - Abbott Laboratories; pg. 1484, pg. 551
Glick, Mike, Sr Dir-Global Pediatric Nutrition - Abbott Nutrition; pg. 1485, pg. 1437
Glickman, Brett, Sr Dir-Global Product Dev-Women's Jeanswear - Levi Strauss & Co.; pg. 43, pg. 220
Glickman, Rob, VP-Cloud Mktg - SAP America, Inc.; pg. 466, pg. 1557
Glienke, Mike, Reg VP-Sls & Ops - The Mattress Firm, Inc.; pg. 934, pg. 1711
Glines, David, Mgr-Product Innovation - Wheels Inc.; pg. 1931, pg. 607
Gliniany, Kathryn, Category Mgr-Mktg - Best Buy Co., Inc.; pg. 1761, pg. 954
Glinsman, Derek L., Dir-Mktg Dev-Sleep & CV Disorders Intl - Philips Respironics; pg. 1585, pg. 1555
Glisson, Chip, Dir-Mktg Comm - Datamax Corporation; pg. 1633, pg. 453
Glisson, Geoff, Sr Specialist-Mktg-Digital - Markel Corporation; pg. 1207, pg. 1783
Globe, Brad, Pres-Warner Bros. Consumer Products - Warner Bros. Worldwide Consumer Products; pg. 490, pg. 55
Glock, Dennis, Mgr-Global Digital Mktg Comm - H.B. Fuller Company; pg. 1165, pg. 961
Glock, Jeff, Dir-Mktg Total Hips - Zimmer Biomet Holdings, Inc.; pg. 1611, pg. 699
Gloden, Shawn, Engr-Product Design - Ford Motor Company; pg. 172, pg. 876
Glodoveza, Jeremiah, Sr Dir-Global Comm - Avaya Inc.; pg. 621, pg. 264
Gloekler, Mike, Mgr-Corp Comm & PR - McKee Foods Corporation; pg. 1860, pg. 1630
Glorieux, Justin, Dir-Creative Production - Bright House Networks LLC; pg. 272, pg. 461
Glorioso, Russell, Mgr-Mktg Comm-NAFTA - Bayer Healthcare Consumer Care Division; pg. 1500, pg. 1087
Glotzbach, Matthew, Product Mgr - YouTube, LLC; pg. 1291, pg. 198
Glover, Ashley, VP-Mktg & Comm-Global - Pace; pg. 1918, pg. 553
Glover, Cam, Mng Dir-Mktg - Orkin, Inc.; pg. 1798, pg. 517
Glover, Carson, Grp Dir-PR & Comm-Global - Tiffany & Co.; pg. 13, pg. 1299
Glover, Delia, Product Mgr-Warrior & New Balance Team Apparel - New Balance Athletic Shoe, Inc.; pg. 1811, pg. 798
Glover, Gail, Project Coord-Interactive Mktg - Ameriprise Financial, Inc.; pg. 715, pg. 930
Glover, Greg, Mgr-Merrell Product Line-North America - Wolverine World Wide, Inc.; pg. 1822, pg. 905
Glover, James, Sr Mgr-Global Strategic Partnerships - Johnson & Johnson; pg. 1549, pg. 1091
Glover, Jamie, Brand Mgr-Adv - 3M Company; pg. 1142, pg. 956
Glover, Laura, Sr Mgr-Product & Solutions Mktg Enablement - NetApp, Inc.; pg. 444, pg. 287
Glover, Valerie, Sr Mgr-Global Mktg Campaign - Hewlett-Packard Company; pg. 404, pg. 175
Glowacki, Alan, Sr Mgr-Technical Mktg - Cisco Systems, Inc.; pg. 372, pg. 240
Glowacki, Matthew, Dir-Mktg & Loyalty - Sears Holdings Corporation; pg. 1784, pg. 618
Glowicki, Jeri, Dir-Mktg - The Bradford Group; pg. 1763, pg. 637
Gluck, Moshe, Rep-Mktg-MassMutual Fin Grp - Massachusetts Mutual Life Insurance Company; pg. 1207, pg. 845
Glucki, Mark, Sr Mgr-Social Media & Digital Mktg - MTS Allstream, Inc.; pg. 1946, pg. 1940
Glueck, Edmund, Mgr-Mktg & New Product Dev - Bodine Electric Company; pg. 1318, pg. 641
Glusman, Andres, VP-Strategy, Product & Community -

First page reference indicates Business Class Edition
Second page reference indicates Geographic Edition

Meetup Inc.; pg. 1266, pg. 1258
Glynn, Barbara, Sr Mgr-Digital Production - Boston Scientific Corporation; pg. 1508, pg. 831
Glynn, Brittany, Sr Rep-Mktg & Adv - United Airlines, Inc.; pg. 1927, pg. 593
Glynn, Kara, Sr Mgr-Field Mktg & Training - Sharp Electronics Corporation; pg. 672, pg. 1082
Gmelich, Alisa, Exec Dir-US Field Mktg - International House of Pancakes, Inc.; pg. 1732, pg. 96
Gmerek, Jay, VP-Mktg - Rich Products Corporation; pg. 892, pg. 1150
Go, Cynthia, Mgr-Global Mktg-Partnerships & Promos - Netflix, Inc.; pg. 1269, pg. 141
Gobao, Jami, Mgr-Sports Mktg-Men's Run & Train - Under Armour, Inc.; pg. 49, pg. 759
Gobbi, Alexandra, Sr VP-Corp Mktg & Comm - EarthLink Holdings Corp.; pg. 1240, pg. 504
Gobbo, Kristen, Dir-Global Mktg Comm, Food, Beverage & Laboratory - Pall Corporation; pg. 232, pg. 1323
Gobs, Tim, Dir-Sls - Philadelphia Flyers, L.P.; pg. 575, pg. 1569
Gochee, Jim, Chief Product Officer - New Relic, Inc.; pg. 445, pg. 224
Goco, Jenny, Sr Dir-Partnership Strategy - International Speedway Corporation; pg. 553, pg. 420
Goczan, Christopher, Product Mgr-Natl - Mercedes-Benz Canada Inc.; pg. 184, pg. 1940
Godard, Patrick, Dir-Mktg & Product Dev-Compact Line - Caterpillar, Inc.; pg. 1321, pg. 650
Godbey, Kecia, Brand Mgr-Dulaglutide-Global - Eli Lilly and Company; pg. 1527, pg. 684
Godbout, Matt, VP-Sponsorship Sls - Indianapolis Colts, Inc.; pg. 553, pg. 687
Godby, Brandon, Dir-Mktg Ops - HealthSouth Corporation; pg. 1540, pg. 3
Goddard, Courtney, Sr Mgr-Sls - Marriott International, Inc.; pg. 1102, pg. 764
Goddard, Janie, Exec VP-Strategic Bus Units & Mktg-Global - Welch Allyn Inc.; pg. 1436, pg. 1342
Goddard, Kevin, Mgr-Social Media Mktg-Amazon Web Svcs - Amazon.com, Inc.; pg. 1226, pg. 1831
Goddard, Kim, Mgr-Retail Mktg-Best Buy Americas - Bose Corporation; pg. 626, pg. 820
Goddard, Lori, Brand Mgr - Zale Corporation; pg. 16, pg. 1724
Goddard, Michael, Dir-Mktg & New Bus Dev - Schlumberger Limited; pg. 801, pg. 1714
Goddard, Peter A., Sr Mgr-Mktg - Medtronic, Inc.; pg. 1564, pg. 939
Godderidge, Ryan, Vp-Sls & Mktg - Browning; pg. 1828, pg. 1752
Goddu, Maureen, Sr Program Mgr-Social Media - NutriSystem, Inc.; pg. 1577, pg. 1533
Godell, Peam, Mgr-Production - White's Electronics; pg. 688, pg. 1509
Godfrey, Anna, Dir-Creative - Gentiva Health Services, Inc.; pg. 1534, pg. 506
Godfrey, David, Sr VP-Sls-Global - Gartner, Inc.; pg. 1248, pg. 374
Godfrey, Ken, Dir-Digital Mktg-North America - Philips Electronics North America; pg. 662, pg. 782
Godfrey, Kerry, Brand Mktg Dir-Global DTC - NIKE, Inc.; pg. 1812, pg. 1492
Godfrey, Lawrence, Dir-Global Category & Shopper Mktg - GlaxoSmithKline Consumer Healthcare; pg. 510, pg. 1554
Godin, Steve, Exec VP-Sls & Bus Dev - International Fiber Corp.; pg. 865, pg. 1317
Godlewski, Khristina, Sr Mgr-Integrated Mktg - Meredith Corporation; pg. 1663, pg. 705
Godlewski, Marcin, Product Mgr - Cisco Systems, Inc.; pg. 372, pg. 240
Godlove, Becky, Brand Mgr-NA Salon Pro Exclusives Brands - The Procter & Gamble Company; pg. 1129, pg. 1418
Godon, Julie, VP-Global Mktg Svcs - ALERE INC.; pg. 1488, pg. 849
Godsey, Dustin, VP-Mktg - Milwaukee Bucks, Inc.; pg. 563, pg. 1878
Godsick, Jeff, Pres-20th Century Fox Consumer Products - 20th Century Fox Film Corp.; pg. 267, pg. 124
Godwin, David L., VP-Minerals & Energy Products - Weyerhaeuser Company; pg. 121, pg. 1820
Godwin, Mallory, Mgr-Mktg - American Express Company; pg. 712, pg. 1190
Godwin, Natalie, Mgr-Global PR-Retail - United Parcel Service, Inc.; pg. 1928, pg. 522
Goebel, Amanda, Mgr-Product & Mktg - Hotwire, Inc.; pg. 1912, pg. 219
Goedde, Tom, VP-Mktg - Electronic Arts Inc.; pg. 951, pg. 189
Goedecke, Glenn, Exec VP-Sls & Mktg - Mayer Electric Supply Company Inc.; pg. 653, pg. 3
Goeke, Brian, Dir-Mktg & Online - Cumulus Media Inc.; pg. 280, pg. 503
Goel, Himani, Sr Specialist-Mktg - Siemens Process Industries and Drives; pg. 673, pg. 485
Goel, Kavi, Sr Product Mgr-Google Search - Google Inc.; pg. 1249, pg. 153
Goel, Vaibhav, Sr Product Mgr - LinkedIn Corporation; pg. 1262, pg. 160
Goel, Vinay, Mgr-Privacy Product - Adobe Systems Incorporated; pg. 342, pg. 235
Goeld, Heather, Dir-Sls - Kayak; pg. 1260, pg. 363
Goeller, George, Sr Dir-Ops - LVMH Inc.; pg. 9, pg. 1254
Goenka, Carey, Sr Assoc Brand Mgr - Popchips; pg. 890, pg. 182
Goenka, Manish, Sr Mgr-Engagement - Cisco Systems, Inc.; pg. 372, pg. 240
Goenka, Vishal, Sr Product Mgr - Google Inc.; pg. 1249, pg. 153
Goering, Richard, Sr Mgr-Technical Comm - Cadence Design Systems, Inc.; pg. 367, pg. 239
Goerisch, Florian, Product Mgr - Google Inc.; pg. 1249, pg. 153
Goerner, Rick, Sr VP-Sls-Worldwide - Microsemi Corporation; pg. 435, pg. 41
Goers, Jim, Mgr-Media Delivery - Valassis; pg. 1698, pg. 386
Goertz, Paul von, Sr Mgr-Global Channel Mktg-Fossil Brand - Fossil Group, Inc.; pg. 5, pg. 1735
Goertzen, Jami, Mgr-Brand & Mktg - Florida Power & Light Company; pg. 1943, pg. 435
Goesele, Bettina, Mgr-Mktg - Sotheby's Inc.; pg. 472, pg. 1294
Goettel, Tim, Dir-Online Mktg - Spark Networks, Inc.; pg. 472, pg. 140
Goetz, Amy, Sr Specialist-PR - Target Corporation; pg. 1786, pg. 942
Goetz, Debra, Sr VP-Corp Mktg & Global Comm - Hyatt Hotels Corporation; pg. 1096, pg. 577
Goetz, Laura, Sr Mgr-Adv - Cooper Tire & Rubber Company; pg. 1881, pg. 1453
Goetz, William W., CMO & Sr VP-Mktg - Sysco Corporation; pg. 1035, pg. 1716
Goetzinger, Dave, Mgr-Technical Mktg - Curries Company; pg. 77, pg. 709
Goetzman, Robyn, Mgr-Digital Mktg-KC Pro - Kimberly-Clark Corporation; pg. 1461, pg. 1720
Goewey, Alexandria, Brand Mgr-Integration - AARP; pg. 124, pg. 393
Goff, Annabella, Sr Mgr-CRM - Disney Interactive Media Group; pg. 1239, pg. 95
Goff, Donna, Mgr-Leisure Sls Bus Dev - MGM Resorts International; pg. 1105, pg. 1028
Goff, Marlo, Exec Assistant-Mktg & Comm - University Of Denver; pg. 609, pg. 323
Goff, Virginia, Mgr-Partnership Mktg & Indus Rels - Tourism Ireland; pg. 1007, pg. 1303
Gogan, Julie, Sr Coord-Brdcst Media - Kohl's Corporation; pg. 1775, pg. 1870
Goh, NaYoung, Dir-Mktg - Pfizer Inc.; pg. 1581, pg. 1278
Gohil, Netesh, Sr Dir-Pricing & Quotations - Philips Electronics North America; pg. 662, pg. 782
Gohil, Netesh, Head-Pricing & Quotations & Sr Dir - Philips Lighting; pg. 1303, pg. 806
Gohman, Sharon, Principal & Product Mgr - Boston Scientific Corporation; pg. 1508, pg. 831
Gohr, Martin, Sr Dir-Pur - Airbus Helicopters, Inc.; pg. 223, pg. 1698
Gohring, Eric, Product Mgr & Engr-Life Safety Products - Mestek, Inc.; pg. 1074, pg. 857
Gohs, Eric, VP-Digital Mktg & Loyalty - Express, Inc.; pg. 24, pg. 1440
Goines, Beverly, Specialist-Mktg - FedEx Corporation; pg. 1907, pg. 1642
Goines, Joshua, Sr Dir-Bus Dev-Global - PayPal Inc.; pg. 1274, pg. 248
Goins, Reginald, VP-Market Unit Sls Ops - The Coca-Cola Company; pg. 240, pg. 493
Goins, Terry, Brand Mgr-Windex - S.C. Johnson & Son, Inc.; pg. 334, pg. 1889
Gokey, Lydia, Mgr-Mktg - PepsiCo, Inc.; pg. 259, pg. 1327
Gokhale, Ajit, VP-Sls & Mktg - National Instruments Corporation; pg. 443, pg. 1664
Gokhale, Neeraj, VP-Products & Comm Global Bus Unit - Oracle Corporation; pg. 450, pg. 191
Gokhale, Yashodhan, Sr Dir-Product EA Access - Electronic Arts Inc.; pg. 951, pg. 189
Golash, Terry, Sr Dir-Medical - Aetna Inc.; pg. 1187, pg. 351
Golatt, Brandon, Planner-Event Mktg - GEICO Corporation; pg. 1200, pg. 399
Gold, Barbara, Sr Strategist-Mktg-Loyalty & CRM - Brooks Brothers Group, Inc.; pg. 39, pg. 1208
Gold, Edward, Dir-Adv - State Farm Mutual Automobile Insurance Co.; pg. 1218, pg. 557
Gold, Jack, Sr Dir-Trng-North America - NIKE, Inc.; pg. 1812, pg. 1492
Gold, Lor, Chief Creative Officer-Global - SGK; pg. 1686, pg. 590
Gold, Meredith, Sr Dir-Multiplatform Program Plng, Sponsorships & Acq - NBC Universal, Inc.; pg. 300, pg. 1266
Gold, Michael, VP-Global Product Dev - PHARMACEUTICAL PRODUCT DEVELOPMENT, INC.; pg. 1584, pg. 1393
Gold, Noah, Sr Mgr-Comm - The Gatorade Company; pg. 251, pg. 574
Gold, Randy, Sr VP-Sls - NuCO2 Inc.; pg. 1175, pg. 468
Gold, Susana, Mgr-Mktg-Latin American Div - Samsung Electronics America, Inc.; pg. 669, pg. 1115
Gold, Timothy, Dir-Mktg - Wells Fargo & Company; pg. 819, pg. 232
Goldbarg, Claudio, Sr VP-Publ & Digital Media Ops - MARTHA STEWART LIVING OMNIMEDIA, INC.; pg. 1661, pg. 1256
Goldberg, Andrew, VP-Programmatic & Digital Media Sls - Synacor, Inc.; pg. 1283, pg. 1151
Goldberg, Andy, Dir-Creative-Global - General Electric Company; pg. 1297, pg. 347
Goldberg, Arleen, Sr Mgr-Digital Delivery - Discover Financial Services; pg. 744, pg. 653
Goldberg, Ashley, Brand Mgr-Natl Value Delivery & New Market Dev-Ethnic Mktg - Procter & Gamble Inc.; pg. 333, pg. 1929
Goldberg, Beverly, VP-Sls-Florsheim Brand - Weyco Group, Inc.; pg. 1822, pg. 1858
Goldberg, Brad, VP-Mktg - MGM Grand Hotel, LLC; pg. 1104, pg. 1028
Goldberg, Bruce, Dir-Technical & Plant Mgr - Stanbee Company, Inc.; pg. 1819, pg. 1050
Goldberg, Inna, Product Mgr - FactSet Research Systems Inc.; pg. 1247, pg. 361
Goldberg, Jesse, Specialist-Product - LG Electronics U.S.A., Inc.; pg. 651, pg. 1060
Goldberg, Jessica, Brand Mgr-Birds Eye Reg Vegetables, Fruit & New Platforms - Pinnacle Foods Group LLC; pg. 889, pg. 1104
Goldberg, Keith, Corp VP-Sls & Mktg - Case Paper Company Inc.; pg. 1455, pg. 1163
Goldberg, Kristen, Mgr-Product Plng & Mktg - Canon U.S.A., Inc.; pg. 1404, pg. 1178
Goldberg, Laurie, Exec VP-PR - Discovery Communications, Inc.; pg. 282, pg. 777
Goldberg, Lev I., Dir-Mktg Comm & Brand Mgmt - Constellation Energy Resources, LLC; pg. 1938, pg. 756
Goldberg, Lewis, Mgr-Sls & Mktg-Natl - Fine Organics Corporation; pg. 330, pg. 1052
Goldberg, Rivka, Dir-Mktg - Stila Cosmetics; pg. 523, pg. 99
Goldberg, Rob, Exec VP-Mktg & Creative-Restaurants - Tommy Bahama; pg. 48, pg. 1842
Goldberg, Ross, Sr Dir-Mktg-Diabetes Mktg & Head-Payer - Sanofi US; pg. 1592, pg. 1046
Goldberg, Sandy, Sr Mgr-Corp Comm - Electronic Arts Inc.; pg. 951, pg. 189
Goldberg, Simon A., Dir-Global Mktg, Digital Mobile & Social - Abbott Laboratories; pg. 1484, pg. 551
Goldberg, Yana, Product Mgr-Mktg - Anixter International Inc.; pg. 1313, pg. 614
Goldberger, Chaya, Sr Dir-Digital Mktg - Fandango Media, LLC; pg. 1247, pg. 130
Goldberger, Seth, Sr Dir-Global Mktg-Ck Color Cosmetics & Calvin Klein Fragrances - Coty, Inc.; pg. 506, pg. 1219
Goldblatt, Ari, Dir-Pro Tennis Mktg - United States Tennis Association; pg. 160, pg. 1354
Goldblatt, Barry, VP-Mktg Res - Church & Dwight Co., Inc.; pg. 1153, pg. 1063
Goldblatt, David, Dir-Channel Mktg & Category Mgmt - Graco Children's Products Inc.; pg. 954, pg. 1531
Golden, Ali, Mgr-PR - Ameriprise Financial, Inc.; pg. 715, pg.

930
Golden, Jenna, Mgr-Sls-Politics & Advocacy - Twitter, Inc.; *pg.* 1285, *pg.* 228
Golden, Jonathan, Product Head - Airbnb, Inc.; *pg.* 1226, *pg.* 211
Golden, Josh, Global VP-Mktg - Xerox Corporation; *pg.* 494, *pg.* 365
Golden, Ken, Dir-PR-Global - Deere & Company; *pg.* 703, *pg.* 632
Golden, Kyle, Product Mgr & Brand Mgr - Lennox International Inc.; *pg.* 1073, *pg.* 1736
Golden, Lisa, Sr Mgr-Intake, Publ & Bus Mgmt - Canadian Imperial Bank of Commerce; *pg.* 729, *pg.* 1935
Golden, Matthew, Dir-Mktg - Pfizer Inc.; *pg.* 1581, *pg.* 1278
Golden, Michael, Sr Asst Brand Mgr - Philip Morris USA Inc.; *pg.* 1894, *pg.* 1803
Golden, Molly, Dir-Mktg - New York Apple Association, Inc.; *pg.* 152, *pg.* 1160
Golden, Whitney, Dir-PR - AT&T Mobility LLC; *pg.* 619, *pg.* 488
Goldenbaum, Jeff, Dir-Mktg - Dataram Corporation; *pg.* 383, *pg.* 1111
Goldenberg, Glenn, Head-Sls & Customer Success - Cerora, Inc.; *pg.* 1405, *pg.* 1516
Goldenstern, Christoph, VP-Corp Strategy, Mktg & Products-Global - Kepner-Tregoe, Inc.; *pg.* 424, *pg.* 1112
Goldfarb, Evan, Sr VP-Sls - Rentrak Corporation; *pg.* 306, *pg.* 1506
Goldfarb, Judy, Dir-Brand & Customer Mktg - British Airways; *pg.* 1901, *pg.* 1207
Goldfarb, Michael, Dir-Media Rels - Doctors Without Borders USA, Inc.; *pg.* 139, *pg.* 1225
Goldfein, Miriam, Sr Dir-Strategy, Store Expansion, Forecasting & Data Analysis - Best Buy Co., Inc.; *pg.* 1761, *pg.* 954
Goldfeld, Eric, Asst VP-Natl Consumer Mktg - AT&T Mobility LLC; *pg.* 619, *pg.* 488
Goldfinch, Jay, Engr-Technical Mktg - NetApp, Inc.; *pg.* 444, *pg.* 287
Goldflam, Rachel, Exec Dir-Mktg - Yurman Design, Inc.; *pg.* 15, *pg.* 1316
Goldhaber, Steve, Sr Dir-Interactive Mktg & Brand-Global - Aon Risk Services Inc.; *pg.* 1193, *pg.* 564
Goldhardt, Meagan, Mgr-Digital Mktg - White Castle Management Co.; *pg.* 1756, *pg.* 1444
Goldin, Hilary, Mgr-Digital Media - Google Inc.; *pg.* 1249, *pg.* 153
Goldkamp, Asa, Rep-Outside Sls - Graybar Electric Company, Inc.; *pg.* 1299, *pg.* 997
Goldman, Aaron, VP-Brand Creative - Lifetime Entertainment Services LLC; *pg.* 296, *pg.* 1251
Goldman, Adina, Sr Mgr-Events Mktg & Special Projects - The Hearst Corporation; *pg.* 1649, *pg.* 1239
Goldman, Billie, Mgr-Partner Mktg - Intel Corporation; *pg.* 645, *pg.* 266
Goldman, Cathy, VP-Mktg, Intl Distr & Production - Sony Pictures Entertainment Inc.; *pg.* 309, *pg.* 72
Goldman, Danielle, Sr Mgr-Trade Mktg - Lavazza Premium Coffees Corp.; *pg.* 874, *pg.* 1250
Goldman, Danielle, Mgr-Adv - XO Group Inc.; *pg.* 1289, *pg.* 1316
Goldman, David, Head-Insights-Paid Search & Product Mgr - Target Corporation; *pg.* 1786, *pg.* 942
Goldman, Jeff, Sls Mgr-Major Accounts-Automotive & Tech - The Washington Post; *pg.* 1701, *pg.* 407
Goldman, Jeffrey, Mgr-Tech & Natl Automotive Adv - Graham Holdings Company; *pg.* 1645, *pg.* 1773
Goldman, JoAnne P., Mgr-Product Mktg - Honeywell International Inc.; *pg.* 407, *pg.* 1088
Goldman, Michelle, Sr Mgr-Promos - DreamWorks Animation SKG, Inc.; *pg.* 284, *pg.* 96
Goldman, Rich, Dir-Products - Miller Heiman Inc.; *pg.* 440, *pg.* 1031
Goldner, Karen, Brand Mgr-Acne Care North America - Neutrogena Corporation; *pg.* 517, *pg.* 137
Goldrick, Rebecca, Dir-Media & Comm - American Society for the Prevention of Cruelty to Animals; *pg.* 131, *pg.* 1193
Goldsand, Lauren, Brand Mgr-Bayer Aspirin & Midol - Bayer Healthcare Consumer Care Division; *pg.* 1500, *pg.* 1087
Goldsand, Lauren, Product Mgr - Merck & Co., Inc.; *pg.* 1566, *pg.* 1077
Goldsborough, Erin, Sr Mgr-Ad Ops - WebMD Health Corporation; *pg.* 1288, *pg.* 1313
Goldschmidt, Andrew, Head-Global Offering & Americas Sls-RPO - International Business Machines Corporation; *pg.* 418, *pg.* 1138
Goldsmith, Alex, Sr Mgr-Global Comm-Cloud, Mobile & Big Data - NetApp, Inc.; *pg.* 444, *pg.* 287
Goldsmith, Andy, VP-Creative Strategy - American Cancer Society, Inc.; *pg.* 126, *pg.* 487
Goldsmith, Keith, Sr Product Mgr - Ingram Micro Inc.; *pg.* 415, *pg.* 261
Goldsmith, Michael, VP-Sls-Intl - Las Vegas Convention & Visitors Authority; *pg.* 997, *pg.* 1027
Goldsmith, Richard, Exec VP-Global Distr & Intl Consumer Products - The Jim Henson Company; *pg.* 293, *pg.* 103
Goldsmith, Richard, Dir-Digital & Social Media - Mike's Hard Lemonade Co.; *pg.* 1966, *pg.* 582
Goldsmith, Robert, Sr Mgr-Sls - Kayak; *pg.* 1260, *pg.* 363
Goldstein, Alon, Dir-Product Mgmt - Harmonic, Inc.; *pg.* 402, *pg.* 246
Goldstein, Alyson, Brand Mgr-Lysol - Reckitt Benckiser Inc.; *pg.* 1136, *pg.* 1105
Goldstein, Brian, Product Dir-Propel SSP - Fairmount Santrol; *pg.* 1162, *pg.* 1409
Goldstein, Carol A., Acct Mgr-Enterprise Creative Solution - Bank of America Corporation; *pg.* 718, *pg.* 1362
Goldstein, Carrie, Sr Mgr-USPR - Pfizer Inc.; *pg.* 1581, *pg.* 1278
Goldstein, Cassie, Specialist-Mktg - T.J. Maxx; *pg.* 1788, *pg.* 822
Goldstein, Cassie, Specialist-Adv - The TJX Companies, Inc.; *pg.* 1788, *pg.* 822
Goldstein, Evan, Mgr-Creative & Adv - Barnes & Noble, Inc.; *pg.* 1619, *pg.* 1201
Goldstein, Nicole, Dir-Mktg-Tech & Engrg - Randstad USA; *pg.* 459, *pg.* 941
Goldstein, Rachel, Dir-Adv Production & Layout Sys - The New York Times Company; *pg.* 1668, *pg.* 1270
Goldstein, Ross, Mng Dir-Retail Annuities Mktg - New York Life Insurance Company; *pg.* 1211, *pg.* 1268
Goldstein, Sandy, Sr Product Mgr-OMNI Channel - Staples, Inc.; *pg.* 474, *pg.* 821
Goldstein, Sherri, Sr Specialist-Mktg & Event - Tyco International (US) Inc.; *pg.* 1891, *pg.* 1113
Goldstein, Sheryl, Sr Category Dir-Sls - Yahoo! Inc.; *pg.* 1289, *pg.* 289
Goldstein, Stacey, Mgr-Mktg-Garnier Skincare Product Innovation - L'Oreal USA; *pg.* 514, *pg.* 1252
Goldstein, Stephen, VP & Gen Mgr-Sls & Mktg - Samsung Electronics America, Inc.; *pg.* 669, *pg.* 1115
Goldstein, Susan, Brand Mgr - Macy's East; *pg.* 1777, *pg.* 1254
Goldstein, Suzanne, Sr Dir-Mktg Beauty-GFO North America - Johnson & Johnson; *pg.* 1549, *pg.* 1091
Goldstein, Tara, VP-Mktg - Brookfield Financial Properties, Inc.; *pg.* 1083, *pg.* 1207
Goldston, Bob, Sr Mgr-Bus Dev-Specialty Markets - Dana Holding Corporation; *pg.* 203, *pg.* 1461
Goldstone, Lisa, Mgr-Mktg Comm-Global - BASF Corporation; *pg.* 1149, *pg.* 1066
Goldwater, Shari, Mgr-Retail Adv-Chevrolet - General Motors Company; *pg.* 175, *pg.* 881
Goldweitz, Elyse, Brand Mgr-Clearasil - Reckitt Benckiser Inc.; *pg.* 1136, *pg.* 1105
Goldy, Christie, Reg Mgr-Sls - Dr Pepper Snapple Group, Inc.; *pg.* 250, *pg.* 1729
Gole, Samir, Sr Dir-Product Mgmt - Viacom Inc.; *pg.* 316, *pg.* 1310
Golembieski, Darlene, Mgr-Shopper Mktg - PepsiCo, Inc.; *pg.* 259, *pg.* 1327
Golen, Frederic, Head-Global Automotive Mktg - Facebook, Inc.; *pg.* 1245, *pg.* 143
Golenbock, Justin, Specialist-PR-47North & Thomas & Mercer-Amazon Publ - Amazon.com, Inc.; *pg.* 1226, *pg.* 1831
Goletz, Rebecca, Sr Analyst-Mktg - American International Group, Inc.; *pg.* 1190, *pg.* 1193
Golier, Christopher, VP-Mobile Mktg & Strategy - National Hockey League; *pg.* 568, *pg.* 1265
Golis, Nadine, Sr Mgr-Mktg - Advance Realty Group, LLC; *pg.* 1079, *pg.* 1045
Golla, Bernice A., Dir-Global Mktg GU - Merck & Co., Inc.; *pg.* 1566, *pg.* 1077
Gollaher, Brian, Product Mgmt-Platform Bus Unit - Red Hat, Inc.; *pg.* 460, *pg.* 1388
Gollaher, Nicholas S., Specialist-Enterprise-Demand Gen & Lifecycle Mktg - Windstream Corporation; *pg.* 321, *pg.* 34
Gollat, Brandon, Planner-Event Mktg - GEICO Corporation; *pg.* 1200, *pg.* 399
Gollehur, Bob, Specialist-Product-Collision Product Lines - General Motors Company; *pg.* 175, *pg.* 881
Golloti, Tammy, Dir-Mktg & Corp Comm - Cisco Systems, Inc.; *pg.* 372, *pg.* 240
Golobich, Russ, Sr Mgr-Asset - OPUS Corporation; *pg.* 101, *pg.* 949
Golod, Margarita, Dir-Product Mktg - Return Path, Inc.; *pg.* 461, *pg.* 1285
Golomb, Adam, Dir-Mktg - Giant Eagle, Inc.; *pg.* 1020, *pg.* 1575
Golonka, Anna, Mgr-Sls - CareerBuilder, LLC; *pg.* 1234, *pg.* 568
Golshan, Diane, Sr Mgr-Digital & Social Mktg - Microsoft Corporation; *pg.* 435, *pg.* 1824
Golshmit, Inna, Acct Mgr-Comml Print & Promotional Products - Staples, Inc.; *pg.* 474, *pg.* 821
Goltra, Andrew, Dir-Mdsg - Uline Shipping Supplies; *pg.* 1385, *pg.* 666
Goltra, Tad, VP-Product Mgmt - EBSCO Information Services Walpole; *pg.* 1638, *pg.* 849
Golzar, Nedah, Coord-Production-Soft Accessories - American Eagle Outfitters, Inc.; *pg.* 37, *pg.* 1572
Gomatam, Sampath, Sr VP-Product - support.com, inc.; *pg.* 1283, *pg.* 192
Gomel, Monique, VP-Global Mktg & Comm - Rocky Mountaineer; *pg.* 1921, *pg.* 1912
Gomes, Anita, Dir-Mktg - QUALCOMM Incorporated; *pg.* 1873, *pg.* 207
Gomes, Jennifer, Sr Mgr-Social Media - Anthem, Inc.; *pg.* 1192, *pg.* 683
Gomes, Kelly, Dir-Natl Field Mktg - Burger King Corporation; *pg.* 1719, *pg.* 440
Gomes, Rodrigo, Sr Mgr-Product Mktg - Bose Corporation; *pg.* 626, *pg.* 820
Gomes-Casseres, Carolina, Dir-Ad Product & Monetization - TheHuffingtonPost.com, Inc.; *pg.* 1692, *pg.* 1298
Gomes-Oliveira, Lisa, Brand Mgr-Men's Shavers - BIC Corporation; *pg.* 501, *pg.* 369
Gomez, Anthony, VP-Sls & Mktg - PNY Technologies, Inc.; *pg.* 455, *pg.* 1105
Gomez, Carolina, Brand Mgr - Newell Rubbermaid Inc.; *pg.* 1128, *pg.* 515
Gomez, Erika, Sr Mgr-Primary Care Mktg - Pfizer Inc.; *pg.* 1581, *pg.* 1278
Gomez, Henry, CMO & Chief Comm Officer - Hewlett-Packard Company; *pg.* 404, *pg.* 175
Gomez, Lizette, Coord-Mktg - Fresh & Easy Neighborhood Market Inc; *pg.* 1020, *pg.* 80
Gomez, Lucia, Assoc Mgr-Hispanic Mktg - Aflac Incorporated; *pg.* 1188, *pg.* 527
Gomez, Marcia, Dir-Titan Mktg Strategy - Nationwide Mutual Insurance Company; *pg.* 1210, *pg.* 1442
Gomez, Miguel, Specialist-Customer Mktg Sls - Bank of America Corporation; *pg.* 718, *pg.* 1362
Gomez, Miguel, Sr VP-Sls - WireCo WorldGroup; *pg.* 1389, *pg.* 987
Gomez, Nancy, Analyst-SAP PR & PO - Hess Corporation; *pg.* 979, *pg.* 1240
Gomez, Rick, Sr VP-Mktg - Target Corporation; *pg.* 1786, *pg.* 942
Gomez, Roberto, Mgr-Technical Mktg - Rayonier Inc.; *pg.* 1179, *pg.* 434
Gomez, Sam, VP-Digital Mktg - Feld Entertainment, Inc.; *pg.* 547, *pg.* 458
Gomez, Susanne, Mgr-Enterprise Channel & Field Mktg - Plantronics, Inc.; *pg.* 663, *pg.* 270
Gomez-Ortigoza, Anaid, Product Mgr - Facebook, Inc.; *pg.* 1245, *pg.* 143
Gomia, Kellie, Dir-Mktg - Anthem, Inc.; *pg.* 1192, *pg.* 683
Gomm, Jack B., Dir-Global Mktg-HCV Launch Team - Gilead Sciences, Inc.; *pg.* 1535, *pg.* 88
Gomprecht, Paula, Brand Mgr-Westin & Sheraton Hotels - Starwood Hotels & Resorts Worldwide, Inc.; *pg.* 1114, *pg.* 378
Goncalves, Leandro, Reg Sr Mgr-Category Mktg-Global Travel - Diageo North America, Inc.; *pg.* 1961, *pg.* 361
Goncalves, Tony, Sr VP-Digital Entertainment Products Grp - DIRECTV Group Holdings, LLC; *pg.* 281, *pg.* 79
Gonczy, Gary, Dir-Mktg & Adv - Kwik Trip Inc.; *pg.* 1026, *pg.* 1864
Gonder, Gary, COO & Dir-Mktg, Sls & Comm - Missouri Lottery; *pg.* 999, *pg.* 979
Gonedes, Jim, Exec VP-Mktg - CCA Industries, Inc.; *pg.* 503, *pg.* 1114
Gong, Brian, Sr Mgr-Pub & Analyst Rels - Netscout Systems, Inc.; *pg.* 1270, *pg.* 858

Gong, River, Exec VP-Sls-Worldwide - Oplink Communications, Inc.; pg. 660, pg. 91
Gonsalves, Daniel, Analyst-Product Line-Mobile & Comm Grp - Intel Corporation; pg. 645, pg. 266
Gonsior, Jennifer, Mgr-Mktg Solutions - National Basketball Association; pg. 566, pg. 1264
Gonsman, Lindsay, Supvr-Central Adv Ops - Gannett Co., Inc.; pg. 1643, pg. 1790
Gonyo, Jeff, Sr Dir-Mktg-ESPN - ESPN, Inc.; pg. 285, pg. 340
Gonzaga, Tania, Sr Mgr-Mktg-Girls Mktg - Mattel Games/Puzzles; pg. 962, pg. 80
Gonzaga, Tania, Sr Mgr-Mktg-Girls Mktg - MATTEL, INC.; pg. 962, pg. 81
Gonzalaz, George, Mgr-Import Sls - Dave Syverson Inc.; pg. 168, pg. 915
Gonzales, Adolfo, Product Mgr - Halliburton Company; pg. 978, pg. 1707
Gonzales, Cristian, Mgr-Social Media - Nautilus, Inc.; pg. 1840, pg. 1846
Gonzales, Esther, Sr Mgr-Mktg Diversity - AT&T Communications Corp.; pg. 1866, pg. 1043
Gonzales, Esther, Sr Mgr-Diversity Mktg - AT&T Mobility LLC; pg. 620, pg. 1152
Gonzales, Frank, Mgr-Mktg - Cinemark Holdings, Inc.; pg. 540, pg. 1729
Gonzales, Kimberly, Dir-Media - Cost Plus World Market; pg. 921, pg. 170
Gonzales, Lisa, Sr Mgr-HR Comm - Iron Mountain Incorporated; pg. 421, pg. 796
Gonzales, Marco Antonio, Sr Dir-Corp Comm-North America - Herbalife International of America, Inc.; pg. 1541, pg. 132
Gonzales, Michael, Sr Mgr-Mktg-Interactive Product Dev - American Express Company; pg. 712, pg. 1190
Gonzales, Nick, Dir-Mktg-Racquet Sports-Global - Wilson Sporting Goods Co.; pg. 1848, pg. 596
Gonzales, Robert, Mgr-Adv - Friedrich Air Conditioning Co.; pg. 1072, pg. 1740
Gonzales, Ruth A., Head-North America Mktg, Gap Specialty - The Gap, Inc.; pg. 1770, pg. 218
Gonzalez, Abelardo, Dir-Product Mgmt-Monitoring - Keynote Systems Incorporated; pg. 425, pg. 255
Gonzalez, Abelardo, Product Mgr-Global - Parker Hannifin Corporation; pg. 1368, pg. 1434
Gonzalez, Alex, Product Mgr - PeopleFluent; pg. 453, pg. 853
Gonzalez, Alexandro, Mgr-Partnership Mktg - Teleflora LLC; pg. 1801, pg. 140
Gonzalez, Allison, Mgr-Ecommerce Mktg-Social & Events - Carter's, Inc.; pg. 21, pg. 491
Gonzalez, Ana, Specialist-Adv Acct Relationship - The Walton Sun; pg. 1701, pg. 465
Gonzalez, Ana M., Product Mgr-Intl - Kissimmee-St. Cloud Convention & Visitors Bureau; pg. 997, pg. 436
Gonzalez, Andres, Dir-Mktg - Holistic Life Foundation, Inc.; pg. 143, pg. 757
Gonzalez, Angel, Dir-Creative - Lumber Liquidators Holdings, Inc.; pg. 94, pg. 1808
Gonzalez, Anique, Assoc Mgr-Interactive Mktg - bebe stores, inc.; pg. 19, pg. 49
Gonzalez, Anthony, Mgr-Sls - Deluxe Corporation; pg. 1634, pg. 964
Gonzalez, Antonio, Mgr-Mktg - Scholastic Corporation; pg. 1683, pg. 1288
Gonzalez, Aurora, Sr Dir-Comm, Issues & Crisis Mgmt - PepsiCo, Inc.; pg. 259, pg. 1327
Gonzalez, Carrie, Dir-Mktg Strategy - Macy's East; pg. 1777, pg. 1254
Gonzalez, Christopher, Dir-Mobile Product Mgmt - Gilt Groupe Inc.; pg. 24, pg. 1234
Gonzalez, Cuitlahuac, Brand Mgr-Engagement & Social Media - BCBG Max Azria Group LLC; pg. 19, pg. 301
Gonzalez, Daniel, Grp Brand Dir-Modern Liqueurs-Southern Comfort & Tuaca - Brown-Forman Corporation; pg. 1958, pg. 732
Gonzalez, Daniel, Sr Dir-Media Strategy - Burger King Corporation; pg. 1719, pg. 440
Gonzalez, Doreen, Sr Mgr-Pur - Gulfstream Aerospace Corporation; pg. 228, pg. 540
Gonzalez, Francis X., VP-Property Mgmt-PR - DDR Corp.; pg. 1089, pg. 1405
Gonzalez, Genie, Brand Mgr - Susser Holdings Corporation; pg. 985, pg. 1671
Gonzalez, George, Asst Coord-Product - Chiquita Brands International, Inc.; pg. 847, pg. 1365
Gonzalez, Irene, Coord-Adv Ops - TEN: The Enthusiast Network; pg. 1691, pg. 1298
Gonzalez, Iris, Mgr-Mktg Comm-LATAM - Burger King Corporation; pg. 1719, pg. 440
Gonzalez, Jack, Dir-Mktg & Sls - American Public Transportation Association; pg. 130, pg. 395
Gonzalez, Jessica, Specialist-Social Media - Pitney Bowes Inc.; pg. 454, pg. 376
Gonzalez, Juan, Dir-Strategic Sls - ChyronHego; pg. 371, pg. 1179
Gonzalez, Juan Pablo, Sr Brand Mgr-Hispanic Mktg - The Coca-Cola Company; pg. 240, pg. 493
Gonzalez, Liane, Sr Dir-Consumer Insights & New Products Mktg - Potbelly Sandwich Works LLC; pg. 1746, pg. 587
Gonzalez, Manny, Sr Dir-Multicultural - Moet Hennessy; pg. 1966, pg. 1260
Gonzalez, Manuel, Mgr-Channel Mktg-IT Miami Exporters - Schneider Electric; pg. 467, pg. 1609
Gonzalez, Mark, Dir-Creative-Intl - Under Armour, Inc.; pg. 49, pg. 759
Gonzalez, Maya, Sr Assoc Brand Mgr-Digital Mktg - Capital One Financial Corporation; pg. 730, pg. 1789
Gonzalez, Miguel, VP-Mktg-Food Products Div - Reckitt Benckiser Inc.; pg. 1136, pg. 1105
Gonzalez, Noemi, Mgr-Sls-Intl - ITW Magnaflux; pg. 1418, pg. 615
Gonzalez, Nora, VP-Sls & Acq - MTI Home Video; pg. 298, pg. 444
Gonzalez, Patricia, Sr VP-In-Theatre Mktg - Paramount Pictures Corporation; pg. 304, pg. 138
Gonzalez, Rebecca, Dir-IS Digital Mktg Svcs - Allergan, Inc.; pg. 1491, pg. 106
Gonzalez, Sasha, Product Mgr-Value Added Sls - FRESH DEL MONTE PRODUCE INC.; pg. 856, pg. 418
Gonzalez, Timothy, Product Mgr - Standard Motor Products, Inc.; pg. 218, pg. 1176
Gonzalez, Veronica S., Asst Dir-Mktg - The Reader's Digest Association, Inc.; pg. 1679, pg. 1322
Gonzalez, Wendy, Assoc Mgr-Product Mktg - Google Inc.; pg. 1249, pg. 153
Gonzalez, Yadira, Partner-Bus & Rep-Sls-Bus Analytics - IBM; pg. 410, pg. 1449
Gonzalves, Jeanne, Dir-Product Mgmt - Local.com Corporation; pg. 1264, pg. 113
Good, Alicia, Dir-Enterprise Solutions-Mktg Optimization - Hewlett-Packard Company; pg. 404, pg. 175
Good, Amy, Mgr-Media Centers of Excellence-Digital, Mobile, Print & DOOH - Nestle Purina PetCare Company; pg. 1479, pg. 1000
Good, David, Sr Mgr-Brand & Vendor Mktg - Academy Sports & Outdoors, Ltd.; pg. 1824, pg. 1724
Good, Kelsey, Acct Dir-Sls - AOL Inc.; pg. 1229, pg. 1195
Good, Rachel, Specialist-Mktg Analytics - Nationwide Mutual Insurance Company; pg. 1210, pg. 1442
Good, Steve, VP-Sls - The Terminix International Company Limited Partnership; pg. 337, pg. 1646
Good, Trent, Dir-Creative-Global - Netflix, Inc.; pg. 1269, pg. 141
Good, Waylon, Sr Mgr-Mktg - General Mills, Inc.; pg. 828, pg. 933
Goodale, Mike, Mgr-Sls - Valley Truck Parts, Inc.; pg. 221, pg. 913
Goodchild, Allie, Mgr-MTV & LOGO Integrated Mktg - MTV Networks Company; pg. 298, pg. 1262
Goodchild, Tom, Reg Mgr-Sls-Middle East & Indian Subcontinent - Reliable Automatic Sprinkler Co., Inc.; pg. 1137, pg. 1158
Goode, Anita, Specialist-Adv - Ducks Unlimited, Inc.; pg. 139, pg. 1642
Goode, Catherine, Mgr-Mktg - The Walt Disney Company; pg. 317, pg. 52
Goode, Lori, Mgr-Product Mktg - Facebook, Inc.; pg. 1245, pg. 143
Goode, Michelle, Mgr-Sls Mktg - Arrow Electronics, Inc.; pg. 619, pg. 325
Goodell, Cindy, Sr Product Mktg Mgr - EMC Corporation; pg. 391, pg. 825
Gooden, Clarence W., Chief Comml Officer & Exec VP-Sls & Mktg - CSX Transportation, Inc.; pg. 1904, pg. 432
Gooden, Monika, Head-Mktg Comm - Federal Home Loan Mortgage Corporation; pg. 751, pg. 1790
Gooden, Patricia, Dir-Product Dev - Unified Brands Inc.; pg. 1385, pg. 970
Goodenough, Kyle, Product Mktg Mgr-Android & Chrome Brand - Google Inc.; pg. 1249, pg. 153
Gooderham, Justin, Mgr-Digital Mktg - Intuit Inc.; pg. 769, pg. 158
Goodeve, Eric, Specialist-Brand Sls-NetApp - Arrow Electronics, Inc.; pg. 619, pg. 325
Goodfellow, Robert, Mgr-Mktg-Oral Care Innovation - Colgate-Palmolive Company; pg. 504, pg. 1215
Goodhart, Chris, Dir-Mktg Comm - Samsung Electronics America, Inc.; pg. 669, pg. 1115
Goodhue, Carol, Sr VP-Wholesale Sls - Aerogroup International, Inc.; pg. 1803, pg. 1055
Goodhue, Shae, Sr Mgr-Enterprise Brand Mktg - CVS Health Corporation; pg. 1765, pg. 1610
Goodin, Stephanie, Dir-Mktg - Gold Medal Products Co.; pg. 55, pg. 1414
Gooding, Jeff, Sr Dir-Consumer Mktg - Ace Hardware Corporation; pg. 1040, pg. 644
Goodliffe, Will, Sr Specialist-Audience Sls-Performance & Programmatic - Yahoo! Inc.; pg. 1289, pg. 289
Goodling, Rob, Sr VP & Mgr-Mktg - Bank of America Corporation; pg. 718, pg. 1362
Goodmacher, Chris, Product Mgr - Justworks, Inc.; pg. 424, pg. 1247
Goodman, Amy, Mgr-Media Svcs - Sterling Jewelers Inc.; pg. 13, pg. 1402
Goodman, Barbara, Bus Mgr - Trend Magazines, Inc.; pg. 1696, pg. 465
Goodman, Daniel E., VP-Sls - Surface Combustion, Inc.; pg. 1077, pg. 1462
Goodman, David, Dir-Mktg - Bayer Healthcare Consumer Care Division; pg. 1500, pg. 1087
Goodman, Grace, Specialist-Digital Mktg - Destination DC; pg. 991, pg. 398
Goodman, Joel, Sr Mgr-Shopper Mktg Insights - The Coca-Cola Company; pg. 240, pg. 493
Goodman, Kate, Sr Dir-Retail Digital - CVS Health Corporation; pg. 1765, pg. 1610
Goodman, Margaret, Sr Mgr-Mktg-Global Loyalty Program - MoneyGram International, Inc.; pg. 783, pg. 1684
Goodman, Milda C., Asst VP-Corp Adv - Pacific Life Insurance Company; pg. 1213, pg. 166
Goodman, Roy, Dir-IT, Energy Mktg & Generation Mgmt - PPL Corporation; pg. 1950, pg. 1514
Goodman, Seth, Head-Comml Cards Product Mgmt & Dir-North America - Citigroup Inc.; pg. 735, pg. 1212
Goodman, Wendy, Mgr-Product Mgmt & New Product Dev - Varitronics, LLC; pg. 487, pg. 954
Goodman, William, Mgr-Digital Mktg - American Diabetes Association; pg. 127, pg. 1770
Goodney, Teresa, Mgr-Social Media - Deere & Company; pg. 703, pg. 632
Goodnight, Nathan D., Rep-Enterprise Content Mgmt Inside Sls - IBM; pg. 410, pg. 1449
Goodnow, Mark, Mgr-Production - Twisted Scholar, Inc.; pg. 315, pg. 1842
Goodridge, Matt, Product Mgr-Google Play - Google Inc.; pg. 1249, pg. 153
Goodrow, Jason, Dir-Mktg-Ninety Nine Restaurants - American Blue Ribbon Holdings; pg. 1714, pg. 1648
Goodson, John, Sr VP & Gen Mgr-Products-Enterprise Intelligence Solutions - Verint Witness Actionable Solutions; pg. 488, pg. 539
Goodspeed, Meghan, Specialist-Mktg - Brookshire Grocery Company; pg. 1016, pg. 1748
Goodwillie, Fiona J., Sr Mgr - Accenture; pg. 1392, pg. 1186
Goodwin, Amber, Supvr-Sls & Admin - National Oilwell Varco, Inc.; pg. 1364, pg. 1712
Goodwin, Barbara, Project Mgr-Standard Products & Customer Svc - Litecontrol Corporation; pg. 1301, pg. 841
Goodwin, Bruce, VP-Sls & Global Mktg-US - CryoLife, Inc.; pg. 1520, pg. 534
Goodwin, Chris, Mgr-Mktg - Land O'Lakes, Inc.; pg. 873, pg. 915
Goodwin, David C., Dir-Product Mgmt - Arris Group, Inc.; pg. 353, pg. 541
Goodwin, Debbie, Analyst-Mktg - Bombardier Inc.; pg. 1318, pg. 1953
Goodwin, Gabe, Sr Dir-Social Production & Producer-Coordinating - ESPN, Inc.; pg. 285, pg. 340
Goodwin, Kurt, Sr Dir - Crutchfield Corporation; pg. 1237, pg. 1777
Goodwin, Milton, VP-Product - Armstrong World Industries, Inc.; pg. 914, pg. 1545
Goodwin, Richard, Product Mgr-Mobile Applications - RACKSPACE HOSTING, INC.; pg. 1277, pg. 1742
Goodwin, Rob, VP-Mktg & New Product Dev-Private Brands Grp - Energizer Holdings, Inc.; pg. 637, pg. 996
Goodwin, Ryder, Dir-Mktg Art - Wells Fargo & Company; pg.

819, *pg.* 232
Goodwin, Scott, Dir-Customer Mktg - Kayak; *pg.* 1260, *pg.* 363
Goodwin, Sean, Specialist-Mktg-Strategic Partnerships - Marks Work Wearhouse Ltd.; *pg.* 44, *pg.* 1903
Goodwin, Talah, Mgr-Mktg Channel - Coca-Cola Bottling Co. Consolidated; *pg.* 240, *pg.* 1365
Goodwin, Valerie, Dir-Mktg - Abaxis, Inc.; *pg.* 1483, *pg.* 298
Goody, Lauren, Head-Creative Content Dev-Brands-The ZOO - Google Inc.; *pg.* 1249, *pg.* 153
Goodyear, Jamie, Dir-Experiential Mktg - Dolby Laboratories, Inc.; *pg.* 284, *pg.* 217
Goon, Jessica, Dir-Social Media-Global - Avon Products, Inc.; *pg.* 500, *pg.* 1198
Goone, David S., Chief Strategy Officer & Sr VP - INTERCONTINENTALEXCHANGE, INC.; *pg.* 769, *pg.* 512
Goose, Michael, Dir-Mktg - The Hain Celestial Group, Inc.; *pg.* 860, *pg.* 1172
Goostree, Jon, Coord Casino Mktg - MGM Resorts International; *pg.* 1105, *pg.* 1028
Goott, Paul, VP-Strategic Mktg Initiatives & Head-Digital-US & Canada - American International Group, Inc.; *pg.* 1190, *pg.* 1193
Gopal, Achala, Specialist-Integrated Mktg-Chex & Cinnamon Toast Crunch Portfolio - General Mills, Inc.; *pg.* 828, *pg.* 933
Gopal, Sanjiv, Interim Co-Exec Dir-Greenpeace India - Greenpeace; *pg.* 142, *pg.* 400
Gopal, Vinuta, Interim Co-Exec Dir-Greenpeace India - Greenpeace; *pg.* 142, *pg.* 400
Gopalakrishnan, Ram, Sr Asst Brand Mgr - The Procter & Gamble Company; *pg.* 1129, *pg.* 1418
Gopalakrishnan, Vishy, Product Mgr-Unified Comm & Collaboration - AT&T Inc.; *pg.* 1867, *pg.* 1674
Gopinath, Dash, Chief Product Officer - IF(WE); *pg.* 1258, *pg.* 219
Gora, Barbara, Mgr-Mktg - Echo Incorporated; *pg.* 1046, *pg.* 626
Gorcey, Eden, Head-Branded Content, Digital Sls & Strategy-Entertainment - Conde Nast Publications, Inc.; *pg.* 1629, *pg.* 1217
Gorder, Genevieve, Designer-Interior & Product - QVC Inc; *pg.* 305, *pg.* 1593
Gordineer, John, Dir-Product Mktg-Dell Security - Dell, Inc.; *pg.* 385, *pg.* 1037
Gordon, Ama, Brand Mgr-PR & Events - Bacardi USA, Inc.; *pg.* 1956, *pg.* 417
Gordon, Anthony, Sr Mgr-Artist Rels - Avid Technology, Inc.; *pg.* 622, *pg.* 804
Gordon, Bill, Mgr-Mktg-Natl - Mazda North American Operations; *pg.* 183, *pg.* 113
Gordon, Brian, Mng Dir-Mktg & USOC Productions - United States Olympic Committee; *pg.* 589, *pg.* 315
Gordon, Chad, Mgr-Sls-Midwest Region - Sabra Dipping Company LLC; *pg.* 893, *pg.* 1686
Gordon, Corey, Sr Product Mgr-Field Engagement - H&R Block, Inc.; *pg.* 764, *pg.* 983
Gordon, Dan, Reg Mgr-Premium Offerings Sls - Yara N America, Inc.; *pg.* 1802, *pg.* 477
Gordon, David, Mng Dir-Sls - Audio Research Corporation; *pg.* 621, *pg.* 953
Gordon, David, Mgr-Mktg-Intl - The Weinstein Company; *pg.* 591, *pg.* 1314
Gordon, Derek, Coord-Social Mktg - Jos. A. Bank Clothiers, Inc.; *pg.* 42, *pg.* 771
Gordon, Elise, Second VP-Creative & Media Svcs - The Travelers Companies, Inc.; *pg.* 1220, *pg.* 352
Gordon, Elise L., Second VP-Creative & Media Svcs - Travelers Insurance; *pg.* 1220, *pg.* 963
Gordon, Erin, Dir-Digital Mktg - Belk, Inc.; *pg.* 1760, *pg.* 1364
Gordon, Gary, Sr Mgr-Bus Continuity - The Boeing Company; *pg.* 225, *pg.* 567
Gordon, Geoff, Mgr-Mktg - QUALCOMM Incorporated; *pg.* 1873, *pg.* 207
Gordon, Gregg, Sr Dir-Strategic Workforce Practice - Kronos Incorporated; *pg.* 425, *pg.* 813
Gordon, Jane, VP-Sls Ops-West Reg - AT&T Mobility LLC; *pg.* 619, *pg.* 488
Gordon, Jessica, Sr Mgr-Digital Mktg Consulting - American Express Company; *pg.* 712, *pg.* 1190
Gordon, Jim, Dir-IT Product - Herff Jones, Inc.; *pg.* 7, *pg.* 686
Gordon, Jon, Dir-Creative - Moe's Southwest Grill, LLC; *pg.* 1027, *pg.* 514
Gordon, Katherine, Coord-Brand Mktg - Kohl's Corporation; *pg.* 1775, *pg.* 1870
Gordon, Kylee Swenson, Editor-in-Chief & Mgr-Content Mktg - Autodesk Inc.; *pg.* 356, *pg.* 257
Gordon, Laura, VP-Mktg & Brand Innovation - 7-Eleven, Inc.; *pg.* 1012, *pg.* 1672
Gordon, Lee, Dir-PR - Mercury Marine; *pg.* 1709, *pg.* 1857
Gordon, Marcel, Product Mgr - Google Inc.; *pg.* 1249, *pg.* 153
Gordon, Mariquita Patterson, Bus Mgr-DLP Embedded Products - Texas Instruments Incorporated; *pg.* 679, *pg.* 1688
Gordon, Philip L., Dir-Mktg - Superior Essex, Inc.; *pg.* 676, *pg.* 521
Gordon, Ricky, Sr Dir-Product Mgmt - Ticketmaster Entertainment LLC; *pg.* 1284, *pg.* 48
Gordon, Robert, Mgr-Sls-NY - National Spinning Company, Inc.; *pg.* 697, *pg.* 1265
Gordon, Sara, Dir-Mktg-Scotts LawnService - The Scotts Miracle-Gro Company; *pg.* 1799, *pg.* 1459
Gordon, Spencer, Mgr-Content & Media-Bud Light - Anheuser-Busch Companies, LLC; *pg.* 237, *pg.* 991
Gordon, Stephanie, Coord-Mktg - The Kroger Co.; *pg.* 1025, *pg.* 1416
Gordon, Steve, Dir-Mktg - ACH Food Companies, Inc.; *pg.* 835, *pg.* 1631
Gordon, SuSu, Sr Mgr-Design-Global - Kimberly-Clark Corporation; *pg.* 1461, *pg.* 1720
Gordon, Tinka, VP-Mktg - Round Table Pizza; *pg.* 1748, *pg.* 69
Gordon, Todd, VP-Sls-CBIZ Benefits & Insurance Svcs, Inc. - CBIZ, INC.; *pg.* 733, *pg.* 1429
Gore, Amit, Strategist-Comml Digital Mktg-ESG Solutions - Dell Inc.; *pg.* 383, *pg.* 1737
Gore, Larry, Dir-Sls & Mktg - AMF Bakery Systems; *pg.* 1313, *pg.* 1800
Gorecki, Steve, Sr Mgr-Media Rels - Motorola Solutions, Inc.; *pg.* 657, *pg.* 659
Gorelik, Michael, Head-Video Sls Strategy-Americas - Google Inc.; *pg.* 1249, *pg.* 153
Goren, Becca, Sr Dir-Customer Experience Applications Product Mktg - Oracle Corporation; *pg.* 450, *pg.* 191
Goren, Bruce, District Sls Mgr & Mgr-Natl Adv - Kia Motors America Inc.; *pg.* 181, *pg.* 112
Gorenberg, Rita, Mgr-PR - Peet's Coffee & Tea, Inc.; *pg.* 1029, *pg.* 85
Gorenshteyn, Vlad, Mgr-Digital Mktg - Cable News Network LP; *pg.* 1624, *pg.* 1208
Gorenstein, Andrew, Chief Revenue Officer - Gawker Media LLC; *pg.* 1248, *pg.* 1234
Gorga, Carly, Asst Dir-Mktg - Penguin Random House; *pg.* 1675, *pg.* 1276
Gorga, Nick, VP-Sls-Asia Pacific - Cray Inc.; *pg.* 380, *pg.* 1834
Gorgonzola, David, Dir-Integrated Media Sls - Valassis; *pg.* 1698, *pg.* 386
Gorham, Christine, Asst VP & Mgr-Mktg - T. Rowe Price Group Inc.; *pg.* 808, *pg.* 759
Gori, Fabio, Dir-Cloud Mktg-Worldwide - Cisco Systems, Inc.; *pg.* 372, *pg.* 240
Gorke, Tom, Exec VP-Sls & Bus Dev - Viacom Inc.; *pg.* 316, *pg.* 1310
Gorlesky, David, Sr Product Mgr - Wells Fargo & Company; *pg.* 819, *pg.* 232
Gormally, Pat, Dir-Prod Mktg - Vishay Americas; *pg.* 686, *pg.* 371
Gorman, Ashley, Head-Refreshments Category & Mgr-Shopper Mktg - Unilever United States, Inc.; *pg.* 904, *pg.* 1061
Gorman, Bob, Sr Dir-Mktg-Southern Reg & Natl Accts - Beam Suntory Inc.; *pg.* 1957, *pg.* 599
Gorman, Heather, Sr Dir-Mktg, Comm & Media-Global - Tumi, Inc.; *pg.* 15, *pg.* 1123
Gorman, Jaime, Brand Mgr-Innovation - William Grant & Sons, Inc.; *pg.* 1972, *pg.* 1057
Gorman, Kathryn, Assoc Mgr-Mktg-Taste of Home - The Reader's Digest Association, Inc.; *pg.* 1679, *pg.* 1322
Gorman, Keith, VP-Mktg Analytics - Comcast Cable Communications, Inc.; *pg.* 276, *pg.* 1560
Gorman, Megan, Sr Mgr-Mktg-Watson Pharmaceuticals - Allergan; *pg.* 1490, *pg.* 1101
Gorman, Mike, Sr Mgr-Natl Partner Mktg - NetApp, Inc.; *pg.* 444, *pg.* 287
Gorman, Mike, Sr Specialist-Mktg Comm - Teleflex Incorporated; *pg.* 48, *pg.* 1548
Gormley, Mary, Assoc Mgr-Shopper Mktg - Unilever United States, Inc.; *pg.* 904, *pg.* 1061
Gormont, Corrine, VP-Mktg Comm - L-3 Communications Holdings Inc.; *pg.* 650, *pg.* 1250
Gorney, Matt, Project Mgr-Mktg - Chipotle Mexican Grill, Inc.; *pg.* 1722, *pg.* 317
Gornick, Emily, Assoc Mgr-Fisher Price US Mktg - Mattel Games/Puzzles; *pg.* 962, *pg.* 80
Gornick, Emily, Assoc Mgr-Fisher Price US Mktg - MATTEL, INC.; *pg.* 962, *pg.* 81
Gornick, Mary Ellen, Sr VP-Products-Global - Workplace Options; *pg.* 493, *pg.* 1389
Gorrin, Andrew, Sr VP-Mktg - Web.com, Inc.; *pg.* 1288, *pg.* 524
Gortaire, Fausto, Mgr-Online Mktg - Xoom Corporation; *pg.* 1289, *pg.* 234
Gorter, Dirk, Dir-Product Mgmt - Environmental Systems Research Institute Inc.; *pg.* 393, *pg.* 188
Gory, Eric, Product Mktg-Industrial Comm - Molex Incorporated; *pg.* 655, *pg.* 628
Gorz, Christine, VP-Mktg & Comm - Moody Bible Institute; *pg.* 605, *pg.* 583
Gosden, Whitney, Sr Mgr-Strategic Plng-New Bus Ventures - Mattel Games/Puzzles; *pg.* 962, *pg.* 80
Gosden, Whitney, Sr Mgr-Strategic Plng-New Bus Ventures - MATTEL, INC.; *pg.* 962, *pg.* 81
Goss, James M., VP-PR & Mktg - CentraState Healthcare System Inc.; *pg.* 1514, *pg.* 1071
Goss, Michael, Mgr-Channel Mktg-Sls Chat - Intuit Inc.; *pg.* 769, *pg.* 158
Goss, Patrick, Head-Mktg-CHC ROPU South America - Boehringer Ingelheim Pharmaceuticals, Inc.; *pg.* 1507, *pg.* 368
Goss, Vivian, Designer-Trng - Merck & Co., Inc.; *pg.* 1566, *pg.* 1077
Gosselin, Matthew, Dir-Mktg-Florida - McGladrey, LLP; *pg.* 781, *pg.* 938
Gosselin, McCall, Dir-PR - PFIP, LLC; *pg.* 1842, *pg.* 1037
Gosselin, Nick, Mgr-Social Media - The Boston Beer Company, Inc.; *pg.* 239, *pg.* 790
Gosser, Allison, Product Mgr-Mktg-Swingline Stapling & Punches - ACCO Brands Corporation; *pg.* 340, *pg.* 626
Gossett, Annie, Brand Mgr-Scott - Kimberly-Clark Corporation; *pg.* 1461, *pg.* 1720
Gossett, Forrest S., Sr Mgr-Comm - The Boeing Company; *pg.* 225, *pg.* 567
Gosule, Erik D., Sr VP & Head-Mktg & Product Dev - Pioneer Investments; *pg.* 794, *pg.* 800
Goswami, Rajat, Sr Dir-Insights & Innovation - DeVry Education Group Inc.; *pg.* 600, *pg.* 607
Goswami, Ranjan, VP-Sls-West - Delta Air Lines, Inc.; *pg.* 1905, *pg.* 503
Gotay, Edwin, Dir-Multicultural Mktg - National Association for Stock Car Auto Racing; *pg.* 566, *pg.* 420
Gotch, Marylee, VP & Mgr-PR & Social Media - KeyCorp; *pg.* 774, *pg.* 1432
Goteh, Nu, Mgr-Culture Mktg-Sonos Studio - Sonos, Inc.; *pg.* 675, *pg.* 263
Goteh, Nuwoe, Sr Mgr-Global Brand Mktg-Lifestyle - Puma North America, Inc.; *pg.* 1816, *pg.* 858
Gotfredson, Sara, VP-West Coast Multimedia Sls & Mktg - ESPN, Inc.; *pg.* 285, *pg.* 340
Gotham, Megan, Mgr-Shopper Mktg-Walmart Team - The J.M. Smucker Company; *pg.* 865, *pg.* 1468
Gotling, Gary, Dir-Sls & Mktg - Hyatt Hotels Corporation; *pg.* 1096, *pg.* 577
Goto, Erick, Sr Designer-Product Graphic - NIKE, Inc.; *pg.* 1812, *pg.* 1492
Goto, Jennifer N., Mgr-West Div Mktg - Comcast Corporation; *pg.* 276, *pg.* 1560
Goto, Mark, Specialist-IT Product - PG&E Corporation; *pg.* 1949, *pg.* 224
Gotreau, Jon, Reg Mgr-Mktg - BUFFALO WILD WINGS, INC.; *pg.* 1718, *pg.* 931
Gotschlich, Chandler, Brand Mgr - Sabra Dipping Company LLC; *pg.* 893, *pg.* 1686
Gotshall, Lisa, Dir-Sls-Bus Gift Svcs - The Popcorn Factory; *pg.* 1861, *pg.* 625
Gottbrath, Chris, Principal & Product Mgr - Rogue Wave Software, Inc.; *pg.* 462, *pg.* 311
Gottehrer, Richard, Founder & Chief Creative Officer - The Orchard Enterprises, Inc.; *pg.* 572, *pg.* 1274
Gottesman, David, Sr Mgr-Digital Mktg - American Express Company; *pg.* 712, *pg.* 1190
Gottfried, Alexandra, Media Planner - The New York Times Company; *pg.* 1668, *pg.* 1270
Gottfried, Kelly, Sr Dir-Mktg-JOHNSON'S Baby & DESITIN - Johnson & Johnson; *pg.* 1549, *pg.* 1091

First page reference indicates Business Class Edition
Second page reference indicates Geographic Edition

Gottipati, Ramana, VP-Product Mgmt & Adoption - 8x8, Inc.; pg. 1865, pg. 282
Gottlieb, Robert, Exec VP & Head-Mktg - Fox Sports Net; pg. 288, pg. 131
Gottloeb, Eric, Sr Mgr-Social Ads Mktg - Amazon.com, Inc.; pg. 1226, pg. 1831
Gottschalk, Lisa, Dir-Mktg - The McGraw-Hill Companies Inc.; pg. 1663, pg. 1257
Gottstein, John, Mgr-Social Media Mktg - Verizon Communications Inc.; pg. 1875, pg. 1309
Gottwals, Steve, Grp Product Mgr-Adobe Reader - Adobe Systems Incorporated; pg. 342, pg. 235
Goubeaux, Annette, Mgr-PR - Neiman Marcus, Inc.; pg. 30, pg. 1684
Goudge, David A., VP-Comml Sls - AutoZone, Inc.; pg. 200, pg. 1641
Goudreau, Lori, Strategist-Mktg - Thrivent Financial for Lutherans; pg. 1219, pg. 944
Goudreault, Salena, Sr Program Mgr-Retail Mktg-Global - Apple Inc.; pg. 350, pg. 73
Gouge, Carlie S., Project Mgr-Interactive Adv - The Home Depot, Inc.; pg. 1050, pg. 510
Gouge, Sean, Sr Mgr-eDell Online North America - Dell Inc.; pg. 383, pg. 1737
Gough, Hope, Mgr-Mktg - Laura Ashley, Inc.; pg. 29, pg. 1615
Gouin, Jeannette, Mgr-Mktg - Electro Standards Laboratories Inc.; pg. 390, pg. 1600
Goulart, Pam, Mgr-Mktg Svcs - Fabreeka International, Inc.; pg. 1882, pg. 847
Goulbourne, Raymond, Exec VP-Brdcst Media Sls - BET Holdings LLC; pg. 271, pg. 396
Gould, Alissa, Mgr-PR - Boiron USA Inc.; pg. 1507, pg. 1556
Gould, Bill, Dir-Mktg - Kwiat Inc.; pg. 8, pg. 1249
Gould, Chris, Mgr-Digital Mktg - Starkey Laboratories, Inc.; pg. 1597, pg. 923
Gould, Doug, Exec Dir-Creative - Boston University; pg. 598, pg. 791
Gould, Emily, Sr VP-Consumer Mktg - Showtime Networks Inc.; pg. 308, pg. 1291
Gould, James, Product Mgr-Digital Aftermarket - Sun Chemical Ink; pg. 1182, pg. 643
Gould, Jay, Sr Product Mgr-Mktg - Cray Inc.; pg. 380, pg. 1834
Gould, Jennifer, Dir-Care Mgmt Interactive Solutions & Mktg - GlaxoSmithKline; pg. 1536, pg. 1565
Gould, Jessica, Sr Mgr-Comm - Corel Corporation; pg. 380, pg. 1931
Gould, Jillian, Mgr-Customer Mktg - The Yankee Candle Company, Inc.; pg. 1792, pg. 843
Gould, Matt, Sr Mgr-Mktg - Naked Juice Company, Inc.; pg. 882, pg. 150
Gould, Megan, Planner-Interactive Mktg - General Mills, Inc.; pg. 828, pg. 933
Gould, Natalie, Dir-Sls-WSJ Weekend, Mansion & Greater New York - Dow Jones & Company, Inc.; pg. 1637, pg. 1225
Gould, Paul, Dir-Sls & Mktg-Six Flags Great Adventure - Six Flags Entertainment Corporation; pg. 583, pg. 1698
Goulding, Pete, Sr Product Mgr - Medtronic; pg. 1563, pg. 830
Goulding, Rob, Dir-Sls-Natl - Twitter, Inc.; pg. 1285, pg. 228
Goulet, Alain, Brand Head-Banzel, Inovelon & Zonegran-Global - Eisai Inc.; pg. 1526, pg. 1133
Goulet, Matthew, Sr VP-Sls & Mktg - GlobalSCAPE Inc.; pg. 401, pg. 1740
Goult, Kevin, Gen Mgr-Mktg-Audi Australia Pty Ltd - Audi of America, Inc.; pg. 164, pg. 1784
Gountanis, Effie, Reg Mgr-Mktg - Mercedes-Benz USA, LLC; pg. 184, pg. 514
Gourhant, Beatrice, Dir-Intl Kindle PR - Amazon.com, Inc.; pg. 1226, pg. 1831
Gourley, Gina, Brand Mgr-Mktg Capability - The Procter & Gamble Company; pg. 1129, pg. 1418
Gous, Eras, Dir-Creative - Aqua America, Inc.; pg. 1935, pg. 1518
Govan, Chris, Coord-Digital Media-On Air Promo - CBS Corporation; pg. 273, pg. 1210
Govan, Julie, Brand Mgr - Crutchfield Corporation; pg. 1237, pg. 1777
Gove, Alan, VP-Mktg & Sls - Vancouver Symphony Orchestra; pg. 590, pg. 1913
Gove, Tom, VP-Sls & Mktg-Telco Div - Starz Entertainment, LLC; pg. 310, pg. 327
Govender, Saigin, Sr Product Mgr-Amazon Echo & Digital Products - Amazon.com, Inc.; pg. 1226, pg. 1831
Governanti, Anthony, Mgr-Technical Mktg - Autodesk Inc.; pg. 356, pg. 257
Govin, Charles T., III, Dir-Field Sls Ops - J.J. Keller & Associates, Inc.; pg. 1654, pg. 1883
Govindarajan, Priya, Team Head-Sls Plng-Glad Waste Mgmt - The Clorox Company; pg. 327, pg. 169
Govorun, Olesya, Sr Mgr-Strategy & Insights - The Dannon Company, Inc.; pg. 851, pg. 1351
Gowan, Jay, VP-Domestic Sls & Mktg - Harsco Rail; pg. 1345, pg. 1623
Goward, Ed, Sr Mgr-Park Ops - Detroit Tigers Baseball Club, Inc.; pg. 545, pg. 880
Gowdy, Wayne D., Sr Product Mgr - Aetna Inc.; pg. 1187, pg. 351
Gowen, Anne, Dir-Mktg-Miracle Ear Div - Miracle-Ear, Inc.; pg. 1568, pg. 940
Goyal, Priyank, Sr Product Mgr - Ericsson; pg. 395, pg. 1108
Goyda, Tom, VP & Mgr-Media Rels - Wells Fargo & Company; pg. 819, pg. 232
Goyenechea, Ximena, Mgr-Shopper Mktg - The Procter & Gamble Company; pg. 1129, pg. 1418
Goyer, Rob, Sr Mgr-Strategic Mktg - HARRIS CORPORATION; pg. 642, pg. 439
Goyer, Susan, Product Mgr-Trade Fin - Royal Bank of Canada; pg. 800, pg. 1942
Goyer, Todd, Head-Jeep Brand & Product Plng Comm - FCA US LLC; pg. 170, pg. 868
Goza, Angelica, Specialist-Mktg - The Procter & Gamble Company; pg. 1129, pg. 1418
Goza, Beth, Sr Mgr-Social Media Mktg - Microsoft Corporation; pg. 435, pg. 1824
Gozenput, Angela, Product Mgr - Pfizer Inc.; pg. 1581, pg. 1278
Gozzi, Erica, Reg Specialist-Mktg - Nordstrom, Inc.; pg. 1779, pg. 1837
Gozzi, Karen, Dir-Corp Adv - Wakefern Food Corporation; pg. 1037, pg. 1058
Graaskamp, Dan, VP-Sls - Eau Claire Press Company; pg. 1638, pg. 1857
Grab, Joshua, Mgr-Trade Mktg - The Boston Beer Company, Inc.; pg. 239, pg. 790
Grabania-Dailerian, Monika, Sr Dir-Consumer Mktg, Media & Brand Strategy-Lifetime - A&E Television Networks, LLC, pg. 267, pg. 1185
Grabarkewitz, Julie, Sr Mgr - American Heart Association Inc.; pg. 128, pg. 1673
Grabarkiewicz, Chris, Dir-Consumer Insights & Mktg Analytics - Luxottica Retail; pg. 8, pg. 1460
Grabeel, Julie, Sr Mgr-Mktg Programs - VMware, Inc.; pg. 490, pg. 179
Graber, Jessica, Mgr-Campaign & Media Mktg - Sonos, Inc.; pg. 675, pg. 263
Graber, Shane, VP-Mktg-House-Grey Goose & House-Bombay - Bacardi USA, Inc.; pg. 1956, pg. 417
Graber, Stephen, Specialist-Area Adv & Promos-East - Chevron Corporation; pg. 974, pg. 259
Grabijas, Marty, VP & Dir-Mktg - HCR ManorCare, Inc.; pg. 1539, pg. 1476
Graboff, Marc, Pres-Global Bus, Legal Affairs, Production Mgmt & Studios - Discovery Communications, Inc.; pg. 282, pg. 777
Grabowich, George, VP-Intl Product Mgmt - Vonage Holdings Corp.; pg. 686, pg. 1074
Grabowski, Bryan, Product Mgr-Skin Cleansing & Bathing-Intl - GOJO Industries, Inc.; pg. 330, pg. 1401
Grabowski, Megan, Sr Mgr-Corp Partnerships - Chicago Professional Sports Limited Partnership; pg. 539, pg. 570
Grabscheid, Michael, Exec Dir-Mktg & New Bus Dev - University of Massachusetts; pg. 609, pg. 781
Grace, Charlie, Chief Revenue Officer-Pro Products - 3D Systems Corporation; pg. 339, pg. 1621
Grace, Frank, Dir-Product Dev - Harodite Industries, Inc.; pg 693, pg. 847
Grace, Greg, Mgr-Product Line-Lumber - Plum Creek Timber Company, Inc.; pg. 105, pg. 1838
Grace, Patrick, Reg Mgr-Sls - TRUMPF Inc.; pg. 1385, pg. 349
Grace, Peter, Sr VP-Sls & Fin - Clean Energy Fuels Corp.; pg. 974, pg. 165
Grace, Tina, Dir-Mktg & Comm-Xerox Federal Solutions, LLC - Xerox Corporation; pg. 494, pg. 365
Gracey, Matthew, Sr Mgr-Comm, Media & Tech - Accenture; pg. 1392, pg. 1186
Gracia, Julie, Sr Mgr-Integrated Mktg & Synergy - The Walt Disney Company; pg. 317, pg. 52
Graciani, Gil, Mgr-Mktg Ops - Intel Corporation; pg. 645, pg. 266
Graciano, Steven, VP-Mktg - National Football League; pg. 567, pg. 1264
Grad, Johannes, Engr-Product - Cadence Design Systems, Inc.; pg. 367, pg. 239
Grady, Amanda, Sr Product Mgr-Messaging & Web Security - Symantec Corporation; pg. 478, pg. 161
Grady, Brendan R., Dir-Market Strategy & Portfolio Mktg - International Business Machines Corporation; pg. 418, pg. 1138
Grady, Cleveland, Sr Dir-Mktg-Promo Mgmt - GlaxoSmithKline; pg. 1536, pg. 1565
Grady, Dennis, Principal & Product Mgr-Developer Experience - Pegasystems Inc.; pg. 453, pg. 74
Graeff, Scott A., Chief Strategy Officer & Treas - Luna Innovations Inc.; pg. 1557, pg. 1806
Graf, Daniel, Head-Product - Twitter, Inc.; pg. 1285, pg. 228
Graf, John D., Mgr-Graphic Comm Sls - Xerox Corporation; pg. 494, pg. 365
Graf, Michael, VP-Adv Sls-BBC World News - AMC Networks Inc.; pg. 269, pg. 1189
Grafanakis, George, Sr Mgr-Product Plng & Mktg - Sharp Electronics Corporation; pg. 672, pg. 1082
Grafer, Katie, Sr VP & Mgr-Mktg-Integrated Campaigns - Bank of America Corporation; pg. 718, pg. 1362
Graff, Brad, Dir-Mktg - Intel Corporation; pg. 645, pg. 266
Graff, Jeremy, Dir-Mktg-Global Comml Dev - AbbVie Inc.; pg. 1486, pg. 638
Graffam, Meghan O., Specialist-Media Rels & Social Media - Tyler Technologies, Inc.; pg. 486, pg. 1690
Graffigna, Paul, VP-Mktg - Virginia Dare Extract Co., Inc.; pg. 908, pg. 1147
Grafham, Ken, Sr Reg Mgr-Mktg - The Allstate Corporation; pg. 1189, pg. 639
Grager, Dave, Mgr-Branding & Adv-Global - Parker Hannifin Corporation; pg. 1368, pg. 1434
Grah, Judy, Brand Mgr-Fisher-Price - MATTEL, INC.; pg. 962, pg. 81
Graham, Aaron, Sr Dir-Strategic Comm - CIENA Corporation; pg. 628, pg. 771
Graham, Alicia, Dir-Global Sls & Mktg Effectiveness - Kimberly-Clark Corporation; pg. 1461, pg. 1720
Graham, Ann, Specialist-Mktg - Schlumberger Limited; pg. 801, pg. 1714
Graham, April A., Planner-Digital Mktg - W.W. Grainger, Inc.; pg. 1390, pg. 625
Graham, Beth, VP-Mktg - Republic Services, Inc.; pg. 107, pg. 19
Graham, Bobby, Dir-Adv-Intl Fashion-GQ - Conde Nast Publications, Inc.; pg. 1629, pg. 1217
Graham, Brian, Sr Dir-Consumer Products - Brunswick Corporation; pg. 1828, pg. 623
Graham, Chad, Brand Mgr-Pkg & Mktg - Cabela's Incorporated; pg. 535, pg. 1019
Graham, Chip, Dir-eBusiness Strategy & Solutions-EBSCO Media - EBSCO Industries, Inc.; pg. 1638, pg. 2
Graham, David, Sr Dir-Product Mgmt & Emerging Buses & Gen Mgr-Archivescom - Ancestry.com LLC; pg. 1228, pg. 1754
Graham, E-Quana, Principal & Designer-Interface - AbbVie Inc.; pg. 1486, pg. 638
Graham, Gabe, Dir-Retail Client Mktg - H&R Block, Inc.; pg. 764, pg. 983
Graham, Glenn, Mgr-Mktg-Svc Provider - Cisco Systems, Inc.; pg. 372, pg. 240
Graham, Gregory, Bus Mgr-Analytics - DIRECTV Group Holdings, LLC; pg. 281, pg. 79
Graham, Ian, VP-Sls & Svcs-EMEA - Harmonic, Inc.; pg. 402, pg. 246
Graham, Jake, Coord-Mktg - Sun Life Financial Inc.; pg. 806, pg. 1944
Graham, Jamie, Dir-Creative - Constant Contact, Inc.; pg. 379, pg. 850
Graham, Jeffrey, Dir-Adv Res-Global - Twitter, Inc.; pg. 1285, pg. 228
Graham, Jennifer, VP-Mktg - Kastle Systems LLC; pg. 648, pg. 1773
Graham, Jim, Sr Mgr-Corp Media Rels - Walgreen Co.; pg. 1608, pg. 605
Graham, John, Dir-Res & Mgr-Mktg & Res - Paddock Publications, Inc.; pg. 1674, pg. 554
Graham, John, Sr VP-Wholesale Sls-North America - Quiksilver, Inc.; pg. 31, pg. 104

Graham, Leah, Mgr-Field Mktg-Los Angeles - Kind LLC; *pg.* 868, *pg.* 1249
Graham, Linda, Sr Mgr-Mktg - NEC Corporation of America, Inc.; *pg.* 658, *pg.* 1723
Graham, Lisa, Mgr-Channel Svcs Mktg-North American Reseller Sls - Xerox Corporation; *pg.* 494, *pg.* 365
Graham, Liz, VP-Sls & Svcs - Wayfair LLC; *pg.* 1288, *pg.* 801
Graham, Matt, Dir-Mktg-Trauma - Zimmer Biomet Holdings, Inc.; *pg.* 1611, *pg.* 699
Graham, Melissa, Coord-Mktg - Perficient, Inc.; *pg.* 1274, *pg.* 1002
Graham, Millie, VP-Mktg - Peter Millar; *pg.* 46, *pg.* 1372
Graham, Nancy, Editor-in-Chief & Exec Producer-Digital Media-Life Reimagined - AARP; *pg.* 124, *pg.* 393
Graham, Nicholas, Sr Mgr-Mktg & ECommerce - Marriott International, Inc.; *pg.* 1102, *pg.* 764
Graham, Nicole, Dir-Internal Media - Luxottica Retail; *pg.* 8, *pg.* 1460
Graham, Phil, VP-Production - Krause Publications, Inc.; *pg.* 1657, *pg.* 1861
Graham, Rachael, Head & Specialist-Mktg - Welch's International; *pg.* 909, *pg.* 816
Graham, Rachel, Specialist-Mktg - Bentley University; *pg.* 598, *pg.* 850
Graham, Shannon, Program Dir-Mktg-Microsoft - Polycom, Inc.; *pg.* 664, *pg.* 249
Graham, Swen, Sr Dir-Creative & Brand Strategy - FourSquare Labs, Inc; *pg.* 1248, *pg.* 1232
Graham, Yogiraj, Dir-Production - Intel Corporation; *pg.* 645, *pg.* 266
Graham-Mason, Sandra, Sr Mgr-Product Mktg - Eisai Inc.; *pg.* 1526, *pg.* 1133
Grahn, Jeffrey E., VP-Product Mgmt - STEPAN COMPANY; *pg.* 1182, *pg.* 643
Grailer, Timothy, Sr Product Mgr-Luminate CRM - Blackbaud, Inc.; *pg.* 361, *pg.* 1613
Grainger, Lacey, Sr Dir-Sls Comm & Client Experience - Xerox Corporation; *pg.* 494, *pg.* 365
Grair, Steve, Mgr-Production - Opera Omaha Inc.; *pg.* 572, *pg.* 1017
Gram, Clark, Sr Mgr-Pur - Church & Dwight Co., Inc.; *pg.* 1153, *pg.* 1063
Graml, Kara, Mgr-Digital Product & Content Mktg - Electrolux Home Products North America; *pg.* 54, *pg.* 1366
Grammar, Leah, Sr Mgr-ECommerce-Shiseido & Cle de Peau Beaute - Shiseido Cosmetics America of SAC; *pg.* 522, *pg.* 1291
Grampp, Elizabeth, Sr Dir-Mktg-Barbie USA - Mattel Games/Puzzles; *pg.* 962, *pg.* 80
Grampp, Elizabeth, Sr Dir-Mktg-Barbie USA - MATTEL, INC.; *pg.* 962, *pg.* 81
Gramz, Jamie, Dir-Global Mktg-POC Informatics - Siemens Healthcare Diagnostics; *pg.* 673, *pg.* 604
Granack, Sara, Sr Dir-Global Comm - W.W. Grainger, Inc.; *pg.* 1390, *pg.* 625
Granadier, Nicki, Asst Mgr-Mktg - PepsiCo, Inc.; *pg.* 259, *pg.* 1327
Granadino, Carlos, Mgr-Product Dev - Valent U.S.A. Corp.; *pg.* 708, *pg.* 305
Granata, Jessica, Sr Mgr-Intl Mktg & PR - Brooks Brothers Group, Inc.; *pg.* 39, *pg.* 1208
Granata, Joseph, Dir-Product Mktg - Samsonite Corporation; *pg.* 11, *pg.* 830
Granath, Derek, Sr Dir-Product Mgmt - Extreme Networks Inc; *pg.* 287, *pg.* 245
Granatiero, Nino, VP-Mktg & Safety - W.W. Grainger, Inc.; *pg.* 1390, *pg.* 625
Grancher, Jim, Assoc Dir-Sls Comm & Strategy - Starwood Hotels & Resorts Worldwide, Inc.; *pg.* 1114, *pg.* 378
Grand, Aurelie, Dir-Product Mktg - Tupperware Brands Corporation; *pg.* 1139, *pg.* 456
Grande, Tony, Sr Mgr-Inventory & Mktg Acctg - Ingram Micro Inc.; *pg.* 415, *pg.* 261
Grandolfo, Alexa, Sr Coord-Mktg - Pacific Sunwear of California, Inc.; *pg.* 1781, *pg.* 43
Grandy, Amanda, Mgr-Mktg - Briggs & Stratton Corporation; *pg.* 201, *pg.* 1899
Grandy, Leslie, Sr Dir-Mobile Apps - Best Buy Co., Inc.; *pg.* 1761, *pg.* 954
Grandy, Patrick, Mgr-Mktg Comm - Zippo Manufacturing Company, Inc.; *pg.* 1895, *pg.* 1518
Granese, Nicole Davis, Sr Dir-Brand Mktg-Global - Visa Inc.; *pg.* 816, *pg.* 230
Graney, Dan, Mgr-Interactive Creative Dev - Caleres, Inc.; *pg.* 1805, *pg.* 993
Grange, Brady, VP & Dir-Global Mktg & Innovation Capability - Diageo North America Inc.; *pg.* 248, *pg.* 1223
Granger, David, Specialist-Mktg Comm - Amway Corporation; *pg.* 326, *pg.* 864
Granger, Dennis, Mgr-Sls - Micropac Industries Inc.; *pg.* 654, *pg.* 1698
Granger, Jim, Dir-Creative-Mobile Ux & Design - Intel Corporation; *pg.* 645, *pg.* 266
Granger, Joseph F., Exec VP-Consumer Products & UFPD - Universal Forest Products, Inc.; *pg.* 117, *pg.* 890
Granha, Danielle, Mgr-Strategic Mktg - Tyco International (US) Inc.; *pg.* 1891, *pg.* 1113
Granit, Carrie, VP-Prospect & Cardmember Digital Mktg - American Express Company; *pg.* 712, *pg.* 1190
Grano, Sarah, Dir-PR - The American Bankers Association; *pg.* 126, *pg.* 394
Granquist, Sue, Sr Mgr-Mktg PMO - CDW Corporation; *pg.* 370, *pg.* 663
Grant, Andrea, Dir-Digital Mktg - Cabela's Incorporated; *pg.* 535, *pg.* 1019
Grant, Beth, Coord-Local Mktg - Chick-fil-A, Inc.; *pg.* 1721, *pg.* 492
Grant, Dave, VP-Indus Content & Mktg - Teradata Corporation; *pg.* 483, *pg.* 1447
Grant, David, Product Mgr - GEICO Corporation; *pg.* 1200, *pg.* 399
Grant, Grady, VP-Medical Sls - Mead Johnson Nutrition Company; *pg.* 1561, *pg.* 615
Grant, Karen, Mgr-Sls Ops-Natl - William Grant & Sons, Inc.; *pg.* 1972, *pg.* 1057
Grant, Kimberly, Sr VP-Enterprise Media - Bank of America Corporation; *pg.* 718, *pg.* 1362
Grant, Kristen, Dir-Comm & Mktg - American Cancer Society, Inc.; *pg.* 126, *pg.* 487
Grant, Lindsay, Dir-Product Promos - National Hockey League; *pg.* 568, *pg.* 1265
Grant, Matt, Sr Dir-Global Mktg & PR - Cloudmark, Inc.; *pg.* 376, *pg.* 216
Grant, Melissa, Sr Mgr-Sls Mktg, Promos & Events - Hulu LLC; *pg.* 1257, *pg.* 274
Grant, Olivia, Designer-eHub Interactive - 3M Company; *pg.* 1142, *pg.* 956
Grant, Taylor, Sr Copywriter-Direct Response - J2 Global Communications, Inc.; *pg.* 1260, *pg.* 133
Grant, Yasmin, Brand Mgr-Amp Energy - PepsiCo, Inc.; *pg.* 259, *pg.* 1327
Granter, Tim, Mgr-Global Mktg-Calvin Klein - Coty, Inc.; *pg.* 506, *pg.* 1219
Grantham, Marna, Sr VP & Head-TV Sls North & South America - Miramax Film Corp.; *pg.* 298, *pg.* 275
Granuzzo, Melanie, Asst Mgr-Social Media-Global - Chanel, Inc.; *pg.* 503, *pg.* 1211
Granzetto, Staci, Dir-Strategic Mktg & Distr - Travelers Insurance; *pg.* 1220, *pg.* 963
Grapenthin, Carrie, Sr VP-Mktg & Comm-Global - Brookfield Global Relocation Services; *pg.* 1083, *pg.* 560
Graseck, Marlene, Sr Mgr-Global Mktg Insights - Electronic Arts Inc.; *pg.* 951, *pg.* 189
Grasman, Jeroen, Sr Dir-Fin-Global Biologics Mfg - Genentech, Inc.; *pg.* 1533, *pg.* 279
Grass, Jim, VP-Pub Sector Sls - Zones, Inc.; *pg.* 1292, *pg.* 1813
Grassian, Doug, Sr Mgr-Airship Comm - The Goodyear Tire & Rubber Company; *pg.* 1883, *pg.* 1401
Grassmann, Larry, VP-Sls & Mktg - NABCO Entrances, Inc.; *pg.* 99, *pg.* 1882
Grasso, Davide, VP-Brand Mktg-Global - NIKE, Inc.; *pg.* 1812, *pg.* 1492
Grasso, Paul, Mgr-Mktg Analytics - Chico's FAS, Inc.; *pg.* 21, *pg.* 427
Grasso, Tina, Sr Specialist-Product, Pipeline & Supply Comm - Merck & Co., Inc.; *pg.* 1566, *pg.* 1077
Grasty, Kevin, Asst VP-Creative Svcs - American University; *pg.* 597, *pg.* 395
Grathwohl, Kate, Mgr-Product Mktg - Graco, Inc.; *pg.* 1342, *pg.* 935
Gratz, Stacy, VP-Mktg, Digital Partnerships & Dev - American Express Company; *pg.* 712, *pg.* 1190
Grau, Lee, Gen Mgr-Sls - Beasley Broadcast Group, Inc.; *pg.* 271, *pg.* 450
Graubart, Ed, VP-Sls-West - NuVasive, Inc.; *pg.* 1577, *pg.* 205
Graul, Melissa, Sr Mgr-Intl Digital Offers Product Mgmt & Strategy - American Express Company; *pg.* 712, *pg.* 1190
Graul, Michelle R., Exec VP-Stores & Mdsg - Kirkland's Inc.; *pg.* 1126, *pg.* 1652
Graumenz, Carlyn, Acct Planner-Digital-Charter Media - Charter Communications, Inc.; *pg.* 274, *pg.* 372
Gravely, Alan, Sr Dir-Brand Comm - Moen Incorporated; *pg.* 1056, *pg.* 1468
Gravely, Amber, Sr Mgr-Consumer Channel Mktg - Plantronics, Inc.; *pg.* 663, *pg.* 270
Graver, Angie, Supvr-Sls Svc - General Mills, Inc.; *pg.* 828, *pg.* 933
Graver, Fred, Head-TV Creative - Twitter, Inc.; *pg.* 1285, *pg.* 228
Graves, Cyndee, Asst Dir-University Mktg & Adv - Penn State University; *pg.* 606, *pg.* 1589
Graves, HyunMee, Dir-Product Mktg & Innovation - General Mills, Inc.; *pg.* 828, *pg.* 933
Graves, Katrina, Brand Mgr-Beverage - Ocean Spray Cranberries, Inc.; *pg.* 887, *pg.* 827
Graves, Rod, Sr Dir-Football Admin - New York Jets Football Club, Inc.; *pg.* 570, *pg.* 1067
Graves, Timothy, Sr Mgr-Client Solutions-Tech & Mobile - Nielsen Business Media; *pg.* 1671, *pg.* 1272
Gravino, Doug, Sr Dir-Video Product Dev - Cox Communications, Inc.; *pg.* 279, *pg.* 501
Gravitt, Sarah, VP-Brand Mktg - Capital One Financial Corporation; *pg.* 730, *pg.* 1789
Gravitt-Baese, Sarah, VP-Brand Mktg - Capital One Financial Corporation; *pg.* 730, *pg.* 1789
Gray, Andy, VP & Dir-Creative-Brand Design - Cole-Haan LLC; *pg.* 1806, *pg.* 1034
Gray, Angie, Brand Mgr-Lawn Fertilizer Mktg - The Scotts Miracle-Gro Company; *pg.* 1799, *pg.* 1459
Gray, Ashley, Coord-Retail Mktg - Under Armour, Inc.; *pg.* 49, *pg.* 759
Gray, Bill, Sr Mgr-Franchise Mktg-East Africa Franchise - The Coca-Cola Company; *pg.* 240, *pg.* 493
Gray, Chris, Sr Dir-Institutions, Corp Responsibility-Global - Pfizer Inc.; *pg.* 1581, *pg.* 1278
Gray, Darrin, Dir-Sls-Contact for Sponsorships - Family First; *pg.* 140, *pg.* 472
Gray, David, Mgr-Global Search Engine Mktg - Analog Devices, Inc.; *pg.* 617, *pg.* 839
Gray, David M., Sr Product Mgr-Mettler-Toledo Thornton, Inc - Mettler-Toledo International Inc.; *pg.* 1423, *pg.* 1441
Gray, Elizabeth, Sr Mgr-Partner Mktg - Red Hat, Inc.; *pg.* 460, *pg.* 1388
Gray, Glenn, Sr Dir-Project Mgmt-Global - Roche Diagnostics Corporation; *pg.* 1590, *pg.* 689
Gray, Gwen, VP-Mktg - The Kraft Heinz Company; *pg.* 871, *pg.* 641
Gray, Heidi, Exec VP-Central Div Sls - News America Incorporated; *pg.* 1669, *pg.* 1271
Gray, Ivor, Mgr-Capital Equipment Sls-Global - Schlumberger Limited; *pg.* 801, *pg.* 1714
Gray, Jason, Sr Mgr-Mobile & Experience Strategy - Philips Healthcare; *pg.* 1585, *pg.* 783
Gray, Jill, Dir-Global Mktg-Pro Hair - Aveda Corporation; *pg.* 499, *pg.* 917
Gray, Jim, Reg Mgr-Sls - Miether Bearing Products, Inc.; *pg.* 1361, *pg.* 1728
Gray, Justin, Assoc Mgr-Media - MillerCoors LLC; *pg.* 255, *pg.* 582
Gray, Kathleen, Assoc Mgr-Mktg - Frontera Foods, Inc.; *pg.* 857, *pg.* 574
Gray, Kelsey, Specialist-Mktg - Amazon.com, Inc.; *pg.* 1226, *pg.* 1831
Gray, Larry H., VP-Consumer Sls & Mktg - The Fuller Brush Company; *pg.* 330, *pg.* 715
Gray, Laura, Dir-Retail Mktg - Cabela's Incorporated; *pg.* 535, *pg.* 1019
Gray, Lynn, Dir-Field Mktg-East Reg - General Growth Properties, Inc.; *pg.* 1093, *pg.* 574
Gray, Marcy, Product Mgr - The Progressive Corporation; *pg.* 1214, *pg.* 1463
Gray, Marjorie, Brand Mgr-Digital - DISH Network Corporation; *pg.* 283, *pg.* 325
Gray, Matt, VP-Product Innovation - Allianz Life Insurance Company of North America; *pg.* 1188, *pg.* 929
Gray, Matt, Brand Mgr-Global - AstraZeneca Pharmaceuticals LP; *pg.* 1497, *pg.* 389
Gray, Matt, Sr Copywriter-Creative - IRIS International, Inc.; *pg.* 1547, *pg.* 64
Gray, Matthew, Planner-Ad Sls - DIRECTV Group Holdings, LLC; *pg.* 281, *pg.* 79
Gray, Megan, Brand Mgr-Xbox - Microsoft Corporation; *pg.* 435, *pg.* 1824

Gray, Michael, Coord-Comm & Social Media - Fox Sports Net; pg. 288, pg. 131
Gray, Renee, Mgr-Mktg - True Value Company; pg. 1065, pg. 592
Gray, Rob, Mgr-Global Product Mktg-Google Maps - Google Inc.; pg. 1249, pg. 153
Gray, Steve, VP-Mktg - Kronos Incorporated; pg. 425, pg. 813
Gray, Steve, VP-Mktg - Kronos International, Inc.; pg. 980, pg. 1683
Gray, Stevie, Sr Dir-Ticket Ops - Golden State Warriors, LLC; pg. 550, pg. 171
Gray, Tom, Sr Dir-Mktg - Interstate Battery System of America Inc.; pg. 208, pg. 1682
Graycar, Holly, Sr Mgr-Email Mktg - LinkedIn Corporation; pg. 1262, pg. 160
Graylish, Gordon, VP & Gen Mgr-Enterprise Solutions Sls - Intel Corporation; pg. 645, pg. 266
Grayson, Bob, VP-The Media Center - Life Care Centers of America; pg. 1555, pg. 1630
Grayton, Sharon D., Assoc Dir-Sls & Res - Cincinnati Symphony Orchestra; pg. 540, pg. 1411
Grazewski, Paul H., Sr VP-Product Mgmt & Strategic Plng - American Science and Engineering, Inc.; pg. 1399, pg. 787
Graziano, Anthony P., Sr Mgr-Mktg - Tech Data Corporation; pg. 482, pg. 416
Graziano, Chris, Brand Mgr - Campbell Soup Company; pg. 844, pg. 1048
Graziano, Patrick, Dir-IT Mktg & Comm - Merck & Co., Inc.; pg. 1566, pg. 1077
Grbic, Alex, Dir-Product Mktg - Altera Corporation; pg. 348, pg. 237
Greaney, Thomas, Product Mgr - Business Insider; pg. 1233, pg. 1208
Greatbanks, Laura, Mgr-Mktg-Team Sports - ASICS America Corporation; pg. 1826, pg. 106
Greatrex, Mark, CMO & Chief Sls Officer - Cox Communications, Inc.; pg. 279, pg. 501
Greaux, Denise, Mgr-Online Mktg-Affiliate & Display - Toys "R" Us, Inc.; pg. 968, pg. 1130
Greaves, Ronald, Head-Diversity & Mgr-Healthcare Vertical Mktg - Siemens Process Industries and Drives; pg. 673, pg. 485
Greb, Brook, Mgr-Mktg-Audience Engagement - Allrecipes.com; pg. 1226, pg. 1831
Grebe, Linda, Dir-Consumer, Product & Mktg - Johnson Outdoors Inc.; pg. 1837, pg. 1888
Grebenc, Jane, Pres/Chief Revenue Officer-First Commonwealth Bank - First Commonwealth Financial Corporation; pg. 754, pg. 1541
Greber, Erika, Asst Dir-Mktg-Digital Publ - Penguin Random House; pg. 1675, pg. 1276
Grebstein, Marci, VP-Mktg, Brand Strategy & External Comm - Food Lion, LLC; pg. 1019, pg. 1390
Grech, Estelle, Sr Specialist-Mktg - Canon U.S.A., Inc.; pg. 1404, pg. 1178
Grech, George, Mgr-Intl Sls-Canada & Caribbean - AMX Corporation; pg. 349, pg. 1735
Greci, David, Sr Assoc Brand Mgr-Trident - Mondelez International, Inc.; pg. 878, pg. 601
Greco, Christy, Assoc Mgr-Mktg - The Timberland Company; pg. 1821, pg. 1039
Greco, German, Dir-Sls - Motorola Mobility LLC; pg. 657, pg. 627
Greco, Jessica, Asst Mgr-PR - Mars, Incorporated; pg. 1858, pg. 1792
Greco, Joseph D., Sr VP-Advanced Tech Grp - NVIDIA Corporation; pg. 447, pg. 268
Greco, Kristen, Dir-Customer Engagement Mktg - Comcast Cable Communications, Inc.; pg. 276, pg. 1560
Greco, Mary, Asst Brand Mgr-Global Mktg-Matrix - L'Oreal USA; pg. 514, pg. 1252
Greco, Morgan, Sr Dir-Social Media & Fan Engagement-A&E, HISTORY & H2 - A&E Television Networks, LLC; pg. 267, pg. 1185
Greco, Peter, Dir-Multi-Channel Mktg - Bristol-Myers Squibb U.S. Pharmaceutical Group; pg. 1511, pg. 1110
Greco, Steve, VP-Sls - DepoMed, Inc.; pg. 1523, pg. 143
Grecula, Joe, VP-Food Service Sls-US & Canada - Cooper-Atkins Corporation; pg. 1407, pg. 355
Greczyn, Brian, Sr Dir-Sls - MATTEL, INC.; pg. 962, pg. 81
Greden, Daniel, Head-eHealth Product & Clinical Innovation - Aetna Inc.; pg. 1187, pg. 351
Greeby, Jennifer, Sr Dir-Diabetes & Obesity Mktg - Takeda Pharmaceuticals USA, Inc.; pg. 1600, pg. 605
Green, Al, VP-Mktg - Southeast Toyota Distributors, LLC; pg. 190, pg. 421
Green, Alex, VP-Mktg - Boston Pizza International, Inc.; pg. 1016, pg. 1908
Green, Alexis, Brand Mgr-Tazo Tea - Starbucks Corporation; pg. 897, pg. 1840
Green, Amy, Specialist-Mktg Dev-Boston, New York, Philadelphia & Washington - Ford Motor Company; pg. 172, pg. 876
Green, Amy, Sr Product Mgr - LKQ Corp.; pg. 210, pg. 185
Green, Angella, Dir-Mktg - Yoshinoya America Inc.; pg. 1756, pg. 297
Green, Ann, Sr Mgr-Shopper Mktg - Keurig Green Mountain, Inc.; pg. 868, pg. 1768
Green, Avery, Planner-Digital Sls - Emmis Communications Corporation; pg. 285, pg. 685
Green, Bill, Engr-Outside Sls - Standard Wire & Cable Co.; pg. 1306, pg. 187
Green, Blair, Sr VP-Creative Adv - Focus Features; pg. 287, pg. 273
Green, Crista, Mgr-Strategic Mktg Plng - Lennox International Inc.; pg. 1073, pg. 1736
Green, Daniel, Mgr-Digital & Social Mktg - Columbia Sportswear Company; pg. 1830, pg. 1501
Green, David, Mgr-Retail Mktg Support - Kia Motors America Inc.; pg. 181, pg. 112
Green, David, Dir-Mktg, Prescription Pharmaceuticals - Valeant Pharmaceuticals International; pg. 1605, pg. 1047
Green, Dennis, Sr VP-Affiliate Sls & Brdcst Ops - Cumulus Media Inc.; pg. 280, pg. 503
Green, Ellen, Sr Mgr-Customer Relationship Mktg - ACE Cash Express, Inc.; pg. 710, pg. 1717
Green, Eric, Category Mgr-Global Retail Product Demonstration - Bose Corporation; pg. 626, pg. 820
Green, Erica, Sr Mgr-Mktg - Society of Chemical Mnaufacturers & Affiliates, Inc.; pg. 156, pg. 404
Green, Erin, Dir-Social & Digital Analytics - Visa Inc.; pg. 816, pg. 230
Green, Floyd W., Corp VP & Head-Community Rels & Urban Mktg - Aetna Inc.; pg. 1187, pg. 351
Green, Gregory, Sr Mgr-Security - Arizona Diamondbacks; pg. 529, pg. 14
Green, Jason, VP-Americas Sls & Applications Global Distr - Maxim Integrated Products, Inc.; pg. 653, pg. 247
Green, Jennifer, Mgr-Media & Ops - Bristol-Myers Squibb Company; pg. 1509, pg. 1206
Green, John, VP-Mktg & ECommerce - Matco Tools Corporation; pg. 1055, pg. 1474
Green, Joseph, Brand Mgr-Nexcare Brand - 3M; pg. 339, pg. 179
Green, Kathryn, Product Mgr-Online - Capella Education Company; pg. 599, pg. 931
Green, Kelly, Mgr-Production - Publix Super Markets, Inc.; pg. 1031, pg. 437
Green, Kevin, Exec Dir-Mktg - Dell Inc.; pg. 383, pg. 1737
Green, Kyle, Mgr-Programmatic Sls - About, Inc.; pg. 1225, pg. 1186
Green, Laura, Brand Mgr-Nuevo Grille - Tyson Foods, Inc.; pg. 902, pg. 35
Green, Lynette, Mgr-Digital Mktg-Vodkas - Brown-Forman Corporation; pg. 1958, pg. 732
Green, Marissa, Sr Specialist-Mktg - Liberty Mutual Insurance Group Inc.; pg. 1205, pg. 797
Green, Melissa, Mgr-Strategic Mktg - Honeywell International Inc.; pg. 407, pg. 1088
Green, Michael, Sr Mgr-Mktg Ops & Global Demand Center - Level 3 Communications, Inc.; pg. 1262, pg. 312
Green, Mike, Sr Dir - ESPN, Inc.; pg. 285, pg. 340
Green, Mike, VP-Sls & Svc-North America - Flint Group, Inc.; pg. 1163, pg. 904
Green, Mitchell, Brand Mgr - Kobrand Corporation; pg. 1965, pg. 1325
Green, Monica, Mgr-Sls-Natl Acct - Atlanta Convention & Visitors Bureau; pg. 989, pg. 489
Green, Natasha Calder, Sr Mgr-Market Dev - LivaNova; pg. 1557, pg. 1710
Green, Randy, Mgr-Adv Sls - The Newark Advocate; pg. 1669, pg. 1467
Green, Richard, District Sls Mgr-Southeast Reg - INCONTACT, INC.; pg. 413, pg. 1752
Green, Scott, Sr VP-Mktg & Sls-North America - Marnier-Lapostolle Inc.; pg. 1966, pg. 1256
Green, Shaun Hunter, Sr VP-Preferred Segment Mktg - Bank of America Corporation; pg. 718, pg. 1362
Green, Ted, Dir-ECommerce & Digital Media - Payless Shoesource, Inc.; pg. 31, pg. 722
Green, Terry, Mgr-Solutions Sls-Graphic Comm Grp - Eastman Kodak Company; pg. 1408, pg. 1333
Green, Tiziana, Mgr-Social Media - TD Ameritrade Holding Corporation; pg. 808, pg. 1018
Green, Travis, VP-Schools Mktg - AdvancePierre Foods, Inc.; pg. 1714, pg. 1409
Green, Travis, Product Mgr-Google Wallet Send Money - Google Inc.; pg. 1249, pg. 153
Green, Valerie, Sr VP-Mktg-Cablevision Systems Corp - Cablevision Systems Corporation; pg. 272, pg. 1141
Green, Victoria, Sr Dir-Art - Asimov's Science Fiction Magazine; pg. 1618, pg. 1197
Greenbaum, Robert, Sr Dir-Mktg & Strategy - Federal National Mortgage Association; pg. 751, pg. 399
Greenberg, Aaron, Product Mgr - Xbox; pg. 970, pg. 1829
Greenberg, Andrew, Sr Dir-Bus Dev - Yahoo! Inc.; pg. 1289, pg. 289
Greenberg, Benjamin, VP-Product Mgmt & User Experience - WebMD Health Corporation; pg. 1288, pg. 1313
Greenberg, Charlie, Head-Global Media Strategy - Merck & Co., Inc.; pg. 1566, pg. 1077
Greenberg, Glenn, Dir-Media Rels & Sponsorship PR - Liberty Mutual Insurance Group Inc.; pg. 1205, pg. 797
Greenberg, Jack, VP-Pricing & Product Dev - Columbian Mutual Life Insurance Company; pg. 1198, pg. 1142
Greenberg, Jason, Sr VP-Mktg - SKECHERS U.S.A., INC.; pg. 1819, pg. 143
Greenberg, Jordan, VP-Mktg - B&G Foods, Inc.; pg. 838, pg. 1102
Greenberg, Kevin, Assoc Dir-Media - Apollo Education Group Inc.; pg. 597, pg. 14
Greenberg, Michael, Sr Acct Exec-Bus Dev-Media & Adv - NeuStar, Inc.; pg. 1872, pg. 1807
Greenberg, Paul, VP-Media Svcs - NYC & Company, Inc.; pg. 1002, pg. 1274
Greenberg, Raquel Bledsoe, Assoc Mgr-eMail Mktg - Chico's FAS, Inc.; pg. 21, pg. 427
Greenberg, Robert, VP-Brand Mktg - Panasonic Corporation of North America; pg. 661, pg. 1120
Greenberg, Shelley, Sr Asst Brand Mgr-Direct - DISH Network Corporation; pg. 283, pg. 325
Greenberg, Suzy M., Sr Mgr-PR - Intel Corporation; pg. 645, pg. 266
Greenberg, Warren, Sls Dir-Large Enterprise - Level 3 Communications, Inc.; pg. 1262, pg. 312
Greenday, Laura, Sr Mgr-Mktg-Customer Programs & Channel Strategy - McKesson Corporation; pg. 1560, pg. 222
Greene, Allen R., VP-Sls & Mktg-Global - Hewlett-Packard Company; pg. 404, pg. 175
Greene, Beth, Exec VP-Mktg & Strategic Branding - Kravet Fabrics Inc.; pg. 932, pg. 1142
Greene, Beth, Exec VP-Mktg & Strategic Branding - Lee Jofa, Inc.; pg. 933, pg. 1142
Greene, C. Scott, Exec VP-Mktg - Universal Forest Products, Inc.; pg. 117, pg. 890
Greene, Chris, Mgr-Production - A.T. Ferrell Company, Inc.; pg. 701, pg. 674
Greene, David, Mgr-Mobile Mktg & Natural Search - Tween Brands Inc.; pg. 34, pg. 1467
Greene, Geneva, Rep-Media Rels - Lockheed Martin Corporation; pg. 229, pg. 762
Greene, Gregory, Dir-Mktg - Sabra Dipping Company LLC; pg. 893, pg. 1686
Greene, Harvey, Sr VP-Media Rels - Miami Dolphins, Ltd.; pg. 562, pg. 419
Greene, Ira, VP-Sls - A.H. Schreiber Co., Inc.; pg. 17, pg. 1188
Greene, Julie, Specialist-Sls & Mktg Solutions - The Dun & Bradstreet Corp.; pg. 1637, pg. 1120
Greene, Kate, Brand Mgr & Product Mgr - Hunter Douglas, Inc.; pg. 928, pg. 1320
Greene, Matthew C, Sr Dir-Mktg-Americas - Siemens PLM Software; pg. 469, pg. 1734
Greene, Scott, Dir-Creative - Fairway Outdoor Advertising of Georgia-Alabama; pg. 1640, pg. 486
Greene, Stephanie Evans, VP-Mktg - Carnival Cruise Lines; pg. 1902, pg. 441
Greene, T. J., Jr., VP-Sls - Buffalo Wire Works Co., Inc.; pg. 72, pg. 1147
Greenfeather, Lynne, Mgr-Mktg Comm-Global - Automated Packaging Systems Inc.; pg. 1452, pg. 1474
Greenfield, Brad, Sr Dir-Mktg-Acne Div - Valeant Pharmaceuticals International; pg. 1605, pg. 1047

Greenhalgh, Shelly, Mgr-Global Partner Mktg-Cloud & Data Center - Cisco Systems, Inc.; pg. 372, pg. 240
Greenhaw, Mark, VP-Mktg - Bank of the Ozarks, Inc.; pg. 721, pg. 33
Greenhill, Gemma, Assoc Mgr-Social Media - Constellation Brands, Inc.; pg. 1960, pg. 1348
Greenholtz, Amy, Coord-Adv Svcs - Hearst Magazines; pg. 1649, pg. 1239
Greenhut, Richard, Dir-Brdcst Sls-US - iBiquity Digital Corporation; pg. 409, pg. 767
Greenia, Kimberly, Dir-Adv - The Home Depot, Inc.; pg. 1050, pg. 510
Greeninger, Butch, Dir-Sls-SWS Div - The Toro Company; pg. 1065, pg. 918
Greenlee, Al, Dir-Mktg - Blue Diamond Growers; pg. 840, pg. 195
Greenlee, Daniel, Gen Mgr-Natl Sls Center - DISH Network Corporation; pg. 283, pg. 325
Greenler, Jeff, VP-Brand & Adv-Global - Monster Worldwide, Inc.; pg. 1268, pg. 859
Greenman, Samuel, Product Mgr-Schwinn Bicycles - Pacific Cycle Inc.; pg. 1709, pg. 1867
Greenman, Stacey, Exec Dir-Mktg - Meredith Corporation; pg. 1663, pg. 705
Greenspan, Alyssa, Dir-Media - Cotton Incorporated Consumer Marketing Headquarters; pg. 692, pg. 1218
Greenspan, Heather, Dir-Mktg-Immunology - Valeant Pharmaceuticals International; pg. 1605, pg. 1047
Greenspan, Janis, Sr Dir-Global Mktg Strategy - Banana Republic; pg. 1760, pg. 212
Greenstein, Charles, Sr VP-Sponsorship Mktg-Global - Bank of America Corporation; pg. 718, pg. 1362
Greenstein, Jordan, Dir-Entertainment Mktg & Product Dev - The Topps Company, Inc.; pg. 588, pg. 1302
Greenstein, Marc, Dir-Creative - NBC News; pg. 300, pg. 1265
Greenwald, Eric, VP-Digital Video Strategy & Production - Bank of America Corporation; pg. 718, pg. 1362
Greenwald, Lisa, VP-Mdsg-Madewell - J. Crew Group, Inc.; pg. 1773, pg. 1245
Greenwald, Stacey, Mgr-Customer Relationship Mktg - Things Remembered, Inc.; pg. 1788, pg. 1455
Greenwood, Bruce, Dir-Product Mktg - Hewlett-Packard Company; pg. 404, pg. 175
Greenwood, David, VP-Sls & Mktg - JS International, Inc.; pg. 931, pg. 818
Greenwood, David, Project Mgr & Product Mgr - Pitney Bowes Inc.; pg. 454, pg. 376
Greenwood, Jason, VP-Mktg - Peter Piper, Inc.; pg. 1744, pg. 18
Greer, Bill, VP-Mktg-KY & Mid-States Div - Atmos Energy Corporation; pg. 1935, pg. 1675
Greer, Gary, Project Mgr-Customer Product Dev - Avery Dennison Corporation; pg. 1452, pg. 95
Greer, Jeffrey, VP-Ops-Satellite Products - KVH Industries Inc; pg. 650, pg. 1602
Greer, John, Chief Creative Officer & Exec VP - FRANKLIN RESOURCES, INC.; pg. 760, pg. 254
Greer, Rick, Dir-Sls - Automotive News; pg. 1618, pg. 879
Greevy, Shannon, Mgr-Social Media - Esurance, Inc.; pg. 1243, pg. 217
Greff, Matt, Product Mgr & Principal - Marchex, Inc.; pg. 1395, pg. 1837
Greficz, Misty, Mgr-Mktg - Magellan Health Services, Inc.; pg. 1557, pg. 337
Gregersen, Ariel, Specialist-RBP-US Mktg-Nike Golf - NIKE, Inc.; pg. 1812, pg. 1492
Gregersen, Steve, Sr Dir-Adv-Natl - Century 21 Real Estate LLC; pg. 1085, pg. 1080
Gregg, Scott, Exec VP-Sls Ops-20th Century Fox Television Distr - FX Networks, LLC; pg. 288, pg. 131
Gregoire, Alyce, Mgr-Mktg Events - McKesson Corporation; pg. 1560, pg. 222
Gregor, Marisa, Specialist-Mktg - American Medical Systems Holdings, Inc.; pg. 1493, pg. 947
Gregorio, Alex, Specialist-Mktg Comm - Upromise, Inc.; pg. 815, pg. 837
Gregorovic, Elvis, Dir-Product Dev - AXA Equitable Life Insurance Company; pg. 1194, pg. 1199
Gregory, Alex, Dir-Sls & Mktg - Sea Island Acquisition LLC; pg. 1111, pg. 540
Gregory, Catherine, Mgr-Social Media Mktg - Red Bull North America, Inc.; pg. 264, pg. 275
Gregory, Chris, Dir-Mktg Tech & Innovation - Electronic Arts Inc.; pg. 951, pg. 189
Gregory, Glenn A., Product Mgr-Global - Microsoft Corporation; pg. 435, pg. 1824
Gregory, Jay, Writer-Mktg Comm - Agilent Technologies, Inc.; pg. 614, pg. 264
Gregory, Jill, Sr VP-Mktg - National Association for Stock Car Auto Racing; pg. 566, pg. 420
Gregory, Kim, Mgr-Mktg Comm - Cubic Transportation Systems, Inc.; pg. 1905, pg. 202
Gregory, Kristina E., Dir-Mktg - Constellation Energy Resources, LLC; pg. 1938, pg. 756
Gregory, Marc, VP-Digital Mktg & Media - Columbus Blue Jackets; pg. 542, pg. 1439
Gregory, Matt, VP-Sls-Specialty Div - The Clorox Company; pg. 327, pg. 169
Gregory, Michael, Mgr-Global Sports Mktg - Beats Electronics LLC; pg. 624, pg. 272
Gregory, Steve, Sr Mgr-Sourcing-Indirect - The Clorox Company; pg. 327, pg. 169
Gregory, Todd, Dir-Mktg & Demand Generation - Hewlett-Packard Company; pg. 404, pg. 175
Gregory, Trisha, Dir-Mktg - Wagner Spray Tech Corporation; pg. 1449, pg. 954
Greif, Kathy, Dir-Mktg - Salvador Dali Museum; pg. 580, pg. 464
Greiff, David, VP-Sls-Insurance & Healthcare Solutions-Americas - Oracle Corporation; pg. 1272, pg. 786
Greig, Steve, Sr Dir-Mktg, Brand, Product & Football-Global - Visa Inc.; pg. 816, pg. 230
Grein, Jeremy, Brand Mgr-Bus Dev - Capital One Bank (USA), N.A.; pg. 730, pg. 1789
Greiner, Amber, Coord-Convention-Mktg - Daktronics, Inc.; pg. 633, pg. 1624
Greiner, Gary G., Reg Mgr-Mktg - Public Service Enterprise Group Incorporated; pg. 1950, pg. 1097
Greiner, Lindsay, Specialist-Mktg - Henry Schein, Inc.; pg. 1541, pg. 1180
Greiner, Meredith, Mgr-Mktg - Nordic Naturals, Inc.; pg. 1573, pg. 305
Greis, Allison A., Program Mgr-Channel Mktg - International Business Machines Corporation; pg. 418, pg. 1138
Greiss, Adam, VP, Head-Global Creative Svcs & Dir-Creative - Morgan Stanley; pg. 783, pg. 1261
Grelewicz, Rick, Sr VP-Mktg - TracFone Wireless, Inc.; pg. 681, pg. 447
Gremley, Rob, Exec VP-Product Dev & Corp Mktg - Parametric Technology Corporation; pg. 452, pg. 835
Grenier, Adam, Head-Performance Mktg - Uber USA, LLC; pg. 1286, pg. 229
Grenier, Christina, Sr Program Mgr-Voice of the Customer Mktg - Cisco Systems, Inc.; pg. 372, pg. 240
Grenier, Elizabeth, Mgr-Mktg-Social Media & Member Svcs - Upromise, Inc.; pg. 815, pg. 837
Grenier, Gerry, Sr Dir-Publ Technologies - Institute of Electrical and Electronics Engineers, Inc.; pg. 144, pg. 1109
Grenier, Guy, VP-Sls & Mktg-Indus - Richelieu Hardware Ltd.; pg. 1060, pg. 1961
Grenier, Kathy, Dir-Mktg - Imperial-Deltah, Inc.; pg. 7, pg. 1601
Grenke, Bob, Product Mgr - Molex Incorporated; pg. 655, pg. 628
Grenz, Dianne, Exec VP & Dir-Sls - Valley National Bancorp; pg. 815, pg. 1130
Grenz, Scott, Acting VP & Head-Media-Global - GlaxoSmithKline; pg. 1536, pg. 1565
Grenz, Scott, Acting VP & Head-Media-Global - GlaxoSmithKline Consumer Healthcare; pg. 510, pg. 1554
Gresham, Cheryl, Dir-Media - Taco Bell Corp.; pg. 1752, pg. 117
Gresham, Ian, VP-Mktg-Diversified Brands - The Sherwin-Williams Company; pg. 1447, pg. 1435
Gresham, Ian, Sr VP-Mktg-Diversified Brands Div - Sherwin Williams; pg. 1448, pg. 1436
Gresko, Marcia, Sr Product Mgr - Educational Insights, Inc.; pg. 951, pg. 187
Greteman, Kevin, Sr Mgr-Product & Mktg - Xilinx, Inc.; pg. 496, pg. 252
Grethen, Suzanne, VP-Mktg & Promo - The Hearst Corporation; pg. 1649, pg. 1239
Greve, Dan, Mgr-Design & Creative Studio - TD Ameritrade Holding Corporation; pg. 808, pg. 1018
Grevelding, Haley, Dir-Digital Mktg-Global - Levi Strauss & Co.; pg. 43, pg. 220
Grevenstuk, Ryan, Product Mgr - Flexible Steel Lacing Company; pg. 1337, pg. 608
Grew, Lauren, Analyst-Digital Mktg Analytics - Liberty Mutual Insurance Group Inc.; pg. 1205, pg. 797
Grewal, Aman, Head-Lifecycle Strategy & Mktg - Sears Holdings Corporation; pg. 1784, pg. 618
Grewal, Tanu, VP-Global Mktg-Baker Furniture - Kohler Co.; pg. 91, pg. 1862
Grewal, TJ, Chief Product Officer - Beats Electronics LLC; pg. 624, pg. 272
Grey, Harry, Head-Digital Mktg Ops-Global - Boston Scientific Corporation; pg. 1508, pg. 831
Grey, Hillary, Sr Analyst-Res-Brand & Product Mktg - United Airlines, Inc.; pg. 1927, pg. 593
Greygor, Heidi, Specialist-Mktg - FedEx Corporation; pg. 1907, pg. 1642
Greyson, Stephanie, Sr Mgr-Talent Engagement - Intuit Inc.; pg. 769, pg. 158
Gribas, Despina, Mgr-Mktg Comm - Pfizer Inc.; pg. 1581, pg. 1278
Grice, Lee, Product Mgr - Equifax Inc.; pg. 748, pg. 504
Grice-Livingston, Dawn, Sr Mgr-Integrated Mktg Comm-Latin America - IBM; pg. 410, pg. 1449
Grider, Jonathan, Mgr-Digital Mktg - Snapfish; pg. 1687, pg. 228
Grieb, Michael, Mgr-Mktg-Natl - Sprint Corporation; pg. 1874, pg. 719
Griebling, Anne, Mgr-Mktg - Exclusive Resorts, LLC; pg. 1091, pg. 319
Grieco, Anthony, Area Dir-Sls-East Americas - Cree Inc.; pg. 631, pg. 1371
Grieco, Dan, Dir-Corp Creative - GF Health Products, Inc.; pg. 1535, pg. 508
Grieco, Irene, Dir-Integrated Sls-Good Housekeeping - The Hearst Corporation; pg. 1649, pg. 1239
Grieco, Mark, VP-Sls - TradeStation Group, Inc.; pg. 811, pg. 459
Grieco, Todd, Brand Mgr - Mercedes-Benz USA, LLC; pg. 184, pg. 514
Griep, Kay, VP & Product Mgr-Mktg - Bank of America Corporation; pg. 718, pg. 1362
Grier, Howard, Assoc Publr-Mktg - The Hearst Corporation; pg. 1649, pg. 1239
Grier, Nicole, Product Mgr-Gifts & Decor - Hallmark Cards, Inc.; pg. 1646, pg. 983
Griesbaum, Dan, Jr., Mgr-Suite Sls & Svc - Detroit Tigers Baseball Club, Inc.; pg. 545, pg. 880
Griesbeck, Katie, Brand Mgr-Spirits - E&J Gallo Winery; pg. 1962, pg. 149
Grieshaber, Michele, CMO - Silicon Laboratories Inc.; pg. 674, pg. 1666
Griesing, Jim, VP-Mktg & Sls - The Hanover Insurance Company; pg. 1202, pg. 862
Griess, Ron, Product Mgr - KPI-JCI; pg. 1354, pg. 1626
Griffanti, Meredith, Sr Dir-PR - Equifax Inc.; pg. 748, pg. 504
Griffey, Brad, Mgr-Internet Mktg Ops - Dollar Thrifty Automotive Group, Inc.; pg. 169, pg. 1489
Griffin, Alyson, VP-Mktg-Worldwide - Hewlett-Packard Company; pg. 404, pg. 175
Griffin, Amber, Sr Mgr-Mktg-Global Stored Value & CRM - The Western Union Company; pg. 822, pg. 327
Griffin, Bridget, Dir-Mktg - Rent-A-Center, Inc.; pg. 940, pg. 1734
Griffin, Brighid, Specialist-Mktg - GEICO Corporation; pg. 1200, pg. 399
Griffin, Chere, Specialist-Mktg Comm & Copywriter - Philips Lighting; pg. 1303, pg. 806
Griffin, Clayton, Sr Mgr-HR-Workplace Practices - American Snuff Company; pg. 1893, pg. 1641
Griffin, Colleen, VP-Adv Sls - Scripps Networks Interactive, Inc.; pg. 1279, pg. 1638
Griffin, Dan, Sr Dir-Global Football Sponsorship Mktg - Visa Inc.; pg. 816, pg. 230
Griffin, Dan, Sr Dir-Global Football Sponsorship Mktg - Visa U.S.A., Inc.; pg. 817, pg. 231
Griffin, Daniel, Mgr-Product Mktg - International Business Machines Corporation; pg. 418, pg. 1138
Griffin, Dennis, Dir-Product Mgmt, Adobe Document Products & Mobile - Adobe Systems Incorporated; pg. 342, pg. 235
Griffin, Emily, Strategist-Digital Media & Partnership - The Detroit Lions, Inc.; pg. 544, pg. 864
Griffin, Erin, Mgr-Mktg Comm - Nautilus, Inc.; pg. 1840, pg. 1846
Griffin, Gary W., Sr Dir-Bus Comm - Travelers Insurance; pg. 1220, pg. 963
Griffin, Greg, VP-Customer Mktg, Global Mass & Mid-Tier - Elizabeth Arden, Inc.; pg. 507, pg. 448
Griffin, Howard, Sr VP-Natl Sls & US Community Publ -

First page reference indicates Business Class Edition
Second page reference indicates Geographic Edition

Gannett Co., Inc.; *pg.* 1643, *pg.* 1790
Griffin, Jack, Product Mgr - Champlain Cable Corp.; *pg.* 1044, *pg.* 1765
Griffin, Jack, Sr Dir-Corp Fin - Mediacom Communications Corporation; *pg.* 653, *pg.* 1182
Griffin, James Michael, VP-Sls - BTU International, Inc.; *pg.* 1320, *pg.* 838
Griffin, Jean, Sr VP-Special Sls-Intl - HBG Books, Inc.; *pg.* 1648, *pg.* 1238
Griffin, Jennifer Duchman, Mgr-Local Retail Sls - The Baltimore Sun Company; *pg.* 1619, *pg.* 755
Griffin, John, Sr Dir-Online Media - Dolby Laboratories, Inc.; *pg.* 284, *pg.* 217
Griffin, Katie, Mgr-Mktg-Meredith 360 - Meredith Corporation; *pg.* 1663, *pg.* 705
Griffin, Kim, Assoc Dir-HCV Mktg - Boehringer Ingelheim Pharmaceuticals, Inc.; *pg.* 1507, *pg.* 368
Griffin, Kristen, Brand Mgr-Mktg-Furniture Medic - The ServiceMaster Company, LLC; *pg.* 335, *pg.* 1646
Griffin, Larry L., Sr VP-Mktg - EIS, Inc.; *pg.* 80, *pg.* 504
Griffin, Maureen, Sr Mgr-Adv & Corp Mktg - Chevron Corporation; *pg.* 974, *pg.* 259
Griffin, Michael, Chief Product Officer - Lucky Brand Dungarees, Inc.; *pg.* 29, *pg.* 301
Griffin, Randy, Exec VP-Sls & Mktg - Western Sizzlin Corporation; *pg.* 1755, *pg.* 1806
Griffin, Tren, Sr Dir - Microsoft Corporation; *pg.* 435, *pg.* 1824
Griffis, Dan, VP-Experiential Mktg, Mgmt & Alliances - Target Corporation; *pg.* 1786, *pg.* 942
Griffith, Ann, Mgr-Interactive Mktg - PUBLIC STORAGE; *pg.* 1467, *pg.* 98
Griffith, Ben, Mgr-Interactive Mktg - Rite Aid Corporation; *pg.* 1590, *pg.* 1519
Griffith, Cary J., Writer-Mktg Comm - Ceridian Corporation; *pg.* 371, *pg.* 932
Griffith, David, Head-Digital Mktg & Media Solutions - Scripps Networks Interactive, Inc.; *pg.* 1279, *pg.* 1638
Griffith, Elaine, Sr Dir-Global Strategic Sourcing-Pur & Procurement Grp - Sirius XM Holdings Inc.; *pg.* 308, *pg.* 1292
Griffith, Greg, Mgr-Foodservice Products Sls - Consolidated Catfish Companies, LLC; *pg.* 850, *pg.* 969
Griffith, Jeff, Sr Dir-Programming & Production - Miami Dolphins, Ltd.; *pg.* 562, *pg.* 419
Griffith, Jennifer, Area Mgr-Sls - United Parcel Service, Inc.; *pg.* 1928, *pg.* 522
Griffith, Jonathan, Coord-Media Inventory & Traffic - Home Box Office, Inc.; *pg.* 290, *pg.* 1240
Griffith, Kristin, Sr Mgr-Mktg-QuickBooks In-Product Mktg - Intuit Inc.; *pg.* 769, *pg.* 158
Griffith, Matt, Brand Mgr-Pampers Global Leading Edge - The Procter & Gamble Company; *pg.* 1129, *pg.* 1418
Griffith, Michael, Exec VP-Sls - Enesco, LLC; *pg.* 1124, *pg.* 620
Griffith, Rod, Dir-Mktg-Americas - Conductix Inc.; *pg.* 1295, *pg.* 1015
Griffith, Todd, VP-Sls & Mktg - Alto-Shaam Inc.; *pg.* 836, *pg.* 1869
Griffiths, Francis, Sr VP-Reg Sls & Mktg - National Instruments Corporation; *pg.* 443, *pg.* 1664
Griffiths, Jailan, VP-Mktg - Dow Jones & Company, Inc.; *pg.* 1637, *pg.* 1225
Griffiths, Julia, Product Mgr - Anthro Corporation; *pg.* 913, *pg.* 1509
Griffiths, Linda, Mgr-Indus Mktg-Smart & Connected Communities - Cisco Systems, Inc.; *pg.* 372, *pg.* 240
Griffiths, Richard, Sr Dir - Pfizer Inc.; *pg.* 1581, *pg.* 1278
Griffiths, Tom, Co-Founder & Chief Product Officer - FanDuel, Inc.; *pg.* 547, *pg.* 1231
Griger, Kimberly D., Mgr-Mktg-Data Center Markets - 3M Company; *pg.* 1142, *pg.* 956
Grigg, Caitlin, Head-Global Media-Tablets & Sr Mgr-Mktg - Microsoft Corporation; *pg.* 435, *pg.* 1824
Griggs, Guy, Mgr-Sls-East Coast - The Washington Post; *pg.* 1701, *pg.* 407
Griggs, Melissa, Supvr-Direct Sls-Genesee County - Comcast Corporation; *pg.* 276, *pg.* 1560
Griggs, Pam, Mgr-Mktg Events - AT&T; *pg.* 1865, *pg.* 258
Griggs, Sara, Sr Mgr-PR & Social Media Mgr - Avid Technology, Inc.; *pg.* 622, *pg.* 804
Grigoriou, Jessica, Dir-Mktg-Axe - Unilever Canada Inc.; *pg.* 903, *pg.* 1946
Grigsby, Keena, Mgr-Mktg-Internet Sls & Mktg - Cellco Partnership; *pg.* 1869, *pg.* 1042
Grigsby, Keena, Mgr-Mktg-Internet Sls & Mktg - Verizon Communications Inc.; *pg.* 1875, *pg.* 1309
Grill, Scott, Dir-Sls, Mktg & 3rd Party Applications - Enventis; *pg.* 637, *pg.* 927
Grill, Talie, Sr Mgr-Digital Mktg - The Walt Disney Company; *pg.* 317, *pg.* 52
Grill, Tom, Mgr-Sls & Mktg-US Western Reg - Ford Motor Company; *pg.* 172, *pg.* 876
Grilli, Mark, VP-Product Mktg & Document Solutions - Adobe Systems Incorporated; *pg.* 342, *pg.* 235
Grillo, Derek, Product Mgr-Global - Thermo Fisher Scientific Inc.; *pg.* 1431, *pg.* 854
Grillon, Fleur, Dir-Consumer Mktg - The Procter & Gamble Company; *pg.* 1129, *pg.* 1418
Grills, Denise E., Sr Dir-Product Strategy & Mktg - Oracle Corporation; *pg.* 450, *pg.* 191
Grim, Ashley, Specialist-Mktg Content - Dick's Sporting Goods, Inc.; *pg.* 1832, *pg.* 1524
Grim, John, Sr Brand Mgr-North America Shopper Mktg - The Procter & Gamble Company; *pg.* 1129, *pg.* 1418
Grimaldi, Michelle, Mgr-Mktg-Mass Media - Recreational Equipment, Inc.; *pg.* 1843, *pg.* 1821
Grimaldi, Sara, Dir-Sport & Platform Sls Res - ESPN, Inc.; *pg.* 285, *pg.* 340
Grimes, Jonathan, Dir-Retail Sls & Mktg - Microsoft Corporation; *pg.* 435, *pg.* 1824
Grimes, Michael, VP-Omni-Channel Mktg - The Finish Line, Inc.; *pg.* 1769, *pg.* 686
Grimes, Peter, Dir-Mktg-Caribbean & Latin America - Arris Group, Inc.; *pg.* 353, *pg.* 541
Grimes, Sally, Head-Innovation, Sls & Global Brand Strategy - Tyson Foods, Inc.; *pg.* 902, *pg.* 35
Grimes, Sandie, VP-Sls - Stahl & Associates Insurance; *pg.* 1217, *pg.* 464
Grimes, Sharon, Assoc Mgr-Reg Mktg - The Allstate Corporation; *pg.* 1189, *pg.* 639
Grimes, Will, VP-Sls & Mktg - Lennar Homes, Inc.; *pg.* 93, *pg.* 1710
Grimm, Andrew, VP-Sls-Indus & Heavy Duty - Peerless Chain Company; *pg.* 1887, *pg.* 967
Grimm, Anne, Sr Product Mgr - GlaxoSmithKline Consumer Healthcare; *pg.* 510, *pg.* 1554
Grimm, Jacob, Sr Mgr-AR & PR - Microsoft Corporation; *pg.* 435, *pg.* 1824
Grimm, Jessoca, Sr Specialist-Creative & Media Mktg - Enterprise Holdings, Inc.; *pg.* 1906, *pg.* 996
Grimm, Leah, Brand Mgr - Johnson & Johnson; *pg.* 1549, *pg.* 1091
Grimm, Lisa, Assoc Dir-Social Media - Whole Foods Market, Inc.; *pg.* 1038, *pg.* 1667
Grimm, Wes, Dir-Sls & Mktg - Anaheim Manufacturing Company; *pg.* 51, *pg.* 48
Grimm, William R., Reg Mgr-Sls - ELECTROMED, INC.; *pg.* 1527, *pg.* 951
Grimme, Paulette, Brand Mgr - Sherwin Williams; *pg.* 1448, *pg.* 1436
Grimshaw, Caroline, Brand Mgr-Building-Ice Cream - Unilever United States, Inc.; *pg.* 904, *pg.* 1061
Grimshaw, Courtney, Sr Mgr-Global Oncology Internal Comm - Novartis Pharmaceuticals Corp.; *pg.* 1575, *pg.* 1054
Grindle, Caleb, Sr Mgr-Mktg, Brand & Digital Adv - Pegasystems Inc.; *pg.* 453, *pg.* 809
Grindrod, Tamara, Dir-Global Brand Strategy & Mktg - Hasbro, Inc.; *pg.* 954, *pg.* 1603
Grinstead, Jan, Brand Mgr-Cadbury, Snacking & Sugar Free Portfolio - The Hershey Co.; *pg.* 1855, *pg.* 1538
Grinstead, Megan, Sr Mgr-Mktg-Farm Rich - Rich Products Corporation; *pg.* 892, *pg.* 1150
Grinthal, Karen, Sr VP-Adv Sls Food Network & Cooking Channel - Scripps Networks Interactive, Inc.; *pg.* 1279, *pg.* 1638
Grio, Michael, Specialist-Adv Ops - Amazon.com, Inc.; *pg.* 1226, *pg.* 1831
Grip, David, Sr Dir-Comm - ASPEN TECHNOLOGY, INC.; *pg.* 354, *pg.* 804
Gripentrog, Eric, VP-DSD Sls & Ops - Kellogg Company; *pg.* 831, *pg.* 870
Grisafi, Stephanie, Mgr-Mktg Dev - Intel Corporation; *pg.* 645, *pg.* 266
Grisales, Monica, Brand Mgr - Gruma Corporation; *pg.* 860, *pg.* 1720
Grise, Emily, Coord-Mktg & Comm - Webster University; *pg.* 610, *pg.* 1004
Grisham, Hannah, Brand Mgr- Digital Mktg-Employer - Marriott International, Inc.; *pg.* 1102, *pg.* 764
Grisham, Robert, Sr VP-Sls - HP Enterprise Services, LLC; *pg.* 409, *pg.* 1731
Grishaver, Alex, Sr Dir-Design - IDEO, Inc.; *pg.* 411, *pg.* 178
Grishaver, Mike, Sr VP-Product - Etsy, Inc.; *pg.* 1768, *pg.* 1230
Griskel, Renita, Dir-Emerging Media Content - Scripps Networks Interactive, Inc.; *pg.* 1279, *pg.* 1638
Grisley, Colleen, Sr Mgr-Global Mktg Campaigns - Hewlett-Packard Company; *pg.* 404, *pg.* 175
Grissinger, Stan, Dir-Sls-Global - NIKE, Inc.; *pg.* 1812, *pg.* 1492
Grissom, Shannon, Mgr-Mktg - Cintas Corporation; *pg.* 372, *pg.* 1411
Griswold, Elizabeth, Dir-Mktg - Quinnipiac University; *pg.* 607, *pg.* 351
Gritzbaugh, Andrew, Mgr-Mktg Comm - Gerber Legendary Blades; *pg.* 1834, *pg.* 1503
Grivas, Diane, Mgr-Interactive Brand Mktg - The Hertz Corporation; *pg.* 1911, *pg.* 450
Groah, Jackie, Dir-Natl Partnerships & Cause Mktg - March of Dimes Birth Defects Foundation; *pg.* 146, *pg.* 1354
Grobe, Stacy, Mgr-Partnership Mktg - Macy's, Inc.; *pg.* 1778, *pg.* 1417
Grobey, Alan, Sr Product Mgr - A-Dec, Inc.; *pg.* 1483, *pg.* 1500
Grode, Travis, Corp Dir-Mktg & Player Dev - Pinnacle Entertainment, Inc.; *pg.* 576, *pg.* 1029
Groehler, Richard, Dir-Mktg & Product Line Mgr-North America - H.B. Fuller Company; *pg.* 1165, *pg.* 961
Groendyke, Melanie, VP & Sr Mgr-Mktg Analytics - Fifth Third Bancorp; *pg.* 752, *pg.* 1413
Groenewegen, Jeanine, Mgr-Mktg-Sponsor Mktg - Manulife Financial Corporation; *pg.* 778, *pg* 1939
Groenke, Evan, Sr Product Mgr-Desktop Graphics - Advanced Micro Devices, Inc.; *pg.* 613, *pg.* 282
Groff, Andy, Dir-Mdsg & Mktg Analytics - Harris Teeter, Inc.; *pg.* 1022, *pg.* 1383
Grofik, Heather, Acct Mgr-Mktg - Ingram Micro Inc.; *pg.* 415, *pg.* 261
Grogan, Brenda, Project Mgr-Mktg - The Coca-Cola Company; *pg.* 240, *pg.* 493
Grogan, Brian N., CTO & Dir-Product Mgmt & Mktg - Siemens PLM Software; *pg.* 469, *pg.* 1734
Grogan, Denise, Product Mgr - Fidelity National Information Services; *pg.* 397, *pg.* 1549
Grogan, Jill, Mgr-Mktg Svcs - Papa Ginos-Deangelo Holding Corporation, Inc.; *pg.* 1743, *pg.* 817
Grogan, Katie, Reg Dir-Sls - Ziff Davis, LLC; *pg.* 1703, *pg.* 1316
Grogan, Kelli, Specialist-Adv - The TJX Companies, Inc.; *pg.* 1788, *pg.* 822
Grogan, Tracy, Mgr-Brand Digital Mktg - Hanesbrands Inc.; *pg.* 26, *pg.* 1394
Grogan, Vince, Head-Institutional & Retirement Mktg - OppenheimerFunds, Inc.; *pg.* 790, *pg.* 1274
Groh, Irene, Dir-Mktg & Sls - The Masterson Company, Inc.; *pg.* 876, *pg.* 1877
Groh, Kari, VP-Comm & PR - The Timken Company; *pg.* 218, *pg.* 1408
Groh, Patti, Dir-Mktg Comm - Sappi Fine Paper North America; *pg.* 1468, *pg.* 801
Grohe, Joan, Sr Mgr-Comm - Avaya Inc.; *pg.* 621, *pg.* 264
Grohe, Ken, Sr VP & Gen Mgr-Emerging Products - Barracuda Networks, Inc.; *pg.* 360, *pg.* 58
Grohmann, Christoph, Sr Mgr-HR - Amgen Inc.; *pg.* 1493, *pg.* 291
Grohs, Bob, Sr Mgr-Mktg - PayPal Inc.; *pg.* 1274, *pg.* 248
Grol, Benjamin, Product Mgr - Facebook, Inc.; *pg.* 1245, *pg.* 143
Grom, Mary E., VP-Mktg - SYNNEX Corporation; *pg.* 480, *pg.* 92
Grommon, Jason, Pres-AZEK Building Products - CPG International, Inc.; *pg.* 1881, *pg.* 1586
Gromosaik, Mark, Grp Product Mgr-Trojan - Church & Dwight Co., Inc.; *pg.* 1153, *pg.* 1063
Gronberg, John, Product Mgr - Yahoo! Inc.; *pg.* 1289, *pg.* 289
Gronberg, Jonathan, Brand Mgr-Corp Gift Cards - Amazon.com, Inc.; *pg.* 1226, *pg.* 1831
Grondahl, Ed, Exec VP-Sls-Global - Tidel Engineering, L.P.; *pg.* 1382, *pg.* 1670
Grondzki, Todd, Sr Coord-Mktg Events - Yamaha Motor Corporation USA; *pg.* 1713, *pg.* 76
Gronfein, Hal, VP-Global Mktg Svcs & Exec Head-Mktg - MoneyGram International, Inc.; *pg.* 783, *pg.* 1684
Gronlund, Keith, Dir-Mktg - Brion Technologies Inc.; *pg.* 1319, *pg.* 265

Gronowicz, Fiona, Sr Mgr-Mktg & Sls - Ford Motor Company; *pg.* 172, *pg.* 876
Groom, Andrew, Strategist-Digital Mktg - E&J Gallo Winery; *pg.* 1962, *pg.* 149
Groom, Lauren, Specialist-Mktg-Digital Media - Doctor's Associates Inc.; *pg.* 1726, *pg.* 356
Grooms, Tim, Dir-YSI Mktg - YSI Incorporated; *pg.* 1438, *pg.* 1483
Grooms, Tom, Dir-Mktg - Frontier Communications of New York, Inc.; *pg.* 398, *pg.* 1335
Groover, Randy, Reg Mgr-Mktg - BUFFALO WILD WINGS, INC.; *pg.* 1718, *pg.* 931
Groppa, Briton, Brand Mgr-Coors Banquet - MillerCoors LLC; *pg.* 255, *pg.* 582
Grosbois, Eric, Reg Mgr-Sls-France & Northern Africa - Reliable Automatic Sprinkler Co., Inc.; *pg.* 1137, *pg.* 1158
Grosch, Stephanie, Rep-Olefins Mktg - The Williams Companies, Inc.; *pg.* 987, *pg.* 1491
Grosel, Dennis, Mgr-Product Delivery & Admin Sys - HAR Adhesive Technologies; *pg.* 1442, *pg.* 1405
Grosik, Dawn T., Asst VP & Branch Mgr-Sls-Courthouse - Village Bank & Trust Financial Corp.; *pg.* 816, *pg.* 1796
Grosjean, Angie, Sr Specialist-Mktg - Owens Corning; *pg.* 102, *pg.* 1476
Gross, Andrew, Sr VP-Mktg - Serta, Inc.; *pg.* 942, *pg.* 619
Gross, April, Mgr-Adv Ops - Meredith Corporation; *pg.* 1663, *pg.* 705
Gross, David, Partner-IT Strategic Bus-Performance & Product - GlaxoSmithKline; *pg.* 1536, *pg.* 1565
Gross, Don, VP-Global Promos Mktg-Walt Disney Studios - The Walt Disney Company; *pg.* 317, *pg.* 52
Gross, Holly, Mgr-Loyalty & Digital Mktg - Fresh & Easy Neighborhood Market Inc; *pg.* 1020, *pg.* 80
Gross, Howie, Mgr-Mktg - Alcatel-Lucent; *pg.* 615, *pg.* 38
Gross, Jason, VP-Strategy & Mktg - VeriFone Systems, Inc.; *pg.* 487, *pg.* 251
Gross, John, Dir-Sls - ShopLocal, LLC; *pg.* 1280, *pg.* 590
Gross, Joshua, Mgr-Product Line-Variable Frequency Drives - Eaton Corporation; *pg.* 1331, *pg.* 1429
Gross, Judith, Dir-Global Mktg-Naturals, Corp R&D - International Flavors & Fragrances Inc.; *pg.* 512, *pg.* 1244
Gross, Kelly, Head-Food Content Mktg Ops - General Mills, Inc.; *pg.* 828, *pg.* 933
Gross, Laura, VP-Res & Media - Warner Bros. Entertainment Inc.; *pg.* 319, *pg.* 54
Gross, Lisa, Sr Dir-Mktg Ops - Comcast Corporation; *pg.* 276, *pg.* 1560
Gross, Michelle L., Program Mgr-Sls-Leasing & North America Sls - The Boeing Company; *pg.* 225, *pg.* 567
Gross, Mitch, Dir-Mobile Adv - eBay Inc.; *pg.* 1240, *pg.* 243
Gross, Paul, Sr VP-Mktg - National Vision, Inc.; *pg.* 1423, *pg.* 534
Gross, Rachel, Sr VP-Event Mktg - Univision Communications Inc.; *pg.* 683, *pg.* 1307
Gross, Rae Anne, Mgr-Mktg - Bee-Alive Inc.; *pg.* 1503, *pg.* 1348
Gross, Steve, Dir-Sls-Worldwide - FlightSafety International, Inc.; *pg.* 601, *pg.* 1160
Gross, Susan M., Dir-Media Rels & Brand-Global - Honeywell International Inc.; *pg.* 407, *pg.* 1088
Gross, Whitney, Engr-Technical Mktg - Intel Corporation; *pg.* 645, *pg.* 266
Grosskopf, Richard, Head-Digital Mktg - Wells Fargo & Company; *pg.* 819, *pg.* 232
Grosskreuz, James, Product Mgr-Global - Rockwell Automation, Inc.; *pg.* 668, *pg.* 1880
Grosskurth, Justin, Mgr-Digital Mktg - Canon U.S.A., Inc.; *pg.* 1404, *pg.* 1178
Grossman, Adam, Sr VP-Mktg & Brand Dev - Boston Red Sox Baseball Club Limited Partnership; *pg.* 534, *pg.* 791
Grossman, Ben, Sls Mgr-Oncology Area-Denver & Phoenix - Novartis Corporation; *pg.* 1574, *pg.* 1273
Grossman, Daniel B., VP-Mktg - Nashville Symphony Association; *pg.* 565, *pg.* 1653
Grossman, Eileen, Dir-Customer Dev Mktg-Consumer - Boehringer Ingelheim Pharmaceuticals, Inc.; *pg.* 1507, *pg.* 368
Grossman, Elisa, Mgr-Email Mktg - AutoNation, Inc.; *pg.* 165, *pg.* 423
Grossman, Emily, Head-Mktg & Mgr-Strategic Plng - Target Corporation; *pg.* 1786, *pg.* 942
Grossman, Jay, VP-Sls & Acq - MTI Home Video; *pg.* 298, *pg.* 444
Grossman, Leslie, Sr Mgr-Mktg-Digital Subscriptions Retention & Winback - The New York Times; *pg.* 1668, *pg.* 1270
Grossman, Paige, Sr Dir-Creative - Ancestry.com LLC; *pg.* 1228, *pg.* 1754
Grossman, Sam, Dir-Mktg - The Sharper Image; *pg.* 1785, *pg.* 886
Grossman, Susan, Sr VP & Grp Head-Media Solutions-MasterCard Advisors - MasterCard Worldwide Inc.; *pg.* 780, *pg.* 988
Grossman, Yan, Program Mgr-Digital Mktg - Apple Inc.; *pg.* 350, *pg.* 73
Grossman-Cohen, Rebecca, Exec Dir-Consumer Mktg - The New York Times; *pg.* 1668, *pg.* 1270
Grossman-Cohen, Rebecca, Exec Dir-Consumer Mktg - The New York Times Company; *pg.* 1668, *pg.* 1270
Grossmith, Krystal, Brand Mgr-Vegetables - Del Monte Foods, Inc.; *pg.* 852, *pg.* 304
Grosso, Kelly, Dir-Mktg - Natural Decorations, Inc.; *pg.* 936, *pg.* 5
Grote, Michael, Dir-Channel Mktg-Americas - Juniper Networks, Inc.; *pg.* 1260, *pg.* 286
Groth, Lindsay, Sr Mgr-Mktg - University of Michigan; *pg.* 609, *pg.* 867
Groth, Terri, Mgr-Mktg Comm - Bemis Healthcare Packaging; *pg.* 1453, *pg.* 1885
Groth, Terri V., Mgr-Mktg Comm - Bemis Company, Inc.; *pg.* 1453, *pg.* 1882
Groth, Urs, Head-Mktg Comm RXE - Mettler-Toledo International Inc.; *pg.* 1423, *pg.* 1441
Grothaus, Cheri, Mgr-Creative Svcs - Ceridian Corporation; *pg.* 371, *pg.* 932
Grothe, Nathan, Category Mgr-Mdse - Recreational Equipment, Inc.; *pg.* 1843, *pg.* 1821
Grotheer, Bill, Mgr-Procurement & Adv - Bristol-Myers Squibb Company; *pg.* 1509, *pg.* 1206
Groty, Amanda, Sr Dir & Head-Comm-PayPal EMEA - PayPal Inc.; *pg.* 1274, *pg.* 248
Ground, Kelly, Sr Mgr-Digital Mktg - HSN, Inc.; *pg.* 291, *pg.* 462
Grouw, Lauren Van, Specialist-Comm-Social Media & Online Mktg - International Paper Company; *pg.* 1460, *pg.* 1644
Grove, Bob, VP-PR-Keystone Reg - Comcast Cable Communications, Inc.; *pg.* 276, *pg.* 1560
Grove, Loring, Brand Mgr-Global - Streamlight Inc.; *pg.* 1306, *pg.* 1527
Grove, Lucinda, Mgr-Adv & Media - Helzberg's Diamond Shops, Inc.; *pg.* 6, *pg.* 984
Grover, Betsey, VP-Investment Product & Strategy - FMR LLC (Fidelity Investments); *pg.* 759, *pg.* 794
Grover, Chase, Dir-Interactive Mktg - Ameriprise Financial, Inc.; *pg.* 715, *pg.* 930
Grover, Jyotsna, Mgr-PR-Infrastructure & Networking Grp - Broadcom Corporation; *pg.* 364, *pg.* 108
Grover, Kelley, Sr Mgr-Global Brand Operational Governance - Deloitte & Touche USA LLP; *pg.* 743, *pg.* 1222
Grover, Matt, Dir-Online Mktg - CareerBuilder, LLC; *pg.* 1234, *pg.* 568
Grover, Matthew, VP & Gen Mgr-Comml Sls - Cablevision Systems Corporation; *pg.* 272, *pg.* 1141
Grover, Peri, Dir-Product Mgmt - Overland Storage, Inc.; *pg.* 451, *pg.* 205
Groves, Brian, Mgr-Mktg - Ventura Foods, LLC; *pg.* 908, *pg.* 49
Groves, Eva, Sr Mgr-Comm - Amgen Inc.; *pg.* 1493, *pg.* 291
Groves, Sarah, Sr Mgr-Brand Mktg & Integrated Mktg - AT&T Mobility LLC; *pg.* 619, *pg.* 488
Groves, Tina, Product Mgr - IBM Canada Limited; *pg.* 411, *pg.* 1923
Grow, Matthew, Dir-Mktg-Sys & Life Sciences - Luminex Corporation; *pg.* 1421, *pg.* 1664
Growdon, John, Sr Dir-Channel Bus Dev-Data Center & Enterprise Networking - Cisco Systems, Inc.; *pg.* 372, *pg.* 240
Grubb, Jim, VP-Emerging Technologies Mktg - Cisco Systems, Inc.; *pg.* 372, *pg.* 240
Grubbs, Molly, Strategist-Creative - Tumblr, Inc.; *pg.* 1285, *pg.* 1305
Grubbs, Todd A, Sr Dir-People Dev & Sys-Field Ops - Chick-fil-A, Inc.; *pg.* 1721, *pg.* 492
Grube, Nancy, VP & Sr Dir-Art - Bank of America Corporation; *pg.* 718, *pg.* 1362
Gruber, Ian, Sr Mgr-Customer Insights & Analytics - Adobe Systems Incorporated; *pg.* 342, *pg.* 235
Gruber, Jodi, Assoc VP-Mktg - MARTHA STEWART LIVING OMNIMEDIA, INC.; *pg.* 1661, *pg.* 1256
Gruber, Sara, Sr Brand Mgr-Mktg & Comm - San Antonio Convention & Visitors Bureau; *pg.* 1004, *pg.* 1742
Gruber, Tom, Mgr-Sls-Natl - KLW Plastics, Inc.; *pg.* 1463, *pg.* 1465
Gruber, Tom, Sr Mgr-Sls Strategy & Reporting - StarKist Foods Inc.; *pg.* 898, *pg.* 1581
Grubnich, Ann, Sr Dir-Sls-Midwest - VeriFone Systems, Inc.; *pg.* 487, *pg.* 251
Grudt, Heather, Dir-Digital Mktg Strategy-Global Mktg - Carlson Wagonlit Travel; *pg.* 1902, *pg.* 948
Gruen, Shera, Head-Prevnar 13 Pediatrics & Dir-Mktg - Pfizer Inc.; *pg.* 1581, *pg.* 1278
Grueneberg, David, Sr VP-Adv & Mktg & Head-Strategic Sourcing - Citigroup Inc.; *pg.* 735, *pg.* 1212
Gruener, Elaine A., VP-Mktg & HR - Hannay Reels Inc.; *pg.* 1344, *pg.* 1351
Grueter, Janet, Sr Mgr-Media Plng & Buying - Cincinnati Bell Inc.; *pg.* 1871, *pg.* 1410
Gruezo, Kimberly, Mgr-Mktg - Hill-Rom Holdings, Inc.; *pg.* 1542, *pg.* 673
Grum, Darci, Sr Mgr-Mktg - Sears Holdings Corporation; *pg.* 1784, *pg.* 618
Grummert, Traci, VP-Mktg - Complete Nutrition; *pg.* 1517, *pg.* 1014
Grundy, Leslie, Sr Mgr-PR - The Timberland Company; *pg.* 1821, *pg.* 1039
Grundy, Mary, Sr Dir-Global Innovation Mktg - Visa Inc.; *pg.* 816, *pg.* 230
Grundy, Mary, Sr Dir-Global Innovation Mktg - Visa U.S.A., Inc.; *pg.* 817, *pg.* 231
Grunkraut, Ariel, Dir-Mktg-Brazil - Burger King Corporation; *pg.* 1719, *pg.* 440
Grusman, Joe, Head-Search Engine Mktg & Emerging Platforms - Zappos.com, Inc.; *pg.* 1291, *pg.* 1030
Gruss, Helga, Dir-Trade Mktg - Pinnacle Foods Group LLC; *pg.* 889, *pg.* 1104
Gruszka, Angela, Dir-Mktg & Comm - ABC Carpet & Home Inc.; *pg.* 912, *pg.* 1185
Grylls, Jonathan A.R., Chief Strategy Officer, Sec, VP & Dir - Dover Saddlery, Inc.; *pg.* 1833, *pg.* 829
Gryp, Catherine, Mgr-PR - CarMax, Inc.; *pg.* 167, *pg.* 1800
Gryzwa, Natalie, Sr Mgr-Mktg-Global Retail - The Donna Karan Company LLC; *pg.* 23, *pg.* 1225
Grzanowski, Cynthia, Dir-Mktg-Single Ticket Sls - Minnesota Orchestra; *pg.* 563, *pg.* 940
Grzesiak, Christie, Project Specialist-Global Product Commercialization - Beam Suntory Inc.; *pg.* 1957, *pg.* 599
Grzeslo, Ken, Mgr-Events Mktg - Chicago Zoological Society, Inc.; *pg.* 539, *pg.* 559
Gschwender, Ashley, Specialist-Mktg - Consumers Energy Company; *pg.* 1938, *pg.* 893
Gschwind, Michael, VP-Sls & Mktg - Bodine Electric Company; *pg.* 1318, *pg.* 641
Gu, Lucy, Engr-Technical Mktg - Intel Corporation; *pg.* 645, *pg.* 266
Gu, W., Dir-Engrg-Power Products - Microsemi Corporation; *pg.* 435, *pg.* 41
Guadagni, Gualtiero, VP-Sls & Mktg - Spectral Diagnostics Inc.; *pg.* 1430, *pg.* 1943
Guadalupe, Loreani, Specialist-PR - Molina Healthcare, Inc.; *pg.* 1569, *pg.* 123
Guaderrama, Julie, Mgr-Event Mktg - Save the Queen, LLC.; *pg.* 1111, *pg.* 124
Guagliano, John, VP-Mktg & Brdcst - Washington Nationals, L.P.; *pg.* 591, *pg.* 407
Guajardo, Marcel, Sr Product Mgr - DISH Network Corporation; *pg.* 283, *pg.* 325
Guanella, Michael, Sr Product Mgr - Hormel Foods Corporation; *pg.* 863, *pg.* 915
Guarasi, Karen, Reg VP-Adv - Daily Record; *pg.* 1633, *pg.* 1103
Guardia, Laura D., Brand Mgr - Pfizer Inc.; *pg.* 1581, *pg.* 1278
Guargena, John, VP-Sls & Mktg-Global - Laird & Company, Inc.; *pg.* 1966, *pg.* 1119
Guastaferro, Nicholas, Dir-Mktg-ABSOLUT - Pernod Ricard USA, Inc.; *pg.* 1968, *pg.* 1332
Gubasta, Dan, Brand Mgr-Dodge - FCA US LLC; *pg.* 170, *pg.* 868
Guberer, Len, Sr Mgr-Sls Ops - Church & Dwight Co., Inc.; *pg.* 1153, *pg.* 1063
Gubitosi, Laura, Mgr-Mktg - Fisher-Price, Inc.; *pg.* 953, *pg.* 1156
Gubrud, Scott, Dir-Sls & Mktg - Four Seasons Hotels Limited; *pg.* 1092, *pg.* 1938
Gubser, Charles, Specialist-Mktg Product-Gearing - Baldor Electric Company; *pg.* 1316, *pg.* 32

First page reference indicates Business Class Edition
Second page reference indicates Geographic Edition

Gubser, Urs, Product Mgr-Emerging Payments COE - Citigroup Inc.; *pg.* 735, *pg.* 1212
Gucker, Cody, Planner-Media Sls - CBS Corporation; *pg.* 273, *pg.* 1210
Guckian, Dale, Mgr-Product Support-North America - Clark Material Handling Company; *pg.* 1323, *pg.* 729
Gudahl, Kelley, Dir-Digital Mktg - The Hearst Corporation; *pg.* 1649, *pg.* 1239
Gudat, Sylvia, Dir-Mktg Tech & Svcs - Citrix Systems, Inc.; *pg.* 375, *pg.* 424
Gudell, Svenja, Sr Dir-Economic Res - Zillow Group, Inc.; *pg.* 1292, *pg.* 1843
Gudgel, Pam, Dir-Policy Watch Product Dev - LexisNexis Group; *pg.* 1658, *pg.* 1446
Gudipudi, Rohit, Mgr-Mktg Automation - The Dun & Bradstreet Corp.; *pg.* 1637, *pg.* 1120
Gudorf, Craig, Dir-Product Mktg-LifeWorks-EAP & Wellness - Ceridian Corporation; *pg.* 371, *pg.* 932
Guellnitz, Lou, Dir-North American Sls - Air Techniques, Inc.; *pg.* 1487, *pg.* 1178
Guelzim, Anna, Mgr-Global Mktg-Tennis - Wilson Sporting Goods Co.; *pg.* 1848, *pg.* 596
Guempel, Eric, VP-Product Strategy & Program Mgmt - ImmunoGen, Inc.; *pg.* 1544, *pg.* 851
Guenette, Isabel, Product Mgr-Nest - Google Inc.; *pg.* 1249, *pg.* 153
Guenther, Caitlyn, Dir-Mktg-The Lincoln Group - The Northwestern Mutual Life Insurance Company; *pg.* 1212, *pg.* 1879
Guenther, Eric, Gen Mgr-Mktg - Ford Motor Company; *pg.* 172, *pg.* 876
Guerin, Aude, Sr Dir-Product Mktg - Zynga Inc.; *pg.* 1292, *pg.* 235
Guerin, Cheryl, Exec VP-Grp Exec Global Products & Solutions-US Markets - MasterCard Incorporated; *pg.* 779, *pg.* 1325
Guerin, Cheryl, Exec VP-Grp Exec Global Products & Solutions-US Markets - MasterCard Worldwide Inc.; *pg.* 780, *pg.* 988
Guerin, Jean, Sr VP-Media Rels - Sony Pictures Entertainment Inc.; *pg.* 309, *pg.* 72
Guerino, Patrick, Specialist-Mktg - MetLife, Inc.; *pg.* 1208, *pg.* 1258
Guerra, Andre, Sr Dir-Reg Therapeutic Area Pain & CNS Latin America - Pfizer Inc.; *pg.* 1581, *pg.* 1278
Guerra, Angelica, Sr VP & Mng Dir-Production-Latin America & US - Sony Pictures Entertainment Inc.; *pg.* 309, *pg.* 72
Guerra, Edna, Program Mgr-Comml-Integrated Mktg Plng - Kimberly-Clark Corporation; *pg.* 1461, *pg.* 1720
Guerra, Jose, Analyst-Fin-Product Control - Citigroup Inc.; *pg.* 735, *pg.* 1212
Guerra, Marcelo, VP-Digital Mktg - Showtime Networks Inc.; *pg.* 308, *pg.* 1291
Guerra, Olavo, Dir-Latin American Sls & Mktg-Annuities - Lexmark International, Inc.; *pg.* 427, *pg.* 730
Guerrasio, Emily, Sr Mgr-Digital Mktg - American Express Company; *pg.* 712, *pg.* 1190
Guerrero, Ariana, Office Mgr & Coord-Mktg - State Farm Mutual Automobile Insurance Co.; *pg.* 1218, *pg.* 557
Guerrero, Armando, VP-Integrated Sls Mktg - Entravision Communications Corporation; *pg.* 285, *pg.* 273
Guerrero, Chris, Mgr-Mktg-Global - Shell Lubricants; *pg.* 217, *pg.* 1714
Guerrero, Gabriel, Mgr-Mktg - Nu Skin Enterprises, Inc.; *pg.* 518, *pg.* 1755
Guerrero, Glafiro, Sr Engr-Product - Corning Incorporated; *pg.* 1122, *pg.* 1154
Guerrier, Fabrice, Mgr-Mktg - STMicroelectronics, Inc.; *pg.* 676, *pg.* 1671
Guerrieri, John, VP-Sls-Central Reg - Hill Phoenix Inc.; *pg.* 1072, *pg.* 528
Guerrieri, Nicholas, Sr Mgr-Mktg - JPMorgan Chase & Co.; *pg.* 772, *pg.* 1246
Guerriero, Zach, Asst VP-Sls & Bus Dev-Media Solutions-MasterCard Advisors - MasterCard Worldwide Inc.; *pg.* 780, *pg.* 988
Guerro, Jose, Product Mgr-BMW i, BMW M, BMW Individual & Alpina Vehicles - BMW of North America, LLC; *pg.* 166, *pg.* 1133
Guerten, Nick, Sr Assoc Brand Mgr - The Kraft Heinz Company; *pg.* 871, *pg.* 641
Guertin, Courtney, Dir-Mktg & Comm - Media General, Inc.; *pg.* 297, *pg.* 1803
Guest, Tammy, Dir-Digital Sls - KTRK Television, Inc.; *pg.* 295, *pg.* 1709
Guether, Rachel, Sr Dir-Fin & Global Supply Chain - Pfizer Inc.; *pg.* 1581, *pg.* 1278
Guetzke, Julie, Mgr-Technical Sls - Super Sky Products, Inc.; *pg.* 113, *pg.* 1871
Guffey, Brent, Dir-Sls & Mktg Special Products Div - Winegard Company; *pg.* 688, *pg.* 702
Guggenbickler, Vicki, Head-Mktg Program - General Electric Company; *pg.* 1297, *pg.* 347
Guggenheim, Stephanie, Sr Dir-Mktg - Neutrogena Corporation; *pg.* 517, *pg.* 137
Guggino, Jon, VP-Mktg-Robert Mondavi & Premium Wines - Constellation Brands, Inc.; *pg.* 1960, *pg.* 1348
Guglielmino, Peter, CTO-Media & Entertainment - International Business Machines Corporation; *pg.* 418, *pg.* 1138
Guglielmo, Michael, Dir-Digital Sls - Answers Corporation; *pg.* 1229, *pg.* 1195
Guida, Chris, Sr Dir-Sls - Merck & Co., Inc.; *pg.* 1566, *pg.* 1077
Guida, Renee, Sr Mgr-Retail Mktg - LEGO Systems, Inc.; *pg.* 961, *pg.* 346
Guidetti, Allison, Sr Mgr-Mktg - The Weather Channel LLC; *pg.* 320, *pg.* 523
Guido, Frank C., Dir-Mktg Comm - Windstream Corporation; *pg.* 321, *pg.* 34
Guido, Rosalyn, Analyst-Global Mktg Data - Thermo Fisher Scientific Inc.; *pg.* 1431, *pg.* 854
Guidotti, Greg, Sr Dir-Mktg-Ready-to-Drink Beverages - The Kraft Heinz Company; *pg.* 871, *pg.* 641
Guidry, Bianca, Dir-Mktg - Real Mex Restaurants, Inc.; *pg.* 1746, *pg.* 75
Guidry, Steven, VP-Asset Mgmt & Mktg - The Reynolds & Reynolds Company; *pg.* 461, *pg.* 1457
Guignard, Gayla H., Chief Strategy Officer - Alexander Graham Bell Association for the Deaf and Hard of Hearing; *pg.* 126, *pg.* 393
Guilbault, Laura, Dir-Global Brand Strategy & Mktg-Disney Princess - Hasbro, Inc.; *pg.* 954, *pg.* 1603
Guiles, Cindy, Sr Product Mgr - Datamax Corporation; *pg.* 1633, *pg.* 453
Guilfoyle, Anne, Sr Mgr-Brand Building-Dove Masterbrand & Personal Wash - Unilever Canada Inc.; *pg.* 903, *pg.* 1946
Guilfoyle, Ellen, Sr Mgr-Performance Excellence - Ocean Spray Cranberries, Inc.; *pg.* 887, *pg.* 827
Guill, Christopher, Graphic Designer & Planner-Sls - Six Flags Entertainment Corporation; *pg.* 583, *pg.* 1698
Guillemette, Gilles, VP & Gen Mgr-Animal Health Pharmaceutical & Nutritional Product - Henry Schein, Inc.; *pg.* 1541, *pg.* 1180
Guillemette, Lucie, VP-Revenue Mgmt & Intl Sls - Air Canada; *pg.* 1896, *pg.* 1902
Guillen, Jerome, VP-Svc & Sls Ops - Tesla Motors, Inc.; *pg.* 191, *pg.* 178
Guimond, Leah, Mgr-Internal Mktg & Enterprise Comm - Target Corporation; *pg.* 1786, *pg.* 942
Guimond, Paul, Sr Mgr-Mktg - Salomon North America, Inc.; *pg.* 1844, *pg.* 1753
Guimont, Jill, Sr Mgr-Neurology Mktg-DBS Therapy - Medtronic, Inc.; *pg.* 1564, *pg.* 939
Guinan, Kristin, Dir-Mktg-FITNESS Magazine - Meredith Corporation; *pg.* 1663, *pg.* 705
Guinand, Maria, Sr Mgr-Consumer Mktg-Oral Health Care Whitening - Philips Electronics North America; *pg.* 662, *pg.* 782
Guinup, Jean, VP-Mktg-Northeast Reg - Simon Property Group, Inc.; *pg.* 1112, *pg.* 690
Guise, Katherine, Brand Mgr & Specialist-HR - Capital One Financial Corporation; *pg.* 730, *pg.* 1789
Guitano, Anton, COO-Local Media, Radio & TV Stations - CBS Corporation; *pg.* 273, *pg.* 1210
Guitard, Jessica R., Mgr-Product Mktg-WFO Software - Hewlett-Packard Company; *pg.* 404, *pg.* 175
Gujarati, Shailendra, Sr Dir-Mktg & Gen Mgr-on GoSmart Mobile & Univision Mobile - T-Mobile US, Inc.; *pg.* 676, *pg.* 1816
Gulbrandsen, Sarah, Sr Mgr-Global HQ & Field Comm - The Gap, Inc.; *pg.* 1770, *pg.* 218
Gulersen, Kobi, Head-Digital Mktg-Global & Dir - MasterCard International, Inc.; *pg.* 780, *pg.* 1326
Guljord, Jon, Sr Dir-Mobile Mktg - Expedia, Inc.; *pg.* 1244, *pg.* 1814
Gulla, Peter, VP-Mktg - Hughes Network Systems LLC; *pg.* 643, *pg.* 770
Gullapalli, Neelima, Sr Dir-Product Mgmt - EZCORP, Inc.; *pg.* 750, *pg.* 1662
Gullerian, Daniel, Mgr-Sls-Latin American - AMF Bakery Systems; *pg.* 1313, *pg.* 1800
Gullett, Craig, Mgr-Comml & OEM Mktg - Old World Industries, Inc.; *pg.* 1175, *pg.* 641
Gulliksen, Vance, Mgr-PR - Carnival Corporation; *pg.* 1902, *pg.* 441
Gullo, Gaye, Sr VP-Corp Mktg - Penn National Gaming, Inc.; *pg.* 574, *pg.* 1595
Gullotta, Michele, Mgr-Digital Mktg - Toys "R" Us, Inc.; *pg.* 968, *pg.* 1130
Gulotta, Steve, VP-Sls - Lennar Homes, Inc.; *pg.* 1101, *pg.* 443
Gultekin, Baris, Dir-Product Mgmt-Android - Google Inc.; *pg.* 1249, *pg.* 153
Gulvik, Jennifer, Sr VP-Mktg & Dir-Creative - Houlihan's Restaurants, Inc.; *pg.* 1731, *pg.* 716
Gumahad, Allison, Sr Mgr-Bus Dev-Proposal - Amazon.com, Inc.; *pg.* 1226, *pg.* 1831
Gumbs, Alex, Sr Rep-Sls - Medtronic, Inc.; *pg.* 1564, *pg.* 939
Gumbs, Karen, Sr Mgr-PR - Loblaw Companies Limited; *pg.* 1026, *pg.* 1918
Gump, Kevin, VP-Enterprise Mktg Ops - Anthem, Inc.; *pg.* 1192, *pg.* 683
Gumpert, Ben, Sr VP-Mktg & Strategy - Sacramento Kings; *pg.* 579, *pg.* 197
Gumpf, Rob, VP-Sls - Summit Plastic Co.; *pg.* 1470, *pg.* 1403
Gumudavelly, Srinivas, Engr-Product Dev - Ford Motor Company; *pg.* 172, *pg.* 876
Gunaca, James, Mgr-Digital Mktg - Amazon.com, Inc.; *pg.* 1226, *pg.* 1831
Gunawan, Stacy, Sr Analyst-Global Mktg Res - Allergan, Inc.; *pg.* 1491, *pg.* 106
Gunderson, Ash Hans, Sr Dir-ECommerce Ops-US - Expedia, Inc.; *pg.* 1244, *pg.* 1814
Gunderson, Brady, Dir-Product Dev - Netflix, Inc.; *pg.* 1269, *pg.* 141
Gunderson, Cory, Mgr-Mktg Comm - Donaldson Company, Inc.; *pg.* 1329, *pg.* 917
Gunderson, Jenna, Mgr-Sls Mktg - Pandora Media Inc.; *pg.* 1273, *pg.* 172
Gunderson, Lynda S., Program Mgr-Mktg & Channel Enablement - Hewlett-Packard Company; *pg.* 404, *pg.* 175
Gunderson, Tanya, Coord-Experienced Mktg - S.C. Johnson & Son, Inc.; *pg.* 334, *pg.* 1889
Gundert, Reagan, Program Mgr-Mktg - MasterCard International, Inc.; *pg.* 780, *pg.* 1326
Gundler, Daniel, Dir-Global Mktg-Informatics - Siemens Healthcare Diagnostics; *pg.* 673, *pg.* 604
Gundler, Lauren, Sr Mgr-Mktg & Sls Ops - Luxottica Retail; *pg.* 8, *pg.* 1460
Gunduz, Sean, Sr Product Mgr-Large Venue & Corp Projectors - Epson America Inc.; *pg.* 394, *pg.* 122
Gune, Aniket, Dir-Product Mktg-Amazon - Audible, Inc.; *pg.* 1230, *pg.* 1095
Gunn, Andrew, Mgr-Natl Mktg-iGeneral & Color Press - Xerox Canada Inc.; *pg.* 494, *pg.* 1930
Gunn, Erica, VP-Mktg - Equifax Inc.; *pg.* 748, *pg.* 504
Gunn, Richard, Sr VP-Mdsg & Mktg - Weis Markets, Inc.; *pg.* 1037, *pg.* 1588
Gunnell, Ray, Mgr-Social Media - Liberty Tax Service; *pg.* 776, *pg.* 1810
Gunnufson, Scott R., VP-Comml Sls, Mktg & Customer Support - Rockwell Collins, Inc.; *pg.* 234, *pg.* 702
Gunsberg, Joanne, Dir-Networks Mktg - Sony Pictures Entertainment Inc.; *pg.* 309, *pg.* 72
Gunter, Rembert, Sr Mgr-Pur-Capital, MRO & Ops Pur - Boehringer Ingelheim Pharmaceuticals, Inc.; *pg.* 1507, *pg.* 368
Gunther, Adam, Program Dir-Cloud Platform Svcs Product Mgmt & Developer Advocacy - IBM; *pg.* 410, *pg.* 1449
Gunther, Nicole, Dir-Creative - DIRECTV Group Holdings, LLC; *pg.* 281, *pg.* 79
Gunther, Rachel, Mgr-Mktg - Starbucks Corporation; *pg.* 897, *pg.* 1840
Guntrum, Kryssa, Sr Dir-Innovation & Tech Corp Comm - Visa Inc.; *pg.* 816, *pg.* 230
Gunzenheiser, Janet, Asst VP & Strategist-Social Media - BOK Financial Corporation; *pg.* 726, *pg.* 1489
Guo, Christina, Mgr-Product Mktg-Mobile Apps - Microsoft Corporation; *pg.* 435, *pg.* 1824
Guo, Jack, Sr Mgr-US Channel Sls Programs & Enablement - Apple Inc.; *pg.* 350, *pg.* 73
Guo, Lydia, Dir-Mktg - Medtronic, Inc.; *pg.* 1564, *pg.* 939
Guo, Xin, Principal & Engr-SSD Media Sys Engrg - Intel Corporation; *pg.* 645, *pg.* 266
Guomundsson, Atli B., Sr Mgr-Corp Fin - Century Aluminum of

West Virginia, Inc.; *pg.* 74, *pg.* 1851
Guppenberger, Lauren, Specialist-PR - CACI International Inc.; *pg.* 367, *pg.* 1773
Gupta, Amita, Mgr-Channel Mktg - Toshiba America, Inc.; *pg.* 681, *pg.* 1302
Gupta, Ankit, Product Mgr - LinkedIn Corporation; *pg.* 1262, *pg.* 160
Gupta, Ashish, Mgr-Product Line - Intel Corporation; *pg.* 645, *pg.* 266
Gupta, Devyani, Head-Reg Mktg-Americas - Rakuten.com Shopping; *pg.* 1277, *pg.* 41
Gupta, Dipayan, Head-Social Media Mktg & Strategy - New York Life Insurance Company; *pg.* 1211, *pg.* 1268
Gupta, Girish, Sr Dir-Sls-Starbucks Brands North America Beverages - PepsiCo, Inc.; *pg.* 259, *pg.* 1327
Gupta, Kampta, Rep-Technical Sls-South Asia - Petroferm Inc.; *pg.* 1177, *pg.* 616
Gupta, Manik, Dir-Product Mgmt-Google Maps - Google Inc.; *pg.* 1249, *pg.* 153
Gupta, Manish, Exec VP & Gen Mgr-OPEN Products - American Express Company; *pg.* 712, *pg.* 1190
Gupta, Sanjay, CMO & Exec VP - The Allstate Corporation; *pg.* 1189, *pg.* 639
Gupta, Saurabh, Product Mgr - Google Inc.; *pg.* 1249, *pg.* 153
Gupta, Sean, Sr Dir-Bus Dev - Time Warner Cable Inc.; *pg.* 312, *pg.* 1301
Gupta, Shantanu, Dir-Solutions Mktg & Bus Plng - Intel Corporation; *pg.* 645, *pg.* 266
Gupta, Sonia, Sr Mgr-Mktg - Penguin Random House; *pg.* 1675, *pg.* 1276
Gupta, Sonia, Assoc Dir-Mktg-Random House Children's Books - Penguin Random House Children's Books; *pg.* 1676, *pg.* 1277
Gupta, Upasana, Mgr-Mktg Comm-Global - Microsoft Corporation; *pg.* 435, *pg.* 1824
Gupta, Vikram, Specialist-Product Mktg - Canon U.S.A., Inc.; *pg.* 1404, *pg.* 1178
Gupta, Yamini, Mgr-Product Mktg - Google Inc.; *pg.* 1249, *pg.* 153
Guran, Jennifer, Sr Mgr - Herbalife International of America, Inc.; *pg.* 1541, *pg.* 132
Gurchiek, Chris, Head-Shopper Mktg Team - Newell Rubbermaid Inc.; *pg.* 1128, *pg.* 515
Gurdgiel, Anne, Mgr-Mktg Svcs - ClubCorp, Inc.; *pg.* 1086, *pg.* 1677
Gurgel, Autumn, Mgr-Category Mktg - Target Corporation; *pg.* 1786, *pg.* 942
Gurion, Hope, Chief Product Officer - CareerBuilder, LLC; *pg.* 1234, *pg.* 568
Guritza, Elisa C., Dir-Mktg Comm - Applied Industrial Technologies, Inc.; *pg.* 199, *pg.* 1428
Gurjar, Rajesh, Mgr-Bus Partner Mktg - IBM; *pg.* 410, *pg.* 1449
Gurkar, Deepti, Brand Mgr-Vodka & Liqueurs Portfolio - Beam Suntory Inc.; *pg.* 1957, *pg.* 599
Gurley, Greg W., VP-Product Mgmt & Natl Accounts - Huttig Building Products, Inc.; *pg.* 88, *pg.* 998
Gurley, Richard T., Sr Dir-Mktg & OEM Mgmt - STERIS Corporation; *pg.* 1597, *pg.* 1464
Gurner, Rosita, Coord-Mktg - Pfizer Inc.; *pg.* 1581, *pg.* 1278
Gurnett, Kendra, Sr Mgr-Mktg-Brand Strategy - Nordstrom, Inc.; *pg.* 1779, *pg.* 1837
Gurney, Andrew, Mgr-Sls - Vilter Manufacturing LLC; *pg.* 1078, *pg.* 1856
Guro, Dave, Product Mgr-Hydrogen Generation & Purification-Global - Air Products and Chemicals, Inc.; *pg.* 1145, *pg.* 1513
Gurry, Lisa, Sr Dir-PR-Xbox - Microsoft Corporation; *pg.* 435, *pg.* 1824
Gursha, Rob, VP-Consumer Mktg - Gannett Co., Inc.; *pg.* 1643, *pg.* 1790
Gurstein, Barry, Sr VP-Television Mktg-Worldwide - Metro-Goldwyn-Mayer Inc.; *pg.* 298, *pg.* 47
Gurule, Alex, Sr Mgr-Mktg - Vogue Magazine; *pg.* 1700, *pg.* 1311
Gurumoorthy, Bala, Dir-Mktg Intelligence - Ferrero U.S.A., Inc.; *pg.* 1852, *pg.* 1121
Gusarov, Sergey, Mgr-Digital Mktg - CELSIUS HOLDINGS, INC.; *pg.* 239, *pg.* 411
Gusella, John, Dir-Sls & Southern Zone - Lightolier; *pg.* 1301, *pg.* 819
Gushurst, Don, Dir-Global Mktg Ops Svcs - Molex Incorporated; *pg.* 655, *pg.* 628
Guss, Lee, Sr Mgr-Mktg - Amgen Inc.; *pg.* 1493, *pg.* 291
Gusse, Angela, Assoc Dir-Mktg - Kellogg Company; *pg.* 831, *pg.* 870
Gust, Angela, Mgr-Global Mktg-ALPR Tech - 3M Company; *pg.* 1142, *pg.* 956
Gust, Jonathan, Dir-Media Rels - Villanova University; *pg.* 610, *pg.* 1589
Gust, Kim, Mgr-Social Media - The Vanguard Group, Inc.; *pg.* 816, *pg.* 1550
Gust, Lou, VP-Sls & Mktg-Electricity - Itron Inc.; *pg.* 422, *pg.* 1822
Gustafson, Laura, Head-ECommerce Shopper Mktg Baby & Child Care Brands - Kimberly-Clark Corporation; *pg.* 1461, *pg.* 1720
Gustafson, Lori, Dir-Digital Mktg & ECommerce - SeaWorld Parks & Entertainment LLC; *pg.* 582, *pg.* 456
Gustafson, Marc, Sr Dir-Scouting Ops - Colorado Rockies Baseball Club, Ltd.; *pg.* 542, *pg.* 317
Gustavson, Steve, Grp Dir-Creative-Enterprise - Adobe Systems Incorporated; *pg.* 342, *pg.* 235
Gustin, Rick, Product Mgr-EPDM - Johns Manville Corporation; *pg.* 89, *pg.* 320
Gutbezahl, Shaunmarie, Dir-Creative - Fred Meyer Stores, Inc.; *pg.* 1769, *pg.* 1502
Gutelius, Robert, Principal-Mktg Analytics & Svcs - IMS Health, Inc.; *pg.* 1544, *pg.* 344
Guter, Pia, Dir-Mktg - Xoom Corporation; *pg.* 1289, *pg.* 234
Guter, Pia Palpal-latoc, Dir-Mktg - Xerox Corporation; *pg.* 494, *pg.* 365
Guterman, Sofya, Mgr-Mktg-Brand Campaigns - Best Buy Co., Inc.; *pg.* 1761, *pg.* 954
Guth, Michael, Exec VP-Sls & Mktg - Madison Square Garden Network; *pg.* 297, *pg.* 1255
Guthrie, Ben, Brand Mgr-Chrysler Town & Country - FCA US LLC; *pg.* 170, *pg.* 868
Guthrie, John, VP-Sls Bus Dev & Partnerships - Daytona Beach Resort Area Convention & Visitors Bureau; *pg.* 991, *pg.* 420
Guthrie, Marjorie, Dir-Creative - Advanced Beauty Systems Inc.; *pg.* 498, *pg.* 1672
Guthrie, Mark, VP-Mobile Broadband Sls-Global - KVH Industries Inc; *pg.* 650, *pg.* 1602
Gutierrez, Ana, Asst Project Mgr-Adv - Macy's East; *pg.* 1777, *pg.* 1254
Gutierrez, Arinda, Mgr-Bus Svcs Mktg - Comcast Corporation; *pg.* 276, *pg.* 1560
Gutierrez, Becky, Dir-Mktg - Cardinal Health, Inc.; *pg.* 1512, *pg.* 1448
Gutierrez, Carol, Mgr-Hispanic Mktg & Brand Promotions - The Boston Beer Company, Inc.; *pg.* 239, *pg.* 790
Gutierrez, Derek, Reg Mgr-Mktg - PepsiCo, Inc.; *pg.* 259, *pg.* 1327
Gutierrez, Dianna, Head-SRT, Design & Motorsports PR - FCA US LLC; *pg.* 170, *pg.* 868
Gutierrez, Janelle, Asst Mgr-Channel Mktg - Janus Capital Group, Inc.; *pg.* 772, *pg.* 320
Gutierrez, Karen, Dir-Social Media-Corp Mktg-US Bank - U.S. Bancorp; *pg.* 815, *pg.* 945
Gutierrez, Katie, Mgr-Mktg - Bell Flavors & Fragrances, Inc.; *pg.* 501, *pg.* 640
Gutierrez, Maria, Mgr-Media, Integration & Comm - The Coca-Cola Company; *pg.* 240, *pg.* 493
Gutierrez, Michael, Dir-PR - Herbalife International of America, Inc.; *pg.* 1541, *pg.* 132
Gutierrez, Noemi, Program Mgr-Mktg - IBM Canada Limited; *pg.* 411, *pg.* 1923
Gutierrez, Patricia, VP & Head-PR - GFI Group Inc.; *pg.* 762, *pg.* 1234
Gutierrez, Stephanie, VP-Retail Mktg - Office Depot, Inc.; *pg.* 448, *pg.* 412
Gutierrez, Wendy, Mgr-Digital Mktg - The Valspar Corporation; *pg.* 1449, *pg.* 945
Gutierrez-Cook, Naomi, Dir-Channel Mktg - McKesson Corporation; *pg.* 1560, *pg.* 222
Gutman, Maria A., HR-Global Mktg & Design Groups - PepsiCo, Inc.; *pg.* 259, *pg.* 1327
Gutmann, Jaclyn E., Head-Intl & Mktg Comm Bus - Raytheon Company; *pg.* 233, *pg.* 854
Gutmore, Ryan, Dir-Mktg Ops - Chico's FAS, Inc.; *pg.* 21, *pg.* 427
Gutowski, Bob, VP-Mktg & ECommerce - Beall's, Inc.; *pg.* 1760, *pg.* 414
Gutsche, Manny, VP-Mktg - RF Industries, Ltd.; *pg.* 461, *pg.* 208
Gutstein, Pancho, Sr VP-Mdsg-North America - Puma North America, Inc.; *pg.* 1816, *pg.* 858
Gutterman, Marc, Planner-Digital Media - The New York Times Company; *pg.* 1668, *pg.* 1270
Guy, Donnell, Mgr-Mktg - Chemtura Corporation; *pg.* 1152, *pg.* 355
Guy, Gary W., Exec Dir-Sls, ECommerce, Omni-Channel & Mgmt Consulting - Hewlett-Packard Company; *pg.* 404, *pg.* 175
Guy, Melissa, Exec Dir-Sls - Cosmopolitan; *pg.* 1630, *pg.* 1218
Guyer, Courtney, Dir-Strategic Mktg-Global - LifeCell Corporation; *pg.* 1556, *pg.* 1045
Guyer, Lisa, Sr Dir-Adv Ops - comScore, Inc; *pg.* 1236, *pg.* 1798
Guymon, Wayne, VP & Gen Mgr-Sls - Fox Sports Net; *pg.* 288, *pg.* 131
Guyton, Penny, Sr Dir & Gen Mgr-Digital Imaging - IDEXX Laboratories, Inc.; *pg.* 1543, *pg.* 753
Guziec, Douglas A., Chief Strategy Officer & Sr VP-Strategy & Bus Dev - Rent-A-Center, Inc.; *pg.* 940, *pg.* 1734
Guzman, Cisoll, Specialist-Mktg - Pfizer Inc.; *pg.* 1581, *pg.* 1278
Guzman, Hugo, VP-Digital Mktg Grp - JPMorgan Chase & Co.; *pg.* 772, *pg.* 1246
Guzman, Josefina, Coord-Mktg - The Goldman Sachs Group, Inc.; *pg.* 762, *pg.* 1236
Guzman, Krystle, Specialist-Strategic Mktg - Nikon Inc.; *pg.* 1424, *pg.* 1181
Guzman, Lenis, Assoc Dir-Enterprises Mktg - Univision Communications Inc.; *pg.* 683, *pg.* 1307
Guzman, Mark, Dir-West Mktg - Calpine Corporation; *pg.* 1936, *pg.* 1702
Guzman, Michelle, Dir-Mktg - In-N-Out Burgers, Inc.; *pg.* 1732, *pg.* 111
Guzman, Natalie, Sr VP & Grp Dir-Affiliate Mktg - Fifth Third Bank, Indiana (Southern); *pg.* 753, *pg.* 678
Guzman, Rob, Mgr-Mktg - Penguin Random House; *pg.* 1675, *pg.* 1276
Guzman, Rob, Mgr-Mktg - Penguin Random House; *pg.* 1675, *pg.* 1276
Guzman, Sarah, Sr Dir-Mktg - PepsiCo, Inc.; *pg.* 259, *pg.* 1327
Guzman, Sherrie De, Dir-Creative - McKesson Corporation; *pg.* 1560, *pg.* 222
Guzman-Blanco, Bernardo, Asst Mgr-PR & Events-Latin America - Nintendo of America, Inc.; *pg.* 965, *pg.* 1829
Guzowski, Stephen, Reg Mgr-Sls - EAO Switch Corporation; *pg.* 1046, *pg.* 356
Guzzi, Michael, Dir-Digital Product Dev - Merriam-Webster, Inc.; *pg.* 1664, *pg.* 846
Gwizdz, Greg, Exec VP & Mgr-Sls-Natl - Wells Fargo & Company; *pg.* 819, *pg.* 232
Gwizdz, Holly, Program Mgr-Mktg-Distr Revenue Mktg - Cisco Systems, Inc.; *pg.* 372, *pg.* 240
Gwyn, Christy, Mgr-Mktg & Bus Dev - Costco Wholesale Corporation; *pg.* 1765, *pg.* 1820
Gwyn, Jennifer, Dir-Mktg & Promos - Southern States Cooperative, Inc.; *pg.* 1482, *pg.* 1804
Gyarmathy, Danielle, Mgr-Natl Sls-Baltimore Market - Comcast Corporation; *pg.* 276, *pg.* 1560

H

Ha, Lee, Dir-Product Mgmt & ECommerce - Live Nation Entertainment, Inc.; *pg.* 558, *pg.* 47
Ha, Thuy, Dir-Product Mgmt - CenturyLink, Inc.; *pg.* 1870, *pg.* 746
Haack, John, Pres-Enterprise Sls-Global - UPS Supply Chain Solutions, Inc.; *pg.* 1929, *pg.* 485
Haag, Anne, Asst Mgr-Mktg - Neiman Marcus, Inc.; *pg.* 30, *pg.* 1684
Haag, Jen, Dir-Segment Mktg - AdvancePierre Foods, Inc.; *pg.* 1714, *pg.* 1409
Haag, Rachel, Mgr-Channel Mktg - Symantec Corporation; *pg.* 479, *pg.* 1753
Haaksma, Barbara, VP-Corp Mktg & Comm - Milliken & Company; *pg.* 696, *pg.* 1622
Haarstad, Bill, Sr Dir-Mktg-Chicago Reg - Comcast Corporation; *pg.* 276, *pg.* 1560
Haas, Brad C., VP-Production - National Band & Tag Co.; *pg.* 1479, *pg.* 739
Haas, Janett, VP-Sls, Western & Central Reg - Forbes, Inc.; *pg.* 1641, *pg.* 1232
Haas, Jeff, VP-Specialty Products & Managed Healthcare - AbbVie Inc.; *pg.* 1486, *pg.* 638

Haas, Jennifer, Mgr-Mktg-Catering - McAlister's Deli; pg. 1737, pg. 484
Haas, Josiah, VP-Sls - Bud Industries, Inc.; pg. 627, pg. 1482
Haas, Karl, Mgr-Natl Sls-Architecturals - Electronic Theatre Controls, Inc.; pg. 1296, pg. 1872
Haas, Lauren, Asst Mgr-Mktg - Pepsi Beverages Company; pg. 258, pg. 1342
Haas, Mary, Strategist-Database Mktg - IBM; pg. 410, pg. 1449
Haas, Regina, Dir-Media Rels - LexisNexis Group; pg. 1658, pg. 1446
Haas, Sean C., VP-Production - National Band & Tag Co.; pg. 1479, pg. 739
Haas, Stacie, VP & Mgr-PR - Fifth Third Bancorp; pg. 752, pg. 1413
Haas, Tana Barton, Sr Dir-Residential Mktg - The ADT Corporation; pg. 612, pg. 409
Haas, Tara, VP-Products - LOGMEIN, INC.; pg. 428, pg. 861
Habben, David, Sr Strategist-Media-APJ - Akamai Technologies, Inc.; pg. 1226, pg. 807
Habbershaw, Sally, VP-Intl Programming, Production & Ops - A&E Television Networks, LLC; pg. 267, pg. 1185
Habberstad, Scott, Dir-Sls & Community Mktg - Alaska Airlines, Inc.; pg. 1897, pg. 1830
Haber, Jack J., VP-Adv & Digital-Global - Colgate-Palmolive Company; pg. 504, pg. 1215
Haberacker, Eric, Strategist-Mktg - The Vanguard Group, Inc.; pg. 816, pg. 1550
Haberkorn, B. J., Dir-Product Mgmt - Microsoft Corporation; pg. 435, pg. 1824
Haberlein, Steven C., VP-Sls - FUJIFILM Medical Systems USA, Inc.; pg. 1531, pg. 374
Haberman, Kasi M., Mgr-Mktg - General Growth Properties, Inc.; pg. 1093, pg. 574
Habib, Lori Abou, Dir-Calendar & Creative - SONIC Corp.; pg. 1750, pg. 1487
Habibi, Richard, VP-Mktg - Citigroup Inc.; pg. 735, pg. 1212
Habig, Jim, Mgr-Product Mktg - YouTube, LLC; pg. 1291, pg. 198
Habig, Lauren, Mgr-Mktg - salesforce.com, inc.; pg. 1278, pg. 226
Hable, James, Dir-Product Dev - Cox Communications, Inc.; pg. 279, pg. 501
Habouri, Georges, Engr-Mktg-Medium Voltage Power Products-Western & Central Canada - ABB Inc.; pg. 64, pg. 1959
Haby, Marissa, Specialist-Mktg - Philips Lighting; pg. 1303, pg. 806
Hace, Brian, VP-Products - Concur Technologies, Inc.; pg. 1236, pg. 1813
Hacherian Hofstede, Sona, Exec Dir-Creative & Mktg Svcs - New York Magazine; pg. 1667, pg. 1269
Hacherian, Sona, Exec Dir-Creative & Mktg Svcs - New York Magazine; pg. 1667, pg. 1269
Hachey, Shawna, Sr Mgr-Product Delivery & Insurance - Canadian Imperial Bank of Commerce; pg. 729, pg. 1935
Hachtel, Greg, Dir-Product Mktg - Siemens Process Industries and Drives; pg. 673, pg. 485
Hack, Jessica, Supvr-Mktg Comm - 3M Company; pg. 1142, pg. 956
Hacker, Chris, VP-Mktg & Design - Herman Miller, Inc.; pg. 926, pg. 913
Hacker, Holly, Dir-Direct Sls & Customer Experience - Vita-Mix Corporation; pg. 1139, pg. 1436
Hackerson, Charles, VP-Sls - SPS COMMERCE, INC.; pg. 472, pg. 942
Hackett, Alicia, Sr Dir-Digital Sls - The E.W. Scripps Company; pg. 1639, pg. 1412
Hackett, Christine, Dir-Adv Production - Barneys New York, Inc.; pg. 38, pg. 1201
Hackett, John, Sr VP-Global Juices & Still Beverages-Global Mktg - The Coca-Cola Company; pg. 240, pg. 493
Hackett, Kelly, Dir-Adv, Digital, Youth & Sponsorships - AT&T Mobility LLC; pg. 619, pg. 488
Hackett, Kerry, Dir-Mktg - The Allstate Corporation; pg. 1189, pg. 639
Hackett, Laura, Sr Dir-Learning & Dev - MillerCoors LLC; pg. 255, pg. 582
Hackett, Lisa, First VP & Dir-Brand & Mktg Comm - First Niagara Bank; pg. 756, pg. 1174
Hackett, Tracy, VP-Mktg - Royal Bank of Canada; pg. 800, pg. 1942
Hackney, Ashlee, Coord-Adv Ops - Scripps Networks Interactive, Inc.; pg. 1279, pg. 1638
Hackney, Bill, VP-Mdsg - AutoZone, Inc.; pg. 200, pg. 1641
Hackney, R. Hodges, Pres-Sls-Intl - Kidron, Inc.; pg. 181, pg. 1457
Haddad, Matt, Sr Dir-Groups, Suites & Outbound Sls - Colorado Rockies Baseball Club, Ltd.; pg. 542, pg. 317
Haddock, Casey, Product Mgr - General Electric Company; pg. 1297, pg. 347
Haderer, Jessica, Coord-Sls & Mktg - IAC Industries, Inc.; pg. 929, pg. 48
Hadiaris, Regis, Dir-Internet Mktg - Quicken Loans, Inc.; pg. 797, pg. 884
Hadiatmodjo, Ari, Coord-Adv - Barnes & Noble, Inc.; pg. 1619, pg. 1201
Hadipanah, Arash, Sr Product Mgr-Mobile - Rue La La; pg. 1278, pg. 800
Hadley, Kirsten, Sr Dir-Innovation - Georgia-Pacific LLC; pg. 1458, pg. 507
Haeberle, Brad, VP-Mktg - Siemens Building Technologies, Inc.; pg. 1376, pg. 560
Haeberle, Brad, VP-Mktg - Siemens Corporation; pg. 803, pg. 1291
Haeflein, Rich, Acct Mgr-Adv - SUPERVALU, Inc.; pg. 1035, pg. 924
Haener, Kenneth, Dir-Media - Pfizer Inc.; pg. 1581, pg. 1278
Haener, Steve, Sr Mgr-Chevrolet Media Ops - General Motors Company; pg. 175, pg. 881
Haenggi, Jamie ROSAND, CMO - Protection One, Inc.; pg. 665, pg. 715
Haenisch, Julie, Sr Mgr-Text Promo - Princeton University Press; pg. 1678, pg. 1112
Haer, Gary, VP-Sls & Mktg - Renewable Energy Group, Inc.; pg. 984, pg. 701
Haergin, Megan, Asst Mgr-Social Intelligence - Brown-Forman Corporation; pg. 1958, pg. 732
Haering, Linda, Sr Dir-HR - WILD Flavors, Inc.; pg. 910, pg. 728
Haesemeyer, Robert, Dir-Global Biologics Mktg - Hospira, Inc.; pg. 1542, pg. 623
Hafer, Jennifer, Specialist-PR - Kennesaw State University; pg. 603, pg. 534
Hafer, Michael, Sr VP-Global CRM, Loyalty & Social Media - The Western Union Company; pg. 822, pg. 327
Haff, Gordon, Sr Mgr-Cloud Strategy Mktg & Evangelism - Red Hat, Inc.; pg. 460, pg. 1388
Hafner, Pam, Mgr-Install Base Mktg - General Electric Company; pg. 1297, pg. 347
Hafner, Rachel, Sr Mgr-Bus Dev-Hotel - Kayak; pg. 1260, pg. 363
Hafstad, Nancy, Reg Dir-Sls - Gilead Sciences, Inc.; pg. 1535, pg. 88
Haftchenary, Ata, Brand Mgr - Procter & Gamble Inc.; pg. 333, pg. 1929
Hagan, Brent, Sr Planner-Product Plng - Nissan North America, Inc.; pg. 186, pg. 1633
Hagan, Carrie, Sr Mgr-Global Strategic Mktg & Internal Digital - Abbott Laboratories; pg. 1484, pg. 551
Hagan, Deb, Sr Dir-Creative - Wal-Mart Stores, Inc.; pg. 1790, pg. 29
Hagan, John, VP-Sls-Natl - Kumho Tire USA, Inc.; pg. 182, pg. 187
Hagan, Ken, Global Product Mgr - DE-STA-CO Industries; pg. 1045, pg. 867
Hagan, Natalie, Product Mgr - Swagelok Company; pg. 1064, pg. 1473
Hagarty, Erin, Sr Assoc Brand Mgr - Church & Dwight Co., Inc.; pg. 1153, pg. 1063
Hagberg, Erika, Head-Fin Svcs Adv-Credit Cards - Google Inc.; pg. 1249, pg. 153
Hage, Henry, COO & Mgr-Sls - Croll-Reynolds Company, Inc.; pg. 1326, pg. 1103
Hage, Siiri, Dir-Mktg Comm & Mgr-Mktg Programs & Creative Svcs - Anritsu Company; pg. 618, pg. 152
Hagedorn, Derk, Sr Mgr-Mktg-Live Sys - Avid Technology, Inc.; pg. 622, pg. 804
Hagedorn, Mandy, Product Mgr-Global - Blount International, Inc.; pg. 1043, pg. 1501
Hagemeier, Marvin, Dir-C&I Sls Western Reg - Leviton Manufacturing Company, Inc.; pg. 1301, pg. 1180
Hagen, Gary, Sr Mgr-End User Technologies - Amgen Inc.; pg. 1493, pg. 291
Hagen, Jamie, Rep-Social Media - Luxottica Retail; pg. 8, pg. 1460
Hagen, Mark, Sr Product Dir - 7-Eleven, Inc.; pg. 1012, pg. 1672
Hagen, Michelle, Specialist-Mktg Ops - Juniper Networks, Inc.; pg. 1260, pg. 286
Hagen, Per, Sr Engr-Technical Mktg - Cisco Systems, Inc.; pg. 372, pg. 240
Hagen, Scott, Chief Sls Officer-Sound United - DEI Holdings, Inc.; pg. 633, pg. 302
Hagen, Tanya, Mgr-Mktg - Quality Dining, Inc.; pg. 1746, pg. 695
Hagen, William, Sr Mgr-Intellectual Property Rights - Institute of Electrical and Electronics Engineers, Inc.; pg. 144, pg. 1109
Hagener, Suzanne, Sr Mgr-Mktg-NonDairy Prods - Blue Diamond Growers; pg. 840, pg. 195
Hagerty, Dan, Sr VP-Sls & Mktg - Tree Top, Inc.; pg. 901, pg. 1843
Hagg, Kelly, VP & Head-Product Dev - Janus Capital Group, Inc.; pg. 772, pg. 320
Haggerty, Bruce G., Dir-Mktg Res - Nestle USA, Inc.; pg. 883, pg. 96
Haggerty, Colleen, Sr VP-Global Mktg & Corp Affairs - Bank of America Corporation; pg. 718, pg. 1362
Haggerty, Megan, Sr Dir-Natl Brdcst & Digital - Combe Incorporated; pg. 1516, pg. 1351
Haggerty, Paul, Mgr-Adv Resources - General Motors Company; pg. 175, pg. 881
Haggith, Dave, Sr Dir-Comm - Maple Leaf Sports & Entertainment Ltd.; pg. 560, pg. 1940
Haghighi, Farshad, Sr VP-Sls Ops, Bus Dev, Field Engrg & Customer Svc - Amkor Technology, Inc.; pg. 67, pg. 25
Hagist, Megan, Mgr-Social Media & Strategist-Digital - Kashi Company; pg. 830, pg. 119
Hagler, Aaron, Dir-Sls & Bus Dev - Agilysys, Inc.; pg. 614, pg. 1409
Haglund, Yuri, Assoc Brand Mgr-Shopper Mktg - Henkel Corporation; pg. 1049, pg. 369
Hagmaier, Mike, Mgr-A&G-LSR Global Mktg Programs - Agilent Technologies, Inc.; pg. 614, pg. 264
Hagn, James, Mgr-Customer Intelligence Analytics & Mktg Innovations - Susquehanna Bank; pg. 807, pg. 1548
Hagney, Morgan, Sr Mgr-Mktg-L'Oreal Paris Cosmetics - L'Oreal USA; pg. 514, pg. 1252
Hagopian, Jacques, Assoc Dir-Mktg-Global Walmart Inc - The Procter & Gamble Company; pg. 1129, pg. 1418
Hagopian, Vartan, VP-Sls - MicroFinancial Incorporated; pg. 782, pg. 805
Hagy, Jeffrey, Sr Mgr-Brand Curriculum Dev & Comml Ops-Global - Pfizer Inc.; pg. 1581, pg. 1278
Hahn, Amber, Sr Mgr-Campaign - Expedia, Inc.; pg. 1244, pg. 1814
Hahn, Daniel, VP & Mgr-Sls-Natl - Discovery Communications, Inc.; pg. 282, pg. 777
Hahn, Erin, Dir-Adv - Carroll County Times; pg. 1626, pg. 780
Hahn, Jim, Sr Mgr-Transportation Security & Supplier Svcs - Johnson & Johnson; pg. 1549, pg. 1091
Hahn, Jon, Mgr-Mktg - General Motors Company; pg 175, pg. 881
Hahn, Nicole, Sr Mgr-Mktg-Strategic Accounts - Samsung Telecommunications America, LLC; pg. 670, pg. 1736
Hahn, Randall, VP-Database Mktg - Citigroup Inc.; pg. 735, pg. 1212
Hahn, Ryan, Assoc Mgr-Mktg - Home Box Office, Inc.; pg. 290, pg. 1240
Hahne, Sarah, Mgr-PR - Palm Springs Desert Resorts Convention & Visitors Authority; pg. 1003, pg. 187
Haidek, Larry, Mgr-Internet Sls - Sanderson Ford Inc.; pg. 190, pg. 13
Haider, Susan, VP-Product Mgmt & Mktg - Deluxe Corporation; pg. 1634, pg. 964
Haies, Jennifer, Sr Mgr-Emerging Solutions - Google Inc.; pg. 1249, pg. 153
Haig, Keith, Sr Mgr-Strategic Content - 3M Company; pg. 1142, pg. 956
Haight, Brenda, Mgr-Sls-Michigan State Associations - Boyne USA Resorts Inc.; pg. 1082, pg. 874
Haile-Selassie, Fanna, Mgr-Media-Global - 3M Company; pg. 1142, pg. 956
Hailey, Janelle, Brand Mgr-Innovation & Strategy-North America - Neutrogena Corporation; pg. 517, pg. 137
Haim, Noam Ben, Sr Product Mgr - Google Inc.; pg. 1249, pg. 153
Haimbach, Andrew S., Analyst-Mktg - Carpenter Technology Corporation; pg. 73, pg. 1584
Hain, Gordon, Product Mgr-Excavator Sys-Trimble LOADRITE - Trimble Navigation Limited; pg. 1384, pg. 288
Hainault, Patrick, Grp VP-Mktg - Inc.com LLC; pg. 1258, pg. 1243
Haines, Gary, Sr VP, Team Head & Sr Mgr-Relationship -

Washington Federal Inc.; *pg.* 818, *pg.* 1842
Haines, Hudson, Head-Creative - Citrix Systems, Inc.; *pg.* 375, *pg.* 424
Haines, Lisa, Mgr-Natl Sls-Hartell - Milton Roy Company; *pg.* 1361, *pg.* 1542
Haines, Sara, Dir-Mktg - Belle Tire Inc.; *pg.* 200, *pg.* 864
Hainlin, Kari, Sr Dir-Ops-Demand & Portfolio Mgmt - Allianz Life Insurance Company of North America; *pg.* 1188, *pg.* 929
Hairston, Mike, Engr-Technical Mktg-Enterprise Backbone BU - Cisco Systems, Inc.; *pg.* 372, *pg.* 240
Haisley, Tracy, Mgr-Product & Enrollment Comm - Aflac Incorporated; *pg.* 1188, *pg.* 527
Hajakian, Nina, Dir-Mktg Trng & Dev - Association of National Advertisers, Inc.; *pg.* 133, *pg.* 1197
Hajdinyak, Claudia, Sr Mgr-Comm-Pub Affairs - Pfizer Inc.; *pg.* 1581, *pg.* 1278
Hajdu, Erika, Sr Mgr-Mktg - Baxter International Inc.; *pg.* 1499, *pg.* 599
Hajduk, Ricky, Specialist-Mdse-ECommerce - Henry Modell & Company, Inc.; *pg.* 1836, *pg.* 1240
Hake, Erin, Mgr-Interactive Mktg Programs - InterContinental Hotels Corporation; *pg.* 1097, *pg.* 511
Hake, Laurie, Strategist-Digital Marketer & Social Media - Halliburton Company; *pg.* 978, *pg.* 1707
Hake, Lisa, Dir-Mktg-Geek Squad - Best Buy Co., Inc.; *pg.* 1761, *pg.* 954
Hakeman, Darren, Sr VP-Product & Strategy - 8x8, Inc.; *pg.* 1865, *pg.* 282
Hakenson, Aaron S., VP-Online Sls - Lionbridge Technologies Inc.; *pg.* 428, *pg.* 851
Hakes, Kent, Sr Dir-Ticket Svcs, Fin & Tech - Colorado Rockies Baseball Club, Ltd.; *pg.* 542, *pg.* 317
Hakes, Sharon E., Sr Dir-Global Oncology Medical Rels - Pfizer Inc.; *pg.* 1581, *pg.* 1278
Hakim, Laila, Sr Dir-Content, Creative Media Solutions & B2B Mktg - Quebecor Media Inc.; *pg.* 1679, *pg.* 1956
Hakki, Fadi, Sr Mgr-Regulatory Affairs - MedImmune LLC; *pg.* 1562, *pg.* 770
Hakl, Shawn, VP-Product & New Bus Innovation - Verizon Communications Inc.; *pg.* 1875, *pg.* 1309
Halabisky, Darren, Mgr-Mktg Plans Grp - Ford Motor Company of Canada, Limited; *pg.* 174, *pg.* 1930
Haladner, Tania M., Sr Dir-Mktg-PepsiCo - PepsiCo, Inc.; *pg.* 259, *pg.* 1327
Halbert, Dawn, Dir-Midwest Adv-Hispanic Ventures - Meredith Corporation; *pg.* 1663, *pg.* 705
Halbert, Don, Product Mgr - Avery Weigh-Tronix, Inc.; *pg.* 1315, *pg.* 925
Halcomb, Sharon, Mgr-Integrated Mktg - West Marine, Inc.; *pg.* 1712, *pg.* 305
Haldeman, Scott, Mgr-Brand Engagement-Integrated Media Solutions - PepsiCo, Inc.; *pg.* 259, *pg.* 1327
Halder Hansen, Kellie, Mgr-Digital Mktg - American Girl LLC; *pg.* 949, *pg.* 1871
Halder, Tuhin, Sr Dir-Strategy & Corp Dev - Bimbo Bakeries USA; *pg.* 840, *pg.* 151
Hale, Anna, Area Dir-Mktg-Oral Health-Central & Eastern Europe - GlaxoSmithKline Consumer Healthcare; *pg.* 510, *pg.* 1554
Hale, Ashley N., Mgr-Mktg - Tyson Foods, Inc.; *pg.* 902, *pg.* 35
Hale, Don, VP-Mktg Comm & Pub Rels - Georgia State University; *pg.* 602, *pg.* 508
Hale, Ellen, VP & Dir-Mktg & Corp Comm - The Associated Press, Inc.; *pg.* 270, *pg.* 1197
Hale, Glenn P., Dir-Sls-Natl Restaurant Chain Accounts - F.W. Bryce, Inc.; *pg.* 857, *pg.* 823
Hale, Jeffrey, Dir-Mktg - Gema USA Inc.; *pg.* 1339, *pg.* 686
Hale, Justin, Reg Dir-Product Mktg - The Boeing Company; *pg.* 225, *pg.* 567
Hale, Justin, Reg Dir-Product Mktg - The Boeing Company - Helicopter Division; *pg.* 226, *pg.* 13
Hale, Katie, Mgr-Event-Mktg & Strategy - Ericsson, Inc.; *pg.* 638, *pg.* 1730
Hale, Kevin, Mgr-Adv & Media - J.P. Morgan Asset Management Holdings Inc.; *pg.* 772, *pg.* 1246
Hale, Lorraine, Dir-Mktg-Entenmanns & Sara Lee - Bimbo Bakeries USA; *pg.* 840, *pg.* 151
Hale, Lynne, Head-PR-Global - Lucasfilm, Ltd.; *pg.* 297, *pg.* 222
Hale, Matthew, Sr Mgr-Mktg - Playtex Apparel, Inc.; *pg.* 31, *pg.* 1395
Hale, Virginia, Project Analyst-Comml Product Dev - Humana, Inc.; *pg.* 1204, *pg.* 734
Hales, Ben, Sr VP-Mktg & Bus Dev - New Orleans Saints L.P.; *pg.* 569, *pg.* 745
Haleua, Chris, Sr Mgr-Product Mktg - Adobe Systems Incorporated; *pg.* 342, *pg.* 235
Haley, Brad, CMO - CKE Restaurants Inc.; *pg.* 1723, *pg.* 63
Haley, Brent, Sr Mgr-WW Digital Content & Customer References-HP Helion - Hewlett-Packard Company; *pg.* 404, *pg.* 175
Haley, Christina, Mgr & Head-Sls Support & Plng-Wealth Sls & Retail Markets - Manulife Financial Corporation; *pg.* 778, *pg.* 1939
Haley, Christopher, Sr VP-Products - PAR Technology Corporation; *pg.* 452, *pg.* 1183
Haley, Darren, Mgr-Product Line - FLIR Systems, Inc.; *pg.* 1413, *pg.* 1510
Haley, Joe, Mgr-Retail Mktg - Mazda North American Operations; *pg.* 183, *pg.* 113
Haley, John, Dir-Mktg & Bus Dev - W.R. Grace & Co.; *pg.* 123, *pg.* 810
Haley, Kevin, Exec-Sls - FedEx Corporation; *pg.* 1907, *pg.* 1642
Haley, Kurt, Gen Mgr-Sls - Magnetic Metals Corp.; *pg.* 1358, *pg.* 1049
Haley, Meg, Brand Mgr-Coca Cola Brand - The Coca-Cola Company; *pg.* 240, *pg.* 493
Haley, Mike, Dir-Mktg - Kimberly-Clark Corporation; *pg.* 1461, *pg.* 1720
Haley, Sean, Program Mgr-Mktg Ops - Amgen Inc.; *pg.* 1493, *pg.* 291
Halfman, Lisa, Dir-Mktg - MetLife, Inc.; *pg.* 1208, *pg.* 1258
Halford, Amy, Dir-Digital Mktg & Media - General Mills, Inc.; *pg.* 828, *pg.* 933
Halgren, Chris, Mgr-Interactive Mktg - Ameriprise Financial, Inc.; *pg.* 715, *pg.* 930
Halicy, Melissa, Sr Mgr-Mktg - GEICO Corporation; *pg.* 1200, *pg.* 399
Halilovic, Fadila, Mgr-Mktg Coordination - ABB Inc.; *pg.* 1309, *pg.* 1359
Haljun, Alison, VP-Retail Mktg & PR - Benefit Cosmetics LLC; *pg.* 501, *pg.* 213
Halkuff, Dawn, VP-Women's Health-Mktg & Sls - Pfizer Inc.; *pg.* 1581, *pg.* 1278
Hall Reinerth, Regan, Dir-Mktg & Comm - National Marrow Donor Program, Inc.; *pg.* 150, *pg.* 941
Hall, Abram, Mgr-Sourcing-Global Procurement-Print, Mktg & Adv - MetLife, Inc.; *pg.* 1208, *pg.* 1258
Hall, Addie, Mgr-Mktg Comm - CSX Corporation; *pg.* 1904, *pg.* 432
Hall, Alison C., Sr Exec Dir-Digital Mktg & Ops - Salix Pharmaceuticals, Inc.; *pg.* 1591, *pg.* 1388
Hall, Amanda, Sr Mgr-Event - Juniper Networks, Inc.; *pg.* 1260, *pg.* 286
Hall, Boderick, Dir-Adv Production-Global - PepsiCo, Inc.; *pg.* 259, *pg.* 1327
Hall, Brian, Dir-Product Dev-Vasque - Red Wing Shoe Company, Inc.; *pg.* 1817, *pg.* 954
Hall, Carla, Mgr-Mktg Production - McGladrey, LLP; *pg.* 781, *pg.* 938
Hall, Cathy, Mgr-Mktg - Hilton Worldwide, Inc.; *pg.* 1094, *pg.* 1791
Hall, Chip, Dir-Programmatic Media & Platform Sls - Google Inc.; *pg.* 1249, *pg.* 153
Hall, Cindy, VP-Mdsg - Hooker Furniture Corporation; *pg.* 928, *pg.* 1788
Hall, Colleen, Assoc Dir-Adv Resources - Bristol-Myers Squibb Company; *pg.* 1509, *pg.* 1206
Hall, David M., Sr VP-Sls & Mktg - Waste Connections, Inc.; *pg.* 1954, *pg.* 1747
Hall, Eric, VP-Adv & Dir-Natl Sls - The Rough Notes Company, Inc.; *pg.* 1681, *pg.* 675
Hall, Garrett, Mgr-Digital Mktg - International Business Machines Corporation; *pg.* 418, *pg.* 1138
Hall, Graeme, Head-Creative-Google Creative Labs - Google Inc.; *pg.* 1249, *pg.* 153
Hall, Greg, Sr VP-Mdsg - Wal-Mart Stores, Inc.; *pg.* 1790, *pg.* 29
Hall, Heather, Mgr-Mktg - Ameriprise Financial, Inc.; *pg.* 715, *pg.* 930
Hall, Hillary, Acct Dir-Natl Sls - The Bonne Bell Company; *pg.* 502, *pg.* 1480
Hall, Jackie, Asst Mgr-Adv - The Kroger Co.; *pg.* 1025, *pg.* 1416
Hall, Jason, VP-Retail Sls - Generac Power Systems Inc.; *pg.* 1340, *pg.* 1898
Hall, Jason, Brand Head-FluMist - MedImmune LLC; *pg.* 1562, *pg.* 770
Hall, Jeannice, Sr Strategist-Media Rels - Southern Company; *pg.* 1952, *pg.* 520
Hall, Jessica, Mgr-Mktg & Loyalty Programs - Office Depot, Inc.; *pg.* 448, *pg.* 412
Hall, John, Sr VP-PR - The American Bankers Association; *pg.* 126, *pg.* 394
Hall, Jonathan, Strategist-Mktg - 3M Company; *pg.* 1142, *pg.* 956
Hall, Julianne, Sr Mgr-Local Mktg-East Div - Wal-Mart Stores, Inc.; *pg.* 1790, *pg.* 29
Hall, Kathleen, Gen Mgr-Windows Consumer Global Campaigns & Product Mktg - Microsoft Corporation; *pg.* 435, *pg.* 1824
Hall, Katie, Sr Specialist-Mobile Mktg - Cabela's Incorporated; *pg.* 535, *pg.* 1019
Hall, Kelsey, Asst Mgr-Mktg-Experiential - Ghirardelli Chocolate Company; *pg.* 1854, *pg.* 252
Hall, Kent, Product Mgr - Stihl, Inc.; *pg.* 1064, *pg.* 1810
Hall, Kimberly, Area Dir-Mktg & Bus Dev - Simon Property Group, Inc.; *pg.* 1112, *pg.* 690
Hall, Kristen, Dir-Mktg Automation - Ameriprise Financial, Inc.; *pg.* 715, *pg.* 930
Hall, Laura, Specialist-Mktg-Lubrizol Advanced Materials - The Lubrizol Corporation; *pg.* 1171, *pg.* 1481
Hall, Lindsey, Brand Mgr - Abbott Laboratories; *pg.* 1484, *pg.* 551
Hall, Lindsey, Brand Mgr - Abbott Nutrition; *pg.* 1485, *pg.* 1437
Hall, Lori, Dir-Mktg - Radio One, Inc.; *pg.* 305, *pg.* 778
Hall, Lydia, Mgr-Media Rels - The American Dental Association; *pg.* 127, *pg.* 564
Hall, Margaret, Exec Dir-Creative Strategy - University of Maryland; *pg.* 609, *pg.* 767
Hall, Marta, Pres & Chief Mktg & Bus Dev Officer - Velodyne Acoustics, Inc.; *pg.* 685, *pg.* 152
Hall, Megan, Brand Mgr - Capital One Financial Corporation; *pg.* 730, *pg.* 1789
Hall, Michael, Sr VP & Mgr-Sls-Natl - Lincoln Financial Group; *pg.* 1206, *pg.* 1375
Hall, Monique, Mgr-Global Sourcing-Mktg - Apple Inc.; *pg.* 350, *pg.* 73
Hall, Niki, VP-Corp Mktg - Polycom, Inc.; *pg.* 664, *pg.* 249
Hall, Rich, VP-Sls-Central Area - Information Builders Inc.; *pg.* 415, *pg.* 1243
Hall, Ryan, Sr Product Mgr - Newell Rubbermaid Inc.; *pg.* 1128, *pg.* 515
Hall, Tiffany, VP-Mktg Transactions Counsel - MasterCard Worldwide Inc.; *pg.* 780, *pg.* 988
Hall, William M., Sr VP & Gen Mgr-Standard Products Grp - ON Semiconductor Corporation; *pg.* 101, *pg.* 18
Hall-Shelton, Geneva, Sr Mgr-Sponsorship - Habitat for Humanity International, Inc.; *pg.* 143, *pg.* 486
Halladay, Gail, Analyst-Mktg - McKesson Corporation; *pg.* 1560, *pg.* 222
Hallahan, Jennifer, Dir-Corp Pub Rels - CA Technologies; *pg.* 366, *pg.* 1168
Hallam, Tim, Sr Dir-Pub & Media Rels - Chicago Professional Sports Limited Partnership; *pg.* 539, *pg.* 570
Hallberg, Alan, CMO & Corp VP - RF Micro Devices, Inc.; *pg.* 667, *pg.* 1376
Hallberg, Victoria, VP-Key Accts & Brand Sls - Marchon Eyewear, Inc.; *pg.* 1421, *pg.* 1180
Halle, Timothy, Asst Mgr-Global Mktg-Marc Jacobs Fragrances - Coty, Inc.; *pg.* 506, *pg.* 1219
Hallengren, Bob, Product Dir-Caterpillar Marine Power Systems - Caterpillar, Inc.; *pg.* 1321, *pg.* 650
Haller Smith, Julie, Mgr-Mdse & Dept Stores - Bare Escentuals, Inc.; *pg.* 500, *pg.* 213
Haller, Douglas, Product Mgr-Treevix & Altrevin Fire Ant Bait Insecticide - BASF Corporation; *pg.* 1149, *pg.* 1066
Haller, Lindsay, Sr Mgr-Mktg-CRM - Vail Resorts, Inc.; *pg.* 1117, *pg.* 313
Haller, Terry, Mgr-Creative Svcs - Harley-Davidson, Inc.; *pg.* 178, *pg.* 1874
Hallett, Josh, Strategist-Digital Mktg - Publix Super Markets, Inc.; *pg.* 1031, *pg.* 437
Halley, John, COO-Ad Sls-Viacom Media Networks & Exec VP - Viacom Inc.; *pg.* 316, *pg.* 1310
Halliburton, Jelena, Brand Mgr - Tura L.P.; *pg.* 1433, *pg.* 1555
Halliday, Ian, Mgr-Media Analytics - Carnival Corporation; *pg.* 1902, *pg.* 441
Halliday, Kent, VP-Sls & Mktg - ZCL Composites Inc.; *pg.* 1892, *pg.* 1906

First page reference indicates Business Class Edition
Second page reference indicates Geographic Edition

Halliday, Richard, VP-Channel Sls-Americas - Digi International Inc.; pg. 387, pg. 948
Halligan, Rob, Grp VP-Strategy & Mktg Nortek Tech Solutions Grp - Nortek, Inc.; pg. 100, pg. 1607
Halliwell, Nicholas, Mgr-PR - Groupon, Inc.; pg. 1255, pg. 575
Hallock, Amanda, Specialist-Mktg - Honeywell International Inc.; pg. 407, pg. 1088
Hallock, Anne, VP-Mktg - The Trade Desk, Inc.; pg. 1284, pg. 301
Hallock, Jayne, Dir-Editorial & Social Media - Network Communications Inc.; pg. 1271, pg. 534
Halloran, Kim, Sr Assoc Brand Mgr - The Kraft Heinz Company; pg. 871, pg. 641
Halloran, Sean, Reg Mgr-Sls - Riverbed Technology, Inc.; pg. 1277, pg. 225
Hallowell, Jan, Analyst-Mktg - IBM; pg. 410, pg. 1449
Halls, Kristie, Sr Product Mgr-Medical Device - Allergan, Inc.; pg. 1491, pg. 106
Halls, Pat, Sr Dir-Sponsorship Sls - Calgary Flames Limited Partnership; pg. 535, pg. 1902
Hallum, Chris, Sr Product Mgr - Microsoft Corporation; pg. 435, pg. 1824
Halpin, Chris, Dir-Sls-Global - Siemens Healthcare Diagnostics; pg. 673, pg. 604
Halpin, Christopher, Sr VP-Licensing & Consumer Products - National Football League; pg. 567, pg. 1264
Halpin, Michael, Sr Mgr-Mktg - The Allstate Corporation; pg. 1189, pg. 639
Halsey, Charlie, Specialist-Mktg - GEICO Corporation; pg. 1200, pg. 399
Halsey, Farlin, VP-Strategic Mktg - Murata Electronics North America, Inc.; pg. 658, pg. 540
Halsey, Nathaniel, Sr VP-Digital Svcs Mktg & Infrastructure - Citigroup Inc.; pg. 735, pg. 1212
Halstead, Cassie, Acct Exec-Digital Media - NBC Universal, Inc.; pg. 300, pg. 1266
Haluska, Scott, VP-Sls-Global - Materion Microelectronics & Services; pg. 1559, pg. 1149
Halverson, Aubrey, VP-Mktg-Pacific Midwest Reg - Wells Fargo & Company; pg. 819, pg. 232
Halverson, J.J., Mgr-Mktg - Bernatello's Pizza Inc.; pg. 840, pg. 928
Halvorsen, Al, Sr Dir-Environmental Sustainability - PepsiCo, Inc.; pg. 259, pg. 1327
Halvorsen, Cindy, Brand Mgr - The Kraft Heinz Company; pg. 871, pg. 641
Halvorsen, Erik, VP-Sls-America - WatchGuard Technologies, Inc.; pg. 491, pg. 1842
Halvorson, Jonathan, Dir-Media Strategy & Entertainment-Global - General Motors Company; pg. 175, pg. 881
Ham, Joe, Mgr-Corp Brand & Media Comm - Las Vegas Sands Corp.; pg. 1100, pg. 1027
Ham, Kristi, Dir-Mktg - The Glik Company; pg. 1771, pg. 615
Hama, Charlene, Sr Mgr-Channel Mktg - SanDisk Corporation; pg. 465, pg. 147
Hamada, Rhonya, Head-Creative & UX Engrg - Microsoft Corporation; pg. 435, pg. 1824
Hamade, Karen, Mgr-Retail Mktg-Natl - Jaguar Land Rover North America LLC; pg. 180, pg. 1081
Hamandi, Rola, Sr VP-US Govt & Intl Sls - ABnote North America; pg. 1878, pg. 789
Hamandi, Rola, Sr VP-US Govt & Intl Sls - American Banknote Corporation; pg. 1615, pg. 1067
Hamann, Hardy, VP-Mktg & Bus Dev - Starrett; pg. 1064, pg. 1621
Hamberlin, Deborah, VP-Affiliate Mktg - The CW Television Network; pg. 632, pg. 52
Hamblen, Benjamin, Sr Dir-Corp Media Svcs - Kate Spade & Company; pg. 27, pg. 1248
Hamblin, Diana, Sr Mgr-Mktg Comm - Instron Corporation; pg. 1349, pg. 839
Hamblin, Mark A., VP-Sls-Western Div - Saia, Inc.; pg. 1922, pg. 533
Hamburger, Adam, Mgr-Mktg - FedEx Corporation; pg. 1907, pg. 1642
Hamburger, John, Dir-Mktg Comm - Linear Technology Corp.; pg. 652, pg. 147
Hamby, Stuart, Acct Exec-Sls - Comcast Sportsnet; pg. 278, pg. 1562
Hamdy, Esmat, Sr VP-Tech Dev & New Product Integration - Microsemi Corporation; pg. 435, pg. 41
Hameed, Saad, Head-Mktg Tech - LinkedIn Corporation; pg. 1262, pg. 160
Hamel, Danielle, Sr Dir-Global Corp Comm - Juniper Networks, Inc.; pg. 1260, pg. 286
Hamel, Karen, Dir-Global & US PR - Novartis Corporation; pg. 1574, pg. 1273
Hamel, Nancy, Mgr-Sls - Hyatt Hotels Corporation; pg. 1096, pg. 577
Hamel, Sean, Mgr-PR-Yahoo! Sports & Games - Yahoo! Inc.; pg. 1289, pg. 289
Hamelinck, Kristin, Analyst-Mktg Events - Huron Consulting Group Inc.; pg. 768, pg. 577
Hamer, Craig, Engr-Product Support - Hewlett-Packard Company; pg. 404, pg. 175
Hamera, Kevin, Sr Mgr-Pur - Ford Motor Company; pg. 172, pg. 876
Hames, Scott, VP-Mktg & Analytics - Bed Bath & Beyond Inc.; pg. 1121, pg. 1127
Hamid, Zatil, Mgr-Internet Mktg-Signal Chain - Texas Instruments Incorporated; pg. 679, pg. 1688
Hamidi, Ridha, Engr-Technical Mktg - Brocade Corporation; pg. 365, pg. 312
Hamidi, Sanaz, Head-Digital Mktg - Amway Corporation; pg. 326, pg. 864
Hamill, Jay, Mgr-Mktg Ops - Volvo Cars of North America LLC; pg. 195, pg. 1117
Hamill, Meera, Sr Mgr-Ingredients Procurement - The Kraft Heinz Company; pg. 871, pg. 641
Hamilton, Beth, Sr Product Mgr-Vyvanse Brand Team - Shire; pg. 1593, pg. 1532
Hamilton, Bryan, Head-Brand-Global Tampax & Assoc Dir-Mktg - The Procter & Gamble Company; pg. 1129, pg. 1418
Hamilton, Carol, Pres-Luxury Products Div - L'Oreal USA; pg. 514, pg. 1252
Hamilton, Carol L., Mgr-Mktg - Hewlett-Packard Company; pg. 404, pg. 175
Hamilton, Cassidy, Mgr-Mktg-Sunglass Hut - Luxottica Retail; pg. 8, pg. 1460
Hamilton, Craig, Product Mgr - Armored AutoGroup Inc.; pg. 199, pg. 342
Hamilton, Cynthia, Sr Mgr-Customer & Brand Dev - Del Monte Foods, Inc.; pg. 852, pg. 304
Hamilton, George, Mgr-Mktg - Jamison Door Company; pg. 89, pg. 771
Hamilton, Greg, Mgr-Media - The Wendy's Company; pg. 1755, pg. 1450
Hamilton, Greg, Mgr-Media - Wendy's International, Inc.; pg. 1755, pg. 1451
Hamilton, Jamie, Dir-ISV Audience Mktg - Microsoft Corporation; pg. 435, pg. 1824
Hamilton, Jillian, Mgr-Product Mktg - Facebook, Inc.; pg. 1245, pg. 143
Hamilton, Joanna, Sr Mgr-Mktg - Intuit Inc.; pg. 769, pg. 158
Hamilton, Kevin, Program Mgr-Mktg-Pkg - General Electric Company; pg. 1297, pg. 347
Hamilton, Lisa, Dir-PR-Robert Half Legal - Robert Half International Inc.; pg. 462, pg. 145
Hamilton, Mark, Head-Mktg-CEEMEA - Facebook, Inc.; pg. 1245, pg. 143
Hamilton, Mark, Sr Mgr-Corp Comm - Travelport Limited; pg. 1925, pg. 521
Hamilton, Maya, Sr Mgr-ECommerce - V.F. Corporation; pg. 34, pg. 1376
Hamilton, Michael, VP & Head-Institutional Product Solutions - Lincoln Financial Group; pg. 1206, pg. 1375
Hamilton, Nancy, Sr Mgr-Mdse - Colony Brands Inc.; pg. 849, pg. 1881
Hamilton, Nick, Sr Acct Exec-Partnership Mktg - Brooklyn Nets; pg. 534, pg. 1145
Hamilton, Nick, Asst VP-Fifth Third Bank Creative Svcs - Fifth Third Bancorp; pg. 752, pg. 1413
Hamilton, Rob, Mgr-Field Mktg-New England - Heineken USA Inc.; pg. 252, pg. 1352
Hamilton, S. Kristie, VP-Medicaid & Medicare Mktg - Anthem, Inc.; pg. 1192, pg. 683
Hamilton, Sarah, Coord-Mktg - Rue La La; pg. 1278, pg. 800
Hamilton, Stacey, Dir-Mktg - PulteGroup, Inc.; pg. 1109, pg. 873
Hamilton, Stacy, Dir-PR - MGM Resorts International; pg. 1105, pg. 1028
Hamilton, Ted, Product Mgr - Google Inc.; pg. 1249, pg. 153
Hamilton, Terence J., VP-Sls & Dir - OptimizeRx Corporation; pg. 1673, pg. 905
Hamilton, Tom, Mgr-Fin-Consumer Foods Sls Div - General Mills, Inc.; pg. 828, pg. 933
Hamilton, Warren, Mgr-Product Dev - Virgin America Inc.; pg. 1930, pg. 55
Hamilton, Will, Mgr-Mktg - SunTrust Banks, Inc.; pg. 807, pg. 520
Hamlar, Jocelyn, Mgr-Mktg Comm - Blue Cross & Blue Shield Association; pg. 1195, pg. 566
Hamlet, Diane, Coord-Creative Svcs - WPVI-TV Inc.; pg. 323, pg. 1572
Hamlett, David, Sr Mgr-Online Communities & Social Media - TD Ameritrade Holding Corporation; pg. 808, pg. 1018
Hamley, Alexandra, Mgr-Digital Mktg & Social Media - The Hertz Corporation; pg. 1911, pg. 450
Hamlin, Ben, Bus Mgr-Fresh Express Retail Salads - Chiquita Brands International, Inc.; pg. 847, pg. 1365
Hamlin, Jake, Coord-Social Media - Yamaha Motor Corporation USA; pg. 1713, pg. 76
Hamlin, Mona, Analyst-Mktg Res - Syracuse University Press; pg. 1690, pg. 1344
Hamm, Amy, Sr Dir-Mktg - Theater League Inc.; pg. 587, pg. 986
Hamm, Claudine C., CEO & Dir-Creative & Fashion - ALYCE Paris; pg. 18, pg. 634
Hamm, Gary D., Dir-Mktg & Govt - Tyson Foods, Inc.; pg. 902, pg. 35
Hamm, Jennifer, Brand Mgr - Kellogg Company; pg. 831, pg. 870
Hamm, Rebecca, Sr Dir-Strategy, Portfolio & Comml Ops Comm - Pfizer Inc.; pg. 1581, pg. 1278
Hammarstrom, David, Dir-PR - MetLife, Inc.; pg. 1208, pg. 1258
Hammer, Keri, Dir-Sls-New York - Inc.com LLC; pg. 1258, pg. 1243
Hammers, Darin, Sr VP-Sls & Mktg-Global & Gen Mgr-Intl - Cogentix Medical, Inc.; pg. 1516, pg. 948
Hammerstein, Greg, Dir-Product Support Svcs - Gulfstream Aerospace Corporation; pg. 228, pg. 540
Hammes, Emily, Coord-Mdse - Wolverine World Wide, Inc.; pg. 1822, pg. 905
Hammes, Susan, VP-Social Media Mktg - American Express Company; pg. 712, pg. 1190
Hammitt, Nicholas, Sr Dir-Mktg-Incubation Brands - PepsiCo, Inc.; pg. 259, pg. 1327
Hammitt, Rebekah, Dir-Creative-Park Bus Newsroom - Capital One Financial Corporation; pg. 730, pg. 1789
Hammond, Anna, Rep-Mktg & Donor Recruitment Sls - American Red Cross; pg. 130, pg. 395
Hammond, Bob, VP-Mktg - Sherwin Williams; pg. 1448, pg. 1436
Hammond, Carrie, Mgr-Mktg - R.C. Bigelow, Inc.; pg. 891, pg. 348
Hammond, Doug, Gen Mgr-Sls - Golf Galaxy, Inc.; pg. 1835, pg. 1525
Hammond, Jacqueline, Dir-Mktg & Enrollment Svcs - Blackboard Inc.; pg. 1232, pg. 396
Hammond, Kim, Product Mgr-Asset - ScanSource, Inc.; pg. 671, pg. 1618
Hammond, Marilyn, VP-Brdcst Sls & Mktg - Media General, Inc.; pg. 297, pg. 1803
Hammond, Michael, VP-Mktg & Creative - Gordmans Stores Inc.; pg. 1771, pg. 1016
Hammond, Rick, Bus Mgr-Health Care Support & Svc Ops-Global - 3M Company; pg. 1142, pg. 956
Hammond, Sandra, Sr Dir-Revenue Optimization-Radio - The Canadian Broadcasting Corporation; pg. 272, pg. 1931
Hammond, Stacy, VP-Retail Acq Mktg - Charles Schwab; pg. 1235, pg. 1661
Hamouly, Mona, VP-Social Media Comm - American Express Company; pg. 712, pg. 1190
Hampton, Bob, VP-Mktg - Crosman Corporation; pg. 951, pg. 1143
Hampton, Bryan, Mgr-Sls-Natl - Trans Ocean Products Inc.; pg. 901, pg. 1818
Hampton, Clay, Sr Dir-Ops - New York Jets Football Club, Inc.; pg. 570, pg. 1067
Hampton, Cynthia, VP-Mktg & Comm - Environmental Defense Fund; pg. 140, pg. 1228
Hampton, Kelly, Sr Dir-Brand Strategy-Global - Hewlett-Packard Company; pg. 404, pg. 175
Hampton, Phil, Dir-Media Rels - UCLA; pg. 608, pg. 141
Hampton, Russell, Exec VP-Franchise Mgmt & Global Consumer Products - NBC Universal, Inc.; pg. 300, pg. 1266
Hampton, Sean, Sr Dir-Digital Mktg - Janus Capital Group, Inc.; pg. 772, pg. 320
Hamrick, Kim, Mgr-Mdsg & Trade Show - The Dixie Group, Inc.; pg. 692, pg. 1629
Hamshaw, Chuck, Div Mgr-Corp, Post & New Media - Megatrax Production Music, Inc.; pg. 297, pg. 167

Hamstead, Amy, Sr Dir-Corp Comm - Host Hotels & Resorts, Inc.; *pg.* 1096, *pg.* 762
Hamstra, Kirsten, Mgr-Social Media - SAS Institute Inc.; *pg.* 466, *pg.* 1361
Hamza, Fuad, Gen Mgr-Brand Mktg - DISH Network Corporation; *pg.* 283, *pg.* 325
Han, Bo, Sr Mgr-Reg Medical Liaisons-Oncology - Amgen Inc.; *pg.* 1493, *pg.* 291
Han, Calvin, Brand Mgr-Consumer Health Care - Boehringer Ingelheim Pharmaceuticals, Inc.; *pg.* 1507, *pg.* 368
Han, Daniel, Mgr-Advanced Product Strategy - Hyundai Motor America; *pg.* 179, *pg.* 89
Han, John, Sr Mgr-Mktg - Samsung Electronics America, Inc.; *pg.* 669, *pg.* 1115
Han, Mike, Sr Mgr-Imaging Partnership & Bus Dev - NVIDIA Corporation; *pg.* 447, *pg.* 268
Han, Ming, Mgr-Comml Mobile Mktg - Cummins Power Generation; *pg.* 1326, *pg.* 932
Han, Paulina, Brand Mgr - LG Electronics U.S.A., Inc.; *pg.* 651, *pg.* 1060
Han, Sang, Assoc Dir-Creative - Apple Inc.; *pg.* 350, *pg.* 73
Han, Sang, Brand Mgr-KENMORE - Sears Holdings Corporation; *pg.* 1784, *pg.* 618
Han, Susan, Dir-Mktg Acq & Retention - Comcast Cable Communications, Inc.; *pg.* 276, *pg.* 1560
Han, Tricia, Chief Product Officer - About, Inc.; *pg.* 1225, *pg.* 1186
Hanahan, Jeanne, Sr Dir & Dir-Media Dept - MATTEL, INC.; *pg.* 962, *pg.* 81
Hanan, Leanne, Sr Mgr-Men's & Women's Corp Mdsg - Cole-Haan LLC; *pg.* 1806, *pg.* 1034
Hanan, Marci, Sr Dir-Consumer Mktg - Microsoft Corporation; *pg.* 435, *pg.* 1824
Hanasik, Janet, Mgr-Mktg - United States Tennis Association; *pg.* 160, *pg.* 1354
Hanavan, William, Mgr-Indus Sls - Niagara Transformer Corp.; *pg.* 1302, *pg.* 1150
Hanba, Craig, Grp Brand Mgr-Skilsaw Power Tools - Robert Bosch Tool Corp; *pg.* 1060, *pg.* 634
Hancart, Ray, Mgr-Social Media - The J.M. Smucker Company; *pg.* 865, *pg.* 1468
Hanchey, Holly, Dir-Mktg & Customer Experience - Atlanta Symphony Orchestra; *pg.* 531, *pg.* 490
Hancock, Andy, Reg Mgr-Commodity & Premium Offerings Sls - Yara N America, Inc.; *pg.* 1802, *pg.* 477
Hancock, Charlene, Mgr-Personalized & Local Area Mktg - Sun Life Financial Inc.; *pg.* 806, *pg.* 1944
Hancock, Gerald, Product Mgr - The Telx Group, Inc.; *pg.* 483, *pg.* 1298
Hancock, Keith, VP-Production - The Wooster Brush Company; *pg.* 1450, *pg.* 1482
Hancock, Kevin, Dir-Sls-Natl Retail Accts - Graham Holdings Company; *pg.* 1645, *pg.* 1773
Hancock, Matthew, Sr Dir-IR - Dollar General Corporation; *pg.* 1767, *pg.* 1635
Hancock, Nancy, Sr Mgr-Mktg Comm - Putnam Investments, LLC; *pg.* 797, *pg.* 800
Hancock, Pete, VP-Sls-Natl - Yelp! Inc.; *pg.* 1291, *pg.* 235
Hand, Derek, Asst Media Buyer - Palisades Media Group, Inc.; *pg.* 452, *pg.* 275
Hand, Orion, Sr Dir-Digital Mktg - John Paul Mitchell Systems; *pg.* 512, *pg.* 133
Hand, Tim, VP-OEM Sls-West - Kelley Blue Book Co., Inc.; *pg.* 1656, *pg.* 112
Handa, Hidetomo, Gen Mgr-Sls & Dir - Yahoo! Inc.; *pg.* 1289, *pg.* 289
Handal, Karla, Mgr-Mktg - Diageo North America, Inc.; *pg.* 1961, *pg.* 361
Handel, Jeremy, Sr Mgr-Pub Affairs - Las Vegas Convention & Visitors Authority; *pg.* 997, *pg.* 1027
Handel, Ray, Dir-Mktg & Promos - Millennium Radio New Jersey; *pg.* 298, *pg.* 1126
Handi, Jenn, Dir-Mktg - The Travelers Companies, Inc.; *pg.* 1220, *pg.* 352
Handler, Devin, Dir-Field Mktg - Qdoba Mexican Grill Inc.; *pg.* 1031, *pg.* 336
Handley, Sarah, VP-Mktg - Fisher-Price, Inc.; *pg.* 953, *pg.* 1156
Handmaker, Pam, Product Mgr - Northern Trust Corporation; *pg.* 787, *pg.* 585
Handspiker, Dean, Dir-Retail Sls, Mktg, Store Design & Mdsg - Indochino; *pg.* 42, *pg.* 1911
Handy, Josh, VP-Product Experience-Global - Method Products Inc.; *pg.* 332, *pg.* 223
Handy, Nicole, Sr Mgr-Mktg-Christian Dior - Parfums Christian Dior, Inc; *pg.* 519, *pg.* 1276
Handy, Sheri, Analyst-Mktg - Xerox Canada Inc.; *pg.* 494, *pg.* 1930
Haner, Evan, Dir-Digital Mktg & ECommerce - Specialized Bicycle Components, Inc.; *pg.* 1711, *pg.* 152
Hanewinckel, Nancy A., Mgr-East Reg Media Rels - Humana, Inc.; *pg.* 1204, *pg.* 734
Haney, Carl, Exec VP-R&D, Product Innovation & Brand Product Dev - The Estee Lauder Companies Inc.; *pg.* 508, *pg.* 1229
Haney, Carrie A., Mgr-Mktg Svcs - Acuity Brands, Inc.; *pg.* 1294, *pg.* 487
Haney, Jessica, Dir-Mktg & Product Mgmt - AT&T Mobility LLC; *pg.* 620, *pg.* 1152
Haney, Kim, Mgr-Event Mktg-Natl - Pernod Ricard USA, Inc.; *pg.* 1968, *pg.* 1332
Haney, Megan, Sr Mgr-Brand Comm-Americas Simple Meals & Beverages - Campbell Soup Company; *pg.* 844, *pg.* 1048
Haney, Shannon, VP-Integrated Brand Mktg - Morgan Stanley; *pg.* 783, *pg.* 1261
Haney, Susan, VP-Mktg - Gaiam, Inc.; *pg.* 1532, *pg.* 334
Hanfling, Jeanette, Dir-PR - Liquidity Services, Inc.; *pg.* 1263, *pg.* 401
Hang, Jennifer, Sr Mgr-Mktg-Vietnam - Dell Inc.; *pg.* 383, *pg.* 1737
Haniffy, Katie, Dir-Media Strategy & Investment - PepsiCo, Inc.; *pg.* 259, *pg.* 1327
Hanighen, John, VP-Comml Mktg - Advance Auto Parts, Inc.; *pg.* 197, *pg.* 1805
Hanka, Disney, Coord-Partnership Mktg Event - Houston Texans, L.P.; *pg.* 553, *pg.* 1708
Hankard, Brendan, Sr Mgr-Premium Sls & Svcs - Boston Red Sox Baseball Club Limited Partnership; *pg.* 534, *pg.* 791
Hanke, John, VP-Product-Niantic Labs - Google Inc.; *pg.* 1249, *pg.* 153
Hankins, Dewayne, VP-Mktg & Digital - Portland Trail Blazers; *pg.* 577, *pg.* 1505
Hankins, Joel, VP-Adv & Mktg - The Cato Corporation; *pg.* 21, *pg.* 1364
Hankins, Mike, Dir-Adv - News-Leader; *pg.* 1670, *pg.* 422
Hanks, Jessica, Mgr-Comm & PR - TheHuffingtonPost.com, Inc.; *pg.* 1692, *pg.* 1298
Hanley, Chuck, Dir-Production - PPG Industries, Inc.; *pg.* 1445, *pg.* 1579
Hanley, Jennifer Lambert, Sr VP-Nationwide Insurance Brand Mktg - Nationwide Mutual Insurance Company; *pg.* 1210, *pg.* 1442
Hanley, Jon, VP-Retail Sls - Country Pure Foods, Inc.; *pg.* 247, *pg.* 1400
Hanley, Michael J., Sr Dir-Fin - Natus Medical Incorporated; *pg.* 1572, *pg.* 199
Hanley, Michael J., VP-Sls - Vail Rubber Works, Inc.; *pg.* 1891, *pg.* 906
Hanlin, Kyle, Sr Dir-Comm & Team Svcs - Carolina Hurricanes Hockey Club; *pg.* 537, *pg.* 1386
Hanlon, Anne, Reg VP-Sls - Health Net, Inc.; *pg.* 1540, *pg.* 308
Hanlon, Kaileen, Sr Mgr-Retail Digital Mktg - CVS Health Corporation; *pg.* 1765, *pg.* 1610
Hanlon, Lindsey, Sr Analyst-Procurement-Mktg Svcs - Unilever United States, Inc.; *pg.* 904, *pg.* 1061
Hanlon, Paul, VP & Gen Mgr-SCC Cement Products - W.R. Grace & Co.; *pg.* 123, *pg.* 810
Hanly, Kathy, Head-Adv - Aetna Inc.; *pg.* 1187, *pg.* 351
Hanna, Eileen, Brand Mgr-Smirnoff Global - Diageo North America, Inc.; *pg.* 1961, *pg.* 361
Hanna, Eileen, Brand Mgr-Smirnoff Global - Diageo North America Inc.; *pg.* 248, *pg.* 1223
Hanna, Mary, Assoc Mgr-Mktg & Brand Mgmt - Toys "R" Us, Inc.; *pg.* 968, *pg.* 1130
Hanna, Melinda, Coord-ECommerce Product - Extended Stay Hotels LLC; *pg.* 1091, *pg.* 1622
Hanna, Sherif, Sr Mgr-Technical Mktg-LTE Modems - QUALCOMM Incorporated; *pg.* 1873, *pg.* 207
Hanna, Steve, VP-Global Matls Sls & Mktg - 3D Systems Corporation; *pg.* 339, *pg.* 1621
Hannaford, Kim, Dir-Mktg - Morgan Foods, Inc.; *pg.* 881, *pg.* 673
Hannan, Andrew, Dir-Mktg & Bus Dev - ACP Marketing, Inc.; *pg.* 1896, *pg.* 1953
Hannan, Barbara, Strategist-Social Media-Global SMB Market - Pitney Bowes Inc.; *pg.* 454, *pg.* 376
Hannan, Carolyne, VP-Sls & Mktg - Comcast Cable Communications, Inc.; *pg.* 276, *pg.* 1560
Hanneke, Kristin, Mgr-Creative Svcs - Panera Bread Company; *pg.* 1029, *pg.* 1001
Hannel, Allison, Dir-Mktg Comm - AT&T Mobility LLC; *pg.* 619, *pg.* 488
Hannemann, Christopher, Dir-Consumer Mktg - American Pop Corn Company; *pg.* 825, *pg.* 712
Hannen, Geoff, Dir-Mktg - Red Bull North America, Inc.; *pg.* 264, *pg.* 275
Hanney, Tara, Mgr-PR-Worldwide - Hewlett-Packard Company; *pg.* 404, *pg.* 175
Hanni, Bill, VP-Ticket Sls & Svc, Washington Wizards & Mystics - Washington Wizards; *pg.* 591, *pg.* 408
Hannigan, Kelly, Sr Mgr-Travel Partnerships in Loyalty & Membership Benefits - American Express Company; *pg.* 712, *pg.* 1190
Hannigan, Tom, Dir-Global Mktg Platforms - International Business Machines Corporation; *pg.* 418, *pg.* 1138
Hanning, Natalie, Planner-Sls-Natl - Pandora Media Inc.; *pg.* 1273, *pg.* 172
Hannock, Melanee, Sr VP-Mktg - St. Jude Children's Research Hospital; *pg.* 1596, *pg.* 1646
Hannon, Bill, Mgr-Inside Sls - Zephyr Manufacturing Co., Inc.; *pg.* 1391, *pg.* 105
Hannon, Cole, Sr Mgr-Regulatory Affairs - Medtronic, Inc.; *pg.* 1564, *pg.* 939
Hannon, Keith, Assoc Dir-Social Media - Cornell University Press; *pg.* 1630, *pg.* 1169
Hannon, Shelly, Grp Acct Dir - H-E-B; *pg.* 1022, *pg.* 1740
Hannon, Terry, Chief Strategy Officer & Chief Bus Dev Officer - Adept Technology, Inc.; *pg.* 1310, *pg.* 182
Hannon, Todd, Mgr-US Regulatory Adv - Pfizer Inc.; *pg.* 1581, *pg.* 1278
Hanns, Sharill, Specialist-Mktg Comm - Epson America Inc.; *pg.* 394, *pg.* 122
Hannula, Mara, VP-Brand Mktg-Global - Marriott International, Inc.; *pg.* 1102, *pg.* 764
Hanrahan, Greg, Sr Dir-Premium Seating - Chicago Professional Sports Limited Partnership; *pg.* 539, *pg.* 570
Hanrahan, Kelly, Mgr-Mktg Brand - Lake Austin Spa Resort; *pg.* 1100, *pg.* 1663
Hanrahan, Sean, Sr VP-Mktg Solutions-ESPN Customer Mktg & Sls - ESPN, Inc.; *pg.* 285, *pg.* 340
Hanrahan, Susan K., Dir-Global Product & Portfolio Strategy - MedImmune LLC; *pg.* 1562, *pg.* 770
Hanras, Charlotte, VP & Mgr-Mktg - Bank of the West; *pg.* 721, *pg.* 213
Hans, Judy E., VP-Mktg - Liberty National Life Insurance Co.; *pg.* 1206, *pg.* 5
Hansberry, Kathy, Mgr-PR - Outrigger Enterprises, Inc.; *pg.* 1107, *pg.* 544
Hansee, Donna, Sr Dir-Mktg & Dir-Comm-Global - WILD Flavors, Inc.; *pg.* 910, *pg.* 728
Hansel, Sandra, VP-Sls - Design Within Reach, Inc.; *pg.* 923, *pg.* 216
Hansen, Alexander, VP-Sls-Enterprise Connectivity-US - Belden, Inc.; *pg.* 624, *pg.* 993
Hansen, Alison, Mgr-Corp Consumer Mktg - Mary Kay Inc.; *pg.* 516, *pg.* 1657
Hansen, Burt, Mgr-Mktg - Aetna Inc.; *pg.* 1187, *pg.* 351
Hansen, Carol, Sr VP & Reg Dir-Mktg-Texas - Wells Fargo & Company; *pg.* 819, *pg.* 232
Hansen, Chad, Dir-Mktg - Weiman Products, LLC; *pg.* 337, *pg.* 616
Hansen, Chuck, Grp VP-Mktg Tech & Production - Macy's East; *pg.* 1777, *pg.* 1254
Hansen, Chuck, Grp VP-Mktg Tech & Production - Macy's, Inc.; *pg.* 1778, *pg.* 1417
Hansen, Dain, Dir-Product Mktg - Oracle Corporation; *pg.* 450, *pg.* 191
Hansen, Dixie, Bus Mgr - KSTP-TV, LLC; *pg.* 295, *pg.* 962
Hansen, Ellen, Mgr-Mktg - Capella Education Company; *pg.* 599, *pg.* 931
Hansen, Emily, Dir-Mktg-ProCare - Stryker Corporation; *pg.* 1598, *pg.* 894
Hansen, Jessica L., Mgr-Consumer Media Rels - Intel Corporation; *pg.* 645, *pg.* 266
Hansen, Joan, Dir-Mktg - BJ'S RESTAURANTS, INC.; *pg.* 1716, *pg.* 104
Hansen, Jon, VP-Energy Production & Mktg - Omaha Public Power District; *pg.* 1948, *pg.* 1017
Hansen, Justin, Dir-Interactive Mktg - Ameriprise Financial, Inc.; *pg.* 715, *pg.* 930
Hansen, Kai, Product Mgr - Google Inc.; *pg.* 1249, *pg.* 153
Hansen, Kara, Dir-Digital Media - The Walt Disney Company; *pg.* 317, *pg.* 52

First page reference indicates Business Class Edition
Second page reference indicates Geographic Edition

Hansen, Karen, Product Mgr-Digital - VITAMIN SHOPPE, INC.; pg. 1608, pg. 1098
Hansen, Kristin, Coord-Mktg - M/I Homes, Inc.; pg. 95, pg. 1441
Hansen, Lonnie G., Sr Dir-Customer Experience - DIRECTV Group Holdings, LLC; pg. 281, pg. 79
Hansen, Marcia, Mgr-Mktg - Intel Corporation; pg. 645, pg. 266
Hansen, Mark, Dir-OEM Sls HVAC & R - Danfoss Graham; pg. 203, pg. 1874
Hansen, Mary, Brand Mgr - McIlhenny Company; pg. 876, pg. 741
Hansen, Matt, Sr Product Mgr - Rockwell Automation, Inc.; pg. 668, pg. 1880
Hansen, Miriam, Dir-Brand, Adv & Design-Natl - American Heart Association Inc.; pg. 128, pg. 1673
Hansen, Mollie, VP-Mktg - Airstream, Inc.; pg. 163, pg. 1456
Hansen, Naomi Chan, Dir-Mktg - DOLE FOOD COMPANY, INC.; pg. 853, pg. 306
Hansen, Peter, Mgr-Instrument Product Line - Teradyne Inc.; pg. 679, pg. 838
Hansen, Scott, Mgr-Bus Mktg & Event - Aetna Inc.; pg. 1187, pg. 351
Hansen, Tima, Mgr-Mktg - TBC Corporation; pg. 1889, pg. 457
Hansen, Tina, Sr Rep-Mktg Comm - Port Authority of New York & New Jersey; pg. 1919, pg. 1283
Hansen, Tonie, Sr Dir-CSR & Sustainability - NVIDIA Corporation; pg. 447, pg. 268
Hanshaw, Madison, Asst Media Planner - Turner Broadcasting System, Inc.; pg. 314, pg. 521
Hansing, Scott, Dir-Mktg-Indochina Cluster - S.C. Johnson & Son, Inc.; pg. 334, pg. 1889
Hansinger, Mark, VP-Sls-US - Oki Data Americas, Inc.; pg. 449, pg. 1090
Hansmann, Bob, Dir-Product Mktg - Websense, Inc.; pg. 491, pg. 210
Hanson, Daniel G., VP-Mktg-Global - Columbia Sportswear Company; pg. 1830, pg. 1501
Hanson, Denise, Mgr-Mobility Mktg - AT&T; pg. 1865, pg. 258
Hanson, Greta, Mgr-Media Strategy - General Mills, Inc.; pg. 828, pg. 933
Hanson, Heather, Dir-Mktg & Program Dev - Cardinal Health, Inc.; pg. 1512, pg. 1448
Hanson, James C., Sr Mgr-Customer Mktg - Abbott Laboratories; pg. 1484, pg. 551
Hanson, Jeff, Mgr-Manufactured Product Sls - Wellmaster Carts; pg. 1388, pg. 1934
Hanson, Krista, Mgr-Digital Mktg - Colgate-Palmolive Company; pg. 504, pg. 1215
Hanson, Linda, Dir-Integrated Mktg - Citrix Systems, Inc.; pg. 375, pg. 424
Hanson, Marc, Dir-Beverage Portfolio Mktg Strategy - Pepsi Beverages Company; pg. 258, pg. 1342
Hanson, Marc, Sr Dir-Global Beverage Portfolio Transformation - PepsiCo, Inc.; pg. 259, pg. 1327
Hanson, Mary, Mgr-PR - The Boeing Company; pg. 225, pg. 567
Hanson, Michael, Sr Mgr-IT - UnitedHealth Group Incorporated; pg. 1221, pg. 950
Hanson, Rhonda, Dir-Platform Engrg, Search & Social-Tech & Product Engrg - Time Inc.; pg. 1693, pg. 1300
Hanson, Rob, Associate-Mktg - DraftKings, Inc.; pg. 545, pg. 793
Hanson, Tim, Mgr-Mktg - United Services Automobile Association; pg. 1221, pg. 1743
Hanson, Timothy P., VP-Sls - Danfoss Power Solutions Company; pg. 1328, pg. 701
Hanson, Tom, VP-Mktg - Quality Dining, Inc.; pg. 1746, pg. 695
Hanson, Troy, Dir-Product Mgmt - Cardinal Health, Inc.; pg. 1512, pg. 1448
Hanson, Vicki L., Mgr-MR Mktg - General Electric Company; pg. 1297, pg. 347
Hanson, Wayne, Sr Mgr-Mktg - Dell Inc.; pg. 383, pg. 1737
Hansotia, Eric, Sr VP-Global Harvesting & Advanced Tech Solutions - AGCO Corporation; pg. 700, pg. 530
Hanspal, Amar, Sr VP-IPG Product Grp - Autodesk Inc.; pg. 356, pg. 257
Hanulec, Ken, VP-Mktg-Inkjet Solutions - Electronics For Imaging, Inc.; pg. 390, pg. 88
Hanvichid, Sam, Sr Mgr-Bus Dev - Analysts International Corporation; pg. 350, pg. 930
Happel, Branden, Sr Mgr-PR & Mktg Comm - The Toro Company Irrigation Products; pg. 1065, pg. 194
Haq, Tariq, Sr Product Mgr-Global - GE Healthcare; pg. 399, pg. 1765
Haqqani, Rafi, Dir-Mktg-Supplies & Accessories - Brother International Corporation - USA; pg. 53, pg. 1046
Harada, Akira, Deputy Div Mng Dir-Overseas Sls & Bus Dev - Ikegami Electronics (U.S.A.), Inc.; pg. 644, pg. 1083
Haran, Jim, VP & Sr Product Mgr-Investment Risk & Analytical Svcs, C&IS - Northern Trust Corporation; pg. 787, pg. 585
Harant, Sarah, Specialist-Ecommerce Mktg - The Bradford Group; pg. 1763, pg. 637
Haras, Shauna, Reg Dir-Sls - Forbes, Inc.; pg. 1641, pg. 1232
Harasti, Lucille, Dir-Corp Mktg & Branding - Credit Suisse Securities (USA) LLC; pg. 742, pg. 1220
Harb, Trey, Dir-Sls-Natl - Time Warner Cable Inc.; pg. 312, pg. 1301
Harbaugh, Odile, Brand Mgr & Reg Mgr-Mktg - The Scotts Miracle-Gro Company; pg. 1799, pg. 1459
Harbeck, Jamie, Dir-Digital Brand Mktg, Luxury & Lifestyle - Hilton Worldwide, Inc.; pg. 1094, pg. 1791
Harbert, Rand, CMO & Chief Sls Officer - State Farm Mutual Automobile Insurance Co.; pg. 1218, pg. 557
Harbin, Beth, Sr Dir-Comm - Southwest Airlines Co.; pg. 1923, pg. 1687
Harbison, William, Engr-Voice & Designer - Alliance Data Systems Corporation; pg. 347, pg. 1729
Harbour, Mike, Product Mgr - Jewell Instruments, LLC; pg. 1418, pg. 1036
Harbrecht, Douglas, Dir-New Media - The Kiplinger Washington Editors, Inc.; pg. 1657, pg. 401
Harbun, Kelvin T., VP-Sls-Asia - Gleason - M&M Precision Systems Corporation; pg. 1341, pg. 1479
Harceg, Nate, Assoc Mgr-Mktg-Pricing Innovations - Wal-Mart Stores, Inc.; pg. 1790, pg. 29
Hardcastle, Jennifer, Mgr-Air Medical Sls - Airbus Helicopters, Inc.; pg. 223, pg. 1698
Harden, Nat, VP-Ticket Sls - Nashville Predators, LLC; pg. 565, pg. 1652
Harden, Sonya E., Dir-Comm-Global Primary Products - Alcoa Inc.; pg. 65, pg. 1188
Harder, Emily, Dir-ECommerce Mktg - Foot Locker, Inc.; pg. 1808, pg. 1231
Harder, Jimena, Sr Mgr-Hispanic Segment - Sysco Corporation; pg. 1035, pg. 1716
Harder, Kyle, Brand Mgr-1800 Tequila & Zarco - Proximo Spirits, Inc.; pg. 1969, pg. 1076
Harder, Scot, VP-Sls & Mktg - ODL Incorporated; pg. 101, pg. 914
Hardesty, Crystal, Dir-Mktg - Goodwill Industries International, Inc.; pg. 1771, pg. 776
Hardesty, David, VP-Sls & Mktg - Aeroflex Incorporated; pg. 614, pg. 1321
Hardesty, Nicole, Assoc Mgr-Product Line-Hush Puppies - Wolverine World Wide, Inc.; pg. 1822, pg. 905
Hardie, Ashley, Sr Mgr-Supplier Dev & Diversity-Realty - Wal-Mart.com; pg. 1287, pg. 50
Hardie, Byron, Sr Dir-SEO - Angie's List Inc; pg. 1228, pg. 682
Hardie, Karen, VP-Global Sls - Rocky Mountaineer; pg. 1921, pg. 1912
Hardigg, Kirsten, Exec Dir-Mdsg - Hunter Boot USA; pg. 1810, pg. 1242
Hardiman, Alex, VP-Product - The New York Times Company; pg. 1668, pg. 1270
Hardiman, Alexandra, VP-Product - The New York Times; pg. 1668, pg. 1270
Hardin, James, VP-Sls & Field Ops - CDK Global, Inc.; pg. 370, pg. 617
Hardin, Jeff, VP-Sls - Cal-Maine Foods, Inc.; pg. 843, pg. 969
Hardin, John L, Mgr-PR - Atlus USA, Inc.; pg. 949, pg. 107
Harding, Bryan, Dir-Mktg Partnerships - The Nature Conservancy; pg. 151, pg. 1774
Harding, Courtney, Sr Mgr-Mktg Reporting & Analytics - F5 Networks, Inc.; pg. 396, pg. 1835
Harding, Michael, Mgr-Product Mktg - NetApp, Inc.; pg. 444, pg. 287
Hardison, Mark, VP-Mktg - El Pollo Loco, Inc.; pg. 1728, pg. 70
Hardison, Matthew F., CMO & Chief Sls Officer - National Railroad Passenger Corporation; pg. 1916, pg. 403
Hardman-Sytar, Cherilyn, VP-Mktg - COUNTRY Financial; pg. 1198, pg. 557
Hardwick, Jennifer, Assoc Dir-Mktg-Chattem Skin Care Brands - Chattem, Inc.; pg. 1515, pg. 1628
Hardwick, Kristin, Head-Bus & Product Comm - Uber USA, LLC; pg. 1286, pg. 229
Hardwick, Masae, Mgr-Pkg Creative & Brand Mgr - Pier 1 Imports, Inc.; pg. 940, pg. 1695
Hardy, Carey, Mgr-Interactive Mktg - InterContinental Hotels Corporation; pg. 1097, pg. 511
Hardy, Elisabet, VP-Product Mgmt & Mktg - Thomson Elite; pg. 484, pg. 72
Hardy, Erika, Dir-Mktg & Men's Health - Eli Lilly and Company; pg. 1527, pg. 684
Hardy, Gina, Dir-Mktg-Propel - PepsiCo, Inc.; pg. 259, pg. 1327
Hardy, John, Dir-Mktg Sourcing - The Walt Disney Company; pg. 317, pg. 52
Hardy, Matthew, Mgr-Sls - McKesson Corporation; pg. 1560, pg. 222
Hardy, Trudy, VP-Mktg - BMW of North America, LLC; pg. 166, pg. 1133
Hardy, Whitney, VP-Mktg - CVS Health Corporation; pg. 1765, pg. 1610
Hare, Dan, Sr Dir-Comm & External Rels - ConAgra Foods, Inc.; pg. 826, pg. 1014
Hare, Georgia, Mgr-Mdsg - Interface, Inc.; pg. 695, pg. 512
Haren, Jamie, Brand Mgr - Bacardi USA, Inc.; pg. 1956, pg. 417
Harger, James N., CMO - Clean Energy Fuels Corp.; pg. 974, pg. 165
Harges, Chris, Dir-Mktg-Global - Mountain Hardwear, Inc.; pg. 1839, pg. 193
Hargis, Jonathan, CMO & Exec VP - Charter Communications, Inc.; pg. 274, pg. 372
Hargreaves, Evan, Product Dir-Wilson Racquet Sports-Global - Wilson Sporting Goods Co.; pg. 1848, pg. 596
Hargreaves, Jeffrey R., Community Sls Mgr - D.R. Horton, Inc.; pg. 1090, pg. 1694
Hargrove, George, VP-Sls & Mktg - Barnhardt Manufacturing Company; pg. 1498, pg. 1364
Hargrove, Randy, Dir-Natl Media Rels - Wal-Mart.com; pg. 1287, pg. 50
Hariasz, Faustyna, Mgr-Sponsorships & Mktg - AIGA, the professional association for design; pg. 125, pg. 1188
Harichandran, Karen, Sr Product Mgr-Mobile - Sephora USA Inc; pg. 522, pg. 227
Hariramani, Prakash, Sr Product Mgr-Google Wallet - Google Inc.; pg. 1249, pg. 153
Harish, Manu, Sr Product Mgr - Go Daddy Inc.; pg. 1249, pg. 21
Harjo, Brandon, Gen Mgr-Sls - Oak Farms Dairy; pg. 887, pg. 1685
Harkcom, M. Kay, Brand Mgr & Mgr-Comm - 3M Company; pg. 1142, pg. 956
Harkins, Bert, Sr VP-Sls & Mktg - Fiserv, Inc.; pg. 397, pg. 1855
Harkins, Charles F., Jr., VP-Sls & Mktg - Hudson Technologies, Inc.; pg. 1073, pg. 1320
Harkins, Megan, Mgr-Digital Mktg & Media-LOFT - Ann Inc.; pg. 18, pg. 1195
Harkins, Scott, VP-Domestic Svcs Mktg-FedEx Express - FedEx Corporation; pg. 1907, pg. 1642
Harkins, Tara, VP-Mktg - Lincoln Financial Group; pg. 1206, pg. 1375
Harkness, Kim, Dir-Mktg-Bus Insurance - The Travelers Companies, Inc.; pg. 1220, pg. 352
Harkness, Renee, Mgr-Mktg-Global - Hewlett-Packard Company; pg. 404, pg. 175
Harkness, Susan, Brand Mgr-Corp Strategy & Mktg - OGE Energy Corp.; pg. 1948, pg. 1486
Harkness, Trent, Dir-Mktg - Polyair Inter Pack Inc.; pg. 1467, pg. 1941
Harkness, Whitney, Sr Asst Brand Mgr - DISH Network Corporation; pg. 283, pg. 325
Harlacher, Denise, Sr Category Mgr-Global Sourcing-Consumer Creative Relationships - Boehringer Ingelheim Pharmaceuticals, Inc.; pg. 1507, pg. 368
Harlam, Bari, Exec VP-Membership, Mktg & Analytics - BJ's Wholesale Club, Inc.; pg. 1762, pg. 857
Harlan, Scott, Product Mgr - Rockwell Automation, Inc.; pg. 668, pg. 1880
Harles, Robert, Mng Dir & Head-Social Bus-Global - Accenture; pg. 1392, pg. 1186
Harley, Tahia, Partner & Mgr-Brand Mktg - Discovery Communications, Inc.; pg. 282, pg. 777
Harlin, Kwame, Producer-Technical-Creative Solutions - LinkedIn Corporation; pg. 1262, pg. 160
Harlin, Scott, Dir-Mktg Comm-Enterprise - OCZ Storage Solutions; pg. 448, pg. 248

Harling, Karen, Sr Mgr & Assoc Comm-U S - Wal-Mart Stores, Inc.; *pg.* 1790, *pg.* 29
Harlow, Lori, Reg Dir-Sls - salesforce.com, inc.; *pg.* 1278, *pg.* 226
Harm, Raymond T., Sr VP-Sls - Hooker Furniture Corporation; *pg.* 928, *pg.* 1788
Harman, Ashley, Sr Program Head-Global Mktg - Whole Foods Market, Inc.; *pg.* 1038, *pg.* 1667
Harman, Cameran, Head-Demand Sls EMEA-LiveRail - Facebook, Inc.; *pg.* 1245, *pg.* 143
Harman, DJ, Mgr-Online Mktg - Hotels.com, L.P.; *pg.* 1257, *pg.* 1682
Harman, Jon, Dir-Asian Sls & Mktg - Precitech, Inc.; *pg.* 1427, *pg.* 1035
Harmeling, Ashley, Dir-Daily Sls & Integrated Promos - Wayfair LLC; *pg.* 1288, *pg.* 801
Harmeling, John T., Sr VP-Mktg - Aflac Incorporated; *pg.* 1188, *pg.* 527
Harmon, Aaron, Sr Dir-Mobile App Platform Product - Viacom Inc.; *pg.* 316, *pg.* 1310
Harmon, Amy, Brand Mgr-Sls Plng-Customer Mktg Grp - The Clorox Company; *pg.* 327, *pg.* 169
Harmon, Brad, Pres/Publr-Dispatch Media Grp - GateHouse Media, Inc.; *pg.* 1644, *pg.* 1159
Harmon, Charles, Sr Dir-Corp Procurement & Corp Svcs - American Honda Motor Co., Inc.; *pg.* 163, *pg.* 292
Harmon, Dan, Mgr-Sensing Products Bus Dev - Texas Instruments Incorporated; *pg.* 679, *pg.* 1688
Harmon, Edith, VP-Advanced Products - New Balance Athletic Shoe, Inc.; *pg.* 1811, *pg.* 798
Harmon, Heather M., Sr Mgr-Trade Mktg-All Channels-Birds Eye - Pinnacle Foods Group LLC; *pg.* 889, *pg.* 1104
Harmon, Jennifer, Sr Mgr-Media - Post Holdings, Inc.; *pg.* 833, *pg.* 1002
Harmon, Nikki, Mgr-Social Media - Mattel Games/Puzzles; *pg.* 962, *pg.* 80
Harms, Kelli, Mgr-Mktg & Sls Promo - Winnebago Industries, Inc.; *pg.* 1712, *pg.* 707
Harms, Tom, VP-Sls, Mktg & Distributor Svcs - Herbalife International of America, Inc.; *pg.* 1541, *pg.* 132
Harn, Angela, Dir-Mktg & Adv - Georgia Southern University; *pg.* 602, *pg.* 541
Harned, John, Dir-Interactive Web Mktg & Production - VMware, Inc.; *pg.* 490, *pg.* 179
Harner, Scott, Reg Mgr-Svc Sls - American Crane & Equipment Corporation; *pg.* 1312, *pg.* 1526
Harness, Ashley, Product Mgr-Steward & Regulatory Affairs - E.I. du Pont de Nemours & Company; *pg.* 1159, *pg.* 390
Harness, Heather, Mgr-Mktg, Adv & Game Entertainment - Baltimore Ravens Limited Partnership; *pg.* 532, *pg.* 755
Harnetiaux, Katie, Dir-Teavana Mktg - Starbucks Corporation; *pg.* 897, *pg.* 1840
Harnett, Alexa, Reg Mgr-Mktg - Mercedes-Benz USA, LLC; *pg.* 184, *pg.* 514
Harnett, Suzanne, Sr Dir-IR - Pfizer Inc.; *pg.* 1581, *pg.* 1278
Harney, Aimee, Sr Mgr-Purchases - The Procter & Gamble Company; *pg.* 1129, *pg.* 1418
Harney, Richard, Sr VP-Mktg - School Specialty, Inc.; *pg.* 467, *pg.* 1860
Harnist, Charlie L., VP-Grocery Sls - Skyline Chili, Inc.; *pg.* 1033, *pg.* 1452
Haro, Steve, Dir-777X Mktg - The Boeing Company - Helicopter Division; *pg.* 226, *pg.* 13
Harof, Terri, Dir-Franchise Sls - Shoney's North America, LLC; *pg.* 1749, *pg.* 1654
Harold, Dan, Dir-Mktg & Sls - Nupla Corporation; *pg.* 101, *pg.* 281
Harold, John, Dir-Creative - The Ratner Companies; *pg.* 520, *pg.* 1809
Harold, Sara, Mgr-Mktg - Carbonite, Inc.; *pg.* 368, *pg.* 792
Harp, Andy, Product Mgr-MPSE - Xerox Corporation; *pg.* 494, *pg.* 365
Harp, Joanna, Dir-Adv - Crain's New York Business; *pg.* 1631, *pg.* 1220
Harpalani, Sandeep, Dir-Product Mktg & Mgmt - NETGEAR, Inc.; *pg.* 444, *pg.* 247
Harpaz, Ran, Sr Dir-Strategy-Consumer & Mobile Products - PayPal Inc.; *pg.* 1274, *pg.* 248
Harpenau, Jan, Coord-Inside Sls - IAC Industries, Inc.; *pg.* 929, *pg.* 48
Harper, Blake, Sr Mgr-Mktg - Ebix Inc.; *pg.* 1241, *pg.* 504
Harper, Brittany, Coord-Shopper Mktg - Brookshire Grocery Company; *pg.* 1016, *pg.* 1748
Harper, Bryan, Sr Mgr-Mktg & Exec Producer-Vikings Entertainment Network - Minnesota Vikings Football Club, Inc.; *pg.* 563, *pg.* 923
Harper, Chelsea, Reg Specialist-Adv - Popeyes Louisiana Kitchen, Inc.; *pg.* 1745, *pg.* 517
Harper, Denine, Reg Dir-Mktg - MetroPCS, Inc.; *pg.* 1872, *pg.* 1683
Harper, Jim, Mgr-Creative - Winn Dixie Stores, Inc.; *pg.* 1038, *pg.* 435
Harper, Jim, Product Mgr-Sls - Zephyr Manufacturing Co., Inc.; *pg.* 1391, *pg.* 105
Harper, Julius, Sr Mgr-Content Strategy-Disney ABC Television Grp - The Walt Disney Company; *pg.* 317, *pg.* 52
Harper, Kenneth, Dir-Product Mgmt & Mktg-Mobile Speech - Nuance Communications, Inc.; *pg.* 447, *pg.* 806
Harper, Kim, Program Mgr-Mktg - Citigroup Inc.; *pg.* 735, *pg.* 1212
Harper, Kristin, VP-Brand Mgmt & Mktg - Cardinal Health, Inc.; *pg.* 1512, *pg.* 1448
Harper, Lauren, Sr Mgr-Mktg-UL Brand & Scale - Unilever United States, Inc.; *pg.* 904, *pg.* 1061
Harper, Michelle, VP-Sls - Cox Media Group; *pg.* 280, *pg.* 502
Harper, Peter, VP-Direct Mktg Centralized Production - Bank of America Corporation; *pg.* 718, *pg.* 1362
Harper, Peter, VP-Strategic Mktg & Brand Dev - General Tools & Instruments LLC; *pg.* 1048, *pg.* 1234
Harper, Robyn, Mgr-Sls Promo - State Automobile Mutual Insurance Company; *pg.* 1217, *pg.* 1444
Harper, Steven, Dir-Strategic Mktg & Comm - Arizona State University; *pg.* 597, *pg.* 25
Harpine, Bryan, Dir-New Products-Global - Church & Dwight Co., Inc.; *pg.* 1153, *pg.* 1063
Harr, Mark, Reg Mgr-Sls - Dover Chemical Corporation; *pg.* 1156, *pg.* 1447
Harralson, Stephanie, Sr Product Mgr - Sunsweet Growers, Inc.; *pg.* 900, *pg.* 309
Harrell, Ben, VP-Mktg, Plng & Analysis - The Priceline Group Inc.; *pg.* 1276, *pg.* 364
Harrell, Henry E., Exec VP-Sls & Mktg - Broder Bros., Co.; *pg.* 1828, *pg.* 1588
Harrell, Joanne, Sr Dir-Citizenship & Pub Affairs-US - Microsoft Corporation; *pg.* 435, *pg.* 1824
Harrell, Joe, Sr Dir-Digital Strategy - WNET.org; *pg.* 322, *pg.* 1315
Harrell, Malinda, Assoc Dir-Convention Sls - Greater Raleigh Convention & Visitors Bureau; *pg.* 994, *pg.* 1387
Harrell, Patrick, Mgr-Creative Strategy - Blue Cross & Blue Shield of Florida, Inc.; *pg.* 1507, *pg.* 432
Harrell, Wendy, Analyst-Sls Ops - Honeywell International Inc.; *pg.* 407, *pg.* 1088
Harres, Victoria, VP-Digital & Events Mktg - PR Newswire Association LLC; *pg.* 1678, *pg.* 1283
Harriett, Todd, Dir-Mktg - Nalco Co.; *pg.* 1174, *pg.* 636
Harriman, Allan, Dir-Natl Sls Ops - Hyundai Motor America; *pg.* 179, *pg.* 89
Harrington, Adam, Product Mgr - Varian Medical Systems, Inc.; *pg.* 1434, *pg.* 178
Harrington, Christine, Mgr-Internet Mktg - Olympus America Inc.; *pg.* 1425, *pg.* 1521
Harrington, Ed, Dir-Creative - Style Weekly Inc.; *pg.* 1690, *pg.* 1804
Harrington, Heather, VP-Mktg-Staples Advantage - Staples, Inc.; *pg.* 474, *pg.* 821
Harrington, Jason, Mgr-Sls-Natl - Snyder Industries, Inc.; *pg.* 1377, *pg.* 1012
Harrington, Leigh, Dir-Mktg Strategy & Comm - Clean Harbors, Inc.; *pg.* 376, *pg.* 839
Harrington, Mary, Sr Strategist-Digital Mktg - Highmark Blue Cross Blue Shield; *pg.* 1203, *pg.* 1576
Harrington, Mike, Assoc Dir-Mktg Comm - Merck & Co., Inc.; *pg.* 1566, *pg.* 1077
Harrington, Sarah, Mgr-Mktg - Hologic, Inc.; *pg.* 1416, *pg.* 784
Harrington, Taryn, Media Buyer - The Progressive Corporation; *pg.* 1214, *pg.* 1463
Harris, Aaron, Sr Dir-PR - Brooklyn Nets; *pg.* 534, *pg.* 1145
Harris, Amber, VP-Comm & Social Media - Discovery Communications, Inc.; *pg.* 282, *pg.* 777
Harris, Andrew, Sr VP-Advisory Svcs - Binswanger Corporation; *pg.* 1082, *pg.* 1559
Harris, Ann, Sr Dir-Turner Sports Digital Res & Analytics - Turner Broadcasting System, Inc.; *pg.* 314, *pg.* 521
Harris, Anna, Sr Dir-Digital Mktg & Analytics - St. Jude Children's Research Hospital; *pg.* 1596, *pg.* 1646
Harris, Anya, Mgr-Mktg-Campaigns-Global - Juniper Networks, Inc.; *pg.* 1260, *pg.* 286
Harris, Barry, Mgr-Product, Cataloging & Mktg-Global - The Timken Company; *pg.* 218, *pg.* 1408
Harris, Bruce, Mgr-Mktg - Q A Group LLC.; *pg.* 1427, *pg.* 89
Harris, Carron, Sr Dir-Ops - Papa Murphy's International, LLC; *pg.* 1743, *pg.* 1846
Harris, Chad, Exec Dir-Mktg & Adv - AT&T Mobility LLC; *pg.* 619, *pg.* 488
Harris, Charles, Sr VP-Mktg - Anaheim/Orange County Visitor & Convention Bureau; *pg.* 988, *pg.* 42
Harris, Chris, Mgr-Trade Mktg - Kao Brands Co. Inc.; *pg.* 513, *pg.* 1415
Harris, Chuck, VP-Sls & Ops-Midwest - Intelligrated, Inc.; *pg.* 1349, *pg.* 1460
Harris, Claudette Carmine, Mgr-Mktg Comm - Solar Turbines Incorporated; *pg.* 1377, *pg.* 209
Harris, Corey, Product Mgr-Label - Ecolab Inc.; *pg.* 329, *pg.* 960
Harris, Dave, Mgr-Natl Acct Sls - Kidron, Inc.; *pg.* 181, *pg.* 1457
Harris, David, Head-Digital Mktg - GE Water & Process Technologies; *pg.* 1339, *pg.* 1588
Harris, Donna, Dir-Retail Adv - Daily Times Leader; *pg.* 1633, *pg.* 972
Harris, Emily, Analyst-Mktg-Regional - Orange Leaf Frozen Yogurt; *pg.* 1742, *pg.* 1487
Harris, Eric, Dir-Mktg Comm-Nikon-Trimble - Trimble Navigation Limited; *pg.* 1384, *pg.* 288
Harris, Felita, Sr Dir-Sls - The Donna Karan Company LLC; *pg.* 23, *pg.* 1225
Harris, Ford, Sr Mgr-BD-Amazon Appstore - Amazon.com, Inc.; *pg.* 1226, *pg.* 1831
Harris, Glenn, Sr Dir-Wholesale Mktg - Markel Corporation; *pg.* 1207, *pg.* 1783
Harris, Graham, Sr Dir-Advanced Creative - Yahoo! Inc.; *pg.* 1289, *pg.* 289
Harris, Horland, Sr Mgr-Engagement - Diageo North America Inc.; *pg.* 248, *pg.* 1223
Harris, Jamie, Analyst-Partnership Mktg - American Express Company; *pg.* 712, *pg.* 1190
Harris, Jeff, Reg Mgr-Sls - Genuine Parts Company; *pg.* 206, *pg.* 506
Harris, Jeff, Sr VP-Global Sls & Mktg - ImageWare Systems, Inc.; *pg.* 412, *pg.* 203
Harris, Jennifer, Reg VP-Mktg - Simon Property Group, Inc.; *pg.* 1112, *pg.* 690
Harris, Jonathan, Sr VP-Intergalactic Sls - GoPro; *pg.* 1414, *pg.* 255
Harris, Kellie, Analyst-Product Mktg - Tyler Technologies, Inc.; *pg.* 486, *pg.* 1690
Harris, Kerry, Mgr-Mktg - TD Ameritrade Holding Corporation; *pg.* 808, *pg.* 1018
Harris, Kim, Product Mgr-Mktg - Bank of America Global Wealth & Investment Management; *pg.* 720, *pg.* 789
Harris, Kyle, Sr Mgr-Design - The Procter & Gamble Company; *pg.* 1129, *pg.* 1418
Harris, Larry, VP & Dir-Mktg - The Bank of New York Mellon Corporation; *pg.* 720, *pg.* 1200
Harris, Mary, Mgr-Agri Food Sls - Watt Publishing Company; *pg.* 1701, *pg.* 655
Harris, Mat, Sr Dir-Adv Products - Tapjoy, Inc.; *pg.* 1396, *pg.* 228
Harris, Matthew, Dir-Sls-US Hispanic - Yahoo! Inc.; *pg.* 1289, *pg.* 289
Harris, Michael, Sr Mgr - Accenture; *pg.* 1392, *pg.* 1186
Harris, Michael J., Dir-Art, Specialist & Designer-Target Creative Studio - Target Corporation; *pg.* 1786, *pg.* 942
Harris, Michelle, Dir-Sls & Mktg - Godwin's Gatorland, Inc.; *pg.* 550, *pg.* 453
Harris, Myrta, Sr Mgr-Mktg Ops - LinkedIn Corporation; *pg.* 1262, *pg.* 160
Harris, Nell, Specialist-Sls - United States Postal Service; *pg.* 1009, *pg.* 406
Harris, Nick, VP-Mktg - Benjamin Moore & Co.; *pg.* 1440, *pg.* 1085
Harris, Nick, Head-Global Brand Mktg-Bloomberg Media - Bloomberg L.P.; *pg.* 725, *pg.* 1204
Harris, Nicole, Coord-Social Media-Adv & Global Brand Mgmt - Liberty Mutual Insurance Group Inc.; *pg.* 1205, *pg.* 797
Harris, Racquel, Sr VP-Member Strategy & Mktg - Sam's Club; *pg.* 1783, *pg.* 29
Harris, Rebecca, Sr Mgr-Global Social Media Strategy - General Motors Company; *pg.* 175, *pg.* 881
Harris, Rita, Sr Mgr-Global Fleet Ops - Vertex Pharmaceuticals Incorporated; *pg.* 1606, *pg.* 801

Harris, Scott, Dir-Campaign & Demand Mktg - Adobe Systems Incorporated; pg. 342, pg. 235
Harris, Scott, Mgr-Media - Hobby Lobby Stores Inc.; pg. 927, pg. 1486
Harris, Sean, Dir-Cause-Related Mktg - Bozzuto's Inc.; pg. 1016, pg. 342
Harris, Simon, Chief Strategy Officer - Oliver Wyman, Inc.; pg. 790, pg. 1274
Harris, Stacey, Mgr-Mktg - GlaxoSmithKline; pg. 1536, pg. 1565
Harris, Stacey, Mgr-Mktg - GlaxoSmithKline Consumer Healthcare; pg. 510, pg. 1554
Harris, Surayyah, Sr Mgr-Consumer Mktg - R.J. Reynolds Tobacco Co.; pg. 1895, pg. 1395
Harris, Terry, VP-Sls - Riceland Foods, Inc.; pg. 892, pg. 36
Harris, Tim, VP-Sls & Mktg - Delta Apparel, Inc.; pg. 39, pg. 1617
Harris, Veronica, Sr Product Mgr - Novartis Pharmaceuticals Corp.; pg. 1575, pg. 1054
Harris, Wes, Sr Dir-Product Mktg - Yahoo! Inc.; pg. 1289, pg. 289
Harris, William B., Sr Mgr-Generation Comm-South & West - Exelon Corporation; pg. 1942, pg. 573
Harrison, Cameron, Dir-Mktg - Americo Manufacturing Co., Inc.; pg. 325, pg. 482
Harrison, Catherine A., Dir-Mktg - The Hanover Insurance Company; pg. 1202, pg. 862
Harrison, Darryll, Mgr-Brand & PR - Volkswagen Group of America, Inc.; pg. 194, pg. 1785
Harrison, Doug, VP-Mktg-Age 50+ Segment - T. Rowe Price Group Inc.; pg. 808, pg. 759
Harrison, Heather, Head-Transfer Pricing Mktg - PricewaterhouseCoopers LLP; pg. 795, pg. 1283
Harrison, Helen, Mgr-Corp & Recruitment Mktg - Accenture; pg. 1392, pg. 1186
Harrison, Jessica, Dir-Natl Mktg Programs - Chipotle Mexican Grill, Inc.; pg. 1722, pg. 317
Harrison, Jim, Dir-Creative Svcs - University Of Florida; pg. 609, pg. 429
Harrison, John, Bus Mgr - The Willamette Valley Company; pg. 1186, pg. 1497
Harrison, Kristina, Dir-Digital Mktg-Europe - Netflix, Inc.; pg. 1269, pg. 141
Harrison, Meghan, Mgr-Digital Mktg - Welch Allyn Inc.; pg. 1436, pg. 1342
Harrison, Nathania, Brand Mgr-Women's-Canada - NIKE, Inc.; pg. 1812, pg. 1492
Harrison, Pamela, Head-ANI Pub Affairs & Sr Dir - Abbott Laboratories; pg. 1484, pg. 551
Harrison, Peter, Head-Mktg Insights-Global - Cigna Corporation; pg. 1197, pg. 338
Harrison, Ray, VP-Center Store Sls - Brookshire Grocery Company; pg. 1016, pg. 1748
Harrison, Soleil, Sr Mgr-Pub Affairs - Gilead Sciences, Inc.; pg. 1535, pg. 88
Harrison, Sonia, Sr Mgr-PR - Mentor Graphics Corporation; pg. 432, pg. 1510
Harrison, Steve P., VP-B2B Mktg - MasterCard Incorporated; pg. 779, pg. 1325
Harrison, Steven, VP-B2B Mktg - MasterCard Worldwide Inc.; pg. 780, pg. 988
Harrison, Tammi, VP-Product Mktg - GrubHub Inc.; pg. 1255, pg. 576
Harrison, Wade, Chief Product Officer & Sr VP - Protective Life Insurance Company; pg. 1215, pg. 4
Harrison, Yadira, Coord-Adv & Mktg - Macy's, Inc.; pg. 1778, pg. 1417
Harrison-Senter, Kimberly, Grp Brand Mgr-Personal Care Global Innovation - Church & Dwight Co., Inc.; pg. 1153, pg. 1063
Harrold, Chris, VP-Bus Dev & Dir-Creative - Mohawk Fine Papers, Inc.; pg. 1464, pg. 1153
Harrop, Jeff, Sr Dir-Mktg - Molson Coors Canada Inc.; pg. 256, pg. 1955
Harrower, Scott, Dir-Mktg - AMC Networks Inc.; pg. 269, pg. 1189
Harrsen, Laurie, Dir-PR & Consumer Comm - McCormick & Company, Incorporated; pg. 1027, pg. 779
Harry, Amy, Gen Mgr-Digital Mktg - Delta Air Lines, Inc.; pg. 1905, pg. 503
Harshaw, Kevin, Sr Dir-Mktg-Thailand Cluster - Reckitt Benckiser Inc.; pg. 1136, pg. 1105
Harshbarger, Tom, Sr Partner & Mgr-Sls - Microsoft Corporation; pg. 435, pg. 1824
Harsini, Francine, Dir-Mktg & PR - Mitsubishi Motors North America, Inc.; pg. 185, pg. 75
Harston, Mark, Mgr-Event & Motorsports Mktg - Universal Technical Institute, Inc.; pg. 608, pg. 24
Hart, Alix, VP-Brand, Digital & Adv - Symantec Corporation; pg. 478, pg. 161
Hart, Bonnie, Assoc Mgr-Online Mktg - Charlotte Russe, Inc.; pg. 21, pg. 201
Hart, Brett J, Interim CEO - United Airlines, Inc.; pg. 1927, pg. 593
Hart, Cindy, Exec Dir-Suite Sls & Svcs - New Orleans Saints L.P.; pg. 569, pg. 745
Hart, Cynthia, Mgr-Mktg-Kenwood Towne Centre - General Growth Properties, Inc.; pg. 1093, pg. 574
Hart, Dave, VP-Distr Sls - Zep Inc.; pg. 338, pg. 524
Hart, James G., VP-Sls-Global - Mirror Image Internet, Inc.; pg. 1267, pg. 848
Hart, Jason, Product Mgr & Program Mgr - AOL Inc.; pg. 1229, pg. 1195
Hart, Jennifer, Sr VP, Assoc Publr & Grp Dir-Mktg-William Morrow - HarperCollins Publishers Inc.; pg. 1647, pg. 1237
Hart, John, Mng Dir-Trading Products - TD Ameritrade Holding Corporation; pg. 808, pg. 1018
Hart, Kim, Mgr-Channel Mktg - Medifast, Inc.; pg. 1562, pg. 774
Hart, Melissa, Mgr-Mktg - Transamerica Insurance & Investment Group; pg. 1219, pg. 141
Hart, Pam, Rep-Sls Events & Trng - United Airlines, Inc.; pg. 1927, pg. 593
Hart, Shannon, Assoc Product Mgr - Graco Children's Products Inc.; pg. 954, pg. 1531
Hart, Teresa, Specialist-Mktg Matls - The Northwestern Mutual Life Insurance Company; pg. 1212, pg. 1879
Hart, Tonya, Controller & Bus Mgr - The Roanoke Times; pg. 1680, pg. 1806
Harte, Susannah, Head-Events-Bloomberg Media Grp - Bloomberg L.P.; pg. 725, pg. 1204
Hartel, Charles, Sr Product Mgr-Fin - Yahoo! Inc.; pg. 1289, pg. 289
Harter, Sherren, Dir-Mktg - Green Mountain Energy Company; pg. 1944, pg. 1663
Hartfield, John, Mgr-Intl Sls-LP-Gas Distributed Products - Algas-SDI; pg. 1311, pg. 1831
Harting, Betsy, Mgr-Mktg Comm & Adv - Olympus America Inc.; pg. 1425, pg. 1521
Hartley, Chris, VP-Mktg - Blue Rhino Corporation; pg. 1318, pg. 1393
Hartley, Christina, Mgr-Mktg Ops - Blackboard Inc.; pg. 1232, pg. 396
Hartley, Jack, Brand Mgr-Customer Mktg - Ocean Spray Cranberries, Inc.; pg. 887, pg. 827
Hartley, Jeffrey L., VP-Consumer Revenue - Morris Publishing Group, LLC; pg. 1666, pg. 525
Hartley, Jessica, Sr Mgr-Digital Mktg Strategy - Accenture; pg. 1392, pg. 1186
Hartley, Julie, Product Mgr-Credit Card - Wells Fargo & Company; pg. 819, pg. 232
Hartley, Sara, VP-Sls - Guideline, Inc.; pg. 402, pg. 1237
Hartling, Eva, VP-Mktg & Comm - Birks & Mayors Inc.; pg. 1, pg. 1953
Hartman, Eddie, Chief Strategy Officer & Pres-Attorney Svcs - LegalZoom.com, Inc.; pg. 1261, pg. 96
Hartman, Emily, Sr Dir - FTI CONSULTING, INC.; pg. 760, pg. 478
Hartman, Eric, Sr Dir-Logistics - Papa John's International, Inc.; pg. 1743, pg. 737
Hartman, Harrison, Dir-Mktg - CoorsTek, Inc.; pg. 77, pg. 330
Hartman, Heather, Dir-Natl Mktg - Meritage Homes Corporation; pg. 97, pg. 23
Hartman, John, Sr Mgr-Sourcing-Strategic Sourcing & Procurement - Georgia-Pacific LLC; pg. 1458, pg. 507
Hartman, Josh, Sr Mgr-Suite Sls & Svcs - Baltimore Ravens Limited Partnership; pg. 532, pg. 755
Hartman, Kate, Sr Mgr-PR-Global - The Coca-Cola Company; pg. 240, pg. 493
Hartman, Kristen, VP-Mktg - Cinnabon, Inc.; pg. 1723, pg. 493
Hartman, Mark, Dir-Mktg - Fruit of the Loom, Inc.; pg. 41, pg. 725
Hartman, Matt, Dir-Creative - La-Z-Boy Incorporated; pg. 932, pg. 901
Hartman, Rebecca Norr, Dir-Mktg Comm & Branding-Global - Welch Allyn Inc.; pg. 1436, pg. 1342
Hartman, Robert C., Sr Product Mgr-Mktg - Hewlett-Packard Company; pg. 404, pg. 175
Hartman, Susan, Assoc Publr-Mktg - Rodale, Inc.; pg. 1681, pg. 1530
Hartman, Tom, Sr Dir-Lean Consulting & Dir-Ops - Autoliv North America, American Technical Center; pg. 200, pg. 867
Hartmann, Corey, Mgr-Mktg - JVC Americas Corp.; pg. 648, pg. 1129
Hartmann, Kristin, Brand Mgr-Licensing - Tommy Hilfiger USA; pg. 48, pg. 1302
Hartnagle, Carol Ann, VP-Sls - TAB Products Co. LLC; pg. 481, pg. 1869
Hartnett, Christopher, Sr Dir-Technical Dev & CMC - The Medicines Company; pg. 1561, pg. 1104
Hartnett, Jeff, Dir-Mktg-Americas - Lennox International Inc.; pg. 1073, pg. 1736
Hartnett, Mark, Dir-Integrated Mktg-VOGUE - Conde Nast Publications, Inc.; pg. 1629, pg. 1217
Hartnett, Mark, Dir-Integrated Mktg-VOGUE - Vogue Magazine; pg. 1700, pg. 1311
Hartquist, Karen, Sr Mgr-Corp Comm - Oracle Corporation; pg. 450, pg. 191
Hartung, Joseph, Brand Mgr-Miller Family of Brands-Innovation - MillerCoors LLC; pg. 255, pg. 582
Hartunian, Greg, VP-Sls - Smart Software, Inc.; pg. 470, pg. 787
Hartvigson, Lisa, Sr Product Mgr - Nordstrom, Inc.; pg. 1779, pg. 1837
Hartwell, Rondel, Dir-Adv & Branding - Winn Dixie Stores, Inc.; pg. 1038, pg. 435
Hartwell, Samantha, Mgr-PR - Neiman Marcus, Inc.; pg. 30, pg. 1684
Hartwell, William, VP-Federal Govt Sls - Sonus Networks Inc.; pg. 1281, pg. 858
Hartwig, Denny, Dir-Media Rels - Live Nation Entertainment, Inc.; pg. 558, pg. 47
Harty, Thomas, Pres-Media Grp-Natl - The Association of Magazine Media; pg. 133, pg. 1197
Harty, Tom, Pres-Meredith Natl Media Grp - Meredith Corporation; pg. 1663, pg. 705
Hartz, Laura A., Mgr-Integrated Mktg Comm & Corp Benefit Funding - MetLife, Inc.; pg. 1208, pg. 1258
Hartzell, Dane, Dir-Digital Mktg-Global - Honeywell International Inc.; pg. 407, pg. 1088
Hartzell, Ron, VP & Product Mgr - National Penn Bancshares, Inc.; pg. 786, pg. 1517
Harubin, Emily, Coord-Brand Mktg - Stanley Black & Decker, Inc.; pg. 1063, pg. 358
Harvey, Brigid, Assoc-Brand Mktg - John B. Sanfilippo & Son, Inc.; pg. 1024, pg. 610
Harvey, Chris, Sr Dir-Inside Sls - The Ultimate Software Group, Inc.; pg. 486, pg. 479
Harvey, Dion, Dir-Sls - SAS Institute Inc.; pg. 466, pg. 1361
Harvey, Emily, Sr Mgr-Digital & Online Mktg - Macy's East; pg. 1777, pg. 1254
Harvey, Emily, Sr Mgr-Digital & Online Mktg - Macy's, Inc.; pg. 1778, pg. 1417
Harvey, Gary, Dir-Creative - True Religion Brand Jeans; pg. 49, pg. 143
Harvey, JC, Brand Mgr-Old Spice - The Procter & Gamble Company; pg. 1129, pg. 1418
Harvey, Kelly, Sr Mgr-Brand & Event Mktg-Modell's Sporting Goods - Henry Modell & Company, Inc.; pg. 1836, pg. 1240
Harvey, Kenny, VP-Intl Sls & Corp Events - Jazzercise, Inc.; pg. 554, pg. 59
Harvey, Laura, Product Mgr-Healthcare - Herman Miller, Inc.; pg. 926, pg. 913
Harvey, Lynn, Dir-Mktg - Aerogroup International, Inc.; pg. 1803, pg. 1055
Harvey, Mike, Brand Mgr - Affinia Group Intermediate Holdings Inc.; pg. 197, pg. 1373
Harvey, Mike, Mgr-Sls-Natl - Affinia Wix Filtration Products; pg. 198, pg. 1373
Harvey, Neil, VP-Sls-Europe, Middle East & Africa - TRIPWIRE, INC.; pg. 485, pg. 1507
Harvey, Prentiss, VP-Sls - Wheels Inc.; pg. 1931, pg. 607
Harvey, Roy, Pres-Global Primary Products - Alcoa Inc.; pg. 65, pg. 1188
Harvey, Sean, Sr Product Mgr - Google Inc.; pg. 1249, pg. 153
Harvey, Steve, Div Dir-Mdse - Wal-Mart Stores, Inc.; pg. 1790, pg. 29
Harvey, Todd, Sr VP-Consumer Mktg - Activision Blizzard, Inc.; pg. 948, pg. 271
Harvey, Wayne, Mgr-Mktg - AT&T; pg. 1865, pg. 258
Harvieux, Craig, Program Mgr-Mktg - Applied Industrial

First page reference indicates Business Class Edition
Second page reference indicates Geographic Edition

Technologies, Inc.; *pg.* 199, *pg.* 1428
Harvin, Michael, Sr Mgr-Agency Rels-Global - American Express Company; *pg.* 712, *pg.* 1190
Harvison, Deborah, VP-Mktg-Mid Atlantic - Simon Property Group, Inc.; *pg.* 1112, *pg.* 690
Harwell, Marc, Dir-Mktg-US - Alexion Pharmaceuticals, Inc.; *pg.* 1489, *pg.* 341
Harwood, Gretchen, Sr Mgr-Product Mktg - Digital River, Inc.; *pg.* 1238, *pg.* 948
Harwood, Jack, Sr Mgr-Global Mktg-Diagnostics - Siemens Healthcare Diagnostics; *pg.* 673, *pg.* 604
Hary, Rebecca, Dir-Media Rels-Global - McDonald's Corporation; *pg.* 1737, *pg.* 645
Hasan, Syed, Pres-Global Sls-Academic & Govt - Springer Science+Business Media, LLC; *pg.* 1688, *pg.* 1295
Hasegawa, Jan, Sr Mgr-Applications - Toyota Motor Sales, U.S.A., Inc.; *pg.* 193, *pg.* 296
Haserot, Linda, VP-Sls & Mktg - Ocean Properties, Ltd.; *pg.* 1106, *pg.* 422
Hashemi, Brian, Dir-Mktg - UncommonGoods LLC; *pg.* 1286, *pg.* 1147
Haskell, Todd, Sr VP & Chief Revenue Officer-Hearst Magazines Digital Media - Hearst Magazines; *pg.* 1649, *pg.* 1239
Haskin, Danny, Dir-Mid-Mktg & Origination-ERCOT - Calpine Corporation; *pg.* 1936, *pg.* 1702
Haskin, Mary, VP-Mktg & Sls Dev - Time Inc.; *pg.* 1693, *pg.* 1300
Haskins, Gwyn, Sr Mgr-Quality Assurance - Express Scripts, Inc.; *pg.* 1530, *pg.* 997
Haskins, Susan, Sr Mgr-Strategic Mktg - FRANKLIN RESOURCES, INC.; *pg.* 760, *pg.* 254
Haskins, Theresa, Bus Mgr-Markets - Portland General Electric Company; *pg.* 1950, *pg.* 1505
Haslag, Jane, Dir-Mktg & Sls - News Tribune Co.; *pg.* 1670, *pg.* 980
Haslam, Christine L., Dir-Mktg-Specialty Businesses - Aetna Inc.; *pg.* 1187, *pg.* 351
Haslam, David, Exec VP-Sls - Martin Door Manufacturing, Inc.; *pg.* 96, *pg.* 1759
Haslanger, Elias, Sr Mgr-Product Mktg-Tablets - Dell Inc.; *pg.* 383, *pg.* 1737
Hasnoo, Sarah, Mgr-Sls-Theatre Dev - Imax Corporation; *pg.* 1417, *pg.* 1926
Hass, Amanda, Mgr-Mktg - Casino Queen, Inc.; *pg.* 537, *pg.* 609
Hass, Erik, Acct Exec-Digital Mktg - Gartner, Inc.; *pg.* 1248, *pg.* 374
Hass, Lauren, Mgr-Retail Adv & Comm Plng - Yurman Design, Inc.; *pg.* 15, *pg.* 1316
Hassan, Sameer, VP-ECommerce & Mktg Tech - Williams-Sonoma, Inc.; *pg.* 1140, *pg.* 234
Hassan, Stacey, Asst Dir-Partnership Mktg - Liberty Mutual Insurance Group Inc.; *pg.* 1205, *pg.* 797
Hassard, James, Exec Dir-Oncology Mktg - Amgen Inc.; *pg.* 1493, *pg.* 291
Hassay, Ron, Sr Specialist-Mktg-Online-Lowe's Home Improvement - Lowe's Companies, Inc.; *pg.* 1053, *pg.* 1383
Hasse, Katie, Sr Specialist-PR - Steelcase Inc.; *pg.* 475, *pg.* 889
Hasselberger, Rich, Dir-Creative - Penguin Random House; *pg.* 1675, *pg.* 1276
Hasselbring, Wally, Mgr-Mktg-Retail Food & Beverage - Amcor Flexibles Inc.; *pg.* 1492, *pg.* 635
Hassell, Greg, VP-Reg Media Rels - JPMorgan Chase & Co.; *pg.* 772, *pg.* 1246
Hassen, Pete, Sr Exec Dir-Mktg - Chicago Blackhawk Hockey Team, Inc.; *pg.* 538, *pg.* 569
Hassett, Matt, Sr Mgr-Channel Program - Tellabs, Inc.; *pg.* 678, *pg.* 637
Hassfurther, Thomas A., Exec VP-Corrugated Products - Packaging Corporation of America; *pg.* 1466, *pg.* 624
Hassoldt, Cheryl, Head-Mktg-Quicken - Intuit Inc.; *pg.* 769, *pg.* 158
Hasson, Barbara, Product Mgr - Sumitomo Electric; *pg.* 1599, *pg.* 1297
Hastings, Jason, Product Mgr-3rd Party Large & Programmatic Sourcing - Microsoft Corporation; *pg.* 435, *pg.* 1824
Hastings, Jeff, Sr VP-Domestic Sls - Paramount Pictures Corporation; *pg.* 304, *pg.* 138
Hastings, Kimberly, Sr Mgr-Corp Comm - The Macerich Company; *pg.* 1101, *pg.* 275
Hastings, Linda, VP-Adv - The Baltimore Sun Company; *pg.* 1619, *pg.* 755
Hastings, Taylor, Dir-ECommerce Mktg-Americas - Quiksilver, Inc.; *pg.* 31, *pg.* 104
Hasty, Alan, Sr VP-Mdsg - Sysco Corporation; *pg.* 1035, *pg.* 1716
Hasty, Denice, Sr VP-Product Mgmt & Mktg-Comcast Bus - Comcast Corporation; *pg.* 276, *pg.* 1560
Hasty, Sherry, Sr Mgr-Creative - Hanesbrands Inc.; *pg.* 26, *pg.* 1394
Hata, Allison, Analyst-Mktg - Intel Corporation; *pg.* 645, *pg.* 266
Hatami, Derrick, VP-Natl Sls - Hyundai Motor America; *pg.* 179, *pg.* 89
Hatami, Derrick, VP-Sls-US - Nissan North America, Inc.; *pg.* 186, *pg.* 1633
Hatamiya, Kim, Exec VP-Mktg - Sony Pictures Entertainment Inc.; *pg.* 309, *pg.* 72
Hatch, Diane, Dir-Brand & Media Performance - Canadian Imperial Bank of Commerce; *pg.* 729, *pg.* 1935
Hatch, John, Sr Dir-Plng, Pricing & Modular Dev - Wal-Mart Stores, Inc.; *pg.* 1790, *pg.* 29
Hatch, Liane, Sr Mgr-Web & New Media - HealthPartners, Inc.; *pg.* 1203, *pg.* 918
Hatch, Michelle, Mgr-Partnership Mktg-Americas - Tourism Australia; *pg.* 1007, *pg.* 140
Hatcher, Cari, Dir-Mktg & Publicity - University of Minnesota; *pg.* 609, *pg.* 945
Hatenschweiler, Mike, Dir-In-store Mktg Design - Walgreen Co.; *pg.* 1608, *pg.* 605
Hatfield, Amy, Specialist-Mdsg - Lowe's Companies, Inc.; *pg.* 1053, *pg.* 1383
Hatfield, Brent, Product Mgr-High Speed I&O Cables - Molex Incorporated; *pg.* 655, *pg.* 628
Hatfield, John D., First VP & Dir-Mktg - Chemical Financial Corporation; *pg.* 734, *pg.* 898
Hathaway, Allison, Sr Mgr-Mktg - The Hearst Corporation; *pg.* 1649, *pg.* 1239
Hathaway, Ashley, Product Mgr - IBM; *pg.* 410, *pg.* 1449
Hathcoat, Emily D., Asst VP-Mktg - CNA Insurance Companies; *pg.* 1198, *pg.* 571
Hatherill, Mark, Sr VP-Product Dev - Munchkin, Inc.; *pg.* 964, *pg.* 300
Hatlestad, Halee, Dir-Creative-Global - Bare Escentuals, Inc.; *pg.* 500, *pg.* 213
Hatrak, Kathleen, Dir-Mktg - Sysco Guest Supply, LLC; *pg.* 336, *pg.* 1085
Hatter, Nathalie, Mgr-Mktg-Events & Sponsorships - Acklands-Grainger Inc.; *pg.* 197, *pg.* 1933
Hatzenbichler-Durchschlag, Iris, Dir-Mktg-EMEA - FalconStor Software, Inc.; *pg.* 396, *pg.* 1179
Hatzey, Bana, Assoc Mgr-Mktg - The Clorox Company; *pg.* 327, *pg.* 169
Hatzis, Mia, Mgr-Adv, Mktg Comm & Trade Mktg - Olympus America Inc.; *pg.* 1425, *pg.* 1521
Hatzopoulos, Phillip, Mng Dir-Client Dev & Sls - CME Group Inc.; *pg.* 738, *pg.* 571
Hau, Colleen, Sr Mgr-Co-Creation - Carhartt, Inc.; *pg.* 39, *pg.* 875
Haubein, Jennifer, Specialist-Social Media - BP America Inc.; *pg.* 972, *pg.* 1702
Hauck, Paul, VP-Worldwide Sls & Support - Liquidmetal Technologies, Inc.; *pg.* 1356, *pg.* 188
Hauenstein, Glen W, Exec VP-Network Plng, Revenue Mgmt & Mktg - Delta Air Lines, Inc.; *pg.* 1905, *pg.* 503
Haug, Bernard, Head-Global Affiliate Mktg - Autodesk Inc.; *pg.* 356, *pg.* 257
Haug, Katherine A., Mgr-Comm, Media & Americas Mktg - CB Richard Ellis, Inc.; *pg.* 1085, *pg.* 1210
Haugarth, Julia, Specialist-Mktg - Insight Enterprises, Inc.; *pg.* 415, *pg.* 26
Hauge, Bridget, Mgr-Mktg - Aveda Corporation; *pg.* 499, *pg.* 917
Hauge, Caroline, Sr Mgr-Mktg-Payments - Amazon.com, Inc.; *pg.* 1226, *pg.* 1831
Hauge, Kari-Michele, VP-Digital Sls & Mktg - AMC Networks Inc.; *pg.* 269, *pg.* 1189
Haugen, Brian, Mgr-Digital Mktg - Boston Scientific Corporation; *pg.* 1508, *pg.* 831
Haugen, Brigitte, District Supvr-Mktg & Cafe-Sodexo Inc. - Principal Financial Group, Inc.; *pg.* 796, *pg.* 706
Haugen, Erik M., Dir-Integrated Mktg - Tribune Media Company; *pg.* 1696, *pg.* 592
Haugen, Sherri, Supvr-Mktg Comm - 3M Company; *pg.* 1142, *pg.* 956
Haugen, Will, Product Mgr - Hy-Vee, Inc.; *pg.* 1023, *pg.* 713
Haugh, Mike, Dir-Product Mktg - Ixia; *pg.* 422, *pg.* 56
Haughie, Michael, Sr Mgr-Sls & Ops - The New York Times; *pg.* 1668, *pg.* 1270
Haughton, Christen, Exec Rep-Sls - GlaxoSmithKline; *pg.* 1536, *pg.* 1565
Hauke, Steve, VP-Sls-Western Family Foods - Western Family Holding Co., Inc.; *pg.* 1037, *pg.* 1509
Haun, Bernard, VP-Mktg - Allegra Network LLC; *pg.* 1614, *pg.* 904
Haun, Glenn, Dir-Sls-North America - Arkema Inc.; *pg.* 1147, *pg.* 1543
Haun, Kristen, Brand Mgr-North America ECommerce - The Procter & Gamble Company; *pg.* 1129, *pg.* 1418
Hausauer, Katherine, Specialist-Content Distr & Mktg - Scripps Networks Interactive, Inc.; *pg.* 1279, *pg.* 1638
Hauser, Amy, Gen Mgr-Mktg & Comm - Maersk Inc.; *pg.* 1914, *pg.* 1080
Hauser, David, Sr Dir-Channel Sls & Mktg - Carbonite, Inc.; *pg.* 368, *pg.* 792
Hauser, Eric, Dir-Sls - Summer Infant, Inc.; *pg.* 1139, *pg.* 1610
Hauser, Jamison, Planner-Sls - Pandora Media Inc.; *pg.* 1273, *pg.* 172
Hauser, Kelly, Mgr-Mktg-Media - T-Mobile US, Inc.; *pg.* 676, *pg.* 1816
Hauser, Polly, Sr VP & Dir-Sls-WMG - Heartland Financial USA, Inc.; *pg.* 765, *pg.* 707
Hauser, Rachel, Coord-Mktg - REBBL INC.; *pg.* 264, *pg.* 225
Hauter, John, Brand Mgr-Dremel - Dremel; *pg.* 1046, *pg.* 634
Hauter, John E, Brand Mgr-Dremel - Robert Bosch Tool Corp; *pg.* 1060, *pg.* 634
Hauze, Ralph, Div VP & Dir-Mktg-Creative - Beall's, Inc.; *pg.* 1760, *pg.* 414
Havaldar, Christina, Mgr-Mktg - Colgate-Palmolive Company; *pg.* 504, *pg.* 1215
Have, Manon Ten, Mgr-Sls & Mktg - IceLandAir North America; *pg.* 1912, *pg.* 841
Havel, Kip, VP-Integrated Mktg - Aflac Incorporated; *pg.* 1188, *pg.* 527
Havens, Scott, Global Head-Digital-Bloomberg Media - Bloomberg L.P.; *pg.* 725, *pg.* 1204
Haviland, Denise, Dir-Mktg & Strategic Comm - Duke University; *pg.* 600, *pg.* 1371
Haviland, Esther, Coord-Mktg - Michigan Apple Committee; *pg.* 147, *pg.* 895
Haviland, Jackie, VP-Channel Mktg - Nuveen Investments, Inc.; *pg.* 788, *pg.* 586
Havlik, Chris, VP-Sls - Hubbell Power Systems, Inc.; *pg.* 643, *pg.* 1614
Havlik, Stephanie, Sr Mgr-Social Media Mktg - AT&T Communications Corp.; *pg.* 1866, *pg.* 1043
Havlik, Stephanie, Sr Mgr-Social Media Mktg - AT&T Mobility LLC; *pg.* 619, *pg.* 488
Havrilla, John, Dir-Mktg Ops - AmerisourceBergen Corporation; *pg.* 1493, *pg.* 1522
Hawbaker, Karrie, Mgr-PR-Diabetes - Medtronic, Inc.; *pg.* 1564, *pg.* 939
Hawes, Alan, Grp Acct Dir - Onion, Inc.; *pg.* 1673, *pg.* 586
Hawes, Chris, VP-PR & Mktg - HCA HOLDINGS, INC.; *pg.* 1539, *pg.* 1651
Hawit-Rivera, Odalis, Brand Mgr - DOLE FOOD COMPANY, INC.; *pg.* 853, *pg.* 306
Hawk, Don, Co-Founder & Exec Dir-Product Innovation - TechTarget, Inc.; *pg.* 482, *pg.* 837
Hawk, James T., VP-Sls-North America - SKF USA; *pg.* 217, *pg.* 1535
Hawk, Kathy, VP-Mktg - Funrise Toy Corp.; *pg.* 549, *pg.* 300
Hawk, Keith, Sr VP-Sls-North American Res Solutions - LexisNexis Group; *pg.* 1658, *pg.* 1446
Hawkes, Melinda, Specialist-Sls & Mktg - The Dallas Morning News Co.; *pg.* 1633, *pg.* 1679
Hawkey, Michael, VP & Gen Mgr-Media Discovery Bus - Rovi Corporation; *pg.* 463, *pg.* 269
Hawkey, Summer, Mgr-Digital Mktg - Rolling Stone Magazine; *pg.* 1681, *pg.* 1287
Hawkins, Angela, Dir-Mktg - Hanesbrands Inc.; *pg.* 26, *pg.* 1394
Hawkins, Ashley, Coord-Media Rels-Global - Whole Foods Market, Inc.; *pg.* 1038, *pg.* 1667
Hawkins, Brettan, Mgr-Social Media - Tractor Supply Company; *pg.* 708, *pg.* 1627
Hawkins, Daniel, Sr Product Mgr - TripAdvisor, Inc.; *pg.* 1926, *pg.* 835
Hawkins, Ed, Dir-Sls & Mktg Sys - Central Garden & Pet Company; *pg.* 1475, *pg.* 303
Hawkins, Jacob, Mgr-Media Rels - Georgia Power Company;

First page reference indicates Business Class Edition
Second page reference indicates Geographic Edition

pg. 1943, *pg.* 508
Hawkins, Jay L., VP-Micron Consumer Products Grp - Micron Technology, Inc.; *pg.* 435, *pg.* 547
Hawkins, Kelly, VP-Loyalty Mktg - Regal Entertainment Group; *pg.* 579, *pg.* 1638
Hawkins, Kristy, Dir-Online Mktg & Analytics - Jewelry Television; *pg.* 7, *pg.* 1637
Hawkins, Liza, Analyst-Social - State Farm Mutual Automobile Insurance Co.; *pg.* 1218, *pg.* 557
Hawkins, Megan, Sr Mgr-Integrated Mktg - McKesson Corporation; *pg.* 1560, *pg.* 222
Hawkins, Molly, Sr Mgr-PR - Lands' End, Inc.; *pg.* 1776, *pg.* 1857
Hawkins, Rodney, VP-Mktg-Cancer Detection Bus - iCad, Inc.; *pg.* 643, *pg.* 1037
Hawkins, Tiffany, Mgr-Mktg Comm - Jazzercise, Inc.; *pg.* 554, *pg.* 59
Hawkins, Toby, VP-Mktg - H&E Equipment Services, Inc.; *pg.* 85, *pg.* 742
Hawkins, Watson, Brand Mgr-DIYnetwork.com - Scripps Networks Interactive, Inc.; *pg.* 1279, *pg.* 1638
Hawkinson, Chad, Sr VP-Product Design Solutions - IHS Inc.; *pg.* 1652, *pg.* 326
Hawks, Kathy, Specialist-Mktg - Associated Food Stores, Inc.; *pg.* 1014, *pg.* 1756
Hawley, Ross, Sr Mgr-Mktg - The Toro Company; *pg.* 1065, *pg.* 918
Hawley, Rusty, VP-Mktg - The New York Giants; *pg.* 570, *pg.* 1055
Hawley, Ryan, Dir-Mktg Plng & Analysis - El Pollo Loco, Inc.; *pg.* 1728, *pg.* 70
Haworth, Erin, Dir-PR-Cooking Light, Real Simple, Health & MyRecipes.com - Time Inc.; *pg.* 1693, *pg.* 1300
Haws, Jay B., VP-Creative - Rocky Mountain Chocolate Factory, Inc.; *pg.* 1032, *pg.* 324
Hawsey, Dave, Dir-Mktg - Anthem, Inc.; *pg.* 1192, *pg.* 683
Hay, Anne, Mgr-Healthcare Mktg - IBM Canada Limited; *pg.* 411, *pg.* 1923
Hay, Anne Z., Mgr-Principal Mktg-EBPP - ACI Worldwide; *pg.* 710, *pg.* 1777
Hay, P., Mgr-Bus Plng-Enterprise Sls - Hewlett-Packard Company; *pg.* 404, *pg.* 175
Hay, Thomas R., Sr VP & Dir-Product Mgmt - BOK Financial Corporation; *pg.* 726, *pg.* 1489
Hayashi, Justin, Dir-Customer Acq Mktg - Zulily; *pg.* 1792, *pg.* 1843
Hayashida, Dave, Specialist-Mktg Proposal - Toshiba America, Inc.; *pg.* 681, *pg.* 1302
Haydamack, Brent, Mgr-Sls & Mktg Analysis - Princess Cruise Lines Ltd.; *pg.* 1920, *pg.* 270
Hayden, Amelia, Mgr-Partner Integration-Mobile, Social & Smart TV Software - Samsung Electronics America, Inc.; *pg.* 669, *pg.* 1115
Hayden, Courtney, Specialist-Brand Mktg Program - The Ritz-Carlton Hotel Company LLC; *pg.* 1110, *pg.* 766
Hayden, Mark, Dir-Integrated Segment Mktg - Ryder System, Inc.; *pg.* 1922, *pg.* 446
Hayden, Michael, Corp VP-Mktg & New Bus Dev - New York Life Insurance Company; *pg.* 1211, *pg.* 1268
Hayden, Thomas K., VP-Mktg - National Notary Association; *pg.* 150, *pg.* 64
Hayden, Tim, Dir-Adv - The Evansville Courier & Press; *pg.* 1639, *pg.* 678
Haydock, Jeff, Dir-PR & Comm - Best Buy Co., Inc.; *pg.* 1761, *pg.* 954
Hayes, Andrew, VP & Dir-Mktg & PR - Fifth Third Bancorp; *pg.* 752, *pg.* 1413
Hayes, Betsy, Sr Mgr-Mktg Comm - Deluxe Corporation; *pg.* 1634, *pg.* 964
Hayes, Billy, VP-Sls - Southeast Toyota Distributors, LLC; *pg.* 190, *pg.* 421
Hayes, Brian, Dir-Digital Sls & Mktg - MTV Networks Company; *pg.* 298, *pg.* 1262
Hayes, Charles, Sr Product Mgr-Mktg - Belkin International, Inc.; *pg.* 361, *pg.* 182
Hayes, David, VP-Mktg & Dir-Adv - C Spire Wireless; *pg.* 628, *pg.* 971
Hayes, David, Head-Creative Strategy - Tumblr, Inc.; *pg.* 1285, *pg.* 1305
Hayes, Dustin, Exec Dir-Mktg Comm - Comcast Corporation; *pg.* 276, *pg.* 1560
Hayes, Garet, Dir-PR - AARON'S, INC.; *pg.* 912, *pg.* 486
Hayes, Heather, Acct Planner-Charter Media - Charter Communications, Inc.; *pg.* 274, *pg.* 372
Hayes, Heather, Sr Mgr-Digital Mktg - Epicor Software Corporation; *pg.* 393, *pg.* 110
Hayes, Heidi, Mgr-PR - Las Vegas Convention & Visitors Authority; *pg.* 997, *pg.* 1027
Hayes, Howard, Sr VP-Product, Svc Innovation & Dev - The Allstate Corporation; *pg.* 1189, *pg.* 639
Hayes, Jennifer, Dir-Strategic Mktg - Schneider Electric; *pg.* 467, *pg.* 1609
Hayes, John D., CMO & Exec VP - American Express Company; *pg.* 712, *pg.* 1190
Hayes, Justin, Product Mgr-Tire Ops - Bridgestone Americas, Inc.; *pg.* 1879, *pg.* 1648
Hayes, Katharina, VP-Sls-North America - 3D Systems Corporation; *pg.* 339, *pg.* 1621
Hayes, Marc, VP-Sls - Munchkin, Inc.; *pg.* 964, *pg.* 300
Hayes, Michael, Mgr-Digital Mktg - Ben & Jerry's Homemade, Inc.; *pg.* 1850, *pg.* 1767
Hayes, Michael, Sr VP-Sls & Sls Strategy - Georgia-Pacific LLC; *pg.* 1458, *pg.* 507
Hayes, Michael, Product Mgr - NaviSite, Inc.; *pg.* 1269, *pg.* 782
Hayes, Michele, VP-Global Partner Programs & Mktg Ops - Riverbed Technology, Inc.; *pg.* 1277, *pg.* 225
Hayes, Nick, Dir-Adv - Hotels.com, L.P.; *pg.* 1257, *pg.* 1682
Hayes, Nicole, Asst Mgr-Consumer PR - Toys "R" Us, Inc.; *pg.* 968, *pg.* 1130
Hayes, Pete, Chief Sls Officer - Equinix, Inc.; *pg.* 394, *pg.* 190
Hayes, Rachel, Brand Mgr-Dev - Unilever United States, Inc.; *pg.* 904, *pg.* 1061
Hayes, Robert, Exec VP-Digital Media - NBC Universal, Inc.; *pg.* 300, *pg.* 1266
Hayes, Timothy, District Mgr-Sls - Bayer Healthcare Consumer Care Division; *pg.* 1500, *pg.* 1087
Haymaker, Bridgette, Grp Product Mgr-QuickBooks Online Growth - Intuit Inc.; *pg.* 769, *pg.* 158
Hayman, Angel, Coord-Mktg - Sigma-Aldrich Corporation; *pg.* 1181, *pg.* 1003
Haynes, Brandt, VP-Product Mgmt, Worldwide Plng & Analysis - Home Box Office, Inc.; *pg.* 290, *pg.* 1240
Haynes, Bryan, Grp Product Mgr-Interactive Mktg-GIO Respiratory - Genentech, Inc.; *pg.* 1533, *pg.* 279
Haynes, Ian, Brand Mgr-Client & Mobility-Dell Federal - Dell Inc.; *pg.* 383, *pg.* 1737
Haynes, Madeline, Product Mgr - Virbac Corporation; *pg.* 1606, *pg.* 1696
Haynes, Tiffany, Specialist-Reg Mktg-Federal - Brocade Communications Systems, Inc.; *pg.* 365, *pg.* 239
Haynie, Chris, Dir-Mktg - Verengo, Inc.; *pg.* 1954, *pg.* 297
Haynie, Pamela J., Sr Mgr-Mktg Comm - Verizon Communications Inc.; *pg.* 1875, *pg.* 1309
Hays, Christina, Sr Dir-US Pediatric Specialty Nutrition, Mktg & Sls - Abbott Nutrition; *pg.* 1485, *pg.* 1437
Hays, John, VP & Dir-Sls & Mktg - Inner Traditions International; *pg.* 1653, *pg.* 1767
Hays, Joy, Dir-Digital & Social Media - AT&T Inc.; *pg.* 1867, *pg.* 1674
Hays, Joy, Program Mgr-Social Media-Worldwide - Texas Instruments Incorporated; *pg.* 679, *pg.* 1688
Hays, Lori L., Dir-Mktg Comm - Anthem, Inc.; *pg.* 1192, *pg.* 683
Hays, Suzy, Sr VP-Mktg - C Spire Wireless; *pg.* 628, *pg.* 971
Hayslip, Deb, Sr Mgr-Medical Comm - Amgen Inc.; *pg.* 1493, *pg.* 291
Hayter, Stephanie, Sr Dir-Mktg - Coty, Inc.; *pg.* 506, *pg.* 1219
Hayward, Paul, Div VP-Brdcst & Digital Mktg - Sears Holdings Corporation; *pg.* 1784, *pg.* 618
Hayward, Wayne, Dir-Mktg - Tinius Olsen, Inc.; *pg.* 1432, *pg.* 1541
Haywood Brown, Mary, VP-Sls - Battle Creek Equipment Co.; *pg.* 1499, *pg.* 870
Hayzlip, Ashley, Sr Mgr-Mktg - Hanesbrands Inc.; *pg.* 26, *pg.* 1394
Hazard, Sarah E., Mgr-Mktg - Vail Resorts, Inc.; *pg.* 1117, *pg.* 313
Hazel, Brent, Mgr-Sls Ops - LifeLock Inc.; *pg.* 776, *pg.* 26
Hazelrig, Mike, Sr Assoc Brand Mgr - The Kraft Heinz Company; *pg.* 871, *pg.* 641
Hazeltine, Richard, Sr Mgr-Tech University - Zappos.com, Inc.; *pg.* 1291, *pg.* 1030
Hazelton, Matthew, Assoc Dir-Mktg-Online - Quinnipiac University; *pg.* 607, *pg.* 351
Hazelton, Scott, Dir-Respiratory Care Solutions Mktg - GlaxoSmithKline; *pg.* 1536, *pg.* 1389
Hazelton, Scott, Dir-Respiratory Care Solutions Mktg - GlaxoSmithKline Consumer Healthcare; *pg.* 510, *pg.* 1554
Hazen, Jeff, Sr VP-Sls & Ops - Mediabistro, Inc.; *pg.* 1266, *pg.* 1258
Hazen, Tammy, VP-Field Mktg - Kind LLC; *pg.* 868, *pg.* 1249
Hazle, Michele, Mgr-Customer Experience Mktg - HP Enterprise Services, LLC; *pg.* 409, *pg.* 1731
Hazlett, Stephen, Mgr-Shopper Mktg-Walmart - Merck & Co., Inc.; *pg.* 1566, *pg.* 1077
Headley, Jay, Dir-Mktg - Cigna Corporation; *pg.* 1197, *pg.* 338
Headley, Jay, Dir-Mktg - CIGNA Tel-Drug, Inc.; *pg.* 1515, *pg.* 1625
Headley, Scott, Sr Mgr-Mktg - Water Pik, Inc.; *pg.* 1609, *pg.* 329
Headly, Michael G., Sr VP-Global Mktg, Sls & Svc - Allison Transmission, Inc.; *pg.* 198, *pg.* 682
Headrick, Maureen, Sr Mgr-Brand Mktg Asset Activation - The Coca-Cola Company; *pg.* 240, *pg.* 493
Heady, Cindy, Analyst-Pharmacy Mktg Support - Fred's Inc.; *pg.* 1769, *pg.* 1644
Heagle, Scott, Mgr-Global Product Category & Launch Comm - Steelcase Inc.; *pg.* 475, *pg.* 889
Heald, John, Sr Dir-Cruise - Carnival Corporation; *pg.* 1902, *pg.* 441
Heald, Steve, Dir-Mktg - AT&T Mobility LLC; *pg.* 619, *pg.* 488
Healey, Brian, Acct Mgr-Sponsorship Sls - Indianapolis Colts, Inc.; *pg.* 553, *pg.* 687
Healey, Jennifer, Asst Mgr-Mktg - Air Techniques, Inc.; *pg.* 1487, *pg.* 1178
Healy, Anoushka, Chief Strategy Officer - News Corporation; *pg.* 1669, *pg.* 1271
Healy, Barbara A., Sr VP-Digital Adv Ops - Tribune Media Company; *pg.* 1696, *pg.* 592
Healy, Douglas M., Sr Mgr-Innovation Architecture & Snacking Consumer Insights - PepsiCo, Inc.; *pg.* 259, *pg.* 1327
Healy, Edward J., VP-Mktg - Buffalo Niagara Convention & Visitors Bureau, Inc.; *pg.* 1901, *pg.* 1147
Healy, Ellen, Sr Dir-Mktg & Consumer Engagement-Global - PepsiCo, Inc.; *pg.* 259, *pg.* 1327
Healy, Gerard, Product Mgr-Power Bus Unit - Pulse Electronics Corporation; *pg.* 666, *pg.* 206
Healy, Greg, Sr Mgr-External Comm - CSL Behring LLC; *pg.* 1520, *pg.* 1543
Healy, Greg, Chief Product Officer - Encyclopaedia Britannica, Inc.; *pg.* 1638, *pg.* 573
Healy, Jennifer, Reg Mgr-Mktg - Ricoh Americas Corporation; *pg.* 461, *pg.* 1131
Healy, Jennifer, Sr Dir-Mktg-Hair Care - Unilever United States, Inc.; *pg.* 904, *pg.* 1061
Healy, Joie, Sr Mgr-Social Media Comm - Cisco Systems, Inc.; *pg.* 372, *pg.* 240
Healy, Kimberly, VP-Consumer Products Div - Solo Cup Company; *pg.* 1469, *pg.* 625
Healy, Lynn, Sr Specialist-Mktg - Cigna Corporation; *pg.* 1197, *pg.* 338
Healy, Shaun, Mgr-Media - United States Cellular Corporation; *pg.* 1875, *pg.* 594
Heaphy, Kevin, Dir-Global Product Mgmt & Comml Sys - Superior Tube Company Inc.; *pg.* 113, *pg.* 1522
Heaphy, Kimberly, Sr Acct Mgr-B2B Sls - T-Mobile US, Inc.; *pg.* 676, *pg.* 1816
Heaps, Kelly, Brand Mgr-Oral Care Global Expansion - The Procter & Gamble Company; *pg.* 1129, *pg.* 1418
Heard, Chad, Mgr-PR - Hyundai Auto Canada; *pg.* 179, *pg.* 1923
Heard, Hilary, Sr Mgr-PR - Bulgari Corporation of America; *pg.* 2, *pg.* 1208
Heard, Kimberli, Mgr-Digital Media - Valassis; *pg.* 1698, *pg.* 386
Heard, Liz, Mgr-Social Media Mktg - AT&T Mobility LLC; *pg.* 619, *pg.* 488
Heard, Mairin, Specialist-Social Media - HomeAway, Inc.; *pg.* 1911, *pg.* 1663
Hearn, Kelly, Dir-Comml Dev & Mktg US Injectables - Pfizer Inc.; *pg.* 1581, *pg.* 1278
Hearn, Sairah, Mgr-Global Social Media & Digital Engagement - lululemon athletica inc.; *pg.* 44, *pg.* 1911
Hearn, Sue, Sr Dir-Comm - Clif Bar Inc.; *pg.* 848, *pg.* 83
Hearne, Michael, Mgr-Corp Mktg Strategy - Land O'Lakes, Inc.; *pg.* 873, *pg.* 915
Hearne, Steve, VP-Sls & Dealer Dev - Toyota Motor Sales, U.S.A., Inc.; *pg.* 193, *pg.* 296
Hearst, Caroline, Sr Mktg Assoc - Jet.com, Inc.; *pg.* 1260, *pg.* 1073
Hearst, Susii, Gen Mgr-Sls - KHON-TV; *pg.* 294, *pg.* 544
Heath, Brian, Sls Mgr-Oncology - Amgen Inc.; *pg.* 1493, *pg.* 291

Heath, Carlene, Sr Mgr-Mktg Comm-Cloud Security, Privacy & Compliance - Microsoft Corporation; *pg.* 435, *pg.* 1824
Heath, Donald, Dir-Mktg-Dell Printing & Imaging - Dell Inc.; *pg.* 383, *pg.* 1737
Heath, Erin, Exec Dir-Worldwide Brand & Creative Content - Lenovo Group Ltd; *pg.* 427, *pg.* 1384
Heath, Kathy, Specialist-Mktg Svcs - Fluor Corporation; *pg.* 82, *pg.* 1719
Heath, Renee, Dir-Digital Mktg - Prestige Brands Holdings, Inc.; *pg.* 520, *pg.* 1345
Heath, Ronald, Mng Dir-Sls & Mktg - Morley Financial Services; *pg.* 784, *pg.* 1504
Heath, Samuel, Sr Dir-Innovation - Burger King Corporation; *pg.* 1719, *pg.* 440
Heath, Stephanie, Mgr-Shopper Mktg - Kellogg Company; *pg.* 831, *pg.* 870
Heath, William F., Sr VP-Product & Clinical-Design, Dev & Delivery - Eli Lilly and Company; *pg.* 1527, *pg.* 684
Heath-Schuttenberg, Tina, Mgr-Mdse - Dean & DeLuca, Inc.; *pg.* 1018, *pg.* 723
Heatley, Nancy, Mgr-Mktg - Bryant Grinder; *pg.* 1320, *pg.* 1768
Heaton, Nancy, Dir-Global Mktg-Bus Machines - Fellowes, Inc.; *pg.* 397, *pg.* 620
Heavey, Rhiannon, Brand Mgr-Market-Developing Brands - Brown-Forman Corporation; *pg.* 1958, *pg.* 732
Hebar, Ray, Dir-Sls & Mktg - Fiserv, Inc.; *pg.* 758, *pg.* 537
Hebel, David, Head-Partner Enablement-Adobe Digital Mktg Solutions - Adobe Systems Incorporated; *pg.* 342, *pg.* 235
Hebel, Richard, Product Mgr-FA-Eagle Product Inspection - Mettler-Toledo International Inc.; *pg.* 1423, *pg.* 1441
Heber, Mark, Reg Mgr-Mktg & Incentives - FCA US LLC; *pg.* 170, *pg.* 868
Heberling, Teresa, Dir-Sls - Screenvision Cinema Network LLC; *pg.* 581, *pg.* 1290
Hebert, Anne, Assoc Product Mgr - Merck & Co., Inc.; *pg.* 1566, *pg.* 1077
Hebert, Bertrand, VP-Mktg Telecom - Videotron Ltd.; *pg.* 317, *pg.* 1957
Hebert, Jenny, Bus Mgr-FCC VGO Bus-Global - Albemarle Corporation; *pg.* 1146, *pg.* 741
Hebert, Myron, Dir-Mktg-New Product Dev - Regeneron Pharmaceuticals, Inc.; *pg.* 1588, *pg.* 1345
Hebert, Shannon, Mgr-Mktg - Meritage Homes Corporation; *pg.* 97, *pg.* 23
Hebner, Kristi, Sr Dir-Segment Brand Strategy - Capital One Financial Corporation; *pg.* 730, *pg.* 1789
Hebner, Scott, VP-Mktg & Events-Global - IBM; *pg.* 410, *pg.* 1449
Hechanova, Wayne, Sr Dir-Mktg - Allianz Life Insurance Company of North America; *pg.* 1188, *pg.* 929
Hecht, Kathy, VP-Mktg & Bus Dev - Silver Star Brands; *pg.* 1785, *pg.* 1886
Hecht, Reed, Product Mgr-Printers-Pro Imaging Div - Epson America Inc.; *pg.* 394, *pg.* 122
Hecht, Tom, VP-Corp Mktg - Milwaukee Brewers Baseball Club, Inc.; *pg.* 562, *pg.* 1878
Heck, Ben, Exec Dir-Sls & Mktg - AT&T Inc.; *pg.* 1867, *pg.* 1674
Heck, Geoff, Sr VP-Sls & Mktg - Signature Flight Support Corp.; *pg.* 234, *pg.* 456
Heck, Jeanine, Sr Dir-Product Mgmt-Comcast Cable - Comcast Corporation; *pg.* 276, *pg.* 1560
Heck, Lee, Coord-Mktg-KB Home-Phoenix - KB Home; *pg.* 90, *pg.* 134
Heck, Ray, VP-Mktg-Chemicals - M-D Building Products, Inc.; *pg.* 95, *pg.* 1486
Heck, Ryan, Sr Mgr-Mktg & Analysis - Texas Roadhouse, Inc.; *pg.* 1753, *pg.* 738
Heckart, Christine, CMO - Brocade Communications Systems, Inc.; *pg.* 365, *pg.* 239
Heckelmann, Richard, Sr Mgr-Mktg-Advanced Programs - Hewlett-Packard Company; *pg.* 404, *pg.* 175
Hecker, Jody, Mgr-Category & Strategic Sourcing-Global Mktg Svcs Procurement - Merck & Co., Inc.; *pg.* 1566, *pg.* 1077
Heckman, Mark, Dir-Mktg - Anthem, Inc.; *pg.* 1192, *pg.* 683
Hecox, Sarah, Brand Mgr - Cargill Meat Solutions; *pg.* 846, *pg.* 722
Hedayati, Ali, Sr VP & Gen Mgr-Network Visibility Products - Emulex Corporation; *pg.* 392, *pg.* 70
Hedayati, Brian, VP-Mktg & Bus Dev-Analog & Power Solutions Grp - Micrel, Inc.; *pg.* 654, *pg.* 247
Hedgecock, Debra, VP-Ops-Worldwide Mktg - MasterCard International, Inc.; *pg.* 780, *pg.* 1326
Hedgecock, Debra, VP-Ops & Worldwide Mktg - MasterCard Worldwide Inc.; *pg.* 780, *pg.* 988
Hedgecock, Ken, VP-Sls, Mktg & Svc - Thomas Built Buses, Inc.; *pg.* 191, *pg.* 1379
Hedgepeth, Dawn, Dir-Mktg-US Skin Care - Unilever United States, Inc.; *pg.* 904, *pg.* 1061
Hedges, Barbara, VP-Mktg Comm - Comcast Cable Communications, Inc.; *pg.* 276, *pg.* 1560
Hedges, Leland, Sr Mgr-Strategy & Innovation - Sony Computer Entertainment America LLC; *pg.* 966, *pg.* 256
Hedman, Eric, Mgr-Mktg - 3M Company; *pg.* 1142, *pg.* 956
Hedrick, Clyde D., Mgr-Software Partner Mktg - Intel Corporation; *pg.* 645, *pg.* 266
Hedrick, Orth, Dir-Product Plng - Kia Motors America Inc.; *pg.* 181, *pg.* 112
Hee, Richard, Dir-Sls - Mokulele Flight Service, Inc.; *pg.* 1916, *pg.* 545
Heede, David, Interim CFO-Global - Molson Coors Brewing Company; *pg.* 256, *pg.* 321
Heegard, Dave, Exec Dir-Sls & Mktg - Lebanon Seaboard Corporation; *pg.* 1797, *pg.* 1547
Heel, Joachim, Sr VP-Sls - Zebra Technologies Corporation; *pg.* 690, *pg.* 628
Heemskerk, Marieke, Mgr-Sls Support & Change - Heineken USA Inc.; *pg.* 252, *pg.* 1352
Heeringa, Nicholas, Specialist-ECommerce Mktg - Topbulb.com LLC; *pg.* 1307, *pg.* 677
Heerlein, Lauren, Dir-Web Mktg & Interactive - John Hancock Financial Services; *pg.* 1205, *pg.* 796
Heerwald, Paul, Mgr-Sls & Mktg - 3M Company; *pg.* 1142, *pg.* 956
Heffern, Lindsey, Mgr-Social Media & Acct Exec - University of Minnesota; *pg.* 609, *pg.* 945
Heffernan, C. Gamble, Sr VP-Product Mgmt - Health Grades, Inc.; *pg.* 1256, *pg.* 319
Heffernan, Chelsea, Sr Mgr-IR - Cirrus Logic, Inc.; *pg.* 629, *pg.* 1661
Heffler, Mava, CMO & VP-Mktg & Comm - EMCOR Group, Inc.; *pg.* 80, *pg.* 361
Heffner, Andrea, Dir-Sls & Mktg-Hotel Jerome - Auberge Resorts, LLC; *pg.* 1080, *pg.* 145
Heffner, Mike, Sr Dir-Ad Ops, Client Svcs & Ops - AOL Inc.; *pg.* 1229, *pg.* 1195
Heffner, Scott T., Asst VP & Asst Dir-Mktg - Chemung Financial Corporation; *pg.* 734, *pg.* 1157
Heffron, Denise, VP-Natl Sls & Comml - Transat A.T., Inc.; *pg.* 1925, *pg.* 1957
Hefner, Brian, Mgr-Mdsg-Intl - Lowe's Companies, Inc.; *pg.* 1053, *pg.* 1383
Hefner, Elizabeth, Program Mgr-Mktg - ASI Corporation; *pg.* 354, *pg.* 90
Hegeman, Michael, Dir-Product Mktg - AT&T Mobility LLC; *pg.* 620, *pg.* 1152
Hegemann, Amber, Mgr-Comml Vertical Mktg - Generac Power Systems Inc.; *pg.* 1340, *pg.* 1898
Hegener, Michael, Assoc Dir-Global Analytics & Mktg Effectiveness - General Motors Company; *pg.* 175, *pg.* 881
Hegg, Trisha, VP-Global Product-Sanuk - Deckers Outdoor Corporation; *pg.* 1807, *pg.* 100
Heggelke, Steve, Exec VP-Mdsg - Bozzuto's Inc.; *pg.* 1016, *pg.* 342
Heggernes, Hans, Specialist-Mktg Comm - Ecolab Inc.; *pg.* 329, *pg.* 960
Hegleman, Lindsay, Dir-Client Rels & Indus Mktg - IHeartMedia Inc.; *pg.* 292, *pg.* 1741
Hegwood, Camille, Mgr-Channel Mktg-Global Scientific Bus - Kimberly-Clark Corporation; *pg.* 1461, *pg.* 1720
Hehman, Jeff, Mgr-Global Mktg-Skincare - Kao Brands Co. Inc.; *pg.* 513, *pg.* 1415
Hehman, Rick, Dir-Mktg - Remy International, Inc.; *pg.* 216, *pg.* 696
Heiber, Bryan, Mgr-Sls - Cinequipt Inc.; *pg.* 629, *pg.* 932
Heiberger, John, Chief Strategy Officer - PrivateBancorp Inc.; *pg.* 796, *pg.* 587
Heick, Dan, Mng Dir-Technical Mktg - Adobe Systems Incorporated; *pg.* 342, *pg.* 235
Heid, Francis, VP-Media Ops - UBM Advanstar; *pg.* 1697, *pg.* 1306
Heiden, Kurt, Mgr-Technical Product Mktg - Bose Corporation; *pg.* 626, *pg.* 820
Heig, Angie, Dir-Mktg - Ruby Tuesday, Inc.; *pg.* 1748, *pg.* 1640
Heigel, Julie, Mgr-Mktg - Toledo Symphony; *pg.* 588, *pg.* 1477
Height, Hilary, Mgr-Adv Sls - The Record; *pg.* 1680, *pg.* 281
Heiken, Laurie, Mgr-Mktg - First Data Corporation; *pg.* 754, *pg.* 505
Heikka, Colleen Woods, Dir-Brand Mktg - TripAdvisor, Inc.; *pg.* 1926, *pg.* 835
Heikkinen, Mika, Head-Metro & Backhaul Routers Product Line - Ericsson, Inc.; *pg.* 638, *pg.* 1730
Heil, Anna, Project Mgr-Mktg - Eagle Point Software Corporation; *pg.* 389, *pg.* 707
Heil, Brad, VP-Products & Svcs - Eagle Point Software Corporation; *pg.* 389, *pg.* 707
Heilbronner, David, Sr Mgr-Brand Strategy - Cumberland Farms, Inc.; *pg.* 1018, *pg.* 820
Heilbrunn, Marybeth, Brand Mgr-CHANEL Eyewear - Luxottica Retail; *pg.* 8, *pg.* 1460
Heilman, Sandy, VP-Sls & Mktg - Aramark; *pg.* 1013, *pg.* 1558
Heim, Ralph, VP-Media & Sponsorships - SONIC Corp.; *pg.* 1750, *pg.* 1487
Heim, Todd, Product Mgr-Brake - Stemco Inc; *pg.* 1182, *pg.* 1726
Heiman, Gregg, Mgr-Software Sls-Distr, Comm & Industrial Sector - IBM; *pg.* 410, *pg.* 1449
Heimensen, Collin, Mgr-Sls & Brokerage - MarineMax, Inc.; *pg.* 1709, *pg.* 416
Heimer, Carly, Specialist-PR - Siemens Medical Solutions USA, Inc.; *pg.* 469, *pg.* 1550
Heimes, Scott, CMO - Digital River, Inc.; *pg.* 1238, *pg.* 948
Heimpel, Ashley, Mgr-Wealth Mktg - Sun Life Financial Inc.; *pg.* 806, *pg.* 1944
Hein, Bryce, VP-Mktg - Quantum Corporation; *pg.* 458, *pg.* 250
Hein, Lacey W., Sr Mgr-Event Mktg - Concur Technologies; *pg.* 1903, *pg.* 501
Heine, Pia, Team Head-Rite Aid Sls - Mars, Incorporated; *pg.* 1858, *pg.* 1792
Heinecke, John, Sr Dir-Brand Mgmt-Global - Blizzard Entertainment; *pg.* 950, *pg.* 107
Heineman, Barbara, Mgr-Creative Svcs - Nikon Inc.; *pg.* 1424, *pg.* 1181
Heineman, Monique, brand Mgr-Intl Mktg Ops - Starbucks Corporation; *pg.* 897, *pg.* 1840
Heinemann, Tanya, Specialist-Mktg - Costco Wholesale Corporation; *pg.* 1765, *pg.* 1820
Heinicke, Krista, Mgr-Food, Beverage Mktg & PR - Broadmoor Hotel, Inc.; *pg.* 1083, *pg.* 315
Heinig, Sandra, Dir-PR - Regal Entertainment Group; *pg.* 579, *pg.* 1638
Heinlein, Andy, Sr Mgr-Mktg - Golf Galaxy, Inc.; *pg.* 1835, *pg.* 1525
Heinlein, Jim, Specialist-Mktg Comm & Graphics - Alstom Signaling, Inc.; *pg.* 1312, *pg.* 1350
Heinlein, Kirk D., Dir-Mktg Comm & Global Markets Adv - AT&T Inc.; *pg.* 1867, *pg.* 1674
Heinmiller, Laura, Mgr-Mktg - American Electric Power Company, Inc.; *pg.* 1934, *pg.* 1437
Heinrich, Doug, Sr VP-Product-Equipment - Black Diamond, Inc.; *pg.* 1827, *pg.* 1756
Heinrich, Rick, Acct Mgr-Sls-NASCAR - The Goodyear Tire & Rubber Company; *pg.* 1883, *pg.* 1401
Heins, James W, Sr Dir-Pub Affairs - Purdue Pharma LP; *pg.* 1587, *pg.* 377
Heinsman, Rusty, Mgr-Sls-Natl - Americo Manufacturing Co., Inc.; *pg.* 325, *pg.* 482
Heinsohn, Bonnie, Dir-Mktg Svcs & Consumer Div - The Valspar Corporation; *pg.* 1449, *pg.* 945
Heintz, Christa, Head-Mktg-Lifecycle Mgmt Saxagliptin Franchise - AstraZeneca Pharmaceuticals LP; *pg.* 1497, *pg.* 389
Heintz, Michael J., Sr Dir-Mktg Comm - E&J Gallo Winery; *pg.* 1962, *pg.* 149
Heintz, Robert, Dir-Mktg - Applied Industrial Technologies, Inc.; *pg.* 199, *pg.* 1428
Heinz, Cheryl, Reg Mgr-Sls - Trans Ocean Products Inc.; *pg.* 901, *pg.* 1818
Heinz, Kelli, Dir-Mktg & Indus Affairs - Bell Flavors & Fragrances, Inc.; *pg.* 501, *pg.* 640
Heinz, Roger J., Exec VP-Sls & Svcs-Global - Tellabs, Inc.; *pg.* 678, *pg.* 637
Heinze, Harold, Sr Dir-Mktg - Tyson Foods, Inc.; *pg.* 902, *pg.* 35
Heinze, Jamey, CMO - CDS Global, Inc.; *pg.* 370, *pg.* 704
Heiple, Rod, Dir-Technical-Engineered Products & Solutions - Alcoa Inc.; *pg.* 65, *pg.* 1188
Heirigs, Jodi, Product Mgr-Material Handling - KPI-JCI; *pg.* 1354, *pg.* 1626

Heirtzler, Lisa, Sr Mgr-Mktg-Intuit Mobile Apps - Intuit Inc.; *pg.* 769, *pg.* 158
Heiser, Jim, Sr Head-Adobe Photoshop Product Mktg Grp - Adobe Systems Incorporated; *pg.* 342, *pg.* 235
Heiser, Julia, Sr VP-Digital Media-US Concerts - Live Nation Entertainment, Inc.; *pg.* 558, *pg.* 47
Heiser, Thomas, VP-Product Mktg - HID Global Corporation; *pg.* 1416, *pg.* 111
Heisey, Sarah, Mgr-Mktg-Cura Hospitality - Eat'n Park Hospitality Group; *pg.* 1728, *pg.* 1539
Heisler, Jill, Dir-Prestige Mktg Consultant - Pernod Ricard USA, Inc.; *pg.* 1968, *pg.* 1332
Heiss, Amy, Mgr-Global Program-Social Media Trng & Activation - Dell Inc.; *pg.* 383, *pg.* 1737
Heitke, Samantha, Head-Mktg & Brand Adv - Best Buy Co., Inc.; *pg.* 1761, *pg.* 954
Heitman, Emily, Specialist-Social Media Svc - Edward D. Jones & Co., LP; *pg.* 746, *pg.* 995
Heitmann, Molly, Coord-Creative Svcs-Brand Mktg - Panera Bread Company; *pg.* 1029, *pg.* 1001
Heitsman, Cindy, Dir-Mktg - Time Warner Cable Inc.; *pg.* 312, *pg.* 1301
Hejnicki, Mark, Dir-Product Mgmt - CommScope, Inc.; *pg.* 278, *pg.* 1378
Hekmat, Laurie, Dir-Mktg-Global - Bayer Healthcare Consumer Care Division; *pg.* 1500, *pg.* 1087
Helander, Diana, Sr Dir-Product Mktg - Lithium Technologies; *pg.* 1263, *pg.* 221
Helbing, Kevin, Interim CFO, Controller & Asst VP - United Fire Group, Inc; *pg.* 1220, *pg.* 703
Helbling, Darci, Mgr-Mktg - Charles River Laboratories, Inc.; *pg.* 1475, *pg.* 360
Held, Jackie, Mgr-Cause Mktg & Special Events - American Red Cross; *pg.* 130, *pg.* 395
Held, Jennifer, Mgr-Federal Mktg - NetApp, Inc.; *pg.* 444, *pg.* 287
Heldman, Mike S., Mgr-Mktg-Product Innovation & Sustainability - International Paper Company; *pg.* 1460, *pg.* 1644
Heleniak, Kristen, Sr Product Mgr-Mktg - La Cie McCormick Canada Co.; *pg.* 872, *pg.* 1922
Helfer, Peter, Dir-Corp Sponsorships & Media Sls - New York Jets Football Club, Inc.; *pg.* 570, *pg.* 1067
Helgerson, Ann, Mgr-Mktg & Psychology - The McGraw-Hill Companies Inc.; *pg.* 1663, *pg.* 1257
Helgeson, Carly, Mgr-Creative Svcs Production - Del Monte Foods, Inc.; *pg.* 852, *pg.* 304
Helle, Chris, Exec Dir-Brand Mktg & Strategy-XFINITY - Comcast Corporation; *pg.* 276, *pg.* 1560
Heller, Georgette, Sr Mgr-Mktg - Allstar Products Group LLC; *pg.* 17, *pg.* 1166
Heller, Gregory, VP-Product Mktg, Dev & Visual Display - Baker Knapp & Tubbs Inc.; *pg.* 916, *pg.* 566
Heller, Ian, VP-Mktg & eBiz - HD SUPPLY, INC.; *pg.* 86, *pg.* 509
Heller, Laurie, Mgr-Mktg - Coach, Inc.; *pg.* 3, *pg.* 1214
Heller, Michelle, Sr Mgr-Digital Strategy & User Experience - American Express Company; *pg.* 712, *pg.* 1190
Heller, Neil, Dir-Mktg - Fleet Laboratories; *pg.* 1531, *pg.* 1787
Heller, Paulette, VP-Mktg - Conair Corporation; *pg.* 505, *pg.* 1055
Hellman, Charlie, VP-Product Dev - Spotify; *pg.* 1282, *pg.* 1295
Hellman, Stacey, Analyst-Email Mktg - The Sports Authority, Inc.; *pg.* 1846, *pg.* 326
Hellmann, Rebecca, VP-Mktg - Cardinal Health, Inc.; *pg.* 1512, *pg.* 1448
Hellmold, Grace, Assoc Dir-Mktg Comm & Events - Sharp Electronics Corporation; *pg.* 672, *pg.* 1082
Hellstern, Adam, Category Mgr-Mktg - Ventura Foods, LLC; *pg.* 908, *pg.* 49
Hellyar, Mary Jane, Pres-Tredegar Film Products & Corp VP - Tredegar Corporation; *pg.* 1890, *pg.* 1804
Helm, Amanda, Dir-Mktg-Sports - Pepsi-Cola North America; *pg.* 259, *pg.* 1327
Helm, Amy, Mgr-Field Mktg-East-HP Software & Enterprise Security - Hewlett-Packard Company; *pg.* 404, *pg.* 175
Helm, Clay, Dir-Global PR - Autodesk Inc.; *pg.* 356, *pg.* 257
Helm, Kevin, Sr Mgr-Customer Strategy & Dev - Del Monte Foods, Inc.; *pg.* 852, *pg.* 304
Helm, Mike, Dir-Mktg - Epson America Inc.; *pg.* 394, *pg.* 122
Helm, Tori, Assoc Brand Mgr-Mktg-Global - Hasbro, Inc.; *pg.* 954, *pg.* 1603
Helmer, Emily, Asst Product Mgr - Hormel Foods Corporation; *pg.* 863, *pg.* 915
Helmer, Emily, Asst Product Mgr - Hormel Foods Corporation - Foodservice Division; *pg.* 864, *pg.* 916
Helmers, Maik D., VP-Central Europe & Sls - LeMaitre Vascular, Inc.; *pg.* 1555, *pg.* 805
Helmes, C. Tucker, Sr Dir - Society of Chemical Mnaufacturers & Affiliates, Inc.; *pg.* 156, *pg.* 404
Helmick, Bryan, Product Mgr-Protocol & Sys - Rohde & Schwarz, Inc.; *pg.* 1428, *pg.* 768
Helmick, Myra, Mgr-Adv & Media - Nestle USA, Inc.; *pg.* 883, *pg.* 96
Helmink, Kristin, Sr Mgr-District Mktg - Aramark; *pg.* 1013, *pg.* 1558
Helminski, Khadra, Mgr-Integrated Mktg - Emerson Process Management; *pg.* 1334, *pg.* 1636
Helmreich, Doug, Dir-Mktg Res & Customer Experience - Cardinal Health, Inc.; *pg.* 1512, *pg.* 1448
Helmrich, Annika, Dir-Mktg-Americas - Amber Road, Inc.; *pg.* 348, *pg.* 1054
Helms, Colin, Sr VP-Digital Media - MTV Networks Company; *pg.* 298, *pg.* 1262
Helms, David, Mgr-Inside Sls - Edd Helms Group, Inc.; *pg.* 1071, *pg.* 442
Helms, Jared L., Exec Engr-Sls - Schneider Electric USA, Inc.; *pg.* 1306, *pg.* 650
Helms, Jenny Earp, Sr VP & Product Mgr-Mktg - Bank of America Corporation; *pg.* 718, *pg.* 1362
Helms, Justin, Brand Mgr-Digital - Logan's Roadhouse, Inc.; *pg.* 1736, *pg.* 1652
Helms, Ty, Sr VP-Sls-Global - Hyatt Hotels Corporation; *pg.* 1096, *pg.* 577
Helper, Gerry, Sr VP-Hockey Comm & PR - Nashville Predators, LLC; *pg.* 565, *pg.* 1652
Helstab, Susan J., Exec VP-Mktg - Four Seasons Hotels Limited; *pg.* 1092, *pg.* 1938
Helthall, Kelly, VP-ECommerce & Digital Mktg - The Men's Wearhouse, Inc.; *pg.* 44, *pg.* 1711
Helton, Christie, Mgr-Mktg - Jacksonville Symphony Association; *pg.* 554, *pg.* 434
Helton, Robin, Mgr-Retail Sls - Knoxville News-Sentinel Company; *pg.* 1657, *pg.* 1637
Heltsley, Andrew, Brand Mgr - Old Dominion Freight Line, Inc.; *pg.* 1918, *pg.* 1391
Heman, Mary F., Mgr-Shopper Mktg - Abbott Laboratories; *pg.* 1484, *pg.* 551
Hembd, Derek, Designer-Digital & UX - The Florida Times-Union; *pg.* 1641, *pg.* 433
Hembree, Allie, Mgr-PR - International Spa Association; *pg.* 145, *pg.* 730
Hembree, Rick, Reg Mgr-Sls - Liquid Controls, Inc.; *pg.* 1356, *pg.* 622
Hembree, Tommy, Coord-Natl Adv - The Home Depot, Inc.; *pg.* 1050, *pg.* 510
Hemlepp, Pat, Dir-Corp Media Rels - American Electric Power Company, Inc.; *pg.* 1934, *pg.* 1437
Hemmelgarn, Tony, Exec VP-Sls, Mktg & Svcs-Global - Siemens PLM Software; *pg.* 469, *pg.* 1734
Hemmer, J., Dir-Sls-On Board Svcs - Cuisine Solutions, Inc.; *pg.* 850, *pg.* 1770
Hemmer, Jason, Specialist-Product - W.L. Gore & Associates, Inc.; *pg.* 122, *pg.* 388
Hemming, Katherine, Mgr-Mktg Comm - Pella Corporation; *pg.* 104, *pg.* 711
Hemmings, Stuart, Dir-Digital Mktg, UX & Connected Technologies - The Chamberlain Group, Inc.; *pg.* 75, *pg.* 611
Hemond, Rick, Dir-Bus Grp-Mktg-Electronic Matls - THE DOW CHEMICAL COMPANY; *pg.* 1157, *pg.* 898
Hempe, Lynn, Grp VP-Softlines, Baby Center & Product Dev - Meijer, Inc.; *pg.* 1779, *pg.* 888
Hempfield, Clarence, Dir-Product Mgmt - Pitney Bowes Inc.; *pg.* 454, *pg.* 376
Hemphill, Garry, VP-Sls & Ops - Intrusion Inc.; *pg.* 1259, *pg.* 1736
Hemphill, Terry, Sr Mgr-Product Mktg - Adobe Systems Incorporated; *pg.* 342, *pg.* 235
Henaire, Pat, VP-Mktg - Broan-NuTone LLC; *pg.* 1069, *pg.* 1860
Henao, Sandra, Dir-Mktg & Comm - Golden Gate University; *pg.* 602, *pg.* 219
Henault, Tammy, Sr Dir-Audience Dev & Bus Intelligence - CBS Interactive, Inc.; *pg.* 369, *pg.* 215
Hendee, Ric, Sr VP-Consumer Mktg - Cotton Incorporated Consumer Marketing Headquarters; *pg.* 692, *pg.* 1218
Henderson, Allie, Specialist-PR - USANA Health Sciences, Inc.; *pg.* 1605, *pg.* 1761
Henderson, Bill, VP-Mktg - Brother International Corporation - USA; *pg.* 53, *pg.* 1046
Henderson, Brett, Dir-Individual Insurance Sls - Manulife Financial Corporation; *pg.* 778, *pg.* 1939
Henderson, Chad, Sr Mgr-Design - Wal-Mart Stores, Inc.; *pg.* 1790, *pg.* 29
Henderson, Dave, Sr VP-US Sls & Customer Strategic Mktg - Hasbro, Inc.; *pg.* 954, *pg.* 1603
Henderson, Dave, VP & Strategist-Social Bus - Wells Fargo Advisors, LLC; *pg.* 819, *pg.* 1005
Henderson, Dayton, Sr Dir-Global Design - Kimberly-Clark Corporation; *pg.* 1461, *pg.* 1720
Henderson, Emily, Exec Specialist-Sls - Eli Lilly and Company; *pg.* 1527, *pg.* 684
Henderson, Frank, Dir-Product Reporting & Analysis - Molina Healthcare, Inc.; *pg.* 1569, *pg.* 123
Henderson, Jamal, Dir-Brand Mktg-Mountain Dew - PepsiCo, Inc.; *pg.* 259, *pg.* 1327
Henderson, Jason, VP-Product Innovation - Captain D's, LLC; *pg.* 1720, *pg.* 1649
Henderson, Jason, Sr Product Mgr-Video Entertainment & Mktg - DISH Network Corporation; *pg.* 283, *pg.* 325
Henderson, Jeff, Mgr-Defense & Federal Products Engine Div - Caterpillar, Inc.; *pg.* 1321, *pg.* 650
Henderson, Laura, Head-Content & Media Monetization-Global - Mondelez International; *pg.* 877, *pg.* 1344
Henderson, Lee, Mgr-PR - Target Corporation; *pg.* 1786, *pg.* 942
Henderson, Marshall, Gen Mgr-Sls - Fairway Outdoor Advertising of Georgia-Alabama; *pg.* 1640, *pg.* 486
Henderson, Matt, Product Mgr - Google Inc.; *pg.* 1249, *pg.* 153
Henderson, Stephanie, Sr Mgr-Mktg Comm - AT&T Mobility LLC; *pg.* 619, *pg.* 488
Henderson, Stewart, Mgr-In-Store Mktg & Brand Mktg - LG Electronics U.S.A., Inc.; *pg.* 651, *pg.* 1060
Henderson, Tom, Mgr-Technical Sls - Honeywell Aerospace Electronic Systems; *pg.* 228, *pg.* 17
Henderson, Trisha, Coord-Mktg - Ann Inc.; *pg.* 18, *pg.* 1195
Henderson, Zenita, Sr Mgr-Mktg-Global - Motorola Solutions, Inc.; *pg.* 657, *pg.* 659
Hendery, Suzanne B., VP-Mktg & Comm - Baystate Health System, Inc.; *pg.* 1501, *pg.* 845
Hendley, Audrey, Sr VP-Mktg & Head-Products & New Product Dev - American Express Company; *pg.* 712, *pg.* 1190
Hendley, David, Asst VP-Honda Natl Sls - American Honda Motor Co., Inc.; *pg.* 163, *pg.* 292
Hendlish, Ilana, VP-Innovation-Product Strategy - The Dun & Bradstreet Corp.; *pg.* 1637, *pg.* 1120
Hendra, Julie, Sr Mgr-Comm - 99 Cents Only Stores LLC; *pg.* 1759, *pg.* 66
Hendra, Tim, Dir-Sls - Neogen Corporation; *pg.* 883, *pg.* 896
Hendren, Abby, Dir-Mktg & Comm - First Busey Corporation; *pg.* 754, *pg.* 562
Hendrick, Jim, Dir-Natl Sls-EAFM - Donaldson Company, Inc.; *pg.* 1329, *pg.* 917
Hendrick, Peter, VP-Mktg - Kyocera Document Solutions America; *pg.* 426, *pg.* 1065
Hendrick, Sallie, Specialist-Mktg Comm - FMC Lithium Division; *pg.* 1163, *pg.* 1366
Hendricks Sullivan, Jennifer, Dir-External Comm & Media Rels - American International Group, Inc.; *pg.* 1190, *pg.* 1193
Hendricks, Christian, Corp VP-Products, Mktg & Innovation - The McClatchy Company; *pg.* 1662, *pg.* 196
Hendricks, Christian A., Corp VP-Products, Mktg & Innovation - McClatchy Newspapers, Inc.; *pg.* 1662, *pg.* 197
Hendricks, John, Exec VP-Sls - Weigel Broadcasting Co.; *pg.* 320, *pg.* 595
Hendrickson, Courtney, Sr Mgr-Bus Dev - Ocean Spray Cranberries, Inc.; *pg.* 887, *pg.* 827
Hendrickson, Harlan, VP-Mktg - Detroit Pistons Basketball Company; *pg.* 544, *pg.* 868
Hendrickson, Kate, Mgr-Media Rels - National Aquarium in Baltimore Inc.; *pg.* 565, *pg.* 758
Hendrickson, Lisa, Sr VP-Mdsg & Design - Destination Maternity Corporation; *pg.* 23, *pg.* 1563
Hendrickson, Scott, Head-Adv Solutions - PayPal Inc.; *pg.* 1274, *pg.* 248
Hendriks, Beth, CTO-Engrg, Product Ops & IT-Global - SCIQUEST, INC.; *pg.* 468, *pg.* 1361
Hendrix, Bernard, Coord-PR - Chick-fil-A, Inc.; *pg.* 1721, *pg.* 492
Hendrix, Darrell, Pres-Sls - Milwaukee Electric Tool Corp.; *pg.* 1056, *pg.* 1855
Hendrixson, Lisa, Mgr-Property Mktg-Flamingo Hotel & Casino

- Caesars Entertainment Corporation; *pg.* 1083, *pg.* 1023
Hendry, Alec, Dir-Digital Media Ops & Dev - MTV Networks Company; *pg.* 298, *pg.* 1262
Hendry, Andrew, Sr Mgr-Product Mktg - F5 Networks, Inc.; *pg.* 396, *pg.* 1835
Henehan, Tom, Mgr-Distributor Sls - MillerCoors; *pg.* 254, *pg.* 1877
Henehan, Tom, Mgr-Distributor Sls - MillerCoors LLC; *pg.* 255, *pg.* 582
Henely, Jessica R., Reg Dir-Mktg - Coventry Health Care, Inc.; *pg.* 1519, *pg.* 761
Heneman, Herb, Dir-Field Mktg - MillerCoors LLC; *pg.* 255, *pg.* 582
Henestrosa, Christine De, Analyst-Mktg & Comm - Xerox Canada Inc.; *pg.* 494, *pg.* 1930
Heng, Elina, Sr Mgr-US Mktg-Boys Action Figures - MATTEL, INC.; *pg.* 962, *pg.* 81
Heninger, Mark, Product Mgr - Ipsen International, Inc.; *pg.* 1073, *pg.* 582
Henke, Becky, VP-Food Mktg, Mdsg & Ops - Colony Brands Inc.; *pg.* 849, *pg.* 1881
Henke, Paul, Dir-Tech & Product Mgmt - Dataram Corporation; *pg.* 383, *pg.* 1111
Henke, Steve, Mgr-Sls - INVISTA B.V.; *pg.* 1168, *pg.* 723
Henkus, Jennifer, Assoc Publr-Mktg - Mansueto Ventures LLC; *pg.* 1661, *pg.* 1256
Henley, Cristina, Dir-PR - Strayer Education Inc.; *pg.* 607, *pg.* 1785
Henley, Cristina, Dir-PR - Strayer University; *pg.* 607, *pg.* 405
Henley, Heather, Writer-Mktg Bus - Lexmark International, Inc.; *pg.* 427, *pg.* 730
Henley, Sharon, Sr Mgr-Mktg - Nikon Inc.; *pg.* 1424, *pg.* 1181
Henn, Steve, VP-Mktg-Ethicon, Inc. - Johnson & Johnson; *pg.* 1549, *pg.* 1091
Hennebry, Mandy, Category Dir-Mktg-Nutrition - GlaxoSmithKline Consumer Healthcare; *pg.* 510, *pg.* 1554
Hennel, Michael, Engr-Technical Mktg - Motorola Mobility LLC; *pg.* 657, *pg.* 627
Hennenhoefer, Gerald J., VP-Sls - Columbian Mutual Life Insurance Company; *pg.* 1198, *pg.* 1142
Hennessey, Barbara, Mgr-Mdsg - Heineken USA Inc.; *pg.* 252, *pg.* 1352
Hennessey, Jennifer, Head-Lake Erie Mktg & Sr Mgr-Mktg Comm - PricewaterhouseCoopers LLP; *pg.* 795, *pg.* 1283
Hennessey, Megan, Mgr-Social Media Comm - Hilton Worldwide, Inc.; *pg.* 1094, *pg.* 1791
Hennessy, Christopher, Specialist-Global Social Media Strategy - Starwood Hotels & Resorts Worldwide, Inc.; *pg.* 1114, *pg.* 378
Hennessy, Dan, VP-Mktg - MillerCoors LLC; *pg.* 255, *pg.* 582
Hennessy, Daniel, Sr Dir-Interactive Art & Designer - Target Corporation; *pg.* 1786, *pg.* 942
Hennessy, Jeff, Sr Dir-Art - Capital One Financial Corporation; *pg.* 730, *pg.* 1789
Hennessy, Jessica, Mgr-Events & Sponsorships, Mktg & Comm - OhioHealth; *pg.* 1578, *pg.* 1443
Hennessy, Sheila, Area Dir-Mall Mktg & Bus Dev - Simon Property Group, Inc.; *pg.* 1112, *pg.* 690
Henney, Jim, Sr VP-Mktg - Wells Fargo & Company; *pg.* 819, *pg.* 232
Hennigan, Megan, Sr Mgr-Shopper Experience - Campbell Soup Company; *pg.* 844, *pg.* 1048
Hennin, Vicki, Sr VP-Mktg & eMedia - Diversified Communications; *pg.* 284, *pg.* 751
Henning, Chris, Exec VP-Sls & Mktg - King Koil Licensing Company Inc.; *pg.* 932, *pg.* 671
Henning, Kyle, Dir-Mktg-Global - Tennant Company; *pg.* 1381, *pg.* 944
Henning, Steve, Dir-Mktg for Cloud, Cybersecurity & Big Data-Global - Computer Sciences Corporation; *pg.* 378, *pg.* 1780
Henninger, Brooke, VP-Brand Delivery-UHNW Mktg - Bank of America Corporation; *pg.* 718, *pg.* 1362
Henricks, Gwenne A., VP-Product Dev & Global Tech Div - Caterpillar, Inc.; *pg.* 1321, *pg.* 650
Henricks, Rod, Dir-Sls - Bunting Magnetics Co.; *pg.* 1320, *pg.* 717
Henricksen, Suzanne, Sr Dir-Brand Insights, Digital Insights & Consumer Affairs - The Clorox Company; *pg.* 327, *pg.* 169
Henriksen, Lisa, Sr VP-Mktg & Own Brands - Giant Eagle, Inc.; *pg.* 1020, *pg.* 1575
Henrikson, Lisa, VP-Brand Strategy & Mktg - 1-800-Flowers.com, Inc.; *pg.* 1758, *pg.* 1151
Henriques, Sandra, Mgr-Global Social Media-Platforms & Tools - Starwood Hotels & Resorts Worldwide, Inc.; *pg.* 1114, *pg.* 378
Henriquez, Allison, Dir-Mktg-Activation - Rue La La; *pg.* 1278, *pg.* 800
Henriquez, Logan, Product Mgr-Cloud Platform - Google Inc.; *pg.* 1249, *pg.* 153
Henriquez, Zoe, Dir-Cause Mktg - March of Dimes Birth Defects Foundation; *pg.* 146, *pg.* 1354
Henry, Adam, Dir-Mktg Sciences - Hologic, Inc.; *pg.* 1416, *pg.* 784
Henry, Alyssa, Head-Advanced Media Platforms - CBS Broadcasting Inc.; *pg.* 273, *pg.* 1210
Henry, Alyssa, Head-Advanced Media Platforms - CBS Corporation; *pg.* 273, *pg.* 1210
Henry, Andrew C., Mgr-Security Mktg - Intel Corporation; *pg.* 645, *pg.* 266
Henry, Ann, Sr VP-Fin & Mdsg - MARTHA STEWART LIVING OMNIMEDIA, INC.; *pg.* 1661, *pg.* 1256
Henry, Beth, VP-Mktg-Global - Cigna Corporation; *pg.* 1197, *pg.* 338
Henry, Bill, Dir-Sls-Eastern US Convenience Channel - Kellogg Company; *pg.* 831, *pg.* 870
Henry, Candace, Mgr-Digital Mktg - Genuine Parts Company; *pg.* 206, *pg.* 506
Henry, Carlissa, VP-Sls & Ops - Phoenix Suns; *pg.* 576, *pg.* 19
Henry, Corey, Mgr-Media Rels - Philip Morris USA Inc.; *pg.* 1894, *pg.* 1803
Henry, David, VP-Product Mgmt & Retail Bus - NETGEAR, Inc.; *pg.* 444, *pg.* 247
Henry, Geoff, Grp Dir-Mktg-Tea Portfolio - The Coca-Cola Company; *pg.* 240, *pg.* 493
Henry, Janice, VP-Mktg - Superior Uniform Group, Inc.; *pg.* 33, *pg.* 468
Henry, John, Sr Dir-Digital Bus & Strategy - Golf Channel; *pg.* 551, *pg.* 454
Henry, Kara, Sr Dir-Mktg Comm & Rels - The Kraft Heinz Company; *pg.* 871, *pg.* 641
Henry, Kindra, Media Buyer - Casey's General Stores, Inc.; *pg.* 1017, *pg.* 701
Henry, Lindsey, Mgr-Mktg Dev - Dell Inc.; *pg.* 383, *pg.* 1737
Henry, Mary Jo, Dir-Mktg - Joe Machens Ford Inc.; *pg.* 180, *pg.* 976
Henry, Michael, Sr Dir-Retail Ops-MIDWEST MARKET - Time Warner Cable Inc.; *pg.* 312, *pg.* 1301
Henry, Mike, Dir-Customer Mktg - Diageo Canada, Inc.; *pg.* 1961, *pg.* 1937
Henry, Steven, Sr Mgr-Mktg-Lighting-EGS Electrical Grp - Emerson Industrial Automation; *pg.* 1296, *pg.* 657
Henry, Thomas, Sr Mgr-NNA Customer Quality & Dealer Network Dev - Nissan North America, Inc.; *pg.* 186, *pg.* 1633
Henry, Tina, Specialist-Mktg-Loyalty Programs - Safeway Inc.; *pg.* 1032, *pg.* 184
Henry, Tom, Corp Dir-Sls-Global - Armstrong International, Inc.; *pg.* 1069, *pg.* 909
Henry, Tom, Head-Indus, Media & Entertainment - Google Inc.; *pg.* 1249, *pg.* 153
Henschel, Tim, Mgr-PR - NCR Corporation; *pg.* 443, *pg.* 531
Hensel, Bill, Dir-Media Rels - Invesco Ltd.; *pg.* 771, *pg.* 513
Henshaw, Jeff, Sr Dir-Web Analytics & Bus Intelligence - Time Warner Cable Inc.; *pg.* 312, *pg.* 1301
Henslee, Nissa, Sr Mgr-Multi-Channel Comm Enablement - Adobe Systems Incorporated; *pg.* 342, *pg.* 235
Hensley, Bryan P., Acct Exec-Charter Media - Charter Communications, Inc.; *pg.* 274, *pg.* 372
Hensley, Ennie, Pres-Intl Sls & Distr - The Weinstein Company; *pg.* 591, *pg.* 1314
Hensley, Steve, Sr Dir-Regulatory Affairs - USA Rice Federation; *pg.* 160, *pg.* 1775
Henson, Brett, Product Mgr - KALO, Inc.; *pg.* 1796, *pg.* 719
Henson, Erin, Specialist-Social Media Mktg - The Home Depot, Inc.; *pg.* 1050, *pg.* 510
Henson, Jerry, Reg Mgr-Sls - Mark Andy, Inc.; *pg.* 1359, *pg.* 975
Henson, Jesse, Dir-Product Mgmt - Baldor Electric Company; *pg.* 1316, *pg.* 32
Henson, Karen, Dir-Internal Comm & Creative Svcs - Republic Services, Inc.; *pg.* 107, *pg.* 19
Henson, Pamela, Reg Pres-Gannett Wisconsin Media - Gannett Co., Inc.; *pg.* 289, *pg.* 1681
Henson, Tara, Dir-Mktg & PR - Oklahoma City Zoological Park; *pg.* 572, *pg.* 1487
Henson, Tim, VP-Product Dev - Da-Lite Screen Company; *pg.* 632, *pg.* 698
Hentnik, Kris, Sr Mgr-Mktg Ops & Print Production-LOFT - Ann Inc.; *pg.* 18, *pg.* 1195
Henze, John, VP-Mktg - Electronics For Imaging, Inc.; *pg.* 390, *pg.* 88
Hepburn, Dave, Sr Mgr-Strategic Alliances - Lenovo Group Ltd; *pg.* 427, *pg.* 1384
Herald, Allison M., Assoc Dir-Global Mktg Comm & Channels - Merck & Co., Inc.; *pg.* 1566, *pg.* 1077
Heran, Doug, Product Mgr-Linear Motion & Seals - Applied Industrial Technologies, Inc.; *pg.* 199, *pg.* 1428
Herard, Melissa, Dir-Digital Mktg - MetLife, Inc.; *pg.* 1208, *pg.* 1258
Heraty, Kevin, Dir-Sls - Aidells Sausage Company; *pg.* 836, *pg.* 253
Herb, Jeff, Mgr-Sls - Setra Systems, Inc.; *pg.* 1428, *pg.* 802
Herb, Lindsey, Brand Mgr-Crest 3DWhite-Global - The Procter & Gamble Company; *pg.* 1129, *pg.* 1418
Herbert, Chris, Mgr-PR-Global - NetJets Inc.; *pg.* 1917, *pg.* 1442
Herbert, Chris, COO-Product & Tech - The Weather Channel LLC, *pg.* 320, *pg.* 523
Herbold, Andrea, Dir-Creative Svcs & Production - Puma North America, Inc.; *pg.* 1816, *pg.* 858
Herbs, Bobbie J., VP-Mktg - Rovi Corporation; *pg.* 463, *pg.* 269
Herbst, Judy, Head-Mktg - Alexander Doll Company, Inc.; *pg.* 949, *pg.* 1545
Herbst, Richard, Sr Dir-Market Access & Patient Strategies - AstraZeneca Pharmaceuticals LP; *pg.* 1497, *pg.* 389
Herbst, Steve, Sr VP-Brdcst & Production - National Association for Stock Car Auto Racing; *pg.* 566, *pg.* 420
Herceg, Julie, Sr Mgr-Retail Mktg - American Greetings Corporation; *pg.* 1615, *pg.* 1428
Hercik, Chris, VP-Native Studio & Dir-Creative-Sports Illustrated Grp - Time Inc.; *pg.* 1693, *pg.* 1300
Herd, Julie, Dir-Product Mgmt - NetApp, Inc.; *pg.* 444, *pg.* 287
Herd, Teresa, VP & Dir-Creative-Global - Intel Corporation; *pg.* 645, *pg.* 266
Herdeman, Steve, Product Mgr - Huffy Corporation; *pg.* 1836, *pg.* 1409
Herdener, Drew, VP-PR - Amazon.com, Inc.; *pg.* 1226, *pg.* 1831
Herdman, Georgina, Sr Mgr-Bus Dev - PricewaterhouseCoopers LLP; *pg.* 795, *pg.* 1283
Herdrich, Madeline, Sr VP-Digital & New Media Distr - Paramount Pictures Corporation; *pg.* 304, *pg.* 138
Heredia, Charles, Head-Web Mktg - salesforce.com, inc.; *pg.* 1278, *pg.* 226
Heredia, Omar, Brand Mgr - Colgate-Palmolive Company; *pg.* 504, *pg.* 1215
Herf, Brian, Sr Dir-Mktg - Revlon, Inc.; *pg.* 521, *pg.* 1286
Hergianto, Justin, Sr Dir-Digital Mktg - ESPN, Inc.; *pg.* 285, *pg.* 340
Hering, Chris, Head-Vertical Market, Adv, Media & Publ - NetSuite, Inc.; *pg.* 1270, *pg.* 255
Herington, Brian, Pres-North America Low Voltage Products & Reg Div Mgr - Thomas & Betts Corporation; *pg.* 680, *pg.* 1646
Herkrath, Dirk, VP-Sls & Mktg - Westinghouse Air Brake Technologies Corporation; *pg.* 1388, *pg.* 1595
Herlihy, Brian, Dir-Mktg - Bacardi USA, Inc.; *pg.* 1956, *pg.* 417
Hermack, Steve, Sr Mgr-Category Strategy - Campbell Soup Company; *pg.* 844, *pg.* 1048
Herman, Greg, Product Mgr-Enidine Brand - ITT Corporation; *pg.* 1351, *pg.* 1354
Herman, Greg, Mktg Dir-Pepsi & Starbucks North American Coffee Partnership - PepsiCo, Inc.; *pg.* 259, *pg.* 1327
Herman, Jake, Mgr-Sls-Natl - McKeon Products, Inc.; *pg.* 1559, *pg.* 912
Herman, John, Sr Dir-Mdsg-Sports Nutrition - GNC Holdings Inc.; *pg.* 1537, *pg.* 1576
Herman, Josh, Partner-ITS Integrated Mktg & Analytics Bus - Kimberly-Clark Corporation; *pg.* 1461, *pg.* 1720
Herman, Sara, Mgr-Mktg-Mid-Atlantic Reg - PepsiCo, Inc.; *pg.* 259, *pg.* 1327
Hermann, Mike, VP-Sls-Wine & Champagne - Pernod Ricard USA, Inc.; *pg.* 1968, *pg.* 1332
Hermans, Tracy, Mgr-Digital Mktg - The Wet Seal, LLC; *pg.* 35, *pg.* 88
Hermes, Tim, Sr Mgr-Display & Search - Xoom Corporation; *pg.* 1289, *pg.* 234
Herms, Larry, Asst Dir-Media Rels - Reds Baseball Partners, LLC; *pg.* 578, *pg.* 1425
Hernandez, Ana, Exec Dir-Intl Mktg-Applebee's & IHOP - DineEquity, Inc.; *pg.* 1725, *pg.* 95

First page reference indicates Business Class Edition
Second page reference indicates Geographic Edition

Hernandez, Aurora, Mgr-Mktg-NBC Digital Branded Entertainment - NBC Universal, Inc.; *pg.* 300, *pg.* 1266
Hernandez, Diana, Mgr-Sls Plng Bus-Ecommerce - The Clorox Company; *pg.* 327, *pg.* 169
Hernandez, Dominique, Mgr-Film Mktg - AMC Entertainment Inc.; *pg.* 527, *pg.* 716
Hernandez, Edgar, VP-Sls - Complex Media, Inc.; *pg.* 1628, *pg.* 1217
Hernandez, Eric, Mgr-Digital Mktg - Citrix Systems, Inc.; *pg.* 375, *pg.* 424
Hernandez, Fernando Delgado, Dir-Mktg - Olive Garden Italian Restaurant; *pg.* 1742, *pg.* 454
Hernandez, Itzel, Supvr-Mktg - Fresh & Easy Neighborhood Market Inc; *pg.* 1020, *pg.* 80
Hernandez, Ivan, Dir-Mktg - Cytosport, Inc.; *pg.* 1018, *pg.* 45
Hernandez, Joel, Coord-Mktg - Tetra Tech, Inc.; *pg.* 115, *pg.* 181
Hernandez, Jose, Sr Mgr-Memory - Samsung Electronics America, Inc.; *pg.* 669, *pg.* 1115
Hernandez, Karol, Specialist-Home Svcs Mktg - The Lee Company; *pg.* 1420, *pg.* 383
Hernandez, Katherine, Mgr-Social Media - Hot Topic, Inc.; *pg.* 42, *pg.* 67
Hernandez, Keith, Planner-Sls - Cable News Network LP; *pg.* 1624, *pg.* 1208
Hernandez, Laura, Exec Dir-Multicultural Mktg - AT&T Communications Corp.; *pg.* 1866, *pg.* 1043
Hernandez, Laura, Exec Dir-Multicultural Mktg - AT&T Inc.; *pg.* 1867, *pg.* 1674
Hernandez, Laura, Exec Dir-Multicultural Mktg - AT&T Inc.; *pg.* 1868, *pg.* 358
Hernandez, Linda, Rep-Telesales Direct Mktg - Humana, Inc.; *pg.* 1204, *pg.* 734
Hernandez, Megan, VP-Loyalty, Product Mktg & Consumer Insights - NCL Corporation Ltd.; *pg.* 1916, *pg.* 444
Hernandez, Olga, Mgr-Mktg - Sanofi US; *pg.* 1592, *pg.* 1046
Hernandez, Paul, VP-Sls - VIZIO, Inc.; *pg.* 686, *pg.* 118
Hernandez, Peter, Coord-Email Mktg - American Apparel, Inc.; *pg.* 18, *pg.* 126
Hernandez, Prospero, Bus Mgr - U.S. Naval Institute; *pg.* 1698, *pg.* 754
Hernandez, Ralph, VP-Sls & Mktg - Triangle Package Machinery Co.; *pg.* 1383, *pg.* 592
Hernandez, Richard, Planner-Adv & Media-Scion - Toyota Motor Sales, U.S.A., Inc.; *pg.* 193, *pg.* 296
Hernandez, Roland, Pres-Consumer Products Div - Monticello Drug Co.; *pg.* 1569, *pg.* 434
Hernandez, Solana, Producer-Digital Media - MTV Networks Company; *pg.* 298, *pg.* 1262
Hernandez, Suzan, Brand Mgr-Mdsg - NIKE, Inc.; *pg.* 1812, *pg.* 1492
Hernandez, Tamara, Mgr-Global Mktg Comm-Brand & Solutions - Dell Inc.; *pg.* 383, *pg.* 1737
Hernandez-Orendain, Saul, Assoc Mgr-Mktg - MATTEL, INC.; *pg.* 962, *pg.* 81
Hernando, Alanna, Acct Mgr-Creative Svcs - Coach, Inc.; *pg.* 3, *pg.* 1214
Herncane, Eileen, Dir-Mktg - Apple Vacations Inc.; *pg.* 1899, *pg.* 1556
Herndon, Chris, Sr Dir-Corp Mktg - VHA Inc.; *pg.* 1606, *pg.* 1724
Herndon, Justin, Assoc Mgr-Corp Rels-Natl Media Team - The Allstate Corporation; *pg.* 1189, *pg.* 639
Herndon, Kristin, Sr Analyst-Media-Consumer Mktg - Ace Hardware Corporation; *pg.* 1040, *pg.* 644
Herndon, Mindy, Sr Mgr - AT&T Communications Corp.; *pg.* 1866, *pg.* 1043
Herndon, Mindy, Sr Mgr - AT&T Inc.; *pg.* 1868, *pg.* 358
Herndon, Sandy, Dir-Advantage Mktg Comm - American Airlines Inc.; *pg.* 1898, *pg.* 1693
Herndon, Wendy, Second VP-Product Dev & Implementation - Aflac Incorporated; *pg.* 1188, *pg.* 527
Herner, Jenny, VP-Mktg Admin - Arch Coal, Inc.; *pg.* 68, *pg.* 992
Herod, Maury, VP-Sls - Hostess Brands LLC; *pg.* 1856, *pg.* 984
Heron, Megan, Dir-Domestic Mktg & Sls - Kissimmee-St. Cloud Convention & Visitors Bureau; *pg.* 997, *pg.* 436
Herr, Ariel C., VP-Comm & Mktg Svcs - Pegasus Solutions, Inc.; *pg.* 452, *pg.* 1685
Herr, Betheny, Mgr-Online Mktg - Siemens Corporation; *pg.* 803, *pg.* 1291
Herr, Dan, VP-Annuity Product Mgmt - Lincoln Financial Group; *pg.* 1206, *pg.* 1375
Herr, Nicole, Mgr-Mktg & Events - The Washington Post; *pg.* 1701, *pg.* 407
Herr, Tracy, VP-Adv - Fred's Inc.; *pg.* 1769, *pg.* 1644
Herrada, Oscar, Dir-Shopper Mktg - The Hershey Co.; *pg.* 1855, *pg.* 1538
Herran, Javier, Mgr-Adv & IT - Sedano's Management, Inc.; *pg.* 1033, *pg.* 430
Herrera, Ana, VP-Adv Sls - Discovery Communications, Inc.; *pg.* 282, *pg.* 777
Herrera, Maurice, Sr VP-Mktg - Weight Watchers International, Inc.; *pg.* 1609, *pg.* 1313
Herrera, Michelle, Sr Mgr-PR - AT&T; *pg.* 1865, *pg.* 258
Herrera, Sonia, Sr Mgr-Mktg - Pfizer Inc.; *pg.* 1581, *pg.* 1278
Herrera-Castillo, Audrey, Dir-Mktg Outreach Programs - New Mexico Tourism Department; *pg.* 1001, *pg.* 1136
Herrera-Davila, Nina, Sr Dir-PR - Marriott International, Inc.; *pg.* 1102, *pg.* 764
Herrera-Lasso, Rafael, Dir-Mktg - Reckitt Benckiser Inc.; *pg.* 1136, *pg.* 1105
Herrera-Malone, Ana, Sr Mgr-Mktg & Comm - Accenture; *pg.* 1392, *pg.* 1186
Herrero, Beatriz, Mgr-Mktg-Intl - StarKist Foods Inc.; *pg.* 898, *pg.* 1581
Herrick, Ann, Dir-Natl Mktg-Omnichannel Retail & Gift Solutions - Hallmark Cards, Inc.; *pg.* 1646, *pg.* 983
Herrick, Jacqueline, Sr Mgr-Consumer Promos - Reckitt Benckiser Inc.; *pg.* 1136, *pg.* 1105
Herrick, Melanie, Sr Mgr-Consumer Insights - Prestige Brands Holdings, Inc.; *pg.* 520, *pg.* 1345
Herriman, Harvey, Gen Mgr-Sls - Dean Arbour Chevrolet Cadillac; *pg.* 169, *pg.* 885
Herrin, Charlie, Sr VP-Product Dev & Design-Comcast Cable - Comcast Corporation; *pg.* 276, *pg.* 1560
Herrin, Parker, Sr Analyst-Product-Consumer Products - CareerBuilder, LLC; *pg.* 1234, *pg.* 568
Herrin, Sarah, Mgr-Digital Adv Campaign - Bose Corporation; *pg.* 626, *pg.* 820
Herring, Bart, Product Mgr-E, S, CL, CLS & SL-Class - Mercedes-Benz USA, LLC; *pg.* 184, *pg.* 514
Herring, JeJuan, Assoc Mgr-Mktg-Cookies & Crackers Portfolio - PepsiCo, Inc.; *pg.* 259, *pg.* 1327
Herring, Kanata A., Mgr-Customer Mktg, Lodging & Entertainment - Brown-Forman Corporation; *pg.* 1958, *pg.* 732
Herring, Lauren, Dir-Mktg - GlaxoSmithKline; *pg.* 1536, *pg.* 1389
Herring, Lauren, Dir-Mktg - GlaxoSmithKline Consumer Healthcare; *pg.* 510, *pg.* 1554
Herring, Michelle, Mgr-Mktg Res - Deere & Company; *pg.* 703, *pg.* 632
Herring, Nate, Sr Product Mgr-Copper Datacom & AV Connectivity - Hubbell Incorporated; *pg.* 1299, *pg.* 370
Herring, Tonya, Sr VP-Mdsg-Non-Perishables - Ahold USA, Inc.; *pg.* 1013, *pg.* 1520
Herrington, Robin, Mgr-Consumer Experience Mktg-US - NIKE, Inc.; *pg.* 1812, *pg.* 1492
Herrling, Derek, Sr Mgr-Brand Solutions-East - Electronic Arts Inc.; *pg.* 951, *pg.* 189
Herrmann, Janice, Mgr-Mktg - The Metropolitan Museum of Art; *pg.* 561, *pg.* 1259
Herrmann, Lars, Sr Dir-Product & Bus Strategy - Red Hat, Inc.; *pg.* 460, *pg.* 1388
Herrmann, Terri, Dir-Mktg - Manpower Group; *pg.* 430, *pg.* 1710
HerrmannRatz, Kristin, Dir-Mktg - ConAgra Foods, Inc.; *pg.* 826, *pg.* 1014
Herrmanns, Christian, VP-Mktg & Sls - MonoSol, LLC; *pg.* 59, *pg.* 694
Herrold, Andy, Mgr-Search Engine Mktg - Caesars Entertainment Corporation; *pg.* 1083, *pg.* 1023
Herron, Gauri, Dir-Shopper Mktg - PepsiCo, Inc.; *pg.* 259, *pg.* 1327
Herron, Gordon, Mgr-Sls & Market Support MR - Philips Electronics North America; *pg.* 662, *pg.* 782
Herron, Lindsey, Planner-Digital Corp Sls - Conde Nast Publications, Inc.; *pg.* 1630, *pg.* 128
Herron, Mark, Sr Dir-Ops - 7-Eleven, Inc.; *pg.* 1012, *pg.* 1672
Herron, Mike, Mgr-Social Media - United States Cellular Corporation; *pg.* 1875, *pg.* 594
Herschberg, Leah, Dir-Sls-Strategic Channels - Kind LLC; *pg.* 868, *pg.* 1249
Herschkowitz, Jodi, Dir-Customer Mktg - Barnes & Noble, Inc.; *pg.* 1619, *pg.* 1201
Hersey, Galen, Sr Mgr-Category & Indirect Sourcing - Land O'Lakes, Inc.; *pg.* 873, *pg.* 915
Hersey, Sherry L., VP-Mktg Dev - Travelers Insurance; *pg.* 1220, *pg.* 963
Hershberger, David, Product Mgr-Storage - Matco Tools Corporation; *pg.* 1055, *pg.* 1474
Hershberger, Lincoln, VP-Mktg-Global - Electronic Arts Inc.; *pg.* 951, *pg.* 189
Herskind, Jennifer, VP-Mktg - Gold's Gym; *pg.* 550, *pg.* 1681
Herskovitz, Rachel, Mgr-Global Adv & Brand Mgmt - American Express Company; *pg.* 712, *pg.* 1190
Herstoff, Tammy, Brand Mktg Mgr - Del Taco Restaurants, Inc.; *pg.* 1725, *pg.* 121
Herter, Caroline, Mgr-Digital Mktg & Co-Op - The Sports Authority, Inc.; *pg.* 1846, *pg.* 326
Hertig, Nancy B., Mgr-Mktg Comm - PerkinElmer, Inc.; *pg.* 1426, *pg.* 853
Herty, Eddy, Dir-Creative-Southeast - Outfront Media; *pg.* 1465, *pg.* 1275
Hertz, William, Dir-Mktg - Cardinal Health, Inc.; *pg.* 1512, *pg.* 1448
Hervatin, Linda, Dir-Shopper Mktg - Nestle Purina PetCare Company; *pg.* 1479, *pg.* 1000
Herwig, Matthew J., VP-Sls & Mktg-Global - CAS Medical Systems, Inc.; *pg.* 1513, *pg.* 339
Herzhauser, Mark, Mgr-Sls Comm - MetLife, Inc.; *pg.* 1208, *pg.* 1258
Herzig, Jake, Rep-Olefins Mktg - The Williams Companies, Inc.; *pg.* 987, *pg.* 1491
Herzog, Eric, VP-Mktg-Storage Sys - IBM; *pg.* 410, *pg.* 1449
Herzog, Jeff, Sr Coord-PR - Kawasaki Motors Corp., U.S.A.; *pg.* 1708, *pg.* 111
Hesburgh, Mary, Sr Mgr-Client Mktg - Valassis Communications, Inc.; *pg.* 1287, *pg.* 897
Hesley, Kirsten, Supvr-Social Media - The Wet Seal, LLC; *pg.* 35, *pg.* 88
Hess, Carol, VP-Comml PC Product Mgmt - Hewlett-Packard Company; *pg.* 404, *pg.* 175
Hess, Constance, VP-Cash Mgmt Sls - CFG Community Bank; *pg.* 734, *pg.* 756
Hess, Dale, VP-Creative - The WhiteWave Foods Company; *pg.* 1037, *pg.* 324
Hess, David, Dir-Sls - Perficient, Inc.; *pg.* 1274, *pg.* 1002
Hess, Dayne, Dir-Sls - Wigwam Mills, Inc.; *pg.* 15, *pg.* 1894
Hess, Mike, Exec VP-Data Fusion & Social TV Analytics - The Nielsen Company B.V.; *pg.* 1671, *pg.* 1272
Hess, Paul, Mgr-Adv Sls - Derrick Publishing Co.; *pg.* 1635, *pg.* 1558
Hess, Sherry, VP-Mktg-WR Grp-Natl Instruments - AWR Corporation; *pg.* 623, *pg.* 78
Hessenius, Chris, Reg Mgr-Sls - Bamberger Polymers, Inc.; *pg.* 1148, *pg.* 1171
Hession, Chris, Sr Mgr-Film & TV Indus Mktg - Autodesk Inc.; *pg.* 356, *pg.* 257
Hession, Dan, Sr Dir-Global Partner Mktg - Cisco Systems, Inc.; *pg.* 372, *pg.* 240
Hessler, Matthew, Sr VP & Dir-Mktg - Bank of the Sierra, Inc.; *pg.* 721, *pg.* 185
Hesson, Gabriel, Mgr-Customer Mktg-Toys R Us - Mattel Games/Puzzles; *pg.* 962, *pg.* 80
Hesson, Gabriel, Mgr-Customer Mktg-Toys"R"Us - MATTEL, INC.; *pg.* 962, *pg.* 81
Hester, Jeff, Mgr-Mktg-North American Papers - International Paper Company; *pg.* 1460, *pg.* 1644
Hester, Jonelle, Mgr-PR - Barracuda Networks, Inc.; *pg.* 360, *pg.* 58
Hester, Sara, Sr Mgr-Mktg-Connected Fitness - Under Armour, Inc.; *pg.* 49, *pg.* 759
Hester, Steve, Sr Dir-Strategic Initiatives - Chick-fil-A, Inc.; *pg.* 1721, *pg.* 492
Hetke, Meghan, Dir-Retail Mktg - Bare Escentuals, Inc.; *pg.* 500, *pg.* 213
Hetman, Yaro, Brand Mgr-Transit, Transit Connect & E-Series - Ford Motor Company; *pg.* 172, *pg.* 876
Hett, Jennifer Glickman, Mgr-Corp Sls - Portland Trail Blazers; *pg.* 577, *pg.* 1505
Hette, Dana, Sr Product Mgr-Transport & Global Product - Expedia, Inc.; *pg.* 1244, *pg.* 1814
Hettema, James, VP-Strategic Sls - Renesas Electronics America Inc.; *pg.* 667, *pg.* 269
Hetzel, Cathy S., Pres-Advanced Media & Info - Rentrak Corporation; *pg.* 306, *pg.* 1506
Hetzel, Stephanie S., Mgr-Trade PR & Events - Caterpillar, Inc.; *pg.* 1321, *pg.* 650
Heuer, Mike, Exec Dir-Field Sls - HBG Books, Inc.; *pg.* 1648, *pg.* 1238
Heumann, Mike, VP-Product Mktg & Alliances - Emulex Corporation; *pg.* 392, *pg.* 70

Heusen, Susan Van, Sr Mgr-Search Mktg - Sally Beauty Holdings, Inc.; pg. 522, pg. 1691
Heuvel, Tammy Vanden, Analyst-Digital Mktg-Global - Brady Corporation; pg. 363, pg. 1873
Hevia, Jorge, Sr VP-Corp Sls & Mktg - Napco Security Systems, Inc.; pg. 658, pg. 1138
Hew, Ling-Wei, Assoc Mgr-Product & Res, ETF Managed Portfolios - MORNINGSTAR, INC.; pg. 784, pg. 583
Hewitt, Bob, Mgr-Sls-Natl - WRGB-TV; pg. 323, pg. 1341
Hewitt, Dave, VP-Domestic Sls - Hufcor Incorporated; pg. 87, pg. 1861
Hewitt, Gary, Mgr-Asphalt Mktg - Marathon Petroleum Company LLC; pg. 981, pg. 1454
Hewitt, Glenn H., Sr Dir-Tax Acctg - Chick-fil-A, Inc.; pg. 1721, pg. 492
Hewitt, Jack, VP-Mktg Svcs - Kraft Canada Inc.; pg. 869, pg. 1939
Hewitt, Melissa, Specialist-Mktg & Graphic Designer - White's Electronics; pg. 688, pg. 1509
Hewitt, Nathan, Mgr-Digital Mktg - ACCO Brands Corporation; pg. 340, pg. 626
Hewitt, Paul, Product Mgr - General Motors of Canada Ltd.; pg. 177, pg. 1931
Hewitt, Ruth, Sr Mgr-Online Mktg-Att.com - AT&T Inc.; pg. 1868, pg. 358
Hext, Emily, Dir-Mktg-Individual Products - Humana, Inc.; pg. 1204, pg. 734
Heydenberk, Connie, Media Buyer - Apple Vacations Inc.; pg. 1899, pg. 1556
Heydenreich, Mary A., Mgr-Mktg - Digital Insight; pg. 744, pg. 189
Heydt, Ellen, Specialist-PR - Canon U.S.A., Inc.; pg. 1404, pg. 1178
Heyl, Nicole, Sr Dir-Emerging Brands - Guthy-Renker LLC; pg. 289, pg. 273
Heyman, Jennifer, VP-Social Media - Wells Fargo & Company; pg. 819, pg. 232
Heyman, Jodi, Brand Mgr-The Company Store - Hanover Direct, Inc.; pg. 1772, pg. 1130
Heyman, Leigh, Dir-New Media Technologies - White House Historical Association; pg. 1702, pg. 408
Heynike, Lorna, Sr VP-Mktg - Callidus Software Inc.; pg. 368, pg. 183
Hibbard, Stacy, Sr Specialist-Social Media Mktg - MAXIMUS, Inc.; pg. 780, pg. 1799
Hibberd, Robin S., Exec VP-Retail Products & Svcs-Canadian Banking - The Bank of Nova Scotia; pg. 721, pg. 1935
Hibbert, Ariel, Mgr-Mktg-New Restaurants - Qdoba Mexican Grill Inc.; pg. 1031, pg. 336
Hibbert, Donna, Controller-Mktg - Castle Brands Inc.; pg. 239, pg. 1209
Hibbison, Michael, VP-Mktg - The Home Depot, Inc.; pg. 1050, pg. 510
Hibbitts, Kirt, Sr VP-Brand & Adv - Wells Fargo & Company; pg. 819, pg. 232
Hibbs, Chris, VP-Sls & Mktg - Chicago Bears Football Club, Inc.; pg. 538, pg. 623
Hibdon, Marcus, Mgr-Comm & PR-Natl - Travel Portland; pg. 1008, pg. 1507
Hibicke, Konni, Dir-Mktg Promos - Milwaukee Bucks, Inc.; pg. 563, pg. 1878
Hibner, Kristin, Sr Mgr-Mktg - PepsiCo, Inc.; pg. 259, pg. 1327
Hichkad, Ravi, Mgr-Channel Mktg - ADTRAN, Inc.; pg. 344, pg. 6
Hickel, April, Sr Mgr-Product Mgmt - BMC Software, Inc.; pg. 362, pg. 1701
Hickenbottom, Trisha, Asst Mgr-Adv - Nintendo of America, Inc.; pg. 965, pg. 1829
Hickerson, Elizabeth, Mgr-Mktg - Astara, Inc.; pg. 1618, pg. 186
Hickey, Ben, VP-Immuno-Oncology Mktg - Bristol-Myers Squibb Company; pg. 1509, pg. 1206
Hickey, Elisa, Specialist-PR - Apple Inc.; pg. 350, pg. 73
Hickey, Erin, Dir-Integrated Mktg-Nickelodeon - Viacom Inc.; pg. 316, pg. 1310
Hickey, Jon, Product Mgr-Mktg-OneDrive - Microsoft Corporation; pg. 435, pg. 1824
Hickey, Kathy, Exec Dir-Mktg-Comcast Bus - Comcast Corporation; pg. 276, pg. 1560
Hickey, Kevin, Dir-Global Direct Mktg - InterContinental Hotels Corporation; pg. 1097, pg. 511
Hickey, Margie, Sr Dir-Patient Advocacy-Global - Novartis Pharmaceuticals Corp.; pg. 1575, pg. 1054
Hickey, Maureen, Mgr-Online Program-Direct Sls - Bose Corporation; pg. 626, pg. 820
Hickey, Sarah, Sr Mgr-Insights - Hillshire Brands; pg. 862, pg. 576
Hickey, Sean, VP-Sls & Bus Dev - Naxos of America Inc.; pg. 1779, pg. 1633
Hicklin, Andrea, Mgr-Mktg - Athleta; pg. 19, pg. 181
Hickman, Andrea, Brand Mgr - The Wendy's Company; pg. 1755, pg. 1450
Hickman, Heidi, Dir-Mktg - Gannett Co., Inc.; pg. 1643, pg. 1790
Hickman, Laura, Brand Mgr - Rust-Oleum Corporation; pg. 1447, pg. 664
Hickman, Matt, VP-Brand Strategies, Sls, Mktg & Bus Dev - Bonnier Corporation; pg. 1622, pg. 480
Hickman, Scott, Product Mgr-Support - McCauley Propeller Systems; pg. 231, pg. 724
Hickox, Feather, Sr Dir-Integrated Mktg-Global - Fair Isaac Corporation; pg. 1247, pg. 955
Hickox, Marin, Mgr-Mktg & Brand - Maple Leaf Sports & Entertainment Ltd.; pg. 560, pg. 1940
Hicks Bowman, Angie, Co-Founder & CMO - Angie's List Inc; pg. 1228, pg. 682
Hicks, Alan R., VP-Admin & Mgr-Area Sls-Mortgage Div - M&T Bank Corporation; pg. 777, pg. 1149
Hicks, Arty, Dir-Adv - The Arkansas City Traveler; pg. 1617, pg. 714
Hicks, David, VP-ISV, OEM, & Java Bus Dev & Mktg-Worldwide - Oracle Corporation; pg. 1272, pg. 786
Hicks, Gwendolyn, Project Mgr-Creative Grp - Constellation Brands, Inc.; pg. 1960, pg. 1348
Hicks, Janet, Mgr-Market-Nonferrous Products - CSX Corporation; pg. 1904, pg. 432
Hicks, Jessica, Analyst-Mktg - The Reynolds & Reynolds Company; pg. 461, pg. 1457
Hicks, Kimberly, Dir-Product Mgmt-Multiplatform Product Mgmt - MTV Networks Company; pg. 298, pg. 1262
Hicks, Lauren, Sr Mgr-Worldwide Mktg Partnerships - Paramount Pictures Corporation; pg. 304, pg. 138
Hicks, Lisa, Sr Mgr-Digital Mktg-Worldwide, Cloud & Smarter Infrastructure - International Business Machines Corporation; pg. 418, pg. 1138
Hicks, Liz, Sr Dir-Brand Mgmt-Global - Marriott International, Inc.; pg. 1102, pg. 764
Hicks, Russell, Pres-Content Dev & Production - Nickelodeon Direct Inc.; pg. 303, pg. 1271
Hicks, Tiara, Product Mgr-Capital One Home Loans - Capital One Financial Corporation; pg. 730, pg. 1789
Hidalgo, Lorena, Mgr-Hispanic Mktg-Wrangler - V.F. Corporation; pg. 34, pg. 1376
Hidalgo, Patricia, Chief Creative Officer, Chief Content Officer & Sr VP-EMEA - Turner Broadcasting System, Inc.; pg. 314, pg. 521
Hidek, Theone, Mgr-Retail & Local Mktg - Guitar Center, Inc.; pg. 1771, pg. 306
Hiebert, Lindsay, Sr Mgr-Mktg-Internet of Things Solutions Mktg - Cisco Systems, Inc.; pg. 372, pg. 240
Hielscher, Nancy, Mgr-Mktg - John Cannon Homes Inc.; pg. 89, pg. 466
Hiemenz, Joe, Mgr-Corp PR - Stratasys, Inc.; pg. 476, pg. 923
Hien, David, Mgr-Product Mktg - Texas Instruments Incorporated; pg. 679, pg. 1688
Hierro, Giraldo, Head-Sls Engrg-Google Apps - Google Inc.; pg. 1249, pg. 153
Higashikawa, Mike, Reg Product Mgr - Molex Incorporated; pg. 655, pg. 628
Higbie, Allison, VP-Mktg - The Coca-Cola Company; pg. 240, pg. 493
Higby, Eva, VP-Segment Mktg & Global Consumer Insights - Avery Dennison Corporation; pg. 1452, pg. 95
Higby, Shane, Dir-Mktg-LCD & LED TV - Samsung Electronics America, Inc.; pg. 669, pg. 1115
Higdon, David, Mng Dir-Integrated Mktg Comm - National Association for Stock Car Auto Racing; pg. 566, pg. 420
Higginbotham, Katherine, Bus Mgr-Corp Accounts-Multi-Vendor Svc - Philips Electronics North America; pg. 662, pg. 782
Higginbotham, Kelly, Strategist-Mktg-Sponsorships - Quicken Loans, Inc.; pg. 797, pg. 884
Higgins, Allison, Dir-Mktg - Sony Pictures Entertainment Inc.; pg. 309, pg. 72
Higgins, Amy L., Mgr-Worldwide PR & Brand - Tektronix, Inc.; pg. 1431, pg. 1496
Higgins, Brian, Sr Mgr-Customer - General Mills, Inc.; pg. 828, pg. 933
Higgins, Brian, VP-Indus Sls - Hydrotex Partners Ltd.; pg. 979, pg. 1692
Higgins, Bridget M., Assoc Dir-Mktg-Partnerships SSB Portfolio - Starwood Hotels & Resorts Worldwide, Inc.; pg. 1114, pg. 378
Higgins, Casey, Specialist-Digital Mktg Content - Virginia Tourism Authority; pg. 1010, pg. 1804
Higgins, Dan, VP-Sls & Mktg - Metalfab, Inc.; pg. 1360, pg. 1127
Higgins, Erica, Dir-Field Sls-Catalog Furniture - Staples, Inc.; pg. 474, pg. 821
Higgins, Gary, Sr Mgr-Product Plng - American Honda Motor Co., Inc.; pg. 163, pg. 292
Higgins, Henry, Dir-Land Sls - Crescent Communities, LLC; pg. 702, pg. 1365
Higgins, John, VP & Dir-Mktg - Brown-Forman Corporation; pg. 1958, pg. 732
Higgins, LaTanya, Dir-Mktg-Louisiana Reg - Gannett Co., Inc.; pg. 289, pg. 1681
Higgins, Lee, Sr Mgr-PR - Active Power, Inc.; pg. 1310, pg. 1660
Higgins, Louise, Reg Mktg Dir-Global Travel Western Reg - Diageo North America, Inc.; pg. 1961, pg. 361
Higgins, Nick, Dir-Glad Mktg - The Procter & Gamble Company; pg. 1129, pg. 1418
Higgins, Niki, Dir-Luxury Sls - Seaside Properties Group, Inc.; pg. 1112, pg. 426
Higgins, Rick, Sr VP-Mdsg & Mktg Skechers Performance - SKECHERS U.S.A., INC.; pg. 1819, pg. 143
Higgins, Scott, Dir-Product Mgmt - Arris Group, Inc.; pg. 353, pg. 541
Higgins, Shawn, Sr Dir-Mktg - TEN: The Enthusiast Network; pg. 1691, pg. 1298
Higgins, Stephen, Mgr-Social Media - TBC Corporation; pg. 1889, pg. 457
Higgins, Susan S., Mgr-Mktg Comm - Verizon Communications Inc.; pg. 1875, pg. 1309
Higgins, Teri, Sr Mgr-Media & Events - Sega of America Inc.; pg. 966, pg. 227
Higgs, Chris, Territory Mgr-Sls - Altria Group, Inc.; pg. 1893, pg. 1800
Higgs, Eve, Dir-Corp Mktg & Dir-Content & Community - Market Leader, Inc.; pg. 1102, pg. 1822
Higgs, Vince, Mgr-Retail Mktg & Sls - Cherry Central Cooperative, Inc.; pg. 847, pg. 909
High, Lori L., Sr VP & Chief Sls & Mktg Officer - The Hartford Financial Services Group, Inc.; pg. 1202, pg. 352
High, Matt, Sr Dir-Ops - Coventry Health Care, Inc.; pg. 1519, pg. 761
Highland, Kim, Mgr-Mktg Promos & Graphics - Beall's, Inc.; pg. 1760, pg. 414
Highley, Ian, VP & Gen Mgr-Semiconductor Bus Products - Littelfuse, Inc.; pg. 1301, pg. 580
Highsmith, Savannah, Specialist-External Comm & Social Media - The Home Depot, Inc.; pg. 1050, pg. 510
Hight, Terry, Dir-Creative - Hitachi Data Systems Corporation; pg. 407, pg. 265
Hight, Thomas, Dir-Oncology Global Mktg Strategy - Astellas Pharma US, Inc.; pg. 1496, pg. 640
Hightower, Glorious, Specialist-Mktg Comm - Airgas, Inc.; pg. 1146, pg. 1583
Higuera, Malena, Dir-Mktg-Global - Maybelline LLC; pg. 516, pg. 1257
Hii, Jeannie, Sr Mgr-Mktg - American Express Company; pg. 712, pg. 1190
Hilbert, Jay, Sr VP-Sls & Bus Dev-Global - Airvana, Inc.; pg. 268, pg. 812
Hilbert, Megan, Sr Analyst-Northeast Area Mktg - Verizon Communications Inc.; pg. 1875, pg. 1309
Hilburger, Mark, Bus Mgr-Automotive OEM-Global - Firestone Industrial Products Division; pg. 1882, pg. 686
Hilburn, Jimmy, Dir-Original Series Mktg - Netflix, Inc.; pg. 1269, pg. 141
Hild, Beth, Sr Mgr-Digital Signage Sls-Central Reg - Samsung Electronics America, Inc.; pg. 669, pg. 1115
Hildale, Philip, VP-Sls - Insulet Corporation; pg. 644, pg. 785
Hildebrand, Jim, VP-Export Sls - Coker Tire Company; pg. 1880, pg. 1628
Hildebrandt, Hilarie, VP-Retail Mktg - 20th Century Fox Film Corp.; pg. 267, pg. 124
Hilderbrand, Carey, VP-Mktg - Western Governors University; pg. 610, pg. 1762
Hildreth, Troy, Corp VP-Mktg, Sls & Bus Dev - WellCare Health Plans Inc.; pg. 1223, pg. 476
Hildyard, Theo, Mgr-Product Mktg - Software AG, Inc.; pg.

First page reference indicates Business Class Edition
Second page reference indicates Geographic Edition

471, *pg.* 1799
Hile, Jennifer, Coord-Sls & Mktg - General Electric Company; *pg.* 1297, *pg.* 347
Hileman, Brad, Dir-Digital, Creative & Brand Dev - Meijer, Inc.; *pg.* 1779, *pg.* 888
Hilf, Bill, Sr VP-Product Mgmt-Helion Cloud - Hewlett-Packard Company; *pg.* 404, *pg.* 175
Hilfman, Dave, Sr VP-Sls - United Continental Holdings, Inc.; *pg.* 1927, *pg.* 593
Hilgeman, Erica, Dir-Americas Mktg - Dell, Inc.; *pg.* 385, *pg.* 1037
Hilgenberg, Lynette, VP & Mgr-Adv - Bank of American Fork; *pg.* 720, *pg.* 1751
Hilger, Lauren, Sr Mgr-Digital Mktg - Mattel Games/Puzzles; *pg.* 962, *pg.* 80
Hilger, Lauren, Mgr-Digital Mktg & Social Media-Barbie & Girls, Inc - MATTEL, INC.; *pg.* 962, *pg.* 81
Hilkemeier, Kami, Mgr-Software Grp Mktg - IBM; *pg.* 410, *pg.* 1449
Hilker, Stephen, Brand Mgr-Frozen & Artisan Bread - Pepperidge Farm, Inc.; *pg.* 888, *pg.* 363
Hill, Amanda, Chief Creative Officer-Intl-A&E Networks - A&E Television Networks, LLC; *pg.* 267, *pg.* 1185
Hill, Amanda, Assoc Mgr-Digital Mktg - The Allstate Corporation; *pg.* 1189, *pg.* 639
Hill, Amanda, Assoc Mgr-Mktg - General Mills, Inc.; *pg.* 828, *pg.* 933
Hill, Amy H., Sr Dir-Pub Affairs - Wal-Mart Stores, Inc.; *pg.* 1790, *pg.* 29
Hill, Angie, Gen Mgr-Audience Mktg-Consumer App & Svcs - Microsoft Corporation; *pg.* 435, *pg.* 1824
Hill, Antony, Head-Creative Agency Partnerships - Google Inc.; *pg.* 1249, *pg.* 153
Hill, Barton, Head-Mktg & Comm-Citi Treasury & Trade Solutions-Global - Citigroup Inc.; *pg.* 735, *pg.* 1212
Hill, Betty A, Dir-Americas Mktg Programs - Siemens Corporation; *pg.* 803, *pg.* 1291
Hill, Brenda D., Mgr-PR - Verizon Communications Inc.; *pg.* 1875, *pg.* 1309
Hill, Caleb, Dir-Adv Svcs EU - Amazon.com, Inc.; *pg.* 1226, *pg.* 1831
Hill, Carl, Dir-Mktg - Clayton Homes, Inc.; *pg.* 1086, *pg.* 1640
Hill, Ceres, Dir-Mktg - The Mob Museum; *pg.* 564, *pg.* 1028
Hill, Chris, Mgr-Model Line-Mktg & Brand Comm - Mazda North American Operations; *pg.* 183, *pg.* 113
Hill, Corliss, Dir-Mktg-Natl - UnitedHealth Group Incorporated; *pg.* 1221, *pg.* 950
Hill, Donna, Mgr-Mktg Comm - Trane Inc.; *pg.* 116, *pg.* 1109
Hill, Eddie, Sr VP-Consumer Mktg & Brand Strategy - BET Holdings LLC; *pg.* 271, *pg.* 396
Hill, Elliott, Pres-Geographies & Sls-Nike Brand - NIKE, Inc.; *pg.* 1812, *pg.* 1492
Hill, Emily, Specialist-Sls Promo Mktg - Target Corporation; *pg.* 1786, *pg.* 942
Hill, Gary R., Sr Mgr-Global Channel Mktg & Programs - Tellabs, Inc.; *pg.* 678, *pg.* 637
Hill, Gerard, Reg VP-Beacon Sls - Beacon Roofing Supply, Inc.; *pg.* 70, *pg.* 840
Hill, Gregory, COO & Pres-Exploration & Production - Hess Corporation; *pg.* 979, *pg.* 1240
Hill, Guy, Exec VP-Product-West Territory - The Allstate Corporation; *pg.* 1189, *pg.* 639
Hill, Ina, Brand Mgr - Gucci America Inc.; *pg.* 6, *pg.* 1237
Hill, Jack, VP-Sls - Minuteman International, Inc.; *pg.* 332, *pg.* 652
Hill, Jason, Dir-Media & Content Strategy-Global - General Electric Company; *pg.* 1297, *pg.* 347
Hill, Jason, Mgr-Sls-Electrical Wholesaling-Natl - HellermannTyton; *pg.* 642, *pg.* 1875
Hill, Jennifer, Sr Dir-Mktg & Oncology - Eli Lilly and Company; *pg.* 1527, *pg.* 684
Hill, Jon, Dir-Sls & Ops-Americas - Bray International, Inc.; *pg.* 52, *pg.* 1702
Hill, Jonathan, VP-Mktg & Technique-PathFinder - Schlumberger Limited; *pg.* 801, *pg.* 1714
Hill, Kaitlin, Media Planner - Marshalls of MA, Inc.; *pg.* 1778, *pg.* 821
Hill, Kaitlin, Media Planner - T.J. Maxx; *pg.* 1788, *pg.* 822
Hill, Kaitlin, Media Planner - The TJX Companies, Inc.; *pg.* 1788, *pg.* 822
Hill, Katie, Sr Dir-Mktg - SAP; *pg.* 465, *pg.* 78
Hill, Kendra, Sr Assoc Brand Mgr-SCOTT 1000 Tissue - Kimberly-Clark Corporation; *pg.* 1461, *pg.* 1720
Hill, Kevin, Sr Dir-Sponsorship Activation - Washington Nationals, L.P.; *pg.* 591, *pg.* 407
Hill, Kevin N., Pres-Paychex Insurance Agency & VP-Insurance Sls & Ops - Paychex, Inc.; *pg.* 792, *pg.* 1336
Hill, Krista, Category Mgr-Mktg Svcs-North American - The Goodyear Tire & Rubber Company; *pg.* 1883, *pg.* 1401
Hill, Kristina, Analyst-Mktg Svcs - Graybar Electric Company, Inc.; *pg.* 1299, *pg.* 997
Hill, Laurie, Assoc Dir-Product Dev & Mgmt-Device Recycling Program - Verizon Communications Inc.; *pg.* 1875, *pg.* 1309
Hill, Leah, Mgr-Experience Mktg Ops - Clif Bar Inc.; *pg.* 848, *pg.* 83
Hill, Lisa, Dir-PR - Saratoga Performing Arts Center, Inc.; *pg.* 581, *pg.* 1340
Hill, Mark, Dir-Life Mktg - Massachusetts Mutual Life Insurance Company; *pg.* 1207, *pg.* 845
Hill, Marvin, Mgr-PR-Natl - Humana, Inc.; *pg.* 1204, *pg.* 734
Hill, McKenzie, Media Buyer-Natl Television - Palisades Media Group, Inc.; *pg.* 452, *pg.* 275
Hill, Michael L., Sr Mgr-Brand Dev-Global - Hasbro, Inc.; *pg.* 954, *pg.* 1603
Hill, Mike, Reg Mgr-Mktg - Lithia Motors Inc; *pg.* 183, *pg.* 1499
Hill, Nathan, Head-Mktg-Petcare - Nestle Purina PetCare Company; *pg.* 1479, *pg.* 1000
Hill, Nicole, Mgr-Global Mktg-Lifestyle Sun - Oakley, Inc.; *pg.* 1840, *pg.* 86
Hill, Rachel, Coord-Premium Seat Sls - Live Nation Entertainment, Inc.; *pg.* 558, *pg.* 47
Hill, Rachel, Acct Exec-Digital Vendor Mktg - Target Corporation; *pg.* 1786, *pg.* 942
Hill, Richard, Sr Dir-Contact Center Sls & Svc - The Terminix International Company Limited Partnership; *pg.* 337, *pg.* 1646
Hill, Roy, Engr-Technical Mktg - Intel Corporation; *pg.* 645, *pg.* 266
Hill, Sarah, Asst Mgr-Mktg - E&J Gallo Winery; *pg.* 1962, *pg.* 149
Hill, Stephanie, Assoc Mgr-Adv - Long John Silver's, LLC; *pg.* 1736, *pg.* 736
Hill, Steven, VP-Mdsg - Zappos.com, Inc.; *pg.* 1291, *pg.* 1030
Hill, Teri, Dir-Media - Lexus Division; *pg.* 182, *pg.* 294
Hill, Teri, Mgr-Media-Lexus USA - Toyota Motor Sales, U.S.A., Inc.; *pg.* 193, *pg.* 296
Hill, Tom, Mgr-Svc-Internal Social Media - Bristol-Myers Squibb Company; *pg.* 1509, *pg.* 1206
Hill, Tonya, Mgr-Product Mktg-Hosting & Cloud Solutions - AT&T Inc.; *pg.* 1868, *pg.* 358
Hill, Zack, Sr Dir-Comm - Philadelphia Flyers, L.P.; *pg.* 575, *pg.* 1569
Hillebrecht, Chris, Sr Mgr-Sls Strategy - Pfizer Inc.; *pg.* 1581, *pg.* 1278
Hiller, Alexis Phillips, Dir-Mktg Comm - Baker Knapp & Tubbs Inc.; *pg.* 916, *pg.* 566
Hiller, Drew, Sr Specialist-Product - Bristol Myers Squibb Company; *pg.* 1509, *pg.* 1206
Hiller, Sara, Mgr-Mktg-Global - Nautica Apparel, Inc.; *pg.* 45, *pg.* 1265
Hillger, Brian, Sr Dir - Microsoft Corporation; *pg.* 435, *pg.* 1824
Hilliard, Kurt, CMO & Exec VP-Sls - DirectBuy, Inc.; *pg.* 1766, *pg.* 694
Hilliard, Maggie, VP-Digital Mktg Strategy - JPMorgan Chase & Co.; *pg.* 772, *pg.* 1246
Hilliard, Melissa, Mgr-Media Rels - Lockheed Martin Corporation; *pg.* 229, *pg.* 762
Hilliard, Michael, Specialist-Trade Sls & Events - Presbyterian Publishing Corporation; *pg.* 1678, *pg.* 737
Hillier, Colson, VP-Precision Mktg - Verizon Communications Inc.; *pg.* 1875, *pg.* 1309
Hillins, Brian, Dir-Mktg-Consumables - PetSmart, Inc.; *pg.* 1481, *pg.* 18
Hillman, Chris, VP-Mktg - Melitta USA Inc.; *pg.* 781, *pg.* 416
Hillman, David, Gen Mgr-Vocational Product Line - Navistar International Corporation; *pg.* 186, *pg.* 630
Hillman, Karyn, Chief Product Officer - Levi Strauss & Co.; *pg.* 43, *pg.* 220
Hills, Jackie, Dir-Retail Creative - BUYSEASONS, Inc.; *pg.* 20, *pg.* 1883
Hillsman, Michael, Sr Dir-Mktg - McDonald's Corporation; *pg.* 1737, *pg.* 645
Hillyer, Chris, Sr Mgr-Innovation - Deckers Outdoor Corporation; *pg.* 1807, *pg.* 100
Hilpertshauser, John, Sr Mgr - Georgia-Pacific LLC; *pg.* 1458, *pg.* 507
Hilpl, Pat Kraft, Exec Dir-Citywide Sls - Philadelphia Convention & Visitors Bureau; *pg.* 1004, *pg.* 1568
Hilston, Sarah, Mgr-Mktg - Gilt Groupe Inc.; *pg.* 24, *pg.* 1234
Hilton, Mike, Head-Global Mktg & Pricing Strategy - Monsanto Company; *pg.* 1173, *pg.* 999
Hiltunen, Peter A., VP & Mgr-Production - United-Guardian, Inc.; *pg.* 1184, *pg.* 1165
Hiltz, Marilla, Mgr-Mktg - Clinique Laboratories LLC; *pg.* 503, *pg.* 1214
Himstedt, Brian, Sr Dir-Info Sys - Kansas City Royals Baseball Corporation; *pg.* 555, *pg.* 985
Himwich, Josh, VP-Product - XO Group Inc.; *pg.* 1289, *pg.* 1316
Hincapie, Edwin, Mgr-Multicultural Comml Mktg - Heineken USA Inc.; *pg.* 252, *pg.* 1352
Hinchman, Jennifer, Mgr-Mktg - Lee Enterprises, Incorporated; *pg.* 1658, *pg.* 704
Hinckley, Fran, Sr Dir-Duncan Hines - Pinnacle Foods Group LLC; *pg.* 889, *pg.* 1104
Hinckley, Lucy, Dir-Bus Partner Mktg-Software Grp - International Business Machines Corporation; *pg.* 418, *pg.* 1138
Hindle, Michelle, Mgr-Adv - Coach, Inc.; *pg.* 3, *pg.* 1214
Hindle, Tacy, Assoc Dir-Mktg - AT&T Mobility LLC; *pg.* 620, *pg.* 1824
Hindley, Lynn, Mgr-Mktg-Corp Accounts-Global - Butler Manufacturing Company; *pg.* 72, *pg.* 981
Hindley, Scott A., VP-Sls & Mktg - Hindley Manufacturing Company, Inc.; *pg.* 1049, *pg.* 1601
Hindman, Meghan, Sr Dir-Oncology Comm - Pfizer Inc.; *pg.* 1581, *pg.* 1278
Hindorff, Marc, Sr Mgr-Corp Responsibility - Brown-Forman Corporation; *pg.* 1958, *pg.* 732
Hinds, Ashley, Specialist-Global PR - Bare Escentuals, Inc.; *pg.* 500, *pg.* 213
Hinds, Ben, Product Mgr-Quantis & Tigear-2 - Baldor Electric Company; *pg.* 1316, *pg.* 32
Hinds, Odette F., Mgr-Alliance Mktg - IBM Canada Limited; *pg.* 411, *pg.* 1923
Hine, Anna, Mgr-Mktg-Global Imports - Constellation Brands, Inc.; *pg.* 1960, *pg.* 1348
Hine, John, Specialist-Tech Sls - Samsung Telecommunications America, LLC; *pg.* 670, *pg.* 1736
Hineman, Stefanie, Mgr-Online Adv Assoc Mktg - Intuit Inc.; *pg.* 769, *pg.* 158
Hiner, David, Dir-Advanced Product Dev - Amkor Technology, Inc.; *pg.* 67, *pg.* 25
Hines, Clarissa, Coord-Mktg-Dom Perignon & Moet & Chandon - Moet Hennessy; *pg.* 1966, *pg.* 1260
Hines, Darius, Brand Mgr-Gins - Pernod Ricard USA, Inc.; *pg.* 1968, *pg.* 1332
Hines, Denise, Mgr-Mktg - Crown Prince, Inc.; *pg.* 850, *pg.* 67
Hines, Jeana, VP-Sls & Mktg - Imperial Sugar Company; *pg.* 864, *pg.* 1746
Hines, Jeff, VP-Global Retention Mktg - Rosetta Stone Inc.; *pg.* 462, *pg.* 1774
Hines, Lisa, Mgr-Digital Mktg - G&K Services Inc.; *pg.* 693, *pg.* 949
Hines, Myra, Sr Product Mgr - PNY Technologies, Inc.; *pg.* 455, *pg.* 1105
Hines, Nina, Sr Mgr-Point of Sale Capability - Alliance Data Systems Corporation; *pg.* 347, *pg.* 1729
Hines, Thomas, Dir-Creative & Promos - J.J. Keller & Associates, Inc.; *pg.* 1654, *pg.* 1883
Hiney, Kathryn, Sr Dir-Product Strategy & Process - The Timberland Company; *pg.* 1821, *pg.* 1039
Hinge, Claus, VP-Sls-EMEA - Printronix, Inc.; *pg.* 456, *pg.* 115
Hingher, Kimmra, Dir-Mktg - Mars Petcare; *pg.* 1478, *pg.* 1633
Hinkle, Kurt, Sr Mgr-Mktg-Brand Mgmt - NBC Universal, Inc.; *pg.* 300, *pg.* 1266
Hinkle, Pamela, Asst Mgr-Mktg - Knouse Foods Cooperative Inc.; *pg.* 869, *pg.* 1558
Hinksman, Darryl, Head-On Trade Customer Mktg - Heineken USA Inc.; *pg.* 252, *pg.* 1352
Hinkson, Tom, Mgr-Sls-Porter - Killark Electric; *pg.* 1300, *pg.* 998
Hinojosa, Mark, Dir-Interactive Media - The Detroit News, Inc.; *pg.* 1635, *pg.* 880
Hinson, Chad, VP-Brand Creative-Global - Levi Strauss & Co.; *pg.* 43, *pg.* 220
Hinson, Gina Young, Dir-Creative Svcs - KFDM-TV; *pg.* 294, *pg.* 1668
Hinterleitner, Guenther, VP-Intl Sls & Mktg - Natus Medical Incorporated; *pg.* 1572, *pg.* 199

Hinton, Charlie, Exec Dir-Mktg Analytics - AT&T Mobility LLC; *pg.* 619, *pg.* 488
Hinton, Charlie, Exec Dir-Mktg Analytics - AT&T Mobility LLC; *pg.* 620, *pg.* 1824
Hinton, Lisa, Dir-Mktg Ops - HealthSouth Corporation; *pg.* 1540, *pg.* 3
Hinton, Michael, Mgr-Mktg-US Feed Ops - Hubbard Feeds Inc.; *pg.* 1477, *pg.* 928
Hinz, Dustin, Exec VP-Mktg - Ernie Ball Inc.; *pg.* 1768, *pg.* 68
Hiole, Reynald, Mgr-Mktg - Blue Shield of California; *pg.* 1195, *pg.* 214
Hipp, Stephanie, Assoc Mgr-Mktg - Time Inc.; *pg.* 1693, *pg.* 1300
Hiranaga, Brad, Head-Bus Unit-Value Brands & Dir-Mktg - General Mills, Inc.; *pg.* 828, *pg.* 933
Hirano, Jennifer, Brand Mgr - Colgate-Palmolive Company; *pg.* 504, *pg.* 1215
Hirano, Takuya, Gen Mgr-Mktg & Ops - Microsoft Corporation; *pg.* 435, *pg.* 1024
Hirapara, Manish, Sr Dir-ECommerce - Office Depot, Inc.; *pg.* 448, *pg.* 412
Hiras, Stacie, VP-Mktg & Comm - Synchronoss Technologies, Inc.; *pg.* 479, *pg.* 1047
Hirji, Asif, Sr Dir-Mktg - Frito-Lay North America, Inc.; *pg.* 1853, *pg.* 1730
Hirji, Asif, Sr Dir-Mktg - PepsiCo, Inc.; *pg.* 259, *pg.* 1327
Hirnikl, John, Mgr-Production & Supvr-IT - Babcox Media; *pg.* 1619, *pg.* 1400
Hirota, Naoko, Specialist-Mktg - Procter & Gamble Inc.; *pg.* 333, *pg.* 1929
Hirsch, Deborah, Sr Dir-Dev - Houston Grand Opera Association; *pg.* 552, *pg.* 1707
Hirsch, Jeffrey A., Pres-Global Mktg & Product Plng-Beverly Hills - Starz Entertainment, LLC; *pg.* 310, *pg.* 327
Hirsch, Kayla, Mgr-Mktg - Magellan Health Services, Inc.; *pg.* 1557, *pg.* 337
Hirsch, Kristin, Dir-Digital Mktg - The Dun & Bradstreet Corp.; *pg.* 1637, *pg.* 1120
Hirsch, Lars, Grp Product Mgr-Search Monetization - Microsoft Corporation; *pg.* 435, *pg.* 1824
Hirsch, Lee, Dir-Mktg - NVIDIA Corporation; *pg.* 447, *pg.* 268
Hirsch, Marcelo, VP-Sls-Latin America - ScanSource, Inc.; *pg.* 671, *pg.* 1618
Hirsch, Martin, Sr Mgr-Credit & Collections - Meredith Corporation; *pg.* 1663, *pg.* 705
Hirsch, Michael, Sr Dir-US Market Access-Strategic Accounts & Managed Care - CUBIST PHARMACEUTICALS, INC.; *pg.* 1521, *pg.* 828
Hirsch, Neil, Sr Mgr-North America Comm - Novelis Inc.; *pg.* 100, *pg.* 516
Hirschbach, Lauren, Exec Dir-Mktg Ops - Shiseido Cosmetics America of SAC; *pg.* 522, *pg.* 1291
Hirschberg, Danielle, Assoc Mgr-PR & Events - Kenneth Cole Productions, Inc.; *pg.* 1810, *pg.* 1248
Hirschfeld, Jennifer, Dir-Mktg - Advanced Beauty Systems Inc.; *pg.* 498, *pg.* 1672
Hirschhorn, Jonathan, Exec VP-Brand & Mktg-Global - MetLife, Inc.; *pg.* 1208, *pg.* 1258
Hirsh, Rich, Mgr-Natl Acct Direct Sls - The Penn Companies; *pg.* 10, *pg.* 1568
Hirshfield, Jessica, Supvr-Digital Global Social Mktg - FRANKLIN RESOURCES, INC.; *pg.* 760, *pg.* 254
Hirst, Beth Ann, Head-Mktg - AstraZeneca Pharmaceuticals LP; *pg.* 1497, *pg.* 389
Hirst, Brant, Dir-Mktg-Asia Pacific - NIKE, Inc.; *pg.* 1812, *pg.* 1492
Hirt, Susan, Mgr-Adv - Trump Entertainment Resorts, Inc.; *pg.* 1117, *pg.* 1041
Hirten, Marc, VP-Channel Mktg - William Grant & Sons, Inc.; *pg.* 1972, *pg.* 1057
Hirtenstein, Edie, Sr Dir-Product Mgmt-Auto - Equifax Inc.; *pg.* 748, *pg.* 504
Hiscar, Kaitlin, Brand Mktg Mgr - Marriott International, Inc.; *pg.* 1102, *pg.* 764
Hiscock, David, Sr VP-Sls EMEA - Genband, Inc.; *pg.* 640, *pg.* 1731
Hisey, Brad, Dir-Digital Mktg - Warner Bros. Entertainment Inc.; *pg.* 319, *pg.* 54
Hiskey, Bernadette, Brand Mktg Dir - Carl Zeiss, Inc.; *pg.* 1405, *pg.* 1345
Hiss, Fielder, VP-Product Mgmt - EnerNOC, Inc.; *pg.* 976, *pg.* 794
Hiss, Tiffini, VP-Sls - comScore, Inc; *pg.* 1236, *pg.* 1798
Hissong, Erica, VP-Direct Mktg & Lead Generation-Anthem - Anthem, Inc.; *pg.* 1192, *pg.* 683
Hitch, Erin, Mgr-PR - Cisco Systems, Inc.; *pg.* 372, *pg.* 240
Hitchcock, Elizabeth, Dir-Social Bus & Digital Platforms - AT&T Inc.; *pg.* 1868, *pg.* 358
Hitchman, Jennifer, Sr Mgr-Partner Svcs - Local.com Corporation; *pg.* 1264, *pg.* 113
Hite, Blair, Mgr-Mktg Channel - Volt Information Sciences, Inc.; *pg.* 490, *pg.* 1312
Hite, Calli, Sr Mgr-Corp Comm - Union Pacific Corporation; *pg.* 1927, *pg.* 1018
Hite, Calli, Sr Mgr-Corp Comm - Union Pacific Railroad Company; *pg.* 1927, *pg.* 1019
Hite, Nicole, VP-Creative Studios - Hallmark Cards, Inc.; *pg.* 1646, *pg.* 983
Hite, Rob, Dir-Mktg - The J.M. Smucker Company; *pg.* 865, *pg.* 1468
Hite-Wadler, Lisa, Dir-Adv Ops - Indianapolis Star; *pg.* 1652, *pg.* 687
Hites, Marshall, Sr VP-Mktg & Creative Svcs - Tribune Media Company; *pg.* 1696, *pg.* 592
Hittie, Mark, Dir-Mktg - Sappi Fine Paper North America; *pg.* 1468, *pg.* 801
Hittle, Robert, Dir-Mktg - Mamma Ilardo's Corp.; *pg.* 1737, *pg.* 779
Hittman, Jill, VP-Mktg-Global - The Nielsen Company B.V.; *pg.* 1671, *pg.* 1272
Hitzeman, Scott, Sr Mgr-IT-Global Network Comm - Plantronics, Inc.; *pg.* 663, *pg.* 270
Hixson, Harry F., Interim CEO - Arena Pharmaceuticals, Inc.; *pg.* 1495, *pg.* 200
Hixson, Josh O., Mgr-PR - AT&T; *pg.* 1865, *pg.* 258
Hiyoshi, Ray, Sr Mgr-Intl Bus-Konami Digital Entertainment - Konami Corporation of America Inc.; *pg.* 960, *pg.* 80
Hizer, Brittany, Mgr-Tech Sls - Brunswick Corporation; *pg.* 1828, *pg.* 623
Hjorth, Chris, Sr Dir-Philadelphia Cream Cheese - The Kraft Heinz Company; *pg.* 871, *pg.* 641
Hlaing, Miranda, Mgr-Mktg - ZIPCAR, INC.; *pg.* 1931, *pg.* 810
Hlebasko, Ginger, Dir-Mktg-One to One Comm & Opportunity Mgmt - State Farm Mutual Automobile Insurance Co.; *pg.* 1218, *pg.* 557
Hluchan, Erik, Dir-Creative - Structural Graphics, LLC; *pg.* 1689, *pg.* 346
Hmura, Steve, Asst Dir-Broad Media - The Hartford Financial Services Group, Inc.; *pg.* 1202, *pg.* 352
Hnath, Erin, Mgr-Adv - National Instruments Corporation; *pg.* 443, *pg.* 1664
Hnetynka, Wendy, Specialist-Channel Mktg & Enterprise Networks Div - ADTRAN, Inc.; *pg.* 344, *pg.* 6
Ho, Alan, Sr Mgr-Mktg Comm-TV - Samsung Electronics America, Inc.; *pg.* 669, *pg.* 1115
Ho, Alex, Exec Dir-Mktg - American Greetings Corporation; *pg.* 1615, *pg.* 1428
Ho, Antony, Mgr-Mktg - Google Inc.; *pg.* 1249, *pg.* 153
Ho, Cheryl, Mgr-Mktg-Arm & Hammer & OxiClean - Church & Dwight Canada Corp.; *pg.* 503, *pg.* 1925
Ho, Clifton, VP-Sls-Asia Pacific - Intersil Corporation; *pg.* 647, *pg.* 146
Ho, Eileen, Asst VP & Sr Mgr-Corp Events - Wells Fargo & Company; *pg.* 819, *pg.* 232
Ho, Florence, Sr Dir-Brand Mktg, Loyalty & Partnerships - Wyndham Worldwide Corporation; *pg.* 1119, *pg.* 1107
Ho, Franklin, Sr Specialist-Product - Twitter, Inc.; *pg.* 1285, *pg.* 228
Ho, Gordon, Sr VP-Global Mktg & Sls-North America - Princess Cruise Lines Ltd.; *pg.* 1920, *pg.* 270
Ho, Jenny, Mgr-Mktg-Consumer Cross Border Mktg - PayPal Inc.; *pg.* 1274, *pg.* 248
Ho, Juliann, Mgr-Mktg-Components - Ingram Micro Inc.; *pg.* 415, *pg.* 261
Ho, Linda, Mgr-Mktg - Hong Kong Tourism Board - New York; *pg.* 1911, *pg.* 1241
Ho, Loretta, Sr Dir-Digital Res-USA Network - NBC Universal, Inc.; *pg.* 300, *pg.* 1266
Ho, Michelle, Sr Mgr-Mktg Ops - McKesson Corporation; *pg.* 1560, *pg.* 222
Ho, Nicky, Coord-Sponsorship Mktg - FMR LLC (Fidelity Investments); *pg.* 759, *pg.* 794
Ho, Peter, VP & Product Mgr - Wells Fargo & Company; *pg.* 819, *pg.* 232
Ho, Ronald, Product Mgr - Google Inc.; *pg.* 1249, *pg.* 153
Hoag, Cathy, Sr Dir-Strategic Media Mgmt - Marriott International, Inc.; *pg.* 1102, *pg.* 764
Hoagland, Rachel, Sr Dir-Digital Mktg & Gaming - Hasbro, Inc.; *pg.* 954, *pg.* 1603
Hoaglun, Brad, Dir-PR & Comm - St. Alphonsus Regional Medical Center; *pg.* 1596, *pg.* 548
Hoak, Keller, VP-Integrated Adv - T. Rowe Price Group Inc.; *pg.* 808, *pg.* 759
Hoang, Chantal, Assoc-Database Mktg - Fandango Media, LLC; *pg.* 1247, *pg.* 130
Hoban, Liam, Category Mgr-Soccer - adidas America Inc.; *pg.* 1803, *pg.* 1500
Hoban, William G., Mgr-Sls - Cooper Tire & Rubber Company; *pg.* 1881, *pg.* 1453
Hobart, Charlie, Sr Rep-Media Rels - United Continental Holdings, Inc.; *pg.* 1927, *pg.* 593
Hobbs, Glen, Exec Dir-Creative - National CineMedia, Inc.; *pg.* 567, *pg.* 314
Hobbs, Holley, Coord-Mktg - Fluor Corporation; *pg.* 82, *pg.* 1719
Hobbs, Jack, Exec VP-Corp Sls - Spanish Broadcasting System Inc.; *pg.* 310, *pg.* 446
Hobbs, Laurie, VP-Mktg - The Marcus Corporation; *pg.* 1102, *pg.* 1877
Hobby, Elizabeth, VP-EDI & Digital Media Adv Ops - Discovery Communications, Inc.; *pg.* 282, *pg.* 777
Hobe, Barbara, Dir-Preferred Partner Relationships & Med D Product - Coventry Health Care, Inc.; *pg.* 1519, *pg.* 761
Hobin, Tanner, Mgr-Digital Shopper Mktg-Nestle Purina North America - Nestle Purina PetCare Company; *pg.* 1479, *pg.* 1000
Hoblit, Robert, Sr Dir-Product Mgmt - Symantec Corporation; *pg.* 478, *pg.* 161
Hobson, Cristin, Mgr-Digital Mktg-Amazon Web Svcs - Amazon.com, Inc.; *pg.* 1226, *pg.* 1831
Hobson, Jim, Reg Mgr-Sls - Alumacraft Boat Company; *pg.* 1705, *pg.* 964
Hobson, Joel, Dir-Mktg - Anaheim Ducks Hockey Club, LLC; *pg.* 528, *pg.* 42
Hobson, Karen, VP-Global Distr, Digital Media & Res Comm - The Walt Disney Company; *pg.* 317, *pg.* 52
Hobson, Ryan, Sr Mgr-Enterprise Demand Mktg Modeling - Adobe Systems Incorporated; *pg.* 342, *pg.* 235
Hoch, Barry, Gen Mgr-Product Plng - Audi of America, Inc.; *pg.* 164, *pg.* 1784
Hoch, Carey, Sr VP & Head-Mktg - Manulife Financial Corporation; *pg.* 778, *pg.* 1939
Hoch, Jeff, Sr Product Dir-Urology Franchise - GlaxoSmithKline; *pg.* 1536, *pg.* 1565
Hoch, Jeff, Sr Product Dir-Urology Franchise - GlaxoSmithKline Consumer Healthcare; *pg.* 510, *pg.* 1554
Hoch, Nattalie, Exec VP-Sls Ops - Miller Heiman Inc.; *pg.* 440, *pg.* 1031
Hochberg, Ali, Coord-Program Adv - Home Box Office, Inc.; *pg.* 290, *pg.* 1240
Hochberg, Jessica, Brand Mgr - Pernod Ricard USA, Inc.; *pg.* 1968, *pg.* 1332
Hochleutner, Alexis, Mgr-Client Solutions-Programmatic Creative-Doubleclick Platform - Google Inc.; *pg.* 1249, *pg.* 153
Hochschild, Melanie, Coord-PR - Kohl's Corporation; *pg.* 1775, *pg.* 1870
Hock, Jeff, Product Mgr-Digital - The Kroger Co.; *pg.* 1025, *pg.* 1416
Hockens, Terry, Brand Mgr-Diet Dr Pepper - Dr Pepper Snapple Group, Inc.; *pg.* 250, *pg.* 1729
Hockett, Chris, Product Mgr-Global Hardware & Software - Snap-on Incorporated; *pg.* 1062, *pg.* 1862
Hockey, Steve, VP-Sls & Mktg - Western Family Holding Co., Inc.; *pg.* 1037, *pg.* 1509
Hockman, Evan, Product Dir-Brimonidine Franchise - Allergan, Inc.; *pg.* 1491, *pg.* 106
Hockman, Joel, Mgr-Interactive Mktg-Retail Ops - Nissan North America, Inc.; *pg.* 186, *pg.* 1633
Hodack, Shindy, Sr Dir-Brand Mgmt & Innovation - YUM! Brands, Inc.; *pg.* 1756, *pg.* 738
Hodapp, Mike, Dir-Digital Mktg & ECommerce - Dillard's, Inc.; *pg.* 1766, *pg.* 34
Hodder, Melissa, Specialist-Digital Mktg - Colgate-Palmolive Company; *pg.* 504, *pg.* 1215
Hodgden, Adam, Mgr-Mktg Automation - Blackbaud, Inc.; *pg.* 361, *pg.* 1613
Hodge, Bryan R., VP-Sls & Ops-Intl - Paychex, Inc.; *pg.* 792, *pg.* 1336
Hodge, Mark, Dir-Mktg - McCain Foods Limited; *pg.* 876, *pg.* 1915
Hodge, Robin, Coord-Reg Mktg - The Allstate Corporation; *pg.* 1189, *pg.* 639
Hodges, Carissa, Sr Program Mgr-Sls Enablement-Demand Generation - CDW Corporation; *pg.* 370, *pg.* 663

First page reference indicates Business Class Edition
Second page reference indicates Geographic Edition

Hodges, Drew, Assoc Dir-Mktg & Innovation-Global - Kellogg Company; *pg.* 831, *pg.* 870
Hodges, Gene, Dir-Mktg - Bed Bath & Beyond Inc.; *pg.* 1121, *pg.* 1127
Hodges, Jennifer, Dir-PR - Loews Hotels Holding Corporation; *pg.* 1101, *pg.* 1252
Hodges, Katie, Mgr-Social Media Mktg - Web.com Group, Inc.; *pg.* 1288, *pg.* 435
Hodges, Katie, Mgr-Social Media Mktg - Web.com, Inc.; *pg.* 1288, *pg.* 524
Hodges, Kimberlee, Mgr-Mktg Comm - Randstad USA; *pg.* 459, *pg.* 941
Hodges, Louise, Head-PR-Europe - Travelzoo Inc; *pg.* 1926, *pg.* 1304
Hodges, Matt, VP-PR & IR - GameStop Corp.; *pg.* 399, *pg.* 1699
Hodges, Sarah, Sr Mgr-Indus Mktg-Autodesk - Autodesk Inc.; *pg.* 356, *pg.* 257
Hodges, Shane, Dir-Global Online Sls & Distr - Starwood Hotels & Resorts Worldwide, Inc.; *pg.* 1114, *pg.* 378
Hodges, Virginia, Dir-Mktg - Dell Inc.; *pg.* 383, *pg.* 1737
Hodgeson, Patrick, Mgr-Social Media & Multimedia Comm - American Golf Corporation; *pg.* 528, *pg.* 272
Hodgins, Becky, Specialist-Inside Sls-Dow Building Solutions Residential Bus Unit - THE DOW CHEMICAL COMPANY; *pg.* 1157, *pg.* 898
Hodgson, Adrian, Sr Mgr-Bus Dev - ASI Corporation; *pg.* 354, *pg.* 90
Hodgson, Jenny, Sr Mgr-Mktg & Digital Innovation - AT&T Inc.; *pg.* 1868, *pg.* 358
Hodgson, Paul, Product Mgr - Piksel; *pg.* 1275, *pg.* 1282
Hoding, Sabine, Mgr-Mktg & Comm - Mercer Inc.; *pg.* 1395, *pg.* 1258
Hodrick, Mary, Dir-Mktg - American Bank Incorporated; *pg.* 711, *pg.* 1513
Hodson, Eric, Mgr-Strategic PR - Deere & Company; *pg.* 703, *pg.* 632
Hoefer, Kate, Brand Mgr-Global - AngioDynamics, Inc.; *pg.* 1495, *pg.* 1173
Hoefflinger, Mike, Dir-Bus Mktg-Global - Facebook, Inc.; *pg.* 1245, *pg.* 143
Hoefling, Ken, VP-Construction Products Div - Caterpillar, Inc.; *pg.* 1321, *pg.* 650
Hoeft, John, Dir-Power Solutions Mgmt & Industrial Sls - Generac Power Systems Inc.; *pg.* 1340, *pg.* 1898
Hoehler, Sharleen, Sr Dir-Mktg - Wyndham Worldwide Corporation; *pg.* 1119, *pg.* 1107
Hoehn, Klaus G., VP-Adv, Tech & Engrg - Deere & Company; *pg.* 703, *pg.* 632
Hoehn, Thomas, Sr Dir-Digital & Social Mktg - Wal-Mart Stores, Inc.; *pg.* 1790, *pg.* 29
Hoekstra, Erin, Assoc Mgr-Mktg - Land O'Lakes, Inc.; *pg.* 873, *pg.* 915
Hoekstra, Mallory, Rep-Sls - Suncor Energy Inc.; *pg.* 985, *pg.* 1905
Hoekwater, Wendy, VP-Mktg & ECommerce - Marriott International, Inc.; *pg.* 1102, *pg.* 764
Hoelting, Azalia, Mgr-Field Mktg - Massage Heights Corporate, LLC; *pg.* 561, *pg.* 1741
Hoelzeman, Larry, VP-Sls-Worldwide - Cray Inc.; *pg.* 380, *pg.* 1834
Hoem, Steve, Mgr-Media & Comm - Anaheim Ducks Hockey Club, LLC; *pg.* 528, *pg.* 42
Hoene, Lisa, VP-Brand & Mktg Svcs - Allianz Life Insurance Company of North America; *pg.* 1188, *pg.* 929
Hoene, Reinhard, Sr Product Mgr - SAS Institute Inc.; *pg.* 466, *pg.* 1361
Hoenick, Robb, Sr Dir-Digital - CVS Health Corporation; *pg.* 1765, *pg.* 1610
Hoeppner, Gerard, VP-Mktg - Busch Gardens Tampa Bay; *pg.* 535, *pg.* 472
Hoerbelt, Jaime, Mgr-Integrated Mktg - Nickelodeon Direct Inc.; *pg.* 303, *pg.* 1271
Hoerner, Bill, Sr Dir-Mktg - Neogen Corporation; *pg.* 883, *pg.* 896
Hoersten, Mark A., VP-Mktg - Keithley Instruments, Inc.; *pg.* 1418, *pg.* 1473
Hoerter, Dirk, Dir-Digital Mktg Excellence - Abbott Laboratories; *pg.* 1484, *pg.* 551
Hoesch, Jackie, Sr Mgr-US Mktg-Philosophy - Coty, Inc.; *pg.* 506, *pg.* 1219
Hoeschen, Mandy, Specialist-Social Media - TD Ameritrade Holding Corporation; *pg.* 808, *pg.* 1018
Hoetmer, Ken, Product Mgr-Google Maps - Google Inc.; *pg.* 1249, *pg.* 153
Hoey, David, Sr Dir - Bergdorf Goodman, Inc.; *pg.* 1761, *pg.* 1202
Hoey, Edward, Dir-Mktg-Ig - CSL Behring LLC; *pg.* 1520, *pg.* 1543
Hoey, Kimberly, Brand Mktg Dir-Running Div-Footwear & Apparel - Mizuno USA, Inc.; *pg.* 1839, *pg.* 538
Hof, Colin, Mgr-Beer Mktg - Republic National Distributing Company; *pg.* 264, *pg.* 1713
Hofberg, Mark, Sr Engr-Sls - RSA Security Inc.; *pg.* 463, *pg.* 786
Hofer, Sydney, Asst Mgr-Corp PR - Kohl's Corporation; *pg.* 1775, *pg.* 1870
Hoff, Alan, VP-Strategic Mktg - SeaChange International, Inc.; *pg.* 1279, *pg.* 781
Hoff, Johnna, Sr Mgr-Comm-BRIC & Emerging Markets - eBay Inc.; *pg.* 1240, *pg.* 243
Hoff, Kurt, Sr VP-Worldwide Sls - Conexant Systems, Inc.; *pg.* 379, *pg.* 165
Hoffberg, Kevin, Mng Dir-Mktg-Private Client Svcs - Russell Investment Group; *pg.* 800, *pg.* 1845
Hoffecker, Joe, Dir-Mktg, Subscriber Svcs & Audience Dev - Cincinnati Business Courier; *pg.* 1627, *pg.* 1411
Hoffelt, Brad, Sr VP & Gen Mgr-Products & Svcs - GE Capital; *pg.* 761, *pg.* 362
Hoffins, Steven, Dir-Mktg-Unitary Products - Johnson Controls, Inc.; *pg.* 209, *pg.* 1876
Hoffman, Alison, Exec VP-Mktg-Beverly Hills - Starz Entertainment, LLC; *pg.* 310, *pg.* 327
Hoffman, Allan, Brand Mgr - Bimbo Bakeries USA; *pg.* 840, *pg.* 151
Hoffman, Amy, Sr Dir-HR - Medtronic, Inc.; *pg.* 1564, *pg.* 939
Hoffman, Brett, Mgr-Mktg Innovation-Beer 2.0 Team - Anheuser-Busch Companies, LLC; *pg.* 237, *pg.* 991
Hoffman, Carrie, Dir-Sls Strategy - CBS Interactive, Inc.; *pg.* 369, *pg.* 215
Hoffman, Christine, Sr Mgr-Digital Mktg Comm - The J.M. Smucker Company; *pg.* 865, *pg.* 1468
Hoffman, Cristina, Sr Mgr-Mktg - CBS Sports Division; *pg.* 274, *pg.* 1211
Hoffman, David, Dir-Mktg & Pricing-Global - Tecumseh Products Company; *pg.* 1381, *pg.* 866
Hoffman, Doug, Mgr-Digital Sls - American Honda Motor Co., Inc.; *pg.* 163, *pg.* 292
Hoffman, Frank, Sr Mgr-Mktg-Brand Retail NA - LEGO Systems, Inc.; *pg.* 961, *pg.* 346
Hoffman, Greg, VP-Global Brand Creative & Experience - NIKE, Inc.; *pg.* 1812, *pg.* 1492
Hoffman, Gustav, Sr Dir-Global IT Comml Bus Solutions - Kellogg Company; *pg.* 831, *pg.* 870
Hoffman, Heather, Rep-Retail Sls - The Hershey Co.; *pg.* 1855, *pg.* 1538
Hoffman, Hilary, Exec VP-Mktg - Universal Studios, Inc.; *pg.* 315, *pg.* 298
Hoffman, Jason, Mgr-Annuity Mktg - Lincoln Financial Group; *pg.* 1206, *pg.* 1375
Hoffman, Jeff, Sr VP-Comml Strategic Mktg - The Chubb Corporation; *pg.* 1196, *pg.* 1128
Hoffman, Jennifer, Sr Mgr-PR - Iconix Brand Group, Inc.; *pg.* 26, *pg.* 1243
Hoffman, Jim, Sr VP-Sls & Mktg - NBC Universal, Inc.; *pg.* 300, *pg.* 1266
Hoffman, John, Exec VP-Sls & Market Dev - Wiremold/LeGrand; *pg.* 689, *pg.* 383
Hoffman, Joshua, Rep-Adv Sls - The New York Times Company; *pg.* 1668, *pg.* 1270
Hoffman, Keane, Dir-Sls & Svc - The Penn Companies; *pg.* 10, *pg.* 1568
Hoffman, Kim, Sr Mgr-Brand Activation-Global - Newell Rubbermaid Inc.; *pg.* 1128, *pg.* 515
Hoffman, Kristal, Sr Mgr-Mktg-Social Media Mktg - The Allstate Corporation; *pg.* 1189, *pg.* 639
Hoffman, Larry L., VP-Production - Dow Jones & Company, Inc.; *pg.* 1637, *pg.* 1225
Hoffman, Lee, Head-New Media & Promos-OnBd Revenue - NCL Corporation Ltd.; *pg.* 1916, *pg.* 444
Hoffman, Lindsay Lawson, Sr Mgr-Programmatic Supply Strategy - Yahoo! Inc.; *pg.* 1289, *pg.* 289
Hoffman, Mark, Dir-Mktg & Innovation - Just Born, Inc.; *pg.* 1857, *pg.* 1516
Hoffman, Matt, Sr Dir-People Ops - Return Path, Inc.; *pg.* 461, *pg.* 1285
Hoffman, Michelle, VP-Sls - The Buckle, Inc.; *pg.* 1764, *pg.* 1011
Hoffman, Michelle, Mgr-Starkey Retail Mktg - Starkey Laboratories, Inc.; *pg.* 1597, *pg.* 923
Hoffman, Niki, Sr Specialist-Mktg Comm - Panasonic Electric Works Corporation of America; *pg.* 661, *pg.* 1095
Hoffman, Sam, Corp Dir-Mktg - Outrigger Enterprises, Inc.; *pg.* 1107, *pg.* 544
Hoffman, Scott, Chief Mdsg Officer - Trans World Entertainment Corporation; *pg.* 313, *pg.* 1137
Hoffman, Sharon, Dir-Mktg - Tyler Technologies, Inc.; *pg.* 486, *pg.* 1690
Hoffman-Jones, Jennifer, Sr Dir-Brand Mktg Luxury & Lifestyle Brands - Hilton Worldwide, Inc.; *pg.* 1094, *pg.* 1791
Hoffmann, Brant, Sr Product Mgr-Young Men's & Boys 8-20 - Kohl's Corporation; *pg.* 1775, *pg.* 1870
Hoffmann, Christine, Sr Mgr-Global Sls Plng - BabyCenter, LLC; *pg.* 1231, *pg.* 212
Hoffmann, Lisa, Mgr-Social Media - Duke Energy Corporation; *pg.* 1940, *pg.* 1366
Hoffmann, Rae, Gen Mgr-Mktg Comm - Port Authority of New York & New Jersey; *pg.* 1919, *pg.* 1283
Hoffmann, Robin, Specialist-Mktg - The Procter & Gamble Company; *pg.* 1129, *pg.* 1418
Hoffmann, W. Josh, Brand Mgr-RAV4 & Highlander-Natl - Toyota Motor Sales, U.S.A., Inc.; *pg.* 193, *pg.* 296
Hoffmeyer, Matthew, VP-Consumer Mktg - Conde Nast Publications, Inc.; *pg.* 1629, *pg.* 1217
Hoffner, Cyndi, Mgr-Adv - The Gorman-Rupp Company; *pg.* 1341, *pg.* 1458
Hoffstein, Paige, Brand Mgr-Captain Morgan Rum - Diageo North America Inc.; *pg.* 248, *pg.* 1223
Hofkens, Keith, Product Mgr-Global - Image Sensing Systems, Inc.; *pg.* 412, *pg.* 961
Hofmann, Allison, VP-Acct Mgmt & Mktg - Qualcare, Inc.; *pg.* 1215, *pg.* 1109
Hofmann, Andy, Dir-Mktg-Sears Optical - Luxottica Retail; *pg.* 8, *pg.* 1460
Hofmann, Regan, Assoc Dir-Mktg & Audience Dev - Emusic.com, Inc.; *pg.* 1243, *pg.* 1227
Hofmeister, Dan, Dir-Mktg - Bumble Bee Foods LLC; *pg.* 842, *pg.* 201
Hogan, Amanda Stephens, Product Mgr-Mktg Dept - Purdue Pharma LP; *pg.* 1587, *pg.* 377
Hogan, Andrea, Dir-Global Partner Mktg - QUALCOMM Incorporated; *pg.* 1873, *pg.* 207
Hogan, Christopher, VP-Mktg Analytics - Macy's, Inc.; *pg.* 1778, *pg.* 1417
Hogan, David, Mgr-eBusiness Mktg - Blue Cross & Blue Shield Association; *pg.* 1195, *pg.* 566
Hogan, Jenny, Head-Chase's Brand Creative Agency-InnerCircle & Exec Dir - JPMorgan Chase & Co.; *pg.* 772, *pg.* 1246
Hogan, Julie, Head-Global Events Mktg - Facebook, Inc.; *pg.* 1245, *pg.* 143
Hogan, Karen, Mgr-Recruitment Sls - The Orange County Register; *pg.* 1673, *pg.* 262
Hogan, Laurin, Brand Mgr-Digital - Benefit Cosmetics LLC; *pg.* 501, *pg.* 213
Hogan, Mike, Sr VP-Secondary Mktg Tech - Bank of America Global Wealth & Investment Management; *pg.* 720, *pg.* 789
Hogan, Patrick, VP-Strategic Mktg - Honeywell International Inc.; *pg.* 407, *pg.* 1088
Hogan, Rick, Sr Dir-Ad Sls Res-Viacom Media Networks - Viacom Inc.; *pg.* 316, *pg.* 1310
Hogan, Sarah, Dir-Mktg - Milwaukee Symphony Orchestra Inc.; *pg.* 563, *pg.* 1878
Hogan, Thomas, Jr., Pres-Unisphere Media & Exec VP-Mktg - Information Today Inc.; *pg.* 1653, *pg.* 1084
Hogarty, Tom, Dir-Product Mgmt - Adobe Systems Incorporated; *pg.* 342, *pg.* 235
Hogben, Andrea, Sr VP-Sls & Mktg - Plain Dealer Publishing Co.; *pg.* 1677, *pg.* 1434
Hoge, Colleen, Sr Mgr-Enterprise Mktg - SanDisk Corporation; *pg.* 465, *pg.* 147
Hogg, Allen, Sr Mgr-Res - MetrixLab; *pg.* 1266, *pg.* 223
Hogg, David, Strategist-Lead Mktg - Highmark Blue Cross Blue Shield; *pg.* 1203, *pg.* 1576
Hogg, Kimberly, Mgr-Mktg-Southeast Reg - PepsiCo, Inc.; *pg.* 259, *pg.* 1327
Hogge, Peggy, Project Mgr-Mktg-Northern California Reg - Whole Foods Market, Inc.; *pg.* 1038, *pg.* 1667
Hogikyan, Edward, Sr VP-Mktg - NYC & Company, Inc.; *pg.* 1002, *pg.* 1274
Hogrefe, Tyler, Sr Product Mgr-Technical - John Deere Consumer & Commercial Equipment, Inc.; *pg.* 705, *pg.* 1360
Hogue, Jared, Mgr-Worldwide Product Strategy Mktg - United

Parcel Service, Inc.; *pg.* 1928, *pg.* 522
Hogue, Karen, Dir-Product Mgmt & Mktg-Desktop Solutions - MORNINGSTAR, INC.; *pg.* 784, *pg.* 583
Hohman, Tess, Sr Mgr-Indus Initiatives - General Mills, Inc.; *pg.* 828, *pg.* 933
Hohnstein, Eleanor, Mgr-Mktg - Reily Foods Company; *pg.* 891, *pg.* 747
Hoidas, Angela, Head-Mktg - Deloitte & Touche USA LLP; *pg.* 743, *pg.* 1222
Hoit, Samantha, Media Buyer - Ruby Tuesday, Inc.; *pg.* 1748, *pg.* 1640
Hojel, Michael, Reg Sls Mgr-Mexico, Central & South America - Algas-SDI; *pg.* 1311, *pg.* 1831
Hojnacki, Christine, VP-PR & Special Events - Bon Ton Stores, Inc.; *pg.* 1763, *pg.* 1596
Hokanson, Maria, VP-Product & Brand Mktg-US - International Dairy Queen, Inc.; *pg.* 1732, *pg.* 938
Hoke, David, Mgr-Product Mktg - Emerson Process Management; *pg.* 1334, *pg.* 1636
Hoke, Wendy, Sr Dir-Mktg & Comm - St. Vincent Medical Center; *pg.* 1597, *pg.* 140
Holahan Myles, Mary, Mgr-Digital Mktg - Dick's Sporting Goods, Inc.; *pg.* 1832, *pg.* 1524
Holahan, Kristen, Mgr-Brand Mktg-Holiday Inn Americas - InterContinental Hotels Corporation; *pg.* 1097, *pg.* 511
Holan, Julie A., Dir-Mktg & Comm - First Data Corporation; *pg.* 754, *pg.* 505
Holas, Janell, Dir-Mktg - Henkel Consumer Adhesives, Inc.; *pg.* 403, *pg.* 1480
Holben, Barry, VP-Sls - Allen Organ Company; *pg.* 527, *pg.* 1549
Holbert, Geordie, Sr Dir-Programmatic Partnerships - Tremor Video; *pg.* 682, *pg.* 1305
Holbrook, Nicole, Mgr-Mktg Comm - Microsoft Corporation; *pg.* 435, *pg.* 1824
Holcomb, Kate, VP-Mktg - Briggs & Riley Travelware; *pg.* 2, *pg.* 1164
Holcomb, Kevin, Engr-Technical Mktg - Cisco Systems, Inc.; *pg.* 372, *pg.* 240
Holcombe, Julie, Dir-LOE Mktg - Pfizer Inc.; *pg.* 1581, *pg.* 1278
Holcombe, Nita, Dir-Mktg - Logility, Inc.; *pg.* 428, *pg.* 513
Holden, Berny, Reg Mgr-Sls-Western Europe - Reliable Automatic Sprinkler Co., Inc.; *pg.* 1137, *pg.* 1158
Holden, Chrissy, Sr Product Mgr - Zebra Technologies Corporation; *pg.* 690, *pg.* 628
Holden, Julie, Mgr-Mktg - Squarespace Inc.; *pg.* 1282, *pg.* 1295
Holden, Justin, Dir-PR - Musical Arts Association; *pg.* 565, *pg.* 1433
Holden, Vanessa, Sr VP & Dir-Creative-West Elm - Williams-Sonoma, Inc.; *pg.* 1140, *pg.* 234
Holder, Matt, Dir-Digital Mktg - Gold's Gym; *pg.* 550, *pg.* 1681
Holding, Jon, Dir-Brand & Adv - BlackRock, Inc.; *pg.* 724, *pg.* 1203
Holdsworth, Amanda, Mgr-Mktg Comm - University of Michigan; *pg.* 609, *pg.* 867
Holdsworth, David, Dir-Mktg - Eggland's Best, Inc.; *pg.* 854, *pg.* 1542
Holdsworth, Kim, Grp Brand Dir - Johnson & Johnson; *pg.* 1549, *pg.* 1091
Holecko, Jeff, Mgr-Media-North America - Kimberly-Clark Corporation; *pg.* 1461, *pg.* 1720
Holets, Len, Sr Mgr-Sls - Megger Inc.; *pg.* 1422, *pg.* 1557
Holgate, Gabrielle, Mgr-In-Store Mktg-KitchenAid Brand - Whirlpool Corporation; *pg.* 62, *pg.* 872
Holguin, Eliana, Mgr-Mktg-Global - Quaker Chemical Corp.; *pg.* 1178, *pg.* 1524
Holifield, Mark, Exec VP-Supply Chain & Product Dev - The Home Depot, Inc.; *pg.* 1050, *pg.* 510
Holl, Tim, Mgr-Product Mktg & Solutions - Konica Minolta Business Solutions USA, Inc.; *pg.* 1419, *pg.* 1113
Holland, Amy, Dir-Adv & Mktg Programs - Boston Ballet Inc.; *pg.* 533, *pg.* 790
Holland, Anne, Mgr-Sls Ops - Toyo Tire (U.S.A.) Corporation; *pg.* 1890, *pg.* 76
Holland, Bill, Mgr-Bus Analytics Sls - International Business Machines Corporation; *pg.* 418, *pg.* 1138
Holland, Chris, Asst Dir-Ticket Sls - Buffalo Bills, Inc.; *pg.* 535, *pg.* 1319
Holland, David R., Co-Founder & Sr VP-Sls & Mktg - ALIMERA SCIENCES, INC.; *pg.* 1490, *pg.* 482
Holland, Frank, Corp VP-Microsoft Adv & Online - Microsoft Corporation; *pg.* 435, *pg.* 1824
Holland, Gary, VP-Adv & Publr-Barron's Magazine - Dow Jones & Company, Inc.; *pg.* 1637, *pg.* 1225
Holland, Jamie, Sr Mgr-Mktg-Oncology - Amgen Inc.; *pg.* 1493, *pg.* 291
Holland, Jennifer, Analyst-Zone Mktg - State Farm Mutual Automobile Insurance Co.; *pg.* 1218, *pg.* 557
Holland, Julie, VP-Analog Products-Worldwide - Diodes Incorporated; *pg.* 634, *pg.* 1729
Holland, Karima, Brand Mgr - Neutrogena Corporation; *pg.* 517, *pg.* 137
Holland, Laura, Dir-Mktg-Luxury Brands - Hickory Chair Company; *pg.* 927, *pg.* 1378
Holland, Rebecca, Mgr-Mktg - American Greetings Corporation; *pg.* 1615, *pg.* 1428
Holland, Russell, Dir-Sls & Mktg - Checkpoint Systems, Inc.; *pg.* 628, *pg.* 1559
Holland, Scott, Dir-Product Mgmt - Johnson Controls, Inc.; *pg.* 209, *pg.* 1876
Hollander, Chris, VP-Mktg - Panera Bread Company; *pg.* 1029, *pg.* 1001
Hollander, Julie, Dir-Media Strategy & Innovation-Global - PepsiCo, Inc.; *pg.* 259, *pg.* 1327
Hollander, Michael, Mgr-Integrated Sls & Events - Univision Communications Inc.; *pg.* 683, *pg.* 1307
Hollander, Pam, VP-Integrated Mktg Comm - The Allstate Corporation; *pg.* 1189, *pg.* 639
Hollands, Sara, Specialist-Search Engine Mktg - Jos. A. Bank Clothiers, Inc.; *pg.* 42, *pg.* 771
Hollek, Darrell E., Exec VP-US Onshore Exploration & Production - Anadarko Petroleum Corporation; *pg.* 971, *pg.* 1746
Hollen, John, VP-Sls-OEM Appliance - LG Electronics U.S.A., Inc.; *pg.* 651, *pg.* 1060
Hollenbeck, Ryan, Sr VP-Mktg-Global - Verint Witness Actionable Solutions; *pg.* 488, *pg.* 539
Hollenkamp, Jennifer, Dir-Mktg - St. Louis Convention & Visitors Commission; *pg.* 1006, *pg.* 1003
Hollenkamp, Kristen, Dir-Sls Strategy - Cox Communications, Inc.; *pg.* 279, *pg.* 501
Hollenkamp, Matthew, Sr Brand Mgr-North America Sports Mktg - The Procter & Gamble Company; *pg.* 1129, *pg.* 1418
Holler, Martha, Sr VP-Corp Mktg & Comm - SLM Corporation; *pg.* 804, *pg.* 388
Holler, Thomas R., Chief Strategy Officer & Exec VP - Virtusa Corporation; *pg.* 490, *pg.* 857
Holley, Christine, Sr Dir-Market Comm - Interactive Intelligence, Inc.; *pg.* 417, *pg.* 687
Holley, Craig, Dir-Consumer Mktg - Tampa Bay Times; *pg.* 1691, *pg.* 464
Holley, Don, Program Mgr-Mktg - Emerson Process Management; *pg.* 1334, *pg.* 1636
Holley, Erin K., Coord-Consumer Mktg - SUPERVALU, Inc.; *pg.* 1035, *pg.* 924
Holley, Kris, Dir-Field Mktg - Domino's Pizza, Inc.; *pg.* 1726, *pg.* 865
Holliday, David, Dir-Sls Plng & Dev - Chattem, Inc.; *pg.* 1515, *pg.* 1628
Holliday-Woodard, Anne, Assoc Dir-Integrated Mktg - Architectural Digest; *pg.* 1617, *pg.* 1196
Hollimon, Katie, Assoc Mgr-Product & Brand Mktg - International Dairy Queen, Inc.; *pg.* 1732, *pg.* 938
Hollingsworth, Greg, Mgr-Mktg Ops & Analytics - Go Daddy Inc.; *pg.* 1249, *pg.* 21
Hollingsworth, Jill, Sr Dir-Internal & Exec Comm - Molson Coors Brewing Company; *pg.* 256, *pg.* 321
Hollingsworth, Samantha, Media Planner-Execution-Media Client Team - Valassis; *pg.* 1698, *pg.* 386
Hollington, Erica, Brand Mgr-Innovation - Dr Pepper Snapple Group, Inc.; *pg.* 250, *pg.* 1729
Hollingworth, Alex, Sr Mgr-Product Mktg & Ops-EMEA - Hitachi Data Systems Corporation; *pg.* 407, *pg.* 265
Hollis, Heather, VP-Product Design & User Experience - Comcast Corporation; *pg.* 276, *pg.* 1560
Hollis, Jack, Grp VP-Mktg - Toyota Motor Sales, U.S.A., Inc.; *pg.* 193, *pg.* 296
Hollis, Sinead, Mgr-Content & Creative-ECommerce - Reebok International Ltd.; *pg.* 1817, *pg.* 811
Hollister, Amy, Product Mgr - Hamilton Beach Brands, Inc.; *pg.* 56, *pg.* 1783
Hollister, Michael, Sr VP-Sls & Mktg - Driscoll Strawberry Associates Inc.; *pg.* 854, *pg.* 305
Hollobaugh, Aaron, VP-Mktg & Comm - Hostway Corporation; *pg.* 1256, *pg.* 577
Holloway, Brenda, Mgr-Mktg - CEC Entertainment, Inc.; *pg.* 1721, *pg.* 1717
Holloway, Daniel, Mgr-Mktg & Webmaster - Children's Hospital Los Angeles; *pg.* 275, *pg.* 128
Holloway, Darnell, Sr Mgr-Local Bus Outreach - Yelp! Inc.; *pg.* 1291, *pg.* 235
Holloway, Keith, Sr Mgr-Portfolio Strategy - Safeway Inc.; *pg.* 1032, *pg.* 184
Holloway, Teresa V., Dir-Mktg & Bus Dev - Simon Property Group, Inc.; *pg.* 1112, *pg.* 690
Holly, Brandie, Mgr-Mktg Svcs & Brand Dev - J.R. Simplot Company; *pg.* 867, *pg.* 547
Holm, Amber, Brand Dir-Adv, Promotions, & Retail Branding - Bridgestone Americas, Inc.; *pg.* 201, *pg.* 1649
Holm, Sharon, Dir-Corp Events & Worldwide Mktg - Avid Technology, Inc.; *pg.* 622, *pg.* 804
Holma, Brad, Dir-Pur & Mktg - Institution Food House, Inc.; *pg.* 864, *pg.* 1378
Holman, Dave, Product Mgr - La Cie McCormick Canada Co.; *pg.* 872, *pg.* 1922
Holman, David C., Chief Strategy Officer - American Family Mutual Insurance Company; *pg.* 1190, *pg.* 1864
Holman, Joseph, Mgr-Adv & Media - Eli Lilly and Company; *pg.* 1527, *pg.* 684
Holman, Lee, Exec VP & Dir-Creative - lululemon athletica inc.; *pg.* 44, *pg.* 1911
Holmberg, Lisa A., Sr Mgr-Product Solutions Market - DataCard Corporation; *pg.* 382, *pg.* 948
Holmblad, David, Dir-Mktg Ops - IDEXX Laboratories, Inc.; *pg.* 1543, *pg.* 753
Holmer, Elizabeth, Mgr-Local Store Mktg - Cardinal Health, Inc.; *pg.* 1512, *pg.* 1448
Holmerud, Justin, Mgr-Global Mktg-Mdsg, Social Commerce & Personalization - Starwood Hotels & Resorts Worldwide, Inc.; *pg.* 1114, *pg.* 378
Holmes, Anthony, Rep-O-Force Northwest Sls - adidas America Inc.; *pg.* 1803, *pg.* 1500
Holmes, Bill, Reg Mgr-Sls - Micropac Industries Inc.; *pg.* 654, *pg.* 1698
Holmes, Carol, VP-HR-Times Union Media - The Florida Times-Union; *pg.* 1641, *pg.* 433
Holmes, Chris, Acct Supvr-Digital & Social Media - Bose Corporation; *pg.* 626, *pg.* 820
Holmes, Christina, Sr Mgr-Online Mktg - LEGO Systems, Inc.; *pg.* 961, *pg.* 346
Holmes, Erica, Sr Mgr-Adv Svcs - CVS Health Corporation; *pg.* 1765, *pg.* 1610
Holmes, Gail, Mgr-Retail Mktg - Energizer Holdings, Inc.; *pg.* 637, *pg.* 996
Holmes, Jennifer, Dir-Mktg-Vaccines Pediatric Comml Strategy - GlaxoSmithKline; *pg.* 1536, *pg.* 1565
Holmes, Jim, Sr Dir-Retail Fin - Office Depot, Inc.; *pg.* 448, *pg.* 412
Holmes, Joe, Dir-Mktg & Comm - Arkansas Department of Economic Development; *pg.* 988, *pg.* 33
Holmes, Jonathan, Mgr-Sls-Natl - Union Bank, N.A.; *pg.* 813, *pg.* 230
Holmes, Julia, Sr Mgr-Campaign-Talent Solutions - LinkedIn Corporation; *pg.* 1262, *pg.* 160
Holmes, Kevin, Mgr-Mktg Comm-Coffee-Mate - Nestle USA, Inc.; *pg.* 883, *pg.* 96
Holmes, Laura, Product Mgr - Google Inc.; *pg.* 1249, *pg.* 153
Holmes, Lisa, Mgr-Mktg-Dell Info Tech & Svcs Company - Dell Inc.; *pg.* 383, *pg.* 1737
Holmes, Matthew, Specialist-Mktg - BB&T Corporation; *pg.* 723, *pg.* 1393
Holmes, Melanie, Sr Mgr-Mktg-State & Local Pub Sector - Deloitte & Touche USA LLP; *pg.* 743, *pg.* 1222
Holmes, Melodie, Dir-Creative Comm & Design, Mktg Promo & Comm - Manulife Financial Corporation; *pg.* 778, *pg.* 1939
Holmes, Michelle, VP-Digital, Media & Customer Acq - Choice Hotels International, Inc.; *pg.* 1086, *pg.* 775
Holmes, Quentin, Strategist-Integrated Mktg & Media - Toyota Motor Sales, U.S.A., Inc.; *pg.* 193, *pg.* 296
Holmes, Rob, VP-Advanced Adv - Comcast Cable Communications, Inc.; *pg.* 276, *pg.* 1560
Holmes, Rob, VP-Advanced Adv - Comcast Corporation; *pg.* 276, *pg.* 1560
Holmes, Shawn, Mgr-District Sls & Natl Acct Sls - Automatic Data Processing, Inc.; *pg.* 357, *pg.* 1117
Holmes, Shawn, Dir-B2B Mktg, Brand & Innovation Mktg - Visa Inc.; *pg.* 816, *pg.* 230
Holmes, Steve, Sr Mgr-Architecture & Engrg - Taco Bell Corp.; *pg.* 1752, *pg.* 117
Holmes, William G, VP-Sls Ops - Lawson Products, Inc.; *pg.* 1355, *pg.* 580
Holmes, Yasha, Dir-Adv - Indianapolis Star; *pg.* 1652, *pg.* 687

First page reference indicates Business Class Edition
Second page reference indicates Geographic Edition

Holmgren, Sara, VP-Mktg-Storewide & OmniChannel - Macy's East; *pg.* 1777, *pg.* 1254
Holmgren, Sara A, VP-Mktg-Storewide & OmniChannel - Macy's, Inc.; *pg.* 1778, *pg.* 1417
Holmlund, Lynn, Sr Mgr-Mktg & PR - IDG Enterprise; *pg.* 1258, *pg.* 821
Holmquist, Jon, Sr VP-Direct Mktg - Boscov's Department Store, LLC; *pg.* 1763, *pg.* 1583
Holnback, Coley, Mgr-Global Brand & Sponsorship Mktg - Visa Inc.; *pg.* 816, *pg.* 230
Holnback, Coley, Mgr-Global Brand & Sponsorship Mktg - Visa U.S.A., Inc.; *pg.* 817, *pg.* 231
Holowicki, Kevin, Sr Dir-Consumer Multi Channel Mktg - GlaxoSmithKline; *pg.* 1536, *pg.* 1565
Holowicki, Kevin, Sr Dir-Consumer Multi Channel Mktg & Media - GlaxoSmithKline Consumer Healthcare; *pg.* 510, *pg.* 1554
Holst, Robert, Specialist-Mktg - Meijer, Inc.; *pg.* 1779, *pg.* 888
Holstein, Chris, VP-Mktg - Universal Lighting Technologies; *pg.* 1307, *pg.* 1655
Holstein, David, Sr Mgr-Promo - Abbott Laboratories; *pg.* 1484, *pg.* 551
Holstein, Rex, Sr Dir-Commodity Pur - Tyson Foods, Inc.; *pg.* 902, *pg.* 35
Holston, Connie, VP-SE Sls - Awrey Bakeries, Inc.; *pg.* 1015, *pg.* 896
Holston, Dave, Sr Dir-Creative Strategy & Brand Mgmt - Georgia Institute Of Technology; *pg.* 602, *pg.* 506
Holt, Brian, Mgr-Trade Mktg - General Mills, Inc.; *pg.* 828, *pg.* 933
Holt, Brian, VP-Mktg - Weis Markets, Inc.; *pg.* 1037, *pg.* 1588
Holt, Carrie, Brand Mgr - Chevron Corporation; *pg.* 974, *pg.* 259
Holt, Casey, Mgr-Insurance Sls - State Farm Mutual Automobile Insurance Co.; *pg.* 1218, *pg.* 557
Holt, Charley, VP-Mktg - Mitchell Gold & Bob Williams; *pg.* 935, *pg.* 1391
Holt, Emily, Coord-Mktg & Sls - AliMed, Inc.; *pg.* 1490, *pg.* 816
Holt, Greg, Mgr-Mktg - LANGUAGE LINE SERVICES HOLDINGS, INC.; *pg.* 426, *pg.* 151
Holt, Lauren, Coord-Wholesale Mktg-Johnston & Murphy - Genesco Inc.; *pg.* 1809, *pg.* 1650
Holt, Linda, Mgr-Pur & Specialist-Mktg - Cummins Inc.; *pg.* 1326, *pg.* 676
Holt, Morgan, Coord-Omnichannel Mktg-Social Media - American Eagle Outfitters, Inc.; *pg.* 37, *pg.* 1572
Holt, Natalia Mezin, Sr Mgr-Mktg & Brand Experience - Sony Electronics, Inc.; *pg.* 676, *pg.* 209
Holt, Neil, Exec VP-Adv Sls - Country Music Television, Inc.; *pg.* 279, *pg.* 1649
Holt, Rachel, Mgr-Web Adv - Neiman Marcus, Inc.; *pg.* 30, *pg.* 1684
Holt, Sarah, Sr Mgr-Retail Mktg - Peet's Coffee & Tea, Inc.; *pg.* 1029, *pg.* 85
Holt, Shelly, Sr Dir-Global Leadership Dev & Internal Comm - Concur Technologies, Inc.; *pg.* 1236, *pg.* 1813
Holt, Steve, VP-Brand & Corp Mktg - The Coast Distribution System, Inc.; *pg.* 1706, *pg.* 152
Holt, Tim, Mgr-Mktg Comm - UniFirst Corporation; *pg.* 50, *pg.* 860
Holtan, Ramer, Head-Mktg-Digital Music - Amazon.com, Inc.; *pg.* 1226, *pg.* 1831
Holthouse, Ross, Sr Mgr-Comm-Global Bus Svcs - The Procter & Gamble Company; *pg.* 1129, *pg.* 1418
Holtschneider, Alan, Dir-Mktg - Yokohama Tire Corporation; *pg.* 1892, *pg.* 94
Holttum, Kim, Sr Dir-Americas Field Mktg IS Programs - Philips Electronics North America; *pg.* 662, *pg.* 782
Holtz, Alex, Dir-Segment Mktg & Digital Media - Grass Valley, Inc.; *pg.* 641, *pg.* 164
Holtz, Tracy, Sr Mgr-Mktg-Software Div - Tech Data Corporation; *pg.* 482, *pg.* 416
Holubec, Orest, Sr VP-Mktg & Comm - Providence Health System; *pg.* 1587, *pg.* 1829
Holwell, Richard J., Interim Gen Counsel - Port Authority of New York & New Jersey; *pg.* 1919, *pg.* 1283
Holyoak, McKelle, Mgr-Social Media & Acct Strategist - Google Inc.; *pg.* 1249, *pg.* 153
Holzer, Alex, Head-App Category Mktg Team-Windows Store & Developer Mktg - Microsoft Corporation; *pg.* 435, *pg.* 1824
Holzer, Lindsey, Mgr-Mktg - LivingSocial, Inc.; *pg.* 1264, *pg.* 401
Holzman, Jason, Sr VP-Brand Creative - USA Networks; *pg.* 315, *pg.* 1308
Hom, Grace, Mgr-Mktg Programs-Autodesk Gallery - Autodesk Inc.; *pg.* 356, *pg.* 257
Hom, Irene, Sr Dir-Digital Mktg - Ralph Lauren Corporation; *pg.* 46, *pg.* 1284
Homan, Susan, Mgr-Mktg-Comml Surfaces-DuPont Building Innovations - E.I. du Pont de Nemours & Company; *pg.* 1159, *pg.* 390
Homchick, Paul, Sr Dir-Applications Product Mktg - Oracle Corporation; *pg.* 450, *pg.* 191
Homen, Chris, Mgr-Mktg - Autodesk Inc.; *pg.* 356, *pg.* 257
Homer, Karyn L., Sr Mgr-Event-Americas Reg - Alcatel-Lucent; *pg.* 615, *pg.* 38
Homet, Dave, Mgr-Sls-PowerSmart Energy Solutions - Graybar Electric Company, Inc.; *pg.* 1299, *pg.* 997
Homiller, Jacob, Chief Sls Officer & Sr VP-Global Bus Mgmt - A.W. Chesterton Company; *pg.* 1315, *pg.* 861
Homler, Kevin, Asst VP & Category Dir-Intl Mktg Advil - Pfizer Inc.; *pg.* 1581, *pg.* 1278
Homlish, Caroline, Dir-Digital Mktg - Chanel, Inc.; *pg.* 503, *pg.* 1211
Homolka, Megan, Sr Specialist-Social Media - Cabela's Incorporated; *pg.* 535, *pg.* 1019
Homsany, Georgia, Brand Mgr - United States Beverage LLC; *pg.* 266, *pg.* 379
Homsher, Kerri, Specialist-Adv - Ikea North America Services LLC; *pg.* 929, *pg.* 1523
Homsy, Sam, Reg Mgr-Mktg-Cadillac - General Motors Company; *pg.* 175, *pg.* 881
Hon, Barbara, Sr Mgr-Mktg - Digital Insight; *pg.* 744, *pg.* 189
Honan, Brendan, Dir-Mktg-Global - John B. Sanfilippo & Son, Inc.; *pg.* 1024, *pg.* 610
Honan, Marc, Sr VP-Content & Media - Buffalo Bills, Inc.; *pg.* 535, *pg.* 1319
Honeker, Stefanie, Sr Mgr-Consumer, Customer Strategy & Insights - Del Monte Foods, Inc.; *pg.* 852, *pg.* 304
Honer, Lori, Specialist-Mktg Comm - Cigna Corporation; *pg.* 1197, *pg.* 338
Honeycutt, David C., Dir-Mktg Comm-Global - PolyOne Corporation; *pg.* 1177, *pg.* 1404
Honeycutt, Jonathan, Brand Mktg Mgr-Fleet-Car, CUV, SUV & Police - Ford Motor Company; *pg.* 172, *pg.* 876
Honeycutt, Lo, Specialist-Mktg-Americas - Fossil Group, Inc.; *pg.* 5, *pg.* 1735
Hong, Chenda, Reg Mgr-Mktg - Websense, Inc.; *pg.* 491, *pg.* 210
Hong, Diana, VP & Dir-Creative-Digital Mktg - Tiffany & Co.; *pg.* 13, *pg.* 1299
Hong, Hani, Dir-Mktg - Shutterstock, Inc.; *pg.* 1280, *pg.* 1291
Hong, Jennie, Sr Dir-Mktg - Church's Chicken, Inc.; *pg.* 1722, *pg.* 493
Hong, Peter, Mgr-Mdse - adidas America Inc.; *pg.* 1803, *pg.* 1500
Hong, Richard, VP-Brand & Mktg-Global - MetLife, Inc.; *pg.* 1208, *pg.* 1258
Honjiyo, Sharon, Dir-Mktg Comm - Holland America Line Inc.; *pg.* 1911, *pg.* 1836
Honjo, Kenta, Product Mgr-Alpha Camera - Sony Electronics, Inc.; *pg.* 676, *pg.* 209
Honnavalli, Kiran, Sr Mgr-Enterprise Applications - Brocade Communications Systems, Inc.; *pg.* 365, *pg.* 239
Honza, Laurie, Dir-Product Dev - VTech Electronics North America, LLC; *pg.* 969, *pg.* 554
Hood Balazs, Lara, Sr VP & Head-Mktg-North America - Visa Inc.; *pg.* 816, *pg.* 230
Hood Balazs, Lara, Sr VP & Head-Mktg-North America - Visa U.S.A., Inc.; *pg.* 817, *pg.* 231
Hood, Brian, Dir-Digital Mktg - Intuit Inc.; *pg.* 769, *pg.* 158
Hood, Devin, Sr Mgr-Demand Generation - Cisco Systems, Inc.; *pg.* 372, *pg.* 240
Hood, Linda, Brand Mgr-Healthcare Quality - American Heart Association Inc.; *pg.* 128, *pg.* 1673
Hood, Marshall G., Specialist-Web Content-Digital Mktg - Nationwide Mutual Insurance Company; *pg.* 1210, *pg.* 1442
Hoodack, Douglas, Dir-Enterprise Sls - CareerBuilder, LLC; *pg.* 1234, *pg.* 568
Hoof, Laura Van, Sr Dir-Insights-Global - PepsiCo, Inc.; *pg.* 259, *pg.* 1327
Hoogenboom, Jeff, Sr VP-Sls-Worldwide - Emulex Corporation; *pg.* 392, *pg.* 70
Hoogenstryd, Robert, Sr Dir-Mktg - Synopsys, Inc.; *pg.* 480, *pg.* 162
Hoogstraten, Jack, Mgr-Plasti-Fab Products - Plasti-Fab Ltd.; *pg.* 1888, *pg.* 1904
Hook, Amy, VP-Mktg & Creative Svcs - Boston University; *pg.* 598, *pg.* 791
Hook, Chris, Dir-Global Mktg, Computing & Graphics - Advanced Micro Devices, Inc.; *pg.* 613, *pg.* 282
Hook, Cynthia, Sr VP-Comcast Assurance & Advisory Team - Comcast Corporation; *pg.* 276, *pg.* 1560
Hook, John, Sr Mgr-Programmatic Ops - Conde Nast Publications, Inc.; *pg.* 1629, *pg.* 1217
HooK, Larry, VP-Sls & Mktg - Gay Lea Foods Co-operative Limited; *pg.* 858, *pg.* 1926
Hooker, Kathleen, Dir-Mktg-PURELL Consumer, ECommerce & Shopper Mktg - GOJO Industries, Inc.; *pg.* 330, *pg.* 1401
Hooker, Troy, Mgr-Sls - Edelbrock Corporation; *pg.* 204, *pg.* 293
Hooks, Judd, Mgr-Social Media & Brand Partnerships - Delta Air Lines, Inc.; *pg.* 1905, *pg.* 503
Hooks, Sylvia, Sr Dir-Americas Mktg-IRA Imaging - Aruba Networks, Inc.; *pg.* 353, *pg.* 284
Hooley, Kevin, Reg Mgr-Mktg-Indus Adhesives & Tapes Western - 3M Company; *pg.* 1142, *pg.* 956
Hooper, Jacqueline, VP & Sr Project Mgr-Adv - Regions Financial Corporation; *pg.* 798, *pg.* 4
Hooper, Jesse, Sr Mgr-Global Media Solutions - Electronic Arts Inc.; *pg.* 951, *pg.* 189
Hooper, Melissa, Specialist-Optimization Product - Google Inc.; *pg.* 1249, *pg.* 153
Hooper, Michelle, Exec VP-Mktg-Fox Searchlight Pictures - Fox Entertainment Group, Inc.; *pg.* 288, *pg.* 131
Hooper, Mike, Dir-Mktg - Trouw Nutrition USA; *pg.* 1482, *pg.* 616
Hoopes, Amy, Exec VP-Sls-Global - Wente Vineyards; *pg.* 1972, *pg.* 122
Hoopes, Drew, Sr Mgr - 3M Company; *pg.* 1142, *pg.* 956
Hoopes, Mack, Sr Mgr-Shopper Insights & Category Mgmt - Henkel Corporation; *pg.* 1165, *pg.* 1535
Hoopes, Robert, Sr Dir-FERC-NERC Compliance - PPL Corporation; *pg.* 1950, *pg.* 1514
Hoover, Erin, Sr Mgr-Channel Mktg-Oil & Gas - Honeywell International Inc.; *pg.* 407, *pg.* 1088
Hoover, Jonathan, Brand Mgr-Deployment - W.W. Grainger, Inc.; *pg.* 1390, *pg.* 625
Hoover, Mark, Dir-Promos & Mktg - Times-Shamrock, Inc.; *pg.* 313, *pg.* 1586
Hoover, Robert, Mgr-Mktg - The Hershey Co.; *pg.* 1855, *pg.* 1538
Hoover, T. Wayne, Sr Dir-Field Ops-West Reg - Chick-fil-A, Inc.; *pg.* 1721, *pg.* 492
Hooykaas, Gerben, Dir-Creative & Brand Mgr - Chase Card Services, Inc.; *pg.* 734, *pg.* 215
Hopcus, Russ, Sr VP-Sls-North America - Columbia Sportswear Company; *pg.* 1830, *pg.* 1501
Hope, Tonya, Mgr-PR - San Antonio Convention & Visitors Bureau; *pg.* 1004, *pg.* 1742
Hopfinger, Michael, Sr Mgr-Americas Distr Mktg - Cisco Systems, Inc.; *pg.* 372, *pg.* 240
Hopkins, Adam, Dir-PR & Corp Comm - World Wrestling Entertainment, Inc.; *pg.* 595, *pg.* 380
Hopkins, Alison, Dir-Mktg - Bacardi USA, Inc.; *pg.* 1956, *pg.* 417
Hopkins, Andrew, VP-Consumer Banking & Lending & Head-Product & Mktg - Discover Financial Services; *pg.* 744, *pg.* 653
Hopkins, Beth, Product Mgr-Svc Mktg - Siemens Medical Solutions USA, Inc.; *pg.* 469, *pg.* 1550
Hopkins, Billy, Mgr-Internet Mktg - Sheplers, Inc.; *pg.* 1785, *pg.* 724
Hopkins, Cliff, Dir-Mktg - Google Inc.; *pg.* 1249, *pg.* 153
Hopkins, Darren, VP-Mktg - Slim-Fast Foods Company; *pg.* 896, *pg.* 1061
Hopkins, Darryl, Sr Product Mgr-netFORUM - Abila, Inc.; *pg.* 340, *pg.* 1660
Hopkins, Derek, Sr VP & Head-Comml & Sls - Bacardi USA, Inc.; *pg.* 1956, *pg.* 417
Hopkins, Dharika, Sr Dir-Enterprise BI-Analytics, Visualization & Info Mgmt - Cox Communications, Inc.; *pg.* 279, *pg.* 501
Hopkins, Howard, Mng Dir-Energy Products - CME Group Inc.; *pg.* 738, *pg.* 571
Hopkins, Jeff, Dir-Sls-Intl - FiberMark Inc.; *pg.* 1457, *pg.* 1764
Hopkins, Jeff, Mgr-Video-Disney Corp Creative Resources - The Walt Disney Company; *pg.* 317, *pg.* 52
Hopkins, Jen, Brand Mgr - Kellogg Company; *pg.* 831, *pg.* 870
Hopkins, Josh, Mgr-Digital Mktg-Molecular Diagnostics - Roche Diagnostics Corporation; *pg.* 1590, *pg.* 689
Hopkins, Kerry, Brand Mgr-Innovation & Outshine Fruit Bars -

Dreyer's Grand Ice Cream Holdings, Inc.; *pg.* 1852, *pg.* 171
Hopkins, Lori, Sr Product Mgr-Mobile & Search - Time Warner Cable Inc.; *pg.* 312, *pg.* 1301
Hopkins, Mark, Dir-Media Rels - OhioHealth; *pg.* 1578, *pg.* 1443
Hopkins, Sandy, Corp Mgr-Mktg Comm - Teknor Apex Company; *pg.* 1889, *pg.* 1605
Hopkins, Scott, Dir-Mktg - Performance Food Group Company, LLC; *pg.* 1030, *pg.* 1803
Hopkins, Spencer, Assoc Product Mgr-Local Content - MapQuest, Inc.; *pg.* 1265, *pg.* 321
Hopkins, Sylvia, VP-Mktg - Make-A-Wish Foundation of Greater Los Angeles; *pg.* 146, *pg.* 136
Hopkins, Tom, Dir-PR - AT&T; *pg.* 1865, *pg.* 258
Hopmeyer, Jacqueline, Mgr-Mktg - Aldo Group; *pg.* 1804, *pg.* 1959
Hopp, Frank, Product Mgr-Software - Lockheed Martin Corporation; *pg.* 229, *pg.* 762
Hopp, Tiffany, Mgr-Retail Mktg - Gerber Legendary Blades; *pg.* 1834, *pg.* 1503
Hopp-Michlosky, Kelli C., Mgr-Mktg & Exec Comm-Environmental Technologies - Corning Incorporated; *pg.* 1122, *pg.* 1154
Hopper, Kristen, Mgr-Product Line-Automotive SSD & SLC NAND - Micron Technology, Inc.; *pg.* 435, *pg.* 547
Hopping, Kelly V., Dir-Bus Ops & Mktg - Advanced Micro Devices, Inc.; *pg.* 613, *pg.* 282
Hopps, Michael, Sr Analyst-Digital Mktg - salesforce.com, inc.; *pg.* 1278, *pg.* 226
Hopson, Frances, Mgr-Creative Svcs - The Clorox Company; *pg.* 327, *pg.* 169
Horan, Brian, Dir-Payer & Health Sys Mktg-Lilly USA - Eli Lilly and Company; *pg.* 1527, *pg.* 684
Horan, Caitlin, Assoc Mgr-Mktg-Digital - Frito-Lay North America, Inc.; *pg.* 1853, *pg.* 1730
Horan, Christopher, Sr VP & Head-Product & Global Supply Chain Mgmt - Genentech, Inc.; *pg.* 1533, *pg.* 279
Horan, Daniel, Exec VP - LIGHTING SCIENCE GROUP CORPORATION; *pg.* 1301, *pg.* 467
Horan, Kai, VP-Prepaid Product Solutions-Global - MasterCard Incorporated; *pg.* 779, *pg.* 1325
Horan, Mary, VP & Dir-Mktg & PR - LAKELAND FINANCIAL CORPORATION; *pg.* 775, *pg.* 699
Horgan, Christine, Sr Mgr-Digital Mktg - MetLife, Inc.; *pg.* 1208, *pg.* 1258
Horgan, Darrah, Dir-PR & Mgr-Mktg - Whole Foods Market, Inc.; *pg.* 1038, *pg.* 1667
Horine, Marc, VP-Revenue & Ops-ESPN Digital & Print Media - ESPN, Inc.; *pg.* 285, *pg.* 340
Horjus, Frans, Mgr-Global Aviation Sls - Exxon Mobil Corporation; *pg.* 977, *pg.* 1718
Hork, Meredith, Mgr-Mktg-Tropicana Farmstand - PepsiCo, Inc.; *pg.* 259, *pg.* 1327
Horkan, Angela, Dir-Mktg - Wisconsin Beef Council, Inc.; *pg.* 161, *pg.* 1867
Horlacher, Christopher, Sr Dir-Art - The Valspar Corporation; *pg.* 1449, *pg.* 945
Horlick, Adrienne, Dir-Mktg Comm - Jack in the Box Inc.; *pg.* 1732, *pg.* 204
Horman, Mike, Dir-Sls - United Parcel Service, Inc.; *pg.* 1928, *pg.* 522
Horn, Chris, Acct Mgr-Sls - Corpus Christi Caller-Times; *pg.* 1630, *pg.* 1671
Horn, Clare, Assoc Dir-Mktg - Northeastern University; *pg.* 605, *pg.* 799
Horn, Doug, Sr Mgr-Catering Sls - Aramark; *pg.* 1013, *pg.* 1558
Horn, Ina, Mgr-Mktg - Wells Fargo & Company; *pg.* 819, *pg.* 232
Horn, Jon, Sr Dir-Mktg - S.C. Johnson & Son, Inc.; *pg.* 334, *pg.* 1889
Horn, Kieran, Brand Mgr - O'Neill Inc.; *pg.* 1842, *pg.* 270
Horn, Kimberly, Dir-Utilization Mgmt & Social Svcs - Kaiser Permanente; *pg.* 1552, *pg.* 171
Horn, Michael, Pres-Intl Mktg - Sony Pictures Entertainment Inc.; *pg.* 309, *pg.* 72
Horn, Sara Van, Supvr-Mktg Comm - The Reynolds & Reynolds Company; *pg.* 461, *pg.* 1457
Horn, Tammy Von, Mgr-Field Mktg-Worldwide - Synopsys, Inc.; *pg.* 480, *pg.* 162
Hornai, Andrew, Dir-Product Mktg - Anixter International Inc.; *pg.* 1313, *pg.* 614
Hornberger, Karen, Sr Mgr-Mktg - The Allstate Corporation; *pg.* 1189, *pg.* 639
Horne, Caitlin, Mgr-Wholesale Mktg - St. John Knits International, Inc.; *pg.* 33, *pg.* 116
Horne, Jack, Sr VP-Sls - Hyatt Hotels Corporation; *pg.* 1096, *pg.* 577
Horne, Renee, VP-Social Bus, Enterprise Strategy & Mktg - United Services Automobile Association; *pg.* 1221, *pg.* 1743
Horne, Steve, Sr Mgr-Mktg Res - The American Dental Association; *pg.* 127, *pg.* 564
Horne, Tina L., Mgr-Mktg-Case Mgmt-Software Grp - IBM; *pg.* 410, *pg.* 1449
Horner, Andrea, VP-Mktg - Magline, Inc.; *pg.* 1358, *pg.* 908
Horner, Bruce, Dir-Media & Alliances - Travelocity, Inc.; *pg.* 1284, *pg.* 1745
Horner, Mark, Sr Mgr-Comm-Global - Eaton Corporation; *pg.* 1331, *pg.* 1429
Hornfeck, Daniel D., Chief Creative Officer & Exec VP - Carolina Bank Holdings, Inc.; *pg.* 732, *pg.* 1374
Hornish, Don, Dir-Mktg & Segment Activation-North America - The Kraft Heinz Company; *pg.* 870, *pg.* 1577
Hornor, Will, Dir-Mktg-Global - Newell Rubbermaid Inc.; *pg.* 1128, *pg.* 515
Hornsby, Robert, Assoc VP-Media Rels - Columbia University; *pg.* 600, *pg.* 1216
Hornsby, Todd, VP-Sls - Bovie Medical Corporation; *pg.* 1402, *pg.* 1178
Hornyak, Pina, Sr Mgr-Digital Mktg - Pfizer Inc.; *pg.* 1581, *pg.* 1278
Horowitz, Bradley, VP-Product-Google+ - Google Inc.; *pg.* 1249, *pg.* 153
Horowitz, Dean, VP-Amos Media Co - Amos Press, Inc.; *pg.* 1616, *pg.* 1472
Horowitz, Diana, Dir-Digital Ad Sls-Northeast - Scripps Networks Interactive, Inc.; *pg.* 1279, *pg.* 1638
Horowitz, Elizabeth, Sr Analyst-Mktg & Digital Acq - American Express Company; *pg.* 712, *pg.* 1190
Horowitz, Eric, Dir-Mktg - Deep Eddy Vodka; *pg.* 1961, *pg.* 1691
Horowitz, Jason, VP-Global Brand & Product Mktg-Hot Wheels - Mattel Games/Puzzles; *pg.* 962, *pg.* 80
Horowitz, Michelle, Sr VP-Mktg-LOFT & Lou & Grey - Ann Inc.; *pg.* 18, *pg.* 1195
Horrigan, Kathleen D., Mgr-Mktg - The Hartford Financial Services Group, Inc.; *pg.* 1202, *pg.* 352
Horrisberger, Mary K., Sr Mgr-Mktg-Educational Programs - IDEXX Laboratories, Inc.; *pg.* 1543, *pg.* 753
Horsch, Randy, Dir-Integrated Mktg - Emerson Process Management; *pg.* 1334, *pg.* 1636
Horsham-Bertels, Helen, Sr Dir-Consumer Affairs - Starwood Hotels & Resorts Worldwide, Inc.; *pg.* 1114, *pg.* 378
Horst, Kayla, Program Mgr-Mktg Automation - Schneider Electric; *pg.* 467, *pg.* 1609
Horstmann, Angela, Dir-Mktg - GlaxoSmithKline; *pg.* 1536, *pg.* 1565
Horstmann, Angela, Sr Product Mgr - GlaxoSmithKline Consumer Healthcare; *pg.* 510, *pg.* 1554
Horta, Darlene, Specialist-Social Media & Email Mktg - TBC Corporation; *pg.* 1889, *pg.* 457
Horton, Jeffrey, Brand Mgr - Kawasaki Motors Corp., U.S.A.; *pg.* 1708, *pg.* 111
Horton, Keith, Mgr-Sls - Fairway Outdoor Advertising; *pg.* 1640, *pg.* 525
Horton, Matt, Coord-Mktg - Brookshire Grocery Company; *pg.* 1016, *pg.* 1748
Horton, Rob, Head-Mktg-Consumer - PPG Industries, Inc.; *pg.* 1445, *pg.* 1579
Horton, Ron, COO-Mktg & HR Tech - Bank of America Corporation; *pg.* 718, *pg.* 1362
Horton, Roy, Dir-Product Mktg - Mack Trucks, Inc.; *pg.* 183, *pg.* 1375
Horton, Stan, Sr Dir-Global Mktg-VEGF TRAP-EYE - Bayer Corporation; *pg.* 1499, *pg.* 1573
Horton, Tom, Dir-Mktg-Global - Fushi Copperweld; *pg.* 1296, *pg.* 1632
Horton, Whitney, Sr Bus Head-Digital Sls Food & Beverage Vertical - Google Inc.; *pg.* 1249, *pg.* 153
Horvat, Gregg, Brand Mgr-Country Time Lemonade - Mondelez International, Inc.; *pg.* 878, *pg.* 601
Horvat, Lori, VP-Mktg - ARIAD Pharmaceuticals, Inc.; *pg.* 1496, *pg.* 807
Horvath, Chris, Dir-Mktg - Dendreon Corporation; *pg.* 1522, *pg.* 1835
Horvath, Kathleen, Coord-Digital Mktg - Anthropologie, Inc.; *pg.* 18, *pg.* 1558
Horwitz, Alex, Reg VP-PR - Comcast Corporation; *pg.* 276, *pg.* 1560
Horwitz, Ashley, Specialist-Mktg - M-I SWACO; *pg.* 980, *pg.* 1710
Horwitz, Jay, VP-Media Rels - Sterling Mets, L.P.; *pg.* 586, *pg.* 1160
Horwitz, Joan, Mgr-Mktg Comm - Agilent Technologies, Inc.; *pg.* 614, *pg.* 264
Horwitz, Rachel, Sr Mgr-HR - Wyndham Vacation Ownership; *pg.* 1119, *pg.* 457
Hosch, Kyle, Dir-Mktg Execution & Ops - Verizon Communications Inc.; *pg.* 1875, *pg.* 1309
Hosch, Mike, VP-Indus Products - Dorner Manufacturing Corp.; *pg.* 1329, *pg.* 1861
Hosea, Emily, Sr Mgr-Global Compensation - Brown-Forman Corporation; *pg.* 1958, *pg.* 732
Hosein, Roxanne, Mgr-Mktg - United States Postal Service; *pg.* 1009, *pg.* 406
Hosey, Kelly, Head-Photography-Adv & Project Mgr - The Home Depot, Inc.; *pg.* 1050, *pg.* 510
Hosford, Shannon, VP-Mktg & Comm - Maple Leaf Sports & Entertainment Ltd.; *pg.* 560, *pg.* 1940
Hosford, Shannon, VP-Mktg & Comm - Toronto Maple Leaf Hockey Club; *pg.* 588, *pg.* 1945
Hoshiko, Jim, Dir-Mktg, Aerospace & Extra Precision Products - Regal Power Transmission Solutions; *pg.* 216, *pg.* 698
Hosking, Ross, Exec VP-Sls-Global - Wyndham Worldwide Corporation; *pg.* 1119, *pg.* 1107
Hoskins, Barbara, Dir-Mktg - PulteGroup, Inc.; *pg.* 1109, *pg.* 873
Hoskins, Erin, VP-Audience Dev & Digital Media - Meredith Corporation; *pg.* 1663, *pg.* 705
Hoskins, Gregg, Sr Acct Mgr-Inside Sls - Dell Inc.; *pg.* 383, *pg.* 1737
Hoskins, John, Sr Mgr-BD-Amazon AppStore-Echo SDK - Amazon.com, Inc.; *pg.* 1226, *pg.* 1831
Hosler, Anne-Marie, Dir-Mktg - Dental One, Inc.; *pg.* 1522, *pg.* 1462
Hospodka, Jason, Reg Mgr-Mktg-Central Reg - Heineken USA Inc.; *pg.* 252, *pg.* 1352
Hosseini, Pasha, Mgr-Multicultural Mktg - H&R Block, Inc.; *pg.* 764, *pg.* 983
Hosto, Raynie, Dir-Sls - Arizona Lottery; *pg.* 988, *pg.* 14
Hota, Nachiketa, Sr Mgr-Fin - Microsoft Corporation; *pg.* 435, *pg.* 1824
Hott, Lisa, Mgr-Adv Production - Boys' Life Magazine; *pg.* 1623, *pg.* 1206
Hotz, Zach, Brand Mgr-Shock Top - Anheuser-Busch Companies, LLC; *pg.* 237, *pg.* 991
Hou, Annie, Dir-Mktg Strategy & Insights-Global - The Coca-Cola Company; *pg.* 240, *pg.* 493
Hou, Wendy, Principal & Product Mgr - Rogue Wave Software, Inc.; *pg.* 462, *pg.* 311
Houck, Zach, Mgr-Mktg - Uber USA, LLC; *pg.* 1286, *pg.* 229
Houde, Tom, Brand Mgr-Kleenex - Kimberly-Clark Inc.; *pg.* 1463, *pg.* 1927
Hough, Alison, Sr Mgr-Adv-Global - The Boeing Company; *pg.* 225, *pg.* 567
Hough, Kym, Dir-Mktg - Ghirardelli Chocolate Company; *pg.* 1854, *pg.* 252
Houghland, Sara J., Dir-Govt Affairs & PR - Comcast Corporation; *pg.* 276, *pg.* 1560
Houghtaling, Ron, VP-Americas Mktg - CB Richard Ellis, Inc.; *pg.* 1085, *pg.* 1210
Houghton, Heath, Product Mgr - Autodesk Inc.; *pg.* 356, *pg.* 257
Houghton, Laura, Dir-Digital Shopper Mktg - The Coca-Cola Company; *pg.* 240, *pg.* 493
Houghton, Michael, VP-Strategic Sls - Avnet Technology Solutions; *pg.* 359, *pg.* 25
Houghton, Pete, Sr Mgr-Airport Affairs - Southwest Airlines Co.; *pg.* 1923, *pg.* 1687
Houlden, Brent, Interim CFO - Danier Leather, Inc.; *pg.* 22, *pg.* 1937
Houle, Brandon, Mgr-ECommerce & Digital Mktg - 3M Company; *pg.* 1142, *pg.* 956
Houlemard, Keith, Dir-Mdsg - NIKE, Inc.; *pg.* 1812, *pg.* 1492
Houlihan Roussel, Jennifer, Sr Dir-Publicity - WQXR FM; *pg.* 595, *pg.* 1316
Houlihan, Laurie, VP-Promotional Dev & Procurement Consumer Products Div - L'Oreal USA; *pg.* 514, *pg.* 1252
Houlihan, Rachel, Sr Mgr-Mktg-Info Mgmt - IDEXX Laboratories, Inc.; *pg.* 1543, *pg.* 753
Houlihan, Robert, Chief Product Officer - Mercury Insurance Company; *pg.* 1208, *pg.* 136
Houpe, Monic J, Head-Multicultural & Brand Mgr - Hallmark

First page reference indicates Business Class Edition
Second page reference indicates Geographic Edition

Cards, Inc.; *pg.* 1646, *pg.* 983
Hourigan, Cindy, VP-Sponsorships, Travel & Events-Mktg Capabilities - Dr Pepper Snapple Group, Inc.; *pg.* 250, *pg.* 1729
Hourihan, Kathleen, Assoc Mgr-Mktg - Rich Products Corporation; *pg.* 892, *pg.* 1150
House, Ann, Sr Mgr-Customer Mktg - The Coca-Cola Company; *pg.* 240, *pg.* 493
House, Annie, VP-Partnership Mktg - The Weather Channel LLC; *pg.* 320, *pg.* 523
House, Beverly, Exec VP-Mdsg Design & Product Dev - Spanx Inc.; *pg.* 32, *pg.* 520
House, Chip, VP-Relationship Mktg-Salesforce Mktg Cloud - ExactTarget Inc.; *pg.* 1244, *pg.* 685
House, Giles, CMO & Sr VP - Callidus Software Inc.; *pg.* 368, *pg.* 183
House, Gina, Dir-Digital Mktg & Strategy - Edward D. Jones & Co., LP; *pg.* 746, *pg.* 995
House, Kim Adams, Head-Jeep Adv - FCA US LLC; *pg.* 170, *pg.* 868
Houseknecht, Sarah, Mgr-PR - Foot Locker, Inc.; *pg.* 1808, *pg.* 1231
Houser, Danielle, Mgr-Production-Global - Toys "R" Us, Inc.; *pg.* 968, *pg.* 1130
Houser, Mike, Analyst-Truck Tire Mktg - Michelin North America Inc.; *pg.* 1886, *pg.* 1618
Houska, Joy, Sr Mgr-Social Media Content Strategy - Target Corporation; *pg.* 1786, *pg.* 942
Houston, Denise, Sr Mgr-Plng - Luxottica Retail; *pg.* 8, *pg.* 1460
Houston, Donald, Sr VP-Sls - Plantronics, Inc.; *pg.* 663, *pg.* 270
Houston, Gail, Head-Recruiting, Product Mgr & Recruiter-Intuit - Intuit Inc.; *pg.* 769, *pg.* 158
Houston, Kevin, Sr Dir-R&D - Church's Chicken, Inc.; *pg.* 1722, *pg.* 493
Houston, Rita, Dir-Global Mktg Capability - The Coca-Cola Company; *pg.* 240, *pg.* 493
Houtzer, Chris, Head-Sls-Bay Area-Cloud Platform - Google Inc.; *pg.* 1249, *pg.* 153
Hovanissian, Teni, Dir-Mktg-Aranesp, EPOGEN & Sensipar Access - Amgen Inc.; *pg.* 1493, *pg.* 291
Hovi, Marie, Mgr-ECommerce Mktg - J.C. Whitney & Co.; *pg.* 209, *pg.* 621
Hovish, Larry, Sr Mgr-Comm - AngioDynamics, Inc.; *pg.* 1495, *pg.* 1173
Hovland, Adrienne, Mgr-Mktg - 3M Company; *pg.* 1142, *pg.* 956
Hovland, Zach, Coord-Mktg & Promos - GameStop Corp.; *pg.* 399, *pg.* 1699
Hovorka, Jeff, Dir-Media & Mktg - Denver Center for the Performing Arts Inc.; *pg.* 544, *pg.* 318
Howard, Ashley, Sr Product Mgr - Amazon.com, Inc.; *pg.* 1226, *pg.* 1831
Howard, Ashley, Sr Strategist-Creative - Yahoo! Inc.; *pg.* 1289, *pg.* 289
Howard, Ben, Sr VP-Mktg & Sls - Sony Music Entertainment; *pg.* 309, *pg.* 1294
Howard, Bill, Sr Product Mgr-Identity - Adobe Systems Incorporated; *pg.* 342, *pg.* 235
Howard, Blain, Sr Mgr-PR-Xbox - Microsoft Corporation; *pg.* 435, *pg.* 1824
Howard, Bridgette, Mgr-Brand & Product Dev - Bluemercury, Inc.; *pg.* 502, *pg.* 396
Howard, Charlie, VP-Mktg & Brand Dev - Gold Star Chili Inc.; *pg.* 1021, *pg.* 1414
Howard, Christian, VP-Mktg & Brdcst - Los Angeles Clippers; *pg.* 558, *pg.* 135
Howard, Drew, Product Mgr-Mobile - Starwood Hotels & Resorts Worldwide, Inc.; *pg.* 1114, *pg.* 378
Howard, Elysia, VP-Mktg & Licensing - American Society for the Prevention of Cruelty to Animals; *pg.* 131, *pg.* 1193
Howard, Fara, VP-Mktg-Global - Vans, Inc.; *pg.* 1821, *pg.* 76
Howard, Gen, Sr Mgr-Sls - Louisville Convention & Visitors Bureau; *pg.* 998, *pg.* 736
Howard, Jason, VP-Ticket Sls & Svc - Houston Astros Baseball Club; *pg.* 552, *pg.* 1707
Howard, Jason J., Dir-Retail Mktg & Consumer Product Dev - Cardinal Health, Inc.; *pg.* 1512, *pg.* 1448
Howard, Jay, Dir-Field Mktg - Zimmer Biomet Holdings, Inc.; *pg.* 1611, *pg.* 699
Howard, Jeff, Pres-Natl Sls - IHeartMedia Inc.; *pg.* 292, *pg.* 1741
Howard, Jessica, Planner-Mktg Strategy - Nordstrom, Inc.; *pg.* 1779, *pg.* 1837
Howard, Joy, VP-Mktg - Patagonia; *pg.* 31, *pg.* 301
Howard, Kara, VP-Mdsg-Global - VistaPrint USA, Incorporated; *pg.* 1700, *pg.* 829
Howard, Kenneth, Project Mgr-Mktg - Staples; *pg.* 474, *pg.* 313
Howard, Kevin, Sr Mgr-Digital Mktg - Ally Financial Inc.; *pg.* 711, *pg.* 878
Howard, Kevin, Dir-Mktg & Community Engagement - Cape Cod Five Cents Savings Bank; *pg.* 730, *pg.* 840
Howard, Kevin J., Sr VP & Chief Actuary-Product - Protective Life Corporation; *pg.* 1215, *pg.* 4
Howard, Kirstan, Dir-Social & Digital Comm - United Parcel Service, Inc.; *pg.* 1928, *pg.* 522
Howard, Kristal, Mgr-PR - The Kroger Co.; *pg.* 1025, *pg.* 1416
Howard, Kristi, Product Mgr - Elkay Manufacturing Company; *pg.* 80, *pg.* 645
Howard, Lisa, Mgr-Mktg Comm - The Toro Company; *pg.* 1065, *pg.* 918
Howard, Mark, Reg Mgr-Sls - Forbes, Inc.; *pg.* 1641, *pg.* 1232
Howard, Meredith, Dir-Publicity & Asst Dir-Mktg - Columbia University Press; *pg.* 1628, *pg.* 1216
Howard, Michael, Sr Mgr-Medical Scientific Comm-Global - Sanofi US; *pg.* 1592, *pg.* 1046
Howard, Paul, Dir-Mktg Comm Global Events - Oracle Corporation; *pg.* 450, *pg.* 191
Howard, Peggy, VP-Mktg & Mgr-Programs - Bank of America Global Wealth & Investment Management; *pg.* 720, *pg.* 789
Howard, Peter, Exec Dir-Comm & Mktg - University of Miami; *pg.* 609, *pg.* 418
Howard, Ron, Dir-Sls-Middle East - The Beverly Hills Hotel; *pg.* 1082, *pg.* 46
Howard, Ruth, Dir-Sls & Mktg Svcs - Steelcase Inc.; *pg.* 475, *pg.* 889
Howard, Sandra, Asst VP-Adv - AT&T Communications Corp.; *pg.* 1866, *pg.* 1043
Howard, Sandra, Asst VP-Adv - AT&T Inc.; *pg.* 1867, *pg.* 1674
Howard, Sarah, Brand Mgr-Global - Novartis Corporation; *pg.* 1574, *pg.* 1273
Howard, Sharon, Brand Mgr-Ketel One & Ciroc Vodka - Diageo Canada, Inc.; *pg.* 1961, *pg.* 1937
Howard, Steve, Sr Mgr-Comm Strategy-Customer Mktg - TELUS CORPORATION; *pg.* 1952, *pg.* 1912
Howard, Steven M., Head-Sls-IBM Worldwide Software Svcs-Commerce Bus Unit - International Business Machines Corporation; *pg.* 418, *pg.* 1138
Howard, Tracy, VP-Mktg & Strategic Plng - Cardinal Health, Inc.; *pg.* 1512, *pg.* 1448
Howard-Glaspie, Regina, Dir-Sls Retention & Mktg - News & Record; *pg.* 1669, *pg.* 1375
Howard-Sarin, Stephen, Head-Display Adv - eBay Inc.; *pg.* 1240, *pg.* 243
Howard-Sarin, Stephen, Sr Dir-Display Adv-North America - Shopping.com, Ltd.; *pg.* 1280, *pg.* 50
Howard-Wallis, Nancy, Writer-Enhanced Product Content - W.W. Grainger, Inc.; *pg.* 1390, *pg.* 625
Howarth, Ellen, Specialist-Social Media - Toms Shoe's Inc; *pg.* 1821, *pg.* 276
Howdle, Lucy, Sr Mgr-Global Brand Dev-Dove Skincare - Unilever United States, Inc.; *pg.* 904, *pg.* 1061
Howe, Brendon, Sr VP-Emerging Products - NetApp, Inc.; *pg.* 444, *pg.* 287
Howe, Carmyn, Community Mgr-Social Media - Humana, Inc.; *pg.* 1204, *pg.* 734
Howe, Connie, Sr Mgr-Technical Svcs - The Adhesive and Sealant Council, Inc.; *pg.* 125, *pg.* 761
Howe, Darienne, VP-Integrated Mktg Comm-Redken & Pureology - L'Oreal USA; *pg.* 514, *pg.* 1252
Howe, Darienne, VP-Integrated Mktg Comm-Redken & Pureology - Redken Laboratories LLC; *pg.* 520, *pg.* 1285
Howe, Greg, Sr VP-Sls-Worldwide - Zilliant, Inc.; *pg.* 497, *pg.* 1668
Howe, Jeffery, Exec VP-Enterprise Sls - Windstream Corporation; *pg.* 321, *pg.* 34
Howe, Laura, VP-Media & Communities - Pearson Education; *pg.* 1675, *pg.* 800
Howe, Louise, Director of Marketing Communications - Quinnipiac University; *pg.* 607, *pg.* 351
Howe, Michael, Dir-Automotive Strategy & Sls Dev - Pandora Media Inc.; *pg.* 1273, *pg.* 172
Howe, Rachael, Dir-Natl Consumer Promos & Sports Mktg - PepsiCo, Inc.; *pg.* 259, *pg.* 1327
Howe, Sandra K., Sr VP-Mktg-Global - Arris Group, Inc.; *pg.* 353, *pg.* 541
Howe, Tamara, Head-Mktg-Australia & New Zealand - Kellogg Company; *pg.* 831, *pg.* 870
Howell, Abbey, Project Mgr-Comml Mktg - AutoZone, Inc.; *pg.* 200, *pg.* 1641
Howell, Angie, Sr Mgr-Mktg - Knoxville News-Sentinel Company; *pg.* 1657, *pg.* 1637
Howell, Dane, VP-Sls & Mktg-North America - SmartWool; *pg.* 32, *pg.* 335
Howell, Darren, Product Mgr-IT - Intel Corporation; *pg.* 645, *pg.* 266
Howell, Jeff, Dir-Sls - JAKKS Pacific, Inc.; *pg.* 960, *pg.* 142
Howell, Jenny, Dir-Brand & Adv - Farmers Group, Inc.; *pg.* 1199, *pg.* 130
Howell, Kira, Reg VP-Mktg - Frontier Communications Corporation; *pg.* 1871, *pg.* 362
Howell, Martin, Dir-Mktg Comm-Worldwide - Cubic Transportation Systems, Inc.; *pg.* 1905, *pg.* 202
Howell, Peter, Sr Product Mgr - GameFly, Inc.; *pg.* 953, *pg.* 132
Howell, Rebecca, VP-Digital Mktg - BlackRock, Inc.; *pg.* 724, *pg.* 1203
Howell, Simon J., Sr Mgr-Brand Engagement - Mercury Insurance Company; *pg.* 1208, *pg.* 136
Howell, Stephanie, Mgr-Content Mktg-Talent Solutions - LinkedIn Corporation; *pg.* 1262, *pg.* 160
Howell, Tyler, VP-Ticket Sls & Svc - Portland Trail Blazers; *pg.* 577, *pg.* 1505
Hower, Stacy, Dir-Mktg-Global Bus Segment - Dell Inc.; *pg.* 383, *pg.* 1737
Hower, Tara, Mgr-Mktg - JPMorgan Chase & Co.; *pg.* 772, *pg.* 1246
Hower, Tim, Sr Mgr-Rigid Plastics - The Hershey Co.; *pg.* 1855, *pg.* 1538
Howerton, Rebekah, Specialist-Comm-Global Mktg - VeriFone Systems, Inc.; *pg.* 487, *pg.* 251
Howeth, John, Sr VP-Foodservice & Egg Product Mktg - American Egg Board; *pg.* 128, *pg.* 650
Howland, Dave, Asst VP-Creative & Digital Strategy - The NASDAQ OMX Group, Inc.; *pg.* 785, *pg.* 1263
Howland, Jon, Dir-Mktg - DeWALT Industrial Tool Company; *pg.* 1328, *pg.* 757
Howland, Jon, VP-Sls - Jameson Publishing Inc.; *pg.* 1654, *pg.* 1530
Howlett, Dodie L., Mgr-Adv & Promos - Kentucky Derby Festival, Inc.; *pg.* 556, *pg.* 735
Howley, Katherine, Strategist-Social Media - Ralph Lauren Corporation; *pg.* 46, *pg.* 1284
Howley, Suzanne, Product Mgr-Digital - Hilton Worldwide, Inc.; *pg.* 1094, *pg.* 1791
Howze, Drea, VP & Head-Healthcare Product - Kelly Services, Inc.; *pg.* 424, *pg.* 911
Hoy, Elizabeth, Sr Mgr-Original Series Mktg - Netflix, Inc.; *pg.* 1269, *pg.* 141
Hoy, Katharine, Sr Mgr-North America EMO & Global Analytics - Brown-Forman Corporation; *pg.* 1958, *pg.* 732
Hoyas, Paula, VP-Mdsg - La-Z-Boy Incorporated; *pg.* 932, *pg.* 901
Hoyh, Dave, Dir-Mktg & Sls - Systron Donner Inertial Division; *pg.* 1430, *pg.* 69
Hoyland, Britt, Coord-Mktg & Events - Meredith Corporation; *pg.* 1663, *pg.* 705
Hoylman, Betsy, Dir-Media & PR - The Northwestern Mutual Life Insurance Company; *pg.* 1212, *pg.* 1879
Hoyne, Carrie, Supvr-Creative - The Home Depot, Inc.; *pg.* 1050, *pg.* 510
Hoyt, Alyssa, Dir-Mktg-Consumer Products - 3D Systems Corporation; *pg.* 339, *pg.* 1621
Hoyt, Amy, Coord-Online Mktg - The Mattress Firm, Inc.; *pg.* 934, *pg.* 1711
Hoyt, Craig, Sr Mgr-MTB Product-Global - Cannondale Bicycle Corporation; *pg.* 1705, *pg.* 1515
Hoyt, Robert, Brand Mgr - Keurig Green Mountain, Inc.; *pg.* 868, *pg.* 1768
Hoyt, Samantha, Product Mgr-Mktg-Emerging Market Svcs - Ford Motor Company; *pg.* 172, *pg.* 876
Hoyt, Scott, Dir-Mktg Comm - Safeway Inc.; *pg.* 1032, *pg.* 184
Hoyt-Pack, Kerri, VP-Brand Mktg-Women's Training-Global - NIKE, Inc.; *pg.* 1812, *pg.* 1492
Hrabak, DeAnne, Mgr-Mktg Svcs - The J.M. Smucker Company; *pg.* 865, *pg.* 1468
Hrdlicka, Kathleen, Mgr-Events Mktg - Emerson Process Management; *pg.* 1334, *pg.* 1636

Hrdlicka, Vit, Sr Dir-Mktg - Canadian Imperial Bank of Commerce; *pg.* 729, *pg.* 1935
Hreniuk, Pam, Mgr-Product Dev - Toys "R" Us, Inc.; *pg.* 968, *pg.* 1130
Hriciga, Mark, Chief Creative Officer & VP-Adv - Experian Consumer Direct; *pg.* 1245, *pg.* 71
Hritcko, John , Jr., Sr VP-Natl Mktg & Sls-Oil & Gas - TRC Companies, Inc.; *pg.* 1383, *pg.* 386
Hritz, Keith, VP-Production - Fox Sports Net; *pg.* 288, *pg.* 131
Hritz, Monica, Sr Assoc Mgr-Mktg - General Mills, Inc.; *pg.* 828, *pg.* 933
Hritzuk, Natasha, Sr Dir-Insights-Global - Microsoft Corporation; *pg.* 435, *pg.* 1824
Hroch, Jackie, Sr Mgr-Brand Activation - Coca-Cola North America; *pg.* 848, *pg.* 500
Hrozencik, Diane, Product Dir-Innovation & Consumer Insight - Johnson & Johnson; *pg.* 1549, *pg.* 1091
Hruby, Emily, Brand Mgr-Strategy-Local Legends Brands - Pabst Brewing Company; *pg.* 258, *pg.* 137
Hruska, Jack, Exec VP-Creative Svcs - Bloomingdale's, Inc.; *pg.* 1763, *pg.* 1204
Hrybenko, Ed, Sr VP-Mktg Ops & Execution - OppenheimerFunds, Inc.; *pg.* 790, *pg.* 1274
Hrycyk, Gillian, Mgr-Mktg - Spring-Green Lawn Care Corporation; *pg.* 1800, *pg.* 652
Hrynewycz, Jeremy, Brand Mgr - The Procter & Gamble Company; *pg.* 1129, *pg.* 1418
Hsia, Danny, Sr Mgr-eMail Experience - LivingSocial, Inc.; *pg.* 1264, *pg.* 401
Hsia, Lisa, Exec VP-Digital, Bravo & Oxygen Media - Bravo Media LLC; *pg.* 271, *pg.* 1206
Hsia, Lisa, Exec VP-Digital, Bravo & Oxygen Media - NBC Universal, Inc.; *pg.* 300, *pg.* 1266
Hsieh, Deborah, Product Mgr - Google Inc.; *pg.* 1249, *pg.* 153
Hsieh, Jeffrey, Sr Product Mgr-Projector - ViewSonic Corporation; *pg.* 489, *pg.* 303
Hsieh, Rossa, Mgr-Product Mktg - Google Inc.; *pg.* 1249, *pg.* 153
Hsieh, Stephen, Sr Mgr-Demand & Supply Plng Wish-Bone - Pinnacle Foods Group LLC; *pg.* 889, *pg.* 1104
Hsu, Angela, VP-Internet Bus & Mktg - Lamps Plus Inc.; *pg.* 1300, *pg.* 64
Hsu, Chi-Ping, Chief Strategy Officer-EDA & Sr VP-Digital & Signoff Grp - Cadence Design Systems, Inc.; *pg.* 367, *pg.* 239
Hsu, Christina, Dir-Online Mktg - Tommy Hilfiger USA; *pg.* 48, *pg.* 1302
Hsu, Dennis, Dir-Brand Mktg - The University of Phoenix, Inc.; *pg.* 610, *pg.* 27
Hsu, Ed, Dir-Product Mktg - VMware, Inc.; *pg.* 490, *pg.* 179
Hsu, Irena, Dir-Mobile Mktg & Engrg - Groupon, Inc.; *pg.* 1255, *pg.* 575
Hsu, Jason, Dir-Mktg Procurement-Global - NIKE, Inc.; *pg.* 1812, *pg.* 1492
Hsu, Jovan, Brand Mgr - Hasbro, Inc.; *pg.* 954, *pg.* 1603
Hsu, Michael, Grp Pres-North America Consumer Products - Kimberly-Clark Corporation; *pg.* 1461, *pg.* 1720
Hsu, Pei-Wen, Mgr-Taurus & MKS Mktg - Ford Motor Company; *pg.* 172, *pg.* 876
Hsu, Stanley, Assoc Product Mgr - Makita U.S.A., Inc.; *pg.* 1358, *pg.* 120
Hsu, Tim, Dir-Mktg - Twitter, Inc.; *pg.* 1285, *pg.* 228
Hsu, Wendy, Brand Mgr-Global - Energizer Holdings, Inc.; *pg.* 637, *pg.* 996
Hsu, William, VP-News Adv Sls-Asia Pacific - Cable News Network LP; *pg.* 1624, *pg.* 1208
Hsueh, Alice, Dir-Brand Mktg-Global - CooperVision, Inc.; *pg.* 1407, *pg.* 1159
Hu, Amy, Dir-Interactive Mktg - H&R Block, Inc.; *pg.* 764, *pg.* 983
Hu, David, Dir-Global Mktg & Comml Leadership - The Coca-Cola Company; *pg.* 240, *pg.* 493
Hu, David, Head-Developer Products & Rels - FourSquare Labs, Inc; *pg.* 1248, *pg.* 1232
Hu, Henry, Sr Mgr-Fin-Growth Initiatives, Strategy & Mktg - IBM; *pg.* 410, *pg.* 1449
Hu, Jen, Brand Mktg Mgr - Verizon Communications Inc.; *pg.* 1875, *pg.* 1309
Hu, Keith, Dir-Mktg-Intl - Washington State Fruit Commission; *pg.* 161, *pg.* 1847
Hu, Michael, Mgr-Sls-China - Algas-SDI; *pg.* 1311, *pg.* 1831
Hu, Walter, Mgr-Product Mktg - Cisco Systems, Inc.; *pg.* 372, *pg.* 240
Hua, Gia, Mgr-Database Mktg-Digital Mktg - BlackRock, Inc.; *pg.* 724, *pg.* 1203
Hua, Sonya, Sr Analyst-Media Mgmt - Accenture; *pg.* 1392, *pg.* 1186
Huang, Allen, Product Mgr - Google Inc.; *pg.* 1249, *pg.* 153
Huang, Ava, Sr VP-Fragrance & Beauty Mktg - Chanel, Inc.; *pg.* 503, *pg.* 1211
Huang, Barry, Product Mgr-Consumer-Growth - LinkedIn Corporation; *pg.* 1262, *pg.* 160
Huang, Ben, VP-Mktg - Ericsson, Inc.; *pg.* 638, *pg.* 1730
Huang, Billy, Dir-PR - Amazon.com, Inc.; *pg.* 1226, *pg.* 1831
Huang, Brian, Sr Product Mgr - ViewSonic Corporation; *pg.* 489, *pg.* 303
Huang, Didi, Sr Dir-North America Mktg Ops & Mgmt - eBay Inc.; *pg.* 1240, *pg.* 243
Huang, Emily, Dir-Mktg-Bonne Bell - Markwins International Corp.; *pg.* 516, *pg.* 67
Huang, Jean, Mgr-Mktg-Plng & Forecasting - Abbott Diabetes Care, Inc.; *pg.* 1483, *pg.* 38
Huang, Kevin, VP-Mktg - ASUSTeK Computer Inc; *pg.* 355, *pg.* 90
Huang, Landy, Head-Export Sls & Gen Mgr-Large Customer Sls - Google Inc.; *pg.* 1249, *pg.* 153
Huang, Lee, Dir-Product Mgmt & Publ Solutions-Global - Barnes & Noble, Inc.; *pg.* 1619, *pg.* 1201
Huang, Lena, Sr Mgr-Digital Guest Experience - 7-Eleven, Inc.; *pg.* 1012, *pg.* 1672
Huang, Linda, Assoc Mgr-Mktg-Intl - Rich Products Corporation; *pg.* 892, *pg.* 1150
Huang, Lynn, Assoc Dir-Mktg-Global - Merck & Co., Inc.; *pg.* 1566, *pg.* 1077
Huang, Michelle, Mgr-Mktg-Vichy - L'Oreal USA; *pg.* 514, *pg.* 1252
Huang, Mike, Sr Mgr-Mktg - The Gap, Inc.; *pg.* 1770, *pg.* 218
Huang, Shell, Sr Dir-External Tech Acq - The Coca-Cola Company; *pg.* 240, *pg.* 493
Huang, Teresa, Assoc Mgr-Mktg-Yoplait - General Mills, Inc.; *pg.* 828, *pg.* 933
Huang, Wanlin, Brand Mgr-Global Svcs - Benefit Cosmetics LLC; *pg.* 501, *pg.* 213
Hubbard, Dan, Sr Dir-Retail Svcs-Commerce-Las Vegas - Cushman & Wakefield, Inc.; *pg.* 1088, *pg.* 1220
Hubbard, David A., Exec VP-Sls & Mktg - Alliance Fiber Optic Products, Inc.; *pg.* 1399, *pg.* 283
Hubbard, Lindsay, Specialist-Mktg Comm - Emerson Climate Technologies, Inc.; *pg.* 1333, *pg.* 1472
Hubbard, Sandy, Sr Specialist-Bus Mktg Comm - Windstream Corporation; *pg.* 321, *pg.* 34
Hubbard, Sarah, Brand Mgr-Nature Made Vitamins, Minerals & Supplements - Nature Made Nutritional Products Inc.; *pg.* 883, *pg.* 148
Hubbard, Steve, VP-Mktg & Innovation-Global - Griffith Laboratories, Inc.; *pg.* 860, *pg.* 552
Hubbard, Tammy, Head-Social Media Mktg-Novartis MS Franchise & Assoc Dir - Novartis Pharmaceuticals Corp.; *pg.* 1575, *pg.* 1054
Hubbard-Miller, Holly, Dir-Mktg - Kingston Technology Company, Inc.; *pg.* 425, *pg.* 90
Hubbell, Alan, Sr Mgr-Mktg-Building Innovations - E.I. du Pont de Nemours & Company; *pg.* 1159, *pg.* 390
Hubbell, Tim, Dir-Brand Mktg - ESPN, Inc.; *pg.* 285, *pg.* 340
Hubbly, Ravi, Sr Mgr-Technical - Lockheed Martin Corporation; *pg.* 229, *pg.* 762
Huber, Derek, Asst Mgr-Sls - Amica Mutual Insurance Co.; *pg.* 1192, *pg.* 1602
Huber, Matt, Sr Mgr-Mktg Premedia - J.C. Penney Company, Inc.; *pg.* 1774, *pg.* 1732
Huber, Thomas, Sr Dir - Quantros, Inc.; *pg.* 1587, *pg.* 147
Huber, Tina, Mgr-Global Social Mktg - Converse Inc.; *pg.* 1831, *pg.* 793
Huberfeld, Brian, Sr Coord-Mktg-Perishables - The Kroger Co.; *pg.* 1025, *pg.* 1416
Huberman, Susan, Dir-Mktg - Amgen Inc.; *pg.* 1493, *pg.* 291
Hubers Haspert, Jill, Sr Assoc Mgr-Mktg - General Mills, Inc.; *pg.* 828, *pg.* 933
Hubert, Jacob, Product Mgr - Google Inc.; *pg.* 1249, *pg.* 153
Huberty, Paul F., Sr VP-Strategic Plng & Mktg - Chester County Hospital; *pg.* 1515, *pg.* 1593
Hubler, Deirdre, Mgr-Internet Mktg - Intel Corporation; *pg.* 645, *pg.* 266
Hubregsen, Carol, Mgr-Product Mktg - Jelly Belly Candy Company; *pg.* 1857, *pg.* 86
Hucal, Melissa, Dir-Mktg-PR - PSB Holdings, Inc.; *pg.* 797, *pg.* 1898
Huck, Krista A., Mgr-Mktg - Express Scripts, Inc.; *pg.* 1530, *pg.* 997
Huckleberry, David, Sr Mgr-Mktg - Pepsi Beverages Company; *pg.* 258, *pg.* 1342
Hucks, Heather, Dir-Mktg Sponsorships - Coca-Cola Bottling Co. Consolidated; *pg.* 240, *pg.* 1365
Huculak, Ed, Publr & Dir-Sls - The Calgary Sun; *pg.* 1625, *pg.* 1903
Hudack, Mike, Dir-Product Mgmt - Facebook, Inc.; *pg.* 1245, *pg.* 143
Hudack, Raymond A., Mgr-Global Strategic Mktg-Lubricants - THE DOW CHEMICAL COMPANY; *pg.* 1157, *pg.* 898
Hudacko, Christine, Dir-iShares Connect Mktg & PR - BlackRock, Inc.; *pg.* 724, *pg.* 1203
Hudak, Lisa, Mgr-Digital Mktg Comm - The J.M. Smucker Company; *pg.* 865, *pg.* 1468
Hudak, Monica, Brand Mgr-Shopper Mktg - Kimberly-Clark Corporation; *pg.* 1461, *pg.* 1720
Hudda, Shiesta, Sr Mgr-Digital Media - BET Holdings LLC; *pg.* 271, *pg.* 396
Huddleston, Jerilyn, Sr Head-Digital Product - Match.Com, LLC; *pg.* 1265, *pg.* 1683
Huddleston, Laura, Dir-Mktg - Prestige Brands Holdings, Inc.; *pg.* 520, *pg.* 1345
Huddleston, Megan, Brand Mgr - Nestle Purina PetCare Company; *pg.* 1479, *pg.* 1000
Hudetz, Rita, Dir-Mktg, Innovation, Strategy, Dairy & Global Nutrition Grp - PepsiCo, Inc.; *pg.* 259, *pg.* 1327
Hudgin, Bryan, Mgr-Mktg - Yamaha Motor Canada Ltd.; *pg.* 1712, *pg.* 1947
Hudgins, Josh, Product Mgr - Google Inc.; *pg.* 1249, *pg.* 153
Hudon, Henri, Dir-Mktg - Pratt & Whitney Canada Corp.; *pg.* 1370, *pg.* 1952
Hudson, Bill, Sr VP-Sls & Customer Svc - Aurora Casket Company, Inc.; *pg.* 1393, *pg.* 673
Hudson, Brenda, Dir-Mktg-Media - AutoZone, Inc.; *pg.* 200, *pg.* 1641
Hudson, Cory, Sr Dir-Creative Tech - AOL Inc.; *pg.* 1229, *pg.* 1195
Hudson, Eric, Dir-Season Sls & Svcs - Minnesota Twins, LLC; *pg.* 563, *pg.* 940
Hudson, Kirk, Dir-Western Market Sls-Client Mgmt - Deluxe Corporation; *pg.* 1634, *pg.* 964
Hudson, Lisa, Specialist-Creative Svcs-Popeyes Louisiana Kitchen - Popeye's Chicken & Biscuits; *pg.* 1745, *pg.* 517
Hudson, Lisa, Specialist-Creative Svcs - Popeyes Louisiana Kitchen, Inc.; *pg.* 1745, *pg.* 517
Hudson, Melody, Mgr-PR - Gila River Gaming Enterprises, Inc.; *pg.* 1093, *pg.* 12
Hudson, Morgan, Sr Dir-Global Solutions & Innovation Mktg - Visa Inc.; *pg.* 816, *pg.* 230
Hudson, Renita, Product Mgr - Sysco Corporation; *pg.* 1035, *pg.* 1716
Hudson, Robert, Gen Mgr-Sls - Tom Bush Regency Motors Inc.; *pg.* 192, *pg.* 435
Hudson, Sheryl, Sr Mgr-Media & Mktg-Microsoft Studios & Devices - Microsoft Corporation; *pg.* 435, *pg.* 1824
Hudson-Maggio, Love, Dir-Digital Products - Cox Media Group; *pg.* 280, *pg.* 502
Hudspeth, Kandace, VP-Mktg - BodyBuilding.com LLC; *pg.* 1232, *pg.* 549
Huebner, Denny, Mgr-Product Mktg - Applied Materials, Inc.; *pg.* 618, *pg.* 264
Huebscher, Agnes, Dir-Mktg-Europe - Edmund Industrial Optics Inc.; *pg.* 1411, *pg.* 1041
Hueser, David, Portfolio Mgr-Product - Xcel Energy Inc.; *pg.* 1955, *pg.* 946
Huey, Amy, Mgr-Adv & Clearances - Dark Horse Comics, Inc.; *pg.* 1633, *pg.* 1500
Huey, Cherie, Mgr-Brand Mktg - Randstad USA; *pg.* 459, *pg.* 941
Huey, Kim, VP-Sls & Ops - Books-A-Million, Inc.; *pg.* 1623, *pg.* 2
Huey, Tiffany, Mgr-Shopper Mktg-NACP - Starbucks Corporation; *pg.* 897, *pg.* 1840
Huezo, Richard, Specialist-Digital Mktg - The Western & Southern Financial Group; *pg.* 1223, *pg.* 1427
Hufcut, Lisa, Dir-PR - Town Sports International Holdings, Inc.; *pg.* 589, *pg.* 1303
Huff, Darla, Product Mgr-Rice - Dow AgroSciences LLC; *pg.* 1156, *pg.* 684
Huff, Della, Sr Product Mgr-Mktg-OS X Photo Apps - Apple Inc.; *pg.* 350, *pg.* 73
Huff, Heidi, Dir-Mktg - IGA, Inc.; *pg.* 1023, *pg.* 578
Huff, John, Gen Mgr-Sls - KWWL-TV; *pg.* 295, *pg.* 712
Huff, Katie, Sr Mgr-Mktg-Wholesale.com - Levi Strauss & Co.; *pg.* 43, *pg.* 220
Huff, Matt, Sr Mgr-Technical Svcs & Comm - Whirlpool

Corporation; pg. 62, pg. 872
Huff, Maureen, VP-PR - Time Warner Cable Inc.; pg. 312, pg. 1301
Huffaker, Meredith, Coord-Mktg - Scripps Networks Interactive, Inc.; pg. 1279, pg. 1638
Huffman, Allison, Mgr-Indus Initiative Mktg - Autodesk Inc.; pg. 356, pg. 257
Huffman, Chris, Mgr-Digital Mktg - Stage Stores, Inc.; pg. 33, pg. 1715
Huffman, Jasmine, Dir-Digital & Social Loyalty Community Dev - Marriott International, Inc.; pg. 1102, pg. 764
Huffman, Josh, Dir-Product Mktg-Global - Blount International, Inc.; pg. 1043, pg. 1501
Huffman, Malin, Dir-Product Mgmt - NetSuite, Inc.; pg. 1270, pg. 255
Huffman, Marc, Pres-Worldwide Sls & Distribution - NetSuite, Inc.; pg. 1270, pg. 255
Huffmyer, Douglas, VP & Dir-Creative-Global - Elizabeth Arden, Inc.; pg. 507, pg. 448
Hufford, David, Sr Dir-Interactive Entertainment - Microsoft Corporation; pg. 435, pg. 1824
Huggins, Kimberly, Mgr-Mktg - HD Electric Company; pg. 1299, pg. 666
Huggins, Stratton, VP & Mgr-Mktg Comm - Renasant Bank; pg. 798, pg. 533
Hugh, Ronell, Product Mgr-Xbox Games-Global - Microsoft Corporation; pg. 435, pg. 1824
Hughes, Andrea, Exec Dir-Product Dev & Mgmt - Cox Communications, Inc.; pg. 279, pg. 501
Hughes, Andrea, Supvr-Mktg Comm Svcs - Honeywell North Safety Products; pg. 42, pg. 1600
Hughes, Anna, Sr Mgr-Product Mktg-Mobile & Local - Microsoft Corporation; pg. 435, pg. 1824
Hughes, Bill, Dir-Global Mktg & Product Dev - Bare Escentuals, Inc.; pg. 500, pg. 213
Hughes, Bill D., Mgr-Mktg - Overly Manufacturing Company; pg. 102, pg. 1534
Hughes, Brian, Sr VP-Cardmember Mktg - Discover Financial Services; pg. 744, pg. 653
Hughes, Celeste, Sr Mgr-Comm & Shareholder Rels - The McGraw-Hill Companies Inc.; pg. 1663, pg. 1257
Hughes, Cherrie, Mgr-Mktg - Singer Sewing Company; pg. 698, pg. 1639
Hughes, Chris, Sr Mgr-Sls - EarthLink Holdings Corp.; pg. 1240, pg. 504
Hughes, Emily, Supvr-Mktg Comm-Post-it Brand - 3M Company; pg. 1142, pg. 956
Hughes, Eric, Dir-Product & Program Mktg - CARIBOU COFFEE COMPANY, INC.; pg. 1764, pg. 932
Hughes, Gina, VP-Mktg - AMC Networks Inc.; pg. 269, pg. 1189
Hughes, Graham, VP-Sls & Mktg - Taylor Morrison; pg. 1116, pg. 24
Hughes, Jared, Sr Mgr-Mktg - Scarecrow Press, Inc.; pg. 1683, pg. 773
Hughes, Jennie, Assoc Mgr-Social Media Mktg - The WhiteWave Foods Company; pg. 1037, pg. 324
Hughes, Jennifer, Dir-Sls-Chains - Diageo North America, Inc.; pg. 1961, pg. 361
Hughes, Jennifer Quintero, Dir-Brand PR Focused Svc & Extended Stay Brands - Hilton Worldwide, Inc.; pg. 1094, pg. 1791
Hughes, Jim, Sr VP & Head-Media Rels - Citizens Financial Group, Inc.; pg. 737, pg. 1606
Hughes, Jim, Sr VP-Broadband Sls-Worldwide - CommScope, Inc.; pg. 278, pg. 1378
Hughes, John, Sr VP-Product Mgmt - Silvon Software Inc.; pg. 470, pg. 669
Hughes, Kay, Sr Specialist-Mktg Programs - ACI Worldwide Inc.; pg. 341, pg. 1010
Hughes, Keith, Dir-Mktg-Polymer Additives - Chemtura Corporation; pg. 1152, pg. 355
Hughes, Linda, Mgr-PR & Mktg - Dayton International Airport; pg. 227, pg. 1478
Hughes, Magdalena, Mktg Dir-Latin America Reg - Mary Kay Inc.; pg. 516, pg. 1657
Hughes, Magdalena, Dir-Mktg-Latin America Reg - Mary Kay Inc.; pg. 516, pg. 1657
Hughes, Margaret, Sr Dir-Mktg-Global - Dell Inc.; pg. 383, pg. 1737
Hughes, Megan, Dir-Product Mgmt-Mobile - Orbitz Worldwide, Inc.; pg. 1918, pg. 586
Hughes, Michael, Sr VP-Sls-Worldwide - Barracuda Networks, Inc.; pg. 360, pg. 58
Hughes, Oliver, Sr Dir & Head-Intl Mktg - Electronic Arts Inc.; pg. 951, pg. 189
Hughes, Rhonda, Mgr-Corp Social Media - Citrix Systems, Inc.; pg. 375, pg. 424
Hughes, Ronda, Sr Dir-Mktg & Audience Data - UBM Advanstar; pg. 1697, pg. 1306
Hughes, Sarah, Mgr-Mktg - Intuit Inc.; pg. 769, pg. 158
Hughes, Scott, Mgr-Software Sls - International Business Machines Corporation; pg. 418, pg. 1138
Hughes, Shannon, Product Mgr-Svcs & Customer Experience - Weyerhaeuser Company; pg. 121, pg. 1820
Hughes, Shelley, VP-PR - IRI Group; pg. 421, pg. 579
Hughes, Susanna Boman, Sr Mgr-Customer Dev-Wal-Mart - LEGO Systems, Inc.; pg. 961, pg. 346
Hughes, Terry, VP-Sls & Mktg - Green Spot, Inc.; pg. 251, pg. 68
Hughes-Rowlands, Richard, Product Mgr - Zebra Technologies Corporation; pg. 690, pg. 628
Hughey, Jim, VP-Production - Fastline Publications Inc.; pg. 1641, pg. 726
Hugo, Sara, Product Mgr - Safeway Inc.; pg. 1032, pg. 184
Hugon, Natalie, Project Mgr-Media Plng & PR - VERA BRADLEY, INC.; pg. 15, pg. 697
Huguely, Andrea, Dir-Media Rels & Comm - American Airlines Inc.; pg. 1898, pg. 1693
Hui, Anna, Mgr-Global Mktg-Maybelline - L'Oreal USA; pg. 514, pg. 1252
Hui, Greg, Dir-Mktg-Axis-L'Oreal Paris Hairstyling - Maybelline LLC; pg. 516, pg. 1257
Hui, Jeanne, Brand Mgr - Reckitt Benckiser Inc.; pg. 1136, pg. 1105
Hui, Raymond, Reg Mgr-Sls-Asia Pacific - NBS Technologies Inc.; pg. 786, pg. 1941
Huie-Roy, Christine, Mgr-Collaborative Mktg - The Kraft Heinz Company; pg. 871, pg. 641
Huiet, Kelly, Mgr-Digital CRM Mktg - Verizon Communications Inc.; pg. 1875, pg. 1309
Huizenga, Amy, Dir-Mktg Vertical Markets & Global Accounts - Anixter International Inc.; pg. 1313, pg. 614
Hulet, Kendall, Sr VP-Product - Ancestry.com LLC; pg. 1228, pg. 1754
Hulick, David, Dir-Mktg - Osram Sylvania, Inc.; pg. 1302, pg. 816
Hulighan, Larry, VP-Sls & Mgr-Hospitality Grp - Copland Fabrics, Inc.; pg. 692, pg. 1359
Hulke, Jennifer, Mgr-Mktg-Camera, Photo & Video - Amazon.com, Inc.; pg. 1226, pg. 1831
Hull, Arne, Mgr-Experiential Mktg - FCA US LLC; pg. 170, pg. 868
Hull, Dan, Dir-Mktg - Giordano's Enterprises, Inc.; pg. 1729, pg. 575
Hull, Dave, Sr VP-Sls & Mktg - Manitowoc Crane Shady Grove; pg. 1359, pg. 1586
Hull, Dennis, Sr Mgr-Consumer & Market Insights - Wm. Wrigley Jr. Company; pg. 1863, pg. 596
Hull, Jim, VP-Egg Products - Cal-Maine Foods, Inc.; pg. 843, pg. 969
Hull, Kimberly A., VP-Strategic Mktg & Comm-Bus Insurance - The Travelers Companies, Inc.; pg. 1220, pg. 352
Hull, Mark, Dir-Product Mgmt - LinkedIn Corporation; pg. 1262, pg. 160
Hull, Stephen, Exec Dir-Mktg-Global - Merck & Co., Inc.; pg. 1566, pg. 1077
Hulquist, Dane, Sr VP & Head-Digital Adv - Wells Fargo & Company; pg. 819, pg. 232
Huls, Sean, Assoc Mgr-Mktg - PepsiCo, Inc.; pg. 259, pg. 1327
Hulse, Gerald, Sr Dir-Sls Strategy - Diamond Foods, Inc.; pg. 1851, pg. 216
Hulsey, Clare, Dir-Mktg Strategy & Insights - The Coca-Cola Company; pg. 240, pg. 493
Hulsey, Jesmine, Asst VP-Mktg - The Doctors Company; pg. 1199, pg. 163
Hulsey, Melissa, Coord-Mktg - Fisher Manufacturing Company; pg. 81, pg. 297
Hulskotter, Dannon, Dir-Mktg & Bus Dev - Minnesota Vikings Football Club, Inc.; pg. 563, pg. 923
Hultgen, Maureen, Grp Mgr-Partner Mktg & Media Sls - Orbitz Worldwide, Inc.; pg. 1918, pg. 586
Hultgren, Alex, Dir-Mktg-Victory Motorcycles - Polaris Industries Inc.; pg. 1709, pg. 928
Hulton, Dominic, Dir-Mktg - Insulet Corporation; pg. 644, pg. 785
Hulvat, Sandy, Project Mgr-Integrated Mktg Comm - IBM; pg. 410, pg. 1449
Humann, Kimberly, Mgr-Shopper Mktg - Barilla America, Inc.; pg. 839, pg. 555
Humble, Stacey, VP-Mktg-Global - The Almond Board of California; pg. 1013, pg. 149
Humes, Tim, Sr Brand Mgr-Strategic Mktg Partnerships & PR - Carhartt, Inc.; pg. 39, pg. 875
Humfleet, Amy, VP-Product Dev & Innovation - Aveda Corporation; pg. 499, pg. 917
Humiston, Richard, VP-Sls - WireCo WorldGroup; pg. 1389, pg. 987
Huml, David W., Sr VP-Mktg-Global - Tennant Company; pg. 1381, pg. 944
Hummel, Hans, Mgr-Mktg-Global - Lonza Inc.; pg. 1171, pg. 1041
Humphrey, Alice, Sr Mgr-Mktg-Kroger - PepsiCo, Inc.; pg. 259, pg. 1327
Humphrey, Chris, VP-Strategy, Mktg & Bus Dev - Maxwell Technologies, Inc.; pg. 653, pg. 204
Humphrey, David, Dir-Product Mgmt - ABB; pg. 340, pg. 486
Humphrey, Elisa, Sr Dir-Brand Mktg - Hotwire, Inc.; pg. 1912, pg. 219
Humphrey, Elizabeth A., Bus Mgr-Enterprise Tech Solutions - Cigna Corporation; pg. 1197, pg. 338
Humphrey, Jim, Dir-Foodservice Mktg - Speedway LLC; pg. 985, pg. 1452
Humphrey, Kitty, Mgr-Natl Accts Sls-Southern Atlantic Reg - Phillips Foods Inc.; pg. 1030, pg. 758
Humphrey, Matt, Sr Mgr-Competition Comm - National Association for Stock Car Auto Racing; pg. 566, pg. 420
Humphrey, Meliza, Mgr-Mktg-Honda Svc - American Honda Motor Co., Inc.; pg. 163, pg. 292
Humphrey, Mike, Mgr-Field Sls - Samsung Telecommunications America, LLC; pg. 670, pg. 1736
Humphrey, Rose, Dir-Mktg - Lennar Corporation; pg. 1100, pg. 443
Humphreys, Antonio, Sr Mgr-Global Procurement - Adobe Systems Incorporated; pg. 342, pg. 235
Humphreys, Denise, Sr Dir-Partnership Mgmt - PGA Tour, Inc.; pg. 574, pg. 460
Humphreys, John, VP-Sls & Mktg - Egenera, Inc.; pg. 390, pg. 802
Humphreys, Justin, VP-Sls - Airstream, Inc.; pg. 163, pg. 1456
Humphreys, Laura, Mgr-Mktg & Partnership Activation - Baltimore Ravens Limited Partnership; pg. 532, pg. 755
Humphries, Craig, Dir-Mktg Res - The Scotts Miracle-Gro Company; pg. 1799, pg. 1459
Humphries, Erin, Sr Mgr-Comml Programs - DigitalGlobe; pg. 227, pg. 1785
Humphries, G. Kent, Sr VP-Contract Sls - Sysco Corporation; pg. 1035, pg. 1716
Humphries, Jamie, Mgr-Mktg-Natl - Toyota Canada, Inc.; pg. 192, pg. 1934
Humphries, Jeremy, Mgr-Social Media - Farmers Group, Inc.; pg. 1199, pg. 130
Humphries, Martyn, VP & Gen Mgr-Media Processors - Freescale Semiconductor, Inc.; pg. 398, pg. 1662
Humston, Erica, Brand Mgr-Online - Vail Resorts, Inc.; pg. 1117, pg. 313
Hund, Diane, VP-Mktg - Essendant Inc.; pg. 1907, pg. 600
Hundelt, Eric, Dir-Field Mktg - Bacardi USA, Inc.; pg. 1956, pg. 417
Hundgen, Stephen, VP-Sls & Mktg - Glen Raven, Inc.; pg. 693, pg. 1373
Hundley, William, Dir-Sys Clinical Svcs Mktg - Indiana University Health Methodist Hospital; pg. 1545, pg. 687
Hundrev, Maria, Mgr-Natl Mktg Comm-BDO USA, LLP - BDO Seidman, LLP; pg. 724, pg. 1202
Hunewill, John, VP-Brand Mktg - Academy Sports & Outdoors, Ltd.; pg. 1824, pg. 1724
Hung, Christine, Assoc Dir-Mktg - Penguin Random House; pg. 1675, pg. 1276
Hung, Justin, Sr Mgr-Fin - J.C. Penney Company, Inc.; pg. 1774, pg. 1732
Hung, Richard, Sr Product Mgr - Google Inc.; pg. 1249, pg. 153
Hung, Tze, Brand Mgr - LEGO Systems, Inc.; pg. 961, pg. 346
Hungerford, Ameda, VP-Mktg - NetSuite, Inc.; pg. 1270, pg. 255
Hungerford, Libby, Reg Mgr-Sls - Tensar Corporation; pg. 114, pg. 485
Hungerford, Sean, Dir-BBM Product Mgmt - BlackBerry Limited; pg. 625, pg. 1947
Hungsberg, Steve, Dir-Mktg - Jarden Home Brands; pg. 1126, pg. 920

Hunking, John, Coord-Mktg & Production - Manulife Financial Corporation; *pg.* 778, *pg.* 1939
Hunn, Jennifer, Coord-Mdse Mktg - The Home Depot, Inc.; *pg.* 1050, *pg.* 510
Hunnicutt, Hal, VP & Dir-Mktg - Glen Raven, Inc.; *pg.* 693, *pg.* 1373
Hunnicutt-Wolfe, Tammy, Head-Traffic & Sr Mgr-Mktg - AT&T Mobility LLC; *pg.* 619, *pg.* 488
Hunsberger, Deron, Sr VP-North America Sls-WMS Gaming - Scientific Games Corporation; *pg.* 468, *pg.* 1029
Hunsel, Rebecca, Mgr-Mktg - Franchise Concepts, Inc.; *pg.* 1769, *pg.* 1005
Hunsinger, John L., II, Mgr-Production & Stage - South Carolina Philharmonic Association Inc.; *pg.* 584, *pg.* 1615
Hunt, Adrijana, Mgr-Mktg Res - Florida's Natural Growers; *pg.* 855, *pg.* 437
Hunt, Ben, Dir-Digital Media - Denver Broncos Football Club; *pg.* 544, *pg.* 325
Hunt, Cherylann, Dir-Product Solutions - Cooper-Atkins Corporation; *pg.* 1407, *pg.* 355
Hunt, Darren, Sr Mgr-Mktg - Applebee's International, Inc.; *pg.* 1715, *pg.* 980
Hunt, Eileen, Sr Mgr-Events Mktg-Global - Synopsys, Inc.; *pg.* 480, *pg.* 162
Hunt, George, Sr VP-Sls - Comverge, Inc.; *pg.* 1325, *pg.* 536
Hunt, Gordon, Dir-Mktg & Comm - National Watermelon Promotion Board; *pg.* 151, *pg.* 454
Hunt, John, VP-Sls - Quiksilver, Inc.; *pg.* 31, *pg.* 104
Hunt, Kellie, Assoc Product Mgr-INC Men's - Macy's East; *pg.* 1777, *pg.* 1254
Hunt, Kevin, Mgr-Social Media - General Mills, Inc.; *pg.* 828, *pg.* 933
Hunt, Kristine, Mgr-Mktg Programs-Healthcare - Dell Inc.; *pg.* 383, *pg.* 1737
Hunt, Lionel, Engr-Technical Mktg - Cisco Systems, Inc.; *pg.* 372, *pg.* 240
Hunt, Lisa, Coord-Mktg - McCarthy Building Companies, Inc.; *pg.* 96, *pg.* 999
Hunt, Neil, Chief Product Officer - Netflix, Inc.; *pg.* 1269, *pg.* 141
Hunt, Sarah, Dir-Natl Field Mktg - T-Mobile US, Inc.; *pg.* 676, *pg.* 1816
Hunt, Teri, Acting CFO - Lakeland Industries, Inc.; *pg.* 1354, *pg.* 1338
Hunt-Boes, Yolanda, Mgr-Mktg Comm - Sony Electronics, Inc.; *pg.* 676, *pg.* 209
Hunter, Adrienne, Dir-Mktg-North America Sls & Distr - International Business Machines Corporation; *pg.* 418, *pg.* 1138
Hunter, Alexander, Sr Producer-Worldwide Mktg Comm - Apple Inc.; *pg.* 350, *pg.* 73
Hunter, Anne, Sr VP-Mktg Strategy-Global - comScore, Inc; *pg.* 1236, *pg.* 1798
Hunter, Caroline, Specialist-Interactive Mktg - Kawasaki Motors Corp., U.S.A.; *pg.* 1708, *pg.* 111
Hunter, Chris, Chief Strategy Officer - Humana, Inc.; *pg.* 1204, *pg.* 734
Hunter, Connie, Sr Dir-Sls - Palm Beach County Convention & Visitors Bureau; *pg.* 1003, *pg.* 479
Hunter, Doug, Mgr-Sls-Natl - Escalade Inc.; *pg.* 1833, *pg.* 678
Hunter, Douglas, Sr Dir-Corp Mktg - Lattice Semiconductor Corporation; *pg.* 651, *pg.* 1498
Hunter, Eric, Exec VP-Mktg - Pier 1 Imports, Inc.; *pg.* 940, *pg.* 1695
Hunter, Erin, VP-ECommerce & Mdsg - Live Nation Entertainment, Inc.; *pg.* 558, *pg.* 47
Hunter, Heather, Dir-Mktg Comm - Safeguard Scientifics, Inc.; *pg.* 464, *pg.* 1592
Hunter, Jesse, Mgr-Field Mktg - Atmel Corporation; *pg.* 621, *pg.* 238
Hunter, Laura, Head-Product Area & Exec Mgr-Comm - Google Inc.; *pg.* 1249, *pg.* 153
Hunter, Lisa, Assoc Dir-Mktg-Global - Brown-Forman Corporation; *pg.* 1958, *pg.* 732
Hunter, Marissa, Head-Ram Adv - FCA US LLC; *pg.* 170, *pg.* 868
Hunter, Pia, Sr Dir-Channel - Apple Inc.; *pg.* 350, *pg.* 73
Hunter, Ruth, Sr VP-Sls & Mktg - Mobile Mini, Inc.; *pg.* 1362, *pg.* 26
Hunter, Scott, Dir-Sls-Worldwide - FlightSafety International, Inc.; *pg.* 601, *pg.* 1160
Hunter, Scott, Mgr-Mktg-Global - Milliken & Company; *pg.* 696, *pg.* 1622
Hunter, Scott, Head-US Mktg-Ophthalmics - Shire; *pg.* 1593, *pg.* 1532
Hunter, Stephen, VP-Dev & Production-Natl Geographic Television Intl - National Geographic Channel; *pg.* 299, *pg.* 402
Hunter, Suzi, Mgr-Product Mktg - Windstar Cruises; *pg.* 1931, *pg.* 1843
Hunter, T.J, Dir-Digital Mktg - Rosetta Stone Inc.; *pg.* 462, *pg.* 1774
Hunter, Tara, Dir-PR - QVC Inc; *pg.* 305, *pg.* 1593
Huntimer, Jody, Mgr-Strategic Mktg - Daktronics, Inc.; *pg.* 633, *pg.* 1624
Huntley, Erica, Mgr-Relationship Mktg Strategy - Choice Hotels International, Inc.; *pg.* 1086, *pg.* 775
Huntoon, Karen, VP-Mktg-North America - Elizabeth Arden, Inc.; *pg.* 507, *pg.* 448
Huntsinger, Stephanie, Mgr-Social Media Ops - NCR Corporation; *pg.* 443, *pg.* 531
Huntsman, James H., Pres-Advanced Matls Div - Huntsman Corporation; *pg.* 1167, *pg.* 1758
Huntsman, Justin, Strategist-Digital Mktg-Internet of Things - Intel Corporation; *pg.* 645, *pg.* 266
Huoponen, Jani, Product Mgr - Google Inc.; *pg.* 1249, *pg.* 153
Hupalo, Christine, Exec Dir-Brand Mktg - 20th Century Fox Film Corp.; *pg.* 267, *pg.* 124
Huppert, Blane, Mgr-Mktg Comm - 3M Company; *pg.* 1142, *pg.* 956
Huppertz, Jeffrey, VP-Mktg & Bus Dev - Espial Group Inc.; *pg.* 1243, *pg.* 1932
Hurd, Alex, Sr Dir-Product Dev, Growth & Payer Innovation-Health & Wellness - Wal-Mart.com; *pg.* 1287, *pg.* 50
Hurd, Bob, Product Mgr-Standby Power Products - Briggs & Stratton Corporation; *pg.* 201, *pg.* 1899
Hurd, Brian, Specialist-Mktg - VeriFone Systems, Inc.; *pg.* 487, *pg.* 251
Hurd, Joyce, Dir-Mktg Comm - Comcast Corporation; *pg.* 276, *pg.* 1560
Hurff, Kerry, Asst VP-Mktg - Safelite Solutions LLC; *pg.* 109, *pg.* 1443
Hurlbut, Karen, Mgr-Comm-Creative Lab - Environmental Systems Research Institute Inc.; *pg.* 393, *pg.* 188
Hurlbutt, Kasey, Brand Mgr-Global - CH2M HILL Companies, Ltd.; *pg.* 75, *pg.* 325
Hurley, Edward, VP-Sls - Spire Corporation; *pg.* 1378, *pg.* 786
Hurley, Heather, Dir-Mktg - Famous Dave's of America, Inc.; *pg.* 1728, *pg.* 926
Hurley, Kim, Mgr-Inside Sls - The Frog, Switch & Manufacturing Company; *pg.* 1338, *pg.* 1520
Hurley, Lee, VP-Digital & Social - Weight Watchers International, Inc.; *pg.* 1609, *pg.* 1313
Hurley, Mark A., Sr Mgr-Partner Relationship-Pub Sector - Citrix Systems, Inc.; *pg.* 375, *pg.* 424
Hurley, Michael, Dir-Mktg - Lindt & Sprungli (USA) Inc.; *pg.* 1857, *pg.* 1039
Hurley, Nicole, Specialist-Product - W.L. Gore & Associates, Inc.; *pg.* 122, *pg.* 388
Hurley, Stasia, Sr Mgr-Solutions Mktg - NetApp, Inc.; *pg.* 444, *pg.* 287
Hurn, Jake, Sr Mgr-Music & Entertainment - Beats Electronics LLC; *pg.* 624, *pg.* 272
Hurn, Matt, Head-Local Consumer Mktg-Mobile Payments - PayPal Inc.; *pg.* 1274, *pg.* 248
Hurn, Tom, Mgr-Local Sls - KCRG TV Station; *pg.* 293, *pg.* 702
Hurp, Sarah, Mgr-Mktg - Evolving Systems, Inc.; *pg.* 395, *pg.* 326
Hurson, Tom, Pres-Northwest Naturals & Sr VP-Ingredient & Food Service Sls - Tree Top, Inc.; *pg.* 901, *pg.* 1843
Hurst, Chuck, VP-Media & Content Delivery - Scripps Networks Interactive, Inc.; *pg.* 1279, *pg.* 1638
Hurst, Jeff, Chief Strategy Officer - HomeAway, Inc.; *pg.* 1911, *pg.* 1663
Hurst, Lori Davidson, Sr Mgr-Ops & Mktg Sys - Autodesk Inc.; *pg.* 356, *pg.* 257
Hurst, Tanya, Sr Mgr-Content & Ops-LN Corp Affiliations-EEMG - LexisNexis Corporate Affiliations; *pg.* 1658, *pg.* 1095
Hurt, Damoni, Bus Mgr-Mktg & Sls-US - Ford Motor Company; *pg.* 172, *pg.* 876
Hurtak, Brian, Dir-Mktg-Enterprise - United Services Automobile Association; *pg.* 1221, *pg.* 1743
Hurtt, Lauren, Supvr-PR - South Jersey Gas Company; *pg.* 1951, *pg.* 1067
Hurvitz, Lauren, Chief Comm & Corp Mktg Officer & Exec VP - Turner Broadcasting System, Inc.; *pg.* 314, *pg.* 521
Hurwitz, Ellyn, Dir-Mktg - Smithsonian Magazine; *pg.* 1687, *pg.* 404
Hurwitz, Freya, Sr Product Mgr-TripAdvisor for Bus - TripAdvisor, Inc.; *pg.* 1926, *pg.* 835
Hurwitz, Nicole, Asst VP-Digital Mktg-Maybelline & Essie - L'Oreal USA; *pg.* 514, *pg.* 1252
Hurwitz, Nicole, Asst VP-Digital Mktg-Maybelline & Essie - Maybelline LLC; *pg.* 516, *pg.* 1257
Hurwitz, Wendy, Dir-Consumer Mktg-Clipper Magazine - Gannett Co., Inc.; *pg.* 1643, *pg.* 1790
Husain, Marc, VP-Sls-Vendor Mgmt System - PeopleFluent; *pg.* 453, *pg.* 853
Husain, Rizwan, Gen Mgr & Dir-Product Mgmt & Innovation - Symantec Corporation; *pg.* 478, *pg.* 161
Husak, Denise, Dir-Product & Dealer Products Team - Kelley Blue Book Co., Inc.; *pg.* 1656, *pg.* 112
Huse, Dan, Mgr-Mktg-Post-it Notes - 3M Company; *pg.* 1142, *pg.* 956
Huse, Susan, Mgr-Titanium Sls - ATI Wah Chang; *pg.* 1314, *pg.* 1492
Hushen, Lauren, Assoc Mgr-Mktg - American Eagle Outfitters, Inc.; *pg.* 37, *pg.* 1572
Hushen, Tom, Sr Mgr-External Comm - Campbell Soup Company; *pg.* 844, *pg.* 1048
Husmann, Carola, Dir-Adv & Mktg Production-Europe - Ralph Lauren Corporation; *pg.* 46, *pg.* 1284
Husnick, Mark, CIO-Alcoa Engineered Products & Solutions - Alcoa Inc.; *pg.* 65, *pg.* 1188
Hussain, Akhtar, Mgr-CHS Refined Fuels Mktg - CHS INC.; *pg.* 702, *pg.* 926
Hussain, Debra, Sr Dir-Mktg-Men's Health Bus Unit - Eli Lilly and Company; *pg.* 1527, *pg.* 684
Hussain, Farah, Sr Mgr-Mktg, Partnerships & New Ventures - PayPal Inc.; *pg.* 1274, *pg.* 248
Hussain, Kathy, Sr Dir-Institutional Mktg - Teachers Insurance & Annuity Association - College Retirement Equities Fund; *pg.* 1219, *pg.* 1297
Hussain, Nadir, Sr Dir & Dir-Online Mktg - SHUTTERFLY, INC.; *pg.* 1280, *pg.* 192
Hussain, Sheeza, Exec Dir-Comml Mktg & Market Dev - Hill-Rom Holdings, Inc.; *pg.* 1542, *pg.* 673
Hussar, Jane, Asst Mgr-Digital Mktg - General Motors Company; *pg.* 175, *pg.* 881
Hussein, Yitzhak, Assoc Mgr-Mktg-Miller Lite Multicultural - MillerCoors; *pg.* 254, *pg.* 1877
Hussein, Yitzhak, Assoc Mgr-Mktg-Miller Lite Multicultural - MillerCoors LLC; *pg.* 255, *pg.* 582
Husseini, Nouhad, Sr Dir-Bus Dev - Regeneron Pharmaceuticals, Inc.; *pg.* 1588, *pg.* 1345
Hussey, Chris, Dir-Mktg - KWWL-TV; *pg.* 295, *pg.* 712
Hussmann, Morten, Dir-Brand, Mktg & Comm - Ernst & Young Global Limited; *pg.* 748, *pg.* 1228
Hust, Katherine L., VP-Sls-Mid-Central Reg - United States Cellular Corporation; *pg.* 1875, *pg.* 594
Husted, Perri, Dir-PMO-Franchise & Global Mktg Support - Merck & Co., Inc.; *pg.* 1566, *pg.* 1077
Huston, Amyas A., Sr Mgr-Medical Affairs - CUBIST PHARMACEUTICALS, INC.; *pg.* 1521, *pg.* 828
Huston, Brian, Mgr-Mktg-Baking & Breakfast - The J.M. Smucker Company; *pg.* 865, *pg.* 1468
Huston, Dennis, VP-Sls & Mktg-Engineered Wood Products - Boise Cascade Holdings, L.L.C.; *pg.* 1453, *pg.* 546
Huszarik, Liz, Sr VP-Media Res - Warner Bros. Entertainment Inc.; *pg.* 319, *pg.* 54
Hutaff, Stephanie, Dir-Product Mktg & Product Mgmt-Dish Care - BSH Home Appliances Corporation; *pg.* 53, *pg.* 108
Hutagalung, Virgil, Mgr-Mktg Ops - Cisco Systems, Inc.; *pg.* 372, *pg.* 240
Hutchens, Phil, VP-Mktg - Standard Motor Products, Inc.; *pg.* 218, *pg.* 1176
Hutcheson, Deborah, Dir-Mktg-North America - Agfa Corporation; *pg.* 1398, *pg.* 1114
Hutcheson, Stephani, Specialist-Mktg Comm - Aviall, Inc.; *pg.* 224, *pg.* 1676
Hutchings, Debbie, Sr Dir-Media - John Wiley & Sons, Inc.; *pg.* 1655, *pg.* 1073
Hutchings, Scott, Dir-Sls - SFS intec, Inc.; *pg.* 1061, *pg.* 1596
Hutchinson, David, Exec VP-Program Ops & Digital Media - Program Partners, Inc.; *pg.* 305, *pg.* 301
Hutchinson, Emily Shipman, Sr Mgr-Digital Mktg - DeVry University Inc.; *pg.* 600, *pg.* 649
Hutchinson, Harrison, Mgr-Loyalty Mktg - K-VA-T Food Stores, Inc.; *pg.* 1025, *pg.* 1770
Hutchinson, James, VP-Mktg - Georgia Lottery Corporation; *pg.* 993, *pg.* 506
Hutchinson, Kara, Dir-Strategic Mktg - Boston Celtics Limited

First page reference indicates Business Class Edition
Second page reference indicates Geographic Edition

Partnership; *pg.* 533, *pg.* 790

Hutchinson, Rod, Mgr-Strategic Demand Plng & Mdsg - Bridgestone Americas, Inc.; *pg.* 201, *pg.* 1649

Hutchinson, Samantha, Assoc Mgr-Mktg - W.W. Grainger, Inc.; *pg.* 1390, *pg.* 625

Hutchinson, Tom, Dir-Mktg, Customer Experience, CRM & Analytics - Raley's Inc.; *pg.* 1031, *pg.* 305

Hutchison, David, Sr VP-Mktg - SAP America, Inc.; *pg.* 466, *pg.* 1557

Hutchison, Halle, Mng Dir-Brand & Mktg Comm - Alaska Airlines, Inc.; *pg.* 1897, *pg.* 1830

Hutchison, Jeff, Sr Dir-Strategic Svcs - Stryker Corporation; *pg.* 1598, *pg.* 894

Hutchison, Jennifer, VP-Mktg-Digital & Brand - First Citizens BancShares, Inc.; *pg.* 754, *pg.* 1387

Hutchisson, Kim, Coord-Sls - Mentor Graphics Corporation; *pg.* 432, *pg.* 1510

Huter, Andrea L., Mgr-Mktg-Integrated Mktg Comm - Rockwell Automation, Inc.; *pg.* 668, *pg.* 1880

Huther, Leigh, Brand Mgr-Enterprise - Ingersoll-Rand Company; *pg.* 1349, *pg.* 1370

Hutler, Craig, Product Mgr - Sears Holdings Corporation; *pg.* 1784, *pg.* 618

Hutson, Heather, Dir-Mktg - McGladrey, LLP; *pg.* 781, *pg.* 938

Hutt, Mary L., Assoc Dir-Payer Strategy & Mktg - Vertex Pharmaceuticals Incorporated; *pg.* 1606, *pg.* 801

Hutter, Gretchen, Sr Mgr-Growth Segment Res - National Association for Stock Car Auto Racing; *pg.* 566, *pg.* 420

Huttner, Taylor, VP-Product Mktg - Audible, Inc.; *pg.* 1230, *pg.* 1095

Hutto, Josh, Dir-Global Mktg-Xbox Hardware & Platform Mktg - Microsoft Corporation; *pg.* 435, *pg.* 1824

Hutton, Liz, Specialist-Mktg Comm-OMC - Schlumberger Limited; *pg.* 801, *pg.* 1714

Hutton, Paul, Sr Dir-Digital Intelligence - The Weather Channel LLC; *pg.* 320, *pg.* 523

Hutton, Richard, Dir-Channel Mktg - Samsung Electronics America, Inc.; *pg.* 669, *pg.* 1115

Hutzler, David, VP-Market & Mgr-Sls - Bank of America Global Wealth & Investment Management; *pg.* 720, *pg.* 789

Huvane, Michael, VP-Mktg - New York Power Authority, Inc.; *pg.* 1947, *pg.* 1137

Huy, Jean, VP-Product Mktg-Global - Sage Software, Inc.; *pg.* 464, *pg.* 116

Huyard, Wayne, Exec VP-Sls, Mktg & Svcs - Fair Isaac Corporation; *pg.* 1247, *pg.* 955

Huygen, Yvette, Dir-PR & Internal Comm-Worldwide - Synopsys, Inc.; *pg.* 480, *pg.* 162

Huyler, Kelly, Brand Mgr-Intl Mktg - S.C. Johnson & Son, Inc.; *pg.* 334, *pg.* 1889

Huynh, Minh, Product Mgr - Starbucks Corporation; *pg.* 897, *pg.* 1840

Huynh, Nghi, Mgr-Adv Ops-Gannett Digital - Gannett Co., Inc.; *pg.* 1643, *pg.* 1790

Huynh, Nicole, VP & Head-Mktg Strategy & Ops-Global - JPMorgan Chase & Co.; *pg.* 772, *pg.* 1246

Huynh, Noelle, Sr Mgr-Res Strategy & Insights - Hulu LLC; *pg.* 1257, *pg.* 274

Huynh, Tony, Sr Mgr-Product Mktg - Hitachi Data Systems Corporation; *pg.* 407, *pg.* 265

Huzjak, Ryan, Dir-Corp Partnerships & Sls - Pittsburgh Steelers Sports Inc.; *pg.* 577, *pg.* 1578

Hwang, Albert, VP-Digital & Shopper Mktg-Household Cleaning Brands - Prestige Brands Holdings, Inc.; *pg.* 520, *pg.* 1345

Hwang, Frank, Sr Mgr-Social Media - The Timberland Company; *pg.* 1821, *pg.* 1039

Hwang, Shui, Mgr-Mktg-Global - Elizabeth Arden, Inc.; *pg.* 507, *pg.* 448

Hyatt, Atosa, Sr Mgr-Channel Mktg - Sage Software, Inc.; *pg.* 464, *pg.* 116

Hyatt, Rob, Exec Dir-Mktg Mgmt - AT&T; *pg.* 1865, *pg.* 258

Hyatt, Sara, Sr Mgr-Comm - Microsoft Corporation; *pg.* 435, *pg.* 1824

Hyde, Alicia, Dir-Sls-Intl - Qualstar Corporation; *pg.* 458, *pg.* 279

Hyde, April, Mgr-Adv & Promos - Grand Ole Opry; *pg.* 289, *pg.* 1651

Hyde, Jeannine Ginivan, Sr Mgr-Corp & Internal Comm - Volkswagen Group of America, Inc.; *pg.* 194, *pg.* 1785

Hyde, Russ, Sr Mgr-New Bus - Cigna Corporation; *pg.* 1197, *pg.* 338

Hyde, Tony, Sr Mgr-Publ - Chicago Professional Sports Limited Partnership; *pg.* 539, *pg.* 570

Hyder, Zeba, Head-Digital Mktg-Global Consumer Lines - American International Group, Inc.; *pg.* 1190, *pg.* 1193

Hydorn, Bret, VP-Mktg - CyberSource Corporation; *pg.* 381, *pg.* 216

Hyer, Tracy, Mgr-Direct Mktg - Sprint Corporation; *pg.* 1874, *pg.* 719

Hyland, Chris, Partner-Sls Bus & Mgr-Employee Comm - SanDisk Corporation; *pg.* 465, *pg.* 147

Hyland, Kelly, Mgr-Affiliate Mktg - AMC Networks Inc.; *pg.* 269, *pg.* 1189

Hyland, Mark, Sr VP-Sls-Global - QuickPlay Media Inc.; *pg.* 666, *pg.* 1941

Hyland, Mary, Mgr-Mktg - Nathan's Famous Inc.; *pg.* 1741, *pg.* 1171

Hyland, Scott, Dir-Mktg - The Davey Tree Expert Company; *pg.* 1794, *pg.* 1456

Hylek, Kristin, Mgr-Alliances & Brands-Brand PR & Reputation - McDonald's Corporation; *pg.* 1737, *pg.* 645

Hyler, Gerald C., Specialist-Field Mktg - The Northwestern Mutual Life Insurance Company; *pg.* 1212, *pg.* 1879

Hylton, Greg, VP-Premium Seating & Ticket Sls - Indianapolis Colts, Inc.; *pg.* 553, *pg.* 687

Hylton, Patrick, Assoc Dir-Immuno-Oncology Mktg-Melanoma - Bristol-Myers Squibb Company; *pg.* 1509, *pg.* 1206

Hyman, Danielle, Product Mgr-Mktg - Den-Mat Corporation; *pg.* 1522, *pg.* 271

Hyman, Michael, Sr VP-Sls - Scott's Liquid Gold-Inc.; *pg.* 335, *pg.* 323

Hyman, Ria, Sr Mgr-Mktg - Cisco Systems, Inc.; *pg.* 372, *pg.* 240

Hymas, Eric, Sr VP-Mdsg - SUPERVALU, Inc.; *pg.* 1035, *pg.* 924

Hynd, Jim, Div VP-Sls & Mktg - Abbott Laboratories; *pg.* 1484, *pg.* 551

Hynes, Matthew, Mgr-Production - Aerogroup International, Inc.; *pg.* 1803, *pg.* 1055

Hynes, Melissa, Mgr-Mktg - Citizens Financial Group, Inc.; *pg.* 737, *pg.* 1606

Hynes, Sean, VP-Sls - VTech Electronics North America, LLC; *pg.* 969, *pg.* 554

Hynes, Wade, Gen Mgr-Community Products & Svcs Canada-Sun Media - Quebecor Media Inc.; *pg.* 1679, *pg.* 1956

Hynninen, Kiera, Head-Mktg - Redbox Automated Retail, LLC; *pg.* 306, *pg.* 649

Hys, Darek, Mgr-Digital Mktg - Checkers Drive-In Restaurants, Inc.; *pg.* 1017, *pg.* 472

I

Iacovelli, Christopher, Sr Mgr-Digital Channels-North American Bus Analysis - TD Bank US Holding Company; *pg.* 809, *pg.* 1051

Iacoviello, John, Sr VP-Sls - BSH Home Appliances Corporation; *pg.* 53, *pg.* 108

Iacuzzo, Christine, VP-Adv & Mktg - Gucci America Inc.; *pg.* 6, *pg.* 1237

Iagnocco, Paul, Sr Dir-Digital Mktg Ops-Global - Kellogg Company; *pg.* 831, *pg.* 870

Iakoubianova-Lavery, Dessislava, Area Dir-Mktg-Oral Health & Nutrition - GlaxoSmithKline Consumer Healthcare; *pg.* 510, *pg.* 1554

Iams, Bryan, VP-Corp Comm, Mktg, Govt & Community Affairs - PPG Industries, Inc.; *pg.* 1445, *pg.* 1579

Ianello, Jeff, VP-Team Mktg & Bus Ops - National Basketball Association; *pg.* 566, *pg.* 1264

Iannello, Stephanie, Specialist-PR & Social Media - North Shore-LIJ Health System; *pg.* 1573, *pg.* 1162

Iannone, Kellie, Sr Mgr-Comm-Global - Newell Rubbermaid Inc.; *pg.* 1128, *pg.* 515

Iannucci, Donna, Sr VP-Mktg - The Hain Celestial Group, Inc.; *pg.* 860, *pg.* 1172

Iannuzzelli, Lisa, Sr Dir-Inquiry Optimization & Digital Mktg - DeVry Education Group Inc.; *pg.* 600, *pg.* 607

Iaquinto, Kevin, CMO & Exec VP - JDA Software Group, Inc.; *pg.* 423, *pg.* 22

Ibach, Nancy, Dir-Patient Strategy-Oncology Mktg - GlaxoSmithKline; *pg.* 1536, *pg.* 1565

Ibarra, Oscar, Dir-Intl Infrastructure Sls - LIGHTING SCIENCE GROUP CORPORATION; *pg.* 1301, *pg.* 467

Ibarra, Renato, Exec Mgr-Production - The Procter & Gamble Company; *pg.* 1129, *pg.* 1418

Ibe, Funbi, Sr Assoc Brand Mgr-Kraft Foods - Mondelez International; *pg.* 877, *pg.* 1344

Ibri, Thierry, VP-Mktg Foodservice Div - General Mills, Inc.; *pg.* 828, *pg.* 933

Ickovic, Caleb, Dir-Database Mktg - Pinnacle Entertainment, Inc.; *pg.* 576, *pg.* 1029

Iddings, Drew, Dir-Mktg-Promos & Plng - The Hershey Co.; *pg.* 1855, *pg.* 1538

Iddings, Drew, Dir-Mktg-Promos & Plng - Hershey Entertainment & Resorts Company; *pg.* 1094, *pg.* 1539

Iengo, Lauren, Mgr-Mktg Ops-Print, Pkg & eMail - J. Crew Group, Inc.; *pg.* 1773, *pg.* 1245

Ienna, Mike, Dir-Detroit Adv - Conde Nast Publications, Inc.; *pg.* 1629, *pg.* 1217

Ienna, Mike, Dir-Detroit Adv - Vogue Magazine; *pg.* 1700, *pg.* 1311

Ieradi, Tony, Sr Dir-Data Center Mgmt - AmerisourceBergen Corporation; *pg.* 1493, *pg.* 1522

Ierubino, Tony, CMO - Merichem Company; *pg.* 1172, *pg.* 1711

Ifcher, Nicole, Sr Dir-Worldwide Product Mktg - Herbalife International of America, Inc.; *pg.* 1541, *pg.* 132

Iglesias, Jorge, Mgr-Trade Mktg - Bacardi USA, Inc.; *pg.* 1956, *pg.* 417

Ignaszak, Jeffrey, VP-Mktg & Comm-Global - Kroll Inc.; *pg.* 425, *pg.* 1249

Ignatova, Yana, Head-Mktg-Northern Europe - Johnson & Johnson Inc.; *pg.* 1552, *pg.* 1923

Igoe, Brian, VP-Sls-ViewSonic Americas - ViewSonic Corporation; *pg.* 489, *pg.* 303

Igoe, Jessica, Head-Global Media & Mktg Partnerships-Google Play - Google Inc.; *pg.* 1249, *pg.* 153

Igrec, Frank, Dir-Mktg - Dick's Sporting Goods, Inc.; *pg.* 1832, *pg.* 1524

Ihler, Jon, VP-Sls, Mktg & Quality Control - MFA Oil Company; *pg.* 981, *pg.* 976

Ihrke, Jennifer L., Dir-Mktg & Affiliate Rels - DIRECTV Group Holdings, LLC; *pg.* 281, *pg.* 79

Ikanowicz, Aleksandra, Head-North America Mktg & Comml Markets - Motorola Solutions, Inc.; *pg.* 657, *pg.* 659

Ike, Tam, Specialist-Franchise Mktg - United States Postal Service; *pg.* 1009, *pg.* 406

Ikesaki, Scott, Mgr-Sls - Downtown Ford Sales Inc.; *pg.* 169, *pg.* 196

Ilagan, Ariel, Sr Mgr-Mktg Analytics - Ubisoft Inc.; *pg.* 589, *pg.* 229

Iler, Steve, Asst Dir-Mktg Tools - The Northwestern Mutual Life Insurance Company; *pg.* 1212, *pg.* 1879

Iles, David, Dir-Product Mgmt & Technical Mktg - Lenovo Group Ltd; *pg.* 427, *pg.* 1384

Iles, Gary, Sr VP-Sls & Mktg - GlowPoint, Inc.; *pg.* 401, *pg.* 1094

Ilg, Garrett J., Sr VP & Head-World Wide Enterprise Sls & Field Ops - Adobe Systems Incorporated; *pg.* 342, *pg.* 235

Ilias, Evan, Dir-Application Platform Sls & Mktg-Worldwide - Microsoft Corporation; *pg.* 435, *pg.* 1824

Iliffe-Moon, Sona, Mgr-PR Brand Affairs - Nestle USA, Inc.; *pg.* 883, *pg.* 96

Illingworth, James, Assoc Dir-Mktg-Shopper Mktg Target - The Procter & Gamble Company; *pg.* 1129, *pg.* 1418

Ilstrup, Tina, Acct Mgr-Integrated Mktg Comm - Land O'Lakes, Inc.; *pg.* 873, *pg.* 915

Im, Carol, Brand Mgr - DISH Network Corporation; *pg.* 283, *pg.* 325

Im, Cyrus, Acct Mgr-Global Sls - Starwood Hotels & Resorts Worldwide, Inc.; *pg.* 1114, *pg.* 378

Imai, Tsuneo, Gen Mgr & Sr Dir - Canon U.S.A., Inc.; *pg.* 1404, *pg.* 1178

Imam, Muhammad, Engr-Technical Mktg - Cisco Systems, Inc.; *pg.* 372, *pg.* 240

Imam, Mustafa, Strategist-Creative - Facebook, Inc.; *pg.* 1245, *pg.* 143

Imamura, Hiro, VP & Gen Mgr-Mktg - Canon U.S.A., Inc.; *pg.* 1404, *pg.* 1178

Imbao, Leslie, Category Mgr-Safety Products, Construction & Home Improvement - 3M Company; *pg.* 1142, *pg.* 956

Imbres, Megan, Dir-Mktg-North America - Netflix, Inc.; *pg.* 1269, *pg.* 141

Imbriaco, Alissa, Mgr-Field Mktg - Philips Lighting; *pg.* 1303, *pg.* 806

Imbrogno, Michelle, Exec Dir-Print & Integrated Sls - New York Magazine; *pg.* 1667, *pg.* 1269

Imhoff, Tim, Mgr-Mktg - Nestle USA, Inc.; *pg.* 883, *pg.* 96

Immaraju, John A., Dir-Comml Product Dev - American Vanguard Corporation; *pg.* 1793, *pg.* 165

Imperial, Johanna, Sr Acct Exec-Grp Sls - Arizona Diamondbacks; *pg.* 529, *pg.* 14

Imus, Ron, Corp Mgr-Mktg & Brand - Toyota Motor Sales,

U.S.A., Inc.; *pg.* 193, *pg.* 296
Inacker, Steve, Pres-Hospital Sls & Svcs - Cardinal Health, Inc.; *pg.* 1512, *pg.* 1448
Inderhees, Cora, Specialist-Brand Mktg-Head & Shoulders - The Procter & Gamble Company; *pg.* 1129, *pg.* 1418
Indianer, Brian, Analyst-Cheetos Mktg - PepsiCo, Inc.; *pg.* 259, *pg.* 1327
Indresovde, Erik, Global Product Mgr-AV - Black Box Corporation; *pg.* 361, *pg.* 1547
Inerfeld, Jonathan M., Mgr-Adv & Media - Ameriprise Financial, Inc.; *pg.* 715, *pg.* 930
Infante, Dominick, Mgr-Product Comm-Natl - Subaru of America, Inc.; *pg.* 191, *pg.* 1050
Infante, Nick, Sr Dir-Pub Affairs & Govt Rels - Wal-Mart Stores, Inc.; *pg.* 1790, *pg.* 29
Infanti, Daniel, Sr VP-Mktg & Adv - CIT GROUP INC.; *pg.* 735, *pg.* 1212
Ing, Olivia, Dir-Digital Mktg-Global - Tiffany & Co.; *pg.* 13, *pg.* 1299
Ing, Susan, Dir-Mktg - Bank of Hawaii Corporation; *pg.* 720, *pg.* 543
Ingala, Janine, Mgr-CRM Mktg - BMW of North America, LLC; *pg.* 166, *pg.* 1133
Ingalls, Nancy C., Head-Mktg Comm - Genworth Financial, Inc.; *pg.* 761, *pg.* 1802
Ingegneri, Paul, VP-Adv - The San Diego Union-Tribune, LLC; *pg.* 1682, *pg.* 208
Ingenito, Renee, Exec Dir-Natl Sls - Comcast Corporation; *pg.* 276, *pg.* 1560
Ingle, Casey, Sr Dir-Global Innovation - Libbey, Inc.; *pg.* 1126, *pg.* 1476
Ingle, Robin, Sr VP-Adv - TripAdvisor, Inc.; *pg.* 1926, *pg.* 835
Ingle, Stephanie, Sr Dir-Global Event Mktg & Customer Influence - Allscripts Healthcare Solutions, Inc.; *pg.* 1492, *pg.* 563
Ingles, Michelle, Sr Mgr-Digital Mktg - Experian Consumer Direct; *pg.* 1245, *pg.* 71
Inglis, Andrew, Sr VP-Card Products - Bank of America Global Wealth & Investment Management; *pg.* 720, *pg.* 789
Inglis, Greg, Sr Dir - National Hockey League; *pg.* 568, *pg.* 1265
Inglis, Jill, Mgr-Global Digital Mktg-Email Mktg, Mobile & Emerging Platforms - Accenture; *pg.* 1392, *pg.* 1186
Inglis, Traci, Sr VP-Mktg - JustFab, Inc.; *pg.* 27, *pg.* 80
Ingmire, Steve, Brand Mgr-Sheba & Wet Cat - Mars Petcare; *pg.* 1478, *pg.* 1633
Ingold, Kristin L., Coord-Mktg - Community Health Systems, Inc.; *pg.* 1516, *pg.* 1632
Ingols, Robin, Dir-Mktg Components - Forging Industry Association; *pg.* 141, *pg.* 1431
Ingraham, Bret, Assoc Mgr-PR - MATTEL, INC.; *pg.* 962, *pg.* 81
Ingraham, Meg, Dir-Mktg Svcs - The University of Virginia; *pg.* 610, *pg.* 1778
Ingram, Bev, Sr Dir-CMC Biopharma - Pfizer Inc.; *pg.* 1581, *pg.* 1278
Ingram, Bill, VP-Adobe Social & Adobe Analytics - Adobe Systems Incorporated; *pg.* 342, *pg.* 235
Ingram, Charlie, VP-Sls & Mktg - Eriez Manufacturing Co. Inc.; *pg.* 1335, *pg.* 1530
Ingram, Clark, Specialist-ECommerce Mktg - Zale Corporation; *pg.* 16, *pg.* 1724
Ingram, Randi, VP-Sls - Multimedia Games Inc.; *pg.* 442, *pg.* 1664
Ingram, Vimala, Mgr-Digital Media & Mktg - The ServiceMaster Company, LLC; *pg.* 335, *pg.* 1646
Ingrassia, Donna M., Mgr-Production-Mktg Svcs - The New York Times Company; *pg.* 1668, *pg.* 1270
Inman, Lauren, Specialist-Customer Mktg - Diageo North America Inc.; *pg.* 248, *pg.* 1223
Inman, Mike, Mgr-Production & Engrg - USG Corporation; *pg.* 118, *pg.* 594
Inman, Paul, VP-Customer Svc & Sls Centers - Camping World, Inc.; *pg.* 1830, *pg.* 725
Innes, Diana, Mgr-Online Mktg-Global Generation-Laureate Online Education - Laureate Education, Inc.; *pg.* 603, *pg.* 757
Innes, Rob, Sr Dir-Adv & CRM Sys - Time Inc.; *pg.* 1693, *pg.* 1300
Innes, Robin, Dir-PR - Cedar Point; *pg.* 537, *pg.* 1472
Inoff, Debbie, Sr Mgr-Mktg Comm - Leviton Manufacturing Company, Inc.; *pg.* 1301, *pg.* 1180
Inoue, Minoru, Engr-Mktg-Medium Voltage Power Products - ABB Inc.; *pg.* 64, *pg.* 1959
Inouye, Nancy, Mgr-Natl Mktg Comm-Scion - Toyota Motor Sales, U.S.A., Inc.; *pg.* 193, *pg.* 296
Inquimboy, Jon, Product Mgr - Esurance, Inc.; *pg.* 1243, *pg.* 217
Inselmann, Clinton, Grp Dir-Creative - State Farm Mutual Automobile Insurance Co.; *pg.* 1218, *pg.* 557
Insetta, Robyn, Coord-Admin-Customer Mktg - Unilever United States, Inc.; *pg.* 904, *pg.* 1061
Inskip, Paul, Exec VP-Sls & Mktg - Prym Consumer USA; *pg.* 698, *pg.* 1622
Intihar, Chris, VP-Mktg & Bus Dev - The Scotts Miracle-Gro Company; *pg.* 1799, *pg.* 1459
Intihar, Jessica, VP-Digital Mktg - The Walt Disney Company; *pg.* 317, *pg.* 52
Intihar, Katie, Sr Asst Brand Mgr-Skoal - Altria Group, Inc.; *pg.* 1893, *pg.* 1800
Intili, Dawn, Mgr-Natl Mktg-IoT Solutions-Emerging Devices & Apple - AT&T Mobility LLC; *pg.* 619, *pg.* 488
Inton, Maria, Mgr-Mktg Comm - Alcatel-Lucent; *pg.* 615, *pg.* 38
Intrieri, Frank, Jr., VP-Sls - Goodway Technologies Corporation; *pg.* 1341, *pg.* 374
Inwood, Greg, VP-Standby Power Products - Briggs & Stratton Corporation; *pg.* 201, *pg.* 1899
Inyart, Heather, Dir-Mktg - Lindt & Sprungli (USA) Inc.; *pg.* 1857, *pg.* 1039
Ioannides, Nektarios, Program Mgr-Bing Identity & Bing Social - Microsoft Corporation; *pg.* 435, *pg.* 1824
Ion, Michaela, Sr Mgr-CRM & Lifetime Value Mktg - Sony Electronics, Inc.; *pg.* 676, *pg.* 209
Iooss, Sarah, Sr VP-Partnerships & Client Strategy-Ad Sls - Viacom Inc.; *pg.* 316, *pg.* 1310
Ioriatti, Valerie C., Specialist-Mktg - Wells Fargo & Company; *pg.* 819, *pg.* 232
Iorio, Vincent, Mgr-Mktg Comm-Natl - Kubota Tractor Corporation; *pg.* 705, *pg.* 294
Ippolito, Ralph, Engr-Sls - EMCOR Services Northeast CommAir/BALCO; *pg.* 1071, *pg.* 847
Ippolito, Robert, Sr Dir-Comml Procurement - Johnson & Johnson; *pg.* 1549, *pg.* 1091
Iqbal, Arif M., Sr Mgr-Global Web Architecture - Avon Products, Inc.; *pg.* 500, *pg.* 1198
Iraca, Sean, Sr Dir-Cloud Innovation - Equinix, Inc.; *pg.* 394, *pg.* 190
Irani, Omar, Dir-Strategic Mktg - Honeywell International Inc.; *pg.* 407, *pg.* 1088
Irbe, Trisha, VP-Sls - Coleman Cable, Inc.; *pg.* 1324, *pg.* 665
Irby, Carri, Mgr-Mktg Svcs - Tenneco, Inc.; *pg.* 985, *pg.* 625
Irby, Mark, VP-Mktg - Publix Super Markets, Inc.; *pg.* 1031, *pg.* 437
Irby, Sarah, VP-Global Mktg-Tom Ford Beauty - The Estee Lauder Companies Inc.; *pg.* 508, *pg.* 1229
Irby, Tim, Dir-Mktg - University of Arkansas for Medical Sciences; *pg.* 608, *pg.* 34
Ireland, Anne B., VP-Sls Plng & Ops - CDW Corporation; *pg.* 370, *pg.* 663
Ireland, Lou, Sr Mgr-Mktg Comm - Dupont Pioneer; *pg.* 1795, *pg.* 708
Ireton, Daniel, Sr Mgr-Digital B2B & Corp Mktg - Vita-Mix Corporation; *pg.* 1139, *pg.* 1436
Ireton, Sean, Specialist-Digital Mktg - hhgregg, Inc.; *pg.* 56, *pg.* 686
Irizarry, Jose, Dir-News, Production & Community Rels - Univision Communications Inc.; *pg.* 683, *pg.* 1307
Irland, Daryl, Mgr-Mktg - Lands' End, Inc.; *pg.* 1776, *pg.* 1857
Irons, Kari Aront, Sr VP-Mktg-Journeys Grp - Genesco Inc.; *pg.* 1809, *pg.* 1650
Irons, Lisa M., Sr Mgr-Community Rels - Capital One Financial Corporation; *pg.* 730, *pg.* 1789
Irvin, Leslie, Asst Gen Mgr-Mdsg - The Gap, Inc.; *pg.* 1770, *pg.* 218
Irvin, Yvette, Head-Social Media & Mktg Innovations - Blue Cross & Blue Shield Association; *pg.* 1195, *pg.* 566
Irvine, Lori, Dir-Mktg & Comm - CH2M HILL Companies, Ltd.; *pg.* 75, *pg.* 325
Irving, Andy, Mgr-Partner Mktg - Xbox; *pg.* 970, *pg.* 1829
Irving, Anna Tolosa, VP & Mgr-Mdsg-Handbags-Omni Divisional - Saks Fifth Avenue, Inc.; *pg.* 1783, *pg.* 1287
Irving, Brian, Dir-Global Mktg - Airbnb, Inc.; *pg.* 1226, *pg.* 211
Irving, Drew, Dir-Innovation Svcs & Trade Mktg - Diageo North America Inc.; *pg.* 248, *pg.* 1223
Irving, Jack, Sr VP & Dir-Media - The Partnership at Drugfree.org; *pg.* 153, *pg.* 1276
Irving, Jenny, Mgr-Mktg - Autodesk Inc.; *pg.* 356, *pg.* 257
Irving, Susan, Sr Dir-Mktg - PepsiCo, Inc.; *pg.* 259, *pg.* 1327
Irwin, Brian, Dir-Mktg-Family Bus & Brand Trust - McDonald's Corporation; *pg.* 1737, *pg.* 645
Irwin, Evan, Sr Mgr-Digital Mktg-Europe - Netflix, Inc.; *pg.* 1269, *pg.* 141
Irwin, James, Sr Dir-Corp Bus Dev - A. Schulman, Inc.; *pg.* 1144, *pg.* 1452
Irwin, Libby, Dir-Product Mktg, CVS & Specialty - CVS Health Corporation; *pg.* 1765, *pg.* 1610
Irwin, Raymond James, Coord-Mktg & Comm - Sacramento Philharmonic Orchestra; *pg.* 579, *pg.* 197
Irwin, Tom, Mgr-Sls - J.D. Streett & Co., Inc.; *pg.* 980, *pg.* 988
Isaacs, Martin, Mgr-Mktg Comm & Wireline - Schlumberger Limited; *pg.* 801, *pg.* 1714
Isaacson, Gunnar, District Mgr-Sls - MiTek, Inc.; *pg.* 1056, *pg.* 975
Isaacson, Nate, Mgr-Social Enablement & Digital Mktg - The Guardian Life Insurance Company of America; *pg.* 1202, *pg.* 1237
Isaacson, Stephanie, Sr Mgr - PG&E Corporation; *pg.* 1949, *pg.* 224
Isaia, Peter, Category Dir-Global Procurement Creative Ideation Agencies - Diageo North America, Inc.; *pg.* 1961, *pg.* 361
Isaza, Diego, Sr Dir-Mktg-Twizzlers, Lancaster & Jolly Rancher - The Hershey Co.; *pg.* 1855, *pg.* 1538
Isenberg, Jason, Team Head-Retail & Trade-Comml Mktg - Puma North America, Inc.; *pg.* 1816, *pg.* 858
Isetts, Rodger, Product Mgr - Snap-on Incorporated; *pg.* 1062, *pg.* 1862
Isgrig, Mike, VP-Consumer Sls & Mktg-North America - Epson America Inc.; *pg.* 394, *pg.* 122
Isham, Ali, Dir-Mktg - Overhead Door Corporation; *pg.* 102, *pg.* 1725
Ishbia, Howard, Exec VP-Sls - Sherwood Food Distributors; *pg.* 1033, *pg.* 884
Isherwood, Kathy, Dir-Integrated Mktg - Dick's Sporting Goods, Inc.; *pg.* 1832, *pg.* 1524
Ishigami, Tak, Sr Mgr-Engrg-Kawasaki Rail Car - Kawasaki Heavy Industries (U.S.A.), Inc.; *pg.* 1352, *pg.* 1248
Isip, Vicki, VP-Mktg - Ghirardelli Chocolate Company; *pg.* 1854, *pg.* 252
Islam, Saqib, Chief Strategy Officer & Sr VP - Alexion Pharmaceuticals, Inc.; *pg.* 1489, *pg.* 341
Isler, Lanita, Sr Mgr-Channel Dev-Progressive Markets - Mars, Incorporated; *pg.* 1858, *pg.* 1792
Isley, Bill, Sr Mgr-Innovation Sys-Coffee R&D - The J.M. Smucker Company; *pg.* 865, *pg.* 1468
Isley, Don, Dir-Sls - WD-40 Company; *pg.* 337, *pg.* 210
Isley, Mary, Mgr-Media - Eden Foods Inc.; *pg.* 1019, *pg.* 875
Isling, Marvin, Sr Mgr-Digital Mktg - Accenture; *pg.* 1392, *pg.* 1186
Ismail, Rubina S., Sr Mgr-Medical Comm - Amgen Inc.; *pg.* 1493, *pg.* 291
Ismail, Sammy, Mgr-Mktg - The Lubrizol Corporation; *pg.* 1171, *pg.* 1481
Ismail, Ziad, Sr VP-Product & Engrg - Marchex, Inc.; *pg.* 1395, *pg.* 1837
Isom, Jeff, Sr Mgr-Mdse - V.F. Corporation; *pg.* 34, *pg.* 1376
Isom, Ron, Sr VP-Sls & Mktg - Naterra International Inc.; *pg.* 59, *pg.* 1684
Ison, Bryant, Dir-Brand Mktg-Global - PepsiCo, Inc.; *pg.* 259, *pg.* 1327
Israel, Carrie, Sr Dir - Yahoo! Inc.; *pg.* 1289, *pg.* 289
Israel, Laura, Brand Mgr-Dinner & Lunch LongHorn Steakhouse - Darden Restaurants, Inc.; *pg.* 1724, *pg.* 453
Israel, Laura, Brand Mgr - Olive Garden Italian Restaurant; *pg.* 1742, *pg.* 454
Israel, Tasha, Sr Mgr-B2B Mktg - Yahoo! Inc.; *pg.* 1289, *pg.* 289
Israll, Nicole, Brand Mgr-Colgate Toothpaste & Mouthwash - Colgate-Palmolive Company; *pg.* 504, *pg.* 1215
Isselmann, Erin, Dir-PR - Xerox Corporation; *pg.* 494, *pg.* 365
Isusi, Ignacio de, Dir-Sls Ops-LATAM - Harley-Davidson, Inc.; *pg.* 178, *pg.* 1874
Iten, Ann, Mgr-Product Mktg-Printer Supplies - Datamax Corporation; *pg.* 1633, *pg.* 453
Ito, Cameron, Mgr-Mktg - The Bartell Drug Company; *pg.* 1499, *pg.* 1833
Ito, Ken, Gen Mgr & Sr Dir - Canon U.S.A., Inc.; *pg.* 1404, *pg.* 1178
Ito, Kimberly, Mgr-Integrated Mktg - Qantas Airways - USA; *pg.* 1920, *pg.* 139
Ito, Stacie, Assoc Dir-Online Mktg - AT&T Mobility LLC; *pg.* 619, *pg.* 488
Ito, Stacie L., Assoc Dir-Online Mktg - AT&T; *pg.* 1865, *pg.* 258

First page reference indicates Business Class Edition
Second page reference indicates Geographic Edition

Ittel, Jeff, Sr VP-Supplier Mktg Avnet Embedded - Avnet, Inc.; *pg.* 622, *pg.* 15
Iturriaga-Yosifi, Mabel, Analyst-Mktg - State Farm Mutual Automobile Insurance Co.; *pg.* 1218, *pg.* 557
Itwaru, Ganesh, Specialist-Internet Mktg-Affiliate Mktg - Google Inc.; *pg.* 1249, *pg.* 153
Iuorio, Alex, Sr VP-Supplier Mktg - Avnet Electronics Marketing; *pg.* 622, *pg.* 15
Iverson, Alice, Sr Mgr-Print Production - The Boston Beer Company, Inc.; *pg.* 239, *pg.* 790
Iverson, Kayleigh, Asst Acct Mgr-Creative Svcs - Coach, Inc.; *pg.* 3, *pg.* 1214
Iverson, Kurt, Sr Mgr-Comm - The Gillette Company; *pg.* 509, *pg.* 795
Ives, Nat, Exec Editor - Advertising Age; *pg.* 1613, *pg.* 1187
Ives, Tobi Elizabeth, Sr Mgr-Production-New Mexico State Film Office - New Mexico Economic Development Department; *pg.* 1001, *pg.* 1136
Ivester, Devin, Dir-Mktg - Google Inc.; *pg.* 1249, *pg.* 153
Ivey, Angela, Dir-Mktg - World Golf Hall of Fame; *pg.* 595, *pg.* 461
Ivie, Koren, Brand Mgr-Mike & Ike & Hot Tamales - Just Born, Inc.; *pg.* 1857, *pg.* 1516
Ivins, David, Product Mgr-Global - Checkpoint Systems, Inc.; *pg.* 628, *pg.* 1559
Ivler, Loren, VP & Head-Bus-US Mktg - MasterCard Worldwide Inc.; *pg.* 780, *pg.* 988
Ivy, Greg, Product Mgr - Level 3 Communications, Inc.; *pg.* 1262, *pg.* 312
Iwami, Cindy, Coord-Mktg - Anaheim Ducks Hockey Club, LLC; *pg.* 528, *pg.* 42
Iwaniuk, Shannon, Sr Mgr-Internal Comm & Design Studio - Galderma Laboratories, L.P.; *pg.* 1532, *pg.* 1695
Iwata, Jon, Sr VP-Mktg, Comm & Citizenship - International Business Machines Corporation; *pg.* 418, *pg.* 1138
Iwata, Tomiko, Sr VP-Special Events-Creative Svcs Grp - Fox Broadcasting Company; *pg.* 287, *pg.* 130
Iyengar, Raj, Product Mgr - Google Inc.; *pg.* 1249, *pg.* 153
Iyer, Adith, Sr Product Mgr - eBay Inc.; *pg.* 1240, *pg.* 243
Iyer, Anjali, Sr Mgr-Rewards Mktg - Marriott International, Inc.; *pg.* 1102, *pg.* 764
Iyer, Jay, Sr Dir-IR - SanDisk Corporation; *pg.* 465, *pg.* 147
Iyer, Shankar, VP-Products-End User Computing - VMware, Inc.; *pg.* 490, *pg.* 179
Iyer, Venkat, VP-Product Mgmt-Cloud for Industries - SAP America, Inc.; *pg.* 466, *pg.* 1557
Izaguirre, Roberto, VP-Sls-Global - Arrow Fastener Company, Inc.; *pg.* 1042, *pg.* 1118
Izatt, Matthew, Product Mgr - Google Inc.; *pg.* 1249, *pg.* 153
Izmirlian, Alex, VP-Global Plng Sls & Trading - Golden Peanut Company, L.L.C.; *pg.* 1854, *pg.* 484
Izurieta, Deanna, Reg Media Buyer - AMERICAN TIRE DISTRIBUTORS HOLDINGS, INC.; *pg.* 199, *pg.* 1379
Izzo, Lenny, Pres-Legal Media - American Lawyer Media, Inc.; *pg.* 1615, *pg.* 1193

J

Jabbour, Hind, Coord-Mktg - Williamsport Symphony Orchestra; *pg.* 592, *pg.* 1595
Jabcon, Jessica, Dir-Mktg - Thermos L.L.C.; *pg.* 61, *pg.* 660
Jaber, Lloyd, Dir-Mdsg - BeautiControl Cosmetics, Inc.; *pg.* 501, *pg.* 1669
Jabes, Gillian, Brand Mgr-Oral Care Innovation - Colgate-Palmolive Company; *pg.* 504, *pg.* 1215
Jablonski, Ilene, VP-Mktg - Mack-Cali Realty Corporation; *pg.* 1102, *pg.* 1056
Jablonski, Jennifer D., Sr Specialist-Product Mktg - Valassis Communications, Inc.; *pg.* 1287, *pg.* 897
Jacabacci, Michele, Mgr-Strategic Mktg - Bauer Publishing USA; *pg.* 1620, *pg.* 1059
Jachino, Randi, Dir-Mktg-Global Toothbrushes Div - Colgate-Palmolive Company; *pg.* 504, *pg.* 1215
Jachowicz, Lisa, Dir-Mktg-Comml Bus - Cigna Corporation; *pg.* 1197, *pg.* 338
Jacinto, Matthew, Sr Designer-Creative Svcs - American Airlines Inc.; *pg.* 1898, *pg.* 1693
Jack, Steven, Mgr-Americas Sls - PPG Industries, Inc.; *pg.* 1445, *pg.* 1579
Jackman, Boris, Exec VP-Refining & Mktg - Suncor Energy Inc.; *pg.* 985, *pg.* 1905
Jackman, Gina, Sr Mgr-Mktg - Align Technology, Inc.; *pg.* 1489, *pg.* 237
Jackman, Katie, Dir-Mktg & Comm - Alley Theatre; *pg.* 527, *pg.* 1699
Jacko, John H., Jr., CMO & VP - Kennametal Inc.; *pg.* 1052, *pg.* 1547
Jackovitz, Joyce, Sr Mgr-Events Mktg - DIRECTV Group Holdings, LLC; *pg.* 281, *pg.* 79
Jackse, Tina, VP-Sls - Henkel Corporation; *pg.* 1165, *pg.* 1535
Jackson, Allan, VP-Sls - Bumble Bee Foods LLC; *pg.* 842, *pg.* 201
Jackson, Amanda, Mgr-Social Media - Bonnier Corporation; *pg.* 1622, *pg.* 480
Jackson, Amy Flynn, Sr Dir-Brand Strategy & Consumer Mktg-TripIt & ExpenseIt - Concur Technologies, Inc.; *pg.* 1236, *pg.* 1813
Jackson, Andrea, Mgr-Mktg-Tire Pros - AMERICAN TIRE DISTRIBUTORS HOLDINGS, INC.; *pg.* 199, *pg.* 1379
Jackson, Annie, Mgr-Brdcst Creative - The Home Depot, Inc.; *pg.* 1050, *pg.* 510
Jackson, Anthony, Dir-Wireless & RF Product Mktg - GigOptix, Inc.; *pg.* 400, *pg.* 245
Jackson, Ashley, Coord- & Mktg Comm - BROOKDALE SENIOR LIVING INC.; *pg.* 1511, *pg.* 1627
Jackson, Beth, Dir-Media & IT - Scripps Networks Interactive, Inc.; *pg.* 1279, *pg.* 1638
Jackson, Brian, Dir-Sls & Mktg - CSX Transportation, Inc.; *pg.* 1904, *pg.* 432
Jackson, Brooks, Assoc Dir-Creative - Apple Inc.; *pg.* 350, *pg.* 73
Jackson, Candice, Mgr-Sls Ops Broker Sls - Aflac Incorporated; *pg.* 1188, *pg.* 527
Jackson, Chris, Mgr-Mktg & Customer Rels - Dahle USA; *pg.* 382, *pg.* 1038
Jackson, Chris, Sr Mgr-Product-Decorative Home - Target Corporation; *pg.* 1786, *pg.* 942
Jackson, Christopher Brett, VP-Sls & Mktg-Oncology Sys - Varian Medical Systems, Inc.; *pg.* 1434, *pg.* 178
Jackson, Daniel, Sr VP-Sls - NetMotion Wireless, Inc.; *pg.* 445, *pg.* 1837
Jackson, Danielle, Dir-Mktg - QUALCOMM Incorporated; *pg.* 1873, *pg.* 207
Jackson, Dave, Mgr-Mktg - Manulife Financial Corporation; *pg.* 778, *pg.* 1939
Jackson, David, Dir-Sls & Mktg-Stanford University Press - Stanford University; *pg.* 607, *pg.* 280
Jackson, Dayna, Sr Mgr-Field Mktg-Pub Sector & Alternate Channels - Level 3 Communications, Inc.; *pg.* 1262, *pg.* 312
Jackson, Diego, Area Dir-Mktg-Latin America - GlaxoSmithKline; *pg.* 1536, *pg.* 1389
Jackson, Diego, Area Dir-Mktg-Latin America - GlaxoSmithKline Consumer Healthcare; *pg.* 510, *pg.* 1554
Jackson, Harold L., Sr Mgr-Analyst Rels-Worldwide - Hewlett-Packard Company; *pg.* 404, *pg.* 175
Jackson, Holly, Brand Mgr-Activia - The Dannon Company, Inc.; *pg.* 851, *pg.* 1351
Jackson, Janelle, Mgr-Digital Mktg & E-commerce - Polar Electro Inc.; *pg.* 664, *pg.* 1173
Jackson, Janna, Mgr-Adv - Neiman Marcus, Inc.; *pg.* 30, *pg.* 1684
Jackson, Jeanne, Pres-Global Product & Mdsg - NIKE, Inc.; *pg.* 1812, *pg.* 1492
Jackson, Jeff, VP-US Mktg-Boys - Hasbro, Inc.; *pg.* 954, *pg.* 1603
Jackson, Jerri, Mgr-Media Rels - University of Arkansas for Medical Sciences; *pg.* 608, *pg.* 34
Jackson, Justin, Mgr-Mktg Programs - Advance Auto Parts, Inc.; *pg.* 197, *pg.* 1805
Jackson, Kelly, Brand Mgr-COTTONELLE - Kimberly-Clark Corporation; *pg.* 1461, *pg.* 1720
Jackson, Kelsey, Coord-PR-Pottery Barn Brands - Williams-Sonoma, Inc.; *pg.* 1140, *pg.* 234
Jackson, Korri R., Sr Mgr-Mktg - Laureate Education, Inc.; *pg.* 603, *pg.* 757
Jackson, Kristi, Specialist-Digital Mktg-North America Digital Commerce - NIKE, Inc.; *pg.* 1812, *pg.* 1492
Jackson, Kristin, Mgr-Mdse - Neiman Marcus, Inc.; *pg.* 30, *pg.* 1684
Jackson, Kristine, Dir-Strategic Comm & Partnership Mktg - Touchstone Energy Cooperatives; *pg.* 1953, *pg.* 1775
Jackson, Luciana, Sr Mgr-Online Mktg - Match.Com, LLC; *pg.* 1265, *pg.* 1683
Jackson, Marques, Brand Mgr-Sports & Entertainment Mktg - MillerCoors LLC; *pg.* 255, *pg.* 582
Jackson, Meredith, Specialist-eMail Mktg - The Sports Authority, Inc.; *pg.* 1846, *pg.* 326
Jackson, Mike, VP-Sls Effectiveness - McKesson Corporation; *pg.* 1560, *pg.* 222
Jackson, Mike, VP-Sls - Wright & McGill Co.; *pg.* 1848, *pg.* 324
Jackson, Monique, Brand Mgr - Pepperidge Farm, Inc.; *pg.* 888, *pg.* 363
Jackson, Patrick L., Dir-Promos & Mktg-Cumulus Brdcst San Francisco Branch - Cumulus Media Inc.; *pg.* 280, *pg.* 503
Jackson, Regina, VP-Product Dev & Mktg - Warner Press, Inc.; *pg.* 1701, *pg.* 673
Jackson, Rex, Dir-Mktg & Sls-LEGOLAND Florida - LEGOLAND California LLC; *pg.* 557, *pg.* 59
Jackson, Rob, VP-Sls - Gaming Partners International Corporation; *pg.* 954, *pg.* 1024
Jackson, Rob, Dir-Mktg - McDonald's Corporation; *pg.* 1737, *pg.* 645
Jackson, Rosie Nagra, Dir-Mktg-UK Food - Mars, Incorporated; *pg.* 1858, *pg.* 1792
Jackson, Sherita, VP-Digital Sls - Meredith Corporation; *pg.* 1663, *pg.* 705
Jackson, Stephanie, Dir-Field Mktg-West & Reg Mgr-Mktg - General Growth Properties, Inc.; *pg.* 1093, *pg.* 574
Jackson, Stephen, Sr Mgr-Sls-Natl - Greater Raleigh Convention & Visitors Bureau; *pg.* 994, *pg.* 1387
Jackson, Ted, Sr Dir-Direct to Consumer - Under Armour, Inc.; *pg.* 49, *pg.* 759
Jackson, Tiffany, Mgr-B2B Mktg Strategy & Corp Products-Global Sls - Delta Air Lines, Inc.; *pg.* 1905, *pg.* 503
Jackson-Luth, Jennifer, Mgr-Mktg Comm - Wm. Wrigley Jr. Company; *pg.* 1863, *pg.* 596
Jacob, Sally, Sr Dir-Comm - Pfizer Inc.; *pg.* 1581, *pg.* 1278
Jacobs, Amy, Area Head-Field Mktg - Domino's Pizza, Inc.; *pg.* 1726, *pg.* 865
Jacobs, Andrea, Mgr-Mktg-American Blue Ribbon Holdings - O'Charley's Inc.; *pg.* 1742, *pg.* 1653
Jacobs, Bob, Dir-Creative - Lands' End, Inc.; *pg.* 1776, *pg.* 1857
Jacobs, David, Sr VP-Publr Sls & Bus Dev - AOL Inc.; *pg.* 1229, *pg.* 1195
Jacobs, Debi, Sr Mgr-Sls & Procurement - The Kroger Co.; *pg.* 1025, *pg.* 1416
Jacobs, Gerry, Sr Mgr-Field Mktg - Checkers Drive-In Restaurants, Inc.; *pg.* 1017, *pg.* 472
Jacobs, Howard, Exec VP-Mktg & Sls - New York Rangers Hockey Club; *pg.* 570, *pg.* 1269
Jacobs, Jack H., VP-Mktg & Product Mgmt - Honeywell Aerospace Electronic Systems; *pg.* 228, *pg.* 17
Jacobs, John, Dir-PR - Sacramento Kings; *pg.* 579, *pg.* 197
Jacobs, Jolene, Assoc Dir-Mktg-Nutrition - Leprino Foods Company; *pg.* 874, *pg.* 320
Jacobs, Joshua, Asst Media Planner-Digital - Palisades Media Group, Inc.; *pg.* 452, *pg.* 275
Jacobs, Jurjen, VP-Mktg-Global - Velcro USA Inc.; *pg.* 699, *pg.* 1036
Jacobs, Katie, Specialist-Mktg-MileagePlus Loyalty Programs - United Airlines, Inc.; *pg.* 1927, *pg.* 593
Jacobs, Linda, Mgr-Mdse - Johnson Smith Company; *pg.* 1774, *pg.* 414
Jacobs, Lindsay, Sr Mgr-Pkg Procurement & Beverages - The Kraft Heinz Company; *pg.* 871, *pg.* 641
Jacobs, Marc, VP-Sls - Redco Foods, Inc.; *pg.* 891, *pg.* 1174
Jacobs, Mark, VP-Digital Mktg Strategy-Umpqua Bank - Umpqua Holdings Corporation; *pg.* 813, *pg.* 1507
Jacobs, Matthew, VP-Mktg & Digital Strategy - salesforce.com, inc.; *pg.* 1278, *pg.* 226
Jacobs, Melissa, Dir-Mktg Comm-Global - Sigma-Aldrich Corporation; *pg.* 1181, *pg.* 1003
Jacobs, Michael, Mgr-Govt & Fleet Sls - Kawasaki Motors Corp., U.S.A.; *pg.* 1708, *pg.* 111
Jacobs, Michele L., Sr Mgr-Mktg - IBM; *pg.* 410, *pg.* 1449
Jacobs, Naomi, Mgr-Social Mktg - QVC Inc; *pg.* 305, *pg.* 1593
Jacobs, Neil, Engr-New Product Introduction - Polycom, Inc.; *pg.* 664, *pg.* 249
Jacobs, Pamela, Head-Digital Mktg Strategy-Ecosystem Dev - International Business Machines Corporation; *pg.* 418, *pg.* 1138
Jacobs, Peter, Sr VP-Mutual Fund Product Mgmt - Northern Trust Corporation; *pg.* 787, *pg.* 585
Jacobs, Phil, VP-Sls-Bandai America - Bandai America Incorporated; *pg.* 950, *pg.* 75
Jacobs, Shelby, Specialist-Social Media Customer Engagement - Toms Shoe's Inc; *pg.* 1821, *pg.* 276
Jacobs, Stacy, Area Dir-Mktg & Bus Dev - Simon Property Group, Inc.; *pg.* 1112, *pg.* 690

Jacobsen, Amy, Mgr-Sls - Naples Beach Hotel & Golf Club; *pg.* 1106, *pg.* 451
Jacobsen, Chris, VP-Mktg - Texas Roadhouse, Inc.; *pg.* 1753, *pg.* 738
Jacobsen, Michael, Sr Dir-Corp Comm - Diebold, Incorporated; *pg.* 387, *pg.* 1407
Jacobsen, Rich, Pres/CEO-Time Warner Retail Sls & Mktg - Time Inc.; *pg.* 1693, *pg.* 1300
Jacobson, Andrew, Mgr-Mobile Mktg - Neiman Marcus, Inc.; *pg.* 30, *pg.* 1684
Jacobson, Angela, Sr Mgr-Mktg & Mdse - GameStop Corp.; *pg.* 399, *pg.* 1699
Jacobson, Candice, Mgr-PR - Mattel Games/Puzzles; *pg.* 962, *pg.* 80
Jacobson, Candice, Mgr-PR - MATTEL, INC.; *pg.* 962, *pg.* 81
Jacobson, Carrie, Dir-Natl Distr Ops & Mktg - Cellco Partnership; *pg.* 1869, *pg.* 1042
Jacobson, Emily, Mgr-Media-Global - Calvin Klein, Inc.; *pg.* 20, *pg.* 1209
Jacobson, Jennifer, Specialist-eMail Mktg - GNC Holdings Inc.; *pg.* 1537, *pg.* 1576
Jacobson, Joe, Dir-Mktg - Concur Technologies, Inc.; *pg.* 1236, *pg.* 1813
Jacobson, John, VP-Sls & Mktg - The DoALL Company; *pg.* 1329, *pg.* 670
Jacobson, Patricia M., Specialist-Reporting-Mktg Automation - ABB Inc.; *pg.* 1309, *pg.* 1359
Jacobson, Priya, VP-Sls - A.H. Schreiber Co., Inc.; *pg.* 17, *pg.* 1188
Jacobson, Violette, Product Mgr-Intl - United States Postal Service; *pg.* 1009, *pg.* 406
Jacobus, Brad, Sr Dir-Mktg - O'Charley's Inc.; *pg.* 1742, *pg.* 1653
Jacoby, Alisa, Dir-Mktg-Tata Global Beverages - Eight O'Clock Coffee; *pg.* 250, *pg.* 1086
Jacoby, Chad, Sr Mgr-Mktg-Nissan Crossover SUVs - Nissan North America, Inc.; *pg.* 186, *pg.* 1633
Jacoby, Judy, Dir-Adv - The Knopf Doubleday Group; *pg.* 1657, *pg.* 1249
Jacoby, Julie, Sr Mgr-Event Mktg-Fairchild Fashion Media - Conde Nast Publications, Inc.; *pg.* 1629, *pg.* 1217
Jacot, Stan, VP-Mktg - Gruma Corporation; *pg.* 860, *pg.* 1720
Jacques, Attica Alexis, VP-Global Mktg-Gap, Inc - The Gap, Inc.; *pg.* 1770, *pg.* 218
Jacques, Sue, Dir-Comml Bank Mktg Res - Capital One Financial Corporation; *pg.* 730, *pg.* 1789
Jadan, Tommy, Dir-Mktg - Happy's Pizza LLC; *pg.* 1730, *pg.* 886
Jadon, Abhishek, Sr Mgr-Digital Mktg - The Gatorade Company; *pg.* 251, *pg.* 574
Jaeckel, Bonnie, Mgr-Comm & Mktg Svcs-Global - Xerox Corporation; *pg.* 494, *pg.* 365
Jaeger, Steve, Pers-Direct Mktg & Exec VP - Quad/Graphics, Inc.; *pg.* 1468, *pg.* 1896
Jafari, Ali, VP-Direct Sls-Europe - Twitter, Inc.; *pg.* 1285, *pg.* 228
Jaffe, Chris, VP-Product Innovation - Netflix, Inc.; *pg.* 1269, *pg.* 141
Jaffe, Lee, Chief Creative Officer - Brilliant Digital; *pg.* 1233, *pg.* 281
Jaffin, Jay, VP-Mktg Comm - Verizon Communications Inc.; *pg.* 1875, *pg.* 1309
Jaffke, John, Sr Dir-Sls Ops - The Kraft Heinz Company; *pg.* 871, *pg.* 641
Jagannath, A L, Dir-Mktg-India & SAARC - VMware, Inc.; *pg.* 490, *pg.* 179
Jagels, Heather, VP-Creative-Home Category - Scripps Networks Interactive, Inc.; *pg.* 1279, *pg.* 1638
Jagger, Norm, Sr VP-Sls & Mktg - Holcim (U.S.) Inc.; *pg.* 1346, *pg.* 885
Jagher, Christine, Dir-Mktg - E&J Gallo Winery; *pg.* 1962, *pg.* 149
Jagielski, Monica, Coord-Mktg-Global - Calvin Klein, Inc.; *pg.* 20, *pg.* 1209
Jagoda, Steve, Sr Mgr-Customer Strategy & Dev - Del Monte Foods, Inc.; *pg.* 852, *pg.* 304
Jagpal, Shireen, Sr Dir - Valeant Pharmaceuticals International; *pg.* 1605, *pg.* 1047
Jahn, Alison, Dir-Global Mktg & Comm OGM-PR - Univar Inc.; *pg.* 1184, *pg.* 1829
Jahn, Mark, Mgr-Product & Mktg-Natl - Toyota Motor Sales, U.S.A., Inc.; *pg.* 193, *pg.* 296
Jahnke, Doug, Mgr-Product Mktg - Eaton Corporation; *pg.* 1331, *pg.* 1429
Jahnke, Kim, Mgr-Channel Mktg - Honeywell International Inc.; *pg.* 407, *pg.* 1088
Jahnke, Tim, Mgr-Natl Sls-SG Retail - Mueller Sports Medicine, Inc.; *pg.* 1570, *pg.* 1887
Jahns, Kathy, VP-Western Sls Reg - Metro Newspapers Advertising Services, Inc.; *pg.* 1665, *pg.* 223
Jain, Ajay, Dir-Product Mktg - Rambus Inc.; *pg.* 459, *pg.* 288
Jain, Akash, Sr Dir-Bus Dev & Partnerships-India - National Basketball Association; *pg.* 566, *pg.* 1264
Jain, Amit, Sr VP-Sls & Mktg - Omnicare, Inc; *pg.* 1578, *pg.* 1418
Jain, Amit, Sr Mgr-Design-SMTS - Texas Instruments Incorporated; *pg.* 679, *pg.* 1688
Jain, Anjali, Head-Mktg-USA & Dir-Canada & Investment - Australian Trade Commission; *pg.* 989, *pg.* 1198
Jain, Dilip C., VP-Tech & Asia Sls - Kyanite Mining Corporation; *pg.* 1170, *pg.* 1779
Jain, Gaurav, Head-Product Mktg & Sls-Mobile Adv - eBay Inc.; *pg.* 1240, *pg.* 243
Jain, Jay, Sr VP-Mktg - Citigroup Inc.; *pg.* 735, *pg.* 1212
Jain, Naveen, Mng Dir-Product Industries Digital Customer - Accenture; *pg.* 1392, *pg.* 1186
Jain, Neeta, Product Mgr-Ad Platform - Amazon.com, Inc.; *pg.* 1226, *pg.* 1831
Jain, Raj, Dir-Global Mktg-Footcare - Bayer Healthcare Consumer Care Division; *pg.* 1500, *pg.* 1087
Jain, Rikhi, Product Mktg Mgr-Mobile Monetization - Facebook, Inc.; *pg.* 1245, *pg.* 143
Jain, Susan M., VP-Worldwide Portfolio & Content Mktg-Global Tech Svcs - IBM; *pg.* 410, *pg.* 1449
Jain, Tarun, Grp Product Mgr - Twitter, Inc.; *pg.* 1285, *pg.* 228
Jain, Tina, Coord-Social Media - National Hockey League; *pg.* 568, *pg.* 1265
Jaitly, Rishi, VP-Media-Asia Pacific & Middle East - Twitter, Inc.; *pg.* 1285, *pg.* 228
Jakab, Shauntinez L., Mgr-Product Mktg - F5 Networks, Inc.; *pg.* 396, *pg.* 1835
Jaknunas, Greg, Sr Product Mgr-Tech - IHS Inc.; *pg.* 1652, *pg.* 326
Jakober, Lorenz, Sr Mgr-Product Mktg - Akamai Technologies, Inc.; *pg.* 1226, *pg.* 807
Jakosalem, Karl, Product Mgr - CDW Corporation; *pg.* 370, *pg.* 663
Jaksch, George, Sr Dir-Corp Responsibility & Pub Affairs - Chiquita Brands International, Inc.; *pg.* 847, *pg.* 1365
Jakubick, Jake, Specialist-Adv Graphics - The Gorman-Rupp Company; *pg.* 1341, *pg.* 1458
Jakubowski, Thomas, Dir-Sls - EDGAR Online, Inc.; *pg.* 746, *pg.* 776
Jalil, Arzinda, Mgr-Adv & Pub Svc Campaign - The Humane Society of the United States; *pg.* 143, *pg.* 400
Jamal, Safir, Sr Asst Brand Mgr-Global - Gillette; *pg.* 1536, *pg.* 795
Jamerson, Hank, VP-Sls & Mktg - Kyanite Mining Corporation; *pg.* 1170, *pg.* 1779
James, Angela F., Mgr-Mktg-Atlanta Reg - Comcast Corporation; *pg.* 276, *pg.* 1560
James, Anne, Mgr-Mktg-Social Media Adv - Amazon.com, Inc.; *pg.* 1226, *pg.* 1831
James, Ben, Mgr-Product Mktg - CompassLearning, Inc.; *pg.* 1628, *pg.* 1661
James, Chou, Analyst-Mktg - Intel Corporation; *pg.* 645, *pg.* 266
James, David, VP-Mktg - CARSTAR; *pg.* 168, *pg.* 718
James, David, Dir-Product Mktg - Lithium Technologies; *pg.* 1263, *pg.* 221
James, Ephraim, Mgr-Production - Ancient American; *pg.* 1616, *pg.* 1856
James, Freddy, Sr VP-Program Dev & Production - Home & Garden Television; *pg.* 290, *pg.* 1637
James, George, Mgr-Retail Adv - Athens Banner-Herald; *pg.* 1618, *pg.* 486
James, J. Todd, VP-Sls-Global - Haworth, Inc.; *pg.* 402, *pg.* 891
James, Jeff, VP-Mktg - Thomas Nelson Inc.; *pg.* 1692, *pg.* 1654
James, Julie, Dir-Adv & Comm - Frontier Airlines, Inc.; *pg.* 1909, *pg.* 319
James, Karen, Mgr-Mktg-Dealer Svcs - Bass Pro Shops, Inc.; *pg.* 1826, *pg.* 1006
James, Kenne, Sr Mgr-Golf Bus Dev - The Toro Company; *pg.* 1065, *pg.* 918
James, Lara, VP-Brand Mktg - Massachusetts Mutual Life Insurance Company; *pg.* 1207, *pg.* 845
James, Laurence, Product Mgr - NetApp, Inc.; *pg.* 444, *pg.* 287
James, Lori L., Acct Exec-Charter Media - Charter Communications, Inc.; *pg.* 274, *pg.* 372
James, Marilyn, Mgr-Sls Support & Special Sections - The Daily Breeze; *pg.* 1632, *pg.* 293
James, Marq, Sr VP-Sls - GuideOne Insurance Company; *pg.* 1202, *pg.* 713
James, Matt, Sr VP-Ops & Mdsg - Redbox Automated Retail, LLC; *pg.* 306, *pg.* 649
James, Megan, Mgr-Sls & Mktg Solutions-Global - Facebook, Inc.; *pg.* 1245, *pg.* 143
James, Michael, Sr Mgr-UX Information Architecture - American Airlines Inc.; *pg.* 1898, *pg.* 1693
James, Nicholas, VP-Mktg - Shaw Ross International Importers; *pg.* 1970, *pg.* 449
James, Paul P., Dir-Motorcycle Product Plng - Harley-Davidson, Inc.; *pg.* 178, *pg.* 1874
James, Ryan, Team Head-US Mass Merchant Channel & Sr Dir-Sls - Electronic Arts Inc.; *pg.* 951, *pg.* 189
James, Sherianne, VP-Mktg-Global - Transitions Optical, Inc.; *pg.* 1432, *pg.* 458
James, Talia, Assoc Coord-PR - QUALCOMM Incorporated; *pg.* 1873, *pg.* 207
James, Terri, Dir-Mktg - American Drew; *pg.* 912, *pg.* 1374
James, Tonya, VP-Product Mgmt - Equifax Inc.; *pg.* 748, *pg.* 504
James, Trevor, Head-Mktg-Zappos Insights - Zappos.com, Inc.; *pg.* 1291, *pg.* 1030
Jameson, Fiona, Dir-Media - Turner Broadcasting System, Inc.; *pg.* 314, *pg.* 521
Jamias, Chris, Mgr-Mktg-CRM - 24 Hour Fitness Worldwide Inc.; *pg.* 526, *pg.* 258
Jamieson, Scott, Dir-Product Mgmt-NATO - Cooper Tire & Rubber Company; *pg.* 1881, *pg.* 1453
Jamison, Dan, Mgr-Mktg Comm - Dupont Pioneer; *pg.* 1795, *pg.* 708
Jamison, Linda, Exec Dir-Mass Merchant Sls - HBG Books, Inc.; *pg.* 1648, *pg.* 1238
Jamison, Rachel, Mgr-Mktg-CRM - Cost Plus World Market; *pg.* 921, *pg.* 170
Jamison, Shivika, Brand Mgr-Smithfield Foods - John Morrell Food Group; *pg.* 866, *pg.* 628
Jamison, Tanya, Dir-Mktg-Worldwide - Electro Rent Corporation; *pg.* 390, *pg.* 300
Jamison, Tim, Product Mgr - Confluence Watersports Co. Inc.; *pg.* 1706, *pg.* 1617
Jampol, Scott, Sr VP-Mktg - OpenTable, Inc.; *pg.* 450, *pg.* 224
Jamshed, Muhammad Shayan, Specialist-Digital Mktg - HSBC Bank USA; *pg.* 767, *pg.* 1241
Janasz, Kathleen, Dir-PR-Cardiac & Vascular Grp - Medtronic, Inc.; *pg.* 1564, *pg.* 939
Janco, Kevin, VP-Corp Mktg - Terex Corporation; *pg.* 1381, *pg.* 384
Janczewski, Lindsay, Sr Mgr-News Digital Sponsorship Strategy - Cable News Network LP; *pg.* 1624, *pg.* 1208
Jandrain, Jay, Exec VP-Sls - Butterball, LLC; *pg.* 843, *pg.* 1385
Jandrain, Molly Mckenna, Dir-PR - McDonald's Corporation; *pg.* 1737, *pg.* 645
Jandris, Julie, Coord-Mdsg - Eby-Brown Co.; *pg.* 1767, *pg.* 636
Janendo, Janice, Mgr-Adv Mktg Ops - Investors Business Daily, Inc.; *pg.* 1653, *pg.* 133
Janes, Grace, Brand Mgr - The Procter & Gamble Company; *pg.* 1129, *pg.* 1418
Janes, Todd, Dir-Product Dev - Lexmark International, Inc.; *pg.* 427, *pg.* 730
Janetos, Marlene, VP-Visitor Svcs, Mktg & Comm - Museum of Discovery & Science, Inc.; *pg.* 565, *pg.* 425
Jang, Rose, Engr-Technical Mktg - Cisco Systems, Inc.; *pg.* 372, *pg.* 240
Jangro, Kristin, Sr Mgr-Mktg & MarketPlace - Constant Contact, Inc.; *pg.* 379, *pg.* 850
Jani, Nileem, Dir-Consumer Insight, New Product Strategy & Innovation - Cellco Partnership; *pg.* 1869, *pg.* 1042
Janik, Jem, Mgr-Social Media Mktg - Alcatel-Lucent; *pg.* 615, *pg.* 1094
Janis, Amy, Sr Mgr-B2B Market Res - Yahoo! Inc.; *pg.* 1289, *pg.* 289
Janis, Andrew, Sr Mgr-Digital Analytics - Ameriprise Financial, Inc.; *pg.* 715, *pg.* 930
Janisch, Susan, Supvr-Sls - A.J. Jersey Inc.; *pg.* 1310, *pg.* 1123
Janke, Melissa K., Sr Mgr-HR & Mktg - Whirlpool Corporation; *pg.* 62, *pg.* 872

First page reference indicates Business Class Edition
Second page reference indicates Geographic Edition

Janke, Rick A., Brand Mgr-Premium - Tyson Foods, Inc.; *pg.* 902, *pg.* 35
Jankoski, Joseph, VP-Mdsg - Hunter Douglas, Inc.; *pg.* 928, *pg.* 1320
Jankovsky, Brian, Head-Publr Sls-Entertainment Partnerships - Google Inc.; *pg.* 1249, *pg.* 153
Jankowski, Ben, Grp Head-Media-Global - MasterCard Incorporated; *pg.* 779, *pg.* 1325
Jankowski, Benjamin, Grp Head-Media-Global - MasterCard International, Inc.; *pg.* 780, *pg.* 1326
Jankowski, Benjamin, Grp Head-Media-Global - MasterCard Worldwide Inc.; *pg.* 780, *pg.* 988
Jankowski, Kristin, Mgr-Mktg Comm - Johnson Outdoors Inc.; *pg.* 1837, *pg.* 1888
Jankowski, Rich, Sr Dir-Media Rels & Team Svcs - St. Louis Blues Hockey Club, LLC; *pg.* 585, *pg.* 1003
Jankowsky, Paul Von, Mgr-Mktg-Chevrolet Crossovers - General Motors Company; *pg.* 175, *pg.* 881
Jannasch, Jim, Mgr-Strategic Operational Dev-Firestone Building Products - Firestone Industrial Products Division; *pg.* 1882, *pg.* 686
Janneau, Laurent, Dir-Adv-Europe - Netflix, Inc.; *pg.* 1269, *pg.* 141
Janness, Laura, Chief Strategy Officer - Bai Brands; *pg.* 238, *pg.* 1073
Jannetty, Megan, Acct Mgr-Enterprise-Mktg Solutions - LinkedIn Corporation; *pg.* 1262, *pg.* 160
Janosch, Maureen, Mgr-Mktg - Littelfuse, Inc.; *pg.* 1301, *pg.* 580
Janow, Suzanne, Sr Mgr-Integrated Mktg - American Media, Inc.; *pg.* 1615, *pg.* 410
Janowich, Stephanie, Media Buyer - Jo-Ann Stores LLC; *pg.* 696, *pg.* 1455
Janowski, Jennifer, Dir-Product Mgmt - GE Healthcare Technologies; *pg.* 1533, *pg.* 1897
Jansen, David, VP-Mktg - Vermillion, Inc.; *pg.* 1435, *pg.* 1667
Jansen, Jim, Head-Industry-Buy-Side Sls-USA - Google Inc.; *pg.* 1249, *pg.* 153
Jansen, Katherine M., Sr Mgr-Bus Dev - Digital Insight; *pg.* 744, *pg.* 189
Jansen, Knud, Product Mgr-Machinery Controls & Automation - ABB Inc. - Automation Technologies Instrumentation Products; *pg.* 1398, *pg.* 1590
Jansen, Laurie, Dir-Global Indus Mktg - Siemens Process Industries and Drives; *pg.* 673, *pg.* 485
Jansen, Matt, Mgr-Web Mktg - Gordon Food Service Inc.; *pg.* 1021, *pg.* 913
Jansen, Svend, Mgr-Global PR-Southern Comfort & Tuaca - Brown-Forman Corporation; *pg.* 1958, *pg.* 732
Janson, Angela, Sr Specialist-Mktg Comm - Ceridian Corporation; *pg.* 371, *pg.* 932
Janssen, Hallie, VP-Mktg - Oregonian Publishing Co.; *pg.* 1673, *pg.* 1504
Janssen, Michael, Mgr-Oracle CRM Application Sls - Oracle Corporation; *pg.* 450, *pg.* 191
Jantos, Jackie, VP-Creative & Brand Strategy - Spotify; *pg.* 1282, *pg.* 1295
Jantzi, Kara, Sr Mgr-Retail Mktg - Nintendo of America, Inc.; *pg.* 965, *pg.* 1829
January, Michelle, Brand Mgr-Pur - L Brands, Inc.; *pg.* 1776, *pg.* 1441
Janveja, Saloni, Dir-Mktg-CRM & Social - Ally Financial Inc.; *pg.* 711, *pg.* 878
Janvier, Jamie, Sr Mgr-Mktg - MAXIMUS, Inc.; *pg.* 780, *pg.* 1799
Janz, Greta, VP-Mktg - Foster Farms; *pg.* 856, *pg.* 122
Janzen, Steve, Mgr-Mktg Comm - Micron Technology, Inc.; *pg.* 435, *pg.* 547
Jaquez, Frank, Sr Dir-Learning & Dev-Global - Flextronics International Ltd.; *pg.* 81, *pg.* 245
Jaquez, Frank, Sr Mgr-Learning & Dev - The Kraft Heinz Company; *pg.* 870, *pg.* 1577
Jaquez, Jessica, Coord-Mktg-Intl - JAKKS Pacific, Inc.; *pg.* 960, *pg.* 142
Jaramillo, Juan, VP-Product - Skulpt Inc.; *pg.* 1594, *pg.* 419
Jaramillo, Maria, Mgr-Mktg - General Mills, Inc.; *pg.* 828, *pg.* 933
Jaramillo, Victor, Sr Mgr-Mktg - MoneyGram International, Inc.; *pg.* 783, *pg.* 1684
Jaramillo-Saa, Karina, Dir-Mktg Ops-Latin America - Harley-Davidson, Inc.; *pg.* 178, *pg.* 1874
Jaras, Dainius, Sr VP & Dir-Creative - Pace; *pg.* 1918, *pg.* 553
Jarcik, Kasey, Sr Dir-Fin - Oakland Athletics Limited Partnership; *pg.* 571, *pg.* 172
Jardine, Milene, Product Dir-Men's Tailored, Shoes & Accessories - Macy's East; *pg.* 1777, *pg.* 1254
Jardon, Ryan, Product Mgr-Seeding - Deere & Company; *pg.* 703, *pg.* 632
Jarer, Jaime, Brand Mgr-ZICAM - Matrixx Initiatives, Inc.; *pg.* 1559, *pg.* 23
Jarjosa, Chris, Mgr-Engineered Wood Products - Boise Cascade; *pg.* 1453, *pg.* 788
Jarlock, Danielle O., Sr Mgr-Brand Dev - The Home Depot, Inc.; *pg.* 1050, *pg.* 510
Jarman, Ian, Mgr-Enterprise Sys Mktg - International Business Machines Corporation; *pg.* 418, *pg.* 1138
Jarman, Jim, Dir-Mktg - Nilfisk-Advance, Inc.; *pg.* 332, *pg.* 953
Jarosch, Ali, Mgr-Digital & Tech Mktg - Andersen Corporation; *pg.* 67, *pg.* 916
Jaroslawski, Gayle, Brand Mgr - Valeant Pharmaceuticals International, Inc.; *pg.* 1605, *pg.* 1957
Jarosz, Tracey, Sr Dir-Bus Intelligence & Analytics - Canadian Imperial Bank of Commerce; *pg.* 729, *pg.* 1935
Jaroszewski, Brian, Sr Mgr-Product Line - Vitesse Semiconductor Corporation; *pg.* 686, *pg.* 57
Jarquin, Darling, Mgr-Multicultural Mktg - Florida Marlins, L.P.; *pg.* 548, *pg.* 442
Jarrard, Leslie, Dir-Interactive Mktg - Premium Franchise Brands LLC; *pg.* 333, *pg.* 485
Jarratt, John, Exec VP-Sls & Mktg - PVH Neckwear Group; *pg.* 46, *pg.* 139
Jarratt, Marissa, Sr Dir-Innovation Mktg - PepsiCo, Inc.; *pg.* 259, *pg.* 1327
Jarrault, Olivier M., Grp Pres-Engineered Products & Solutions & Exec VP - Alcoa Inc.; *pg.* 65, *pg.* 1188
Jarrell, Bill, VP-Ops & Mktg - Brennan Industries Inc.; *pg.* 1319, *pg.* 1429
Jarrell, Dayle, Product Dir - GlaxoSmithKline; *pg.* 1536, *pg.* 1389
Jarrell, Laura, Mgr-Adv - United Bankshares, Inc.; *pg.* 813, *pg.* 1849
Jarrett, Jeff, Dir-Mktg-Duracell - The Procter & Gamble Company; *pg.* 1129, *pg.* 1418
Jarrett, Jennifer Gibb, Mgr-Sls - Waldorf Astoria Naples; *pg.* 1118, *pg.* 451
Jarrett, Joy, Sr Dir-Mktg Svcs - Community Health Systems, Inc.; *pg.* 1516, *pg.* 1632
Jarrett, Paul, VP & Sr Product Mgr - JPMorgan Chase & Co.; *pg.* 772, *pg.* 1246
Jarrett, Richard, Dir-Mktg & Bus Dev-Global - Praxair, Inc.; *pg.* 1178, *pg.* 344
Jarvey, Natalie, Writer-Digital Media - The Hollywood Reporter Inc.; *pg.* 1650, *pg.* 133
Jarvis, Angela, Sr Mgr-Integrated Media - Capella Education Company; *pg.* 599, *pg.* 931
Jarvis, Patrick, Sr VP-Mktg & Comm - Battelle Memorial Institute; *pg.* 1401, *pg.* 1437
Jarvis, Ron, VP-Mdsg & Sustainability - The Home Depot, Inc.; *pg.* 1050, *pg.* 510
Jarvis, Scott, Mgr-Mktg & Bus Dev - PostNet International Franchise Corporation; *pg.* 456, *pg.* 322
Jarzab, Anna, Sr Mgr-Digital & Social Mktg - Penguin Random House; *pg.* 1675, *pg.* 1276
Jarzab, Anna, Sr Mgr-Digital & Social Mktg-Penguin Grp USA - Penguin Random House; *pg.* 1675, *pg.* 1276
Jarzabek, Christina, VP & Mgr-Private Banking Product & Channel - BMO Harris Bank N.A.; *pg.* 725, *pg.* 567
Jarzabek, Marcy, Asst Mgr-Mktg - Rich Products Corporation; *pg.* 892, *pg.* 1150
Jasco, Tricia, Sr Mgr-Adv - Dassault Falcon Jet Corp.; *pg.* 227, *pg.* 1122
Jashnani, Yogi, Sr Dir - Capital One Financial Corporation; *pg.* 730, *pg.* 1789
Jasinek, Matthew, Specialist-Mktg - Omnicell Inc.; *pg.* 1578, *pg.* 161
Jasinski, Christopher, Head-Mktg Technologist & Social Media - Amway Corporation; *pg.* 326, *pg.* 864
Jasinski, Jennifer, Mgr-Content Mktg - SPS COMMERCE, INC.; *pg.* 472, *pg.* 942
Jasmin, Karen, Dir-Mktg-Americas - iRobot Corp.; *pg.* 1418, *pg.* 785
Jasmin, Kevin, Sr Mgr-Brand Strategy - TD Ameritrade Holding Corporation; *pg.* 808, *pg.* 1018
Jason, Dianna, VP-Mktg - KPWR-FM; *pg.* 294, *pg.* 52
Jason, Julie, Sr Mgr-Mktg - T-Mobile US, Inc.; *pg.* 676, *pg.* 1816
Jass, Kelsey, Specialist-Product Mktg - Deluxe Corporation; *pg.* 1634, *pg.* 964
Jassal, Manpreet, Mgr-Mktg - Gartner, Inc.; *pg.* 1248, *pg.* 374
Jasuja, Amit, Sr VP-Dev Identity Mgmt & Security Products - Oracle Corporation; *pg.* 450, *pg.* 191
Jasyk, Andrew, Mgr-Mktg - The Major Automotive Companies, Inc.; *pg.* 183, *pg.* 1175
Jatania, Madhavi, Mgr-Oncology Mktg - Pfizer Inc.; *pg.* 1581, *pg.* 1278
Jatia, Sid, VP-Direct-To-Consumer, Products & Strategy - Under Armour, Inc.; *pg.* 49, *pg.* 759
Jatkevicius, Patricia D., Sr VP-Mktg - Liberty Bank Inc.; *pg.* 776, *pg.* 356
Jaubert, Frederic, Reg Mgr-Sls-France Spain ME - Dynisco Instruments LLC; *pg.* 1526, *pg.* 823
Jauquet, Kevin, Sr Mgr-Global Mktg Res & Analytics - Kimberly-Clark Corporation; *pg.* 1461, *pg.* 1720
Javaid, Omar, Chief Product Officer - Vonage Holdings Corp.; *pg.* 686, *pg.* 1074
Javor, Andrea, Sr Dir-Global Digital & Media - Beam Suntory Inc.; *pg.* 1957, *pg.* 599
Jawetz, Gil, Designer-Digital Media-Global Investment Svcs - T. Rowe Price Group Inc.; *pg.* 808, *pg.* 759
Jawor, Jennifer, Principal Mgr-Field Mktg-Fin Svcs - Informatica Corporation; *pg.* 414, *pg.* 190
Jaworski, Susan, Specialist-Mktg - La-Z-Boy Incorporated; *pg.* 932, *pg.* 901
Jax, Tim, Brand Mgr-HK Anderson & Private Brand Pretzels - ConAgra Foods, Inc.; *pg.* 826, *pg.* 1014
Jaxheimer, Sarah, Dir-Wholesale Online Strategy & Mktg - Ralph Lauren Corporation; *pg.* 46, *pg.* 1284
Jay, Caleb, Sr Dir-Legal Affairs & Assoc Gen Counsel - Arizona Diamondbacks; *pg.* 529, *pg.* 14
Jay, Stephen, Mgr-Field Mktg & Promos - Shell Oil Company; *pg.* 984, *pg.* 1714
Jayanth, Vignesh, Sr Product Mgr - Bose Corporation; *pg.* 626, *pg.* 820
Jayaraman, Jay, VP-Global Mktg-Oral Care - Colgate-Palmolive Company; *pg.* 504, *pg.* 1215
Jaynes, Mike, VP-Sls & Product Integrity - Marcos Pizza Inc.; *pg.* 1737, *pg.* 1476
Jayson, Erica, Assoc Dir-Mktg-Women & Co - Citigroup Inc.; *pg.* 735, *pg.* 1212
Jazayeri, Mike, Product Dir-Cardboard - Google Inc.; *pg.* 1249, *pg.* 153
Jean-Jacques, Michele, Brand Mgr-Emilio Pucci, Chloe & Salvatore Ferragamo - Marchon Eyewear, Inc.; *pg.* 1421, *pg.* 1180
Jeancolas, Hugues, Sr Product Mgr-Apex - MSC Software Corporation; *pg.* 441, *pg.* 262
Jeckell, Barry, Specialist-Social Media - ShopRite Supermarkets, Inc.; *pg.* 1033, *pg.* 1160
Jecki, Chantal, Coord-Mktg & Sls - Valeant Pharmaceuticals International, Inc.; *pg.* 1605, *pg.* 1957
Jedrzejek, Steve, Mgr-Mktg - Nufarm Americas Inc; *pg.* 1798, *pg.* 552
Jee, Dan, Dir-Intl Mktg - Gilt Groupe Inc.; *pg.* 24, *pg.* 1234
Jeff, Steven, VP-Integrated & Strategic Mktg-CBS Television Stations - CBS Broadcasting Inc.; *pg.* 273, *pg.* 1210
Jeff, Steven, VP-Integrated & Strategic Mktg-CBS Television Stations - CBS Corporation; *pg.* 273, *pg.* 1210
Jefferies, Sandra, Specialist-Mktg & Proposal - BE Aerospace, Inc.; *pg.* 224, *pg.* 478
Jefferis, Lori, Product Mgr-Enwisen Product Strategy - Infor; *pg.* 414, *pg.* 484
Jeffers, Alan, Mgr-Media Rels - Exxon Mobil Corporation; *pg.* 977, *pg.* 1718
Jeffers, Chris, VP-Mktg - Keeney Manufacturing Company; *pg.* 90, *pg.* 360
Jeffers, Karen H., Specialist-Mktg Comm - UTC Aerospace Systems; *pg.* 236, *pg.* 1369
Jeffers, Rich, Dir-Media Rels - Darden Restaurants, Inc.; *pg.* 1724, *pg.* 453
Jeffers, Terry, Mgr-Mktg - ABB Inc.; *pg.* 1309, *pg.* 1359
Jefferson, Elwood, Reg Mgr-Sls-Western - Flanders Corporation; *pg.* 1336, *pg.* 1392
Jeffrey, Ashley, Brand Mgr-Private - Michaels Stores, Inc.; *pg.* 1127, *pg.* 1722
Jeffrey, Laura, Dir-Mktg - bebe stores, inc.; *pg.* 19, *pg.* 49
Jeffrey, Rick, Sls Dir-Completions & Production - Baker Hughes Incorporated; *pg.* 1315, *pg.* 1700
Jeffreys, Mark, Assoc Dir-Mktg-Gillette North America - The Procter & Gamble Company; *pg.* 1129, *pg.* 1418
Jeffries, Bryan, Dir-Mktg - Cinemark Holdings, Inc.; *pg.* 540, *pg.* 1729
Jeffries, David, Mgr-Mktg-ANZ - Invacare Corporation; *pg.* 1546, *pg.* 1451

Jeffries, Jon, VP & Gen Mgr-Sls - Great Dane Trailers; pg. 1707, pg. 539
Jeffs, Ryan, Specialist-Sls & Mktg Support - Affymetrix, Inc.; pg. 1487, pg. 263
Jeffs, Tony, Dir-Mktg - Cisco Systems, Inc.; pg. 372, pg. 240
Jefson, Sam, Specialist-PR - Winnebago Industries, Inc.; pg. 1712, pg. 707
Jelenic, Lee, Mgr-Lincoln Mktg - Ford Motor Company; pg. 172, pg. 876
Jelinek, Rich, Dir-Commodity Product Mktg - CME Group, Inc.; pg. 738, pg. 571
Jenest, Shannon, Dir-Mktg Comm & Strategy - Philips Electronics North America; pg. 662, pg. 782
Jeniece, Vaughn, Sr Mgr-Mktg - AMC, Inc.; pg. 1759, pg. 487
Jenkins, Abigail, Mgr-Mktg - Pfizer Inc.; pg. 1581, pg. 1278
Jenkins, Adam, Dir-Digital Mktg - SunPower Corporation; pg. 1952, pg. 250
Jenkins, Anne, Dir-Shopper Mktg - Kimberly-Clark Corporation; pg. 1461, pg. 1720
Jenkins, Bill, Exec VP-Sls - Kawasaki Motors Corp., U.S.A.; pg. 1708, pg. 111
Jenkins, Carol, Mgr-Sls - Beach Products, Inc.; pg. 1501, pg. 471
Jenkins, Cassie, Sr Mgr-Customer Mktg - T-Mobile US, Inc.; pg. 676, pg. 1816
Jenkins, Chris, Exec Dir-Media Rels - Buffalo Bills, Inc.; pg. 535, pg. 1319
Jenkins, Cindy, Supvr-Mktg Dev - 3M Company; pg. 1142, pg. 956
Jenkins, David, Dir-Digital Mktg - EIS, Inc.; pg. 80, pg. 504
Jenkins, Doug, Sr VP-Products & Svcs Engrg - EBSCO Information Services Walpole; pg. 1638, pg. 849
Jenkins, Eben, Gen Mgr-Video Product Line-Tektronix - Danaher Corporation; pg. 1044, pg. 397
Jenkins, Fred, Exec VP-Sls - Mergent, Inc.; pg. 1664, pg. 1616
Jenkins, Glynn, Dir-Comm & PR - The Kroger Co.; pg. 1025, pg. 1416
Jenkins, Jamey, Mgr-Adv - The Gaston Gazette; pg. 1644, pg. 1373
Jenkins, Joel, Dir-Corp Mktg - Community Newspapers Inc.; pg. 1628, pg. 486
Jenkins, Julienne, Mgr-Social Media Mktg - TELENAV, INC.; pg. 678, pg. 288
Jenkins, Lauren, Acct Mgr-Mktg - Ingram Micro Inc.; pg. 415, pg. 261
Jenkins, Mark, Mgr-Field Mktg-Chevrolet - General Motors Company; pg. 175, pg. 881
Jenkins, Mary A., Sr Dir-Sls Ops - AT&T; pg. 1865, pg. 258
Jenkins, Matt, Sr Mgr-Mktg Bus Performance & Sale Plng - Southwest Airlines Co.; pg. 1923, pg. 1687
Jenkins, Patricia Trish, Mgr-Adv - Cynthiana Publishing Co.; pg. 1632, pg. 726
Jenkins, Richie, Sr Dir-Foodservice Mktg - Butterball, LLC; pg. 843, pg. 1385
Jenkins, Rob, Dir-Mktg & Consumer Sls - Rev-A-Shelf; pg. 1060, pg. 738
Jenkins, Russell, Reg Mgr-Sls - Bassett Furniture Industries, Incorporated; pg. 916, pg. 1776
Jenkins, Sophia C., Sr Mgr-Clinical Comm - Baxter International Inc.; pg. 1499, pg. 599
Jenkins, Stuart, Sr VP-Innovation & Product Dev - Deckers Outdoor Corporation; pg. 1807, pg. 100
Jenkins, Tim, Sr VP-Sls & Mktg-Europe - Symmetry Medical Inc.; pg. 1600, pg. 699
Jenkins, Tricia, Mgr-Media & Comm - The Procter & Gamble Company; pg. 1129, pg. 1418
Jenkins-Blum, Robyn, Corp Mgr-PR - Cisco Systems, Inc.; pg. 372, pg. 240
Jenner, Stephen H., VP-Mktg - Zogenix, Inc.; pg. 1612, pg. 211
Jennings, Allan L., Sr VP-Products & Solutions Dev - Stratus Technologies, Inc.; pg. 477, pg. 832
Jennings, Ashley, Brand Mgr - Long John Silver's, LLC; pg. 1736, pg. 736
Jennings, Ben, Dir-Events & Mktg - The Wichita Eagle; pg. 1702, pg. 724
Jennings, Brian, Exec VP-Mktg - National Hockey League; pg. 568, pg. 1265
Jennings, Brigette, Sr Mgr-Mktg - Genesco Inc.; pg. 1809, pg. 1650
Jennings, Carolyn, Sr Mgr-Adv-Global - Avon Products, Inc.; pg. 500, pg. 1198
Jennings, Charlie, Mgr-Sls-Natl - DIT-MCO International Corporation; pg. 634, pg. 982
Jennings, David, Dir-Creative & Digital - Fossil Group, Inc.; pg. 5, pg. 1735
Jennings, Evelyn, VP-Sls Comml - Acme United Corporation; pg. 1040, pg. 346
Jennings, Jean, Dir-Sls-Intl - Institute of Electrical and Electronics Engineers, Inc.; pg. 144, pg. 1109
Jennings, Stacy, Dir-Mktg - Savannah Morning News; pg. 1683, pg. 540
Jennings, Steve, VP-Sls - Goody Products, Inc.; pg. 510, pg. 509
Jennings, Susan, VP-Corp Comm & Mktg - EdR Trust; pg. 1090, pg. 1642
Jennison, Paul, VP-Govt Sls & New Bus Dev - L-3 Wescam Inc.; pg. 1419, pg. 1919
Jenny, Jennifer, Mgr-Mktg-Retail Natl Accounts - McKesson Corporation; pg. 1560, pg. 222
Jensen, Brett C., Asst VP-Sls - The Kansas City Southern Railway Company; pg. 1913, pg. 985
Jensen, Brian, Sr VP-Mktg - Firstbank Holding Company of Colorado, Inc.; pg. 758, pg. 333
Jensen, Carrol, VP-Product Implementation - Assurant Health; pg. 1193, pg. 1873
Jensen, Clay, VP-Ticket Sls & VIP Svcs - Jazz Basketball Investors, Inc.; pg. 554, pg. 1759
Jensen, Doug, VP-CRM & Corp Mktg Analytics - The Estee Lauder Companies Inc.; pg. 508, pg. 1229
Jensen, Eric, Sr Mgr-Mktg - Amgen Inc.; pg. 1493, pg. 291
Jensen, Eric, Mgr-Mktg-HGTV, DIY Network & Great American Country - Scripps Networks Interactive, Inc.; pg. 1279, pg. 1638
Jensen, Erica, Sr Mgr-Integrated Mktg Comm - General Mills, Inc.; pg. 828, pg. 933
Jensen, Erik, Sr Dir-Brand Engagement - Denny's, Inc.; pg. 1725, pg. 1622
Jensen, Flemming, Mgr-Mktg & PR - CenturyLink, Inc; pg. 1870, pg. 317
Jensen, Jen, Dir-Mktg - Best Buy Co., Inc.; pg. 1761, pg. 954
Jensen, Jeremy, Program Mgr-Worldwide Tech Mktg-HP Indigo - Hewlett-Packard Company; pg. 404, pg. 175
Jensen, Jerry, Dir-Sls & Mktg - Benchmark Hospitality International Inc.; pg. 1081, pg. 1747
Jensen, Jessica, Dir-Social Media-Global - QUALCOMM Incorporated; pg. 1873, pg. 207
Jensen, Julia, VP-Intl PR - MATTEL, INC.; pg. 962, pg. 81
Jensen, Leticia, Dir-Sls-Brazil - THE DOW CHEMICAL COMPANY; pg. 1157, pg. 898
Jensen, Linda, Dir-Mktg - Six Flags Over Georgia, Inc.; pg. 583, pg. 525
Jensen, Mark A., Dir-Platform Mktg - Xilinx, Inc.; pg. 496, pg. 252
Jensen, Marn, Dir-Creative - Hallmark Cards, Inc.; pg. 1646, pg. 983
Jensen, Pamela H., Dir-Natl Sls-Western Reg & Principal-Registered - MetLife, Inc.; pg. 1208, pg. 1258
Jensen, Ryan, Engr-PR Test Sys - Medtronic, Inc.; pg. 1564, pg. 939
Jensen, Sarah, Dir-Mktg - Unilever United States, Inc.; pg. 904, pg. 1061
Jenssen, Dave, VP & Mgr-OOH Adv & Digital Signage - Truven Health Analytics; pg. 486, pg. 331
Jentgen, Fred, Mgr-PC Mktg - Intel Corporation; pg. 645, pg. 266
Jeo, Nate, Dir-Online Mktg, Paid Search Mktg & Display Retargeting - Overstock.com, Inc.; pg. 1273, pg. 1760
Jerald, Mitra, Sr Dir-Bus Dev & Strategic Plng - Turner Broadcasting System, Inc.; pg. 314, pg. 521
Jeremiah, John, Sr Mgr-Product Mktg - Hewlett-Packard Company; pg. 404, pg. 175
Jernejec, Adam, Specialist-Mobile Mktg - WebMD Health Corporation; pg. 1288, pg. 1313
Jerome, Cathy, Sr Mgr-Partnership Mktg - Baltimore Orioles, L.P.; pg. 532, pg. 755
Jerscheid, Todd, Dir-Mall Mktg & Bus Dev - Simon Property Group, Inc.; pg. 1112, pg. 690
Jerse, Rachael, Rep-Sls Dev - Citrix Online LLC; pg. 1235, pg. 99
Jesko, Mark, VP-Sls, Mktg & Svcs-Network Power-GNB Industrial Power - Exide Technologies; pg. 204, pg. 483
Jesse, Sam, Mgr-Product Mktg - Google Inc.; pg. 1249, pg. 153
Jessen, Paul, Brand Mgr-Personal Care Innovation - Tom's of Maine, Inc.; pg. 523, pg. 750
Jessup, Chris, Sr VP-Sls & Mktg-MRO Div - AAR Corp.; pg. 223, pg. 671
Jessup, Edward J., Jr., VP-Mktg & Sls - W.R. Case & Sons Cutlery Company; pg. 1141, pg. 1518
Jessup, Jennifer, Dir-Sls - Jacksonville Symphony Association; pg. 554, pg. 434
Jessup, Shannon, Sr VP-Sls - Tapjoy, Inc.; pg. 1396, pg. 228
Jesus, Manuel De, Mgr-Digital Mktg Delivery - Johnson & Johnson; pg. 1549, pg. 1091
Jesus, Yvette De, Sr Mgr-Mktg-Multicultural Market - The Allstate Corporation; pg. 1189, pg. 639
Jeszenszky, Paul, Dir-Online Mktg & Media - Airbnb, Inc.; pg. 1226, pg. 211
Jetley, Nupur, Assoc Mgr-Retail Mktg - Activision Blizzard, Inc.; pg. 948, pg. 271
Jett, Raymond, Engr-Technical Mktg - Cisco Systems, Inc.; pg. 372, pg. 240
Jett, Steve, Mgr-Mktg-Natl - Lexus Division; pg. 182, pg. 294
Jette, Chris, Dir-Corp Mktg-Digital - American Media, Inc.; pg. 1615, pg. 410
Jette, Julie, Dir-Media Rels & Publications - Tufts Medical Center; pg. 1603, pg. 801
Jew, Christine, Asst Mgr-Product Plng - Hyundai Motor America; pg. 179, pg. 89
Jewel, Jerry, Sr VP-Ops & Sls - Sun Communities, Inc.; pg. 1115, pg. 907
Jewell, Rand, Mgr-Mktg-Southeastern Zone - Canon U.S.A., Inc.; pg. 1404, pg. 1178
Jewell, Tiara, Mgr-Digital Mktg-AnnTaylor.com - Ann Inc.; pg. 18, pg. 1195
Jewett, Adrienne, Media Buyer - Valassis; pg. 1698, pg. 386
Jewett, Daniel, VP-Product Mgmt - Tableau Software, Inc.; pg. 481, pg. 1841
Jewett, Tara, Reg Sls Dir-Immunology - Genentech, Inc.; pg. 1533, pg. 279
Jeziorowski, Nicole, Asst Mgr-Mktg-Baseball - New Era Cap Company Inc.; pg. 1840, pg. 1155
Jeznach, Christopher, Mgr-Automotive Sls-US - Spirol International Corporation; pg. 1378, pg. 345
Jezyk, Matt, Sr Mgr-Product Line-AEC Conceptual Design Products - Autodesk Inc.; pg. 356, pg. 257
Jha, Miku, Product Mgr - International Business Machines Corporation; pg. 418, pg. 1138
Jhaveri, Kate, Sr Dir-Consumer Mktg - Twitter, Inc.; pg. 1285, pg. 228
Jhung, Daniel, Dir-Mktg - Nestle USA, Inc.; pg. 883, pg. 96
Jia, James, Sr Mgr - Microsemi Corporation; pg. 435, pg. 41
Jiang, James, Mgr-Product Res - The Progressive Corporation; pg. 1214, pg. 1463
Jiang, Michelle, Dir-Mktg-China - The J.M. Smucker Company; pg. 865, pg. 1468
Jiang, Minyang, Mgr-Sls Zone-Detroit - Ford Motor Company; pg. 172, pg. 876
Jiannas, Nick, VP-Sls & Mktg - Stihl, Inc.; pg. 1064, pg. 1810
Jikaria, Neha, Brand Mgr - The Dannon Company, Inc.; pg. 851, pg. 1351
Jilek, Kristen, VP-Sls Pro - Boston Private; pg. 726, pg. 791
Jillson, Lisa, Dir-Mktg - The Allstate Corporation; pg. 1189, pg. 639
Jimenez, Edgar, Mgr-Sls-Western Zone - Hitachi America, Ltd.; pg. 642, pg. 1344
Jimenez, Frank, Sr Dir-Insights Driven Performance & Retail Evolution - The Hershey Co.; pg. 1855, pg. 1538
Jimenez, Jaime, Pres-Univision Local Media - Univision Communications Inc.; pg. 683, pg. 1307
Jimenez, Kristen, Sr Mgr-Leadership Comm - Coca-Cola Refreshments USA, Inc.; pg. 247, pg. 500
Jimenez, Matthew, Mgr-Media & Brand Adv - Capital One Bank (USA), N.A.; pg. 730, pg. 1789
Jimenez, Micaela, Coord-PR - eHealth, Inc.; pg. 1242, pg. 153
Jimenez, Michael, Mgr-Design, Product Dev, Mktg & Creative Svc - Jada Toys, Inc.; pg. 960, pg. 67
Jimenez, Nikki, Dir-Mktg & Promos - Cumulus Media Inc.; pg. 280, pg. 503
Jimenez, Sandra, Project Mgr-SMB Website Mktg - PayPal Inc.; pg. 1274, pg. 248
Jimenez, Veronica, Mgr-Mktg - Whataburger, Inc.; pg. 1755, pg. 1744
Jimenez-Belen, Karina, Specialist-Mktg & Sponsorship - Horizon Blue Cross Blue Shield of New Jersey; pg. 1203, pg. 1096
Jimeson, Mackay, Dir-Media Rels - Pfizer Inc.; pg. 1581, pg. 1278
Jiongo, Greg, Dir-Mktg-Pricing & Demand Plng - Dell Inc.; pg. 383, pg. 1737
Jivoin, Jerry, Sr Dir-Mktg-Toy Dev & Mktg - Hasbro, Inc.; pg. 954, pg. 1603

Jo, Jonghee, Head-Analytics, Website Testing & Targeting-Digital Mktg Grp - JPMorgan Chase & Co.; *pg.* 772, *pg.* 1246
Joachim, Bernadette, VP-Insert Media - American List Counsel, Inc.; *pg.* 349, *pg.* 1110
Joakim, Hani, Sr VP-Hospitality Solutions Product Dev - Sabre Corporation; *pg.* 1710, *pg.* 752
Joannou, Dion, Sr VP-Sls - Viavi Solutions Inc.; *pg.* 1435, *pg.* 148
Jobb, Karen, VP-Sls - Clif Bar Inc.; *pg.* 848, *pg.* 83
Jobst, Michael, Mgr-Mktg-Natl - BMW of North America, LLC; *pg.* 166, *pg.* 1133
Jochum, Brian, Sr Dir-Mktg - Sears Holdings Corporation; *pg.* 1784, *pg.* 618
Jochum, Shane, Sr Dir-Mktg - adidas America Inc.; *pg.* 1803, *pg.* 1500
Jocson, Vince, Mgr-Loyalty Mktg & CRM - Cost Plus World Market; *pg.* 921, *pg.* 170
Joe, Pat, VP-Global Outsource Ops-Customer Care, Chat & Social Media - DISH Network Corporation; *pg.* 283, *pg.* 325
Joe, Roxanne, Dir-Mktg Strategy - Orchard Supply Hardware Stores Corp.; *pg.* 1058, *pg.* 248
Joedecke, Jessica, Reg Dir-Mktg-Eastern Europe, Middle East, Africa-Vaccines - Merck & Co., Inc.; *pg.* 1566, *pg.* 1077
Joffer, Andrew, VP-Sls - Jelly Belly Candy Company; *pg.* 1857, *pg.* 86
Jofriet, Peter, Dir-Sls Enablement - Honeywell Aerospace Electronic Systems; *pg.* 228, *pg.* 17
Jogis, Chris, Dir-iShares Brand & Adv - BlackRock, Inc.; *pg.* 724, *pg.* 1203
Joglekar, Samir, Exec VP-Sls - Renaissance Learning, Inc.; *pg.* 607, *pg.* 1899
Johanesen, Chris, Product VP - Buzzfeed; *pg.* 1233, *pg.* 1208
Johannesen, Heidi, Dir-Mktg-Intl - Virginia Tourism Authority; *pg.* 1010, *pg.* 1804
Johanneson, Christian, Dir-Worldwide Retail Channel Mktg-Digital - Microsoft Corporation; *pg.* 435, *pg.* 1824
Johanni, Chip, Dir-NF Mktg Ops - Nationwide Mutual Insurance Company; *pg.* 1210, *pg.* 1442
Johannsen, Heather, Mgr-Database Mktg - Texas Instruments Incorporated; *pg.* 679, *pg.* 1688
Johansen, Brian, Reg Mgr-Sls-Western - Southwestern Industries, Inc.; *pg.* 1429, *pg.* 69
Johansen, Christine, Mgr-PR-Collaboration - Cisco Systems, Inc.; *pg.* 372, *pg.* 240
Johansen, Melissa, Sr Planner-Integrated Shopper Mktg - General Mills, Inc.; *pg.* 828, *pg.* 933
Johanson, John, Dir-Mdsg-Direct Mktg - Crate & Barrel, Inc.; *pg.* 922, *pg.* 640
Johanson, Terri, Reg Mgr-Channel Sls - Oakley, Inc.; *pg.* 1840, *pg.* 86
Johansson, Daniel, Product Mgr-Software & Solutions-Nordic - Sharp Electronics Corporation; *pg.* 672, *pg.* 1082
Johantgen, Dayna, Planner-Mktg Comm-Social - General Mills, Inc.; *pg.* 828, *pg.* 933
Johl, Goge, Sr Mgr-Mktg-Alumni Chapters & Events-East - The University of Phoenix, Inc.; *pg.* 610, *pg.* 27
Johler, Carrie, Brand Mgr - Energizer Holdings, Inc.; *pg.* 637, *pg.* 996
John, Ann, Sr Mgr-Education - Mediabistro, Inc.; *pg.* 1266, *pg.* 1258
John, Doug, Dir-Sls & Mktg - KALO, Inc.; *pg.* 1796, *pg.* 719
John, Duane, Brand Mgr-Online & Sr Designer-Mktg - LABORATORY CORPORATION OF AMERICA HOLDINGS; *pg.* 1554, *pg.* 1359
John, Jonathan, Supvr-Sls - GEICO Corporation; *pg.* 1200, *pg.* 399
John, Ricky, Bus Mgr-Comml - Sunoco Inc.; *pg.* 985, *pg.* 1571
Johne, Ryan, Mgr-Mktg-Campaign Analytics - Expedia, Inc.; *pg.* 1244, *pg.* 1814
Johns, Amy, Div Mgr-Mktg-Absolut Vodka - Pernod Ricard USA, Inc.; *pg.* 1968, *pg.* 1332
Johns, Bryan, Sr Mgr-Worldwide Developer Rels - Apple Inc.; *pg.* 350, *pg.* 73
Johns, David, Brand Mgr-Pampers Global Digital Mktg & Ecommerce - The Procter & Gamble Company; *pg.* 1129, *pg.* 1418
Johns, Geoff, Chief Creative Officer - DC Comics, Inc.; *pg.* 1633, *pg.* 1221
Johns, Michael, Product Mgr - Shure Incorporated; *pg.* 672, *pg.* 638
Johns, Peter, Mgr-Mktg-Market Access - Abbott Diabetes Care, Inc.; *pg.* 1483, *pg.* 38
Johns, Trevor, Mgr-Mktg - Rockstar, Inc.; *pg.* 265, *pg.* 1029
Johnsen, Elissa, Sr Dir-Head-Product & Pipeline Comm - Takeda Pharmaceuticals USA, Inc.; *pg.* 1600, *pg.* 605
Johnsen, Jeremiah, Mgr-Live Events & Mktg - Townsquare Media, Inc.; *pg.* 313, *pg.* 350
Johnson, Aaron, Dir-Digital Mktg - Kohl's Corporation; *pg.* 1775, *pg.* 1870
Johnson, Alicia, Program Mgr-Digital Mktg - Brown-Forman Corporation; *pg.* 1958, *pg.* 732
Johnson, Alisha, Product Mgr-Mktg-Sport Beans & Jelly Belly - Jelly Belly Candy Company; *pg.* 1857, *pg.* 86
Johnson, Alison, Sr Planner-Mktg Comm - General Mills, Inc.; *pg.* 828, *pg.* 933
Johnson, Amanda, VP-Integrated Mktg - Here Media Inc.; *pg.* 290, *pg.* 132
Johnson, Amanda, Dir-Customer Relationship Mktg - Herschend Family Entertainment Corp.; *pg.* 552, *pg.* 973
Johnson, Amanda, Mgr-Mktg-Member Mktg - ZIPCAR, INC.; *pg.* 1931, *pg.* 810
Johnson, Amy, Area Dir-Sls - Crestline Hotels & Resorts, Inc.; *pg.* 1088, *pg.* 1779
Johnson, Andrew, Interim Pres & Interim CEO - 3D Systems Corporation; *pg.* 339, *pg.* 1621
Johnson, Angela, Dir-Product Strategy & Mktg Ops - Habitat for Humanity International, Inc.; *pg.* 143, *pg.* 486
Johnson, Angela, Dir-Mktg Comm - The Krystal Company; *pg.* 1734, *pg.* 1629
Johnson, Anne, Mgr-Social Media-Vogue.com - Conde Nast Publications, Inc.; *pg.* 1629, *pg.* 1217
Johnson, Anne, Mgr-Social Media-Vogue.com - Vogue Magazine; *pg.* 1700, *pg.* 1311
Johnson, Anthony, Specialist-Mktg Comm - A. Schulman, Inc.; *pg.* 1144, *pg.* 1452
Johnson, April, Dir-Customer Mktg - Acuity Brands, Inc.; *pg.* 1294, *pg.* 487
Johnson, April, Dir-Mktg - Ameriprise Financial, Inc.; *pg.* 715, *pg.* 930
Johnson, Ashley, Assoc Mgr-Mktg, Digital & Social Media - Jamba, Inc.; *pg.* 1024, *pg.* 84
Johnson, Ashley, Assoc Mgr-Mktg-Engagement - OpenTable, Inc.; *pg.* 450, *pg.* 224
Johnson, Benjamin, VP-Enterprise Media - Bank of America Global Wealth & Investment Management; *pg.* 720, *pg.* 789
Johnson, Benjamin, Sr Assoc Mgr-Mktg-Pillsbury Grands! Biscuits - General Mills, Inc.; *pg.* 828, *pg.* 933
Johnson, Beth, VP-Digital Media & Content - ABC Cable Networks Group; *pg.* 268, *pg.* 51
Johnson, Bill, Sr Dir-Pub Affairs - Potash Corp.; *pg.* 1177, *pg.* 641
Johnson, Brad, VP-Partner Sls & Ops - Wayfair LLC; *pg.* 1288, *pg.* 801
Johnson, Brian, Sr Mgr-Campaign - Amazon.com, Inc.; *pg.* 1226, *pg.* 1831
Johnson, Brian, VP-Mktg - Q.E.P. CO., INC.; *pg.* 1371, *pg.* 413
Johnson, Brown, Exec VP & Dir-Creative - Sesame Workshop; *pg.* 307, *pg.* 1290
Johnson, Bruce, Dir-Consumer Mktg - Tyson Foods, Inc.; *pg.* 902, *pg.* 35
Johnson, Buster, Dir-Sls - Harsco Rail; *pg.* 1345, *pg.* 1623
Johnson, Camille, Sr Mgr-Product Mktg-Global - Medtronic; *pg.* 1563, *pg.* 183
Johnson, Carol, VP-Digital Mktg & Ops - AMN Healthcare Services, Inc.; *pg.* 1494, *pg.* 200
Johnson, Carrie, Dir-Corp & Mktg Comm - Graybar Electric Company, Inc.; *pg.* 1299, *pg.* 997
Johnson, Casey, Sr Specialist-Mktg - The Schwan Food Company; *pg.* 894, *pg.* 928
Johnson, Catherine, Assoc Mgr-Mktg - MATTEL, INC.; *pg.* 962, *pg.* 81
Johnson, Chela, VP-Mktg - Lions Gate Entertainment Corp.; *pg.* 296, *pg.* 274
Johnson, Cheryl, Supvr & Coord-Mktg - Arctic Cat Inc.; *pg.* 1705, *pg.* 953
Johnson, Chris, Sr VP-Mktg & Enterprise Learning - Factory Mutual Insurance Company; *pg.* 1199, *pg.* 1601
Johnson, Chris, Grp Product Mgr-Office 365 - Microsoft Corporation; *pg.* 435, *pg.* 1824
Johnson, Christina R., Mgr-Mktg Programs - CyberSource Corporation; *pg.* 381, *pg.* 216
Johnson, Christopher, Product Mgr-Beyond Mass Retail - Fruit of the Loom, Inc.; *pg.* 41, *pg.* 725
Johnson, Chuck, Dir-Product Dev - Hill's Pet Nutrition, Inc.; *pg.* 1476, *pg.* 721
Johnson, Craig, VP-Global Mktg-Malibu & Kahlua - The Absolut Spirits Company Inc.; *pg.* 1956, *pg.* 1325
Johnson, Cynthia, Sr Mgr-Economic Dev - Pinellas County Economic Development; *pg.* 1004, *pg.* 416
Johnson, Dale, Div Mgr-Mdse-Regulated Products, Adult Beverages & Tobacco - Walgreen Co.; *pg.* 1608, *pg.* 605
Johnson, Dan, Dir-Produce, Floral Sls & Mktg - The Kroger Co.; *pg.* 1025, *pg.* 1416
Johnson, Darin, VP-Mktg-Extremities - Exactech, Inc.; *pg.* 1529, *pg.* 428
Johnson, David, Product Mgr - Fiserv, Inc.; *pg.* 397, *pg.* 1855
Johnson, David H., Mgr-Mktg Comm - Twin Disc, Incorporated; *pg.* 220, *pg.* 1889
Johnson, Dean, Sr VP-Sls & Mktg - Gentiva Health Services, Inc.; *pg.* 1534, *pg.* 506
Johnson, Deanna, Mgr-Mktg-Global - Emerson Process Management; *pg.* 1334, *pg.* 1636
Johnson, Deborah, Sr Analyst-Strategic Project Mktg - FedEx Corporation; *pg.* 1907, *pg.* 1642
Johnson, Dennis, Exec VP-Policy & Advocacy - The Children's Health Fund; *pg.* 137, *pg.* 1211
Johnson, Dennis, Dir-Media Rels - Time Warner Cable Inc.; *pg.* 312, *pg.* 1301
Johnson, Derek, Sr Mgr-Mktg-Agile - AT&T; *pg.* 1865, *pg.* 258
Johnson, Derek, Supvr-Digital Mktg Platforms - Mercedes-Benz USA, LLC; *pg.* 184, *pg.* 514
Johnson, Derrick, VP-Mktg - United Parcel Service, Inc.; *pg.* 1928, *pg.* 522
Johnson, Devin, VP-Publicity-BBC AMERICA & Consumer Products - BBC Worldwide America Inc.; *pg.* 271, *pg.* 1201
Johnson, Devin, Head-Digital Media - Tribune Media Company; *pg.* 1696, *pg.* 592
Johnson, Dina, Dir-Relationship Mktg - Wolverine World Wide, Inc.; *pg.* 1822, *pg.* 905
Johnson, Don, Sr VP-US Media Ops - Discovery Communications, Inc.; *pg.* 282, *pg.* 777
Johnson, Donald E., VP-Sls - The Ferry Cap & Set Screw Company; *pg.* 1047, *pg.* 1457
Johnson, Dorothy, Brand Mgr-DreamWorks, Weight Watchers, Natural & Organic Cereals - Post Consumer Brands; *pg.* 833, *pg.* 927
Johnson, Douglas E., Sr VP-Mktg - The Sportsman's Guide, Inc.; *pg.* 1846, *pg.* 965
Johnson, Elisabeth, Planner-Product & Svcs - Motorola Solutions, Inc.; *pg.* 657, *pg.* 659
Johnson, Ellie, Dir-Digital Mktg - Red Hat, Inc.; *pg.* 460, *pg.* 1388
Johnson, Emily, Mgr-Social Media Mktg - National Grid USA; *pg.* 1946, *pg.* 852
Johnson, Eric, Exec VP & Gen Mgr-Tech, Games & Media - CBS Interactive, Inc.; *pg.* 369, *pg.* 215
Johnson, Eric, Assoc Publr-Integrated Mktg - Conde Nast Publications, Inc.; *pg.* 1629, *pg.* 1217
Johnson, Eric, Exec VP-Global Multimedia Sls - ESPN, Inc.; *pg.* 285, *pg.* 340
Johnson, Eric, Sr Mgr-Mktg - The Orvis Company, Inc.; *pg.* 1781, *pg.* 1764
Johnson, Eric, Brand Strategist - Pinterest; *pg.* 1275, *pg.* 225
Johnson, Eric, Assoc Publr-Mktg - Self Magazine; *pg.* 1686, *pg.* 1290
Johnson, Fern, CIO-Global Procurement & Legal & Sr Dir - PepsiCo, Inc.; *pg.* 259, *pg.* 1327
Johnson, Gabriel, Sr Mgr-Product Mktg - Sony Electronics, Inc.; *pg.* 676, *pg.* 209
Johnson, Gary, Sr Mgr-Motorsports - FCA US LLC; *pg.* 170, *pg.* 868
Johnson, Geoff, Dir-Media Plng & Buying - General Mills, Inc.; *pg.* 828, *pg.* 933
Johnson, Greg, Sr Dir-Fin & IR - Amkor Technology, Inc.; *pg.* 67, *pg.* 25
Johnson, Greg, VP-Health & Beauty Care Products - Fred Meyer Stores, Inc.; *pg.* 1769, *pg.* 1502
Johnson, Greg, VP-Mktg-TurboTax - Intuit Inc.; *pg.* 769, *pg.* 158
Johnson, Heath, VP-Mktg Ops - Workiva; *pg.* 493, *pg.* 701
Johnson, Heavenly, Brand Mgr - Pharmavite LLC; *pg.* 1584, *pg.* 167
Johnson, James, Sr VP-Mktg & Bus Dev - Virco Manufacturing Corporation; *pg.* 946, *pg.* 297
Johnson, Jamie, Mgr-Sls Comm - Kinetic Concepts, Inc.; *pg.* 1553, *pg.* 1741
Johnson, Jane, Sr VP-Sls & Mktg - Wireless Ronin Technologies Inc.; *pg.* 689, *pg.* 951

Johnson, Janet, Dir-Mktg & Poultry-Global - Cargill, Inc.; *pg.* 845, *pg.* 965
Johnson, Janice, Sr Dir-Global Customer Ops Events - SAP America, Inc.; *pg.* 466, *pg.* 1557
Johnson, Jared, Dir-Mktg - Frito-Lay North America, Inc.; *pg.* 1853, *pg.* 1730
Johnson, Jason, Dir-Product Mgmt - Life Technologies; *pg.* 1420, *pg.* 1497
Johnson, Jason, Mgr-Sls-North America - Marine Travelift, Inc.; *pg.* 1359, *pg.* 1895
Johnson, Jeff, Mgr-Sls - AMPAC Enterprises, Inc.; *pg.* 1825, *pg.* 843
Johnson, Jeff L., Assoc Dir-Mktg-Watson Pharmaceuticals - Allergan; *pg.* 1490, *pg.* 1101
Johnson, Jeff M., Mgr-Mktg - Ameriprise Financial, Inc.; *pg.* 715, *pg.* 930
Johnson, Jeffrey, Dir-Digital Mktg - Dermalogica, Inc.; *pg.* 1523, *pg.* 63
Johnson, Jeffrey J., Sr Dir-PMO - LexisNexis Litigation Solutions; *pg.* 1659, *pg.* 1446
Johnson, Jennifer, Dir-Mktg - Hormel Foods Corporation; *pg.* 863, *pg.* 915
Johnson, Jeremy, Sr Mgr-Engrg - Ancestry.com LLC; *pg.* 1228, *pg.* 1754
Johnson, Jerry, Sr Dir-Channel Media - Carlson Companies Inc.; *pg.* 1084, *pg.* 947
Johnson, Jessica, Dir-Mktg - Extra Space Storage, Inc.; *pg.* 1091, *pg.* 1757
Johnson, Jill, Brand Mgr-Social Media & Brand Integration - Boost Mobile; *pg.* 1869, *pg.* 107
Johnson, Jill, VP-Mktg - Jewelry Television; *pg.* 7, *pg.* 1637
Johnson, John, Corp Sec & Dir-PR & Legislative Affairs - Plains Cotton Cooperative Association; *pg.* 697, *pg.* 1726
Johnson, Jonathan, Sr VP & Dir-Creative - HSN, Inc.; *pg.* 291, *pg.* 462
Johnson, Jonathan Eric, Dir-Trade & Channel Mktg - Logitech Inc.; *pg.* 1264, *pg.* 164
Johnson, Jordan, Mgr-Digital Optimization & Mdsg - Southwest Airlines Co.; *pg.* 1923, *pg.* 1687
Johnson, Joy, Mgr-Sls-Natl - Metropolitan Tucson Convention & Visitors Bureau; *pg.* 998, *pg.* 27
Johnson, Julie, Mgr-Classified Sls-Capital Newspapers - Madison Newspapers, Inc.; *pg.* 1661, *pg.* 1866
Johnson, Juliet, Mgr-Media & PR-Corp Comm - Whirlpool Corporation; *pg.* 62, *pg.* 872
Johnson, Karry, VP-Sls - Wolverine World Wide, Inc.; *pg.* 1822, *pg.* 905
Johnson, Kate, Dir-Sls-Central Reg - Clif Bar Inc.; *pg.* 848, *pg.* 83
Johnson, Kate, Head-Integrated Mktg Comml ProgramU by Kotex - Kimberly-Clark Corporation; *pg.* 1461, *pg.* 1720
Johnson, Kate, Sr Dir-Global Sponsorship Mktg - Visa Inc.; *pg.* 816, *pg.* 230
Johnson, Kate, Sr Dir-Global Sponsorship Mktg - Visa U.S.A., Inc.; *pg.* 817, *pg.* 231
Johnson, Katie, VP-Digital Mktg-Global - First Data Corporation; *pg.* 754, *pg.* 505
Johnson, Keith, Dir-New Bus Dev & Mktg - Hutchinson Technology Inc.; *pg.* 409, *pg.* 926
Johnson, Kelly, Mgr-Mktg & Consumer Comm - Nestle Waters North America Inc.; *pg.* 257, *pg.* 375
Johnson, Ken, Sr VP-Sls - Rug Doctor, LP; *pg.* 1373, *pg.* 1734
Johnson, Kerry, Product Mgr - QNX Software Systems Ltd; *pg.* 458, *pg.* 1932
Johnson, Kevin, Dir-Svcs Product Mgmt & Mktg - Mitel Networks Corporation; *pg.* 654, *pg.* 1921
Johnson, Kristin, Mgr-Mktg - McGladrey, LLP; *pg.* 781, *pg.* 938
Johnson, Kristy J., Mgr-Medical Mktg - Mead Johnson Nutrition Company; *pg.* 1561, *pg.* 615
Johnson, Kyle, Dir-Wireless Products - Charter Communications, Inc.; *pg.* 274, *pg.* 372
Johnson, Laela, Brand Mgr-Pet Food Innovation - Del Monte Foods, Inc.; *pg.* 852, *pg.* 304
Johnson, Lance, Mgr-Product & Design-Ultimate Direction - Exxel Outdoors LLC; *pg.* 1833, *pg.* 311
Johnson, Laura, Dir-Creative Svcs - University of Minnesota; *pg.* 609, *pg.* 945
Johnson, Lauren, Grp Dir-Adv-Hearst Integrated & Digital Media - Hearst Magazines; *pg.* 1649, *pg.* 1239
Johnson, Lauren, Dir-PR - Neiman Marcus, Inc.; *pg.* 30, *pg.* 1684
Johnson, Lauren, Mgr-Customer Mktg - TXU Energy Retail Company LLC; *pg.* 1953, *pg.* 1690
Johnson, LeLaine, Mgr-FedEx Office Integrated Mktg & Sls Mktg - FedEx Corporation; *pg.* 1907, *pg.* 1642
Johnson, Libby, Sr Asst Brand Mgr-Tresemme - Unilever United States, Inc.; *pg.* 904, *pg.* 1061
Johnson, Lisa, Dir-Ticket Sls & Svc - Anaheim Ducks Hockey Club, LLC; *pg.* 528, *pg.* 42
Johnson, Lisa, Brand Mgr-Sparkling ICE - TalkingRain Beverage Company; *pg.* 266, *pg.* 1823
Johnson, Lloyd, Chief Sls Officer & Exec VP - Diamond Foods, Inc.; *pg.* 1851, *pg.* 216
Johnson, M. Carl, III, Chief Growth Officer & Exec VP-Mktg - Big Heart Pet Brands; *pg.* 1474, *pg.* 213
Johnson, Mark, Sr Mgr-Digital Customer Experience - American Express Company; *pg.* 712, *pg.* 1190
Johnson, Mark, Mgr-European Mktg - Megger Inc.; *pg.* 1422, *pg.* 1557
Johnson, Mark, VP-Mktg - Navistar International Corporation; *pg.* 186, *pg.* 630
Johnson, Mark, Mgr-Enterprise-Product Suite - Oracle Corporation; *pg.* 450, *pg.* 191
Johnson, Mark, VP-Sls & Mktg - Osborn International; *pg.* 1367, *pg.* 1406
Johnson, Mark, VP-Integrated Media Sls - Valassis Communications, Inc.; *pg.* 1287, *pg.* 897
Johnson, Mark, Mgr-Product Line-Mobile Satcom Sys - ViaSat, Inc.; *pg.* 489, *pg.* 62
Johnson, Matt, Sr Head-Product - Apple Inc.; *pg.* 350, *pg.* 73
Johnson, Matt, VP-Sls - Beaulieu Group, LLC; *pg.* 917, *pg.* 529
Johnson, Matt, Dir-Sls-Metro New York - Diageo North America Inc.; *pg.* 248, *pg.* 1223
Johnson, Matt, Dir-Adv - Safelite Solutions LLC; *pg.* 109, *pg.* 1443
Johnson, Matthew, Mgr-Mktg Commercialization-Glade - S.C. Johnson & Son, Inc.; *pg.* 334, *pg.* 1889
Johnson, Matthew S., VP-Product Dev - Bassett Furniture Industries, Incorporated; *pg.* 916, *pg.* 1776
Johnson, Melinda, Brand Mgr-Frederic Fekkai Hair Care-Global - The Procter & Gamble Company; *pg.* 1129, *pg.* 1418
Johnson, Melissa, Producer-Sls - The Allstate Corporation; *pg.* 1189, *pg.* 639
Johnson, Michael, Mgr-Mktg-Tachycardia & Heart Failure - Boston Scientific Corporation; *pg.* 1508, *pg.* 831
Johnson, Michael, Dir-Sls, Comml & Aftermarket-Worldwide - Eaton Corporation; *pg.* 1331, *pg.* 1429
Johnson, Michael, VP-Mktg - V.F. Corporation; *pg.* 34, *pg.* 1376
Johnson, Michael E., Specialist-Comm & Collaboration Product Sls - Cisco Systems, Inc.; *pg.* 372, *pg.* 240
Johnson, Michele Dowling, Sr VP-Mktg - New York & Company, Inc.; *pg.* 1779, *pg.* 1268
Johnson, Mike, VP-Sls & Mktg - KPI-JCI; *pg.* 1354, *pg.* 1626
Johnson, Mike, Sr Dir-Mktg-Intl - Krispy Kreme Doughnuts, Inc.; *pg.* 1734, *pg.* 1394
Johnson, Miles, Mgr-Product Mktg - Google Inc.; *pg.* 1249, *pg.* 153
Johnson, Miles C., Mgr-Product PR - Hyundai Motor America; *pg.* 179, *pg.* 89
Johnson, Natali, Sr Mgr-Mktg-TNT Scripted Originals - Turner Broadcasting System, Inc.; *pg.* 314, *pg.* 521
Johnson, Natalie, Sr Mgr-Digital Comm & Social Media - The Coca-Cola Company; *pg.* 240, *pg.* 493
Johnson, Natalie, Dir-Integrated Mktg & Salesforce Platform - salesforce.com, inc.; *pg.* 1278, *pg.* 226
Johnson, Nick, VP-Mktg - Fairmount Santrol; *pg.* 1162, *pg.* 1409
Johnson, Nick, Sr VP-Natl Sls-NBC Sports Digital - NBC Universal, Inc.; *pg.* 300, *pg.* 1266
Johnson, Nigel P., VP-Bus Dev & Product Mgmt - Zix Corporation; *pg.* 497, *pg.* 1691
Johnson, Paige, Analyst-Product - Berry Plastics; *pg.* 1879, *pg.* 678
Johnson, Parker, Mng Dir-Sls & Mktg-Ramius - Cowen Group, Inc.; *pg.* 742, *pg.* 1219
Johnson, Paul, Dir-Sls-Midwest - Essence Magazine; *pg.* 1639, *pg.* 1229
Johnson, Pete, Dir-Product Mgmt - Flexera Software Inc.; *pg.* 398, *pg.* 658
Johnson, Philip, Sr VP-Sls & Mktg - Carmeuse North America; *pg.* 73, *pg.* 1574
Johnson, Rachael, VP-Digital Strategy, Media & ECommerce-Luxury Products Div - L'Oreal USA; *pg.* 514, *pg.* 1252
Johnson, Ralph, Sr Dir-Visual Mdsg & Store Plng - Benefit Cosmetics LLC; *pg.* 501, *pg.* 213
Johnson, Randy, VP-Sls - Barrel O'Fun Snack Foods Co.; *pg.* 1850, *pg.* 952
Johnson, Randy, Sr VP-Mdsg - BrandsMart USA; *pg.* 627, *pg.* 430
Johnson, Randy, VP-N2Power Sls - Qualstar Corporation; *pg.* 458, *pg.* 279
Johnson, Rebeca M., Sr VP-Mktg & Culinary - DineEquity, Inc.; *pg.* 1725, *pg.* 95
Johnson, Rich, Head-Programmatic Media & Strategic Partnerships - Conversant, Inc.; *pg.* 1393, *pg.* 306
Johnson, Richard, Mgr-Interactive Mktg - MetroPCS, Inc.; *pg.* 1872, *pg.* 1683
Johnson, Rina, Sr Dir-Mktg Svcs - 24 Hour Fitness Worldwide Inc.; *pg.* 526, *pg.* 258
Johnson, Robert, Reg Mgr-Mktg-Precision Solutions & Telematics - CNH America LLC; *pg.* 702, *pg.* 560
Johnson, Ryan, Coord-Mktg - Anaheim Ducks Hockey Club, LLC; *pg.* 528, *pg.* 42
Johnson, Ryan, Mgr-Brand Mktg - RetailMeNot Inc.; *pg.* 1782, *pg.* 1665
Johnson, Ryan, Specialist-Reg Mktg-Eastern Region - Subaru of America, Inc.; *pg.* 191, *pg.* 1050
Johnson, Sara, Specialist-PR - Move, Inc.; *pg.* 1268, *pg.* 247
Johnson, Sarah, Mgr-Mktg-Americas - Hilton Worldwide, Inc.; *pg.* 1094, *pg.* 1791
Johnson, Scott, Product Mgr - Caterpillar, Inc.; *pg.* 1321, *pg.* 650
Johnson, Scott, Sr Dir-Strategic Plng & Mktg-Div I - Community Health Systems, Inc.; *pg.* 1516, *pg.* 1632
Johnson, Scott, Product Mgr-Google Drive - Google Inc.; *pg.* 1249, *pg.* 153
Johnson, Scott, Mgr-Retail IT Product - McDonald's Corporation; *pg.* 1737, *pg.* 645
Johnson, Shauna, Sr Dir-Comm - Kindred Healthcare, Inc.; *pg.* 1553, *pg.* 736
Johnson, Sid, Dir-Mktg - Jayco Inc.; *pg.* 1708, *pg.* 695
Johnson, Sonia, Mgr-Mktg-Eggs - Michael Foods, Inc.; *pg.* 877, *pg.* 949
Johnson, Stephanie, Sr Mgr-Internal Comm - Apollo Education Group Inc.; *pg.* 597, *pg.* 14
Johnson, Stephen, Reg Dir-Sls-NorthEast - Barcoding Inc.; *pg.* 360, *pg.* 755
Johnson, Stephen, Dir-Social Media - Teachers Insurance & Annuity Association - College Retirement Equities Fund; *pg.* 1219, *pg.* 1297
Johnson, Steve, Sr Dir-Strategic Insights & Analytics - Frito-Lay North America, Inc.; *pg.* 1853, *pg.* 1730
Johnson, Steve, Dir-Product Dev - Hubbell Incorporated; *pg.* 1299, *pg.* 370
Johnson, Steve, Sr Dir-Sls & Mktg - Key Technology, Inc.; *pg.* 868, *pg.* 1847
Johnson, Steven, Mgr-Truck Product Portfolio Plng - FCA US LLC; *pg.* 170, *pg.* 868
Johnson, Tamara, Sr Dir-Global Brand - Medtronic, Inc.; *pg.* 1564, *pg.* 939
Johnson, Tara, Mgr-Incentives-Central Mktg Org - General Mills, Inc.; *pg.* 828, *pg.* 933
Johnson, Tim, Sr Mgr-Mktg-CRM - The Gap, Inc.; *pg.* 1770, *pg.* 218
Johnson, Tim, Mgr-Mktg & eCommerce - Marriott International, Inc.; *pg.* 1102, *pg.* 764
Johnson, Tina, Mgr-Channel Mktg - Trex Company, Inc.; *pg.* 116, *pg.* 1812
Johnson, TJ, Bus Mgr-Frozen Products - Foster Farms; *pg.* 856, *pg.* 122
Johnson, Todd, Sr Assoc Brand Mgr - The Kraft Heinz Company; *pg.* 871, *pg.* 641
Johnson, Tom, Sr Mgr-Mktg - Mammoth Mountain Ski Area; *pg.* 1102, *pg.* 142
Johnson, Tom, Mgr-Media & Events - Nebraska Lottery; *pg.* 1000, *pg.* 1012
Johnson, Tommy, VP-Govt & PR - CONSOL ENERGY INC.; *pg.* 1154, *pg.* 1520
Johnson, Tony, Mgr-Mktg-Colorado - General Motors Company; *pg.* 175, *pg.* 881
Johnson, Tracey, Brand Mgr-Tuaca Liqueur - Brown-Forman Corporation; *pg.* 1958, *pg.* 732
Johnson, Trey, Sr VP & Gen Mgr-Mdse-Food & Consumables - Big Lots, Inc.; *pg.* 1762, *pg.* 1438
Johnson, Ty A., Sr Dir-Pops & Presentations - Indianapolis Symphony Orchestra; *pg.* 553, *pg.* 687
Johnson, Venus Bivins, Sr Mgr-Sls Strategy-Chicago - AOL Inc.; *pg.* 1229, *pg.* 1195
Johnson, Warren, VP-Adv - Burlington Coat Factory; *pg.* 1764, *pg.* 1047

Johnson, Wes, Reg Mgr-Premium Offerings Sls - Yara N America, Inc.; *pg.* 1802, *pg.* 477
Johnson-Balentine, Dee, Officer-Mktg & HR - First Western Bank & Trust; *pg.* 757, *pg.* 1398
Johnson-Jones, Yvonne, Sr Mgr-Comm - The Boeing Company; *pg.* 225, *pg.* 567
Johnston, Aaron, Head-Sls & Acct Mgmt-Media Platforms - Google Inc.; *pg.* 1249, *pg.* 153
Johnston, Alan, Product Mgr-Global - Molex Incorporated; *pg.* 655, *pg.* 628
Johnston, Allison, Mgr-Mktg-Global - Mode Media; *pg.* 1267, *pg.* 50
Johnston, Bill, Dir-PR - San Diego Chargers Football Co.; *pg.* 580, *pg.* 208
Johnston, Charles M., Interim CEO - HAMPTON ROADS BANKSHARES, INC.; *pg.* 765, *pg.* 1796
Johnston, Cindy, Dir-Corp Mktg Ops - Xerox Corporation; *pg.* 494, *pg.* 365
Johnston, David, Mgr-Mktg - Nestle USA, Inc.; *pg.* 883, *pg.* 96
Johnston, Dennis, VP-Sls - Oklahoma City Convention & Visitors Bureau; *pg.* 1002, *pg.* 1487
Johnston, Elizabeth, Coord-Electronic Mktg - Brookshire Grocery Company; *pg.* 1016, *pg.* 1748
Johnston, Fritz, Dir-Brand & Adv - The Boeing Company; *pg.* 225, *pg.* 567
Johnston, Hayley, Coord-PR - QUALCOMM Incorporated; *pg.* 1873, *pg.* 207
Johnston, Heather Litus, Product Mgr - Epson America Inc.; *pg.* 394, *pg.* 122
Johnston, Jack, Mgr-Mktg Comm - Texas Instruments Incorporated; *pg.* 679, *pg.* 1688
Johnston, Jenn, COO & CMO - Global Franchise Management LLC; *pg.* 1771, *pg.* 537
Johnston, Jennifer, Mgr-Mktg - Zoll Medical Corporation; *pg.* 1612, *pg.* 814
Johnston, Jerry, Mgr-Sys Sls-West Reg - Cooper Wheelock; *pg.* 630, *pg.* 1080
Johnston, Jim, Pres-Concentrate Sls - Dr Pepper Snapple Group, Inc.; *pg.* 250, *pg.* 1729
Johnston, Kellee, Dir-Mktg - Alto-Shaam Inc.; *pg.* 836, *pg.* 1869
Johnston, Kyle, Dir-Creative - Garmin International, Inc.; *pg.* 1414, *pg.* 717
Johnston, Les, Mgr-Natl OEM Technical Sls - Cole Hersee Company; *pg.* 202, *pg.* 792
Johnston, Lisa L., Mgr-Mktg Comm-Medicare Bus - Anthem, Inc.; *pg.* 1192, *pg.* 683
Johnston, Lisa S., CMO & Exec VP-Mktg - EverBank Financial Corp.; *pg.* 749, *pg.* 432
Johnston, Mary, VP & Mgr-Mktg Comm - Sun Trust Bank, Atlanta; *pg.* 806, *pg.* 520
Johnston, Mary, VP & Mgr-Mktg Comm - SunTrust Banks, Inc.; *pg.* 807, *pg.* 520
Johnston, Robert, Chief Strategy Officer & Exec VP - The InterTech Group, Inc.; *pg.* 1350, *pg.* 1613
Johnston, Robert, Dir-Mktg - NCR Corporation; *pg.* 443, *pg.* 531
Johnston, Russ, Exec VP-Mktg & Corp Comm - Pioneer Electronics (USA) Inc.; *pg.* 663, *pg.* 124
Johnston, Ryan, Assoc Mgr-Brand Mktg - Taco Bell Corp.; *pg.* 1752, *pg.* 117
Johnston, Scott, Sr VP-Product - Dockers Brand; *pg.* 40, *pg.* 217
Johnston, Skip, Mgr-Content Team-Digital Mktg - Sigma-Aldrich Corporation; *pg.* 1181, *pg.* 1003
Johnston, Thomas, Sr VP-Creative & Mdsg - American Greetings Corporation; *pg.* 1615, *pg.* 1428
Johnston, Tory, VP-Mktg - Chattanooga Bakery Inc.; *pg.* 847, *pg.* 1628
Johnston, Walt, VP-Mktg & Strategic New Product Plng - Astellas Pharma US, Inc.; *pg.* 1496, *pg.* 640
Johnstone, Chris D., VP & Mgr-Production - Regions Financial Corporation; *pg.* 798, *pg.* 4
Johnstone, Katherine, Mgr-Media Rels - French Government Tourist Office; *pg.* 992, *pg.* 1233
Johnstone, Lisa, Dir-Digital Mktg - VIZIO, Inc.; *pg.* 686, *pg.* 118
Johnstone, Rick, VP-Employee Benefits Sls - Standard Insurance Company; *pg.* 1217, *pg.* 1506
Joiner, Amy, Mgr-PR - Target Corporation; *pg.* 1786, *pg.* 942
Joiner, Kyra, Mgr-Activation-Mktg Partnerships - Phoenix Suns; *pg.* 576, *pg.* 19
Joiner, Mike, Mgr-Mktg-US - McDonald's Corporation; *pg.* 1737, *pg.* 645
Joines, Martin, Sr VP-Sls - Aquatic; *pg.* 68, *pg.* 42
Jokisch, Jack, Analyst-Mktg Fin - Horace Mann Companies; *pg.* 1203, *pg.* 662
Jollay, Jeff, VP-Mktg & Product Dev - BrassCraft Manufacturing Company; *pg.* 1043, *pg.* 902
Jollay, Jeffrey L., VP-Mktg & Product Dev - Wenger Corporation; *pg.* 1307, *pg.* 952
Jolliff, Michael, Mgr-Mktg-New Customer Acq - CVS Health Corporation; *pg.* 1765, *pg.* 1610
Jolly, Diya, Grp Product Mgr - Google Inc.; *pg.* 1249, *pg.* 153
Jolly, Mike, Bus Mgr-Global - Google Inc.; *pg.* 1249, *pg.* 153
Joly, Denise, Mgr-Customer Mktg - Coty, Inc.; *pg.* 506, *pg.* 1219
Jonas, Lilli, Sr Mgr-Integrated Brand Mktg - Levi Strauss & Co.; *pg.* 43, *pg.* 220
Jones, Abigail, Dir-Product Mgmt - American Express Company; *pg.* 712, *pg.* 1190
Jones, Adrian, Exec VP-Worldwide Sls - Symantec Corporation; *pg.* 478, *pg.* 161
Jones, Alan S., Sr Mgr-Channel Mktg - SanDisk Corporation; *pg.* 465, *pg.* 147
Jones, Alexander R, Reg Mgr-Sls-Corp Bus Solutions - AT&T Inc.; *pg.* 1867, *pg.* 1674
Jones, Alicia, Head-Honda & Acura Social Media Mktg - American Honda Motor Co., Inc.; *pg.* 163, *pg.* 292
Jones, Alison, Dir-Mktg Creative Svcs Project Mgmt - Teachers Insurance & Annuity Association - College Retirement Equities Fund; *pg.* 1219, *pg.* 1297
Jones, Alyssa, Mgr-PR & Social Media - Assurant, Inc.; *pg.* 1193, *pg.* 1198
Jones, Amber, Mgr-Mktg Comm - Dunn-Edwards Corporation; *pg.* 1442, *pg.* 129
Jones, Amy, Sr Specialist-PR-Nordstrom Corp Affairs - Nordstrom, Inc.; *pg.* 1779, *pg.* 1837
Jones, Andrew, Dir-Govt Programs Medicaid Mktg - Anthem, Inc.; *pg.* 1192, *pg.* 683
Jones, Ben, Dir-Creative - Google Inc.; *pg.* 1249, *pg.* 153
Jones, Benjamin, Dir-Mktg & Analytics-Venture Card - Capital One Bank (USA), N.A.; *pg.* 730, *pg.* 1789
Jones, Biege, Dir-Internal Art & Mgr-Adv - Sport Obermeyer Ltd.; *pg.* 1846, *pg.* 310
Jones, Bradley, VP-Sls-Natl Accts - Eby-Brown Co.; *pg.* 1767, *pg.* 636
Jones, Brendan, Dir-Electric Vehicle Sls & Infrastructure Deployment - Nissan North America, Inc.; *pg.* 186, *pg.* 1633
Jones, Britt, VP-Sls-Homecenter, Hardware & Mass - Zep Inc.; *pg.* 338, *pg.* 524
Jones, Brooke, VP-Corp Mktg - Weber-Stephen Products LLC; *pg.* 62, *pg.* 650
Jones, Bryan, Sr Dir-Shopper Mktg - PepsiCo, Inc.; *pg.* 259, *pg.* 1327
Jones, Bryan E., VP-Comml Mktg-North America - Dell Inc.; *pg.* 383, *pg.* 1737
Jones, Candace, Mgr-Engagement Strategies Mktg - Health Fitness Corporation; *pg.* 1539, *pg.* 937
Jones, Carmen, Head-Mktg-Eco, A & V Solutions - Panasonic Corporation of North America; *pg.* 661, *pg.* 1120
Jones, Carmen, Head-Mktg-Eco & A/V Solutions - Panasonic Electric Works Corporation of America; *pg.* 661, *pg.* 1095
Jones, Casey, Mgr-Social Media - Eileen Fisher, Inc.; *pg.* 24, *pg.* 1168
Jones, Ceil, Mgr-Sls-Stamford - Coldwell Banker Residential Brokerage; *pg.* 1087, *pg.* 850
Jones, Chandra, Reg Dir-Mktg - Papa John's International, Inc.; *pg.* 1743, *pg.* 737
Jones, Chip, Sr Dir-Footwear Innovation - NIKE, Inc.; *pg.* 1812, *pg.* 1492
Jones, Chris, Mgr-Mktg - Boston Scientific Corporation; *pg.* 1508, *pg.* 831
Jones, Chris, Head-Ontario Retail Dev Sls - Nestle Canada Inc.; *pg.* 883, *pg.* 1929
Jones, Clark, VP-Fin, Mktg, Sls, Travel Ops, WDPRO & Walt Disney Parks - The Walt Disney Company; *pg.* 317, *pg.* 52
Jones, Clayton, Product Mgr - Google Inc.; *pg.* 1249, *pg.* 153
Jones, Corey, VP-Mktg - Globe Life & Accident Insurance Company; *pg.* 1201, *pg.* 1486
Jones, Craig, VP-Mktg - Sotheby's International Realty, Inc.; *pg.* 1113, *pg.* 1294
Jones, Dan, Sr Dir-HR - Kubota Tractor Corporation; *pg.* 705, *pg.* 294
Jones, Darden, Mgr-Southwest Reg Sls - Summit Plastic Co.; *pg.* 1470, *pg.* 1403
Jones, Darryl, Exec VP-Sls, Mktg, Tech Svcs & Bus Dev-Global - Implant Sciences Corporation; *pg.* 1348, *pg.* 860
Jones, Dave, Mgr-Solution Mktg - Hyland Software, Inc.; *pg.* 409, *pg.* 1480
Jones, David, Sr Mgr-Proposal & Mktg - Fluor Corporation; *pg.* 82, *pg.* 1719
Jones, David B., Dir-Sls & Mktg - Northrop Grumman Corporation; *pg.* 231, *pg.* 1781
Jones, Del, Mgr-Sls & Mktg - Morris Communications Company LLC; *pg.* 1666, *pg.* 525
Jones, Dennis, Mgr-Mktg - Jack Henry & Associates, Inc.; *pg.* 422, *pg.* 988
Jones, Doug, Grp Product Mgr-CPD - Molex Incorporated; *pg.* 655, *pg.* 628
Jones, Doug, Mgr-Corp Comm & PR - Pharmavite LLC; *pg.* 1584, *pg.* 167
Jones, Doug, Sr Product Mgr - Smith Micro Software, Inc.; *pg.* 471, *pg.* 41
Jones, Doug, Sr VP-Mdsg - VITAMIN SHOPPE, INC.; *pg.* 1608, *pg.* 1098
Jones, Ed, Product Mgr - KEMET Corporation; *pg.* 649, *pg.* 1621
Jones, Eddie, Principal & Designer-Product - Avid Technology, Inc.; *pg.* 622, *pg.* 804
Jones, Eddie, Mgr-Sls - Fairway Outdoor Advertising of the Piedmont Triad; *pg.* 1640, *pg.* 1374
Jones, Felice, Asst VP-Mktg & Events - National Football League Players Incorporated; *pg.* 149, *pg.* 401
Jones, Gannon, Head-Brand Mktg - MillerCoors LLC; *pg.* 255, *pg.* 582
Jones, Gareth, VP-Sls-EMEA - Fitbit Inc.; *pg.* 639, *pg.* 218
Jones, Gary, VP-Mktg - Armstrong Garden Centers, Inc.; *pg.* 1793, *pg.* 99
Jones, Gary, VP-Product Dev, R&D - BeautiControl Cosmetics, Inc.; *pg.* 501, *pg.* 1669
Jones, Gary, Dir-Sls Plng - Starbucks Corporation; *pg.* 897, *pg.* 1840
Jones, George, Mgr-Mktg-GMC Acadia & Terrain - General Motors Company; *pg.* 175, *pg.* 881
Jones, Gil A., Dir-Mktg & Promos - Cumulus Media Inc.; *pg.* 280, *pg.* 503
Jones, Greg, Sr Product Mgr-Mktg - Cardinal Health, Inc.; *pg.* 1512, *pg.* 1448
Jones, Greg, Dir-Res & Platform Sls - New York Life Insurance Company; *pg.* 1211, *pg.* 1268
Jones, Greg, Dir-Channel Mktg & Market Insights - Newell Rubbermaid Inc.; *pg.* 1128, *pg.* 515
Jones, Gregory, Dir-Mktg & Brand Strategy - Massachusetts Mutual Life Insurance Company; *pg.* 1207, *pg.* 845
Jones, Harry, Dir-Mktg-Pediatric Nutrition Innovation - Abbott Laboratories; *pg.* 1484, *pg.* 551
Jones, Holly, Mgr-Mktg Plng & Strategy - Family Dollar Stores, Inc.; *pg.* 1768, *pg.* 1382
Jones, Holly, Dir-Creative Svcs - WICD-TV; *pg.* 321, *pg.* 562
Jones, J., District Mgr-Sls - The Harris Products Group; *pg.* 1345, *pg.* 533
Jones, James, Dir-Sls - Elmer's Products, Inc.; *pg.* 1442, *pg.* 1479
Jones, Janice M., VP-Mdsg - PulteGroup, Inc.; *pg.* 1109, *pg.* 873
Jones, Jason, Bus Mgr - 3M Company; *pg.* 1142, *pg.* 956
Jones, Jayne, Dir-Mktg Comm - Medtronic, Inc.; *pg.* 1564, *pg.* 939
Jones, Jean S., Dir-Mktg & Wireless - Alcatel-Lucent; *pg.* 615, *pg.* 38
Jones, Jeff, Exec VP-Boxed Beef & Trim Sls-Fresh Meat Div - American Foods Group, LLC; *pg.* 837, *pg.* 1859
Jones, Jeff, Mgr-Brand Mktg - Lenovo Group Ltd; *pg.* 427, *pg.* 1384
Jones, Jenni, Dir-Field Mktg - McDonald's Corporation; *pg.* 1737, *pg.* 645
Jones, Jennifer, VP-Creative Adv-Worldwide - Warner Home Video Inc.; *pg.* 319, *pg.* 55
Jones, Jennifer Carlsen, Dir-Digital Mktg - The Sports Authority, Inc.; *pg.* 1846, *pg.* 326
Jones, Jeremy, Sr VP-Sls - MegaPath, Inc.; *pg.* 432, *pg.* 71
Jones, Jill, Mgr-Sls & Mktg - Lennar Corporation; *pg.* 1100, *pg.* 443
Jones, Jimmy, Dir-Creative - Capital One Bank (USA), N.A.; *pg.* 730, *pg.* 1789
Jones, Joel, VP-Sls Plng & Ops - Facebook, Inc.; *pg.* 1245, *pg.* 143
Jones, John, Sr VP-Comml Mktg & Strategy - American International Group, Inc.; *pg.* 1190, *pg.* 1193
Jones, John D., VP-Product Support - H&E Equipment Services, Inc.; *pg.* 85, *pg.* 742
Jones, Joseph, Sr Dir-Global Comm - BASF Corporation; *pg.*

1149, *pg.* 1066
Jones, Justin, Sr Dir-Pricing & Plng - Southwest Airlines Co.; *pg.* 1923, *pg.* 1687
Jones, Kathleen, Mgr-Retail Mktg - Zippo Manufacturing Company, Inc.; *pg.* 1895, *pg.* 1518
Jones, Katie, Specialist-Video Sls Ops - Yahoo! Inc.; *pg.* 1289, *pg.* 289
Jones, Keith, Sr Dir-Governmental Affairs - 7-Eleven, Inc.; *pg.* 1012, *pg.* 1672
Jones, Kelly, Grp Dir-Production - The Hollywood Reporter Inc.; *pg.* 1650, *pg.* 133
Jones, Kelly, Reg Sls Mgr-Individual Market - Premera Blue Cross; *pg.* 1214, *pg.* 1823
Jones, Kenneth, VP-Corp Mktg - Carnival Corporation; *pg.* 1902, *pg.* 441
Jones, Kevin, Brand Mgr - Overhead Door Corporation; *pg.* 102, *pg.* 1725
Jones, Kim, Sr Reg Mgr-Mktg - Pepsi Beverages Company; *pg.* 258, *pg.* 1342
Jones, Kristen, Mgr-Product Mktg - Facebook, Inc.; *pg.* 1245, *pg.* 143
Jones, Larry, Dir-Medicaid Implementation & Sr Products - Humana, Inc.; *pg.* 1204, *pg.* 734
Jones, Latica, Sr Specialist-Mktg - FedEx Corporation; *pg.* 1907, *pg.* 1642
Jones, Laura, Mgr-Product Mktg-Commerce - Google Inc.; *pg.* 1249, *pg.* 153
Jones, Laura, Sr Mgr-PR - Microsoft Corporation; *pg.* 435, *pg.* 1824
Jones, Leah, Sr Acct Mgr-Creative Svcs & Global Licensed Categories - Coach, Inc.; *pg.* 3, *pg.* 1214
Jones, Marjorie, Sr Specialist-Mktg - FedEx Corporation; *pg.* 1907, *pg.* 1642
Jones, Martin, Sr Mgr-Mktg-Social Media & Content Mktg - Cox Communications, Inc.; *pg.* 279, *pg.* 501
Jones, Matt, VP-Sls & Mktg - Dorner Manufacturing Corp.; *pg.* 1329, *pg.* 1861
Jones, Matthew, Brand Mgr-Sportswear, Skateboarding & Basketball - NIKE, Inc.; *pg.* 1812, *pg.* 1492
Jones, Meghan, Coord-Mktg - Knott's Berry Farm; *pg.* 556, *pg.* 50
Jones, Meghan, Sr Mgr-Brand Building-Deodorants - Unilever Canada Inc.; *pg.* 903, *pg.* 1946
Jones, Melissa, Sr Dir-PMO-Global Tech Org - LexisNexis Group; *pg.* 1658, *pg.* 1446
Jones, Michael, Product Mgr-Mid-Pickups - General Motors Company; *pg.* 175, *pg.* 881
Jones, Michael, Program Mgr-Outdoor Mktg-Mississippi Tourism - Mississippi Development Authority; *pg.* 999, *pg.* 969
Jones, Mike, Sr VP-Sls & Trade Mktg - Aidells Sausage Company; *pg.* 836, *pg.* 253
Jones, Nancy, CMO - Allianz Life Insurance Company of North America; *pg.* 1188, *pg.* 929
Jones, Nancy, Sr Mgr-Pub Safety Solutions Mktg - Hitachi Data Systems Corporation; *pg.* 407, *pg.* 265
Jones, Natalie, VP-Brand Dev & Creative Product - Mannington Mills, Inc.; *pg.* 934, *pg.* 1119
Jones, Natalie, Sr Product Mgr - National Geographic Society; *pg.* 1667, *pg.* 402
Jones, Natalie Z., Dir-Mktg & Events - DreamWorks Animation SKG, Inc.; *pg.* 284, *pg.* 96
Jones, Nate, VP & Publ-Mobile, Social & Emerging Platforms - Warner Bros. Entertainment Inc.; *pg.* 319, *pg.* 54
Jones, Neal, Chief Sales & Marketing Officer-Middle East & Africa - Marriott International, Inc.; *pg.* 1102, *pg.* 764
Jones, Nicole, Gen Mgr-Content Strategy & Digital Mktg Optimization - Delta Air Lines, Inc.; *pg.* 1905, *pg.* 503
Jones, Nikki, Mgr-Special Event Sls - Dave & Buster's Entertainment, Inc.; *pg.* 1724, *pg.* 1679
Jones, Nooka, Mgr-Mktg-Creative Lab - Google Inc.; *pg.* 1249, *pg.* 153
Jones, Olga Osminkina, VP-Mktg-Water Div - The Dannon Company, Inc.; *pg.* 851, *pg.* 1351
Jones, Patrick, VP-Corp Hospitality, Sls & Svcs - Madison Square Garden Network; *pg.* 297, *pg.* 1255
Jones, Patrick, Mgr-Digital Mktg Knowledge - Unilever United States, Inc.; *pg.* 904, *pg.* 1061
Jones, Paul, VP-Brand & Digital Mktg - Mary Kay Inc.; *pg.* 516, *pg.* 1657
Jones, Paula, Grp Dir-Mktg - Cadence Design Systems, Inc.; *pg.* 367, *pg.* 239
Jones, Phil, Mgr-Brand Mktg-North America - AGCO Corporation; *pg.* 700, *pg.* 530
Jones, Phil, Sr VP-Sls-North America - The Scotts Miracle-Gro Company; *pg.* 1799, *pg.* 1459
Jones, Polly, Product Mgr - Nutraceutical International Corporation; *pg.* 1576, *pg.* 1753
Jones, Rachel, Asst VP-Direct Response & Analytical Mktg - Bank of America Corporation; *pg.* 718, *pg.* 1362
Jones, Richard, Gen Mgr-Digital & Automotive Sls - The Dallas Morning News Co.; *pg.* 1633, *pg.* 1679
Jones, Richard W., Mgr-Mktg Comm - Corken, Inc.; *pg.* 1325, *pg.* 1485
Jones, Rob, Co-Founder & Creative Dir - FanDuel, Inc.; *pg.* 547, *pg.* 1231
Jones, Robin, Mgr-Adv & Traffic - NBTY, Inc.; *pg.* 1572, *pg.* 1338
Jones, Rodney S., Sr Dir-Engrg & Construction - Great Wolf Resorts, Inc.; *pg.* 1093, *pg.* 1866
Jones, Russell, VP-Mktg & Membership Dev - American Symphony Orchestra League; *pg.* 528, *pg.* 1194
Jones, Samantha, Sr Dir-Bus Dev - Assurant, Inc.; *pg.* 1193, *pg.* 1198
Jones, Sarah, Dir-Field Mktg - American Red Cross; *pg.* 130, *pg.* 395
Jones, Scott, VP-Sls & Mktg - Dixon Valve & Coupling Company; *pg.* 1045, *pg.* 766
Jones, Scott, Sr Mgr-Brand Mktg-Global - Yahoo! Inc.; *pg.* 1289, *pg.* 289
Jones, Scott H., Dir-Strategic Mktg-Global - Johnson & Johnson; *pg.* 1549, *pg.* 1091
Jones, Seamus, Mgr-Mktg-NA - Dell Inc.; *pg.* 383, *pg.* 1737
Jones, Sophie, Mgr-Mktg Comm & PathFinder - Schlumberger Limited; *pg.* 801, *pg.* 1714
Jones, Stacey, Sr Dir-Corp Mktg - Accenture; *pg.* 1392, *pg.* 1186
Jones, Stephanie, Specialist-Mktg Comm-Chemical, Oil & Gas Indus Grp - ABB Inc. - Automation Technologies Instrumentation Products; *pg.* 1398, *pg.* 1590
Jones, Steven A., Mgr-Mktg-America - Six Flags Entertainment Corporation; *pg.* 583, *pg.* 1698
Jones, Steven F., Mgr-Mktg-Low Voltage Products - ABB Inc.; *pg.* 1309, *pg.* 1359
Jones, Susan, Dir-Media - Diageo North America Inc.; *pg.* 248, *pg.* 1223
Jones, Suzanne, Sr Dir-Global Chocolate Innovation - The Hershey Co.; *pg.* 1855, *pg.* 1538
Jones, Tami, Sr Dir - Ohio State University; *pg.* 606, *pg.* 1443
Jones, Ted, Mgr-Sls - Textile Rubber & Chemical Company; *pg.* 1890, *pg.* 530
Jones, Thomas, Sr Mgr-Transactions - Federal National Mortgage Association; *pg.* 751, *pg.* 399
Jones, Thomas A., VP-Sls - EIS, Inc.; *pg.* 80, *pg.* 504
Jones, Tiffanie, Exec Dir-Global Brand Mktg Color Cosmetics - Avon Products, Inc.; *pg.* 500, *pg.* 1198
Jones, Tina Dempsey, Sr Head-Mktg & Mgr - CenturyLink, Inc; *pg.* 1870, *pg.* 317
Jones, Todd, Mgr-Ecommerce Mktg & Design - Bass Pro Shops, Inc.; *pg.* 1826, *pg.* 1006
Jones, Tom, Mgr-Applications Sls - Oracle Corporation; *pg.* 1272, *pg.* 786
Jones, Toni, Dir-Social Media - U-Haul International, Inc.; *pg.* 1926, *pg.* 20
Jones, Wade, Dir-Online Mktg - Golfsmith International Holdings, Inc.; *pg.* 1835, *pg.* 1662
Jones, Wade, Sr VP-Mktg & Strategy-Sabre Travel Network - Sabre Corporation; *pg.* 1710, *pg.* 752
Jones, Yardise, VP & Sr Mgr-Chase Retail Mktg - JPMorgan Chase & Co.; *pg.* 772, *pg.* 1246
Jones-Cervantes, Colleen, VP-Product Supply & Trading - Chevron Corporation; *pg.* 974, *pg.* 259
Jones-Olson, Logan, Dir-Mktg - Overstock.com, Inc.; *pg.* 1273, *pg.* 1760
Jonez, Jim, VP-Mktg - Dot Hill Systems Corp.; *pg.* 388, *pg.* 333
Jonsson, Johan, Product Mgr-Construction Boomers - Atlas Copco Comptec LLC; *pg.* 1314, *pg.* 1349
Jooma, Imran, Pres-Mktg, Online & Fin Svcs & Exec VP - Sears, Roebuck & Co.; *pg.* 1785, *pg.* 619
Joost, Cheryl, Mgr-Social Media Mktg - Benjamin Moore & Co.; *pg.* 1440, *pg.* 1085
Joosten, Steve, Reg Mgr-Sls - Campbell Wrapper Corporation; *pg.* 1454, *pg.* 1856
Jopek, Larry, VP-Mktg & Community Partnerships - Florida West Coast Public Broadcasting, Inc.; *pg.* 287, *pg.* 473
Jorda, Maria-Victoria, Assoc Dir-Mktg - Merck & Co., Inc.; *pg.* 1566, *pg.* 1077
Jordan, Brooke, Assoc Mgr-Mktg Geek Squad - Best Buy Co., Inc.; *pg.* 1761, *pg.* 954
Jordan, Chris, Mgr-Sls & Customer Svc - The Flinchbaugh Co., Inc.; *pg.* 82, *pg.* 1551
Jordan, Emily, Head-Global Retail Mktg Initiatives - Google Inc.; *pg.* 1249, *pg.* 153
Jordan, Emily, Brand Mgr - NIKE, Inc.; *pg.* 1812, *pg.* 1492
Jordan, Heather, Dir-Global Mktg & Product Dev - Bare Escentuals, Inc.; *pg.* 500, *pg.* 213
Jordan, Jackie, Dir-Color Mktg - Sherwin Williams; *pg.* 1448, *pg.* 1436
Jordan, Jeanne, VP & Reg Mgr-Sls - Yadkin Valley Financial Corporation; *pg.* 824, *pg.* 1372
Jordan, Karen, Mgr-Mktg-Sls Tech Org - Verizon Communications Inc.; *pg.* 1875, *pg.* 1309
Jordan, Leslie, Dir-Product Mgmt - Lithium Technologies; *pg.* 1263, *pg.* 221
Jordan, Linn, Dir-Mktg Strategy & Plng - Walgreen Co.; *pg.* 1608, *pg.* 605
Jordan, Mark, Sr Dir-News & Sports Programming - NBC Sports Network; *pg.* 300, *pg.* 375
Jordan, Phil, Mgr-Mktg & Pub Affairs - Journal Star, Inc.; *pg.* 1656, *pg.* 651
Jordan, Staci, Corp Dir-Digital Mktg - D.R. Horton, Inc.; *pg.* 1090, *pg.* 1694
Jordan, Teresa, Mgr-Digital Mktg - True Value Company; *pg.* 1065, *pg.* 592
Jordan, Victor, Mgr-Mktg Svcs - McKee Foods Corporation; *pg.* 1860, *pg.* 1630
Jordan-Deen, Kevin, Dir-Mktg - Colgate-Palmolive Company; *pg.* 504, *pg.* 1215
Jorge, Gina, Mgr-Multicultural Mktg - American Honda Motor Co., Inc.; *pg.* 163, *pg.* 292
Jorge, Kathleen, VP-Aftermarket Sls-North America - Delphi Automotive LLP; *pg.* 204, *pg.* 910
Jorgensen, Amanda, Assoc Dir-Zantac Mktg - Boehringer Ingelheim Pharmaceuticals, Inc.; *pg.* 1507, *pg.* 368
Jorgensen, Ken, Dir-Media Rels - Sturm, Ruger & Company, Inc.; *pg.* 1846, *pg.* 371
Jorgensen, Mark, Sr Mgr-Mktg - Consolidated Metco Inc.; *pg.* 1325, *pg.* 1846
Jorgensen, Michael, Sr VP-Creative - L'Oreal USA; *pg.* 514, *pg.* 1252
Jorgenson, Britt, Acct Dir-Mktg - adidas America Inc.; *pg.* 1803, *pg.* 1500
Jose, Jacob, Product Mgr - Texas Instruments Incorporated; *pg.* 679, *pg.* 1688
Jose, Sarah, Head-Brand Mktg Mgmt - S.C. Johnson & Son, Inc.; *pg.* 334, *pg.* 1889
Josefsberg, Isabella, Strategist-Social Media-Global - Starwood Hotels & Resorts Worldwide, Inc.; *pg.* 1114, *pg.* 378
Joseph, Aj, Exec Dir-Creative - Adobe Systems Incorporated; *pg.* 342, *pg.* 235
Joseph, Angie, Dir-Mktg & Circulation - Tampa Bay Business Journal; *pg.* 1691, *pg.* 476
Joseph, Dennis, Sr Mgr-Strategic-Global - Kimberly-Clark Corporation; *pg.* 1461, *pg.* 1720
Joseph, Jon, Sr VP-Sls & Bus Dev - The Penn Companies; *pg.* 10, *pg.* 1568
Joseph, Mark, Dir-Integrated Mktg - USG Corporation; *pg.* 118, *pg.* 594
Joseph, Neil, Mgr-Offer Mktg Ecobusiness - Schneider Canada, Inc.; *pg.* 1374, *pg.* 1928
Joseph, Sarah, Mgr-Mktg - Church & Dwight Canada Corp.; *pg.* 503, *pg.* 1925
Joseph, Sharon, VP-Sls-Walmart & Club - Newell Rubbermaid Inc.; *pg.* 1128, *pg.* 515
Joseph, Tim, Product Mgr-1.5 T MR Bus Unit - Toshiba America, Inc.; *pg.* 681, *pg.* 1302
Josephakis, John, VP-Sls-Worldwide - Cray Inc.; *pg.* 380, *pg.* 1834
Josephson, Mark, Chief Sls Officer & VP - The Reader's Digest Association, Inc.; *pg.* 1679, *pg.* 1322
Josephson, Robert, Assoc Dir-Media Rels - Purdue Pharma LP; *pg.* 1587, *pg.* 377
Joshi, Aditya, Exec VP-Products - Intralinks Inc.; *pg.* 420, *pg.* 1244
Joshi, Mohini, Brand Mgr-Jack's & Growth Channels - Nestle USA, Inc.; *pg.* 883, *pg.* 96
Joshi, Shirish, Dir-Channel Sls-APAC - Polycom, Inc.; *pg.* 664, *pg.* 249
Joshi, Umesh, Sr Product Mgr - VMware, Inc.; *pg.* 490, *pg.* 179
Jost, Jennifer, Dir-Omni Channel Mktg - PetSmart, Inc.; *pg.* 1481, *pg.* 18
Jost, Patrick, Sr VP-Licensing & Mktg Intl - BMG/Music; *pg.*

First page reference indicates Business Class Edition
Second page reference indicates Geographic Edition

533, *pg.* 1205
Joukoff, Stephanie, Sr Acct Mgr-Wearables, Retail & Partner Mktg-Cause Mktg - Intel Corporation; *pg.* 645, *pg.* 266
Jouve, Yen, Dir-Mktg Strategy & Plng - The Coca-Cola Company; *pg.* 240, *pg.* 493
Jovanovic, Traci, Reg VP-Microsoft Mobile Device Sls-North America - Microsoft Corporation; *pg.* 435, *pg.* 1824
Jow, Steve, Sr VP-Sls - SYNNEX Corporation; *pg.* 480, *pg.* 92
Jowaisas, Kate, Supvr-Sports Adv - GEICO Corporation; *pg.* 1200, *pg.* 399
Joy, Benjamin, Dir-Product Mgmt - InFocus Corporation; *pg.* 644, *pg.* 1503
Joy, Christine, Sr Mgr-Mktg - Comcast Corporation; *pg.* 276, *pg.* 1560
Joy, Pam, Sr Mgr-Mktg Channel - Wright Express Corporation; *pg.* 493, *pg.* 753
Joy, Ryan, Sr Dir-R&D - Checkers Drive-In Restaurants, Inc.; *pg.* 1017, *pg.* 472
Joy, Susan, Sr Media Planner-Mktg-Journeys Grp - Genesco Inc.; *pg.* 1809, *pg.* 1650
Joyce, Alan, Product Mgr - YouTube, LLC; *pg.* 1291, *pg.* 198
Joyce, Brian, VP- Sls-A + E Networks - The History Channel; *pg.* 290, *pg.* 1240
Joyce, Claire, Product Mgr-Global Apparel & Running - New Balance Athletic Shoe, Inc.; *pg.* 1811, *pg.* 798
Joyce, Derek, Mgr-Product PR - Hyundai Motor America; *pg.* 179, *pg.* 89
Joyce, Gavin, Dir-Mktg, Loyalty & CRM - Destination Maternity Corporation; *pg.* 23, *pg.* 1563
Joyce, Jennifer, Product Dir-Global - Flint Group, Inc.; *pg.* 1163, *pg.* 904
Joyce, Jessica, Mgr-PR - Bed Bath & Beyond Inc.; *pg.* 1121, *pg.* 1127
Joyce, Kelsey, Sr Dir-Legal Affairs - T-Mobile US, Inc.; *pg.* 676, *pg.* 1816
Joyce, Kevin, Product Dir-Performance - The North Face, Inc.; *pg.* 1840, *pg.* 252
Joyce, Paul, Product Dir-Mgmt - Google Inc.; *pg.* 1249, *pg.* 153
Joyce, Todd, Sr VP-East Coast Sls - DefyMedia; *pg.* 1237, *pg.* 1222
Joyner, David, Exec VP-Sls & Mktg - CVS Health Corporation; *pg.* 1765, *pg.* 1610
Joyner, Jessica, Project Mgr-Mktg - Ingersoll-Rand Company; *pg.* 1349, *pg.* 1370
Joyner, Kenneth, Dir-Coal Mktg - Norfolk Southern Corporation; *pg.* 1917, *pg.* 1797
Joyner, Shannon, Brand Mgr - Electrolux Home Products North America; *pg.* 54, *pg.* 1366
Jozwiak, Laura, Sr VP-Sls & Client Rels - Wheels Inc.; *pg.* 1931, *pg.* 607
Jozwik, Julie, Mgr-Franchise Mktg - Matco Tools Corporation; *pg.* 1055, *pg.* 1474
Juarez, Abel, Mgr-Inside Sls - Viking Door & Window; *pg.* 119, *pg.* 251
Juarez, Jenifer, Sr Head-Integrated Mktg - NetApp, Inc.; *pg.* 444, *pg.* 287
Juarez, Karla Nadieska, Mgr-Merchant Adv - Academy Sports & Outdoors, Ltd.; *pg.* 1824, *pg.* 1724
Juarez, Mike, Mgr-Mktg Strategy - American Airlines Inc.; *pg.* 1898, *pg.* 1693
Juarez, Sophia, Sr Mgr-Mktg - Latina Media Ventures, LLC; *pg.* 1657, *pg.* 1250
Juarez-Mrazek, Ivan, VP-Digital Mktg-Paid Search & Social Media - Bank of America Corporation; *pg.* 718, *pg.* 1362
Juba, Mark, Dir-Customer Mktg - Tractor Supply Company; *pg.* 708, *pg.* 1627
Jubb, Mary, Specialist-Retail Mktg - Kikkoman International Inc.; *pg.* 868, *pg.* 220
Jubelirer, Matt, Principal & Mgr-Product Mktg-Office Labs - Microsoft Corporation; *pg.* 435, *pg.* 1824
Juber, Nico, Sr Mgr-Mktg & Digital Media - Adobe Systems Incorporated; *pg.* 342, *pg.* 235
Jucha, Sandi Willis, Dir-Field Mktg - BUFFALO WILD WINGS, INC.; *pg.* 1718, *pg.* 931
Jucker, Emmanuelle, Brand Mgr-Consumer Products Div-North America - Ansell; *pg.* 1495, *pg.* 1114
Juda, Monique, Mgr-Product & Mktg Svcs - Applied Industrial Technologies, Inc.; *pg.* 199, *pg.* 1428
Judah, Natalie, Sr Specialist-Email Mktg - Nordstrom, Inc.; *pg.* 1779, *pg.* 1837
Judal, Jay, Dir-Outside Sls - Zoological Society of San Diego; *pg.* 595, *pg.* 211
Judd, Dennis, Dir-Mktg - Dupont Pioneer; *pg.* 1795, *pg.* 708
Judd, Shane, Dir-Digital Mktg - Kohler Co.; *pg.* 91, *pg.* 1862
Judge, Garth, Sr Dir-Mobile R&D - 8x8, Inc.; *pg.* 1865, *pg.* 282
Judge, Patrick, Buyer-Mktg - GEICO Corporation; *pg.* 1200, *pg.* 399
Judkins, John, Dir-Mktg - Comcast Cable Communications, Inc.; *pg.* 276, *pg.* 1560
Judkins, Kathleen, Brand Mgr-Pro Oral Health - The Procter & Gamble Company; *pg.* 1129, *pg.* 1418
Judkins, Rosemary, Mgr-Sls - Alabama Bureau of Tourism & Travel; *pg.* 988, *pg.* 7
Judkowitz, Jay, Product Mgr-Cloud Platform Storage - Google Inc.; *pg.* 1249, *pg.* 153
Judy, Cortese, Bus Mgr-Pricing - ACCO Brands Corporation; *pg.* 340, *pg.* 626
Judy, Dave, VP-Retail Sls-Retail Svcs - Alliance Data Systems Corporation; *pg.* 347, *pg.* 1729
Jue, Laurine, Sr Mgr-Comm - Avista Corporation; *pg.* 1935, *pg.* 1843
Juenger, Steve, Dir-Mktg - Reliance Medical Products, Inc.; *pg.* 1589, *pg.* 1461
Juhas, Gina, Sr Mgr-Mktg-CDT - Cox Communications, Inc.; *pg.* 279, *pg.* 501
Juhasz, Diana, VP-Specialty Merchant Mktg - Citigroup Inc.; *pg.* 735, *pg.* 1212
Juhl, Andrea, Mgr-Mktg Comm - MTS Systems Corporation; *pg.* 442, *pg.* 923
Juhnke, Mike, Program Mgr-Product - Lochinvar Corporation; *pg.* 1073, *pg.* 1640
Juisenga, Steve, VP-Sls - American Pop Corn Company; *pg.* 825, *pg.* 712
Jukes, Lindsey, Dir-Mktg & Morningstar Investment Svcs - MORNINGSTAR, INC.; *pg.* 784, *pg.* 583
Jules, Francis, Rep-Sls Dev - salesforce.com, inc.; *pg.* 1278, *pg.* 226
Julian, Anna H., Mgr-Mktg Ops-Americas Field Mktg - Cisco Systems, Inc.; *pg.* 372, *pg.* 240
Julian, Christina, Dir-Midwest Mktg - Toll Brothers, Inc.; *pg.* 115, *pg.* 1541
Julian, Kendrick, Mgr-Product Mktg - eBags, Inc.; *pg.* 1240, *pg.* 331
Julian, Kenneth, Sr Dir-Corp Comm - Harsco Corporation; *pg.* 86, *pg.* 1519
Julian, Marian, Brand Mktg Mgr - Overstock.com, Inc.; *pg.* 1273, *pg.* 1760
Juliano, Auburn, Brand Mgr - The J.M. Smucker Company; *pg.* 865, *pg.* 1468
Juliano, Dina, Sr VP-Consumer Product Strategy-TV Everywhere - NBC Universal, Inc.; *pg.* 300, *pg.* 1266
Juliano, Lily, Head-Multicultural Mktg - Cellco Partnership; *pg.* 1869, *pg.* 1042
Juliano, Stacey, Dir-Mktg Comm & Branding-Natl - Verizon Communications Inc.; *pg.* 1875, *pg.* 1309
Juliano, Virginia, VP-Multi-Platform Mktg - Showtime Networks Inc.; *pg.* 308, *pg.* 1291
Julius, Jennee, Dir-Mktg Strategy - ITAGroup, Inc.; *pg.* 422, *pg.* 713
Julius, Maxwell, Mgr-Digital Mktg - Abbott Laboratories; *pg.* 1484, *pg.* 551
Jump, Jeannie S., Coord-PR - Saia, Inc.; *pg.* 1922, *pg.* 533
Jump, John, Brand Mgr-Powersports Div - K&N Engineering Inc.; *pg.* 210, *pg.* 194
Jump, Monte, VP-Global Mktg-Lotz Better - Schlotzsky's, Ltd.; *pg.* 1749, *pg.* 1665
Junca, Stephanie, Specialist-Digital Mktg & Web Content - Elkay Manufacturing Company; *pg.* 80, *pg.* 645
Juneau, Christopher A., Sr Dir-Mktg-Global Accounts - Concur Technologies, Inc.; *pg.* 1236, *pg.* 1813
Juneja, Abhivarun, Dir-Customer Mktg - American Express Company; *pg.* 712, *pg.* 1190
Jung, Cyndi A., Dir-Mktg - Markel Corporation; *pg.* 1207, *pg.* 1783
Jung, Peter, Sr Dir-Growth Segment Mktg - National Association for Stock Car Auto Racing; *pg.* 566, *pg.* 420
Jung, Sarah, Program Mgr-Cultural & Traditional Media - Liberty Mutual Insurance Group Inc.; *pg.* 1205, *pg.* 797
Junge, Bob, VP-Airport Solutions & Product Mgmt - PASSUR Aerospace, Inc.; *pg.* 233, *pg.* 376
Junghans, Chris, Sr VP-Sls - Nashville Predators, LLC; *pg.* 565, *pg.* 1652
Jungreis, Benjamin, Assoc Dir-Indirect Procurement-Media - Colgate-Palmolive Company; *pg.* 504, *pg.* 1215
Junkins, Cara, Dir-Sls & Mktg - Titan International, Inc.; *pg.* 219, *pg.* 653
Junkunc, Theresa, Dir-Mktg Comm - Bissell Homecare, Inc.; *pg.* 52, *pg.* 887
Jupe, Jennifer, Reg Dir-Mktg - KB Home; *pg.* 90, *pg.* 134
Jurczak, Deborah, Asst Media Buyer - IBM; *pg.* 410, *pg.* 1449
Jurczyk, Rita, Dir-Major Media Sls - The San Diego Union-Tribune, LLC; *pg.* 1682, *pg.* 208
Jurgella, Jeff, Sr Dir-Corp Partnerships - Minnesota Twins, LLC; *pg.* 563, *pg.* 940
Juriga, Jesse, Dir-Creative - Google Inc.; *pg.* 1249, *pg.* 153
Juris, Lisa, VP-Mktg - Cybex International, Inc.; *pg.* 1521, *pg.* 832
Jurkiewicz, Matthew, Specialist-Mktg Comm - Eppendorf North America; *pg.* 1412, *pg.* 1164
Jurney, Scott, Reg Dir-Sls - Sanofi US; *pg.* 1592, *pg.* 1046
Jurries, Valerie, VP-Mktg - Hasbro, Inc.; *pg.* 954, *pg.* 1603
Juster, Maxwell, Brand Mgr - Anheuser-Busch Companies, LLC; *pg.* 237, *pg.* 991
Justh, Tiffani, Brand Mgr - Utz Quality Foods, Inc.; *pg.* 907, *pg.* 1536
Justice, Lonnie, VP-Sls, Mktg & Svcs - Agilent Technologies, Inc.; *pg.* 614, *pg.* 264
Justice, Troy, Sr Dir-Basketball Ops-Intl - National Basketball Association; *pg.* 566, *pg.* 1264
Justiniano, Jaime, Brand Mgr-Online-Social Media - TracFone Wireless, Inc.; *pg.* 681, *pg.* 447
Justman, Anthony, Sr Dir-Legal & Bus Affairs - Sony Computer Entertainment America LLC; *pg.* 966, *pg.* 256
Juszak, Brian, Dir-Retail Mktg-North America - Carhartt, Inc.; *pg.* 39, *pg.* 875
Jutt, Salma, Sr Dir-Mktg-LATISSE - Allergan, Inc.; *pg.* 1491, *pg.* 106
Jutteau-Casagrande, Valerie, Brand Mgr-OxiClean - Church & Dwight Co., Inc.; *pg.* 1153, *pg.* 1063
Juzeszyn, Michelle, Mgr-Event Mktg & Sponsorship - Porsche Cars North America, Inc.; *pg.* 189, *pg.* 518

K

Kabakoff, Drew, Dir-Brand Mktg - Sunoco Inc.; *pg.* 985, *pg.* 1571
Kabb, Julie, Rep-Sls & Bus Dev-Natl - General Growth Properties, Inc.; *pg.* 1093, *pg.* 574
Kacala, Jacquelyn, Sr Coord-PR - Kohl's Corporation; *pg.* 1775, *pg.* 1870
Kacala, Karan, Mgr-Online Mktg - Illumina, Inc.; *pg.* 412, *pg.* 203
Kacergis, Jeff, Bus Mgr-Dev - BDO Seidman, LLP; *pg.* 724, *pg.* 1202
Kachru, Amit, Mgr-Offer Mktg-Indus Svcs Canada-Schneider Electric - Schneider Canada, Inc.; *pg.* 1374, *pg.* 1928
Kacur, Petro, Dir-Media Rels - The Coca-Cola Company; *pg.* 240, *pg.* 493
Kaczka-Rivera, Kirsten, Mgr-GTM & Launch-PPS Worldwide Mktg - Hewlett-Packard Company; *pg.* 404, *pg.* 175
Kaczmarski, Joe, Mgr-Sls-Natl - Godiva Chocolatier, Inc.; *pg.* 1854, *pg.* 1235
Kadambi, Kiran, Sr Product Mgr - eBay Inc.; *pg.* 1240, *pg.* 243
Kaderabek, Brooke, Div Mgr-Mktg - William Grant & Sons, Inc.; *pg.* 1972, *pg.* 1057
Kadir, Razia, Asst Mgr-Mktg - AMEX Bank of Canada; *pg.* 715, *pg.* 1923
Kadivar, Sylvie, Sr Dir-Strategic Mktg - Samsung Electronics America, Inc.; *pg.* 669, *pg.* 1115
Kadrmas, Stacey, Sr Mgr-Brand Dev - The Home Depot, Inc.; *pg.* 1050, *pg.* 510
Kaduk, Andrea, Mgr-SEM & Paid Social - Walgreen Co.; *pg.* 1608, *pg.* 605
Kadyan, Anurag, Sr Dir-eCommerce & Digital Mktg - Tourneau Inc.; *pg.* 14, *pg.* 1303
Kadylak, Judy, VP-Mktg - Bruegger's Corporation; *pg.* 1718, *pg.* 1764
Kae, Diana, Coord-Mktg - Asiana Airlines; *pg.* 1899, *pg.* 126
Kaelin, Melissa, Dir-Sls - The Libman Company; *pg.* 331, *pg.* 553
Kaestner, Mark, Dir-Learning & Dev-Sls Capability - The Coca-Cola Company; *pg.* 240, *pg.* 493
Kafantaris, Lou, Grp Brand Mgr-Global Aftermarket - Federal-Mogul Holdings Corporation; *pg.* 205, *pg.* 907
Kagan, Adina, Sr VP-Media & Customer Insights - Chanel, Inc.; *pg.* 503, *pg.* 1211
Kagele, Jerry, Sr VP-Sls-Worldwide - HGST; *pg.* 406, *pg.* 260
Kagen, Brian, CMO & Exec VP - Medifast, Inc.; *pg.* 1562, *pg.* 774
Kagey, Tara, Mgr-Direct Response Mktg - Genworth Financial,

Inc.; *pg.* 761, *pg.* 1802
Kahaly, Cara, Dir-Shopper Mktg & Insights-Grocery & Alternate Channel - Novartis Corporation; *pg.* 1574, *pg.* 1273
Kahan, Michelle, Dir-Mktg - GREAT AMERICAN GROUP, INC.; *pg.* 1394, *pg.* 308
Kaharick, Allison E., Coord-Corp Mktg - Black Box Corporation; *pg.* 361, *pg.* 1547
Kahen, Robin, Sr Brand Mgr-Mktg-Global - Abbott Laboratories; *pg.* 1484, *pg.* 551
Kahler, Dylan, Sr Project Mgr-Creative - Brooks Sports Inc.; *pg.* 1805, *pg.* 1818
Kahn, Alan, VP-Foodservice Sls-Prepared Foods - Pilgrim's Pride Corporation; *pg.* 889, *pg.* 330
Kahn, Karen, VP-Corp Mktg & Comm - Broadcom Corporation; *pg.* 364, *pg.* 108
Kahn, Lisa, Dir-Global Adv & Brand Mgmt Bus Plng - American Express Company; *pg.* 712, *pg.* 1190
Kahn, Mary, Sr Mgr-Brand Innovation - PepsiCo, Inc.; *pg.* 250, *pg.* 1327
Kahn, Matt, Dir-Corp Mktg - Energy Brands, Inc.; *pg.* 854, *pg.* 1227
Kahn, Melanie, Sr Dir-Puppy Mills Campaign - The Humane Society of the United States; *pg.* 143, *pg.* 400
Kahn, Stuart, Brand Mktg Mgr-Retail Design & Experience - American Greetings Corporation; *pg.* 1615, *pg.* 1428
Kaihatu, Walter, VP-Outdoor Products - Browning; *pg.* 1828, *pg.* 1752
Kail, Aaron, Brand Mgr - The Procter & Gamble Company; *pg.* 1129, *pg.* 1418
Kaim, Karen, Reg Mgr-Sls - Babcox Media; *pg.* 1619, *pg.* 1400
Kainec, Sean, Head-SEO & Sr Mgr - The Home Depot, Inc.; *pg.* 1050, *pg.* 510
Kainer, Adam, Mgr-Energy Mktg-Indirect Sls - NRG Energy, Inc.; *pg.* 1948, *pg.* 1712
Kainer, Karen, Mgr-Consumer & Digital Mktg - Merck Animal Health; *pg.* 1478, *pg.* 1124
Kairis, Margaret, VP-Sls, Bus Plng & Strategy - Sony Electronics, Inc.; *pg.* 676, *pg.* 209
Kairys, George, Mgr-Product Mktg-Global - Molex Incorporated; *pg.* 655, *pg.* 628
Kaiser, Jim, Mgr-Sls & Svc - Hougen Manufacturing Inc.; *pg.* 1347, *pg.* 908
Kaiser, Karen, VP-Adv-Natl - Domino's Pizza, Inc.; *pg.* 1726, *pg.* 865
Kaiser, Kurtis, Sr Mgr-Media Mktg & Pro - Cabela's Incorporated; *pg.* 535, *pg.* 1019
Kaiser, Liz, Head-Product Innovation Mktg - Visa Inc.; *pg.* 816, *pg.* 230
Kaiser, Liz, Dir-US Mktg-Apple Pay - Visa U.S.A., Inc.; *pg.* 817, *pg.* 231
Kaiser, Louis, Mgr-Mktg-Partner Card Svcs EMEA - American Express Company; *pg.* 712, *pg.* 1190
Kaiser, Patrick, Dir-Mktg - Nationwide Mutual Insurance Company; *pg.* 1210, *pg.* 1442
Kaiser, Renee, Dir-Natl Field Sls - Electrolux Home Products North America; *pg.* 54, *pg.* 1366
Kaiser, Rhett, Brand Mgr-No America-IBM Flash & SAN - International Business Machines Corporation; *pg.* 418, *pg.* 1138
Kaiser, Vikki, Dir-Mktg & PR - Panera Bread Company; *pg.* 1029, *pg.* 1001
Kajcienski, Sean, Chief Sales Officer - Coverall North America, Inc.; *pg.* 329, *pg.* 421
Kajfez, Greg, Sr Mgr-Web Mktg - FileMaker, Inc.; *pg.* 639, *pg.* 265
Kajihara, Claudia, Coord-Mktg-Catalog & estore - Guthy-Renker LLC; *pg.* 289, *pg.* 273
Kajiwara, Hitoshi, Mng Dir-Production & Pur - Alpine Electronics of America, Inc.; *pg.* 616, *pg.* 292
Kajshmanan, Anand, Product Mgr - Intel Corporation; *pg.* 645, *pg.* 266
Kajuch, Zuzana, VP-Sls Support - Trunk Club; *pg.* 49, *pg.* 593
Kakkar, Samir, Product Mgr - ADTRAN, Inc.; *pg.* 344, *pg.* 6
Kalaf, Alex, Dir-Strategy & Sls Plng - U.S. News & World Report, L.P.; *pg.* 1698, *pg.* 1308
Kalaijakis, Anthony, Mgr-Strategic Medical Mktg - Molex Incorporated; *pg.* 655, *pg.* 628
Kalakuntla, Ron, VP-Mktg - Integrated Silicon Solution, Inc.; *pg.* 645, *pg.* 145
Kalamajka, Traci, Mgr-Interactive Mktg - The Goodyear Tire & Rubber Company; *pg.* 1883, *pg.* 1401
Kalani, Neeraj, Sr Dir-Global Strategy & Insights - PepsiCo, Inc.; *pg.* 259, *pg.* 1327
Kalb, Bill, Dir-Sls - ELECTROMED, INC.; *pg.* 1527, *pg.* 951
Kalbacher, Kori, Dir-Media Specialists - MFA Incorporated; *pg.* 1479, *pg.* 976
Kaldor, Erik, Specialist-Mktg Comm - Medtronic, Inc.; *pg.* 1564, *pg.* 939
Kalec, Katherine, Buyer-Mktg - GEICO Corporation; *pg.* 1200, *pg.* 399
Kalember, Jen, Specialist-Sls & Mktg-Strategic Customers - The Dun & Bradstreet Corp.; *pg.* 1637, *pg.* 1120
Kaleta, Tom, VP-Mktg - Benelli USA Corporation; *pg.* 1827, *pg.* 754
Kaley, Peggi, Dir-Mktg-Global - Dell Inc.; *pg.* 383, *pg.* 1737
Kalezic, Dragana, Dir-Adv Ops - Salon Media Group, Inc.; *pg.* 1278, *pg.* 226
Kalfus, Lisa, Sr Dir-Mktg - Wente Vineyards; *pg.* 1972, *pg.* 122
Kalis, David, VP-Mktg - FMR LLC (Fidelity Investments); *pg.* 759, *pg.* 794
Kaljaj, Victor, Mgr-Digital Mktg Tech-GMIT Global Sls & Mktg - General Motors Company; *pg.* 175, *pg.* 881
Kallenberg, Vicki, Analyst-Mktg - Safeway Inc.; *pg.* 1032, *pg.* 184
Kalles, Susi, Mgr-ECommerce Mktg-Social Media Mktg - AT&T Mobility LLC; *pg.* 619, *pg.* 488
Kallman, Rena, Project Mgr-Mktg Comm - International Business Machines Corporation; *pg.* 418, *pg.* 1138
Kallner, Bruce, Sr VP-Strategic Sls & Mktg - NBC Universal, Inc.; *pg.* 300, *pg.* 1266
Kalmanowicz, Diane, Sr Dir-Web Mktg & Dev - Citrix Systems, Inc.; *pg.* 375, *pg.* 424
Kalmanowicz, Joel, Assoc Product Mgr - Google Inc.; *pg.* 1249, *pg.* 153
Kalmbach, Kelly, Dir-Mktg - Chicago Convention & Tourism Bureau; *pg.* 990, *pg.* 569
Kalmus, Jocelyn, Assoc Mgr-Mktg - General Mills, Inc.; *pg.* 828, *pg.* 933
Kalna, Terry, Sr VP-Sls & Brdcst - Pittsburgh Penguins LLC; *pg.* 577, *pg.* 1578
Kalodner, Elizabeth, Exec VP & Gen Mgr-CBS Consumer Products - CBS Broadcasting Inc.; *pg.* 273, *pg.* 1210
Kalodner, Elizabeth, Exec VP & Gen Mgr-CBS Consumer Products - CBS Corporation; *pg.* 273, *pg.* 1210
Kalra, Nikhilesh, Reg Dir-Mktg-Middle East - Reckitt Benckiser Inc.; *pg.* 1136, *pg.* 1105
Kalra, Sachin, Grp Mgr-Mktg & Student Bus - Adobe Systems Incorporated; *pg.* 342, *pg.* 235
Kalra, Vipin, Sr VP & Head-Merchant Sls & Solutions-Asia Pacific - Visa Inc.; *pg.* 816, *pg.* 230
Kalsi, Monu, VP & Head-Digital Mktg - Zurich Holding Company of America, Inc.; *pg.* 1224, *pg.* 660
Kaltabanis, Ginny, Sr Dir-HR - Hermes of Paris, Inc.; *pg.* 7, *pg.* 1240
Kaltenbach, Brian, Planner-Mktg - GEICO Corporation; *pg.* 1200, *pg.* 399
Kaltreider, Jeffrey, VP-Mktg - Munchkin, Inc.; *pg.* 964, *pg.* 300
Kalus, Mark, VP-Product Mgmt-Buy-Side - Tremor Video; *pg.* 682, *pg.* 1305
Kamal, Asad, Dir-Strategic Mktg-Global - Honeywell International Inc.; *pg.* 407, *pg.* 1088
Kamat, Mayur, Product Mgr-Google Talk-Real Time Comm - Google Inc.; *pg.* 1249, *pg.* 153
Kamath, Amar, VP-Mktg - Bio-Reference Laboratories, Inc.; *pg.* 1402, *pg.* 1058
Kambol, Bill, Sr Specialist-Mdsg & Display - Nestle Purina PetCare Company; *pg.* 1479, *pg.* 1000
Kamchatov, Rebecca, Specialist-Mktg - Toll Brothers, Inc.; *pg.* 115, *pg.* 1541
Kamdar, Jinen, Product Mgr - Twitter, Inc.; *pg.* 1285, *pg.* 228
Kamdar, Sagar, Dir-Product Mgmt-Google Loon - Google Inc.; *pg.* 1249, *pg.* 153
Kamel, Karen, Product Mgr - Jarden Consumer Solutions; *pg.* 57, *pg.* 412
Kamenoff, Brooke, Coord-Social Media & Digital Dev - J. Crew Group, Inc.; *pg.* 1773, *pg.* 1245
Kamieniecki, Marta, Dir-Product Dev-Jewelry - Harry Winston, Inc.; *pg.* 6, *pg.* 1238
Kamienski, Tim, Dir-Brand Mktg - Sony Corporation of America; *pg.* 675, *pg.* 1293
Kaminska, Mike, Dir-Mdse - Hockey Western New York, LLC; *pg.* 552, *pg.* 1149
Kaminski, Jeffrey, Dir-Mktg Ops & Strategy-New Comml Channels - Novartis Corporation; *pg.* 1574, *pg.* 1273
Kaminski, Julie, Dir-Mktg & Comm - Christianity Today International; *pg.* 1627, *pg.* 561
Kaminsky, Jody, VP-Mktg - The Ultimate Software Group, Inc.; *pg.* 486, *pg.* 479
Kaminsky, Steve, Dir-Mktg & Comm - EMCOR Group, Inc.; *pg.* 80, *pg.* 361
Kamis, David, VP-Media Svcs & Distr - Crain Communications, Inc.; *pg.* 1631, *pg.* 879
Kamkhalia, Pranav, VP-Product Dev - NBC Universal, Inc.; *pg.* 300, *pg.* 1266
Kammerer, Mark, Sr VP-Mktg & Sls - Holland America Line Inc.; *pg.* 1911, *pg.* 1836
Kamp, Melody, Dir-Mktg - Simon Property Group, Inc.; *pg.* 1112, *pg.* 690
Kamp, Robert, VP & Head-Global Sls & Intl Ops - PlayNetwork, Inc.; *pg.* 577, *pg.* 1829
Kampelman, Ben, Mgr-Dicamba Mktg-US - Monsanto Company; *pg.* 1173, *pg.* 999
Kamper, Chris, VP-Offline Media - NutriSystem, Inc.; *pg.* 1577, *pg.* 1533
Kampf, Tom, Product Mgr-Trailer - Thermo King Corporation; *pg.* 1077, *pg.* 918
Kamrad, Colleen K., Sr Dir-Telesales & Ops - GlaxoSmithKline; *pg.* 1536, *pg.* 1565
Kamras, Paul, Sr Dir-Game Presentation - Brooklyn Nets; *pg.* 534, *pg.* 1145
Kan, Boky, Mgr-Mktg - Health Net, Inc.; *pg.* 1540, *pg.* 308
Kanabis, Debra, VP-Retail Mktg - Ralph Lauren Corporation; *pg.* 46, *pg.* 1284
Kanae, Tad, Strategist-Internal Social Bus - Mercer Inc.; *pg.* 1395, *pg.* 1258
Kanakarajan, Pavithra, Product Mgr-Map Maker - Google Inc.; *pg.* 1249, *pg.* 153
Kanalas, Kimberly, Brand Mgr-Media - Zurich Holding Company of America, Inc.; *pg.* 1224, *pg.* 660
Kanaley, Michael, Sr Mgr-Market Res - Capital One Financial Corporation; *pg.* 730, *pg.* 1789
Kanama, Michelle, Project Mgr-Digital Adv & Analytics - KB Home; *pg.* 90, *pg.* 134
Kanama, Rami, VP-Clock & Timing Products - Micrel, Inc.; *pg.* 654, *pg.* 247
Kanan, Matthew R., Exec VP-Sls & Mktg - Kanan Enterprises, Inc.; *pg.* 1857, *pg.* 1473
Kanapi, Randy, Mgr-Philippines Mktg - Intel Corporation; *pg.* 645, *pg.* 266
Kanaplue, Tom, Mgr-US Wholesale & Latin America Sls - Younger Optics; *pg.* 1437, *pg.* 297
Kanary, Kimberly, VP-PR & Social Media - Sterling Jewelers Inc.; *pg.* 13, *pg.* 1402
Kandel, Daniel, Sr Dir-Advanced Dev - KLA-Tencor Corporation; *pg.* 1353, *pg.* 146
Kandel, Keri, Head-Cross-Product Mktg-Google Brand - Google Inc.; *pg.* 1249, *pg.* 153
Kandikonda, Ravi, VP-Mktg Intelligence & Insight - Comcast Cable Communications, Inc.; *pg.* 276, *pg.* 1560
Kane Arturi, Liz, Dir-Adv - Dooney & Bourke, Inc.; *pg.* 24, *pg.* 361
Kane, Brian, Dir-Annuity Product Mgmt - MetLife, Inc.; *pg.* 1208, *pg.* 1258
Kane, Cara, Sr Dir-Corp Comm - KB Home; *pg.* 90, *pg.* 134
Kane, Chris, Dir-Media - Safeway Inc.; *pg.* 1032, *pg.* 184
Kane, David, Sr Mgr-Interactive Mktg - FCA US LLC; *pg.* 170, *pg.* 868
Kane, David, Sr Mgr-Interactive Mktg - TD Auto Finance; *pg.* 809, *pg.* 886
Kane, Gary, Dir-Mktg & Licensed Brands - Disney Theatrical Productions; *pg.* 545, *pg.* 1224
Kane, James, VP-Mktg Solutions - Live Nation Entertainment, Inc.; *pg.* 558, *pg.* 47
Kane, James, VP-Mktg Solutions - Live Nation Worldwide - Times Square Office; *pg.* 558, *pg.* 1252
Kane, Kathryn, Dir-Norton Global Mktg Campaigns - Symantec Corporation; *pg.* 478, *pg.* 161
Kane, Kelly, Dir-Integrated Mktg - Discovery Communications, Inc.; *pg.* 282, *pg.* 777
Kane, Kevin, Mgr-PR - Subway Restaurants; *pg.* 1751, *pg.* 356
Kane, Kim, Assoc Brand Mktg Mgr-Dunkin' Donuts Intl - Dunkin' Brands Group, Inc.; *pg.* 1727, *pg.* 810
Kane, Kurt, Chief Concept & Mktg Officer - The Wendy's Company; *pg.* 1755, *pg.* 1450
Kane, Leo, Sr VP-Consumer Products - National Football League; *pg.* 567, *pg.* 1264
Kane, Robert, Sr VP-Product Mgmt - Insight Enterprises, Inc.; *pg.* 415, *pg.* 26
Kane, Stephen, Sr VP-Mktg - Fidelity Information Services, Inc.; *pg.* 397, *pg.* 433
Kane, Steve, Head-Digital Sls - Barnes & Noble, Inc.; *pg.*

1619, *pg.* 1201
Kanfer, Elizabeth, Sr Dir-Fashion-Accessories - Saks Fifth Avenue, Inc.; *pg.* 1783, *pg.* 1287
Kang, Betsy, Reg Dir-Sls & Catering-Great Wolf Lodge - Great Wolf Resorts, Inc.; *pg.* 1093, *pg.* 1866
Kang, George, VP-OEM, Inside Sls & Dealer Dev - Edmunds, Inc.; *pg.* 1241, *pg.* 273
Kang, Jay, Mgr-Mktg - LG Electronics U.S.A., Inc.; *pg.* 651, *pg.* 1060
Kang, John, Mgr-Sls & China - House of Raeford Farms, Inc.; *pg.* 864, *pg.* 1386
Kang, Steve, Dir-Product Mgmt - Visa Inc.; *pg.* 816, *pg.* 230
Kaniewski, Tom, Dir-Creative-History Partnership - A&E Television Networks, LLC; *pg.* 267, *pg.* 1185
Kanios, Jan, Grp VP-Mktg - Ross Stores, Inc.; *pg.* 1783, *pg.* 78
Kannady, William, Coord-Mktg-Multicultural - Coca-Cola Bottling Co. Consolidated; *pg.* 240, *pg.* 1365
Kanneganti, Shivani, Brand Mgr-Downy Lenor Global - The Procter & Gamble Company; *pg.* 1129, *pg.* 1418
Kannengieszer, Steve, Dir-Product Mktg - Brooks Instrument, LLC; *pg.* 1403, *pg.* 1537
Kano, Wendy, Dir-Mktg Ops - LinkedIn Corporation; *pg.* 1262, *pg.* 160
Kanter, Maurissa, Dir-PR - Aon Hewitt; *pg.* 350, *pg.* 627
Kantor, Cynthia, Sr Gen Mgr-Product Mgmt & Mktg - General Electric Company; *pg.* 1297, *pg.* 347
Kantor, Susan, Sr VP-Mktg - Warner Bros. Entertainment Inc.; *pg.* 319, *pg.* 54
Kanwar, Kusum, Product Mgr - salesforce.com, inc.; *pg.* 1278, *pg.* 226
Kao, Evelyn, Product Mgr - Google Inc.; *pg.* 1249, *pg.* 153
Kao, Grace, Dir-Mktg - Yahoo! Inc.; *pg.* 1289, *pg.* 289
Kao, Helen, Brand Mgr-Fall, Holiday Mktg & Promos - Starbucks Corporation; *pg.* 897, *pg.* 1840
Kapas, Mukulika, Sr Product Mgr - Hewlett-Packard Company; *pg.* 404, *pg.* 175
Kapferer, Kathryn, Mgr-Mktg Res - The Sherwin-Williams Company; *pg.* 1447, *pg.* 1435
Kapferer, Kathryn, Mgr-Mktg Res - Sherwin Williams; *pg.* 1448, *pg.* 1436
Kaplan, Alex, Sr VP-Revenue & Mktg - DIRECTV Group Holdings, LLC; *pg.* 281, *pg.* 79
Kaplan, Alexander, Mktg Mgr-Americas - Dell Inc.; *pg.* 383, *pg.* 1737
Kaplan, Alyssa, Planner-Sls-CBS Television Network - CBS Corporation; *pg.* 273, *pg.* 1210
Kaplan, Amanda, Product Mgr-Membership Mktg - BJ's Wholesale Club, Inc.; *pg.* 1762, *pg.* 857
Kaplan, Andrew, Sr Product Mgr-Mktg - LinkedIn Corporation; *pg.* 1262, *pg.* 160
Kaplan, David, Sr VP-Res & Insights-Bravo & Oxygen Media - Bravo Media LLC; *pg.* 271, *pg.* 1206
Kaplan, David, Specialist-Bus Sls - Microsoft Corporation; *pg.* 435, *pg.* 1824
Kaplan, David, Jr., Sr VP & Gen Mgr-Mdse - HomeGoods, Inc.; *pg.* 1125, *pg.* 821
Kaplan, Glenn, Dir-Creative - Barnes & Noble, Inc.; *pg.* 1619, *pg.* 1201
Kaplan, Howard, Dir-Mktg Svcs - Schiller-Pfeiffer, Inc.; *pg.* 1061, *pg.* 1587
Kaplan, Jennifer, Mgr-Product Mktg - GovDelivery, Inc.; *pg.* 1255, *pg.* 961
Kaplan, Jennifer Camac, Brand Mgr-Dev-Global - Unilever United States, Inc.; *pg.* 904, *pg.* 1061
Kaplan, Jon, VP-Sls & Ops-US - Google Inc.; *pg.* 1249, *pg.* 153
Kaplan, Julia, Dir-Mktg-Home Care Div - The Clorox Company; *pg.* 327, *pg.* 169
Kaplan, Julia, Analyst-Retention Mktg - JAND, Inc.; *pg.* 1418, *pg.* 1245
Kaplan, Laurie, Project Mgr-Mktg Comm - Broadridge Financial Solutions Inc.; *pg.* 727, *pg.* 1172
Kaplan, Rachel, Mgr-Mktg Comm - WestRock Company; *pg.* 1472, *pg.* 1805
Kaplan, Sherrill, Dir-Digital & Loyalty Mktg - Dunkin' Brands Group, Inc.; *pg.* 1727, *pg.* 810
Kaplan, Steve, Dir-Sls-Northeast Reg - Interactive Intelligence, Inc.; *pg.* 417, *pg.* 687
Kaplan, Todd, Sr Dir-Mktg - PepsiCo, Inc.; *pg.* 259, *pg.* 1327
Kaplan, Tony, Dir-Trade Mktg - adidas America Inc.; *pg.* 1803, *pg.* 1500
Kapler, Jason, VP-Mktg - LiveWorld, Inc.; *pg.* 1264, *pg.* 246
Kaplinski, April, Mgr-Social Media & Digital Comm-Global Corp Affairs - Amgen Inc.; *pg.* 1493, *pg.* 291
Kaplun, James, Dir-Creative-Retail Mktg - Hess Corporation; *pg.* 979, *pg.* 1240
Kapoor, Kunal, Head-Products & Client Solutions - MORNINGSTAR, INC.; *pg.* 784, *pg.* 583
Kapoor, Sean, VP-Mktg-Global - Harman International Industries, Incorporated; *pg.* 641, *pg.* 374
Kapoor, Sumit, Sr Mgr-Brand Mktg-Amazon & Junglee - Amazon.com, Inc.; *pg.* 1226, *pg.* 1831
Kappel, Jason, Dir-Customer Relationship Mktg - GameStop Corp.; *pg.* 399, *pg.* 1699
Kappelman, Kanan, Mgr-Mktg - Iowa Department of Economic Development; *pg.* 995, *pg.* 705
Kappenstein, Dave, VP-Tech-Crossbeam Media - Comcast Interactive Media, LLC; *pg.* 1236, *pg.* 1562
Kappitt, Michael, CMO-Global & Sr VP - Bloomin' Brands, Inc.; *pg.* 1716, *pg.* 471
Kappos, Beth, Mgr-Mktg Comm-DirecTV - Hewlett-Packard Company; *pg.* 404, *pg.* 175
Kapsimalis, Jim, Mgr-Digital Mktg - The Walt Disney Company; *pg.* 317, *pg.* 52
Kaptzan, Alex, VP-Convention Sls & Svcs - Tampa Bay & Co.; *pg.* 1007, *pg.* 476
Kapuscinski, Chris, Dir-Wireless Mktg - Alcatel-Lucent USA, Inc.; *pg.* 615, *pg.* 1728
Kar, Ashish, Sr Mgr-Worldwide Mktg Strategy, Analytics & Ops - Hewlett-Packard Company; *pg.* 404, *pg.* 175
Karac, Tom, Sr Dir-Event Ops - Tampa Bay Rays Baseball, Ltd.; *pg.* 586, *pg.* 464
Karachalios, Aleka, Brand Dir-Creative & Adv-Global - Dell Inc.; *pg.* 383, *pg.* 1737
Karadimas, Kait, Analyst-Digital Mktg - Bloomingdale's, Inc.; *pg.* 1763, *pg.* 1204
Karais, Pamela, Sr Mgr-Consumer Experience - Samsung Electronics America, Inc.; *pg.* 669, *pg.* 1115
Karame, Melissa, Sr VP-Pro Mktg Medscape - WebMD Health Corporation; *pg.* 1288, *pg.* 1313
Karamzadeh, Bobak, Mgr-Media - Discovery Communications, Inc.; *pg.* 282, *pg.* 777
Karas, Julie, Mgr-Relationship-Creative Svcs - Massachusetts Mutual Life Insurance Company; *pg.* 1207, *pg.* 845
Karassik, Roni, Sr Mgr-Campaign Res-Custom Media Res & Consumer Listening - Microsoft Corp.; *pg.* 440, *pg.* 321
Karazim, Andrew J., Sr Dir-Global PRA & CA Capabilities - Eli Lilly and Company; *pg.* 1527, *pg.* 684
Karbowiak, Rich, Mgr-Mktg - Thomas Engineering Inc.; *pg.* 1382, *pg.* 619
Karches, Dan, Sr Dir-Global Tea Category & Innovation - Starbucks Corporation; *pg.* 897, *pg.* 1840
Karcz, Joe, VP-Global Product Commercialization - Beam Suntory Inc.; *pg.* 1957, *pg.* 599
Kardesh, Eric, Mgr-Mktg & Comm - Universal Technical Institute, Inc.; *pg.* 608, *pg.* 24
Kare, Susan, Sr Designer-Product - Pinterest; *pg.* 1275, *pg.* 225
Karelse, Linda, Coord-Mktg - Mlive Media Group; *pg.* 1665, *pg.* 888
Karem, Keith, Dir-Bus Mktg - Hyatt Hotels Corporation; *pg.* 1096, *pg.* 577
Karen, Jayson, Assoc Dir-CRM Mktg - Sharp Electronics Corporation; *pg.* 672, *pg.* 1082
Karens, Kristi, Dir-Media & Consumer Engagement-Digital & Agency Partnerships - Mondelez International, Inc.; *pg.* 878, *pg.* 601
Karesh, Howard N., Dir-Internal Comm & Creative Media - Exelon Corporation; *pg.* 1942, *pg.* 573
Kargas, David, Head-Mktg Comm Plng - The Clorox Company; *pg.* 327, *pg.* 169
Karidis, George, Chief Strategy Officer - Softlayer Technologies Inc; *pg.* 471, *pg.* 1686
Karim, Taseen, Mgr-Sls - Milton Roy Company; *pg.* 1361, *pg.* 1542
Karimzada, Zoey, Mgr-Email Mktg - ZAGG INCORPORATED; *pg.* 690, *pg.* 1762
Karipides, Larry, Sr Dir-New Bus Dev N.A. - Return Path, Inc.; *pg.* 461, *pg.* 1285
Karkosak, Franny, Dir-Media & Digital Mktg - Carlson Companies Inc.; *pg.* 1084, *pg.* 947
Karlen, Susan, Dir-Mktg - CBC Restaurant Corp.; *pg.* 1721, *pg.* 1677
Karlesky, John, Dir-Mktg Support - Lowe's Companies, Inc.; *pg.* 1053, *pg.* 1383
Karlowski, Jason, Mgr-Sports Mktg & PR - Henry Modell & Company, Inc.; *pg.* 1836, *pg.* 1240
Karls, Elizabeth, Analyst-ECommerce Mktg - Weyco Group, Inc.; *pg.* 1822, *pg.* 1858
Karlsson, Peter U, Sr VP-Sls-Global - CommScope, Inc.; *pg.* 278, *pg.* 1378
Karminski, Brett, Brand Mgr - Frontier Natural Products Co-op; *pg.* 509, *pg.* 710
Karmosky, Andrew, Assoc Mgr-Mktg - OppenheimerFunds, Inc.; *pg.* 790, *pg.* 1274
Karnes, Dave, VP-Sls-Truck NA - Eaton Corporation; *pg.* 1331, *pg.* 1429
Karney, Megan, Mgr-Digital Mktg - Extended Stay Hotels LLC; *pg.* 1091, *pg.* 1622
Karode, Kavita, Mgr-Mktg-NAM Mobile App Dev - Microsoft Corporation; *pg.* 435, *pg.* 1824
Karolian, Matt, Dir-Social Media - The Boston Globe; *pg.* 1623, *pg.* 790
Karp McHugh, Nadine, VP-Media-Global - Colgate-Palmolive Company; *pg.* 504, *pg.* 1215
Karp, Eric, Sr Dir-Brand Mktg - Tommy Bahama; *pg.* 48, *pg.* 1842
Karp, Ken J., VP-Mktg & PR - The F.A. Bartlett Tree Expert Company; *pg.* 1795, *pg.* 373
Karp, Marcelle, VP-Brand Strategy & Creative Svcs - Madison Square Garden Network; *pg.* 297, *pg.* 1255
Karper, Ed, Mgr-North American Mktg-Coil Coatings - Akzo Nobel Coatings Inc.; *pg.* 1439, *pg.* 1437
Karpf, Josh, Dir-Social Mktg-Global - Spotify; *pg.* 1282, *pg.* 1295
Karpo-DeVillier, Lauren, VP-Digital Media-Disney ABC Television Grp - The Walt Disney Company; *pg.* 317, *pg.* 52
Karpos, Tim, Sr Mgr-Comml Notebook Mktg - Dell Inc.; *pg.* 383, *pg.* 1737
Karpowicz, Paul, Pres-Meredith Local Media Grp - Meredith Corporation; *pg.* 1663, *pg.* 705
Karrick, Sherry, Mgr-Media Svcs - Kentucky Lottery Corporation; *pg.* 996, *pg.* 735
Karron, Jonathan, VP-Mktg & Consumer Tech - Herschend Family Entertainment Corp.; *pg.* 552, *pg.* 973
Karsant, Alexis, Sr Mgr-Shopper Mktg - Unilever United States, Inc.; *pg.* 904, *pg.* 1061
Karschney, Charles, Mgr-Production - Spokane Symphony Orchestra; *pg.* 584, *pg.* 1844
Karstensen, Eirik, Mgr-PR & Comm - Treasury Wine Estates; *pg.* 1971, *pg.* 164
Karter, Nick, VP-Bus Dev & Product Mgmt - QUALCOMM Incorporated; *pg.* 1873, *pg.* 207
Karuga, Sharon, Dir-Africa Mktg - Philips Healthcare; *pg.* 1585, *pg.* 783
Karwoski, Anthony, Head-Adv Strategic Sls & Alliances - Travelport Limited; *pg.* 1925, *pg.* 521
Kasel, Erica, VP-Mktg-Fashion, Watches & Fine Jewelry - Chanel, Inc.; *pg.* 503, *pg.* 1211
Kashimer, Bill, Dir-Media, Production & Mgmt - The Sun Products Corporation; *pg.* 336, *pg.* 385
Kashman, Mark, Sr Product Mgr - Microsoft Corporation; *pg.* 435, *pg.* 1824
Kashner, Heather, Sr Mgr-Integrated Comm & Partnerships - Burt's Bees Inc.; *pg.* 502, *pg.* 1370
Kasinger, Jason, Mgr-Application Sls-Enterprise-HCM - Oracle Corporation; *pg.* 450, *pg.* 191
Kaskavitch, Matthew, Mgr-Social Media-Denver & Anschutz Medical Campus - University Of Colorado; *pg.* 608, *pg.* 323
Kasle, Jon, VP-Comm & External Affairs & VP-Corp PR - Raytheon Company; *pg.* 233, *pg.* 854
Kasmier, Lindsay, Product Mgr - Valassis Communications, Inc.; *pg.* 1287, *pg.* 897
Kasnic, Andrea, Dir-Sls & Mktg - Hyatt Hotels Corporation; *pg.* 1096, *pg.* 577
Kasoff, Barry L., Interim Pres - Imation Corp.; *pg.* 413, *pg.* 952
Kasper, Carol, Dir-Mktg - University of Chicago Press; *pg.* 1698, *pg.* 594
Kasper, Laurie, Mgr-Digital Mktg - Intel Corporation; *pg.* 645, *pg.* 266
Kasper, Noreen, Sr Dir-HR - The Timberland Company; *pg.* 1821, *pg.* 1039
Kass, Amy, Sr Mgr-Customer Relationship Mktg - Constant Contact, Inc.; *pg.* 379, *pg.* 850
Kassab, Alexander, Brand Mgr-CVS Customer Team - The Procter & Gamble Company; *pg.* 1129, *pg.* 1418
Kassan, Matt, Dir-NOOK CRM Mktg - Barnes & Noble, Inc.; *pg.* 1619, *pg.* 1201
Kassner, Danielle, Mgr-Dept Store Mktg & Ops - Aveda Corporation; *pg.* 499, *pg.* 917
Kastalsky, Daniel, Mgr-Performance Mktg - The Western

Union Company; pg. 822, pg. 327
Kaster, Heather, Sr Mgr-Mktg Svcs - The Kraft Heinz Company; pg. 871, pg. 641
Kastl, John, Product Mgr-Equipment - Valmont Industries, Inc.; pg. 1387, pg. 1019
Kastner, Deseret, Coord-Mktg - California Strawberry Commission; pg. 135, pg. 305
Kastrinakis, Mary Ellen, Sr Mgr-Mktg-Campaigns & Category Mktg - Office Depot, Inc.; pg. 448, pg. 412
Kastritis, Bill, Sr Product Dir - Cars.com; pg. 1234, pg. 568
Katan, Yaniv, Sr Mgr-Creative Product Mktg, Sls & Channel Enablement - Cisco Systems, Inc.; pg. 372, pg. 240
Kataoka, Alex, Product Mgr - Grass Valley, Inc.; pg. 641, pg. 164
Katcher, Jamie, Sr Dir - Cushman & Wakefield, Inc.; pg. 1088, pg. 1220
Katerndahl, Carl, Exec VP & Head-Retail Sls & Distr - Nuveen Investments, Inc.; pg. 788, pg. 586
Kates, Gian Pablo, VP-Network Sls - Telemundo Network Inc.; pg. 311, pg. 430
Katien, P.J., Dir-Mktg-John Frieda - Kao Brands Co. Inc.; pg. 513, pg. 1415
Katkhouda, Nadine, Brand Mgr-Away-From-Home - Peet's Coffee & Tea, Inc.; pg. 1029, pg. 85
Kato, Linda, Sr Mgr-Mktg Budgets - Nissan North America, Inc.; pg. 186, pg. 1633
Katopis, Christopher, VP-Sls & Mktg - Cains Foods, L.P.; pg. 843, pg. 784
Katsapis, Christina, Dir-Mktg - Comcast Cable Communications, Inc.; pg. 276, pg. 1560
Katsch, Christine, Sr Assoc Mgr-Integrated Mktg - Unilever United States, Inc.; pg. 904, pg. 1061
Katsuleres, Chris, Dir-Olympic Mktg & Sports Programs - General Electric Company; pg. 1297, pg. 347
Kattula, Jennifer, Head-Mktg-Atlas - Facebook, Inc.; pg. 1245, pg. 143
Kattwinkel, Sergio, Gen Mgr-Trade Mktg - LG Electronics Canada, Inc.; pg. 651, pg. 1927
Katyal, Sabina, Segment Mgr-Mktg Comm - McKesson Corporation; pg. 1560, pg. 222
Katz, Alana, Specialist-Mktg - E*TRADE Financial Corporation; pg. 749, pg. 1230
Katz, Andrew, VP-Mktg Dos Equis - Heineken USA Inc.; pg. 252, pg. 1352
Katz, Carole, VP-Mktg - Watertown Savings Bank Inc.; pg. 818, pg. 855
Katz, Craig, Sr Mgr-Web Dev - Crate & Barrel, Inc.; pg. 922, pg. 640
Katz, David J., Chief Mktg Officer & Exec VP - Randa Accessories, LLC; pg. 47, pg. 657
Katz, David M., Sr VP-Sls & Mktg - UniFirst Corporation; pg. 50, pg. 860
Katz, Ed, VP-Sls-Natl - Software AG, Inc.; pg. 471, pg. 1799
Katz, Etienne, Sr VP-Global Sls & Exec Conferences - The Wall Street Journal; pg. 1700, pg. 1312
Katz, Evan, Mgr-Mktg-Branding & Adv - E*TRADE Financial Corporation; pg. 749, pg. 1230
Katz, Glori, Sr VP-Mktg & Adv - Stein Mart, Inc.; pg. 1786, pg. 435
Katz, Jordan, Sr VP-Sls & Channel Mktg - Take-Two Interactive Software, Inc.; pg. 481, pg. 1297
Katz, Juliana, Sr Assoc Brand Mgr-Big Heart Pet Brands - Del Monte Foods, Inc.; pg. 852, pg. 304
Katz, Kathleen, VP-Mktg-Westinghouse Brand - CBS Corporation; pg. 273, pg. 1210
Katz, Kelly, VP & Sr Mgr-Retirement Plan Svcs - T. Rowe Price Group Inc.; pg. 808, pg. 759
Katz, Lauren, Acct Mgr-Adv-Travel Vertical - Google Inc.; pg. 1249, pg. 153
Katz, Marla, Dir-Corp Mktg-Brand - Lincoln Financial Group; pg. 1206, pg. 1375
Katz, Matthew, Sr Dir-Digital Adv Ops & Client Svcs - Cable News Network LP; pg. 1624, pg. 1208
Katz, Michael, VP-Intl Programming & Production - A&E Television Networks, LLC; pg. 267, pg. 1185
Katz, Mike, VP-Brand, Acq & Channel Mktg - T-Mobile US, Inc.; pg. 676, pg. 1816
Katz, Nancy, Sr Mgr-Pub Customer - GlaxoSmithKline; pg. 1536, pg. 1565
Katz, Nancy J., VP & Gen Mgr-Mdse - Bed Bath & Beyond Inc.; pg. 1121, pg. 1127
Katz, Richard, VP-Direct Mktg & Sls - American National Insurance Company; pg. 1191, pg. 1697
Katz, Samantha, Brand Mgr-Dev & Promos - Aramark; pg. 1013, pg. 1558
Katz, Sharon, Dir-Mktg - Coty, Inc.; pg. 506, pg. 1219
Katzen, Sondi J., Dir-PR - Chicago Zoological Society, Inc.; pg. 539, pg. 559
Katzke, Larry, Mgr-Mktg-Natl Auto Incentives - American Honda Motor Co., Inc.; pg. 163, pg. 292
Katzki, Sara, Sr Mgr-Integrated Mktg - Rolling Stone Magazine; pg. 1681, pg. 1287
Katzman, Ken, VP-Mktg - Dover Publications, Inc.; pg. 1636, pg. 1182
Katzman, Stephanie, Sr Acct Exec-Mktg Solutions - LinkedIn Corporation; pg. 1262, pg. 160
Kauffman, Carol, Sr Dir-Procurement - Family Dollar Stores, Inc.; pg. 1768, pg. 1382
Kauffman, Cary, Dir-Creative Svcs - Waddell & Reed Financial, Inc.; pg. 818, pg. 721
Kauffman, Chris, Head-Global Mktg-BELSOMRA - Merck & Co., Inc.; pg. 1566, pg. 1077
Kauffman, Kathleen, Specialist-Mktg-Personal Lines - Selective Insurance Group, Inc.; pg. 1216, pg. 1045
Kauffman, Kathy, Mgr-Database Mktg Automation, Segmentation & Plng - Entrust, Inc.; pg. 393, pg. 1680
Kauffman, Lisa, Specialist-Mktg, Comml Flooring - Armstrong World Industries, Inc.; pg. 914, pg. 1545
Kauffman, Russell, Mgr-Production - David Michael & Co. Inc.; pg. 852, pg. 1563
Kauffmann, Ken, Mgr-Product Mgmt - Cisco Systems, Inc.; pg. 372, pg. 240
Kaufman, Alexa G., Dir-PR - AT&T Inc.; pg. 1867, pg. 1674
Kaufman, Harvey W., Sr Dir-Medical - Quest Diagnostics Incorporated; pg. 1587, pg. 1080
Kaufman, Jennifer, VP-Mktg - Blue Cross & Blue Shield Association; pg. 1195, pg. 566
Kaufman, Jessica, Sr Mgr-Voice Channel - Blue Shield of California; pg. 1195, pg. 214
Kaufman, Joanna, Specialist-Digital Mktg-Laureate Online Education - Laureate Education, Inc.; pg. 603, pg. 757
Kaufman, Larry, Product Mgr-Pro Imaging - Epson America Inc.; pg. 394, pg. 122
Kaufman, Pamela, CMO, Pres-Consumer Products & Specialist-Product - Nickelodeon Direct Inc.; pg. 303, pg. 1271
Kaufman, Rachel, Sr Mgr-Global Sustainability Mktg - Johnson & Johnson; pg. 1549, pg. 1091
Kaufman, Steven D., Dir-Mktg, Promos & PR - Kaufman Financial Group, Inc.; pg. 1205, pg. 886
Kaufmann, Ken, Sr Dir-Mktg Innovation - Ahold USA, Inc.; pg. 1013, pg. 1520
Kaul, Kimberly, VP-Brand & Adv - Nuveen Investments, Inc.; pg. 788, pg. 586
Kaupinen, Pamela, Dir-Mktg-GQ - Conde Nast Publications, Inc.; pg. 1629, pg. 1217
Kaupinen, Pamela, Sr Dir-Mktg-GQ - Vogue Magazine; pg. 1700, pg. 1311
Kaushik, Deepak, Sr Product Mgr-Kindle Content - Amazon.com, Inc.; pg. 1226, pg. 1831
Kaushik, Mukund, VP-IT Svcs & Global Mktg - Kimberly-Clark Corporation; pg. 1461, pg. 1720
Kauzlaric, Jeff, Mgr-Adv & Comm - Furuno USA, Inc.; pg. 640, pg. 1819
Kavalerchik, Fannet, Mgr-Digital Media - Stage Stores, Inc.; pg. 33, pg. 1715
Kavanagh, John, Sr Dir-Platform Product Mgmt - Synacor, Inc.; pg. 1283, pg. 1151
Kavanaugh, David, Sr Specialist-Mktg - Windstream Corporation; pg. 321, pg. 34
Kavanaugh, Lara, Sr Strategist-Mktg Digital-Global - Medtronic, Inc.; pg. 1564, pg. 939
Kavanaugh, Tim, Assoc VP-Product Plng & Mktg - Sharp Electronics Corporation; pg. 672, pg. 1082
Kavege, Jackie A., Dir-Field Mktg-Mid-Atlantic - General Growth Properties, Inc.; pg. 1093, pg. 574
Kavett, Susan, Head-Digital Mktg-Multi-Channel Mktg - Sanofi US; pg. 1592, pg. 1046
Kawaguchi, Mai, Sr Mgr-Digital Mktg - Sega of America Inc.; pg. 966, pg. 227
Kawahata, Keith, VP-Product & Gen Mgr - GREE International, Inc.; pg. 1255, pg. 219
Kawamoto, Jamie, Dir-Mktg Comm - Hawaiian Telcom Communications, Inc.; pg. 1872, pg. 544
Kawchack, Mary Ellen, Mgr-Mktg - Nevada Commission on Tourism; pg. 1000, pg. 1021
Kawlewski, Glen, Dir-Sls-Asia Pacific - Mead Johnson Nutrition Company; pg. 1561, pg. 615
Kay, Colleen, Sr Mgr-Acq Mktg - Cars.com; pg. 1234, pg. 568
Kay, George, Sr Mgr-Mktg-New Brands - Mars Petcare; pg. 1478, pg. 1633
Kay, Katie, Sr Mgr-Mktg - Guthy-Renker LLC; pg. 289, pg. 273
Kay, Peyton, Head-Mktg-Global - MSCI Inc.; pg. 785, pg. 1262
Kay, Peyton, Sr VP & Head-Mktg & Investors-Global - Truven Health Analytics; pg. 486, pg. 331
Kay, Sarah, Sr Dir-Global Brand Innovation - NIKE, Inc.; pg. 1812, pg. 1492
Kay, Shane, Sr Mgr-Sls - Kelley Blue Book Co., Inc.; pg. 1656, pg. 112
Kay, Tara, Planner-Sls - Spotify; pg. 1282, pg. 1295
Kay, Warren, VP-Global Adv - Under Armour, Inc.; pg. 49, pg. 759
Kaykas-Wolff, Rebecca, Dir-Product Mktg - Oracle Corporation; pg. 450, pg. 191
Kaylor, Debora, Dir-Mktg - Gorilla Glue Co.; pg. 1048, pg. 1414
Kayman, Brian, Interim CFO - Groupon, Inc.; pg. 1255, pg. 575
Kayse, Kathy, VP-Sls Strategy & Solutions - Yahoo! Inc.; pg. 1289, pg. 289
Kazan, David, Dir-Mktg - General Electric Company; pg. 1297, pg. 347
Kazan, Elina, VP-Media Rels & Cause Mktg - Macy's East; pg. 1777, pg. 1254
Kazdan, Elizabeth, Analyst-Mktg - eBags, Inc.; pg. 1240, pg. 331
Kazee, Derek, Dir-Retention Mktg - Ebates.com; pg. 1240, pg. 217
Kazerman, Keith, Sr VP-Adv Sls - DIRECTV Group Holdings, LLC; pg. 281, pg. 79
Kazi, Rousseau, Product Mgr - Facebook, Inc.; pg. 1245, pg. 143
Kazimour, Kory, Sr Mgr-Data & Res - Frontier Natural Products Co-op; pg. 509, pg. 710
Kazlauskas, Ashley, Sr Mgr-Consumer Mktg & Fundraising - American Red Cross; pg. 130, pg. 395
Kazmerski, Leonard, VP-Mktg & Bus Dev - HAECO Americas; pg. 228, pg. 1374
Kazmierczak, Thomas, Jr., Head-Retirement & College Products - T. Rowe Price Group Inc.; pg. 808, pg. 759
Ke, Doris, Mgr-Social Comm-APAC - Unilever United States, Inc.; pg. 904, pg. 1061
Keane, Carol, Dir-Sls Ops - ChyronHego; pg. 371, pg. 1179
Keane, John J., Sr VP-Advanced Tech Sys - Nordson Corporation; pg. 1365, pg. 1480
Kear, Brie, Mgr-Sls - Boyne USA Resorts Inc.; pg. 1082, pg. 874
Kear, Robert, Partner & CMO - Sales Performance International, Inc.; pg. 464, pg. 1368
Kearey, Rebecca, Exec VP-Intl Mktg & Distr Fox Filmed Entertainment - 20th Century Fox Film Corp.; pg. 267, pg. 124
Kearin, Stacey, Dir-Mktg-Superspreads - Land O'Lakes, Inc.; pg. 873, pg. 915
Kearney, Candace, Div Mgr-Mdsg-Bebe.com - bebe stores, inc.; pg. 19, pg. 49
Kearney, Jeff, Sr Dir-Sports Mktg - The Gatorade Company; pg. 251, pg. 574
Kearney, Sean, VP & Reg Mgr-Multi-Platform Sls - The Weather Channel LLC; pg. 320, pg. 523
Kearns, Patrick, Mgr-Mktg-GBU-Indus Standard Servers & Software Mktg - Hewlett-Packard Company; pg. 404, pg. 175
Kearns, Sarah, Dir-Mktg Comm - ViewSonic Corporation; pg. 489, pg. 303
Keast, Rob, Dir-Mktg Channels & Transformation - Royal Bank of Canada; pg. 800, pg. 1942
Keates, Hilary, Dir-Global Mktg & Brand Mgmt - New Balance Athletic Shoe, Inc.; pg. 1811, pg. 798
Keating, Elizabeth, VP-Mktg - Acorda Therapeutics, Inc.; pg. 1486, pg. 1138
Keating, Roy, VP-Sls & Gen Mgr - MTD Products, Inc.; pg. 1057, pg. 1478
Keats, Dan, Dir-Sponsorship Mktg - The Allstate Corporation; pg. 1189, pg. 639
Keaveny, Sean, Sr VP-Rewards Product Mgmt - Upromise, Inc.; pg. 815, pg. 837
Kebalo, Andrea, Product Mgr-Analytics - Univision Communications Inc.; pg. 683, pg. 1307
Kechichian, Mike, VP-Advertiser Mktg & Client Solutions - Los Angeles Times Communications, LLC; pg. 1660, pg. 135
Keckeisen, Brett, Analyst-Adv & Media-Scion - Toyota Motor Sales, U.S.A., Inc.; pg. 193, pg. 296

First page reference indicates Business Class Edition
Second page reference indicates Geographic Edition

Keckler, Michelle, Coord-Digital Mktg - Bridgestone Americas, Inc.; *pg.* 201, *pg.* 1649
Kee, Bill, Sr Product Mgr - Google Inc.; *pg.* 1249, *pg.* 153
Kee, Jim, Mgr-Events & Mktg-Global - Schneider Electric; *pg.* 467, *pg.* 1609
Kee, Shelley, Sr VP-Sls & Grp Client Dev - PBC Health Benefits Society; *pg.* 1214, *pg.* 1911
Keefe, Ashley, Analyst-Digital Mktg - The Reader's Digest Association, Inc.; *pg.* 1679, *pg.* 1322
Keefe, Cathy, Mgr-Media Rels - Travel Industry Association of America; *pg.* 158, *pg.* 405
Keefe, Gary, Dir-Global Sls-Comml Vehicle Products - Littelfuse, Inc.; *pg.* 1301, *pg.* 580
Keefe, Kevin, VP-Svc & Sls Support - Hennessy Industries, Inc.; *pg.* 207, *pg.* 1639
Keefer, Missy, Mgr-Adv - Abilene Reporter News; *pg.* 1613, *pg.* 1657
Keegan, Aubrey, Sr Mgr-Promos - Honest Tea; *pg.* 253, *pg.* 762
Keegan, Beth, Sr VP-Mktg Solutions - Valassis Communications, Inc.; *pg.* 1287, *pg.* 897
Keegan, Keith, VP-Mktg - Aeropostale, Inc.; *pg.* 17, *pg.* 1188
Keehner, Bill, Grp Head-Sustain-Sls & Mktg - General Motors Company; *pg.* 175, *pg.* 881
Keeler, Lisa, Sr Mgr-Bus Dev Team - Ceridian Corporation; *pg.* 371, *pg.* 932
Keeler, Martha, Dir-Mktg - Greene County Bancorp, Inc.; *pg.* 764, *pg.* 1152
Keeler, Mike, VP-Advance Tech - Hendrickson International; *pg.* 207, *pg.* 672
Keeley, Kara, Mgr-Field & Experiential Mktg - The Coca-Cola Company; *pg.* 240, *pg.* 493
Keeley, Murphy, VP-Mktg & Svcs - X-Rite, Incorporated; *pg.* 1437, *pg.* 891
Keen, Bruce, Sr Dir-Engrg Dev-Global - Wm. Wrigley Jr. Company; *pg.* 1863, *pg.* 596
Keen, Liz, Sr Dir-Comm & Special Projects - Conde Nast Publications, Inc.; *pg.* 1629, *pg.* 1217
Keenan, Brian, Mgr-Mktg-Global - 3M Company; *pg.* 1142, *pg.* 956
Keenan, Caroline, Sr Product Mgr-Paid Svcs - AOL Inc.; *pg.* 1229, *pg.* 1195
Keenan, Drew, Dir-Media Strategy & Plng - The Home Depot, Inc.; *pg.* 1050, *pg.* 510
Keenan, James, Sr VP-Sls & Mktg - ABF Freight System, Inc.; *pg.* 1896, *pg.* 31
Keenan, John, Sr Mgr-Mktg - Cisco Systems, Inc.; *pg.* 372, *pg.* 240
Keenan, Kali, Sr Mgr-Mdsg - Tupperware Brands Corporation; *pg.* 1139, *pg.* 456
Keenan, Mary, Sr Dir-Sourcing Strategy & Ops-Global - Lands' End, Inc.; *pg.* 1776, *pg.* 1857
Keenan, Nicki, Sr VP-Sls - Landry's, Inc.; *pg.* 1735, *pg.* 1709
Keenan, Tyler, Dir-Mktg - NIKE Canada Ltd.; *pg.* 1840, *pg.* 1934
Keene, Darrin, Mgr-Digital Mktg-Apple Online Retail - Apple Inc.; *pg.* 350, *pg.* 73
Keery Callahan, Katherine, Sr Mgr-Digital Media - Wayfair LLC; *pg.* 1288, *pg.* 801
Kees, Lyndsey, Dir-Mktg & Bus Dev - Simon Property Group, Inc.; *pg.* 1112, *pg.* 690
Keese, Carol, Deputy Chief-Mktg - The University of Virginia; *pg.* 610, *pg.* 1778
Keeshan, John, Media Planner - BET Holdings LLC; *pg.* 271, *pg.* 396
Keeshan, Tracie, Mgr-Mktg - SCANA Corporation; *pg.* 1951, *pg.* 1612
Keesler, Barbara, Media Buyer - Educational Testing Service Inc.; *pg.* 1394, *pg.* 1111
Keetell, Theo, Dir-Consumer & Retail Mktg - Levi Strauss & Co.; *pg.* 43, *pg.* 220
Keeton, Jencey, Mgr-Global Mktg-Social Media - Fossil Group, Inc.; *pg.* 5, *pg.* 1735
Keevan, Danielle, Sr Specialist-Mktg Production - Chico's FAS, Inc.; *pg.* 21, *pg.* 427
Keevers, Mary, Specialist-Mktg - First Merchants Corporation; *pg.* 756, *pg.* 695
Kefale, Makeda, Dir-Mktg Svcs - Outdoor Advertising Association of America; *pg.* 152, *pg.* 403
Kefferstan, John, Dir-Production - The Atlantic Monthly Group; *pg.* 1618, *pg.* 396
Kefor, Anh-Dao, Brand Mgr - Dunkin' Brands Group, Inc.; *pg.* 1727, *pg.* 810
Kegg, Liz, Sr Mgr-Organizational Readiness - Citrix Systems, Inc.; *pg.* 375, *pg.* 424
Kegley, Scott, Dir-Digital & Social Media - San Francisco Forty Niners, Ltd.; *pg.* 581, *pg.* 270
Kehley, Todd, Dir-Trade Mktg & Shopper Insights - BIC Corporation; *pg.* 501, *pg.* 369
Kehoe, Chase, Sr Mgr-Integrated Mktg - Time Inc.; *pg.* 1693, *pg.* 1300
Kehoe, Diane, Acct Mgr-Creative Svcs - Bentley University; *pg.* 598, *pg.* 850
Kehoe, Louise, VP & Dir-Media Rels - Eastman Kodak Company; *pg.* 1408, *pg.* 1333
Kehoe, Mike, VP-Mktg-Intl - Bloomin' Brands, Inc.; *pg.* 1716, *pg.* 471
Keib, Michelle, Mgr-Natl Sls - F.E. Hale Manufacturing Company; *pg.* 925, *pg.* 1160
Keigher, Terry, Dir-Brand Strategy & Mktg Svcs - Blue Cross & Blue Shield Association; *pg.* 1195, *pg.* 566
Keil, Katherine, Dir-Mktg-Burt's Bees Innovation - The Clorox Company; *pg.* 327, *pg.* 169
Keilen, Steven, VP-Corp Sls-North America - Compuware Corporation; *pg.* 379, *pg.* 879
Keilly, Chris, Dir-Mdsg-Non Foods - Giant Eagle, Inc.; *pg.* 1020, *pg.* 1575
Keilty, Rick, Dir-Product Mgmt & Global Svcs Software Dev - EMC Corporation; *pg.* 391, *pg.* 825
Keim, Katy, CMO & Gen Mgr-Lithium Social Web - Lithium Technologies; *pg.* 1263, *pg.* 221
Keimach, Andrew, Exec VP-Sls - Munchkin, Inc.; *pg.* 964, *pg.* 300
Keir, Jeannette, Sr Mgr-Mktg - Procter & Gamble Inc.; *pg.* 333, *pg.* 1929
Keirouz, Tony, VP-Mktg & Applications - STMicroelectronics, Inc.; *pg.* 676, *pg.* 1671
Keirsey, Frankie, Mgr-Online Mktg - Pennwell Publishing Company Inc.; *pg.* 1676, *pg.* 1490
Keister, Kristi, Supvr-Mktg - Six Flags Entertainment Corporation; *pg.* 583, *pg.* 1698
Keister, Paul, Chief Creative Officer - Carvana LLC; *pg.* 168, *pg.* 16
Keith, Amy, Brand Mgr - Mars, Incorporated; *pg.* 1858, *pg.* 1792
Keith, Bill, Product Mgr-Road - SRAM Corporation; *pg.* 967, *pg.* 590
Keith, Christine, Head-Creative - The Coca-Cola Company; *pg.* 240, *pg.* 493
Keith, Corey, Sr Dir-Brand Adv & Paid Search - BMC Software, Inc.; *pg.* 362, *pg.* 1701
Keith, Melinda, Sr Dir-Customer Satisfaction & Bus Svcs-Field Ops - DIRECTV Group Holdings, LLC; *pg.* 281, *pg.* 79
Keith, Shana, Mgr-PR - Cox Communications, Inc.; *pg.* 279, *pg.* 501
Keitt, Kristen, Dir-Mktg-Cosmetics - L'Oreal USA; *pg.* 514, *pg.* 1252
Kelban, Russell, VP-Digital Mktg - Universal Studios, Inc.; *pg.* 315, *pg.* 298
Kelbley, Jay, Sr Mgr-Mktg-Digital Imaging - Samsung Electronics America, Inc.; *pg.* 669, *pg.* 1115
Kelepouris, Amber A., Sr Specialist-Mktg Comm - Hewlett-Packard Company; *pg.* 404, *pg.* 175
Kell, Melissa, Mgr-Integrated Shopper Mktg - General Mills, Inc.; *pg.* 828, *pg.* 933
Kellam, Richard, Sr VP-Sls & Mktg-Global - The Goodyear Tire & Rubber Company; *pg.* 1883, *pg.* 1401
Kellar, Denise, Dir-Events & Sls Admin - West Corporation; *pg.* 492, *pg.* 1019
Kelleher, Christina, Acct Supvr-Digital & Social Media - Bose Corporation; *pg.* 626, *pg.* 820
Kelleher, Christine, Mgr-Mktg - Aris Horticulture, Inc.; *pg.* 1793, *pg.* 1404
Kelleher, Dan, Dir-Ad Sls Mktg AMC - AMC Networks Inc.; *pg.* 269, *pg.* 1189
Kelleher, David, Sr Mgr - Whirlpool Corporation; *pg.* 62, *pg.* 872
Kelleher, Laura, VP-Mktg Product Finishes Div - The Sherwin-Williams Company; *pg.* 1447, *pg.* 1435
Kelleher, Meghan, Sr Mgr-Comm - Kind LLC; *pg.* 868, *pg.* 1249
Kelleher, Sean, Assoc Program Mgr-Social Media - Liberty Mutual Insurance Group Inc.; *pg.* 1205, *pg.* 797
Keller, Andrea, Coord-Consumer Mktg - Bonnier Corporation; *pg.* 1622, *pg.* 480
Keller, Cathy, Dir-Sls - Omaha Convention and Visitors Bureau; *pg.* 152, *pg.* 1017
Keller, Cynthia A., Mgr-Technical Comm-Global Mktg Comm - Honeywell International Inc.; *pg.* 407, *pg.* 1088
Keller, David, Sr Dir-eBusiness - Leviton Manufacturing Company, Inc.; *pg.* 1301, *pg.* 1180
Keller, Elizabeth, Coord-Digital Media - Delaware Tourism Office; *pg.* 991, *pg.* 387
Keller, Gregory, Dir-Sls - Frontera Foods, Inc.; *pg.* 857, *pg.* 574
Keller, Janet, Mgr-Adv, Social Media, CRM & Digital - General Motors Company; *pg.* 175, *pg.* 881
Keller, Jim, VP-Sls - Hulu LLC; *pg.* 1257, *pg.* 274
Keller, John, Dir-Product Mgmt-Data Center - Comcast Corporation; *pg.* 276, *pg.* 1560
Keller, Lisa, Mng Editor-Social Media Community Mgmt Team - Nestle Purina PetCare Company; *pg.* 1479, *pg.* 1000
Keller, Mark, Mgr-Mktg - The Chamberlain Group, Inc.; *pg.* 75, *pg.* 611
Keller, Matthew A., CMO-Capstone - Capstone Press, Inc.; *pg.* 1625, *pg.* 951
Keller, Meghan, Mgr-Ad Sls Mktg-Food Network & Cooking Channel - Scripps Networks Interactive, Inc.; *pg.* 1279, *pg.* 1638
Keller, Meredith, Dir-PR - Van Cleef & Arpels, Inc.; *pg.* 15, *pg.* 1308
Keller, Michael R., Dir-Aftermarket Sls - Stemco Inc; *pg.* 1182, *pg.* 1726
Keller, Robert, Mgr-Global Advanced Product Mktg-Cross Vehicle Mktg - Ford Motor Company; *pg.* 172, *pg.* 876
Keller, Stacey, Sr Mgr-PR - Amazon.com, Inc.; *pg.* 1226, *pg.* 1831
Keller, Tom, Dir-Mktg-North America Displays - Dell Inc.; *pg.* 383, *pg.* 1737
Kelley, Allison, Dir-Digital & Mobile Mktg - National Railroad Passenger Corporation; *pg.* 1916, *pg.* 403
Kelley, Brian, Reg Mgr-Sls - Bostik Inc.; *pg.* 1150, *pg.* 833
Kelley, Chris, Product Mgr-Exec Compensation Analytics - Aon Hewitt; *pg.* 350, *pg.* 627
Kelley, Chris, VP-Online Mktg - Siemens Process Industries and Drives; *pg.* 673, *pg.* 485
Kelley, Craig, VP-PR - Indianapolis Colts, Inc.; *pg.* 553, *pg.* 687
Kelley, Dan, Mgr-Natl Trade Mktg - Brown-Forman Corporation; *pg.* 1958, *pg.* 732
Kelley, Daniel, VP-Mktg - D-Link Systems, Inc.; *pg.* 381, *pg.* 89
Kelley, Jacki, COO-Bloomberg Media - Bloomberg L.P.; *pg.* 725, *pg.* 1204
Kelley, Jay, Sr Mgr-Product Mktg - F5 Networks, Inc.; *pg.* 396, *pg.* 1835
Kelley, Kari, Dir-Mktg-Bakers Square Restaurants - American Blue Ribbon Holdings; *pg.* 1714, *pg.* 1648
Kelley, Leigh Anne, Sr VP-Database & Direct Mktg - Regions Financial Corporation; *pg.* 798, *pg.* 4
Kelley, Mark J., Sr Mgr-Software Dev - Dell Storage; *pg.* 386, *pg.* 922
Kelley, Megan, Specialist-Products Mktg - Accenture; *pg.* 1392, *pg.* 1186
Kelley, Melanie, Mgr-Mktg - Zale Corporation; *pg.* 16, *pg.* 1724
Kelley, Niki, Sr Mgr-CSR Program Office - Campbell Soup Company; *pg.* 844, *pg.* 1048
Kelley, Rob, VP-Brand Mktg-FJ - Acushnet Company; *pg.* 1824, *pg.* 818
Kelley, Sean, Sr Mgr-Mktg Analytics - McKesson Corporation; *pg.* 1560, *pg.* 222
Kelley, Suzy, Mgr-Field Mktg-North Central Reg - MetroPCS, Inc.; *pg.* 1872, *pg.* 1683
Kelley, Ted, Sr VP-Global Sls - Summer Infant, Inc.; *pg.* 1139, *pg.* 1610
Kelley, Terry, Mgr-Product Dev - Harris Moran Seed Co.; *pg.* 1796, *pg.* 150
Kelley, Thomas M., Sr VP-Mktg - Marathon Petroleum Company LLC; *pg.* 981, *pg.* 1454
Kelley, Tom, Sr VP-Mktg - Marathon Oil Corporation; *pg.* 981, *pg.* 1710
Kelley, Tom, Sr Dir-North American Brand Mgmt-Brand Jordan - NIKE, Inc.; *pg.* 1812, *pg.* 1492
Kelley, Trevor, Sr VP-Digital Mktg - The Walt Disney Company; *pg.* 317, *pg.* 52
Kelliher, Doug, VP-Product Mgmt - Polartec LLC; *pg.* 697, *pg.* 827
Kelliher, Michael, Exec VP-Sls & Mktg - FLEXcon Corporation; *pg.* 1457, *pg.* 844
Kellis, David, Dir-PR & Social Media - The Clorox Company; *pg.* 327, *pg.* 169
Kellmanson, Mary, Sr VP-Mktg - Winn Dixie Stores, Inc.; *pg.* 1038, *pg.* 435
Kellogg, Catherine, Mgr-Digital Mktg - Bluefly, Inc.; *pg.* 1232,

pg. 1205
Kellogg, Kathleen, Mgr-Production-Global Comm-Novartis Institutes-Biomedical Res - Novartis Corporation; *pg.* 1574, *pg.* 1273
Kellogg, Ken, Sr Dir-Digital Res - Marriott International, Inc.; *pg.* 1102, *pg.* 764
Kellogg, Melissa, Dir-Product Mktg - Freightliner Trucks; *pg.* 174, *pg.* 1502
Kellogg, Mike, VP-Revenue Mgmt & Sls Strategy - Cars.com; *pg.* 1234, *pg.* 568
Kells, Chris, Engr-Technical Mktg - Cisco Systems, Inc.; *pg.* 372, *pg.* 240
Kelly, A. J., Pres-ExxonMobil Fuels, Lubricants & Specialties Mktg - Exxon Mobil Corporation; *pg.* 977, *pg.* 1718
Kelly, Allison, VP-Partnership Mktg - Major League Soccer LLC; *pg.* 560, *pg.* 1256
Kelly, Andy, Specialist-Mktg Comm - Cummins Inc.; *pg.* 1326, *pg.* 676
Kelly, Anne, VP-Sls - BuyerZone.com, LLC, *pg.* 1200, *pg.* 850
Kelly, Anne-Mari, Dir-Sls & Mktg - WMF of America, Inc.; *pg.* 1140, *pg.* 1380
Kelly, Becky, Sr Mgr-Mktg - 7-Eleven, Inc.; *pg.* 1012, *pg.* 1672
Kelly, Bill, VP-Global Mktg-Juice - The Coca-Cola Company; *pg.* 240, *pg.* 493
Kelly, Bob, Sr VP-Sls & Mktg - R.C. Bigelow, Inc.; *pg.* 891, *pg.* 348
Kelly, Brendan, Mng Dir-Ad Sls & Partnerships-Meredith Video Studios - Meredith Corporation; *pg.* 1663, *pg.* 705
Kelly, Brian, Dir-Eastern Reg Sls-Spalding Team Div - Spalding; *pg.* 1845, *pg.* 846
Kelly, Britta, Mgr-Mktg-Adoptions - PetSmart, Inc.; *pg.* 1481, *pg.* 18
Kelly, Cambria, Sr Mgr-Global Staffing & HR Optimization - Amazon.com, Inc.; *pg.* 1226, *pg.* 1831
Kelly, Carla, Gen Mgr-Multicultural Mktg - Colgate-Palmolive Company; *pg.* 504, *pg.* 1215
Kelly, Charlie, Mgr-Mktg Program-Demand Programs - International Business Machines Corporation; *pg.* 418, *pg.* 1138
Kelly, Chip, Sr Dir-Comml Strategy-Europe - Kellogg Company; *pg.* 831, *pg.* 870
Kelly, Chris, Sr Mgr-Mktg - Regeneron Pharmaceuticals, Inc.; *pg.* 1588, *pg.* 1345
Kelly, Christina, Mgr-Mktg - Sprint Corporation; *pg.* 1874, *pg.* 719
Kelly, Cindy, Sr VP-Natl Adv Sls - Crown Media Holdings Inc.; *pg.* 280, *pg.* 281
Kelly, Dan, VP-Sls - Musco Family Olive Company; *pg.* 882, *pg.* 297
Kelly, Dana, Exec Dir-Mktg-Branded Solutions - Time Inc.; *pg.* 1693, *pg.* 1300
Kelly, Daniel, Dir-Sls & Revenue - Cox Media Group; *pg.* 280, *pg.* 502
Kelly, Deborah, Mgr-PR - Boiron USA Inc.; *pg.* 1507, *pg.* 1556
Kelly, Dervla, VP-Mktg & Comm - Shaw Media Inc.; *pg.* 308, *pg.* 1943
Kelly, Erin, Sr Dir-Omnichannel Customer Experience - DSW, Inc.; *pg.* 1807, *pg.* 1439
Kelly, Eron, Gen Mgr-WW Productivity Sls - Microsoft Corporation; *pg.* 435, *pg.* 1824
Kelly, Frances, Sr Mgr-Events-Global - Bank of America Corporation; *pg.* 718, *pg.* 1362
Kelly, Heather, Sr Mgr-Comm - Lockheed Martin Corporation; *pg.* 229, *pg.* 762
Kelly, Jack, Mgr-Digital & Social Mktg - Subaru of America, Inc.; *pg.* 191, *pg.* 1050
Kelly, Jamie, Mgr-Product Mktg - Fitbit Inc.; *pg.* 639, *pg.* 218
Kelly, Jeff, VP & Exec Dir-Creative-Digital Mktg - 20th Century Fox Film Corp.; *pg.* 267, *pg.* 124
Kelly, Jenine, Sr Dir-Global Sponsorship Mktg - Save the Children Federation, Inc.; *pg.* 156, *pg.* 384
Kelly, Joe, Sr Mgr-Sls & Project - Edd Helms Group, Inc.; *pg.* 1071, *pg.* 442
Kelly, John, Sr Dir-Mktg - ACH Food Companies, Inc.; *pg.* 835, *pg.* 1631
Kelly, John, Mgr-Mktg - City Sports; *pg.* 1830, *pg.* 860
Kelly, John, Sr VP-Ad Sls - NBC Universal, Inc.; *pg.* 300, *pg.* 1266
Kelly, John, Head-Confections Mktg-US & Sr Dir - Wm. Wrigley Jr. Company; *pg.* 1863, *pg.* 596
Kelly, Kara, Brand Mgr - Hasbro, Inc.; *pg.* 954, *pg.* 1603
Kelly, Kathleen, VP-Sls-Cancer Detection Bus - iCad, Inc.; *pg.* 643, *pg.* 1037
Kelly, Keith, Assoc Mgr-Integrated Mktg - New Balance Athletic Shoe, Inc.; *pg.* 1811, *pg.* 798
Kelly, Kerry, Sr Dir-Federal Affairs - Waste Management, Inc.; *pg.* 1954, *pg.* 1716
Kelly, Lauren, Sr Dir-Oncology Mktg - McKesson Corporation; *pg.* 1560, *pg.* 222
Kelly, Lauren, Brand Mgr - Smithfield Foods, Inc.; *pg.* 896, *pg.* 1806
Kelly, Leanna, Mgr-Mdsg & E-commerce - Kenneth Cole Productions, Inc.; *pg.* 1810, *pg.* 1248
Kelly, Maggie, VP-Mktg - The American Bankers Association; *pg.* 126, *pg.* 394
Kelly, Mary, Dir-Natl Adv & Major Retail - The Boston Globe; *pg.* 1623, *pg.* 790
Kelly, Matt, Sr Dir-Senate - National Railroad Passenger Corporation; *pg.* 1916, *pg.* 403
Kelly, Maureen, Mgr-Mktg - Grant Thornton International Ltd.; *pg.* 763, *pg.* 575
Kelly, Michael, Sr Mgr-Media & Consumer Comm - American Licorice Co. Inc.; *pg.* 1850, *pg.* 692
Kelly, Michael, VP-Sls - Media General, Inc.; *pg.* 297, *pg.* 1803
Kelly, Michael, Sr Mgr-Product Mgmt & Delivery - Mood Media; *pg.* 298, *pg.* 1616
Kelly, Michael, Sr Dir-Mktg - Time Out New York; *pg.* 1694, *pg.* 1301
Kelly, Mike, VP-North America Brand Mktg-Central - NIKE, Inc.; *pg.* 1812, *pg.* 1492
Kelly, Mike, Exec VP-Mktg - PVH Corp.; *pg.* 46, *pg.* 1283
Kelly, Nick, Dir-Experiential Mktg-Sports - Anheuser-Busch Companies, LLC; *pg.* 237, *pg.* 991
Kelly, Patty, Reg Mgr-Sls - ASICS America Corporation; *pg.* 1826, *pg.* 106
Kelly, Paul, Sr Dir-Procurement Dept-Contracts Unit - NJ Transit Corporation; *pg.* 1917, *pg.* 1097
Kelly, Ronan, Mgr-Product Mktg - Pulse Electronics Corporation; *pg.* 666, *pg.* 206
Kelly, Russell, Brand Mgr-TUDOR Watch USA LLC - Rolex Watch U.S.A., Inc.; *pg.* 11, *pg.* 1286
Kelly, Ryan, Dir-Mktg Ops - Dell Inc.; *pg.* 383, *pg.* 1737
Kelly, Ryan, Specialist-Product - Facebook, Inc.; *pg.* 1245, *pg.* 143
Kelly, Scott, Mgr-Adv-US - Ford Motor Company; *pg.* 172, *pg.* 876
Kelly, Shawn, VP-Media Tech - Shaw Media Inc.; *pg.* 308, *pg.* 1943
Kelly, Sonia, Mgr-Mktg Comm - Trimble Navigation Limited; *pg.* 1384, *pg.* 288
Kelly, Stacie, Coord-Field Mktg - Exxon Mobil Corporation; *pg.* 977, *pg.* 1718
Kelly, Susan, Gen Mgr-Sls - Renda Broadcasting Corporation; *pg.* 306, *pg.* 1581
Kelly, Timothy, Mgr-Sports & Event Mktg - Bridgestone Americas, Inc.; *pg.* 1879, *pg.* 1648
Kelly, Tony, Mng Dir-Product Dev - The Goldman Sachs Group, Inc.; *pg.* 762, *pg.* 1236
Kelly, Vikki Valencia, Mgr-Citywide Sls - Denver Metro Convention & Visitors Bureau; *pg.* 991, *pg.* 318
Kelly, Whitney, Mgr-Social Strategy & Activation - Hyatt Hotels Corporation; *pg.* 1096, *pg.* 577
Kelly-Bartley, Kim, VP-Mktg & Site Dev - White Castle Management Co.; *pg.* 1756, *pg.* 1444
Kelman, Ariel, VP-Worldwide Mktg-Amazon Web Svcs - Amazon.com, Inc.; *pg.* 1226, *pg.* 1831
Kelman, Melanie, VP & Mgr-Event Mktg - Sun Trust Bank, Atlanta; *pg.* 806, *pg.* 520
Kelman, Melanie, Mgr-Event Mktg - SunTrust Banks, Inc.; *pg.* 807, *pg.* 520
Kelner, Donner, Dir-Mktg - American Louver Company; *pg.* 1294, *pg.* 660
Kelner, Michael, Sr Dir-Sponsorship Mktg - FMR LLC (Fidelity Investments); *pg.* 759, *pg.* 794
Kelsay, Dan, Mgr-Field Mktg - Red Bull North America, Inc.; *pg.* 264, *pg.* 275
Kelsch, Jenelle, Head-Specialty & Consumer Mktg - Herman Miller, Inc.; *pg.* 926, *pg.* 913
Kelsey, Chuck, Dir-Sls - Mission Inn Resorts Inc.; *pg.* 1105, *pg.* 431
Kelsey, Ernie, Mgr-Honda Reg Mktg - American Honda Motor Co., Inc.; *pg.* 163, *pg.* 292
Kelsey, Sue, Dir-US Mktg-Wellness & Skin health - GlaxoSmithKline; *pg.* 1536, *pg.* 1389
Kelsey, Sue, Dir-US Mktg-Wellness & Skin health - GlaxoSmithKline Consumer Healthcare; *pg.* 510, *pg.* 1554
Kelso, Anita Edson, Sr Dir-Media & Comm - American Society for the Prevention of Cruelty to Animals; *pg.* 131, *pg.* 1193
Kelso, Christy, Dir-Mktg - Samsung Telecommunications America, LLC; *pg.* 670, *pg.* 1736
Kelso, Courtney, Sr VP-Product & Mktg-Enterprise Growth Grp - American Express Company; *pg.* 712, *pg.* 1190
Kelso, Michael, Dir-Mktg - Rockstar, Inc.; *pg.* 265, *pg.* 1029
Kelty, Cat, Mgr-PR - Amazon.com, Inc.; *pg.* 1226, *pg.* 1831
Keltz, Heather L., VP-Ad Ops & Ad Product Dev - The Hearst Corporation; *pg.* 1649, *pg.* 1239
Kelvin, John, Exec VP-Mktg & Bus Dev-Intl - TimberWest Forest Corp.; *pg.* 1470, *pg.* 1912
Kelyman, Scott, Sr Dir-Building Ops - Tampa Bay Rays Baseball, Ltd.; *pg.* 586, *pg.* 464
Kemet, Alia, Dir-Mktg & Strategist-Brand - Ikea North America Services LLC; *pg.* 929, *pg.* 1523
Kemler, Brian, Product Mgr - Google Inc.; *pg.* 1249, *pg.* 153
Kemm, Ron, Dir-Mktg - XTRA Lease LLC; *pg.* 195, *pg.* 1005
Kemme, Matt, VP-Product Mktg - Shaklee Corporation; *pg.* 1593, *pg.* 184
Kemmerer, Janet, Reg VP-Mktg - William Lyon Homes; *pg.* 122, *pg.* 166
Kemmitz, Lucy, Mgr-Social Media, Hilton Hotels & Resorts - Hilton Worldwide, Inc.; *pg.* 1094, *pg.* 1791
Kemp, Aidan, VP & Dir-Creative-Adv - Bergdorf Goodman, Inc.; *pg.* 1761, *pg.* 1202
Kemp, Brian, VP-Sls Ops-GolfNow - Golf Channel; *pg.* 551, *pg.* 454
Kemp, Ed, VP-Sls - R.G. Barry Corporation; *pg.* 1818, *pg.* 1470
Kemp, Julie, VP-Mktg - Vital Images, Inc.; *pg.* 1607, *pg.* 950
Kemp, Tony R., Sr Dir-HR, Fin & Back Office Solutions - LexisNexis Group; *pg.* 1658, *pg.* 1446
Kempenaar, Adam, Sr Dir-New Media & Creative Svcs - Chicago Blackhawk Hockey Team, Inc.; *pg.* 538, *pg.* 569
Kempf, Whitney, Strategist-Social Media-Global Digital Mktg - Mary Kay Inc.; *pg.* 516, *pg.* 1657
Kempf, Whitney, Strategist-Social Media-Global Digital Mktg - Mary Kay Inc.; *pg.* 516, *pg.* 1657
Kemps, Jennifer, Asst Mgr-Grp Sls - Denver Center for the Performing Arts Inc.; *pg.* 544, *pg.* 318
Kempskie, Kevin M., Dir-PR - RSA Security Inc.; *pg.* 463, *pg.* 786
Kempton, Joice, VP-Retail Mktg - PetSmart, Inc.; *pg.* 1481, *pg.* 18
Kenan, Steve, Sr Mgr-Channel & End User Mktg - Welch Allyn Inc.; *pg.* 1436, *pg.* 1342
Kendall, Ali, Mgr-Digital Mktg - KB Home; *pg.* 90, *pg.* 134
Kendall, Jenna, Coord-Media Info-PR - Bass Pro Shops, Inc.; *pg.* 1826, *pg.* 1006
Kendall, Katie, Mgr-Enterprise Social Monitoring-Customer Care Ops - Walgreen Co.; *pg.* 1608, *pg.* 605
Kendall, Kerry, Mgr-Digital Mktg - Sony Pictures Entertainment Inc.; *pg.* 309, *pg.* 72
Kendall, Kris, Mgr-Mktg-Interface Products - NXP Semiconductors; *pg.* 660, *pg.* 248
Kendall, Maggie, Sr Dir-Global Benefits Comm, Tech & UX - Comcast Corporation; *pg.* 276, *pg.* 1560
Kendall, Michael, Dir-Product Mgmt & Mktg - Lenovo Group Ltd; *pg.* 427, *pg.* 1384
Kendall, Michelle, Bus Mgr-Orlando - Parsons Brinckerhoff Inc.; *pg.* 103, *pg.* 1276
Kendall, Scott, Dir-Cross Media Strategy - Adobe Systems Incorporated; *pg.* 342, *pg.* 235
Kendall, Steve, VP-Dedicated Sls - USA Truck, Inc.; *pg.* 1929, *pg.* 36
Kendig, Chuck, Asst VP-Sls & Production Plng-Logistics - American Honda Motor Co., Inc.; *pg.* 163, *pg.* 292
Kendrick, Craig, Sr Rep-Mktg - Mercury Insurance Company; *pg.* 1208, *pg.* 136
Kendrick, Karen, Dir-Mktg - Fruit of the Loom, Inc.; *pg.* 41, *pg.* 725
Kendrick, Machelle, Dir-Mktg - Simon Property Group, Inc.; *pg.* 1112, *pg.* 690
Kendzierski, Karen, Mgr-Online Mktg - Animal Health International, Inc.; *pg.* 1474, *pg.* 1749
Keneally, Kayleen J., Sr Dir-Corp Comm - Bankrate, Inc.; *pg.* 1231, *pg.* 451
Kenealy, Michelle, Specialist-Email Mktg - Caesars Entertainment Corporation; *pg.* 1083, *pg.* 1023
Kenehan, Vera, Mgr-Strategic Product-LTE Brdcst - Ericsson; *pg.* 395, *pg.* 1108
Kenemer, JoAn, Mgr-Mktg Procurement - Coca-Cola Bottling Co. Consolidated; *pg.* 240, *pg.* 1365
Kenepp, Lori, Mgr-Mktg Comm - Flextronics International Ltd.; *pg.* 81, *pg.* 245

First page reference indicates Business Class Edition
Second page reference indicates Geographic Edition

Kenghe, Ambarish, Grp Product Mgr-Chromecast - Google Inc.; *pg.* 1249, *pg.* 153
Kenig, Jason, Product Dir-Mktg - Johnson & Johnson; *pg.* 1549, *pg.* 1091
Kenison, Stephanie, Specialist-Mktg-Bus Svcs - Comcast Corporation; *pg.* 276, *pg.* 1560
Kenler, James, Dir-Mktg Tech & Ops - CareerBuilder, LLC; *pg.* 1234, *pg.* 568
Kenley, Blake, Mgr-Mktg - D&H Distributing Co., Inc.; *pg.* 381, *pg.* 1536
Kenneally, Anne Marie, Sr VP-Global Enterprise Sls - CommScope, Inc.; *pg.* 278, *pg.* 1378
Kenneally, Stacy, Sr Mgr-HR Comm - ITT Corporation; *pg.* 1351, *pg.* 1354
Kennedy, Adam, Sr Mgr-Digital Mktg - Scripps Networks Interactive, Inc.; *pg.* 1279, *pg.* 1638
Kennedy, Adam, Dir-Brand Mktg - Uber USA, LLC; *pg.* 1286, *pg.* 229
Kennedy, Barry, Mgr-Sls-Natl - BMC Industrial Educational Services; *pg.* 362, *pg.* 902
Kennedy, Bill, Sr Mgr-Pilot Hiring Programs - United Airlines, Inc.; *pg.* 1927, *pg.* 593
Kennedy, Breta, Mgr-Growth Mktg - Uber USA, LLC; *pg.* 1286, *pg.* 229
Kennedy, Brian, Mng Dir-India & VP-Mktg-Intl - The Reader's Digest Association, Inc.; *pg.* 1679, *pg.* 1322
Kennedy, Brian, Brand Mgr-Dove Hair - Unilever United States, Inc.; *pg.* 904, *pg.* 1061
Kennedy, Dan, Brand Mgr-Global Sourcing & Private - Michaels Stores, Inc.; *pg.* 1127, *pg.* 1722
Kennedy, Daniel, Head-Digital & Sr Mgr-Digital Mktg - Stanley Black & Decker, Inc.; *pg.* 1063, *pg.* 358
Kennedy, Debra, Sr Strategist-Media - Southwest Airlines Co.; *pg.* 1923, *pg.* 1687
Kennedy, Don, Sr VP-Revenue & Strategy - AOL Inc.; *pg.* 1229, *pg.* 1195
Kennedy, Gavin, Dir-Consumer Mktg - The Gorton Group; *pg.* 859, *pg.* 823
Kennedy, Iain, Sr Dir-Product Mgmt & Commerce Platform Strategy - Microsoft Corporation; *pg.* 435, *pg.* 1824
Kennedy, Jean, Assoc Dir-Brand Mktg - Time Inc.; *pg.* 1693, *pg.* 1300
Kennedy, Jennifer, Mgr-Partner Mktg - Match.Com, LLC; *pg.* 1265, *pg.* 1683
Kennedy, Jim, Sr VP-Digital Strategy & Products - The Associated Press, Inc.; *pg.* 270, *pg.* 1197
Kennedy, Jolynn, Sr Product Specialist - BROADWIND ENERGY, INC.; *pg.* 1319, *pg.* 598
Kennedy, Katherine, Mgr-Mktg - Eaton Vance Corp.; *pg.* 746, *pg.* 794
Kennedy, Kathryn, Dir-Mktg-Pure Leaf & Brisk - PepsiCo, Inc.; *pg.* 259, *pg.* 1327
Kennedy, Liz, Dir-Content Strategy & Social Media - FreshDirect, LLC; *pg.* 857, *pg.* 1174
Kennedy, Lynsey, Mgr-Mktg-Intl - Pear Bureau Northwest; *pg.* 153, *pg.* 1500
Kennedy, Maury, VP-Sls & Mktg - Palm Harbor Homes, Inc.; *pg.* 1107, *pg.* 1658
Kennedy, Renata, Assoc Mgr-Mktg - Penguin Random House; *pg.* 1675, *pg.* 1276
Kennedy, Rosalie, Specialist-Brand Mktg-Angry Orchard Hard Cider - The Boston Beer Company, Inc.; *pg.* 239, *pg.* 790
Kennedy, Shawn, Coord-Natl Mktg Trade Show - LifeCell Corporation; *pg.* 1556, *pg.* 1045
Kennedy, Shawn, Dir-Mktg-Brokerage - Transamerica Insurance & Investment Group; *pg.* 1219, *pg.* 141
Kennedy, Tim, Mgr-Mktg - Yamaha Motor Canada Ltd.; *pg.* 1712, *pg.* 1947
Kennelty, Tim, VP-Product Strategy & Dev - American Lawyer Media, Inc.; *pg.* 1615, *pg.* 1193
Kennemer, Andy, VP-Omnichannel Mktg - ABERCROMBIE & FITCH CO.; *pg.* 37, *pg.* 1466
Kenneth, Amy Mondschein, Sr Product Mgr - Levenger Company; *pg.* 1776, *pg.* 421
Kenneth, Susan, Dir-Creative - Museum of Discovery & Science, Inc.; *pg.* 565, *pg.* 425
Kenneway, Matt, Head-Mktg-Canada - Amazon.com, Inc.; *pg.* 1226, *pg.* 1831
Kenney, Brian T., VP-Sls & Mktg - Trimedyne, Inc.; *pg.* 1432, *pg.* 121
Kenney, Chris, Sr Mgr-Pricing & Promotions - VistaPrint USA, Incorporated; *pg.* 1700, *pg.* 829
Kenney, Joe, Mgr-eMail Mktg - MetroPCS, Inc.; *pg.* 1872, *pg.* 1683
Kenney, Katie, Media Buyer - Les Schwab Tire Centers of Oregon, Inc.; *pg.* 210, *pg.* 1508
Kenney, Stephanie, Coord-Domestic Sls Mktg - Virginia Tourism Authority; *pg.* 1010, *pg.* 1804
Kennington, Justin, Mgr-Product Line-Digital Media - Crestron Electronics Inc.; *pg.* 631, *pg.* 1116
Kenny, Brian, Sr Mgr-Comm & Design-Global Sls Portfolio Leadership & Innovation - NIKE, Inc.; *pg.* 1812, *pg.* 1492
Kenny, Colleen, VP-Mktg-CBS Television Network - CBS Broadcasting Inc.; *pg.* 273, *pg.* 1210
Kenny, Colleen, VP-Mktg Comm-CBS Television Network - CBS Corporation; *pg.* 273, *pg.* 1210
Kenny, Colleen, VP-Mktg Comm - CBS Entertainment Division; *pg.* 274, *pg.* 1211
Kenny, Kelly, Dir-Product & Brand Mktg-Food - American Dairy Queen Corporation; *pg.* 1714, *pg.* 930
Kenny, Kelly, Dir-Product & Brand Mktg-Food - Dairy Queen Corporate Store; *pg.* 1724, *pg.* 932
Kenny, Kelly, Dir-Product & Brand Mktg-Food - International Dairy Queen, Inc.; *pg.* 1732, *pg.* 938
Kenny, Pat, Dir-Mktg & Construction Market Team - PPG Industries, Inc.; *pg.* 1445, *pg.* 1579
Kenny, Thomas, Exec VP & Gen Mgr-Sls & Mktg-Worldwide - Absolute Software Corporation; *pg.* 340, *pg.* 1909
Kenoly, Deitra R., Dir-Adv - The Record; *pg.* 1680, *pg.* 281
Kensinger, Edward, Dir-Creative Strategies - Siemens Corporation; *pg.* 803, *pg.* 1291
Kent, Bradley, Chief Sls Officer & Chief Svcs Officer - Dallas Convention & Visitors Bureau; *pg.* 991, *pg.* 1678
Kent, Candice, Mgr-Mktg-Creative Svcs - PRAHealth Sciences; *pg.* 1585, *pg.* 1388
Kent, Elise, Sr Mgr-Global Mktg Ops - Levi Strauss & Co.; *pg.* 43, *pg.* 220
Kent, Greg, Analyst-Natl Customer Mktg-Gum - Wm. Wrigley Jr. Company; *pg.* 1863, *pg.* 596
Kent, Jody, VP-Mktg Comm - Universal Technical Institute, Inc.; *pg.* 608, *pg.* 24
Kent, John R., Sr Mgr-Media Rels-Lockheed Martin Missiles & Fire Control - Lockheed Martin Corporation; *pg.* 229, *pg.* 762
Kent, Jon, Brand Mgr-Innovation - Diageo North America, Inc.; *pg.* 1961, *pg.* 361
Kent, Jon, Brand Mgr-Innovation - Diageo North America Inc.; *pg.* 248, *pg.* 1223
Kent, Julie, Dir-Digital Mktg - Arizona State University; *pg.* 597, *pg.* 25
Kent, Laurie, Reg Mgr-Mktg - Beazer Homes USA, Inc.; *pg.* 1081, *pg.* 491
Kent, Nicole, Coord-Digital Mktg - Albertson's LLC; *pg.* 1013, *pg.* 546
Kent, Richard, Sr Mgr - American Honda Motor Co., Inc.; *pg.* 163, *pg.* 292
Kent, Steve, Dir-Adv & Creative - Harris Teeter, Inc.; *pg.* 1022, *pg.* 1383
Kenyon, Jessica, Sr Coord-Mktg Comm - QUALCOMM Incorporated; *pg.* 1873, *pg.* 207
Kenyon, Miranda, Mgr-Mktg-North America Field Mktg - Level 3 Communications, Inc.; *pg.* 1262, *pg.* 312
Keogh, Vicki, Dir-Bank Brand Mktg - Capital One Financial Corporation; *pg.* 730, *pg.* 1789
Keough, Mike, Sr Dir-Logistics, Goods & Svcs Pur - Arkema Inc.; *pg.* 1147, *pg.* 1543
Keown, Brad, Dir-Sls-Natl - Twitter, Inc.; *pg.* 1285, *pg.* 228
Keown, Jacqueline, Sr Mgr-Field Mktg - Dunkin' Brands Group, Inc.; *pg.* 1727, *pg.* 810
Keown, Jason, Sr Dir-Mktg - Shaw Media Inc.; *pg.* 308, *pg.* 1943
Kephart, Alex, Mgr-Catalog Processors Mktg Comm - Texas Instruments Incorporated; *pg.* 679, *pg.* 1688
Kephart, Michael, VP-Sls & Mktg-Intl - Dal-Tile Corporation; *pg.* 78, *pg.* 1678
Kepner, Stephanie, Dir-Mktg - Lift Brands; *pg.* 557, *pg.* 920
Kerbel, Christina, Specialist-Trade Mktg - Rust-Oleum Corporation; *pg.* 1447, *pg* 664
Kerbel, Daniel, Brand Mgr-Beauty & Grooming - The Procter & Gamble Company; *pg.* 1129, *pg.* 1418
Kerchner, Stephanie, Assoc Mgr-Mktg-Innovation - MillerCoors LLC; *pg.* 255, *pg.* 582
Kerdock, Steve, Dir-Online Mktg - Avnet, Inc.; *pg.* 622, *pg.* 15
Kerekes, Kristen, Mgr-Email Mktg - Sleepy's, Inc.; *pg.* 943, *pg.* 1167
Kerkmeijer, William, Mgr-Sls-EMEA & India - Interphase Corporation; *pg.* 420, *pg.* 1732
Kerley, Bob, VP-Mktg - Atmos Energy Corporation; *pg.* 1935, *pg.* 1675
Kerley, Mallory, Mgr-Media & Comm - American Society for the Prevention of Cruelty to Animals; *pg.* 131, *pg.* 1193
Kerlik, Lisa, Brand Mgr-Digital - American Eagle Outfitters, Inc.; *pg.* 37, *pg.* 1572
Kermalli, Samina, Bus Mgr-Adv - The Walt Disney Company; *pg.* 317, *pg.* 52
Kerman, Kay, Sr Mgr-Digital Mktg - American Airlines Inc.; *pg.* 1898, *pg.* 1693
Kermisch, Pam, Dir-Mktg-Indian & Victory Motorcycles - Polaris Industries Inc.; *pg.* 1709, *pg.* 928
Kern, Byron, Product Mktg Mgr-Wilson Jones Brand - ACCO Brands Corporation; *pg.* 340, *pg.* 626
Kern, Doug, Dir-Digital Mktg - Sharp Electronics Corporation; *pg.* 672, *pg.* 1082
Kern, Heather, Product Mgr-Fumigants - Dow AgroSciences LLC; *pg.* 1156, *pg.* 684
Kern, Inna, Dir-Global Integrated Mktg Comm - Johnson & Johnson; *pg.* 1549, *pg.* 1091
Kern, Jeff, Sr Mgr-Product & Mktg - General Motors Company; *pg.* 175, *pg.* 881
Kern, Jodi, Dir-Digital Brand Mktg, Portfolio & HHonors - Hilton Worldwide, Inc.; *pg.* 1094, *pg.* 1791
Kern, Kevin, Dir-PR - Elvis Presley Enterprises, Inc.; *pg.* 1090, *pg.* 1642
Kern, Kevin P., Sr VP-Mktg - Konica Minolta Business Solutions USA, Inc.; *pg.* 1419, *pg.* 1113
Kern, Sara, Dir-Mktg & Promos - Turner Broadcasting System, Inc.; *pg.* 314, *pg.* 521
Kern, Tom, Project Mgr-Sls Analytics - Discover Financial Services; *pg.* 744, *pg.* 653
Kernan, Dan, Global Product Dir-Aftermarket Solutions-Industrial Process Bus - ITT Corporation; *pg.* 1351, *pg.* 1354
Kernan, Deborah, Mgr-Mktg Comm - Bio-Rad Laboratories, Inc.; *pg.* 1504, *pg.* 101
Kerner, Hilary, Dir-Mktg & Comm-IBM Watson - IBM; *pg.* 410, *pg.* 1449
Kerner, Lizzie, Sr Dir-Dev & Original Series - Cable News Network LP; *pg.* 1624, *pg.* 1208
Kerns, Ken, Mgr-Mktg - Siemens Process Industries and Drives; *pg.* 673, *pg.* 485
Kerr, Becca, Sr Dir-Brand Mktg-Brand Pepsi - PepsiCo, Inc.; *pg.* 259, *pg.* 1327
Kerr, Corey, Dir-PR - Cardinal Health, Inc.; *pg* 1512, *pg.* 1448
Kerr, Deborah, Chief Product & Tech Officer - Sabre Corporation; *pg.* 1710, *pg.* 752
Kerr, Jamie, Sr Mgr-Natl Sponsorships - AT&T Mobility LLC; *pg.* 619, *pg.* 488
Kerr, Megan, Media Planner - Sleepy's, Inc.; *pg.* 943, *pg.* 1167
Kerr, Patrick, Product Mgr-Technical-Unified Workflow Solutions - Eastman Kodak Company; *pg.* 1408, *pg.* 1333
Kerr, Rachel, Asst Mgr-Experiential Mktg - Kraft Foods Oscar Mayer; *pg.* 870, *pg.* 1866
Kerr, Tyler, Sr Mgr-Digital Comm - V.F. Corporation; *pg.* 34, *pg.* 1376
Kerschbaum, Jenna, Specialist-Mktg-Dealership Online Svcs - Ally Financial Inc.; *pg.* 711, *pg.* 878
Kerscher, Chris, Mgr-Mktg-Masterbatch - A. Schulman, Inc.; *pg.* 1144, *pg.* 1452
Kersh, Carter A., Sr Dir-Americas Field & Partner Mktg - Juniper Networks, Inc.; *pg.* 1260, *pg.* 286
Kershner, Ryan, Mgr-Mktg-Immunodiagnostic Sys - Beckman Coulter, Inc.; *pg.* 1402, *pg.* 48
Kershteyn, Yana, Mgr-Media & Integrations - The Home Depot, Inc.; *pg.* 1050, *pg.* 510
Kerslake, Scott, Interim Pres - Mountain Hardwear, Inc.; *pg.* 1839, *pg.* 193
Kerson, Aaron, Product Mgr - Marin Bikes; *pg.* 1708, *pg.* 168
Kersten, Drew, Sr Mgr-Online Mktg - Best Buy Co., Inc.; *pg.* 1761, *pg.* 954
Kerviche, Arnaud, Sr Mgr-Mktg-North American Div - MATTEL, INC.; *pg.* 962, *pg.* 81
Kerwin, James J., CMO & Exec VP - Security Mutual Life Insurance Company of New York; *pg.* 1216, *pg.* 1142
Kesapragada, Sree, Product Mgr-Global - Applied Materials, Inc.; *pg.* 618, *pg.* 264
Keshav, Kiran, Sr Dir-Res Technologies - Yale University Press; *pg.* 1703, *pg.* 359
Keshi, Nneka, Dir-Digital Mktg, African & Middle East Zone - L'Oreal USA; *pg.* 514, *pg.* 1252
Kesler, Adrian, VP-Consumer & Small Bus Mktg - CenturyLink, Inc.; *pg.* 1870, *pg.* 746
Kesliker, Himani, Mgr-Mktg - PepsiCo, Inc.; *pg.* 259, *pg.* 1327
Kessel, Eran, Dir-Intl Mktg-Europe, Africa & Asia & Sls-Sub-

Saharan Africa - Trippe Manufacturing Company; pg. 220, pg. 592
Kesselman, Rachel, Specialist-Mktg - FedEx Corporation; pg. 1907, pg. 1642
Kessen, Heather, Specialist-Mktg Comm-Comml - Moen Incorporated; pg. 1056, pg. 1468
Kesser, Susan, VP-Media Rels - FX Networks, LLC; pg. 288, pg. 131
Kesserwani, Paul, Mgr-Sls Ops - Twitter, Inc.; pg. 1285, pg. 228
Kessler, Adam, Sr Mgr-Mktg-Production - American Eagle Outfitters, Inc.; pg. 37, pg. 1572
Kessler, Jeff, VP-Sls & Mktg-Retail - Therma-Tru Corp.; pg. 115, pg. 1462
Kessler, John, Dir-Sls - University of Chicago Press; pg. 1698, pg. 594
Kessler, Thomas, Exec VP-Global Sls & European Ops - Edmund Industrial Optics Inc.; pg. 1411, pg. 1041
Kessler, Thomas, Sr Dir-Franchise Sls - SONIC Corp.; pg. 1750, pg. 1487
Kester, Amy, Mgr-Strategic Mktg-Worldwide Digital & Customer Insights - Hewlett-Packard Company; pg. 404, pg. 175
Kesting, Bill, Mgr-Fire Protection Products, Indus Adhesives & Tapes - 3M Company; pg. 1142, pg. 956
Ketchell, David, Mgr-Global Market Segment-Inside Sls Svcs - IBM Canada Limited; pg. 411, pg. 1923
Ketchen, Emily, VP-Mktg-PPS APJ - Hewlett-Packard Company; pg. 404, pg. 175
Ketelsen, Trish, Dir-Mktg - Vornado Realty Trust; pg. 1118, pg. 1312
Kettelhodt, Jill, Mgr-Sls Plng & Strategy - The Clorox Company; pg. 327, pg. 169
Kettelhut, Mary Ellen, VP-Mktg-North America - Herman Miller, Inc.; pg. 926, pg. 913
Ketter, Andy, VP-Mktg - Answers Corporation; pg. 1229, pg. 1195
Ketter, Nick, Mgr-Digital Mktg-Xbox - Microsoft Corporation; pg. 435, pg. 1824
Ketterer, Ted, Brand Mgr-FUZE - The Coca-Cola Company; pg. 240, pg. 493
Kettmann, Heather, Grp Mgr-Mktg Comm - Synopsys, Inc.; pg. 480, pg. 162
Kettunen, Eric, VP-Mktg & Client Mgmt - Publishers Group West; pg. 1679, pg. 46
Ketvertis, Heidi, Sr Dir-Mktg - MTD Products, Inc.; pg. 1057, pg. 1478
Keung, Michael P., Mgr-Technical Mktg-Sasol Chemicals USA LLC - Sasol North America Inc.; pg. 984, pg. 1713
Kevish, Dana, Mgr-ECommerce Shopper Mktg - Kimberly-Clark Corporation; pg. 1461, pg. 1720
Kew, Anita, Mgr-Social & Digital Comm - United Parcel Service, Inc.; pg. 1928, pg. 522
Key, Gary, Dir-Mktg - ASUSTeK Computer Inc; pg. 355, pg. 90
Key, John, Dir-Collaboration Technologies & Social Media Dev - Coca-Cola Refreshments USA, Inc.; pg. 247, pg. 500
Key, Scott, Sr Mgr-Comm & Change Mgmt-Brand, Mktg, Sls & Consumer Svcs - Marriott International, Inc.; pg. 1102, pg. 764
Key, Shreya, Dir-Mktg - Anthro Corporation; pg. 913, pg. 1509
Key, Tony, Sr VP-Mktg & Sls - Ubisoft Inc.; pg. 589, pg. 229
Keyes, Norman, Dir-Media Rels - Philadelphia Museum of Art; pg. 575, pg. 1569
Keyes, Sharon, Sr Dir-Product Dev - Fossil Group, Inc.; pg. 5, pg. 1735
Keys, David, VP-Sls & Mktg-East - Hilton Worldwide, Inc.; pg. 1094, pg. 1791
Keyser, Ariana, Brand Mgr - LEGO Systems, Inc.; pg. 961, pg. 346
Keyser, Chandra, Dir-Global Mktg & Branding - NYSE Euronext; pg. 789, pg. 1274
Keyser, Kent, VP-Sls & Mktg - Garden of Life, Inc.; pg. 1532, pg. 478
Keyser, Vicki, Reg Dir-Sls - Palm Springs Desert Resorts Convention & Visitors Authority; pg. 1003, pg. 187
Keyt, Jim, Sr Mgr-Global Tech Strategy - Ben & Jerry's Homemade, Inc.; pg. 1850, pg. 1767
Kgonare, Boitumelo, Mgr-Product Mktg - Dell Inc.; pg. 383, pg. 1737
Khachatoorian, Armineh, Brand Mgr-3M Unitek - 3M Company; pg. 1142, pg. 956
Khachatoorian, Armineh, Brand Mgr - 3M Unitek Corporation; pg. 1483, pg. 150
Khaitan, Laxmikant, Bus Mgr - Multisorb Technologies, Inc.; pg. 1570, pg. 1150
Khalaf, Heather, Specialist-Mktg - FedEx Corporation; pg. 1907, pg. 1642
Khaleel, Richard, CMO-Global & Mng Dir - Jefferies Group, Inc.; pg. 772, pg. 1246
Khalil, Talea, Dir-Consumer Mktg - Allergan, Inc.; pg. 1491, pg. 106
Khalilollahi, Yousef, Sr Dir - Xilinx, Inc.; pg. 496, pg. 252
Khan, Adam, VP-Social Media Strategy & Analytics - Citi Trends Inc.; pg. 22, pg. 539
Khan, Adam, VP-Social Media Strategy & Analytics - Citigroup Inc.; pg. 735, pg. 1212
Khan, Ammar H., Mgr-Social Media - Ford Motor Company of Canada, Limited; pg. 174, pg. 1930
Khan, Farhana, Head-Product Mktg & Analyst-Global Market - Cabot Microelectronics Corporation; pg. 1151, pg. 554
Khan, Imran, Chief Strategy Officer - Snapchat, Inc.; pg. 1281, pg. 301
Khan, Kamal, Reg Mgr-Sls - SOR, Inc.; pg. 1306, pg. 716
Khan, Lisa, Sr Dir-Pro Svcs - Mylan, Inc.; pg. 1570, pg. 1520
Khan, Mishaal, Sr Mgr-Digital Mktg - Career Education Corporation; pg. 599, pg. 658
Khan, Muhammad, Product Mgr - Pulse Electronics Corporation; pg. 666, pg. 206
Khan, Najia, Project Mgr-Mktg - VMware, Inc.; pg. 490, pg. 179
Khan, Nazish, Mgr-Database Mktg - Gartner, Inc.; pg. 1248, pg. 374
Khan, Noman, Sr Mgr-Innovation R&D-Global - Ocean Spray Cranberries, Inc.; pg. 887, pg. 827
Khan, Nyron, Sr Dir & Head-Global Mktg-Metabolics Disorders Franchise - Alexion Pharmaceuticals, Inc.; pg. 1489, pg. 341
Khan, Rizwan, Exec VP-Mktg - Tellabs, Inc.; pg. 678, pg. 637
Khan, Sahar, Sr Mgr-Mktg - Johnson & Johnson; pg. 1549, pg. 1091
Khan, Shelby, Mgr-Digital Mktg-HP Software IT Experts Community - Hewlett-Packard Company; pg. 404, pg. 175
Khan, Sherri D., Dir-Mktg Comm & Bus Adv - AT&T; pg. 1865, pg. 258
Khan, Sumara, Mgr-Mktg-Federal & Natl - CenturyLink, Inc.; pg. 1870, pg. 746
Khan, Umair, Principal & Product Mgr-Mktg - CA Technologies; pg. 366, pg. 1168
Khan, Zahid, Head-Mktg-New Initiatives - Amazon.com, Inc.; pg. 1226, pg. 1831
Khanijow, Rakesh, Mgr-Mktg - KLA-Tencor Corporation; pg. 1353, pg. 146
Khanna, Rohit, VP-Informatics & Worldwide Mktg - Waters Corporation; pg. 1436, pg. 834
Khanna, Sheetal, Sr Dir-Mktg & Emerging Brands - SHUTTERFLY, INC.; pg. 1280, pg. 192
Khanna, Smita, Sr Mgr-Adv - Holland America Line Inc.; pg. 1911, pg. 1836
Khara, Sushmita, Sr Mgr-Programmatic Mktg - Netflix, Inc.; pg. 1269, pg. 141
Kharbanda, Sumit, Sr Product Mgr-Wireless Connectivity Mktg - Broadcom Corporation; pg. 364, pg. 108
Khare, Rohit, Product Mgr - Google Inc.; pg. 1249, pg. 153
Khatod, Rahul, Assoc Dir-Digital Mktg-Worldwide - LifeScan Inc; pg. 1556, pg. 146
Khavinson, Lana, Grp Product Mgr - LinkedIn Corporation; pg. 1262, pg. 160
Khemani, Victoria, Product Mgr-ECommerce-On-Site Search - Staples, Inc.; pg. 474, pg. 821
Khetty, Sarah, Brand Mgr - McCain Foods Limited; pg. 876, pg. 1915
Khiem, Dustin, Sr Mgr-Medical Comm - Amgen Inc.; pg. 1493, pg. 291
Kho, Julie, Mgr-PR - Applied Industrial Technologies, Inc.; pg. 199, pg. 1428
Khodabandeh, Julia, Brand Mgr - Stonyfield Farm, Inc.; pg. 899, pg. 1035
Khoja, Nur, Mgr-Customer Growth Initiatives-CIBC Card Products - Canadian Imperial Bank of Commerce; pg. 729, pg. 1935
Khoo, Anastasia, Dir-Mktg - Human Rights Campaign; pg. 143, pg. 400
Khoo, Ben, Sr Mgr-Mktg - Intuit Inc.; pg. 769, pg. 158
Khorana, Anil, Sr Mgr-IR - United Continental Holdings, Inc.; pg. 1927, pg. 593
Khorana, Shami, Exec VP-Corp Strategy & Mktg - HTC Global Services Inc.; pg. 409, pg. 911
Khoubian, Anna, Assoc Mgr-Mktg - Mattel Games/Puzzles; pg. 962, pg. 80
Khouri, Amer, VP-Mktg & Bus Dev - Orbital ATK; pg. 1425, pg. 1779
Khouri, Mike, VP-Bus Dev, Retail Strategy & Media Distr - Sesame Workshop; pg. 307, pg. 1290
Khurana, Bipin, Controller-US iPhone Sls - Apple Inc.; pg. 350, pg. 73
Khurana, Chumi, Head-Brand-US Oncology Mktg - GlaxoSmithKline; pg. 1536, pg. 1565
Khurana, Chumi, Head-Brand-US Oncology Mktg - GlaxoSmithKline Consumer Healthcare; pg. 510, pg. 1554
Khvostichenko, Boris, Product Mgr - Google Inc.; pg. 1249, pg. 153
Ki Woo, Mung, Exec VP-Digital Products & Solutions - MasterCard Worldwide Inc.; pg. 780, pg. 988
Kiachian, Jon, Dir-Product Line - Texas Instruments Incorporated; pg. 679, pg. 1688
Kiat, Elizabeth, Product Mgr - Jet.com, Inc.; pg. 1260, pg. 1073
Kibbey, Lowinn, VP-Mktg-JNJ Consumer - Johnson & Johnson; pg. 1549, pg. 1091
Kibler, Kate, Sr Dir-Mdsg, Visual & Specialty Retail - Under Armour, Inc.; pg. 49, pg. 759
Kibort, Laura B., Mgr-Corp Brand & Adv - Unum Group; pg. 1222, pg. 1629
Kibrick, Brooke, Mgr-Mktg - Restonic Mattress Corporation; pg. 941, pg. 553
Kickham, Leslie, Sr Mgr-PR & Events - Beiersdorf North America Inc.; pg. 501, pg. 385
Kidambi, Sanjay, Head-Product Mktg & Plng - Microsoft Corporation; pg. 435, pg. 1824
Kidd, Alistair, Dir-Mktg-Whisky & Rum - Diageo Canada, Inc.; pg. 1961, pg. 1937
Kidd, Chris, Sr Mgr-Market Res - Capital One Financial Corporation; pg. 730, pg. 1789
Kidd, Dawn, Grp Product Dir - Johnson & Johnson; pg. 1549, pg. 1091
Kidd, Jonel, Acct Exec-Adv - The Arizona Republic; pg. 1617, pg. 14
Kidd, Joshua, Sr Mgr-Digital Mktg & Brand Comm - Siemens Corporation; pg. 803, pg. 1291
Kidd, Stacey, Mgr-Sls Support & Mktg - Blommer Chocolate Company; pg. 1851, pg. 566
Kidder, Todd, Mgr-Sls-Intl - Federal Foam Technologies Inc.; pg. 692, pg. 1884
Kidera, Stephen, Mgr-Media Rels - Gannett Co., Inc.; pg. 1643, pg. 1790
Kidrowski, Adam, Mgr-Sls - Makita U.S.A., Inc.; pg. 1358, pg. 120
Kidwell, Eddie, Assoc-Sls - Semonin Realtors; pg. 1112, pg. 738
Kidwell, Robert, Dir-Internal Comm & Social Media - Waste Management, Inc.; pg. 1954, pg. 1716
Kiefer, Gary, Mng Editor-New Media - The Dispatch Printing Company; pg. 1636, pg. 1439
Kiefer, Stan, Sr Product Mgr-Cyber Security Svcs - Symantec Corporation; pg. 478, pg. 161
Kiefert, Jack, Mgr-Customer Mktg - Honeywell International Inc.; pg. 407, pg. 1088
Kieffer, Brian, Asst Mgr-Mktg - Briggs & Stratton Corporation; pg. 201, pg. 1899
Kieffer, Erica, Asst Dir-Mktg Integration & Support - The Northwestern Mutual Life Insurance Company; pg. 1212, pg. 1879
Kieffer, Kevin, VP-Sls & Mktg - Encore Wire Corporation; pg. 637, pg. 1726
Kieffer, Kim, Mgr-Mktg-Franchise Dev - Spring-Green Lawn Care Corporation; pg. 1800, pg. 652
Kiehner, Elizabeth, Sr Mgr-Design - International Business Machines Corporation; pg. 418, pg. 1138
Kiekbusch, Nikki, Mgr-Bus Mktg - Sprint Corporation; pg. 1874, pg. 719
Kiel, Hollis, Reg Mgr-Sls - Harris Moran Seed Co.; pg. 1796, pg. 150
Kiel, Mark, Mgr-Production & Strategist-Digital - Adco, Inc.; pg. 325, pg. 482
Kielar, Katherine L., Brand Mgr-Mktg-SIX:02 & Lady Foot Locker - Foot Locker, Inc.; pg. 1808, pg. 1231
Kielarowski, Ray, Sr VP-Mktg & Sls - Bush Brothers & Company; pg. 843, pg. 1636
Kielblock, Paola, Exec VP-Retail Products - Fairway Independent Mortgage Corporation; pg. 750, pg. 1866
Kielt, Angie, Sr Mgr-PR & Social Media - Hearts on Fire Company; pg. 6, pg. 796
Kielty, Cathy, Principal & Designer-Interactive - American

First page reference indicates Business Class Edition
Second page reference indicates Geographic Edition

Electric Power Company, Inc.; *pg.* 1934, *pg.* 1437
Kierce, Tina, Mgr-Mktg-Idaho & Wyoming Properties - General Growth Properties, Inc.; *pg.* 1093, *pg.* 574
Kiernan, Matthew, Product Mgr - Pella Corporation; *pg.* 104, *pg.* 711
Kiernan, Melanie, Specialist-Mktg - Fluor Corporation; *pg.* 82, *pg.* 1719
Kiernan, Pam, Mgr-Trade Mktg - Saucony, Inc.; *pg.* 1818, *pg.* 828
Kiernan, Paul, Sr Dir-Mktg Res & Plng-Central Div - Comcast Cable Communications, Inc.; *pg.* 276, *pg.* 1560
Kiernan, Rebecca, Mgr-Creative Production-Interactive Design - Macy's East; *pg.* 1777, *pg.* 1254
Kieschnick, Bart, Mgr-Omni-Channel Product - 7-Eleven, Inc.; *pg.* 1012, *pg.* 1672
Kiffer, Jennifer, Exec Dir-Mktg-Conde Nast Traveler - Conde Nast Publications, Inc.; *pg.* 1629, *pg.* 1217
Kigel, Luke, Dir-Media - Johnson & Johnson; *pg.* 1549, *pg.* 1091
Kiger, Kathryn, Asst Brand Mktg Mgr - LexisNexis Group; *pg.* 1658, *pg.* 1446
Kiger, Matt, VP-Sls & Trng - Townsquare Media, Inc.; *pg.* 313, *pg.* 350
Kight, Laura, Mgr-Trade Mktg - Cytosport, Inc.; *pg.* 1018, *pg.* 45
Kightlinger, Brian, VP-Corp Sls - Meredith Corporation; *pg.* 1663, *pg.* 705
Kihara, Melissa, Head-Bus Dev & Adv Product Strategy-SmartTVs - Samsung Electronics America, Inc.; *pg.* 669, *pg.* 1115
Kihn, Manfred, Reg Mgr-Sls - E.D. Bullard Company; *pg.* 1332, *pg.* 727
Kiisk, Krista, Brand Mgr-Smirnoff Ice - Diageo North America Inc.; *pg.* 248, *pg.* 1223
Kikuma, James, Product Engr - Toyota Motor Sales, U.S.A., Inc.; *pg.* 193, *pg.* 296
Kilareski, Cassandra, Sr Mgr-Mktg Comm & Digital Strategy - Bridgestone Americas, Inc.; *pg.* 201, *pg.* 1649
Kilberg-Walsh, Beth Ann, VP-Mktg Comm - Xerox Corporation; *pg.* 494, *pg.* 365
Kilborn, Lisa, Sr Dir-Corp Comm - Avid Technology, Inc.; *pg.* 622, *pg.* 804
Kilbride, Lindsey, VP-Sls - Trunk Club; *pg.* 49, *pg.* 593
Kilbride, Megan, Sr Dir-Global Strategic Mktg-Vodka Category - Campari America; *pg.* 1960, *pg.* 214
Kilbride, Sean, Mgr-Technical Mktg - NVIDIA Corporation; *pg.* 447, *pg.* 268
Kilburn, Jessica, Mgr-Sls - Newport Aquarium; *pg.* 571, *pg.* 739
Kilby, Gina, Sr Mgr-Digital Mktg - Stonyfield Farm, Inc.; *pg.* 899, *pg.* 1035
Kilcoyne, Keith, Producer-Creative Svcs - Comcast Cable Communications, Inc.; *pg.* 276, *pg.* 1560
Kilday, Frank, Product Mgr - W.L. Gore & Associates, Inc.; *pg.* 122, *pg.* 388
Kildea, Tim, VP-Sls - Toledo Commutator Co.; *pg.* 1383, *pg.* 903
Kilgarriff, Rob, Sr VP-Sls - Monster Worldwide, Inc.; *pg.* 1268, *pg.* 859
Kilgore, Laura, Dir-Mktg - Lennar Corporation; *pg.* 1100, *pg.* 443
Kilgore, Randy, Pres-Natl Sls - Gannett Co., Inc.; *pg.* 1643, *pg.* 1790
Kilgour, Ian, Dir-Sls - Stanley Black & Decker, Inc.; *pg.* 1063, *pg.* 358
Kill, Theodore P., VP-Sls-Global - Methode Electronics, Inc.; *pg.* 654, *pg.* 581
Kille, Julie, Sr Project Mgr-Mktg - Urban Outfitters, Inc.; *pg.* 1789, *pg.* 1571
Killebrew, Michelle, Program Dir-Strategy & Solutions-Social Bus - IBM; *pg.* 410, *pg.* 1449
Killebrew, Michelle, Program Dir-Strategy & Solutions-Social Bus - International Business Machines Corporation; *pg.* 418, *pg.* 1138
Killeen, Leigh, Deputy Exec Dir-Mktg & PR - State of Florida Department of Citrus; *pg.* 1006, *pg.* 437
Killen, Wayne, Gen Mgr-Product Strategy & Launch - Audi of America, Inc.; *pg.* 164, *pg.* 1784
Killgore, Ashley, Coord-Product Mgmt - Attwood Corporation; *pg.* 1705, *pg.* 897
Killingsworth, Laura, Project Mgr-Co-Op Mktg - Lithia Motors Inc; *pg.* 183, *pg.* 1499
Killion, Wendy Olson, Dir-Product Mgmt - Expedia, Inc.; *pg.* 1244, *pg.* 1814
Kilmartin, Philip, Sr Acct Mgr-Inside Sls - Informatica Corporation; *pg.* 414, *pg.* 190
Kilmer, Casey, Mgr-Mktg Comm - Nissan North America, Inc.; *pg.* 186, *pg.* 1633
Kilroy, Thomas M., Exec VP-Sls & Mktg - Intel Corporation; *pg.* 645, *pg.* 266
Kim, Aaron, Assoc Dir-Adv Ops - IGN Entertainment, Inc.; *pg.* 1258, *pg.* 220
Kim, Adrienne, Brand Mktg Mgr - LG Electronics U.S.A., Inc.; *pg.* 651, *pg.* 1060
Kim, Alison, Dir-Mktg & Food Svcs - WestRock Company; *pg.* 1472, *pg.* 1805
Kim, Amanda, Analyst-Social Media - Under Armour, Inc.; *pg.* 49, *pg.* 759
Kim, Amy, Sr Dir-Mktg-Charter Bus - Charter Communications, Inc.; *pg.* 274, *pg.* 372
Kim, Annette Y., Mgr-Mktg - E.I. du Pont de Nemours & Company; *pg.* 1159, *pg.* 390
Kim, Borin, Sr Analyst-Bus & Mktg Ops - Liberty Mutual Insurance Group Inc.; *pg.* 1205, *pg.* 797
Kim, Charles, Sr Mgr-Strategy, M&A, Category Fin & Decision Support - Diageo North America Inc.; *pg.* 248, *pg.* 1223
Kim, Clara, Dir-Adv Solutions - Microsoft Corporation; *pg.* 435, *pg.* 1824
Kim, Cliff, Mgr-Digital Mktg & Analytics - Ticketmaster Entertainment LLC; *pg.* 1284, *pg.* 48
Kim, Dan, Head-Mktg-Global - Solera Holdings, Inc.; *pg.* 1217, *pg.* 1749
Kim, David, Mgr-Sls & Ultrasound Res - Analogic Corporation; *pg.* 1399, *pg.* 840
Kim, David, Sr Mgr-CRM Ops - T-Mobile US, Inc.; *pg.* 676, *pg.* 1816
Kim, DongWook, Global Product Mgr - Molex Incorporated; *pg.* 655, *pg.* 628
Kim, Esther, Brand Mgr - Ghirardelli Chocolate Company; *pg.* 1854, *pg.* 252
Kim, Eunice, Product Mgr-Google Play - Google Inc.; *pg.* 1249, *pg.* 153
Kim, Gina, Mgr-Mktg - El Pollo Loco, Inc.; *pg.* 1728, *pg.* 70
Kim, Grace, Brand Mgr - Dr Pepper Snapple Group, Inc.; *pg.* 250, *pg.* 1729
Kim, Grace, Sr Dir-Res - Twitter, Inc.; *pg.* 1285, *pg.* 228
Kim, Guemmy, Product Mgr-Acct Controls & Settings - Google Inc.; *pg.* 1249, *pg.* 153
Kim, Hannah, Coord-Mktg & Book Dev - The Museum of Modern Art; *pg.* 565, *pg.* 1263
Kim, Ike, Brand Mgr-Red Baron Pizza - The Schwan Food Company; *pg.* 894, *pg.* 928
Kim, James, Mgr-Product Mktg - Anixter International Inc.; *pg.* 1313, *pg.* 614
Kim, James J., Sr VP-Sls & Mktg-Worldwide - Semtech Corporation; *pg.* 671, *pg.* 57
Kim, Janet, Producer-Photoshoot, Mktg & Creative Svcs - Hot Topic, Inc.; *pg.* 42, *pg.* 67
Kim, Jason, Mgr-Digital Mktg & Intl - J. Crew Group, Inc.; *pg.* 1773, *pg.* 1245
Kim, Jayson, Div VP-Consumer Mktg - BCBG Max Azria Group LLC; *pg.* 19, *pg.* 301
Kim, Jhun, Sr Product Mgr - Panasonic Corporation of North America; *pg.* 661, *pg.* 1120
Kim, Jinnie, Reg Mgr-Mktg-APAC - Bose Corporation; *pg.* 626, *pg.* 820
Kim, Joanne, Sr Specialist-Digital Adv - TD Ameritrade Holding Corporation; *pg.* 808, *pg.* 1018
Kim, John, Mgr-Mktg Analytics - PUBLIC STORAGE; *pg.* 1467, *pg.* 98
Kim, Joon, Head-Global Trade Processing Products-Treasury Svcs - The Bank of New York Mellon Corporation; *pg.* 720, *pg.* 1200
Kim, Jr, Product Mgr-Reporting Enablement - Adobe Systems Incorporated; *pg.* 342, *pg.* 235
Kim, Karen, Asst Mgr-Acura Reg Mktg - American Honda Motor Co., Inc.; *pg.* 163, *pg.* 292
Kim, Krysten E., Specialist-PR & Community Affairs - Samsung Electronics America, Inc.; *pg.* 669, *pg.* 1115
Kim, Mira, Sr Dir-New Bus Dev - The Clorox Company; *pg.* 327, *pg.* 169
Kim, Richard, Dir-Brand Mktg - Hulu LLC; *pg.* 1257, *pg.* 274
Kim, Richard, VP-Sls & Gen Mgr-Asia - Neonode, Inc.; *pg.* 659, *pg.* 268
Kim, Ricky, Sr Mgr-Consumer Promos - Nintendo of America, Inc.; *pg.* 965, *pg.* 1829
Kim, Roy, Grp Mgr-Product Mktg - NVIDIA Corporation; *pg.* 447, *pg.* 268
Kim, Saehee, Specialist-Digital Mktg - Oakley, Inc.; *pg.* 1840, *pg.* 86
Kim, Sam, Mgr-Mktg - CB Richard Ellis Group, Inc.; *pg.* 1085, *pg.* 127
Kim, Sara, Product Mgr-Projectors - Epson America Inc.; *pg.* 394, *pg.* 122
Kim, Scott, Gen Mgr-Search Engine Mktg & Search Engine Optimization - IAC Search & Media, Inc.; *pg.* 1257, *pg.* 171
Kim, Shin, Brand Mgr-Utility Bedding & Trim - Macy's East; *pg.* 1777, *pg.* 1254
Kim, Shin, Brand Mgr-Utility Bedding & Trim - Macy's, Inc.; *pg.* 1778, *pg.* 1417
Kim, SK, Sr Dir-Product Strategy & Mktg - Samsung Electronics America, Inc.; *pg.* 669, *pg.* 1115
Kim, Son, Dir-Mktg - The Gap, Inc.; *pg.* 1770, *pg.* 218
Kim, Stephen, Product Engr - Mentor Graphics Corporation; *pg.* 432, *pg.* 1510
Kim, Steve, Product Mgr-Enterprise Platforms - Netflix, Inc.; *pg.* 1269, *pg.* 141
Kim, Taehoon, Head-Japan Mktg Team-Semiconductor & Display - Samsung Electronics America, Inc.; *pg.* 669, *pg.* 1115
Kim, Tom, Sr Mgr-Mktg - Intuit Inc.; *pg.* 769, *pg.* 158
Kim, Woo, Mgr-Mktg & Branding-OEM - Microsoft Corporation; *pg.* 435, *pg.* 1824
Kim, Woojong, Sr Mgr-Adv Collateral - Hyundai Motor America; *pg.* 179, *pg.* 89
Kim, YeJin, Dir-Creative-Global - Blissworld LLC; *pg.* 501, *pg.* 1204
Kim, Young, Dir-Product Dev - Caleres, Inc.; *pg.* 1805, *pg.* 993
Kim, Yuna, Specialist-Search Engine Mktg - Expedia, Inc.; *pg.* 1244, *pg.* 1814
Kim-Williams, Anna, Dir-Global Mktg, PR & AR & Bus Mgr - Microsoft Corporation; *pg.* 435, *pg.* 1824
Kimball, Harry, Dir-Database Mktg - Big Y Foods, Inc.; *pg.* 1015, *pg.* 845
Kimbell, David, CMO - Ulta Salon, Cosmetics & Fragrance, Inc.; *pg.* 524, *pg.* 559
Kimberl, Mary D., Sr Mgr-Mktg - AT&T Mobility LLC; *pg.* 619, *pg.* 488
Kimble, KaNeeTa, Brand Mgr-North America Brand Ops - The Procter & Gamble Company; *pg.* 1129, *pg.* 1418
Kimble, Michael, Dir-Global Mktg-Enterprise Solutions - Dell Inc.; *pg.* 383, *pg.* 1737
Kimbrel, Jesse, Specialist-PR-Barracuda - Barracuda Networks, Inc.; *pg.* 360, *pg.* 58
Kimbro, Becky, VP-Mktg - Rangers Baseball LLC; *pg.* 578, *pg.* 1659
Kimbro, Julie S., Dir-Mktg - Truven Health Analytics; *pg.* 486, *pg.* 331
Kimbro, Robert, VP-Distr Sls - Standard Motor Products, Inc.; *pg.* 218, *pg.* 1176
Kimener, Pat, Sr VP-Sls - The Chicago Faucet Company; *pg.* 1044, *pg.* 606
Kimhorak, Michelle, Mgr-Digital Mktg-Global - The Procter & Gamble Company; *pg.* 1129, *pg.* 1418
Kimlinger, Ashley, Brand Mgr - Deluxe Corporation; *pg.* 1634, *pg.* 964
Kimmel, Kris, Product Mgr-YZ Sys - Milton Roy Company; *pg.* 1361, *pg.* 1542
Kimmell, Arwen, Sr Mgr-Consumer Insights - Kashi Company; *pg.* 830, *pg.* 119
Kin, Richard, Product Mgr-Enterprise Digital - Darden Restaurants, Inc.; *pg.* 1724, *pg.* 453
Kin, Richard, Product Mgr-Enterprise Digital - Olive Garden Italian Restaurant; *pg.* 1742, *pg.* 454
Kinas, Scott, Sr Mgr-Reg Brand Mktg - Pfizer Inc.; *pg.* 1581, *pg.* 1278
Kincaid, Jennifer, Mgr-Commodity, Direct & Digital Mktg - The Allstate Corporation; *pg.* 1189, *pg.* 639
Kincaid, Kayla, Specialist-ECommerce Mktg Content - Big Lots, Inc.; *pg.* 1762, *pg.* 1438
Kincaid, Susie, Bus Mgr - The Arkansas City Traveler; *pg.* 1617, *pg.* 714
Kinch, Stephen, Sr Product Mgr-Mobile & API - 7-Eleven, Inc.; *pg.* 1012, *pg.* 1672
Kindig, Beth A., Mgr-Mktg - United Parcel Service, Inc.; *pg.* 1928, *pg.* 522
Kindig, Jeff, VP-Mktg Strategy - AMX Corporation; *pg.* 349, *pg.* 1735
Kinerk, Beth A., Sr VP-Sls-North America - Avis Budget Group, Inc.; *pg.* 1900, *pg.* 1102
King, Aaron, Specialist-Bus Products - Sentry Insurance Group; *pg.* 1217, *pg.* 1895
King, Adrian, Reg Dir-Mktg - Boyd Gaming Corporation; *pg.* 1082, *pg.* 1022

King, Aleta, Sr Dir-Patron Dev - Pittsburgh Symphony Inc.; *pg.* 577, *pg.* 1579
King, Bernadette, Dir-Mktg - The Procter & Gamble Company; *pg.* 1129, *pg.* 1418
King, Bill, Dir-Product R&D - Samsonite Corporation; *pg.* 11, *pg.* 830
King, Carla, Analyst-Mktg-Pet Foods - Del Monte Foods, Inc.; *pg.* 852, *pg.* 304
King, Catherine, Sr Mgr- Design-women's C9 for Target - Hanesbrands Inc.; *pg.* 26, *pg.* 1394
King, Charles, Exec VP-Mktg - Alere Health Systems, Inc.; *pg.* 1488, *pg.* 535
King, Charles, Dir-Online Mktg - Softlayer Technologies Inc; *pg.* 471, *pg.* 1686
King, Charles G., VP-Sls Tubular - Northwest Pipe Company; *pg.* 100, *pg.* 1846
King, Crystal, Specialist-Mktg - Susan G. Komen for the Cure; *pg.* 158, *pg.* 1688
King, Curt, Sr VP-Publicity, Mktg & Corp Comm - NBC Universal, Inc.; *pg.* 300, *pg.* 1266
King, Daniel, Head-Media Plng-Australia - Facebook, Inc.; *pg.* 1245, *pg.* 143
King, Daniella, Mgr-eMail Mktg - Quiksilver, Inc.; *pg.* 31, *pg.* 104
King, David, VP-Strategic Mktg, Tax & Acctg - CCH Inc.; *pg.* 1626, *pg.* 653
King, David, Grp Product Mgr-Music Insights - YouTube, LLC; *pg.* 1291, *pg.* 198
King, Debbie, Mgr-Product Line - Teledyne Benthos, Inc.; *pg.* 1431, *pg.* 838
King, Debra, Mgr-Retail Fuels Mktg-Americas - Exxon Mobil Corporation; *pg.* 977, *pg.* 1718
King, Denise, Sr Coord-Adv - Society of Manufacturing Engineers; *pg.* 157, *pg.* 878
King, Don, VP-Sls - BiNW; *pg.* 918, *pg.* 1833
King, Emily, Reg Mgr-Mktg - CKE Restaurants Inc.; *pg.* 1723, *pg.* 63
King, Emily, Sr VP-Media & On-Air Plng - Fox Broadcasting Company; *pg.* 287, *pg.* 130
King, Hal, Dir-Food & Product Safety - Chick-fil-A, Inc.; *pg.* 1721, *pg.* 492
King, Heather R., Assoc Dir-Mktg Comm - Merck & Co., Inc.; *pg.* 1566, *pg.* 1077
King, Howie, Dir-Bus Dev & Product Innovation - PASSUR Aerospace, Inc.; *pg.* 233, *pg.* 376
King, Jade, Sr Mgr-Comm - GlaxoSmithKline; *pg.* 1536, *pg.* 1565
King, Jake, Sr Dir-Adv Ops - comScore, Inc; *pg.* 1236, *pg.* 1798
King, Janice, VP & Project Mgr-Mktg - Bank of the West; *pg.* 721, *pg.* 213
King, Janine, Dir-Procurement, Sls & Mktg - Sanofi US; *pg.* 1592, *pg.* 1046
King, Jill, Sr Mgr-Mktg-Dept Store Hosiery Brands - Hanesbrands Inc.; *pg.* 26, *pg.* 1394
King, Joe, Principal Product Mgr-Kindle - Amazon.com, Inc.; *pg.* 1226, *pg.* 1831
King, John, VP-Global Mktg-SBL - MasterCard International, Inc.; *pg.* 780, *pg.* 1326
King, Julian, Sr VP-Mktg & Corp Dev - Xoom Corporation; *pg.* 1289, *pg.* 234
King, Kari, Dir-Integrated Mktg Plng - Allianz Life Insurance Company of North America; *pg.* 1188, *pg.* 929
King, Kari, Sr VP-Sls Strategy & VP-Sls - Mode Media; *pg.* 1267, *pg.* 50
King, Kathy, Mgr-Product Mktg - Insperity, Inc.; *pg.* 416, *pg.* 1725
King, Katrina, Reg Mgr-Sls - Ilpea Industries, Inc.; *pg.* 1348, *pg.* 697
King, Kendall, Mgr-Integrated Sls Plng - World Wrestling Entertainment, Inc.; *pg.* 595, *pg.* 380
King, Kim, Reg Head-Mktg - Humana, Inc.; *pg.* 1204, *pg.* 734
King, Laraine, Sr Mgr-Corp Comm - Amgen Inc.; *pg.* 1493, *pg.* 291
King, Laura, Sr Dir-Employee Comm - Microsoft Corporation; *pg.* 435, *pg.* 1824
King, Leighsa, VP-Adv - Citigroup Inc.; *pg.* 735, *pg.* 1212
King, Louis, Dir-Adv & Mktg - Hutchens Industries Inc.; *pg.* 208, *pg.* 1006
King, Maria, Mgr-Brand Mktg - Hickory Farms, Inc.; *pg.* 862, *pg.* 1462
King, Mark, Head-Diversity, Inclusion & HR Policy & Sr Dir-Global - Kellogg Company; *pg.* 831, *pg.* 870
King, Mark A., Sr VP-Sls & Mktg - Diodes Incorporated; *pg.* 634, *pg.* 1729
King, Matt, Assoc Dir-Mktg-Intl - Burt's Bees Inc.; *pg.* 502, *pg.* 1370
King, Melanie, Coord-Digital Mktg - Saks Fifth Avenue, Inc.; *pg.* 1783, *pg.* 1287
King, Michelle, Sr Dir-PR-Global - Dunkin' Brands Group, Inc.; *pg.* 1727, *pg.* 810
King, Mike, Mgr-Global Product Line - Eaton's Crouse-Hinds; *pg.* 1296, *pg.* 1344
King, Mindy, Mgr-Social & Mobile Mktg - Intuit Inc.; *pg.* 769, *pg.* 158
King, Nick, Head-Mktg & Devices for Work - Google Inc.; *pg.* 1249, *pg.* 153
King, Paul, Dir-Product Design - MATTEL, INC.; *pg.* 962, *pg.* 81
King, Princess, Mgr-Global Mktg Launch - Ford Motor Company; *pg.* 172, *pg.* 876
King, Rachel, Product Mgr-Global - AstraZeneca Pharmaceuticals LP; *pg.* 1497, *pg.* 389
King, Randy, Sr Mgr-Comm - McKesson Corporation; *pg.* 1560, *pg.* 222
King, Ryan, Product Mgr - The Upper Deck Company, LLC; *pg.* 969, *pg.* 62
King, Shanise, Dir-US Mktg Reg - Revlon, Inc.; *pg.* 521, *pg.* 1286
King, Shari, Brand Mgr-Hunt's Condiments & Pasta Sauce - ConAgra Foods, Inc.; *pg.* 826, *pg.* 1014
King, Susan, Sr Mgr - Capital One Financial Corporation; *pg.* 730, *pg.* 1789
King, Tina, Sr Product Mgr - Rejuvenation Inc.; *pg.* 1304, *pg.* 1506
King, Wayne, VP-Sls & Mktg - CRC Industries, Inc.; *pg.* 329, *pg.* 1590
King, William, Sr VP-Sls - Fujitsu Computer Systems Corporation; *pg.* 398, *pg.* 285
King-Roberson, Shanea, Product Mgr - Google Inc.; *pg.* 1249, *pg.* 153
Kingery, Andrew, Dir-Shopper & Customer Mktg - Beiersdorf North America Inc.; *pg.* 501, *pg.* 385
Kinghorn, Daniel, Sr Mgr-Natl Sponsorships - Crown Imports LLC; *pg.* 248, *pg.* 572
Kingra, Mahinder S., Mgr-Mktg - Cornell University Press; *pg.* 1630, *pg.* 1169
Kingsmill, Inese, Dir-Partner Strategy, Mktg & Programs - Microsoft Corporation; *pg.* 435, *pg.* 1824
Kingston, Patrick, Mgr-Sls Strategy & Plng - Hillshire Brands; *pg.* 862, *pg.* 576
Kingston, Richard, Dir-Mktg & IR - CEVA, Inc.; *pg.* 628, *pg.* 153
Kingston, Shannon, Specialist-Mktg - Finger Lakes Racing Association Inc.; *pg.* 548, *pg.* 1160
Kington, Damian, Head-Mktg-Global - Liquidnet Holdings, Inc.; *pg.* 776, *pg.* 1251
Kingzett, Traci, Brand Mgr - Revlon Consumer Products Corporation; *pg.* 521, *pg.* 1286
Kinkade, Brendan, Sr Mgr-vCloud Air Partner Sls - VMware, Inc.; *pg.* 490, *pg.* 179
Kinkade, Roxann M., Dir-Media Rels & Pub Affairs - Pinnacle Entertainment, Inc.; *pg.* 576, *pg.* 1029
Kinnaird, Tim, Mgr-Mktg Comm - Arrow Electronics, Inc.; *pg.* 619, *pg.* 325
Kinnaman, Julie, Acct Exec-Charter Media - Charter Communications, Inc.; *pg.* 274, *pg.* 372
Kinnaman, Micah J., Sr Mgr-Product Mktg - AT&T Mobility LLC; *pg.* 620, *pg.* 1152
Kinnear, Jamie, Dir-Mktg - Land O'Lakes, Inc.; *pg.* 873, *pg.* 915
Kinney, David, Dir-Midwest Convention Sls - Louisville Convention & Visitors Bureau; *pg.* 998, *pg.* 736
Kinney, Debra, Mgr-Mktg Comm - Siemens Process Industries and Drives; *pg.* 673, *pg.* 485
Kinney, Kelly, Product Mgr-Mktg-Global - IDEX Corporation; *pg.* 1347, *pg.* 623
Kinney, Lorrie, Mgr-Mktg & Comm - Federal-Mogul Holdings Corporation; *pg.* 205, *pg.* 907
Kinney, Mike, VP-Sls - Asure Software, Inc.; *pg.* 355, *pg.* 1660
Kinney, Patricia, Sr VP-Digital User Centered Product Dev - BB&T Corporation; *pg.* 723, *pg.* 1393
Kinnsch, Gary, VP-Sls - 505 Games (US), Inc.; *pg.* 948, *pg.* 38
Kinross, Kevin, Mgr-Creative Svcs - Cardinal Health, Inc.; *pg.* 1512, *pg.* 1448
Kinsella, Angela, Sr Dir-Programmatic Sls Ops - Demand Media, Inc.; *pg.* 1238, *pg.* 273
Kinsella, Molly, Sr Dir-Brand Mktg - Best Buy Co., Inc.; *pg.* 1761, *pg.* 954
Kinsey, Christopher, Mgr-PR & Social Media-Europe - Banana Republic; *pg.* 1760, *pg.* 212
Kinsey, Steve, Mgr-Customer Sls-Amazon.com - GlaxoSmithKline; *pg.* 1536, *pg.* 1389
Kinsey, Steve, Mgr-Customer Sls-Amazon.com - GlaxoSmithKline; *pg.* 1536, *pg.* 1565
Kinsey, Steve, Mgr-Customer Sls-Amazon.com - GlaxoSmithKline Consumer Healthcare; *pg.* 510, *pg.* 1554
Kinsley, Sarah, Mgr-Mktg - Reebok International Ltd.; *pg.* 1817, *pg.* 811
Kinsman, Todd, Sr Mgr-Analytics & Americas Sls - Bose Corporation; *pg.* 626, *pg.* 820
Kinstedt, Paul, Acting COO - Republic Airways Holdings Inc.; *pg.* 1894, *pg.* 689
Kint, Daniel, Mgr-Sls - Haco-Atlantic, Inc.; *pg.* 1344, *pg.* 1707
Kintigh, Luke, Strategist-Global Content & Media - Intel Corporation; *pg.* 645, *pg.* 266
Kintner, Mike, Dir-Mktg & Ops - Caesars Entertainment Corporation; *pg.* 1083, *pg.* 1023
Kintzler, Bill, Dir-Product Dev - Cracker Barrel Old Country Store, Inc.; *pg.* 1723, *pg.* 1639
Kinzel, Lisa, Brand Mgr - Stonyfield Farm, Inc.; *pg.* 899, *pg.* 1035
Kinzer, Elizabeth, Sr Mgr-Mktg - United Parcel Service, Inc.; *pg.* 1928, *pg.* 522
Kinzler, Philip, Sr Mgr-Brand Activation - Newell Rubbermaid Inc.; *pg.* 1128, *pg.* 515
Kinzy, Jason F., Mgr-Specialty Bus Mktg - Anthem, Inc.; *pg.* 1192, *pg.* 683
Kiong, Poon Wai, Product Mgr-Global - Molex Incorporated; *pg.* 655, *pg.* 628
Kiple, Bob, Strategist-Chevrolet Global Adv & Brand - General Motors Company; *pg.* 175, *pg.* 881
Kipness, Megan L., Assoc Dir-Mktg - Allergan; *pg.* 1490, *pg.* 1101
Kipp, Bryan, Dir-Digital Mktg & CRM - Jo-Ann Stores LLC; *pg.* 696, *pg.* 1455
Kipper, Fulvia, Sr Mgr-Corp Comm - Amgen Inc.; *pg.* 1493, *pg.* 291
Kirbow, Donna W., Sr Dir-Fin Svcs - Chick-fil-A, Inc.; *pg.* 1721, *pg.* 492
Kirby, Amy, VP-Mktg - Albertson's LLC; *pg.* 1013, *pg.* 546
Kirby, Brian, Mgr-Digital Mktg - Wendy's International, Inc.; *pg.* 1755, *pg.* 1451
Kirby, Bruce, Mgr-Adv Production - The Mattress Firm, Inc.; *pg.* 934, *pg.* 1711
Kirby, David W., VP-Sls - Monrovia Growers; *pg.* 1797, *pg.* 44
Kirby, Kim, Mgr-Media - Capital One Financial Corporation; *pg.* 730, *pg.* 1789
Kirby, Sue, Project Mgr & Coord-Mktg - Massachusetts Mutual Life Insurance Company; *pg.* 1207, *pg.* 845
Kirby, Timothy G., Territory Mgr-Sls - Caterpillar, Inc.; *pg.* 1321, *pg.* 650
Kircher, Maggie, Reg Dir-Field Mktg - Hyatt Hotels Corporation; *pg.* 1096, *pg.* 577
Kirchgessner, Daniel, Reg Product Mgr-Mktg - Facebook, Inc.; *pg.* 1245, *pg.* 143
Kirchhardt, Debbie, Dir-Sls Ops - Amkor Technology, Inc.; *pg.* 67, *pg.* 25
Kirchler, Jennifer L., Specialist-PR Supply Chain Source - Raytheon; *pg.* 459, *pg.* 115
Kirchmeier, Desirae, Mgr-Mktg - Ulta Salon, Cosmetics & Fragrance, Inc.; *pg.* 524, *pg.* 559
Kirchmeier, Kathi, Mgr-Mktg Programs - Thermo Fisher Scientific Inc.; *pg.* 1602, *pg.* 61
Kirchner, Melissa, Mgr-Mktg-Plant Nutrition - Compass Minerals International, Inc.; *pg.* 1154, *pg.* 718
Kirchoff, Gary, Product Mgr-Composite Machining - Dormer Pramet; *pg.* 1329, *pg.* 609
Kirimca, Irfan, Sr Dir-Ticket Ops - New York Yankees; *pg.* 570, *pg.* 1144
Kiristis, Cristi, Mgr-Mktg-NA - VeriFone Systems, Inc.; *pg.* 487, *pg.* 251
Kiritsis, Kathryn, Dir-Digital Mktg & ECommerce - Bayer HealthCare Pharmaceutical Division; *pg.* 1500, *pg.* 1132
Kirk, Alexis, Mgr-Retail Mktg - Michael Kors (USA), Inc.; *pg.* 29, *pg.* 1260
Kirk, Jami, Mgr-Sls - Starwood Hotels & Resorts Worldwide, Inc.; *pg.* 1114, *pg.* 378
Kirk, Jason, Sr Analyst-Mktg - Renaissance Learning, Inc.; *pg.* 607, *pg.* 1899
Kirk, Katharine, Dir-Customer Loyalty Mktg - American Express Company; *pg.* 712, *pg.* 1190
Kirk, Stephanie, Mgr-Mktg-CRM TRU - Toys "R" Us, Inc.; *pg.*

First page reference indicates Business Class Edition
Second page reference indicates Geographic Edition

968, *pg.* 1130
Kirk, Trisha, Dir-Mktg - Guthrie Theater Foundation; *pg.* 551, *pg.* 937
Kirkby, Heather, Dir-Product Mgmt-QuickBooks Online Accountant - Intuit Inc.; *pg.* 769, *pg.* 158
Kirkendall, Eric, Sr VP-Retail Sls - New Age Electronics, Inc.; *pg.* 659, *pg.* 63
Kirkham, Mark, Sr Dir-Mktg-Global Pepsi - PepsiCo, Inc.; *pg.* 259, *pg.* 1327
Kirkiris, Nectar, Dir-Product Mgmt - Intel Corporation; *pg.* 645, *pg.* 266
Kirkland, Danny, Mgr-Digital Mktg-Fabric Care-Global - Vidal Sassoon Co.; *pg.* 524, *pg.* 1426
Kirkland, Heather, Dir-Event Mktg - MARTHA STEWART LIVING OMNIMEDIA, INC.; *pg.* 1661, *pg.* 1256
Kirkland, Wandee, Category Mgr-Purchased Products - Wright & McGill Co.; *pg.* 1848, *pg.* 324
Kirkman, Chris, VP-Product Ops - Replacements, Ltd.; *pg.* 1138, *pg.* 1383
Kirkman, Janet, Product Mgr - Nalco Co.; *pg.* 1174, *pg.* 636
Kirkman, John, Dir-Pro Mktg-Consumer Healthcare - Johnson & Johnson; *pg.* 1549, *pg.* 1091
Kirkman, Rian, VP-Mktg-The Venetian - Las Vegas Sands Corp.; *pg.* 1100, *pg.* 1027
Kirkpatrick, Alana, Sr Mgr-Mktg Programs - Nuance Communications, Inc.; *pg.* 447, *pg.* 806
Kirkpatrick, Kathryn, Mgr-Corp Media Rels - Ace Hardware Corporation; *pg.* 1040, *pg.* 644
Kirkpatrick, Katie, Sr Mgr-Comm-PPG Architectural Coatings - PPG Industries, Inc.; *pg.* 1445, *pg.* 1579
Kirkpatrick, Matthew, Head-Geographic Mktg - Monsanto Company; *pg.* 1173, *pg.* 999
Kirkpatrick, Renee, Exec Administrator-Mktg - Access National Corporation; *pg.* 710, *pg.* 1798
Kirksey, Greg, Dir-Mktg Comm Solutions - Acuity Brands, Inc.; *pg.* 1294, *pg.* 487
Kirksey, Heather, Mgr-PR - Atlanta Convention & Visitors Bureau; *pg.* 989, *pg.* 489
Kirkwood, Bob, Exec VP-Tech & Mktg - INVISTA B.V.; *pg.* 1168, *pg.* 723
Kirn, Brian, Sr Mgr-Mktg-Siding Products Grp - CertainTeed Corporation; *pg.* 74, *pg.* 1589
Kirn, Matthew, Mgr-ECommerce Mobile Product Dev - Marriott International, Inc.; *pg.* 1102, *pg.* 764
Kiroff, Gina, Mgr-Mktg-Knorr & Hellmann's - Unilever Canada Inc.; *pg.* 903, *pg.* 1946
Kirsch, Mary Ann, Head-Sls & Mktg Pur & Head-North America & Global - FCA US LLC; *pg.* 170, *pg.* 868
Kirsch, Meghan, VP-Brand Creative - A&E Television Networks, LLC; *pg.* 267, *pg.* 1185
Kirsch, Vicky A., Grp VP-Worldwide Events Mktg - Gartner, Inc.; *pg.* 1248, *pg.* 374
Kirschman, Philip, Mgr-Mktg-Bus Insights Grp - The Clorox Company; *pg.* 327, *pg.* 169
Kirschner, Ruth, Dir-Natl Advertiser Sls - DoubleClick, Inc.; *pg.* 1239, *pg.* 1225
Kirschner, Ruth, Dir-Natl Advertiser Sls - Google Inc.; *pg.* 1249, *pg.* 153
Kirscht, Rachel, Mgr-Mktg-Mobile - The New York Times; *pg.* 1668, *pg.* 1270
Kirsten, Keith, Dir-Sls - Detroit Metro Convention & Visitors Bureau; *pg.* 139, *pg.* 880
Kirsten, Kluepfel, Mgr-Corp Mktg - National Oilwell Varco, Inc.; *pg.* 1364, *pg.* 1712
Kirtikar, Komal, Dir-Local & Product Mktg - Lyft; *pg.* 429, *pg.* 222
Kirtland, James, Dir-Strategy-Global Mktg - American Express Company; *pg.* 712, *pg.* 1190
Kirtman, Michael, Brand Mgr-Kroger Customer Team - The Procter & Gamble Company; *pg.* 1129, *pg.* 1418
Kirvan, Susan, Sr Mgr-Mktg & Mktg Comm - Oki Data Americas, Inc.; *pg.* 449, *pg.* 1090
Kirwan, Tom, Dir-Natl Sls-People Digital - People Magazine; *pg.* 1676, *pg.* 1278
Kirwin, Beatrix, Mgr-Customer Mktg - Kayak; *pg.* 1260, *pg.* 363
Kiser, Jeff, VP-Sls & Mktg - Aetna Inc.; *pg.* 1187, *pg.* 351
Kiser, Tess, Mgr-Mktg - Georgia Southern University; *pg.* 602, *pg.* 541
Kish, Allison, Sr Mgr - American Express Company; *pg.* 712, *pg.* 1190
Kishimoto, Ashlee, Sr Dir-IR - Hawaiian Airlines, Inc.; *pg.* 1910, *pg.* 543
Kisker, Brooke C., Brand Mgr-Comm-North America - Monsanto Company; *pg.* 1173, *pg.* 999
Kispert, Kimberly, VP-Mktg & Comm Ops - International Business Machines Corporation; *pg.* 418, *pg.* 1138
Kispert, Leann, Dir-Brand Mktg - Explore Minnesota Tourism; *pg.* 992, *pg.* 960
Kiss, Bill, Chief Digital Mktg Officer-Sears & Kmart - Kmart Corporation; *pg.* 1775, *pg.* 617
Kiss, Bill, Chief Digital Mktg Officer-Sears & Kmart - Sears Holdings Corporation; *pg.* 1784, *pg.* 618
Kiss, Geza, Mgr-Production - KraftMaid Cabinetry, Inc.; *pg.* 1053, *pg.* 1465
Kissane, Jonathan, Chief Strategy Officer - NetApp, Inc.; *pg.* 444, *pg.* 287
Kissell, Jason, VP-Adv Sls - The Boston Globe; *pg.* 1623, *pg.* 790
Kissin, Daniel, Sr Mgr-Analytics-US Reg - Expedia, Inc.; *pg.* 1244, *pg.* 1814
Kissinger, Jim, VP-Convention Sls - Anaheim/Orange County Visitor & Convention Bureau; *pg.* 988, *pg.* 42
Kissko, Edie, Sr Dir-Corp Comm-Global - The Gap, Inc.; *pg.* 1770, *pg.* 218
Kissner, Josh, Product Mgr - Santa Cruz Bicycles; *pg.* 1710, *pg.* 271
Kist, Karen, Mgr-Mktg Ops - Airstream, Inc.; *pg.* 163, *pg.* 1456
Kistler, Eric, Mgr-Premium Sls - Atlanta Falcons Football Club, LLC; *pg.* 530, *pg.* 532
Kistner, Jamie, VP-Mktg-STP - Armored AutoGroup Inc.; *pg.* 199, *pg.* 342
Kiszka, Jim, Sr Mgr-Paid Digital Media-North America - Kellogg Company; *pg.* 831, *pg.* 870
Kitchen, Kimberly, Mgr-Metallurgical Coal Mktg - Norfolk Southern Corporation; *pg.* 1917, *pg.* 1797
Kitson, Rosie, Asst VP-Channel Mktg-AT&T - AT&T Mobility LLC; *pg.* 619, *pg.* 488
Kittelson, Brian, Dir-Integrated Shopper Mktg - General Mills, Inc.; *pg.* 828, *pg.* 933
Kitten, Marcia B., Dir-Mktg & Star-Education - Valley Morning Star; *pg.* 1699, *pg.* 1699
Kittenplan, Susan, VP & Editor-New Media Initiatives - Yahoo! Inc.; *pg.* 1289, *pg.* 289
Kitto, David J, VP-Mktg & Sls - John F. Kennedy Center for the Performing Arts; *pg.* 555, *pg.* 401
Kittoe, Patrick, Mgr-Adv - AmerisourceBergen Corporation; *pg.* 1493, *pg.* 1522
Kittredge, Tad, Assoc Dir-Mktg - Burt's Bees Inc.; *pg.* 502, *pg.* 1370
Kittredge, Tad, Assoc Dir-Mktg-Burt's Bees - The Clorox Company; *pg.* 327, *pg.* 169
Kitzie, Erin, Coord-PR - CNBC; *pg.* 275, *pg.* 1059
Kitzmiller, Karen, Asst Sls Mgr-Consultants - Century 21 Real Estate LLC; *pg.* 1085, *pg.* 1080
Kivioja, Rod, Dir-Sls - Super Sky Products, Inc.; *pg.* 113, *pg.* 1871
Kiyokane, Kari, Assoc Mgr-Mktg - Live Nation Entertainment, Inc.; *pg.* 558, *pg.* 47
Kiyota, Travis, VP-Corp Affairs & Sr Dir-Governmental Rels - PG&E Corporation; *pg.* 1949, *pg.* 224
Kizielewicz, James, CMO & Sr VP - Kronos Incorporated; *pg.* 425, *pg.* 813
Kizner, Francine, Mgr-Social Media - Mattel Games/Puzzles; *pg.* 962, *pg.* 80
Kizner, Francine, Mgr-Social Media - MATTEL, INC.; *pg.* 962, *pg.* 81
Kizzar, Mark, Head-New Media & Commerce - GlobalLogic, Inc.; *pg.* 400, *pg.* 1791
Kjeldsen, Cassidy, Sr Specialist-SMB Mktg-Global - Plantronics, Inc.; *pg.* 663, *pg.* 270
Kjolaas-Holland, Kari Anne, Mgr-Sls & Mktg-Europe & Africa - Schlumberger Limited; *pg.* 801, *pg.* 1714
Klaassens, Maggie, Mgr-Search Engine Mktg - Starwood Hotels & Resorts Worldwide, Inc.; *pg.* 1114, *pg.* 378
Klaey, Hans-Peter, Sr VP-Global Sls - Ixia; *pg.* 422, *pg.* 56
Klaft, Robert, Sr Mgr-Honda Power Equipment Ops - American Honda Motor Co., Inc.; *pg.* 163, *pg.* 292
Klages, Renee, Sr Specialist-Mktg - Anadarko Petroleum Corporation; *pg.* 971, *pg.* 1746
Klages, Timo, Product Mgr-Brdcst Solutions - Rohde & Schwarz, Inc.; *pg.* 1428, *pg.* 768
Klahr, Shari, Sr Dir-Market & Competitive Strategy - Teachers Insurance & Annuity Association - College Retirement Equities Fund; *pg.* 1219, *pg.* 1297
Klair, Erica, VP-US Customer Mktg & Issuer - MasterCard International, Inc.; *pg.* 780, *pg.* 1326
Klapisch, Geoff, Dir-Comm & Media - Destination XL Group, Inc.; *pg.* 40, *pg.* 810
Klapper, Suzanne, VP-Mktg - Strayer University; *pg.* 607, *pg.* 405
Klasen, Michael, Product Mgr-SurePower Brand Products - Eaton Corporation; *pg.* 1331, *pg.* 1429
Klashinsky, Rod, VP-Sls & Special Projects - International Road Dynamics Inc.; *pg.* 1912, *pg.* 1962
Klasmeier, Gary, Product Mgr-D-ILA Projectors - JVC Americas Corp.; *pg.* 648, *pg.* 1129
Klassen, Melina, Mgr-Channel Mktg & Alliance Mktg - Plantronics, Inc.; *pg.* 663, *pg.* 270
Klatka, Kyle, Mgr-Mktg-Microcontroller & Consumer Digital - Teradyne Inc.; *pg.* 679, *pg.* 838
Klatt, Kim, VP-Sls - American Chemet Corporation; *pg.* 1147, *pg.* 599
Klause, Tonya N., Dir-PR - Microsoft Corporation; *pg.* 435, *pg.* 1824
Klavas, Sarah, Brand Mgr - Wisconsin Department of Tourism; *pg.* 1011, *pg.* 1868
Klavins, Maris, Mgr-Mktg-Integrated Crop Platform - Bayer CropScience; *pg.* 1149, *pg.* 981
Klawans, Jan, Mgr-Retail Mktg - World's Finest Chocolate, Inc.; *pg.* 1864, *pg.* 597
Kleber, Klee, Sr VP-Mktg & Product Dev - RACKSPACE HOSTING, INC.; *pg.* 1277, *pg.* 1742
Klecker, Amanda, Dir-Mktg - MARTHA STEWART LIVING OMNIMEDIA, INC.; *pg.* 1661, *pg.* 1256
Kleczka, Karen, Analyst-Mktg Effectiveness - Kohl's Corporation; *pg.* 1775, *pg.* 1870
Klee, Joanna, Dir-Mktg - Guardian Building Products Distribution; *pg.* 85, *pg.* 1619
Kleeman, Mike, Sr Mgr-Process - Capital One Financial Corporation; *pg.* 730, *pg.* 1789
Kleffner, Jim, Mgr-Product, Program & Product Dev Engrg - Advanced Micro Devices, Inc.; *pg.* 613, *pg.* 282
Klei-Schlosser, Karen, Assoc Dir-Mktg-NA Laundry - The Procter & Gamble Company; *pg.* 1129, *pg.* 1418
Kleiman, Danny, Grp VP-Repair & Engrg-Tech Products - AAR Corp.; *pg.* 223, *pg.* 671
Kleiman, Michael, Div Dir-Mktg - Tyler Technologies, Inc.; *pg.* 486, *pg.* 1690
Klein, Adam, VP-US Sls & Independent Retail - Dimplex North America Limited; *pg.* 54, *pg.* 1920
Klein, Allyson, Dir-Mktg - Intel Corporation; *pg.* 645, *pg.* 266
Klein, Andrew J., Dir-Mktg - Conair Corporation; *pg.* 505, *pg.* 1055
Klein, Bob, Sr Dir-Corp Reputation - Harley-Davidson, Inc.; *pg.* 178, *pg.* 1874
Klein, Daniel, Product Mgr - Macy's, Inc.; *pg.* 1778, *pg.* 1417
Klein, David, Product Mgr - Klein Tools Inc.; *pg.* 1052, *pg.* 627
Klein, Eric, Brand Mgr - Chobani LLC; *pg.* 847, *pg.* 1318
Klein, Giselle, Brand Mgr - Munchkin, Inc.; *pg.* 964, *pg.* 300
Klein, Jaclyn, Mgr-Loyalty Program & Mktg - JetBlue Airways Corporation; *pg.* 1913, *pg.* 1174
Klein, Jeff, VP-Brand Mktg - Frito-Lay North America, Inc.; *pg.* 1853, *pg.* 1730
Klein, JoEllen, Asst Product Mgr - Trippe Manufacturing Company; *pg.* 220, *pg.* 592
Klein, John, Dir-Federal Sls - TRIPWIRE, INC.; *pg.* 485, *pg.* 1507
Klein, Karen, Dir-Product Mgmt & Mdsg-ECommerce - Ticketmaster Entertainment LLC; *pg.* 1284, *pg.* 48
Klein, Kerrie, Mgr-Fin Product Comm - CME Group Inc.; *pg.* 738, *pg.* 571
Klein, Linda, Sr Product Mgr-Chinaware - AS America, Inc.; *pg.* 68, *pg.* 1108
Klein, Maggie, Dir-PR & Brand - Spanx Inc.; *pg.* 32, *pg.* 520
Klein, Mario, Dir-Mktg - NXP Semiconductors; *pg.* 660, *pg.* 248
Klein, Matt, VP-Media Rels - CIT GROUP INC.; *pg.* 735, *pg.* 1212
Klein, Michelle, Head-Global Mktg - Facebook, Inc.; *pg.* 1245, *pg.* 143
Klein, Samantha, Mgr-Mktg-Digital & Editorial Content - IBM; *pg.* 410, *pg.* 1449
Klein, Scott, Sr Dir-Mktg-Cardiac Diagnostics & Monitoring - Medtronic, Inc.; *pg.* 1564, *pg.* 939
Klein, Shannon, VP-Mktg & Comm - HealthPartners, Inc.; *pg.* 1203, *pg.* 918
Klein, Tim, VP-PR - Equifax Inc.; *pg.* 748, *pg.* 504
Klein, Tom, VP-Mktg - The Rocket Science Group, LLC; *pg.* 1278, *pg.* 519
Klein-Lepore, Mindel, Dir-Digital Mktg-Worldwide - Colgate-Palmolive Company; *pg.* 504, *pg.* 1215
Kleinbaum, Cynthia, Sr Dir-Mktg - Gilt Groupe Inc.; *pg.* 24,

pg. 1234
Kleinberg, Sarah, Grp Mgr-Mktg-Creative Partnerships - Google Inc.; pg. 1249, pg. 153
Kleinberg, Scott, Editor-Social Media - Tribune Media Company; pg. 1696, pg. 592
Kleinebreil, Anna, Product Mgr-CLA, GLA & SLK - Mercedes-Benz USA, LLC; pg. 184, pg. 514
Kleinerman, Lori, Dir-Mktg & PR - Chicago Theatre Group Inc.; pg. 539, pg. 570
Kleinman, Dan, VP-Mktg-Rums Portfolio - Diageo North America Inc.; pg. 248, pg. 1223
Kleinman, Gary, Dir-Brand Strategy, Adv, Natl Media & Direct Response - Intuit Inc.; pg. 769, pg. 158
Kleinman, Peter, Dir-Mktg - Leviton Manufacturing Company, Inc.; pg. 1301, pg. 1180
Kleinschmidt, Gary, Dir-Retirement Sls - Legg Mason, Inc.; pg. 775, pg. 758
Kleinsmith, Jordan, Product Mgr-Tax - Thomson Reuters Tax & Accounting; pg. 484, pg. 905
Kleiwer, Art, Mng Dir-Intl Vertical Rig Sls - The George E. Failing Company; pg. 1340, pg. 1484
Klem, Chris, Dir-Mktg Comm - The Chamberlain Group, Inc.; pg. 75, pg. 611
Klemm, Amanda, Dir-Mktg-Hill's Science Diet - Colgate-Palmolive Company; pg. 504, pg. 1215
Klene, Ed, Assoc Dir-Mktg - Sunny Delight Beverages Co.; pg. 899, pg. 1426
Klenk, Donald, VP-Ops-Turf & Consumer Products - Briggs & Stratton Corporation; pg. 201, pg. 1899
Klenke, Joseph L., Exec VP-Advanced Tech & Channels - The Standard Register Company; pg. 473, pg. 1446
Kleto, Thomas, Coord-Mktg Programs - AMERICAN TIRE DISTRIBUTORS HOLDINGS, INC.; pg. 199, pg. 1379
Klettke, Scott, Gen Mgr-RF Products - Murata Electronics North America, Inc.; pg. 658, pg. 540
Klicsu, Joe, Sr Mgr-Digital Comm - Energizer Holdings, Inc.; pg. 637, pg. 996
Kliegerman, Lisa, Brand Mgr - Diageo North America, Inc.; pg. 1961, pg. 361
Kliegerman, Lisa, Brand Mgr - Diageo North America Inc.; pg. 248, pg. 1223
Klier, Katrina, Mng Dir-Digital Mktg & Comm-Global - Accenture; pg. 1392, pg. 1186
Kligman, Rob, VP-Digital & Integrated Sls - World Wrestling Entertainment, Inc.; pg. 595, pg. 380
Klim, Jodi, Sr Mgr-Mktg - Equifax Inc.; pg. 748, pg. 504
Klima, Jill, Dir-Site Mktg - Sephora USA Inc; pg. 522, pg. 227
Klimas, Carolyn, Dir-Mktg-Medical Solutions Div - Olympus America Inc.; pg. 1425, pg. 1521
Klimczak, Karen, Dir-Mktg-Denver & Anschutz Medical Campus - University Of Colorado; pg. 608, pg. 323
Klimek, Clarissa, Key Acct Mgr-Mktg-SOREL - Columbia Sportswear Company; pg. 1830, pg. 1501
Klimek, Kate, Mgr-Mktg Strategy - W.W. Grainger, Inc.; pg. 1390, pg. 625
Klimke, Dan, Mgr-Product Mktg - Netscout Systems, Inc.; pg. 1270, pg. 858
Kline, Adam, Sr Dir - Manhattan Associates, Inc.; pg. 430, pg. 513
Kline, Anne-Marie, VP-Mktg - Living Proof, Inc.; pg. 514, pg. 809
Kline, Christina, VP-Brand Mktg-AIU - Career Education Corporation; pg. 599, pg. 658
Kline, Chuck, Exec VP-Sls-Properties Grp - MDI Entertainment LLC; pg. 964, pg. 484
Kline, Clifford, Sr VP-Customer & Product Support Ops - John Wiley & Sons, Inc.; pg. 1655, pg. 1073
Kline, David, Pres-Media Sls & Exec VP - Charter Communications, Inc.; pg. 274, pg. 372
Kline, Ed, Dir-Mktg - Church & Dwight Co., Inc.; pg. 1153, pg. 1063
Kline, Jason, Dir-Mktg Plng - Dick's Sporting Goods, Inc.; pg. 1832, pg. 1524
Kling, Marian, Coord-Online Mktg - Helzberg's Diamond Shops, Inc.; pg. 6, pg. 984
Klinge, John, Product Mgr-Metal Detection - Eriez Manufacturing Co. Inc.; pg. 1335, pg. 1530
Klingelhofer, Grace, Product Mgr-ABC News Digital - ABC, Inc.; pg. 268, pg. 1185
Klingensmith, Michele, Mgr-Shopper Mktg - GlaxoSmithKline Consumer Healthcare; pg. 510, pg. 1554
Klinger, Dan, Sr Mgr-Global Info Security - The Hershey Co.; pg. 1855, pg. 1538
Klinger, Jonathan, VP-Mktg - Masco Corporation; pg. 96, pg. 909
Klinghoffer, Dawn, Sr Dir-HR Bus Insights - Microsoft Corporation; pg. 435, pg. 1824
Klinghoffer, Rachel, Mgr-Mktg - Time Inc.; pg. 1693, pg. 1300
Klink, Jonas O., Dir-Product Mgmt-Shopping Experience - eBay Inc.; pg. 1240, pg. 243
Klinter, Denise, Sr Project Mgr-US Mktg Ops - Harley-Davidson, Inc.; pg. 178, pg. 1874
Klipfel, Peter W., Dir-Mktg - Gardner Denver Nash; pg. 1338, pg. 381
Klootwyk, Kent, Mgr-Mdsg - Ag Processing Inc.; pg. 835, pg. 1013
Klooz Thompson, Natalie, Brand Mgr-Fresh, Frozen & Seasonal - Butterball, LLC; pg. 843, pg. 1385
Klopfer, Edward, Mgr-Revenue - Finch Paper LLC; pg. 1457, pg. 1161
Klopstad, Barry D., Dir-Global Mktg-Oncology - Eli Lilly and Company; pg. 1527, pg. 684
Klose, Nathan, Dir-Creative - Books-A-Million, Inc.; pg. 1623, pg. 2
Klosen, Chris, Mgr-Sls & Mktg - Balchem Corporation; pg. 839, pg. 1183
Kloss, Terry, Analyst-Bus-Global Mktg - Exxon Mobil Corporation; pg. 977, pg. 1718
Kloster, Nicole, Mgr-Brand Mktg - Panera Bread Company; pg. 1029, pg. 1001
Klouda, Michael, VP-Mktg - Toll Brothers, Inc.; pg. 115, pg. 1541
Kluberspies, Lisa, Head-Gen Programs & Mgr-Mktg Campaign - NaviSite, Inc.; pg. 1269, pg. 782
Klug, Brittany, Coord-Local Mktg Strategy - CarMax, Inc.; pg. 167, pg. 1800
Klug, Kathleen, Sr Dir-Retail Mktg - Carter's, Inc.; pg. 21, pg. 491
Kluge, Pete, Sr Product Mktg Mgr-Media & Adv Solutions - Adobe Systems Incorporated; pg. 342, pg. 235
Kluger, Robert, Sr Mgr-Real Estate - Panera Bread Company; pg. 1029, pg. 1001
Klugman, Jeffrey, Exec VP & Gen Mgr-Products & Revenue - TiVo Inc.; pg. 313, pg. 251
Kluka, Julie, Sr Assoc Brand Mgr-POISE Brand - Kimberly-Clark Corporation; pg. 1461, pg. 1720
Klumb, Begonya, Chief Strategy Officer & Exec VP - UMB Financial Corporation; pg. 812, pg. 987
Klund, Jamie, Mgr-Retail Mktg - Cabela's Incorporated; pg. 535, pg. 1019
Klutho, Bill, Mgr-Strategic PR - Deere & Company; pg. 703, pg. 632
Kmiotek, Alison, Mgr-Media Rels - Macy's East; pg. 1777, pg. 1254
Knaak-Stuart, Lindsay, Sr Dir-Mktg Strategy - Kate Spade LLC; pg. 28, pg. 1248
Knabe, Jeff, Mgr-Mktg - McCormick & Company, Incorporated; pg. 1027, pg. 779
Knabenbauer, Ron, Coord-Website & Media Rels - Colorado Avalanche, LLC; pg. 541, pg. 317
Knapp, Andrea, Mgr-Media Rels - Delphi Automotive LLP; pg. 204, pg. 910
Knapp, Chris, Brand Mgr-Procurement-Global - ABERCROMBIE & FITCH CO.; pg. 37, pg. 1466
Knapp, David, Bus Mgr-Marine - Mitsubishi Rayon Carbon Fiber and Composites, Inc.,; pg. 1173, pg. 113
Knapp, Laura, Sr Writer & Sr Analyst-Mktg Comm - Coventry Health Care, Inc.; pg. 1519, pg. 761
Knasin, Julia, Sr Coord-PR & Brand Mgmt - Cheesecake Factory Incorporated; pg. 1017, pg. 56
Knauer, Linda F., Mgr-Mktg - Cisco Systems, Inc.; pg. 372, pg. 240
Knauf, Vicki, Product Mgr-Haystack & PriceEdge - IHS Inc.; pg. 1652, pg. 326
Knauff, Chris, Sls Enterprise Accounts - Staples, Inc.; pg. 474, pg. 821
Knaus, Mary Ann, Sr VP-Strategic Dev & Global Mktg - Jarden Consumer Solutions; pg. 57, pg. 412
Knecht, Frederick, Dir-Mktg Production - Association of National Advertisers, Inc.; pg. 133, pg. 1197
Knecht, Ronald, VP & Product Dir - Princeton Financial Systems, Inc.; pg. 795, pg. 1112
Knee, Mitchell, Reg Mgr-Sls-Northeast - Harodite Industries, Inc.; pg. 693, pg. 847
Kneeland, Samantha, Sr Specialist-Online Adv - Nordstrom, Inc.; pg. 1779, pg. 1837
Kneeshaw, Dan, Sr Dir-Global Associate Comm-Digital & Enterprise Initiatives - Wal-Mart.com; pg. 1287, pg. 50
Kneisel, Donald, VP-IT & Mktg Analysis - Resorts Atlantic City; pg. 1110, pg. 1041
Kneller, Ben, Sr Mgr-Mktg - DIRECTV Group Holdings, LLC; pg. 281, pg. 79
Knese, Allisyn, Brand Mktg Mgr - Carhartt, Inc.; pg. 39, pg. 875
Knewitz, Ernie, VP-Media Rels-Global - Johnson & Johnson; pg. 1549, pg. 1091
Knewitz, Jim, Dir-Mktg - Gilead Sciences, Inc.; pg. 1535, pg. 88
Knick, Randy, Dir-Sls, Mktg Latin America & US Govt - Abaxis, Inc.; pg. 1483, pg. 298
Knieriem, Rob, Mgr-Sls-Regional - Specialty Foods Group-Field Packing Div.; pg. 897, pg. 739
Knight, Blake, Mgr-Global Mktg-Advanced Concepts - Mattel Games/Puzzles; pg. 962, pg. 80
Knight, Blake, Mgr-Global Mktg-Advanced Concepts - MATTEL, INC.; pg. 962, pg. 81
Knight, Cara R., Mgr-Product Mktg - AT&T; pg. 1865, pg. 258
Knight, Fintan, Dir-Sls & Mktg - Rolls-Royce Corporation; pg. 216, pg. 689
Knight, Jerry, Mgr-Mktg Equipment Hub - Pepsi Beverages Company; pg. 258, pg. 1342
Knight, Jim, VP-Mktg, ECommerce & IT - Spangler Candy Company; pg. 1862, pg. 1407
Knight, Kelli, Mgr-Mktg - Anthem, Inc.; pg. 1192, pg. 683
Knight, Lischele, Mgr-Mktg-Online & Targeted Channels - JPMorgan Chase & Co.; pg. 772, pg. 1246
Knight, Moyra, Sr Dir-Employee & Corp Comm-Corp Affairs - Astellas Pharma US, Inc.; pg. 1496, pg. 640
Knight, Robert, VP-Film, TV & Adv - Music Sales Corporation; pg. 1666, pg. 1263
Knighten, Karina, Sr Mgr-Project Mgmt-Brand & Events - Nickelodeon Direct Inc.; pg. 303, pg. 1271
Knipp, Julie, Sr Planner-Integrated Mktg Comm - General Mills, Inc.; pg. 828, pg. 933
Knitowski, Mark, VP-Product Innovation - Victoria's Secret Stores, LLC; pg. 1789, pg. 1471
Knodt, Steve, Assoc Mgr-Mktg - Great Clips, Inc.; pg. 510, pg. 937
Knolhoff, Jackie, Sr Specialist-Media Rels - Edward D. Jones & Co., LP; pg. 746, pg. 995
Knoll, Bill, Exec VP-Product Mgmt - Cardtronics, Inc.; pg. 732, pg. 1703
Knoll, John, Chief Creative Officer & Sr Supvr-Visual Effects - Lucasfilm, Ltd.; pg. 297, pg. 222
Knoll, Katie, Mgr-Merchant Mktg-RTW Div - Bon Ton Stores, Inc.; pg. 1763, pg. 1596
Knoll, Lindsay, Dir-Mktg-Olympics & Corp Initiatives - Ralph Lauren Corporation; pg. 46, pg. 1284
Knollmiller, Brittany, Asst Mgr-Mktg, Adv & Media - El Pollo Loco, Inc.; pg. 1728, pg. 70
Knolls, Lee, Vp-Sls - Makita U.S.A., Inc.; pg. 1358, pg. 120
Knook, Cor N., Mgr-Sls - NAO, Inc.; pg. 1074, pg. 1567
Knopf, Vikki, Mgr-Mdse - Seattle Seahawks; pg. 582, pg. 1830
Knotaitis, Melissa, Mgr-Mktg & Global Accts - TechTarget, Inc.; pg. 482, pg. 837
Knotek, John, Grp VP-Adobe Mktg Cloud-East Reg - Adobe Systems Incorporated; pg. 342, pg. 235
Knotts, J., Div Mgr-Mktg-Europe, CIS, ANME - Deere & Company; pg. 703, pg. 632
Knotts, Olivia, Planner-Sls - ESPN, Inc.; pg. 285, pg. 340
Knouft, David, Sr Dir-US Mktg-Endocrine - Pfizer Inc.; pg. 1581, pg. 1278
Knowler, Carl, Dir-Mktg & Adv - Canadian Western Bank; pg. 729, pg. 1906
Knowles, Debra R., CMO-Health Mktg & VP - Standard Life & Accident Insurance Company; pg. 1217, pg. 1725
Knowles, Jen, VP-Mktg-Babies"R"Us - Toys "R" Us, Inc.; pg. 968, pg. 1130
Knowles, John, Sr VP-Sls - Point.360, Inc.; pg. 305, pg. 52
Knowles, Kenneth A., III, Exec VP-Product Mgmt - OpenLink Financial, Inc.; pg. 449, pg. 1346
Knowles, Lily, Vp-Product Mktg - VIZIO, Inc.; pg. 686, pg. 118
Knowlson, Cathy, VP & Mgr-Bankcard Mktg - Zions Bancorporation; pg. 824, pg. 1762
Knowlton, Kylie, Analyst-Sls & Mktg - Abercrombie & Kent USA, LLC; pg. 1896, pg. 607
Knowlton, Lee, Sr VP-Global Franchise Sls & Intl Div - Massage Envy Limited, LLC; pg. 516, pg. 23
Knowlton, Scott, Sr Product Mgr-Mktg - Synopsys, Inc.; pg. 480, pg. 162
Knowlton, Tim, VP-Sls Ops - Saucony, Inc.; pg. 1818, pg. 828
Knox, Brett, Sr VP-Mktg - ABM Industries, Inc.; pg. 64, pg. 1186
Knox, Carolyn, Mgr-Mktg Matls - TracFone Wireless, Inc.; pg.

681, *pg.* 447
Knox, Cherry, Sr Dir-Mktg, Strategy & Plng - St. Jude Children's Research Hospital; *pg.* 1596, *pg.* 1646
Knox, Emilie, Mgr-Mktg-Liberte & Mountain High Yogurt - General Mills, Inc.; *pg.* 828, *pg.* 933
Knox, Eric, Mgr-Reg Sls & Bus Dev - Do It Best Corp.; *pg.* 1045, *pg.* 680
Knox, Eric, Specialist-Mktg Comm-B2B - Groupon, Inc.; *pg.* 1255, *pg.* 575
Knox, Heather C., Sr Dir-Comml Comm - Microsoft Corporation; *pg.* 435, *pg.* 1824
Knox, Laura, Dir-Mktg - State Farm Mutual Automobile Insurance Co.; *pg.* 1218, *pg.* 557
Knox, Michele C., Mgr-Mktg Program-Indirect Channels - Direct Energy; *pg.* 1939, *pg.* 1704
Knox, Sarah, Mgr-Natl Shopper Mktg - The Clorox Company; *pg.* 327, *pg.* 169
Knoy, Cheri, Dir-Adv - Delta Farm Press; *pg.* 1634, *pg.* 968
Knudsen, Brian, VP-Strategic Mktg-Large Law Firms - Truven Health Analytics; *pg.* 486, *pg.* 331
Knudsen, Dana, Dir- Mktg & Graphic Design - Dippin' Dots LLC; *pg.* 853, *pg.* 739
Knudtson, Tamara, Analyst-Media - Menard, Inc.; *pg.* 1055, *pg.* 1857
Knutson, Diane C., Mgr-IBM Global Mktg Ops - Imation Corp.; *pg.* 413, *pg.* 952
Knutson, Herb, Dir-Mktg - Inline Plastics Corp.; *pg.* 1460, *pg.* 370
Knutson, Marianne, VP-Mktg-Global - Aveda Corporation; *pg.* 499, *pg.* 917
Knutson, Matthew, Sr Planner-Digital Media - Esurance, Inc.; *pg.* 1243, *pg.* 217
Knutson, Scott, VP-Sls & Mktg - Costa Cruise Lines N.V.; *pg.* 1904, *pg.* 431
Knutzen, Josef, Dir-New Product Dev - Prestige Brands Holdings, Inc.; *pg.* 520, *pg.* 1345
Knutzen, Matt, Dir-Humanities & Social Sciences Res Div - The New York Public Library; *pg.* 605, *pg.* 1269
Knysheva, Inna, Dir-Creative Svcs - Polycom, Inc.; *pg.* 664, *pg.* 249
Ko, Jamie, Sr Mktg Mgr-Fresh Inc. - LVMH Inc.; *pg.* 9, *pg.* 1254
Ko-Baek, Cynthia, VP-Brand & Mktg-Global - MetLife, Inc.; *pg.* 1208, *pg.* 1258
Kobak, Deb, Dir-Product Dev & Adv-Bradford Exchange - The Bradford Group; *pg.* 1763, *pg.* 637
Kobashigawa, Lori, Exec Dir-Interactive Mktg - Wynn Las Vegas, LLC; *pg.* 1119, *pg.* 1030
Kobayashi, Thomas, Mgr-Mdsg-Confection & Snacks - Nestle USA, Inc.; *pg.* 883, *pg.* 96
Kobayashi, Toshinori, Dir-Mktg & Sls - Alpine Electronics of America, Inc.; *pg.* 616, *pg.* 292
Kobelski, Stacey, Sr Mgr-Comm-Global - Bulova Corporation; *pg.* 2, *pg.* 1356
Koble, Russ, Brand Mgr-Comm - Toyota Motor Sales, U.S.A., Inc.; *pg.* 193, *pg.* 296
Koblin, Aaron, Dir-Creative Lab - Google Inc.; *pg.* 1249, *pg.* 153
Kobuszewski, Dave, Dir-Mktg Platforms - National Association for Stock Car Auto Racing; *pg.* 566, *pg.* 420
Koc Maurer, Elissa, Sr Mgr-External & Fin Comm - Abbott Laboratories; *pg.* 1484, *pg.* 551
Koc, Elissa, Sr Mgr-External & Fin Comm - Abbott Laboratories; *pg.* 1484, *pg.* 551
Kocer, Kim, Mgr-Mktg Ops & Market Facing Org-Global - 3M Company; *pg.* 1142, *pg.* 956
Kocer, Lori, Mgr-Corp Mktg Strategy - Land O'Lakes, Inc.; *pg.* 873, *pg.* 915
Koch, Amy, Mgr-Mdsg - One Step Ahead; *pg.* 1780, *pg.* 1881
Koch, Barbara, Mgr-Americas Partner Mktg - Cisco Systems, Inc.; *pg.* 372, *pg.* 240
Koch, Diane L., Mgr-Mktg - 3M Company; *pg.* 1142, *pg.* 956
Koch, Douglas, Chief Strategy Officer, Chief Talent Officer & Sr VP - Caleres, Inc.; *pg.* 1805, *pg.* 993
Koch, Jerry, Dir-Corp Mktg & Product Mgmt - Intelligrated Systems LLC; *pg.* 1350, *pg.* 998
Koch, Joe, Dir-Mktg - Country Pure Foods, Inc.; *pg.* 247, *pg.* 1400
Koch, John H., Dir-Sls-Metals - CSX Transportation, Inc.; *pg.* 1904, *pg.* 432
Koch, Kimberly, Mgr-Social Media Visual Platforms-Enterprise Mktg - Wells Fargo & Company; *pg.* 819, *pg.* 232
Koch, Lisa, Specialist-Mktg - Raven Industries, Inc.; *pg.* 1888, *pg.* 1625
Koch, Mark, Mgr-Nebraska Reg Sls - Grossenburg Implement, Inc.; *pg.* 1344, *pg.* 1626
Koch, Matt, Mgr-New Media - Chicago Bears Football Club, Inc.; *pg.* 538, *pg.* 623
Koch, Nate, Mgr-Social Mktg - Kohl's Corporation; *pg.* 1775, *pg.* 1870
Koch, Ordell, Dir-Sls - Harsco Rail; *pg.* 1345, *pg.* 1623
Koch, Suz, Sr Mgr-Mktg & Social Media - Amazon.com, Inc.; *pg.* 1226, *pg.* 1831
Koch, William F., Mgr-Mktg-Employment Mktg - Ameriprise Financial, Inc.; *pg.* 715, *pg.* 930
Koch, Zeke, Sr Dir-Product Mgmt & Design - Adobe Systems Incorporated; *pg.* 342, *pg.* 235
Kochaver, Kim, Head-Trade Mktg-Mktg Solutions - LinkedIn Corporation; *pg.* 1262, *pg.* 160
Kochendarfer, Lauren, Specialist-Media Rels-AIG Property Casualty - American International Group, Inc.; *pg.* 1190, *pg.* 1193
Kocher, Debbie, Mgr-Reseller Mktg - SYNNEX Corporation; *pg.* 480, *pg.* 92
Kocher, Patrick, Sr Dir-RDQ - The Kraft Heinz Company; *pg.* 871, *pg.* 641
Kochhar, Vinita, Head-Events & Field Mktg - JPMorgan Chase & Co.; *pg.* 772, *pg.* 1246
Kock, Peter, Dir-Mktg & Sls - LEGOLAND California LLC; *pg.* 557, *pg.* 59
Kockos, Kelly, Sr VP & Product Mgr-Home Equity - Wells Fargo & Company; *pg.* 819, *pg.* 232
Kocon, Lori, Mgr-Media Strategy-Global - Google Inc.; *pg.* 1249, *pg.* 153
Kocon, Stan, Dir-Mktg & Proposals - Voith Hydro Inc.; *pg.* 1387, *pg.* 1598
Kocurek, Mark, Reg Mgr-Sls-Textron - Bell Helicopter Textron, Inc.; *pg.* 224, *pg.* 1693
Kodak, Skip, Sr VP-Shopper Mktg & Channel Dev - LEGO Systems, Inc.; *pg.* 961, *pg.* 346
Kodjabacheva, Kristina, Specialist-Digital Media - Best Buy Canada Ltd.; *pg.* 1761, *pg.* 1907
Koe, Kristen, Sr Dir-Mktg-Children's Entertainment, Sporting Goods & Fitness - Sears Holdings Corporation; *pg.* 1784, *pg.* 618
Koeck, Magnus, VP-Mktg & Brand Mgmt - Volvo Trucks North America, Inc.; *pg.* 195, *pg.* 1377
Koedijk, Jochen, Head-Social Media Adv - Amazon.com, Inc.; *pg.* 1226, *pg.* 1831
Koehler, Bob, Reg Mgr-Mktg-Northeast US & Canada - Pear Bureau Northwest; *pg.* 153, *pg.* 1500
Koehler, Jamey, Product Mgr - LIGHTING SCIENCE GROUP CORPORATION; *pg.* 1301, *pg.* 467
Koehler, Justin, Strategist-Digital Mktg - Lenovo Group Ltd; *pg.* 427, *pg.* 1384
Koehler, Kristine, Mgr-Mdsg & Display - Energizer Holdings, Inc.; *pg.* 637, *pg.* 996
Koehler, Laurie, Mgr-Consumer Campaigns Activation-Americas Mktg Grp - Intel Corporation; *pg.* 645, *pg.* 266
Koehler, Rich, Dir-Product & Mktg-Amazon Payments - Amazon.com, Inc.; *pg.* 1226, *pg.* 1831
Koehler, Roger, Dir-Sls Western Reg & Mgr-Product Mktg - Iteris, Inc.; *pg.* 293, *pg.* 261
Koehler, Steffen, Sr Mgr-Product Line - Finisar Corporation; *pg.* 639, *pg.* 285
koehler, susan, Sr Mgr-Community Involvement - Sam's Club; *pg.* 1783, *pg.* 29
Koehne, Christine, Sr Planner-Sls - Pandora Media Inc.; *pg.* 1273, *pg.* 172
Koellmer, Marko, Mgr-Spare Parts Sls - Arburg, Inc.; *pg.* 1314, *pg.* 359
Koellner, Scott, Mgr-ECommerce Mktg - W.B. Mason Company; *pg.* 491, *pg.* 803
Koen, Jennifer, Sr Mgr-Mktg & Digital Strategies - Sport Clips, Inc.; *pg.* 523, *pg.* 1698
Koen, Lisa, Program Mgr-Demand Generation Mktg - Adobe Systems Incorporated; *pg.* 342, *pg.* 235
Koen, Robert, Head-Marketplace Sls - Amazon.com, Inc.; *pg.* 1226, *pg.* 1831
Koenen, Katherine, Sr Mgr-Mktg - Ameriprise Financial, Inc.; *pg.* 715, *pg.* 930
Koenen, Mark S., VP-Sls & Mktg - Williams Controls, Inc.; *pg.* 222, *pg.* 1508
Koenig, Bill, Pres-Global Media Distr - National Basketball Association; *pg.* 566, *pg.* 1264
Koenig, Christian, VP-PR - Porsche Cars North America, Inc.; *pg.* 189, *pg.* 518
Koenig, Derek, Sr VP & Head-Creative - Discovery Communications, Inc.; *pg.* 282, *pg.* 777
Koenig, Gina, Dir-Adv - Pacific Palisades Post Inc.; *pg.* 1673, *pg.* 174
Koenig, Kyle, District Sls Mgr-Mid-West - Champlain Cable Corp.; *pg.* 1044, *pg.* 1765
Koenig, Stefka, Dir-Product Mgmt & Global Ultrasound Mktg - Philips Electronics North America; *pg.* 662, *pg.* 782
Koeninger, Tom, VP-Sls - Ellenbee-Leggett Company Inc.; *pg.* 854, *pg.* 1452
Koenitzer, Jay G., VP-Mktg - Helwig Carbon Products, Inc.; *pg.* 1346, *pg.* 1875
Koepele, Eric, Sr VP-Sls - Ziff Davis, LLC; *pg.* 1703, *pg.* 1316
Koepke, Mike, Acct Mgr & Mgr-Tech Sls - Texas Instruments Incorporated; *pg.* 679, *pg.* 1688
Koeppen, Keith, Mgr-Mktg Comm-US - Ford Motor Company; *pg.* 172, *pg.* 876
Koerte, Peter, VP-Mktg-Global - Siemens Healthcare Diagnostics; *pg.* 673, *pg.* 604
Koester, Jennifer, Sr VP-Advanced Adv Products & Data Analytics - Cablevision Systems Corporation; *pg.* 272, *pg.* 1141
Koester, Josef, Dir-Mktg-HPC, Product Mgmt & Sustainability-North America - BASF Corporation; *pg.* 1149, *pg.* 1066
Koester, Rob, VP-Consumer Product Mktg - Consolidated Communications Holdings, Inc.; *pg.* 630, *pg.* 631
Koester, Rob, Sr Dir-Product Mgmt - Consolidated Communications, Inc.; *pg.* 1871, *pg.* 1534
Koester, Tim, Brand Mgr - Nestle Purina PetCare Company; *pg.* 1479, *pg.* 1000
Koeter, John, VP-Mktg & Solutions Grp - Synopsys, Inc.; *pg.* 480, *pg.* 162
Koetter, Sam, Sr Product Mgr-Ethernet Svcs - XO Communications; *pg.* 497, *pg.* 1786
Koewler, Julie, Mng Dir-Adv-Global - Accenture; *pg.* 1392, *pg.* 1186
Koff, Noah, Sr Mgr-Global Mktg & Media - AliphCom, Inc.; *pg.* 616, *pg.* 212
Koffler, Gregg, VP-Franchise Sls - CBC Restaurant Corp.; *pg.* 1721, *pg.* 1677
Kogan, Leslie, Sr Mgr-Production - The Reader's Digest Association, Inc.; *pg.* 1679, *pg.* 1322
Kohara, Brice, Brand Mgr-HP Networking - Zones, Inc.; *pg.* 1292, *pg.* 1813
Kohari, Jason, Sr Mgr-Interactive Mktg - Genentech, Inc.; *pg.* 1533, *pg.* 279
Koharik, Nicole, Dir-Sustainability Mktg-Global - GOJO Industries, Inc.; *pg.* 330, *pg.* 1401
Kohl, Kevin, Product Mgr-Comml - Pass & Seymour/Legrand; *pg.* 1303, *pg.* 1344
Kohl, Portia, Mgr-Media - Vail Resorts, Inc.; *pg.* 1117, *pg.* 313
Kohler, Andrew, Sr Mgr-Category Leadership - Pinnacle Foods Group LLC; *pg.* 889, *pg.* 1104
Kohler, Paul, Sr Product Mgr-VSAN Partner Ecosystem - VMware, Inc.; *pg.* 490, *pg.* 179
Kohler, Stephen, Sr Dir-Mktg-Americas Bus Unit - Shure Incorporated; *pg.* 672, *pg.* 638
Kohli, Kanika, Acct Exec-Mktg Solutions - LinkedIn Corporation; *pg.* 1262, *pg.* 160
Kohli, Lauren, Assoc Mgr-Sls Mktg - Hulu LLC; *pg.* 1257, *pg.* 274
Kohli, Nidhi, Exec Dir-Media-Fashion, Watches & Fine Jewelry & Digital - Chanel, Inc.; *pg.* 503, *pg.* 1211
Kohn, Allison, Mgr-PR - Samsung Electronics America, Inc.; *pg.* 669, *pg.* 1115
Kohn, Scott, Grp Sr VP-Natl Adv Sls - Discovery Communications, Inc.; *pg.* 282, *pg.* 777
Kohn, Scott, VP-Adv Sls-Midwest Reg - Travel Channel LLC; *pg.* 313, *pg.* 766
Kohndrow, Heather, Mgr-Media - Cost Plus World Market; *pg.* 921, *pg.* 170
Kohnstamm, Abby F., CMO & Exec VP - Pitney Bowes Inc.; *pg.* 454, *pg.* 376
Kohout, Fred, VP-Partner Mktg-Worldwide - EMC Corporation; *pg.* 391, *pg.* 825
Kohr, Todd, Mgr-Mktg - The Hershey Co.; *pg.* 1855, *pg.* 1538
Kohyama, Leo, Mgr-Mktg Comm - Hamamatsu Corporation; *pg.* 1415, *pg.* 1046
Koide, Hiroko, Sr VP-Global Mktg-Fine Writing - Newell Rubbermaid Inc.; *pg.* 1128, *pg.* 515
Koiner, Shaun, Chief Product Officer - The Sporting News; *pg.* 1688, *pg.* 1295
Koizim, Gregory, Mgr-eMail Mktg - Barnes & Noble, Inc.; *pg.* 1619, *pg.* 1201
Koizumi, Yoshi, Dir-Sls-Asia Pacific - GigOptix, Inc.; *pg.* 400, *pg.* 245
Kokell, Jennifer, Mgr-Media Rels-Global - Pfizer Inc.; *pg.* 1581, *pg.* 1278

Kokes, Brian, VP-Adv - Seattle Times Company; *pg.* 1685, *pg.* 1840
Kokes, Nathan, Brand Mgr-Advanced Tech Vehicles - Toyota Motor Sales, U.S.A., Inc.; *pg.* 193, *pg.* 296
Kokolis, Tom, Mgr-Sls & Mktg-Natl - Hays Fluid Controls; *pg.* 1049, *pg.* 1370
Kokon, Fatma, Brand Mgr - Pinnacle Foods Group LLC; *pg.* 889, *pg.* 1104
Kokoska, Megan, Dir-ECommerce & Mktg - Dollar General Corporation; *pg.* 1767, *pg.* 1635
Kokoska, Megan, Dir-ECommerce & Mktg - Dollar Tree, Inc.; *pg.* 1767, *pg.* 1778
Kokotajlo, Elizabeth, Sr Dir-Design - LensCrafters, Inc.; *pg.* 1420, *pg.* 1460
Kolander, Connie, Dir-Educational Sls - Nasco International, Inc.; *pg.* 1779, *pg.* 1858
Kolander, Natalie, Mgr-Corp Sls - Minnesota Vikings Football Club, Inc.; *pg.* 563, *pg.* 923
Kolar, Alex, Reg VP-Intl Govt Sls - Gulfstream Aerospace Corporation; *pg.* 228, *pg.* 540
Kolar, Marisa, Sr Mgr-Consumer Relationship Mktg - Kraft Chemical Company; *pg.* 1170, *pg.* 632
Kolasa, George, VP-Mktg & Comm - Burberry Limited; *pg.* 20, *pg.* 1208
Kolb, Jill, Product Mgr - Sabre Holdings Corporation; *pg.* 1922, *pg.* 1745
Kolb, Karen, Dir-Direct Mktg - Gilt Groupe Inc.; *pg.* 24, *pg.* 1234
Kolbe, Brittany, Brand Mgr-In-Store Experience - rue21, inc.; *pg.* 32, *pg.* 1591
Kolbe, Jerry, Dir-Mktg - Murata Electronics North America, Inc.; *pg.* 658, *pg.* 540
Kolbe, Linda, Mgr-ECommerce Product Line - W.W. Grainger, Inc.; *pg.* 1390, *pg.* 625
Kolbe, Scott, Sr Mgr-Mktg - BJ'S RESTAURANTS, INC.; *pg.* 1716, *pg.* 104
Kolbert, Lori, Dir-Sls & Mktg-Wells Fargo - Wells Fargo & Company; *pg.* 819, *pg.* 232
Kolbert-Hyle, Kate, Product Mgr-Mktg-Glass - Google Inc.; *pg.* 1249, *pg.* 153
Kolega, Janette, VP-Mktg - LPL Financial Corporation; *pg.* 777, *pg.* 798
Kolesar, Kimberly, Partner-Mktg-Global - Red Hat, Inc.; *pg.* 460, *pg.* 1388
Kolev, Eileen, Program Mgr-Mktg - MicroStrategy, Inc.; *pg.* 1266, *pg.* 1809
Kolich, Anna, Mgr-Mktg-Media - MillerCoors LLC; *pg.* 255, *pg.* 582
Kolker, Roger R., Mgr-Mktg - Xerox Corporation; *pg.* 494, *pg.* 365
Kollappallil, Patricia, VP-Comm-Animal Planet & Discovery Kids Media - Discovery Communications, Inc.; *pg.* 282, *pg.* 777
Koller, John, VP-Mktg - Sony Computer Entertainment America LLC; *pg.* 966, *pg.* 256
Kolleth, Mike, Dir-Corp Adv & Branding - THE DOW CHEMICAL COMPANY; *pg.* 1157, *pg.* 898
Kollm, John, District Mgr-Sls - Golf Galaxy, Inc.; *pg.* 1835, *pg.* 1525
Kollman, Amber, Dir-Consumer Mktg - Colorado Tourism Office; *pg.* 991, *pg.* 318
Kollman, Kelli, Sr Dir-Fin - Detroit Tigers Baseball Club, Inc.; *pg.* 545, *pg.* 880
Kollmann, Jerry, Sr VP-Sls, Mktg & Customer Support-Worldwide - Axxcelera Broadband Wireless Inc.; *pg.* 623, *pg.* 263
Kolmar, Doug, Analyst-Mktg-Social Media & Brand Advocates - L.L. Bean, Inc.; *pg.* 1777, *pg.* 750
Kolodny, Brad I., Acct Mgr-Travel Adv - The New York Times Company; *pg.* 1668, *pg.* 1270
Kolodny, Lisa, VP-Brand Mktg & Comm - FreshDirect, LLC; *pg.* 857, *pg.* 1174
Kolody, Lynda, Controller & Sr Dir - Toronto Blue Jays Baseball Club; *pg.* 588, *pg.* 1945
Kolodzinski, Jeffrey, Brand Mgr-Humminbird - Johnson Outdoors Inc.; *pg.* 1837, *pg.* 1888
Kolondzic, Kova, Brand Mgr-Strategy & Innovation Depend - Kimberly-Clark Corporation; *pg.* 1461, *pg.* 1720
Kolpack, Andrea, VP-Creative-Orchard Brands - Blair Corporation; *pg.* 1762, *pg.* 1590
Kolpek, Jeanne, Dir-Mktg Programs - Universal Technical Institute, Inc.; *pg.* 608, *pg.* 24
Kolstad, Andrea M., Sr Dir-Web Strategy & Mktg Sys - Polycom, Inc.; *pg.* 664, *pg.* 249
Kolstad, James, Dir-Social Innovation & Mktg-Corp Social Responsibility - NBC Universal, Inc.; *pg.* 300, *pg.* 1266
Kolton, Matthew, Mgr-Integrated Brand & Retail Mktg - Bridgestone Americas, Inc.; *pg.* 201, *pg.* 1649
Koman, Roger, Dir-Mktg & New Media - Eggland's Best, Inc.; *pg.* 854, *pg.* 1542
Komarnicki, Russell, Mgr-Interactive, Social Media & PR - Old World Industries, Inc.; *pg.* 1175, *pg.* 641
Komiega, Samantha, Sr Mgr-PR & Comm - The Timberland Company; *pg.* 1821, *pg.* 1039
Kominski, Ursula, Brand Mgr-Heaters - Kaz, Inc.; *pg.* 58, *pg.* 844
Komoroske, Alex, Sr Product Mgr - Google Inc.; *pg.* 1249, *pg.* 153
Komoroski, Bernard, Dir-Product Mktg-LifeVest - Zoll Medical Corporation; *pg.* 1612, *pg.* 814
Kon, Kelvin, VP-Mktg Ops - Focus Features; *pg.* 287, *pg.* 273
Kondos, Adam, Dir-Creative Svcs - The Pep Boys - Manny, Moe & Jack; *pg.* 215, *pg.* 1568
Kondritz, Greg, Sr Dir & Assoc Gen Counsel - Houston Texans, L.P.; *pg.* 553, *pg.* 1708
Konduru, Vijay, Head-Digital Mktg & Analytics - Citigroup Inc.; *pg.* 735, *pg.* 1212
Konecny, Karen, VP-Mktg & Comm - Rush Enterprises Inc.; *pg.* 189, *pg.* 1728
Kong, Cynthia, Mgr-PR - Robert Half International Inc.; *pg.* 462, *pg.* 145
Kong, Sean, Dir-Mktg Analytics - Discover Financial Services; *pg.* 744, *pg.* 653
Koniak, Adam, Sr Product Mgr - Dolby Laboratories, Inc.; *pg.* 284, *pg.* 217
Konicoff, Honey, Dir-Brand Mktg - Marriott International, Inc.; *pg.* 1102, *pg.* 764
Konieczka, Ken, VP-Sls Ops - Mitsubishi Motors North America, Inc.; *pg.* 185, *pg.* 75
Konieczna, Bibianna, Dir-Mktg-Jack Daniel's - Brown-Forman Corporation; *pg.* 1958, *pg.* 732
Konig, Stephen, Product Mgr - Google Inc.; *pg.* 1249, *pg.* 153
Koning, Johan, Mgr-Mktg - Intel Corporation; *pg.* 645, *pg.* 266
Konnecke, Michelle, Mgr-Mktg Comm - Bayer Healthcare Consumer Care Division; *pg.* 1500, *pg.* 1087
Konrad, Ayelet, Acct Exec-Mktg Solutions - LinkedIn Corporation; *pg.* 1262, *pg.* 160
Konsoer, Julie, Asst Mgr-Adv Ops - Sinclair Broadcast Group, Inc.; *pg.* 308, *pg.* 773
Konstant, Kimberly, Sr Mgr-Mktg Comm - Beiersdorf North America Inc.; *pg.* 501, *pg.* 385
Konstantopoulos, Gus, VP-Sls & Mktg - Citigroup Inc.; *pg.* 735, *pg.* 1212
Kontowicz, Rebecca, Coord-PR & Specialist-PR - Kohl's Corporation; *pg.* 1775, *pg.* 1870
Kontranowski, Michael J., VP-Sls - LaPolla Industries, Inc.; *pg.* 1444, *pg.* 1710
Konzel, Michele, Mgr-Mktg - Paychex, Inc.; *pg.* 792, *pg.* 1336
Koo, Jayne, Sr Mgr-Client Rels & Mktg Ops - NBC Universal, Inc.; *pg.* 300, *pg.* 1266
Koo, Katia, Brand Mgr-Private-Global Sourcing - Michaels Stores, Inc.; *pg.* 1127, *pg.* 1722
Koodray, Diane, Dir-Mktg-Dupilumab - Regeneron Pharmaceuticals, Inc.; *pg.* 1588, *pg.* 1345
Kooistra, Chris, Dir-Mktg Svcs - Cobra Electronics Corporation; *pg.* 629, *pg.* 572
Kooistra, Richard, VP-Sls & Consulting - Swisslog Logistics; *pg.* 1380, *pg.* 1796
Kooker, Dennis, Pres-Global Digital Bus & US Sls - Sony Music Entertainment; *pg.* 309, *pg.* 1294
Koolwal, Aditya, Product Mgr - Facebook, Inc.; *pg.* 1245, *pg.* 143
Koomey, Melissa Grigorieff, Sr Dir-Comml Plng-Cardiovascular & Respiratory - Gilead Sciences, Inc.; *pg.* 1535, *pg.* 88
Koong, Victor, Product Mgr-EMD Millipore - Millipore Corporation; *pg.* 1423, *pg.* 788
Koontz, Steven, Product Mgr-Digital Media - Pennwell Publishing Company Inc.; *pg.* 1676, *pg.* 1490
Koos, Jeff, Mgr-Star Brand & Mktg - Star Building Systems; *pg.* 112, *pg.* 1488
Koosmann, Brent, Product Mgr - Jennie-O Turkey Store, LLC; *pg.* 865, *pg.* 966
Kopac, Matt, Mgr-Social & Environmental Responsibility - Burt's Bees Inc.; *pg.* 502, *pg.* 1370
Kopas, Frank, Sr VP-Sls - Ecora Software Corporation; *pg.* 389, *pg.* 1662
Kopcinski, Mariola, Dir-Strategic Mktg-Global - FMC Corporation; *pg.* 1163, *pg.* 1564
Kopech, Michael, Dir-Mktg - ESPN, Inc.; *pg.* 285, *pg.* 340
Kopecky, Michelle, Mgr-Product Mktg - Ariens Company Inc.; *pg.* 700, *pg.* 1855
Kopecky, Tina, Dir-Sls & Mktg - Hannibal Courier-Post; *pg.* 1647, *pg.* 978
Kopenec, Christopher, Mgr-Digital Mktg - Brinker International, Inc.; *pg.* 1718, *pg.* 1676
Kopercinski, Nathalie, Asst Mgr-Sls & Mktg Ops - Sidney Frank Importing Co., Inc.; *pg.* 1970, *pg.* 1184
Kopf, Brian, Mgr-Market Res & Media Strategy - Empire Today, LLC; *pg.* 923, *pg.* 643
Kopf, Mary Kay, CMO - Electrolux Home Products North America; *pg.* 54, *pg.* 1366
Kopfmann, Michelle, Dir-Adv - Bayard Inc.; *pg.* 1620, *pg.* 359
Kopiasz, Tennille, Sr VP-US Mktg-Coty Prestige - Coty, Inc.; *pg.* 506, *pg.* 1219
Kopko, Agatha, Category Mgr-Mktg - Publix Super Markets, Inc.; *pg.* 1031, *pg.* 437
Kopkowski, Renee, Sr Dir-Global External Comm - Mars North America; *pg.* 1859, *pg.* 1072
Koplan, Elizabeth, Sr Dir-Adv - Monster Worldwide, Inc.; *pg.* 1268, *pg.* 859
Koplin, Ann, Dir-Annuity Product Mktg - Thrivent Financial for Lutherans; *pg.* 1219, *pg.* 944
Koplin, Fred, Dir-Mktg - Yokohama Tire Corporation; *pg.* 1892, *pg.* 94
Kopp, Emilie, Sr Mgr-Content Mktg - SOLARWINDS, INC.; *pg.* 471, *pg.* 1666
Kopp, Erik, Sr Dir-Corp Comm - PAREXEL International Corporation; *pg.* 1580, *pg.* 853
Kopp, Katy, Product Mgr - Boston Scientific Corporation; *pg.* 1508, *pg.* 831
Kopp, Kerri, Dir-Mktg & Social Commitment - The Coca-Cola Company; *pg.* 240, *pg.* 493
Koppel, Christie, Sr Specialist-Mktg - Georgia Southern University; *pg.* 602, *pg.* 541
Koppel, Evan, Reg Dir-Sls - United Airlines, Inc.; *pg.* 1927, *pg.* 593
Koppelman, Baker, VP-Ticket Sls & Ops - Baltimore Ravens Limited Partnership; *pg.* 532, *pg.* 755
Kopper, Lynn, Dir-Media - Chanel, Inc.; *pg.* 503, *pg.* 1211
Kopple, Jim, Dir-Mktg - Camerican International; *pg.* 844, *pg.* 1101
Kopsick, Kimmie, Analyst-Global Online Mktg-Social Media - Claire's Stores, Inc.; *pg.* 1764, *pg.* 617
Korach, Sarah, Mgr-Mktg - Expedia, Inc.; *pg.* 1244, *pg.* 1814
Korankyi, Ama, Planner-Sls - Pandora Media Inc.; *pg.* 1273, *pg.* 172
Korbas, Greg, Product Mgr-Classics Footwear-Global - Reebok International Ltd.; *pg.* 1817, *pg.* 811
Korbelak, Dawn Boggio, Dir-Corp Product Dev - Hovnanian Enterprises, Inc.; *pg.* 1096, *pg.* 1114
Korch, Dana, Mgr-Mktg Comm - Attachmate Corporation; *pg.* 356, *pg.* 1833
Korch, Jennifer, Dir-Global Digital Mktg-Specialty Medicine - Bayer Corporation; *pg.* 1499, *pg.* 1573
Kordes, Charles, VP-Mktg-Customer Demand & Head-Experience - SafeAuto Insurance Company; *pg.* 1216, *pg.* 1443
Kordosky, Julie, Sr Mgr-Product Mktg - Boston Scientific Corporation; *pg.* 1508, *pg.* 831
Koren, Greg, Sr VP-Sls - Comdata Corporation; *pg.* 739, *pg.* 1627
Korenthal, Christopher W., Area Mgr-Sls - D.R. Horton, Inc.; *pg.* 1090, *pg.* 1694
Korff, Suzanne, Head-Mktg Comm - Princess Cruise Lines Ltd.; *pg.* 1920, *pg.* 270
Koris, Sally J., Sr Mgr-Comm - Northrop Grumman Corporation; *pg.* 231, *pg.* 1781
Korizno, Michael A., VP-Strategic Acct Mgmt, New Bus Dev & Sls Ops-Worldwide - Eastman Kodak Company; *pg.* 1408, *pg.* 1333
Korman, Paul, Sr Specialist-Internet Adv - ITT Educational Services, Inc.; *pg.* 603, *pg.* 675
Korn, Joanna, Sr Mgr-Online Mktg - Penguin Random House; *pg.* 1675, *pg.* 1276
Korner, Sean, Head-Projections & Product Mgr - Bloomberg L.P.; *pg.* 725, *pg.* 1204
Korney, Brian, Acct Exec-Immuno-Oncology-CV, Metabolics & Mktg Svcs - Bristol-Myers Squibb Company; *pg.* 1509, *pg.* 1206
Kornman, Kelly, Brand Mgr-Strategic - Capital One Financial Corporation; *pg.* 730, *pg.* 1789
Koro, Fuat, Dir-Global Mktg & Bus Dev - Bose Corporation; *pg.* 626, *pg.* 820
Korotzer, Gary M., Exec VP & Head-Mktg Consumer Credit Solutions - Wells Fargo & Company; *pg.* 819, *pg.* 232

Korous, Erin, Mgr-Loyalty Mktg - True Value Company; *pg.* 1065, *pg.* 592
Korpics, John, VP & Dir-Creative-Digital & Print - ESPN, Inc.; *pg.* 285, *pg.* 340
Kors, Michael, Chief Creative Officer & Dir - Michael Kors (USA), Inc.; *pg.* 29, *pg.* 1260
Korshunova, Kseniya, Mgr-Small Bus Segment-Intl Mktg - FedEx Corporation; *pg.* 1907, *pg.* 1642
Korst, Jeremy, Gen Mgr-Windows Product Mktg - Microsoft Corporation; *pg.* 435, *pg.* 1824
Kort, Jennifer, Assoc Mgr-Mktg - Jamba, Inc.; *pg.* 1024, *pg.* 84
Korte, Brent, Sr VP & Head-Advisor & Channel Mktg - LPL Financial Corporation; *pg.* 777, *pg.* 798
Korte, Kristin, Brand Mgr-Budweiser Brand Team - Anheuser-Busch Companies, LLC; *pg.* 237, *pg.* 991
Kortemeyer, Timothy M., Pres-Penford Products - Penford Corporation; *pg.* 1177, *pg.* 314
Korynski, Jessica, Product Mgr-Accessory-Cadillac - General Motors Company; *pg.* 175, *pg.* 881
Korzekwa, Christi, Sr VP-Mktg - Tractor Supply Company; *pg.* 708, *pg.* 1627
Kosanke, John, VP-Media & Mgmt-Worldwide - International Business Machines Corporation; *pg.* 418, *pg.* 1138
Kosaris, Toni, Dir-Sls - Denver Metro Convention & Visitors Bureau; *pg.* 991, *pg.* 318
Kosek, Kristen, Mgr-Mktg-Natl - CBIZ, INC.; *pg.* 733, *pg.* 1429
Kosenkova, Virginia, Product Mgr-High Performance Lubricants & Greases - Castrol North America Inc.; *pg.* 973, *pg.* 1129
Koserowski, Phil, VP-Interactive Mktg - The Leading Hotels of the World, Ltd.; *pg.* 1100, *pg.* 1250
Koshi, Robyn Mukai, Sr Mgr-Mktg - Atlus USA, Inc.; *pg.* 949, *pg.* 107
Kosiak, Mike, Mgr-Natl Sls - Quadion Corporation; *pg.* 1888, *pg.* 941
Kosier, Audrey, Strategist-Social Media - Infor; *pg.* 414, *pg.* 484
Kosinski, Justin, Mgr-Mktg - Aetna Inc.; *pg.* 1187, *pg.* 351
Koskovolis, Lou, Sr VP-Golf Media Sls-NBC Sports Group - NBC Sports Network; *pg.* 300, *pg.* 375
Koskovolis, Lou, Sr VP-Golf Media Sls-NBC Sports Group - NBC Universal, Inc.; *pg.* 300, *pg.* 1266
Kosner, John, Exec VP-Digital & Print Media-ESPN - ESPN, Inc.; *pg.* 285, *pg.* 340
Kosnick, Terry, Brand Mgr-Design - 3M Company; *pg.* 1142, *pg.* 956
Kosobucki, Alix Reisinger, Sr Assoc Brand Mgr-The Laughing Cow - Bel Brands USA; *pg.* 839, *pg.* 566
Kosofsky, Larry, VP-Merchant Mktg-Home - Macy's East; *pg.* 1777, *pg.* 1254
Kosovalic, Maya, Mgr-Digital & Media Comm - L'Oreal USA; *pg.* 514, *pg.* 1252
Koss Zoog, Jennifer, Head-Integrated Mktg - Conde Nast Publications, Inc.; *pg.* 1629, *pg.* 1217
Koss Zoog, Jennifer, VP-Creative Solutions - Vogue Magazine; *pg.* 1700, *pg.* 1311
Koss, Ashleigh, Dir-Media Rels-Global - Amgen Inc.; *pg.* 1493, *pg.* 291
Kossally, Brenton, Mgr-Interactive Mktg & ECommerce - TracFone Wireless, Inc.; *pg.* 681, *pg.* 447
Kosse, Jennifer, Brand Mgr-Athenos & Churny Portfolio-Base - Mondelez International; *pg.* 877, *pg.* 1344
Kosseim, Mona, Mng VP-Channel Mktg - Gartner, Inc.; *pg.* 1248, *pg.* 374
Kosslyn, Justin, Product Mgr - Google Inc.; *pg.* 1249, *pg.* 153
Kossoss, David, Dir-Mktg-Global - Kepner-Tregoe, Inc.; *pg.* 424, *pg.* 1112
Kossow, Joe, VP-New Product Dev-Global - Church & Dwight Co., Inc.; *pg.* 1153, *pg.* 1063
Kost, Fred, VP-Security Solutions Mktg - Ixia; *pg.* 422, *pg.* 56
Kost, Susan, Dir-Tax & Legal Mktg-Global - Deloitte & Touche USA LLP; *pg.* 743, *pg.* 1222
Kost, Trish, Sr Dir-Mktg Comm & Content Dev - American Girl LLC; *pg.* 949, *pg.* 1871
Kostich, Rob, Sr VP-Product Mgmt-Call of Duty - Activision Blizzard, Inc.; *pg.* 948, *pg.* 271
Kostiw, Kimberley, Coord-Special Events & Mktg - Mount Sinai Medical Center; *pg.* 1569, *pg.* 448
Kostiw, Lorraine, Mgr-Event Mktg - The New York Times; *pg.* 1668, *pg.* 1270
Kostuck, Katie, Mgr-Creative - Kohl's Corporation; *pg.* 1775, *pg.* 1870
Koszi, Nichole, Dir-Mktg - Sure Fit Inc.; *pg.* 944, *pg.* 1514
Kota, Ajith, Sr Mgr-Product Line Mgmt - Applied Materials, Inc.; *pg.* 618, *pg.* 264
Kotaniemi, Brandon, Dir-HIV Mktg - Gilead Sciences, Inc.; *pg.* 1535, *pg.* 88
Kotas, Paul, Sr VP-Adv-Worldwide - Amazon.com, Inc.; *pg.* 1226, *pg.* 1831
Kotcher, Mark, Sr Dir-Category Mgmt-Center Store - Save-A-Lot, Ltd.; *pg.* 894, *pg.* 977
Kotchka, Katie, Dir-PR-Global Themed Entertainment - Warner Bros. Entertainment Inc.; *pg.* 319, *pg.* 54
Kothari, Akshay, Product Head - LinkedIn Corporation; *pg.* 1262, *pg.* 160
Kothari, Christina, Brand Mgr - The Clorox Company; *pg.* 327, *pg.* 169
Kothari, Sourabh, Sr Mgr-Rich Media Mktg - Cisco Systems, Inc.; *pg.* 372, *pg.* 240
Kothavala, Sarvar, VP-Mktg-The Americas-Syneron - Candela Corporation; *pg.* 1404, *pg.* 855
Kotik, Andrey, Dir-Sls-Russia, CIS & Ukraine - X-Rite, Incorporated; *pg.* 1437, *pg.* 891
Kotikalapudi, Vizay, Sr Mgr-Product Mktg - Symantec Corporation; *pg.* 478, *pg.* 161
Kotrba, Bill, VP-Mktg Analytics & Pricing - Regis Corporation; *pg.* 521, *pg.* 941
Kottke, Mariah, Brand Mgr-Shopper Mktg - Kimberly-Clark Corporation; *pg.* 1461, *pg.* 1720
Kotz, Bruce, VP-Specialty Products - Golden Peanut Company, L.L.C.; *pg.* 1854, *pg.* 484
Kouchoukos, Thomas, Dir-Mktg - Vascular Solutions, Inc.; *pg.* 1434, *pg.* 946
Kougias, Stephen, Dir-PR - San Diego Symphony Orchestra Association; *pg.* 580, *pg.* 208
Kouletsis, Denee, Mgr-Mktg Procurement - Hershey Entertainment & Resorts Company; *pg.* 1094, *pg.* 1539
Kounalakis, Nickolas, Reg Dir-Sls-Natl West - AOL Inc.; *pg.* 1229, *pg.* 1195
Koupal, Brian, Mgr-Mktg Analytics - Citrix Systems, Inc.; *pg.* 375, *pg.* 424
Koupas, Andy, Mgr-Sls - Abaxis, Inc.; *pg.* 1483, *pg.* 298
Kourlis Samuelson, Rita, Dir-Wool & Pelt Mktg-Intl - American Sheep Industry Association, Inc.; *pg.* 131, *pg.* 325
Koussoulis, Lea, VP-Global Media & Comm-Redken, Pureology & Mizani - L'Oreal USA; *pg.* 514, *pg.* 1252
Koutolakis, Susan, Mgr-Global Mktg Programs - Progress Software Corporation; *pg.* 457, *pg.* 786
Koutros, Gina, Mgr-Experiential Mktg - BMW of North America, LLC; *pg.* 166, *pg.* 1133
Kovac, Charles F., Sr VP-Freight Products - Westinghouse Air Brake Technologies Corporation; *pg.* 1388, *pg.* 1595
Kovac, Michelle, Dir-Java Mktg & Ops - Oracle Corporation; *pg.* 450, *pg.* 191
Kovach, John, Dir-Product Mgmt - Honeywell International Inc.; *pg.* 407, *pg.* 1088
Kovach, Marty, Head-Global Content & Creative Evolution - Merck & Co., Inc.; *pg.* 1566, *pg.* 1077
Koval, Amanda, Sr Mgr-Shopper Mktg - Unilever United States, Inc.; *pg.* 904, *pg.* 1061
Koval, Nora, Mgr-Digital Mktg - The Dun & Bradstreet Corp.; *pg.* 1637, *pg.* 1120
Kovarsky, Cyril, Sr VP-Sls-Global - Accor; *pg.* 1079, *pg.* 1657
Koven, Stephen, Dir-Mktg - Henkel Consumer Adhesives, Inc.; *pg.* 403, *pg.* 1480
Koven, Stephen, Dir-Mktg - Henkel Consumer Goods; *pg.* 511, *pg.* 22
Koves, Sarah, Dir-Brand Mktg - Wyndham Worldwide Corporation; *pg.* 1119, *pg.* 1107
Kovich, Mark, VP-Sls & Mktg - American Woodmark Corporation; *pg.* 913, *pg.* 1811
Kovisars, Fil, Mgr-Community Mktg - Stonyfield Farm, Inc.; *pg.* 899, *pg.* 1035
Kovnats, Jen, Product Mgr - Google Inc.; *pg.* 1249, *pg.* 153
Kowalchuk, Tavia, Sr Dir-Mktg-William Morrow & Cookbooks - HarperCollins Publishers Inc.; *pg.* 1647, *pg.* 1237
Kowalchyk, Michael, Coord-Digital Mktg - Belk, Inc.; *pg.* 1760, *pg.* 1364
Kowalczyk, Nadia, Dir-Global Mktg-Batteries - Energizer Holdings, Inc.; *pg.* 637, *pg.* 996
Kowalczyk, Oriane, Mgr-Global Brand Mktg-Innovation-Scholl - Reckitt Benckiser Inc.; *pg.* 1136, *pg.* 1105
Kowalczyk, Ryan, Dir-Product Strategy - Orbitz Worldwide, Inc.; *pg.* 1918, *pg.* 586
Kowalske, Renee, Dir-Mktg Comm - L-3 Communications Holdings Inc.; *pg.* 650, *pg.* 1250
Kowalski, David A., Pres-Indus Products, Svcs Bus Grp & SPX Global Mfg Ops - SPX Corporation; *pg.* 218, *pg.* 1369
Kowalski, Dean, Dir-Co-Brand Mktg - Alliance Data Systems Corporation; *pg.* 347, *pg.* 1729
Kowalski, Gail, Sr Product Mgr - XO Holdings, Inc.; *pg.* 689, *pg.* 1786
Kowalski, Maureen, VP-Mktg Info - Kelly Services, Inc.; *pg.* 424, *pg.* 911
Kowalski, Sandra Lee, Dir-Mktg - Northern Arizona University; *pg.* 606, *pg.* 12
Kowalski, Tommy, Sr Mgr-Acq Mktg - adidas America Inc.; *pg.* 1803, *pg.* 1500
Kowalski, Wayne, VP-Specialty Products - Southwire Company; *pg.* 1063, *pg.* 527
Kowalsky, Francine, Asst VP & Dir-Mktg - Frederick Wildman & Sons Ltd.; *pg.* 1963, *pg.* 1233
Kowalyk, Kirsten Leppert, Brand Mgr-Innovation - Abbott Nutrition; *pg.* 1485, *pg.* 1437
Kowitz, Stephanie, Sr Mgr-Shopper Insights-Convenience Retail - Coca-Cola North America; *pg.* 848, *pg.* 500
Koyama, Debora, VP-Mktg Stella Artois & Craft-Global - Anheuser-Busch Companies, LLC; *pg.* 237, *pg.* 991
Koyama, Heather, Exec Product Mgr-Microwave & Ventilation - GE Consumer & Industrial; *pg.* 55, *pg.* 733
Koyama, Jason, Sr Specialist-Mktg - Canon U.S.A., Inc.; *pg.* 1404, *pg.* 1178
Koyfman, Alina, Sr Mgr-Consumer Plng & Res - Diageo North America Inc.; *pg.* 248, *pg.* 1223
Koyrakh, Rachel, Specialist-Mktg & Branding - New York Life Insurance Company; *pg.* 1211, *pg.* 1268
Kozak, Adam, Product Mgr-Client & Graphics Bus - Advanced Micro Devices, Inc.; *pg.* 613, *pg.* 282
Kozak, David, VP-Mktg - Direct Energy; *pg.* 1939, *pg.* 1704
Kozak, Jim, Sr Dir-Mktg-B2B & Sports Partnerships - The Canadian Broadcasting Corporation; *pg.* 272, *pg.* 1931
Kozanian, Hagop, VP-Analog Mktg - Texas Instruments Incorporated; *pg.* 679, *pg.* 1688
Kozek, Ed, Sr VP-Product & Engrg - The Weather Channel LLC; *pg.* 320, *pg.* 523
Kozel, Kristy, Asst Mgr-Retail Mktg - American Greetings Corporation; *pg.* 1615, *pg.* 1428
Kozera, Heather, Dir-Digital Mktg - Sidney Frank Importing Co., Inc.; *pg.* 1970, *pg.* 1184
Koziara, Dave, Mgr-Mktg Ops-Buick & GMC - General Motors Company; *pg.* 175, *pg.* 881
Kozielski, Ken, Assoc VP-Sls Effectiveness - Aramark; *pg.* 1013, *pg.* 1558
Kozikowski, Laura, Dir-Brand Mktg - Solidworks Corporation; *pg.* 472, *pg.* 815
Kozinski, Alexandra, Specialist-Social Media & Content - Coldwell Banker Real Estate LLC; *pg.* 1087, *pg.* 1103
Kozlen, Kevin, Dir-Pub Affairs & Mktg - Advocate Health Care; *pg.* 1487, *pg.* 607
Kozleski, Angie, Mgr-Mktg & Digital Comm-Global - Ford Motor Company; *pg.* 172, *pg.* 876
Kozloski, Julie, Product Mgr - Intuit Inc.; *pg.* 769, *pg.* 158
Kozlowski, Lucas, Mgr-eMail Mktg - Express, Inc.; *pg.* 24, *pg.* 1440
Kozlowski, Tracy, Coord-Mktg - Kao Brands Co. Inc.; *pg.* 513, *pg.* 1415
Kozol, George B., Sr VP-Mktg - Security Mutual Life Insurance Company of New York; *pg.* 1216, *pg.* 1142
Kozolchyk, Erika, Brand Mgr-Personal Care Innovation - Colgate-Palmolive Company; *pg.* 504, *pg.* 1215
Kra-Oz, Ophir, Product Mgr - Google Inc.; *pg.* 1249, *pg.* 153
Kraatz, Sarah, Writer-Creative - Time Warner Cable Inc.; *pg.* 312, *pg.* 1301
Kraayenbrink, Lisa, Sr Mgr-Mktg - Best Buy Co., Inc.; *pg.* 1761, *pg.* 954
Krabbe, Jack, Acct Exec-Corp Sls - Baltimore Ravens Limited Partnership; *pg.* 532, *pg.* 755
Kraemer, Bernard, Sr Product Mgr - TE Connectivity Ltd.; *pg.* 677, *pg.* 1515
Kraemer, Debbie, Mgr-Digital Mktg - Sun Life Financial Inc.; *pg.* 806, *pg.* 1944
Kraemer, John, Mgr-Mktg - General Motors Company; *pg.* 175, *pg.* 881
Krafcik, Jonathan, Sr Product Mgr - Google Inc.; *pg.* 1249, *pg.* 153
Kraff, Kevin, VP-Mktg-Global - 505 Games (US), Inc.; *pg.* 948, *pg.* 38
Krafka-Harkema, Kathy, Mgr-Interactive Mktg & Digital Strategy - Vermeer Manufacturing Company; *pg.* 708, *pg.* 711
Kraft, Chris, Sr Dir-Global Assoc Comm - Wal-Mart Stores, Inc.; *pg.* 1790, *pg.* 29
Kraft, Claudia, Reg Mgr-Mktg - H&R Block, Inc.; *pg.* 764, *pg.*

983
Kraft, Jennifer, Sr Dir-Mktg Comm - Diebold, Incorporated; *pg.* 387, *pg.* 1407
Kraft, Ken, VP-Mktg-Cox Bus - Cox Communications, Inc.; *pg.* 279, *pg.* 501
Kraft, Lauren, Mgr-Mktg Comm - Siemens Process Industries and Drives; *pg.* 673, *pg.* 485
Kraham, Brendon, Dir-Emerging Ads Sls & Product Strategy - Google Inc.; *pg.* 1249, *pg.* 153
Krahel, Karol, Sr Mgr-Mktg-Customer Brands Tissue - Georgia-Pacific LLC; *pg.* 1458, *pg.* 507
Krainer, Ana, Mgr-Mktg-Pepsi - PepsiCo, Inc.; *pg.* 259, *pg.* 1327
Krajewski, Mike, Dir-Sls & Agriculture - Shur-Co, Inc.; *pg.* 110, *pg.* 1626
Krakoff, Reed, Exec Dir-Creative & Sr VP - Coach, Inc.; *pg.* 3, *pg.* 1214
Krakovsky, Dmitri, Sr VP-Product Mgmt-Global - SuccessFactors, Inc.; *pg.* 477, *pg.* 228
Krakow, Janet, VP-Mktg & Diversified Brands Div-Retail Brands - Sherwin-Williams Wood Care Group; *pg.* 1448, *pg.* 1127
Krakow, Janet, VP-Mktg-Retail Brands & Diversified Brands Div - Sherwin Williams; *pg.* 1448, *pg.* 1436
Krakowski, Jill, Sr Dir-Mktg - Revlon Consumer Products Corporation; *pg.* 521, *pg.* 1286
Krakowski, Jill, Sr Dir-Mktg - Revlon, Inc.; *pg.* 521, *pg.* 1286
Krakowski, Rick, Product Mgr-iCloud-Worldwide Product Mktg - Apple Inc.; *pg.* 350, *pg.* 73
Kralj, Zora, Mgr-Shopper Mktg - Glaxo Smith Kline Inc.; *pg.* 1536, *pg.* 1926
Kramer, Bruce, VP-Consumer Sls & Mktg - Wahl Clipper Corporation; *pg.* 524, *pg.* 662
Kramer, David A., Exec VP-Sls & Mktg - CR England, Inc.; *pg.* 1904, *pg.* 1756
Kramer, Erica, Mgr-Mktg - NutriSystem, Inc.; *pg.* 1577, *pg.* 1533
Kramer, Ira, VP-Mktg - D.R. Horton, Inc.; *pg.* 1090, *pg.* 1694
Kramer, Jamie, Sr VP-Digital Mktg - Sony Pictures Home Entertainment; *pg.* 310, *pg.* 72
Kramer, Leslie, Analyst-Mktg - 3M Company; *pg.* 1142, *pg.* 956
Kramer, Margie, Mgr-Adv - Jewel-Osco; *pg.* 1024, *pg.* 620
Kramer, Mindy, VP-PR-Florida Reg - Comcast Corporation; *pg.* 276, *pg.* 1560
Kramer, Monica, Mgr-Field Mktg-Ingram Micro - Juniper Networks, Inc.; *pg.* 1260, *pg.* 286
Kramer, Peter, Exec Dir-Sls & Mktg-Watches & Fine Jewelry - Chanel, Inc.; *pg.* 503, *pg.* 1211
Kramer, Rachel, Sr Planner-Digital Sls - Conde Nast Publications, Inc.; *pg.* 1629, *pg.* 1217
Kramer, Rachel, Mgr-Sls Plng - Vogue Magazine; *pg.* 1700, *pg.* 1311
Kramer, Ryan, Sr Mgr-Digital Mktg - VeriFone Systems, Inc.; *pg.* 487, *pg.* 251
Kramer, Stephanie, Exec Dir-Skincare Mktg - Chanel, Inc.; *pg.* 503, *pg.* 1211
Kramer, Tim, Mgr-Sls - Eberhard Manufacturing Division; *pg.* 1046, *pg.* 1475
Kramnic, Kevin, VP-Promotional Mktg - Crown Imports LLC; *pg.* 248, *pg.* 572
Krandel, Frank, VP-Adv - Boscov's Department Store, LLC; *pg.* 1763, *pg.* 1583
Kranich, Hannah, Dir-Mktg - Bloomberg L.P.; *pg.* 725, *pg.* 1204
Kranitz, Adam E., Sr Mgr-Worldwide Mktg - Avid Technology, Inc.; *pg.* 622, *pg.* 804
Kranz, Jennifer, VP-Mktg, Promotional Strategy & Plng-WE TV - AMC Networks Inc.; *pg.* 269, *pg.* 1189
Kranz, Rick, Editor-Product - Automotive News; *pg.* 1618, *pg.* 879
Kraselsky, Lynne, VP-CNBC US & Intl Sls - NBC Universal, Inc.; *pg.* 300, *pg.* 1266
Kraska, Ashley Bowling, VP-NBCUniversal Television & New Media Distr - NBC Universal, Inc.; *pg.* 300, *pg.* 1266
Krasnigor, Keith, Sr Dir-Asset Team-Oncology - AbbVie Inc.; *pg.* 1486, *pg.* 638
Krasnow, Kate, Coord-Mktg - Bentley University; *pg.* 598, *pg.* 850
Krasovetz, Kristi, Sr Specialist-Mktg Comm - Siemens Corporation; *pg.* 803, *pg.* 1291
Krasovetz, Kristi, Sr Specialist-Mktg Comm - Siemens Healthcare Diagnostics; *pg.* 673, *pg.* 604
Kratka, Harris, Dir-Integrated Mktg - Time Inc.; *pg.* 1693, *pg.* 1300
Kratt, Dwayne, Sr Dir-Govt Affairs - Diageo North America, Inc.; *pg.* 1961, *pg.* 361
Kratz, Dave, Mgr-Sls Admin - Curries Company; *pg.* 77, *pg.* 709
Kratz, Hannah, Mgr-Mktg - McDonald's Corporation; *pg.* 1737, *pg.* 645
Kratz, Kayla, Product Mgr - Boral Roofing; *pg.* 71, *pg.* 107
Kratzberg, Keith, Sr VP-Sls & Mktg - Epson America Inc.; *pg.* 394, *pg.* 122
Kraudel, Ryan, VP-Mktg - Valencell, Inc.; *pg.* 684, *pg.* 1389
Kraus, Amanda, Mgr-Channel Mktg - Tumi, Inc.; *pg.* 15, *pg.* 1123
Kraus, Andy, Brand Mgr-Plantronics - CDW Corporation; *pg.* 370, *pg.* 663
Kraus, Kerri, Mng Dir-Digital Mktg - Charles Schwab & Company, Inc.; *pg.* 734, *pg.* 215
Kraus, Matt, Sr Mgr-Search Engine Mktg - Sears Holdings Corporation; *pg.* 1784, *pg.* 618
Kraus, Patrick, Assoc Dir-Mktg - The Procter & Gamble Company; *pg.* 1129, *pg.* 1418
Kraus, Suzanne, Dir-Mktg & Bus - Comcast Corporation; *pg.* 276, *pg.* 1560
Kraus, Tim, Supvr-Product Mgmt - Intelligrated, Inc.; *pg.* 1349, *pg.* 1460
Kraus, Tom, Dir-Budweiser Brand Mktg - Anheuser-Busch Companies, LLC; *pg.* 237, *pg.* 991
Krause, Adam, Sr Mgr-Online Media - Ubisoft Inc.; *pg.* 589, *pg.* 229
Krause, Brian, VP-Mktg & Comm-Global - Molex Incorporated; *pg.* 655, *pg.* 628
Krause, Erin, Dir-Product Mktg - Atkins Nutritionals, Inc.; *pg.* 1498, *pg.* 316
Krause, Marion, Sr Mgr-Ops, Brand & Channel Mgmt - Siemens Healthcare Diagnostics; *pg.* 673, *pg.* 604
Krause, Paul, Bus Mgr-Architecture Drives - Rockwell Automation, Inc.; *pg.* 668, *pg.* 1880
Kraushaar, Gabriella, Mgr-Mktg - Sun Life Financial Inc.; *pg.* 806, *pg.* 1944
Krausnick, Dale, VP-Mktg & Product Dev - NSS Enterprises, Inc.; *pg.* 59, *pg.* 1476
Krauss, Beth, Coord-PR-Northern California & Reno - Whole Foods Market, Inc.; *pg.* 1038, *pg.* 1667
Krauss, Douglas, Sr Mgr-Integrated Shopper Mktg - Campbell Soup Company; *pg.* 844, *pg.* 1048
Kraut, Michael, VP-Sls-Natl - Cars.com; *pg.* 1234, *pg.* 568
Krauthause, Kathy, Mgr-Adv - Trump Entertainment Resorts, Inc.; *pg.* 1117, *pg.* 1041
Kravec, Saul, VP-Sls - Elizabeth Arden, Inc.; *pg.* 507, *pg.* 448
Kravetz, Steve, VP-Ad Sls & Bus Dev - AMC Networks Inc.; *pg.* 269, *pg.* 1189
Kravitz, Brian, Product Mgr-Google Docs - Google Inc.; *pg.* 1249, *pg.* 153
Kravitz, Terri Abril, Sr Mgr-Convention Sls - Greater Miami Convention & Visitors Bureau; *pg.* 993, *pg.* 442
Krawczyk, Jack, VP-Product Mgmt - Pandora Media Inc.; *pg.* 1273, *pg.* 172
Krawll, Jordan, Sr Mgr-Customer Mktg - Bacardi USA, Inc.; *pg.* 1956, *pg.* 417
Kraycik, Mike, Mgr-Digital Mktg - Comcast Cable Communications, Inc.; *pg.* 276, *pg.* 1560
Kraynak, Mark, Chief Product Officer - Imperva, Inc.; *pg.* 413, *pg.* 193
Krebs, Jody, Mgr-Mktg - MarineMax, Inc.; *pg.* 1709, *pg.* 416
Krebs, Joe, Dir-Mktg-Comml Segments-Global - The Sherwin-Williams Company; *pg.* 1447, *pg.* 1435
Krebs, Joe, Dir-Mktg-Warehouse Distr - Sherwin Williams; *pg.* 1448, *pg.* 1436
Krebs, Michael, Sls Dir-Content Solutions - Time Inc.; *pg.* 1693, *pg.* 1300
Krebs, Shaunna, Mgr-Mktg Comm - LOUD Technologies Inc.; *pg.* 652, *pg.* 1847
Krebs, Shayne, Product Mgr - A-Dec, Inc.; *pg.* 1483, *pg.* 1500
Krebs, Tom, VP-Sls - Lennox Hearth Products; *pg.* 93, *pg.* 1652
Krebsbach, Michael, Dir-Channel Mktg - The Kraft Heinz Company; *pg.* 871, *pg.* 641
Kreger, Dan, Product Mgr-Global - Molex Incorporated; *pg.* 655, *pg.* 628
Kreger, Mike, Reg Mgr-Sls-South Central - Wheatland Tube Company; *pg.* 121, *pg.* 1594
Krehbiel, Amy, Brand Mgr-Tide Delivery - The Procter & Gamble Company; *pg.* 1129, *pg.* 1418
Kreidell, Walter, Dir-Correctional Sls & Product Dev - Point Blank Solutions, Inc.; *pg.* 1467, *pg.* 460
Kreider, Nicole, Dir-Mktg & Strategy - CorVel Corporation; *pg.* 1198, *pg.* 109
Kreiger, Steve, VP-Sls - Ingram Micro Mobility; *pg.* 415, *pg.* 697
Kreinbrink, Rodney A., Sr Mgr-Mfg Reliability - Cooper Tire & Rubber Company; *pg.* 1881, *pg.* 1453
Kreindler, Tony, Sr Dir-Strategic Comm - Environmental Defense Fund; *pg.* 140, *pg.* 1228
Kreiser, Kevin, Analyst-Field Sls-CVS - Unilever United States, Inc.; *pg.* 904, *pg.* 1061
Kreiser, Mary, VP-Sls - M.Z. Berger & Co., Inc.; *pg.* 10, *pg.* 1175
Kreiter, Kevin B., Corp VP-Mktg & Engrg - Cascade Corporation; *pg.* 1321, *pg.* 1497
Krekoukis, Ted, Sr Mgr-Bus Ops-Digital Newsstand - Barnes & Noble, Inc.; *pg.* 1619, *pg.* 1201
Krembs, Angelique, VP-Mktg-Pepsi Beverages North America - PepsiCo, Inc.; *pg.* 259, *pg.* 1327
Kreml, Shelly, Dir-Mktg - International Foods and Ingredients Inc.; *pg.* 865, *pg.* 616
Krempasky, Aaron, Specialist-US Channel Mktg - Oakley, Inc.; *pg.* 1840, *pg.* 86
Kremposky, Kevin, Mgr-Sls-Eastern Reg - Napco Security Systems, Inc.; *pg.* 658, *pg.* 1138
Krenek, Debby, Sr VP-Cablevision Local Media & Dir-Newsday Editorial - Newsday Media Group; *pg.* 1670, *pg.* 1181
Kresch, Matt, Dir-Product Mktg-Microsoft Dynamics CRM-Svc - Microsoft Corp.; *pg.* 440, *pg.* 321
Kresge, Ali, Assoc Dir-Mktg Comm-Merck Oncology - Merck & Co., Inc.; *pg.* 1566, *pg.* 1077
Kresha, Dan, Mgr-Internet Mktg - Mutual of Omaha Insurance Company; *pg.* 1210, *pg.* 1016
Kress, Scott, VP-Sls - Volvo Trucks North America, Inc.; *pg.* 195, *pg.* 1377
Kressin, Thomas, Dir-Product Mktg - Itron Inc.; *pg.* 422, *pg.* 1822
Kressler, Bill, Reg Mgr-Sls-Northeast - Litecontrol Corporation; *pg.* 1301, *pg.* 841
Kreter, Sarah, Mgr-Product Category - Swarovski North America Limited Inc.; *pg.* 13, *pg.* 1600
Kretz, Cathy, Mgr-Convention Sls - Travel Portland; *pg.* 1008, *pg.* 1507
Kreul-Starr, Elizabeth, Dir-Mktg-1-DAY ACUVUE DEFINE-Beauty Platform - Johnson & Johnson; *pg.* 1549, *pg.* 1091
Krevans, Jerry, Sr Dir - Nathan's Famous Inc.; *pg.* 1741, *pg.* 1171
Krever, Jason, Dir-IT-Mktg & Comm - Campbell Soup Company; *pg.* 844, *pg.* 1048
Kreyling, Colleen, Brand Mgr-Global Card & Loyalty-EMEA - Starbucks Corporation; *pg.* 897, *pg.* 1840
Krider, Michael, Assoc Mgr-Content Mktg - Hulu LLC; *pg.* 1257, *pg.* 274
Krieger, Dave, Mgr-Direct Mktg - AutoZone, Inc.; *pg.* 200, *pg.* 1641
Krieger, Kevin, Mgr-Product Design & Dev - Marlite, Inc.; *pg.* 95, *pg.* 1448
Krieger, Louise, Sr Mgr-Mktg - AT&T Mobility LLC; *pg.* 619, *pg.* 488
Krieger, Randy, Dir-ASEAN Mktg & Sls - Ford Motor Company; *pg.* 172, *pg.* 876
Krienke, Scott, Sr VP-Product & Mktg - Assurant Health; *pg.* 1193, *pg.* 1873
Kriete, Ed, Sr VP-Integrated Mktg - Hasbro, Inc.; *pg.* 954, *pg.* 1603
Krigel, Beth, Brand Mgr-Jim Beam-Global - Beam Suntory Inc.; *pg.* 1957, *pg.* 599
Kringelis, Cindy Tyler, Assoc Dir-Mktg - Cellco Partnership; *pg.* 1869, *pg.* 1042
Krinn, Doug, VP-Mktg - UnitedHealth Group Incorporated; *pg.* 1221, *pg.* 950
Krippinger, Michael, Mgr-Mktg - US Foods; *pg.* 1036, *pg.* 703
Krisay, Amy, Mgr-Mktg Svcs Delivery - Accenture; *pg.* 1392, *pg.* 1186
Krischer, Kelly, Brand Mgr - Blackbaud, Inc.; *pg.* 361, *pg.* 1613
Krisewicz, Brant, Mgr-Online Mktg - CenturyLink, Inc; *pg.* 1870, *pg.* 317
Krishan, Ami, Sr Dir-Mktg - PepsiCo, Inc.; *pg.* 259, *pg.* 1327
Krishna, Rekha, Product Mgr - Cisco Systems, Inc.; *pg.* 372, *pg.* 240
Krishna, Varun, Sr Dir-Retail Products - PayPal Inc.; *pg.* 1274, *pg.* 248
Krishna-Kumar, Kalpana, Specialist-Mktg - Coldwell Banker Real Estate LLC; *pg.* 1087, *pg.* 1103
Krishnan, Sophie, VP-Product & Mktg-Global - Expedia, Inc.; *pg.* 1244, *pg.* 1814

Krishnan, Sriram, Product Mgr - Facebook, Inc.; *pg.* 1245, *pg.* 143
Krisko, Diane, Dir-Mktg Ops - Pfizer Inc.; *pg.* 1581, *pg.* 1278
Krisko, Jennifer, Mgr-Mktg - Wells Fargo & Company; *pg.* 819, *pg.* 232
Krist, James, Mgr-Key Acct Sls & Svc - Omaha Public Power District; *pg.* 1948, *pg.* 1017
Kristel-Smith, Kerith, Mgr-Adv - Harvard Pilgrim Health Care, Inc.; *pg.* 1539, *pg.* 856
Kristensen, Bryce, VP-Social & Interactive - E! Online, Inc.; *pg.* 1239, *pg.* 129
Kristinsson, Andri, Product Mgr-SlideShare Mobile Apps - LinkedIn Corporation; *pg.* 1262, *pg.* 160
Kristle, Jill, Mgr-Interactive Mktg - ConAgra Foods, Inc.; *pg.* 826, *pg.* 1014
Kristo, Nathalie, Sr VP-Mktg & Global Bus Dev - L'Oreal USA; *pg.* 514, *pg.* 1252
Kristofferson, Deborah, VP-Brand & Creative Strategy - Peet's Coffee & Tea, Inc.; *pg.* 1029, *pg.* 85
Kritikos, Marianne, Coord-Mktg & Sr Planner-Mktg - Office Depot, Inc.; *pg.* 448, *pg.* 412
Kritsinger, Sheri, Brand Mgr - John B. Sanfilippo & Son, Inc.; *pg.* 1024, *pg.* 610
Kritzer, Andrew, Sr Dir-Committees & Conferences - Association of National Advertisers, Inc.; *pg.* 133, *pg.* 1197
Kritzer, Raelyn, Dir-Channel Mktg-WW - Brocade Communications Systems, Inc.; *pg.* 365, *pg.* 239
Kritzler, Aliya, Dir-Mktg Comm - Morgans Hotel Group Co.; *pg.* 1105, *pg.* 1262
Kritzman, Steven, Sr VP-Sls - Pandora Media Inc.; *pg.* 1273, *pg.* 172
Kritzmire, Anne, Mng Dir-Closed-End Funds & Global Structured Products - Nuveen Investments, Inc.; *pg.* 788, *pg.* 586
Krizman, Steve, Sr Dir-Comm, PR & Mktg - Kaiser Permanente; *pg.* 1552, *pg.* 171
Krob, Jennifer M., Mgr-Database Mktg - Meredith Corporation; *pg.* 1663, *pg.* 705
Kroeger, Chris, Sr VP-Mktg - Sabre Holdings Corporation; *pg.* 1922, *pg.* 1745
Kroeger, Dawn, Dir-Mktg & Comm - Two Men And A Truck International, Inc.; *pg.* 1926, *pg.* 896
Kroger, Frank E., VP-Shopper Mktg - Valassis; *pg.* 1698, *pg.* 386
Krohlow, Pat, Dir-Mktg - WLUK-TV; *pg.* 322, *pg.* 1860
Krohn, Darlene, Gen Mgr & Product Mgr - W.L. Gore & Associates, Inc.; *pg.* 122, *pg.* 388
Krohn, James V., Bus Mgr-Wire & Cable Global - LyondellBasell Industries; *pg.* 980, *pg.* 1710
Krohn, Karl, Dir-Mktg-Spreads Category - Ferrero U.S.A., Inc.; *pg.* 1852, *pg.* 1121
Kroitoro, Yosef, Sr Dir-Sls & Mktg IS-DS Div - Samsung Electronics America, Inc.; *pg.* 669, *pg.* 1115
Krojansky, Mark, VP-Mktg - Stamps.com Inc.; *pg.* 1282, *pg.* 82
Krok, Marc, Sr VP-Ad Sls - AMC Networks Inc.; *pg.* 269, *pg.* 1189
Krol, Christina, Coord-Mktg - Glaxo Smith Kline Inc.; *pg.* 1536, *pg.* 1926
Krolick, Mark, Mng Dir-Mktg & Product Dev - United Airlines, Inc.; *pg.* 1927, *pg.* 593
Kroll, Beth, Mgr-Channel Mktg - Symantec Corporation; *pg.* 478, *pg.* 161
Kroll, Jeffrey, Assoc Dir-Mktg Science - Gilead Sciences, Inc.; *pg.* 1535, *pg.* 88
Kroll, Shawn, Sr Mgr-Hip Engrg - Stryker Corporation; *pg.* 1598, *pg.* 894
Kroll, Shawn, Sr Mgr-Hip Engrg - Stryker Orthopaedics; *pg.* 1599, *pg.* 1082
Kroll, Sue, Pres-Worldwide Mktg & Intl Distr-Warner Bros Pictures - Warner Bros. Entertainment Inc.; *pg.* 319, *pg.* 54
Kronauge, Stuart, Sr VP-Customer Mktg - Coca-Cola North America; *pg.* 848, *pg.* 500
Kronby, Miles, Chief Product Officer-Digital - Merriam-Webster, Inc.; *pg.* 1664, *pg.* 846
Krone, Samantha, Media Buyer - Lightning Hockey LP; *pg.* 557, *pg.* 474
Kronenburger, Rick, Dir-Mktg-Content & Partnerships - General Growth Properties, Inc.; *pg.* 1093, *pg.* 574
Kronenfeld, Robert, Sr Dir-Mktg - KB Home; *pg.* 90, *pg.* 134
Kronthal-Sacco, Randi, CMO-Interim - Rodan + Fields, LLC; *pg.* 522, *pg.* 225
Kroog, Joe, Dir-Product Mgmt - BioSpace, Inc.; *pg.* 1231, *pg.* 1082
Kroon, Jennifer, Sr Mgr-Mktg - NetApp, Inc.; *pg.* 444, *pg.* 287
Kroon, Michael, Assoc Mgr-Mktg - Wal-Mart Stores, Inc.; *pg.* 1790, *pg.* 29
Kroon, Robert, Assoc VP & Dir-Strategic Product & Ops - HomeGoods, Inc.; *pg.* 1125, *pg.* 821
Kroplewski, Patrick V., Mgr-Channel Mktg - Robert Bosch Tool Corp; *pg.* 1060, *pg.* 634
Krows, Nicole, Specialist-Sls-Xbox LIVE - Microsoft Corporation; *pg.* 435, *pg.* 1824
Krueger, Jill, Sr Mgr-Mktg Programs - IBM; *pg.* 410, *pg.* 1449
Krueger, Kenneth W., Interim Chm, Interim Pres & Interim CEO - The Manitowoc Company, Inc.; *pg.* 1358, *pg.* 1868
Krueger, Tamara, Dir-Corp Mktg - United Dairy Farmers, Inc.; *pg.* 906, *pg.* 1426
Krueger, Terry, Coord-Mktg - PODS Enterprises, Inc.; *pg.* 1919, *pg.* 416
Kruempel, Leslie, Mgr-Interactive Mktg - Cooperative Regions of Organic Producer Pools; *pg.* 850, *pg.* 1864
Kruepke, Mary, Media Planner & Media Buyer - Batteries Plus Bulbs LLC; *pg.* 360, *pg.* 1860
Kruesi, Jonathan, Brand Mgr-Kleenex - Kimberly-Clark Corporation; *pg.* 1461, *pg.* 1720
Krug, Carey Collins, VP-Mktg-Global - Ralph Lauren Corporation; *pg.* 46, *pg.* 1284
Krug, Dana, VP-Sls & Bus Dev - Redbox Automated Retail, LLC; *pg.* 306, *pg.* 649
Krug, Johannes, Product Mgr-Laboratory Hardware CAD & CAM Sys - Sirona Dental Systems, Inc.; *pg.* 1429, *pg.* 1175
Krug, Kelly, Asst Dir-Integrated Mktg - The Hartford Financial Services Group, Inc.; *pg.* 1202, *pg.* 352
Krug, Marven, Dir-Digital Product Mgmt - Scripps Networks Interactive, Inc.; *pg.* 1279, *pg.* 1638
Kruger, Jack, Brand Mgr - Kellogg Company; *pg.* 831, *pg.* 870
Kruger, Jim, CMO & Exec VP - Polycom, Inc.; *pg.* 664, *pg.* 249
Kruger, Nathan, Sr Dir-Mktg - GREEN DOT CORPORATION; *pg.* 763, *pg.* 180
Kruger, Steve, Dir-Brand Mktg - Briggs & Stratton Corporation; *pg.* 201, *pg.* 1899
Krugman, Kendra Baker, VP-Sls & Mdsg-Mass Channel - OshKosh B'Gosh, Inc.; *pg.* 45, *pg.* 1885
Kruh, David, Mgr-Direct Mktg & Eloqua - Analog Devices, Inc.; *pg.* 617, *pg.* 839
Krull, Ann, Mgr-Redemption Sls - A&A Global Industries Inc.; *pg.* 948, *pg.* 767
Krumlauf, Bruce, Mgr-Indirect Tax Product Line-CCH Tax & Acctg - CCH Inc.; *pg.* 1626, *pg.* 653
Krumm, Michael, Dir-Mktg - Brother International Corporation - USA; *pg.* 53, *pg.* 1046
Krump, Kristine, Mgr-Mktg - The Travelers Companies, Inc.; *pg.* 1220, *pg.* 352
Krupa, Foster, Sr Dir-Product Innovation - International Game Technology; *pg.* 420, *pg.* 1606
Krupinski, Marybeth, Sr Dir-Bus Intell & Strategy-North East Div - Comcast Corporation; *pg.* 276, *pg.* 1560
Krupp, Bryan, Brand Mgr - Altria Group, Inc.; *pg.* 1893, *pg.* 1800
Kruse, Jason, Sr Mgr-Web Analytics - Dice.com; *pg.* 1238, *pg.* 712
Kruse, Martha, Sr Dir-Multicultural Mktg - Rooms To Go.com, Inc.; *pg.* 941, *pg.* 468
Kruseck, Pam, Mgr-Grp Sls & Tourism - Atlanta Symphony Orchestra; *pg.* 531, *pg.* 490
Krusewski, Jonathan, Mgr-Mktg Brand - Champs Sports; *pg.* 1806, *pg.* 414
Krusmark, Kristina, Product Mgr-Info Svcs - EBSCO Industries, Inc.; *pg.* 1638, *pg.* 2
Krut, Sandra, Dir-Mktg Svcs - Banfi Vintners; *pg.* 1957, *pg.* 1161
Kruusi, Natascha, Sr Mgr-Mktg-Gaggenau - BSH Home Appliances Corporation; *pg.* 53, *pg.* 108
Krygiel, Colleen, Mgr-Mktg - Dunkin' Brands Group, Inc.; *pg.* 1727, *pg.* 810
Krynock, Lorrie, Mgr-Mktg Graphics - Kimberly-Clark Corporation; *pg.* 1461, *pg.* 1720
Krywicki, Gerald, VP-Sls - Heatbath Corporation; *pg.* 1165, *pg.* 826
Krzys, Alison, Mgr-PR & Special Events-Midwest - Bloomingdale's, Inc.; *pg.* 1763, *pg.* 1204
Ksiezyk, Mark, Dir-DIY Mktg - The Sherwin-Williams Company; *pg.* 1447, *pg.* 1435
Ksiezyk, Mark, Dir-DIY Mktg - Sherwin Williams; *pg.* 1448, *pg.* 1436
Kuan, Nolan, Mgr-Mktg Intelligence - Cisco Systems, Inc.; *pg.* 372, *pg.* 240
Kubacki, Megan, Brand Mgr - Activision Blizzard, Inc.; *pg.* 948, *pg.* 271
Kubalok, Tara N., Sr Reg Mgr-Mdsg-AT&T Mobility - AT&T; *pg.* 1865, *pg.* 258
Kubera, Dan, Dir-Media Rels - Brunswick Corporation; *pg.* 1828, *pg.* 623
Kubera, Julie, Mgr-Adv & Mktg Comm - United Technologies Corporation; *pg.* 235, *pg.* 353
Kubicek, Amanda, Specialist-Mktg-Global Projects - Brinker International, Inc.; *pg.* 1718, *pg.* 1676
Kubinski, Steve, VP-Mktg - American Eagle Outfitters, Inc.; *pg.* 37, *pg.* 1572
Kubitschek, Evan, Specialist-Online Mktg - Cree Inc.; *pg.* 631, *pg.* 1371
Kublo, Yan, Sr Analyst-Mktg - Honeywell International Inc.; *pg.* 407, *pg.* 1088
Kubota, Kent, Product Mgr-Enterprise Flash Storage Sys - Toshiba America, Inc.; *pg.* 681, *pg.* 1302
Kucera, Trip, Sr Dir-North America Mktg-Center of Excellence - Oracle Corporation; *pg.* 1272, *pg.* 786
Kuch, Kelly, Sr Mgr-Consumer Mktg - Conde Nast Publications, Inc.; *pg.* 1629, *pg.* 1217
Kuch, Kelly, Sr Mgr-Partnership Mktg - Vogue Magazine; *pg.* 1700, *pg.* 1311
Kucharski, Angie, VP-Media Strategies - CBS Corporation; *pg.* 273, *pg.* 1210
Kucharski, Mark, VP & Sr Dir-Creative - Chico's FAS, Inc.; *pg.* 21, *pg.* 427
Kucharz, Ezra, Pres-Local Digital Media - CBS Corporation; *pg.* 273, *pg.* 1210
Kuchuris, Greg, Mgr-Mktg-Printed Circuit Products - Molex Incorporated; *pg.* 655, *pg.* 628
Kucich, Robert, VP-Retirement Mktg - FMR LLC (Fidelity Investments); *pg.* 759, *pg.* 794
Kucyk, Jay, Mgr-Retail Sls - Country Pure Foods, Inc.; *pg.* 247, *pg.* 1400
Kuczynski, Thomas M., Chief Dev Officer & Chief Strategy Officer - Viad Corp.; *pg.* 816, *pg.* 20
Kuda, Kohposh, Strategist-Tech Evangelist & Mktg - Sprint Corporation; *pg.* 1874, *pg.* 719
Kudowitz, Brian, Product Mgr - Bloomberg BNA; *pg.* 1621, *pg.* 1772
Kudva, Abhijeet, Mgr-Strategic Mktg-Turkey & India - Honeywell International Inc.; *pg.* 407, *pg.* 1088
Kuebitz, Tasha, Mgr-Online Mktg - Amazon.com, Inc.; *pg.* 1226, *pg.* 1831
Kuechenmeister, Chris, VP-Comm - Frito-Lay North America, Inc.; *pg.* 1853, *pg.* 1730
Kuehl, John, Mgr-Digital Mktg - Sub Zero Wolf; *pg.* 60, *pg.* 1867
Kuehne, Mike, Gen Mgr-Inflates Mktg - Wilson Sporting Goods Co.; *pg.* 1848, *pg.* 596
Kuehner, Joe, Mgr-Southern Distributor Sls - Herr Foods Inc.; *pg.* 861, *pg.* 1557
Kuehnle, Edward, Pres-Mktg - Catalina Marketing Corporation; *pg.* 369, *pg.* 462
Kuenzie, Kevin, Mgr-Powersports Sls - ROCKFORD CORPORATION; *pg.* 667, *pg.* 26
Kuerbis, Lisa, Coord-Mktg - Syracuse University Press; *pg.* 1690, *pg.* 1344
Kuerbis, Tate, Sr Designer-Footwear-Brand Jordan - NIKE, Inc.; *pg.* 1812, *pg.* 1492
Kuester, Joe, Sr Mgr-Bus Dev - Kimberly-Clark Corporation; *pg.* 1461, *pg.* 1720
Kuftinec, Lisa, Sr Mgr-Mktg - USANA Health Sciences, Inc.; *pg.* 1605, *pg.* 1761
Kuharski, Tim, Sr Dir-Fin - Carlson Real Estate Company; *pg.* 1084, *pg.* 947
Kuhl, Bryan, First Asst VP & Mgr-Strategic Mktg - Astoria Financial Corporation; *pg.* 717, *pg.* 1172
Kuhl, Erica, Sr Dir-Community - salesforce.com, inc.; *pg.* 1278, *pg.* 226
Kuhlman, Jerry, Head-Global Channel-Enterprise MultiChannel Mktg - Pfizer Inc.; *pg.* 1581, *pg.* 1278
Kuhlman, Russell B., VP-Sls Dev - Retractable Technologies Inc.; *pg.* 1590, *pg.* 1725
Kuhlmann, Erin, Mgr-Global Mktg-Media - ConAgra Foods, Inc.; *pg.* 826, *pg.* 1014
Kuhn, Breanna, Brand Mgr-Poise - Kimberly-Clark Corporation; *pg.* 1461, *pg.* 1720
Kuhn, Bruce, Dir-Product Dev - Klein Tools Inc.; *pg.* 1052, *pg.* 627
Kuhn, Bryan, Div VP-Sls-Eastern Div - Bar-S Foods Co.; *pg.* 839, *pg.* 15

Kuhn, Christian, VP-Mktg-Homewood Suites & Home2 - Hilton Worldwide, Inc.; *pg.* 1094, *pg.* 1791
Kuhn, Colleen, Brand Mgr-Vlasic - Pinnacle Foods Group LLC; *pg.* 889, *pg.* 1104
Kuhn, Derek, VP-Sls-BlackBerry Tech Solutions - BlackBerry Limited; *pg.* 625, *pg.* 1947
Kuhn, Jonathan, Sr Dir-Brand Mktg-Global - Acorda Therapeutics, Inc.; *pg.* 1486, *pg.* 1138
Kuhn, Kelly, Mgr-Product Mgmt-Mobile - Macy's East; *pg.* 1777, *pg.* 1254
Kuhn, Kim, Mgr-Mktg - Smead Manufacturing Company; *pg.* 470, *pg.* 926
Kuhn, Ryan, Sr Dir-Mktg - Goodwill Industries International, Inc.; *pg.* 1771, *pg.* 776
Kuhn, Tom, VP-Bus Dev & Media Sls - PGA Tour, Inc.; *pg.* 574, *pg.* 460
Kuhnert, Hans-Peter, VP-Sls-EMEA - Black Box Corporation; *pg.* 361, *pg.* 1547
Kuhr, Peter, Mgr-Product Dev - Lund Food Holdings, Inc.; *pg.* 875, *pg.* 924
Kuhrt, Kate Paalandi, Sr Dir-Regulatory & Product Plng - Thomson Reuters - Corporate Headquarters; *pg.* 1693, *pg.* 1299
Kuiper, Cindy, Dir-Mktg - Welch Allyn Inc.; *pg.* 1436, *pg.* 1342
Kujawski, Joe, Dir-Wholesale Mktg - The Sherwin-Williams Company; *pg.* 1447, *pg.* 1435
Kuker, Donna, Dir-Global Partner Mktg - VMware, Inc.; *pg.* 490, *pg.* 179
Kukesh, Natalie, Specialist-Mktg-North America - The Almond Board of California; *pg.* 1013, *pg.* 149
Kukla, Jodi, Dir-Mktg - BizFilings; *pg.* 724, *pg.* 1865
Kuklinski, Kyle, Mgr-Mktg Strategy & Consumer Insights - CarMax, Inc.; *pg.* 167, *pg.* 1800
Kukreja, Umesh, Sr Dir-Global Alliances Solutions & Sys Engrg - Juniper Networks, Inc.; *pg.* 1260, *pg.* 286
Kulaga, Tom, Dir-Creative & Mktg - The New York Times; *pg.* 1668, *pg.* 1270
Kule, Amy, VP-Mktg-Macy's Parade & Annual Events - Macy's East; *pg.* 1777, *pg.* 1254
Kulesa, Kelley, Mgr-Mktg & Player Dev - Ameristar Casinos, Inc.; *pg.* 528, *pg.* 1022
Kulesa, Sharon, Rep-Digital Printing Sls - Hewlett-Packard Company; *pg.* 404, *pg.* 175
Kulick, Matthew, Product Mgr - Google Inc.; *pg.* 1249, *pg.* 153
Kulkarni, Madhura, Sr Mgr-Mktg-Digital Strategy Shopper Conversion - PepsiCo, Inc.; *pg.* 259, *pg.* 1327
Kulkarni, Neha, Dir-New Product Dev-Global - American Express Company; *pg.* 712, *pg.* 1190
Kulkarni, Rajeev, Chief Product Officer & VP - 3D Systems Corporation; *pg.* 339, *pg.* 1621
Kulkarni, Shefali, Editor-Social Media & Engagement - Newsweek Daily Beast Co.; *pg.* 1670, *pg.* 1271
Kull, Larry, Sr Dir-Sls & Consumer Products - Yokohama Tire Corporation; *pg.* 1892, *pg.* 94
Kull, Marcia, VP-Marine Sls - Volvo Penta of the Americas, Inc.; *pg.* 1712, *pg.* 1778
Kullberg, Christine M., Dir-Mktg-Specialty Solutions - Cardinal Health, Inc.; *pg.* 1512, *pg.* 1448
Kullhem, Andrea Cornejo, Assoc Mgr-Mktg-Spirits - E&J Gallo Winery; *pg.* 1962, *pg.* 149
Kulok, Lisa A., Sr Dir-Plng-Global - Columbia Sportswear Company; *pg.* 1830, *pg.* 1501
Kuly, Helena, Sr Mgr-Worldwide Partner Comm - Juniper Networks, Inc.; *pg.* 1260, *pg.* 286
Kumagai, Les, Dir & Analyst-Indus-Rels & PR - Verizon Communications Inc.; *pg.* 1875, *pg.* 1309
Kumar, Akarshan, Product Mgr - Twitter, Inc.; *pg.* 1285, *pg.* 228
Kumar, Arun, Sr Product Mgr-Multimedia - BlackBerry Limited; *pg.* 625, *pg.* 1947
Kumar, Dhiraj, Sr Dir-Consumer Strategy-North America - PayPal Inc.; *pg.* 1274, *pg.* 248
Kumar, Divya, Sr Product Mktg Mgr-IE - Microsoft Corporation; *pg.* 435, *pg.* 1824
Kumar, Manisha, Sr Mgr-Digital Mktg - salesforce.com, inc.; *pg.* 1278, *pg.* 226
Kumar, Monica, Sr Dir-Database Product Mktg - Oracle Corporation; *pg.* 450, *pg.* 191
Kumar, Navin, Sr Mgr-Product Mktg-XBOX Accessories - Microsoft Corporation; *pg.* 435, *pg.* 1824
Kumar, Niranjan, Sr Mgr-Product Mktg-3D IC TSV & WLP Tech-Silicon Sys Grp - Applied Materials, Inc; *pg.* 618, *pg.* 1009
Kumar, Nisha, Sr Mgr-Product Mktg - Cars.com; *pg.* 1234, *pg.* 568
Kumar, Nitin, Sr Dir-Acct Mgmt - Yahoo! Inc.; *pg.* 1289, *pg.* 289
Kumar, Praveen, Sr Mgr - American Airlines Inc.; *pg.* 1898, *pg.* 1693
Kumar, Rohan, VP-Digital Mktg - Charter Communications, Inc.; *pg.* 274, *pg.* 372
Kumar, Sushil, VP-Product Strategy & Bus Dev - Oracle Corporation; *pg.* 450, *pg.* 191
Kume, Allyson, VP-Product & Design-Children's - Macy's East; *pg.* 1777, *pg.* 1254
Kummer, Judy, Sr Specialist-Product Sls-Mobile & Kindle - Amazon.com, Inc.; *pg.* 1226, *pg.* 1831
Kump, Suzanne M., Mgr-Mktg - Patterson Dental Supply, Inc.; *pg.* 1580, *pg.* 963
Kumpis, Monique, Sr Mgr-Adv - Hyundai Motor America; *pg.* 179, *pg.* 89
Kunberger, George A., Jr., Exec VP-Global Sls & Mktg - Jacobs Engineering Group, Inc.; *pg.* 88, *pg.* 180
Kuncl, Sharon, VP-Mdsg - Eby-Brown Co.; *pg.* 1767, *pg.* 636
Kunemoto, Max, Sr Mgr-Event Mktg & Bus - Dick's Sporting Goods, Inc.; *pg.* 1832, *pg.* 1524
Kunkel, Emily, Sr Mgr-Consumer Mktg Brand - LinkedIn Corporation; *pg.* 1262, *pg.* 160
Kunkel, Jennifer, Mgr-ECommerce Mktg - Foot Locker, Inc.; *pg.* 1808, *pg.* 1231
Kunkel, John, Brand Mgr-Lowe's - American Woodmark Corporation; *pg.* 913, *pg.* 1811
Kunkel, Thomas M., Exec VP & Pres-Bond & Fin Products - The Travelers Companies, Inc.; *pg.* 1220, *pg.* 352
Kunkle, Vickie, Sr VP-Mdsg - Hard Rock Cafe International, Inc.; *pg.* 1730, *pg.* 454
Kunning, Cody, Dir-Search Engine Mktg - Marchex, Inc.; *pg.* 1395, *pg.* 1837
Kuns, Gary, Dir-Mktg Support & Tobacco - Speedway LLC; *pg.* 985, *pg.* 1452
Kunst, Greg, Dir-Mktg-Retina Pharmaceuticals-Global - Alcon; *pg.* 1399, *pg.* 530
Kuntz, Alan, Mgr-Mktg-Product Line - Schneider Electric USA, Inc.; *pg.* 1306, *pg.* 650
Kunz, Donald L., VP-Mktg Svcs - DMI Furniture, Inc.; *pg.* 923, *pg.* 733
Kunz, Scott M., Dir-Adv - The New York Times; *pg.* 1668, *pg.* 1270
Kunz, Tori, Mgr-Mktg-Bus Dev & Strategy - Intuit Inc.; *pg.* 769, *pg.* 158
Kunze, Ken, CMO - Craft Brewers Alliance, Inc; *pg.* 247, *pg.* 1502
Kuo, Anthony, Dir-Product Mgmt - Newegg Inc.; *pg.* 1271, *pg.* 67
Kuo, Karen, Sr Mgr - Pfizer Inc.; *pg.* 1581, *pg.* 1278
Kuo, Lydia, Sr Assoc Brand Mgr-RITZ Crackers - Mondelez International; *pg.* 877, *pg.* 1344
Kup, Marc, Sr Dir-Fleet Transactions - Hawaiian Airlines, Inc.; *pg.* 1910, *pg.* 543
Kuperstein, Kenneth, Dir-Mktg Brand Plng & Dev - Cybex International, Inc.; *pg.* 1521, *pg.* 832
Kupferman, Alon, VP-Admin-Digital Banking Product Mgmt - M&T Bank Corporation; *pg.* 777, *pg.* 1149
Kupferman, Mark, VP-Insights & Interactive Mktg - Six Flags Entertainment Corporation; *pg.* 583, *pg.* 1698
Kuphal, Betty, Dir-Media-Southeast Reg - Coca-Cola North America; *pg.* 848, *pg.* 500
Kupka, Luann, Mgr-Mktg & Sls Admin - Davis-Standard LLC; *pg.* 1328, *pg.* 368
Kurapati, Kaushal, VP-Products - MasterCard Incorporated; *pg.* 779, *pg.* 1325
Kurata, Koji, Sr Mgr-PR-Corp Comm - Sony Electronics, Inc.; *pg.* 676, *pg.* 209
Kurciski, Sashko, Mgr-Mktg - Siemens PLM Software; *pg.* 469, *pg.* 1734
Kurdziel, Courtney, Mgr-Mktg - Straw Hat Cooperative Corporation; *pg.* 1751, *pg.* 260
Kurgan, Tom, VP-Sls & Mktg-Smallwares - Lincoln Foodservice Products, LLC; *pg.* 1127, *pg.* 1432
Kuri, Yussef, Mgr-Mktg - The Hershey Co.; *pg.* 1855, *pg.* 1538
Kurick, Staci, Dir-Digital Mktg - Ann Inc.; *pg.* 18, *pg.* 1195
Kurimsky, Carol, VP-Corp Mktg - SanDisk Corporation; *pg.* 465, *pg.* 147
Kurisu, Warren, Product Dir-Embedded Software Div - Mentor Graphics Corporation; *pg.* 432, *pg.* 1510
Kurkowski, George, Dir-Brand Mktg - Sears, Roebuck & Co.; *pg.* 1785, *pg.* 619
Kurlon, Sara, Assoc Mgr-Mktg-Innovation & New Bus Dev - Land O'Lakes, Inc.; *pg.* 873, *pg.* 915
Kurolapnik, Geno, Mgr-Mktg - Eby-Brown Co.; *pg.* 1767, *pg.* 636
Kuronen, Elizabeth, VP-Strategic Comm, Mktg & Pub Affairs - PHARMACEUTICAL PRODUCT DEVELOPMENT, INC.; *pg.* 1584, *pg.* 1393
Kurr, Greg, VP-Sls - Kemps LLC; *pg.* 867, *pg.* 961
Kurschner, Dan, Sr Mgr-SP Mobility Mktg - Cisco Systems, Inc.; *pg.* 372, *pg.* 240
Kurt, David, Sr Mgr-Corp Comm - USG Corporation; *pg.* 118, *pg.* 594
Kurtz, Ericka, Acct Mgr-Adv - MGM Resorts International; *pg.* 1105, *pg.* 1028
Kurtz, Helen, VP & Dir-Mktg-Yoplait - General Mills, Inc.; *pg.* 828, *pg.* 933
Kurtz, Jared, Assoc Dir-Respiratory Mktg - Boehringer Ingelheim Pharmaceuticals, Inc.; *pg.* 1507, *pg.* 368
Kurtz, Pam, Sr Mgr-Mktg - American Express Company; *pg.* 712, *pg.* 1190
Kurtz, William, Sr Mgr-Bus Dev & Strategy - Whirlpool Corporation; *pg.* 62, *pg.* 872
Kurtzman, Wayne, Mgr-Social Media Mktg Insights & Monitoring - Pitney Bowes Inc.; *pg.* 454, *pg.* 376
Kurumbail, Sankar, Product Mgr-Off-Highway Trucks & Wheel Tractor Scrapers - Caterpillar, Inc.; *pg.* 1321, *pg.* 650
Kurutz, Dean, Mgr-Mktg - Furuno USA, Inc.; *pg.* 640, *pg.* 1819
Kurysh, Justin, Mgr-Segment Mktg - Andersen Corporation; *pg.* 67, *pg.* 916
Kusa, Ralph, Engr-Sls - EMCOR Services Northeast CommAir/BALCO; *pg.* 1071, *pg.* 847
Kusak, Karen, Mgr-Web Mktg - Cisco Systems, Inc.; *pg.* 372, *pg.* 240
Kusch, Aaron, Brand Mgr - Vail Resorts, Inc.; *pg.* 1117, *pg.* 313
Kushner, Chris, Assoc Dir-Mktg - John Wiley & Sons, Inc.; *pg.* 1655, *pg.* 1073
Kushner, Yana, Sr Dir-Mktg - Clif Bar Inc.; *pg.* 848, *pg.* 83
Kusior, Patrick, Mgr-Social Media, Webcast & Video - Analog Devices, Inc.; *pg.* 617, *pg.* 839
Kuske, Bridget, Assoc Product Mgr-Sterilization - Kimberly-Clark Corporation; *pg.* 1461, *pg.* 1720
Kussmann, Erika, Dir-Brand Mktg - Rodan + Fields, LLC; *pg.* 522, *pg.* 225
Kustantini, Sami, Brand Mgr-Zabiha Halal - Maple Lodge Farms Ltd.; *pg.* 876, *pg.* 1918
Kustell, Melissa, VP-Global Mktg-Fisher-Price Baby - MATTEL, INC.; *pg.* 962, *pg.* 81
Kuster, John, Sr Product Mgr-AD&M - TE Connectivity Ltd.; *pg.* 677, *pg.* 1515
Kustiak, Tandy, Sr Dir-HR & People - Edmonton Oilers Hockey Club; *pg.* 546, *pg.* 1906
Kustu, Deniz, Dir-Product Mktg & eCommerce - AT&T Inc.; *pg.* 1867, *pg.* 1674
Kusumoto, Mariko, Mgr-Natl Mktg Comm-Lexus - Toyota Motor Sales, U.S.A., Inc.; *pg.* 193, *pg.* 296
Kusz, Bob, Mgr-Sls - Worcester Telegram & Gazette Corp.; *pg.* 1702, *pg.* 863
Kutchma, Brian, VP-Sls Mktg - Black Box Corporation; *pg.* 361, *pg.* 1547
Kutina, Maria, Sr Mgr-Category Dev - Diageo North America, Inc.; *pg.* 1961, *pg.* 361
Kutrieh, Nejim, Dir-Casino Mktg - Station Casinos, Inc.; *pg.* 585, *pg.* 1030
Kutsche, Bill, Mgr-Strategic Mktg - Murata Electronics North America, Inc.; *pg.* 658, *pg.* 540
Kutscher, Adelheid, Sr Head-Field Engagement-Adv & Online - Microsoft Corporation; *pg.* 435, *pg.* 1824
Kutzik, Paul, Dir-Circulation Sls - San Antonio Express News; *pg.* 1682, *pg.* 1742
Kuwabara, Kathryn, Sr Mgr-Proposal - EA Engineering, Science & Technology, Inc.; *pg.* 389, *pg.* 772
Kuwahara, Teresa, Mgr-Mktg-Intl - National Potato Promotion Board; *pg.* 150, *pg.* 322
Kuypers, Patrick, Mgr-Engagement Mktg - American Heart Association Inc.; *pg.* 128, *pg.* 1673
Kuypers, Tom, VP-Digital Mktg & CRM - Bed Bath & Beyond Inc.; *pg.* 1121, *pg.* 1127
Kuzara, Patty, Coord-Mktg - Cellino & Barnes; *pg.* 1293, *pg.* 1147
Kuzemchak, Steve, Analyst-Adv - Volkswagen Group of America, Inc.; *pg.* 194, *pg.* 1785
Kuzler, Danna, Sr Dir-Nonprofit & Govt Rels - The Advertising Council, Inc.; *pg.* 125, *pg.* 1187
Kuzujanakis, Aimee, Designer-Media & Graphics - Accenture; *pg.* 1392, *pg.* 1186

First page reference indicates Business Class Edition
Second page reference indicates Geographic Edition

Kvasnicka, Jay, Corp VP-Sls & Mktg - Gleason Industrial Products Inc.; pg. 1341, pg. 1874
Kwait, Eric, Dir-Partnership Sls - Golden State Warriors, LLC; pg. 550, pg. 171
Kwak, Grace, Product Mgr - Google Inc.; pg. 1249, pg. 153
Kwan, Agnes C., Mgr-Intl & Mktg Programs-Global Comm Grp - Intel Corporation; pg. 645, pg. 266
Kwan, Carissa T., Mgr-Mktg, Social Media & Digital Influencers - The Gymboree Corporation; pg. 25, pg. 77
Kwan, Shirley, Brand Mgr-People Magazine - Time Inc.; pg. 1693, pg. 1300
Kwasnick, Kristen, Asst VP & Mgr-IBD Mktg - Nuveen Investments, Inc.; pg. 788, pg. 586
Kwasniewski, Maribeth, Dir-Retail Mktg - Moen Incorporated; pg. 1056, pg. 1468
Kweskin, Alisa, Sr Mgr-Mktg-Affiliates & Shopping Channel - Office Depot, Inc.; pg. 448, pg. 412
Kwiatkowski, Charlie, VP-Comml & Indus Sls - Flanders Corporation; pg. 1336, pg. 1392
Kwiatkowski, Holly, Analyst-Mktg-Sls Ops - Automatic Data Processing, Inc.; pg. 357, pg. 1117
Kwiatkowski, Lauren, Dir-Mktg-Ralph Lauren Home - Ralph Lauren Corporation; pg. 46, pg. 1284
Kwok, Carrie, Mgr-Integrated Mktg - Major League Baseball; pg. 560, pg. 1255
Kwok, Kurt, Head-Corp Mktg - Applied Materials, Inc.; pg. 618, pg. 264
Kwolek, Sarah, Sr Analyst-Social Media Insights - Disney Interactive Media Group; pg. 1239, pg. 95
Kwon, Cathi, Principal & Product Mgr-Experience Design Studio - Adobe Systems Incorporated; pg. 342, pg. 235
Kwong, Alison, Specialist-Social Media - Wyndham Worldwide Corporation; pg. 1119, pg. 1107
Kwong, Caroline, Brand Mgr-Innovation - Del Monte Foods, Inc.; pg. 852, pg. 304
Kwong, Lisette, Sr Mgr-Corp Comm - BlackBerry; pg. 625, pg. 1717
Kwong-Joon, Leong, Reg Product Mgr-Tower Crane-APAC - The Manitowoc Company, Inc.; pg. 1358, pg. 1868
Kyaw, Kim, Mgr-Digital Mktg & Social Media - Jaguar Land Rover North America LLC; pg. 180, pg. 1081
Kydd, Tom, Brand Mgr-Global Football Digital - NIKE, Inc.; pg. 1812, pg. 1492
Kylberg, Rich, VP-Global Mktg & Comm - Arrow Electronics, Inc.; pg. 619, pg. 325
Kyle, Anne, Mgr-Product Dev - Maryland Office of Tourism Development; pg. 998, pg. 758
Kyle, Brendan, Sr Mgr-ECommerce Online - AT&T Mobility LLC; pg. 619, pg. 488
Kyle, William, Dir-Mktg - General Electric Company; pg. 1297, pg. 347
Kyles, Heather, Sr Mgr-Sls Events - F5 Networks, Inc.; pg. 396, pg. 1835
Kyllo, Rachel, VP-Mktg - Kemps LLC; pg. 867, pg. 961
Kyrychynskyi, Roman, Dir-Memory Products - Advanced Micro Devices, Inc.; pg. 613, pg. 282

L

L'Abate, John, Mgr-PR - Crawford & Company; pg. 1199, pg. 502
La Gesse, Rob, VP-Social Strategy - RACKSPACE HOSTING, INC.; pg. 1277, pg. 1742
La Penta, Paul, Mgr-Product & Brand-AMG, Maybach, Designo & S-Class - Mercedes-Benz USA, LLC; pg. 184, pg. 514
La Plain, Keith, Sr Dir-Product Commercialization - Varian Medical Systems, Inc.; pg. 1434, pg. 178
La Porte, R.J, Sr Mgr-District Mktg - Aramark; pg. 1013, pg. 1558
La, Vicki, Assoc Mgr-Integrated Mktg - Hulu LLC; pg. 1257, pg. 274
Laabs, Dinorah, Mgr-Intl Sls-Global Dairy Ingredients - Land O'Lakes, Inc.; pg. 873, pg. 915
Laabs, Sylvia A., Mgr-Direct-Response Mktg-Retention - Aetna Inc.; pg. 1187, pg. 351
Laabs, Tom, Sr Dir-Pur & Distr - Cousins Submarines, Inc.; pg. 1017, pg. 1870
Laakko, Betsy G., Sr Dir-Brand Mktg & Strategy - Save-A-Lot, Ltd.; pg. 894, pg. 977
Laatsch, Mike, VP-PR - The Western & Southern Financial Group; pg. 1223, pg. 1427
Labadini, Kenneth, Sr VP-Mktg & Corp Affairs Ops-Global - Bank of America Corporation; pg. 718, pg. 1362
LaBarre, Michael J., VP-Product Dev - Halozyme Therapeutics, Inc.; pg. 1539, pg. 203
Labay, Jerry, Sr Program Mgr-Mktg - Autodesk Inc.; pg. 356, pg. 257
Labbate, Marco, Mgr-Sls-Intl - Reed Exhibitions USA; pg. 460, pg. 364
Labbett, Bob, VP-Comm & Channel Mktg - Emerson Climate Technologies, Inc.; pg. 1333, pg. 1472
LaBella, Steve, Sr VP-Mktg-Global - Fisher-Price, Inc.; pg. 953, pg. 1156
Laberge, Anne-Sophie, Coord-Mktg - Bombardier Recreational Products, Inc.; pg. 201, pg. 1960
Laberge, Diane, Mgr-Mktg-Skin Care Grp - Unilever Canada Inc.; pg. 903, pg. 1946
Labesque, Laurie, VP-US Mktg philosophy - Coty, Inc.; pg. 506, pg. 1219
Labiak, Eric, Sr VP-Sls ACI On Demand - ACI Worldwide; pg. 710, pg. 1777
Labocki, James, Mgr-Cloud Computing Technical Product Mktg - Red Hat, Inc.; pg. 460, pg. 1388
Labonia, Mike, Sr VP-Adv - San Francisco Chronicle; pg. 1683, pg. 226
Labonte, Robert, Brand Mgr-Online Mktg - Hasbro, Inc.; pg. 954, pg. 1603
Labovitz, Jeff, Dir-Global Mktg-Star Wars - Hasbro, Inc.; pg. 954, pg. 1603
Labrador, Rafael W., Sr Dir-Brand Payer, Access Mktg & Oncology - GlaxoSmithKline; pg. 1536, pg. 1565
LaBreche, Beth, VP-Enterprise Mktg & Comm - CHS INC.; pg. 702, pg. 926
LaBrecque, Mark, VP-Mktg-US Activation - Krispy Kreme Doughnuts, Inc.; pg. 1734, pg. 1394
LaBree, Lucas, Mgr-Mktg Comm - Johnson Outdoors Inc.; pg. 1837, pg. 1888
Labroo, Amy, Sr Dir-Emerging Tech - Wyndham Worldwide Corporation; pg. 1119, pg. 1107
LaBroscian, Amanda, Mgr-Mobile Media - Experian Consumer Direct; pg. 1245, pg. 71
LaBuzzetta, Lisa, Mgr-Content Mktg - Aflac Incorporated; pg. 1188, pg. 527
Lacanienta, Ranny, Dir-Product Mgmt - SirsiDynix Corporation; pg. 470, pg. 1751
LaCaria, Robert, Assoc Dir-Mktg - Novartis Corporation; pg. 1574, pg. 1273
Lacasse, Mary-Ellen, Dir-Shaver Mktg - BIC Corporation; pg. 501, pg. 369
Lacasse, Nicolas, Mgr-Mktg-Ontario & Atlantic - Ford Motor Company of Canada, Limited; pg. 174, pg. 1930
Lacasse, Stephanie, Mgr-Mktg Retail Svcs - Parfums Christian Dior, Inc; pg. 519, pg. 1276
Lacayo, Silvia, Brand Mgr - Unilever United States, Inc.; pg. 904, pg. 1061
Lacey, Colin, VP-Product Mgmt & Managed Svcs - Unisys Corporation; pg. 487, pg. 1517
Lacey, Jim, VP-Media, PR & Strategic Comm - Massachusetts Mutual Life Insurance Company; pg. 1207, pg. 845
LaChance, Brandon, Dir- & Digital Mktg - Carl Karcher Enterprises, Inc.; pg. 1720, pg. 63
LaChance, Brandon, Dir-Adv & Digital Mktg - CKE Restaurants Inc.; pg. 1723, pg. 63
Lachance, Brian, Interim Head-Brand Strategy & Mktg - United Way Worldwide; pg. 160, pg. 1772
Lachapelle, Richard, Mgr-Sls-Intl - Scintrex Ltd.; pg. 1374, pg. 1920
Lacheur, Tamina, Mgr-Mktg-Investments - Royal Bank of Canada; pg. 800, pg. 1942
Lachowetz, Lisa, Exec Dir-Mktg-Hearst Design Grp - The Hearst Corporation; pg. 1649, pg. 1239
Lachowetz, Lisa A., Exec Dir-Mktg - House Beautiful; pg. 1651, pg. 1241
Lachut, Suzie, Mgr-Mktg-Parkhurst Dining - Eat'n Park Hospitality Group; pg. 1728, pg. 1539
Lacina, Kim, VP-Mktg & Comm - American Lung Association; pg. 129, pg. 395
Lackey, Brandon, VP-Mktg & Tech - Telsco Industries, Inc.; pg. 1381, pg. 1698
Lackey, Sarah, Specialist-Sls & Analyst-Market - LyondellBasell Industries; pg. 980, pg. 1710
Lacombe, Ron, VP-Traditional Sls - Motorcar Parts of America, Inc.; pg. 213, pg. 295
LaConti, Jonathan, Sr VP-Ad Sls-Northeast Reg-Travel Channel & GAC - Scripps Networks Interactive, Inc.; pg. 1279, pg. 1638
LaConti, Jonathan, Sr VP-Ad Sls-Northeast Reg-Travel Channel & GAC - Travel Channel LLC; pg. 313, pg. 766
Lacorazza, Michael, Exec VP & Head-Integrated Mktg - Wells Fargo & Company; pg. 819, pg. 232
LaCroix, Brigitte, Mgr-Global Mktg-Specialty Bus - GE Healthcare; pg. 399, pg. 1765
LaCroix, Patrick, Strategist-Media - Bose Corporation; pg. 626, pg. 820
LaCroix, Steve, CMO & VP-Sls & Mktg - Minnesota Vikings Football Club, Inc.; pg. 563, pg. 923
LaCruz, Rogger, VP & Sr Product Mgr - Union Bank, N.A.; pg. 813, pg. 230
Lacson, Chuck, Mgr-Product Mktg - Sony Computer Entertainment America LLC; pg. 966, pg. 256
Lacy, Christina, Planner-Flat Products - Special Metals Corporation; pg. 1377, pg. 1850
Lacy, David L., Mgr-Sls - Toho Tenax America, Inc.; pg. 1184, pg. 1655
Lacy, Dawn, Dir-Mktg Plng & Ops-Footlocker.com & Eastbay - Foot Locker, Inc.; pg. 1808, pg. 1231
Lacy, Jane, Bus Mgr-Contracts - Amazon.com, Inc.; pg. 1226, pg. 1831
Lacy, John, Chief Product Officer & Exec VP - Burton Snowboard Company; pg. 1829, pg. 1765
Laczi, Christopher, Dir-Mktg - Sovran Self Storage, Inc.; pg. 472, pg. 1355
Laczi, Christopher, Dir-Mktg - Uncle Bobs Self-Storage; pg. 1471, pg. 1151
Lad, Suneet, Asst Brand Mgr-Jimmy Dean Mktg Innovation - Tyson Foods, Inc.; pg. 902, pg. 35
Ladd, Carter, Dir-Bus Dev-Soccer United Mktg - Major League Soccer LLC; pg. 560, pg. 1256
Ladd, Ted, Sr Dir-PR - salesforce.com, inc.; pg. 1278, pg. 226
Ladd, Tim, VP-TM & Comml Card Sls - Fifth Third Bancorp; pg. 752, pg. 1413
Ladd-Reinfrank, Courtney, Brand Mgr-Home Ent & TV Distribution Mktg - Lions Gate Entertainment Corp.; pg. 296, pg. 274
Laderer, Alicia, Assoc Product Mgr - Bed Bath & Beyond Inc.; pg. 1121, pg. 1127
Laderman, Gerry, Interim CFO - United Airlines, Inc.; pg. 1927, pg. 593
Ladestro, Sal, Exec VP-Mktg - Sony Pictures Releasing Corporation; pg. 310, pg. 72
Ladetsky, Seth, Sr VP-Sls-Turner Sports Digital - Turner Broadcasting System, Inc.; pg. 314, pg. 521
Ladewig, Torin, Mgr-Creative Activation - The Coca-Cola Company; pg. 240, pg. 493
Ladha, Alykhan, Coord-Products Mktg - NOVA Chemicals Corporation; pg. 1175, pg. 1904
Ladner, Jeff, Sr Dir-Operational Excellence & Risk Mgmt - IHS Inc.; pg. 1652, pg. 326
Ladolcetta, Lauren, Mgr-Mktg - J. Crew Group, Inc.; pg. 1773, pg. 1245
Ladolcetta, Matthew, Dir-Digital Mktg & Strategy - The Trump Organization, LLC; pg. 1117, pg. 1305
Laesser, Jerald, VP-Mktg & Franchise Dev - Martin Franchises Inc.; pg. 332, pg. 1458
Lafemina, Leonard M., Head-Svcs Sls - IBM; pg. 410, pg. 1449
LaFevre, Janet, Sr Mgr-Mktg - General Growth Properties, Inc.; pg. 1093, pg. 574
Laffey, Tom, Exec VP-Products & Tech - TIBCO Software Inc.; pg. 484, pg. 178
Laffoon, Jodi, Mgr-Email Mktg-Lowesforpros.com - Lowe's Companies, Inc.; pg. 1053, pg. 1383
LaFlamme, Connie, Mgr-Mktg Comm - Caterpillar, Inc.; pg. 1321, pg. 650
Laflin, Michelle, Mgr-Media - Brown-Forman Corporation; pg. 1958, pg. 732
Lafon, Elaine, Coord-Natl Sls - NBC Universal, Inc.; pg. 300, pg. 1266
LaFond, Anne, Sr Mgr-Mktg Alliances - Monster Worldwide, Inc.; pg. 1268, pg. 859
LaFontaine, Chris, Sr Mgr-Corp Comm - Boston Scientific Corporation; pg. 1508, pg. 831
Lafontaine, Felix, Sr Mgr-DTS - Wm. Wrigley Jr. Company; pg. 1863, pg. 596
Lafontaine, Richard, Mgr-Mktg - Blinds To Go Inc.; pg. 918, pg. 1953
Lafontaine, Tim N., VP-Mdsg - A. M. Castle & Co.; pg. 64, pg. 644
LaFontant, Alain, VP-Bus Dev & Brand Mgr - Sean John Clothing, Inc.; pg. 48, pg. 1290
Laforest, Mathieu, Dir-Global Mktg-Ski-Doo - Bombardier Recreational Products, Inc.; pg. 201, pg. 1960

Lafortune, Alain, Exec VP-Pur & Mktg - The Jean Coutu Group (PJC) Inc.; pg. 1548, pg. 1952
LaFrance, Greg, Mgr-Classified & Online Adv - Gannett Co., Inc.; pg. 1643, pg. 1790
LaFrank, Amy, Dir-Field Mktg - The Krystal Company; pg. 1734, pg. 1629
LaFratta, Michelle R., Sr Specialist-Mktg - The Hanover Insurance Company; pg. 1202, pg. 862
Lafuente, Tanya, Dir-Mktg - Lord & Taylor LLC; pg. 1777, pg. 1252
Lagana, Angela, Mgr-Interactive Mktg - Scripps Networks Interactive, Inc.; pg. 1279, pg. 1638
Lagana, Sherri, Dir-Pro Association & Partnership Mktg - Liberty Mutual Insurance Group Inc.; pg. 1205, pg. 797
Lagatol, Shauna, Reg Mgr-Spring Waters Grp Mktg - Nestle Waters North America Inc.; pg. 257, pg. 375
LaGattuta, Lynn, Mgr-Procurement, Mktg & Comm - International Business Machines Corporation; pg. 418, pg. 1138
Lager, Ira, Dir-Creative Ops - David's Bridal, Inc.; pg. 23, pg. 1523
Lagno, Marissa, Assoc Mgr-Channel Mktg - iRobot Corp.; pg. 1418, pg. 785
Lagos, Isidora, Principal & Head-Brand Mktg & Comm - William Blair & Company LLC; pg. 822, pg. 596
Lagos, Linda, Brand Dir-Mktg & Digital - PepsiCo, Inc.; pg. 259, pg. 1327
Lagos, Lindsay, Mgr-Media Sls - Best Buy Co., Inc.; pg. 1761, pg. 954
Lagos, Steven, Chm & Dir-Creative - Lagos Inc.; pg. 8, pg. 1566
Lagrone, Marlene D., Sr Mgr-Events - AT&T; pg. 1865, pg. 258
LaGrotta, Christy, Specialist-Digital Mktg - Champion Enterprises Holdings, LLC; pg. 75, pg. 910
Laguardia, Tom, VP-Mktg - Hammond Valve Corp.; pg. 1049, pg. 1883
LaGuardia, Tom, VP-Mktg - Milwaukee Valve Company, Inc.; pg. 1361, pg. 1884
Lagunas, Claudia, Sr Dir-Global Digital Mktg - Visa Inc.; pg. 816, pg. 230
LaHaie, Sara, Mgr-Brand Mktg & PR-US - Dr. Martens AirWair USA LLC; pg. 1807, pg. 1502
Lahat, Avner, Sr Dir - Vishay Intertechnology, Inc.; pg. 1435, pg. 1551
Lahey, Elizabeth, Dir-Mktg Acq J Crew Direct - J. Crew Group, Inc.; pg. 1773, pg. 1245
Lahl, Daniel, VP-Product Mktg - SAP; pg. 465, pg. 78
Lahl, Emily, Mgr-Mktg - The Allstate Corporation; pg. 1189, pg. 639
Lahlum, Brian, Mgr-Creative Svcs - Baker & Taylor, Inc.; pg. 1619, pg. 1362
Lahr, Carl, Sr VP-Mktg & Sls - Los Angeles Clippers; pg. 558, pg. 135
Lahti, Mike, VP-Sls - Lochinvar Corporation; pg. 1073, pg. 1640
Lai, Aaron, Sr Mgr-Market Analytics - Blue Shield of California; pg. 1195, pg. 214
Lai, Boon, CMO & VP-Mktg Health & Wellness - Philips Electronics North America; pg. 662, pg. 782
Lai, Gigi, Sr Dir-Strategic Mktg - Applied Materials, Inc; pg. 618, pg. 1009
Lai, Jean, Sr Analyst-Bus & Media Software Engrg - L'Oreal USA; pg. 514, pg. 1252
Lai, Julius, Sr Dir-CRM - Activision Blizzard, Inc.; pg. 948, pg. 271
Laib, Kari, Project Mgr-Mktg - Recreational Equipment, Inc.; pg. 1843, pg. 1821
Laide, John, VP & Sr Product Mgr-Corp Governance - FactSet Research Systems Inc.; pg. 1247, pg. 361
Laier, Tom, Mgr-Interactive Mktg - 3M Company; pg. 1142, pg. 956
Laine, Amy, Dir-Integrated Mktg & Promo - The Hearst Corporation; pg. 1649, pg. 1239
Laine, Jordan, Sr Mgr - AMC Entertainment Inc.; pg. 527, pg. 716
Lainey, Garcia, Mgr-Brand PR & Engagement - McDonald's Corporation; pg. 1737, pg. 645
Laing, Scott, Product Head - Under Armour, Inc.; pg. 49, pg. 759
Laino, Nicholas, Planner-Sls-MTV, MTV2, mtvU, Tr3s & Logo - Viacom Inc.; pg. 316, pg. 1310
Laird, Chris, Dir-Brand Ops & Mktg Innovation - The Procter & Gamble Company; pg. 1129, pg. 1418
Laird, Valerie, Dir-Mktg - AMERICAN REPROGRAPHICS COMPANY; pg. 1616, pg. 303
Laird-Williams, Michele, Mgr-Worldwide Customer Mktg-Flexographic Pkg Div - Eastman Kodak Company; pg. 1408, pg. 1333
Lajeunesse, Carl, Dir-Charter Sls - Peter Pan Bus Lines, Inc.; pg. 1919, pg. 846
Lajoie, Lori M., Specialist-Mktg-MassMutual Fin Grp - Massachusetts Mutual Life Insurance Company; pg. 1207, pg. 845
Lakatos, Debbie, Sr Mgr-Demand Generation-Global - Hach Company; pg. 1415, pg. 334
Lake, Colleen, Sr Assoc Brand Mgr-Valentine's Season - Mars North America; pg. 1859, pg. 1072
Lake, Matt, Sr VP-Mktg & Adv - Cablevision Systems Corporation; pg. 272, pg. 1141
Lake, Peter J., Exec VP-Sls & Bus Dev - ZF TRW; pg. 222, pg. 897
Lake, Sarah, Sr Mgr-Process-Digital Extended Ops - Capital One Financial Corporation; pg. 730, pg. 1789
Lake, Steve, Reg Mgr-Sls-Natl - KCRG TV Station; pg. 293, pg. 702
Lakhani, Sandy, Principal & Product Mgr - AOL Inc.; pg. 1229, pg. 1195
Lakkas, George, Mgr-Strategic OEM Mktg-High Power Solutions - Texas Instruments Incorporated; pg. 679, pg. 1688
Lakritz, Stephanie, Sr Dir-Consumer & Market Insights-North America - Reckitt Benckiser Inc.; pg. 1136, pg. 1105
Lal, Prashant, Dir-Mktg - Reckitt Benckiser Inc.; pg. 1136, pg. 1105
Lalani, Sharmeen, Sr Mgr-Channel Mktg - SanDisk Corporation; pg. 465, pg. 147
Lalazari, Georgia, Mgr-Mktg - Hewlett-Packard Company; pg. 404, pg. 175
Laleman, Marybeth, Sls Mgr & Mgr-Venison Import - New Zealand Lamb Cooperative, Inc.; pg. 886, pg. 385
Lalich, Sara, Mgr-Global Loyalty Mktg & Acq - Hotels.com, L.P.; pg. 1257, pg. 1682
Lalin, Jerome, VP-Mktg - Wizards of the Coast, Inc.; pg. 970, pg. 1830
Lalji, Alysha, Mgr-Social Media - Anthem, Inc.; pg. 1192, pg. 683
Lalka, Ted, VP-Product Plng & Mktg - Subaru Canada, Inc.; pg. 190, pg. 1929
Lall, Kris, Sr Product Mgr - Attachmate Corporation; pg. 356, pg. 1833
Lalla, Ronald, Exec VP-Mdsg - Office Depot, Inc.; pg. 448, pg. 412
Lalley, Joe, Dir-Creative Engagement - PricewaterhouseCoopers LLP; pg. 795, pg. 1283
Lallouz, Joe, Product Mgr - Etsy, Inc.; pg. 1768, pg. 1230
Lally, Amy, Mgr-Mktg-Cloud Svcs - Ingram Micro Inc.; pg. 415, pg. 261
Lally, Dave, VP-Sls - Federal Hose Manufacturing Inc.; pg. 1047, pg. 1469
Lalonde, Sabrina, Mgr-External Mktg - Marks Work Wearhouse Ltd.; pg. 44, pg. 1903
Laluz, Arnaldo, Sr Dir-Pharmaceutical Pur & Pharmacy Programs - Rite Aid Corporation; pg. 1590, pg. 1519
Lalwaney, Rajesh, Sr Mgr - Capital One Financial Corporation; pg. 730, pg. 1789
Lalwani, Lalchand S., VP-Sls-Intl - Red Peacock International, Inc.; pg. 667, pg. 168
Lam, Carmen, VP-Hotel Sls & Mktg-Asia Pacific - Fairmont Hotels & Resorts Inc.; pg. 1091, pg. 1938
Lam, Danielle, Sr Mgr-Promo Dev - Publishers Clearing House; pg. 1782, pg. 1324
Lam, Derek, VP-Product Dev - Ericsson; pg. 395, pg. 1108
Lam, Ella, VP & Sr Mgr-Mktg - UnionBanCal Corporation; pg. 813, pg. 230
Lam, Fiona, Sr Dir-Mktg-Asia Pacific - Brocade Communications Systems, Inc.; pg. 365, pg. 239
Lam, Jessica, Specialist-Digital Media - Michaels Stores, Inc.; pg. 1127, pg. 1722
Lam, Jinny, Dir-Mktg - Ghirardelli Chocolate Company; pg. 1854, pg. 252
Lam, Joey, Specialist-Sls Technical Ops - Google Inc.; pg. 1249, pg. 153
Lam, Linh, Sr Mgr-IT - Hitachi Data Systems Corporation; pg. 407, pg. 265
Lam, Vanessa, Specialist-Interactive Mktg - Mitsubishi Motors North America, Inc.; pg. 185, pg. 75
Lamanette, Michelle, Head-Mktg - Humana, Inc.; pg. 1204, pg. 734
Lamar, Joe, Sr VP-Product Mgmt - Bank of America Corporation; pg. 718, pg. 1362
Lamar, Michelle, Mgr-Acq Mktg - Sprint Corporation; pg. 1874, pg. 719
Lamas, Karla, Sr Mgr-Product Dev - NYDJ Apparel, LLC; pg. 30, pg. 302
Lamb, Chris, Mgr-Mobile Products - InterContinental Hotels Corporation; pg. 1097, pg. 511
Lamb, David, Sr Dir-Developed Markets - Baxter International Inc.; pg. 1499, pg. 599
Lamb, Dean, Dir-Mktg - CDW Corporation; pg. 370, pg. 663
Lamb, Dwight, Sr., Assoc Publr-Production - Saturday Evening Post Society; pg. 1683, pg. 690
Lamb, Ellen, Dir-Corp Mktg - NTS Development Company; pg. 1106, pg. 737
Lamb, James, Brand Mgr-Mentos Gum - Perfetti Van Melle USA, Inc.; pg. 1860, pg. 727
Lamb, Jamie, Mgr-Sls Ops - Accenture; pg. 1392, pg. 1186
Lamb, Michele, Mgr-Energy Efficiency Mktg - South Jersey Gas Company; pg. 1951, pg. 1067
Lamb, Stephen, Dir-Mktg & Digital Commerce - Chico's FAS, Inc.; pg. 21, pg. 427
Lamb, Tracy, Dir-Sls Field Training & Ops - Miller and Smith Homes, Inc.; pg. 97, pg. 1794
Lamb, Travis, Area Sls Mgr-Boston Branch - 3M Company; pg. 1142, pg. 956
Lambatos, Stacy, Sr Dir-Corp Events - AOL Inc.; pg. 1229, pg. 1195
Lambert, Adam, VP-Sls - Dogfish Head Craft Brewery, Inc.; pg. 249, pg. 388
Lambert, Bob, Mgr-Online Mktg - Abt Electronics, Inc.; pg. 612, pg. 614
Lambert, Gail, Coord-Mktg - Pepsi Beverages Company; pg. 258, pg. 1342
Lambert, Jeff, Sr Dir-Mktg - Bright House Networks LLC; pg. 272, pg. 461
Lambert, Jennifer, VP-Mktg - Crosman Corporation; pg. 951, pg. 1143
Lambert, Kathryn, Dir-Mktg Comm & Customer Retention - Hawaiian Telcom Communications, Inc.; pg. 1872, pg. 544
Lambert, Kellie, Dir-Mktg - Kerstin Florian, Inc.; pg. 513, pg. 121
Lambert, Kim, Mgr-Product Mktg & Content Strategy - Verizon Communications Inc.; pg. 1875, pg. 1309
Lambert, Kristina, Mgr-Mktg-Info Mgmt - IDEXX Laboratories, Inc.; pg. 1543, pg. 753
Lambert, Michael, Dir-Mktg & Bus Dev - Dell Inc.; pg. 383, pg. 1737
Lambert, Natalie, Sr Dir-Integrated Product Mktg - Citrix Systems, Inc.; pg. 375, pg. 424
Lambert, Neal, Dir-Payor Segment & Value Mktg-Oncology - Amgen Inc.; pg. 1493, pg. 291
Lambert, Nick, VP-Sls & Mktg - Sunday River Skiway Corp.; pg. 586, pg. 749
Lambert, Raymond D., Sr., Reg Mgr-Sls-Retail Banking Grp - M&T Bank Corporation; pg. 777, pg. 1149
Lambert, Rebecca, Dir-Media Strategy - Best Buy Co., Inc.; pg. 1761, pg. 954
Lambert, Robert, Sr VP-Comml Sls - Budget Rent A Car System, Inc.; pg. 1901, pg. 1102
Lambert, Ryan, Mgr-Mktg - Neiman Marcus, Inc.; pg. 30, pg. 1684
Lambert, Sara, Sr Product Mgr - Batteries Plus Bulbs LLC; pg. 360, pg. 1860
Lambert, Todd, VP-Ticketing & Suite Sls - The Detroit Lions, Inc.; pg. 544, pg. 864
Lambertsen, Kate, Mgr-Trade & Mktg - Norwegian Cruise Line; pg. 1917, pg. 444
Lambeth, Deborah, Mgr-Mktg-Intl - Glen Raven, Inc.; pg. 693, pg. 1373
Lambing, Dwayne, Reg Mgr-Sls-East - Nordco, Inc.; pg. 1365, pg. 1884
Lambis, Jorge, Sr Analyst-Mktg - Amica Mutual Insurance Co.; pg. 1192, pg. 1602
Lamble, Karen, Sr Product Mgr-CV Ultrasound - Philips Electronics North America; pg. 662, pg. 782
Lambrecht, Steven, Brand Mgr-French's Mustard - Reckitt Benckiser Inc.; pg. 1136, pg. 1105
Lambright Sauder, Mike, Dir-Mktg - Sauder Woodworking Co.; pg. 941, pg. 1403
Lambright, Lisa, Dir-Mktg - JHB International, Inc.; pg. 696, pg. 320
Lambros, Jennifer, Dir-Integrated Mktg - The Hearst Corporation; pg. 1649, pg. 1239
Lamendola, Ronnie, Mgr-Mktg Comm - Garmin International, Inc.; pg. 1414, pg. 717

First page reference indicates Business Class Edition
Second page reference indicates Geographic Edition

LaMere, Jessica, Planner-Ad Sls - The Outdoor Channel; *pg.* 303, *pg.* 291

Lamey, Kristen, VP-Mktg - Nordstrom, Inc.; *pg.* 1779, *pg.* 1837

Lamey, Misty, Specialist-Digital Media - The Hershey Co.; *pg.* 1855, *pg.* 1538

Laming, Rebecca, Sr Dir-Mktg & Comm - Christopher & Dana Reeve Foundation; *pg.* 137, *pg.* 1120

Lamir, Deborah, Mgr-Brand, Creative Svcs, Corp Comm & Pub Affairs - CSX Corporation; *pg.* 1904, *pg.* 432

Lamka, Breanne, Assoc Mgr-Mktg - Trinchero Family Estates; *pg.* 1971, *pg.* 197

Lamm, Tammy, Mgr-Sls-Natl - Tampa Bay & Co.; *pg.* 1007, *pg.* 476

Lammers, Cassidy, Mgr-Workstation Mktg-Worldwide - Lenovo Group Ltd; *pg.* 427, *pg.* 1384

Lammers, Dale, VP-Sls & Program Mgmt-Global Metals & Mechanisms - Lear Corporation; *pg.* 229, *pg.* 907

Lammers, John, Div Product Dir - Advance Auto Parts, Inc.; *pg.* 197, *pg.* 1805

Lammert, Shannon, Sr Specialist-PR - Build-A-Bear Workshop, Inc.; *pg.* 950, *pg.* 993

LaMonica, Bryna, Brand Mgr-Caltrate - Pfizer Inc.; *pg.* 1581, *pg.* 1278

Lamont, Anita, Sr Dir-Comm - Charter Communications, Inc.; *pg.* 274, *pg.* 372

LaMontagne, Grant, Pres-Consumer Sls & Customer - Kimberly-Clark Corporation; *pg.* 1461, *pg.* 1720

LaMontagne, Jennifer, Mgr-Local Sls - Inner City Broadcasting Corporation; *pg.* 292, *pg.* 1243

LaMore, RuthAnn, Dir-Retail Mktg - Boar's Head Provisions Co., Inc.; *pg.* 841, *pg.* 465

Lamoreaux, Erika, Assoc Dir-Digital Media - The Clorox Company; *pg.* 327, *pg.* 169

Lamoreaux, Michelle, Mgr-Mktg - Arrow Electronics, Inc.; *pg.* 619, *pg.* 325

Lamothe, Nick, Sr Mgr-Retention Mktg - adidas America Inc.; *pg.* 1803, *pg.* 1500

LaMothe, Sheila, Mgr-Mktg - TRUMPF Inc.; *pg.* 1385, *pg.* 349

LaMotte, Molly, Sr Mgr-Campaign Mktg - Sonos, Inc.; *pg.* 675, *pg.* 263

Lamoureux, Robert, Sr VP & Head-Mktg-Asia Pacific-CIT Aerospace - CIT GROUP INC.; *pg.* 735, *pg.* 1212

Lamoureux, Tom, Mgr-Mktg - General Electric Company; *pg.* 1297, *pg.* 347

Lamp, Carmen, Sr Mgr-Med Affairs - Amgen Inc.; *pg.* 1493, *pg.* 291

Lamparske, Amy, Dir-Digital & Social Media - General Mills, Inc.; *pg.* 828, *pg.* 933

Lampe, Jeff, Dir-Mktg - Arrow Electronics, Inc.; *pg.* 619, *pg.* 325

Lampe, Jerry, Mgr-US Channel Partner Mktg - Hewlett-Packard Company; *pg.* 404, *pg.* 175

Lampe, Katie, Head-Adv Ops & Partner Mgr-Sls Ops - Twitter, Inc.; *pg.* 1285, *pg.* 228

Lampey, Todd, VP-Distr Sls - M&G Dura-Vent, Inc.; *pg.* 95, *pg.* 298

Lampon, Rafael, Sr Dir-Mktg & Product Mgmt - Applegate; *pg.* 837, *pg.* 1045

Lamport, Hollie, Dir-Media - Bloomingdale's, Inc.; *pg.* 1763, *pg.* 1204

Lamprey, Rich, Dir-Sports Mktg - AARON'S, INC.; *pg.* 912, *pg.* 486

Lamson, Pete, Sr VP-Sls & Mktg - Carbonite, Inc.; *pg.* 368, *pg.* 792

Lamy, Patrick, Sr Dir-Comml Plng-Liver Disease Therapeutic Area - Gilead Sciences, Inc.; *pg.* 1535, *pg.* 88

Lancaster, Darlene, Sr Dir-HR - Canadian Imperial Bank of Commerce; *pg.* 729, *pg.* 1935

Lancaster, Greg, Sr Mgr-Category Mgmt - LEGO Systems, Inc.; *pg.* 961, *pg.* 346

Lancaster, Michelle, Sr Mgr-PR - Microsoft Corporation; *pg.* 435, *pg.* 1824

Lance, Dan, Sr VP-Sls & Mktg - Kalmbach Publishing Co.; *pg.* 1656, *pg.* 1898

Lancellotti, Christina, Sr Analyst-Mktg - Ricoh Americas Corp.; *pg.* 462, *pg.* 538

Lancelot, James, Head-Digital Media Mgmt - Google Inc.; *pg.* 1249, *pg.* 153

Lancia, Mark, VP-Mktg & Adv-The Art Institutes - Education Management Corporation; *pg.* 601, *pg.* 1575

Lancia, Pete, Sr Dir-Mktg - QUALCOMM Incorporated; *pg.* 1873, *pg.* 207

Land, Ashley, Sr Mgr-HR - Lockheed Martin Corporation; *pg.* 229, *pg.* 762

Land, Dorothy, Specialist-Adv - Wynn Resorts Limited; *pg.* 1119, *pg.* 1030

Land, Elizabeth, Partner-Mktg & Bus Dev - Intel Corporation; *pg.* 645, *pg.* 266

Land, George, Sr VP-Programming & Production-NBA China - National Basketball Association; *pg.* 566, *pg.* 1264

Landan, Kim, Analyst-Mktg - American Honda Motor Co., Inc.; *pg.* 163, *pg.* 292

Landau, Adam, Brand Mgr-Lipton Tea - Unilever United States, Inc.; *pg.* 904, *pg.* 1061

Landau, Agnes, Sr VP-Mktg-Global - Clinique Laboratories LLC; *pg.* 503, *pg.* 1214

Landau, Beth, Supvr-Mktg - Reinke Manufacturing Company, Inc.; *pg.* 707, *pg.* 1010

Landau, Blake, Program Mgr-Social Media-Digital Support - Intel Corporation; *pg.* 645, *pg.* 266

Landau, Keith, Chief Product Officer & Exec VP - Genband, Inc.; *pg.* 640, *pg.* 1731

Landau, Laurie, Sr Dir-Oncology & Neuroscience PR - Eisai Inc.; *pg.* 1526, *pg.* 1133

Landau, Leo, VP-Sls & Mktg - Etronics, Inc.; *pg.* 1244, *pg.* 1146

Landers, Billy, Mgr-Solutions Mktg - Emerson Process Management; *pg.* 1334, *pg.* 1636

Landers, David, Brand Mgr-Tampax - The Procter & Gamble Company; *pg.* 1129, *pg.* 1418

Landers, Tim, VP-Mdsg - Hollander Sleep Products; *pg.* 927, *pg.* 411

Landes, Joseph, Gen Mgr-India Developer, Platform Evangelism & Sls - Microsoft Corporation; *pg.* 435, *pg.* 1824

Landfair, Joe, VP-Sls - ACH Food Companies, Inc.; *pg.* 835, *pg.* 1631

Landin, Hans, VP-Bus Advancement - The Timken Company; *pg.* 218, *pg.* 1408

Landis, Jennifer, Specialist-US Mktg - Pfizer Inc.; *pg.* 1581, *pg.* 1278

Landis, Jodi, Mgr-Product Comm - BlackRock, Inc.; *pg.* 724, *pg.* 1203

Landoll, Laura Tankersley, Mgr-PR-B2B Mktg - National Cattlemen's Beef Association; *pg.* 148, *pg.* 314

Landolt, Danielle, Mgr-Mktg & Comm - American Axle & Manufacturing Holdings, Inc.; *pg.* 198, *pg.* 879

Landolt, Noelle, Mgr-Online Mktg - David's Bridal, Inc.; *pg.* 23, *pg.* 1523

Landon, Clay, Mgr-District Sls - Makita U.S.A., Inc.; *pg.* 1358, *pg.* 120

Landon, Kristen N., Dir-Women's Health Mktg-Watson Pharmaceuticals - Allergan; *pg.* 1490, *pg.* 1101

Landowski, Ben, Sr Mgr-Mktg Ops - Capella Education Company; *pg.* 599, *pg.* 931

Landrieu, Mike, Sr Mgr-Consumer Insights - Brinker International, Inc.; *pg.* 1718, *pg.* 1676

Landro, Blake, Head-Global Brand Product - Google Inc.; *pg.* 1249, *pg.* 153

Landry, Alicia, Product Mgr - PC Connection, Inc.; *pg.* 452, *pg.* 1036

Landry, Diane, Dir-Mktg - National Arts Centre Corporation; *pg.* 566, *pg.* 1932

Landry, Ed, VP-Sls-US - McCormick & Company, Incorporated; *pg.* 1027, *pg.* 779

Landry, Mallory, Acct Mgr-Adv - Emmis Communications Corporation; *pg.* 285, *pg.* 685

Landry, Sheri, Asst VP-Global Event Mktg - Citigroup Inc.; *pg.* 735, *pg.* 1212

Landskron, Justin, VP-Digital Mktg & Online Production - Ubisoft Inc.; *pg.* 589, *pg.* 229

Landsman, Sarah, Mgr-Customer Team Mktg - The Procter & Gamble Company; *pg.* 1129, *pg.* 1418

Landt, Richard, VP-Aerospace Quality & Product Engrg-Global - PCC SPS Fastener Division; *pg.* 1059, *pg.* 1542

Landwehr, Rachel, Mgr-Mktg - Supercuts, Inc.; *pg.* 523, *pg.* 942

Lane, Allison, Mgr-Mktg Ops - ASICS America Corporation; *pg.* 1826, *pg.* 106

Lane, Ann, Coord-Mktg Comm - Theragenics Corporation; *pg.* 1431, *pg.* 527

Lane, Caitlin, VP-Direct Mktg - Citizens Financial Group, Inc.; *pg.* 737, *pg.* 1606

Lane, Christopher, Dir-Mktg & Bus Dev - Simon Property Group, Inc.; *pg.* 1112, *pg.* 690

Lane, Chuck, Dir-Incentive Travel & PR - Humana, Inc.; *pg.* 1204, *pg.* 734

Lane, Daniel, Mgr-Retail Mktg - Clarks Companies; *pg.* 1806, *pg.* 836

Lane, Gahn, VP-Svc Provider Sls - Westcon Group, Inc.; *pg.* 492, *pg.* 1345

Lane, Jennifer, Coord-Mktg-DuPont Industrial Biosciences - E.I. du Pont de Nemours & Company; *pg.* 1159, *pg.* 390

Lane, Katherine, Mgr-Apparel, ACC & EQT Product Mktg - Columbia Sportswear Company; *pg.* 1830, *pg.* 1501

Lane, Katherine, Sr Dir-Mktg & Corp Comm - Emulex Corporation; *pg.* 392, *pg.* 70

Lane, Katrina R., Exec VP & Gen Mgr-Consumer Mktg & Ops-US Consumer Cards - American Express Company; *pg.* 712, *pg.* 1190

Lane, Kelli, Assoc Vice Chancellor-Media & PR - Keiser University; *pg.* 603, *pg.* 443

Lane, Larry, Reg Mgr-Sls-Northern - GSC Enterprises, Inc.; *pg.* 1021, *pg.* 1746

Lane, LaTonya, Sr Acct Exec-Sls - Memphis Grizzlies; *pg.* 561, *pg.* 1645

Lane, Lisa, VP-Mktg - Automatic Data Processing, Inc.; *pg.* 357, *pg.* 1117

Lane, Matt, Sr Dir-Tournament Revenue - PGA Tour, Inc.; *pg.* 574, *pg.* 460

Lane, Michelle, Dir-Road Mktg - Bridgestone Americas, Inc.; *pg.* 201, *pg.* 1649

Lane, Mike, VP-Sls & Mktg-US - 3M Unitek Corporation; *pg.* 1483, *pg.* 150

Lane, Mike, Dir-PR - Steamboat Ski & Resort Corporation; *pg.* 1115, *pg.* 336

Lane, Nick, Asst VP-Adv & Mgr-Design - Westamerica Bancorporation; *pg.* 821, *pg.* 258

Lane, Nicki, Supvr-Mktg Recruiting & Dev - Caterpillar, Inc.; *pg.* 1321, *pg.* 650

Lane, Peter, Dir-Product Mgmt - Aruba Networks, Inc.; *pg.* 353, *pg.* 284

Lane, Sarah, Asst VP-Mktg & Sls Strategy - CarMax, Inc.; *pg.* 167, *pg.* 1800

Lane, Scott, Product Mgr - Zebra Technologies Corporation; *pg.* 690, *pg.* 628

Lane, Stacey, VP-Corp Mktg - Marshalls of MA, Inc.; *pg.* 1778, *pg.* 821

Lane, Stacey, VP-Corp Mktg - T.J. Maxx; *pg.* 1788, *pg.* 822

Lane, Stacey, VP-Corp Mktg - The TJX Companies, Inc.; *pg.* 1788, *pg.* 822

Lane, Susan, Sr Mgr-Mktg - Juniper Networks, Inc.; *pg.* 1260, *pg.* 286

Lane, Wendy, Brand Mgr-Lincoln Certified Pre-Owned-Ford Motor Company - The Lincoln Motor Company; *pg.* 182, *pg.* 878

LaNeve, Mark, VP-Mktg, Sls & Svc-US - Ford Motor Company; *pg.* 172, *pg.* 876

Laney, Micah, Sr Mgr-Assoc Comm-Global - Wal-Mart Stores, Inc.; *pg.* 1790, *pg.* 29

Laney, Scott, Product Mgr-Liquid Indus Coatings - PPG Industries, Inc.; *pg.* 1445, *pg.* 1579

Lang, Andras, VP-Data Mgmt Products - LOGMEIN, INC.; *pg.* 428, *pg.* 861

Lang, Audrey, Product Mgr - BrassCraft Manufacturing Company; *pg.* 1043, *pg.* 902

Lang, Cecilia, VP-Adv-Global - The Washington Post; *pg.* 1701, *pg.* 407

Lang, Dave, Sr Mgr-Digital Media - Baltimore Ravens Limited Partnership; *pg.* 532, *pg.* 755

Lang, Ed, Sr Dir-External Comm - Genentech, Inc.; *pg.* 1533, *pg.* 279

Lang, Germaine, Mgr-Mktg Programs - Bottomline Technologies Inc.; *pg.* 363, *pg.* 483

Lang, Jim, Bus Mgr-Global - Rock Valley Oil & Chemical Company; *pg.* 1179, *pg.* 631

Lang, John, Dir-Sls-Rosemount-North America - Emerson Process Management; *pg.* 1334, *pg.* 1636

Lang, Karena, Mgr-Mktg & Programs - Toshiba America, Inc.; *pg.* 681, *pg.* 1302

Lang, Kevin, Dir-Mktg Comm - Publix Super Markets, Inc.; *pg* 1031, *pg.* 437

Lang, Maggie, Sr Dir-Consumer Mktg & Engagement - Kimpton Hotel & Restaurant Group; *pg.* 1099, *pg.* 220

Lang, Marshall, Sr VP-Mktg - AGL Resources Inc.; *pg.* 1933, *pg.* 487

Lang, Max, Mgr-ECommerce Mktg - The Ritz-Carlton Hotel Company LLC; *pg.* 1110, *pg.* 766

Lang, Rick, Sr VP-Mktg & Sls-Central Div - Comcast Corporation; *pg.* 276, *pg.* 1560

Lang, Sarah R., Mgr-Mktg - Hewlett-Packard Company; *pg.* 404, *pg.* 175

Lang, Stuart, VP-North America Mktg - Electronic Arts Inc.; *pg.* 951, *pg.* 189

Lang, Tia, Dir-Media & Digital Strategy - Bacardi USA, Inc.; pg. 1956, pg. 417
Langan, Ed, Dir-Mktg-Displays & Client Peripherals Product Line Mgmt - Dell Inc.; pg. 383, pg. 1737
Langan, Jennifer, Dir-Mobility Product Mktg-Enterprise Bus Div - Samsung Electronics America, Inc.; pg. 669, pg. 1115
Langan, Kara, Sr VP-Mktg-Global - Elizabeth Arden, Inc.; pg. 507, pg. 448
Langan, Mark, Dir-Mktg - Endless Pools, Inc.; pg. 1833, pg. 1515
Langbein, Christian, VP-PR - Prada U.S.A. Corp.; pg. 31, pg. 1283
Langdon, Jacquelyn, Assoc Mgr-Promos-Customer Mktg - General Mills Canada Corp.; pg. 828, pg. 1926
Lange Engel, Alison, Sr Dir-Mktg-Global - LinkedIn Corporation; pg. 1262, pg. 160
Lange, Beth, Mgr-Brand, Digital & Media-Comml Vehicles - Mercedes-Benz USA, LLC; pg. 184, pg. 514
Lange, Brian, Dir-Mktg-Respiratory - GlaxoSmithKline; pg. 1536, pg. 1389
Lange, Jessica, Mgr-PR - The North Face, Inc.; pg. 1840, pg. 252
Lange, Nicole, Mgr-Mktg-Global - Fossil Group, Inc.; pg. 5, pg. 1735
Lange, Sara E., Mgr-PR - Neiman Marcus, Inc.; pg. 30, pg. 1684
Lange, Scott, Head-Creative - Google Inc.; pg. 1249, pg. 153
Lange, Terese, Supvr-Mktg Ops - True Value Company; pg. 1065, pg. 592
Langer, Bernd, Specialist-Consumables Sls - The Harris Products Group; pg. 1345, pg. 533
Langer, Eli, Producer-Social Media - CNBC; pg. 275, pg. 1059
Langer, Megan E., Mgr-PR - Intel Corporation; pg. 645, pg. 266
Langert, Dan, Mgr-Media & Digital - MillerCoors; pg. 254, pg. 1877
Langert, Dan, Mgr-Media & Digital - MillerCoors LLC; pg. 255, pg. 582
Langevin, Luc, Pres/COO-Specialty Products Grp - Cascades, Inc.; pg. 73, pg. 1950
Langfeldt, Leslie, Mgr-Mktg Comm - Jayco Inc.; pg. 1708, pg. 695
Langfield, Allan, Sr Dir-Product Dev - Comcast Corporation; pg. 276, pg. 1560
Langford, Holly, Mgr-Mktg - 7-Eleven, Inc.; pg. 1012, pg. 1672
Langford, Johanna, VP-Mktg Creative - J. Crew Group, Inc.; pg. 1773, pg. 1245
Langford, Kara, Mgr-Mktg-Pure Leaf - PepsiCo, Inc.; pg. 259, pg. 1327
Langford, William, Sr Dir-Field & Franchise Mktg - PepsiCo, Inc.; pg. 259, pg. 1327
Langhorst, Cynthia, Sr Dir-Comm & Mktg - Trammell Crow Company; pg. 1116, pg. 1689
Langin, Kevin, Sr Dir-PR - First National Bank; pg. 756, pg. 1553
Langin, Stacy, Asst VP-Mktg - Aramark; pg. 1013, pg. 1558
Langley, Andy, Reg Mgr-Technical & Mktg - Halliburton Company; pg. 978, pg. 1707
Langley, Cait, Coord-PR & Comm - Tahiti Tourisme North America, Inc.; pg. 1007, pg. 83
Langlie, Dawn, Specialist-Principal Mktg Comm - Medtronic, Inc.; pg. 1564, pg. 939
Langlois, Francois, Sr VP-Exploration & Production - Suncor Energy Inc.; pg. 985, pg. 1905
Langmann, Angela, Head-Buying, Sports & Outdoors & Sr Mgr - Amazon.com, Inc.; pg. 1226, pg. 1831
Langner, Colleen Mckay, Sr VP-Mktg Ops - Cox Communications, Inc.; pg. 279, pg. 501
Langner, Jake, Sr Dir-Global Channel Mktg - AliphCom, Inc.; pg. 616, pg. 212
Langona, Lori, Dir-Consumer Mktg - Plantronics, Inc.; pg. 663, pg. 270
Langsenkamp, Carl, VP-PR-Global - Xerox Corporation; pg. 494, pg. 365
Langston, John, Grp Product Mgr - Duke Energy Corporation; pg. 1940, pg. 1366
Langston, Mitch, Dir-Mktg-Intl - Popeye's Chicken & Biscuits; pg. 1745, pg. 517
Langston, Mitch, Dir-Mktg-Intl - Popeyes Louisiana Kitchen, Inc.; pg. 1745, pg. 517
Langtry, Paul, Sr Mgr-Acct Mgmt - Adobe Systems Incorporated; pg. 342, pg. 235
Lania, Kelly, Jr Coord-Mktg - Toys "R" Us, Inc.; pg. 968, pg. 1130
LaNiear, Charlotte, Brand Mgr-Clairol Global Fashion House - The Procter & Gamble Company; pg. 1129, pg. 1418
Lanka, Murali, COO-India-Store Ops, Sls, Bus Dev & Mktg - Wal-Mart Stores, Inc.; pg. 1790, pg. 29
Lankford, Doug, Dir-Home Theater Product Mktg - Bose Corporation; pg. 626, pg. 820
Lankford, Robert, Rep-Territory Sls-North & South Carolina - Honeywell International Inc.; pg. 407, pg. 1088
Lankford, Timothy, Mgr-Franchise Recruiting & Mktg - 7-Eleven, Inc.; pg. 1012, pg. 1672
Lanman, Mike, Sr VP-Enterprise Product Mgmt - Verizon Communications Inc.; pg. 1875, pg. 1309
Lann, Jessica, Mgr-Target Brand Product Dev - American Greetings Corporation; pg. 1615, pg. 1428
Lann, Loic, Brand Mgr-Air Wick - Reckitt Benckiser Inc.; pg. 1136, pg. 1105
Lannie, P. Anthony, Interim CFO - Apache Corporation; pg. 1034, pg. 1700
Lannon, Kirsten, Sr Mgr-Mktg-North America - The Timberland Company; pg. 1821, pg. 1039
Lanoue, Bob, Sr Mgr-IC Design - Vicor Corporation; pg. 1435, pg. 783
Lanphear, Charles, Dir-Media - United Services Automobile Association; pg. 1221, pg. 1743
Lanphear, Clare, Specialist-Digital Mktg - The Sherwin-Williams Company; pg. 1447, pg. 1435
Lanphear, Clare, Mgr-Social Media Mktg - Sherwin Williams; pg. 1448, pg. 1436
Lanpher, Gordon, Sr Dir-Digital Innovation - adidas America Inc.; pg. 1803, pg. 1500
Lans, Marty, Sr Dir-R&D, Storage, Networking & Interoperability - Hewlett-Packard Company; pg. 404, pg. 175
Lansche, Allan, Planner-Social Media - Turner Broadcasting System, Inc.; pg. 314, pg. 521
Lansing, Allen, Dir-Creative Svcs - KENS-TV; pg. 294, pg. 1741
Lansing, Susan, VP-Mktg & Branding - QUALCOMM Incorporated; pg. 1873, pg. 207
Lanson, Jim, Sr Engr-Technical Mktg - NetApp, Inc.; pg. 444, pg. 287
Lanthier Bandy, Julie, Assoc Vice Chancellor-Mktg - National University; pg. 605, pg. 119
Lanthier, Melissa, Sr Mgr-Mktg - VeriSign, Inc.; pg. 488, pg. 1799
Lantigua, Alvaro, Sr Mgr - AXA Equitable Life Insurance Company; pg. 1194, pg. 1199
Lantosca, Isabela, Sr Dir-Digital Mktg - ESPN, Inc.; pg. 285, pg. 340
Lantz-Rickard, Diane F., Brand Mktg Mgr-Global - Caterpillar, Inc.; pg. 1321, pg. 650
Lanuza, Jose Q., Dir-Sls-West Coast - Pressure BioSciences, Inc.; pg. 1586, pg. 844
Lanza, Alessandra, Dir-Corp PR - American Student Assistance; pg. 714, pg. 789
Lanzaro, Dana, Planner-Mdse - Levi Strauss & Co.; pg. 43, pg. 220
Lanzetta, Augie, VP-Sls - Inline Plastics Corp.; pg. 1460, pg. 370
Lanzi, Paul, Sr Mgr-Mobile, Web & Portal - Gilead Sciences, Inc.; pg. 1535, pg. 88
Lanzillotti, John, Dir-Mktg - Benjamin Moore & Co.; pg. 1440, pg. 1085
Lanzit, Kristi, Product Mgr-Projectors - Epson America Inc.; pg. 394, pg. 122
Lao, Norman, Dir-Creative - Sunshine Makers, Inc.; pg. 336, pg. 105
Lapa, Warren, Grp VP-Digital Products & Bus Dev - Time Warner Cable Inc.; pg. 312, pg. 1301
Lapeyre, Tre, Mgr-Product Mktg - Intralox LLC; pg. 1350, pg. 744
Lapierre, Kevin, Sr Dir-Product Mktg - CME Group Inc.; pg. 738, pg. 571
Lapierre, Kevin, Sr Dir-Product Mktg - CME Group, Inc.; pg. 738, pg. 571
Lapine, Kim, VP-Mktg - The Smith & Wollensky Restaurant Group, Inc.; pg. 1750, pg. 1293
Lapinski, Anne, Sr Mgr-Global IT Mktg Solutions - The Valspar Corporation; pg. 1449, pg. 945
Lapiska, Evan, Sr Specialist-PR - Target Corporation; pg. 1786, pg. 942
LaPlante, Marie, VP-Brand Mktg - Orbitz Worldwide, Inc.; pg. 1918, pg. 586
LaPoint, Chris, VP-Product Mgmt - SOLARWINDS, INC.; pg. 471, pg. 1666
LaPort, Kelsey McMurray, Mgr-Media - NBTY, Inc.; pg. 1572, pg. 1338
LaPorte, Patrick, Dir-Outbound Segment Mktg-Datacenter Networking - Brocade Communications Systems, Inc.; pg. 365, pg. 239
Laporte, Rick, VP-Sls-Worldwide - Fluke Corporation; pg. 1413, pg. 1819
Lapp, Melissa, Mgr-Adv-US - American Express Company; pg. 712, pg. 1190
Lappetito, Caroline, Dir-Media Rels-Global - Merck & Co., Inc.; pg. 1566, pg. 1077
Lara, Al, Specialist-Media Rels-Northeast Utilities - Eversource; pg. 1942, pg. 845
Lara, Albania, Mgr-Mktg Comm-Chemical Intermediates - BASF Corporation; pg. 1149, pg. 1066
Lara, Emilia, Sr Mgr-Hispanic Mktg Strategy & Plng - J.C. Penney Company, Inc.; pg. 1774, pg. 1732
Lara, Jesus L., Exec VP-Digital Media - Spanish Broadcasting System Inc.; pg. 310, pg. 440
Lara, Laura, Mgr-Creative Design & Mktg Comm - W.W. Grainger, Inc.; pg. 1390, pg. 625
Laraway, Russ, Sr Dir-SMB - Twitter, Inc.; pg. 1285, pg. 228
Larch, Gary, Mgr-Sls-North Texas - Jones-Blair Company; pg. 1443, pg. 1682
Lardi, Brian, Mgr-Online Mktg - Shell Lubricants; pg. 217, pg. 1714
Lares, Sofia, Mgr-PR, Media & Integrate Comm-Matrix - L'Oreal USA; pg. 514, pg. 1252
Larew, Kristin, Reg Mgr-Mktg - Public Service Enterprise Group Incorporated; pg. 1950, pg. 1097
Larian, Jason, Mgr-Bus Dev & Mktg - MGA Entertainment, Inc.; pg. 964, pg. 300
Larimore, Nikki, Coord-Adv - MFA Incorporated; pg. 1479, pg. 976
Lariviere, Jacinthe, Dir-Mktg of Innovative Products-Away-Home Canada - Cascades, Inc.; pg. 73, pg. 1950
Lark, John, Sr Dir-Global Cloud Solutions Mktg - Ariba, Inc.; pg. 353, pg. 283
Larke, Priscilla, Mgr-Mktg & ECommerce - Fossil Group, Inc.; pg. 5, pg. 1735
Larkin, Jaya, Mgr-Sls & Svcs - St. Augustine, Ponte Vedra & The Beaches Visitors & Convention Bureau; pg. 1006, pg. 461
Larkin, Katie, Exec VP-Adv Sls Res & Strategy - NBC Universal, Inc.; pg. 300, pg. 1266
Larkin, Peter, Publr-Channel Media & Assoc Publr-TechTarget Networking - TechTarget, Inc.; pg. 482, pg. 837
Larnder, Greg, VP-Sls - TeraGo Inc.; pg. 1284, pg. 1934
LaRocca, Paul, VP-Brand Mktg - Foxwoods Resort Casino; pg. 549, pg. 353
Larocca, Sal, Pres-Global Ops & Mdsg - National Basketball Association; pg. 566, pg. 1264
Larocca, Tracee, Brand Dir-Creative - Taco Bell Corp.; pg. 1752, pg. 117
Laroche, Bernard, Dir-Cloud Mgmt Product Mktg - VMware, Inc.; pg. 490, pg. 179
Laroche, Emmanuel, VP-Mktg & Consumer Insights & Head-Mktg-Global - Symrise, Inc.; pg. 1183, pg. 1125
LaRocque, Charisse, Coord-Online Media-Digital Mktg Svcs - Sabre Holdings Corporation; pg. 1922, pg. 1745
Larocque, Ed, Mgr-Mktg-Natl - Toyota Motor Sales, U.S.A., Inc.; pg. 193, pg. 296
LaRosa, Carol, Mgr-Mktg Comm-Global - Schneider Electric USA, Inc.; pg. 1306, pg. 650
Larose, James, VP-Digital Mktg-Home Lending - Wells Fargo & Company; pg. 819, pg. 232
LaRose, Joseph, Mgr-Bus Products - Sentry Insurance Group; pg. 1217, pg. 1895
Larot, Linda, Specialist-Mktg - Philips Lighting; pg. 1303, pg. 806
Larrazabal, Melissa, Product Mgr-Hispanic Program - Janssen Pharmaceutica Products, L.P.; pg. 1548, pg. 1125
Larrea, Dan, Sr Dir-Team Travel - Milwaukee Brewers Baseball Club, Inc.; pg. 562, pg. 1878
Larsen, Brad, VP-Sls & Mktg - Telluride Ski & Golf Company LLP; pg. 587, pg. 336
Larsen, Britany, VP-Mktg - Bluefly, Inc.; pg. 1232, pg. 1205
Larsen, Chris, Product Mgr-Surfacing - Harsco Rail; pg. 1345, pg. 1623
Larsen, Dana, Brand Mgr-Adv & Mktg - Ace Hardware Corporation; pg. 1040, pg. 644
Larsen, Dane, Mgr-Mktg-Creative Lab - Google Inc.; pg. 1249, pg. 153
Larsen, Deborah, Head-Brand & Dir-Global Mktg-Weight

Control - GlaxoSmithKline; *pg.* 1536, *pg.* 1565
Larsen, Deborah, Head-Brand & Dir-Global Mktg-Weight Control - GlaxoSmithKline Consumer Healthcare; *pg.* 510, *pg.* 1554
Larsen, Emily, Sr VP-Mktg - Kohl's Corporation; *pg.* 1775, *pg.* 1870
Larsen, Jennifer, Sr Dir-Brand & Reputation - Maritz Inc.; *pg.* 1914, *pg.* 977
Larsen, Kristin E., Mgr-Mktg Comm - Cardinal Health, Inc.; *pg.* 1512, *pg.* 1448
Larsen, Rick D., Mgr-Sls & Mktg Dev - Intel Corporation; *pg.* 645, *pg.* 266
Larsen, Roger, Brand Mgr - PNM Resources, Inc.; *pg.* 1949, *pg.* 1135
Larsen, Sandra, Specialist-Mktg-Comml Print, Mdsg & Premiums - Nestle USA, Inc.; *pg.* 883, *pg.* 96
Larsen, Sara, VP-Mktg & Comm-North America - Dassault Systems Enovia; *pg.* 382, *pg.* 851
Larsen, Stephanie, VP-Mktg-Men's & Kid's - Macy's, Inc.; *pg.* 1778, *pg.* 1417
Larsen, Walter F., Jr., Mgr-Natl Sls-Elenco Electronics Toy Div - Elenco Electronics, Inc.; *pg.* 953, *pg.* 670
Larson, Amanda, Assoc Mgr-Mktg & Events - Hulu LLC; *pg.* 1257, *pg.* 274
Larson, Amy, VP-Digital Mktg - The Children's Place, Inc.; *pg.* 22, *pg.* 1119
Larson, Amy, VP-Mktg & ECommerce-Glasses.com - Luxottica Retail; *pg.* 8, *pg.* 1460
Larson, Beth, VP-Advisor Mktg - Thrivent Financial for Lutherans; *pg.* 1219, *pg.* 944
Larson, Daniel, Assoc Dir-Mktg - Merck & Co., Inc.; *pg.* 1566, *pg.* 1077
Larson, Dena, Mgr-Mktg - General Mills, Inc.; *pg.* 828, *pg.* 933
Larson, Doug, Sr Mgr-Employee Comm - Symantec Corporation; *pg.* 478, *pg.* 161
Larson, Dylan, Dir-Server Platform Mktg - Intel Corporation; *pg.* 645, *pg.* 266
Larson, Erik, Sr Strategist-Social Media - AT&T Inc.; *pg.* 1868, *pg.* 358
Larson, Jack, Dir-Creative - Avatar Studios; *pg.* 270, *pg.* 992
Larson, Kathy, Mgr-Adv - The York News-Times; *pg.* 1703, *pg.* 1020
Larson, Keith, Mgr-Consumer Products Sls-North America - Winegard Company; *pg.* 688, *pg.* 702
Larson, Kim, Dir-Bus, Mktg & Ops-Worldwide - Microsoft Corporation; *pg.* 435, *pg.* 1824
Larson, Laura, Brand Mgr-Shopper Mktg - Kimberly-Clark Corporation; *pg.* 1461, *pg.* 1720
Larson, Leah, VP & Dir-Creative-UGG AUSTRALIA - Deckers Outdoor Corporation; *pg.* 1807, *pg.* 100
Larson, Robert, Product Mgr-Core News - Bloomberg L.P.; *pg.* 725, *pg.* 1204
Larson, Scott, Dir-Global Campaigns Creative - MoneyGram International, Inc.; *pg.* 783, *pg.* 1684
Larson, Scott, Brand Mgr - Noosa Yoghurt; *pg.* 886, *pg.* 310
Larson, Scott, Sr Dir-Sls-Wal-Mart Team - Pinnacle Foods Group LLC; *pg.* 889, *pg.* 1104
Larson, Sheryl, Head-Mktg Comm - Northern Trust Corporation; *pg.* 787, *pg.* 585
Larson, Stefanie, Principal-Mktg - FedEx Corporation; *pg.* 1907, *pg.* 1642
Larson, Thomas, Specialist-Integrated Mktg - Lucky Brand Dungarees, Inc.; *pg.* 29, *pg.* 301
Larson, Thomas, Mgr-Retail Mktg-NTB, Tire Kingdom & Merchant's - TBC Corporation; *pg.* 1889, *pg.* 457
Larter, Stacey, Dir-Mktg, Oil & Gas-Global Solutions-Schneider Electric - Schneider Canada, Inc.; *pg.* 1374, *pg.* 1928
Larue, Jennifer, VP-Product Dev - MARTHA STEWART LIVING OMNIMEDIA, INC.; *pg.* 1661, *pg.* 1256
LaRussa, Gina, Sr VP-HR & Ad Sls - NBC Universal, Inc.; *pg.* 300, *pg.* 1266
Las, Emily, VP & Head-Bus-US Digital Mktg - MasterCard Worldwide Inc.; *pg.* 780, *pg.* 988
Lasala, Chris, Dir-New Products & Solutions-Publr Bus Grp - Google Inc.; *pg.* 1249, *pg.* 153
Lasala, Fran, Acct Exec-New Media - WABC-TV Inc.; *pg.* 317, *pg.* 1312
Lasater, Mike, VP-Sls & Mktg-MGP Ingredients - MGP Ingredients, Inc.; *pg.* 877, *pg.* 714
LaScala, Chris, VP-Mktg - Great Wolf Resorts, Inc.; *pg.* 1093, *pg.* 1866
Laschansky, Steven C., Mgr-Mktg - 3M Company; *pg.* 1142, *pg.* 956
Lasche, Krista, Brand Mgr-Private-Seasonal - Michaels Stores, Inc.; *pg.* 1127, *pg.* 1722
LaScolea, Gabby, Mgr-Online Mktg & Media - Ann Inc.; *pg.* 18, *pg.* 1195
Laseca, Erick, Head-Corp Data Strategy & Mktg Info Sys - The Kraft Heinz Company; *pg.* 871, *pg.* 641
Laserstein, Diana, Mgr-Reg Mktg Plng - Kohl's Corporation; *pg.* 1775, *pg.* 1870
Lash, Brian, Dir-Mktg - Scott's Liquid Gold-Inc.; *pg.* 335, *pg.* 323
Lashaway, Cassidy, Mgr-Interactive Mktg-Intl - Paramount Pictures Corporation; *pg.* 304, *pg.* 138
Lasker, John, VP-Programming & Acq-Digital Media - ESPN, Inc.; *pg.* 285, *pg.* 340
Laskiewicz, Lynn, Dir-Strategic Sourcing-Mktg - Walgreen Co.; *pg.* 1608, *pg.* 605
Laskin, Eliad, Assoc Dir-Social Media Strategies - The Hartford Financial Services Group, Inc.; *pg.* 1202, *pg.* 352
Laskoski, Shawn, VP-Product Mgmt-Residential Solutions - Ingersoll-Rand Company; *pg.* 1349, *pg.* 1370
Laskowski, Joe, Sr Dir-Global Mktg, Comm & eBusiness - Haemonetics Corporation; *pg.* 1538, *pg.* 802
Lasky, Emily, Supvr-Digital Media - Essence Magazine; *pg.* 1639, *pg.* 1229
Laspe, Forrest, Sr Dir-Ops Analysis - 7-Eleven, Inc.; *pg.* 1012, *pg.* 1672
Lassel, Karim, VP-Sls & Mktg - CGGVeritas Services (U.S.) Inc.; *pg.* 973, *pg.* 1703
Lassen-Hoch, Marjorie, Dir-Mktg-Comcast Bus - Comcast Corporation; *pg.* 276, *pg.* 1560
Lasseter, John, Chief Creative Officer-Walt Disney - Pixar Animation Studios; *pg.* 304, *pg.* 85
Lasso, Carolina, Mgr-Product Mktg - Google Inc.; *pg.* 1249, *pg.* 153
Last, Anna, Dir-Creative - Williams-Sonoma, Inc.; *pg.* 1140, *pg.* 234
Last, Keith, Brand Mgr-Lighters - BIC Corporation; *pg.* 501, *pg.* 369
LaStella, Andrea L., Asst Mgr-Mktg - Toll Brothers, Inc.; *pg.* 115, *pg.* 1541
Lastrapes, Shavon, Mgr-Mktg - Sam's Club; *pg.* 1783, *pg.* 29
Lasure-Roy, Sharon, Sr Mgr-Social Media & Digital Comm - Blue Cross & Blue Shield of Florida, Inc.; *pg.* 1507, *pg.* 432
Laszcz, Linda, Dir-Strategic Mktg & Interactive Mktg - MTD Products, Inc.; *pg.* 1057, *pg.* 1478
Laszlo, Deana, Brand Mgr-Experience - The Gap, Inc.; *pg.* 1770, *pg.* 218
Latasa, Fred, Sr VP-Mktg - WebMD Health Corporation; *pg.* 1288, *pg.* 1313
Lateef, Jarama, Product Mgr-GI Mktg - Shire; *pg.* 1593, *pg.* 1532
Latendresse, Ann, Dir-Brand Mktg - Great Clips, Inc.; *pg.* 510, *pg.* 937
Later, Jeffrey P., Area VP-Comm Sls - General Cable Corporation; *pg.* 83, *pg.* 729
Later, Jill, Brand Mgr-Dove Body Wash - Unilever United States, Inc.; *pg.* 904, *pg.* 1061
Latham, Adam, Sr Mgr-Corp Brand - Intersil Corporation; *pg.* 647, *pg.* 146
Latham, Chris, Asst VP & Mgr-Mktg - CB&S Bank; *pg.* 732, *pg.* 8
Latham, JoAnne, Exec Dir-Mktg - Excelsior College; *pg.* 601, *pg.* 1137
Latham, Megan, Sr Dir-Sls Plng & Strategy-People.com - Time Inc.; *pg.* 1693, *pg.* 1300
Latham, Paul, VP-Membership, Mktg, Svcs & Travel - Costco Wholesale Corporation; *pg.* 1765, *pg.* 1820
Lathan, Kris Hunter, Dir-Pub & Media Rels - Northwestern Memorial HealthCare; *pg.* 1574, *pg.* 585
Lathers, Elizabeth, Mgr-Experiential Mktg - FCA US LLC; *pg.* 170, *pg.* 868
Lathrop, John, Mgr-Market-Retail Sls - Samsung Telecommunications America, LLC; *pg.* 670, *pg.* 1736
Laties, Michelle, Dir-Mktg Comm-Novartis Oncology - Novartis Corporation; *pg.* 1574, *pg.* 1273
Latino, Dominick, Dir-Internet Strategy & Mktg - Pool Corporation; *pg.* 1843, *pg.* 743
Latlip, David, Dir & Project Mgr-Mktg - Waddell & Reed Financial, Inc.; *pg.* 818, *pg.* 721
LaTorre, Lou, Pres-Fox Cable Adv Sls - FX Networks, LLC; *pg.* 288, *pg.* 131
Latta, Jill, Sr Mgr-Americas Field Mktg - Cisco Systems, Inc.; *pg.* 372, *pg.* 240
Lattina, Alan, Reg Product Mgr-West & Mgr-Sls-Intl - Centrifugal & Mechanical Industries, Inc.; *pg.* 1322, *pg.* 994
Lattman, Matt, Sr Dir-Bus-Small Bus Banking - Capital One Financial Corporation; *pg.* 730, *pg.* 1789
Latts, Kate, VP-Mktg - Heaven Hill Distilleries, Inc.; *pg.* 1964, *pg.* 725
Latty, Joe, Mgr-Mktg Ops - Arrow Electronics, Inc.; *pg.* 619, *pg.* 325
Lau, Ashley, Mgr-Digital Media - Esurance, Inc.; *pg.* 1243, *pg.* 217
Lau, Jason, Sr Mgr-Market Res - DIRECTV Group Holdings, LLC; *pg.* 281, *pg.* 79
Lau, Jonathan, Mgr-Mktg-Sponsorships - Aon Risk Services Inc.; *pg.* 1193, *pg.* 564
Lau, Linda, Assoc Mgr-Mktg - Inc.com LLC; *pg.* 1258, *pg.* 1243
Lau, Mark, Brand Mgr-Global - NIKE, Inc.; *pg.* 1812, *pg.* 1492
Lau, Melissa, Dir-Adv Solutions - United Online, Inc.; *pg.* 1286, *pg.* 308
Lau, O. Daryn, VP & Gen Mgr-Comm Product Div - PMC-Sierra, Inc.; *pg.* 664, *pg.* 287
Lau, Paul, Engr-PR SW QA - EMC Corporation; *pg.* 391, *pg.* 825
Lau, Tony, Sr VP-Staff & Product Mgmt - MetroPCS, Inc.; *pg.* 1872, *pg.* 1683
Lauber, Ernie, VP-Sls-Americas - Fluke Corporation; *pg.* 1413, *pg.* 1819
Lauber, Kimberly, Dir-Mktg-Random House Children's Books - Penguin Random House; *pg.* 1675, *pg.* 1276
Lauber, Kimberly, Dir-Mktg-Random House Children's Books - Penguin Random House; *pg.* 1675, *pg.* 1276
Lauber, Steve, VP-Corp Adv - The Hearst Corporation; *pg.* 1649, *pg.* 1239
Laubusch, Christa, Supvr-Adv Promotion - Kalmbach Publishing Co.; *pg.* 1656, *pg.* 1898
Lauchaire, Nicole, VP-Corp Mktg & Comm - Varsity Brands, Inc.; *pg.* 1847, *pg.* 1647
Laucht, Lucy, Sr Mgr-Digital Dev & Social Media - J. Crew Group, Inc.; *pg.* 1773, *pg.* 1245
Lauck, Jenny, VP-Influencer Svcs-SheKnows Media - Blogher Inc.; *pg.* 1232, *pg.* 45
Laudano, Julie, Analyst-Mktg & Pricing - Honeywell International Inc.; *pg.* 407, *pg.* 1088
Laudenslayer, Sandy N., Dir-Mktg - McKesson Corporation; *pg.* 1560, *pg.* 222
Lauderdale, Debbie, Media Planner & Buyer - Jelly Belly Candy Company; *pg.* 1857, *pg.* 86
Lauer, Allyson, Mgr-Membership Sls & Mktg - Maryland Zoological Society, Inc.; *pg.* 561, *pg.* 758
Lauer, Heather, Brand Mgr - Cargill Meat Solutions; *pg.* 846, *pg.* 722
Lauer, Kenny, VP-Digital & Mktg - Golden State Warriors, LLC; *pg.* 550, *pg.* 171
Lauer, Mark, Mgr-Mktg Ops - General Motors Company; *pg.* 175, *pg.* 881
Lauf, Jay, Sr VP, Publr-Quartz-The Atlantic Media Grp - The Atlantic Monthly Group; *pg.* 1618, *pg.* 396
Laufer, Kate, VP-PR - Sidney Frank Importing Co., Inc.; *pg.* 1970, *pg.* 1184
Laufer, Patricia, Mgr-Mktg - Samsung Electronics America, Inc.; *pg.* 669, *pg.* 1115
Laughlin, Anne, Area Dir-PR & Field Comm - Republic Services, Inc.; *pg.* 107, *pg.* 19
Laughlin, Gary, Dir-Mktg & Comm-Grp Benefits - Sun Life Financial Inc.; *pg.* 806, *pg.* 1944
Laughlin, Kiernan, Brand Mgr-Innovation-Lysol - Reckitt Benckiser Inc.; *pg.* 1136, *pg.* 1105
Laughlin, Linda A., Dir-Media Rels - Verizon Communications Inc.; *pg.* 1875, *pg.* 1309
Laughlin, Nicole, VP-Mktg - Meijer, Inc.; *pg.* 1779, *pg.* 888
Laughlin, Patrick, Dir-Mktg & Project Mgmt - Fuchs North America.; *pg.* 857, *pg.* 774
Laughlin, Sean, Dir-Mktg Strategy - Harley-Davidson, Inc.; *pg.* 178, *pg.* 1874
Laughlin, Tim, Mgr-Social Media, Adv & Brand Strategy - Xcel Energy Inc.; *pg.* 1955, *pg.* 946
Lauher, Thomas, Dir-Mktg & Media Plng - Webster University; *pg.* 610, *pg.* 1004
Laukes, Edward, VP-Mktg - Toyota Motor Sales, U.S.A., Inc.; *pg.* 193, *pg.* 296
Laundre, Kelly, Sr Mgr-Home2 Suites by Hilton - Hilton Worldwide, Inc.; *pg.* 1094, *pg.* 1791
Laure, Julianne, Analyst-Mktg - Pepsi Beverages Company; *pg.* 258, *pg.* 1342
Laureano, Paul, VP-Integrated Sls & Mktg - FX Networks, LLC; *pg.* 288, *pg.* 131

Lauren, Ralph, Chm & Chief Creative Officer - Ralph Lauren Corporation; *pg.* 46, *pg.* 1284
Laurence, Jolie, Sr Mgr-Mktg-Multipack - Frito-Lay North America, Inc.; *pg.* 1853, *pg.* 1730
Laurence, Suzanne, Sr Dir-Comm - Aeropostale, Inc.; *pg.* 17, *pg.* 1188
Laurento, Patty, Sr Mgr-Mktg - Nobel Learning Communities, Inc.; *pg.* 605, *pg.* 1593
Lauria, Jessica, Sr Dir-Brand Comm - Chobani LLC; *pg.* 847, *pg.* 1318
Lauria, Kristen, VP-Mktg & Global Bus Svcs - International Business Machines Corporation; *pg.* 418, *pg.* 1138
Lauria, Lynnette, VP-Portfolio-Mktg - Simon Property Group, Inc.; *pg.* 1112, *pg.* 690
Lauria, Wendy, Assoc Publr-Mktg-Harper's Bazaar - The Hearst Corporation; *pg.* 1649, *pg.* 1239
Laurich, Frank, Sr Strategist-Mktg Comm - Principal Financial Group, Inc.; *pg.* 796, *pg.* 706
Laurita, Suzanne, Asst VP-Retailer Mktg - Simon Property Group, Inc.; *pg.* 1112, *pg.* 690
Lauritzen, Cara, Assoc Mgr-Mktg - MillerCoors LLC; *pg.* 255, *pg.* 582
Lauro, Cathy, Mgr-Shopper Mktg - Unilever United States, Inc.; *pg.* 904, *pg.* 1061
Laurora, Massimo, Area Mgr-Sls-Europe - Setra Systems, Inc.; *pg.* 1428, *pg.* 802
Laursen, Chelsea, Mgr-Experience Mktg - Clif Bar Inc.; *pg.* 848, *pg.* 83
Lauschke, Scott M., VP-Sls & Customer Svc - AK Steel Holding Corporation; *pg.* 1311, *pg.* 1479
Lauten, Russell, Sr Mgr-IR - Hanesbrands Inc.; *pg.* 26, *pg.* 1394
Lautenschlager, Fred, Reg Sls Mgr-Central Reg - General Motors of Canada Ltd.; *pg.* 177, *pg.* 1931
Lautier, Amber, Mgr-Sls - Sumner Communications Inc.; *pg.* 1690, *pg.* 338
Laux, Geoffrey, Mgr-Brand Mktg-Credit Card Acq - Capital One Financial Corporation; *pg.* 730, *pg.* 1789
Laux, Melissa, VP-NBC Sports Sls Mktg - NBC Universal, Inc.; *pg.* 300, *pg.* 1266
Lauzon, Bruno, Rep-Sls - Sleeman Unibroue Quebec; *pg.* 265, *pg.* 1950
Lauzon, Philip, Dir-Creative - MC2; *pg.* 431, *pg.* 1153
Lavachek, Chad, Mgr-Retail Mktg-TOMS Eyewear - Toms Shoe's Inc; *pg.* 1821, *pg.* 276
LaVallee, Courtney, Dir-Mktg Comm - Chick-fil-A, Inc.; *pg.* 1721, *pg.* 492
LaVallee, Liz, Mgr-Digital Mktg - The Vermont Teddy Bear Company; *pg.* 969, *pg.* 1767
Lavallee, Michelle M., Head-Sls & Mktg-Global - Raven Industries, Inc.; *pg.* 1888, *pg.* 1625
Lavallee, Stephanie, Product Mgr & Mgr-Market-MIS Instrumentation - Cardinal Health, Inc.; *pg.* 1512, *pg.* 1448
Lavariere-Sanchez, Karen J., Dir-PR - Massachusetts Mutual Life Insurance Company; *pg.* 1207, *pg.* 845
Lavelle, Desmond, Strategist-Creative - Facebook, Inc.; *pg.* 1245, *pg.* 143
Lavelle, Stewart, CMO & Chief Sls Officer - Magellan Health Services, Inc.; *pg.* 1557, *pg.* 337
Lavender, Michelle, Sr Mgr-Mktg-Activation - Turner Broadcasting System, Inc.; *pg.* 314, *pg.* 521
Lavengood, Carol, Dir-Mktg Comm - Cummins Inc.; *pg.* 1326, *pg.* 676
Laverde, Roberto Ramirez, Dir-Mktg-Mexico - Bacardi USA, Inc.; *pg.* 1956, *pg.* 417
Laverentz, Holly, Mgr-Sls-Natl - Tampa Bay & Co.; *pg.* 1007, *pg.* 476
Laverick, Tim, Sr VP-Infrastructure Products - ANADIGICS, Inc.; *pg.* 617, *pg.* 1128
Lavers, Glen, Sr Engr-Technical Mktg - Cisco Systems, Inc.; *pg.* 372, *pg.* 240
Laverty, Dave, VP-Mktg & Big Data & Analytics - IBM; *pg.* 410, *pg.* 1449
Lavi, Daniella, Media Buyer-Natl Television - Palisades Media Group, Inc.; *pg.* 452, *pg.* 275
Lavi, Elana, Reg Dir-Mktg - KB Home; *pg.* 90, *pg.* 134
Lavi, Yonatan, Product Dir - Lavi Industries Inc.; *pg.* 93, *pg.* 299
Lavigna, Chris, Mgr-Retail & Contractor Segment Mktg - CertainTeed Corporation; *pg.* 74, *pg.* 1589
Lavigne, Larry, Acct Mgr-Sls - 3M Company; *pg.* 1142, *pg.* 956
Lavigne, Mary, Specialist-Mktg Comm-Body Protection - Honeywell International Inc.; *pg.* 407, *pg.* 1088
Lavin, Jason, Dir-Mktg-Dr. Scholl's - Bayer Healthcare Consumer Care Division; *pg.* 1500, *pg.* 1087
Lavin, Joseph, Mgr-Section-Freshness Gum Product Dev Platform Head - Mondelez International; *pg.* 877, *pg.* 1344
Lavin, Lauren L, Mgr-Mktg-Direct Mail & CRM - The Gymboree Corporation; *pg.* 25, *pg.* 77
Lavin, Mike, Sr Mgr-Global Product Mktg-Xbox Live Svc - Microsoft Corporation; *pg.* 435, *pg.* 1824
Lavis, Benjamin, Dir-Sls-Intl - Megger Inc.; *pg.* 1422, *pg.* 1557
Lavoie, Denise, Mgr-Mktg Comm - Henkel Corporation; *pg.* 1165, *pg.* 1535
Lavoie, John, Dir-Brand & Consumer Mktg Comm - Samsung Electronics America, Inc.; *pg.* 669, *pg.* 1115
Lavorante, Jennifer, Dir-Mktg - John Hardy USA, Inc.; *pg.* 7, *pg.* 1246
Lavrusik, Vadim, Product Mgr - Facebook, Inc.; *pg.* 1245, *pg.* 143
Lavsi, Nitasha, Dir-Digital Mktg - L'Oreal USA; *pg.* 514, *pg.* 1252
Law, Doneen, Dir-Global Mktg & Innovation-Pharmaceutical & Nutrition - Ashland Inc.; *pg.* 972, *pg.* 726
Law, Evelyn, Brand Mgr-Retail - NIKE, Inc.; *pg.* 1812, *pg.* 1492
Law, Jamie, Reg Dir-PR - Kimpton Hotel & Restaurant Group; *pg.* 1099, *pg.* 220
Law, John J., VP-Global OE Sls - The Timken Company; *pg.* 218, *pg.* 1408
Law, Karen, Sr Mgr-Client Mktg-Grocery, Drug & Mass - Valassis Communications, Inc.; *pg.* 1287, *pg.* 897
Law, Leonard, Product Mgr - Google Inc.; *pg.* 1249, *pg.* 153
Law, Matt, Brand Mgr-Teavana - Starbucks Corporation; *pg.* 897, *pg.* 1840
Law, Todd, Head-Global Brand-Opioid Products - Pfizer Inc.; *pg.* 1581, *pg.* 1278
Law, Veronica, Dir-Product Mgmt - Expedia, Inc.; *pg.* 1244, *pg.* 1814
Law, Will, Chief Architect-Media Cloud Engrg - Akamai Technologies, Inc.; *pg.* 1226, *pg.* 807
Lawall, Kevin, Dir-Global Mktg-Maternal & Neonatal Health - GlaxoSmithKline Consumer Healthcare; *pg.* 510, *pg.* 1554
Lawee, Ian, Dir-Product & Tech-Precision Converters - Analog Devices, Inc.; *pg.* 617, *pg.* 839
Lawenda, David, Head-US Global Mktg Solutions - Facebook, Inc.; *pg.* 1245, *pg.* 143
Lawing, John, Pres, COO & VP-Advanced Products - AVX Corporation; *pg.* 623, *pg.* 1616
Lawinger, Mark, Mgr-Product Line-Fixtures - Sloan Valve Company; *pg.* 1062, *pg.* 613
Lawkins, Bob, Dir-Interactive Mktg - 1-800-Flowers.com, Inc.; *pg.* 1758, *pg.* 1151
Lawler, Angela, VP-Field Mktg-Merrill Lynch - Bank of America Corporation; *pg.* 718, *pg.* 1362
Lawler, Colleen, VP-Membership Bus Ops & Mktg Strategy - American Medical Association; *pg.* 130, *pg.* 564
Lawler, Danielle, Dir-Social Media - Adorama Camera Inc.; *pg.* 1398, *pg.* 1187
Lawler, Joseph, Mgr-Field Mktg - MillerCoors; *pg.* 254, *pg.* 1877
Lawler, Logan S., Mgr-Social Media Dev - Dell Inc.; *pg.* 383, *pg.* 1737
Lawless, Jennifer, Mgr-Sls Comm - Anheuser-Busch Companies, LLC; *pg.* 237, *pg.* 991
Lawless, Nola, Sr Mgr-Mktg-L'Oreal Paris Hair Color - L'Oreal USA; *pg.* 514, *pg.* 1252
Lawless, Nola, Sr Mgr-Mktg-L'Oreal Paris Hair Color - Maybelline LLC; *pg.* 516, *pg.* 1257
Lawley, Pat, Mgr-Mktg Tech - Dr Pepper Snapple Group, Inc.; *pg.* 250, *pg.* 1729
Lawlor, Brian, Sr Dir-HR - The Hain Celestial Group, Inc.; *pg.* 860, *pg.* 1172
Lawlor, David, Dir-Sls & Mktg - International Paper Company; *pg.* 1460, *pg.* 1644
Lawlor, Mary, Mgr-Color Mktg - Kelly-Moore Paint Company, Inc.; *pg.* 1443, *pg.* 198
Lawnicki, Benjamin, Brand Mgr-Strategy & Innovation, Pull-ups & GoodNites Brands - Kimberly-Clark Corporation; *pg.* 1461, *pg.* 1720
Lawrence, Anne, Dir-Mktg & Dev - South Dakota Symphony Orchestra; *pg.* 584, *pg.* 1625
Lawrence, Barb, Assoc Mgr-Mktg - American Girl LLC; *pg.* 949, *pg.* 1871
Lawrence, Benny, Mgr-Media & Brand Innovation - Audi of America, Inc.; *pg.* 164, *pg.* 1784
Lawrence, Beth, Exec VP-Digital Adv Sls - Scripps Networks Interactive, Inc.; *pg.* 1279, *pg.* 1638
Lawrence, David, Div Mgr-Mdse & ECommerce - The Men's Wearhouse, Inc.; *pg.* 44, *pg.* 1711
Lawrence, David, Sr VP & Reg Mgr-Sls-Northeast - NetJets Inc.; *pg.* 1917, *pg.* 1442
Lawrence, David, Product Mgr - Shimano American Corporation; *pg.* 1845, *pg.* 116
Lawrence, Gary, Sr Dir-Pur - Colorado Rockies Baseball Club, Ltd.; *pg.* 542, *pg.* 317
Lawrence, Gaysha, Dir-US Consumer Mktg-Prepaid - MasterCard Worldwide Inc.; *pg.* 780, *pg.* 988
Lawrence, Jennifer, Mgr-CRM Mktg - Select Comfort Corporation; *pg.* 942, *pg.* 942
Lawrence, Jill, Dir-Mktg - Cosi, Inc.; *pg.* 1723, *pg.* 600
Lawrence, Julie, Sr Specialist-Mdsg-Cooking Products - General Electric Company; *pg.* 1297, *pg.* 347
Lawrence, Kelly, Mgr-Global Mktg-Digital Print Solutions - The Lubrizol Corporation; *pg.* 1171, *pg.* 1481
Lawrence, Lesli, Sr VP & Dir-Creative-Print Adv - CBS Broadcasting Inc.; *pg.* 273, *pg.* 1210
Lawrence, Lesli, Sr VP & Dir-Creative-Print Adv - CBS Corporation; *pg.* 273, *pg.* 1210
Lawrence, Meredith, Dir-Field Mktg-North America - Polycom, Inc.; *pg.* 664, *pg.* 249
Lawrence, Nathan P., VP-Mktg & Bus Dev - Pressure BioSciences, Inc.; *pg.* 1586, *pg.* 844
Lawrence, Randal, Dir-Content Mktg - AT&T Inc.; *pg.* 1867, *pg.* 1674
Lawrence, Ronette, Sr Dir-Plng & User Res - Microsoft Corporation; *pg.* 435, *pg.* 1824
Lawrence, Sarah, Brand Mgr-Retail - NIKE, Inc.; *pg.* 1812, *pg.* 1492
Lawrence, Tara, VP-User Experience & Creative - Quidsi, Inc.; *pg.* 1276, *pg.* 1076
Lawrence, Todd, Mgr-Field Mktg - Subaru of America, Inc.; *pg.* 191, *pg.* 1050
Lawrence, Tom, Sr VP-Sls & Mktg - Taco Incorporated; *pg.* 1077, *pg.* 1601
Lawrenz, John, Head-Sls Team & Dir - Del Monte Foods, Inc.; *pg.* 852, *pg.* 304
Lawson, Byron, Dir-Worldwide IBM Software One Sls & Bus Partners - International Business Machines Corporation; *pg.* 418, *pg.* 1138
Lawson, Christine, Sr VP-Sls & Catering - Kimpton Hotel & Restaurant Group; *pg.* 1099, *pg.* 220
Lawson, Cory, Assoc Mgr-Mktg - Transitions Optical, Inc.; *pg.* 1432, *pg.* 458
Lawson, Cynthia, VP-PR & Comm - DePaul University; *pg.* 600, *pg.* 572
Lawson, Deanna, Bus Mgr - Riverside Ford; *pg.* 189, *pg.* 885
Lawson, Elaine, VP & Head-Bus-US Digital Mktg - MasterCard International, Inc.; *pg.* 780, *pg.* 1326
Lawson, Elaine, VP & Head-Bus-US Digital Mktg - MasterCard Worldwide Inc.; *pg.* 780, *pg.* 988
Lawson, Jenna, Specialist-Events Mktg, Industry & Customer Engagement - LinkedIn Corporation; *pg.* 1262, *pg.* 160
Lawson, Josh, VP-Intl Interactive Mktg - Paramount Pictures Corporation; *pg.* 304, *pg.* 138
Lawson, Karen, Sr Dir-Product Tech - NIKE, Inc.; *pg.* 1812, *pg.* 1492
Lawson, Larry, Mgr-Mktg & Mdsg - Dr Pepper Snapple Group, Inc.; *pg.* 250, *pg.* 1729
Lawson, Libby, VP-PR - Tyson Foods, Inc.; *pg.* 902, *pg.* 35
Lawson, Mark, VP-Digital Mktg & Sls - Cox Communications, Inc.; *pg.* 279, *pg.* 501
Lawson, Matt, Mng Dir-Ads Mktg - Google Inc.; *pg.* 1249, *pg.* 153
Lawson, Matthew C, Acct Dir-Partnership Mktg - International Speedway Corporation; *pg.* 553, *pg.* 420
Lawson, Rachel, Brand Mgr - Mondelez International; *pg.* 877, *pg.* 1344
Lawson, Rowan, Sr Mgr-Mktg & Market Dev-OEMs, Bose Ride Team-Worldwide - Bose Corporation; *pg.* 626, *pg.* 820
Lawson, Sam, Mgr-Corp Dev & Ticket Sls - Chicago White Sox Ltd.; *pg.* 539, *pg.* 570
Lawson, Scott, Gen Dir-Mktg - General Motors Company; *pg.* 175, *pg.* 881
Lawson, Shawn, Brand Mgr - International Paper Company; *pg.* 1460, *pg.* 1644
Lawson, Terry, Mgr-Mktg - Allen & Hoshall, Inc.; *pg.* 66, *pg.* 1641
Lawson-Zilai, Lauren, Dir-PR - Goodwill Industries International, Inc.; *pg.* 1771, *pg.* 776
Lawton, Aana, Dir-Mktg - L'Oreal USA; *pg.* 514, *pg.* 1252
Lawton, John, Dir-Mktg - EnerSys Inc.; *pg.* 1334, *pg.* 1584
Lawton, Kerry, Mgr-Global Mktg-SEBAGO - Wolverine World Wide, Inc.; *pg.* 1822, *pg.* 905

First page reference indicates Business Class Edition
Second page reference indicates Geographic Edition

Lawton, Laura, Head-PR & Social Media - PRAHealth Sciences; *pg.* 1585, *pg.* 1388
Lawton, Michael, Dir-Creative - Fortune; *pg.* 1642, *pg.* 1232
Lawton, Suzanne, Head-Strategic Mktg - Greene, Tweed & Co.; *pg.* 1344, *pg.* 1544
Lawyer, Justin, Sr Product Mgr - Google Inc.; *pg.* 1249, *pg.* 153
Lax, Jon, Dir-Product Design - Facebook, Inc.; *pg.* 1245, *pg.* 143
Lay, Erica, Dir-Worldwide Mktg Comm - Apple Inc.; *pg.* 350, *pg.* 73
Lay, Katie, Sr Mgr-Product Mgmt-Amazon Elements - Amazon.com, Inc.; *pg.* 1226, *pg.* 1831
Lay-Flurrie, Jenny, Sr Dir-Accessibility, Online Safety & Privacy - Microsoft Corporation; *pg.* 435, *pg.* 1824
Laycock, Dan, Sr Mgr-PR-Microsoft Surface & Microsoft Hardware - Microsoft Corporation; *pg.* 435, *pg.* 1824
Laycock, Rob, VP-Mktg - Pacers Basketball, LLC; *pg.* 573, *pg.* 689
Layfield, Mike, Dir-Dairy Strategy-US Cattle Mktg - Zoetis Inc.; *pg.* 1611, *pg.* 1067
Laylin, Carla, Dir-Mktg - T. Marzetti Company; *pg.* 900, *pg.* 1444
Layman, Chuck, Sr Mgr-Mktg-Customer Experience - United Parcel Service, Inc.; *pg.* 1928, *pg.* 522
Layman, Emily, Sr Coord-Product Mktg - CarMax, Inc.; *pg.* 167, *pg.* 1800
Layman, Heather, Assoc Dir-Mktg - The Nature Conservancy; *pg.* 151, *pg.* 1774
Layne, Elizabeth Trongone, Dir-Mktg - Bonobos; *pg.* 39, *pg.* 1205
Layne, Paige C., Mgr-Corp Comm-Customer Billing, Payments & Products-Smart Grid - Duke Energy Corporation; *pg.* 1940, *pg.* 1366
Laytham, Amelia, Supvr-Mktg - United Parcel Service, Inc.; *pg.* 1928, *pg.* 522
Layton, Ann, Dir-Inland Marine-Trng & Mktg - The Travelers Companies, Inc.; *pg.* 1220, *pg.* 352
Layton, Joel, Sr Dir-Digital Commerce - Lands' End, Inc.; *pg.* 1776, *pg.* 1857
Layton, Krista, Mgr-Sls - Plano Molding Company; *pg.* 1887, *pg.* 652
Layton, Louis, Dir-Product Mgmt - Fiserv, Inc.; *pg.* 397, *pg.* 1855
Layton, Wade, Mng Dir-CIT Comm, Media & Entertainment & Co-Head - CIT GROUP INC.; *pg.* 735, *pg.* 1212
Lazar, Colleen, Sr Dir-Corp Mktg - CME Group, Inc.; *pg.* 738, *pg.* 571
Lazaroff, Bill, Exec VP-Product Dev & Design - LIFETIME BRANDS, INC.; *pg.* 1127, *pg.* 1161
Lazarus, Kyle, Mgr-Social Media-Consumer Bus Div - Samsung Electronics America, Inc.; *pg.* 669, *pg.* 1115
Lazarus, Peter, Sr VP-Adv Sls - NBC Universal, Inc.; *pg.* 300, *pg.* 1266
Lazarus, Steven, Dir-Digital Mktg & Customer Acq - The Children's Place, Inc.; *pg.* 22, *pg.* 1119
Lazarz, Peter, Dir-Mktg - Angie's List Inc; *pg.* 1228, *pg.* 682
Lazatin, Miguel, Sr Mgr-Mktg-Security Sys Div - Sony Electronics, Inc.; *pg.* 676, *pg.* 209
Lazerow, Michael, Chief Strategy Officer - salesforce.com, inc.; *pg.* 1278, *pg.* 226
Lazopoulos, Emanuel, Sr VP-Sls, Mktg & Product Mgmt-North America - FRESH DEL MONTE PRODUCE INC.; *pg.* 856, *pg.* 418
Lazorisak, Paul, VP-Customer Mktg & Analytics - The Talbots, Inc.; *pg.* 34, *pg.* 824
Lazowski, John, Sr Dir-Mktg, Insights & Innovation - ACH Food Companies, Inc.; *pg.* 835, *pg.* 1631
Lazzara, Steve, Sr VP-Sls & Mktg - Kraco Enterprises, LLC; *pg.* 210, *pg.* 68
Lazzareschi, Matthew, Specialist-Mktg - Amica Mutual Insurance Co.; *pg.* 1192, *pg.* 1602
Lazzaro, Joseph, Dir-Digital Sls - Gannett Co., Inc.; *pg.* 1643, *pg.* 1790
Lazzaro, Nick, Exec VP-Strategy & Product Dev - Synchronoss Technologies, Inc.; *pg.* 479, *pg.* 1047
Lazzaroni, Deanna, Mgr-Global Content Mktg & Social Media Strategy - LinkedIn Corporation; *pg.* 1262, *pg.* 160
Le Bras-Brown, Rob, Sr VP-Mktg, Printing & Personal Sys - Hewlett-Packard Company; *pg.* 404, *pg.* 175
Le Fave, Marta, Mgr-Northeast Sls - Tri-K Industries, Inc.; *pg.* 523, *pg.* 1099
Le, Amelia, Mgr-Digital Mktg - MATTEL, INC.; *pg.* 962, *pg.* 81
Le, Emmie, Mgr-Field Mktg - Advanced Micro Devices, Inc.; *pg.* 613, *pg.* 282
Le, Heather, Product Mgr - RetailMeNot Inc.; *pg.* 1782, *pg.* 1665
Le, John, Mgr-Mktg - Softlayer Technologies Inc; *pg.* 471, *pg.* 1686
Le, Leslie, Asst Mgr-Mktg - Neiman Marcus, Inc.; *pg.* 30, *pg.* 1684
Le, Monique, Program Mgr-Relationship Mktg-US Retail - BlackRock, Inc.; *pg.* 724, *pg.* 1203
Le, Stephanie, Sr Coord-Mktg Comm - QUALCOMM Incorporated; *pg.* 1873, *pg.* 207
Leach, Michelle, Mgr-PR - Brocade Communications Systems, Inc.; *pg.* 365, *pg.* 239
Leach-Kemon, Erin, Producer-Social Media-Global Digital Mktg - Starbucks Corporation; *pg.* 897, *pg.* 1840
Leach-Rouvi, Amanda, VP-Mktg-North America - Robert Half International Inc.; *pg.* 462, *pg.* 145
Leachman, Melissa, Sr Mgr-Demand Generation-Digital Strategy - Citrix Online LLC; *pg.* 1235, *pg.* 99
Leader, Adam, Product Mgr-Local Listings Freshness & Provider Data - Google Inc.; *pg.* 1249, *pg.* 153
Leader, Ian, Product Head-Google Calendar - Google Inc.; *pg.* 1249, *pg.* 153
Leadley, Kim, Mgr-Media & Analyst Rels - Progress Software Corporation; *pg.* 457, *pg.* 786
Leaf, Lynne, Dir-Digital Mktg - Merrill Corporation; *pg.* 1664, *pg.* 962
League, Jennifer, Sr Mgr-Content - F5 Networks, Inc.; *pg.* 396, *pg.* 1835
Leahey, Jim, VP-Sls & Mktg - Oakland Athletics Limited Partnership; *pg.* 571, *pg.* 172
Leahy, John David, Mgr-New Product Dev - Kind LLC; *pg.* 868, *pg.* 1249
Leahy, Mackenzie, Assoc Mgr-Social Media-US - Reebok International Ltd.; *pg.* 1817, *pg.* 811
Leak, Latria, Asst Dir-Community Rels & Cause Mktg - Orlando Magic; *pg.* 572, *pg.* 455
Leal, Mabel, Sr Strategist-Adv - Salt River Project; *pg.* 707, *pg.* 26
Leaming, Kim, Sr Mgr-Direct Mktg & Global Promos - Holland America Line Inc.; *pg.* 1911, *pg.* 1836
Leamon, Kevin, Asst VP-Acct Mgmt & Creative Svcs - Horace Mann Companies; *pg.* 1203, *pg.* 662
Leamon, Roy, III, VP-Production & Tech - Texas Monthly; *pg.* 1692, *pg.* 1666
Leander, Felix, Dir-Digital Mktg - Visa Inc.; *pg.* 816, *pg.* 230
Leander, Felix, Dir-Digital Mktg - Visa U.S.A., Inc.; *pg.* 817, *pg.* 231
Leano, Jonathan, Mgr-Retail Experience Mktg-US - Hewlett-Packard Company; *pg.* 404, *pg.* 175
Leapley, Jason, Mgr-Product Line Bus - Emerson Process Management; *pg.* 1334, *pg.* 1636
Leard, Christian, VP-Trade Mktg & Writing Segment - Newell Rubbermaid Inc.; *pg.* 1128, *pg.* 515
Learish, John, Sr VP-Mktg - Rite Aid Corporation; *pg.* 1590, *pg.* 1519
Leary, Jennifer, Dir-Brand Strategy, Innovation & Social Media - Electrolux Home Products North America; *pg.* 54, *pg.* 1366
Leary, Lisa, VP-Bus Sls - FairPoint Communications, Inc.; *pg.* 1871, *pg.* 1366
Leary, Mary, Sr Specialist-Weekly Adv Mktg - Target Corporation; *pg.* 1786, *pg.* 942
Leary, Tom, Dir-Strategic Mktg - Alcoa Inc.; *pg.* 65, *pg.* 1188
Lease, Brendan, Mgr-Mktg - United Parcel Service, Inc.; *pg.* 1928, *pg.* 522
Leask, Bill, Product Dir - PR Newswire Association LLC; *pg.* 1678, *pg.* 1283
Leath, Sharon, Dir-Integrated Content Mktg - Dr Pepper Snapple Group, Inc.; *pg.* 250, *pg.* 1729
Leatherby, Jim, Product Mgr - Halliburton Company; *pg.* 978, *pg.* 1707
Leatherwood, Steve, VP-Mktg - Anixter International Inc.; *pg.* 1313, *pg.* 614
Leavell, Melissa, Dir-Adv - Ingles Markets, Incorporated; *pg.* 1023, *pg.* 1358
Leavengood, Marty, Area VP-Sls - CenturyLink, Inc; *pg.* 1870, *pg.* 317
Leavister, Ed, Mgr-Sls-Eastern Reg - Crown Prince, Inc.; *pg.* 850, *pg.* 67
Leavitt, Kim, Dir-Global Partner Mktg - Red Hat, Inc.; *pg.* 460, *pg.* 1388
Leavitt, Mark, Global Head-Tech, Media & Telcomm Investment Banking Grp - Piper Jaffray Companies; *pg.* 794, *pg.* 941
Leavitt, Stephanie, Dir-Social Media & Branded Content - Carnival Corporation; *pg.* 1902, *pg.* 441
Leavy, David, Chief Comm Officer & Sr Exec VP-Corp Mktg & Affairs - Discovery Communications, Inc.; *pg.* 282, *pg.* 777
LeBard, Amy, Coord-North America Applied Mktg - Aveda Corporation; *pg.* 499, *pg.* 917
LeBeau, Andrew, Dir-Product Mktg-BIOVIA - Dassault Systems Enovia; *pg.* 382, *pg.* 851
LeBeau, Mike, Product Mgr - Facebook, Inc.; *pg.* 1245, *pg.* 143
LeBel, Tim, Sr VP-Sls-Mars Chocolate North America - Mars North America; *pg.* 1859, *pg.* 1072
Leber-Bell, Jennifer, Dir-Website Mktg & Corp PR - Lettuce Entertain You Enterprises, Inc.; *pg.* 1735, *pg.* 580
Lebert, Shelley, Brand Mgr - Rust-Oleum Corporation; *pg.* 1447, *pg.* 664
Lebess, Charlie, Head-Creative Agency - Google Inc.; *pg.* 1249, *pg.* 153
LeBlanc, Brandon, Sr Mgr-Mktg Comm - Microsoft Corporation; *pg.* 435, *pg.* 1824
Leblanc, Carol, Sr VP-Consumer & Education Products - Smithsonian Magazine; *pg.* 1687, *pg.* 404
LeBlanc, Deborah Armanino, Dir-Sls & Mktg - Armanino Foods of Distinction, Inc.; *pg.* 837, *pg.* 100
LeBlanc, Diane, Sr Dir-Visa Comml Solutions - Visa Inc.; *pg.* 816, *pg.* 230
LeBlanc, Dick, Exec VP-Sls-Global - Flow International Corporation; *pg.* 1337, *pg.* 1821
LeBlanc, Erica, Dir-Mktg-Home Cleaning Innovation - S.C. Johnson & Son, Inc.; *pg.* 334, *pg.* 1889
LeBlanc, Katherine, Mgr-Mktg & Comm - Smoothie King Franchises, Inc.; *pg.* 1750, *pg.* 743
Leblanc, Keith, Mgr-Mktg - Sterilite Corporation; *pg.* 1138, *pg.* 848
LeBloch, Denise, VP-Mktg & Comm - Marianjoy Rehabilitation Hospital; *pg.* 1558, *pg.* 669
Leblond, Ryan, Coord-Allied Brands Mktg - The Boston Beer Company, Inc.; *pg.* 239, *pg.* 790
LeBoeuf, Nicole, Sr Mgr-ECommerce Ops - The Dress Barn, Inc.; *pg.* 1767, *pg.* 1343
Lebotesis, Sheri, Asst Mgr-Adv - Toll Brothers, Inc.; *pg.* 115, *pg.* 1541
Lebovitz, Jamie, Sr Mgr-Reg Mktg & Field Mdsg - AT&T Mobility LLC; *pg.* 619, *pg.* 488
Lebow, Jodi, Sr Mgr-Mktg-Demand Generation - Teradata Corporation; *pg.* 483, *pg.* 1447
Lebowitz, Jackie, Product Mgr-People.com - Time Inc.; *pg.* 1693, *pg.* 1300
Lecarpentier Assor, Charlotte, Dir-Global Mktg-DAVIDOFF Perfumes & JOOP Perfumes - Coty, Inc.; *pg.* 506, *pg.* 1219
Lechan, Jeremy, Specialist-Media Rels - Tufts Medical Center; *pg.* 1603, *pg.* 801
Leciejewski, Brent, Mgr-Mktg-Global - Flextronics International Ltd.; *pg.* 81, *pg.* 245
Lecker, Lori, Dir-Comm-Global Rolled Products & Global Innovation - Alcoa Inc.; *pg.* 65, *pg.* 1188
Leckey, David, Exec VP-Consumer Mktg - American Media, Inc.; *pg.* 1615, *pg.* 410
Leckie, Sarah, Dir-Programs & New Product Dev - Canlan Ice Sports Corporation; *pg.* 536, *pg.* 1907
LeClair, Joe, Brand Mgr-Mktg-Adv, Brand Mgmt & Interactive - Liberty Mutual Insurance Group Inc.; *pg.* 1205, *pg.* 797
LeClare, Phil, Dir-PR - Forrester Research, Inc.; *pg.* 1642, *pg.* 807
Leclerc, Manon, Head-Bus Travel, Mktg & Comm - IBM Canada Limited; *pg.* 411, *pg.* 1923
LeCount, Andy, Exec Dir-Chain Sls - HBG Books, Inc.; *pg.* 1648, *pg.* 1238
Lecours, Bernard, Dir-Strategic Mktg-Adjacent Markets - General Electric Company; *pg.* 1297, *pg.* 347
Ledanski, Nick, Mgr-Military Sls - Rose Packing Company; *pg.* 892, *pg.* 556
Ledbetter, Letty, VP-Global Product & Svcs PR - Oracle Corporation; *pg.* 450, *pg.* 191
Ledbetter, Stacey, Dir-Brand & Integrated Mktg - The Ratner Companies; *pg.* 520, *pg.* 1809
Lederer, Matt, Sr Dir-Sports Strategic Mktg - Comcast Corporation; *pg.* 276, *pg.* 1560
Lederer, Matthew, Sr Dir-Sports Strategic Mktg - Comcast Cable Communications, Inc.; *pg.* 276, *pg.* 1560
Lederer, Valerie, Dir-Traditional Creative - PetSmart, Inc.; *pg.* 1481, *pg.* 18
Lederman, Mark, Sr Dir-Product Mgmt - Synchronoss Technologies, Inc.; *pg.* 479, *pg.* 1047
Lederman, Michelle, Acct Mgr-Media Solutions - LinkedIn

Corporation; *pg.* 1262, *pg.* 160
Ledesma, Rosalind, Brand Mgr-Multicultural - Boost Mobile; *pg.* 1869, *pg.* 107
Ledford, Michael, Sr Mgr-Product Dev-Freestanding Ranges - Whirlpool Corporation; *pg.* 62, *pg.* 872
Ledgar, Peter A., Mgr-Sls - Waterous Company; *pg.* 1387, *pg.* 965
Ledgerwood Noble, Jill, Mgr-Digital Mktg-North America - Shell Lubricants; *pg.* 217, *pg.* 1714
Ledieu, Eric, Dir-Chief Mktg-Sedans, Sports Cars & NISMO - Nissan North America, Inc.; *pg.* 186, *pg.* 1633
LeDoux, Chamain, Sr Mgr-Mktg-MLB Sponsorship - T-Mobile US, Inc.; *pg.* 676, *pg.* 1816
Leduc, Katherine, Sr Mgr-Customer Analytics - CVS Health Corporation; *pg.* 1765, *pg.* 1610
Leduc, Natacha, Brand Mgr-Imodium, Lactaid, Anusol, Combantrin & Microlax - Johnson & Johnson Inc.; *pg.* 1552, *pg.* 1923
Lee, Aaron, Mgr-Adv Insertion & Ops - AT&T; *pg.* 1865, *pg.* 258
Lee, Aaron, Dir-Product Mktg - Lexar Media, Inc.; *pg.* 1262, *pg.* 146
Lee, Agnes, Sr Dir-IR - ResMed Inc.; *pg.* 1589, *pg.* 207
Lee, Alex, Sr Mgr-Mktg - E&J Gallo Winery; *pg.* 1962, *pg.* 149
Lee, Allen, Mgr-Sls - Advanced Micro Devices, Inc.-Markham; *pg.* 345, *pg.* 1922
Lee, Alyssa, Assoc Mgr-Mktg-Instore Bakery Div - Rich Products Corporation; *pg.* 892, *pg.* 1150
Lee, Amanda, Mgr-PR - Tech Data Corporation; *pg.* 482, *pg.* 416
Lee, Amy, Specialist-Mktg - Jaguar Land Rover North America LLC; *pg.* 180, *pg.* 1081
Lee, Andrea, Head-Mktg & Seller Marketplace-Home Improvement & Home Automation - Amazon.com, Inc.; *pg.* 1226, *pg.* 1831
Lee, Angela, Assoc Mgr-Mktg - Ocean Spray Cranberries, Inc.; *pg.* 887, *pg.* 827
Lee, Barry L., Product Dir - Cumberland Pharmaceuticals, Inc.; *pg.* 1521, *pg.* 1650
Lee, Ben, Sr Mgr-Product Support & Customer Experience - Yahoo! Inc.; *pg.* 1289, *pg.* 289
Lee, Bennett, Analyst-Product Mktg - United Parcel Service, Inc.; *pg.* 1928, *pg.* 522
Lee, Billy, Mgr-Sls & Mktg - Owens Corning; *pg.* 102, *pg.* 1476
Lee, Bob, Mgr-Creative - Daktronics, Inc.; *pg.* 633, *pg.* 1624
Lee, Brandon, Mgr-Digital Media Ops - Williams-Sonoma, Inc.; *pg.* 1140, *pg.* 234
Lee, Brian, Dir-Digital Media - Guthy-Renker LLC; *pg.* 289, *pg.* 273
Lee, Brian, Brand Mgr-Eggo - Kellogg Company; *pg.* 831, *pg.* 870
Lee, Bryan, Dir-Indus Solutions & Sls - salesforce.com, inc.; *pg.* 1278, *pg.* 226
Lee, Cary, Sr Product Mgr - Kohl's Corporation; *pg.* 1775, *pg.* 1870
Lee, Chris, Reg Mgr-Sls - Bacardi USA, Inc.; *pg.* 1956, *pg.* 417
Lee, Chris, Dir-Brand Partnerships & Social Media Engagement - Esurance, Inc.; *pg.* 1243, *pg.* 217
Lee, Christina, Assoc Mgr-CRM Mktg - Sony Corporation of America; *pg.* 675, *pg.* 1293
Lee, Christine, Sr Dir-US Trends & Innovation - McDonald's Corporation; *pg.* 1737, *pg.* 645
Lee, Christine, Sr Product Mgr - Twitter, Inc.; *pg.* 1285, *pg.* 228
Lee, Chung, Product Mgr-Mktg-Global - Skyworks Solutions, Inc.; *pg.* 674, *pg.* 862
Lee, Cindy, Sr Mgr-Mktg - Intuit Inc.; *pg.* 769, *pg.* 158
Lee, Cynthia, VP-Integrated Sls & Mktg - Warner Bros. Entertainment Inc.; *pg.* 319, *pg.* 54
Lee, Dae, Dir-Integrated Mktg Strategy - PETCO Animal Supplies, Inc.; *pg.* 1480, *pg.* 206
Lee, Dan, Product Mgr-Cloud Svcs - Accusoft; *pg.* 1398, *pg.* 470
Lee, Daniel, Dir-Product Mgmt-Digital Adv Effectiveness - The Nielsen Company B.V.; *pg.* 1671, *pg.* 1272
Lee, Danielle, Dir-Media Innovation - AT&T; *pg.* 1865, *pg.* 258
Lee, David, VP-Mktg Specialist IV - BB&T Corporation; *pg.* 723, *pg.* 1393
Lee, David, Mgr-Reg Sls & Mktg-Central Reg - BMW of North America, LLC; *pg.* 166, *pg.* 1133
Lee, David, Sr Mgr-Ticket Ops - Cleveland Browns Football Company LLC; *pg.* 541, *pg.* 1406
Lee, David, Sr Dir-New Bus Mktg - DirectBuy, Inc.; *pg.* 1766, *pg.* 694
Lee, David, Chief Creative Officer - Squarespace Inc.; *pg.* 1282, *pg.* 1295
Lee, Debbie, Mgr-Creative Production - Plum Organics; *pg.* 890, *pg.* 85
Lee, Donald, Sr Mgr-Category Sourcing Mktg & Adv - The Walt Disney Company; *pg.* 317, *pg.* 52
Lee, Erica Stock, Dir-ECommerce & Mktg - O'Reilly Auto Parts; *pg.* 214, *pg.* 872
Lee, Florence, Sr Dir-Creative Svcs - Giorgio Armani Corporation; *pg.* 25, *pg.* 1234
Lee, Frank, Client Partner-Global Mktg Solutions - Facebook, Inc.; *pg.* 1245, *pg.* 143
Lee, Gail, Asst VP-Global Mktg Skincare - L'Oreal USA; *pg.* 514, *pg.* 1252
Lee, H. Travis, Sr VP-Mktg-Global - Cynosure, Inc.; *pg.* 1521, *pg.* 858
Lee, Helen, Dir-Social Media - Athleta; *pg.* 19, *pg.* 181
Lee, Howard, Mgr-Digital Mktg-Ahnu & Hoka One One - Deckers Outdoor Corporation; *pg.* 1807, *pg.* 100
Lee, Hwa Shih, VP-Digital Media - Palisades Media Group, Inc.; *pg.* 452, *pg.* 275
Lee, Hyuk, VP-Mktg Intelligence - Time Warner Cable Inc.; *pg.* 312, *pg.* 1301
Lee, Jacalyn, Dir-PR - Care.com; *pg.* 1960, *pg.* 850
Lee, Jackie, Brand Mgr-Innovation - Welch Foods Inc.; *pg.* 909, *pg.* 815
Lee, Jacklyn, Mgr-Fragrance Mktg - Parfums Christian Dior, Inc; *pg.* 519, *pg.* 1276
Lee, Jae Young, Coord-Mktg-Global - Coty, Inc.; *pg.* 506, *pg.* 1219
Lee, Jaeho, Sr Mgr-Mktg - The Allstate Corporation; *pg.* 1189, *pg.* 639
Lee, Jaison, Dir-Mktg Strategy - AutoNation, Inc.; *pg.* 165, *pg.* 423
Lee, James, Head-Mktg-Life Sciences - Cognizant Technology Solutions Corporation; *pg.* 377, *pg.* 1124
Lee, Jamille, Mgr-Sls - Apartment Investment and Management Company; *pg.* 1079, *pg.* 316
Lee, Jane, Brand Mktg Dir-Fin - Heineken USA Inc.; *pg.* 252, *pg.* 1352
Lee, Jane, Brand Mgr-Dremel - Robert Bosch Tool Corp; *pg.* 1060, *pg.* 634
Lee, Jason, Mgr-Sls - House of Raeford Farms, Inc.; *pg.* 864, *pg.* 1386
Lee, Jay, Head-Category Experiences Product, Nike+ - NIKE, Inc.; *pg.* 1812, *pg.* 1492
Lee, Jeanice, Dir-Digital, Social & Relationship Mktg - Lexus Division; *pg.* 182, *pg.* 294
Lee, Jennifer, Brand Mgr-Plng - Levi Strauss & Co.; *pg.* 43, *pg.* 220
Lee, Jennifer, VP & Mgr-Direct Mktg - Wells Fargo & Company; *pg.* 819, *pg.* 232
Lee, Jenny, Dir-Mktg-Global - The Donna Karan Company LLC; *pg.* 23, *pg.* 1225
Lee, Jenny, Sr Mgr-Education Tech Innovation - Johnson & Johnson; *pg.* 1549, *pg.* 1091
Lee, Jenny, Sr Dir-Fin - TEN: The Enthusiast Network; *pg.* 1691, *pg.* 1298
Lee, Jenny, Sr Mgr - The Walt Disney Company; *pg.* 317, *pg.* 52
Lee, Jessica, Mgr-Mktg-SEM - Macy's East; *pg.* 1777, *pg.* 1254
Lee, Jiyoung, Product Mgr-Global - GE Healthcare Technologies; *pg.* 1533, *pg.* 1897
Lee, John, Dir-Sports Mktg - GoPro; *pg.* 1414, *pg.* 255
Lee, John, Dir-Mktg & Innovation - Whataburger, Inc.; *pg.* 1755, *pg.* 1744
Lee, John T., Dir-Investment Product Dev - FMR LLC (Fidelity Investments); *pg.* 759, *pg.* 794
Lee, John T.C., Sr VP-Controls, PFMC & HPS Products - MKS INSTRUMENTS, INC.; *pg.* 1362, *pg.* 781
Lee, Jonathan, Brand Mgr-Comm - BP America Inc.; *pg.* 972, *pg.* 1702
Lee, Joseph, Sr VP-Commerce & Mktg-Global - MyWebGrocer.com Corp.; *pg.* 1269, *pg.* 1769
Lee, Joyce, VP-Mktg - Cosi, Inc.; *pg.* 1723, *pg.* 600
Lee, Judy, Mgr-Worldwide Channel Mktg - NetApp, Inc.; *pg.* 444, *pg.* 287
Lee, Kamenna, VP-Bus Mktg - American Red Cross; *pg.* 130, *pg.* 395
Lee, Katie, Sr Mgr-Mktg-Consumer Campaigns - Intel Corporation; *pg.* 645, *pg.* 266
Lee, Katy, Specialist-Digital Mktg - Ikea North America Services LLC; *pg.* 929, *pg.* 1523
Lee, Kennie, Second VP-Product Dev & Actuary - Security Mutual Life Insurance Company of New York; *pg.* 1216, *pg.* 1142
Lee, Kenny, Dir-Worldwide Demand Mktg - Lithium Technologies; *pg.* 1263, *pg.* 221
Lee, Kevin, Mgr-Digital Mktg - Hulu LLC; *pg.* 1257, *pg.* 274
Lee, Kirk L., Vice Chm & Chief Creative Officer - Guaranty Bancshares, Inc.; *pg.* 764, *pg.* 1728
Lee, Kris, Designer-Digital - Clinique Laboratories LLC; *pg.* 503, *pg.* 1214
Lee, Kristin, Bus Mgr - Microsoft Corporation; *pg.* 435, *pg.* 1824
Lee, Laura, Mgr-Social Media & Corp Comm - Nestle Purina PetCare Company; *pg.* 1479, *pg.* 1000
Lee, Leslee, Specialist-Shopper Mktg-Coupon - E&J Gallo Winery; *pg.* 1962, *pg.* 149
Lee, Linda, Dir-Mktg - Alfred Angelo, Inc.; *pg.* 17, *pg.* 1532
Lee, Linda, Sr Dir-Cracker-North America - Mondelez International, Inc.; *pg.* 878, *pg.* 601
Lee, Lisa, Brand Mgr - Diageo North America, Inc.; *pg.* 1961, *pg.* 361
Lee, Lisa, Brand Mgr - Diageo North America Inc.; *pg.* 248, *pg.* 1223
Lee, Lois, Project Specialist-Integrated Mktg Comm - Cisco Systems, Inc.; *pg.* 372, *pg.* 240
Lee, Lori, Sr Exec VP & Officer-Mktg-Global - AT&T Inc.; *pg.* 1867, *pg.* 1674
Lee, Marvin, Specialist-Internet Mktg - Asiana Airlines; *pg.* 1899, *pg.* 126
Lee, Mary, Sr Mgr-IR - Flextronics International Ltd.; *pg.* 81, *pg.* 245
Lee, Megan, Sr Mgr-Community Outreach - Southwest Airlines Co.; *pg.* 1923, *pg.* 1687
Lee, Megan, Specialist-Adv Production - Subaru of America, Inc.; *pg.* 191, *pg.* 1050
Lee, Michael, Sr Mgr-Campaign - Electronic Arts Inc.; *pg.* 951, *pg.* 189
Lee, Michelle, Sr Product Mgr-Oncology & MS - AbbVie Inc.; *pg.* 1486, *pg.* 638
Lee, Mike, CIO-Mktg-Global - GE Capital; *pg.* 761, *pg.* 362
Lee, Mitch, Head-Media & Sponsorships-Global - Motorola Mobility LLC; *pg.* 657, *pg.* 627
Lee, Nancy, Mgr-Adv Product Mktg - eBay Inc.; *pg.* 1240, *pg.* 243
Lee, Nancy, Dir-Mktg - Intuit Inc.; *pg.* 769, *pg.* 158
Lee, Peter, Sr Assoc Mgr-Mktg - General Mills, Inc.; *pg.* 828, *pg.* 933
Lee, Raymond, Dir-Mktg Ops - The New York Times Company; *pg.* 1668, *pg.* 1270
Lee, Ricky, Mgr-Gaming Mktg - Logitech Inc.; *pg.* 1264, *pg.* 164
Lee, Rob, Area Mgr-Sls - Farmers Group, Inc.; *pg.* 1199, *pg.* 130
Lee, Robert, Dir-Sls & Mktg - Younger Optics; *pg.* 1437, *pg.* 297
Lee, Robynne, Dir-Product Mktg - VIZIO, Inc.; *pg.* 686, *pg.* 118
Lee, Roger, VP-Brand Mktg - Kaplan, Inc.; *pg.* 603, *pg.* 425
Lee, Ryan, Sr Mgr-Product Mktg - AT&T Mobility LLC; *pg.* 620, *pg.* 1824
Lee, Ryan, Sr Mgr-Digital Experience - Select Comfort Corporation; *pg.* 942, *pg.* 942
Lee, Sam, Sr Mgr-Dev, WebEx Social & Enterprise Collaboration Platform - Cisco Systems, Inc.; *pg.* 372, *pg.* 240
Lee, Sarah, Dir-PR - Choice Hotels International, Inc.; *pg.* 1086, *pg.* 775
Lee, Sean M., Brand Mgr-P&G Global Digital Innovation - The Procter & Gamble Company; *pg.* 1129, *pg.* 1418
Lee, Sky, Mgr-Mktg-Engagement - Amazon.com, Inc.; *pg.* 1226, *pg.* 1831
Lee, Stella, Dir-Media-China - LVMH Inc.; *pg.* 9, *pg.* 1254
Lee, Stuart, Sr VP & Gen Mgr-Mdsg - Sterling Jewelers Inc.; *pg.* 13, *pg.* 1402
Lee, Suk, Dir-Sls-Intl - Publishers Group West; *pg.* 1679, *pg.* 46
Lee, Susan, Mgr-Mktg-Program Trng & Engagement-Carlson Rezidor Hotel Grp - Carlson Companies Inc.; *pg.* 1084, *pg.* 947
Lee, Terry, Dir-Mktg-TV - Sharp Electronics Corporation; *pg.* 672, *pg.* 1082
Lee, Tiffany, Brand Mgr-Talent - HomeAway, Inc.; *pg.* 1911, *pg.* 1663
Lee, Tim, Acct Mgr-Sls - OMNOVA Solutions Inc; *pg.* 1176,

pg. 1453
Lee, Tommy, Partner - Habif, Arogeti & Wynne, LLP; pg. 764, pg. 509
Lee, Trent, Sr Mgr-Mktg-Global Nutrition Grp - PepsiCo, Inc.; pg. 259, pg. 1327
Lee, Vanessa, Mgr-Mktg & Brand Mgr-Consumer Products - National Football League; pg. 567, pg. 1264
Lee, Victor, Sr Mgr-Mktg Strategy - CVS Health Corporation; pg. 1765, pg. 1610
Lee, Victor, Sr VP-Digital Mktg - Hasbro, Inc.; pg. 954, pg. 1603
Lee, Victoria, Brand Mgr-Brand Engagement - Coldwell Banker Real Estate LLC; pg. 1087, pg. 1103
Lee, Vivian, Sr Analyst-Mktg-OPEN Merchant Cross-Sell Acq - American Express Company; pg. 712, pg. 1190
Lee, Younghee, Exec VP & Head-Global Mktg - Samsung Electronics America, Inc.; pg. 669, pg. 1115
Lee-Lim, Meg, Dir-Mktg Strategy - Cost Plus World Market; pg. 921, pg. 170
Lee-Olsen, Mindy, VP-Mktg Svcs - Affymetrix, Inc.; pg. 1487, pg. 263
Lee-Pearce, Charl, Head-Digital & Social Mktg - Microsoft Corporation; pg. 435, pg. 1824
Leebaw, Jeff, VP-Corp Media Rels - Johnson & Johnson; pg. 1549, pg. 1091
Leece, Evelina, Sr Mgr-Mktg-Chemical Portfolio of Products - Sunstar Americas Inc.; pg. 1599, pg. 591
Leech, Grant, VP-Brand Mktg - United States Cellular Corporation; pg. 1875, pg. 594
Leeds, Christina, Mgr-Media Rels - National Railroad Passenger Corporation; pg. 1916, pg. 403
Leedy, Justin, Dir-Product Mktg - Web.com Group, Inc.; pg. 1288, pg. 435
Leedy, Justin, Dir-Product Mktg - Web.com, Inc.; pg. 1288, pg. 524
Leedy, Mark, Dir-Sls - Vicon Industries, Inc.; pg. 685, pg. 1166
Leeloy, Wayne, Sr Dir-Strategic Mktg & Partnerships - Warner Music Group Corp.; pg. 590, pg. 1313
Leem, Robert, Sr Analyst-Mktg - Pacific Life Insurance Company; pg. 1213, pg. 166
Leemis, Jen, Sr Mgr-Consumer Mktg - Cars.com; pg. 1234, pg. 568
Leemis, Jen, Sr Mgr-Consumer Mktg-Cars.com - Classified Ventures, LLC; pg. 1235, pg. 571
Leeper, Laura, Sr Mgr-Event Mktg & Strategy - Brocade Corporation; pg. 365, pg. 312
Leepson, Susan, Grp VP-Comm Strategy & PR - Time Warner Cable Inc.; pg. 312, pg. 1301
Lees, Brent, Sr Mgr-Product Mktg - Riverbed Technology, Inc.; pg. 1277, pg. 225
Leesemann, Patty, Sr Mgr-Assoc Comm - The Kroger Co.; pg. 1025, pg. 1416
Leever, Karen, VP & Gen Mgr-Digital Media-New York - Discovery Communications, Inc.; pg. 282, pg. 777
Lefco, Daniel, Sr Product Mgr-Wearables & IoT - Hewlett-Packard Company; pg. 404, pg. 175
Lefebvre, Martha, Mgr-Mktg-Equine Products - Central Garden & Pet Company; pg. 1475, pg. 303
Lefever, Kim, Mgr-Social Media & Copywriter - Armstrong World Industries, Inc.; pg. 914, pg. 1545
Lefevre, Florence, Head-Institutional Sls-Europe - Dow Jones & Company, Inc.; pg. 1637, pg. 1225
Leff, Alan, VP-Quality & Production - PRIMO WATER CORPORATION; pg. 1030, pg. 1395
Leffel, Janet, Specialist-Mktg-EcoBusiness - Schneider Electric USA, Inc.; pg. 1306, pg. 650
Leffew, Kevin, VP-Field Sls-US & Canada - EBSCO Information Services Walpole; pg. 1638, pg. 849
Leffler, Greg, Sr Mgr-Site Reliability Engrg - LinkedIn Corporation; pg. 1262, pg. 160
Lefko, Kim, Exec VP-Mktg - Weber-Stephen Products LLC; pg. 62, pg. 650
Lefort, Jackie, Programs Mgr-Mktg - PACCAR Inc.; pg. 187, pg. 1816
Lefrano, Jaimie, Dir-Mktg - Safilo USA Inc.; pg. 11, pg. 1106
Lefthes, Stuart, Sr VP-Sls - Medical Information Technology, Inc.; pg. 431, pg. 859
Legan, Ann, VP-Brand Mktg - Constellation Brands, Inc.; pg. 1960, pg. 1348
Legare, Leslie, Sr Dir-Creative-On & Off Air Promos - Country Music Television, Inc.; pg. 279, pg. 1649
Legato, Anne, Sr Mgr-Product Mktg-Engrg Excellence - Microsoft Corporation; pg. 435, pg. 1824
Legato, Denise, Specialist-Mktg Comm - Honeywell International Inc.; pg. 407, pg. 1088
Legault, Lori, Sr VP-Sls Cineplex Media - Cineplex Entertainment LP; pg. 275, pg. 1936
Lege, Curtis, Bus Mgr - Dover Chemical Corporation; pg. 1156, pg. 1447
Legelis, Kim, VP-Mktg - Lockheed Martin Corporation; pg. 229, pg. 762
Legentil, Chris, Assoc Dir-Mktg Comm - National Basketball Association; pg. 566, pg. 1264
Leger, Jim St., Mgr-Mktg - Intel Corporation; pg. 645, pg. 266
Leger, Kyley, Mgr-Mktg Comm-Global - Emerson Process Management; pg. 1334, pg. 1636
Leger, Lynne, VP-Mktg - David's Bridal, Inc.; pg. 23, pg. 1523
Leger, Thierry, Head-L&H Products - Swiss Reinsurance America Corporation; pg. 1218, pg. 1140
Legere, Troy, Sr Mgr-Program & Pub Sector - SYNNEX Corporation; pg. 480, pg. 92
LeGette, Suzanne, Mgr-CRM Mktg - Raley's Inc.; pg. 1031, pg. 305
Leggett, Ihsan, Brand Mgr-New Bus Creation - The Procter & Gamble Company; pg. 1129, pg. 1418
Leggio, Denise, Sr Mgr-Adv Ops - Publishers Clearing House; pg. 1782, pg. 1324
Leggio, Jennifer, Sr Dir-Security Market Strategy & Mktg - Cisco Systems, Inc.; pg. 372, pg. 240
Legrand, Olivier, Mng Dir-Asia Pacific & Head-Mktg Solutions - LinkedIn Corporation; pg. 1262, pg. 160
Legros, Jean, VP-Sls & Mktg - The Mentholatum Company; pg. 1565, pg. 1320
Legters, Bob, Sr VP-Product - Fidelity National Information Services; pg. 397, pg. 1549
Lehanski, Alison Roselli, Head-Mktg-US & Dir - Pfizer Inc.; pg. 1581, pg. 1278
Lehanski, David, Sr VP-Integrated Sls - National Hockey League; pg. 568, pg. 1265
Lehaut, Benoit, Product Mgr-Global - Molex Incorporated; pg. 655, pg. 628
Lehet, Anna, Brand Mgr-HP PSG - CDW Corporation; pg. 370, pg. 663
Lehigh, Ed, VP-Mktg - Colorado Serum Co.; pg. 1516, pg. 318
Lehky, Matt, Sr Mgr-Mktg-Hospital Segment - Cardinal Health, Inc.; pg. 1512, pg. 1448
Lehman, Ashley, Sr Brand Mgr-Mktg - Jayco Inc.; pg. 1708, pg. 695
Lehman, Charles, Product Mgr - Mood Media; pg. 298, pg. 1616
Lehman, David, Mng Dir-Commodity Res & Product Dev - CME Group Inc.; pg. 738, pg. 571
Lehman, Eric, Pres-Retail Sls - Gildan Activewear Inc.; pg. 1835, pg. 1955
Lehman, Gregg, Sr Product Mgr-Fin & Risk Mgmt - Fiserv, Inc.; pg. 397, pg. 1855
Lehman, Julie, Dir Mktg-Lean Cuisine - Nestle USA, Inc.; pg. 883, pg. 96
Lehman, Lindsay, Sr Dir-Mktg Analytics - NCL Corporation Ltd.; pg. 1916, pg. 444
Lehman, Lindsay, Dir-Relationship Mktg - Norwegian Cruise Line; pg. 1917, pg. 444
Lehmann, Bob, Sr Dir-Mktg Strategy, Res & Analysis - ASPEN TECHNOLOGY, INC.; pg. 354, pg. 804
Lehmann, Michael, VP-Product Mgmt - Oracle Corporation; pg. 450, pg. 191
Lehmann, Ryan, Specialist-Loyalty Mktg - Restaurants Unlimited, Inc.; pg. 1748, pg. 1839
Lehmkuhl, Tom, Dir-Sls-Intl - Elkay Manufacturing Company; pg. 80, pg. 645
Lehner, Dustin, Head-Shopper Mktg Team - Mars, Incorporated; pg. 1858, pg. 1792
Lehner, Steve, Product Mgr - PPG Industries, Inc.; pg. 1445, pg. 1579
Lehner, Teri, Mgr-Mktg - Thrivent Financial for Lutherans; pg. 1219, pg. 944
Lehnert, Donald, III, Mgr-Digital Media, Sls & Mktg - Gund, Inc.; pg. 954, pg. 1056
Lehnhoff, Jesse, Dir-Mktg - Handi-Craft Company; pg. 954, pg. 998
Lehotsky, Anne, Coord-Mktg - WCI Communities, Inc.; pg. 1118, pg. 414
Lehr, Jonathan, Sr Mgr-Shopper Mktg - The Dannon Company, Inc.; pg. 851, pg. 1351
Lehr, Meredith, Sr Dir & Asst Gen Counsel - Holland America Line Inc.; pg. 1911, pg. 1836
Lehr, Sheila, Mng Counsel-Mktg & Intellectual Property - McDonald's Corporation; pg. 1737, pg. 645
Lehrer, Christine, Sr Mgr-Product Mktg & Consumer Video Comm - AT&T Mobility LLC; pg. 619, pg. 488
Lehrfeld, Rich, VP-Global Media, Sponsorship & Experiential Mktg - American Express Company; pg. 712, pg. 1190
Lehrmann, Ashley, Sr Dir-Brand Mktg - Rust-Oleum Corporation; pg. 1447, pg. 664
Lei, Ben, Assoc Dir-Transplant Mktg - Genentech, Inc.; pg. 1533, pg. 279
Leibowitz, Josh, Chief Strategy Officer - Carnival Corporation; pg. 1902, pg. 441
Leicht, Amanda, Sr Product Mgr-Google Maps - Google Inc.; pg. 1249, pg. 153
Leichter, Pamela, Dir-Consumer Mktg - Memorial Sloan-Kettering Cancer Center Inc.; pg. 1565, pg. 1258
Leichtling, Jake, Product Mgr-Extensions Platform - Google Inc.; pg. 1249, pg. 153
Leiderman, Breeanna, Mgr-Sls-Intl - O.F. Mossberg & Sons, Inc.; pg. 1842, pg. 360
Leidt, Beth, Second VP-Mktg - The Guardian Life Insurance Company of America; pg. 1202, pg. 1237
Leier, Pam R., VP-Mktg - Lampert Yards, Inc.; pg. 1053, pg. 962
Leiferman, Heather, Dir-PR - BUFFALO WILD WINGS, INC.; pg. 1718, pg. 931
Leigh, Ben, Sr Mgr-Partnership & Event Activation - Under Armour, Inc.; pg. 49, pg. 759
Leigh, Jason, Dir-Insights-Global Mktg Solutions - LinkedIn Corporation; pg. 1262, pg. 160
Leigh, Robert, Sr Mgr-Plng & Distr - Mercedes-Benz USA, LLC; pg. 184, pg. 514
Leigh, Susan, VP-Adv Sls - Scripps Networks Interactive, Inc.; pg. 1279, pg. 1638
Leigh, Vince, Brand Mgr-Nike Retail - NIKE, Inc.; pg. 1812, pg. 1492
Leightell, Karen, Sr Mgr-Mktg & Social Media Strategy - IBM Canada Limited; pg. 411, pg. 1923
Leighton, Carolyn, Sr Product Mgr-Immunology Mktg - CSL Behring LLC; pg. 1520, pg. 1543
Leighton, Ethan, Brand Mgr-Strategy - Toyota Motor Sales, U.S.A., Inc.; pg. 193, pg. 296
Leighton, Helen, Area Dir-PR - Starwood Hotels & Resorts Worldwide, Inc.; pg. 1114, pg. 378
Leighton, James B., Interim CEO - Boulder Brands, Inc.; pg. 1016, pg. 310
Leighton, William, Sr Dir-Strategic Accounts & Ops Recruitment - Kelly Services, Inc.; pg. 424, pg. 911
Leigon, David E., Sr Specialist-Trng Dev-Tyco Safety Products - Tyco International (US) Inc.; pg. 1891, pg. 1113
Leiman, Scott, Sr Dir-Small Bus Product Mktg - Automatic Data Processing, Inc.; pg. 357, pg. 1117
Leiman, Seth, Brand Mgr-Emergen-C - Pfizer Inc.; pg. 1581, pg. 1278
Leimbach, Bryan, Assoc Product Mgr - McKesson Corporation; pg. 1560, pg. 222
Leimbach, Peter, VP-Sports Sls Res - Fox Sports Net; pg. 288, pg. 131
Leimer, George, VP-Fantasy Sports & Premium Products - ESPN, Inc.; pg. 285, pg. 340
Leimkuhler, Eric, Sr VP-Mktg - loanDepot LLC; pg. 776, pg. 86
Leines, Eric, VP-Sls & Mktg - Wausau Paper Bay West; pg. 1471, pg. 1465
Leinicke, Andy, Sr Mgr-Mktg - Intuit Inc.; pg. 769, pg. 158
Leinwand, Neil, Sr VP-Mktg - Applegate; pg. 837, pg. 1045
Leinweber, Carl, Reg Mgr-Sls-Northeast - Eastman Machine Company; pg. 1331, pg. 1148
Leinweber, Tabetha, Dir-Direct Mktg & Donor Svcs - Susan G. Komen for the Cure; pg. 158, pg. 1688
Leipert, Rebecca, Dir-Mktg Ops-Global - Keurig Green Mountain, Inc.; pg. 868, pg. 1768
Leisen, Michael J., VP-Interactive Mktg - Ameriprise Financial, Inc.; pg. 715, pg. 930
Leishman, Ginger, Mgr-Mobile Product Mktg & Community Mgr - eBay Inc.; pg. 1240, pg. 243
Leisinger, Megan, Dir-Retail Brand Mktg - NIKE, Inc.; pg. 1812, pg. 1492
Leisman, Heather, VP-Indus Mktg - TripAdvisor, Inc.; pg. 1926, pg. 835
Leisner, John, Sr Product Mgr - Miller Electric Manufacturing Co.; pg. 1361, pg. 1852
Leist, Amanda, VP-Acq Mktg Strategy-Credit Card - Wells Fargo & Company; pg. 819, pg. 232
Leistikow, Kimberly, Dir-Mktg - Best Buy Co., Inc.; pg. 1761, pg. 954
Leitch, Jason, Brand Mgr-Fungicides - BASF Corporation; pg.

1149, *pg.* 1066

Leite, Sharon M., Exec VP-Sls & Customer Experience - Pier 1 Imports, Inc.; *pg.* 940, *pg.* 1695

Leiter, Mark, Chief Strategy Officer - The Nielsen Company B.V.; *pg.* 1671, *pg.* 1272

Leitess, James, Dir-Mktg Tech - Intrawest ULC; *pg.* 1098, *pg.* 320

Leith, Amy, Head-Global Markets Mktg - Bank of America Corporation; *pg.* 718, *pg.* 1362

Leithner, Jill A., Mgr-Worldwide Consumer Mktg - Intel Corporation; *pg.* 645, *pg.* 266

Leitner, Catherine C., Dir-Area & PR-Caribbean & Latin America - The Ritz-Carlton Hotel Company LLC; *pg.* 1110, *pg.* 766

Leitner, Holly, Specialist-Creative Mktg - The Terlato Wine Group; *pg.* 1971, *pg.* 555

Leitner, Jenn, Brand Mgr - Red Lobster; *pg.* 1747, *pg.* 455

Leitner, Mimi, Sr Dir-Mktg-US Retail Experience - Revlon Consumer Products Corporation; *pg.* 521, *pg.* 1286

Leitner, Mimi, Sr Dir-Mktg-US Retail Experience - Revlon, Inc.; *pg.* 521, *pg.* 1286

Leiva, Lily, Dir-Digital Mktg - Atlanta Convention & Visitors Bureau; *pg.* 989, *pg.* 489

LeJeune, Judi, VP & Dir-PR - IBERIABANK Corporation; *pg.* 768, *pg.* 744

Leland, Steve, Dir-Mktg - Accenture; *pg.* 1392, *pg.* 1186

Leljedal, Tim, Mgr-Media Rels - Southern Company; *pg.* 1952, *pg.* 520

Lema-Hallauer, Lily, Mgr-Mktg - Amazon.com, Inc.; *pg.* 1226, *pg.* 1831

Lemaire, Jerome, Dir-Mktg-UK - Reckitt Benckiser Inc.; *pg.* 1136, *pg.* 1105

Leman, Dan, Mgr-Sls - Besser Company; *pg.* 1317, *pg.* 865

Lemant, Valerie, Dir-Mktg-Strategy - Kraft Canada Inc.; *pg.* 869, *pg.* 1939

LeMasters, Heather, Sr Mgr-Digital Mktg - Trinchero Family Estates; *pg.* 1971, *pg.* 197

Lemasters, Michael, Sr Mgr-Mktg-Medical Consumables - Cardinal Health, Inc.; *pg.* 1512, *pg.* 1448

LeMay, Ed, Sr VP-Mktg Svcs - Constellation Brands, Inc.; *pg.* 1960, *pg.* 1348

Lemberger, Mike, Head-Loyalty, Offers, & Data Solutions-Global Info Products - Visa U.S.A., Inc.; *pg.* 817, *pg.* 231

Lemcke, Randy, Sr VP-Sls - Plano Molding Company; *pg.* 1887, *pg.* 652

LeMelle, Tammy, Dir-Digital Mktg Natl Tour Promos - Live Nation Entertainment, Inc.; *pg.* 558, *pg.* 47

Lemery, Jean-Marc, Mgr-Sls-Export & Industrial Covers - Building Products of Canada Corp.; *pg.* 72, *pg.* 1951

Lemieux, Kevin, Mgr-Sls - Nutting; *pg.* 1366, *pg.* 1626

Lemire, Francois, Sr Dir-HR-Comm-Internal Svcs - L-3 MAS Canada; *pg.* 229, *pg.* 1952

Lemke, Katja, Specialist-Mktg-Shop Your Way - Sears Holdings Corporation; *pg.* 1784, *pg.* 618

Lemke, Wendy, Corp Mgr-Mktg - C.R. Bard, Inc.; *pg.* 1519, *pg.* 1094

Lemley, Greg, Reg Coord-Adv - The Home Depot, Inc.; *pg.* 1050, *pg.* 510

Lemley, Steve, VP-Field Mktg, Media & Mdsg - Hardees Food Systems, Inc.; *pg.* 1731, *pg.* 998

LeMoine, Chris, Mgr-Production - North Dakota Mill & Elevator Association; *pg.* 833, *pg.* 1398

LeMoine, Heather, Mgr-Mktg - North Dakota Department of Commerce Tourism Division; *pg.* 1002, *pg.* 1397

Lemon, Laurel, Assoc Mgr-Product Dev - Avon Products, Inc.; *pg.* 500, *pg.* 1198

Lemons, Jenna, Mgr-Sls - Aramark; *pg.* 1013, *pg.* 1558

Lemos, Anabela, Product Mgr-Worldwide-LFP - Hewlett-Packard Company; *pg.* 404, *pg.* 175

Lemus, Hector Silva, Mgr-Mktg - General Mills, Inc.; *pg.* 828, *pg.* 933

Lemyze, Christine, VP-Mktg-Global Tech Svcs & Cloud Computing-North America - International Business Machines Corporation; *pg.* 418, *pg.* 1138

Lenard, Chantel, Dir-Mktg-US - Ford Motor Company; *pg.* 172, *pg.* 876

Lenart, Mary, Coord-Sls & Mktg - Mayfran International, Inc.; *pg.* 1359, *pg.* 1432

Lenchus, Kim, Coord-Mktg -Finish, Fabric, Carpet & Personal Care - Reckitt Benckiser Inc.; *pg.* 1136, *pg.* 1105

Lendler, Jennifer K., Assoc VP-Consumer Insights & Mktg Center of Excellence - Aramark; *pg.* 1013, *pg.* 1558

Lendzinski, Matthew, Mgr-Field Mktg-Dow Construction Chemicals - THE DOW CHEMICAL COMPANY; *pg.* 1157, *pg.* 898

Lene, Dian, VP-Mktg - P&H Mining Equipment; *pg.* 103, *pg.* 1879

Lenge, Chris, VP-Sls Strategy - A&E Television Networks, LLC; *pg.* 267, *pg.* 1185

Lengkong, Monica, Corp Mgr-Mktg - Robb Report; *pg.* 1681, *pg.* 142

Lenhart, Brian, Dir-Digital Mktg, Travel & Lifestyle Svcs - American Express Company; *pg.* 712, *pg.* 1190

Lenhart, Tracy, VP-Consumer Mktg - Lifetime Entertainment Services LLC; *pg.* 296, *pg.* 1251

Lenker, Scott, Sr Mgr-Product & Pricing - Intel Corporation; *pg.* 645, *pg.* 266

Lenko, Peter, Mgr-Mktg - Lafarge Canada Inc.; *pg.* 92, *pg.* 1958

Lenney, Mary A., Sr Mgr-Customer Mktg - Alcatel-Lucent; *pg.* 615, *pg.* 38

Lennon, Gene, Dir-Interactive, IT & Production - Greater Media Newspapers, Inc.; *pg.* 1646, *pg.* 1071

Lennon, Heather J., Mgr-Component PR & Strategist-Social Media - Advanced Micro Devices, Inc.-Markham; *pg.* 345, *pg.* 1922

Lennon, Lori, Dir-Sls - The Clorox Company; *pg.* 327, *pg.* 169

Lennon, Miles, Head-Product - Spotify; *pg.* 1282, *pg.* 1295

Lennox, Diane, Mgr-PR Svcs - SAS Institute Inc.; *pg.* 466, *pg.* 1361

Lennox, Gregory, Sr Mgr-Digital Comm - Aramark; *pg.* 1013, *pg.* 1558

Lenny, Don, Dir-Sls-North America - Zippo Manufacturing Company, Inc.; *pg.* 1895, *pg.* 1518

Lenow, Patrick, VP-PR - SONIC Corp.; *pg.* 1750, *pg.* 1487

Lensing, Kevin, Sr Dir-Mobility Solutions - Advanced Micro Devices, Inc.; *pg.* 613, *pg.* 282

Lensner, Don, Sr Mgr-Business - Johnson Matthey Process Technologies; *pg.* 1169, *pg.* 1083

Lentini, Kathy, Dir-Energy & Mktg Svcs - PECO Energy Company; *pg.* 1949, *pg.* 1568

Lentner, Jennifer, Sr Dir-Mktg Comm - Stryker Corporation; *pg.* 1598, *pg.* 894

Lentner, Kurt, Sr Dir-Corp Quality Sys - Stryker Corporation; *pg.* 1598, *pg.* 894

Lentz, Stacey C., Mgr-PR - Lowe's Companies, Inc.; *pg.* 1053, *pg.* 1383

Lenz, Doug, VP-Product Mgmt, Mktg & Bus Dev - Thermo King Corporation; *pg.* 1077, *pg.* 918

Lenz, Ian, Bus Mgr-Customer - The Dannon Company, Inc.; *pg.* 851, *pg.* 1351

Lenz, Vicki, Dir-Mktg Comm - Anixter International Inc.; *pg.* 1313, *pg.* 614

Lenzie, Brian T., Sr Dir-Comml, Telco & MDU Mktg - DIRECTV Group Holdings, LLC; *pg.* 281, *pg.* 79

Leo, Arthur, Mgr-Customer Mktg - Johnson & Johnson; *pg.* 1549, *pg.* 1091

Leo, Brian, Dir-Mktg Tech - Essendant Inc.; *pg.* 1907, *pg.* 600

Leo, Jerry, Exec VP-Program Strategy & Production-Bravo TV - NBC Universal, Inc.; *pg.* 300, *pg.* 1266

Leoce, Kristen, Exec Dir-Live Media - Time Inc.; *pg.* 1693, *pg.* 1300

Leon, Angela, Sr Mgr-Mktg-Pkg & Mdsg - Intuit Inc.; *pg.* 769, *pg.* 158

Leon, Cecile de, Mgr-Mktg-Global - F5 Networks, Inc.; *pg.* 396, *pg.* 1835

Leon, Edward, VP-Mdsg & Dir - Leon's Furniture Limited; *pg.* 933, *pg.* 1948

Leon, George, Exec VP-Consumer Mktg - Sony Corporation of America; *pg.* 675, *pg.* 1293

Leon, George, Exec VP-Consumer Mktg - Sony Pictures Entertainment Inc.; *pg.* 309, *pg.* 72

Leon, J P, VP-Advanced Tech - Stamps.com Inc.; *pg.* 1282, *pg.* 82

Leon, Kimberlie, Sr Dir-Mktg & Content - Reed Exhibitions USA; *pg.* 460, *pg.* 364

Leon, Rosie, Asst Mgr-Mktg - Black Box Corporation; *pg.* 361, *pg.* 1547

Leonard, Anne, Client Svcs Dir-Fairchild Fashion Media - Conde Nast Publications, Inc.; *pg.* 1629, *pg.* 1217

Leonard, Becki, Dir-PR - Good Technology, Inc.; *pg.* 1249, *pg.* 285

Leonard, Caitlin, Head-Mktg Ops & Hot Sys-Global - Keurig Green Mountain, Inc.; *pg.* 868, *pg.* 1768

Leonard, Caroline, Sr Assoc Brand Mgr-Campbell's Organic - Campbell Soup Company; *pg.* 844, *pg.* 1048

Leonard, Christopher, Sr Mgr-Comml Sls Strategy - General Motors Company; *pg.* 175, *pg.* 881

Leonard, Jeff, Sr VP-Mktg - Wells Fargo Advisors, LLC; *pg.* 819, *pg.* 1005

Leonard, Jennifer, Sr Mgr-Product PR & Events - Hanesbrands Inc.; *pg.* 26, *pg.* 1394

Leonard, Kaelin, Brand Mktg Mgr-OshKosh B'gosh - Carter's, Inc.; *pg.* 21, *pg.* 491

Leonard, Karen, Mgr-Centralized Sls Mktg - Wells Fargo & Company; *pg.* 819, *pg.* 232

Leonard, Lauren, Mgr-Integrated Mktg-Redbook - The Hearst Corporation; *pg.* 1649, *pg.* 1239

Leonard, Nancy, Mgr-Mktg-Water Microbiology - IDEXX Laboratories, Inc.; *pg.* 1543, *pg.* 753

Leonard, Nicole, Sr Product Mgr - Intrado Inc.; *pg.* 420, *pg.* 334

Leonard, Paul, VP-Brand Mktg - Expedia, Inc.; *pg.* 1244, *pg.* 1814

Leonard, Polly, Sr Mgr-Integrated Mktg - Motorola Solutions, Inc.; *pg.* 657, *pg.* 659

Leonard, Rebecca, Assoc VP & Dir-PR - T.J. Maxx; *pg.* 1788, *pg.* 822

Leonard, Rebecca, Assoc VP & Dir-PR - The TJX Companies, Inc.; *pg.* 1788, *pg.* 822

Leonard, Tara, Exec Dir-Clinique North America Mktg - The Estee Lauder Companies Inc.; *pg.* 508, *pg.* 1229

Leonardo, John, Exec-Mktg - Grecian Delight Foods Inc.; *pg.* 859, *pg.* 610

Leonarz, Richard, Sr Mgr-Mktg - Samsung Electronics America, Inc.; *pg.* 669, *pg.* 1115

Leonauskas, John, Mgr-Mktg - Menard, Inc.; *pg.* 1055, *pg.* 1857

Leone, Beth Ann, Sr Mgr-Strategic Sourcing-Ethicon - Johnson & Johnson; *pg.* 1549, *pg.* 1091

Leone, Denise, Dir-Online Mktg & Affiliates - SHUTTERFLY, INC.; *pg.* 1280, *pg.* 192

Leone, Roxanne, Mgr-Mktg - New Age Electronics, Inc.; *pg.* 659, *pg.* 63

Leonetti, Donato, Rep-Tech Sls-Fin & Comm - Oracle Corporation; *pg.* 450, *pg.* 191

Leonetti, Elaine, Sr Mgr-Mktg Comm - Blue Cross & Blue Shield Association; *pg.* 1195, *pg.* 566

Leonetti, Laura, Product Dir-Oncology - GlaxoSmithKline; *pg.* 1536, *pg.* 1389

Leonetti, Laura, Product Dir-Oncology - GlaxoSmithKline Consumer Healthcare; *pg.* 510, *pg.* 1554

Leonetti, Matilde, Dir-Mktg - The Gap, Inc.; *pg.* 1770, *pg.* 218

Leong, Aaron, Mgr-Sls - TripAdvisor, Inc.; *pg.* 1926, *pg.* 835

Leong, Adeline, VP-Integrated Mktg - Sephora USA Inc; *pg.* 522, *pg.* 227

Leong, David, Mgr-PR - Kingston Technology Company, Inc.; *pg.* 425, *pg.* 90

Leong, Jiti, Program Mgr-Mktg - Dell Inc.; *pg.* 383, *pg.* 1737

Leopold, Alexander, Sr Specialist-Social Media - Klipsch Group, Inc.; *pg.* 649, *pg.* 688

Leos, Lyris, Brand Mktg Dir-Strategy - J.C. Penney Company, Inc.; *pg.* 1774, *pg.* 1732

Lepage, Marie Ginette, VP-Mktg, Content & Brdcst - Videotron Ltd.; *pg.* 317, *pg.* 1957

Lepard, Ashley, Sr Specialist-Mktg - Comcast Cable Communications, Inc.; *pg.* 276, *pg.* 1560

Lepera, Steve, Dir-Mktg-Mailorder-Schiller Grounds Care, Inc - Schiller-Pfeiffer, Inc.; *pg.* 1061, *pg.* 1587

Lepicier, Ryan, Sr VP-Mktg & Comm - National Peanut Board; *pg.* 150, *pg.* 515

Lepine, Gilles, Sr VP-Sls & Mktg - Uniboard Canada Inc.; *pg.* 117, *pg.* 1952

Lepkowsky, Michael, Dir-IT-Digital Mktg - Unilever United States, Inc.; *pg.* 904, *pg.* 1061

Lepore, Melissa, Mgr-Corp Bus Mktg - Hyatt Hotels Corporation; *pg.* 1096, *pg.* 577

LeQuire, Miranda, Sr Analyst-Mktg Strategy - Level 3 Communications, Inc.; *pg.* 1262, *pg.* 312

Lerch, Chuck, Mgr-Mktg - Stenhouse Publishers; *pg.* 1689, *pg.* 752

Lerman, Scott, Mgr-Global PR & Medical Diagnostics - General Electric Company; *pg.* 1297, *pg.* 347

Lerner, Doug, Sr Dir-Mktg-Velocity - Discovery Communications, Inc.; *pg.* 282, *pg.* 777

Lerner, Julia, Coord-Mktg - GEICO Corporation; *pg.* 1200, *pg.* 399

Lerner, Meg, VP-Mktg-North America - Avon Products, Inc.; *pg.* 500, *pg.* 1198

LeRoux, Brian, Product Mgr-PhoneGap & Topcoat - Adobe Systems Incorporated; *pg.* 342, *pg.* 235

Leroux, Marc, Mgr-Mktg - ABB Inc.; *pg.* 1309, *pg.* 1359

Leroux, Paul, Mgr-PR - BlackBerry Limited; *pg.* 625, *pg.* 1947

Leroy, Jean Marc, VP-Product Mktg - Essilor of America, Inc.; *pg.* 1412, *pg.* 1680

LeRoy, Karen, Engr-Technical Mktg - Cisco Systems, Inc.; *pg.* 372, *pg.* 240
Leroy, Xavier, VP-Sls-EMEA-MPT Grp - IDEX Corporation; *pg.* 1347, *pg.* 623
Lerz, Sarah, Sr Mgr-Media - Nautilus, Inc.; *pg.* 1840, *pg.* 1846
LeSage, Lora, Sr VP-Digital Media-NBC Owned Television Stations - NBC Universal Television Networks Group; *pg.* 302, *pg.* 1267
Lesage, Martin, Dir-Sls Dev & Execution - Pepsi Beverages Company; *pg.* 258, *pg.* 1342
Lesage, Philippe, Sr Mgr-Mktg-Digital Mktg, Bus Intelligence & Bus Ops - Hewlett-Packard Company; *pg.* 404, *pg.* 175
LeSane, Suzette, VP-Product Dev - CoreLogic, Inc.; *pg.* 1198, *pg.* 109
Lescaille, Rob, Sr Mgr-MyHyundai & Blue Link - Hyundai Motor America; *pg.* 179, *pg.* 89
Lesch, Brendan, VP-Sls & Mktg - Monadnock Paper Mills, Inc.; *pg.* 1464, *pg.* 1033
Lesher, Melissa, Sr Mgr-Corp Comm - Accenture; *pg.* 1392, *pg.* 1186
Lesikar, Tori, Specialist-Social Media - Columbia Sportswear Company; *pg.* 1830, *pg.* 1501
Lesinski, Rhonda, CMO & Sr VP-Product Mgmt - Del Monte Foods, Inc.; *pg.* 852, *pg.* 304
Lesinski, Thomas, Interim CEO - Sonar Entertainment; *pg.* 309, *pg.* 140
Leska, Shawn, Dir-Sls - Sturm, Ruger & Company, Inc.; *pg.* 1846, *pg.* 371
Leske, Matt, Sr Product Mgr - Google Inc.; *pg.* 1249, *pg.* 153
Lesko, Christine, Dir-Adv - Cleveland Cavaliers/Quicken Loans Arena; *pg.* 541, *pg.* 1429
Lesko, Dennis, VP-Sls & Mktg - Broadmoor Hotel, Inc.; *pg.* 1083, *pg.* 315
Leslie, Amy, Dir-Mktg & Bus Dev - Olympus America Inc.; *pg.* 1425, *pg.* 1521
Leslie, Brian, Dir-Sls Ops - Helly-Hansen (US), Inc.; *pg.* 26, *pg.* 1813
Leslie, Cynthia A., Sr Dir-Mktg - Travelers Insurance; *pg.* 1220, *pg.* 963
Leslie, Jon, Asst Vice Chancellor-Strategic Mktg-Boulder - University Of Colorado; *pg.* 608, *pg.* 323
Leslie, Scott, Supvr-Adv - United Parcel Service, Inc.; *pg.* 1928, *pg.* 522
Leslie, Steve, Sr VP-Sls & Mktg - Softchoice Corporation; *pg.* 471, *pg.* 1943
Lesmeister, Emily, Mgr-Pricing & Mktg Strategy - Regis Corporation; *pg.* 521, *pg.* 941
Lesmeister, Tim, VP-Mktg - WD-40 Company; *pg.* 337, *pg.* 210
Lesnak, Elaine, Sr Mgr-US Mktg - Philips Respironics; *pg.* 1585, *pg.* 1555
Lesniak, Jim J., VP-Sls & Mktg - Zix Corporation; *pg.* 497, *pg.* 1691
Lesperance, Mimish, Sr Mgr-Worldwide Channel Partner Mktg - Cisco Systems, Inc.; *pg.* 372, *pg.* 240
Lessem, Sarah, Mgr-Mktg - Aon Risk Services Inc.; *pg.* 1193, *pg.* 564
Lesser, James M., VP-Mktg & Sls - Oakhurst Dairy; *pg.* 887, *pg.* 752
Lesser, Jon, Dir-Mktg - Kind LLC; *pg.* 868, *pg.* 1249
Lesser, Tammi, Sr Dir-Mktg - IDEXX Laboratories, Inc.; *pg.* 1543, *pg.* 753
Lessor, Mark A., VP-Sls - Gibraltar Packaging Group, Inc.; *pg.* 1459, *pg.* 1011
Lestan, Jake, Head-Sponsorships, Brand Ops & Banking & Lending Adv - Discover Financial Services; *pg.* 744, *pg.* 653
Lester, Arlene J., Specialist-Pub Affairs & Media Rels - State Farm Mutual Automobile Insurance Co.; *pg.* 1218, *pg.* 557
Lester, Brian, Dir-Mktg, Innovation & Emerging Growth Grp - Nestle Purina PetCare Company; *pg.* 1479, *pg.* 1000
Lester, Chris, Mgr-Market-AT&T Media Rels-Kansas-Missouri - AT&T; *pg.* 1865, *pg.* 258
Lester, Katie, Sr Mgr-Adv - AT&T Inc.; *pg.* 1868, *pg.* 358
Lester, Keith, Mgr-PR - Rockwell Automation, Inc.; *pg.* 668, *pg.* 1880
LeStrange, Judy, Sr Product Mgr - General Electric Company; *pg.* 1297, *pg.* 347
Lestrud, Sydney, Mgr-Digital Mktg-Global - General Electric Company; *pg.* 1297, *pg.* 347
Leszcynski, Laura, Mgr-Mktg - General Mills, Inc.; *pg.* 828, *pg.* 933
Letang, Lisa, Supvr-Adv & Media - The Gorman-Rupp Company; *pg.* 1341, *pg.* 1458
Letch, Monica, Head-Digital & Social Adv-Verizon Fios - Verizon Communications Inc.; *pg.* 1875, *pg.* 1309
Letcher, Gregg, Program Mgr-Mktg - Wells Fargo & Company; *pg.* 819, *pg.* 232
Letter, Matthew, VP-Sls - ABF Freight System, Inc.; *pg.* 1896, *pg.* 31
Letterio, Vince, Dir-Direct Sls - DC Comics, Inc.; *pg.* 1633, *pg.* 1221
Lettman, Maria, Dir-Social Media - Cargill, Inc.; *pg.* 845, *pg.* 965
Lettow, Kris, Sr Dir-Ops-Honeycomb Bus Unit - Hunter Douglas, Inc.; *pg.* 928, *pg.* 1320
Leuer, Katherine, Sr Analyst-Affiliate Mktg - Bloomingdale's, Inc.; *pg.* 1763, *pg.* 1204
Leung, Alicia, Mgr-Social Media - Warner Bros. Entertainment Inc.; *pg.* 319, *pg.* 54
Leung, Amy S., Dir-Loyalty Mktg & Channel Mgmt - American Express Company; *pg.* 712, *pg.* 1190
Leung, Curtis, Mgr-Web Mktg-Strategic Initiatives - Autodesk Inc.; *pg.* 356, *pg.* 257
Leung, Joanna, Mgr-Mktg, Mergers, Acq & Private Brands Strategy - 7-Eleven, Inc.; *pg.* 1012, *pg.* 1672
Leung, Kenneth, Dir-Enterprise Indus Mktg - Avaya Inc.; *pg.* 621, *pg.* 264
Leung, Kevin, Mgr-Product Mktg - AT&T; *pg.* 1865, *pg.* 258
Leung, Kristy, Sr Mgr-Consumer Mktg - Reynolds American Inc.; *pg.* 1894, *pg.* 1395
Leung, Matthew, Dir-Adv - Reckitt Benckiser Inc.; *pg.* 1136, *pg.* 1105
Leung, Mayee, Sr VP-Mktg - Tupperware Brands Corporation; *pg.* 1139, *pg.* 456
Leung, Sofia, Sr Product Mgr-Mktg Innovations Grp - Intuit Inc.; *pg.* 769, *pg.* 158
Leunissen, Marc, Dir-Sls-Louisiana - Cox Communications, Inc.; *pg.* 279, *pg.* 501
Leupold, Phil, Dir-Sls-Global - Weyerhaeuser Company; *pg.* 121, *pg.* 1820
Leuschner, Carl, VP-Internet/Phone Products - Charter Communications, Inc.; *pg.* 274, *pg.* 372
Leuthe, Paul, Corp Mgr-Mktg - Sub Zero Wolf; *pg.* 60, *pg.* 1867
Leuzarder, Jennie, Mgr-On Premise Strategy & Multicultural Mktg - Diageo North America Inc.; *pg.* 248, *pg.* 1223
Levak, Dan, Dir-Digital Media - Atlanta Falcons Football Club, LLC; *pg.* 530, *pg.* 532
Levan, Marnie, Dir-Digital Mktg Maybelline - L'Oreal USA; *pg.* 514, *pg.* 1252
LeVasseur, Armand, Dir-Curio Brand Mktg - Hilton Worldwide, Inc.; *pg.* 1094, *pg.* 1791
Levchenko, Mariya, Strategist-Social Media - John Hancock Financial Services; *pg.* 1205, *pg.* 796
LeVeau, Steve, Dir-Mktg - Central Garden & Pet Company; *pg.* 1475, *pg.* 303
Leveck, Colleen, Brand Mgr - Continental Mills, Inc.; *pg.* 827, *pg.* 1845
Levee, Brian, Product Mgr - Google Inc.; *pg.* 1249, *pg.* 153
Leveen, Jami, Dir-Mktg & Environmental Stewardship - Aramark; *pg.* 1013, *pg.* 1558
Leveille, Craig, Exec Dir-FX Products - CME Group Inc.; *pg.* 738, *pg.* 571
Leven, Bari, Reg Sls Mgr-Advanced Products-Comcast Bus - Comcast Corporation; *pg.* 276, *pg.* 1560
Levenson, Alexis, Sr Dir-Enterprise Comm - Pfizer Inc.; *pg.* 1581, *pg.* 1278
Levenson, David, Acct Dir-Adv Sls - Sirius XM Holdings Inc.; *pg.* 308, *pg.* 1292
Levenson, Rodger, Interim CFO - WSFS Financial Corporation; *pg.* 823, *pg.* 392
Leventhal, Dan, Sr Mgr-Digital Content Syndication - Showtime Networks Inc.; *pg.* 308, *pg.* 1291
Leventhal, Susan, Dir-Mktg - A&E Stores, Inc.; *pg.* 17, *pg.* 1124
Leverenz, Julie, Dir-Mktg - Cisco Systems, Inc.; *pg.* 372, *pg.* 240
Leverenz, Julie, Dir-Mktg-Americas Enterprise - NetApp, Inc.; *pg.* 444, *pg.* 287
Leverette, Kate, VP-Mktg - Kentucky Lottery Corporation; *pg.* 996, *pg.* 735
Levesque, Aubrey, Mgr-Mktg - The Travelers Companies, Inc.; *pg.* 1220, *pg.* 352
Levesque, Christopher, VP-Mktg & Mdsg - Anvil Holdings, Inc.; *pg.* 18, *pg.* 1195
Levesque, Louise, VP-Corp Mktg - Cirque du Soleil Inc.; *pg.* 540, *pg.* 1954
Levey, Andy, Dir-Mktg, 360 & Content - Cirque du Soleil Inc.; *pg.* 540, *pg.* 1954
Levi, Karin, VP-B2B Digital Mktg-US - MasterCard Incorporated; *pg.* 779, *pg.* 1325
Levi, Libby, Designer-Brand Vision - Red Hat, Inc.; *pg.* 460, *pg.* 1388
Levi, Natalie, Asst Mgr-Global Mktg-Philosophy Fragrances - Coty, Inc.; *pg.* 506, *pg.* 1219
Levi, Ross, VP-Mktg Initiatives - Empire State Development-Division of Tourism; *pg.* 992, *pg.* 1227
Levia, Jim, Sr Mgr-Sls - Mitchel-Lincoln Packaging Ltd; *pg.* 1464, *pg.* 1960
Levien, Meredith Kopit, Exec VP-Adv - The New York Times Company; *pg.* 1668, *pg.* 1270
Levin, Carolyn, Assoc Dir-Consumer Mktg - Bristol-Myers Squibb Company; *pg.* 1509, *pg.* 1206
Levin, Olga, VP-Corp Mktg & Adv - CNA Insurance Companies; *pg.* 1198, *pg.* 571
Levin, Per H., Pres/Chief Sls Officer-Shrink Mgmt Solutions & Mdse Visibility - Checkpoint Systems, Inc.; *pg.* 628, *pg.* 1559
Levin, Roberto, Sr Mgr-ECommerce Mktg - World Wrestling Entertainment, Inc.; *pg.* 595, *pg.* 380
Levin, Wayne, Chief Strategic Officer & Gen Counsel - Lions Gate Entertainment Corp.; *pg.* 296, *pg.* 274
Levin-Scherz, Josh, Mgr-Mktg - DraftKings, Inc.; *pg.* 545, *pg.* 793
Levine, Aaron, Sr Mgr-Product Mktg - Sony Corporation of America; *pg.* 675, *pg.* 1293
Levine, Aaron, Sr Mgr-Product Mktg - Sony Electronics, Inc.; *pg.* 676, *pg.* 209
Levine, Carole, VP-Mktg-Global - Mattel Games/Puzzles; *pg.* 962, *pg.* 80
Levine, Carole, VP-Mktg-Global - MATTEL, INC.; *pg.* 962, *pg.* 81
Levine, Christa, Brand Mgr-Bashas Family of Stores - Bashas' Supermarkets; *pg.* 1015, *pg.* 12
Levine, Dara, Dir-Product Mgmt - Tumi, Inc.; *pg.* 15, *pg.* 1123
Levine, Debby, Brand Mgr - Macy's East; *pg.* 1777, *pg.* 1254
Levine, Deidre, Sr Mgr-Acct Mgmt Adv & Direct Mail - The Gap, Inc.; *pg.* 1770, *pg.* 218
Levine, Greg, Analyst-Sls - The NASDAQ OMX Group, Inc.; *pg.* 785, *pg.* 1263
Levine, Harry, Mgr-Product Mktg - Hewlett-Packard Company; *pg.* 404, *pg.* 175
Levine, Holli, Assoc Dir-Mktg Procurement - The Kraft Heinz Company; *pg.* 871, *pg.* 641
Levine, Jason, Sr Dir-Mktg - Gilead Sciences, Inc.; *pg.* 1535, *pg.* 88
Levine, Jeremy, Sr VP-Digital Sls - Live Nation Entertainment, Inc.; *pg.* 558, *pg.* 47
Levine, Jeremy, Sr VP-Digital Sls - Live Nation Worldwide - Times Square Office; *pg.* 558, *pg.* 1252
Levine, Josh, Mgr-Product Mktg - Google Inc.; *pg.* 1249, *pg.* 153
Levine, Kevin, Dir-Mktg Svcs-Europe - Bose Corporation; *pg.* 626, *pg.* 820
Levine, Neil, Sr Dir-Mktg-Ophthalmology - Regeneron Pharmaceuticals, Inc.; *pg.* 1588, *pg.* 1345
Levine, Pamela, Exec VP-Mktg - Home Box Office, Inc.; *pg.* 290, *pg.* 1240
Levine, Robyn Mait, VP-Sls Dev - WebMD Health Corporation; *pg.* 1288, *pg.* 1313
Levine, Rory, Dir-Mktg & Comm - AIGA, the professional association for design; *pg.* 125, *pg.* 1188
Levine, Sandi, Sr Assoc Brand Mgr - BIC Corporation; *pg.* 501, *pg.* 369
Levine, Tammy, VP-PR - Electronic Arts Inc.; *pg.* 951, *pg.* 189
Levine, Whitney, Mgr-Pay for Performance-Digital Mktg - The Sports Authority, Inc.; *pg.* 1846, *pg.* 326
Levings, Richard, Product Mgr - Charles Machine Works, Inc.; *pg.* 1322, *pg.* 1488
Levinson, Howard, Sr VP-Adv Sls - Yankees Entertainment & Sports Network, LLC; *pg.* 324, *pg.* 1316
Levinson, Jen, Sr Dir-NBA Creative Svcs - NBA Properties, Inc.; *pg.* 569, *pg.* 1120
Levinson, Peter, Sr VP-Product & Tech - LifeLock Inc.; *pg.* 776, *pg.* 26
Levinson, Toru, Mgr-PR - Absolute Software Corporation; *pg.* 340, *pg.* 1909
Levinthal, Phyllis, Sr VP & Head-Global Category Mktg & Adv - Citigroup Inc.; *pg.* 735, *pg.* 1212
Levinton, Jennifer, Specialist-Mktg & Comm - Xerox Corporation; *pg.* 494, *pg.* 365
Levitskaya-Lecue, Elena, Dir-Mktg - The Dannon Company, Inc.; *pg.* 851, *pg.* 1351

Levitt, Laurie, Assoc Dir-Integrated Mktg - AARP Publications; *pg.* 1613, *pg.* 1185
Levitt, Liza, Deputy Gen Counsel-Products & Dir - Intuit Inc.; *pg.* 769, *pg.* 158
Levitt, Walter, Exec VP-Mktg-Comedy Central - Comedy Partners; *pg.* 278, *pg.* 1216
Levitz, Alyssa, Product Mgr - Facebook, Inc.; *pg.* 1245, *pg.* 143
Levos, Taylor, Acct Exec-Sls - Telemundo Network Inc.; *pg.* 311, *pg.* 430
Levy, Andrew, Assoc Mgr-Product Mktg - G&K Services Inc.; *pg.* 693, *pg.* 949
Levy, Brian, Dir-Direct Response Sls - NBC Universal, Inc.; *pg.* 300, *pg.* 1266
Levy, Daniella, Acct Mgr-Marriott Creative & Content Mktg - Marriott International, Inc.; *pg.* 1102, *pg.* 764
Levy, Eric, Sr VP & Head-Product & Solutions Mgmt-Retirement Plan Svcs - Lincoln Financial Group; *pg.* 1206, *pg.* 1375
Levy, Jon, Brand Mgr - The Kraft Heinz Company; *pg.* 871, *pg.* 641
Levy, Justin, Dir-Social Mktg - Citrix Systems, Inc.; *pg.* 375, *pg.* 424
Levy, Linda, Grp VP & Div Mgr-Mdse-Cosmetics - Macy's, Inc.; *pg.* 1778, *pg.* 1417
Levy, Mark, Dir-Natl Medical, Medicare & Medicaid Products - Anthem, Inc.; *pg.* 1192, *pg.* 683
Levy, Melissa, Mgr-Content Mktg - BUFFALO WILD WINGS, INC.; *pg.* 1718, *pg.* 931
Levy, Michael, Product Mgr-Colocation - CenturyLink, Inc.; *pg.* 1870, *pg.* 746
Levy, Patrick, Product Mgr - Pall Corporation; *pg.* 232, *pg.* 1323
Levy, Sid, Sr Dir-Comm & Community Rels - Snyder's-Lance, Inc.; *pg.* 896, *pg.* 1368
Levy-Lamoreaux, Jo-Anne, Mgr-Adv & Internet Svcs - The Phillies, L.P.; *pg.* 575, *pg.* 1569
Levzow, Erin, VP-Mktg - Freebirds World Burrito; *pg.* 1729, *pg.* 1662
Lew, Ashleigh, Mgr-Originals Mktg - Netflix, Inc.; *pg.* 1269, *pg.* 141
Lew, Daisy, Dir-Product Dev & Res - Manulife Financial Corporation; *pg.* 778, *pg.* 1939
Lew, Dave, Dir-Brand Mktg-Writing-Global - Newell Rubbermaid Inc.; *pg.* 1128, *pg.* 515
Lew, Kim H., Sr Mgr-Oncology Scientific Affairs - Amgen Inc.; *pg.* 1493, *pg.* 291
Lewallen, Jimmie, Mgr-Email Mktg - Blue Nile, Inc.; *pg.* 2, *pg.* 1834
Lewan, Dave, VP-Sls-Answers Cloud Svcs - Answers Corporation; *pg.* 1229, *pg.* 1195
Lewandowski, Cathy, Sr Mgr-PR-AT&T Corp Comm - AT&T Inc.; *pg.* 1867, *pg.* 1674
Lewandowski, Kelly, Specialist-Mktg, PR & Comm - Flextronics International Ltd.; *pg.* 81, *pg.* 245
Lewbart, Brian, Sr Mgr-PR - T. Rowe Price Group Inc.; *pg.* 808, *pg.* 759
Lewchuk, Rick, Sr VP-Creative Mktg - Cable News Network LP; *pg.* 1624, *pg.* 1208
Lewczyk, Rob, Head-Creative - eBay Inc.; *pg.* 1240, *pg.* 243
Lewellyn, Teca, Sr Mgr-Brand Comm - Kellogg Company; *pg.* 831, *pg.* 870
Lewenthal, Lisa L., Dir-Mktg Comm & Dir-Event Mktg - Convergys Corporation; *pg.* 379, *pg.* 1412
Lewiecki, Mark, Sr Product Mgr - Adobe Systems Incorporated; *pg.* 342, *pg.* 235
Lewin, Catharina, Producer-Creative Resources-Global Mktg Comm - MATTEL, INC.; *pg.* 962, *pg.* 81
Lewin, Lysa, VP-Convention Sls - San Francisco Travel Association; *pg.* 1005, *pg.* 227
Lewinson, Hilary, Mgr-Global Trade Mktg-Performance Sports - Oakley, Inc.; *pg.* 1840, *pg.* 86
Lewis, Alexander, Sr Assoc Brand Mgr - The Kraft Heinz Company; *pg.* 871, *pg.* 641
Lewis, Amy, Dir-Web Mktg - Forrester Research, Inc.; *pg.* 1642, *pg.* 807
Lewis, Anthony, Sr Dir - QUALCOMM Incorporated; *pg.* 1873, *pg.* 207
Lewis, Arthur, VP-Client Solutions Sls-Americas - Dell Inc.; *pg.* 383, *pg.* 1737
Lewis, Arthur, Exec VP-Product Dev & Head-Design-New York - Kohl's Corporation; *pg.* 1775, *pg.* 1870
Lewis, Bill, Sr VP-Sls & Mktg - Frosty Acres Brands, Inc.; *pg.* 1020, *pg.* 484
Lewis, Casey, Sr Mgr-Corp Comm - Nintendo of America, Inc.; *pg.* 965, *pg.* 1829
Lewis, Dal, Asst Dir-Sls - The Calgary Sun; *pg.* 1625, *pg.* 1903
Lewis, Daniel, Dir-New Media Comm - Sesame Workshop; *pg.* 307, *pg.* 1290
Lewis, David, Exec VP-Sls & Mktg - Baker Publishing Group; *pg.* 1619, *pg.* 864
Lewis, Debra, Brand Mgr - BrassCraft Manufacturing Company; *pg.* 1043, *pg.* 902
Lewis, Dijuana, Exec VP-Consumer Products & Enterprise Mktg - Aetna Inc.; *pg.* 1187, *pg.* 351
Lewis, Dwain, Dir-Grp Sls - Detroit Tigers Baseball Club, Inc.; *pg.* 545, *pg.* 880
Lewis, Ed, Chief Strategy Officer - Syniverse Holdings, Inc.; *pg.* 479, *pg.* 475
Lewis, Elizabeth, Sr Assoc Brand Mgr - Bridgestone Americas, Inc.; *pg.* 1879, *pg.* 1648
Lewis, Elizabeth, Sr Assoc Brand Mgr - Bridgestone Americas, Inc.; *pg.* 201, *pg.* 1649
Lewis, Erika, Sr Mgr-Press-Entertainment Publicity - NBC Universal, Inc.; *pg.* 300, *pg.* 1266
Lewis, Guy, VP-Strategic Mktg & Plng - Honeywell International Inc.; *pg.* 407, *pg.* 1088
Lewis, Hannah, Assoc Dir-Mktg-Ketchup, Condiments & Sauces - The Kraft Heinz Company; *pg.* 870, *pg.* 1577
Lewis, Haston, VP-Customer Mktg - PepsiCo, Inc.; *pg.* 259, *pg.* 1327
Lewis, Haston , II, Sr Dir-Mktg - Frito-Lay North America, Inc.; *pg.* 1853, *pg.* 1730
Lewis, Janel, Mgr-Mktg-Global - BIC Corporation; *pg.* 501, *pg.* 369
Lewis, Jeanine, Sr Mgr-Mktg-Multicultural Mktg - The Coca-Cola Company; *pg.* 240, *pg.* 493
Lewis, Jenn, Dir-Mktg & ILS - Cardinal Health, Inc.; *pg.* 1512, *pg.* 1448
Lewis, Jenna, Mgr-Mdse - Lowe's Companies, Inc.; *pg.* 1053, *pg.* 1383
Lewis, Jennifer, VP-Mktg - Digital Insight; *pg.* 744, *pg.* 189
Lewis, Jenny M., Sr Mgr-Innovation - Nestle Healthcare Nutrition; *pg.* 1572, *pg.* 941
Lewis, Johanna K., Sr VP & Gen Mgr-Mdse-Decorative Home - Ross Stores, Inc.; *pg.* 1783, *pg.* 78
Lewis, John, Mgr-Mktg - Praxair, Inc.; *pg.* 1178, *pg.* 344
Lewis, John, Dir-Global Analytics & Consumer Mktg - The Scotts Miracle-Gro Company; *pg.* 1799, *pg.* 1459
Lewis, Julie, VP & Product Mgr-Mktg - Bank of America Corporation; *pg.* 718, *pg.* 1362
Lewis, Karin, Mgr-Parts Sls - Bryant Grinder; *pg.* 1320, *pg.* 1768
Lewis, Kate, Head-Mktg Programs & Events - Aetna Inc.; *pg.* 1187, *pg.* 351
Lewis, Kevin T., Dir-Global Mktg-Dow Plastics Additives - THE DOW CHEMICAL COMPANY; *pg.* 1157, *pg.* 898
Lewis, Kim, Sr VP-Sls-West Coast & Midwest - BET Holdings LLC; *pg.* 271, *pg.* 396
Lewis, Kirk M., Dir-Mktg-Software & Peripherals - Dell Inc.; *pg.* 383, *pg.* 1737
Lewis, Lena, Sr Mgr-Shopper Mktg - Wm. Wrigley Jr. Company; *pg.* 1863, *pg.* 596
Lewis, Lindsey, Brand Mgr-Global Jergens Skin Care - Kao Brands Co. Inc.; *pg.* 513, *pg.* 1415
Lewis, Lori, VP-Social Media - Cumulus Media Inc.; *pg.* 280, *pg.* 503
Lewis, Lori, Coord-Mktg - State Farm Mutual Automobile Insurance Co.; *pg.* 1218, *pg.* 557
Lewis, Mark, VP-Integrated Mktg - Discovery Communications, Inc.; *pg.* 282, *pg.* 777
Lewis, Martyn, Dir-Mktg-EMEA-CIT Aerospace - CIT GROUP INC.; *pg.* 735, *pg.* 1212
Lewis, Mary, Sr Mgr-Promotional Matl Mgmt - Sanofi US; *pg.* 1592, *pg.* 1046
Lewis, Melinda, VP-Mktg - Ferrara Candy Co.; *pg.* 1852, *pg.* 612
Lewis, Michael, Analyst-Consumer Product Strategic - Bank of America Corporation; *pg.* 718, *pg.* 1362
Lewis, Michael, Sr Mgr-Comm - Midas International, Inc.; *pg.* 212, *pg.* 620
Lewis, Mike, Product Mgr-Bus Travel - Airbnb, Inc.; *pg.* 1226, *pg.* 211
Lewis, Monte, VP-Sls - Dunn-Edwards Corporation; *pg.* 1442, *pg.* 129
Lewis, Nicole M., VP-Mktg-Global - Kelly Services, Inc.; *pg.* 424, *pg.* 911
Lewis, Nitsa, VP-Mktg - Crystal Cruises LLC; *pg.* 1904, *pg.* 128
Lewis, Paige, Dir-Mktg Programs - Red Hat, Inc.; *pg.* 460, *pg.* 1388
Lewis, Paige, VP-Mktg - Universal Studios, Inc.; *pg.* 315, *pg.* 298
Lewis, Pete, Sr Dir-Mktg - Stonyfield Farm, Inc.; *pg.* 899, *pg.* 1035
Lewis, Preston, Dir-Product - BodyBuilding.com LLC; *pg.* 1232, *pg.* 549
Lewis, Randy, VP-Mktg-Global - Brooklyn Nets; *pg.* 534, *pg.* 1145
Lewis, Randy, Mgr-Sls-Natl - Featherlite, Inc.; *pg.* 1707, *pg.* 704
Lewis, Sarah, Mgr-Mktg Comm - Meridian Bioscience Inc.; *pg.* 1422, *pg.* 1417
Lewis, Shaun L., Dir-PR & Strategic Partnerships-Global - Levi Strauss & Co.; *pg.* 43, *pg.* 220
Lewis, Susan, VP-Investor & Media Rels - Aeropostale, Inc.; *pg.* 17, *pg.* 1188
Lewis, Thom, VP-Mktg - Target Corporation; *pg.* 1786, *pg.* 912
Lewis, Tina, Sr Mgr-Market Analysis - The Boeing Company; *pg.* 225, *pg.* 567
Lewis, Vince, Mgr-Global Mktg Comm - Bell Helicopter Textron, Inc.; *pg.* 224, *pg.* 1693
Lewis-Parks, April, Dir-Community & PR - Consolidated Credit Counseling Services, Inc.; *pg.* 741, *pg.* 424
Ley, Brandon M., Coord-Mktg & Comm - Ameriprise Financial, Inc.; *pg.* 715, *pg.* 930
Leyba, Lisa, Mgr-Digital Mktg - The WhiteWave Foods Company; *pg.* 1037, *pg.* 324
Leyden, Melanie, Dir-Mktg - Ghirardelli Chocolate Company; *pg.* 1854, *pg.* 252
Leyden, Nicole Pezzola, VP-Digital Sls - Scripps Networks Interactive, Inc.; *pg.* 1279, *pg.* 1638
Leymon, Melissa Walters, Mgr-Mktg Program & Plng - PNM Resources, Inc.; *pg.* 1949, *pg.* 1135
Lezynski, Jerry, Mng Dir-Mktg & Comm - SEI Investments Company; *pg.* 802, *pg.* 1558
Lhotka, Deborah, Sr Mgr-Category & Trade Mktg - Sunstar Americas Inc.; *pg.* 1599, *pg.* 591
Li, Amy, Sr Mgr-Bus Strategy & Process - American Express Company; *pg.* 712, *pg.* 1190
Li, Becky, Mgr-Mktg Plng & Forecasting - Esurance, Inc.; *pg.* 1243, *pg.* 217
Li, Carol, Sr Mgr-Customer Lifecycle Analytics - Gilt Groupe Inc.; *pg.* 24, *pg.* 1234
Li, Henry, Sr Dir-Mobile Strategic Partnerships - NeuStar, Inc.; *pg.* 1872, *pg.* 1807
Li, Jennifer, Assoc Mgr-Mktg-Small Bus Grp - Intuit Inc.; *pg.* 769, *pg.* 158
Li, Jia, Brand Mgr - Nestle USA, Inc.; *pg.* 883, *pg.* 96
Li, John, Sr Mgr-Online Mktg-Sls Solutions - LinkedIn Corporation; *pg.* 1262, *pg.* 160
Li, Julia, Program Head-CRM & Email Mktg - Nintendo of America, Inc.; *pg.* 965, *pg.* 1829
Li, Lana, Mgr-Sls Mktg - Pandora Media Inc.; *pg.* 1273, *pg.* 172
Li, Pavan, Product Mgr - Microsoft Corporation; *pg.* 435, *pg.* 1824
Li, Raymond, Sr Dir-Engrg Multimedia ASIC - Advanced Micro Devices, Inc.-Markham; *pg.* 345, *pg.* 1922
Li, Stephen, Product Mgr-Global - Littelfuse, Inc.; *pg.* 1301, *pg.* 580
Li, Susan, Sr Mgr-Subject Matter Expert-UPS Temperature True Pkg - United Parcel Service, Inc.; *pg.* 1928, *pg.* 522
Li, Tina, Sr Mgr-Customer Valuation - DIRECTV Group Holdings, LLC; *pg.* 281, *pg.* 79
Li, Ting, Sr VP-Sls-China - Broadcom Corporation; *pg.* 364, *pg.* 108
Li, Xue Yun, Sr Mgr-Mdsg-ECommerce Philosophy.com - Coty, Inc.; *pg.* 506, *pg.* 1219
Li, Yan, Sr Dir-Memory Strategy - SanDisk Corporation; *pg.* 465, *pg.* 147
Li, Yu, Sr Designer-Product - Citrix Systems, Inc.; *pg.* 375, *pg.* 424
Li, Yue, Sr Mgr-QA - EMC Corporation; *pg.* 391, *pg.* 825
LiaBraaten, Julie, Sr Dir-Brand, Market & Consumer Insights - T-Mobile US, Inc.; *pg.* 676, *pg.* 1816
Liang, Joyce, Dir-SMB Mktg - Box Inc.; *pg.* 1232, *pg.* 124
Liang, June, Sr Mgr-Strategic Partnerships - Kayak; *pg.* 1260, *pg.* 363
Liang, Lingzi, Sr Mgr-Workforce Optimization - PepsiCo, Inc.; *pg.* 259, *pg.* 1327
Liao, Jackie, Sr Mgr-Community Investments - Starbucks Corporation; *pg.* 897, *pg.* 1840

First page reference indicates Business Class Edition
Second page reference indicates Geographic Edition

Liaw, Wally Yih-Shyan, VP-Sls - Super Micro Computer, Inc.; *pg.* 478, *pg.* 251
Libbe, Katie, VP-Consumer Mktg & Solutions - Allianz Life Insurance Company of North America; *pg.* 1188, *pg.* 929
Libbey, Robert, Head-Digital & Social Comm - Pfizer Inc.; *pg.* 1581, *pg.* 1278
Libby, Allie, VP & Dir-PR-The Private Bank - Wells Fargo & Company; *pg.* 819, *pg.* 232
Liberato, Bill, Head-Primary Care Sls-Natl Bus Grp - Merck & Co., Inc.; *pg.* 1566, *pg.* 1077
Liberto, Andrea, Sr Mgr-Trade Mktg - AS America, Inc.; *pg.* 68, *pg.* 1108
Liberty, Luke, Sr Specialist-Mktg-Global - Thermo Fisher Scientific Inc.; *pg.* 1431, *pg.* 854
Libonati, Pamela, Assoc Dir-Creative - Bloomingdale's, Inc.; *pg.* 1763, *pg.* 1204
Librach, Jeffrey R., Sr Mgr-Construction - NewGround Resources; *pg.* 99, *pg.* 975
Librett, Craig, Sr Dir-PR-Global - Westcon Group, Inc.; *pg.* 492, *pg.* 1345
Librett, Mauri, VP-Mktg - Arett Sales Corporation; *pg.* 700, *pg.* 1107
LiCalzi, Dave, VP-Product Mktg-CBS Sports - CBS Interactive, Inc.; *pg.* 369, *pg.* 215
Licari, Joe, Sr Dir-Sls - Yahoo! Inc.; *pg.* 1289, *pg.* 289
Licata, Patricia, Sr Rep-PR - United States Postal Service; *pg.* 1009, *pg.* 406
Licata, Rachel, Mgr-Digital Media - Buffalo Bills, Inc.; *pg.* 535, *pg.* 1319
Licato, Jim, Sr Product Mgr-Fiduciary Svcs - MORNINGSTAR, INC.; *pg.* 784, *pg.* 583
Liceaga, Marco, VP-Mktg & Promo-Univision Deportes - Univision Communications Inc.; *pg.* 683, *pg.* 1307
Licht, Lisa, Sr VP-Mktg Partnerships & Platforms - Yahoo! Inc.; *pg.* 1289, *pg.* 289
Lichthart, Kris, Mgr-Digital Mktg - Monrovia Growers; *pg.* 1797, *pg.* 44
Lichtinshtein, Emanuel, Mgr-Natl Fleet Sls, CPO & Remarketing - Volvo Cars of Canada Ltd.; *pg.* 195, *pg.* 1946
Lichtman, Seth, Dir-Mktg - Hamilton Beach Brands, Inc.; *pg.* 56, *pg.* 1783
Lichtmess, Eric, VP-Adv & Integrated Media-The Americas - Tommy Hilfiger USA; *pg.* 48, *pg.* 1302
Lichtner, Jenny, Sr Dir-Comml Dev & Inflammation - Pfizer Inc.; *pg.* 1581, *pg.* 1278
Lick, Neil, VP & Div Mgr-Mdse-Retail Mdsg - Williams-Sonoma, Inc.; *pg.* 1140, *pg.* 234
Liddiard, Michele, Mgr-Strategic Sourcing-Mktg - Sony Pictures Entertainment Inc.; *pg.* 309, *pg.* 72
Liddle, Don, Mgr-Product Comm - Siemens Canada Ltd.; *pg.* 1306, *pg.* 1921
Lidow, Arel, VP-Product Mgmt - AppNexus; *pg.* 352, *pg.* 1196
Lidrbauch, David, Sr Product Mktg Mgr-Functional Verification - Cadence Design Systems, Inc.; *pg.* 367, *pg.* 239
Lieb, Dave, Product Mgr-Google Photos - Google Inc.; *pg.* 1249, *pg.* 153
Lieber, Nathalie, Grp Product Mktg Mgr-Content & Community - LinkedIn Corporation; *pg.* 1262, *pg.* 160
Lieberman, Carrie, Sr Dir-Content Distr - NBC Universal, Inc.; *pg.* 300, *pg.* 1266
Lieberman, Josh, VP-Digital Mktg - Barneys New York, Inc.; *pg.* 38, *pg.* 1201
Lieberman, Rita, Dir-Mktg Comm - Thomas Register of American Manufacturers; *pg.* 1692, *pg.* 1299
Lieberman, Sarah, VP & Dir-Mktg - Simon & Schuster, Inc.; *pg.* 1687, *pg.* 1292
Lieberman, Scott, Mgr-Bus Dev & Mktg-Ingersoll Rand Fin Svcs - Ingersoll-Rand Company; *pg.* 1349, *pg.* 1370
Lieberman, Tressie, Sr Dir-Digital Experience & Social Engagement - Taco Bell Corp.; *pg.* 1752, *pg.* 117
Liebert, Mark, VP-Mktg Education - Association of National Advertisers, Inc.; *pg.* 133, *pg.* 1197
Liebeskind, Howard, Sr Mgr-Mktg Svcs - 505 Games (US), Inc.; *pg.* 948, *pg.* 38
Liebig, Jennifer, Dir-Dev Mktg-Global - Starwood Hotels & Resorts Worldwide, Inc.; *pg.* 1114, *pg.* 378
Liebl, Jeff, CMO & VP - Digi International Inc.; *pg.* 387, *pg.* 948
Liebler, Brian, VP-Adv Sls & Bus Dev - ooVoo LLC; *pg.* 1272, *pg.* 1274
Liebman, Christina N., Dir-Integrated Mktg-Global - Emerson Process Management; *pg.* 1334, *pg.* 1636
Liebman, Gregg, Sr VP-Adv Sls Insights & Strategy - Telemundo Network Inc.; *pg.* 311, *pg.* 430
Liebman, Jeremy, Assoc Mgr-Social Media - Constellation Brands, Inc.; *pg.* 1960, *pg.* 1348
Liebman, Paul, Mgr-Mktg - Coilcraft, Inc.; *pg.* 1324, *pg.* 562
Liebo, Sherri L., VP-Mktg - Cisco Systems, Inc.; *pg.* 372, *pg.* 240
Liebowitz, Jason, VP-Sls - LiveWorld, Inc.; *pg.* 1264, *pg.* 246
Lief, Sophia, Asst Mgr-Social Media Mktg - Coach, Inc.; *pg.* 3, *pg.* 1214
Liem, Bing, VP-Sls & Mktg - FUJIFILM U.S.A., Inc.; *pg.* 1414, *pg.* 1348
Lien Kralevich, Vivian, VP-Mktg & Bus Dev - ASUSTeK Computer Inc; *pg.* 355, *pg.* 90
Lien, Nick, Sr Product Mgr - The Kroger Co.; *pg.* 1025, *pg.* 1416
Liese, Donna, Mgr-Adv - Princeton University Press; *pg.* 1678, *pg.* 1112
Lieszkovszky, Michelle, Brand Mgr - Butterball, LLC; *pg.* 843, *pg.* 1385
Lietz, Corinna, Designer-Interactive-Mobile Apps, Set Top Box & Web - DIRECTV Group Holdings, LLC; *pg.* 281, *pg.* 79
Lietzke-Nastuk, Kristin, Dir-Campaign Mktg - Cadence Design Systems, Inc.; *pg.* 367, *pg.* 239
Lieu, Hansen, Dir-Solution Mktg - SAP America, Inc.; *pg.* 466, *pg.* 1557
Lifgren, Ashley, Acct Mgr-Inside Sls - Dell Storage; *pg.* 386, *pg.* 922
Lifshitz, Laura, Mgr-Digital Media - Colavita USA, Inc.; *pg.* 849, *pg.* 1056
Lifsitz, David, Dir-Creative - Liberty Mutual Insurance Group Inc.; *pg.* 1205, *pg.* 797
Light, Gary, Dir-Retail Sls-Selkirk, Hart & Cooley - Selkirk Corporation; *pg.* 1076, *pg.* 1736
Light, Geoff, VP-New Product Dev - United Parcel Service, Inc.; *pg.* 1928, *pg.* 522
Lightbody, Jennifer, Dir-Mktg Strategy - Nordstrom, Inc.; *pg.* 1779, *pg.* 1837
Lihwa, John, Product Mgr - Graco, Inc.; *pg.* 1342, *pg.* 935
Liipfert, Jeff, Assoc Dir-Media - AT&T Southeast; *pg.* 1868, *pg.* 489
Likens, John, Sr VP-Mdsg - Moran Foods, Inc.; *pg.* 1028, *pg.* 976
Likens, John, Sr VP-Mdsg - Save-A-Lot, Ltd.; *pg.* 894, *pg.* 977
Likoray, Peter, Sr VP-Sls-Bus Aircraft - Bombardier Inc.; *pg.* 1318, *pg.* 1953
Liles, Sheila, Coord-Adv Production - Harris Teeter, Inc.; *pg.* 1022, *pg.* 1383
Lilienthal, Rainer, Sr Mgr-Trade Dev - Port of Houston Authority; *pg.* 1920, *pg.* 1713
Liljeberg, Thomas, Exec VP-Product Line Mgmt - Source Photonics, Inc.; *pg.* 1429, *pg.* 305
Lillard, Brooke, Dir-Sls - Gannett Co., Inc.; *pg.* 1643, *pg.* 1790
Lilleboe, Laura A., Product Mgr-Mktg - UnitedHealth Group Incorporated; *pg.* 1221, *pg.* 950
Lilley, Andy, Product Dir - Bottomline Technologies (de), Inc.; *pg.* 727, *pg.* 1038
Lilley, Derek, Sr Mgr-Consumer & Market Insights - Wm. Wrigley Jr. Company; *pg.* 1863, *pg.* 596
Lilley, Karen, Sr Mgr-Innovation - Diageo North America Inc.; *pg.* 248, *pg.* 1223
Lilley, May, Sr Mgr-Intl Comm - Vail Resorts, Inc.; *pg.* 1117, *pg.* 313
Lilley, Michelle, Mgr-Mktg-Little Tikes - MGA Entertainment, Inc.; *pg.* 964, *pg.* 300
Lillis, Kristen, Sr Specialist-Mktg - Brooks Brothers Group, Inc.; *pg.* 39, *pg.* 1208
Lillis, Lauren, Mgr-Social Media - U.S. Bancorp; *pg.* 815, *pg.* 945
Lilly, Adam, Dir-Digital, New Media & Global Mktg - The Donna Karan Company LLC; *pg.* 23, *pg.* 1225
Lilly, Danna, Dir-Sls - Myrtle Beach Area Convention and Visitors Bureau; *pg.* 565, *pg.* 1621
Lilly, Melissa, Brand Mgr-Mktg - DISH Network Corporation; *pg.* 283, *pg.* 325
Lilly, Russel, Dir-Mktg-Dressings US - Unilever United States, Inc.; *pg.* 904, *pg.* 1061
Lim, Aik Leong, Sr Mgr-Mdsg - NIKE, Inc.; *pg.* 1812, *pg.* 1492
Lim, Andrea, Mgr-Engagement Mktg - Lexus Division; *pg.* 182, *pg.* 294
Lim, Christina, Sr Mgr-Creative Design, Global Retail & Corp Mktg - SanDisk Corporation; *pg.* 465, *pg.* 147
Lim, Clara, Sr Mgr-Mktg-Digital Acq & Strategy - Intuit Inc.; *pg.* 769, *pg.* 158
Lim, Dennis, Assoc Mgr-ECommerce Mktg - Cost Plus World Market; *pg.* 921, *pg.* 170
Lim, Jason, Dir-Creative Svcs - Golden State Warriors, LLC; *pg.* 550, *pg.* 171
Lim, Jennifer, Mgr-Social Media & Brand Content Mktg - Hyundai Motor America; *pg.* 179, *pg.* 89
Lim, Jihae, Assoc Brand Mktg Mgr - Papa Murphy's International, LLC; *pg.* 1743, *pg.* 1846
Lim, Karissa, Brand Mgr-Horizon Organic - The WhiteWave Foods Company; *pg.* 1037, *pg.* 324
Lim, Kelly, Specialist-Relationship Mktg - StubHub, Inc.; *pg.* 586, *pg.* 228
Lim, Victor A., Mgr-Product Mktg-Digital Audience - Tribune Media Company; *pg.* 1696, *pg.* 592
Lima, Jessica, Sr Mgr-Loyalty Strategy - Sears Holdings Corporation; *pg.* 1784, *pg.* 618
Lima, Stephen, Sr Mgr-Mktg - Cigna Corporation; *pg.* 1197, *pg.* 338
Limes, Randy, Brand Mgr-NA Fabric Care Digital & Ecommerce - The Procter & Gamble Company; *pg.* 1129, *pg.* 1418
Limper, Hank, Mgr-Mktg - Houghton International Inc.; *pg.* 1167, *pg.* 1589
Limpert, Leslie, Dir-CRM & Mktg Sys - The Men's Wearhouse, Inc.; *pg.* 44, *pg.* 1711
Lin, Brian, Sr Product Mgr - Cablevision Systems Corporation; *pg.* 272, *pg.* 1141
Lin, Elizabeth, Dir-Worldwide Campaign-Partner Mktg - Intel Corporation; *pg.* 645, *pg.* 266
Lin, Henry, Product Mgr - NVIDIA Corporation; *pg.* 447, *pg.* 268
Lin, Jean, Dir-Customer Lifecycle Mktg - United States Cellular Corporation; *pg.* 1875, *pg.* 594
Lin, Kenneth, Dir-Product Mgmt - Subaru of America, Inc.; *pg.* 191, *pg.* 1050
Lin, Marilyn, Dir-Product Intelligence & Enablement - salesforce.com, inc.; *pg.* 1278, *pg.* 226
Lin, Nan, Mgr-NA Field Mktg - THE DOW CHEMICAL COMPANY; *pg.* 1157, *pg.* 898
Lin, Richard, VP-Sls-APAC & Japan - Atmel Corporation; *pg.* 621, *pg.* 238
Lin, Shawn, VP-Mktg - Oplink Communications, Inc.; *pg.* 660, *pg.* 91
Lin, Talis, Dir-Consumer Mktg & Digital Products - The New York Times; *pg.* 1668, *pg.* 1270
Linabarger, Scott, Sr Dir-Multichannel Content Mktg - Cleveland Clinic; *pg.* 1516, *pg.* 1429
Linardos, George, Sr VP-Product Strategy - Time Inc.; *pg.* 1693, *pg.* 1300
Linares, Alyshia, Dir-Creative & Consumer Mktg - National Geographic Channel; *pg.* 299, *pg.* 402
Linares, Jess, Dir-Mktg Creative Svcs - DreamWorks Animation SKG, Inc.; *pg.* 284, *pg.* 96
Lincoln, Brittany, Specialist-Social Media - Frontier Airlines, Inc.; *pg.* 1909, *pg.* 319
Lincoln, David, Sr Product Mgr - Generac Power Systems Inc.; *pg.* 1340, *pg.* 1898
Lincoln, Davin, Sr Mgr-IR - Vail Resorts, Inc.; *pg.* 1117, *pg.* 313
Lincoln, Howard A., Mgr-Mktg - The Baseball Club of Seattle, L.P.; *pg.* 532, *pg.* 1833
Lincoln, Mandy, Mgr-Mktg - The Baseball Club of Seattle, L.P.; *pg.* 532, *pg.* 1833
Lincoln, Stephen B., Exec VP-Sls - Garelick Farms, LLC; *pg.* 858, *pg.* 823
Lind, Jennifer, Analyst-Trade Mktg-National Accounts - B&G Foods, Inc.; *pg.* 838, *pg.* 1102
Lind, Ken, Sr Mgr-Mktg-Channels Strategy - Cisco Systems, Inc.; *pg.* 372, *pg.* 240
Lindal, Christina, Mgr-Sls-Natl - Lindal Cedar Homes, Inc.; *pg.* 94, *pg.* 1837
Lindal, Martin J., Mgr-Online Mktg - Lindal Cedar Homes, Inc.; *pg.* 94, *pg.* 1837
Lindauer, Jennifer, Sr VP & Dir-Adv-North America Consumer-Global CMO Grp - Citi Trends Inc.; *pg.* 22, *pg.* 539
Lindbeck, Troy, Dir-Mktg Programs - RaceTrac Petroleum, Inc.; *pg.* 983, *pg.* 519
Lindbloom, Katie, Mgr-Experis Brand Mktg - MANPOWER INC.; *pg.* 430, *pg.* 1877
Linde, Alex, VP-Adv & Monetization - eBay Inc.; *pg.* 1240, *pg.* 243
Linde, Koen Ter, VP-Sls-Europe - CommScope, Inc.; *pg.* 278, *pg.* 1378
Linde, Monica, Dir-Global Mktg-Alzheimer's Disease - Eli Lilly and Company; *pg.* 1527, *pg.* 684
Lindeberg, Marcella, Dir-Creative-Fashion - Sequential Brands Group, Inc.; *pg.* 1395, *pg.* 1290

Lindeen, Heather, Assoc Mgr-Mktg - Burt's Bees Inc.; *pg.* 502, *pg.* 1370
Lindemulder, Lindsey, Specialist-Mktg - Wolverine World Wide, Inc.; *pg.* 1822, *pg.* 905
Linden, Erik R., Head-Media & PR-NRG Home Solar - NRG Energy, Inc.; *pg.* 1948, *pg.* 1712
Linden, Kathy, Mgr-Media & Events-Americas MarCom - Kennametal Inc.; *pg.* 1052, *pg.* 1547
Lindenbaum, Kenneth, Brand Mgr - Paramount Pictures Corporation; *pg.* 304, *pg.* 138
Linder, Cathy, Dir-Mktg Res-Tempur Sealy Intl - Tempur Sealy International, Inc.; *pg.* 944, *pg.* 731
Linder, Joanna, Dir-Retail Mktg - Clarks Companies; *pg.* 1806, *pg.* 836
Lindgren, Madonna, Sr Mgr-Interactive Mktg - Polaris Industries Inc.; *pg.* 1709, *pg.* 928
Lindgren, Steve, VP-Sls - KSB Inc.; *pg.* 1354, *pg.* 1802
Lindheimer, David, Head-Product & Programs-Mechanical Turk - Amazon.com, Inc.; *pg.* 1226, *pg.* 1831
Lindholm, Chad, VP-Sls Natl Accts - Clean Energy Fuels Corp.; *pg.* 974, *pg.* 165
Lindley, Greg, Designer-Product - Facebook, Inc.; *pg.* 1245, *pg.* 143
Lindley, Katelin, Mgr-Mktg - Storck USA, L.P.; *pg.* 1862, *pg.* 591
Lindley, Shaun, VP-Sls - Spirax Sarco, Inc.; *pg.* 1076, *pg.* 1612
Lindmark, Julie, Product Mgr - Boston Scientific Corporation; *pg.* 1508, *pg.* 831
Lindner, Gerald, Sr Mgr-Print Mfg Process Tech - Medtronic, Inc.; *pg.* 1564, *pg.* 939
Lindorff, Beth, Sr Analyst-Mktg Res - American Family Mutual Insurance Company; *pg.* 1190, *pg.* 1864
Lindquist, Christopher, Sr VP-Natl Sls - Warner Bros. Entertainment Inc.; *pg.* 319, *pg.* 54
Lindquist, James, Mgr-Major Accounts & Sls Mgr-Natl Sponsorship - Dow Jones & Company, Inc.; *pg.* 1637, *pg.* 1225
Lindsay, Anne, Dir-Mktg-Michelin Tweel Technologies - Michelin North America Inc.; *pg.* 1886, *pg.* 1618
Lindsay, David, Sr Product Mgr - Gilead Sciences, Inc.; *pg.* 1535, *pg.* 88
Lindsay, Katie L., Sr Mgr-Mktg - The Macerich Company; *pg.* 1101, *pg.* 275
Lindsay, Matt, Head-Comml-Health & Wellness & Sr Dir - Kellogg Company; *pg.* 831, *pg.* 870
Lindsay, Neil, VP-Mktg - Amazon.com, Inc.; *pg.* 1226, *pg.* 1831
Lindsay, Steve, Product Mgr-Instrument Transformers, Sensors & Cutouts - ABB Inc.; *pg.* 1309, *pg.* 1359
Lindsey, Benjamin, Mgr-Mktg-Refining - Alcoa Inc.; *pg.* 65, *pg.* 1188
Lindsey, Bill, VP-Mktg - Starbrite Corp.; *pg.* 336, *pg.* 426
Lindsey, Derek, Specialist-Interactive & Retail Mktg - Mazda North American Operations; *pg.* 183, *pg.* 113
Lindsey, Troy, Sr Rep-Sls-Wholesale Mktg - ConocoPhillips; *pg.* 975, *pg.* 1703
Lindsey-Houston, Teresa, Dir-Snacks Mktg-Pringles - Kellogg Company; *pg.* 831, *pg.* 870
Lindstrom Brun, Annette, VP-Cause Mktg & Social Responsibility - Scripps Networks Interactive, Inc.; *pg.* 1279, *pg.* 1638
Lindstrom, Chelsey, Brand Mgr - Whirlpool Corporation; *pg.* 62, *pg.* 872
Lindstrom, Erik, Sr Analyst-Mktg - Darden Restaurants, Inc.; *pg.* 1724, *pg.* 453
Lindstrom, John, Reg Dir-Sls - Siemens Process Industries and Drive; *pg.* 1376, *pg.* 1587
Lindstrom, Peter, Product Mgr-North America - Videojet Technologies Inc.; *pg.* 489, *pg.* 671
Lindt, Don, Sr Mgr-Web Mktg - Brocade Communications Systems, Inc.; *pg.* 365, *pg.* 239
Lineberry, Rebecca, Sr Recruiter-Mktg - Kohl's Corporation; *pg.* 1775, *pg.* 1870
Liner, Drew, Specialist-Mktg Automation - F5 Networks, Inc.; *pg.* 396, *pg.* 1835
Lines, Luke, Specialist-Reg Sls - Balchem Corporation; *pg.* 839, *pg.* 1183
Linet, Danielle, Sr VP-Creative Svcs & Distr - The Advertising Council, Inc.; *pg.* 125, *pg.* 1187
Linford, Sarah A., Mgr-Channel Mktg - Windstream Corporation; *pg.* 321, *pg.* 34
Ling, C. Clifton, Dir-Advanced Clinical Res - Varian Medical Systems, Inc.; *pg.* 1434, *pg.* 178
Ling, Daymond, Sr Dir-Advanced Analytics - Canadian Imperial Bank of Commerce; *pg.* 729, *pg.* 1935
Ling, Gary, Product Mgr - Google Inc.; *pg.* 1249, *pg.* 153
Ling, Lei, VP-Product Dev - Afexa Life Sciences Inc.; *pg.* 1487, *pg.* 1905
Ling, Steve, Mgr-Ford Car Mktg - Ford Motor Company; *pg.* 172, *pg.* 876
Ling, Yun, Sr Mgr-Market Intelligence - Burger King Corporation; *pg.* 1719, *pg.* 440
Ling-Tse, Sook, Dir-Adv - Nautica Apparel, Inc.; *pg.* 45, *pg.* 1265
Lingamfelter, Chris, VP-Integrated Sys Sls & Strategy - Intelligrated, Inc.; *pg.* 1349, *pg.* 1460
Lingen, Daniel, Sr Mgr-Digital Comm - Electronic Arts Inc.; *pg.* 951, *pg.* 189
Lingeris, Anna, Sr Mgr-Brand PR & Consumer Engagement - The Hershey Co.; *pg.* 1855, *pg.* 1538
Linggo, Colin, Dir-Mktg & Media - Paramount Pictures Corporation; *pg.* 304, *pg.* 138
Link, Kim, Sr Mgr Issues Preparedness & Engagement - Monsanto Company; *pg.* 1173, *pg.* 999
Link, Laurin, Coord-Mktg-Comml Sls - Advance Auto Parts, Inc.; *pg.* 197, *pg.* 1805
Link, Lisa, Mgr-Mktg & Adv - Illinois Bureau of Tourism; *pg.* 995, *pg.* 578
Link, Richard, Dir-Mktg - Bimbo Bakeries USA; *pg.* 840, *pg.* 151
Link, Ryan P., Sr Mgr-Fin - LifeCell Corporation; *pg.* 1556, *pg.* 1045
Link, William, VP-Sls-Food Processing Market Segment - Hydrotex Partners Ltd.; *pg.* 979, *pg.* 1692
Linke, Scott, Brand Mktg Mgr - Rawlings Sporting Goods Co., Inc.; *pg.* 1843, *pg.* 1002
Linker, Rusty, Dir-Mktg-Economic Dev - Tulsa Metro Chamber; *pg.* 1008, *pg.* 1491
Linker, Stephanie, Mgr-Digital Mktg - BlackRock, Inc.; *pg.* 724, *pg.* 1203
Linkh, Frank, Sr Mgr-Member Experience - Audible, Inc.; *pg.* 1230, *pg.* 1095
Linn, Carrie, Assoc Mgr-Mktg & Customer Analytics - Tractor Supply Company; *pg.* 708, *pg.* 1627
Linn, Jennifer, Sr Dir-Corp Partnerships - New York Jets Football Club, Inc.; *pg.* 570, *pg.* 1067
Linnane, Fran, Assoc VP-Product Dev, Mergers & Integrations - AT&T Mobility LLC; *pg.* 619, *pg.* 488
Linnartz, Bruce, Sr Mgr-Svc Ops - Xplore Technologies Corp.; *pg.* 497, *pg.* 1667
Linnington, Max, Exec VP-Sls - CoStar Group, Inc.; *pg.* 742, *pg.* 397
Lino, Tiffany, VP-Creative Svcs - ABC Cable Networks Group; *pg.* 268, *pg.* 51
Linquist, Todd C., VP-Product Mgmt - MetroPCS, Inc.; *pg.* 1872, *pg.* 1683
Linse, Kara, Dir-Global Sponsorship Mktg-Olympic Games - Visa Inc.; *pg.* 816, *pg.* 230
Linse, Kara, Dir-Global Sponsorship Mktg-Olympic Games - Visa U.S.A., Inc.; *pg.* 817, *pg.* 231
Linskens, Jason, Planner-Mktg - Humana, Inc.; *pg.* 1204, *pg.* 734
Linskey, Kelly, Coord-Mktg - DIRECTV Group Holdings, LLC; *pg.* 281, *pg.* 79
Linsky, Stuart T., VP-Engrg & Global Product Dev-Aerospace Sys - Northrop Grumman Corporation; *pg.* 231, *pg.* 1781
Linsky, Wendy, VP-Mktg - Tech Data Corporation; *pg.* 482, *pg.* 416
Linsley, Peter, Sr Product Mgr - Google Inc.; *pg.* 1249, *pg.* 153
Linsley, Robin, VP-Mktg - Conair Corporation; *pg.* 505, *pg.* 1055
Lintner, Todd, Sr Copywriter-Target.com & Mobile Product Team - Target Corporation; *pg.* 1786, *pg.* 942
Linton, Andrea, Mgr-Natural Products Sls - Crown Prince, Inc.; *pg.* 850, *pg.* 67
Linton, Cathy, Sr VP & Dir-Adv & Brand Comm - Sun Trust Bank, Atlanta; *pg.* 806, *pg.* 520
Linton, Cathy, Sr VP & Dir-Adv & Brand Comm - SunTrust Banks, Inc.; *pg.* 807, *pg.* 520
Lintz, Connie, Mgr-Mktg Svcs - Snyder Industries, Inc.; *pg.* 1377, *pg.* 1012
Lintz, Justin S., Brand Mgr-Hormel & Stagg Chili - Hormel Foods Corporation; *pg.* 863, *pg.* 915
Lion, Cynthia, Sr Coord-Mktg - Alexion Pharmaceuticals, Inc.; *pg.* 1489, *pg.* 341
Lip, Bryan, Sr Dir-Partnerships & Head-Search-Global - Expedia, Inc.; *pg.* 1244, *pg.* 1814
Lipari, Patricia, Mgr-Worldwide Mktg Comm-Retail Sys Solutions - Eastman Kodak Company; *pg.* 1408, *pg.* 1333
Lipinski, Bart, Sr Mgr-Integrated Mktg Comm-Global - Motorola Solutions, Inc.; *pg.* 657, *pg.* 659
Lipinski, Mary A., Product Dir - Expedia, Inc.; *pg.* 1244, *pg.* 1814
Lipinski, Pat, Dir-Sls - Cytosport, Inc.; *pg.* 1018, *pg.* 45
Lipman, Jennifer, Assoc Mgr-Sls - Penguin Random House; *pg.* 1675, *pg.* 1276
Lipman, M. Benjamin, Sr Exec VP-Sls - Guardsmark, LLC; *pg.* 401, *pg.* 1237
Lipnisky, Alex, Sr Mgr-Digital Channel - Follett Higher Education Group; *pg.* 1769, *pg.* 669
Lipp, Jaclyn, Specialist-Social Media - Safelite Solutions LLC; *pg.* 109, *pg.* 1443
Lippard, Gregory W., VP-Rail Product Sls - L.B. Foster Company; *pg.* 1355, *pg.* 1578
Lippe Davis, Patricia, VP-Mktg & Media Sls - AARP; *pg.* 124, *pg.* 393
Lippe, Nathan, Product Dir-CareerRookie - CareerBuilder, LLC; *pg.* 1234, *pg.* 568
Lippelman, Stan, VP-Mktg - Bass Pro Shops, Inc.; *pg.* 1826, *pg.* 1006
Lippert, Ernst, Dir-Mktg-Global - Lonza Inc.; *pg.* 1171, *pg.* 1041
Lippert, James, VP-Sls - Hamilton Caster & Mfg. Co.; *pg.* 206, *pg.* 1454
Lippert, Mark J., VP-Mktg - Hamilton Caster & Mfg. Co.; *pg.* 206, *pg.* 1454
Lippman, Adam, Product Mgr-Payments - Meetup Inc.; *pg.* 1266, *pg.* 1258
Lippman, Blair, Mgr-Ad Sls & Content Mktg-AMC - AMC Networks Inc.; *pg.* 269, *pg.* 1189
Lippman, Eli, Dir-Social Media - American Media, Inc.; *pg.* 1615, *pg.* 410
Lippman, Joel S., Chief Medical Officer & Exec VP-Product Dev - Noven Pharmaceuticals, Inc.; *pg.* 1576, *pg.* 445
Lippolis, John, Sr Dir-Customer Mktg - Mondelez International, Inc.; *pg.* 878, *pg.* 601
Lips, Anne, Mgr-Retail Mktg & Visual Mdsg - Sony Electronics, Inc.; *pg.* 676, *pg.* 209
Lipsey, David, Mgr-Mktg-Intel Security Group - Intel Corporation; *pg.* 645, *pg.* 266
Lipsin, Bill, VP-Worldwide Channel Sls - NetApp, Inc.; *pg.* 444, *pg.* 287
Lipski, Kathy V., Specialist-Mktg - UOP LLC; *pg.* 1386, *pg.* 606
Lipsky, David, Dir-Audible Studios Mktg - Audible, Inc.; *pg.* 1230, *pg.* 1095
Lipsky, Debbie, Sr Mgr & Sr Planner-Meeting - SEI Investments Company; *pg.* 802, *pg.* 1558
Lipsman, Andrew, VP-Mktg & Insights - comScore, Inc; *pg.* 1236, *pg.* 1798
Lipson, Matthew, Sr VP-Digital Mktg - Focus Features; *pg.* 287, *pg.* 273
Liriano, Edward, Reg Acct Mgr-East Client Mktg - BabyCenter, LLC; *pg.* 1231, *pg.* 212
Lis, Gana, Sr Program Mgr-Customer & Product Support - Honeywell Aerospace Electronic Systems; *pg.* 228, *pg.* 17
Lisa, Kristen, Mgr-PR - Advanced Micro Devices, Inc.; *pg.* 613, *pg.* 282
Lishinski, Jodi J., Mgr-Mktg Ops Info & Sys - NetApp, Inc.; *pg.* 444, *pg.* 287
Lishok, Kyle, Mgr-Mktg - Surfrider Foundation; *pg.* 158, *pg.* 199
Lisiecki, Jean, Sr Mgr-Plng & Comm-NAFS - Campbell Soup Company; *pg.* 844, *pg.* 1048
Lisk, Matthew, Sr Dir-Brokerage - Cushman & Wakefield, Inc.; *pg.* 1088, *pg.* 1220
Liskey, Anita, Mng Dir-Corp Mktg & Comm - CME Group, Inc.; *pg.* 738, *pg.* 571
Liskey, Anita S., Mng Dir-Corp Mktg & Comm - CME Group Inc.; *pg.* 738, *pg.* 571
Liss, Barbara, Sr Dir-Social Media - Motorola Mobility LLC; *pg.* 657, *pg.* 627
Liss, Diana, Dir-Digital Media Adv Ops - Discovery Communications, Inc.; *pg.* 282, *pg.* 777
Liss, Jessica, Mgr-Mktg - Lifetime Entertainment Services LLC; *pg.* 296, *pg.* 1251
Liss-Levinson, William, COO, Chief Strategy Officer & VP - Castle Connolly Medical Ltd.; *pg.* 1626, *pg.* 1210
Lissandrello, Kevin, Mgr-Segment Mktg - Vertafore Inc.; *pg.* 1222, *pg.* 386
List, Karen, Exec Dir-Agency, Indus Rels & Sports Mktg - The New York Times; *pg.* 1668, *pg.* 1270
List, Karen, Exec Dir-Agency, Indus Rels & Sports Mktg - The

New York Times Company; pg. 1668, pg. 1270
Lista, Blanca, VP-Feature Film Production - The Jim Henson Company; pg. 293, pg. 103
Listanski, Lindsay, Sr Mgr-Media Engagement - Coldwell Banker Real Estate LLC; pg. 1087, pg. 1103
Lister, Chris, VP-Sls Americas & EMEA - Intersil Corporation; pg. 647, pg. 146
Lister, Jonathan, VP-North America Sls & Mktg Solutions - LinkedIn Corporation; pg. 1262, pg. 160
Listgarten, Sherry, Dir-Product Mgmt - YouTube, LLC; pg. 1291, pg. 198
Liston, Keith, VP-Sls - Gleason - M&M Precision Systems Corporation; pg. 1341, pg. 1479
Liszczak, Jaime, Mgr-Mktg-Hess Toy Truck - Hess Corporation; pg. 979, pg. 1240
Liszewski, Adam, Project Dir-Brand Mktg - Choice Hotels International, Inc.; pg. 1086, pg. 775
Liszka, James, Mgr-Mktg - The Allstate Corporation; pg. 1189, pg. 639
Liszt, Robert M., VP-Worldwide Sls, Bus Mktg & Ops - PMC-Sierra, Inc.; pg. 664, pg. 287
Litam, Darlene, Sr Brand Mgr-Mktg-Global - Revlon, Inc.; pg. 521, pg. 1286
Litchfield, Meghan, Sr Dir-ECommerce-Global - GoPro; pg. 1414, pg. 255
Litchfield, Steven, Chief Strategy Officer & Exec VP - Microsemi Corporation; pg. 435, pg. 41
Litchfield, Vicki, VP & Mgr-Mktg - BOK Financial Corporation; pg. 726, pg. 1489
Litfin, Heather, Dir-Mktg-North America - Mattel Games/Puzzles; pg. 962, pg. 80
Litfin, Heather, Dir-Mktg-North America - MATTEL, INC.; pg. 962, pg. 81
Lithgow, Karen, Sr VP-Corp Mktg - The ADT Corporation; pg. 612, pg. 409
Litow, Debbie, Brand Mgr-Mars Ice Cream - Mars North America; pg. 1859, pg. 1072
Litster, Christopher, Chief Revenue Officer & Sr VP-Sls & Mktg - Constant Contact, Inc.; pg. 379, pg. 850
Litt, Neil, Dir-Editing, Design & Production - Princeton University Press; pg. 1678, pg. 1112
Litteken, Kimberly, Specialist-Mktg Project-Agri - Trouw Nutrition USA; pg. 1482, pg. 616
Litterer, Karen, Sr Dir-PR - Community Health Systems, Inc.; pg. 1516, pg. 1632
Litterio, John, Dir-Renewable Fuels Mktg - CHS INC.; pg. 702, pg. 926
Little, Andrea M., Dir-Mktg & Mgr-Design Studio-Model Home Merchandiser - D.R. Horton, Inc.; pg. 1090, pg. 1694
Little, Angela, Planner-Multi Media - The Atlanta Journal-Constitution; pg. 1618, pg. 490
Little, Brandon, Chief Creative Officer & Sr VP - Fossil Group, Inc.; pg. 5, pg. 1735
Little, Brooke, Assoc Mgr-Mktg-Channel Mktg - MillerCoors, pg. 254, pg. 1877
Little, Brooke, Brand Mgr-Innovations - MillerCoors LLC; pg. 255, pg. 582
Little, Carolyn, Dir-Mktg Ops - MacNeil Automotive Products, Ltd.; pg. 211, pg. 559
Little, Dennis, Chm-Production - Lockheed Martin Corporation; pg. 229, pg. 762
Little, Fawn, Brand Mgr-IT-Horizon Organic - The WhiteWave Foods Company; pg. 1037, pg. 324
Little, Gary, Mgr-Digital Mktg - CBS Interactive, Inc.; pg. 369, pg. 215
Little, Ian, Dir-Mktg & ECommerce - Hi-Tec Sports USA, Inc.; pg. 1809, pg. 150
Little, James M., Rep-Outside Sls-Mission Drilling Products - National Oilwell Varco, Inc.; pg. 1364, pg. 1712
Little, Jim, CMO - Shaw Communications Inc.; pg. 307, pg. 1904
Little, Keith D., Sr Mgr-Media Rels - Lockheed Martin Corporation; pg. 229, pg. 762
Little, Ken, VP-Product Engrg - Tumblr, Inc.; pg. 1285, pg. 1305
Little, Kevin, Dir-Editorial-Turner Entertainment Networks PR - Turner Broadcasting System, Inc.; pg. 314, pg. 521
Little, Lisa, Head-Digital Mktg-SEM - TXU Energy Retail Company LLC; pg. 1953, pg. 1690
Little, Megan, Sr Dir-Adv & Event Mktg - St. Louis Blues Hockey Club, LLC; pg. 585, pg. 1003
Little, Michael J., CFO & COO - Premier Exhibitions, Inc.; pg. 577, pg. 518
Little, Rob, Dir-Mktg-RLC Div - The Toro Company; pg. 1065, pg. 918
Little, Steve, VP-Product Dev - Automatic Data Processing, Inc.; pg. 357, pg. 1117
Little, Tim, Product Mgr-Siemens Milltronics - Siemens Canada Ltd.; pg. 1306, pg. 1921
Littlefield, Brian, Dir-Indus & Automotive Segment Mktg - United Parcel Service, Inc.; pg. 1928, pg. 522
Littlefield, Charles, Dir-Mktg - Bacardi USA, Inc.; pg. 1956, pg. 417
Littlejohn, Courtney, Sr Mgr-Mktg Svcs - Gulfstream Aerospace Corporation; pg. 228, pg. 540
Littlejohn, Jennifer, Dir-Mktg - Tennessee Department of Tourist Development; pg. 1007, pg. 1654
Littlejohn, Marla, Sr Product Mgr-Immunology - AbbVie Inc.; pg. 1486, pg. 638
Littleson, Randy, Sr VP-Mktg - Flexera Software Inc.; pg. 398, pg. 658
Littman, Kaitlin, Coord-New Media - Genesco Inc.; pg. 1809, pg. 1650
Littrell, Tom, Product Mgr-Fixtures - Electronic Theatre Controls, Inc.; pg. 1296, pg. 1872
Litvack, Samara, Rep-Mktg Comm - Eastman Chemical Company; pg. 1159, pg. 1636
Litwin, Rich, Mgr-Mktg - Aetna Inc.; pg. 1187, pg. 351
Litz, Brian, Reg Mgr-Sls - Cars.com; pg. 1234, pg. 568
Litz, Kyle, Specialist-Digital Mktg - Lands' End, Inc.; pg. 1776, pg. 1857
Liu Huang, Sandra, Product Mgr - Quora, Inc.; pg. 1277, pg. 178
Liu, Adrian, Mgr-Product Line-Svc Provider Video - Cisco Systems, Inc.; pg. 372, pg. 240
Liu, Aline, Mgr-Content Mktg - Ricoh Americas Corporation; pg. 461, pg. 1131
Liu, Benjamin, Sr Mgr-Web Mktg - Adobe Systems Incorporated; pg. 342, pg. 235
Liu, Brittany, Sr Mgr-Mktg Programs-Global - Epicor Software Corporation; pg. 393, pg. 110
Liu, Christina, Mgr-Integrated Mktg - Viacom Inc.; pg. 316, pg. 1310
Liu, Cynthia, Dir-Mktg-Global Brand Excellence & Equity - The Hershey Co.; pg. 1855, pg. 1538
Liu, Deb, Dir-Product Mgmt-Platform Monetization - Facebook, Inc.; pg. 1245, pg. 143
Liu, Ellen, Dir-Media - The Clorox Company; pg. 327, pg. 169
Liu, Emily, Dir-Innovation-Mktg - Continental Mills, Inc.; pg. 827, pg. 1845
Liu, Gary, Mgr-Community-Knowledge Mgmt & Unified Social Bus - Unisys Corporation; pg. 487, pg. 1517
Liu, George, Dir-Airline Global Brand & Mktg - The Boeing Company - Helicopter Division; pg. 226, pg. 13
Liu, Henry, Exec Dir-New Brand Dev & Global Mktg - The Estee Lauder Companies Inc.; pg. 508, pg. 1229
Liu, Jade, Specialist-Social Discovery - Buzzfeed; pg. 1233, pg. 1208
Liu, Janice M., Mgr-Consumer Svcs Mktg-Americas Reg - Hewlett-Packard Company; pg. 404, pg. 175
Liu, Jennifer, Grp Product Mgr - Google Inc.; pg. 1249, pg. 153
Liu, Julie, Sr Dir-New Ventures, Mktg & Strategy - Jamba, Inc.; pg. 1024, pg. 84
Liu, Kelvin, Mgr-PR-Global - Activision Blizzard, Inc.; pg. 948, pg. 271
Liu, Kun, VP-Product Line Mgmt & Bus Dev - Oplink Communications, Inc.; pg. 660, pg. 91
Liu, Lillian, Supvr-Mktg - 3M Company; pg. 1142, pg. 956
Liu, Lisa, Sr Mgr-IT - The Gap, Inc.; pg. 1770, pg. 218
Liu, Lynn, Sr Mgr-New Media Dev - PR Newswire Association LLC; pg. 1678, pg. 1283
Liu, Nathan, Sr Dir-Mdse Plng - Pacific Sunwear of California, Inc.; pg. 1781, pg. 43
Liu, Noriko, Reg VP-Brand & Field Mktg-Asia Pacific - Hyatt Hotels Corporation; pg. 1096, pg. 577
Liu, Phillip, Sr Product Mgr - 8x8, Inc.; pg. 1865, pg. 282
Liu, Steven, Dir-Consumer Prod Mktg - The Hercules Tire & Rubber Company; pg. 1884, pg. 1454
Liu, Taiyang, Head-Global Sls Plng - Google Inc.; pg. 1249, pg. 153
Liu, Timothy, Sr Dir-Comml Strategy - Air Canada; pg. 1896, pg. 1902
Liu, Tingting, Specialist-Mktg Comm - ABB Inc.; pg. 1309, pg. 1359
Liu, Wei, Mgr-Sls - Caterpillar, Inc.; pg. 1321, pg. 650
Liu, Wendy, Dir-Mktg - Medtronic, Inc.; pg. 1564, pg. 939
Liu, Wensui, VP & Sr Mgr-Risk Analytics - Fifth Third Bank, Indiana (Southern); pg. 753, pg. 678
Liuzzi, John, Dir-Sls - Plews/Edelmann; pg. 215, pg. 607
Livdahl, Todd, Dir-Media Tech & Ops - The Walt Disney Company; pg. 317, pg. 52
Livermore, Allison, Sr Mgr-Integrated Mktg - Time Inc.; pg. 1693, pg. 1300
Livermore, April, VP-Online Mktg - TechTarget, Inc.; pg. 482, pg. 837
Livesay, Kristen, Mgr-Interactive Mktg - Wm. Wrigley Jr. Company; pg. 1863, pg. 596
Livi, Bianca, Bus Mgr-Tech-Global - Google Inc.; pg. 1249, pg. 153
Livingston, Adam, Sr Product Mgr-Cordless - Makita U.S.A., Inc.; pg. 1358, pg. 120
Livingston, Cindy, Sr Mgr-Brand Strategy & Campaign - Plantronics, Inc.; pg. 663, pg. 270
Livingston, Corey, Sr Dir-Digital & Integrated Mktg Campaigns - Level 3 Communications, Inc.; pg. 1262, pg. 1664
Livingston, Jennifer, Mgr-PR - Atkins Nutritionals, Inc.; pg. 1498, pg. 316
Livingston, Kathleen, Grp VP-Mktg Ops & Comm - PVH Corp.; pg. 46, pg. 1283
Livingston, Lesley, Dir-Mktg Sourcing - Johnson & Johnson; pg. 1549, pg. 1091
Livingston, Melissa, Mgr-Mktg - The Walt Disney Company; pg. 317, pg. 52
Livingston, Philip B., CEO-Mktg & Bus Solutions - LexisNexis Litigation Solutions; pg. 1659, pg. 1446
Livingston, Ryan, Mgr-Mktg Matls Compliance - The Northwestern Mutual Life Insurance Company; pg. 1212, pg. 1879
Livingston, Terry, Gen Mgr-Global Product Mgmt Aftermarket & Trailer - Meritor, Inc.; pg. 212, pg. 911
Livingston, Troy, Sr Mgr-Mktg - Panasonic Corporation of North America; pg. 661, pg. 1120
Livingstone, Andrew, Specialist-Mktg - Charles River Laboratories, Inc.; pg. 1475, pg. 360
Livingstone, Steve, Sr Mgr-Bus Dev & Sls Ops - Jacksonville Jaguars, Ltd.; pg. 554, pg. 433
Livne, Roy, Product Mgr-Google Now - Google Inc.; pg. 1249, pg. 153
Livore, Mariana, Head-Global Mktg-Equity & Innovation - Mead Johnson Nutrition Company; pg. 1561, pg. 615
Liwag, Luis, Designer-Digital - NIKE, Inc.; pg. 1812, pg. 1492
Lizano, Antonio, Mgr-Corp Multicultural Mktg - Paychex, Inc.; pg. 792, pg. 1336
Ljubicich, Lauren, Dir-Mktg - Pfizer Inc.; pg. 1581, pg. 1278
Llaury, Claudia, Mgr-GNS Mktg-LAC - American Express Company; pg. 712, pg. 1190
Llenza, Mariel, Dir-Hispanic Adv - AT&T Mobility LLC; pg. 619, pg. 488
Llereza, Janice, Sr Mgr-Real Estate & Real Assets - The Boeing Company; pg. 225, pg. 567
Llewellyn, Joe, Dir-Corp Mktg - Mayer Electric Supply Company Inc.; pg. 653, pg. 3
Llorca, Maria E., Sr Mgr-Mktg - General Growth Properties, Inc.; pg. 1093, pg. 574
Llorens, Hector, Mgr-Mktg - Intel Corporation; pg. 645, pg. 266
Lloyd, Alexis, Dir-Creative - The New York Times; pg. 1668, pg. 1270
Lloyd, Andy, Gen Mgr-Commerce Products - NetSuite, Inc.; pg. 1270, pg. 255
Lloyd, Dave, Sr Mgr-Search Mktg-Global - Adobe Systems Incorporated; pg. 342, pg. 235
Lloyd, David, Analyst-Mktg Promo-Consumer Reports - Consumers Union of the United States, Inc.; pg. 1630, pg. 1356
Lloyd, Deborah, Chief Creative Officer - Kate Spade & Company; pg. 27, pg. 1248
Lloyd, James, Dir-Sls & New Bus Dev-Kalama Chemicals Flavor & Fragrance - Emerald Performance Materials, LLC; pg. 1161, pg. 1445
Lloyd, Kalshelia, Brand Mgr-Gum Innovation - Mondelez International, Inc.; pg. 878, pg. 601
Lloyd, Kelly, Principal-Mktg - Constellation Energy Resources, LLC; pg. 1938, pg. 756
Lloyd, Laura, Sr Dir-Video Svcs - Comcast Corporation; pg. 276, pg. 1560
Lloyd, Linda, Product Mgr-Bio-HPLC Columns & Media - Agilent Technologies, Inc.; pg. 614, pg. 264
Lloyd, Michael, Interim Pres-Mktg Svcs - Acxiom Corporation; pg. 342, pg. 33
Lloyd, Michelle, Dir-Digital Sls - I-5 Publishing LLC; pg. 1651, pg. 133
Lloyd, Rick, VP-Adv - Schroeder Publishing Company; pg. 1685, pg. 739

Lloyd, Stephanie L., Reg Mgr-Mktg - Pepsi Beverages Company; pg. 258, pg. 1342
Lloyd-Smith, Kenneth, Mgr-Vehicle Sls-Lexus Div - Toyota Canada, Inc.; pg. 192, pg. 1934
Llull, Barbara, Sr Mgr-Mktg Comm & Brand - Philips Electronics North America; pg. 662, pg. 782
Llull, Barbara, Sr Mgr-Mktg Comm & Brand - Philips Lighting; pg. 1303, pg. 806
Lo, Cherish, Asst Dir-Mktg & Planned Giving - City of Hope National Medical Center; pg. 1516, pg. 77
Lo, Katherine, Brand Mgr-CLIF Builder's - Clif Bar Inc.; pg. 848, pg. 83
Lo, Sean, Designer-Creative - General Motors Company; pg. 175, pg. 881
Lo, Vicky, Sr Mgr-CRM Data Mktg & Analysis - The Walt Disney Company; pg. 317, pg. 52
Lo, Victoria, Brand Mgr-Children's TYLENOL & MOTRIN - Johnson & Johnson Inc.; pg. 1552, pg. 1923
Lo, YingJui, Assoc Dir-Sls Force Effectiveness - Novartis Pharmaceuticals Corp.; pg. 1575, pg. 1054
Loach, Chris, Mgr-Finished Products - International Paper Company; pg. 1460, pg. 1644
Loadman, Thomas D., VP & Gen Mgr-Railroad Products & Svcs - Koppers Holdings Inc.; pg. 1170, pg. 1577
Loaiza, Aristobulo, Sr Mgr-BASF New Bus - BASF Corporation; pg. 1149, pg. 1066
Lobb, Laura E., VP & Product Mgr - Cardinal Bank N.A.; pg. 732, pg. 1790
Lobeiras, Andres, Product Mgr - Beckman Coulter, Inc.; pg. 1402, pg. 48
Lober, Dianne, Brand Mgr-Comm - INVISTA B.V.; pg. 1168, pg. 723
Loberg, Christopher, Sr Dir-Mktg - Tektronix, Inc.; pg. 1431, pg. 1496
Lobo, Carolina, VP-Mktg - AmerisourceBergen Corporation; pg. 1493, pg. 1522
Lobo, Clifford, Assoc Mgr-Mktg-Fin Performance Mgmt - IBM Canada Limited; pg. 411, pg. 1923
Lobo, Kay K., Dir-Mktg Insights - Abbott Laboratories; pg. 1484, pg. 551
Lobo, Philomena, Sr Mgr-Mobile Client Engrg - Twitter, Inc.; pg. 1285, pg. 228
Lobpries, Lawrence, VP-Consumer Mktg - Lowe's Companies, Inc.; pg. 1053, pg. 1383
Lobsiger, Ryan, Acct Mgr-Sponsorship Sls - Indianapolis Colts, Inc.; pg. 553, pg. 687
Locascio, Len, CFO & Dir-Sls - ALYCE Paris; pg. 18, pg. 634
Loch, Jeffrey, Founder, Pres, CMO & Dir - Green Earth Technologies, Inc.; pg. 704, pg. 1352
Loch, Joseph, VP-Franchise & Retail Sls - Hickory Farms, Inc.; pg. 862, pg. 1462
Loch, Pat, Sr VP-Sls & Mktg - Leggett & Platt, Incorporated; pg. 933, pg. 974
Lochner, Lisa, Mgr-PR - LIFETIME BRANDS, INC.; pg. 1127, pg. 1161
LoCicero, Nina, Mgr-Digital Mktg-Global - Rockwell Automation, Inc.; pg. 668, pg. 1880
Lock, Kyle, Sr Dir-Retail Mktg - Butterball, LLC; pg. 843, pg. 1385
Lock, Melissa, Mgr-Mktg-New Ventures - Jamba, Inc.; pg. 1024, pg. 84
Lockard, Kim, Sr Mgr-Mktg-Open Bus Unit - Allscripts Healthcare Solutions, Inc.; pg. 1492, pg. 563
Locke, Brad, Dir-Mktg - Mars Petcare; pg. 1478, pg. 1633
Locke, Candice, Mgr-Channel Mktg - Blue Coat Systems, Inc.; pg. 362, pg. 284
Locke, Jim, Dir-Creative - Del Monte Foods, Inc.; pg. 852, pg. 304
Locke, Molly, Mgr-Mktg - Clover Stornetta Farms Inc.; pg. 848, pg. 182
Locke, Nancy, Sr Dir-Admin - Time Warner Cable Inc.; pg. 312, pg. 1301
Locker, Tony, Dir-Product Mgmt - G&W Electric Company; pg. 1338, pg. 558
Lockett, Dale, Dir-Creative Svcs & Community Mktg - KHOU-TV, Inc.; pg. 294, pg. 1709
Lockett, Nikki, Sr Mgr-Mktg-KitchenAid Small Appliances - Whirlpool Corporation; pg. 62, pg. 872
Lockett, Rachel J., Dir-Mktg - L'Oreal USA; pg. 514, pg. 1252
Lockhart, David, VP-Creative, Design & UX - Citigroup Inc.; pg. 735, pg. 1212
Lockhart, Paul, Dir-HP Software Mktg - Hewlett-Packard Company; pg. 404, pg. 175
Lockhart-Triolo, June, Dir-Art & Mgr-Mktg - J. Robert Scott Inc.; pg. 930, pg. 105
Lockwood, Angela, Dir-PR - Itron Inc.; pg. 422, pg. 1822
Lockwood, Ann, Mgr-Mktg - TD Bank US Holding Company; pg. 809, pg. 1051
Lockwood, Dan, Mgr-PR - South Jersey Gas Company; pg. 1951, pg. 1067
Lockwood, Diane, Mgr-Field Mktg-NA - International Business Machines Corporation; pg. 418, pg. 1138
Lockwood, Ed, Sr Dir-IR - KLA-Tencor Corporation; pg. 1353, pg. 146
Lockwood, Heather, Dir-Digital Mktg-Global - Aveda Corporation; pg. 499, pg. 917
Lockwood, Jane, Asst VP-ECommerce & Digital Mktg - L'Oreal USA; pg. 514, pg. 1252
Lockwood, Kenneth H., VP-Sls Ops - Oakley, Inc.; pg. 1840, pg. 86
Lockwood, Rachel, Dir-Mktg - Ralph Lauren Corporation; pg. 46, pg. 1284
Locoh-Donou, Francois, Sr VP & COO - CIENA Corporation; pg. 628, pg. 771
Lodato, Chuck, Grp Dir-Production - The Hearst Corporation; pg. 1649, pg. 1239
LoDebole, Ed, Dir-Demand, Mktg & Procurement - Diageo North America, Inc.; pg. 1961, pg. 361
Lodha, Kriti, Sr Asst Brand Mgr-Gillette - The Procter & Gamble Company; pg. 1129, pg. 1418
Lodi, Shakeel, Strategist-Mktg-Enterprise Client Solutions - Dell Inc.; pg. 383, pg. 1737
Loebach, Beth F., Sr Mgr-Server Sys Mgmt Software Dev - Lenovo Group Ltd; pg. 427, pg. 1384
Loebman, Lee, Dir-Mktg-Medline University - Medline Industries, Inc.; pg. 1562, pg. 635
Loeffl, Jim, Reg VP-Sls - Bumble Bee Foods LLC; pg. 842, pg. 201
Loehle, Alicia, Coord-PR - Ralph Lauren Corporation; pg. 46, pg. 1284
Loehnis, Barney, Head-Digital Mktg-Global - Mercer Inc.; pg. 1395, pg. 1258
Loehr, Jason, VP & Dir-Media & Insights-Global - Brown-Forman Corporation; pg. 1958, pg. 732
Loeper, Mark, VP & Gen Mgr-Creative Specialties Intl - Moen Incorporated; pg. 1056, pg. 1468
Loercher, Shane, Category Mgr-Agencies, Media & Mktg Svcs - Johnson & Johnson; pg. 1549, pg. 1091
Loerzel, Christy, Sr Mgr-NAM Channel Mktg - Symantec Corporation; pg. 478, pg. 161
Loesch, George, VP-Natl Sls-Emerging Channels - Campbell Soup Company; pg. 844, pg. 1048
Loesch, Paris, VP-Markets & Digital Mktg Svcs-Global - Lionbridge Technologies Inc.; pg. 428, pg. 851
Loesch, Rachele, Acct Mgr-Mktg - Under Armour, Inc.; pg. 49, pg. 759
Loesel, Mark, Mgr-Cloud Mktg - Cisco Systems, Inc.; pg. 372, pg. 240
Loew, Christie, Mgr-Digital Mktg - Amazon.com, Inc.; pg. 1226, pg. 1831
Loew, Mrinalini, VP-Digital Product Mgmt - Weight Watchers International, Inc.; pg. 1609, pg. 1313
Loewe, Nancy, Chief Strategy Officer - Kimberly-Clark Corporation; pg. 1461, pg. 1720
Loewenthal, Elana, Dir-Mktg-Intl - Home Box Office, Inc.; pg. 290, pg. 1240
Loewy, Emily, Mgr-Mktg Svcs - NCL Corporation Ltd.; pg. 1916, pg. 444
Lofaso, Rick, Corp Mgr-Car Mktg - Toyota Motor Sales, U.S.A., Inc.; pg. 193, pg. 296
Loferski, Eric J., VP-Mktg - Wigwam Mills, Inc.; pg. 15, pg. 1894
Loffredo, Jessica, Sr Mgr-Email Mktg Ops - Penguin Random House; pg. 1675, pg. 1276
Lofgren, Rayme, Sr Specialist-Mktg & Media - Arizona Diamondbacks; pg. 529, pg. 14
Loft, Scott, VP-Ticket Sls, Retention & Database Ops - Oklahoma City Thunder; pg. 571, pg. 1487
Loftiss, Heather, Dir-Creative - NRG Energy, Inc.; pg. 1948, pg. 1712
Lofton, Adrienne, Sr VP-Global Brand Mktg - Under Armour, Inc.; pg. 49, pg. 759
Lofton, Brittany, Coord-Adv - Delta Air Lines, Inc.; pg. 1905, pg. 503
Loftus, Kari, Mgr-Global Mktg-Demand Generation, Acq & Retention - Pitney Bowes Software Inc.; pg. 455, pg. 1346
Loftus, Kathleen, Assoc Brand Mgr-Mktg - Shiseido Cosmetics America of SAC; pg. 522, pg. 1291
Lofty, Keven, Sr Analyst-Mktg Res - Jockey International, Inc.; pg. 27, pg. 1861
Lofurno, Alan, VP-Mktg - Blount International, Inc.; pg. 1043, pg. 1501
Logan, Aaron, Engr-Product Support - Lam Research Corporation; pg. 1354, pg. 91
Logan, Alicia, Dir-Mktg - Endo Pharmaceuticals Holdings, Inc.; pg. 1528, pg. 1549
Logan, Angus, Head-Product Mgmt & Product Mktg-OneDrive - Microsoft Corporation; pg. 435, pg. 1824
Logan, Colleen, VP-Mktg - Icon Health & Fitness, Inc.; pg. 1837, pg. 1752
Logan, Deb, Sr Dir-Partnership Sls - Milwaukee Bucks, Inc.; pg. 563, pg. 1878
Logan, Erin, Brand Mgr-Pet Care - The Procter & Gamble Company; pg. 1129, pg. 1418
Logan, Jamie, Assoc Publr & Dir-Creative - Florida Family Magazine; pg. 1641, pg. 466
Logan, Jeff, VP-Mktg Plng & Strategy - Anthem, Inc.; pg. 1192, pg. 683
Logan, John, Sr Mgr-Sensor Engrg - Atmel Corporation; pg. 621, pg. 238
Logan, Joseph W., Sr VP-Sls-Worldwide - Synopsys, Inc.; pg. 480, pg. 162
Logan, Joshua, Mgr-PR & Comm Strategy - Standard Insurance Company; pg. 1217, pg. 1506
Logan, Katie, Mgr-Media Rels - OhioHealth; pg. 1578, pg. 1443
Logan, Kirsten, VP-Sls & Mktg - Santa Fe Leather Corporation; pg. 12, pg. 1059
Logan, Lorna, Dir-Lifecycle Mktg-Digital & Print - HSN, Inc.; pg. 291, pg. 462
Logan, Margaux, Sr Mgr-Global Brand Dev-Caress & Lux Skin Cleansing - Unilever United States, Inc.; pg. 904, pg. 1061
Logan, Sean, Sr Mgr-Editorial-Creative Svcs - Fair Isaac Corporation; pg. 1247, pg. 955
Logee, Bill, Mgr-Mktg - ASICS America Corporation; pg. 1826, pg. 106
Loggins, Robert, Brand Mgr - Bush Brothers & Company; pg. 843, pg. 1636
Lograsso, Angela, Grp Mgr-Mktg Comm - Verizon Communications Inc.; pg. 1875, pg. 1309
Logsdon, Andrea, Assoc Dir-Sls Comm - ESPN, Inc.; pg. 285, pg. 340
Logsdon, Desiree, Sr VP-Mktg Comm & Corp Citizenship - Bunn-O-Matic Corporation; pg. 53, pg. 661
Loh, Helen, Sr VP-Owned Media, Content & Digital Mktg - Charles Schwab & Company, Inc.; pg. 734, pg. 215
Lohela, Marc, Sr Mgr-Market - Herman Miller, Inc.; pg. 926, pg. 913
Lohier, Marie-Rose, Dir-Sls - Academic Travel Abroad, Inc.; pg. 1896, pg. 393
Lohman, Francesca, Sr Mgr-Product Mktg-Digital Mktg Suite - Adobe Systems Incorporated; pg. 342, pg. 235
Lohman, Jeff, Dir-Interactive Strategy & Mktg - Medtronic, Inc.; pg. 1564, pg. 939
Lohmann, Katie, Sr Planner-Digital Vendor Mktg-Electronics - Target Corporation; pg. 1786, pg. 942
Lohnes, George R., VP-Mktg - UGL Services; pg. 486, pg. 784
Lohr, Dave, Pres-Trade Sls - California Products Corporation; pg. 1441, pg. 781
Lohr, Jennifer, Dir-Mktg - Crystal Cruises LLC; pg. 1904, pg. 128
Lohse, Pat, VP-Mktg - Clopay Building Products Company; pg. 76, pg. 1459
Loiacono, Leo, Sr Dir-Program Mgmt & Customer Svc - Valcor Engineering Corporation; pg. 1386, pg. 1123
Loing, Pierre, VP-Product Strategy & Plng - Nissan North America, Inc.; pg. 186, pg. 1633
Loiselle, Joanna, Mgr-Channel Mktg-Pub Sector - Red Hat, Inc.; pg. 460, pg. 1388
Lojewski, Robert J., Sr Dir-Brand Payer Mktg - Pfizer Inc.; pg. 1581, pg. 1278
Loken, John, Exec VP-Mktg-Ticketmaster North America - Ticketmaster Entertainment LLC; pg. 1284, pg. 48
Lokes, Brendan, Specialist-Digital Mktg - Carhartt, Inc.; pg. 39, pg. 875
Lokes, David, VP-Mktg - Champs Sports; pg. 1806, pg. 414
Lokken, Dawn, Dir-Channel Mktg - Boston Scientific Corporation; pg. 1508, pg. 831
Lollie, Shawn, Specialist-Mktg - Ford Motor Company; pg. 172, pg. 876
Lollini, Claudio, Sr VP-Global Sls & Mktg-Fort Lauderdale - KEMET Corporation; pg. 649, pg. 1621
Loman, Jeff, Grp Product Mgr-Mobile - PayPal Inc.; pg. 1274, pg. 248

First page reference indicates Business Class Edition
Second page reference indicates Geographic Edition

Lomas, Jamie, Dir-Adv Sls - Amazon.com, Inc.; *pg.* 1226, *pg.* 1831
Lomax, Tony, Mgr-Product Mktg-UK & IRL - Lexmark International, Inc.; *pg.* 427, *pg.* 730
Lomba, Ennvoy, Mgr-Digital Mktg - Carnival Cruise Lines; *pg.* 1902, *pg.* 441
Lombard, Steve, Dir-Creative - KCRA-TV; *pg.* 293, *pg.* 196
Lombardi, Doug, VP-Mktg - Valve Corporation; *pg.* 487, *pg.* 1817
Lombardi, Michael J., Exec VP-Sls - TravelCenters of America, LLC; *pg.* 1925, *pg.* 1481
Lombardi, Molly M., Mgr-Worldwide PPS Integrated Mktg - Hewlett-Packard Company; *pg.* 404, *pg.* 175
Lombardi, Robbie, Mgr-Promotional Review & Mktg Svcs - Johnson & Johnson; *pg.* 1549, *pg.* 1091
Lombardi, Sheila, Dir-Reg Promotional Mktg - CVS Health Corporation; *pg.* 1765, *pg.* 1610
Lombardo, Alexa, Dir-Intl Mktg - Gilt Groupe Inc.; *pg.* 24, *pg.* 1234
Lombardo, Greg, VP-Global Brand Mktg & Strategy - Hasbro, Inc.; *pg.* 954, *pg.* 1603
Lombardo, Jon, Head-Content Mktg - LinkedIn Corporation; *pg.* 1262, *pg.* 160
Lombardo, Steve, Chief Comm & Mktg Officer - Koch Industries, Inc.; *pg.* 1463, *pg.* 724
Lombera, Juan, Dir-Mktg-Latin America Personal Care - Colgate-Palmolive Company; *pg.* 504, *pg.* 1215
Lomicky, Joey, Sr Specialist-PR & Comm - Medtronic, Inc.; *pg.* 1564, *pg.* 939
LoMonaco, Traci, Mgr-Consumer Mktg-LaCroix Sparkling Water - National Beverage Corp.; *pg.* 257, *pg.* 425
Lomow, Samantha, Sr VP-Mktg-Global - Hasbro, Inc.; *pg.* 954, *pg.* 1603
Loncto, Chris, Dir Brand Mktg & Comm - Sharp Electronics Corporation; *pg.* 672, *pg.* 1082
London, Aimee, Sr Mgr-Customer Mktg - MATTEL, INC.; *pg.* 962, *pg.* 81
London, Anita, Editor-Mktg - VITACOST.COM, INC.; *pg.* 1607, *pg.* 414
London, Charles, Sr Dir-Creative - Zynga Inc.; *pg.* 1292, *pg.* 235
London, Dennis, Dir-Sls-Europe - ACR Electronics, Inc.; *pg.* 612, *pg.* 422
London, Jon, Head-Mktg-Cider Div - The Boston Beer Company, Inc.; *pg.* 239, *pg.* 790
London, Rob, Sr Product Mgr - Gay Lea Foods Co-operative Limited; *pg.* 858, *pg.* 1926
Londono, Jorge, Mgr-Product Launch - Bose Corporation; *pg.* 626, *pg.* 820
Lonergan, Jeff, Mgr-Production - Jacksonville Journal-Courier; *pg.* 1654, *pg.* 621
Lonergan, Jullia, Head-Adv & Promos-Point of Care Ultrasound - GE Healthcare; *pg.* 399, *pg.* 1765
Long, Abby, Assoc Specialist-Product Dev - Brown-Forman Corporation; *pg.* 1958, *pg.* 732
Long, Ajaa, Exec Dir-Global Mktg Makeup & Fragrance - Clinique Laboratories LLC; *pg.* 503, *pg.* 1214
Long, Amy, Dir-Digital Product Mgmt - J.C. Penney Company, Inc.; *pg.* 1774, *pg.* 1732
Long, Barry, Mgr-Production - Reading Symphony Orchestra Association; *pg.* 578, *pg.* 1585
Long, Beth, Dir-Partnerships, Comml & Consumer Bank Mktg - Capital One Financial Corporation; *pg.* 730, *pg.* 1789
Long, Brian, Sr Dir-Global Pro Svcs - Masimo Corporation; *pg.* 1558, *pg.* 113
Long, Bridget L., Mgr-Sls & Ops Plng - Lowe's Companies, Inc.; *pg.* 1053, *pg.* 1383
Long, Caitlin, Coord-Mktg Budget - Grand Canyon Education, Inc.; *pg.* 602, *pg.* 16
Long, Cheryl, Sr Mgr-Mktg - Verizon Communications Inc.; *pg.* 1875, *pg.* 1309
Long, Cindy, Sr VP & Gen Mgr-Mdse - Dollar General Corporation; *pg.* 1767, *pg.* 1635
Long, Cleo N., Sr Assoc Mgr-Mktg-Emerging Brands, Soy Vay & Nueva Cocina - The Clorox Company; *pg.* 327, *pg.* 169
Long, Cory, Brand Mgr-Sport Archive & Onitsuka - ASICS America Corporation; *pg.* 1826, *pg.* 106
Long, Eric, Mgr-Sls Plng - Starbucks Corporation; *pg.* 897, *pg.* 1840
Long, Garrett, Sr Dir-Mktg-Connected Home - SanDisk Corporation; *pg.* 465, *pg.* 147
Long, Gary, Sr Dir-Transactional Comm - Teachers Insurance & Annuity Association - College Retirement Equities Fund; *pg.* 1219, *pg.* 1297
Long, Heather, Mgr-Channel-Mktg - T. Rowe Price Group Inc.; *pg.* 808, *pg.* 759
Long, Helen, Sr Analyst-Strategic Project Mktg - FedEx Corporation; *pg.* 1907, *pg.* 1642
Long, Henry P., Sr VP-Mdsg & Design - Hooker Furniture Corporation; *pg.* 928, *pg.* 1788
Long, Jeannette, VP-Brand Mktg - AS America, Inc.; *pg.* 68, *pg.* 1108
Long, Jerry, Dir-Intl Mktg-Urology & Women's Health Div - Boston Scientific Corporation; *pg.* 1508, *pg.* 831
Long, Karin, Mgr-Mktg Svcs - Rite Aid Corporation; *pg.* 1590, *pg.* 1519
Long, Katie, Sr Specialist-Global Digital Adv - Accenture; *pg.* 1392, *pg.* 1186
Long, Keri, Sr Specialist-Internet Mktg - Enterprise Holdings, Inc.; *pg.* 1906, *pg.* 996
Long, Kevin, Head-Mktg & Ops - The Hartford Financial Services Group, Inc.; *pg.* 1202, *pg.* 352
Long, Kirsten, Dir-Mktg Comm - Lynx Software Technologies; *pg.* 429, *pg.* 247
Long, Mark, Chief Strategy Officer & Exec VP - Western Digital Corporation; *pg.* 492, *pg.* 118
Long, Michelle, Sr Dir-Inventory Control - Academy Sports & Outdoors, Ltd.; *pg.* 1824, *pg.* 1724
Long, Mike B, VP-Sustainable Dev & Social Performance - Shell Oil Company; *pg.* 984, *pg.* 1714
Long, Monique, Mgr-Mktg Resources Ops - GlaxoSmithKline; *pg.* 1536, *pg.* 1565
Long, Nancy, Sr Mgr-Mktg - Brother International Corporation - USA; *pg.* 53, *pg.* 1046
Long, Nicholas, Sr Mgr-Retail Ops - Orlando Magic; *pg.* 572, *pg.* 455
Long, Nick, Mgr-Product Mktg-Global - Graco, Inc.; *pg.* 1342, *pg.* 935
Long, Paul M., Jr., VP-Sls-Natl - Paradise, Inc.; *pg.* 888, *pg.* 458
Long, Peter, Brand Mgr - The Kraft Heinz Company; *pg.* 871, *pg.* 641
Long, Rian, Dir-Online Mktg - Teleflora LLC; *pg.* 1801, *pg.* 140
Long, Robin, VP-Product Mktg & Bus Dev - Replacements, Ltd.; *pg.* 1138, *pg.* 1383
Long, Rodney, VP-Sls - Cooper Wiring Devices; *pg.* 1295, *pg.* 538
Long, Scott, Mgr-Channel Bus Sls - Sprint Corporation; *pg.* 1874, *pg.* 719
Long, Sean, Product Mgr-Macy's Mdsg Grp - Macy's East; *pg.* 1777, *pg.* 1254
Long, Sean, Dir-Mktg & Applications - Maxim Integrated Products, Inc.; *pg.* 653, *pg.* 247
Long, Spencer, Assoc Mgr-Mktg - Expedia, Inc.; *pg.* 1244, *pg.* 1814
Long, Tracy, VP-Mktg - Baldor Electric Company; *pg.* 1316, *pg.* 32
Longan, Kip, Pres & Mgr-Sls - Long Realty Company; *pg.* 1101, *pg.* 27
Longden, Larry, VP & Gen Mgr-Microelectronics Products - Maxwell Technologies, Inc.; *pg.* 653, *pg.* 204
Longenderfer, Megan, Dir-PR & Comm - Olympus America Inc.; *pg.* 1425, *pg.* 1521
Longendyke, Rob, Sr VP-Mktg & Comm - Medica, Inc.; *pg.* 1208, *pg.* 949
Longenecker, Lauren, Brand Mgr-Trade Mktg - Stoli Group USA LLC; *pg.* 1970, *pg.* 1296
Longfellow, Audrey, Sr VP-Emerging Payments Mktg - Bank of America Corporation; *pg.* 718, *pg.* 1362
Longford, Nicholas, Mgr-Channel Mktg, Retail, Online & New Distr - Robert Bosch Tool Corp; *pg.* 1060, *pg.* 634
Longfritz, David, Head-Mktg & Bus Dev - National Life Insurance Company; *pg.* 1210, *pg.* 1766
Longhi, Amy, Sr Dir-Sls Strategy - Activision Blizzard, Inc.; *pg.* 948, *pg.* 271
Longhi, Lou, Dir-Sls-Global - Broadridge Financial Solutions Inc.; *pg.* 727, *pg.* 1172
Longhini-Mcelroy, Nicole, Brand Mgr-Fiat North America - FCA US LLC; *pg.* 170, *pg.* 868
Longin, Tracy, Dir-Email Mktg & Customer Comm - The Ultimate Software Group, Inc.; *pg.* 486, *pg.* 479
Longley, Rachel, Product Mgr-Mobile - Weight Watchers International, Inc.; *pg.* 1609, *pg.* 1313
Longmire, Hu, Sr Mgr-Interactive Mktg - Dollar General Corporation; *pg.* 1767, *pg.* 1635
Longmire, Julie, Dir-Sls Mktg - Pandora Media Inc.; *pg.* 1273, *pg.* 172
Longoria, Dani, VP-Adv & Dir-Corp Natl Media - Journal Sentinel, Inc.; *pg.* 1655, *pg.* 1876
Longphee, Terri Parnell, Sr Dir-Sls & Mktg - Florida State Fair Authority; *pg.* 549, *pg.* 473
Longwood, Caitlin, Mgr-Social Mktg - Ebates.com; *pg.* 1240, *pg.* 217
Longworth, Guy, Sr VP-Mktg & PlayStation Network - Sony Computer Entertainment America LLC; *pg.* 966, *pg.* 256
Lonner, Matt, Mgr-Global Social Performance-Pub Policy & Corp Responsibility - Chevron Corporation; *pg.* 974, *pg.* 259
Lonnett, Chris, VP-Sls Ops & Learning - Motorola Solutions, Inc.; *pg.* 657, *pg.* 659
Lonsbury, Kristin, Sr Strategist-Digital-Paid Media - UnitedHealth Group Incorporated; *pg.* 1221, *pg.* 950
Lonsdale, Paul, Mgr-Drilling Grp Mktg & Comm - Schlumberger Limited; *pg.* 801, *pg.* 1714
Loo, Mei K., Sr Mgr-Mktg - Marriott International, Inc.; *pg.* 1102, *pg.* 764
Lookretis, Dan, Reg Mgr-Sls - Post Consumer Brands; *pg.* 833, *pg.* 927
Loomis, Greg, Asst Mgr-Mktg-Women's Mass Underwear - Hanesbrands Inc.; *pg.* 26, *pg.* 1394
Loonan, Seth, Sr Dir-Mktg - Authentidate Holding Corp.; *pg.* 356, *pg.* 1044
Looney, Sean, Planner-Production - Clariant Corporation; *pg.* 1153, *pg.* 1365
Loos, Matthew, Dir-Truck & Bus Mktg - Bridgestone Americas, Inc.; *pg.* 1879, *pg.* 1648
Loos, Matthew, Dir-Truck & Bus Mktg - Bridgestone Americas, Inc.; *pg.* 201, *pg.* 1649
Looze, Amy, Sr Mgr-Mktg-Video & Branded Entertainment - Macy's East; *pg.* 1777, *pg.* 1254
Lopacki, Richard, VP-Mktg Dev - Johnson & Johnson; *pg.* 1549, *pg.* 1091
Loparco, Lindsey, Asst VP-Mktg - Urban Financial of America, LLC.; *pg.* 815, *pg.* 1491
Lopdrup, Jennifer, Sr Product Mgr - Intuit Inc.; *pg.* 769, *pg.* 158
Loper, Larry, Sr Brand Mktg Dir - Juniper Networks, Inc.; *pg.* 1260, *pg.* 286
Lopes, Maria, Sr Product Mgr-Transplant Franchise - Novartis Corporation; *pg.* 1574, *pg.* 1273
Lopez, Abraham, Product Mgr-Engine Mgmt - Robert Bosch Tool Corp; *pg.* 1060, *pg.* 634
Lopez, Alejandro, Mgr-Adv - MetLife, Inc.; *pg.* 1208, *pg.* 1258
Lopez, Ana Maria, VP-Digital Sls Mktg & Solutions - Discovery Communications, Inc.; *pg.* 282, *pg.* 777
Lopez, Art, VP-Media Plng & Production - NBC Universal, Inc.; *pg.* 300, *pg.* 1266
Lopez, Brianna, Head-Originals Marketing - Amazon.com, Inc.; *pg.* 1226, *pg.* 1831
Lopez, Cassie, Sr Mgr-Consumer Insight - Under Armour, Inc.; *pg.* 49, *pg.* 759
Lopez, Catalina, Brand Mgr-Counter Skincare-RoC & KORRES - Johnson & Johnson Inc.; *pg.* 1552, *pg.* 1923
Lopez, Claudina, Mgr-Mktg - Alienware Corporation; *pg.* 346, *pg.* 439
Lopez, Claudina, Mgr-Mktg - Dell, Inc.; *pg.* 385, *pg.* 1037
Lopez, Coral, Specialist-Digital Mktg - Guthy-Renker LLC; *pg.* 289, *pg.* 273
Lopez, Edgardo A., Exec Bus Process Mgr-HP Converged Sys Mktg Grp - Hewlett-Packard Company; *pg.* 404, *pg.* 175
Lopez, Erick, Asst VP & Mgr-Sls & Adv Compliance - Eaton Vance Corp.; *pg.* 746, *pg.* 794
Lopez, Georgia Manolas, Sr Dir-Mktg - Playmates Toys Inc.; *pg.* 965, *pg.* 82
Lopez, James, VP-Mktg & Bus Dev - Socket Mobile, Inc.; *pg.* 471, *pg.* 164
Lopez, Janette, Sr Assoc Brand Mgr - Campbell Soup Company; *pg.* 844, *pg.* 1048
Lopez, Javier, Brand Mgr - Bristol-Myers Squibb Company; *pg.* 1509, *pg.* 1206
Lopez, Jennie, Coord-Channel Mktg - Zebra Technologies Corporation; *pg.* 690, *pg.* 628
Lopez, Jerry, Coord-Mktg - Air France, USA; *pg.* 1897, *pg.* 1188
Lopez, Jesse, Sr Mgr-Latin America Strategy - Mondelez International, Inc.; *pg.* 878, *pg.* 601
Lopez, Karen, Mgr-Social Media - L'Oreal USA; *pg.* 514, *pg.* 1252
Lopez, Kristin, Mgr-Media - PETCO Animal Supplies, Inc.; *pg.* 1480, *pg.* 206
Lopez, Leola, Coord-Media - Jarden Consumer Solutions; *pg.* 57, *pg.* 412
Lopez, Lincoln, VP & Gen Mgr-Social Media - Univision Communications Inc.; *pg.* 683, *pg.* 1307

Lopez, Luis, Dir-Product Dev - Whirlpool Corporation; *pg.* 62, *pg.* 872
Lopez, Mario, Product Category Mgr - Harbor Freight Tools; *pg.* 1772, *pg.* 55
Lopez, Mark, Exec VP & Gen Mgr-Univision Interactive Media - Univision Communications Inc.; *pg.* 683, *pg.* 1307
Lopez, Modesto, Brand Mgr-Mktg & Comml Dept - The Procter & Gamble Company; *pg.* 1129, *pg.* 1418
Lopez, Nathalie, Mgr-Client Mktg - Assurant, Inc.; *pg.* 1193, *pg.* 1198
Lopez, Olga, Coord-Mktg - Popchips; *pg.* 890, *pg.* 182
Lopez, Raul Esquer, Brand Mgr-Tecate & Indio Brands - Heineken USA Inc.; *pg.* 252, *pg.* 1352
Lopez, Revecca, Specialist-Channel Mktg-NA Mktg & PR Programs - Polycom, Inc.; *pg.* 664, *pg.* 249
Lopez, Robert, Sr Mgr-Comm-Innovation Campaign - Cisco Systems, Inc.; *pg.* 372, *pg.* 240
Lopez, Theresa, Mgr-Intl Customer Mktg - Elizabeth Arden, Inc.; *pg.* 507, *pg.* 448
Lopez, Thomas, VP-Mktg-US Growth Channels - The Kraft Heinz Company; *pg.* 871, *pg.* 641
Lopiccolo, Deborah Dacey, Dir-Mktg Strategy, Programs & Risk Consulting - KPMG LLP; *pg.* 774, *pg.* 1086
Lopinto, Joanne, Assoc Publr-Mktg - The Family Circle, Inc.; *pg.* 1640, *pg.* 1230
LoPinto, Joanne, Assoc Publr-Mktg - Meredith Corporation; *pg.* 1663, *pg.* 705
Lopis, Josephine, Mgr-Comml Mktg - Avis Rent A Car System, LLC; *pg.* 165, *pg.* 1102
Lopreato, Nicole, Brand Mktg Mgr - Dunkin' Brands Group, Inc.; *pg.* 1727, *pg.* 810
LoPresti, Lana, Program Mgr-Mktg - The Great Atlantic & Pacific Tea Company, Inc.; *pg.* 1021, *pg.* 1086
Lopriore, Randae, Dir-Digital Mktg - Time Inc.; *pg.* 1693, *pg.* 1300
Loran, Jennifer, Asst Mgr-Mktg - Briggs & Stratton Corporation; *pg.* 201, *pg.* 1899
Loranger, Cathy, Dir-Mktg - Shenandoah University; *pg.* 607, *pg.* 1812
Lorango, David, Sr Mgr-Digital Mktg-Roll Global - POM Wonderful, LLC; *pg.* 890, *pg.* 139
Lord, Alex, Sr Dir-Global Ad Creative Tech - Yahoo! Inc.; *pg.* 1289, *pg.* 289
Lord, Anthony, Mgr-Mktg - CASCADE MICROTECH, INC.; *pg.* 1405, *pg.* 1492
Lord, Ashley, Reg Mgr-Mktg - Kia Motors America Inc.; *pg.* 181, *pg.* 112
Lord, Lyndsay, Sr Mgr-Ad Ops & Performance - MyWebGrocer.com Corp.; *pg.* 1269, *pg.* 1769
Lord, Pete, Mgr-Product Line - Autodesk Inc.; *pg.* 356, *pg.* 257
Lord, Rob, Area Dir-Sls - YRC Worldwide Inc.; *pg.* 1931, *pg.* 720
Lorden, Andrew, Brand Mgr-Special K - Kellogg Company; *pg.* 831, *pg.* 870
Lordi, Mike, Head-Sls Support-AXA Advisors - AXA Equitable Life Insurance Company; *pg.* 1194, *pg.* 1199
Loredo, Julio, Dir-Digital Mktg - SolarCity Corporation; *pg.* 111, *pg.* 256
Loredo, Susan, Dir-Mktg - Audubon Magazine; *pg.* 1618, *pg.* 1198
Loren-Gulla, Linda, VP-Mktg - CELSIUS HOLDINGS, INC.; *pg.* 239, *pg.* 411
Lorenson, Claude, Dir-Product Mgmt-SQL Server Mktg Grp - Microsoft Corporation; *pg.* 435, *pg.* 1824
Lorentsen, Soren, Dir-Product Mktg - Sigma Designs, Inc.; *pg.* 469, *pg.* 148
Lorentson, Karen, Dir-Americas Partner Mktg - Autodesk Inc.; *pg.* 356, *pg.* 257
Lorentzen, Keira, Sr Dir-Acq Mktg - Constant Contact, Inc.; *pg.* 379, *pg.* 850
Lorenz, Andrew, VP & Mgr-Mktg Strategy - JPMorgan Chase & Co.; *pg.* 772, *pg.* 1246
Lorenz, Liza, Dir-Comm & Mktg - Ford's Theatre Society Inc.; *pg.* 549, *pg.* 399
Lorenz, Lori, Dir-Mktg & Bus Dev - Hewlett-Packard Company; *pg.* 404, *pg.* 175
Lorenzana, Myriam, Reg Coord-Mktg-Latin America - Hasbro, Inc.; *pg.* 954, *pg.* 1603
Lorenze, Caitlyn, Sr Mgr-Mktg Ops - Gilead Sciences, Inc.; *pg.* 1535, *pg.* 88
Lorenzo, Dora, Dir-Diverse Mktg - AT&T; *pg.* 1865, *pg.* 258
Lorenzo, Dora, Dir-Diverse Mktg - AT&T Communications Corp.; *pg.* 1866, *pg.* 1043
Lorenzo, Marissa, Analyst-Social Media Community Mgmt - Kia Motors America Inc.; *pg.* 181, *pg.* 112
Loreski, Joe, VP-Affiliate Sls & Mktg - National Hockey League; *pg.* 568, *pg.* 1265
Lorge, John, Sr Mgr-Customer Acq - Electronic Arts Inc.; *pg.* 951, *pg.* 189
Loria, Mauricio, Sr Dir-Bus Intelligence & Consumer Insights - CARIBOU COFFEE COMPANY, INC.; *pg.* 1764, *pg.* 932
Lorimer, Dylan, Sr Product Mgr - Google Inc.; *pg.* 1249, *pg.* 153
Lorimer, Skip, Mgr-Sourcing-Global Mktg & Sls - Amway Corporation; *pg.* 326, *pg.* 864
Lorimor, Randy, Mgr-Adv - COUNTRY Financial; *pg.* 1198, *pg.* 557
Lorion, Mark, VP-Bus Dev & Mktg - United States Cold Storage, Inc.; *pg.* 61, *pg.* 1051
Loro, Malcolm, Dir-Indus Mktg - CIENA Corporation; *pg.* 628, *pg.* 771
LoRusso, Lana, Publr-Adv Sls - Entertainment Weekly Inc.; *pg.* 1639, *pg.* 1228
Losacco, Dominic, VP-Global Mktg - Moe's Southwest Grill, LLC; *pg.* 1027, *pg.* 514
Losacco, Vinicius, VP-Mktg-Latin America - Netflix, Inc.; *pg.* 1269, *pg.* 141
Losardo, Joe, Exec Brand Dir-Taste of Home - The Reader's Digest Association, Inc.; *pg.* 1679, *pg.* 1322
Losavio, Dana, Mgr-Social Media Strategic Svcs - Bristol-Myers Squibb Company; *pg.* 1509, *pg.* 1206
Loschelder, Todd, Dir-Sls & Mktg - Schneller, Inc.; *pg.* 234, *pg.* 1456
Losco, Janiene, Mng Dir-Digital, Adv & Creative Svcs - New York Life Insurance Company; *pg.* 1211, *pg.* 1268
Losh, Mike, Area Mgr-Direct Mail Adv - Gannett Co., Inc.; *pg.* 1643, *pg.* 1790
Lossing, Steve, Sr VP-Mdsg - PETCO Animal Supplies, Inc.; *pg.* 1480, *pg.* 206
Losson, Caroline, VP-Mktg - Agropur Cooperative; *pg.* 836, *pg.* 1950
LoSurdo, Tosha, Assoc Program Mgr-Mktg Insights - Liberty Mutual Insurance Group Inc.; *pg.* 1205, *pg.* 797
Loten, Moira, VP-Mktg-Global - Colgate-Palmolive Company; *pg.* 504, *pg.* 1215
Lotfi, Shaheen, Acct Exec-Adv-Bing - Microsoft Corporation; *pg.* 435, *pg.* 1824
Lotgering, Anne-Sophie, VP-Sls & Mktg-Europe Reg - Orange Business Services; *pg.* 1273, *pg.* 1785
Lothian, David, Sr Dir-Sls Strategy & Plng - Frito-Lay North America, Inc.; *pg.* 1853, *pg.* 1730
Lotking, Makoto, Mgr-Mktg - Honest Tea; *pg.* 253, *pg.* 762
Lotkowictz, Lynn, Dir-Adv - Trend Magazines, Inc.; *pg.* 1696, *pg.* 465
Lott, Christine, Mgr-Mktg-Intl Retail - Blue Diamond Growers; *pg.* 840, *pg.* 195
Lott, Marissa E., Sr Mgr-Strategy & Bus Plng - American Express Company; *pg.* 712, *pg.* 1190
Lotti, Martin, VP & Dir-Creative-Global - NIKE, Inc.; *pg.* 1812, *pg.* 1492
Lotts, Liz, Editor-Mktg - VITACOST.COM, INC.; *pg.* 1607, *pg.* 414
Lotz, Adam, Principal & Product Mgr-ShareFile - Citrix Systems, Inc.; *pg.* 375, *pg.* 424
Lotz, Jeff, Sr Dir-Xeljanz US Mktg - Pfizer Inc.; *pg.* 1581, *pg.* 1278
Loucks, Tammy, Product Mgr-Progressive Insurance - The Progressive Corporation; *pg.* 1214, *pg.* 1463
Loud, Ingrid, Brand Mgr-Alice & Olivia - Saks Fifth Avenue, Inc.; *pg.* 1783, *pg.* 1287
Louey, Allison, Sr Mgr-PR - Feld Entertainment, Inc.; *pg.* 547, *pg.* 458
Lougee, Dave, Pres-Tegna Media - Gannett Co., Inc.; *pg.* 1643, *pg.* 1790
Lougee, Melanie, Head-Product Strategy-Workforce Applications - Intuit Inc.; *pg.* 769, *pg.* 158
Loughery, Mike, Dir-Corp Mktg Comm - CertainTeed Corporation; *pg.* 74, *pg.* 1589
Loughmiller, Megan, Specialist-Electronic Mktg - Brookshire Grocery Company; *pg.* 1016, *pg.* 1748
Loughney, Mark, VP-Animation, Young Adults & Kids Media Res - Turner Broadcasting System, Inc.; *pg.* 314, *pg.* 521
Loughran, Margaret, VP & Sr Head-Bus-Global Affluent Products & Travel Svcs - MasterCard Incorporated; *pg.* 779, *pg.* 1325
Louie, Daniel, Mgr-Sports & Experiential Mktg - Kia Motors America Inc.; *pg.* 181, *pg.* 112
Louie, Douglas, Sr Dir-Product Mktg Enterprise - Smith Micro Software, Inc.; *pg.* 471, *pg.* 41
Louie, Lonny, Sr Mgr-Quality - Systron Donner Inertial Division; *pg.* 1430, *pg.* 69
Louis, Jenifer, Brand Mgr-Protection Ops - Cisco Systems, Inc.; *pg.* 372, *pg.* 240
Loulakis, Andrea, Brand Mgr - Johnson & Johnson; *pg.* 1549, *pg.* 1091
Lourenco, Christine, Sr Dir-Talent Strategy & Digital - Ann Inc.; *pg.* 18, *pg.* 1195
Lourenco, Fernando, Mgr-Sls & Mktg - 3M Company; *pg.* 1142, *pg.* 956
Loustaunau, Aline, Asst Dir-Cause Related Mktg - City of Hope National Medical Center; *pg.* 1516, *pg.* 77
Louviere, Jill R., Analyst-BCA Mktg CAS Value Analysis - The Boeing Company; *pg.* 225, *pg.* 567
Louwagie, Julie A., Coord-Mktg-Baune Fin - The Northwestern Mutual Life Insurance Company; *pg.* 1212, *pg.* 1879
Lovaas, John, Dir-Sls & Mktg - Harrington & King Perforating Company, Inc.; *pg.* 1164, *pg.* 576
Lovato, Joanne, VP-Brand & Entertainment Mktg - Samsung Electronics America, Inc.; *pg.* 669, *pg.* 1115
Love, Angela, Acct Exec-Charter Media - Charter Communications, Inc.; *pg.* 274, *pg.* 372
Love, Bari, Sr VP-Comm & Mktg - Metro Atlanta Chamber of Commerce; *pg.* 998, *pg.* 514
Love, Carlos, Sr Brand Mgr-Mktg-LATAM - Dell Inc.; *pg.* 383, *pg.* 1737
Love, Cathy, VP-Mktg & Comm - SCANA Corporation; *pg.* 1951, *pg.* 1612
Love, John, Exec VP-R&D Travel & Expense Product Bus Unit - Concur Technologies, Inc.; *pg.* 1236, *pg.* 1813
Love, Karen, Sr Mgr-Creative Svcs - Hanesbrands Inc.; *pg.* 26, *pg.* 1394
Love, Katie, Mgr-Online Mktg - Southwest Airlines Co.; *pg.* 1923, *pg.* 1687
Love, Kelsey, Strategist-Corp Digital Mktg - Clayton Homes, Inc.; *pg.* 1086, *pg.* 1640
Love, Mark, District Mgr-Mktg-Atlanta - Federated Mutual Insurance Company; *pg.* 1200, *pg.* 952
Love, Melanie, Sr Product Mgr-Kelty - Exxel Outdoors LLC; *pg.* 1833, *pg.* 311
Love, Melissa, Mgr-Social Bus - IBM; *pg.* 410, *pg.* 1449
Love, Rhena, Dir-Customer Mktg-Natl Restaurants-PepsiCo Foodservice - PepsiCo, Inc.; *pg.* 259, *pg.* 1327
Love, Vanessa, Dir-Mktg Tech - Protective Life Insurance Company; *pg.* 1215, *pg.* 4
Loveday, Melody, Media Planner & Media Buyer - Zappos.com, Inc.; *pg.* 1291, *pg.* 1030
Lovei, Krisztina, Sr Assoc Brand Mgr - Wm. Wrigley Jr. Company; *pg.* 1863, *pg.* 596
Lovejoy, Ann, Dir-Creative - Pier 1 Imports, Inc.; *pg.* 940, *pg.* 1695
Lovelace, Eric, Asst Mgr-Production - Forrest Keeling Nursery, Inc.; *pg.* 1795, *pg.* 977
Lovelace, Greg, Dir-Mktg & Bus Dev-Cargo & Cruise - Tampa Port Authority Inc.; *pg.* 1925, *pg.* 476
Lovelace, Kelsea, Brand Mgr - Rocky Mountain Chocolate Factory, Inc.; *pg.* 1032, *pg.* 324
Loveless, Brad, Mgr-Mktg & Product Dev - Simpson Door Company; *pg.* 110, *pg.* 1823
Loveless, Dawn, Acct Exec-Mktg - Bank of America Corporation; *pg.* 718, *pg.* 1362
Lovell, Jenn, Brand Mgr-Children's ZYRTEC - Johnson & Johnson; *pg.* 1549, *pg.* 1091
Lovell, Ken, Sr VP-Media Dev - PGA Tour, Inc.; *pg.* 574, *pg.* 460
Lovell, Rob, Sr Mgr-Channel Strategy & Innovation - Bath & Body Works, LLC; *pg.* 500, *pg.* 1471
Lovell, Zach, Sr Product Mgr - Airvana, Inc.; *pg.* 268, *pg.* 812
Lovely-Lin, Barbara, Mgr-Tech Svcs Mktg - Hewlett-Packard Company; *pg.* 404, *pg.* 175
Loverde, Mike, Reg Dir-Adv & PR - MetroPCS, Inc.; *pg.* 1872, *pg.* 1683
LoVerde, Paul, Dir-US Pituitary Mktg-Rare Diseases - Novartis Pharmaceuticals Corp.; *pg.* 1575, *pg.* 1054
LoVerme, Chris, Brand Mgr-Snack Nuts - Blue Diamond Growers; *pg.* 840, *pg.* 195
Lovette, Kelley, Sr Mgr-Sls Ops - Waste Management, Inc.; *pg.* 1954, *pg.* 1716
Lovin, Melissa, Dir-Integrated Mktg-The Hartford - The Hartford Financial Services Group, Inc.; *pg.* 1202, *pg.* 352
Loving, Melissa, Sr Mgr-Mobility-Global - TD Auto Finance; *pg.* 809, *pg.* 886
Lovinger, Dan, Exec VP-Sls-NBCUniversal Entertainment Grp - NBC Universal, Inc.; *pg.* 300, *pg.* 1266
Lovinger, Dan, Exec VP-Sls-NBCUniversal Entertainment Grp

First page reference indicates Business Class Edition
Second page reference indicates Geographic Edition

- Telemundo Network Inc.; pg. 311, pg. 430
Lovins, Julie, Sr Mgr-Customer Svc - Chicago Blackhawk Hockey Team, Inc.; pg. 538, pg. 569
Lovinsky, Noam, Dir-Product Mgmt - YouTube, LLC; pg. 1291, pg. 198
Low, Cassie, Mgr-Direct TV Sls-Clinical Skin Care - Peter Thomas Roth Labs LLC; pg. 520, pg. 1278
Low, Jim, Sr Dir-US Gum Category - Mondelez International; pg. 877, pg. 1344
Low, Tad, Sr Mgr-Field Mktg-Emerging Markets - Moe's Southwest Grill, LLC; pg. 1027, pg. 514
Lowden, Tom, Territory Mgr-Eastern Reg Sls - Blonder Tongue Laboratories, Inc.; pg. 625, pg. 1100
Lowe, Brooke, Brand Mgr-Retail - NIKE, Inc.; pg. 1812, pg. 1492
Lowe, David, VP & Div Mgr-Mdse-Proprietary Brands - Golfsmith International Holdings, Inc.; pg. 1835, pg. 1662
Lowe, David M., Exec VP-Indus Products Div - Graco, Inc.; pg. 1342, pg. 935
Lowe, Donna, Dir-Product Adv - Henry Schein, Inc.; pg. 1541, pg. 1180
Lowe, Greg, Mgr-Product Mktg-AT& T Bus Solutions - AT&T Inc.; pg. 1867, pg. 1674
Lowe, Kathy, Mgr-Corp Sls-Key Accts - American Airlines Inc.; pg. 1898, pg. 1693
Lowe, Kenneth, VP-Strategic Mktg - Sigma Designs, Inc.; pg. 469, pg. 148
Lowe, Leslie, Sr Mgr-Global Adv - United Airlines, Inc.; pg. 1927, pg. 593
Lowe, Mark, Mgr-ECommerce Mktg & Digital Dept - Ace Hardware Corporation; pg. 1040, pg. 644
Lowe, Matt, VP-Retail Mktg - McKesson Corporation; pg. 1560, pg. 222
Lowe, Melissa, Mgr-Mktg HR-Global - Brown-Forman Corporation; pg. 1958, pg. 732
Lowe, Monte, Exec VP-Sls & Mktg - National Beef Packing Company, LLC; pg. 882, pg. 985
Lowe, Tammy, Dir-Mktg - ROCKFORD CORPORATION; pg. 667, pg. 26
Lowell, Rett, Sr Specialist-Mktg, Media & Entertainment Indus - Deloitte & Touche USA LLP; pg. 743, pg. 1222
Lowell, Victoria, Exec VP-Mktg - Animal Planet, LLC; pg. 270, pg. 777
Lowell, Zach, Brand Mgr-Retail Dev-Men's Wholesale - Ralph Lauren Corporation; pg. 46, pg. 1284
Lowenstein, Jeremy, VP-Global Mktg-Sally Hansen - Coty, Inc.; pg. 506, pg. 1219
Lower, Rob, Dir-Sls-Premium Seats - Live Nation Entertainment, Inc.; pg. 558, pg. 47
Lowery, Jason, Dir-Strategic Acct & Territory Mktg - Adobe Systems Incorporated; pg. 342, pg. 235
Lowery, Kate, Dir-PR-Global - Whole Foods Market, Inc.; pg. 1038, pg. 1667
Lowitz, Kevin, Sr Product Mgr-Protein Biology - Thermo Fisher Scientific Inc.; pg. 1431, pg. 854
Lowman, Dave, Mgr-Market Sls - Deluxe Corporation; pg. 1634, pg. 964
Lowman, Hal, Mgr-Segment Mktg - United Parcel Service, Inc.; pg. 1928, pg. 522
Lowney, Jenny, Project Mgr-Mktg - Harley-Davidson, Inc.; pg. 178, pg. 1874
Lowrey, Cecile, Mgr-Mktg - Saks Fifth Avenue, Inc.; pg. 1783, pg. 1287
Lowry, Kelly, Reg Mgr-Mktg - Pepsi Beverages Company; pg. 258, pg. 1342
Lowry, Kelly M., Program Mgr-Mktg - Intel Corporation; pg. 645, pg. 266
Lowry, Marion, Dir-Adv-Western - Robb Report; pg. 1681, pg. 142
Lowsky, David, Product Mgr - Google Inc.; pg. 1249, pg. 153
Lowthion, Magda, Dir-Global Mktg Anti Infectives-Global Established Pharma - Pfizer Inc.; pg. 1581, pg. 1278
Loyed, Robin, Dir-Operator Mktg-Global - International Game Technology; pg. 957, pg. 1024
Loyka, Eric, Dir-Mktg - The Okonite Company; pg. 1302, pg. 1113
Loza, Ivonne, Mgr-Mktg - McDonald's Corporation; pg. 1737, pg. 645
Lozado, Karen, Mgr-Mktg & Comm - Kindred Healthcare, Inc.; pg. 1553, pg. 736
Lozan, Jai, Mgr-Brand Mktg-Global - Western Digital Corporation; pg. 492, pg. 118
Lozano, Karla, Mgr-Multicultural Mktg - Home Box Office, Inc.; pg. 290, pg. 1240
Lozyniak, Richard, Interim CEO - Heritage Home Group; pg. 926, pg. 1379
Lu, Alice, Sr Product Mgr-Oncology Mktg - Regeneron Pharmaceuticals, Inc.; pg. 1588, pg. 1345
Lu, Annie, Mgr-Inside Sls - ASUSTeK Computer Inc; pg. 355, pg. 90
Lu, Denise, Dir-Global Mktg-Automotive Refinish - PPG Industries, Inc.; pg. 1445, pg. 1579
Lu, Fei, Sr Product Mgr - Microsoft Corporation; pg. 435, pg. 1824
Lu, Flora, Mgr-Mktg Forecasting & Analysis - Netflix, Inc.; pg. 1269, pg. 141
Lu, Joan, Head-Section-Global R&D-Product Supply - The Procter & Gamble Company; pg. 1129, pg. 1418
Lu, Lisa, Mgr-Mktg - PepsiCo, Inc.; pg. 259, pg. 1327
Lu, Marianne, Sr Mgr-Product Mktg - Intuit Inc.; pg. 769, pg. 158
Lu, Mike, VP-Product Mgmt - GREE International, Inc.; pg. 1255, pg. 219
Lu, Nanqian, Sr Assoc Brand Mgr - Unilever United States, Inc.; pg. 904, pg. 1061
Lu, Wenqing, Sr Dir-Advanced Analytics - Orbitz Worldwide, Inc.; pg. 1918, pg. 586
Lubacz, Jennifer, Assoc Dir-US Diabetes Mktg - Merck & Co., Inc.; pg. 1566, pg. 1077
Lubatti, John L., Mgr-Mktg-MidAtlantic Reg - USI Holdings Corporation; pg. 1222, pg. 1144
Lubbers, Paul, Head-Sls-Allstate B2B - The Allstate Corporation; pg. 1189, pg. 639
Lubelczyk, Steven, Bus Mgr-Analytics - F.W. Bryce, Inc.; pg. 857, pg. 823
Lubetkin, Greg, Dir-Digital Adv Ops - ABC, Inc.; pg. 268, pg. 1185
Lubets, Andrew, Brand Mgr-Apparel - New Balance Athletic Shoe, Inc.; pg. 1811, pg. 798
Lubig, John, Mgr-IT, Mktg & Comm - Ford Motor Company; pg. 172, pg. 876
Lubin, Steven L., VP & Gen Mgr-Mdse - Walgreen Co.; pg. 1608, pg. 605
Lubitz, Debra, Specialist-Adv - Toll Brothers, Inc.; pg. 115, pg. 1541
Lubitz, Mitch, Head-East Reg Media Rels - Humana, Inc.; pg. 1204, pg. 734
Lublin, Meghan, Sr VP-Corp Mktg & Comm - Sunrise Senior Living, Inc.; pg. 1599, pg. 1795
Lubliner, Jourdann, Mgr-PR - Gilt Groupe Inc.; pg. 24, pg. 1234
Lubold, Patty N., Dir-Media Rels & Field Comm - Massachusetts Mutual Life Insurance Company; pg. 1207, pg. 845
Lubomski, Steve, VP-Mktg - Aeropostale, Inc.; pg. 17, pg. 1188
Luby, Elizabeth, Sr Mgr-PR & Womenswear-Americas - Burberry Limited; pg. 20, pg. 1208
Luc, Connie, Asst VP-Events Mktg - City National Bank; pg. 737, pg. 725
Luca, Carla, Sr Mgr-Global Bus-Women's Systems - Edgewell Personal Care; pg. 1526, pg. 995
Lucas, Amy, Mgr-Mktg - Round Table Pizza; pg. 1748, pg. 69
Lucas, Andrea, Dir-Mktg Innovation-Global & New Products - Alcon; pg. 1399, pg. 530
Lucas, Bryan, VP-Corp Sls - St. Louis Blues Hockey Club, LLC; pg. 585, pg. 1003
Lucas, Candice, Dir-Commodity Products - CME Group Inc.; pg. 738, pg. 571
Lucas, Jeff, VP-Global Bus Svcs-Advanced Media - Raytheon Company; pg. 233, pg. 854
Lucas, Jeff, Head-Sls & Mktg - Viacom Inc.; pg. 316, pg. 1310
Lucas, Jessica, Sr Planner & Buyer-Media - Sleep Country USA, Inc.; pg. 943, pg. 1822
Lucas, John E., Sr Mgr-PR - Samsung Electronics America, Inc.; pg. 669, pg. 1115
Lucas, Lynn, CMO - Good Technology, Inc.; pg. 1249, pg. 285
Lucas, Nicole, Exec Dir-Mktg-Global - The Estee Lauder Companies Inc.; pg. 508, pg. 1229
Lucas, Rob, Dir-Mktg - The Nolan Company; pg. 1365, pg. 1408
Lucas, Shelly, Sr Mgr-Mktg-Content - The Dun & Bradstreet Corp.; pg. 1637, pg. 1120
Lucchesi, Mary Ann, Mgr-Midwest Event Mktg - Nordstrom, Inc.; pg. 1779, pg. 1837
Lucci, Emily, Dir-Mktg - The J.M. Smucker Company; pg. 865, pg. 1468
Lucente, Dean, Sr Dir-Advanced & Programmatic Media Solutions-CM 360 - Comcast Corporation; pg. 276, pg. 1560
Lucente, Janice, Mgr-Mktg - The Allstate Corporation; pg. 1189, pg. 639
Lucero, Leticia, Mgr-Convention Sls - San Francisco Travel Association; pg. 1005, pg. 227
Lucero, Louie, Specialist-Adv & Pub Affairs - Pacific Life Insurance Company; pg. 1213, pg. 166
Lucero, Nadine, Program Mgr-Mktg - Cisco Systems, Inc.; pg. 372, pg. 240
Lucey, Jeffrey, Specialist-Mktg - Massachusetts Mutual Life Insurance Company; pg. 1207, pg. 845
Luchini, Umberto, VP-Mktg - Campari America; pg. 1960, pg. 214
Luci, Gino, Asst VP-Mktg-Ralph Lauren Fragrances - L'Oreal USA; pg. 514, pg. 1252
Lucia, Allison, Sr Mgr-Partner Svcs & Activation - StubHub, Inc.; pg. 586, pg. 228
Luciano, Elizabeth, VP-Mktg & Brand Strategy, A&E, History & H2 - A&E Television Networks, LLC; pg. 267, pg. 1185
Luciano, Kelly, Sr Mgr-Social Media - Anthropologie, Inc.; pg. 18, pg. 1558
Lucio, Antonio, Chief Mktg & Comm Officer-Personal Sys Grp - Hewlett-Packard Company; pg. 404, pg. 175
Lucion, Lori, Head-Mktg Comm-Honda Aircraft Company - American Honda Motor Co., Inc.; pg. 163, pg. 292
Luck, John, Dir-Mdsg - Motorcar Parts of America, Inc.; pg. 213, pg. 295
Luckadoo, Ben, Mgr-Digital Mktg - Equinox Fitness Clubs; pg. 546, pg. 1228
Lucker, John, Partner & Head-Global Advanced Analytics & Modeling - Deloitte & Touche USA LLP; pg. 743, pg. 1222
Luckett, Jennifer, Specialist-Mktg - KFC Corporation; pg. 1733, pg. 735
Luckett, Robert, Specialist-PR - Canon U.S.A., Inc.; pg. 1404, pg. 1178
Luckey, Tyler, Assoc Mgr-Product Line-Core NSW Footwear - NIKE, Inc.; pg. 1812, pg. 1492
Ludecker, Scott, VP-Sls & Mktg-Global - Misonix Inc.; pg. 1568, pg. 1159
Ludka, Steve, Supvr-Sls - Republic Services, Inc.; pg. 107, pg. 19
Ludke, Greg, Product Mgr-Customer Experience - Intuit Inc.; pg. 769, pg. 158
Ludlow, Andy, Mgr-Mktg - The J.M. Smucker Company; pg. 865, pg. 1468
Ludlow, Ron, Sr Mgr-Channel Mktg - Autodesk Inc.; pg. 356, pg. 257
Ludlow, Shawna, Mgr-Outside Sls - The State Journal-Register; pg. 1689, pg. 662
Ludmer, Sarah, Sr Partner-Nutrition Mktg - Kellogg Company; pg. 831, pg. 870
Ludwick, Kelly D., Sr Dir-Corp Legal - Chick-fil-A, Inc.; pg. 1721, pg. 492
Ludwig, Alexis H., Sr VP-Citi Cards Sls Growth Mktg Execution - Citigroup Inc.; pg. 735, pg. 1212
Ludwig, Beth, VP-Sls & Mktg-Europe Reg - Mary Kay Inc.; pg. 516, pg. 1657
Ludwig, Brianna, Mgr-Mktg & Internal Comm - North Dakota Department of Commerce Tourism Division; pg. 1002, pg. 1397
Ludwig, James, VP-Design & Product Engrg-Global - Steelcase Inc.; pg. 475, pg. 889
Ludwig, Michael, Head-Social Media-Customer Svc - Hulu LLC; pg. 1257, pg. 274
Ludwig, Peter, Product Mgr - Google Inc.; pg. 1249, pg. 153
Ludwig, Stephen, VP-Mktg, Comm & Strategy - CH2M HILL Companies, Ltd.; pg. 75, pg. 325
Ludwig, Steve, Mgr-Mktg Programs-Global - Rockwell Automation, Inc.; pg. 668, pg. 1880
Luebbers, John, VP-Sls & Mktg - United Dairy Farmers, Inc.; pg. 906, pg. 1426
Luebke, David, Dir-Digital Mktg - Wal-Mart Stores, Inc.; pg. 1790, pg. 29
Luebke, Mark, Brand Mgr - Nutraceutical International Corporation; pg. 1576, pg. 1753
Lueck, Nancy, Reg Dir-PR - Bloomingdale's, Inc.; pg. 1763, pg. 1204
Lueck, Tim, Mgr-Adv - Federated Mutual Insurance Company; pg. 1200, pg. 952
Lueckenotte, Barb, Brand Mgr-Licensing - Energizer Holdings, Inc.; pg. 637, pg. 996
Luedeke, Jeff, VP-Sls & Mktg - HAECO Americas; pg. 228, pg. 1374
Lueder, Laura, Mgr-Corp PR - MDU Resources Group, Inc.; pg. 981, pg. 1397

Luedke, Danny, Mgr-Product Mktg - F5 Networks, Inc.; *pg.* 396, *pg.* 1835

Luelo, Donna, Dir-Adv - The Record; *pg.* 1680, *pg.* 1922

Luengo, Frank, Sr Mgr-Mktg - American Express Company; *pg.* 712, *pg.* 1190

Luetkemeyer, Michael, Interim Pres - Forward Industries, Inc.; *pg.* 5, *pg.* 478

Luetters, Mark, Exec VP-Building Products - Georgia-Pacific LLC; *pg.* 1458, *pg.* 507

Luft, Debbie, Brand Strategist - Tumblr, Inc.; *pg.* 1285, *pg.* 1305

Lug, Aaron, Dir-Adv Sls-Western Reg - Sony Pictures Entertainment Inc.; *pg.* 309, *pg.* 72

Luginbill, Amanda, Assoc Dir-Integrated Mktg - The Hearst Corporation; *pg.* 1649, *pg.* 1239

Lugo, Lisa L., VP-Mktg Solutions - Live Nation Worldwide - Times Square Office; *pg.* 558, *pg.* 1252

Lugo, Mark, Sr Specialist-Mktg Svcs - New York Life Insurance Company; *pg.* 1211, *pg.* 1268

Lugo, Pedro, Mgr-Digital Mktg - Visa Inc.; *pg.* 816, *pg.* 230

Lugo, Pedro, Mgr-Digital Mktg - Visa U.S.A., Inc.; *pg.* 817, *pg.* 231

Lui, John, Rep-Application Sls-Customer Experience - Oracle Corporation; *pg.* 1272, *pg.* 786

Lui, Linda, VP-Channel Sls-World Wide - Altera Corporation; *pg.* 348, *pg.* 237

Luib, Erika, Mgr-Mktg - Ligand Pharmaceuticals Inc.; *pg.* 1556, *pg.* 119

Luisa, Jennifer, VP-Mktg & Comm - The Hanover Insurance Company; *pg.* 1202, *pg.* 862

Lujan, Veronica, Acct Exec-Adv - AT&T; *pg.* 1865, *pg.* 258

Lukach, Giulia, Sr Mgr-ECommerce Mktg - Cost Plus World Market; *pg.* 921, *pg.* 170

Lukaitis, Scott, Brand Mgr - Bel-Ray Company, Inc.; *pg.* 972, *pg.* 1128

Lukanich, Andrew, Dir-Partnership Sls - International Speedway Corporation; *pg.* 553, *pg.* 420

Lukasik, Emily, Mgr-Mktg - Barneys New York, Inc.; *pg.* 38, *pg.* 1201

Lukavsky, Joe, VP-Integrated Mktg - Belk, Inc.; *pg.* 1760, *pg.* 1364

Luke, Erin, Mgr-Mktg Digital Svcs - Peterbilt Motors Co.; *pg.* 188, *pg.* 1691

Luken, Jessica, Dir-Mktg Comm - OCZ Storage Solutions; *pg.* 448, *pg.* 248

Luken, Michael, Sr Product Mgr - Cisco Systems, Inc.; *pg.* 372, *pg.* 240

Lukin, Janda, Sr Dir-OREO & Chips Ahoy! - Mondelez International, Inc.; *pg.* 878, *pg.* 601

Lukmani, Murtaza, Product Ops Mgr-Google Analytics - Google Inc.; *pg.* 1249, *pg.* 153

Luksan, Mike, VP-Sls, Magazines & Media - CDS Global, Inc.; *pg.* 370, *pg.* 704

Lula, Marirose, Sr Mgr-Corp Comm - Michael Kors (USA), Inc.; *pg.* 29, *pg.* 1260

Lulie, Alyssa, Dir-Adv - Raley's Inc.; *pg.* 1031, *pg.* 305

Lull, Travis, Product Mgr - Twitter, Inc.; *pg.* 1285, *pg.* 228

Lum, Andrew, Sr Mgr-Product Mktg - Sony Computer Entertainment America LLC; *pg.* 966, *pg.* 256

Lum, Elliot, VP-Strategic Mktg-Columbia Records - Sony Music Entertainment; *pg.* 309, *pg.* 1294

Lum, Morris, Sr Specialist-Product Mktg - FRANKLIN RESOURCES, INC.; *pg.* 760, *pg.* 254

Lum, Stephen, Mgr-Product Mktg - Samsung Semiconductor, Inc.; *pg.* 670, *pg.* 250

Lumabas, William S., Specialist-Web Mktg - Brocade Corporation; *pg.* 365, *pg.* 312

Lumba, Ena, Dir-Mktg-Baby Franchise-Global - Johnson & Johnson; *pg.* 1549, *pg.* 1091

Lumnah, Aaron, Specialist-Database Mktg - Carbonite, Inc.; *pg.* 368, *pg.* 792

Lumpinski, Kristine, VP-Mktg - Timex Corporation; *pg.* 14, *pg.* 355

Lumsden, Gretchen, Sr Mgr-Organizational Dev - The Home Depot, Inc.; *pg.* 1050, *pg.* 510

Lumsden, Jason, Sr VP-Sls - OPI Products Inc.; *pg.* 518, *pg.* 167

Lumsden, Larry, VP-Products - TECSYS, Inc.; *pg.* 482, *pg.* 1956

Lumumba, Mwanza, Sr Mgr-Mktg-Miller Family Brands - MillerCoors LLC; *pg.* 255, *pg.* 582

Luna, Armando, Jr., Head-Individual Medicare Sls & Mktg - Aetna Inc.; *pg.* 1187, *pg.* 351

Luna, Gloria, VP-Rusk Mktg & Education - Conair Corporation; *pg.* 505, *pg.* 1055

Luna, Heather, Mgr-Natl Shopper Mktg Team - The Clorox Company; *pg.* 327, *pg.* 169

Lunardini, Abby, VP-Brand Mktg & Comm - Virgin America Inc.; *pg.* 1930, *pg.* 55

Lunau, Dwain, Sr Mgr-Bus Dev - Motorola Mobility LLC; *pg.* 657, *pg.* 627

Lund, Debra S., Dir-Corp PR-Global - Franklin Covey Co.; *pg.* 1642, *pg.* 1758

Lund, Jan, Sr Mgr-Outbound - Quality Bicycle Products; *pg.* 1710, *pg.* 918

Lund, John, VP-Sls-North America - Tennant Company; *pg.* 1381, *pg.* 944

Lund, Kevin, Grp Mgr-Product Mktg - Deere & Company; *pg.* 703, *pg.* 632

Lund, Maggie, Asst Mgr-PR - Kohl's Corporation; *pg.* 1775, *pg.* 1870

Lund, Megan, Mgr-Mktg Strategy - Nordstrom, Inc.; *pg.* 1779, *pg.* 1837

Lund, Tom, Dir-Sls & Mktg - Llewellyn Worldwide Limited; *pg.* 1660, *pg.* 967

Lundberg, Ann, Sr VP-Digital Sls, Food & Cooking - The E.W. Scripps Company; *pg.* 1639, *pg.* 1412

Lundberg, Ann, Sr VP-Digital Sls-Food & Cooking - Scripps Networks Interactive, Inc.; *pg.* 1279, *pg.* 1638

Lundblad, Jackie, Analyst-Social Adv - Buzzfeed; *pg.* 1233, *pg.* 1208

Lundblad, Mathias, Mgr-Global Product Line-Premium Golf Equipment - Wilson Sporting Goods Co.; *pg.* 1848, *pg.* 596

Lundeen, Jim, VP & Gen Mgr-Retail Sls - Cyanotech Corporation; *pg.* 1154, *pg.* 545

Lundell, Alyson, Dir-PR - Universal Orlando; *pg.* 590, *pg.* 456

Lundgren, Ginger M., Sr Mgr-Consumer Engagement-Radio Disney - The Walt Disney Company; *pg.* 317, *pg.* 52

Lundgren, Regan, Mgr-Mining Parts Mktg-Americas Distr Svcs Div - Caterpillar, Inc.; *pg.* 1321, *pg.* 650

Lundgren, Susan S., Dir-Mktg Comm - Schlumberger Limited; *pg.* 801, *pg.* 1714

Lundgren, Vicki, Assoc Dir-Adv Ops - Meredith Corporation; *pg.* 1663, *pg.* 705

Lundmark, Gary, Dir-Digital Mktg - Guitar Center, Inc.; *pg.* 1771, *pg.* 306

Lundsberg, Suann, Dir-Media Rels - Burlington Northern Santa Fe, LLC; *pg.* 1901, *pg.* 1694

Lundstrom, Matt, Dir-Digital Creative - Palisades Media Group, Inc.; *pg.* 452, *pg.* 275

Lundstrom, Tanya, Head-Project & Specialist-Fit & Wear Test-Product Dev-VASQUE - Red Wing Shoe Company, Inc.; *pg.* 1817, *pg.* 954

Lung, Donald, VP-Sls-Asia - KEMET Corporation; *pg.* 649, *pg.* 1621

Lung, Frank, Product Mgr - NetApp, Inc.; *pg.* 444, *pg.* 287

Lung, Ruth A., Mgr-Relationship Mktg - Siemens PLM Software; *pg.* 469, *pg.* 1734

Lunn, Michelle, Mgr-Mktg & Ops - Applied Industrial Technologies, Inc.; *pg.* 199, *pg.* 1428

Lunsford, Jim, Dir-Relationship Mktg - CareerBuilder, LLC; *pg.* 1234, *pg.* 568

Lunt, Jessica, Analyst-Trade Mktg-Costco, Sam's Club & Wholesale Club - Reckitt Benckiser Inc.; *pg.* 1136, *pg.* 1105

Lunt, Mike, VP-Sls-EMEA - SCIQUEST, INC.; *pg.* 468, *pg.* 1361

Lunter, Mark, VP-Mktg - Caesars Entertainment Corporation; *pg.* 1083, *pg.* 1023

Lunzer, Laurie, Mgr-Production - The Spokesman-Review; *pg.* 1687, *pg.* 1844

Luo, Michelle, Assoc Product Mgr - Google Inc.; *pg.* 1249, *pg.* 153

Luong, Nancy, Sr Mgr-Digital Mktg - American Apparel, Inc.; *pg.* 18, *pg.* 126

Luong, Nancy, Supvr-Email & Digital Mktg - Fresh & Easy Neighborhood Market Inc; *pg.* 1020, *pg.* 80

Luongo, Dominic, Sr Dir-Ad Sls Res-A&E Networks - A&E Television Networks, LLC; *pg.* 267, *pg.* 1185

Luongo, Salvatore, Dir-Creative & UX Global Ops-Product Strategy & Design - Aon Risk Services Inc.; *pg.* 1193, *pg.* 564

Luongo, Tami, Brand Mgr - Lindt & Sprungli (USA) Inc.; *pg.* 1857, *pg.* 1039

Lupatkin, Judith, Specialist-Mktg - Home Box Office, Inc.; *pg.* 290, *pg.* 1240

Lupetin, Michael, VP-Mktg & Brand - KQED Inc.; *pg.* 294, *pg.* 220

Lupinacci, Craig, Sr VP-Sls-Global - Author Solutions, Inc.; *pg.* 1618, *pg.* 674

Luraschi, Clay, VP-Product Dev - The Topps Company, Inc.; *pg.* 588, *pg.* 1302

Lurie, Zander, Sr VP-Media - GoPro; *pg.* 1414, *pg.* 255

Luse, Jonathan, Sr Product Dir - Intel Corporation; *pg.* 645, *pg.* 266

Lusetti, Terry, Mgr-Club Sls - YoCream International Inc.; *pg.* 1039, *pg.* 1508

Lush, Melissa, Sr Dir-Brand Mktg-Global - Staples, Inc.; *pg.* 474, *pg.* 821

Lusk, Jason, Dir-Sls - Denver Metro Convention & Visitors Bureau; *pg.* 991, *pg.* 318

Lussenhop, Rick, Sr Mgr-Mktg - The Allstate Corporation; *pg.* 1189, *pg.* 639

Lust, Lee, Product Mgr-Roast, Ground Coffee & Foodservice - The J.M. Smucker Company; *pg.* 865, *pg.* 1468

Lustberg, Alex, CMO - Lyris, Inc.; *pg.* 429, *pg.* 84

Lustberg, Tama, VP-Sls Leather Div - Fossil Group, Inc.; *pg.* 5, *pg.* 1735

Lustig, Christine, VP-Media-US - MasterCard Worldwide Inc.; *pg.* 780, *pg.* 988

Lustig, Erin, Brand Mgr-Global - MATTEL, INC.; *pg.* 962, *pg.* 81

Lusty, Greg, Dir-Product Mgmt, R&D - CENTRIA, Inc.; *pg.* 74, *pg.* 1554

Luth, Ethan, Mgr-Global Segment-Seed Growth Corn Products - Bayer CropScience; *pg.* 1149, *pg.* 981

Luther, Ashley, Brand Mgr-Digital-Nike Women-North America - NIKE, Inc.; *pg.* 1812, *pg.* 1492

Luther, Justin, Supvr-PR - United Parcel Service, Inc.; *pg.* 1928, *pg.* 522

Luther, Kyle, VP-Sls-Eastern US & Canada - Grass Valley, Inc.; *pg.* 641, *pg.* 164

Luthi, Francesca, Chief Comm & Mktg Officer & Exec VP - Assurant, Inc.; *pg.* 1193, *pg.* 1198

Luthringer, Paul, VP-Corp & Mktg Comm - Hearst Magazines; *pg.* 1649, *pg.* 1239

Luthy, John, Product Mgr-Global - Molex Incorporated; *pg.* 655, *pg.* 628

Luthy, P., VP-Sls - Brown Paper Goods Company; *pg.* 1454, *pg.* 665

Lutte, Abigail, Mgr-Mktg - The Dun & Bradstreet Corp.; *pg.* 1637, *pg.* 1120

Lutter, Brian, Sr Mgr-New Product Dev - Kind LLC; *pg.* 868, *pg.* 1249

Lutter, Paige, Sr Mgr-Global Brand Dev - Logitech Inc.; *pg.* 1264, *pg.* 164

Luttrell, Landon, Dir-Sls - THE DOW CHEMICAL COMPANY; *pg.* 1157, *pg.* 898

Luttrell, Monique, Dir-Client Mktg-Bus Tech Media - United Business Media LLC; *pg.* 1697, *pg.* 1177

Luttschwager, Keith, Sr Mgr-Audience Mktg - Microsoft Corporation; *pg.* 435, *pg.* 1824

Lutz, Ann, Mgr-Lead Product - CenturyLink, Inc.; *pg.* 1870, *pg.* 746

Lutz, Carolyn, Mgr-Brdcst Media - Staples, Inc.; *pg.* 474, *pg.* 821

Lutz, Emily, Specialist-Vendor Mktg-Golf & Racquet Sports - Dick's Sporting Goods, Inc.; *pg.* 1832, *pg.* 1524

Lutz, Jeff, Asst Dir-Ticket Sls - Detroit Tigers Baseball Club, Inc.; *pg.* 545, *pg.* 880

Lutz, Lisa, VP-Product - Allegiant Travel Company; *pg.* 346, *pg.* 1022

Lutz, Mark, VP-Technical Sls & Engrg - HCS Corporation; *pg.* 86, *pg.* 1821

Lutz, Monte, Head-PR-Global - Activision Blizzard, Inc.; *pg.* 948, *pg.* 271

Lutz, Steve, Sr VP-Sls-USA - Maybelline LLC; *pg.* 516, *pg.* 1257

Lutz, William, Sr Dir-Comm - Defenders of Wildlife; *pg.* 138, *pg.* 398

Luu, Frederic, VP-Sls & Mktg-Asia & EMEA - Digi International Inc.; *pg.* 387, *pg.* 948

Luu, Quynh, Mgr-Channel Mktg - Hewlett-Packard Company; *pg.* 404, *pg.* 175

Luu, Sang, Product Mgr-Mktg-Americas - Google Inc.; *pg.* 1249, *pg.* 153

Luu, Thi, Sr Mgr-Product Mgmt - Amazon.com, Inc.; *pg.* 1226, *pg.* 1831

Luu-Van, Melissa, Product Mgr-Security - Facebook, Inc.; *pg.* 1245, *pg.* 143

Lux, Bruce, Head-Mktg, Global Digital & ECommerce - The Procter & Gamble Company; *pg.* 1129, *pg.* 1418

Lux, Mary, VP-Product Mgmt - U.S. Bancorp; *pg.* 815, *pg.* 945

Luxemburg, Rachel, Principal & Strategist-Community & Social Media - Adobe Systems Incorporated; *pg.* 342, *pg.* 235
Luz, Zachary, Assoc Mgr-Adv - Dunkin' Brands Group, Inc.; *pg.* 1727, *pg.* 810
Luzano, Theresa, Sr Mgr-Adv & Promos-Northstar New Jersey Lottery - New Jersey State Lottery; *pg.* 1000, *pg.* 1126
Luzar, Alison, Dir-Mktg - Accenture; *pg.* 1392, *pg.* 1186
Ly, Julie, Mgr-PR - Kate Spade LLC; *pg.* 28, *pg.* 1248
Ly, Stephanie, Project Mgr-Global Experience Mktg - Herman Miller, Inc.; *pg.* 926, *pg.* 913
Lyckman, Anders, Dir-Creative-Lingerie - Victoria's Secret Stores, LLC; *pg.* 1789, *pg.* 1471
Lyendecker, Evan, Mgr-Mktg - Confluence Watersports Co. Inc.; *pg.* 1706, *pg.* 1617
Lyke, James, Exec VP-Integrated Mktg Solutions - Entravision Communications Corporation; *pg.* 285, *pg.* 273
Lyle, Dustin, Dir-Strategic Sourcing Commodity-Mktg - Sony Pictures Entertainment Inc.; *pg.* 309, *pg.* 72
Lyle, Karen, Analyst-Sls - The Scotts Miracle-Gro Company; *pg.* 1799, *pg.* 1459
Lyle, Paul, VP-Product Dev & Sourcing - HomeGoods, Inc.; *pg.* 1125, *pg.* 821
Lyle, Rebekah, Dir-Mktg & Innovation-Yogurt - The WhiteWave Foods Company; *pg.* 1037, *pg.* 324
Lyman, John, Head-Partnerships & Mktg - Google Inc.; *pg.* 1249, *pg.* 153
Lyman, Kristin, Assoc Dir-Mktg Comm - Novartis Pharmaceuticals Corp.; *pg.* 1575, *pg.* 1054
Lynam, Terry, Chief PR Officer & VP - North Shore-LIJ Health System; *pg.* 1573, *pg.* 1162
Lynch, Amanda, Brand Mgr-Mktg - PPG Industries, Inc.; *pg.* 1445, *pg.* 1579
Lynch, Amy, Dir-Reg Mktg - FMR LLC (Fidelity Investments); *pg.* 759, *pg.* 794
Lynch, Cara E., Program Mgr-WHIM Mktg & Sls - Xerox Corporation; *pg.* 494, *pg.* 365
Lynch, Carol, VP-Sls & Mktg - Leviton Manufacturing Company, Inc.; *pg.* 1301, *pg.* 1180
Lynch, Dan, VP-Media & Partnerships - The New York Giants; *pg.* 570, *pg.* 1055
Lynch, Diane, Sr Mgr-Mktg - Ingram Micro Inc.; *pg.* 415, *pg.* 261
Lynch, Eileen, Sr VP-Brand Mktg-Global - Truven Health Analytics; *pg.* 486, *pg.* 331
Lynch, Elizabeth, Mgr-Media Rels - March of Dimes Birth Defects Foundation; *pg.* 146, *pg.* 1354
Lynch, Frank, Exec VP-Sls & Mktg - Faribault Foods, Inc.; *pg.* 855, *pg.* 925
Lynch, Jennifer, Sr Product Mgr - New Balance Athletic Shoe, Inc.; *pg.* 1811, *pg.* 798
Lynch, Jim, VP-Building Products Grp - Autodesk Inc.; *pg.* 356, *pg.* 257
Lynch, Joani, Dir-Brand Mktg - Mammoth Mountain Ski Area; *pg.* 1102, *pg.* 142
Lynch, Joe, VP-Mktg-Global Markets - Omnicell Inc.; *pg.* 1578, *pg.* 161
Lynch, John, Dir-Sls-East - Honeywell Salisbury Electrical Safety; *pg.* 1884, *pg.* 558
Lynch, John, VP & Head-US Mktg - Reebok International Ltd.; *pg.* 1817, *pg.* 811
Lynch, Julie, Sr Mgr-AfterSls - Nissan North America, Inc.; *pg.* 186, *pg.* 1633
Lynch, Kevin, Chief Strategy Officer & Exec VP - AECOM; *pg.* 64, *pg.* 173
Lynch, Kevin, Chief Strategy Officer & Exec VP - AECOM Technology Corporation; *pg.* 65, *pg.* 125
Lynch, Kristin, VP-Mktg & Product Dev - World Kitchen LLC; *pg.* 1141, *pg.* 657
Lynch, Lila, Sr VP-Bus Integration Mktg - Bank of America Corporation; *pg.* 718, *pg.* 1362
Lynch, Lisa, Mgr-Comm & Media - CB Richard Ellis, Inc.; *pg.* 1085, *pg.* 1210
Lynch, Martha, Sr Dir-Software Engrg - Progress Software Corporation; *pg.* 457, *pg.* 786
Lynch, Melissa, VP-Intl Mktg-EMEA & ASIA - Avis Budget Group, Inc.; *pg.* 1900, *pg.* 1102
Lynch, Michelle, Sr Dir-IT Strategy & Plng - Liberty Mutual Insurance Group Inc.; *pg.* 1205, *pg.* 797
Lynch, Patrick, Sr Dir-Acctg & Ops - Boston Celtics Limited Partnership; *pg.* 533, *pg.* 790
Lynch, Rich, VP-Mktg - Do It Best Corp.; *pg.* 1045, *pg.* 680
Lynch, Sean, Specialist-Mktg & PR - Fila USA; *pg.* 1808, *pg.* 779
Lynch, Steve, Mgr-Social Media Mktg - Guitar Center, Inc.; *pg.* 1771, *pg.* 306
Lynch, Thomas, VP-Sls - Advantage Business Media; *pg.* 1613, *pg.* 1116
Lynch, Torie, Dir-Social Media - Tilted Kilt Franchise Operating LLC; *pg.* 1754, *pg.* 27
Lynde, Dan, Dir-ECommerce Mktg - Staples, Inc.; *pg.* 474, *pg.* 821
Lynde, Jim, Gen Mgr-Sls - Nordco, Inc.; *pg.* 1365, *pg.* 1884
Lyne, Carey Dietz, Sr Mgr-Mobile Shopping Product Mgmt - Amazon.com, Inc.; *pg.* 1226, *pg.* 1831
Lynes, Kim, Mgr-Mktg - Time Inc.; *pg.* 1693, *pg.* 1300
Lyngdal, Janet, Mgr-Mktg & Indirects Procurement - Beiersdorf North America Inc.; *pg.* 501, *pg.* 385
Lynn, Christine, VP-Adv & Mktg Comm - Choice Hotels International, Inc.; *pg.* 1086, *pg.* 775
Lynn, Dawn, Dir-Global Product Dev & Brand Mgmt-Girls World - Toys "R" Us, Inc.; *pg.* 968, *pg.* 1130
Lynn, Frank, Sr Mgr-Global Mktg & Corp Comm - Cisco Systems, Inc.; *pg.* 372, *pg.* 240
Lynn, Haniel, Gen Mgr-Sls & Mktg - CEB Inc.; *pg.* 733, *pg.* 1773
Lynn, Jason, Sr VP-Product - AppNexus; *pg.* 352, *pg.* 1196
Lynn, Katharine, Assoc Dir-Mktg & Comm - Universum USA; *pg.* 1286, *pg.* 1307
Lynn, Stephanie, Sr Dir-Ecommerce - Vineyard Vines LLC; *pg.* 50, *pg.* 379
Lynum, Mary, Sr Dir-Strategic Mktg & Sls - Cenveo Inc.; *pg.* 1626, *pg.* 372
Lyon, Craig, Brand Mgr-Global Basketball - NIKE, Inc.; *pg.* 1812, *pg.* 1492
Lyon, Heather, Program Mgr-Technical Mktg & Engrg - Hewlett-Packard Company; *pg.* 404, *pg.* 175
Lyon, Jamie, Assoc Mgr-Mktg-Wheaties, Fiber One, Total, Fruit & Nut Cereals - General Mills, Inc.; *pg.* 828, *pg.* 933
Lyon, Rick, Bus Unit Mgr-Power & Energy - Conax Technologies LLC; *pg.* 1325, *pg.* 1148
Lyons, Aidan, VP-Database Mktg - NFL Films, Inc.; *pg.* 303, *pg.* 1090
Lyons, Archie J., Exec Producer & Dir-Creative - Caterpillar, Inc.; *pg.* 1321, *pg.* 650
Lyons, Bruce, Sr VP-Employer Sls & Acct Svcs - Caremark Pharmacy Services; *pg.* 1513, *pg.* 1649
Lyons, Greg, VP-Mktg-Mountain Dew & Energy - Pepsi Beverages Company; *pg.* 258, *pg.* 1342
Lyons, Jack, Sr Dir-Americas Healthcare ISV's - Citrix Systems, Inc.; *pg.* 375, *pg.* 424
Lyons, Jeffrey, Sr VP-Mdsg-Fresh Foods - Costco Wholesale Corporation; *pg.* 1765, *pg.* 1820
Lyons, Jenna, Pres & Exec Dir-Creative - J. Crew Group, Inc.; *pg.* 1773, *pg.* 1245
Lyons, Julie, Sr Mgr-Internal Comm - Equinix, Inc.; *pg.* 394, *pg.* 190
Lyons, Kyle, Dir-Mktg - Mars Canada Inc.; *pg.* 1478, *pg.* 1918
Lyons, Lucy, Dir-Comm & PR - U.S. News & World Report, L.P.; *pg.* 1698, *pg.* 1308
Lyons, Michael, Dir-Mktg-Walmart, Sam's Retailer Brands & Group Innovation - The Sun Products Corporation; *pg.* 336, *pg.* 385
Lyons, Nora, Dir-Mktg & Sls - American Express Company; *pg.* 712, *pg.* 1190
Lyons, Rebecca, Dir-Mktg-Intl - Washington State Apple Commission; *pg.* 160, *pg.* 1847
Lyons, Robert, Product Mgr - Mersen; *pg.* 1302, *pg.* 836
Lyons-Williams, Lori, VP-Sls & Mktg-Urology - Allergan, Inc.; *pg.* 1491, *pg.* 106
Lysaght, Michael, Sr VP-Digital Product Engrg - Weight Watchers International, Inc.; *pg.* 1609, *pg.* 1313
Lyst, Nathan, Sr Mgr-Mktg Ops-North America - Nissan North America, Inc.; *pg.* 186, *pg.* 1633
Lytle, James, Div Mgr-Mdse - Genesco Inc.; *pg.* 1809, *pg.* 1650
Lytle, Mike, Sr Dir-Sls - NuVasive, Inc.; *pg.* 1577, *pg.* 205
Lytle, Vivian, Sr VP-Digital Mktg Strategy & Execution - Wells Fargo & Company; *pg.* 819, *pg.* 232

M

Ma, Catherine, Brand Mgr-TRESemme-Global - Unilever United States, Inc.; *pg.* 904, *pg.* 1061
Ma, Frankie, Mgr-Customer Mktg - Diageo Canada, Inc.; *pg.* 1961, *pg.* 1937
Ma, Nat, Dir-Digital Mktg - Burberry Limited; *pg.* 20, *pg.* 1208
Ma, Olivia, Sr Mgr-News Lab - Google Inc.; *pg.* 1249, *pg.* 153
Maahs, Fred, Sr Dir-Community Investment & Natl Partnerships - Comcast Corporation; *pg.* 276, *pg.* 1560
Maas, Ali, Brand Mgr - Stearns & Foster Bedding Company; *pg.* 944, *pg.* 1392
Maas, Anne, Dir-Mktg - Bare Necessities, Inc.; *pg.* 19, *pg.* 1056
Maas, H. Joseph, Pres-Sls & Mktg-Global - Kronos Worldwide, Inc.; *pg.* 980, *pg.* 1053
Maas, Karlene, Brand Mgr-Private - Michaels Stores, Inc.; *pg.* 1127, *pg.* 1722
Maas, Lori, VP-Sls - Wenger Corporation; *pg.* 1307, *pg.* 952
Maas, Robert, Sr Dir-ECommerce Tech - Nordstrom, Inc.; *pg.* 1779, *pg.* 1837
Mabry, Barbara A., Mgr-Mktg Ops - The Boeing Company; *pg.* 225, *pg.* 567
Macaione, Allison, Rep-Product Mktg - Caterpillar, Inc.; *pg.* 1321, *pg.* 650
Macaluso, Danielle, Asst VP-PR - L'Oreal USA; *pg.* 514, *pg.* 1252
Macaluso, Kim, Mgr-PR - Neiman Marcus, Inc.; *pg.* 30, *pg.* 1684
Macaluso, Melody, Mgr-Mktg Innovation - Frito-Lay North America, Inc.; *pg.* 1853, *pg.* 1730
Macaluso, Melody, Mgr-Mktg Innovation - PepsiCo, Inc.; *pg.* 259, *pg.* 1327
Macapagal, Arend, Mgr-Branded Sls Operation - T-Mobile US, Inc.; *pg.* 676, *pg.* 1816
MacArthur, Andrew, Mgr-Partner Mktg - Boingo Wireless, Inc.; *pg.* 625, *pg.* 127
Macarthy, Jon, Dir-Consumer Mktg - Meredith Corporation; *pg.* 1663, *pg.* 705
Macasa, Shiena, Mgr-Creative Svcs Traffic - Bank of the West; *pg.* 721, *pg.* 213
Macaulay, Lisa, Brand Mgr-Healthy Essentials - Johnson & Johnson; *pg.* 1549, *pg.* 1091
Macauley, Kelly, VP-Global Direct & Digital Mktg - NetJets Inc.; *pg.* 1917, *pg.* 1442
Macauley, Sarah, Asst Coord-Adv - Toll Brothers, Inc.; *pg.* 115, *pg.* 1541
MacAvery, Sarah, Sr Mgr-Special Events - Rodale, Inc.; *pg.* 1681, *pg.* 1530
Macayan, Alex, Mgr-Email Mktg-Partnership Mktg - Teleflora LLC; *pg.* 1801, *pg.* 140
MacBeth, Shirley, VP-Corp Mktg - ACI Worldwide Inc.; *pg.* 341, *pg.* 1010
Macca, Jon, VP-Media & Customer Engagement - J.C. Penney Company, Inc.; *pg.* 1774, *pg.* 1732
Maccabe, Ellen, Sr Mgr-Consumer Insights - Vonage Holdings Corp.; *pg.* 686, *pg.* 1074
MacCallum, Alex, Asst Editor-Masthead-Audience Dev & Product - The New York Times; *pg.* 1668, *pg.* 1270
MacCallum, Cori, Second VP-Bus Insurance Mktg - Travelers Insurance; *pg.* 1220, *pg.* 963
Maccari, Michael, Dir-Creative - Perry Ellis International, Inc.; *pg.* 45, *pg.* 445
Maccaro, Chris, VP-Sls & Category Head-Fin - Yahoo! Inc.; *pg.* 1289, *pg.* 289
Macchia, Anthony, Sr Dir-Mktg - Bright House Networks LLC; *pg.* 272, *pg.* 461
Maccio, Chris, Dir-Sls - Ryder System, Inc.; *pg.* 1922, *pg.* 446
MacClellan, Clare, Sr Mgr-Events - National Hockey League; *pg.* 568, *pg.* 1265
MacColl, Sarah, Brand Mgr-OxiClean Laundry Detergent - Church & Dwight Co., Inc.; *pg.* 1153, *pg.* 1063
Maccormack, Gillian, VP-PR-Global - SNC-Lavalin Group Inc.; *pg.* 111, *pg.* 1956
MacCormack, Patrick, Coord-Digital Mktg - Vermont Department of Tourism & Marketing; *pg.* 1010, *pg.* 1767
Macdonald, Ben, Pres-Bloomberg SEF LLC & Head-Product-Global - Bloomberg L.P.; *pg.* 725, *pg.* 1204
MacDonald, Dan, Sr Dir-Corp Comm - Dollar General Corporation; *pg.* 1767, *pg.* 1635
Macdonald, David J., Head-Mktg-Belk Client - General Electric Company; *pg.* 1297, *pg.* 347
MacDonald, Dean, Dir-Creative - Mondo Media Corporation; *pg.* 1268, *pg.* 223
MacDonald, Doug, VP-Indus Products - Canadian National Railway Company; *pg.* 1902, *pg.* 1953
Macdonald, Gordon, Dir-Microsoft Dynamics SMB Product Mktg - Microsoft Corporation; *pg.* 435, *pg.* 1824
MacDonald, Greg, Sr Dir-Programmatic Supply & Marketplace Dev - Yahoo! Inc.; *pg.* 1289, *pg.* 289
Macdonald, Greta, Mgr-Email Mktg - The ServiceMaster Company, LLC; *pg.* 335, *pg.* 1646
Macdonald, Ian, Brand Mgr-AVEENO Lotions & LUBRIDERM - Johnson & Johnson Inc.; *pg.* 1552, *pg.* 1923
MacDonald, Jeanne, Chief Sls Officer-Global - Futurestep; *pg.*

399, *pg.* 131
MacDonald, Jennifer, Grp Product Mgr-Product Comm & Sls Support - Canadian Imperial Bank of Commerce; *pg.* 729, *pg.* 1935
MacDonald, Katie, Dir-Mktg - WOW! World of Wonder Children's Museum; *pg.* 595, *pg.* 332
MacDonald, Kelly, Sr Mgr-Infiniti Media Plng & Strategy-Nissan Motor Corporation - Nissan North America, Inc.; *pg.* 186, *pg.* 1633
Macdonald, Mary, Dir-Sls & Trade Mktg Ops - Electronic Arts Inc.; *pg.* 951, *pg.* 189
Macdonald, Morgan, Mgr-Federal Mktg - Deloitte & Touche USA LLP; *pg.* 743, *pg.* 1222
Macdonald, Ruth, Mgr-Mktg Comm - Dot Hill Systems Corp.; *pg.* 388, *pg.* 333
Macdonald, Scott, VP-Indus Sls - Siemens; *pg.* 1376, *pg.* 1466
MacDonald, Steve, Bus Mgr-Meetings & Events - Doctor's Associates Inc.; *pg.* 1726, *pg.* 356
MacDonald, Stew, Chief Revenue Officer - Edmonton Oilers Hockey Club; *pg.* 546, *pg.* 1906
MacDonald, Tom, VP-Sls & Customer Svc - MacLean Power Systems; *pg.* 1054, *pg.* 1615
MacDonell, Glen, Mng Dir-Loyalty & Partnership Mktg - Best Western International, Inc.; *pg.* 1081, *pg.* 15
Mace, Hayden, Mgr-Mktg - Amazon.com, Inc.; *pg.* 1226, *pg.* 1831
Mace, Lynn, Specialist-Mktg - Omaha Convention and Visitors Bureau; *pg.* 152, *pg.* 1017
Macedo, Dulcidio, Dir-Product Mgmt & Strategy-Mobile - Samsung Telecommunications America, LLC; *pg.* 670, *pg.* 1736
Macejko, Stephanie, VP-Mktg - Reeves International, Inc.; *pg.* 966, *pg.* 1108
Macero, Kevin, Sr Dir-Shopper & Category Insights - Pfizer Inc.; *pg.* 1581, *pg.* 1278
Macey, Andrea Bell, VP-Digital Media & Bus Dev-WE TV - AMC Networks Inc.; *pg.* 269, *pg.* 1189
Macey, Nick, Sr VP & Head-Product - LivingSocial, Inc.; *pg.* 1264, *pg.* 401
Macey, Scott, Mgr-Mktg Production Ops - Teachers Insurance & Annuity Association - College Retirement Equities Fund; *pg.* 1219, *pg.* 1297
Macey, Shawn, Dir-Digital Media Svcs - Bonnier Corporation; *pg.* 1622, *pg.* 480
Macfarlane, Hunter, Product Mgr - PGT, Inc.; *pg.* 104, *pg.* 452
Machalski, John, Sr VP-Residential Sls - Cablevision Systems Corporation; *pg.* 272, *pg.* 1141
Machamer, Dan, Sr Mgr-Sls - Samsung Electronics America, Inc.; *pg.* 669, *pg.* 1115
Machasic, Jason, Mgr-Mktg Strategy - Blue Cross & Blue Shield of Michigan; *pg.* 1195, *pg.* 879
Maches, Jennifer, Mgr-Mktg - Toms Shoe's Inc; *pg.* 1821, *pg.* 276
Machin, Kelly, Specialist-Mktg & Graphic Designer - Assurant, Inc.; *pg.* 1193, *pg.* 1198
Machiz, Joshua, Dir-Integrated Mktg - The NASDAQ OMX Group, Inc.; *pg.* 785, *pg.* 1263
Macholz, Karina, Mgr-Mktg Programs & Comm-Global - Richardson Electronics, Ltd.; *pg.* 667, *pg.* 622
Machovec, Dax, Sr Mgr-Product Mktg-Sterling Brand Bathing - Kohler Co.; *pg.* 91, *pg.* 1862
Machuca, Michael, Dir-Upstream O&G Mktg-North America - Emerson Process Management; *pg.* 1334, *pg.* 1636
Machuzak, Kathy, Assoc Dir-Payer Mktg - Bristol-Myers Squibb Company; *pg.* 1509, *pg.* 1206
Maciejewski, Carrie, VP-Admin & Mgr-Mktg & Retail - M&T Bank Corporation; *pg.* 777, *pg.* 1149
Maciel, Claudia, Supvr-Mktg Production - Jacuzzi Brands Corporation; *pg.* 554, *pg.* 65
Maciel, Jason, Dir-Media & Adv - VIZIO, Inc.; *pg.* 686, *pg.* 118
Maciel, Leanne, Brand Mgr-Sponsorships & Events - Heineken USA Inc.; *pg.* 252, *pg.* 1352
Macik, Ashley, Specialist-Integrated Supply Mktg - WESCO International Inc.; *pg.* 687, *pg.* 1582
MacInnes, Eva, Rep-Mktg - Comcast Corporation; *pg.* 276, *pg.* 1560
Macios, Peter, Product Mgr-Exec - GE Water & Process Technologies; *pg.* 1339, *pg.* 1588
MacIsaac, Andy, Sr Mgr-Mktg - International Business Machines Corporation; *pg.* 418, *pg.* 1138
Mack, Beth, Pres-Sls & Mdsg - Hollander Sleep Products; *pg.* 927, *pg.* 411
Mack, Brian, VP-Insurance & Product Mgr-Annuity - Citigroup Inc.; *pg.* 735, *pg.* 1212
Mack, Greg, Dir-Mktg - Lund Food Holdings, Inc.; *pg.* 875, *pg.* 924
Mack, John, Reg Mgr-Mktg - FCA US LLC; *pg.* 170, *pg.* 868
Mack, Joseph, VP-Sls-Americas - GatesAir, Inc.; *pg.* 640, *pg.* 1460
Mack, Kelly Kennedy, Pres-Corcoran Sunshine Mktg Grp - Corcoran Sunshine Marketing Group; *pg.* 1088, *pg.* 1218
Mack, Lauren, Specialist-Mktg-Wolverine Brand - Wolverine World Wide, Inc.; *pg.* 1822, *pg.* 905
Mack, Nancy, Mgr-Mktg - Cisco Systems, Inc.; *pg.* 372, *pg.* 240
Mackar, Amit, Dir-Mktg - The Dannon Company, Inc.; *pg.* 851, *pg.* 1351
MacKay, Mary, Dir-Mktg Strategy - American Library Association; *pg.* 1615, *pg.* 564
Macke, Jim, Controller-Mktg & Comm - Enterprise Holdings, Inc.; *pg.* 1900, *pg.* 006
MacKenzie Miller, Lauren, Mgr-Production - Anchorage Symphony Orchestra; *pg.* 528, *pg.* 10
MacKenzie, Chris, VP-Sls - BPI Sports, LLC; *pg.* 842, *pg.* 430
Mackenzie, Doug, Sr Dir-Sls-Intl - The W.E. Bassett Company; *pg.* 524, *pg.* 371
MacKenzie, Heather, Sr Mgr-Events - Autodesk Inc.; *pg.* 356, *pg.* 257
Mackenzie, Jennifer, Sr VP-Mktg - Nationwide Mutual Insurance Company; *pg.* 1210, *pg.* 1442
MacKenzie, Jim, Mgr-Integrated Mktg - New Balance Athletic Shoe, Inc.; *pg.* 1811, *pg.* 798
MacKenzie, Karen, Mgr-Consumer Mktg-Content-Lowe's Home Improvement - Lowe's Companies, Inc.; *pg.* 1053, *pg.* 1383
Mackenzie, Sarah, Sr Mgr - The Boston Beer Company, Inc.; *pg.* 239, *pg.* 790
Mackenzie, Simon, Rep-Enterprise Sls Dev - SPS COMMERCE, INC.; *pg.* 472, *pg.* 942
MacKenzie, Warren, VP-Mktg & Sls - PTC Alliance Corp.; *pg.* 1370, *pg.* 1594
Mackenzie-Heyboer, Mariska, Dir-Global Paid Search Adv - Oracle Corporation; *pg.* 1272, *pg.* 786
MacKenzie-Neill, Rachael, Sr Dir-Sponsorships & Mktg Comm - Canadian Imperial Bank of Commerce; *pg.* 729, *pg.* 1935
Mackey, Danielle, Dir-Mktg - Jacoby & Meyers LLP; *pg.* 423, *pg.* 1317
Mackey, Edmund, Sr Dir-Mktg - DIRECTV Group Holdings, LLC; *pg.* 281, *pg.* 79
Mackey, Elizabeth, Mgr-Strategic Mktg - W.W. Grainger, Inc.; *pg.* 1390, *pg.* 625
Mackey, Ryan, Sr Dir-Corp Sponsorships - Dallas Mavericks; *pg.* 543, *pg.* 1678
Mackey, Tracey S., VP-Mktg Procurement & Sustainable Procurement-Global - The Coca-Cola Company; *pg.* 240, *pg.* 493
Macki, Evelyn, Mgr-Social Media - NCL Corporation Ltd.; *pg.* 1916, *pg.* 444
Mackiewicz, Kevin, VP & Sr Mgr-Mktg-De Novo Strategy - Fifth Third Bancorp; *pg.* 752, *pg.* 1413
Mackiewicz, Regina, Bus Mgr-Zone - Siemens Healthcare Diagnostics; *pg.* 673, *pg.* 604
Mackinlay, Molly, Product Mgr-Google Classroom - Google Inc.; *pg.* 1249, *pg.* 153
MacKinnon, Kelli, Dir-Sls - Marquis Who's Who, LLC; *pg.* 1661, *pg.* 1044
MacKinzie, Echo, VP-Mktg & Design - Edelman Leather, LLC; *pg.* 923, *pg.* 359
Mackle, Ryan, Dir-Global Expansion & Product Mgmt - Amazon.com, Inc.; *pg.* 1226, *pg.* 1831
Macklin, Kevin, Sr Analyst-Mktg - Polaris Industries Inc.; *pg.* 1709, *pg.* 928
Macko, Pat, Dir-Mktg - Sherwin Williams; *pg.* 1448, *pg.* 1436
Macko, Patricia, Dir-Mktg - Sherwin-Williams Diversified Brands Division; *pg.* 1448, *pg.* 1435
Macko, Philip, Sr VP-Sls - Megatrax Production Music, Inc.; *pg.* 297, *pg.* 167
Macko, Terry, Sr VP-Comm & Mktg - World Wildlife Fund, Inc.; *pg.* 162, *pg.* 408
Mackow, Natasha, Dir-Mktg Comm - The Second Cup Ltd.; *pg.* 1749, *pg.* 1928
Mackrell, Warwick, VP-Sls - Ritchie Bros. Auctioneers Incorporated; *pg.* 1372, *pg.* 1907
Mackrory, Jared, Brand Mgr-Scott Naturals Brand-Brand Plng & Execution - Kimberly-Clark Corporation; *pg.* 1461, *pg.* 1720
Maclaga, Katy B., Sr Mgr-Benefits - The Home Depot, Inc.; *pg.* 1050, *pg.* 510
MacLaughlin, Chris, VP-Mktg & Comm - International Business Machines Corporation; *pg.* 418, *pg.* 1138
MacLean, Tavish, Dir-Product Mgmt - T-Mobile US, Inc.; *pg.* 676, *pg.* 1816
MacLean, Tom, Dir-Mktg & Sls - The Guardian Life Insurance Company of America; *pg.* 1202, *pg.* 1237
Maclellan, John, VP-Sls & Mktg - O.F. Mossberg & Sons, Inc.; *pg.* 1842, *pg.* 360
Maclellan, Lisa, Mgr-New Product Mktg - Arby's Restaurant Group, Inc.; *pg.* 1014, *pg.* 488
MacLeod, Edward A., VP-Consumer Mktg - Toronto Star Newspapers Ltd.; *pg.* 1695, *pg.* 1945
Macleod, John, Sr VP-Plng & Sls - Virgin America Inc.; *pg.* 1930, *pg.* 55
MacLeod, Roger, Sr Dir-Mktg-Endocrinology - Endo Pharmaceuticals Holdings, Inc.; *pg.* 1528, *pg.* 1549
Maclin, Alisa, VP-Mktg-Mobile Enterprise - International Business Machines Corporation; *pg.* 418, *pg.* 1138
Macmanus Funke, Kelly, VP-Mktg-US - Fila USA; *pg.* 1800, *pg.* 779
Macmillan, Bruce, Dir-Online Mktg - AT&T Inc.; *pg.* 1867, *pg.* 1674
Macmillan, Diane, Sr Dir-Mktg - SAP America, Inc.; *pg.* 466, *pg.* 1557
MacMillan, Scot, Mgr-Promos Mktg-Natl - Keurig Green Mountain, Inc.; *pg.* 868, *pg.* 1768
MacNair, Dave, VP-Mktg - Hayward Pool Products; *pg.* 1049, *pg.* 1057
MacNair, Elizabeth, Coord-Digital Mktg - Briggs & Stratton Corporation; *pg.* 201, *pg.* 1899
Macnamara, Kelly, Sr Mgr-Sls Dev & Field Mktg Comm - The Western Union Company; *pg.* 822, *pg.* 327
MacNeil, Heather, VP-Mktg - Suja Juice; *pg.* 265, *pg.* 210
MacNeill, Mike, Mgr-Mktg-Xerox Global Svcs - Xerox Canada Inc.; *pg.* 494, *pg.* 1930
MacNelly, Robert J., VP-Mktg - Leon's Furniture Limited; *pg.* 933, *pg.* 1948
MacNichol, Lucy, Sr Mgr-Content Dev & Editor - Philadelphia Convention & Visitors Bureau; *pg.* 1004, *pg.* 1568
Macolino, Debra, Sr Mgr-Customer Insights - Alexion Pharmaceuticals, Inc.; *pg.* 1489, *pg.* 341
MacPherson, Andy, Mgr-Field Mktg - EMC Corporation; *pg.* 391, *pg.* 825
MacPherson, Scott, Mgr-Global Mktg-Tech Consulting - Hewlett-Packard Company; *pg.* 404, *pg.* 175
Macri, Ed, Sr VP-Marketing & Analytics - Wayfair LLC; *pg.* 1288, *pg.* 801
Macri, Michael, Mgr-Mktg Sciences - Ford Motor Company; *pg.* 172, *pg.* 876
Macsuga, Todd, Dir-Mktg - Nestle USA, Inc.; *pg.* 883, *pg.* 96
Macune, Meryl Truffelman, VP-Digital Mktg-Global - The Estee Lauder Companies Inc.; *pg.* 508, *pg.* 1229
Macwan, Sanjay, CTO-Media Labs & Sr VP - NBC Universal, Inc.; *pg.* 300, *pg.* 1266
MacWilliams, Lori, Sr Mgr-Mktg Ops Dept - R.J. Reynolds Tobacco Co.; *pg.* 1895, *pg.* 1395
MacWilliams, Patricia, Head-Healthcare Adv Sls - Google Inc.; *pg.* 1249, *pg.* 153
Macy, Bill, VP-Sls - Information Builders Inc.; *pg.* 415, *pg.* 1243
Madaio, Melissa, Dir-Digital Mktg-Garnier Brand - L'Oreal USA; *pg.* 514, *pg.* 1252
Madan, Natasha, Dir-Mktg-Chocolate - Nestle USA, Inc.; *pg.* 883, *pg.* 96
Madara, Steve, VP-Global Thermal Sls - Emerson Network Power Liebert; *pg.* 1071, *pg.* 1439
Maday, R. John, Mgr-Production - Retractable Technologies Inc.; *pg.* 1590, *pg.* 1725
Madden, Dave, Sr VP-Media Solutions-Global - Electronic Arts Inc.; *pg.* 951, *pg.* 189
Madden, Dre, Dir-Global Mktg, Display & Mobile - OpenTable, Inc.; *pg.* 450, *pg.* 224
Madden, Kelly, Mgr-Mktg-Dental & Vision Products - Aetna Inc.; *pg.* 1187, *pg.* 351
Madden, Kevin R., Assoc Mgr-Multicultural Mktg - Moet Hennessy; *pg.* 1966, *pg.* 1260
Madden, Robert, VP-Sls - Bridon American Corp.; *pg.* 1319, *pg.* 1594
Madden, Robert, Sr VP-Mktg, Creative, Comm & Brand Strategy - Travel Channel LLC; *pg.* 313, *pg.* 766
Madden, Shannon, Sr Specialist-Mktg Svcs - 24 Hour Fitness Worldwide Inc.; *pg.* 526, *pg.* 258
Madden, Sheila, Mgr-eBusiness Display Media - Discover Financial Services; *pg.* 744, *pg.* 653

First page reference indicates Business Class Edition
Second page reference indicates Geographic Edition

Madden, Steve, Product Mgr-Software - Agilent Technologies, Inc.; pg. 614, pg. 264
Maddock, Jeffrey, Dir-Mktg - FedEx Corporation; pg. 1907, pg. 1642
Maddox, Dwayne, Reg Mgr-Media - American Family Mutual Insurance Company; pg. 1190, pg. 1864
Maddox, Ivan, Product Mgr-InsitePro - Intermap Technologies Corporation; pg. 417, pg. 1903
Maddox, Katrina, Mgr-Digital Mktg, Social Media & Email Mktg - Grand Ole Opry; pg. 289, pg. 1651
Maddox, Rick, Sr Mgr-Mktg - Adobe Systems Incorporated; pg. 342, pg. 235
Madej, Michael, Dir-Digital Media - Babcox Media; pg. 1619, pg. 1400
Madeley, Hunter, Sr VP-Sls - HubSpot, Inc.; pg. 409, pg. 808
Madenwald, Marc, Dir-Sls Process & Productivity - Adobe Systems Incorporated; pg. 342, pg. 235
Mader, Michelle, Sr Mgr-Digital Media - PetSmart, Inc.; pg. 1481, pg. 18
Mader, Wendi, Sr Product Mgr-Health Svcs - Quest Diagnostics Incorporated; pg. 1587, pg. 1080
Madera, Sandy, Mgr-Mktg - Tourneau Inc.; pg. 14, pg. 1303
Maderer, Jason, Representative-Media Rels - Georgia Institute Of Technology; pg. 602, pg. 506
Madge, Sharon, Sr Mgr-Digital Ops-UK & Ireland - Warner Music Group Corp.; pg. 590, pg. 1313
Madha, Fatima, Dir-Sls - Rainmaker Systems Inc.; pg. 458, pg. 58
Madhavan, Nitya, Sr Dir-Global Barbie Mktg - Mattel Games/Puzzles; pg. 962, pg. 80
Madhavan, Nitya, Sr Dir-Barbie Mktg-Global - MATTEL, INC.; pg. 962, pg. 81
Madigan, Eileen, VP-Creative - Four Seasons Hotels Limited; pg. 1092, pg. 1938
Madigan, Joan E., Bus Mgr-Medical Sls - 3M Company; pg. 1142, pg. 956
Madigan, Lisa, Specialist-Mktg - American Medical Systems Holdings, Inc.; pg. 1493, pg. 947
Madison, Eliza, Dir-Mktg - Sea Island Clothiers, LLC; pg. 32, pg. 1146
Madison, Felicia, Dir-Sls - San Antonio Convention & Visitors Bureau; pg. 1004, pg. 1742
Madison, Shari, Producer-Global Brands-Mktg Comm - MATTEL, INC.; pg. 962, pg. 81
Madole, Rebecca, Sr Mgr-Digital Mktg Strategy - Discover Financial Services; pg. 744, pg. 653
Madonna, Lia, Dir-Client Svcs & Mktg - David's Bridal, Inc.; pg. 23, pg. 1523
Madrid, Ken, Mgr-Sls - Crown Prince, Inc.; pg. 850, pg. 67
Madrid, Oscar, Dir-Multicultural Mktg - Verizon Communications Inc.; pg. 1875, pg. 1309
Madsen, Amy, Sr Coord-Mktg-Wells Fargo Home Mortgage - Wells Fargo & Company; pg. 819, pg. 232
Madson, Paul, Sr Dir-US Enterprise Strategy - Johnson & Johnson; pg. 1549, pg. 1091
Maeder, Frank, Product Mgr-PantoneLIVE-Global - X-Rite, Incorporated; pg. 1437, pg. 891
Maeder, Jason, Sr Product Mgr - Microsystems; pg. 440, pg. 608
Maercklein, Andy, Asst VP & Dir-Mktg - T.J. Maxx; pg. 1788, pg. 822
Maestas, Kate, Mgr-Convention Sls - Denver Metro Convention & Visitors Bureau; pg. 991, pg. 318
Maffei, Steph, Product Mgr - Fender Musical Instruments Corporation; pg. 547, pg. 21
Maffett, Dionne, Head-Customer Insights & Experience Mktg - Eli Lilly and Company; pg. 1527, pg. 684
Magalei, Raymond, Dir-Mktg - Polynesian Cultural Center; pg. 577, pg. 545
Magallon, Becky, Coord-In-Store Mktg Strategy - Kohl's Corporation; pg. 1775, pg. 1870
Magana, Chris, Dir-Customer Mktg - The Goodyear Tire & Rubber Company; pg. 1883, pg. 1401
Magardician, Madeleine, Mgr-Adv & Partnership Mktg - Macy's, Inc.; pg. 1778, pg. 1417
Magee, Dave, Sr Dir - Cushman & Wakefield, Inc.; pg. 1088, pg. 1220
Magee, Jacky, Sr Product Mgr-Mktg-Skype for Bus - Microsoft Corporation; pg. 435, pg. 1824
Magee, Liza, Grp Mgr-Mktg-Web UX & eMail Mktg - Microsoft Corporation; pg. 435, pg. 1824
Magee, Marianna, Dir-Mktg Calendar & Plng - Popeye's Chicken & Biscuits; pg. 1745, pg. 517
Magee, Marianna, Dir-Mktg Calendar & Plng - Popeyes Louisiana Kitchen, Inc.; pg. 1745, pg. 517
Magee, Rawles, Mgr-Legal Adv - Inside Business Inc.; pg. 1653, pg. 1797
Magee, Rebecca, Coord-Social Consciousness - Eileen Fisher, Inc.; pg. 24, pg. 1168
Magel, Robert W., Jr., Dir-Mktg - Lancaster Newspapers Inc.; pg. 1657, pg. 1546
Mager, Kim, Dir-Mktg - Hinkley Lighting Inc.; pg. 1299, pg. 1404
Maggard, Susan, Dir-Digital Media - Luxottica Retail; pg. 8, pg. 1460
Maggiolino, Gary, Mgr-Mktg Programs-North America - InterSystems; pg. 1350, pg. 1016
Maghakian, Emil, Sr Dir-Hardware Dev & Mfg Test Engrg - Microsoft Corporation; pg. 435, pg. 1824
Magida, Brian, Dir-Digital Mktg - JAND, Inc.; pg. 1418, pg. 1245
Magill, Drew, Dir-Mktg-Europe - The Boeing Company; pg. 225, pg. 567
Magill, Drew, Dir-Mktg-Europe - The Boeing Company - Helicopter Division; pg. 226, pg. 13
Magill, Jennifer, Mgr-Social Media Mktg - Cotton Incorporated Consumer Marketing Headquarters; pg. 692, pg. 1218
Magill, Patrick, Mgr-Natl Mktg-Foodservice - The Coca-Cola Company; pg. 240, pg. 493
Magilligan, Jay, Mng Dir-Mktg - American Student Assistance; pg. 714, pg. 789
Maglalang, Aileen, Mgr-Channel Mktg Programs - Brocade Communications Systems, Inc.; pg. 365, pg. 239
Maglaras, Kathy, Dir-Regulatory Affairs-Adv & Promo - Novartis Corporation; pg. 1574, pg. 1273
Magnani, Matt, Sr Dir-Sls Promos & Mktg - Performance Direct, Inc.; pg. 1781, pg. 1361
Magnano-Damm, Joan, Acct Dir-Convention Sls-Natl - Seattle Convention & Visitors Bureau; pg. 1005, pg. 1839
Magnarelli, Amandah, Dir-Database Mktg - Forrester Research, Inc.; pg. 1642, pg. 807
Magner, Alix, Mgr-Sls-Natl - Quality Bicycle Products; pg. 1710, pg. 918
Magner, Hilary, Rep-Sls & Mktg - NRG Energy, Inc.; pg. 1948, pg. 1712
Magni, Giovanni, Chief Strategy Officer & Exec VP - Bio-Rad Laboratories, Inc.; pg. 1504, pg. 101
Magnini, Michael, Sr Mgr-Events - AT&T Inc.; pg. 1867, pg. 1674
Magno, Jess, Mgr-Product Mktg - Sunstar Americas Inc.; pg. 1599, pg. 591
Magnus, Bryan, Mgr-Mktg, Bus Dev & Insulating Materials-Global - Honeywell International Inc.; pg. 407, pg. 1088
Magnuson, Rod, Product Dir-Sinks & Faucets - Elkay Manufacturing Company; pg. 80, pg. 645
Magnussen, Stephanie, Sr Mgr-Database Mktg - TD Ameritrade Holding Corporation; pg. 808, pg. 1018
Magnusson, Andreas, Mgr-Mktg Comm - Alimak Hek Inc; pg. 66, pg. 1749
Magnusson, Marjorie, Mgr-PR - Arizona Office of Tourism; pg. 988, pg. 14
Magoc, Kate, Mgr-Mktg - Uber USA, LLC; pg. 1286, pg. 229
Magon, Laura, Brand Mgr-Global P&G Brand - The Procter & Gamble Company; pg. 1129, pg. 1418
Magstadt, Barbara, Sr Dir-In Store Presentation - Wal-Mart Stores, Inc.; pg. 1790, pg. 29
Maguire, Christine, District Mgr-Sls - Office Depot, Inc.; pg. 448, pg. 412
Maguire, Mark, Sr Dir-Tax - General Electric Company; pg. 1297, pg. 347
Maguire, Rob, Dir-AutoCAD Platform Product Line Grp - Autodesk Inc.; pg. 356, pg. 257
Maguire, Sean, Sr Dir-Security - Arizona Diamondbacks; pg. 529, pg. 14
Maguire, Sue Ellen, Dir-Mktg - Wisconsin Chamber Orchestra; pg. 593, pg. 1867
Maguire-Ott, Kathleen, Mgr-Mktg - The Western & Southern Financial Group; pg. 1223, pg. 1427
Magyar, Jennifer, Dir-Global Contracts & Adv - Subway Restaurants; pg. 1751, pg. 356
Mah, Amy, Mgr-Channel Mktg - Acer America Corporation; pg. 341, pg. 235
Mah, Lorenzo, Sr Mgr-Revenue Ops & Analytics - Yahoo! Inc.; pg. 1289, pg. 289
Mah, Theresa, Accountant-Mktg - EnCana Corp.; pg. 976, pg. 1903
Mahajan, Ruchi, Sr Product Mgr - Cox Communications, Inc.; pg. 279, pg. 501
Mahal, Tina, Sr Dir-Mktg, SunChips, Rold Gold & Baked - Frito-Lay North America, Inc.; pg. 1853, pg. 1730
Mahan, Amanda, Dir-Creative, Digital, Content & Social - The Clorox Company; pg. 327, pg. 169
Mahan, Bekah, Mgr-Mktg Comm - Bayer CropScience; pg. 1149, pg. 981
Mahan, Kay, Mgr-Shopper Mktg-Baby & Child Care-Walmart Bus Dev - Kimberly-Clark Corporation; pg. 1461, pg. 1720
Mahan, Sara, Acct Coord-Media & Events-Natl - Life Time Fitness, Inc.; pg. 1556, pg. 920
Mahange, Matimba, Dir-Sls & Mktg - Joy Mining Machinery; pg. 1352, pg. 1591
Mahany, Kevin J., VP-Mdsg - Susser Holdings Corporation; pg. 985, pg. 1671
Mahdik, Christopher, VP-Customer Lifecycle Mktg - American Express Company; pg. 712, pg. 1190
Maher, Bill, Sr Dir-New Product Commercialization-CVM - Novartis Pharmaceuticals Corp.; pg. 1575, pg. 1054
Maher, Ed, VP-Sls - Outfront Media; pg. 1465, pg. 1275
Maher, Jill, VP-Digital Mktg - FMR LLC (Fidelity Investments); pg. 759, pg. 794
Maher, Joe, Product Mgr - Continental Tire North America, Inc.; pg. 1880, pg. 1615
Maher, John, Strategist-On-Air Media-Investigation Discovery - Discovery Communications, Inc.; pg. 282, pg. 777
Maher, Kathy, Sr VP-Revenue Mgmt - Wyndham Worldwide Corporation; pg. 1119, pg. 1107
Maher, Kevin, Sr Dir & Head-Consumer Insight & Mktg Analytics-Global - Electronic Arts Inc.; pg. 951, pg. 189
Maher, Marie, Bus Mgr - Scientific American, Inc.; pg. 1685, pg. 1290
Maher, Tom, Sr Mgr-In Store Mktg - Electrolux Home Products North America; pg. 54, pg. 1366
Mahesh, Shrikirti, Brand Mgr-Keurig Cold Beverage Sys-Innovation - Keurig Green Mountain, Inc.; pg. 868, pg. 1768
Maheshwary, Sonu, Sr Mgr-Product Mktg - KLA-Tencor Corporation; pg. 1353, pg. 146
Mahieu, Frans, Dir-Mktg-Global - Kimberly-Clark Corporation; pg. 1461, pg. 1720
Mahler, Peggy, Mgr-Mktg-Intel Intelligent Sys Alliance - Intel Corporation; pg. 645, pg. 266
Mahler, Ross, Product Mgr-Drilling Comml - General Electric Company; pg. 1297, pg. 347
Mahler, Steve, Dir-Mktg - Turning Stone Resort Casino LLC, pg. 1117, pg. 1348
Mahlman, Jessica, VP & Mgr-Mktg - Sun Bancorp, Inc.; pg. 806, pg. 1127
Mahlmeister, Bryan M., Sr Mgr-Global Mktg Effectiveness & Insights - General Motors Company; pg. 175, pg. 881
Mahlow, Karen, Brand Mgr - Jennie-O Turkey Store, LLC; pg. 865, pg. 966
Mahlum, Dan, VP-Secondary Mktg-Nationwide Advantage Mortgage Company - Nationwide Mutual Insurance Company; pg. 1210, pg. 1442
Mahmood, Amir, Dir-Product Mgmt-Advanced Solutions - AT&T Inc.; pg. 1867, pg. 1674
Mahn, Michael, Specialist-PR Field Svc - Honeywell International Inc.; pg. 407, pg. 1088
Mahnesmith, Cindy, Specialist-Mktg Svcs - Graybar Electric Company, Inc.; pg. 1299, pg. 997
Mahon, Brian, Sr Assoc Brand Mgr-VELVEETA Meals - The Kraft Heinz Company; pg. 871, pg. 641
Mahon, Diane, Mgr-Mktg - W.W. Grainger, Inc.; pg. 1390, pg. 625
Mahon, Janice K., VP-Tech Commlization & Gen Mgr-PHOLED Material Sls Bus - Universal Display Corporation; pg. 683, pg. 1064
Mahone, Jessica, Dir-Art-Creative Pkg - J.C. Penney Company, Inc.; pg. 1774, pg. 1732
Mahoney, Brian, Dir-Adv Sls - The Phillies, L.P.; pg. 575, pg. 1569
Mahoney, Brian, Mgr-Mktg - Saucony, Inc.; pg. 1818, pg. 828
Mahoney, Cheryl, VP-Mdsg-Promo & Bus Dev - CVS Health Corporation; pg. 1765, pg. 1610
Mahoney, Christina, Sr Mgr-Bus Dev - Smarter Travel Media LLC; pg. 1687, pg. 801
Mahoney, Dan, Sr VP-Sls, Strategy & Vendor Fin-Global - CIT GROUP INC.; pg. 735, pg. 1212
Mahoney, David, VP-Sls & Mktg - Sapporo U.S.A., Inc.; pg. 1969, pg. 295
Mahoney, Francesca, Mgr-Multicultural-Brand Mktg - Target Corporation; pg. 1786, pg. 942
Mahoney, Gerard, Sr Dir - Nathan's Famous Inc.; pg. 1741, pg. 1171
Mahoney, Laura, Mgr-Global Media Insights - Unilever United States, Inc.; pg. 904, pg. 1061

Mahoney, Lisa, Assoc Mgr-Channel Mktg - New Balance Athletic Shoe, Inc.; *pg.* 1811, *pg.* 798
Mahoney, Mark, Exec VP-Sls - Extended Stay Hotels LLC; *pg.* 1091, *pg.* 1622
Mahoney, Mark, VP & Gen Mgr-Sls - KTRK Television, Inc.; *pg.* 295, *pg.* 1709
Mahoney, Michael, Dir-Golf Ball Product Mgmt - Acushnet Company; *pg.* 1824, *pg.* 818
Mahoney, Nina, Dir-Mktg & Sponsorship - International Plaza & Bay Street; *pg.* 1773, *pg.* 473
Mahoney, Patrick D., CMO - Institute of Electrical and Electronics Engineers, Inc.; *pg.* 144, *pg.* 1109
Mahoney, Paul M., Pres-Indus Sls - Rhode Island Textile Company, Inc.; *pg.* 698, *pg.* 1605
Mahoney, Peter, CMO & Gen Mgr-Dragon Desktop - Nuance Communications, Inc.; *pg.* 447, *pg.* 806
Mahoney, Renee, Strategist-Creative - The Valspar Corporation; *pg.* 1449, *pg.* 945
Mahoney, Tom, Sr VP-Sls - Trans-Lux Corporation; *pg.* 881, *pg.* 365
Mahoney, Tyrrell Hammer, VP-Sls, Mktg & Bus Dev - Chronicle Books; *pg.* 1627, *pg.* 216
Mahoney-Demars, Regina, Dir-Integrated Mktg - ConAgra Foods, Inc.; *pg.* 826, *pg.* 1014
Mahood, Tracy, Sr Mgr-Mktg - Education Management Corporation; *pg.* 601, *pg.* 1575
Mahop, Xaverie, Sr Assoc Brand Mgr-A 1 & Grey Poupon - The Kraft Heinz Company; *pg.* 871, *pg.* 641
Mahtab, Ajoy, VP-Mktg & Strategy-Worldwide - Becton, Dickinson & Company; *pg.* 1501, *pg.* 1068
Mahtani, Rahul, Mgr-Social Media - Jack in the Box Inc.; *pg.* 1732, *pg.* 204
Mai, Alfred, Mgr-Mobile Mktg - Zoosk Inc.; *pg.* 1292, *pg.* 235
Maicher, Lorie, Sr Specialist-Mktg Svcs - Endo Pharmaceuticals Holdings, Inc.; *pg.* 1528, *pg.* 1549
Maiden, Lisa, Dir-Retail & Natl Adv - Cape Cod Times; *pg.* 1625, *pg.* 826
Maidenberg, Shawn, Mgr-Mktg Analytics - Sun Life Financial Inc.; *pg.* 806, *pg.* 1944
Maier, D. J., Mgr-Sls - Wisco Products, Inc.; *pg.* 1389, *pg.* 1447
Maier, Donald R., CEO-Flooring Products & Exec VP - Armstrong World Industries, Inc.; *pg.* 914, *pg.* 1545
Maier, Julia, Dir-Sls & Mktg-Bus Div - Blue Cross & Blue Shield of Michigan; *pg.* 1195, *pg.* 879
Maier, Susan, Dir-PR - The Ritz-Carlton Chicago; *pg.* 1110, *pg.* 589
Maier, Zach, Product Mgr - Google Inc.; *pg.* 1249, *pg.* 153
Maierle, Dan, Mgr-Social Media-Puritan's Pride - NBTY, Inc.; *pg.* 1572, *pg.* 1338
Maiers, Marty, Dir-Mktg - Diamond Jo, LLC; *pg.* 1089, *pg.* 707
Maietta, Jasmine, Sr Dir-Global Brand Mktg - Under Armour, Inc.; *pg.* 49, *pg.* 759
Maile, Richard, Dir-Creative-Bus Comm - Assurant, Inc.; *pg.* 1193, *pg.* 1198
Mailhot, Nick, Mgr-Channel Solutions Mktg - Schneider Canada, Inc.; *pg.* 1374, *pg.* 1928
Mailloux, Drew, Mgr-Mktg - Loews Hotels Holding Corporation; *pg.* 1101, *pg.* 1252
Maiman, Janice, Sr VP-Comm, Media, News & Pro Pathways - American Institute of Certified Public Accountants Inc.; *pg.* 129, *pg.* 1192
Main, George, VP-Mdsg - Eby-Brown Co.; *pg.* 1767, *pg.* 636
Maines, Duke, Sr Dir-Organizational Dev - Heineken USA Inc.; *pg.* 252, *pg.* 1352
Mains, Jim, Sr VP-Products & Programs - Smith Micro Software, Inc.; *pg.* 471, *pg.* 41
Mainz, Bob, VP-Sls & Mktg - Zero-Max, Inc.; *pg.* 222, *pg.* 954
Mainz, Chris, Sr Specialist-PR - Southwest Airlines Co.; *pg.* 1923, *pg.* 1687
Maio, Missy, Sr Mgr-Retail Mdsg - Dunkin' Brands Group, Inc.; *pg.* 1727, *pg.* 810
Maise, Meg, Sr Mgr-Internal Comm - American International Group, Inc.; *pg.* 1190, *pg.* 1193
Maiser, Brock, Mgr-Corp Sls - Minnesota Twins, LLC; *pg.* 563, *pg.* 940
Maitino, Edward, Mng Dir-Mktg, Adv & Tourism - Empire State Development-Division of Tourism; *pg.* 992, *pg.* 1227
Maitra, Tara, Sr VP & Gen Mgr-Content & Media Sls - TiVo Inc.; *pg.* 313, *pg.* 251
Maiura, Colleen, Sr Specialist-Category Mktg - Lowe's Companies, Inc.; *pg.* 1053, *pg.* 1383
Maizel, Ari, Dir-Mktg - Allergan; *pg.* 1490, *pg.* 1101
Majeau, Bernard, Dir-Product Dev - eBags, Inc.; *pg.* 1240, *pg.* 331
Majeed, Liliahn, VP-Team Mktg & Bus Ops - National Basketball Association; *pg.* 566, *pg.* 1264
Majeski, Glenn T., Sr Dir-Comm - Quest Diagnostics Incorporated; *pg.* 1587, *pg.* 1080
Majikes, Matthew G., District Head-Sls - Genworth Financial, Inc.; *pg.* 761, *pg.* 1802
Majmudar, Sonal, Sr Mgr-Brand Mktg-Global - Hasbro, Inc.; *pg.* 954, *pg.* 1603
Majno, Lorenzo, VP-Mktg - Instron Corporation; *pg.* 1349, *pg.* 839
Major, Cameron, Producer-Digital Mktg - Beats Electronics LLC; *pg.* 624, *pg.* 272
Major, Danny, Sr Mgr-Mktg - American Express Company; *pg.* 712, *pg.* 1190
Major, Michael, VP-Corp Mktg - Applied Micro Circuits Corporation; *pg.* 618, *pg.* 283
Major, Raymond, Sr Mgr-Sustainability Initiatives - The Hershey Co.; *pg.* 1855, *pg.* 1538
Majure, Ronda, VP-Global Bus Segment Sls - Thomson CompuMark; *pg.* 484, *pg.* 838
Mak, Alex, Sr Dir-Memory Design - SanDisk Corporation; *pg.* 465, *pg.* 147
Mak, Becca, Brand Mgr-Baskin-Robbins - Dunkin' Brands Group, Inc.; *pg.* 1727, *pg.* 810
Mak, Lawrence, Mgr-Product Mktg - Facebook, Inc.; *pg.* 1245, *pg.* 143
Mak, Lisa, Dir-Mktg - Oil-Dri Corporation of America; *pg.* 1480, *pg.* 586
Mak, Sabrina, Dir-Sls - Galaxy Nutritional Foods, Inc.; *pg.* 857, *pg.* 1603
Makar, Mina, Sr Dir-Global Mktg-Lesinurad - AstraZeneca Pharmaceuticals LP; *pg.* 1497, *pg.* 389
Makara, Chris, Strategist-Interactive Mktg & Digital - Insperity, Inc.; *pg.* 416, *pg.* 1725
Makarek-Baez, Nancy, VP-Sls - Carter's, Inc.; *pg.* 21, *pg.* 491
Makarigakis, Nestor, Grp Dir-Mktg Comm - Mistras Group, Inc.; *pg.* 1362, *pg.* 1113
Makavy, Ran, Product Dir - Facebook, Inc.; *pg.* 1245, *pg.* 143
Makhatadze, Nick, Grp Dir-Global Media - Tiffany & Co.; *pg.* 13, *pg.* 1299
Maki, Evelyn, Dir-Mktg Comm - Joy Global, Inc.; *pg.* 1351, *pg.* 1876
Maki, Kimberly, Corp VP-Corp Comm & PR - Bright House Networks LLC; *pg.* 272, *pg.* 461
Maki, Nancy E., Dir-Mktg Comm - Boston Scientific Corporation; *pg.* 1508, *pg.* 831
Makinen, Jill, Rep-Key Acct Sls - Carhartt, Inc.; *pg.* 39, *pg.* 875
Makofske, Lauren, Brand Mgr-Global - Marchon Eyewear, Inc.; *pg.* 1421, *pg.* 1180
Makransky, Karen, Mgr-Product Mktg - Dell Inc.; *pg.* 383, *pg.* 1737
Makri, Helen, Assoc Mgr-Mktg-B2B2C - Wyndham Worldwide Corporation; *pg.* 1119, *pg.* 1107
Makris, George, Product Mgr-Global - Corsair Components, Inc.; *pg.* 380, *pg.* 90
Maks, Holly, Sr Specialist-Automotive Mktg - Ally Financial Inc.; *pg.* 711, *pg.* 878
Malaby, Kristen, Mgr-Media - Tourism Australia; *pg.* 1007, *pg.* 140
Maladra, Keith, VP-Digital Mktg & Strategy - Forest City Enterprises, Inc.; *pg.* 1092, *pg.* 1430
Malaga, Scott, Sr Dir-Sls-Natl - Learfield Communications, Inc.; *pg.* 296, *pg.* 979
Malamud, Jason, Gen Mgr-Adv Sls - Verizon Communications Inc.; *pg.* 1875, *pg.* 1309
Malanga, Gregg, Product Mgr - Arrow Fastener Company, Inc.; *pg.* 1042, *pg.* 1118
Malanga, Gregg, Product Mgr - Masco Corporation; *pg.* 96, *pg.* 909
Malaspina, Kristin, VP-Partnership Mktg & Corp Mktg - Time Warner Cable Inc.; *pg.* 312, *pg.* 1301
Malaszenko, Natalie, VP-Mktg - Omni Hotels & Resorts; *pg.* 1107, *pg.* 1685
Malatesta, John, VP-Bus & Mktg Operational Transformation-Global - Schneider Electric; *pg.* 467, *pg.* 1609
Malave, Iveliesse, VP-Consumer & Entertainment PR - Univision Communications Inc.; *pg.* 683, *pg.* 1307
Malaviya, Sonali, Head-Bus Mktg-India - Twitter, Inc.; *pg.* 1285, *pg.* 228
Malbari, Rubina, Exec Dir-Global Media & Mktg - The Estee Lauder Companies Inc.; *pg.* 508, *pg.* 1229
Malbon, Ben, Dir-Creative Partnerships - Google Inc.; *pg.* 1249, *pg.* 153
Malburg, Jeff, Media Buyer - Valassis; *pg.* 1698, *pg.* 386
Malcolm, Gail B., Mgr-Mktg-SYNGO Americas - Siemens Medical Solutions USA, Inc.; *pg.* 469, *pg.* 1550
Malcolm, Gayle, VP-Adv & Design - Best Buy Co., Inc.; *pg.* 1761, *pg.* 954
Malcolm, MaryBeth Cloutman, Sr Dir-Category Dev & Mktg Solutions - Yahoo! Inc.; *pg.* 1289, *pg.* 289
Malcolm, Michelle, Dir-Customer Mktg - CME Group Inc.; *pg.* 738, *pg.* 571
Malcom-Kerr, Brandy, Mgr-B2B Mktg - Zulily; *pg.* 1792, *pg.* 1843
Malcuit, Jennifer, Product Mgr-Overhead Door Corporation - Wayne-Dalton Corp.; *pg.* 120, *pg.* 1465
Maldonado, Danny, Exec VP-Sls & Mktg - Bell Helicopter Textron, Inc.; *pg.* 224, *pg.* 1693
Maldonado, Len, Mgr-Media - Simon Property Group, Inc.; *pg.* 1112, *pg.* 690
Maldonado, Marty, Specialist-Product - Philips Electronics North America; *pg.* 662, *pg.* 782
Male, Bill, Mgr-Sls-Intl - Scintrex Ltd.; *pg.* 1374, *pg.* 1920
Male, Les, Sr Dir-Energy Products - CME Group Inc.; *pg.* 738, *pg.* 571
Malec, Rachel, Mgr-Adv - FCA US LLC; *pg.* 170, *pg.* 868
Malecha, Peter, Mgr-Digital Mktg - ASICS America Corporation; *pg.* 1826, *pg.* 106
Malecki, Florian, Dir-Intl Product Mktg-Network Security - Dell Inc.; *pg.* 383, *pg.* 1737
Malek, Nathan, Dir-Mktg-Engine Products - Donaldson Company, Inc.; *pg.* 1329, *pg.* 917
Maleknia, Jasmine, Mgr-Social Media - Airbnb, Inc.; *pg.* 1226, *pg.* 211
Maletsky, Kerry, Dir-Crypto Product Line - Atmel Corporation; *pg.* 621, *pg.* 238
Malfa, Susan, Sr VP-Natl Adv Sls - NBC Universal, Inc.; *pg.* 300, *pg.* 1266
Malfa, Susan, Sr VP-Sls - Oxygen Media LLC; *pg.* 303, *pg.* 1275
Malfitano, Gissell, Mgr-Mktg - ASUSTeK Computer Inc; *pg.* 355, *pg.* 90
Malfy, Laura, Mgr-Entertainment Mktg & Promos - National Football League; *pg.* 567, *pg.* 1264
Malgesini, Michelle, Sr Mgr-Mktg - McKesson Corporation; *pg.* 1560, *pg.* 222
Malhotra, Anupam, Sr Mgr-Connected Vehicle - Audi of America, Inc.; *pg.* 164, *pg.* 1784
Malhotra, Kanuj, CFO-Nook Media & VP-Corp Dev - Barnes & Noble, Inc.; *pg.* 1619, *pg.* 1201
Malhotra, Paayal, Mng Dir-Integrated Mktg & Promos - American Diabetes Association; *pg.* 127, *pg.* 1770
Malhotra, Raju, Sr VP-Products - Conversant, Inc.; *pg.* 1393, *pg.* 306
Malhotra, Sajid, Chief Strategy Officer - Limelight Networks, Inc.; *pg.* 1262, *pg.* 26
Malick, Scott, Mgr-Digital Adv - Scottrade, Inc.; *pg.* 802, *pg.* 1003
Malik, Haseeb, Mgr-Mktg - Amazon.com, Inc.; *pg.* 1226, *pg.* 1831
Malik, Megha, Sr Mgr-Strategic Sourcing - Vertex Pharmaceuticals Incorporated; *pg.* 1606, *pg.* 801
Malik, Piyush, Mgr-Market-Mktg Strategy - IBM Canada Limited; *pg.* 411, *pg.* 1923
Malik, Salma, Analyst-Mktg Ops - Safeway Inc.; *pg.* 1032, *pg.* 184
Malin, Bob, Mng Dir-Intl Sls & VP-Licensing - Serta, Inc.; *pg.* 942, *pg.* 619
Malin, Carla, Dir-Shopper Mktg-Supermarkets - Unilever United States, Inc.; *pg.* 904, *pg.* 1061
Malin, Christopher, Head-Mobile Mktg - Citrix Systems, Inc.; *pg.* 375, *pg.* 424
Malinick, Kathryn, Dir-Consumer Mktg - Kashi Company; *pg.* 830, *pg.* 119
Malinoski, Mallory, Head-Sls Acct Mgmt - S.C. Johnson & Son, Inc.; *pg.* 334, *pg.* 1889
Malinosky, Louise, Mgr-Channel Mktg-Global - Citrix Systems, Inc.; *pg.* 375, *pg.* 424
Malinowski, John, Sr Mgr-Indus Affairs - Baldor Electric Company; *pg.* 1316, *pg.* 32
Malinowski, Susan, VP-Mktg - Wacoal America Inc.; *pg.* 35, *pg.* 1312
Malis, Vickie, Dir-Product & Solutions Mktg - Iron Mountain Incorporated; *pg.* 421, *pg.* 796
Malish, Michelle, Sr Dir-Loyalty & Relationship Mktg - T.G.I. Friday's Inc.; *pg.* 1754, *pg.* 1669
Malish, Rachel, Coord-Media & Community Rels - Whole Foods Market, Inc.; *pg.* 1038, *pg.* 1667
Malkani, Nicholas, Brand Mktg Mgr-End User Computing - Dell

Inc.; pg. 383, pg. 1737
Malkiewicz, Steve, Dir-Mktg & Comm-IBM Res & IP - International Business Machines Corporation; pg. 418, pg. 1138
Malkosky, Mark, Asst Dir-Maintenance Trng, Bus Dev & Sls - FlightSafety International, Inc.; pg. 601, pg. 1160
Malkovich, Kristen, Specialist-Mktg Automation - New Relic, Inc.; pg. 445, pg. 224
Mallahan, Alison, Sr Specialist-PR - Itron Inc.; pg. 422, pg. 1822
Mallard, Daren J., Mgr-SPVTG Mktg & Bus Dev - Cisco Systems, Inc.; pg. 372, pg. 240
Mallea, Ana, Bus Mgr-Intl - Jelly Belly Candy Company; pg. 1857, pg. 86
Mallela, Bala, Sr Dir-Consumer & Shopper Insights - Kimberly-Clark Corporation; pg. 1461, pg. 1720
Mallen, Chris, Mgr-Mktg - Outfront Media; pg. 1465, pg. 1275
Maller, Katie, Sr Mgr-Comm - ShoreTel, Inc.; pg. 469, pg. 288
Mallett, Erica, Product Mgr - Dorel Juvenile Group, Inc.; pg. 923, pg. 676
Malley, Cullen, Mgr-Customer Mktg-Breyers & Popsicle - Unilever United States, Inc.; pg. 904, pg. 1061
Mallick, Brooke, Mgr-Mktg-Gatorade Thirst Quencher - PepsiCo, Inc.; pg. 259, pg. 1327
Mallie, Mark, Head-Product Plng-Comml Vehicles - FCA Canada Inc.; pg. 170, pg. 1948
Mallie, Mark, Sr Mgr-Portfolio Plng - FCA US LLC; pg. 170, pg. 868
Malloch, Richard P., Pres-Hearst Bus Media - The Hearst Corporation; pg. 1649, pg. 1239
Mallon, Kevin, Sr Mgr-PR - FileMaker, Inc.; pg. 639, pg. 265
Mallon, Lauren, Sr Mgr-Mktg-Global - Fila USA; pg. 1808, pg. 779
Malloris, Libby, Mgr-Mktg & Pricing-Pulp Bus - International Paper Company; pg. 1460, pg. 1644
Mallory, Don, VP & Mgr-Mktg - BOK Financial Corporation; pg. 726, pg. 1489
Mallory, Kristin, Mgr-Online Mktg - Bose Corporation; pg. 626, pg. 820
Mallory, Tiffany, Brand Mgr - Stryker Orthopaedics; pg. 1599, pg. 1082
Malloy, Carey, Sr Mgr-Brand Mktg - eBay Inc.; pg. 1240, pg. 243
Malloy, Janet, Sr Specialist-Mktg Comm-Provider Experience - Cigna Corporation; pg. 1197, pg. 338
Malloy, Lisa I., Sr Mgr-Media Rels - Intel Corporation; pg. 645, pg. 266
Malloy, Michael, Exec VP-Products & Strategy - Webroot Software, Inc.; pg. 1289, pg. 313
Malloy, Paula, Div VP & Dir-Mdse Mktg-JCP Salon - J.C. Penney Company, Inc.; pg. 1774, pg. 1732
Mallozzi, Frank, Sr VP-Worldwide Sls & Mktg - Electronics For Imaging, Inc.; pg. 390, pg. 88
Malmed, Dan, VP & Dir-Sls-USMedia - Nielsen Audio; pg. 446, pg. 768
Malmqvist, Ana, Sr Dir-Product Mktg - Bloomin' Brands, Inc.; pg. 1716, pg. 471
Malmstead, Mark, Head-Dodge Mktg & Comm - FCA US LLC; pg. 170, pg. 868
Malo, Lisa, Dir-Mktg-Creative Svcs - Edible Arrangements International, Inc.; pg. 1768, pg. 382
Maloberti, Elisa, Dir-Egg Product Mktg - American Egg Board; pg. 128, pg. 650
Malone, Brett, Dir-Search & Media Product - Smarter Travel Media LLC; pg. 1687, pg. 801
Malone, Caitlin, Dir-PR & Social Media-Audiovox - Voxx International; pg. 686, pg. 1166
Malone, Gene, Product Mgr-Emerging Technologies - TE Connectivity Ltd.; pg. 677, pg. 1515
Malone, Jaimey, VP-Sls - USA Truck, Inc.; pg. 1929, pg. 36
Malone, James, Product Mgr - Google Inc.; pg. 1249, pg. 153
Malone, Jasmin, Brand Mgr - Truth Initiative; pg. 158, pg. 405
Malone, Jill, Sr Mgr-Digital Mktg - MoneyGram International, Inc.; pg. 783, pg. 1684
Malone, John A., Sr VP-Sls - Escort, Inc.; pg. 1412, pg. 1479
Malone, Myrtle D., Mgr-Mktg Comm - Stewart & Stevenson, LLC; pg. 985, pg. 1715
Malone, Shandy, Dir-Sls - Super Micro Computer, Inc.; pg. 478, pg. 251
Malone, Shannon, Dir-Product Strategy-Warby Parker - JAND, Inc.; pg. 1418, pg. 1245
Malone, Tim, Sr Mgr-Global Mktg-Lifestyle Design - New Balance Athletic Shoe, Inc.; pg. 1811, pg. 798
Malone, Valerie, Dir-Mktg - LG Electronics Canada, Inc.; pg. 651, pg. 1927
Maloney, Catherine, Sr Mgr-Govt & Community Rels - Comcast Cable Communications, Inc.; pg. 276, pg. 1560
Maloney, Joe, VP-Sls-Intl - Baldor Electric Company; pg. 1316, pg. 32
Maloney, Katarina, Sr Mgr-PR - Kobrand Corporation; pg. 1965, pg. 1325
Maloney, Kevin, VP-Sls - Smarter Travel Media LLC; pg. 1687, pg. 801
Maloney, Mary, Dir-Mktg - Federal Agricultural Mortgage Corporation; pg. 751, pg. 399
Maloney, Mary D., Sr Dir-Benefits & HR, Asst Sec & Assoc Gen Counsel - NACCO Industries, Inc.; pg. 1174, pg. 1433
Maloney, Paul, VP-Sls & Svc - Solidscape, Inc.; pg. 1063, pg. 1037
Maloney, Robert J., Sr VP-Affinity Mktg - Liberty Mutual Insurance Group Inc.; pg. 1205, pg. 797
Malott, Mark, Mgr-Mktg-Intl - Reliv International, Inc.; pg. 1589, pg. 975
Malouf, Cindy, Mgr-Brand, Creative Mktg Digital & eLearning - The Walt Disney Company; pg. 317, pg. 52
Maloy, Flynn, VP-Global Acct Mktg - Hewlett-Packard Company; pg. 404, pg. 175
Maltese, Joanna, Product Mgr-American Rag Young Men's, Knits & Sweaters - Macy's East; pg. 1777, pg. 1254
Maltin, Samantha, Sr VP-Mktg Innovations - A&E Television Networks, LLC; pg. 267, pg. 1185
Maltrud, Sarah, Coord-Mktg-Global - Arrow Electronics, Inc.; pg. 619, pg. 325
Maltry, Heather, Specialist-Mktg Mgmt - Nationwide Mutual Insurance Company; pg. 1210, pg. 1442
Malz, Nick, Area Mgr-Sls-Southeast - Abaxis, Inc.; pg. 1483, pg. 298
Malzahn, John, Head-Data Center & Cloud Solutions Mktg - Cisco Systems, Inc.; pg. 372, pg. 240
Mamann, Nancy, VP-Global Mktg-UGG Australia - Deckers Outdoor Corporation; pg. 1807, pg. 100
Mamaradlo Kahanna, Danielle, Dir-Mktg - Golden Franchising Corporation; pg. 1730, pg. 1736
Mameesh, Mona, Mgr-Mktg-Security Svcs-Ultrabook - Intel Corporation; pg. 645, pg. 266
Mamet, Matthew, Sr Dir-Product & Instant Booking - TripAdvisor, Inc.; pg. 1926, pg. 835
Mamizuka, Brandy, Sr Mgr-Bus Dev - Micron Technology, Inc.; pg. 435, pg. 547
Mamuric, Nikki, Dir-Mktg-Global - L'Oreal USA; pg. 514, pg. 1252
Man, Jacqueline, Media Planner - Shaw Communications Inc.; pg. 307, pg. 1904
Manall, John, Media Buyer-Digital & Strategist-Search - GEICO Corporation; pg. 1200, pg. 399
Manalo, Kristine, Assoc Mgr-Mktg - The Children's Place, Inc.; pg. 22, pg. 1119
Manby, Jeff, Exec VP & Gen Mgr-Mdse-Men's & Kids - Kohl's Corporation; pg. 1775, pg. 1870
Mancasola, Colby, VP-Content Products - Mode Media; pg. 1267, pg. 50
Mance, Jennifer, Dir-Sls & Mktg - Six Flags Entertainment Corporation; pg. 583, pg. 1698
Manchepalli, Precious, Dir-Mktg-Strategic Partnerships - The Cartoon Network; pg. 273, pg. 492
Mancher, Audrey, Mgr-Mktg Comm - Port Authority of New York & New Jersey; pg. 1919, pg. 1283
Manchess, Mary, Specialist-Social Content - Bloomin' Brands, Inc.; pg. 1716, pg. 471
Manchester, Jill, Sr VP-Mktg & Branding Strategy - Ferrara Candy Co.; pg. 1852, pg. 612
Manchester, Tom, VP-Field Mktg - Dunkin' Brands Group, Inc.; pg. 1727, pg. 810
Manchuso, Scott, Dir-Product Mktg - LoJack Corporation; pg. 210, pg. 811
Mancini, Jennifer, Supvr-Natl Adv & Media - CDW Corporation; pg. 370, pg. 663
Mancini, Marisa, Corp Mgr Mktg - Bankrate, Inc.; pg. 1231, pg. 451
Mancini, Michka, VP-Media Sls-Digital & Multiplatform Sls - Rogers Media Inc.; pg. 1681, pg. 1942
Mancino, Tonia, Dir-Mktg - Lavazza Premium Coffees Corp.; pg. 874, pg. 1250
Mancuso, Amanda, Product Mgr-Residential Sensors - Leviton Manufacturing Company, Inc.; pg. 1301, pg. 1180
Mancuso, Kevin, Dir-Global Creative-Nexxus Salon Hair Care - Unilever United States, Inc.; pg. 904, pg. 1061
Mancuso, Lauren, Strategist-Mktg - Chipotle Mexican Grill, Inc.; pg. 1722, pg. 317
Mancuso, Lisa, Sr VP-Mktg-Baby - Fisher-Price, Inc.; pg. 953, pg. 1156
Mancuso, Natalie, Sr Product Mgr-Anaphylaxis Mktg - Sanofi US; pg. 1592, pg. 1046
Mancuso-Horn, Lisa, Mgr-Advanced Product Mktg & Strategy-Global - Ford Motor Company; pg. 172, pg. 876
Mandacina, Joe, VP-Corp Comm & PR - Sprint Corporation; pg. 1874, pg. 719
Mandala, Angela, Specialist-Social Media - Jo-Ann Stores LLC; pg. 696, pg. 1455
Mandala, Steve, Exec VP-Sls - Univision Communications Inc.; pg. 683, pg. 1307
Mandara, Kim, Assoc Dir-Mktg Comm - National Basketball Association; pg. 566, pg. 1264
Mandel Dunsche, Maria, VP-Mktg & Adv Strategy - AT&T Inc.; pg. 1867, pg. 1674
Mandel, Adam, Mgr-Interactive & US Mktg - Allianz Life Insurance Company of North America; pg. 1188, pg. 929
Mandel, Jay, VP-Digital Mktg-Global - MasterCard Incorporated; pg. 779, pg. 1325
Mandel, Kristen, Mgr-Mktg-Skinny Cow Candy - Nestle USA, Inc.; pg. 883, pg. 96
Mandel, Max, Brand Mgr-Digital - The Finish Line, Inc.; pg. 1769, pg. 686
Mandell, Sarah, Brand Mgr-Remy Martin VS & VSOP - Remy Cointreau USA Inc.; pg. 1969, pg. 1285
Mandelstein, Kathy, Dir-Social Bus Strategy - PricewaterhouseCoopers LLP; pg. 795, pg. 1283
Mandich, Monya, Dir-Mktg-Global - Expedia, Inc.; pg. 1244, pg. 1814
Mandinach, Jason, Product Mgr - Pacific Investment Management Company LLC; pg. 791, pg. 165
Mandir, Laurie, Exec VP-Secondary Mktg - Stearns Lending, LLC.; pg. 805, pg. 262
Mandle, Gary, Sr Product Mgr - Sony Electronics, Inc.; pg. 676, pg. 209
Mandler, Rick, VP-Digital Media Adv - ABC, Inc.; pg. 268, pg. 1185
Mandrillo, Jay, Dir-Bakery Sls & Mdsg-Price Chopper Supermarkets - Golub Corporation; pg. 1021, pg. 1340
Mandujano, Mayra, Specialist-Mktg - The Sports Authority, Inc.; pg. 1846, pg. 326
Manea, Irene, Mgr-Tivoli Worldwide Mktg - International Business Machines Corporation; pg. 418, pg. 1138
Manegold, Todd, Head-Product Mktg-LED, Lamps & Home - Philips Electronics North America; pg. 662, pg. 782
Manegold, Todd, Head-Product Mktg-LED-Lamps & Home - Philips Lighting; pg. 1303, pg. 806
Maneri, Giovanni, Mgr-Mktg Info - Standard Motor Products, Inc.; pg. 218, pg. 1176
Maness, Anne, Sr Mgr-Digital Personalization - The Kroger Co.; pg. 1025, pg. 1416
Maness, Tinsley, Mgr-Mktg - ScanSource, Inc.; pg. 671, pg. 1618
Maney, Tom, Exec VP-Fox Hispanic Media - 20th Century Fox Film Corp.; pg. 267, pg. 124
Manfredi, Frances, Pres-Cable & New Media Distr - NBC Universal, Inc.; pg. 300, pg. 1266
Manfredi, Frances, Pres-Cable & New Media Distr - NBC Universal Television Networks Group; pg. 302, pg. 1267
Manfredi, Justin, Sr Dir-Digital Mktg - Activision Blizzard, Inc.; pg. 948, pg. 271
Mangahis, Roland, Asst Mgr-Mktg - The Allstate Corporation; pg. 1189, pg. 639
Mangalick, Sharad, Sr Product Mgr-Digital Imaging - Adobe Systems Incorporated; pg. 342, pg. 235
Mangalindan, Yvette, Sr Dir-Banana Republic Global CRM - Banana Republic; pg. 1760, pg. 212
Mangan, Jocelyn, Sr VP-Product Mgmt - OpenTable, Inc.; pg. 450, pg. 224
Manganaro, Christina, Sr Mgr-Brand Activation - The Coca-Cola Company; pg. 240, pg. 493
Manganaro, Katie, Reg VP-Mktg - Caesars Entertainment Corporation; pg. 1083, pg. 1023
Manganaro, Yvonne, Sr Dir-Mktg - Gelson's Markets; pg. 1020, pg. 85
Manganello, Christine, Sr Mgr-Enterprise NAR Field Mktg - Alcatel-Lucent USA, Inc.; pg. 615, pg. 1728
Mangano, Claudine A., Dir-Mobile Computing Solutions Media Rels Team - Intel Corporation; pg. 645, pg. 266
Mangano, Liz, Asst Mgr-Production-Boys Apparel - Toys "R" Us, Inc.; pg. 968, pg. 1130
Mangas, Lucy, Dir-Strategic Partner Mktg-Sys Integrators & Outsourcers - EMC Corporation; pg. 391, pg. 825
Mangas, Tim, Mgr-Midwest Sls - Symmetry Medical Inc.; pg. 1600, pg. 699

Mangels, Tonya, VP-Food & Beverage Mktg - AMC Entertainment Inc.; *pg.* 527, *pg.* 716
Mangelsdorf, Kristina, Sr Dir-Global Citizenship & PepsiCo Foundation - PepsiCo, Inc.; *pg.* 259, *pg.* 1327
Mangen, Karly, Assoc Mgr-Mktg - General Mills, Inc.; *pg.* 828, *pg.* 933
Mangeot, Mike, Mgr-PR - United Parcel Service, Inc.; *pg.* 1928, *pg.* 522
Mangham, Melissa, Dir-New Media - The Daily Ardmoreite; *pg.* 1632, *pg.* 1484
Mangia, Karen, Sr Dir & Dir-Global Voice of Customer - Cisco Systems, Inc.; *pg.* 372, *pg.* 240
Mangialardi, Gregg, Grp Product Mgr - Robert Bosch Tool Corp; *pg.* 1060, *pg.* 634
Mangino, Michelle, Mgr-Social Media - athenahealth, Inc.; *pg.* 1497, *pg.* 855
Mangione, Michael, Dir-Consumer Mktg - Bose Corporation; *pg.* 626, *pg.* 820
Manglod, Tina, Sr Mgr-Mktg & Sponsorships - AT&T Mobility LLC; *pg.* 620, *pg.* 1824
Mangold, Elizabeth, Brand Mgr - The Topps Company, Inc.; *pg.* 588, *pg.* 1302
Mangold, Marty, Sr Coord-Mktg - Vascular Solutions, Inc.; *pg.* 1434, *pg.* 946
Mangon, Nicolas, Sr Dir-AEC Indus & Bus Strategy - Autodesk Inc.; *pg.* 356, *pg.* 257
Mangum, Adam, Mgr-Mktg-Plant Nutrition - Land O'Lakes, Inc.; *pg.* 873, *pg.* 915
Mangum, William, Mgr-Utility Sls - Niagara Transformer Corp.; *pg.* 1302, *pg.* 1150
Mangus, Dan, Dir-Mktg - Hobie Cat Company; *pg.* 1708, *pg.* 173
Mani, Divya, Dir-Brand Mktg - The Procter & Gamble Company; *pg.* 1129, *pg.* 1418
Mani, Sumita, Product Mgr - Microsoft Corporation; *pg.* 435, *pg.* 1824
Maniar, Paras, Chief Strategy Officer - ReachLocal, Inc.; *pg.* 1277, *pg.* 308
Manila, Kristen, Coord-Mktg - GEICO Corporation; *pg.* 1200, *pg.* 399
Manin, David, Sr Dir-Mktg - First DataBank, Inc.; *pg.* 397, *pg.* 217
Maniscalco, Michelle, Mgr-Mktg Comm-Media Rels-Global - PolyOne Corporation; *pg.* 1177, *pg.* 1404
Maniscalco, Ralph, Dir-Mktg Comm - Honeywell International Inc.; *pg.* 407, *pg.* 1088
Manista, Stephanie, Mgr-Mktg-Consumer - General Electric Company; *pg.* 1297, *pg.* 347
Manley, Justin, Sr Dir-Bus Dev - Teledyne Benthos, Inc.; *pg.* 1431, *pg.* 838
Manley, Sarah M., Mgr-Talent Community & Mktg - UnitedHealth Group Incorporated; *pg.* 1221, *pg.* 950
Mann, Beverly A., Mgr-Event Mktg - Aetna Inc.; *pg.* 1187, *pg.* 351
Mann, Carrie, Sr Mgr-Mktg - ZIPCAR, INC.; *pg.* 1931, *pg.* 810
Mann, Cathy G., Sr Dir-Mktg & Strategy-Global - Halliburton Company; *pg.* 978, *pg.* 1707
Mann, Garrett, Dir-Content Mktg - TechTarget, Inc.; *pg.* 482, *pg.* 837
Mann, Jessica, Sr Specialist-Social Media - Gilt Groupe Inc.; *pg.* 24, *pg.* 1234
Mann, Laurie, Sr VP-Search Products - Yahoo! Inc.; *pg.* 1289, *pg.* 289
Mann, Lisa, Exec VP-Mktg - Kind LLC; *pg.* 868, *pg.* 1249
Mann, Marissa, Assoc Mgr-Mktg - The Clorox Company; *pg.* 327, *pg.* 169
Mann, Mike, VP & Sr Mgr-Strategy & Plng Digital Channels - TD Bank US Holding Company; *pg.* 809, *pg.* 1051
Mann, Robert, Product Mgr - Robert Half International Inc.; *pg.* 462, *pg.* 145
Mann, Tanya, VP-Design-Global Consumer Products - Mattel Games/Puzzles; *pg.* 962, *pg.* 80
Mann, Tanya, VP-Design-Global Consumer Products - MATTEL, INC.; *pg.* 962, *pg.* 81
Mann, Timothy , Jr., Interim Pres & Interim CEO - Axiall Corporation; *pg.* 69, *pg.* 491
Manna, Julia, Brand Mgr-Global Fragrance Product Innovation - Avon Products, Inc.; *pg.* 500, *pg.* 1198
Manna, Mike, VP-Product Mgmt, Batteries & Energy - Ultralife Corporation; *pg.* 1385, *pg.* 1317
Mannapperuma, Samita, Sr Dir-Bus Dev - NBC Sports Network; *pg.* 300, *pg.* 375
Mannard, Kelly, CMO, Chief Strategy Officer & Exec VP - Northern Trust Corporation; *pg.* 787, *pg.* 585
Manne, Lavanya, Mgr-Digital Mktg - Discover Financial Services; *pg.* 744, *pg.* 653
Mannebach, Liz, Specialist-Comm & Digital Media - Grant Thornton International Ltd.; *pg.* 763, *pg.* 575
Mannheim, Dianna, VP-Creative Adv - Sony Pictures Home Entertainment; *pg.* 310, *pg.* 72
Mannina, Scott, Sr Mgr-Channel Mktg-West - Hewlett-Packard Company; *pg.* 404, *pg.* 175
Manning, Kathleen, Head-Media & Pub Affairs - Monsanto Company; *pg.* 1173, *pg.* 999
Manning, Kristen, Head-Digital Mktg & CRM - Mercedes-Benz USA, LLC; *pg.* 184, *pg.* 514
Manning, Linda A., VP-Sls & Mktg-Minnesota Div - D.R. Horton, Inc.; *pg.* 1090, *pg.* 1694
Manning, Lisa, VP-Mktg - Arizona Cardinals Football Club, Inc.; *pg.* 529, *pg.* 25
Manning, Loretta, Mgr-Mktg Programs-Molecular Pathology, Diagnostics & Genomics - Agilent Technologies, Inc.; *pg.* 614, *pg.* 264
Manning, Lorraine, Sr Planner-Mdse - Barnes & Noble, Inc.; *pg.* 1619, *pg.* 1201
Manning, Mary Ann, VP & Dir-Mktg Comm - Boston Private; *pg.* 726, *pg.* 791
Manning, Melissa, Coord-Mktg - Harley-Davidson, Inc.; *pg.* 178, *pg.* 1874
Manning, Meredith, VP-Global Hemophilia Mktg - Baxter International Inc.; *pg.* 1499, *pg.* 599
Manning, Shandin, Supvr-Media - The Home Depot, Inc.; *pg.* 1050, *pg.* 510
Manning, Stuart, Assoc Mgr-Mktg - Sargento Foods Inc.; *pg.* 894, *pg.* 1886
Manning, Treg, VP-Sls & Mktg-North America - Airbus Helicopters, Inc.; *pg.* 223, *pg.* 1698
Manning, Vicki, Asst VP-Media - The TJX Companies, Inc.; *pg.* 1788, *pg.* 822
Mannis, Avi, Sr VP-Mktg - Hawaiian Airlines, Inc.; *pg.* 1910, *pg.* 543
Mannix, Laura, Mgr-Mktg Effectiveness - Mercer Inc.; *pg.* 1395, *pg.* 1258
Manns, Dennis, Asst VP-Sls & Logistics Plng - American Honda Motor Co., Inc.; *pg.* 163, *pg.* 292
Manohar, Neville, Sr Mgr-Mktg - FCA US LLC; *pg.* 170, *pg.* 868
Manolis, Maggie, Reg Specialist-Mktg-Midwest - US Foods; *pg.* 1036, *pg.* 703
Manoog, Sarah L., Dir-Mktg - Boston Symphony Orchestra Inc.; *pg.* 534, *pg.* 791
Manos, Arlene, Pres-Natl Adv Sls - AMC Networks Inc.; *pg.* 269, *pg.* 1189
Manoufar, Sally, Sr Mgr-Health & Wellness - Johnson & Johnson; *pg.* 1549, *pg.* 1091
Manowitz, Neal, VP-Digital Imaging, Consumer Sls & Mktg - Sony Electronics, Inc.; *pg.* 676, *pg.* 209
Mansergh, Alice, Dir-Consumer Mktg-UK - Google Inc.; *pg.* 1249, *pg.* 153
Mansfield, Aimee, Head-Product Dev - GE Capital; *pg.* 761, *pg.* 362
Mansfield, Catherine, Dir-Mktg Comm-Heavy Civil Construction Div - Trimble Navigation Limited; *pg.* 1384, *pg.* 288
Mansfield, Craig, Sr Mgr-CRM Analytics-Online Store - Apple Inc.; *pg.* 350, *pg.* 73
Mansfield, Matt, VP-Product Innovation - CQ Roll Call; *pg.* 1631, *pg.* 397
Manso, Richard, VP-Interactive Mktg & ECommerce - L'Oreal USA; *pg.* 514, *pg.* 1252
Manson, Julie, Brand Mgr - The Goodyear Tire & Rubber Company; *pg.* 1883, *pg.* 1401
Mantakounis, Irene, Brand Mgr-Pop-Tarts Brand Mktg - Kellogg Company; *pg.* 831, *pg.* 870
Manteau, Carl, Sr Dir-Grp Sls - Milwaukee Bucks, Inc.; *pg.* 563, *pg.* 1878
Mantell, Jon, VP-Digital Products & Video - CBS Interactive, Inc.; *pg.* 369, *pg.* 215
Mantero, Frank, Sr VP-Corp Comm & Mktg - Ansell; *pg.* 1495, *pg.* 1114
Manthorp, John, Dir-US Mktg-Endocrine Care - Pfizer Inc.; *pg.* 1581, *pg.* 1278
Manu, Daniel, Sr Dir-Digital Programming - TruTV; *pg.* 314, *pg.* 1305
Manuel, David, Mgr-Mktg & Sls - Medieval Times Inc.; *pg.* 561, *pg.* 51
Manuel, Mike, Sr Mgr-Mktg-Content & Social Consumer - LinkedIn Corporation; *pg.* 1262, *pg.* 160
Manus, Roger, Mgr-Segment Mktg-Sys Integrators - Schneider Electric; *pg.* 467, *pg.* 1609
Manwarren, Adam, Brand Mgr-Mktg - FMC Corporation; *pg.* 1163, *pg.* 1564
Manzanilla, Nicole, Mgr-Shopper Mktg - Hill's Pet Nutrition, Inc.; *pg.* 1476, *pg.* 721
Manzanilla, Sandra, Mgr-Mktg & Recruiting - New York Life Insurance Company; *pg.* 1211, *pg.* 1268
Manzano, Grace, Dir-Mktg-Sports Nutrition - Natrol, Inc.; *pg.* 1570, *pg.* 64
Manzano, Laura, VP-Sls-Auberge Resorts Collection - Auberge Resorts, LLC; *pg.* 1080, *pg.* 145
Manzi, Danielle, Coord-Mktg - The Hearst Corporation; *pg.* 1649, *pg.* 1239
Manzo, Cindy, Mgr-Mktg Svcs - Church & Dwight Co., Inc.; *pg.* 1153, *pg.* 1063
Mao, Veronica, Mgr-Digital Brand Mktg - Under Armour, Inc.; *pg.* 49, *pg.* 759
Mapes, Tim, Sr VP-Mktg - Delta Air Lines, Inc.; *pg.* 1905, *pg.* 503
Maphumolo, Sithabile, Brand Mgr-Yum! Restaurants International - KFC Corporation; *pg.* 1733, *pg.* 705
Maples, Elizabeth, Sr Mgr-Product Mktg - LinkedIn Corporation; *pg.* 1262, *pg.* 160
Mapleston, Rob, Mgr-Mktg Comm-Measurement Products-Global - ABB Inc. - Automation Technologies Instrumentation Products; *pg.* 1398, *pg.* 1590
Mapleston, Robert, Mgr-Mktg Comm-Measurement Products-Global - ABB Inc.; *pg.* 1309, *pg.* 1359
Maquivar, Memo, VP-Mktg - Altria Group, Inc.; *pg.* 1893, *pg.* 1800
Mara, Bernard M., VP-Mfg-Performance Engineered Products - Carpenter Technology Corporation; *pg.* 73, *pg.* 1584
Marado, Annette, Dir-Mktg - Carpenter Technology Corporation; *pg.* 73, *pg.* 1584
Marafioti, Nathan, Dir-Mktg & ECommerce - Reckitt Benckiser Inc.; *pg.* 1136, *pg.* 1105
Maragno, Brian, Sr Mgr-Large Dealer Groups - Nissan North America, Inc.; *pg.* 186, *pg.* 1633
Maramba, Theresa, Sr Acct Mgr-Adv - Concur Technologies, Inc.; *pg.* 1236, *pg.* 1813
Marandi, Mary, Sr Mgr-Corp Comm - National Association of Professional Baseball Leagues, Inc.; *pg.* 566, *pg.* 463
Marano, Lauren, Brand Mgr - Banfi Vintners; *pg.* 1957, *pg.* 1161
Marasch, Michael, VP-Roll Product Mktg & Sls - Spinnaker Coating, LLC; *pg.* 1470, *pg.* 1477
Marasco, Angelo, Dir-Corp Product Dev - ODL Incorporated; *pg.* 101, *pg.* 914
Marashio, Pete, Acct Mgr-Sls - Parker Chomerics; *pg.* 662, *pg.* 862
Marasigan, Princess, Category Mgr-Mktg - Newegg Inc.; *pg.* 1271, *pg.* 67
Maratea, Joe, VP-Mktg - Valero Energy Corporation; *pg.* 986, *pg.* 1743
Maravich, Sam , Jr., VP-Sls & Mktg - Perseon Corporation; *pg.* 1581, *pg.* 1760
Maravilla, Emelyn, Dir-Peer to Peer Mktg - Boehringer Ingelheim Pharmaceuticals, Inc.; *pg.* 1507, *pg.* 368
Marban, Lesly, VP-Corp Mktg - Medline Industries, Inc.; *pg.* 1562, *pg.* 635
Marburger, Donald, Asst Mgr-Email Mktg - Toys "R" Us, Inc.; *pg.* 968, *pg.* 1130
Marcais, Vincent, Exec VP-Brand & Digital Customer Mktg-Home Entertainment - 20th Century Fox Home Entertainment, Inc.; *pg.* 267, *pg.* 125
Marcantonio, Mike, Dir-Online Mktg - LendingTree, LLC; *pg.* 775, *pg.* 1367
Marcellin, Mike, Sr VP-Strategy, Mktg & Platform Sys Div - Juniper Networks, Inc.; *pg.* 1260, *pg.* 286
March, Jason, Dir-Mktg - Hamilton Co., Inc.; *pg.* 1415, *pg.* 1031
March, Justin, Rep-Product Sls - Weyerhaeuser Company; *pg.* 121, *pg.* 1820
Marchand, Chantale, VP-Mktg - Rand A Technology Corporation; *pg.* 459, *pg.* 774
Marchand, Chantale, VP-Mktg - RAND WORLDWIDE, INC.; *pg.* 459, *pg.* 821
Marchand, Hector, VP-Mktg - NDC Technologies; *pg.* 1423, *pg.* 118
Marchant, Al, VP-After Sls Div - Alimak Hek Inc; *pg.* 66, *pg.* 1749
Marchant, Cathy, Dir-Brand Mktg - Champion Athleticwear Inc.; *pg.* 39, *pg.* 1394
Marchant, Cathy, Dir-Brand Mktg-Champion Athleticwear - Hanesbrands Inc.; *pg.* 26, *pg.* 1394
Marchant, Jennifer, VP-Customer Mktg - Time Inc.; *pg.* 1693,

First page reference indicates Business Class Edition
Second page reference indicates Geographic Edition

pg. 1300
Marchant, Joseph, Mgr-Sls-National - Gerber Legendary Blades; *pg.* 1834, *pg.* 1503
Marchant, Leigh, VP & Dir-Mktg - Penguin Random House; *pg.* 1675, *pg.* 1276
Marchbanks, LeAnn, Mgr-Cause Mktg - American Airlines Group Inc.; *pg.* 224, *pg.* 1693
Marchesano, Serena, Dir-Oral Care Mktg-Colgate Palmolive Canada - Colgate-Palmolive Canada Inc.; *pg.* 503, *pg.* 1937
Marcheschi, Erick, Mgr-Mktg-Global - Specialized Bicycle Components, Inc.; *pg.* 1711, *pg.* 152
Marcheschi, Paula, Mgr-Creative Svcs - KGO Television, Inc.; *pg.* 294, *pg.* 220
Marchese, Amy, Sr Dir-Corp Functions Bus Tech - Pfizer Inc.; *pg.* 1581, *pg.* 1278
Marchese, Anthony, VP-Sls & Mktg - Bush Hog, Inc.; *pg.* 702, *pg.* 8
Marchese, Joe, Pres-Advanced Adv Products-Fox Networks Grp - Twenty-First Century Fox, Inc.; *pg.* 315, *pg.* 1305
Marchetti, Antonella, Category Mgr-Global Procurement Mktg Svcs - Bristol-Myers Squibb Company; *pg.* 1509, *pg.* 1206
Marchioni, Jason, Mgr-Media-Fiat NA - FCA US LLC; *pg.* 170, *pg.* 868
Marchionna, Melissa, Sr Mgr-Digital Programming - New York Jets Football Club, Inc.; *pg.* 570, *pg.* 1067
Marchlik, Michael, Partner & Dir-Natl Sls, Mktg, GA Advisory & Valuation Svcs - GREAT AMERICAN GROUP, INC.; *pg.* 1394, *pg.* 308
Marchwicki, Julius, Product Mgr-SYNC AppLink-Global - Ford Motor Company; *pg.* 172, *pg.* 876
Marciano, Andre, Dir-Media & Integrated Comm - Pernod Ricard USA, Inc.; *pg.* 1968, *pg.* 1332
Marciano, Paul, Chm & Chief Creative Officer - Guess?, Inc.; *pg.* 25, *pg.* 132
Marcinek, John, Dir-Integrated Mktg - National Marine Manufacturers Association; *pg.* 149, *pg.* 584
Marco, Philip, VP-Creative - Chicago Show Inc.; *pg.* 371, *pg.* 560
Marcolini, Heather, Sr Mgr-Acct Mktg - Intuit Inc.; *pg.* 769, *pg.* 158
Marcolla, David, Dir-Product Mktg - AT&T; *pg.* 1865, *pg.* 258
Marconi, Luis G., VP-Mktg - Hormel Foods Corporation; *pg.* 863, *pg.* 915
Marconi, Luis G., VP-Mktg - Hormel Foods Corporation - Foodservice Division; *pg.* 864, *pg.* 916
Marcoon, Barbara, Dir-ECommerce & Digital Mktg - The Robert Allen Group, Inc.; *pg.* 698, *pg.* 819
Marcotte, Eric, Reg Mgr-Sls - Stedman Machine Company; *pg.* 1379, *pg.* 673
Marcotte, Lori, Product Mgr-Readers - FGX International, Inc.; *pg.* 5, *pg.* 1608
Marcotte, Shannon, Mgr-Mktg & Audience Reach - The New York Times; *pg.* 1668, *pg.* 1270
Marcou, Jennifer, Sr Dir-Customer Experience Mktg - Microsoft Corporation; *pg.* 435, *pg.* 1824
Marcoux, Christian, Sr Dir-Legal, Mergers, Acq & Financing - Quebecor Media Inc.; *pg.* 1679, *pg.* 1956
Marcoux, Jeff, CMO-Worldwide Enterprise Mktg - Microsoft Corp.; *pg.* 440, *pg.* 321
Marcoux, Richard F., Pres-Sls - R.R. Donnelley & Sons Company; *pg.* 1682, *pg.* 589
Marcroft, Darlene, VP-PR & Comm - The Ultimate Software Group, Inc.; *pg.* 486, *pg.* 479
Marcucci, Peggy, Sr Mgr-Mktg Comm - Applied Materials, Inc.; *pg.* 618, *pg.* 264
Marcucci, Tom, VP-Sls & Mktg - Gonnella Baking Company; *pg.* 859, *pg.* 575
Marcus, Amanda, Sr Specialist-Mktg - American International Group, Inc.; *pg.* 1190, *pg.* 1193
Marcus, David, VP-Messaging Products - Facebook, Inc.; *pg.* 1245, *pg.* 143
Marcus, Elisa, Mgr-Mktg-Intl - Illinois Bureau of Tourism; *pg.* 995, *pg.* 578
Marcus, Gustavo, Mgr-Natl Sls-Social & Info - Google Inc.; *pg.* 1249, *pg.* 153
Marcus, Lori Tauber, Chief Product Officer & Chief Brand Officer-Global - Keurig Green Mountain, Inc.; *pg.* 868, *pg.* 1768
Marcus, Melanie, VP-Strategic Mktg - McKesson Corporation; *pg.* 1560, *pg.* 222
Marcus, Mike, Dir-Digital Ad Sls Mktg - NBC Sports Network; *pg.* 300, *pg.* 375
Marcus, Mike, Dir-Digital Ad Sls Mktg - NBC Universal, Inc.; *pg.* 300, *pg.* 1266
Marcus, Scott, Brand Mktg Dir-Ritz Franchise - Mondelez International; *pg.* 877, *pg.* 1344
Marcus, Scott, Dir-Mktg-Savory Brands-North America - Mondelez International, Inc.; *pg.* 878, *pg.* 601
Marcy, Maximillian J., Sr Mgr-Treasury & IR - H.B. Fuller Company; *pg.* 1165, *pg.* 961
Marcyes, Lisa, Mgr-Social Media Mktg Channel - Cisco Systems, Inc.; *pg.* 372, *pg.* 240
Marden, Scott, Sr VP-Mktg & Res - Captivate; *pg.* 272, *pg.* 1209
Marder, Alice, Sr Mgr-B2B Brand Strategy - Cars.com; *pg.* 1234, *pg.* 568
Marder, Kalie, Specialist-Mktg - Chevron Corporation; *pg.* 974, *pg.* 259
Marderosian, Karen, VP-Cross-Platform Sls - The Weather Channel LLC; *pg.* 320, *pg.* 523
Mardini, Abdel Karim, Product Mgr - Google Inc.; *pg.* 1249, *pg.* 153
Mardis, Michael, Mgr-Online Mktg - InterCall, Inc.; *pg.* 417, *pg.* 578
Mardon, Susan, Coord-Mktg - Logan's Roadhouse, Inc.; *pg.* 1736, *pg.* 1652
Marecic, Dave, Brand Mgr-Aquafresh - GlaxoSmithKline Consumer Healthcare; *pg.* 510, *pg.* 1554
Marek, Elysse, Sr Assoc Brand Mgr - Georgia-Pacific LLC; *pg.* 1458, *pg.* 507
Marek, Mary-Irene E., Mgr-Social Media - Toys "R" Us, Inc.; *pg.* 968, *pg.* 1130
Marek, Tracy, CMO & Sr VP-Mktg - Cleveland Cavaliers/Quicken Loans Arena; *pg.* 541, *pg.* 1429
Marentic, Amy, Mgr-Global Car & Crossover Grp Mktg - Ford Motor Company; *pg.* 172, *pg.* 876
Marentic, Jeff, Dir-US Sls Ops - Ford Motor Company; *pg.* 172, *pg.* 876
Maresca, Geoff, Reg Dir-Sls - Microsoft Corporation; *pg.* 435, *pg.* 1824
Maresca, Rob, Dir-Mktg-Respiratory - AstraZeneca Pharmaceuticals LP; *pg.* 1497, *pg.* 389
Margan, Kim, Assoc Dir-Publ & Adv - New York Institute of Technology; *pg.* 605, *pg.* 1318
Margaronis, Vitor, Dir-Mktg - BASF Corporation; *pg.* 1149, *pg.* 1066
Margason, Scott, Dir-Product Plng - Hyundai Motor America; *pg.* 179, *pg.* 89
Margavage, Joel, Strategist-Digital Mktg & Media Planner - Bayada Nurses Inc.; *pg.* 1499, *pg.* 1087
Margerum, Barry, Chief Strategy Officer - Plantronics, Inc.; *pg.* 663, *pg.* 270
Margeson, Georgia, Sr Dir-Adv - Church's Chicken, Inc.; *pg.* 1722, *pg.* 493
Margetic, Richard, Dir-Social-Small Bus Grp - Intuit Inc.; *pg.* 769, *pg.* 158
Margida, Vince, Brand Mgr - Johnson & Johnson; *pg.* 1549, *pg.* 1091
Margison, Paul, Product Mgr-Cloud Web Security Svcs - AT&T; *pg.* 1865, *pg.* 258
Margold, John, Sr VP-Sls & Mktg - Rowe International Corp; *pg.* 669, *pg.* 889
Margolis, Laura, Sr Mgr-Corp Rels - The Allstate Corporation; *pg.* 1189, *pg.* 639
Margosian, Steve, Sr VP-Enterprise Sls & Mktg-NBC Sports Grp - NBC Universal, Inc.; *pg.* 300, *pg.* 1266
Mari, Kathleen, Mgr-Mktg - Lackmann Culinary Services; *pg.* 1026, *pg.* 1356
Maria, Carla De, Asst Dir-Mktg & Bus Dev - Simon Property Group, Inc.; *pg.* 1112, *pg.* 690
Maria, Pollock, Sr Coord-Mktg - Southeast Toyota Distributors, LLC; *pg.* 190, *pg.* 421
Mariani, Kristin, Sr Mgr-Corp Comm - Amazon.com, Inc.; *pg.* 1226, *pg.* 1831
Mariano, Bob, Mgr-Digital Mktg - Raley's Inc.; *pg.* 1031, *pg.* 305
Mariano, Jim, Product Mgr-Donations - Constant Contact, Inc.; *pg.* 379, *pg.* 850
Mariano, Lori, Sr Dir-Global Fragrance Mktg - Elizabeth Arden, Inc.; *pg.* 507, *pg.* 448
Mariano, Sandra, Product Mgr-Payments - Google Inc.; *pg.* 1249, *pg.* 153
Marie, Sage, Sr Mgr-Automobile PR - American Honda Motor Co., Inc.; *pg.* 163, *pg.* 292
Marik, Sandor, Sr VP-Mktg - Business Insider; *pg.* 1233, *pg.* 1208
Marill, Edward, Mgr-Sls-Intl - Air Techniques, Inc.; *pg.* 1487, *pg.* 1178
Marin, Francisco, Sr Dir-Product Plng-Dry Grocery - Pinnacle Foods Group LLC; *pg.* 889, *pg.* 1104
Marin, Frank D., Engr-Technical Sls - AT&T; *pg.* 1865, *pg.* 258
Marinaro, Roseanne, Sr Dir-Xfinity Home Field Ops - Comcast Corporation; *pg.* 276, *pg.* 1560
Marine, Bill, Sr Mgr-HR-North America - SI Group, Inc.; *pg.* 1181, *pg.* 1341
Marineau, Dana, VP-Global Creative Team - Electronic Arts Inc.; *pg.* 951, *pg.* 189
Marinelli, Dolores, Asst VP & Mgr-Mktg Comm - The Chubb Corporation; *pg.* 1196, *pg.* 1128
Marini, Rick, Gen Mgr-Digital Product Dev - Hearst Magazines; *pg.* 1649, *pg.* 1239
Marinis, Lisa De, Dir-Mktg - HearUSA, Inc.; *pg.* 1541, *pg.* 457
Marino, Frank, VP-Mktg - Atmos Energy Corporation; *pg.* 1935, *pg.* 1675
Marino, Megan, Dir-Strategic Plng & Mktg-Catalyst Div - BASF Corporation; *pg.* 1149, *pg.* 1066
Marino, Rebecca, Mgr-Design & Production - Factory Mutual Insurance Company; *pg.* 1199, *pg.* 1601
Marino, Robert A., VP-Network Sls - ION Media Networks, Inc.; *pg.* 293, *pg.* 479
Marino, Sara, Sr Analyst-Mktg Comm - CA Technologies; *pg.* 366, *pg.* 1168
Marinos, Alexa, Head-PR & Comm - Hyland Software, Inc.; *pg.* 409, *pg.* 1480
Marion, Kevin, Mgr-South Central US & Canadian Natl Sls - Tech Spray, L.P.; *pg.* 1183, *pg.* 1659
Mark, Alisha, Sr Mgr-PR-Xbox - Microsoft Corporation; *pg.* 435, *pg.* 1824
Mark, Andrew, Product Mgr - Panasonic Corporation of North America; *pg.* 661, *pg.* 1120
Mark, David, Chief Strategy Officer - Flextronics International Ltd.; *pg.* 81, *pg.* 245
Mark, Isaac, Dir-Mktg - JPMorgan Chase & Co.; *pg.* 772, *pg.* 1246
Mark, Jorie, Mgr-Social Media - The Kroger Co.; *pg.* 1025, *pg.* 1416
Mark, Stephane, Dir-Mktg-Individual Insurance & Wealth - Sun Life Financial Inc.; *pg.* 806, *pg.* 1944
Mark, Susy, Dir-Segmentation & Indus Mktg - Xerox Corporation; *pg.* 494, *pg.* 365
Markee, Colleen, Coord-Social Media & Online Content - VITAMIN SHOPPE, INC.; *pg.* 1608, *pg.* 1098
Markel, Elise, Mgr-Mktg Programs - Cisco Systems, Inc.; *pg.* 372, *pg.* 240
Markert, Lauren, Sr Specialist-Mktg - McKesson Corporation; *pg.* 1560, *pg.* 222
Market, Regina, VP-Mktg - IRONPLANET, INC.; *pg.* 1259, *pg.* 183
Markey, Julie, Mktg-Gen Mdse Mission Trips - Wal-Mart Stores, Inc.; *pg.* 1790, *pg.* 29
Markey, Timothy, Sr Mgr-Sls Plng & Alignments - Janssen Pharmaceutica Products, L.P.; *pg.* 1548, *pg.* 1125
Markfield, Roger, Exec Creative Dir - American Eagle Outfitters, Inc.; *pg.* 37, *pg.* 1572
Markgraf, Herb, VP-Mktg - PRT Forest Regeneration Income Fund; *pg.* 1799, *pg.* 1913
Markham, Debbie, Mgr-Field Mktg - NetApp, Inc.; *pg.* 444, *pg.* 287
Markle, Kelly, Product Mgr-Indus Bus Grp - Rust-Oleum Corporation; *pg.* 1447, *pg.* 664
Markle, Martin, Sr Dir-Children's Content - The Canadian Broadcasting Corporation; *pg.* 272, *pg.* 1931
Markle, Pam, Mgr-Pub Sector Field Mktg-Healthcare - Polycom, Inc.; *pg.* 664, *pg.* 249
Markley, Steve, VP-Mdsg - Do It Best Corp.; *pg.* 1045, *pg.* 680
Markovitz, Bill, Mgr-Mktg - 3M Company; *pg.* 1142, *pg.* 956
Markovitz, Catherine, Mgr-Auto Care Mktg - 3M Company; *pg.* 1142, *pg.* 956
Markowicz, Susan, Mgr-Adv-Global - Ford Motor Company; *pg.* 172, *pg.* 876
Markowitz, Andrew, VP-Sls & Mktg-Specialty Metals - Olympic Steel Inc.; *pg.* 101, *pg.* 1433
Markowitz, Andy, Gen Mgr-Performance Mktg Labs - GE Capital; *pg.* 761, *pg.* 362
Markowitz, Michael, Dir-Technical Media Rels - STMicroelectronics, Inc.; *pg.* 676, *pg.* 1671
Markowski, Lisa S., VP-Adv Brand Mgmt & Accessories Global Mktg - Ralph Lauren Corporation; *pg.* 46, *pg.* 1284
Markowski, Sherri M., Sr Dir-Strategy & Bus Dev - LexisNexis Litigation Solutions; *pg.* 1659, *pg.* 1446
Marks, Abby, Dir-Strategic Mktg Partnerships - NBC News; *pg.* 300, *pg.* 1265

Marks, Alan J., Sr Mgr-Product Mktg - Alcatel-Lucent; *pg.* 615, *pg.* 38
Marks, Brian, Dir-Digital & Web Mktg - Aramark; *pg.* 1013, *pg.* 1558
Marks, Cliff, Pres-Sls & Mktg - National CineMedia, Inc.; *pg.* 567, *pg.* 314
Marks, Dawn, VP-Mktg Comm-Global - Anixter International Inc.; *pg.* 1313, *pg.* 614
Marks, Ellen, Mng Dir-Mktg & Comm, Accenture Digital & Accenture Interactive - Accenture; *pg.* 1392, *pg.* 1186
Marks, Janey, Sr Dir-Strategic Alliances - Getty Images, Inc.; *pg.* 1645, *pg.* 1836
Marks, Jeff, Sr Mgr-Customer Mktg - Kashi Company; *pg.* 830, *pg.* 119
Marks, John, Dir-PR - Medline Industries, Inc.; *pg.* 1562, *pg.* 635
Marks, Karen, Dir-Integrated Mktg - Pepperidge Farm, Inc.; *pg.* 888, *pg.* 363
Marks, Kelli, Mgr-CRM Partner Mktg-Retail Web Div - Hewlett-Packard Company; *pg.* 404, *pg.* 175
Marks, Michelle, Sr VP-Mktg & Feature Film Promos - Fox Entertainment Group, Inc.; *pg.* 288, *pg.* 131
Marks, Nancy, Dir-Solution Provider Program Mktg - Constant Contact, Inc.; *pg.* 379, *pg.* 850
Marks, Sean, Sr Dir-Mktg - Kraft Foods Oscar Mayer; *pg.* 870, *pg.* 1866
Markson, Rosemary, Sr VP-TV Mktg-Warner Bros Home Entertainment - Warner Home Video Inc.; *pg.* 319, *pg.* 55
Markus, Dara, Dir-Adv - American Media, Inc.; *pg.* 1615, *pg.* 410
Markus, Eric, Sr Asst Brand Mgr - The Procter & Gamble Company; *pg.* 1129, *pg.* 1418
Markus, Matias, Sr Mgr-Strategic Mktg - Honeywell Aerospace Electronic Systems; *pg.* 228, *pg.* 17
Markus, Rick, VP-Sls & Acct Mgmt - MultiPlan, Inc.; *pg.* 1570, *pg.* 852
Markusen, Lisa, Dir-Event Mktg - adidas America Inc.; *pg.* 1803, *pg.* 1500
Markway Shaw, Kristin, Mgr-Social Media Content - H&R Block, Inc.; *pg.* 764, *pg.* 983
Markway-Meyer, Gerry, Mgr-Corp Sls - Build-A-Bear Workshop, Inc.; *pg.* 950, *pg.* 993
Marlborough, Michelle, VP-Product Strategy - Medidata Solutions, Inc.; *pg.* 431, *pg.* 1258
Marletta, David, Dir-Sls - Smarter Travel Media LLC; *pg.* 1687, *pg.* 801
Marley, Joshua, Mgr-Market-Builder & Retail Sls - Whirlpool Corporation; *pg.* 62, *pg.* 872
Marmer, Daria Axelrod, Product Mgr - LinkedIn Corporation; *pg.* 1262, *pg.* 160
Marmer, Michele, Mgr-Mktg Events - Allscripts Healthcare Solutions, Inc.; *pg.* 1492, *pg.* 563
Marmion, Shane, VP-Product Dev - William S. Hein & Co., Inc.; *pg.* 1702, *pg.* 1151
Marmor-Peters, Stephanie, Mgr-Retail Mktg - adidas America Inc.; *pg.* 1803, *pg.* 1500
Marnell, Sean, Sr Mgr-Customer Solutions - Pernod Ricard USA, Inc.; *pg.* 1968, *pg.* 1332
Maro, Meghan, Sr Mgr-Corp Brand Mgmt - The Walt Disney Company; *pg.* 317, *pg.* 52
Marois, Yann, Exec Dir-Global Mktg-Origins & Ojon - The Estee Lauder Companies Inc.; *pg.* 508, *pg.* 1229
Maron, Jane, Mgr-Mktg - Hewlett-Packard Company; *pg.* 404, *pg.* 175
Marone, Lisa, Mgr-Mktg - RadiSys Corporation; *pg.* 458, *pg.* 1498
Maroney, Claudia, Gen Mgr-Ops & Sls-Rochester West - Frontier Communications Corporation; *pg.* 1871, *pg.* 362
Maroniene, Fernando, Dir-Mktg-Latin America & Caribbean - Adobe Systems Incorporated; *pg.* 342, *pg.* 235
Marovich, Dina, Sr VP-Worldwide Media & Interactive Mktg - Paramount Pictures Corporation; *pg.* 304, *pg.* 138
Marple, Sandy, VP-PR - Neiman Marcus, Inc.; *pg.* 30, *pg.* 1684
Marquard, Callie, Mgr-Mktg & Acct Exec - State Farm Mutual Automobile Insurance Co.; *pg.* 1218, *pg.* 557
Marquard, Donna, Dir-PR-Neuromodulation - Medtronic, Inc.; *pg.* 1564, *pg.* 939
Marquardt, Brian, Grp Product Mgr-Ads & Shopping - Google Inc.; *pg.* 1249, *pg.* 153
Marquardt, Jack, Sr Dir-Strategic Insights, Portfolio & Brand Strategy - Frito-Lay North America, Inc.; *pg.* 1853, *pg.* 1730
Marquardt, Randy, VP-Mktg-Global - Club Car, Inc.; *pg.* 1830, *pg.* 532
Marquart, Brian, Grp Product Mgr-video - YouTube, LLC; *pg.* 1291, *pg.* 198
Marquart, Seth, Specialist-Demand Generation Performance Mktg - International Business Machines Corporation; *pg.* 418, *pg.* 1138
Marques, Daniel, Dir-Online Mktg - The Talbots, Inc.; *pg.* 34, *pg.* 824
Marques, Mari, Mgr-Mktg-Global - P.F. Chang's China Bistro, Inc.; *pg.* 1030, *pg.* 24
Marques, Ricardo, VP-Mktg - Anheuser-Busch Companies, LLC; *pg.* 237, *pg.* 991
Marques, Sonya, Assoc Mgr-Customer Mktg - General Mills Canada Corp.; *pg.* 828, *pg.* 1926
Marquez, Angelique, Mgr-Media - Apollo Education Group Inc.; *pg.* 597, *pg.* 14
Marquez, Elizabell Rivera, Dir-Mktg - Nestle USA, Inc.; *pg.* 883, *pg.* 96
Marquez, Eva, Brand Dir-Global Product-Autoimmune - Eli Lilly and Company; *pg.* 1527, *pg.* 684
Marquez, Lorenzo, VP-Mktg-North America - Cosentino USA; *pg.* 77, *pg.* 1745
Marquez, Lourdes, Mgr-Media-Offline - Universal Orlando; *pg.* 590, *pg.* 456
Marquina, Stewart, Dir-Mktg-Red Lobster - Olive Garden Italian Restaurant; *pg.* 1742, *pg.* 454
Marquina, Stewart, Dir-Mktg - Red Lobster; *pg.* 1747, *pg.* 455
Marquis, C. Decker, Sr VP & Dir-Digital, Social Media & Multi-Channel Mktg - SANTANDER HOLDINGS USA, INC.; *pg.* 801, *pg.* 800
Marr, Sue, Mgr-Mktg-Australia - Thai Airways International Ltd.; *pg.* 1925, *pg.* 83
Marra, Bob, Gen Mgr-Sls - WPIX, Inc.; *pg.* 322, *pg.* 1316
Marra, Greg, Product Mgr-News Feed - Facebook, Inc.; *pg.* 1245, *pg.* 143
Marraccini, Damon, Dir-Product Mgmt, Mobile Commerce & User Experience - Dick's Sporting Goods, Inc.; *pg.* 1832, *pg.* 1524
Marrara, Jennifer, Mgr-ECommerce Mktg - rue21, inc.; *pg.* 32, *pg.* 1591
Marraro, Francesca, VP-Mktg & Comm - Health Management Systems, Inc.; *pg.* 1540, *pg.* 1238
Marrero, Luis, Dir-Sls - Oracle Corporation; *pg.* 1272, *pg.* 786
Marrin, Amy, Mgr-Mktg Comm - Eastman Chemical Company; *pg.* 1159, *pg.* 1636
Marrin, Laura, Specialist-Internet Mktg - Canon U.S.A., Inc.; *pg.* 1404, *pg.* 1178
Marriott, Bill, Mgr-Corp Partnership Sls - Baltimore Orioles, L.P.; *pg.* 532, *pg.* 755
Marron, Matthew, Sr Mgr-Acct Mgmt-Mktg Solutions - LinkedIn Corporation; *pg.* 1262, *pg.* 160
Marron, Tim, Sr Mgr-Site Plng - Expedia, Inc.; *pg.* 1244, *pg.* 1814
Marroquin, Juan Carlos, VP-Sls & Mktg-Fiber Glass Sys - National Oilwell Varco, Inc.; *pg.* 1364, *pg.* 1712
Marroquin, Tracine, VP-Mktg & Product - Jacuzzi Brands Corporation; *pg.* 554, *pg.* 65
Marrus, Christopher R., Sr VP-Sls - Stryker Mako; *pg.* 1598, *pg.* 427
Mars, Steve, VP-Mktg - Madison Square Garden Network; *pg.* 297, *pg.* 1255
Marsal, Kalle, VP-Product Mgmt-Inkjet Printing - Hewlett-Packard Company; *pg.* 404, *pg.* 175
Marsaud, Didier, Sr Mgr-Corp Comm - Nissan Canada Inc.; *pg.* 214, *pg.* 1928
Marschner, Steve, Sr Mgr-R&D - General Mills, Inc.; *pg.* 828, *pg.* 933
Marsden, Graeme, Mgr-Mktg Comm - Cole Hersee Company; *pg.* 202, *pg.* 792
Marsden, Maggie, Acct Mgr-Mktg - Accenture; *pg.* 1392, *pg.* 1186
Marsh, Charlene, Sr Mgr-Mktg Comm - Microsoft Corporation; *pg.* 435, *pg.* 1824
Marsh, Chuck, Dir-Mktg - Jarco/U.S. Castings; *pg.* 1051, *pg.* 1127
Marsh, Deborah, Specialist-Mktg - PerkinElmer, Inc.; *pg.* 1426, *pg.* 853
Marsh, Isabel, VP-Display Adv-Global Digital Mktg - Citigroup Inc.; *pg.* 735, *pg.* 1212
Marsh, Jake, VP-Sls - Frosty Acres Brands, Inc.; *pg.* 1020, *pg.* 484
Marsh, Jim, Dir-Digital & Social Media - Home Box Office, Inc.; *pg.* 290, *pg.* 1240
Marsh, Jim, Mgr-Content & Brand Mgr - Moog Inc.; *pg.* 231, *pg.* 1156
Marsh, Lawrence C., Exec VP & Chief Strategy Officer-New Market Dev - AmerisourceBergen Corporation; *pg.* 1493, *pg.* 1522
Marsh, Melissa, Sr Dir-Go-To-Market - Rogers Communications Inc.; *pg.* 668, *pg.* 1942
Marsh, Roger, Mgr-Mktg-Corp & Independent Accounts - GlaxoSmithKline; *pg.* 1536, *pg.* 1565
Marsh, Roger, Mgr-Mktg-Corp & Independent Accounts - GlaxoSmithKline Consumer Healthcare; *pg.* 510, *pg.* 1554
Marsh, Stacey, Sr Dir-Mktg & Comm - Fossil Group, Inc.; *pg.* 5, *pg.* 1735
Marsh, Troy, Reg Mgr-Gas Mktg - Anadarko Petroleum Corporation; *pg.* 971, *pg.* 1746
Marshall, Amy, Specialist-Global Revision Knee Mktg Comm - Zimmer Biomet Holdings, Inc.; *pg.* 1611, *pg.* 699
Marshall, Beth, Mgr-Mktg - Cisco Systems, Inc.; *pg.* 372, *pg.* 240
Marshall, Beth, Dir-Email Mktg - Zurich Holding Company of America, Inc.; *pg.* 1224, *pg.* 660
Marshall, Chris, Dir-Creative, Brand & Client Integration - Rogers Communications Inc.; *pg.* 000, *pg.* 1942
Marshall, Chuck, Dir-US Surgical Mktg - Alcon; *pg.* 1399, *pg.* 530
Marshall, Daniel, Dir-Mktg - Levenger Company; *pg.* 1776, *pg.* 421
Marshall, Debra, VP-Mktg - Health Fitness Corporation; *pg.* 1539, *pg.* 937
Marshall, Eddie, Dir-Media - Fred's Inc.; *pg.* 1769, *pg.* 1644
Marshall, Erin, Sr Asst Brand Mgr - P&G-Clairol, Inc.; *pg.* 519, *pg.* 1418
Marshall, Jennifer, Dir-PR - Apollo Education Group Inc.; *pg.* 597, *pg.* 14
Marshall, Joanne, Mgr-Mktg-Batiste Dry Shampoo - Church & Dwight Co., Inc.; *pg.* 1153, *pg.* 1063
Marshall, Kari, Sr Dir-Media - T-Mobile US, Inc.; *pg.* 676, *pg.* 1816
Marshall, Kim A., Reg Mgr-Mdsg - Wal-Mart Stores, Inc.; *pg.* 1790, *pg.* 29
Marshall, Laura, Asst Mgr-Mktg - Knouse Foods Cooperative Inc.; *pg.* 869, *pg.* 1558
Marshall, Leslie, Dir-Events, Magazine & Social Media - MORNINGSTAR, INC.; *pg.* 784, *pg.* 583
Marshall, Linda, Bus Mgr - Wichita Symphony Society Inc.; *pg.* 592, *pg.* 724
Marshall, Loraine, Mgr-Retail Adv - The News-Times; *pg.* 1670, *pg.* 344
Marshall, Markeisha, Mgr-Media Rels - Walgreen Co.; *pg.* 1608, *pg.* 605
Marshall, Paige, Brand Mgr - Bush Brothers & Company; *pg.* 843, *pg.* 1636
Marshall, Robby, Brand Mgr-Digital-Emerging Markets - NIKE, Inc.; *pg.* 1812, *pg.* 1492
Marshall, Robert, Product Mgr-Fisher Science Education - Thermo Fisher Scientific Inc.; *pg.* 1431, *pg.* 854
Marshall, Sarah, Mgr-PR - RealPage, Inc.; *pg.* 1277, *pg.* 1669
Marshall, Shellie, Dir-Media - Discovery Communications, Inc.; *pg.* 282, *pg.* 777
Marshall, Stacey, Sr Mgr-Field Mktg - Oracle Corporation; *pg.* 450, *pg.* 191
Marshall, Stacie, Brand Mgr - Salem Media Group, Inc.; *pg.* 307, *pg.* 57
Marshall, Steve, Mgr-Mktg - Sturtevant Inc.; *pg.* 1379, *pg.* 824
Marshall, Todd, Sr Mgr-Mktg - ACCO Brands Corporation; *pg.* 340, *pg.* 626
Marshall, Todd, Sr VP-Mktg - Target Corporation; *pg.* 1786, *pg.* 942
Marshall, Trever, Mgr-Ops-Mktg & Employer Solutions - Capella Education Company; *pg.* 599, *pg.* 931
Marshburn, Catherine, Dir-Consumer Activation & Interactive Mktg - Busch Gardens Tampa Bay; *pg.* 535, *pg.* 472
Marshiano, Lea, Sr Mgr-Mktg - Nine West Holdings, Inc.; *pg.* 1815, *pg.* 1272
Marsinach, Olivia, Dir-Mktg-Global - Merck Animal Health; *pg.* 1478, *pg.* 1124
Marso, Pete, Product Mgr - MICO, Incorporated; *pg.* 212, *pg.* 951
Marson, John, Sr Mgr-Media Plng - The Kraft Heinz Company; *pg.* 871, *pg.* 641
Marston, Marguerite, Mgr-PR - Ikea North America Services LLC; *pg.* 929, *pg.* 1523
Martel, Alfredo V., Sr VP-Mktg - CARIBOU COFFEE COMPANY, INC.; *pg.* 1764, *pg.* 932
Martel, Frederick, VP-Sls & Mktg - Audemars Piguet (North America); *pg.* 1, *pg.* 1198
Martel, Michael L., Engr-Product Mktg - Speedline Technologies, Inc.; *pg.* 1378, *pg.* 823

First page reference indicates Business Class Edition
Second page reference indicates Geographic Edition

Martell, Bridget A., Chief Medical Officer & VP-Clinical Product Dev - Juniper Pharmaceuticals; pg. 1552, pg. 797
Martell, Fran, Product Mgr-Trade Capabilities-Global - Citigroup Inc.; pg. 735, pg. 1212
Martell, Jose, Sr Mgr-Technical Mktg - Brocade Communications Systems, Inc.; pg. 365, pg. 239
Martell, Karen, Head-Local Mktg - Square Inc.; pg. 473, pg. 228
Martell, Matt, Mgr-Product Mktg - Columbia Sportswear Company; pg. 1830, pg. 1501
Martell, Pat, Dir-Health Sciences Mktg - Waters Corporation; pg. 1436, pg. 834
Martelle, Brandon, Specialist-Mktg Capability - Alliance Data Systems Corporation; pg. 347, pg. 1729
Martellotti, Melissa, Dir-PR & Mktg Comm-Pet Specialty - Mars Petcare; pg. 1478, pg. 1633
Martens, Bonnie, Specialist-Mktg Comm - Humphrey Products Corporation; pg. 1300, pg. 894
Martens, Dick, Mgr-Sls-Intl - Weinbrenner Shoe Company, Inc.; pg. 1822, pg. 1871
Martens, Michael, VP-Trade Book Sls - Dark Horse Comics, Inc.; pg. 1633, pg. 1500
Martens, Scott, Bus Mgr - Milwaukee Brewers Baseball Club, Inc.; pg. 562, pg. 1878
Martens, Theresa, Mgr-Mktg-Global - Fisher-Price, Inc.; pg. 953, pg. 1156
Marti, Elizabeth Beltran, Dir-Mktg Activation - Build-A-Bear Workshop, Inc.; pg. 950, pg. 993
Martignetti, Charles A., Exec Dir-eServices, eSupport & Social Media Care - AT&T Inc.; pg. 1867, pg. 1674
Martin, Aaron, VP-Sls - Radiator Specialty Company; pg. 215, pg. 1380
Martin, Alisha, Sr Mgr-External Comm - AstraZeneca Pharmaceuticals LP; pg. 1497, pg. 389
Martin, Allyson, Sr Dir-Shopper Mktg - Wilton Products, Inc.; pg. 1140, pg. 672
Martin, Alvaro, VP-Sls Latin America - Harmonic, Inc.; pg. 402, pg. 246
Martin, Amy, Dir-Mktg - Constellation Brands, Inc.; pg. 1960, pg. 1348
Martin, Andrea, Mgr-Conference Mktg - The New York Times Company; pg. 1668, pg. 1270
Martin, Andrea Fleming, Dir-Americas Channel Mktg Programs, SMB & Cloud - Symantec Corporation; pg. 478, pg. 161
Martin, Angela, Sr Dir-Mktg - Dollar General Corporation; pg. 1767, pg. 1635
Martin, April, Dir-Claim Mktg & Comm - The Travelers Companies, Inc.; pg. 1220, pg. 352
Martin, August, VP-Mktg & Digital Content Partnerships - 20th Century Fox Film Corp.; pg. 267, pg. 124
Martin, Beth, Sr Writer-Mktg - Mentor Graphics Corporation; pg. 432, pg. 1510
Martin, Bill, Product Mgr - Rockwell Automation, Inc.; pg. 668, pg. 1880
Martin, Carolyn, Dir-Mktg Program - IBM Canada Limited; pg. 411, pg. 1923
Martin, Chris, Sr Planner-Comml Vehicle Bus Unit Strategy & Sls Ops Support - Nissan North America, Inc.; pg. 186, pg. 1633
Martin, Christie, Product Mgr-Thornton BU - Mettler-Toledo International Inc.; pg. 1423, pg. 1441
Martin, Christina, VP-Digital Mktg - MoneyGram International, Inc.; pg. 783, pg. 1684
Martin, Christine, Sr Mgr-Strategic Plng - American Express Company; pg. 712, pg. 1190
Martin, Crystal, Product Mgr - Crosman Corporation; pg. 951, pg. 1143
Martin, Dan, VP-Sls & Liberator Foodservice - Carolina Beverage Corporation; pg. 239, pg. 1390
Martin, Daniele, Mgr-Mktg - The Muralo Company; pg. 1444, pg. 1042
Martin, David, Dir-Sls Tire Supply & Specialty Rubber - AMERICAN TIRE DISTRIBUTORS HOLDINGS, INC.; pg. 199, pg. 1379
Martin, David, Sr VP & Head-Sls, Mktg & Ops-Global - CoreLogic, Inc.; pg. 1198, pg. 109
Martin, Dianne, Dir-Concept Dev & Global Strategic Mktg - LifeCell Corporation; pg. 1556, pg. 1045
Martin, Dina, Sr Project Mgr-Digital & Social Media - Macy's, Inc.; pg. 1778, pg. 1417
Martin, Ed, Sr Mgr-Indus Strategy - Autodesk Inc.; pg. 356, pg. 257
Martin, Emily, Sr Acct Exec-Digital Mktg - Adobe Systems Incorporated; pg. 342, pg. 235
Martin, Emily, Assoc-Mktg Supervising-Energy Sector - Ernst & Young Global Limited; pg. 748, pg. 1228
Martin, Eric, Coord-Mktg - The CW Television Network; pg. 632, pg. 52
Martin, Eve, Assoc Mgr-Mktg Ops Support - Sigma-Aldrich Corporation; pg. 1181, pg. 1003
Martin, Ezra, Dir-North America Brand Mktg-Energy & Concepts - NIKE, Inc.; pg. 1812, pg. 1492
Martin, Federico San, VP-Global Consumer Products - The Jim Henson Company; pg. 293, pg. 103
Martin, Gary, VP-Sls, Mktg & Svc Programs-Bombardier Aerospace - Bombardier Inc.; pg. 1318, pg. 1953
Martin, Gina, Sr Mgr-Mktg Comm-Customer Mktg - Bausch & Lomb Incorporated; pg. 1401, pg. 1045
Martin, Grady, Dir-Sls - Plains Cotton Cooperative Association; pg. 697, pg. 1726
Martin, Greg, Mgr-Retail Mktg - FCA US LLC; pg. 170, pg. 868
Martin, Jack M., Dir-PR - Northrop Grumman Corporation; pg. 231, pg. 1781
Martin, Jacob, Brand Mgr-Digestive Health - Prestige Brands Holdings, Inc.; pg. 520, pg. 1345
Martin, Jamal, Mgr-Mktg & Electronics - Wal-Mart Stores, Inc.; pg. 1790, pg. 29
Martin, James, Dir-Product Line-Instant Comm-Enterprise Cloud Applications - Alcatel-Lucent; pg. 615, pg. 38
Martin, Jane, Dir-Mktg - Castle Brands Inc.; pg. 239, pg. 1209
Martin, Jasmine, Mgr-Mktg - Sony Music Entertainment; pg. 309, pg. 1294
Martin, Jeff, Exec VP-Sls & Mktg - Utz Quality Foods, Inc.; pg. 907, pg. 1536
Martin, Jennifer, Dir-Sls - American Licorice Co. Inc.; pg. 1850, pg. 692
Martin, Jennifer, Sr Strategist-Social Media - Sony Electronics, Inc.; pg. 676, pg. 209
Martin, Jenny, Assoc Dir-Creative & Copy - Wells Fargo & Company; pg. 819, pg. 232
Martin, Jill, Creative Dir-GILI Collection - QVC Inc; pg. 305, pg. 1593
Martin, Jim, VP-Mktg & Mgr-Adv - Richlee Shoe Company; pg. 1818, pg. 769
Martin, John A., VP-Sls-North America - Gildan Activewear Inc.; pg. 1835, pg. 1955
Martin, Jon, Dir-Managed Care & Brand Mktg - Merck & Co., Inc.; pg. 1566, pg. 1077
Martin, Josh, Dir-Digital & Social Media - Arby's Restaurant Group, Inc.; pg. 1014, pg. 488
Martin, Kenny, Sr VP-Digital Mktg-Paid Search - Bank of America Corporation; pg. 718, pg. 1362
Martin, Kenyata, Dir-Mktg-Innovation-Pizza - Nestle USA, Inc.; pg. 883, pg. 96
Martin, Kim, Chief Strategy Officer - Meredith Corporation; pg. 1663, pg. 705
Martin, Kimberly, VP-Partner Strategy & Sls - Citrix Systems, Inc.; pg. 375, pg. 424
Martin, Kyle, Dir-Mktg-Brand & Shopper Mktg Integration - Frito-Lay North America, Inc.; pg. 1853, pg. 1730
Martin, Lee, Sr VP-Sls-Europe - Getty Images, Inc.; pg. 1645, pg. 1836
Martin, Leigh, Sr Mgr-Strategy & Plng-Global Partner Mktg - Cisco Systems, Inc.; pg. 372, pg. 240
Martin, Linda M., Mgr-Adv - Wright & McGill Co.; pg. 1848, pg. 324
Martin, Lindsay, Media Planner - Graham Holdings Company; pg. 1645, pg. 1773
Martin, Luis Alfonso, Sr Mgr-Global Comml Strategy HCV - AbbVie Inc.; pg. 1486, pg. 638
Martin, Mark, VP-Mktg & Intl Markets - S.C. Johnson & Son, Inc.; pg. 334, pg. 1889
Martin, Matt, VP-Mktg - Family Dollar Stores, Inc.; pg. 1768, pg. 1382
Martin, Matt, Sr Mgr - Home Box Office, Inc.; pg. 290, pg. 1240
Martin, Matt, Sr Dir-Strategy & Ops - Sam's Club; pg. 1783, pg. 29
Martin, Megan, Mgr-Mktg-Accenture Credit Svcs - Accenture; pg. 1392, pg. 1186
Martin, Megan, Brand Mgr-Campbell's Homestyle - Campbell Soup Company; pg. 844, pg. 1048
Martin, Michele, Sr Mgr-Sls Performance Mgmt - TD Bank US Holding Company; pg. 809, pg. 1051
Martin, Mike, Mgr-Sls-FOX 5 Local & Digital - Tribune Media Company; pg. 1696, pg. 592
Martin, Nathaniel, III, Sr Mgr-Sourcing & Procurement, Food & Beverage - The Walt Disney Company; pg. 317, pg. 52
Martin, Nicki, Coord-Mktg - Jack Schwartz Shoes, Inc.; pg. 1810, pg. 1245
Martin, Patricia, Sr VP & Gen Mgr-Mktg - Boston Proper, Inc.; pg. 20, pg. 410
Martin, Peter, Sr Product Mgr-Risk - Google Inc.; pg. 1249, pg. 153
Martin, Quinton R., VP-Community Mktg - Coca-Cola North America; pg. 848, pg. 500
Martin, Ramon, Head-Global Merchant Sls & Solutions - Visa Inc.; pg. 816, pg. 230
Martin, Ric, VP-Sls-Western Zone - Bunn-O-Matic Corporation; pg. 53, pg. 661
Martin, Ricardo, VP-Mktg-Unilever Canada - Unilever Canada Inc.; pg. 903, pg. 1946
Martin, Ronda, Acct Exec-Adv-Charter Media - Charter Communications, Inc.; pg. 274, pg. 372
Martin, Ross, Exec VP-Mktg Strategy & Engagement - Viacom Inc.; pg. 316, pg. 1310
Martin, Ryan, Dir-Mktg - E&J Gallo Winery; pg. 1962, pg. 149
Martin, Sam, Sr Dir-Digital Mktg & Sls-Global - Timex Corporation; pg. 14, pg. 355
Martin, Sam, Dir-Trade Mktg - The WhiteWave Foods Company; pg. 1037, pg. 324
Martin, Samantha, Dir-Mktg - CB Richard Ellis Group, Inc.; pg. 1085, pg. 127
Martin, Scott, Sr Mgr - The Boeing Company; pg. 225, pg. 567
Martin, Scott, Dir-Adv Ops - The New York Times; pg. 1668, pg. 1270
Martin, Serge, VP-Mktg & Strategic Plng - AGC Glass North America, Inc.; pg. 65, pg. 482
Martin, Sherry, Mgr-Natl Adv Copy - The Home Depot, Inc.; pg. 1050, pg. 510
Martin, Silvia San, Dir-Sls-Omni Nashville Hotel - Omni Hotels & Resorts; pg. 1107, pg. 1685
Martin, Steven, Sr Dir-Mktg - Finger Lakes Racing Association Inc.; pg. 548, pg. 1160
Martin, Stuart, VP-Mktg - Zumiez Inc.; pg. 16, pg. 1822
Martin, Suzanne, Head-Global People Dev, Brand & Mktg - Google Inc.; pg. 1249, pg. 153
Martin, Tambra, VP-Mktg - Medline Industries, Inc.; pg. 1562, pg. 635
Martin, Ted, Asst VP & Sr Mgr-RIA Channel Mktg - T. Rowe Price Group Inc.; pg. 808, pg. 759
Martin, Tim, Mgr-Suite Sls - Arizona Diamondbacks; pg. 529, pg. 14
Martin, Tim, Dir-Mktg - The Scotts Miracle-Gro Company; pg. 1799, pg. 1459
Martin, Todd, Sr Mgr-Mktg Ops - Wal-Mart Stores, Inc.; pg. 1790, pg. 29
Martin, Tony, Mgr-Mktg Comm - Honeywell International Inc.; pg. 407, pg. 1088
Martin, Trevor, Mgr-Social Media Mktg - The Nature Conservancy; pg. 151, pg. 1774
Martin, Wes, Deputy Gen Mgr-Product Support - Hensley Industries, Inc.; pg. 1166, pg. 1682
Martin, Whitney, Mgr-Mktg-Wholesale & Outlet - Kate Spade LLC; pg. 28, pg. 1248
Martin, Yvahn, Sr Mgr-Digital Mktg - V.F. Corporation; pg. 34, pg. 1376
Martin, Yvette, Product Mgr - Quorum Information Technologies Inc.; pg. 458, pg. 1904
Martin-Hill, Felicia, Sr Brand Mgr-Social Engagement & Cause Mktg - Sprint Corporation; pg. 1874, pg. 719
Martinage, Lou, Sr Product Mgr-Alert Customer Engagement Platform - MicroStrategy, Inc.; pg. 1266, pg. 1809
Martinazzi, Peter, Dir-Product Mgmt - Facebook, Inc.; pg. 1245, pg. 143
Martindill, Darren, Mgr-Sls - Hamamatsu Corporation; pg. 1415, pg. 1046
Martinek, Katie, Mgr-Mktg & ECommerce - Harley-Davidson, Inc.; pg. 178, pg. 1874
Martinek, Rich, Mgr-Adv-Chevrolet - General Motors Company; pg. 175, pg. 881
Martinelli, Carrie, Mgr-Mktg Comm - Cree Inc.; pg. 631, pg. 1371
Martinelli, David, Mgr-Digital Mktg - McDonald's Corporation; pg. 1737, pg. 645
Martinelli, John, Mgr-Sls-Natl - KCRA-TV; pg. 293, pg. 196
Martinette, Jill, Mgr-Mktg-Western Reg - Mercedes-Benz USA, LLC; pg. 184, pg. 514
Martinez, Adriana, Specialist-Mktg - Rosetta Stone Inc.; pg. 462, pg. 1774
Martinez, Adriana, Analyst-Natl Customer Mktg - Wm. Wrigley Jr. Company; pg. 1863, pg. 596

Martinez, Alejandra, Sr Product Specialist-Private Brands-Juniors Apparel - J.C. Penney Company, Inc.; *pg.* 1774, *pg.* 1732
Martinez, Alejandro, Mgr-Intl Strategic Mktg - Honeywell International Inc.; *pg.* 407, *pg.* 1088
Martinez, Alisa, Sr Mgr-Brand PR-Global - Starbucks Corporation; *pg.* 897, *pg.* 1840
Martinez, Argelia, Mgr-Media-Snacks & Morning Star Farms - Kellogg Company; *pg.* 831, *pg.* 870
Martinez, Audrey, Mgr-Mktg - Jacuzzi Brands Corporation; *pg.* 554, *pg.* 65
Martinez, Chela, Sr Mgr-Mktg & Sls Ops - DIRECTV Group Holdings, LLC; *pg.* 281, *pg.* 79
Martinez, Christian, Head-Sls-US Hispanic - Facebook, Inc.; *pg.* 1245, *pg.* 143
Martinez, Cosette, Specialist-Digital & Social Media Partnerships - Telemundo Network Inc.; *pg.* 311, *pg.* 430
Martinez, Dan, Sr Dir-PR - Golden State Warriors, LLC; *pg.* 550, *pg.* 171
Martinez, Dave, VP-Sls - D'Arrigo Bros. Company; *pg.* 852, *pg.* 197
Martinez, Deyanira, Office Mgr-Adv & Sls Support - The New York Times Company; *pg.* 1668, *pg.* 1270
Martinez, Dinna, VP & Product Mgr - Wells Fargo & Company; *pg.* 819, *pg.* 232
Martinez, Erma, Mgr-Inside Sls - Allfast Fastening Systems, Inc.; *pg.* 1041, *pg.* 66
Martinez, Felix, Sr VP-Intl Offshore Sls - Pan-American Life Insurance Company; *pg.* 1213, *pg.* 747
Martinez, Fernanda, Dir-Sls Promos - Univision Communications Inc.; *pg.* 683, *pg.* 1307
Martinez, Gabriel T., Corp Counsel-Adv & Mktg - The Clorox Company; *pg.* 327, *pg.* 169
Martinez, George, VP-Corp Mktg & Security Products Grp - Mace Security International, Inc.; *pg.* 1172, *pg.* 1541
Martinez, Helena, Dir-Mktg - Continucare Corporation; *pg.* 1518, *pg.* 442
Martinez, Ingrid, VP-Mktg - Pollo Campero; *pg.* 1782, *pg.* 1685
Martinez, Jennifer, Dir-Media Rels-Corp Comm - CNA Insurance Companies; *pg.* 1198, *pg.* 571
Martinez, Jesus, Mgr-Mktg-Latin America - Brown-Forman Corporation; *pg.* 1958, *pg.* 732
Martinez, Joanna, Mgr-Media Solutions - Yahoo! Inc.; *pg.* 1289, *pg.* 289
Martinez, Joel, Sr Mgr-Product Plng - Altera Corporation; *pg.* 348, *pg.* 237
Martinez, John, Mgr-Sls - TCI Precision Metals, Inc.; *pg.* 1380, *pg.* 95
Martinez, Juan, Sr Mgr-Tech - Sony Corporation of America; *pg.* 675, *pg.* 1293
Martinez, Kevin, VP-Mktg - The Baseball Club of Seattle, L.P.; *pg.* 532, *pg.* 1833
Martinez, Kris, Mgr-Digital Mktg - Greater Milwaukee Convention & Visitors Bureau; *pg.* 993, *pg.* 1874
Martinez, Lucas, Mgr-Mktg-TEVA - Deckers Outdoor Corporation; *pg.* 1807, *pg.* 100
Martinez, Lucinda, Sr VP-Multicultural Mktg - Home Box Office, Inc.; *pg.* 290, *pg.* 1240
Martinez, Luis, Asst Mgr-Product Mktg-Core - Belkin International, Inc.; *pg.* 361, *pg.* 182
Martinez, Marta, Head-Video Sls-Global - AOL Inc.; *pg.* 1229, *pg.* 1195
Martinez, Melissa, Sr Analyst-Mktg-Media Strategy - American Honda Motor Co., Inc.; *pg.* 163, *pg.* 292
Martinez, Melissa E., VP-New Product Dev - Allegheny Technologies Incorporated; *pg.* 66, *pg.* 1572
Martinez, Michael, Mgr-On-Premise Sls Activation - Anheuser-Busch Companies, LLC; *pg.* 237, *pg.* 991
Martinez, Roxanna, Assoc Mgr-Mktg-Chili's Grill & Bar - Brinker International, Inc.; *pg.* 1718, *pg.* 1676
Martinez, Roxanna, Assoc Mgr-Mktg-Chili's Grill & Bar - Chili's, Inc.; *pg.* 1722, *pg.* 1677
Martinez, Sonia, VP-Mktg - United Business Media LLC; *pg.* 1697, *pg.* 1177
Martinez, Trisha Kunst, Mgr-Digital Mktg Strategy - Ford Motor Company; *pg.* 172, *pg.* 876
Martinez-Escobar, Christine, VP & Dir-Sls - Univision Communications Inc.; *pg.* 683, *pg.* 1307
Martinez-Interiano, Alberto, Head-Developer Mktg & Comms - Microsoft Corporation; *pg.* 435, *pg.* 1824
Martinez-Lopez, Ruben E., Rep-Mktg Dev - Blackboard Inc.; *pg.* 1232, *pg.* 396
Martini, Anibal, Dir-Mktg-Global - Mars, Incorporated; *pg.* 1858, *pg.* 1792
Martini, Anibal, Dir-Global Mktg-M & M's - Mars North America; *pg.* 1859, *pg.* 1072
Martini, Erika, Assoc Mgr-Mktg - Storck USA, L.P.; *pg.* 1862, *pg.* 591
Martino, Christine, VP-Natl Ad Sls-Eastern - Screenvision Cinema Network LLC; *pg.* 581, *pg.* 1290
Martino, David, Dir-Creative Svcs - Schlotzsky's, Ltd.; *pg.* 1749, *pg.* 1665
Martino, Karen, Specialist-Mktg Matls Review - The Northwestern Mutual Life Insurance Company; *pg.* 1212, *pg.* 1879
Martino, Scott, Head-Mktg Analytics - Mercedes-Benz USA, LLC; *pg.* 184, *pg.* 514
Martinovic, Marin, Dir-Acq & Retention Mktg - Sprint Corporation; *pg.* 1874, *pg.* 719
Martins, Stephanie, Mgr-Coronary Mktg-Latin America - Medtronic, Inc.; *pg.* 1564, *pg.* 939
Martir, Michael, Dir-Customer Tech Mktg - McKesson Corporation; *pg.* 1560, *pg.* 222
Martire, Leonard, VP-Mktg - Frequency Electronics, Inc.; *pg.* 639, *pg.* 1182
Martiz, Erik Gabriel, Mgr-Americas Reg Parts Sls-Caterpillar Marine - Caterpillar, Inc.; *pg.* 1321, *pg.* 650
Marton, Simon, CMO - Treasury Wine Estates; *pg.* 1971, *pg.* 164
Martone, Kindra, VP-Global Collocation Sls - CenturyLink, Inc.; *pg.* 1870, *pg.* 746
Martorano, Dennis, Dir-Mktg Sciences - Comcast Cable Communications, Inc.; *pg.* 276, *pg.* 1560
Martos, D'Arianne, Asst Mgr-Mktg Svcs - Norwegian Cruise Line; *pg.* 1917, *pg.* 444
Martson, Paul, Sr Mgr-Corp Mktg - Cisco Systems, Inc.; *pg.* 372, *pg.* 240
Marty, Daniel, Dir-Sls Ops - Automatic Data Processing, Inc.; *pg.* 357, *pg.* 1117
Marty, Michael, VP & Gen Mgr-Ops, Sls & B2B - Care.com; *pg.* 1960, *pg.* 850
Martz, Doug, Sr VP-Adv Sls - The Tennis Channel, Inc.; *pg.* 679, *pg.* 276
Martz, Greg, Dir-Mktg - L-3 Interstate Electronics Corporation; *pg.* 650, *pg.* 43
Martz, Wes, VP-Mktg - KADANT INC.; *pg.* 1352, *pg.* 858
Martz, Wesley, VP-Mktg - Kadant Johnson Inc.; *pg.* 1073, *pg.* 909
Marusak, Jeffrey, Sr Product Mgr-Mktg-Cisco Cloud Collaboration Tech Grp - Cisco Systems, Inc.; *pg.* 372, *pg.* 240
Marusarz, Kathy, Bus Mgr - National Association of Realtors; *pg.* 1666, *pg.* 584
Marusic, Mike, Sr VP-Mktg & Ops - Sharp Electronics Corporation; *pg.* 672, *pg.* 1082
Maruska, John, Specialist-Consult Channel Mktg - EMC Corporation; *pg.* 391, *pg.* 825
Maruszak, Patricia, Mgr-Mktg Comm - Justrite Manufacturing Company, LLC; *pg.* 1394, *pg.* 606
Marvin, Christine, Dir-Mktg - Marvin Windows & Doors; *pg.* 934, *pg.* 965
Marvin, Jacob, Sr Mgr-Engrg - Motorola Mobility LLC; *pg.* 657, *pg.* 627
Marvin, Lisa, Mgr-Social Innovation - eBay Inc.; *pg.* 1240, *pg.* 243
Marvin, Tim, Exec Dir-Retail Sls - Mizkan Americas, Inc.; *pg.* 877, *pg.* 634
Marwell, Josh, Pres-Sls - HarperCollins Publishers Inc.; *pg.* 1647, *pg.* 1237
Marx, Brian, Mgr-Digital Mktg - Cargill, Inc.; *pg.* 845, *pg.* 965
Marx, Jonathan, Sr Dir-Mktg & Comm - Nashville Symphony Association; *pg.* 565, *pg.* 1653
Marx, Laura, Sr Dir-Alliances Mktg - Polycom, Inc.; *pg.* 664, *pg.* 249
Marx, Michael, Sr Dir - Visa Inc.; *pg.* 816, *pg.* 230
Marx, Michael, Sr Dir - Visa U.S.A., Inc.; *pg.* 817, *pg.* 231
Marx, Stephanie, Mgr-Social Bus - Starbucks Corporation; *pg.* 897, *pg.* 1840
Marxen, Jake, VP-Broker Dealer Sls Dev - Allianz Life Insurance Company of North America; *pg.* 1188, *pg.* 929
Maryniak, Stefan, Assoc Dir-Product Mgmt - Catalina Marketing Corporation; *pg.* 369, *pg.* 462
Marzec, John L., III, Dir-Product Mgmt - ECRM Imaging Systems, Inc.; *pg.* 1410, *pg.* 848
Marzullo, Matthew, Mgr-Capital Sls Equipment - C.I. Hayes; *pg.* 1070, *pg.* 1600
Marzullo, Michelle, Specialist-Mktg - PrivateBancorp Inc.; *pg.* 796, *pg.* 587
Mascari, Charlie, Mgr-Product Line - Cisco Systems, Inc.; *pg.* 372, *pg.* 240
Mascarin, Anne, Product Mgr-Hardware - Red Hat, Inc.; *pg.* 460, *pg.* 1388
Mascaro, Holly, Coord-Integrated Mktg-Hearst Men's Grp - The Hearst Corporation; *pg.* 1649, *pg.* 1239
Mascatello, Chris, Exec VP-Tech Sls - ANC Sports Enterprises, LLC; *pg.* 1825, *pg.* 1325
Masch, Sol, Exec Dir-Video & Mobile Sls - Time Inc.; *pg.* 1693, *pg.* 1300
Masden, Kelly, Coord-Mktg - Texas Roadhouse, Inc.; *pg.* 1753, *pg.* 738
Mash, Stephanie, Sr Specialist-Mktg - Owens Corning; *pg.* 102, *pg.* 1476
Masheder, Tom, Dir-Global Multi-Channel Mktg - GlaxoSmithKline Consumer Healthcare; *pg.* 510, *pg.* 1554
Mashek, Tom, Mgr-Suite Sls & Svcs - The Phillies, L.P.; *pg.* 575, *pg.* 1569
Masi, Vince, VP-Sls, Distr & Brand Acctg-Global - IBM; *pg.* 410, *pg.* 1449
Masle, Jennifer, Sr Mgr Mktg - 7-Eleven, Inc.; *pg.* 1012, *pg.* 1672
Masilionis, Brian, Brand Mgr - Applebee's International, Inc.; *pg.* 1715, *pg.* 980
Masilionis, Krista, Dir-Creative Studio - Hallmark Cards, Inc.; *pg.* 1646, *pg.* 983
Maska, Johanna, VP-Mktg & Comm - Los Angeles Times Communications, LLC; *pg.* 1660, *pg.* 135
Maskal, Vanessa, Exec VP-Sls & Mktg - B&G Foods, Inc.; *pg.* 838, *pg.* 1102
Masker, Susan, Acct Exec-Media Sls-Charter Media - Charter Communications, Inc.; *pg.* 274, *pg.* 372
Maslanyk, Bo, VP-Sls & Mktg - Clark Material Handling Company; *pg.* 1323, *pg.* 729
Maslowsky, Craig, VP-Enrollment Mgmt & Mktg - Excelsior College; *pg.* 601, *pg.* 1137
Mason, Allison, Sr Mgr-Pub Sector Mktg - Red Hat, Inc.; *pg.* 460, *pg.* 1388
Mason, Anthony, VP-Strategic Mktg - Foxwoods Resort Casino; *pg.* 549, *pg.* 353
Mason, Chardia, Brand Mgr-Retail Dev - Ralph Lauren Corporation; *pg.* 46, *pg.* 1284
Mason, Dan, Mgr-Mktg - 3M Company; *pg.* 1142, *pg.* 956
Mason, David, Sr Mgr-PR - AT&T; *pg.* 1865, *pg.* 258
Mason, Emily, Dir-Consumer Mktg-Urology Portfolio - Astellas Pharma US, Inc.; *pg.* 1496, *pg.* 640
Mason, Erik, Head-Mktg Program-Adv - Quicken Loans, Inc.; *pg.* 797, *pg.* 884
Mason, Frank, Sls Dir-Engineered Field Solutions-Americas - Honeywell International Inc.; *pg.* 407, *pg.* 1088
Mason, Jeff, VP-Product - ESM Solutions Corporation; *pg.* 1243, *pg.* 1591
Mason, Paul, Product Mgr - Google Inc.; *pg.* 1249, *pg.* 153
Mason, Paul, Dir-Sls-Global - Wyndham Worldwide Corporation; *pg.* 1119, *pg.* 1107
Mason, Rob, VP-Global Mktg-Jim Beam - Beam Suntory Inc.; *pg.* 1957, *pg.* 599
Mason, Robin, Sr VP-Mktg-Global - Elizabeth Arden, Inc.; *pg.* 507, *pg.* 448
Mason, Rodney, VP-Mktg-Global - Blackhawk Engagement Solutions, Inc.; *pg.* 1232, *pg.* 1725
Mason, Scott, Mgr-Sls - Thetford Corporation; *pg.* 337, *pg.* 867
Mason, Tyler, VP-PR - UnitedHealth Group Incorporated; *pg.* 1221, *pg.* 950
Mason-Veronelli, Jessica, Specialist-Mktg Comm-Temperature Mgmt Solutions - Zoll Medical Corporation; *pg.* 1612, *pg.* 814
Masood, James, Sr VP-Sls & Mktg - FieldBrook Foods Inc.; *pg.* 1852, *pg.* 1156
Masoom, Zia, Dir-Product Mktg US Ops - Xerox Corporation; *pg.* 494, *pg.* 365
Masotto, Tom, VP-Product Mgmt - ON24, Inc.; *pg.* 1272, *pg.* 224
Massa, Mike, VP-Sls - Hayward Pool Products; *pg.* 1049, *pg.* 1057
Massafra, Lino, VP-Sls & Mktg - North Atlantic Industries Inc.; *pg.* 1424, *pg.* 1143
Massanova, Chris, Dir-Fuel Coke Mktg - ConocoPhillips; *pg.* 975, *pg.* 1703
Massar, Kevin, Dir-Product Line - Converse Inc.; *pg.* 1831, *pg.* 793
Massarella, Linda, Dir-Mktg - Lennar Corporation; *pg.* 1100, *pg.* 443
Massarelli, John P., VP-Sls & Mktg - Beacon Roofing Supply, Inc.; *pg.* 70, *pg.* 840

First page reference indicates Business Class Edition
Second page reference indicates Geographic Edition

Masse, Ann, Mgr-Natl Vehicle Mktg & Comm - Toyota Motor Sales, U.S.A., Inc.; pg. 193, pg. 296

Masse, Carole, Assoc Dir-Creative - Aon Hewitt; pg. 350, pg. 627

Massenzio, Melanie, Sr Product Mgr - Novartis Pharmaceuticals Corp.; pg. 1575, pg. 1054

Masseria, Kaitlin, Specialist-Mktg Comm - The Progressive Corporation; pg. 1214, pg. 1463

Massey, Andrea, Sr VP-Mktg - RealPage, Inc.; pg. 1277, pg. 1669

Massey, Angela, Sr Product Mgr & Sr Mgr-Market - Cardinal Health, Inc.; pg. 1512, pg. 1448

Massey, Christen, Coord-Mktg - LEGOLAND California LLC; pg. 557, pg. 59

Massey, Daniel, Dir-Mktg - Dell Inc.; pg. 383, pg. 1737

Massey, Krista, Sr VP-Mktg Activation & Engagement - Sun Trust Bank, Atlanta; pg. 806, pg. 520

Massey, Krista, Sr VP-Mktg Activation & Engagement - SunTrust Banks, Inc.; pg. 807, pg. 520

Massey, Lori, Dir-Creative - Fossil Group, Inc.; pg. 5, pg. 1735

Massey, Whitney, Specialist-Adv - Alabama Power Company; pg. 1933, pg. 1

Massi, Rich, VP-Product Deployment - Comcast Corporation; pg. 276, pg. 1560

Massimilla, Jeffrey, Chief Product Cybersecurity Officer - General Motors Company; pg. 175, pg. 881

Massimini, Kelly, Sr Mgr-Mktg Comm - IMS Health, Inc.; pg. 1544, pg. 344

Massimo, Ryan, Dir-Mktg - Dell Inc.; pg. 383, pg. 1737

Massing, Diana K., Sr Mgr-Comm - Citigroup Inc.; pg. 735, pg. 1212

Masson, Sylvain, Dir-Digital & Media Intelligence - Heineken USA Inc.; pg. 252, pg. 1352

Mast, Olivia, Program Head-Mktg Comm - General Electric Company; pg. 1297, pg. 347

Mastanduno, Joe, Acct Mgr-Rental Mktg - John Deere Consumer & Commercial Equipment, Inc.; pg. 705, pg. 1360

Mastantuono, Christina, Mgr-Mktg - Party City Corporation; pg. 1781, pg. 1116

Mastascusa, Stacey, Mgr-Circulation Sls & Mktg - The News-Herald; pg. 1670, pg. 908

Master, Rob, VP-Global Media-Americas & Europe - Unilever United States, Inc.; pg. 904, pg. 1061

Master, Sarah, Brand Mgr - Bayer Corporation; pg. 1499, pg. 1573

Masters, Allison, Dir-Mktg - Preferred Hotel Group; pg. 1108, pg. 587

Masters, Andrew, Sr VP-Global Product Dev & Tech - BioClinica, Inc.; pg. 1506, pg. 1556

Masters, Jenny, Mgr-Mktg - Lennar Corporation; pg. 1100, pg. 443

Masters, Katie, Sr Mgr-Social Engagement - EMC Corporation; pg. 391, pg. 825

Masters, Lucy, Asst VP-Mktg - Northeastern University; pg. 605, pg. 799

Masterson, Patrick, Sr Mgr-Channel Mktg - Intuit Inc.; pg. 769, pg. 158

Masterson, William, Mgr-Mktg & Technical Svcs-Americas - Cabot Corporation; pg. 1151, pg. 792

Mastrandrea, Kristin, VP-PR - MSCI Inc.; pg. 785, pg. 1262

Mastrangelo, Andrew, Dir-Media Rels - Lahey Clinic; pg. 1554, pg. 805

Mastrocola, Roberto, Sr Mgr-Integrated Comm-Connections Plng & Investment - The Coca-Cola Company; pg. 240, pg. 493

Mastrogiacomo, Susan, Dir-Comml Mktg Svcs - Heineken USA Inc.; pg. 252, pg. 1352

Mastroianni, Mark, Dir-Mktg Comm & Special Programs - Henry Schein, Inc.; pg. 1541, pg. 1180

Mastrojohn, Dean, Dir-Media Rels-Global - Pfizer Inc.; pg. 1581, pg. 1278

Masuda, Dana, Sr Mgr-Employee Engagement - NetApp, Inc.; pg. 444, pg. 287

Masullo, Caroline, Sr Dir-US Digital Engagement - McDonald's Corporation; pg. 1737, pg. 645

Matalamaki, Cindy, Mgr-Mktg Comm - Ceridian Corporation; pg. 371, pg. 932

Matanle, Lynn, Mgr-Digital Media - Macy's, Inc.; pg. 1778, pg. 1417

Matarazzo, Vinicius, Reg Mgr-Sls - NBS Technologies Inc.; pg. 786, pg. 1941

Matasich, Kevin, Head-Sls Ops-US - Merck & Co., Inc.; pg. 1566, pg. 1077

Mataya, David, Mgr-Creative Svcs - Honeywell International Inc.; pg. 407, pg. 1088

Matchett, Dorothy, Mgr-Strategic Sls-Subsea & Submersibles - Cooper Interconnect; pg. 630, pg. 1118

Matchette, Rita, Mgr-Customer Mktg - Avago Technologies; pg. 358, pg. 238

Mateer, Erin, Supvr-Adv Acct - MGM Resorts International; pg. 1105, pg. 1028

Mateja, Kristin, Head-Mktg Svcs - MORNINGSTAR, INC.; pg. 784, pg. 583

Matejka, Stacey, Specialist-Mktg - At Home Stores LLC; pg. 1760, pg. 1729

Matejko, Donald M., Sr VP-Americas Digital Mktg Comml Sls - Adobe Systems Incorporated; pg. 342, pg. 235

Mateo, Jennifer, Mgr-Mktg Comm - Verizon Communications Inc.; pg. 1875, pg. 1309

Materazzo, Lisa, Corp Mgr-Media Strategy & Digital Engagement - Toyota Motor Sales, U.S.A., Inc.; pg. 193, pg. 296

Matero, Cindy, Dir-Brand Mktg - Home Box Office, Inc.; pg. 290, pg. 1240

Matev, Peter D., Mgr-Mktg - FedEx Corporation; pg. 1907, pg. 1642

Matharu, Harpinder, Sr Product Mgr - Xilinx, Inc.; pg. 496, pg. 252

Matheney, Jenny, Dir-Product Mktg - Blackbaud, Inc.; pg. 361, pg. 1613

Matheny, Gregg, Mgr-Sls - Terral Seed, Inc.; pg. 1801, pg. 748

Matheny, Kelly, Mgr-Channel Mktg - Rinnai America Corp.; pg. 1076, pg. 538

Matheny, Liz, Dir-Mktg - Woodcraft Supply Corp.; pg. 1390, pg. 1850

Matheny, Tom, Mgr-Database Mktg - Hockey Western New York, LLC; pg. 552, pg. 1149

Mather, Kedesh, Sr Mgr-Comm-UK & Ireland - MasterCard Incorporated; pg. 779, pg. 1325

Matherne, Rich, Sr Dir-Field Mktg - Chick-fil-A, Inc.; pg. 1721, pg. 492

Mathers, Kevin, Country Dir-Sls-Google UK - Google Inc.; pg. 1249, pg. 153

Mathers, Trevor, Sr Dir-HCM Cloud Technical Solutions - Oracle Corporation; pg. 1272, pg. 786

Mathes Yep, Brooke, VP-Mktg Strategy & Comm - NCI BUILDING SYSTEMS, INC.; pg. 1364, pg. 1712

Mathes, Kim, Dir-Mktg - HCA HOLDINGS, INC.; pg. 1539, pg. 1651

Mathes, Ralph, Dir-Creative Svcs - Media General, Inc.; pg. 297, pg. 1803

Matheu, Sara, Dir-Media Dev & Comm - Hillshire Brands; pg. 862, pg. 576

Mathew, Anne K., Dir-Mktg - Gilead Sciences, Inc.; pg. 1535, pg. 88

Mathew, Liza, Dir-Product Mktg-Delta Retail & Peerless - Delta Faucet Company; pg. 78, pg. 684

Mathew, Priyanka, Mgr-Digital Mktg-Burberry Beauty & Hermes Parfums - Shiseido Cosmetics America of SAC; pg. 522, pg. 1291

Mathew, Roshen, Exec Dir-Emerging Media - AT&T; pg. 1865, pg. 258

Mathew, Susan, Sr Mgr-Innovation & Commlization - Diageo North America Inc.; pg. 248, pg. 1223

Mathews, Anne Marie, VP-PR - Norwegian Cruise Line; pg. 1917, pg. 444

Mathews, Beth, Dir-Mktg-Retail Ship Centers - United Parcel Service, Inc.; pg. 1928, pg. 522

Mathews, Jennifer, Mgr-PR - ZIPCAR, INC.; pg. 1931, pg. 810

Mathews, Julie, Assoc Mgr-Global Digital Mktg - The Hershey Co.; pg. 1855, pg. 1538

Mathews, Kim, Exec Mgr-Briefing & Sr Mgr-Mktg - CommVault Systems, Inc.; pg. 377, pg. 1125

Mathews, Leslie, Mgr-Convention Sls - Pensacola Bay Area Convention & Visitors Bureau; pg. 1004, pg. 458

Mathews, Scott, Pres-Digital Mktg - CDK Global, Inc.; pg. 370, pg. 617

Mathews, Sean, Dir-Mktg Comm-Outback Steakhouse - Bloomin' Brands, Inc.; pg. 1716, pg. 471

Mathewson, James, Program Dir-Global Search Mktg - International Business Machines Corporation; pg. 418, pg. 1138

Mathias, T.J., Mgr-Natl Event Mktg - Fifth Generation, Inc.; pg. 1963, pg. 1662

Mathieson, Derek, Chief Strategy Officer & VP - Baker Hughes Incorporated; pg. 1315, pg. 1700

Mathieux, Daniel, Dir-Mktg Insights & eBusiness - American Automobile Association; pg. 1190, pg. 429

Mathis, Brad, Sr Dir-Market Access - Alexion Pharmaceuticals, Inc.; pg. 1489, pg. 341

Mathis, Dave, Sr VP-Sls & Mktg - Golden Heritage Foods, LLC; pg. 858, pg. 715

Mathis, Tanya, Dir-Creative Asset Mgmt - FMR LLC (Fidelity Investments); pg. 759, pg. 794

Mathisen, Sheryle, Mgr-Mktg Comm - 3M Company; pg. 1142, pg. 956

Mathisen, Todd, Sr Mgr-Bus Dev - 3M Company; pg. 1142, pg. 956

Mathison, Lisa, Dir-Media Strategy - Walgreen Co.; pg. 1608, pg. 605

Mathur, Bikash, Sr Dir - Cognizant Technology Solutions Corporation; pg. 377, pg. 1124

Mathur, Kinjil, VP & Head-Mktg - FourSquare Labs, Inc; pg. 1248, pg. 1232

Mathur, Ritu, Brand Mgr-Luna - Clif Bar Inc.; pg. 848, pg. 83

Mathur, Rohit, Product Mgr-Line Sls-Drilling Svcs - Baker Hughes Incorporated; pg. 1315, pg. 1700

Mathur, Shana, VP-Mktg & Comm - Los Angeles Philharmonic Association; pg. 559, pg. 135

Mathuran, Neal, Dir-Mktg - L'Oreal USA; pg. 514, pg. 1252

Mathy, Christophe, Sr Dir-Comm-Honeywell Transportation Sys - Honeywell International Inc.; pg. 407, pg. 1088

Mathy, Lisa, Project Mgr-Mktg - The Northwestern Mutual Life Insurance Company; pg. 1212, pg. 1879

Matijcio, Justin, Brand Mgr-Innovation - Pepperidge Farm, Inc.; pg. 888, pg. 363

Matin, Tara, Sr Acct Mgr-Media-Talent Brand - LinkedIn Corporation; pg. 1262, pg. 160

Matisko, David E., Mgr-Sls - Cargill, Inc.; pg. 845, pg. 965

Matison, Jennifer, Sr Mgr-Consumer Info - Texas Beef Council; pg. 158, pg. 1666

Matits, William, Sr VP-Sls-ROI - HealthPort, Inc.; pg. 403, pg. 484

Matiyow, Ryan, Sr Dir-Mktg-Frito Lay - PepsiCo, Inc.; pg. 259, pg. 1327

Matles, Justin, Gen Mgr-Customer Mktg Strategy - DISH Network Corporation; pg. 283, pg. 325

Matlock, Benjamin, Mgr-Mktg - T-Mobile US, Inc.; pg. 676, pg. 1816

Matlock, Cathy, Dir-Mktg-DeVry University - DeVry Education Group Inc.; pg. 600, pg. 607

Matlock, Kim, VP-Digital Mktg & Customer Relationship Mgmt - Hard Rock Cafe International, Inc.; pg. 1730, pg. 454

Matlock, Robin, VP-Corp Mktg - VMware, Inc.; pg. 490, pg. 179

Matlock, Sherry, Dir-Mktg-Southwest Reg - Charter Communications, Inc.; pg. 274, pg. 372

Matlow, Annie, Dir-Mktg & PR - Spokane Symphony Orchestra; pg. 584, pg. 1844

Maton, Marnie, Mgr-Mktg - TrueCar Inc.; pg. 1284, pg. 276

Matousek, Matt, Sr Dir-Member Mktg - UnitedHealth Group Incorporated; pg. 1221, pg. 950

Matras, Shari, Dir-Mktg - Wm. Wrigley Jr. Company; pg. 1863, pg. 596

Matray, Jeff, Brand Mgr-Brand Dev - Olive Garden Italian Restaurant; pg. 1742, pg. 454

Matray, Jeff, Brand Mgr-Digital Mktg - Red Lobster; pg. 1747, pg. 455

Matsler, Todd, Mgr-Segment Mktg & Intelligent Sys Grp - Intel Corporation; pg. 645, pg. 266

Matson, Bruce, Sr Dir-Dairy Procurement - Dean Foods Company; pg. 852, pg. 1679

Matson, Holly, Mgr-Interactive Media & Content - Polaris Industries Inc.; pg. 1709, pg. 928

Matson, Jennifer, Brand Mgr - Darden Restaurants, Inc.; pg. 1724, pg. 453

Matson, Kelly, Mgr-Mktg Comm - Henkel Corporation; pg. 1165, pg. 1535

Matsueda, Jay, Sr Dir-Strategic Mktg & Comm-Lighting Solutions - LSI Industries Inc.; pg. 58, pg. 1416

Matsui, Yukio, Sr VP & Head-Mktg Strategy - Astellas Pharma US, Inc.; pg. 1496, pg. 640

Matsumoto, Asaka, Sr Mgr-New Bus Dev - Ricoh Americas Corp.; pg. 462, pg. 538

Matsumoto, Kevin, Coord-Mktg - Armstrong Garden Centers, Inc.; pg. 1793, pg. 99

Matsumura, Emili, Sr Assoc Mgr-Brand Mktg - Taco Bell Corp.; pg. 1752, pg. 117

Matsuo, Jaci, Dir-Online Mktg & Digital Asset Mgmt - Hawaii Visitors & Convention Bureau; pg. 994, pg. 543

Matsuoka, Dave, Mgr-Mktg - Orchard Supply Hardware Stores

Corp.; *pg.* 1058, *pg.* 248

Matsuzawa, Masaaki, Chief Strategic Officer & Head-Corp Dev-China - National Basketball Association; *pg.* 566, *pg.* 1264

Mattacchione, Anthony L., Interim CFO - Bruker Corporation; *pg.* 1511, *pg.* 788

Mattappally, Nidhin, Sr Mgr-Mktg-Discover it Portfolio Experience - Discover Financial Services; *pg.* 744, *pg.* 653

Mattas, Proscovia, Mgr-Sls-Natl - Louisville Convention & Visitors Bureau; *pg.* 998, *pg.* 736

Matteo, Derek, Dir-Mktg-Posterior Thoracolumbar Fixation - NuVasive, Inc.; *pg.* 1577, *pg.* 205

Matteo, Jeanine, Mgr-Mktg & Visual Production - Ann Inc.; *pg.* 18, *pg.* 1195

Mattera, Larry, Exec VP-Commerce, Digital Mktg & Strategy - Warner Bros. Records, Inc.; *pg.* 1791, *pg.* 55

Mattern, Jason, Sr Dir-Sls - MTD Products, Inc.; *pg.* 1057, *pg.* 1478

Mattes, Leanne, VP-Mktg - Relax the Back Corporation; *pg.* 940, *pg.* 120

Matteson, Rich, Dir-Natl Mktg, Sls Plng & Forecasting - Pizza Hut, Inc.; *pg.* 1744, *pg.* 1733

Matthew, Ian, Sr Mgr-Sls Enablement-Oil & Gas & Utilities - Autodesk Inc.; *pg.* 356, *pg.* 257

Matthews, Angelica, Brand Mgr & Mgr-Sam's Club Mktg - The Procter & Gamble Company; *pg.* 1129, *pg.* 1418

Matthews, Barry, Sr Mgr-Print Production - BCBG Max Azria Group LLC; *pg.* 19, *pg.* 301

Matthews, Brad, Sr Dir-Social Commerce - eBay Inc.; *pg.* 1240, *pg.* 243

Matthews, Colleen, Dir-WW Comml & Distr Programs, Mktg & Comm - Juniper Networks, Inc.; *pg.* 1260, *pg.* 286

Matthews, David, Mgr-Production - Banana Republic; *pg.* 1760, *pg.* 212

Matthews, Glen, Sr Mgr-Product Mgmt - Advanced Micro Devices, Inc.; *pg.* 613, *pg.* 282

Matthews, Kimarie, Sr VP-Virtual Channels Social Care & Capabilities - Wells Fargo & Company; *pg.* 819, *pg.* 232

Matthews, Lauren, Coord-Mktg-EVOL Foods - Boulder Brands, Inc.; *pg.* 1016, *pg.* 310

Matthews, Liz, Dir-Product Dev - Taco Bell Corp.; *pg.* 1752, *pg.* 117

Matthews, Mathew, Dir-European Cloud Sls - Computer Sciences Corporation; *pg.* 378, *pg.* 1780

Matthews, Mike, Sr Mgr-IT-Global Network & Comm Implementations - Cisco Systems, Inc.; *pg.* 372, *pg.* 240

Matthews, Paul, Dir-Trade Mktg - Bumble Bee Foods LLC; *pg.* 842, *pg.* 201

Matthews, Robert, Gen Mgr-Consumer Mktg-Global - Microsoft Corp.; *pg.* 440, *pg.* 321

Matthews-Smith, Minda, Dir-Mktg - LSI Industries Inc.; *pg.* 58, *pg.* 1416

Mattia, Joann, Area Mgr-Mktg - Sunoco Inc.; *pg.* 985, *pg.* 1571

Mattila, Juha, Product Mgr - STERIS Corporation; *pg.* 1597, *pg.* 1464

Mattilio, Melissa, Mgr-Consumer Mktg - Turkey Hill Dairy, Inc.; *pg.* 902, *pg.* 1522

Mattimoe, Betsy, VP, Sr Mgr-Mktg & Product Mgr-Bus Debit - JPMorgan Chase & Co.; *pg.* 772, *pg.* 1246

Mattimore, Mary, VP-Mktg Svcs - News America Incorporated; *pg.* 1669, *pg.* 1271

Mattina, Lori La, Mgr-Sls & Mktg - Pfizer Inc.; *pg.* 1581, *pg.* 1278

Mattina, Rob, VP-Mktg - Detroit Red Wings, Inc.; *pg.* 544, *pg.* 880

Mattingly, Michael, Exec Product Mgr-Refrigeration - GE Consumer & Industrial; *pg.* 55, *pg.* 733

Mattioli, John, Mgr-Sponsorships & Event Mktg - Chick-fil-A, Inc.; *pg.* 1721, *pg.* 492

Mattner, Mary, Specialist-Customer Mktg - Johnsonville Sausage, LLC; *pg.* 867, *pg.* 1894

Mattsoff, Arita, VP-Mktg - Stratasys, Inc.; *pg.* 476, *pg.* 923

Mattson, Courtney, Partner-Sls-Acct Mgmt & Mgr-Mktg-Online Learning - Franklin Covey Co.; *pg.* 1642, *pg.* 1758

Mattson, Kristin, Sr Specialist-PR - Digital River, Inc.; *pg.* 1238, *pg.* 948

Mattson, Michael D., Dir-Adv - Aubuchon Hardware; *pg.* 1043, *pg.* 859

Mattson, Michelle, Dir-Social Media - T-Mobile US, Inc.; *pg.* 676, *pg.* 1816

Mattus, Milton, Dir-Sls Snacks Metro-Atlantic BBU - Bimbo Bakeries USA; *pg.* 840, *pg.* 151

Matty, Rick, VP-Product Mgmt - LegalZoom.com, Inc.; *pg.* 1261, *pg.* 96

Matula, Valentine, Gen Mgr-Emerging Products & Tech & Sr Dir - Avaya Inc.; *pg.* 621, *pg.* 264

Maturo, Pat, Sr Dir-Fin - Einstein Noah Restaurant Group, Inc.; *pg.* 1019, *pg.* 332

Matus, Mark, Product Mgr-Global-Ruggedized Fiber Optic Interconnects - Molex Incorporated; *pg.* 655, *pg.* 628

Matusic, Karen P., Sr Dir-Federal Rels - Exxon Mobil Corporation; *pg.* 977, *pg.* 1718

Matuzek, Betsy, Sr Mgr-Sourcing & Procurement - Staples, Inc.; *pg.* 474, *pg.* 821

Matyja, Amy, Coord-Social Media Mktg - Zenni Optical, Inc.; *pg.* 1438, *pg.* 168

Matzke, Richard D., Reg Mgr-Sls-Eastern US-Masonry/Landscape - Besser Company; *pg.* 1317, *pg.* 865

Mauceri, Ben, VP-Mdsg-Intl - Lowe's Companies, Inc.; *pg.* 1053, *pg.* 1383

Mauk, Wil, Mgr-Global Procurement-Mktg Svcs - The Coca-Cola Company; *pg.* 240, *pg.* 493

Maul, Brohan, VP-Brand Mgmt & Mktg - Bandai America Incorporated; *pg.* 950, *pg.* 75

Mauloff, Gregory J., Corp VP-Sls - National Wine & Spirits, Inc.; *pg.* 1967, *pg.* 689

Maupas, Gary, Mgr-Sls - Pelican Products; *pg.* 1467, *pg.* 843

Maupin, Matt, Product Mgr-Wireless Embedded Sys - Silicon Laboratories Inc.; *pg.* 674, *pg.* 1666

Maurer, Donna, Dir-Consumer Mktg - School Specialty, Inc.; *pg.* 467, *pg.* 1860

Maurer, Jessica, Specialist-Mktg - Insight Enterprises, Inc.; *pg.* 415, *pg.* 26

Maurer, Matthew, Mgr-Mktg & Brand Strategy - United Airlines, Inc.; *pg.* 1927, *pg.* 593

Maurer, Sean, VP-Mdsg - Ahold USA, Inc.; *pg.* 1013, *pg.* 1520

Mauri, Brendan, Sr Mgr-Brand Mktg - Applebee's International, Inc.; *pg.* 1715, *pg.* 980

Mauricio, Luke G., Mgr-Small Bus Segment Mktg - United Parcel Service, Inc.; *pg.* 1928, *pg.* 522

Mauro, Nicholas, Sr Mgr-Mktg - PNY Technologies, Inc.; *pg.* 455, *pg.* 1105

Mauro, Ron, Mgr-Customer Sls - GlaxoSmithKline; *pg.* 1536, *pg.* 1389

Mauro, Ron, Mgr-Customer Sls-Family Dollar, Dollar Tree & 99 cent only - GlaxoSmithKline Consumer Healthcare; *pg.* 510, *pg.* 1554

Maurrasse, Jeanne, Brand Mgr - Unilever United States, Inc.; *pg.* 904, *pg.* 1061

Maus, Trudy, Exec Dir-Creative & Production Svcs - Banner Direct; *pg.* 1619, *pg.* 1200

Mauser, Shawn, Reg Dir-Sls - The Northwestern Mutual Life Insurance Company; *pg.* 1212, *pg.* 1879

Mautz, John, Sr Mgr-Data Center LAN Svcs - Xerox Corporation; *pg.* 494, *pg.* 365

Mautz, Robert, Dir-Natl Adv - Sonic Automotive, Inc.; *pg.* 190, *pg.* 1369

Mautz, Scott, Dir-Mktg - The Procter & Gamble Company; *pg.* 1129, *pg.* 1418

Maver, Jenna, Sr Mgr-Social Media - Kronos Incorporated; *pg.* 425, *pg.* 813

Maverick, Carly, Dir-Digital Sls Plng - Time Inc.; *pg.* 1693, *pg.* 1300

Maverick, Kristin, Sr Dir-Emerging Media - Bravo Media LLC; *pg.* 271, *pg.* 1206

Mavrodin, Julia, Dir-Digital Mktg - L'Oreal USA; *pg.* 514, *pg.* 1252

Mavros, Popi, Sr Dir-Client Dev & Mktg Strategy - Ticketmaster Entertainment LLC; *pg.* 1284, *pg.* 48

Mawer, Mark, VP-Sls & Mktg - Tekra Corporation; *pg.* 1184, *pg.* 1884

Max, Cheryl, Sr Dir-Mktg - Juniper Networks, Inc.; *pg.* 1260, *pg.* 286

Maximini, Kendall, Mgr-Mdsg & Mktg - Birchbox; *pg.* 1762, *pg.* 1203

Maxson, David, Sr Dir-Digital Mktg & Software - Avery Dennison Corporation; *pg.* 1452, *pg.* 95

Maxwell, Joan, VP-Mdsg - VERA BRADLEY, INC.; *pg.* 15, *pg.* 697

Maxwell, Kimberly, Sr Dir-Strategic Insights Res - MTV Networks Company; *pg.* 298, *pg.* 1262

Maxwell, Laura, Dir-Mktg - MapQuest, Inc.; *pg.* 1265, *pg.* 321

Maxwell, Lauren, VP & Dir-Local Sls & Mktg Strategies - Susquehanna Bank; *pg.* 807, *pg.* 1548

Maxwell, Liam, VP-Product Dev - Oracle Corporation; *pg.* 450, *pg.* 191

Maxwell, Marcus, Product Mgr - Eaton Corporation; *pg.* 1331, *pg.* 1429

Maxwell, Mark, VP-Products - Military Advantage, Inc.; *pg.* 1267, *pg.* 223

Maxwell, Michelle, Mgr-Mktg Comm - Microsoft Corporation; *pg.* 435, *pg.* 1824

Maxwell, Robert, VP-Production - PRT Forest Regeneration Income Fund; *pg.* 1799, *pg.* 1913

Maxwell, Sonja, Sr Mgr-Mktg - Microsoft Corporation; *pg.* 435, *pg.* 1824

Maxwell, Theresa, Designer-Adv - Lee Enterprises, Incorporated; *pg.* 1658, *pg.* 704

Maxwell, Wendy, Coord-Mktg - Rich Products Corporation; *pg.* 892, *pg.* 1150

May, Andrew, Dir-Sls Strategy & Plng - PepsiCo, Inc.; *pg.* 259, *pg.* 1327

May, Chrisitne, Mgr-Digital Media Buying - Apple Vacations Inc.; *pg.* 1899, *pg.* 1556

May, David, Dir-Web & Interactive Mktg - Chapman University; *pg.* 599, *pg.* 174

May, David, Sr Dir-Direct to Consumer Bus - Pure Fishing, Inc.; *pg.* 1843, *pg.* 1614

May, Doug, VP-Piston Products-Textron Aviation - Textron Inc.; *pg.* 235, *pg.* 1607

May, Elaine, Exec Dir-Mktg-Novartis Animal Health - Novartis Corporation; *pg.* 1574, *pg.* 1273

May, Jaren, Product Mgr-Global - TE Connectivity Ltd.; *pg.* 677, *pg.* 1515

May, Jeff, Sr VP-Mktg - Universal Technical Institute, Inc.; *pg.* 608, *pg.* 24

May, Jessica, Sr Analyst-Mktg Ops - Constellation Energy Resources, LLC; *pg.* 1938, *pg.* 756

May, Jillian, Sr Dir-Design Integration - Best Buy Co., Inc.; *pg.* 1761, *pg.* 954

May, Karen, Mgr-PR - United Airlines, Inc.; *pg.* 1927, *pg.* 593

May, Karen Twigg, Dir-PR - Ulta Salon, Cosmetics & Fragrance, Inc.; *pg.* 524, *pg.* 559

May, Kirk R., VP-Corp Sls - ABF Freight System, Inc.; *pg.* 1896, *pg.* 31

May, Laura, Dir-Mktg - Danaher Corporation; *pg.* 1044, *pg.* 397

May, Laura, Brand Mgr-North America Dish Care Design - The Procter & Gamble Company; *pg.* 1129, *pg.* 1418

May, Maya, Sr Dir-Retail Optical CRM & Loyalty - Luxottica Retail; *pg.* 8, *pg.* 1460

May, Ralph, Sr Mgr-Bus Dev-Walmart Global - The Hershey Co.; *pg.* 1855, *pg.* 1538

May, Rochelle, Sr Mgr-Benefits & HRIS - Aeropostale, Inc.; *pg.* 17, *pg.* 1188

May, Susan V., Sr Mgr - Broadcom Corporation; *pg.* 364, *pg.* 108

May, Tom, Dir-PR - MFA Oil Company; *pg.* 981, *pg.* 976

May, Wayne N., Publr & Mgr-Adv - Ancient American; *pg.* 1616, *pg.* 1856

Mayer, Brian, Brand Mgr-EAS & Zone Perfect - Abbott Nutrition; *pg.* 1485, *pg.* 1437

Mayer, Diane, VP-Residence Inn & Brand Mgr-Global - Marriott International, Inc.; *pg.* 1102, *pg.* 764

Mayer, Jill, Controller-Fin & Dir-Mktg - Bead Industries Inc.; *pg.* 200, *pg.* 356

Mayer, John F., VP-Retail Sls-US - The J.M. Smucker Company; *pg.* 865, *pg.* 1468

Mayer, Julia, Specialist-Mktg-HP PSG - SYNNEX Corporation; *pg.* 480, *pg.* 92

Mayer, Justin, Dir-Brand Mktg & Gen Mgr-Hess Toy Truck - Hess Corporation; *pg.* 979, *pg.* 1240

Mayer, Kenny, Mgr-Mktg - United Parcel Service, Inc.; *pg.* 1928, *pg.* 522

Mayer, Kevin, Chief Strategy Officer & Sr Exec VP - The Walt Disney Company; *pg.* 317, *pg.* 52

Mayer, Liz, Product Mgr-Coffee Mktg - The J.M. Smucker Company; *pg.* 865, *pg.* 1468

Mayer, Matt, Product Mgr-Cross Border Pooling - Northern Trust Corporation; *pg.* 787, *pg.* 585

Mayer, Mike, Exec VP-Sls Solutions - NBC Universal, Inc.; *pg.* 300, *pg.* 1266

Mayer, Rose, Product Mgr - Autobytel Inc.; *pg.* 1230, *pg.* 107

Mayer, Sarah, Dir-Technical Assurance-IT Product Sys - The Boeing Company; *pg.* 225, *pg.* 567

Mayer, Sonja, Specialist-Mktg - The Procter & Gamble Company; *pg.* 1129, *pg.* 1418

Mayeri, Elizabeth, Dir-PR-Intl - Orange Business Services; *pg.* 1273, *pg.* 1785

Mayerick, Joseph , Jr., Sr VP-Mktg - Bolt Technology Corporation; *pg.* 1318, *pg.* 360

Mayers, Hannah, Coord-Mktg - Rich Products Corporation; *pg.* 892, *pg.* 1150

Mayers, Peter, Sr Mgr-Bus Dev - Barbados Tourism Authority; *pg.* 1900, *pg.* 1200
Mayes, Kelly, Product Mgr - Facebook, Inc.; *pg.* 1245, *pg.* 143
Mayes, Maureen, Mgr-Mktg - Flextronics International Ltd.; *pg.* 81, *pg.* 245
Mayes, Ryan, Brand Mgr - Carrier Corporation; *pg.* 1070, *pg.* 349
Mayew, Julie C., Dir-Mktg - Abbott Laboratories; *pg.* 1484, *pg.* 551
Mayfield, Dale, VP & Product Head-Residential Products - Masonite International Corporation; *pg.* 1054, *pg.* 1920
Mayfield, Heather, Mgr-Comml Mktg Comm-Global - Dell Inc.; *pg.* 383, *pg.* 1737
Mayfield, Jonathan, Product Mgr-Mobile - Delta Air Lines, Inc.; *pg.* 1905, *pg.* 503
Mayfield, Kristina, Mgr-CRM & Digital Mktg - Jenny Craig Operations, Inc.; *pg.* 1548, *pg.* 59
Mayforth, Shannon, Mgr-Natl Assurance Mktg - PricewaterhouseCoopers LLP; *pg.* 795, *pg.* 1283
Mayko, Kathleen, Dir-Social Media-MassMutual Fin Grp - Massachusetts Mutual Life Insurance Company; *pg.* 1207, *pg.* 845
Mayle, Steve, VP-Trade & Mktg - General Mills, Inc.; *pg.* 828, *pg.* 933
Maylor, Ken, VP-Sls & Mktg - Orbotech Inc.; *pg.* 1367, *pg.* 788
Mayman, Avrum, Dir-Product Mgmt & Mktg - Segway Inc.; *pg.* 1923, *pg.* 1033
Mayman, Gemma, Dir-Mktg-Chantix - Pfizer Inc.; *pg.* 1581, *pg.* 1278
Maynard, Brett, Product Mgr - Automatic Data Processing, Inc.; *pg.* 357, *pg.* 1117
Maynard, Chris, VP-Membership Mktg - BJ's Wholesale Club, Inc.; *pg.* 1762, *pg.* 857
Maynard, Deb, Dir-Mktg-Special Projects - United Natural Foods, Inc.; *pg.* 907, *pg.* 1608
Maynard, Don, Sr Product Mgr-Dell Precision Workstations - Dell Inc.; *pg.* 383, *pg.* 1737
Maynard, Jared, Acct Dir-Programmatic Sls-Natl - Demand Media, Inc.; *pg.* 1238, *pg.* 273
Mayne, Dena, VP-Mktg-Food & Beverage-Asia Pacific & Latin America - Ecolab Inc.; *pg.* 329, *pg.* 960
Mayo, Beth, Dir-Digital Mktg - Tanger Factory Outlet Centers, Inc.; *pg.* 1116, *pg.* 1376
Mayo, Tiffany, Sr Mgr-Mktg - L'Oreal USA; *pg.* 514, *pg.* 1252
Mayora, Virginia, Sr Specialist-Adv Compliance - The Guardian Life Insurance Company of America; *pg.* 1202, *pg.* 1237
Mayoralgo, Tom, Mgr-Customer Mktg - The Yankee Candle Company, Inc.; *pg.* 1792, *pg.* 843
Mays, Charley, Dir-Mktg - Dr Pepper Snapple Group, Inc.; *pg.* 250, *pg.* 1729
Mays, Jim, Chief Creative Officer-Design & Grp VP-Design - Ford Motor Company; *pg.* 172, *pg.* 876
Mays, Karen, Head-B2B Mktg - E*TRADE Financial Corporation; *pg.* 749, *pg.* 1230
Mays, Susan, VP-Mktg & Strategic Initiatives - CH2M HILL Companies, Ltd.; *pg.* 75, *pg.* 325
Mazakas, Michele, Mgr-Product Ops - General Electric Company; *pg.* 1297, *pg.* 347
Mazey, Gia, Sr Mgr-Mktg-Integrated Comm - The Western Union Company; *pg.* 822, *pg.* 327
Mazhukhina, Irina, District Coord-Mktg - H&R Block, Inc.; *pg.* 764, *pg.* 983
Maziarz, Gary, Mgr-Global Product Data Mgmt - Bose Corporation; *pg.* 626, *pg.* 820
Mazick, Mark, Dir-Global Retail Brand Mktg - The Hershey Co.; *pg.* 1855, *pg.* 1538
Mazur, Gary F., Sr Assoc Brand Mgr-Beverages - Campbell Soup Company; *pg.* 844, *pg.* 1048
Mazuranic, Jordan, Graphic Designer-Digital Media - Schnuck Markets, Inc.; *pg.* 1033, *pg.* 1002
Mazza, AJ, Mgr-Mktg - ESPN, Inc.; *pg.* 285, *pg.* 340
Mazza, Lou, Sr Assoc VP-Sls & Mktg - Amica Mutual Insurance Co.; *pg.* 1192, *pg.* 1602
Mazza, Mary J., Client Partner-IT, Mktg & Sls - Alcatel-Lucent; *pg.* 615, *pg.* 38
Mazza, Maurizio, Product Mgr-Brazed & Gasket Heat Exchanger - Alfa Laval Inc.; *pg.* 700, *pg.* 1800
Mazzei, Carole, Mgr-Mktg Programs & Svcs - Arrow Electronics, Inc.; *pg.* 619, *pg.* 325
Mazzeo, Genevieve, Mgr-Integrated Mktg - ConAgra Foods, Inc.; *pg.* 826, *pg.* 1014
Mazzini, Scott, Sr VP-Product Mgmt - Bunn-O-Matic Corporation; *pg.* 53, *pg.* 661
Mazzocco, Len, Sr VP-Creative - The Walt Disney Company; *pg.* 317, *pg.* 52
Mazzoli, Bob, Chief Creative Officer - Calvin Klein, Inc.; *pg.* 20, *pg.* 1209
Mbugua, Martin, Dir-Media Rels & University Spokesperson - Princeton University Press; *pg.* 1678, *pg.* 1112
Mburu, Miriam, Natl Dir-Mktg - Aon Risk Services Inc.; *pg.* 1193, *pg.* 564
McAdams, Jeff, Head-Global Running Mktg - New Balance Athletic Shoe, Inc.; *pg.* 1811, *pg.* 798
McAffee, Michele, Dir-Mktg - Rockford Symphony Orchestra; *pg.* 579, *pg.* 655
Mcalear, Matt, Brand Mgr-Dodge - FCA US LLC; *pg.* 170, *pg.* 868
McAleenan, Kathleen, Bus Mgr-Specialty Crops - Monsanto Company; *pg.* 1173, *pg.* 999
McAleer, Bryan, Assoc Dir-Mktg-Sports - ESPN, Inc.; *pg.* 285, *pg.* 340
McAlister, Larry, Dir-Sls & Mktg Comm - Hanesbrands Inc.; *pg.* 26, *pg.* 1394
McAllen, Rob, Mgr-Interactive Products-Blackbaud Europe - Blackbaud, Inc.; *pg.* 361, *pg.* 1613
McAllister, Amanda, Sr Dir-Strategy & Ops - Microsoft Corporation; *pg.* 435, *pg.* 1824
McAllister, Beth, Reg Sls Mgr & Sr Rep-Applications Sls - Oracle Corporation; *pg.* 450, *pg.* 191
McAllister, Curt, Mgr-Product News - Toyota Motor Sales, U.S.A., Inc.; *pg.* 193, *pg.* 296
McAllister, Diana, Dir-Mktg - Papa Murphy's International, LLC; *pg.* 1743, *pg.* 1846
McAllister, Ian, Dir-Product - Airbnb, Inc.; *pg.* 1226, *pg.* 211
Mcallister, Jackie, Sr Dir-Brand Mktg & Extended Stay Brands - Marriott International, Inc.; *pg.* 1102, *pg.* 764
McAllister, Jeff, Sr Mgr-Asset-Soccer Sports Mktg - adidas America Inc.; *pg.* 1803, *pg.* 1500
McAllister, Matthew, Sr Mgr-Product Mgmt, Prime & Delivery Experience - Amazon.com, Inc.; *pg.* 1226, *pg.* 1831
McAllister, Mike, Dir-Residential Mktg - Beaulieu Group, LLC; *pg.* 917, *pg.* 529
McAllister, Patrick, Sr Mgr-Mktg - E*TRADE Financial Corporation; *pg.* 749, *pg.* 1230
McAllister, Ryan, Mgr-Mktg - Amazon.com, Inc.; *pg.* 1226, *pg.* 1831
McAllister, Scott, Sr VP-Consumer Digital Mktg & Revenue - Time Inc.; *pg.* 1693, *pg.* 1300
McAllister, Stacey, Sr Dir-Stored Value & Emerging Payments - The Gap, Inc.; *pg.* 1770, *pg.* 218
McAlpin, Tom, Mgr-Mktg-AgChem Additives - BASF Corporation; *pg.* 1149, *pg.* 1066
McAlpine, Peter, Sr Dir-APAC-Education Sls & Channel - Adobe Systems Incorporated; *pg.* 342, *pg.* 235
McAnally, Bryce, Brand Mgr-Adv - California Travel & Tourism Commission; *pg.* 990, *pg.* 196
McAndrew, John, Sr Mgr-Mktg - PepsiCo, Inc.; *pg.* 259, *pg.* 1327
McAndrew, Tom, Mgr-Technical Mktg-Content Creation - Dolby Laboratories, Inc.; *pg.* 284, *pg.* 217
McAndrews, Bailey, Brand Mgr-Assassin's Creed - Ubisoft Inc.; *pg.* 589, *pg.* 229
McAndrews, Tom, VP-Mktg - Rodney Hunt Company; *pg.* 1372, *pg.* 840
McAneany, Kathleen, Mgr-Product Mgmt-Productivity Applications - BlackBerry; *pg.* 625, *pg.* 1717
McAninch, Becky, Sr Dir-Beverage Innovation - The Kraft Heinz Company; *pg.* 871, *pg.* 641
McArdle, Chris, VP-Mktg Svcs - NeuStar, Inc.; *pg.* 1872, *pg.* 1807
McArdle, Janine J., VP-Oil & Gas Mktg-Worldwide - Apache Corporation; *pg.* 1934, *pg.* 1700
McArdle, Justin, Product Mgr-Adv Products - Kelley Blue Book Co., Inc.; *pg.* 1656, *pg.* 112
McArdle, Moira, VP-Mktg - Market Data Retrieval; *pg.* 1661, *pg.* 370
McAree, Guy, Dir-Corp Comm & Mktg - Ballard Power Systems, Inc.; *pg.* 70, *pg.* 1907
McArthur, Judy, Mgr-Customer Mktg - McCain Foods Limited; *pg.* 876, *pg.* 1915
McArthur, Stephanie, Program Mgr-Integrated Mktg-Global - CA Technologies; *pg.* 366, *pg.* 1168
McAteer, Brian D., VP-Sls Ops - CommVault Systems, Inc.; *pg.* 377, *pg.* 1125
Mcateer, John, Gen Mgr-Sls - Domtar Corporation; *pg.* 1456, *pg.* 1954
McAteer, John, VP-US Sls, Retail & Tech - Google Inc.; *pg.* 1249, *pg.* 153
McAulay, Chuck, Dir-Local Mktg - Bonefish Grill; *pg.* 1717, *pg.* 471
McAuley, Sarah, Sr Dir-Mktg - EnerNOC, Inc.; *pg.* 976, *pg.* 794
Mcauliffe, Carolanne, VP-Mktg - National Basketball Association; *pg.* 566, *pg.* 1264
McAuliffe, Heather, VP-PR - J. Crew Group, Inc.; *pg.* 1773, *pg.* 1245
McAuliffe, Kelley, Mgr-Mdsg-Intl - Under Armour, Inc.; *pg.* 49, *pg.* 759
McAuslan, Grant, Sr Mgr-Digital Mktg & eCommerce Dev - The Rockport Group; *pg.* 1818, *pg.* 812
McAvoy, Dawn, Head-Branding & Adv - Aetna Inc.; *pg.* 1187, *pg.* 351
McAvoy, Holly, Mgr-Mktg Comm Plng - Deere & Company; *pg.* 703, *pg.* 632
Mcavoy, Lisa, Mgr-Interactive Mktg - ConAgra Foods, Inc.; *pg.* 826, *pg.* 1014
McAvoy, Lisa, Mgr-Product Dev - CQ Roll Call; *pg.* 1631, *pg.* 397
McAvoy, Susanne, Exec VP-Mktg - Crown Media Holdings Inc.; *pg.* 280, *pg.* 281
McAvoy, Susanne, Exec VP-Mktg, Creative & Comm - The Hallmark Channel; *pg.* 290, *pg.* 281
McAward, Melissa, Sr Rep-Mktg - Kelly Services, Inc.; *pg.* 424, *pg.* 911
McBath, Andrew, Sr Dir-Product & Strategic Mktg - Internap Network Services Corporation; *pg.* 417, *pg.* 513
McBee, Kim, VP-Mktg & Adv - Big O Tires, Inc.; *pg.* 201, *pg.* 314
McBennett, Maggie, Sr Dir-HR - LinkedIn Corporation; *pg.* 1262, *pg.* 160
McBratney, Brent, Dir-Airline Mktg - Airbus North America Holdings, Inc.; *pg.* 1897, *pg.* 1784
McBratney, Kt, Sr Mgr-Bus Dev - Newegg Inc.; *pg.* 1271, *pg.* 67
Mcbride, Laura, Brand Mgr-Coffee - The J.M. Smucker Company; *pg.* 865, *pg.* 1468
McBrien, Bob, Product Mgr - Bel Fuse Inc.; *pg.* 624, *pg.* 1075
Mcburnett, Chad, Sr Specialist-Product - Southwire Company; *pg.* 1063, *pg.* 527
McBurney, Matthew J., VP-Comml Products Grp - Modine Manufacturing Company; *pg.* 1074, *pg.* 1888
McCabe, Caitlin, Sr Mgr-PR - Microsoft Corporation; *pg.* 435, *pg.* 1824
McCabe, Claire, Sr Mgr-Licensing - American Society for the Prevention of Cruelty to Animals; *pg.* 131, *pg.* 1193
McCabe, Clare, Assoc Dir-Mktg - Bristol-Myers Squibb Company; *pg.* 1509, *pg.* 1206
McCabe, Colleen, Sr Dir-External Comm - Getty Images, Inc.; *pg.* 1645, *pg.* 1836
McCabe, Daniel, Sr VP-Sls & Mktg-US & Canada - Deere & Company; *pg.* 703, *pg.* 632
McCabe, Jamie, Coord-Product Mktg - Plantronics, Inc.; *pg.* 663, *pg.* 270
McCabe, Jenny, Dir-Media Rels-Global - Netflix, Inc.; *pg.* 1269, *pg.* 141
McCabe, Kaitlin, Asst Mgr-Products & ECommerce - Weight Watchers International, Inc.; *pg.* 1609, *pg.* 1313
McCabe, Kristen, Asst VP-Product - Luxottica Retail; *pg.* 8, *pg.* 1460
McCabe, Larry, Sr Dir-Brdcst - Tampa Bay Rays Baseball, Ltd.; *pg.* 586, *pg.* 464
Mccabe, Patricia, Sr Mgr-Mktg - Benjamin Moore & Co.; *pg.* 1440, *pg.* 1085
McCadden, Leticia, Specialist-PR - The Gallup Organization; *pg.* 399, *pg.* 399
McCadney, Lauren, Dir-Digital Engagement & Social Media - CDW Corporation; *pg.* 370, *pg.* 663
McCafferty, Brianne, Planner-Sls - Turner Broadcasting System, Inc.; *pg.* 314, *pg.* 521
McCafferty, Christine, Reg Dir-PR & Comm - Comcast Cable Communications, Inc.; *pg.* 276, *pg.* 1560
McCaffree, Matt, Sr Dir-Regulatory Strategy - Comverge, Inc.; *pg.* 1325, *pg.* 536
McCaffrey, Michael, Sr Dir-Reputation Strategy & Insights - Johnson & Johnson; *pg.* 1549, *pg.* 1091
McCaffrey, Sara, Dir-Sls Ops - Tremor Video; *pg.* 682, *pg.* 1305
McCaffrey, Shirley, Specialist-Mktg - McKesson Corporation; *pg.* 1560, *pg.* 222
McCaffrey, Tom, Product Dir-Enterprise Solutions - Kroll Inc.; *pg.* 425, *pg.* 1249
McCaffrey, William, Dir-Mktg - Meredith Corporation; *pg.*

1663, *pg.* 705
Mccain, Ron, VP-Sls Dev - Reliv International, Inc.; *pg.* 1589, *pg.* 975
McCain, Shawne, Product Mgr-Ladies, Men's & Kids Basic Accessories - Bon Ton Stores, Inc.; *pg.* 1763, *pg.* 1596
McCalister, Brad, Mgr-Digital Mktg-Global - Ford Motor Company; *pg.* 172, *pg.* 876
McCall, Rob, VP-Adv Sls - Scripps Networks Interactive, Inc.; *pg.* 1279, *pg.* 1638
McCall, Shane, VP-Mktg Comm - PetSmart, Inc.; *pg.* 1481, *pg.* 18
McCall, Tracie, Mgr-Specialties Mktg - Marathon Petroleum Company LLC; *pg.* 981, *pg.* 1454
Mccalla, Bridget, Mgr-Acq Online Mktg - JPMorgan Chase & Co.; *pg.* 772, *pg.* 1246
McCallister, Michael, Mgr-Creative-Mktg Brand Mgmt - Cabela's Incorporated; *pg.* 535, *pg.* 1019
McCallson, Karen, VP-PR - PHH Corporation; *pg.* 793, *pg.* 1090
Mccallum, Katrinka, VP-Product & Tech Ops - Red Hat, Inc.; *pg.* 460, *pg.* 1388
McCamant, Kimberly, Sr Mgr-Mktg-Siemens Building Technologies - Siemens Process Industries and Drives; *pg.* 673, *pg.* 485
McCambridge, Christine, Mgr-Shopper Mktg - ConAgra Foods, Inc.; *pg.* 826, *pg.* 1014
McCambridge, Dennis, VP-Sls & Mktg - CTP Transportation Products; *pg.* 203, *pg.* 1006
McCambridge, Megan, VP-Global Brand & Mktg Customer Centricity - MetLife, Inc.; *pg.* 1208, *pg.* 1258
McCamley, Maren, Sr Mgr-Subsidiary Rights - Penguin Random House; *pg.* 1675, *pg.* 1276
McCammon, Scott, Product Mgr-Mktg-Global - Hewlett-Packard Company; *pg.* 404, *pg.* 175
McCann, Lauren, Mgr-Segment Mktg - T-Mobile US, Inc.; *pg.* 676, *pg.* 1816
McCann, Lisa, Dir-Global Mktg-Tequila - Pernod Ricard USA, Inc.; *pg.* 1968, *pg.* 1332
McCann, Mark, Product Mgr-Rx Lenses - Oakley, Inc.; *pg.* 1840, *pg.* 86
McCann, Maureen, VP-Sls & Mktg - Caleres, Inc.; *pg.* 1805, *pg.* 993
McCann, Michael, Dir-Consumer Mktg - True Value Company; *pg.* 1065, *pg.* 592
McCann, Paul W., VP & Head-Production-Global - Monsanto Company; *pg.* 1173, *pg.* 999
McCann, Rich, Dir-Mktg - Nice-Pak Products, Inc.; *pg.* 1465, *pg.* 1319
McCann, Tracy, Sr Mgr-Fleet-North America - Mylan, Inc.; *pg.* 1570, *pg.* 1520
McCardell, Roger, Sr Mgr-Sls - Kidde Fire Fighting; *pg.* 1170, *pg.* 1531
McCarey, Brett, Sr Mgr-Mktg - AutoTrader, Inc.; *pg.* 1230, *pg.* 490
McCarron, Hilary, Mgr-Port Mktg - Port Authority of New York & New Jersey; *pg.* 1919, *pg.* 1283
McCarron, Tom, VP-Sls & Mktg-Oil & Gas - Eaton Corporation; *pg.* 1331, *pg.* 1429
McCarthy, Alanna, Assoc Mgr-Mktg - MATTEL, INC.; *pg.* 962, *pg.* 81
McCarthy, Brian J., Rep-Adv Sls - The New York Times Company; *pg.* 1668, *pg.* 1270
McCarthy, Christine, Mgr-Direct Mktg - Foxwoods Resort Casino; *pg.* 549, *pg.* 353
McCarthy, Christopher, Dir-Mktg - Sargento Foods Inc.; *pg.* 894, *pg.* 1886
McCarthy, Craig, Dir-Partnership Mktg - Major League Soccer LLC; *pg.* 560, *pg.* 1256
McCarthy, Dan, Dir-Bus & Mktg Strategy - Intuit Inc.; *pg.* 769, *pg.* 158
McCarthy, Denise, Mgr-Adv & PR - Brother International Corporation - USA; *pg.* 53, *pg.* 1046
McCarthy, Elizabeth, Sr Brand Mktg Mgr - Lee Jofa, Inc.; *pg.* 933, *pg.* 1142
McCarthy, Elizabeth, Rep-Mktg Svcs-Atlantic Gulf - The Williams Companies, Inc.; *pg.* 987, *pg.* 1491
McCarthy, Jackie, Sr Mgr-DTC Sls & Mktg - The Valspar Corporation; *pg.* 1449, *pg.* 945
McCarthy, Jj, Head-Local Mktg - eBay Inc.; *pg.* 1240, *pg.* 243
McCarthy, John, Sr Product Mgr-Annuity Products - MORNINGSTAR, INC.; *pg.* 784, *pg.* 583
McCarthy, John, VP-Mktg-Puritan's Pride & Direct Digital - NBTY, Inc.; *pg.* 1572, *pg.* 1338
McCarthy, Kara, Dir-Mktg Partnerships & Bus Dev - The Clorox Company; *pg.* 327, *pg.* 169
McCarthy, Kerri, Sr Assoc Brand Mgr-OREO - Mondelez International; *pg.* 877, *pg.* 1344
McCarthy, Kerri, Sr Assoc Brand Mgr-OREO - Mondelez North America; *pg.* 881, *pg.* 1054
McCarthy, Kevin, Sr Mgr-PR - Workiva; *pg.* 493, *pg.* 701
McCarthy, Kristine, Mgr-Mktg Budget - Zoll Medical Corporation; *pg.* 1612, *pg.* 814
McCarthy, Maria, VP-Midwest-Corp Sls - Time Inc.; *pg.* 1693, *pg.* 1300
McCarthy, Marisa, Dir-Mktg & PR - Pasadena Symphony Association; *pg.* 574, *pg.* 181
McCarthy, Mary, Mgr-Mktg, Pub & Analyst Rels-Mainframe Solutions - Compuware Corporation; *pg.* 379, *pg.* 879
McCarthy, Matthew, Sr Dir-Brand Dev - Unilever United States, Inc.; *pg.* 904, *pg.* 1061
McCarthy, Megan, Analyst-Social Media Comm - Hilton Worldwide, Inc.; *pg.* 1094, *pg.* 1791
McCarthy, Michael, VP & Sr Mgr-Comml Real Estate Relationship - M&T Bank Corporation; *pg.* 777, *pg.* 1149
McCarthy, Mike, Dir-Adv & Mdsg - DineEquity, Inc.; *pg.* 1725, *pg.* 95
McCarthy, Mike, Acct Mgr-Sls - Intelligrated, Inc.; *pg.* 1349, *pg.* 1460
McCarthy, Pat, Sr VP-Corp Mktg - AppNexus; *pg.* 352, *pg.* 1196
McCarthy, Patrick, Dir-Sls - Ariba, Inc.; *pg.* 353, *pg.* 283
Mccarthy, R. Casey, Dir-Integrated Mktg-Bon Appetit & Epicurious - Conde Nast Publications, Inc.; *pg.* 1629, *pg.* 1217
McCarthy, Ryan, Specialist-Field Mktg - Papa Ginos-Deangelo Holding Corporation, Inc.; *pg.* 1743, *pg.* 817
McCarthy, Scott, VP-Sls-Asia Pacific - Gaming Partners International Corporation; *pg.* 954, *pg.* 1024
McCarthy, Sue, Div VP-Global Digital Mktg - Coach, Inc.; *pg.* 3, *pg.* 1214
McCarthy, Tim, Dir-Technical Mktg - Juniper Networks, Inc.; *pg.* 1260, *pg.* 286
McCartin, Brian, Exec VP-Convention & Tourism Sls - Travel Portland; *pg.* 1008, *pg.* 1507
McCartin, Matthew, CMO & VP-Mktg - Williamson-Dickie Manufacturing Company; *pg.* 50, *pg.* 1696
McCartney, Amanda, Sr Specialist-Mktg - Covered California; *pg.* 1519, *pg.* 196
McCartney, Barbara, VP-Mktg North America-Nestle Health Science - Nestle USA, Inc.; *pg.* 883, *pg.* 96
McCarty, Gavin, Sr Sls Mgr-Carrier Sls - Samsung Electronics America, Inc.; *pg.* 669, *pg.* 1115
McCarty, Geoffrey R., VP-Mktg - Luna Innovations Inc.; *pg.* 1557, *pg.* 1806
McCarty, Jami, Sr Mgr-Mktg - Red Hat, Inc.; *pg.* 460, *pg.* 1388
Mccarty, Karen, Dir-Creative-Community Programs - Big Apple Circus Ltd.; *pg.* 533, *pg.* 1145
McCarus, John, Chief Strategy Officer - Media General, Inc.; *pg.* 297, *pg.* 1803
McCarver, MacKenzie, Mgr-Social Media Comm - Hilton Worldwide, Inc.; *pg.* 1094, *pg.* 1791
McCarville, Brendon, Sr Coord-Mktg - Atmos Energy Corporation; *pg.* 1935, *pg.* 1675
McCaskey, Daniel, Sr Dir-Brand Adv - Capital One Financial Corporation; *pg.* 730, *pg.* 1789
McCasland, Amber, Sr Dir-Corp Affairs - Levi Strauss & Co.; *pg.* 43, *pg.* 220
McCasland, Mitch, Sr Dir-Global Consumer Insights - T.G.I. Friday's Inc.; *pg.* 1754, *pg.* 1669
Mccathren, Michael, Mgr-Interactive Digital Mktg - Chick-fil-A, Inc.; *pg.* 1721, *pg.* 492
McCaughan, Sandy, Specialist-Adv - American Honda Motor Co., Inc.; *pg.* 163, *pg.* 292
McCaughey, Jennifer F., Sr Dir-IR & Fin Comm - Transcontinental Inc.; *pg.* 1695, *pg.* 1957
McCaul, Brian, Sr VP & Product Mgr-Credit Card - Zions Bancorporation; *pg.* 824, *pg.* 1762
McCauley, John, Sr Dir-Mktg - Maple Leaf Sports & Entertainment Ltd.; *pg.* 560, *pg.* 1940
McCauley, Kieran, Sr Dir-Brand Mktg - Marcos Pizza Inc.; *pg.* 1737, *pg.* 1476
McCauley, Steve, Sr Dir-Mktg-Frozen Pizza & Snacks - Nestle USA, Inc.; *pg.* 883, *pg.* 96
McCauley, Tim, Sr Dir-Mobile Commerce - Walgreen Co.; *pg.* 1608, *pg.* 605
Mccaulley, Brad, VP-Sls - Entertainment Publications, Inc.; *pg.* 1639, *pg.* 910
McCausland, Doug, Dir & Head-Product Mktg & Digital Media-CDN Svcs - AT&T Inc.; *pg.* 1867, *pg.* 1674
McCausland, Joel, Dir-Product Mgmt - Sport Court International Inc.; *pg.* 1846, *pg.* 1761
McChrystal, Bill, Reg VP-Mdsg - CarMax, Inc.; *pg.* 167, *pg.* 1800
McClain, Ann, Sr Dir-Bus Intelligence Effectiveness - Sanofi US; *pg.* 1592, *pg.* 1046
McClain, Clint, Sr Dir-Mktg Content - Wal-Mart Stores, Inc.; *pg.* 1790, *pg.* 29
McClain, Robin, VP-Mktg & Comm - Destination DC; *pg.* 991, *pg.* 398
McClamroch, Dave, Mgr-Partnership Mktg - Chicago Bears Football Club, Inc.; *pg.* 538, *pg.* 623
McClanahan, Brad, Dir-Mktg - Tennessee Football, Inc.; *pg.* 587, *pg.* 1654
McClaren, Sue Ann, VP-Ticket Sls, Ops & Svcs - Colorado Rockies Baseball Club, Ltd.; *pg.* 542, *pg.* 317
McClarren, Andrea, Mgr-Retail Mktg - The Children's Place, Inc.; *pg.* 22, *pg.* 1119
McClary, Brian, Brand Mgr-Ford Fiesta - Ford Motor Company; *pg.* 172, *pg.* 876
McClary-Ransier, Rachel, Dir-Mktg BRMC - Community Health Systems, Inc.; *pg.* 1516, *pg.* 1632
McClaskey, Chad F., Mgr-Mktg - Telsmith, Inc.; *pg.* 1381, *pg.* 1871
McClay, Ileana, Mgr-Mktg Integration - The Florida Lottery; *pg.* 992, *pg.* 469
McClean, Natasha, Product Dir - Neutrogena Corporation; *pg.* 517, *pg.* 137
McClear, Rebecca, Specialist-Mktg Comm - THE DOW CHEMICAL COMPANY; *pg.* 1157, *pg.* 898
McCleary, Kelly, Sr Dir-Mdse Fin - Wal-Mart Stores, Inc.; *pg.* 1790, *pg.* 29
McCleave, Bill, Brand Mgr-Mktg - Marathon Petroleum Company LLC; *pg.* 981, *pg.* 1454
Mcclellan, Michael R., VP-Indus Products - Norfolk Southern Corporation; *pg.* 1917, *pg.* 1797
McClelland, Alex, Designer-Product - American Greetings Corporation; *pg.* 1615, *pg.* 1428
McClelland, Andy, Mgr-Mktg Personalization - L.L. Bean, Inc.; *pg.* 1777, *pg.* 750
Mcclelland, Christina, Brand Mgr-Barefoot Wine & Bubbly Field-Virginia - E&J Gallo Winery; *pg.* 1962, *pg.* 149
McClelland, Lisa, Sr Mgr-Audit - Donaldson Company, Inc.; *pg.* 1329, *pg.* 917
McClelland, Scott, Dir-Product Mgmt-Global - Branson Ultrasonics Corporation - Plastics Joining Division; *pg.* 1403, *pg.* 343
McClement, Christopher, Sr Dir-Mktg & Mainstream Coffee - The Kraft Heinz Company; *pg.* 871, *pg.* 641
McClement, Kristin, Asst Mgr-Corp PR - Chico's FAS, Inc.; *pg.* 21, *pg.* 427
McClemmy, Richard, VP-Corp Sls - Angels Baseball, L.P.; *pg.* 529, *pg.* 42
McClenahan, Taylor, Mgr-Sls-Natl - DealerTrack Holdings, Inc.; *pg.* 743, *pg.* 1172
Mcclennan, Kim, Mgr-Social Media - Home Hardware Stores Limited; *pg.* 1051, *pg.* 1933
McClennen, Lindsey, Dir-Mktg - AstraZeneca Pharmaceuticals LP; *pg.* 1497, *pg.* 389
McClew, Brad, Mgr-Traffic-Adv Production - Michaels Stores, Inc.; *pg.* 1127, *pg.* 1722
McCloskey, Brian, Sr VP-Sourcing & Digital Mktg - AMN Healthcare Services, Inc.; *pg.* 1494, *pg.* 200
McCloskey, Carly, Mgr-Tourism Sls & Mktg - The Museum of Modern Art; *pg.* 565, *pg.* 1263
McCloskey, Holly, Dir-Media - Dillard's, Inc.; *pg.* 1766, *pg.* 34
McCloy, Kristen, Coord-PR - RE/MAX International, Inc.; *pg.* 1109, *pg.* 322
McClune, Paul, Product Mgr - ITT Corporation; *pg.* 1351, *pg.* 1354
Mcclung, Bruce, VP-Sls - PFSweb, Inc.; *pg.* 1275, *pg.* 1733
McClung, Kathleen, Sr Dir-Advice & Wealth Mgmt PR - Ameriprise Financial, Inc.; *pg.* 715, *pg.* 930
McClung, Laura, Head-Audience & Product Mktg-You Tube, B2B - Google Inc.; *pg.* 1249, *pg.* 153
McClung, Reed, Sr Dir-Customer Mktg Oncology Managed Markets US - Novartis Pharmaceuticals Corp.; *pg.* 1575, *pg.* 1054
McClure, Beth, Dir-Mktg & Comm - Agilysys, Inc.; *pg.* 614, *pg.* 1409
McClure, Doug, Sr Dir-Bus Intelligence - Genuine Parts Company; *pg.* 206, *pg.* 506
Mcclure, Eliza, Brand Mgr-LOUIS XIII & QSS - Remy Cointreau USA Inc.; *pg.* 1969, *pg.* 1285
McClure, Jennifer, Mgr-Integration, Comm & Media - Coca-

First page reference indicates Business Class Edition
Second page reference indicates Geographic Edition

Cola Refreshments USA, Inc.; *pg.* 247, *pg.* 500
McClure, John, Assoc VP-Convention Sls - Anaheim/Orange County Visitor & Convention Bureau; *pg.* 988, *pg.* 42
McClure, Marc, VP-Field Sls-Eastern US - Tech Data Corporation; *pg.* 482, *pg.* 416
McClurg, Maurice, Mgr-Work & Hunt Mktg - Red Wing Shoe Company, Inc.; *pg.* 1817, *pg.* 954
McCluskey, Kerri, Mgr-Creative Adv Copy - J.C. Penney Company, Inc.; *pg.* 1774, *pg.* 1732
McCluskey, Tara, Planner-Sls - NBC Universal, Inc.; *pg.* 300, *pg.* 1266
McColl, Alastair, Dir-Mdsg-Running Footwear North America - NIKE, Inc.; *pg.* 1812, *pg.* 1492
McColley, Cindy, Mgr-Mktg-Branded Fin & Insurance Products - General Motors Company; *pg.* 175, *pg.* 881
McCollin, Terri, Sr Mgr-PR-EMEA - Preferred Hotel Group; *pg.* 1108, *pg.* 587
McCollum, Adam, Dir-PR & Comm - Bally North America, Inc.; *pg.* 1804, *pg.* 1200
McCollum, James, Dir-Mktg - Big Heart Pet Brands; *pg.* 1474, *pg.* 213
McCollum, Tom, Global Product Mgr - Molex Incorporated; *pg.* 655, *pg.* 628
Mccomb, Lisa, Dir-Media Rels - McDonald's Corporation; *pg.* 1737, *pg.* 645
McComb, Shawn, Mgr-Mktg-Global - CNH America LLC; *pg.* 702, *pg.* 560
McConeghey, Theresa, Asst VP-SBD Products - Principal Financial Group, Inc.; *pg.* 796, *pg.* 706
McConnell, Bernie, VP-Product Grp & Svcs-WIDIA - Kennametal Inc.; *pg.* 1052, *pg.* 1547
McConnell, Brent, Dir-Interactive Mktg - Kelly Services, Inc.; *pg.* 424, *pg.* 911
McConnell, Christine, Dir-Mktg - Travelzoo Inc; *pg.* 1926, *pg.* 1304
McConnell, Colin, Dir-Product & Bus Products - ZipRealty, Inc.; *pg.* 1120, *pg.* 85
McConnell, Deborah, Mgr-Mobility Product - AT&T; *pg.* 1865, *pg.* 258
McConnell, Fred, Dir-Mktg - Susser Holdings Corporation; *pg.* 985, *pg.* 1671
McConnell, Jager, VP-Product-Work.com - salesforce.com, inc.; *pg.* 1278, *pg.* 226
Mcconnell, Jason, Sr Mgr-Product Mktg - Microsoft Corporation; *pg.* 435, *pg.* 1824
McConnell, Phil, VP & Div Mgr-Mdse - Hastings Entertainment, Inc.; *pg.* 1773, *pg.* 1659
McConnell, Rick M., Pres-Products & Dev - Akamai Technologies, Inc.; *pg.* 1226, *pg.* 807
Mcconnell, Ryan, VP-Corp Mktg - Atlas Van Lines, Inc.; *pg.* 1900, *pg.* 678
McConnell, Susan A., Mgr-Mktg Comm - McKesson Corporation; *pg.* 1560, *pg.* 222
McConville, Ray, Mgr-Media Rels - Verizon Communications Inc.; *pg.* 1875, *pg.* 1309
McConville, Sarah, VP-Mktg & Publr-HBR PRESS - Harvard Business Review; *pg.* 1648, *pg.* 1238
McCooey, John M., Dir-Mktg-Global - E.I. du Pont de Nemours & Company; *pg.* 1159, *pg.* 390
McCooey, Sharon, Sr Dir-Intl Ops - LinkedIn Corporation; *pg.* 1262, *pg.* 160
McCook, George M., VP-Mktg & Sls - Purcell Co., Inc.; *pg.* 1109, *pg.* 968
McCord, Carrie M., Dir-Mktg Svcs - American National Insurance Company; *pg.* 1191, *pg.* 1697
McCorison, Shannon, VP-Mktg-The Americas - ProLogis; *pg.* 1108, *pg.* 322
McCorkell, Emma, Dir-Original Film PR - Netflix, Inc.; *pg.* 1269, *pg.* 141
McCormack, Emma, Dir-Mktg-Asia Pacific - ShoreTel, Inc.; *pg.* 469, *pg.* 288
Mccormack, JoAnn, Sr Mgr-Digital Strategy - Novartis Corporation; *pg.* 1574, *pg.* 1273
McCormack, Maureen, Mgr-Segment & Media Rels - Deere & Company; *pg.* 703, *pg.* 632
McCormack, Richard, VP-Mktg Strategy & Ops - Fujitsu Computer Systems Corporation; *pg.* 398, *pg.* 285
McCormack, Roger, Dir-Accessories, Performance Parts Strategy, Plng & Mktg - General Motors Company; *pg.* 175, *pg.* 881
McCormick, Cathleen, Sr Mgr-Trade Mktg - Turkey Hill Dairy, Inc.; *pg.* 902, *pg.* 1522
McCormick, Chris, VP-Mktg - Starkey Laboratories, Inc.; *pg.* 1597, *pg.* 923
McCormick, Ginny, VP-Integrated Media & Promos - Hasbro, Inc.; *pg.* 954, *pg.* 1603
McCormick, Greg, Sr VP-Mktg & Bus Dev - Ranir LLC; *pg.* 520, *pg.* 888
McCormick, John, Exec VP-Sls - McNeil & NRM Inc.; *pg.* 1360, *pg.* 1402
McCormick, John, Exec Dir-Sls Dev - The New Yorker Magazine, Inc.; *pg.* 1669, *pg.* 1271
Mccormick, Ken, Product Mgr-SLS Core Stage - The Boeing Company; *pg.* 225, *pg.* 567
McCormick, Kristin, Assoc Product Mgr-Celestial Seasonings - The Hain Celestial Group, Inc.; *pg.* 860, *pg.* 1172
McCormick, Marc, Mgr-Field Mktg - Polycom, Inc.; *pg.* 664, *pg.* 249
McCormick, Melissa, VP-Sls-The Americas - Taylor Company; *pg.* 901, *pg.* 655
McCormick, Shane, Sr Mgr-Mktg - Cessna Aircraft Company; *pg.* 226, *pg.* 723
McCorvey, Susan, Specialist-Mktg - Evoqua Water Technologies; *pg.* 1162, *pg.* 541
McCotter, Rose, VP-Digital Mktg - Sony Pictures Entertainment Inc.; *pg.* 309, *pg.* 72
McCowan, Ryan, Product Mgr - ADTRAN, Inc.; *pg.* 344, *pg.* 6
McCown, Chris, VP-Video Product Mgmt - Scripps Networks Interactive, Inc.; *pg.* 1279, *pg.* 1638
Mccown, Sue, Product Mgr-Dev & R&D - Seattle Coffee Company; *pg.* 265, *pg.* 1839
McCoy, Holly, Mgr-Adv - Candid Color Systems, Inc.; *pg.* 1404, *pg.* 1485
McCoy, Jim, Dir-Sports Mktg - Nationwide Mutual Insurance Company; *pg.* 1210, *pg.* 1442
McCoy, Justin, VP-Mktg - Cousins Submarines, Inc.; *pg.* 1017, *pg.* 1870
McCoy, Katayun, Brand Mgr-John Frieda Hair Care Products - Kao Brands Co. Inc.; *pg.* 513, *pg.* 1415
McCoy, Laura, VP-Mktg & Comm - OhioHealth; *pg.* 1578, *pg.* 1443
McCoy, Leslie, Assoc Mgr-Mktg - Wente Vineyards; *pg.* 1972, *pg.* 122
McCoy, Marc, Dir-Crude Oil Mktg - Occidental Petroleum Corporation; *pg.* 1175, *pg.* 137
McCoy, Megan, Product Mgr-Mktg-Global - Emerson Process Management; *pg.* 1334, *pg.* 1636
McCoy, Mike, VP-Mktg & Comml Roofing - G-P Gypsum Corporation; *pg.* 978, *pg.* 505
McCoy, Scott, Brand Mgr-Pet Snacks Innovation - Big Heart Pet Brands; *pg.* 1474, *pg.* 213
McCoy, Travis, Product Mgr - Google Inc.; *pg.* 1249, *pg.* 153
Mccracken, Kelly, Assoc Product Mgr - Sun Life Financial Inc.; *pg.* 806, *pg.* 1944
McCracken, Shannon, Sr Dir-Direct Response Mktg - Special Olympics International, Inc.; *pg.* 157, *pg.* 405
Mccrary, David, Sr VP-Product Mgmt - Cardtronics, Inc.; *pg.* 732, *pg.* 1703
McCrary, Elissa, Sr Dir-Media Rels - American Cancer Society, Inc.; *pg.* 126, *pg.* 487
Mccray, Loren, Brand Mgr - The Procter & Gamble Company; *pg.* 1129, *pg.* 1418
McCray, Ronald D., Chm & Interim CEO - Career Education Corporation; *pg.* 599, *pg.* 658
McCrea, Jeffrey, VP-Sls & Mktg Grp & Dir-Consumer Channels Grp - Intel Corporation; *pg.* 645, *pg.* 266
McCreath, Damien, Sr Asst Brand Mgr - P&G-Clairol, Inc.; *pg.* 519, *pg.* 1418
McCreery, Clay, Sr VP-Sls & Svc-Worldwide - Concurrent Computer Corporation; *pg.* 379, *pg.* 531
McCreery, Michelle, Product Mgr - AS America, Inc.; *pg.* 68, *pg.* 1108
McCrehan, Arlene, Sr Dir-Online Media - Goodwill Industries International, Inc.; *pg.* 1771, *pg.* 776
McCreight, Tim, Dir-Mktg - American Institute of Chemical Engineers; *pg.* 129, *pg.* 1193
McCrocklin, Melinda, Sr Mgr-Brand-Global - American Girl LLC; *pg.* 949, *pg.* 1871
McCrory, Dale, Dir-Product Strategy & Innovation - First Data Corporation; *pg.* 754, *pg.* 505
McCrory, K.C., Supvr-PR - PPG Industries, Inc.; *pg.* 1445, *pg.* 1579
McCroskery, Amanda, Sr Producer-Creative Team-Global - Twitter, Inc.; *pg.* 1285, *pg.* 228
McCrumb, MaryBeth, Product Mgr - Affymetrix, Inc.; *pg.* 1487, *pg.* 263
McCue, Sandra, Mgr-Mktg Comm - Cardinal Health, Inc.; *pg.* 1512, *pg.* 1448
McCuiston, Adam, Dir-Mktg-Scotts - The Scotts Miracle-Gro Company; *pg.* 1799, *pg.* 1459
McCuiston, Anna, Dir-Mktg-Similac - Abbott Nutrition; *pg.* 1485, *pg.* 1437
McCullagh, Marc, Brand Mgr-Kettle Brand - Diamond Foods, Inc.; *pg.* 1851, *pg.* 216
McCullers, Derrica, Dir-Mktg - Salon Media Group, Inc.; *pg.* 1278, *pg.* 226
McCullers, Marissa, Sr Specialist-Mktg - Chico's FAS, Inc.; *pg.* 21, *pg.* 427
Mcculloch, David W., Sr Dir-Corp Comm - Cisco Systems, Inc.; *pg.* 372, *pg.* 240
McCulloch, Jay, VP-Global Mktg-Oral Care Products - Water Pik, Inc.; *pg.* 1609, *pg.* 329
McCulloch, Michelle, Dir-Mktg-West Div - Comcast Cable Communications, Inc.; *pg.* 276, *pg.* 1560
Mccullom, Candace, VP & Mgr-Brand & Adv - Wells Fargo & Company; *pg.* 819, *pg.* 232
McCullough, Cindy, Mgr-Product Mktg - Planar Systems, Inc.; *pg.* 455, *pg.* 1495
McCullough, Daniel, Mgr-Online Mktg - AARP; *pg.* 124, *pg.* 393
McCullough, Jacqueline, Graphic Designer & Coord-Production - Merck & Co., Inc.; *pg.* 1566, *pg.* 1077
McCullough, Katherine Stiel, Coord-Recruiting & Mktg - AXA Equitable Life Insurance Company; *pg.* 1194, *pg.* 1199
McCullough, Kim, VP-Mktg - Jaguar Land Rover North America LLC; *pg.* 180, *pg.* 1081
McCullough, Marilyn S., VP-Comml Mktg - Anthem, Inc.; *pg.* 1192, *pg.* 683
McCullough, Michael, CMO & Exec VP - Miami Heat Limited Partnership; *pg.* 562, *pg.* 444
Mccullough, Mike, Sr Dir-Media & Adv - The Travelers Companies, Inc.; *pg.* 1220, *pg.* 352
McCullough, Mike, Sr Dir-Media & Adv - Travelers Insurance; *pg.* 1220, *pg.* 963
McCullough, Patrick, Sr Product Mgr - Olympus America Inc.; *pg.* 1425, *pg.* 1521
McCumiskey, Andrew, Dir-Technical Mktg - NetApp, Inc.; *pg.* 444, *pg.* 287
McCune, Scott, VP-Global Partnerships & Experiential Mktg - The Coca-Cola Company; *pg.* 240, *pg.* 493
Mccurdy, Rachel C., Analyst-Mktg - Intel Corporation; *pg.* 645, *pg.* 266
McCurry, Mike, Product Mgr-Global - Black Box Corporation; *pg.* 361, *pg.* 1547
McCutchen, Kristi, Sr Dir-Mktg-vCloud Air - VMware, Inc.; *pg.* 490, *pg.* 179
McCutcheon, Kyle, Mgr-New Media - Corus Entertainment Inc.; *pg.* 279, *pg.* 1937
McDade, Tracy, Sr Mgr-Mktg Comm - AT&T Inc.; *pg.* 1867, *pg.* 1674
McDaniel, Carrie, Mgr-Product Mktg - Imperva, Inc.; *pg.* 413, *pg.* 193
McDaniel, Julie, VP-Mktg - Perle Systems Limited; *pg.* 454, *pg.* 1924
McDaniel, Max, CMO-Display Bus Grp & Sr Dir - Applied Materials, Inc; *pg.* 618, *pg.* 1009
McDaniel, Max, CMO-Display Bus Grp & Sr Dir - Applied Materials, Inc.; *pg.* 618, *pg.* 264
McDermed, Kevin, COO-Engineered Products - Bradken; *pg.* 1150, *pg.* 714
Mcdermott, Bill, Mgr-Product Svc-Global Mobility & Comm Svcs - The Boeing Company; *pg.* 225, *pg.* 567
McDermott, Chris, Mgr-Key Events & Sponsorship Mktg-IBM Sls & Distr - International Business Machines Corporation; *pg.* 418, *pg.* 1138
McDermott, Christine, Mgr-Mktg - CB Richard Ellis Group, Inc.; *pg.* 1085, *pg.* 127
McDermott, Gary, Dir-Product Mktg - Skyworks Solutions, Inc.; *pg.* 674, *pg.* 862
McDermott, Jim, Sr VP-Mktg - Amica Mutual Insurance Co.; *pg.* 1192, *pg.* 1602
McDermott, John P., Sr VP-Sls & Mktg-Global - Rockwell Automation, Inc.; *pg.* 668, *pg.* 1880
Mcdermott, Megan, Product Mgr-Macy's Mdsg Grp - Macy's East; *pg.* 1777, *pg.* 1254
McDermott, Patrick, Sr Mgr-Adv-Global - Accenture; *pg.* 1392, *pg.* 1186
McDermott, Paula, Mgr-Mktg - WPVI-TV Inc.; *pg.* 323, *pg.* 1572
McDevitt, Bryce L., Specialist-PR - Northrop Grumman Corporation; *pg.* 231, *pg.* 1781
McDevitt, Julie, Sr Mgr-Online Mktg - NutriSystem, Inc.; *pg.* 1577, *pg.* 1533
McDevitt, Paul, Sr Mgr-ECommerce Mktg - Spencer Gifts LLC; *pg.* 1786, *pg.* 1057

McDonagh, Lena, Dir-Publ & Creative Svcs - Chicago National League Ball Club, LLC; *pg.* 539, *pg.* 569
McDonagh, Mariann, CMO & Exec VP - INCONTACT, INC.; *pg.* 413, *pg.* 1752
McDonagh, Matt, VP-Sls-Natl - Onion, Inc.; *pg.* 1673, *pg.* 586
McDonagh, Megan O., Dir-Global Consumer Mktg Strategy & Campaigns - Intel Corporation; *pg.* 645, *pg.* 266
McDonald, Andrew, Sr Product Mgr - Yahoo! Inc.; *pg.* 1289, *pg.* 289
McDonald, Betsy, Mgr-Sls - Angela Adams; *pg.* 913, *pg.* 751
McDonald, Beverly, Dir-Mktg - Automatic Data Processing, Inc.; *pg.* 357, *pg.* 1117
McDonald, Bobbie, Dir-Product Mktg - Boston Market Corporation; *pg.* 1717, *pg.* 329
McDonald, Brandon P., Sr Specialist-Digital Mktg - AMN Healthcare Services, Inc.; *pg.* 1494, *pg.* 200
McDonald, Bruce, VP-Strategic Partnership Mktg - The Coca-Cola Company; *pg.* 240, *pg.* 493
McDonald, Christopher, Product Mgr-Regulation & Compliance-TOMS - Bloomberg L.P.; *pg.* 725, *pg.* 1204
Mcdonald, Darryl D., Chief Strategy Officer - Teradata Corporation; *pg.* 483, *pg.* 1447
McDonald, Diana, Principal-Mktg Analytics & Svcs - IMS Health, Inc.; *pg.* 1544, *pg.* 344
McDonald, Edward, Dir-Sls - SAS Institute Inc.; *pg.* 466, *pg.* 1361
McDonald, George E., Sr Mgr-Field Ops - Dawson Geophysical Company; *pg.* 383, *pg.* 1727
McDonald, Jennifer, Sr VP-Digital Sls & Mktg - Bank of America Corporation; *pg.* 718, *pg.* 1362
McDonald, Jennifer, Mgr-NY Sls - Time Inc.; *pg.* 1693, *pg.* 1300
McDonald, Jim, Mgr-Mktg - United Parcel Service, Inc.; *pg.* 1928, *pg.* 522
McDonald, Katherinn, Dir-Product Mgmt-Mobile & Free-to-Play - 505 Games (US), Inc.; *pg.* 948, *pg.* 38
McDonald, Keith, Mgr-European Sls - Parker Chomerics; *pg.* 662, *pg.* 862
McDonald, Lisa, Mgr-Creative Svcs - SUPERVALU, Inc.; *pg.* 1035, *pg.* 924
McDonald, Mark, Mgr-Advisor Mktg - Manulife Financial Corporation; *pg.* 778, *pg.* 1939
McDonald, Mary, Sr Mgr-Editorial Assets & Rights - Conde Nast Publications, Inc.; *pg.* 1629, *pg.* 1217
Mcdonald, Paul, Sr Brand Mgr-Social Media - BCBG Max Azria Group LLC; *pg.* 19, *pg.* 301
Mcdonald, Paul, Product Mgr - Google Inc.; *pg.* 1249, *pg.* 153
McDonald, Rob, Sr VP-Sls & Mktg Music - E1 Entertainment U.S. LP; *pg.* 284, *pg.* 1323
McDonald, Susan, Bus Mgr-David Yurman - Neiman Marcus, Inc.; *pg.* 30, *pg.* 1684
McDonald, Todd, Mgr-Online Brand Mktg - Toys "R" Us, Inc.; *pg.* 968, *pg.* 1130
McDonald, Tom, Sr VP-Mktg - San Francisco Giants Baseball Club; *pg.* 581, *pg.* 226
McDonell, Deanne, Sr Mgr-Customer & Shopper Mktg - Rich Products Corporation; *pg.* 892, *pg.* 1150
Mcdoniel, George, Dir-Corp Partnerships Sls - Chicago White Sox Ltd.; *pg.* 539, *pg.* 570
McDonnell, Brian, Dir-Mktg-Global Product Ops - Dell Inc.; *pg.* 383, *pg.* 1737
McDonnell, Finola, VP-Intl Mktg & Comm - CNBC; *pg.* 275, *pg.* 1059
McDonnell, Jim, Dir-Digital Mktg - Papa John's International, Inc.; *pg.* 1743, *pg.* 737
McDonnell, Matt, Dir-Brand Mktg - World Kitchen LLC; *pg.* 1141, *pg.* 657
Mcdonnell, Phil, Product Mgr - Google Inc.; *pg.* 1249, *pg.* 153
McDonnell, Theresa, Dir-Integrated Mktg - Unilever United States, Inc.; *pg.* 904, *pg.* 1061
McDonogh, Ann, Mgr-Customer & Channel Assoc Sls Promo - Brown-Forman Corporation; *pg.* 1958, *pg.* 732
McDonough, Barb, Mgr-New Product Dev - CertainTeed Corporation; *pg.* 74, *pg.* 1589
McDonough, David, VP-Mktg-Acute Care - Medline Industries, Inc.; *pg.* 1562, *pg.* 635
McDonough, Janae, Sr Dir-MoPub - Twitter, Inc.; *pg.* 1285, *pg.* 228
McDonough, Joanne, Sr Dir-Strategy & Insights - Heineken USA Inc.; *pg.* 252, *pg.* 1352
McDonough, John, VP-Sls & Mktg - The Protectoseal Company; *pg.* 1370, *pg.* 556
McDonough, Katie, Dir-Sls Plng & Acct Exec - CBS Corporation; *pg.* 273, *pg.* 1210
Mcdonough, Kelley, Dir-PR-NY - Distilled Spirits Council of the United States, Inc.; *pg.* 139, *pg.* 398
Mcdonough, Larry, Dir-Product Mgmt - VMware, Inc.; *pg.* 490, *pg.* 179
McDonough, Tim, VP-Brand Mktg-Global - Moen Incorporated; *pg.* 1056, *pg.* 1468
McDonough, Tim, VP-Mktg-Worldwide - QUALCOMM Incorporated; *pg.* 1873, *pg.* 207
McDonough, Tina, Sr Mgr-Mktg - Papa Ginos-Deangelo Holding Corporation, Inc.; *pg.* 1743, *pg.* 817
McDonough, William, Dir-Mktg-KICKTV - Major League Soccer LLC; *pg.* 560, *pg.* 1256
McDougal, Julia, Mgr-Brand & Adv-Boeing Defense, Space & Security - The Boeing Company; *pg.* 225, *pg.* 567
McDougal, Krista, Sr Dir-Market Mgmt-North America - Expedia, Inc.; *pg.* 1244, *pg.* 1814
McDougall, Ryan, Mgr-Mktg - LinkedIn Corporation; *pg.* 1262, *pg.* 160
McDowell, Bert E., Sr Mgr-Mktg Insights - EarthLink Holdings Corp.; *pg.* 1240, *pg.* 504
McDowell, Danyall, Sr Product Mgr-Internet Svcs Grp - Wells Fargo & Company; *pg.* 819, *pg.* 232
McDowell, Darren, Mgr-Product Mktg - Eaton Bussmann, Inc.; *pg.* 1331, *pg.* 977
McDowell, James, Dir-Event Mktg - Softlayer Technologies Inc; *pg.* 471, *pg.* 1686
McDowell, Laura, Mgr-Pub & Media Rels-TJ Maxx & Marshalls Stores - Marshalls of MA, Inc.; *pg.* 1778, *pg.* 821
McDowell, Laura, Mgr-Media & PR - T.J. Maxx; *pg.* 1788, *pg.* 822
McDowell, Robert, Sr VP-Mktg & Distr - Choice Hotels International, Inc.; *pg.* 1086, *pg.* 775
McDuffee, Joey, Head-Sls & Mktg - Wipro Gallagher Solutions; *pg.* 823, *pg.* 447
McElhatton, Kate, Specialist-Digital Mktg - E.I. du Pont de Nemours & Company; *pg.* 1159, *pg.* 390
McElligott, Brian J., Mng Dir & Head-Info Products-Global - CME Group Inc.; *pg.* 738, *pg.* 571
McElligott, Leeanne, Planner-Digital Media - PGA Tour, Inc.; *pg.* 574, *pg.* 460
McElman, Michelle, Assoc Program Mgr-Mktg Comm, Meeting Mgmt & Event Strategy - Liberty Mutual Insurance Group Inc.; *pg.* 1205, *pg.* 797
Mcelroy, Ben, VP-Sls - Dr Pepper Snapple Group, Inc.; *pg.* 250, *pg.* 1729
McElroy, Cory, Dir-Product Mgmt & Mktg-Retail Solutions - Hewlett-Packard Company; *pg.* 404, *pg.* 175
McElroy, Vanessa, Product Dir-Women's Casual Footwear - The Timberland Company; *pg.* 1821, *pg.* 1039
McElvogue, Gregor, Mgr-Global Solutions-Media & Entertainment - International Business Machines Corporation; *pg.* 418, *pg.* 1138
McElwee, Carrie, Dir-PR - Staples, Inc.; *pg.* 474, *pg.* 821
McElyea, Shawn, Dir-Product Line-PowerSoak & Warewashing - Unified Brands Inc.; *pg.* 1385, *pg.* 970
McEnaney, Mike, Sr VP-Mktg & Strategy - Angelica Corporation; *pg.* 38, *pg.* 483
McEnaney, Sarah, Mgr-Mktg-ACDelco - General Motors of Canada Ltd.; *pg.* 177, *pg.* 1931
McEnery, Christine, Assoc Mgr-Mktg-Every Day-Rachael Ray - Meredith Corporation; *pg.* 1663, *pg.* 705
McEnroe, Keith, Dir-Sls - GlaxoSmithKline Consumer Healthcare; *pg.* 510, *pg.* 1554
McEown, John, Assoc Dir-Creative - Garmin International, Inc.; *pg.* 1414, *pg.* 717
Mceuen, Llyn, Reg Mgr-Sls - American Rice, Inc.; *pg.* 837, *pg.* 1700
McEver, John, Brand Mgr-Boating Magazine & Publr - Yachting Magazine; *pg.* 1703, *pg.* 1602
McEvoy, Erin, Dir-Mktg & Event Strategy - AmerisourceBergen Corporation; *pg.* 1493, *pg.* 1522
McEvoy, James, Dir-Intl Media Distr & Sponsorship - World Wrestling Entertainment, Inc.; *pg.* 595, *pg.* 380
McEvoy, Sue, Mgr-Retail Mktg-Corp Accts - The Goodyear Tire & Rubber Company; *pg.* 1883, *pg.* 1401
Mcevoy, Thomas J., Pres-Enterprise Sls - CenturyLink, Inc.; *pg.* 1870, *pg.* 746
McEwen, Drew, VP-Sls & Mktg - Piper Aircraft, Inc.; *pg.* 233, *pg.* 477
McFadden, Beth, VP-Image Events & Media - Giorgio Armani Corporation; *pg.* 25, *pg.* 1234
McFadden, John, Sr Dir-Finance - Myers Industries, Inc.; *pg.* 1887, *pg.* 1402
McFadden, Michael E., VP-Sls & Managed Markets-US - AVANIR Pharmaceuticals; *pg.* 1498, *pg.* 40
McFadden, Rebo, Mgr-Mktg-Fitness Grp - SKECHERS U.S.A., INC.; *pg.* 1819, *pg.* 143
McFadden, Suzanne, Sr VP-Mktg & Strategy - Comcast Cable Communications, Inc.; *pg.* 276, *pg.* 1560
McFall, Finbar, VP-Mktg-Land Rover North America - Jaguar Land Rover North America LLC; *pg.* 180, *pg.* 1081
Mcfall-Metz, Jenifer, Sr Mgr-Digital Marketing Demand Generation-Global - Computer Sciences Corporation; *pg.* 378, *pg.* 1780
McFarland, Bonnie L., Dir-Creative Svcs - Del Monte Foods, Inc.; *pg.* 852, *pg.* 304
McFarland, Carol, Sr VP-Adv - Staples, Inc.; *pg.* 474, *pg.* 821
McFarland, Cheryl, Mgr-Trade Mktg - All-Clad Metalcrafters LLC; *pg.* 1121, *pg.* 1519
McFarland, Chris, Sr Graphic Designer-Mktg-Global - CommScope; *pg.* 630, *pg.* 668
McFarland, Jill, Sr Mgr-Digital & Social Media - Applebee's International, Inc.; *pg.* 1715, *pg.* 980
McFarland, John, Dir-Mktg & Innovation-Global - General Motors Company; *pg.* 175, *pg.* 881
McFarland, Randy L., Mgr-Utility Coal Mktg - Norfolk Southern Corporation; *pg.* 1917, *pg.* 1797
Mcfarlane, Roe, Sr VP-ECommerce, Academic Tools Product Dev & Strategic Mktg - Follett Higher Education Group; *pg.* 1769, *pg.* 669
McGahey, Jason, Mgr-Sls-Indus Sys - Dynapower Corporation; *pg.* 1330, *pg.* 1768
Mcgallian, Rachel, Dir-Sls & Mktg - Verizon Communications Inc.; *pg.* 1875, *pg.* 1309
McGann, John P., Exec VP & Dir-HR & Mktg - Bank Leumi USA; *pg.* 718, *pg.* 1200
McGarrell, Michael, Mgr-Mktg Comm - Ford Motor Company of Canada, Limited; *pg.* 174, *pg.* 1930
McGarry, Heather, Sr Mgr-Mktg - Lane Bryant; *pg.* 1776, *pg.* 1441
McGarry, Meghan, Specialist-Media Solution - Google Inc.; *pg.* 1249, *pg.* 153
McGarvey, Jamie, Sr Mgr-Employee Comm - Astellas Pharma US, Inc.; *pg.* 1496, *pg.* 640
McGavock, Megan, Sr Mgr-Applied Mktg-North America - Aveda Corporation; *pg.* 499, *pg.* 917
Mcgaw, Robert A., Dir-Consumer Mktg - SUPERVALU, Inc. - Eastern Region; *pg.* 1035, *pg.* 1795
McGeachie, Mike, Engr-Product - Cornell Dubilier Electronics; *pg.* 630, *pg.* 1620
McGeary, Chris, VP-Mktg - Realogy Corporation; *pg.* 1109, *pg.* 1081
McGee, Adam, Supvr-OOH Media - Brown-Forman Corporation; *pg.* 1958, *pg.* 732
McGee, Christine R., Sr VP-Mktg-Oil & Gas - Clean Harbors, Inc.; *pg.* 376, *pg.* 839
McGee, Elissa, Brand Mgr-Portfolio Digital Strategy - Diageo North America Inc.; *pg.* 248, *pg.* 1223
McGee, Heather, Dir-Creative & Production Svcs - Banner Direct; *pg.* 1619, *pg.* 1200
McGee, James, VP-Sls, Mktg & Bus Dev - Brand Energy, Inc.; *pg.* 71, *pg.* 533
McGee, Michael, Sr Analyst-Search Engine Mktg - HSN, Inc.; *pg.* 291, *pg.* 462
McGee, Ronald M., Sr VP-Property, Casualty Products & Svcs - Insperity, Inc.; *pg.* 416, *pg.* 1725
Mcgee, Tracy, Mgr-Customer Mktg - Hallmark Cards, Inc.; *pg.* 1646, *pg.* 983
McGee, Viki, Project Mgr-Mktg - Taco John's International, Inc.; *pg.* 1753, *pg.* 1901
Mcgehee, Shawn, VP-Product Mktg - ClassMates Online, Inc.; *pg.* 1235, *pg.* 1834
McGettigan, Iesa, Sr Dir-Brand Mktg-TripAdvisor for Bus - TripAdvisor, Inc.; *pg.* 1926, *pg.* 835
McGhee, Billie, Designer-Digital - The TJX Companies, Inc.; *pg.* 1788, *pg.* 822
Mcghee, Erin, Mgr-PR - Cray Inc.; *pg.* 380, *pg.* 1834
McGill, James W., Pres-Electrical Products Grp - Eaton Corporation; *pg.* 1331, *pg.* 1429
McGill, Laura, Mgr-Content-Social Media - Delta Air Lines, Inc.; *pg.* 1905, *pg.* 503
Mcgill, Paul, Exec Dir-Sls-Europe - Chem-Trend Limited Partnership; *pg.* 973, *pg.* 892
McGillan, Dina M., Mgr-Mktg Ops - Incyte Corporation; *pg.* 1545, *pg.* 392
McGillicuddy, Annie, Sr Mgr-Integrated Mktg-Harper's Bazaar - The Hearst Corporation; *pg.* 1649, *pg.* 1239
McGillivray, Daniel, Assoc Mgr-Digital Adv - Coach, Inc.; *pg.* 3, *pg.* 1214
McGillivray, Doug, VP-Sls - General Mills Canada Corp.; *pg.* 828, *pg.* 1926

First page reference indicates Business Class Edition
Second page reference indicates Geographic Edition

McGillivray, Sarah, Mgr-Completions Sls - Baker Hughes Incorporated; pg. 1315, pg. 1700
McGinley, Chris, VP-Mktg-Titleist Golf Clubs - Acushnet Company; pg. 1824, pg. 818
McGinn, Joe, Sr Mgr-Pub Affairs - Sunoco Inc.; pg. 985, pg. 1571
Mcginnis, Kevin, VP-Dev & Ops-Pinsight Media - Sprint Corporation; pg. 1874, pg. 719
McGinnis, Mara, Exec Dir-PR & Comm - Pratt Institute; pg. 606, pg. 1146
McGinnis, Martin, Mgr-Global Market Offer & Mktg Complexity - Ford Motor Company; pg. 172, pg. 876
Mcginnis, Tiffany, Product Mgr-Hips - Exactech, Inc.; pg. 1529, pg. 428
McGiverin, Todd, Dir-Sls & Mktg - Haggen, Inc.; pg. 1022, pg. 1817
McGlothlin, Chad, Mgr-Sls-US - Dover Chemical Corporation; pg. 1156, pg. 1447
McGlumphy, Kelly, Mgr-PR - GOJO Industries, Inc.; pg. 330, pg. 1401
McGlynn, Tim, Mgr-Channel Mktg & CFM-3M Personal Safety Div - 3M Company; pg. 1142, pg. 956
McGoldrick, Mark, Planner-Sls - Cable News Network LP; pg. 1624, pg. 1208
McGoldrick, Shawn, Designer-Online Adv-AT&T Consumer Digital Experience - AT&T; pg. 1865, pg. 258
McGougan, Nicole, Specialist-PR - Blackbaud, Inc.; pg. 361, pg. 1613
McGough, Kim, Sr Mgr-Integrated Mktg - Campbell Soup Company; pg. 844, pg. 1048
McGovern, Andrew, Acct Exec-Corp Sls UK Market - salesforce.com, inc.; pg. 1278, pg. 226
Mcgovern, Brian, Sr Mgr-Mktg-North America - The Timberland Company; pg. 1821, pg. 1039
McGovern, Casey, Dir-Digital Mktg - Regis Corporation; pg. 521, pg. 941
McGovern, Cathy, Sr Mgr-Adv - AT&T Inc.; pg. 1867, pg. 1674
McGovern, Chelsea, Mgr-Creative Adv - Focus Features; pg. 287, pg. 273
McGovern, Jamie, Sr Dir-Art - Capital One Financial Corporation; pg. 730, pg. 1789
McGovern, Linda, VP-Mktg - USG Corporation; pg. 118, pg. 594
McGovern, Patrick J., Sr VP-Sls, Strategic Plng & Digital Media - ABC, Inc.; pg. 268, pg. 1185
Mcgowan, Andrew, Dir-Media Rels-Global - United Parcel Service, Inc.; pg. 1928, pg. 522
McGowan, Bret M., Sr VP-Sls & Mktg - Vicon Industries, Inc.; pg. 685, pg. 1166
McGowan, J. Kelly, Sr Dir - American Securities LLC; pg. 714, pg. 1193
McGowan, Kim C., Dir-Mktg Svcs - International Paper Company; pg. 1460, pg. 1644
McGowan, Laura, Sr Dir-Mktg - LG Electronics Canada, Inc.; pg. 651, pg. 1927
McGowan, Scott A., Mgr-Mktg-Consumables & ECommerce - Mark Andy, Inc.; pg. 1359, pg. 975
McGowan, Steve, Dir-Shopper Mktg - Mondelez International, Inc.; pg. 878, pg. 601
McGowan, Tim, Deputy VP-Mktg & Comm-Alumni & Dev - Columbia University; pg. 600, pg. 1216
McGowan, Tim, Deputy VP-Alumni, Dev Mktg & Comm - Columbia University Press; pg. 1628, pg. 1216
McGowen, John, Sr Analyst-Product - HCA HOLDINGS, INC.; pg. 1539, pg. 1651
McGown, Chris, Sr Mgr-Category & Brand Mktg - Kohl's Corporation; pg. 1775, pg. 1870
McGrail, Nam, Sr Dir-Partnership Activation - Los Angeles Kings Hockey Club L.P.; pg. 559, pg. 135
McGranahan, Eric, Dir-Online Mktg - Monster Worldwide, Inc.; pg. 1268, pg. 859
McGrath, Bob, Sr Dir-Corp Comm - CB Richard Ellis, Inc.; pg. 1085, pg. 1210
McGrath, Chris, VP-Mktg - Country Kitchen International, Inc.; pg. 1723, pg. 1865
McGrath, Elizabeth, Dir-Mktg - Sterling Jewelers Inc.; pg. 13, pg. 1402
McGrath, Glenn, Dir-Trade Mktg - The Libman Company; pg. 331, pg. 553
Mcgrath, Gretchen, Mgr-Mktg - Paychex, Inc.; pg. 792, pg. 1336
McGrath, Jenna, Assoc Mgr-Mktg-Pillsbury Innovation - General Mills, Inc.; pg. 828, pg. 933
McGrath, Jim, Sr VP-Media Engrg-Global - Discovery Communications, Inc.; pg. 282, pg. 777
McGrath, Joe, Sr VP & Gen Mgr-Mdse, Housewares, Small Appliances & Tabletop - Boscov's Department Store, LLC; pg. 1763, pg. 1583
McGrath, Kelly, Product Mgr-Digital Mktg-User Experience, SEO & Analytics - Johnson & Johnson; pg. 1549, pg. 1091
McGrath, Paula, VP & Mgr-Channel Mktg-Wirehouse - Nuveen Investments, Inc.; pg. 788, pg. 586
McGrath, Rachel, Specialist-Mktg - HEICO Corporation; pg. 228, pg. 431
McGrath, Stephanie, Sr Mgr-Brand Mktg Readiness - Capital One Financial Corporation; pg. 730, pg. 1789
McGrath, Tracey, Mgr-Mktg-Minute Clinic - CVS Health Corporation; pg. 1765, pg. 1610
McGraw, Anne, Sr Mgr-Global Digital Assets - Nissan North America, Inc.; pg. 186, pg. 1633
McGraw, Brandon, Brand Mktg Mgr - Facebook, Inc.; pg. 1245, pg. 143
McGraw, Eric, Dir-Museum Ops & Mktg - Harley-Davidson, Inc.; pg. 178, pg. 1874
McGraw, Joseph M., Dir-Mktg & Adv - United Gilsonite Laboratories; pg. 1449, pg. 1527
McGraw, Philip , Jr., Dir-Sls-Natl - Sabra Dipping Company LLC; pg. 893, pg. 1686
McGray, Don, Asst Mgr-Customer Svcs Social Media - Peet's Coffee & Tea, Inc.; pg. 1029, pg. 85
McGreevy, Phyllis, Producer-Creative - Target Corporation; pg. 1786, pg. 942
McGregor-Fonteix, Deb, Sr Mgr-Comm - Honeywell International Inc.; pg. 407, pg. 1088
McGrew, Mike, Sr Dir-Comm-Beer Div - Constellation Brands, Inc.; pg. 1960, pg. 1348
McGriff, Deborah K, Sr Dir-Fin - Teledyne Brown Engineering, Inc.; pg. 235, pg. 6
McGriff, Marlo, Product Mgr - Google Inc.; pg. 1249, pg. 153
McGriff, Sam, Coord-Sls Promo-Western US Reg - John Deere Consumer & Commercial Equipment, Inc.; pg. 705, pg. 1360
McGrogan, Amber, Mgr-Mktg-Mktg Connections - MillerCoors; pg. 254, pg. 1877
McGruder, Elizabeth Hagen, Mgr-Mktg - Eastman Machine Company; pg. 1331, pg. 1148
Mcguigan, Steve, Head-App Store Mktg - Apple Inc.; pg. 350, pg. 73
McGuiness, Jeff, Chief Sales Officer - Embrace Home Loans, Inc.; pg. 747, pg. 1603
McGuiness, Ward, Assoc Mgr-Adv Svcs - Barron's; pg. 1620, pg. 1201
McGuinness, Keith, Brand Mgr-Gerber - Gerber Life Insurance Company; pg. 1201, pg. 1352
McGuinness, Keith, Brand Mgr-Gerber - Nestle USA, Inc.; pg. 883, pg. 96
McGuinness, Steve, Mgr-Intl Product & Pricing - The Chubb Corporation; pg. 1196, pg. 1128
McGuire, Chris, Dir-Sports Mktg - adidas America Inc.; pg. 1803, pg. 1500
McGuire, Chris, Mgr-Digital Mktg - Starwood Hotels & Resorts Worldwide, Inc.; pg. 1114, pg. 378
Mcguire, David, Sr Dir-Mktg Ops-Global - SunPower Corporation; pg. 1952, pg. 250
McGuire, James, Sr VP-Sls & Svc-Worldwide - FormFactor, Inc.; pg. 1882, pg. 122
McGuire, John, Asst Brand Mgr-PEEPS & Seasonal Products - Just Born, Inc.; pg. 1857, pg. 1516
McGuire, Kara, Mgr-Mktg-Activation - Doctor's Associates Inc.; pg. 1726, pg. 356
McGuire, Kitri, Sr Specialist-Mktg Comm - Leatherman Tool Group, Inc.; pg. 1053, pg. 1504
McGuire, Martha, Sr VP & Sr Mgr-Loan Capital Markets - First Banks, Inc.; pg. 754, pg. 976
McGuire, Nicole, VP-Consumer Mktg - Kalmbach Publishing Co.; pg. 1656, pg. 1898
McGuire, Raymond, Head-Advisory Bus - Citigroup Inc.; pg. 735, pg. 1212
McGuire, Ryan, Coord-Construction Mktg - Daktronics, Inc.; pg. 633, pg. 1624
McGuire, Shannon, VP-Sls - A.D.A.M., INC.; pg. 1225, pg. 487
McGuire, Shian-Li, Dir-Brand Mktg - American Sports Licensing, Inc.; pg. 1825, pg. 1524
McGuire, Shian-Li, Dir-Brand Mktg, Field & Stream - Dick's Sporting Goods, Inc.; pg. 1832, pg. 1524
McGuire, Stephen, Sr Mgr-Policy, External Affairs & Comm - Pfizer Inc.; pg. 1581, pg. 1278
McGuire, Steve, Mgr-Brand Licensing & Global Mktg Ops - General Motors Company; pg. 175, pg. 881
Mcguire, Therese, Brand Mgr-Standard Bourbons - Brown-Forman Corporation; pg. 1958, pg. 732
McGuire, Tina, Dir-Mktg & Mdsg-Walmart - Hallmark Cards, Inc.; pg. 1646, pg. 983
McGuirl, Jennifer, Mgr-Sls Plng-People.com - Time Inc.; pg. 1693, pg. 1300
McGurn, Edward, VP-Production - Phoenix Pictures Inc.; pg. 304, pg. 138
McGurrin, Jennifer, Assoc Dir-Mktg-Global Design to Value - Kellogg Company; pg. 831, pg. 870
McHatton, Heather, VP-Brand Mktg & Comm & Head-US Sponsorships - Morgan Stanley; pg. 783, pg. 1261
McHenry, Bob, Head-Global Client-Centric Mktg - Accenture; pg. 1392, pg. 1186
McHenry, Nancy, VP-Grp Sls Ops-The Americas - Marriott International, Inc.; pg. 1102, pg. 764
Mchood, Tammy P., Sr Product Mgr - Henry Schein, Inc.; pg. 1541, pg. 1180
McHugh, Barbara, VP-Mktg - Major League Baseball; pg. 560, pg. 1255
McHugh, Cris, Sr Mgr-Comm-Boeing Comml Airplanes - The Boeing Company; pg. 225, pg. 567
McHugh, Kathleen, Sr Mgr-Product Mktg-Windows - Microsoft Corporation; pg. 435, pg. 1824
McHugh, Kristin, Mgr-PR - Randstad USA; pg. 459, pg. 941
McHugh, Nadine Karp, Sr VP-Omni Media - L'Oreal USA; pg. 514, pg. 1252
McHugh, Tom, Sr Dir-Product Supply - Beiersdorf North America Inc.; pg. 501, pg. 385
McIlduff, Kenneth, Mgr-Florida Mktg-CBS - Aetna Inc.; pg. 1187, pg. 351
McIlvain, Pat, VP-Sports Mktg-Global - Oakley, Inc.; pg. 1840, pg. 86
Mcilvaine, Jennifer, Head-Mktg & Market Access - AstraZeneca Pharmaceuticals LP; pg. 1497, pg. 389
McIndoe, John, Sr VP-Mktg - IRI Group; pg. 421, pg. 579
McInerney, Chris, Sr VP-Sls & Mktg - FiberMark Inc.; pg. 1457, pg. 1764
Mcinerney, Emily, Dir-Mktg - Tapjoy, Inc.; pg. 1396, pg. 228
McInnis, Keilan, Mgr-Natl Pre-Owned Sls Ops - Mercedes-Benz Canada Inc.; pg. 184, pg. 1940
McInnis, Noreen, Mgr-Product Mktg - Disney Interactive Media Group; pg. 1239, pg. 95
Mcinnis, Scott, Brand Mgr-Global Dell Outlet-Enterprise Product - Dell, Inc.; pg. 385, pg. 1037
Mcinnis, Scott, Brand Mgr-Global Dell Outlet-Enterprise Product - Dell Inc.; pg. 383, pg. 1737
McIntosh, Audra, VP & Mgr-Mktg-Comml Segments-Huntington National Bank - Huntington Bancshares Incorporated; pg. 767, pg. 1440
Mcintosh, Clara, Brand Mgr - Nestle Purina PetCare Company; pg. 1479, pg. 1000
McIntosh, Helen, Dir-Mktg Comm-Global - Ingredion; pg. 864, pg. 669
McIntosh, Jill, VP-Mdsg-Natural Foods - The Kroger Co.; pg. 1025, pg. 1416
McIntosh, Kelli, Sr Mgr-Mktg-Digital Customer Solutions - PepsiCo, Inc.; pg. 259, pg. 1327
McIntosh, Mark, Mgr-Web Mktg - Empire Today, LLC; pg. 923, pg. 643
McIntosh, Merle, Sr VP-Mdsg & Product Mgmt - Newegg Inc.; pg. 1271, pg. 67
McIntyre, Cynthia, Sr Head-Bus & Mktg - Visa Inc.; pg. 816, pg. 230
McIntyre, Cynthia, Sr Head-Bus & Mktg - Visa U.S.A., Inc.; pg. 817, pg. 231
McIntyre, Diane, Mgr-PR - Dreyer's Grand Ice Cream Holdings, Inc.; pg. 1852, pg. 171
McIntyre, Guillaume, Mgr-Programmatic Mktg & Partnerships-Latin America - Netflix, Inc.; pg. 1269, pg. 141
McIntyre, John T., VP-Mdsg-Sls & Brand Dev - Sysco Corporation; pg. 1035, pg. 1716
McIntyre, Megan, Sr Mgr-Emerging Media & Print - Anheuser-Busch Companies, LLC; pg. 237, pg. 991
McIntyre, Shaun, Specialist-Sls & Svc - TD Bank US Holding Company; pg. 809, pg. 1051
McKaig, Brian, VP-Mktg & Comm - United Way Worldwide; pg. 160, pg. 1772
McKay, Andrew, Specialist-Corp Sls Representative & Platform - salesforce.com, inc.; pg. 1278, pg. 226
McKay, Erin, Dir-ECommerce Mktg & Mdsg - The Life Is Good Company; pg. 44, pg. 1034
McKay, Jonathan, Product Mgr-Browser Partnerships - Facebook, Inc.; pg. 1245, pg. 143

McKay, Kristin, Dir-Mktg-US - Hasbro, Inc.; pg. 954, pg. 1603
McKay, Laura, Brand Mktg Mgr-North American Van Lines - SIRVA, Inc.; pg. 1923, pg. 669
McKay, Maureen, Dir-Natl Accounts Mktg-Grp Benefits - Sun Life Financial Inc.; pg. 806, pg. 1944
McKay, Sunny, Mgr-CLIF Kid Experience Mktg - Clif Bar Inc.; pg. 848, pg. 83
Mckean, Chris, Sr Engr-Product - Parker Hannifin - Webster Plastics Inc; pg. 1887, pg. 1159
McKean, Kyle, Dir-Mktg - The Conard-Pyle Company; pg. 1794, pg. 1594
McKean, Mac, Sr VP-Digital Media-AMC & SundanceTV - AMC Networks Inc.; pg. 269, pg. 1189
McKeaney, Ed, Sr Exec VP-Mdsg & Adv - Boscov's Department Store, LLC; pg. 1763, pg. 1583
McKechnie, Andrew, Grp Dir-Creative - Apple Inc.; pg. 350, pg. 73
McKechnie, Duncan, VP-Global Mktg-CF - Vertex Pharmaceuticals Incorporated; pg. 1606, pg. 801
McKee, April, Mgr-Event Mktg-Xbox - Microsoft Corporation; pg. 435, pg. 1824
McKee, Bill, Mgr-Corp PR - Xerox Corporation; pg. 494, pg. 365
McKee, Bob, Sr VP-Mktg & Comm - ConvaTec Ltd.; pg. 1518, pg. 1121
Mckee, Kaitlyn, Sr Mgr-ECommerce-Global - Newell Rubbermaid Inc.; pg. 1128, pg. 515
McKee, Na'im, Dir-Digital Mktg - University Of Denver; pg. 609, pg. 323
McKee, Scott, Dir-PR - Kia Motors America Inc.; pg. 181, pg. 112
McKee, Tyler, Mgr-Direct & Digital Mktg - National Hockey League; pg. 568, pg. 1265
McKeegan, Mary, Sr VP-Brand Strategy & Creative Svcs - Bank of the West; pg. 721, pg. 213
McKeever, Harold, VP-Mktg - Aflac Incorporated; pg. 1188, pg. 527
McKeithen, Beth A., Mgr-Mktg - International Paper Company; pg. 1460, pg. 1644
McKell, Debra, Dir-Mktg - HCA HOLDINGS, INC.; pg. 1539, pg. 1651
McKellar, Lori, Dir-Solution Mktg-Life Sciences - EMC Corporation; pg. 391, pg. 825
McKellar, Shannon, VP-Mktg - Harrah's Louisiana Downs Casino & Racetrack; pg. 551, pg. 743
McKellips, Paul, Exec VP-Pub Affairs & Media - Foundation for Biomedical Research; pg. 141, pg. 399
McKelvey, Greg, CMO, Chief Strategy Officer & Exec VP - Fossil Group, Inc.; pg. 5, pg. 1735
McKelvey, Kerry, VP-Mktg & Sls-Big South Reg - Comcast Cable Communications, Inc.; pg. 276, pg. 1560
McKelvie, Genny, Program Mgr-Dealer Adv - John Deere Consumer & Commercial Equipment, Inc.; pg. 705, pg. 1360
Mckendrick, Leron, Dir-Brand Mktg - AARON'S, INC.; pg. 912, pg. 486
Mckendry, Jesse, Mgr-Mktg-Media & Acq - The Progressive Corporation; pg. 1214, pg. 1463
McKenna, Alysa, Mgr-PR, Hamilton & Rado Brands - Swatch Group USA; pg. 13, pg. 1131
McKenna, Colleen, Sr Dir-Mktg - Allergan, Inc.; pg. 1491, pg. 106
McKenna, Danielle, Coord-Email Mktg - Alaska Air Group, Inc.; pg. 1897, pg. 1830
McKenna, David, Dir-Sls Dev - Mack Trucks, Inc.; pg. 183, pg. 1375
Mckenna, Dennis F., VP-Mktg & Bus Dev - Preformed Line Products Company; pg. 1370, pg. 1434
McKenna, Diane M., Dir-Mktg - Pfizer Inc.; pg. 1581, pg. 1278
McKenna, Heather, Dir-Brand Mktg - The J. Jill Group, Inc.; pg. 1774, pg. 842
Mckenna, Kathleen, Product Mgr-Indus IoT - AT&T; pg. 1865, pg. 258
McKenna, Katie, Coord-Online Mktg & Social Media - FalconStor Software, Inc.; pg. 396, pg. 1179
McKenna, Mark, Head-Mktg-Global - Putnam Investments, LLC; pg. 797, pg. 800
McKenna, Megan, Project Mgr-Mktg - Empire State Development Corporation; pg. 747, pg. 1227
McKenna, Melanie, Mgr-Sls - Toll Brothers, Inc.; pg. 115, pg. 1541
McKenna, Nancy, VP-Production - TruTV; pg. 314, pg. 1305
McKenna, Neil, Dir-Interactive Mktg - 1-800-Flowers.com, Inc.; pg. 1758, pg. 1151
McKenna, Sheri, Sr Mgr-Field Mktg & Sls Ops - XO Communications; pg. 497, pg. 1786
McKenna, Tara, Specialist-Media & Partnerships-US - MasterCard Worldwide Inc.; pg. 780, pg. 988
McKenna, Toby, Sr VP-Sls - Answers Corporation; pg. 1229, pg. 1195
Mckenna, Tom, Dir-Digital Mktg & Channel Strategy - Verizon Communications Inc.; pg. 1875, pg. 1309
McKenney, Bree, Exec Dir-Creative Strategy - Vogue Magazine; pg. 1700, pg. 1311
Mckenney, Cecilia K, Exec VP-HR & Sls Ops - Frontier Communications of New York, Inc.; pg. 398, pg. 1335
McKenney, Cecilia K., Exec VP-HR & Sls Ops - Frontier Communications Corporation; pg. 1871, pg. 362
McKenty, Tara, Dir-Creative - Google Inc.; pg. 1249, pg. 153
McKenzie, Carrie, Sr Mgr-US Customer Insights & Analytics - Mattel Games/Puzzles; pg. 962, pg. 80
McKenzie, Carrie, Sr Mgr-US Customer Insights & Analytics - MATTEL, INC.; pg. 962, pg. 81
McKenzie, Dawn, Head-Dallas Local Mktg-Geographic Mktg - Accenture; pg. 1392, pg. 1186
McKenzie, Julie, Sr VP-Softlines & Packaged Good-Nickelodeon Consumer Products - Viacom Inc.; pg. 316, pg. 1310
McKenzie, Kathryn, Sr Dir-Pub Affairs Brand Comm - Abbott Laboratories; pg. 1484, pg. 551
McKenzie, Keisha, Program Dir-Branding, Social Media & Client Programs - International Business Machines Corporation; pg. 418, pg. 1138
McKenzie, Kelly, Sr Mgr-Portfolio Mktg-Sports - Marriott International, Inc.; pg. 1102, pg. 764
McKenzie, Rob, Mgr-Mktg-Global - THE DOW CHEMICAL COMPANY; pg. 1157, pg. 898
McKenzie, Yvette, VP-Mdsg-Latin America - ScanSource, Inc.; pg. 671, pg. 1618
McKeon, Andy, Head-Global Customer Mktg-Facebook & Instagram - Facebook, Inc.; pg. 1245, pg. 143
McKeon, Emily, Sr Mgr-Mktg Comm - Microsoft Corporation; pg. 435, pg. 1824
McKeon, Jamie, VP-Mktg-Foodservice Div - Rich Products Corporation; pg. 892, pg. 1150
McKeon, Molly, Coord-Digital Mktg - GEICO Corporation; pg. 1200, pg. 399
McKeon, Nikki, Mgr-Mktg - 3M Company; pg. 1142, pg. 956
McKeon, Sara, Mgr-Product Mktg - Graco, Inc.; pg. 1342, pg. 935
McKeon, Suzanne, Mgr-Mktg & Creative Svcs - G4S Secure Solutions USA; pg. 399, pg. 436
McKeone, Kelly, VP-Partnership & Florist Mktg - Teleflora LLC; pg. 1801, pg. 140
McKeown, Kelly, Dir-Mktg & Brand Mgmt - Oklahoma City Thunder; pg. 571, pg. 1487
Mckeown, Pat, Sr Mgr-Field Activities-Kawasaki Rail Car - Kawasaki Heavy Industries (U.S.A.), Inc.; pg. 1352, pg. 1248
McKernan, Michelle, Mgr-Mktg & Social Media - Godiva Chocolatier, Inc.; pg. 1854, pg. 1235
McKernan, Richard, Mgr-Pro Console Sls-Western Reg - Avid Technology, Inc.; pg. 622, pg. 804
McKessar, Liam, Mgr-Integrated Mktg-VOGUE - Vogue Magazine; pg. 1700, pg. 1311
McKibben, William, Sr Product Mgr - Affinity Gaming LLC; pg. 526, pg. 1022
McKibbins, Phil, Sr Dir-Emerging Tech - ESPN, Inc.; pg. 285, pg. 340
Mckie, Matt, Sr Mgr-Global Product Mktg-FIFA - Electronic Arts Inc.; pg. 951, pg. 189
McKiernan, Irene, Dir-Mktg - Simon Property Group, Inc.; pg. 1112, pg. 690
McKiernan, Meg, Specialist-Mktg-Intl - Rust-Oleum Corporation; pg. 1447, pg. 664
McKiernan, Myles, Sr Dir-Design for Launch - AstraZeneca Pharmaceuticals LP; pg. 1497, pg. 389
McKillen, Jason, Sr Coord-Mktg - MetroPCS, Inc.; pg. 1872, pg. 1683
McKinlay, Jamie, VP-Global Mktg-EASPORTS & RACING - Electronic Arts Inc.; pg. 951, pg. 189
McKinley, Forrest, Mgr-Mktg Ops - Hewlett-Packard Company; pg. 404, pg. 175
McKinley, Ida, Sr Dir-IT Process & Governance - Dean Foods Company; pg. 852, pg. 1679
McKinley, Jeremy, Mgr-Retail Mktg & Training - Trek Bicycle Corporation; pg. 1847, pg. 1896
McKinley, John, Dir-Mktg & Product Mgmt - Cardinal Health, Inc.; pg. 1512, pg. 1448
McKinley, Stephanie, Mgr-Digital Mktg - Lands' End, Inc.; pg. 1776, pg. 1857
Mckinney, Ashton, Dir-Mktg-US - CryoLife, Inc.; pg. 1520, pg. 534
McKinney, Christine A., Dir-Channel Mktg & SCS Network Ops - McKesson Corporation; pg. 1560, pg. 222
McKinney, Clifford P., Dir-Sls - The Washington Post; pg. 1701, pg. 407
McKinney, Jessica, Sr Mgr-Brand Mktg - AT&T Inc.; pg. 1867, pg. 1674
McKinney, Kim, Sr Dir-Bus Dev - American Quarter Horse Association; pg. 130, pg. 1658
McKinney, Matt, Strategist-Content Mktg - Texas Instruments Incorporated; pg. 679, pg. 1688
McKinney, Sarah Gaskin, Sr Program Mgr-Mktg - SOLARWINDS, INC.; pg. 471, pg. 1666
McKinney, Simone, Mgr-Media & Community Rels - SCANA Corporation; pg. 1951, pg. 1612
McKinney, Sydney, Coord-Mktg - Stanley Furniture Co., Inc.; pg. 943, pg. 1379
McKinney, Terri, Dir-Mktg - Nelnet, Inc.; pg. 786, pg. 1012
McKinney, Toney, Mgr-Mktg Ops-Global - Polycom, Inc.; pg. 664, pg. 249
McKinney, Tracy, Sr Mgr-Strategic Partnerships - American Express Company; pg. 712, pg. 1190
McKinnie, Joseph, Mgr-Mktg-New Product Dev - United Parcel Service, Inc.; pg. 1928, pg. 522
McKinnis, Arnie, Mgr-Product Mktg-MatrixIT - TANGOE, INC.; pg. 481, pg. 368
McKinnon, Rebecca, Dir-Sponsorship & Integrated Media Sls-Natl - Life Time Fitness, Inc.; pg. 1556, pg. 920
McKnight, Caitlin, Planner-Sls-The Food Network - Food Network; pg. 287, pg. 1231
McKnight, Jim, Sr VP-Sls & Mktg - Intelligrated, Inc.; pg. 1349, pg. 1460
McKnight, Lisa, Sr VP-Mktg-North America - Mattel Games/Puzzles; pg. 962, pg. 80
McKnight, Lisa, Sr VP-Mktg-North America - MATTEL, INC.; pg. 962, pg. 81
McKnight-Goelz, Kelly, VP-Sls & Mktg - Unilens Vision Inc.; pg. 1433, pg. 438
Mclachlan, Danielle Effenberger, Mgr-Mktg-Global - MATTEL, INC.; pg. 962, pg. 81
McLachlan, Jason, Sr Mgr-Mktg - TELUS CORPORATION; pg. 1952, pg. 1912
McLafferty, Meighan, Mgr-PR-Amazon Fashion - Amazon.com, Inc.; pg. 1226, pg. 1831
Mclain, Jessica, Analyst-Field Mktg - Pizza Hut, Inc.; pg. 1744, pg. 1733
McLain, Melissa, Sr Mgr-Channel Mktg - Brother International Corporation - USA; pg. 53, pg. 1046
McLane, W. Greg, Sr VP-Sls & Mktg - CATASYS, INC.; pg. 1514, pg. 127
Mclaney, John, Product Mgr-Reinforcing-Natl - Meadow Burke; pg. 96, pg. 474
McLaren, David, Div VP-Sls & Mktg - Insperity, Inc.; pg. 416, pg. 1725
McLaren, Michael, Brand Mgr-Scotch - Pernod Ricard USA, Inc.; pg. 1968, pg. 1332
McLaren, Sarah, Brand Mgr-US Morning Foods Mktg-Froot Loops & Apple Jacks - Kellogg Company; pg. 831, pg. 870
McLaud, Tiffany, Dir-Air Wick Mktg-Europe & North America - Reckitt Benckiser Inc.; pg. 1136, pg. 1105
McLaughlin, Andrea L., Sr Mgr-PR - AT&T Communications Corp.; pg. 1866, pg. 1043
Mclaughlin, Ben, Sr Brand Mgr-Kroger Shopper Mktg - Colgate-Palmolive Company; pg. 504, pg. 1215
McLaughlin, Ben, Sr Mgr-Brand Comm-Global - Converse Inc.; pg. 1831, pg. 793
McLaughlin, Brenna, Dir-Mktg & Comm - Association of American University Presses; pg. 133, pg. 1197
Mclaughlin, Chris, Brand Mgr-Global - AstraZeneca Pharmaceuticals LP; pg. 1497, pg. 389
McLaughlin, Danielle, Dir-PR-Food Network & Cooking Channel - Scripps Networks Interactive, Inc.; pg. 1279, pg. 1638
McLaughlin, Erin, Mgr-Mktg-Social Media & PR - Bare Necessities, Inc.; pg. 19, pg. 1056
McLaughlin, Heather, Exec Dir-PR - Apollo Education Group Inc.; pg. 597, pg. 14
Mclaughlin, Jacqueline, Mgr-Digital Mktg & Inside Sls - IBM; pg. 410, pg. 1449
McLaughlin, Jerry, Sr Mgr-Ticket Acctg - Minnesota Twins, LLC; pg. 563, pg. 940
McLaughlin, Kathy, VP-Sls Support & Admin-Adv Sls - Discovery Communications, Inc.; pg. 282, pg. 777

McLaughlin, Kathy, Mng Editor, Mgr-Custom Publ & Editor-Social Media & SEO - Watt Publishing Company; *pg.* 1701, *pg.* 655
McLaughlin, Kevin, Specialist-Strategic Mktg & Adv - Shimadzu Scientific Instruments, Inc.; *pg.* 1428, *pg.* 768
McLaughlin, Michael, Mgr-Product Dev - Wawa, Inc.; *pg.* 1037, *pg.* 1552
Mclaughlin, Mike, VP-Agriculture Sls - Hydrotex Partners Ltd.; *pg.* 979, *pg.* 1692
McLaughlin, Patrick, Mgr-Sys Sls - Intelligrated, Inc.; *pg.* 1349, *pg.* 1460
Mclaughlin, Robert, Dir-Mktg Svcs - Chick-fil-A, Inc.; *pg.* 1721, *pg.* 492
McLaughlin, Sanarr, Mgr-Interactive Mktg - InterContinental Hotels Corporation; *pg.* 1097, *pg.* 511
McLaughlin, Thomas M., Dir-Mktg - Cartridge World North America, Llc.; *pg.* 369, *pg.* 661
McLaughlin, Todd, Sr VP-Sls Strategy & Ops-Enterprise Grp - Hewlett-Packard Company; *pg.* 404, *pg.* 175
McLaurin, Ken, Mgr-Strategic Mktg - Red Hat, Inc.; *pg.* 460, *pg.* 1388
McLead, Kari, Planner-Product Mktg - Baker Hughes Incorporated; *pg.* 1315, *pg.* 1700
McLean, Catherine, Mgr-Mktg - Nestle Waters North America Inc.; *pg.* 257, *pg.* 375
Mclean, Jasmine, Dir-Mktg - Stowe Area Association, Inc.; *pg.* 1115, *pg.* 1768
Mclean, Junior, Acct Mgr-Adv - Graham Holdings Company; *pg.* 1645, *pg.* 1773
McLean, Lynn, VP-Sls - Hitachi Data Systems Corporation; *pg.* 407, *pg.* 265
McLean, Marie, Mgr-Mktg Comm - General Mills, Inc.; *pg.* 828, *pg.* 933
McLean, Patrick, Sr VP & Head-Brand & Product Mktg - TD Bank US Holding Company; *pg.* 809, *pg.* 1051
McLean, Roddy, Mgr-ECommerce Mktg-Worldwide - Crucial Technology Div of Micron; *pg.* 1237, *pg.* 550
McLean, Ryan, VP & Gen Mgr-Global Mktg - Bissell Homecare, Inc.; *pg.* 52, *pg.* 887
McLean, Scot B., VP-Sls - Haws Corporation; *pg.* 56, *pg.* 1032
McLean, Simon, VP-Sls & Mktg - NXP Semiconductors; *pg.* 660, *pg.* 248
Mclean, Wendy, VP-Sls - Infantino, LLC; *pg.* 957, *pg.* 203
McLeanas, Melissa, Dir-Partnership Mktg - Six Flags Entertainment Corporation; *pg.* 583, *pg.* 1698
McLeish, Chuck, Dir-Mktg - LEGO Systems, Inc.; *pg.* 961, *pg.* 346
McLelland, Greg, VP-Sls - Shaw Media Inc.; *pg.* 308, *pg.* 1943
Mclelland, Shawn, VP-Media & Events - USANA Health Sciences, Inc.; *pg.* 1605, *pg.* 1761
McLemore, Jeff, VP-Mktg-North America - Sunsweet Growers, Inc.; *pg.* 900, *pg.* 309
Mclemore, Todd, Product Brand Mgr-Passenger Car & Small Engine Oils - Citgo Petroleum Corporation; *pg.* 974, *pg.* 1703
Mclendon, Diane, Mgr-Mktg & Sls - The Kansas City Star Company; *pg.* 1656, *pg.* 985
Mclenon, Hal, Sr Mgr-Product Mktg-Pkg Solutions - Eastman Kodak Company; *pg.* 1408, *pg.* 1333
McLeod, Annie, Assoc Dir-Adv - Neiman Marcus, Inc.; *pg.* 30, *pg.* 1684
McLeod, Ben, Sr VP-Corp Mktg - Regions Financial Corporation; *pg.* 798, *pg.* 4
Mcleod, Devron, Mgr-Mktg-IVM, Greenhouse & Nursery - Nufarm Americas Inc; *pg.* 1798, *pg.* 552
McLeod, Greg, VP-Trade Channel Mktg Chains - Anheuser-Busch Companies, LLC; *pg.* 237, *pg.* 991
Mcleod, Mike, Sr Mgr-Digital Adv Products & Tech - PGA Tour, Inc.; *pg.* 574, *pg.* 460
McLeod, Richard, Dir-Mktg-North American Whisky - Pernod Ricard USA, Inc.; *pg.* 1968, *pg.* 1332
McLeod, Ron, Dir-Sls & Software - Siemens Process Industries and Drive; *pg.* 1376, *pg.* 1587
McLeod, Sherry, Program Mgr-Mktg - Acxiom Corporation; *pg.* 342, *pg.* 33
McLeroy, Kerri, Sr Mgr-Mktg - Cheddar's, Inc; *pg.* 1721, *pg.* 1718
McLerran, Ross, Mgr-Media Rels-West Reg - Humana, Inc.; *pg.* 1204, *pg.* 734
McLoughlin, Tim, Mgr-Sls-Southern California - Purcell Murray Company Inc.; *pg.* 59, *pg.* 50
McLucas, Brian, Product Mgr - Affymetrix, Inc.; *pg.* 1487, *pg.* 263
McLuckie, Craig, Sr Product Mgr - Google Inc.; *pg.* 1249, *pg.* 153
McMackin, Dan, Mgr-PR - United Parcel Service, Inc.; *pg.* 1928, *pg.* 522
McMahon, Ashley, Sr Mgr-Consumer Tax & Ecosystem - Intuit Inc.; *pg.* 769, *pg.* 158
McMahon, Bert, Corp VP-Sls - W.F. Young, Inc.; *pg.* 1610, *pg.* 817
McMahon, Brian, Engr-Technical Mktg - Cisco Systems, Inc.; *pg.* 372, *pg.* 240
McMahon, Jennifer, Mgr-PR & Mktg Comm - WestRock Company; *pg.* 1472, *pg.* 1805
McMahon, Jim, Mgr-Sls-Natl - Houghton International Inc.; *pg.* 1167, *pg.* 1589
McMahon, Jim, Sr Mgr-Brand Mktg-Global - Marriott International, Inc.; *pg.* 1102, *pg.* 764
McMahon, John, Sr Mgr-Mktg - Intuit Inc.; *pg.* 769, *pg.* 158
McMahon, Ken, VP-Mountain West Enterprise Sls - CenturyLink, Inc.; *pg.* 1870, *pg.* 746
McMahon, Ken, Sr Dir-Customer Svc, Mohawk Grp, Domestic & Intl - Mohawk Industries, Inc.; *pg.* 935, *pg.* 527
Mcmahon, Linda, Dir-Grp Sls - Daytona Beach Resort Area Convention & Visitors Bureau; *pg.* 991, *pg.* 420
McMahon, Lori B., Sr Mgr-Consumer Mktg Strategy - Intel Corporation; *pg.* 645, *pg.* 266
McMahon, Matthew, VP-Corp Mktg & Comm - IBM; *pg.* 410, *pg.* 1449
McMahon, Meghan, Mgr-Brand Mktg - TripAdvisor, Inc.; *pg.* 1926, *pg.* 835
McMahon, Michael, Dir-Sls & Mktg-Austin - Fairmont Hotels & Resorts Inc.; *pg.* 1091, *pg.* 1938
McMahon, Michelle, VP-Franchise Sls - La Rosa's, Inc.; *pg.* 1735, *pg.* 1416
McMahon, Rob, Product Mgr - Komatsu America Corp.; *pg.* 92, *pg.* 655
McMahon, Ryan, Sr Product Mgr - Autodesk Inc.; *pg.* 356, *pg.* 257
McMahon-Kopp, Amy, VP-Programs & Consumer Products - Mode Media; *pg.* 1267, *pg.* 50
McManigal, Suzanne, Mgr-Digital Mktg - MATTEL, INC.; *pg.* 962, *pg.* 81
McManners, Donna H., Asst Mgr-Adv - The Kroger Co.; *pg.* 1025, *pg.* 1416
McManus, Becky, Dir-Integrated Mktg Comm & Brand Design - Land O'Lakes, Inc.; *pg.* 873, *pg.* 915
McManus, Brendan, Sr Mgr-Comm & Public Affairs - TD Ameritrade Holding Corporation; *pg.* 808, *pg.* 1018
McManus, Brian, Dir-Mktg-Oncology Customer Strategy - GlaxoSmithKline; *pg.* 1536, *pg.* 1565
McManus, Dawn B., Reg Mgr-Mktg - Atmos Energy Corporation; *pg.* 1935, *pg.* 1675
McManus, Katherine, Dir-Mktg & Comm - EMC Corporation; *pg.* 391, *pg.* 825
McManus, Matt, VP-Sls & Mktg Channel & Direct - Fujitsu Computer Systems Corporation; *pg.* 398, *pg.* 285
McManus, Phillip, Coord-Electronic Mktg - Brookshire Grocery Company; *pg.* 1016, *pg.* 1748
Mcmanus, Tony, Dir-Sls - WNYT-TV; *pg.* 322, *pg.* 1137
McManus, Victoria, Mgr-Trade Mktg - Elizabeth Arden, Inc.; *pg.* 507, *pg.* 448
McMaster, Cheri, Sr Mgr-Beauty Care Comm - The Procter & Gamble Company; *pg.* 1129, *pg.* 1418
McMenamin, Jim, Sr Dir & Head-Mktg-LA Reg - Siemens Healthcare Diagnostics; *pg.* 673, *pg.* 604
McMenamy, Barry, Sr Dir-Corp Fin - Winn Dixie Stores, Inc.; *pg.* 1038, *pg.* 435
McMennamy, Shelby, Mgr-Mktg Production - Krispy Kreme Doughnuts, Inc.; *pg.* 1734, *pg.* 1394
McMichael, Katie, Sr Mgr-Mktg-Channel Accounts - BlackBerry Limited; *pg.* 625, *pg.* 1947
McMichael, Noel, VP-Product-Data Science Safe Haven - Acxiom Corporation; *pg.* 342, *pg.* 33
McMichael, Travis, Head-Mktg Strategy - Beats Electronics LLC; *pg.* 624, *pg.* 272
McMillan, Ed, Sr Mgr-Fin - Fifth Third Bancorp; *pg.* 752, *pg.* 1413
McMillan, Henry W., Dir-Respiratory Mktg - Sunovion Pharmaceuticals Inc.; *pg.* 1599, *pg.* 832
McMillan, Michael T., Sr Dir-Franchise Dev - Pepsi-Cola North America; *pg.* 259, *pg.* 1327
McMillan, Shermon, Dir-Mktg - Chattem, Inc.; *pg.* 1515, *pg.* 1628
McMillin, Jesse, Creative Dir - Lyft; *pg.* 429, *pg.* 222
Mcminn, Mark, Dir-Sls - San Jose Convention/Visitors Bureau; *pg.* 1005, *pg.* 250
McMinn, Stacey, Mgr-Mktg Svcs - McAlister's Deli; *pg.* 1737, *pg.* 484
McMorris, Brian, VP-Sls-North America-Fixed Robotics - Adept Technology, Inc.; *pg.* 1310, *pg.* 182
McMorrow, Joanne M., Dir-Digital Mktg & Accenture Strategy - Accenture; *pg.* 1392, *pg.* 1186
McMullan, Bridget, Mgr-Product Line - Foot Locker, Inc.; *pg.* 1808, *pg.* 1231
McMullan, Roger, Designer-Interactive Visual - John Wiley & Sons, Inc.; *pg.* 1655, *pg.* 1073
McMullen, Jim, Product Mgr - Materion Microelectronics & Services; *pg.* 1559, *pg.* 1149
McMullen, Neal, Dir-Corp Sls - Buffalo Bills, Inc.; *pg.* 535, *pg.* 1319
McMullin, Barry, Sr VP-Integrated Sls - World Wrestling Entertainment, Inc.; *pg.* 595, *pg.* 380
Mcmurdy, Sarah, Dir-Mktg - Animal Planet, LLC; *pg.* 270, *pg.* 777
McMurdy, Sarah, Dir-Mktg-Animal Planet - Discovery Communications, Inc.; *pg.* 282, *pg.* 777
McMurray, Monty, Mgr-Integrated Sls - Health Magazine; *pg.* 1648, *pg.* 1238
McMurrey, Doug, VP-Mktg & Bus Dev - Kinder Morgan; *pg.* 1945, *pg.* 1709
McMurtry, Gabriel, Brand Mgr - DISH Network Corporation; *pg.* 283, *pg.* 325
McNab, Paul, CMO & Chief Strategy Officer - Viavi Solutions Inc.; *pg.* 1435, *pg.* 148
McNabb, David, Sr Dir-Multisport - adidas America Inc.; *pg.* 1803, *pg.* 1500
Mcnabb, Donald, Mgr-Mktg - AMERISAFE, Inc.; *pg.* 1191, *pg.* 743
Mcnabb, Dustin, Dir-Mktg - Computer Sciences Corporation; *pg.* 378, *pg.* 1780
McNabb, Lea Ann, Mgr-PR - Trimble Navigation Limited; *pg.* 1384, *pg.* 288
McNair, Courtney, Mgr-Mktg - Honest Tea; *pg.* 253, *pg.* 762
McNair, Deborah, Mgr-Corp PR - Dell Inc.; *pg.* 383, *pg.* 1737
Mcnalis, Andrew, Sr Mgr-Big Data & Data Warehouse Admin - Sears Holdings Corporation; *pg.* 1784, *pg.* 618
McNally, Aimee, Mgr-Digital Mktg - Cigna Corporation; *pg.* 1197, *pg.* 338
McNally, Danielle, Dir-Global Product PR - Motorola Mobility LLC; *pg.* 657, *pg.* 627
McNally, Jennifer, Mgr-Retail Mktg & Events - Polar Electro Inc.; *pg.* 664, *pg.* 1173
McNally, Laura, Sr Mgr-Mktg Comm-Healthcare Transformation Svcs - Philips Electronics North America; *pg.* 662, *pg.* 782
Mcnally, Meghann, Dir-Dealer Mktg Excellence - AGCO Corporation; *pg.* 700, *pg.* 530
McNally, Melissa, Sr Dir-Mktg-Americas - Hugo Boss Fashions Inc.; *pg.* 42, *pg.* 1242
McNally, Michael, Sr Dir-Brand Rels - LEGO Systems, Inc.; *pg.* 961, *pg.* 346
McNamara, Alan, Sr Mgr-Corp Comm - Barnes & Noble, Inc.; *pg.* 1619, *pg.* 1201
McNamara, Jack, Mgr-Product Mktg - Bosch Security Systems, Inc.; *pg.* 626, *pg.* 1158
McNamara, James, Mgr-Digital Mktg - Aubuchon Hardware; *pg.* 1043, *pg.* 859
McNamara, John, VP-Multimedia Sls - ESPN, Inc.; *pg.* 285, *pg.* 340
McNamara, John, VP-Corp Sls - Reliable Automatic Sprinkler Co., Inc.; *pg.* 1137, *pg.* 1158
McNamara, Karen, Sr Mgr-Campaign-Mktg-Creative Cloud for Bus - Adobe Systems Incorporated; *pg.* 342, *pg.* 235
McNamara, Katie, Sr Specialist-Social Media - Jo-Ann Stores LLC; *pg.* 696, *pg.* 1455
McNamara, Kelly, Sr Product Mgr-Xolair Mktg - Genentech, Inc.; *pg.* 1533, *pg.* 279
McNamara, Kevin, Sr VP-Sls & Ops-Air Conditioning Sys - LG Electronics U.S.A., Inc.; *pg.* 651, *pg.* 1060
Mcnamara, Kevin J., Dir-Mktg - The Hanover Insurance Company; *pg.* 1202, *pg.* 862
McNamara, Kristin L., Dir-Mktg-Comml & New Residential Segments - The Sherwin-Williams Company; *pg.* 1447, *pg.* 1435
McNamara, Michael, Sr Mgr-Core Software Product Mktg - NetApp, Inc.; *pg.* 444, *pg.* 287
McNamara, Patrick, Brand Mgr-Hillshire Farm-Lunchmeat - Tyson Foods, Inc.; *pg.* 902, *pg.* 35
Mcnamara, Richard, VP-Integrated Media Sls - Madison Square Garden Network; *pg.* 297, *pg.* 1255
McNamara, Tricia, Brand Mktg Mgr-Global - Caleres, Inc.; *pg.*

1805, pg. 993
McNamara, Wendy, Mgr-Product Dev Mktg - FedEx Corporation; pg. 1907, pg. 1642
Mcnamee, Dave, Sr Product Mgr-Platform - Adobe Systems Incorporated; pg. 342, pg. 235
Mcnamee, Michael, VP-Mktg - Stratosphere Corporation; pg. 1115, pg. 1030
McNaughton, David, CMO & Sr VP-Mktg - Mediacom LLC; pg. 297, pg. 1182
McNaul, Carol, Dir-Convention Sls - Anaheim/Orange County Visitor & Convention Bureau; pg. 988, pg. 42
McNaull, Cindy, Dir-Brand & Mktg-Global - INVISTA B.V.; pg. 1168, pg. 723
McNeal, Trevor, Mgr-Digital & Social Media Mktg - Home Box Office, Inc.; pg. 290, pg. 1240
McNease, Patty, Dir-Mktg - Homes.com, Inc.; pg. 1256, pg. 203
McNeely, Mark, Mgr-Mktg - Toshiba America, Inc.; pg. 681, pg. 1302
McNeely, Rick, Sr VP-Mdsg - Dollar Tree, Inc.; pg. 1767, pg. 1778
McNeil, Don, Sr Product Mgr - Parker Hannifin Corporation; pg. 1368, pg. 1434
McNeil, Fatima, VP-Mktg - SunTrust Banks, Inc.; pg. 807, pg. 520
McNeill, Annie, Coord-Mktg - Winmark Corporation; pg. 1792, pg. 946
McNeill, Christi, Mgr-Social & Digital Strategy - The Patron Spirits Company; pg. 1967, pg. 1029
McNeill, Jon, Pres-Global Sls & Svc - Tesla Motors, Inc.; pg. 191, pg. 178
Mcneill, Kathleen, Gen Mgr-Mdse-Beauty - Urban Outfitters, Inc.; pg. 1789, pg. 1571
McNeilly, Linda, Sr Mgr-Product & Svcs Mktg - Cardinal Health, Inc.; pg. 1512, pg. 1448
McNerney, Carol, VP-Mktg Strategy & Plng - Pitney Bowes Inc.; pg. 454, pg. 376
McNicholas, Brendan, Exec Dir-Media Svcs - Colorado Avalanche, LLC; pg. 541, pg. 317
McNiel, Caroline, VP-Media-Global - Activision Blizzard, Inc.; pg. 948, pg. 271
McNitt, Ali, Mgr-Mktg - Houlihan's Restaurants, Inc.; pg. 1731, pg. 716
McNorton, Lesley A., Brand Mktg Mgr - Hewlett-Packard Company; pg. 404, pg. 175
McNulty, Dave, Dir-Influencer Entertainment Mktg - Diageo North America Inc.; pg. 248, pg. 1223
McNulty, Diane C., Exec Dir-Community Affairs & Media Rels - The New York Times Company; pg. 1668, pg. 1270
McNulty, Kevin, Dir-Creative - ACCO Brands Corporation; pg. 340, pg. 626
McNulty, Lauren A., Dir-Mktg & Bus Dev-Lenox Square - Simon Property Group, Inc.; pg. 1112, pg. 690
McNulty, Meredith, Mgr-Field Mktg - Level 3 Communications, Inc.; pg. 1262, pg. 312
McNulty, Stephen H., VP-Sls - SigmaTron International, Inc.; pg. 674, pg. 611
Mcnulty, Tina, Mgr-Mktg - The F.A. Bartlett Tree Expert Company; pg. 1795, pg. 373
McNutt, Myckey, Brand Mgr-Fin - The Yankee Candle Company, Inc.; pg. 1792, pg. 843
McPartland, Brian, Sr Dir-IT - Washington Capitals; pg. 591, pg. 1775
McPeek, Shari, Mgr-Mktg - Rev-A-Shelf; pg. 1060, pg. 738
McPhee, Katie, Sr Mgr-Mktg - Intuit Inc.; pg. 769, pg. 158
McPherson, Jeannie, Sr Mgr-Corp Comm - VeriSign, Inc.; pg. 488, pg. 1799
McPherson, John, Chief Fin & Strategy Officer & Exec VP - Vulcan Materials Company; pg. 119, pg. 4
McPherson, Kevin M., Global Head-Sls - MARKETAXESS HOLDINGS INC.; pg. 778, pg. 1256
McPherson, Lindsay, Brand Mgr-Tom's of Maine - Colgate-Palmolive Company; pg. 504, pg. 1215
McPherson, Mary, Mgr-Brand Ops-Media - Procter & Gamble Inc.; pg. 333, pg. 1929
McPhillips, David, Mgr-Trade Mktg - Heineken USA Inc.; pg. 252, pg. 1352
McQuade, Gina, Dir-Convention Sls - Anaheim/Orange County Visitor & Convention Bureau; pg. 988, pg. 42
McQueen, Jade, Mng Dir-Media & Entertainment - Box Inc.; pg. 1232, pg. 124
McQuenn, Katie, Sr Mgr-Online Mktg - Hilton Worldwide, Inc.; pg. 1094, pg. 1791
McQuillan, Brianne, VP-Mktg & Solution Strategies - Aerco International Inc.; pg. 1068, pg. 1142
McQuillan, Lucy, Exec VP-Global Sls - Alto-Shaam Inc.; pg. 836, pg. 1869
McQuinn, Matthew, VP-Mktg - SkinnyPop Popcorn LLC; pg. 895, pg. 661
McQuiston, Ed, VP-Sls-Global - Hyland Software, Inc.; pg. 409, pg. 1480
McQuiston, Kelly, Dir-Comml Products - Kelly Services, Inc.; pg. 424, pg. 911
McRae, Matt, CTO & Head-Mktg - VIZIO, Inc.; pg. 686, pg. 118
McRae, Tara, Sr VP-Brand & Mktg - Puma North America, Inc.; pg. 1816, pg. 858
McReynolds, Drew, Mng Dir-Global Res, Telecommunications & Media - Royal Bank of Canada; pg. 800, pg. 1942
McReynolds, Joan, Chief Creative Officer - Hanesbrands Inc.; pg. 26, pg. 1394
McShera, Tara, Sr Mgr-Mktg - Upromise, Inc.; pg. 815, pg. 837
McSpadden, Dan, Dir-Mktg - Florida's Natural Growers; pg. 855, pg. 437
McSpadden, David, Sr VP-Global Client Mktg - FRANKLIN RESOURCES, INC.; pg. 760, pg. 254
McSpadden, Roxanne, Dir-Mktg-Graphics for Matls Grp North America - Avery Dennison Corporation; pg. 1452, pg. 95
McSunas, Michael, Sr Counsel-Adv, Mktg & Promos - FCA US LLC; pg. 170, pg. 868
McTier, Karen, Exec VP-Domestic Licensing & Worldwide Mktg - Warner Bros. Worldwide Consumer Products; pg. 490, pg. 55
McUmber, John, Reg Mgr-Sls-Midwest - Morris Coupling Company; pg. 1057, pg. 1530
Mcvey, Jane, Dir-Creative Svcs - Texas Monthly; pg. 1692, pg. 1666
McWeeney, Gerry, VP-Sls Ops - Captivate; pg. 272, pg. 1209
McWhinney, Ariele, Specialist-Mktg-Continuing Education Div - Harvard University Press; pg. 1648, pg. 808
McWhorter, Nick, VP-Media Licensing - Dark Horse Comics, Inc.; pg. 1633, pg. 1500
McWilliam, Gail, VP-Mktg-Perdue Brand - Perdue Farms Incorporated; pg. 889, pg. 777
McWilliams, Stacy, VP-Team Mktg & Bus Ops - National Basketball Association; pg. 566, pg. 1264
McWilson, Jim, VP-Strategic Channel Partner Sls - Zebra Technologies Corporation; pg. 690, pg. 628
Meacham, Anna, Dir-PR & Social Media - Sea Island Clothiers, LLC; pg. 32, pg. 1146
Mead, Ashley, Dir-Mktg & Social Media Strategy - American Express Company; pg. 712, pg. 1190
Mead, Brian, Product Mgr - Yahoo! Inc.; pg. 1289, pg. 289
Mead, Cara, Mgr-Integrated Sls - National Football League; pg. 567, pg. 1264
Mead, Chris, Mng Dir-Mktg Div - CME Group Inc.; pg. 738, pg. 571
Mead, Christopher, Mng Dir-Mktg Div - CME Group, Inc.; pg. 738, pg. 571
Mead, Heather, Mgr-Web Mktg - T-Mobile US, Inc.; pg. 676, pg. 1816
Mead, Joy, Assoc Dir-Mktg - The Procter & Gamble Company; pg. 1129, pg. 1418
Mead, Kimberly, Mgr-Adv - Dunkin' Brands Group, Inc.; pg. 1727, pg. 810
Meade, Emma, Sr Dir-US Comm - BP America Inc.; pg. 972, pg. 1702
Meade, Evelyn, Dir-Adv & Brand Comm - Cancer Treatment Centers of America; pg. 1511, pg. 410
Meade, Joni, Asst VP-Mktg Production - New York Life Insurance Company; pg. 1211, pg. 1268
Meade, Mary, Mgr-Sls-Natl - Metropolitan Tucson Convention & Visitors Bureau; pg. 998, pg. 27
Meade, Robert, Dir-Mktg Strategy & Asset Sls-CIT Aerospace - CIT GROUP INC.; pg. 735, pg. 1212
Meade, Sharon, Sr Mgr-Corp Comm - Brown-Forman Corporation; pg. 1958, pg. 732
Meade, Shawn P., Sr Mgr-Network Ops & Common Infrastructure - DIRECTV Group Holdings, LLC; pg. 281, pg. 79
Meadows, Jeremy, Mgr-Mktg Comm - Nissan North America, Inc.; pg. 186, pg. 1633
Meadows, Joe, Mgr-Emerging Media - The Progressive Corporation; pg. 1214, pg. 1463
Meadows, Mandy, Mgr-Digital & Social Media - Cinemark Holdings, Inc.; pg. 540, pg. 1729
Meadows, Maria, VP-Local Digital Sls - Gannett Co., Inc.; pg. 1643, pg. 1790
Meadows, Michael, Mgr-Mktg & Comm - Warner Press, Inc.; pg. 1701, pg. 673
Meadows, Richard D., Exec VP-Mktg, Sls & Guest Programs - Holland America Line Inc.; pg. 1911, pg. 1836
Meadows, Theresa, Bus Mgr - Downtown Ford Sales Inc.; pg. 169, pg. 196
Mealiea, Wallace, Mgr-Customer Res & Adv - Edison Electric Institute; pg. 1941, pg. 398
Mealiffe, Gavin, VP-Sls - Tropicana Products, Inc.; pg. 902, pg. 592
Mealt, Tim, VP-Sls & Mktg - A. Finkl & Sons Co.; pg. 1309, pg. 563
Meaney, Benjamin, Sr VP & Mgr-Mass Adv - Bank of America Corporation; pg. 718, pg. 1362
Means, Jeannie, VP-Mktg - Benihana Inc.; pg. 1716, pg. 409
Means, Kassie, Chief Revenue Officer-Woman's Day & Publr - The Hearst Corporation; pg. 1649, pg. 1239
Mearls, Mike, Sr Mgr-Dungeons & Dragons Res & Design - Wizards of the Coast, Inc.; pg. 970, pg. 1830
Mears, Katherine, VP-Corp Mktg - Regions Financial Corporation; pg. 708, pg. 1
Mease, Adam, Head-Product Line-Low Voltage Distr Equipment - GE Energy; pg. 1338, pg. 506
Meberg, Anna-Louise, Specialist-Social Media & Mktg - The Hain Celestial Group, Inc.; pg. 860, pg. 1172
Mecca, Ann, Dir-Adv-US - American Express Company; pg. 712, pg. 1190
Mecca, Lindsay, Sr Mgr-Brand Comm - OXO; pg. 1058, pg. 1275
Mecham, Blake, Mgr-Sls-National - Browning; pg. 1828, pg. 1752
Mechler, Autumn, Brand Mktg Mgr - Landry's, Inc.; pg. 1735, pg. 1709
Mechler, Tom, Mgr-Product Mktg - Bosch Security Systems, Inc.; pg. 626, pg. 1158
Meck, Andrea M., Dir-Mktg - Toll Brothers, Inc.; pg. 115, pg. 1541
Meck, Lally, Sr Rep-Mktg-Sponsorships - United Continental Holdings, Inc.; pg. 1927, pg. 593
Meckfessel, John, Dir-Strategic Mktg-Global - Johnson & Johnson; pg. 1549, pg. 1091
Mecs, Andy, Dir-Trade Mktg & Military Sls - StarKist Foods Inc.; pg. 898, pg. 1581
Medalis, Gary, Dir-Mktg-Goodyear Comml - The Goodyear Tire & Rubber Company; pg. 1883, pg. 1401
Medcraft, Justin, Brand Mgr-Smirnoff-Global - Diageo North America Inc.; pg. 248, pg. 1223
Meddin, Marisa, Assoc Mgr-Mktg-Music Partnerships - PepsiCo, Inc.; pg. 259, pg. 1327
Medeiros, Geoff, VP-Brand Mgmt & Product Dev - The Yankee Candle Company, Inc.; pg. 1792, pg. 843
Medeiros, Jeff, Dir-Mktg - PNY Technologies, Inc.; pg. 455, pg. 1105
Medel, Linda, Brand Mgr-Oracle - CDW Corporation; pg. 370, pg. 663
Medema, Dana, Dir-Mktg - Colgate-Palmolive Company; pg. 504, pg. 1215
Meden, Scott A., Exec VP & Gen Mgr-Mdse & Shoe Div - Nordstrom, Inc.; pg. 1779, pg. 1837
Medero, Evelyn, Sr Dir-Multicultural Mktg & Bus Dev - St. Jude Children's Research Hospital; pg. 1596, pg. 1646
Medhurst, Brian, Bus Mgr - Sanderson Ford Inc.; pg. 190, pg. 13
Medici, Lori, VP-Mktg - Perry Ellis International, Inc.; pg. 45, pg. 445
Medina, Angela, Dir-Mktg - Anthem, Inc.; pg. 1192, pg. 683
Medina, Christine, Sr Asst Brand Mgr-ARPU Digital Strategy - DISH Network Corporation; pg. 283, pg. 325
Medina, Julie, Dir-Mktg - Career Education Corporation; pg. 599, pg. 658
Medina, Kathy, Sr Mgr-Media-Global - American Express Company; pg. 712, pg. 1190
Medina, Rachel, Sr Specialist-Comm-Social Media - UnitedHealth Group Incorporated; pg. 1221, pg. 950
Medina, Rafael, Dir-Mktg & Comm-Colorado Markets - Entravision Communications Corporation; pg. 285, pg. 273
Medina, Rosita, Sr Mgr-Mktg-Monster High, Ever After High & My Password - MATTEL, INC.; pg. 962, pg. 81
Medina, Sharni, Sr Mgr-Customer Mktg - Hewlett-Packard Company; pg. 404, pg. 175
Medina, Tara Olson, Mgr-Social Mktg-Global - Aveda Corporation; pg. 499, pg. 917
Medine, Ryan, Mgr-US Mktg-Action Figures - Mattel Games/Puzzles; pg. 962, pg. 80
Medinger, Jeff, Dir-Retail Sls - MetroPCS, Inc.; pg. 1872, pg. 1683

First page reference indicates Business Class Edition
Second page reference indicates Geographic Edition

Mediratta, Pavan, VP-Mktg - LexisNexis Litigation Solutions; *pg.* 1659, *pg.* 1446
Medler, Catherine, Mgr-Mktg & Promo - Siemens Process Industries and Drives; *pg.* 673, *pg.* 485
Medlicott, Stephen, Dir-Mktg Grp-Natl - Boy Scouts of America; *pg.* 134, *pg.* 1717
Medori, Melissa, Mgr-PR - The Weather Channel LLC; *pg.* 320, *pg.* 523
Medrano, Roberto, Exec VP-Mktg, Product Mgmt, Bus Dev & Channels - Akana; *pg.* 346, *pg.* 125
Medros, Adam, VP-Product - TripAdvisor, Inc.; *pg.* 1926, *pg.* 835
Medvidofsky, Sol, Mgr-Email Mktg-Global Digital Svcs - American International Group, Inc.; *pg.* 1190, *pg.* 1193
Medway, Roy, Sr Mgr-Comm Delivery - Royal Bank of Canada; *pg.* 800, *pg.* 1942
Mee, Allison, Mgr-Brdcst Creative - The Home Depot, Inc.; *pg.* 1050, *pg.* 510
Mee, Julia, Sr Dir-Adv, Media & Sponsorships-Global - Cisco Systems, Inc.; *pg.* 372, *pg.* 240
Meegan, Jeannine, Mgr-Mktg Comm - Becton, Dickinson & Company; *pg.* 1501, *pg.* 1068
Meehan, Christine, Mgr-Field Mktg - Aetna Inc.; *pg.* 1187, *pg.* 351
Meehan, Eric, Mgr-Institutional Mktg - SEI Investments Company; *pg.* 802, *pg.* 1558
Meehan, Michelle, Exec Dir-Integrated Mktg - Rodale, Inc.; *pg.* 1681, *pg.* 1530
Meehan, Richard, Exec VP-Ops & Mktg - Heartland Express, Inc.; *pg.* 1910, *pg.* 710
Meehan, Tara, Mgr-Online Media - Alaska Airlines, Inc.; *pg.* 1897, *pg.* 1830
Meek, Scott, Dir-Mktg-Indian Motorcycle - Polaris Industries Inc.; *pg.* 1709, *pg.* 928
Meeks, Andrew, Mgr-Mktg - Beam Suntory Inc.; *pg.* 1957, *pg.* 599
Meeks, Brian, Dir-Bus Analytics-Natl Retail Sls - Bacardi USA, Inc.; *pg.* 1956, *pg.* 417
Meeks, Meghan, Asst Mgr-PR - Neiman Marcus, Inc.; *pg.* 30, *pg.* 1684
Meenaghan, Jill, Grp Dir-Mktg-Hearst Men's Grp & Assoc Publr - The Hearst Corporation; *pg.* 1649, *pg.* 1239
Meese, Dolly, Chief Strategy Officer & Exec VP - Bright House Networks LLC; *pg.* 272, *pg.* 461
Meetz, Jennifer, VP-Consumer Brands Mktg - Rich Products Corporation; *pg.* 892, *pg.* 1150
Meeus, Alan, Sr Mgr-Product Mktg - Microsoft Corporation; *pg.* 435, *pg.* 1824
Mefford, Greg, VP-Distr Sls-Worldwide - Vishay Intertechnology, Inc.; *pg.* 1435, *pg.* 1551
Megchiani, Prakash, Reg Dir-Mktg-Middle East - Eaton Corporation - Industrial Controls; *pg.* 1296, *pg.* 1874
Megee, Janet, Dir-SEO & Social Media - Autobytel Inc.; *pg.* 1230, *pg.* 107
Meggers, Kay, Pres-Global Rolled Products Global & Exec VP - Alcoa Inc.; *pg.* 65, *pg.* 1188
Mehdi, Ranjini, Program Mgr-Mktg - PayPal Inc.; *pg.* 1274, *pg.* 248
Mehdi, Yusuf, Corp VP-Mktg, Bus & Strategy-Interactive Entertainment Div - Microsoft Corp.; *pg.* 440, *pg.* 321
Mehlman, Jenny, Sr Mgr-Mktg & Sls - Barilla America, Inc.; *pg.* 839, *pg.* 555
Mehra, Anu, Mgr-Mktg Comm - Eaton Corporation; *pg.* 1331, *pg.* 1429
Mehra, Divya, Principal & Product Mgr - Red Hat, Inc.; *pg.* 460, *pg.* 1388
Mehra, Mandira, Sr VP-Mktg - Internap Network Services Corporation; *pg.* 417, *pg.* 513
Mehra, Vineet, Pres-Global Mktg Svcs - Johnson & Johnson; *pg.* 1549, *pg.* 1091
Mehranfshani, Sara, Mgr-Partnership Mktg - Zoological Society of San Diego; *pg.* 595, *pg.* 211
Mehren, Victor, Dir-Mktg - Wm. Wrigley Jr. Company; *pg.* 1863, *pg.* 596
Mehrmann, Cheryl, Dir-Mktg Comm - Newell Rubbermaid Inc.; *pg.* 1128, *pg.* 515
Mehrmann, Drew, Specialist-Mktg, Promos & Brand Delivery - DISH Network Corporation; *pg.* 283, *pg.* 325
Mehrotra, Payal, Product Mgr - EMC Corporation; *pg.* 391, *pg.* 825
Mehta, Anurag, VP-Wireless & New Media - NeuStar, Inc.; *pg.* 1872, *pg.* 1807
Mehta, Devi, Sr Mgr-Brand, Adv & Mktg - Teachers Insurance & Annuity Association - College Retirement Equities Fund; *pg.* 1219, *pg.* 1297
Mehta, Hemali, Brand Mgr - Colgate-Palmolive Company; *pg.* 504, *pg.* 1215
Mehta, Jatin, Mgr-Strategic Market & Product Analytics - FedEx Corporation; *pg.* 1907, *pg.* 1642
Mehta, Kaushal, Sr Mgr-New Product Dev & Innovation - American Express Company; *pg.* 712, *pg.* 1190
Mehta, Ketan, Sr Mgr-Global Product Mktg - Honeywell International Inc.; *pg.* 407, *pg.* 1088
Mehta, Ketan, Sr Mgr-IP Product Mktg - Xilinx, Inc.; *pg.* 496, *pg.* 252
Mehta, Manish, Chief Product Officer - Spredfast; *pg.* 1282, *pg.* 1666
Mehta, Mansi, Brand Mktg Mgr-Obesity Mktg - Takeda Pharmaceuticals USA, Inc.; *pg.* 1600, *pg.* 605
Mehta, Rebecca Gerben, Head-Bus & Strategist-Mktg & Brand - Adobe Systems Incorporated; *pg.* 342, *pg.* 235
Mehta, Rishi, Dir-Mobile Product Strategy & Dev - Wyndham Worldwide Corporation; *pg.* 1119, *pg.* 1107
Mehta, Tina, Mgr-Shopper Mktg-Drugstore Channel - Mars, Incorporated; *pg.* 1858, *pg.* 1792
Mehta, Vaishali H., Mgr-Mktg - Ameriprise Financial, Inc.; *pg.* 715, *pg.* 930
Mehto, Merja, Product Mgr - Thermo Fisher Scientific Inc.; *pg.* 1431, *pg.* 854
Mei, Alex, CMO & Exec VP - OCZ Storage Solutions; *pg.* 448, *pg.* 248
Mei, Ting, Strategist-Social Media-Global - Intel Corporation; *pg.* 645, *pg.* 266
Meidinger, Monica, Brand Mgr-Skin Care - Mary Kay Inc.; *pg.* 516, *pg.* 1657
Meier, David, VP-Bus Dev, Mktg & Sls - Aero Systems Engineering Inc.; *pg.* 223, *pg.* 959
Meier, Hillery, Dir-Product & Brand Mgmt - Hunter Douglas, Inc.; *pg.* 928, *pg.* 1320
Meier, Jim, Sr Dir-Localization - Frito-Lay North America, Inc.; *pg.* 1853, *pg.* 1730
Meier, Jim, Sr Dir-Mktg Fin - MillerCoors LLC; *pg.* 255, *pg.* 582
Meier, John J., Mgr-Mktg - LyondellBasell Industries; *pg.* 980, *pg.* 1710
Meier, Lisa, Grp VP-Time Warner Cable Media - Time Warner Cable Inc.; *pg.* 312, *pg.* 1301
Meigs, Lara, Coord-Social Media - Abbott Nutrition; *pg.* 1485, *pg.* 1437
Meiland-Shaw, Lara, Dir-Mdsg-RTW - LVMH Inc.; *pg.* 9, *pg.* 1254
Meindl, Bob, Dir-Mktg - Cisco Systems, Inc.; *pg.* 372, *pg.* 240
Meiners, Grace, Specialist-Integrated Mktg - The Wall Street Journal; *pg.* 1700, *pg.* 1312
Meiners, Steve, VP-Corp Sls - Crest Foods Co. Inc.; *pg.* 850, *pg.* 554
Meinhardt, Karl, VP-Social & Digital Mktg - Albertson's LLC; *pg.* 1013, *pg.* 546
Meinheit, Krista P., Sr Mgr-Co-Mktg-Svc Providers - Alcatel-Lucent USA, Inc.; *pg.* 615, *pg.* 1728
Meins, Dan, Dir-Mktg & Food Ingredients - Riceland Foods, Inc.; *pg.* 892, *pg.* 36
Meisel, Jackie, Specialist-Mktg - Red Wing Shoe Company, Inc.; *pg.* 1817, *pg.* 954
Meisel, Robert, Sr Analyst-Mktg-Co-Brand Acq - American Express Company; *pg.* 712, *pg.* 1190
Meiser, Leanna, Sr Mgr-Mktg Trng & Capabilities - The Hershey Co.; *pg.* 1855, *pg.* 1538
Meissner, Michal, VP-Sls-Intl - Jelly Belly Candy Company; *pg.* 1857, *pg.* 86
Meister, Ed, VP & Reg Mgr-Sls & Mktg - Wells Fargo & Company; *pg.* 819, *pg.* 232
Meister, Tim, Div Mgr-Mktg - Deere & Company; *pg.* 703, *pg.* 632
Meitzner, Jennifer, Sr Mgr-Pepsi TM Digital & Integrated Media Solutions - PepsiCo, Inc.; *pg.* 259, *pg.* 1327
Meixner, Amanda, Strategist-Social Media - Beachbody, LLC; *pg.* 271, *pg.* 272
Mejia, Juan, Mgr-Digital Mktg-Global - Colgate-Palmolive Company; *pg.* 504, *pg.* 1215
Mejstrik, Joseph, Mgr-Mktg - Wal-Mart Stores, Inc.; *pg.* 1790, *pg.* 29
Mekdusadeerom, Ploy, Program Mgr-Mobile Mktg - Cabela's Incorporated; *pg.* 535, *pg.* 1019
Melamed, Mara, Sr Brand Mgr-Brand Mgr-Whiskey - Beam Suntory Inc.; *pg.* 1957, *pg.* 599
Melander, Amanda, Dir-Mktg - athenahealth, Inc.; *pg.* 1497, *pg.* 855
Melani, Kristi, Dir-Web & Digital Mktg - Plantronics, Inc.; *pg.* 663, *pg.* 270
Melanson, Beth, Sr Mgr-Convention Sls-Eastern Reg - San Francisco Travel Association; *pg.* 1005, *pg.* 227
Melantoni, Guillermo, Mgr-Product Line - Autodesk Inc.; *pg.* 356, *pg.* 257
Melbourne, David F., Sr VP-Mktg & Corp Social Responsibility - Bumble Bee Foods LLC; *pg.* 842, *pg.* 201
Melby, Crystal, Mgr-Mktg-Direct Acq - T-Mobile US, Inc.; *pg.* 676, *pg.* 1816
Melcher, Charlotte, Dir-PR - The Ritz-Carlton Chicago; *pg.* 1110, *pg.* 589
Meldahl, Susan, Mgr-Principal Solutions-Sls & Reporting Platform - Microsoft Corporation; *pg.* 435, *pg.* 1824
Meldrum, Innes, Mgr-Mktg - Novartis Pharmaceuticals Corp.; *pg.* 1575, *pg.* 1054
Mele, Alessandra, Coord-Mktg - W.F. Young, Inc.; *pg.* 1610, *pg.* 817
Melendez, Delimar, Assoc Dir-Creative Svcs - Cellco Partnership; *pg.* 1869, *pg.* 1042
Melendez, Edward, Exec VP-Integrated Mktg Solutions, Natl Sls & Hispanic Mktg - Entravision Communications Corporation; *pg.* 285, *pg.* 273
Melendez, William, Assoc Mgr-Mktg - Burt's Bees Inc.; *pg.* 502, *pg.* 1370
Melero, Marcela, Dir-Mktg - Unilever United States, Inc.; *pg.* 904, *pg.* 1061
Melesky, Kristen, Sr Mgr-Customer Comm Channel - Cigna Corporation; *pg.* 1197, *pg.* 338
Melfi, Joe, Mgr-Cloud Solutions Product Mktg & Dir - D-Link Systems, Inc.; *pg.* 381, *pg.* 89
Melfi, Robert, Reg Sls Mgr-Northeast - Ateeco, Inc.; *pg.* 838, *pg.* 1586
Melikhov, Olivia, Sr Mgr-Social Media - American Society for the Prevention of Cruelty to Animals; *pg.* 131, *pg.* 1193
Melillo, Ben, Sr Mgr-Loyalty-Digital Personalization - The Kroger Co.; *pg.* 1025, *pg.* 1416
Melillo, Gerald R., Jr., Pres-Sls Svcs - PDI, Inc.; *pg.* 1580, *pg.* 1104
Meline, Tristan, Brand Mgr-Global Brands - MillerCoors LLC; *pg.* 255, *pg.* 582
Melissinos, Chris, Dir-Corp Strategy-Media & Entertainment - Verizon Communications Inc.; *pg.* 1875, *pg.* 1309
Melkote, Keerti, Co-Founder & Head-Products & Partnerships - Aruba Networks, Inc.; *pg.* 353, *pg.* 284
Melle, Stacy, VP-Mktg - NBC Universal, Inc.; *pg.* 300, *pg.* 1266
Mellein, John, Dir-Mktg & Sls - Minnesota State Lottery; *pg.* 999, *pg.* 956
Mellen, Amanda Lomont, Sr Dir-Integrated Mktg - LifeLock Inc.; *pg.* 776, *pg.* 26
Mellen, Meaghann, Coord-Social Media - University of Massachusetts; *pg.* 609, *pg.* 781
Melliere, Gary, Gen Mgr-Sponsorships & Mktg Assets - The Goodyear Tire & Rubber Company; *pg.* 1883, *pg.* 1401
Melling, Alan, Sr Dir-RFID Product & Program Mgmt - Motorola Enterprise Mobility; *pg.* 441, *pg.* 1167
Mellman, Staci, Brand Mgr - Visit Florida Inc.; *pg.* 1010, *pg.* 470
Mello, Andy, Mgr-Event Mktg - Cisco Systems, Inc.; *pg.* 372, *pg.* 240
Mello, Jeff, Mgr-Mktg - Cellco Partnership; *pg.* 1869, *pg.* 1042
Mello, Jeff, Mgr-Mktg - Verizon Communications Inc.; *pg.* 1875, *pg.* 1309
Mello, Lynne, VP-Mktg Comm - Tomy; *pg.* 968, *pg.* 648
Mellor, Gretchen, Brand Mgr - StarKist Foods Inc.; *pg.* 898, *pg.* 1581
Mellor, Jon, Sr Dir-Corp Comm - Automatic Data Processing, Inc.; *pg.* 357, *pg.* 1117
Mellor, Lindsay, Mgr-Mktg - Citizen Watch Co. of America, Inc.; *pg.* 3, *pg.* 293
Mellott, Kerianne, Mgr-Social Media - eHarmony.com, Inc.; *pg.* 1242, *pg.* 180
Mellott, Russ, VP-Software Sls - Intelligrated, Inc.; *pg.* 1349, *pg.* 1460
Mellozzi, Jo, Mgr-Mobility Product Mktg - AT&T; *pg.* 1865, *pg.* 258
Melnick, Steven, Sr VP-Mktg & Brand Mgmt - 20th Century Fox Film Corp.; *pg.* 267, *pg.* 124
Melnick, Wendy, Mgr-Production - Trade Press Media Group; *pg.* 1695, *pg.* 1881
Melnyk, Doug, Mgr-Corp Sls - Minnesota Vikings Football Club, Inc.; *pg.* 563, *pg.* 923
Melo, Bernardo, VP-Sls & Mktg-Global - The Singing Machine Company, Inc.; *pg.* 674, *pg.* 426
Meloro, J.R., Sr Dir & Head-Global Medical Comm - Pfizer Inc.; *pg.* 1581, *pg.* 1278

Melser, Harold, Dir-Ministry Advancement Lutheran Hour Ministries - International Lutheran Laymen's League; *pg.* 293, *pg.* 998

Melson, Don, Sr Dir-US Consumer & Bus Insights - McDonald's Corporation; *pg.* 1737, *pg.* 645

Melton, Adrienne, Sr Mgr-Plng & Execution - Genentech, Inc.; *pg.* 1533, *pg.* 279

Melton, Ben, Brand Mgr - Cisco Systems, Inc.; *pg.* 372, *pg.* 240

Melton, Chad, Mgr-Web & Digital Media - Ingersoll-Rand Company; *pg.* 1349, *pg.* 1370

Melton, Greg, Dir-Adv - Long John Silver's, LLC; *pg.* 1736, *pg.* 736

Melton, Jessica, Coord-Mktg - The University of Texas System; *pg.* 610, *pg.* 1667

Melton, Julie, Mgr-Media & Integrated Mktg - Henkel Consumer Adhesives, Inc.; *pg.* 403, *pg.* 1480

Melton, Mike, Exec Dir-Mktg Res & Analysis - Cox Communications, Inc.; *pg.* 279, *pg.* 501

Melton, Sarah, Dir-PR - Dallas Mavericks; *pg.* 543, *pg.* 1678

Meltsner, Angie, Mgr-Sls Plng - The Wall Street Journal; *pg.* 1700, *pg.* 1312

Meltzer, Pamela, Pres & Designer-Creative-Jewelry - PuppyPaws, Inc.; *pg.* 11, *pg.* 1463

Meltzer-Paul, Stephanie, VP-Membership Rewards & Cobrand Products - BJ's Wholesale Club, Inc.; *pg.* 1762, *pg.* 857

Meluso, Ginette, Dir-Comm & Sls Enablement - AmerisourceBergen Corporation; *pg.* 1493, *pg.* 1522

Melville, Graham, Sr Dir-Product Mktg-Cloud Networking - Citrix Systems, Inc.; *pg.* 375, *pg.* 424

Melville, Greg, Head-Mobile Products & Payments - Regions Financial Corporation; *pg.* 798, *pg.* 4

Melvin, Chris, Dir-Media Rels - Arizona Cardinals Football Club, Inc.; *pg.* 529, *pg.* 25

Melvin, Emil, Dir-Sls & Mktg - Del-Tron Precision, Inc.; *pg.* 1328, *pg.* 337

Memon, Farhan, VP-Mobile Products & Strategy - JPMorgan Chase & Co.; *pg.* 772, *pg.* 1246

Memon, Jawwad, Engr-Technical Mktg-NetApp - NetApp, Inc.; *pg.* 444, *pg.* 287

Mena, Susan, Dir-Mktg - The Allstate Corporation; *pg.* 1189, *pg.* 639

Menard, Anne Marie, Bus Mgr - WLNE-TV; *pg.* 322, *pg.* 1608

Menard, Brian, Sr Dir-Sls & Mktg - Mediacom LLC; *pg.* 297, *pg.* 1182

Menard, Maria, Dir-Global Products Mktg - SVB Financial Group; *pg.* 808, *pg.* 270

Menard, Nathan, Mgr-Mktg - Zoosk Inc.; *pg.* 1292, *pg.* 235

Mencia, Susana, Head-Interactive Mktg & ECommerce - 3M Company; *pg.* 1142, *pg.* 956

Mencken, Scott, VP-Mktg - Move, Inc.; *pg.* 1268, *pg.* 247

Mendel, Jori, Assoc Dir-Mktg - AT&T Mobility LLC; *pg.* 619, *pg.* 488

Mendel, Sherry, Acct Mgr & Mgr-Pursuit Mktg - Hewlett-Packard Company; *pg.* 404, *pg.* 175

Mendell, Benita, Gen Mgr-Rio Grande Valley Media Network - The Monitor; *pg.* 1665, *pg.* 1726

Mendell, Marc, VP-Product Design & Dir-Creative - CBS Interactive, Inc.; *pg.* 369, *pg.* 215

Mendelowitz, Dana, Sr Mgr-Integrated Mktg-Harper's Bazaar - The Hearst Corporation; *pg.* 1649, *pg.* 1239

Mendelsohn, Adam, Sr Mgr-Media & Mktg - Anaheim Ducks Hockey Club, LLC; *pg.* 528, *pg.* 42

Mender, Tom, Sr Mgr - Whirlpool Corporation; *pg.* 62, *pg.* 872

Mendez, Alejandra, Rep-Cat Rental Power Mktg - Caterpillar, Inc.; *pg.* 1321, *pg.* 650

Mendez, Arturo, Sr Dir - Kroll Inc.; *pg.* 425, *pg.* 1249

Mendez, Bernardo, Product Mgr - Active Power, Inc.; *pg.* 1310, *pg.* 1660

Mendez, Deborah, Assoc Mgr-Mktg-Insights - Wm. Wrigley Jr. Company; *pg.* 1863, *pg.* 596

Mendez, Kurstin, Assoc Dir-Product Mktg & Strategy Dev - WebMD Health Corporation; *pg.* 1288, *pg.* 1313

Mendini, Douglas A., Dir-Sls - Kensington Publishing Corp.; *pg.* 1656, *pg.* 1248

Mendisabal, Rick, Sr Rep-Mktg - The Williams Companies, Inc.; *pg.* 987, *pg.* 1491

Mendonca, Jose, Product Dir-Payer Mktg - Johnson & Johnson; *pg.* 1549, *pg.* 1091

Mendoza, Alfredo, Project Mgr-Digital Mktg - 24 Hour Fitness Worldwide Inc.; *pg.* 526, *pg.* 258

Mendoza, Alvaro, Mgr-Product Mktg - The Goodyear Tire & Rubber Company; *pg.* 1883, *pg.* 1401

Mendoza, Angela, Sr Program Mgr-Mktg - Cisco Systems, Inc.; *pg.* 372, *pg.* 240

Mendoza, Ashley E., Sr Mgr-Strategic Comm - Albemarle Corporation; *pg.* 1146, *pg.* 741

Mendoza, Jacinth, Mgr-Mktg - L'Oreal USA; *pg.* 514, *pg.* 1252

Mendoza, Leslie, Dir-Mktg - Real Mex Restaurants, Inc.; *pg.* 1746, *pg.* 75

Mendoza, Mary B., Mgr-Creative Activation - The Coca-Cola Company; *pg.* 240, *pg.* 493

Mendoza, Miko, Brand Mgr-Mktg-Global - The Gap, Inc.; *pg.* 1770, *pg.* 218

Mendoza, Paul, Brand Mgr - Taco Bell Corp.; *pg.* 1752, *pg.* 117

Mendoza, Will, Mgr-Mktg - W.R. Grace & Co.; *pg.* 123, *pg.* 810

Menendez, Christina, VP-Shopper Mktg & ECommerce Sls-Walmart Inc - PepsiCo, Inc.; *pg.* 259, *pg.* 1327

Menendez, Hector E., Sr Mgr-Mktg-Wireless Solutions Mktg - Alcatel-Lucent; *pg.* 615, *pg.* 38

Menesguen, Marc, Pres-Consumer Products Div - L'Oreal USA; *pg.* 514, *pg.* 1252

Menezes, Brian, Dir-Product Mgmt - VMware, Inc.; *pg.* 490, *pg.* 179

Menezes, Sheldon, Sr Product Mgr-Xbox Live - Microsoft Corporation; *pg.* 435, *pg.* 1824

Mengler, Nancy, Mgr-Creative Svcs - The News-Times; *pg.* 1670, *pg.* 344

Mengwasser, Kyle, Head-Mktg Strategy-Family Care - Kimberly-Clark Corporation; *pg.* 1461, *pg.* 1720

Meniai, Nordine, Sls Mgr-Pkg-EMEA - ITW Dynatec; *pg.* 1351, *pg.* 1635

Menicheschi, Edward, CMO & Pres-Conde Nast Media Grp - Conde Nast Publications, Inc.; *pg.* 1629, *pg.* 1217

Menikoff, Grant, Mgr-Loyalty & Credit Card Mktg - Barnes & Noble, Inc.; *pg.* 1619, *pg.* 1201

Menk, Laura, Mgr-Mktg-Intl - Popeyes Louisiana Kitchen, Inc.; *pg.* 1745, *pg.* 517

Menke, Brandon, Specialist-Product Mktg - Caterpillar, Inc.; *pg.* 1321, *pg.* 650

Menke, Linda, Mgr-Social Media & Event Mktg - FSC Franchise Co., LLC; *pg.* 1729, *pg.* 473

Menke-Watts, Monica, Dir-Pharmacy Mktg - Anthem, Inc.; *pg.* 1192, *pg.* 683

Menking, Sharon, Exec Dir-Sls Dev & Mktg - ABC, Inc.; *pg.* 268, *pg.* 1185

Mennenga, Catherine M., Counsel-Adv & Brand Mgmt - General Electric Company; *pg.* 1297, *pg.* 347

Mennone-Preisner, Paula, Specialist-Mktg & Comm - Radio Frequency Systems, Inc.; *pg.* 666, *pg.* 354

Menon, Bindi, VP-Mktg Strategy & Insights - Captain D's, LLC; *pg.* 1720, *pg.* 1649

Menon, Jyoti, Dir-Mktg Solutions - eBay Inc.; *pg.* 1240, *pg.* 243

Mensing, Gretchen, Mgr-Comm & Mktg - Michigan Apple Committee; *pg.* 147, *pg.* 895

Menter, Aurora, Dir-Mktg Ops - Northeastern University; *pg.* 605, *pg.* 799

Menter, Debra, Mgr-Events Mktg - Gartner, Inc.; *pg.* 1248, *pg.* 374

Mentry, Marc, Sr VP-Brand Mktg - Capital One Financial Corporation; *pg.* 730, *pg.* 1789

Mentzer, Shannon, Dir-Internet Mktg - SHUTTERFLY, INC.; *pg.* 1280, *pg.* 192

Menuet, Beth, Exec VP & Gen Mgr-Mdse - Academy Sports & Outdoors, Ltd.; *pg.* 1824, *pg.* 1724

Menuskin, Lisa, Mgr-Mktg - FedEx Corporation; *pg.* 1907, *pg.* 1642

Menz, Carolyn, VP-Digital Mktg & Social Media - CIT GROUP INC.; *pg.* 735, *pg.* 1212

Menzel, Courtney, Sr VP-Domestic Distr & Partner Mktg - Discovery Communications, Inc.; *pg.* 282, *pg.* 777

Menzel, Jack, Dir-Product Mgmt-Google Search - Google Inc.; *pg.* 1249, *pg.* 153

Menzella, Danielle, Mgr-Mktg-Movado & ESQ by Movado - Movado Group, Inc.; *pg.* 10, *pg.* 1101

Menzies, Tracey, VP-Creative Ops & Production - HarperCollins Publishers Inc.; *pg.* 1647, *pg.* 1237

Mepham, Dan, Product Mgr-Accessories - General Motors Company; *pg.* 175, *pg.* 881

Mepham, Dan, Product Mgr-Accessories - General Motors of Canada Ltd.; *pg.* 177, *pg.* 1931

Mequet, Brian, VP-Mktg - Pernod Ricard USA, Inc.; *pg.* 1968, *pg.* 1332

Mera, Pilar, Mgr-Consumer Mktg - Home Box Office, Inc.; *pg.* 290, *pg.* 1240

Merbler, Ron, Mgr-Digital Mktg-Enterprise Platform - Ford Motor Company; *pg.* 172, *pg.* 876

Mercadante, Damon, Dir-Programmatic Mktg & Revenue - CBS Interactive, Inc.; *pg.* 369, *pg.* 215

Mercado, Eddie, Sr Mgr-Digital Mktg-B2B Acq & Current Customer - DIRECTV Group Holdings, LLC; *pg.* 281, *pg.* 79

Mercado, Tony, Mgr-Mktg - Kenwood USA Corporation; *pg.* 649, *pg.* 123

Mercaldi, Lauren, Strategist-Digital Mktg-Global - Cigna Corporation; *pg.* 1197, *pg.* 338

Mercer, Dolly, Mgr-Consumer Promos & Natl Events Mktg - Golden Corral Corporation; *pg.* 1730, *pg.* 1387

Mercer, Donna, VP-Adv & Consumer Insights - Golden Corral Corporation; *pg.* 1730, *pg.* 1387

Mercer, Jaimie, Dir-Retail Sls & Ops - The Orvis Company, Inc.; *pg.* 1781, *pg.* 1764

Mercer, Jeffrey, Sr Dir - Microsoft Corp.; *pg.* 440, *pg.* 321

Mercer, Jeremy, Supvr-Mktg-Online & Mobile Solutions - Jack Henry & Associates, Inc.; *pg.* 422, *pg.* 988

Mercer, Lori, Mgr-Mktg-Global Sourcing - Apple Inc.; *pg.* 350, *pg.* 73

Mercer, Robert, Sr Dir-PR - DIRECTV Group Holdings, LLC; *pg.* 281, *pg.* 79

Mercer, Robin, Sr Mgr-Mktg - Canadian Imperial Bank of Commerce; *pg.* 729, *pg.* 1935

Mercer, Scott, VP & Dir-Creative - The Orvis Company, Inc.; *pg.* 1781, *pg.* 1764

Mercer, Tess, VP-Mktg Tech - The Dun & Bradstreet Corp.; *pg.* 1637, *pg.* 1120

Merchant, Abbas, Grp VP-Mktg & Comm - M&T Bank Corporation; *pg.* 777, *pg.* 1149

Merchant, Amy, Mgr-Digital Mktg - Hallmark Cards, Inc.; *pg.* 1646, *pg.* 983

Merciel, Aileen Angulo, Sr VP-Mktg & Creative - Telemundo Network Inc.; *pg.* 311, *pg.* 430

Mercil, Lacey, Supvr-Mktg - 3M Company; *pg.* 1142, *pg.* 956

Mercolini, Shannon, Head-Global Internal Channels-Brand, Comm & Mktg - Ernst & Young Global Limited; *pg.* 748, *pg.* 1228

Mercuri, Dominic J., CMO & Exec VP-Community & Environment - The Toronto-Dominion Bank; *pg.* 810, *pg.* 1945

Mercurio, Dennis, Mgr-Sls & Telesales Ops-Internet Mktg - Deluxe Corporation; *pg.* 1634, *pg.* 964

Mercurio, Mark A., VP-Mktg & Innovation - Gorilla Glue Co.; *pg.* 1048, *pg.* 1414

Meredith, Carissa, Dir-Mktg - Workiva; *pg.* 493, *pg.* 701

Meredith, James, VP & Head-Mktg & Comm - Cinemark Holdings, Inc.; *pg.* 540, *pg.* 1729

Meredith, Jeff, VP-Mktg-Lenovo Bus Grp - Lenovo Group Ltd; *pg.* 427, *pg.* 1384

Meredith, Kate, Mgr-Mktg-Natl - Aramark; *pg.* 1013, *pg.* 1558

Merem, Mike, Dir-Production - The Blade Co.; *pg.* 1621, *pg.* 1476

Meretakis, Dimitris, Product Mgr - Google Inc.; *pg.* 1249, *pg.* 153

Mergentime, Brian, Specialist-Reg Sls - Air Techniques, Inc.; *pg.* 1487, *pg.* 1178

Merheb, Pablo, Dir-Mktg-Fritos Brand & Dips Portfolio - Frito-Lay North America, Inc.; *pg.* 1853, *pg.* 1730

Merheb, Pablo, Dir-Mktg, Fritos Brand & Dips Portfolio - PepsiCo, Inc.; *pg.* 259, *pg.* 1327

Meriam, Steve, Mgr-Sls-Natl - Stihl, Inc.; *pg.* 1064, *pg.* 1810

Merickel, Justin, Sr Dir-Media Optimizer - Adobe Systems Incorporated; *pg.* 342, *pg.* 235

Merida, Marco, VP-Mktg Alliances - Bluegreen Corporation; *pg.* 1082, *pg.* 410

Merideth, Jason, Brand Mgr-Dreyer's & Edy's - Dreyer's Grand Ice Cream Holdings, Inc.; *pg.* 1852, *pg.* 171

Meridor, Nathaniel, Sr Mgr-Global Scientific Comm-Managed Care Sys - Amgen Inc.; *pg.* 1493, *pg.* 291

Merino, Alejandro, Reg Mgr-Sls-Africa, Middle East & Latin America - Hutchinson/Mayrath Industries Inc.; *pg.* 704, *pg.* 714

Merino, Marc A., Supvr-Mktg - Six Flags Entertainment Corporation; *pg.* 583, *pg.* 1698

Meritt, Jaime, VP-Product Mgmt - Progress DataDirect; *pg.* 457, *pg.* 1385

Meriwether, Brad, Dir-Consumer Mktg - Atlanta National League Baseball Club, Inc.; *pg.* 530, *pg.* 490

Merk, Janice, Dir-North America Mktg - Limelight Networks, Inc.; *pg.* 1262, *pg.* 26

Merkel, Cindy, Sr Mgr-Trade Promos - Kellogg Company; *pg.* 831, *pg.* 870

Merker, Kayla, Mgr-Mktg - CoreLogic, Inc.; *pg.* 1198, *pg.* 109

Merker, Kit, Product Mgr - Google Inc.; pg. 1249, pg. 153
Merkerson, Shonda, Specialist-Social Media - Valassis Communications, Inc.; pg. 1287, pg. 897
Merket, Danielle, Sr Assoc Mgr-Mktg-Global Chocolate Innovation - The Hershey Co.; pg. 1855, pg. 1538
Merkle, Katherine, Brand Mgr - The Sherwin-Williams Company; pg. 1447, pg. 1435
Merklin, Alice, Dir-Creative Strategy - Nordstrom, Inc.; pg. 1779, pg. 1837
Merksamer, Amy, Dir-Digital Mktg - L'Oreal USA; pg. 514, pg. 1252
Merkulov, Peter, VP-Product Strategy & Tech Alliances - GlobalSCAPE Inc.; pg. 401, pg. 1740
Merle, Andrew, Sr Mgr-Sports Mktg - Clif Bar Inc.; pg. 848, pg. 83
Merle-Lieberman, Sharon, VP-Mktg - 20th Century Fox Film Corp.; pg. 267, pg. 124
Merline, Tom, Dir-Sls-North America - Everett Charles Technologies; pg. 638, pg. 185
Merlo, Greg, Brand Mgr-Michelob ULTRA & Value Brands - Anheuser-Busch Companies, LLC; pg. 237, pg. 991
Meron, Guy, Sr Dir-Technical Mktg & Solution-RBU - Juniper Networks, Inc.; pg. 1260, pg. 286
Merrell, Bryan, VP-Sls - Vertical Communications, Inc.; pg. 488, pg. 270
Merrick, Ed, District Mgr-Sls - AutoTrader, Inc.; pg. 1230, pg. 490
Merrick, Jennifer, Strategist-Social Media - Mercer Inc.; pg. 1395, pg. 1258
Merrick, Jim, Dir-Mktg-Gaming & Graphics - QUALCOMM Incorporated; pg. 1873, pg. 207
Merrifield, John, Head-Project-Google for Work Inside Sls - Google Inc.; pg. 1249, pg. 153
Merrill, Bob, Exec VP-Sls & Mktg - Jeld-Wen, Inc.; pg. 1051, pg. 1499
Merrill, Caron, Sr Mgr-Customer Res & Customer Experience Grp - CVS Health Corporation; pg. 1765, pg. 1610
Merrill, Chuck, Specialist-Sls & Mktg Solutions - The Dun & Bradstreet Corp.; pg. 1637, pg. 1120
Merrill, Mark G., Sr VP-Advanced Engrg - NETGEAR, Inc.; pg. 444, pg. 247
Merrill, Ryan, Brand Mgr-Innovation - Continental Mills, Inc.; pg. 827, pg. 1845
Merritt, Bill, VP-Sls & Mktg-Global - Tecumseh Products Company; pg. 1381, pg. 866
Merritt, Carrie, Dir-PR - SVB Financial Group; pg. 808, pg. 270
Merritt, Dan, Reg Mgr-Sls - Reliable Automatic Sprinkler Co., Inc.; pg. 1137, pg. 1158
Merritt, Daniel, Mgr-Mktg - Badger Meter, Inc.; pg. 1401, pg. 1873
Merritt, Daniel, Sr Analyst-Domestic & Intl Mktg - Wynn Resorts Limited; pg. 1119, pg. 1030
Merritt, Greg, VP-Mktg - Cree Inc.; pg. 631, pg. 1371
Merritt, Jane, Mgr-Mktg & Specialty Products - Aetna Inc.; pg. 1187, pg. 351
Merritt, Janelle, Brand Mgr-Paid Social Media - Capital One Financial Corporation; pg. 730, pg. 1789
Merritt, John, Sr Dir-Advancement - University of Minnesota; pg. 609, pg. 945
Merritt, Teri, VP-Brand Mktg & ECommerce-Americas - Marriott International, Inc.; pg. 1102, pg. 764
Merry, Tara, Sr Product Head-Mktg & Comml - General Electric Company; pg. 1297, pg. 347
Merryman, Corrina, Reg Mgr-Sls - Galaxy Nutritional Foods, Inc.; pg. 857, pg. 1603
Mershon, Brian, Dir-Media Rels & External Comm-Global - Fluor Corporation; pg. 82, pg. 1719
Merten, Brian, Analyst-Trade Mktg & Distr - Altria Group, Inc.; pg. 1893, pg. 1800
Mertens, Connie, Dir-Digital Mktg - AT&T; pg. 1865, pg. 258
Mervis, Rebecca, Dir-Brand Strategy, Mktg & Cambria Suites - Choice Hotels International, Inc.; pg. 1086, pg. 775
Merwin, Alyssa, Head-Sls-SMB Relationship Mgmt-North America & Dir - LinkedIn Corporation; pg. 1262, pg. 160
Merwitz, Harmony, VP-Global Mktg-OEM Supply Fasteners - Anixter International Inc.; pg. 1313, pg. 614
Merz, Jennifer, Mgr-Corp Sponsorship Mktg - PetSmart, Inc.; pg. 1481, pg. 18
Merzbacher, Peg, VP-Reg Mktg - Peapod, LLC; pg. 1029, pg. 661
Mesa, Matt, Coord-Social Media - Los Angeles Dodgers Inc.; pg. 559, pg. 135
Meserve, Mercedes, VP-Mktg - Brookfield Homes Corporation; pg. 72, pg. 1779
Mesharer, Mike, Dir-RV Sls - Thetford Corporation; pg. 337, pg. 867
Mesick, Kari, Sr Product Mgr-Market Strategy - Deluxe Corporation; pg. 1634, pg. 964
Meskin, Barbara, Brand Mgr-Froot Loops & Apple Jacks - Kellogg Company; pg. 831, pg. 870
Mesko, Mike, VP-Production - Lost Arrow Corporation; pg. 44, pg. 301
Meskunas, Stefanie, Assoc Mgr-Mktg - Ateeco, Inc.; pg. 838, pg. 1586
Mesloh, Debbie, Sr Dir-Global Pub & Govt Affairs - The Gap, Inc.; pg. 1770, pg. 218
Mesnik, Michael, Dir-Mktg-US - CareFusion Corporation; pg. 1513, pg. 201
Messenger, Wade, VP-Sls - PulteGroup, Inc.; pg. 1109, pg. 873
Messer, Anne C., Dir-Mktg - Wilmington Trust Corporation; pg. 822, pg. 392
Messerschmidt, Eric, VP-Mktg Strategy, Loyalty & CRM - Ulta Salon, Cosmetics & Fragrance, Inc.; pg. 524, pg. 559
Messick, Mark, Mgr-Mktg-Intl - Club Car, Inc.; pg. 1830, pg. 532
Messick, Pamela, Specialist-Media Production - Jacuzzi Brands Corporation; pg. 554, pg. 65
Messier, Jessica, Dir-Strategic Mktg - Sony Music Entertainment; pg. 309, pg. 1294
Messina, Erin, Specialist-Channel Mktg - Stratasys, Inc.; pg. 476, pg. 923
Messina, Giovanna, Mgr-Online Partnership Mktg - The Hearst Corporation; pg. 1649, pg. 1239
Messina, Jacob, Dir-Internet Mktg - Loews Hotels Holding Corporation; pg. 1101, pg. 1252
Messina, Kristin, Project Mgr-Mktg - Sports Illustrated; pg. 1688, pg. 1295
Messina, Rebecca, VP-Mktg Capability & Integration-Global - The Coca-Cola Company; pg. 240, pg. 493
Messina, Scott, Sr Mgr-Acq Mktg - LOGMEIN, INC.; pg. 428, pg. 861
Messina, Vince, Dir-Sls-Natl - Microsoft Corporation; pg. 435, pg. 1824
Messing, Barbara, CMO - TripAdvisor, Inc.; pg. 1926, pg. 835
Messinger, Scott, Corp VP-Adv & Brand Mgmt - Las Vegas Sands Corp.; pg. 1100, pg. 1027
Messner, Cody, Product Mgr - Leggett & Platt, Incorporated; pg. 933, pg. 974
Messuti, Esteban, Mgr-Mktg-Global Procurement - Unilever United States, Inc.; pg. 904, pg. 1061
Mestemaker, Heather, Dir-Global Mktg Cardiovascular New Products - GlaxoSmithKline; pg. 1536, pg. 1389
Mestemaker, Heather, Dir-Global Mktg Cardiovascular New Products - GlaxoSmithKline Consumer Healthcare; pg. 510, pg. 1554
Meszaros, Mark, VP-Core Product Mgmt & Innovation - Carolina Biological Supply Company; pg. 1513, pg. 1359
Metallo, Jeffrey, Assoc Mgr-Mktg Comm - LifeCell Corporation; pg. 1556, pg. 1045
Metcalf, David, VP-Mktg - PODS Enterprises, Inc.; pg. 1919, pg. 416
Metcalf, Don, Dir-Product Mktg - Penske Truck Leasing Company, L.P.; pg. 188, pg. 1585
Metcalf, John, VP-Customer Mktg - Huntington Bancshares Incorporated; pg. 767, pg. 1440
Metcalf, Mary, Dir-Digital Mktg - The Walt Disney Company; pg. 317, pg. 52
Metcalfe, Andrea, Coord-Sls & Mktg - State Farm Mutual Automobile Insurance Co.; pg. 1218, pg. 557
Metheny, Kevin, Program Dir-WJR Radio-Cumulus Media - WJR-AM Radio; pg. 322, pg. 884
Metherd, Jeff, Mgr-Brand Mktg-Govt, Pub Safety & Emergency Preparedness - W.W. Grainger, Inc.; pg. 1390, pg. 625
Metoyer, Candace N., Mgr-Mktg - Intel Corporation; pg. 645, pg. 266
Metros, Wendy, Dir-PR - Henry Ford Museum and Greenfield Village; pg. 552, pg. 878
Metselaar, Gerard, VP-Sls & Mktg Intl Grp-Corp Brand Dev - Henry Schein, Inc.; pg. 1541, pg. 1180
Mettler, Mark, Sr VP & Gen Mgr-Mdsg - Staples, Inc.; pg. 474, pg. 821
Metwalli, Sharif, Dir-Media & Comm Investment Banking - SunTrust Banks, Inc.; pg. 807, pg. 520
Metz, Jenny, Specialist-Mktg & Brand - The Sports Authority, Inc.; pg. 1846, pg. 326
Metz, Jenny, Mgr-Sls-Hotel & Local Corp Market - Zoological Society of San Diego; pg. 595, pg. 211
Metz, Judy, Assist Dir-Print & Production - Bentley University; pg. 598, pg. 850
Metz, Kendra, Sr Mgr-Digital Engagement - National Association for Stock Car Auto Racing; pg. 566, pg. 420
Metzer, Eran, Sr Dir-Solution Dev - Yahoo! Inc.; pg. 1289, pg. 289
Metzger, Greg, Dir-Mktg - Red Gold, Inc.; pg. 891, pg. 677
Metzger, Julie, Mgr-Sls-Natl - LANGUAGE LINE SERVICES HOLDINGS, INC.; pg. 426, pg. 151
Metzger, Melina, Mgr-PR-Safelite AutoGlass - Safelite Solutions LLC; pg. 109, pg. 1443
Metzger, Nick, Specialist-PR - State Farm Mutual Automobile Insurance Co.; pg. 1218, pg. 557
Metzinger, Bruce A., Sr Dir & Asst Sec - Halliburton Company; pg. 978, pg. 1707
Metzinger, Kate, Sr Mgr-Mktg, Comm Strategy, Innovation & Plng - Georgia-Pacific LLC; pg. 1458, pg. 507
Metzler, Maria del Pilar, Sr Mgr-PR - Avaya Inc.; pg. 621, pg. 264
Metzler, Marissa, Specialist-Social Media-FTD Companies, Inc - Provide Commerce, Inc.; pg. 1276, pg. 206
Metzner, Jeff, Brand Mgr-Global Always - The Procter & Gamble Company; pg. 1129, pg. 1418
Meucci, Lindsay, Mgr-Targeted Mktg - Giant Eagle, Inc.; pg. 1020, pg. 1575
Meurer, Erik, Assoc Mgr-Mktg Comm-Global & US Markets - LifeCell Corporation; pg. 1556, pg. 1045
Meusch, Monty, Area Mgr-Sls - Farmers National Company; pg. 703, pg. 1015
Meves, Brandon, Sr Specialist-Mktg - The Northwestern Mutual Life Insurance Company; pg. 1212, pg. 1879
Mevorah, Dave, VP-Sls-Targeted Media Health - Time Inc.; pg. 1693, pg. 1300
Meye, Tricia, Reg Head-Inside Sls-Central - ABB Inc. - Automation Technologies Instrumentation Products; pg. 1398, pg. 1590
Meyer, Alex, Designer-New Media & Social Mktg - Live Nation Entertainment, Inc.; pg. 558, pg. 47
Meyer, Amy J., Dir-Corp Media Rels - Johnson & Johnson; pg. 1549, pg. 1091
Meyer, Andrew, Head-Creative-Global Mktg - Facebook, Inc.; pg. 1245, pg. 143
Meyer, Benjamin A., Sr Mgr-Mktg Programs - International Business Machines Corporation; pg. 418, pg. 1138
Meyer, Beth, VP-Mktg, Product & Innovation-Global - Powermat USA, LLC; pg. 665, pg. 875
Meyer, Beth, Dir-Creative, Video Svcs & Archival Assets - United States Tennis Association; pg. 160, pg. 1354
Meyer, Brent, Dir-Team Sls - adidas America Inc.; pg. 1803, pg. 1500
Meyer, Carla, Mgr-Social Media - Garmin International, Inc.; pg. 1414, pg. 717
Meyer, Cathy, Mgr-Mktg - General Mills, Inc.; pg. 828, pg. 933
Meyer, Chris, VP-Bus Sls-Global - Las Vegas Convention & Visitors Authority; pg. 997, pg. 1027
Meyer, Cindy, Mgr-Retail Brand Product Presentation - NIKE, Inc.; pg. 1812, pg. 1492
Meyer, Denise, Mgr-Social Media Comm - Interactive Intelligence, Inc.; pg. 417, pg. 687
Meyer, Drew, Sr Dir-Product Mktg & Info Mgmt - Symantec Corporation; pg. 478, pg. 161
Meyer, Elizabeth, Sr Asst Brand Mgr-Downy-North America Delivery - The Procter & Gamble Company; pg. 1129, pg. 1418
Meyer, Eric, Analyst-Mktg Support - The Northwestern Mutual Life Insurance Company; pg. 1212, pg. 1879
Meyer, Erica, Mgr-Mktg-North America - Elizabeth Arden, Inc.; pg. 507, pg. 448
Meyer, Erik, Dir-Entertainment & Production - Padres L.P.; pg. 573, pg. 206
Meyer, Gordon, Dir-Digital Mktg - Sirius XM Holdings Inc.; pg. 308, pg. 1292
Meyer, Heath R., Sr Mgr-Mktg-Global - QUALCOMM Incorporated; pg. 1873, pg. 207
Meyer, Jason, Sr Product Mgr - Epson America Inc.; pg. 394, pg. 122
Meyer, Jena, Sr Brand Mgr-Global Mktg-Youth & Accessories - Under Armour, Inc.; pg. 49, pg. 759
Meyer, Jennifer, Dir-Market Res & Product Dev - Universal Forest Products, Inc.; pg. 117, pg. 890
Meyer, Jill, Dir-PR & Comm - Healthways, Inc.; pg. 1540, pg. 1632
Meyer, John, Head-Strategic Partnerships & Mktg Team - Corporation Service Company; pg. 380, pg. 390
Meyer, Josh, Product Mgr - Apple Inc.; pg. 350, pg. 73

Meyer, Kara, Dir-Adv Sls Mktg & Promos - The Walt Disney Company; *pg.* 317, *pg.* 52
Meyer, Karen, VP-Products - Qvidian; *pg.* 458, *pg.* 829
Meyer, Kirby, Mgr-Creative Content-Brand Mktg - Panera Bread Company; *pg.* 1029, *pg.* 1001
Meyer, Kristina, Specialist-Product Mktg - FRANKLIN RESOURCES, INC.; *pg.* 760, *pg.* 254
Meyer, Lauren, Specialist-Mktg - Toll Brothers, Inc.; *pg.* 115, *pg.* 1541
Meyer, Lee, Sr Mgr-Mktg-Equipment Innovation - PepsiCo, Inc.; *pg.* 259, *pg.* 1327
Meyer, Mark, Sr Mgr-Technical Solutions - Yahoo! Inc.; *pg.* 1289, *pg.* 289
Meyer, Scott, Product Mgr - Huttig Building Products, Inc.; *pg.* 88, *pg.* 998
Meyer, Sheree, Sr Mgr-Procurement Solutions - Wyndham Worldwide Corporation; *pg.* 1119, *pg.* 1107
Meyer, Sleighton, Sr Mgr-Mktg Comm - HARRIS CORPORATION; *pg.* 642, *pg.* 439
Meyer, Stephanie, Sr Mgr-Mktg-Core Bus - Sargento Foods Inc.; *pg.* 894, *pg.* 1886
Meyer, Tara, VP-Digital Adv Sls-Family Networks - Crown Media Holdings Inc.; *pg.* 280, *pg.* 281
Meyer-Ravelli, Shawna, Sr Dir-Mktg Strategy & Programs - NetApp, Inc.; *pg.* 444, *pg.* 287
Meyerkopf, Rick, VP-Mdsg-Hannaford Supermarkets - Hannaford Brothers Co.; *pg.* 1022, *pg.* 752
Meyers, Daniel, VP-Sls, Comml & Strategic Mgmt - Vertex Pharmaceuticals Incorporated; *pg.* 1606, *pg.* 801
Meyers, Jaclyn, Mgr-Trade Mktg & Team Head-Lysol & Dettol-Europe & North America - Reckitt Benckiser Inc.; *pg.* 1136, *pg.* 1105
Meyers, Jay, Mgr-Interactive Sls - KTVI-TV; *pg.* 295, *pg.* 999
Meyers, John, Exec Dir-Sls Ops & Comml Info Mgmt - Amgen Inc.; *pg.* 1493, *pg.* 291
Meyers, Lauren, Assoc Dir-Mktg Solutions - Conde Nast Publications, Inc.; *pg.* 1629, *pg.* 1217
Meyers, Lisa, Sr Dir-Creative Svcs-North America - Nice-Pak Products, Inc.; *pg.* 1465, *pg.* 1319
Meyers, Paul, Mgr-Social Media - Pabst Brewing Company; *pg.* 258, *pg.* 137
Meyers, Paul, Dir-Sls - Valcor Engineering Corporation; *pg.* 1386, *pg.* 1123
Meyers, Sara, Product Mgr-Cloud & Internet VAS - Cincinnati Bell Inc.; *pg.* 1871, *pg.* 1410
Meyers, Stephanie, Editor-Social Media - Inc.com LLC; *pg.* 1258, *pg.* 1243
Meyers, Zach, Brand Mgr - The Kraft Heinz Company; *pg.* 871, *pg.* 641
Meyerson, Andrew, Dir-Sls - Time Inc.; *pg.* 1693, *pg.* 1300
Meyerson, Gabrielle, Brand Mgr-Oral Care - Colgate-Palmolive Company; *pg.* 504, *pg.* 1215
Meyerson, Randy, Sr Dir-Product & Svc Innovation - T-Mobile US, Inc.; *pg.* 676, *pg.* 1816
Meynier, Dixie G., Project Mgr-Municipal Mktg - Waste Management, Inc.; *pg.* 1954, *pg.* 1716
Meza, Randy, Dir-Mktg - Carhartt, Inc.; *pg.* 39, *pg.* 875
Mezheritsky, Ilya, Product Mgr - Google Inc.; *pg.* 1249, *pg.* 153
Mezle, Erin, Dir-Mktg - Fujitsu General America, Inc.; *pg.* 55, *pg.* 1065
Mezza, Sandra, Mgr-Print & Sign Adv - The Kroger Co.; *pg.* 1025, *pg.* 1416
Mhley, Colleen, Mgr-Mktg-Alliance - BDO Seidman, LLP; *pg.* 724, *pg.* 1202
Micali, Jack, Dir-Oncology Mktg - Merck & Co., Inc.; *pg.* 1566, *pg.* 1077
Micali, Sara, Specialist-Online Mktg - Brooks Brothers Group, Inc.; *pg.* 39, *pg.* 1208
Micciulla, Alissa, Strategist-Social Media - Starwood Hotels & Resorts Worldwide, Inc.; *pg.* 1114, *pg.* 378
Micek, Chad, Mgr-Sls - Chief Industries, Inc.; *pg.* 1323, *pg.* 1010
Michael, Douglas, Sr VP-Mktg - 3M Company; *pg.* 1142, *pg.* 956
Michael, Shana, Sr Mgr-Digital Billing & Renewal - Meredith Corporation; *pg.* 1663, *pg.* 705
Michael, Tod, Product Mgr-Underground - Vermeer Manufacturing Company; *pg.* 708, *pg.* 711
Michaelian, Bob, Sr VP-Consumer Product - BizRate.com; *pg.* 1231, *pg.* 126
Michaelis, Kevin B., VP-Products & Tech - Air Products and Chemicals, Inc.; *pg.* 1145, *pg.* 1513
Michaelis, Ryan, Mgr-East & Central Sls-Tech Vertical-Mktg Solutions - LinkedIn Corporation; *pg.* 1262, *pg.* 160
Michaels, Andrea, Mgr-Major Market Sls - Hyatt Hotels Corporation; *pg.* 1096, *pg.* 577
Michaels, Jennifer, Sr VP-PR - MGM Resorts International; *pg.* 1105, *pg.* 1028
Michaels, Paige, Specialist-Mktg Programs-ITCG Camera & Video Mktg Div - Canon U.S.A., Inc.; *pg.* 1404, *pg.* 1178
Michaels, Richard, Asst VP, Branch Sls Mgr - United Community Financial Corp.; *pg.* 814, *pg.* 1483
Michaels, Robin, Sr Mgr-IT - Johnson & Johnson; *pg.* 1549, *pg.* 1091
Michaels, Vicki, Acct Mgr-Adv - MGM Resorts International; *pg.* 1105, *pg.* 1028
Michaelsen, Kim, Project Mgr-IT & Mktg - HNI Corporation; *pg.* 927, *pg.* 709
Michaelson, Julie, VP-Sls-North America - BabyCenter, LLC; *pg.* 1231, *pg.* 212
Michalak, CJ, Mgr-Mktg - Constellation Energy Resources, LLC; *pg.* 1938, *pg.* 756
Michalak, Rob, Dir-Social Mission-Global - Ben & Jerry's Homemade, Inc.; *pg.* 1850, *pg.* 1767
Michalopoulos, Will, Sr Dir-Retail Sls - Hearst Magazines; *pg.* 1649, *pg.* 1239
Michalovich, Steve, Mgr-Digital Mktg - The Scotts Miracle-Gro Company; *pg.* 1799, *pg.* 1459
Michalsen, Tom, Dir-Mktg - Weber Packaging Solutions, Inc.; *pg.* 491, *pg.* 554
Michaud, Caroline, VP-Corp Comm & PR - Preferred Hotel Group; *pg.* 1108, *pg.* 587
Michaud, France, Sr Mgr-Mdsg-E-Commerce - Keds LLC; *pg.* 1810, *pg.* 828
Michaud, Ginny, Sr Media Buyer - Pearson Education; *pg.* 1675, *pg.* 800
Michaud, Helene, Asst VP-Mktg & Comm Svcs - Sun Life Financial Inc.; *pg.* 806, *pg.* 1944
Michaud, John, VP-Sls & Mktg - Tufco Technologies, Inc.; *pg.* 1697, *pg.* 1860
Michaud, Todd, VP-Global & Gen Mgr-NCR Global Enterprise, Mdsg & SCM Solutions - NCR Corporation; *pg.* 443, *pg.* 531
Michaylira, Mark, Sr Mgr-Pkg & Brand Creative - Mattel Games/Puzzles; *pg.* 962, *pg.* 80
Michaylira, Mark, Sr Mgr-Pkg & Brand Creative - MATTEL, INC.; *pg.* 962, *pg.* 81
Micheau, Traci A., Sr Reg Mgr-Mktg - BUFFALO WILD WINGS, INC.; *pg.* 1718, *pg.* 931
Michel, Andrea, Specialist-Channel Mktg - Schneider Electric USA, Inc.; *pg.* 1306, *pg.* 650
Michel, Dawn, Dir-Mktg - Barona Resort & Casino; *pg.* 1080, *pg.* 121
Michel, Jennifer, Sr Acct Mgr-Mktg - Ingram Micro Inc.; *pg.* 415, *pg.* 261
Michel, Steven, Asst VP-Mktg - Farmers Rice Cooperative; *pg.* 855, *pg.* 196
Michel, Yves R., Dir-Global Sls & Mktg - PureSafe Water Systems, Inc.; *pg.* 333, *pg.* 1322
Michelassi, Roberto, Product Mgr-Consumer Mktg-CV & Met - Bristol-Myers Squibb U.S. Pharmaceutical Group; *pg.* 1511, *pg.* 1110
Michele, Cherie, Mgr-Adv - Paramount Fitness Corp.; *pg.* 1842, *pg.* 138
Michelet, Christelle, Dir-Mktg-L'Oreal Professional - L'Oreal USA; *pg.* 514, *pg.* 1252
Michelet, Philippe, Sr Dir-Product Mgmt & Data Center & Orchestration-Global - Hewlett-Packard Company; *pg.* 404, *pg.* 175
Michell, Steve, Product Mgr - Epson America Inc.; *pg.* 394, *pg.* 122
Michels, Ashley, Sr Mgr-Mktg - GameStop Corp.; *pg.* 399, *pg.* 1699
Michels, Erin, Coord-Mktg-Intl - Home Box Office, Inc.; *pg.* 290, *pg.* 1240
Michels, Jim, Dir-Internet & Mgr-Adv Sls - The Evansville Courier & Press; *pg.* 1639, *pg.* 678
Michels, Shawn, Sr Product Mgr - Akamai Technologies, Inc.; *pg.* 1226, *pg.* 807
Michener, Mark, Sr Dir - Microsoft Corporation; *pg.* 435, *pg.* 1824
Michielini, Michele, Sr Dir-Consumer Insights - NBTY, Inc.; *pg.* 1572, *pg.* 1338
Michl, Heike, Specialist-Conferences & Events-Event Mktg - UBS Financial Services Inc.; *pg.* 812, *pg.* 1306
Michmershuizen, Peggy, Project Mgr-ELA & Global Experience Mktg - Herman Miller, Inc.; *pg.* 926, *pg.* 913
Mick, Jennifer, Mgr-Mktg Channel & Sr Specialist-Strategic Comm - Waddell & Reed Financial, Inc.; *pg.* 818, *pg.* 721
Mickel, Clint, Brand Mgr - Pinnacle Foods Group LLC; *pg.* 889, *pg.* 1104
Mickelberg, Beth, VP-Corp Mktg - JPMorgan Chase & Co.; *pg.* 772, *pg.* 1246
Mickelson, Gary, Sr Dir-PR - Tyson Foods, Inc.; *pg.* 902, *pg.* 35
Mickey, Kristin, Coord-Market Level Mktg & Integrated Media - Chick-fil-A, Inc.; *pg.* 1721, *pg.* 492
Mickle, J. Douglas, Grp Dir-Adv & Mktg Svcs - Reynolds Consumer Products; *pg.* 1138, *pg.* 625
Mickle, Shannon, Program Mgr-Direct Mktg - Wells Fargo & Company; *pg.* 819, *pg.* 232
Micko, Brandon, Dir-Mktg Comm - Burger King Corporation; *pg.* 1719, *pg.* 440
Mickschl, Amy, Brand Mgr-High Performance Coatings - Rust-Oleum Corporation; *pg.* 1447, *pg.* 664
Miclot, Mike D., VP-Mktg - Belden, Inc.; *pg.* 624, *pg.* 993
Micolo, Steve, Dir-Mktg Dev - Subway Restaurants; *pg.* 1751, *pg.* 356
Micucci, Joe, Dir-Media Rels - W.W. Grainger, Inc.; *pg.* 1390, *pg.* 625
Micun, Tim, Product Mgr-TVS Diode Arrays line - Littelfuse, Inc.; *pg.* 1301, *pg.* 580
Middlebrook, George, Mgr-Product Line-Global - IBM; *pg.* 410, *pg.* 1449
Middleton, Jay, Sr Mgr-Worldwide Search Mktg - Adobe Systems Incorporated; *pg.* 342, *pg.* 235
Middleton, Jim, Exec Dir-North American Solutions Mktg - Dell Inc.; *pg.* 383, *pg.* 1737
Middleton, Renee, Dir-Field Mktg - Taco John's International, Inc.; *pg.* 1753, *pg.* 1901
Middleton, Sarah, Exec VP-National Production & Mktg - Fairway Independent Mortgage Corporation; *pg.* 750, *pg.* 1866
Midgley, Stephen, VP-Mktg-Global - Absolute Software Corporation; *pg.* 340, *pg.* 1909
Midha, Pooja, Sr VP-Digital Ad Sls & Ops - ABC, Inc.; *pg.* 268, *pg.* 1185
Midha, Rajesh, Chief Product Officer - ooVoo LLC; *pg.* 1272, *pg.* 1274
Midura, Todd, Dir-Mktg-Tic Tac - Ferrero U.S.A., Inc.; *pg.* 1852, *pg.* 1121
Miebach, Michael, Chief Product Officer - MasterCard Incorporated; *pg.* 779, *pg.* 1325
Miedlar, Matthew, Analyst-SAS-Mktg - CIT GROUP INC.; *pg.* 735, *pg.* 1212
Miele, Laura, Sr VP-Global Mktg EA Games - Electronic Arts Inc.; *pg.* 951, *pg.* 189
Miele, Stanley G., Pres-Sls & Mktg-Sucampo Pharma Americas, Inc & Sr VP - Sucampo Pharmaceuticals, Inc.; *pg.* 1599, *pg.* 765
Mielke, Shawn, Dir-Small Bus Mktg-Global - Google Inc.; *pg.* 1249, *pg.* 153
Mier, Joel, VP-Product & Svcs Mktg - Genworth Financial, Inc.; *pg.* 761, *pg.* 1802
Mier, Rafael, Mgr-IR & Global Mktg - Cytec Industries, Inc.; *pg.* 1155, *pg.* 1131
Miers, Elizabeth, Mgr-Mktg - The Vanguard Group, Inc.; *pg.* 816, *pg.* 1550
Miesner, John, Mng Dir & Head-Global Sls-GTX - GAIN CAPITAL HOLDINGS, INC.; *pg.* 760, *pg.* 1043
Miffleton, Taylor, Sr Mgr - The Coca-Cola Company; *pg.* 240, *pg.* 493
Miget, Heidi, Mgr-Digital Mktg - SUPERVALU, Inc.; *pg.* 1035, *pg.* 924
Migias, George, Dir-Worldwide Mktg-Orencia - Bristol-Myers Squibb Company; *pg.* 1509, *pg.* 1206
Miglionico-Poulsen, Jennifer, Dir-Mktg Argosy Alton - Penn National Gaming, Inc.; *pg.* 574, *pg.* 1595
Migliore, Maria, Mgr-Mktg - In-N-Out Burgers, Inc.; *pg.* 1732, *pg.* 111
Migliorino, Michael, Brand Mgr - Checkers Drive-In Restaurants, Inc.; *pg.* 1017, *pg.* 472
Migliozzi, Kerrie, Asst Mgr-Mktg-CRM - Toys "R" Us, Inc.; *pg.* 968, *pg.* 1130
Mignone, Marissa, Sr Assoc Brand Mgr - Pepperidge Farm, Inc.; *pg.* 888, *pg.* 363
Miguez, Lisa, Sr Mgr-Employee Comm - HSBC Bank USA; *pg.* 767, *pg.* 1241
Mihail, Marie, Sr Program Mgr-Microsoft Mktg Academy - Microsoft Corporation; *pg.* 435, *pg.* 1824
Mihalko, Rob, VP-Mktg & Bus Networks - Ariba, Inc.; *pg.* 353, *pg.* 283
Mihalop, Andy, Head-Network Agencies-Media Platforms UK - Google Inc.; *pg.* 1249, *pg.* 153

First page reference indicates Business Class Edition
Second page reference indicates Geographic Edition

Mihara, Makiko, Sr Mgr - Yanmar America Corporation; *pg.* 196, *pg.* 482
Mihm, Wendy, Dir-Mktg - Truth Initiative; *pg.* 158, *pg.* 405
Mihok, Tim, Sr Dir-Global Shared Svcs - Yahoo! Inc.; *pg.* 1289, *pg.* 289
Miiller, Ron, VP-Sls-Americas - CommVault Systems, Inc.; *pg.* 377, *pg.* 1125
Mijlin, Eileen, VP & Program Mgr-Mktg - Wells Fargo & Company; *pg.* 819, *pg.* 232
Mikalauskas, Andy, VP-Sls & Mktg - ZCL Composites Inc.; *pg.* 1892, *pg.* 1906
Mikalis, Brian, Sr VP-Monetization & Mid-Market Sls - Pandora Media Inc.; *pg.* 1273, *pg.* 172
Mikami, Mindy, Coord-Mktg - Okuma America Corporation; *pg.* 1366, *pg.* 1368
Mikardos, Joan, Sr Dir & Head-Connected Mktg - Sanofi US; *pg.* 1592, *pg.* 1046
Mikesell, Kelly, VP-Mktg - Simon Property Group, Inc.; *pg.* 1112, *pg.* 690
Mikeska, Devon, Brand Mktg Mgr - Landry's, Inc.; *pg.* 1735, *pg.* 1709
Mikita, Trish, VP-Digital Media Strategy - AccuWeather, Inc.; *pg.* 268, *pg.* 1587
Miklos, Karin, Dir-Consumer Strategy & Mktg - Sutter Health; *pg.* 1600, *pg.* 197
Miklusak, Neil, Sr Head-Sls-North America-B2B - LinkedIn Corporation; *pg.* 1262, *pg.* 160
Miklush, Jeffrey, Dir-Design & Production - Bosch Inspection Technology Inc.; *pg.* 1319, *pg.* 1041
Miko, John, Corp Reg VP-Sls - Sysco Corporation; *pg.* 1035, *pg.* 1716
Mikolajczak, Stephen, Brand Mktg Mgr-Team Sports Div - Mizuno USA, Inc.; *pg.* 1839, *pg.* 538
Mikos, Adam, Mgr-Sls-Intl - Associated Research Inc.; *pg.* 1400, *pg.* 622
Mikovch, Cheryl, Sr Mgr-Mktg & Cloud Computing - International Business Machines Corporation; *pg.* 418, *pg.* 1138
Mikowski, Russell, VP-Sls - iCIMS, Inc.; *pg.* 411, *pg.* 1083
Miks, Ron, Grp Mgr-Experiential Mktg - Mazda North American Operations; *pg.* 183, *pg.* 113
Mikschl, Andy, VP-Sls - San Diego Convention & Visitors Bureau; *pg.* 1004, *pg.* 208
Mikulenka, Mike, Dir-Mktg Svcs - Cameron Drilling & Production Systems; *pg.* 1321, *pg.* 1702
Mikulinsky, Regina, Program Mgr-Mktg Insights - Liberty Mutual Insurance Group Inc.; *pg.* 1205, *pg.* 797
Mikutel, Rachel, Assoc Mgr-Sls & Mktg Dev - The Walt Disney Company; *pg.* 317, *pg.* 52
Milam, Greg, Sr Brand Mgr-Mktg - CDW Corporation; *pg.* 370, *pg.* 663
Milan, Norberto, VP-Sls-Caribbean & Latin America - F5 Networks, Inc.; *pg.* 396, *pg.* 1835
Milanes, Lucie, Dir-Mktg Strategy & Comm-North & Latin America - Epson America Inc.; *pg.* 394, *pg.* 122
Milanese, Barry, Dir-Sls & Mktg - Costa Fruit & Produce Inc.; *pg.* 850, *pg.* 793
Milani, Mark, Sr VP-Product Engrg - Actian Corporation; *pg.* 342, *pg.* 188
Milanian, Bita, Sr VP-Mktg Comm - Genband, Inc.; *pg.* 640, *pg.* 1731
Milano, Anthony, Sr Dir-ECommerce - Hugo Boss Fashions Inc.; *pg.* 42, *pg.* 1242
Milano, Donna L., Mgr-Mktg - IBM; *pg.* 410, *pg.* 1449
Milano, Michele, Specialist-Mktg - University of Pennsylvania; *pg.* 609, *pg.* 1571
Milardo, Matthew, Dir-ADM & Bus-Griffin Hospital - Griffin Health Services Corporation; *pg.* 1538, *pg.* 345
Milazzo, Jamie, Mgr-Visual Mktg Plng - Sears Holdings Corporation; *pg.* 1784, *pg.* 618
Milazzo, Jessica, Mgr-Mdsg-Gourmet Food & Gift Baskets - 1-800-Flowers.com, Inc.; *pg.* 1758, *pg.* 1151
Milbank, Michael, Specialist-VW Accessories Product Plng - Volkswagen Group of America, Inc.; *pg.* 194, *pg.* 1785
Milbourn, Lana, Project Mgr & Mgr-Rotational Product - Facebook, Inc.; *pg.* 1245, *pg.* 143
Milbourn, Tess, VP-HR-Cardiac & Vascular Grp Sls - Mallinckrodt Pharmaceuticals; *pg.* 1557, *pg.* 978
Milburn, Reginald, Mgr-Creative & Technical Svcs - Sprint Corporation; *pg.* 1874, *pg.* 719
Milcarek, Heather, Dir-Pro Channel Mktg - Philips Electronics North America; *pg.* 662, *pg.* 782
Milcarek, Heather, Dir-Pro Channel Mktg - Philips Lighting; *pg.* 1303, *pg.* 806
Milder, Andrew, Bus Mgr-Global - 3M Company; *pg.* 1142, *pg.* 956
Mileos, Demetra, Mgr-Acq Mktg Partnerships - American Express Company; *pg.* 712, *pg.* 1190
Miles, Amy, Sr Mgr-Comml Ops & Digital-Global - Libbey, Inc.; *pg.* 1126, *pg.* 1476
Miles, Chris, Sr Dir-Mktg Comm - The Kraft Heinz Company; *pg.* 871, *pg.* 641
Miles, David, Grp VP-Sls & Mktg - Simonds International Corporation; *pg.* 1376, *pg.* 819
Miles, Jennifer, Dir-Mktg Mgmt - AT&T; *pg.* 1865, *pg.* 258
Miles, Jennifer, Dir-Mktg Mgmt-U-verse Video Dev - AT&T Communications Corp.; *pg.* 1866, *pg.* 1043
Miles, Larry K., VP-Product Support-Global - Gencor Industries, Inc.; *pg.* 1339, *pg.* 453
Miles, Marc, Mgr-Digital Sls & Mktg - BB&T Corporation; *pg.* 723, *pg.* 1393
Miles, Ron, Sr Mgr-Events - AT&T; *pg.* 1865, *pg.* 258
Miles, Ron, VP-Aftermarket Sls-White-Rodgers - Emerson White-Rodgers; *pg.* 1071, *pg.* 996
Miletic, Janine, Assoc Dir-Mktg - The Procter & Gamble Company; *pg.* 1129, *pg.* 1418
Miletic, Vedran, Assoc Dir-Mktg-North America Fabric Care Delivery - The Procter & Gamble Company; *pg.* 1129, *pg.* 1418
Milette, Danielle, Brand Mgr-Scotch & Rum Portfolio - Beam Suntory Inc.; *pg.* 1957, *pg.* 599
Milette, Steve, Head-Sls - Hyundai Auto Canada; *pg.* 179, *pg.* 1923
Milewski, Matthew, Brand Mgr-Olive Garden - Darden Restaurants, Inc.; *pg.* 1724, *pg.* 453
Milewski, Matthew, Brand Mgr-Olive Garden - Olive Garden Italian Restaurant; *pg.* 1742, *pg.* 454
Miley, Allison, Exec VP & Head-Wealth, Brokerage & Retirement Mktg Comm - Wells Fargo Advisors, LLC; *pg.* 819, *pg.* 1005
Miley, Greg, VP-Media Rels - Sanofi US; *pg.* 1592, *pg.* 1046
Milford, Susan, Sr VP-Strategic Mktg, Plng & Foundation - Centegra Northern Illinois Medical Center; *pg.* 1196, *pg.* 632
Milhoan, Cathy, Dir-Production - DoD News; *pg.* 1239, *pg.* 769
Milici, Kevin T., Head-Mktg-Global - General Electric Company; *pg.* 1297, *pg.* 347
Milke, Karen, Dir-Creative Agency Buying - Mars, Incorporated; *pg.* 1858, *pg.* 1792
Millage, Ken, Mgr-Mktg - Knouse Foods Cooperative Inc.; *pg.* 869, *pg.* 1558
Millar, Aoife, Brand Mgr-Global - Revlon Consumer Products Corporation; *pg.* 521, *pg.* 1286
Millar, Aoife, Brand Mgr-Global - Revlon, Inc.; *pg.* 521, *pg.* 1286
Millar, Timothy, Dir-Sls - Werner Holding Co.; *pg.* 121, *pg.* 1534
Millard, Patrick, Dir-Mktg Comm - Fiserv, Inc.; *pg.* 758, *pg.* 537
Millen, Matt, VP-Bus Sls - T-Mobile US, Inc.; *pg.* 676, *pg.* 1816
Miller, Alan, Mgr-Global Mktg-Safety Devices - Smiths Medical MD, Inc.; *pg.* 1594, *pg.* 963
Miller, Alanna, Assoc Mgr-Mktg - Mattel Games/Puzzles; *pg.* 962, *pg.* 80
Miller, Alex, Mgr-Product Mktg-WiFi Products - ANADIGICS, Inc.; *pg.* 617, *pg.* 1128
Miller, Alison, Sr Dir-Mktg - Chicago National League Ball Club, LLC; *pg.* 539, *pg.* 569
Miller, Alison, Sr Mgr-Adv - Tempur Sealy International, Inc.; *pg.* 944, *pg.* 731
Miller, Allison, Product Mgr - Google Inc.; *pg.* 1249, *pg.* 153
Miller, Allison, Coord-Local Mktg - Meineke Car Care Centers, Inc.; *pg.* 212, *pg.* 1367
Miller, Amanda, VP-Mktg - The Trump Organization, LLC; *pg.* 1117, *pg.* 1305
Miller, Amy T., Dir-Software Product Mgmt - Dell Inc.; *pg.* 383, *pg.* 1737
Miller, Andrea, Program Mgr-Mktg-Treasury Mgmt - Wells Fargo & Company; *pg.* 819, *pg.* 232
Miller, Andrew, VP-Corp Mktg & Comm - Aon Risk Services Inc.; *pg.* 1193, *pg.* 564
Miller, Andrew, Product Mgr-Mobile App - United Airlines, Inc.; *pg.* 1927, *pg.* 593
Miller, Andrew, Product Mgr-Mobile App - United Continental Holdings, Inc.; *pg.* 1927, *pg.* 593
Miller, Andrew J., Mgr-Adv - FedEx Corporation; *pg.* 1907, *pg.* 1642
Miller, Andy, Mgr-Medical Products - 3D Systems Corporation; *pg.* 339, *pg.* 1621
Miller, Anita, Product Mgr - The Progressive Corporation; *pg.* 1214, *pg.* 1463
Miller, Anita L., Dir-Mktg - Education Management Corporation; *pg.* 601, *pg.* 1575
Miller, Ashley, Specialist-Mktg Comm - Baldor Electric Company; *pg.* 1316, *pg.* 32
Miller, Barbara, Sr Mgr-Customer Mktg-SAS - Canadian Imperial Bank of Commerce; *pg.* 729, *pg.* 1935
Miller, Barbara Ross, Head-Sony Direct Sls - Sony Electronics, Inc.; *pg.* 676, *pg.* 209
Miller, Ben, VP-Product Dev - Sinclair Broadcast Group, Inc.; *pg.* 308, *pg.* 773
Miller, Bill, Sr VP-Creative Mktg - The Talbots, Inc.; *pg.* 34, *pg.* 824
Miller, Brad, Mgr-Mktg Comm - American Heart Association Inc.; *pg.* 128, *pg.* 1673
Miller, Brandon, Brand Mgr - The Upper Deck Company, LLC; *pg.* 969, *pg.* 62
Miller, Brent, VP-Aftermarket Sls-North America - JLG Industries, Inc.; *pg.* 1351, *pg.* 1551
Miller, Brian, Sr Acct Exec-Natl Sls - Cars.com; *pg.* 1234, *pg.* 568
Miller, Brian, Reg VP-Sls - Sprint Corporation; *pg.* 1874, *pg.* 719
Miller, Brian, Sr Mgr-Sls Comm & Policies - United Airlines, Inc.; *pg.* 1927, *pg.* 593
Miller, Bridgette, Dir-Mktg - The Sun Products Corporation; *pg.* 336, *pg.* 385
Miller, Bryan G., VP & Mng Dir-Sls - LexisNexis Litigation Solutions; *pg.* 1659, *pg.* 1446
Miller, Cameron, Reg Mgr-Mktg - AMERICAN TIRE DISTRIBUTORS HOLDINGS, INC.; *pg.* 199, *pg.* 1379
Miller, Cara, Sr Dir-Pub Affairs - Gilead Sciences, Inc.; *pg.* 1535, *pg.* 88
Miller, Carly, Assoc Product Mgr - Intuit Inc.; *pg.* 769, *pg.* 158
Miller, Carrie, Mgr-Mktg Commodity - Intel Corporation; *pg.* 645, *pg.* 266
Miller, Charles, Dir-Digital Care & Social Media-Mobile Support Strategy - DIRECTV Group Holdings, LLC; *pg.* 281, *pg.* 79
Miller, Chip, VP-Poultry Sls - Simmons Foods Inc.; *pg.* 895, *pg.* 35
Miller, Chris, Dir-Product Mktg - Bose Corporation; *pg.* 626, *pg.* 820
Miller, Chris, VP-Strategy & Mktg - THE FRESH MARKET, INC.; *pg.* 1020, *pg.* 1374
Miller, Chris, District Mgr-Sls - Sysco Corporation; *pg.* 1035, *pg.* 1716
Miller, Chris, VP-Sls - The Terlato Wine Group; *pg.* 1971, *pg.* 555
Miller, Christie, Asst Mgr-Product Dev - Sephora USA Inc; *pg.* 522, *pg.* 227
Miller, Christine, Sr Coord-Mktg - Bausch & Lomb Incorporated; *pg.* 1401, *pg.* 1045
Miller, Chuck, Dir-Agriculture Sls - Nasco International, Inc.; *pg.* 1779, *pg.* 1858
Miller, Claire, VP-Mktg-Honeywell First Responders - Honeywell International Inc.; *pg.* 407, *pg.* 1088
Miller, Claire, Coord-Mktg & Brdcst - Los Angeles Dodgers Inc.; *pg.* 559, *pg.* 135
Miller, Claire, Product Dir-Vaccines - Pfizer Inc.; *pg.* 1581, *pg.* 1278
Miller, Cliff, VP-Creative Svcs - Eat'n Park Hospitality Group; *pg.* 1728, *pg.* 1539
Miller, Daniel M., Exec VP-Mktg-Mutual Funds - GAMCO Investors, Inc.; *pg.* 761, *pg.* 1339
Miller, Danny, Sr Mgr-PR & Comm - Esurance, Inc.; *pg.* 1243, *pg.* 217
Miller, Daryl, Dir-Mktg - Rich Products Corporation; *pg.* 892, *pg.* 1150
Miller, Dave, VP-Mktg & Product - The Gates Corporation; *pg.* 205, *pg.* 319
Miller, Dave, Sr Dir-Market Plng & Res - Walgreen Co.; *pg.* 1608, *pg.* 605
Miller, David, Sr Dir-Corp Comm - CSR; *pg.* 280, *pg.* 284
Miller, David, Dir-Mktg & Sls - Four Seasons Hotels Limited; *pg.* 1092, *pg.* 1938
Miller, David, VP-Adv Sls - Fox Sports Net; *pg.* 288, *pg.* 131
Miller, Dawn Adams, Program Mgr-Oracle Sls Academy - Oracle Corporation; *pg.* 1272, *pg.* 786
Miller, Dayna, Dir-Sls-Travel Trade - The Greater Vancouver Convention & Visitor Bureau; *pg.* 994, *pg.* 1910
Miller, Deanna W., Mgr-Mktg - The Home Depot, Inc.; *pg.* 1050, *pg.* 510
Miller, Deb, VP-Global Mktg & Comm - Brightstar Corporation;

pg. 627, *pg.* 440

Miller, Debbie, Exec VP-Domestic Theatrical Mktg - 20th Century Fox Film Corp.; *pg.* 267, *pg.* 124

Miller, Donald, Gen Mgr-Sls - Starrett; *pg.* 1064, *pg.* 1621

Miller, Donna, Sr Mgr-Digital Mktg - Partners HealthCare System, Inc.; *pg.* 1580, *pg.* 800

Miller, Doug, Dir-Mktg - Crescent Cardboard Company, L.L.C.; *pg.* 1456, *pg.* 670

Miller, Eli, Product Mgr - Roger Cleveland Golf Company, Inc.; *pg.* 1844, *pg.* 105

Miller, Eric, Sr VP-Sls - Applegate; *pg.* 837, *pg.* 1045

Miller, Evan, Sr Strategist-PR & Social Media - Target Corporation; *pg.* 1786, *pg.* 942

Miller, Gavin, VP & Gen Mgr-Sls & Mktg Solutions - Avnet Technology Solutions; *pg.* 359, *pg.* 25

Miller, Greg, Mgr-Western Reg Sls-Bulk Markets - Charter Communications, Inc.; *pg.* 274, *pg.* 372

Miller, Gretchen, Mgr-Media Rels - Johnson Controls, Inc.; *pg.* 209, *pg.* 1876

Miller, Heather, Sr Dir-Digital Mktg - MATTEL, INC.; *pg.* 962, *pg.* 81

Miller, Heather, Exec VP-Mktg Comm - UMB Financial Corporation; *pg.* 812, *pg.* 987

Miller, Jacqueline, Dir-Digital & New Media - Honeywell International Inc.; *pg.* 407, *pg.* 1088

Miller, James, Dir-Loyalty Mktg - Ann Inc.; *pg.* 18, *pg.* 1195

Miller, Jane, Supvr-Media - MAACO Franchising, Inc.; *pg.* 211, *pg.* 1367

Miller, Jane, Sr Dir-Strategic Mktg - The Pampered Chef; *pg.* 1129, *pg.* 552

Miller, Jason, Mgr-Mktg-Credit, Loyalty & Gift Cards - Eddie Bauer, Inc.; *pg.* 40, *pg.* 1814

Miller, Jason, Exec VP-Ad Sls & Integrated Mktg - FUSE Networks LLC; *pg.* 288, *pg.* 1233

Miller, Jason, Sr Mgr-Content Mktg & Mktg Solutions - LinkedIn Corporation; *pg.* 1262, *pg.* 160

Miller, Jeff, VP-Sls - DePuy Synthes; *pg.* 1523, *pg.* 1593

Miller, Jeff, VP-Product Innovation - Dunkin' Brands Group, Inc.; *pg.* 1727, *pg.* 810

Miller, Jeff, VP-Product Dev - Nintendo of America, Inc.; *pg.* 965, *pg.* 1829

Miller, Jeff, Dir-Mktg Programs-Americas - Siemens PLM Software; *pg.* 469, *pg.* 1734

Miller, Jeffrey A., Sr VP-Global Sls - PCTEL, Inc.; *pg.* 452, *pg.* 557

Miller, Jen, Area Mgr-Sls - The Coca-Cola Company; *pg.* 240, *pg.* 493

Miller, Jenna, Analyst-Sls Comm-Sls Ops & Grp Segment - Humana, Inc.; *pg.* 1204, *pg.* 734

Miller, Jennifer, Mgr-Solutions Sls - Avnet, Inc.; *pg.* 622, *pg.* 15

Miller, Jennifer E., Dir-Mktg - The Clorox Company; *pg.* 327, *pg.* 169

Miller, Jess, Sr Dir-Retention Ops - DIRECTV Group Holdings, LLC; *pg.* 281, *pg.* 79

Miller, Jim, Sr VP-Production & Dev - Lions Gate Entertainment Corp.; *pg.* 296, *pg.* 274

Miller, Joanna, Sr Dir-Art - Capital One Financial Corporation; *pg.* 730, *pg.* 1789

Miller, John, Exec VP-Sls & Mktg - Americo Manufacturing Co., Inc.; *pg.* 325, *pg.* 482

Miller, John, Dir-Brand Insight-Global Mktg - AstraZeneca Pharmaceuticals LP; *pg.* 1497, *pg.* 389

Miller, Jonathan, VP-Sls & Mktg - Chicago White Metal Casting, Inc.; *pg.* 1153, *pg.* 556

Miller, Julia, Dir-Content & Engagement Mktg - Benjamin Moore & Co.; *pg.* 1440, *pg.* 1085

Miller, Julia, Sr Mgr-Branding & Content - M.D.C. Holdings, Inc.; *pg.* 1104, *pg.* 321

Miller, Justin, Mgr-Direct Sls - Charter Communications, Inc.; *pg.* 274, *pg.* 372

Miller, Justin, Dir-Mktg-Mixable Spirits - William Grant & Sons, Inc.; *pg.* 1972, *pg.* 1057

Miller, Karina, Coord-Mktg - Pfizer Inc.; *pg.* 1581, *pg.* 1278

Miller, Kate, Dir-Mktg & Bus Dev - Simon Property Group, Inc.; *pg.* 1112, *pg.* 690

Miller, Kathy, Project Mgr-Mktg-Global - Energizer Holdings, Inc.; *pg.* 637, *pg.* 996

Miller, Katie, Sr Product Mgr - MoneyGram International, Inc.; *pg.* 783, *pg.* 1684

Miller, Katie Baillie, Grp Dir-Sports Mktg - The Coca-Cola Company; *pg.* 240, *pg.* 493

Miller, Kellee, Sr Mgr-Shopper Mktg - DOLE FOOD COMPANY, INC.; *pg.* 853, *pg.* 306

Miller, Kristin, Sr Assoc Brand Mgr-Goldfish - Pepperidge Farm, Inc.; *pg.* 888, *pg.* 363

Miller, Kristy, Portfolio Mgr-College Sports Mktg & Affinity Partnerships - GEICO Corporation; *pg.* 1200, *pg.* 399

Miller, Laura, Mgr-Digital Mktg - Cullen/Frost Bankers, Inc.; *pg.* 742, *pg.* 1740

Miller, Lauren, Coord-Production-Dr. Scholl's Shoes - Caleres, Inc.; *pg.* 1805, *pg.* 993

Miller, Lauren, Coord-PR-Intl - QUALCOMM Incorporated; *pg.* 1873, *pg.* 207

Miller, Leslie, Brand Mgr - Unilever United States, Inc.; *pg.* 904, *pg.* 1061

Miller, Leslie S., Reg Mgr-Mktg - Atmos Energy Corporation; *pg.* 1935, *pg.* 1675

Miller, Lisa, Dir-Adv - The Sun; *pg.* 1690, *pg.* 28

Miller, Lorin, Dir-FIELDVUE Mktg - Emerson Process Management; *pg.* 1334, *pg.* 1636

Miller, Luke, Sr Editor-Xcelerated Mktg - Meredith Corporation; *pg.* 1663, *pg.* 705

Miller, Mandy, Coord-Mktg - Diamond Jo, LLC; *pg.* 1089, *pg.* 707

Miller, Marc, Sr Mgr-Deployment & Itinerary Plng - Royal Caribbean Cruises Ltd; *pg.* 1921, *pg.* 446

Miller, Maria, Sr VP-Mktg - NCL Corporation Ltd.; *pg.* 1916, *pg.* 444

Miller, Maria, Sr VP-Mktg - Norwegian Cruise Line; *pg.* 1917, *pg.* 444

Miller, Mark, VP-Sls & Gen Mgr-Analogic Ultrasound - Analogic Corporation; *pg.* 1399, *pg.* 840

Miller, Mark, VP-Corp & Mktg Comm-Corp Svcs-Jacksonville - Crowley Maritime Corporation; *pg.* 1904, *pg.* 170

Miller, Mark, Dir-Mktg-Salty Snack Portfolio - Kellogg Company; *pg.* 831, *pg.* 870

Miller, Mark, Exec Dir-Mktg Svcs - Olympus America Inc.; *pg.* 1425, *pg.* 1521

Miller, Matt, Chief Strategy Officer & VP - Interface, Inc.; *pg.* 695, *pg.* 512

Miller, Matthew, VP-Adv Sls & Mktg - 4Licensing Corporation; *pg.* 948, *pg.* 1185

Miller, Max, Sr Mgr-Alliance - Concur Technologies; *pg.* 1903, *pg.* 501

Miller, Meg, Dir-PR - Produce Marketing Association; *pg.* 154, *pg.* 388

Miller, Melinda, Analyst-Mktg - State Farm Mutual Automobile Insurance Co.; *pg.* 1218, *pg.* 557

Miller, Michael, Product Mgr-DBS - CenturyLink, Inc; *pg.* 1870, *pg.* 317

Miller, Michael, Sr VP-Sls & Mktg - PVH Corp.; *pg.* 46, *pg.* 1283

Miller, Mike, Sr VP-Mktg & Res-Global - National Cattlemen's Beef Association; *pg.* 148, *pg.* 314

Miller, Mike, Dir-Strategy, Sls Ops & New Market Dev Unit - Time Warner Cable Inc.; *pg.* 312, *pg.* 1301

Miller, Mira, Specialist-Mktg - California Lottery; *pg.* 990, *pg.* 196

Miller, Morgan, Reg Mgr-Sls-Specialty Accts - Toms Shoe's Inc; *pg.* 1821, *pg.* 276

Miller, Nate, VP-Ecommerce Mktg & Web Design - Northern Tool + Equipment; *pg.* 1366, *pg.* 919

Miller, Nicole, Product Mgr - Air Techniques, Inc.; *pg.* 1487, *pg.* 1178

Miller, Nicole, Mgr-Adv - Padres L.P.; *pg.* 573, *pg.* 206

Miller, Pam, Mgr-Mktg - H&R Block, Inc.; *pg.* 764, *pg.* 983

Miller, Paul C., Analyst-Mktg-Steel - Canadian National Railway Company; *pg.* 1902, *pg.* 1953

Miller, Paula, Dir-Creative Content & Lowe's Creative Ideas - Lowe's Companies, Inc.; *pg.* 1053, *pg.* 1383

Miller, Paulette, Dir-Mktg - Western Piedmont Symphony; *pg.* 592, *pg.* 1379

Miller, Peg, Mgr-Corp Sls - Lee Enterprises, Incorporated; *pg.* 1658, *pg.* 704

Miller, Rebecca, Dir-Brand Mktg - Pizza Hut, Inc.; *pg.* 1744, *pg.* 1733

Miller, Renee, Specialist-Experiential Mktg - American Honda Motor Co., Inc.; *pg.* 163, *pg.* 292

Miller, Renee, Asst VP-Mktg Comm - Flagstar Bancorp, Inc.; *pg.* 758, *pg.* 910

Miller, Rich, Mgr-Mktg Ops - Diamond Jo, LLC; *pg.* 1089, *pg.* 707

Miller, Rich, Dir-Product Plng - Nissan North America, Inc.; *pg.* 186, *pg.* 1633

Miller, Richard, Dir-Product Mgmt - Epson America Inc.; *pg.* 394, *pg.* 122

Miller, Robyn, Sr VP-Mktg - The Tennis Channel, Inc.; *pg.* 679, *pg.* 276

Miller, Rodney, Dir-Mktg - Boyd Gaming Corporation; *pg.* 1082, *pg.* 1022

Miller, Rodney, Sr Dir-Ops & HR - Professional Education Institute; *pg.* 457, *pg.* 561

Miller, Ross, Dir-Mktg - Pittsburgh Penguins LLC; *pg.* 577, *pg.* 1578

Miller, Sarah, Assoc Mgr-Shopper Mktg - PepsiCo, Inc.; *pg.* 259, *pg.* 1327

Miller, Scott, Interim Exec VP-Fresh Formats - Ahold USA, Inc.; *pg.* 1013, *pg.* 1520

Miller, Seth, Coord-Mktg - Major League Baseball; *pg.* 560, *pg.* 1255

Miller, Silvana, VP-Global B2B Product Mktg - MasterCard Incorporated; *pg.* 779, *pg.* 1325

Miller, Stacy, Mgr-Mktg - Eli Lilly and Company; *pg.* 1527, *pg.* 684

Miller, Stefan L., Sr Assoc Mgr-Mktg-Larabar Innovation - General Mills, Inc.; *pg.* 828, *pg.* 933

Miller, Stefanie, Grp VP-Strategic Partnership Mktg - The Coca-Cola Company; *pg.* 240, *pg.* 493

Millor, Stuart, VP-Mktg & Bus Dev - Emerson Process Management; *pg.* 1334, *pg.* 1636

Miller, Susan, Brand Mgr - Alliance Laundry Holdings LLC; *pg.* 51, *pg.* 1890

Miller, Susan, Dir-Adv - Stein Mart, Inc.; *pg.* 1786, *pg.* 435

Miller, Suzanne, VP-Field Mktg & Media - Popeye's Chicken & Biscuits; *pg.* 1745, *pg.* 517

Miller, Suzanne, VP-Field Mktg & Media - Popeyes Louisiana Kitchen, Inc.; *pg.* 1745, *pg.* 517

Miller, Tameika, Mgr-Mktg-Pepperidge Farm Portfolio - Pepperidge Farm, Inc.; *pg.* 888, *pg.* 363

Miller, Tami, Dir-Mktg - Heritage Sportswear, LLC; *pg.* 26, *pg.* 1455

Miller, Terry, Sr Mgr-Mktg Programs - Citrix Systems, Inc.; *pg.* 375, *pg.* 424

Miller, Terry, VP-Mktg & Comm - Great Clips, Inc.; *pg.* 510, *pg.* 937

Miller, Thomas, VP-Brand Mktg-USA Today & Gannett - Gannett Co., Inc.; *pg.* 1643, *pg.* 1790

Miller, Tom, Sr Mgr-Key Acct Mktg - Columbia Sportswear Company; *pg.* 1830, *pg.* 1501

Miller, Tom, Dir-Mktg-Optics Grp - Newport Corporation; *pg.* 1424, *pg.* 114

Miller, Tomm, VP-Mktg - Barneys New York, Inc.; *pg.* 38, *pg.* 1201

Miller, Tracy, Product Mgr-New Products Dev - Gold'n Plump Poultry, Inc.; *pg.* 858, *pg.* 956

Miller, Wendy C., Dir-Mobility Sls & West Reg-AT&T Signature Client Grp - AT&T; *pg.* 1865, *pg.* 258

Miller, William B., Pres-Print Media - Flint Group, Inc.; *pg.* 1163, *pg.* 904

Milleson, Julie, Sr Dir-Brand Mktg - National Geographic Society; *pg.* 1667, *pg.* 402

Millet, Jen, Dir-Customer Acq & Brand Mktg - StubHub, Inc.; *pg.* 586, *pg.* 228

Millet, Tim, Sr Dir-Platform Architecture - Apple Inc.; *pg.* 350, *pg.* 73

Millette, Andrea, Area Rep-Mktg - Performance Food Group Company, LLC; *pg.* 1030, *pg.* 1803

Millette, Matt, Sr Dir-Mktg & Brand Mgmt - Simms Fishing Products Corp.; *pg.* 1845, *pg.* 1008

Milligan, Joshua, Sr Dir-Customer Mgmt - Ubisoft Inc.; *pg.* 589, *pg.* 229

Milligan, Kelly, Assist Dir-Creative Svcs - Bentley University; *pg.* 598, *pg.* 850

Milligan, Kimberly, Mgr-California Mktg - Verizon Communications Inc.; *pg.* 1875, *pg.* 1309

Milligan, Louisa, VP-Mktg - Marshalls of MA, Inc.; *pg.* 1778, *pg.* 821

Milligan, Lynette, Sr Mgr-Channel Mktg-SMB - Concur Technologies, Inc.; *pg.* 1236, *pg.* 1813

Milligan, Peter, Sr Mgr-Mktg-Customer Collaboration Solutions - Cisco Systems, Inc.; *pg.* 372, *pg.* 240

Millikan, Phyllis M., VP-Americas Engrg Solutions Sls - IHS Inc.; *pg.* 1652, *pg.* 326

Milliken, Danielle, Brand Mgr-Innovation - Kellogg Company; *pg.* 831, *pg.* 870

Milliken, Mark, VP-Sls - The Commercial Furniture Group; *pg.* 920, *pg.* 994

Millikin, Stephen, Sr Dir-PR-Global - Steinway & Sons; *pg.* 586, *pg.* 1176

Millis, John, Product Mgr-Class A Gas - Winnebago Industries, Inc.; *pg.* 1712, *pg.* 707

Millman, Anna, Mgr-Social Media-Content & Community - Ariba, Inc.; *pg.* 353, *pg.* 283

Millman, Dan, Sr Mgr-Premium Partnerships - New York Jets

First page reference indicates Business Class Edition
Second page reference indicates Geographic Edition

Football Club, Inc.; pg. 570, pg. 1067
Millman, Melissa, Sr Project Mgr-Retention Mktg - DIRECTV Group Holdings, LLC; pg. 281, pg. 79
Mills, Angela, Mgr-Sls-Meeting Connections - Hyatt Hotels Corporation; pg. 1096, pg. 577
Mills, Clay, Sr Dir-Mktg Comm-EMEIA - Apple Inc.; pg. 350, pg. 73
Mills, Gilma, Mgr-Mktg-Store Design - Verizon Communications Inc.; pg. 1875, pg. 1309
Mills, Greg, VP-Intl Sls Svc & Corp Ops - Cincom Systems, Inc.; pg. 372, pg. 1411
Mills, Greg, Dir-Mktg Strategy - Intel Corporation; pg. 645, pg. 266
Mills, Helena, Sr Dir-Global Brand Creative - Mattel Games/Puzzles; pg. 962, pg. 80
Mills, Helena, Sr Dir-Creative-Global Mktg Comm - MATTEL, INC.; pg. 962, pg. 81
Mills, Jeffrey, Dir-Product Mktg - Sage Software, Inc.; pg. 464, pg. 116
Mills, Jessica, Mgr-Comml Sls Implementation & Life-Cycle - Advance Auto Parts, Inc.; pg. 197, pg. 1805
Mills, Justin, Dir-Adv & PR - Flexsteel Industries, Inc.; pg. 925, pg. 707
Mills, Kim, Assoc-Sls - Semonin Realtors; pg. 1112, pg. 738
Mills, Kurt, VP-Channel Sls & Ops-Worldwide - Blue Coat Systems, Inc.; pg. 362, pg. 284
Mills, Lee A., Sr Dir-Shows & Events Strategy - Wal-Mart Stores, Inc.; pg. 1790, pg. 29
Mills, Nelson, VP & Div Mgr-Mdse - VITAMIN SHOPPE, INC.; pg. 1608, pg. 1098
Mills, Regina, Sr Mgr-Mktg - Wal-Mart Stores, Inc.; pg. 1790, pg. 29
Mills, Steve, Sr Dir - Aetna Inc.; pg. 1187, pg. 351
Mills, Steve, Mgr-Local Sls - KTVI-TV; pg. 295, pg. 999
Mills, Tim, Product Mgr-Kaydon Filtration - Kaydon Corporation; pg. 1352, pg. 866
Milne, Lisa, Head-Mktg Platform-Emerging Markets - Pfizer Inc.; pg. 1581, pg. 1278
Milne, Rob, Dir-Mktg Ops - Mazda North American Operations; pg. 183, pg. 113
Milne, Stacey, VP-Portfolio Mktg Strategy & Plng - Marriott International, Inc.; pg. 1102, pg. 764
Milner, David, Product Mgr - Megger Inc.; pg. 1422, pg. 1557
Milner, Diane, Mgr-Mktg - Noah Technologies Corporation; pg. 1175, pg. 1742
Milner, Gary, Dir-Digital Mktg-Global - Lenovo Group Ltd; pg. 427, pg. 1384
Milner, Sarah, Dir-Mktg & Studio-Jacksonville Div - KB Home; pg. 90, pg. 134
Milo, Udi, Product Head-Discover & Distribute Platforms - LinkedIn Corporation; pg. 1262, pg. 160
Milo-Slagle, Gia, Product Dir - McKesson Corporation; pg. 1560, pg. 222
Milone, Christina, Event Mktg - General Mills Canada Corp.; pg. 828, pg. 1926
Milot, Katie, Dir-Sls, Strategy & Dev - The Atlantic Monthly Group; pg. 1618, pg. 396
Milrad, Danny, Dir-Product Mktg-Archiving & Info Mgmt - Barracuda Networks, Inc.; pg. 360, pg. 58
Milstein, Lauren, Dir-Global Online Mktg - Michael Kors (USA), Inc.; pg. 29, pg. 1260
Milsten, Melissa, Dir-Mktg & Partnerships - Penguin Random House; pg. 1675, pg. 1276
Miltenis, John, VP-Mktg-Intl - United Parcel Service, Inc.; pg. 1928, pg. 522
Milton, Allison, Specialist-PR - Tableau Software, Inc.; pg. 481, pg. 1841
Milton, Greg, Dir-Sls & Mktg Strategy - The Dannon Company, Inc.; pg. 851, pg. 1351
Milton, Jessica, Dir-PR-Florida - Benchmark Hospitality International Inc.; pg. 1081, pg. 1747
Milton, Yeara, Mgr-E-Media Comm - Lehman College; pg. 604, pg. 1144
Miltz, Melanie, Dir-Mktg - KSTP-FM, LLC; pg. 295, pg. 962
Milum, Julie, Sr Mgr-Consumer Insights & Strategy - Whirlpool Corporation; pg. 62, pg. 872
Milus, Jeanne, Dir-Sls - Anthem, Inc.; pg. 1192, pg. 683
Milway, Colleen, Dir-Media - JPMorgan Chase & Co.; pg. 772, pg. 1246
Mimran, Joe, Dir-Creative-Joe Fresh Brand & Pres-Joseph Mimran & Associates - Loblaw Companies Limited; pg. 1026, pg. 1918
Mims, Cyle, Coord-Media & External Comm - Total System Services, Inc.; pg. 484, pg. 528
Mims, Monique, Brand Mgr-Brand Dev-Global - Harman International Industries, Incorporated; pg. 641, pg. 374
Mimun, Joy, Head-Product Mgmt-Reuters Consumer Media-Global - Thomson Reuters - Corporate Headquarters; pg. 1693, pg. 1299
Mina, George, Mgr-Mktg - IBM; pg. 410, pg. 1449
Mina, Gregor, Dir-Brand Mktg-Bushmills Irish Whiskey - Proximo Spirits, Inc.; pg. 1969, pg. 1076
Minafri, Jennifer, Dir-Mktg-Client Comm & Customer Experience - Automatic Data Processing, Inc.; pg. 357, pg. 1117
Minaldi, Troy, Dir-Adv - Rent-A-Center, Inc.; pg. 940, pg. 1734
Minamyer, Mark, VP-Product Dev & Quality Assurance - Dunn-Edwards Corporation; pg. 1442, pg. 129
Minardi, Sam, Assoc Dir-Mktg Innovation - Kellogg Company; pg. 831, pg. 870
Minari, Keita, Brand Mgr-Europe - Beam Suntory Inc.; pg. 1957, pg. 599
Minas, Nick, Product Mgr - John Deere Consumer & Commercial Equipment, Inc.; pg. 705, pg. 1360
Minas, Norma, Mgr-Online Mktg - California Lottery; pg. 990, pg. 196
Minassian, Patti, Sr Mgr-Comm Strategist - Southern California Edison Company; pg. 1952, pg. 194
Mincks, Jay E., Exec VP-Sls & Mktg - Insperity, Inc.; pg. 416, pg. 1725
Mindeck, Krystal, Product Mgr-Mktg - The Sherwin-Williams Company; pg. 1447, pg. 1435
Mindeck, Krystal, Assoc Mgr-Mktg - Sherwin Williams; pg. 1448, pg. 1436
Mindel, Michael, Sr VP-Mktg - Il Fornaio (America) Corporation; pg. 1731, pg. 70
Mindrup, Shawn, Acct Exec-Sls & Mktg - The Kansas City Southern Railway Company; pg. 1913, pg. 985
Minea, Andrew, Brand Mgr - Treasury Wine Estates; pg. 1971, pg. 164
Minear, Jason, VP-Mdsg - FitLife Brands; pg. 1531, pg. 1015
Mineo, Nancy E., Dir-Mktg - AT&T; pg. 1865, pg. 258
Miner, Jennifer, Mgr-Digital Mktg - The Pampered Chef; pg. 1129, pg. 552
Miner, Kathleen, VP-Product Mktg - Thomson Reuters - Corporate Headquarters; pg. 1693, pg. 1299
Ming, Elizabeth, Sr Mgr-Comm & Brand PR-Home Care - The Procter & Gamble Company; pg. 1129, pg. 1418
Minger, Mandy, VP-Mktg - Daily Racing Form, LLC; pg. 1632, pg. 1221
Mingos, Adam, Reg Dir-Adv - GateHouse Media, Inc.; pg. 1644, pg. 1159
Minh, Drew, Mgr-Digital Mktg - NBC Universal, Inc.; pg. 300, pg. 1266
Minich, Dee, Sr VP-Sls & Mktg - Hovnanian Enterprises, Inc.; pg. 1096, pg. 1114
Minick, Russell S., Exec VP-Residential Products - GENERAC HOLDINGS INC.; pg. 1340, pg. 1897
Minick, Russell S., Exec VP-Residential Products - Generac Power Systems Inc.; pg. 1340, pg. 1898
Minifee, Marcus, Sr Mgr-Consumer Promos-Channel Mktg Strategy - Samsung Electronics America, Inc.; pg. 669, pg. 1115
Mininger, Lucas, Dir-Mktg-Topical Pain Care - Chattem, Inc.; pg. 1515, pg. 1628
Minister, Katie, Mgr-Digital Mktg - Cardinal Health, Inc.; pg. 1512, pg. 1448
Miniutti, Sandra, VP-Mktg - Charity Navigator; pg. 136, pg. 1071
Mink, Geoff, Mgr-Mktg Comm - AT&T Mobility LLC; pg. 620, pg. 1152
Minkel, Maureen, Dir-Consumer Mktg-Natl - Aramark; pg. 1013, pg. 1558
Minner, Jamie, VP-Sls - Momentum Telecom, Inc.; pg. 1872, pg. 3
Minnich, Brandt, VP-Mktg - Mercury Insurance Company; pg. 1208, pg. 136
Minnick, Amy, Sr VP-IHS Tech, Media & Telecom - IHS Inc.; pg. 1652, pg. 326
Minnick, Jill M., Sr VP-Mktg - ITT Educational Services, Inc.; pg. 603, pg. 675
Mino, Terri M., Mgr-PR - Neiman Marcus, Inc.; pg. 30, pg. 1684
Minogue, John, Sr Mgr-Central Reg Sls-Fire Protection Products - Ansul, Incorporated; pg. 1147, pg. 1869
Minogue, Patrick, VP-Customer Mktg - Bacardi USA, Inc.; pg. 1956, pg. 417
Minogue, Terry, Sr VP-Brand Mktg & Creative - Viacom Inc.; pg. 316, pg. 1310
Minor, Chelsea, Dir-PR & Pub Affairs - Raley's Inc.; pg. 1031, pg. 305
Minor, Eric, Sr Dir-Mktg - The Libman Company; pg. 331, pg. 553
Minor, Jon, Sls Mgr-Asia Pacific Reg - Daktronics, Inc.; pg. 633, pg. 1624
Minor, Scott, Dir-Online Mktg - ZipRealty, Inc.; pg. 1120, pg. 85
Minor, Trevor, Brand Mgr - Capital One Financial Corporation; pg. 730, pg. 1789
Minsk, Helayna, VP-Mktg-Johnson & Johnson Consumer China - Johnson & Johnson; pg. 1549, pg. 1091
Minskoff, Evan, Head-Mktg Strategy & Ops - Tumblr, Inc.; pg. 1285, pg. 1305
Minsky, Jeff, Sr VP-Innovation & Integrated Media - NYC & Company, Inc.; pg. 1002, pg. 1274
Minter, Jessica, Asst Mgr-Mktg Comm - Jeld-Wen, Inc.; pg. 1051, pg. 1499
Minter, Marcia, VP-Creative - L.L. Bean, Inc.; pg. 1777, pg. 750
Minton, Amy, Dir-Campaign & Mktg Tech - Wyndham Vacation Ownership; pg. 1119, pg. 457
Mintun, Michael S., VP-Sls - Lincoln Electric Holdings, Inc.; pg. 1355, pg. 1432
Mintz, Danielle, VP-Distributor Mktg & Strategy - AMC Networks Inc.; pg. 269, pg. 1189
Mintzer, Andrew, Exec VP-Product Strategy & Customer Delivery - Bottomline Technologies (de), Inc.; pg. 727, pg. 1038
Mintzer, Andrew, Exec VP-Product Strategy & Customer Delivery - Bottomline Technologies Inc.; pg. 363, pg. 483
Mips-Medugno, Melissa, Asst VP-Digital & Creative Svcs - BJ's Wholesale Club, Inc.; pg. 1762, pg. 857
Mir, Emily, Dir-PR - Halliburton Company; pg. 978, pg. 1707
Mirabella, Rob, Sr Dir & Head-Office of Alliances - The Clorox Company; pg. 327, pg. 169
Mirabelli, John, Sr Dir-Scouting Ops - Cleveland Indians Baseball Company, Inc.; pg. 541, pg. 1429
Mirakian, Ashley, Dir-Mktg & PR - Toledo Symphony; pg. 588, pg. 1477
Miranda, Katherine, Mgr-PR - Vans, Inc.; pg. 1821, pg. 76
Miranda, Melissa, Sr Mgr-Mktg-TM Pepsi-Cultural Brand Engagement - PepsiCo, Inc.; pg. 259, pg. 1327
Miranda, Nelson, Sr Dir-North America Reg Mktg - Elizabeth Arden, Inc.; pg. 507, pg. 448
Miranda, Pete, Dir-Sls & Mktg - NRG Energy, Inc.; pg. 1948, pg. 1712
Miras, Camille, Analyst-Bus-Sls Ops - Pandora Media Inc.; pg. 1273, pg. 172
Mirel, Catherine, Sr Dir-Fin - Starwood Hotels & Resorts Worldwide, Inc.; pg. 1114, pg. 378
Mirelez, Sara, VP-Mktg Svcs - The WhiteWave Foods Company; pg. 1037, pg. 324
Mirich, Marci D., Mgr-Channel Mktg - Xerox Corporation; pg. 494, pg. 365
Miriello, Ann M., Mgr-Mktg Ops - Comcast Cable Communications, Inc.; pg. 276, pg. 1560
Mirks, Michelle, VP & Gen Mgr-Tape Products - American Biltrite Inc.; pg. 1878, pg. 856
Mironoff, Melinda, Dir-Unbranded Mktg - Valero Energy Corporation; pg. 986, pg. 1743
Mironova, Mila, Mgr-Mktg Comm - Siemens Canada Ltd.; pg. 1306, pg. 1921
Mirrer, Richard, Sr Specialist-Accessory & Event Mktg - BMW of North America, LLC; pg. 166, pg. 1133
Mirro, Monica, VP-Sls - Under Armour, Inc.; pg. 49, pg. 759
Mirshafiei, Sean, VP-Electronics Mktg-Global - Enthone Inc.; pg. 1161, pg. 381
Mirsky, Mitch, Mgr-Global Mktg-Social - Fisher-Price, Inc.; pg. 953, pg. 1156
Mirt, Kelly, VP-Adv - The Charlotte Observer Publishing Co.; pg. 1627, pg. 1364
Mirus Bates, Donna, Sr VP-Mktg Comm & Content Dev - Universal Orlando; pg. 590, pg. 456
Mirza, Jafar, Analyst-Digital Mktg - General Motors Company; pg. 175, pg. 881
Misa, Greg, Dir-Social Media & Brand Engagement - Bolthouse Farms; pg. 841, pg. 44
Misawa, Hisao Victor, VP-Mktg-Global-Writing - Newell Rubbermaid Inc.; pg. 1128, pg. 515
Misch, John, Sr Mgr-Corp Hospitality Sls - Arizona Cardinals Football Club, Inc.; pg. 529, pg. 25
Mischka, Cynthia, Sr Project Mgr-Sls & Mktg Ops - DIRECTV Group Holdings, LLC; pg. 281, pg. 79
Miscisin, Michael, Sr Mgr - Ernst & Young Global Limited; pg.

748, *pg.* 1228
Misdom, Laura, Dir-Global Brand Mgmt & Integrated Mktg - Avaya Inc.; *pg.* 621, *pg.* 264
Misenheimer, Heather D., Mgr-Mktg-DXR GSSNA - Philips Electronics North America; *pg.* 662, *pg.* 782
Mishan, Jeff, Dir-Adv - E. Mishan & Sons, Inc.; *pg.* 1767, *pg.* 1226
Mishizen, Gary, Sr Mgr - Waste Management, Inc.; *pg.* 1954, *pg.* 1716
Mishkin, Nina, Dir-Digital Brand & Social Media Mktg - American Express Company; *pg.* 712, *pg.* 1190
Mishler, Naysa, Mgr-Advocate Mktg - LinkedIn Corporation; *pg.* 1262, *pg.* 160
Mishra, Rajeev, VP-Comml Mktg & New Bus Dev-North America - Epson America Inc.; *pg.* 394, *pg.* 122
Misiewicz, Jerome, Coord-Mktg - H&R Block, Inc.; *pg.* 764, *pg.* 983
Misilewich, Dan, Specialist-Mktg-Enterprise Sys Plng & Product Mgmt Div - Canon U.S.A., Inc.; *pg.* 1401, *pg.* 1178
Misiti, Vincent S., Bus Mgr-Personal Care-Global - The Lubrizol Corporation; *pg.* 1171, *pg.* 1481
Miske, Myron, Dir-Product Line - Fairchild Semiconductor Corporation; *pg.* 638, *pg.* 245
Miskovsky, Sandra, Dir-Mktg - Manulife Financial Corporation; *pg.* 778, *pg.* 1939
Misner, Nathan, Dir-Global Integrated Comm & Social Mktg - F5 Networks, Inc.; *pg.* 396, *pg.* 1835
Misquez, Traci, Reg Mgr-Mktg - CKE Restaurants Inc.; *pg.* 1723, *pg.* 63
Missey, Joy, Sr Mgr-Digital Sls - Build-A-Bear Workshop, Inc.; *pg.* 950, *pg.* 993
Mistretta, Crystal, Brand Mgr & Mgr-Adv - Hubbell Incorporated; *pg.* 1299, *pg.* 370
Mistry, Cyrus, Sr Product Mgr - Google Inc.; *pg.* 1249, *pg.* 153
Mitarai, Rocky, Dir-Product Mktg - Saba Software, Inc.; *pg.* 464, *pg.* 192
Mitcham, Erin, Mgr-Brand Pkg Production & Designer-Production - Pier 1 Imports, Inc.; *pg.* 940, *pg.* 1695
Mitchel, Jim, VP-Mktg - CDW Corporation; *pg.* 370, *pg.* 663
Mitchell, Aiden, VP-Mktg - Arrow Electronics, Inc.; *pg.* 619, *pg.* 325
Mitchell, Allison, Dir-Adv Sls & Cause Mktg - National Geographic Channel; *pg.* 299, *pg.* 402
Mitchell, Andre, Mgr-Mktg Procurement Team - Nestle USA, Inc.; *pg.* 883, *pg.* 96
Mitchell, Anglea, Dir-Mktg - Whirlpool Corporation; *pg.* 62, *pg.* 872
Mitchell, Bernard, Supvr-Mktg - Kroll Inc.; *pg.* 425, *pg.* 1249
Mitchell, Bill, Sr Dir-Corp Investment - Jabil Circuit, Inc.; *pg.* 422, *pg.* 463
Mitchell, Bob, Mgr-Sls-North America - Replogle Globes, Inc.; *pg.* 461, *pg.* 559
Mitchell, Brent, VP-Mktg-E! & Esquire Network - NBC Universal, Inc.; *pg.* 300, *pg.* 1266
Mitchell, Brie, Mgr-Digital Media - Bloomingdale's, Inc.; *pg.* 1763, *pg.* 1204
Mitchell, Brittany, Analyst-Adv - State Farm Mutual Automobile Insurance Co.; *pg.* 1218, *pg.* 557
Mitchell, Brittnay, Sr Specialist-Mktg & Comm - Federal Home Loan Mortgage Corporation; *pg.* 751, *pg.* 1790
Mitchell, Brittney, Assoc Mgr-Mktg - PepsiCo, Inc.; *pg.* 259, *pg.* 1327
Mitchell, Caitlin, Social & Digital Content Mgr, Integrated Mktg Content - The Coca-Cola Company; *pg.* 240, *pg.* 493
Mitchell, Catherine, Exec Dir-Video Product Mgmt - Cox Communications, Inc.; *pg.* 279, *pg.* 501
Mitchell, Cathy, VP-Mdsg - Hickory Chair Company; *pg.* 927, *pg.* 1378
Mitchell, Chad, Sr Dir-Digital Comm - Wal-Mart Stores, Inc.; *pg.* 1790, *pg.* 29
Mitchell, Chris, Dir-Membership Mktg - The American Dental Association; *pg.* 127, *pg.* 564
Mitchell, Chris, Dir-Mktg - CRYSTAL ROCK HOLDINGS, INC.; *pg.* 248, *pg.* 382
Mitchell, Cynthia, Mgr-ECommerce Mktg & Digital Mktg - Interstate Battery System of America Inc.; *pg.* 208, *pg.* 1682
Mitchell, Daniel, Dir-Sls-Pan Pacific - Conax Technologies LLC; *pg.* 1325, *pg.* 1148
Mitchell, David, Dir-Mktg-Global - THE DOW CHEMICAL COMPANY; *pg.* 1157, *pg.* 898
Mitchell, Debbie, Sr VP-PR - Cardinal Health, Inc.; *pg.* 1512, *pg.* 1448
Mitchell, Drew, Dir-US Field Mktg - Golfsmith International Holdings, Inc.; *pg.* 1835, *pg.* 1662
Mitchell, Ed, VP-Sls - Melitta USA Inc.; *pg.* 781, *pg.* 416
Mitchell, Elicia, Coord-Mktg & Tradeshow - Cross Country Healthcare, Inc.; *pg.* 1520, *pg.* 411
Mitchell, Georgia, Mgr-PR & Internal Comm - Robert Bosch Tool Corp; *pg.* 1060, *pg.* 634
Mitchell, Heather, Specialist-Mktg - Hy-Vee, Inc.; *pg.* 1023, *pg.* 713
Mitchell, Janelda R., VP-Mktg - Farmers Capital Bank Corporation; *pg.* 750, *pg.* 728
Mitchell, Janine, VP-Mdsg - GNC Holdings Inc.; *pg.* 1537, *pg.* 1576
Mitchell, Jeanette, Sr Mgr-Mktg, Media & Adv - Crate & Barrel, Inc.; *pg.* 922, *pg.* 640
Mitchell, Jennifer, Dir-Social Enablement - The Hartford Financial Services Group, Inc.; *pg.* 1202, *pg.* 352
Mitchell, Jennifer, Sr Specialist-Mktg - School Specialty, Inc.; *pg.* 467, *pg.* 1860
Mitchell, Jerrod, Sr Mgr-Mktg Comm - Applebee's International, Inc.; *pg.* 1715, *pg.* 980
Mitchell, Joan, VP-Pub Rels - Western Governors University; *pg.* 610, *pg.* 1762
Mitchell, John W., VP & Mgr-Sls - Eagle Manufacturing Company; *pg.* 79, *pg.* 1851
Mitchell, Joseph, Interim Pres, Interim CEO & COO - UQM Technologies, Inc.; *pg.* 684, *pg.* 334
Mitchell, Kathy, Mgr-Comm & Media - Trammell Crow Company; *pg.* 1116, *pg.* 1689
Mitchell, Katie, VP-Intl Mktg - J. Crew Group, Inc.; *pg.* 1773, *pg.* 1245
Mitchell, Kenneth, Mng Dir-Brand & Consumer Mktg - National Association for Stock Car Auto Racing; *pg.* 566, *pg.* 420
Mitchell, Kenny, Sr Dir-Consumer Engagement - The Gatorade Company; *pg.* 251, *pg.* 574
Mitchell, Lauren, Sr Mgr-Media - NutriSystem, Inc.; *pg.* 1577, *pg.* 1533
Mitchell, Lisa, Dir-Mktg - Caleres, Inc.; *pg.* 1805, *pg.* 993
Mitchell, Lisa A., Mgr-Mktg Comm - Sherwin Williams; *pg.* 1448, *pg.* 1436
Mitchell, Matthew, Sr Mgr-Brand Mktg - Newell Rubbermaid Inc.; *pg.* 1128, *pg.* 515
Mitchell, Melissa, Dir-Multicultural Mktg - The Coca-Cola Company; *pg.* 240, *pg.* 493
Mitchell, Micah, Dir-Adv - The Arkansas City Traveler; *pg.* 1617, *pg.* 714
Mitchell, Michael, Sr Dir-Corp External Comm - Mondelez International, Inc.; *pg.* 878, *pg.* 601
Mitchell, Michael, VP-Strategic Mktg, Partnerships, Live Entertainment & Cruises - Time Inc.; *pg.* 1693, *pg.* 1300
Mitchell, Michael R., Sr Dir - The Medicines Company; *pg.* 1561, *pg.* 1104
Mitchell, Mike, Sr Dir - Cisco Systems, Inc.; *pg.* 372, *pg.* 240
Mitchell, Mitzi, Mgr-Mktg Comm - MetroPCS, Inc.; *pg.* 1872, *pg.* 1683
Mitchell, Nikki, VP-PR - Baylor Health Care System; *pg.* 1500, *pg.* 1676
Mitchell, Patricia, Exec VP-Retail & Sls Ops - IBW Financial Corp.; *pg.* 768, *pg.* 401
Mitchell, Ralph, VP-Comm & Mktg - Reds Baseball Partners, LLC; *pg.* 578, *pg.* 1425
Mitchell, Rhonda, Dir-Mktg - Interface, Inc.; *pg.* 695, *pg.* 512
Mitchell, Rick, Sr Mgr-Product Mktg - Amazon.com, Inc.; *pg.* 1226, *pg.* 1831
Mitchell, Ryan, Dir-Mktg - Tavistock Restaurant Group; *pg.* 1753, *pg.* 803
Mitchell, Samantha, Specialist-Mktg - Luminex Corporation; *pg.* 1421, *pg.* 1664
Mitchell, Sarah, Mgr-Mktg & Global Nutrition Grp - PepsiCo, Inc.; *pg.* 259, *pg.* 1327
Mitchell, Sono, VP-Program Adv & Mktg - Home Box Office, Inc.; *pg.* 290, *pg.* 1240
Mitchell, Stephan, Specialist-Indexed UL Product Mktg - Pacific Life Insurance Company; *pg.* 1213, *pg.* 166
Mitchell, Stephanie, Sr Brand Mgr-Rubbermaid Comml Products - Newell Rubbermaid Inc.; *pg.* 1128, *pg.* 515
Mitchell, Taryn, VP-Sls & Digital Channel-Global - Reckitt Benckiser Inc.; *pg.* 1136, *pg.* 1105
Mitchell, Terri, Mgr-Mktg Comm - Bayer CropScience; *pg.* 1149, *pg.* 981
Mitchell, Thor, Product Mgr-Google Developer Platform - Google Inc.; *pg.* 1249, *pg.* 153
Mitchell, Tom, Sr Dir-Procure To Pay & Corp Svcs-Retail Ops - Nintendo of America, Inc.; *pg.* 965, *pg.* 1829
Mitchell, Victoria, Specialist-Mktg Comm - Thermo Fisher Scientific Inc.; *pg.* 1431, *pg.* 854
Mitcheol, Sean, Sr VP-Mktg - L.A. Gear, Inc.; *pg.* 1811, *pg.* 134
Mitchum, Paige, Asst Mgr-Mktg - Boulder Brands, Inc.; *pg.* 1016, *pg.* 310
Mitra, Abhik, Sr Mgr-Solutions - Imation Corp.; *pg.* 413, *pg.* 952
Mitra, Amal, Sr Dir-LTE Solutions - Alcatel-Lucent; *pg.* 615, *pg.* 1094
Mitrevski, Michael, Specialist-Mktg - E*TRADE Financial Corporation; *pg.* 749, *pg.* 1230
Mitro, Monica, Exec VP-PR - L Brands, Inc.; *pg.* 1776, *pg.* 1441
Mitro, Monica, Exec VP-PR - Victoria's Secret Stores, LLC; *pg.* 1789, *pg.* 1471
Mitropoulos, Maria, VP-Mktg-Asia & Oceania - Gruma Corporation; *pg.* 860, *pg.* 951
Mitsock, Mike, VP-Mktg - KVH Industries Inc; *pg.* 650, *pg.* 1602
Mitsui, Katie, Sr Product Mgr - The Bradford Group; *pg.* 1763, *pg.* 637
Mittal, Ritu, Category Head & Brand Mgr - The Procter & Gamble Company; *pg.* 1129, *pg.* 1418
Mittelbrun, Susan, VP-Mktg-Rinnai America Corporation - Rinnai America Corp.; *pg.* 1076, *pg.* 538
Mittelman, Dove, Mgr-Mdse - Phoenix Suns; *pg.* 576, *pg.* 19
Mittleman, Ileene, Sr VP-Adv & Creative Svcs-CBS Television - CBS Broadcasting Inc.; *pg.* 273, *pg.* 1210
Mittleman, Ileene, Sr VP-Adv & Creative Svcs-CBS Television - CBS Corporation; *pg.* 273, *pg.* 1210
Mitton, Ryan, Mgr-Global Advanced Product Mktg - Ford Motor Company; *pg.* 172, *pg.* 876
Miu, Edward, Mgr-Sls & Logistics - Happy's Pizza LLC; *pg.* 1730, *pg.* 886
Miu, Jennifer, Sr Mgr-PR - Juniper Networks, Inc.; *pg.* 1260, *pg.* 286
Miura, Natsuko, Mgr-Mktg - IBM; *pg.* 410, *pg.* 1449
Mix, Joy L., Sr Mgr-HR Comm - Abbott Laboratories; *pg.* 1484, *pg.* 551
Mixon, Tim, Dir-Mktg Talent & Capabilities-Social Media Activation - Dell Inc.; *pg.* 383, *pg.* 1737
Miyazono, Max, Sr Dir-Strategic Initiatives, Corp Bus Dev - SAP America, Inc.; *pg.* 466, *pg.* 1557
Miyoshi, Joyce, Brand Mgr-Emerging Markets Running - NIKE, Inc.; *pg.* 1812, *pg.* 1492
Mize, Greg, Dir-Digital Mktg - Atlanta National League Baseball Club, Inc.; *pg.* 530, *pg.* 490
Mize, Kelly, Mgr-PR - Invacare Corporation; *pg.* 1546, *pg.* 1451
Mizek, Robert, VP-Foodservice Sls - High Liner Foods (USA) Incorporated; *pg.* 862, *pg.* 816
Mizenko, Paul W., Sr Designer-Adv - The Home Depot, Inc.; *pg.* 1050, *pg.* 510
Mizufuka, Eric, Product Mgr - Epson America Inc.; *pg.* 394, *pg.* 122
Mizuno, Rachel, Sr VP-Distr Mktg-US - Sony Pictures Entertainment Inc.; *pg.* 309, *pg.* 72
Mlodozeniec, Susan, Sr Mgr-Mktg-Demand Generation - Forrester Research, Inc.; *pg.* 1642, *pg.* 807
Mlutkowski, Kevin P., Dir-Mktg - American Concrete Institute; *pg.* 127, *pg.* 885
Mlynarczyk, Karen, VP-Integrated Mktg Comm - L'Oreal USA; *pg.* 514, *pg.* 1252
Mlynek, Nina, Sr Assoc Brand Mgr-Pasta - Barilla America, Inc.; *pg.* 839, *pg.* 555
Moak, Ashley, Program Mgr-Media-Entertainment Content - YouTube, LLC; *pg.* 1291, *pg.* 198
Moatazedi, David, VP-Sls & Mktg-Facial Aesthetics - Allergan, Inc.; *pg.* 1491, *pg.* 106
Mobley, Elmer, Dir-Digital & Social Strategies - ACS Industries, Inc.; *pg.* 1040, *pg.* 1602
Mochulsky, Rick, Sr VP-Sls - Motorcar Parts of America, Inc.; *pg.* 213, *pg.* 295
Mock, Christopher, Product Mgr-Global Trauma - Zimmer Biomet Holdings, Inc.; *pg.* 1611, *pg.* 699
Mockridge, Staci, Sr Mgr-Media - PulteGroup, Inc.; *pg.* 1109, *pg.* 873
Modaff, Steve, Mgr-Mktg - Tootsie Roll Industries, Inc.; *pg.* 1863, *pg.* 591
Model, Justin M., Dir-East Reg Mktg & Comm - Accenture; *pg.* 1392, *pg.* 1186
Modelski, Kasia, Product Mgr - Skullcandy, Inc.; *pg.* 674, *pg.* 1754
Modi, Rooshina, Sr Mgr-Digital Mktg - Barnes & Noble, Inc.; *pg.* 1619, *pg.* 1201
Modirzadeh, Soheil, Mgr-Mktg Programs - Synopsys, Inc.; *pg.*

480, *pg.* 162
Modolo, Kate, Sr Mgr-Corp Comm - Delta Air Lines, Inc.; *pg.* 1905, *pg.* 503
Modur, Subha, Dir-Media-North America - Kayak; *pg.* 1260, *pg.* 363
Moe, Rich, VP-Sls - Wolverine World Wide, Inc.; *pg.* 1822, *pg.* 905
Moe, Tom, Dir-Mktg - Nestle USA, Inc.; *pg.* 883, *pg.* 96
Moeckel, Jennifer, Mgr-Sls - Buca, Inc.; *pg.* 1718, *pg.* 931
Moeggenberg, Katy, Head-Global Social Media Platform - The Procter & Gamble Company; *pg.* 1129, *pg.* 1418
Moehn, Alex, Coord-Email Mktg - Milwaukee Bucks, Inc.; *pg.* 563, *pg.* 1878
Moeller, Craig, VP-Mktg - ClosetMaid Corporation; *pg.* 920, *pg.* 452
Moeller, Jeff, Sr Dir-Comm & Content - Los Angeles Kings Hockey Club L.P.; *pg.* 559, *pg.* 135
Moeller, Julie, VP-Media Strategy & Bus Dev-US - National Football League; *pg.* 567, *pg.* 1264
Moeller, Nancy, Dir-Mktg - Merrill Corporation; *pg.* 1664, *pg.* 962
Moeller, Shay, Product Mgr - Wahl Clipper Corporation; *pg.* 524, *pg.* 662
Moen, Jon, Product Mgr-Treasury Mgmt - First Banks, Inc.; *pg.* 754, *pg.* 976
Moffat, Rebecca, Bus Mgr-Americas Supplies Mktg - Hewlett-Packard Company; *pg.* 404, *pg.* 175
Moffatt, Catherine, VP-Shopper Plng & Customer Mktg Centre of Excellence-Global - Diageo North America Inc.; *pg.* 248, *pg.* 1223
Moffatt, Steve, CTO-Front End Products - Applied Materials, Inc.; *pg.* 618, *pg.* 264
Moffett, T. J., VP-Mktg-Movies - Redbox Automated Retail, LLC; *pg.* 306, *pg.* 649
Moffit, Bob, Product Mgr - Ashland Performance Materials; *pg.* 1147, *pg.* 1448
Moffitt, Adam, Mgr-ECommerce Mktg - Northern Tool + Equipment; *pg.* 1366, *pg.* 919
Moffitt, Ian, Sr Dir-Programming, Strategy & Acq-Yahoo Screen - Yahoo! Inc.; *pg.* 1289, *pg.* 289
Moffitt, Scott, Exec VP-Sls & Mktg - Nintendo of America, Inc.; *pg.* 965, *pg.* 1829
Mogan, Sarah, Acct Coord-Media Sls - Rogers Communications Inc.; *pg.* 668, *pg.* 1942
Mogel, Melinda, Sr Mgr-Field & Customer Mktg Programs - Pegasystems Inc.; *pg.* 453, *pg.* 809
Mogen, Christopher, Mgr-Creative Digital - Toys "R" Us, Inc.; *pg.* 968, *pg.* 1130
Mogensen, David, Head-B2B Product Mktg-YouTube & Google Display - Google Inc.; *pg.* 1249, *pg.* 153
Mogensen, Jill, Mgr-Mktg - E*TRADE Financial Corporation; *pg.* 749, *pg.* 1230
Moger, Mallory, Specialist-PR - USANA Health Sciences, Inc.; *pg.* 1605, *pg.* 1761
Moghe, Kshitij, Dir-Product Mktg - Nuance Communications, Inc.; *pg.* 447, *pg.* 806
Mohamed, Mohamed, Supvr-Retention Mktg Ops - Provide Commerce, Inc.; *pg.* 1276, *pg.* 206
Mohamed, Shazad, Product Mgr - Facebook, Inc.; *pg.* 1245, *pg.* 143
Mohan, Ankur, Sr Product Mgr-Games Grp - Autodesk Inc.; *pg.* 356, *pg.* 257
Mohan, Rajan, VP-Mdsg & Booking-Marriott.com - Marriott International, Inc.; *pg.* 1102, *pg.* 764
Mohan, Samir, Head-Trade Mktg-Europe & North America - Reckitt Benckiser Inc.; *pg.* 1136, *pg.* 1105
Mohanty, Bobby, Sr VP & Gen Mgr-Products - Vertical Communications, Inc.; *pg.* 488, *pg.* 270
Mohel, Jill Lobliner, Sr Dir-Mktg Plng & Execution - Hilton Worldwide, Inc.; *pg.* 1094, *pg.* 1791
Mohii, Arman, Product Dir - The NASDAQ OMX Group, Inc.; *pg.* 785, *pg.* 1263
Mohl, Anna, VP-US Institutional Sls-HealthCare Nutrition - Nestle Healthcare Nutrition; *pg.* 1572, *pg.* 941
Mohl, Anna, VP-US Institutional Sls-HealthCare Nutrition - Nestle USA, Inc.; *pg.* 883, *pg.* 96
Mohl, Jeff, VP-Sports Mktg - NYC & Company, Inc.; *pg.* 1002, *pg.* 1274
Mohle, Lisa, Sr Mgr-Direct Mktg & Consumer Mktg - Bonnier Corporation; *pg.* 1622, *pg.* 480
Mohler, Bob, Sr VP-Digital Media-Telepictures - Warner Bros. Entertainment Inc.; *pg.* 319, *pg.* 54
Mohler, Keith, Mgr-Brand Mktg - Community Coffee Company LLC; *pg.* 849, *pg.* 741
Mohler, Susan, VP-Mktg - MultiPlan, Inc.; *pg.* 1570, *pg.* 852
Mohnke, Dan, VP-Sls & Mktg Ops & Sr Mgr-Mktg & Ops - Nissan North America, Inc.; *pg.* 186, *pg.* 1633
Mohnshine, Daniel, Dir-Mktg - The Hershey Co.; *pg.* 1855, *pg.* 1538
Mohon, Jane, Sr VP-Mktg Svcs - Sony Pictures Home Entertainment; *pg.* 310, *pg.* 72
Mohr, Leslie, Head-Mktg-Sustainability & Nutrition - Nestle USA, Inc.; *pg.* 883, *pg.* 96
Moin, Anjie, Dir-eCommerce Digital Mktg - Office Depot, Inc.; *pg.* 448, *pg.* 412
Moiz, Khurram, Sr Mgr-Mktg Analytics - The Home Depot, Inc.; *pg.* 1050, *pg.* 510
Moke, Nicole, Sr Mgr-PR - Equinox Fitness Clubs; *pg.* 546, *pg.* 1228
Mokros, Carrie, Specialist-Store Mktg - DSW, Inc.; *pg.* 1807, *pg.* 1439
Moldin, Cindy, Brand Mgr-Gillette Venus - The Procter & Gamble Company; *pg.* 1129, *pg.* 1418
Moldovan, Jane, Sr Mgr-Online Retailing - Wyndham Worldwide Corporation; *pg.* 1119, *pg.* 1107
Molen, Laura, Exec VP-Cable Adv Sls - NBC Universal, Inc.; *pg.* 300, *pg.* 1266
Molenda, James, Co-Founder & Exec VP-Sls Ops-Global - Imation Nexsan Solutions; *pg.* 413, *pg.* 292
Molette, Andrea, VP-Media - Stage Stores, Inc.; *pg.* 33, *pg.* 1715
Molina, Loyda, Mgr-Recruiting & Mktg-Latino Market - New York Life Insurance Company; *pg.* 1211, *pg.* 1268
Molina, Solangelee, Sr Dir-Video Programming - Univision Communications Inc.; *pg.* 683, *pg.* 1307
Molina, Stella, VP-Mktg - Taco Bueno Restaurants, L.P.; *pg.* 1753, *pg.* 1692
Molinari, Caitlin, Specialist-Digital Mktg - Pacific Sunwear of California, Inc.; *pg.* 1781, *pg.* 43
Molinaro, Art, Dir-Technical & Sr Mgr-Stage - The Florida Orchestra; *pg.* 548, *pg.* 462
Molinaro, Joe, Mgr-Natl Sls-Ameristar - Ingersoll-Rand Company; *pg.* 1349, *pg.* 1370
Molinaro, Zach, Mgr-Digital Media-Pretzel Crisps - Snyder's-Lance, Inc.; *pg.* 896, *pg.* 1368
Moline-Ashby, Michele, Sr Project Mgr-Mktg - Trinchero Family Estates; *pg.* 1971, *pg.* 197
Molinello, Mara, Sr Mgr-Mktg-Global - Baxter International Inc.; *pg.* 1499, *pg.* 599
Moll, Jack, Gen Mgr & Sr Dir - Ethan Allen Interiors Inc.; *pg.* 924, *pg.* 343
Moll, Sandra, Mgr-Corp Web Mktg - Liberty Mutual Insurance Group Inc.; *pg.* 1205, *pg.* 797
Mollat, Amy, Dir-Product Mktg-Software Networking Div - Brocade Corporation; *pg.* 365, *pg.* 312
Moller, Julia Gutz, Asst VP-Mktg, Brand & Creative Svcs-Mktg - Allianz Life Insurance Company of North America; *pg.* 1188, *pg.* 929
Moller-Hansen, Maiken, Principal & Product Mgr-Amazon Fire TV - Amazon.com, Inc.; *pg.* 1226, *pg.* 1831
Mollere, Marc, Sr VP-Sls - Dymatize Enterprises, Inc.; *pg.* 1525, *pg.* 1692
Mollerus, Kristin, VP-Digital Mktg - Citizens Financial Group, Inc.; *pg.* 737, *pg.* 1606
Mollet, Sean, VP-Product Mgmt - PC Mall, Inc.; *pg.* 452, *pg.* 295
Mollica, Jim, Head-Digital Mktg & Content - Under Armour, Inc.; *pg.* 49, *pg.* 759
Mollins, Candace, Mgr-Mktg & Comm - Sun Life Financial Inc.; *pg.* 806, *pg.* 1944
Mollison, Amy, Mgr-Americas Field Mktg-AEC Construction - Autodesk Inc.; *pg.* 356, *pg.* 257
Molloy, Corina, Sr Dir-Format Optimization - Office Depot, Inc.; *pg.* 448, *pg.* 412
Molloy, Glenn, Mgr-Strategic Platform-Sls - Intel Corporation; *pg.* 645, *pg.* 266
Molloy, Jack, Sr VP-Sls-North America - Motorola Solutions, Inc.; *pg.* 657, *pg.* 659
Molloy, Meghan T., Sr Mgr-Promotional Mktg-Early Launch Oncology - MedImmune LLC; *pg.* 1562, *pg.* 770
Molnar, Doug, Sr VP-Mktg - WesBanco, Inc.; *pg.* 821, *pg.* 1851
Molnar, Laura, Brand Mgr - Gruma Corporation; *pg.* 860, *pg.* 1720
Molock, Angela, Product Mgr-Technical - RACKSPACE HOSTING, INC.; *pg.* 1277, *pg.* 1742
Moloff, Jason, Brand Mgr-Dannon Packaged Frozen Yogurt - The Dannon Company, Inc.; *pg.* 851, *pg.* 1351
Moloney, Chris X., CMO & Sr VP-Mktg - Wells Fargo Advisors, LLC; *pg.* 819, *pg.* 1005
Moloney, Jim, Dir-Mktg - Albany International Corp.; *pg.* 691, *pg.* 1038
Molthen, Bridget, Dir-Mktg - Jones Dairy Farm; *pg.* 867, *pg.* 1858
Molyet, John, Reg Mgr-Sls-HM Clause - Harris Moran Seed Co.; *pg.* 1796, *pg.* 150
Molyneux, Braden, Specialist-Mktg Technical-Acrobat.com - Adobe Systems Incorporated; *pg.* 342, *pg.* 235
Momon, Caroline, Sr Mgr-R&D-Quaker Foods North America - PepsiCo, Inc.; *pg.* 259, *pg.* 1327
Momsen, Chris, Exec VP-Sls & Solutions Mgmt - Advent Software, Inc.; *pg.* 345, *pg.* 211
Monaco, Christina, Dir-Corp Media & Events - Moet Hennessy; *pg.* 1966, *pg.* 1260
Monaco, Nicholas, Sr Product Mgr - Panasonic Corporation of North America; *pg.* 661, *pg.* 1120
Monaco, Tierney, Head-Bus Ops & Mktg Integration - Mars Petcare; *pg.* 1478, *pg.* 1633
Monaghan, Barry, VP-Retail Sls & Mktg - National Hockey League; *pg.* 568, *pg.* 1265
Monaghan, Brendan, Sr VP-Adv - The New York Times Company; *pg.* 1668, *pg.* 1270
Monaghan, John, Dir-Sls Culture & Events - Marriott International, Inc.; *pg.* 1102, *pg.* 764
Monaghan, Kathy, Brand Mktg Mgr - Pendleton Woolen Mills, Inc.; *pg.* 697, *pg.* 1505
Monahan, Brian, VP-Mktg - Wal-Mart Stores, Inc.; *pg.* 1790, *pg.* 29
Monahan, Joe, Sr VP-Sls - Carhartt, Inc.; *pg.* 39, *pg.* 875
Monahan, Matt, Dir-Channel Mktg - Comcast Corporation; *pg.* 276, *pg.* 1560
Monahan, Shelly, Mgr-Mktg Comm - Boston Scientific Corporation; *pg.* 1508, *pg.* 831
Monahan, Susan, Reg Mgr-Sls - Sunovion Pharmaceuticals Inc.; *pg.* 1599, *pg.* 832
Monasmith, Brad, Mgr-Mktg Ops - Medtronic, Inc.; *pg.* 1564, *pg.* 939
Moncayo, Chris, Exec VP-Integrated Mktg Solutions-Texas Reg - Entravision Communications Corporation; *pg.* 285, *pg.* 273
Moncini, Kurt, Product Mgr - Komatsu America Corp.; *pg.* 92, *pg.* 655
Monckton, Mark, Area Mgr-Mktg - Sunoco Inc.; *pg.* 985, *pg.* 1571
Monczka, Tom, Product Mgr - Brother International Corporation - USA; *pg.* 53, *pg.* 1046
Monda, Beth, VP-Mktg & ECommerce - BCBG Max Azria Group LLC; *pg.* 19, *pg.* 301
Mondragon, Dan, Grp Mgr-Product Innovation, Optimization & Mktg Cloud - Adobe Systems Incorporated; *pg.* 342, *pg.* 235
Mondy, Joseph, Dir-PR - Cigna Corporation; *pg.* 1197, *pg.* 338
Mondzelewski, Chris, VP-Mktg - Mars Petcare; *pg.* 1478, *pg.* 1633
Monestime, Michael, Dir-Sponsorship Sls - Live Nation Entertainment, Inc.; *pg.* 558, *pg.* 47
Monetti, Kathy, Sr VP-Mktg - American Girl LLC; *pg.* 949, *pg.* 1871
Monge, Cristina, Mgr-Mktg-CruiseOne & Cruises Inc - World Travel Holdings; *pg.* 1931, *pg.* 860
Monge, Jonathan, Brand Mgr-Hefty - Reynolds Consumer Products; *pg.* 1138, *pg.* 625
Mongole, Gloria, Mgr-Sls & Mktg Ops - McKesson Corporation; *pg.* 1560, *pg.* 222
Monico, Dominick, Exec Dir-Sls, Mktg & Bus Dev-Global - Waterous Company; *pg.* 1387, *pg.* 965
Monin, Monica, Mgr-Mktg Comm - Corning Incorporated; *pg.* 1122, *pg.* 1154
Monin, Pauline, Product Mgr-EMEA PC Components - PNY Technologies, Inc.; *pg.* 455, *pg.* 1105
Moninger, John K., Mng Dir-Retail Sls - Eaton Vance Corp.; *pg.* 746, *pg.* 794
Moninghoff, Bruce, VP-Sls - Spirax Sarco, Inc.; *pg.* 1076, *pg.* 1612
Monis, Ralph, Sr Mgr-IM Allocation & Replenishment-Kmart Menswear - Kmart Corporation; *pg.* 1775, *pg.* 617
Moniz, Garret, Sr Mgr-Bus Dev - NetSuite, Inc.; *pg.* 1270, *pg.* 255
Moniz, Vangie, Mgr-Adv - Fry's Electronics, Inc.; *pg.* 640, *pg.* 245
Monkiewicz, Matt, VP-Mktg - Kayem Foods, Inc.; *pg.* 867, *pg.* 814
Monkman, Christina, Mgr-Mktg - David's Bridal, Inc.; *pg.* 23, *pg.* 1523

Monkman, Holly, Dir-Roxy Sports Mktg - Quiksilver, Inc.; *pg.* 31, *pg.* 104
Monnie, Samuel, Dir-Mktg Capability & Mktg Excellence-Global - Campbell Soup Company; *pg.* 844, *pg.* 1048
Monnier, Olivier, Dir-Mktg, Connectivity & Internet of Things - Texas Instruments Incorporated; *pg.* 679, *pg.* 1688
Monnin, Nikki, Mgr-Mktg-Bluebird Comm & Engagement - American Express Company; *pg.* 712, *pg.* 1190
Monninger, Bryan, Dir-Prescription Diet Mktg Hill's Pet Nutrition - Colgate-Palmolive Company; *pg.* 504, *pg.* 1215
Monreal, Mariana, Head-Programmatic & Audience Adv & Mgr - Yahoo! Inc.; *pg.* 1289, *pg.* 289
Monroe, Amy, Dir-Brand Mktg - The Yankee Candle Company, Inc.; *pg.* 1792, *pg.* 843
Monroe, Jessica, Product Mgr - Standard Motor Products, Inc.; *pg.* 218, *pg.* 1176
Monroe, Michael, Exec Dir-Mktg - Forbes, Inc.; *pg.* 1641, *pg.* 1232
Monroe, Sue, Dir-Mktg - Cigna Corporation; *pg.* 1107, *pg.* 338
Monroe, Terisa, Asst VP-Customer Mktg - The Coca-Cola Company; *pg.* 240, *pg.* 493
Monson, Elizabeth, Dir-Social Media - Ann Inc.; *pg.* 18, *pg.* 1195
Monson, John, Mgr-Social Media & Mktg - Country Music Television, Inc.; *pg.* 279, *pg.* 1649
Monson, John, VP-Mktg - MoSys Inc.; *pg.* 657, *pg.* 268
Monsowitz, Eric, Principal & Product Mgr - Amazon.com, Inc.; *pg.* 1226, *pg.* 1831
Monstrola, Davena, Mgr-Mktg - Lowe's Companies, Inc.; *pg.* 1053, *pg.* 1383
Montagna, Deborah A., VP-Bus & Product Dev - Ocean Power Technologies, Inc.; *pg.* 1948, *pg.* 1107
Montagna, Lisa, District Mgr-PR - Robert Half International Inc.; *pg.* 462, *pg.* 145
Montague, Kelly, VP-Adv - The Hamilton Spectator; *pg.* 1647, *pg.* 1921
Montague, Kyle, Mgr-Product Line - Parker Hannifin - Webster Plastics Inc; *pg.* 1887, *pg.* 1159
Montague, Michelle Lynn, Exec Dir-Mktg & Publicity - Abrams; *pg.* 1613, *pg.* 1186
Montague, Monty, Mgr-Mdse - Cincinnati Bengals, Inc.; *pg.* 540, *pg.* 1410
Montague, Sarah, VP-Consumer Mktg - Bright Horizons Family Solutions Inc.; *pg.* 598, *pg.* 855
Montalto, Crystal, Mgr-Media Svcs & Brand Mktg - PGA Tour, Inc.; *pg.* 574, *pg.* 460
Montalvo, Michelle, Brand Mgr-Lauren, Denim & Supply - Ralph Lauren Corporation; *pg.* 46, *pg.* 1284
Montana, Michael, Mgr-Inside Sls & Estimating - Summit Corporation of America; *pg.* 1182, *pg.* 380
Montanez, Gina, Sr Mgr-Web Mktg - T-Mobile US, Inc.; *pg.* 676, *pg.* 1816
Montani, Rick, Sr VP-Construction Products Div - Sika Corporation; *pg.* 110, *pg.* 1080
Montano, Ben, Dir-Brand Mktg - Hasbro, Inc.; *pg.* 954, *pg.* 1603
Montbriand, Alissa, Sr Dir-Digital - Bloomin' Brands, Inc.; *pg.* 1716, *pg.* 471
Monte, Valentina, Assoc Mgr-Digital & Social Media Mktg - Home Box Office, Inc.; *pg.* 290, *pg.* 1240
Monteagudo, Graciela I., Sr VP & Gen Mgr-Mktg - Mead Johnson Nutrition Company; *pg.* 1561, *pg.* 615
Montecinos, Kathleen, Sr Supvr-Digital Mktg - GEICO Corporation; *pg.* 1200, *pg.* 399
Montefusco, Linda, Mgr-Adv & Video Production - Ricoh Americas Corp.; *pg.* 462, *pg.* 538
Montei, Matt, Sr Dir-Mktg-Skittles, Starburst & Lifesavers - Wm. Wrigley Jr. Company; *pg.* 1863, *pg.* 596
Monteiro, Jean-marc, Dir-Sls, Mktg & Customer Support - BE Aerospace, Inc.; *pg.* 224, *pg.* 478
Monteleone, Michael, Brand Mgr - The Sun Products Corporation; *pg.* 336, *pg.* 385
Monteleone, Michele, Sr Dir-Video Content & Dev - Rodale, Inc.; *pg.* 1681, *pg.* 1530
Montella, Christopher, VP-Mktg - Perry Ellis International, Inc.; *pg.* 45, *pg.* 445
Montella, Kim, Mgr-Sls - Coldwell Banker Residential Brokerage; *pg.* 1087, *pg.* 850
Montella, Richard A., VP-Sls & Customer Svc - Bloomberg BNA; *pg.* 1621, *pg.* 1772
Montemayor, Donna, Sr Dir-Rx Pro Svcs, Mktg & Strategic Initiatives - H-E-B; *pg.* 1022, *pg.* 1740
Montemayor, Marilyn, Assoc Dir-Hispanic Consumer Adv - AT&T; *pg.* 1865, *pg.* 258
Monterio, Frank, CFO-Platform Specialty Products - MacDermid, Inc.; *pg.* 1172, *pg.* 321
Montero Harting, Olivia, Head-Social Media - Chevron Corporation; *pg.* 974, *pg.* 259
Montero, Veronica, Mgr-Digital Mktg-Accenture Interactive - Accenture; *pg.* 1392, *pg.* 1186
Montesano, Jennifer A., Dir-Mktg & PR - General Dynamics Corporation; *pg.* 228, *pg.* 1781
Monteverde, Miguel, Sr VP-Digital Media - Discovery Communications, Inc.; *pg.* 282, *pg.* 777
Montez, Ramon, Analyst-Digital Mktg - Las Vegas Convention & Visitors Authority; *pg.* 997, *pg.* 1027
Montgomery, Bill, Dir-Adv & Promos - Prairie Farms Dairy, Inc.; *pg.* 890, *pg.* 561
Montgomery, Bruce, VP-Sls-North & South America - Fleet Laboratories; *pg.* 1531, *pg.* 1787
Montgomery, Celeste, Mgr-Channel Mktg - The Vanguard Group, Inc.; *pg.* 816, *pg.* 1550
Montgomery, Chip, Sr Specialist-Mktg - Honeywell International Inc.; *pg.* 407, *pg.* 1088
Montgomery, Danny, Sr VP-Mfg & Engineered Products - Alpha Pro Tech, Ltd.; *pg.* 1492, *pg.* 1922
Montgomery, Erin, Dir-Corp PR - Charles Schwab & Company, Inc.; *pg.* 734, *pg.* 215
Montgomery, Gordon, VP-Mktg & Pub Affairs - The Art Institute of Chicago; *pg.* 530, *pg.* 565
Montgomery, Howard M., Dir-Creative Design - Armstrong World Industries, Inc.; *pg.* 914, *pg.* 1545
Montgomery, Karina, VP-Sls Dev - Pandora Media Inc.; *pg.* 1273, *pg.* 172
Montgomery, Kellee, Mgr-Social & Emerging Digital Mktg - Ford Motor Company; *pg.* 172, *pg.* 876
Montgomery, Lawrence, Dir-Adv-Natl - Kaiser Permanente; *pg.* 1552, *pg.* 171
Montgomery, Lynnette, Dir-Global eCommerce & Digital Mktg - Burt's Bees Inc.; *pg.* 502, *pg.* 1370
Montgomery, Max, Mgr-Mktg - MDI Entertainment LLC; *pg.* 964, *pg.* 484
Montgomery, Michelle, Mgr-Mktg - Kansas City Chiefs Football Club, Inc.; *pg.* 555, *pg.* 984
Montgomery, Monica, Mgr-Mktg - American Dairy Queen Corporation; *pg.* 1714, *pg.* 930
Montgomery, Monica, Mgr-Mktg - Dairy Queen Corporate Store; *pg.* 1724, *pg.* 932
Montgomery, Myra W., Specialist-Mktg Comm & Event - Evonik Corporation; *pg.* 1162, *pg.* 1103
Montgomery, Nancy, Sr Dir-1 to 1 Consumer Comm - R.J. Reynolds Tobacco Co.; *pg.* 1895, *pg.* 1395
Montgomery, Niki, Mgr-Mktg-Global - 3M Company; *pg.* 1142, *pg.* 956
Montgomery, Paige, Head-Mktg-Cross-Audit Svcs - Deloitte & Touche USA LLP; *pg.* 743, *pg.* 1222
Montgomery, Stephanie, Assoc Dir-Media & Talent Rels - National Geographic Channel; *pg.* 299, *pg.* 402
Montgomery, Susan, Sr Specialist-Mktg Comm - Schneider Electric; *pg.* 467, *pg.* 1609
Montgomery, Tricia, VP-Product Mgmt & Consumer Experience - Outerwall Inc.; *pg.* 1367, *pg.* 1816
Monti, Daniele, VP-Global Creative-Teavana & Emerging Brands - Starbucks Corporation; *pg.* 897, *pg.* 1840
Monticelli, Mark, Assoc Dir-Health Sys Mktg - Astellas Pharma US, Inc.; *pg.* 1496, *pg.* 640
Monticolo, Marissa, Dir-Media - Capital Brands, LLC; *pg.* 53, *pg.* 127
Montini, Tony, Exec VP-Mdsg & Distr - Rite Aid Corporation; *pg.* 1590, *pg.* 1519
Montler, Joe, VP-Mktg, Strategy & Bus Dev - McKesson Corporation; *pg.* 1560, *pg.* 222
Montone, Al, Assoc Mgr-Social Media - Tervis Tumbler Company; *pg.* 1890, *pg.* 477
Montopoli, Paul, Dir-Mktg - Ferrari North America, Inc.; *pg.* 171, *pg.* 1060
Montour, Carol, Mgr-Channel Mktg - Multi-Tech Systems Inc.; *pg.* 442, *pg.* 951
Montour, Michael, Sr VP-Sls-North America - LivePerson, Inc.; *pg.* 1264, *pg.* 1252
Montoya, Alejandro, Dir-Mktg-High Growth Markets - Veeder-Root Company; *pg.* 61, *pg.* 371
Montoya, Paul, Pres-Media Sls-CBS Television Distr - CBS Broadcasting Inc.; *pg.* 273, *pg.* 1210
Montroy, Lisa, Asst Mgr-Product Mktg-Golf Balls - Acushnet Company; *pg.* 1824, *pg.* 818
Monturo, Celeste, Brand Mgr-Breakfast - Johnsonville Sausage, LLC; *pg.* 867, *pg.* 1894
Monument, Jennifer, Coord-Mktg Comm - Dollar Tree, Inc.; *pg.* 1767, *pg.* 1778
Monville, Charles, Specialist-Hematology Sls & Rotational Dev program - Novartis Corporation; *pg.* 1574, *pg.* 1273
Monzo, Julie, Sr Mgr-Global Medical & Dev-Corp Affairs - Astellas Pharma US, Inc.; *pg.* 1496, *pg.* 640
Mooberry, Derik, Sr VP-Products & Ops - Bally Technologies, Inc.; *pg.* 531, *pg.* 1022
Moodhe, Chris, Mgr-Mktg Res - Anthem, Inc.; *pg.* 1192, *pg.* 683
Moody, Alex, Mgr-Mktg-LAM - Schlumberger Limited; *pg.* 801, *pg.* 1714
Moody, Brooke, Dir-Strategic Product Initiatives - Cox Media Group; *pg.* 280, *pg.* 502
Moody, Chris, Dir-Mktg-Content & Social - Oracle Corporation; *pg.* 450, *pg.* 191
Moody, Elizabeth, Mgr-Product Mktg - Sun Trust Bank, Atlanta; *pg.* 806, *pg.* 520
Moody, Elizabeth, Mgr-Product Mktg - SunTrust Banks, Inc.; *pg.* 807, *pg.* 520
Moody, JD, Dir-Mktg-Intl - SKECHERS U.S.A., INC.; *pg.* 1819, *pg.* 143
Moody, Jessica, VP-Mktg - Grey House Publishing Corp.; *pg.* 1646, *pg.* 1137
Moody, Michelle, Mgr-Connected Vehicle Mktg - Ford Motor Company; *pg.* 172, *pg.* 876
Moody, Randy, Mgr-Ice Cream Sls - Purity Dairies, LLC; *pg.* 891, *pg.* 1653
Moody, Sandi T., Sr Dir-Bus Analysis - Chick-fil-A, Inc.; *pg.* 1721, *pg.* 492
Moody-Byrd, Gail, Sr Dir & Head-Integrated Plan Mktg-Integrated Digital - SAP America, Inc.; *pg.* 466, *pg.* 1557
Moody-St Clair, Sherie, Dir-Mktg - Idaho Lottery; *pg.* 995, *pg.* 547
Moolla, Roohi, Sr VP-Social Strategy & Trends-Enterprise Social Media - Wells Fargo & Company; *pg.* 819, *pg.* 232
Moomaw, Scott, Assoc VP-Mktg - United Therapeutics Corporation; *pg.* 1604, *pg.* 778
Moon, Andy, VP-Sls - Power Equipment Company inc; *pg.* 1369, *pg.* 1637
Moon, Annie, Mgr-Mktg-Sally Hansen & New York Color Cosmetics - Coty, Inc.; *pg.* 506, *pg.* 1219
Moon, Anthony, Sr Dir - PepsiCo, Inc.; *pg.* 259, *pg.* 1327
Moon, Grace, Coord-Creative & Mktg Svcs - New York Magazine; *pg.* 1667, *pg.* 1269
Moon, H. Christopher, Bus Mgr-USA - Purafil, Inc.; *pg.* 333, *pg.* 530
Moon, Kathy, Sr Dir-Plng, Analysis & Data Ops - Symantec Corporation; *pg.* 478, *pg.* 161
Moon, Leslie, Sr Specialist-Mktg - FedEx Corporation; *pg.* 1907, *pg.* 1642
Moon, Mark F., Pres-Sls & Product Ops & Exec VP - Motorola Solutions, Inc.; *pg.* 657, *pg.* 659
Moon, Pam, Sr Mgr-Global Named Accts Mktg - Autodesk Inc.; *pg.* 356, *pg.* 257
Moon, Seung H., Dir-Global aHUS Medical Mktg - Alexion Pharmaceuticals, Inc.; *pg.* 1489, *pg.* 341
Moon, Shawn D., Exec VP-Sls & Delivery-Global - Franklin Covey Co.; *pg.* 1642, *pg.* 1758
Moon, Tom, VP-Sls - Cosmopolitan; *pg.* 1630, *pg.* 1218
Moon, Virgina, Sr Assoc Brand Mgr - Del Monte Foods, Inc.; *pg.* 852, *pg.* 304
Moona, Tamara, Product Mgr-BlackBerry App World - BlackBerry Limited; *pg.* 625, *pg.* 1947
Mooney, Al, Product Mgr-Premiere Pro - Adobe Systems Incorporated; *pg.* 342, *pg.* 235
Mooney, Allison, Head-Trends & Insights, Mktg & Editor-in-Chief-Think with Google - Google Inc.; *pg.* 1249, *pg.* 153
Mooney, Dennis, Grp VP-Product Dev - Navistar International Corporation; *pg.* 186, *pg.* 630
Mooney, Jim, Corp Mgr-Toyota & Scion Dealer Product & Sls Engagement - Toyota Motor Sales, U.S.A., Inc.; *pg.* 193, *pg.* 296
Mooney, Kara, Dir-Creative Svcs - New York Yankees; *pg.* 570, *pg.* 1144
Mooney, Mark, VP-Digital & TV Ad Sls - The Weather Channel LLC; *pg.* 320, *pg.* 523
Mooney, Orla, Mgr-Product Line - Intel Corporation; *pg.* 645, *pg.* 266
Moonka, Rajas, Product Mgr-Grp Bus - Google Inc.; *pg.* 1249, *pg.* 153
Moor, Anthony, Dir-Product Mgmt - Yahoo! Inc.; *pg.* 1289, *pg.* 289
Moore, A. Scott, VP-Mktg-Worldwide - Anadarko Petroleum Corporation; *pg.* 971, *pg.* 1746
Moore, Alan, Dir-Sls & Mktg - Lippincott Williams & Wilkins,

First page reference indicates Business Class Edition
Second page reference indicates Geographic Edition

Inc.; pg. 1659, pg. 1567
Moore, Ashley, Mgr-Mktg-Hardgoods - PetSmart, Inc.; pg. 1481, pg. 18
Moore, Barbara Zinn, Sr VP & Gen Mgr-Mdsg-Cosmetics, Gifts & Gourmet - Lord & Taylor LLC; pg. 1777, pg. 1252
Moore, Billy, Dir-Adv - Kinston Free Press; pg. 1656, pg. 1380
Moore, Brad, Dir-Digital Adv Sls - Meredith Corporation; pg. 1663, pg. 705
Moore, Brenda, Product Mgr-CPG - Tree Top, Inc.; pg. 901, pg. 1843
Moore, Brent, Div VP-New Product Innovation & Supply Chain-Pharmavite - Nature Made Nutritional Products Inc.; pg. 883, pg. 148
Moore, Carolee Ettline, VP-Sls & Mktg - Crestline Hotels & Resorts, Inc.; pg. 1088, pg. 1779
Moore, Carrie, Mgr-Sls - Hyatt Hotels Corporation; pg. 1096, pg. 577
Moore, Carrie Foster, Sr Mgr-Corp Comm - Wal-Mart.com; pg. 1287, pg. 50
Moore, Chris, Sr Product Mgr-Product Svcs & Innovation - T-Mobile US, Inc.; pg. 676, pg. 1816
Moore, Chris, Brand Mgr - The Tire Rack Inc.; pg. 1890, pg. 697
Moore, Cory, VP-Creative & Original Content-Global - Gibson Guitar Corp.; pg. 550, pg. 1650
Moore, Deborah, Sr VP & Dir-Mktg-Home Lending - EverBank Financial Corp.; pg. 749, pg. 432
Moore, Declan, Chief Media Officer - National Geographic Society; pg. 1667, pg. 402
Moore, Dennis, VP-Sls & Mktg - Denver Broncos Football Club; pg. 544, pg. 325
Moore, Erin, Sr Mgr-Mktg - Hanesbrands Inc.; pg. 26, pg. 1394
Moore, Jaime, Mgr-Sls - Desert European Motorcars, Ltd.; pg. 169, pg. 187
Moore, James, Sr Product Mgr - IBM; pg. 410, pg. 1449
Moore, Jane, Head-Advancement - National Arts Centre Corporation; pg. 566, pg. 1932
Moore, Jeff, VP-Mechanical Sls-North America - Baldor Electric Company; pg. 1316, pg. 32
Moore, Jerry, VP-Mktg - Altec Industries Inc.; pg. 1312, pg. 1
Moore, Jessica, Brand Mgr - ACH Food Companies, Inc.; pg. 835, pg. 1631
Moore, John C, Head-Institutional Equity Sls & Trading - William Blair & Company LLC; pg. 822, pg. 596
Moore, Jon, VP-Mktg & eCommerce-Core Hotels-America's - Marriott International, Inc.; pg. 1102, pg. 764
Moore, Justin, Dir-Mktg - Weatherby, Inc.; pg. 1848, pg. 181
Moore, Karen L., Mgr-Adv - DMI Furniture, Inc.; pg. 923, pg. 733
Moore, Kate, VP-Mktg & PR - Grand Rapids Symphony Society; pg. 551, pg. 887
Moore, Kathleen, Mgr-Mktg & Exec Comm - Hewlett-Packard Company; pg. 404, pg. 175
Moore, Kathryn, Dir-Media - Raymour & Flanigan Furniture Co.; pg. 940, pg. 1174
Moore, Kelly, VP-Sls - Mohawk Home; pg. 935, pg. 541
Moore, Kelly, Brand Mgr - Sally Beauty Holdings, Inc.; pg. 522, pg. 1691
Moore, Ken, VP-Sls - ACS Industries, Inc.; pg. 1040, pg. 1602
Moore, Ken, Sr Mgr-Conversion Product Mgmt - Ancestry.com LLC; pg. 1228, pg. 1754
Moore, Ken, Dir-Retail Ops & Mdsg - Aubuchon Hardware; pg. 1043, pg. 859
Moore, Kenny, Reg Mgr-Mktg-Belvedere - LVMH Inc.; pg. 9, pg. 1254
Moore, Kimberly Williams, VP-Mktg & External Rels - North Carolina Mutual Life Insurance Company; pg. 1212, pg. 1372
Moore, Larry, VP-Mktg - Jeld-Wen, Inc.; pg. 1051, pg. 1499
Moore, Lindsay, Mgr-Brand Mktg Strategies - DSW, Inc.; pg. 1807, pg. 1439
Moore, Lindsey, Mgr-Corp Sponsorships Mktg & Activation - The PNC Financial Services Group, Inc.; pg. 795, pg. 1579
Moore, Lorien, Sr Dir & Head Intl Alliance & Project Mgmt - CUBIST PHARMACEUTICALS, INC.; pg. 1521, pg. 828
Moore, Mallory, Mgr-Media Optimization - DSW, Inc.; pg. 1807, pg. 1439
Moore, Marcia, VP-Mktg - Transamerica Insurance & Investment Group; pg. 1219, pg. 141
Moore, Mary, Mgr-Integrated Mktg - Inc.com LLC; pg. 1258, pg. 1243
Moore, Maureen, VP-Mktg & Comm - Fellowes, Inc.; pg. 397, pg. 620
Moore, Michael, Dir-Natl Fleet Sls - Aamco Transmissions, Inc.; pg. 197, pg. 1540
Moore, Michael, Head-Digital Mktg - Nestle Purina PetCare Company; pg. 1479, pg. 1000
Moore, Michael, VP & Gen Mgr-Call Center & Sls Ops - Sirius XM Holdings Inc.; pg. 308, pg. 1292
Moore, Michael J., Sr Dir-Comm & External Affairs - BP America Inc.; pg. 972, pg. 1702
Moore, Michele, Mgr-Media Buying-Progressive Insurance - The Progressive Corporation; pg. 1214, pg. 1463
Moore, Michelle, Dir-Mktg & Events - TradeStation Group, Inc.; pg. 811, pg. 459
Moore, Muneer, Sr Mgr-Player Svcs - National Football League Players Incorporated; pg. 149, pg. 401
Moore, Natalie, Dir-Mktg & Sls - Henkels & McCoy, Inc.; pg. 86, pg. 1517
Moore, Nicola, Product Mgr - Starbucks Corporation; pg. 897, pg. 1840
Moore, Owen Campbell, Assoc Product Mgr - Google Inc.; pg. 1249, pg. 153
Moore, Patricia, Program Mgr-Mktg Comm - Liberty Mutual Insurance Group Inc.; pg. 1205, pg. 797
Moore, Rachel, Assoc Dir-Media - Palisades Media Group, Inc.; pg. 452, pg. 275
Moore, Robert, Dir-Product Platforms & Svcs - The ADT Corporation; pg. 612, pg. 409
Moore, Robin, Mgr-Mktg - Huffy Corporation; pg. 1836, pg. 1409
Moore, Ron, Sr Product Mgr-MetLife Auto & Home - MetLife, Inc.; pg. 1208, pg. 1258
Moore, Ryan, Dir-Mktg Channel - Enterprise Holdings, Inc.; pg. 1906, pg. 996
Moore, Ryan, VP-Digital Sls - Sinclair Broadcast Group, Inc.; pg. 308, pg. 773
Moore, Ryan, Sr Mgr-Dev - Twitter, Inc.; pg. 1285, pg. 228
Moore, Scott, Sr VP-Mktg-US - Best Buy Co., Inc.; pg. 1761, pg. 954
Moore, Scott, Product Mgr-IT, Digital Asset Mgmt, Production & Inventory - Discovery Communications, Inc.; pg. 282, pg. 777
Moore, Scott P., Dir-Security Mktg-Americas - Hewlett-Packard Company; pg. 404, pg. 175
Moore, Serena, Brand Mgr-Shopper Mktg - Colgate-Palmolive Company; pg. 504, pg. 1215
Moore, Seth, VP-Mktg-Website & Mobile - Overstock.com, Inc.; pg. 1273, pg. 1760
Moore, Sharelynn, VP-Corp Mktg & Pub Affairs - Itron Inc.; pg. 422, pg. 1822
Moore, Sophie, Mgr-PR & Comm - Community Health Systems, Inc.; pg. 1516, pg. 1632
Moore, Stacey, VP-Legal Affairs-Global Supply Chain & Comml Products - Newell Rubbermaid Inc.; pg. 1128, pg. 515
Moore, Stephanie, Head-Digital Mktg-Consumer Goods & Svcs - Accenture; pg. 1392, pg. 1186
Moore, Susan, Product Mgr-Mobile Channel - Sun Trust Bank, Atlanta; pg. 806, pg. 520
Moore, Timothy, Sr Mgr-Mktg Activation & ECommerce - adidas America Inc.; pg. 1803, pg. 1500
Moore, Tracy, Sr VP-Mdsg - C&S Wholesale Grocers, Inc.; pg. 1016, pg. 1035
Moore, Vanessa, Analyst-Mktg Svcs - 3M Company; pg. 1142, pg. 956
Moore, Wesley, Dir-Mktg-Americas - FLIR Systems, Inc.; pg. 1413, pg. 1510
Moore, Wesley, VP-Mktg - Teradata Corporation; pg. 483, pg. 1447
Moore-Dreby, Kacey, Grp Brand Dir - Johnson & Johnson; pg. 1549, pg. 1091
Moorehead, Denise M., Dir-Digital Media Ops & Optimization - Electronic Arts Inc.; pg. 951, pg. 189
Moorehead, Paul, VP & Dir-Creative-Mktg - United States Beverage LLC; pg. 266, pg. 379
Moorhead, John, Brand Mgr - Seventh Generation, Inc.; pg. 335, pg. 1765
Moorhead, Linda, Dir-Corp Mktg - Bergstrom Automotive; pg. 166, pg. 1883
Mooring, Joey, Dir-PR - GameStop Corp.; pg. 399, pg. 1699
Moorlag, Ryan, Mgr-Assoc Mktg - The Toro Company; pg. 1065, pg. 918
Moosher, Kenneth, Sr Mgr-Sls & Mktg Compliance - TracFone Wireless, Inc.; pg. 681, pg. 447
Mora, Claudia, Mgr-Mktg - Savaria Concord Lifts Inc.; pg. 1592, pg. 1919
Mora, Duane, Sr VP-Sls & New Bus Dev - Jackson Hewitt Tax Service Inc.; pg. 771, pg. 1103
Mora, Randy, Sr Dir-US Sls Natl Retail - New Age Electronics, Inc.; pg. 659, pg. 63
Morain, Vicki, Brand Mgr-Shopper Mktg - SUPERVALU, Inc.; pg. 1035, pg. 924
Moraitakis, Mark, Sr Dir-Hospitality & Svc Design - Chick-fil-A, Inc.; pg. 1721, pg. 492
Morakis, Tony, Sr Dir-Shared Brand Building Svcs - Georgia-Pacific LLC; pg. 1458, pg. 507
Morales, Amanda, Coord-Mktg - AutoNation, Inc.; pg. 165, pg. 423
Morales, Cody, Assoc Brand Mgr-PlayStation Platform Mktg - Sony Computer Entertainment America LLC; pg. 966, pg. 256
Morales, Denise, Sr Dir-Mktg - Live Nation Entertainment, Inc.; pg. 558, pg. 47
Morales, Haydee, Dir-Wardrobe & Designer-Costume - Miami City Ballet, Inc.; pg. 562, pg. 448
Morales, Juan, Product Mgr-UL Compliant Fuse - Littelfuse, Inc.; pg. 1301, pg. 580
Morales, Kim, Mgr-Mktg & Media Strategy - Bloomin' Brands, Inc.; pg. 1716, pg. 471
Morales, Lorenzo, Mgr-Digital Mktg Tech - Electrolux Home Products North America; pg. 54, pg. 1366
Morales, Lucia, Dir-Mktg & Pro Svcs - Brady/TISCOR, Inc.; pg. 364, pg. 200
Morales, Lucio, Assoc Product Mgr - Hitachi Koki USA, Ltd.; pg. 1050, pg. 537
Morales, Natalia, Sr Mgr-Strategy & Bus Plng - American Express Company; pg. 712, pg. 1190
Morales, Rachel, Mgr-Mktg & Brand Dev - Goodwill Industries International, Inc.; pg. 1771, pg. 776
Morales, Sara, Sr Mgr-Corp Partnership Activation - Anaheim Ducks Hockey Club, LLC; pg. 528, pg. 42
Morales, Sergio, Dir-Retail & Brand Ready Packaging Sls - Genuine Parts Company; pg. 206, pg. 506
Morales, Sergio, Dir-Product & Brand Dev - Georgia-Pacific LLC; pg. 1458, pg. 507
Morales, Yuri, Head-Sponsorships LAC & Sr Dir - Visa Inc.; pg. 816, pg. 230
Morales, Yuri, Head-Sponsorships LAC & Sr Dir - Visa U.S.A., Inc.; pg. 817, pg. 231
Moran, Amy L., Sr Specialist-Mktg & Comm - WNET.org; pg. 322, pg. 1315
Moran, Chelsea, Sr Specialist-Mktg Project Mgmt - Target Corporation; pg. 1786, pg. 942
Moran, Chris, Specialist-PR - Nevada Commission on Tourism; pg. 1000, pg. 1021
Moran, Christine, Analyst-Mktg-Swing line - ACCO Brands Corporation; pg. 340, pg. 626
Moran, Coline, Specialist-Mktg - Zale Corporation; pg. 16, pg. 1724
Moran, David, Exec VP-Mktg & Strategy-Global - Carlson Wagonlit Travel; pg. 1902, pg. 948
Moran, Diana, VP-Media - Movado Group, Inc.; pg. 10, pg. 1101
Moran, Eileen, VP-Adv - MAACO Franchising, Inc.; pg. 211, pg. 1367
Moran, Gerry, Head-Social Media & Content-Global - Cognizant Technology Solutions Corporation; pg. 377, pg. 1124
Moran, Jeffrey, VP-PR, Events & Lifestyle Mktg - Pernod Ricard USA, Inc.; pg. 1968, pg. 1332
Moran, Jessica, Specialist-Interactive Mktg - Marshalls of MA, Inc.; pg. 1778, pg. 821
Moran, Jessica, Supvr-Interactive Mktg - T.J. Maxx; pg. 1788, pg. 822
Moran, Jessica, Specialist-Interactive Mktg - The TJX Companies, Inc.; pg. 1788, pg. 822
Moran, John, Dir-PR - United Technologies Corporation; pg. 235, pg. 353
Moran, Laura, Mgr-Media Rels - HubSpot, Inc.; pg. 409, pg. 808
Moran, Margaret, Brand Mgr-Westin & Sheraton - Starwood Hotels & Resorts Worldwide, Inc.; pg. 1114, pg. 378
Moran, Mark, Sr VP-Mktg & Distr - Ebates.com; pg. 1240, pg. 217
Moran, Patrick, Sr Dir-Mktg - TiVo Inc.; pg. 313, pg. 251
Moran, Patti, Dir-Mktg - Avaya Inc.; pg. 621, pg. 264
Moran, Russ, VP-Mktg - MarkWest Energy Partners, L.P.; pg. 981, pg. 321
Moran, Sean, Exec VP-Ad Sls & Integrated Mktg-Music & Entertainment - MTVN Video Hits Inc.; pg. 299, pg. 1263

Moran, Sean, Exec VP-Linear & Digital Ad Sls & Integrated Mktg - Viacom Inc.; *pg.* 316, *pg.* 1310
Moran, Todd, Dir-Social Enterprise - Schneider Electric USA, Inc.; *pg.* 1306, *pg.* 650
Moran, Tofer, Creative Dir - Combe Incorporated; *pg.* 1516, *pg.* 1351
Moran, Tracy, Product Mgr-Stanley Black & Decker, Inc - DeWALT Industrial Tool Company; *pg.* 1328, *pg.* 757
Morant, Mark, Pres-Products & Tech - EnergySolutions Inc.; *pg.* 1941, *pg.* 1757
Morante, Steve, VP-Field Sls - Bayer Healthcare Consumer Care Division; *pg.* 1500, *pg.* 1087
Morato, Nina, Coord-Multi- Market Mktg - Univision Communications Inc.; *pg.* 683, *pg.* 1307
Morawetz, Carolina, Mgr-Mktg-Collaboration Solutions-Latin America - Cisco Systems, Inc.; *pg.* 372, *pg.* 240
Mordekai, Jodi, Brand Mgr - Post Holdings, Inc.; *pg.* 833, *pg.* 1002
Morden, Christopher, Mgr-Mktg Comm - Ford Motor Company of Canada, Limited; *pg.* 174, *pg.* 1930
Morea, Liz, Coord-Mktg, Print - Jeffers, Inc.; *pg.* 1477, *pg.* 5
Moreau, Brandy, Coord-Media - Abt Electronics, Inc.; *pg.* 612, *pg.* 614
Moreau, Ellen, VP-Mktg Comm - Sherwin Williams; *pg.* 1448, *pg.* 1436
Morehart, Susan, Dir-Sls & Mktg - Stearns Products Inc.; *pg.* 523, *pg.* 279
Morehead, Don, Mgr-Sls-Natl - KWWL-TV; *pg.* 295, *pg.* 712
Morehead, James, Product Mgr - Google Inc.; *pg.* 1249, *pg.* 153
Morehouse, Alicia, Mgr-Channel Mktg - Western Digital Corporation; *pg.* 492, *pg.* 118
Morehouse, Susan, Sr Mgr-Mktg - Alcatel-Lucent USA, Inc.; *pg.* 615, *pg.* 1728
Moreira, Carla, Mgr-Mktg - Cost Plus World Market; *pg.* 921, *pg.* 170
Moreira, Jessica, VP-Mktg - Citizens Financial Group, Inc.; *pg.* 737, *pg.* 1606
Morel, Joy, Sr Dir-Global Branding, Adv & Creative Svcs - VeriSign, Inc.; *pg.* 488, *pg.* 1799
Moreland, Anthony, VP-Sls-North America - Bell Helicopter Textron, Inc.; *pg.* 224, *pg.* 1693
Moreland, Antonieta, Brand Mgr - YUM! Brands, Inc.; *pg.* 1756, *pg.* 738
Morell, Kelly, Sr Mgr - Meredith Corporation; *pg.* 1663, *pg.* 705
Morell, Tanya, Dir-Direct & Loyalty Mktg - Holland America Line Inc.; *pg.* 1911, *pg.* 1836
Morelli, Andreia, Dir-Mktg LAC - American Express Company; *pg.* 712, *pg.* 1190
Morelli, Maryellen, Sr Mgr-Conference - Gartner, Inc.; *pg.* 1248, *pg.* 374
Morelli, Michele, VP-Bus & Consumer Mktg - AOL Inc.; *pg.* 1229, *pg.* 1195
Morelli, Tim, Mgr-Emerging Media & Content - Zumiez Inc.; *pg.* 16, *pg.* 1822
Moren, Cassandra, Sr Dir-CG & Retail Solutions Indus Mktg - Oracle Corporation; *pg.* 450, *pg.* 191
Morena, Jessica, Brand Mgr-Innovation - Colgate-Palmolive Company; *pg.* 504, *pg.* 1215
Moreno, Aracely, Sr Dir-Mktg - Frito-Lay North America, Inc.; *pg.* 1853, *pg.* 1730
Moreno, Brianna, Brand Mgr-Comm - Reebok International Ltd.; *pg.* 1817, *pg.* 811
Moreno, Emi, Brand Mgr - The Procter & Gamble Company; *pg.* 1129, *pg.* 1418
Moreno, Monse, Mgr-Multicultural Sls Dev - Pandora Media Inc.; *pg.* 1273, *pg.* 172
Moreno, Neil, Sr Producer-Creative Media Svcs-Natl Mktg - BMW of North America, LLC; *pg.* 166, *pg.* 1133
Moreno, Orlando, Mgr-Mktg-Ophthalmology - Abbott Medical Optics, Inc.; *pg.* 1485, *pg.* 260
Moreno-Nickerson, Federico, Dir-Product Dev Caribbean, Costa Rica & Mexico - Classic Vacations, LLC; *pg.* 1903, *pg.* 242
Morentin, Liz, Sr VP-Corp Comm, Publicity & Mktg - dick clark productions, inc.; *pg.* 281, *pg.* 273
Morera, Ofelia, Grp Mgr-Mktg Comm - Verizon Communications Inc.; *pg.* 1875, *pg.* 1309
Moret, Blake, Sr VP-Control Products & Solutions - Rockwell Automation, Inc.; *pg.* 668, *pg.* 1880
Moreton, William W., Interim CFO - Panera Bread Company; *pg.* 1029, *pg.* 1001
Moretti, Joanne, VP & Head-Global Software Mktg - Dell Inc.; *pg.* 383, *pg.* 1737
Moretti, Joanne, Sr VP-Mktg & Sls Enablement - Jabil Circuit, Inc.; *pg.* 422, *pg.* 463
Moretz, Linda, Mgr-Product Dev - Broyhill Furniture Industries, Inc.; *pg.* 919, *pg.* 1381
Morey, Mark E., Dir-Mktg - Hormel Foods Corporation; *pg.* 863, *pg.* 915
Morey-Reuner, Margaret, Dir-Strategic Partnerships, Bus Dev & Values Mktg - The Timberland Company; *pg.* 1821, *pg.* 1039
Moreyra, Christina, Mgr-Mktg-Web Analytics - Ally Financial Inc.; *pg.* 711, *pg.* 878
Morga, Jason S., VP-Mktg-Americas - Kelly Services, Inc.; *pg.* 424, *pg.* 911
Morgan, Aaron, Sr Mgr-Social Media - Pandora Media Inc.; *pg.* 1273, *pg.* 172
Morgan, Adrian, Mgr-Mktg Ops - Riverbed Technology, Inc.; *pg.* 1277, *pg.* 225
Morgan, Amy, Mgr-Digital Mktg & PR - ConAgra Foods, Inc.; *pg.* 826, *pg.* 1014
Morgan, Andrea, Mgr-Affiliate Mktg - Sephora USA Inc; *pg.* 522, *pg.* 227
Morgan, Andrea, Sr Mgr-New Products Mktg - Varian Medical Systems, Inc.; *pg.* 1434, *pg.* 178
Morgan, Ashley, Coord-PR - IBERIABANK Corporation; *pg.* 768, *pg.* 744
Morgan, Bill, Sr VP-Mktg - Motorola Mobility LLC; *pg.* 657, *pg.* 627
Morgan, Blake, Program Mgr-Social Media-Digital Support - Intel Corporation; *pg.* 645, *pg.* 266
Morgan, Brad, Sr Dir-Protein - Performance Food Group Company, LLC; *pg.* 1030, *pg.* 1803
Morgan, Bryce, Mgr-Strategic Mktg - Atmel Corporation; *pg.* 621, *pg.* 238
Morgan, Chris, Product Dir-Mgmt-OpenShift Partner Ecosystem - Red Hat, Inc.; *pg.* 460, *pg.* 1388
Morgan, Christopher, District Mgr-Sls-New England - Mohawk Fine Papers, Inc.; *pg.* 1464, *pg.* 1153
Morgan, Cindy, Sr Mgr-Adv, Mktg & Acq - ChildFund International; *pg.* 137, *pg.* 1801
Morgan, Colin, Reg Product Mgr-Bus Solutions - Videojet Technologies Inc.; *pg.* 489, *pg.* 671
Morgan, Dan, Chief Sls Officer - Snyder's-Lance, Inc.; *pg.* 896, *pg.* 1368
Morgan, David, Sr Mgr-Ad Valorem Tax - Murphy Oil Corporation; *pg.* 982, *pg.* 31
Morgan, David L., Mgr-Mktg Res - Delphi Automotive LLP; *pg.* 204, *pg.* 910
Morgan, Evelyn, Sr Mgr-Ops & Sr Community - Microsoft Corporation; *pg.* 435, *pg.* 1824
Morgan, Grace, Dir-Mktg Ops & Partnerships-Global - General Motors Company; *pg.* 175, *pg.* 881
Morgan, Heather, Dir-Products, Risk & Compliance - Dow Jones & Company, Inc.; *pg.* 1637, *pg.* 1225
Morgan, Jeremy, Sr VP-Mktg & Consumer Insights - Smashburger Master LLC; *pg.* 1750, *pg.* 323
Morgan, Jim, Dir-Sls & Ops-Global - Fike Corporation; *pg.* 1047, *pg.* 973
Morgan, Jim, Brand Mgr-Fin - Heineken USA Inc.; *pg.* 252, *pg.* 1352
Morgan, John, S Dir-Sls - Tyson Foods, Inc.; *pg.* 902, *pg.* 35
Morgan, Justin, Dir-Mktg Technologies - Comcast Cable Communications, Inc.; *pg.* 276, *pg.* 1560
Morgan, Kamaria, Head-Project-Media - Delta Air Lines, Inc.; *pg.* 1905, *pg.* 503
Morgan, Kevin, Dir-Mktg Comm - ADTRAN, Inc.; *pg.* 344, *pg.* 6
Morgan, Linda, Mgr-Creative Dev - MetroPCS, Inc.; *pg.* 1872, *pg.* 1683
Morgan, Lindsey, Brand Mgr-Horizon Organic - The WhiteWave Foods Company; *pg.* 1037, *pg.* 324
Morgan, Mark A., VP-Sls & Comm - ScanSource, Inc.; *pg.* 671, *pg.* 1618
Morgan, Neil, Dir-Sls - Sanderson Farms, Inc.; *pg.* 893, *pg.* 970
Morgan, Pam, Project Mgr-Mktg - Medtronic, Inc.; *pg.* 1564, *pg.* 939
Morgan, Patty, Sr Dir-Security & Risk - Wal-Mart Stores, Inc.; *pg.* 1790, *pg.* 29
Morgan, Paula, Mgr-Retail Mktg - SKECHERS U.S.A., INC.; *pg.* 1819, *pg.* 143
Morgan, Rachael, Assoc Dir-Sls - Hyatt Hotels Corporation; *pg.* 1096, *pg.* 577
Morgan, Rhonda, Sr Dir-Employee Comm - Parametric Technology Corporation; *pg.* 452, *pg.* 835
Morgan, Sylvia, Category Mgr-Global Procurement-Mktg Svcs - InterContinental Hotels Corporation; *pg.* 1097, *pg.* 511
Morgan, Tara, Mgr-PR & Comm - SI Group, Inc.; *pg.* 1181, *pg.* 1341
Morgan, Tom, Mgr-Mktg - Netflix, Inc.; *pg.* 1269, *pg.* 141
Morgan, Tracy, Mgr-In House Mktg - Bluegreen Corporation; *pg.* 1082, *pg.* 410
Morgan, Wes, Dir-Product Mgmt-ITT Cannon - ITT Corporation; *pg.* 1351, *pg.* 1354
Morgan-Moscowitz, Sara, Sr VP-Brand & Strategic Mktg - Syfy; *pg.* 311, *pg.* 1297
Morgenstein, Lauren, Brand Mgr-NA Ecommerce - The Procter & Gamble Company; *pg.* 1129, *pg.* 1418
Morgenstern, Harold, Sr VP-Adv Sls, Digital Media - Discovery Communications, Inc.; *pg.* 282, *pg.* 777
Morgenstern, Harold, Sr VP-Adv Sls-Eastern Reg - Travel Channel LLC; *pg.* 313, *pg.* 766
Morgenstern, Roger C., Sr Dir-Pub Info - CMS Energy Corporation; *pg.* 1937, *pg.* 893
Morhardt, Connor, Sr Mgr-ECommerce & Digital Activation - Nestle Waters North America Inc.; *pg.* 257, *pg.* 375
Mori, Janelle, Mgr-Digital Mktg - Alfred Angelo, Inc.; *pg.* 17, *pg.* 1532
Mori, Michael, Dir-Sls - The Blade Co.; *pg.* 1621, *pg.* 1476
Moriarity, Betty, VP-Mktg - National Penn Bancshares, Inc.; *pg.* 786, *pg.* 1517
Moriarty, Allison B., VP-Sls & Mktg Raleigh Div - M/I Homes, Inc.; *pg.* 95, *pg.* 1441
Moriarty, Ita, Sr VP-Convention Sls - Greater Miami Convention & Visitors Bureau; *pg.* 993, *pg.* 442
Moriarty, Thomas M., Chief Health Care Strategy Officer, Gen Counsel & Exec VP - CVS Health Corporation; *pg.* 1765, *pg.* 1610
Moriber, Samantha, Coord-Media - Chanel, Inc.; *pg.* 503, *pg.* 1211
Morici, Antonio, Dir-Premium Sls & Svcs - Los Angeles Dodgers Inc.; *pg.* 559, *pg.* 135
Morikawa, Darlene, Dir-PR & Comm - Hawaii Visitors & Convention Bureau; *pg.* 994, *pg.* 543
Morin, Barry, Sr VP-Mktg - Amscan Holdings, Inc.; *pg.* 1760, *pg.* 1158
Morin, Christine, Sr Specialist-Mktg Comm - American International Group, Inc.; *pg.* 1190, *pg.* 1193
Morin, Claude, VP-Sls-Global - Air Canada; *pg.* 1896, *pg.* 1902
Morin, Courtney, Mgr-Digital Mktg - Saks Fifth Avenue, Inc.; *pg.* 1783, *pg.* 1287
Morin, Dianne, Dir-Mktg & Comm - Fiserv, Inc.; *pg.* 758, *pg.* 537
Morin, Noelle, Reg Dir-Mktg - Anheuser-Busch Companies, LLC; *pg.* 237, *pg.* 991
Morishita, Eric, Sr Product Mgr - Abbott Laboratories; *pg.* 1484, *pg.* 551
Moritz, Stephanie, Chief Comm Officer-Mktg & Comm - The American Dental Association; *pg.* 127, *pg.* 564
Morkri, Christopher, Sr Dir-Art-Digital & Interactive - Lands' End, Inc.; *pg.* 1776, *pg.* 1857
Morley, Adam, Dir-Intl Mktg - Electronic Arts Inc.; *pg.* 951, *pg.* 189
Morley, Jean, Dir-Creative Svcs-Wiley Content Mgmt & Tech - John Wiley & Sons, Inc.; *pg.* 1655, *pg.* 1073
Morley, Larry, Dir-Sls - Edison Properties, LLC; *pg.* 1906, *pg.* 1096
Mormack, Paul, Sr Program Mgr-Mktg Comm - The Hanover Insurance Company; *pg.* 1202, *pg.* 862
Mormoris, Steve, CMO & Sr VP-Global Mktg Fragrances - Coty, Inc.; *pg.* 506, *pg.* 1219
Morningstar, Bill, Sr VP-Sponsorship Sls - MLB Network; *pg.* 298, *pg.* 1120
Morningstar, Jamie, VP-Ticket Sls & Svc - Milwaukee Bucks, Inc.; *pg.* 563, *pg.* 1878
Moro, Barb, Sr Mgr-Adv Support - Microsoft Corporation; *pg.* 435, *pg.* 1824
Morog, Jessica, Product Mgr-HCP Mktg-Abbott Diabetes Care - Abbott Laboratories; *pg.* 1484, *pg.* 551
Moroney, Eileen, VP-Digital Adv Bus & Ops - National Geographic Society; *pg.* 1667, *pg.* 402
Morosanu, Catalin, VP-Sls & Mktg-Europe Middle East & Africa - Cray Inc.; *pg.* 380, *pg.* 1834
Moroz, Brian, Sr Mgr-Agency Relationship-Creative - Google Inc.; *pg.* 1249, *pg.* 153
Moroze, Wendy, Mgr-Mktg - Party City Corporation; *pg.* 1781, *pg.* 1116
Morphew, Juliet, Mgr-Comml Sls - Protection One, Inc.; *pg.* 665, *pg.* 715
Morr, Tania, Dir-Database Mktg - Williams-Sonoma, Inc.; *pg.*

1140, *pg.* 234
Morra, Sarah, Assoc Mgr-Mktg - The Clorox Company; *pg.* 327, *pg.* 169
Morreal, Bill, VP-Mktg - Juno Lighting Group; *pg.* 648, *pg.* 679
Morreale, Tony, Mgr-PR - Turner Broadcasting System, Inc.; *pg.* 314, *pg.* 521
Morrell, Amy, Assoc Dir-Mktg & HCP Promos-Women's Health - Merck & Co., Inc.; *pg.* 1566, *pg.* 1077
Morrell, Blyth, Asst Dir-Mktg & Strategic Comm - Duke University; *pg.* 600, *pg.* 1371
Morrell, Carly, Sr Specialist-Digital Mktg - The ADT Corporation; *pg.* 612, *pg.* 409
Morris, Aaron, Product Mgr-Reality Capture - Autodesk Inc.; *pg.* 356, *pg.* 257
Morris, Andrea, Mgr-Mktg - Frito-Lay North America, Inc.; *pg.* 1853, *pg.* 1730
Morris, Brad, VP-Sls - Milan Express Co., Inc.; *pg.* 1916, *pg.* 1647
Morris, Carly, Sr Specialist-PR - Best Buy Co., Inc.; *pg.* 1761, *pg.* 954
Morris, Catherine, Chief Strategy Officer & Sr VP - Arrow Electronics, Inc.; *pg.* 619, *pg.* 325
Morris, Craig, Dir-Mktg - GlaxoSmithKline; *pg.* 1536, *pg.* 1389
Morris, Daniel, Dir-Product Mgmt - RACKSPACE HOSTING, INC.; *pg.* 1277, *pg.* 1742
Morris, Haley, Specialist-Mktg Ops - Pegasystems Inc.; *pg.* 453, *pg.* 74
Morris, Jim, Mgr-Strategic Sls - Cars.com; *pg.* 1234, *pg.* 568
Morris, John, Mgr-Mktg - Foot Locker, Inc.; *pg.* 1808, *pg.* 1231
Morris, John, VP-Adv & Media - Travelers Insurance; *pg.* 1220, *pg.* 963
Morris, Joshua, Sr Mgr-Digital Media - Ubisoft Inc.; *pg.* 589, *pg.* 229
Morris, Juliette, Exec VP-Partner Mktg & Comm - NBC Universal, Inc.; *pg.* 300, *pg.* 1266
Morris, Kit, Dir-College Sports Mktg - NIKE, Inc.; *pg.* 1812, *pg.* 1492
Morris, Laure, Sr Mgr-Digital Mktg & Media - Mondelez International, Inc.; *pg.* 878, *pg.* 601
Morris, Les, Dir-Corp PR - Simon Property Group, Inc.; *pg.* 1112, *pg.* 690
Morris, Lisa, VP-Mktg - L'Oreal USA; *pg.* 514, *pg.* 1252
Morris, Lydia, VP-Consumer Mktg - Time Inc.; *pg.* 1693, *pg.* 1300
Morris, Maria, Mgr-Integrated Mktg Campaign - American Family Mutual Insurance Company; *pg.* 1190, *pg.* 1864
Morris, Mark, Sr Product Mgr-Archtics - Ticketmaster Entertainment LLC; *pg.* 1284, *pg.* 48
Morris, Patrick, Coord-Mktg-Sports Mgmt-SEC Network - ESPN, Inc.; *pg.* 285, *pg.* 340
Morris, Patty, Dir-Mktg & Brand Content - State Farm Mutual Automobile Insurance Co.; *pg.* 1218, *pg.* 557
Morris, Rachel, Head-Makeup Mktg - L'Oreal USA; *pg.* 514, *pg.* 1252
Morris, Rebecca, Dir-Mktg - KB Home; *pg.* 90, *pg.* 134
Morris, Richard, VP-Consumer Products Plng & Partnerships - Viacom Inc.; *pg.* 316, *pg.* 1310
Morris, Roberta, VP & Gen Mgr-Water & Lab Products - Thermo Fisher Scientific Inc.; *pg.* 1431, *pg.* 854
Morris, Scott, Sr Dir-Mktg-Creative Cloud & Creative Suite - Adobe Systems Incorporated; *pg.* 342, *pg.* 235
Morris, Seth, Mgr-Online Media - Penguin Random House; *pg.* 1675, *pg.* 1276
Morris, Seth, Mgr-Online Media - Penguin Random House; *pg.* 1675, *pg.* 1276
Morris, Shelley M., Chief Strategy Officer & Exec VP - New Horizons Worldwide, Inc.; *pg.* 445, *pg.* 43
Morris, Susan, Brand Mgr - Chattem, Inc.; *pg.* 1515, *pg.* 1628
Morris, Thomas, Mgr-Channel Sls - Hitachi America, Ltd.; *pg.* 642, *pg.* 1344
Morris, Tim, Sr VP-Sls, Mkt Dev & Customer Support-Americas Region - JLG Industries, Inc.; *pg.* 1351, *pg.* 1551
Morrish, Lydia, Mgr-Mktg-Asset Mgmt - PricewaterhouseCoopers LLP; *pg.* 795, *pg.* 1283
Morrish, Ruth, Specialist-Mktg - Honeywell International Inc.; *pg.* 407, *pg.* 1088
Morrison, Anna, Sr Strategist-Digital Mktg - Penn State University; *pg.* 606, *pg.* 1589
Morrison, Bill, VP-Mktg Comm-Global - Emerson Process Management; *pg.* 1334, *pg.* 1636
Morrison, Bob, Sr Dir-Ad Product Solutions - Yahoo! Inc.; *pg.* 1289, *pg.* 289
Morrison, Brad, Dir-Sls & Mktg - Total System Services, Inc.; *pg.* 484, *pg.* 528
Morrison, Brian, Assoc Dir-Digital Adv - John Wiley & Sons, Inc.; *pg.* 1655, *pg.* 1073
Morrison, Bruce, Exec VP-Global Sls & Licensing - MGA Entertainment, Inc.; *pg.* 964, *pg.* 300
Morrison, Caroline, VP-Creative Mktg - The Children's Place, Inc.; *pg.* 22, *pg.* 1119
Morrison, Dana, Mgr-Field Mktg Ops-North America - CA Technologies; *pg.* 366, *pg.* 1168
Morrison, Devlin O., Assoc Dir-Mktg-US HIV - Merck & Co., Inc.; *pg.* 1566, *pg.* 1077
Morrison, Diane L., VP-Sls & Mktg-Natl Homebuilding - CalAtlantic Group, Inc.; *pg.* 1084, *pg.* 108
Morrison, Emily, Asst Mgr-Mktg - The Gatorade Company; *pg.* 251, *pg.* 574
Morrison, Geraldine, Sr Head-Mktg-Emerging Trials & Brand Partnerships - Sprint Corporation; *pg.* 1874, *pg.* 719
Morrison, Glenda, Sr Dir-HR - Houston Texans, L.P.; *pg.* 553, *pg.* 1708
Morrison, Jason, Head-Mktg & Comm-Hublot - LVMH Inc.; *pg.* 9, *pg.* 1254
Morrison, Jennifer, Mgr-Music & Social Media Promos-CMT Digital Media - Country Music Television, Inc.; *pg.* 279, *pg.* 1649
Morrison, Jennifer, Area Dir-Mktg & Bus Dev - Simon Property Group, Inc.; *pg.* 1112, *pg.* 690
Morrison, Jim, Dir-Jeep Mktg - FCA US LLC; *pg.* 170, *pg.* 868
Morrison, Kelly, Dir-Mktg & Product Mgmt - Cardinal Health, Inc.; *pg.* 1512, *pg.* 1448
Morrison, Kevin, VP-Mktg Comm - Equifax Inc.; *pg.* 748, *pg.* 504
Morrison, Marin, Brand Mgr-Robert Half Mgmt Resources, Fin & Acctg - Robert Half International Inc.; *pg.* 462, *pg.* 145
Morrison, Patty, Mgr-Product Mktg - Panasonic Electric Works Corporation of America; *pg.* 661, *pg.* 1095
Morrison, Pete, VP-Mktg - Bassett Furniture Industries, Incorporated; *pg.* 916, *pg.* 1776
Morrison, Rachael, Dir-Sls-Personal Care Div - The Hain Celestial Group, Inc.; *pg.* 860, *pg.* 1172
Morrison, Scott, Mgr-Local Sls - WMOR; *pg.* 322, *pg.* 476
Morrison, Terry, Mgr-Mktg & Comm-North America - CNH America LLC; *pg.* 702, *pg.* 560
Morrison, William, Sr Mgr-Global Packaging - Microsoft Corporation; *pg.* 435, *pg.* 1824
Morrissey, Chelsea, Brand Mgr-Nerf Global - Hasbro, Inc.; *pg.* 954, *pg.* 1603
Morrissey, John A., Dir-Bus Ops & Mktg - Chicago Rivet & Machine Company; *pg.* 1323, *pg.* 636
Morrissey, Julie, Mgr-Digital Mktg Strategy-Natl - BDO Seidman, LLP; *pg.* 724, *pg.* 1202
Morrissey, Lyndell, Dir-Central Reg Media & Commercialization - Coca-Cola North America; *pg.* 848, *pg.* 500
Morrissey, Megan, VP-Mktg - Thule, Inc.; *pg.* 218, *pg.* 369
Morrissey, Patrick, VP-Sls - Electronics For Imaging, Inc.; *pg.* 390, *pg.* 88
Morrissey, Ryan, Sr Dir-Product Strategy - 8x8, Inc.; *pg.* 1865, *pg.* 282
Morrissey, Stephen, Dir-Mktg & Comm - Intelligentsia Coffee, Inc.; *pg.* 865, *pg.* 578
Morrissey, Tom, Sr Dir-Legal Ops & eDiscovery - Purdue Pharma LP; *pg.* 1587, *pg.* 377
Morrissey, Victoria, Dir-Brand & Content Mktg - W.W. Grainger, Inc.; *pg.* 1390, *pg.* 625
Morrone, Peter, Sr VP-Product Engrg - ChyronHego; *pg.* 371, *pg.* 1179
Morros, Jason, Dir-Mktg & Mdsg-My M&Ms - Mars, Incorporated; *pg.* 1858, *pg.* 1792
Morrow, Barbara, Mgr-Digital Media & Conference Svcs - RAND WORLDWIDE, INC.; *pg.* 459, *pg.* 821
Morrow, Branden, Coord-Mktg Svcs - Oklahoma City Thunder; *pg.* 571, *pg.* 1487
Morrow, Brenda, Mgr-PR-Northeast & Midwest Regions - Chick-fil-A, Inc.; *pg.* 1721, *pg.* 492
Morrow, Scott, Engr-Sys Sls - Edlund Company, Inc.; *pg.* 1123, *pg.* 1765
Morrow, Steve, VP-Sls - Fiske Brothers Refining Company; *pg.* 978, *pg.* 1096
Morsches, Gary, Mng Dir-Energy Products - CME Group Inc.; *pg.* 738, *pg.* 571
Morse, Berit, Sr Mgr-Loyalty Platforms - General Mills, Inc.; *pg.* 828, *pg.* 933
Morse, Lisa, Sr Mgr-Mktg Svcs - Marvin Windows & Doors; *pg.* 934, *pg.* 965
Morse, Mark, Dir-Mktg-Hot Wheels - MATTEL, INC.; *pg.* 962, *pg.* 81
Morse, Robb, Dir-Mktg - Magellan Diagnostics; *pg.* 1557, *pg.* 838
Morse, Stephen, VP-Mktg-Global - Boston Scientific Corporation; *pg.* 1508, *pg.* 831
Morse, Steve, Product Mgr-New Bus Solutions - Accenture; *pg.* 1392, *pg.* 1186
Morseman, Kristin, Sr VP-Ecommerce, Digital & Social - D.V.F. Studios; *pg.* 24, *pg.* 1226
Morstadt, Dave, Sr Dir-Fin - Luxottica Retail; *pg.* 8, *pg.* 1460
Mortada, Dina, Project Mgr-Mktg - Staples, Inc.; *pg.* 474, *pg.* 821
Mortensen, Pam, Sr VP & Gen Mgr-Mdse-Fine Jewelry & Accessories - J.C. Penney Company, Inc.; *pg.* 1774, *pg.* 1732
Mortensen, Randy, Sr VP-Mktg-Enterprise Cabling & Security Solutions - Anixter International Inc.; *pg.* 1313, *pg.* 614
Mortensen, Steve, Assoc Dir-Creative Svcs - Affymetrix, Inc.; *pg.* 1487, *pg.* 263
Mortimer, Courtney, Brand Mgr-Innovation - Diageo North America Inc.; *pg.* 248, *pg.* 1223
Mortimer, Tod, Dir-Gas & Power Mktg - CMS Energy Corporation; *pg.* 1937, *pg.* 893
Morton, Blaine, Dir-Sls & Bus Dev-Food-NE USA & Canada - Zep Inc.; *pg.* 338, *pg.* 524
Morton, Brad, Sr VP-Sls - Sport Chalet, Inc.; *pg.* 1846, *pg.* 119
Morton, Daniel, Dir-Product & Tech - Bose Corporation; *pg.* 626, *pg.* 820
Morton, David, Sr VP-Sls & Mktg - AMERISAFE, Inc.; *pg.* 1191, *pg.* 743
Morton, Dianna, Sr Mgr-Mktg - Digital Insight; *pg.* 744, *pg.* 189
Morton, Donna, Dir-Joint Bus Mktg - British Airways; *pg.* 1901, *pg.* 1207
Morton, Jeff, Dir-Adv - National Hot Rod Association; *pg.* 149, *pg.* 99
Morton, Lisa S., Sr Mgr-Mktg - The Boeing Company; *pg.* 225, *pg.* 567
Morton, Rob, Dir-PR - Akamai Technologies, Inc.; *pg.* 1226, *pg.* 807
Morton, Stacey, Mgr-Global Mktg - The Estee Lauder Companies Inc.; *pg.* 508, *pg.* 1229
Morton, Trent, Dir-Mktg - Dallas Stars L.P.; *pg.* 543, *pg.* 1697
Mosbach, Elizabeth, Mgr-Creative Boutique Production - Rue La La; *pg.* 1278, *pg.* 800
Mosby, Christel, Sr VP-Mktg - Grand Canyon Education, Inc.; *pg.* 602, *pg.* 16
Mosca, Peter, Dir-PR & Exec Comm-Global - Century 21 Real Estate LLC; *pg.* 1085, *pg.* 1080
Moscicki, Ann, Acct Exec-Creative Comm - Xerox Corporation; *pg.* 494, *pg.* 365
Moscone, Joseph, Sr Mgr-PR Americas-Booking.com - The Priceline Group Inc.; *pg.* 1276, *pg.* 364
Moscovic, Courtney, Assoc Mgr-PR - Pizza Hut, Inc.; *pg.* 1744, *pg.* 1733
Moseley, Bill, Dir-Mktg Comm - AT&T Inc.; *pg.* 1867, *pg.* 1674
Moseley, Matthew, Mgr-Natl Product Sls - Honeywell International Inc.; *pg.* 407, *pg.* 1088
Moser, Adam, Head-Adv Ops - Hulu LLC; *pg.* 1257, *pg.* 274
Moser, Don, Head-North America Lubricants Mktg Operation Team - Shell Lubricants; *pg.* 217, *pg.* 1714
Moser, Joe, VP-Sls - Xerox Corporation; *pg.* 494, *pg.* 365
Moser, Paul, Sr Writer & Sr Specialist-Media & PR - Sun Life Financial Inc.; *pg.* 806, *pg.* 1944
Moser, Stephanie, Mgr-Brand Adv, Graphics & Identity-Embassy Suites - Hilton Worldwide, Inc.; *pg.* 1094, *pg.* 1791
Moses, Cathey, VP-Booking & Mktg & Gen Mgr - Grand Canyon Education, Inc.; *pg.* 602, *pg.* 16
Moses, Doug, Mgr-Mktg-US Active Comm - 3M Company; *pg.* 1142, *pg.* 956
Moses, Halyn, Mgr-Partnership Mktg - Time Warner Cable Inc.; *pg.* 312, *pg.* 1301
Moses, Jeff, Sr VP-Cloud Sls - Informatica Corporation; *pg.* 414, *pg.* 190
Moses, Jennifer, Brand Mgr - Campbell Soup Company; *pg.* 844, *pg.* 1048
Moses, Julie, Dir-Creative Svcs - Protective Life Insurance Company; *pg.* 1215, *pg.* 4
Moses, Kathy, Sr Mgr-Bus Change - Anthem, Inc.; *pg.* 1192, *pg.* 683
Moses, Kevin, Sr Assoc Brand Mgr - The Kraft Heinz Company; *pg.* 871, *pg.* 641
Moses, Michael, VP-Sls - Dynaric, Inc.; *pg.* 1882, *pg.* 1810

Moses, Paige, Sr Dir-Foundation Svcs - Inova Health System; *pg.* 1545, *pg.* 1781
Moses, Sam, Sr Dir-WM Global Tech Svcs - Wal-Mart Stores, Inc.; *pg.* 1790, *pg.* 29
Moses, Tiffani, Brand Mgr-AVEENO Body Care - Johnson & Johnson; *pg.* 1549, *pg.* 1091
Moses, Tracy, Sr VP-Mktg, Analytics, Comm & Foundation - SMILE BRANDS GROUP INC.; *pg.* 1594, *pg.* 116
Mosey, Nav, Mgr-Sls-Natl - Implant Sciences Corporation; *pg.* 1348, *pg.* 860
Moshe, Rachel, Brand Mgr - MGA Entertainment, Inc.; *pg.* 964, *pg.* 300
Mosher, Cari, Brand Mgr-Design - General Mills, Inc.; *pg.* 828, *pg.* 933
Mosher, Catherine, Brand Mgr-Mktg - Sabre Holdings Corporation; *pg.* 1922, *pg.* 1745
Mosher, Constance, VP & Mgr-Mktg - Wells Fargo & Company; *pg.* 819, *pg.* 232
Moshfegh, Lisa, Sr Mgr-Mktg-Yahoo Media Network - Yahoo! Inc.; *pg.* 1289, *pg.* 289
Moshier, Elizabeth K., Dir-Mktg - GlaxoSmithKline; *pg.* 1536, *pg.* 1565
Moskal, T.E., Dir-Mktg - Diamond Power International, Inc.; *pg.* 1070, *pg.* 1457
Moskitis, Lauren, Sr Specialist-Cause Mktg - Goodwill Industries International, Inc.; *pg.* 1771, *pg.* 776
Moskowitz, Jake, Sr Mgr-Consumer Mktg - AT&T Communications Corp.; *pg.* 1866, *pg.* 1043
Moskowitz, Todd, VP-Sls - Townsquare Media, Inc.; *pg.* 313, *pg.* 350
Moslak, Katie, Brand Mgr - Tequila Avion; *pg.* 1971, *pg.* 1298
Mosley, Dawn, Mgr-Channel Mktg - The Valspar Corporation; *pg.* 1449, *pg.* 945
Mosley, Patricia, Dir-Product Mktg - CME Group Inc.; *pg.* 738, *pg.* 571
Mosley, Patricia, Dir-Product Mktg - CME Group, Inc.; *pg.* 738, *pg.* 571
Mosley, Stephanie Wu, Reg Mgr-Mktg - McDonald's Corporation; *pg.* 1737, *pg.* 645
Moss, Alan, VP-Online Sls-Americas - Google Inc.; *pg.* 1249, *pg.* 153
Moss, Jodi, Dir-Mktg & Branding-Natl - USI Holdings Corporation; *pg.* 1222, *pg.* 1144
Moss, Peter, Dir-Sls-Europe & Asia - Greater Miami Convention & Visitors Bureau; *pg.* 993, *pg.* 442
Moss, Phillip, Dir-Global ECommerce Product Mgmt-Bus Tools - Levi Strauss & Co.; *pg.* 43, *pg.* 220
Moss, Randal, Mgr-Digital Mktg - ACCO Brands Corporation; *pg.* 340, *pg.* 626
Moss, Ron, Project Mgmt Dir-Content Mktg & Strategies - Time Inc.; *pg.* 1693, *pg.* 1300
Moss, Susan E., Sr VP-Mktg & Comm - Kindred Healthcare, Inc.; *pg.* 1553, *pg.* 736
Moss, Tim, Mgr-Natl Foodservice Sls - American Blue Ribbon Holdings; *pg.* 1714, *pg.* 1648
Mossbeck, Thomas, Product Mgr - McKee Foods Corporation; *pg.* 1860, *pg.* 1630
Mosseri, Adam, Product Dir - Facebook, Inc.; *pg.* 1245, *pg.* 143
Mossler, Fred, Sr VP-Mdsg - Zappos.com, Inc.; *pg.* 1291, *pg.* 1030
Mossman, Bruce, Specialist-Digital Mktg-Worldwide - Intel Corporation; *pg.* 645, *pg.* 266
Mossman, Sean, VP-Mktg-Weatherization - M-D Building Products, Inc.; *pg.* 95, *pg.* 1486
Most, Brandon, Product Mgr-Mktg-Capture & Integration Products - Perceptive Software; *pg.* 453, *pg.* 1775
Mosteko, Nancy, Mgr-Mktg & Admin - Waters Corporation; *pg.* 1436, *pg.* 834
Mosteller, Kate, Sr Dir-Mktg - Penn Foster Education Group, Inc.; *pg.* 606, *pg.* 1586
Mota, David, Sr Mgr-Product Mktg - The Chamberlain Group, Inc.; *pg.* 75, *pg.* 611
Mota, Erika, Sr Coord-Mktg Production - Pacific Sunwear of California, Inc.; *pg.* 1781, *pg.* 43
Motard, Vanessa, Asst Mgr-Mktg Ops - Comcast Cable Communications, Inc.; *pg.* 276, *pg.* 1560
Mothershed, Juliet, Mgr-Field Mktg - Grill Concepts, Inc.; *pg.* 1730, *pg.* 308
Motley, Carol, Dir-Convention Sls - Destination DC; *pg.* 991, *pg.* 398
Motley, Kathleen, Mgr-Adv-Natl - Conde Nast Publications, Inc.; *pg.* 1629, *pg.* 1217
Motley, Kathleen, Mgr-Natl Adv-Golf Digest - Vogue Magazine; *pg.* 1700, *pg.* 1311
Motley, Robyn, Sr VP & Gen Mgr-AARP Media - AARP; *pg.* 124, *pg.* 393
Motsick, Stacy, VP & Dir-Channel Mktg - Waddell & Reed Financial, Inc.; *pg.* 818, *pg.* 721
Mott, Charlie, Mgr-Product & Mktg - General Motors Company; *pg.* 175, *pg.* 881
Mott, Douglas, VP-Mdsg & Product Mgmt - Geeknet, Inc.; *pg.* 1248, *pg.* 1780
Mott, Greg, Mgr-Sls Comm & Capabilities - Canadian Imperial Bank of Commerce; *pg.* 729, *pg.* 1935
Motta, Danielle, Product Mgr-Global Exclusives - Hasbro, Inc.; *pg.* 954, *pg.* 1603
Motta, Elizabeth, Mgr-Social Media Insights - World Wrestling Entertainment, Inc.; *pg.* 595, *pg.* 380
Motta, Erin, Sr Analyst-Strategic Mktg & Implementation - National Grid USA; *pg.* 1946, *pg.* 852
Motta, Roberto, Sr Mgr-Bus Unit - Whirlpool Corporation; *pg.* 62, *pg.* 872
Mottet, Nick, Mgr-Product Mgmt-Global Marketplace-Used Products - Amazon.com, Inc.; *pg.* 1226, *pg.* 1831
Mottiwala, Aziz, VP-US Eye Care Mktg - Allergan, Inc.; *pg.* 1491, *pg.* 106
Mottola, Paolo, Mgr-Content Mktg - Recreational Equipment, Inc.; *pg.* 1843, *pg.* 1821
Motts, Dave, VP-Mktg & Sponsorship - National Football Museum, Inc.; *pg.* 568, *pg.* 1408
Mou, Kye, Product Mgr-Mktg-AdWords - Google Inc.; *pg.* 1249, *pg.* 153
Moulds, Jami, Sr Mgr-Brand & Creative Svcs - Hitachi Data Systems Corporation; *pg.* 407, *pg.* 265
Moulin, Kristen, Asst VP-Shopper Mktg - The Coca-Cola Company; *pg.* 240, *pg.* 493
Moulster, Ian, Product Mgr-Windows - Microsoft Corporation; *pg.* 435, *pg.* 1824
Moulton, Jeff, Dir-Mktg-Grp - Humana, Inc.; *pg.* 1204, *pg.* 734
Moulton, Sandra, Sr Engr-Technical Mktg - NetApp, Inc.; *pg.* 444, *pg.* 287
Mounajed, Yasmin, Brand Mgr - DISH Network Corporation; *pg.* 283, *pg.* 325
Mound, Kimberly M., Sr Coord-PR - Safilo USA Inc.; *pg.* 11, *pg.* 1106
Mounier, Raymond, Mgr-Mktg Comm - Johnson & Johnson; *pg.* 1549, *pg.* 1091
Mount, Marie, Brand Mgr-Global Pantene - The Procter & Gamble Company; *pg.* 1129, *pg.* 1418
Mountford, Paul, Chief Sls Officer - Riverbed Technology, Inc.; *pg.* 1277, *pg.* 225
Mountjoy, Talla, Brand Mgr - Deloitte & Touche USA LLP; *pg.* 743, *pg.* 1222
Mounts, Sandy Lesko, Deputy Dir-Mktg Comm - Ohio Lottery Commission; *pg.* 1002, *pg.* 1433
Moura, Daniela, Project Mgr-Mktg - Dell Inc.; *pg.* 383, *pg.* 1737
Moura, Jerusa, Dir-Mktg-Global - Revlon, Inc.; *pg.* 521, *pg.* 1286
Mourad, Kristen, Sr Mgr-Synergy & Promos-Radio Disney - The Walt Disney Company; *pg.* 317, *pg.* 52
Mourier, Aurore, Sr Product Mgr-San Jose - eBay Inc.; *pg.* 1240, *pg.* 243
Mouritsen, Linda, Grp Mgr-Mktg Comm - Jeld-Wen, Inc.; *pg.* 1051, *pg.* 1499
Mouser, Bobby, Dir-Customer Svcs & Mktg - Public Service Company of Oklahoma; *pg.* 1950, *pg.* 1443
Mousigian, Barbara, VP-Product - Cars.com; *pg.* 1234, *pg.* 568
Mout, Kasi, Sr Mgr-Mktg - Amazon.com, Inc.; *pg.* 1226, *pg.* 1831
Mouyal, Simon, VP-Solutions & North America Mktg-Global - RACKSPACE HOSTING, INC.; *pg.* 1277, *pg.* 1742
Movrich, Jason, Specialist-Product Mktg - FRANKLIN RESOURCES, INC.; *pg.* 760, *pg.* 254
Mowat, Karl, Mgr-Engine Mktg - PACCAR Inc.; *pg.* 187, *pg.* 1816
Mowbray, Anabella, Mgr-Mktg & Product Dev - American Kennel Club, Inc.; *pg.* 129, *pg.* 1193
Mower, Kris, Sr Mgr-Mktg-Epic Story Program - NetApp, Inc.; *pg.* 444, *pg.* 287
Mower, Steven, Analyst-Mktg - The Travelers Companies, Inc.; *pg.* 1220, *pg.* 352
Mowery, Jim, Product Specialist-Fixed Gas Detection - Bacharach Inc.; *pg.* 1400, *pg.* 1556
Mowery, Keith, Sr Dir-Transportation & Logistics - United States Cold Storage, Inc.; *pg.* 61, *pg.* 1051
Mowrey, Rick, Dir-Mktg & Bus Dev - CENTRIA, Inc.; *pg.* 74, *pg.* 1554
Moxley, Emily, Product Mgr-Google Search - Google Inc.; *pg.* 1249, *pg.* 153
Moxley, Erin Walsh, Sr Dir-Sls Enablement - TripAdvisor, Inc.; *pg.* 1926, *pg.* 835
Moxy, Deniece, Sr Mgr-Product Mgmt - Actuate Corporation; *pg.* 342, *pg.* 253
Moy, Dennis, Dir-Mktg - Avago Technologies; *pg.* 358, *pg.* 238
Moy, Dennis, Sr Mgr-Mktg-Comml Natl Accounts & Custom Innovation - Kellogg Company; *pg.* 831, *pg.* 870
Moy, Esther, Mgr-Retail Mktg - Oakley, Inc.; *pg.* 1840, *pg.* 86
Moy, Kenley, VP-Sls-Natl - San Francisco Travel Association; *pg.* 1005, *pg.* 227
Moya, Adam, Dir-Mktg & Product Mgmt - Honeywell International Inc.; *pg.* 407, *pg.* 1088
Moya, Jane F., Specialist-Mktg Comm - Federal Home Loan Mortgage Corporation; *pg.* 751, *pg.* 1790
Moye, Angie, Gen Mgr-Sls - WHBF-TV; *pg.* 321, *pg.* 654
Moye, Jay, Sr Writer-Digital Comm & Social Media - The Coca-Cola Company; *pg.* 240, *pg.* 493
Moye, Patrick, Product Dir-Global Career Site Platform - CareerBuilder, LLC; *pg.* 1234, *pg.* 568
Moyer, Caitlin, Dir-New Media - Milwaukee Brewers Baseball Club, Inc.; *pg.* 562, *pg.* 1878
Moyer, Catherine Holmes, Dir-Consumer Comm, Integrated Mktg & Consumer Mktg Grp - Safeway Inc.; *pg.* 1032, *pg.* 184
Moyer, Emily, VP-Mktg & Digital Strategies - Michael J. Fox Foundation for Parkinson's Research; *pg.* 147, *pg.* 1260
Moyer, Jenni, Sr Dir-Corp Comm, Network & Ops - Comcast Corporation; *pg.* 276, *pg.* 1560
Moyer, Kevin W., Dir-Product Mktg Performance Surfaces - USG Corporation; *pg.* 118, *pg.* 594
Moyer, Matthew, Sr Dir-Customer Experience Mktg - Comcast Cable Communications, Inc.; *pg.* 276, *pg.* 1560
Moyer, Maureen C., Dir-Wholesale Mktg - AT&T Mobility LLC; *pg.* 619, *pg.* 488
Moyer, Patricia, Sr Mgr-Channel Mktg - Symantec Corporation; *pg.* 478, *pg.* 161
Moyer, Tom, Reg Mgr-Sls-Midwest - Bell Helicopter Textron, Inc.; *pg.* 224, *pg.* 1693
Moylan, Steve, VP-Shopper Mktg & Health-Wellness Innovation - Safeway Inc.; *pg.* 1032, *pg.* 184
Moynhian, Brian, Head-Product - Panjo; *pg.* 1274, *pg.* 275
Moynihan, Michael, VP-Mktg - LEGO Systems, Inc.; *pg.* 961, *pg.* 346
Moynihan, Tim, Brand Mgr-Post-it Brand-Global - 3M Company; *pg.* 1142, *pg.* 956
Mozilo, Cori, Sr Mgr-Mktg-Diner Engagement - OpenTable, Inc.; *pg.* 450, *pg.* 224
Mozina, Bojana, Sr Mgr-Brand Partnership - Amazon.com, Inc.; *pg.* 1226, *pg.* 1831
Mozingo, Sara, Specialist-Mktg & Comm - Sprint Corporation; *pg.* 1874, *pg.* 719
Mozingo, Scott, Product Mgr-Burpee Home Gardens - Ball Horticultural Company; *pg.* 1793, *pg.* 668
Mrjenovich, Jay, Product Mgr - Edgewave Inc; *pg.* 390, *pg.* 202
Mroczkowski, Gina, Program Mgr-Copy & Print Mktg - Staples, Inc.; *pg.* 474, *pg.* 821
Mrugacz, Linda, Dir-Mktg & Comm - GEA Farm Technologies; *pg.* 704, *pg.* 636
Muasher, Jena, Mgr-ECommerce Mktg-Skin Care Products - Sunstar Americas Inc.; *pg.* 1599, *pg.* 591
Muashsher, Jamal K., Dir-Mktg-Valvoline - Ashland Inc.; *pg.* 972, *pg.* 726
Muche, Ken, Mgr-PR - Cellco Partnership; *pg.* 1869, *pg.* 1042
Muckleston, Paul, Gen Mgr-Worldwide Surface Channel Sls - Microsoft Corporation; *pg.* 435, *pg.* 1824
Mudd, Angeline, Bus Mgr - News-Leader; *pg.* 1670, *pg.* 422
Mudd, Graham, Dir-Ads Product Mktg - Facebook, Inc.; *pg.* 1245, *pg.* 143
Mudd, Susan, Dir-Client Mktg - Valassis Communications, Inc.; *pg.* 1287, *pg.* 897
Mudgett, John, Dir-Natl Strategic Sls-Restorative Therapies Grp - Medtronic, Inc.; *pg.* 1564, *pg.* 939
Mudway, Deb, VP-Mktg-Home Environment USA, Consumer Rels & Trade Mktg - Kaz, Inc.; *pg.* 58, *pg.* 844
Muecke, Milanka, Dir-PR & Comm - Lenovo Group Ltd; *pg.* 427, *pg.* 1384
Mueckler, Rob, VP-Sls & Mktg - BOMAG Americas, Inc.; *pg.* 1318, *pg.* 621
Muehl, Mark, Sr VP-Product Engrg - Comcast Corporation; *pg.* 276, *pg.* 1560
Muelleman, Sarah, Mgr-Digital Media - Hostess Brands LLC;

pg. 1856, *pg.* 984

Mueller, Bernadette M., Exec VP & Dir-Sls & Client Dev - Valley National Bancorp; *pg.* 815, *pg.* 1130

Mueller, Bob, Exec Dir-PR - AT&T Inc.; *pg.* 1867, *pg.* 1674

Mueller, Bob, Sr Mgr-Pur-Global Brand Building Purchases-Talent & Entertainment - The Procter & Gamble Company; *pg.* 1129, *pg.* 1418

Mueller, Danielle, Mgr-Digital Mktg - Agfa Corporation; *pg.* 1398, *pg.* 1114

Mueller, Dave, Sr Product Mgr - Klein Tools Inc.; *pg.* 1052, *pg.* 627

Mueller, Eric, Specialist-Bus Dev-Ford Sls - Ford Motor Company; *pg.* 172, *pg.* 876

Mueller, Jim, Gen Mgr & Grp Dir-Mktg - Johnsonville Sausage, LLC; *pg.* 867, *pg.* 1894

Mueller, Kurt F., Sr VP-Sls - Hormel Foods Corporation; *pg.* 863, *pg.* 915

Mueller, Leah, Dir-Tourism & Sls - Buffalo Niagara Convention & Visitors Bureau, Inc.; *pg.* 1901, *pg.* 1147

Mueller, Linda, Mgr-Digital Mktg - Robert Bosch Tool Corp; *pg.* 1060, *pg.* 634

Mueller, Lyndon, Sr Dir-Product Mgmt - The Home Depot, Inc.; *pg.* 1050, *pg.* 510

Mueller, Rebecca, Dir-Production & Traffic Svcs - Coach, Inc.; *pg.* 3, *pg.* 1214

Mueller, Rebekah, Sr Product Mgr-Mobile Entertainment Apps - Comcast Corporation; *pg.* 276, *pg.* 1560

Mueller, Susan, VP-Mktg & Dir-Strategic Mktg & Critical Care - Cardinal Health, Inc.; *pg.* 1512, *pg.* 1448

Mueller, Thilo, Sr Product Mgr - Kennametal Inc.; *pg.* 1052, *pg.* 1547

Mueller, Tracy, Brand Mgr - Monsanto Company; *pg.* 1173, *pg.* 999

Mueller-Sim, Anthony, Sr Mgr-Mktg Production - Ann Inc.; *pg.* 18, *pg.* 1195

Muendel, Jeff, Head-Digital Mktg - Amazon.com, Inc.; *pg.* 1226, *pg.* 1831

Muguerza, Andrea, Mgr-Mktg - L'Oreal USA; *pg.* 514, *pg.* 1252

Muhlenkamp, Lisa, Dir-Mktg Programs - Cincinnati Business Courier; *pg.* 1627, *pg.* 1411

Muhlenkamp, Paige, Brand Mgr-Schlage - Ingersoll-Rand Company; *pg.* 1349, *pg.* 1370

Muhtar, Jonathan, CMO & Exec VP - Captain D's, LLC; *pg.* 1720, *pg.* 1649

Mui, John, Sr Mgr-Product Line - Broadcom Corporation; *pg.* 364, *pg.* 108

Muilenburg, Crystal, Product Dir-Pro Mktg - Allergan, Inc.; *pg.* 1491, *pg.* 106

Muir, Tim, VP-Franchise Sls & Dev - Choice Hotels International, Inc.; *pg.* 1086, *pg.* 775

Mukherjee, Michelle, Head-Consumer Media-Global - Intel Corporation; *pg.* 645, *pg.* 266

Mukherjee, Sanjoy, VP-Sls - Broadridge Financial Solutions Inc.; *pg.* 727, *pg.* 1172

Mukherjee, Uttam, Sr Asst Brand Mgr-Tide - The Procter & Gamble Company; *pg.* 1129, *pg.* 1418

Mukhi, Rishi, Acct Mgr-Mktg-Dick's Sporting Goods - adidas America Inc.; *pg.* 1803, *pg.* 1500

Mulargia, Nicholas, VP-Sls & Mktg - Crystal World, Inc.; *pg.* 4, *pg.* 1122

Mulato, Dennis, Dir-Digital & Consumer Mktg - The McGraw-Hill Companies Inc.; *pg.* 1663, *pg.* 1257

Mulbry, Monique, Sr Dir-Brand Strategy, Adv & Marcom-Global - Plantronics, Inc.; *pg.* 663, *pg.* 270

Mulcahy, Fawn, Sr Mgr-Sponsorship Mktg - Royal Bank of Canada; *pg.* 800, *pg.* 1942

Mulcahy, Joyce, Mgr-Mktg - Cisco Systems, Inc.; *pg.* 372, *pg.* 240

Mulcahy, Neil, Exec VP-Sls-Fox Sports Media Grp - Fox Entertainment Group, Inc.; *pg.* 288, *pg.* 131

Mulcahy, Renee, Sr Mgr-Customer Mktg - Del Monte Foods, Inc.; *pg.* 852, *pg.* 304

Mulchan, Crisha, Specialist-Partner Mktg-Bus Analytics-Worldwide - IBM Canada Limited; *pg.* 411, *pg.* 1923

Mulder, Dave, Mgr-Product Mktg - Deere & Company; *pg.* 703, *pg.* 632

Mulder, Erik, Sr Mgr-Solutions-Energy & High-Tech - NetApp, Inc.; *pg.* 444, *pg.* 287

Muldoon, Brian, Specialist-Mktg - Comcast Cable Communications, Inc.; *pg.* 276, *pg.* 1560

Muldoon, Lara, Mgr-Device Mktg-Connected & Emerging Device Categories - United States Cellular Corporation; *pg.* 1875, *pg.* 594

Muldoon, Maureen, Dir-Sls-Intl - Trek Bicycle Corporation; *pg.* 1847, *pg.* 1896

Muldoon, Ryan, Sr Dir-New Bus Dev - Johnson & Johnson; *pg.* 1549, *pg.* 1091

Muldrow, James, Dir-Product Mgmt - comScore, Inc; *pg.* 1236, *pg.* 1798

Mulford, Kristine, Mgr-PR-Global - Motorola Mobility LLC; *pg.* 657, *pg.* 627

Mulford, Marty, Sr Dir-Ticket Sls - Nashville Predators, LLC; *pg.* 565, *pg.* 1652

Mulhall, Neil, VP & Div Mgr-Mdse-Apparel - Toys "R" Us, Inc.; *pg.* 968, *pg.* 1130

Mulholland, Lindsay, Mgr-Digital Mktg & Partnerships - Scripps Networks Interactive, Inc.; *pg.* 1279, *pg.* 1638

Mulholland, Niall, Dir-Media Mktg - Cineplex Entertainment LP; *pg.* 275, *pg.* 1936

Mulic, Gina, Sr Mgr-Social Bus - Rogers Communications Inc.; *pg.* 668, *pg.* 1942

Mulica, Mike, Pres-Worldwide Sls & Bus Dev - RealNetworks, Inc.; *pg.* 460, *pg.* 1839

Muligano, Michael, VP-Creative - Timex Corporation; *pg.* 14, *pg.* 355

Mullaly, David, Brand Mgr-Walmart Customer Team - The Procter & Gamble Company; *pg.* 1129, *pg.* 1418

Mullaney, Andria, Sr Mgr-Mktg-Education Solutions-K-12 Schools & Small Colleges - Blackbaud, Inc.; *pg.* 361, *pg.* 1613

Mullaney, Laura S., Sr Mgr-Event Mktg - Allscripts Healthcare Solutions, Inc.; *pg.* 1492, *pg.* 563

Mullapudi, Sridhar, Dir-Product Mgmt - Citrix Systems, Inc.; *pg.* 375, *pg.* 424

Mullen, Brenna, Product Mgr - AVANIR Pharmaceuticals; *pg.* 1498, *pg.* 40

Mullen, Christina, Sr Mgr-Online Mktg - David's Bridal, Inc.; *pg.* 23, *pg.* 1523

Mullen, Enza, Assoc Dir-Creative - Combe Incorporated; *pg.* 1516, *pg.* 1351

Mullen, Jack, Sr VP-Mktg - ShopKo; *pg.* 1785, *pg.* 1860

Mullen, Jeanniey, VP-Mktg - Barnes & Noble, Inc.; *pg.* 1619, *pg.* 1201

Mullen, Patrick, VP-Mktg - Nestle Purina PetCare Company; *pg.* 1479, *pg.* 1000

Mullen, Tom, Mgr-Sls & Bus Accounts - Charter Communications, Inc.; *pg.* 274, *pg.* 372

Mullenholz, Lauren, Sr Mgr-Product Mktg - LinkedIn Corporation; *pg.* 1262, *pg.* 160

Muller, George, Dir-Mktg Svcs - Cleveland Browns Football Company LLC; *pg.* 541, *pg.* 1406

Muller, Levi, Mgr-Mktg-Global - Tupperware Brands Corporation; *pg.* 1139, *pg.* 456

Muller, Mikkel, Project Mgr-Mktg - Texas Instruments Incorporated; *pg.* 679, *pg.* 1688

Muller, Rob, Mgr-Digital Mktg - Roche Diagnostics Corporation; *pg.* 1590, *pg.* 689

Muller, Stewart, VP-Intl Sls & Mktg - Cisco Systems, Inc.; *pg.* 372, *pg.* 240

Muller, Tracy, Sr Product Mgr - Q.E.P. CO., INC.; *pg.* 1371, *pg.* 413

Muller, Veronica, Brand Mgr-Licensing-Latin America - Perry Ellis International, Inc.; *pg.* 45, *pg.* 445

Muller-Stotser, Jodi, Exec Dir-Retention Mktg - Cox Communications, Inc.; *pg.* 279, *pg.* 501

Mullery, Karen, Sr Dir-Global Women's Health Mktg - American Medical Systems Holdings, Inc.; *pg.* 1493, *pg.* 947

Mulligan, Arthur R., Mgr-Product Line-Svcs - Eaton Corporation - Industrial Controls; *pg.* 1296, *pg.* 1874

Mulligan, Brian, Asst VP-PR - North Shore-LIJ Health System; *pg.* 1573, *pg.* 1162

Mulligan, Colin, Sr VP-Sls Mgmt - Bank of America Global Wealth & Investment Management; *pg.* 720, *pg.* 789

Mulligan, Julie, Sr VP-Mdsg, Product Dev & Photography - 1-800-Flowers.com, Inc.; *pg.* 1758, *pg.* 1151

Mullin, Adrian, Dir-Mktg - The Northwestern Mutual Life Insurance Company; *pg.* 1212, *pg.* 1879

Mullin, Danielle, VP-Mktg - ABC Family Channel; *pg.* 268, *pg.* 51

Mullin, Dave, VP-Sls & Mktg - Lear Corporation; *pg.* 229, *pg.* 907

Mullin, James, Product Mgr-MembranePlus - Simulations Plus, Inc.; *pg.* 470, *pg.* 121

Mullin, Matt, Sr Mgr-Digital Content - Barnes & Noble, Inc.; *pg.* 1619, *pg.* 1201

Mullin, Sarah, Brand Mgr-Hills Bros Coffee & Cappuccino - Massimo Zanetti Beverage USA; *pg.* 876, *pg.* 1808

Mullin, Tricia D., Sr Mgr-Customer Mktg - Coca-Cola North America; *pg.* 848, *pg.* 500

Mullins, Chris, Mgr-Search & Paid Online Mktg - Sandals Resorts International; *pg.* 1111, *pg.* 446

Mullins, Leslie, Sr Dir-Retail Brand-Global Marketplace Mgmt - NIKE, Inc.; *pg.* 1812, *pg.* 1492

Mullins, Marc, VP-Warehouse Sls - Hiland Dairy Foods Company; *pg.* 862, *pg.* 1006

Mullins, Michelle M., Dir-Corp & Adv - Six Flags Entertainment Corporation; *pg.* 583, *pg.* 1698

Mullins, Miles, Product Mgr - Knape & Vogt Manufacturing Company; *pg.* 1052, *pg.* 913

Mullins, Samantha, Asst Product Mgr-Waring Div - Conair Corporation; *pg.* 505, *pg.* 1055

Mullnaey, Mandy, Sr Product Mgr-Collections Bedding - Macy's East; *pg.* 1777, *pg.* 1254

Mulloy, Cheryl, Sr Mgr-Strategic Mktg & Head-New Bus Dev - THE DOW CHEMICAL COMPANY; *pg.* 1157, *pg.* 898

Mulnix, Brian, VP-Mktg-US Prescription Bus - Galderma Laboratories, L.P.; *pg.* 1532, *pg.* 1695

Multer, Thomas, VP-Product Tech - Reliable Automatic Sprinkler Co., Inc.; *pg.* 1137, *pg.* 1158

Mulvaney, Luke, Specialist-Mktg Comm - Polaris Industries Inc.; *pg.* 1709, *pg.* 928

Mulvihill, Madeline, Coord-Ad Sls Mktg, Travel Channel & Great American Country - Scripps Networks Interactive, Inc.; *pg.* 1279, *pg.* 1638

Mulvihill, Morgan, Mgr-Mktg-Kroger Customer Team - The Procter & Gamble Company; *pg.* 1129, *pg.* 1418

Mumm, Paul, VP-Mktg - Lawn Doctor Inc.; *pg.* 1796, *pg.* 1074

Mumman, Patrick, Mgr-Acq & Franchise Dev Sls-East Market - H&R Block, Inc.; *pg.* 764, *pg.* 983

Mumper-Dickerson, Melanie, Sr Mgr-Comm - Whirlpool Corporation; *pg.* 62, *pg.* 872

Munch, William D., VP-Sls & Mktg - Pyramid Mouldings; *pg.* 105, *pg.* 429

Mund, Matthew, Sr VP-Product Mgmt - Monster Worldwide, Inc.; *pg.* 1268, *pg.* 859

Mundinger, Amber, Dir-Sponsorship-Fairchild Fashion Media, Fairchild Summits - Conde Nast Publications, Inc.; *pg.* 1629, *pg.* 1217

Mundo-Dainas, Victoria Del, Mgr-Global Customer Success Mktg-Demand Generation & Digital Mktg - Cisco Systems, Inc.; *pg.* 372, *pg.* 240

Mundt, Jeff A., Sr Mgr-Mktg & Tech-Advanced Innovation Center of Excellence - The Hershey Co.; *pg.* 1855, *pg.* 1538

Mundy, Michael, Reg Mgr-Sls-North America - NBS Technologies Inc.; *pg.* 786, *pg.* 1941

Mundy, Renee, Dir-Mktg-Global - MedImmune LLC; *pg.* 1562, *pg.* 770

Mundy, William T., Dir-Sls & Bus Dev - Cardinal Bank N.A.; *pg.* 732, *pg.* 1790

Mungara, Ajay, Sr Product Mgr-Internet of Things & Developer Experience - Intel Corporation; *pg.* 645, *pg.* 266

Mungiello, Anthony, Product Mgr-Laptops - Panasonic Corporation of North America; *pg.* 661, *pg.* 1120

Mungovan, Billy, Dir-Product Strategy & Advertiser Solutions - Adobe Systems Incorporated; *pg.* 342, *pg.* 235

Mungovan, Dave, Sr Mgr-Global Procurement & Travel - Monster Worldwide, Inc.; *pg.* 1268, *pg.* 859

Muniz, Alaina, Mgr-Digital Mktg - Subway Restaurants; *pg.* 1751, *pg.* 356

Muniz, Dan, Coord-Global Mktg-Tommy Hilfiger Watches & Jewelry - Tommy Hilfiger USA; *pg.* 48, *pg.* 1302

Munk, Eric, Mgr-Chrysler-Jeep-Dodge Mktg - FCA US LLC; *pg.* 170, *pg.* 868

Munk, Janne, Coord-Mktg - Fresenius Medical Care North America; *pg.* 1531, *pg.* 851

Munn, Louisa Kramer, Program Mgr-Mktg - AutoZone, Inc.; *pg.* 200, *pg.* 1641

Munnelly, Christine, Exec VP-Mdsg - New York & Company, Inc.; *pg.* 1779, *pg.* 1268

Munoz, Andres, VP-Mktg - San Antonio Convention & Visitors Bureau; *pg.* 1004, *pg.* 1742

Munoz, Anna, Acct Mgr-Natl & Natl Sls Mgr - Univision Communications Inc.; *pg.* 683, *pg.* 1307

Munoz, Hillary, Brand Mgr-Digital Mktg - DISH Network Corporation; *pg.* 283, *pg.* 325

Munoz, Jenna, Sr Mgr-Consumer Insights - Academy Sports & Outdoors, Ltd.; *pg.* 1824, *pg.* 1724

Munoz, Jose Mario, Brand Mgr - Bacardi USA, Inc.; *pg.* 1956, *pg.* 417

Munoz, Vianey, Mgr-Worldwide Mktg Plng & Ops - Hewlett-Packard Company; *pg.* 404, *pg.* 175

Munroe, Carole, Dir-Walt Disney World PR-Disney

Destinations - The Walt Disney Company; *pg.* 317, *pg.* 52
Munroe, Dwight, Dir-Mktg - Theodore Presser Co.; *pg.* 1692, *pg.* 1544
Munroe, Nicole, Mgr-Mktg - United States Tennis Association; *pg.* 160, *pg.* 1354
Munroe, Vicki, Dir-Product Dev - The Florida Lottery; *pg.* 992, *pg.* 469
Munsee, Josh, Mgr-Mktg-Global - Microsoft Corporation; *pg.* 435, *pg.* 1824
Munson, Amy, VP-Sls & Mktg Tech - Medline Industries, Inc.; *pg.* 1562, *pg.* 635
Munson, Kelly, Div Pres-Product & Sr VP - WellCare Health Plans Inc.; *pg.* 1223, *pg.* 476
Munster, Greg, Sr Dir-Global Sls Productivity - Red Hat, Inc.; *pg.* 460, *pg.* 1388
Munteanu, Amalia, VP-Digital Mktg-NBC Entertainment - NBC Universal, Inc.; *pg.* 300, *pg.* 1266
Munusamy, Thilakavathy, Dir-Sls & Mktg - LEGOLAND California LLC; *pg.* 557, *pg.* 59
Munzer, James, Sr Mgr-Mktg, Media & Adv - Vans, Inc.; *pg.* 1821, *pg.* 76
Mura, Libby Oberpriller, Dir-Mktg & Sls-PG&A - Polaris Industries Inc.; *pg.* 1709, *pg.* 928
Mura, Veronique, Sr Mgr-Global Brand Dev-Dove Men+Care Face - Unilever United States, Inc.; *pg.* 904, *pg.* 1061
Murad, Mohammed, VP-Global Sls, Mktg & Bus Dev - LG Electronics U.S.A., Inc.; *pg.* 651, *pg.* 1060
Murakami, Jim, Sr Product Mgr-Tablet Accessories-Global - Kensington Technology Group; *pg.* 424, *pg.* 191
Murali, Anand, Mgr-Global Product & Pricing - Eastman Chemical Company; *pg.* 1159, *pg.* 1636
Murali, Gayathri, Engr-Technical Mktg - Intel Corporation; *pg.* 645, *pg.* 266
Muramoto, Dan, Mgr-CRM & Reg Mktg - Kubota Tractor Corporation; *pg.* 705, *pg.* 294
Murasko, Paul, Sr Dir-Multi Channel Mktg - Sunovion Pharmaceuticals Inc.; *pg.* 1599, *pg.* 832
Murata, Koichi, Dir-Telecom Mktg - GigOptix, Inc.; *pg.* 400, *pg.* 245
Muratore, Jeremy, Strategist-Social Media - PerkinElmer, Inc.; *pg.* 1426, *pg.* 853
Muratore, Kylie, Specialist-PR - T. Rowe Price Group Inc.; *pg.* 808, *pg.* 759
Murchison, Carole, Dir-Mktg Comm-Worldwide - Synopsys, Inc.; *pg.* 480, *pg.* 162
Murchison, Rod, VP-Products - TRIPWIRE, INC.; *pg.* 485, *pg.* 1507
Murchland Luecke, Suzanne, Exec Dir-Rays Baseball Foundation & Sr Dir-Community Rels - Tampa Bay Rays Baseball, Ltd.; *pg.* 586, *pg.* 464
Murden, Oscar, Mgr-Sls Dev - About, Inc.; *pg.* 1225, *pg.* 1186
Murdoch, Cheryl, Head-Mktg Dev - Herman Miller, Inc.; *pg.* 926, *pg.* 913
Murdoch, Kyle, Sr Dir-ECommerce Mktg - The Ritz-Carlton Hotel Company LLC; *pg.* 1110, *pg.* 766
Murdock, Robert A., Reg Mgr-Sls - Murdock, Inc.; *pg.* 98, *pg.* 67
Murguia, Raul, Dir-Mktg & Innovation - Pharmavite LLC; *pg.* 1584, *pg.* 167
Murillo, Eliana, Head-Multicultural Mktg - Google Inc.; *pg.* 1249, *pg.* 153
Murley, Shila, Brand Mgr - Johnson & Johnson Inc.; *pg.* 1552, *pg.* 1923
Murnan, Shawn, Sr Dir-Mktg & Brand Adv - Best Buy Co., Inc.; *pg.* 1761, *pg.* 954
Murnane, Claire, Brand Mgr-Similac - Abbott Nutrition; *pg.* 1485, *pg.* 1437
Murnane, Jonathan, Dir-Experiential Mktg-Global - Activision Blizzard, Inc.; *pg.* 948, *pg.* 271
Murnen, Peter, VP-Mktg - Motorcar Parts of America, Inc.; *pg.* 213, *pg.* 295
Murnick, Cynthia, Dir-Sls - Xplore Technologies Corp.; *pg.* 497, *pg.* 1667
Murov, Sarah, Dir-PR & Mktg Comm - Loews Hotels Holding Corporation; *pg.* 1101, *pg.* 1252
Murphey, Dave, Dir-Corp Partnerships & Integrated Media - Miami Dolphins, Ltd.; *pg.* 562, *pg.* 419
Murphy, Adam, VP-Mktg-Michelin Americas Truck Tires - Michelin North America Inc.; *pg.* 1886, *pg.* 1618
Murphy, Aideen, Dir-Mktg & Sr Brand Mgr - Kellogg Company; *pg.* 831, *pg.* 870
Murphy, Andrea, Coord-Mktg - Church & Dwight Canada Corp.; *pg.* 503, *pg.* 1925
Murphy, Anne, Brand Mgr-Consumer Foods-Beans Portfolio - ConAgra Foods, Inc.; *pg.* 826, *pg.* 1014
Murphy, Becky, Mgr-Mktg - Aveda Corporation; *pg.* 499, *pg.* 917
Murphy, Brendan E., Mgr-Sls-DC Field - Unum Group; *pg.* 1222, *pg.* 1629
Murphy, Brent, Mgr-Mktg-Vital Signs & Cardiopulmonary - Welch Allyn Inc.; *pg.* 1436, *pg.* 1342
Murphy, Brent, Mgr-Mktg-Vital Signs & Cardiopulmonary - Welch's International; *pg.* 909, *pg.* 816
Murphy, Brian, Sr Dir-Bus Dev-Emerging Markets-Menlo Logistics - Menlo Worldwide, LLC; *pg.* 1915, *pg.* 255
Murphy, Brian J., Mgr-PR - Waters Corporation; *pg.* 1436, *pg.* 834
Murphy, Caitlin, Brand Strategist-ZOO - Google Inc.; *pg.* 1249, *pg.* 153
Murphy, Carter, Mgr-Local Sls - WJBF-TV; *pg.* 321, *pg.* 525
Murphy, Casey, Brand Mgr-cat.com - Caterpillar, Inc.; *pg.* 1321, *pg.* 650
Murphy, Catherine, Grp Product Dir-Global - Johnson & Johnson; *pg.* 1549, *pg.* 1091
Murphy, Chris, Sr Dir & Mng Editor - adidas America Inc.; *pg.* 1803, *pg.* 1500
Murphy, Chris, Sr Dir-Grp Sls - Golden State Warriors, LLC; *pg.* 550, *pg.* 171
Murphy, Chris, Head-Sls - HBG Books, Inc.; *pg.* 1648, *pg.* 1238
Murphy, Christina, VP & Mgr-Market Sls - Bank of America Corporation; *pg.* 718, *pg.* 1362
Murphy, Cynthia, Mgr-Mktg - Independent Publishers Group; *pg.* 1652, *pg.* 578
Murphy, Dan, Exec VP-Sls & Mktg - Bridgestone Golf, Inc.; *pg.* 1828, *pg.* 528
Murphy, David, Sr VP-Sls, Mktg & Mdsg - Barco Uniforms, Inc.; *pg.* 19, *pg.* 94
Murphy, David, Sr Mgr - BDO Seidman, LLP; *pg.* 724, *pg.* 1202
Murphy, David, VP-Sls & Mktg - Lind Electronics, Inc.; *pg.* 1355, *pg.* 938
Murphy, Debra, Mgr-Creative Mktg - University of Pennsylvania; *pg.* 609, *pg.* 1571
Murphy, Dennis, Exec VP-Sls & Mktg-Global - CooperVision, Inc.; *pg.* 1407, *pg.* 1159
Murphy, Dennis J., Exec VP-Global Sls & Mktg - The Cooper Companies, Inc.; *pg.* 1518, *pg.* 183
Murphy, Doug, Dir-Creative Svcs - The New York Giants; *pg.* 570, *pg.* 1055
Murphy, Ellen M., Dir-Boston & Hartford Mktg & Comm - Accenture; *pg.* 1392, *pg.* 1186
Murphy, Erin, Sr Mgr-Comm - Noodles & Company; *pg.* 1742, *pg.* 313
Murphy, Jacqueline, Mgr-Worldwide & AG Mktg Programs - IBM; *pg.* 410, *pg.* 1449
Murphy, Jennifer, Sr VP-Sls - ALERE INC.; *pg.* 1488, *pg.* 849
Murphy, Jim, Dir-Mktg Capabilities & Bus Plng - Brown-Forman Corporation; *pg.* 1958, *pg.* 732
Murphy, Jim, Sr VP & Gen Mgr-Digital Adv - Catalina Marketing Corporation; *pg.* 369, *pg.* 462
Murphy, Jim, Product Mgr - Quaker Chemical Corp.; *pg.* 1178, *pg.* 1524
Murphy, Joanne, Dir-Mktg - Tom's of Maine, Inc.; *pg.* 523, *pg.* 750
Murphy, Joe, VP-Sls-US - Franklin Sports, Inc.; *pg.* 1834, *pg.* 847
Murphy, John, Sr Product Mgr-Datamax-O'Neil - Datamax Corporation; *pg.* 1633, *pg.* 453
Murphy, Julie, Dir-Mktg - Okuma America Corporation; *pg.* 1366, *pg.* 1368
Murphy, Kate, Sr Dir-Global Adv Campaigns & Brand - Microsoft Corporation; *pg.* 435, *pg.* 1824
Murphy, Kathleen, Mgr-Mktg Programs - Thermo Fisher Scientific Inc.; *pg.* 1602, *pg.* 61
Murphy, Kevin, Mgr-Pub & Govt Affairs-Natural Gas & Power Mktg Company - Exxon Mobil Corporation; *pg.* 977, *pg.* 1718
Murphy, Lauren, Mgr-Sls Admin - Bonnier Corporation; *pg.* 1622, *pg.* 480
Murphy, Lauren, Sr Product Mgr - MARTHA STEWART LIVING OMNIMEDIA, INC.; *pg.* 1661, *pg.* 1256
Murphy, Lisa, Mgr-Convention Sls - Greater Miami Convention & Visitors Bureau; *pg.* 993, *pg.* 442
Murphy, Lyndsey, Sr Mgr-Search - Williams-Sonoma, Inc.; *pg.* 1140, *pg.* 234
Murphy, Mairead, Dir-Worldwide Mktg Ops-Sys & Tech Grp - IBM; *pg.* 410, *pg.* 1449
Murphy, Matt, Sr VP-Digital Video Distr-Disney & ESPN Media Networks - ESPN, Inc.; *pg.* 285, *pg.* 340
Murphy, Michael P., Dir-Bank Mktg - TriCo Bancshares; *pg.* 811, *pg.* 65
Murphy, Michaela, Reg Mgr-Sls & Bus Dev - Oracle Corporation; *pg.* 450, *pg.* 191
Murphy, Michelle, Mgr-Mktg - Terex Corporation; *pg.* 1381, *pg.* 384
Murphy, Mick, Dir-Creative - Michaels Stores, Inc.; *pg.* 1127, *pg.* 1722
Murphy, Mike, Coord-Production - Captivate; *pg.* 272, *pg.* 1209
Murphy, Mike, Mgr-Retail Mktg - Ford Motor Company; *pg.* 172, *pg.* 876
Murphy, Mike, VP-Sls - General Cable Corporation; *pg.* 83, *pg.* 729
Murphy, Mike, Specialist-Multimedia Adv - Hamilton-Wenham Chronicle; *pg.* 1647, *pg.* 816
Murphy, Mike, Head-Media & Entertainment Partnerships - Intel Corporation; *pg.* 645, *pg.* 266
Murphy, Mike, Dir-Digital Mktg - VCA Inc.; *pg.* 1606, *pg.* 141
Murphy, Molly, Sr VP-Sls & Mktg - Eaton Corporation; *pg.* 1331, *pg.* 1429
Murphy, Molly, Dir-Mktg & Sls - Quality Chekd Dairies, Inc.; *pg.* 154, *pg.* 630
Murphy, Stacey, Dir-Mktg - Brainstorm Group, Inc.; *pg.* 364, *pg.* 838
Murphy, Stephen, Exec VP-Sls, Mktg & Intl Comml Bus - DJO Incorporated; *pg.* 1524, *pg.* 302
Murphy, Tim, VP-Mktg-ABSOLUT Vodka, Beefeater Gin, Plymouth Gin & FRIS Vodka - Pernod Ricard USA, Inc.; *pg.* 1968, *pg.* 1332
Murphy, Tom, Mgr-Mktg - UPS Ground Freight, Inc.; *pg.* 1929, *pg.* 1804
Murphy, Tracy, VP-Strategic Mktg - Sutter Health; *pg.* 1600, *pg.* 197
Murphy, W. Robert, Exec VP-Sls & Mktg - Hubbell Incorporated; *pg.* 1299, *pg.* 370
Murphy, Will, Sr VP-Sls - Farm Journal Media; *pg.* 1640, *pg.* 1564
Murrain, Basil L., VP-Mktg & Promo - American Urban Radio Networks; *pg.* 269, *pg.* 1573
Murray, Adam, Mgr-Pre-Owned Sls - Kuni Enterprises Inc.; *pg.* 182, *pg.* 1846
Murray, Andrew, Head-PMD Partner Mktg - Facebook, Inc.; *pg.* 1245, *pg.* 143
Murray, Andy, Sr VP-Creative - Wal-Mart Stores, Inc.; *pg.* 1790, *pg.* 29
Murray, Anne, Sr Dir-Mktg Comm - Southwest Airlines Co.; *pg.* 1923, *pg.* 1687
Murray, Ashley, Brand Mgr-HP IPG Printing Supplies - CDW Corporation; *pg.* 370, *pg.* 663
Murray, Bart, VP-Mktg - GlaxoSmithKline; *pg.* 1536, *pg.* 1389
Murray, Caroline, Acting Dir-Mktg & Comm - Miami City Ballet, Inc.; *pg.* 562, *pg.* 448
Murray, Carrie, Specialist-Digital Media - Audi of America, Inc.; *pg.* 164, *pg.* 1784
Murray, David, Mgr-Social Media - Blue Cross & Blue Shield of Michigan; *pg.* 1195, *pg.* 879
Murray, Dennis L., Sr Analyst-Mktg - CA Technologies; *pg.* 366, *pg.* 1168
Murray, Fiona, VP-Corp Mktg - Canadian National Railway Company; *pg.* 1902, *pg.* 1953
Murray, Glenn, Reg Mgr-Mktg - Airbus Helicopters, Inc.; *pg.* 223, *pg.* 1698
Murray, Grant, VP-Sls - Concord Pacific Group; *pg.* 1087, *pg.* 1910
Murray, Grif, Mgr-Mktg - BodyBuilding.com LLC; *pg.* 1232, *pg.* 549
Murray, Heather, VP-Product Mktg-HP Solutions Grp - Tech Data Corporation; *pg.* 482, *pg.* 416
Murray, Jeff, Sr Mgr-Mktg - Philips Electronics North America; *pg.* 662, *pg.* 782
Murray, Ken, Head-Digital Products - Farmers Group, Inc.; *pg.* 1199, *pg.* 130
Murray, Kevin, Dir-Mktg - Purcell Murray Company Inc.; *pg.* 59, *pg.* 50
Murray, Kristine, VP-Creative Svcs-Global - Bare Escentuals, Inc.; *pg.* 500, *pg.* 213
Murray, Lana, Mgr-Mktg - The Allstate Corporation; *pg.* 1189, *pg.* 639
Murray, Leslie, Dir-Mktg - Acklands-Grainger Inc.; *pg.* 197, *pg.* 1933
Murray, Lisa, VP-Mktg - Entrepreneur Media, Inc.; *pg.* 1639, *pg.* 110
Murray, Melanie, Sr Mgr-Mktg - Panera Bread Company; *pg.* 1029, *pg.* 1001

First page reference indicates Business Class Edition
Second page reference indicates Geographic Edition

Murray, Michael, Chief Product Officer & Exec VP - Catalina Marketing Corporation; *pg.* 369, *pg.* 462
Murray, Page, VP-Pan-Worldwide Channel Mktg - Hewlett-Packard Company; *pg.* 404, *pg.* 175
Murray, Paul, Sr Mgr-Loyalty & Payments Mktg - Dunkin' Brands Group, Inc.; *pg.* 1727, *pg.* 810
Murray, Peter, VP-Global Brand & Sports Mktg - Under Armour, Inc.; *pg.* 49, *pg.* 759
Murray, Rod, Sr Dir-Event Presentation & Production Ops - Pittsburgh Penguins LLC; *pg.* 577, *pg.* 1578
Murray, Ryan, Brand Mgr-Digital & US Surgical Mktg - Alcon; *pg.* 1399, *pg.* 530
Murray, Shannon, Sr Acct Mgr-Mktg - Ingram Micro Inc.; *pg.* 415, *pg.* 261
Murray, Sue, Mgr-Brand Design-Corp Mktg Svcs - Land O'Lakes, Inc.; *pg.* 873, *pg.* 915
Murray, Terence, Sr Mgr-Mktg Insights-Northstar Lottery Grp, LLC - New Jersey State Lottery; *pg.* 1000, *pg.* 1126
Murray, Tim, Mgr-Comml Fleet-Natl Sls-USA - Shell Lubricants; *pg.* 217, *pg.* 1714
Murray, Todd, VP-Mktg & Licensing-Wholesale - Caleres, Inc.; *pg.* 1805, *pg.* 993
Murray, Tom, VP-Residential Mktg - The ADT Corporation; *pg.* 612, *pg.* 409
Murray, Virginia, Mgr-Mktg - Active Parenting Publishers; *pg.* 1613, *pg.* 535
Murray, Wendy, Specialist-Mktg - Adobe Systems Incorporated; *pg.* 342, *pg.* 235
Murrell, Imani, Analyst-Digital Mktg-Mobile - Canadian Tire Corporation Limited; *pg.* 202, *pg.* 1936
Murri, Mike, Dir-Sls - WXYZ-TV; *pg.* 323, *pg.* 908
Murrin, Dan, Assoc Dir-Creative-Photography - L.L. Bean, Inc.; *pg.* 1777, *pg.* 750
Murrin, Ryan, Dir-Adv, Res & Direct - Chipotle Mexican Grill, Inc.; *pg.* 1722, *pg.* 317
Murtha, Joli, Grp VP & Mgr-Adv - Sun Trust Bank, Atlanta; *pg.* 806, *pg.* 520
Murtha, Joli, Grp VP & Mgr-Adv - SunTrust Banks, Inc.; *pg.* 807, *pg.* 520
Murtha, Kerri, Sr Dir - Teachers Insurance & Annuity Association - College Retirement Equities Fund; *pg.* 1219, *pg.* 1297
Murty, Jayant, Dir-Strategy, Media & Integrated Mktg-Asia Pacific - Intel Corporation; *pg.* 645, *pg.* 266
Musa, Henrietta, Mgr-Field Mktg-North America - Philips Electronics North America; *pg.* 662, *pg.* 782
Musale, Laura, Asst Mgr-Mktg - Neiman Marcus, Inc.; *pg.* 30, *pg.* 1684
Musante, Kenneth, Sr Dir & Controller-Mfg - Ethan Allen Interiors Inc.; *pg.* 924, *pg.* 343
Musbach, Michael, Mgr-Mktg Dev-Govt-Grainger - General Electric Company; *pg.* 1297, *pg.* 347
Muscarella, Silvester, Sr Mgr-Internal Audit - M&T Bank Corporation; *pg.* 777, *pg.* 1149
Muscarello, Tony, Exec VP-Sls-US - Cardtronics, Inc.; *pg.* 732, *pg.* 1703
Muscat, Michael K., Jr., Sr VP-Product Dev Svcs - Computer Programs & Systems, Inc.; *pg.* 378, *pg.* 7
Musci, Larry, Mgr-Sls & Mktg - W.J. Ruscoe Company; *pg.* 122, *pg.* 1403
Musco, Nicole, Mgr-Product Dev - Revlon Consumer Products Corporation; *pg.* 521, *pg.* 1286
Musgrove, Marc, Dir-Internet of Everything & Industries PR-Global Corp Comm - Cisco Systems, Inc.; *pg.* 372, *pg.* 240
Musgrove, Melissa, Head-Social Media - Regions Financial Corporation; *pg.* 798, *pg.* 4
Mushro, Aaron, Dir-Mktg - Truth Initiative; *pg.* 158, *pg.* 405
Music, Melissa Byrd, Sr Mgr-Brand Dev & US Mktg-Enterprise Growth Prepaid - American Express Company; *pg.* 712, *pg.* 1190
Muskopf, Karin, Sr Mgr-PR - Microsoft Corporation; *pg.* 435, *pg.* 1824
Muskus, Gerard, Dir & Head-US Hispanic Mktg - Rosetta Stone Inc.; *pg.* 462, *pg.* 1774
Musler, Monet, Brand Mgr-Intimate Apparel - Macy's East; *pg.* 1777, *pg.* 1254
Musler, Monet, Brand Mgr-Intimate Apparel - Macy's, Inc.; *pg.* 1778, *pg.* 1417
Musmeci, Eleni, Specialist-Internet Mktg-ECommerce - Canon U.S.A., Inc.; *pg.* 1404, *pg.* 1178
Musmeci, Len, Mgr-Mktg Outreach, Pro Engrg & Solutions Div - Canon U.S.A., Inc.; *pg.* 1404, *pg.* 1178
Mussaw, Adam, Mgr-Market Plng & Mktg Analytics - CareFirst BlueCross BlueShield; *pg.* 1196, *pg.* 397
Musselman, Katie, Mgr-Lifecycle Mktg-Consumer Apps & Svcs - Microsoft Corporation; *pg.* 435, *pg.* 1824
Musselman, Michael, Dir-Mktg & Analytics - American National Insurance Company; *pg.* 1191, *pg.* 1697
Musselwhite, Donna, Dir-Mktg Comm - Anthem, Inc.; *pg.* 1192, *pg.* 683
Musser, Megan, Mgr-Mdsg - Carl Karcher Enterprises, Inc.; *pg.* 1720, *pg.* 63
Musser, Megan, Mgr-Mdsg - CKE Restaurants Inc.; *pg.* 1723, *pg.* 63
Musser, Michele L, Sr Mgr-Mktg - AT&T Mobility LLC; *pg.* 619, *pg.* 488
Mustafa-Bowne, Dee, Dir-Creative - The Weather Channel LLC; *pg.* 320, *pg.* 523
Mustee, Kevin, VP-Mktg - E.L. Mustee & Sons, Inc.; *pg.* 1124, *pg.* 1430
Mustin, David, Dir-Media Svcs - PepsiCo, Inc.; *pg.* 259, *pg.* 1327
Mutchnik, Renee, Dir-Mktg & Comm - The Baltimore Sun Company; *pg.* 1619, *pg.* 755
Mutebi, Bru, Mgr-Mktg-Global - Facebook, Inc.; *pg.* 1245, *pg.* 143
Muth, Chuck, Sr VP-Sls Venturing & Emerging Brands - The Coca-Cola Company; *pg.* 240, *pg.* 493
Mutty, Dan, Dir-Online Mktg - Lionbridge Technologies Inc.; *pg.* 428, *pg.* 851
Mutuc, Eins, Mgr-Product Mktg - La Cie McCormick Canada Co.; *pg.* 872, *pg.* 1922
Mutuc, Eins, Product Mgr - McCormick & Company, Incorporated; *pg.* 1027, *pg.* 779
Mutz, Christopher, Exec Dir-US Mktg - Alexion Pharmaceuticals, Inc.; *pg.* 1489, *pg.* 341
Mutzman, Stephanie, Mgr-Mktg - Big Lots, Inc.; *pg.* 1762, *pg.* 1438
Muysson, Hans, VP-Product Dev-Brand Dev Grp - SGK; *pg.* 1686, *pg.* 590
Muzilla, Craig, Sr VP-Application Platform Products Bus Grp - Red Hat, Inc.; *pg.* 460, *pg.* 1388
Muzumdar, Maha, VP-Mktg - Oracle Corporation; *pg.* 450, *pg.* 191
Mydlach, Mark F., VP-Sls-Global - STEPAN COMPANY; *pg.* 1182, *pg.* 643
Myer, Jeff, Sr Dir-Natl Adv & Brand Mgmt - Nationwide Mutual Insurance Company; *pg.* 1210, *pg.* 1442
Myers, Amey, Sr VP-Mktg - Gordmans Stores Inc.; *pg.* 1771, *pg.* 1016
Myers, Anne, Brand Dir-Global Mktg-Autoimmune - Eli Lilly and Company; *pg.* 1527, *pg.* 684
Myers, Anne, Sr Coord-Mktg - MetroPCS, Inc.; *pg.* 1872, *pg.* 1683
Myers, Bart, Product Mgr - Caterpillar, Inc.; *pg.* 1321, *pg.* 650
Myers, Chris, Product Mgr-Heating Cable - Chromalox, Inc.; *pg.* 1070, *pg.* 1574
Myers, Dan, Sr Dir-Customer Mktg & Sls Plng - Diamond Foods, Inc.; *pg.* 1851, *pg.* 216
Myers, Eric, VP-Adv Sls - The Atlanta Journal-Constitution; *pg.* 1618, *pg.* 490
Myers, Gary, VP-Circulation & Mktg - The Hamilton Spectator; *pg.* 1647, *pg.* 1921
Myers, Glen, Dir-Creative Brand Svcs - Amway Corporation; *pg.* 326, *pg.* 864
Myers, Greg, Mgr-Mktg - Emerson Network Power; *pg.* 1071, *pg.* 1479
Myers, Heter, Mgr-Media Rels-North America - NIKE, Inc.; *pg.* 1812, *pg.* 1492
Myers, Jay, Mgr-Technical Product-Global ECommerce Dev - Best Buy Co., Inc.; *pg.* 1761, *pg.* 954
Myers, Jeff, VP-Consumer Mktg & Sls-West Reg - Gannett Co., Inc.; *pg.* 1643, *pg.* 1790
Myers, Jeff, CMO & Chief Sls Officer - Wyndham Vacation Ownership; *pg.* 1119, *pg.* 457
Myers, Justin, Mgr-Mktg & Comm - Windstream Corporation; *pg.* 321, *pg.* 34
Myers, Kathy, Coord-Sls & Project - The Homer Laughlin China Company; *pg.* 1125, *pg.* 1850
Myers, Kelley, Dir-Digital Products Category Brand Mgmt - Starbucks Corporation; *pg.* 897, *pg.* 1840
Myers, Kelly Singleton, Sr VP-Sls - Sunrise Senior Living, Inc.; *pg.* 1599, *pg.* 1795
Myers, Ken, Mgr-Mktg Brand - Affinia Group Intermediate Holdings Inc.; *pg.* 197, *pg.* 1373
Myers, Kurt, VP-Mktg - Clear Springs Foods, Inc.; *pg.* 848, *pg.* 548
Myers, Leigh, Dir-Brand & Patient Mktg - EXACT SCIENCES CORPORATION; *pg.* 1529, *pg.* 1865
Myers, Margaret, Exec VP & Gen Mgr-Mdse-Accessories & Women's Specialties - Nordstrom, Inc.; *pg.* 1779, *pg.* 1837
Myers, Megan, Sr Mgr-Mktg - American Express Company; *pg.* 712, *pg.* 1190
Myers, Morie, Dir-Sls - Stemco Inc; *pg.* 1182, *pg.* 1726
Myers, Pam, Strategist-Social Media - HCA HOLDINGS, INC.; *pg.* 1539, *pg.* 1651
Myers, Randy, Mgr-Product Dev - Bayer CropScience; *pg.* 1149, *pg.* 981
Myers, Rick, Dir-Brand & Mktg - Advent Software, Inc.; *pg.* 345, *pg.* 211
Myers, Rob, Brand Mgr-CravOn - J.R. Simplot Company; *pg.* 867, *pg.* 547
Myers, Rob, Dir-PR - Wyndham Worldwide Corporation; *pg.* 1119, *pg.* 1107
Myers, Therese, VP & Dir-PR - KeyCorp; *pg.* 774, *pg.* 1432
Myers, Thomas, Chief Strategy Officer & VP-Market Ops - The SSI Group, Inc.; *pg.* 473, *pg.* 7
Myers, Tim D., Pres-Wheel & Transportation Products - Alcoa Wheel & Forged Products; *pg.* 66, *pg.* 1427
Myers, Todd, Sr Mgr-Capacity Mgmt - Nissan North America, Inc.; *pg.* 186, *pg.* 1633
Myers, Tom, Dir-Mktg-Global - Gogo Business Air; *pg.* 1871, *pg.* 312
Myerson, Tracy, Dir-US Mktg - Fisher-Price, Inc.; *pg.* 953, *pg.* 1156
Myftiu, Matt, Dir-Michigan Production Hub-Digital First Media - Digital First Media; *pg.* 1238, *pg.* 1224
Myhre, Julie, Asst Mgr-Mktg - Kemps LLC; *pg.* 867, *pg.* 961
Myhrwold, Angela, Dir-Mktg-Three Rivers Medical Center - Community Health Systems, Inc.; *pg.* 1516, *pg.* 1632
Mykyta, Valeria, Mgr-Integrated Mktg - Dow Jones & Company, Inc.; *pg.* 1637, *pg.* 1225
Myland, Linette, Mgr-Mktg-Voice of the Customer - Siemens Process Industries and Drives; *pg.* 673, *pg.* 485
Myler, Jason, Mng Dir-Tech, Media & Telecom Investment Banking Grp-Boston - Piper Jaffray Companies; *pg.* 794, *pg.* 941
Mynders, Veronica, Mgr-Mktg - DraftKings, Inc.; *pg.* 545, *pg.* 793
Myohanen, Sami, Dir-Mktg - Henkel Corporation; *pg.* 1165, *pg.* 1535
Myrick, Dave, Sr VP-Sls-North America - The Hertz Corporation; *pg.* 1911, *pg.* 450
Myrick-Estelle, Erin, Mgr-Mktg - 99 Cents Only Stores LLC; *pg.* 1759, *pg.* 66
Myron, Dave, Sr Dir-FPGA Product Mgmt & Mktg - Xilinx, Inc.; *pg.* 496, *pg.* 252
Mysak, Liz, Brand Mktg Mgr - Wakefern Food Corporation; *pg.* 1037, *pg.* 1058
Myslinski, David, Dir-Creative - Arizona Diamondbacks; *pg.* 529, *pg.* 14
Mysore, Jayanth, Sr Product Mgr - Google Inc.; *pg.* 1249, *pg.* 153
Mytrowitz, Kelly, Mgr-Integrated Mktg-DEPARTURES - Time Inc.; *pg.* 1693, *pg.* 1300

N

Nabbefeldt, Drew, Brand Mgr-Activation-North America - Newell Rubbermaid Inc.; *pg.* 1128, *pg.* 515
Nabea, Anthony, Specialist-Online Mktg - DriveTime Automotive Group, Inc.; *pg.* 169, *pg.* 16
Naber, Lindsey, Mgr-Mktg-Key Accounts - Rawlings Sporting Goods Co., Inc.; *pg.* 1843, *pg.* 1002
Nace, Kathy, Sr Mgr-Res - Luxottica Retail; *pg.* 8, *pg.* 1460
Nachlas, Adam, Sr Dir-Brokerage - Cushman & Wakefield, Inc.; *pg.* 1088, *pg.* 1220
Nachum, David, Product Mgr - Google Inc.; *pg.* 1249, *pg.* 153
Nacif, Victor, Head-Product Comm-Global - Nissan North America, Inc.; *pg.* 186, *pg.* 1633
Nadal, Brad, Dir-Field Mktg - MillerCoors LLC; *pg.* 255, *pg.* 582
Nadali, Michael, VP-Sls & Sls Ops - Empire Today, LLC; *pg.* 923, *pg.* 643
Nadboy, Michael, VP-Online Mktg & Strategic Dev - FragranceNet.com, Inc.; *pg.* 1248, *pg.* 1155
Nader, Julia, Dir-Mktg - E&J Gallo Winery; *pg.* 1962, *pg.* 149
Naderi, Angela, Mgr-Retail Mktg - Highmark Blue Cross Blue Shield; *pg.* 1203, *pg.* 1576
Nadig, Craig, Mgr-Global Sls, Mktg, CRM & Bus Intelligence Sys - Armstrong World Industries, Inc.; *pg.* 914, *pg.* 1545
Nadile, Zac, Brand Mgr-Colt 45 & Malts - Pabst Brewing Company; *pg.* 258, *pg.* 137
Nadkarni, Tushar, Head-Product Mktg-Atlas - Facebook, Inc.;

pg. 1245, *pg.* 143
Nadler, Lesley, Head-Digital Sls & Exec Dir - Vogue Magazine; *pg.* 1700, *pg.* 1311
Naffier, Victoria, Acct Mgr-Mktg - Hewlett-Packard Company; *pg.* 404, *pg.* 175
Nafman, Joshua, Sr Dir-Brand Mktg & Digital, Social & Content - Kind LLC; *pg.* 868, *pg.* 1249
Naftzger, Alan, Dir-Email & Onsite Mktg - Ancestry.com LLC; *pg.* 1228, *pg.* 1754
Nafziger, Dwight, VP-Sls & Mktg - Marsh Bellofram Corporation; *pg.* 1885, *pg.* 1850
Nafziger, Nancy, Mgr-Natl Mktg & Tech Consulting - McGladrey, LLP; *pg.* 781, *pg.* 938
Nag, Aditya, Product Mgr-Wearables - Intel Corporation; *pg.* 645, *pg.* 266
Nagaraj, Sriram, Dir-Global Mktg-Inflammatory Bowel Disease - AstraZeneca Pharmaceuticals LP; *pg.* 1497, *pg.* 389
Nagarajan, Vidya, Product Mgr-Chrome Devices-Enterprise - Google Inc.; *pg.* 1249, *pg.* 153
Nagarkar, Shaila, Mgr-Adv - Cellco Partnership; *pg.* 1869, *pg.* 1042
Nagata, Taryn, Sr Media Planner-Digital - Palisades Media Group, Inc.; *pg.* 452, *pg.* 275
Nagel, Amanda, Assoc Mgr-Mktg - Great Clips, Inc.; *pg.* 510, *pg.* 937
Nagel, Larry, Dir-Online Mktg & Global eBusiness - MetLife, Inc.; *pg.* 1208, *pg.* 1258
Nagel, Mark, Exec Dir-Mktg-AT&T Foundry - AT&T West; *pg.* 1869, *pg.* 212
Nagel, Suzanne, Exec Dir-Brand Mktg - Edmunds, Inc.; *pg.* 1241, *pg.* 273
Nagele, Kim, Sr Mgr-Pur-Print Media - J.C. Penney Company, Inc.; *pg.* 1774, *pg.* 1732
Naggiar, Caroline, Sr VP-Mktg - Tiffany & Co.; *pg.* 13, *pg.* 1299
Naghdy, Nabil, Product Mgr-Maps - Google Inc.; *pg.* 1249, *pg.* 153
Nagle, Monica, Mgr-Interactive & Web Mktg - Hewlett-Packard Company; *pg.* 404, *pg.* 175
Nagle, Sarah, Dir-Programmatic Sls - Tremor Video; *pg.* 682, *pg.* 1305
Nagy, Ingrid, Dir-Mktg - Bristol-Myers Squibb Company; *pg.* 1509, *pg.* 1206
Nagy, Jeff, Product Mgr-Global - Molex Incorporated; *pg.* 655, *pg.* 628
Nahas, Stephanie, Specialist-Social Media - Caleres, Inc.; *pg.* 1805, *pg.* 993
Nahass, Pasha, Product Mgr-Mobile Display Ads - Google Inc.; *pg.* 1249, *pg.* 153
Nahon, Claude, Pres-Mood Media Intl - Mood Media; *pg.* 298, *pg.* 1616
Nahoum, Kathryne, Dir-Mktg - Kind LLC; *pg.* 868, *pg.* 1249
Nahrgang, Taylor, Mgr-Mktg - Weatherby, Inc.; *pg.* 1848, *pg.* 181
Nahuz, Sergio, Head-Sls-US - The Kraft Heinz Company; *pg.* 870, *pg.* 1577
Naide, Adam, Head-Social Media - Cox Communications, Inc.; *pg.* 279, *pg.* 501
Naidish, Joan, Sr Mgr-Americas Svcs Mktg - Juniper Networks, Inc.; *pg.* 1260, *pg.* 286
Naig, Gretchen, Mgr-Ops Design & Product Dev - CARIBOU COFFEE COMPANY, INC.; *pg.* 1764, *pg.* 932
Naigeon, Virginie, Dir-Internal Comm & PR-USA - Galderma Laboratories, L.P.; *pg.* 1532, *pg.* 1695
Naik, Mitesh, Dir-Sls & Mktg Admin - Peterbilt Motors Co.; *pg.* 188, *pg.* 1691
Naik, Purvi, Mgr-Mktg Comm - Varian Medical Systems, Inc.; *pg.* 1434, *pg.* 178
Naik, Rithika, Brand Mgr - Church & Dwight Co., Inc.; *pg.* 1153, *pg.* 1063
Nail, Joe, Mgr-Product Mktg-Risk Mgmt - Monsanto; *pg.* 1798, *pg.* 1399
Nail, Joe, Mktg Mgr-Risk Mgmt - Monsanto Company; *pg.* 1173, *pg.* 999
Nail, Jonathan, Sr Mgr-Mktg-DVD - Netflix, Inc.; *pg.* 1269, *pg.* 141
Naiman, Amanda, Mgr-Media Rels - Siemens Medical Solutions USA, Inc.; *pg.* 469, *pg.* 1550
Naiman, Kristen, VP-Brand Creative - Kate Spade & Company; *pg.* 27, *pg.* 1248
Naimoli, Ray, Sr Mgr-Corp Partnership Sls - Baltimore Orioles, L.P.; *pg.* 532, *pg.* 755
Nair, Daya, Mgr-Digital Mktg - Kimberly-Clark Corporation; *pg.* 1461, *pg.* 1720
Nair, Manoj, Sr Mgr-Global Cloud Program - Ingram Micro Inc.; *pg.* 415, *pg.* 261
Nair, Raj, CTO & Grp VP-Product Dev-Global - Ford Motor Company; *pg.* 172, *pg.* 876
Naito, Take, Head-Oregon State Sls - Diageo North America, Inc.; *pg.* 1961, *pg.* 361
Najat, Joseph, Sr Mgr-Category Insights - Diamond Foods, Inc.; *pg.* 1851, *pg.* 216
Najera, Armando , Jr., Product Mgr - Komatsu America Corp.; *pg.* 92, *pg.* 655
Najjar, Tony, Grp VP-Sls & Mktg-Aerospace & Defense - CIRCOR Aerospace, Inc.; *pg.* 226, *pg.* 69
Najman, Allison, Sr Community Mgr & Sr Mgr-Social Media - NetApp, Inc.; *pg.* 444, *pg.* 287
Najoan, Allison, Brand Mgr-JM Collection - Macy's East; *pg.* 1777, *pg.* 1254
Najoan, Allison, Brand Mgr-JM Collection - Macy's, Inc.; *pg.* 1778, *pg.* 1417
Nakai, Rudy, Founder & Designer - Crystal World, Inc.; *pg.* 4, *pg.* 1122
Nakajima, Jun, Dir-Sls - Taiyo Yuden (U.S.A.), Inc.; *pg.* 1080, *pg.* 279
Nakamura, Christina, Assoc Mgr-Digital Mktg - HD SUPPLY, INC.; *pg.* 86, *pg.* 509
Nakamura, Grant, Product Mgr - Wells Fargo & Company; *pg.* 819, *pg.* 232
Nakashima, Jill, Sr Mgr-Mktg-Mint - Intuit Inc.; *pg.* 769, *pg.* 158
Nakasone, Bob, Sr Dir-Bus Dev - Naked Juice Company, Inc.; *pg.* 882, *pg.* 150
Nakata, Vicki, VP-Loyalty & Travel Products - Hawaiian Airlines, Inc.; *pg.* 1910, *pg.* 543
Nakhwa, Lissa, Program Mgr-Mktg-Global - Agilent Technologies, Inc.; *pg.* 614, *pg.* 264
Nakonechny, Oleg, Sr Mgr-Convention Svcs - San Francisco Travel Association; *pg.* 1005, *pg.* 227
Nalezny, Jessie, Assoc Product Mgr & Brand Mgr-Food - Dairy Queen Corporate Store; *pg.* 1724, *pg.* 932
Nalezny, Jessie, Assoc Mgr-Product & Brand-Food - International Dairy Queen, Inc.; *pg.* 1732, *pg.* 938
Nalley, Allen, Mgr-Sls & Bus Dev-Military & Defense - Oshkosh Specialty Vehicles; *pg.* 1918, *pg.* 561
Nallur, Girish, Principal-Mktg - FedEx Corporation; *pg.* 1907, *pg.* 1642
Nally, Jennifer, VP-Event Mktg-Global - Citigroup Inc.; *pg.* 735, *pg.* 1212
Nam, Virginia, Dir-Social Media-Lucky Magazine - Vogue Magazine; *pg.* 1700, *pg.* 1311
Namboori, Lakshmi, Sr Mgr-Product Line - Juniper Networks, Inc.; *pg.* 1260, *pg.* 286
Namias, Linda, Sr Dir-Corp Comm - Broadridge Financial Solutions Inc.; *pg.* 727, *pg.* 1172
Namineni, Srini, Sr Dir-Fin Plng & Analysis - salesforce.com, inc.; *pg.* 1278, *pg.* 226
Namiot, Keith, Head-Employer Sponsored Markets Product Dev & Dir - AXA Equitable Life Insurance Company; *pg.* 1194, *pg.* 1199
Nanakdewa, Lisa, Assoc Mgr-Mktg-Ice Breakers & Lancaster - Hershey Canada, Inc.; *pg.* 1855, *pg.* 1926
Nance, Sunshine, Dir-Mktg& Comm-Global - Boxlight Corporation; *pg.* 627, *pg.* 1813
Nanclares, Monique, Sr Mgr-Digital Campaign - Samsung Electronics America, Inc.; *pg.* 669, *pg.* 1115
Nandra, Navraj, Sr Dir-Mktg Analog & Mixed Signal IP - Synopsys, Inc.; *pg.* 480, *pg.* 162
Nanduri, Anil, Dir-Solutions & Products-Perceptual Computing Grp - Intel Corporation; *pg.* 645, *pg.* 266
Nandwani, Suneet, Sr Dir-Cloud Engrg - eBay Inc.; *pg.* 1240, *pg.* 243
Nanes, Ezra, Sr Dir-Digital Media Product - AccuWeather, Inc.; *pg.* 268, *pg.* 1587
Nangle, David J., Pres/CEO-The Harris Products Grp & Sr VP - Lincoln Electric Holdings, Inc.; *pg.* 1355, *pg.* 1432
Nangle, Leslie, Assoc Dir-Mktg - Princeton University Press; *pg.* 1678, *pg.* 1112
Nankervis, Carolyn, VP-Mktg - Fox Valley Symphony Association Inc.; *pg.* 549, *pg.* 1852
Nankil, Natalie M., Mgr-Media Rels - General Motors of Canada Ltd.; *pg.* 177, *pg.* 1931
Nanni, Margaret, Sr VP-Product Dev & Sourcing - Sure Fit Inc.; *pg.* 944, *pg.* 1514
Nanton, Elton, Designer-Brand, Stationery & Pkg - A. T. CROSS COMPANY; *pg.* 339, *pg.* 1602
Nanus, Wendy, Dir-Adv - Self Magazine; *pg.* 1686, *pg.* 1290
Naoum, John, Sr Mgr-Global Mktg-Global Bus Dev - Brinker International, Inc.; *pg.* 1718, *pg.* 1676
Napierski, Ryan, Pres-Global Sls & Ops - Nu Skin Enterprises, Inc.; *pg.* 518, *pg.* 1755
Naples, Mike, Bus Mgr-Alliance - United States Postal Service; *pg.* 1009, *pg.* 406
Napleton, Chris, Gen Mgr-Sls - Napleton Schaumburg Motors, Inc.; *pg.* 185, *pg.* 659
Napoli, Stefanie, Exec VP-Media - Columbia TriStar Motion Picture Group; *pg.* 275, *pg.* 72
Napolitano, Mike, VP-Consumer Products-Hard Goods - Major League Baseball; *pg.* 560, *pg.* 1255
Nappa, Mary, Rep-Mktg Svcs - Columbian Mutual Life Insurance Company; *pg.* 1198, *pg.* 1142
Naquin, Dana, Mgr-Mktg-CareerBuilder Healthcare - CareerBuilder, LLC; *pg.* 1234, *pg.* 568
Narang, Priya, Sr VP-Mktg & Sls Dev - Time Inc.; *pg.* 1693, *pg.* 1300
Narang, Promod, Sr VP-Products - eGain Communications Corporation; *pg.* 1242, *pg.* 284
Narang, Radhika, Dir-Media Strategy & Plng - Cisco Systems, Inc.; *pg.* 372, *pg.* 240
Narang, Rajiv, Sr Dir-Customer Optimization - eBay Inc.; *pg.* 1240, *pg.* 243
Narasimhan, Kris, Product Mgr-Nuclear - Superior Tube Company Inc.; *pg.* 113, *pg.* 1522
Narasimhan, Ravi, Grp Product Mgr - Google Inc.; *pg.* 1249, *pg.* 153
Narasimhan, Shar, Sr Product Mgr-Touch Mktg - Atmel Corporation; *pg.* 621, *pg.* 238
Narayanan, Revathi, Sr Mgr-Bus Dev & Networking Bus unit - Micron Technology, Inc.; *pg.* 435, *pg.* 547
Nardella, Cindy, Sr Mgr-Channel Mktg-ADI & Loyalty - Honeywell International Inc.; *pg.* 407, *pg.* 1088
Nardi, Lisa, VP-Mktg - Nipro Diagnostics, Inc.; *pg.* 1573, *pg.* 426
Nardini, Robert, Mgr-Mktg, Promos & Event - Dominick's Finer Foods, LLC; *pg.* 1019, *pg.* 644
Nardini, Trevor, Dir-Brand Adv - TripAdvisor, Inc.; *pg.* 1926, *pg.* 835
Narendra, Naren, Sr Product Mgr - Cisco Systems, Inc.; *pg.* 372, *pg.* 240
Naresh, Rakshith, Product Mgr - Adobe Systems Incorporated; *pg.* 342, *pg.* 235
Naretto, Nancy, Sr Mgr-Strategic Alliances - Agilysys, Inc.; *pg.* 614, *pg.* 1409
Narod, Kenneth D., VP-Construction Sls - Eaton Corporation; *pg.* 1331, *pg.* 1429
Naroff, Neil, Chief Strategy Officer - Max & Erma's Restaurants, Inc.; *pg.* 1737, *pg.* 1652
Naroo-Pucci, Noreen Naz, Sr Dir-Creative-Apparel Design - Under Armour, Inc.; *pg.* 49, *pg.* 759
Nartker, Andrew, Product Mgr - Google Inc.; *pg.* 1249, *pg.* 153
Narula, Ayesha, Brand Mgr-Cetaphil - Galderma Laboratories, L.P.; *pg.* 1532, *pg.* 1695
Naruse, Taro, Sr Dir-Product Mgmt - RetailMeNot Inc.; *pg.* 1782, *pg.* 1665
Narvaez, Ed, Mgr-Channel Mktg - Dot Hill Systems Corp.; *pg.* 388, *pg.* 333
Narvaez, Tricia, Sr Specialist-Digital Mktg & Retail Mktg - Volkswagen Group of America, Inc.; *pg.* 194, *pg.* 1785
Nasamu-Odior, Vivian, Brand Mgr-TYLENOL Owned & Earned Media - Johnson & Johnson; *pg.* 1549, *pg.* 1091
Nasca, Susan M., Sr Planner-Mdse - Levi Strauss & Co.; *pg.* 43, *pg.* 220
Nascimento, Alexis, Strategist-Digital Mktg - E&J Gallo Winery; *pg.* 1962, *pg.* 149
Nasgovitz, Sheila M., Strategist-Mktg-Digital Interactions - Thrivent Financial for Lutherans; *pg.* 1219, *pg.* 944
Nash, Andrew, Category Dir-Mktg-Scotch & North American Whiskies - William Grant & Sons, Inc.; *pg.* 1972, *pg.* 1057
Nash, Ann, Sr Dir-Mktg-Consulting - PricewaterhouseCoopers LLP; *pg.* 795, *pg.* 1283
Nash, Brian, VP-Mktg & Sls - NuSil Technology LLC; *pg.* 1887, *pg.* 63
Nash, Christy, Specialist-Mktg - Toll Brothers, Inc.; *pg.* 115, *pg.* 1541
Nash, Eric, Sr Dir-Online Mktg - Stamps.com Inc.; *pg.* 1282, *pg.* 82
Nash, Gary, VP-OTR Sls USA Mexico - Yokohama Tire Corporation; *pg.* 1892, *pg.* 94
Nash, Jeff, Interim Mng Editor - CNBC; *pg.* 275, *pg.* 1059
Nash, Kerri, Brand Mktg Mgr - BJ's Wholesale Club, Inc.; *pg.* 1762, *pg.* 857
Nash, Paul, Sr Product Mgr-Compute Engine - Google Inc.; *pg.* 1249, *pg.* 153

First page reference indicates Business Class Edition
Second page reference indicates Geographic Edition

Nash, Seth, Dir-Product Mgmt-Hips - Zimmer Biomet Holdings, Inc.; *pg.* 1611, *pg.* 699
Nasher, Rasha, Product Mgr-Mobility - Hewlett-Packard Company; *pg.* 404, *pg.* 175
Nasmyth, Ibrahim, Program Mgr-Digital Sls & Mktg-Deposits - Wells Fargo & Company; *pg.* 819, *pg.* 232
Nasomyont, Jui Chairit, Brand Mgr-Color Cosmetics-Global - Avon Products, Inc.; *pg.* 500, *pg.* 1198
Nason, Anna, Specialist-Online Mktg - Provide Commerce, Inc.; *pg.* 1276, *pg.* 206
Nason, Jennifer, Global Chm-Tech, Media & Telecom - JPMorgan Chase & Co.; *pg.* 772, *pg.* 1246
Nasri, Jennifer, Mgr-Digital Mktg - Lexus Division; *pg.* 182, *pg.* 294
Nass, Erin, Mgr-Mktg-Travel Agency Engagement - Mark Travel Corporation; *pg.* 1915, *pg.* 1877
Nass, Julia, Specialist-Mktg-Broadcast Production - GEICO Corporation; *pg.* 1200, *pg.* 399
Nassar, Lara, Product Mgr-Import Knits - Macy's East; *pg.* 1777, *pg.* 1254
Nassayan, Deb, Sr Mgr-Media Production - Chico's FAS, Inc.; *pg.* 21, *pg.* 427
Nasser, Mohamad, Sr Dir-M2M Product, Platform & Mktg - Sprint Corporation; *pg.* 1874, *pg.* 719
Nasser, Selma, Dir-PR & Adv - Corcoran Sunshine Marketing Group; *pg.* 1088, *pg.* 1218
Nasso, Dominic, Exec VP-Sls - Buffalo Wire Works Co., Inc.; *pg.* 72, *pg.* 1147
Nassr, Christine, Asst Dir-Mktg & Bus Dev - City of Hope National Medical Center; *pg.* 1516, *pg.* 77
Nastasia, Vic, Sr VP-Sls & Mktg - Monster Beverage Corporation; *pg.* 257, *pg.* 69
Nastro, Ken, Dir-Adv & HR - Key Food Stores Co-Operative, Inc.; *pg.* 1025, *pg.* 1343
Natarajan, Nat, CTO & Sr VP-Product & Tech-Consumer Tax Grp - Intuit Inc.; *pg.* 769, *pg.* 158
Nathan, Ashwin, Sr Dir-Mktg, Digital, ECommerce & D3 Studios - Frito-Lay North America, Inc.; *pg.* 1853, *pg.* 1730
Nathan, Ashwin, Sr Dir-Digital, ECommerce & D3 Studios - PepsiCo, Inc.; *pg.* 259, *pg.* 1327
Nathan, Betsy, Mgr-Mktg - Harvard Pilgrim Health Care, Inc.; *pg.* 1539, *pg.* 856
Nathan, Elango, Mgr-Mktg & Strategic Mktg-Global - Abbott Diabetes Care, Inc.; *pg.* 1483, *pg.* 38
Nathan, Senthil, Mgr-Product & Program & Analyst-Bus Sys - Intuitive Surgical, Inc.; *pg.* 1546, *pg.* 286
Nathan, Stacy, Assoc Publr-Adv - Hearst Magazines; *pg.* 1649, *pg.* 1239
Nathanson, Alex, Brand Mgr-Corp Mktg - Rain Bird Corporation; *pg.* 707, *pg.* 44
Nathanson, Joel, Sr VP & Head-Social Media - Bank of the West; *pg.* 721, *pg.* 213
Nathanson, Robert, Sr Dir-Platform Sls - AppNexus; *pg.* 352, *pg.* 1196
Nation, Desmond, Mgr-Mktg-Cardiac Rhythm Mgmt Diagnostics - Medtronic, Inc.; *pg.* 1564, *pg.* 939
Natowitz, Alan J., Gen Mgr-Mdse - Bed Bath & Beyond Inc.; *pg.* 1121, *pg.* 1127
Nau, Kimberly, Dir-Mktg - Ocean Spray Cranberries, Inc.; *pg.* 887, *pg.* 827
Naude, El-Deane, Sr Mgr-Product Info - Sony Electronics, Inc.; *pg.* 676, *pg.* 209
Naughton, Chad, Reg Sls Dir-Digital & Implants-Western - 3M Company; *pg.* 1142, *pg.* 956
Naughton, Eileen, Mng Dir & VP-UK-Ireland Sls & Ops - Google Inc.; *pg.* 1249, *pg.* 153
Naugle, Bob, Dir-Mktg Sys - Las Vegas Convention & Visitors Authority; *pg.* 997, *pg.* 1027
Naumann, Rachael, Specialist-Mktg Matls Compliance - The Northwestern Mutual Life Insurance Company; *pg.* 1212, *pg.* 1879
Naumes, Pamela, Sr Dir-Brand Engagement - Bolthouse Farms; *pg.* 841, *pg.* 44
Nava, Adam, Sr Mgr-Mktg-Demand Generation - Brocade Corporation; *pg.* 365, *pg.* 312
Nava, Edmundo, VP-Mktg Ops - Adecco USA, Inc.; *pg.* 342, *pg.* 1178
Nava, James, Mgr-Mktg-Ontario - General Motors of Canada Ltd.; *pg.* 177, *pg.* 1931
Navab, Alexander , Jr., Head-Media & Comm Team - KKR & CO. L.P.; *pg.* 774, *pg.* 1249
Navaid, Omer, Assoc Mgr-Acq Mktg - Cars.com; *pg.* 1234, *pg.* 568
Navarra Marusak, Ashley, Mgr-Corp Mktg-Global Sponsorships Mktg - Cisco Systems, Inc.; *pg.* 372, *pg.* 240
Navarrete, Alida, Sr Mgr-Mktg-Customer Acq & Retention - Yahoo! Inc.; *pg.* 1289, *pg.* 289
Navarro, Heather, Sr Mgr-Online Mktg - LeapFrog Enterprises, Inc.; *pg.* 961, *pg.* 84
Navarro, Luis, Sr Product Mgr - New Balance Athletic Shoe, Inc.; *pg.* 1811, *pg.* 798
Navarro, Michele, Sr Mgr-Mktg Comm - Boston Scientific Corporation; *pg.* 1508, *pg.* 831
Navarro, Rafael , III, VP-Comm, Media Rels & Motorsports - Pirelli Tire North America; *pg.* 1887, *pg.* 539
Navarro, Xaila, Brand Mgr-Mktg & Dev-Global - Hasbro, Inc.; *pg.* 954, *pg.* 1603
Navas, Antonio, Dir-Legal, Mktg Sls & Distr Grp - Nissan North America, Inc.; *pg.* 186, *pg.* 1633
Nave, Ross, Brand Mgr - Stryker Corporation; *pg.* 1598, *pg.* 894
Navejas, Gabriela, Dir-Mktg - Accor; *pg.* 1079, *pg.* 1657
Naven, Ron, Reg Mgr-Commodity & Premium Offerings Sls - Yara N America, Inc.; *pg.* 1802, *pg.* 477
Naves, Karen L., Dir-Global Integrated Mktg & Mobility - CA Technologies; *pg.* 366, *pg.* 1168
Navia, Anthony, Analyst-Bus-Tactical Mktg - John Deere Consumer & Commercial Equipment, Inc.; *pg.* 705, *pg.* 1360
Naviaux, Jeffrey, Mgr-Mktg Automation-North America - Ceridian Corporation; *pg.* 371, *pg.* 932
Nawalaniec, Chris, Mgr-Sls-Natl - Stedman Machine Company; *pg.* 1379, *pg.* 673
Nawrocki, Laura, Sr Dir-ECommerce - BCBG Max Azria Group LLC; *pg.* 19, *pg.* 301
Nayak, Vandan, Sr Product Mgr-Lifecycle Mgmt Suite - Hewlett-Packard Company; *pg.* 404, *pg.* 175
Nayanar, Deepesh, Dir-Product Mgmt-Connected Vehicle Bus - Navistar International Corporation; *pg.* 186, *pg.* 630
Nayar, Anuj, Sr Dir-Global Initiatives - PayPal Inc.; *pg.* 1274, *pg.* 248
Naye, Jen, Assoc Mgr-Mktg-Upstream Innovation - MillerCoors; *pg.* 254, *pg.* 1877
Naylor, Mark, Mgr-Customer Sls - GlaxoSmithKline Consumer Healthcare; *pg.* 510, *pg.* 1554
Naylor, Peter, Sr VP-Adv Sls - Hulu LLC; *pg.* 1257, *pg.* 274
Naylor, Philip, Project Coord-Multi-Channel Mktg - Teachers Insurance & Annuity Association - College Retirement Equities Fund; *pg.* 1219, *pg.* 1297
Naylor, Shannon, Dir-Mktg - Palm Beach Tan, Inc.; *pg.* 519, *pg.* 1671
Nazareth, Lisa, Dir-Mktg - Pfizer Inc.; *pg.* 1581, *pg.* 1278
Nazarewicz, Eva, Sr Mgr-Customer Mktg - LinkedIn Corporation; *pg.* 1262, *pg.* 160
Nazarian, Dana, Exec VP-Memory Products Div - Cypress Semiconductor Corporation; *pg.* 1326, *pg.* 243
Nazarian, Sara, Specialist-Brand, External Comm & PR - Ernst & Young Global Limited; *pg.* 748, *pg.* 1228
Nazee, Hoglund, VP-Product Mgmt - Johnson Controls, Inc.; *pg.* 209, *pg.* 1876
Nazemzadeh, Tania, Specialist-Mktg Comm - Beckman Coulter, Inc.; *pg.* 1402, *pg.* 48
Nazzal, Tamara, Partner-Mktg & Mgr-Mktg - athenahealth, Inc.; *pg.* 1497, *pg.* 855
Neal, Aaron, Product Mgr-PSU-Global - Corsair Components, Inc.; *pg.* 380, *pg.* 90
Neal, David, Sr VP-Sls & Mktg - Comverge, Inc.; *pg.* 1325, *pg.* 536
Neal, Hollie, Sr Mgr-Comm-Global - Fossil Group, Inc.; *pg.* 5, *pg.* 1735
Neal, Holly, Mgr-Mktg-Global Programs - Red Hat, Inc.; *pg.* 460, *pg.* 1388
Neal, Jen, Exec VP-Mktg-E! Entertainment - E! Online, Inc.; *pg.* 1239, *pg.* 129
Neal, Peter, Acct Mgr-College Sports Mktg - NIKE, Inc.; *pg.* 1812, *pg.* 1492
Neal, Scott, Sr VP-Sls & Mktg - Gulfstream Aerospace Corporation; *pg.* 228, *pg.* 540
Neale, Dan, Dir-Shopper Mktg & Concept Dev - Safeway Inc.; *pg.* 1032, *pg.* 184
Neale, Russ, Dir-Product Mgmt & Innovation - The Valspar Corporation; *pg.* 1449, *pg.* 945
Near, Dan, Dir-Consumer Products Licensing - National Hockey League; *pg.* 568, *pg.* 1265
Nearing, Janice, Dir-PR - Save the Manatee Club, Inc.; *pg.* 156, *pg.* 439
Nearing, Nicole, Mgr-Comm & Media Rels - Kaman Music Corporation; *pg.* 555, *pg.* 339
Neary, Kara, Mgr-Global Email Mktg - Columbia Sportswear Company; *pg.* 1830, *pg.* 1501
Necessary, Steve, VP-Video Product Dev & Mgmt - Cox Communications, Inc.; *pg.* 279, *pg.* 501
Nedeau, John, VP-Sls-Global - SRAM Corporation; *pg.* 967, *pg.* 590
Neder, Steve, Gen Mgr-Brand Strategy, Media & Retail Mktg - Volkswagen Group of America, Inc.; *pg.* 194, *pg.* 1785
Nedvidek, Steve, Dir-Mktg - Chick-fil-A, Inc.; *pg.* 1721, *pg.* 492
Neebe, Margot, Mgr-Product Mktg - Google Inc.; *pg.* 1249, *pg.* 153
Needham, MaryEllen, VP-Creative Svcs - Macy's East; *pg.* 1777, *pg.* 1254
Needle, Allen, Mgr-Sls Ops - Giant Bicycle Inc.; *pg.* 1707, *pg.* 164
Needleman, Jesse, Asst VP & Dir-Mktg - Marshalls of MA, Inc.; *pg.* 1778, *pg.* 821
Needleman, Jesse, Asst VP & Dir-Mktg - T.J. Maxx; *pg.* 1788, *pg.* 822
Needleman, Jesse, Asst VP & Dir-Mktg - The TJX Companies, Inc.; *pg.* 1788, *pg.* 822
Neeley, Dwayne, Mgr-Casino Mktg - Norwegian Cruise Line; *pg.* 1917, *pg.* 444
Neely, Craig, Dir-Mktg - Mars Petcare; *pg.* 1478, *pg.* 1633
Neely, Elena, Mgr-Sls & Major Accts - United States Postal Service; *pg.* 1009, *pg.* 406
Neely, Laura, Mgr-Field Mktg - Starwood Hotels & Resorts Worldwide, Inc.; *pg.* 1114, *pg.* 378
Neely, Renate, Dir-Mktg - Telos Corporation; *pg.* 483, *pg.* 1776
Nees, Peter, Product Mgr - Interactive Intelligence, Inc.; *pg.* 417, *pg.* 687
Neese, Jessica, Mgr-Mktg Comm - McKesson Corporation; *pg.* 1560, *pg.* 222
Neeser, Timothy, Dir-New Product Dev & Mktg - Chart Industries, Inc.; *pg.* 1405, *pg.* 1454
Neesley, Michele, Sr Dir-Mktg - DIRECTV Group Holdings, LLC; *pg.* 281, *pg.* 79
Neff, Christopher, VP-Mktg - NIC Inc.; *pg.* 445, *pg.* 718
Neff, Douglas, Sr Mgr-US Olympic Programs - Deloitte & Touche USA LLP; *pg.* 743, *pg.* 1222
Negaard, Kim, Product Mgr - Google Inc.; *pg.* 1249, *pg.* 153
Negri, Joe, Sr Dir-Mktg - AutoNation, Inc.; *pg.* 165, *pg.* 423
Negron, Gabriel, Coord-Mktg - Pfizer Inc.; *pg.* 1581, *pg.* 1278
Neidermire, Troy, Grp Mgr-Digital Media, SEO & SEM - Target Corporation; *pg.* 1786, *pg.* 942
Neidert, Angela, Mgr-Mktg - CB Richard Ellis Group, Inc.; *pg.* 1085, *pg.* 127
Neil, Fred, Head-Lifecycle Mktg & BI-Global - Amazon.com, Inc.; *pg.* 1226, *pg.* 1831
Neiley, Donna M., Chief Strategy Officer - W.P. Carey & Co., LLC; *pg.* 823, *pg.* 1315
Neill, Cliff, VP-Sls - Oakley, Inc.; *pg.* 1840, *pg.* 86
Neilson, Glenn P., Dir-Private Label Brand Mktg - The Scotts Miracle-Gro Company; *pg.* 1799, *pg.* 1459
Neiman, Peter, VP-Brand & Adv - Unum Group; *pg.* 1222, *pg.* 1629
Neipp, Nancy, Sr Dir-Global Events - Cisco Systems, Inc.; *pg.* 372, *pg.* 240
Neira, Marisa, Sr Mgr-Mktg-Jewelry & Timepieces - Van Cleef & Arpels, Inc.; *pg.* 15, *pg.* 1308
Neis, Tracey, Sr Mgr-Strategy & Insights-Global - PepsiCo, Inc.; *pg.* 259, *pg.* 1327
Neitlich, Scott, Dir-Mktg - JAKKS Pacific, Inc.; *pg.* 960, *pg.* 142
Neivert, Deb, Sr Dir-Portfolio Strategy & Mgmt - AstraZeneca Pharmaceuticals LP; *pg.* 1497, *pg.* 389
Nekrasov, Ivan, Brand Mgr-Dell Enterprise - Dell Inc.; *pg.* 383, *pg.* 1737
Nelan, Tony, Dir-Sls - Twitter, Inc.; *pg.* 1285, *pg.* 228
Nelder, Mason, Dir-Social Media & Digital Strategy - Cellco Partnership; *pg.* 1869, *pg.* 1042
Nelder, Mason, Sr Dir & Dir-Central Insights & Social Bus - Verizon Communications Inc.; *pg.* 1875, *pg.* 1309
Nella, Jamie, Mgr-Sls-Natl - Embassy Industries, Inc.; *pg.* 1071, *pg.* 1164
Nelles, Andrew, Sr Mgr-Mktg - Sony Corporation of America; *pg.* 675, *pg.* 1293
Nelligan, Barb, Sr VP & Product Mgr-Global Fund Svcs - The Northern Trust Company; *pg.* 787, *pg.* 585
Nelligan, John, Gen Mgr-OEM & Natl Acct Sls - Meritor, Inc.; *pg.* 212, *pg.* 911
Nellis, Randy, VP-Creative & Consumer Mktg - Sony Pictures Entertainment Inc.; *pg.* 309, *pg.* 72
Nelsen, Mark, Sr Mgr-Mktg & Retail Mktg - Cabela's Incorporated; *pg.* 535, *pg.* 1019

Nelsen, Scott, Sr Dir-Oracle Grp - Arrow Electronics, Inc.; *pg.* 619, *pg.* 325
Nelson, Andrea, Dir-Product Mktg - Intel Corporation; *pg.* 645, *pg.* 266
Nelson, Anita, VP-Sls & Licensing - Dark Horse Comics, Inc.; *pg.* 1633, *pg.* 1500
Nelson, Anne, VP & Mgr-Corp Sponsorship Mktg - UnionBanCal Corporation; *pg.* 813, *pg.* 230
Nelson, Benjamin, Sr Product Mgr-Mktg - AT&T Inc.; *pg.* 1867, *pg.* 1674
Nelson, Bruce, Sr VP & Gen Mgr-Mdse - Ross Stores, Inc.; *pg.* 1783, *pg.* 78
Nelson, Bryan, Dir-Product Mgmt-Lodge, Outdoor, Bikes & Fitness - Dick's Sporting Goods, Inc.; *pg.* 1832, *pg.* 1524
Nelson, Charles, Analyst-Trade Mktg-Target Team - Unilever United States, Inc.; *pg.* 904, *pg.* 1061
Nelson, Chip, Mgr-Sls-North America - The George E. Failing Company; *pg.* 1340, *pg.* 1484
Nelson, Chris, Dir-Social Mktg - Country Music Television, Inc.; *pg.* 279, *pg.* 1649
Nelson, Clint, Mgr-Web Creative - Sierra Trading Post Inc.; *pg.* 1819, *pg.* 1901
Nelson, Craig, Mgr-Product Mktg - Siemens Process Industries and Drives; *pg.* 673, *pg.* 485
Nelson, Cynthia, Coord-Media Sls - Time Warner Cable Inc.; *pg.* 312, *pg.* 1301
Nelson, Dan, VP-Worldwide Media Rels - Lockheed Martin Corporation; *pg.* 229, *pg.* 762
Nelson, Daniel, Product Mgr-Integrated Solutions - Thermo Fisher Scientific Inc.; *pg.* 1431, *pg.* 854
Nelson, Dawn Bowen, Sr Mgr-Content Curation - Charter Communications, Inc.; *pg.* 274, *pg.* 372
Nelson, Derek, Mgr-Creative Svcs - Anytime Fitness; *pg.* 529, *pg.* 926
Nelson, Desiree, Product Mgr-Air Guns, Cutlery, Dog Trng & Hunting Electronics - Gander Mountain Company; *pg.* 1834, *pg.* 960
Nelson, Elizabeth, Mgr-Mktg - Land O'Lakes, Inc.; *pg.* 873, *pg.* 915
Nelson, Gary, Analyst-Interactive Mktg - Xerox Corporation; *pg.* 494, *pg.* 365
Nelson, George D., Mgr-Sls - Bryant Grinder; *pg.* 1320, *pg.* 1768
Nelson, Greg, Dir-Mktg Plng & Ops - McKesson Corporation; *pg.* 1560, *pg.* 222
Nelson, Jennifer, Reg Analyst-Mktg-Customer Care & Aftersales - General Motors Company; *pg.* 175, *pg.* 881
Nelson, Jim, Sr Mgr-Mktg - B.C. Hydro; *pg.* 1936, *pg.* 1909
Nelson, Joshua, Brand Mgr - E&J Gallo Winery; *pg.* 1962, *pg.* 149
Nelson, Justin, Mgr-Mktg - Jo-Ann Stores LLC; *pg.* 696, *pg.* 1455
Nelson, Kelly, Mgr-Sls-Deli Mdsg - The Kroger Co.; *pg.* 1025, *pg.* 1416
Nelson, Lamont, Sr Mgr-Corp Partnerships - Memphis Grizzlies; *pg.* 561, *pg.* 1645
Nelson, Lori, Mgr-Mktg Comm - Ecolab Inc.; *pg.* 329, *pg.* 960
Nelson, Mark, Sr VP-Worldwide Sls & Technical Svcs - Altera Corporation; *pg.* 348, *pg.* 237
Nelson, Maura, VP-Mktg & Comm-Schumacher Grp - F. Schumacher & Co.; *pg.* 925, *pg.* 1230
Nelson, Mike, Dir-Own Brand Product Mgmt - Staples; *pg.* 474, *pg.* 313
Nelson, Nate, Mgr-PR - ZAGG INCORPORATED; *pg.* 690, *pg.* 1762
Nelson, Nathan, Sr Mgr-Pur - The Procter & Gamble Company; *pg.* 1129, *pg.* 1418
Nelson, Qiana, Mgr-Legal Sls Team - CDW Corporation; *pg.* 370, *pg.* 663
Nelson, Rachel, Dir-PR - Lowry Park Zoological Society of Tampa Inc.; *pg.* 559, *pg.* 474
Nelson, Rhonda, Dir-Brand, Mktg & Comm-Northeast Reg - Ernst & Young Global Limited; *pg.* 748, *pg.* 1228
Nelson, Rich, Sr VP-Mktg - Broadcom Corporation; *pg.* 364, *pg.* 108
Nelson, Scott, Sr Mgr-Medical Device & Mktg - Medtronic, Inc.; *pg.* 1564, *pg.* 939
Nelson, Sharon, Dir-Mktg - The Northwestern Mutual Life Insurance Company; *pg.* 1212, *pg.* 1879
Nelson, Shelly, VP-Sls - Hooper Holmes, Inc.; *pg.* 1542, *pg.* 718
Nelson, Steven, Sr VP-Health Svcs, Strategy, Product & Mktg - Highmark Blue Cross Blue Shield; *pg.* 1203, *pg.* 1576
Nelson, Ted, Sr Mgr-Customer Mktg - Kellogg Company; *pg.* 831, *pg.* 870
Nelson, Thomas M., Analyst-Mktg - BNC BANCORP; *pg.* 726, *pg.* 1379
Nemani, Ramani, Mgr-Multicultural Mktg - American Heart Association Inc.; *pg.* 128, *pg.* 1673
Nemann, Haley, Sr Mgr-Global eCommerce User Experience - Crocs, Inc.; *pg.* 1806, *pg.* 335
Nemaric, Tania, Dir-Brand Strategy & Offline Mktg - 1-800-Flowers.com, Inc.; *pg.* 1758, *pg.* 1151
Nemechek, Monica, Dir-Mktg - DeVry University Inc.; *pg.* 600, *pg.* 649
Nemechek, Victor, Sr Mgr-Product Mktg - Hitachi Data Systems Corporation; *pg.* 407, *pg.* 265
Nemeckay, Brian, Mgr-Virtual Product Dev - Crayola LLC; *pg.* 951, *pg.* 1528
Nemer, Julia, Product Mgr-MYHABIT - Amazon.com, Inc.; *pg.* 1226, *pg.* 1831
Nemeroff, Julie, Coord-Hospitality & Global Mktg Partnerships - National Basketball Association; *pg.* 566, *pg.* 1264
Nemkovich, Kathryn McIlwee, VP-Product Mgmt - Penn Foster Education Group, Inc.; *pg.* 606, *pg.* 1586
Nenning, Adam, Dir-Mktg Decision Sciences & Customer Analytics - Kohl's Corporation; *pg.* 1775, *pg.* 1870
Neoh, Cheryl, Specialist-Mktg Insights - Electronic Arts Inc.; *pg.* 951, *pg.* 189
Neoh, Erin, Assoc Product Dir-OneTouch - Johnson & Johnson Inc.; *pg.* 1552, *pg.* 1923
Nepean, Ross, VP-Mktg-Worldwide - TAB Products Co. LLC; *pg.* 481, *pg.* 1869
Nepon, Ari, Sr Mgr-Site Reliability Engrg-Apple Pay, Device & Carrier Svcs - Apple Inc.; *pg.* 350, *pg.* 73
Neppl, Christina, Exec VP-Mdsg & Logistics - BJ's Wholesale Club, Inc.; *pg.* 1762, *pg.* 857
Nercesian, Armen, Specialist-Mktg, Digital & SEM - DISH Network Corporation; *pg.* 283, *pg.* 325
Neret, Gabriela, Specialist-Product Mktg - Sony Electronics, Inc.; *pg.* 676, *pg.* 209
Neri, David, Exec VP & Gen Mgr-Mdse - Belk, Inc.; *pg.* 1760, *pg.* 1364
Neri, Emilie, Mgr-Americas Mktg & Comm-ZENITH-Watch & Jewelry USA - LVMH Inc.; *pg.* 9, *pg.* 1254
Nerviani, Emily, Coord-Mktg - Lucasfilm, Ltd.; *pg.* 297, *pg.* 222
Nesbit, Yelena Gitlin, Sr Dir-Comm - Rodale, Inc.; *pg.* 1681, *pg.* 1530
Nesbitt, Fred, Specialist-Inside Sls - Southern Lumber & Millwork Corp.; *pg.* 112, *pg.* 1613
Nescio, Elena, Reg Brand Mgr-East Grp - Gannett Co., Inc.; *pg.* 1643, *pg.* 1790
Nespeca, Matt, Bus Mgr-IVM - Bayer CropScience; *pg.* 1149, *pg.* 981
Nespole, Terri, Dir-Digital & Creative Svcs - New York Life Insurance Company; *pg.* 1211, *pg.* 1268
Nespoli, J.D., VP-Mdsg - Relax the Back Corporation; *pg.* 940, *pg.* 120
Nessl, Steve, Mgr-Mktg - Yamaha Motor Corporation USA; *pg.* 1713, *pg.* 76
Nester, Holly, Dir-Product Dev - Pennwell Publishing Company Inc.; *pg.* 1676, *pg.* 1490
Nestler, Andrew, VP-Sls-US - Bayer Healthcare Consumer Care Division; *pg.* 1500, *pg.* 1087
Nestor, David, Dir-Adv - The Fred W. Albrecht Grocery Co.; *pg.* 1020, *pg.* 1400
Nestor, Peggy, Dir-Sls - Oleg Cassini, Inc.; *pg.* 30, *pg.* 1274
Nestorick, Matt, Dir-Sls - Stanley Black & Decker, Inc.; *pg.* 1063, *pg.* 358
Nesvacil, Nicola, Mgr-Production - Del Monte Foods, Inc.; *pg.* 852, *pg.* 304
Netelenbos, Derek, Sr Dir-Adv Sls & Acct Mgmt-Global - Expedia, Inc.; *pg.* 1244, *pg.* 1814
Nethercoat, Stacy, VP-Product Mktg-Software - Tech Data Corporation; *pg.* 482, *pg.* 416
Netherton, Jeff, VP-Product Mgmt - Graybar Electric Company, Inc.; *pg.* 1299, *pg.* 997
Netivi, Neil, Dir-Media - NEOC; *pg.* 1395, *pg.* 459
Neu, Kate, Assoc Coord-Mktg - Whole Foods Market, Inc.; *pg.* 1038, *pg.* 1667
Neubauer, Kyra, VP & Dir-Eastern Reg Mktg-Commerce Bank - Commerce Bancshares, Inc.; *pg.* 740, *pg.* 982
Neubecker, Lindsay, Sr Mgr-Global Tools & Storage - Stanley Black & Decker, Inc.; *pg.* 1063, *pg.* 358
Neuberger, Christopher B., Pres-NutraBrands & VP-Mktg & Sls - Nutraceutical International Corporation; *pg.* 1576, *pg.* 1753
Neudeck, Dave, Dir-Digital Mktg - Virginia Tourism Authority; *pg.* 1010, *pg.* 1804
Neufeld, Abner, Dir-Grp & Arena Sls - Brooklyn Nets; *pg.* 534, *pg.* 1145
Neufeld, Rebecca, Mgr-PR - Yahoo! Inc.; *pg.* 1289, *pg.* 289
Neuhaus, Erin, Mgr-Mktg - Provide Commerce, Inc.; *pg.* 1276, *pg.* 206
Neuhaus, Krista, Sr Mgr-Digital Mktg - Kate Spade & Company; *pg.* 27, *pg.* 1248
Neuhaus, Stacey, Brand Mgr-Rum Portfolio-Global - Campari America; *pg.* 1960, *pg.* 214
Neuman, Chris, VP-Mktg - Cardinal Health, Inc.; *pg.* 1512, *pg.* 1448
Neuman, Cindy, Sr Dir-Advanced Analytics - ConAgra Foods, Inc.; *pg.* 826, *pg.* 1014
Neuman, Jeff, Dir-Mktg-Frank's RedHot - Reckitt Benckiser Inc.; *pg.* 1136, *pg.* 1105
Neuman, Lisa, Sr Mgr-Worldwide Field Enablement & Comm - Adobe Systems Incorporated; *pg.* 342, *pg.* 235
Neuman, Mark, Mgr-Integrated Mktg - CARIBOU COFFEE COMPANY, INC.; *pg.* 1764, *pg.* 932
Neuman, Ninveh, VP Comml Mktg-Global - Rockwell Automation, Inc.; *pg.* 668, *pg.* 1880
Neumann, Emily, Dir-WW & AMS AR & PR - Hewlett-Packard Company; *pg.* 404, *pg.* 175
Neumann, Kathleen, Sr Media Buyer-Adv - National Instruments Corporation; *pg.* 443, *pg.* 1664
Neumann, Mark, VP-Mktg-Bone Health & Cardiology - Amgen Inc.; *pg.* 1493, *pg.* 291
Neumann, Matt, Sr Dir-Leasing & Dev-Illinois & Wisconsin - Liberty Property Trust; *pg.* 1101, *pg.* 1550
Neumann, R. Stephen, VP-Mktg Ops-Consumer Insights & Consumer Rels - Bayer Corporation; *pg.* 1499, *pg.* 1573
Neumann, Sandy, Sr Dir-Employment Mktg - Ameriprise Financial, Inc.; *pg.* 715, *pg.* 930
Neumeier, Debra, Dir-Product Mktg - Tech Data Corporation; *pg.* 482, *pg.* 416
Neuroth, Julia, Sr Mgr-Trade Mktg - Newell Rubbermaid Inc.; *pg.* 1128, *pg.* 515
Neusner, Robert D., Head-Global Mktg-Diagnostics - Johnson & Johnson; *pg.* 1549, *pg.* 1091
Neustel, Larry, Mgr-Adv Production - Kohler Co.; *pg.* 91, *pg.* 1862
Neuwirth, Brian, VP-Sls & Mktg - Unex Manufacturing, Inc.; *pg.* 1385, *pg.* 1075
Neuwirth, Michael, Sr Dir-PR - The Dannon Company, Inc.; *pg.* 851, *pg.* 1351
Nevel, Sarah Van, Sr Specialist-PR - Target Corporation; *pg.* 1786, *pg.* 942
Nevers, Eliza, VP-Product, Demand Platform & AOL Platforms - AOL Inc.; *pg.* 1229, *pg.* 1195
Nevers, Lacey, Sr Mgr-Mktg-Global - American Apparel, Inc.; *pg.* 18, *pg.* 126
Neves, Erica, Mgr-Travel Trade Mktg - Hawaii Visitors & Convention Bureau; *pg.* 994, *pg.* 543
Neves, Larissa, Coord-Sls - Harris Moran Seed Co.; *pg.* 1796, *pg.* 150
Neves, Nicole, Dir-PR, Special Events & Mktg - Guess?, Inc.; *pg.* 25, *pg.* 132
Neveux, Paul, Dir-Global Premises Fiber Product Mgmt - Superior Essex, Inc.; *pg.* 676, *pg.* 521
Nevill, Dan, Reg Dir-Airline Mktg - The Boeing Company; *pg.* 225, *pg.* 567
Neville, Jodie, Sr Dir-Strategic Initiatives - Hasbro, Inc.; *pg.* 954, *pg.* 1603
Neville, Karla, Mgr-Event Mktg-Natl - Pernod Ricard USA, Inc.; *pg.* 1968, *pg.* 1332
Neville, Molly, Sr Analyst-Mktg - Brown & Brown, Inc.; *pg.* 1196, *pg.* 419
Neville, Moya, Sr VP-Sls & Mktg - The Atlanta Journal-Constitution; *pg.* 1618, *pg.* 490
Neville, Pam, VP-Digital Mktg - FMR LLC (Fidelity Investments); *pg.* 759, *pg.* 794
Neville, Ryan, Dir-Internet & New Media - Hy-Vee, Inc.; *pg.* 1023, *pg.* 713
Nevin, Kelli, Mgr-Contract Ops-ISV & Channel Sls - salesforce.com, inc.; *pg.* 1278, *pg.* 226
Nevin, Mike, Sr Mgr-Procurement Grp-Dairy Commodity Risk Mgmt - Starbucks Corporation; *pg.* 897, *pg.* 1840
Nevins, Jeff, Head-Media Rels - FairPoint Communications, Inc.; *pg.* 1871, *pg.* 1366
Nevins, Jennifer, Sr Dir-Grp Sls - St. Louis Blues Hockey Club, LLC; *pg.* 585, *pg.* 1003
Nevosh, Christine, Mgr-Western Mktg - E.I. du Pont de Nemours & Company; *pg.* 1159, *pg.* 390
Nevoso, Christina, Brand Mgr-Intl Brands - Safilo USA Inc.; *pg.* 11, *pg.* 1106

First page reference indicates Business Class Edition
Second page reference indicates Geographic Edition

New, Michele, Dir-Mktg - Saks Fifth Avenue, Inc.; *pg.* 1783, *pg.* 1287
Newberger, Charlie, Sr Dir-Mktg - McDonald's Corporation; *pg.* 1737, *pg.* 645
Newberry, Allison, Mgr-Mktg - Comcast Sportsnet; *pg.* 278, *pg.* 1562
Newberry, Daniel, Dir-Ad Ops-MLB Advanced Media - Major League Baseball; *pg.* 560, *pg.* 1255
Newberry, Tina, Mgr-Mktg - Newport Aquarium; *pg.* 571, *pg.* 739
Newboe, Betty, Sr Dir-Technical Comm - Applied Materials, Inc; *pg.* 618, *pg.* 1009
Newbold, Heather, Mgr-Mktg - PRAHealth Sciences; *pg.* 1585, *pg.* 1388
Newbold, Kevin, Sr Product Mgr-Handsets & Devices - Cincinnati Bell Inc.; *pg.* 1871, *pg.* 1410
Newborn, Joanne, Mgr-Field Mktg-Excelsior Wines - Banfi Vintners; *pg.* 1957, *pg.* 1161
Newbrough, Greg, VP-Sls - Sleeman Breweries, Ltd.; *pg.* 265, *pg.* 1920
Newbury, Scott A., Second VP-Bus Insurance Sls Support - The Travelers Companies, Inc.; *pg.* 1220, *pg.* 352
Newby, Beth, Principal-Mktg-FedEx Mobile Solutions - FedEx Corporation; *pg.* 1907, *pg.* 1642
Newby, Taylor, Mgr-Social Media - The Metropolitan Museum of Art; *pg.* 561, *pg.* 1259
Newby-Robson, Edd, Sr Dir-Mktg - Electronic Arts Inc.; *pg.* 951, *pg.* 189
Newcomb, Eliza, Analyst-Social Media - The Sports Authority, Inc.; *pg.* 1846, *pg.* 326
Newcomb, James, Sr Dir-Global Brand Mgmt & Digital Strategies - The Boeing Company; *pg.* 225, *pg.* 567
Newcomb, Jim, Sr Dir-Global Brand Mgmt & Digital Strategies - The Boeing Company - Helicopter Division; *pg.* 226, *pg.* 13
Newcomb, Lucinda, VP-Site & Mobile Product Mgmt - Sephora USA Inc; *pg.* 522, *pg.* 227
Newcomb, Michelle, Sr Media Planner - Bose Corporation; *pg.* 626, *pg.* 820
Newcombe, Mike, Mgr-Products & Svcs Portfolio - OGE Energy Corp.; *pg.* 1948, *pg.* 1486
Newell, Diana M., Sr Dir-Supply Chain Product Ops - Brocade Communications Systems, Inc.; *pg.* 365, *pg.* 239
Newell, Matthew, Mgr-Digital Mktg - State Farm Mutual Automobile Insurance Co.; *pg.* 1218, *pg.* 557
Newell, Melissa, Specialist-Mktg-Vehicle Sls & Mktg - Mercedes-Benz USA, LLC; *pg.* 184, *pg.* 514
Newell, Nancy, Head-IPG Worldwide Media Ops - Hewlett-Packard Company; *pg.* 404, *pg.* 175
Newell, Randall, Dir-Dev Ops Mktg - IBM; *pg.* 410, *pg.* 1449
Newhart, Thomas L., VP-Sls-Americas - Digital Lightwave, Inc.; *pg.* 634, *pg.* 462
Newhoff, Mary, Mgr-Digital Mktg - Tommy Bahama; *pg.* 48, *pg.* 1842
Newhouse, Samuel I., Jr., Mgr-Mktg - Conde Nast Publications, Inc.; *pg.* 1629, *pg.* 1217
Newhuis, Robert, Dir-Sls - Middle Atlantic Products Inc.; *pg.* 1360, *pg.* 1065
Newkirk, Shelley, Sr Mgr-Exec Comm & Engrg - Cisco Systems, Inc.; *pg.* 372, *pg.* 240
Newland, Greg, Exec VP-Mktg & PR - Travel Portland; *pg.* 1008, *pg.* 1507
Newlands, Ellen, Sr Product Mgr-Security - Red Hat, Inc.; *pg.* 460, *pg.* 1388
Newlon, Don, VP-Mktg & Gen Mgr-Integrated Products Div - Emerson Climate Technologies, Inc.; *pg.* 1333, *pg.* 1472
Newlove, Jo Anne, Mgr-Sls Admin - Americo Manufacturing Co., Inc.; *pg.* 325, *pg.* 482
Newman Weldon, Stacey, Dir-Natl Adv Sls - Weight Watchers International, Inc.; *pg.* 1609, *pg.* 1313
Newman, Brad, Sr Dir-US Mktg-Specialty Pharmaceuticals Div - Baxter International Inc.; *pg.* 1499, *pg.* 599
Newman, Craig, Sr Product Mgr-Global - Becton, Dickinson & Company; *pg.* 1501, *pg.* 1068
Newman, Danielle, Mgr-Media Buying - Pfizer Inc.; *pg.* 1581, *pg.* 1278
Newman, David, Dir-Sls & Mktg-Home Center & Hardware-Worldwide - Graco, Inc.; *pg.* 1342, *pg.* 935
Newman, David, Sr VP-Mktg & Comm - Sterling Mets, L.P.; *pg.* 586, *pg.* 1160
Newman, Del, Mgr-Mktg Comm-Global - Tennant Company; *pg.* 1381, *pg.* 944
Newman, Diane, Sr VP-Sls-Natl - Digital First Media; *pg.* 1238, *pg.* 1224
Newman, Dobbie, VP-Global Mktg-Beverage - WestRock Company; *pg.* 1472, *pg.* 1805
Newman, Ed, Mgr-Adv - Amsoil Inc.; *pg.* 971, *pg.* 1896
Newman, Eric, VP-Sls - Cooperative Regions of Organic Producer Pools; *pg.* 850, *pg.* 1864
Newman, Gary, Mgr-Inside Sls-Graphic Comm - Xerox Canada Inc.; *pg.* 494, *pg.* 1930
Newman, Jason E., VP-Sports Sls - Univision Communications Inc.; *pg.* 683, *pg.* 1307
Newman, Jon, Mgr-Performance Mktg - Zynga Inc.; *pg.* 1292, *pg.* 235
Newman, Julie, Sr Mgr-Industries Strategy & Plng-Global - Cisco Systems, Inc.; *pg.* 372, *pg.* 240
Newman, Kristi B., Specialist-Mktg - United States Postal Service; *pg.* 1009, *pg.* 406
Newman, Kristin, Dir-Mktg & Strategy Converting Papers - International Paper Company; *pg.* 1460, *pg.* 1644
Newman, Lauren, VP-Corp Sls-East Coast - Time Inc.; *pg.* 1693, *pg.* 1300
Newman, Liz, Dir-Mktg - Merz Aesthetics; *pg.* 1567, *pg.* 255
Newman, Margaret, Sr VP-HR, Mktg & Comm - HD SUPPLY, INC.; *pg.* 86, *pg.* 509
Newman, Nancy, Sr Dir-Shopper Mktg & CPG - ShopLocal, LLC; *pg.* 1280, *pg.* 590
Newman, Patricia, Sr Rep-Exec Sls - GlaxoSmithKline; *pg.* 1536, *pg.* 1565
Newman, Richard, Exec VP-Mktg & State Strategy - Empire State Development Corporation; *pg.* 747, *pg.* 1227
Newman, Ryan, Brand Mgr - Ralph Lauren Corporation; *pg.* 46, *pg.* 1284
Newman, Samantha, VP-Integrated Mktg, Music & Entertainment - MTV Networks Company; *pg.* 298, *pg.* 1262
Newman, Samantha, Sr Mgr-Event - Univision Communications Inc.; *pg.* 683, *pg.* 1307
Newman, Sondra, Sr Dir-IR - Repligen Corporation; *pg.* 1589, *pg.* 854
Newman, Victoria, Coord-Mktg-Synergy - ESPN, Inc.; *pg.* 285, *pg.* 340
Newmark, Andrew, Exec VP-Sls & Mktg-Global - TransAct Technologies Incorporated; *pg.* 484, *pg.* 351
Newnes, Johnny, Coord-Social Media Mktg - BJ'S RESTAURANTS, INC.; *pg.* 1716, *pg.* 104
Newport, Hillary, Sr Product Mgr-Microsite Products - PR Newswire Association LLC; *pg.* 1678, *pg.* 1283
Newsom, Jeremy, Exec VP & Sr Mgr-Comml Lending - Amegy Bank, N.A.; *pg.* 711, *pg.* 1700
Newsom, Tyler, Product Mgr & Specialist-North America - Flint Group, Inc.; *pg.* 1163, *pg.* 904
Newstadt, Todd, Corp VP-Mktg - World Finer Foods, Inc.; *pg.* 910, *pg.* 1044
Newton, Anita, VP-Mktg - Hallmark Cards, Inc.; *pg.* 1646, *pg.* 983
Newton, Bill, Chief Sls Officer & Chief Bus Officer - Fruit of the Loom, Inc.; *pg.* 41, *pg.* 725
Newton, Blythe, Specialist-Mktg-Proposal Dev - Grant Thornton International Ltd.; *pg.* 763, *pg.* 575
Newton, Brice, Sr Product Mgr-Running Footwear - ASICS America Corporation; *pg.* 1826, *pg.* 106
Newton, Debra, VP-Mktg Comm - Transamerica Insurance & Investment Group; *pg.* 1219, *pg.* 141
Newton, Jonathan, Sr Mgr-SCM - Eaton Corporation; *pg.* 1331, *pg.* 1429
Newton, Kris, Sr Dir-IR - NetApp, Inc.; *pg.* 444, *pg.* 287
Newton, Latondra, Grp VP-Social Innovation - Toyota Motor North America, Inc.; *pg.* 192, *pg.* 1303
Newton, Lynn, Asst VP & Mgr-Mktg-Americas - Liberty Mutual Insurance Group Inc.; *pg.* 1205, *pg.* 797
Newton, Miriam, Dir-Product Mktg-Adobe Document Solutions - Adobe Systems Incorporated; *pg.* 342, *pg.* 235
Newton, Peter, CEO-GateHouse Media Ventures - GateHouse Media, Inc.; *pg.* 1644, *pg.* 1159
Newton, Peter, Sr Dir-Product Mgmt & Mktg - NETGEAR, Inc.; *pg.* 444, *pg.* 247
Newton, Robin, Analyst-Adv Placement - Valassis Communications, Inc.; *pg.* 1287, *pg.* 897
Newton, Steven, Coord-Mktg Distr - Globe Life & Accident Insurance Company; *pg.* 1201, *pg.* 1486
Newton, Todd, Sr Dir-Mktg - Apartment Investment and Management Company; *pg.* 1079, *pg.* 316
Newvine, Colleen, Product Mgr-AP Stylebook - The Associated Press, Inc.; *pg.* 270, *pg.* 1197
Newvine, Jamie, Mgr-ECommerce Mktg - Ulta Salon, Cosmetics & Fragrance, Inc.; *pg.* 524, *pg.* 559
Neyer, Natalie, Mgr-PR - Metro Bancorp, Inc.; *pg.* 782, *pg.* 1537
Neylon, Bryan, Sr Product Mgr - Richardson Electronics, Ltd.; *pg.* 667, *pg.* 622
Ng, Brian, Head-Mktg-Pet Specialty Brands-Big Heart Pet Brands - Del Monte Foods, Inc.; *pg.* 852, *pg.* 304
Ng, Carol, Mgr-Sls & Promo - Manulife Financial Corporation; *pg.* 778, *pg.* 1939
Ng, Dave, Product Mgr-Mobile Computing - Samsung Electronics America, Inc.; *pg.* 669, *pg.* 1115
Ng, Della, VP-Integrated Mktg - Wells Fargo & Company; *pg.* 819, *pg.* 232
Ng, Henry, Sr VP-Citi Cards & Product Dir - Citigroup Inc.; *pg.* 735, *pg.* 1212
Ng, James, Engr-Technical Mktg - Cisco Systems, Inc.; *pg.* 372, *pg.* 240
Ng, Joey, Mgr-Mktg - American Apparel, Inc.; *pg.* 18, *pg.* 126
Ng, Michael, Brand Mgr-Hot Wheels, Matchbox & Tyco - MATTEL, INC.; *pg.* 962, *pg.* 81
Ng, Peter, Head-Mktg Excellence-Novartis Oncology - Novartis Corporation; *pg.* 1574, *pg.* 1273
Ng, Rany, Product Dir-Mgmt - Google Inc.; *pg.* 1249, *pg.* 153
Ngo, Kate, Product Mgr - XO Group Inc.; *pg.* 1289, *pg.* 1316
Ngo, Michelle, Sr Dir-Corp Fin - Kilroy Realty Corporation; *pg.* 1099, *pg.* 134
Ngo, Timothy, Sr Mgr-Mktg - PepsiCo, Inc.; *pg.* 259, *pg.* 1327
Ngo, Tran, Assoc Mgr-Product Mktg-Performance Ads - Google Inc.; *pg.* 1249, *pg.* 153
Nguyen, Amy, Sr Specialist-Mktg-North America - Bare Escentuals, Inc.; *pg.* 500, *pg.* 213
Nguyen, Anh T., Mgr-Mktg Campaign - Wells Fargo & Company; *pg.* 819, *pg.* 232
Nguyen, Ann, Rep-Sls - Liberty Mutual Insurance Group Inc.; *pg.* 1205, *pg.* 797
Nguyen, Anthony, Brand Mgr-Global - P.F. Chang's China Bistro, Inc.; *pg.* 1030, *pg.* 24
Nguyen, Bao T., VP-R&D Large Scale Analytics & Online Adv Technologies - AOL Inc.; *pg.* 1229, *pg.* 1195
Nguyen, Cammie, Sr Mgr-Breakthrough Innovation - Barilla America, Inc.; *pg.* 839, *pg.* 555
Nguyen, Casey, Mgr-Americas Revenue Mktg - Cisco Systems, Inc.; *pg.* 372, *pg.* 240
Nguyen, Cecilia, Sr Mgr-Publicity-Disney Television Animation - The Walt Disney Company; *pg.* 317, *pg.* 52
Nguyen, Cheryl L., Sr Mgr-CFRST & AC Hotels Franchising - Marriott International, Inc.; *pg.* 1102, *pg.* 764
Nguyen, Chris, Mgr-Mktg - Zoosk Inc.; *pg.* 1292, *pg.* 235
Nguyen, Dang, Sr Mgr-Cloud Svcs & Digital Products - Toshiba America, Inc.; *pg.* 681, *pg.* 1302
Nguyen, Debra, Sr Mgr-Global Media Strategy-Levi's Brand Mktg - Levi Strauss & Co.; *pg.* 43, *pg.* 220
Nguyen, Hoang-Oanh, Sr Program Mgr-Social Media-Consumer Ops - Google Inc.; *pg.* 1249, *pg.* 153
Nguyen, James, Principal & Product Mgr - Symantec Corporation; *pg.* 478, *pg.* 161
Nguyen, Kevin, Engr-Technical Mktg - Cisco Systems, Inc.; *pg.* 372, *pg.* 240
Nguyen, Lan H., Assoc Dir-Product Mktg - McKesson Corporation; *pg.* 1560, *pg.* 222
Nguyen, Melissa, Brand Mgr - Hotels.com, L.P.; *pg.* 1257, *pg.* 1682
Nguyen, Michael, Coord-Digital & Social Media-Media Impact & Brand Mktg - Arby's Restaurant Group, Inc.; *pg.* 1014, *pg.* 488
Nguyen, Michael, Sr Mgr-Product Mktg-Adv - eBay Inc.; *pg.* 1240, *pg.* 243
Nguyen, Phong, Dir-Adv UK - eBay Inc.; *pg.* 1240, *pg.* 243
Nguyen, Quan, VP-Mktg - Lennox International Inc.; *pg.* 1073, *pg.* 1736
Nguyen, Richard, Head-Adv Ops - Pinterest; *pg.* 1275, *pg.* 225
Nguyen, Tammy, Sr Specialist-Brand Adv - Volkswagen Group of America, Inc.; *pg.* 194, *pg.* 1785
Nguyen, Thai P., Dir-Mktg Strategy - Anthem, Inc.; *pg.* 1192, *pg.* 683
Nguyen, Thao, Product Mgr - Amazon.com, Inc.; *pg.* 1226, *pg.* 1831
Nguyen, Theresa, Mgr-Mktg Insights-Global Media Solutions - Electronic Arts Inc.; *pg.* 951, *pg.* 189
Nguyen, Tina, Sr Mgr-Brand Engagement & Pub Affairs - Taco Bell Corp.; *pg.* 1752, *pg.* 117
Nguyen, Tri, Sr Mgr-Product Mgmt - Dell Software; *pg.* 385, *pg.* 40
Nguyen, Vanessa Crie, Mgr-Mktg-ALDO - Aldo Group; *pg.* 1804, *pg.* 1959
Nguyen, Vinh, Sr Mgr-ECommerce & Web - Michael Stars, Inc.; *pg.* 29, *pg.* 100

Nha, Victoria, Mgr-Mktg - American International Group, Inc.; *pg.* 1190, *pg.* 1193
Ni Eideain, Louisa, Dir-Sales & Trade Mktg-Macy's for P&G Prestige - The Procter & Gamble Company; *pg.* 1129, *pg.* 1418
Niakoulov, Stanislava, Sr Analyst-Sls-Bundles Sls Ops - DIRECTV Group Holdings, LLC; *pg.* 281, *pg.* 79
Niaz, Fahim, Dir-Product Mgmt - Smith Micro Software, Inc.; *pg.* 471, *pg.* 41
Niazmand, Colette, Dir-Mktg-Global - Tesla Motors, Inc.; *pg.* 191, *pg.* 178
Nibert, Rhonda, Sr Mgr-Brand Portfolio Programs - Marriott International, Inc.; *pg.* 1102, *pg.* 764
Nicastro, Robert, Brand Mgr-Lambert Kay Pet Products - Church & Dwight Co., Inc.; *pg.* 1153, *pg.* 1063
Nicastro, Tahryn, Mgr-Sponsorship Adv - Sprint Corporation; *pg.* 1874, *pg.* 719
Niccolls, Phil, VP-Indus Mktg & Applications - Emerson Process Management; *pg.* 1334, *pg.* 1636
Niceberg, Peter K., Dir-Design Production & Product Mgr-Huffington Magazine - TheHuffingtonPost.com, Inc.; *pg.* 1692, *pg.* 1298
Nichol, Aaron, Mgr-Sls & Pur - Olympic Steel Inc.; *pg.* 101, *pg.* 1433
Nicholas, Amanda, Acct Exec-Digital Adv Sls - Univision Communications Inc.; *pg.* 683, *pg.* 1307
Nicholas, Dan, VP-Sls - The Standard Register Company; *pg.* 473, *pg.* 1446
Nicholas, Georgette, Sr VP-IR, PR & Ratings Agencies - Genworth Financial, Inc.; *pg.* 761, *pg.* 1802
Nicholas, Jeremy, VP-Digital Product Mktg - Visa Inc.; *pg.* 816, *pg.* 230
Nicholas, Melissa, Dir-Acct Mktg - HBG Books, Inc.; *pg.* 1648, *pg.* 1238
Nicholas, Roman, Specialist-IT Mktg-Global Mktg & Comm Tech Mobile - Campbell Soup Company; *pg.* 844, *pg.* 1048
Nicholas, Val, VP & Dir-Creative-NBC News - NBC Universal, Inc.; *pg.* 300, *pg.* 1266
Nicholls, Mike, Dir-Mktg Ops - Anthem, Inc.; *pg.* 1192, *pg.* 683
Nichols, Bill, Sr Mgr-Strategic EHS Svcs - Applied Materials, Inc; *pg.* 618, *pg.* 1009
Nichols, Bill, Jr., Dir-Natl Sls-Viral Hepatitis - Bristol-Myers Squibb Company; *pg.* 1509, *pg.* 1206
Nichols, Colleen, Sr Mgr-Comm - Citrix Systems, Inc.; *pg.* 375, *pg.* 424
Nichols, David, Dir-Product Mgmt - Dacor; *pg.* 54, *pg.* 67
Nichols, Dean, Gen Mgr-Sls & Store Ops - Kelly-Moore Paint Company, Inc.; *pg.* 1443, *pg.* 198
Nichols, Diana, Dir-Sls - Lagos Inc.; *pg.* 8, *pg.* 1566
Nichols, Glenn, Mgr-Mktg Comm - Thomas & Betts Corporation; *pg.* 680, *pg.* 1646
Nichols, Helene, VP & Coord-Adv - Wilt-Pruf Products, Inc.; *pg.* 1801, *pg.* 346
Nichols, Jeff, Sr Mgr-Mktg - Cracker Barrel Old Country Store, Inc.; *pg.* 1723, *pg.* 1639
Nichols, Jeff, VP-Sls & Mktg - Standard Bent Glass Corporation; *pg.* 218, *pg.* 1519
Nichols, Jenna, Mgr-PR & Social Media - Huron Consulting Group Inc.; *pg.* 768, *pg.* 577
Nichols, Jennifer, Mgr-Adv - National Association of Convenience Stores; *pg.* 148, *pg.* 1771
Nichols, Jerry, Head-Performance Mgmt-Worldwide Bus Mgmt Office-Corp Mktg - SAP America, Inc.; *pg.* 466, *pg.* 1557
Nichols, Joe, Dir-Comml-Lifetime & Brand Creative - Lifetime Entertainment Services LLC; *pg.* 296, *pg.* 1251
Nichols, Josh, Dir-Creative - Fox Sports Net; *pg.* 288, *pg.* 131
Nichols, Melissa, Mgr-Interactive Mktg Ops - The Scotts Miracle-Gro Company; *pg.* 1799, *pg.* 1459
Nichols, Michael L., Sr Dir-R&D - Key Technology, Inc.; *pg.* 868, *pg.* 1847
Nichols, Naaz, Sr Dir-Integrated Mktg Comm - Travelocity, Inc.; *pg.* 1284, *pg.* 1745
Nichols, Robert, Sr Dir-Agronomy, Weed Control, Sticky Cotton & Nematology - Cotton Incorporated Consumer Marketing Headquarters; *pg.* 692, *pg.* 1218
Nichols, Sarah, Dir-Mktg Svcs - Brown-Forman Corporation; *pg.* 1958, *pg.* 732
Nichols, Sharman, Sr Dir-User Experience & User Assistance - Websense, Inc.; *pg.* 491, *pg.* 210
Nichols, Tessa, Mgr-Mktg-Strategy-MACYS.COM - Macy's East; *pg.* 1777, *pg.* 1254
Nichols, Todd, Dir-Sls -Americas - A. Schulman, Inc.; *pg.* 1144, *pg.* 1452
Nichols, Tricia, Sr Dir-Consumer Engagement, Media & Brand Partnerships - Banana Republic; *pg.* 1760, *pg.* 212
Nichols, Tricia, Sr Dir-Consumer Engagement, Media & Brand Partnerships - The Gap, Inc.; *pg.* 1770, *pg.* 218
Nichols, Watson, Sr Mgr-Comm - Digital Insight; *pg.* 744, *pg.* 189
Nicholson, Alexandra, Dir-Social Media - Pegasystems Inc.; *pg.* 453, *pg.* 809
Nicholson, Allison, Brand Mgr - Newell Rubbermaid Inc.; *pg.* 1128, *pg.* 515
Nicholson, Brooke, Mgr-Product Mktg - Siemens Canada Ltd.; *pg.* 1306, *pg.* 1921
Nicholson, Chris, Sr Mgr-PR - Akamai Technologies, Inc.; *pg.* 1226, *pg.* 807
Nicholson, Dave, VP-Sls - The Euclid Chemical Company; *pg.* 81, *pg.* 1430
Nicholson, Francine, Sr Product Mgr - eHarmony.com, Inc.; *pg.* 1242, *pg.* 180
Nicholson, James, Sr Product Mgr-Surface - Microsoft Corporation; *pg.* 435, *pg.* 1824
Nicholson, Jason, Dir-Mktg - Austin Symphony Orchestra; *pg.* 531, *pg.* 1660
Nicholson, Kelli, Mgr-Creative Content-Brand Mktg - Panera Bread Company; *pg.* 1029, *pg.* 1001
Nicholson, Marilyn, VP-Media & Promotions - Long John Silver's, LLC; *pg.* 1736, *pg.* 736
Nicholson, Myron D., VP-New Products & Tech - Viskase Companies, Inc.; *pg.* 1471, *pg.* 599
Nicholson, Paul, SVP-Production & Technology - Showtime Networks Inc.; *pg.* 308, *pg.* 1291
Nicholson, Tim, VP-Mktg & Technical Svcs - Fort Dearborn Company; *pg.* 1457, *pg.* 610
Nick, Brian, Dir-Media Rels-Natl - Wal-Mart.com; *pg.* 1287, *pg.* 50
Nick, Diane, VP-Contract & Direct Customer Mktg - Office Depot, Inc.; *pg.* 448, *pg.* 412
Nick, Kistner, Sr Product Mgr - The Nielsen Company B.V.; *pg.* 1671, *pg.* 1272
Nickel, Amy, Mgr-Mktg - Ruth's Hospitality Group, Inc.; *pg.* 1748, *pg.* 480
Nickel, Jason, Mgr-Social Media Mktg - Amazon.com, Inc.; *pg.* 1226, *pg.* 1831
Nickele, Christopher J., Pres-CNO Bus & Exec VP-Product Mgmt - CNO Financial Group, Inc.; *pg.* 1198, *pg.* 675
Nickell, Jennifer B., Dir-Global Mktg Comm & Integrated Comml Plng - Kimberly-Clark Corporation; *pg.* 1461, *pg.* 1720
Nickerson, Mary, Mgr-Mktg-Natl - Toyota Motor Sales, U.S.A., Inc.; *pg.* 193, *pg.* 296
Nickerson, Rena, Dir-Mktg - Church & Dwight Canada Corp.; *pg.* 503, *pg.* 1925
Nicklas, Chris, Product Mgr - Klein Tools Inc.; *pg.* 1052, *pg.* 627
Nicklin, Steve, VP-Mktg - Outdoor Advertising Association of America; *pg.* 152, *pg.* 403
Nicks, Keith, Dir-Customer Loyalty & Retail Mktg-Food Lion - Food Lion, LLC; *pg.* 1019, *pg.* 1390
Nickson, Richard, VP-Sls - Linear Technology Corp.; *pg.* 652, *pg.* 147
Nicol, C. Greg, Product Mgr-Pur - Speedway Motors Inc.; *pg.* 218, *pg.* 1012
Nicol, Donna, Mgr-Creative Svcs - Rosco Laboratories, Inc.; *pg.* 1782, *pg.* 378
Nicol, Ron, Head-Tech, Media & Telecom Practice-Global - The Boston Consulting Group, Inc.; *pg.* 363, *pg.* 790
Nicol, Thomas, Dir-Mktg & Customer Experience - Abebooks Inc.; *pg.* 1613, *pg.* 1913
Nicolaescu, Marissa, Mgr-Media Rels - Macy's, Inc.; *pg.* 1778, *pg.* 1417
Nicolaidis, Tony, VP-Mktg - DeWALT Industrial Tool Company; *pg.* 1328, *pg.* 757
Nicolini, Janet, Sr Mgr-Integrated Mktg - Pepperidge Farm, Inc.; *pg.* 888, *pg.* 363
Nicoll, Derek, VP-Brand, Adv, Interactive & Partnerships - UnitedHealth Group Incorporated; *pg.* 1221, *pg.* 950
Nicolson, Jamie, Project Mgr-Mktg - Apartment Investment and Management Company; *pg.* 1079, *pg.* 316
Nicosia, Diane, Sr Dir-Mktg - Conair Corporation; *pg.* 505, *pg.* 1055
Nicosia, Shannon, Mgr-Mktg & Promos - Pixar Animation Studios; *pg.* 304, *pg.* 85
Nidamanuri, Hari, Grp Product Mgr - Sears Holdings Corporation; *pg.* 1784, *pg.* 618
Niday, Danielle, Sr Mgr-Mktg - AbbVie Inc.; *pg.* 1486, *pg.* 638
Niebaum, Katie Laning, VP-Comm & Media Rels - National Restaurant Association; *pg.* 150, *pg.* 403
Niece, Toni, VP-Mktg - Luby's, Inc.; *pg.* 1736, *pg.* 1710
Nieckar, Chris, Mgr-Mktg - 4iiii Innovations Inc.; *pg.* 64, *pg.* 1905
Niedbalski, Dave, VP-Mktg - Live Nation Entertainment, Inc.; *pg.* 558, *pg.* 47
Niederhaus, Tara, Assoc Mgr-Creative-Brdcst TV - PetSmart, Inc.; *pg.* 1481, *pg.* 18
Niederpruem, Gary, VP-Mktg Global-Emerson Network Power - Emerson Network Power; *pg.* 1071, *pg.* 1479
Niehaus, Chris, Sr Dir-Natl Cloud Programs - Microsoft Corporation; *pg.* 435, *pg.* 1824
Niehaus, Michael, Sr Mgr-Product Mktg - Microsoft Corporation; *pg.* 435, *pg.* 1824
Niehaus, Tracy, Mgr-Mktg - Intelligrated Systems Inc.; *pg.* 1349, *pg.* 1414
Niehoff, Chelsie, Assoc Mgr-Mktg-Club Channel - Sargento Foods Inc.; *pg.* 894, *pg.* 1886
Niekamp, Cynthia L., Sr Dir - LexisNexis Group; *pg.* 1658, *pg.* 1446
Niekelski, Jefferey J., Sr Dir-Brand Mktg-Payer - Merck & Co., Inc.; *pg.* 1566, *pg.* 1077
Nielsen, Alan, Exec VP-Dealer Sls - Konica Minolta Business Solutions USA, Inc.; *pg.* 1419, *pg.* 1113
Nielsen, Amy, Sr Specialist-Mktg - Thrivent Financial for Lutherans; *pg.* 1219, *pg.* 944
Nielsen, Callette, VP & Brand Mgr-Global - Marriott International, Inc.; *pg.* 1102, *pg.* 764
Nielsen, Chris, Assoc Dir-Mktg - The Clorox Company; *pg.* 327, *pg.* 169
Nielsen, Christina, Mgr-Mktg Comm & Brand - Lawson Products, Inc.; *pg.* 1355, *pg.* 580
Nielsen, Erika, Dir-Mktg & PR - BorgWarner Inc.; *pg.* 167, *pg.* 867
Nielsen, Jeff, Dir-Mktg - Abbott Laboratories; *pg.* 1484, *pg.* 551
Nielsen, Jessica, VP-Comm & Mktg - Lockheed Martin Corporation; *pg.* 229, *pg.* 762
Nielsen, Kathy, Mgr-Platform-Comml Notebook Product Mktg - Hewlett-Packard Company; *pg.* 404, *pg.* 175
Nielsen, Kelly, Sr VP-Creative Adv-Worldwide - Sony Pictures Entertainment Inc.; *pg.* 309, *pg.* 72
Nielsen, Kristina, VP-Digital Mktg - Bank of the West; *pg.* 721, *pg.* 213
Nielsen, Layla, Dir-Integrated Mktg-Natl - Radio One, Inc.; *pg.* 305, *pg.* 778
Nielsen, Mark, Dir-Creative - Publix Super Markets, Inc.; *pg.* 1031, *pg.* 437
Nielsen, Patrick, Mgr-Mktg - Broan-NuTone LLC; *pg.* 1069, *pg.* 1860
Nielsen, Roy, Sr Engr-Product - Freescale Semiconductor, Inc.; *pg.* 398, *pg.* 1662
Nielson, Jamie, Product Mgr - Valent U.S.A. Corp.; *pg.* 708, *pg.* 305
Nielson, Stephen, Sr Product Mgr-Photoshop - Adobe Systems Incorporated; *pg.* 342, *pg.* 235
Niemann, Thomas, Mgr-Social Sustainability - Ford Motor Company; *pg.* 172, *pg.* 876
Niemczyk, Mike, Sr Strategist-Social Media Content - Groupon, Inc.; *pg.* 1255, *pg.* 575
Niemeyer, Chalmers, Area Mgr-Mktg - Porsche Cars North America, Inc.; *pg.* 189, *pg.* 518
Niemi, Jean, Sr Dir-Corp Comm - True Value Company; *pg.* 1065, *pg.* 592
Niemiec, Jacquie, Dir-Digital Media - Penton Media, Inc.; *pg.* 1676, *pg.* 1277
Nieminen, Antti, Head-Brand & Mktg Comm - Finnair Oyj-New York; *pg.* 1909, *pg.* 1231
Nieminen, Kaisa, Mgr-Global Brand Mktg Entertainment, Games & Consumer Products - Mattel Games/Puzzles; *pg.* 962, *pg.* 80
Nienaber, Gina, Mgr-Mktg-SP Routing & Switching - Cisco Systems, Inc.; *pg.* 372, *pg.* 240
Nienhaus, Andrew, Mgr-Mktg - Amazon.com, Inc.; *pg.* 1226, *pg.* 1831
Nientimp, Elizabeth, Dir-Creative Content, Design & Production - General Mills, Inc.; *pg.* 828, *pg.* 933
Niersbach, Bob, Sr Mgr-Comm - DeVry Education Group Inc.; *pg.* 600, *pg.* 607
Niese, Ken, Dir-Sls Ops - Angie's List Inc; *pg.* 1228, *pg.* 682
Niess, Anna, Designer-Product - Tumblr, Inc.; *pg.* 1285, *pg.* 1305
Niethammer, Mike, Dir-Mktg-Hot Pockets, Lean Pockets & Buitoni - Nestle Purina PetCare Company; *pg.* 1479, *pg.* 1000

First page reference indicates Business Class Edition
Second page reference indicates Geographic Edition

Nieva, Jennifer, Dir-Product Innovation - Netflix, Inc.; *pg.* 1269, *pg.* 141
Nieves, Beatriz, Specialist-Email Mktg - Gartner, Inc.; *pg.* 1248, *pg.* 374
Nieves, Kimberly J., Brand Mgr - CVS Health Corporation; *pg.* 1765, *pg.* 1610
Nigg, Amy R., Sr Acct Mgr-Database Mktg Svcs - Meredith Corporation; *pg.* 1663, *pg.* 705
Nightingale, Liz, VP-Mktg & Comm - F. Schumacher & Co.; *pg.* 925, *pg.* 1230
Nigrinis, Miguel, Dir-Mktg-Southwest - Anheuser-Busch Companies, LLC; *pg.* 237, *pg.* 991
Nigro, Michael F., Dir-Mktg-AT&T Bus Svcs - AT&T Mobility LLC; *pg.* 620, *pg.* 1152
Nigro, Zachary, Coord-Brand Mktg - Burton Snowboard Company; *pg.* 1829, *pg.* 1765
Nihalani, Abhay, Mgr-Product Mktg - GE Healthcare; *pg.* 399, *pg.* 1765
Nihalani, Vishay, Product Mgr-Google Shopping Express - Google Inc.; *pg.* 1249, *pg.* 153
Nikezi, Aida, Mgr-Adv Media - Bloomingdale's, Inc.; *pg.* 1763, *pg.* 1204
Nikolaus, Andrea, Coord-PR & Promos - Turkey Hill Dairy, Inc.; *pg.* 902, *pg.* 1522
Nikolenko, Marina, Dir-Mktg - Lifeway Foods, Inc.; *pg.* 874, *pg.* 634
Nikoloff, Corina, Sr Product Mgr - Affymetrix, Inc.; *pg.* 1487, *pg.* 263
Niles, Shari A., Exec VP-Mktg - Andrew Peller Limited; *pg.* 1956, *pg.* 1920
Niles-Lane, Sharifah, Dir-Social Media - Houghton Mifflin Harcourt Publishing Company; *pg.* 1651, *pg.* 796
Nilsen, Teresa, Coord-Mktg - Reckitt Benckiser Inc.; *pg.* 1136, *pg.* 1105
Nilssen, Meggin, VP-Treasury Mgmt Sls - Blue Valley Ban Corp; *pg.* 725, *pg.* 718
Nilsson, Bob, Dir-Solutions Mktg - Extreme Networks Inc; *pg.* 287, *pg.* 245
Nino, Denise, Specialist-Mktg Comm - Shure Incorporated; *pg.* 672, *pg.* 638
Nino, Jose, VP-ECommerce & Mktg - Perry Ellis International, Inc.; *pg.* 45, *pg.* 445
Nipper, Paige, Coord-Mktg Events - Comcast Cable Communications, Inc.; *pg.* 276, *pg.* 1560
Nir, Shuki, Sr VP-Corp Mktg & Gen Mgr-Retail BU - SanDisk Corporation; *pg.* 465, *pg.* 147
Nirenberg, Dan, Dir-Mktg - Georgia-Pacific LLC; *pg.* 1458, *pg.* 507
Niro, Jeannette, Reg Mgr-Sls - The J.M. Smucker Company; *pg.* 865, *pg.* 1468
Niro, Lucy, Mgr-Mktg & Comm - Fujitsu Consulting; *pg.* 398, *pg.* 1955
Nischol, Karan, Head-Mobile Product - Hulu LLC; *pg.* 1257, *pg.* 274
Nishida, Ann, Sr Mgr Corp Comm - Hawaiian Telcom Communications, Inc.; *pg.* 1872, *pg.* 544
Nishimoto, Susan, Sr Dir-Mktg Ops - Box Inc.; *pg.* 1232, *pg.* 124
Nishita, Kimi, Sr Dir-Corp Comm - Intuitive Surgical, Inc.; *pg.* 1546, *pg.* 286
Nisivocci, Kathy, Sr VP-Digital Sls & Mktg - Bank of America Corporation; *pg.* 718, *pg.* 1362
Nissan, Ryan, Dir-PR - New York Rangers Hockey Club; *pg.* 570, *pg.* 1269
Nissim, Julia, Mgr-Media Rels - The American Dental Association; *pg.* 127, *pg.* 564
Niszczak, Kelly, Specialist-Media - Ikea North America Services LLC; *pg.* 929, *pg.* 1523
Niven, Michelle, Sr VP-Affiliate Ad Sls - Oxygen Media LLC; *pg.* 303, *pg.* 1275
Nix, Gary, Dir-Mktg & Product Mgmt - AP Exhaust Products, Inc.; *pg.* 199, *pg.* 1373
Nix, Kelli, Asst VP & Area Mgr-Mktg - Regions Financial Corporation; *pg.* 798, *pg.* 4
Nix, Traci, Coord-Social Media - Hobby Lobby Stores Inc.; *pg.* 927, *pg.* 1486
Nixon, Hilary, Sr Specialist-PR - RE/MAX International, Inc.; *pg.* 1109, *pg.* 322
Nixon, Tammy, Mgr-Product-Global - Singer Sewing Company; *pg.* 698, *pg.* 1639
Niziak, Drew J., Sr VP-Broker Sls & Aflac Benefit Solutions - Aflac Incorporated; *pg.* 1188, *pg.* 527
Nizielski, Rob, VP-Network Sls - Captivate; *pg.* 272, *pg.* 1209
Njaka, Chima, Mgr-Product Line - VMware, Inc.; *pg.* 490, *pg.* 179
Njowoka, Maurice, Brand Mgr-Tanzania - The Coca-Cola Company; *pg.* 240, *pg.* 493
Noain, Alfonso, Dir-Mktg - DIRECTV Group Holdings, LLC; *pg.* 281, *pg.* 79
Nobay, Frances, Dir-Digital Media - Teachers Insurance & Annuity Association - College Retirement Equities Fund; *pg.* 1219, *pg.* 1297
Noble, Amaris, Mgr-Integrated Mktg Comm-Brdcst, Entertainment & Digital - National Association for Stock Car Auto Racing; *pg.* 566, *pg.* 420
Noble, Andrew, Sr Brand Dir-Dixie Consumer Products - Georgia-Pacific LLC; *pg.* 1458, *pg.* 507
Noble, Beatrice, Sr Mgr-Education Field Mktg - Adobe Systems Incorporated; *pg.* 342, *pg.* 235
Noble, Jonathan, Analyst-Mktg - Amica Mutual Insurance Co.; *pg.* 1192, *pg.* 1602
Noble, Julien, VP-Intl Digital Mktg & Publicity - The Walt Disney Company; *pg.* 317, *pg.* 52
Noble, Paula, Specialist-Mktg Sls Support - Humana, Inc.; *pg.* 1204, *pg.* 734
Noble, Scott, Dir-Integrated Mktg - Del Monte Foods, Inc.; *pg.* 852, *pg.* 304
Noble, Scott P., Sr Portfolio Mgr-Mktg - FedEx Express Corporation; *pg.* 1908, *pg.* 1644
Noble, Shawn, Sr Dir-Media - Giorgio Armani Corporation; *pg.* 25, *pg.* 1234
Noble, Tonya, Sr Assoc Brand Mgr - E&J Gallo Winery; *pg.* 1962, *pg.* 149
Nobliski, Rich, Dir-Channel Mktg - Siemens PLM Software; *pg.* 469, *pg.* 1734
Nobui, Jennifer, Brand Mgr-Huggies - Kimberly-Clark Corporation; *pg.* 1461, *pg.* 1720
Nobui, Sean, Sr Brand Mgr-Viva - Kimberly-Clark Corporation; *pg.* 1461, *pg.* 1720
Nocar, Geoff, Dir-Mktg-Respiratory Mktg-BREO - GlaxoSmithKline; *pg.* 1536, *pg.* 1565
Nocco, Corey, Sr Mgr-Digital Strategy - Under Armour, Inc.; *pg.* 49, *pg.* 759
Nocera, Bruce, Dir-Sls - Associated Fabrics Corporation; *pg.* 691, *pg.* 1064
Noceti, Moriah, Reg Dir-Mktg - MetroPCS, Inc.; *pg.* 1872, *pg.* 1683
Nockels, Jennifer, Mgr-Mktg - L'Oreal USA; *pg.* 514, *pg.* 1252
Nockleby, Kristie, Sr VP-Small Bus Product Strategies - The Columbia Bank; *pg.* 739, *pg.* 767
Nodzak, Lauren, Dir-PR - Pernod Ricard USA, Inc.; *pg.* 1968, *pg.* 1332
Noe, David P., VP-Sls & Mktg & Gen Mgr - Rev-A-Shelf; *pg.* 1060, *pg.* 738
Noel, Karen, Gen Mgr-Bus Mktg - Sprint Corporation; *pg.* 1874, *pg.* 719
Noel, Karen, Mgr-Adv - State Farm Mutual Automobile Insurance Co.; *pg.* 1218, *pg.* 557
Noel, Katherine, Sr Asst Brand Mgr Marlboro - Altria Group, Inc.; *pg.* 1893, *pg.* 1800
Noel, Meghan, Sr Dir-Media Solutions - Concur Technologies, Inc.; *pg.* 1236, *pg.* 1813
Noelck, Jess, Sr Specialist-PR - CUNA Mutual Insurance Society; *pg.* 743, *pg.* 1865
Noering, Siri, Mgr-WebSphere Channel Mktg-North America - IBM; *pg.* 410, *pg.* 1449
Noeth, Kerri, Strategist-B2B Principle Content Mktg - Cars.com; *pg.* 1234, *pg.* 568
Noetzel, Kimberly, Sr Mgr-Comm - Charter Communications, Inc.; *pg.* 274, *pg.* 372
Noffke, Luke, Dir-Digital Mktg - Ernie Ball Inc.; *pg.* 1768, *pg.* 68
Nofi, Leigh, Mgr-PR - Canon U.S.A., Inc.; *pg.* 1404, *pg.* 1178
Noh, John, Sr Dir - Brocade Communications Systems, Inc.; *pg.* 365, *pg.* 239
Nohe, Brad, Sr Dir-Norovirus Vaccine Global Mktg - Takeda Pharmaceuticals USA, Inc.; *pg.* 1600, *pg.* 605
Noisette, Louis, Specialist-Mktg - FedEx Corporation; *pg.* 1907, *pg.* 1642
Noiseux, Moira, Mgr-Field Mktg-Northern California - Kind LLC; *pg.* 868, *pg.* 1249
Nojaim, Kelly Thomas, Dir-Partner Sls - Microsoft Corporation; *pg.* 435, *pg.* 1824
Nolan, Daniel, Sr Mgr-Mktg-Digital Experience Team - Vail Resorts, Inc.; *pg.* 1117, *pg.* 313
Nolan, Fiona, Sr VP-Mktg - CommScope, Inc.; *pg.* 278, *pg.* 1378
Nolan, George, Pres-Great Northern Products - Great Northern Products, Ltd.; *pg.* 859, *pg.* 1609
Nolan, John, VP & Dir-Sls - The Nielsen Company B.V.; *pg.* 1671, *pg.* 1272
Nolan, Joseph, Exec Dir-Social Media - Beachbody, LLC; *pg.* 271, *pg.* 272
Nolan, Kathleen D., Supvr-Mktg Comm - Constellation Energy Resources, LLC; *pg.* 1938, *pg.* 756
Nolan, Michael, Sr Mgr-Mktg, Comm, Event & Sponsorship Mktg-Global - Accenture; *pg.* 1392, *pg.* 1186
Nolan, Nancy A., Assoc Dir-Global Mktg Comm-Mktg Comm & Channels - Merck & Co., Inc.; *pg.* 1566, *pg.* 1077
Nolda, Rhonda, Acct Exec-Charter Media - Charter Communications, Inc.; *pg.* 274, *pg.* 372
Nolen, Brad, Dir-Product Strategy & Market Dev-Bombardier Aerospace - Bombardier Inc.; *pg.* 1318, *pg.* 1953
Nolen, Brad, Mgr-Global Category & Transformation New Product Introductions - Hewlett-Packard Company; *pg.* 404, *pg.* 175
Nolet, Jason, Sr VP & Gen Mgr-Switching, Routing & Analytics Products Grp - Brocade Corporation; *pg.* 365, *pg.* 312
Noll, Amy M, Sr Dir-Mktg - Simon Property Group, Inc.; *pg.* 1112, *pg.* 690
Noll, Jens, Product Dir-Europe & Intl - Jockey International, Inc.; *pg.* 27, *pg.* 1861
Nolting, Andrea, Brand Mgr-Tide Design-North America - The Procter & Gamble Company; *pg.* 1129, *pg.* 1418
Nomoto, Kenichi, Sr Dir - Eisai Inc.; *pg.* 1526, *pg.* 1133
Nonnemacher, Kristen, Mgr-Education Mktg - Crayola LLC; *pg.* 951, *pg.* 1528
Nook, Greg, CMO & Exec VP - J.E. Dunn Construction Group, Inc.; *pg.* 89, *pg.* 984
Noonan, Brendan, Dir-Channel Mktg-Small Format - MillerCoors; *pg.* 254, *pg.* 1877
Noonan, Brendan, Dir-Channel Mktg - MillerCoors LLC; *pg.* 255, *pg.* 582
Noonan, Chris, VP-Media - Charter Communications, Inc.; *pg.* 274, *pg.* 372
Noonan, Colleen, VP-Mktg & Creative Svcs - Daily News, L.P.; *pg.* 1632, *pg.* 1221
Nooney, Mary Beth, Product Mgr - STERIS Corporation; *pg.* 1597, *pg.* 1464
Norbis, Mario, Brand Mgr-Global - Honeywell International Inc.; *pg.* 407, *pg.* 1088
Nord, Joey T., Exec Dir-Mktg Comm & PR - McKesson Corporation; *pg.* 1560, *pg.* 222
Nordberg, John W., Asst VP-Bus Mktg - AT&T; *pg.* 1865, *pg.* 258
Nordeen, Nicole, Sr Specialist-Internal Mktg & Enterprise Comm - Target Corporation; *pg.* 1786, *pg.* 942
Norder, Kari, Sr Mgr-Exec Comm - Adobe Systems Incorporated; *pg.* 342, *pg.* 235
Nordquist, Jill, Sr VP-Mktg - JAKKS Pacific, Inc.; *pg.* 960, *pg.* 142
Nordstrom, David, VP-Social Media - Toyota Motor Sales, U.S.A., Inc.; *pg.* 193, *pg.* 296
Nordstrom, Peter E., Co-Pres, Pres-Mdsg & Exec VP - Nordstrom, Inc.; *pg.* 1779, *pg.* 1837
Nordstrum, Chris, Sr Mgr-Adv-Global - Cisco Systems, Inc.; *pg.* 372, *pg.* 240
Noren, Adam, Head-Platform-Large Advertiser & Agency Mktg - Google Inc.; *pg.* 1249, *pg.* 153
Noren, Lindsay, Mgr-Digital Mktg - The North Face, Inc.; *pg.* 1840, *pg.* 252
Norene-Behles, Cady, Mgr-Social Strategy Consulting - Oracle Corporation; *pg.* 1272, *pg.* 786
Norian, Lori, VP-Mktg - Matrixx Initiatives, Inc.; *pg.* 1559, *pg.* 23
Noriega, Lauren, Mgr-Media Mktg - Visionworks of America, Inc.; *pg.* 1436, *pg.* 1744
Norkiewicz, Jeff, VP-Mktg - Dominick's Finer Foods, LLC; *pg.* 1019, *pg.* 644
Norman, Anne, Mgr-Brand, Creative & Content - American Family Mutual Insurance Company; *pg.* 1190, *pg.* 1864
Norman, Hiram, VP-Digital Media & Gen Mgr-CWTV.com - Warner Bros. Entertainment Inc.; *pg.* 319, *pg.* 54
Norman, Ian G., Dir-Sls-Capital Area - Astellas Pharma US, Inc.; *pg.* 1496, *pg.* 640
Norman, Jake, Head-Agency Dev-Canada - Facebook, Inc.; *pg.* 1245, *pg.* 143
Norman, Jennifer, VP-Mktg - Stearns Products Inc.; *pg.* 523, *pg.* 279
Norman, Jessica, Mgr-Mktg - Siemens Process Industries and Drive; *pg.* 1376, *pg.* 1587
Norman, Julie, Brand Mgr-Celebrity Fragrance Portfolio - Coty, Inc.; *pg.* 506, *pg.* 1219
Norman, Mark, VP-Americas Sls & Mktg-Worldwide Distr - Fairchild Semiconductor Corporation; *pg.* 638, *pg.* 245

Norman, Matthew, Div Mgr-Mdse-Home Entertainment - Amazon.com, Inc.; *pg.* 1226, *pg.* 1831

Norman, Michael, Mgr-Technical, Mktg, Software & Tools Strategy - Freescale Semiconductor, Inc.; *pg.* 398, *pg.* 1662

Norman, Stephen P., Dir-Banking & Capital Markets Mktg - PricewaterhouseCoopers LLP; *pg.* 795, *pg.* 1283

Normand, Marc C., VP-Res, Disney Media Sls & Mktg - The Walt Disney Company; *pg.* 317, *pg.* 52

Normand, Philippe, Dir-Global Mktg-Can-Am Off Road Vehicles - Bombardier Recreational Products, Inc.; *pg.* 201, *pg.* 1960

Normart, Mike, Sr Dir-Casual Lifestyle - Zappos.com, Inc.; *pg.* 1291, *pg.* 1030

Norment, Lindsey, Mgr-Adv & Promos - Virginia Tourism Authority; *pg.* 1010, *pg.* 1804

Norpel, Sam, VP-Digital Mktg, ECommerce & Customer Acq - Lands' End, Inc.; *pg.* 1776, *pg.* 1857

Norr, Cynde, Product Mgr - Recreational Equipment, Inc.; *pg.* 1843, *pg.* 1821

Norris, Brian, Dir-Natl Adv Sls-Direct Response & Latino - DISH Network Corporation; *pg.* 283, *pg.* 325

Norris, Cody, Mgr-Mktg-Gaming - Alienware Corporation; *pg.* 346, *pg.* 439

Norris, David, Head-Mktg - Pfizer Inc.; *pg.* 1581, *pg.* 1278

Norris, Dean, Sr VP-Mktg & Special Ops - Fox Broadcasting Company; *pg.* 287, *pg.* 130

Norris, Matthew, Mgr-Digital Media Mktg - Charter Communications, Inc.; *pg.* 274, *pg.* 372

Norris, Paula J., Supvr-Mktg - SYNNEX Corporation; *pg.* 480, *pg.* 92

Norris, Scott, Exec VP & Gen Mgr-Mdse - The Men's Wearhouse, Inc.; *pg.* 44, *pg.* 1711

Norris, Stephanie, Dir-Product Mgmt-Infrastructure Svcs - The Weather Channel LLC; *pg.* 320, *pg.* 523

Norris, Steven, Coord-Social Media - Georgia Institute Of Technology; *pg.* 602, *pg.* 506

Norris-Howser, Natalie, Head-Mktg - Vein Clinics of America Inc; *pg.* 1606, *pg.* 609

Norsworthy, Alice, Exec VP-Mktg & Sls - Universal Orlando; *pg.* 590, *pg.* 456

North, Aron, Dir-Adv - Taco Bell Corp.; *pg.* 1752, *pg.* 117

North, Chris, Sr Dir-Bus Dev - AVANIR Pharmaceuticals; *pg.* 1498, *pg.* 40

North, Cynthia, Dir-Consumer Mktg - Bayer Healthcare Consumer Care Division; *pg.* 1500, *pg.* 1087

North, David, VP-Mktg-ExCell, Glenoit & Croscill Companies - Croscill, Inc.; *pg.* 1122, *pg.* 1220

North, Diana, Specialist-Product Dev - 3M Company; *pg.* 1142, *pg.* 956

North, Erin, Sr Assoc Brand Mgr - Central Garden & Pet Company; *pg.* 1475, *pg.* 303

North, Kenn, Principal & Product Mgr - National Instruments Corporation; *pg.* 443, *pg.* 1664

North, Larry, Dir-Mktg - Nortek Security & Control LLC; *pg.* 659, *pg.* 59

Northcott, John, VP-Mktg, Comml Strategy & Ops - Lexicon Pharmaceuticals, Inc.; *pg.* 1555, *pg.* 1747

Northcutt, Christa, Mgr-Mktg Production - Gordmans Stores Inc.; *pg.* 1771, *pg.* 1016

Northcutt, Justin, Dir-Mktg-North America - Dell Inc.; *pg.* 383, *pg.* 1737

Northcutt, Todd, VP-Product - IGN Entertainment, Inc.; *pg.* 1258, *pg.* 220

Northing, Richard, Sr VP-Products & Svcs - Flexera Software Inc.; *pg.* 398, *pg.* 658

Northrup, Jeff, Product Mgr - DPL Inc.; *pg.* 1939, *pg.* 1445

Norton, Amy, Dir-Online Mktg - Costco Wholesale Corporation; *pg.* 1765, *pg.* 1820

Norton, Charlotte, Sr Mgr-Mktg Comm - Zoll Medical Corporation; *pg.* 1612, *pg.* 814

Norton, Diane, Strategist-Mktg-Deluxe Cornerstone Solutions - Deluxe Corporation; *pg.* 1634, *pg.* 964

Norton, Jason, VP-Product Dev - TransUnion Corp.; *pg.* 811, *pg.* 591

Norton, Jeff, Asst VP & Sr Mgr-Mktg - Eaton Vance Corp.; *pg.* 746, *pg.* 794

Norton, Jeff, Dir-Mktg - The Viking Group; *pg.* 119, *pg.* 891

Norton, Jennifer, Sr Dir-Comm-North America - Janssen Pharmaceutica Products, L.P.; *pg.* 1548, *pg.* 1125

Norton, Jennifer, Sr Dir-Comm-North America - Johnson & Johnson Inc.; *pg.* 1552, *pg.* 1923

Norton, Jim, Head-Media Sls-Global - AOL Inc.; *pg.* 1229, *pg.* 1195

Norton, Joe, Dir-PR - American International Group, Inc.; *pg.* 1190, *pg.* 1193

Norton, John, Dir-PR - National Community Pharmacists Association; *pg.* 148, *pg.* 1771

Norton, Patricia, Sr Dir-Bus Plng & Ops - Best Buy Co., Inc.; *pg.* 1761, *pg.* 954

Norton, Rodney, Sr Mgr-Digital Mktg-Footlocker.com & Eastbay - Foot Locker, Inc.; *pg.* 1808, *pg.* 1231

Norton, Stephen, Sr Dir-Corp Comm - STERIS Corporation; *pg.* 1597, *pg.* 1464

Norvell, Amanda, Sr Dir-Online Mktg - Golf Channel; *pg.* 551, *pg.* 454

Norvell, Marcus, Rep-Smith Bits Technical Sls - Smith International, Inc.; *pg.* 1377, *pg.* 1715

Norvelle, Jim, Dir-Media Rels-Dominion Energy - Dominion Resources, Inc.; *pg.* 1939, *pg.* 1802

Norville, Julie Kim, Sr Mgr-Compliance - Northern Trust Corporation; *pg.* 787, *pg.* 585

Norville, Marina Hoffmann, VP-Corp & Fin PR - American Express Company; *pg.* 712, *pg.* 1190

Norway, Michele, Mgr-Vendor Mktg-IBM Software - Ingram Micro Inc.; *pg.* 415, *pg.* 261

Norwood, Danielle, Sr Mgr-Mktg-North American Toy Div - VTech Electronics North America, LLC; *pg.* 969, *pg.* 554

Nosal, Marc, Brand Mgr-Private - SUPERVALU, Inc. - Eastern Region; *pg.* 1035, *pg.* 1795

Nosal, Mary, Sr Brand Mgr-Mktg - American Eagle Outfitters, Inc.; *pg.* 37, *pg.* 1572

Nosler, Brad, VP-Mktg & Sls - Comcast Cable Communications, Inc.; *pg.* 276, *pg.* 1560

Nosov, Xenia, Mgr-Product Mktg - Pinterest; *pg.* 1275, *pg.* 225

Noss, Erin, Sr Mgr-Comm - Aramark; *pg.* 1013, *pg.* 1558

Nota, Ralph, Mgr-NE Sls & Distr - NABCO Entrances, Inc.; *pg.* 99, *pg.* 1882

Notes, Zack, Mgr-Digital Mktg - UncommonGoods LLC; *pg.* 1286, *pg.* 1147

Notis, Nancy E., Assoc Dir-Mktg & Pub Affairs - HCA HOLDINGS, INC.; *pg.* 1539, *pg.* 1651

Notley, Patrick, VP-Sls - NBC Universal, Inc.; *pg.* 300, *pg.* 1266

Noto, Anthony, CFO & CMO-Interim - Twitter, Inc.; *pg.* 1285, *pg.* 228

Noto, Terry, Gen Mgr-Sls-The Americas - Hensley Industries, Inc.; *pg.* 1166, *pg.* 1682

Nottingham, Allison, Mgr-Digital Sls Ops - The Dallas Morning News Co.; *pg.* 1633, *pg.* 1679

Nottonson, Eric, Head-Institutional Retirement Product Mktg - Teachers Insurance & Annuity Association - College Retirement Equities Fund; *pg.* 1219, *pg.* 1297

Nouri, Suzanne, Sr VP-Digital Product Mgmt - Citigroup Inc.; *pg.* 735, *pg.* 1212

Noursalehi, Saum, Sr VP-Mktg - Overstock.com, Inc.; *pg.* 1273, *pg.* 1760

Nourse, Scott, VP-Digital Product Dev - Public Broadcasting Service; *pg.* 305, *pg.* 1774

Novacek, Jack, Area Mgr-Sls - J.R. Simplot Company; *pg.* 867, *pg.* 547

Novacek, Nancy, Mgr-Mktg Dev - PepsiCo, Inc.; *pg.* 259, *pg.* 1327

Novack, Nicole, Mgr-Mktg Ops - Novartis Pharmaceuticals Corp.; *pg.* 1575, *pg.* 1054

Novak, Brett, Sr VP-Sls & Mktg - Akorn, Inc.; *pg.* 1488, *pg.* 622

Novak, Chris, Global Product Mgr-DEUTSCH - TE Connectivity Ltd.; *pg.* 677, *pg.* 1515

Novak, Dan, VP-Global Mktg, PR & Comm - QUALCOMM Incorporated; *pg.* 1873, *pg.* 207

Novak, David J., Jr., Exec VP-Sls & Bus Dev - SPS COMMERCE, INC.; *pg.* 472, *pg.* 942

Novak, Elizabeth, Coord-Field Mktg & Mdsg - PVH Corp.; *pg.* 46, *pg.* 1283

Novak, Eugene, Mgr-Dev & Product-Radio Controls - Magnetek, Inc.; *pg.* 1301, *pg.* 1870

Novak, Jamie, VP-Product Mktg - JPMorgan Chase & Co.; *pg.* 772, *pg.* 1246

Novak, Kent, Sr VP & Gen Mgr-DLP Products - Texas Instruments Incorporated; *pg.* 679, *pg.* 1688

Novak, Kirk, VP-Strategy & Mktg - Merichem Company; *pg.* 1172, *pg.* 1711

Novak, Mike, Mgr-Product Mktg-Uconnect Access - FCA US LLC; *pg.* 170, *pg.* 868

Novak, Stephanie, Mgr-Mktg-Aerie Brand, Digital & Intl - American Eagle Outfitters, Inc.; *pg.* 37, *pg.* 1572

Novak, Susan, Sr Dir-PepsiCo Global Brand Comm - PepsiCo, Inc.; *pg.* 259, *pg.* 1327

Novalski, Philip, Rep-Mktg - Hess Corporation; *pg.* 979, *pg.* 1240

Novarro, Doug, Dir-Corp PR & Compliance Comm-Global - Pall Corporation; *pg.* 232, *pg.* 1323

Novella, Sophia, VP-Mktg - Campbell Soup Company; *pg.* 844, *pg.* 1048

Novelli, Christina, Mgr-Creative Svcs - Potbelly Sandwich Works LLC; *pg.* 1746, *pg.* 587

Novi, Nicole, Sr Mgr-Mktg - Adobe Systems Incorporated; *pg.* 342, *pg.* 235

Novia, Joe, Div VP-Sls - Extended Stay Hotels LLC; *pg.* 1091, *pg.* 1622

Novick, Steven, Mgr-Mktg & Membership Solutions - BJ's Wholesale Club, Inc.; *pg.* 1762, *pg.* 857

Novickas, Adam, VP-Mktg - Ubisoft Inc.; *pg.* 589, *pg.* 229

Novoa, Noelle, Mgr-PR - ASICS America Corporation; *pg.* 1826, *pg.* 106

Novosel, Michael, VP-Client Sls - iMODULES Software, Inc.; *pg.* 1258, *pg.* 716

Novotney, Jeremy, District VP-Sls - Eaton Corporation; *pg.* 1331, *pg.* 1429

Novotny, Mark, Mgr-Mktg-Global - Nordson Corporation; *pg.* 1365, *pg.* 1480

Novy, Mike, Sr VP-Sls - Constellation Brands, Inc.; *pg.* 1960, *pg.* 1348

Nowak, Christopher, Sr Mgr-Product Dev-Mopar - FCA US LLC; *pg.* 170, *pg.* 868

Nowak, Lisa, Dir-Global Sls Enablement - Zebra Technologies Corporation; *pg.* 690, *pg.* 628

Nowak, Matt, Dir-Sls-Natl - Valeant Pharmaceuticals International, Inc.; *pg.* 1605, *pg.* 1957

Nowak, Michael, Product Mgr - Facebook, Inc.; *pg.* 1245, *pg.* 143

Nowak, Thomas, Sr VP-Mktg & Mdsg Europe - Staples, Inc.; *pg.* 474, *pg.* 821

Nowicki, Kathy, Sr Mgr-Mktg - Dunkin' Brands Group, Inc.; *pg.* 1727, *pg.* 810

Nowik, Michael, Mgr-Mktg - The Allstate Corporation; *pg.* 1189, *pg.* 639

Nowik, Tom, Area Product Mgr-Base Station Antennas & Brdcst - Radio Frequency Systems, Inc.; *pg.* 666, *pg.* 354

Nowlin, Brandy, Dir-Mktg - Deli Management Inc.; *pg.* 1725, *pg.* 1668

Noyes, Brian, VP-Mktg - SONOSITE, INC.; *pg.* 1429, *pg.* 1818

Noyes, Diane, Brand Mgr - ConAgra Foods, Inc.; *pg.* 826, *pg.* 1014

Noyes, Gareth, Chief Strategy Officer & VP-Strategy & Corp Dev - Wind River Systems, Inc.; *pg.* 493, *pg.* 38

Noyes, Glenn, Dir-Mdse-Drums & Percussion - Guitar Center, Inc.; *pg.* 1771, *pg.* 306

Noyle, Dave, Dir-Creative Svcs - Sun Life Financial Inc.; *pg.* 806, *pg.* 1944

Nozaki, Mitch, Mgr-Tech Mktg - Murata Electronics North America, Inc.; *pg.* 658, *pg.* 540

Ntseoane, Thabo, Brand Mgr-Namibia - KFC Corporation; *pg.* 1733, *pg.* 735

Nucci, Jim, Brand Mgr-Mktg - Intel Corporation; *pg.* 645, *pg.* 266

Nuce, Russell, Chief Strategy Officer - EVINE Live Inc.; *pg.* 1768, *pg.* 922

Nuevo-Celeste, Victoria, VP-Mktg - Califia Farms LLC; *pg.* 843, *pg.* 179

Nugent, Allison, Sr Mgr-Mktg - Toll Brothers, Inc.; *pg.* 115, *pg.* 1541

Nugent, Anne, VP-PR - Coty, Inc.; *pg.* 506, *pg.* 1219

Nugent, Bill, Gen Mgr-Sls - Steve Foley Cadillac; *pg.* 190, *pg.* 641

Nugent, Brian, Sr VP & Gen Mgr-Mdse - Boscov's Department Store, LLC; *pg.* 1763, *pg.* 1583

Nugent, Ginny, VP-Production - Home Box Office, Inc.; *pg.* 290, *pg.* 1240

Nugent, Katelyn, Sr Mgr-Brand Mktg - Converse Inc.; *pg.* 1831, *pg.* 793

Nugent, Kevin, Mgr-Sls-Bulk Plant & Terminal Solutions - Liquid Controls, Inc.; *pg.* 1356, *pg.* 622

Nugent, Steve, Dir-Sls-IQF & MicroDried - Milne Food Products, Inc.; *pg.* 877, *pg.* 1824

Nugroshchel, Esta, Dir-PR - Boscov's Department Store, LLC; *pg.* 1763, *pg.* 1583

Nuich, Jeff, Sr Dir-Comm - Comcast Sportsnet; *pg.* 278, *pg.* 1562

Nukho, Kristine, Sr Mgr-Pricing & Inventory - ION Media Networks, Inc.; *pg.* 293, *pg.* 479

Nukunya, John, Sr Mgr-Market Res-App & Device Ecosystems

First page reference indicates Business Class Edition
Second page reference indicates Geographic Edition

- Microsoft Corporation; pg. 435, pg. 1824
Null, Larry, Dir-Retail Sls - Rose Packing Company; pg. 892, pg. 556
Nulsen, Jeff, Sr Dir-Global Prod Mktg - VistaPrint USA, Incorporated; pg. 1700, pg. 829
Numsuwan, Alan, Head-Comml Mktg - Booz Allen Hamilton Inc; pg. 363, pg. 1788
Nunes, Craig S., VP-Global Mktg-HP Storage - Hewlett-Packard Company; pg. 404, pg. 175
Nunes, James, Mng Dir-Mktg Hi Res Headshot - Trinchero Family Estates; pg. 1971, pg. 197
Nunes, Kevin, Dir-Production - Weatherby, Inc.; pg. 1848, pg. 181
Nunez, Arturo, Head-Mktg-ALAC - Apple Inc.; pg. 350, pg. 73
Nunez, Diego, Sr Dir-Digital Mktg & ECommerce - Skullcandy, Inc.; pg. 674, pg. 1754
Nunez, German, Sr Mgr-Mktg-Hematology Platforms - Beckman Coulter, Inc.; pg. 1402, pg. 48
Nunez, Maurice, Sr Mgr-Monetization - OpenX Technologies, Inc.; pg. 1272, pg. 180
Nunn, Matt, Dir-US Developer Tools Product Mktg - Microsoft Corporation; pg. 435, pg. 1824
Nunn, Summer, Dir-Digital Mktg - Meineke Car Care Centers, Inc.; pg. 212, pg. 1367
Nunziata, Ben, Mgr-Mdsg & Plng - Burton Snowboard Company; pg. 1829, pg. 1765
Nunziati, John, Sr Dir-IR - Avaya Inc.; pg. 621, pg. 264
Nuss, Michael, Mgr-ECommerce Mktg - Shoe Carnival, Inc.; pg. 1819, pg. 679
Nussbaum, Hazel, Brand Mgr-AXE - Unilever United States, Inc.; pg. 904, pg. 1061
Nussbaum, Jason, VP-Intl Mktg - The Patron Spirits Company; pg. 1967, pg. 1029
Nussbaum, Kim, VP-Adv - The McClatchy Company; pg. 1662, pg. 196
Nutley, Patrick, Sr Dir-Bus Analytics & Admin - Sharp Electronics Corporation; pg. 672, pg. 1082
Nutsugah, Philip, VP-Data, Voice Product Dev & Mgmt - Cox Communications, Inc.; pg. 279, pg. 501
Nuttall, Gary, Mgr-Mktg - Xerox Canada Inc.; pg. 494, pg. 1930
Nutter-Wiersbitzky, Shannon, Principal & Head-Institutional Mktg - The Vanguard Group, Inc.; pg. 816, pg. 1550
Nutting, Charlie, Sr Asst Brand Mgr-Old Spice - The Procter & Gamble Company; pg. 1129, pg. 1418
Nuys, Cheryl Van, Mgr-Mktg Comm-Global - Hospira, Inc.; pg. 1542, pg. 623
Nuzzo, Phil, VP-OEM Sls - Philips Respironics; pg. 1585, pg. 1555
Nwamadi, Tresia, Sr Dir-HR Sls & Customer Dev - ConAgra Foods, Inc.; pg. 826, pg. 1014
Nyberg, Dave, Sr Mgr-External Affairs-Twin Cities - Comcast Corporation; pg. 276, pg. 1560
Nyberg, Goran, Pres-Volvo Sls & Mktg - Volvo Trucks North America, Inc.; pg. 195, pg. 1377
Nyberg, Wendy, Sr Dir-Mktg - Trinchero Family Estates; pg. 1971, pg. 197
Nyborg, Jacquelyn, VP-Mktg - Wayside Technology Group, Inc.; pg. 491, pg. 1121
Nye, Bryan, Analyst-Social Media - Henry Schein, Inc.; pg. 1541, pg. 1180
Nyer, Joanne, VP-Mktg & Dir - The TJX Companies, Inc.; pg. 1788, pg. 822
Nygaard, Bridget, Mgr-Mktg - Schneider; pg. 1922, pg. 1859
Nygaard, Kurt, Chief Sls Officer - Harwick Standard Distribution Corporation; pg. 1164, pg. 1402
Nyholm, Mark, Product Mgr-Technical-Heavy Duty - Amsoil Inc.; pg. 971, pg. 1896
Nyikes, Nancy, Mgr-Mktg Comm - General Electric Company; pg. 1297, pg. 347
Nykaza, Russ, Sr Dir-Talent Mgmt - United States Cellular Corporation; pg. 1875, pg. 594
Nyman, Eric, Sr VP-Mktg - Hasbro, Inc.; pg. 954, pg. 1603
Nyman, Jacob A., Dir-Office of Promo & Adv Review - Merck & Co., Inc.; pg. 1566, pg. 1077
Nymark, Marcie, Sr Mgr-Marcom - Microsoft Corporation; pg. 435, pg. 1824
Nyquist, John, Dir-Sls & Bus Dev - American Axle & Manufacturing Holdings, Inc.; pg. 198, pg. 879

O

O Brien, Michael, Dir-Sls - Bemis Healthcare Packaging; pg. 1453, pg. 1885
O Hara, Thom, Head-Medical Div Mktg - W.L. Gore & Associates, Inc.; pg. 122, pg. 388
O Reilly, Patrick, Mgr-Technical & Mktg - Eberhard Manufacturing Division; pg. 1046, pg. 1475
O'Beirne, Jennifer, Dir-Bus Svcs Mktg - Staples, Inc.; pg. 474, pg. 821
O'Beirne, Kieran, Brand Mgr-Scotch, Gin & Tequila - Diageo Canada, Inc.; pg. 1961, pg. 1937
O'Boyle, Kristin, VP-Mktg Ops - E*TRADE Financial Corporation; pg. 749, pg. 1230
O'Brian, Peter, VP-Mktg Comm - Xerox Corporation; pg. 494, pg. 365
O'Brien, Ashleigh, Sr Mgr-Mktg-Agency Mgmt - Microsoft Corporation; pg. 435, pg. 1824
O'Brien, Brad, Mgr-Social Media Mktg - Provide Commerce, Inc.; pg. 1276, pg. 206
O'Brien, Bradley, Exec VP-Design & Product Dev - Tommy Bahama; pg. 48, pg. 1842
O'Brien, Brendan, Head-Global Software Solutions Sls - Cisco Systems, Inc.; pg. 372, pg. 240
O'Brien, Brice, Exec VP-Consumer Mktg-R.J. Reynolds Tobacco Company - Reynolds American Inc.; pg. 1894, pg. 1395
O'Brien, Brice, Exec VP-Consumer Mktg - R.J. Reynolds Tobacco Co.; pg. 1895, pg. 1395
O'Brien, Bridget, VP-Brand, Comm & Creative - VistaPrint USA, Incorporated; pg. 1700, pg. 829
O'Brien, Christine, Coord-Consumer Mktg & Promos - NBC Universal, Inc.; pg. 300, pg. 1266
O'Brien, Conor, Dir-Mktg-Lysol, Dettol & Sagrotan - Reckitt Benckiser Inc.; pg. 1136, pg. 1105
O'Brien, Courtney, Dir-Mktg - E&J Gallo Winery; pg. 1962, pg. 149
O'Brien, Danica, Dir-Creative Mktg Svcs - Toms Shoe's Inc; pg. 1821, pg. 276
O'Brien, Deirdre, Exec-Adv, Brand & Social Media - Tourism Ireland; pg. 1007, pg. 1303
O'Brien, Ed, VP-Healthcare Sls - Dimensional Insight, Inc.; pg. 387, pg. 805
O'Brien, Edward, Sr VP-Tech Product Mgmt - FMR LLC (Fidelity Investments); pg. 759, pg. 794
O'Brien, Erin, Sr Mgr-Digital & CRM Strategy - Best Buy Co., Inc.; pg. 1761, pg. 954
O'Brien, Erin, Mgr-Social Media - Omaha Convention and Visitors Bureau; pg. 152, pg. 1017
O'Brien, Felicity, Head-Mktg-EMEA - ACI Worldwide; pg. 341, pg. 449
O'Brien, Jay, Mgr-Production - Baltimore Ravens Limited Partnership; pg. 532, pg. 755
O'Brien, Jay, VP & Gen Mgr-Mdsg-Footwear - Henry Modell & Company, Inc.; pg. 1836, pg. 1240
O'Brien, Jerry, Mgr-Adv - Allen Organ Company; pg. 527, pg. 1549
O'Brien, Jim, CMO - Geeknet, Inc.; pg. 1248, pg. 1780
O'Brien, Joan, Mgr-Mktg Comm - ABB Inc. - Automation Technologies Instrumentation Products; pg. 1398, pg. 1590
O'Brien, Karen, VP-Social Media-Global - The Western Union Company; pg. 822, pg. 327
O'Brien, Kathleen, VP-Sls - Seventh Generation, Inc.; pg. 335, pg. 1765
O'Brien, Kathryn, Sr Dir-Branded Mktg & Ops - Gulf Oil Limited Partnership; pg. 978, pg. 814
O'Brien, Kathy, VP-Skin & Mktg Svcs - Unilever United States, Inc.; pg. 904, pg. 1061
O'Brien, Kelley, Dir-Interactive, Digital & Social - Krispy Kreme Doughnuts, Inc.; pg. 1734, pg. 1394
O'Brien, Ken, Sr VP-Mdsg - QVC Inc; pg. 305, pg. 1593
O'Brien, Kevin, VP-Sls - Manischewitz Company; pg. 875, pg. 1097
O'Brien, Kolleen, Mgr-Mktg Channel - Ivy Funds Distributor Inc.; pg. 771, pg. 719
O'Brien, Kristen, Mgr-E-mail Mktg Ops - Wayfair LLC; pg. 1288, pg. 801
O'Brien, Lauren, Planner-Mktg - Family Dollar Stores, Inc.; pg. 1768, pg. 1382
O'Brien, Lua, Product Mgr - OXO; pg. 1058, pg. 1275
O'Brien, Lyra, Coord-PR - Kohl's Corporation; pg. 1775, pg. 1870
O'Brien, Mallory, Specialist-Comm-Social Media - Kohler Co.; pg. 91, pg. 1862
O'Brien, Mark M., VP-Brand Mktg & Mgmt - Mizuno USA, Inc.; pg. 1839, pg. 538
O'Brien, Mary, VP-Mktg-Global - Saucony, Inc.; pg. 1818, pg. 828
O'Brien, Matt, Dir-Field Mktg - Honest Tea; pg. 253, pg. 762
O'Brien, Melissa, Sr Mgr-Category Mktg - Sam's Club; pg. 1783, pg. 29
O'Brien, Michael, Sr Mgr-Mktg - Chase Card Services, Inc.; pg. 734, pg. 215
O'Brien, Michael, VP & Dir-Sls - The E.W. Scripps Company; pg. 1639, pg. 1412
O'Brien, Mick, Dir-Mktg Comm-Global - Bose Corporation; pg. 626, pg. 820
O'Brien, Mike, VP-Corp & Product Plng - Hyundai Motor America; pg. 179, pg. 89
O'Brien, Nancy, VP-Brand Mktg - Minnesota Twins, LLC; pg. 563, pg. 940
O'Brien, Shelley P., Mgr-Product Mktg - AT&T; pg. 1865, pg. 258
O'Brien, Susan, VP-Mktg - Canadian Tire Corporation Limited; pg. 202, pg. 1936
O'Brien, Tipper, Brand Mgr-Digital-Innovation & Hispanic Brands - Anheuser-Busch Companies, LLC; pg. 237, pg. 991
O'Brien, Tom, Chief Revenue Officer & Exec VP-Digital Media - Nexstar Broadcasting Group, Inc.; pg. 303, pg. 1723
O'Brien, Tom, VP-Automotive Sls - SKF Sealing Solutions; pg. 217, pg. 610
O'Bryan, Lora, Asst VP & Mgr-Investment Advisors Mktg - Fifth Third Bancorp; pg. 752, pg. 1413
O'Carmody, Leslie, Sr Dir-Mktg - PerkinElmer, Inc.; pg. 1426, pg. 853
O'Carroll, Tammy, Mgr-Enterprise Demand Mktg - Adobe Systems Incorporated; pg. 342, pg. 235
O'Clair, Joan, Mgr-Corp Comm & Social Media - TravelCenters of America, LLC; pg. 1925, pg. 1481
O'Connell, Christine, Head-Digital Mktg & Social Media-Mopar - FCA US LLC; pg. 170, pg. 868
O'Connell, Colin, VP-Sls & Mktg-Trion & IAQ - Trion, Inc.; pg. 682, pg. 1390
O'Connell, Jim, Chief Sls Officer - National Association for Stock Car Auto Racing; pg. 566, pg. 420
O'Connell, Kevin, Sr VP-Mktg - Eat'n Park Hospitality Group; pg. 1728, pg. 1539
O'Connell, Kimberly, Sr Dir-Interactive Mktg & ECommerce - TracFone Wireless, Inc.; pg. 681, pg. 447
O'Connell, Mary, Dir-Brand PR - The Clorox Company; pg. 327, pg. 169
O'Connell, Matthew, Mgr-Production - Martindale-Hubbell, Inc.; pg. 1662, pg. 1095
O'Connell, Michael D., Brand Mgr - Neenah Paper, Inc.; pg. 1465, pg. 484
O'Connell, Olivia, Mgr-Recruiting Program Mktg - Oracle Corporation; pg. 450, pg. 191
O'Connell, Pat, Mgr-Player & Media Rels - Arizona Diamondbacks; pg. 529, pg. 14
O'Connell, Patrick, Dir-Mktg & Comm - KONE Inc.; pg. 1353, pg. 633
O'Conner, Jasmine, Specialist-Mktg Comm - Cummins Inc.; pg. 1326, pg. 676
O'Connor, Ashley E., Analyst-Digital Sls-Central Pacific-Spectrum Reach - Charter Communications, Inc.; pg. 274, pg. 372
O'Connor, Brian, VP-Global Jordan Brand Mktg - NIKE, Inc.; pg. 1812, pg. 1492
O'Connor, Brian, VP-PR - Princess Cruise Lines Ltd.; pg. 1920, pg. 270
O'Connor, Cory, Product Mgr - Google Inc.; pg. 1249, pg. 153
O'Connor, Craig W., Mgr-Digital Access Mktg - FedEx Express Corporation; pg. 1908, pg. 1644
O'Connor, Deb, VP-Mktg Strategy & Branding - Trustmark Corporation; pg. 812, pg. 969
O'Connor, Dennis, VP-Ticket Sls & Svc - Memphis Grizzlies; pg. 561, pg. 1645
O'Connor, Edward H., Jr., VP-Sls-Connecticut - Frontier Communications Corporation; pg. 1871, pg. 362
O'Connor, F. Joseph, Sr VP-Sls, Corp Accounts & Intl - Mohawk Fine Papers, Inc.; pg. 1464, pg. 1153
O'Connor, Fran, Sr Dir-Online Mktg - Holland America Line Inc.; pg. 1911, pg. 1836
O'Connor, Fritz, Mgr-Contract Mktg - GE Consumer & Industrial; pg. 55, pg. 733
O'Connor, Fritz, Mgr-Contract Mktg - General Electric Company; pg. 1297, pg. 347
O'Connor, James, Mgr-Global Mktg-Drambuie - William Blair & Company LLC; pg. 822, pg. 596
O'Connor, Jenna, Sr Mgr-Direct Mktg - GNC Holdings Inc.; pg. 1537, pg. 1576
O'Connor, Kate, Exec Dir-PR - Boehringer Ingelheim

Pharmaceuticals, Inc.; *pg.* 1507, *pg.* 368
O'Connor, Kathleen, Strategist-Dynamic Mktg & Comm - Aflac Incorporated; *pg.* 1188, *pg.* 527
O'Connor, Kevin, Sr Dir-Mktg - Beats Electronics LLC; *pg.* 624, *pg.* 272
O'Connor, Kim, Sr VP & Sr Mgr-Media - Citigroup Inc.; *pg.* 735, *pg.* 1212
O'Connor, Kim, Sr Dir-Sls & Mktg Svcs - Sanofi US; *pg.* 1592, *pg.* 1046
O'Connor, Lorne, Brand Mgr-Mktg - Enesco, LLC; *pg.* 1124, *pg.* 620
O'Connor, Mannix, Dir-Technical Mktg - MRV Communications, Inc.; *pg.* 441, *pg.* 64
O'Connor, Matthew, Product Mgr - Google Inc.; *pg.* 1249, *pg.* 153
O'Connor, Meghan, Assoc Mgr-Consumer Mktg - Rodale, Inc.; *pg.* 1681, *pg.* 1530
O'Connor, Melanie, Sr Mgr-Voice & Data Product Mgmt - Cox Communications, Inc.; *pg.* 279, *pg.* 501
O'Connor, Meredith, Mgr-Digital Media - Google Inc.; *pg.* 1249, *pg.* 153
O'Connor, Mike, Dir-Production - Amarillo Globe-News; *pg.* 1614, *pg.* 1658
O'Connor, Pamela, Sr Mgr-Mktg Comm - EarthLink Holdings Corp.; *pg.* 1240, *pg.* 504
O'Connor, Phil, Dir & Sr Mgr-Mktg-Nissan Motor Company - Nissan North America, Inc.; *pg.* 186, *pg.* 1633
O'Connor, Sean M., Dir-Wealth Mgmt Mktg - Teachers Insurance & Annuity Association - College Retirement Equities Fund; *pg.* 1219, *pg.* 1297
O'Connor, Suchi, Brand Mgr-Ecommerce - The Clorox Company; *pg.* 327, *pg.* 169
O'Connor, Tim, Dir-Sterling Brand Mdsg & Channel Mktg - Kohler Co.; *pg.* 91, *pg.* 1862
O'Connor, Tina, Rep-Sls-Natl - General Growth Properties, Inc.; *pg.* 1093, *pg.* 574
O'Connor, Tonia, Pres-Distr Sls & Mktg - Univision Communications Inc.; *pg.* 683, *pg.* 1307
O'Daniel-Munger, Rick, Mgr-Mktg-Humana Military - Humana, Inc.; *pg.* 1204, *pg.* 734
O'Dell, Ashley, Mgr-Mktg-Content & Creative - Atlanta Convention & Visitors Bureau; *pg.* 989, *pg.* 489
O'Dell, Ashley, Mgr-Integrated Mktg - Dolby Laboratories, Inc.; *pg.* 284, *pg.* 217
O'Dell, Dione, Dir-Mktg - rue21, inc.; *pg.* 32, *pg.* 1591
O'Dell, Julie, Dir-PR - Hallmark Cards, Inc.; *pg.* 1646, *pg.* 983
O'Donnell, Alice, VP-Mktg - Massage Heights Corporate, LLC; *pg.* 561, *pg.* 1741
O'Donnell, Caren, Coord-Mktg, Trng & Dev - The Clorox Company; *pg.* 327, *pg.* 169
O'Donnell, Diane, Sr Specialist-PR - North Shore-LIJ Health System; *pg.* 1573, *pg.* 1162
O'Donnell, Frank, VP-Adv Tech - The New York Times Company; *pg.* 1668, *pg.* 1270
O'Donnell, Jim, VP-West Coast Adv Sls & Ad Sls Ops - Hulu LLC; *pg.* 1257, *pg.* 274
O'Donnell, Kelley, VP-Mktg-PEAK - Old World Industries, Inc.; *pg.* 1175, *pg.* 641
O'Donnell, Kelly, Mgr-Global Product & ETF Mktg - The Vanguard Group, Inc.; *pg.* 816, *pg.* 1550
O'Donnell, Krissy, Assoc Mgr-Mktg Ops - The Children's Place, Inc.; *pg.* 22, *pg.* 1119
O'Donnell, Kristin, Mgr-Trade Mktg - Constellation Brands, Inc.; *pg.* 1960, *pg.* 1348
O'Donnell, Marjorie, Dir-Special Markets & Asst Dir-Adv - The Washington Times, LLC; *pg.* 1701, *pg.* 408
O'Donnell, Mary, VP-Retail Mktg - Alliance Data Systems Corporation; *pg.* 347, *pg.* 1729
O'Donnell, Molly, Dir-Influencer Mktg & Windows Phone - Microsoft Corporation; *pg.* 435, *pg.* 1824
O'Donnell, Pat, Brand Mgr - The Procter & Gamble Company; *pg.* 1129, *pg.* 1418
O'Donnell, Ryan, Mgr-Vendor Mktg - Ingram Micro Inc.; *pg.* 415, *pg.* 261
O'Donnell, Shaun T., Sr Mgr-Mktg Comm - AT&T; *pg.* 1865, *pg.* 258
O'Donnell, Tara, Sr Mgr-Digital Mktg - Universal Studios, Inc.; *pg.* 315, *pg.* 298
O'Donnell, Tom, Dir-Partnership Dev Media Sls & Acct Exec-Media Sls - Madison Square Garden Network; *pg.* 297, *pg.* 1255
O'Donoghue, Mark, Dir-Mktg Comm-Global - Avery Dennison Corporation; *pg.* 1452, *pg.* 95
O'Donovan, Terrence J., VP-Mktg & Sls - Core Molding Technologies, Inc.; *pg.* 1881, *pg.* 1439
O'Dowd, Rylee, Mgr-Mktg - Franklin Covey Co.; *pg.* 1642, *pg.* 1758
O'Fallon, Rick, Dir-Mktg - California Raisin Marketing Board; *pg.* 1017, *pg.* 93
O'Farrell, Paul, Sr VP & Gen Mgr-Steelhead Products Grp - Riverbed Technology, Inc.; *pg.* 1277, *pg.* 225
O'Flaherty, Sean, Sr Product Mgr - Klein Tools Inc.; *pg.* 1052, *pg.* 627
O'Furey, Mitchell, Asst Mgr-Mktg - The Clorox Company; *pg.* 327, *pg.* 169
O'Gara, Brian, Sr Dir-Special Events - Major League Baseball; *pg.* 560, *pg.* 1255
O'Gorman, Ian, Brand Mktg Mgr - Sprint Corporation; *pg.* 1874, *pg.* 719
O'Guin, Kathleen, Dir-PR - Molina Healthcare, Inc.; *pg.* 1569, *pg.* 123
O'Halloran, Megan, Specialist-Retail Mktg - Honeywell International Inc.; *pg.* 407, *pg.* 1088
O'Halloran, Michael, Mgr-Product Mktg - Samsung Electronics America, Inc.; *pg.* 669, *pg.* 1115
O'Halloran, Sean, Mgr-Product Mktg - The Toro Company; *pg.* 1065, *pg.* 918
O'Hanlon, Holly, Sr Mgr-Natl Media - Select Comfort Corporation; *pg.* 942, *pg.* 942
O'Hara, Adrienne, Dir-Consumer PR - Toys "R" Us, Inc.; *pg.* 968, *pg.* 1130
O'Hara, Danielle, Dir-Strategy & Plng, Mktg Integration & Customer Insights - American Express Company; *pg.* 712, *pg.* 1190
O'Hara, Gavin, Publr-Social Media-Global - Lenovo Group Ltd; *pg.* 427, *pg.* 1384
O'Hara, Kathleen, VP-Mktg - Direct Energy; *pg.* 1939, *pg.* 1704
O'Hara, Kristen, CMO-Global Media - Time Warner Inc.; *pg.* 312, *pg.* 1302
O'Hara, Molly, Assoc Mgr-Brand Mktg-Accessories - Under Armour, Inc.; *pg.* 49, *pg.* 759
O'Hare, Caroline Corrigan, Head-Content Mktg Strategy - Bloomberg L.P.; *pg.* 725, *pg.* 1204
O'Hare, Kim, VP-Product Mktg - Automatic Data Processing, Inc.; *pg.* 357, *pg.* 1117
O'Hare, Marissa, Sr Dir-Audience Dev - Wenner Media LLC; *pg.* 1701, *pg.* 1314
O'Haver, Lora, Mgr-Solutions Mktg - Cisco Systems, Inc.; *pg.* 372, *pg.* 240
O'Hea, Crystal, Corp Dir-Mktg & Consumer Activation-Media Enterprises Div - SeaWorld Orlando; *pg.* 582, *pg.* 455
O'Hea, Crystal, Corp Dir-Mktg & Consumer Activation-Media Enterprises Div - SeaWorld Parks & Entertainment LLC; *pg.* 582, *pg.* 456
O'Hearn, Kevin, Mgr-Sls-Gulf Coast Reg - Tanknology Inc; *pg.* 114, *pg.* 1666
O'Herron, Jennifer, Asst VP & Dir-North America Mktg Comm - AECOM Technology Corporation; *pg.* 65, *pg.* 125
O'Kane, Patricia, Mgr-Mktg - Honeywell International Inc.; *pg.* 407, *pg.* 1088
O'Keefe Hendricks, Lauren, VP-Sls - Conde Nast Publications, Inc.; *pg.* 1629, *pg.* 1217
O'Keefe, Brittany, Sr Digital Mktg Specialist - Yoplait USA, Inc.; *pg.* 910, *pg.* 947
O'Keefe, Jim, VP-Mdsg - DirectBuy, Inc.; *pg.* 1766, *pg.* 694
O'Keefe, Molly, Dir-Adv Ops - Tribune Media Company; *pg.* 1696, *pg.* 592
O'Kelly, Meghan, Sr Mgr-Corp Rels-Midwest Reg - The Allstate Corporation; *pg.* 1189, *pg.* 639
O'Leary, Dan, VP-Mktg-R&B Foods - Mizkan Americas, Inc.; *pg.* 877, *pg.* 634
O'Leary, Dennis, VP-Mktg Partnerships - San Diego Chargers Football Co.; *pg.* 580, *pg.* 208
O'Leary, Jim, Sr Mgr-Mobile Solutions Mktg - Cisco Systems, Inc.; *pg.* 372, *pg.* 240
O'Leary, Joe, Acct Exec-Comml Dev Sls - Comcast Cable Communications, Inc.; *pg.* 276, *pg.* 1560
O'Leary, Kasey, Sr Dir-Portfolio & Loyalty Mktg - Hilton Worldwide, Inc.; *pg.* 1094, *pg.* 1791
O'Leary, Kate, Head-Tech Mktg Solutions-Emerging & Mgr-Sls - LinkedIn Corporation; *pg.* 1262, *pg.* 160
O'Leary, Kevin, Sr Mgr-Mktg & Product Mgmt-DOCSIS CPE - Arris Group, Inc.; *pg.* 353, *pg.* 541
O'Leary, Patrick, VP-Emerging Markets Sls & Mktg - Elanco Animal Health; *pg.* 1475, *pg.* 681
O'Leary, William J., VP-Product Dev - Winnebago Industries, Inc.; *pg.* 1712, *pg.* 707
O'Loughlin, Dena, Dir-Mktg-Disney Princess & Frozen - JAKKS Pacific, Inc.; *pg.* 960, *pg.* 142
O'Mahony, Robert E., Mgr-Customer Experience Mktg - Hewlett-Packard Company; *pg.* 404, *pg.* 175
O'Malley, Chris, Mgr-Segment Mktg - Intel Corporation; *pg.* 645, *pg.* 266
O'Malley, Lynne, Supvr-Promos & Mdsg - Kia Motors America Inc.; *pg.* 181, *pg.* 112
O'Malley, Patrick, CMO, Chief Comml Officer & VP - Landstar System, Inc.; *pg.* 1914, *pg.* 434
O'Malley, Patrick, Sr VP-Product-Global - Saucony, Inc.; *pg.* 1818, *pg.* 828
O'Malley, Sean, VP-Advisory Mktg Svcs - FRANKLIN RESOURCES, INC.; *pg.* 760, *pg.* 254
O'Mary, Scott, Sr Specialist-Mktg - FedEx Corporation; *pg.* 1907, *pg.* 1642
O'Murchu, Liam, Sr Mgr-Dev - Symantec Corporation; *pg.* 478, *pg.* 161
O'Neal, Jim, Dir-Partner Mktg - FTD Group, Inc.; *pg.* 1795, *pg.* 608
O'Neal, Kim, Specialist-Channel Mktg - Honeywell International Inc.; *pg.* 407, *pg.* 1088
O'Neal, Lisa, Mgr-Field Mktg - Philips Electronics North America; *pg.* 662, *pg.* 782
O'Neal, Randy, Exec Dir-Mktg Ops - Cox Communications, Inc.; *pg.* 279, *pg.* 501
O'Neil, Brendan, Project Mgr-Creative Svcs - Coach, Inc.; *pg.* 3, *pg.* 1214
O'Neil, Danielle, VP-Mktg - Lindt & Sprungli (USA) Inc.; *pg.* 1857, *pg.* 1039
O'Neil, Eddie, Product Mgr-Platform - Facebook, Inc.; *pg.* 1245, *pg.* 143
O'Neil, Melissa, Product Mgr-HealthVault - Microsoft Corporation; *pg.* 435, *pg.* 1824
O'Neil, Michael, Sr Dir-Emerging Bus - Constant Contact, Inc.; *pg.* 379, *pg.* 850
O'Neil, Terry, Mgr-PR - Ralphs Grocery Company; *pg.* 1031, *pg.* 69
O'Neill, Chris, Dir-PR - Capital One Bank (USA), N.A.; *pg.* 730, *pg.* 1789
o'neill, chris, Dir-PR - Capital One Financial Corporation; *pg.* 730, *pg.* 1789
O'Neill, Cindy, Specialist-Mktg Comm - Armstrong World Industries, Inc.; *pg.* 914, *pg.* 1545
O'Neill, Dan, Dir-Vehicle Mktg - General Motors of Canada Ltd.; *pg.* 177, *pg.* 1931
O'Neill, Danielle, Specialist-Email Mktg - TripAdvisor, Inc.; *pg.* 1926, *pg.* 835
O'Neill, J. J., VP-Sls & Mktg-Retail - High Liner Foods Incorporated; *pg.* 862, *pg.* 1917
O'Neill, Jennifer, Sr Mgr-Corp Employee Comm - Intuit Inc.; *pg.* 769, *pg.* 158
O'Neill, Jessica T., Dir-Mktg - Georgia Southern University; *pg.* 602, *pg.* 541
O'Neill, Karen L., Dir-HPS Svcs Mktg - Honeywell International Inc.; *pg.* 407, *pg.* 1088
O'Neill, Kate, Dir-Product Mktg - Facebook, Inc.; *pg.* 1245, *pg.* 143
O'Neill, Katie, Dir-Mktg & Comm - Boingo Wireless, Inc.; *pg.* 625, *pg.* 127
O'Neill, Keely, Coord-Event-Mktg-Brooks Running Company - Brooks Sports Inc.; *pg.* 1805, *pg.* 1818
O'Neill, Marie, Sr VP-Mktg - Ameriprise Financial, Inc.; *pg.* 715, *pg.* 930
O'Neill, Megan, Mgr-Mktg - CB Richard Ellis, Inc.; *pg.* 1085, *pg.* 1210
O'Neill, Mike, Reg Mgr-Sls - Vapor Bus International; *pg.* 221, *pg.* 560
O'Neill, Patrick M, Mgr-Sls - Art's-Way Manufacturing Co., Inc.; *pg.* 701, *pg.* 701
O'Neill, Scott, VP-Sls-Acute Sls - The SSI Group, Inc.; *pg.* 473, *pg.* 7
O'Neill, Tricia, Reg VP-Specialty Products-North America - Zurich Holding Company of America, Inc.; *pg.* 1224, *pg.* 660
O'Neill, Wendy, Asst VP & Sr Mgr-PR - Astoria Financial Corporation; *pg.* 717, *pg.* 1172
O'Niones, Katie, Specialist-Mktg - Atlas Van Lines, Inc.; *pg.* 1900, *pg.* 678
O'Pray, Liz, Sr Mgr-Sports Sponsorships - American Express Company; *pg.* 712, *pg.* 1190
O'Reilly, Breda, Dir-Adv - The New Yorker Magazine, Inc.; *pg.* 1669, *pg.* 1271
O'Reilly, Chris, Sr Dir-Mktg - Broadcom Corporation; *pg.* 364, *pg.* 108
O'Reilly, Hannah, Product Mgr-Digital Mktg - Abbott Diabetes Care, Inc.; *pg.* 1483, *pg.* 38

First page reference indicates Business Class Edition
Second page reference indicates Geographic Edition

O'Reilly, Jeffrey, Sr Mgr-Digital Shopper Conversion - Pepsi Beverages Company; *pg.* 258, *pg.* 1342
O'Reilly, Larry, Exec VP-Sls-Worldwide - Imax Corporation; *pg.* 1417, *pg.* 1926
O'Reilly, Philip, VP-Sls & Advanced Architectures-Worldwide - Brocade Corporation; *pg.* 365, *pg.* 312
O'Reilly, Rob, Dir-Creative-Central Ontario - Xerox Canada Inc.; *pg.* 494, *pg.* 1930
O'Reilly, Shay, Sr Mgr-Bus Analytics - Adobe Systems Incorporated; *pg.* 342, *pg.* 235
O'Rourke, Kelly, Mgr-Mktg-Team Sports - ASICS America Corporation; *pg.* 1826, *pg.* 106
O'Rourke, Sarah, Sr Mgr-Product Mktg-Consumer & 3D Printing - Autodesk Inc.; *pg.* 356, *pg.* 257
O'Rourke, Toby, Sr VP-Mktg - Kampgrounds of America, Inc.; *pg.* 555, *pg.* 1008
O'Shaughnessy, Jim, Dir-Mktg & Bus Dev - ACCO Brands Corporation; *pg.* 340, *pg.* 626
O'Shaughnessy, Mike, Sr Mgr-Technical - Sigmund Cohn Corp.; *pg.* 1062, *pg.* 1183
O'Shea, Carmen, Sr VP-Mktg Engagement - SAP; *pg.* 465, *pg.* 78
O'Shea, Michael, Sr Mgr-Digital & Media Platforms - Best Buy Co., Inc.; *pg.* 1761, *pg.* 954
O'Shea, Nancy, Dir-PR - The Field Museum; *pg.* 548, *pg.* 573
O'Sullivan, David, Sr Dir-Design & Energy - The Great Atlantic & Pacific Tea Company, Inc.; *pg.* 1021, *pg.* 1086
O'Sullivan, Denis, Product Mgr-Global - Molex Incorporated; *pg.* 655, *pg.* 628
O'Sullivan, Diane, Dir-Mktg & Branding-Performance Films-Global - Eastman Chemical Company; *pg.* 1159, *pg.* 1636
O'Sullivan, Sharon, Exec VP-Adv Sls - Discovery Communications, Inc.; *pg.* 282, *pg.* 777
O'Toole, Tom, Dir-Creative - Marchon Eyewear, Inc.; *pg.* 1421, *pg.* 1180
O'Toole, Tom, Pres-MileagePlus & Sr VP-Mktg & Loyalty - United Airlines, Inc.; *pg.* 1927, *pg.* 593
O`Neill, Martin, Exec Dir-Global Media Grp - Time Warner Inc.; *pg.* 312, *pg.* 1302
Oakcrum, Brenda, Strategist-Media-Off-Air - Discovery Communications, Inc.; *pg.* 282, *pg.* 777
Oakes, Joy, Sr Dir-Mid-Atlantic Reg - National Parks Conservation Association; *pg.* 150, *pg.* 403
Oakes, Karin G., Specialist-Mktg Comm-America's Reg - Thermo Fisher Scientific Inc.; *pg.* 1431, *pg.* 854
Oakes, Melissa, VP-Sls - Hair Club for Men, Ltd., Inc.; *pg.* 511, *pg.* 411
Oakhill, Tim, Strategist-Mktg-Worldwide - International Business Machines Corporation; *pg.* 418, *pg.* 1138
Oakley, Adam, VP-High-End Mktg - Anheuser-Busch Companies, LLC; *pg.* 237, *pg.* 991
Oakley, David B., Sr Dir-Licensing - LexisNexis Group; *pg.* 1658, *pg.* 1446
Oakley, Glenn C., Exec VP-Media Tech, Production & Ops - Discovery Communications, Inc.; *pg.* 282, *pg.* 777
Oakley, Scott, Product Mgr-Global - Rockwell Automation, Inc.; *pg.* 668, *pg.* 1880
Oakley, Tracey, Coord-Field Mktg - Publix Super Markets, Inc.; *pg.* 1031, *pg.* 437
Oakman, Paula, Reg Rep-Mktg - Commerce Bancshares, Inc.; *pg.* 740, *pg.* 982
Oare, Amy, Mgr-Mktg Programs - Oklahoma City Thunder; *pg.* 571, *pg.* 1487
Oas, Jennifer, Dir-Mdsg- Private Label - THE FRESH MARKET, INC.; *pg.* 1020, *pg.* 1374
Oates, Doug, VP-Sls-Asia-Pacific - Equinix, Inc.; *pg.* 394, *pg.* 190
Oates, Elizabeth K., Sr Mgr-Consumer & Brand Insights - Kohl's Corporation; *pg.* 1775, *pg.* 1870
Oates, Matt, Dir-Brand Mktg - St. Jude Children's Research Hospital; *pg.* 1596, *pg.* 1646
Oates, Rebecca, Coord-Mktg Production & Promos - Shoe Carnival, Inc.; *pg.* 1819, *pg.* 679
Oathout, Doug, VP-Channel Partner, Alliances & OEM Mktg - Hewlett-Packard Company; *pg.* 404, *pg.* 175
Obara, Milissa, Dir-Product Mgmt - Fallon Community Health Plan; *pg.* 1530, *pg.* 862
Obembe, Sarah, Brand Mgr-3rd Party Brands - William Grant & Sons, Inc.; *pg.* 1972, *pg.* 1057
Obendorf, Chuck, Dir-Product Mktg - MTD Products, Inc.; *pg.* 1057, *pg.* 1478
Obeng, Elliot, Designer-Product - Adobe Systems Incorporated; *pg.* 342, *pg.* 235
Obeng, Pashington, Sr Mgr-Brand Comm & Digital Mktg-Soccer - adidas America Inc.; *pg.* 1803, *pg.* 1500
Obenshain, Elaine, Mgr-Retail Mktg - Williamson-Dickie Manufacturing Company; *pg.* 50, *pg.* 1696
Oberman, Michele, Specialist-Mktg Comm - Newport Corporation; *pg.* 1424, *pg.* 114
Obermeier, Ron, Mgr-Retail Adv - The Evansville Courier & Press; *pg.* 1639, *pg.* 678
Obermoller, Bethany, Program Mgr-Mktg - Wells Fargo & Company; *pg.* 819, *pg.* 232
Oberoi, Arun, Exec VP-Sls & Svcs-Global - Red Hat, Inc.; *pg.* 460, *pg.* 1388
Oberoi, Pallavi, Sr Product Mgr - Wal-Mart.com; *pg.* 1287, *pg.* 50
Oberrender, Maggie, Asst Mgr-Mktg - Penguin Random House; *pg.* 1675, *pg.* 1276
Oblak, Chad, Product Mgr - Pulse Electronics Corporation; *pg.* 666, *pg.* 206
Oblak, Steve, Sr VP-Mdsg & Gen Mgr - Wayfair LLC; *pg.* 1288, *pg.* 801
Oblin, Steve, Sr Mgr-Mktg - Fujitsu Consulting; *pg.* 398, *pg.* 1955
Obourn-Guarente, Modesty, Category Specialist-Mktg-Residential Flooring - Armstrong World Industries, Inc.; *pg.* 914, *pg.* 1545
Obradovic-Sarkic, Katarina, Sr Product Mgr-Data Visualization Components - Oracle Corporation; *pg.* 450, *pg.* 191
Obray, Chris, Mgr-Channel Mktg Programs - Medtronic, Inc.; *pg.* 1564, *pg.* 939
Obsitnikv, Paul, VP-Svc Provider Mktg - Juniper Networks, Inc.; *pg.* 1260, *pg.* 286
Obuszewski, Mark, Mgr-Mktg Ops-Global - AVX Corporation; *pg.* 623, *pg.* 1616
Ocampo, Joaquin, Product Mgr - Bosch Rexroth Corporation; *pg.* 1319, *pg.* 1516
Ocean, Jennifer, Dir-Mktg-Global - Godiva Chocolatier, Inc.; *pg.* 1854, *pg.* 1235
Ochiltree, Andy, Sr Mgr-Global Brand Mktg-Action Figures & Outdoor - Mattel Games/Puzzles; *pg.* 962, *pg.* 80
Ochiltree, Andy, Brand Mgr-BOOMco-Global - MATTEL, INC.; *pg.* 962, *pg.* 81
Ochoa, Diana, Mgr-Mktg-Hispanic Consumer Strategy - Univision Communications Inc.; *pg.* 683, *pg.* 1307
Ochoa, Joe, VP-Strategic Mktg, Roofing & Asphalt - Owens Corning; *pg.* 102, *pg.* 1476
Ochoa, Jonathan K., Analyst-Mktg - Tropicana Products, Inc.; *pg.* 902, *pg.* 592
Ochoa, Margaret, Sr Dir-Online Mktg - Match.Com, LLC; *pg.* 1265, *pg.* 1683
Ochoa, Mauricio, Sr Mgr-Category Insights - Georgia-Pacific LLC; *pg.* 1458, *pg.* 507
Ochrym, Robert G., VP-Bus Dev, Strategic Sls & Mktg - AXT, Inc.; *pg.* 1400, *pg.* 90
Ochs, Stephen, Sr VP-Mktg - National CineMedia, Inc.; *pg.* 567, *pg.* 314
Ockenfels, Ralph, VP-Mktg - Tennessee Football, Inc.; *pg.* 587, *pg.* 1654
Ockerman, Leslie, Coord-Mktg - Kellogg Company; *pg.* 831, *pg.* 870
Ocon, Nina, Coord-Social Media - Telemundo Network Inc.; *pg.* 311, *pg.* 430
OConnell, Jennifer, Mgr-ECommerce Mktg - The Timberland Company; *pg.* 1821, *pg.* 1039
Oddo, David J., Interim Co-CFO & Sr VP-Fin - National CineMedia, Inc.; *pg.* 567, *pg.* 314
Oddo, Jim, VP-Mktg - Sealed Air Corporation; *pg.* 1468, *pg.* 1058
Odeh, Omar, Mgr-Ford Focus, Focus ST & Focus RS Product Mktg - Ford Motor Company; *pg.* 172, *pg.* 876
Odell, Stephen T., Exec VP-Mktg, Sls & Svc-Global - Ford Motor Company; *pg.* 172, *pg.* 876
Oden, Aaron J., Engr-Technical Mktg - Cisco Systems, Inc.; *pg.* 372, *pg.* 240
Odenbach, Jessica, Mgr-Social Media-Quaker - PepsiCo, Inc.; *pg.* 259, *pg.* 1327
Odenthal, Shelley, Mgr-Digital Mktg Strategy-US Skincare - Johnson & Johnson; *pg.* 1549, *pg.* 1091
Odenwald, Thomas, Sr VP & Sr Strategist-Products & Innovation Board Area - SAP America, Inc.; *pg.* 466, *pg.* 1557
Odiamar, Sasha, Specialist-Integrated Mktg - Live Nation Worldwide - Times Square Office; *pg.* 558, *pg.* 1252
Odom, Justin, Mgr-Digital Mktg Activation - Crayola LLC; *pg.* 951, *pg.* 1528
Odom, Tina, Head-Shopper Mktg Team - Unilever United States, Inc.; *pg.* 904, *pg.* 1061
Odore, Joseph, Product Mgr - Panasonic Corporation of North America; *pg.* 661, *pg.* 1120
Oefinger, Haley, Specialist-Social Media Comm - Esurance, Inc.; *pg.* 1243, *pg.* 217
Oehler, David, Mgr-Mktg-Nature Valley, Wheaties & Fiber One Cereals - General Mills, Inc.; *pg.* 828, *pg.* 933
Oei, Natalie, Assoc Mgr-Mobile Mktg - Coach, Inc.; *pg.* 3, *pg.* 1214
Oei, Sabrina, Sr Dir-Corp Comm - NIKE, Inc.; *pg.* 1812, *pg.* 1492
Oelschlaeger, Tom, Dir-Mktg & Comm - Avnet, Inc.; *pg.* 622, *pg.* 15
Oesch, Jenna, Head-Mktg-North America-Monsanto Vegetable Seeds - Monsanto; *pg.* 1798, *pg.* 1399
Oesch, Jenna, Head-Mktg-Monsanto Vegetable Seeds-North America - Monsanto Company; *pg.* 1173, *pg.* 999
Oesterle, Karl, Dir-Adv - Tops Markets, LLC; *pg.* 1036, *pg.* 1355
Oetjens, Paul, Sr Dir-Customer Mktg-ECommerce & Life Cycle Mktg - Carbonite, Inc.; *pg.* 368, *pg.* 792
Offenberg, Jennette, Product Mgr & Brand Mgr - Church & Dwight Co., Inc.; *pg.* 1153, *pg.* 1063
Offerdahl, Stephanie, Sr Mgr-Trade Show & Mktg - Airbus North America Holdings, Inc.; *pg.* 1897, *pg.* 1784
Offerjost, Jessica, Coord-Consumer PR - Toys "R" Us, Inc.; *pg.* 968, *pg.* 1130
Offermann, Stephan, Dir-PR - Adobe Systems Incorporated; *pg.* 342, *pg.* 235
Offord, Julie, Dir-Mktg Ops, Eastern Mountain Sports & Bob's Stores - Bob's Stores Corp.; *pg.* 38, *pg.* 354
Offutt, Denise, Sr Mgr-Market Res - Epson America Inc.; *pg.* 394, *pg.* 122
Offutt, Tim, Sr Analyst-Social Media - eHarmony.com, Inc.; *pg.* 1242, *pg.* 180
Ofner, Sara, Brand Mgr - The Coca-Cola Company; *pg.* 240, *pg.* 493
Ofodile, Emeka, Sr Dir-Consumer Mktg - ESPN, Inc.; *pg.* 285, *pg.* 340
Ofstein, Anna, Acct Exec-Mktg Solutions - LinkedIn Corporation; *pg.* 1262, *pg.* 160
Ogbogu, Vicky, Dir-Mktg-Intl - Choice Hotels International, Inc.; *pg.* 1086, *pg.* 775
Ogburn, Chris, VP-Worldwide Channel Mktg - Hewlett-Packard Company; *pg.* 404, *pg.* 175
Ogburn, Lynn, Mgr-New Product Mktg - 3M; *pg.* 339, *pg.* 179
Ogburn, Lynn, Mgr-New Product Mktg - 3M Company; *pg.* 1142, *pg.* 956
Ogden, Eddie, Mgr-PR - The Goodyear Tire & Rubber Company; *pg.* 1883, *pg.* 1401
Ogden, Ryan, Specialist-Consumer & Mktg Res - Associated Food Stores, Inc.; *pg.* 1014, *pg.* 1756
Oggerino, Chris, Sr Mgr-Svcs Mktg - Cisco Systems, Inc.; *pg.* 372, *pg.* 240
Ogle, Bryan, Sr Dir-Sports Mktg & Digital Strategy - K-Swiss; *pg.* 1837, *pg.* 306
Ogle, Michelle, Assoc Dir-North America Digital Mktg - Starwood Hotels & Resorts Worldwide, Inc.; *pg.* 1114, *pg.* 378
Oglesby, Leslie, Exec Dir-Mktg-Global - The Estee Lauder Companies Inc.; *pg.* 508, *pg.* 1229
Ogof, Alex, VP-Mdsg & Div Mgr-Mdsg-Home - Gilt Groupe Inc.; *pg.* 24, *pg.* 1234
Ogorek, Keith, Sr VP-Mktg - Author Solutions, Inc.; *pg.* 1618, *pg.* 674
Ogorek, Keith, Sr VP-Mktg - iUniverse, Inc.; *pg.* 1259, *pg.* 674
OGrady, Paul, Sr Dir-Afinitor-Scientific Comm - Novartis Pharmaceuticals Corp.; *pg.* 1575, *pg.* 1054
Oguche, Susan, Sr Mgr-Pub Affairs-Abbott Nutrition-Pediatrics - Abbott Laboratories; *pg.* 1484, *pg.* 551
Ogundiyun, Babatunde, Principal & Designer-Multimedia Web - Capital One Financial Corporation; *pg.* 730, *pg.* 1789
Ogunneye, Joy Doyin, Sr Mgr-Global Mktg-Beyonce Fragrances - Coty, Inc.; *pg.* 506, *pg.* 1219
Oh, Julii, Dir-Mktg - Philharmonic Symphony Society of New York Inc.; *pg.* 575, *pg.* 1282
Oh, Mike, VP-Creative Adv - Paramount Pictures Corporation; *pg.* 304, *pg.* 138
Ohana, Issachar, Exec VP-Sls-Worldwide - CEVA, Inc.; *pg.* 628, *pg.* 153
Ohaus, Kristin, Sr Assoc Brand Mgr - Mars Petcare; *pg.* 1478, *pg.* 1633
Ohearn, Claudine, Dir-Digital Product Mgmt - Citigroup Inc.; *pg.* 735, *pg.* 1212
Ohlen, Mark Von, Brand Mgr-Entertainment - The Topps Company, Inc.; *pg.* 588, *pg.* 1302
Ohlrich, Dale, Mgr-Specialty Products-IBC & Dry Handling Div

- Snyder Industries, Inc.; pg. 1377, pg. 1012
Ohnemus, Kevin, Specialist-Sls-Hyundai Motor Mfg Alabama - Hyundai Motor America; pg. 179, pg. 89
Ohno, Rob, Sr VP-Corp Mktg - PGA Tour, Inc.; pg. 574, pg. 460
Ohrnberger, Joan A., Dir-Adv Production - The New York Times Company; pg. 1668, pg. 1270
Ohta, Derek, Sr Mgr-Corp Partnerships - Anaheim Ducks Hockey Club, LLC; pg. 528, pg. 42
Oja, Rachel, Assoc Mgr-PR & Consumer Engagement - Newell Rubbermaid Inc.; pg. 1128, pg. 515
Ojagh, Sasha, Mgr-Mktg - Which Wich, Inc.; pg. 1756, pg. 1690
Ojakovo, Rukky, Brand Mgr-COSTCO Customer Team - The Procter & Gamble Company; pg. 1129, pg. 1418
Ojanen, Matti, Sr Dir-Lat Am Comm - Pfizer Inc.; pg. 1581, pg. 1278
Ojeda-Orranti, Armando, Mgr-Field Mktg - Heineken USA Inc.; pg. 252, pg. 1352
Ojerholm, Barbara, Mgr-Product Mktg - Juniper Networks, Inc.; pg. 1260, pg. 286
Ojiri, Danny, VP-Sls & Mktg - Outrigger Enterprises, Inc.; pg. 1107, pg. 544
Ojo, Tina I., Mgr-Mktg - Clean Harbors, Inc.; pg. 376, pg. 839
Oka, Masashi, Exec Chm, Pres-Acting & CEO - Union Bank, N.A.; pg. 813, pg. 230
Oka, Masashi, Exec Chm, Pres-Acting & CEO - UnionBanCal Corporation; pg. 813, pg. 230
Okamoto, Satoshi, Mgr-Product Mktg - Akamai Technologies, Inc.; pg. 1226, pg. 807
Okayama, Lauren, Mgr-Mktg - AT&T; pg. 1865, pg. 258
Okenquist, David, Sr Brand Mgr-Global Mktg & Centrum Core - Pfizer Inc.; pg. 1581, pg. 1278
Okkinga, Klaas, Dir-Strategic Mktg-Cattle Biologicals & Infectious Diseases - Pfizer Inc.; pg. 1581, pg. 1278
Okland, Julie, Sr Mgr-Mktg & Promos - Minnesota Twins, LLC; pg. 563, pg. 940
Okonkwo, Aneto, Product Mgr - Google Inc.; pg. 1249, pg. 153
Okoth, Didacus, Brand Mgr - The Monitor; pg. 1665, pg. 1726
Oksenkrug, Margarita, Mgr-Media Rels - Lenox Hill Hospital; pg. 1555, pg. 1251
Okui, Glen, Sr Specialist-Mktg - FedEx Corporation; pg. 1907, pg. 1642
Okumura, Kenji, Sr Dir-Digital Strategy - UnitedHealth Group Incorporated; pg. 1221, pg. 950
Olach, Trisha, Mgr-Sls-Natl Accounts - Boyne USA Resorts Inc.; pg. 1082, pg. 874
Olack, Jordan, Sr VP & Head-Product Mgmt Team - KeyCorp; pg. 774, pg. 1432
Olah, Teresa, Dir-Mktg - Sensient Flavors Inc.; pg. 895, pg. 690
Olazaba, E. Zeke, Dir-Bus Dev Global-Sls & Mktg Latin America - OCZ Storage Solutions; pg. 448, pg. 248
Olbrycht, Andy, Dir-Sls & Mktg - Cambridge Brass; pg. 73, pg. 1919
Olcott, Deanna, Mgr-Global Mktg Content Strategies - ALERE INC.; pg. 1488, pg. 849
Olden, Matthew, Product Mgr-Multi-Media Solutions - Bally Technologies, Inc.; pg. 531, pg. 1022
Oldenburg, Mark, Mgr-Natl Fleet Mktg, Mobility & Strategic Plng - Toyota Motor Sales, U.S.A., Inc.; pg. 193, pg. 296
Older, Dale, Dir-Mobile Products - AOL Inc.; pg. 1229, pg. 1195
Oldham, Kate, Sr VP & Gen Mgr-Mdse - Saks Incorporated; pg. 1783, pg. 1288
Oldham, Lisa, Mgr-Digital Mktg-North America - The Procter & Gamble Company; pg. 1129, pg. 1418
Oldham, Michael ann, Mgr-Mktg Comm - Fresh & Easy Neighborhood Market Inc; pg. 1020, pg. 80
Oldrin, Eric, Strategist-Creative - Facebook, Inc.; pg. 1245, pg. 143
Oldroyd, Daniel, Portfolio Dir-Global Support & Deployment Product Grp - Dell Inc.; pg. 383, pg. 1737
Olecki, Katie, Dir-Mktg-Men's & Kid's Div - J.C. Penney Company, Inc.; pg. 1774, pg. 1732
Olejarz, David, Mgr-Media Rels - Henry Ford Health System; pg. 1541, pg. 883
Olejniczak, Rob, Head-Mktg-Comml Learning & Dev - MillerCoors LLC; pg. 255, pg. 582
Oleksik, Darlene, Mgr-Branding & Comm-Automotive Products - Eaton Corporation; pg. 1331, pg. 1429
Oles, Jessica, Coord-Mktg - A Book Company, LLC; pg. 1225, pg. 729
Oleskiewicz, Julie, Sr Mgr-Loyalty Mktg - The Leading Hotels of the World, Ltd.; pg. 1100, pg. 1250
Oleson, Brett, Sr Mgr-Sls Training - Whirlpool Corporation; pg. 62, pg. 872
Oleson, Christian, Dir-Creative Svcs & Global Brand Mgmt - Patterson Companies, Inc.; pg. 1580, pg. 962
Oleson, Tim, Media Planner & Media Buyer-Programmatic - The Star Tribune Company; pg. 1689, pg. 942
Olguin, Andrea, Dir-Shopper Mktg & Plng - Safeway Inc.; pg. 1032, pg. 184
Oliande, Sylvia, Mgr-Media Rels - Kissimmee-St. Cloud Convention & Visitors Bureau; pg. 997, pg. 436
Olinger, Chris, Dir-Sports Sls - Young Electric Sign Company; pg. 1308, pg. 1762
Olinger, Lori, Mgr-Western Reg Strategic Sls & Healthcare - Kelly Services, Inc.; pg. 424, pg. 911
Oliphant, Rence, VP-Sls & Mktg-Global - Hendrickson International; pg. 207, pg. 672
Oliva, Jim, Dir-Sls - Real Goods Solar, Inc.; pg. 1075, pg. 334
Oliva, Melanie, Dir-Integrated Mktg - Time Inc.; pg. 1693, pg. 1300
Oliva, Monica, Brand Mgr-Sweet'N Low - Cumberland Packing Corp.; pg. 851, pg. 1146
Olivares, Karen, Dir-Brand Mktg-Marriott Hotels & Resorts - Marriott International, Inc.; pg. 1102, pg. 764
Olive, Mark, Sr Reg Dir-Mktg - Papa John's International, Inc.; pg. 1743, pg. 737
Olive, Mark, VP-Mktg - Sun Tan City, LLC; pg. 523, pg. 738
Oliveira, Kelly, Sr Mgr-Digital Mktg - Staples, Inc.; pg. 474, pg. 821
Oliveira, Paulo, Mgr-Mktg-Global - Caterpillar, Inc.; pg. 1321, pg. 650
Oliver, Eric, Dir-Digital Mktg - The North Face, Inc.; pg. 1840, pg. 252
Oliver, Geoff, Brand Mgr - Spin Master Ltd.; pg. 967, pg. 1943
Oliver, Heather L., Program Mgr-PSS Mktg - Hewlett-Packard Company; pg. 404, pg. 175
Oliver, John, Mgr-Mktg - Six Flags Entertainment Corporation; pg. 583, pg. 1698
Oliver, Kevin, Strategist-Mktg & Solutions - Dell Inc.; pg. 383, pg. 1737
Oliver, Lauren, Brand Mgr-Shopper Mktg - The Clorox Company; pg. 327, pg. 169
Oliver, Melanie, Mgr-Charleston Local Sls - WSAZ-TV; pg. 323, pg. 1850
Oliver, Nikki, Mgr-Corp Comm & Global Social Newsroom Community - The Procter & Gamble Company; pg. 1129, pg. 1418
Oliver, Ramona, Sr Dir-Center for Comm - National Education Association; pg. 148, pg. 401
Oliver, Tracy A., Dir-Media-Ohio - Dominion Resources, Inc.; pg. 1939, pg. 1802
Oliveri, Jarrett, Head-Mktg Team - Whole Foods Market, Inc.; pg. 1038, pg. 1667
Oliveri, Liz, Head-Mktg for Prime Fin-Global & Dir - Citigroup Inc.; pg. 735, pg. 1212
Oliveri, Tom, VP-Mktg-Android, Chrome & Enterprise - Google Inc.; pg. 1249, pg. 153
Olivia, Marianne, Brand Mgr - Dentsply International Inc.; pg. 1522, pg. 1596
Olivier, Joe, Dir-Comm Delivery Gateway-Sls Strategy & Effectiveness - Royal Bank of Canada; pg. 800, pg. 1942
Olivieri, Mark, Sr Mgr-Mktg-Innovation - PepsiCo, Inc.; pg. 259, pg. 1327
Olivieri, Ryan, Sr Coord-Search Engine Mktg - Zappos.com, Inc.; pg. 1291, pg. 1030
Olivieri, Sally E., Partner-Global Bus-Sls Enablement-Channel Sls - Hewlett-Packard Company; pg. 404, pg. 175
Ollison, Fitz, Sr Dir-Football Comm - New Orleans Saints L.P.; pg. 569, pg. 745
Ollivier, Caroline, Dir-Mktg - Knoll, Inc.; pg. 425, pg. 1527
Olm, Myra T., Dir-Brand Protection Res & Product Dev - Eastman Kodak Company; pg. 1408, pg. 1333
Olmstead, George, Sr Dir & Principal-Healthcare Practice Grp - Cushman & Wakefield, Inc.; pg. 1088, pg. 1220
Olmstead, Kelly, Dir-Brand Mktg-Sport Style Div - adidas America Inc.; pg. 1803, pg. 1500
Olmsted, Christina, Dir-Mktg & Corp Comm-Global - Cisco Systems, Inc.; pg. 372, pg. 240
Olney, Brian, Dir-Brand Mktg - All Market, Inc.; pg. 237, pg. 1189
Olree, Julia, Mgr-Mktg Insights & Strategy - Audi of America, Inc.; pg. 164, pg. 1784
Olsen, Greg, Sr Mgr-Digital Product-Commerce Checkout - Best Buy Co., Inc.; pg. 1761, pg. 954
Olsen, James, Dir-Mktg Comm - Edward D. Jones & Co., LP; pg. 746, pg. 995
Olsen, John, VP-Sls - Ungerer & Company; pg. 524, pg. 1079
Olsen, Karl, VP & Mgr-Divisional Mdse - Tractor Supply Company; pg. 708, pg. 1627
Olsen, Kate, Strategist-Social Mktg - The Pampered Chef; pg. 1129, pg. 552
Olsen, Lindsey, Specialist-Social Media - The Scotts Miracle-Gro Company; pg. 1799, pg. 1459
Olsen, Martin T., Exec VP-Sls & Mktg - TSS, Inc.; pg. 117, pg. 768
Olsen, Michael, Sr Dir-Leasing-Anchor Store Leasing - DDR Corp.; pg. 1089, pg. 1405
Olsen, Nancy, Dir-Mass Mktg - Cablevision Systems Corporation; pg. 272, pg. 1141
Olsen, Steve, Sr VP & Gen Mgr-Mdse - Total Wine & More; pg. 1971, pg. 775
Olshan, Bruce, Sr Dir-Global Supply Chain - Avery Dennison Corporation; pg. 1452, pg. 95
Olshove-Newman, Kelly, Dir-Mktg - Honours Golf Company, LLC; pg. 1090, pg. 3
Olslund, Rune, Sr Dir-Mktg, Demand Generation, Inbound, Digital & Revenue Mgmt - Cisco Systems, Inc.; pg. 372, pg. 240
Olson Benedict, Amy, VP-Mktg & Customer Experience - Maids International Inc.; pg. 1395, pg. 1016
Olson Rokhsar, Julia, Dir-Mktg & Res-Harper's Bazaar - The Hearst Corporation; pg. 1649, pg. 1239
Olson, Andee, Mgr-Production-Vogue - Conde Nast Publications, Inc.; pg. 1629, pg. 1217
Olson, Andee, Mgr-Production - Vogue Magazine; pg. 1700, pg. 1311
Olson, Angie, Mgr-Mktg-Global - 3M Company; pg. 1142, pg. 956
Olson, Carrie, Sr Specialist-Mktg & Ops - Deluxe Corporation; pg. 1634, pg. 964
Olson, Christine, VP-Natl Ad Sls-Lifetime - A&E Television Networks, LLC; pg. 267, pg. 1185
Olson, Craig, Mgr-Sls Admin - Putzmeister America; pg. 1371, pg. 1896
Olson, Danielle, Sr Mgr-Mktg - Insight Enterprises, Inc.; pg. 415, pg. 26
Olson, Danielle, Assoc Mgr-Adv - Regis Corporation; pg. 521, pg. 941
Olson, Debra, Sr Mgr-Recipe Dev - Golden Corral Corporation; pg. 1730, pg. 1387
Olson, Ellen, Sr Dir-Art-Adv-Polo Ralph Lauren - Ralph Lauren Corporation; pg. 46, pg. 1284
Olson, Eric, Product Mgr - ABB Inc. - Automation Technologies Instrumentation Products; pg. 1398, pg. 1590
Olson, Gary, Sr VP-Mktg - Breeze-Eastern Corporation; pg. 1319, pg. 1132
Olson, Gary, Sr VP-Worldwide Sls & Ops - Edgewave Inc; pg. 390, pg. 202
Olson, Greg, VP-Sls - Toho Tenax America, Inc.; pg. 1184, pg. 1655
Olson, Greg, Product Mgr-Health & Safety - TSI Incorporated; pg. 1432, pg. 965
Olson, Jane, Sr VP-Mktg & Brand Strategy - Oxygen Media LLC; pg. 303, pg. 1275
Olson, Jason, Dir-Mktg - Rust-Oleum Corporation; pg. 1447, pg. 664
Olson, Jeff, Sr Dir-Comm-US - McDonald's Corporation; pg. 1737, pg. 645
Olson, Jessica, Project Mgr & Media Planner-Multi - The Atlanta Journal-Constitution; pg. 1618, pg. 490
Olson, Jim, Sr VP-Sls & Mktg - Jazz Basketball Investors, Inc.; pg. 554, pg. 1759
Olson, Jimmy, Assoc Dir-Creative - Apple Inc.; pg. 350, pg. 73
Olson, Kenton, Dir-Digital Media & Emerging Media - Seattle Seahawks; pg. 582, pg. 1830
Olson, Knut, Sr VP-Mission Advancement - Thrivent Financial for Lutherans; pg. 1219, pg. 944
Olson, Kristen, Brand Mktg Mgr - Great Wolf Resorts, Inc.; pg. 1093, pg. 1866
Olson, Lance, Supvr-Mktg-Infection Prevention Div - 3M Company; pg. 1142, pg. 956
Olson, Lauren, Dir-Product Mgmt-App Experiences - NBC Universal, Inc.; pg. 300, pg. 1266
Olson, Michael, Head-Music Industry Strategy & Sr Dir - Pandora Media Inc.; pg. 1273, pg. 172
Olson, Pauline, Sr Mgr-Pur - Brinker International, Inc.; pg. 1718, pg. 1676
Olson, Rachel, Mgr-Retail Mktg - LG Electronics U.S.A., Inc.; pg. 651, pg. 1060

Olson, Randy, VP-Mktg - Miller Industries, Inc.; pg. 185, pg. 1655
Olson, Rebecca, Dir-Tri-Channel Mktg - Eddie Bauer, Inc.; pg. 40, pg. 1814
Olson, Sally, Corp Mgr-Mktg - Fastenal Company; pg. 396, pg. 966
Olson, Stephanie, Sr Mgr-Mktg - Teachers Insurance & Annuity Association - College Retirement Equities Fund; pg. 1219, pg. 1297
Olson, Tay, Project Mgr-Creative Svcs - Seventh Generation, Inc.; pg. 335, pg. 1765
Olson, Tim, VP-Digital Media & Education - KQED Inc.; pg. 294, pg. 220
Olson, Uyen P., Dir-Product Mktg - Jack in the Box Inc.; pg. 1732, pg. 204
Olson-Stevens, Karmen, Brand Mgr-Redhook - Craft Brewers Alliance, Inc; pg. 247, pg. 1502
Olsson, Kaitlyn, Asst Mgr-Mktg - Teleflora LLC; pg. 1801, pg. 140
Olszewska, Magdalena, Mgr-Mktg, Brand Innovation & Global Mktg - Colgate-Palmolive Company; pg. 504, pg. 1215
Olszewski, Andrzej, Sr Mgr-Verbal Branding - Autodesk Inc.; pg. 356, pg. 257
Olt, Betty, Dir-PR & Special Projects - North Shore-LIJ Health System; pg. 1573, pg. 1162
Oltman, Zanny, VP-Mktg & Mktg Partnerships - Destination Maternity Corporation; pg. 23, pg. 1563
Oluwole, Morin, VP-Global Mktg Solutions - Facebook, Inc.; pg. 1245, pg. 143
Olvera, Adrian Xavier, Sr Mgr-Global Innovation - Dell Inc.; pg. 383, pg. 1737
Olvera, Claudia, Mgr-Mktg Comm - VeriFone Systems, Inc.; pg. 487, pg. 251
Olvera, Eduardo, Head-Global Emerging Tech-UI Design & Sr Mgr - Nuance Communications, Inc.; pg. 447, pg. 806
Olwig, Barbara J., Dir-Creative - Express Scripts, Inc.; pg. 1530, pg. 997
Olwig, Joe, Reg Dir-Enterprise Sls - World Wide Technology Holding Co., Inc.; pg. 493, pg. 988
Olwine, Betsy, Dir-Sls & Mktg - The Ritz-Carlton Hotel Company LLC; pg. 1110, pg. 766
Oman, Dave, Reg Mgr-Sls - Hi-Vac Corporation; pg. 56, pg. 1458
OMara, Tim, VP-Sls - Gibraltar Industries, Inc.; pg. 1340, pg. 1148
Ommen, Chuck, Dir-Mktg & Comm - Universal Hospital Services, Inc.; pg. 1604, pg. 945
Ommen, Tony, Sr Dir-Team Svcs - Chicago Blackhawk Hockey Team, Inc.; pg. 538, pg. 569
Omori, Sue, Exec Dir-Reg Mktg - Cleveland Clinic; pg. 1516, pg. 1429
Onagoruwa, Ebun, Product Mgr - Microsoft Corporation; pg. 435, pg. 1824
Ondrejko, Matt, VP-Mktg-Global - Valmont Industries, Inc.; pg. 1387, pg. 1019
Oneill, Bill, Dir-Bus Dev & Sls - Buehler, Ltd.; pg. 1403, pg. 622
Oneto Gamiotea, Angela, Specialist-Mktg - Chiquita Brands International, Inc.; pg. 847, pg. 1365
Ong, Adeline, Sr Dir-Corp & Brand Comm - Viacom Inc.; pg. 316, pg. 1310
Ong, Edward, Mgr-Product Mktg - Power Integrations, Inc.; pg. 1369, pg. 249
Ong, Ee-Ping, Head-China Country & Sr Dir - American Securities LLC; pg. 714, pg. 1193
Ong, Vincent, Sr Dir-Brand Mgmt - Starwood Hotels & Resorts Worldwide, Inc.; pg. 1114, pg. 378
Onigbanjo, Adebayo, Dir-Mktg - Zebra Technologies Corporation; pg. 690, pg. 628
Onken, Brad, VP-Strategic Mktg & Bus Dev - Zaner-Bloser, Inc.; pg. 970, pg. 1445
Onkey, Emily, Sr Mgr-Brand Mktg - Bonobos; pg. 39, pg. 1205
Ono, Mike, Mgr-Creative Svcs - Oakland Athletics Limited Partnership; pg. 571, pg. 172
Onofre, Gabriela, Dir-Mktg & Comm - The Procter & Gamble Company; pg. 1129, pg. 1418
Onorato, David, VP-Convenience Sls - The Hershey Co.; pg. 1855, pg. 1538
Ontanon, Lauren, Specialist-Adv & New Media - Paramount Pictures Corporation; pg. 304, pg. 138
Ooka, Akemi, Sr Dir-Formulation - Method Products Inc.; pg. 332, pg. 223
Oosterveld, Leanne M., Sr Mgr-Mktg-Co-Brand Banking - Royal Bank of Canada; pg. 800, pg. 1942
Oosthuizen, Andre, Dir-Mktg - Porsche Cars North America, Inc.; pg. 189, pg. 518
Opallo, Dan, Mgr-Mktg & Social Media - Cablevision Systems Corporation; pg. 272, pg. 1141
Opdenaker, Mike, Dir-Sls - Bimbo Bakeries USA; pg. 840, pg. 151
Opel, Eric, Dir-E2E Exp & Sr Mgr-Mktg Comm - Microsoft Corporation; pg. 435, pg. 1824
Opie, Lindsay, Sr Specialist-Industry Mktg - BDO Seidman, LLP; pg. 724, pg. 1202
Opiola, Denise, Mgr-Integrated Mktg - ConAgra Foods, Inc.; pg. 826, pg. 1014
Oplustil, Kaz, VP-Sls, East & Central - CBS Corporation; pg. 273, pg. 1210
Opong, Natasha, Sr Mgr-Mktg Partnerships-Global - National Basketball Association; pg. 566, pg. 1264
Oppenheim, Lee, VP-Franchise Sls - Precision Auto Care, Inc.; pg. 215, pg. 1787
Oppenheimer, Howard, Dir-Mktg & Strategic Svcs - Blue Cross & Blue Shield Association; pg. 1195, pg. 566
Oppenheimer, Wendy, Dir-Solutions Mktg - SAS Institute Inc.; pg. 466, pg. 1361
Oprendek, Trey, Sr Mgr-Bus Mktg - PMC-Sierra, Inc.; pg. 664, pg. 287
Oputa, Elizabeth, Assoc Product Mgr - Pfizer Inc.; pg. 1581, pg. 1278
Oravez, Kate, VP-PR-West Div - Comcast Corporation; pg. 276, pg. 1560
Orazi, Philip, III, Sr Dir-Trng & Dev - Chick-fil-A, Inc.; pg. 1721, pg. 492
Orchard, Dallas, Sr VP-Global Premium Products - International Game Technology; pg. 957, pg. 1024
Orcutt, Jodi, Acct Mgr-Svcs Sls - Avaya Inc.; pg. 621, pg. 264
Orcutt, Mark J., Exec VP-Building Products - Axiall Corporation; pg. 69, pg. 491
Orcutt, Nikki, Deputy Dir-Mktg - West Virginia Lottery; pg. 1011, pg. 1849
Ordal, Peter, Sr Dir-Partnership Mktg - The Hertz Corporation; pg. 1911, pg. 450
Ordaz, Lorena, Mgr-Consumer Mktg Rels - Ace Hardware Corporation; pg. 1040, pg. 644
Ordlock, Cherise, Sr Dir-ECommerce Plng & Analysis - Walgreen Co.; pg. 1608, pg. 605
Ordman, Marty, VP-Mktg & Comm - DOLE FOOD COMPANY, INC.; pg. 853, pg. 306
Ordonez, Bernardo, Reg Mgr-Sls - ITW Magnaflux; pg. 1418, pg. 615
Ordway, Greg, Dir-Franchise Sls - PepsiCo, Inc.; pg. 259, pg. 1327
Ore, John, Sr VP-Product - Business Insider; pg. 1233, pg. 1208
Orear, Andrew, VP-Stop Loss & Limited Benefit Medical Sls - Reliance Standard Life Insurance Company; pg. 1215, pg. 1570
Orecchio, Stacey, Mgr-PR-Conair Corp - Conair Corporation; pg. 505, pg. 1055
OReilly, Paul, Sr Mgr-Plng, Procurement & Inventory - Acushnet Company; pg. 1824, pg. 818
Orelind, Greger, Sr Product Mgr - Alexa Internet, Inc.; pg. 1226, pg. 212
Orellana, Juan Jose, VP-IR & Mktg - Molina Healthcare, Inc.; pg. 1569, pg. 123
Orellana, Patty, Mgr-Production - NYDJ Apparel, LLC; pg. 30, pg. 302
Orendorff, Al, Sr VP-PR - Genworth Financial, Inc.; pg. 761, pg. 1802
Orenstein, Jeff, Acct Exec-Ticket Sls - Arizona Cardinals Football Club, Inc.; pg. 529, pg. 25
Orf, Michelle, Mgr-Social Media - Lennar Corporation; pg. 1100, pg. 443
Orford, Rob, Mgr-European Sls - Anaren, Inc.; pg. 617, pg. 1157
Oria, Eric, Sr Dir-Mktg & Strategy - GameStop Corp.; pg. 399, pg. 1699
Oria, Laura, Mgr-Customer Relationship Mktg - Michaels Stores, Inc.; pg. 1127, pg. 1722
Oriatti, Dave, VP-Sls & Mktg-Cord & Electronic Products - Coleman Cable, Inc.; pg. 1324, pg. 665
Orie, Rob, Mgr-Mktg Comm - Eaton Corporation; pg. 1331, pg. 1429
Oriedo, Sang'ona, Assoc Dir-Mktg-North America New Product Commercialization - LifeScan Inc; pg. 1556, pg. 146
Oriji, Ndidi, Sr VP-Adv Standards - NBC Universal, Inc.; pg. 300, pg. 1266
Oringer, Mike, Sr VP-Innovation & Trade Mktg - Stoli Group USA LLC; pg. 1970, pg. 1296
Orlandi, Mario, VP-Sls - Avnet, Inc.; pg. 622, pg. 15
Orlando, Danielle, Dir-Mktg & Brand Mgmt - Trico Products Corporation; pg. 220, pg. 905
Orlando, Nancy, Mgr-Pub Rels - SANTANDER HOLDINGS USA, INC.; pg. 801, pg. 800
Orlando, Pam, Chief Creative Officer - Humana, Inc.; pg. 1204, pg. 734
Orlando, Steve, Sr Dir-Media Rels - University Of Florida; pg. 609, pg. 429
Orlich, Daryl, VP-Eastern Reg Sls - StanChem, Inc.; pg. 1449, pg. 345
Orloff, Jeffrey, Sr Mgr-ECommerce-Global - SanDisk Corporation; pg. 465, pg. 147
Orlowsky, Fabiola, Mgr-Corp Brand & Adv - Anthem, Inc.; pg. 1192, pg. 683
Ormberg, Bob, VP-Mktg & Sls - General Communication, Inc.; pg. 1871, pg. 10
Orme, Natalie Hosea, Sr Mgr-Mktg Res - Kao Brands Co. Inc.; pg. 513, pg. 1415
Ormsby, Gregory, Mgr-Mktg Comm - Microsoft Corporation; pg. 435, pg. 1824
Ormseth, Holly, Product Mgr - Facebook, Inc.; pg. 1245, pg. 143
Ornburg, Todd, Dir-Mktg-Global - NVIDIA Corporation; pg. 447, pg. 268
Orona, Dan, VP-Mktg - Foxworth-Galbraith Lumber Company; pg. 1047, pg. 1730
Oros, Brenda, Sr Mgr-Retail Mktg - ASICS America Corporation; pg. 1826, pg. 106
Oros, John, Dir-Category Mgmt & Shopper Mktg - Anheuser-Busch Companies, LLC; pg. 237, pg. 991
Orosco, M. Jane, Mgr-Mktg Data - Houston Grand Opera Association; pg. 552, pg. 1707
Orozco, Laura, Sr Analyst-Fin-Global Adv - Xerox Corporation; pg. 494, pg. 365
Orpello, Arianna, Sr Dir-Mktg - Capital One Financial Corporation; pg. 730, pg. 1789
Orr, Andy, Brand Mgr - Red Gold, Inc.; pg. 891, pg. 677
Orr, Dan, Sr VP-Mktg - W.B. Mason Company; pg. 491, pg. 803
Orr, Jamaal, Mgr-Mktg - Viacom Inc.; pg. 316, pg. 1310
Orr, Kristen, Brand Mgr-Commercialization - Smithfield Foods, Inc.; pg. 896, pg. 1806
Orr, Melissa, Mgr-Integrated Mktg-Enterprise Mobility - Symantec Corporation; pg. 478, pg. 161
Orr, Nicole, Sr Mgr-Mktg-LaCrosse Brand - LaCrosse Footwear, Inc.; pg. 1811, pg. 1503
Orr, Roxie, Sls Mgr-CPOV-Southwest Reg - FCA US LLC; pg. 170, pg. 868
Orsi, Kevin, VP-Digital Sls & Customer Experience - Wells Fargo & Company; pg. 819, pg. 232
Orsi, Sara J., Sr Analyst-Digital & Social Media - ConocoPhillips; pg. 975, pg. 1703
Orsini, Heidi, Dir-Mktg-Intl - Wendy's International, Inc.; pg. 1755, pg. 1451
Orsini, Jacqueline, Product Mgr-Generation Plan & Product Road Map - Electrolux Home Products North America; pg. 54, pg. 1366
Ortale, Mike, VP-Sls - The Evercare Company; pg. 1124, pg. 483
Ortega, Belia, Mgr-Comm-Investor & Media Rels - DeVry Education Group Inc.; pg. 600, pg. 607
Ortega, Ernie, Pres-Sls - XO Holdings, Inc.; pg. 689, pg. 1786
Ortega, Natalia, Planner-Interactive Mktg - General Mills, Inc.; pg. 828, pg. 933
Orth, Kevin, VP-Sls - Cree Inc.; pg. 631, pg. 1371
Orth, Robyn, Dir-Digital & Social Media Comm - Eli Lilly and Company; pg. 1527, pg. 684
Orth, Tanya, Mgr-Sls Dev - Hewlett-Packard Company; pg. 404, pg. 175
Orth, Tiffany, Brand Mktg Mgr-Market Dev - Rubbermaid Home Products; pg. 1138, pg. 1453
Orthman, Wendy, Mgr-Midwest PR - FCA US LLC; pg. 170, pg. 868
Ortiz, Christian, Category Mgr-Mktg, Brand, Trade & Shopper Mktg - Reckitt Benckiser Inc.; pg. 1136, pg. 1105
Ortiz, Claudivel, Mgr-Sls Dev - L'Oreal USA; pg. 514, pg. 1252
Ortiz, Edie, Mgr-Adv Scheduling & Ops - AT&T; pg. 1865, pg. 258
Ortiz, Enrique, Reg Mgr-Bus Dev & Mktg - Hewlett-Packard Company; pg. 404, pg. 175
Ortiz, Evyette, Dir-Mktg - Ark Restaurants Corp.; pg. 1715, pg. 1196

Ortiz, Fernando, Dir-Mktg-HEINEKEN Mexico-Cuauhtemoc Moctezuma - Heineken USA Inc.; *pg.* 252, *pg.* 1352
Ortiz, Katherine, Mgr-Mktg - eBay Inc.; *pg.* 1240, *pg.* 243
Ortiz, Lesly, Supvr-Mktg Comm - Pollo Tropical Inc.; *pg.* 1745, *pg.* 445
Ortiz, Luis, Mgr-Mktg Innovation - PepsiCo, Inc.; *pg.* 259, *pg.* 1327
Ortiz, Mark, Mgr-Interactive Mktg-Natl - American Honda Motor Co., Inc.; *pg.* 163, *pg.* 292
Ortiz, Randy, Head-Adv & Comm-Dodge & SRT - FCA US LLC; *pg.* 170, *pg.* 868
Ortiz, Vanessa, Mgr-Field Mktg-On Premise - Bacardi USA, Inc.; *pg.* 1956, *pg.* 417
Ortiz, Victor, Dir-Mobile Product Mgmt - Toys "R" Us, Inc.; *pg.* 968, *pg.* 1130
Ortley, Steven, Sr Mgr-Product Mktg - Honeywell International Inc.; *pg.* 407, *pg.* 1088
Ortman, Margarete, Sr Mgr-ECommerce - hhgregg, Inc.; *pg.* 56, *pg.* 686
Ortman, Sarah, Assoc Dir-Mktg Comm - The Clorox Company; *pg.* 327, *pg.* 169
Ortolani, Christie, Assoc Mgr-Digital Mktg Analytics - CNBC; *pg.* 275, *pg.* 1059
Ortolano, Alex, Dir-Segment Mktg - United Parcel Service, Inc.; *pg.* 1928, *pg.* 522
Orton, Adam, Mgr-Mktg - Outerwall Inc.; *pg.* 1367, *pg.* 1816
Orton, Deb, Sr Dir-Mktg - SAS Institute Inc.; *pg.* 466, *pg.* 1361
Orullian, Peter, Grp Product Mgr - Xbox; *pg.* 970, *pg.* 1829
Osadchy, Luba, Mgr-Walmart US Stores Fabric, Home & Family Care Mktg - The Procter & Gamble Company; *pg.* 1129, *pg.* 1418
Osakada, Val, Dir-Creative - Earth Friendly Products; *pg.* 329, *pg.* 552
Osberg, Diana, Dir-Mktg & Brand Integration - BUFFALO WILD WINGS, INC.; *pg.* 1718, *pg.* 931
Osberg, Ken, Grp Product Mgr-Accessories - Robert Bosch Tool Corp; *pg.* 1060, *pg.* 634
Osberg, Kristina, Assoc Mgr-Mktg-Convenience - MillerCoors; *pg.* 254, *pg.* 1877
Osborn, Amy, VP-Treasury Svcs Mktg - JPMorgan Chase & Co.; *pg.* 772, *pg.* 1246
Osborn, Brian, VP-Brand Mktg - SHUTTERFLY, INC.; *pg.* 1280, *pg.* 192
Osborn, Debra, Sr Dir-Reporting & Analytics - Aetna Inc.; *pg.* 1187, *pg.* 351
Osborn, Duncan, Product Mgr - Google Inc.; *pg.* 1249, *pg.* 153
Osborn, Meredith, Sr Dir-Comm & Social Responsibility - Bare Escentuals, Inc.; *pg.* 500, *pg.* 213
Osborn, Michael J., Founder & VP-Mdsg - Wine.com, Inc.; *pg.* 1972, *pg.* 234
Osborn, Shalee, Reg Mgr-Mktg-West Market - H&R Block, Inc.; *pg.* 764, *pg.* 983
Osborne, Aaron, Mgr-Mktg Asset & Professional Sports - Coca-Cola Bottling Co. Consolidated; *pg.* 240, *pg.* 1365
Osborne, Anne, Sr Mgr-Contracts-Corp Vendor Mgmt - Charles Schwab; *pg.* 1235, *pg.* 1661
Osborne, Bob, Mgr-Shopper Mktg - Pepperidge Farm, Inc.; *pg.* 888, *pg.* 363
Osborne, Cassy, Product Mgr - Moen Incorporated; *pg.* 1056, *pg.* 1468
Osborne, Claire, Dir-Solutions Sls - Travelport Limited; *pg.* 1925, *pg.* 521
Osborne, Jackie, Mgr-Mktg - CIRCOR Aerospace, Inc.; *pg.* 226, *pg.* 69
Osborne, Jonathan, Brand Mgr-Global - Eli Lilly and Company; *pg.* 1527, *pg.* 684
Osborne, Lance, Product Mgr & Mgr-Technical Sls - Meadow Burke; *pg.* 96, *pg.* 474
Osborne, Richard L., Chief-Creative Svcs - Metropolitan Transportation Authority; *pg.* 1915, *pg.* 1260
Osburn, Gina, Mgr-Product Dev - The Hain Celestial Group, Inc.; *pg.* 860, *pg.* 1172
Osburn, Sara, Sr Specialist-Consumer Mktg - Lowe's Companies, Inc.; *pg.* 1053, *pg.* 1383
Osburn, Stacey, Dir-Pub & Media Rels - National Collegiate Athletic Association; *pg.* 567, *pg.* 688
Oshirak, Leigh, VP-PR & Mktg Comm - Williams-Sonoma, Inc.; *pg.* 1140, *pg.* 234
Oshita, Jill, Campaign Mgr & Mgr-Product Mktg - Hewlett-Packard Company; *pg.* 404, *pg.* 175
Osielski, Matthew, Sr Mgr-Mktg - CenturyLink, Inc.; *pg.* 1870, *pg.* 746
Osilia, Peter, Sr Dir-Mktg-Latin America - Astellas Pharma US, Inc.; *pg.* 1496, *pg.* 640
Osinski, Bob, Dir-Key Sls Accts - Exide Technologies; *pg.* 204, *pg.* 483
Osinski, Caroline, Coord-ECommerce Mktg - Ann Inc.; *pg.* 18, *pg.* 1195
Osiol, Amanda, Mgr-Creative Dev, Online & Event Mktg - SeaWorld Parks & Entertainment LLC; *pg.* 582, *pg.* 456
Oskin, Desiree, VP-Corp Mktg - Amegy Bank, N.A.; *pg.* 711, *pg.* 1700
Osley, Lori, Sr Dir-Franchise Sls & Dev Mktg - SONIC Corp.; *pg.* 1750, *pg.* 1487
Osmanski, Lauren, Gen Mgr-Card & Mgr-Mktg - General Motors Company; *pg.* 175, *pg.* 881
Osmer, Justin, Sr Partner Mgr-Mktg-Xbox Games - Microsoft Corporation; *pg.* 435, *pg.* 1824
Osner-Hackett, Chris, Sr Dir-Media-North America - Kellogg Company; *pg.* 831, *pg.* 870
Osofsky, Justin, VP-Global Ops & Media Partnerships - Facebook, Inc.; *pg.* 1245, *pg.* 143
Osofsky, Marc D., Sr VP-Mktg - Lionbridge Technologies Inc.; *pg.* 428, *pg.* 851
Osorio, Lisa, Gen Mgr-Mktg - Nikon Inc.; *pg.* 1424, *pg.* 1181
Osowski, Nicole, Dir-Web Sls & Mdsg - Lenovo Group Ltd; *pg.* 427, *pg.* 1384
Osowski, Rick, Product Mgr-Technical - IBM; *pg.* 410, *pg.* 1449
Osowski, Teresa, Coord-Mktg Svcs - Mestek, Inc.; *pg.* 1074, *pg.* 857
Ossa, Pamela, Assoc Dir-Mktg - Allergan; *pg.* 1490, *pg.* 1101
Ossi, Terri, Sr Mgr-Mktg - Costa Del Mar Sunglasses, Inc.; *pg.* 1407, *pg.* 419
Osso, Dave, Brand Mgr - The Genie Company; *pg.* 55, *pg.* 1403
Ostaffe, Harry, Dir-Mktg - Black Box Corporation; *pg.* 361, *pg.* 1547
Ostahowski, Jay M., Sr Mgr-Innovation Res - General Motors Company; *pg.* 175, *pg.* 881
Ostenberg, Herb, Sr VP-North American Sls - Electro Rent Corporation; *pg.* 390, *pg.* 300
Ostenkamp, Laura, Sr Mgr-Mktg Comm-US Wholesale - Moen Incorporated; *pg.* 1056, *pg.* 1468
Osterbeck, Ryan, Sr Mgr-Digital Mktg-Global - Equinix, Inc.; *pg.* 394, *pg.* 190
Osterberg, Julie, Dir-Mktg - American Medical Systems Holdings, Inc.; *pg.* 1493, *pg.* 947
Osterhoff, Doug, Mgr-Mktg-Natl - General Motors Company; *pg.* 175, *pg.* 881
Osterloh, Steve, VP-Mktg - Ennis, Inc.; *pg.* 393, *pg.* 1727
Osterman, Steve, Sr VP-Sls - Merrill Corporation; *pg.* 1664, *pg.* 962
Ostermann, Courtney, Sr Dir-Corp Mktg - Imperva, Inc.; *pg.* 413, *pg.* 193
Ostermann, Ken, Gen Mgr-Outreach Customer Mktg - Harley-Davidson, Inc.; *pg.* 178, *pg.* 1874
Ostern, Eric, Sr Mgr-Global Partnerships - Unilever United States, Inc.; *pg.* 904, *pg.* 1061
Ostgard, Gayle I., Dir-Mktg-Bus Mobile Solutions, Software & Svcs Grp - Intel Corporation; *pg.* 645, *pg.* 266
Ostler, Clint, Mgr-Media & Market Strategy - Alaska Airlines, Inc.; *pg.* 1897, *pg.* 1830
Ostoich, Vladimir E., VP-Govt Affairs & Mktg-Pacific Rim - Abaxis, Inc.; *pg.* 1483, *pg.* 298
Ostos, Pia, Brand Mgr-Mktg-Global - Hasbro, Inc.; *pg.* 954, *pg.* 1603
Ostrander, Lonny C., VP-HR Svcs Sls-Natl - Paychex, Inc.; *pg.* 792, *pg.* 1336
Ostreko, Katie, Mgr-Category Furniture Mktg - Steelcase Inc.; *pg.* 475, *pg.* 889
Ostrer, Brian, VP-Mktg-Armor All - Armored AutoGroup Inc.; *pg.* 199, *pg.* 342
Ostrower, Sarh, Dir-Mktg-North America - Clinique Laboratories LLC; *pg.* 503, *pg.* 1214
Ostrowski, Carol, Specialist-Mktg - The Northwestern Mutual Life Insurance Company; *pg.* 1212, *pg.* 1879
Ostrowski, Emily, Sr Mgr-Mktg-HGTV Magazine - Hearst Magazines; *pg.* 1649, *pg.* 1239
Ostrowski, Michelle, Mgr-Sls Integration & Dealer Rels - General Motors Company; *pg.* 175, *pg.* 881
Ostrowski, Susan, Exec VP-Sls & Mktg - The Female Health Company; *pg.* 1530, *pg.* 573
Ostryniec, Robert P., Chief Product Supply Officer - Keurig Green Mountain, Inc.; *pg.* 868, *pg.* 1768
Ostvoll, Jean M., Mng Dir-Health & Public Svc, Mktg & Comm - Accenture; *pg.* 1392, *pg.* 1186
Ostwald, Kevin, Dir-Sls & Mktg - Sure Fit Inc.; *pg.* 944, *pg.* 1514
Osumi, Jina, Dir-Brand Strategy & Mktg Activation - Del Monte Foods, Inc.; *pg.* 852, *pg.* 304
Oswal, Shreya, Mgr-Product Mktg - LinkedIn Corporation; *pg.* 1262, *pg.* 160
Oswald, Tami, Head-Mktg - Zappos.com, Inc.; *pg.* 1291, *pg.* 1030
Oswald, Wolfgang, Sr VP-Sls-Eastern Hemisphere - WireCo WorldGroup; *pg.* 1389, *pg.* 987
Oswalt, Jonathon, Mgr-Platform Sls-Regions Investment Svcs - Regions Financial Corporation; *pg.* 798, *pg.* 4
Otaki, Kaoru, Dir-Critical Infectious Diseases-Global Mktg - Cepheid; *pg.* 1514, *pg.* 284
Otero-Reiss, Alessandra, VP-Customer Relship Mktg - Time Warner Cable Inc.; *pg.* 312, *pg.* 1301
Otey, Brent, Dir-Mktg - Veterinary Pet Insurance Co.; *pg.* 1222, *pg.* 49
Otis, Christie A., Sr Dir-Worldwide Mktg - Immucor, Inc.; *pg.* 1544, *pg.* 537
Otis, Evan, Asst Mgr-Product Mktg & Distr - The Walt Disney Company; *pg.* 317, *pg.* 52
Otley, Elizabeth Warren, Product Mgr-Web & Mobile - Quicken Loans, Inc.; *pg.* 797, *pg.* 884
Otoo, Andrew, Head-EU Vaccines Mktg Reg Brand Team-Prevenar 13 Adult - Pfizer Inc.; *pg.* 1581, *pg.* 1278
Otranto, Deanna, Mgr-Content Mktg - NutriSystem, Inc.; *pg.* 1577, *pg.* 1533
Otremba, Jerry, Head-Retail Sls - The Star Tribune Company; *pg.* 1689, *pg.* 942
Ott, Bart, VP-Mktg & Bus Dev - Materion Advanced Chemicals; *pg.* 1172, *pg.* 1877
Ott, Chris, Sr Dir-Product Mktg - FMR LLC (Fidelity Investments); *pg.* 759, *pg.* 794
Ott, Melissa, Program Mgr-Mktg - WESCO International Inc.; *pg.* 687, *pg.* 1582
Ottenbreit, Shawn, CFO-HP Mktg - Hewlett-Packard Company; *pg.* 404, *pg.* 175
Ottenweller, Scott, VP-Customer Acq Mktg - JPMorgan Chase & Co.; *pg.* 772, *pg.* 1246
Otter, Thomas, VP-Product Mgmt-Employee Central - SuccessFactors, Inc.; *pg.* 477, *pg.* 228
Otto, Donna, Mgr-Digital Engagement-Interactive Mktg - Ameriprise Financial, Inc.; *pg.* 715, *pg.* 930
Otto, Greg, VP-Secondary Mktg - M/I Homes, Inc.; *pg.* 95, *pg.* 1441
Otto, Jennifer, Dir-Creative - McKesson Corporation; *pg.* 1560, *pg.* 222
Otto, Shannon, Mgr-Global Social Media - Clinique Laboratories LLC; *pg.* 503, *pg.* 1214
Otway, Marci, Mgr-Mktg & Execution & Optimization - Pitney Bowes Inc.; *pg.* 454, *pg.* 376
Ou, Francisco, Mgr-Mktg-Intl - Boston Scientific Corporation; *pg.* 1508, *pg.* 831
Ouderkirk, Eric, Dir-Global Mktg-Mfg Strategic Bus Unit - Ecolab Inc.; *pg.* 329, *pg.* 960
Oudewaal, John, Mgr-SP Cloud Channel Sls - Cisco Systems, Inc.; *pg.* 372, *pg.* 240
Ouellet, Serge, Asst VP-Mktg Pur - The Jean Coutu Group (PJC) Inc.; *pg.* 1548, *pg.* 1952
Ouellette, Thomas, Assoc Dir-Global Antibiotic Mktg Team - Merck & Co., Inc.; *pg.* 1566, *pg.* 1077
Oujiri, Steve, VP-Military Sls - Standard Bent Glass Corporation; *pg.* 218, *pg.* 1519
Oulton, Brian, VP-Strategic & Initiative Mktg - Belden, Inc.; *pg.* 624, *pg.* 993
Ourmieres-Widener, Christine, Chief Sls Officer-Global - American Express Company; *pg.* 712, *pg.* 1190
Outlaw, Tom, VP-Sls - Ingles Markets, Incorporated; *pg.* 1023, *pg.* 1358
Overbeck, Mayo, Dir-Sls - Rantec Microwave Systems, Inc.; *pg.* 666, *pg.* 307
Overbeek, Ryan, Principal & Product Mgr - Medtronic, Inc.; *pg.* 1564, *pg.* 939
Overby, Katherine, Brand Mgr-787 Dreamliner - The Boeing Company; *pg.* 225, *pg.* 567
Overcash, Sarah, Sr VP-Digital Product Mgmt - Bank of America Corporation; *pg.* 718, *pg.* 1362
Overend, Mary, Mgr-Digital Mktg - Country Music Association; *pg.* 138, *pg.* 1649
Overly, Erin, Sr Dir-Global Innovation - Mondelez International, Inc.; *pg.* 878, *pg.* 601
Overmyer, Brian, Sr Mgr-Partner Programs - Cisco Systems, Inc.; *pg.* 372, *pg.* 240
Overos, David, Dir-Product Mktg - Software AG, Inc.; *pg.* 471, *pg.* 1799

First page reference indicates Business Class Edition
Second page reference indicates Geographic Edition

Overson, Mike, Sr Analyst-Mktg Res - Arizona Public Service Company; pg. 1935, pg. 14
Overstreet, Jason, Mng Dir-Mktg & Comm - United States Bowling Congress; pg. 159, pg. 1660
Overstreet, Myrna, Mgr-Mktg-Global Branded Entertainment - The Procter & Gamble Company; pg. 1129, pg. 1418
Overstreet, Todd, VP-Adv Ops - Scripps Networks Interactive, Inc.; pg. 1279, pg. 1638
Overturf, James, Sr VP-Mktg & IR - Extra Space Storage, Inc.; pg. 1091, pg. 1757
Oviatt, Jared, VP-Sls - Wigwam Mills, Inc.; pg. 15, pg. 1894
Ovuka, Phil, Dir-Creative Media Svcs - GEICO Corporation; pg. 1200, pg. 399
Owen, Alan, Mgr-Mktg - Sensient Technologies Corporation; pg. 895, pg. 1881
Owen, Allison, Mgr-Mktg - Inspirato LLC; pg. 1912, pg. 320
Owen, Chris, Dir-Global Integrated Media - Monster Worldwide, Inc.; pg. 1268, pg. 859
Owen, Chris, VP-Integrated Mktg - United Services Automobile Association; pg. 1221, pg. 1743
Owen, Dan, VP-Adv Sls - The Weather Channel LLC; pg. 320, pg. 523
Owen, Jasen X., Product Mgr-Rheumatology Mktg - Abbott Laboratories; pg. 1484, pg. 551
Owen, Kerri, Brand Mgr-Kahlua - Pernod Ricard USA, Inc.; pg. 1968, pg. 1332
Owen, Lorina, Coord-Sls & Mktg-Digital Solutions - John Wiley & Sons, Inc.; pg. 1655, pg. 1073
Owen, Ray, VP-Sls & Mktg - TDK-Lambda High Power Division; pg. 1380, pg. 1090
Owen, Tim, Dir-Engrg & Product Dev - Continental Motors; pg. 227, pg. 7
Owens, Ann, Officer-Natl Adv - National Railroad Passenger Corporation; pg. 1916, pg. 403
Owens, Benjamin L., VP-Mktg & Strategy - Honeywell North Safety Products; pg. 42, pg. 1600
Owens, Blair, VP-Mktg - Monster Beverage Corporation; pg. 257, pg. 69
Owens, Carlye, Mgr-Bus Dev & Mktg Campaign - Black Box Corporation; pg. 361, pg. 1547
Owens, Craig, Sr Dir-Mktg-Global - Electronic Arts Inc.; pg. 951, pg. 189
Owens, George J., Mng Dir-Customer Engagement-Mktg Dept - Service Corporation International; pg. 1395, pg. 1714
Owens, Janet, Partner-Brand-Institutional, Branding & Creative Svcs - Manulife Financial Corporation; pg. 778, pg. 1939
Owens, Kim, Sr VP-Adv Strategy & Media Rels - The Men's Wearhouse, Inc.; pg. 44, pg. 1711
Owens, Kristine, Mgr-PR-Online & Retail - Staples, Inc.; pg. 474, pg. 821
Owens, Lianna, Brand Mgr-Innovation & Strategy - The WhiteWave Foods Company; pg. 1037, pg. 324
Owens, Maggie, Dir-Mktg - Burris Logistics; pg. 843, pg. 387
Owens, Nina, Specialist-Social Media - Michaels Stores, Inc.; pg. 1127, pg. 1722
Owens, Parker, Mgr-Mktg - Colorado Symphony Association Inc.; pg. 542, pg. 318
Owens, Patrick, Sr Mgr-Interactive Mktg - Acushnet Company; pg. 1824, pg. 818
Owens, Peg, Specialist-Mktg - Idaho Department of Commerce; pg. 995, pg. 547
Owens, Stephen, Sr Dir-Procurement-Global - eBay Inc.; pg. 1240, pg. 243
Owins, Tammy, Mgr-Shopper Mktg - Pepsi Beverages Company; pg. 258, pg. 1342
Owsinski, Jerry, Mgr-Mktg, Comm & Trng - Steelcase Inc.; pg. 475, pg. 889
Oxford, Kathy, Sr Mgr-Intl Trade - Georgia Department of Economic Development; pg. 992, pg. 506
Oxford, Megan, Specialist-Mktg Comm - PETCO Animal Supplies, Inc.; pg. 1480, pg. 206
Oxley, Gregory L., Mgr-Mktg Comm-Americas - Air Products and Chemicals, Inc.; pg. 1145, pg. 1513
Oyadomari, Marissa, Mgr-Mktg - The Gap, Inc.; pg. 1770, pg. 218
Oyanedel, Alejandra, Dir-Mktg Fin - PepsiCo, Inc.; pg. 259, pg. 1327
Oyharcabal, Jack, Mgr-Enterprise Mktg - Apple Inc.; pg. 350, pg. 73
Ozeri, Lea, Dir-Mktg - Scholastic Corporation; pg. 1683, pg. 1288
Ozga, Sarah, Product Mgr - ABB Inc.; pg. 1309, pg. 1359
Ozias, Rachel, Dir-Mktg - Comcast Cable Communications, Inc.; pg. 276, pg. 1560
Ozimek, Joe, VP-Mktg - The Boeing Company; pg. 225, pg. 567
Ozimek, Mark, Brand Mgr-SunnyD - Sunny Delight Beverages Co.; pg. 899, pg. 1426
Ozisikyilmaz, Nil, Asst Dir-Mktg Sciences - Astellas Pharma US, Inc.; pg. 1496, pg. 640

P

Paap, Sue, Mgr-Mktg - Norse Dairy Systems LLC; pg. 886, pg. 1442
Paar, Jessica, Dir-PR - The Boston Beer Company, Inc.; pg. 239, pg. 790
Paavonpera, Jay, Sr Mgr-PR-Dior Homme - Parfums Christian Dior, Inc; pg. 519, pg. 1276
Pabst, Matt, Mgr-Shopper Mktg - ConAgra Foods, Inc.; pg. 826, pg. 1014
Paccione, Lisa, VP-Sls & Dev-Global - Syniverse Holdings, Inc.; pg. 479, pg. 475
Paccione, Tracy, VP-Mdsg - Ethan Allen Interiors Inc.; pg. 924, pg. 343
Pace, Alicia, Mgr-Mdsg & Web Content-Global ECommerce Ops - Toys "R" Us, Inc.; pg. 968, pg. 1130
Pace, Jon A., Mng Dir & Head-Health & Benefits Sls - Aon Hewitt; pg. 350, pg. 627
Pace, Mark J., VP-Sls & Mktg - Westinghouse Air Brake Technologies Corporation; pg. 1388, pg. 1595
Pace, Paige, Sr Mgr-Indus Analyst Rels - Adobe Systems Incorporated; pg. 342, pg. 235
Pace-Sanders, Denise M., VP & Dir-Brand & Mktg - Peapack-Gladstone Bank; pg. 792, pg. 1071
Pacelli, Anthony, VP-Trade Mktg - B&G Foods, Inc.; pg. 838, pg. 1102
Pacelli, Bob, Sr Mgr-Comm - Boral Roofing; pg. 71, pg. 107
Pacenza, Lisa, Sr Mgr-Mktg - Deloitte & Touche USA LLP; pg. 743, pg. 1222
Pacewicz, Roman, Sr VP-Mktg & Strategy-Global - AT&T Inc.; pg. 1867, pg. 1674
Pacheco, Eddie, Product Mgr - Goya Foods, Inc.; pg. 859, pg. 1075
Pacheco, John, Mng Dir-Institutional Mktg - Charles Schwab & Company, Inc.; pg. 734, pg. 215
Pacheco, Maria, Mgr-Product Mktg - Google Inc.; pg. 1249, pg. 153
Pacheco, Melody, Sr Acct Exec-Sls - Deluxe Corporation; pg. 1634, pg. 964
Pacheco, Ron, Dir-Product Mgmt - Red Hat, Inc.; pg. 460, pg. 1388
Pacheco, Stacie, VP-Strategic Mktg - Acuity Brands, Inc.; pg. 1294, pg. 487
Pacheco, Steve, Dir-Adv & Sponsorship Mktg - FedEx Corporation; pg. 1907, pg. 1642
Pacheco, Steve, Dir-Adv & Sponsorship Mktg - FedEx Office & Print Services, Inc.; pg. 396, pg. 1681
Pachelli, Anthony, Rep-Enterprise Sls - Amazon.com, Inc.; pg. 1226, pg. 1831
Pachetti, Alex, Mng Dir-Mktg & Comm - Accenture; pg. 1392, pg. 1186
Pachucki, Alicia, Assoc Mgr-Digital Mktg, Search & Content - Darden Restaurants, Inc.; pg. 1724, pg. 453
Pachucki, Alicia, Assoc Mgr-Digital Mktg, Search & Content - Olive Garden Italian Restaurant; pg. 1742, pg. 454
Pacific, Barbara, Specialist-Mktg - Boston Scientific Corporation; pg. 1508, pg. 831
Pacifico, Terry, Dir-Creative Ops-Global Comm - The Lubrizol Corporation; pg. 1171, pg. 1481
Pacilio, Marleine, Dir-Interactive Media & Adv - OPI Products Inc.; pg. 518, pg. 167
Pacino, John, VP-Product Dev & Social Media - National Hockey League; pg. 568, pg. 1265
Paciorka, Allison, Assoc Analyst-Mktg, Digital Media Programmatic & Display - Target Corporation; pg. 1786, pg. 942
Packard, Mark Stanfield, Sr Dir-Treasury - Hawaiian Airlines, Inc.; pg. 1910, pg. 543
Packer, Curtis, Sr Specialist-Mktg - Associated Food Stores, Inc.; pg. 1014, pg. 1756
Packer, Mike, VP-Sls - Club Car, Inc.; pg. 1830, pg. 532
Packham, Maura, VP-Mktg & Comm - Quad/Graphics, Inc.; pg. 1468, pg. 1896
Packingham, Kevin, Exec VP-Product Mgmt - Cablevision Systems Corporation; pg. 272, pg. 1141
Packles, Michael, Specialist-Online Mktg - Airbnb, Inc.; pg. 1226, pg. 211
Pacsi, Phil, VP-Consumer Mktg - Bridgestone Americas, Inc.; pg. 201, pg. 1649
Padden, Stephanie, Dir-Retail Mktg - La-Z-Boy Incorporated; pg. 932, pg. 901
Padfield, Naomi, Mgr-Channel Mktg & Comml - Unilever United States, Inc.; pg. 904, pg. 1061
Padgett, Chris, VP-Mktg & Head-Digital - Nestle Purina PetCare Company; pg. 1479, pg. 1000
Padgett, Chris, VP-Mktg & Head-Digital - Nestle USA, Inc.; pg. 883, pg. 96
Padgett, Jeffery, Sr Dir & Engr-Distinguished Software - The Gap, Inc.; pg. 1770, pg. 218
Padgett, John, Mgr-Sls - Jessup's Appliances; pg. 58, pg. 477
Padgett, Ken, Brand Mgr - The Kraft Heinz Company; pg. 871, pg. 641
Padgitt, Jason, Sr VP-Mktg & Comm - Fender Musical Instruments Corporation; pg. 547, pg. 21
Padgitt, Rj, Dir-Channel Partner Sls - Emdeon, Inc.; pg. 747, pg. 1650
Padian, John, COO-Pelican Products - Pelican Products, Inc.; pg. 1842, pg. 295
Padian, Michael, Sr Mgr-Digital & Social Comm - Southern California Edison Company; pg. 1952, pg. 194
Padilla, Carolina, Dir-Multicultural Mktg - DISH Network Corporation; pg. 283, pg. 325
Padilla, Martine, Mgr-Mktg Comm & Retail Production - Sprint Corporation; pg. 1874, pg. 719
Padilla, Sandra, Mgr-Digital Mktg - Dell Inc.; pg. 383, pg. 1737
Padiyar, Preeti, Product Mgr-Indus Cloud Applications - SAP America, Inc.; pg. 466, pg. 1557
Padmanabhan, Jayram, VP-Global Product Mgmt & Dev-Enterprise Growth - American Express Company; pg. 712, pg. 1190
Padmanabhan, Sandhya, Brand Mgr-Smirnoff Vodka - Diageo North America, Inc.; pg. 1961, pg. 361
Padro, Estela, Brand Mgr - GlaxoSmithKline; pg. 1536, pg. 1389
Padro, Michael, Mgr-Sls & Mktg-HV Gas Insulated Substations - ABB Inc.; pg. 1309, pg. 1359
Padua, Reinaldo, Asst VP-Hispanic Mktg - The Coca-Cola Company; pg. 240, pg. 493
Paduchik, Jason, Sr Dir-Legislative Affairs-Ohio - AT&T Inc.; pg. 1867, pg. 1674
Padula, Tony, Mgr-Mktg Comm - Amphenol Corporation; pg. 616, pg. 381
Padwal, Sachin, Sr Dir-Multichannel & Mobile - Sam's Club; pg. 1783, pg. 29
Paek, Dottie, Sr Dir-Mktg - Toll Brothers, Inc.; pg. 115, pg. 1541
Paeseler, Dee Dee, Mgr-Product Mktg-Chromecast - Google Inc.; pg. 1249, pg. 153
Paessler, Konstantin, Brand Mgr-COVERGIRL & MAX FACTOR Global Design - The Procter & Gamble Company; pg. 1129, pg. 1418
Pagan, Robert, Mgr-Creative - Makita U.S.A., Inc.; pg. 1358, pg. 120
Pagano, Kristin, Dir-Mktg - Munchkin, Inc.; pg. 964, pg. 300
Pagano, Mary, Mgr-Community-Global Digital Mktg - The Estee Lauder Companies Inc.; pg. 508, pg. 1229
Pagano, Michael A., VP-Sls - Stahl & Associates Insurance; pg. 1217, pg. 464
Page, Andrew, Product Mgr - NVIDIA Corporation; pg. 447, pg. 268
Page, Catherine, Mgr-Mktg Programs - Texas Instruments Incorporated; pg. 679, pg. 1688
Page, David, Mgr-Field Mktg-Tequilas - Brown-Forman Corporation; pg. 1958, pg. 732
Page, Doreen J., Dir-Media-Audio - Macy's, Inc.; pg. 1778, pg. 1417
Page, Ed, Sr Dir-Ad Sls-CPG - MyWebGrocer.com Corp.; pg. 1269, pg. 1769
Page, Kathy, Sr VP-Production, Distr & Creative Svcs - Hasbro, Inc.; pg. 954, pg. 1603
Page, Larry, Sr Dir-Mktg-US Oral Care - Johnson & Johnson; pg. 1549, pg. 1091
Page, Matt, Sr Dir-Outdoor Performance - Under Armour, Inc.; pg. 49, pg. 759
Page, Ray, Mgr-Adv & Promos - Texas Lottery Commission; pg. 1007, pg. 1666
Page, Robin, Dir-Mktg - Barneys New York, Inc.; pg. 38, pg. 1201
Page, Sandra, VP-Ad Sls Plng & Strategy - The History Channel; pg. 290, pg. 1240
Pagel, Shelly Niebur, Mgr-Mktg Comm - 3M Company; pg. 1142, pg. 956

Pagendam, Mike, Exec VP & Head-Bus Area After Sls-Global - Alimak Hek Inc; *pg.* 66, *pg.* 1749
Pagenkopf, Pam, Sr Mgr-Data Mgmt & Bus Intelligence - Thomas & Betts Corporation; *pg.* 680, *pg.* 1646
Pagliarello, Dino, Mgr-Product Mktg - Konica Minolta Business Solutions USA, Inc.; *pg.* 1419, *pg.* 1113
Pagliero, Christina, Sr Mgr-Integrated Mktg - Mansueto Ventures LLC; *pg.* 1661, *pg.* 1256
Pahl, Greg, Dir-Retail Mktg Execution - La-Z-Boy Incorporated; *pg.* 932, *pg.* 901
Pahl, Lisa, Dir-Product Mgmt - DATATRAK International, Inc.; *pg.* 383, *pg.* 1462
Pahlavan, Babak, Dir-Product Mgmt-Google Analytics - Google Inc.; *pg.* 1249, *pg.* 153
Paige, Christine, Sr VP-Mktg & Digital Svcs - Kaiser Foundation Health Plan of the Mid-Atlantic States, Inc.; *pg.* 1205, *pg.* 776
Paige, Sandra, Brand Mgr - B&G Foods, Inc.; *pg.* 838, *pg.* 1102
Paik, Lou, Head-Digital Strategy & Mgr-Shopper Mktg - The Dannon Company, Inc.; *pg.* 851, *pg.* 1351
Paine, Alyson, Sr Mgr-Digital Strategy - salesforce.com, inc.; *pg.* 1278, *pg.* 226
Paine, Kate, Mgr-Strategic Comm & Brand Mgr - The Hershey Co.; *pg.* 1855, *pg.* 1538
Painter, Brad, VP-Worldwide Disk Sls - Quantum Corporation; *pg.* 458, *pg.* 250
Painter, Emily, Mgr-Global Digital & Social Media - Banana Republic; *pg.* 1760, *pg.* 212
Painter, Robert, VP-Corp Mktg - Cognizant Technology Solutions Corporation; *pg.* 377, *pg.* 1124
Painting, Jeffrey, Chief Sls Officer-Bus & Sr VP - Time Warner Cable Inc.; *pg.* 312, *pg.* 1301
Paiva, Nathalie, Dir-Mktg & PR - AmorePacific US, Inc.; *pg.* 498, *pg.* 1195
Pajerski, Maureen, CMO & Chief Sls Officer - Rauland-Borg Corporation; *pg.* 666, *pg.* 634
Paka, Anand, Product Mgr - Google Inc.; *pg.* 1249, *pg.* 153
Pal, Ayan, Dir-Creative - Deloitte & Touche USA LLP; *pg.* 743, *pg.* 1222
Pal, Greg, VP-Mktg, Strategy & Bus Dev-Enterprise Div - Nuance Communications, Inc.; *pg.* 447, *pg.* 806
Palacio, Mark, Mgr-Mktg Comm, Computed Tomography & Radiation Oncology - Siemens Medical Solutions USA, Inc.; *pg.* 469, *pg.* 1550
Palacios, Fiorella, Brand Mgr-Global Digital Mktg - Starbucks Corporation; *pg.* 897, *pg.* 1840
Palacios, Raul, Sr Product Mgr - Brother International Corporation - USA; *pg.* 53, *pg.* 1046
Paladino, Justin, Engr-Product Dev - Intel Corporation; *pg.* 645, *pg.* 266
Palamara, Anthony, Dir-Product Mgmt - WebMD Health Corporation; *pg.* 1288, *pg.* 1313
Palamountain, Mark, Sr Dir-Agricultural Ops - Limoneira Company; *pg.* 705, *pg.* 276
Palande, Gaurav, Sr Specialist-Mktg Automation - Synopsys, Inc.; *pg.* 480, *pg.* 162
Palang, Theresa, Mgr-PR & Digital Mktg - Yokohama Tire Corporation; *pg.* 1892, *pg.* 94
Palathinkara, Vinod, Mgr-Mktg-Installed Base & Margin - General Electric Company; *pg.* 1297, *pg.* 347
Palavalli, Naveen, Principal & Product Mgr - Symantec Corporation; *pg.* 478, *pg.* 161
Palazzolo, Jack, Dir-Global Advanced Product Mktg - Ford Motor Company of Canada, Limited; *pg.* 174, *pg.* 1930
Palazzolo, John, Sr VP-Sls - Clopay Building Products Company; *pg.* 76, *pg.* 1459
Palefsky, Elisa, VP-Sls-MJ Soffe LLC - Delta Apparel, Inc.; *pg.* 39, *pg.* 1617
Palekar, Rohan, Chief Comml Officer & Sr VP-Mktg & Sls - AVANIR Pharmaceuticals; *pg.* 1498, *pg.* 40
Palen, Irene, Sr Mgr-Mktg - Verizon Communications Inc.; *pg.* 1875, *pg.* 1309
Palen, Kris, Mgr-Mktg Comm-Sys - Johnson Controls, Inc.; *pg.* 209, *pg.* 1876
Palenbaum, Gary, Sr VP-Product Mgmt, Consumer Electronics & Gaming - SYNNEX Corporation; *pg.* 480, *pg.* 92
Palese, Greg, VP-Mktg - Klein Tools Inc.; *pg.* 1052, *pg.* 627
Paleski, Katrina, Sr Mgr-Mktg-Mtn Dew Brand Team - PepsiCo, Inc.; *pg.* 259, *pg.* 1327
Paletz, Stefanie D., Dir-Adv - The New York Times Company; *pg.* 1668, *pg.* 1270
Paley, Meredith, VP-PR - The Talbots, Inc.; *pg.* 34, *pg.* 824
Palin, Carrie, VP-Mktg-Cloud Data Svcs - IBM; *pg.* 410, *pg.* 1449
Palin, Drew, Sr Mgr-Mktg-Gatorade Technology & Equipment Innovation - PepsiCo, Inc.; *pg.* 259, *pg.* 1327
Palka, Monica, Rep-Inside Sls - World Wide Technology Holding Co., Inc.; *pg.* 493, *pg.* 988
Pallad, Mike, Sr VP-Natl & Network Sls - Cumulus Media Inc.; *pg.* 280, *pg.* 503
Palladino, Amy, Sr Dir-Corp Comm - Heineken USA Inc.; *pg.* 252, *pg.* 1352
Palladino, Anne, Specialist-Mktg - Siemens Corporation; *pg.* 803, *pg.* 1291
Palladino, Stacy, Product Dev Mgr-Children's wear - Toys "R" Us, Inc.; *pg.* 968, *pg.* 1130
Paller, Craig, VP-Worldwide Sls & Signal Processing & Sr Dir - Harman International Industries, Incorporated; *pg.* 641, *pg.* 374
Pallotta, Herbie, Mgr-Social Media - Caesars Entertainment Corporation; *pg.* 1083, *pg.* 1023
Pallotta, Jim, Strategist-Creative Mktg - ASM International; *pg.* 132, *pg.* 1461
Palludan, Nina, Sr Dir-IT - Tillamook County Creamery Association; *pg.* 901, *pg.* 1509
Palm, Greg, VP-Sls & Mktg - Mark Andy, Inc.; *pg.* 1359, *pg.* 975
Palm, Lisa, Mgr-Mktg, Media & Digital - McDonald's Corporation; *pg.* 1737, *pg.* 645
Palm, Stacey, Sr VP-Synchronization & Mktg - Music Sales Corporation; *pg.* 1666, *pg.* 1263
Palm, Stephen, Sr Dir-Technical - Broadcom Corporation; *pg.* 364, *pg.* 108
Palm, Vicki, Dir-Mktg - The Vernon Company; *pg.* 488, *pg.* 710
Palma, Al, Exec VP-Sls - Eby-Brown Co.; *pg.* 1767, *pg.* 636
Palma, Alexander, Mgr-Online Mktg - The Priceline Group Inc.; *pg.* 1276, *pg.* 364
Palma, Dawn, Sr Mgr-ECommerce Mktg - Staples, Inc.; *pg.* 474, *pg.* 821
Palmer, Andy, Dir-Product Mgmt - eBay Inc.; *pg.* 1240, *pg.* 243
Palmer, Ann, Program Mgr-Adv & New Media - American Honda Motor Co., Inc.; *pg.* 163, *pg.* 292
Palmer, Barbara M., Mgr-Mktg & Sls IM Engagement - Xerox Corporation; *pg.* 494, *pg.* 365
Palmer, Brenda, Product Mgr-Digital - FIRST NIAGARA FINANCIAL GROUP, INC.; *pg.* 757, *pg.* 1148
Palmer, Carolyn, Sr VP-Mktg-Global - Kelly Services, Inc.; *pg.* 424, *pg.* 911
Palmer, Catherine, Sr Mgr-Thought Leadership Mktg - Autodesk Inc.; *pg.* 356, *pg.* 257
Palmer, Danielle, Brand Mgr-Brand Comm - Chobani LLC; *pg.* 847, *pg.* 1318
Palmer, Dave, Sr Product Mgr-Implements - Kubota Tractor Corporation; *pg.* 705, *pg.* 294
Palmer, Jackson, Mgr-Product Mktg - Adobe Systems Incorporated; *pg.* 342, *pg.* 235
Palmer, Jason, Mgr-Mktg-Epson America - Epson America Inc.; *pg.* 394, *pg.* 122
Palmer, Jeffrey, Mgr-Sls & Mktg - IBM; *pg.* 410, *pg.* 1449
Palmer, Jennifer, Sr Dir-Natl Accounts-Target Corporation - Mohawk Home; *pg.* 935, *pg.* 541
Palmer, Jeremiah, Sr Mgr-Mktg - Mars Petcare; *pg.* 1478, *pg.* 1633
Palmer, John, Sr Product Mgr - Angie's List Inc; *pg.* 1228, *pg.* 682
Palmer, Judy, Sr Dir-Mktg Comm - The Stop & Shop Supermarket Company LLC; *pg.* 1034, *pg.* 842
Palmer, Kevin, Mgr-Retail Sls-Natl - Ocean Beauty Seafoods, Inc.; *pg.* 1028, *pg.* 1838
Palmer, Laura, Sr VP-Distributor Mktg - Showtime Networks Inc.; *pg.* 308, *pg.* 1291
Palmer, Maria, Brand Mgr - Starbucks Corporation; *pg.* 897, *pg.* 1840
Palmer, Michelle, Sr Mgr-Brand Comm-Global - Reebok International Ltd.; *pg.* 1817, *pg.* 811
Palmer, Rich, VP-Sls - CLARCOR, Inc.; *pg.* 1455, *pg.* 1632
Palmer, Richard W., Jr., Mgr-Pre Sls Sys Engrg - Juniper Networks, Inc.; *pg.* 1260, *pg.* 286
Palmer, Sarah, VP-Mktg-Attraction & Head-Generation - Adecco USA, Inc.; *pg.* 342, *pg.* 1178
Palmer, Tracy, Dir-Adv - Sprint Corporation; *pg.* 1874, *pg.* 719
Palmersheim, Richard, Grp VP-Mktg - Broan-NuTone LLC; *pg.* 1069, *pg.* 1860
Palmet, Darren, Dir-Mktg-Eye, Ear & Skin - Prestige Brands Holdings, Inc.; *pg.* 520, *pg.* 1345
Palmieri, Anita, Mgr-Mktg Intelligence & Comm - FMC Corporation; *pg.* 1163, *pg.* 1564
Palmieri, Frank, Mgr-Search Creative Dev - Yahoo! Inc.; *pg.* 1289, *pg.* 289
Palmieri-Zannella, Karin, Sr Mgr-Consumer Mktg & Promos - Keurig Green Mountain, Inc.; *pg.* 868, *pg.* 1768
Palmquist, Melissa, Assoc Mgr-Mktg - W.W. Grainger, Inc.; *pg.* 1390, *pg.* 625
Palombini, Marina, Dir-Global Mktg-Diversified Brands - Pfizer Inc.; *pg.* 1581, *pg.* 1278
Palombo, Domenico, Engr-Technical Mktg - Cisco Systems, Inc.; *pg.* 372, *pg.* 240
Palonsky, Paul, VP-Sls - Hynix Semiconductor America Inc.; *pg.* 409, *pg.* 246
Palopoli, Bina, Sr Mgr-Partner Mktg - Hotels.com, L.P.; *pg.* 1257, *pg.* 1682
Palozzi, Gino A., Sr Mgr - IBM; *pg.* 410, *pg.* 1449
Palsrok, Emily Gerkin, Mng Dir-PR - The Michigan Economic Development Corporation, Tourism & Marketing; *pg.* 999, *pg.* 895
Palter, Kimberly, Mgr Mktg - Detroit Red Wings, Inc.; *pg.* 544, *pg.* 880
Paluck, Anne, Dir-Mktg & Menu Innovation - McDonald's Corporation; *pg.* 1737, *pg.* 645
Paluso, Anne, Mgr-Mktg Comm-Construction-North America - CNH America LLC; *pg.* 702, *pg.* 560
Pamon, Steve, Head-Sports & Entertainment Mktg - JPMorgan Chase & Co.; *pg.* 772, *pg.* 1246
Pampati, Ashwin, Strategist-Mktg - Spotify; *pg.* 1282, *pg.* 1295
Pan, Alan, Sr Dir-Product Mgmt - Synchronoss Technologies, Inc.; *pg.* 479, *pg.* 1047
Pan, David, Product Mgr-Enhanced Mktg Svcs - Amazon.com, Inc.; *pg.* 1226, *pg.* 1831
Pan, Pattie, VP & Sr Head-Bus & Mktg-Global - MasterCard Incorporated; *pg.* 779, *pg.* 1325
Panagiotoulias, Theo, Sr VP-Global Sls & Alliances - Hawaiian Airlines, Inc.; *pg.* 1910, *pg.* 543
Panagrossi, Brenda Scariot, Sr Dir-Digital Distr - Ubisoft Inc.; *pg.* 589, *pg.* 229
Panara, David, Dir-Adv-US & Intl Sls - Information Today Inc.; *pg.* 1653, *pg.* 1084
Panaro, Ann, Mgr-Event Mktg - Lenovo Group Ltd; *pg.* 427, *pg.* 1384
Panasewicz, Stan, Sr Dir-IR - Johnson & Johnson; *pg.* 1549, *pg.* 1091
Panat, Julu, VP & Product Mgr-Digital - JPMorgan Chase & Co.; *pg.* 772, *pg.* 1246
Panattoni, Dan, Dir-Digital Mktg & eCommerce Strategy - Anixter International Inc.; *pg.* 1313, *pg.* 614
Panay, Panos, Product Mgr-Surface - Microsoft Corporation; *pg.* 435, *pg.* 1824
Panchak, Tom, Head-Bus-Digital Mktg & Patient Comm - Intuitive Surgical, Inc.; *pg.* 1546, *pg.* 286
Panchapakesan, Chithra P., Sr Mgr-Product Dev-Global - Mars, Incorporated; *pg.* 1858, *pg.* 1792
Panchot, Bernie, VP-Product Dev - AdvancePierre Foods, Inc.; *pg.* 1714, *pg.* 1409
Panczak, Carl, Head-Products-Fjord - Accenture; *pg.* 1392, *pg.* 1186
Pandey, Deepika, Grp VP-Customer Experience, Direct & Digital Mktg - Walgreen Co.; *pg.* 1608, *pg.* 605
Pandey, Gunjan, Gen Mgr-Mktg - McCain Foods Limited; *pg.* 876, *pg.* 1915
Pandiscia, Dana, Project Mgr-Mktg Ops - The Dun & Bradstreet Corp.; *pg.* 1637, *pg.* 1120
Pando, Anne, Assoc Mgr-Mktg-Coors Banquet - MillerCoors LLC; *pg.* 255, *pg.* 582
Pandolfo, Rebecca, Dir-Mktg - The Hartford Financial Services Group, Inc.; *pg.* 1202, *pg.* 352
Pandya, Bhavesh, Dir-Mktg Analytics & Insights - TD Ameritrade Holding Corporation; *pg.* 808, *pg.* 1018
Pandya, Liz, Brand Mgr - Johnson & Johnson; *pg.* 1549, *pg.* 1091
Panek, David, VP-Product Mktg - Teradata Corporation; *pg.* 483, *pg.* 1447
Panek, John, Mgr-Channel Mktg-Americas - Zebra Technologies Corporation; *pg.* 690, *pg.* 628
Panepinto, Cheryl M., Specialist-Events Mktg - Avid Technology, Inc.; *pg.* 622, *pg.* 804
Panetta, Jim, Dir-Premium Sls & Svc - Anaheim Ducks Hockey Club, LLC; *pg.* 528, *pg.* 42
Panfil, Claudia, VP-Adv, Brand & Media - Norwegian Cruise Line; *pg.* 1917, *pg.* 444
Panfil, Derek, Sr VP-Mdsg - Pet Supplies Plus; *pg.* 1781, *pg.* 897

Panfilio, Christa, Mgr-Global Brand Mktg-Media Content - NIKE, Inc.; pg. 1812, pg. 1492
Pang, Joyce, Mgr-Sls Plng - Canon U.S.A., Inc.; pg. 1404, pg. 1178
Pang, Roger, VP-Sls & Mktg - Westinghouse Solar; pg. 688, pg. 58
Pang, Tiffany, Sr Mgr-Partnership Mktg & Strategy - American Express Company; pg. 712, pg. 1190
Panganiban, Susan, VP & Program Mgr-Mktg-Sls Effectiveness - Wells Fargo & Company; pg. 819, pg. 232
Panico, Susan, VP-Sls Mktg - Pandora Media Inc.; pg. 1273, pg. 172
Panik, Laura, Sr Mgr-Mktg - WebMD Health Corporation; pg. 1288, pg. 1313
Panizza, Florencia, Head-Mktg & Comm - MARKETAXESS HOLDINGS INC.; pg. 778, pg. 1256
Panjwani, Javed, Head-Practice & Sr Dir-Cloud ERP - Cognizant Technology Solutions Corporation; pg. 377, pg. 1124
Pankhania, Brittany, Dir-Mktg - The Cartoon Network; pg. 273, pg. 492
Pankowski, Steve, Sr Mgr-Ticket Sls - San Diego Chargers Football Co.; pg. 580, pg. 208
Pankratz, Michael, Mgr-Mktg - Comcast Cable Communications, Inc.; pg. 276, pg. 1560
Pannell, Marcellus, VP-Digital Mktg - Bank of America Corporation; pg. 718, pg. 1362
Pannell, Marvin, Dir-Digital Mktg - New York Life Insurance Company; pg. 1211, pg. 1268
Pannozzo, Vincent, Mgr-Social Media - Miami Dolphins, Ltd.; pg. 562, pg. 419
Pannu, Ajitpal, Chief Strategy Officer - Smaato Inc.; pg. 1281, pg. 228
Panoncialman, Mark, Mgr-Digital Mktg - American Honda Motor Co., Inc.; pg. 163, pg. 292
Panora, Robert, Acting Dir-Ops - AMERICAN DG ENERGY INC.; pg. 1068, pg. 850
Panos, Andy, VP-Field Sls-US - G&K Services Inc.; pg. 693, pg. 949
Pansini, Anna, Mgr-Mktg Comm - Bogen Communications International Inc.; pg. 625, pg. 1113
Pansini, Jessica, Sr Mgr-Internal Comm - Novartis Pharmaceuticals Corp.; pg. 1575, pg. 1054
Pantani, Chris, Dir-Mktg-UHP Mktg, Event Mgmt, Sponsorships & Motorsports - Cooper Tire & Rubber Company; pg. 1881, pg. 1453
Pantel, Lori, VP-Mktg-US - Mattel Games/Puzzles; pg. 962, pg. 80
Pantel, Lori, VP-Mktg-US - MATTEL, INC.; pg. 962, pg. 81
Pantin, Christina, VP-PR - Samsung Telecommunications America, LLC; pg. 670, pg. 1736
Pantoja, Michael, Dir-Creative - The Nielsen Company B.V.; pg. 1671, pg. 1272
Panyik-Dale, Denise, Dir-Sls Media Rels-Global - Alcatel-Lucent USA, Inc.; pg. 615, pg. 1728
Panza, Paul, Dir-Mktg - DOLE FOOD COMPANY, INC.; pg. 853, pg. 306
Panzera, Andrea, Coord-Sls - Olympus America Inc.; pg. 1425, pg. 1521
Panziera, David C., Mgr-Segment Mktg - Intel Corporation; pg. 645, pg. 266
Paola, Alessandra, Specialist-eBusiness-Mktg Comm - Ford Motor Company of Canada, Limited; pg. 174, pg. 1930
Paola, Mike, Sr Dir-Product Mktg - SAP; pg. 465, pg. 78
Paolercio, Anthony, Jr., VP-Sls-HSN - Michael Anthony Jewelers, Inc.; pg. 10, pg. 1183
Paoli, Arina, Mgr-Mktg-Global - 3M Company; pg. 1142, pg. 956
Paolin, John P., Sr VP-Mktg & Corp Comm - Hill International Inc.; pg. 87, pg. 1083
Paolini, Amy Summers, Mgr-Digital Media & Comm - DOLE FOOD COMPANY, INC.; pg. 853, pg. 306
Paolini, Ben, Coord-Adv & Promos - Sovran Self Storage, Inc.; pg. 472, pg. 1355
Paolino, Leah, Mgr-Integrated Mktg-Men's Health - Rodale, Inc.; pg. 1681, pg. 1530
Paolino, Michelle, Dir-Mktg-Girls - Hasbro, Inc.; pg. 954, pg. 1603
Papacek, Kevin, Dir-Mktg-Jack Links - Link Snacks, Inc.; pg. 874, pg. 1881
Papachristou, Nicholas, Dir-Digital Mktg & Customer Insight - BBVA Compass Bank; pg. 723, pg. 2
Papadakis, James, Brand Mgr-Icelandic Seafood - High Liner Foods (USA) Incorporated; pg. 862, pg. 816
Papadakis, Jim, Brand Mgr - High Liner Foods; pg. 862, pg. 1796
Papadonta, Popi, Mgr-Mktg-Seasons & Plng - Staples, Inc.; pg. 474, pg. 821
Papageorgiou, Lisa, Dir-Enterprise Mktg-Comcast Bus Svcs - Comcast Corporation; pg. 276, pg. 1560
Papandreou, Jennifer, Dir-Mktg Innovation Centre - Johnson & Johnson Inc.; pg. 1552, pg. 1923
Paparello, John, VP & Mgr-Adv - Sandy Spring Bancorp, Inc.; pg. 801, pg. 774
Papazian, Kirk, Div VP-Sls-Western Div - Kumho Tire USA, Inc.; pg. 182, pg. 187
Papazian, Ruth, CMO & Head-Bus Dev - H.D. Vest, Inc.; pg. 765, pg. 1720
Pape, Jamie, Sr Coord-Mktg - SRS Real Estate Partners; pg. 1113, pg. 1687
Pape, Robert J., Sr VP-Sls - J&J Snack Foods Corporation; pg. 865, pg. 1107
Papile, Yesenia, Mgr-Retail Mktg - Brookfield Financial Properties, Inc.; pg. 1083, pg. 1207
Papile, Yesenia, Mgr-Mktg-Burberry Beauty - Shiseido Cosmetics America of SAC; pg. 522, pg. 1291
Papp, Istvan, VP-Sls, Mktg & Svcs-APAC - Microsoft Corporation; pg. 435, pg. 1824
Pappas, Christos N, Dir-Mktg Innovation - UBS Financial Services Inc.; pg. 812, pg. 1306
Pappas, Jamie, Dir-Global Brand Comm & Social Media Mktg - Akamai Technologies, Inc.; pg. 1226, pg. 807
Pappas, Jim, Dir-Mktg - Intel Corporation; pg. 645, pg. 266
Pappas, Linda, VP-Mktg - AECOM; pg. 64, pg. 173
Pappas, Lisa, Sr Mgr-Reg Mktg - Tommy Hilfiger USA; pg. 48, pg. 1302
Pappas, Philo, Exec VP-Mdsg - Michaels Stores, Inc.; pg. 1127, pg. 1722
Pappathopoulos, Nick, Dir-PR & Corp Comm - Cardtronics, Inc.; pg. 732, pg. 1703
Pappenheimer, Andrea, Assoc Publr, Sr VP & Dir-Sls - HarperCollins Publishers Inc.; pg. 1647, pg. 1237
Pappion, Melissa, Mgr-Online Mktg - Spanx Inc.; pg. 32, pg. 520
Paquay, Christine, Product Mgr-Global - Kronos Incorporated; pg. 425, pg. 813
Paquet, Jacqueline, Mgr-Retail Digital Mktg - Boscov's Department Store, LLC; pg. 1763, pg. 1583
Paquette, Alexandra, Brand Mgr - H.J. Heinz Co. of Canada Ltd.; pg. 863, pg. 1929
Paquette, Ken, Sr Analyst-Bus, Digital Mktg & ECommerce - Anixter International Inc.; pg. 1313, pg. 614
Paquette-Nelson, Lisa, Sr Dir-Fin-Brocade Capital Solutions - Brocade Communications Systems, Inc.; pg. 365, pg. 239
Paraan, Catherine, Sr Mgr-Loyalty & Direct Mktg - Wyndham Worldwide Corporation; pg. 1119, pg. 1107
Paradise, Jerry, Exec Dir-Product Mktg & Product Ops - Lenovo Group Ltd; pg. 427, pg. 1384
Paradise, Scott E., VP-Mktg & Bus Dev-The America - Magna International Inc.; pg. 211, pg. 1918
Parady, Elizabeth, Mgr-Retail Sls Plng - Energizer Holdings, Inc.; pg. 637, pg. 996
Paragas, Betsye, Dir-Mktg & PR - Omaha Community Playhouse; pg. 572, pg. 1017
Paragas, Betsye, Dir-Dev & Mktg - Opera Omaha Inc.; pg. 572, pg. 1017
Parah, Amanda, Dir-Studio & Mktg - KB Home; pg. 90, pg. 134
Parameswaran, Ananth, Dir-Product Plng & Strategy - ZF TRW; pg. 222, pg. 897
Paranjpe, Kiran, Head-Partner Bus Solutions-Social News & Comm - Google Inc.; pg. 1249, pg. 153
Pardi, Chris, VP-Mktg - Fisher-Price, Inc.; pg. 953, pg. 1156
Pardinas, Maritza, Sr Mgr-Brand Dev - Univision Communications Inc.; pg. 683, pg. 1307
Pardini, Jaclyn, Mgr-PR - Lowe's Companies, Inc.; pg. 1053, pg. 1383
Pardo, Janet, Sr VP-Product Dev - Clinique Laboratories LLC; pg. 503, pg. 1214
Pardo, Patrick, Sr Dir-Design-Handbags, Travel & Accessories - Coach, Inc.; pg. 3, pg. 1214
Parducci, Anne, Exec VP-Mktg & Gen Mgr-Family Entertainment - Lions Gate Entertainment Corp.; pg. 296, pg. 274
Pardue, David, VP-Bus Dev & Soft Products - Volvo Trucks North America, Inc.; pg. 195, pg. 1377
Pare, Brian, Dir-Mktg - Pepsi Beverages Company; pg. 258, pg. 1342
Pare, Charles, VP-Sls & Mktg - Rousseau Metal, Inc.; pg. 463, pg. 1960
Pare, David, VP, Dir-Circulation & Mgr-Mktg - The Record-Journal Publishing Company; pg. 1680, pg. 354
Pare, Dee, Sr Mgr-Solutions Mktg-IoT & Enterprise Networks - Cisco Systems, Inc.; pg. 372, pg. 240
Pare, Paul F., Dir-Mktg - Jacobs Vehicle Systems; pg. 1351, pg. 338
Parekh, Amrish, Product Mgr-Mobile - NBC Universal, Inc.; pg. 300, pg. 1266
Parekh, Bhaumik, Sr Mgr - Accenture; pg. 1392, pg. 1186
Parekh, Pranav, Product Mgr-VMware Practice - RACKSPACE HOSTING, INC.; pg. 1277, pg. 1742
Parent, Brett, Sr Dir-eCommerce - Wolverine World Wide, Inc.; pg. 1822, pg. 905
Parent, Elizabeth, Strategist-Social Media - Capital One Financial Corporation; pg. 730, pg. 1789
Parent, Jeannie, Sr VP-Sls - Digital First Media; pg. 1238, pg. 1224
Parent, Joyce, Sr Mgr-Mktg-Hematology - IDEXX Laboratories, Inc.; pg. 1543, pg. 753
Parent, Libby, Product Mgr-Global Innovation - Keurig Green Mountain, Inc.; pg. 868, pg. 1768
Parente, Christina, Dir-Direct Mktg - Carter's, Inc.; pg. 21, pg. 491
Parente, Marco, Dir-Product Mgmt - The Nielsen Company B.V.; pg. 1671, pg. 1272
Parenty, Pat, Pres-L'Oreal Professional Products Div - L'Oreal USA; pg. 514, pg. 1252
Paretzkin, Jonas, Dir-PR & Social Media - ConAgra Foods, Inc.; pg. 826, pg. 1014
Pargas, Savannah, Specialist-Mktg - Darigold, Inc.; pg. 852, pg. 1835
Parham, Ron, Sr Dir-IR & Corp Comm - Columbia Sportswear Company; pg. 1830, pg. 1501
Parido, Scott, Sr VP-US Retail Sls - FIJI Water; pg. 251, pg. 130
Parikh, Nicki, Mgr-Partnership Mktg - United States Olympic Committee; pg. 589, pg. 315
Parikh, Stootee, Mgr-Mktg - SHUTTERFLY, INC.; pg. 1280, pg. 192
Parimi, Satyanarayana, Grp VP-Product Mgmt - Time Warner Cable Inc.; pg. 312, pg. 1301
Paris, Chris, Mng Dir-Europe & VP-Sls-Worldwide - AWR Corporation; pg. 623, pg. 78
Paris, Craig, Sr Mgr-North America Enterprise Sls Solutions-Fin Svcs - LinkedIn Corporation; pg. 1262, pg. 160
Paris, Tim, Acct Mgr-Creative Svcs - DIRECTV Group Holdings, LLC; pg. 281, pg. 79
Parish, Jann, VP-Mktg-The Americas - Calvin Klein, Inc.; pg. 20, pg. 1209
Parisi, Ashley, Brand Mgr - Newell Rubbermaid Inc.; pg. 1128, pg. 515
Parisi, Bobbie, VP-Mktg-Leatherman - Leatherman Tool Group, Inc.; pg. 1053, pg. 1504
Parisi, Clare, Project Mgr-Mktg - IMS Health, Inc.; pg. 1544, pg. 344
Parisi, Dawn, Dir-Sls & Mktg-Westin St John Resort & Villas - Westin Hotels & Resorts; pg. 1118, pg. 379
Parisi, Dawn, VP-Field Sls - Wyndham Vacation Ownership; pg. 1119, pg. 457
Parisi, Justin, Engr-Technical Mktg-NFS - NetApp, Inc.; pg. 444, pg. 287
Parisi, Lauren, Asst Mgr-Online Mktg & Media - Ann Inc.; pg. 18, pg. 1195
Parizman, Chad, Dir-Convergent Media - Scripps Networks Interactive, Inc.; pg. 1279, pg. 1638
Park, Cherry, Sr Dir-Mktg - QUALCOMM Incorporated; pg. 1873, pg. 207
Park, Crystal, Sr Dir-Mktg - AOL Inc.; pg. 1229, pg. 1195
Park, Dan D., Head-Product Mgmt-Amazon Bus - Amazon.com, Inc.; pg. 1226, pg. 1831
Park, Daniel, Sr Mgr-Product Mktg-Microsoft Store Online - Microsoft Corporation; pg. 435, pg. 1824
Park, Ellise, VP-Digital Mktg-Bloomingdale - Bloomingdale's, Inc.; pg. 1763, pg. 1204
Park, Eugene, Brand Dir-Inlyta US Mktg - Pfizer Inc.; pg. 1581, pg. 1278
Park, Heather, Sr Dir-Portfolio Mktg - Genzyme Corporation; pg. 1534, pg. 808
Park, James, VP-Mktg - Which Wich, Inc.; pg. 1756, pg. 1690
Park, Jay, Asst Mgr-Interactive Mktg - Hyundai Motor America; pg. 179, pg. 89
Park, Jene, Sr Mgr-Personal Savings & Digital Mktg - American Express Company; pg. 712, pg. 1190
Park, Jim, VP-Sls - Hardwick Clothes Inc.; pg. 42, pg. 1630
Park, Joelle Heise, Dir-Brand Mktg-DoubleTree & Embassy

Suites by Hilton Hotels - Hilton Worldwide, Inc.; *pg.* 1094, *pg.* 1791
Park, Jung, VP-Adv Products & Ops - TEN: The Enthusiast Network; *pg.* 1691, *pg.* 1298
Park, Karen, Sr Mgr-Mktg-Internet Banking-Intuit Fin Svcs - Intuit Inc.; *pg.* 769, *pg.* 158
Park, Linda, Sr Mgr-Product Mktg & Data Loss Prevention - Symantec Corporation; *pg.* 478, *pg.* 161
Park, Meridyth, Sr VP-Mktg Strategy & Plng - Bank of America Global Wealth & Investment Management; *pg.* 720, *pg.* 789
Park, Paige, Acct Exec-Grp Sls - Saint Louis Cardinals, L.P.; *pg.* 580, *pg.* 1002
Park, Pamela, Mgr-Adv & Media - Toyota Motor Sales, U.S.A., Inc.; *pg.* 193, *pg.* 296
Park, Richard, Mgr-Product Line Trng Dev - Deere & Company; *pg.* 703, *pg.* 632
Park, Stacia, Brand Mgr - NBTY, Inc.; *pg.* 1572, *pg.* 1338
Park, Susi, Gen Mgr-Adv GQ - Conde Nast Publications, Inc.; *pg.* 1629, *pg.* 1217
Park, Susi, Gen Mgr-Adv-GQ - Vogue Magazine; *pg.* 1700, *pg.* 1311
Park, Tenny, Dir-Adv & Brand Mktg - Red Bull North America, Inc.; *pg.* 264, *pg.* 275
Parke, Bill, Dir-Corp Mktg & Fin Comm - CME Group Inc.; *pg.* 738, *pg.* 571
Parke, Bill, Dir-Corp Mktg & Fin Comm - CME Group, Inc.; *pg.* 738, *pg.* 571
Parke, Julie, Mgr-Product Mktg - comScore, Inc; *pg.* 1236, *pg.* 1798
Parker, Adrian, VP-Digital Mktg - The Patron Spirits Company; *pg.* 1967, *pg.* 1029
Parker, Allan, Specialist-Mktg & Comm-Military & Govt - Zoll Medical Corporation; *pg.* 1612, *pg.* 814
Parker, Barry, Sr VP-Mktg & Comml Svcs - Symmetry Medical Inc.; *pg.* 1600, *pg.* 699
Parker, Candace, Mgr-Mktg - Outfront Media; *pg.* 1465, *pg.* 1275
Parker, Carey, VP & Mgr-Online Adv - Wells Fargo & Company; *pg.* 819, *pg.* 232
Parker, Charma, Coord-ECommerce Mktg-Search - Carter's, Inc.; *pg.* 21, *pg.* 491
Parker, Chris, CMO, Chief Sls Officer & Exec VP - Nashville Predators, LLC; *pg.* 565, *pg.* 1652
Parker, Dan, VP-Strategic Sls Comm - CVS Health Corporation; *pg.* 1765, *pg.* 1610
Parker, Dana, VP-Mdsg - VF Imagewear; *pg.* 50, *pg.* 476
Parker, Dave, VP-Sls & Mktg - M/I Homes, Inc.; *pg.* 95, *pg.* 1441
Parker, Don, Sr Product Mgr - Autodesk Inc.; *pg.* 356, *pg.* 257
Parker, Doug, Partner-Mktg & VP-Global - Intel Corporation; *pg.* 645, *pg.* 266
Parker, Duane, VP-Sls & Mktg - Martin Universal Design, Inc.; *pg.* 430, *pg.* 884
Parker, Erich, Dir-Corp Comm & Creative - E.I. du Pont de Nemours & Company; *pg.* 1159, *pg.* 390
Parker, George, Mgr-Natl Sls-Oral-B & Glide Brands - The Procter & Gamble Company; *pg.* 1129, *pg.* 1418
Parker, Jason, Mgr-Sponsorships & Cause Mktg - Nautica Apparel, Inc.; *pg.* 45, *pg.* 1265
Parker, Jessica, Mgr-Sports Mktg Special Ops - Under Armour, Inc.; *pg.* 49, *pg.* 759
Parker, Jim, Sr Mgr - Cognizant Technology Solutions Corporation; *pg.* 377, *pg.* 1124
Parker, Jim, Dir-Sls-Western Reg - Method Products Inc.; *pg.* 332, *pg.* 223
Parker, Jim, VP-Sls-Intl - Pierce Manufacturing, Inc.; *pg.* 188, *pg.* 1852
Parker, Joann, VP-Mktg Retail Appliances - Helen of Troy L.P.; *pg.* 511, *pg.* 1692
Parker, John S., Mgr-Technical Mktg - NetApp, Inc.; *pg.* 444, *pg.* 287
Parker, Jonah, Dir-SWAT & District Mgr-Market-Sls - The Scotts Miracle-Gro Company; *pg.* 1799, *pg.* 1459
Parker, Kathy, VP-Mktg & Innovation - Just Born, Inc.; *pg.* 1857, *pg.* 1516
Parker, Kiesha, Program Mgr-Mktg - Wells Fargo & Company; *pg.* 819, *pg.* 232
Parker, Mark, Reg Mgr-Sls - Weber Packaging Solutions, Inc.; *pg.* 491, *pg.* 554
Parker, Michael, VP-Mktg & Customer Svc-SAIA Motor Freight Lines - Saia, Inc.; *pg.* 1922, *pg.* 533
Parker, Mike, VP-Sls-Global - Fellowes, Inc.; *pg.* 397, *pg.* 620
Parker, Miriam, Deputy Dir-Mktg - Little, Brown & Company; *pg.* 1660, *pg.* 1251
Parker, Nathaniel, Mgr-Mktg Alliance - Gartner, Inc.; *pg.* 1248, *pg.* 374
Parker, P., Mgr-Sls-Replacement Parts & Svc - C.I. Hayes; *pg.* 1070, *pg.* 1600
Parker, Paul, Sr Mgr-Mktg-Cattle - Pfizer Inc.; *pg.* 1581, *pg.* 1278
Parker, Peter, Mgr-Retail Adv - Woodcraft Supply Corp.; *pg.* 1390, *pg.* 1850
Parker, Regan, Assoc Mgr-Mktg-Brand Loyalty - Williams-Sonoma, Inc.; *pg.* 1140, *pg.* 234
Parker, Richard, Mgr-Div Sls - Telescope Casual Furniture Inc.; *pg.* 944, *pg.* 1162
Parker, Sarah, Exec Dir-Mktg Ops - CME Group Inc.; *pg.* 738, *pg.* 571
Parker, Sarah, Exec Dir-Mktg Ops - CME Group, Inc.; *pg.* 738, *pg.* 571
Parker, Scott, VP-Sports & Brand Mktg - ESPN, Inc.; *pg.* 285, *pg.* 340
Parker, Steven, Co-Publr & Bus Mgr - New Jersey Hills Media Group; *pg.* 1667, *pg.* 1044
Parker, Tivoli, Mgr-Retail Brand Mktg - NIKE, Inc.; *pg.* 1812, *pg.* 1492
Parker, Tom, Sr VP-Global Products-Reston - Kroll Inc.; *pg.* 425, *pg.* 1249
Parker, Toni, Mgr-Mktg Comm - SPX Corporation; *pg.* 218, *pg.* 1369
Parkes, Jacqueline, CMO - Major League Baseball; *pg.* 560, *pg.* 1255
Parkes, Oliver, Dir-Mktg-Consumer Healthcare - GlaxoSmithKline; *pg.* 1536, *pg.* 1565
Parkes, Susan, Sr VP-Mktg & Strategy - People Magazine; *pg.* 1676, *pg.* 1278
Parkes-Cirignano, Susan, Sr VP-Mktg & Strategy - Time Inc.; *pg.* 1693, *pg.* 1300
Parkhill, Clayton, Mgr-Mktg - The Libman Company; *pg.* 331, *pg.* 553
Parkins, Steve, Dir-Bus Dev & Partner Rels & Gen Sls Mgr - AutoNation, Inc.; *pg.* 165, *pg.* 423
Parkinson, Betsy, Dir-Creative-Accessories, Intimate Apparel & Home - Dillard's, Inc.; *pg.* 1766, *pg.* 34
Parkinson, Elizabeth, Sr VP-Mktg & Partnerships - The Detroit Lions, Inc.; *pg.* 544, *pg.* 864
Parks, Alison, Exec VP-Mktg & Gen Mgr - Worth; *pg.* 1702, *pg.* 1315
Parks, Elena, Brand Mgr - Eggland's Best, Inc.; *pg.* 854, *pg.* 1542
Parks, Ian, Sr Product Mgr-Consumer Products - Adobe Systems Incorporated; *pg.* 342, *pg.* 235
Parks, Kim, Mgr-Adv - United States Postal Service; *pg.* 1009, *pg.* 406
Parks, Madeline, Coord-Mktg - Fluor Corporation; *pg.* 82, *pg.* 1719
Parks, Sandra, Sr Dir-Mktg Ops - Comcast Corporation; *pg.* 276, *pg.* 1560
Parks, Sheila, Brand Mgr-Novartis Animal Health - Novartis Corporation; *pg.* 1574, *pg.* 1273
Parks, Susan, Product Mgr-GeoPro - Intermap Technologies Corporation; *pg.* 417, *pg.* 1903
Parks, Whitney, Mgr-Global CTC Mktg Plng - Reebok International Ltd.; *pg.* 1817, *pg.* 811
Parlato, Jason, Sr Mgr-Intl Promo Bus Dev, Calvin Klein Fragrances & ck one color - Coty, Inc.; *pg.* 506, *pg.* 1219
Parlatore, Elena, Head-Quaker Digital & Social - PepsiCo, Inc.; *pg.* 259, *pg.* 1327
Parlett, Kris, Sr Mgr-Comm - The Procter & Gamble Company; *pg.* 1129, *pg.* 1418
Parma, Andy, Mgr-Product Mktg & Server & Workstation Div - Advanced Micro Devices, Inc.; *pg.* 613, *pg.* 282
Parmelee, Lisa, Dir-Sls Ops & Bus Plng-PRO - The Timberland Company; *pg.* 1821, *pg.* 1039
Parmenter, Madeline, Specialist-Comm & Media Rels - Johnson & Wales University; *pg.* 603, *pg.* 1606
Parmentier, Amber, VP-Global Sponsorships & Event Mktg - Citigroup Inc.; *pg.* 735, *pg.* 1212
Parmentier, Jenny, Pres-Engineered Matls Grp & VP - Parker Hannifin Corporation; *pg.* 1368, *pg.* 1434
Parmet, Marc, Sr Dir-IT-F1 Global Transformation - Avery Dennison Corporation; *pg.* 1452, *pg.* 95
Parmiter, Ian, Sr VP-Integrated Adv Sls Mktg - Discovery Communications, Inc.; *pg.* 282, *pg.* 777
Parnell, Chris, Sls Mgr-Consumer Electronics - Skullcandy, Inc.; *pg.* 674, *pg.* 1754
Parnell, Justin, Dir-Global Mktg-Savory Brands - Mondelez International; *pg.* 877, *pg.* 1344
Parnham, Kyle, Mgr-Mktg Projects - ITT Educational Services, Inc.; *pg.* 603, *pg.* 675
Parobek, Patty, Sr Mgr-SEO - American Greetings Corporation; *pg.* 1615, *pg.* 1428
Parpart, Tom, Mgr-Global Product Mktg-MICT Accessories - General Electric Company; *pg.* 1297, *pg.* 347
Parr, Warren, Dir-Ticket Sls - Atlanta Falcons Football Club, LLC; *pg.* 530, *pg.* 532
Parra, Edwin, Sr Engr-Mktg & Sls - ABB Inc.; *pg.* 1309, *pg.* 1359
Parra, Hugo, Dir-Product Mgmt - Symantec Corporation; *pg.* 479, *pg.* 1753
Parra, Sandra, Dir-HR, Comml Intl & Global Mktg - Abbott Laboratories; *pg.* 1484, *pg.* 551
Parra, Shanna, Reg Mgr-Mktg - PepsiCo, Inc.; *pg.* 259, *pg.* 1327
Parran, John, Dir-Mktg-Automotive Refinish USCA - PPG Industries, Inc.; *pg.* 1445, *pg.* 1579
Parrent, Paige, Mgr-Digital Media - Volkswagen Group of America, Inc.; *pg.* 194, *pg.* 1785
Parrett, David, Sr Dir-Motorization - Hunter Douglas, Inc.; *pg.* 928, *pg.* 1320
Parretta, Matt, Analyst-PR & Indus Rels - Dell Inc.; *pg.* 383, *pg.* 1737
Parrilla, Michael, Mgr-Mktg Analytics - Bacardi USA, Inc.; *pg.* 1956, *pg.* 417
Parrillo, Lisa, Mgr-Media - Wynn Resorts Limited; *pg.* 1119, *pg.* 1030
Parris, Suzanne, Mgr-Mktg Database Decision Strategy-Infrastructure & Projects - Wells Fargo & Company; *pg.* 819, *pg.* 232
Parrish, Gloria, Dir-Intl Brand Mgmt-Nickelodeon Viacom Consumer Products - Viacom Inc.; *pg.* 316, *pg.* 1310
Parrish, Julie, Sr Mgr - Accenture; *pg.* 1392, *pg.* 1186
Parrish, Julie, CMO & Sr VP - NetApp, Inc.; *pg.* 444, *pg.* 287
Parrish, Kenda W., Sr Mgr-Mktg - MoneyGram International, Inc.; *pg.* 783, *pg.* 1684
Parrish, Kimber, Mgr-Comml & Industrial Mktg - Ingersoll-Rand Company; *pg.* 1349, *pg.* 1370
Parrish, Laura, Sr Mgr-Association Channel Sls - Constellation; *pg.* 1938, *pg.* 373
Parrish, Meredith, Principal & Officer-Northeast Corridor Adv & Promo - National Railroad Passenger Corporation; *pg.* 1916, *pg.* 403
Parrish, Robert, VP-Global Sls & Strategic Accts - SGS U.S. Testing Company Inc.; *pg.* 1181, *pg.* 1065
Parrish, Vanessa, Dir-Mktg & Comm - Singer Sewing Company; *pg.* 698, *pg.* 1639
Parrish, Vicki, Sr Mgr-Corp Global Events - Itron Inc.; *pg.* 422, *pg.* 1822
Parry, David P., Sr Dir-Comm & Events - Philips Electronics North America; *pg.* 662, *pg.* 782
Parry, Jamie, Mgr-Digital & Social Media - Chevron Corporation; *pg.* 974, *pg.* 259
Parry, Lee J., Sr Dir-Product Mgmt & Mobile Comm - Yahoo! Inc.; *pg.* 1289, *pg.* 289
Parshenov, Margaret, Mgr-Mktg Svcs - Diageo North America Inc.; *pg.* 248, *pg.* 1223
Parsons, Andrea, Dir-PR & Corp Comm - Blue Cross & Blue Shield Association; *pg.* 1195, *pg.* 566
Parsons, Annie, Sr Planner-Social Mktg Comm - General Mills, Inc.; *pg.* 828, *pg.* 933
Parsons, Brooks, Sr Dir-Ops - New York City Ballet; *pg.* 569, *pg.* 1268
Parsons, Cal, Product Mgr-Small Cells - Texas Instruments Incorporated; *pg.* 679, *pg.* 1688
Parsons, Gina, Media Buyer - BROOKDALE SENIOR LIVING INC.; *pg.* 1511, *pg.* 1627
Parsons, Greg, Sr VP & Dir-Creative-Global Work - Herman Miller, Inc.; *pg.* 926, *pg.* 913
Parsons, Jay, Sr VP-Media - VeriFone Systems, Inc.; *pg.* 487, *pg.* 251
Parsons, Julie, Sr VP-Vehicle Product Mgmt - The Allstate Corporation; *pg.* 1189, *pg.* 639
Parsons, Karen, Mgr-Mktg Comm-Global - Eastman Chemical Company; *pg.* 1159, *pg.* 1636
Parsons, Susan, Dir-Direct Mktg - Redbox Automated Retail, LLC; *pg.* 306, *pg.* 649
Parsonson, Greg, Partner & VP-product Mktg - Zones, Inc.; *pg.* 1292, *pg.* 1813
Partch, Rusty, Strategist-Social Media - Chipotle Mexican Grill, Inc.; *pg.* 1722, *pg.* 317
Partello, Wayne, CMO & Sr VP - Padres L.P.; *pg.* 573, *pg.* 206
Partenheimer, David, Mgr-Media Rels - United States Postal Service; *pg.* 1009, *pg.* 406

First page reference indicates Business Class Edition
Second page reference indicates Geographic Edition

Partipilo, Anthony, VP-Mktg & Mdsg - Toronto Blue Jays Baseball Club; pg. 588, pg. 1945
Partner, Jordan, Jr Mgr-Retail & Trade-Comml Mktg - Puma North America, Inc.; pg. 1816, pg. 858
Parton, Betsy, Brand Mgr-Global - MATTEL, INC.; pg. 962, pg. 81
Partridge, John, Sr Mgr-Storage Engrg-Platform OS - Dell Storage; pg. 386, pg. 922
Partridge, Patrick, CMO - Western Governors University; pg. 610, pg. 1762
Partridge, Paul, Dir-GRS Investments Mktg - Manulife Financial Corporation; pg. 778, pg. 1939
Partridge, Victoria M., Specialist-Mktg - FedEx Corporation; pg. 1907, pg. 1642
Parvaiz, Omar, Product Mgr-South Carolina & Tennessee-Progressive Insurance - The Progressive Corporation; pg. 1214, pg. 1463
Parvel, Andrew, Dir-Sls & Mktg - Jenkins Group, Inc.; pg. 1654, pg. 909
Parzych, Christopher, VP & Product Mgr-Digital Customer Experience - Citigroup Inc.; pg. 735, pg. 1212
Parzych, Dawn, Dir-Product & Sls Engrg - Arrow Electronics, Inc.; pg. 619, pg. 325
Pasay, Ashley, Sr Strategist-Digital Mktg - Highmark Blue Cross Blue Shield; pg. 1203, pg. 1576
Pascal, Amy, Sr Dir-North America Digital Mktg - Johnson & Johnson; pg. 1549, pg. 1091
Pascalar, Chuck, VP-Mktg - Payless Shoesource, Inc.; pg. 31, pg. 722
Pascaud, Raphael S., Chief Mktg Portfolio & Bus Dev Officer - Align Technology, Inc.; pg. 1489, pg. 237
Pascente, Donna, Supvr-Digital Mktg - The Pampered Chef; pg. 1129, pg. 552
Paschke, Chuck, Sr Dir-Organizational Health - Galderma Laboratories, L.P.; pg. 1532, pg. 1695
Pascual, Alfred, Sr Mgr-Bus Analytics - DIRECTV Group Holdings, LLC; pg. 281, pg. 79
Pascual, Brian, Dir-Mktg - LexisNexis Group; pg. 1658, pg. 1446
Pascucilla, Maureen A., Dir-Mktg & Sls Sourcing-Global Procurement & Ops - Pfizer Inc.; pg. 1581, pg. 1278
Pasculli, Jamie, Mgr-Integrated Mktg-O The Oprah Magazine - Hearst Magazines; pg. 1649, pg. 1239
Paseiro, Adonis, Bus Mgr-Local - BI-LO, LLC; pg. 1015, pg. 1617
Pasersky, Kristin, Mgr-Mktg & Corp Event - David's Bridal, Inc.; pg. 23, pg. 1523
Pasha, Ali, Product Mgr - Google Inc.; pg. 1249, pg. 153
Pashel, Megan, Assoc Mgr-Brand Mktg - MATTEL, INC.; pg. 962, pg. 81
Pashkevich, Lauren, Mgr-Sports Mktg Customer Svc - Under Armour, Inc.; pg. 49, pg. 759
Pasiakos, Jennifer, VP-Integrated Mktg Comm-Global - Maybelline LLC; pg. 516, pg. 1257
Pasika, Zorian, Product Mgr-Platform & Tools - Redbox Automated Retail, LLC; pg. 306, pg. 649
Pasinosky, Theresa, Sr Dir-Global Brand Mktg - Xoom Corporation; pg. 1289, pg. 234
Pask, John, Dir-Channel Mktg - NRG Energy, Inc.; pg. 1948, pg. 1712
Paska, Paul, Head-Mktg DACH - Puma North America, Inc.; pg. 1816, pg. 858
Paskalis, Lou, Sr VP-Enterprise Media Exec - Bank of America Corporation; pg. 718, pg. 1362
Pasmanik, Steve, VP-Sls Ops & Channel Mktg - AT&T Mobility LLC; pg. 619, pg. 488
Pasos, Michelle, Asst VP-Mktg & Head-Bus - Visa Inc.; pg. 816, pg. 230
Pasos, Michelle, Asst VP-Mktg & Head-Bus - Visa U.S.A., Inc.; pg. 817, pg. 231
Pasqua, Gina, Analyst-Digital Mktg & SEO - LivingSocial, Inc.; pg. 1264, pg. 401
Pasquale, Laura, VP-Mktg Comm - LOGMEIN, INC.; pg. 428, pg. 861
Pasquali, Sonia, Dir-Product Mgmt, US Content & Mobile Apps - BabyCenter, LLC; pg. 1231, pg. 212
Pasqualini, Rico, VP-Sls - JanSport; pg. 1837, pg. 38
Pasqualotti, Luca, Brand Mgr-Global - Newell Rubbermaid Inc.; pg. 1128, pg. 515
Pasqualucci, Dan, Sr Team Head-Reg Sls - GlaxoSmithKline; pg. 1536, pg. 1565
Pasquarette, John, VP-eBusiness & Mktg Ops - National Instruments Corporation; pg. 443, pg. 1664
Pasquet-Geairon, Isabelle, VP-Mktg - Van Houtte, Inc.; pg. 908, pg. 1957
Pasquier, Samuel, Dir-Product Mgmt - Cisco Systems, Inc.; pg. 372, pg. 240
Pass, David, VP-Metabolism Mktg - Boehringer Ingelheim Pharmaceuticals, Inc.; pg. 1507, pg. 368
Passantino, Jamie, Sr Mgr-Internal Corp Comm - Polycom, Inc.; pg. 664, pg. 249
Passe, Tom, Sr Product Mgr - Infor Lawson; pg. 414, pg. 961
Passerello, Cory, Product Mgr & Mgr-Bus Dev - Litecontrol Corporation; pg. 1301, pg. 841
Passios, Tim, VP-Solutions Mktg - Interactive Intelligence, Inc.; pg. 417, pg. 687
Passons, Tory, Sr Product Mgr-Travel Payment Solutions - U.S. Bancorp; pg. 815, pg. 945
Pasterick, Kelly, VP-Global Fin Processes-Global Primary Products - Alcoa Inc.; pg. 65, pg. 1188
Pasteris, German, Dir-Global Mktg-Diabetes - GlaxoSmithKline; pg. 1536, pg. 1389
Pasteris, German, Dir-Global Mktg-Diabetes - GlaxoSmithKline Consumer Healthcare; pg. 510, pg. 1554
Pasternack, Seth, Sr Mgr-Mktg - Robertet, Inc.; pg. 522, pg. 1100
Pasternak, David J., Dir-Mktg - Sony Corporation of America; pg. 675, pg. 1293
Pastor, Kate, Exec VP-Retail Sls - Twinlab Corporation; pg. 1603, pg. 1306
Pastor, Liz, VP-Product-CareerBuilder.com - CareerBuilder, LLC; pg. 1234, pg. 568
Pastore, Gregg, Sr Dir-Digital Media - Buffalo Bills, Inc.; pg. 535, pg. 1319
Pastore, Melissa, Mgr-PR - Swarovski North America Limited Inc.; pg. 13, pg. 1600
Pastore, Tim, Pres-Original Programming & Production - National Geographic Channel; pg. 299, pg. 402
Pastrana, George, VP-Mktg & Innovation - ACH Food Companies, Inc.; pg. 835, pg. 1631
Pastre, Katherine, VP-Media - The Advertising Council, Inc.; pg. 125, pg. 1187
Pastre, Moire, Mgr-Creative Studio - Yurman Design, Inc.; pg. 15, pg. 1316
Pasvogel, Brad, Product Mgr-Tillage - Deere & Company; pg. 703, pg. 632
Paszczykowski, Nathan, VP & Dir-Mktg-Cincinnati Affiliate - Fifth Third Bancorp; pg. 752, pg. 1413
Pasztor, Tom, Sr Dir-Corp & Govt Rels - Potash Corp.; pg. 1177, pg. 641
Pat, Eckerstrom, Exec VP-Mdsg - Crate & Barrel, Inc.; pg. 922, pg. 640
Patadia, Deepal, Mgr-PR-North America - Time Out New York; pg. 1694, pg. 1301
Patak, Stephen, VP-Sls-United States & Canada - Extreme Networks Inc; pg. 287, pg. 245
Pataky, Bill, VP-Product Mgmt - Oracle Corporation; pg. 450, pg. 191
Patalano, Ray, Dir-Bus Dev & Channel Sls - Alcatel-Lucent; pg. 615, pg. 1094
Patanella, Allyson, Mgr-PR - ChyronHego; pg. 371, pg. 1179
Patasnick, Melissa, Assoc Product Mgr - Church & Dwight Co., Inc.; pg. 1153, pg. 1063
Patchett, Jason, Sr Dir-IR - Canadian Imperial Bank of Commerce; pg. 729, pg. 1935
Patchin, Shelley, Dir-Adv - Anthem, Inc.; pg. 1192, pg. 683
Pate, Jack, Dir-Social Media - Tyson Foods, Inc.; pg. 902, pg. 35
Pate, Joanne, Sr Mgr-Adv-Global - American Express Company; pg. 712, pg. 1190
Pate, Stephen, Sr Dir-Community & Governmental Affairs - New Orleans Saints L.P.; pg. 569, pg. 745
Patel, Amit, Dir-Product Mgmt - DIRECTV Group Holdings, LLC; pg. 281, pg. 79
Patel, Ankan, Sr Counsel-Mktg & Sponsorships & VP - MasterCard Incorporated; pg. 779, pg. 1325
Patel, Ankit, Sr Product Mgr-VCA - NVIDIA Corporation; pg. 447, pg. 268
Patel, Ankusha, Sr Analyst-Fin-Trade Mktg - General Mills Canada Corp.; pg. 828, pg. 1926
Patel, Bhavesh S., Dir-Mktg - Emerson Network Power; pg. 1071, pg. 1479
Patel, Bina, Dir-Channel Sls - Asante Technologies, Inc.; pg. 619, pg. 238
Patel, Devanshi, Sr Assoc Brand Mgr - The Hershey Co.; pg. 1855, pg. 1538
Patel, Disha, Mgr-Mktg Comm-Siemens Industry, Inc. - Siemens Process Industries and Drive; pg. 1376, pg. 1587
Patel, Gayatri, Dir-Product Mgmt, Marketplace Analytics & Experimentation - eBay Inc.; pg. 1240, pg. 243
Patel, Hitesh, Product Mgr - Target Corporation; pg. 1786, pg. 942
Patel, Jabir, Sr Dir-BI, DW, Analytics & Big Data - CME Group Inc.; pg. 738, pg. 571
Patel, Jabir, Sr Dir-BI, DW, Analytics & Big Data - CME Group, Inc.; pg. 738, pg. 571
Patel, Jeetu, Chief Strategy Officer & Sr VP-Platform - Box Inc.; pg. 1232, pg. 124
Patel, Malini, Brand Mgr-Degree - Unilever United States, Inc.; pg. 904, pg. 1061
Patel, Mehul, Sr Mgr-Loyalty Strategy & Fin - United Airlines, Inc.; pg. 1927, pg. 593
Patel, Neela, Sr Specialist-Loyalty, Promos & Relationship Mktg - Choice Hotels International, Inc.; pg. 1086, pg. 775
Patel, Nehal, Dir-Mktg-Brookside & Platform Chocolates - The Hershey Co.; pg. 1855, pg. 1538
Patel, Nikul, Chief Product Officer - LendingTree, LLC; pg. 775, pg. 1367
Patel, Nilesh, VP-Product Mgmt & Mktg - Overland Storage, Inc.; pg. 451, pg. 205
Patel, Nivedita, Brand Mgr - Pinnacle Foods Group LLC; pg. 889, pg. 1104
Patel, Nupur, Sr Mgr-Medical Comm - NPS Pharmaceuticals, Inc.; pg. 1576, pg. 1043
Patel, Parag, VP-Worldwide Sls & Software-Defined Storage - VMware, Inc.; pg. 490, pg. 179
Patel, Parvez, VP-ECommerce-Mktg & Mdsg - W.W. Grainger, Inc.; pg. 1390, pg. 625
Patel, Payal, Product Mgr-Crisis - Google Inc.; pg. 1249, pg. 153
Patel, Purvi, Sr Dir-Direct Imports - Ross Stores, Inc.; pg. 1783, pg. 78
Patel, Rachna, Mgr-Product Mktg-Innovation & New Ventures - eBay Inc.; pg. 1240, pg. 243
Patel, Raj, Sr Mgr-Digital Mktg - LG Electronics Canada, Inc.; pg. 651, pg. 1927
Patel, Rita, Dir-Mktg-Grocery - Target Corporation; pg. 1786, pg. 942
Patel, Sameer, Sr VP-Products & Go-To-Market-Networks & Collaboration Software - SAP America, Inc.; pg. 466, pg. 1557
Patel, Sanjay, Mgr-Sls Analytics - Diageo Canada, Inc.; pg. 1961, pg. 1937
Patel, Sapana, Sr Dir-Bus Intelligence - Spirit Airlines, Inc.; pg. 234, pg. 449
Patel, Shashank, Interim CFO - Xylem Inc.; pg. 1078, pg. 1339
Patel, Shefali, Mgr-Mktg - MATTEL, INC.; pg. 962, pg. 81
Patel, Shrineil, Head-Customer Mktg Team-ShopperView - Meijer, Inc.; pg. 1779, pg. 888
Patel, Simone, Product Mgr-Point of Care Ultrasound - Philips Electronics North America; pg. 662, pg. 782
Patel, Sonaly, Brand Mgr - The Home Depot, Inc.; pg. 1050, pg. 510
Patel, Tapan, Mgr-Mktg-Global - SAS Institute Inc.; pg. 466, pg. 1361
Patel, Traci, Mgr-Mktg-Fin Advisor Svcs - The Vanguard Group, Inc.; pg. 816, pg. 1550
Patel, Umi, Dir-Mktg-Mountain Dew Innovation - PepsiCo, Inc.; pg. 259, pg. 1327
Patel, Utkarsh, Head-Digital Mktg & Comm - Humana, Inc.; pg. 1204, pg. 734
Patel, Viraj, Mgr-Mktg-Loyalty Program - The Children's Place, Inc.; pg. 22, pg. 1119
Patel-Hennessey, Christine, Dir-Mktg - AIMCO Properties, L.P.; pg. 1079, pg. 316
Pater, Suzanne, Brand Mgr-Activation - The Coca-Cola Company; pg. 240, pg. 493
Paterson, Deborah, Specialist-Mktg - Honeywell International Inc.; pg. 407, pg. 1088
Patersone, Tami, Mgr-Digital Mktg - Tuesday Morning Corporation; pg. 1789, pg. 1690
Pathak, Akash, Dir-Digital Mktg US - McDonald's Corporation; pg. 1737, pg. 645
Patient, Alison, Sr Dir-Corp Affairs - Coca-Cola Bottling Co. Consolidated; pg. 240, pg. 1365
Patil, Himanshu, Mgr-Online Mktg - Xoom Corporation; pg. 1289, pg. 234
Patil, Rajesh, Sr Specialist-Technical Mktg-Campus & Data Center Products - Juniper Networks, Inc.; pg. 1260, pg. 286
Patin, Sara, Mgr-Mktg-Beauty, Designer Jewellery & Precious Jewellery - Neiman Marcus, Inc.; pg. 30, pg. 1684
Patino, Luis, Sr VP & Gen Mgr-Los Angeles Local Media - Univision Communications Inc.; pg. 683, pg. 1307

Patino, Sylvia, Acct Mgr-Creative Svcs - Coach, Inc.; pg. 3, pg. 1214
Patiri, Theresa, Sr VP-Production & Bus Affairs - AMC Networks Inc.; pg. 269, pg. 1189
Patnaude, Jim, Dir-Sls-Northern Zone - Lightolier; pg. 1301, pg. 819
Patricio, Jamie, Sr Mgr-Global Experiential Mktg - PayPal Inc.; pg. 1274, pg. 248
Patrick, Don, Pres/COO-Enterprise Mktg Solutions - Infogroup Inc.; pg. 1652, pg. 1016
Patrick, Hannah, Asst VP-Consumer & Small Bus Social Media - Bank of America Corporation; pg. 718, pg. 1362
Patrick, James, Mgr-Mktg & Adv - Wal-Mart Stores, Inc.; pg. 1790, pg. 29
Patrick, Joe, Head-Worldwide Sls - Miramax Film Corp.; pg. 298, pg. 275
Patrick, Leonie, Sr Dir-Convention Sls - San Francisco Travel Association; pg. 1005, pg. 227
Patrick, Marc, VP-Global Golf Mktg - NIKE, Inc.; pg. 1812, pg. 1492
Patrick, Michael, Mgr-Media & Entertainment Rels - Audi of America, Inc.; pg. 164, pg. 1784
Patrizio, Ilene, Dir-Integrated Media - CA Technologies; pg. 366, pg. 1168
Patrylak, Christa, Dir-Social Media & Performance Mktg - Home Box Office, Inc.; pg. 290, pg. 1240
Patt, David, Brand Mgr - SONIC Corp.; pg. 1750, pg. 1487
Patt, Kelly, Sr Mgr-Consumer Mktg - Activision Blizzard, Inc.; pg. 948, pg. 271
Pattanayak, Pradhan, Sr Dir-Engrg-Ad Server & Forecasting Engine - Yahoo! Inc.; pg. 1289, pg. 289
Pattani, Paresh, Sr Dir-High Performance Data Solutions - Intel Corporation; pg. 645, pg. 266
Pattat, Emily, Dir-Mktg Res - Saint Jude Children's Research Hospital Inc.; pg. 155, pg. 1646
Patte, Chris, Brand Mgr - Starbucks Corporation; pg. 897, pg. 1840
Pattee, Ryan, Head-Global Product Dev & Dir-Mktg - ACCO Brands Corporation; pg. 340, pg. 626
Pattengale, Stephen, Sr Mgr-Internet Mktg - Career Education Corporation; pg. 599, pg. 658
Patterson, Brendan, Dir-Product Mgmt - WatchGuard Technologies, Inc.; pg. 491, pg. 1842
Patterson, Candace E., Mgr-Personal Lines Mktg - The Chubb Corporation; pg. 1196, pg. 1128
Patterson, Carla, Brand Mgr-Fancy Feast - Nestle Purina PetCare Company; pg. 1479, pg. 1000
Patterson, Chris, Product Mgr-Cloud & Hosting Svcs - NaviSite, Inc.; pg. 1269, pg. 782
Patterson, Clint, Sr Dir-Consumer & Retail Comm - T-Mobile US, Inc.; pg. 676, pg. 1816
Patterson, David, Mgr-Mktg Comm - Deere & Company; pg. 703, pg. 632
Patterson, Deborah, Sr Dir-Product & Tech Mktg - Amkor Technology, Inc.; pg. 67, pg. 25
Patterson, Deron, Mgr-Intl Sls-Latin America & Caribbean - PPG Industries, Inc.; pg. 1445, pg. 1579
Patterson, Diane, Sr Product Mgr - Riviana Foods Inc.; pg. 892, pg. 1713
Patterson, James, Sr Dir-Ops - Bonnier Corporation; pg. 1622, pg. 480
Patterson, James, Planner-Sls - Discovery Communications, Inc.; pg. 282, pg. 777
Patterson, John B., Sr Mgr-PR & Community Rels - Raytheon Company; pg. 233, pg. 854
Patterson, Katherine, Mgr-Global Mktg-DI - GE Healthcare; pg. 399, pg. 1765
Patterson, Keeley, Dir-Sls Strategy & Res - Tumblr, Inc.; pg. 1285, pg. 1305
Patterson, Keith, Mgr-PR & Media Rels - Roger Cleveland Golf Company, Inc.; pg. 1844, pg. 105
Patterson, Kerry, Dir-Product Mktg - The Ultimate Software Group, Inc.; pg. 486, pg. 479
Patterson, Mandy, Brand Mgr - Starbucks Corporation; pg. 897, pg. 1840
Patterson, Nick, Assoc Dir-Mktg - The Procter & Gamble Company; pg. 1129, pg. 1418
Patterson, Paige, Mgr-Mktg-Consumer Insights - Verizon Communications Inc.; pg. 1875, pg. 1309
Patterson, Ron, Sls Mgr - Comcast Corporation; pg. 276, pg. 1560
Patterson, Seth, Mgr-Digital Mktg - Pendleton Woolen Mills, Inc.; pg. 697, pg. 1505
Patterson, Steve, VP-Mktg, Comm & Govt Affairs - Southern States Cooperative, Inc.; pg. 1482, pg. 1804
Patterson, Stewart, Dir-Client Mktg - Valassis; pg. 1698, pg. 386
Patterson, Tasha, Sr Mgr-Customer Experience Mktg - United States Cellular Corporation; pg. 1875, pg. 594
Patterson, Todd, Dir-Consumer Adv-Global - Philips Respironics; pg. 1585, pg. 1555
Patterson, Tom, Mgr-Web Mktg - ADTRAN, Inc.; pg. 344, pg. 6
Patterson-Megarry, Michelle, Acct Mgr-Partner Mktg-Worldwide - Intel Corporation; pg. 645, pg. 266
Patti, Chris, VP-Sls-US - Keystone Automotive Operations, Inc.; pg. 210, pg. 1531
Pattock, Donna Wilksen, Mgr-Mktg - Ingram Micro Inc.; pg. 415, pg. 261
Pattock, Shawn, Sr Mgr-Americas Field Mktg - Emulex Corporation; pg. 392, pg. 70
Patton, Brenna, Sr Mgr-Sls Promo - Saladmaster; pg. 60, pg. 1659
Patton, Cindy, Dir-Sls & Mktg - Cumberland Pharmaceuticals, Inc.; pg. 1521, pg. 1650
Patton, David, Sr Dir-Strategy & Market Insights - Automatic Data Processing, Inc.; pg. 357, pg. 1117
Patton, David, Sr Strategist-Digital Mktg - Vulcan, Inc.; pg. 687, pg. 5
Patton, Katrina, VP-Product Dev - Lexington Home Brands; pg. 933, pg. 1391
Patton, Kris, Head-Media Rels - General Mills, Inc.; pg. 828, pg. 933
Patton, Lindene, Head-Hazard Product Dev-Global - CoreLogic, Inc.; pg. 1198, pg. 109
Patton, Michelle, Sr Coord-Mktg - Wells Fargo & Company; pg. 819, pg. 232
Patton, Molly, Coord-Mktg - Victoria Symphony Society; pg. 590, pg. 1913
Patton, Paul, Sr Mgr-Regulatory, Res & Dev - Delta Faucet Company; pg. 78, pg. 684
Patullo, Jon, Mng Dir-Tech Product Mgmt - TD Ameritrade Holding Corporation; pg. 808, pg. 1018
Paturzo, Stephanie, Acct Exec-Mktg - Bloomingdale's, Inc.; pg. 1763, pg. 1204
Patyk, Amy, Sr Mgr-Multi-Channel Mktg - Alcon; pg. 1399, pg. 530
Patzwaldt, Melissa, Program Mgr-Client Executive Mktg & Global Recognition Events - International Business Machines Corporation; pg. 418, pg. 1138
Pauer, Jay, Sr Dir-Brand Mktg - DeVry Education Group Inc.; pg. 600, pg. 607
Paul, Arata, District Mgr-Sls - General Motors Company; pg. 175, pg. 881
Paul, Brian, Dir-Creative & Producer-Video - USANA Health Sciences, Inc.; pg. 1605, pg. 1761
Paul, Carolyn, Brand Mgr-Consumer - Simon Property Group, Inc.; pg. 1112, pg. 690
Paul, Chad, Sr Dir-R&D Tax Svcs - BDO Seidman, LLP; pg. 724, pg. 1202
Paul, Chris, VP-Media & Acq - Squarespace Inc.; pg. 1282, pg. 1295
Paul, Christiane, Sr Dir-Mktg-Spreads USA - Unilever United States, Inc.; pg. 904, pg. 1061
Paul, Gardner, Reg Mgr-Sls-South Central - Jayco Inc.; pg. 1708, pg. 695
Paul, Heather, Specialist-Pub Affairs, PR & Media - State Farm Mutual Automobile Insurance Co.; pg. 1218, pg. 557
Paul, Jeffrey, Head-Mktg, Consumer Markets & Indus Mfg - KPMG LLP; pg. 774, pg. 1086
Paul, Monica, VP-Sports Mktg - Dallas Convention & Visitors Bureau; pg. 991, pg. 1678
Paul, Shannon, VP-Social Media - Fifth Third Bancorp; pg. 752, pg. 1413
Paul, Tim, VP-Mktg & Distr Mgmt-Zurich Insurance - Zurich Holding Company of America, Inc.; pg. 1224, pg. 660
Paule, Debbie, Sr Dir-Mktg Ops - Equifax Workforce Solutions; pg. 394, pg. 997
Paule, Jhermaine, Analyst-Mktg Ops - Safeway Inc.; pg. 1032, pg. 184
Paules, Gretchen, VP-Field Mktg - Noodles & Company; pg. 1742, pg. 313
Paulino, Dewi, Sr Mgr-Mktg-Brand Strategy - Gannett Co., Inc.; pg. 1643, pg. 1790
Paulisick, Adam, Sr VP-Mktg & Strategy - Nielsen Business Media; pg. 1671, pg. 1272
Paull, Adrian, VP-Customer & Product Support - Honeywell International Inc.; pg. 407, pg. 1088
Paulo, Melissa, Mgr-Social Media - Clif Bar Inc.; pg. 848, pg. 83
Pauls, Andrew, Sr Dir-Corp Mktg - Milwaukee Brewers Baseball Club, Inc.; pg. 562, pg. 1878
Pauls, Greg, Mgr-Mktg & Adv - The Staplex Company, Inc.; pg. 474, pg. 1146
Pauls, Nicole, Principal, Dir-Product Mgmt & Product Mgr - SOLARWINDS, INC.; pg. 471, pg. 1666
Paulsen, Bradley, Sr Dir-Product Dev & Private Brands - The Home Depot, Inc.; pg. 1050, pg. 510
Paulsen, Derek J., Grp VP-Mktg - Gibraltar Industries, Inc.; pg. 1340, pg. 1148
Paulsen, Dylan, Sr VP-Club Mktg - Cabela's Incorporated; pg. 535, pg. 1019
Paulsen, Jennifer, Mgr-Field Mktg-Energy & Life Sciences - Pegasystems Inc.; pg. 453, pg. 809
Paulsen, Nicole, Mgr-Mktg - IBM; pg. 410, pg. 1449
Paulsin, Lyn, Dir-PR - Borghese, Inc.; pg. 502, pg. 1205
Paulson, Andy, Brand Mgr - Ferrara Candy Co.; pg. 1852, pg. 612
Paulson, Jed, Dir-Mktg & Direct-Free People - Urban Outfitters, Inc.; pg. 1789, pg. 1571
Paulson, Larry, VP-Product Mgmt-Qualcomm Device Reference Designs - QUALCOMM Incorporated; pg. 1873, pg. 207
Pauly, Dave, Product Mgr-Alpha Free - Appvion Inc.; pg. 1451, pg. 1852
Pauly, Kristen, Dir-Sls & Mktg-IVD - SurModics, Inc.; pg. 1600, pg. 924
Pauly, Tessa, Mgr-Digital Brand & Social Media Mktg - American Express Company; pg. 712, pg. 1190
Paumen, Richard, Sr VP-Retail Sls & Mktg - Sun-Maid Growers of California; pg. 899, pg. 119
Paurowski, Tracy, Dir-Comm & PR-American Express Travel-Consumer Travel Div - American Express Company; pg. 712, pg. 1190
Paustenbach, Lyanne, Head-Mktg Bus - Cisco Systems, Inc.; pg. 372, pg. 240
Pava, Vicente, VP-Sls-Comm Indus Americas - Hewlett-Packard Company; pg. 404, pg. 175
Pavel, Elizabeth, Dir-Mktg Comm - Lam Research Corporation; pg. 1354, pg. 91
Pavia, Audrey, VP-Mktg - Tura L.P.; pg. 1433, pg. 1555
Pavia, Leigh Anne, VP-Adv Sls-NBCUniversal, Inc. - Esquire Network; pg. 286, pg. 1229
Pavia, LeighAnne, VP-Adv Sls - NBC Universal, Inc.; pg. 300, pg. 1266
Pavillard, Denis, VP-Product Mktg - Logitech Inc.; pg. 1264, pg. 164
Pavlica, Nicole, Mgr-Mktg-Core Bus - Sargento Foods Inc.; pg. 894, pg. 1886
Pavlick, Maria, Sr Dir-Art - Brocade Corporation; pg. 365, pg. 312
Pavlovsky, Lucy, Analyst-Mktg-CHANEL Eyewear - Luxottica Group; pg. 8, pg. 1323
Pavlowski, Sylvain, Sr VP-Sls-Europe - Information Builders Inc.; pg. 415, pg. 1243
Pavol, Stephanie, Mgr-Social Media - Cardinal Health, Inc.; pg. 1512, pg. 1448
Pavon, Cristina, Sr Mgr-Mdsg - Burger King Corporation; pg. 1719, pg. 440
Pawlinski, Carol, Rep-Legal Notice Adv - Naples Daily News; pg. 1666, pg. 451
Pawlitz, Loren, Exec Dir-Mktg & ECommerce - Concordia Publishing House; pg. 1629, pg. 995
Pawlowicz, Melissa, Sr Dir-Promos - Kellogg Company; pg. 831, pg. 870
Pawlowski, John, Brand Mgr - ConAgra Foods, Inc.; pg. 826, pg. 1014
Pawlowski, Kim, Acct Mgr-Broker Mktg - Aetna Inc.; pg. 1187, pg. 351
Pawlowski, Steve, Mgr-Media Rels - PetSmart, Inc.; pg. 1481, pg. 18
Pawluk, Susan, Sr Mgr-Mktg Ops - Deluxe Corporation; pg. 1634, pg. 964
Pawlyshyn, Mark, Sr VP-Mktg - U.S. Bancorp; pg. 815, pg. 945
Pawson, Rob, Reg Mgr-Sls - Haviland Enterprises Inc.; pg. 1165, pg. 887
Paxman, Merrill, Mgr-Indus Sls - Miller's Honey Company; pg. 1860, pg. 1759
Paxson, Cara, Mgr-Client Sls - Alliance Data Systems Corporation; pg. 347, pg. 1729
Paxton, Mickey, Sr VP & Exec Dir-Creative - Cablevision Systems Corporation; pg. 272, pg. 1141
Paxton, Nancy, Sr Dir-IR & Treasury - Apple Inc.; pg. 350, pg. 73

First page reference indicates Business Class Edition
Second page reference indicates Geographic Edition

Paxton, Shelley, VP-Global Mktg & Brand - Harley-Davidson, Inc.; *pg.* 178, *pg.* 1874
Payan, Adriana, Brand Mgr - Helen of Troy L.P.; *pg.* 511, *pg.* 1692
Paye, Matt, VP-Mktg - Los Angeles Clippers; *pg.* 558, *pg.* 135
Payment, Andy, Dir-Global Comm & Media Rels - VeriFone Systems, Inc.; *pg.* 487, *pg.* 251
Payne, Andrea, Sr Dir-Digital Mktg - Gartner, Inc.; *pg.* 1248, *pg.* 374
Payne, Andrew, Mgr-Email Mktg - Fender Musical Instruments Corporation; *pg.* 547, *pg.* 21
Payne, Ashley, Mgr-Email Mktg - Carter's, Inc.; *pg.* 21, *pg.* 491
Payne, Candace, Mgr-Mktg, Community & Social Media - Sephora USA Inc; *pg.* 522, *pg.* 227
Payne, David, Chief Product Officer - Gannett Co., Inc.; *pg.* 1643, *pg.* 1790
Payne, Dustin, Reg Mgr-Mktg-Athletics - Grand Canyon Education, Inc.; *pg.* 602, *pg.* 16
Payne, Elisabeth, Sls Dir-Audience, Programmatic & Mobile - Yahoo! Inc.; *pg.* 1289, *pg.* 289
Payne, Erica, Sr Coord-Mktg - Anthem, Inc.; *pg.* 1192, *pg.* 683
Payne, Frank, Gen Mgr-Fleet Sls - The Goodyear Tire & Rubber Company; *pg.* 1883, *pg.* 1401
Payne, Freddie, Reg Mgr-Sls-Northeast - Crane Carrier Company; *pg.* 168, *pg.* 1489
Payne, Jennifer, Product Mgr - Hallmark Cards, Inc.; *pg.* 1646, *pg.* 983
Payne, John, Product Dir-Test & Measurement - Southwire Company; *pg.* 1063, *pg.* 527
Payne, Kayla, Sr Specialist-Mktg-Managed Care Svcs - Cardinal Health, Inc.; *pg.* 1512, *pg.* 1448
Payne, Louis, Mgr-Mktg-Starboard Cruise Svcs - LVMH Inc.; *pg.* 9, *pg.* 1254
Payne, Raymond M., VP-Sls-Vertical Sls - The SSI Group, Inc.; *pg.* 473, *pg.* 7
Payne, Rob, Category Brand Mgr-P&G Homecare Div - Procter & Gamble Inc.; *pg.* 333, *pg.* 1929
Payne, Ryan, Sr VP-Mktg - TEN: The Enthusiast Network; *pg.* 1691, *pg.* 1298
Payne, Tom, Dir-Mktg - The King Arthur Flour Company, Inc.; *pg.* 833, *pg.* 1767
Paynter, Betsy, Mgr-Digital Media - Heineken USA Inc.; *pg.* 252, *pg.* 1352
Paynter, Tim, Dir-Mktg Comm & Aerospace Sector - Northrop Grumman Corporation; *pg.* 231, *pg.* 1781
Paz, Ariana, Partner-HR Bus-Sls & Mktg - STEPAN COMPANY; *pg.* 1182, *pg.* 643
Paz, Karen, VP & Mgr-Mktg - Comerica Incorporated; *pg.* 740, *pg.* 1677
Paz, Lorena, Sr Mgr-New Product Mktg - NRG Energy, Inc.; *pg.* 1948, *pg.* 1712
Paz, Tania, VP-Digital Media Ops & Tech - Telemundo Network Inc.; *pg.* 311, *pg.* 430
Paz, Toni, Sr Dir-Major & Planned Giving - Jacksonville Symphony Association; *pg.* 554, *pg.* 434
Paz, Tulio, Reg Brand Mgr-Scotch CCA - Diageo North America, Inc.; *pg.* 1961, *pg.* 361
Pchola, Ed, Product Dir - Dremel; *pg.* 1046, *pg.* 634
Peace, Heather, Mgr-e-Tail Channel Mktg - Kimberly-Clark Corporation; *pg.* 1461, *pg.* 1720
Peace, Steve, Sr VP-Media-Intl - Paramount Pictures Corporation; *pg.* 304, *pg.* 138
Peace, Susan, Sr Dir-Beauty Products & Retail - Dessange International, Inc.; *pg.* 506, *pg.* 787
Peacock, Erica, VP-Mktg - QuinStreet, Inc.; *pg.* 1276, *pg.* 89
Peacock, James, Sr Mgr-Website - PulteGroup, Inc.; *pg.* 1109, *pg.* 873
Peacock, Kevin A., Head-Strategic Mktg-Global - Dendreon Corporation; *pg.* 1522, *pg.* 1835
Peacock, Owen, Mgr-Lexus Natl Product Mktg - Toyota Motor Sales, U.S.A., Inc.; *pg.* 193, *pg.* 296
Peacock, Wayne, Exec VP, Enterprise Strategy & Mktg - United Services Automobile Association; *pg.* 1221, *pg.* 1743
Peak, Tamara, Specialist-eBusiness & Web Mktg - Schneider Electric; *pg.* 467, *pg.* 1609
Peake, Adam, Exec VP-Global Mktg - Under Armour, Inc.; *pg.* 49, *pg.* 759
Pealer, Mike, Mgr-Mktg-Mercury Removal - Calgon Carbon Corporation; *pg.* 1151, *pg.* 1574
Pean, Kellie, Brand Mgr-CIROC - Diageo North America Inc.; *pg.* 248, *pg.* 1223
Pearce, Kate, Mgr-Lincoln Mktg - Ford Motor Company; *pg.* 172, *pg.* 876
Pearce, Kristen, Mgr-Mktg - Autodesk Inc.; *pg.* 356, *pg.* 257
Pearce, Lexie, Mgr-PR - Freddy's Frozen Custard & Steakburgers; *pg.* 1729, *pg.* 723
Pearce, Stephen, VP-Leisure Travel & Digital Mktg - The Greater Vancouver Convention & Visitor Bureau; *pg.* 994, *pg.* 1910
Pearl, Bruce, VP-Mktg - The H.T. Hackney Company; *pg.* 1023, *pg.* 1637
Pearl, Jeffrey, VP-Carrier Sls-North America - BroadSoft, Inc.; *pg.* 1233, *pg.* 770
Pearl, Lindsey, Dir-Social Media & Performance Mktg - Home Box Office, Inc.; *pg.* 290, *pg.* 1240
Pearl, Paul S., Sr VP-Sls & Ops Svcs - Arcade Marketing, Inc.; *pg.* 352, *pg.* 1196
Pearlman, Pamela, Dir-Customer Loyalty & Credit Mktg - Barneys New York, Inc.; *pg.* 38, *pg.* 1201
Pearlstein, Jamee, Sr Assoc Brand Mgr - The Kraft Heinz Company; *pg.* 871, *pg.* 641
Pearsall, Bobbie, Dir-Adv - Quoizel Inc.; *pg.* 1304, *pg.* 1616
Pearson, Anne, Mgr-Mktg-Europe - Jarden Consumer Solutions; *pg.* 57, *pg.* 412
Pearson, Carla, Sr Dir-Payer New Product Dev Strategy - GlaxoSmithKline; *pg.* 1536, *pg.* 1565
Pearson, Carolyn, Specialist-Mktg Brand - Bissell Homecare, Inc.; *pg.* 52, *pg.* 887
Pearson, Eric, Mgr-Product Mktg - The Hertz Corporation; *pg.* 1911, *pg.* 450
Pearson, Garth, Product Mgr - Solo Cup Company; *pg.* 1469, *pg.* 625
Pearson, Jeff, Sr VP-Mktg - hhgregg, Inc.; *pg.* 56, *pg.* 686
Pearson, Jonathan, Exec VP-Mktg & Clinical Dev - Cutera, Inc.; *pg.* 1521, *pg.* 49
Pearson, Mark, Exec VP-Brand Mgmt & Digital Media - 20th Century Fox Film Corp.; *pg.* 267, *pg.* 124
Pearson, Mike, Product Engr - Target Corporation; *pg.* 1786, *pg.* 942
Pearson, Sarah, Dir-Mktg - Hess Corporation; *pg.* 979, *pg.* 1240
Pearson, Susan, Mgr-Mktg - MetLife, Inc.; *pg.* 1208, *pg.* 1258
Pearson, Teresa, Sr Dir-Global Brand Mktg & Dev - Hasbro, Inc.; *pg.* 954, *pg.* 1603
Pearson, Toby, Dir-Channel Mktg - AT&T Inc.; *pg.* 1867, *pg.* 1674
Pearson, Tony, Sr Dir-Bus Dev - Finisar Corporation; *pg.* 639, *pg.* 285
Pearson, Tyler, Dir-PR - WellStar Health System, Inc.; *pg.* 161, *pg.* 536
Pearson, Zoe, Mgr-Mktg - Pinterest; *pg.* 1275, *pg.* 225
Peart, Randy, Dir-Mktg Comm - Kenworth Truck Co.; *pg.* 181, *pg.* 1822
Pearton, Elaine, Mgr-Global Digital Mktg-Bayer HealthCare Diabetes Care - Bayer Corporation; *pg.* 1499, *pg.* 1573
Pease, Diane, Mgr Inbound Mktg - Cisco Systems, Inc.; *pg.* 372, *pg.* 240
Pease, Joe, Dir-Mktg-MassMutual Fin Grp - Massachusetts Mutual Life Insurance Company; *pg.* 1207, *pg.* 845
Pease, Tracy, Brand Mgr-North American Architectural Coatings - PPG Industries, Inc.; *pg.* 1445, *pg.* 1579
Peattie, Mark, Bus Mgr-Display Adv - eBay Inc.; *pg.* 1240, *pg.* 243
Peavey, Jordan, Dir-Field Mktg - The Nature Conservancy; *pg.* 151, *pg.* 1774
Peavy, Jim, Asst VP-PR - A.M. Best Company; *pg.* 1614, *pg.* 1101
Peavy, Rachel, Dir-PR - Atlanta Convention & Visitors Bureau; *pg.* 989, *pg.* 489
Pech, Kent, VP-Retail Mktg - Lee Jeans; *pg.* 43, *pg.* 721
Pechar, Brian, Mgr-Sls-Natl - Metpar Corp.; *pg.* 97, *pg.* 1350
Pechstein, Scott, VP-Sls - Autobytel Inc.; *pg.* 1230, *pg.* 107
Peck, Dave, Head-Digital & Social Media Mktg-Global - PayPal Inc.; *pg.* 1274, *pg.* 248
Peck, Gary, Dir-Sls & Mktg - Belden, Inc.; *pg.* 624, *pg.* 993
Peck, John, Product Mgr-Global Tech - Avery Dennison Corporation; *pg.* 1452, *pg.* 95
Peck, Larry, Mgr-Experiential Mktg - General Motors Company; *pg.* 175, *pg.* 881
Peck, Lindsay, Asst Mktg Mgr-Acq - American Greetings Corporation; *pg.* 1615, *pg.* 1428
Peckham, Jim, Mgr-Mktg - Varco Pruden Buildings, Inc.; *pg.* 118, *pg.* 1647
Pecora, Alexandre, Dir-Residential Product Mktg - CertainTeed Corporation; *pg.* 74, *pg.* 1589
Pecora, Chenin, Mgr-Mktg Program - Which Wich, Inc.; *pg.* 1756, *pg.* 1690
Pecoraro, Charles, Mgr-Product Mktg-Edge & Explorer-Asia Pacific CBG - Ford Motor Company; *pg.* 172, *pg.* 876
Peddicord, Mark, Mgr-Mktg - The Blade Co.; *pg.* 1621, *pg.* 1476
Peddie, Tom, VP-Global Sls - NIKE, Inc.; *pg.* 1812, *pg.* 1492
Peddy, Christine, Dir-Global Mktg-Almay Makeup - Revlon Consumer Products Corporation; *pg.* 521, *pg.* 1286
Pedersen, Chris, Sr Product Mgr-Tegra Camera - NVIDIA Corporation; *pg.* 447, *pg.* 268
Pedersen, Paul, Mgr-Search Engine Mktg - The E.W. Scripps Company; *pg.* 1639, *pg.* 1412
Pedersen, Pete, Global Head-PR - Sonos, Inc.; *pg.* 675, *pg.* 263
Pedersen, Shannon, Mgr-Mktg-West Reg - McGladrey, LLP; *pg.* 781, *pg.* 938
Pedersen, Shannon, Dir-Media Strategy - Papa Murphy's International, LLC; *pg.* 1743, *pg.* 1846
Pederson, Bree, Mgr-Procurement & Mktg - Diageo North America Inc.; *pg.* 248, *pg.* 1223
Pederson, Kristin, Sr Planner-Digital Media - Bloomberg L.P.; *pg.* 725, *pg.* 1204
Pederson, Michael, Brand Mgr-Lazer Helmets - Quality Bicycle Products; *pg.* 1710, *pg.* 918
Pederson, Scott, Dir-Mktg - Sleeman Breweries, Ltd.; *pg.* 265, *pg.* 1920
Pederson, Seth, Mgr-Mktg Partnerships - General Mills, Inc.; *pg.* 828, *pg.* 933
Pederson, Terry, VP-Sls - Daiwa Corporation; *pg.* 1832, *pg.* 75
Pedra, Christi M., Sr VP-Mktg, Customer Solutions & Pharmaceutical Distr - Cardinal Health, Inc.; *pg.* 1512, *pg.* 1448
Pedro, Leianne, Mgr-Adv-Local Agencies & Major Accts - The Honolulu Star-Advertiser; *pg.* 1650, *pg.* 544
Pedro, Liz, Dir-Customer Success Mktg - Mitel Networks, Inc.; *pg.* 1872, *pg.* 13
Pedroff, Stephen, Sr Dir-Global Mktg Comm - AngioDynamics, Inc.; *pg.* 1495, *pg.* 1173
Pedroza, Luis, Interactive Mktg-eMail & Membership Programs - eBay Inc.; *pg.* 1240, *pg.* 243
Pedruczny, Jayna, Assoc Mgr-Mktg Intern - General Mills, Inc.; *pg.* 828, *pg.* 933
Pedzwater, Devin, Dir-Creative Italian Vanity Fair - Conde Nast Publications, Inc.; *pg.* 1630, *pg.* 128
Peebles, Ross, Interim CEO - GLOBAL GEOPHYSICAL SERVICES, INC.; *pg.* 1414, *pg.* 1727
Peek, Robert, Project Mgr & Mgr-Social Media - Dell Inc.; *pg.* 383, *pg.* 1737
Peeler, Kat, Sr VP-Mktg - L'Oreal USA; *pg.* 514, *pg.* 1252
Peeler, Ric, Dir-Consumer Mktg Strategy - Intel Corporation; *pg.* 645, *pg.* 266
Peemoller, Britt, Sr Mgr-Comm - Microsoft Corporation; *pg.* 435, *pg.* 1824
Peeples, William, Mng Dir-Mktg & Southern Ops Sls - AGL Resources Inc.; *pg.* 1933, *pg.* 487
Peet, Amy, Head-Digital Mktg & Sr Mgr - FCA US LLC; *pg.* 170, *pg.* 868
Peet, Katie, Dir-Social Media - State Automobile Mutual Insurance Company; *pg.* 1217, *pg.* 1444
Peever, Shane, Brand Mgr-Chevrolet Cars & Crossovers - General Motors of Canada Ltd.; *pg.* 177, *pg.* 1931
Pegas, Lauren, Dir-Global Mktg Excellence - Merck & Co., Inc.; *pg.* 1566, *pg.* 1077
Peichl, Frank, Product Mgr - Sirona Dental Systems, Inc.; *pg.* 1429, *pg.* 1175
Peiffer, Bob, Dir-Creative Svcs - Sargento Foods Inc.; *pg.* 894, *pg.* 1886
Peikert, Christina, Dir-Mktg & Comm-Bombardier Aerospace - Bombardier Inc.; *pg.* 1318, *pg.* 1953
Peikon, Andy, Sr VP-Sls - Live Nation Entertainment, Inc.; *pg.* 558, *pg.* 47
Peimer, Elisa, Sr Dir-Digital Mktg-Sony Masterworks - Sony Music Entertainment; *pg.* 309, *pg.* 1294
Peinert, Anne, Supvr-Inside Sls & Quotations - Litecontrol Corporation; *pg.* 1301, *pg.* 841
Peiris, Keith, Mgr-Product Mgmt - Facebook, Inc.; *pg.* 1245, *pg.* 143
Pekar, Irinia, Sr Assoc Brand Mgr - Del Monte Foods, Inc.; *pg.* 852, *pg.* 304
Pekich, Wendelyn, Dir-Mktg - Wexford Health Sources Inc.; *pg.* 1610, *pg.* 1582
Peksoz, Erkin, Sr Assoc Brand Mgr - ACH Food Companies, Inc.; *pg.* 835, *pg.* 1631
Pekton, Pete, Mgr-Social Media - General Electric Company; *pg.* 1297, *pg.* 347

Pelegio, Jessica, Product Mgr - Google Inc.; *pg.* 1249, *pg.* 153
Pelfrey, Cathy, Product Mgr - The Progressive Corporation; *pg.* 1214, *pg.* 1463
Pelissero, Tom, Mgr-Mktg - 3M Company; *pg.* 1142, *pg.* 956
Pelk, Jim, Dir-Electronic Sls - Ingersoll-Rand Company; *pg.* 1349, *pg.* 1370
Pell, Quentin, Dir-PR & Comm-Mktg - Tanger Factory Outlet Centers, Inc.; *pg.* 1116, *pg.* 1376
Pellack, Tom, VP-Mktg & Creative Svcs - Comcast Sportsnet; *pg.* 278, *pg.* 1562
Pelland, Todd, Dir-Sls-Natl - Cooper Wheelock; *pg.* 630, *pg.* 1080
Pellegrini, Gene, Mgr-Online Mktg - The Pep Boys - Manny, Moe & Jack; *pg.* 215, *pg.* 1568
Pellegrini, Jeff, VP-Adv Sls - Discovery Communications, Inc.; *pg.* 282, *pg.* 777
Pellegrino, Angela, Mgr-Sls Sys - LinkedIn Corporation; *pg.* 1262, *pg.* 160
Pellegrino, Lucy, Sr Mgr-Strategic Mktg - Nikon Inc.; *pg.* 1424, *pg.* 1181
Pellegrino, Michael, Chief Customer Officer & Pres-Consumer Products - Sargento Foods Inc.; *pg.* 894, *pg.* 1886
Pellegrino, Stephen M., Sr VP-Global Sls - Key Technology, Inc.; *pg.* 868, *pg.* 1847
Pellegrino, Timoteo, Mgr-Mktg-Sectors-North America - IBM Canada Limited; *pg.* 411, *pg.* 1923
Pellenttiere, Jim, Dir-Mktg-Latin America, Canada, Australia & New Zealand - Amgen Inc.; *pg.* 1493, *pg.* 291
Pellerin, Keith, VP & Head-Product - Aflac Incorporated; *pg.* 1188, *pg.* 527
Pelletier, James, Dir-Brand Mktg-Best Buy & Future Shop - Best Buy Canada Ltd.; *pg.* 1761, *pg.* 1907
Pelletier, Kate, Assoc Brand Mgr-Global Diabetes Mktg - Eli Lilly and Company; *pg.* 1527, *pg.* 684
Pelletier, Sean, Sr Product Mgr-GeForce Software - NVIDIA Corporation; *pg.* 447, *pg.* 268
Pelliccio, John, Mgr-Technical Product Mktg - Bose Corporation; *pg.* 626, *pg.* 820
Pellicone, Michael, Dir-Sls - Alcatel-Lucent USA, Inc.; *pg.* 615, *pg.* 1728
Pellissier, Joseph, Sr Mgr-Sponsorship Dev - Charles Schwab & Company, Inc.; *pg.* 734, *pg.* 215
Pellman, Mark, Dir-Sls & Mktg - Baumfolder Corporation; *pg.* 360, *pg.* 1472
Peloquin, Samantha, Mgr-Digital Mktg - Lexington Home Brands; *pg.* 933, *pg.* 1391
Pelosi, Lisa, Dir-Comm & Media Rels - Johnson & Wales University; *pg.* 603, *pg.* 1606
Peltier, Betty, Mgr-Sls-Consumables-Intl - The Harris Products Group; *pg.* 1345, *pg.* 533
Peltier, Jim, Sr Mgr-Mktg Comm - HARRIS CORPORATION; *pg.* 642, *pg.* 439
Peltier, Kelli, Mgr-Mktg - 3M Company; *pg.* 1142, *pg.* 956
Pelton, Eric, Sr Mgr-Svcs Product Mgmt-Avid Global Svcs - Avid Technology, Inc.; *pg.* 622, *pg.* 804
Pelton, Nicole, Mgr-Technical Mktg-Solar Bus Grp - Applied Materials, Inc.; *pg.* 618, *pg.* 264
Pelus, Jennifer, Dir-Channel Mktg-Payer - Quest Diagnostics Incorporated; *pg.* 1587, *pg.* 1080
Pelzl, Jeff, Dir-Product Mktg - High End Systems, Inc.; *pg.* 1299, *pg.* 1663
Pemberton, Abby, Mgr-Social Media - Publix Super Markets, Inc.; *pg.* 1031, *pg.* 437
Pemberton, Antoniette, Jr Mgr-PR - Iconix Brand Group, Inc.; *pg.* 26, *pg.* 1243
Pemberton, Chris, Sr Mgr-ECommerce - Ghirardelli Chocolate Company; *pg.* 1854, *pg.* 252
Pemberton, Kendra N., Sr Product Mgr-HCV - Gilead Sciences, Inc.; *pg.* 1535, *pg.* 88
Pemberton, Stephanie, Sr Dir-Mktg - Indianapolis Colts, Inc.; *pg.* 553, *pg.* 687
Pena, Alejandra, Sr VP-Mktg - Castle Brands Inc.; *pg.* 239, *pg.* 1209
Pena, Cynthia, Sr Mgr-Mobile Mktg - Hotwire, Inc.; *pg.* 1912, *pg.* 219
Pena, Derrick, Sr Product Mgr-FUSE - Cardinal Health, Inc.; *pg.* 1512, *pg.* 1448
Pena, Gaby, Mgr-Product & Growth - Twitter, Inc.; *pg.* 1285, *pg.* 228
Pena, Kelly, Mgr-Social Media Program - AutoZone, Inc.; *pg.* 200, *pg.* 1641
Pena, Liznelia, Mgr-Integrated Mktg - The Hearst Corporation; *pg.* 1649, *pg.* 1239
Pena, Maria, Head-Ops-Intuit & Sr Mgr-Mktg - Intuit Inc.; *pg.* 769, *pg.* 158
Pena, Robert, Mgr-Global Product Line-Liner Hangers - Baker Hughes Incorporated; *pg.* 1315, *pg.* 1700
Pena, William, Mgr-Pre-Owned Sls - The Collection, Inc.; *pg.* 168, *pg.* 418
Pena-Bickley, Joanna, Chief Creative Officer-Interactive Experience - International Business Machines Corporation; *pg.* 418, *pg.* 1138
Penagos, Monica, Dir-Mktg - Meridian Bioscience Inc.; *pg.* 1422, *pg.* 1417
Penagos, Ryan, Exec Dir-Editorial-Marvel's Digital Media Grp - Marvel Entertainment, LLC; *pg.* 1662, *pg.* 1257
Penagos, Vanessa, Dir-Content & Inbound Mktg - Toyota Motor Sales, U.S.A., Inc.; *pg.* 193, *pg.* 296
Penaranda, Ana C., Sr Mgr-Site Admin - Society of Chemical Mnaufacturers & Affiliates, Inc.; *pg.* 156, *pg.* 404
Penca, Tony, Dir-Mktg - Rejuvenation Inc.; *pg.* 1304, *pg.* 1506
Pence, Brandon, Head-Global Mktg-BioProcess - GE Healthcare; *pg.* 399, *pg.* 1765
Pence, Michael, Sr Dir-Consumer Insights Global Nutrition Grp - PepsiCo, Inc.; *pg.* 259, *pg.* 1327
Penchina, Lauren, Dir-Mktg & Bus Dev - Simon Property Group, Inc.; *pg.* 1112, *pg.* 690
Pendley, Robert, Supvr-Adv Review Unit - The Guardian Life Insurance Company of America; *pg.* 1202, *pg.* 1237
Pendse, Lisa, Brand Mgr-Intl - Ubisoft Inc.; *pg.* 589, *pg.* 229
Penello, Albert, Sr Dir-Product Plng, Compete & User Res - Microsoft Corporation; *pg.* 435, *pg.* 1824
PeNField, Matt, Sr Dir-Consumer Insights - Zynga Inc.; *pg.* 1292, *pg.* 235
Peng, Andrea, Mgr-Interactive Production & Adv Products - Kelley Blue Book Co., Inc.; *pg.* 1656, *pg.* 112
Peng, Christina, Brand Mgr-Worldwide Cleansing Innovation - Neutrogena Corporation; *pg.* 517, *pg.* 137
Peng, Justin, Mgr-Mktg - Best Buy Co., Inc.; *pg.* 1761, *pg.* 954
Peng, Victor, Exec VP & Gen Mgr-Products - Xilinx, Inc.; *pg.* 496, *pg.* 252
Pengelly, Angela, Asst Mgr-Mktg - Land O'Lakes, Inc.; *pg.* 873, *pg.* 915
Penich, Abby Johnson, Dir-PR & Social Media - ConAgra Foods, Inc.; *pg.* 826, *pg.* 1014
Penich, Tom, Mgr-Media Comm - BMW of North America, LLC; *pg.* 166, *pg.* 1133
Penkala, David, Dir-Mktg-Natl - Aramark; *pg.* 1013, *pg.* 1558
Penman, Patricia, VP-Global Mktg Svcs & Comm - Johnson Outdoors Inc.; *pg.* 1837, *pg.* 1888
Penn, Aaron, Mgr-Product Experience-Global - Anheuser-Busch Companies, LLC; *pg.* 237, *pg.* 991
Penn, Jayson, Exec VP-Sls & Ops - Pilgrim's Pride Corporation; *pg.* 889, *pg.* 330
Penn, Mandy, Dir-Mktg - Universal Orlando; *pg.* 590, *pg.* 456
Pennartz, Will, Sr Mgr-Mktg-Danner - LaCrosse Footwear, Inc.; *pg.* 1811, *pg.* 1503
Penner, Adam, Mgr-Digital Mktg - INVISTA B.V.; *pg.* 1168, *pg.* 723
Penner, Chris, Sr Asst Brand Mgr-Home Care - Procter & Gamble Inc.; *pg.* 333, *pg.* 1929
Penner-Howell, Kae, Grp Dir-Creative - The WhiteWave Foods Company; *pg.* 1037, *pg.* 324
Penning, Jason, Dir-Sls-Premium Seats - Live Nation Entertainment, Inc.; *pg.* 558, *pg.* 47
Pennington, Christine, Mgr-Mktg - Strayer University; *pg.* 607, *pg.* 405
Pennington, Greg, Product Mgr - Google Inc.; *pg.* 1249, *pg.* 153
Pennington, Jeff, Dir-Sls-Telecom - Analog Devices, Inc.; *pg.* 617, *pg.* 839
Pennington, Jeff, Mgr-Consumer Mktg - SpartanNash Co; *pg.* 1034, *pg.* 889
Pennington, Lesley, Reg VP-Sls - William Lyon Homes; *pg.* 122, *pg.* 166
Pennington, Lisa, Sr Mgr-Exec Comm & Support - California Pizza Kitchen Inc.; *pg.* 1720, *pg.* 127
Pennington, Michael, Dir-Ethnic Mktg - Affiliated Foods, Inc.; *pg.* 1012, *pg.* 1658
Pennington, Terry, VP-Sls - Ennis, Inc.; *pg.* 393, *pg.* 1727
Pennix, Alisha, Sr Mgr-IR - Newell Rubbermaid Inc.; *pg.* 1128, *pg.* 515
Pennock, Larry, VP-Mktg - Clayton Corporation; *pg.* 1154, *pg.* 977
Penny, Thomas, Product Mgr-Indus Defoamers & Mgr-Technical Sls - Emerald Performance Materials, LLC; *pg.* 1161, *pg.* 1445
Penrith, Leslie, VP-Mktg - U.S. Bancorp; *pg.* 815, *pg.* 945
Penrose, Anthea, Mgr-PR - Raymond James Financial, Inc.; *pg.* 798, *pg.* 464
Pensa, Erin, Dir-PR - CVS Health Corporation; *pg.* 1765, *pg.* 1610
Pensec, John, Sr Dir-Comm & Pub Affairs - Mueller Water Products, Inc.; *pg.* 98, *pg.* 515
Penso, Juan, Dir-Direct Mktg Comm - Comcast Cable Communications, Inc.; *pg.* 276, *pg.* 1560
Penso, Juan, Dir-Direct Mktg Comm - Comcast Corporation; *pg.* 276, *pg.* 1560
Penta, Michael, VP-Sls - Giga-tronics Incorporated; *pg.* 640, *pg.* 260
Pentecost, Brian, Dir-Creative - General Electric Company; *pg.* 1297, *pg.* 347
Pento, Kevin, Dir-Mktg User Experience - Vonage Holdings Corp.; *pg.* 686, *pg.* 1074
Penumatcha, Raju, Sr VP-Product Dev - Oracle Corporation; *pg.* 450, *pg.* 191
Penzner, Eliana, Mgr-Mktg - Intel Corporation; *pg.* 645, *pg.* 266
Penzone, Shane, Rep-Specialty Sls-Specialty Care - GE Healthcare; *pg.* 399, *pg.* 1765
Peoples, Josh, VP-Lawns Mktg - The Scotts Miracle-Gro Company; *pg.* 1799, *pg.* 1459
Pepe, Steve, Head-Comml Mktg-Global - GE Capital; *pg.* 761, *pg.* 362
Pepe, Steven, Dir-Digital Mktg - GE Water & Process Technologies; *pg.* 1339, *pg.* 1588
Pepe, Steven, Dir-Digital Mktg - General Electric Company; *pg.* 1297, *pg.* 347
Pepin, Dominique, Sr Mgr-Mktg-Dealers Retail Canada - PPG Canada Inc.; *pg.* 1178, *pg.* 1928
Pepitone, Nick, Project Mgr-Paid Media - Discover Financial Services; *pg.* 744, *pg.* 653
Pepper, Amber, VP-Mktg & Comm-Europe - Coach, Inc.; *pg.* 3, *pg.* 1214
Pepper, Bob, VP-Mktg - Hormel Foods Corporation; *pg.* 863, *pg.* 915
Pepper, Janina, Project Mgr-Creative Svcs - Citrix Online LLC; *pg.* 1235, *pg.* 99
Pepper, Janina, Project Mgr-Creative Svcs - Citrix Systems, Inc.; *pg.* 375, *pg.* 424
Pepper, Rick, Sr Mgr-Ops Svcs - Jack in the Box Inc.; *pg.* 1732, *pg.* 204
Peppiatt, Ray, Mgr-Mktg & Consumer Products-SBU - Rain Bird Corporation; *pg.* 707, *pg.* 44
Pepping, Mark, Mgr-Product Mktg - Experian Consumer Direct; *pg.* 1245, *pg.* 71
Pepple, Darin, Sr Mgr-Mktg Plng-Imaging-Consumer Mktg Grp - Panasonic Corporation of North America; *pg.* 661, *pg.* 1120
Peralta, Robert, Sr VP-Sls Ops - NBC Universal, Inc.; *pg.* 300, *pg.* 1266
Peralta, Samantha, Coord-Mktg - Transamerica Insurance & Investment Group; *pg.* 1219, *pg.* 141
Peralta, Tania, Mgr-Online Mktg - Steven Madden, Ltd.; *pg.* 1819, *pg.* 1176
Peranteau, Michelle, Dir-Mktg & Comm - Baume & Mercier, Inc.; *pg.* 1, *pg.* 1201
Perdiguerra, Miles, Dir-Mktg - DHC USA Inc.; *pg.* 507, *pg.* 216
Perdue, Bob, Product Mgr-Engineered Products - Baldor Electric Company; *pg.* 1316, *pg.* 32
Perdue, Jay, Sr Dir-UX Design & Content - St. Jude Children's Research Hospital; *pg.* 1596, *pg.* 1646
Perdue, Stephanie Sotelo, Chief Product Mktg Officer - Taco Bell Corp.; *pg.* 1752, *pg.* 117
Pere, Olga, Sr Mgr-Mktg-Global Category Innovation - Kellogg Company; *pg.* 831, *pg.* 870
Perea, Carlos, VP-Sls Latin America - Extreme Networks Inc; *pg.* 287, *pg.* 245
Peregi, Lisa, Coord-Mktg - Massage Envy Limited, LLC; *pg.* 516, *pg.* 23
Perego, Michelle, Sr Dir-Creative Ops & Dev - Boston Proper, Inc.; *pg.* 20, *pg.* 410
Pereida, Clair, Assoc Specialist-Mktg Comm - SanDisk Corporation; *pg.* 465, *pg.* 147
Pereira, Daryl, Mgr-Social Bus - International Business Machines Corporation; *pg.* 418, *pg.* 1138
Pereira, Fabian, VP-Mktg - Johnsonville Sausage, LLC; *pg.* 867, *pg.* 1894
Pereira, Jorge, Mgr-Sls-Intl - Huffy Corporation; *pg.* 1836, *pg.* 1409
Pereira, Marco, Mgr-Brand & Adv - Hewlett-Packard Company;

First page reference indicates Business Class Edition
Second page reference indicates Geographic Edition

pg. 404, *pg.* 175
Pereira, Nicole, Mgr-Northeast Reg Mktg-Dom Perignon - Moet Hennessy; *pg.* 1966, *pg.* 1260
Pereira, Rich, VP-Sls-Major & Natl Accts - Tech Data Corporation; *pg.* 482, *pg.* 416
Perelman, Andi, Coord-New Media - Pittsburgh Penguins LLC; *pg.* 577, *pg.* 1578
Perentesis, Valerie, Sr Dir-Pharmacovigilance Evaluation, Reporting & Sys - Johnson & Johnson; *pg.* 1549, *pg.* 1091
Perera, Wiren, VP-LAN Solutions Bus Unit & Corp Strategic Mktg - Micrel, Inc.; *pg.* 654, *pg.* 247
Peres, Jessica, Analyst-Sponsorship Mktg - State Farm Mutual Automobile Insurance Co.; *pg.* 1218, *pg.* 557
Peretz, Meir, Mgr-Sls - Harris Moran Seed Co.; *pg.* 1796, *pg.* 150
Perez, Andrea, Brand Mgr - The Procter & Gamble Company; *pg.* 1129, *pg.* 1418
Perez, Andy, Mgr-Social Content - Beam Suntory Inc.; *pg.* 1957, *pg.* 599
Perez, Angel, Dir-Trade Mktg-Frozen Div - Pinnacle Foods Group LLC; *pg.* 889, *pg.* 1104
Perez, Annalisa, Mgr-Contracts-Display Adv - Amazon.com, Inc.; *pg.* 1226, *pg.* 1831
Perez, Anthony, Dir-Creative - Leatherman Tool Group, Inc.; *pg.* 1053, *pg.* 1504
Perez, Borja, Sr VP-Digital & Social Media - Telemundo Network Inc.; *pg.* 311, *pg.* 430
Perez, Cecil, VP-Sls-Latin America - Riverbed Technology, Inc.; *pg.* 1277, *pg.* 225
Perez, Cecilia, Dir-Multicultural Mktg - Chevron Corporation; *pg.* 974, *pg.* 259
Perez, Chris, Sr Specialist-Mktg - McKesson Corporation; *pg.* 1560, *pg.* 222
Perez, Donald, Dir-Channel Mktg - AT&T; *pg.* 1865, *pg.* 258
Perez, Edward, VP-Mktg & Sls Ops - United States Cellular Corporation; *pg.* 1875, *pg.* 594
Perez, Evelyn, Acct Mgr-Sls & Comm Div - ScanSource, Inc.; *pg.* 671, *pg.* 1618
Perez, Jared, Sr Product Mgr - AOL Inc.; *pg.* 1229, *pg.* 1195
Perez, Jennifer, Sr Dir-Go Red For Women - American Heart Association Inc.; *pg.* 128, *pg.* 1673
Perez, Jorge, Dir-Mktg-NA Comml Pricing, Analytics & Strategy - Dell Inc.; *pg.* 383, *pg.* 1737
Perez, Kerry, Brand Mktg Mgr - AMN Healthcare Services, Inc.; *pg.* 1494, *pg.* 200
Perez, Leandro, Dir-Product Mktg-Analytics - salesforce.com, inc.; *pg.* 1278, *pg.* 226
Perez, Lisa, Dir-Mktg - Bayer Healthcare Consumer Care Division; *pg.* 1500, *pg.* 1087
Perez, Lubna, Sr Assoc Brand Mgr - Mondelez International, Inc.; *pg.* 878, *pg.* 601
Perez, Lucia, Product Mgr - Xerox Corporation; *pg.* 494, *pg.* 365
Perez, Luis, Sr Analyst-Mktg - Alliance Data Systems Corporation; *pg.* 347, *pg.* 1729
Perez, Marcie, Mgr-Chrysler Brand Media, CRM & Social - FCA US LLC; *pg.* 170, *pg.* 868
Perez, Marisa, Sr Dir-Shopper Mktg, Digital Conversion & Program Activation - Frito-Lay North America, Inc.; *pg.* 1853, *pg.* 1730
Perez, Marisa, Sr Dir-Shopper Mktg, Digital Conversion & Program Activation - PepsiCo, Inc.; *pg.* 259, *pg.* 1327
Perez, Mercedes, Dir-Media - Consolidated Credit Counseling Services, Inc.; *pg.* 741, *pg.* 424
Perez, Nicole, Coord-Mktg - Univision Communications Inc.; *pg.* 683, *pg.* 1307
Perez, Oliver, Mgr-Mktg - General Mills, Inc.; *pg.* 828, *pg.* 933
Perez, Orlando, Head-Platform & Programmatic Sls-Sector - Google Inc.; *pg.* 1249, *pg.* 153
Perez, Ricardo, Specialist-Digital Mktg - Pinnacle Entertainment, Inc.; *pg.* 576, *pg.* 1029
Perez, Santiago, Category Mgr-Product - Goya Foods, Inc.; *pg.* 859, *pg.* 1075
Perez, Selina, Mgr-Customer Team Mktg-Target Team - The Procter & Gamble Company; *pg.* 1129, *pg.* 1418
Perez, Sonya, Brand Mgr-Bacardi Rums - Bacardi USA, Inc.; *pg.* 1956, *pg.* 417
Perez, Veronica, Dir-Sls & Mktg-Charlotte Div - Lennar Corporation; *pg.* 1100, *pg.* 443
Perfater, Matt, Specialist-Mktg - Advance Auto Parts, Inc.; *pg.* 197, *pg.* 1805
Perham, Charlotte R., Sr Dir-Comm - Plumbing-Heating-Cooling Contractors-National Association; *pg.* 154, *pg.* 1782
Perich, Tom, Dir-Mktg-The Home Depot - American Woodmark Corporation; *pg.* 913, *pg.* 1811
Perino, David, Dir-Mktg-Global Launch Excellence - Merck & Co., Inc.; *pg.* 1566, *pg.* 1077
Perkel, Josh, Sr Mgr-Mktg Comm - Synopsys, Inc.; *pg.* 480, *pg.* 162
Perkel, Rachel, Head-Mktg, Wealth Brokerage & Retirement - Wells Fargo & Company; *pg.* 819, *pg.* 232
Perkin, Chris, VP & Dir-DC & Sub-Advisory - Loomis, Sayles & Company, L.P.; *pg.* 777, *pg.* 798
Perkins, Bob, VP-Mktg - Danaher Corporation; *pg.* 1044, *pg.* 397
Perkins, Brian, VP-Mktg-Budweiser - Anheuser-Busch Companies, LLC; *pg.* 237, *pg.* 991
Perkins, Candace, Mgr-Media - MGM Resorts International; *pg.* 1105, *pg.* 1028
Perkins, Clark, Brand Mgr-Chippewa Boots - Justin Brands, Inc.; *pg.* 1810, *pg.* 1695
Perkins, Courtnay, Brand Mgr - Revlon Consumer Products Corporation; *pg.* 521, *pg.* 1286
Perkins, Courtnay, Brand Mgr - Revlon, Inc.; *pg.* 521, *pg.* 1286
Perkins, Dave, Sr Mgr-Mktg Programs Mgmt-Global - Welch Allyn Inc.; *pg.* 1436, *pg.* 1342
Perkins, Don, VP-Product Mktg - Windstream Corporation; *pg.* 321, *pg.* 34
Perkins, Edie, VP-Product Dev-Intl - Scholastic Corporation; *pg.* 1683, *pg.* 1288
Perkins, Greg, Mgr-Mdsg - Larson-Juhl US LLC; *pg.* 933, *pg.* 537
Perkins, Jaime, Sr Mgr-Learning Experience - Autodesk Inc.; *pg.* 356, *pg.* 257
Perkins, Jeff, Exec Dir-Sls & Mktg - Cellco Partnership; *pg.* 1869, *pg.* 1042
Perkins, Jeff, Exec Dir-Sls & Mktg - Verizon Communications Inc.; *pg.* 1875, *pg.* 1309
Perkins, Jim, Mgr-Channel Mktg North America-Comml Fleets - Shell Oil Company; *pg.* 984, *pg.* 1714
Perkins, Kenneth J., Sr Dir-Corp Real Estate Svcs - United Rentals, Inc.; *pg.* 1386, *pg.* 350
Perkins, Lindsay, Designer-Digital - L.L. Bean, Inc.; *pg.* 1777, *pg.* 750
Perkins, Mallory, Sr Mgr-Digital Strategy - Wal-Mart.com; *pg.* 1287, *pg.* 50
Perkins, Michelle, Dir-Integrated Mktg-E-Media Bus - Dolby Laboratories, Inc.; *pg.* 284, *pg.* 217
Perkins, Rachel, Brand Mgr - Kind LLC; *pg.* 868, *pg.* 1249
Perkins, Robin, Dir-Comm & Mktg - Earth Share; *pg.* 140, *pg.* 762
Perkins, Scott, Asst VP-Adv - AT&T Inc.; *pg.* 1867, *pg.* 1674
Perkins, Sherrie, VP-Mktg & New Bus Dev - LivaNova; *pg.* 1557, *pg.* 1710
Perkins, Susan, VP-Mktg-US & Canada - Tupperware Brands Corporation; *pg.* 1139, *pg.* 456
Perkins, Todd, Mgr Mktg - IMS Health, Inc.; *pg.* 1544, *pg.* 344
Perkins-Roberts, Cynthia, VP-Multicultural Mktg & Sls Dev - Video Advertising Bureau; *pg.* 160, *pg.* 1311
Perler, Ari, VP-Market Res & Strategic Sls Insights - NBC Universal Television Networks Group; *pg.* 302, *pg.* 1267
Perlingos, Julia C., Project Mgr-Mktg Comm & Creative - Apria Healthcare Group Inc.; *pg.* 1495, *pg.* 120
Perlis, Adam, Dir-Creative-AT&T AdWorks - AT&T Inc.; *pg.* 1867, *pg.* 1674
Perlis, Lee, Dir-Mktg - Blackboard Inc.; *pg.* 1232, *pg.* 396
Perlis, Mike, Pres/CEO-Forbes Media - Forbes, Inc.; *pg.* 1641, *pg.* 1232
Perlman, Betsy, Mgr-Digital Mktg - J. Crew Group, Inc.; *pg.* 1773, *pg.* 1245
Perlman, Bruce, Dir-Integrated Mktg - The Progressive Corporation; *pg.* 1214, *pg.* 1463
Perlman, Mark, Sr VP-Field Sls - Ameritas Investment Corp.; *pg.* 1192, *pg.* 1410
Perlman, Michelle, Assoc Dir-HIV Mktg - Bristol-Myers Squibb Company; *pg.* 1509, *pg.* 1206
Perlman, Tracy, VP-Entertainment Mktg & Promos - National Football League; *pg.* 567, *pg.* 1264
Perlmutter, Brett R., Mgr-Mktg Comm-Medicare Programs - Anthem, Inc.; *pg.* 1192, *pg.* 683
Perlow, Adam, VP-Sls Ops, Branding, Mktg, Sls & Aggressive Growth - Kia Motors America Inc.; *pg.* 181, *pg.* 112
Perlozzo, Tom, Buyer-Mktg-Adv Production - GEICO Corporation; *pg.* 1200, *pg.* 399
Perlstein, Julie M., Dir-Adv Promos - The Washington Post; *pg.* 1701, *pg.* 407
Perna, Seda, Sr Mgr-Content-Worldwide - Gucci America Inc.; *pg.* 6, *pg.* 1237
Perodeau, Michael, VP-Mktg - Pratt & Whitney Canada Corp.; *pg.* 1370, *pg.* 1952
Perone, Dino, Reg VP-Sls-B2B Enterprise - AT&T Inc.; *pg.* 1868, *pg.* 358
Perone, Michael, Co-Founder, CMO & Exec VP - Barracuda Networks, Inc.; *pg.* 360, *pg.* 58
Perone, Nick, Sr Mgr-Mktg - Intuit Inc.; *pg.* 769, *pg.* 158
Peros, Shane, Mng Dir-Partner Sls-US - Google Inc.; *pg.* 1249, *pg.* 153
Peroy, Marcel, Brand Mgr-American Crew-Global - Revlon Consumer Products Corporation; *pg.* 521, *pg.* 1286
Peroy, Marcel, Brand Mgr-American Crew-Global - Revlon, Inc.; *pg.* 521, *pg.* 1286
Perpich, David, Sr VP-Product - The New York Times Company; *pg.* 1668, *pg.* 1270
Perras, Jaime, Mgr-Mktg Programs-ARRIS - Motorola Mobility LLC; *pg.* 657, *pg.* 627
Perreault, Kathleen, Dir-Shopper Mktg - Hillshire Brands; *pg.* 862, *pg.* 576
Perrelli, Joyce, Program Mgr-Mktg Comm - Cisco Systems, Inc.; *pg.* 372, *pg.* 240
Perri, Melissa, Head-Shopper Mktg Category - Unilever United States, Inc.; *pg.* 904, *pg.* 1061
Perricelli, Lori, Brand Mgr-Aquafina FlavorSplash - Pepsi-Cola North America; *pg.* 259, *pg.* 1327
Perrill, Susan, Mgr-Product Mktg - Xerox Corporation; *pg.* 494, *pg.* 365
Perrin, Blaine, Dir-Product Mktg - Columbia Sportswear Company; *pg.* 1830, *pg.* 1501
Perrin, Brian, Sr Dir-Mktg & Digital Product Dev-Harper Wave & Harper Bus - HarperCollins Publishers Inc.; *pg.* 1647, *pg.* 1237
Perrin, Kelsey, Planner-Mktg - Nordstrom, Inc.; *pg.* 1779, *pg.* 1837
Perrine, Dave, Mgr-Mktg Intelligence - Valassis; *pg.* 1698, *pg.* 386
Perron, Clermont, Sr VP-Sls - Polycor Inc.; *pg.* 105, *pg.* 1958
Perrotta, Mario, Dir-Sls & Mktg - Norwalk Compressor Company, Inc.; *pg.* 1366, *pg.* 380
Perruso, Catherine, Product Mgr-Small Bus - AT&T; *pg.* 1865, *pg.* 258
Perry, Anthony, VP-Media Sls - Move, Inc.; *pg.* 1268, *pg.* 247
Perry, Brenda, Sr Dir-HR - Amkor Technology, Inc.; *pg.* 67, *pg.* 25
Perry, Bridget, VP-Enterprise Mktg - Adobe Systems Incorporated; *pg.* 342, *pg.* 235
Perry, Christopher J., Pres-Sls, Mktg & Client Solutions - Broadridge Financial Solutions Inc.; *pg.* 727, *pg.* 1172
Perry, Dave, Dir-Mktg - American Medical Systems Holdings, Inc.; *pg.* 1493, *pg.* 947
Perry, Denise, Sr Mgr-Mktg Comm & Adv - FMR LLC (Fidelity Investments); *pg.* 759, *pg.* 794
Perry, Donna C., Mgr-Mktg Comm - Clean Harbors, Inc.; *pg.* 376, *pg.* 839
Perry, Effie, Dir-Mktg - EZCORP, Inc.; *pg.* 750, *pg.* 1662
Perry, George, Sr Dir-Strategic Partnership Mktg-Global - Rosetta Stone Inc.; *pg.* 462, *pg.* 1774
Perry, Grace, Sr Dir-Sls & Mktg - HomeTown Communications Network, Inc.; *pg.* 1650, *pg.* 904
Perry, Hayden, Sr Mgr-Mktg - Peet's Coffee & Tea, Inc.; *pg.* 1029, *pg.* 85
Perry, Heather, Dir-Fragrance Mktg - Chanel, Inc.; *pg.* 503, *pg.* 1211
Perry, Jamie, VP-Brand & Product Dev - JetBlue Airways Corporation; *pg.* 1913, *pg.* 1174
Perry, Jana Sanders, Specialist-PR Media - Jelly Belly Candy Company; *pg.* 1857, *pg.* 86
Perry, Jim, Head-Sls-Nickelodeon Grp-Viacom Media Networks - Viacom Inc.; *pg.* 316, *pg.* 1310
Perry, John, VP-Adv - Valero Energy Corporation; *pg.* 986, *pg.* 1743
Perry, Joseph, Analyst-Digital Mktg-ECommerce - Bluegreen Corporation; *pg.* 1082, *pg.* 410
Perry, Kristen, Sr Mgr-Media & Mktg - Ann Inc.; *pg.* 18, *pg.* 1195
Perry, Kristen, Assoc Mgr-Mktg - HP Hood LLC; *pg.* 864, *pg.* 829
Perry, Lauren, Mgr-Adv-W Magazine - Vogue Magazine; *pg.* 1700, *pg.* 1311
Perry, Lily, Acct Exec-Digital Media Adv - Yahoo! Canada Co.; *pg.* 1289, *pg.* 1947
Perry, Maria, Asst VP & Sr Mgr-Event - MFS Investment Management; *pg.* 782, *pg.* 798
Perry, Mark, Dir-Product Plng - Nissan North America, Inc.; *pg.* 186, *pg.* 1633

Perry, Martha, Dir-PR - Brown & Crouppen, P.C.; *pg.* 1393, *pg.* 993
Perry, Michelle, Dir-Mktg - Constellation Brands, Inc.; *pg.* 1960, *pg.* 1348
Perry, Miles, Mgr-Mktg - FedEx Corporation; *pg.* 1907, *pg.* 1642
Perry, Robin, Sr Mgr-Customer Mktg - Coca-Cola Refreshments USA, Inc.; *pg.* 247, *pg.* 500
Perry, Roger, Mgr-Product & Mktg - Aeroflex Incorporated; *pg.* 614, *pg.* 1321
Perry, Sarah A., Mgr-Creative Svcs - Adobe Systems Incorporated; *pg.* 342, *pg.* 235
Perry, Sean, Mgr-Sls-Natl-Fire & Waterworks - Watts Water Technologies, Inc.; *pg.* 1078, *pg.* 837
Perry, Tim, Dir-Mktg - Norgren, Inc.; *pg.* 231, *pg.* 333
Perry, Toby, Dir & Sr Mgr-Mktg-Electric Vehicles - Nissan North America, Inc.; *pg.* 186, *pg.* 1633
Perry, Tracey, Brand Mgr - IHS Inc.; *pg.* 1652, *pg.* 326
Perry, Trish, Dir-PR-Global - ADTRAN, Inc.; *pg.* 344, *pg.* 6
Persaud, Michael, Dir-Programmatic Adv - Wenner Media LLC; *pg.* 1701, *pg.* 1314
Persie, Ashley, Sr Coord-Mktg - Truth Initiative; *pg.* 158, *pg.* 405
Persky, Jody, VP-Brand Mktg - Career Education Corporation; *pg.* 599, *pg.* 658
Person, Calvin, Mgr & Engr-Technical Mktg - Cisco Systems, Inc.; *pg.* 372, *pg.* 240
Person, Judy, Sr VP-Sls - Randa Corp.; *pg.* 47, *pg.* 1285
Perttu, Tiina, Sr Mgr-Bus Dev - Haworth, Inc.; *pg.* 402, *pg.* 891
Perucho, Irene, Head-Franchise-Immuno-Oncology & Mgr-Mktg - Bristol-Myers Squibb Company; *pg.* 1509, *pg.* 1206
Perusse, Charles, Sr Mgr-Product Analytics-FundsNetwork - FMR LLC (Fidelity Investments); *pg.* 759, *pg.* 794
Pesaturo, Phyllis, VP-Creative & Dir - QuanTuro Publishing, Inc.; *pg.* 1679, *pg.* 445
Pescara, Marco Q., CMO-Mktg & Mdsg - Lumber Liquidators Holdings, Inc.; *pg.* 94, *pg.* 1808
Pesce, Richard, Sr Mgr-Comm - Capital One Financial Corporation; *pg.* 730, *pg.* 1789
Peskin, Timon, Mgr-Trade Mktg - Annie's Inc.; *pg.* 1760, *pg.* 45
Pesoa, Rodrigo, Sr Dir-Sls-Latin America - Dassault Falcon Jet Corp.; *pg.* 227, *pg.* 1122
Pestana, Marina Lima, Mgr-Mktg - Deloitte & Touche USA LLP; *pg.* 743, *pg.* 1222
Pestinger, Greg A., Grp Brand Dir-North America - Brown-Forman Corporation; *pg.* 1958, *pg.* 732
Pestow, Liz, Dir-Mktg - Indiana Crop Improvement Association, Inc.; *pg.* 144, *pg.* 693
Pesut, Elliott, Mgr-Integrated Mktg - Alaska Airlines, Inc.; *pg.* 1897, *pg.* 1830
Petaia, Stephen, Asst VP-Corp Mktg - Comerica Incorporated; *pg.* 740, *pg.* 1677
Pete, Diane, Sr Mgr-Consumer Insights - The Home Depot, Inc.; *pg.* 1050, *pg.* 510
Petee, Laura, Sr Mgr-Contract Channel Mktg - Whirlpool Corporation; *pg.* 62, *pg.* 872
Peter, Aimee St, Mgr-Mktg Comm-Global - Hach Company; *pg.* 1415, *pg.* 334
Peter, Kim, Dir-Mktg - Anderson Erickson Dairy Company; *pg.* 837, *pg.* 704
Peter, Leigh, Dir-Integrated Mktg Solutions & Rels - Bayer Healthcare Consumer Care Division; *pg.* 1500, *pg.* 1087
Peterfeso, Keith, Brand Mgr - Nestle Purina PetCare Company; *pg.* 1479, *pg.* 1000
Peterlin, John G., III, Sr Dir-Mktg - Port of Galveston; *pg.* 1919, *pg.* 1697
Peters, Aaron, Sr Mgr-Market Plng & Res - Walgreen Co.; *pg.* 1608, *pg.* 605
Peters, Brian, Dir-Mktg-Corp Alliances & Capabilities - General Mills, Inc.; *pg.* 828, *pg.* 933
Peters, Brian, Mgr-Plant - Grain Processing Corporation; *pg.* 859, *pg.* 709
Peters, Calvin, Mgr-PR & Digital Comm - Duane Reade, Inc.; *pg.* 1525, *pg.* 1226
Peters, Chris P., Strategist-Global Bus Mktg - Intel Corporation; *pg.* 645, *pg.* 266
Peters, Craig, Sr VP-Bus Dev, Content & Mktg - Getty Images, Inc.; *pg.* 1645, *pg.* 1836
Peters, Dean, Dir-PR & Comm - International Dairy Queen, Inc.; *pg.* 1732, *pg.* 938
Peters, Dennis, Sr Mgr-Procurement & Contracts - Baker Hughes Incorporated; *pg.* 1315, *pg.* 1700
Peters, Dylan, Analyst-Mktg - United Parcel Service, Inc.; *pg.* 1928, *pg.* 522
Peters, Eugene, Dir-Product Mgmt - Automatic Data Processing, Inc.; *pg.* 357, *pg.* 1117
Peters, Gwen, Sr Mgr-Mktg - Digital Insight; *pg.* 744, *pg.* 189
Peters, Jed, VP-Sls & Mktg-US - ACCO Brands Corporation; *pg.* 340, *pg.* 626
Peters, Jeff, Assoc Dir-Letairis HCP Mktg - Gilead Sciences, Inc.; *pg.* 1535, *pg.* 88
Peters, Jessica, Asst VP & Coord-Adv - Banner Corporation; *pg.* 722, *pg.* 1846
Peters, Jim, Mgr-Digital, Social & CRM Mktg-Lincoln Motor Co. - Ford Motor Company; *pg.* 172, *pg.* 876
Peters, Joel, CMO & Sr VP - Toronto Convention & Visitors Association; *pg.* 1007, *pg.* 1945
Peters, Katelyn, Specialist-Adv - Family Dollar Stores, Inc.; *pg.* 1768, *pg.* 1382
Peters, Linh, VP-Mktg - SpartanNash Co; *pg.* 1034, *pg.* 889
Peters, Luke, Product Mgr-Corn Herbicides - Dow AgroSciences LLC; *pg.* 1156, *pg.* 684
Peters, Lynn, Dir-Mktg-Global - Takeda Pharmaceuticals USA, Inc.; *pg.* 1600, *pg.* 605
Peters, Megan, Sr Mgr-Sourcing - Amway Corporation; *pg.* 326, *pg.* 864
Peters, Monique, Sr Mgr-CRM - The Home Depot, Inc.; *pg.* 1050, *pg.* 510
Peters, Rick C., Sr Mgr-Comml Data Org-Global - Eaton Corporation; *pg.* 1331, *pg.* 1429
Peters, Sarah, Coord-Social Media - Carter's, Inc.; *pg.* 21, *pg.* 491
Peters, Sharon, VP-Media & Original Programming - Cablevision Systems Corporation; *pg.* 272, *pg.* 1141
Peters, Sharon, Mgr-PR - Institute of Real Estate Management; *pg.* 144, *pg.* 578
Peters, Stephanie, Mgr-Adv - Nintendo of America, Inc.; *pg.* 965, *pg.* 1829
Peters, Tony, VP-Sls - Bermo Enterprises Inc.; *pg.* 20, *pg.* 906
Petersen Stroud, Kirsten, Specialist-Mktg - Halifax Medical Center; *pg.* 1538, *pg.* 420
Petersen, Barry Daniel, Sr Analyst-Creative & Brand Design - United Airlines, Inc.; *pg.* 1927, *pg.* 593
Petersen, David, VP-Mktg - Stanley Furniture Co., Inc.; *pg.* 943, *pg.* 1379
Petersen, Eric, Head-Sls-Northern Territory - Farmers Group, Inc.; *pg.* 1199, *pg.* 130
Petersen, Erynn, Sr VP-Audience Products & Editorial Tools - Time Inc.; *pg.* 1693, *pg.* 1300
Petersen, Henrik Smith, Pres-Sls-Global - Airspan Networks Inc.; *pg.* 346, *pg.* 410
Petersen, Justin, Brand Mgr-Meta - The Procter & Gamble Company; *pg.* 1129, *pg.* 1418
Petersen, Kelly, Dir-Mktg & Market Tech-Global - The NASDAQ OMX Group, Inc.; *pg.* 785, *pg.* 1263
Petersen, Kelly, Head-Product - Tremor Video; *pg.* 682, *pg.* 1305
Petersen, Kristen, Dir-Demand Center & Global Mktg Ops - F5 Networks, Inc.; *pg.* 396, *pg.* 1835
Petersen, Nick, Brand Mgr - Amazon.com, Inc.; *pg.* 1226, *pg.* 1831
Petersen, Rich, Dir-Mktg Mgmt - SanDisk Corporation; *pg.* 465, *pg.* 147
Petersen, Robin, Specialist-Mktg - American Medical Systems Holdings, Inc.; *pg.* 1493, *pg.* 947
Petersen, Stephanie A., Mgr-Sls & Mktg-Natl - JPMorgan Chase & Co.; *pg.* 772, *pg.* 1246
Petershagen, Joel, Product Mgr-Mktg-Bus Ops - Advanced Micro Devices, Inc.; *pg.* 613, *pg.* 282
Petersmarck, Lynn, Dir-Adv - Living Essentials, LLC; *pg.* 1026, *pg.* 886
Petersohn, Walter, Exec VP-Sls - Sirona Dental Systems, Inc.; *pg.* 1429, *pg.* 1175
Peterson, Alea L., Specialist-Mktg - Thrivent Financial for Lutherans; *pg.* 1219, *pg.* 944
Peterson, Allison, VP-Mktg - Best Buy Co., Inc.; *pg.* 1761, *pg.* 954
Peterson, Bruce, Sr Mgr - Intuit Inc.; *pg.* 769, *pg.* 158
Peterson, Caitlin, Mgr-Social Media-North America - Netflix, Inc.; *pg.* 1269, *pg.* 141
Peterson, Christopher H., Sr Mgr-Mktg Insights-ECommerce Europe - Ralph Lauren Corporation; *pg.* 46, *pg.* 1284
Peterson, David, Dir-Digital Vendor Mktg - Target Corporation; *pg.* 1786, *pg.* 942
Peterson, Dean, Dir-Sls Admin - Curries Company; *pg.* 77, *pg.* 709
Peterson, Deborah, Dir-Customer Relationship Mktg - American Family Mutual Insurance Company; *pg.* 1190, *pg.* 1864
Peterson, Dylan, Mgr-Sls - Amazon.com, Inc.; *pg.* 1226, *pg.* 1831
Peterson, Emily, Dir-Mktg Comm & Events - FTD.com Inc.; *pg.* 1770, *pg.* 608
Peterson, Emily, Analyst-Mktg & Shopper Mktg-Walmart - PepsiCo, Inc.; *pg.* 259, *pg.* 1327
Peterson, Eric, Mgr-Mktg - Ford Motor Company; *pg.* 172, *pg.* 876
Peterson, Eric, VP-Sls - Gerber Plumbing Fixtures Corporation; *pg.* 84, *pg.* 672
Peterson, Hanna, Product Mgr-Mobile - Target Corporation; *pg.* 1786, *pg.* 942
Peterson, Heather, Sr Mgr-Mktg-Licensed Partners - CafePress.com, Inc.; *pg.* 1234, *pg.* 254
Peterson, Jeff, VP-Online Mktg & Sls - Go Daddy Inc.; *pg.* 1249, *pg.* 21
Peterson, Jeff, VP-Comml Sls & Customer Svc - Matco Tools Corporation; *pg.* 1065, *pg.* 1474
Peterson, Jim, COO-Metal Food & Household Products Pkg & Sr VP - Ball Corporation; *pg.* 1452, *pg.* 311
Peterson, John, Product Mgr-Technical - Cisco Systems, Inc.; *pg.* 372, *pg.* 240
Peterson, Jon, Mgr-Mktg Comm - GSI Group Inc.; *pg.* 1415, *pg.* 784
Peterson, Kaleigh, Rep-Application Sls-DC/VA/NC & Federal - Oracle Corporation; *pg.* 1272, *pg.* 786
Peterson, Karen, VP-Mktg - Ancestry.com LLC; *pg.* 1228, *pg.* 1754
Peterson, Keith, VP-Mktg - Ceridian Corporation; *pg.* 371, *pg.* 932
Peterson, Keith, Reg Mgr-Mktg - Lithia Motors Inc; *pg.* 183, *pg.* 1499
Peterson, Keith, Mgr-Web Mktg - Sprint Corporation; *pg.* 1874, *pg.* 719
Peterson, Kent, Mgr-Mktg-ECommerce & Video - Milwaukee School of Engineering; *pg.* 605, *pg.* 1878
Peterson, Kim, CMO, Chief Strategy Officer & Sr VP - Alta Resources Corporation; *pg.* 347, *pg.* 1882
Peterson, Kirk, Sr Mgr-Institutional Adv, Branding & Sponsorships - TD Ameritrade Holding Corporation; *pg.* 808, *pg.* 1018
Peterson, Kurt, VP-Sls - Nilodor, Inc.; *pg.* 332, *pg.* 1406
Peterson, Kyle, Mgr-Digital Mktg-Global - Ingram Micro Inc.; *pg.* 415, *pg.* 261
Peterson, Lara, VP-Mktg - Kaz, Inc.; *pg.* 58, *pg.* 844
Peterson, Lori, Strategist-Co-Op & Reg Mktg - Explore Minnesota Tourism; *pg.* 992, *pg.* 960
Peterson, Mary E., Sr Dir-Networking & Tech Svcs-Content Strategy & Programs - Hewlett-Packard Company; *pg.* 404, *pg.* 175
Peterson, Megan, Specialist-Social Media Mktg - The Home Depot, Inc.; *pg.* 1050, *pg.* 510
Peterson, Melissa, Mgr-Media - The Allstate Corporation; *pg.* 1189, *pg.* 639
Peterson, Michelle, Mgr-Mktg - General Mills, Inc.; *pg.* 828, *pg.* 933
Peterson, Mike, Dir-PR - Charles Schwab; *pg.* 1235, *pg.* 1661
Peterson, Monica Womack, Dir-Social Media Strategy & Ops - Toyota Motor Sales, U.S.A., Inc.; *pg.* 193, *pg.* 296
Peterson, Nye, Dir-Global Mktg-Global B2B Campaigns & Creative - Dell Inc.; *pg.* 383, *pg.* 1737
Peterson, RJ, Mgr-Digital Mktg-Global - Michael Kors (USA), Inc.; *pg.* 29, *pg.* 1260
Peterson, Robyn, CTO & Sr VP-Product Mgmt - PC Magazine; *pg.* 1674, *pg.* 1276
Peterson, Rod, Mgr-Adv Sls - Ogden Publications, Inc.; *pg.* 1672, *pg.* 722
Peterson, Ron, VP-Sls-Corp Brands - Paradise, Inc.; *pg.* 888, *pg.* 458
Peterson, Sarah, Sr Mgr-Internal & External Tech Comm - Intuit Inc.; *pg.* 769, *pg.* 158
Peterson, Stacey, Sr Mgr-Mktg-Segment & Field - Quantum Corporation; *pg.* 458, *pg.* 250
Peterson, Steven, Mgr-Mktg - The Toro Company; *pg.* 1065, *pg.* 918
Peterson, Susan, Specialist-Trade Media Mktg - Alaska Airlines, Inc.; *pg.* 1897, *pg.* 1830
Peterson, Susan M., Sr Mgr-Mktg-Bus Analysis & Insight-IBM Security Sys - IBM; *pg.* 410, *pg.* 1449
Peterson, Tony, Sr Product Mgr - McKesson Corporation; *pg.* 1560, *pg.* 222
Peth, Charlie, VP-Sls - Wausau Paper; *pg.* 1471, *pg.* 1855
Peth, Megan, Dir-Brand Mktg-Troy-Bilt - MTD Products, Inc.;

pg. 1057, pg. 1478
Petherbridge, Jo, Exec VP-PR & Digital-BBC America - BBC Worldwide America Inc.; pg. 271, pg. 1201
Petillo, Bruce, Dir-Mktg - Insight Enterprises, Inc.; pg. 415, pg. 26
Petillo, Katherine, Sr Dir-Creative Svcs - Warner Music Group Corp.; pg. 590, pg. 1313
Petit, Brett, Sr VP-Mktg & Sls - Six Flags Entertainment Corporation; pg. 583, pg. 1698
Petit, Todd, Asst VP-Actuarial Product Dev - Allianz Life Insurance Company of North America; pg. 1188, pg. 929
Petit-Frere, Ryann, Mgr-Mktg - IGT; pg. 412, pg. 1031
Petite, Damon, Sr Mgr-Product Mktg - Pandora Media Inc.; pg. 1273, pg. 172
Petito, Fred, Chief Strategy Officer & Chief Analytics Officer - Eveo Inc.; pg. 1244, pg. 217
Petkov, Plamen, VP-Mktg & Bus Dev - Datamax Corporation; pg. 1633, pg. 453
Petrak, Michael R., VP-Sls & Digital Svcs-LDD - GateHouse Media, Inc.; pg. 1644, pg. 1159
Petralia, John, Head-Mktg-Bloomberg Media, Indus Verticals & Recruiting - Bloomberg L.P.; pg. 725, pg. 1204
Petrangelo, J. Geoffrey, Dir-Sls & Bus Dev - Fallbrook Technologies Inc.; pg. 1336, pg. 203
Petranoff, Shannon, Sr VP-Interactive Mktg - Paramount Pictures Corporation; pg. 304, pg. 138
Petrauskas, Ren, Dir-Mktg & Creative - ALYCE Paris; pg. 18, pg. 634
Petrecca, Steve, Mgr-Interactive Mktg - Nissan North America, Inc.; pg. 186, pg. 1633
Petri, Brian, Mgr-Annuity Mktg - The Guardian Life Insurance Company of America; pg. 1202, pg. 1237
Petrick, Adam, Dir-Brand & Mktg-Global - Puma North America, Inc.; pg. 1816, pg. 858
Petrick, Ray, VP-Sls-USA & Canada - Boiron USA Inc.; pg. 1507, pg. 1556
Petrillo, Chris, Category Mgr-Product - Oakley, Inc.; pg. 1840, pg. 86
Petrillo, Joe, VP-Sls Dev - MARTHA STEWART LIVING OMNIMEDIA, INC.; pg. 1661, pg. 1256
Petrillo, Letitia, Sr Mgr-Partnership Mktg - Washington Capitals; pg. 591, pg. 1775
Petrillo, Roberto, VP-Sls-Worldwide - Teledyne LeCroy; pg. 1431, pg. 1153
Petrinec, Mike, Dir-Creative Svcs - State Farm Mutual Automobile Insurance Co.; pg. 1218, pg. 557
Petro, Tracy, Coord-Entertainment Mktg & Promos - National Football League; pg. 567, pg. 1264
Petrocelli, Neil, VP-Sls, Mktg & Ops - Borghese, Inc.; pg. 502, pg. 1205
Petroff, Chris, Mgr-Sls - Gold Medal Products Co.; pg. 55, pg. 1414
Petronio, Simone, Sr Mgr-Mktg-Intl - Blistex, Inc.; pg. 502, pg. 644
Petronzio, Gwen, Sr Mgr-Integrated Mktg - FreshDirect, LLC; pg. 857, pg. 1174
Petrovic, Mary Kate, Dir-Consumer Mktg - Country Music Television, Inc.; pg. 279, pg. 1649
Petrovich, Emily, Sr Specialist-Mktg & Target Team - The Procter & Gamble Company; pg. 1129, pg. 1418
Petrucci, Paul, Mgr-Sls & Mktg - BorgWarner Inc.; pg. 167, pg. 867
Petrunich, Mike, Dir-Sls & Mktg-Clinical Res Market - Abaxis, Inc.; pg. 1483, pg. 298
Petrushchak, Suzy, Dir-Mktg - E&J Gallo Winery; pg. 1962, pg. 149
Petrusic, Mato, VP-Sls-EMEA & Asia Pacific - iPass, Inc.; pg. 1259, pg. 193
Petruska, Linda, Sr Dir-Corp HR - TBC Corporation; pg. 1889, pg. 457
Petry, Laura, Dir-Mktg-Jack Daniel's - Brown-Forman Corporation; pg. 1958, pg. 732
Petry, Michael, Creative Dir - Tumi, Inc.; pg. 15, pg. 1123
Petry, Michael, Product Mgr-Mobile - Weight Watchers International, Inc.; pg. 1609, pg. 1313
Petschow, Kevin R., Sr Mgr - Cisco Systems, Inc.; pg. 372, pg. 240
Pett, Scot, VP-Ticket & Suite Sls - Detroit Tigers Baseball Club, Inc.; pg. 545, pg. 880
Pettersen, Faith, Coord-Online Mktg - Costco Wholesale Corporation; pg. 1765, pg. 1820
Pettey, Christy, Dir-PR - Gartner, Inc.; pg. 1248, pg. 374
Petti, Samantha, Mgr-Mktg Comm - United Airlines, Inc.; pg. 1927, pg. 593
Pettigrew, Steve, Sr Product Mgr-Technical - OpenText; pg. 1272, pg. 1956
Pettinato, Crystal, Mgr-Mktg & Comm - American Express Company; pg. 712, pg. 1190
Pettine, Spencer, Dir-Mktg-Biologics - NuVasive, Inc.; pg. 1577, pg. 205
Pettit, Ashley, Mgr-Social Bus - Southwest Airlines Co.; pg. 1923, pg. 1687
Pettit, Sarah, Specialist-Mktg, PR & Social Media - Associated Food Stores, Inc.; pg. 1014, pg. 1756
Petts, Dale, Product Mgr-Global - Simonds International Corporation; pg. 1376, pg. 819
Petts, David, Sr VP-Sls-Worldwide - ShoreTel, Inc.; pg. 469, pg. 288
Pettus, Jeff, Dir-Sls - Pleasant Holidays LLC; pg. 1919, pg. 307
Pettus, Randy, Dir-Production - Sanderson Farms, Inc.; pg. 893, pg. 970
Petty, Jenny, Brand Mgr-Jackpots - International Game Technology; pg. 957, pg. 1024
Petty, Richard, Sr VP-Production - Power Music, Inc.; pg. 305, pg. 1751
Pettyjohn, Lindsey, Mgr-Integrated Mktg Comm - AGCO Corporation; pg. 700, pg. 530
Pettyjohn, Thad, VP-Sls - Jamison Bedding, Inc.; pg. 930, pg. 1651
Petzelt, Kai, Sr Dir-Solution Mktg - SAP America, Inc.; pg. 466, pg. 1557
Petzinger, Stefan, VP-EU Brand Mktg - Kayak; pg. 1260, pg. 363
Peurach, Jack, Exec VP-Products - SunPower Corporation; pg. 1952, pg. 250
Peykar, Shirin, VP-DR Ad Sls - Univision Communications Inc.; pg. 683, pg. 1307
Peyton, Carla, Sr VP-Licensed Consumer Products-The Americas - BBC Worldwide America Inc.; pg. 271, pg. 1201
Peyton, Doug, Product Mgr - Alliant Energy Corporation; pg. 1933, pg. 1864
Peyton, Tom, Asst VP-Adv & Mktg - American Honda Motor Co., Inc.; pg. 163, pg. 292
Pezdek, Laura, Sr Mgr-OPEN Acq - American Express Company; pg. 712, pg. 1190
Pezzi, Millet, Sr Media Planner & Media Buyer - MGM Resorts International; pg. 1105, pg. 1028
Pezzi, Renee, Sr VP & Dir-Customer Experience, Product & Online - CB&S Bank; pg. 732, pg. 8
Pfaendler, Shelley, Sr Mgr-PR - Deloitte & Touche USA LLP; pg. 743, pg. 1222
Pfaff, Diana, VP-Mktg & Comm - Irving Convention & Visitors Bureau; pg. 996, pg. 1720
Pfannenstiel, Bruce, VP-Mktg Ops - Payless Shoesource, Inc.; pg. 31, pg. 722
Pfau, Liz, Asst Dir-New Product Plng - Astellas Pharma US, Inc.; pg. 1496, pg. 640
Pfeffer, Bob, Dir-Sls - Harris Waste Management Group, Inc.; pg. 1345, pg. 526
Pfeffer, Evan, Exec Dir-Programmatic Sls - Time Inc.; pg. 1693, pg. 1300
Pfeffer, Matt, Dir-Digital Sls-North East & Mid-Atlantic - Live Nation Entertainment, Inc.; pg. 558, pg. 47
Pfeifer, David, Dir-Mktg - The Seibels Bruce Group, Inc.; pg. 1216, pg. 1614
Pfeifer, Donovan, Program Mgr-Product Dev - Fluke Corporation; pg. 1413, pg. 1819
Pfeifer, Emily, Assoc Mgr-Trade Mktg - Constellation Brands, Inc.; pg. 1960, pg. 1348
Pfeifer, Jim, VP-Revenue - Hawks Basketball, Inc.; pg. 551, pg. 509
Pfeifer, Kathrin, Product Mgr - Miele Inc.; pg. 59, pg. 1112
Pfeiffer, Gary, VP-Global Brand Mktg-DISNEY INFINITY - Disney Interactive Media Group; pg. 1239, pg. 95
Pfeiffer, Joe, Mgr-Corp Sls Acct Svcs & Sr Acct Exec - Saint Louis Cardinals, L.P.; pg. 580, pg. 1002
Pfeiffer, Tristi, Dir-Mktg - MillerCoors LLC; pg. 255, pg. 582
Pfenning, Lisa, Category Dir-Mktg-North America Innovation - William Grant & Sons, Inc.; pg. 1972, pg. 1057
Pfingston, Robert, Dir-Creative - Camping World, Inc.; pg. 1830, pg. 725
Pfister, Brent, VP-Mktg-Tempur-Pedic Brand - Tempur Sealy International, Inc.; pg. 944, pg. 731
Pfister, David, Mgr-Media & Acq Ops - Electronic Arts Inc.; pg. 951, pg. 189
Pfitzer, Gary, Mgr-Mktg - Cisco Systems, Inc.; pg. 372, pg. 240
Pfitzner, Michael, Exec VP & Head-Mktg & Comml Coordination - ArcelorMittal Steel USA Inc.; pg. 68, pg. 564
Pflaum, Tana M., Mgr-Mktg Comm - Diebold, Incorporated; pg. 387, pg. 1407
Pfluegl, Michael, Dir-Sls-Sponsorship - Live Nation Entertainment, Inc.; pg. 558, pg. 47
Pfluger, Brian, Mgr-Product Line-EDM - Makino Inc.; pg. 1358, pg. 1461
Pfordresher, Suzanne, Dir-Adv & Brand Mgmt - SeaWorld Parks & Entertainment LLC; pg. 582, pg. 456
Pfund, Ann, Dir-Integrated Mktg - Lord & Taylor LLC; pg. 1777, pg. 1252
Pfund, Jessica, Product Mgr - Google Inc.; pg. 1249, pg. 153
Pfund, Ryan, Sr Product Mgr - Bradley Corporation; pg. 71, pg. 1870
Phadke, Harish, Brand Mgr-Europe & North America-Airwick - Reckitt Benckiser Inc.; pg. 1136, pg. 1105
Phalen, H. Todd, Dir-Sls - Black Brothers Company; pg. 70, pg. 632
Pham, Christina, Mgr-Field Mktg - T-Mobile US, Inc.; pg. 676, pg. 1816
Pham, Cuong, Mgr-Mktg Analytics - LegalZoom.com, Inc.; pg. 1261, pg. 96
Pham, Cuong, Sr Product Mgr - Microsoft Corporation; pg. 435, pg. 1824
Pham, Hung, Mgr-Strategic Mktg - BASF Corporation; pg. 1149, pg. 1066
Pham, Hung, Mgr-Mktg - CVS Health Corporation; pg. 1765, pg. 1610
Pham, Mary, Mgr-Toyota Mdsg & Brand Mgr - Toyota Motor Sales, U.S.A., Inc.; pg. 193, pg. 296
Pham, Schuyler, Dir-Social Media Strategy - Getty Images, Inc.; pg. 1645, pg. 1836
Pham, Tish, Acct Mgr-Adv - Edmunds, Inc.; pg. 1241, pg. 273
Pham, Trinh, Mgr-ECommerce Product Grp - Esurance, Inc.; pg. 1243, pg. 217
Pham, Yen, Analyst-Sls Compensation - McKesson Corporation; pg. 1560, pg. 222
Phan, Anh, VP & Gen Mgr-Medical Technologies & Distr Sls - ITT Corporation; pg. 1351, pg. 1354
Phan, Baohuong, Sr Strategist-Web Mktg - Citrix Systems, Inc.; pg. 375, pg. 424
Phan, Francis, Sr Mgr-Adv UX - Yahoo! Inc.; pg. 1289, pg. 289
Phan, Victor, Sr Dir-Ops & Supply Chain - Bumble Bee Foods LLC; pg. 842, pg. 201
Phanel, Phong, Product Mgr-Pro AV - Epson America Inc.; pg. 394, pg. 122
Phares, Chuck, Exec VP-Sls - L.A. T Sportswear, LLC; pg. 1838, pg. 526
Phares, Joan, Mgr-Mktg - Genworth Financial, Inc.; pg. 761, pg. 1802
Phaup, Wayne, Mgr-Social Media Mktg - United Continental Holdings, Inc.; pg. 1927, pg. 593
Phelan, Dan, VP-Mktg-Residential Div - The Dixie Group, Inc.; pg. 692, pg. 1629
Phelan, Rich, Assoc VP-Media - Marshalls of MA, Inc.; pg. 1778, pg. 821
Phelan, Rich, Assoc VP-Media - T.J. Maxx; pg. 1788, pg. 822
Phelan, Rich, Assoc VP-Media - The TJX Companies, Inc.; pg. 1788, pg. 822
Phelan, Steve, Partner & Exec VP-Sls - Bush Industries Inc.; pg. 919, pg. 1170
Phelps, Amy, Area Dir-Mktg - PulteGroup, Inc.; pg. 1109, pg. 873
Phelps, Andrew, Sr Product Mgr - The New York Times Company; pg. 1668, pg. 1270
Phelps, Ashley R., Mgr-Mktg - HCA HOLDINGS, INC.; pg. 1539, pg. 1651
Phelps, Craig, Sr Asst VP & Dir-Mktg - Amica Mutual Insurance Co.; pg. 1192, pg. 1602
Phelps, David, Chief Sls Officer - Lifevantage Corporation; pg. 1556, pg. 1762
Phelps, Debra, Mgr-Field Mktg-Americas Global Mktg Team - TIBCO Software Inc.; pg. 484, pg. 178
Phelps, Holly, Assoc Mgr-Mktg-Retail & Partner Promos - SeaWorld Parks & Entertainment LLC; pg. 582, pg. 456
Phelps, Jackie, Mgr-Adv Sls - Worcester Telegram & Gazette Corp.; pg. 1702, pg. 863
Phelps, Max, Dir-Outdoor Sls & Natl Book Network - The Globe Pequot Press, Inc.; pg. 1645, pg. 350
Phelps, Selena, Coord-Mktg - Colonial Williamsburg Foundation; pg. 541, pg. 1811
Phibbs, Mark, VP-Mktg-EMEA - Adobe Systems Incorporated; pg. 342, pg. 235

Philbin, Kaitlin, Planner-Digital Sls - Sun-Times Media Group, Inc.; *pg.* 1690, *pg.* 591
Philbin, Tim, VP-Adv Sls-Wetv - AMC Networks Inc.; *pg.* 269, *pg.* 1189
Philbrick, Lindsay, Mgr-Mktg - Hologic, Inc.; *pg.* 1416, *pg.* 784
Philip, Kristen, Mgr-Field Mktg - Ceridian Corporation; *pg.* 371, *pg.* 932
Philip, Rich, Sr Mgr-Products & Svcs - Duke Energy Corporation; *pg.* 1940, *pg.* 1366
Philips, Adam, Mgr-Mktg Comm - DC Comics, Inc.; *pg.* 1633, *pg.* 1221
Philips, Julie, Product Mgr - Barnes & Noble, Inc.; *pg.* 1619, *pg.* 1201
Philips, Kevin, Mgr-Retail & Experiential Mktg - BMW of North America, LLC; *pg.* 166, *pg.* 1133
Philips, Liz, Sr Mgr-Mktg & Strategy - QUALCOMM Incorporated; *pg.* 1873, *pg.* 207
Philips, Sarah, Mgr-Digital Media - Michaels Stores, Inc.; *pg.* 1127, *pg.* 1722
Phillimore, Tiago, Head-Mktg Intelligence - TAP Portugal; *pg.* 1925, *pg.* 1098
Phillip, Curlis, Sr Mgr-Mktg-Mobility Solutions - AT&T Inc.; *pg.* 1867, *pg.* 1674
Phillipp, John, Dir-Sls-Wire Products - Special Metals Corporation; *pg.* 1377, *pg.* 1850
Phillipps, Ben, Sr Dir-CXO Comm - VMware, Inc.; *pg.* 490, *pg.* 179
Phillips, Amanda, VP-Consumer Mktg - Country Music Television, Inc.; *pg.* 279, *pg.* 1649
Phillips, Amy, Sr Dir-Comm - ESPN, Inc.; *pg.* 285, *pg.* 340
Phillips, Amy, Brand Mgr-Hammermill - International Paper Company; *pg.* 1460, *pg.* 1644
Phillips, Andrew, Engr-Technical Mktg - Cisco Systems, Inc.; *pg.* 372, *pg.* 240
Phillips, Angie, Sr Mgr-Acq Mktg & Small Bus Svcs - American Express Company; *pg.* 712, *pg.* 1190
Phillips, Benjamin J., Dir-Technical & Mgr-Production - Boston Ballet Inc.; *pg.* 533, *pg.* 790
Phillips, Billy, Sr Dir-Corp Sponsorship - Dallas Mavericks; *pg.* 543, *pg.* 1678
Phillips, Brandon, Dir-Mktg - Anixter International Inc.; *pg.* 1313, *pg.* 614
Phillips, Catherine L., VP-Sustainable Forests & Products - Weyerhaeuser Company; *pg.* 121, *pg.* 1820
Phillips, Charlie, Exec VP-Mdsg - J. Crew Group, Inc.; *pg.* 1773, *pg.* 1245
Phillips, Chris, Chief Product Officer - Pandora Media Inc.; *pg.* 1273, *pg.* 172
Phillips, Cindy, Mgr-Mktg Comm-Global - Thomas & Betts Corporation; *pg.* 680, *pg.* 1646
Phillips, Claire, Mgr-Mktg-BREO ELLIPTA - GlaxoSmithKline; *pg.* 1536, *pg.* 1565
Phillips, David, VP-Brand Mktg & Creative - MTV Networks Company; *pg.* 298, *pg.* 1262
Phillips, David, VP-Brand Mktg & Creative - Spike TV; *pg.* 310, *pg.* 1295
Phillips, David A., Dir-Software Customer Svcs Mktg & Sls - Philips Electronics North America; *pg.* 662, *pg.* 782
Phillips, Eric, Mgr-Mktg - Armaly Brands; *pg.* 326, *pg.* 912
Phillips, Erin, Specialist-Adv & Mktg - U.S. Bancorp; *pg.* 815, *pg.* 945
Phillips, Feon, Dir-Mktg Analytics - Popeyes Louisiana Kitchen, Inc.; *pg.* 1745, *pg.* 517
Phillips, Gabby, Sr VP-Content & Social-US - Citigroup Inc.; *pg.* 735, *pg.* 1212
Phillips, Heather, Asst Dir-Media Rels - Cleveland Clinic; *pg.* 1516, *pg.* 1429
Phillips, Jason, Mgr-Mktg - Charles Schwab & Company, Inc.; *pg.* 734, *pg.* 215
Phillips, John, Mng Dir-Comm, Media & Tech - Accenture; *pg.* 1392, *pg.* 1186
Phillips, Jon, Principal & Product Mgr-Search & Discovery - Amazon.com, Inc.; *pg.* 1226, *pg.* 1831
Phillips, Jon, Reg Mgr-Sls - Tyler Technologies, Inc.; *pg.* 486, *pg.* 1690
Phillips, Juan, Creative Dir - Travelpro International, Inc.; *pg.* 14, *pg.* 413
Phillips, Karen, Program Mgr-Mktg - Quantum Fuel Systems Technologies Worldwide, Inc.; *pg.* 1371, *pg.* 115
Phillips, Karianne, Coord-PR - Neiman Marcus, Inc.; *pg.* 30, *pg.* 1684
Phillips, Kate, Analyst-Mktg Bus - Sprint Corporation; *pg.* 1874, *pg.* 719
Phillips, Kati, Brand Mgr-Activation - Newell Rubbermaid Inc.; *pg.* 1128, *pg.* 515
Phillips, Keary, Dir-Digital Mktg - The Allstate Corporation; *pg.* 1189, *pg.* 639
Phillips, Kelsey, Mgr-Acq Mktg - Intuit Inc.; *pg.* 769, *pg.* 158
Phillips, Kimberly, Mgr-PR - Design Within Reach, Inc.; *pg.* 923, *pg.* 216
Phillips, Laura, Sr VP & Gen Mgr-Mdse - Wal-Mart Stores, Inc.; *pg.* 1790, *pg.* 29
Phillips, Mark, VP-Pharmacy Mdsg - Wal-Mart Stores, Inc.; *pg.* 1790, *pg.* 29
Phillips, Nedelka Tejada, Sr Dir-Mktg - Hughes Network Systems LLC; *pg.* 643, *pg.* 770
Phillips, Reggie, Product Mgr - KEMET Corporation; *pg.* 649, *pg.* 1621
Phillips, Rick, Sr Dir-Sls, Comml & OTR Product - Yokohama Tire Corporation; *pg.* 1892, *pg.* 94
Phillips, Ross, Reg Mgr-Mktg - Pepsi Beverages Company; *pg.* 258, *pg.* 1342
Phillips, Susan, Dir-Mktg - Myrtle Beach Area Convention and Visitors Bureau; *pg.* 565, *pg.* 1621
Phillips, Susan, Dir-Mktg - Universal Lighting Technologies; *pg.* 1307, *pg.* 1655
Phillips-Luther, Rachel, VP-Mktg - Zoes Kitchen, Inc.; *pg.* 1757, *pg.* 1735
Philo, Tony, Mgr-Mktg Partnership Activation - Coca-Cola Refreshments USA, Inc.; *pg.* 247, *pg.* 500
Philp, Brian, Specialist-Digital Mktg-Staples Advantage Canada - Staples, Inc.; *pg.* 474, *pg.* 821
Philp, Dave, Mgr-Digital Mktg - Amy's Kitchen, Inc.; *pg.* 837, *pg.* 276
Phipps, Amanda, Reg Mgr-Adv - Popeyes Louisiana Kitchen, Inc.; *pg.* 1745, *pg.* 517
Phipps, Jason, Sr VP-Digital Media - FX Networks, LLC; *pg.* 288, *pg.* 131
Phipps, Kim, Dir-Mktg & Brand-Global - Acer America Corporation; *pg.* 341, *pg.* 235
Phipps, Marcus, Sr Mgr-Data Center & Cloud Mktg - Cisco Systems, Inc.; *pg.* 372, *pg.* 240
Phipps, Paul, CMO - Visit Florida Inc.; *pg.* 1010, *pg.* 470
Phipps, Paula, Head-Product Mktg-Software Portfolio - Hitachi Data Systems Corporation; *pg.* 407, *pg.* 265
Phipps, Sander, Grp Product Mgr - Sony Electronics, Inc.; *pg.* 676, *pg.* 209
Phipps, Tanya, Coord-Mktg-Red Lobster - Olive Garden Italian Restaurant; *pg.* 1742, *pg.* 454
Phipps, Tanya, Coord-Mktg-Red Lobster - Red Lobster; *pg.* 1747, *pg.* 455
Phlipot, Thomas, Exec VP-New Products - Progressive Dynamics, Inc.; *pg.* 665, *pg.* 898
Phung, Allen, Dir-Sls-Americas - CyberOptics Corporation; *pg.* 1408, *pg.* 925
Phung, My, Mgr-ISG Mktg - Western Digital Corporation; *pg.* 492, *pg.* 118
Piacentini, Caitlin, Media Planner - Marshalls of MA, Inc.; *pg.* 1778, *pg.* 821
Piacentini, Caitlin, Media Planner - T.J. Maxx; *pg.* 1788, *pg.* 822
Piacentini, Caitlin, Media Planner - The TJX Companies, Inc.; *pg.* 1788, *pg.* 822
Piasek, Michal, Brand Mgr-Fin - Heineken USA Inc.; *pg.* 252, *pg.* 1352
Piatek, Luke, Coord-Mktg - State Farm Mutual Automobile Insurance Co.; *pg.* 1218, *pg.* 557
Piatkowski, Tom, Sr Mgr & Project Mgr-Client Svcs - Epicor Software Corporation; *pg.* 393, *pg.* 110
Piazza, Gabriele Di, VP & Gen Mgr-Mktg Optimization - Hewlett-Packard Company; *pg.* 404, *pg.* 175
Piazza, Nicole, Mgr-Mktg Comm - Cardinal Health, Inc.; *pg.* 1512, *pg.* 1448
Pica, Lauren, Specialist-Mktg-Coloredge - Eastman Kodak Company; *pg.* 1408, *pg.* 1333
Picard, Leslie, Sr VP-Sls & Branded Solutions - Turner Broadcasting System, Inc.; *pg.* 314, *pg.* 521
Picard, Lindsay, Dir-Mktg - W.B. Mason Company; *pg.* 491, *pg.* 803
Picard, Ray, Exec VP-Sls - Move, Inc.; *pg.* 1268, *pg.* 247
Picasso, Lauren, Assoc Dir-Mktg - Jet.com, Inc.; *pg.* 1260, *pg.* 1073
Piccardo, Gina, Mgr-WorldWide Retail Mktg - SanDisk Corporation; *pg.* 465, *pg.* 147
Picciano, Patra, Dir-Distr Partnership Mktg - Univision Communications Inc.; *pg.* 683, *pg.* 1307
Piccinotti, Alberto, VP-Sls & Tech-EMEA - Reichhold, Inc.; *pg.* 1179, *pg.* 1372
Picciolo, Bret, Mgr-PR - Time Warner Cable Inc.; *pg.* 312, *pg.* 1301
Piccione, Michele, Chief Creative Officer - Alfred Angelo, Inc.; *pg.* 17, *pg.* 1532
Piccirillo, Chuck, Sr Product Mgr-Mktg - Osram Sylvania, Inc.; *pg.* 1302, *pg.* 816
Piccirillo, Joe, VP-Cross Networks Ad Sls Res - Discovery Communications, Inc.; *pg.* 282, *pg.* 777
Picco, Dion, Sr Dir-Product Mgmt & Mktg - Progress DataDirect; *pg.* 457, *pg.* 1385
Piccolo, Andrea, Brand Mgr - Swiss Water Decaffeinated Coffee Income Fund; *pg.* 900, *pg.* 1907
Piccolo, Brian, Sr Dir-Digital Strategic Svcs - Liberty Mutual Insurance Group Inc.; *pg.* 1205, *pg.* 797
Picconatto, Jay, Assoc Dir-Mktg - General Mills, Inc.; *pg.* 828, *pg.* 933
Pichamuthu, Joseph, Sr Dir-Oncology Global Mktg - Regeneron Pharmaceuticals, Inc.; *pg.* 1588, *pg.* 1345
Piche, Kate, Sr Product Mgr - Stanley Black & Decker, Inc.; *pg.* 1063, *pg.* 358
Pickard, Grace, Dir-Strategic Mktg - Manulife Financial Corporation; *pg.* 778, *pg.* 1939
Pickard, Mark, Sr Product Mgr-Scanners - Epson America Inc.; *pg.* 394, *pg.* 122
Pickel, Virginia, Sr Mgr-Adv Svcs - Robb Report; *pg.* 1681, *pg.* 142
Pickelsimer, Lisa, Exec Dir-Video Product Dev - Cox Communications, Inc.; *pg.* 279, *pg.* 501
Pickering, Ben, Sr VP-Strategic Mktg - Bank of America Corporation; *pg.* 718, *pg.* 1362
Pickering, Chris, Sr Dir & Dept Head-Mobile Engrg Lab - Samsung Telecommunications America, LLC; *pg.* 670, *pg.* 1736
Pickett, Beth, Mgr-Mktg Comm - The Hanover Insurance Company; *pg.* 1202, *pg.* 862
Pickett, Dan, VP-Home & Comml Products - Knape & Vogt Manufacturing Company; *pg.* 1052, *pg.* 913
Pickett, Mark, Mgr-Product Mktg - CareerBuilder, LLC; *pg.* 1234, *pg.* 568
Pickett, Mark, Dir-Worldwide Sls-Armor & Structural Ceramics - Saint-Gobain Abrasives, Inc. - Philadelphia; *pg.* 1180, *pg.* 1553
Pickrell, Shiyi, Sr Mgr-Digital Analytics - Microsoft Corporation; *pg.* 435, *pg.* 1824
Pickrell, William, Dir-Sls-Fire Safety Solutions-The Americas - Albemarle Corporation; *pg.* 1146, *pg.* 741
Picoli, Patty, VP-NA Payments, Mktg Comm & Mktg Sciences - Pitney Bowes Inc.; *pg.* 454, *pg.* 376
Picone, Tom, VP-Sls & Mktg - Hyer Industries Inc.; *pg.* 1051, *pg.* 841
Picone, Zeny, Head-Creative - Google Inc.; *pg.* 1249, *pg.* 153
Picott, Carrie, Brand Mgr-Strategy - Citgo Petroleum Corporation; *pg.* 974, *pg.* 1703
Pidgeon, Dave, Mgr-PR - Norfolk Southern Corporation; *pg.* 1917, *pg.* 1797
Pidgeon, Ewan, Dir-Creative - Ingram Micro Inc.; *pg.* 415, *pg.* 261
Pidgeon, Shane, Sr Mgr-Product Mktg-Lenovo - Lenovo Group Ltd; *pg.* 427, *pg.* 1384
Piedrahita, John, Mgr-Mktg - Bozzuto's Inc.; *pg.* 1016, *pg.* 342
Pieh, Darren, Mgr-Local Sls - WTVD-TV Inc.; *pg.* 323, *pg.* 1372
Piehl, Jason, Mgr-Production - The Saint Paul Chamber Orchestra; *pg.* 580, *pg.* 963
Piehl, Suzanne, VP-Creative Admin - Conair Corporation; *pg.* 505, *pg.* 1055
Pieja, Tiffany, Mgr-Mdsg - Burt's Bees Inc.; *pg.* 502, *pg.* 1370
Piekos, Lauren, Dir-Product Line - Berry Plastics; *pg.* 1879, *pg.* 678
Piell, Terrie, Sr Mgr-Mktg - A.M. Best Company; *pg.* 1614, *pg.* 1101
Pien, Will, Sr Product Mgr-vSphere - VMware, Inc.; *pg.* 490, *pg.* 179
Pienkowski, Deborah, Dir-Mktg - General Electric Company; *pg.* 1297, *pg.* 347
Pieper, Bryan, Corp VP-Internet Mktg Strategy & Plng - New York Life Insurance Company; *pg.* 1211, *pg.* 1268
Piepgrass, Brian, Dir-Growth Mktg - Facebook, Inc.; *pg.* 1245, *pg.* 143
Piepiora, Katie, Mgr-Adv & Innovation - The Boston Beer Company, Inc.; *pg.* 239, *pg.* 790
Pierantoni, MaryBeth, Sr Product Mgr-Performance - Oracle Corporation; *pg.* 450, *pg.* 191
Pierburg, Karl, Sr Dir-Football Sys - Atlanta Falcons Football Club, LLC; *pg.* 530, *pg.* 532
Pierce, Andrew, Mgr-Outdoor Digital Mktg & Mdsg - The Orvis

First page reference indicates Business Class Edition
Second page reference indicates Geographic Edition

Company, Inc.; *pg.* 1781, *pg.* 1764
Pierce, Brett, Mgr-Digital Mktg & Social Media - The Travelers Companies, Inc.; *pg.* 1220, *pg.* 352
Pierce, Christopher, Head-RCC Therapy-US Mktg - Pfizer Inc.; *pg.* 1581, *pg.* 1278
Pierce, Darrah, Mgr-Mktg - Delta Farm Press; *pg.* 1634, *pg.* 968
Pierce, Doug, Dir-Sls-APAC - International Datacasting Corporation; *pg.* 419, *pg.* 1921
Pierce, Douglas, Specialist-Mining Product & Mgr-Global Accts - ESCO Corporation; *pg.* 1335, *pg.* 1502
Pierce, John, Dir-Product Mktg - Cadence Design Systems, Inc.; *pg.* 367, *pg.* 239
Pierce, Jonathan, Dir-Social Media & Creative Svcs - American Airlines Inc.; *pg.* 1898, *pg.* 1693
pierce, kara, Sr Producer-TV & Content-Global Mktg - Netflix, Inc.; *pg.* 1269, *pg.* 141
Pierce, Kristin, Dir-Reg Mktg-Americas - Brocade Corporation; *pg.* 365, *pg.* 312
Pierce, Michael, Brand Mgr - The Scotts Miracle-Gro Company; *pg.* 1799, *pg.* 1459
Pierce, Mike, Sr Mgr-Sls - Mitsubishi Rayon Carbon Fiber and Composites, Inc.,; *pg.* 1173, *pg.* 113
Pierce, Pat, Dir-Mktg & Diagnostic Tools - SPX Corporation; *pg.* 218, *pg.* 1369
Pierce, Sonja, Coord-Classified Adv - American Society of Cinematographers; *pg.* 1616, *pg.* 103
Pierce, Stu, Mgr-Mktg -GMC Sierra Pick-Up - General Motors Company; *pg.* 175, *pg.* 881
Pierce, Thomas, VP-Mktg - Comcast Cable Communications, Inc.; *pg.* 276, *pg.* 1560
Pierdant, Jennifer, Brand Mgr-Seagram's Gin - Pernod Ricard USA, Inc.; *pg.* 1968, *pg.* 1332
Piereck, Louis, Sr Mgr-Global Mktg-Dove Body Wash - Unilever United States, Inc.; *pg.* 904, *pg.* 1061
Pieri, Philippe, Mgr-Global Web Mktg & Strategy - Cisco Systems, Inc.; *pg.* 372, *pg.* 240
Pierluisi, Anthony, Brand Mgr-Procter & Gamble - Duracell; *pg.* 635, *pg.* 337
Piero, Kelly, Mgr-Media Rels - Diebold, Incorporated; *pg.* 387, *pg.* 1407
Pieronek, Tara, Mgr-Mktg - Accenture; *pg.* 1392, *pg.* 1186
Pierre, Nancy St., Dir-Corp & Bus Unit PR - Sabre Holdings Corporation; *pg.* 1922, *pg.* 1745
Pierre-Louis, Jude, Sr Dir-Product Dev & Innovations - Walgreen Co.; *pg.* 1608, *pg.* 605
Pierro, Dave, Dir-Fin-Mktg Funds - American Dairy Queen Corporation; *pg.* 1714, *pg.* 930
Pierro, Dave, Dir-Fin-Mktg Funds - International Dairy Queen, Inc.; *pg.* 1732, *pg.* 938
Piersanti, Valerio, Brand Mgr - Ferrari North America, Inc.; *pg.* 171, *pg.* 1060
Pierskalla, Lori, Mgr-Indus Mktg - Hitachi Data Systems Corporation; *pg.* 407, *pg.* 265
Piersma, Craig, Dir-Mktg - Gentex Corporation; *pg.* 206, *pg.* 913
Pierson, Lydia, Dir-Digital Mktg & CRM - The Buckle, Inc.; *pg.* 1764, *pg.* 1011
Pierson, Natalie, Program Mgr-Online Adv - Amazon.com, Inc.; *pg.* 1226, *pg.* 1831
Pierson, Yuko Y., Sr Engr-Sls-Ad Tech - Yahoo! Inc.; *pg.* 1289, *pg.* 289
Pierucci, Joe, Mgr-Product Strategy-Global - Ford Motor Company; *pg.* 172, *pg.* 876
Pierz, Michele E., Dir-Mktg - The Northwestern Mutual Life Insurance Company; *pg.* 1212, *pg.* 1879
Pietkiewicz, Steve, VP & Gen Mgr-Power Products - Linear Technology Corp.; *pg.* 652, *pg.* 147
Pietro, Tony, Brand Mgr-Americas Holiday Inn Resort Brand - InterContinental Hotels Corporation; *pg.* 1097, *pg.* 511
Pietrowski, Madison, Brand Mgr-Bud Light - Anheuser-Busch Companies, LLC; *pg.* 237, *pg.* 991
Pietsch, Robert, Dir-Sls-West - Twitter, Inc.; *pg.* 1285, *pg.* 228
Piette, Lynne, Brand Mgr - Volkswagen Canada, Inc.; *pg.* 194, *pg.* 1918
Pigeaire, Yann, Dir-Mktg - Similasan Corporation; *pg.* 1594, *pg.* 332
Pignataro, Ben, Exec VP & Sls Mgr-Natl - Capezio Ballet Makers Inc.; *pg.* 1805, *pg.* 1125
Pignatelli, Cassandra, Specialist-Mktg Comm - BMW of North America, LLC; *pg.* 166, *pg.* 1133
Pignatiello, Jody, Mgr-Private Brands & Category Mktg - Lowe's Companies, Inc.; *pg.* 1053, *pg.* 1383
Pigot, Tim, Sr Dir-Mktg - Gilead Sciences, Inc.; *pg.* 1535, *pg.* 88
Pihaly, Christina, Specialist-Brand Sls - Arrow Electronics, Inc.; *pg.* 619, *pg.* 325
Pihl, Steve, Mgr-Customer Mktg - McCain Foods Limited; *pg.* 876, *pg.* 1915
Pike, Eric, Dir-Creative - MARTHA STEWART LIVING OMNIMEDIA, INC.; *pg.* 1661, *pg.* 1256
Pike, Josh, Reg VP-Sls - Frosty Acres Brands, Inc.; *pg.* 1020, *pg.* 484
Pike, Kelly, Acct Exec-Charter Media - Charter Communications, Inc.; *pg.* 274, *pg.* 372
Pike, Lora, Sr Dir-IR - Keryx Biopharmaceuticals, Inc.; *pg.* 1553, *pg.* 1248
Pike, Reed, Dir-Product Dev & Design - Huffy Corporation; *pg.* 1836, *pg.* 1409
Pikel, Andy, Sr Dir-Brand Mktg - Rust-Oleum Corporation; *pg.* 1447, *pg.* 664
Pikelny, Philip, CMO & VP - The Dispatch Printing Company; *pg.* 1636, *pg.* 1439
Pikus, Patrick, Mgr-Heavy Truck Mktg - The Timken Company; *pg.* 218, *pg.* 1408
Piland, Drew, Mgr-Digital Mktg - The Pantry, Inc.; *pg.* 1029, *pg.* 1360
Pilare, Ariel, Graphic Designer-Wealth Mgmt Mktg - Wells Fargo & Company; *pg.* 819, *pg.* 232
Pilarz, Kitty, Sr Dir-Product Safety - MATTEL, INC.; *pg.* 962, *pg.* 81
Pilcher, Todd, Product Mgr - Dow AgroSciences LLC; *pg.* 1156, *pg.* 684
Pileski, Mark, Mgr-Sls - Hollister Staffing, Inc.; *pg.* 1394, *pg.* 796
Pilichowski, Alexandra, Mgr-Studio & Coord-Media Production - MacNeil Automotive Products, Ltd.; *pg.* 211, *pg.* 559
Piliero, Jennifer, Sr Product Mgr - Ceridian Corporation; *pg.* 371, *pg.* 932
Pilkington, Jon, VP-Products - Datawatch Corporation; *pg.* 383, *pg.* 813
Pilkington, Mary Winn, VP-IR & PR - Dollar General Corporation; *pg.* 1767, *pg.* 1635
Pilkonis, Pat, Head-Adv-Americas - UBS Financial Services Inc.; *pg.* 812, *pg.* 1306
Pillai, Ravi, Sr Dir-Cosmetic Ingredients - Symrise, Inc.; *pg.* 1183, *pg.* 1125
Pillers, Mark, VP-Cab Sls & Mktg - Crenlo, LLC; *pg.* 77, *pg.* 955
Pillette, Lisa, VP-Mktg-Global - Ralph Lauren Corporation; *pg.* 46, *pg.* 1284
Pilli, Franco, VP-Casino Mktg - Foxwoods Resort Casino; *pg.* 549, *pg.* 353
Pillion, Dean, Assoc Dir-Creative - Merck & Co., Inc.; *pg.* 1566, *pg.* 1077
Pilmanis, Kalon, Gen Mgr-Product-Multi-Tools & Gear - Fiskars Brands, Inc.; *pg.* 1124, *pg.* 1866
Pilnacek, Gina, Sr Dir-Mktg - Polar Electro Inc.; *pg.* 664, *pg.* 1173
Pilon, Lauren, Sr Mgr-Mktg - LendingTree, LLC; *pg.* 775, *pg.* 1367
Pilukas, Ron, Dir-Product Mgmt - F5 Networks, Inc.; *pg.* 396, *pg.* 1835
Pimentel, Andre, Assoc Product Mgr - Sharp Electronics Corporation; *pg.* 672, *pg.* 1082
Pimentel, Roger, Sr Product Mgr-Mktg - Amazon.com, Inc.; *pg.* 1226, *pg.* 1831
Pinakatt, Elena, Dir-Global Brand Mktg-Juice & Dairy-Far East - The Coca-Cola Company; *pg.* 240, *pg.* 493
Pinckney, Quiana, Sr Mgr-PR - HD SUPPLY, INC.; *pg.* 86, *pg.* 509
Pinckney, Wendy, VP-Global Branding & Mktg Comm - 3D Systems Corporation; *pg.* 339, *pg.* 1621
Pinder, Beth, VP-Sls & Mktg-EdR Collegiate Housing - EdR Trust; *pg.* 1090, *pg.* 1642
Pine, Matthew, VP-Mktg-Carrier Residential HVAC - United Technologies Corporation; *pg.* 235, *pg.* 353
Pineda, Alexei, Dir-Product Mgmt-Xbox - Microsoft Corporation; *pg.* 435, *pg.* 1824
Pineda, Kimberly, Dir-Comm-Oracle Mktg - Oracle Corporation; *pg.* 450, *pg.* 191
Pineda, Luis, Sr VP-Product Mgmt, Bus Dev & Mobile Computing - QUALCOMM Incorporated; *pg.* 1873, *pg.* 207
Pineda, Ramiro, Mgr-Adv & Digital Mktg - Bridgestone Americas, Inc.; *pg.* 201, *pg.* 1649
Pineiro, Eileen, Dir-Mktg & Comm-Latin America & US Hispanic - Discovery Communications, Inc.; *pg.* 282, *pg.* 777
Pinell, Nadine, Sr Mgr-External Comm - Genentech, Inc.; *pg.* 1533, *pg.* 279
Pinero, Jeff, Mgr-Global IPV New Bus Dev & Svcs Mktg - Arris Group, Inc.; *pg.* 353, *pg.* 541
Pinero, Jose, Sr Dir-PR & Entertainment Svcs - Microsoft Corporation; *pg.* 435, *pg.* 1824
Pines, Marissa, Sr Mgr-Mktg - PepsiCo, Inc.; *pg.* 259, *pg.* 1327
Pineux, Nora, Dir-Digital Mktg - Ancestry.com LLC; *pg.* 1228, *pg.* 1754
Pingeton, Scott, Sr Product Mgr-Core Data - TripAdvisor, Inc.; *pg.* 1926, *pg.* 835
Pingle, Jan, Dir-Product Mktg - Honeywell International Inc.; *pg.* 407, *pg.* 1088
Pingpank, Anne, Mgr-Mktg Program-Liberty Intl Underwriters - Liberty Mutual Insurance Group Inc.; *pg.* 1205, *pg.* 797
Pingree, Ben, Dir-Mktg - Sonic Automotive, Inc.; *pg.* 190, *pg.* 1369
Pings, Greg, Mgr-Content Mktg - Xerox Corporation; *pg.* 494, *pg.* 365
Pinhasi, Ileen, Product Mgr-Mobile - Constant Contact, Inc.; *pg.* 379, *pg.* 850
Pinho, Jennifer, Rep-Pharmaceutical Sls - Takeda Pharmaceuticals USA, Inc.; *pg.* 1600, *pg.* 605
Pini, Carolina, Brand Mgr-Mobile Comm - LG Electronics Canada, Inc.; *pg.* 651, *pg.* 1927
Pinkas, Debra, Brand Mgr - Toys "R" Us, Inc.; *pg.* 968, *pg.* 1130
Pinkert, Chris, Dir-Digital Media - St. Louis Blues Hockey Club, LLC; *pg.* 585, *pg.* 1003
Pinkerton, Blaine, Dir-Turf Sls - Nufarm Americas Inc; *pg.* 1798, *pg.* 552
Pinkett-Carter, Laura, Dir-Mktg-Global - Johnson & Johnson; *pg.* 1549, *pg.* 1091
Pinkovezky, Aviad, Sr Product Mgr-LinkedIn Company Pages - LinkedIn Corporation; *pg.* 1262, *pg.* 160
Pinner, Diantha, Head-Americas Digital Strategist-Americas Field Mktg - Cisco Systems, Inc.; *pg.* 372, *pg.* 240
Pinney, Alyson, Sr Mgr-Digital Mktg - Intuit Inc.; *pg.* 769, *pg.* 158
Pinnock, Alicia, Sr Mgr-Ops Dev-Gap Franchise - The Gap, Inc.; *pg.* 1770, *pg.* 218
Pinon, Esther, Mgr-Sls-Latin America - International Paper Company; *pg.* 1460, *pg.* 1644
Pinon, Natalie, Mgr-Integrated Mktg - FedEx Corporation; *pg.* 1907, *pg.* 1642
Pinsky, Yury, Product Mgr - Google Inc.; *pg.* 1249, *pg.* 153
Pintauro, Frank, Gen Mgr-Red Grp & Exec Dir-Creative - Showtime Networks Inc.; *pg.* 308, *pg.* 1291
Pinto, Carl, Dir-Mktg - Bradford-White Corporation; *pg.* 1069, *pg.* 1514
Pinto, Michelle, Dir-Media Rels - North Shore-LIJ Health System; *pg.* 1573, *pg.* 1162
Pionati, Nino, Chief Strategy & Mktg Officer - Alliqua, Inc.; *pg.* 1492, *pg.* 1189
Piontkowski, John, Gen Mgr-East Reg & Sr Dir-Reg Sls - Microsoft Corp.; *pg.* 440, *pg.* 321
Piotrowski, Andrea, Mgr-Sls - Toho Tenax America, Inc.; *pg.* 1184, *pg.* 1655
Piparsania, Vinay K., Dir-Mktg, Sls & Svc - Ford Motor Company; *pg.* 172, *pg.* 876
Piper, Amanda, Sr Mgr-Mktg - PepsiCo, Inc.; *pg.* 259, *pg.* 1327
Piper, Blake, Dir-Mdsg-Greater China Running - NIKE, Inc.; *pg.* 1812, *pg.* 1492
Piper, Chuck, Mgr-Product Mktg - Intel Corporation; *pg.* 645, *pg.* 266
Piper, Dale, Dir-Design & Creative - Texas Roadhouse, Inc.; *pg.* 1753, *pg.* 738
Piper, Gretchen, Mgr-Multimedia Adv - Journal Star, Inc.; *pg.* 1656, *pg.* 651
Piper, Tara, Head-Entertainment Mktg-North America - Coca-Cola North America; *pg.* 848, *pg.* 500
Pipitone, Nick, Project Mgr-Paid Media - Discover Financial Services; *pg.* 744, *pg.* 653
Pipkin, Georgi M., Mgr-Media Rels-Home, Cause, Community, Diversity & Branding - Macy's, Inc.; *pg.* 1778, *pg.* 1417
Pipkorn, Jillian L., Sr Mgr-Category & Brand Mktg-Home Div - Kohl's Corporation; *pg.* 1775, *pg.* 1870
Pippin, Joey, Dir-Pharmacy Segment Mktg & Community Pharmacy Team - GlaxoSmithKline; *pg.* 1536, *pg.* 1565
Pippin, Mark, Dir-Product Dev - Electra Bicycle Company; *pg.* 1706, *pg.* 303
Pippin, Robert, Brand Mgr-WJBF WAGT - Media General, Inc.; *pg.* 297, *pg.* 1803
Pippin, Robert, Brand Mgr-WJBF WAGT - WJBF-TV; *pg.* 321,

pg. 525
Piquette, Kristen, Mgr-Social Media - The PNC Financial Services Group, Inc.; pg. 795, pg. 1579
Piraino, Kim, Mgr-Strategic Mktg - Centegra Northern Illinois Medical Center; pg. 1196, pg. 632
Pirard, Pierre, Exec VP-Product Innovation & Global Supply Chain - Elizabeth Arden, Inc.; pg. 507, pg. 448
Pires, Amanda, VP-Comm, Global Solutions & Innovation Mktg - Visa Inc.; pg. 816, pg. 230
Pirone, Jackie, Dir-Mktg - OraSure Technologies Inc; pg. 1578, pg. 1516
Pirozzoli, Meghan, Brand Mgr-Global - Symantec Corporation; pg. 478, pg. 161
Pirrello, Nikki, Assoc Grp Publr-Mktg & Conferences - Crain Communications, Inc.; pg. 1631, pg. 879
Pirri, Sue, VP-Fin-Sls Fin - Autodesk Inc.; pg. 356, pg. 257
Pirrone, Carmelo, Sr VP-Mktg - Sony Corporation of America; pg. 675, pg. 1293
Pirtle, Dwight, Sr Specialist-Digital Mktg - Caesars Entertainment Corporation; pg. 1083, pg. 1023
Pirtle, Kimberly, Analyst-Loyalty Mktg - Gilt Groupe Inc.; pg. 24, pg. 1234
Pirtle, Sara, Mgr-Mktg - Dollar General Corporation; pg. 1767, pg. 1635
Pirtle, William L., Sr VP-Sls & Mktg - Shenandoah Telecommunications Co.; pg. 672, pg. 1779
Pirttinen, Cia, Sr Mgr-Mktg-Nordics - Hotels.com, L.P.; pg. 1257, pg. 1682
Pisarra, Shelley, Sr Dir-Shopper Insights & Analytics - Frito-Lay North America, Inc.; pg. 1853, pg. 1730
Pisarra, Shelley, Sr Dir-Shopper Insights & Analytics - PepsiCo, Inc.; pg. 259, pg. 1327
Pisca, Erin, Assoc Mgr-Mktg - General Mills, Inc.; pg. 828, pg. 933
Piscadlo, Kaitlyn, Asst Mgr-Mktg - Cotton Incorporated Consumer Marketing Headquarters; pg. 692, pg. 1218
Pisciotta, Dominick, Sr VP-Sls & Mktg - Sherwin-Williams Wood Care Group; pg. 1448, pg. 1127
Pisciotta, Jennifer, VP-Mktg - The Patron Spirits Company; pg. 1967, pg. 1029
Piscopo, Jill, Brand Mgr-Innovation - Keurig Green Mountain, Inc.; pg. 868, pg. 1768
Piskadlo, Mark, Dir-Sls & Western Reg - Interactive Intelligence, Inc.; pg. 417, pg. 687
Pisone, Cassandra, Coord-Social Media Mktg - American Eagle Outfitters, Inc.; pg. 37, pg. 1572
Pisors, Shelly, VP-Field Mktg - Comerica Incorporated; pg. 740, pg. 1677
Pistilli, James, Brand Mgr-Social & Digital - International Business Machines Corporation; pg. 418, pg. 1138
Pistone, Paige, Dir-Mktg - Friendship Dairies, Inc.; pg. 857, pg. 1171
Pistore, Tom, VP-Ticket Sls & Svc - Maple Leaf Sports & Entertainment Ltd.; pg. 560, pg. 1940
Pistore, Tom, VP-Sls & Svc - Toronto Maple Leaf Hockey Club; pg. 588, pg. 1945
Piszar, Sandor, Dir-Mktg-Chevy Trucks - General Motors Company; pg. 175, pg. 881
Pitaro, Regina M., Head-Institutional Mktg - GAMCO Investors, Inc.; pg. 761, pg. 1339
Pitas, Paul, Dir-PR & Comm - Culver Franchising System, Inc.; pg. 1724, pg. 1887
Pitas, Sara, Sr Planner-Integrated Shopper Mktg-Safeway - General Mills, Inc.; pg. 828, pg. 933
Pitchford, Mark, Mng Dir-Sls & Svc - Esurance, Inc.; pg. 1243, pg. 217
Pitcock, Jeff, Mgr-Creative Svcs - Chicago Professional Sports Limited Partnership; pg. 539, pg. 570
Pithis, Dan, Mgr-Sls - Cedar Farms Company, Inc.; pg. 846, pg. 1559
Pitigoi, Cosmin, Sr Dir-Global Analytics - PayPal Inc.; pg. 1274, pg. 248
Pitmon, Melissa, Mgr-Mktg Ops - The Procter & Gamble Company; pg. 1129, pg. 1418
Pitner, Michele, Mgr-Channel Sls, Mobile & Global ECommerce - Fellowes, Inc.; pg. 397, pg. 620
Pitt, Jerry, Sr Dir-Mktg-Original Content - TEN: The Enthusiast Network; pg. 1691, pg. 1298
Pittel, Bill, Dir-Adv - Architectural Digest; pg. 1617, pg. 1196
Pittel, Bill, Dir-Adv-Architectural Digest - Conde Nast Publications, Inc.; pg. 1629, pg. 1217
Pittman, Erin, Project Mgr-Mktg - ScanSource, Inc.; pg. 671, pg. 1618
Pittman, Marian, Exec VP-Digital Strategy, Content & Sls - Cox Media Group; pg. 280, pg. 502
Pittman, Mauresa, Mgr-Mktg & Client Relationship - United States Postal Service; pg. 1009, pg. 406
Pittman, R. J., Sr VP & Chief Product Officer-Marketplaces - eBay Inc.; pg. 1240, pg. 243
Pittner, Susan, Assoc Dir-Shopper Mktg - Mondelez International, Inc.; pg. 878, pg. 601
Pitts, John, VP & Dir-Mktg - The Knopf Doubleday Group; pg. 1657, pg. 1249
Pitts, Megan, Brand Mgr-Listerine - Johnson & Johnson; pg. 1549, pg. 1091
Pitts, Randy, Sr Principal & Engr-Mktg - Intersil Corporation; pg. 647, pg. 146
Pitts, Rhonda, Sr Mgr-Online Mktg - AT&T; pg. 1865, pg. 258
Pittson, Tyler, Product Mgr - Kubota Tractor Corporation; pg. 705, pg. 294
Pivnicny, Tim, VP-Sls & Mktg - Atlus USA, Inc.; pg. 949, pg. 107
Pizano, Amber, Sr Mgr-Comm-University Program & Engrg Workforce Dev Worldwide - Texas Instruments Incorporated; pg. 679, pg. 1688
Pizzelanti, Kristine, Dir-Mktg-Asia - Kate Spade LLC; pg. 28, pg. 1248
Pizzimenti, James, Engr-Product Design - Ford Motor Company; pg. 172, pg. 876
Pizzinato, Elizabeth, Sr VP-Mktg & Comm - Four Seasons Hotels Limited; pg. 1092, pg. 1938
Pizzuti, Brian D., VP-Sls - National Wine & Spirits, Inc.; pg. 1967, pg. 689
Pizzutti, Dena, Mgr-Mktg - Wawa, Inc.; pg. 1037, pg. 1552
Pla, Christophe, Dir-Bus & End User Mktg - Adobe Systems Incorporated; pg. 342, pg. 235
Place, Bud, Sr Mgr - FCA US LLC; pg. 170, pg. 868
Place, Jeffrey, Sr VP & Mgr-Sls-Natl - Ivy Funds Distributor Inc.; pg. 771, pg. 719
Placidi, Laurent, Sr Dir-US Mktg-LEMTRADA - Genzyme Corporation; pg. 1534, pg. 808
Placke, Kathy, Sr Mgr-Mktg-Strategic Industries - Alcatel-Lucent USA, Inc.; pg. 615, pg. 1728
Plageman-Davis, Jenifer, Head-Product Innovation - Bush Brothers & Company; pg. 843, pg. 1636
Planck, Kirsten, Brand Mgr-Employer - SAP America, Inc.; pg. 466, pg. 1557
Planek, Jerry, Dir-Sls - Kraft Chemical Company; pg. 1170, pg. 632
Plant, David, Dir-Product Dev - PGA Tour, Inc.; pg. 574, pg. 460
Plant, Heather, Grp Dir-Consumer Mktg - The Hearst Corporation; pg. 1649, pg. 1239
Plant, John, Brand Mgr-Casa Sauza US & Global - Beam Suntory Inc.; pg. 1957, pg. 599
Plant, Leslie, Sr Mgr-PR - IBM Canada Limited; pg. 411, pg. 1923
Plante, Dale N., Pres-Forest Products Div & Exec VP - Hexion; pg. 1166, pg. 1440
Plante, Walter, Sr Dir-Res, Dev & Engrg - ENTEGRIS, INC.; pg. 1882, pg. 788
Plas, Jim, Chief Product Officer - CDS Global, Inc.; pg. 370, pg. 704
Plaskett, Kim, VP-Mktg - Greyhound Lines, Inc.; pg. 1910, pg. 1681
Plaszcz, Brittany, Specialist-Reg Mktg - FindLaw; pg. 1641, pg. 285
Platek, Allen, VP-New Product Dev - Tempur Sealy International, Inc.; pg. 944, pg. 731
Plater, Solomon, Brand Mgr - Altria Group, Inc.; pg. 1893, pg. 1800
Plater, Tiffany, Mgr-Mktg - L'Oreal USA; pg. 514, pg. 1252
Plati, Corinna, Sr Mng Dir-Events & Ad Sls - SYS-Con Media, Inc.; pg. 1690, pg. 1134
Platt, Amanda, Specialist-Social Media & PR - Domino's Pizza, Inc.; pg. 1726, pg. 865
Platt, Craig, Sr VP & Dir-Creative - Showtime Networks Inc.; pg. 308, pg. 1291
Platt, Jennie, Dir-Global New Product Dev Citi Cards - Citigroup Inc.; pg. 735, pg. 1212
Platt, Judith, Dir-Free Expression Advocacy - Association of American Publishers, Inc.; pg. 133, pg. 1197
Platt, Julie, Mgr-Digital Mktg - Susquehanna Bank; pg. 807, pg. 1548
Platte-Pantazakos, Anna, Dir-Mktg & Retailer Rels - Tanger Factory Outlet Centers, Inc.; pg. 1116, pg. 1376
Plavac, Dave, Mgr-Online Mktg - AT&T; pg. 1865, pg. 258
Plaza, Angel, Asst VP-Product Mgmt - Horace Mann Companies; pg. 1203, pg. 662
Plazas, Diana, VP-Brands, Mktg & Digital-CALA - Marriott International, Inc.; pg. 1102, pg. 764
Ple, Yannick, Coord-Mktg-Creative Svcs - Lord & Taylor LLC; pg. 1777, pg. 1252
Pleas, John, Dir-Sls - Seattle Seahawks; pg. 582, pg. 1830
Pleasant, Elissa, Specialist-Mktg - Polycom, Inc.; pg. 664, pg. 249
Pleasant, Lisa, Dir-Digital Strategy & Product Plng - American Airlines Inc.; pg. 1898, pg. 1693
Pleasants, John, Pres-Disney Interactive Media Grp - The Walt Disney Company; pg. 317, pg. 52
Plehn, Stephanie, Mgr-Shopper Mktg - Johnsonville Sausage, LLC; pg. 867, pg. 1894
Pleiman, Scott, Sr VP-Fin, Strategy, Mdsg, Mktg, & US Strategy - Wal-Mart.com; pg. 1287, pg. 50
Plemmons, Kim, Reg Mgr-Sls & Mktg - Wells Fargo & Company; pg. 819, pg. 232
Plemons, Chad, Mgr-Corp Mktg Comm - Publix Super Markets, Inc.; pg. 1031, pg. 437
Plescia, Anthony, Analyst-Social Media - BlackBerry Limited; pg. 625, pg. 1947
Plesser, Jamie, Dir-Interactive Mktg Strategy & Execution - Allianz Life Insurance Company of North America; pg. 1188, pg. 929
Pleszewicz, Shannon, Mgr-Mktg Events & Creative Svcs - Cablevision Systems Corporation; pg. 272, pg. 1141
Pleus, Iness, Sr VP-Ops, Brand Mktg & Creative - Spike TV; pg. 310, pg. 1295
Plews, Stacy, Sr Dir-Direct Consumer Plng - Tommy Bahama; pg. 48, pg. 1842
Plishner, Elias, Sr VP-Worldwide Digital Mktg - Sony Pictures Entertainment Inc.; pg. 309, pg. 72
Pliszka, Nicole, Head-Sls & Customer Mktg - S.C. Johnson & Son, Inc.; pg. 334, pg. 1889
Ploszaj, Terence, Dir-Mktg Execution & Insights - The Northwestern Mutual Life Insurance Company; pg. 1212, pg. 1879
Plotch, Alison, Brand Mgr - The University of Phoenix, Inc.; pg. 610, pg. 27
Plotnick, Larry, Sr Mgr-Fin - Amazon.com, Inc.; pg. 1226, pg. 1831
Plouffe, Robbin Jorgensen, Reg Dir-Sls-Media Grp Interactive-Connecticut - The News-Times; pg. 1670, pg. 344
Plourde, Julia, Dir-Media - AT&T Mobility LLC; pg. 619, pg. 488
Plourde, Julia, Dir-Media - AT&T Mobility LLC; pg. 620, pg. 1824
Pluckhorn, Eric, Dir-Mktg - Allergan; pg. 1490, pg. 1101
Pluff, Katie, Mgr-Marketing Campaign & Brand Mktg - BUFFALO WILD WINGS, INC.; pg. 1718, pg. 931
Pluff, Paul, Dir-Mktg - Smith & Wesson Holding Corporation; pg. 1845, pg. 846
Plumb, Noah, Brand Mgr-Social Media - Go Daddy Inc.; pg. 1249, pg. 21
Plumby, Glenn, VP-Mktg - Speedway LLC; pg. 985, pg. 1452
Plumlee, Dan, Dir-Interactive Media - Indianapolis Colts, Inc.; pg. 553, pg. 687
Plummer, Becky, Assoc Mgr-Mktg-Snacks - Sargento Foods Inc.; pg. 894, pg. 1886
Plummer, Cindy, VP-Domestic Mktg - California Table Grape Commission; pg. 135, pg. 93
Plummer, Dana, Coord-Mktg - The Zippertubing Company; pg. 1892, pg. 12
Plummer, Julie, Dir-Mktg & PR - HCA HOLDINGS, INC.; pg. 1539, pg. 1651
Plummer, Marilyn, Mgr-Adv Projects - Texas Monthly; pg. 1692, pg. 1666
Plungy, Mark, Dir-PR - Cadence Design Systems, Inc.; pg. 367, pg. 239
Plunkett, Andrew, Sr Mgr-Mktg & Digital Media - FMR LLC (Fidelity Investments); pg. 759, pg. 794
Poblocki, Paul B., Dir-Strategic Mktg-Energy Solutions - Johnson Controls, Inc.; pg. 209, pg. 1876
Poce, Valerio, Mgr-Product Mktg-Retail - Google Inc.; pg. 1249, pg. 153
Pochodylo, Laura, Coord-Digital Mktg - Grand Ole Opry; pg. 289, pg. 1651
Pocialik, Graham, Mgr-Trade Mktg - Electrolux Home Products North America; pg. 54, pg. 1366
Pociask, Ryan, Dir-Grp Mktg - Johnsonville Sausage, LLC; pg. 867, pg. 1894
Pocino, Allison, Mgr-Product Mktg - Carl Karcher Enterprises, Inc.; pg. 1720, pg. 63
Podber, Alissa, Asst Mgr-Global Mktg-Marc Jacobs Fragrances - Coty, Inc.; pg. 506, pg. 1219
Podbielak, Joseph, Sr Dir-Brand Fin - Marchon Eyewear, Inc.;

pg. 1421, *pg.* 1180
Podhayny, Lisa, Assoc Brand Mgr-One-A-Day New Product Dev - Bayer Healthcare Consumer Care Division; *pg.* 1500, *pg.* 1087
Podiak, Dick, Sr Dir-Mktg-Cracker Portfolio - Kellogg Company; *pg.* 831, *pg.* 870
Podlas, Steve, Brand Mgr-Comml Coatings - PPG Industries, Inc.; *pg.* 1445, *pg.* 1579
Podolsky, Corey, VP-Bus Dev-CBS Local Digital Media - CBS Broadcasting Inc.; *pg.* 273, *pg.* 1210
Podracky, Steve, Mgr-Mktg - Schulze & Burch Biscuit Company; *pg.* 894, *pg.* 589
Poe, Amy, Mgr-Field Mktg - Starwood Hotels & Resorts Worldwide, Inc.; *pg.* 1114, *pg.* 378
Poehlein, Steve, Dir-Digital Media & Mobility - HP Enterprise Services, LLC; *pg.* 409, *pg.* 1731
Poelstra, Josh, Supvr-Mktg & Sls-Variable Mktg Profit - Ford Motor Company; *pg.* 172, *pg.* 876
Poggi, Joanne, Sr Program Mgr-Channel Mktg - Polycom, Inc.; *pg.* 664, *pg.* 249
Pogosova, Natalya, Analyst-Mktg & Mdsg Insights - Ahold USA, Inc.; *pg.* 1013, *pg.* 1520
Pogue, Frank, VP-Innovation, Mktg & Corp Affairs - StarKist Foods Inc.; *pg.* 898, *pg.* 1581
Pogue, Phil, Dir-Sls - The Penn Companies; *pg.* 10, *pg.* 1568
Pogue, Steve, Dir-Mktg - Cardinal Health, Inc.; *pg.* 1512, *pg.* 1448
Pohl, John, Sr Dir-Svcs Mktg - Cisco Systems, Inc.; *pg.* 372, *pg.* 240
Pohl, Kim, Dir-Mktg - W.H. Maze Company; *pg.* 1389, *pg.* 652
Pohl, Steve, Interim CFO - Novelis Inc.; *pg.* 100, *pg.* 516
Pohlman, Brett, Asst VP & Mgr-Social Media Community - Regions Financial Corporation; *pg.* 798, *pg.* 4
Poiesz, Benjamin, Product Mgr - Google Inc.; *pg.* 1249, *pg.* 153
Poindexter, Jennifer, Mgr-Health & Wellness Mktg - Anthem, Inc.; *pg.* 1192, *pg.* 683
Poindexter, Paquita, Sr Mgr-Mktg - Sunstar Americas Inc.; *pg.* 1599, *pg.* 591
Poindexter, Randy, Sr VP-Mktg - Bojangles' Restaurants, Inc.; *pg.* 1717, *pg.* 1364
Poindexter, Sara, Sr Mgr-Mktg Process - Capital One Financial Corporation; *pg.* 730, *pg.* 1789
Poinsotte, Francois, Area Mgr-Sls - Bemis Healthcare Packaging; *pg.* 1453, *pg.* 1885
Pointeau, Kate, Brand Mktg Mgr - NACCO Industries, Inc.; *pg.* 1174, *pg.* 1433
Poirier, Betsy, VP-Mktg & Mdsg - Macy's East; *pg.* 1777, *pg.* 1254
Poirier, Mario, Dir-Sls Ops-Western Canada - Xerox Canada Inc.; *pg.* 494, *pg.* 1930
Pokorny, Brian, Sr Mgr-Digital & Media - MillerCoors LLC; *pg.* 255, *pg.* 582
Pokorny, Robert, Sr Mgr-Mktg Analysis - ALYCE Paris; *pg.* 18, *pg.* 634
Pola, John, VP-Specialty Sls - Jelly Belly Candy Company; *pg.* 1857, *pg.* 86
Polacco, Lorenzo Staunovo, Sr Dir-Sls & Adv Ops - Yahoo! Inc.; *pg.* 1289, *pg.* 289
Polak, Christine, Sr Specialist-Mktg - Cardinal Health, Inc.; *pg.* 1512, *pg.* 1448
Polakovic, Miroslav, Sr Engr-Technical Mktg - Cisco Systems, Inc.; *pg.* 372, *pg.* 240
Polanco, Nancy, Sr Acct Mgr-Mktg - Ingram Micro Inc.; *pg.* 415, *pg.* 261
Polanski, Carolyn, Sr Mgr-Mktg Comm-Global - Avery Dennison Corporation; *pg.* 1452, *pg.* 95
Polansky, David, VP-Sls-Stacy Adams Brand - Weyco Group, Inc.; *pg.* 1822, *pg.* 1858
Polasanapalli, Sindhura, Dir-Mktg & Innovation - Dean Foods Company; *pg.* 852, *pg.* 1679
Polaski, Christina, Mgr-Content & Social Media - Carbonite, Inc.; *pg.* 368, *pg.* 792
Polatty, Eric, Mgr-Digital Mktg - Medifast, Inc.; *pg.* 1562, *pg.* 774
Polcsa, Gregory, Brand Mgr-Nature Made Digital - Pharmavite LLC; *pg.* 1584, *pg.* 167
Polen, Heather, Sr Mgr-Comm & Learning Svcs-Global - General Mills, Inc.; *pg.* 828, *pg.* 933
Polenchar, Joseph, VP-Inside Sls & Demand Generation - Fujitsu Computer Systems Corporation; *pg.* 398, *pg.* 285
Poler, Megan, Mgr-Product Mktg - Valassis; *pg.* 1698, *pg.* 386
Poletti, Gina, Brand Mktg Mgr - Reeves International, Inc.; *pg.* 966, *pg.* 1108
Polevoy, Matt, Dir-Social Media - Sony Corporation of America; *pg.* 675, *pg.* 1293
Polgar, James, Mgr-Sls-East Reg - Technibus LLC; *pg.* 1380, *pg.* 1408
Polhemus, Missy, Mgr-Digital Mktg - Books-A-Million, Inc.; *pg.* 1623, *pg.* 2
Policano, Robert, Product Mgr-Telematics Svcs - Mercedes-Benz USA, LLC; *pg.* 184, *pg.* 514
Polich, Victor, Mgr-Sls-Natl - Bank of the West; *pg.* 721, *pg.* 213
Polinchock, David, Dir-Mktg - AT&T Inc.; *pg.* 1867, *pg.* 1674
Poling, Dustin, Mgr-Digital Mktg-Global - NetJets Inc.; *pg.* 1917, *pg.* 1442
Poling, Kristi, Mgr-Mktg & Comm - Sunrise Senior Living, Inc.; *pg.* 1599, *pg.* 1795
Polinski, Dennis, Product Mgr-Brand Protection Solutions-Global - Brady Corporation; *pg.* 363, *pg.* 1873
Poliseo, Stacy, VP-Digital Mktg - M&T Bank Corporation; *pg.* 777, *pg.* 1149
Polisoto, Jeff, Sr Mgr-Mktg - Rich Products Corporation; *pg.* 892, *pg.* 1150
Polite, Donald, Exec Dir-Mktg, Partner Mgmt, Licensing, Brand Mgmt & Sls Plng - Warner Bros. Records, Inc.; *pg.* 1791, *pg.* 55
Polito, Amanda, Dir-Local Adv & Mktg Programs - The Allstate Corporation; *pg.* 1189, *pg.* 639
Polizano, John, Sr VP-Adv - Daily News, L.P.; *pg.* 1632, *pg.* 1221
Polizzi, Tasha G., Specialist-Adv - The Progressive Corporation; *pg.* 1214, *pg.* 1463
Polizzotto, Susan F., Sr Mgr-Product Mktg-Internet of Everything - QUALCOMM Incorporated; *pg.* 1873, *pg.* 207
Polk, Kim, Mgr-Mktg Comm - Emerson Process Management; *pg.* 1334, *pg.* 1636
Polk, Ryan, VP-Product Mgmt - Rally Software Development Corp.; *pg.* 459, *pg.* 311
Polka, Brittney, Sr Assoc Brand Mgr-Skittles - Wm. Wrigley Jr. Company; *pg.* 1863, *pg.* 596
Polkinghorne, Jennifer, Mgr-Adv & Media - The J.M. Smucker Company; *pg.* 865, *pg.* 1468
Poll, Melissa, Dir-Events Mktg & Special Projects - The Hearst Corporation; *pg.* 1649, *pg.* 1239
Pollack, Aaron, Head-Channel Mktg - Canary Connect, Inc.; *pg.* 628, *pg.* 1209
Pollack, Ben, Exec Dir-Digital Mktg - Sealed Air Corporation; *pg.* 1468, *pg.* 1058
Pollack, Elissa, Mgr-PR - Pentair Water Pool and Spa, Inc.; *pg.* 104, *pg.* 1171
Pollack, Jon, Exec VP-Sls Promo, Mktg & Ecommerce-Belk Stores Svcs - Belk, Inc.; *pg.* 1760, *pg.* 1364
Pollack, Kymm, VP-Mktg-Pillsbury - General Mills, Inc.; *pg.* 828, *pg.* 933
Pollack, Patsy, Sr Exec VP-Mdsg - MARTHA STEWART LIVING OMNIMEDIA, INC.; *pg.* 1661, *pg.* 1256
Pollard, Rachel, Sr Mgr-Mktg-Managed Svcs - Lexmark International, Inc.; *pg.* 427, *pg.* 730
Pollard, Stan, Dir-Electronic & Creative Media - Georgia Power Company; *pg.* 1943, *pg.* 508
Pollet, Tracie, Sr Mgr-Mktg - Valassis; *pg.* 1698, *pg.* 386
Polley, Frank, VP-Spirits Trade Mktg - Pernod Ricard USA, Inc.; *pg.* 1968, *pg.* 1332
Pollis, Steve, Sr Mgr-Mktg - AT&T; *pg.* 1865, *pg.* 258
Pollis, Teri, VP-Mktg - Wells Fargo & Company; *pg.* 819, *pg.* 232
Pollock, Clarissa, Coord-Mktg - Yasutomo & Co.; *pg.* 497, *pg.* 280
Pollock, Don, Sr Dir-Product Ops-COX Bus - Cox Communications, Inc.; *pg.* 279, *pg.* 501
Pollock, Elizabeth, Sr Mgr-Mktg - The Quaker Oats Company; *pg.* 834, *pg.* 588
Pollock, Robert, VP-Sls-Comml-Lamps Channel - Cree Inc.; *pg.* 631, *pg.* 1371
Polly, Richard, Sr Dir-ECommerce - Office Depot, Inc.; *pg.* 448, *pg.* 412
Polo, Ashley, Dir-ECommerce,Social Media & PR - Foxwoods Resort Casino; *pg.* 549, *pg.* 353
Polo, Debi, Mgr-Mktg Comm - Amkor Technology, Inc.; *pg.* 67, *pg.* 25
Polo, Holly, Sr Mgr-Sls & Mktg Events - Bracco Diagnostics, Inc.; *pg.* 1509, *pg.* 1085
Poloha, Michael, Sr Product Mgr-Wholesale Bathroom - Moen Incorporated; *pg.* 1056, *pg.* 1468
Polonka, Jack, Dir-R&D Matl-Product Physical Science - The Estee Lauder Companies Inc.; *pg.* 508, *pg.* 1229
Polonsky, Alex, Dir-Internet Mktg-SEO - SHUTTERFLY, INC.; *pg.* 1280, *pg.* 192
Polsinelli, Andrew, Mgr-Sls Ops-Natl - Jaguar Land Rover North America LLC; *pg.* 180, *pg.* 1081
Polsky, Andrew, VP-Sls - Entravision Communications Corporation; *pg.* 285, *pg.* 273
Polsky, Lori, Dir-Creative Svcs-Global - Bare Escentuals, Inc.; *pg.* 500, *pg.* 213
Polston, Chip, VP-Comm, Govt & PR - Kentucky Lottery Corporation; *pg.* 996, *pg.* 735
Polt, Nicholas, Dir-Mktg Comm - MicroStrategy, Inc.; *pg.* 1266, *pg.* 1809
Polte, Maureen, VP-Product Mgmt - Flexera Software Inc.; *pg.* 398, *pg.* 658
Polton, Tom, Sr Dir-Product Stewardship & Environmental Sustainability - Pfizer Inc.; *pg.* 1581, *pg.* 1278
Polydoroff, Michael, Sr Dir-Brand Mktg - Williamson-Dickie Manufacturing Company; *pg.* 50, *pg.* 1696
Polzin, Ryan, Product Mgr-HVT Emerging Markets - Medtronic, Inc.; *pg.* 1564, *pg.* 939
Poma, Whitney, Mgr-Mktg - Uber USA, LLC; *pg.* 1286, *pg.* 229
Pomeroy, Christine, Sr Dir-Americas Mktg - F5 Networks, Inc.; *pg.* 396, *pg.* 1835
Pomeroy, Stacey, Sr Mgr-Insights & Innovation - Kimberly-Clark Corporation; *pg.* 1461, *pg.* 1720
Ponczoch, John, Sr VP-Food Mktg & Ops - TravelCenters of America, LLC; *pg.* 1925, *pg.* 1481
Pond, Jeff, Reg Mgr-Sls-Stemco Brake Products - Stemco Inc; *pg.* 1182, *pg.* 1726
Ponde, Nikhilesh, Sr Dir-Mobile, Social & Partner Mktg - Hotwire, Inc.; *pg.* 1912, *pg.* 219
Ponder, Jeffrey D , Sr Specialist-Mktg Comm - NuVasive, Inc.; *pg.* 1577, *pg.* 205
Poniatowski, Matthew, Mgr-Digital Mktg - FCA US LLC; *pg.* 170, *pg.* 868
Ponnambalam, Shiva, Mgr-New Product Program-Hardware Engrg - Apple Inc.; *pg.* 350, *pg.* 73
Pontecorvo, Stephen L., VP-Grp Life Products - MetLife, Inc.; *pg.* 1208, *pg.* 1258
Pontikes, Georgia, Product Mgr-HCV - AbbVie Inc.; *pg.* 1486, *pg.* 638
Pontillo, Joan, Mgr-Channel Mktg - Honeywell International Inc.; *pg.* 407, *pg.* 1088
Pontious, Timothy, Sr Mgr-Capability - Alliance Data Systems Corporation; *pg.* 347, *pg.* 1729
Ponto, Andrea, Dir-Mktg-Underclass Portraits - Lifetouch, Inc.; *pg.* 1420, *pg.* 922
Ponton, Diana, VP-Sls & Mktg - San Jose Convention/Visitors Bureau; *pg.* 1005, *pg.* 250
Ponzini, Daniel, Coord-PR - Subaru Canada, Inc.; *pg.* 190, *pg.* 1929
Ponzio, Crystal, Sr Mgr-Global Creative - Netflix, Inc.; *pg.* 1269, *pg.* 141
Ponzoni, Andrew, Sr Mgr-Comm - Dassault Falcon Jet Corp.; *pg.* 227, *pg.* 1122
Poole, Carole, Project Coord-Mktg - Sally Beauty Holdings, Inc.; *pg.* 522, *pg.* 1691
Poole, Clint, VP-Mktg - Lionbridge Technologies Inc.; *pg.* 428, *pg.* 851
Poole, Craig, Coord-Web-PR - United Parcel Service, Inc.; *pg.* 1928, *pg.* 522
Poole, Darrin, Sr Mgr-Svcs Mktg - Adobe Systems Incorporated; *pg.* 342, *pg.* 235
Poole, Delicia, VP-Audience Dev-Grand View Media Grp - EBSCO Industries, Inc.; *pg.* 1638, *pg.* 2
Poole, Greg, VP-Imaging Products - FUJIFILM Canada Inc.; *pg.* 1414, *pg.* 1925
Poole, Jeff, Dir-Sls - Albuquerque Convention & Visitors Bureau; *pg.* 988, *pg.* 1135
Poole, John, Mgr-Sports Sls - Kissimmee-St. Cloud Convention & Visitors Bureau; *pg.* 997, *pg.* 436
Poole, Melissa, Product Mgr - Igloo Products Corporation; *pg.* 1126, *pg.* 1724
Poole, Michelle, Sr VP-Global Product Creation & Mdsg - Crocs, Inc.; *pg.* 1806, *pg.* 335
Poole, Nicolle, Dir-Mktg - Frito-Lay North America, Inc.; *pg.* 1853, *pg.* 1730
Poon, Sarah, Sr Mgr-Global Mktg-Developed Markets - L'Oreal USA; *pg.* 514, *pg.* 1252
Popa, Emil, Dir-Sls - U.S. Bottlers Machinery Company; *pg.* 1386, *pg.* 1369
Popadych, Heather, VP-Mktg & ECommerce-Direct & Web Dev - Harbor Freight Tools; *pg.* 1772, *pg.* 55
Pope, Ava, Dir-Sls - Greensboro Convention & Visitors Bureau; *pg.* 994, *pg.* 1374

Pope, Bryan, Sr Mgr-Comm - Zynga Inc.; *pg.* 1292, *pg.* 235
Pope, Courtney, Assoc Specialist-Integrated Mktg & Svcs - Deluxe Corporation; *pg.* 1634, *pg.* 964
Pope, Jody, Dir-Mktg-Individual Retention-Anthem - Anthem, Inc.; *pg.* 1192, *pg.* 683
Pope, Joe, Dir-Mktg - Rowan Companies, Inc.; *pg.* 984, *pg.* 1713
Pope, Samantha, Sr Mgr-Digital Product Adoption - CVS Health Corporation; *pg.* 1765, *pg.* 1610
Popelka, Heather, Assoc Dir-Media - Education Management Corporation; *pg.* 601, *pg.* 1575
Popen, Sean, Sr Dir-ECommerce Mktg - Office Depot, Inc.; *pg.* 448, *pg.* 412
Poperin, Sharon Van, Mgr-Mktg - Lennar Homes, Inc.; *pg.* 93, *pg.* 1710
Popescu, Monica, Mgr-Trade Mktg - Church & Dwight Canada Corp.; *pg.* 503, *pg.* 1925
Popillion, Nora, Dir-Entertainment & PR - Boyd Gaming Corporation; *pg.* 1082, *pg.* 1022
Popkin, Kimberly, Sr Analyst-Strategic Mktg - FedEx Corporation; *pg.* 1907, *pg.* 1642
Popofsky, Carly, Mgr-Mktg-Wholesale, Men's & Timepieces - Yurman Design, Inc.; *pg.* 15, *pg.* 1316
Popovici, Elena, Mgr-Acq Mktg - DIRECTV Group Holdings, LLC; *pg.* 281, *pg.* 79
Popowitz, Brian, VP & Head-Mktg & Bus Dev - Black Box Corporation; *pg.* 361, *pg.* 1547
Popp, Lisa, Mgr-Adv Records - TEN: The Enthusiast Network; *pg.* 1691, *pg.* 1298
Popp-Hellebuyck, Amy, Mgr-Brand Mktg & PR - La-Z-Boy Incorporated; *pg.* 932, *pg.* 901
Popp-Stahly, Sonja, Dir-Digital Media Comm - Eli Lilly and Company; *pg.* 1527, *pg.* 684
Poppen, Doug, Sr Dir-Mktg - Bojangles' Restaurants, Inc.; *pg.* 1717, *pg.* 1364
Poppen, Lisa, Sr Dir-Brand Mktg-Global - The Ritz-Carlton Hotel Company LLC; *pg.* 1110, *pg.* 766
Poppens, Jim, VP-Mktg-All-Clad - All-Clad Metalcrafters LLC; *pg.* 1121, *pg.* 1519
Popper, Jeff, VP-Mktg-Global - Hasbro, Inc.; *pg.* 954, *pg.* 1603
Popper, Joanna, VP-Mktg - Telemundo Network Inc.; *pg.* 311, *pg.* 430
Popper, Susan, Sr VP-Experience Mktg - Hewlett-Packard Company; *pg.* 404, *pg.* 175
Popper, Susan, Sr VP-Experience Mktg - HP Enterprise Services, LLC; *pg.* 409, *pg.* 1731
Poppers, Jennifer M., Sr Mgr-Comm - The Gap, Inc.; *pg.* 1770, *pg.* 218
Popsie, Joshua, Coord-Online Mktg - IceLandAir North America; *pg.* 1912, *pg.* 841
Popson, Emily, Mgr-Demand Generation Mktg - Blackbaud, Inc.; *pg.* 361, *pg.* 1613
Porcaro, Michael, Sr Mgr-PR & Intuit Global Bus Div - Intuit Inc.; *pg.* 769, *pg.* 158
Porche, Lesa, Sr Mgr - Charles Schwab & Company, Inc.; *pg.* 734, *pg.* 215
Pordash, Donnie, Sr Dir-Customer Svc - Rangers Baseball LLC; *pg.* 578, *pg.* 1659
Pordon, Kenneth, Mgr-Fan Strategy & Mktg - National Football League; *pg.* 567, *pg.* 1264
Pordy, Melissa, Grp Dir-Media Northern America Mktg - Tiffany & Co.; *pg.* 13, *pg.* 1299
Poremba, Barbara, VP-Retail Sls-Natl - Coca-Cola Refreshments USA, Inc.; *pg.* 247, *pg.* 500
Poris, Betsy, VP-Strategic Mktg-Book Clubs - Scholastic Corporation; *pg.* 1683, *pg.* 1288
Poropatich, Jay, Dir-Digital Mktg - Staples, Inc.; *pg.* 474, *pg.* 821
Porras, Leslie I., Dir-PR - Anthem, Inc.; *pg.* 1192, *pg.* 683
Porritt, Andy, Acct Exec-Adv Solutions - AT&T Inc.; *pg.* 1867, *pg.* 1674
Port, Andrea, Dir-Digital & Social Content - Kenneth Cole Productions, Inc.; *pg.* 1810, *pg.* 1248
Port, Bethany, Coord-Adv - Siemens Corporation; *pg.* 803, *pg.* 1291
Portal, Marie-Aude, Brand Mgr-Global Promo-Guess Nautica - Coty, Inc.; *pg.* 506, *pg.* 1219
Portas, Chad, Chief Creative Officer - Bai Brands; *pg.* 238, *pg.* 1073
Portell, Christine T., Mgr-Mktg - Express Scripts, Inc.; *pg.* 1530, *pg.* 997
Portelli, John, VP-Sls & Mktg - Advertising Checking Bureau Incorporated; *pg.* 345, *pg.* 1187
Porter, Brad, Dir-Mktg - Peapod, LLC; *pg.* 1029, *pg.* 661
Porter, Brianne, Mgr-Customer Experience & Bus Dev & Mgr-Natl Sls - The Baby Jogger Company; *pg.* 949, *pg.* 1800
Porter, Chris, Sr Mgr-Comm-Global Product Dev - Genentech, Inc.; *pg.* 1533, *pg.* 279
Porter, Chuck, Sr Dir - Giant Eagle, Inc.; *pg.* 1020, *pg.* 1575
Porter, James, Sr VP-Media Sys & IT Dev - Starz Entertainment, LLC; *pg.* 310, *pg.* 327
Porter, Jen, Dir-Mktg-Intl - Forever 21, Inc.; *pg.* 24, *pg.* 130
Porter, Jessica, Asst VP & Coord-Mktg - IBERIABANK Corporation; *pg.* 768, *pg.* 744
Porter, Karen, Dir-Media Svcs - Camping World, Inc.; *pg.* 1830, *pg.* 725
Porter, Regina, Sr Mgr-Sls - Baton Rouge Area Convention & Visitors Bureau; *pg.* 989, *pg.* 741
Porter, Richard M., Mgr-Product Dev-Midwest Reg - American Vanguard Corporation; *pg.* 1793, *pg.* 165
Porter, Robert C., Sr Dir-Medical - ExamWorks Group, Inc.; *pg.* 1529, *pg.* 505
Porter, Sarah, Rep-PR-Intl - Universal Orlando; *pg.* 590, *pg.* 456
Porter, Sherrie, Sr VP & Gen Mgr-Sls - Esslinger-Wooten-Maxwell Realtors, Inc.; *pg.* 1091, *pg.* 418
Porter, Stephanie A., Mgr-Strategic Mktg - Hasbro, Inc.; *pg.* 954, *pg.* 1603
Porter, Wendy, Sr Mgr-Mktg - UnitedHealth Group Incorporated; *pg.* 1221, *pg.* 950
Porterfield, Lynn, Dir-Enterprise Adv - Hewlett-Packard Company; *pg.* 404, *pg.* 175
Porterfield, Tim, Dir-Mktg - SAP America, Inc.; *pg.* 466, *pg.* 1557
Portet, Nicole, VP-Adv & Media - Charles Schwab; *pg.* 1235, *pg.* 1661
Portet, Nicole, VP-Adv - Charles Schwab & Company, Inc.; *pg.* 734, *pg.* 215
Portilla, Ramon, Sr Dir-Global Customer Insights & Analytics - Sam's Club; *pg.* 1783, *pg.* 29
Portillo Roman, Antonio, Dir-Field Mktg - Remy Cointreau USA Inc.; *pg.* 1969, *pg.* 1285
Porto, Andy, Head-Dermatology Sls - Novartis Pharmaceuticals Corp.; *pg.* 1575, *pg.* 1054
Porto, Jose, Reg Dir-Sls-Caribbean & Central America - Blue Coat Systems, Inc.; *pg.* 362, *pg.* 284
Portu, Mark, Chief Product Officer - Piksel; *pg.* 1275, *pg.* 1282
Portwood, Nicole, VP-Brand Mktg - Fifth Generation, Inc.; *pg.* 1963, *pg.* 1662
Porzucek, Connie, Sr Mgr-Shared Svcs Comm & Trng-Global - The Hershey Co.; *pg.* 1855, *pg.* 1538
Posch, Lisa, Sr Mgr-Mktg - The Bradford Group; *pg.* 1763, *pg.* 637
Posen, Andrew, Sr Dir-IR - Tremor Video; *pg.* 682, *pg.* 1305
Posen, Zac, Dir-Creative - Brooks Brothers Group, Inc.; *pg.* 39, *pg.* 1208
Posey, David, VP-Sls-Central US - CompuCom Systems, Inc.; *pg.* 378, *pg.* 1678
Posey, Sheri, Mgr-Mktg - MC2; *pg.* 431, *pg.* 1153
Posillico, Christina, Mgr-Mktg - Cablevision Systems Corporation; *pg.* 272, *pg.* 1141
Posner, David, Product Mgr - Trippe Manufacturing Company; *pg.* 220, *pg.* 592
Pospischel, Gustavo, Sr Dir-Core Mobile Engrg - Sears Holdings Corporation; *pg.* 1784, *pg.* 618
Pospisil, Joshua, Sr Coord-Vendor Mktg-Digital & Social Content - Academy Sports & Outdoors, Ltd.; *pg.* 1824, *pg.* 1724
Posse, Melissa, Brand Mgr-Chocolate Innovation - The Hershey Co.; *pg.* 1855, *pg.* 1538
Possemato, Karen, Sr Dir-Corp Mktg - Illumina, Inc.; *pg.* 412, *pg.* 203
Post, Julie, Head-US Pediatric Meningitis Vaccine Consumer & Dir-Mktg - Pfizer Inc.; *pg.* 1581, *pg.* 1278
Post, Ryan, Brand Mgr-Global Out-of-Store Card - Starbucks Corporation; *pg.* 897, *pg.* 1840
Post, Shari, Head-Primetime Sls - NBC Universal, Inc.; *pg.* 300, *pg.* 1266
Post, Steven, Dir-Customer Specific Mktg Plng - Ahold USA, Inc.; *pg.* 1013, *pg.* 1520
Posta, Maria Della, Sr VP-Sls & Mktg - Pratt & Whitney Canada Corp.; *pg.* 1370, *pg.* 1952
Posten, Greg, Dir-Digital Mktg & Gen Mgr-SymantecTV - Symantec Corporation; *pg.* 478, *pg.* 161
Posternak, HillaryRoss, Dir-Brand Mktg USA Network - NBC Universal, Inc.; *pg.* 300, *pg.* 1266
Poswilko-McReynolds, Karin, Mgr-Mktg - Acuity Brands, Inc.; *pg.* 1294, *pg.* 487
Potash, Sara, Mgr-Mktg-Lip Category - Maybelline LLC; *pg.* 516, *pg.* 1257
Poteet, Jon, Mgr-Mktg Comm-Worldwide - Diodes Incorporated; *pg.* 634, *pg.* 1729
Potes, Veronica, Mgr-Mktg-E! Network Partnerships - NBC Universal, Inc.; *pg.* 300, *pg.* 1266
Poticny, Jacquelyn G., Sr Mgr-Wireless Bus Ops & Customer Solutions - Alcatel-Lucent USA, Inc.; *pg.* 615, *pg.* 1728
Poto, Lindsey, Mgr-Shopper Mktg - Ubisoft Inc.; *pg.* 589, *pg.* 229
Potocnik, Frank, Dir-Natl Channel Sls-Enterprise Solutions Grp - Dell Inc.; *pg.* 383, *pg.* 1737
Potorski, Michelle, Sr Dir-MinuteClinic Mktg - CVS Health Corporation; *pg.* 1765, *pg.* 1610
Potorski, Michelle, Product Mgr - The Gillette Company; *pg.* 509, *pg.* 795
Potratz, Josh, Sr Mgr-Market & Ventilation - Philips Electronics North America; *pg.* 662, *pg.* 782
Pott, Alistair, Product Mgr-Google Play - Google Inc.; *pg.* 1249, *pg.* 153
Potter, Adam, Sr Mgr-Mktg - IDEXX Laboratories, Inc.; *pg.* 1543, *pg.* 753
Potter, Brian H., Sr Dir-Comm - Comcast Sportsnet; *pg.* 278, *pg.* 1562
Potter, Diane, Dir-Consumer Mktg - Bonnier Corporation; *pg.* 1622, *pg.* 480
Potter, Jeff, VP-Product Dev - Northern Trust Corporation; *pg.* 787, *pg.* 585
Potter, Jim, VP-Product Mgmt - Hostway Corporation; *pg.* 1256, *pg.* 577
Potter, Karen, Coord-PR - Greenville Hospital System Inc.; *pg.* 1538, *pg.* 1617
Potter, Kelly, Mgr-Event Mktg - Houlihan's Restaurants, Inc.; *pg.* 1731, *pg.* 716
Potter, Kris, VP-Mktg & ECommerce - Apple Vacations Inc.; *pg.* 1899, *pg.* 1556
Potter, Richard, Exec VP-Production & Dev - Relativity Media, LLC; *pg.* 306, *pg.* 47
Pottier, Julie, Mgr-Mktg-Cultural Institute - Google Inc.; *pg.* 1249, *pg.* 153
Potts, Amanda, Mgr-Mktg - Fazoli's Management Inc.; *pg.* 1728, *pg.* 729
Potts, Christian T., Sr Mgr-Corp Comm - Iron Mountain Incorporated; *pg.* 421, *pg.* 796
Potts, Jim, Analyst-Mktg - Honeywell International Inc.; *pg.* 407, *pg.* 1088
Potts, John, VP-Sls - World Dryer Corporation; *pg.* 63, *pg.* 556
Potts, Ken, Dir-Mktg-Season & Major Programs - Seattle Theatre Group; *pg.* 582, *pg.* 1840
Potts, Lisa, Sr VP-Sls & Mktg - Trump Entertainment Resorts, Inc.; *pg.* 1117, *pg.* 1041
Potts, Michael, VP-Creative Svcs - The Weather Channel LLC; *pg.* 320, *pg.* 523
Potts, Rachel A., Rep-Media - Caterpillar, Inc.; *pg.* 1321, *pg.* 650
Potts, Randy, Sr VP-Sls - Abila, Inc.; *pg.* 340, *pg.* 1660
Potts, Tony, Sr VP-Finl Advisor Mktg - Wells Fargo & Company; *pg.* 819, *pg.* 232
Potucek, Kevin, VP-Product Mgmt - Hayward Pool Products; *pg.* 1049, *pg.* 1057
Potvin, Michel, VP-Corp Mktg & Strategy - Esterline Technologies Corporation; *pg.* 1412, *pg.* 1814
Pouk, John, VP & Gen Mgr-Worldwide Life Science Sls - Agilent Technologies, Inc.; *pg.* 614, *pg.* 264
Poulin, Cathy, Dir-PR & Outreach - Bob's Discount Furniture Inc.; *pg.* 1763, *pg.* 354
Poulin, Shannon, VP & Gen Mgr-Data Center Mktg & Enterprise - Intel Corporation; *pg.* 645, *pg.* 266
Pouliot, Elisa, Dir-ECommerce Relationship Mktg - Marshalls of MA, Inc.; *pg.* 1778, *pg.* 821
Pouliot, Elisa, Dir-ECommerce Relationship Mktg - T.J. Maxx; *pg.* 1788, *pg.* 822
Pouliot, Elisa, Dir-ECommerce Relationship Mktg - The TJX Companies, Inc.; *pg.* 1788, *pg.* 822
Pouliquen, Dominique, Dir-Mktg & Market Dev-Reality Solution Grp - Autodesk Inc.; *pg.* 356, *pg.* 257
Poulos, Alexandros, VP-Mktg - support.com, inc.; *pg.* 1283, *pg.* 192
Poulos, Anastasia, Assoc Mgr-Co-Brand Mktg - Southwest Airlines Co.; *pg.* 1923, *pg.* 1687
Poulos, Kristen, Mgr-Global Product Line - Belden, Inc.; *pg.* 624, *pg.* 993
Poulsen, Todd, Sr Dir-Ticket Sls & Svcs - San Diego Chargers Football Co.; *pg.* 580, *pg.* 208

First page reference indicates Business Class Edition
Second page reference indicates Geographic Edition

Poulton, Bob, Reg Mgr-Sls - Reliable Automatic Sprinkler Co., Inc.; pg. 1137, pg. 1158
Pouncy, Dwenya, Mgr-Global & Americas Mktg-Skagen Denmark - Fossil Group, Inc.; pg. 5, pg. 1735
Pound, Patty H., Dir-Migraine Mktg - AVANIR Pharmaceuticals; pg. 1498, pg. 40
Pountney, Charles W., Sr Exec VP-Sls & Mktg - Bellisio Foods, Inc.; pg. 840, pg. 931
Pour, Lindsay, Mgr-Corp Mktg - PFIP, LLC; pg. 1842, pg. 1037
Pous, Terri, Editor-Social Media-Brides Magazine - Conde Nast Publications, Inc.; pg. 1629, pg. 1217
Poveda, Cecilia, Project Mgr-Mktg Svcs - Brightstar Corporation; pg. 627, pg. 440
Poveromo, Maria, Sr Dir-AR, PR & Social Media - Adobe Systems Incorporated; pg. 342, pg. 235
Povey, John, VP-Database Mktg - Cablevision Systems Corporation; pg. 272, pg. 1141
Powell, Allison, Sr Rep-Educational Sls - Lippincott Williams & Wilkins, Inc.; pg. 1659, pg. 1567
Powell, Ashley, Coord-Mktg - Indianapolis Colts, Inc.; pg. 553, pg. 687
Powell, Beth, Mgr-Private Label Mktg - John B. Sanfilippo & Son, Inc.; pg. 1024, pg. 610
Powell, Bill, Sr Dir-Culinary - O'Charley's Inc.; pg. 1742, pg. 1653
Powell, Brent, Sr Mgr-Mktg-Hanes, JMS & C9 by Champion Women's UW - Hanesbrands Inc.; pg. 26, pg. 1394
Powell, Brigid, Mgr-Event Plng & Mktg Ops - Gilead Sciences, Inc.; pg. 1535, pg. 88
Powell, Chris, Reg Mgr-Mktg - Whataburger, Inc.; pg. 1755, pg. 1744
Powell, Claire, Exec VP-Mktg - Geneva Watch Group; pg. 5, pg. 1174
Powell, Hobson, Sr Dir-Optimization Svcs - Yahoo! Inc.; pg. 1289, pg. 289
Powell, Jacob, Acct Mgr-Tiers & Mgr-Social Media Community - Hewlett-Packard Company; pg. 404, pg. 175
Powell, Jacqueline, Sr Specialist-Mktg Event - Allscripts Healthcare Solutions, Inc.; pg. 1492, pg. 563
Powell, Jeff, Mgr-Mktg & Promos - Edward Don & Company; pg. 54, pg. 672
Powell, Jeffrey, Mgr-Product & Pro Education - Toyota Canada, Inc.; pg. 192, pg. 1934
Powell, Jessica, Mgr-Media & Integrated Mktg - Henkel Corporation; pg. 1165, pg. 1535
Powell, Jessica, VP-Mktg - The State Lottery Commission of Indiana; pg. 1006, pg. 690
Powell, Lindsay, Mgr-Mktg - 3M Company; pg. 1142, pg. 956
Powell, Lisa, VP-Advanced Sls - The Guardian Life Insurance Company of America; pg. 1202, pg. 1237
Powell, Martin, VP-Sls & Mktg - Guardian Industries Corp.; pg. 85, pg. 869
Powell, Melissa, Sr Mgr-PR - Microsoft Corporation; pg. 435, pg. 1824
Powell, Ray, VP-Global Mktg Partnerships - 20th Century Fox Home Entertainment, Inc.; pg. 267, pg. 125
Powell, Sean, Dir-Sls-North America - The Ripley Company; pg. 1305, pg. 342
Powell, Spencer, Product Mgr - Facebook, Inc.; pg. 1245, pg. 143
Powell, Susan, Specialist-Direct Mktg - Susan G. Komen for the Cure; pg. 158, pg. 1688
Powell, Toyin, Dir-Mktg & Analytics - American Express Company; pg. 712, pg. 1190
Powelson, Bart, Dir-Comml Mktg - Emerson Climate Technologies, Inc.; pg. 1333, pg. 1472
Power, Jeff, Gen Mgr-Sls - Reliable Chevrolet; pg. 189, pg. 1736
Power, Liz, Dir-Media Rels-Global - Novartis Vaccines & Diagnostics, Inc.; pg. 1575, pg. 809
Power, Meg, Exec Dir-Digital Sls - Time Inc.; pg. 1693, pg. 1300
Power, Mike, Sr Dir - Pfizer Inc.; pg. 1581, pg. 1278
Powers, Amy, VP-Adv Sls - Daily Press; pg. 1632, pg. 302
Powers, Bill, Dir-Mktg - Aaon, Inc.; pg. 1068, pg. 1488
Powers, Brian, VP-Sls & Mktg - Wasau Paper Corp.; pg. 1471, pg. 1882
Powers, Carrie, VP-Mktg - Vascular Solutions, Inc.; pg. 1434, pg. 946
Powers, Ellie, Product Mgr-Play - Google Inc.; pg. 1249, pg. 153
Powers, Hugh A., Dir-Media - Anheuser-Busch Companies, LLC; pg. 237, pg. 991
Powers, John, Sr Product Mgr - Echo Incorporated; pg. 1046, pg. 626
Powers, Linda, Reg Dir-Mktg - Wendy's International, Inc.; pg. 1755, pg. 1451
Powers, Lisanne, Mgr-Mktg Comm-Unified Comm - AT&T Communications Corp.; pg. 1866, pg. 1043
Powers, Maureen, VP-Deposit Products Mktg - Discover Financial Services; pg. 744, pg. 653
Powers, Meggan, Sr Dir-Corp Comm - KLA-Tencor Corporation; pg. 1353, pg. 146
Powers, Mindy, Sr VP-Sls - XO Communications; pg. 497, pg. 1786
Powers, Tara, Mgr-US Sls Comm - Avon Products, Inc.; pg. 500, pg. 1198
Powers, Tim, Mgr-Social Media - IBM; pg. 410, pg. 1449
Powers, Will, VP-Mktg - Restaurants Unlimited, Inc.; pg. 1748, pg. 1839
Poy, Russ, VP-Product Dev - Pellerin Milnor Corporation; pg. 1368, pg. 744
Poyser, John, Sr Analyst-Enablement-Mktg Tech Solutions - Adobe Systems Incorporated; pg. 342, pg. 235
Poytress, Emily, Assoc Mgr-Digital Mktg - Intuit Inc.; pg. 769, pg. 158
Poznansky, Mike, Mgr-Collegiate Mktg - Red Bull North America, Inc.; pg. 264, pg. 275
Poznoff, Nancy, Dir-Mktg Promos - Starbucks Corporation; pg. 897, pg. 1840
Prabaker, Madhu, Product Mgr-Mobile - Yelp! Inc.; pg. 1291, pg. 235
Prabhakar, Rohit, Sr Mgr-Digital Mktg - McKesson Corporation; pg. 1560, pg. 222
Prabhakara, Ajith, Sr Mgr-Mktg & Product Mgr - T-Mobile US, Inc.; pg. 676, pg. 1816
Prache, Marine, Mgr-Product Mktg - Jaguar Land Rover North America LLC; pg. 180, pg. 1081
Prade, Konrad La, Dir-Adv - The Gaston Gazette; pg. 1644, pg. 1373
Pradhan, Anir, Sr Officer-Mktg - Equifax Workforce Solutions; pg. 394, pg. 997
Pradhan, Keith, Sr Dir-Pricing & Product Strategy - salesforce.com, inc.; pg. 1278, pg. 226
Pradhan, Lauren, Sr Mgr-Mktg-Chex, Kix & Big G Cereal - General Mills, Inc.; pg. 828, pg. 933
Pradhan, Ranjit, Sr Product Mgr-Mobile Banking & Payments - Bank of the West; pg. 721, pg. 213
Pradhan, Samir, Product Mgr - Google Inc.; pg. 1249, pg. 153
Pradhan, Smriti, Sr Head-Digital Mktg - DISH Network Corporation; pg. 283, pg. 325
Prado, Andrea, Reg Brand Mgr - Entravision Communications Corporation; pg. 285, pg. 273
Prado, Jacqueline, Specialist-Consumer Mktg - Ace Hardware Corporation; pg. 1040, pg. 644
Prado, Lori Ann, Mgr-eMail Mktg - Golfsmith International Holdings, Inc.; pg. 1835, pg. 1662
Prado, Lourdes, Sr Mgr-Consumer Insights-Cross-Portfolio - Bacardi USA, Inc.; pg. 1956, pg. 417
Prado, Yoli, Creative Dir - Headstrong Corporation; pg. 403, pg. 1798
Pradzinski, Bob, VP-Sls - Hyundai Motor America; pg. 179, pg. 89
Praeger, Lisa, VP-Sls & Mktg Ops-US - Alcon; pg. 1399, pg. 530
Prairie, Douglas, Product Mgr - Raven Industries, Inc.; pg. 1888, pg. 1625
Prairie, Kyle, VP-Ticket Sls - Carolina Hurricanes Hockey Club; pg. 537, pg. 1386
Pramuk, Christian, Product Mgr - Autodesk Inc.; pg. 356, pg. 257
Prange, Sarah, Asst Mgr-Mktg & Brand Comm - Sub Zero Wolf; pg. 60, pg. 1867
Pranikoff, Michael, Dir-Emerging Media-Global - PR Newswire Association LLC; pg. 1678, pg. 1283
Pransky, Jordana, Dir-Natl Adv & Brand Partnerships-Food Innovation Grp - Conde Nast Publications, Inc.; pg. 1629, pg. 1217
Prasad, Chandrodaya, Dir-Product Mgmt - Cisco Systems, Inc.; pg. 372, pg. 240
Prasad, Norwin, Dir-Digital Mktg - Gannett Co., Inc.; pg. 1643, pg. 1790
Prasad, Sandeep, Product Mgr - Cisco Systems, Inc.; pg. 372, pg. 240
Prasad, Shail, VP-Mktg - Telebrands, Inc.; pg. 1396, pg. 1066
Prashanth, B., Reg Mgr-Sls - Abbott Laboratories; pg. 1484, pg. 551
Prast, Joseph, Brand Mgr-All Family Savory & Availability - Pepperidge Farm, Inc.; pg. 888, pg. 363
Prater, Robert, Mgr-Sls - Jefferson Chevrolet Co.; pg. 180, pg. 883
Prather, Beth, Dir-Co-Marketing & Tour - TheatreworksUSA; pg. 587, pg. 1298
Prather, Marnie, Dir-PR & Mktg - Bally North America, Inc.; pg. 1804, pg. 1200
Prati, Leila, Brand Mgr-Global - Shell Oil Company; pg. 984, pg. 1714
Pratt, Adam, Sr Mgr-Sls Enablement Mktg - Adobe Systems Incorporated; pg. 342, pg. 235
Pratt, Gavin, Dir-Product Mgmt - Hewlett-Packard Company; pg. 404, pg. 175
Pratt, Heidi, Mgr-Channel Mktg - Dal-Tile Corporation; pg. 78, pg. 1678
Pratt, Heidi, Mgr-Channel Mktg - Mohawk Industries, Inc.; pg. 935, pg. 527
Pratt, Michael, Dir-Content Mktg & Integration - LEGO Systems, Inc.; pg. 961, pg. 346
Pratt, Rebecca, Sr Dir-Comm - Capital One Financial Corporation; pg. 730, pg. 1789
Pratt, Robert, Mgr-CX Product Mgmt-MyHabit.com - Amazon.com, Inc.; pg. 1226, pg. 1831
Pratt, Robert, Mgr-Mktg Growth - Penske Truck Leasing Company, L.P.; pg. 188, pg. 1585
Pratt, Sharon, Mgr-Sls Admin & Planner-Event - Hanesbrands Inc.; pg. 26, pg. 1394
Pratt, Taylor, Sr Product Mgr - HomeAway, Inc.; pg. 1911, pg. 1663
Pratt-Heaney, Judd, Sr Mgr-Global Brand & Media - Harman International Industries, Incorporated; pg. 641, pg. 374
Pravorne, Janice, Reg Mgr-Sls & Mktg - Co-Ex Corp.; pg. 76, pg. 382
Preble, Karen, Sr Dir-Rheumatology Mktg - Sanofi US; pg. 1592, pg. 1046
Precht, Jim, Sr VP-Sls & Mktg - Advanced Environmental Recycling Technologies, Inc.; pg. 1310, pg. 35
Precopio, John , III, Mgr-Product Line-Bus Networks Solutions - Schneider Electric; pg. 467, pg. 1609
Pred, Becky, Mgr-Mktg Comm - Sprint Corporation; pg. 1874, pg. 719
Preece-Davis, Mona, Sr Mgr-eCommerce Mktg - ClosetMaid Corporation; pg. 920, pg. 452
Preest, Dan, VP-HR-The Americas & Global Mktg - ESAB Welding & Cutting Products; pg. 1335, pg. 1615
Preikschat, Steve, Head-Fixed Income Product Strategy-Global - Janus Capital Group, Inc.; pg. 772, pg. 320
Preis, Elizabeth L., VP-Mktg-North America - The Estee Lauder Companies Inc.; pg. 508, pg. 1229
Preisel, Thomas, Dir-Sls & Mktg - Axel Plastics Research Laboratories, Inc.; pg. 326, pg. 1356
Preisser, Dave, VP-Production - Houston Chronicle; pg. 1651, pg. 1707
Preisser, Rosemary, Sr Mgr-Trng - Pfizer Inc.; pg. 1581, pg. 1278
Preissner, Shawn, Mgr-Mktg Automation - NetApp, Inc.; pg. 444, pg. 287
Prelack, Jim, Mgr-Worldwide Channel Mktg - Intel Corporation; pg. 645, pg. 266
Premi, Mike, Mgr-Bus Dev-New Product Innovation - Intel Corporation; pg. 645, pg. 266
Premkumar, Vidya, Dir-Product Line - Fairchild Semiconductor Corporation; pg. 638, pg. 245
Prendergast, Gregg, VP-US Channel Sls - Acer America Corporation; pg. 341, pg. 235
Prendergast, Hayley, Bus Mgr-Customer - Revlon, Inc.; pg. 521, pg. 1286
Prentice, Tony, VP-Mobile Payments & Products - American Express Company; pg. 712, pg. 1190
Prentiss, Mike, Sr Mgr-State Govt Rels & Govt Comm-Global - The Procter & Gamble Company; pg. 1129, pg. 1418
Prescott, Ashley, Asst Mgr-Email Mktg - XO Group Inc.; pg. 1289, pg. 1316
Prescott, Jeff, Asst VP-Comm & Mktg - HCA HOLDINGS, INC.; pg. 1539, pg. 1651
Prescott, Jennifer O., Dir-Creative & Editorial - The Dun & Bradstreet Corp.; pg. 1637, pg. 1120
Presker, Kristen, Mgr-Email Mktg - Build-A-Bear Workshop, Inc.; pg. 950, pg. 993
Presley, Ann, Exec Dir-Product Mgmt-Enterprise Info Solutions - McKesson Corporation; pg. 1560, pg. 222
Press Maguire, Alexandra, Dir-Digital Mktg - Gilt Groupe Inc.; pg. 24, pg. 1234
Press, Eva, Strategist-Mktg - Facebook, Inc.; pg. 1245, pg. 143
Press, Jacqueline, Sr Mgr-Media - Under Armour, Inc.; pg. 49,

pg. 759
Press, Michelle, Mgr-Mktg Comm-Global - Underwriters Laboratories Inc.; *pg.* 1396, *pg.* 641
Press, Natalee, Sr Mgr-Digital Mktg Svcs - Allergan, Inc.; *pg.* 1491, *pg.* 106
Pressas, Wendy, Sr Mgr-Customer Mktg - The Coca-Cola Company; *pg.* 240, *pg.* 493
Pressentin, Cassie, Dir-Meeting Sls-Midwest - Anaheim/Orange County Visitor & Convention Bureau; *pg.* 988, *pg.* 42
Pressentin, Dawn, Mgr-Mktg - Accenture; *pg.* 1392, *pg.* 1186
Presser, Richard, Dir-PR - Hugo Boss Fashions Inc.; *pg.* 42, *pg.* 1242
Pressley, Ellen G., Rep-PR - E.I. du Pont de Nemours & Company; *pg.* 1159, *pg.* 390
Pressman, Brian, Dir-NFL Media - National Football League; *pg.* 567, *pg.* 1264
Pressoir, Gregory, Brand Mgr-Global - Revlon Consumer Products Corporation; *pg.* 521, *pg.* 1286
Pressoir, Gregory, Brand Mgr-Global - Revlon, Inc.; *pg.* 521, *pg.* 1286
Presson, Damion, Product Mgr-Basketball-Allen Iverson Collection - Reebok International Ltd.; *pg.* 1817, *pg.* 811
Prestegaard, Shawn, Mgr-Mktg - 3M Company; *pg.* 1142, *pg.* 956
Prestegord, Adam, Mgr-Segment Mktg - FMC Corporation; *pg.* 1163, *pg.* 1564
Prestianni, John, Sr Dir-Fin - Florida State Fair Authority; *pg.* 549, *pg.* 473
Preston, Debra, Brand Mgr - Wyndham Vacation Ownership; *pg.* 1119, *pg.* 457
Preston, Emily, Specialist-Digital Mktg - SpartanNash Co; *pg.* 1034, *pg.* 889
Preston, Jeff, Sr Mgr-SEO - The Walt Disney Company; *pg.* 317, *pg.* 52
Preston, Joe, Exec VP-Global Footwear & Mktg - New Balance Athletic Shoe, Inc.; *pg.* 1811, *pg.* 798
Preston, Jon, Head-Social Media - Staples, Inc.; *pg.* 474, *pg.* 821
Preston, Kelly, Sr Mgr-Omni Channel Mktg - PetSmart, Inc.; *pg.* 1481, *pg.* 18
Preston, Lauren, Brand Mktg Mgr - Qdoba Mexican Grill Inc.; *pg.* 1031, *pg.* 336
Preston, Mark, VP-Digital Media - Hubbard Broadcasting, Inc.; *pg.* 291, *pg.* 961
Preston, Michael, Dir-PR - Philadelphia 76ers, L.P.; *pg.* 575, *pg.* 1568
Preti, Chris, Dir-Advair & Flovent Mktg - GlaxoSmithKline; *pg.* 1536, *pg.* 1389
Pretotto, Mary, Dir-Social Media Community & Intelligence - Rogers Communications Inc.; *pg.* 668, *pg.* 1942
Prettyman, Mary, VP-Mktg-North America - Airbus North America Holdings, Inc.; *pg.* 1897, *pg.* 1784
Pretyman, Caroline, Dir-Media Rels - Eversource; *pg.* 1942, *pg.* 845
Preuss, Lisa, Sr Dir-PR & Analyst Rels - Epicor Software Corporation; *pg.* 393, *pg.* 110
Previ, Tom, Sr Dir-JW Marriott Brand Mktg - Marriott International, Inc.; *pg.* 1102, *pg.* 764
Prewitt, John, Supvr-Bus Analytics & Digital Media - Arizona Diamondbacks; *pg.* 529, *pg.* 14
Prial, Katherine, Specialist-Media Traffic - Charter Communications, Inc.; *pg.* 274, *pg.* 372
Priblo, Jack, Dir-Corp Mktg - Georgia-Pacific LLC; *pg.* 1458, *pg.* 507
Pribram, Sarah, VP-Mktg Svcs - The Vermont Teddy Bear Company; *pg.* 969, *pg.* 1767
Price, Allan, Dir-Global Digital Mktg - Monster Beverage Corporation; *pg.* 257, *pg.* 69
Price, Anika, Sr Mgr-Product Mktg - Amazon.com, Inc.; *pg.* 1226, *pg.* 1831
Price, Anne M., Dir-Global Mktg Capabilities - United Parcel Service, Inc.; *pg.* 1928, *pg.* 522
Price, Anthy, Sr VP-Media & Integrations - Disney Interactive Media Group; *pg.* 1239, *pg.* 95
Price, April, Coord-PR - The Ritz-Carlton Hotel Company LLC; *pg.* 1110, *pg.* 766
Price, Ben, Exec VP-Natl Ad Sls - Discovery Communications, Inc.; *pg.* 282, *pg.* 777
Price, Ben, Sr VP-Adv Sls-Natl - Travel Channel LLC; *pg.* 313, *pg.* 766
Price, Bob, VP-Mdsg - Art Van Furniture, Inc.; *pg.* 914, *pg.* 912
Price, David, VP-Bus Dev Media - Ericsson, Inc.; *pg.* 638, *pg.* 1730
Price, Debra, Brand Mktg Mgr - Novartis Corporation; *pg.* 1574, *pg.* 1273
Price, Hayden, Dir-Trade Mktg - Musco Family Olive Company; *pg.* 882, *pg.* 297
Price, Heather, Mgr-Mktg - Knoxville News-Sentinel Company; *pg.* 1657, *pg.* 1637
Price, James, Sr VP-Data Insights & Programmatic Product - Outfront Media; *pg.* 1465, *pg.* 1275
Price, Jeff, Product Mgr-Svcs - Cisco Systems, Inc.; *pg.* 372, *pg.* 240
Price, Joel, Sr Mgr-Digital Content - San Diego Chargers Football Co.; *pg.* 580, *pg.* 208
Price, John, Supvr-Mktg Comm-Global - 3M Company; *pg.* 1142, *pg.* 956
Price, John, Exec Dir-Adv Ops - Gawker Media LLC; *pg.* 1248, *pg.* 1234
Price, Joss, Sr Mgr-Global Media Solutions - Electronic Arts Inc.; *pg.* 951, *pg.* 189
Price, Julie V., Mgr-Digital Mktg & Adv-Enterprise Grp - Hewlett-Packard Company; *pg.* 404, *pg.* 175
Price, Katie, Sr Mgr-Mktg Res - The Coca-Cola Company; *pg.* 240, *pg.* 493
Price, Keith, Dir-Natl Media Rels & Bus Comm - The Goodyear Tire & Rubber Company; *pg.* 1883, *pg.* 1401
Price, Kelsey, Coord-Social Media Content - Lord & Taylor LLC; *pg.* 1777, *pg.* 1252
Price, Kevin, Product Dir - Infor; *pg.* 414, *pg.* 484
Price, Kippy, Asst Dir-Mktg & Bus Dev-West Town Mall & Knoxville Center - Simon Property Group, Inc.; *pg.* 1112, *pg.* 690
Price, Leslie, Product Mgr - Acxiom Corporation; *pg.* 342, *pg.* 607
Price, Lisa, Mgr-Digital Mktg Channel - Bank of America Corporation; *pg.* 718, *pg.* 1362
Price, Malissa, Dir-Global Mktg PMO - Mylan, Inc.; *pg.* 1570, *pg.* 1520
Price, Martin, VP-Product Mgmt - OpenX Technologies, Inc.; *pg.* 1272, *pg.* 180
Price, Matthew, Specialist-Digital Mktg - Volkswagen Group of America, Inc.; *pg.* 194, *pg.* 1785
Price, Nancy, Sr Product Mgr - Mission Pharmacal Company Inc.; *pg.* 1568, *pg.* 1742
Price, Nikal, VP-Brand Mktg-Paramount Home Media Distribution - Paramount Pictures Corporation; *pg.* 304, *pg.* 138
Price, Penry, VP-Mktg Solutions - LinkedIn Corporation; *pg.* 1262, *pg.* 160
Price, Rick, Mgr-Food Svc Sls & Customer Svc - Heat Seal LLC; *pg.* 1345, *pg.* 1431
Price, Samantha, Dir-Ad Products - The Weather Channel LLC; *pg.* 320, *pg.* 523
Price, Sandy, Dir-Tourism Sls - Oklahoma City Convention & Visitors Bureau; *pg.* 1002, *pg.* 1487
Price, Sharon, Dir-Svcs Mktg - Cisco Systems, Inc.; *pg.* 372, *pg.* 240
Price, Shawn, Sr Mgr-End-User & Collaboration Applications TS - Cisco Systems, Inc.; *pg.* 372, *pg.* 240
Price, Steve, Sr Mgr-Bus Dev-Global - Blizzard Entertainment; *pg.* 950, *pg.* 107
Price, Steven, Sr Dir-Conservation Science & Practice - World Wildlife Fund Canada; *pg.* 162, *pg.* 1947
Price, Terra, Acct Coord-PR - McCormick & Company, Incorporated; *pg.* 1027, *pg.* 779
Price, Tracy Waxenberg, Head-Adv Team - Wegmans Food Markets, Inc.; *pg.* 1037, *pg.* 1337
Prida, Karla, Sr Mgr-Strategy & Insights-Automotive - Univision Communications Inc.; *pg.* 683, *pg.* 1307
Pridgen, Kim, Mgr-Creative Svcs - Paul Mueller Company; *pg.* 706, *pg.* 1007
Pries, Jim, Mgr-Sls-Natl - Lapp Insulator Company, LLC; *pg.* 1946, *pg.* 1173
Pries, Scott, Mgr-Mktg Comm - Emerson Process Management; *pg.* 1334, *pg.* 1636
Priest, Jason E., Mgr-Mktg - Intel Corporation; *pg.* 645, *pg.* 266
Priest, Meltem, VP-Mktg & ECommerce - Marriott International, Inc.; *pg.* 1102, *pg.* 764
Priester, Christine, VP-Mktg - Advocate Health Care; *pg.* 1487, *pg.* 607
Priester, Jennifer, Coord-Mktg-Center for Connected Health - Partners HealthCare System, Inc.; *pg.* 1580, *pg.* 800
Priestley, Catherine, Engr-PR Design Assurance - Medtronic, Inc.; *pg.* 1564, *pg.* 939
Priestman, Tom, Mgr-Digital Mktg & ECommerce-COP - Colgate-Palmolive Company; *pg.* 504, *pg.* 1215
Prieto, Viola, Coord-Mktg - Kinetic Concepts, Inc.; *pg.* 1553, *pg.* 1741
Prihoda, Kathleen, Sr Mgr-Comm - The Walt Disney Company; *pg.* 317, *pg.* 52
Primard, Mylene, Dir-Sls-Wine - Bacardi USA, Inc.; *pg.* 1956, *pg.* 417
Prime, Milton, Sr VP & Sr Dir-Audit - Bank of America Corporation; *pg.* 718, *pg.* 1362
Primer, Tina, Dir-Creative Svcs - Abbott Laboratories; *pg.* 1484, *pg.* 551
Primola, Nick, Sr VP-Mktg Education & CMO Initiatives - Association of National Advertisers, Inc.; *pg.* 133, *pg.* 1197
Prince, Aikisha, Mgr-Integrated Mktg - Getty Images, Inc.; *pg.* 1645, *pg.* 1836
Prince, Duncan, Product Mgr - Mercedes-Benz USA, LLC; *pg.* 184, *pg.* 514
Prince, Lindsay, Mgr-Mktg-Professional Education - American Heart Association Inc.; *pg.* 128, *pg.* 1673
Prince, Steve, Dir-Sls Ops & Bus Dev - New Balance Athletic Shoe, Inc.; *pg.* 1811, *pg.* 798
Principe, Felicia, Sr Mgr-Brand Adv & Mktg - Major League Baseball; *pg.* 560, *pg.* 1255
Prine, Megan, Sr Product Mgr-Walt Disney Parks & Resorts Online - The Walt Disney Company; *pg.* 317, *pg.* 52
Pringels, Ariane, Reg Mgr-Sls - Audemars Piguet (North America); *pg.* 1, *pg.* 1198
Pringle, Ann, Product Mgr-Wholesale Kitchen - Moen Incorporated; *pg.* 1056, *pg.* 1468
Pringle, Devin, Mgr-Mktg-Performance Div - Air Lift Company; *pg.* 198, *pg.* 895
Pringle, Leah, Mgr-Recruiting, B2B & Local Mktg - Aflac Incorporated; *pg.* 1188, *pg.* 527
Prins, Jamie, Sr Product Mgr - Amazon.com, Inc.; *pg.* 1226, *pg.* 1831
Prins, Kate Watson, Sr Mgr-Mktg - The Hollywood Reporter Inc.; *pg.* 1650, *pg.* 133
Printzian, Jonathan, Sr Dir-Pricing & Strategy - Emdeon, Inc.; *pg.* 747, *pg.* 1650
Priolo, Judy, Sr Dir-Quality - PepsiCo, Inc.; *pg.* 259, *pg.* 1327
Prior, Abby, Dir-Mktg-Premium Bread Brands - Bimbo Bakeries USA Inc.; *pg.* 840, *pg.* 1540
Prior, Jason, Sr Dir-Retail Mktg - Williamson-Dickie Manufacturing Company; *pg.* 50, *pg.* 1696
Prior, Kevin, Mgr-Product Mktg - Facebook, Inc.; *pg.* 1245, *pg.* 143
Prior, Peter J., Specialist-Sls & Mktg Solutions - The Dun & Bradstreet Corp.; *pg.* 1637, *pg.* 1120
Prisbylla, Derek, Dir-Residential Sls & Ops - Guardian Alarm Company; *pg.* 641, *pg.* 907
Prisco, Steven J., Dir-Mktg - Sam Ash Music Corporation; *pg.* 669, *pg.* 1167
Priselac, Meagan, Specialist-Social Media - The Coca-Cola Company; *pg.* 240, *pg.* 493
Pritchard, Ben, Sr Mgr-Corp Comm - Cisco Systems, Inc.; *pg.* 372, *pg.* 240
Pritchard, Lisa M., Head-Mktg-New Bus Div - Intuit Inc.; *pg.* 769, *pg.* 158
Pritchard, Marc S, Officer-Mktg & Brand Building-Global - The Procter & Gamble Company; *pg.* 1129, *pg.* 1418
Pritchard, Matthew, Head-Digital Mktg-Global - Novartis Corporation; *pg.* 1574, *pg.* 1273
Pritchard, Stacy W., Dir-Mktg Sys - Autodesk Inc.; *pg.* 356, *pg.* 257
Pritikin, Liane, Sr Dir-Strategic Insights & Res - MTV Networks Company; *pg.* 298, *pg.* 1262
Pritsker, Alex, Mgr-Online Mktg - The Metropolitan Museum of Art; *pg.* 561, *pg.* 1259
Pritts, Rob, Reg Dir-Tournament Sls - American Golf Corporation; *pg.* 528, *pg.* 272
Prius, Erica Gartsbeyn, Mgr-Prius Product Mktg & Comm - Toyota Motor Sales, U.S.A., Inc.; *pg.* 193, *pg.* 296
Probert, David, Dir-Ingredient Mktg - ADM Alliance Nutrition, Inc.; *pg.* 1474, *pg.* 653
Probert, Tom, Product Mgr-MapInfo Pro Global - Pitney Bowes Inc.; *pg.* 454, *pg.* 376
Probst, Tom, Sr Dir-Medical Ops & Special Projects - Colorado Rockies Baseball Club, Ltd.; *pg.* 542, *pg.* 317
Prociw, Lindsay, Dir-Category Mktg - William Grant & Sons, Inc.; *pg.* 1972, *pg.* 1057
Proctor, Laura, Dir-Customer Mktg-Industrial-North America - Ansell; *pg.* 1495, *pg.* 1114
Proctor, Lauren, Coord-Field Mktg - Panera Bread Company; *pg.* 1029, *pg.* 1001
Proctor, Steven J., Grp VP-Global Sls & Bus Dev - American Axle & Manufacturing Holdings, Inc.; *pg.* 198, *pg.* 879

First page reference indicates Business Class Edition
Second page reference indicates Geographic Edition

Proctor, Taryn, Media Planner-Strategy & Buyer-Digital - Caesars Entertainment Corporation; pg. 1083, pg. 1023
Proefke, Gary, Sr Mgr-Segment Mktg - Avaya Inc.; pg. 621, pg. 264
Profaci, John A., VP-Mktg - Colavita USA, Inc.; pg. 849, pg. 1056
Profetto, Mike, VP-Product Engrg - Gold Eagle Company; pg. 206, pg. 575
Profumo, Frank, Dir-Adv - Intralox LLC; pg. 1350, pg. 744
Profumo, Frank, Dir-Creative - The Laitram LLC; pg. 1354, pg. 744
Prokop, P. J., Dir-Mktg - Providence Performing Arts Center; pg. 578, pg. 1607
Prokos, George, Sr VP-Ticket Sls & Svcs - Dallas Mavericks; pg. 543, pg. 1678
Proot, Kris, Dir-Sls - O'Brien Corporation; pg. 1366, pg. 1001
Proper, David, Exec VP-Media Strategy & Distr - National Hockey League; pg. 568, pg. 1265
Prophet, Tony, Corp VP-Windows & Search Mktg - Microsoft Corporation; pg. 435, pg. 1824
Proshan, Naomi, Dir-Segment Mktg - Teachers Insurance & Annuity Association - College Retirement Equities Fund; pg. 1219, pg. 1297
Prosser, Chelsea, Assoc-Mktg - Legg Mason, Inc.; pg. 775, pg. 758
Prossick, Nancy, Mgr-Mktg-Long Term Care - GF Health Products, Inc.; pg. 1535, pg. 508
Prost, Jamie, Mgr-Svc Mktg-USCAN - GE Healthcare; pg. 399, pg. 1765
Proto, Marie, Sr Mgr-Domestic Money Transfer Mktg - The Western Union Company; pg. 822, pg. 327
Protter, Courtney, Brand Mgr - PayPal Inc.; pg. 1274, pg. 248
Proud, David, VP-Corp Mktg - Clean Harbors, Inc.; pg. 376, pg. 839
Proud, Mike, Dir-Mktg-North America - Federal-Mogul Holdings Corporation; pg. 205, pg. 907
Proudfoot, Kevin, Exec Dir-Creative-Google Creative Lab - Google Inc.; pg. 1249, pg. 153
Prough, Justin, Exec Dir-Creative - Meredith Corporation; pg. 1663, pg. 705
Prout, Danielle, Dir-Mdsg - Tiffany & Co.; pg. 13, pg. 1299
Provansal, Nicole, Sr Acct Exec-Corp Sls - Angels Baseball, L.P.; pg. 529, pg. 42
Provencal, Marjorie A., Analyst-Mktg - Xerox Corporation; pg. 494, pg. 365
Provencher, Leo, Dir-Sls-Asia - Stanbee Company, Inc.; pg. 1819, pg. 1050
Provenza, Salvatore, VP-Sls & Mktg - Eos International, Inc.; pg. 1243, pg. 59
Provine, Corey, Dir-Mktg - The Hain Celestial Group, Inc.; pg. 860, pg. 1172
Provines, Christy, Acct Mgr-Adv - Time Inc.; pg. 1693, pg. 1300
Provinsal, Mark S., Dir-Sls & Mktg-Europe - Vicon Industries, Inc.; pg. 685, pg. 1166
Provost, Dave, Dir-Sls-Natl - Whirlpool Corporation; pg. 62, pg. 872
Provost, Stephanie Coyle, Product Mgr-Accessories-Global - The Timberland Company; pg. 1821, pg. 1039
Pruce, Megan Ferington, Dir-PR - Cleveland Clinic; pg. 1516, pg. 1429
Prud'homme, Sheila, Sr Mgr-Mktg & Strategic Alliances - Dr Pepper Snapple Group, Inc.; pg. 250, pg. 1729
Pruden, Cheryl, Sr VP-Mktg Insights - Citigroup Inc.; pg. 735, pg. 1212
Prudhomme, Jessica, Head-Affluent Consumer Mktg-US - MasterCard International, Inc.; pg. 780, pg. 1326
Prudhomme, Rebecca, VP-Product & Solutions Mktg - Amdocs Inc.; pg. 348, pg. 974
Pruex, Marguerite Saint, Sr Mgr-Tax Mktg & Bus Dev - PricewaterhouseCoopers LLP; pg. 795, pg. 1283
Pruismann, Debby, Coord-Corp Sls & Mktg - American Packaging Corporation; pg. 1451, pg. 1333
Pruitt, Brian, Sr Dir-Brand Media - Arby's Restaurant Group, Inc.; pg. 1014, pg. 488
Pruitt, Dawn, Dir-Consumer Mktg-Dry Eye - Allergan, Inc.; pg. 1491, pg. 106
Pruitt, Mark, VP-Mktg - Dawson Geophysical Company; pg. 383, pg. 1727
Pruitt, Michael, Sr Product Mgr-Indus Markets - Epson America Inc.; pg. 394, pg. 122
Pruitt, Tyson, Sr Mgr-Media Rels - Monsanto Company; pg. 1173, pg. 999
Prunell, Justin, Head-Media Solutions-Mobile - Google Inc.; pg. 1249, pg. 153
Pruner, Todd, Mgr-Mktg Automation - Ixia; pg. 422, pg. 56
Prunty, Kaci, Mgr-Retail Mktg & Brand Activation - Tempur Sealy International, Inc.; pg. 944, pg. 731
Prusak, Leo, VP-Air Traffic Mgmt Products & Strategy - PASSUR Aerospace, Inc.; pg. 233, pg. 376
Prusank, Steve, Sr VP-Sls & Mktg - High Liner Foods (USA) Incorporated; pg. 862, pg. 816
Prusank, Steve M., Sr VP-Sls & Mktg - High Liner Foods; pg. 862, pg. 1796
Prusinski, Sarah, Mgr-Mktg - Conair Corporation; pg. 505, pg. 1055
Pruss, Josh, VP-Partnership Mktg - Brooklyn Nets; pg. 534, pg. 1145
Pruthi, Priyanka, Grp Product Mgr-Digital Video & Audio - Adobe Systems Incorporated; pg. 342, pg. 235
Pryne, Mark A., Corp Sec & Dir-Sls - American Felt & Filter Company; pg. 1312, pg. 1184
Pryne, Scott, Rep-Sls - American Felt & Filter Company; pg. 1312, pg. 1184
Pryor, Ann, Sr Mgr-Publicity - The McGraw-Hill Companies Inc.; pg. 1663, pg. 1257
Pryor, Jessica, Brand Mgr - Arby's Restaurant Group, Inc.; pg. 1014, pg. 488
Pryor, Karin, VP-Mktg-Store Fixtures Grp - Leggett & Platt, Incorporated; pg. 933, pg. 974
Pryor, Kristiana, Mgr-Mktg Assets - Oklahoma City Thunder; pg. 571, pg. 1487
Pryts, Edward J., Sr VP-Sls-North America - Cybex International, Inc.; pg. 1521, pg. 832
Pryzwansky, Scott, Dir-PR-Eastern US Markets - Time Warner Cable Inc.; pg. 312, pg. 1301
Przesiek, David, Chief Sls Officer & Sr VP - Fallon Community Health Plan; pg. 1530, pg. 862
Przybyslawski, Tony, Exec Dir-Mktg - The Boeing Company; pg. 225, pg. 567
Przyklenk, Garry, Sr Mgr-Digital Insights - TD Bank US Holding Company; pg. 809, pg. 1051
Psaltis, Jennifer, Mgr-Product Mktg - Arrow Electronics, Inc.; pg. 619, pg. 325
Psarras, Adrianne, Specialist-PR - Overstock.com, Inc.; pg. 1273, pg. 1760
Psoinos, Katie, Brand Mktg Mgr - Converse Inc.; pg. 1831, pg. 793
Psycharis, George, Sr Dir-Airframe & Engine Maintenance - Air Canada; pg. 1896, pg. 1902
Psyhojos, Ally, Mgr-Mktg - Wyndham Worldwide Corporation; pg. 1119, pg. 1107
Ptalis, Deborah, Sr Mgr-Creative Project Mgmt - Revlon, Inc.; pg. 521, pg. 1286
Pua, Roger, Sr Dir-Corp Comm-Asia Pacific - LinkedIn Corporation; pg. 1262, pg. 160
Puariea, Erin, Gen Mgr-Experiential Mktg & Taste Of Home Cooking School - The Reader's Digest Association, Inc.; pg. 1679, pg. 1322
Pucci, Don, CMO & CTO - Multi-Fineline Electronix, Inc.; pg. 658, pg. 114
Puccino, Alexandra, Mgr-Sls & Mktg - National Railroad Passenger Corporation; pg. 1916, pg. 403
Puckett, Denny, Mgr-Mktg - Intuit Inc.; pg. 769, pg. 158
Puckett, Thomas, Strategist-Creative - Facebook, Inc.; pg. 1245, pg. 143
Puclik, Brian, Mgr-Corp Mktg - The PNC Financial Services Group, Inc.; pg. 795, pg. 1579
Puco, Christopher C., VP-Sls-North America - Align Technology, Inc.; pg. 1489, pg. 237
Pudduck, Andrew, VP-Mktg & Mdsg - Hooters of America LLC; pg. 1731, pg. 511
Pudner, Heejung, Product Mgr-Molded Case Circuit Breaker - Eaton Corporation; pg. 1331, pg. 1429
Puebla, Marco, Head-Global Brand, Digital & Adv - Symantec Corporation; pg. 478, pg. 161
Puebla, Rafael, Head-Mktg Geo Central Div-LAC Reg - MasterCard Incorporated; pg. 779, pg. 1325
Puello, Tania Lia, Brand Mgr-Global Mktg - Calvin Klein, Inc.; pg. 20, pg. 1209
Puente, Laura, Dir-Strategic Mktg & Multicultural Mktg - ConAgra Foods, Inc.; pg. 826, pg. 1014
Puentes, Bill, Sr Dir-Mktg-Oils & Baking - ACH Food Companies, Inc.; pg. 835, pg. 1631
Puerst, Michael, Mgr-Sls - Reliable Automatic Sprinkler Co., Inc.; pg. 1137, pg. 1158
Puetz, Curt, Product Mgr - Daktronics, Inc.; pg. 633, pg. 1624
Puffe, Richard, Sr Product Mgr-Pro - Thomson Reuters - Corporate Headquarters; pg. 1693, pg. 1299
Puffett, Emily, Dir-Intermediary Mktg - Janus Capital Group, Inc.; pg. 772, pg. 320
Puga, Amado, Supvr-Production - Panavise Products, Inc.; pg. 1058, pg. 1032
Pugerude, Mar, Pres-Sls-Global - Genband, Inc.; pg. 640, pg. 1731
Pugh, Brian, Dir-Mktg & Emerging Tech - Meijer, Inc.; pg. 1779, pg. 888
Pugh, Bryan, Chief Mdsg & Mktg Officer - Fred's Inc.; pg. 1769, pg. 1644
Pugh, Gary, Mgr-Customer Mktg - Valassis; pg. 1698, pg. 386
Pugh, Mtu, VP-Mdsg - Family Dollar Stores, Inc.; pg. 1768, pg. 1382
Pugh, Rachel, Sr Dir-Strategic Comm - Georgetown University; pg. 602, pg. 400
Pugliese, David, Sr VP-Mktg - Cox Communications, Inc.; pg. 279, pg. 501
Pugliese, John, VP-Mktg Comm & Brdcst - Memphis Grizzlies; pg. 561, pg. 1645
Puglisi, Francesca, Mgr-Global Mktg-New Media & Experiential - Transitions Optical, Inc.; pg. 1432, pg. 458
Puig, Andrea, Brand Mgr - The Coca-Cola Company; pg. 240, pg. 493
Pujals, Francesca, Sr Mgr-Strategy & Insights - Univision Communications Inc.; pg. 683, pg. 1307
Pujara, Chetan, Sr Dir & Head-Small Molecule Product Dev & Pkg Engrg - Allergan, Inc.; pg. 1491, pg. 106
Puleo, Steve, Product Mgr-Simpactor & Powderizer - Sturtevant Inc.; pg. 1379, pg. 824
Pulford, Seth, Mgr-Mktg-TEVA - Deckers Outdoor Corporation; pg. 1807, pg. 100
Pulicari, Ron, Mgr-Mktg - Cognex Corporation; pg. 1406, pg. 834
Pulido, Joseph, Mgr-Mktg Strategy - Toyota Motor Sales, U.S.A., Inc.; pg. 193, pg. 296
Pullano, Michael, Brand Mgr - Hasbro, Inc.; pg. 954, pg. 1603
Pullen, Mari, Mgr-Bus & Mktg Strategy - Intuit Inc.; pg. 769, pg. 158
Pullen, Steve, VP-Mktg-Global Database & Analytics - Gartner, Inc.; pg. 1248, pg. 374
Pulliam, Bob, Mgr-Sls & Mktg - Clinton Industries, Inc.; pg. 1324, pg. 1079
Pulliam, George, Asst VP & Branch Mgr-Sls-Powhatan - Village Bank & Trust Financial Corp.; pg. 816, pg. 1796
Pulliam, Wheeler, VP-Sls-Central Reg - Universal Lighting Technologies; pg. 1307, pg. 1655
Pullin, Ericka, Sr VP-Mktg - Cullen/Frost Bankers, Inc.; pg. 742, pg. 1740
Pulver, Bob, Sr Analyst-Social Insights-IBM Market Development - International Business Machines Corporation; pg. 418, pg. 1138
Puma, James, Mgr-Strategic Sourcing-Mktg Adv & Res - Verizon Communications Inc.; pg. 1875, pg. 1309
Pummell, Nick, Sr Mgr-Retail Ops - Zappos.com, Inc.; pg. 1291, pg. 1030
Pun, Vincent, Dir-Creative-Anthem, Inc. - Anthem, Inc.; pg. 1192, pg. 683
Punja, Sabrina, Mgr-Mktg-Global - Elizabeth Arden, Inc.; pg. 507, pg. 448
Punwani, Neil, Sr VP & Dir-Mktg-Europe - Brown-Forman Corporation; pg. 1958, pg. 732
Pupel, Sharon, VP-Sls - Post Holdings, Inc.; pg. 833, pg. 1002
Puramsetti, Kristin, Dir-Digital Brand Acq & Alt Sls - Comcast Cable Communications, Inc.; pg. 276, pg. 1560
Puranik, Gautam, VP-Mktg & Analysis - CarMax, Inc.; pg. 167, pg. 1800
Purcell, Byron, Sr Dir-Treasury Svcs & IR - Rite Aid Corporation; pg. 1590, pg. 1519
Purcell, Courtney, Specialist-Internet Mktg - Replacements, Ltd.; pg. 1138, pg. 1383
Purcell, David, VP-Digital & Mktg Transformation - Visa Inc.; pg. 816, pg. 230
Purcell, David, Head-Creative - Zenni Optical, Inc.; pg. 1438, pg. 168
Purcell, Karen, Sr VP-Sls Performance - Bank of America Corporation; pg. 718, pg. 1362
Purcell, Kathryn, Head-Portfolio Team-NA Brand Mktg & Ops - Shell Oil Company; pg. 984, pg. 1714
Purcell, Kels D., Dir-Sls - Purcell Murray Company Inc.; pg. 59, pg. 50
Purcell, Sean, Product Mgr - Google Inc.; pg. 1249, pg. 153
Purcell, Todd, Sr Mgr-Digital Fin Svcs Advisory-EY Digital - Ernst & Young Global Limited; pg. 748, pg. 1228
Purdie Montgomery, Candace, Dir-Event Mktg - Essence

Magazine; *pg.* 1639, *pg.* 1229
Purdon, Jarrod, Mgr-Mktg-Pro & Consumer Svcs Segments - United Parcel Service, Inc.; *pg.* 1928, *pg.* 522
Purdon, Tom, Dir-Store Brands Sls - SpartanNash Co.; *pg.* 1034, *pg.* 925
Purdy, Alexandra, Sr Specialist-Mktg - Dave & Buster's Entertainment, Inc.; *pg.* 1724, *pg.* 1679
Purdy, Elaine Urban, VP-Adv & Promos - National Amusements, Inc.; *pg.* 299, *pg.* 840
Purgess, Linda, Mgr-Channel Mktg - Godiva Chocolatier, Inc.; *pg.* 1854, *pg.* 1235
Puri, Jay K., Exec VP-Sls-Worldwide - NVIDIA Corporation; *pg.* 447, *pg.* 268
Puric, Rob, Dir-Product Mgmt Connected Home - Honeywell International Inc.; *pg.* 407, *pg.* 1088
Purpura, Nate, Dir-Content Mktg - eHealth, Inc.; *pg.* 1242, *pg.* 153
Pursel, Ken, Mgr-Sls-DOM Mechanical Tube - Wheatland Tube Company; *pg.* 121, *pg.* 1594
Purswell, Randy, Sr Mgr-Sls - Baker Hughes Incorporated; *pg.* 1315, *pg.* 1700
Purvis, Alva, VP-Channel Mktg Strategy-Data Mgmt - CA Technologies; *pg.* 366, *pg.* 1168
Purvis, Jim, Mgr-Mktg Strategy & Comml Insurance - Liberty Mutual Insurance Group Inc.; *pg.* 1205, *pg.* 797
Purvis, Mark, Dir-Brand Mktg-Global - Wizards of the Coast, Inc.; *pg.* 970, *pg.* 1830
Purvis, Will, Mgr-Customer Mktg - E&J Gallo Winery; *pg.* 1962, *pg.* 149
Purwar, Ruchir, Dir-Sls-Global Sys Integrators - Dell Inc.; *pg.* 383, *pg.* 1737
Pusateri, Joe, Sr Dir-Mktg - GEICO Corporation; *pg.* 1200, *pg.* 399
Puscar, Marcelo, Dir-Mktg-Reg Americas - Volvo Penta of the Americas, Inc.; *pg.* 1712, *pg.* 1778
Pusey, Meghan, Sr Dir-Integrated Comm - National Cattlemen's Beef Association; *pg.* 148, *pg.* 314
Pustinger, Jenni, Sr Dir-Shopper Mktg Walmart & Sam's Club - The Hershey Co.; *pg.* 1855, *pg.* 1538
Puthussery, Joseph, VP-Global Mktg Demand Center, Mktg Strategy & Ops - Cisco Systems, Inc.; *pg.* 372, *pg.* 240
Putman, Krystal, Dir-Mktg - Public Broadcasting Service; *pg.* 305, *pg.* 1774
Putnam, Matt, Sr Dir-Retail & Shopper Insight - Hasbro, Inc.; *pg.* 954, *pg.* 1603
Putrino, Mia, Assoc Mgr-Product Mktg-Console - Sony Computer Entertainment America LLC; *pg.* 966, *pg.* 256
Putthoff, Angela, Bus Mgr-Intermodal & Specialist-Intermodal Mktg - The Kansas City Southern Railway Company; *pg.* 1913, *pg.* 985
Puttick, Chelsey, Mgr-Mktg-eMail - Bloomingdale's, Inc.; *pg.* 1763, *pg.* 1204
Putz, Duane, Product Mgr - Pella Corporation; *pg.* 104, *pg.* 711
Puzzitiello, Rocco, Reg Sls Mgr-Healthcare-Western US - Insight Enterprises, Inc.; *pg.* 415, *pg.* 26
Pydimukkala, Chai, Sr Dir-Product Mgmt - Oracle Corporation; *pg.* 1272, *pg.* 786
Pye, Darryl, Head-Product-Western & Central Europe - MetLife, Inc.; *pg.* 1208, *pg.* 1258
Pyle, Derrick, Specialist-Web Mktg - Pegasystems Inc.; *pg.* 453, *pg.* 74
Pyle, Kathy, Sr Dir-Mktg-US - McDonald's Corporation; *pg.* 1737, *pg.* 645
Pyle, Mark, Brand Mgr & Mgr-Comm - Shell Lubricants; *pg.* 217, *pg.* 1714
Pyle, Michael, Sr VP-Engrg & Product Dev - Pegasystems Inc.; *pg.* 453, *pg.* 809
Pyle, Rick, VP-Sls-Intl - Alliance Laundry Holdings LLC; *pg.* 51, *pg.* 1890
Pyle, Tara, Dir-Mktg - L'Oreal USA; *pg.* 514, *pg.* 1252
Pyliotis, Marianne, Sr Mgr-Mktg Comm - Dorel Juvenile Group, Inc.; *pg.* 923, *pg.* 676
Pyper, Andrew, Sr Head-Bus-US Merchant Mktg - MasterCard Incorporated; *pg.* 779, *pg.* 1325
Pyper, Andy, Sr Head-Bus-US Merchant Mktg - MasterCard Worldwide Inc.; *pg.* 780, *pg.* 988
Pyron, Kyle, Sr VP-Mktg & Comm - VHA Inc.; *pg.* 1606, *pg.* 1724
Pyszczymuka, Greg, Sr Dir-Mktg - Zogenix, Inc.; *pg.* 1612, *pg.* 211
Pyszkowski, Frank, Sr VP-Sls & Mktg Retail Brands - The C.F. Sauer Company; *pg.* 847, *pg.* 1801

Q

Qaqundah, Nicole, Mgr-Product Mktg-US Retail Desktops - Hewlett-Packard Company; *pg.* 404, *pg.* 175
Qayyum, Sidrah, Sr Mgr-Digital Audience Dev - Time Inc.; *pg.* 1693, *pg.* 1300
Qin, Jifeng, Sr Product Mgr-Automotive Product Bus Unit - International Rectifier Corporation; *pg.* 647, *pg.* 80
Qin, Lake, Dir-Sls-China - GigOptix, Inc.; *pg.* 400, *pg.* 245
Qiu, Yinguang, Dir-Market Res & Officer-Mktg - Amica Mutual Insurance Co.; *pg.* 1192, *pg.* 1602
Qu, Kelly, Sr Mgr-Strategic & Intl Dev - Kind LLC; *pg.* 868, *pg.* 1249
Quaassdorff, Gerardo, Exec Dir-Mktg-Intl - Holstein Association USA, Inc.; *pg.* 143, *pg.* 1764
Quach, Karen, Div Dir-Mktg - Pernod Ricard USA, Inc.; *pg.* 1968, *pg.* 1332
Quach, Rebecca, Mgr-Mktg - Nestle Purina PetCare Canada; *pg.* 1479, *pg.* 1928
Quach, Steven, Dir-Online Mktg - Hotels.com, L.P.; *pg.* 1257, *pg.* 1682
Quadlin, Sean, Mgr-Mktg - Google Inc.; *pg.* 1249, *pg.* 153
Quady, Jill, Brand Mgr - Remy Cointreau USA Inc.; *pg.* 1969, *pg.* 1285
Quaglia, Cindy, Mgr-Catalog Mktg - LEGO Systems, Inc.; *pg.* 961, *pg.* 346
Quaile, Lauren, Grp Mgr-Shopper Mktg - Campbell Soup Company; *pg.* 844, *pg.* 1048
Quale, Matthew, VP-Retail Mktg - MetLife, Inc.; *pg.* 1208, *pg.* 1258
Qualey, Marjorie, VP-Platform & Product Svcs-Desktop Tools - Charles Schwab; *pg.* 1235, *pg.* 1661
Qualey, Marjorie, VP-Platform & Product Mgmt-Desktop Tools - Charles Schwab & Company, Inc.; *pg.* 734, *pg.* 215
Qualkenbush, Paul, Dir-Brand Mktg & High Performance Coatings - Rust-Oleum Corporation; *pg.* 1447, *pg.* 664
Qualls, Erica, Brand Mgr - Tomy; *pg.* 968, *pg.* 648
Qualls, Lisa, Specialist-Storage Brand Sls - International Business Machines Corporation; *pg.* 418, *pg.* 1138
Quam, Brent, Mgr-Partnership Mktg - Macy's, Inc.; *pg.* 1778, *pg.* 1417
Quam, Carol, Dir-Mktg - OPUS Corporation; *pg.* 101, *pg.* 949
Quan, Thao, Dir-Mktg-Plng North America - HSBC Bank USA; *pg.* 767, *pg.* 1241
Quandt, Bernard, Dir-Sls & Svc-Intl - Associated Global Systems, Inc.; *pg.* 1899, *pg.* 1184
Quaranta, Jennifer, Assoc Mgr-Integrated Content Mktg - Dr Pepper Snapple Group, Inc.; *pg.* 250, *pg.* 1729
Quaranta, Mike, CMO & VP - Oxford Life Insurance Company; *pg.* 1213, *pg.* 18
Quarante, Dante, VP-Creative Svcs - E&J Gallo Winery; *pg.* 1962, *pg.* 149
Quaratiello, Frank, VP-Media Rels - Citizens Bank & Trust; *pg.* 737, *pg.* 976
Quaratiello, Frank, VP-Media Rels - Citizens Financial Group, Inc.; *pg.* 737, *pg.* 1606
Quast, Eugene, VP-Sls-Global - Natural Alternatives International, Inc.; *pg.* 1571, *pg.* 253
Quatrini, Tony, Dir-Mktg - Pittsburgh Steelers Sports Inc.; *pg.* 577, *pg.* 1578
Queally, Monica, Sr Mgr-Digital Mktg - Nestle Waters North America Inc.; *pg.* 257, *pg.* 375
Quealy, Christy, Mgr-Media - Taco Bell Corp.; *pg.* 1752, *pg.* 117
Quebbemann, Tony, Product Mgr-Mktg - Molex Incorporated; *pg.* 655, *pg.* 628
Queenan, Tim, Dir-Strategy-Google Creative Lab - Google Inc.; *pg.* 1249, *pg.* 153
Quejado, Michelle, Interim CFO - Zynga Inc.; *pg.* 1292, *pg.* 235
Queller, David, Sr VP-Sls & Acct Mgmt - Express Scripts, Inc.; *pg.* 1530, *pg.* 997
Quenet, Vivian, VP-Sls-Asia Pacific & Dir - KVH Industries Inc; *pg.* 650, *pg.* 1602
Quenneville, Joan, Mgr-Retail Mktg - The Talbots, Inc.; *pg.* 34, *pg.* 824
Querel, Beatrice, Product Mgr - LaneLabs USA Inc.; *pg.* 1554, *pg.* 1128
Query, Dan, Sr VP-Product Dev-Global - Tempur Sealy International, Inc.; *pg.* 944, *pg.* 731
Quesada, Leah, VP-Mktg & Comm-Global - Xerox Corporation; *pg.* 494, *pg.* 365
Quesnel, Norman, Sr Specialist-Mktg - Amica Mutual Insurance Co.; *pg.* 1192, *pg.* 1602
Quesnell, Mary, Dir-Mktg-Ford Customer Svc Div - Ford Motor Company; *pg.* 172, *pg.* 876
Quevedo, Gisele, Sr Mgr-Bus Dev & Mgr-Mktg - Experian Consumer Direct; *pg.* 1245, *pg.* 71
Quick, Cameron, Sr Acct Exec-Ticket Sls - Golden State Warriors, LLC; *pg.* 550, *pg.* 171
Quickert, Kathy, Asst VP-Mktg - Lane Bryant; *pg.* 1776, *pg.* 1441
Quicksilver, Kim, Dir-Global Brand & Mktg - MetLife, Inc.; *pg.* 1208, *pg.* 1258
Quie, Christian, Mgr-Walmart Customer Sls - General Mills, Inc.; *pg.* 828, *pg.* 933
Quig, Deborah, Dir-Mktg-Global - McDonald's Corporation; *pg.* 1737, *pg.* 645
Quigg, Andrew, Head-Media Bus - The Progressive Corporation; *pg.* 1214, *pg.* 1463
Quigley, Bill, Dir-Mktg & Sls-Gunstock Mountain Resort - Gunstock Recreation Area; *pg.* 1094, *pg.* 1034
Quigley, Mark, Bus Mgr-Cloud Platform - Amazon.com, Inc.; *pg.* 1226, *pg.* 1831
Quille, Laura, Assoc Mgr-Mktg-Intl - Rust-Oleum Corporation; *pg.* 1447, *pg.* 664
Quillen, David, VP-Production - Waynesboro Nurseries, Inc.; *pg.* 1801, *pg.* 1811
Quillin, Sue, VP-Sls Svcs - Tyson Foods, Inc.; *pg.* 902, *pg.* 35
Quilter, Maureen C., Sr Dir-Comm - Comcast Sportsnet; *pg.* 278, *pg.* 1562
Quinlan, Nicole, Sr Mgr-Corp Comm - Newell Rubbermaid Inc.; *pg.* 1128, *pg.* 515
Quinlin, Michael, Exec Dir-Marketing - Massachusetts Office of Travel & Tourism; *pg.* 998, *pg.* 798
Quinlisk, Liz, Dir-Global Mktg Strategy-Imaging - X-Rite, Incorporated; *pg.* 1437, *pg.* 891
Quinn, Brett, Sr Dir-System z Product Mgmt - EMC Corporation; *pg.* 391, *pg.* 825
Quinn, Charles, VP-Mktg & Sourcing - Franklin Sports, Inc.; *pg.* 1834, *pg.* 847
Quinn, Christopher, Mgr-Plan & Mktg Analytics - Cablevision Systems Corporation; *pg.* 272, *pg.* 1141
Quinn, Colleen, Dir-Mktg, Comm, Media & Entertainment, ECommerce & Utilities - Teradata Corporation; *pg.* 483, *pg.* 1447
Quinn, Damien, Dir-Payer Mktg & Sr Product Mgr - Pfizer Inc.; *pg.* 1581, *pg.* 1278
Quinn, Elizabeth, Sr Mgr-Customer Strategy & Dev-Target - Del Monte Foods, Inc.; *pg.* 852, *pg.* 304
Quinn, Erin, Sr Mgr-Mktg - Tommy Bahama; *pg.* 48, *pg.* 1842
Quinn, Hilary, Dir-Coca-Cola TM Mktg-Western Europe - The Coca-Cola Company; *pg.* 240, *pg.* 493
Quinn, Jeff, Head-Mktg-CRESTOR - AstraZeneca Pharmaceuticals LP; *pg.* 1497, *pg.* 389
Quinn, Jennifer, Specialist-Search Mktg - Lord & Taylor LLC; *pg.* 1777, *pg.* 1252
Quinn, Jill, Sr Mgr-HR & Employee Comm - Royal Bank of Canada; *pg.* 800, *pg.* 1942
Quinn, Joelle, Sr Dir-Adv Sls & Mktg - Time Warner Inc.; *pg.* 312, *pg.* 1302
Quinn, John, Gen Mgr-East Coast Adv Sls - DISH Network Corporation; *pg.* 283, *pg.* 325
Quinn, Julia, Dir-Social Media - National Railroad Passenger Corporation; *pg.* 1916, *pg.* 403
Quinn, Julie, Sr Mgr-Mktg, Portfolio Mktg & Foodservice - PepsiCo, Inc.; *pg.* 259, *pg.* 1327
Quinn, Kelly, VP-Sls - Townsquare Media, Inc.; *pg.* 313, *pg.* 350
Quinn, Laura, Mgr-Customer Mktg - Johnson & Johnson; *pg.* 1549, *pg.* 1091
Quinn, Patrick, Dir-Sls & Mktg - General Motors of Canada Ltd.; *pg.* 177, *pg.* 1931
Quinn, Patrick, Mgr-Creative Svcs - Hillshire Brands; *pg.* 862, *pg.* 576
Quinn, Patrick, Assoc Mgr-Trade Mktg-Natl Accounts - Ocean Spray Cranberries, Inc.; *pg.* 887, *pg.* 827
Quinn, Paul, VP-Sls - Ellicott Dredges, LLC; *pg.* 1333, *pg.* 757
Quinn, Sean, Reg Mgr-Sls - M&T Bank Corporation; *pg.* 777, *pg.* 1149
Quinn, Stacey, VP-Strategic Mktg - Teachers Insurance & Annuity Association - College Retirement Equities Fund; *pg.* 1219, *pg.* 1297
Quinnette, Denise, Dir-Product Mgmt-Appliances, Power & Signal - TE Connectivity Ltd.; *pg.* 677, *pg.* 1515
Quinones, Denis, Dir-Promos & Dir-Mktg - Entravision Communications Corporation; *pg.* 285, *pg.* 273
Quinones, Patricia, VP-Mktg Svcs & Logistics & ERP - Visa

Inc.; *pg.* 816, *pg.* 230
Quinones, Patricia Levine, VP-Mktg Svcs & Logistics & ERP - Virco Manufacturing Corporation; *pg.* 946, *pg.* 297
Quinones, Widaliz, Brand Mgr - Remy Cointreau USA Inc.; *pg.* 1969, *pg.* 1285
Quintal, Stephanie, Sr Mgr-Search Engine Mktg - Hewlett-Packard Company; *pg.* 404, *pg.* 175
Quintana, Christine, Brand Mgr & Mgr-Strategic Comm - Micron Technology, Inc.; *pg.* 435, *pg.* 547
Quintana, Mariana, Sr Mgr-Product Mktg-Worldwide Svcs - Microsoft Corporation; *pg.* 435, *pg.* 1824
Quintana, Rick, VP-Digital Sls & Mktg - Wells Fargo & Company; *pg.* 819, *pg.* 232
Quintana, Tiffaney, Sr Dir-Mktg - TIBCO Software Inc.; *pg.* 484, *pg.* 178
Quintana, Victoria, Sr Dir-Mktg & Small Bus Solutions - AT&T Inc.; *pg.* 1867, *pg.* 1674
Quintano, Mayra, Analyst-Programmatic Mktg - CBS Interactive, Inc.; *pg.* 369, *pg.* 215
Quintero, Anabella, Reg Brand Mgr - Diageo North America Inc.; *pg.* 248, *pg.* 1223
Quintero, Carlos, Brand Mgr-NA Crest Whitestrips - The Procter & Gamble Company; *pg.* 1129, *pg.* 1418
Quirbach, John, Mgr-Tech Sls - Oracle Corporation; *pg.* 450, *pg.* 191
Quirolgico, Ana-Liza, Sr Mgr-Brand Activation - Beam Suntory Inc.; *pg.* 1957, *pg.* 599
Quiroz, Delia, Dir-Leisure Sls - Tampa Bay & Co.; *pg.* 1007, *pg.* 476
Quiroz, Gina, Head-Social Support Ops - Lenovo Group Ltd; *pg.* 427, *pg.* 1384
Quiroz, Lauren, Mgr-Sls & Mktg-Intl - Justin Brands, Inc.; *pg.* 1810, *pg.* 1695
Quiroz, Melissa, Coord-Mktg - First Cash Financial Services, Inc.; *pg.* 754, *pg.* 1659
Quiroz, Mercedes, Brand Mgr & Assoc Mgr-Synergy - Disney Interactive Media Group; *pg.* 1239, *pg.* 95
Quispe, Alison, Head-Svc Provider Field Mktg-US - Cisco Systems, Inc.; *pg.* 372, *pg.* 240
Quist, Amber, VP-Brand Mktg & Comm - Spredfast; *pg.* 1282, *pg.* 1666
Quizon, Myra, Coord-Mktg - AECOM Technology Corporation; *pg.* 65, *pg.* 125
Quon, Ivy, Sr VP-Mktg & Admin - Zacky Farms, Inc.; *pg.* 911, *pg.* 93
Quon, Norma, Exec Dir-Mktg - Whole Foods Market, Inc.; *pg.* 1038, *pg.* 1667
Quotson, Jennifer, VP-Creative Studios-Global - Starbucks Corporation; *pg.* 897, *pg.* 1840
Qureshi, Samira, Sr Dir-Mktg - Warner Bros. Records, Inc.; *pg.* 1791, *pg.* 55

R

Ra, Samuel, Acct Mgr-Mktg-Pro AV, Peripherals & Physical Security - Ingram Micro Inc.; *pg.* 415, *pg.* 261
Raab, Kurt, Sr Product Mgr - Amkor Technology, Inc.; *pg.* 67, *pg.* 25
Raab, Steven, Product Mgr-Fixed Income - The Dreyfus Corporation; *pg.* 745, *pg.* 1226
Raasch, Gary, Sr Dir-Mktg & Client Svcs - National Hot Rod Association; *pg.* 149, *pg.* 99
Rabasca, Anne, Mgr-Mktg - Toll Brothers, Inc.; *pg.* 115, *pg.* 1541
Rabaut, Paul, Brand Mgr-Hawthorne Garden Co. - The Scotts Miracle-Gro Company; *pg.* 1799, *pg.* 1459
Rabazzi, Diana, Sr Mgr-Media - Vail Resorts, Inc.; *pg.* 1117, *pg.* 313
Rabb, Alan, VP-Sparkling, Strategic Mktg, Bus Affairs & Productivity - The Coca-Cola Company; *pg.* 240, *pg.* 493
Rabbach, Deana, Mgr-Program Mktg-CRM - Sephora USA Inc; *pg.* 522, *pg.* 227
Rabbat, Phil, Mgr-Global Strategic Mktg-Antioxidants & Viscosity Modifiers - BASF Corporation; *pg.* 1149, *pg.* 1066
Rabbu, Chris, VP-Mktg-Lead Generation - Vonage Holdings Corp.; *pg.* 686, *pg.* 1074
Rabe, Steve, VP-Sls & Mktg-ATC - AVX Corporation; *pg.* 623, *pg.* 1616
Rabel, Alyson, Sr Mgr-Digital Mktg - United Services Automobile Association; *pg.* 1221, *pg.* 1743
Rabello, Henry, VP-Mktg & Gen Mgr-Olympics-Nike Brazil - NIKE, Inc.; *pg.* 1812, *pg.* 1492
Rabenovets, Joshua, Sr Dir-Product Mktg - Electronic Arts Inc.; *pg.* 951, *pg.* 189
Rabenovets, Joshua, Dir-Brand & Digital Product Mktg - ESPN, Inc.; *pg.* 285, *pg.* 340
Rabenschlag, Olivier, Head-Creative - Google Inc.; *pg.* 1249, *pg.* 153
Rabin, David, Exec Dir-Mktg - Lenovo Group Ltd; *pg.* 427, *pg.* 1384
Rabin, Harris, VP-Mktg & New Brands-Global - Anheuser-Busch Companies, LLC; *pg.* 237, *pg.* 991
Rabinovitz, Michael, Brand Mgr-Caramels - The Hershey Co.; *pg.* 1855, *pg.* 1538
Rabinowitz, Ilana, VP-Mktg - Lion Brand Yarn Company; *pg.* 696, *pg.* 1050
Rabinowitz, Seth, Sr VP-Mktg & Fan Engagement - New York Jets Football Club, Inc.; *pg.* 570, *pg.* 1067
Rabinowitz, Susan, Mgr-Credit Products - Bank of America Corporation; *pg.* 718, *pg.* 1362
Rabinowitz, Vanessa, Mgr-Mktg-Gift Card & Digital Bus Dev - Sephora USA Inc; *pg.* 522, *pg.* 227
Rabins, Andy, Specialist-Advanced Product Dev - 3M Company; *pg.* 1142, *pg.* 956
Rabizadeh, Vida, Dir-Brand Mktg-Women's & Soccer - NIKE, Inc.; *pg.* 1812, *pg.* 1492
Rabsatt, Simona, Dir-Vendor Mgmt & Procurement-Mktg US - Wal-Mart Stores, Inc.; *pg.* 1790, *pg.* 29
Racanello, Michael, Dir-Sls Ops - Reliable Automatic Sprinkler Co., Inc.; *pg.* 1137, *pg.* 1158
Raccuglia, Joseph, Dir-Product & Solutions Mktg of Network - Alcatel-Lucent USA, Inc.; *pg.* 615, *pg.* 1728
Racela, Rick, Sr Mgr-Web Products - NBC Sports Network; *pg.* 300, *pg.* 375
Rach-Nelson, Alyssa, Mgr-Product Dev-Digital Vendor Mktg - Target Corporation; *pg.* 1786, *pg.* 942
Rachau, Shaun, VP-Mktg Comm - Fender Musical Instruments Corporation; *pg.* 547, *pg.* 21
Racine, Eric, Mgr-Digital Mktg - Georgia-Pacific LLC; *pg.* 1458, *pg.* 507
Racioppi, Glenn, Sr Asst Brand Mgr - Unilever United States, Inc.; *pg.* 904, *pg.* 1061
Racioppo, Neal, Dir-Mktg - Arena Stage; *pg.* 529, *pg.* 395
Raczko, Bill, Head-Mktg-Fin Advisor Svcs - The Vanguard Group, Inc.; *pg.* 816, *pg.* 1550
Rad, Sara, Assoc Publr-Sls & Brand Dev-Good Housekeeping - Good Housekeeping; *pg.* 1645, *pg.* 1236
Rad, Sara, Assoc Publr-Sls & Brand Dev-Good Housekeeping - The Hearst Corporation; *pg.* 1649, *pg.* 1239
Radatovich, Rick, Dir-Sls-Natl Accounts - BIC Corporation; *pg.* 501, *pg.* 369
Radcliff, Deb, Sr VP-Mktg - West Marine, Inc.; *pg.* 1712, *pg.* 305
Radcliff, Patrick, Sr Mgr-Display Mktg - eBay Inc.; *pg.* 1240, *pg.* 243
Radcliffe, Kara, Mgr-Mktg - Honeywell International Inc.; *pg.* 407, *pg.* 1088
Radcliffe, Lauren, VP-Media & Acq - E*TRADE Financial Corporation; *pg.* 749, *pg.* 1230
Radde, David D., Exec VP-Mktg - USA Financial; *pg.* 815, *pg.* 864
Radder, Melissa, Rep-Sls - Ingram Micro Inc.; *pg.* 415, *pg.* 261
Rademaker, Jennifer, Exec VP-US Solutions Sls & Customer Delivery - MasterCard Incorporated; *pg.* 779, *pg.* 1325
Rader, Chad, Project Mgr-Automotive Mktg - Gannett Co., Inc.; *pg.* 1643, *pg.* 1790
Raderman, Alan, Sr Dir-Global Demand Generation Mktg - CA Technologies; *pg.* 366, *pg.* 1168
Radford, Pam, Sr Dir-Engagement Mktg-Global - Electronic Arts Inc.; *pg.* 951, *pg.* 189
Radhakrishna, Sahana, Product Mgr - Sears Holdings Corporation; *pg.* 1784, *pg.* 618
Radhakrishnan, Raj, Product Mgr - IHS Inc.; *pg.* 1652, *pg.* 326
Radigan, Carol, Sr Mgr-Rewards Fin Partnerships - Marriott International, Inc.; *pg.* 1102, *pg.* 764
Radigan, Christina, Dir-Mktg & Comm - OMG, Inc.; *pg.* 1367, *pg.* 781
Radin, Aaron, Sr VP-Partnerships & Portfolio Products - NBC Universal, Inc.; *pg.* 300, *pg.* 1266
Radinzel, Grant, VP-Product Mgmt & Dev - Aero Systems Engineering Inc.; *pg.* 223, *pg.* 959
Radivan, Nicolas, Mgr-Sls & Dev - National FFA Organization; *pg.* 149, *pg.* 688
Radka, Amy, Assoc Product Mgr-Dow Building Solutions - THE DOW CHEMICAL COMPANY; *pg.* 1157, *pg.* 898
Radke, Dorothy, Dir-Mktg - DATATRAK International, Inc.; *pg.* 383, *pg.* 1462
Radke, Shelby, Coord-Mktg - Cargill, Inc.; *pg.* 845, *pg.* 965
Radke, Vicky, Sr Dir-Amtrak Guest Rewards - National Railroad Passenger Corporation; *pg.* 1916, *pg.* 403
Radley, James, Brand Mgr-Safeway Customer Team - The Procter & Gamble Company; *pg.* 1129, *pg.* 1418
Radlo, Dawn, Sr Mgr-Strategic Pricing - Canon U.S.A., Inc.; *pg.* 1404, *pg.* 1178
Radloff, Scott, Coord-Mktg & Publicity - NBC Universal, Inc.; *pg.* 300, *pg.* 1266
Radman, Daniel, Brand Mgr-Bud Light FMB Brands - Anheuser-Busch Companies, LLC; *pg.* 237, *pg.* 991
Rado, Steven, CMO, Sr VP & Interim Mng Dir-Europe - Lands' End, Inc.; *pg.* 1776, *pg.* 1857
Radock, Erik, Mng Dir-Platform & Product Mgmt - Charles Schwab & Company, Inc.; *pg.* 734, *pg.* 215
Radogna, Mark, Grp Product Mgr - Epson America Inc.; *pg.* 394, *pg.* 122
Radous, Jim, VP-Sls & Mktg - Nissan Forklift Corporation, North America; *pg.* 186, *pg.* 631
Radow, Lauren, Brand Mgr-Coke - The Coca-Cola Company; *pg.* 240, *pg.* 493
Raduenz, Kimberly, Asst Mgr-Mktg - Briggs & Stratton Corporation; *pg.* 201, *pg.* 1899
Radwan, Tarek, Assoc Mgr-Product Mktg - Juniper Networks, Inc.; *pg.* 1260, *pg.* 286
Radzik, Gene, Sr Product Mgr - Dolby Laboratories, Inc.; *pg.* 284, *pg.* 217
Rae, D. N., Sr Acct Mgr-Cable Sls-US - Juniper Networks, Inc.; *pg.* 1260, *pg.* 286
Rae-Grant, John, Sr Product Mgr-Gmail - Google Inc.; *pg.* 1249, *pg.* 153
Raeth, Erika, Specialist-Mktg - FedEx Corporation; *pg.* 1907, *pg.* 1642
Raether, Laura, Dir-Mktg-Natl - Jostens, Inc.; *pg.* 7, *pg.* 938
Rafaelian, Carolyn, Founder & Dir-Creative - Alex and Ani; *pg.* 1, *pg.* 1600
Rafani, Massey, Exec VP-Creative Adv - Warner Bros. Entertainment Inc.; *pg.* 319, *pg.* 54
Raffa, Alec, Dir-Sls - Molded Fiber Glass Companies; *pg.* 1886, *pg.* 1403
Raffaele, Kelly A., Mgr-Mktg & Promos - The Walt Disney Company; *pg.* 317, *pg.* 52
Raffaele, Nick, VP-Sports Mktg - Callaway Golf Company; *pg.* 1829, *pg.* 58
Rafferty, Matt, VP-Sls - MORNINGSTAR, INC.; *pg.* 784, *pg.* 583
Raffone, David, Chief Revenue Officer & Chief Sls Officer - Skullcandy, Inc.; *pg.* 674, *pg.* 1754
Rafie, Bill, Sr Dir-Property Maintenance Sls - The Sherwin-Williams Company; *pg.* 1447, *pg.* 1435
Raftery, Ellyn, CMO - Fidelity Information Services, Inc.; *pg.* 397, *pg.* 433
Ragaglia, Alyse, Mgr-Event Mktg-Global - Reebok International Ltd.; *pg.* 1817, *pg.* 811
Ragavan, Sangeetha, Brand Mgr - Wm. Wrigley Jr. Company; *pg.* 1863, *pg.* 596
Ragazzoni, Niccolo, Dir-Mktg-Intl - LVMH Inc.; *pg.* 9, *pg.* 1254
Raghavachari, Usha, Head-European Mktg Comm - Ford Motor Company; *pg.* 172, *pg.* 876
Raghunandanan, Manoj, Grp Brand Dir - Johnson & Johnson; *pg.* 1549, *pg.* 1091
Ragland, Gregory, Dir-Fin-GCOM Div-Consumer Fin & Mktg Innovation - General Mills, Inc.; *pg.* 828, *pg.* 933
Ragland, Keith, Mgr-Solutions Mktg-Heartland District - Microsoft Corporation; *pg.* 435, *pg.* 1824
Raglin, David, Product Mgr-Support - Crane Carrier Company; *pg.* 168, *pg.* 1489
Rago, Joe, Dir-Digital & Mktg Div - Walgreen Co.; *pg.* 1608, *pg.* 605
Ragognetti, Chris, Dir-Mktg-Global - TE Connectivity Ltd.; *pg.* 677, *pg.* 1515
Ragovin, Jeff, Chief Strategy Officer-Salesforce Mktg Cloud - salesforce.com, inc.; *pg.* 1278, *pg.* 226
Ragsdale, Lori, Dir-Mktg Comm - General Electric Company; *pg.* 1297, *pg.* 347
Ragsdill, Dana, Dir-Product Mgmt - Dell Inc.; *pg.* 383, *pg.* 1737
Raguckas, David V., Grp Controller-Motion Control & Filtration Products - Kaydon Corporation; *pg.* 1352, *pg.* 866
Rahaman, Peter, VP-Sls - Rail Europe Inc.; *pg.* 1920, *pg.* 1354
Rahimeh, Victoria, Mgr-Mktg & SEO - Fossil Group, Inc.; *pg.* 5, *pg.* 1735

Rahman, Adnan, Dir-Mktg - Amgen Inc.; *pg.* 1493, *pg.* 291
Rahman, Kate, Mgr-Digital Mktg - Publix Super Markets, Inc.; *pg.* 1031, *pg.* 437
Rahn, Josh, Grp Dir-Global Mktg Solutions - Facebook, Inc.; *pg.* 1245, *pg.* 143
Rahner, Erik, Grp Dir-Mktg - Energizer Holdings, Inc.; *pg.* 637, *pg.* 996
Rahoy, Jody, Mgr-Mktg - Alto-Shaam Inc.; *pg.* 836, *pg.* 1869
Rai, Devi Jaspal, VP-Channel Sls & Ops - MegaPath, Inc.; *pg.* 432, *pg.* 71
Rai, Manish, VP-Mktg - MERU NETWORKS, INC.; *pg.* 434, *pg.* 286
Raiani, Jerome A., Product Mgr-Life - The Guardian Life Insurance Company of America; *pg.* 1202, *pg.* 1237
Raiano, Bridget, Media Planner - Monster Worldwide, Inc.; *pg.* 1268, *pg.* 859
Raible, James J., VP-Sls - Xtek, Inc.; *pg.* 1390, *pg.* 1427
Raible, Marci, Dir-Media-Global - Campbell Soup Company; *pg.* 844, *pg.* 1040
Raider, Jen, Mgr-PR - Walden University; *pg.* 610, *pg.* 946
Raidl, Debi, Mgr-Mktg-Global Comm-Brocade Network Subscription - Brocade Corporation; *pg.* 365, *pg.* 312
Raihan, Irshad, Sr Principal-Product Mktg-Big Data - Red Hat, Inc.; *pg.* 460, *pg.* 1388
Raikundalia, Sheevani, VP-Sls-Northeast - The Washington Post; *pg.* 1701, *pg.* 407
Railey, Lyndsay, Mgr-Mktg - Papa John's International, Inc.; *pg.* 1743, *pg.* 737
Raimondi, Damien, Mgr-Creative Svcs - Visit Florida Inc.; *pg.* 1010, *pg.* 470
Raina, Madhulika, Mgr-Product Mktg-U-verse TV Apps - AT&T Communications Corp.; *pg.* 1866, *pg.* 1043
Raina, Madhulika, Mgr-Product Mktg-U-verse TV Apps - AT&T Inc.; *pg.* 1867, *pg.* 1674
Rainbolt, Doug, VP-Mktg & Corp Dev - Alacritech, Inc.; *pg.* 346, *pg.* 237
Raine, Burke, VP-Mktg-Snacks - Diamond Foods, Inc.; *pg.* 1851, *pg.* 216
Rainer, Leslie, Sr Mgr-Mktg - Combe Incorporated; *pg.* 1516, *pg.* 1351
Raineri, Jaclyn, Community Mgr-Social Media - Volvo Cars of North America LLC; *pg.* 195, *pg.* 1117
Raines, Ron, Mgr-Vertical Sls - Cooper Interconnect; *pg.* 630, *pg.* 1118
Rainey, Lee, VP-Mktg - AccuWeather, Inc.; *pg.* 268, *pg.* 1587
Rainey, Luci, VP-Acq Mktg & Onboarding - Comcast Cable Communications, Inc.; *pg.* 276, *pg.* 1560
Rainey, Patricia, Dir-GSFC Field Mktg - The Boeing Company; *pg.* 225, *pg.* 567
Rains, Courtney, Specialist-PR - Applied Systems Inc.; *pg.* 352, *pg.* 663
Rains, Pam, Dir-Sls & Mktg-Natl - Brookshire Grocery Company; *pg.* 1016, *pg.* 1748
Raish, Tom, Dir-Mktg-Foot & Ankle-Global - Zimmer Biomet Holdings, Inc.; *pg.* 1611, *pg.* 699
Raisl, Lauren, Brand Mgr-Strategy - Capital One Financial Corporation; *pg.* 730, *pg.* 1789
Raiton, Cindy, Pres-Sls - Bookazine Company, Inc.; *pg.* 1622, *pg.* 1042
Raj, James, Product Mgr - Panjo; *pg.* 1274, *pg.* 275
Raja, Natasha, VP-Mktg & Customer Svc - DHI Group, Inc.; *pg.* 1238, *pg.* 1223
Raja, Vijay, Mgr-Mktg-ITO - Amdocs Inc.; *pg.* 348, *pg.* 974
Rajagopal, Ashley Noah, Mgr-Mktg & Marketplace-US Trade Books - Amazon.com, Inc.; *pg.* 1226, *pg.* 1831
Rajagopal, Meghana, Brand Mgr-Thomas English Muffins - Bimbo Bakeries USA; *pg.* 840, *pg.* 151
Rajagopal, Sumana, Dir-Media Strategy - Comcast Corporation; *pg.* 276, *pg.* 1560
Rajala, Chrissy, Dir-Media Plng - National Hockey League; *pg.* 568, *pg.* 1265
Rajamannar, Raja, CMO - MasterCard Incorporated; *pg.* 779, *pg.* 1325
Rajan, Gayathri, Dir-Product Mgmt - Google Inc.; *pg.* 1249, *pg.* 153
Rajani, Tina, Mgr-Mktg-Valentines, Holiday & Pot of Gold - Hershey Canada, Inc.; *pg.* 1855, *pg.* 1926
Rajaraman, Shiva, Product Mgr - Google Inc.; *pg.* 1249, *pg.* 153
Rajendran, Priya, Sr Mgr-Global Solutions-OEM Partnerships - PayPal Inc.; *pg.* 1274, *pg.* 248
Rajeski, Heather, Sr Mgr-Promo & Events - Oakland Athletics Limited Partnership; *pg.* 571, *pg.* 172
Rajkovich, Sam, Dir-Sls & Mktg - Sturtevant Inc.; *pg.* 1379, *pg.* 824
Rajski, Tina, Product Mgr - CCH Inc.; *pg.* 1626, *pg.* 653
Rajwat, Paresh, Product Mgr - Facebook, Inc.; *pg.* 1245, *pg.* 143
Rakes, Brad, Brand Mgr - Dr Pepper Snapple Group, Inc.; *pg.* 250, *pg.* 1729
Rakes, Julie B., Dir-Media Rels - Capital One Financial Corporation; *pg.* 730, *pg.* 1789
Rakova, Maria, Sr Mgr-Mktg - Trane Inc.; *pg.* 116, *pg.* 1109
Rakovec, Bryan, Mgr-Sls - Heat Seal LLC; *pg.* 1345, *pg.* 1431
Rakowski, Brian, VP-Product Mgmt - Google Inc.; *pg.* 1249, *pg.* 153
Raley, Tina, Sr Mgr-Compensation - The E.W. Scripps Company; *pg.* 1639, *pg.* 1412
Ralles, Mary, Sr Mgr-Global Corp Comm & Reputation - The Procter & Gamble Company; *pg.* 1129, *pg.* 1418
Ralls, Jen, Dir-PR - Fitbit Inc.; *pg.* 639, *pg.* 218
Raloff, Valgene E., Product Mgr - Electron Beam Technologies, Inc.; *pg.* 1046, *pg.* 621
Ralph, Lucy, Coord-Adv-The Tennessean - Gannett Co., Inc.; *pg.* 1643, *pg.* 1790
Ralston, Matthew, Sr Specialist-Social Media - Nordstrom, Inc.; *pg.* 1779, *pg.* 1837
Ram, Balaji, Sr Dir-Product Analytics & Experimentation - PayPal Inc.; *pg.* 1274, *pg.* 248
Ramachandran, Bala, Sr Mgr-eMarketing Strategy - W.W. Grainger, Inc.; *pg.* 1390, *pg.* 625
Ramachandran, Subhash, Sr VP-Product Mgmt - Software AG, Inc.; *pg.* 471, *pg.* 1799
Ramachandran, Usha, Sr Product Mgr - Cisco Systems, Inc.; *pg.* 372, *pg.* 240
Ramage, Casey Cook, VP-Mktg & PR - Brown Jordan International Company; *pg.* 919, *pg.* 740
Ramage, Katie, Dir-Sports Mktg - The North Face, Inc.; *pg.* 1840, *pg.* 252
Ramage, Matt, Sr VP-Product Mgmt - VTech Electronics North America, LLC; *pg.* 969, *pg.* 554
Raman, Emily, Dir-Brand Mktg-US - Visa Inc.; *pg.* 816, *pg.* 230
Raman, Priya, Brand Mgr - Ubisoft Inc.; *pg.* 589, *pg.* 229
Raman, Sundar, Dir-Mktg-North America Fabric Care - The Procter & Gamble Company; *pg.* 1129, *pg.* 1418
Ramani, Ashok, Product Head-Big Data - eBay Inc.; *pg.* 1240, *pg.* 243
Ramarao, Rajesh, Sr Mgr-Collaboration Practice - Cisco Systems, Inc.; *pg.* 372, *pg.* 240
Ramasubramanian, Krams, Specialist-Technical Sls-Commerce - International Business Machines Corporation; *pg.* 418, *pg.* 1138
Ramaswami, Prem, Product Mgr - Google Inc.; *pg.* 1249, *pg.* 153
Ramaswami, Rachel, Mgr-Worldwide Supplies Mktg - Hewlett-Packard Company; *pg.* 404, *pg.* 175
Ramaswamy, Raj, Head-Monetization, Product & Revenue - Yahoo! Inc.; *pg.* 1289, *pg.* 289
Ramaswamy, Sridhar, Dir-Technical Product Mktg-NVIDIA Mobile Grp - NVIDIA Corporation; *pg.* 447, *pg.* 268
Rambadran, Bharath, Sr Product Mgr-Content Discovery & Personalization - Amazon.com, Inc.; *pg.* 1226, *pg.* 1831
Rambaud, Stanislas, Brand Mgr-Middle East & India - Baume & Mercier, Inc.; *pg.* 1, *pg.* 1201
Ramberg, Eric, Mgr-Sls - Carlson JPM Store Fixtures; *pg.* 369, *pg.* 919
Ramberg, Mark, Gen Mgr-Media & Entertainment - Amazon.com, Inc.; *pg.* 1226, *pg.* 1831
Rambo, Bethany, VP-Treasury Mgmt Sls - Blue Valley Ban Corp; *pg.* 725, *pg.* 718
Rambo, Dena, Assoc Dir-Sls - Dallas Convention & Visitors Bureau; *pg.* 991, *pg.* 1678
Rambo, Greg, Reg Mgr-Commodity & Premium Offerings Sls - Yara N America, Inc.; *pg.* 1802, *pg.* 477
Ramburn, Satish, Sr Mgr-Comm & Trng Svcs - Canadian Imperial Bank of Commerce; *pg.* 729, *pg.* 1935
Ramesh, Girish, Sr Mgr-Mktg - Atmel Corporation; *pg.* 621, *pg.* 238
Ramey, Blair, VP-Mktg - Chattem, Inc.; *pg.* 1515, *pg.* 1628
Ramey, Edithann, VP-Mktg - Brinker International, Inc.; *pg.* 1718, *pg.* 1676
Ramey, Kelli, VP-Adv & Creative Svcs - H&R Block, Inc.; *pg.* 764, *pg.* 983
Ramge, Abbey, Mgr-Media-Global - Oakley, Inc.; *pg.* 1840, *pg.* 86
Ramhurst, Jaime, Dir-ECommerce & Social Media - Croscill, Inc.; *pg.* 1122, *pg.* 1220
Ramirez, Anthony, Mgr-Mktg - Tribune Media Company; *pg.* 1696, *pg.* 592
Ramirez, Brandon, Sr Grp Mgr-Product Dev - Hyundai Motor America; *pg.* 179, *pg.* 89
Ramirez, Donna, Sr Mgr-Comm - TELUS CORPORATION; *pg.* 1952, *pg.* 1912
Ramirez, Javier, Dir-Media - Focus Features; *pg.* 287, *pg.* 273
Ramirez, Juan, Sr Dir-IT - Tampa Bay Rays Baseball, Ltd.; *pg.* 586, *pg.* 464
Ramirez, Max, VP-Digital Media-SBS Interactive - Spanish Broadcasting System Inc.; *pg.* 310, *pg.* 446
Ramirez, Mickey, Mgr-Pub Affairs & Mktg - Advocate Health Care; *pg.* 1487, *pg.* 607
Ramirez, Rick, Sr VP-Targeted Mktg - Warner Bros. Entertainment Inc.; *pg.* 319, *pg.* 54
Ramirez, Scott, VP-Product Mktg & Dev-Visual Products - Toshiba America Consumer Products, LLC; *pg.* 681, *pg.* 1130
Ramirez, Tita, Sr Product Mgr-Mktg - AT&T Inc.; *pg.* 1867, *pg.* 1674
Ramis, Javier, VP-Mktg-UTG - Univision Communications Inc.; *pg.* 683, *pg.* 1307
Ramjas, Enid, Sr Mgr-Mktg - Office Depot, Inc.; *pg.* 448, *pg.* 412
Ramleth, Geir, Chief Strategy Officer, Sr VP & Gen Mgr-Workspace Svcs - Citrix Systems, Inc.; *pg.* 375, *pg.* 424
Ramlochan, Dianne, Mgr-Digital Mktg - Saks Fifth Avenue, Inc.; *pg.* 1783, *pg.* 1287
Rammer, Anthony, Dir-Creative - Johnsonville Sausage, LLC; *pg.* 867, *pg.* 1894
Ramon, Lourdes, Dir-Corp Mktg - Univision Communications Inc.; *pg.* 683, *pg.* 1307
Ramos, Antonio, Dir-Platform Mktg - Crayola LLC; *pg.* 951, *pg.* 1528
Ramos, Casandra, Coord-Mktg-Cosmetics - L'Oreal USA; *pg.* 514, *pg.* 1252
Ramos, Cristina, Mgr-Mktg & Consumer Activation - SeaWorld Parks & Entertainment LLC; *pg.* 582, *pg.* 456
Ramos, Damaris, Analyst-Social Media - State Farm Mutual Automobile Insurance Co.; *pg.* 1218, *pg.* 557
Ramos, Heather, Mgr-Mktg & Field Comm - The Guardian Life Insurance Company of America; *pg.* 1202, *pg.* 1237
Ramos, Igor, Dir-Sls-LATAM - Speed Commerce, Inc.; *pg.* 967, *pg.* 1737
Ramos, Jasmine, Sr Mgr-PR - Sega of America Inc.; *pg.* 966, *pg.* 227
Ramos, Joe, Sr Mgr-Local Media - Kohl's Corporation; *pg.* 1775, *pg.* 1870
Ramos, Lorna, Reg Mgr-Trade Mktg - 3M Company; *pg.* 1142, *pg.* 956
Ramos, Marie Z., Assoc Mgr-eMail Mktg - Chico's FAS, Inc.; *pg.* 21, *pg.* 427
Ramos, Mike, Product Mgr & Mgr-Mktg - The Timken Company; *pg.* 218, *pg.* 1408
Ramos, Nydia, Dir-Mktg & Media-Goya Puerto Rico - Goya Foods, Inc.; *pg.* 859, *pg.* 1075
Ramos, Oscar, Sr Dir-ESPN Deportes Content - ESPN, Inc.; *pg.* 285, *pg.* 340
Ramos, Rene, Dir-Mktg - Constellation Brands, Inc.; *pg.* 1960, *pg.* 1348
Ramos, Ronald, Asst VP-Strategic Comm & Mktg - Kennesaw State University; *pg.* 603, *pg.* 534
Ramos, Zachary, Sr Mgr-Bus Dev - Kellogg Company; *pg.* 831, *pg.* 870
Ramoz, Mike, Dir-Sls Ops & Customer Svc - AMX Corporation; *pg.* 349, *pg.* 1735
Ramp, Kathy, Mgr-Product Compliance & Plng-John Deere Mdse & Brand Licensing - Deere & Company; *pg.* 703, *pg.* 632
Rampley, Gaetana, Grp VP & Mgr-Mktg Comm - Sun Trust Bank, Atlanta; *pg.* 806, *pg.* 520
Rampley, Gaetana, Grp VP & Mgr-Mktg Comm - SunTrust Banks, Inc.; *pg.* 807, *pg.* 520
Rampley, Mike, Sr VP-Mktg & Bus Dev - Hoosier Energy Rural Electric Cooperative Inc.; *pg.* 1944, *pg.* 674
Rampley, Tom, Mgr-Media Sls Data & Analytics - DISH Network Corporation; *pg.* 283, *pg.* 325
Ramprasad, Ram, Dir-Mktg-Global - Merck & Co., Inc.; *pg.* 1566, *pg.* 1077
Ramsay, Andre, Supvr-Sls Video - DEP Distribution Exclusive Ltd; *pg.* 1766, *pg.* 1954
Ramsay, Dawn L., Dir-Natl Mktg-Private Client Grp - American International Group, Inc.; *pg.* 1190, *pg.* 1193
Ramsay, Jennifer, Mgr-iTunes PR - Apple Inc.; *pg.* 350, *pg.* 73
Ramsdale, Chris, Product Mgr - Google Inc.; *pg.* 1249, *pg.*

153
Ramsey, Beth, Mgr-Mktg Comm-Global - PPG Industries, Inc.; *pg.* 1445, *pg.* 1579
Ramsey, Brad, VP-Sls - Gannett Co., Inc.; *pg.* 1643, *pg.* 1790
Ramsey, Brooke, Brand Mgr - Blistex, Inc.; *pg.* 502, *pg.* 644
Ramsey, Cynthia, VP-Sls - Time Out New York; *pg.* 1694, *pg.* 1301
Ramsey, James, Sr Mgr-Field Sls - Mercury Insurance Company; *pg.* 1208, *pg.* 136
Ramsey, Jamie, Asst Dir-Media Rels & Digital Content - Reds Baseball Partners, LLC; *pg.* 578, *pg.* 1425
Ramsey, Jennifer, Supvr-Social Media - United Parcel Service, Inc.; *pg.* 1928, *pg.* 522
Ramsey, Jordan, Mgr-Trade Mktg - Electrolux Home Products North America; *pg.* 54, *pg.* 1366
Ramsey, Kenneth A., Exec VP-Sls & Bus Dev - MCT Worldwide LLC; *pg.* 653, *pg.* 939
Ramsey, Lauren, Mgr-Mktg-Global - Microsoft Corporation; *pg.* 435, *pg.* 1824
Ramsey, Lindsey, Mgr-Brand Activation Team & Trade Mktg-Bud Light Sports - Anheuser-Busch Companies, LLC; *pg.* 237, *pg.* 991
Ramsey, Nancy, Sr Mgr-Market - Herman Miller, Inc.; *pg.* 926, *pg.* 913
Ramsey, Rob, Sr Product Mgr - Tyson Foods, Inc.; *pg.* 902, *pg.* 35
Ramsey, Tom, VP-Creative Mktg - Bath & Body Works, LLC; *pg.* 500, *pg.* 1471
Ramsey-Macomber, Larry E., Sr Product Mgr-Mktg - Honeywell International Inc.; *pg.* 407, *pg.* 1088
Ramshur, Michele, Mgr-Indus Mktg Comm - Emerson Process Management; *pg.* 1334, *pg.* 1636
Ramsland, Scott, Gen Mgr-Mdsg-Footwear - Sears Holdings Corporation; *pg.* 1784, *pg.* 618
Rana, Taru, Dir-Product Mgmt, Data Science & Engrg - Dow Jones & Company, Inc.; *pg.* 1637, *pg.* 1225
Rana, Vinod, Product Mgr - Belden, Inc.; *pg.* 624, *pg.* 993
Ranadive, Ameet, Sr Dir-Product-Twitter - Twitter, Inc.; *pg.* 1285, *pg.* 228
Ranadive, Meara, Asst VP & Mgr-Digital Mktg-Corp Mktg & Comm - T. Rowe Price Group Inc.; *pg.* 808, *pg.* 759
Ranaldi, Robert D., Exec VP-Sls & Distr-Worldwide - Parametric Technology Corporation; *pg.* 452, *pg.* 835
Rancatore, Erica, Mgr-Mktg-Luxury & Lifestyle Brands - Hilton Worldwide, Inc.; *pg.* 1094, *pg.* 1791
Rancatore, Ryan, Sr Specialist-Adv - FRANKLIN RESOURCES, INC.; *pg.* 760, *pg.* 254
Ranchon, Gaelle, Mgr-Intl Sls & Mktg - Bulova Corporation; *pg.* 2, *pg.* 1356
Rancourt, Carly, Media Planner - Bose Corporation; *pg.* 626, *pg.* 820
Rand, Jason, Acct Mgr-Mid-Market Sls - Twitter, Inc.; *pg.* 1285, *pg.* 228
Rand, Kathy, Mgr-Product Vigilance - The Procter & Gamble Company; *pg.* 1129, *pg.* 1418
Randal, Ryan, Mgr-Mktg Automation - The Dun & Bradstreet Corp.; *pg.* 1637, *pg.* 1120
Randall, Adam, Reg Mgr-Sls-Western - Allfast Fastening Systems, Inc.; *pg.* 1041, *pg.* 66
Randall, Christy, Brand Mgr-Partnerships Brand Mktg - Capital One Bank (USA), N.A.; *pg.* 730, *pg.* 1789
Randall, Dana, Sr Dir-Global Omni-Channel Innovation - Coach, Inc.; *pg.* 3, *pg.* 1214
Randall, Dave, Sr Mgr-Mktg Strategy & Analytics - Great Clips, Inc.; *pg.* 510, *pg.* 937
Randall, Garry, Sr VP-HR, Consumer Products & Disney Interactive - The Walt Disney Company; *pg.* 317, *pg.* 52
Randall, James, Mgr-Sls-Natl - Alvimar Genesis; *pg.* 1825, *pg.* 886
Randall, Jennifer, Asst VP & Corp Specialist-Sports Mktg & Event Plng - BB&T Corporation; *pg.* 723, *pg.* 1393
Randall, Nancy, Mgr-Mktg Svcs - The Toro Company; *pg.* 1065, *pg.* 918
Randall, Nate, Sr Mgr-Global Benefits & Employee Experience - Tesla Motors, Inc.; *pg.* 191, *pg.* 178
Randall, Whitney, VP & Gen Mgr-Mdse - dELiA's, Inc.; *pg.* 23, *pg.* 1222
Randazzo, Denise, VP-PR & Adv - Wynn Resorts Limited; *pg.* 1119, *pg.* 1030
Randell, Anne, VP-Mktg - Sea Island Clothiers, LLC; *pg.* 32, *pg.* 1146
Randell, Marc, Head-Sls - Trane Inc.; *pg.* 116, *pg.* 1109
Randles, Jason, Mgr-Digital Mktg - Deschutes Brewery Inc.; *pg.* 248, *pg.* 1496
Randol, Jeremy, VP-Programmatic Sls Strategy - Pandora Media Inc.; *pg.* 1273, *pg.* 172
Randolph, Gerry, Assoc Mgr-Mktg-Sports - Yahoo! Inc.; *pg.* 1289, *pg.* 289
Randon, Filippo, Dir-Digital & Social Media-Global - Chanel, Inc.; *pg.* 503, *pg.* 1211
Randorf, Roz, VP-Adv - Forum Communications Company; *pg.* 1642, *pg.* 1397
Ranes, Trisha, Sr Mgr-Latino Mktg - H&R Block, Inc.; *pg.* 764, *pg.* 983
Raney, Craig, Dir-Mktg - Hobart Brothers Company; *pg.* 1346, *pg.* 1477
Rangaiah, Babs, VP-Media Innovation-Global - Unilever United States, Inc.; *pg.* 904, *pg.* 1061
Range, Matthew, Dir-Mktg - HATCO, Inc.; *pg.* 6, *pg.* 1698
Rangel, Art, Sr Dir - Apple Inc.; *pg.* 350, *pg.* 73
Rangel, Nick, Mgr-PR - Eastman Kodak Company; *pg.* 1408, *pg.* 1333
Ranger, Marci, VP-Mktg - Caleres, Inc.; *pg.* 1805, *pg.* 993
Rangwala, Faisal, Sr Mgr-ECommerce & Digital Mktg - Johnson & Johnson; *pg.* 1549, *pg.* 1091
Rani, Yin Woon, VP-Mktg Activation - Campbell Soup Company; *pg.* 844, *pg.* 1048
Ranieri, James, VP-Sls-Americas - Silberline Manufacturing Co., Inc.; *pg.* 110, *pg.* 1588
Ranjan, Manish, VP-Product Mktg - Ultratech, Inc.; *pg.* 1433, *pg.* 251
Rank, Vivian E., Sr Mgr-Talent Mgmt - SUPERVALU, Inc.; *pg.* 1035, *pg.* 924
Rankin, Ivy, Sr Mgr-Mktg - DIRECTV Group Holdings, LLC; *pg.* 281, *pg.* 79
Rannazzisi-Gerstein, Christine, Grp Assoc Publr-Mktg-Hearst Magazines - Good Housekeeping; *pg.* 1645, *pg.* 1236
Rannells, Caitlin, Brand Mgr-Activation-Tequila Portfolio - Beam Suntory Inc.; *pg.* 1957, *pg.* 599
Ransom, Chris, Dir-Sls Engrg - Verizon Communications Inc.; *pg.* 1875, *pg.* 1309
Ranta, Rosanne, Sr Assoc Mgr-Mktg - General Mills, Inc.; *pg.* 828, *pg.* 933
Rantz, Glori, Strategist-Partnership Mktg - Explore Minnesota Tourism; *pg.* 992, *pg.* 960
Ranzinger, Rick, VP-Sls & Market - Lyman Products Corporation; *pg.* 1839, *pg.* 356
Rao, Chet, Sr Mgr-Strategy, M&A, Bus Dev-SFG - Hormel Foods Corporation; *pg.* 863, *pg.* 915
Rao, Gautam, Mgr-Product Mgmt-Smart Svcs - Cisco Systems, Inc.; *pg.* 372, *pg.* 240
Rao, Naresh, Engr-Technical Mktg - Cisco Systems, Inc.; *pg.* 372, *pg.* 240
Rao, Rajani, Brand Mgr - Del Monte Foods, Inc.; *pg.* 852, *pg.* 304
Rao, Reema, Dir-Product Mgmt - Home Box Office, Inc.; *pg.* 290, *pg.* 1240
Rao, Vivek, VP & Gen Mgr-Thermal Products Div - SPP Process Technology Systems Limited-Thermal Division; *pg.* 472, *pg.* 250
Raper, Jason, Sr Mgr-Field Mktg & Grand Openings - PetSmart, Inc.; *pg.* 1481, *pg.* 18
Raphael, Alison, Sr Mgr-Pricing & Monetization - eBay Inc.; *pg.* 1240, *pg.* 243
Raphael, Ana, Sr Dir-Sls - Ubisoft Inc.; *pg.* 589, *pg.* 229
Raphael, Brenda, VP-Mktg - Pfizer Inc.; *pg.* 1581, *pg.* 1278
Raphael, Erwin, Dir-Product Quality & Svc Engrg - Hyundai Motor America; *pg.* 179, *pg.* 89
Raphael, Marianne, Sr Dir-Mktg-NBC News - NBC Universal, Inc.; *pg.* 300, *pg.* 1266
Rapisand, Lauren, Mgr-Media Rels-North Central Reg - Macy's, Inc.; *pg.* 1778, *pg.* 1417
Rapoport, Evan, Product Mgr-Google x - Google Inc.; *pg.* 1249, *pg.* 153
Raposo, Peg, Sr Mgr-Quality - PayPal Inc.; *pg.* 1274, *pg.* 248
Rapp, Alicia, Asst Coord-Mktg - Toll Brothers, Inc.; *pg.* 115, *pg.* 1541
Rapp, Alison, Specialist-Product Mktg - Nintendo of America, Inc.; *pg.* 965, *pg.* 1829
Rapp, Jacob, Dir-Technical Product Mgmt - VMware, Inc.; *pg.* 490, *pg.* 179
Rapp, Jennifer, Brand Mgr-Guinness - Diageo North America Inc.; *pg.* 248, *pg.* 1223
Rapp, Matthew, Dir-Sls & Mktg-Clinical Res Markets - Abaxis, Inc.; *pg.* 1483, *pg.* 298
Rapp, Michael, Dir-Mktg - Fujitsu Computer Systems Corporation; *pg.* 398, *pg.* 285
Rapp, Shelly, Media Buyer - Les Schwab Tire Centers of Oregon, Inc.; *pg.* 210, *pg.* 1508
Rappaport, Jessica, VP-Mktg - The E.W. Scripps Company; *pg.* 1639, *pg.* 1412
Rappaport, Michael, Coord-PR - New York Rangers Hockey Club; *pg.* 570, *pg.* 1269
Raptes, Jim, Mgr-Custom Sls - Deco Products Co.; *pg.* 1045, *pg.* 704
Raque, Leigh, Dir-Mktg - Humana, Inc.; *pg.* 1204, *pg.* 734
Raquepaw, Tricia, Dir-Mktg Comm - Independent Bank Corporation; *pg.* 768, *pg.* 893
Rarogiewicz, Mary, Project Mgr-Affiliation Mktg - Massachusetts Mutual Life Insurance Company; *pg.* 1207, *pg.* 845
Rarrick, John, Sr Mgr-Mktg-Northeast Area - T-Mobile US, Inc.; *pg.* 676, *pg.* 1816
Rasa, Mary-Kate, Specialist-Brand & Promotional Adv - Choice Hotels International, Inc.; *pg.* 1086, *pg.* 775
Rasanen, Jodie, Brand Mgr - Dunkin' Brands Group, Inc.; *pg.* 1727, *pg.* 810
Rasberry, Elizabeth, Mgr-PR - Cox Communications, Inc.; *pg.* 279, *pg.* 501
Rasch, Fred, VP-MRO Sls - HAECO Americas; *pg.* 228, *pg.* 1374
Rasch, Ryan, Mgr-Inside Sls-Southwest & West - The Wm. Powell Company; *pg.* 1389, *pg.* 1427
Rasetta, Anthony, VP-Mktg-Canada Confectionery - Mondelez International; *pg.* 877, *pg.* 1344
Rashad, Amira, Head-Brand Adv-Middle East, North Africa & Pakistan - Facebook, Inc.; *pg.* 1245, *pg.* 143
Rashba, Marc, VP-TV & Customer Mktg Grp - Sony Pictures Entertainment Inc.; *pg.* 309, *pg.* 72
Rashdan, Mogeeb, Mgr-Mktg - PepsiCo, Inc.; *pg.* 259, *pg.* 1327
Rasheed, Asim, Engr-Technical Mktg - Ixia; *pg.* 422, *pg.* 56
Rashid, Dalia, Specialist-Comm & Social Media - ABB Inc.; *pg.* 64, *pg.* 1959
Rashid, Renee, Dir-Global Product Dev, Environment & Energy Comm - General Motors Company; *pg.* 175, *pg.* 881
Rashti, Dana, Chief Marketing & Strategy Officer - Neighborhood Health Plan Inc.; *pg.* 1211, *pg.* 798
Rasico, Andy, Mgr-Mktg - Universal Electronics, Inc.; *pg.* 683, *pg.* 262
Rask, Julie, Mgr-Sls - Williams-Sonoma, Inc.; *pg.* 1140, *pg.* 234
Raskin, Seva, Mgr-Geographic Mktg - Accenture; *pg.* 1392, *pg.* 1186
Raskin-Schmitt, Cyndi, Dir-Comm & Mktg - Pinellas Suncoast Transit Authority; *pg.* 1919, *pg.* 463
Rasmussen, Alan, Mgr-Adv Ops - AutoTrader, Inc.; *pg.* 1230, *pg.* 490
Rasmussen, Brent, Dir-Oncology Mktg - Astellas Pharma US, Inc.; *pg.* 1496, *pg.* 640
Rasmussen, Eric, Sr Dir-Telecom, Cable & Cloud Field Mktg - Juniper Networks, Inc.; *pg.* 1260, *pg.* 286
Rasmussen, Judi, Mgr-Sls-Food Svc - The Uhlmann Co.; *pg.* 834, *pg.* 986
Rasmussen, Kara, Sr Mgr-Mktg Comm - Stryker Corporation; *pg.* 1598, *pg.* 894
Rasmussen, Rick, Dir-Customer Loyalty & Mktg Programs - Alaska Airlines, Inc.; *pg.* 1897, *pg.* 1830
Rasmussen, Tim, Mgr-PR - MDU Resources Group, Inc.; *pg.* 981, *pg.* 1397
Rasmussen, Trevor, Sr Mgr-Content Mktg - Deluxe Corporation; *pg.* 1634, *pg.* 964
Rasmussen, Whitney, Mgr-ECommerce & Digital Mktg - Meredith Corporation; *pg.* 1663, *pg.* 705
Rasoul, Muhammad, Chief Product Officer & Exec VP - GAIN CAPITAL HOLDINGS, INC.; *pg.* 760, *pg.* 1043
Raspopovich, Amee, Coord-Mktg - H&R Block, Inc.; *pg.* 764, *pg.* 983
Rassai, Susan, Mgr-Campaign Mktg-Global - Symantec Corporation; *pg.* 478, *pg.* 161
Rastrelli, Ed Buff, Sr Dir-Bus Dev - Johnson & Johnson; *pg.* 1549, *pg.* 1091
Rasure, Ann, VP-Mktg-Retail Ready Care Div - Medline Industries, Inc.; *pg.* 1562, *pg.* 635
Ratajczek, Kristine, Mgr-Direct Mktg - Kaplan, Inc.; *pg.* 603, *pg.* 425
Ratcliffe, Chris, Sr VP-Mktg-EMC Core Technologies - EMC Corporation; *pg.* 391, *pg.* 825
Ratcliffe, Steven, Product Dir-Mdsg - Travelport Limited; *pg.* 1925, *pg.* 521
Rath, Mark, Asst Dir-Sls - Omaha Convention and Visitors Bureau; *pg.* 152, *pg.* 1017
Rath, Meredith, Dir-Mktg & Bus Dev - Vogue Magazine; *pg.* 1700, *pg.* 1311

Rathauser, Michael, Sr VP-Mktg - Lions Gate Entertainment Corp.; *pg.* 296, *pg.* 274

Rathmann, Abigail L., Sr Mgr-Community-Social Media - Abbott Laboratories; *pg.* 1484, *pg.* 551

RathMass, Todd, Dir-Mktg Svcs - Alabama Power Company; *pg.* 1933, *pg.* 1

Rathore, Vinay, Sr Dir-Mktg - Infinera Corporation; *pg.* 644, *pg.* 286

Rathsburg, Brian, Mgr-F-Series Super Duty Mktg - Ford Motor Company; *pg.* 172, *pg.* 876

Rathyen, John, Dir-Sls-East Reg - Kawasaki Motors Corp., U.S.A.; *pg.* 1708, *pg.* 111

Ratliff, Brandon, Mgr-Digital Mktg - QUALCOMM Incorporated; *pg.* 1873, *pg.* 207

Ratliff, Paul, Dir & Mgr-Mktg - The Travelers Companies, Inc.; *pg.* 1220, *pg.* 352

Ratna, Abhishek, Sr Mgr-Bus Program, Mktg Automation & Global Mktg Ops - Microsoft Corp.; *pg.* 440, *pg.* 321

Ratner, William A., Head-Brand-Neuroscience & Sr Dir - Eli Lilly and Company; *pg.* 1527, *pg.* 684

Rattanakhom, Joe, Dir-Sls-Intl - Harsco Rail; *pg.* 1345, *pg.* 1623

Ratte, Tina, Supvr-Mktg - Amy's Kitchen, Inc.; *pg.* 837, *pg.* 276

Ratterman, Chris, Brand Mgr-Evan Williams Bourbon - Heaven Hill Distilleries, Inc.; *pg.* 1964, *pg.* 725

Rattin, Paul, Dir-Mobile Mktg & Bus Dev - Orbitz Worldwide, Inc.; *pg.* 1918, *pg.* 586

Ratushewitz, Dawn, Sr Dir-Bus Process & Integrated Supply Chain - Becton, Dickinson & Company; *pg.* 1501, *pg.* 1068

Ratzmann, Bianca, Mgr-Adv Sls - Daily News, L.P.; *pg.* 1632, *pg.* 1221

Rau, Erica, VP-Mktg - Sacramento Kings; *pg.* 579, *pg.* 197

Rau, John, Mgr-Mktg - Diageo North America, Inc.; *pg.* 1961, *pg.* 361

Raub, Adam, Sr Dir-Bus Intelligence - Assurant, Inc.; *pg.* 1193, *pg.* 1198

Rauch, Jennette, Mgr-Mktg-Wilson, DeMarini & ATEC - Wilson Sporting Goods Co.; *pg.* 1848, *pg.* 596

Rauh, Taylor, Acct Mgr-Sls & Admin - CSPI Technology Solutions; *pg.* 381, *pg.* 421

Raumschuh, Mike, Reg Mgr-Sls - Kia Motors America Inc.; *pg.* 181, *pg.* 112

Rausch, Marianne, Dir-Brand Mktg & Strategic Partnerships - American Express Company; *pg.* 712, *pg.* 1190

Rausch, Sara, Dir-Mktg - Post Consumer Brands; *pg.* 833, *pg.* 927

Rausch, Steve, Head-Enterprise Integrated Mktg Comm-Global - Motorola Solutions, Inc.; *pg.* 657, *pg.* 659

Rauschenberg, Nathan, Mgr-Digital Mktg - The Baseball Club of Seattle, L.P.; *pg.* 532, *pg.* 1833

Rauscher, Walter, VP-Corp Sls & Catering - Ark Restaurants Corp.; *pg.* 1715, *pg.* 1196

Rauschnot, Nicole, Coord-PR - Electronic Arts Inc.; *pg.* 951, *pg.* 189

Raval, Anjali, Dir-Mktg & Promos - Madison Square Garden Network; *pg.* 297, *pg.* 1255

Ravalli, Chiara, Mktg Mgr-Web - The New York Times Company; *pg.* 1668, *pg.* 1270

Ravanpey, Ramin, Sr Dir-Software Dev Support - Nintendo of America, Inc.; *pg.* 965, *pg.* 1829

Ravel, Francoise M., Sr Mgr-Bus & Legal-Worldwide Motion Pictures Grp - Sony Pictures Entertainment Inc.; *pg.* 309, *pg.* 72

Ravela, Mylene, Mgr-Mktg - Intuit Inc.; *pg.* 769, *pg.* 158

Raven, Bryan, Sr Mgr-Media - Charles Schwab & Company, Inc.; *pg.* 734, *pg.* 215

Raven, Kylie, Sr Mgr-Mktg Partnerships - Yahoo! Inc.; *pg.* 1289, *pg.* 289

Raven, Max, Sr VP-Ad Sls - CNBC; *pg.* 275, *pg.* 1059

Ravenelle, Andrea, Supvr-Digital Mktg - Marshalls of MA, Inc.; *pg.* 1778, *pg.* 821

Ravenelle, Andrea, Supvr-Digital Mktg - T.J. Maxx; *pg.* 1788, *pg.* 822

Ravenelle, Andrea, Supvr-Digital Mktg - The TJX Companies, Inc.; *pg.* 1788, *pg.* 822

Ravenna, Luna, Brand Mgr - Cover Girl Cosmetics; *pg.* 506, *pg.* 772

Ravenna, Luna, Brand Mgr-CoverGirl - The Procter & Gamble Company; *pg.* 1129, *pg.* 1418

Ravichandran, Aruna, VP-Product Mktg & Strategy - CA Technologies; *pg.* 366, *pg.* 1168

Ravishunkar, Arvind, Sr Mgr-Corp Strategy - Fairchild Semiconductor Corporation; *pg.* 638, *pg.* 245

Ravitch, Michael, Mgr-Mktg - Sun Life Financial Inc.; *pg.* 806, *pg.* 1944

Rawal, Gunjan, Mgr-Mktg Comm-Intel Software - Intel Corporation; *pg.* 645, *pg.* 266

Rawden, David, Interim CFO - Career Education Corporation; *pg.* 599, *pg.* 658

Rawle, Dennis, Dir-Sls-Europe - Graphite Metallizing Corporation; *pg.* 1343, *pg.* 1356

Rawlings, Allison, Head-PR - DreamWorks Animation SKG, Inc.; *pg.* 284, *pg.* 96

Rawlings, November, Mgr-PR & Events - Ethan Allen Interiors Inc.; *pg.* 924, *pg.* 343

Rawn, Abid, VP-Sls & Mktg - DepoMed, Inc.; *pg.* 1523, *pg.* 143

Rawn, Kimberly, Sr Mgr-Comm, PR & Mktg - Phonak LLC; *pg.* 1585, *pg.* 665

Rawson, Jake, Dir-Sls-Golf-Global - Cutter & Buck, Inc.; *pg.* 39, *pg.* 1835

Ray, A.J., Sr Mgr-Market - Kforce Inc.; *pg.* 1261, *pg.* 473

Ray, Alison, Dir-Mktg - AT&T Mobility LLC; *pg.* 619, *pg.* 488

Ray, Amie Becton, Dir-Database Mktg & Strategy - National Hockey League; *pg.* 568, *pg.* 1265

Ray, Brandi, Dir-Mktg-Digital Shopper Conversion - PepsiCo, Inc.; *pg.* 259, *pg.* 1327

Ray, Carey, VP-Digital Mktg - Wells Fargo & Company; *pg.* 819, *pg.* 232

Ray, Chip, VP-Sls - Aurora Casket Company, Inc.; *pg.* 1393, *pg.* 673

Ray, Christopher, Dir-Digital Mktg - LG Electronics U.S.A., Inc.; *pg.* 651, *pg.* 1060

Ray, Cynthia, Dir-Mktg & Sponsorship - QUALCOMM Incorporated; *pg.* 1873, *pg.* 207

Ray, David, Sr Mgr-Ops - The Boeing Company; *pg.* 225, *pg.* 567

Ray, Dawn, Dir-Trade & Dev PR - Hilton Worldwide, Inc.; *pg.* 1094, *pg.* 1791

Ray, Elaine H., Sr Product Mgr - Gilead Sciences, Inc.; *pg.* 1535, *pg.* 88

Ray, Elizabeth, Mgr-Product Mktg - Oracle Corporation; *pg.* 450, *pg.* 191

Ray, Janet, Mgr-Integrated Mktg Comm - Universal Orlando; *pg.* 590, *pg.* 456

Ray, Juliane, Sr Mgr-Sls Ops-Global - American Medical Systems Holdings, Inc.; *pg.* 1493, *pg.* 947

Ray, Julie, Mgr-Mktg Comm Svcs - Graybar Electric Company, Inc.; *pg.* 1299, *pg.* 997

Ray, Karen, Dir-Field Mktg - Juniper Networks, Inc.; *pg.* 1260, *pg.* 286

Ray, Kayla, Coord-Media Strategies-HGTV - Scripps Networks Interactive, Inc.; *pg.* 1279, *pg.* 1638

Ray, Monica, Exec VP-Consumer Mktg - Conde Nast Publications, Inc.; *pg.* 1629, *pg.* 1217

Ray, Raj, Sr Dir-Product Mgmt - QUALCOMM Incorporated; *pg.* 1873, *pg.* 207

Ray, Robert D., Mng Dir-Commodities, Equities & Intl Sls - CME Group, Inc.; *pg.* 738, *pg.* 571

Ray, Ronnie, Dir-Product Mgmt-Cisco - Cisco Systems, Inc.; *pg.* 372, *pg.* 240

Ray, Sarah, Head-Capital Markets Mktg Comm & Exec Dir - Morgan Stanley; *pg.* 783, *pg.* 1261

Ray, Scott, Designer-Creative-ECommerce - Helzberg's Diamond Shops, Inc.; *pg.* 6, *pg.* 984

Ray, Scott, Sr Dir-US Fuel - Wal-Mart Stores, Inc.; *pg.* 1790, *pg.* 29

Ray, Stephen, Specialist-Mktg - Brookshire Grocery Company; *pg.* 1016, *pg.* 1748

Ray, Vickie, Rep-Field Mktg - Comerica Incorporated; *pg.* 740, *pg.* 1677

Raybould, James, Sr Dir-Mktg - LinkedIn Corporation; *pg.* 1262, *pg.* 160

Rayburn, Christopher, Dir-Global Transformative Mktg - Fluke Corporation; *pg.* 1413, *pg.* 1819

Raym, Carol, Sr Mgr-Exec Comm - Cisco Systems, Inc.; *pg.* 372, *pg.* 240

Raymo, Marissa, Mgr-Global Retail Media Strategy - General Motors Company; *pg.* 175, *pg.* 881

Raymon, Amber, Sr VP & Dir-Mktg & Comml Div - BOK Financial Corporation; *pg.* 726, *pg.* 1489

Raymond, Al, Head-U.S. Privacy & Social Media Compliance - TD Bank US Holding Company; *pg.* 809, *pg.* 1051

Raymond, Christie, VP-Sls - Transport Topics Publishing Group; *pg.* 1696, *pg.* 1772

Raymond, Darcy, VP-Mktg & Entertainment - Tampa Bay Rays Baseball, Ltd.; *pg.* 586, *pg.* 464

Raymond, Debora, Dir-Media Rels - The Hartford Financial Services Group, Inc.; *pg.* 1202, *pg.* 352

Raymond, Don, VP-Mktg-US & Flooring Sls - Uniboard Canada Inc.; *pg.* 117, *pg.* 1952

Raymond, Joe, VP-Product Dev - Xoom Corporation; *pg.* 1289, *pg.* 234

Raymond, John, Mgr-Mktg Sys - Whataburger, Inc.; *pg.* 1755, *pg.* 1744

Raymond, Josh, Product Mgr-Comml Payment Solutions - Comdata Corporation; *pg.* 739, *pg.* 1627

Raymond, Katie, Sr Mgr-Digital & Social Media Mktg-Global - Harman International Industries, Incorporated; *pg.* 641, *pg.* 374

Raymond, Katie E., Mgr-Channel Mktg-Independent Channel - Armstrong World Industries, Inc.; *pg.* 914, *pg.* 1545

Raymond, Meredith, Assoc Dir-Global Sustainability & Product Stewardship - Life Technologies; *pg.* 1420, *pg.* 1497

Raymond, Rob, VP-Fin Sls-Global - Diebold, Incorporated; *pg.* 387, *pg.* 1407

Raymond, Tammy, Dir-Mktg - BioSafe Systems, LLC; *pg.* 1149, *pg.* 345

Raymondo, Paul, Brand Mgr - The Goodyear Tire & Rubber Company; *pg.* 1883, *pg.* 1401

Raynaud, Daniel, Product Mgr - Google Inc.; *pg.* 1249, *pg.* 153

Rayner, Andrew, Rep-Sls - American Automobile Association; *pg.* 1190, *pg.* 429

Raynor, Carla, VP-Strategic Mktg - Blue Cross & Blue Shield Association; *pg.* 1195, *pg.* 566

Raz, Danielle, Acct Exec-Mktg Solutions - LinkedIn Corporation; *pg.* 1262, *pg.* 160

Raza, Syma, Coord-PR - American Eagle Outfitters, Inc.; *pg.* 37, *pg.* 1572

Razek, Edward, Pres/CMO-Brand & Creative Svcs - L Brands, Inc.; *pg.* 1776, *pg.* 1441

Rea, Vicki, Mgr-Mktg - LSI Industries Inc.; *pg.* 58, *pg.* 1416

Read, Amy, Mgr-Database Mktg - Carbonite, Inc.; *pg.* 368, *pg.* 792

Read, Jessica, Specialist-Digital Mktg - AMERIS BANCORP; *pg.* 715, *pg.* 536

Read, Kimberly, Sr Dir-Site Ops - RetailMeNot Inc.; *pg.* 1782, *pg.* 1665

Read, Kit, Product Mgr - Cars.com; *pg.* 1234, *pg.* 568

Read, Mike, Dir-Mktg - Ixia; *pg.* 422, *pg.* 56

Read, Rory P., COO & Pres-Worldwide Comml Sls - Dell Inc.; *pg.* 383, *pg.* 1737

Readence, Jennifer, Specialist-Digital Mktg - The Sherwin-Williams Company; *pg.* 1447, *pg.* 1435

Reading, Catherine, Sr Mgr-Product Mktg - Groupon, Inc.; *pg.* 1255, *pg.* 575

Reading, Katherine A., VP-Sls - Seedburo Equipment Co.; *pg.* 707, *pg.* 590

Reaes, Ashley, Assoc Mgr-Trade Mktg-Office Super Stores - BIC Corporation; *pg.* 501, *pg.* 369

Reagan, Allyson, Dir-Email Mktg - Angie's List Inc; *pg.* 1228, *pg.* 682

Reagan, Courtney, VP-Mktg - Abercrombie & Kent USA, LLC; *pg.* 1896, *pg.* 607

Reagan, Jeff, Sr VP-Mktg - Wakefern Food Corporation; *pg.* 1037, *pg.* 1058

Reagan, Jennifer, Dir-Mktg-Oil & Gas-Canada - General Electric Company; *pg.* 1297, *pg.* 347

Reagan, Liz, Mgr-Mktg & Sls-NA - SCHOTT North America, Inc.; *pg.* 109, *pg.* 698

Reagan, Mike, Sr VP-Brand Mktg - RE/MAX International, Inc.; *pg.* 1109, *pg.* 322

Real, Lindsay, Mgr-Creative Svcs - Coach, Inc.; *pg.* 3, *pg.* 1214

Real, Peter, VP-High Speed Products & Tech - Analog Devices, Inc.; *pg.* 617, *pg.* 839

Reali, D.J., Sr VP-Adv Sls-Natl - The Weather Channel LLC; *pg.* 320, *pg.* 523

Ream, Natalie, VP-Customer Comm & Mktg - The Kroger Co.; *pg.* 1025, *pg.* 1416

Reams, Russell, Mgr-Mktg-Healthcare Segment - United Parcel Service, Inc.; *pg.* 1928, *pg.* 522

Reantaso, Maricris, Dir-Product Mgmt - Expedia, Inc.; *pg.* 1244, *pg.* 1814

Reany, Bob, Sr VP & Grp Head-Authentication Product Strategy - MasterCard Incorporated; *pg.* 779, *pg.* 1325

Reardon, Dan, Head-eCommerce, Mobile Sls, Customer Acq & Engagement - Snapfish; *pg.* 1687, *pg.* 228

Reardon, Kevin, Dir-Retail Sls - Summit Industries, Inc.; *pg.* 1599, *pg.* 535

Reardon, Martine, Exec VP-Mktg-Natl - Macy's, Inc.; *pg.* 1778, *pg.* 1417

Reardon, Michael, Reg VP-Sls Western Reg - Mack Trucks,

Inc.; *pg.* 183, *pg.* 1375
Reashor, Juliette, Sr Mgr-Social Media - Fisher-Price, Inc.; *pg.* 953, *pg.* 1156
Reat, Chris, Mgr-Roundup Mktg - Monsanto; *pg.* 1798, *pg.* 1399
Reat, Chris, Mgr-Roundup Mktg - Monsanto Company; *pg.* 1173, *pg.* 999
Reaves, Brian S., Chief Sls Officer & Sr VP - Destination XL Group, Inc.; *pg.* 40, *pg.* 810
Reaves, Nancy, Sr Mgr-Storage Product Mgmt - Lenovo Group Ltd; *pg.* 427, *pg.* 1384
Reay, Robert L., VP & Gen Mgr-Mixed Signal Products - Linear Technology Corp.; *pg.* 652, *pg.* 147
Rebecca, Rebecca A., Sr Mgr-Mktg - Express Scripts, Inc.; *pg.* 1530, *pg.* 997
Rebele, Elaine, Mgr-Mktg Comm - Varian Medical Systems, Inc.; *pg.* 1434, *pg.* 178
Rebello, Ed, Sr Mgr-Corp Comm & Marcom - Cypress Semiconductor Corporation; *pg.* 1326, *pg.* 243
Rebello, Jagdish, Sr Dir - IHS Inc.; *pg.* 1652, *pg.* 326
Rebelo, Gina, Mgr-Adv-Natl - Daily News, L.P.; *pg.* 1632, *pg.* 1221
Reber, Nicole, Sr Mgr-Integrated Mktg - Apollo Education Group Inc.; *pg.* 597, *pg.* 14
Reber, Sally A., Sr Project Mgr-Mktg Comm - Stryker Corporation; *pg.* 1598, *pg.* 894
Rebimbas, John, VP-Product Dev - Broadridge Financial Solutions Inc.; *pg.* 727, *pg.* 1172
Reblin, Gary, VP-New Products & Innovation - United States Postal Service; *pg.* 1009, *pg.* 406
Rechin, Philip C., VP-Sls - MOD-PAC CORP.; *pg.* 1665, *pg.* 1150
Rechter, Terri, Mgr-Consumer Mktg-Sports Programs - AutoTrader, Inc.; *pg.* 1230, *pg.* 490
Recio, Mark, Dir-Internet Mktg - ITT Educational Services, Inc.; *pg.* 603, *pg.* 675
Reck, Allison M., Assoc Mgr-Mktg & Direct Mktg - G&K Services Inc.; *pg.* 693, *pg.* 949
Reck, Jenna, Mgr-PR - Target Corporation; *pg.* 1786, *pg.* 942
Reck, Karina, Brand Analyst-Central Mktg - Microsoft Corporation; *pg.* 435, *pg.* 1824
Reckamp, Justin, Analyst-Mktg - State Farm Mutual Automobile Insurance Co.; *pg.* 1218, *pg.* 557
Reckerman, Dirk, Head-Mktg-Baby - Amazon.com, Inc.; *pg.* 1226, *pg.* 1831
Reckhow, Michael, Product Mgr-Instant Articles & Paper - Facebook, Inc.; *pg.* 1245, *pg.* 143
Reckson, Allison, Exec Dir-Mktg & Special Projects - Palm Beach Media Group Inc.; *pg.* 1674, *pg.* 457
Recktenwald, Angie, Mgr-Mktg Media - RE/MAX International, Inc.; *pg.* 1109, *pg.* 322
Recoder, Andres, Global Head-Corp Sls & Client Solutions - Citigroup Inc.; *pg.* 735, *pg.* 1212
Record, Chris, VP-Sls Ops - Pandora Media Inc.; *pg.* 1273, *pg.* 172
Records, Heather, Dir-Creative Svcs-Pet Nutrition - Central Garden & Pet Company; *pg.* 1475, *pg.* 303
Rector, Elizabeth, Sr Mgr-Strategic Mktg - Cisco Systems, Inc.; *pg.* 372, *pg.* 240
Reda, Amanda, Asst Mgr-Mktg - Scholastic Inc.; *pg.* 1683, *pg.* 1288
Reda, Eva, Sr VP & Gen Mgr-Membership Mktg - American Express Company; *pg.* 712, *pg.* 1190
Reda, Katharine, Mgr-Mktg - Big Lots, Inc.; *pg.* 1762, *pg.* 1438
Redd, Carrie, Product Mgr-Medicare Product Solutions - Express Scripts, Inc.; *pg.* 1530, *pg.* 997
Reddan, Sarah, Mgr-eMail Mktg-Lord & Taylor - Lord & Taylor LLC; *pg.* 1777, *pg.* 1252
Reddick, Candi, Sr Mgr-Mktg Comm - AT&T Mobility LLC; *pg.* 619, *pg.* 488
Reddick, Hal, VP-Sls - duPont Registry; *pg.* 1637, *pg.* 462
Reddy, Inder, Pres-Honeywell Security Products-Americas - Honeywell International Inc.; *pg.* 407, *pg.* 1088
Reddy, Jim, VP-Sls-Americas - InFocus Corporation; *pg.* 644, *pg.* 1503
Reddy, Niyanthi, Analyst-Mktg - PepsiCo, Inc.; *pg.* 259, *pg.* 1327
Reddy, Pallavi, Dir-Mktg Intelligence - Church's Chicken, Inc.; *pg.* 1722, *pg.* 493
Reddy, Pavan, Mgr-Product Mktg - Red Hat, Inc.; *pg.* 460, *pg.* 1388
Reddy, Pylla Chandrasheker, Mgr-Production - Bactolac Pharmaceutical, Inc.; *pg.* 1498, *pg.* 1163
Reddy, Raj, VP-Mktg & Strategy - Alcoa Inc.; *pg.* 65, *pg.* 1188
Reddy, Sravan, Sr Dir-Gen Acctg - The E.W. Scripps Company; *pg.* 1639, *pg.* 1412
Redell, Amy, Sr Mgr-Product Mktg-Creative Cloud for Enterprise - Adobe Systems Incorporated; *pg.* 342, *pg.* 235
Reder, Stacy, Assoc Product Mgr-Pro Endorsements - Hill's Pet Nutrition, Inc.; *pg.* 1476, *pg.* 721
Redfern, Joff, VP-Mobile Product - LinkedIn Corporation; *pg.* 1262, *pg.* 160
Redfern, Karen, Sr Dir-Mktg Comm - Recreation Vehicle Industry Association; *pg.* 155, *pg.* 1799
Redfield, Charles, Exec VP-Mdsg - Sam's Club; *pg.* 1783, *pg.* 29
Redfield, Charles, Exec VP-Mdsg-Sam's Club - Wal-Mart Stores, Inc.; *pg.* 1790, *pg.* 29
Redgate, Dan, Global Sports Mktg, Media & Strategic Partnerships - Doctor's Associates Inc.; *pg.* 1726, *pg.* 356
Redhair, Fiona, Mgr-Trade & Customer Mktg-Great Lakes Reg - MillerCoors LLC; *pg.* 255, *pg.* 582
Redick, Scott, Mng Dir-Creative Strategy - Charles Schwab; *pg.* 1235, *pg.* 1661
Rediker, Emily, Brand Mgr-Mktg - Copart, Inc.; *pg.* 168, *pg.* 86
Reding, Michael B., VP-Sls Support & Intl Ops - Toyota Motor Sales, U.S.A., Inc.; *pg.* 193, *pg.* 296
Redinger, Kelly, Dir-Mktg - Wolverine World Wide, Inc.; *pg.* 1822, *pg.* 905
Redko, Eugene, Assoc Product Mgr - Leviton Manufacturing Company, Inc.; *pg.* 1301, *pg.* 1180
Redler, Jessica, Mgr-Digital Mktg - Pernod Ricard USA, Inc.; *pg.* 1968, *pg.* 1332
Redlien, Diana, Coord-Mktg & Pro Products - Turtle Wax, Inc.; *pg.* 220, *pg.* 671
Redlinger, Erika N., Specialist-Comml Mktg - ABB Inc.; *pg.* 1309, *pg.* 1359
Redlinger, Kris, Dir-Branding & Sponsorship Mktg - Go Daddy Inc.; *pg.* 1249, *pg.* 21
Redman, Harold L., Pres-Products Grp - Briggs & Stratton Corporation; *pg.* 201, *pg.* 1899
Redmon, Matt, Dir-Channel Mktg-MG Brands - LOUD Technologies Inc.; *pg.* 652, *pg.* 1847
Redmond, Brian, Brand Mgr-NERF US Mktg - Hasbro, Inc.; *pg.* 954, *pg.* 1603
Redmond, Cecilia Garcia, Sr Dir-Corp Mktg - Thor Industries, Inc.; *pg.* 1711, *pg.* 1456
Redmond, Jason, Dir-Enterprise Integrated Mktg Comm - Samsung Electronics America, Inc.; *pg.* 669, *pg.* 1115
Redmond, Joal, VP-PR - Avnet, Inc.; *pg.* 622, *pg.* 15
Redmond, Nan, Dir-Corp Comm & PR - Edible Arrangements International, Inc.; *pg.* 1768, *pg.* 382
Redmond, Patrick, Dir-Interactive Mktg & Analytics - SIRVA, Inc.; *pg.* 1923, *pg.* 669
Redmond, Rich, Chief Product Officer - GatesAir, Inc.; *pg.* 640, *pg.* 1460
Redmond, Thomas, Mgr-Digital Mktg - PayPal Inc.; *pg.* 1274, *pg.* 248
Redohl, Jennifer, Sr Analyst-Global Adv - Accenture; *pg.* 1392, *pg.* 1186
Reece, Andy, Mgr-Sls - Sanderson Ford Inc.; *pg.* 190, *pg.* 13
Reece, Christian, Sr Product Mgr-Global - Affymetrix, Inc.; *pg.* 1487, *pg.* 263
Reece, Jeffrey, Dir-Digital Mktg - Dell Inc.; *pg.* 383, *pg.* 1737
Reece, Marshall, VP-Sls & Mktg - Associated Milk Producers Inc.; *pg.* 838, *pg.* 951
Reece, Tera J., Mgr-Field Mktg-Hewlett-Packard Enterprise Security - Hewlett-Packard Company; *pg.* 404, *pg.* 175
Reed, Adam, Dir-Mktg-Regional - Raising Cane's USA; *pg.* 1746, *pg.* 742
Reed, Alan, Publr-Motor Trend's Truck Trend & Dir-Integrated Sls & Mktg - TEN: The Enthusiast Network; *pg.* 1691, *pg.* 1298
Reed, Allison, Mgr-Consumer Mktg - Harley-Davidson, Inc.; *pg.* 178, *pg.* 1874
Reed, Amy, Brand Mgr - The McGraw-Hill Companies Inc.; *pg.* 1663, *pg.* 1257
Reed, Ann, VP-Mdsg - Fred Meyer Stores, Inc.; *pg.* 1769, *pg.* 1502
Reed, Bart, VP-Brand & Mktg Svcs-UnitedHealthcare Medicare & Retirement - UnitedHealth Group Incorporated; *pg.* 1221, *pg.* 950
Reed, Betty, Head-Media & Social Media Ops - FCA US LLC; *pg.* 170, *pg.* 868
Reed, Cheryl, Reg Dir-Sls-Houston - United Airlines, Inc.; *pg.* 1927, *pg.* 593
Reed, Claudia, Sr VP-Mktg - Weissman Theatrical Supply, Inc.; *pg.* 35, *pg.* 1004
Reed, Dale, VP-Sls-North America - Emerson Network Power; *pg.* 1071, *pg.* 1479
Reed, Danielle, Partner-YouTube & Head-Sls - Google Inc.; *pg.* 1249, *pg.* 153
Reed, David, Dir-Mktg - Bianchi U.S.A., Inc.; *pg.* 1827, *pg.* 100
Reed, David, Sr Mgr-Corp Fin - LyondellBasell Industries; *pg.* 980, *pg.* 1710
Reed, Doug, VP-Mktg - National Association of Convenience Stores; *pg.* 148, *pg.* 1771
Reed, Erin, Brand Mgr - Bissell Homecare, Inc.; *pg.* 52, *pg.* 887
Reed, H.O., Dir-Digital Strategy, Analytics & Social Media - MATTEL, INC.; *pg.* 962, *pg.* 81
Reed, Ivan, Dir-Integrated Mktg - Office Depot, Inc.; *pg.* 448, *pg.* 412
Reed, James, Dir-Media Ops - Discovery Communications, Inc.; *pg.* 282, *pg.* 777
Reed, Jamie, Head-Programmatic Sls Solutions - Google Inc.; *pg.* 1249, *pg.* 153
Reed, Jason, Dir-Sls - Hamilton Beach Brands, Inc.; *pg.* 56, *pg.* 1783
Reed, Jerry, Sr Mgr-Data Center Ops - Brown-Forman Corporation; *pg.* 1958, *pg.* 732
Reed, Jessica, Mgr-Social Media Mktg - Mood Media; *pg.* 298, *pg.* 1616
Reed, Jolee, Mgr-Mktg Comm - Liberty Mutual Insurance Group Inc.; *pg.* 1205, *pg.* 797
Reed, Katie, Dir-Local Restaurant Mktg - Freebirds World Burrito; *pg.* 1729, *pg.* 1662
Reed, Kelly, Dir-Brand, Adv, Customers & Plng - Microsoft Corporation; *pg.* 435, *pg.* 1824
Reed, Kyley, Mgr-Product Mktg-Five-Star - ACCO Brands Corporation; *pg.* 340, *pg.* 626
Reed, Lauren, Dir-Natl Mktg Programs - Sun Life Financial Inc.; *pg.* 806, *pg.* 1944
Reed, Leona, Sr Dir-Mktg-Intl - California Travel & Tourism Commission; *pg.* 990, *pg.* 196
Reed, Mark, Sr Dir-EPM Transformation - The Hackett Group, Inc.; *pg.* 1255, *pg.* 443
Reed, Michael, Sr Dir-Real Estate - Stater Bros. Markets; *pg.* 1034, *pg.* 198
Reed, Mike, Dir-Product Mktg - Paychex, Inc.; *pg.* 792, *pg.* 1336
Reed, Philip, Sr Editor-Consumer Advice - Edmunds, Inc.; *pg.* 1241, *pg.* 273
Reed, Richard, Acct Mgr-Inside Sls - Dell, Inc.; *pg.* 385, *pg.* 1037
Reed, Ron, VP-Sls - SAS Institute (Canada), Inc.; *pg.* 466, *pg.* 1943
Reed, Ted, Mgr-Mktg-Intl - Bose Corporation; *pg.* 626, *pg.* 820
Reed, Terrence M., Sr Dir-HR - Georgia-Pacific Cellulose; *pg.* 1164, *pg.* 1644
Reeder, Annie, Sr Mgr-Adv - Discover Financial Services; *pg.* 744, *pg.* 653
Reeder, Rob, Mgr-Campaign-Natl Mktg - Hallmark Cards, Inc.; *pg.* 1646, *pg.* 983
Reedman, Thomas, Dir-Global Mktg-Kiehl's - L'Oreal USA; *pg.* 514, *pg.* 1252
Reedy, John, Dir-Sls-Natl - Besser Company; *pg.* 1317, *pg.* 865
Reehl, Keith, Mgr-Interactive Mktg-Global - Aon Risk Services Inc.; *pg.* 1193, *pg.* 564
Rees, Dallan, Product Mgr-Mobile Applications - 1-800 CONTACTS, INC.; *pg.* 1758, *pg.* 1753
Rees, Lisa, Mgr-Mktg Comm - Avnet, Inc.; *pg.* 622, *pg.* 15
Reese, Andy, Sr Mgr-Product Mktg - IHS Inc.; *pg.* 1652, *pg.* 326
Reese, Chad, Mgr-Crop Protection Mktg - Monsanto Company; *pg.* 1173, *pg.* 999
Reese, Chris, Sr Dir-Pub Comm - Ameriprise Financial, Inc.; *pg.* 715, *pg.* 930
Reese, Dan, Brand Mgr-Frozen Snacks - The Kraft Heinz Company; *pg.* 870, *pg.* 1577
Reese, David, Dir-Product Mktg - The Goodyear Tire & Rubber Company; *pg.* 1883, *pg.* 1401
Reese, Jason, Sr Product Mgr - Zimmer Biomet Holdings, Inc.; *pg.* 1611, *pg.* 699
Reese, Jeff, Sr Dir-Integrated Mktg - GoPro; *pg.* 1414, *pg.* 255
Reese, Jenifer, Brand Mgr-Global Olay Personal Care - The Procter & Gamble Company; *pg.* 1129, *pg.* 1418
Reese, Jonathan, Sr Mgr-Mktg-Adv & IPM - Concur

Technologies, Inc.; pg. 1236, pg. 1813
Reese, Laura, Sr Mgr-Media Svcs - Church's Chicken, Inc.; pg. 1722, pg. 493
Reese, Michael, Mgr-Mktg-Global - GlaxoSmithKline; pg. 1536, pg. 1565
Reese, Michael, Sr Mgr-Product Mktg - Samsung Electronics America, Inc.; pg. 669, pg. 1115
Reese, Tom, Dir-Sls - Norfolk Southern Corporation; pg. 1917, pg. 1797
Reesor, Kelly, Product Mgr - Michaels Stores, Inc.; pg. 1127, pg. 1722
Reetz, Douglas, Sr VP-Sls - Hormel Foods Corporation; pg. 863, pg. 915
Reeves, Alison, Mgr-Mktg - Krispy Kreme Doughnuts, Inc.; pg. 1734, pg. 1394
Reeves, Charleen, Mgr-Sls-Nevada Sierra District - United States Postal Service; pg. 1009, pg. 406
Reeves, Charlotte, Sr Mgr-Trade Shows & Events - McKesson Corporation; pg. 1500, pg. 222
Reeves, Clair, VP-Mktg-Global - L'Oreal USA; pg. 514, pg. 1252
Reeves, Dawn, VP-Mktg & Relocation - RealtySouth; pg. 1109, pg. 4
Reeves, Elizabeth, Brand Mgr-Breakfast Innovation - Tyson Foods, Inc.; pg. 902, pg. 35
Reeves, Gary, Dir-Mktg Partnerships - AARON'S, INC.; pg. 912, pg. 486
Reeves, Jason, Sr Brand Mgr-Natl Mktg - Applebee's International, Inc.; pg. 1715, pg. 980
Reeves, Julie, Vice Chancellor-Brand Mktg - University Of Denver; pg. 609, pg. 323
Reeves, Kathryne, Sr VP-Enterprise Mktg - Cardinal Health, Inc.; pg. 1512, pg. 1448
Reeves, Kristi, Dir-Consumer Mktg-Respiratory Div - GlaxoSmithKline; pg. 1536, pg. 1389
Reeves, Kristie, Project Mgr-New Media - PGA Tour, Inc.; pg. 574, pg. 460
Reeves, Lindie, Head-Digital Mktg - Owens Corning; pg. 102, pg. 1476
Reeves, Marta C., VP-Corp Mktg & Comm - Pan-American Life Insurance Company; pg. 1213, pg. 747
Reeves, Matt, Sr Mgr-Digital Mktg - Charter Communications, Inc.; pg. 274, pg. 372
Reeves, Renee, Mgr-Global Supplier-Adv & Mktg - Apple Inc.; pg. 350, pg. 73
Reeves, Ron, Strategist-PR & Social - Herman Miller, Inc.; pg. 926, pg. 913
Reeves, Scott, VP-Relationship Mktg - Career Education Corporation; pg. 599, pg. 658
Refaat, Eman, Brand Mgr - The Kraft Heinz Company; pg. 870, pg. 1577
Refaeli, David, Dir-Email Mktg - Ziff Davis, LLC; pg. 1703, pg. 1316
Regan, Beth, VP-Sls - Calvin Klein, Inc.; pg. 20, pg. 1209
Regan, Christine L., Sr Dir-Corp Affairs - Pfizer Inc.; pg. 1581, pg. 1278
Regan, Dave, VP-Sls & Mktg - The Vernon Company; pg. 488, pg. 710
Regan, David, Sr Product Mgr - Twitter, Inc.; pg. 1285, pg. 228
Regan, Devon, Sr Dir-Acq Mktg - LOGMEIN, INC.; pg. 428, pg. 861
Regan, Justin, Sr Mgr-Brand Mktg-Global - Vans, Inc.; pg. 1821, pg. 76
Regan, Maura, Sr VP & Gen Mgr-Global Consumer Products - Sesame Workshop; pg. 307, pg. 1290
Regan, Nadine, Designer-Mktg & Graphic - Blackbaud, Inc.; pg. 361, pg. 1613
Regas, Tracy, VP-Mktg Strategy - Citigroup Inc.; pg. 735, pg. 1212
Rege, Priya, Sr Product Mgr - Johnson & Johnson; pg. 1549, pg. 1091
Reggi, Candice, Dir-Adv-Natl - XO Group Inc.; pg. 1289, pg. 1316
Reggio, John, VP-Sls Ops - XO Group Inc.; pg. 1289, pg. 1316
Regis, Greg, Sr VP-Adv Sls & Media Partnerships - Scripps Networks Interactive, Inc.; pg. 1279, pg. 1638
Regis, Karen, Mgr-Consumer Mktg - Intel Corporation; pg. 645, pg. 266
Register, Mike, Grp VP & Mgr-Database Mktg - Sun Trust Bank, Atlanta; pg. 806, pg. 520
Register, Mike, Grp VP & Mgr-Database Mktg - SunTrust Banks, Inc.; pg. 807, pg. 520
Regniault, Marcella, VP-Digital Sls Plng & Client Svcs - JPMorgan Chase & Co.; pg. 772, pg. 1246
Regnier, Joni, Dir-Adv - The Newton Kansan; pg. 1671, pg. 717
Regules, Pete, Dir-Multifamily Products & Svcs - CORT Business Services Corporation; pg. 921, pg. 1777
Rehbein, Katie, Sr Mgr-Brand Partnership - Amazon.com, Inc.; pg. 1226, pg. 1831
Rehm, Adrienne, Mgr-Mktg - Herman Miller, Inc.; pg. 926, pg. 913
Rehm, Gary, VP-Mktg - Atmos Energy Corporation; pg. 1935, pg. 1675
Rehm, Jeff, Sr Mgr-Corp Facilities & Global Sustainability - W.W. Grainger, Inc.; pg. 1390, pg. 625
Rehman, Rehana, Strategist-Social Media Channel - Cisco Systems, Inc.; pg. 372, pg. 240
Rehner, Denise, Mgr-Event Mktg & Comm - Cisco Systems, Inc.; pg. 372, pg. 240
Rei, Olga, Asst Mgr-Asia Pacific & Global Mktg - Tiffany & Co.; pg. 13, pg. 1299
Rei, Rebecca, Specialist-Mktg - Amica Mutual Insurance Co.; pg. 1192, pg. 1602
Reich, Brian, Specialist-Digital Mktg - Brocade Communications Systems, Inc.; pg. 365, pg. 239
Reich, Brian, Gen Mgr-Product Line - Tektronix, Inc.; pg. 1431, pg. 1496
Reich, Brit, VP-Sls-North America - Arctic Cat Inc.; pg. 1705, pg. 953
Reich, Joel, Sr VP & Gen Mgr-Array Products Bus Unit - NetApp, Inc.; pg. 444, pg. 287
Reich, Russell, Chief Strategy Officer - MC2; pg. 431, pg. 1153
Reichen, Penny, Mgr-Sls Ops - Leupold & Stevens, Inc.; pg. 1420, pg. 1492
Reichenberger, Jared, Brand Mgr-Propellers - Mercury Marine; pg. 1709, pg. 1857
Reichert, Alison, Sr Mgr-Mktg-Celebrex & Flector Patch - Pfizer Inc.; pg. 1581, pg. 1278
Reichert, Chris, Mng Dir-Sls & Mktg-Markel Specialty - Markel Corporation; pg. 1207, pg. 1783
Reichert, Jason, Dir-Mktg - United Services Automobile Association; pg. 1221, pg. 1743
Reichert, John, Dir-Client Solutions & Product Mgr-WMS - TECSYS, Inc.; pg. 482, pg. 1956
Reichert, Kelly C., Head-Global Mktg-Thermal Apparel - E.I. du Pont de Nemours & Company; pg. 1159, pg. 390
Reichert, Michael, Dir-Mktg-National - Which Wich, Inc.; pg. 1756, pg. 1690
Reichgott, Barry, Mgr-Mktg-Oral Care Innovation - Colgate-Palmolive Company; pg. 504, pg. 1215
Reichwald, Nicole, Mgr-Mktg - Allen-Edmonds Shoe Corp.; pg. 1804, pg. 1887
Reid, Brian W., VP-Sls-Intl - OraSure Technologies Inc; pg. 1578, pg. 1516
Reid, Chris, Mgr-Product Plng & Res-Natl - Yamaha Motor Canada Ltd.; pg. 1712, pg. 1947
Reid, Dana, Mgr-Mktg & Customer Svc - Transitions Optical, Inc.; pg. 1432, pg. 458
Reid, Darnell, Principal-Mktg - FedEx Corporation; pg. 1907, pg. 1642
Reid, Denise, Mgr-Mktg-Channel Sls - Samsung Telecommunications America, LLC; pg. 670, pg. 1736
Reid, Ellis, Sr Mgr-Indus Mktg - Dolby Laboratories, Inc.; pg. 284, pg. 217
Reid, Erica, Coord-Social Media - Shell Lubricants; pg. 217, pg. 1714
Reid, Gordon, Mgr-Sls - Chart Industries, Inc.; pg. 1405, pg. 1454
Reid, Jake, Sr Mgr-Social Media - Expedia, Inc.; pg. 1244, pg. 1814
Reid, Jeff, Product Mgr-Mktg-Small Cars - Ford Motor Company; pg. 172, pg. 876
Reid, Jonathan, VP-Sls-APAC - BroadSoft, Inc.; pg. 1233, pg. 770
Reid, Julie, Dir-Sls-Australia & New Zealand - United Airlines, Inc.; pg. 1927, pg. 593
Reid, Kimberly L., Dir-Mall Mktg & Bus Dev - Simon Property Group, Inc.; pg. 1112, pg. 690
Reid, Lisa, Mgr-Beauty Care Mktg - Procter & Gamble Inc.; pg. 333, pg. 1929
Reid, Lynn, Dir-Mktg - Omega Watch Company; pg. 10, pg. 1131
Reid, Philip, Category Mgr-Sls - Philips Lighting; pg. 1303, pg. 806
Reid, Rebecca, Mgr-Product Mktg-Google Brand Ads Mktg - Google Inc.; pg. 1249, pg. 153
Reid, Rob, Media Planner - The Canadian Broadcasting Corporation; pg. 272, pg. 1931
Reid, Robb, Specialist-Mktg & Consumer Relations - Hostess Brands LLC; pg. 1856, pg. 984
Reid, Ryan, Mgr-Social Media - PETCO Animal Supplies, Inc.; pg. 1480, pg. 206
Reid, Sarah, Brand Mgr-Miller Lite - MillerCoors LLC; pg. 255, pg. 582
Reid, Sean, Mgr-Sls-Natl - Escort, Inc.; pg. 1412, pg. 1479
Reid, Tim, Grp VP-Mktg Strategy & Comm - Macy's East; pg. 1777, pg. 1254
Reid, William, VP-Product Dev - Amphenol Fiber Systems International, Inc.; pg. 617, pg. 1658
Reidenbach, Kathleen Sanford, Sr VP-Mktg - Kimpton Hotel & Restaurant Group; pg. 1099, pg. 220
Reider, Abbey, Dir-Global Social & Digital Content Strategy - Starwood Hotels & Resorts Worldwide, Inc.; pg. 1114, pg. 378
Reidt, Amy, Sr Mgr-Retail Mktg - LEGO Systems, Inc.; pg. 961, pg. 346
Reidy, Mike, Dir-Digital Sls - NBC Universal, Inc.; pg. 300, pg. 1266
Reierson, Amanda, Head-Digital Mktg - Farmers Group, Inc.; pg. 1199, pg. 130
Reierson, Jeff, Dir-Mktg-Global - Medtronic, Inc.; pg. 1564, pg. 939
Reif, Bob, Chief Revenue Officer & Exec VP - Saint Louis Rams Football Company; pg. 580, pg. 1002
Reif, Jennifer, Dir-Demand Center, Mktg Strategy & Ops - Equinix, Inc.; pg. 394, pg. 190
Reiff, David, Head-Retail Mktg - Vornado Realty Trust; pg. 1118, pg. 1312
Reiff, Kara, Sr Dir-Integrated Mktg-Global - Wm. Wrigley Jr. Company; pg. 1863, pg. 596
Reifschneider, Dennis, Reg Mgr-Sls - Furst-McNess Company; pg. 1476, pg. 613
Reifschneider, Doug, VP-Mktg - Firehouse Subs; pg. 1728, pg. 433
Reil, Anissa, Sr Mgr-Mktg Dept Plng & Ops - Southwest Airlines Co.; pg. 1923, pg. 1687
Reiley, Brendan, Sr Product Mgr-AOL Mobile Adv Product & Svcs - AOL Inc.; pg. 1229, pg. 1195
Reiling, Ben, Dir-Motorsports Mktg - The Coca-Cola Company; pg. 240, pg. 493
Reilly, Beth, Head-Digital & Social Mktg-Americas Reg & Sr Dir - Barilla America, Inc.; pg. 839, pg. 555
Reilly, Brian, Product Dir-Healthcare Matls - NuSil Technology LLC; pg. 1887, pg. 63
Reilly, Chris, Mgr-Global Media - AliphCom, Inc.; pg. 616, pg. 212
Reilly, Erin, Head-Green Mktg - Google Inc.; pg. 1249, pg. 153
Reilly, Gabe, Head-Vertical Mktg Comm - Facebook, Inc.; pg. 1245, pg. 143
Reilly, James, Dir-Sls Fin - The New York Post; pg. 1668, pg. 1269
Reilly, Jean, Supvr-Mktg Comm-PLP & DPW Solar - Preformed Line Products Company; pg. 1370, pg. 1434
Reilly, Katie, Mgr-Global Consumer Products & Brand Licensing - Warner Music Group Corp.; pg. 590, pg. 1313
Reilly, Kevin, Sls Dir-Indian Motorcycle & Victory Motorcycles - Polaris Industries Inc.; pg. 1709, pg. 928
Reilly, Lisa K., Asst VP-Adv & PR-MassMutual Retirement Svcs - Massachusetts Mutual Life Insurance Company; pg. 1207, pg. 845
Reilly, Mary Ann Fitzmaurice, Sr VP-Customer Mktg & Brand Mgmt - American Express Company; pg. 712, pg. 1190
Reilly, Tom, Exec VP-Reg Sls - National CineMedia, Inc.; pg. 567, pg. 314
Reim, Maia Coven, Dir-Adv Art - Princeton University Press; pg. 1678, pg. 1112
Reimann, Gina, Head-Creative-Accessories - Google Inc.; pg. 1249, pg. 153
Reimann, Jessica, Mgr-Mktg - NKK Switches; pg. 1302, pg. 23
Reimann, Jim, Brand Mgr - The Sun Products Corporation; pg. 336, pg. 385
Reimold, Mark, Sr Mgr-Digital Mktg - EMC Corporation; pg. 391, pg. 825
Rein, Lesa, Dir-Sls Engrg - Scan-Optics, LLC; pg. 467, pg. 354
Rein, Simon, Product Mgr-Cultural Institute - Google Inc.; pg. 1249, pg. 153
Reinberger, Bill, VP-Corp Sls - Reds Baseball Partners, LLC; pg. 578, pg. 1425

First page reference indicates Business Class Edition
Second page reference indicates Geographic Edition

Reinbold, Mark, Dir-Mktg Ops - Hewlett-Packard Company; *pg.* 404, *pg.* 175
Reinders, Gerrit, Exec VP-Sls & Mktg-Global - TELKONET, INC.; *pg.* 678, *pg.* 1881
Reineke, Kevin, Assoc Dir-Mktg - Novartis Corporation; *pg.* 1574, *pg.* 1273
Reiner, Adam, Sr Dir-Sls-Home Care & Corp Bus Plng - The Clorox Company; *pg.* 327, *pg.* 169
Reiner, Sally, VP-Sls-Michael Kors Watch & Jewelry - Fossil Group, Inc.; *pg.* 5, *pg.* 1735
Reinertson, Liz, Sr Mgr-Strategic Comm - G&K Services Inc.; *pg.* 693, *pg.* 949
Reines, Pat, Sr Mgr-SmartPath Ground Based Augmentation Sys - Honeywell Aerospace; *pg.* 228, *pg.* 16
Reinhard, Brenda, Sr Mgr-Loyalty Strategy & Mktg - Sears Holdings Corporation; *pg.* 1784, *pg.* 618
Reinhard, Clark, Dir-Mktg - P&G-Clairol, Inc.; *pg.* 519, *pg.* 1418
Reinhard, Clark, Dir-Mktg - The Procter & Gamble Company; *pg.* 1129, *pg.* 1418
Reinhard, Tess, Sr Dir-Organizational Capability - CDW Corporation; *pg.* 370, *pg.* 663
Reinhardt, Danielle, Brand Mgr - Enesco, LLC; *pg.* 1124, *pg.* 620
Reinhardt, Jeff, Mng Dir-Media & Mktg Svcs - SRDS, Inc.; *pg.* 1688, *pg.* 657
Reinhart, Kerstin, Mgr-Mobile & Social Media - DSW, Inc.; *pg.* 1807, *pg.* 1439
Reinheimer, Emily, Mgr-Mktg - Perfumania Holdings, Inc.; *pg.* 520, *pg.* 1141
Reinke, Justin, Dir-Refrigeration Product Mktg - Samsung Electronics America, Inc.; *pg.* 669, *pg.* 1115
Reinking, Melissa, Dir-Partner Mktg - Provide Commerce, Inc.; *pg.* 1276, *pg.* 206
Reinkober, Brian, Dir-Mass Media - Bon Ton Stores, Inc.; *pg.* 1763, *pg.* 1596
Reinkopf, Dahlia, Sr Dir-Mktg - POM Wonderful, LLC; *pg.* 890, *pg.* 139
Reinlein, Laura, Specialist-Mktg-Comml Trucks - Champion Enterprises Holdings, LLC; *pg.* 75, *pg.* 910
Reinman, Jodi, Mgr-PR & Social Media - California Strawberry Commission; *pg.* 135, *pg.* 305
Reinold, Jeffery, Supvr-Sls & Svc - Oakhurst Dairy; *pg.* 887, *pg.* 752
Reis, Doreen, Mgr-Adv - Boston Symphony Orchestra Inc.; *pg.* 534, *pg.* 791
Reis, Vicky, Mgr-Outside Multi-Media Sls - The Topeka Capital-Journal; *pg.* 1695, *pg.* 722
Reisenauer, Mark, VP-Oncology Sls & Mktg - Astellas Pharma US, Inc.; *pg.* 1496, *pg.* 640
Reisenwitz, Eric, Sr VP-Underwriting, Product & Ops-Grp Protection - Lincoln Financial Group; *pg.* 1206, *pg.* 1375
Reiser, Laura, Brand Mgr - Dick's Sporting Goods, Inc.; *pg.* 1832, *pg.* 1524
Reisman, Gail, Sr Dir-Amtrak - National Railroad Passenger Corporation; *pg.* 1916, *pg.* 403
Reisner, Michael, VP-Mktg - Alva/Amco Pharmacal Companies, Inc.; *pg.* 1492, *pg.* 637
Reiss, Elanna, Brand Mktg Mgr - Bayer CropScience; *pg.* 1149, *pg.* 981
Reiss, Lance, Sr VP-FX Mktg - FX Networks, LLC; *pg.* 288, *pg.* 131
Reiss, Robert, Brand Mgr-North America Fabric Care - The Procter & Gamble Company; *pg.* 1129, *pg.* 1418
Reiss, Victor, Dir-Social, Digital Experience & Innovation Team - Cancer Treatment Centers of America; *pg.* 1511, *pg.* 410
Reiss-Davis, Zachary, Mgr-Product Mktg - salesforce.com, inc.; *pg.* 1278, *pg.* 226
Reiter, Dara, Specialist-PR - Oakley, Inc.; *pg.* 1840, *pg.* 86
Reiter, Kristin, Dir-Creative Concept-Global Football - NIKE, Inc.; *pg.* 1812, *pg.* 1492
Reiter, Shelli, Acct Brand Mgr-Global Mktg Comm-GE Healthcare - GE Healthcare; *pg.* 399, *pg.* 1765
Reitman, Sandra, Sr Mgr-Education Ops - Mediabistro, Inc.; *pg.* 1266, *pg.* 1258
Reitz, Mark, Mgr-Mktg - Eaton Corporation; *pg.* 1331, *pg.* 1429
Reitz, Nicole, Div Mgr-Sls - Stanley Black & Decker, Inc.; *pg.* 1063, *pg.* 358
Rekhi, Sachin, Dir-Product Mgmt - LinkedIn Corporation; *pg.* 1262, *pg.* 160
Rekonen, Heikki, Dir-Sls - AWR Corporation; *pg.* 623, *pg.* 78
Rellihen, Kristine, Mgr-Mktg-Sustainability - Sears Holdings Corporation; *pg.* 1784, *pg.* 618
Rellosa, Eric, VP & Gen Mgr-Mdse - Spencer Gifts LLC; *pg.* 1786, *pg.* 1057
Relyea, Craig, Sr VP-Content Strategy & Mktg - LeapFrog Enterprises, Inc.; *pg.* 961, *pg.* 84
Remar, Pat, Reg Mgr-Sls - Eberhard Manufacturing Division; *pg.* 1046, *pg.* 1475
Rembiszewski, Peter, Head-Application Resource Optimizer Program & Engr-Product Dev - AT&T; *pg.* 1865, *pg.* 258
Remes, Sheila M., Mng Dir-Sls Strategy - The Boeing Company; *pg.* 225, *pg.* 567
Remi-John, Obehi, Brand Mgr-Lysol - Reckitt Benckiser Inc.; *pg.* 1136, *pg.* 1105
Remied, Charles A., Mgr-Central Reg Sls - SERFILCO, Ltd.; *pg.* 1375, *pg.* 641
Remily, Scott A., Mgr-Field Mktg-CT - Philips Electronics North America; *pg.* 662, *pg.* 782
Remondino, Bob, Mgr-Mktg-Global - THE DOW CHEMICAL COMPANY; *pg.* 1157, *pg.* 898
Remoquillo, Dorothy, Sr Mgr-Mktg-Solutions & Alliances - Fujitsu Computer Systems Corporation; *pg.* 398, *pg.* 285
Remsberg, Brian, Dir-PR-TCA - Michelin North America Inc.; *pg.* 1886, *pg.* 1618
Remulla, Paul Kenji, Assoc Mgr-Mktg - MoneyGram International, Inc.; *pg.* 783, *pg.* 1684
Remuzzi, Mary, Sr Dir-Global Direct to Consumer Retail & Comm - NIKE, Inc.; *pg.* 1812, *pg.* 1492
Ren, Anna H., Reg Mgr-Mktg - Direct Energy; *pg.* 1939, *pg.* 1704
Ren, Bo, Product Mgr - Facebook, Inc.; *pg.* 1245, *pg.* 143
Renard, Bastien, Sr Dir-Mktg-France - NIKE, Inc.; *pg.* 1812, *pg.* 1492
Rencher, Brad, Sr VP & Gen Mgr-Digital Mktg Bus Unit - Adobe Systems Incorporated; *pg.* 342, *pg.* 235
Rencher, Jeff, VP-Sls & Mkt-Surgical Products - Bovie Medical Corporation; *pg.* 1402, *pg.* 1178
Renda, Philip A., VP & Gen Mgr-DS Brown & Infrastructure Products Div - Gibraltar Industries, Inc.; *pg.* 1340, *pg.* 1148
Rendall, Erica, Dir-Mktg-Liquid Concentrates-MiO, Kool-Aid & Crystal Light - The Kraft Heinz Company; *pg.* 871, *pg.* 641
Rendall, Kate, Product Mgr-CDW Cloud Collaboration - CDW Corporation; *pg.* 370, *pg.* 663
Rende, Jonathan, Exec VP-Products & Mktg - Keynote Systems Incorporated; *pg.* 425, *pg.* 255
Rendek, Carl, Mgr-Production - Orlando Philharmonic Orchestra Inc.; *pg.* 573, *pg.* 455
Rendek, Pete, Mgr-Digital Mktg - Avnet Technology Solutions; *pg.* 359, *pg.* 25
Rendek, Sandy, Dir-Mktg - Orlando Philharmonic Orchestra Inc.; *pg.* 573, *pg.* 455
Rendon, Veronica, Dir-Field Mktg-West Reg - Dean Foods Company; *pg.* 852, *pg.* 1679
Renehan, Anne, Sr Mgr-Product Mktg - Adobe Systems Incorporated; *pg.* 342, *pg.* 235
Renfro, Dave, Dir-Media - ECPI University; *pg.* 601, *pg.* 1810
Renfro, Rachel, Brand Mgr - Dell, Inc.; *pg.* 385, *pg.* 1037
Renfro, Rachel, Brand Mgr - Dell Inc.; *pg.* 383, *pg.* 1737
Renick-Mayer, Courtney, Planner-Sls - Pandora Media Inc.; *pg.* 1273, *pg.* 172
Renna, Ray, Sr Mgr-Integrated Mktg - Samsung Electronics America, Inc.; *pg.* 669, *pg.* 1115
Renner, Alicia, Dir-Mktg - Little Caesars Enterprises, Inc.; *pg.* 1736, *pg.* 883
Renner, Gary, Dir-Mktg - Setco Sales Company; *pg.* 1061, *pg.* 1426
Renner, Jason, Sr Product Mgr - Bradley Corporation; *pg.* 71, *pg.* 1870
Renner, Joan A., Mgr-Digital Strategy Mktg - IBM; *pg.* 410, *pg.* 1449
Renner, Katherine, Product Mgr-Coffee - Hamilton Beach Brands, Inc.; *pg.* 56, *pg.* 1783
Renner, Marisol, Specialist-Publ & PR - Baltimore Ravens Limited Partnership; *pg.* 532, *pg.* 755
Renner, Stephanie A., Dir-Mktg - Railserve Inc.; *pg.* 1921, *pg.* 519
Rennhoff, Alice, Dir-Mktg Ops-Global - Levi Strauss & Co.; *pg.* 43, *pg.* 220
Renny, Melissa, Brand Mgr-Innovation - Mondelez International, Inc.; *pg.* 878, *pg.* 601
Renouard, Bruce, Sr VP-Sls & Bus Dev-Worldwide - Cree Inc.; *pg.* 631, *pg.* 1371
Rensel, Elizabeth, VP-Product Dev - MasterCard International, Inc.; *pg.* 780, *pg.* 1326
Renshaw, Jordan, Coord-Mktg - Pandora Media Inc.; *pg.* 1273, *pg.* 172
Rensink, Rachael, Sr Mgr-User Experience & Social Media-HR - Delta Air Lines, Inc.; *pg.* 1905, *pg.* 503
Renteria, Nathaniel, Assoc Mgr-Mktg - Dr Pepper Snapple Group, Inc.; *pg.* 250, *pg.* 1729
Rentler, Kimberly, Mgr-Shopper Mktg - GlaxoSmithKline; *pg.* 1536, *pg.* 1565
Rentler, Kimberly, Mgr-Shopper Mktg - GlaxoSmithKline Consumer Healthcare; *pg.* 510, *pg.* 1554
Rentner, Deanna, Specialist-Mktg - W.R. Grace & Co.; *pg.* 123, *pg.* 810
Rentsch, Robert, Brand Mgr - Craft Brewers Alliance, Inc; *pg.* 247, *pg.* 1502
Rentzel, Matthew, Mgr-Horizontal Pump Product - Rentzel Pump Manufacturing, LP; *pg.* 707, *pg.* 1726
Renwick, Frank, Sr Dir-Mktg - NRG Energy, Inc.; *pg.* 1366, *pg.* 1112
Renwick, Frank, Sr Dir-Mktg - NRG Energy, Inc.; *pg.* 1948, *pg.* 1712
Renwick, Lauren, Mgr-Search, Mobile & Emerging Media - Turner Broadcasting System, Inc.; *pg.* 314, *pg.* 521
Renzi, Andrea, Sr Specialist-Internet Adv - ITT Educational Services, Inc.; *pg.* 603, *pg.* 675
Renzi, Jeff, Pres-Sls-Global - Unisys Corporation; *pg.* 487, *pg.* 1517
Repar, Lawrence P., COO & Exec VP-Sls & Mktg-Global - Masonite International Corporation; *pg.* 1054, *pg.* 1920
Repice, Victoria, VP-Product Mgmt - Sirius XM Holdings Inc.; *pg.* 308, *pg.* 1292
Reppenhagen, Paul, Dir-Mktg - Post Consumer Brands; *pg.* 833, *pg.* 927
Requesto, Maria, Sr Dir-Consumer Insights - DIRECTV Group Holdings, LLC; *pg.* 281, *pg.* 79
Resch, Martin, Product Mgr-Outdoor EMEA - Garmin International, Inc.; *pg.* 1414, *pg.* 717
Reseburg, John, Sr Dir-Corp Comm - Electronic Arts Inc.; *pg.* 951, *pg.* 189
Resera, Silvia, Gen Mgr-Sls - Domtar Corporation; *pg.* 1456, *pg.* 1954
Reske, Joe, Dir-Mktg-Cheetos - Frito-Lay North America, Inc.; *pg.* 1853, *pg.* 1730
Reske, Joe, Dir-Mktg-Cheetos - PepsiCo, Inc.; *pg.* 259, *pg.* 1327
Resman, Cindy, Dir-PR & Corp Comm - Medtronic, Inc.; *pg.* 1564, *pg.* 939
Resman, Tess, Sr Mgr-Mktg - PepsiCo, Inc.; *pg.* 259, *pg.* 1327
Resnick, Ann Marie, Sr VP-Mktg & Promos - Scholastic Corporation; *pg.* 1683, *pg.* 1288
Resnick, Ann Marie, Sr VP-Mktg & Promos - Scholastic Inc.; *pg.* 1683, *pg.* 1288
Resnick, Rick, VP-Mktg-Univision Sports Sls - Univision Communications Inc.; *pg.* 683, *pg.* 1307
Resnick, Sara, Sr Mgr-SEO & Digital Mktg - 1-800-Flowers.com, Inc.; *pg.* 1758, *pg.* 1151
Resnik, Barry, Dir-Mktg - Vision-Ease Lens Corporation; *pg.* 1436, *pg.* 954
Ress, Diana, Dir-Mktg - BPI Sports, LLC; *pg.* 842, *pg.* 430
Restaino, Dawn, Mgr-Mktg - Ingram Micro Inc.; *pg.* 415, *pg.* 261
Restaino, Jonathan, Acct Head-Digital & Social Media - Bose Corporation; *pg.* 626, *pg.* 820
Restaino, Mario, Dir-Mktg & Sls - PPL Corporation; *pg.* 1950, *pg.* 1514
Restall, John, Exec VP-Strategic Mktg & Res - Sony Pictures Entertainment Inc.; *pg.* 309, *pg.* 72
Resteghini, Matthew, Sr VP-Mktg - Monster Worldwide, Inc.; *pg.* 1268, *pg.* 859
Restivo, Ashley, Mgr-Social & Digital Engagement - Dick's Sporting Goods, Inc.; *pg.* 1832, *pg.* 1524
Restivo, Nickolas, Mgr-Social Media Mktg - Cytosport, Inc.; *pg.* 1018, *pg.* 45
Restom, Omar, Product Mgr-Mobile - LinkedIn Corporation; *pg.* 1262, *pg.* 160
Restuccia, Lauren, Mgr-PR-North American - Samsung Electronics America, Inc.; *pg.* 669, *pg.* 1115
Retcho, Stephanie, Sr VP-Mktg-North America - Kayak; *pg.* 1260, *pg.* 363
Retelle, Jennifer, Reg Mgr-Mdsg - Redco Foods, Inc.; *pg.* 891, *pg.* 1174
Retlewski, Paul, Mgr-Global Product Line - Hewlett-Packard Company; *pg.* 404, *pg.* 175
Rettberg, Tim, Sr Mgr-Product Mktg - BSH Home Appliances Corporation; *pg.* 53, *pg.* 108
Rettelle, Robert, Mgr-Mktg - Boston Market Corporation; *pg.* 1717, *pg.* 329
Rettig, Kevin, Sr Mgr-Media Mgmt-Global - Accenture; *pg.*

1392, *pg.* 1186
Reuben, Blakely, Mgr-Mktg-Brand Payer & Access-Vaccines - GlaxoSmithKline; *pg.* 1536, *pg.* 1389
Reukers, Bram, Brand Mgr-Heineken - Heineken USA Inc.; *pg.* 252, *pg.* 1352
Reule, Kathryn, Mgr-Digital Mktg - The Procter & Gamble Company; *pg.* 1129, *pg.* 1418
Reusch, Janet, Mgr-Social Media Community - Bankrate, Inc.; *pg.* 1231, *pg.* 451
Reuter, Ken, Sr Dir-Mktg & Branded Novelties - Wells Enterprises, Inc.; *pg.* 909, *pg.* 709
Reuter, Kimberly, Asst Mgr-Email Mktg - Nine West Holdings, Inc.; *pg.* 1815, *pg.* 1272
Reveles, Alexandra, Coord-Mktg - JanSport; *pg.* 1837, *pg.* 38
Revell, Sally, Mgr-Mktg - Intuit Inc.; *pg.* 769, *pg.* 158
Revie, John, VP-Consumer Electronics Sls - Sharp Electronics Corporation; *pg.* 672, *pg.* 1082
Revnew, Steve, VP-Product Dev-Paint Stores Grp Mktg - Sherwin Williams; *pg.* 1440, *pg.* 1400
Rewerts, Kevin, Div VP-Mdsg-Automotive, Pet & Farm & Ranch Products - True Value Company; *pg.* 1065, *pg.* 592
Rewis, Nancy, VP-ECommerce & Digital Mktg - Turner Broadcasting System, Inc.; *pg.* 314, *pg.* 521
Rex, Mariko, Sr VP-Mktg - L'Oreal USA; *pg.* 514, *pg.* 1252
Rexing, Myrna, Brand Mgr - totes Isotoner Corporation; *pg.* 14, *pg.* 1426
Rexroat, Mark, Dir-Retail Comm & Mktg Svcs - Sprint Corporation; *pg.* 1874, *pg.* 719
Rey, Fiona, Brand Mgr - Bayer Corporation; *pg.* 1499, *pg.* 1573
Rey, Jay, Dir-Sls & Adv - Tampa Bay Newspapers, Inc.; *pg.* 1691, *pg.* 468
Rey, Patsy, Dir-Loyalty Mktg - Enterprise Holdings, Inc.; *pg.* 1906, *pg.* 996
Reyen, Jim, Mgr-Sls & Mktg-Natl - Johnson Outdoors Inc.; *pg.* 1837, *pg.* 1888
Reyes, Angela, Assoc Product Mgr-Footwear - New Balance Athletic Shoe, Inc.; *pg.* 1811, *pg.* 798
Reyes, Anhelo, VP-Brand Mktg - Spike TV; *pg.* 310, *pg.* 1295
Reyes, Deborah, Mgr-Dodge Brand Mktg - FCA US LLC; *pg.* 170, *pg.* 868
Reyes, Guillermo, Mgr-Svc Mktg - General Electric Company; *pg.* 1297, *pg.* 347
Reyes, John, Chief Sls Officer & Exec VP - San Francisco Travel Association; *pg.* 1005, *pg.* 227
Reyes, Kevin, Sr Mgr-Digital Mktg - Anthropologie, Inc.; *pg.* 18, *pg.* 1558
Reyes, Kristen, Mgr-Enterprise Social Media - Hewlett-Packard Company; *pg.* 404, *pg.* 175
Reyes, Pedro, Product Mgr-Global - Applied Materials, Inc; *pg.* 618, *pg.* 1009
Reyes, Rafael, Sr Product Mgr-Home Cleaning-Global - Whirlpool Corporation; *pg.* 62, *pg.* 872
Reyes, Raul, Dir-Consumer Mktg - McDonald's Corporation; *pg.* 1737, *pg.* 645
Reyes, Stephen, VP-Sls & Mktg - Olympic Steel Inc.; *pg.* 101, *pg.* 1433
Reynar, Angela, Sr Dir-Res-Strategy & Integration - Yahoo! Inc.; *pg.* 1289, *pg.* 289
Reynish, Steve, Interim CFO & Exec VP-Oil Sands Ventures - Suncor Energy Inc.; *pg.* 985, *pg.* 1905
Reynolds, Adam, Mgr-Email Mktg - The Schwan Food Company; *pg.* 894, *pg.* 928
Reynolds, Al, Gen Mgr-Sls - Modern Track Machinery; *pg.* 98, *pg.* 610
Reynolds, Anthony, Product Mgr-TW & Traction Stores-NAPA Heavy Duty - Genuine Parts Company; *pg.* 206, *pg.* 506
Reynolds, Anthony, Product Mgr-TW & Traction Stores, NAPA Heavy Duty - National Automotive Parts Association; *pg.* 213, *pg.* 515
Reynolds, Ashley, Asst Product Mgr - Conair Corporation; *pg.* 505, *pg.* 1055
Reynolds, Brett W., VP-FE Products - FirstEnergy Corp.; *pg.* 1942, *pg.* 1400
Reynolds, Cami, Sr Mgr-Strategic Partnership Mktg - The Coca-Cola Company; *pg.* 240, *pg.* 493
Reynolds, Cheryl, VP-Comm, Adv & Brand Mgmt - American Institute of Certified Public Accountants Inc.; *pg.* 129, *pg.* 1192
Reynolds, Chris, VP-Data & Mktg Analytics - Conde Nast Publications, Inc.; *pg.* 1629, *pg.* 1217
Reynolds, Chris, Sr Assoc Brand Mgr-DEPEND - Kimberly-Clark Corporation; *pg.* 1461, *pg.* 1720
Reynolds, Chris, Mgr-eMail Mktg - Lands' End, Inc.; *pg.* 1776, *pg.* 1857
Reynolds, Christopher, VP-Data & Mktg Analytics - Conde Nast Digital; *pg.* 1237, *pg.* 1217
Reynolds, Cindy, Dir-Mktg Comm - Attachmate Corporation; *pg.* 356, *pg.* 1833
Reynolds, Dan, Dir-Social Media Strategy - Disney Interactive Media Group; *pg.* 1239, *pg.* 95
Reynolds, Dan, Mgr-Digital Mktg Ops - The Schwan Food Company; *pg.* 894, *pg.* 928
Reynolds, Dana, Sr Mgr-Global Assoc Comm - Wal-Mart.com; *pg.* 1287, *pg.* 50
Reynolds, Deidre, Mgr-Mktg Comm - Mack-Cali Realty Corporation; *pg.* 1102, *pg.* 1056
Reynolds, Gavin, Program Mgr-Mktg - IBM; *pg.* 410, *pg.* 1449
Reynolds, Jennifer, Dir-Integrated Consumer Mktg & ECommerce - eBay Inc.; *pg.* 1240, *pg.* 243
Reynolds, Jim, Sr VP-Mktg, R&D - Wells Enterprises, Inc.; *pg.* 909, *pg.* 709
Reynolds, Katie, Coord-Social Media - Taco Bell Corp.; *pg.* 1752, *pg.* 117
Reynolds, Kim A., Sr VP & Gen Mgr-Mdsg - rue21, inc.; *pg.* 32, *pg.* 1591
Reynolds, Kimberly, Mgr-Media & Community Rels - Publix Super Markets, Inc.; *pg.* 1031, *pg.* 437
Reynolds, Marty, Category Dir-Mktg - TreeHouse Foods, Inc.; *pg.* 901, *pg.* 649
Reynolds, Meg, Sr Mgr-Mktg Campaign Plng - Recreational Equipment, Inc.; *pg.* 1843, *pg.* 1821
Reynolds, Mike, Exec VP-Products & Solutions-Consumer Div - Blackhawk Engagement Solutions, Inc.; *pg.* 1232, *pg.* 1725
Reynolds, Ned, Dir-Media Rels-Americas - GE Capital; *pg.* 761, *pg.* 362
Reynolds, Rich, Chief Strategy Officer-EPG - Microsoft Corporation; *pg.* 435, *pg.* 1824
Reynolds, Sheri, VP-Sls - MicroBilt Corporation; *pg.* 782, *pg.* 534
Reynolds, Terry, Sr Dir-Pro & Global Scouting - Reds Baseball Partners, LLC; *pg.* 578, *pg.* 1425
Reynoso, Beth, Head-Mktg-Signature Client Grp - AT&T Communications Corp.; *pg.* 1866, *pg.* 1043
Rezek, Richard, Mgr-Svcs Mktg-Global - General Electric Company; *pg.* 1297, *pg.* 347
Rezendes, Jon, Mgr-Trade Mktg - Ocean Spray Cranberries, Inc.; *pg.* 887, *pg.* 827
Rezk, Adel, Reg Sr Mgr-Mktg-Retention & Competition - Comcast Corporation; *pg.* 276, *pg.* 1560
Rezka, Kevin, Acct Mgr-Northeast Sls - Dell Inc.; *pg.* 383, *pg.* 1737
Reznicek, David, Mgr-Product Plng - Deere & Company; *pg.* 703, *pg.* 632
Reznick, Mike, Mgr-Social Media Res - ESPN, Inc.; *pg.* 285, *pg.* 340
Rhadigan, Terry, Exec Dir-Product & Tech Comm - General Motors Company; *pg.* 175, *pg.* 881
Rhee, Stephen, VP-Adv Sls-Natl - A&E Television Networks, LLC; *pg.* 267, *pg.* 1185
Rhew, Thuy, Dir-Sls & Insights - Central Garden & Pet Company; *pg.* 1475, *pg.* 303
Rhine, Greg S., VP-Sls & Mktg Americas & Global OEM - Logitech Inc.; *pg.* 1264, *pg.* 164
Rhines, Donna, Dir-Mktg - Nuance Transcription; *pg.* 1576, *pg.* 516
Rhoades, Craig, VP-Customer Svcs, Mktg & Distr Svcs - American Electric Power Service Corporation; *pg.* 1934, *pg.* 1437
Rhoades, David, Dir-Mktg-Consumer Brands - Dawn Food Products, Inc.; *pg.* 1018, *pg.* 893
Rhoades, Jeffrey, Mgr-Mktg Comm-Global - The Lubrizol Corporation; *pg.* 1171, *pg.* 1481
Rhoades, Susan, VP-Retail Sls & Mktg - Armstrong World Industries, Inc.; *pg.* 914, *pg.* 1545
Rhoads, Bryan, Mgr-Social Media-Global - Intel Corporation; *pg.* 645, *pg.* 266
Rhoads, Matthew, Mgr-Dealer Mktg - Mazda North American Operations; *pg.* 183, *pg.* 113
Rhodes, Alison, Head-Promo Compliance-Promotional Matls Compliance - GlaxoSmithKline; *pg.* 1536, *pg.* 1389
Rhodes, Ashley, Sr Coord-Search Engine Mktg-Paid Search - CarMax, Inc.; *pg.* 167, *pg.* 1800
Rhodes, Bob, VP-Sls Plng & Ops - Ricoh Americas Corp.; *pg.* 462, *pg.* 538
Rhodes, Brian, VP-Dev & Product Mgr - TaxSlayer LLC; *pg.* 808, *pg.* 532
Rhodes, Harry, VP-Sls - Maui Jim, Inc.; *pg.* 9, *pg.* 651
Rhodes, Karen, Mgr-Energy Efficiency Mktg - Xcel Energy Inc.; *pg.* 1955, *pg.* 946
Rhodes, Kyle, Sr Mgr-Shopper & Retail Insights - Samsung Telecommunications America, LLC; *pg.* 670, *pg.* 1736
Rhodes, Laura, Mgr-Thought Leadership-Natl Sls Mktg - Genworth Financial, Inc.; *pg.* 761, *pg.* 1802
Rhodes, Paul, VP-Mktg - IDI Composites International; *pg.* 57, *pg.* 696
Rhodes, Rachel, Brand Mgr-Huggies Diapers - Kimberly-Clark Corporation; *pg.* 1461, *pg.* 1720
Rhodes, William H., Reg Mgr-Mktg - McDonald's Corporation; *pg.* 1737, *pg.* 645
Rhonehouse, Eric, VP-Retail Sls - Makita U.S.A., Inc.; *pg.* 1358, *pg.* 120
Rhoten, Brandon, VP-Digital & Social Media - The Wendy's Company; *pg.* 1755, *pg.* 1450
Rhoten, Brandon, VP-Digital & Social Media - Wendy's International, Inc.; *pg.* 1755, *pg.* 1451
Rhoton, Vince, Sr VP-Sls & Mktg - Lifetime Products Inc.; *pg.* 933, *pg.* 1751
Rhy, Amber, Supvr-Mktg - 3M Company; *pg.* 1142, *pg.* 956
Rhyan, Megan, Mgr-Mktg-Branding Programs & Sponsorships - NCR Corporation; *pg.* 443, *pg.* 531
Rhyasen, Dan, Mgr-Campaign Mktg Team-Franklin Templeton Investments - FRANKLIN RESOURCES, INC.; *pg.* 760, *pg.* 254
Rhyne, Daren, Brand Mgr - NIKE, Inc.; *pg.* 1812, *pg.* 1492
Ribaudo, Mark, Sr Dir-Search Mktg-Global - Pitney Bowes Inc.; *pg.* 454, *pg.* 376
Ribeiro, Rita, Sr Mgr-Digital Mktg-Global - Abbott Laboratories; *pg.* 1484, *pg.* 551
Ribet, Blaise, Principal & Product Mgr - Oracle Corporation; *pg.* 450, *pg.* 191
Ribolzi, Lindsay, Mgr-Mktg Innovation - PepsiCo, Inc.; *pg.* 259, *pg.* 1327
Ribolzi, Peter, Mgr-Mktg-Global Brand - Zebra Technologies Corporation; *pg.* 690, *pg.* 628
Ricard, Ron, Sr Mgr-Mktg Analytics - Forrester Research, Inc.; *pg.* 1642, *pg.* 807
Ricardez, Rolando, Mgr-Mktg - Citigroup Inc.; *pg.* 735, *pg.* 1212
Ricca, Arnaldo, VP-Sls-Danfoss Drives North America - Danfoss Graham; *pg.* 203, *pg.* 1874
Riccardi, John J., Dir-Sls-Terahertz - ADVANCED PHOTONIX, INC.; *pg.* 1398, *pg.* 865
Riccardi, Laurie, Supvr-Mktg - Six Flags Entertainment Corporation; *pg.* 583, *pg.* 1698
Ricci, Carolyn, Sr Product Mgr-New Platform Growth Initiatives - Zebra Technologies Corporation; *pg.* 690, *pg.* 628
Ricci, Davide, Dir-Product Mgmt & Open Source Platforms - Wind River Systems, Inc.; *pg.* 493, *pg.* 38
Ricci, Karen, Sr Mgr-Event-Americas - Motorola Mobility LLC; *pg.* 657, *pg.* 627
Ricci, Lisa, VP-Mktg - Interiors by Steven G Inc.; *pg.* 929, *pg.* 459
Ricciardelli, Michael, Sr VP-Bus Dev & Consumer Mktg - Bankrate, Inc.; *pg.* 1231, *pg.* 451
Riccio, Jim, Dir-Creative - Subway Restaurants; *pg.* 1751, *pg.* 356
Riccioni, Jerry, Sr VP-Retail Sls - Old World Industries, Inc.; *pg.* 1175, *pg.* 641
Ricco, Anthony, VP-Demand Mktg-Worldwide - Citrix Systems, Inc.; *pg.* 375, *pg.* 424
Ricco, Whitney, Program Specialist-Mktg - Sunoco Inc.; *pg.* 985, *pg.* 1571
Rice, Betsy, Asst Dir-Field Mktg - The Northwestern Mutual Life Insurance Company; *pg.* 1212, *pg.* 1879
Rice, Christopher, Sr Mgr-Digital Design & Content Strategy - Samsung Electronics America, Inc.; *pg.* 669, *pg.* 1115
Rice, Corianne, Asst VP-Global Sls Trng - Legg Mason, Inc.; *pg.* 775, *pg.* 758
Rice, Dan, Product Mgr-Measuring Tools - Robert Bosch Tool Corp; *pg.* 1060, *pg.* 634
Rice, Eric, Sr Mgr-Sls Ops & Mgr-Customer Mktg-Private Brands - Del Monte Foods, Inc.; *pg.* 852, *pg.* 304
Rice, Jeff, Sr Dir-Ethical Sourcing Governance - Wal-Mart.com; *pg.* 1287, *pg.* 50
Rice, Jenna, Sr Mgr-Social Media - Motorola Mobility LLC; *pg.* 657, *pg.* 627
Rice, Jennifer, VP & Sr Dir-Res - Neogen Corporation; *pg.* 883, *pg.* 896
Rice, Kari, Brand Mgr - Mountain Hardwear, Inc.; *pg.* 1839, *pg.* 193
Rice, Keith, Mgr-Online Mktg - CME Group Inc.; *pg.* 738, *pg.* 571
Rice, Meghan, Sr Assoc Brand Mgr - Wm. Wrigley Jr.

First page reference indicates Business Class Edition
Second page reference indicates Geographic Edition

Company; pg. 1863, pg. 596
Rice, Norman, Exec VP-Global Mktg & Corp Dev - Extreme Networks Inc; pg. 287, pg. 245
Rice, Paul, Sr VP-Consumer Mktg Production - Bank of America Corporation; pg. 718, pg. 1362
Rice, Rich, Sr Dir-Media Rels - Rangers Baseball LLC; pg. 578, pg. 1659
Rice, Roland, VP-Sls-US Comml Bus - Plantronics, Inc.; pg. 663, pg. 270
Rice, Spencer, VP-Mktg - SoulCycle Holdings LLC; pg. 1845, pg. 1294
Rice, Stephanie, Dir-Ad Sls Mktg - Screenvision Cinema Network LLC; pg. 581, pg. 1290
Rice, Tara, Mgr-Interactive Mktg - Tennant Company; pg. 1381, pg. 944
Ricevuto, Asleigh, Asst Mgr-Healthcare Mktg - Kao Brands Co. Inc.; pg. 513, pg. 1415
Rich, Allegra, Sr Dir-Brand Identity - Comcast Cable Communications, Inc.; pg. 276, pg. 1560
Rich, Andre, Gen Mgr-Apparel & Mktg - Kmart Corporation; pg. 1775, pg. 617
Rich, Blair, Exec VP-Mktg - Warner Bros. Entertainment Inc.; pg. 319, pg. 54
Rich, David, Sr VP-Sls, Bus Dev & Info Svcs-Global - MasterCard Worldwide Inc.; pg. 780, pg. 988
Rich, Lisa, Assoc Mgr-Mktg Comm - LifeCell Corporation; pg. 1556, pg. 1045
Rich, Michael, Sr Mgr-Mktg - Cisco Systems, Inc.; pg. 372, pg. 240
Rich, Saundra, Dir-Field Mktg - Jura-Capresso Inc.; pg. 58, pg. 1052
Rich, Scott, VP & Sr Mgr-Mktg-Consumer Banking Digital Mktg - JPMorgan Chase & Co.; pg. 772, pg. 1246
Rich, Tiffany, Sr Media Buyer & Planner - CACI International Inc.; pg. 367, pg. 1773
Richard, Henri, Sr VP-Commercial Sls & Support-Worldwide - SanDisk Corporation; pg. 465, pg. 147
Richard, Lisa, VP-Sls & Customer Rels - Starkey Laboratories, Inc.; pg. 1597, pg. 923
Richard, Michelle J., Mgr-CRM & Loyalty Mktg-Optical Brands - Luxottica Group; pg. 8, pg. 1323
Richard-Craven, Jordan, Brand Mgr-MAKERS - AOL Inc.; pg. 1229, pg. 1195
Richards, Al, Mgr-Info Mgmt & Healthcare Mktg - CommVault Systems, Inc.; pg. 377, pg. 1125
Richards, Ann-Marie, Coord-Mktg - PepsiCo, Inc.; pg. 259, pg. 1327
Richards, Bryan, Dir-Mktg Svcs - Meijer, Inc.; pg. 1779, pg. 888
Richards, Cassidy, Sr Dir-Strategic Alliances - March of Dimes Birth Defects Foundation; pg. 146, pg. 1354
Richards, Cindy, Sr Acct Exec-Adv - Merle Norman Cosmetics, Inc.; pg. 517, pg. 136
Richards, Dane, Dir-Creative-Global - Columbia Sportswear Company; pg. 1830, pg. 1501
Richards, Daniel, Mng Dir & Head-Media-Global - Citigroup Inc.; pg. 735, pg. 1212
Richards, Dawne, Sr VP-Linear Products - Rentrak Corporation; pg. 306, pg. 1506
Richards, Douglas, VP-Sls - Weibel, Inc.; pg. 1972, pg. 122
Richards, Ian, Coord-Mktg Campaign - IBM Canada Limited; pg. 411, pg. 1923
Richards, John E., Sr Dir - Alliance of Confessing Evangelicals, Inc.; pg. 126, pg. 1545
Richards, Julie, Mgr-Mktg & Comm-North America - Raytheon Company; pg. 233, pg. 854
Richards, Kevin, Dir-Mktg-Whiskeys & Specialty Brands - Sazerac Company, Inc.; pg. 1969, pg. 745
Richards, Kris, Dir-Online Sls - Robb Report; pg. 1681, pg. 142
Richards, Laura, Mgr-Comm-Mktg Promos & Comm-Grp Benefits & Retirement Solutions - Manulife Financial Corporation; pg. 778, pg. 1939
Richards, Megan, Mgr-Mktg Strategy - Nordstrom, Inc.; pg. 1779, pg. 1837
Richards, Nicole, Dir-Sls Ops - Smarter Travel Media LLC; pg. 1687, pg. 801
Richards, Paul, Mgr-Sls - Setra Systems, Inc.; pg. 1428, pg. 802
Richards, Susan, Sr Mgr-Internal Comm - Symantec Corporation; pg. 478, pg. 161
Richards, Ticole, Sr VP-Mktg-Intl - The Walt Disney Company; pg. 317, pg. 52
Richards, Todd, VP-Insights & Innovation-Discovery Digital Media - Discovery Communications, Inc.; pg. 282, pg. 777
Richards-Person, Melissa, VP-Global Field Mktg - Papa John's International, Inc.; pg. 1743, pg. 737
Richardsen, Donna, Dir-Integrated Mktg Comm-North America - Colgate-Palmolive Company; pg. 504, pg. 1215
Richardson, Beth, Dir-Creative Content - The Upper Room; pg. 1698, pg. 1655
Richardson, Courtney, Sr Mgr-Brand Strategy & Insights - Carhartt, Inc.; pg. 39, pg. 875
Richardson, Denise, Mgr-Small Bus Mktg - Manulife Financial Corporation; pg. 778, pg. 1939
Richardson, Diane, Sr Mgr-Mktg Category & Strategic Sourcing-Global - Amgen Inc.; pg. 1493, pg. 291
Richardson, Emily, Mgr-Mktg Comm-Global - AGCO Corporation; pg. 700, pg. 530
Richardson, Hal, Pres-Home Media Distr & Paramount Pictures - Paramount Pictures Corporation; pg. 304, pg. 138
Richardson, Karen, Writer-Mktg - Environmental Systems Research Institute Inc.; pg. 393, pg. 188
Richardson, Leisha, Dir-Mktg - ACI Worldwide Inc.; pg. 341, pg. 1010
Richardson, Linda W., Sr Dir-Mktg - MetroPCS, Inc.; pg. 1872, pg. 1683
Richardson, Mark, VP-Adv Sls-Southeast Reg - Scripps Networks Interactive, Inc.; pg. 1279, pg. 1638
Richardson, Marnie, Mgr-New Media - National Arts Centre Corporation; pg. 566, pg. 1932
Richardson, Michael, VP-Mdsg - The Gap, Inc.; pg. 1770, pg. 218
Richardson, Mike, VP-Mktg - Casey's General Stores, Inc.; pg. 1017, pg. 701
Richardson, Patty, Mgr-Sls - Witt Industries, Inc.; pg. 1140, pg. 1461
Richardson, Paul, Sr Dir-Chemistry - CooperVision, Inc.; pg. 1407, pg. 1159
Richardson, Peter C., Dir-Printer Mktg EBD - Samsung Electronics America, Inc.; pg. 669, pg. 1115
Richardson, Ryan, Mgr-Digital Media - BUFFALO WILD WINGS, INC.; pg. 1718, pg. 931
Richardson, Stephanie, Sr Mgr-ECommerce - AT&T Mobility LLC; pg. 619, pg. 488
Richardson, Susan, Mgr-Mktg - Friedrich Air Conditioning Co.; pg. 1072, pg. 1740
Richardson, Tom, VP-Mktg & Sls - Cupid Foundations, Inc.; pg. 22, pg. 1220
Richardson, Tricia D., VP-New Product Dev - Helen of Troy L.P.; pg. 511, pg. 1692
Richardson, Yolanda R., Chief Deputy Exec Dir-Strategy, Mktg & Product Dev - Covered California; pg. 1519, pg. 196
Richenberg, Tim, Sr VP-Sls - Constellation Brands, Inc.; pg. 1960, pg. 1348
Richens, Stuart, Grp VP-Digital Media - Network Communications Inc.; pg. 1271, pg. 534
Richer, Joseph T., Dir-Sls & Mktg Compliance-Medicare - Anthem, Inc.; pg. 1192, pg. 683
Richeson, Brian, VP-Sls & Svc - Tampa Bay Rays Baseball, Ltd.; pg. 586, pg. 464
Richey, Mark, Sr Mgr-Mktg - Skyworks Solutions, Inc.; pg. 674, pg. 862
Richie, Dave, Sr Dir-GSS Sls - KLA-Tencor Corporation; pg. 1353, pg. 146
Richman, Cathy, Dir-Mktg Comm - Zimmer Biomet Holdings, Inc.; pg. 1611, pg. 699
Richman, Donald, Dir-Mktg & Bus Dev - Avant; pg. 717, pg. 566
Richman, Gary, Dir-Product Mgmt - Intel Corporation; pg. 645, pg. 266
Richman, Jason, Head-Product-Monetization - Spotify; pg. 1282, pg. 1295
Richmond, Alison, Dir-Mktg & Comm - On Assignment, Inc.; pg. 449, pg. 56
Richmond, Angela, Dir-PR - St. Jude Children's Research Hospital; pg. 1596, pg. 1646
Richmond, Chris, Dir-Shopper Mktg & Brand Promo - Post Holdings, Inc.; pg. 833, pg. 1002
Richmond, Kara, Mgr-Retail Mktg - The Men's Wearhouse, Inc.; pg. 44, pg. 1711
Richmond, Lauren, Mgr-Mktg - Brown-Forman Corporation; pg. 1958, pg. 732
Richmond, Linda, Media Planner & Media Buyer - SUPERVALU, Inc.; pg. 1035, pg. 924
Richmond, Martha, Mgr-Corp Mktg & Media Rels - Port of Portland; pg. 1920, pg. 1505
Richter, Brandon, Planner-Sls - Pandora Media Inc.; pg. 1273, pg. 172
Richter, Carolyn, Program Mgr-Mktg - International Business Machines Corporation; pg. 418, pg. 1138
Richter, Lisa, Dir-Mktg - ISSA; pg. 145, pg. 640
Richter, Michael, Chief Privacy Officer-Product & Mktg - Facebook, Inc.; pg. 1245, pg. 143
Richter, Paige, Brand Mgr - Kao Brands Co. Inc.; pg. 513, pg. 1415
Richter, Scott, Mgr-Retail Mktg-Dodge - FCA US LLC; pg. 170, pg. 868
Rick, Michele, Dir-Direct Mktg - The ServiceMaster Company, LLC; pg. 335, pg. 1646
Rick, Milissa, Dir-Mktg & Consumer Activation-Global - Pacific Cycle Inc.; pg. 1709, pg. 1867
Rickabaugh, Joe, Dir-Field Mgmt & Seedstock Mktg - American Hereford Association; pg. 129, pg. 980
Ricker, Kacie, Reg VP-Mktg - Coldwell Banker Residential Brokerage; pg. 1087, pg. 850
Rickerd, Nancy, Sr Mgr-Mktg - AT&T Communications Corp.; pg. 1866, pg. 1043
Rickerd, Nancy, Sr Mgr-Mktg - AT&T Inc.; pg. 1867, pg. 1674
Rickerd, Nancy, Sr Mgr-Mktg - AT&T Mobility LLC; pg. 620, pg. 1152
Ricketts, Althea, Sr Dir-Ops-Global Mktg & Sls - Shure Incorporated; pg. 672, pg. 638
Ricketts, Mark, VP-Alcohol Products - Grain Processing Corporation; pg. 859, pg. 709
Ricketts, Russell, Assoc Mgr-Mktg - E&J Gallo Winery; pg. 1962, pg. 149
Rickling, Lelia, Assoc Mgr-Consumer Acq Mktg - Cars.com; pg. 1234, pg. 568
Rickord, Troy F., Head-Customer Mktg - Honeywell International Inc.; pg. 407, pg. 1088
Ricks, Hunter, Strategist-Digital Mktg - Lincoln Financial Group; pg. 1206, pg. 1375
Ricotta, Lindsay, Mgr-Mktg-LensCrafters - Luxottica Retail; pg. 8, pg. 1460
Riddle, Danny, Sr Dir-Field Ops - Coca-Cola Bottling Co. Consolidated; pg. 240, pg. 1365
Riddle, John, VP-Sls - LG Electronics U.S.A., Inc.; pg. 651, pg. 1060
Riddle, Rich, Dir-Mktg-Sensipar Promos - Amgen Inc.; pg. 1493, pg. 291
Ridel, Kim, Brand Mgr-Tactical-Riding Lawn Equipment - Deere & Company; pg. 703, pg. 632
Ridel, Lenny, Sr Dir-Product Dev - F5 Networks, Inc.; pg. 396, pg. 1835
Ridenour, Denise, Analyst-PR - Kelly Services, Inc.; pg. 424, pg. 911
Ridenour, Richard, Mgr-Sls-Natl - ITW Magnaflux; pg. 1418, pg. 615
Ridens, Cortney, Reg Dir-Mktg - Meritage Homes Corporation; pg. 97, pg. 23
Rideout, Dora, Brand Mgr - The Hartz Mountain Corp.; pg. 1476, pg. 1120
Rider, Michelle, Head-Affinity Mktg - Aetna Inc.; pg. 1187, pg. 351
Ridge, Stuart, Sr VP-Site Optimization & Mktg - Provide Commerce, Inc.; pg. 1276, pg. 206
Ridgeway, Rick, VP-Environmental Initiatives & Special Media Projects - Patagonia; pg. 31, pg. 301
Ridgley, Karima, Sr Dir-Global Mktg & Creative-oldnavy.com - The Gap, Inc.; pg. 1770, pg. 218
Ridgway-Barnes, Jessica, Mgr-Mktg-Distr - Philips Electronics North America; pg. 662, pg. 782
Ridinger, Christy, Dir-Adv - Times Record News; pg. 1695, pg. 1749
Ridjaneck, Matt, Mgr-Sls-Global - Smithfield Foods, Inc.; pg. 896, pg. 1806
Ridley, Dave, Sr VP-Mktg & Revenue Mgmt - Southwest Airlines Co.; pg. 1923, pg. 1687
Ridout, Annette, Rep-Adv - PADI Americas; pg. 573, pg. 188
Ridout, Tammy, Mgr-Media Rels & Policy Comm - American Electric Power Company, Inc.; pg. 1934, pg. 1437
Riebau, Timothy, VP-Product Sls - J.J. Keller & Associates, Inc.; pg. 1654, pg. 1883
Riebock, Paul, VP-Enterprise Sls - NetMotion Wireless, Inc.; pg. 445, pg. 1837
Riecks, Stacey, Sr Dir-Category Mgmt & Shopper Insights - Keurig Green Mountain, Inc.; pg. 868, pg. 1768
Riedel, Dennis, Product Mgr - Meritor, Inc.; pg. 212, pg. 911
Rieder, Derek, Sr Product Mgr-CREON - Abbott Laboratories; pg. 1484, pg. 551
Riediger, Jenna, Sr Mgr-Market-Consumer Spend - MTS Systems Corporation; pg. 442, pg. 923
Riegal, Nick, Sr Dir-Brand & Mktg Comm - Tervis Tumbler

Company; *pg.* 1890, *pg.* 477
Riegel, Kelleri, Product Mgr-DIFM Svcs - Web.com Group, Inc.; *pg.* 1288, *pg.* 435
Riegel, Kelleri, Product Mgr-Online Mktg Grp - Web.com, Inc.; *pg.* 1288, *pg.* 524
Riegel, Mark, VP-Brand & Channel Mktg - Ferrara Candy Co.; *pg.* 1852, *pg.* 612
Riegel, Mike, VP-Mktg - Cisco Systems, Inc.; *pg.* 372, *pg.* 240
Riego, Magnolia, Dir-Bus Ops, Global Mktg & Comml Dev - Pfizer Inc.; *pg.* 1581, *pg.* 1278
Riehl, Christian, VP-Production - Telemundo Network Inc.; *pg.* 311, *pg.* 430
Riehl, Larry, Dir-Mktg Svcs & Dev - Manulife Financial Corporation; *pg.* 778, *pg.* 1939
Riehle, Norma, Mgr-Design-B2B Strategic Mktg - NRG Energy, Inc.; *pg.* 1948, *pg.* 1712
Rieke, Diane, Mgr-Mktg Comm - Grain Processing Corporation; *pg.* 859, *pg.* 709
Riemma, Nicolo, Dir-Global Media Strategy & Plng - Clinique Laboratories LLC; *pg.* 503, *pg.* 1214
Riendeau, Brian, Mgr-Adv - General Motors of Canada Ltd.; *pg.* 177, *pg.* 1931
Riera, Shelly, Dir-Consumer Adv - AT&T; *pg.* 1865, *pg.* 258
Ries, Bob, Mgr-Lead Product - Thermo Fisher Scientific Inc.; *pg.* 1431, *pg.* 854
Ries, Brad, Mgr-Channel Mktg - Lenovo Group Ltd; *pg.* 427, *pg.* 1384
Ries, Brian, Sr Mgr-Mktg-Data Tech & Svcs - The Toro Company; *pg.* 1065, *pg.* 918
Ries, Janet, Head-Global Mktg - The Rockport Group; *pg.* 1818, *pg.* 812
Ries, Michael, Mgr-Application Sls-Midwest Oracle Mktg Cloud TeamOracle - Oracle Corporation; *pg.* 1272, *pg.* 786
Ries, Stacy, Sr Dir-Mktg - SAP; *pg.* 465, *pg.* 78
Rieselman, John, Dir-Media - OMG, Inc.; *pg.* 1367, *pg.* 781
Riesenbach, Larry, Mgr-Mktg Intelligence - Nestle USA, Inc.; *pg.* 883, *pg.* 96
Rieser, Susan, Sr Mgr-Print Production - Lane Bryant; *pg.* 1776, *pg.* 1441
Riess, Dan, Exec VP-Integrated Mktg & Branded Content - Turner Broadcasting System, Inc.; *pg.* 314, *pg.* 521
Rietcheck, Jennette, Mgr-Mktg-Food Animal Bus - Bayer Corporation; *pg.* 1499, *pg.* 1573
Riethmiller, Alex, VP-Comm-NFL Media - National Football League; *pg.* 567, *pg.* 1264
Rietze, Paul, Dir-Compute Platform Solutions & Advanced Technical Sls - Intel Corporation; *pg.* 645, *pg.* 266
Rievman, Randi, Dir-Mktg - Bayer HealthCare Pharmaceutical Division; *pg.* 1500, *pg.* 1132
Rife, Justin, Mgr-Mktg - totes Isotoner Corporation; *pg.* 14, *pg.* 1426
Riff, Adam, VP-Digital Mktg - The ADT Corporation; *pg.* 612, *pg.* 409
Rigali, Aniela, Asst Mgr-Social Media - American Honda Motor Co., Inc.; *pg.* 163, *pg.* 292
Rigano Steinberg, Linda, Exec Dir-Media Rels - Thomas Publishing Company LLC; *pg.* 1692, *pg.* 1299
Rigano, Ed, Sr VP-Sls - Stern-Leach; *pg.* 1064, *pg.* 783
Rigazio, Alexander, Rep-Growth Sls - Republic Services, Inc.; *pg.* 107, *pg.* 19
Rigby, Bill, VP-Bus Dev & Digital Media-US Media Grp - International Data Group; *pg.* 1653, *pg.* 796
Rigel, Asten, Mgr-Social Media - Rite Aid Corporation; *pg.* 1590, *pg.* 1519
Riggert, Doug, Reg Mgr-Sls - Lincoln Financial Group; *pg.* 1206, *pg.* 1375
Riggins, Rosy, Program Mgr-Mktg - Wells Fargo & Company; *pg.* 819, *pg.* 232
Riggins, Tom, Sr VP-Mktg & Sls - R.A. Jones & Co.; *pg.* 1371, *pg.* 704
Riggio, John G., Dir-Adv - The New York Times Company; *pg.* 1668, *pg.* 1270
Riggs, Ashley, Coord-Mktg Comm - QUALCOMM Incorporated; *pg.* 1873, *pg.* 207
Riggs, Jennifer L., Sr Product Mgr - J.C. Penney Company, Inc.; *pg.* 1774, *pg.* 1732
Riggs, Jessica, Sr Specialist-PR & Analyst Rels - Epicor Software Corporation; *pg.* 393, *pg.* 110
Riggs, Kelli, Sr Mgr-Mktg - Comcast Corporation; *pg.* 276, *pg.* 1560
Righter, Jonhenry, Sr Designer-Technical-HCI D+E & Digital Products - Home Box Office, Inc.; *pg.* 290, *pg.* 1240
Rigney, Christopher, Brand Dir-Integration-Nike Sports Mktg - NIKE, Inc.; *pg.* 1812, *pg.* 1492
Rigney, James, Dir-Mktg - Red Bull North America, Inc.; *pg.* 264, *pg.* 275
Rigney, Lou, Sr Mgr-Market Mgmt - Cisco Systems, Inc.; *pg.* 372, *pg.* 240
Rigney, Melissa, Sr Mgr-Mktg-Svc Provider - NetApp, Inc.; *pg.* 444, *pg.* 287
Rigodanzo, Joe, Mgr-Svcs Mktg - Cisco Systems, Inc.; *pg.* 372, *pg.* 240
Rigolini, Brandon, Mgr-East Coast Reg Mktg - California Pizza Kitchen Inc.; *pg.* 1720, *pg.* 127
Rigopulos, Alex, Chm & Chief Creative Officer - Harmonix Music Systems, Inc.; *pg.* 1256, *pg.* 808
Rigotti, Kelly, Sr Mgr-Mktg Comm - Microsoft Corporation; *pg.* 435, *pg.* 1824
Rijks, Ralph, Sr VP-Mktg - Heineken USA Inc.; *pg.* 252, *pg.* 1352
Rijsinghani, Vikas, Sr VP-Online Mktg - Web.com Group, Inc.; *pg.* 1288, *pg.* 435
Rijsinghani, Vikas, Sr VP-Online Mktg - Web.com, Inc.; *pg.* 1288, *pg.* 524
Rikkinen, Nicole, VP-Mktg - PlayNetwork, Inc.; *pg.* 577, *pg.* 1829
Riley, Chasity, Coord-Sls & Mktg-Intl - Heaven Hill Distilleries, Inc.; *pg.* 1964, *pg.* 725
Riley, David, Exec Dir-Corp Mktg & PR - The NPD Group, Inc.; *pg.* 1672, *pg.* 1323
Riley, Erin, VP-Mktg-Global - Cole-Haan LLC; *pg.* 1806, *pg.* 1034
Riley, Erin, Dir-Sls - Kind LLC; *pg.* 868, *pg.* 1249
Riley, Francis, Sr VP-Intl Sls & Ops - Norwegian Cruise Line; *pg.* 1917, *pg.* 444
Riley, Jim, Mgr-Mktg - Columbus Blue Jackets; *pg.* 542, *pg.* 1439
Riley, Katie, Specialist-Social & Digital Media Mktg - The Progressive Corporation; *pg.* 1214, *pg.* 1463
Riley, Kellen, Mgr-Market-Crude Oil & Refined Petroleum Products - CSX Corporation; *pg.* 1904, *pg.* 432
Riley, Kevin C., Sr VP-Sls - Digi International Inc.; *pg.* 387, *pg.* 948
Riley, Lisa, Mgr-PR - Orange Leaf Frozen Yogurt; *pg.* 1742, *pg.* 1487
Riley, Lucia, Brand Mgr & Mgr-Creative - SAS Institute Inc.; *pg.* 466, *pg.* 1361
Riley, Martha, Sr VP-Music Grp & Brand Sls - Viacom Inc.; *pg.* 316, *pg.* 1310
Riley, Melissa, VP-Sls & Svcs - Destination DC; *pg.* 991, *pg.* 398
Riley, Mike, VP-Brand Franchise Dev, Content Strategy, Distr & Mktg - MATTEL, INC.; *pg.* 962, *pg.* 81
Riley, Peggy, Dir-Southeast Sls - Louisville Convention & Visitors Bureau; *pg.* 998, *pg.* 736
Riley, Randall H., Dir-Mktg-Intl - Citizens Inc.; *pg.* 1197, *pg.* 1661
Riley, Roger, Sr Dir-Team Travel - Arizona Diamondbacks; *pg.* 529, *pg.* 14
Riley, Sean, VP-Extended Care Mktg - McKesson Corporation; *pg.* 1560, *pg.* 222
Riley, Steve, Dir-Mktg - Dietz & Watson Inc.; *pg.* 853, *pg.* 1563
Riley, Valerie, Specialist-Social Media - Caleres, Inc.; *pg.* 1805, *pg.* 993
Riley, Will, Sr Dir-Brand Mgmt - Zaxby's Franchising, Inc.; *pg.* 1756, *pg.* 486
Rimmington, David, Dir-Sls-EMEA - SCIQUEST, INC.; *pg.* 468, *pg.* 1361
Rimolt, Christopher F., Sr Dir-Sls - Eli Lilly and Company; *pg.* 1527, *pg.* 684
Rinaldi, Bill, Acct Exec-Creative Svcs - E&J Gallo Winery; *pg.* 1962, *pg.* 149
Rinaldi, Frank, Sr Dir-Growth Channels & Ecommerce - Pinnacle Foods Group LLC; *pg.* 889, *pg.* 1104
Rinaldi, Lydia, Mgr-Mktg - The Hearst Corporation; *pg.* 1649, *pg.* 1239
Rincione, Jillian, Mgr-Publicity & PR - Starz Entertainment, LLC; *pg.* 310, *pg.* 327
Rind, Marc, VP-Product Dev - Automatic Data Processing, Inc.; *pg.* 357, *pg.* 1117
Rinder, Jerry, VP-Sls & Mktg - Woolrich, Inc.; *pg.* 699, *pg.* 1595
Rinderle, Robert, Dir-Digital Mktg & Comm - THE DOW CHEMICAL COMPANY; *pg.* 1157, *pg.* 898
Rindo, Richard, Dir-Mktg-Global Offset Solutions - Eastman Kodak Company; *pg.* 1408, *pg.* 1333
Rindoks, Kurt P., VP-Engrg & Product Dev - Kewaunee Scientific Corporation; *pg.* 931, *pg.* 1391
Rinehart, Harold, Mgr-Mktg ES&S - Marathon Petroleum Company LLC; *pg.* 981, *pg.* 1454
Rinehart, Richard, Corp Dir-Production - The McClatchy Company; *pg.* 1662, *pg.* 196
Rinehart, Stebbin, Dir-Mktg - Apollo Education Group Inc.; *pg.* 597, *pg.* 14
Riner, Craig, VP-Mktg - Rite Aid Corporation; *pg.* 1590, *pg.* 1519
Ring, Carolyn, Mgr-Acq Mktg - Copart, Inc.; *pg.* 168, *pg.* 86
Ring, Joshua, Acct Exec-Natl Sls - Gannett Co., Inc.; *pg.* 289, *pg.* 1681
Ring-Mussa, Megan, Dir-Sls & Mktg - SYS-Con Media, Inc.; *pg.* 1690, *pg.* 1134
Ringle, Jennifer, Mgr-Production - San Diego Symphony Orchestra Association; *pg.* 580, *pg.* 208
Ringler, Reed, Asst Dir-Mktg - Fasig-Tipton Co. Inc.; *pg.* 750, *pg.* 729
Ringstad, Jamie, Sr Mgr-Mktg - Microsoft Corporation; *pg.* 435, *pg.* 1824
Rini, Cheryl, Dir-Product Comm Regulatory Affairs - Vertex Pharmaceuticals Incorporated; *pg.* 1606, *pg.* 801
Rinke, Jeff, VP-Mktg - Hungry Howie's Pizza & Subs Inc.; *pg.* 1023, *pg.* 897
Rinkinen, Joseph, Product Mgr - Herman Miller, Inc.; *pg.* 926, *pg.* 913
Rinkus, Eileen, Dir-Mktg Comm - PODS Enterprises, Inc.; *pg.* 1919, *pg.* 416
Rinock, Angie, Specialist-PR - State Farm Mutual Automobile Insurance Co.; *pg.* 1218, *pg.* 557
Rintamaki, Jan, Mgr-Mktg - Polaris Industries Inc.; *pg.* 1709, *pg.* 928
Rioboli, Rick, VP-Metadata Products & Search Svcs-CoMPASS - Comcast Corporation; *pg.* 276, *pg.* 1560
Riojas, Christina, Mgr-Mktg - General Growth Properties, Inc.; *pg.* 1093, *pg.* 574
Riordan, Dennis F., CFO & Interim Pres-Flagstone Foods - TreeHouse Foods, Inc.; *pg.* 901, *pg.* 649
Riordan, Elizabeth, VP-Sls - NIC Inc.; *pg.* 445, *pg.* 718
Riordan, Robert, Sr VP-Sls - DIRECTV Group Holdings, LLC; *pg.* 281, *pg.* 79
Rios, Leslie, Mgr-Mktg Ops-West Div - Comcast Cable Communications, Inc.; *pg.* 276, *pg.* 1560
Rios, Leticia, Bus Mgr-Jaguar - The Collection, Inc.; *pg.* 168, *pg.* 418
Rios, Natashya, Dir-Product Mktg - Web.com Group, Inc.; *pg.* 1288, *pg.* 435
Rios, Ricardo, Mgr-Mktg-New Digital Products & Mobile - The New York Times; *pg.* 1668, *pg.* 1270
Ripani, Chris, Exec Dir-Mktg, Comml Stores - Bridgestone Americas, Inc.; *pg.* 201, *pg.* 1649
Ripke, Susan, VP-Mktg & Creative Svcs - VITAMIN SHOPPE, INC.; *pg.* 1608, *pg.* 1098
Ripley, Ken, Exec VP-Adv Sls - Al Jazeera America, LLC; *pg.* 269, *pg.* 1188
Ripley, Rich, VP-Integrated Mktg Solutions - Entravision Communications Corporation; *pg.* 285, *pg.* 273
Ripperger, Phil, VP-Sls-New Media Solutions - IRI Group; *pg.* 421, *pg.* 579
Rippey, Chris, Head-Indus-Fin Svcs Adv - Google Inc.; *pg.* 1249, *pg.* 153
Rippey, Meredith E., Sr Mgr-Adv-Global - Xerox Corporation; *pg.* 494, *pg.* 365
Ripple, John, Mgr-NGL Mktg - Anadarko Petroleum Corporation; *pg.* 971, *pg.* 1746
Ripps, Josh, VP-Sls & Consumer Markets - WebMD Health Corporation; *pg.* 1288, *pg.* 1313
Rippy, M. Paul, Reg Mgr-Sls - PPL Corporation; *pg.* 1950, *pg.* 1514
Risbrudt, Erik, Reg Mgr-Sls - Dr Pepper Snapple Group, Inc.; *pg.* 250, *pg.* 1729
Rise, Jim, VP & Gen Mgr-Entry Products Bus Unit - Xerox Corporation; *pg.* 494, *pg.* 365
Riser, Dave, VP-External Rels-Trade Mktg - R.J. Reynolds Tobacco Co.; *pg.* 1895, *pg.* 1395
Rishavy, Dave, Product Mgr - Rohde & Schwarz, Inc.; *pg.* 1428, *pg.* 768
Risi, Pete, Gen Mgr-Sls - The Collection, Inc.; *pg.* 168, *pg.* 418
Risinger, John, VP-Sls & Mktg - Discovery Communications, Inc.; *pg.* 282, *pg.* 777
Risis, Mark, Head-Strategy, Bus Dev & Mktg - TiVo Inc.; *pg.* 313, *pg.* 251
Rissmann, Carole, VP-Mktg - Beiersdorf North America Inc.; *pg.* 501, *pg.* 385
Ristow, Randy, Dir-Mktg & Analytics - The Allstate Corporation; *pg.* 1189, *pg.* 639

Ritchey, Dean, Reg Mgr-Sls - ITW Magnaflux; pg. 1418, pg. 615
Ritchie, Anna, Mgr-Social Media - The Sun Products Corporation; pg. 336, pg. 385
Ritchie, Bryan, Mgr-Mktg - Church & Dwight Canada Corp.; pg. 503, pg. 1925
Ritchie, Ian, Dir-Svcs Sls - Microsoft Corporation; pg. 435, pg. 1824
Ritchie, Nicole, Sr Dir-Comm-American Home Shield - The ServiceMaster Company, LLC; pg. 335, pg. 1646
Ritt, Allison, Sr Mgr-Direct Mktg - United States Cellular Corporation; pg. 1875, pg. 594
Rittenhouse, James, Dir-New Product Dev - National Molding, LLC; pg. 1887, pg. 430
Rittenhouse, Tim, Sr Specialist-Experiential Mktg-Sports - BMW of North America, LLC; pg. 166, pg. 1133
Ritter, Brandi J., Sr Program Mgr-Mktg Alliance - Lenovo Group Ltd; pg. 427, pg. 1384
Ritter, Glenn, VP-Sls & Supply Chain-Black Diamond Equipment - Black Diamond, Inc.; pg. 1827, pg. 1756
Ritter, Ingrid, Sr Mgr-Mktg-Healthcare Strategy - United Parcel Service, Inc.; pg. 1928, pg. 522
Ritter, Mike, Dir-Mktg - INVISTA B.V.; pg. 1168, pg. 723
Ritter, Paul, Dir-Creative - Glamour; pg. 1645, pg. 1235
Ritter, Scott, Exec Dir-Mktg Ops Europe-Bus Integration - Merck & Co., Inc.; pg. 1566, pg. 1077
Ritter, Stefanie, Coord-Mktg - Elizabeth Arden, Inc.; pg. 507, pg. 448
Rittmann, Mary, Dir-Travel Indus Mktg - Arizona Office of Tourism; pg. 988, pg. 14
Ritzberger, Carl, Sr Mgr-Strategic Mktg - Honeywell International Inc.; pg. 407, pg. 1088
Ritzel, Amy, Corp Dir-PR - Shriners Hospitals For Children; pg. 1594, pg. 475
Riva, Teresa, Brand Mgr-Global Hair Care Front End Innovation - The Procter & Gamble Company; pg. 1129, pg. 1418
Rivage, Ken, Brand Mgr-Component - Lenovo Group Ltd; pg. 427, pg. 1384
Rivard, Jonathan, Mgr-Mktg Ops - Subaru of America, Inc.; pg. 191, pg. 1050
Rivas, Alexandria, Coord-Mktg - Tommy Bahama; pg. 48, pg. 1842
Rivas, Felipe, Sr Mgr-Bus Analytics - DIRECTV Group Holdings, LLC; pg. 281, pg. 79
Rivas, Nieves, Dir-Creative - Bovie Medical Corporation; pg. 1402, pg. 1178
Riveiro, Jason, Mgr-Multicultural Brand Mktg - Big Lots, Inc.; pg. 1762, pg. 1438
Rivell, Christian, Dir-Online Mktg - QVC Inc; pg. 305, pg. 1593
Rivera, Adrian, VP-Sls & Mktg-Coca-Cola Puerto Rico Bottlers - Coca-Cola North America; pg. 848, pg. 500
Rivera, Casey Harris, Sr Mgr-Online Product Mgmt-Mobile - The Home Depot, Inc.; pg. 1050, pg. 510
Rivera, Christopher, Assoc Dir-Brand Mktg-Global Mktg Assignment - Kellogg Company; pg. 831, pg. 870
Rivera, Erickson, Supvr-Production - National Molding, LLC; pg. 1887, pg. 430
Rivera, Greg, Sr Dir-US Advertiser Solutions, Interactive Content & Experiences - Microsoft Corporation; pg. 435, pg. 1824
Rivera, Janessa, Specialist-PR - Gartner, Inc.; pg. 1248, pg. 374
Rivera, Jovina, Coord-Adv Copy - Comcast Cable Communications, Inc.; pg. 276, pg. 1560
Rivera, Kenyetta, Mgr-Mktg - United Parcel Service, Inc.; pg. 1928, pg. 522
Rivera, Kerry, Mgr-Digital Mktg - Toyota Motor Sales, U.S.A., Inc.; pg. 193, pg. 296
Rivera, Michelle, Sr Mgr-Mktg - Meredith Corporation; pg. 1663, pg. 705
Rivera, Ruben, Analyst-Mktg - State Farm Mutual Automobile Insurance Co.; pg. 1218, pg. 557
Rivera-Guzman, Cesar E., Mgr-Payer Mktg - GlaxoSmithKline; pg. 1536, pg. 1389
Rivera-Kerr, Paula, Mgr-Media Rels - Oakwood Healthcare, Inc.; pg. 1577, pg. 878
Rivero, Ines, Specialist-Mktg Comm-Intl - Caleres, Inc.; pg. 1805, pg. 993
Riveros, Gerry, Sr Principal Mgr-Product Mktg - Red Hat, Inc.; pg. 460, pg. 1388
Rivers, Dennise, Sr Mgr-Trade Mktg - VeeV Acai Spirits; pg. 1972, pg. 141
Rivers, Elisabeth, Mgr-Adv - Sprint Corporation; pg. 1874, pg. 719
Rivers, Erin, Project Mgr-Mktg & Comm - Webster University; pg. 610, pg. 1004
Rivers, Kacy, Brand Mgr - Watkins Manufacturing Corporation; pg. 120, pg. 303
Rivet, Mike, Sr Mgr-Mktg - Intel Corporation; pg. 645, pg. 266
Rizk, Sarah, Specialist-Mktg - FRANKLIN RESOURCES, INC.; pg. 760, pg. 254
Rizvi, Ali, Sr Product Mgr - ShoreTel, Inc.; pg. 469, pg. 288
Rizzo, Adriana, Sr Dir-Mktg - ESPN, Inc.; pg. 285, pg. 340
Rizzo, Anna, Brand Mgr-LG - CDW Corporation; pg. 370, pg. 663
Rizzo, Gilberto, Product Mgr-Global - Molex Incorporated; pg. 655, pg. 628
Rizzo, Joneil, Coord-Meeting Plng Mktg - LifeCell Corporation; pg. 1556, pg. 1045
Rizzuto, Denis, Sr VP-Liquid Sls & Ops - Conair Corporation; pg. 505, pg. 1055
Roa, Julian, Analyst-Email Mktg - Williams-Sonoma, Inc.; pg. 1140, pg. 234
Roach, Bryan, VP-PMO & Lean Ops & Sr Dir-Ops Fin - The Detroit Medical Center; pg. 1524, pg. 880
Roach, Emma, Mgr-Mktg-UK - Saucony, Inc.; pg. 1818, pg. 828
Roach, Gabe, Bus Mgr-ECommerce - H-E-B; pg. 1022, pg. 1740
Roach, John, VP-Mdsg - Eby-Brown Co.; pg. 1767, pg. 636
Roach, Nathan, Mgr-Mdsg & Tennis - adidas America Inc.; pg. 1803, pg. 1500
Roach, Tony, Sr Mgr-Loyalty Partnerships - Southwest Airlines Co.; pg. 1923, pg. 1687
Roach, Turner, Mgr-Social Media Mktg-US - Deloitte & Touche USA LLP; pg. 743, pg. 1222
Roadruck, David K., Mgr-Adv - Flex-O-Glass, Inc.; pg. 1457, pg. 574
Roadruck, David K., Mgr-Adv - Warp Brothers; pg. 1471, pg. 595
Roark, Brock, Brand Mgr-On-The-Go Innovation - Kellogg Company; pg. 831, pg. 870
Robb, Floyd, VP-Comm & Mktg Support - Basin Electric Power Cooperative; pg. 1936, pg. 1397
Robb, Michael, Interim Pres & Interim CEO - AirIQ, Inc.; pg. 346, pg. 1932
Robb, Nishma, Head-Mktg - Google Inc.; pg. 1249, pg. 153
Robb, Tanya, Sr Specialist-Social Media Publ - Canadian Imperial Bank of Commerce; pg. 729, pg. 1935
Robbins, Bill, Exec VP-Sls-Worldwide - Nuance Communications, Inc.; pg. 447, pg. 806
Robbins, Brian, Mgr-Online Mktg - Avon Products, Inc.; pg. 500, pg. 1198
Robbins, Casey, Mgr-Customer Mktg - Kronos Incorporated; pg. 425, pg. 813
Robbins, David, VP-Social Media Strategy - Al Jazeera America, LLC; pg. 269, pg. 1188
Robbins, David, Dir-Sls - The St. Augustine Record; pg. 1688, pg. 461
Robbins, Dineka, Specialist-Email Mktg - Toll Brothers, Inc.; pg. 115, pg. 1541
Robbins, Grant, Dir-Mktg - Heritage Home Group; pg. 926, pg. 1379
Robbins, Jen, Sr Mgr-Editorial, Promos & Radio Production - Apple Inc.; pg. 350, pg. 73
Robbins, Kimberly, Sr Mgr-Mktg & Product Dev-Gorham, Lenox Crystal & Metal - Lenox; pg. 1053, pg. 817
Robbins, Laura, Mgr-Product Mktg - Blackbaud, Inc.; pg. 361, pg. 1613
Robbins, Ryan M, Dir-Premium Sls & Svc - Cleveland Indians Baseball Company, Inc.; pg. 541, pg. 1429
Roberson, Candice, Principal-Mktg - FedEx Office & Print Services, Inc.; pg. 396, pg. 1681
Roberson, Carmen, Dir-Retail Mktg - Gump's Corp.; pg. 1772, pg. 219
Roberson, Charles D., VP-Sls-Intl - Lakeland Industries, Inc.; pg. 1354, pg. 1338
Roberson, Craig, Sls Mgr-Surgical Div-Eastern US - Bovie Medical Corporation; pg. 1402, pg. 1178
Roberson, Dale, Mgr-Tire Pros Mktg-Upper Midwest - AMERICAN TIRE DISTRIBUTORS HOLDINGS, INC.; pg. 199, pg. 1379
Roberson, Erica, Brand Mgr-Dev-Global Multicultural Hair Care - Unilever United States, Inc.; pg. 904, pg. 1061
Roberson, Susan, Gen Mgr & Sr VP-Time Consumer Mktg - Time Inc.; pg. 1693, pg. 1300
Robert, Angie, Mgr-Social Media Comm-TurboTax - Intuit Inc.; pg. 769, pg. 158
Robert-Hunt, Paula, Dir-Mktg Tech - Penn Foster Education Group, Inc.; pg. 606, pg. 1586
Roberti, Ruth, VP-Creative Svcs & Brand Presentation - J. Crew Group, Inc.; pg. 1773, pg. 1245
Roberto, Brion, Dir-Digital Mktg & Social Media-Global - Diageo North America Inc.; pg. 248, pg. 1223
Roberto, Derek, VP-New Media & Entertainment - Iconix Brand Group, Inc.; pg. 26, pg. 1243
Roberts, Ashleigh, Brand Mgr - Mondelez International, Inc.; pg. 878, pg. 601
Roberts, Barret, Sr Dir-CPG Sls Dev - Pandora Media Inc.; pg. 1273, pg. 172
Roberts, Bob, Mgr-Mktg Res - Babcox Media; pg. 1619, pg. 1400
Roberts, Bradley, Corp Mgr-Mktg Comm - Monsanto Company; pg. 1173, pg. 999
Roberts, Carmen H., Sr Mgr-Mktg Matls - The Coca-Cola Company; pg. 240, pg. 493
Roberts, Carrie, Sr Mgr-Global Brand Strategy & Campaigns - Microsoft Corporation; pg. 435, pg. 1824
Roberts, Casey, Specialist-Mktg Svcs & Events - Daybreak Game Company, LLC; pg. 1237, pg. 202
Roberts, Cheryl, Brand Mgr & Mgr-Creative Svcs - Omni Hotels & Resorts; pg. 1107, pg. 1685
Roberts, Christine, Editor-Mobile & Emerging Products - Daily News, L.P.; pg. 1632, pg. 1221
Roberts, Christopher, Sr VP-Home Entertainment Media & Digital - Rentrak Corporation; pg. 306, pg. 1506
Roberts, Christopher, VP-Product Dev - Zillow Group, Inc.; pg. 1292, pg. 1843
Roberts, Corley, Mgr-Mktg-Connected Accessories-Global - Fossil Group, Inc.; pg. 5, pg. 1735
Roberts, Dan, Dir-Product Mktg - Software AG, Inc.; pg. 471, pg. 1799
Roberts, Dana B., Sr Mgr-Acq & Product Mktg - DIRECTV Group Holdings, LLC; pg. 281, pg. 79
Roberts, David, Dir-Sls Central Div - Hurd Windows & Doors Inc; pg. 88, pg. 1869
Roberts, Dick, VP-Mktg - Sony Pictures Home Entertainment; pg. 310, pg. 72
Roberts, Elaine, Sr Mgr-Mktg - PepsiCo, Inc.; pg. 259, pg. 1327
Roberts, Emily, Sr Mgr-Mktg - Amazon.com, Inc.; pg. 1226, pg. 1831
Roberts, Heather V., Counsel-Product Dev - Motorola Mobility LLC; pg. 657, pg. 627
Roberts, Holly, Project Mgr-Global Creative Svcs - Dell Inc.; pg. 383, pg. 1737
Roberts, Irene T., Mgr-PR - Dominion Resources, Inc.; pg. 1939, pg. 1802
Roberts, Jaime, Mgr-PR-Givenchy Beauty & Fragrance - LVMH Inc.; pg. 9, pg. 1254
Roberts, Jean M., Dir-Adv - The New York Times Company; pg. 1668, pg. 1270
Roberts, Jeff, Product Mgr - GE Healthcare; pg. 399, pg. 1765
Roberts, Jessica, Sr Dir-Mktg & Comm-RehabCare - Kindred Healthcare, Inc.; pg. 1553, pg. 736
Roberts, Jill, Brand Mgr-Chef Boyardee - ConAgra Foods, Inc.; pg. 826, pg. 1014
Roberts, Jim, Sr Product Mgr-Studio Sys - Broadcast Electronics, Inc.; pg. 627, pg. 653
Roberts, Jodette, Mgr-Global Product Mktg-Magnetic Resonance Trng - General Electric Company; pg. 1297, pg. 347
Roberts, Kathie J., VP-Brand Mktg - United Community Banks, Inc.; pg. 814, pg. 526
Roberts, Kristen L., VP-PR & Community Investment - Comcast Corporation; pg. 276, pg. 1560
Roberts, Lara, Mktg Dir-Digital Commerce - NIKE, Inc.; pg. 1812, pg. 1492
Roberts, Lynn, VP-Adv & PR - The Echo Design Group, Inc.; pg. 4, pg. 1226
Roberts, Mary, Sr Mgr-Mktg Comm & Email - Cost Plus World Market; pg. 921, pg. 170
Roberts, Matthew, Sr Analyst-Mktg & Digital Index - Adobe Systems Incorporated; pg. 342, pg. 235
Roberts, Michael, Dir-SEM & Digital Adv - AutoNation, Inc.; pg. 165, pg. 423
Roberts, Michael, Dir-Mktg & Customer Experience - Office Depot, Inc.; pg. 448, pg. 412
Roberts, Michael, Sr Mgr-Tech Sls - Oracle Corporation; pg. 1272, pg. 786
Roberts, Michelle, Dir-Digital Plng & Production - The Clorox Company; pg. 327, pg. 169

Roberts, Neil, Exec Dir-Mktg - The Tennis Channel, Inc.; *pg.* 679, *pg.* 276
Roberts, Nigel H., Sr Dir-Associations-Global - LexisNexis Group; *pg.* 1658, *pg.* 1446
Roberts, Paul, VP-Unified Social Bus-Global - Unisys Corporation; *pg.* 487, *pg.* 1517
Roberts, Randi, VP-Sls-Multiple Sclerosis Bus Unit - Novartis Pharmaceuticals Corp.; *pg.* 1575, *pg.* 1054
Roberts, Richard, Dir-Mktg & Bus Dev - Hexcel Corporation; *pg.* 1884, *pg.* 375
Roberts, Rob, Mgr-Community-Consumer Products - Autodesk Inc.; *pg.* 356, *pg.* 257
Roberts, Rochelle, VP-Bus Dev & Sls-North America - Cartesian; *pg.* 369, *pg.* 718
Roberts, Russ, Sr VP-Tax, Fin & Advocacy - Canadian Advanced Technology Alliance; *pg.* 136, *pg.* 1931
Roberts, Shari, Acct Mgr-Mktg - Under Armour, Inc.; *pg.* 49, *pg.* 759
Roberts, Sonya, Sr Mgr-Trade Show - Mentor Graphics Corporation; *pg.* 432, *pg.* 1510
Roberts, Stephanie, Bus Mgr - Commentary; *pg.* 1628, *pg.* 1216
Roberts, Stephen, Brand Mgr-Sustainability - Dell Inc.; *pg.* 383, *pg.* 1737
Roberts, Steve, Mgr-Mktg - Eagle Manufacturing Company; *pg.* 79, *pg.* 1851
Roberts, Suzie, VP-Sls - Glen Raven, Inc.; *pg.* 693, *pg.* 1373
Roberts, Terry, VP-Sls & Mdsg-Nashville - Associated Wholesale Grocers, Inc.; *pg.* 1015, *pg.* 715
Roberts, Tiffany, Coord-Mktg Comm - Andis Company; *pg.* 498, *pg.* 1895
Roberts, Tom, Sr VP-Mktg-Electronic Payments - Fiserv, Inc.; *pg.* 758, *pg.* 537
Roberts, Tom, Dir-Field Sls & Ops-Mfg Sys - Intelligrated Systems LLC; *pg.* 1350, *pg.* 998
Roberts, Tom, Sr VP-Mktg - Sprint Corporation; *pg.* 1874, *pg.* 719
Roberts, Travis, Mgr-Mktg - Windstream Corporation; *pg.* 321, *pg.* 34
Roberts, Ty, Dir-Electricity Product Mktg-EMEA Reg - Itron Inc.; *pg.* 422, *pg.* 1822
Roberts, Whitney, Coord-Mktg - Multimedia Games Inc.; *pg.* 442, *pg.* 1664
Robertshaw, Beth, Specialist-Email Mktg - VITAMIN SHOPPE, INC.; *pg.* 1608, *pg.* 1098
Robertson, Amy M., Mgr-Mktg Svcs - US Oncology, Inc.; *pg.* 1604, *pg.* 1747
Robertson, Barron, Grp Product Mgr - Fiskars Brands, Inc.; *pg.* 1124, *pg.* 1866
Robertson, Casey, Product Mgr-North America - Videojet Technologies Inc.; *pg.* 489, *pg.* 671
Robertson, David, Dir-Product Line - Analog Devices, Inc.; *pg.* 617, *pg.* 839
Robertson, David, Dir-Mktg - Hanesbrands Inc.; *pg.* 26, *pg.* 1394
Robertson, Geoffrey, VP-Product, Innovation & Bus Integration - W.W. Grainger, Inc.; *pg.* 1390, *pg.* 625
Robertson, Jeff, VP-Product, SkyClubs & Mktg Comm - Delta Air Lines, Inc.; *pg.* 1905, *pg.* 503
Robertson, Jeff, Head-US Sls-Pfizer Vaccines - Pfizer Inc.; *pg.* 1581, *pg.* 1278
Robertson, Jeff, VP-CRM Mktg - The Sharper Image; *pg.* 1785, *pg.* 886
Robertson, Jenifer, VP-Mktg & Bus Dev - AT&T Inc.; *pg.* 1868, *pg.* 358
Robertson, Jennifer, Sr VP-Digital Media & Bus Dev - AMC Networks Inc.; *pg.* 269, *pg.* 1189
Robertson, Jennifer, Brand Mgr - Gold Eagle Company; *pg.* 206, *pg.* 575
Robertson, Jim, Brand Mgr-InterContinental Hotels & Resorts-Guest Experience - InterContinental Hotels Corporation; *pg.* 1097, *pg.* 511
Robertson, Jim, VP-Mktg-Flooring Tools & Accessories - M-D Building Products, Inc.; *pg.* 95, *pg.* 1486
Robertson, Joe, Mgr-Adv & PR - Blue Bell Creameries, L.P.; *pg.* 1851, *pg.* 1668
Robertson, K. C., Dir-Creative - WJZ-TV; *pg.* 322, *pg.* 760
Robertson, Kristin, Dir-Mktg & VM-Adidas Concept Stores - adidas America Inc.; *pg.* 1803, *pg.* 1500
Robertson, Laura, Brand Mgr - National Geographic Society; *pg.* 1667, *pg.* 402
Robertson, Linda, Sr Dir - Inova Health System; *pg.* 1545, *pg.* 1781
Robertson, Mike, Sls Dir-UK & Ireland Coated Bd & Acct Mgr-Pan Europe - International Paper Company; *pg.* 1460, *pg.* 1644
Robertson, Paul, Exec VP-Shaw Comm & Pres-Shaw Media - Shaw Communications Inc.; *pg.* 307, *pg.* 1904
Robertson, Robin, Sr VP & Asst Dir-Mktg - Cardinal Bank N.A.; *pg.* 732, *pg.* 1790
Robertson, Samantha, Coord-Social Media - Brookshire Grocery Company; *pg.* 1016, *pg.* 1748
Robertson, Sean, Gen Mgr-Adv Sls-Dish Media Sls - DISH Network Corporation; *pg.* 283, *pg.* 325
Robertson, Stewart, Engr-Technical Mktg Applications - KLA-Tencor Corporation; *pg.* 1353, *pg.* 146
Robertson, Tami, Publr-Adv - Google Inc.; *pg.* 1249, *pg.* 153
Robertson, Tammy, Specialist-PR - Target Corporation; *pg.* 1786, *pg.* 942
Robertson, Tiko, Dir-Mktg - Charles Schwab; *pg.* 1235, *pg.* 1661
Robertson, Tracy, Dir-Mktg-Global - General Electric Company; *pg.* 1297, *pg.* 347
Robertson, Walt, VP Sls - Keeneland Association Inc.; *pg.* 1477, *pg.* 730
Robey, Courtney, Mgr-Mktg Comm - Recreation Vehicle Industry Association; *pg.* 155, *pg.* 1799
Robey, Louis, Accountant-Gas Mktg - ConocoPhillips; *pg.* 975, *pg.* 1703
Robidoux, David, VP-Mktg - PIP Printing, Inc.; *pg.* 1677, *pg.* 149
Robidoux, David, VP-Mktg - Sir Speedy, Inc.; *pg.* 1687, *pg.* 149
Robilliard, Dominic, Dir-Design & Creative - Sony Computer Entertainment America LLC; *pg.* 966, *pg.* 256
Robinett, Eugene, VP-Sls-Intl - Hutchens Industries Inc.; *pg.* 208, *pg.* 1006
Robinett, Sarah, Asst VP-Digital Mktg - Scottrade, Inc.; *pg.* 802, *pg.* 1003
Robinette, Barb, VP-Mktg Comm-Workers' Compensation Managed Care - Coventry Health Care, Inc.; *pg.* 1519, *pg.* 761
Robinette, Victoria, Mgr-PR - Neiman Marcus, Inc.; *pg.* 30, *pg.* 1684
Robino, Mary Goss, Sr VP-Mktg Partnerships-Global - Sony Pictures Entertainment Inc.; *pg.* 309, *pg.* 72
Robins, Callie, Mgr-New Product Dev - American Express Company; *pg.* 712, *pg.* 1190
Robins, Elizabeth, Sr Product Mgr-Solution Incubation - Diebold, Incorporated; *pg.* 387, *pg.* 1407
Robins, Jennifer, Sr Mgr-Enterprise Comm - Cameron International; *pg.* 1151, *pg.* 1702
Robins, Kelsey, Specialist-Mktg-Media Adv - GEICO Corporation; *pg.* 1200, *pg.* 399
Robins, Shawn, VP-Product Support - Power Equipment Company inc; *pg.* 1369, *pg.* 1637
Robinson Hinkle, Alex, Head-Relationship Mktg - eBay Inc.; *pg.* 1240, *pg.* 243
Robinson, Alain, Head-Natl Indus Mktg-Consumer & Indus Products - Deloitte & Touche USA LLP; *pg.* 743, *pg.* 1222
Robinson, Alan, Dir-Mktg - THE DOW CHEMICAL COMPANY; *pg.* 1157, *pg.* 898
Robinson, Andy, Product Mgr-European - Sealed Air Corporation; *pg.* 1468, *pg.* 1058
Robinson, Ashlee, Coord-Retail Mktg - Forever 21, Inc.; *pg.* 24, *pg.* 130
Robinson, Audra D., Mgr-Shopper Mktg - Pfizer Inc.; *pg.* 1581, *pg.* 1278
Robinson, Barbara, Asst VP-Vertical Mktg - The Dun & Bradstreet Corp.; *pg.* 1637, *pg.* 1120
Robinson, Bart, VP-Mktg - Mohawk Fine Papers, Inc.; *pg.* 1464, *pg.* 1153
Robinson, Beth, Sr Mgr-Mktg-Kitchen Aid Brand - Whirlpool Corporation; *pg.* 62, *pg.* 872
Robinson, Bill, Exec VP-Sls - INCONTACT, INC.; *pg.* 413, *pg.* 1752
Robinson, Brenna, Sr Mgr-PR - Kelley Blue Book Co., Inc.; *pg.* 1656, *pg.* 112
Robinson, Brenna, Dir-Global Reputation, Digital, Content & Media Strategy - Pfizer Inc.; *pg.* 1581, *pg.* 1278
Robinson, Cara, VP-Global Mktg, Makeup & Fragrance - Clinique Laboratories LLC; *pg.* 503, *pg.* 1214
Robinson, Caralene, Sr VP-Mktg & Creative - MTVN Video Hits Inc.; *pg.* 299, *pg.* 1263
Robinson, Carol, Dir-Creative Resources - American Red Cross; *pg.* 130, *pg.* 395
Robinson, Carter, Sr Mgr-Mktg - AT&T Inc.; *pg.* 1867, *pg.* 1674
Robinson, Cheri, Mgr-Mktg Comm - Duke Energy Corporation; *pg.* 1940, *pg.* 1366
Robinson, Chris, Mgr-Adv & Media - Carhartt, Inc.; *pg.* 39, *pg.* 875
Robinson, Chris, Dir-Mktg & Comm - Hussey Seating Co.; *pg.* 929, *pg.* 751
Robinson, Chris, Bus Mgr - Lucite International, Inc.; *pg.* 94, *pg.* 1631
Robinson, Cindy, Sr Coord-Mktg - Spirit Airlines, Inc.; *pg.* 234, *pg.* 449
Robinson, Cody, Dir-Production - Denton Publishing Company; *pg.* 1634, *pg.* 1691
Robinson, Dana, Dir-Social Media - Fandango Media, LLC; *pg.* 1247, *pg.* 130
Robinson, Danielle, Mgr-Channel Mktg - Wright Express Corporation; *pg.* 493, *pg.* 753
Robinson, Dave, Sr Mgr-Bus Dev, Derivative Fleet Support & Sustainment - The Boeing Company; *pg.* 225, *pg.* 567
Robinson, David, Sr Mgr-Asst Brand & Brand Delivery - DISH Network Corporation; *pg.* 283, *pg.* 325
Robinson, Debbie, Coord-Mktg - Biltmore Estate Wine Company; *pg.* 1958, *pg.* 1358
Robinson, Deirdre, Exec Dir-Brand Mgmt & Mktg Comm - Verizon Communications Inc.; *pg.* 1875, *pg.* 1309
Robinson, Deryck, VP-Sls-East Reg - Infinera Corporation; *pg.* 644, *pg.* 286
Robinson, Donald T., VP-Retention Mktg & Ops Fulfillment - TEN: The Enthusiast Network; *pg.* 1691, *pg.* 1298
Robinson, Drew J., VP-Valuation & Advisory Grp - CB Richard Ellis Group, Inc.; *pg.* 1085, *pg.* 127
Robinson, Gary, Mgr-Acura Product Plng - American Honda Motor Co., Inc.; *pg.* 163, *pg.* 292
Robinson, Gary, Sr Mgr-Mktg-Lenovo System x Servers-Worldwide - Lenovo Group Ltd; *pg.* 427, *pg.* 1384
Robinson, George, Sr Product Mgr-Interoperabilty - First DataBank, Inc.; *pg.* 397, *pg.* 217
Robinson, Hunter, Mgr-Media Rels - Darden Restaurants, Inc.; *pg.* 1724, *pg.* 453
Robinson, Hunter, Mgr-Media Rels - Olive Garden Italian Restaurant; *pg.* 1742, *pg.* 454
Robinson, Jaimie, Coord-Mktg & Comm - The Coleman Company, Inc.; *pg.* 1830, *pg.* 723
Robinson, Jessica, Mgr-Mktg Comm - THE DOW CHEMICAL COMPANY; *pg.* 1157, *pg.* 898
Robinson, Jessica, Sr Dir-Mktg-Portfolio Brands - Heineken USA Inc.; *pg.* 252, *pg.* 1352
Robinson, Jim, Sr Mgr-User Experience & Requirements - Cox Communications, Inc.; *pg.* 279, *pg.* 501
Robinson, Jordan, Sr Specialist-Creative - Twitter, Inc.; *pg.* 1285, *pg.* 228
Robinson, Kim, Mgr-Creative Solutions - BBC Worldwide America Inc.; *pg.* 271, *pg.* 1201
Robinson, Kirk, Sr VP-Comml Markets & Global Sls - Ingram Micro Inc.; *pg.* 415, *pg.* 261
Robinson, Krystina, Mgr-Comml Mktg-Dutch Brands - Heineken USA Inc.; *pg.* 252, *pg.* 1352
Robinson, Lauren, Mgr-Event Mktg - ESPN, Inc.; *pg.* 285, *pg.* 340
Robinson, Lauventria, VP-Multicultural Mktg - The Coca-Cola Company; *pg.* 240, *pg.* 493
Robinson, Linda Gosden, Head-Mktg & Comm-Global - BlackRock, Inc.; *pg.* 724, *pg.* 1203
Robinson, Liz, VP-Brand Strategy & Creative Svcs - SLM Corporation; *pg.* 804, *pg.* 388
Robinson, Lori, Dir-Acq-Digital Mktg - Sirius XM Holdings Inc.; *pg.* 308, *pg.* 1292
Robinson, Melina, Specialist-Digital Mktg - Pinnacle Entertainment, Inc.; *pg.* 576, *pg.* 1029
Robinson, Michael, Product Mgr-App Lab - Hearst Magazines; *pg.* 1649, *pg.* 1239
Robinson, Michael, Mgr-Creative - Nautilus, Inc.; *pg.* 1840, *pg.* 1846
Robinson, Michael, Dir-Customer Sls & Mktg - Omaha Steaks International, Inc.; *pg.* 1780, *pg.* 1017
Robinson, Mike, Mgr-Sls - Mars, Incorporated; *pg.* 1858, *pg.* 1792
Robinson, Mitch, Dir-Trade Mktg - Zillow Group, Inc.; *pg.* 1292, *pg.* 1843
Robinson, Monique, Principal Mgr-Field Mktg - Informatica Corporation; *pg.* 414, *pg.* 190
Robinson, Nicole, Pres-Mondelez Intl Foundation & Sr Dir-Community Involvement - Mondelez International, Inc.; *pg.* 878, *pg.* 601
Robinson, Paul, Sr Product Mgr - Brother International Corporation - USA; *pg.* 53, *pg.* 1046
Robinson, Raquel, Reg Mgr-Mktg - Essilor of America, Inc.; *pg.* 1412, *pg.* 1680

First page reference indicates Business Class Edition
Second page reference indicates Geographic Edition

Robinson, Rebecca, Mgr-Product Mktg-CRM & Travel Policy - Sabre Holdings Corporation; pg. 1922, pg. 1745
Robinson, Rick, Product Mgr - API Healthcare Corp.; pg. 350, pg. 1860
Robinson, Rick, Mgr-Worldwide Mktg Solutions - Lexmark International, Inc.; pg. 427, pg. 730
Robinson, Rob, Sr Dir-Health Policy Excellence - Johnson & Johnson; pg. 1549, pg. 1091
Robinson, Rob, Sr Specialist-Social Comm - Nissan North America, Inc.; pg. 186, pg. 1633
Robinson, Sarah B., Mgr-PR - Rollins, Inc.; pg. 1179, pg. 519
Robinson, Stacy, Mgr-Digital Mktg - Boyd Gaming Corporation; pg. 1082, pg. 1022
Robinson, Steve, VP-Mktg & Therapeutic Nutrition Div - Abbott Laboratories; pg. 1484, pg. 551
Robinson, Thomas, Dir-Ops & Product Dev-Natural Fibers Div - Barnhardt Manufacturing Company; pg. 1498, pg. 1364
Robinson, Tim, Mgr-Sls-Eastern Reg - Flanders Corporation; pg. 1336, pg. 1392
Robinson, Tim, Sr Dir-US Pricing Strategy & Investment - Wal-Mart.com; pg. 1287, pg. 50
Robinson, Todd, Sr VP-Digital Mktg, Consumer & Small Bus Social Media - Bank of America Corporation; pg. 718, pg. 1362
Robinson, Tony, Mgr-Mktg Dev - The Coca-Cola Company; pg. 240, pg. 493
Robinson, Tracy, Dir-Mktg-Amtrak - National Railroad Passenger Corporation; pg. 1916, pg. 403
Robinson, Will, VP-Mktg - Ledo Pizza System Inc.; pg. 874, pg. 754
Robison, Gary, Dir-Mktg & Customer Svc - Mahr Federal, Inc.; pg. 1358, pg. 1606
Robison, Lindsay, Specialist-Global PR - Whole Foods Market, Inc.; pg. 1038, pg. 1667
Robison, Megan A., Mgr-Social Media Content - General Electric Company; pg. 1297, pg. 347
Robles, Edith, Mgr-PR-Global - Brown-Forman Corporation; pg. 1958, pg. 732
Robles, John, Sr Product Mgr-Plng - Dell Inc.; pg. 383, pg. 1737
Robles, Madel, Mgr-Mktg - RACKSPACE HOSTING, INC.; pg. 1277, pg. 1742
Robles, Rosemarie, Mgr-Media Rels - Macy's, Inc.; pg. 1778, pg. 1417
Robles, Roxanne, Specialist-Social Media - PETCO Animal Supplies, Inc.; pg. 1480, pg. 206
Robles, Ryan, Assoc Mgr-Mktg - Intuit Inc.; pg. 769, pg. 158
Robley, Christopher, Coord-Mktg - CD Baby, Inc.; pg. 1764, pg. 1501
Robling, Jack, Head-Digital Media & Sr Rep-Comm - Lockheed Martin Corporation; pg. 229, pg. 762
Roblyer, Chris, Sr Mng Counsel-Strategic Mktg - The Coca-Cola Company; pg. 240, pg. 493
Robnett, Phil, VP-Mktg & Sls-Cheese - California Milk Advisory Board; pg. 843, pg. 149
Robson, Alexandra, Acct Exec-Sls & Mktg - Kingsley-Bate, Ltd.; pg. 932, pg. 1787
Robson, Sally, Mgr-Adv - Iowa Lottery; pg. 996, pg. 705
Roccabruna, Pamela, VP-Mktg Svcs - Geneva Watch Group; pg. 5, pg. 1174
Roccaforte, Franki, Planner-Sls - Pandora Media Inc.; pg. 1273, pg. 172
Rocchio, Courtney, Brand Mgr-Market Segment - Indiana University Health Methodist Hospital; pg. 1545, pg. 687
Rocco, Amy, Mgr-Digital Mktg - BIC Corporation; pg. 501, pg. 369
Rocha, Chris, Sr Mgr-Digital Mktg - Cabela's Incorporated; pg. 535, pg. 1019
Rocha, Jerry, VP-Cross Platform & Digital Media - Nielsen Business Media; pg. 1671, pg. 1272
Rocha, Jim, Mgr-Mktg Strategies - Safeway Inc.; pg. 1032, pg. 184
Rocha, Ron, Dir-Mktg - Pacific Life Insurance Company; pg. 1213, pg. 166
Roche, Brad, VP-Mktg - Hill Phoenix Inc.; pg. 1072, pg. 528
Roche, Cindy Klein, VP-Mktg - athenahealth, Inc.; pg. 1497, pg. 855
Roche, Dan, Dir-Mktg-Portable Power & Cleaning Sys - Briggs & Stratton Corporation; pg. 201, pg. 1899
Roche, Elodie, Dir-US Mktg-Calvin Klein Fragrances - Coty, Inc.; pg. 506, pg. 1219
Roche, Jason, Dir-Mktg-Global - GOJO Industries, Inc.; pg. 330, pg. 1401
Roche, Karen, Sr Dir-Mktg - Kings Food Markets, Inc.; pg. 1025, pg. 1103
Roche, Maureen, Dir-Mktg & Dev - Goodwill Industries International, Inc.; pg. 1771, pg. 776
Roche, Rob, Project Mgr-Mktg - MetLife, Inc.; pg. 1208, pg. 1258
Rocheleau, Gary, VP-Retail Mktg Execution - Vons A Safeway Company; pg. 1036, pg. 43
Rochelle, Grant, Sr Dir-Global Product Support & Program Offerings - Autodesk Inc.; pg. 356, pg. 257
Rochelle, Jonathan, Dir-Product Mgmt - Google Inc.; pg. 1249, pg. 153
Rochester, Tammeca, Brand Mgr - Colgate-Palmolive Company; pg. 504, pg. 1215
Rochette, Nancy C., Specialist-Mktg & Comm - ABB Inc.; pg. 64, pg. 1959
Rochford, Guy, Dir-Production - America's Test Kitchen; pg. 1616, pg. 803
Rochkind, Jennifer, Sr Mgr-Corp Philanthropy - Toyota Motor North America, Inc.; pg. 192, pg. 1303
Rochlitz, Kevin, VP-Corp Sls & Bus Dev - Baltimore Ravens Limited Partnership; pg. 532, pg. 755
Rochwerg, Denise, Sr Mgr-Brand Design & Prepress - General Mills Canada Corp.; pg. 828, pg. 1926
Rock, Amy D., Sr Dir-Regulatory & Scientific Affairs - Cumberland Pharmaceuticals, Inc.; pg. 1521, pg. 1650
Rock, George R, Dir-Mktg - Press-Republican; pg. 1678, pg. 1322
Rock, Megan, Sr VP-Partnership Mktg - The Weather Channel LLC; pg. 320, pg. 523
Rock, Mitchell C., VP-Sls & Mktg - UFP Technologies, Inc.; pg. 1891, pg. 823
Rockhead, Dean, Sr Mgr-Product - VIA Rail Canada Inc.; pg. 1930, pg. 1957
Rocklewitz, Aaron, Brand Mgr-Keebler Club & Carr's Crackers - Kellogg Company; pg. 831, pg. 870
Rockman, Melissa, Specialist-Channel Mktg - VistaPrint USA, Incorporated; pg. 1700, pg. 829
Rockmore, Adam, VP-Mktg - Fandango Media, LLC; pg. 1247, pg. 130
Rockmore, Bette, Sr VP-Adv Sls - Sirius XM Holdings Inc.; pg. 308, pg. 1292
Rocko, Wojtek, Brand Mgr-Lucerne - Safeway Inc.; pg. 1032, pg. 184
Rockwell, Charles, Coord-Global Marine Lubricants Mktg - Exxon Mobil Corporation; pg. 977, pg. 1718
Rockwell, Michael, Exec VP-Products & Tech - Dolby Laboratories, Inc.; pg. 284, pg. 217
Rodack, Kristin, Dir-Mktg-D23 - The Walt Disney Company; pg. 317, pg. 52
Rodahl, Dawn, Mgr-Mktg Ops-Renewable Energy Div - 3M Company; pg. 1142, pg. 956
Rodak, John, Dir-Integrated Project Mgmt-Mktg - Bridgestone Americas, Inc.; pg. 201, pg. 1649
Rodammer, Kris, Dir-Creative - Putnam Investments, LLC; pg. 797, pg. 800
Rodda, Duke, Strategist-Mktg - 3M Company; pg. 1142, pg. 956
Rodda, Janis, Dir-Media Strategy & Plng - Big Heart Pet Brands; pg. 1474, pg. 213
Rodden, Dana, Head-Enterprise Channel Mktg - GlaxoSmithKline; pg. 1536, pg. 1565
Roddey, James, Mgr-Comm & Media Rels - Embry-Riddle Aeronautical University; pg. 601, pg. 420
Rode, Lisa, VP & Head-Bus-Product Mgmt-MasterPass - MasterCard Incorporated; pg. 779, pg. 1325
Rodeawald, Jenna, Sr Mgr-Consumer Mktg - Amgen Inc.; pg. 1493, pg. 291
Rodemeyer, Traci, Mgr-Mktg Comm-Corn - Dupont Pioneer; pg. 1795, pg. 708
Roden, Andrew, Mgr-Media - Diageo North America Inc.; pg. 248, pg. 1223
Rodenbiker, Kelsey, Assoc Dir-Mktg - Inc.com LLC; pg. 1258, pg. 1243
Rodenburg, Susan Larson, Dir-Mktg - Lincoln Symphony Orchestra; pg. 557, pg. 1012
Rodenhouse, Kate, Dir-Mktg & Comm - Hampton Roads Economic Development Alliance; pg. 994, pg. 1797
Rodenmayer, Nelson, VP-Client Mktg - Valassis; pg. 1698, pg. 386
Rodgers, Abby, Brand Mgr-Global - Exxon Mobil Corporation; pg. 977, pg. 1718
Rodgers, Chip, VP-Experience Mktg - CIENA Corporation; pg. 628, pg. 771
Rodgers, Donna, Mgr-Design & Mdse - Bacova Guild, Ltd.; pg. 916, pg. 1779
Rodgers, Erin, Sr Dir-Corp Comm - Medtronic, Inc.; pg. 1564, pg. 939
Rodgers, Mary, Dir-Mktg Comm - Cuisinart Inc.; pg. 1123, pg. 373
Rodgers, Mary J., Dir-Mktg Comm - Waring Products, Inc.; pg. 62, pg. 379
Rodgers, Randy, Product Mgr-Portfolio - Danfoss Power Solutions Company; pg. 1328, pg. 701
Rodgers, Susan, Dir-Mktg CRM - Pier 1 Imports, Inc.; pg. 940, pg. 1695
Rodgers, Tom, Dir-Sls & Mktg-Firestone Brand Agricultural Tires - Bridgestone Americas, Inc.; pg. 201, pg. 1649
Rodis, Jeff, Mgr-Mktg Ops - Mutual of Omaha Insurance Company; pg. 1210, pg. 1016
Rodman, Andrew, Mgr-Sls-Natl - Galderma Laboratories, L.P.; pg. 1532, pg. 1695
Rodman, Jennifer, Specialist-Mktg - Weatherby, Inc.; pg. 1848, pg. 181
Rodman, Lincoln, Sr VP-Mdsg & Mktg - FTD Group, Inc.; pg. 1795, pg. 608
Rodman, Lisa, Mgr-Mktg - PETCO Animal Supplies, Inc.; pg. 1480, pg. 206
Rodney, Dawn, VP-Creative - National Geographic Society; pg. 1667, pg. 402
Rodney, Natasha, Mgr-Adv - Barnes & Noble, Inc.; pg. 1619, pg. 1201
Rodrigue, Nena, Exec VP-Original Programming, Acq & Production - BBC Worldwide America Inc.; pg. 271, pg. 1201
Rodrigues, Alexandre Norberto, Bus Mgr - 3M Company; pg. 1142, pg. 956
Rodrigues, Ashwin, Dir-Mktg-Global - Majesco; pg. 429, pg. 1089
Rodrigues, Bill, Pres-North America & Global Sls - Dell Inc.; pg. 383, pg. 1737
Rodrigues, Brian, Mgr-Mktg Strategy - The Walt Disney Company; pg. 317, pg. 52
Rodrigues, Joao, Dir-Mktg-VMS - Reckitt Benckiser Inc.; pg. 1136, pg. 1105
Rodriguez, Aileen, Mgr-Mktg - Duane Reade, Inc.; pg. 1525, pg. 1226
Rodriguez, Alex, Specialist-Product Mktg-Latin America - Canon U.S.A., Inc.; pg. 1404, pg. 1178
Rodriguez, Alfredo, VP-Mktg - DISH Network Corporation; pg. 283, pg. 325
Rodriguez, Amy, Sr Mgr-Production Partnership Mktg & Creative Content - ABC Cable Networks Group; pg. 268, pg. 51
Rodriguez, Andrea, Mgr-Sls & Mktg - Winn Dixie Stores, Inc.; pg. 1038, pg. 435
Rodriguez, Ann, Specialist-Mktg-Super 1 Foods - Brookshire Grocery Company; pg. 1016, pg. 1748
Rodriguez, Aylene, Assoc Mgr-Customer Mktg - The Yankee Candle Company, Inc.; pg. 1792, pg. 843
Rodriguez, Calu, Assoc Dir-Sales Mktg - ESPN, Inc.; pg. 285, pg. 340
Rodriguez, Carolina, Sr Mgr-Mktg - DIRECTV Group Holdings, LLC; pg. 281, pg. 79
Rodriguez, Claudio, Brand Mgr-Arroz SOS Mexico - Riviana Foods Inc.; pg. 892, pg. 1713
Rodriguez, Dave, Mgr-Multicultural Mktg - The Lincoln Motor Company; pg. 182, pg. 878
Rodriguez, David, Mgr-Mktg Comm-Multicultural - Ford Motor Company; pg. 172, pg. 876
Rodriguez, David, Mgr-Mktg-NY Metro - McDonald's Corporation; pg. 1737, pg. 645
Rodriguez, David, Brand Mgr-Purina Pro Plan USA - Nestle Purina PetCare Company; pg. 1479, pg. 1000
Rodriguez, Ed, VP-Americas Mktg & Inside Sls - Citrix Systems, Inc.; pg. 375, pg. 424
Rodriguez, Elida, Corp Mgr-Mktg Comm - Publix Super Markets, Inc.; pg. 1031, pg. 437
Rodriguez, Enrique, Chief Sls Officer & Exec VP - JDA Software Group, Inc.; pg. 423, pg. 22
Rodriguez, Gene, Dir-PR - Anthem, Inc.; pg. 1192, pg. 683
Rodriguez, Guillermo, Mgr-Media Plng - Univision Communications Inc.; pg. 683, pg. 1307
Rodriguez, Irasema, Mgr-Mktg & Comm - Barksdale, Inc.; pg. 1317, pg. 126
Rodriguez, Ivelisse, Brand Mgr - Unilever United States, Inc.; pg. 904, pg. 1061
Rodriguez, Jose A., Mgr-Sls - Humana, Inc.; pg. 1204, pg. 734
Rodriguez, Juan, Brand Mgr - Mars Petcare; pg. 1478, pg. 1633
Rodriguez, Leandro, Dir-Sls-Intl - Kidron, Inc.; pg. 181, pg.

1457
Rodriguez, Marco, Mgr-Convention Sls - San Francisco Travel Association; *pg.* 1005, *pg.* 227
Rodriguez, Maria Z., Specialist-PR - DORAL FINANCIAL CORPORATION; *pg.* 744, *pg.* 1599
Rodriguez, Marifer, Sr Mgr-Social Media Mktg - Pitney Bowes Inc.; *pg.* 454, *pg.* 376
Rodriguez, Mary, Specialist-Digital Mktg - The ADT Corporation; *pg.* 612, *pg.* 409
Rodriguez, Michelle, Coord-Trade Show & Mktg - Abaxis, Inc.; *pg.* 1483, *pg.* 298
Rodriguez, Miguel, Program Mgr-Interactive Mktg - Advent Software, Inc.; *pg.* 345, *pg.* 211
Rodriguez, Mildred, Specialist-Corp & Global Mktg HR - Brown-Forman Corporation; *pg.* 1958, *pg.* 732
Rodriguez, Naomi, Sr Dir-External Affairs - Los Angeles Dodgers Inc.; *pg.* 559, *pg.* 135
Rodriguez, Nury, Dir-Mktg - Lennar Corporation; *pg.* 1100, *pg.* 443
Rodriguez, Pamela, Mgr-Mktg Ops - Liberty Home Equity Solutions, Inc.; *pg.* 776, *pg.* 186
Rodriguez, Paula, Mgr-Commodity Mktg-Olefins & NGL - The Williams Companies, Inc.; *pg.* 987, *pg.* 1491
Rodriguez, Porfirio, Sr Mgr-Consumer Insights & Analytics-Global - Wal-Mart Stores, Inc.; *pg.* 1790, *pg.* 29
Rodriguez, Rebecca, Mgr & Strategist-Media - Whataburger, Inc.; *pg.* 1755, *pg.* 1744
Rodriguez, Richard, Sr Mgr-Mktg-Global Beverage Grp-Energy Drinks - PepsiCo, Inc.; *pg.* 259, *pg.* 1327
Rodriguez, Roshelle, Brand Mgr-Global Vicks - The Procter & Gamble Company; *pg.* 1129, *pg.* 1418
Rodriguez, Shari Winet, VP-PR - Bridgepoint Education, Inc.; *pg.* 598, *pg.* 201
Rodriguez, Sherri, VP-Sls - Infor; *pg.* 414, *pg.* 484
Rodriguez, Shirley, Analyst-Mktg Comm - State Farm Mutual Automobile Insurance Co.; *pg.* 1218, *pg.* 557
Rodriguez, Stacie J., Principal-Mktg-Channel Mktg Enablement - EMC Corporation; *pg.* 391, *pg.* 825
Rodriguez, Tara, Brand Mgr - Mars Petcare; *pg.* 1478, *pg.* 1633
Rodriguez, Tatiana, VP-Programming & Creative Strategy - Nickelodeon Direct Inc.; *pg.* 303, *pg.* 1271
Rodriguez, Walter, Dir-Market Plng, Strategy & Mktg Ops - Verizon Communications Inc.; *pg.* 1875, *pg.* 1309
Rodriguez, Wayne, Sr Mgr-Events & Promos - Newell Rubbermaid Inc.; *pg.* 1128, *pg.* 515
Rodriguez-Gutzmer, Ines, Dir-Corp Comm & Global Mktg - Acxiom Corporation; *pg.* 342, *pg.* 607
Roduner, Ted, Sr Mgr-PR - Microsoft Corporation; *pg.* 435, *pg.* 1824
Rodway, Beth, Brand Mgr-Mktg-Ann Taylor Factory & Loft Outlet Stores - Ann Inc.; *pg.* 18, *pg.* 1195
Roe, Peggy Fang, Chief Sls & Mktg Officer-Asia Pacific - Marriott International, Inc.; *pg.* 1102, *pg.* 764
Roebuck, Barry, Dir-Creative - Hamilton Beach Brands, Inc.; *pg.* 56, *pg.* 1783
Roebuck, Eric, Sr Product Mgr - H&R Block, Inc.; *pg.* 764, *pg.* 983
Roecker, Michael, Mgr-Global Mktg-Indus Additives - The Lubrizol Corporation; *pg.* 1171, *pg.* 1481
Roeder, Carey, VP & Program Mgr-Mktg - Wells Fargo Financial, Inc.; *pg.* 821, *pg.* 707
Roeder, Christine A., Assoc Dir-Mktg - AT&T; *pg.* 1865, *pg.* 258
Roeglin, Lauren, Mgr-Retention Mktg - Hewlett-Packard Company; *pg.* 404, *pg.* 175
Roehl, Chris, Product Mgr - Miller Electric Manufacturing Co.; *pg.* 1361, *pg.* 1852
Roehm, Arthur W., VP-Sls - Intel Corporation; *pg.* 645, *pg.* 266
Roell, Jerome, Dir-Bus Dev, Mktg & Plng - John Deere Consumer & Commercial Equipment, Inc.; *pg.* 705, *pg.* 1360
Roell, Madeleine, Assoc Mgr-Mktg - Best Buy Co., Inc.; *pg.* 1761, *pg.* 954
Roeller, Bob, Mgr-Precast Sls-Northeast-Plains - Dayton Superior Corporation; *pg.* 1328, *pg.* 1464
Roenna, Joe, Exec VP-Mdsg, Procurement & Inventory Mgmt - Eby-Brown Co.; *pg.* 1767, *pg.* 636
Roeper, Zachary, Product Mgr-Digital - BBC Worldwide America Inc.; *pg.* 271, *pg.* 1201
Roepke, Jon, Dir-Product Mgmt - Belkin International, Inc.; *pg.* 361, *pg.* 182
Roering, Mike, Mgr-Michelin Sls - Quality Bicycle Products; *pg.* 1710, *pg.* 918
Roesch, Gloria, Mgr-Clinical Mktg - MedImmune LLC; *pg.* 1562, *pg.* 770
Roese, Clinton, Sr Mgr-Media - Bayer Corporation; *pg.* 1499, *pg.* 1573
Roesel, Steven, Dir-Adv & Media-Global - GlaxoSmithKline; *pg.* 1536, *pg.* 1389
Roesler, John, VP-Sls & Mktg - Theragenics Corporation; *pg.* 1431, *pg.* 527
Roesner, Randy, Dir-Pharmacy & Health Care Mktg - Walgreen Co.; *pg.* 1608, *pg.* 605
Roethe, Carrie F., Sr Dir-Internal Comm - Level 3 Communications, Inc.; *pg.* 1262, *pg.* 1664
Roetter, Alex, VP-Engrg & Revenue - Twitter, Inc.; *pg.* 1285, *pg.* 228
Roettger, Linda, Dir-Mktg - Agilent Technologies, Inc.; *pg.* 614, *pg.* 264
Roewe, Jay, Sr VP-Production - Home Box Office, Inc.; *pg.* 290, *pg.* 1240
Roff, Heather, Asst VP-Media - L'Oreal USA; *pg.* 514, *pg.* 1252
Rogal, David, Sr Dir-Sls Res - Pandora Media Inc.; *pg.* 1273, *pg.* 172
Rogalski, Rebecca, Sr Dir-Integrated Mktg-Town & Country - The Hearst Corporation; *pg.* 1649, *pg.* 1239
Rogers, Aaron, Dir-Adv & Publicity - NBC Universal, Inc.; *pg.* 300, *pg.* 1266
Rogers, Adam, Sr Mgr-IR - Workiva; *pg.* 493, *pg.* 701
Rogers, Ashley, Dir-Mktg & Bus Dev-St Augustine Premium Outlets - Simon Property Group, Inc.; *pg.* 1112, *pg.* 690
Rogers, Brian, Brand Mgr-Innovation & Pringles US - Kellogg Company; *pg.* 831, *pg.* 870
Rogers, Charlie, Dir-Sls-Latin America - Fender Musical Instruments Corporation; *pg.* 547, *pg.* 21
Rogers, Dan, Sr Mgr-Mktg - Grand Ole Opry; *pg.* 289, *pg.* 1651
Rogers, Dan, CMO - Symantec Corporation; *pg.* 478, *pg.* 161
Rogers, Ericka, Dir-Mktg Comm - Dell Inc.; *pg.* 383, *pg.* 1737
Rogers, Jack F., VP-Sls & Mktg - Hussey Seating Co.; *pg.* 929, *pg.* 751
Rogers, Jan, Sr Mgr-Brand Mktg Editorial - Oracle Corporation; *pg.* 450, *pg.* 191
Rogers, Jeanine, District Mgr-Sls - Chevron Corporation; *pg.* 974, *pg.* 259
Rogers, Jennifer, VP-Innovation Mktg Team - Univision Communications Inc.; *pg.* 683, *pg.* 1307
Rogers, Jennifer Jossart, Project Mgr-Direct Mail & Email Mktg - Harley-Davidson, Inc.; *pg.* 178, *pg.* 1874
Rogers, Jenny, Sr Product Mgr - Boston Scientific Corporation; *pg.* 1508, *pg.* 831
Rogers, Joe, Mgr-Strategic Mktg - Siemens Process Industries and Drives; *pg.* 673, *pg.* 485
Rogers, Johannah, Brand Mgr-Captain Morgan - Diageo North America Inc.; *pg.* 248, *pg.* 1223
Rogers, John, Sr VP-Product Mgmt & Head-Embassy Suites-Global - Hilton Worldwide, Inc.; *pg.* 1094, *pg.* 1791
Rogers, Jonathan, Dir-Style Brand Mktg-Global - Fossil Group, Inc.; *pg.* 5, *pg.* 1735
Rogers, Karen, Sr Dir-Employee & Exec Comm - BMC Software, Inc.; *pg.* 362, *pg.* 1701
Rogers, Kate, Coord-Mktg - The Dun & Bradstreet Corp.; *pg.* 1637, *pg.* 1120
Rogers, Kirk, Mgr-Sls - Precitech, Inc.; *pg.* 1427, *pg.* 1035
Rogers, Kristie, Dir-Consumer Mktg - Wolverine World Wide, Inc.; *pg.* 1822, *pg.* 905
Rogers, Lingling, Sr Mgr-CMC Regulatory Affairs - Allergan, Inc.; *pg.* 1491, *pg.* 106
Rogers, Lura, Asst VP-Domestic Mktg - NATIONAL WESTERN LIFE INSURANCE COMPANY; *pg.* 1210, *pg.* 1664
Rogers, Mae, Sr Product Mgr-Mktg - AT&T Mobility LLC; *pg.* 620, *pg.* 1824
Rogers, Mark, Sr Mgr-Comml Mktg - DIRECTV Group Holdings, LLC; *pg.* 281, *pg.* 79
Rogers, Matt, Head-Indus-Large Customer Sls - Google Inc.; *pg.* 1249, *pg.* 153
Rogers, Meg, Sr VP & Dir-Creative-Worldwide - Combe Incorporated; *pg.* 1516, *pg.* 1351
Rogers, Nate, VP-Mktg & Comm - OhioHealth; *pg.* 1578, *pg.* 1443
Rogers, Payton, Sr Mgr-Global Agencies & Media - Johnson & Johnson; *pg.* 1549, *pg.* 1091
Rogers, Robyn, Analyst-Mktg Res - AT&T; *pg.* 1865, *pg.* 258
Rogers, Roosevelt, VP-Sls & Mktg - Laser Technology, Inc.; *pg.* 1419, *pg.* 314
Rogers, Sara, Program Mgr-Mktg - Tyler Technologies, Inc.; *pg.* 486, *pg.* 1690
Rogers, Scott, VP-Foodservice Sls - Van's International Foods, Inc.; *pg.* 908, *pg.* 302
Rogers, Shelley, Mgr-Corp Mktg Comm - Publix Super Markets, Inc.; *pg.* 1031, *pg.* 437
Rogers, Susan, Mgr-Inside Sls - ITW Magnaflux; *pg.* 1418, *pg.* 615
Rogers, Tim, Dir-Digital Mktg Fin - Adobe Systems Incorporated; *pg.* 342, *pg.* 235
Rogers, Ty, Sr Mgr-Corp Comm - Amazon.com, Inc.; *pg.* 1226, *pg.* 1831
ROgers, Victoria, Dir-Hotel Sls - Mount Airy Casino Resort; *pg.* 1106, *pg.* 1554
Rogers-Rivera, Carrie, Assoc Mgr-Mktg - HP Hood LLC; *pg.* 864, *pg.* 829
Rogge, Karen, Interim CFO - Applied Micro Circuits Corporation; *pg.* 618, *pg.* 283
Roggemann, Ellen, VP-Mktg - Equinox Fitness Clubs; *pg.* 546, *pg.* 1228
Roggenkamp, Mark, Exec Dir-Channel Mktg - Deluxe Corporation; *pg.* 1634, *pg.* 964
Rogina, Bill, Specialist-Mktg - Red Wing Shoe Company, Inc.; *pg.* 1817, *pg.* 954
Roginski, Glenn, Dir-Media & Connections-Pharmaceuticals - Johnson & Johnson; *pg.* 1549, *pg.* 1091
Rogosheske, Tanya, Mgr-Adv & GRM - Aveda Corporation; *pg.* 499, *pg.* 917
Rogovin, Sarah, Dir-Mktg - The Kraft Heinz Company; *pg.* 871, *pg.* 641
Rogowin, Adam, Dir-PR - Chicago Blackhawk Hockey Team, Inc.; *pg.* 538, *pg.* 569
Rogowski, Ray, Dir-Mktg-Global - Honeywell International Inc.; *pg.* 407, *pg.* 1088
Rohan, Chris, Dir-Institutional & Intl Mktg - Eaton Vance Corp.; *pg.* 746, *pg.* 794
Rohani, Talieh, Sr Product Mgr - Rosetta Stone Inc.; *pg.* 462, *pg.* 1774
Rohatgi, Sanjay, Sr VP-Sls-Asia Pacific & Japan - Symantec Corporation; *pg.* 478, *pg.* 161
Rohde, Chris, Sr Mgr-User Experience & Mechanical Design - Autodesk Inc.; *pg.* 356, *pg.* 257
Rohe, Tim, Mgr-Brdcst Adv Production - Menard, Inc.; *pg.* 1055, *pg.* 1857
Rohlfs, Erin M., Mgr-Bus Mktg Channel - AT&T; *pg.* 1865, *pg.* 258
Rohm, Kelly, Mgr-Mktg & Brand Mgr-Dell Fin Svcs - Dell Inc.; *pg.* 383, *pg.* 1737
Rohmann, Eric, Dir-Sls - Princeton University Press; *pg.* 1678, *pg.* 1112
Rohrbacker, Keith, Product Mgr - Kubota Tractor Corporation; *pg.* 705, *pg.* 294
Rohrbaugh, Jim, Product Mgr-Controls - GEA Refrigeration North America, Inc.; *pg.* 1072, *pg.* 1597
Rohrbaugh, Tracy, Sr Dir-Mktg-Global - Revlon, Inc.; *pg.* 521, *pg.* 1286
Rohrer, Carolyn, Sr Mgr-Exec Comm - Autodesk Inc.; *pg.* 356, *pg.* 257
Rohrer, Danielle, Mgr-Mktg - Kadant Johnson Inc.; *pg.* 1073, *pg.* 909
Rohrer, Neil F., VP-Core Eastern US Sls - Paychex, Inc.; *pg.* 792, *pg.* 1336
Rohrer, Vikki, Mgr-Adv Fin-Global - Ford Motor Company; *pg.* 172, *pg.* 876
Rohrmann, Nicole, Mgr-Global Brand Media - Marquis Jet Partners Inc.; *pg.* 1915, *pg.* 1256
Rohrs, Annie, Sr Mgr-Comm - CBS Interactive, Inc.; *pg.* 369, *pg.* 215
Rohrs, Jeffrey K., VP-Mktg Insights - ExactTarget Inc.; *pg.* 1244, *pg.* 685
Rohy, Eric, Exec VP-Product Mgmt - Questar Assessment, Inc.; *pg.* 1679, *pg.* 1143
Roides, Breana, Product Dir - Johnson & Johnson; *pg.* 1549, *pg.* 1091
Roig, Carmen, Sr VP-Sls & Mktg - Crystal Cruises LLC; *pg.* 1904, *pg.* 128
Roj-Wiedman, Danika, Brand Mgr-GREENIES - Mars Petcare; *pg.* 1478, *pg.* 1633
Rojas, Alfredo, Dir-Digital Product Mgmt & Guest Tech - Carnival Corporation; *pg.* 1902, *pg.* 441
Rojas, Anna, Specialist-Mktg & Social Media - Save the Queen, LLC.; *pg.* 1111, *pg.* 124
Rojas, Aracelis, Product Mgr - Lillian Vernon Corporation; *pg.* 1776, *pg.* 315
Rojas, Beatriz, Sr Dir-Multicultural Mktg - Kaiser Permanente; *pg.* 1552, *pg.* 171

Rojas, Pedro, Producer-Digital Vendor Mktg - Target Corporation; *pg.* 1786, *pg.* 942
Rok, Charly, VP-PR - David's Bridal, Inc.; *pg.* 23, *pg.* 1523
Rokosh, Ervin, Dir-Mktg - Culligan International Company; *pg.* 54, *pg.* 656
Roland, Ed, Mgr-Mobile Mktg - Kraft Foods Oscar Mayer; *pg.* 870, *pg.* 1866
Roland, Larry, Dir-Mktg - Utility Trailer Manufacturing Company; *pg.* 1712, *pg.* 68
Roland, Rick, Sr Mgr-Program Mktg - Red Hat, Inc.; *pg.* 460, *pg.* 1388
Rolapp, Brian, Exec VP-Media & Pres/CEO-NFL Network - National Football League; *pg.* 567, *pg.* 1264
Rolenc, Steven, Mgr-Mktg-Intl - Stryker Corporation; *pg.* 1598, *pg.* 894
Rolfes, Mark, VP-US Sls-Pelican Products - Pelican Products, Inc.; *pg.* 1842, *pg.* 295
Roll, Susan, Principal-Mktg - FedEx Corporation; *pg.* 1907, *pg.* 1642
Roller, Becky, Sr VP-Mktg & Comm-Global - Flextronics International Ltd.; *pg.* 81, *pg.* 245
Roller, Ben, Sr Dir-Ticket Ops & CRM - Miami Dolphins, Ltd.; *pg.* 562, *pg.* 419
Rolleston, Ron, Exec VP-Creative & Bus Dev - Elizabeth Arden, Inc.; *pg.* 507, *pg.* 448
Rollinger, Rob, Program Mgr-Global Mktg - Intel Corporation; *pg.* 645, *pg.* 266
Rollins, Dave, Mgr-Product & Market Dev - Magnetic Metals Corp.; *pg.* 1358, *pg.* 1049
Rollins, Gretchen, Sr Mgr-Mktg & Comm - DIRECTV Group Holdings, LLC; *pg.* 281, *pg.* 79
Rollins, James, VP-Digital Video Distr-ESPN Media-New York - ESPN, Inc.; *pg.* 285, *pg.* 340
Rollins, Kyle, Mgr-Mktg-High Tech & Govt - Honeywell International Inc.; *pg.* 407, *pg.* 1088
Rollins, Nancy, Mgr-Mktg - Missouri Lottery; *pg.* 999, *pg.* 979
Rollins, Stefan, Dir-Strategic Plng & Ops-Indus Strategy Mktg - Autodesk Inc.; *pg.* 356, *pg.* 257
Rollinson, Sandra H., Dir-Field Mktg - General Growth Properties, Inc.; *pg.* 1093, *pg.* 574
Rolofson, Christy, Brand Mgr-Media - DISH Network Corporation; *pg.* 283, *pg.* 325
Rolves, Lisa, Brand Mgr-US Shopper Mktg - Energizer Holdings, Inc.; *pg.* 637, *pg.* 996
Rom, Kimberly, Dir-Mktg - Del Monte Foods, Inc.; *pg.* 852, *pg.* 304
Romagnoli Santore, Jennifer, Dir-Bus Plng Mktg Svcs - Bristol-Myers Squibb Company; *pg.* 1509, *pg.* 1206
Romagnoli, Lucky, Mgr-Pre Owned Sls - Fairway Ford Lincoln; *pg.* 170, *pg.* 1617
Romaine, Edward, Assoc Publr-Integrated Sls Dev-GQ - Vogue Magazine; *pg.* 1700, *pg.* 1311
Roman, Alexandra, Sr Dir-Revenue & Adv Solutions-ESPN Digital Media - ESPN, Inc.; *pg.* 285, *pg.* 340
Roman, Antonio, Sr VP-Natl Sls-Univision Television Grp - Univision Communications Inc.; *pg.* 683, *pg.* 1307
Roman, Blair, Mgr-Creative & Emerging Media - Toys "R" Us, Inc.; *pg.* 968, *pg.* 1130
Roman, Carine, Head-Global Adv Ops - LinkedIn Corporation; *pg.* 1262, *pg.* 160
Roman, Elias, Product Mgr-Google Play Music - Google Inc.; *pg.* 1249, *pg.* 153
Roman, Isis, Asst Mgr-Fragrance & Product Dev - Parlux Fragrances, Inc.; *pg.* 519, *pg.* 426
Roman, Lisa, Dir-Mktg - Breitling USA; *pg.* 2, *pg.* 385
Roman, Rica, Mgr-Media - Procter & Gamble Inc.; *pg.* 333, *pg.* 1929
Roman, Ted, Sr VP-Natl Sls - William Grant & Sons, Inc.; *pg.* 1972, *pg.* 1057
Roman, Ursula, Dir-Mktg - Fred's Inc.; *pg.* 1769, *pg.* 1644
Romanchik, Ron, VP-Sls & Mktg-Recording Tech - AudioCodes USA; *pg.* 356, *pg.* 1121
Romanko, Kimberly A., Mgr-Mktg-Global - 3M Company; *pg.* 1142, *pg.* 956
Romano, Courtney, Mgr-Search & Affiliate Mktg - Coach, Inc.; *pg.* 3, *pg.* 1214
Romano, Jaime, Dir-Sls-Rite Aid - Reckitt Benckiser Inc.; *pg.* 1136, *pg.* 1105
Romano, John, Dir-Internet Media - Vital Pharmaceuticals, Inc.; *pg.* 1607, *pg.* 479
Romano, Kelly, Dir-Creative - Orlando Magic; *pg.* 572, *pg.* 455
Romano, Madeline, Mgr-Experiential Mktg & Events - Groupon, Inc.; *pg.* 1255, *pg.* 575
Romano, Peter, Sr Dir-East Coast Sls - AutoTrader, Inc.; *pg.* 1230, *pg.* 490
Romano, Rich, Mgr-Sls & Mktg - Winn Dixie Stores, Inc.; *pg.* 1038, *pg.* 435
Romanoff, Daniel, Brand Mgr-Innovation - The Kraft Heinz Company; *pg.* 871, *pg.* 641
Romanovich, Maggie, Specialist-Sls Trng - Constellation Brands, Inc.; *pg.* 1960, *pg.* 1348
Romanow, Bryan, Reg Mgr-Mktg-Southeast Reg - WESCO International Inc.; *pg.* 687, *pg.* 1582
Romanow, Sarah, Brand Mgr-Integrated - Brooks Sports Inc.; *pg.* 1805, *pg.* 1818
Romanowicz, Edyta, Acct Mgr-Media-Talent Brand - LinkedIn Corporation; *pg.* 1262, *pg.* 160
Romas, Michele, Brand Mgr-Media - Xerox Corporation; *pg.* 494, *pg.* 365
Romatier, Christophe, Sr Mgr-Strategic Mktg - Honeywell International Inc.; *pg.* 407, *pg.* 1088
Romenesko, Ben, Product Mgr - Miller Electric Manufacturing Co.; *pg.* 1361, *pg.* 1852
Romeo, Dominick, Sr Mgr-Mktg - L'Oreal USA; *pg.* 514, *pg.* 1252
Romeo, Jennie, Dir-Product Mgmt-Global - Levi Strauss & Co.; *pg.* 43, *pg.* 220
Romeo, Russ, Sr Dir-Mktg - Dunkin' Brands Group, Inc.; *pg.* 1727, *pg.* 810
Romer, Allison Young, VP-Enterprise Mktg - American Medical Association; *pg.* 130, *pg.* 564
Romer, Katy, Brand Mgr-Design - 3M Company; *pg.* 1142, *pg.* 956
Romere, Keith, Mgr-Sls Activation - PepsiCo, Inc.; *pg.* 259, *pg.* 1327
Romero, Armando, Dir-Adv - Justin Brands, Inc.; *pg.* 1810, *pg.* 1695
Romero, Colleen, Dir-Digital Mktg-NAPA Auto Parts - Genuine Parts Company; *pg.* 206, *pg.* 506
Romero, Colleen, Dir-Digital Mktg - National Automotive Parts Association; *pg.* 213, *pg.* 515
Romero, Debra, Sr Mgr-Media - Pfizer Inc.; *pg.* 1581, *pg.* 1278
Romero, Emily, VP-Mktg - Penguin Random House; *pg.* 1675, *pg.* 1276
Romero, Emily, VP-Mktg-Penguin Young Readers Grp - Penguin Random House; *pg.* 1675, *pg.* 1276
Romero, Martha L., Mgr-Technical Ocean Mktg - Schlumberger Limited; *pg.* 801, *pg.* 1714
Romero, Patricia, VP-Multicultural Mktg-West - Time Warner Cable Inc.; *pg.* 312, *pg.* 1301
Romero, Stephen, VP-Intl Sls - McIlhenny Company; *pg.* 876, *pg.* 741
Romig, Caitlin, Mgr-Digital Media - Rosetta Stone Inc.; *pg.* 462, *pg.* 1774
Romine, James C., VP-Regulatory & Product Stewardship - E.I. du Pont de Nemours & Company; *pg.* 1159, *pg.* 390
Rominski, Katy, Mgr-Social Media - Hubbard Broadcasting, Inc.; *pg.* 291, *pg.* 961
Romm, Elisa, Exec VP-B2B Mktg - MasterCard Incorporated; *pg.* 779, *pg.* 1325
Romo, Gilbert, VP-Sls Comm Div - Integrated Electrical Services, Inc.; *pg.* 88, *pg.* 1708
Romo, Lauren, Mgr-Mktg-Madewell - J. Crew Group, Inc.; *pg.* 1773, *pg.* 1245
Romoff, Mike, Sr Dir-Global Sls & Adv Ops - LinkedIn Corporation; *pg.* 1262, *pg.* 160
Romoser, Chris, Dir-PR & Worldwide Comm - Lenovo Group Ltd; *pg.* 427, *pg.* 1384
Romoser, Sandy, Sr VP-Sls & Chief Customer Officer - PepsiCo, Inc.; *pg.* 259, *pg.* 1327
Ron, Lior, Corp VP-Product Mgmt - Motorola Mobility LLC; *pg.* 657, *pg.* 627
Ronaghan, Jerry, Sr VP-Product Innovation - The Dun & Bradstreet Corp.; *pg.* 1637, *pg.* 1120
Ronan, Douglas, VP-Mktg - Driscoll Strawberry Associates Inc.; *pg.* 854, *pg.* 305
Ronan, Elizabeth, VP-Alternative Mktg - CBS Corporation; *pg.* 273, *pg.* 1210
Rondeau, Kyle, Mgr-Event Mktg - Nielsen Audio; *pg.* 446, *pg.* 768
Rondina, Lisa, Mgr-Sls - Fairway Outdoor Advertising of the Triangle East; *pg.* 1640, *pg.* 1387
Rondinelli, Karen, Asst Dir-Mktg - The Northwestern Mutual Life Insurance Company; *pg.* 1212, *pg.* 1879
Rondon, Al, Sr Mgr-Mktg-Sports & Entertainment Mktg - Coca-Cola North America; *pg.* 848, *pg.* 500
Rondon, Diego, Sr Dir-Multicultural Mktg - Sysco Corporation; *pg.* 1035, *pg.* 1716
Ronen, Amit, VP & Gen Mgr-Device Mgmt Product Div - Wind River Systems, Inc.; *pg.* 493, *pg.* 38
Roney, Stephen, VP-Product Mktg-Global - DTS, Inc.; *pg.* 634, *pg.* 55
Rongavilla, Joe, Dir-Media - Ubisoft Inc.; *pg.* 589, *pg.* 229
Ronis, Marty, VP-Mktg & Sls - Michigan Wheel Corporation; *pg.* 1709, *pg.* 888
Ronnau, Todd, Sr Mgr-Avaya Managed & Hosted Solutions - Avaya Inc.; *pg.* 621, *pg.* 264
Ronse, Luz, Mgr-Channel Mktg - Schneider Electric; *pg.* 467, *pg.* 1609
Roodman, Adam, Dir-US Sls-Microsoft Adv Exchange - Microsoft Corp.; *pg.* 440, *pg.* 321
Rook, Jennifer, Sr Mgr-Mktg - Elkay Manufacturing Company; *pg.* 80, *pg.* 645
Rooks, Mark, Sr Dir-Pepsi Sports Mktg - PepsiCo, Inc.; *pg.* 259, *pg.* 1327
Rooney, Emily, Coord-Mktg Partnerships - Minnesota Vikings Football Club, Inc.; *pg.* 563, *pg.* 923
Rooney, Joe, Sr VP-Brand Mktg, Adv & Social Media - Cox Communications, Inc.; *pg.* 279, *pg.* 501
Rooney, Kristin M., Dir-Content Mktg - Verizon Communications Inc.; *pg.* 1875, *pg.* 1309
Rooney, Melissa, Asst Media Buyer - Palisades Media Group, Inc.; *pg.* 452, *pg.* 275
Rooney, Mike, VP-Sls & Mktg - Emerson Process Management; *pg.* 1334, *pg.* 1636
Rooney, Peggy A., Specialist-Mktg-Home Depot - Armstrong World Industries, Inc.; *pg.* 914, *pg.* 1545
Rooney, Sharon, Exec Dir-Global New Product Commercialization - Novartis Pharmaceuticals Corp.; *pg.* 1575, *pg.* 1054
Roos, Scott, VP-Product Design - Juno Lighting, Inc.; *pg.* 1300, *pg.* 606
Root, Brooke, Sr Coord-Social Media Mktg - Victoria's Secret Stores, LLC; *pg.* 1789, *pg.* 1471
Root, Mark, Corp Dir-Media Rels - Northrop Grumman Corporation; *pg.* 231, *pg.* 1781
Ropella, Annie, Sr Specialist-Mktg Comm - Brady Corporation; *pg.* 363, *pg.* 1873
Roper, Avis, Sr Dir-Comm - Indianapolis Colts, Inc.; *pg.* 553, *pg.* 687
Roper, Bill, VP & Head-DI Central Creative - Disney Interactive Media Group; *pg.* 1239, *pg.* 95
Roper, Catherine, Dir-Mktg - Delta Faucet Company; *pg.* 78, *pg.* 684
Roper, John, Sr Mgr-Onshore Comm-Global - Hess Corporation; *pg.* 979, *pg.* 1240
Roper, Lauren, Sr Mgr-Mktg-DailyBurn - IAC/InterActiveCorp; *pg.* 292, *pg.* 1242
Roperti, Christina, Mgr-PR - Godiva Chocolatier, Inc.; *pg.* 1854, *pg.* 1235
Roque, Noel, Sr Mgr-Mktg & Bus Dev-Latin America - Coca-Cola North America; *pg.* 848, *pg.* 500
Roques, Liz, Brand Mgr - Chattem, Inc.; *pg.* 1515, *pg.* 1628
Rork, Joe, Sr Engr-Product Dev - Ford Motor Company; *pg.* 172, *pg.* 876
Rosa, Dan, Dir-Sls - Cannon Equipment Company; *pg.* 1321, *pg.* 920
Rosa, Erin, Sr Dir-Retail Digital Customer Engagement - CVS Health Corporation; *pg.* 1765, *pg.* 1610
Rosa, Jennifer, Mgr-PR - Third Federal Savings & Loan Association; *pg.* 810, *pg.* 1436
Rosa, Mike, Dir-Strategy & Technical Mktg-Emerging Technologies - Applied Materials, Inc; *pg.* 618, *pg.* 1009
Rosa, Tim, VP-Mktg - Fitbit Inc.; *pg.* 639, *pg.* 218
Rosack, Mary Kate, Brand Mgr-Olive Garden - Darden Restaurants, Inc.; *pg.* 1724, *pg.* 453
Rosack, Mary Kate, Brand Mgr-Olive Garden - Olive Garden Italian Restaurant; *pg.* 1742, *pg.* 454
Rosal, Monica, Coord-Mktg Comm - QUALCOMM Incorporated; *pg.* 1873, *pg.* 207
Rosalia Eger, Elizabeth, Mgr-Mktg & Comm-Global - The Donna Karan Company LLC; *pg.* 23, *pg.* 1225
Rosania, Paul, Grp Product Mgr - Twitter, Inc.; *pg.* 1285, *pg.* 228
Rosano, Linda, Sr Dir-Bus Insurance Mktg - The Travelers Companies, Inc.; *pg.* 1220, *pg.* 352
Rosario, Annabelle, Mgr-Mktg-Intl - FedEx Corporation; *pg.* 1907, *pg.* 1642
Rosario, Efrain, Dir-Global Shopper Mktg-Global - The Coca-Cola Company; *pg.* 240, *pg.* 493
Rosario, Frideiza, Sr Analyst-Procurement, Mktg & Bus Svcs-North America - Unilever United States, Inc.; *pg.* 904, *pg.* 1061

Rosario, Jonathan del, Sr Asst Brand Mgr-Fabric Care-Alliance Innovation Team - The Procter & Gamble Company; *pg.* 1129, *pg.* 1418
Rosario, Silvian, Sr Dir-Product Plng - LexisNexis Group; *pg.* 1658, *pg.* 1446
Rosarioe, Frank, Sr Mgr-ECommerce - Just Born, Inc.; *pg.* 1857, *pg.* 1516
Rosas, Alicia, VP-Mktg-Confectionary - Bimbo Bakeries USA; *pg.* 840, *pg.* 151
Rosati, Dan, Dir-New Product Dev-Global - Spectrum Brands Holdings, Inc.; *pg.* 60, *pg.* 1867
Roscoe, Elizabeth, Head-Mktg-Global - The Western Union Company; *pg.* 822, *pg.* 327
Roscoe, Leah, VP-Mktg-Global - VeriFone Systems, Inc.; *pg.* 487, *pg.* 251
Roscoe, Lizzie, Mgr-Social Media-Global Digital Comm - McDonald's Corporation; *pg.* 1737, *pg.* 645
Rose, Alan D., Dir-Indus Mktg-Energy & Utilities - Intel Corporation; *pg.* 645, *pg.* 266
Rose, Amy, Dir-Integrated Media - Caleres, Inc.; *pg.* 1805, *pg.* 993
Rose, Andrew, Mgr-Social Media Community - Amica Mutual Insurance Co.; *pg.* 1192, *pg.* 1602
Rose, Andrew, Mgr-Online Mktg - The Vanguard Group, Inc.; *pg.* 816, *pg.* 1550
Rose, Angie, Mgr-Mktg Process Improvement - The Kroger Co.; *pg.* 1025, *pg.* 1416
Rose, Austin, Asst Mgr-Online Mktg - Teleflora LLC; *pg.* 1801, *pg.* 140
Rose, Betsy, Head-Contrast Mktg - Bracco Diagnostics, Inc.; *pg.* 1509, *pg.* 1085
Rose, Bill, Mgr-Media Rels - ABB Inc.; *pg.* 1309, *pg.* 1359
Rose, Bill, Asst VP & Sr Mgr-Product & Mktg Mgmt Bus Svcs - Federated Investors, Inc.; *pg.* 752, *pg.* 1575
Rose, Bill, Sr VP-Local Media Client Solutions - Nielsen Audio; *pg.* 446, *pg.* 768
Rose, Bob, Dir-PR - Oakland Athletics Limited Partnership; *pg.* 571, *pg.* 172
Rose, Brian, Sr Dir-Product Dev - Cox Communications, Inc.; *pg.* 279, *pg.* 501
Rose, Caitlin, Mgr-Wholesale Mktg-Paint Stores Grp - The Sherwin-Williams Company; *pg.* 1447, *pg.* 1435
Rose, Caitlin, Mgr-Wholesale Mktg-Paint Stores Grp - Sherwin Williams; *pg.* 1448, *pg.* 1436
Rose, Cindy, VP-Mktg, Brand & Comm - All Children's Hospital Inc.; *pg.* 1490, *pg.* 461
Rose, Doug, Sr VP-Programming & Mktg - QVC Inc; *pg.* 305, *pg.* 1593
Rose, Greg, Sr Assoc Mgr-Mktg - General Mills, Inc.; *pg.* 828, *pg.* 933
Rose, John, Dir-Retail Mktg & Sls - Dickey's Barbecue Restaurants, Inc.; *pg.* 1725, *pg.* 1680
Rose, John, Product Mgr-Metal Cutting - Robert Bosch Tool Corp; *pg.* 1060, *pg.* 634
Rose, Julie, VP-Mktg Strategy & Comm - Ecolab Inc.; *pg.* 329, *pg.* 960
Rose, Kelly, VP & Sr Mgr-Mktg Relationship - Bank of America Corporation; *pg.* 718, *pg.* 1362
Rose, Kelly, VP-Sls - Nola Media Group; *pg.* 1671, *pg.* 747
Rose, Kelsey, Mgr-Mktg - G.H. Bass & Co.; *pg.* 1809, *pg.* 1234
Rose, Lindsey, Mgr-Mktg - Live Nation Entertainment, Inc.; *pg.* 558, *pg.* 47
Rose, Mark, Mgr-Comml & Mktg-NWS - Chevron Corporation; *pg.* 974, *pg.* 259
Rose, Michelle M., Sr Mgr-Mktg - Accenture; *pg.* 1392, *pg.* 1186
Rose, Nicholas, Mgr-Mktg Analytics & Insight - Dell Inc.; *pg.* 383, *pg.* 1737
Rose, Peter, Dir-Product Dev - Rose Packing Company; *pg.* 892, *pg.* 556
Rose, Randy, Dir-Consumer Products Licensing - National Hockey League; *pg.* 568, *pg.* 1265
Rose, Richard, VP-Sls & Mktg-Titan Tire - Titan International, Inc.; *pg.* 219, *pg.* 653
Rose, Scott, Rep-Primary Care Sls - Eli Lilly and Company; *pg.* 1527, *pg.* 684
Rose, Tip, Dir-Digital Mktg - Cardinal Health, Inc.; *pg.* 1512, *pg.* 1448
Rose, Vanessa, Sr Dir-Intl Ops & Bus Dev - The Gap, Inc.; *pg.* 1770, *pg.* 218
Rose, William, Sr VP-Local Media Client Solutions - The Nielsen Company B.V.; *pg.* 1671, *pg.* 1272
Roseberry, Taylor, Planner-Integrated Mktg Comm-Progresso - General Mills, Inc.; *pg.* 828, *pg.* 933
Roselli, John, Dir-Product Mktg & Mgmt - Bose Corporation; *pg.* 626, *pg.* 820
Roselli, Laura, Dir-Digital Mktg Platforms - Atmel Corporation; *pg.* 621, *pg.* 238
Roselli, Stacey, Dir-Sls & Mktg - Custom Chemical Formulators, Inc.; *pg.* 329, *pg.* 271
Roseman, David, Dir-Digital Mktg & Direct Sls Div - IDT Corporation; *pg.* 643, *pg.* 1096
Rosemann, Bill, Dir-Creative-Marvel Games - Marvel Entertainment, LLC; *pg.* 1662, *pg.* 1257
Rosen, Adam, Exec VP-Mktg - Sidney Frank Importing Co., Inc.; *pg.* 1970, *pg.* 1184
Rosen, Christopher, Sr Dir-News - Entertainment Weekly Inc.; *pg.* 1639, *pg.* 1228
Rosen, Dave, Dir-Adv & Mktg - G. Joannou Cycle Co. Inc.; *pg.* 1707, *pg.* 1098
Rosen, Joshua, Sr Mgr-Mktg-Toys - Amazon.com, Inc.; *pg.* 1226, *pg.* 1831
Rosen, Leah, Assoc VP-Mktg & Creative Svcs - The George Washington University; *pg.* 602, *pg.* 400
Rosen, Maren, VP-Mdsg - Stuller, Inc.; *pg.* 13, *pg.* 745
Rosen, Mike, Exec VP-NBCU Hispanic Group Adv Sale - NBC Universal, Inc.; *pg.* 300, *pg.* 1266
Rosen, Sam, VP-Mktg - The Atlantic Monthly Group; *pg.* 1618, *pg.* 396
Rosen, Tim, Dir-Mktg - Jostens, Inc.; *pg.* 7, *pg.* 938
Rosenbalm, Tracy, Specialist-Mktg Comm - Intel Corporation; *pg.* 645, *pg.* 266
Rosenbaum, Dan, Mgr-Visitor Experience Mktg - San Francisco Travel Association; *pg.* 1005, *pg.* 227
Rosenbaum, Elena, Brand Mktg Mgr-Shopper Sam's Club - The Clorox Company; *pg.* 327, *pg.* 169
Rosenbaum, Jamie, Dir-Mktg Comm - Tomy; *pg.* 968, *pg.* 648
Rosenbaum, Jim, Sr Engr-Technical Mktg - Intel Corporation; *pg.* 645, *pg.* 266
Rosenberg, Adam, Grp Product Mgr - TripAdvisor, Inc.; *pg.* 1926, *pg.* 835
Rosenberg, Amanda, Mgr-Glass Mktg - Google Inc.; *pg.* 1249, *pg.* 153
Rosenberg, David, Dir-Brand Adv - AARP; *pg.* 124, *pg.* 393
Rosenberg, Jeremy, Mgr-Sls-Natl - SureFire, LLC; *pg.* 1307, *pg.* 90
Rosenberg, Josh, Mgr-Social Media - Time Warner Cable Inc.; *pg.* 312, *pg.* 1301
Rosenberg, Leslie, Specialist-Mktg - Office Depot, Inc.; *pg.* 448, *pg.* 412
Rosenberg, Marc, Sr Mgr-Adv - The Washington Post; *pg.* 1701, *pg.* 407
Rosenberg, Maria, Assoc Mgr-Mktg - General Mills, Inc.; *pg.* 828, *pg.* 933
Rosenberg, Mark, Mgr-PR - Milwaukee Bucks, Inc.; *pg.* 563, *pg.* 1878
Rosenberg, Michael, VP-Media & Mobile Mktg - Paramount Pictures Corporation; *pg.* 304, *pg.* 138
Rosenberg, Nikki, Mgr-Shopper Mktg - Procter & Gamble Inc.; *pg.* 333, *pg.* 1929
Rosenberg, Steve, Sr Dir-Respiratory Mktg - Merck & Co., Inc.; *pg.* 1566, *pg.* 1077
Rosenberg, Susan, Mgr-PR - United Parcel Service, Inc.; *pg.* 1928, *pg.* 522
Rosenberger, Rusty, Dir-Global Product Mgmt-Tiered Storage Solutions - Imation Corp.; *pg.* 413, *pg.* 952
Rosenblum, Gary, Sr Dir-Channel Dev-LifeScan, J&J - LifeScan Inc; *pg.* 1556, *pg.* 146
Rosenbluth, David, VP-Product & Consumer Mktg - Gerber Life Insurance Company; *pg.* 1201, *pg.* 1352
Rosenfeld, Janelle, VP-Adv & Comm - Altadis USA, Inc.; *pg.* 1893, *pg.* 423
Rosenfeld, Rich, VP-Sls-Watches & Apparel - Victorinox Swiss Army Inc.; *pg.* 1139, *pg.* 357
Rosenfelt, Rebecca, Product Mgr-Growth - Airbnb, Inc.; *pg.* 1226, *pg.* 211
Rosenfield, Julia, Asst Dir-Digital Mktg Strategy - The Hartford Financial Services Group, Inc.; *pg.* 1202, *pg.* 352
Rosengard, Rebecca Kramer, Head-Indus Mktg-Automotive - Twitter, Inc.; *pg.* 1285, *pg.* 228
Rosengarten, Susie, Mgr-Adv Graphics - The Lima News; *pg.* 1659, *pg.* 1457
Rosengren, Pete, Asst VP & Dir-Adv - The Daily Herald Co.; *pg.* 1632, *pg.* 1819
Rosengren, Pete, Asst VP & Dir-Adv-Daily Herald Media Grp - Paddock Publications, Inc.; *pg.* 1674, *pg.* 554
Rosenkranz, Sherry, Mgr-Adv-Global - General Motors Company; *pg.* 175, *pg.* 881
Rosenlund, Kim, Dir-Mktg - ATI Physical Therapy; *pg.* 1498, *pg.* 558
Rosenson, Stacey A., VP-Sls, Mktg & Ops - DIRECTV Group Holdings, LLC; *pg.* 281, *pg.* 79
Rosenstein, Daniel, Mgr-Internet Mktg - Consolidated Credit Counseling Services, Inc.; *pg.* 741, *pg.* 424
Rosenstein, Howard, Dir-Branded Content, Integrated Sls & Mktg - Meredith Corporation; *pg.* 1663, *pg.* 705
Rosenstein, Michael, VP-Global Product Mgmt & Solutions Enablement - Dell Inc.; *pg.* 383, *pg.* 1737
Rosenstock, Marcie, Mgr-Event Mktg - Inc.com LLC; *pg.* 1258, *pg.* 1243
Rosenthal, Debbie, Sr Specialist-Mktg - FedEx Corporation; *pg.* 1907, *pg.* 1642
Rosenthal, Denny, Dir-Customer Svc & Intl Sls - The Worth Company; *pg.* 1848, *pg.* 1895
Rosenthal, Ellen C., Specialist-Mktg Comm - Eversource; *pg.* 1942, *pg.* 845
Rosenthal, Holly, Head-Global Mktg Comm - Merck & Co., Inc.; *pg.* 1566, *pg.* 1077
Rosenthal, Kurt, Sr Mgr-Mktg & Comm-Global - Cisco Systems, Inc.; *pg.* 372, *pg.* 240
Rosenthal, Larry, Specialist-Sls & Mktg Integration - The Dun & Bradstreet Corp.; *pg.* 1637, *pg.* 1120
Rosenthal, Melissa, Dir-Creative Svcs - Buzzfeed; *pg.* 1233, *pg.* 1208
Rosenthal, Paul, VP-Mktg - Transport Topics Publishing Group; *pg.* 1696, *pg.* 1772
Rosenwald, April, Sr Product Mgr-ECommerce - Dick's Sporting Goods, Inc.; *pg.* 1832, *pg.* 1524
Rosenzweig, Jeff, Sr Dir-CRM - Match.Com, LLC; *pg.* 1265, *pg.* 1683
Roshan, Pejman, VP-Product Mgmt - ShoreTel, Inc.; *pg.* 469, *pg.* 288
Rosich, Carly, Mgr-Partnership Mktg - MGM Resorts International; *pg.* 1105, *pg.* 1028
Rosiello, Rob, Sr VP-Sls-Americas - Riverbed Technology, Inc.; *pg.* 1277, *pg.* 225
Rosier, Amy, Mgr-Comm & Mktg - Tri-State Motor Transit Co.; *pg.* 1926, *pg.* 980
Rosin, Richard, Sr Dir-Mdsg - C&S Wholesale Grocers, Inc.; *pg.* 1016, *pg.* 1035
Roskill, Damian, CMO - AppNeta; *pg.* 352, *pg.* 1909
Rosky, Mark, Mgr-Content & Mktg-Park Avenue Securities - The Guardian Life Insurance Company of America; *pg.* 1202, *pg.* 1237
Rosman, Jennifer, Sr Mgr-Channel Mktg-Unilever Food Solutions - Unilever United States, Inc.; *pg.* 904, *pg.* 1061
Rospenda, John, VP-Mktg - JustFab, Inc.; *pg.* 27, *pg.* 80
Ross, Alexander, Sr VP-Sls - Web.com Group, Inc.; *pg.* 1288, *pg.* 435
Ross, Amy, Dir-Mktg & Video Dev - AT&T Communications Corp.; *pg.* 1866, *pg.* 1043
Ross, Amy, Dir-Mktg & Video Dev - AT&T Inc.; *pg.* 1867, *pg.* 1674
Ross, Andrew, VP & Product Mgr-CitiDirect BE - Citigroup Inc.; *pg.* 735, *pg.* 1212
Ross, Andrew, Chief Strategy Officer & Exec VP - ConAgra Foods, Inc.; *pg.* 826, *pg.* 1014
Ross, Anna, Dir-Global Integrated Mktg Comm - Combe Incorporated; *pg.* 1516, *pg.* 1351
Ross, Chip, Head-Social Media - DIRECTV Group Holdings, LLC; *pg.* 281, *pg.* 79
Ross, Chris, Sr VP-Sls-Global Channels - Barracuda Networks, Inc.; *pg.* 360, *pg.* 58
Ross, Chris, VP-Mktg - HP Hood LLC; *pg.* 864, *pg.* 829
Ross, Christy, Dir-Natl Mktg - M.D.C. Holdings, Inc.; *pg.* 1104, *pg.* 321
Ross, Dana, Dir-Creative Svcs - Continental Mills, Inc.; *pg.* 827, *pg.* 1845
Ross, Donaldson, Chief Revenue Officer & Sr VP - Bankrate, Inc.; *pg.* 1231, *pg.* 451
Ross, Gary, Dir-Sls - Savaria Concord Lifts Inc.; *pg.* 1592, *pg.* 1919
Ross, George, VP-Sls & Mktg - Carolina Biological Supply Company; *pg.* 1513, *pg.* 1359
Ross, Gigi G., Mgr-Corp Social Channels - Johnson & Johnson; *pg.* 1549, *pg.* 1091
Ross, Greg, Dir-Mktg-US Toothpaste & Mouthwash - Colgate-Palmolive Company; *pg.* 504, *pg.* 1215
Ross, Gregory, Dir-Media-Asia - The Procter & Gamble Company; *pg.* 1129, *pg.* 1418
Ross, Gwen K., Sr Analyst-Mdsg-Contract - Staples, Inc.; *pg.* 474, *pg.* 821
Ross, Hannah, Sr Mgr-Mktg - Meineke Car Care Centers, Inc.; *pg.* 212, *pg.* 1367

First page reference indicates Business Class Edition
Second page reference indicates Geographic Edition

Ross, Havilah R., Mgr-Mktg Comm - Six Flags Entertainment Corporation; pg. 583, pg. 1698
Ross, Jazmin, Assoc Mgr-Digital Mktg - Newell Rubbermaid Inc.; pg. 1128, pg. 515
Ross, Jenna, Coord-Social Media - Fender Musical Instruments Corporation; pg. 547, pg. 21
Ross, Jennifer, Sr Mgr-Client & Assoc Experience - TD Ameritrade Holding Corporation; pg. 808, pg. 1018
Ross, Jim, Dir-Sls-Indus Flexible Foam Sys - Span-America Medical Systems, Inc.; pg. 1595, pg. 1618
Ross, Jo Ann, Pres-Sls - CBS Corporation; pg. 273, pg. 1210
Ross, Joel, Sr Mgr-Mktg Comm-Global - Avery Dennison Corporation; pg. 1452, pg. 95
Ross, Johanna, Product Dir - Converse Inc.; pg. 1831, pg. 793
Ross, Jonathan, Sr Mgr-Market Res - Apple Inc.; pg. 350, pg. 73
Ross, Jordana, Mgr-Mktg - Ralph Lauren Corporation; pg. 46, pg. 1284
Ross, Keith, Product Mgr - Black Box Corporation; pg. 361, pg. 1547
Ross, Kerri, Dir-Sls Mktg & Program Mgmt - Advertising Age; pg. 1613, pg. 1187
Ross, Kory, Product Mgr-Mid Tractors - Deere & Company; pg. 703, pg. 632
Ross, Lauren, Product Mgr-Flights - TripAdvisor, Inc.; pg. 1926, pg. 835
Ross, Lisa, Sr Dir-Domestic Brand - Marchon Eyewear, Inc.; pg. 1421, pg. 1180
Ross, Maggie, Asst VP & Mgr-Mktg Channel - Ivy Funds Distributor Inc.; pg. 771, pg. 719
Ross, Marlene, VP-Mktg - Akorn; pg. 1488, pg. 1138
Ross, Matt, Head-Global Brand & Creative Mktg-YouTube - Google Inc.; pg. 1249, pg. 153
Ross, Matthew S., Sr Mgr-Global Mktg-Abbott Animal Health - Abbott Laboratories; pg. 1484, pg. 551
Ross, Mike, Reg Mgr-Sls - Redco Foods, Inc.; pg. 891, pg. 1174
Ross, Nancy B., Mgr-Mktg - United States Postal Service; pg. 1009, pg. 406
Ross, Nicole, VP & Sr Mgr-Relationship-Wealth Mgmt-Northern Indiana - The PNC Financial Services Group, Inc.; pg. 795, pg. 1579
Ross, Peter, VP-Corp Mktg - TechTarget, Inc.; pg. 482, pg. 837
Ross, Richard, VP-Sls & Mktg - Bardahl Manufacturing Corporation; pg. 972, pg. 1833
Ross, Robin, Sr Dir-Corp Mktg - Costco Wholesale Corporation; pg. 1765, pg. 1820
Ross, Robin, VP-Brand Creative Ops - J. Crew Group, Inc.; pg. 1773, pg. 1245
Ross, Sarah, Sr Dir-Coors Family of Brands-Molson & Foster's - MillerCoors LLC; pg. 255, pg. 582
Ross, Suzi, VP-Integrated Mktg - HSN, Inc.; pg. 291, pg. 462
Rosser, Kathryn, Sr Specialist-Mktg - Siemens Process Industries and Drives; pg. 673, pg. 485
Rosser, Troy D., Sr VP-Sls - Computer Programs & Systems, Inc.; pg. 378, pg. 7
Rosset, Jill, Mgr-Channel Mktg - Paslode; pg. 1059, pg. 664
Rosseter, Amanda, Dir-Media Rels & Corp Comm-Global - The Coca-Cola Company; pg. 240, pg. 493
Rosseter, Jolene, Planner-Mktg - Peapod, LLC; pg. 1029, pg. 661
Rossetti, Karen, Mgr-Mktg Svcs - Big Y Foods, Inc.; pg. 1015, pg. 845
Rossi, Alessio, VP-Digital Mktg, ECommerce & CRM-Lancome - L'Oreal USA; pg. 514, pg. 1252
Rossi, Andrew, Acct Exec-Ticket Sls - Golden State Warriors, LLC; pg. 550, pg. 171
Rossi, Bianca, Analyst-Social Media Mktg - eBags, Inc.; pg. 1240, pg. 331
Rossi, Christie C., Sr Dir-Mktg Strategy - Comcast Corporation; pg. 276, pg. 1560
Rossi, Christina, Sr Dir-Corp Mktg & Comm - Fresenius Medical Care North America; pg. 1531, pg. 851
Rossi, David, VP-Mktg - Manischewitz Company; pg. 875, pg. 1097
Rossi, Gina, VP-Mktg & Brand Dev - Oneida Savings Bank; pg. 790, pg. 1319
Rossi, Mark, Sr VP-Enterprise Sls-Western Reg - Merrill Corporation; pg. 1664, pg. 962
Rossick, Scott, Sr Mgr-Digital & Intl Creative - F5 Networks, Inc.; pg. 396, pg. 1835
Rossick, Susie, Sr Mgr-Reg Mktg-Honda & Acura - American Honda Motor Co., Inc.; pg. 163, pg. 292
Rossignol, Jeannine, VP-Mktg-Large Enterprise Ops - Xerox Corporation; pg. 494, pg. 365
Rossini, Tom, Dir-Mktg - The Hartford Financial Services Group, Inc.; pg. 1202, pg. 352
Rossino, Matt, Mgr-Social Media - AARON'S, INC.; pg. 912, pg. 486
Rosskamm, Erica, Brand Mgr - Wm. Wrigley Jr. Company; pg. 1863, pg. 596
Rossman, Julie, Brand Mgr - Constellation Brands, Inc.; pg. 1960, pg. 1348
Rossman, Lyndsay, Dir-Global Tourism Mktg - Simon Property Group, Inc.; pg. 1112, pg. 690
Rossman, Ted, Mgr-PR - Bankrate, Inc.; pg. 1231, pg. 451
Rossman, Tom, VP-Sls - MTD Products, Inc.; pg. 1057, pg. 1478
Rosso, Brent, VP-Digital Media - Target Corporation; pg. 1786, pg. 942
Rosso, David J., Reg Mgr-Sls - Reliable Automatic Sprinkler Co., Inc.; pg. 1137, pg. 1158
Rossomangno, Laura, Program Mgr-Mktg-Luxury Vinyl Tile - Armstrong World Industries, Inc.; pg. 914, pg. 1545
Rosst, Carl W., Sr Mgr-Bus Comm - The Guardian Life Insurance Company of America; pg. 1202, pg. 1237
Rost, Martin, Sr Dir-Market Access-Global - Pfizer Inc.; pg. 1581, pg. 1278
Rostagno, Claudia, Mgr-Mktg-Interactive & Digital Access Mktg - FedEx Express Corporation; pg. 1908, pg. 1644
Roston, Michael, Sr Editor-Social Media - The New York Times Company; pg. 1668, pg. 1270
Rota, Andrea, Sr Mgr-Education & Corp Digital Mktg - The New York Times; pg. 1668, pg. 1270
Rotberg, Adam, Mgr-Sls - Tapjoy, Inc.; pg. 1396, pg. 228
Rotella, Lou , III, VP-Mktg - Rotellas Italian Bakery, Inc.; pg. 892, pg. 1018
Rotem, David, Exec VP-Sls & Mktg - Tribune Media Company; pg. 1696, pg. 592
Rotenberg, Ellen, Dir-Product Strategy - Thomson Reuters Markets; pg. 810, pg. 1299
Roth, Adam, VP-Brand Mktg-Running - NIKE, Inc.; pg. 1812, pg. 1492
Roth, Ashley, Assoc Dir-Adv Ops - Complex Media, Inc.; pg. 1628, pg. 1217
roth, Catherine, Dir-Mktg & ECommerce - Marriott International, Inc.; pg. 1102, pg. 764
Roth, Christina, Mgr-Sls Promo - Kohl's Corporation; pg. 1775, pg. 1870
Roth, Elizabeth, Sr Mgr-New Products Mktg-Global - Kinetic Concepts, Inc.; pg. 1553, pg. 1741
Roth, Erik, Sr Mgr-Tech-Southwest.com - Southwest Airlines Co.; pg. 1923, pg. 1687
Roth, Jen, Mgr-Social Media Content - The Allstate Corporation; pg. 1189, pg. 639
Roth, Jessie, Planner-Digital Media - Bloomberg L.P.; pg. 725, pg. 1204
Roth, Katherine, Sr Mgr-Mktg - The Allstate Corporation; pg. 1189, pg. 639
Roth, Kelly, VP-Mktg - ATI Physical Therapy; pg. 1498, pg. 558
Roth, Kim, Pres-Production - Imagine Entertainment; pg. 292, pg. 46
Roth, Martin, Exec Dir-Mktg, Adv & New Media - National Cattlemen's Beef Association; pg. 148, pg. 314
Roth, Matt, Sr Product Mgr - Zulily; pg. 1792, pg. 1843
Roth, Mike, Mgr-Mktg-Pipe Welding Products - Miller Electric Manufacturing Co.; pg. 1361, pg. 1852
Roth, Nicole M., Program Mgr-Vertical Mktg - Intel Corporation; pg. 645, pg. 266
Roth, Oliver, Sr Mgr-Mktg - Electronic Arts Inc.; pg. 951, pg. 189
Roth, Paul, Pres-Retail Sls - AT&T Inc.; pg. 1867, pg. 1674
Roth, Rob, Sr Dir & Head-Global Mktg-Rare Hematology Diseases - Genzyme Corporation; pg. 1534, pg. 808
Roth, Sheila, Specialist-Media Rels - The Western & Southern Financial Group; pg. 1223, pg. 1427
Roth, Steve, Product Mgr - Third Federal Savings & Loan Association; pg. 810, pg. 1436
Roth, Tim, Dir-Digital Sls-KHOU11 Media Solutions - KHOU-TV, Inc.; pg. 294, pg. 1709
Rothaus, Alex, Mgr-Search Engine Mktg - Provide Commerce, Inc.; pg. 1276, pg. 206
Rothe, Patrick, Dir-Sls - Telluride Ski & Golf Company LLP; pg. 587, pg. 336
Rothenberg, Jennifer, Head-Global Mktg-Corp Solutions - The NASDAQ OMX Group, Inc.; pg. 785, pg. 1263
Rothenberg, Mike, Sr Mgr-Corp Comm - CACI International Inc.; pg. 367, pg. 1773
Rothenburger, Hortense, Brand Mgr-CARTE NOIRE & KENCO Cappuccinos - Mondelez International, Inc.; pg. 878, pg. 601
Rothenhausen, Mark, Dir-Inside Sls - Goodway Technologies Corporation; pg. 1341, pg. 374
Rothermel, Mary, VP-Sls - CooperVision, Inc.; pg. 1407, pg. 1159
Rothgeb, Ken, VP & Gen Mgr-Sls & Mktg-Air Conditioning Div - Rheem Manufacturing - Air Conditioning Div; pg. 1075, pg. 32
Rothgeb, Tim, VP-Comml & OEM Sls - M&G Dura-Vent, Inc.; pg. 95, pg. 298
Rothman, Aaron, Sr Product Mgr - Google Inc.; pg. 1249, pg. 153
Rothman, Greg, Sr Product Dir - Vonage Holdings Corp.; pg. 686, pg. 1074
Rothman, Jeffrey, VP-Mktg & Innovation - The Dannon Company, Inc.; pg. 851, pg. 1351
Rothman, Mike, Planner-Digital Sls - The Wall Street Journal; pg. 1700, pg. 1312
Rothschild, Jim, Dir-Adv - Capitol Broadcasting Company, Inc.; pg. 272, pg. 1386
Rothschild, Jordan, Specialist-Field Mktg - Beam Suntory Inc.; pg. 1957, pg. 599
Rothstein, Sharon, CMO - Starbucks Corporation; pg. 897, pg. 1840
Rothweiler, Dori, Project Coord-Mktg - California Raisin Marketing Board; pg. 1017, pg. 93
Rotolo, Danielle, Specialist-Media Rels - All Children's Hospital Inc.; pg. 1490, pg. 461
Rotolo, Jack, Pres-Sls & Bus Ops-Global - Mode Media; pg. 1267, pg. 50
Rotsch, Carolyn, Sr Mgr-Digital Mktg - NBTY, Inc.; pg. 1572, pg. 1338
Rottenberg, Alan, CMO-Ceridian HCM - Ceridian Corporation; pg. 371, pg. 932
Rotter, Mitch, Sr VP-Brand Mktg - Ticketmaster Entertainment LLC; pg. 1284, pg. 48
Rottier, Jason, Mgr-On-line Category & Sls Plng - Mars Petcare; pg. 1478, pg. 1633
Rottler, Nick, Head-Corp Mktg - Symantec Corporation; pg. 478, pg. 161
Rotunno, Dave, Exec Dir-Mktg - Mizkan Americas, Inc.; pg. 877, pg. 634
Rouaix, Sylvie, VP-Product Dev & Brand Mktg - Sephora USA Inc; pg. 522, pg. 227
Roubicek, Karen, Mgr-Events Mktg - Liberty Mutual Insurance Group Inc.; pg. 1205, pg. 797
Rouch, Tracy, Mgr-PR - St. Louis Post-Dispatch LLC; pg. 1688, pg. 1004
Rouget, Brent, Sr Mgr-Pkg Procurement - Kellogg Company; pg. 831, pg. 870
Roughan, Sarah, Head-Multicultural Mktg - New York Life Insurance Company; pg. 1211, pg. 1268
Rought, Jay, Mgr-Sls-Central US & Canada - Waterous Company; pg. 1387, pg. 965
Roughton, Bert, Mng Editor & Sr Dir-Editorial - The Atlanta Journal-Constitution; pg. 1618, pg. 490
Rougier, Glenn, Sr Dir & Head-Global Strategic Mktg & Radiology Device Svcs Bus - Bayer Corporation; pg. 1499, pg. 1573
Rouhani, Blake, Sr Mgr-PR - Hilton Worldwide, Inc.; pg. 1094, pg. 1791
Rouillard, Andrew, VP-Brand Mgmt & Adv - Mutual of Omaha Insurance Company; pg. 1210, pg. 1016
Roulston, Caitlin, Sr Mgr-PR-Microsoft Comml Comm - Microsoft Corporation; pg. 435, pg. 1824
Roumfort, Mark, VP-Product Mgmt & Dev - The HON Company; pg. 928, pg. 709
Roumian, Jenn, Brand Mgr-Global Talent Acq - Electronic Arts Inc.; pg. 951, pg. 189
Rounce, Justin, CTO & VP-Mktg - Cameron International; pg. 1151, pg. 1702
Round, Cynthia, Sr VP-Mktg & External Rels - The Metropolitan Museum of Art; pg. 561, pg. 1259
Round, John, Asst VP-Sls - Wheels Inc.; pg. 1931, pg. 607
Rounds, Nicole, Mgr-Mktg & Specialist-Mktg-Comml Div - LoJack Corporation; pg. 210, pg. 811
Roundtree, Laura, Dir-Brand Mktg - CBC Restaurant Corp.; pg. 1721, pg. 1677
Rouns, Cameron, VP-Global Mktg-Abbott Medical Optics Div - Abbott Medical Optics, Inc.; pg. 1485, pg. 260
Rountree, Marcus, Sr Specialist-Category Mktg - Lowe's Companies, Inc.; pg. 1053, pg. 1383

First page reference indicates Business Class Edition
Second page reference indicates Geographic Edition

Rourke, Bob, Mgr-Sls & Mktg-Natl - Precision Roll Grinders, Inc.; *pg.* 1370, *pg.* 1514
Rourke, Seth, Dir-Mktg-Global - Honeywell International Inc.; *pg.* 407, *pg.* 1088
Rouse, Michael, Mgr-Sls & Product - Sanden International (USA), Inc.; *pg.* 217, *pg.* 1750
Rouse, Mike, Sr Dir-Sls Ops - Hostess Brands LLC; *pg.* 1856, *pg.* 984
Rousseau, Kara, Sr VP-Ad Sls Mktg - The Walt Disney Company; *pg.* 317, *pg.* 52
Rousseau, Sophie, Sr Mgr-Mktg - The Home Depot, Inc.; *pg.* 1050, *pg.* 510
Roussin, Siping, Sr Mgr-Optimization & Personalization - Lenovo Group Ltd; *pg.* 427, *pg.* 1384
Routhieaux, Bruce, VP-Sls - Carmeuse North America; *pg.* 73, *pg.* 1574
Routhier, Justine, Mgr-Social Media - SANTANDER HOLDINGS USA, INC.; *pg.* 801, *pg.* 800
Roux, Andre, Sr Mgr-Bus Analytics - DIRECTV Group Holdings, LLC; *pg.* 281, *pg.* 79
Roux, Elise, Dir-Global PR & Comm - Benefit Cosmetics LLC; *pg.* 501, *pg.* 213
Roux, Jerome, Head-Mktg-Franchise - The Gap, Inc.; *pg.* 1770, *pg.* 218
Roux, Michael, VP-Product Mgmt - PATIENT SAFETY TECHNOLOGIES, INC.; *pg.* 1580, *pg.* 114
Roux, Olivier, Mng Dir-Corp Mktg & Comm - Accenture; *pg.* 1392, *pg.* 1186
Roux, Pierre, Dir-Mktg-Wireless MCU Solutions - Atmel Corporation; *pg.* 621, *pg.* 238
Roux, Roy, VP-Sls - Bradken; *pg.* 1150, *pg.* 714
Rovak, Don, Dir-Ticket Sls - Atlanta Falcons Football Club, LLC; *pg.* 530, *pg.* 532
Roval, Ofir, Product Mgr-Cloud Platform - Google Inc.; *pg.* 1249, *pg.* 153
Roveto, Peter, Dir-Mktg - Brookline Bancorp, Inc.; *pg.* 727, *pg.* 804
Rowan, Cyndi E., Head-Field Sls & Recruiter - The Allstate Corporation; *pg.* 1189, *pg.* 639
Rowe, Alethea, Sr Dir-PR - Cheesecake Factory Incorporated; *pg.* 1017, *pg.* 56
Rowe, Chris M., Assoc Mgr-Mktg - The Allstate Corporation; *pg.* 1189, *pg.* 639
Rowe, Danny, VP-Market Unit Sls - Coca-Cola Bottling Co. Consolidated; *pg.* 240, *pg.* 1365
Rowe, Darrin, Sr Mgr-Mdsg - Hotels.com, L.P.; *pg.* 1257, *pg.* 1682
Rowe, Denny L., Dir-Sls & Mktg - Weldon Solutions; *pg.* 1388, *pg.* 1598
Rowe, Grant, Product Mgr - E.D. Bullard Company; *pg.* 1332, *pg.* 727
Rowe, Lucie, Mgr-New Media Distr - Scripps Networks Interactive, Inc.; *pg.* 1279, *pg.* 1638
Rowe, Michael, Sr Dir-Strategic Mktg-Global - Allergan, Inc.; *pg.* 1491, *pg.* 106
Rowe, Nicole, Dir-Corp Mktg - RSA Security Inc.; *pg.* 463, *pg.* 786
Rowe, Paul, Specialist-Online Mktg Ops - Intuit Inc.; *pg.* 769, *pg.* 158
Rowe, Shelley, Mgr-Mktg - Samuels Group, Inc.; *pg.* 109, *pg.* 1898
Rowe, Tamora, Media Buyer - Valassis; *pg.* 1698, *pg.* 386
Rowe, Tim, VP-Mktg - Trade Press Media Group; *pg.* 1695, *pg.* 1881
Rowe, Tom, Mgr-Online Media - W.R. Grace & Co.; *pg.* 123, *pg.* 810
Rowicki, Lynn, Specialist-Mktg - The Northwestern Mutual Life Insurance Company; *pg.* 1212, *pg.* 1879
Rowles, Amanda, Sr Mgr-Mktg - CBS Interactive, Inc.; *pg.* 369, *pg.* 215
Rowles, Chet, Mgr-Best Buy & Big Box Retail Mktg - Dell Inc.; *pg.* 383, *pg.* 1737
Rowley, Craig, Dir-Integrated Mktg - Recreational Equipment, Inc.; *pg.* 1843, *pg.* 1821
Rowley, Laura, VP-Video Production & Product - Meredith Corporation; *pg.* 1663, *pg.* 705
Rowley, Lori, Mgr-Mktg-Residential Ceilings - Armstrong World Industries, Inc.; *pg.* 914, *pg.* 1545
Rowley, Storer, Dir-Media Rels - Northwestern University; *pg.* 606, *pg.* 612
Roxin, Amy, VP & Mgr-Sls-Central New York - FIRST NIAGARA FINANCIAL GROUP, INC.; *pg.* 757, *pg.* 1148
Roy, Ashis, VP-Tech & Product Engrg-India - Time Inc.; *pg.* 1693, *pg.* 1300
Roy, Julie, Sr Dir-Customer Mktg & Analytics - DSW, Inc.; *pg.* 1807, *pg.* 1439
Roy, Keya, Dir-Creative & Corp Mktg - Dow Jones & Company, Inc.; *pg.* 1637, *pg.* 1225
Roy, Khosi, Sr Mgr-Asst Brand-COVERGIRL North America - The Procter & Gamble Company; *pg.* 1129, *pg.* 1418
Roy, Michael, Specialist-Social Care - Alaska Air Group, Inc.; *pg.* 1897, *pg.* 1830
Roy, Molly, Dir-Mktg - Res-Care, Inc.; *pg.* 1589, *pg.* 738
Roy, Monique, Sr Specialist-Mktg Comm - Tyler Technologies, Inc.; *pg.* 486, *pg.* 1690
Roy, Monte, Sr VP-Sls - Information Builders Inc.; *pg.* 415, *pg.* 1243
Roy, Nikhil, Product Mgr - Google Inc.; *pg.* 1249, *pg.* 153
Roy, Rajiv, VP-Bus Dev & Dir-Product Mgmt - Rudolph Technologies, Inc.; *pg.* 669, *pg.* 918
Roy, Rick, Sr Mgr-Mktg - Express Scripts, Inc.; *pg.* 1530, *pg.* 997
Roy, Rob, Grp VP & Head-ECommerce & Digital Mktg-Time Warner Cable - Time Warner Cable Inc.; *pg.* 312, *pg.* 1301
Roy, Stephen, Pres-North American Sls & Mktg - Mack Trucks, Inc.; *pg.* 183, *pg.* 1375
Roy, Stephen, Dir-CT, Nuclear Medicine New Product Introduction & Mfg Engrg - Philips Healthcare; *pg.* 1585, *pg.* 783
Royba, Paul A., Dir-Mktg, Natl Sls & Distr - Bayer Corporation; *pg.* 1499, *pg.* 1573
Royce, Anthony, Sr Dir-Product Mktg-Zynga Sports - Zynga Inc.; *pg.* 1292, *pg.* 235
Royer, James, Dir-Digital Media & Strategy - Kansas City Chiefs Football Club, Inc.; *pg.* 555, *pg.* 984
Roylance, Grason, Coord-Email Mktg - Overstock.com, Inc.; *pg.* 1273, *pg.* 1760
Royston, Becky, Sr Analyst-Strategic Mktg - PulteGroup, Inc.; *pg.* 1109, *pg.* 873
Royston, Christine, Dir-Mktg Comm-Global - LinkedIn Corporation; *pg.* 1262, *pg.* 160
Royston, Rob, Mgr-Mktg Intelligence & Infrastructure - FedEx Corporation; *pg.* 1907, *pg.* 1642
Rozan, Michelle, VP-Mktg - Bloomingdale's, Inc.; *pg.* 1763, *pg.* 1204
Rozek, Staci F., Sr Mgr-Mktg - SYNNEX Corporation; *pg.* 480, *pg.* 92
Rozen, Matt, Grp Mgr-Social Media - Adobe Systems Incorporated; *pg.* 342, *pg.* 235
Rozenblat, Dan, Sr Dir-Ticket Sls & Svc - Chicago Blackhawk Hockey Team, Inc.; *pg.* 538, *pg.* 569
Rozier, Bill, VP-Mktg-Global - CIENA Corporation; *pg.* 628, *pg.* 771
Rozin, Randall, Dir-Brand Mgmt & Mktg Comm-Global - Dow Corning Corporation; *pg.* 1159, *pg.* 900
Rozner, Alyson, Mgr-Mktg - WABC-TV Inc.; *pg.* 317, *pg.* 1312
Rozsa, Kevin, VP-Global Distributors & Mktg - Transtar Industries, Inc.; *pg.* 219, *pg.* 1478
Rozwadowski, Christina, Brand Mgr - Rust-Oleum Corporation; *pg.* 1447, *pg.* 664
Ruane, Chris, Exec Dir-Global Sls-North America - Fairmont Hotels & Resorts Inc.; *pg.* 1091, *pg.* 1938
Ruane, Erin, VP-Sls - Homes.com, Inc.; *pg.* 1256, *pg.* 203
Ruane, John, VP-Sls & Mdsg - The Stop & Shop Supermarket Company LLC; *pg.* 1034, *pg.* 842
Ruane, Karen, Mgr-Field Mktg - Autodesk Inc.; *pg.* 356, *pg.* 257
Ruarte, Fernando, Co-Founder, CTO-Platform & Products & Exec VP - Mode Media; *pg.* 1267, *pg.* 50
Ruba, Sarah, Asst VP & Mgr-Mktg - Wells Fargo & Company; *pg.* 819, *pg.* 232
Rubalcaba, Maya, Brand Mgr-Scotch, Japanese Whisky & US - Beam Suntory Inc.; *pg.* 1957, *pg.* 599
Ruben, Keith, Mgr-Mktg-Digital Consumer Mktg - Conde Nast Publications, Inc.; *pg.* 1629, *pg.* 1217
Ruben, Keith, Mgr-Mktg-Digital Consumer Mktg - Vogue Magazine; *pg.* 1700, *pg.* 1311
Ruben, Will, Product Mgr - Facebook, Inc.; *pg.* 1245, *pg.* 143
Rubendall, Tracey, Rep-Sls - Eli Lilly and Company; *pg.* 1527, *pg.* 684
Rubenstein, Jane, Mgr-PR-Global - Brown-Forman Corporation; *pg.* 1958, *pg.* 732
Rubenstein, Jason, Dir-US Agency Ad Sls - Expedia, Inc.; *pg.* 1244, *pg.* 1814
Rubenstein, Paul, Partner & Head-Product Strategy-Talent Solutions - Aon Hewitt; *pg.* 350, *pg.* 627
Rubenstein, Sarah, Sr Mgr-Mktg-US Oncology - Pfizer Inc.; *pg.* 1581, *pg.* 1278
Rubenstein, Stacy, Specialist-Media Rels - Medline Industries, Inc.; *pg.* 1562, *pg.* 635
Rubenzer, Laura, Sr Analyst-Media Optimization - Target Corporation; *pg.* 1786, *pg.* 942
Ruberg, Kerry, VP & Program Mgr-Mktg - Huntington Bancshares Incorporated; *pg.* 767, *pg.* 1440
Ruberg, Kerry, VP & Program Mgr-Mktg - The Huntington National Bank; *pg.* 767, *pg.* 1440
Rubin, Alyssa, Head-Mktg Programs - Direct Energy; *pg.* 1939, *pg.* 1704
Rubin, Ann, VP-Branded Content & Global Creative - International Business Machines Corporation; *pg.* 418, *pg.* 1138
Rubin, Emily, Mgr-Product Mktg - Google Inc.; *pg.* 1249, *pg.* 153
Rubin, Karen N., Sr Product Mgr-Digital Products - Amazon.com, Inc.; *pg.* 1226, *pg.* 1831
Rubin, Matthew, Sr Product Mgr - CommVault Systems, Inc.; *pg.* 377, *pg.* 1125
Rubin, Paul, Chief Medical Officer & Sr VP-R&D - XOMA Corporation; *pg.* 1611, *pg.* 46
Rubin, Scott M., Dir-Payer Mktg & Oncology - Eli Lilly and Company; *pg.* 1527, *pg.* 684
Rubin, Shelley, VP-Adv - Big Lots, Inc.; *pg.* 1762, *pg.* 1438
Rubin, Spencer, Partner-Mktg & Sr Dir-Content Distr - Viacom Inc.; *pg.* 316, *pg.* 1310
Rubin, Tina, Sr Mgr-Mktg - Amazon.com, Inc.; *pg.* 1226, *pg.* 1831
Rubinfeld, Arthur, Chief Creative Officer & Pres-Global Innovation & Evolution Fresh - Starbucks Corporation; *pg.* 897, *pg.* 1840
Rubinger, Robert S., CFO, Sec, Exec VP & Dir-Product Dev - United-Guardian, Inc.; *pg.* 1184, *pg.* 1165
Rubino, Barb, Mgr-Mktg - Anthem, Inc.; *pg.* 1192, *pg.* 683
Rubino, Katharine, Mgr-PR - Neiman Marcus, Inc.; *pg.* 30, *pg.* 1684
Rubino, Lynn, Dir-Creative - L'Oreal USA; *pg.* 514, *pg.* 1252
Rubino, Russell, VP-Mktg-Global - The NASDAQ OMX Group, Inc.; *pg.* 785, *pg.* 1263
Rubino, Tom, Dir-Pub Affairs & Adv - Horizon Blue Cross Blue Shield of New Jersey; *pg.* 1203, *pg.* 1096
Rubino, Vince, Mgr-Event Mktg - LEGO Systems, Inc.; *pg.* 961, *pg.* 346
Rubinstein, Rob, Mgr-Sls Ops-Natl - Heaven Hill Distilleries, Inc.; *pg.* 1964, *pg.* 725
Ruble, Doug, VP-Mktg - O'Reilly Automotive, Inc.; *pg.* 214, *pg.* 1006
Rublowsky, Alexander, Sr Dir-Mktg-Platforms & Licensing - F5 Networks, Inc.; *pg.* 396, *pg.* 1835
Ruby, Carrie, Supvr-Mktg Comm - 3M Company; *pg.* 1142, *pg.* 956
Rucci, Susan, Mgr-Corp Social Media Team - Johnson & Johnson; *pg.* 1549, *pg.* 1091
Ruccolo, Domenic, Sr VP-Worldwide Sls & Mktg-Construction & Forestry Div - Deere & Company; *pg.* 703, *pg.* 632
Ruchman, Jonathan, VP-Brand Mktg - BROOKDALE SENIOR LIVING INC.; *pg.* 1511, *pg.* 1627
Rucinski, Ed, Sr VP-Sls - Nuance Dictaphone Healthcare Solutions; *pg.* 447, *pg.* 806
Rucker, Amber, Specialist-Social Media Customer Relationship - General Motors Company; *pg.* 175, *pg.* 881
Rucker, Andrew G., Reg VP-Sls & Distr - MetroPCS, Inc.; *pg.* 1872, *pg.* 1683
Rucker, Cliff, VP-Sls - United States Postal Service; *pg.* 1009, *pg.* 406
Rucker, Dena, Sr VP-Mdsg & Product Dev-Far East - Geneva Watch Group; *pg.* 5, *pg.* 1174
Rucker, Heather, Sr Mgr-ECommerce - AT&T Communications Corp.; *pg.* 1866, *pg.* 1043
Rucker, Heather, Sr Mgr-ECommerce - AT&T Inc.; *pg.* 1867, *pg.* 1674
Rucker, Jelani, Dir-Bus Dev & Mktg - Wheatland Tube Company; *pg.* 121, *pg.* 1594
Rucker, Mike, VP-Mktg & Digital Solutions-Content Solutions - Time Inc.; *pg.* 1693, *pg.* 1300
Rudd, Corey, Sr Assoc Brand Mgr - The Kraft Heinz Company; *pg.* 871, *pg.* 641
Rudd, Rick, Mgr-Field Technical Sls-East & Canada - Lenovo Group Ltd; *pg.* 427, *pg.* 1384
Ruddell, Katie, Specialist-Global Brand Product-Women's - lululemon athletica inc.; *pg.* 44, *pg.* 1911
Rudder, Kendra, VP-Media Strategies - Scripps Networks Interactive, Inc.; *pg.* 1279, *pg.* 1638
Ruddock, Eda, Dir-Leisure Sls & Destination Weddings-Discover The Palm Beaches - Palm Beach County Convention & Visitors Bureau; *pg.* 1003, *pg.* 479
Rudduck, Gareth, Dir-Global Mktg-Sensodyne -

First page reference indicates Business Class Edition
Second page reference indicates Geographic Edition

GlaxoSmithKline Consumer Healthcare; pg. 510, pg. 1554
Rudduck, Richard, Mgr-Mktg-Global - Liberty Mutual Insurance Group Inc.; pg. 1205, pg. 797
Rude, Mike, Dir-Freight Solutions Mktg-FedEx Svcs - FedEx Corporation; pg. 1907, pg. 1642
Rudecki, Walter, Dir-Life Mktg Sls - American National Insurance Company; pg. 1191, pg. 1697
Rudenstein, Karen, Mgr-Global Brand Mktg & Dev-Gaming - Hasbro, Inc.; pg. 954, pg. 1603
Rudger, Aaron, Owner-Mktg-Web Performance - Keynote Systems Incorporated; pg. 425, pg. 255
Rudin, Melanie, Dir-Mktg & Sls Promos - Tourneau Inc.; pg. 14, pg. 1303
Rudisill, Chris, Dir-Brand Sls - Embassy Suites Hotels; pg. 1090, pg. 1790
Rudman, Lisa, Mgr-Mktg-Innovations & Incubation Brands - MillerCoors LLC; pg. 255, pg. 582
Rudnick, Gary, Dir-Sls - Mutoh America Inc.; pg. 443, pg. 18
Rudnick, Mark, VP-Mktg - AARON'S, INC.; pg. 912, pg. 486
Rudofski, Carol J., Acct Exec-Charter Media-St Louis - Charter Communications, Inc.; pg. 274, pg. 372
Rudolph, Greg, Sr Coord-Adv Ops - CarMax, Inc.; pg. 167, pg. 1800
Rudolph, P.J., Sr Assoc Brand Mgr-Grape Nuts - Post Holdings, Inc.; pg. 833, pg. 1002
Rudy, John, Sr Head-Mktg - Cintas Corporation; pg. 372, pg. 1411
Rue, William, Brand Mgr-Aleve - Bayer Healthcare Consumer Care Division; pg. 1500, pg. 1087
Ruebensaal, Clayton, VP-Mktg-Global - The Ritz-Carlton Hotel Company LLC; pg. 1110, pg. 766
Rueckert, Grayson, Mgr-Mktg - American Express Company; pg. 712, pg. 1190
Rueda, Viviana, Sr Dir Mktg, Brand Mgmt, B2B Mktg, B2C Mktg & GTM Strategy - Experian Consumer Direct; pg. 1245, pg. 71
Ruedisueli, Russ, Dir-SRT & Motorsports Engrg & Vehicle Line Exec-All SRT Products - FCA US LLC; pg. 170, pg. 868
Ruegemer, Meg Sutula, Brand Mgr - Nestle USA, Inc.; pg. 883, pg. 96
Ruel, Roberta, Asst VP-Brand Mktg - Sun Life Financial Inc.; pg. 806, pg. 1944
Rueppel, April, Sr Dir-Member Rels - Association of National Advertisers, Inc.; pg. 133, pg. 1197
Ruesch, Tom, Acct Exec-Charter Media - Charter Communications, Inc.; pg. 274, pg. 372
Ruesink, Sherri, Mgr-Mktg - General Electric Company; pg. 1297, pg. 347
Ruf, Cynthia, Dir-Corp Mktg - North Shore-LIJ Health System; pg. 1573, pg. 1162
Ruf, Simone, VP-Product & Processes - Rail Europe Inc.; pg. 1920, pg. 1354
Rufai, Morin, Specialist-Social Media - Kennesaw State University; pg. 603, pg. 534
Ruff, Brandy, Dir-Brand PR - Kellogg Company; pg. 831, pg. 870
Ruffing, Catherine, Mgr-Sls & Mktg - Genworth Financial, Inc.; pg. 761, pg. 1802
Ruffins, Ebonne, Sr Dir-Diversity Media Comm - Comcast Corporation; pg. 276, pg. 1560
Ruffus, Caitlyn, Asst Mgr-Outreach Mktg - Boulder Brands, Inc.; pg. 1016, pg. 310
Rufo, Tony, Dir-Sls-Office & Education - Elmer's Products, Inc.; pg. 1442, pg. 1479
Ruggiero, Cindy, Sr Specialist-Mktg Ops - Boston Scientific Corporation; pg. 1508, pg. 831
Ruggiero, John, Dir-Media Asset Svcs-NY - The History Channel; pg. 290, pg. 1240
Ruggiero, Lauren, Sr Dir-Scripted Dev - Spike TV; pg. 310, pg. 1295
Ruggiero, Nicolina, Dir-Brand & Digital Mktg - The Great Atlantic & Pacific Tea Company, Inc.; pg. 1021, pg. 1086
Rughwani, Reshma, Exec VP-Commercialization & Product Strategy - eHealth, Inc.; pg. 1242, pg. 153
Ruhge, Kimberly, Dir-New Product Dev - Tupperware Brands Corporation; pg. 1139, pg. 456
Ruhland, Robert, VP-Mktg-North America - BUFFALO WILD WINGS, INC.; pg. 1718, pg. 931
Ruhland, Samantha, Mgr-AT&T Mktg Support - AT&T Mobility LLC; pg. 619, pg. 488
Ruia, Andy, Asst VP-Media - L'Oreal USA; pg. 514, pg. 1252
Ruijssenaars, Robert, Dir-Customer Mktg - E&J Gallo Winery; pg. 1962, pg. 149
Ruim, Randy, Sr VP-Sls & Mktg-Comml Resources - RedBuilt LLC; pg. 106, pg. 548
Ruiz Astorga, Ana Carolina, Sr Mgr-Comm-Baby, Feminine & Family Care-Latin America - The Procter & Gamble Company; pg. 1129, pg. 1418
Ruiz, Adriana Pena, Exec VP-Brand & Sls Dev - Entravision Communications Corporation; pg. 285, pg. 273
Ruiz, Alyssa, Product Mgr - Quicken Loans, Inc.; pg. 797, pg. 884
Ruiz, Isis, Sr Dir-Mktg Svcs - NCL Corporation Ltd.; pg. 1916, pg. 444
Ruiz, Jessica, Coord-Social Media-Guest Rels - Toys "R" Us, Inc.; pg. 968, pg. 1130
Ruiz, Jill, Sr Mgr-Luna Brand - Empire Today, LLC; pg. 923, pg. 643
Ruiz, Joe, VP-Customer-Sls North America-Core Wholesale & New Bus - Godiva Chocolatier, Inc.; pg. 1854, pg. 1235
Ruiz, Luisa, Coord-Mktg - Benihana Inc.; pg. 1716, pg. 409
Ruiz, Ramon, Dir-ECommerce & Mktg - ICE.com, Inc.; pg. 1258, pg. 1955
Ruiz, Teresa Gonzalez, VP-Mktg Fisher-Price - Fisher-Price, Inc.; pg. 953, pg. 1156
Ruiz, Veronica, Mgr-Local Mktg-Sprint Prepaid Grp - Boost Mobile; pg. 1869, pg. 107
Ruiz, Veronica, Mgr-Hispanic Mktg-Sprint Nextel - Sprint Corporation; pg. 1874, pg. 719
Ruk, Marija, Coord-Mktg & Sls-Consumer & OTC - Johnson & Johnson; pg. 1549, pg. 1091
Rukadikar, Manish, Mgr-Mktg Program Mgmt - DTE Energy Company; pg. 1940, pg. 880
Rule, Tom, Sr Product Mgr - Siemens Building Technologies, Inc.; pg. 1376, pg. 560
Rumford, Zoe, Sr Dir-HR - Audible, Inc.; pg. 1230, pg. 1095
Rumley, Skip, VP & Dir-Creative - Hickory Chair Company; pg. 927, pg. 1378
Rumme, Scott, Mgr-Plant - Greer Steel Company; pg. 85, pg. 1447
Rumminger, Jason, VP-Publicity, Media Integrations & Promos - Sony Pictures Entertainment Inc.; pg. 309, pg. 72
Rumph, Crystal, Mgr-Global Mktg Comm & Digital Strategy - Branson Ultrasonics Corporation - Plastics Joining Division; pg. 1403, pg. 343
Rumsey, Pete, Exec VP-Sls & Bus Dev - LIGHTING SCIENCE GROUP CORPORATION; pg. 1301, pg. 467
Runac, Ankica, Brand Mgr - ACH Food Companies, Inc.; pg. 835, pg. 1631
Rund, Brian, Dir-Branding & Mktg Svcs - Nufarm Americas Inc; pg. 1798, pg. 552
Rund, Jim, Chief Revenue Officer-Media - Conversant, Inc.; pg. 1393, pg. 306
Rundell, Rebecca, Mgr-Adv-Natl - J.C. Penney Company, Inc.; pg. 1774, pg. 1732
Rundus, Ken, Sr Dir-IS - Mohawk Industries, Inc.; pg. 935, pg. 527
Runkel, Steve, VP-Sls-North America-TPS - Black Box Corporation; pg. 361, pg. 1547
Runnels, Sheila, VP-Adv - Capital City Press; pg. 1625, pg. 741
Runyan, Cynthia, Brand Mgr-Strategic - 3M Company; pg. 1142, pg. 956
Runyon, Andrew, VP-Intl Interactive Mktg - Paramount Pictures Corporation; pg. 304, pg. 138
Runyon, James, Mgr-Sls - Speedgrip Chuck, Inc.; pg. 1377, pg. 677
Runyon, Jeff, Mgr-Accts & Sls-Natl - Escort, Inc.; pg. 1412, pg. 1479
Runyon, Vicky, Mgr-Mktg - The Allstate Corporation; pg. 1189, pg. 639
Ruot, Lona, Mgr-Mktg & Designer - The Sherwin-Williams Company; pg. 1447, pg. 1435
Ruot, Lona, Mgr-Mktg & Designer - Sherwin Williams; pg. 1448, pg. 1436
Rupczynski, Bob, VP-Media, Data & CRM - The Kraft Heinz Company; pg. 871, pg. 641
Ruppel, Kellsey, Principal & Dir-Product Mktg - Oracle Corporation; pg. 1272, pg. 786
Rusch, Ed, VP-Corp Mktg - Elemica, Inc.; pg. 1242, pg. 1591
Rusch, Thiemo, Gen Mgr-Vehicle Sls - Audi of America, Inc.; pg. 164, pg. 1784
Ruscito, Jessica, Dir-US Media & Digital Branding - Reebok International Ltd.; pg. 1817, pg. 811
Ruse, Tom, Mgr-Mktg Comm - Research Products Corporation; pg. 1075, pg. 1867
Rusev, Peter, Sr Product Mgr - LinkedIn Corporation; pg. 1262, pg. 160
Rush, Ann Kathryn, Dir-Product Dev - Alliance Data Systems Corporation; pg. 347, pg. 1729
Rush, Aussie Josh, Global Dir-Creative - Quiksilver, Inc.; pg. 31, pg. 104
Rush, Corry, Dir-PR - The New York Giants; pg. 570, pg. 1055
Rush, Dorrie, Dir-Mktg-Accessible Tech - Lighthouse International; pg. 1557, pg. 1251
Rush, Jessica, Category Mgr-Mktg - hhgregg, Inc.; pg. 56, pg. 686
Rush, Jozlynn, Sr Specialist-Social Media - Taco Bell Corp.; pg. 1752, pg. 117
Rush, Meg, VP-Consumer Experience & e-Marketing - Anthem, Inc.; pg. 1192, pg. 683
Rush, Sean, Sr Mgr-Mktg - Career Education Corporation; pg. 599, pg. 658
Rushing, Matt, VP-Product Mgmt-Global Advanced Tech Solutions & EFG - AGCO Corporation; pg. 700, pg. 530
Rushing, Tara, Reg Brand Mgr-NorCal - FCA US LLC; pg. 170, pg. 868
Rushmore, Jenny, Dir-Mktg - TripAdvisor, Inc.; pg. 1926, pg. 835
Rusin, William F., VP-Sls & Mktg - W.W. Norton & Company, Inc.; pg. 1702, pg. 1316
Ruskamp, Leanne, Mgr-Creative Svcs - Cabela's Incorporated; pg. 535, pg. 1019
Ruskin, Rick, Head-Mktg-Global Connected Consumer-Commerce Team - General Motors Company; pg. 175, pg. 881
Russ, Anastasia, Mgr-Integrates & Emerging Media - Dr Pepper Snapple Group, Inc.; pg. 250, pg. 1729
Russ, Daren, Brand Mgr-Food & Beverage Enhancers - The Hershey Co.; pg. 1855, pg. 1538
Russart, Laura, Project Mgr-Museum Mktg - Harley-Davidson, Inc.; pg. 178, pg. 1874
Russel, Kristin, Sr Dir-Product Dev & Product Mktg - Omnicell Inc.; pg. 1578, pg. 161
Russell, Charles, Sr Mgr-Mktg, Res & Consumer Insights - Applebee's International, Inc.; pg. 1715, pg. 980
Russell, Cheryl, Dir-Mktg-East Div - McDonald's Corporation; pg. 1737, pg. 645
Russell, Diane, VP-Mktg - Lincoln National Corporation; pg. 776, pg. 1567
Russell, Erin, Mgr-Mktg - VeriFone Systems, Inc.; pg. 487, pg. 251
Russell, Ethan, Product Mgr - Google Inc.; pg. 1249, pg. 153
Russell, Evan, Sr Specialist-Adv-Marine, Aviation & Watersports - Bonnier Corporation; pg. 1622, pg. 480
Russell, Geoffrey, Dir-Sls - Keeneland Association Inc.; pg. 1477, pg. 730
Russell, Holly, Dir-Product Comm - GlaxoSmithKline; pg. 1536, pg. 1389
Russell, Iain, Sr Product Mgr - Thermo Fisher Scientific Inc.; pg. 1602, pg. 61
Russell, John, Product Mgr-Chromebook & Thin Client & VDI - Dell Inc.; pg. 383, pg. 1737
Russell, Jordyn, Mgr-Mktg Comm-Enterprise Products - Plantronics, Inc.; pg. 663, pg. 270
Russell, Juli, Mgr-Digital Mktg - The Kroger Co.; pg. 1025, pg. 1416
Russell, Kenneth, Interim Pres & Interim CEO - Mechanics Bank; pg. 781, pg. 193
Russell, Kristin, Mgr-Mktg - Flextronics International Ltd.; pg. 81, pg. 245
russell, kyle, Sr Dir-Mktg Production Mgmt - Discovery Communications, Inc.; pg. 282, pg. 777
Russell, Matt, Product Mgr & Mgr-Tech Comm - BMW of North America, LLC; pg. 166, pg. 1133
Russell, Meaghan, Sr Mgr-Mktg Activation - Reebok International Ltd.; pg. 1817, pg. 811
Russell, Neil, Rep-Field Sls - LG Electronics Canada, Inc.; pg. 651, pg. 1927
Russell, Rachel, VP-Mktg, BD & Customer Experience Innovation - Liquidity Services, Inc.; pg. 1263, pg. 401
Russell, Richard, Dir-Media Strategy & Mktg Tech - Deckers Outdoor Corporation; pg. 1807, pg. 100
Russell, Rob, Dir-Social, Mobile & Digital Comm - United Parcel Service, Inc.; pg. 1928, pg. 522
Russell, Robin, Analyst-Mktg - E.I. du Pont de Nemours & Company; pg. 1159, pg. 390
Russell, Sanford, Sr Dir-GRID Alliances & Mktg-Enterprise - NVIDIA Corporation; pg. 447, pg. 268
Russell, Stephanie, Mgr-Adv - Pellerin Milnor Corporation; pg. 1368, pg. 744
Russell, Tim, Sr Mng Dir & Head-Sls - Meredith Corporation; pg. 1663, pg. 705
Russell, Travis, Head-Intl Sls-UK Mktg Solutions - LinkedIn

Corporation; pg. 1262, pg. 160
Russell, Victoria, Mgr-Mktg Analysis - Papa John's International, Inc.; pg. 1743, pg. 737
Russeth, Scott H., Sr VP-Pricing Mgmt - Republic Services, Inc.; pg. 107, pg. 19
Russman, Hayley, Dir-Integrated Mktg-Bon Appetit & Epicurious - Conde Nast Publications, Inc.; pg. 1629, pg. 1217
Russman, Hayley, Dir-Integrated Mktg-Bon Appetit & Epicurious - Vogue Magazine; pg. 1700, pg. 1311
Russo, Alfred, Dir-Mktg - Remington Arms Company, LLC; pg. 1844, pg. 1382
Russo, Dan, Mgr-Online Grp Product Mktg - WebEx Communications, Inc.; pg. 491, pg. 270
Russo, James, Mgr-Field Mktg-Northeast Reg - Kind LLC; pg. 868, pg. 1249
Russo, Jennifer, Sr Product Mgr-Health Insurer - Anthem, Inc.; pg. 1192, pg. 683
Russo, Josan J., Sr Product Mgr-Digital & Interactive Adv - DIRECTV Group Holdings, LLC; pg. 281, pg. 79
Russo, Lindsay, Specialist-Mktg - Wyndham Worldwide Corporation; pg. 1119, pg. 1107
Russo, Louis, Gen Mgr & Brand Mgr - Justin Brands, Inc.; pg. 1810, pg. 1695
Russo, Nick, Exec Dir-Digital Mktg - Meredith Corporation; pg. 1663, pg. 705
Russo, Nicole, Asst Mgr-Online Mktg - Ann Inc.; pg. 18, pg. 1195
Russo, Rico, Specialist-Field Mktg-Sacramento & Tahoe - Red Bull North America, Inc.; pg. 264, pg. 275
Russo, Susan, Dir-Product Mktg - Hallmark Cards, Inc.; pg. 1646, pg. 983
Russo, Susan, Dir-Mktg-Advanced Concepts - MATTEL, INC.; pg. 962, pg. 81
Russold, Tracy, Mgr-Sls-Natl - Boyne USA Resorts Inc.; pg. 1082, pg. 874
Russomanno, Carol, Div Mgr-Mktg - William Grant & Sons, Inc.; pg. 1972, pg. 1057
Russomanno, Marcelo, Mgr-LATAM & Specialist-Sls - Microsoft Corporation; pg. 435, pg. 1824
Rust, Christy, Coord-US Mktg Retail - Exxon Mobil Corporation; pg. 977, pg. 1718
Rust, Claire, Sr Mgr-Procurement, Adv & Mktg-PAB Media - PepsiCo, Inc.; pg. 259, pg. 1327
Rust, Janet, Sr Specialist-Mktg Comm - Toshiba America, Inc.; pg. 681, pg. 1302
Rust, Kati, Mgr-Brand & Customer Mktg - Oil-Dri Corporation of America; pg. 1480, pg. 586
Rustico, Dario, Dir-Sls & Mktg-Central Europe, Africa, Middle East & India - Costa Cruise Lines N.V.; pg. 1904, pg. 431
Rustomji, Neville, Mgr-Mktg Strategy, Analytics & CRM - Guitar Center, Inc.; pg. 1771, pg. 306
Ruszkowski, Chris, VP-Adv & Mktg - The Quizno's Master LLC; pg. 1746, pg. 322
Rutenis, Paul, Exec VP-Mdsg, Plng & Allocation - West Marine, Inc.; pg. 1712, pg. 305
Ruth, Allison, Buyer-Digital Mktg - GEICO Corporation; pg. 1200, pg. 399
Ruth, Kaaren, Sr Product Mgr-Consumer Mktg-Neuroscience Bus Unit - Shire; pg. 1593, pg. 1532
Rutherford, Lari, Sr Mgr-EMR Partnerships - Welch Allyn Inc.; pg. 1436, pg. 1342
Rutherford, Steve, Mgr-Mktg - Caterpillar, Inc.; pg. 1321, pg. 650
Rutherford, Todd, Sr Product Mgr-Windows Entertainment - Microsoft Corporation; pg. 435, pg. 1824
Rutland, Trace, Mgr-US Digital Media - The Hershey Co.; pg. 1855, pg. 1538
Rutledge, Amy, Dir-Media - Tempur Sealy International, Inc.; pg. 944, pg. 731
Rutledge, Ashley, Mgr-Residential Product Mgmt - Siemens Corporation; pg. 803, pg. 1291
Rutledge, Christy, Mgr-Relationship Mktg-Global - United Parcel Service, Inc.; pg. 1928, pg. 522
Rutledge, Chuck, Dir-Strategic Mktg & Alliances - Alcatel-Lucent; pg. 615, pg. 38
Rutledge, Merritt, Dir-Digital Mktg - The Western Union Company; pg. 822, pg. 327
Rutledge, Nicole, Mgr-Field Mktg-Customer Events-Ultrasound - Philips Electronics North America; pg. 662, pg. 782
Rutledge, Ryan, Mgr-Sls Excellence & Strategy-Media Analytics Solutions - Microsoft Corporation; pg. 435, pg. 1824
Rutledge, Scott, VP-Mktg - The Wooster Brush Company; pg. 1450, pg. 1482
Rutman, Marshall, Brand Mgr-Men's - lululemon athletica inc.; pg. 44, pg. 1911
Rutstein, William, Sr VP-Sls-Worldwide - Vascular Solutions, Inc.; pg. 1434, pg. 946
Rutter, Ellen, Mgr-Shopper Mktg - Bose Corporation; pg. 626, pg. 820
Ruvalcaba, Jessica, Mgr-Channel Mktg-Americas - Cisco Systems, Inc.; pg. 372, pg. 240
Ruwe, Matt, Product Mgr - Bose Corporation; pg. 626, pg. 820
Ruzal, Carlos, Dir-Sls - INTCOMEX, Inc.; pg. 416, pg. 443
Ruzicka, Brad, Dir-Worldwide Channel Mktg & Distr Comm - Texas Instruments Incorporated; pg. 679, pg. 1688
Ruzicka, Dana, Chief Product Officer - Avid Technology, Inc.; pg. 622, pg. 804
Ruzzo, Marie, Dir-Indus Mktg-Comm & Media - Pegasystems Inc.; pg. 453, pg. 809
Ryan, Aaron, Sr VP-Mktg Solutions & USA Basketball - National Basketball Association; pg. 566, pg. 1264
Ryan, Belinda, Coord-Media - Panera Bread Company; pg. 1029, pg. 1001
Ryan, Bill, Brand Mgr - 3M Company; pg. 1142, pg. 956
Ryan, Bryce, VP-Mktg Partnerships-Worldwide - Paramount Pictures Corporation; pg. 304, pg. 138
Ryan, Caitlin, Dir-Database Mktg - Canadian Imperial Bank of Commerce; pg. 729, pg. 1935
Ryan, Caitlin, Coord-Mktg - GEICO Corporation; pg. 1200, pg. 399
Ryan, Cece, Dir-Sls-Natl - People Magazine; pg. 1676, pg. 1278
Ryan, Chris, Sr Mgr-Fin & Product Support - The Allstate Corporation; pg. 1189, pg. 639
Ryan, Chris, VP-Sls Res & Strategy - Scripps Networks Interactive, Inc.; pg. 1279, pg. 1638
Ryan, Christina, Assoc Mgr-Mktg - FRANKLIN RESOURCES, INC.; pg. 760, pg. 254
Ryan, Christopher, Dir-Product Launch - Chobani LLC; pg. 847, pg. 1318
Ryan, Cody, Sr Asst Brand Mgr - DISH Network Corporation; pg. 283, pg. 325
Ryan, David J., Head-Global Strategy-Multi-Channel Mktg - Pfizer Inc.; pg. 1581, pg. 1278
Ryan, Derek D., Product Mgr-Unified Comm - Intel Corporation; pg. 645, pg. 266
Ryan, Diana, Mgr-Integrated Mktg - The New Republic Inc.; pg. 1667, pg. 403
Ryan, Emily J., VP & Program Mgr-Mktg - Wells Fargo & Company; pg. 819, pg. 232
Ryan, Erin, Sr Mgr-Internal & Corp Comm - Polycom, Inc.; pg. 664, pg. 249
Ryan, Greg, Sr Dir-Mktg & Corp Plng - Canon U.S.A., Inc.; pg. 1404, pg. 1178
Ryan, Jackie, Dir-Science & Analytics-IBM Smarter Workforce Product Mgmt - International Business Machines Corporation; pg. 418, pg. 1138
Ryan, Jake, VP-Sls - Empire Today, LLC; pg. 923, pg. 643
Ryan, Jennifer, Asst Dir-Media & PR - The Northwestern Mutual Life Insurance Company; pg. 1212, pg. 1879
Ryan, Jennifer, Coord-Ops & Analyst-Mktg - Zoll Medical Corporation; pg. 1612, pg. 814
Ryan, Jennifer R., Dir-Media Rels - Atmos Energy Corporation; pg. 1935, pg. 1675
Ryan, Jessica, Dir-Mktg-Heinz Brands - The Kraft Heinz Company; pg. 870, pg. 1577
Ryan, John, Sr VP-Americas Sls - Genband, Inc.; pg. 640, pg. 1731
Ryan, John, VP-Mktg - MWI Veterinary Supply, Inc.; pg. 1570, pg. 548
Ryan, Julie, VP-Mktg - Thermos L.L.C.; pg. 61, pg. 660
Ryan, Kathleen, Sr Mgr-US Channel Mktg & Ops - Avaya Inc.; pg. 621, pg. 264
Ryan, Katie, Sr Mgr-Sustainability - NRG Energy, Inc.; pg. 1948, pg. 1712
Ryan, Kelly, Mgr-Mktg Programs - Epicor Software Corporation; pg. 393, pg. 110
Ryan, Kelly, Sr Mgr-Mktg - Poppin; pg. 1782, pg. 1282
Ryan, Kevin, Mgr-Mktg-Product Strategy Votrient & Tykerb - GlaxoSmithKline; pg. 1536, pg. 1389
Ryan, Kevin C., VP-Bus Dev & Mktg - McKesson Corporation; pg. 1560, pg. 222
Ryan, Krystin, Program Mgr-Mktg - Wells Fargo & Company; pg. 819, pg. 232
Ryan, Lauren, Brand Mgr-elit-Stolichnaya - Stoli Group USA LLC; pg. 1970, pg. 1296
Ryan, Laurie, Dir-Mktg - Motorola Mobility LLC; pg. 657, pg. 627
Ryan, Liz, Mgr-Media-Global - Campbell Soup Company; pg. 844, pg. 1048
Ryan, Matthew, Coord-Digital Mktg - Roots Canada Ltd.; pg. 47, pg. 1942
Ryan, Matthew, Chief Strategy Officer-Global & Exec VP - Starbucks Corporation; pg. 897, pg. 1840
Ryan, Maurice J., Sr VP-Worldwide Sls & Mktg - Viskase Companies, Inc.; pg. 1471, pg. 599
Ryan, Michael, Sr Dir-Reg Comml Mktg - Heineken USA Inc.; pg. 252, pg. 1352
Ryan, Michael, Dir-Online Mktg - Lowe's Companies, Inc.; pg. 1053, pg. 1383
Ryan, Mike, Mgr-ECommerce & Online Mktg - Wyndham Worldwide Corporation; pg. 1119, pg. 1107
Ryan, Nancy, Dir-Media & Integrated Mktg Comm - The Allstate Corporation; pg. 1189, pg. 639
Ryan, Nicholas, Assoc specialist-Mktg - Canon U.S.A., Inc.; pg. 1404, pg. 1178
Ryan, Paula, VP-Product Dev & Exclusive Label Mktg - Sally Beauty Holdings, Inc.; pg. 522, pg. 1691
Ryan, Rusty, Sr Project Mgr-Creative Adv - J.C. Penney Company, Inc.; pg. 1774, pg. 1732
Ryan, Sean, Dir-Bus Rental Sls - Enterprise Holdings, Inc.; pg. 1906, pg. 996
Ryan, Sean, Dir-Digital Mktg - J.C. Penney Company, Inc.; pg. 1774, pg. 1732
Ryan, Steve, Mgr-Bus Dev-Growing Media-Home Depot - The Scotts Miracle-Gro Company; pg. 1799, pg. 1459
Ryan, Tim, Assoc Dir-Creative-Email - Staples; pg. 474, pg. 313
Ryan, Todd, Area Dir-Sls & Mktg-Eastern Canada - Starwood Hotels & Resorts Worldwide, Inc.; pg. 1114, pg. 378
Ryan, Tom, Dir-Media Rels, Employee & Exec Comm-Global - International Paper Company; pg. 1460, pg. 1644
Ryan, Yvonne, Dir-Intl Mktg - Pollo Campero; pg. 1782, pg. 1685
Ryba, James, Dir-Product Mktg - Vishay Americas; pg. 686, pg. 371
Rychter, Jason, Mgr-Mktg - MORNINGSTAR, INC.; pg. 784, pg. 583
Ryckman, Rebecca, VP-Strategic Mktg-Home Fin - Chase Card Services, Inc.; pg. 734, pg. 215
Ryder, Courtney, Mgr-Mktg Ops - Puma North America, Inc.; pg. 1816, pg. 858
Ryder, Jamie, Dir-Digital Mktg - Preferred Hotel Group; pg. 1108, pg. 587
Ryder, Mindy, Sr Mgr-Customer Mktg - Ghirardelli Chocolate Company; pg. 1854, pg. 252
Ryder, Roberto, Jr Brand Mgr-Heineken - Heineken USA Inc.; pg. 252, pg. 1352
Ryder, Timothy, Brand Mgr-Woodford Reserve & North American Whiskeys - Brown-Forman Corporation; pg. 1958, pg. 732
Rydlinski, George, Dir-Mktg - Fairbanks Symphony Association; pg. 547, pg. 10
Rydman, Lisa, VP-Mktg - Spec's Family Partners Ltd.; pg. 1970, pg. 1715
Rye, Beth, Dir-New Media - Yankton Daily Press & Dakotan; pg. 1703, pg. 1626
Rye, Kenneth, Mgr-Mdsg Mktg - The Home Depot, Inc.; pg. 1050, pg. 510
Rygiel, Jana, VP-Portfolio Mktg, IT & Gaming - Caesars Entertainment Corporation; pg. 1083, pg. 1023
Rygol, Pete, Reg Mgr-Sls - Kaeser & Blair Incorporated; pg. 1656, pg. 1405
Rylee, John, Dir-Mktg-Global - Rotary Lift; pg. 216, pg. 694
Ryman, Natalie, Gen Mgr-Sls - NewsChannel 5; pg. 303, pg. 1653
Rynders, Melissa, Product Mgr - Boston Scientific Corporation; pg. 1508, pg. 831
Rynne, Josh, Product Mgr - The Ultimate Software Group, Inc.; pg. 486, pg. 479
Ryno, Amie, Sr Mgr-University Rels - Comcast Corporation; pg. 276, pg. 1560
Rysavy, Tom, Dir-Mktg - BUFFALO WILD WINGS, INC.; pg. 1718, pg. 931
Ryu, Crystal, Mgr-Corp Procurement-Mktg Svcs - Sony Pictures Entertainment Inc.; pg. 309, pg. 72
Rywolt, Kristen, Mgr-Mktg - PerkinElmer, Inc.; pg. 1426, pg. 853
Ryzinski, Tony, VP-Mktg - Highmark Blue Cross Blue Shield; pg. 1203, pg. 1576
Ryznar, Amanda, Dir-Corp Mktg & Mktg Ops - MORNINGSTAR, INC.; pg. 784, pg. 583

First page reference indicates Business Class Edition
Second page reference indicates Geographic Edition

Rzewnicki, Peter, Head-Pricing Strategy & Dir-US Mktg - Novartis Vaccines & Diagnostics, Inc.; *pg.* 1575, *pg.* 809

S

Saad, Jean, Mgr-Sponsorships & Mdsg - Air Canada; *pg.* 1896, *pg.* 1902
Saadeh, Michael, Product Mgr-User Interface - AMX Corporation; *pg.* 349, *pg.* 1735
Saakyan, Violet, Mgr-Mktg - Allergan; *pg.* 1490, *pg.* 1101
Saavedra, Annette, Specialist-Digital Media - Apollo Education Group Inc.; *pg.* 597, *pg.* 14
Saavedra, Carlos, Sr Dir-Culture Mktg & Innovation - PepsiCo, Inc.; *pg.* 259, *pg.* 1327
Saba, Roger, Jr., VP-Mktg & Sls - Sabas Bunch Limited Partnership; *pg.* 47, *pg.* 12
Sabala, Gregory, Dir-Mktg Comm - Den-Mat Corporation; *pg.* 1522, *pg.* 271
Saban, Kirk, Sr Dir-FPGA & SoC Product Mgmt & Mktg - Xilinx, Inc.; *pg.* 496, *pg.* 252
Saban, Shelley, Mgr-Mktg - QUALCOMM Incorporated; *pg.* 1873, *pg.* 207
Saban, Tamara, Program Mgr-Mktg - Ross Stores, Inc.; *pg.* 1783, *pg.* 78
Sabat, John R., Sr VP-Global Sls, Mktg & Natl Accounts - Akorn, Inc.; *pg.* 1488, *pg.* 622
Sabat, Margaret, Product Mgr - Blair Corporation; *pg.* 1762, *pg.* 1590
Sabatelle, Amanda, Dir-PR-Luxury Products Div - L'Oreal USA; *pg.* 514, *pg.* 1252
Sabatino, Joseph, VP-Sls-Central Reg - Adobe Systems Incorporated; *pg.* 342, *pg.* 235
Sabatino, Richard, Assoc Dir-Multiple Sclerosis Mktg - Novartis Pharmaceuticals Corp.; *pg.* 1575, *pg.* 1054
Sabecky, Holly, Dir-Mktg - The New Yorker Magazine, Inc.; *pg.* 1669, *pg.* 1271
Saber, Mike, Dir-Mktg - Belden, Inc.; *pg.* 624, *pg.* 993
Sabet, Nima, Sr Mgr-Sears Incentives-B2B Mktg - Sears Canada Inc.; *pg.* 1784, *pg.* 1943
Sabharwal, Anil, Dir-Product & Engrg-Google Photos - Google Inc.; *pg.* 1249, *pg.* 153
Sabia, Kirsten, VP-Mktg Svcs - PGA Tour, Inc.; *pg.* 574, *pg.* 460
Sabin, Nancy, VP-Brand Mktg-US - Johnson & Johnson; *pg.* 1549, *pg.* 1091
Sable, Lindsay, Mgr-Integrated Mktg-Harper's BAZAAR - Hearst Magazines; *pg.* 1649, *pg.* 1239
Sablone, Wilma, Mgr-Mktg - Manulife Financial Corporation; *pg.* 778, *pg.* 1939
Sabo, Alice, Dir-Mktg - Applied Industrial Technologies, Inc.; *pg.* 199, *pg.* 1428
Sabo, Jonathan, VP-Mktg - Detecto Scale Company; *pg.* 1045, *pg.* 1007
Sabolsky, Emily, Mgr-Social Media & Local Store Mktg - Saladworks, LLC; *pg.* 1749, *pg.* 1524
Saca, Gabriel, Sr VP-Production - Rag & Bone; *pg.* 46, *pg.* 1284
Sacco, Daphne Liska, Dir-Internet Mktg - eBay Inc.; *pg.* 1240, *pg.* 243
Sacco, Natalie, Mgr-Digital Media - Penton Media, Inc.; *pg.* 1676, *pg.* 1277
Sacco, Troy, VP-Sls & Mktg-Private Events & Tournaments - American Golf Corporation; *pg.* 528, *pg.* 272
Saccomano, Ron, Sr VP-Sls & Mktg-Intl - Westinghouse Lighting Corporation; *pg.* 687, *pg.* 1571
Sachs, Amy, VP-Sls - Elizabeth Arden, Inc.; *pg.* 507, *pg.* 448
Sachs, Carly, Sr Assoc Mgr-Mktg - The Hershey Co.; *pg.* 1855, *pg.* 1538
Sachs, Eric, Dir-Product Mgmt-Identity - Google Inc.; *pg.* 1249, *pg.* 153
Sachs, Leslie, Dir-Retail Mktg - Northern Tool + Equipment; *pg.* 1366, *pg.* 919
Sachs, Liz, Coord-Consumer Mktg & Program Adv - Home Box Office, Inc.; *pg.* 290, *pg.* 1240
Sachtleben, Amy, Dir-Fin & Strategy-Consumer Products - Mattel Games/Puzzles; *pg.* 962, *pg.* 80
Sachtleben, Amy, Dir-Fin & Strategy-Consumer Products - MATTEL, INC.; *pg.* 962, *pg.* 81
Sack, Alyson, Specialist-Customer Mktg - Meijer, Inc.; *pg.* 1779, *pg.* 888
Sack, Chris, Reg Mgr-Sls - Sinclair Broadcast Group, Inc.; *pg.* 308, *pg.* 773
Sack, Ethan, Sr Dir-Mktg - LEGO Systems, Inc.; *pg.* 961, *pg.* 346
Sack, Jeanine, Specialist-Mktg-Cincinnati Affiliate Div - Fifth Third Bancorp; *pg.* 752, *pg.* 1413
Sack, Lindsey, Interim Mgr-Mktg & Comm-Asia - CB Richard Ellis, Inc.; *pg.* 1085, *pg.* 1210
Sackenheim, Jimmy, Mgr-Digital Mktg-Victoria's Secret - L Brands, Inc.; *pg.* 1776, *pg.* 1441
Sackett, Drewry, Mgr-PR & Community Rels - THE FRESH MARKET, INC.; *pg.* 1020, *pg.* 1374
Sackett, Erica, Corp VP-Customer Mktg & CRM - New York Life Insurance Company; *pg.* 1211, *pg.* 1268
Sackman, Stuart, VP-Global Product & Tech - Automatic Data Processing, Inc.; *pg.* 357, *pg.* 1117
Sacknoff, Lindsay, Sr VP & Head-Retail Deposit Products & Pricing - TD Bank US Holding Company; *pg.* 809, *pg.* 1051
Sacks, Elissa, Sr Mgr-Brand Activation - Beam Suntory Inc.; *pg.* 1957, *pg.* 599
Sacks, Jonathan, Sr Dir-Global Femoral Brand Mktg - Stryker Orthopaedics; *pg.* 1599, *pg.* 1082
Sadana, Sumit, Chief Strategy Officer & Exec VP - SanDisk Corporation; *pg.* 465, *pg.* 147
Sadberry, Kyle, Mgr Sls-Southeast Reg - Atlas Minerals & Chemicals, Inc.; *pg.* 69, *pg.* 1552
Sadden, Kathy, Sr VP-ITO Mktg & Sls Ops - Xerox Corporation; *pg.* 494, *pg.* 365
Sadeghi, Tina, Exec Dir-Digital Sls & Partnerships - Marvel Entertainment, LLC; *pg.* 1662, *pg.* 1257
Sadeghian, Alex, Dir-Mktg - Yamaha Corporation of America; *pg.* 595, *pg.* 51
Sadeghy, Mary, Assoc VP-Mktg & Bus Dev - City of Hope National Medical Center; *pg.* 1516, *pg.* 77
Sadeh, Talal, Dir-Global Brand Mktg & Design-Toy Box Vehicles - Mattel Games/Puzzles; *pg.* 962, *pg.* 80
Sadeh, Talal, Dir-Global Brand Mktg & Design-Toy Box Vehicles - MATTEL, INC.; *pg.* 962, *pg.* 81
Sadick, Karen, Sr VP-Buying & Mdsg - Clarks Companies; *pg.* 1806, *pg.* 836
Sadler, Ben, Mgr-Mktg-Global Strategy - Starbucks Corporation; *pg.* 897, *pg.* 1840
Sadler, J.C., VP-Mktg & Comm - HCA HOLDINGS, INC.; *pg.* 1539, *pg.* 1651
Sadler, Robert, Product Mgr - DISH Network Corporation; *pg.* 283, *pg.* 325
Sadler, Scott, Category Product Mgr-Integrated Tech - Steelcase Inc.; *pg.* 475, *pg.* 889
Sadler, Tom, Sr Mgr-Ops-Fiber Optic Sys Div - Panduit Corp.; *pg.* 661, *pg.* 663
Sadlis, Steven, Asst VP & Mgr-Mktg - Flushing Financial Corporation; *pg.* 759, *pg.* 1172
Sadofsky, Lynn, VP-Production & Dev - National Geographic Society; *pg.* 1667, *pg.* 402
Sadowski, Bryan, VP-FlowEngine Product Mktg - RadiSys Corporation; *pg.* 458, *pg.* 1498
Sadowski, Kristen, Sr Dir-Pharmacy Mktg - CVS Health Corporation; *pg.* 1765, *pg.* 1610
Sadowski, Laura, Dir-Mktg - Happ Controls Inc.; *pg.* 641, *pg.* 634
Sadowski, Maggie, Brand Mgr - Ocean Spray Cranberries, Inc.; *pg.* 887, *pg.* 827
Sadowski, Rob, Dir-Offer Mktg - RSA Security Inc.; *pg.* 463, *pg.* 786
Sadri, Afsaneh, Mgr-Email Mktg - Sony Electronics, Inc.; *pg.* 676, *pg.* 209
Sadusky, Vincent L., Pres/CEO-LIN Media - Media General; *pg.* 297, *pg.* 1607
Saechou, Farm, Sr Mgr-PR-PlayStation - Sony Computer Entertainment America LLC; *pg.* 966, *pg.* 256
Saeed, Cyma Zulfiqar, Mgr-eBusiness Mktg-Organic Search Strategy - The Allstate Corporation; *pg.* 1189, *pg.* 639
Saenz, Gisela, Sr Mgr-Mktg-Immediate Consumption Portfolio - Frito-Lay North America, Inc.; *pg.* 1853, *pg.* 1730
Saenz, Jennifer, Sr Dir-Mktg - Frito-Lay North America, Inc.; *pg.* 1853, *pg.* 1730
Safarian, Golareh, VP-Production-Special Ops-Film, TV & Sports - Fox Broadcasting Company; *pg.* 287, *pg.* 130
Safchuk, Nathaniel, Mgr-Sponsorship Mktg - Ticketmaster Entertainment LLC; *pg.* 1284, *pg.* 48
Saferin, Steven M., Chief Creative Officer & Pres-Properties Grp - Scientific Games Corporation; *pg.* 468, *pg.* 1029
Saffian, Lisa, VP-Integrated Mktg - MTV Networks Company; *pg.* 298, *pg.* 1262
Safford, Margaret, Dir-Product Mgmt & Strategy - Staples, Inc.; *pg.* 474, *pg.* 821
Safi, Nadia, Analyst-Social Media - Whirlpool Corporation; *pg.* 62, *pg.* 872
Saftler, Bryan, Sr Product Mktg Mgr-Microsoft - Microsoft Corporation; *pg.* 435, *pg.* 1824
Sagar, Nancy, Mgr-PR - Neiman Marcus, Inc.; *pg.* 30, *pg.* 1684
Sagar, Sushma, Sr Mgr-Mktg & PR - Kate Spade LLC; *pg.* 28, *pg.* 1248
Sagarminaga, Macarena, Head-Media & Partnerships - J. Crew Group, Inc.; *pg.* 1773, *pg.* 1245
Sage, Jim, VP-Primary Care Mktg-US - Pfizer Inc.; *pg.* 1581, *pg.* 1278
Sage, Sara, Sr Mgr-Reg Mktg - The Allstate Corporation; *pg.* 1189, *pg.* 639
Sagebiel, Ed, Sr Dir-Corp Comm-Global - Eli Lilly and Company; *pg.* 1527, *pg.* 684
Sagedahl, Sara, Asst Mgr-Integrated Mktg Comm - General Mills, Inc.; *pg.* 828, *pg.* 933
Sager, Michael, Asst Mgr-Mktg - Storck USA, L.P.; *pg.* 1862, *pg.* 591
Sager, Patrick, Dir-Digital Mktg-Global - Disney Interactive Media Group; *pg.* 1239, *pg.* 95
Sagers, Elaine, VP-Mktg - Pella Corporation; *pg.* 104, *pg.* 711
Saglio, Roman, Sr Dir-Mktg - Bausch & Lomb Incorporated; *pg.* 1401, *pg.* 1045
Sagness, Owen, Gen Mgr-Adv & Online-UK - Microsoft Corporation; *pg.* 435, *pg.* 1824
Sagram, Vikki, Assoc Mgr-Mktg - FreshDirect, LLC; *pg.* 857, *pg.* 1174
Sagripanti, Mary, VP-Mktg-Kraft Singles, Natural Cheese & Velveeta - The Kraft Heinz Company; *pg.* 871, *pg.* 641
Sague, Allan, Asst VP-Mktg, Distr, Small Comml, Tech, Pro & Mgmt Liability - The Hanover Insurance Company; *pg.* 1202, *pg.* 862
Sagues, Amy V., Dir-Application Svcs Mktg - Accenture; *pg.* 1392, *pg.* 1186
Saha, Sayandeb, Head-Product Mgmt, Storage & Data Bus - Red Hat, Inc.; *pg.* 460, *pg.* 1388
Sahagian, Glenn, Dir-Brdcst Media & Creative - P.C. Richard & Son; *pg.* 59, *pg.* 1159
Sahagun, Nydia J., Grp Mgr-Multicultural Brand Mktg - Target Corporation; *pg.* 1786, *pg.* 942
Sahasi, Jayesh, CTO & Chief Product Officer - ON24, Inc.; *pg.* 1272, *pg.* 224
Sahay, Loren, Mgr-Media - Discovery Communications, Inc.; *pg.* 282, *pg.* 777
Sahay, Shobhit, Product Mgr-Office 365 - Microsoft Corporation; *pg.* 435, *pg.* 1824
Sahin, Ali, VP-Sls-EMEA - Exar Corporation; *pg.* 395, *pg.* 91
Sahni, Sukhi, Dir-Comm & Mktg PR - Capital One Financial Corporation; *pg.* 730, *pg.* 1789
Sahuc, Philip, Dir-Client Mktg-Team Solutions - Valassis; *pg.* 1698, *pg.* 386
Saia, Tony, Program Mgr-Email Mktg - Quicken Loans, Inc.; *pg.* 797, *pg.* 884
Said, Nadia, Head-Shopper Mktg Team & Sr Brand Mgr-Adult Care - Kimberly-Clark Inc.; *pg.* 1463, *pg.* 1927
Saiki, Laura, Dir-Product Line-Golf - Cutter & Buck, Inc.; *pg.* 39, *pg.* 1835
Sailer, David, Dir-Mktg, Subscription Sls & Audience Svcs - Minnesota Orchestra; *pg.* 563, *pg.* 940
Saillant, Dominick, Dir-Media Rels - Club de hockey Canadien, Inc.; *pg.* 541, *pg.* 1954
Sailors, Shannon, Dir-Adv - Carmike Cinemas, Inc.; *pg.* 273, *pg.* 528
Sain-Dieguez, Vanessa, Dir-Social Media Comm - Hilton Worldwide, Inc.; *pg.* 1094, *pg.* 1791
Saindon, Aimee, Sr Mgr-Customer Mktg - Mattel Games/Puzzles; *pg.* 962, *pg.* 80
Saint John, Bozoma, Head-Global Consumer Mktg, iTunes & Beats Music - Beats Electronics LLC; *pg.* 624, *pg.* 272
Saito, Cheri, Mgr-Product Mktg - Twitter, Inc.; *pg.* 1285, *pg.* 228
Saito, Chris, Sr Dir-Customer Experience-Online Store - Apple Inc.; *pg.* 350, *pg.* 73
Sajewich, John, Sr Mgr-Sls Strategy & Plng-Naked Juice - Pepsi Beverages Company; *pg.* 258, *pg.* 1342
Sajous, Kelly, Specialist-Production - The Greater Boston Food Bank; *pg.* 993, *pg.* 795
Sakaguchi, Jamie, Brand Mgr - Nature Made Nutritional Products Inc.; *pg.* 883, *pg.* 148
Sakalas, Kelly, Mgr-Sponsorships & PR - The J.M. Smucker Company; *pg.* 865, *pg.* 1468
Sakaria, Neela, VP-Program & Mktg Res-History - A&E Television Networks, LLC; *pg.* 267, *pg.* 1185
Sakhnini, Humam, Chief Strategy Officer & Chief Talent Officer - Activision Blizzard, Inc.; *pg.* 948, *pg.* 271

Sakonchick, Beth, Acct Mgr-Mktg Comm - Aetna Inc.; pg. 1187, pg. 351
Sakowicz, Kelly, Sr Product Mgr - Jarden Consumer Solutions; pg. 57, pg. 412
Saksena, Asheesh, Chief Strategy Officer & Exec VP - Cox Communications, Inc.; pg. 279, pg. 501
Salagaj, John, Sr Dir-Mktg & Strategic Brands - The Hertz Corporation; pg. 1911, pg. 450
Salai, John, Sr Mgr-Digital Mktg - Subway Restaurants; pg. 1751, pg. 356
Salameh, Mais, Reg Mgr-Comm & Mktg - Baker Hughes Incorporated; pg. 1315, pg. 1700
Salamon, Jeff, Dir-Mktg & Strategy - MTD Products, Inc.; pg. 1057, pg. 1478
Salas, Francisco, Project Mgr-LatAm, Iberia & US & Sr Graphic Designer-Mktg - BlackRock, Inc.; pg. 724, pg. 1203
Salas, Monique, Supvr-Mktg-Raleigh Reg - McDonald's Corporation; pg. 1737, pg. 645
Salas, Suzanne, Dir-Adv, Brand & Media - NCL Corporation Ltd.; pg. 1916, pg. 444
Salas, Suzanne, Dir-Adv, Brand & Media - Norwegian Cruise Line; pg. 1917, pg. 444
Salas, Tin, Sr VP-Interactive Mktg - Amegy Bank, N.A.; pg. 711, pg. 1700
Salazar, Alma, Sr Mgr-Consumer Mktg-Invisalign Brand - Align Technology, Inc.; pg. 1489, pg. 237
Salazar, Jolene, Head-Digital Content Mktg - 3M Company; pg. 1142, pg. 956
Salazar, Katherine, Dir-Mktg - Valeant Pharmaceuticals International; pg. 1605, pg. 1047
Salazar, Lauren, Assoc Dir & Dir-Social Media - Weight Watchers International, Inc.; pg. 1609, pg. 1313
Salazar, Natalia, Sr Mgr-Mktg - American Express Company; pg. 712, pg. 1190
Salazar, Rosario, Pres, Head-Designer & Architect - Rosario Salazar Design Inc.; pg. 941, pg. 418
Salchert, Julie, Asst Dir-Mktg Integration - The Northwestern Mutual Life Insurance Company; pg. 1212, pg. 1879
Saldana-Chase, Melissa, Sr Planner-Integrated Mktg Comm - General Mills, Inc.; pg. 828, pg. 933
Saldanha, Neela, Sr Dir-Innovation Insights-Global Snacks Grp - PepsiCo, Inc.; pg. 259, pg. 1327
Saldanha, Savio, Sr Product Mgr-Innovation - Halliburton Company; pg. 978, pg. 1707
Saldarriaga, Sebastian, Strategist-Intl Social Media - Michael Kors (USA), Inc.; pg. 29, pg. 1260
Saldivar, Leticia, Head-Consumer Mktg & Adv - California Lottery; pg. 990, pg. 196
Sale, Bob, VP-Sls - Hubbell Lighting - Progress Lighting Division; pg. 1300, pg. 1617
Salehi, Rani, VP-Mktg Comm-Global - HID Global Corporation; pg. 1416, pg. 111
Salek, Mark, VP-Direct Mktg - Lamps Plus Inc.; pg. 1300, pg. 64
Salem, Michael, VP-Product Mktg - Papa Murphy's International, LLC; pg. 1743, pg. 1846
Salerno, Chris, Sls Mgr - Marriott International, Inc.; pg. 1102, pg. 764
Sales, Alessandra, Sr Mgr-Mktg - Zoosk Inc.; pg. 1292, pg. 235
Sales, Karen, VP-Shopper Mktg-Albertsons Safeway - Albertson's LLC; pg. 1013, pg. 546
Sales, Kathleen, Writer-Mktg Content - ACCO Brands Corporation; pg. 340, pg. 626
Salgado, Adam, VP-Multicultural & Field Mktg - McDonald's Corporation; pg. 1737, pg. 645
Salgado, Kirby, VP-Mdsg - AARON'S, INC.; pg. 912, pg. 486
Salgar, Satyajeet, Product Mgr-Search - Google Inc.; pg. 1249, pg. 153
Salguero, Jeff, VP-Adv & Creative Dev-Global - Colgate-Palmolive Company; pg. 504, pg. 1215
Sali, Lisa, Mgr-Digital Mktg - Amazon.com, Inc.; pg. 1226, pg. 1831
Saliba, Jeannette, Mgr-Affiliate & CSE Mktg - Sterling Jewelers Inc.; pg. 13, pg. 1402
Saliba, Julie, Sr Brand Mktg Dir - The Quaker Oats Company; pg. 834, pg. 588
Saliba, Rindala, Sr Mgr-Global Technical Mktg Multi-Media - Motorola Mobility LLC; pg. 657, pg. 627
Salinas, Adrian, Sr Product Mktg Mgr-Personal Sys Grp-Comml Accessories - Hewlett-Packard Company; pg. 404, pg. 175
Salinas, Alex, Mgr-Adv - The Majestic Star Casino, LLC; pg. 560, pg. 1027
Salinas, Sandy, Sr Dir-Bus Plng - Taco Cabana, Inc.; pg. 1753, pg. 1743
Salinas, Vilma, Sr Mgr-Event Logistics - Country Music Association; pg. 138, pg. 1649
Salindong, Jia, Country Mgr-Mktg - The Procter & Gamble Company; pg. 1129, pg. 1418
Sall, Eric, VP-Worldwide Mktg & Bus Analytics - International Business Machines Corporation; pg. 418, pg. 1138
Sall, Lisa, Sr Mgr-Mktg Comm - The American Dental Association; pg. 127, pg. 564
Sallaska, Shana, Sr Mgr-Social Media & Web - Energy Future Holdings Corp.; pg. 1941, pg. 1680
Sallee, Lindsy E., Dir-Land Aftermarket Sls - National Oilwell Varco, Inc.; pg. 1364, pg. 1712
Salleroli, Margaret, Dir-Mktg Comm-Global - PNY Technologies, Inc.; pg. 455, pg. 1105
Sallmen, Brad, Dir-Sls Ops - Herff Jones, Inc.; pg. 7, pg. 686
Salman, Ibrahim, Product Mgr-Bus Fibe TV - Bell Canada; pg. 1936, pg. 1960
Salmanowicz, Kirsten, Specialist Digital Mktg Project - Land O'Lakes, Inc.; pg. 873, pg. 915
Salmanpour, Christopher, Dir-Sls-Europe - Tapjoy, Inc.; pg. 1396, pg. 228
Salmen, Kelsey, Mgr-Mktg-Quaker - PepsiCo, Inc.; pg. 259, pg. 1327
Salmen, Kelsey, Mgr-Mktg - The Quaker Oats Company; pg. 834, pg. 588
Salmieri, Kelly, Mgr-Partnership Mktg - Portland Trail Blazers; pg. 577, pg. 1505
Salmon, Diane, Sr Dir-Offers & Loyalty - Visa Inc.; pg. 816, pg. 230
Salmon, Jessica, Sr Mgr-Strategy & Fin - Wal-Mart Stores, Inc.; pg. 1790, pg. 29
Salmon, Patrick, Sr Mgr-Creative Strategy-Global - Yahoo! Inc.; pg. 1289, pg. 289
Salmond, John, VP-Sls & Mktg - Manulife Financial Corporation; pg. 778, pg. 1939
Salmons, Barry, Sr Mgr-Client Svcs & Web Ops-ECommerce Digital Mktg - Cardinal Health, Inc.; pg. 1512, pg. 1448
Salnier, Erin, Sr VP-Portfolio Sls Mktg - NBC Universal, Inc.; pg. 300, pg. 1266
Salsi, Joshua C., Dir & Team Head-US Mktg & Pfizer Oncology - Pfizer Inc.; pg. 1581, pg. 1278
Salsovic, Dave, Planner-Mktg - Dick's Sporting Goods, Inc.; pg. 1832, pg. 1524
Salter, Mike, Dir-Creative - Chattem, Inc.; pg. 1515, pg. 1628
Salter, Robin, Mgr-Creative & Head Writer-Creative - Banner Direct; pg. 1619, pg. 1200
Salter, Sarah, Head-Mktg - Equinox Fitness Clubs; pg. 546, pg. 1228
Saltiel, Al, Sr VP-Mktg-Customer Satisfaction - AutoZone, Inc.; pg. 200, pg. 1641
Saltonstall, Tom, VP-Sls - Structural Graphics, LLC; pg. 1689, pg. 346
Saltz, Maria, Sr Mgr-Social Media Analytics - Adobe Systems Incorporated; pg. 342, pg. 235
Salvador, Teri, Mgr-Sls & Mktg - Buca, Inc.; pg. 1718, pg. 931
Salvador-Canas, Juan L., Sr Mgr-Trade Mktg-Latin America - Newell Rubbermaid Inc.; pg. 1128, pg. 515
Salvadore, John, Sr Mgr-Mktg - PPG Industries, Inc.; pg. 1445, pg. 1579
Salvati, Regina C., Rep-Mktg - AT&T; pg. 1865, pg. 258
Salvatore, Brad, Acct Exec-Sponsorship Sls - Major League Baseball; pg. 560, pg. 1255
Salvatore, Heather J., Sr Mgr-PR - Philips Electronics North America; pg. 662, pg. 782
Salvatore, Matthew, Assoc Dir-Mktg & Participation - Massachusetts Institute of Technology; pg. 604, pg. 809
Salvatori, Mike, Specialist-Production Print Sls-Graphic Comm - Xerox Corporation; pg. 494, pg. 365
Salvia, Paige, Sr Mgr-Media - FMR LLC (Fidelity Investments); pg. 759, pg. 794
Salvo, Alessandra, Brand Mgr - Ben & Jerry's Homemade, Inc.; pg. 1850, pg. 1767
Salyers, David, VP-Natl & Reg Mktg - Chick-fil-A, Inc.; pg. 1721, pg. 492
Salyers, Jeff, Mgr-Mktg - Zatarain's Brands, Inc.; pg. 911, pg. 744
Salzberg, Kristen, Mgr-Mktg - Intuit Inc.; pg. 769, pg. 158
Salzmann, D'Arcy, Sr Product Mgr-Windows Embedded - Microsoft Corporation; pg. 435, pg. 1824
Sam, Isaias, Mgr-Mktg - Goya Foods, Inc.; pg. 859, pg. 1075
Sam, Ivy, Mgr-Consumer Mktg-Global - Mary Kay Inc.; pg. 516, pg. 1657
Sam, Malene, Dir-Mobile Media Solutions - CBS Interactive, Inc.; pg. 369, pg. 215
Samame, Eduardo, VP-New Products & Gen Mgr-Direct Mktg Solutions - Time Warner Cable Inc.; pg. 312, pg. 1301
Samansky, Valerie, Mgr-Mktg Comm - Oracle Corporation; pg. 1272, pg. 786
Samarasinghe, Dimi, Coord-Mktg-Cross-Border Banking - Royal Bank of Canada; pg. 800, pg. 1942
Samarasinghe, Paba, Brand Mgr - Kind LLC; pg. 868, pg. 1249
Sambataro, Jennifer, Supvr-Print Media - FMR LLC (Fidelity Investments); pg. 759, pg. 794
Samberg, David, Mgr-PR-Natl - Verizon Communications Inc.; pg. 1875, pg. 1309
Sambo, David, VP-OSF Sls - INX International Ink Co.; pg. 421, pg. 658
Sambrotto, Lauren, Dir & Head-Natl Media & PR - UnionBanCal Corporation; pg. 813, pg. 230
Sambusini, Martin, Brand Mgr-Developer-Lipton - Unilever United States, Inc.; pg. 904, pg. 1061
Samel, Joe, Sr Key Acct Mgr-Trade Mktg - Anheuser-Busch Companies, LLC; pg. 237, pg. 991
Samford, Sara, Assoc Mgr-Mktg Res - Capital One Financial Corporation; pg. 730, pg. 1789
Samide, Jamie, Sr Dir-Mktg - Cintas Corporation; pg. 372, pg. 1411
Sammann, Derek, Sr Mng Dir & Head-Commodities & Options Products-Global - CME Group Inc.; pg. 738, pg. 571
Sammons, Brent, Sr Mgr-Mktg - QUALCOMM Incorporated; pg. 1873, pg. 207
Sammons, Jan, Dir-Mktg - Godfather's Pizza, Inc.; pg. 1729, pg. 1015
Sampath, Pradheep, VP-Marketplace Product Mgmt-Global - Liquidity Services, Inc.; pg. 1263, pg. 401
Sampson, Bonnie, Dir-Creative - Capital One Financial Corporation; pg. 730, pg. 1789
Sampson, Caitlin, Mgr-Partner Mktg - Juniper Networks, Inc.; pg. 1260, pg. 286
Sampson, Cat, Mgr-Growth Mktg - Uber USA, LLC; pg. 1286, pg. 229
Sampson, Douglas G., VP-Production, R&D - Dynatronics Corporation; pg. 1526, pg. 1757
Sampson, Ellen, Mgr-Mktg-Global - Siemens Healthcare Diagnostics; pg. 673, pg. 604
Sampson, Najah, Team Head-Worldwide Comml Dev & Hematology Franchise & Sr Dir - Pfizer Inc.; pg. 1581, pg. 1278
Sampson, Savon S., Sr Mgr-Mktg-McKesson Brands - McKesson Corporation; pg. 1560, pg. 222
Sampson, Tina, VP-Grp Sls - Vail Resorts, Inc.; pg. 1117, pg. 313
Sampson, Zaneta, Mgr-Mktg - Swatch Group USA; pg. 13, pg. 1131
Samra, Victor, Mgr-Digital Media Mktg - The Museum of Modern Art; pg. 565, pg. 1263
Sams, Jimmy D., Acct Exec-Charter Media - Charter Communications, Inc.; pg. 274, pg. 372
Sams-Pierson, Heddy, Assoc Publr-Sls - Conde Nast Publications, Inc.; pg. 1629, pg. 1217
Samson, Aaron, Sr Mgr-Mktg - Mattel Games/Puzzles; pg. 962, pg. 80
Samson, Aaron, Sr Mgr-Mktg - MATTEL, INC.; pg. 962, pg. 81
Samudovsky, Joe, Dir-Cargo Sls - Horizon Air Industries; pg. 1912, pg. 1836
Samuel, Dorothy, Program Mgr-Mktg Comm - Atlas Copco Comptec LLC; pg. 1314, pg. 1349
Samuel, Jim, Mgr-Internet Mktg Svcs - Universal Health Services Inc.; pg. 1604, pg. 1544
Samuel, Kavita, Sr Mgr-Mktg Ops - Blue Coat Systems, Inc.; pg. 362, pg. 284
Samuel, Neena, Assoc Dir-PR - Hofstra University; pg. 602, pg. 1166
Samuel, Pam, Mgr-Strategic Mktg-Global - Medtronic, Inc.; pg. 1564, pg. 939
Samuels, Callie, Program Specialist-Mktg - BMC Software, Inc.; pg. 362, pg. 1701
Samuels, Mark, VP-Product Delivery-Intl - LexisNexis Group; pg. 1658, pg. 1446
Samuels, Sofia, Sr Dir-Customer Loyalty & Retention - Ryder System, Inc.; pg. 1922, pg. 446
Samuels, Tiffany, Sr Assoc Mgr-Mktg-Betty Crocker Side Dishes - General Mills, Inc.; pg. 828, pg. 933
Samuelson, Michael, Dir-Mktg & PR - Atlantic Health System Inc.; pg. 1498, pg. 1087
San Miguel, John, Mgr-Mktg - The Hershey Co.; pg. 1855, pg.

First page reference indicates Business Class Edition
Second page reference indicates Geographic Edition

1538
Sanaie, Paymon, Sr Product Mgr - NeuStar, Inc.; *pg.* 1872, *pg.* 1807
Sanborn, Dan, VP-PR & Entertainment Mktg - Diageo North America Inc.; *pg.* 248, *pg.* 1223
Sanchez, Adriel, Head-Mktg-Americas - CommVault Systems, Inc.; *pg.* 377, *pg.* 1125
Sanchez, Amanda, Mgr-PR - Adobe Systems Incorporated; *pg.* 342, *pg.* 235
Sanchez, Amanda N., Mgr-Mktg-Client Svcs-IBM Hardware - Ingram Micro Inc.; *pg.* 415, *pg.* 261
Sanchez, David, VP-Sls - Streaming Media Hosting, Inc.; *pg.* 1283, *pg.* 166
Sanchez, Hugo, Dir-Mktg - O'Reilly Automotive, Inc.; *pg.* 214, *pg.* 1006
Sanchez, Jeannie, Sr Mgr-Wholesale Comm - Van Cleef & Arpels, Inc.; *pg.* 15, *pg.* 1308
Sanchez, Jonfrey, District Head-Sls-Geo - PepsiCo, Inc.; *pg.* 259, *pg.* 1327
Sanchez, Judy C., Sr Dir-Corp Comm & Pub Affairs - United States Sugar Corporation; *pg.* 907, *pg.* 417
Sanchez, Karina, Copywriter-Mktg - J.C. Penney Company, Inc.; *pg.* 1774, *pg.* 1732
Sanchez, Maria, Brand Mgr - Bristol-Myers Squibb Company; *pg.* 1509, *pg.* 1206
Sanchez, Monica L., Mgr-Mktg-Events & Sponsorships - Teachers Insurance & Annuity Association - College Retirement Equities Fund; *pg.* 1219, *pg.* 1297
Sanchez, Nicolas, Product Head-Big Data - eBay Inc.; *pg.* 1240, *pg.* 243
Sanchez, Oscar, Sr Mgr-Mktg - Ixia; *pg.* 422, *pg.* 56
Sanchez, Rachel, Dir-Email Mktg - The Children's Place, Inc.; *pg.* 22, *pg.* 1119
Sanchez, Renee, Brand Mgr-Global Retail-NikeFactory Stores - NIKE, Inc.; *pg.* 1812, *pg.* 1492
Sanchez, Ricardo, Sr Mgr-Category Mktg-Tech & Digital - Office Depot, Inc.; *pg.* 448, *pg.* 412
Sanchez, Rodrigo, VP & Product Head-Comml Cards Bus to Bus-North America - Citigroup Inc.; *pg.* 735, *pg.* 1212
Sanchez, Stella, Dir-Mktg-Starwood Preferred Guest Credit Card - American Express Company; *pg.* 712, *pg.* 1190
Sanchez, Theresa, Sr Mgr-Mktg-Latin America, Canada, Australia & New Zealand - Amgen Inc.; *pg.* 1493, *pg.* 291
Sanchez, Valentina, Mgr-Mktg - The Procter & Gamble Company; *pg.* 1129, *pg.* 1418
Sanchez, Victoria, Mgr-US Channel Mktg, SMB & Comml - Apple Inc.; *pg.* 350, *pg.* 73
Sanchirico, Chris, Sr Dir-Sls & Mktg - BE Aerospace, Inc.; *pg.* 224, *pg.* 478
Sand, Hallie, Dir-Mktg - True Religion Brand Jeans; *pg.* 49, *pg.* 143
Sand, Kayleigh, Mgr-Sls-Private & Corp Events - Newport Aquarium; *pg.* 571, *pg.* 739
Sandager, Emily, Sr Specialist-Mktg - Thrivent Financial for Lutherans; *pg.* 1219, *pg.* 944
Sandberg, Karl, Sr Mgr-Application Ops - Land O'Lakes, Inc.; *pg.* 873, *pg.* 915
Sandblom, Terri, Sr Mgr-Mktg - Swarovski North America Limited Inc.; *pg.* 13, *pg.* 1600
Sandeep, Shrivastava, Mgr-Mktg - Philips Electronics North America; *pg.* 662, *pg.* 782
Sandelli, Allegra, Sr VP & Dir-Mktg Comm - TD Bank US Holding Company; *pg.* 809, *pg.* 1051
Sander, Adam, Sr Mgr-Procurement - Renewable Energy Group, Inc.; *pg.* 984, *pg.* 701
Sanderford, Sherry McGlamory, Sr Dir-Comm & Bus Comm - Aetna Inc.; *pg.* 1187, *pg.* 351
Sanders, Bob, Engr-Sls - iMODULES Software, Inc.; *pg.* 1258, *pg.* 716
Sanders, Cindy, Mgr-Dev-Mktg Cloud - Adobe Systems Incorporated; *pg.* 342, *pg.* 235
Sanders, Dale, Sr Dir-Intl Ops - Briggs & Stratton Corporation; *pg.* 201, *pg.* 1899
Sanders, David, Head-PR & Media-UK - Princess Cruise Lines Ltd.; *pg.* 1920, *pg.* 270
Sanders, Ed, Dir-Mktg-Global-Google Glass - Google Inc.; *pg.* 1249, *pg.* 153
Sanders, Frank, VP-Provider Mktg - GlaxoSmithKline; *pg.* 1536, *pg.* 1565
Sanders, Geoffrey, Sr VP-Digital Mktg-On-Site Mdsg, eMail & Display Media - Citigroup Inc.; *pg.* 735, *pg.* 1212
Sanders, Howard, Mgr-Sls-Southeast Region - Sabra Dipping Company LLC; *pg.* 893, *pg.* 1686
Sanders, Jason, Assoc Mgr-Email Mktg - Ancestry.com LLC; *pg.* 1228, *pg.* 1754
Sanders, Karen Wright, Mgr-Digital Mktg - The Vanguard Group, Inc.; *pg.* 816, *pg.* 1550
Sanders, Katy, Brand Mgr-Grilling Products - Duraflame, Inc.; *pg.* 1123, *pg.* 280
Sanders, Kyle, Sr Mgr-Brand Mgmt & Pkg - Academy Sports & Outdoors, Ltd.; *pg.* 1824, *pg.* 1724
Sanders, Kyle, Mgr-Sls & Bus Dev - Honeywell Aerospace Electronic Systems; *pg.* 228, *pg.* 17
Sanders, Michael, Sr Mgr-Production Engrg, Exploration & Strategic Svcs - Devon Energy Corporation; *pg.* 975, *pg.* 1485
Sanders, Patrick, Mgr-Natl Mktg Programs - Allen-Edmonds Shoe Corp.; *pg.* 1804, *pg.* 1887
Sanders, Rebecca, Dir-PR - Brookshire Grocery Company; *pg.* 1016, *pg.* 1748
Sanders, Tricia, Dir-Mktg & Bus Dev-Battlefield Mall - Simon Property Group, Inc.; *pg.* 1112, *pg.* 690
Sanderson, Briand, Sr Product Mgr-Mktg - Microsoft Corporation; *pg.* 435, *pg.* 1824
Sanderson, Greg, Mgr-Mktg - Young Innovations, Inc.; *pg.* 1611, *pg.* 977
Sanderson, Heather, Sr Dir-Digital Publ Ops & Support - Penguin Random House; *pg.* 1675, *pg.* 1276
Sanderson, Sandra, Exec VP-Mktg - Wal-Mart Canada Corp.; *pg.* 1790, *pg.* 1929
Sandheinrich, Lauren, Mgr-Segment Mktg - Merge eClinical Inc.; *pg.* 1266, *pg.* 1385
Sandhu, Jodi, Mgr-Shopper Mktg - Safeway Inc.; *pg.* 1032, *pg.* 184
Sandiford, Steven, Mgr-Mktg Analytics - LOGMEIN, INC.; *pg.* 428, *pg.* 861
Sandlin, Ed, Mgr-Product Mktg Indus Bus - Schneider Electric USA, Inc.; *pg.* 1306, *pg.* 650
Sando, Jill, VP & Mgr-Mdse - Target Corporation; *pg.* 1786, *pg.* 942
Sandom, Brian, Product Mgr-Digital Weekly Ad - Target Corporation; *pg.* 1786, *pg.* 942
Sandomenico, Nicole, Specialist-Product Stewardship - Honeywell International Inc.; *pg.* 407, *pg.* 1088
Sandor, Daniel, Sr Mgr-Sls Strategy - Kimberly-Clark Corporation; *pg.* 1461, *pg.* 1720
Sandor, George, Dir-Global Organics, Americas Sls & Dev - FMC Lithium Division; *pg.* 1163, *pg.* 1366
Sandoval, Beatriz, Sr Exec Mgr-Mktg-North America - BSH Home Appliances Corporation; *pg.* 53, *pg.* 108
Sandoval, Claudia, Dir-Global Brands & Product Dev - Toys "R" Us, Inc.; *pg.* 968, *pg.* 1130
Sandoval, Lisa, Sr Mgr-Partner Solutions-Exchange - Twitter, Inc.; *pg.* 1285, *pg.* 228
Sandoval, Veronica, Assoc Brand Mgr-Mktg Girls & Preschool - Bandai America Incorporated; *pg.* 950, *pg.* 75
Sandoval-Mulvey, Rose, Sr VP-Strategic Dev & Corp Mktg - Lam Research Corporation; *pg.* 1354, *pg.* 246
Sandrick, Amanda, Reg Specialist-Mktg - CommScope; *pg.* 630, *pg.* 668
Sandru, Diana, Mgr-Mktg - Bank Leumi USA; *pg.* 718, *pg.* 1200
Sands, Alysia, Sr Mgr-Digital Publicity & Corp PR - Showtime Networks Inc.; *pg.* 308, *pg.* 1291
Sands, Kirsten, Reg Dir-Mktg - Texas Roadhouse, Inc.; *pg.* 1753, *pg.* 738
Sands, Michael, Dir-Sls & Product Dev - Capital Brands, LLC; *pg.* 53, *pg.* 127
Sandstedt, Martha, Dir-Mktg - Texas Instruments Incorporated; *pg.* 679, *pg.* 1688
Sandstrom, Kassandra, Mgr-Social Media - Nordstrom, Inc.; *pg.* 1779, *pg.* 1837
Sandulli, Walter, Sr Dir-Mktg - Sanofi US; *pg.* 1592, *pg.* 1046
Sanduski, Jim, Pres-Sharp Electronics Marketing Company of America - Sharp Electronics Corporation; *pg.* 672, *pg.* 1082
Sandvick, Carolyn, Mgr-ECommerce Mktg - Weyco Group, Inc.; *pg.* 1822, *pg.* 1858
Sandvik, Mark S., VP-Sls - Icicle Seafoods, Inc.; *pg.* 864, *pg.* 1836
Sandy, Ann, Dir-Mktg & Comm - Royal Bank of Canada; *pg.* 800, *pg.* 1942
Sanelli, Fred, Sr VP-Mktg, Brands & Sls Dev - Performance Food Group Company, LLC; *pg.* 1030, *pg.* 1803
Sanford, Frank W., VP-Mktg - Sanford & Hawley, Inc.; *pg.* 109, *pg.* 381
Sanford, Justine, Coord-Mktg Comm - Nature's Path Foods Inc.; *pg.* 833, *pg.* 1908
Sanford, Linda, Dir-Mktg - Brother International Corporation - USA; *pg.* 53, *pg.* 1046
Sanford, Marc, Sr Dir-Digital Mktg Analytics - Zillow Group, Inc.; *pg.* 1292, *pg.* 1843
Sanford, Taylor, Mgr-Sls & Bus Dev - FMC Lithium Division; *pg.* 1163, *pg.* 1366
Sangalli, Walter L., VP-Sls & Mktg-Worldwide - Maxim Integrated Products, Inc.; *pg.* 653, *pg.* 247
Sangam, Prakash, Dir-Technical Mktg - QUALCOMM Incorporated; *pg.* 1873, *pg.* 207
Sanger, Sherry, Sr VP-Mktg - Penske Truck Leasing Company, L.P.; *pg.* 188, *pg.* 1585
Sanghvi, Shaily, Sr Dir-Strategy - Del Monte Foods, Inc.; *pg.* 852, *pg.* 304
Sanghvi, Vishal, Mgr-Mktg Strategy & Campaigns - Intel Corporation; *pg.* 645, *pg.* 266
SanGiacomo, Linda, Sr Dir-Adv & Creative - Dunkin' Brands Group, Inc.; *pg.* 1727, *pg.* 810
Sangiuliano, Debra, Dir-Media - Pfizer Inc.; *pg.* 1581, *pg.* 1278
Sanguinetti, Cecilia, Assoc VP-One to One Mktg - Royal Caribbean Cruises Ltd; *pg.* 1921, *pg.* 446
Sanguinetti, Daneyni, Sr Mgr-Center of Excellence Multicultural Mktg - The Coca-Cola Company; *pg.* 240, *pg.* 493
Sangwan, Sarika, Dir-Digital Brand & Social Media Strategy - American Express Company; *pg.* 712, *pg.* 1190
Sanichar, Ashley, Head-Central Govt Sls-Pub Sector - Microsoft Corporation; *pg.* 435, *pg.* 1824
Sanie, Michael, Sr Dir-Verification Mktg - Synopsys, Inc.; *pg.* 480, *pg.* 162
Sankaran, Arvind, Sr Product Mgr-GPM & Product Mktg - Applied Materials, Inc.; *pg.* 618, *pg.* 264
Sankaran, Bharat, Sr Assoc Brand Mgr - Post Holdings, Inc.; *pg.* 833, *pg.* 1002
Sankaran, Karthik, Gen Mgr-Embedded Sys Products & Tech-Bangalore - Analog Devices, Inc.; *pg.* 617, *pg.* 839
Sanker, Donna L., VP-Mktg-ampm & ARCO - BP America Inc.; *pg.* 972, *pg.* 1702
Sankey, Rebecca, Sr Mgr-Mktg-Global Innovation - PepsiCo, Inc.; *pg.* 259, *pg.* 1327
Sanna, Chuck, Product Line Mgr-High Speed Data Converters - Texas Instruments Incorporated; *pg.* 679, *pg.* 1688
Sannes, Steve, Mgr-Sls - North Dakota Mill & Elevator Association; *pg.* 833, *pg.* 1398
Sansanese, Victor, Asst VP-ECommerce & Digital Mktg - L'Oreal USA; *pg.* 514, *pg.* 1252
Sansom, Roger, VP-Sls & Customer Svc - Kraft Food Ingredients; *pg.* 870, *pg.* 1645
Sansone, Perry, VP-Sls-North America-Idelle Labs - Helen of Troy L.P.; *pg.* 511, *pg.* 1692
Sansores, Alfredo, VP-Sls-Intl - A&K Railroad Materials Inc.; *pg.* 1896, *pg.* 1755
Sant, Anjali, Dir-Digital Mktg - Hyatt Hotels Corporation; *pg.* 1096, *pg.* 577
Sant, Don, Dir-Sls-Global - NCR Corporation; *pg.* 443, *pg.* 531
Santaella, Raphael J., VP-Sls & Mktg - Canadian Fish Exporters, Inc.; *pg.* 845, *pg.* 784
Santaella, Rene, VP & Gen Sls Mgr-Sony Pictures Television - Sony Pictures Entertainment Inc.; *pg.* 309, *pg.* 72
Santana Bru, Sebastian, Strategist-Creative - Facebook, Inc.; *pg.* 1245, *pg.* 143
Santana, Lissette, Mgr-Digital Media & Employee Comm - PPL Corporation; *pg.* 1950, *pg.* 1514
Santangelo, Caroline, VP-Mktg Insights & Analytics - Liberty Mutual Insurance Group Inc.; *pg.* 1205, *pg.* 797
Santangelo, John, VP-Inbound & Digital Mktg - Adecco USA, Inc.; *pg.* 342, *pg.* 1178
Santangelo, Mary, Sr Mgr-Mktg - Coty, Inc.; *pg.* 506, *pg.* 1219
Santangelo, Thomas, Dir-Mktg-Pepsi-Lipton Partnership - Pepsi Beverages Company; *pg.* 258, *pg.* 1342
Santeler, Brad, Sr Dir-Mktg Mgmt & Capability Building - Abbott Laboratories; *pg.* 1484, *pg.* 551
Santello, Sandy, Dir-Mktg Comm-Global - LifeCell Corporation; *pg.* 1556, *pg.* 1045
Santer, Tom, VP-Sls - Speakman Company; *pg.* 112, *pg.* 388
Santi, Adrienne, Dir-Social Media - VITAMIN SHOPPE, INC.; *pg.* 1608, *pg.* 1098
Santi, Glen, Acct Mgr-Sls - Brainerd Daily Dispatch; *pg.* 1623, *pg.* 919
Santiago, Cathleen, Mgr-Network Dev & Mktg - Montefiore Medical Center; *pg.* 1569, *pg.* 1144
Santiago, Jennifer, Reg Mgr-Mktg - Hess Corporation; *pg.* 979, *pg.* 1240
Santiago, Jessica, Specialist-Local Mktg - Ikea North America Services LLC; *pg.* 929, *pg.* 1523

Santilli, Andrea, Mgr-Mktg - Audi of America, Inc.; *pg.* 164, *pg.* 1784
Santillo, Michael, VP-Mktg - Flexsteel Industries, Inc.; *pg.* 925, *pg.* 707
Santilo, Gloria, Dir-Mktg Comm-Global - IBM; *pg.* 410, *pg.* 1449
Santin, Gianni, Mgr-Mktg - Expedia, Inc.; *pg.* 1244, *pg.* 1814
Santini, Vince, VP-Sls - Litecontrol Corporation; *pg.* 1301, *pg.* 841
Santo, Stacey, VP-Mktg Comm & Brand Strategy - Rue La La; *pg.* 1278, *pg.* 800
Santora, Anthony, Assoc-Sls - Semonin Realtors; *pg.* 1112, *pg.* 738
Santora, Tom, CMO & Sr VP-Sls - Omni Hotels & Resorts; *pg.* 1107, *pg.* 1685
Santoro, Amanda, Brand Mgr-Rels - LEGO Systems, Inc.; *pg.* 961, *pg.* 346
Santoro, Gregory J., CMO, Chief Strategy Officer & Exec VP - NII Holdings, Inc.; *pg.* 659, *pg.* 1799
Santoro, Lindsay, Mgr-Mktg - Mohegan Tribal Gaming Authority; *pg.* 564, *pg.* 381
Santoro, Lisa, Sr Mgr-Visual Mdsg Ops & Production - Ann Inc.; *pg.* 18, *pg.* 1195
Santoro, Nikki, VP-Product & Design - The Weather Channel LLC; *pg.* 320, *pg.* 523
Santos, Anna, Sr Product Mgr-Fire TV - Amazon.com, Inc.; *pg.* 1226, *pg.* 1831
Santos, Dan, VP-Corp & Channel Sls-Worldwide - LapLink Software, Inc.; *pg.* 426, *pg.* 1815
Santos, Freddy, Sr Mgr-Corp Rels - The Allstate Corporation; *pg.* 1189, *pg.* 639
Santos, Hana, Dir-Mktg-Key Accounts Mktg - Pacific Life Insurance Company; *pg.* 1213, *pg.* 166
Santos, Javier G., Mgr-Mktg - The Western Union Company; *pg.* 822, *pg.* 327
Santos, Jennifer, Product Mgr - Safilo USA Inc.; *pg.* 11, *pg.* 1106
Santos, Kam, Mgr-Mktg - JPMorgan Chase & Co.; *pg.* 772, *pg.* 1246
Santos, Norman, Sr Dir-Procurement - Aramark; *pg.* 1013, *pg.* 1558
Santos, Raul, Mgr-Mktg - Wal-Mart Stores, Inc.; *pg.* 1790, *pg.* 29
Santos, Sonya M., Dir-Mktg-Americas - W.R. Grace & Co.; *pg.* 123, *pg.* 810
Santoyo, Gus, Mgr-PR - Chevron Corporation; *pg.* 974, *pg.* 259
Santschi, Douglas, VP-Mktg - AdvancePierre Foods, Inc.; *pg.* 1714, *pg.* 1409
Sanville, Danielle, Brand Mgr-Thompson Center - Smith & Wesson Holding Corporation; *pg.* 1845, *pg.* 846
Sanz, Gerard, Product Mgr - Google Inc.; *pg.* 1249, *pg.* 153
Sanzo, James, Product Mgr-Advanced Imaging - Olympus America Inc.; *pg.* 1425, *pg.* 1521
Saoji, Mayuresh, Mgr-Lead Product - Google Inc.; *pg.* 1249, *pg.* 153
Sapir, Alex C., Exec VP-Mktg & Sls - United Therapeutics Corporation; *pg.* 1604, *pg.* 778
Sapirstein, Jake, Head-Innovation Lab & Sr Dir-Digital Mktg - SAP America, Inc.; *pg.* 466, *pg.* 1557
Saporito, Andrea, VP-Mktg, Digital Partnerships & Dev - American Express Company; *pg.* 712, *pg.* 1190
Saporito, Joe, Mgr-Sls - AOL Inc.; *pg.* 1229, *pg.* 1195
Saporito, Stefanie, Mgr-Trade Mktg - NBTY, Inc.; *pg.* 1572, *pg.* 1338
Sapos, Judy, Brand Mgr-PR - The Kraft Heinz Company; *pg.* 870, *pg.* 1577
Sappenfield, Scott, Dir-Mktg - Ubisoft Inc.; *pg.* 589, *pg.* 229
Saputo, Sandy, CMO & Sr VP-Mktg-Global - Bare Escentuals, Inc.; *pg.* 500, *pg.* 213
Sara, Rowena, Sr Dir-PR & Global Comm Strategy - Habitat for Humanity International, Inc.; *pg.* 143, *pg.* 486
Saracco, Michael A, Sr VP-Natl Sls - BioScrip, Inc.; *pg.* 1506, *pg.* 1158
Saraceni, Wesley, Sr Assoc Brand Mgr - Mondelez International; *pg.* 877, *pg.* 1344
Saracino, Michael, Dir-Digital Mktg - Eddie Bauer, Inc.; *pg.* 40, *pg.* 1814
Sarajian, Keri, Sr Dir-Mktg, Brand Mgmt & Home Cleaning - S.C. Johnson & Son, Inc.; *pg.* 334, *pg.* 1889
Sarandos, Chris, Acct Mgr-Performance Mktg - Google Inc.; *pg.* 1249, *pg.* 153
Sarasua, Robert, Dir-Mktg Procurement - Luxottica Retail; *pg.* 8, *pg.* 1460
Sarathy, Latha, VP-Telemundo Media Digital Res - Telemundo Network Inc.; *pg.* 311, *pg.* 430
Saratlic, George, Product Mgr-Comm-Canada - General Motors of Canada Ltd.; *pg.* 177, *pg.* 1931
Sarbaugh, Carina, Mgr-Mktg-Brand Gen Mills - General Mills, Inc.; *pg.* 828, *pg.* 933
Sarbinoff, Ryan, Mgr-Sls - Marcus & Millichap Real Estate Investment Company; *pg.* 1102, *pg.* 56
Sardanis, Steven, Mgr-Adv Ops - The New York Times Company; *pg.* 1668, *pg.* 1270
Sardinha, Rob, Assoc Dir-Payer Mktg-Multiple Sclerosis - Novartis Corporation; *pg.* 1574, *pg.* 1273
Sarfraz, Kashif, Dir-Mktg & Sls - Johnson & Johnson Inc.; *pg.* 1552, *pg.* 1923
Sargent, Bob, Dir-Brdcst & Corp Sls - San Francisco Forty Niners, Ltd.; *pg.* 581, *pg.* 270
Sargent, Erayna, Brand Mgr-Flavor Enhancements Core Brands & Private Label - ACH Food Companies, Inc.; *pg.* 835, *pg.* 1631
Sargent, Hajime, Specialist-Digital Mktg - Dynapar; *pg.* 1408, *pg.* 610
Sargent, Joe, Brand Mgr-Multicultural - MillerCoors LLC; *pg.* 255, *pg.* 582
Sargent, Scott, Product Mgr - Victaulic Company; *pg.* 1066, *pg.* 1529
Sarian, Teny, Coord-Mktg & Promos - Universal Studios, Inc.; *pg.* 315, *pg.* 298
Sarin, Punit, VP-Product - LiveRail; *pg.* 1264, *pg.* 145
Sarkis, Pauline, Program Mgr-Mktg - Intel Corporation; *pg.* 645, *pg.* 266
Sarma, Vikram, Sr Dir-Global Insights - The Clorox Company; *pg.* 327, *pg.* 169
Sarna, Ruchika, Sr Mgr-Mktg Analytics & Strategy - Johnson & Johnson; *pg.* 1549, *pg.* 1091
Sarner, Steve, VP-Mktg - IF(WE); *pg.* 1258, *pg.* 219
Sarnoff, Brett, Dir-Rheumatology Product & Sr Mgr-Mktg Dev - Janssen Pharmaceutica Products, L.P.; *pg.* 1548, *pg.* 1125
Saroop, Rohit, Dir-Small Bus Bank Mktg - Capital One Financial Corporation; *pg.* 730, *pg.* 1789
Saroop, Sriram, Product Mgr - Google Inc.; *pg.* 1249, *pg.* 153
Sarraf, Natalie, Mgr-Social Media Mktg - Iconix Brand Group, Inc.; *pg.* 26, *pg.* 1243
Sarria, Angel, Brand Mgr-US Domestic & Multicultural Mktg Strategy - The Walt Disney Company; *pg.* 317, *pg.* 52
Sarro, Jan, VP-Sls & Mktg - FUSION TELECOMMUNICATIONS INTERNATIONAL, INC.; *pg.* 1248, *pg.* 1233
Sarrow, Robert, Mgr-Database Mktg - Bosley Inc.; *pg.* 1508, *pg.* 46
Sartor, Danielle, Sr Dir-Product Dev - Timex Corporation; *pg.* 14, *pg.* 355
Sartorius, Carlos, Sr VP-Worldwide Sls & Svcs - Citrix Systems, Inc.; *pg.* 375, *pg.* 424
Sarubbi, John, Sr Mgr-Mktg - IBM; *pg.* 410, *pg.* 1449
Sarvas, Danelle, Dir-Field Mktg-East - Kind LLC; *pg.* 868, *pg.* 1249
Sarver, Amanda, Coord-PR & New Media - Baltimore Orioles, L.P.; *pg.* 532, *pg.* 755
Sarvey, Amy, Sr Mgr-Mktg - LifeCell Corporation; *pg.* 1556, *pg.* 1045
Sarvis, John, VP-Ceramic Products - AVX Corporation; *pg.* 623, *pg.* 1616
Sarwar, Adil, Head-Tech Mktg-PC Client Grp - Intel Corporation; *pg.* 645, *pg.* 266
Sas, Brian, Reg Mgr-Sls & Mktg-Caribbean & US Exporters - Rich Products Corporation; *pg.* 892, *pg.* 1150
Sass, Jeff, Sr VP-Truck Sls & Mktg-North America - Navistar International Corporation; *pg.* 186, *pg.* 630
Sassano, Lauren, Sr Mgr-Local Store Mktg - Rubio's Restaurants, Inc.; *pg.* 1748, *pg.* 60
Sassano, Rachel, Mgr-Cross Segment Mktg - The Western Union Company; *pg.* 822, *pg.* 327
Sassen, Jennifer, VP-Mktg-North America - Sage Software, Inc.; *pg.* 464, *pg.* 116
Sasser, Rachel, Sr Mgr-Mktg-Global Nutrition Grp Grains Innovation - PepsiCo, Inc.; *pg.* 259, *pg.* 1327
Sassi, Lynda Zuber, Dir-Sls, Mass Market, Premiums & Licensing - Chronicle Books; *pg.* 1627, *pg.* 216
Sasso, Kelly S., Mgr-PR - Lexar Media, Inc.; *pg.* 1262, *pg.* 146
Sasson, Brian, Mgr-Social Investments-Global - The Procter & Gamble Company; *pg.* 1129, *pg.* 1418
Saste, Priya, Project Head-Mdsg - Delta Air Lines, Inc.; *pg.* 1905, *pg.* 503
Sastry, Raj, Sr Mgr-Insights & Strategy - Best Buy Co., Inc.; *pg.* 1761, *pg.* 954
Satanovsky, Oleg, Coord-Product Comm - BMW of North America, LLC; *pg.* 166, *pg.* 1133
Satchell, Chris, Chief Product Officer & Exec VP - Comcast Cable Communications, Inc.; *pg.* 276, *pg.* 1560
Sater, Kim, Dir-Consumer Mktg-US - Mary Kay Inc.; *pg.* 516, *pg.* 1657
Sathe, Saleel, Head-Paid Search Mktg Product-Global - eBay Inc.; *pg.* 1240, *pg.* 243
Sather, Stacey, Mgr-Creative & Adv - St. Augustine, Ponte Vedra & The Beaches Visitors & Convention Bureau; *pg.* 1006, *pg.* 461
Sathyamurthy, Suresh, Head-Product Mktg-Emerging Technologies Div & Sr Dir - EMC Corporation; *pg.* 391, *pg.* 825
Sathyesh, Rajeev, Country Mgr-Mktg & Bus Delivery-Gillette India - The Procter & Gamble Company; *pg.* 1129, *pg.* 1418
Sato, Andrea Hicks, Dir-Sls Trng & Comm - The Dannon Company, Inc.; *pg.* 851, *pg.* 1351
Satran, Laurie, Specialist-Media - Ikea North America Services LLC; *pg.* 929, *pg.* 1523
Satre, Brian, VP-Mktg - Blistex, Inc.; *pg.* 502, *pg.* 644
Satrom, Virginia, Specialist-Channel Mktg - RSA Security Inc.; *pg.* 463, *pg.* 786
Satterfield, David L., Co-COO & Sr VP-Mktg & Originations - First Investors Financial Services Group, Inc.; *pg.* 756, *pg.* 1706
Satterfield, Eric, Program Mgr-Digital Mktg - Automobile Club of Southern California; *pg.* 134, *pg.* 126
Satterfield, Stephanie, Mgr-Mktg Sls - The Society of American Military Engineers; *pg.* 156, *pg.* 1771
Satyal, Vikas, Dir-Comml Mktg US Strategy & Plng - Heineken USA Inc.; *pg.* 252, *pg.* 1352
Satyavolu, Schwark, Exec VP-Product & Tech - LifeLock Inc.; *pg.* 776, *pg.* 26
Saucier, Caroline, Specialist-Comm-Corp Brand & Adv - Johnson Controls, Inc.; *pg.* 209, *pg.* 1876
Saucier, Tony, Dir-Social Media - Life Time Fitness, Inc.; *pg.* 1556, *pg.* 920
Sauder, Don, Grp Dir-Companion Animal New Products Mktg - Zoetis Inc.; *pg.* 1611, *pg.* 1067
Sauer, Denise, Analyst-Strategic Mktg - FedEx Corporation; *pg.* 1907, *pg.* 1642
Sauer, John M., Dir-Technical Mktg-Tellabs - Tellabs, Inc.; *pg.* 678, *pg.* 637
Sauer, Mark, Exec VP-Sls - The C.F. Sauer Company; *pg.* 847, *pg.* 1801
Sauer, Susan, Sr Mgr-Religious Sls - Louisville Convention & Visitors Bureau; *pg.* 998, *pg.* 736
Sauerhoff, Gabriel, VP-Digital Media Distr - Discovery Communications, Inc.; *pg.* 282, *pg.* 777
Sauerman, Suzaan, Sr Dir-Global Mktg - GN Netcom Inc.; *pg.* 640, *pg.* 1037
Sauers, Catherine, Reg Mgr-Client Mktg-Midwest - BabyCenter, LLC; *pg.* 1231, *pg.* 212
Saul, Chris, Mgr-Storwize Family Mktg - International Business Machines Corporation; *pg.* 418, *pg.* 1138
Saul, Robert, Sr Product Mgr-Tire Ops - Bridgestone Americas, Inc.; *pg.* 1879, *pg.* 1648
Saun, Krista Van, Mng Dir-NY Sls - Tribune Media Company; *pg.* 1696, *pg.* 592
Saunders, Andrew, Sr VP-Creative - Getty Images, Inc.; *pg.* 1645, *pg.* 1836
Saunders, Brynn, Project Mgr-Digital-Global Sls - Oakley, Inc.; *pg.* 1840, *pg.* 86
Saunders, Dean, Sr Dir-Pur - G4S Secure Solutions USA; *pg.* 399, *pg.* 436
Saunders, Fred, Sr VP-Mktg & Brand - LendingTree, LLC; *pg.* 775, *pg.* 1367
Saunders, Jamie, Sr Mgr-Mktg Comm - Neenah Paper, Inc.; *pg.* 1465, *pg.* 484
Saunders, JP, Sr Dir-Solution Strategy - Oracle Corporation; *pg.* 450, *pg.* 191
Saunders, Mark, Sr Rep-PR - United States Postal Service; *pg.* 1009, *pg.* 406
Saunders, Rick, Dir-Mktg - Orchard Supply Hardware Stores Corp.; *pg.* 1058, *pg.* 248
Saunders, Sara, Brand Mgr - The Procter & Gamble Company; *pg.* 1129, *pg.* 1418
Sauser, Todd, Dir-Mktg - Nilodor, Inc.; *pg.* 332, *pg.* 1406
Sauter, Leigh, Supvr-Mktg - Comcast Cable Communications, Inc.; *pg.* 276, *pg.* 1560
Sauter, Stephanie, Dir-Comm & Mktg European Customers-Global - Harman International Industries, Incorporated; *pg.*

641, *pg.* 374
Sauve, Danielle, Mgr-Mktg - SGK; *pg.* 1686, *pg.* 590
Sava, Morgan A., Program Mgr-Channel Mktg - Eaton Corporation; *pg.* 1331, *pg.* 1429
Savage, Angela, Mgr-Digital Mktg - Chick-fil-A, Inc.; *pg.* 1721, *pg.* 492
Savage, Beth, Mgr-Mktg Programs - ASPEN TECHNOLOGY, INC.; *pg.* 354, *pg.* 804
Savage, Brandon, Dir-Product Mgmt - Box Inc.; *pg.* 1232, *pg.* 124
Savage, Carl, VP-Sls & Mktg - Micro Corp.; *pg.* 1056, *pg.* 1122
Savage, Cheryl, Mgr-Media Sls - Yahoo! Inc.; *pg.* 1289, *pg.* 289
Savage, Gene, Dir-Franchise Sls & Real Estate - The Johnny Rockets Group, Inc.; *pg.* 1733, *pg.* 41
Savage, Jennifer, VP-Brand Mktg Initiatives-Spike TV - MTV Networks Company; *pg.* 298, *pg.* 1262
Savage, Jennifer, VP-Brand Mktg Initiatives - Spike TV; *pg.* 310, *pg.* 1295
Savage, Jessica, Mgr-Social Media & Online Mktg - International Paper Company; *pg.* 1460, *pg.* 1644
Savage, John, Dir-Mktg-Healthcare - Cintas Corporation; *pg.* 372, *pg.* 1411
Savage, John, Brand Mgr-Walkers Market Deli - PepsiCo, Inc.; *pg.* 259, *pg.* 1327
Savage, Katie, Acct Exec-Enterprise Corp Sls - salesforce.com, inc.; *pg.* 1278, *pg.* 226
Savage, Kristen Barrett, Sr Brand Mktg Mgr - Landry's, Inc.; *pg.* 1735, *pg.* 1709
Savage, Wendy, Mgr-Social & Environmental Responsibility - Patagonia; *pg.* 31, *pg.* 301
Savaiano, Genevieve, Assoc Mgr-Social Media, PR & Content Mktg - Conagra Foods; *pg.* 826, *pg.* 994
Savaiano, Genevieve, Assoc Mgr-Social Media, PR & Content Mktg - ConAgra Foods, Inc.; *pg.* 826, *pg.* 1014
Savant, Matt, Dir-Mktg & Brand Mgmt - Anaheim Ducks Hockey Club, LLC; *pg.* 528, *pg.* 42
Savarese, Brian, Product Mgr-Consumer Retail & Pro AV Home Theater Projectors - Epson America Inc.; *pg.* 394, *pg.* 122
Savarese, Donna, Sr Specialist-Media Rels - Lockheed Martin Corporation; *pg.* 229, *pg.* 762
Savelle, Bill, Exec VP-Products - Telsco Industries, Inc.; *pg.* 1381, *pg.* 1698
Saviano, Claudio, Mgr-Sls-Intl - House of Raeford Farms, Inc.; *pg.* 864, *pg.* 1386
Savic, Alex, Mng Dir-Latin America Sls - United Airlines, Inc.; *pg.* 1927, *pg.* 593
Saville, Bert, Mgr-Trade Mktg - Pernod Ricard USA, Inc.; *pg.* 1968, *pg.* 1332
Savinelli, Daniela, Sr Mgr-Mktg-NA - Netflix, Inc.; *pg.* 1269, *pg.* 141
Savkar, Jaya, Sr Dir-Product Mgmt - SHUTTERFLY, INC.; *pg.* 1280, *pg.* 192
Savoni, Michael, Head-Social Media Bus Process - General Motors Company; *pg.* 175, *pg.* 881
Savory, Patrick, Mgr-Sls-Natl - Waters Corporation; *pg.* 1436, *pg.* 834
Savoye, Frederick, Gen Mgr-Product & Bus Plng - Microsoft Corporation; *pg.* 435, *pg.* 1824
Savstrom, Angela, Assoc Mgr-Mktg - Land O'Lakes, Inc.; *pg.* 873, *pg.* 915
Savvas, George, Dir-PR-Disneyland Resort - The Walt Disney Company; *pg.* 317, *pg.* 52
Savvina, Anastasia, Sr Copywriter-Brand Creative - Kaiser Permanente; *pg.* 1552, *pg.* 171
Sawan-Lara, Nadim, Specialist-Mktg-Airtime & POP - TracFone Wireless, Inc.; *pg.* 681, *pg.* 447
Sawaya, Evan, Sr Specialist-Social Media Customer Relationship - General Motors Company; *pg.* 175, *pg.* 881
Sawaya, Rima, Mgr-Mktg Innovation - Mars, Incorporated; *pg.* 1858, *pg.* 1792
Sawaya, Rima, Mgr-Mktg Innovation - Mars North America; *pg.* 1859, *pg.* 1072
Sawchuk, Lori, Brand Mgr - McDonald's Corporation; *pg.* 1737, *pg.* 645
Sawdon, Stephen, Dir-Mktg - BTM Corporation; *pg.* 1320, *pg.* 898
Sawhny, Vidya, Mgr-Worldwide PR-Cloud - Hewlett-Packard Company; *pg.* 404, *pg.* 175
Sawicki, Becky, Sr Mgr-Sls & Mktg - Jura-Capresso Inc.; *pg.* 58, *pg.* 1052
Sawicki, Chad, Dir-Mktg-Adv & Sponsorship-Northeast Reg - AT&T Communications Corp.; *pg.* 1866, *pg.* 1043
Sawicki, Tom, Sr Mgr-Mktg - IDEXX Laboratories, Inc.; *pg.* 1543, *pg.* 753
Sawyer, Amy, Dir-Product Mgmt Mobile Svcs - Carlson Wagonlit Travel; *pg.* 1902, *pg.* 948
Sawyer, Catherine, Coord-Web Mktg - CB Richard Ellis, Inc.; *pg.* 1085, *pg.* 1210
Sawyer, Cheryl, VP-Corp Mktg - Teradata Corporation; *pg.* 483, *pg.* 1447
Sawyer, Crystal, Dir-Mktg - McDonald's Corporation; *pg.* 1737, *pg.* 645
Sawyer, Kolette, Mgr-Mktg Comm - Dentsply International Inc.; *pg.* 1522, *pg.* 1596
Sawyer, Marina, Mgr-Sls-Intl - Americo Manufacturing Co., Inc.; *pg.* 325, *pg.* 482
Sawyer, Rick, VP & Gen Mgr-Mdse-Auto - Sears Holdings Corporation; *pg.* 1784, *pg.* 618
Saxby, Anthony, Mgr-Product Mktg - Microsoft Corporation; *pg.* 435, *pg.* 1824
Saxena, Apoorv, Product Mgr-Google Apps - Google Inc.; *pg.* 1249, *pg.* 153
Saxena, Monika, Sr Dir-Brand Mktg - Darden Restaurants, Inc.; *pg.* 1724, *pg.* 453
Saxena, Monika, Sr Dir-Brand Mktg - Olive Garden Italian Restaurant; *pg.* 1742, *pg.* 454
Saxon, Amanda, Sr Mgr-Field Mktg - Panera Bread Company; *pg.* 1029, *pg.* 1001
Saxton, George, Product Mgr - J.C. Whitney & Co.; *pg.* 209, *pg.* 621
Saxton, John, Sr Mgr-Trade Mktg - StarKist Foods Inc.; *pg.* 898, *pg.* 1581
Say, Chris, Mgr-Mktg - Rent-A-Center, Inc.; *pg.* 940, *pg.* 1734
Sayan, Eduardo, Dir-Multicultural Mktg - Anthem, Inc.; *pg.* 1192, *pg.* 683
Sayani, Nazzie, Mgr-Guest Svcs & Social Media - Toys "R" Us, Inc.; *pg.* 968, *pg.* 1130
Sayed, Ayman, Chief Product Officer-Santa Clara - CA Technologies; *pg.* 366, *pg.* 1168
Sayen, Jeff, Mgr-Adv - Volkswagen Group of America, Inc.; *pg.* 194, *pg.* 1785
Sayer, Stacey, Mgr-Social Media Mktg - Level 3 Communications, Inc.; *pg.* 1262, *pg.* 312
Sayewitz, Lauren, Mgr-Online Mktg - Brooks Brothers Group, Inc.; *pg.* 39, *pg.* 1208
Sayles, Christina J., Assoc Dir-Global Medical Mktg-PNH - Alexion Pharmaceuticals, Inc.; *pg.* 1489, *pg.* 341
Saylor, Amber, Assoc Mgr-Mktg - Pacific Sunwear of California, Inc.; *pg.* 1781, *pg.* 43
Saylor, Justin, Asst VP-Mktg WDD - ACT Inc.; *pg.* 597, *pg.* 708
Saylor, Mark, Brand Mgr - Toys "R" Us, Inc.; *pg.* 968, *pg.* 1130
Sayward, Adrienne, Mgr-Mktg - Honest Tea; *pg.* 253, *pg.* 762
Sbarra, Rob, Sr Dir-Americas Channel Bus Team-Tech Svcs - Hewlett-Packard Company; *pg.* 404, *pg.* 175
Scafidi, Mike, Dir-Mktg Tech & Digital Ops - PepsiCo, Inc.; *pg.* 259, *pg.* 1327
Scaife, Roy, Engr-Technical Mktg - NetApp, Inc.; *pg.* 444, *pg.* 287
Scala, Peter, Sr VP-Mdsg & Online Marketplace - Staples, Inc.; *pg.* 474, *pg.* 821
Scalera, Buddy, Sr Dir-Content Strategy - The Medicines Company; *pg.* 1561, *pg.* 1104
Scalf, Thomas R., Sr VP-Engine Products - Donaldson Company, Inc.; *pg.* 1329, *pg.* 917
Scalise, Justin, Dir-Live Event Mktg-Midwest Reg - World Wrestling Entertainment, Inc.; *pg.* 595, *pg.* 380
Scallan, Brett, VP-Mktg - Ste. Michelle Wine Estates Ltd.; *pg.* 1970, *pg.* 1847
Scalo, Matthew D., Sr Dir-Strategic Plng - Luminex Corporation; *pg.* 1421, *pg.* 1664
Scalza, Susan, Sr Mgr-Mktg-Acq Mktg Segment Strategy - Teachers Insurance & Annuity Association - College Retirement Equities Fund; *pg.* 1219, *pg.* 1297
Scalzo, Lisa R., Sr Dir-Corp Comm, Video Products & Svcs - Comcast Corporation; *pg.* 276, *pg.* 1560
Scalzo, Terry, Sr Strategist-Mktg - Intel Corporation; *pg.* 645, *pg.* 266
Scanlan, Karla J., Analyst-Mktg - McKesson Corporation; *pg.* 1560, *pg.* 222
Scanlan, Tim, VP-Talent & Production - ESPN, Inc.; *pg.* 285, *pg.* 340
Scanlon, Blake, Dir-Global Sls & Engrg Dev, Bearings & Power Transmission Grp - The Timken Company; *pg.* 218, *pg.* 1408
Scanlon, Brian, Chief Strategy Officer & Exec VP - Thomson Reuters - Corporate Headquarters; *pg.* 1693, *pg.* 1299
Scanlon, Colleen, Exec Dir-Media-North America - The Estee Lauder Companies Inc.; *pg.* 508, *pg.* 1229
Scanlon, Jim, Mgr-Sls-Natl - GAMCO Investors, Inc.; *pg.* 761, *pg.* 1339
Scanlon, Vince, VP & Dir-PR & Media Rels-Wells Fargo Wealth Mgmt - Wells Fargo & Company; *pg.* 819, *pg.* 232
Scannell, Bill, Pres-Sls & Customer Ops-Global - EMC Corporation; *pg.* 391, *pg.* 825
Scannell, Bruce, Acct Mgr-Adv Sls - Investors Business Daily, Inc.; *pg.* 1653, *pg.* 133
Scantlebury, Dwana, Sr Mgr-Sls & Mktg Integration - Avon Products, Inc.; *pg.* 500, *pg.* 1198
Scaravaglione, Frank A., VP-Travel Indus Sls - Carey International, Inc.; *pg.* 1902, *pg.* 397
Scaravaglione, Joe, Sr Mgr-Market - Unum Group; *pg.* 1222, *pg.* 1629
Scaravillo, Michael P., Mgr-Demand Gen & Lifecycle Mktg-Enterprise - Windstream Corporation; *pg.* 321, *pg.* 34
Scarborough, Beverly, Coord-Mktg Comm - Michelin North America Inc.; *pg.* 1886, *pg.* 1618
Scarborough, Randy, VP-Mktg - FedEx Corporation; *pg.* 1907, *pg.* 1642
Scarbrough, Beki, VP-Integrated Mktg-Global - CA Technologies; *pg.* 366, *pg.* 1168
Scarchilli, Isabelle, Dir-Mktg - Lagos Inc.; *pg.* 8, *pg.* 1566
Scardapane, Gail, VP-PR - Saladworks, LLC; *pg.* 1749, *pg.* 1524
Scardillo, Angela, VP-Mktg - Best Buy Canada Ltd.; *pg.* 1761, *pg.* 1907
Scardina, John, Sr VP-Mdsg - Eby-Brown Co.; *pg.* 1767, *pg.* 636
Scardino, Paul, VP-Sls & Mktg - Globecomm Systems Inc.; *pg.* 640, *pg.* 1164
Scarlett, Christine, Asst VP-Interactive Mktg - McKesson Corporation; *pg.* 1560, *pg.* 222
Scarnecchia, Ray, Mgr-Production - The Canton Repository; *pg.* 1625, *pg.* 1407
Scarpa, Joe, VP-Long Term Care In Force Product Mgmt - Genworth Financial, Inc.; *pg.* 761, *pg.* 1802
Scarpa, Kate, Mgr-PR - Amazon.com, Inc.; *pg.* 1226, *pg.* 1831
Scarpelli, Connie, Mgr-Mktg - General Motors Company; *pg.* 175, *pg.* 881
Scarpelli, Shelly B., Sr Mgr-Federal Mktg - Juniper Networks, Inc.; *pg.* 1260, *pg.* 286
Scarsellato, Valerie, Specialist-Segment Mktg-Social Media - Intel Corporation; *pg.* 645, *pg.* 266
Scartozzi, Michelle, Coord-Mktg - Eby-Brown Co.; *pg.* 1767, *pg.* 636
Scates, Dee, Sr Mgr-North American Innovation - Godiva Chocolatier, Inc.; *pg.* 1854, *pg.* 1235
Scatigno, Kevin, VP-Entertainment Adv Sls - NBC Universal, Inc.; *pg.* 300, *pg.* 1266
Scattareggia, Joe, Sr VP-Sls-Carrier Bus Unit - Windstream Corporation; *pg.* 321, *pg.* 34
Scavo, J., Sr VP-Interactive Mktg, ECommerce & Fan Svcs - Warner Bros. Records, Inc.; *pg.* 1791, *pg.* 55
Scelfo, Meghan, Brand Mgr - The Clorox Company; *pg.* 327, *pg.* 169
Scerbo, John, Sr Head-Product Mgmt - VERISK ANALYTICS, INC.; *pg.* 1222, *pg.* 1076
Scerra, Molly Mckenna, Brand Mgr-Halls - Mondelez International, Inc.; *pg.* 878, *pg.* 601
Schaadt, Brian, Product Mgr-Kitchens - Pfister, Inc.; *pg.* 1059, *pg.* 88
Schacher, Debra, Reg Mgr-Mktg & ECommerce - Marriott International, Inc.; *pg.* 1102, *pg.* 764
Schacht, Diane, Sr Mgr-Event Adv & Mktg - Macy's, Inc.; *pg.* 1778, *pg.* 1417
Schachte, Matt, Dir-Creative - Simmons Company; *pg.* 943, *pg.* 520
Schachtel, Jane, Head-Tech & Telecom-Global Vertical Mktg - Facebook, Inc.; *pg.* 1245, *pg.* 143
Schachter, Josh, Sr Product Mgr - Intuit Inc.; *pg.* 769, *pg.* 158
Schade, Karen, Sr Mgr - GlaxoSmithKline Consumer Healthcare; *pg.* 510, *pg.* 1554
Schade, Matt, Dir-Social Strategy-Newsroom - adidas America Inc.; *pg.* 1803, *pg.* 1500
Schader, Ryan, Exec VP-Sls & Mktg - Jelly Belly Candy Company; *pg.* 1857, *pg.* 86
Schadler, Michael, Dir-Mktg-Intl - State of Florida Department of Citrus; *pg.* 1006, *pg.* 437
Schadler, Scott, Mgr-Product Mktg-Utility Tractors - John Deere Consumer & Commercial Equipment, Inc.; *pg.* 705,

pg. 1360
Schaefer, Brendan, Dir-Mktg-Emerging Brands - PepsiCo, Inc.; *pg.* 259, *pg.* 1327
Schaefer, David, Asst VP-Mktg - Liberty Tax Service; *pg.* 776, *pg.* 1810
Schaefer, Jonathan, Dir-Mktg - ConAgra Foods, Inc.; *pg.* 826, *pg.* 1014
Schaefer, Leslye, Sr VP-Mktg - Scholastic Corporation; *pg.* 1683, *pg.* 1288
Schaefer, Lynne, Mgr-Mktg - Tootsie Roll Industries, Inc.; *pg.* 1863, *pg.* 591
Schaefer, Mark, Mgr-Mktg Comm-Digital - Justrite Manufacturing Company, LLC; *pg.* 1394, *pg.* 606
Schaefer, Paul, Mgr-Creative Svcs & Corp Comm - American Airlines Inc.; *pg.* 1898, *pg.* 1693
Schaefer, Rich, Mgr-Variable Speed Mktg - Baldor Electric Company; *pg.* 1316, *pg.* 32
Schaefer, Thomas, Mgr-Mktg & Comm-Global - Hewlett-Packard Company; *pg.* 404, *pg.* 175
Schaefers, Mike, VP-Global Mktg-PPS - West Pharmaceutical Services, Inc.; *pg.* 1472, *pg.* 1532
Schaeffer, Bill, Jr., VP-Sls - Sargento Foods Inc.; *pg.* 894, *pg.* 1886
Schaeffer, Brittney, Sr Mgr-Digital Mktg - Ubisoft Inc.; *pg.* 589, *pg.* 229
Schaeffer, Don, VP-Sls-Mid Atlantic Div - The Ultimate Software Group, Inc.; *pg.* 486, *pg.* 479
Schaeffer, Jason, Exec Dir-Media - Sony Pictures Entertainment Inc.; *pg.* 309, *pg.* 72
Schaeffer, Justin, Product Mgr-Storage Devices - Black Box Corporation; *pg.* 361, *pg.* 1547
Schaeffer, Leticia, Mgr-Channel Mktg - Quantum Corporation; *pg.* 458, *pg.* 250
Schaeffer, Lora, Sr Dir-Integrated Media & Customer Acq - DSW, Inc.; *pg.* 1807, *pg.* 1439
Schaeffer, Marisa, Dir-Brand Adv-Corporate & Pub Affairs - Pacific Life Insurance Company; *pg.* 1213, *pg.* 166
Schaeffer, Tim, Sr Mgr-Search Mktg - Zappos.com, Inc.; *pg.* 1291, *pg.* 1030
Schaeffer, Todd, Product Mgr - Nilfisk-Advance, Inc.; *pg.* 332, *pg.* 953
Schaeper, Cher, Sr Coord-Digital Mktg - Victoria's Secret Stores, LLC; *pg.* 1789, *pg.* 1471
Schafer, Ana, Sr Mgr-Mktg & Ecosystem Rels - QUALCOMM Incorporated; *pg.* 1873, *pg.* 207
Schafer, Bryon, Sr VP-Media Res & Insights - Warner Bros. Entertainment Inc.; *pg.* 319, *pg.* 54
Schafer, Heiko, Sr Dir-Consumer Insights & Analytics-Global - Wal-Mart Stores, Inc.; *pg.* 1790, *pg.* 29
Schafer, Heiko, Sr Dir-Consumer Insights & Analytics-Global - Wal-Mart.com; *pg.* 1287, *pg.* 50
Schafer, Kristie, Mgr-Mktg-Gkdirect - G&K Services Inc.; *pg.* 693, *pg.* 949
Schafer, Lisa Brogan, Assoc Dir-BELSOMRA Mktg Team - Merck & Co., Inc.; *pg.* 1566, *pg.* 1077
Schafer, Mike, VP & Dir-Mktg - Fifth Third Bancorp; *pg.* 752, *pg.* 1413
Schaffart, Ray, Mgr-Mktg & Sls Support - Modine Manufacturing Company; *pg.* 1074, *pg.* 1888
Schaffer, Adrian, VP-Sls & Bus Dev - UQM Technologies, Inc.; *pg.* 684, *pg.* 334
Schaffer, J., Sr Mgr-Mktg - Nissan North America, Inc.; *pg.* 186, *pg.* 1633
Schaffer, Michael, Sr Mgr-Mktg-PD Neuroscience - AbbVie Inc.; *pg.* 1486, *pg.* 638
Schaffner, Carly, Sr Mgr-Corp Comm - TrueCar Inc.; *pg.* 1284, *pg.* 276
Schaffner, Serena, Dir-Mktg Comm - American Egg Board; *pg.* 128, *pg.* 650
Schafman, Merle, Dir-Mktg Svcs - Culligan International Company; *pg.* 54, *pg.* 656
Schaible, Linda, VP-Mktg & Audience Dev - Houston Chronicle; *pg.* 1651, *pg.* 1707
Schain, Trevor, Mgr-eMail Mktg - AMERICAN TIRE DISTRIBUTORS HOLDINGS, INC.; *pg.* 199, *pg.* 1379
Schaknowski, Heather, Dir-Segment Mktg-Global - Concur Technologies, Inc.; *pg.* 1236, *pg.* 1813
Schales, Messina, Sr Mgr-HR - McIlhenny Company; *pg.* 876, *pg.* 741
Schalk, Cindy, Mgr-Mktg Ops - Cisco Systems, Inc.; *pg.* 372, *pg.* 240
Schall, Heather, VP-Mktg Comm - LIFETIME BRANDS, INC.; *pg.* 1127, *pg.* 1161
Schall, Robert, Specialist-Mktg Outreach - Canon U.S.A., Inc.; *pg.* 1404, *pg.* 1178
Schaller, Liz, Mgr-Digital Mktg - Bose Corporation; *pg.* 626, *pg.* 820
Schalow, Terry, Dir-Specialty Sls - ASICS America Corporation; *pg.* 1826, *pg.* 106
Schandl, Charles, Mgr-Dealer Sls-Parts & Svc - Ford Motor Company of Canada, Limited; *pg.* 174, *pg.* 1930
Schank, Jessica, Mgr-Digital Mktg & Social Media, Region Americas - Barilla America, Inc.; *pg.* 839, *pg.* 555
Schanman, Gary, Sr VP-Video Products - Charter Communications, Inc.; *pg.* 274, *pg.* 372
Schanzlin, Chance, Sr Mgr-Indus Mktg - Acxiom Corporation; *pg.* 342, *pg.* 33
Schaper, Chris, Sr Mgr-Brand & Adv - Sears Holdings Corporation; *pg.* 1784, *pg.* 618
Schapman, Liz, Mgr-Adv - Neiman Marcus, Inc.; *pg.* 30, *pg.* 1684
Schardt, Doug, Product Mgr - Komori America Corporation; *pg.* 1353, *pg.* 656
Scharf, Molly, Mgr-Mktg-Cycle for Survival - Memorial Sloan-Kettering Cancer Center Inc.; *pg.* 1565, *pg.* 1258
Scharingson, Jon, Dir-Sls & Mktg - Renewable Energy Group, Inc.; *pg.* 984, *pg.* 701
Scharnhorst, Jana, VP-Mktg - Fox Associates, LLC; *pg.* 549, *pg.* 997
Schastny, Danyell, Dir-Sls & Mktg - Hyatt Hotels Corporation; *pg.* 1096, *pg.* 577
Schatschneider, April, Category Mgr-Mdse - GNC Holdings Inc.; *pg.* 1537, *pg.* 1576
Schaubroeck, Julie, Dir-Product & Sls Mktg - American Family Mutual Insurance Company; *pg.* 1190, *pg.* 1864
Schauder, Paul, VP & Dir-Creative - LOGMEIN, INC.; *pg.* 428, *pg.* 861
Schauer, Darren, Product Mgr - Molex Incorporated; *pg.* 655, *pg.* 628
Schauer, John, Product Mgr - Yamaha Corporation of America; *pg.* 595, *pg.* 51
Schauer, John, Product Mgr - Yamaha Electronics Corporation USA; *pg.* 689, *pg.* 51
Schaumburg, Jerry, Sr Dir-Integration Dev - Jack Henry & Associates, Inc.; *pg.* 422, *pg.* 988
Schaus, James, Reg Sls Mgr-Indus Comm - GE Canada Company; *pg.* 1296, *pg.* 1926
Schauss, Mark, Mgr-Wholesale Mktg - Markel Corporation; *pg.* 1207, *pg.* 1783
Schavocky, Toni, Dir-Mktg - Cigna-HealthSpring; *pg.* 1515, *pg.* 1632
Schechter, Markus, Product Mgr-Global - Leica Microsystems, Inc.; *pg.* 1420, *pg.* 555
Schechtman, Arielle, Mgr-PR - The Walt Disney Company; *pg.* 317, *pg.* 52
Scheele, Stephanie, Coord-Event Mktg - ASICS America Corporation; *pg.* 1826, *pg.* 106
Scheele, Stephanie, VP-Mktg - VERA BRADLEY, INC.; *pg.* 15, *pg.* 697
Scheer, Adam, Sr VP-Product Line Mgmt & Corp Dev - MRV Communications, Inc.; *pg.* 441, *pg.* 64
Scheer, Jen, Dir-Mktg - Garden Fresh Restaurant Corp.; *pg.* 1729, *pg.* 203
Scheerer, Ben, Sr Mgr-Product Line Mktg - VMware, Inc.; *pg.* 490, *pg.* 179
Scheessele, B.J., Sr Dir-Mktg & Country Mgr-Canada - LifeCell Corporation; *pg.* 1556, *pg.* 1045
Scheetz, Leslie, Mgr-Mktg Svcs Procurement - The Kraft Heinz Company; *pg.* 871, *pg.* 641
Scheetz, Mike, Mgr-Sls - Skyline Corporation; *pg.* 1711, *pg.* 677
Scheff, Artie, Sr VP-Mktg - REELZCHANNEL LLC; *pg.* 306, *pg.* 1135
Scheffer, Ramon, Dir-Fin Reporting Advisory Svcs - Habif, Arogeti & Wynne, LLP; *pg.* 764, *pg.* 509
Scheffer, Steve, Brand Mgr - Baker Hughes Incorporated; *pg.* 1315, *pg.* 1700
Scheffers, Todd J., VP-Sls - The Goodheart-Willcox Co., Inc.; *pg.* 1645, *pg.* 663
Scheffki, Mike, Brand Mgr-Pyrex - World Kitchen LLC; *pg.* 1141, *pg.* 657
Scheider, Jacqueline, Mgr-Mktg - Jack Henry & Associates, Inc.; *pg.* 422, *pg.* 988
Scheidler, Rebecca, Sr Dir-US Skin Care Mktg - Kao Brands Co. Inc.; *pg.* 513, *pg.* 1415
Schein, Matt, Sr Dir-Brand Mktg - SONIC Corp.; *pg.* 1750, *pg.* 1487
Schein, Steve, Dir-Product Dev - DIRECTV Group Holdings, LLC; *pg.* 281, *pg.* 79
Scheiner, Michael, Sr Dir-Mktg & PR - ABERCROMBIE & FITCH CO.; *pg.* 37, *pg.* 1466
Scheinkman, Stephanie, Mgr-Reg Mktg-North America - Elizabeth Arden, Inc.; *pg.* 507, *pg.* 448
Scheinrock, Darcie, Product Mgr-eBusiness - MetroPCS, Inc.; *pg.* 1872, *pg.* 1683
Scheiwe, Steven D., Chm/Pres-Ontrac Advisors, Inc. - Hancock Fabrics, Inc.; *pg.* 693, *pg.* 968
Schelble, Jim S., Exec VP-Sls & Mktg - Werner Enterprises, Inc.; *pg.* 1930, *pg.* 1019
Schell, Ellen, Brand Mgr-Silk Innovation - The WhiteWave Foods Company; *pg.* 1037, *pg.* 324
Schell, Jeff, Dir-Adv - The News-Herald; *pg.* 1670, *pg.* 908
Schell, Lisa, Copywriter-Mktg - Gartner, Inc.; *pg.* 1248, *pg.* 374
Schellhammer, Beth, Specialist-Category & Brand Mktg - Kohl's Corporation; *pg.* 1775, *pg.* 1870
Schellin, Jeremy, Assoc Mgr-Mktg - General Mills, Inc.; *pg.* 828, *pg.* 933
Schelpf, Kimberly, Sr Mgr-Mktg - Meredith Corporation; *pg.* 1663, *pg.* 705
Schembri, Bob, Sr Product Mgr - Pandora Media Inc.; *pg.* 1273, *pg.* 172
Schemm, Dennis, VP-Fin-Armstrong Floor Products - Armstrong World Industries, Inc.; *pg.* 914, *pg.* 1545
Schemmel, Jon, Dir-Product Mgmt-Latin America - General Cable Corporation; *pg.* 83, *pg.* 729
Schemmel, Kara, Sr VP & Dir-Creative - Bank of America Corporation; *pg.* 718, *pg.* 1362
Schenck, Cami, Mgr-Media - ConAgra Foods, Inc.; *pg.* 826, *pg.* 1014
Schenck, Chip, VP-Programmatic Sls & Strategy - Meredith Corporation; *pg.* 1663, *pg.* 705
Schenzel, John, VP-Sls Admin - Weinbrenner Shoe Company, Inc.; *pg.* 1822, *pg.* 1871
Scheper, Frans, Exec VP & Gen Mgr-Standard Products Applications - NXP Semiconductors; *pg.* 660, *pg.* 248
Schepisi, Alissa, Sr Mgr-Comm-Water & Process Svcs - Ecolab Inc.; *pg.* 329, *pg.* 960
Schepps, Zoe, Mgr-PR - Revlon Consumer Products Corporation; *pg.* 521, *pg.* 1286
Schepps, Zoe, Mgr-PR - Revlon, Inc.; *pg.* 521, *pg.* 1286
Scheps, Randall, VP & Gen Mgr-Wheel Products - Alcoa Inc.; *pg.* 65, *pg.* 1188
Scher, Herb, Dir-PR - The New York Public Library; *pg.* 605, *pg.* 1269
Scherer, Susan, Mgr-Sls & Sourcing - The Kroger Co.; *pg.* 1025, *pg.* 1416
Scherler, Randy, VP-Sls & Mktg - Freeway Corporation; *pg.* 1338, *pg.* 1431
Schermerhorn, Bill, VP & Dir-Creative - Macy's East; *pg.* 1777, *pg.* 1254
Schermerhorn, Katherine, Sr Mgr-Corp External Affairs - The Coca-Cola Company; *pg.* 240, *pg.* 493
Scherrer, Marianna, Dir-Sls-Force Recognition - Mary Kay Inc.; *pg.* 516, *pg.* 1657
Scherrer, Marianna, Dir-Sls Force Recognition - Mary Kay Inc.; *pg.* 516, *pg.* 1657
Scherschel, Sandy, VP-Sls & Mktg - The Chamberlain Group, Inc.; *pg.* 75, *pg.* 611
Schertell, Julie A., Sr VP-Fine Paper & Technical Products US - Neenah Paper, Inc.; *pg.* 1465, *pg.* 484
Scherz, Andy, Sr Product Mgr - Epson America Inc.; *pg.* 394, *pg.* 122
Scherzer, Matt, Sr Mgr-Customer Mktg - Mars, Incorporated; *pg.* 1858, *pg.* 1792
Scheuber, Venus, Brand Mgr-Southern California Area - Xerox Corporation; *pg.* 494, *pg.* 365
Scheuerlein, Jared, Team Head-Social Media - General Motors Company; *pg.* 175, *pg.* 881
Schewe, Charlie, Gen Mgr-Global Corp Sls - Delta Air Lines, Inc.; *pg.* 1905, *pg.* 503
Schey, Eric, Mgr-Mktg - UPS Supply Chain Solutions, Inc.; *pg.* 1929, *pg.* 485
Schick, Kimberley, Dir-Digital Mktg-Small Business Group - Intuit Inc.; *pg.* 769, *pg.* 158
Schickler, Craig, VP-Hotel Sls & Supplier Rels - The Priceline Group Inc.; *pg.* 1276, *pg.* 364
Schickowski, Rachel, Head-Global Content Mktg - Rockwell Automation, Inc.; *pg.* 668, *pg.* 1880
Schiebel, Erica, Supvr-Mktg Comm - 3M Company; *pg.* 1142, *pg.* 956
Schiebel, Kyle, Analyst-Social Media - State Farm Mutual Automobile Insurance Co.; *pg.* 1218, *pg.* 557
Schieffer, Jeanne, Mgr-Corp Comm & PR - Nebraska Public Power District; *pg.* 1947, *pg.* 1010

First page reference indicates Business Class Edition
Second page reference indicates Geographic Edition

Schiel, Andrew, Sr Mgr-Mktg-Retail & Brand - Lands' End, Inc.; *pg.* 1776, *pg.* 1857
Schieltz, Mary Kay D., Sr Dir-Product Dev-Global - LexisNexis Group; *pg.* 1658, *pg.* 1446
Schievelbein, Micki, Dir-Adv - Yankton Daily Press & Dakotan; *pg.* 1703, *pg.* 1626
Schiffli, Mike, Dir-Area Mktg-Ft Wayne DC - SUPERVALU, Inc., Food Marketing Division; *pg.* 1035, *pg.* 681
Schiffman, Joshua, Product Dir-Mobile Engagement-IBM ExperienceOne - IBM; *pg.* 410, *pg.* 1449
Schiffman, Lynn, Sr Mgr-Media - Verizon Communications Inc.; *pg.* 1875, *pg.* 1309
Schiffman, Matthew R., Mng Dir & Head-Global Mktg & US Retail Distr - Legg Mason, Inc.; *pg.* 775, *pg.* 758
Schiffman, Richard J., Product Mgr & Head-Open Trading - MARKETAXESS HOLDINGS INC.; *pg.* 778, *pg.* 1256
Schild, Bernadette, VP & Brand Mgr - Wells Fargo & Company; *pg.* 819, *pg.* 232
Schild, Tonya, Bus Mgr - Yankton Daily Press & Dakotan; *pg.* 1703, *pg.* 1626
Schildhouse, Suzy, Mgr-Media & Events - Express, Inc.; *pg.* 24, *pg.* 1440
Schill, Allison D., Sr Product Mgr-Comml Dev - Pfizer Inc.; *pg.* 1581, *pg.* 1278
Schiller, Andrew, Sr Mgr-Equipment Innovation Reporting & Advanced Analytics - PepsiCo, Inc.; *pg.* 259, *pg.* 1327
Schiller, Derek L., Exec VP-Sls & Mktg - Atlanta National League Baseball Club, Inc.; *pg.* 530, *pg.* 490
Schiller, Paul, Dir-Product Mktg - Piksel; *pg.* 1275, *pg.* 1282
Schiller, Philip, Sr VP-Mktg-Worldwide - Apple Inc.; *pg.* 350, *pg.* 73
Schiller, Rosann, Dir-Mktg-FCC Comml Strategy - W.R. Grace & Co.; *pg.* 123, *pg.* 810
Schiller, Tobin, Sr Dir-Mktg & Circulation - Restoration Hardware Holdings, Inc.; *pg.* 1060, *pg.* 70
Schillig, Nancy, Sr Strategist-Procurement-Mktg & Banking Svcs - KeyCorp; *pg.* 774, *pg.* 1432
Schilling, John, Gen Mgr-Product Comm - Volkswagen Group of America, Inc.; *pg.* 194, *pg.* 1785
Schilling, Steve, Pres-Digital Media Bus - Ballantyne Strong, Inc.; *pg.* 623, *pg.* 1013
Schiltz, Joseph A., Sr VP-Mktg & Targeted Media - Tribune Media Company; *pg.* 1696, *pg.* 592
Schimmelman, Mary, Sr Mgr-Social Media Mktg - Holland America Line Inc.; *pg.* 1911, *pg.* 1836
Schimmenti, Amanda, Coord-Mktg-Modell's Sporting Goods - Henry Modell & Company, Inc.; *pg.* 1836, *pg.* 1240
Schinabeck, Thomas S., Sr VP & Reg Mgr-Sls-Western - Federated Investors, Inc.; *pg.* 752, *pg.* 1575
Schinasi, Peter, Dir-Relationship Mktg - British Airways; *pg.* 1901, *pg.* 1207
Schindeldecker, Rich, Dir-Creative-Digital - Select Comfort Corporation; *pg.* 942, *pg.* 942
Schindler, Bobby, Specialist-Corp Mktg Comm - PolyOne Corporation; *pg.* 1177, *pg.* 1404
Schindler, Eric, Product Dir-Men's & Women's Golf Apparel-Global - NIKE, Inc.; *pg.* 1812, *pg.* 1492
Schindler, John, VP-Products - VIZIO, Inc.; *pg.* 686, *pg.* 118
Schindler, Lisa, Mgr-Mktg Comm - Arrow Electronics, Inc.; *pg.* 619, *pg.* 325
Schindler, Philip, Sr VP-Global Sls & Ops - Google Inc.; *pg.* 1249, *pg.* 153
Schindler, Robert, VP-Mktg - Associated Materials LLC; *pg.* 69, *pg.* 1445
Schinto, Tyler D., Sr Mgr-Private Equity Investments - Sumitomo Electric; *pg.* 1599, *pg.* 1297
Schioler, Marcus, Sr Mgr-Indus-Video Strategy - Autodesk Inc.; *pg.* 356, *pg.* 257
Schirling, Kathy, Dir-Mktg & Community Svcs - People's United Bank; *pg.* 793, *pg.* 749
Schirmer, Mark, Mgr-Product Comm-Utility Vehicles-North America - Ford Motor Company; *pg.* 172, *pg.* 876
Schirra, Tracey, Dir-Mktg Ops - PetSmart, Inc.; *pg.* 1481, *pg.* 18
Schlachter, Jaime, Assoc Media Planner - Tommy Hilfiger USA; *pg.* 48, *pg.* 1302
Schlachter, Keith, Mgr-Product Mktg - Hewlett-Packard Company; *pg.* 404, *pg.* 175
Schlachternhaufen, Tom, Sr VP-Sls - Stoli Group USA LLC; *pg.* 1970, *pg.* 1296
Schlacter, Robert, VP-Sls & New Channels - Staples, Inc.; *pg.* 474, *pg.* 821
Schlader, Joel, Specialist-Small Bus Sls - FCA US LLC; *pg.* 170, *pg.* 868
Schlaffer, Georg, Product Mgr - Leica Microsystems, Inc.; *pg.* 1420, *pg.* 555
Schlagenhauf, Brad, Head-Fin Svcs Indus Mktg - Hewlett-Packard Company; *pg.* 404, *pg.* 175
Schlangen, Steve, VP-Product Dev - Altec Lansing LLC; *pg.* 348, *pg.* 1553
Schlarb, Brandon, Corp Dir-Partnership Sls - Pacers Basketball, LLC; *pg.* 573, *pg.* 689
Schlarb, Karen, Sr Mgr-Mktg Comm - Intrado Inc.; *pg.* 420, *pg.* 334
Schlauderaff, Mark, Mgr-Americas Customer Mktg - Honeywell International Inc.; *pg.* 407, *pg.* 1088
Schlecht, Jessica, Sr Mgr-Autodesk University Program Strategy - Autodesk Inc.; *pg.* 356, *pg.* 257
Schlee, Josh, Mgr-Product Compliance - Electra Bicycle Company; *pg.* 1706, *pg.* 303
Schlef, Brian, Dir-Mktg - LIFETIME BRANDS, INC.; *pg.* 1127, *pg.* 1161
Schlegel, Gregory, Sr Dir-Store Design & Construction - Chico's FAS, Inc.; *pg.* 21, *pg.* 427
Schlegel, Kelli, Mgr-Media Rels - Hewlett-Packard Company; *pg.* 404, *pg.* 175
Schlegel, Kyle, VP-Mktg-H&B - Hillerich & Bradsby Co., Inc.; *pg.* 1836, *pg.* 576
Schlegel, Mary-Karin, Exec Dir-Branding & Consumer Mktg - Florida Hospital Association; *pg.* 140, *pg.* 469
Schlegel, Mary-Karin, Exec Dir-Branding & Consumer Mktg - Florida Hospital Orlando; *pg.* 1531, *pg.* 453
Schlegel, Tom, Sr VP-Product Dev - Radio Flyer Inc.; *pg.* 966, *pg.* 588
Schleicher, Ryan, Head-Sls - Ocean Spray Cranberries, Inc.; *pg.* 887, *pg.* 827
SchleigerFleet, Lindsey, Mgr-Comml Product Mktg - Sinclair Oil Corporation; *pg.* 984, *pg.* 1760
Schleis, Helen, Mgr-Field Mktg - School Specialty, Inc.; *pg.* 467, *pg.* 1860
Schler, Jaclyn, Sr Coord-Adv - The J.M. Smucker Company; *pg.* 865, *pg.* 1468
Schlesinger, Nicole, Sr Mgr-Enterprise Growth & Intl Payment Options - American Express Company; *pg.* 712, *pg.* 1190
Schlesinger, Robert, Mgr-Sls - Rhode Island Philharmonic Orchestra Inc.; *pg.* 579, *pg.* 1601
Schlessinger-Brett, Deborah, VP-Partnership & Emerging Media Sls - Viacom Inc.; *pg.* 316, *pg.* 1310
Schletewitz, Dave, Specialist-Direct Channel Mktg-Consumer Segment - Chevron Corporation; *pg.* 974, *pg.* 259
Schley, Steve, VP-Mktg - Kroll Inc.; *pg.* 425, *pg.* 1249
Schlichting, Warren, Sr VP-Programming & Media Sls - DISH Network Corporation; *pg.* 283, *pg.* 325
Schlicker, Carl, Pres, CEO & Exec VP-Sls & Mktg - Giant of Maryland LLC; *pg.* 1021, *pg.* 773
Schliemann, Carrie, Dir-Mktg & Pet Food - Del Monte Foods, Inc.; *pg.* 852, *pg.* 304
Schliesman, Dave, Sr VP & District Dir-Sls - Allianz Life Insurance Company of North America; *pg.* 1188, *pg.* 929
Schlitz, Matthew, Dir-Existing Customer Mktg-North America Branded Cards - Citigroup Inc.; *pg.* 735, *pg.* 1212
Schlitzer, Victor, Dir-Brand & Content Mktg - Bentley University; *pg.* 598, *pg.* 850
Schloemer, Annette, Dir-Mktg, Appraisal & Tax Div - Tyler Technologies, Inc.; *pg.* 486, *pg.* 1690
Schloot, Suzanne, Mgr-Social Media - Kate Spade LLC; *pg.* 28, *pg.* 1248
Schloss, James D., Corp VP-Sls & Mktg - The Smithfield Packing Co., Inc.; *pg.* 896, *pg.* 1807
Schloss, Julie, Assoc Mgr-Mktg-Softlines - Mattel Games/Puzzles; *pg.* 962, *pg.* 80
Schloss, Julie, Assoc Mgr-Mktg-Softlines - MATTEL, INC.; *pg.* 962, *pg.* 81
Schloth, Debbie, Sr Product Mgr - AstraZeneca Pharmaceuticals LP; *pg.* 1497, *pg.* 389
Schlotter, Dee Rice, Brand Mgr-Natl Color-PPG Architectural Finishes, Inc. - PPG Industries, Inc.; *pg.* 1445, *pg.* 1579
Schlottmann, Dawn, Analyst-Cross-Media Mktg-NBC News - NBC Universal, Inc.; *pg.* 300, *pg.* 1266
Schluensen, Mandy Bigler, Mgr-Mktg-Social Demand Generation - SunPower Corporation; *pg.* 1952, *pg.* 250
Schlueter, Chris, Sr Mgr-Sls Strategy-OTC - Johnson & Johnson; *pg.* 1549, *pg.* 1091
Schlyer, Penny, Mgr-Indus Solutions Mktg-IBM MobileFirst - IBM; *pg.* 410, *pg.* 1449
Schmadebeck, Ross, Corp Mgr-Interactive Mktg - SeaWorld Parks & Entertainment LLC; *pg.* 582, *pg.* 456
Schmaeling, Amber, Corp Mgr-Digital Mktg - MGM Resorts International; *pg.* 1105, *pg.* 1028
Schmale, Lin, Sr Dir-Govt Rels - Society of American Florists; *pg.* 156, *pg.* 1771
Schmalzle, Aimee, VP-Mktg - Spa Finder, Inc.; *pg.* 1113, *pg.* 1295
Schmeichel, Joni, Mgr-Strategic Mktg - Daktronics, Inc.; *pg.* 633, *pg.* 1624
Schmersey, Shawn, Mgr-Adv Ops - AutoTrader, Inc.; *pg.* 1230, *pg.* 490
Schmertz, Matthew, Sr Mgr-Digital Mktg - 7-Eleven, Inc.; *pg.* 1012, *pg.* 1672
Schmicker, Michael, VP-Mktg & Corp Comm - Pacific Marine & Supply Co. Ltd. Inc.; *pg.* 1918, *pg.* 544
Schmid, Jurgen, Product Mgr - Belden, Inc.; *pg.* 624, *pg.* 993
Schmid, Lindsey, Dir-Mktg - Berkshire Visitors Bureau; *pg.* 989, *pg.* 841
Schmid, Rebecca, Mgr-Mktg Partnership Activation - Coca-Cola Refreshments USA, Inc.; *pg.* 247, *pg.* 500
Schmid, Sara, Grp Dir-Mktg Integration-Global - The Coca-Cola Company; *pg.* 240, *pg.* 493
Schmid, Shelly, Asst VP & Mgr-Direct Mktg - TCF Financial Corporation; *pg.* 808, *pg.* 966
Schmidlin, Carol, Supvr-Tactical Sls Ops - Leupold & Stevens, Inc.; *pg.* 1420, *pg.* 1492
Schmidt Wallace, Katie, Dir-Mktg Solutions - Mode Media; *pg.* 1267, *pg.* 50
Schmidt, Allycia, Sr Product Mgr-Mobile - The Home Depot, Inc.; *pg.* 1050, *pg.* 510
Schmidt, Amy, Brand Mgr-Bushmills - Diageo North America Inc.; *pg.* 248, *pg.* 1223
Schmidt, Amy, Sr Mgr-Campaign - TTI Floor Care North America; *pg.* 61, *pg.* 1473
Schmidt, Anya, Dir-Mktg-Huggies MEA Reg - Kimberly-Clark Corporation; *pg.* 1461, *pg.* 1720
Schmidt, Becky, Coord-Mktg - Williams Patent Crusher & Pulverizer Co., Inc.; *pg.* 1389, *pg.* 1005
Schmidt, Brian, VP-Sls-Global - TripAdvisor, Inc.; *pg.* 1926, *pg.* 835
Schmidt, Cheri, Brand Mgr - The Procter & Gamble Company; *pg.* 1129, *pg.* 1418
Schmidt, David, Sr Mgr-Solutions Mktg - Adobe Systems Incorporated; *pg.* 342, *pg.* 235
Schmidt, David, Sr Mgr-Mktg - Bandai America Incorporated; *pg.* 950, *pg.* 75
Schmidt, Donald, Dir-Creative Mktg-Tab & FSI - Wal-Mart Stores, Inc.; *pg.* 1790, *pg.* 29
Schmidt, Evelyn, Mgr-Projects-Mktg - Meredith Corporation; *pg.* 1663, *pg.* 705
Schmidt, Hinrich, Sr Mgr-Mktg - Motorola Mobility LLC; *pg.* 657, *pg.* 627
Schmidt, John, Dir-Mktg Comm - BASF Corporation; *pg.* 1149, *pg.* 1066
Schmidt, John, Dir-New Product Dev - Ulbrich Stainless Steel & Special Metals, Inc.; *pg.* 117, *pg.* 360
Schmidt, Jon, Mgr-Mktg-Digital Commerce-White House & Black Market - Chico's FAS, Inc.; *pg.* 21, *pg.* 427
Schmidt, Jon, Sr VP-Mobile Sls & GTM - SAP; *pg.* 465, *pg.* 78
Schmidt, Kathleen, VP & Dir-Mktg & Publicity - Running Press; *pg.* 1682, *pg.* 1570
Schmidt, Kim, Dir-Mktg & Event - Escort, Inc.; *pg.* 1412, *pg.* 1479
Schmidt, Kim, Mgr-Pub & Media Rels - North Dakota Department of Commerce Tourism Division; *pg.* 1002, *pg.* 1397
Schmidt, Leah, Mgr-Mktg - Claire's Stores, Inc.; *pg.* 1764, *pg.* 617
Schmidt, Leanne J., VP-Mktg - Dynatex International; *pg.* 635, *pg.* 277
Schmidt, Luiz, Sr Mgr-Mktg-Latin America & Caribbean - Brown-Forman Corporation; *pg.* 1958, *pg.* 732
Schmidt, Matthew, Sr Mgr-Corp Comm - FUJIFILM U.S.A., Inc.; *pg.* 1414, *pg.* 1348
Schmidt, Neal, Product Mgr-Sears.com - Sears Holdings Corporation; *pg.* 1784, *pg.* 618
Schmidt, Patrick, Mgr-Sls-Natl - Pandora Media Inc.; *pg.* 1273, *pg.* 172
Schmidt, Paul, Sr VP-Products - TANGOE, INC.; *pg.* 481, *pg.* 368
Schmidt, Samuel, Mgr-Mktg-Lay's - PepsiCo, Inc.; *pg.* 259, *pg.* 1327
Schmidt, Sarah, Asst Mgr-Mktg - Time Inc.; *pg.* 1693, *pg.* 1300
Schmidt, Todd, Mgr-SRAM Sls-Quality Bicycle Products - SRAM Corporation; *pg.* 967, *pg.* 590
Schmidtke, John, Sr Mgr-Loyalty & Managed Brands - Walgreen Co.; *pg.* 1608, *pg.* 605

Schmidtlin, Shelley, Mgr-Mktg & Comm - Blue Shield of California; *pg.* 1195, *pg.* 214
Schmillen, Sara, Dir-Mktg & Cold Stone Creamery - Kahala Franchising LLC; *pg.* 1025, *pg.* 23
Schmitt, Amanda, Sr Specialist-Mktg - Owens Corning; *pg.* 102, *pg.* 1476
Schmitt, Karl, VP-Mktg Res & Design - Sherwin Williams; *pg.* 1448, *pg.* 1436
Schmitt-Collins, Lisa, Mgr-Digital Mktg Solutions - USG Corporation; *pg.* 118, *pg.* 594
Schmitz, Brant, Mgr-Integrated Mktg - Deluxe Corporation; *pg.* 1634, *pg.* 964
Schmitz, Jeff, Sr Dir-Variety Franchise - The Hershey Co.; *pg.* 1855, *pg.* 1538
Schmitz, Jeremy, Sr Mgr-Mktg-Autodesk Consumer & 3D Printing Grp - Autodesk Inc.; *pg.* 356, *pg.* 257
Schmitz, Tad, Corp Dir-Mktg & Consumer Activation - SeaWorld Parks & Entertainment LLC; *pg.* 582, *pg.* 456
Schmoock, David, Pres-End-User Computing Sls - Dell, Inc.; *pg.* 385, *pg.* 1037
Schmuch, Karen, Supvr-Mktg Comm - Mersen; *pg.* 1302, *pg.* 836
Schmucker, Brian, Dir-Analytics & Sls Process Improvements - Kelly Services, Inc.; *pg.* 424, *pg.* 911
Schmucker, Juliann, Sr Engr-Sls - Kennametal Inc.; *pg.* 1052, *pg.* 1547
Schmundt-Thomas, Georg, CMO-Global Duracell & VP-Mktg - The Procter & Gamble Company; *pg.* 1129, *pg.* 1418
Schnabel, Richard, Exec VP-Sls - Tanknology Inc; *pg.* 114, *pg.* 1666
Schnarr, John, Sr Dir-Sls-Global - Nordson Corporation; *pg.* 1365, *pg.* 1480
Schnarre, Maegan, Sr Specialist-Mktg - Cardinal Health, Inc.; *pg.* 1512, *pg.* 1448
Schnaufer, Erich S., Interim CFO - Ryerson Inc.; *pg.* 1373, *pg.* 589
Schneck, Christie, Analyst-Mktg - Wells Fargo & Company; *pg.* 819, *pg.* 232
Schneck, Kara, Sr Dir-PR - Nu Skin Enterprises, Inc.; *pg.* 518, *pg.* 1755
Schneeberg, Larry, Reg Mgr-Mktg - GlaxoSmithKline; *pg.* 1536, *pg.* 1389
Schneeberg, Larry, Reg Mgr-Mktg - GlaxoSmithKline Consumer Healthcare; *pg.* 510, *pg.* 1554
Schneekloth, Katie, Coord-Direct Mktg Campaign - Green Bay Packers, Inc.; *pg.* 551, *pg.* 1859
Schneider, Angel, Mgr-Mktg-Max & Erma's - American Blue Ribbon Holdings; *pg.* 1714, *pg.* 1648
Schneider, Becky, Specialist-Mktg - QC Holdings, Inc.; *pg.* 797, *pg.* 719
Schneider, Ben, Project Mgr-Mktg Svcs Dept - The New York Times Company; *pg.* 1668, *pg.* 1270
Schneider, Bruce, VP-Sls - Guardian Building Products Distribution; *pg.* 85, *pg.* 1619
Schneider, Christian, Mgr-Enterprise Sls-Amazon Web Svcs - Amazon.com, Inc.; *pg.* 1226, *pg.* 1831
Schneider, Christina, Brand Mgr - Nestle Purina PetCare Company; *pg.* 1479, *pg.* 1000
Schneider, Chuck, Sr Dir-Visual Mdsg - World Kitchen LLC; *pg.* 1141, *pg.* 657
Schneider, Corey, Assoc Mgr-Retention Mktg - Time Inc.; *pg.* 1693, *pg.* 1300
Schneider, Craig, VP-Sector Mktg-North America - Shell Oil Company; *pg.* 984, *pg.* 1714
Schneider, Davis, Mgr-Mktg - LinkedIn Corporation; *pg.* 1262, *pg.* 160
Schneider, Glenn, Sr Analyst-Pricing Mktg - FedEx Corporation; *pg.* 1907, *pg.* 1642
Schneider, Hank, Mgr-Sls - Chicago-Wilcox Mfg. Company, Inc.; *pg.* 202, *pg.* 661
Schneider, Jason, Dir-Product Dev & Mktg - Gamewright; *pg.* 953, *pg.* 836
Schneider, Jeff, Dir-Product Mgmt-VMAX - EMC Corporation; *pg.* 391, *pg.* 825
Schneider, Jennifer, Assoc Dir-Media - Shoe Carnival, Inc.; *pg.* 1819, *pg.* 679
Schneider, Joseph T., Sr VP-Sls & Mktg - Sparton Corporation; *pg.* 1377, *pg.* 660
Schneider, Joshua, Mgr-Brand Comm & Content Mktg - VistaPrint USA, Incorporated; *pg.* 1700, *pg.* 829
Schneider, Kate, Dir-Mktg - Cumberland Packing Corp.; *pg.* 851, *pg.* 1146
Schneider, Ken, Strategist-Content-Social Media - U-Haul International, Inc.; *pg.* 1926, *pg.* 20
Schneider, Kirsten, Specialist-Product - Google Inc.; *pg.* 1249, *pg.* 153
Schneider, Lara, Mgr-Mktg Comm - Toshiba America, Inc.; *pg.* 681, *pg.* 1302
Schneider, Lori, VP-Mktg & Comm - Grease Monkey International, Inc.; *pg.* 84, *pg.* 331
Schneider, Maggie, Mgr-PR - Brown-Forman Corporation; *pg.* 1958, *pg.* 732
Schneider, Melanie J., Mgr-Integrated Mktg Comm - Mondelez International, Inc.; *pg.* 878, *pg.* 601
Schneider, Michael, Reg Mgr-Sls - Mark Andy, Inc.; *pg.* 1359, *pg.* 975
Schneider, Michael G., VP-Corp Mktg - Automatic Data Processing, Inc.; *pg.* 357, *pg.* 1117
Schneider, Michelle D., Project Mgr-Client & Mktg-Creative Svcs - Avid Technology, Inc.; *pg.* 622, *pg.* 804
Schneider, Nicole, Head-Creative & Adv - Deere & Company; *pg.* 703, *pg.* 632
Schneider, Phil, VP-Sls - Big Y Foods, Inc.; *pg.* 1015, *pg.* 845
Schneider, Phillip J., Jr., CMO & Chief Sls Officer - Mike Albert Leasing, Inc.; *pg.* 185, *pg.* 1417
Schneider, Stacey, Specialist-Mktg Comm - Emdeon, Inc.; *pg.* 747, *pg.* 1650
Schneider, Travis, Product Mgr - Parker Hannifin Corporation; *pg.* 1368, *pg.* 1434
Schneiderman, Craig, Dir-Corp Media-US - L'Oreal USA; *pg.* 514, *pg.* 1252
Schneiders, Jennifer M., Dir-Mktg - Hologic, Inc.; *pg.* 1416, *pg.* 784
Schnell, Bill, Mgr-PR - Cirrus Logic, Inc.; *pg.* 629, *pg.* 1661
Schnell, Joanna, Specialist-Mktg-Intl - Anthropologie, Inc.; *pg.* 18, *pg.* 1558
Schnell, Patrik, Sr Mgr-SW Dev - Amazon.com, Inc.; *pg.* 1226, *pg.* 1831
Schnell, Rachael, Dir-Brand Mktg - Foot Locker, Inc.; *pg.* 1808, *pg.* 1231
Schnepp, David, Brand Mgr-North America Consumer & Small Bus Laptops - Dell Inc.; *pg.* 383, *pg.* 1737
Schnepp, John, Dir-Adv - Big Y Foods, Inc.; *pg.* 1015, *pg.* 845
Schnettler, Kale, Sr Assoc Brand Mgr-Maxwell House & Yuban - Kraft Chemical Company; *pg.* 1170, *pg.* 632
Schnettler, Kale, Sr Assoc Brand Mgr-Maxwell House & Yuban - The Kraft Heinz Company; *pg.* 871, *pg.* 641
Schnichels, Lisa, Dir-Mdsg-Meijer.com - Meijer, Inc.; *pg.* 1779, *pg.* 888
Schnip, Hillary, Specialist-Mktg Analytics & Performance - Diageo North America Inc.; *pg.* 248, *pg.* 1223
Schnirel, Mark, Head-Mktg Automation - Thermo Fisher Scientific Inc.; *pg.* 1431, *pg.* 854
Schnobrich, Anne, Brand Mgr-Flavored Vodkas - Campari America; *pg.* 1960, *pg.* 214
Schnupp, Peter, VP-Digital Media Plng & Buying - BlackRock, Inc.; *pg.* 724, *pg.* 1203
Schnur, Eric R., Pres-Lubrizol Advanced Materials & Corp VP - The Lubrizol Corporation; *pg.* 1171, *pg.* 1481
Schnur, Jennifer L., Sr Specialist-Mktg & Analyst-Bus - Markel Corporation; *pg.* 1207, *pg.* 1783
Schnuriger, Melanie, VP-Product Dev - Daily News, L.P.; *pg.* 1632, *pg.* 1221
Schoales, Jeremy, Mgr-Market Dev & Digital Mktg - Thermo Fisher Scientific Inc.; *pg.* 1431, *pg.* 854
Schoch, Kirk, Specialist-Mktg Comm - Comcast Corporation; *pg.* 276, *pg.* 1560
Schock, Bob, Sr Mgr-Print Production - Anthem, Inc.; *pg.* 1192, *pg.* 683
Schock, Carey D., Mgr-Strategic Comm, Web Content & Social Media - Schneider Electric USA, Inc.; *pg.* 1306, *pg.* 650
Schock, Carmen, Assoc Mgr-Mktg-North America Pro Oral Care - The Procter & Gamble Company; *pg.* 1129, *pg.* 1418
Schoder, Lisa, Mgr-Digital Mktg - Ford Motor Company; *pg.* 172, *pg.* 876
Schoen, Michael, VP-Mktg Svcs-San Francisco - NeuStar, Inc.; *pg.* 1872, *pg.* 1807
Schoenberg, Al, Gen Mgr-Production - Travelhost, Inc.; *pg.* 1696, *pg.* 1689
Schoenberg, Jaymie, Dir-Mktg - Constellation Brands, Inc.; *pg.* 1960, *pg.* 1348
Schoenberger, Colin, Assoc Dir-Social Media & Analytics - WNET.org; *pg.* 322, *pg.* 1315
Schoeneberger, Alex, Product Mgr - Kelley Blue Book Co., Inc.; *pg.* 1656, *pg.* 112
Schoenecker, Don, Mgr-USB Product-Digital Debug Solutions - Agilent Technologies, Inc.; *pg.* 614, *pg.* 264
Schoenfeld, Mark, Mgr-Field Mktg-Field & Channel Mktg-ISM - Autodesk Inc.; *pg.* 356, *pg.* 257
Schoenfield, Jeff, Sr Assoc Brand Mgr - Wm. Wrigley Jr. Company; *pg.* 1863, *pg.* 596
Schoenfield, Sam, VP-Integrated Mktg Svcs - MetLife, Inc.; *pg.* 1208, *pg.* 1258
Schoenherr, Faye, Mgr-Customer Mktg-Emerging Channels - MATTEL, INC.; *pg.* 962, *pg.* 81
Schoening, Jared, Brand Mgr-Global-Nike.com & Trng - NIKE, Inc.; *pg.* 1812, *pg.* 1492
Schoeninger, Dick, VP-Adv-Northeast - The Rough Notes Company, Inc.; *pg.* 1681, *pg.* 675
Schoenwaelder, Scott, Mgr-Product Mktg - Jockey International, Inc.; *pg.* 27, *pg.* 1861
Schoenwetter, Joseph, Brand Mgr-Digital-KPNT FM-105.7 The Point - Emmis Communications Corporation; *pg.* 285, *pg.* 685
Schoepflin, Joann, Specialist-Adv Production - Lowe's Companies, Inc.; *pg.* 1053, *pg.* 1383
Schoeppner, Sean, Mgr-Technical Mktg - Xerox Corporation; *pg.* 494, *pg.* 365
Schoettker, Matt, VP & Sr Product Mgr-Dev - Fifth Third Bancorp; *pg.* 752, *pg.* 1413
Schoettle, Catherine, Mgr-Mdse - Sea Island Clothiers, LLC; *pg.* 32, *pg.* 1146
Schoff, Andrea, Sr Mgr-Corp Comm - The Procter & Gamble Company; *pg.* 1129, *pg.* 1418
Schofield-Sevey, Andrea, Mgr-Shopper Mktg - Safeway Inc.; *pg.* 1032, *pg.* 184
Scholes, George D., VP-US Sls, Svc & Applications - FEI Company; *pg.* 1413, *pg.* 1498
Scholl, Daniela, Mgr-PR-St. John Providence Health System - St. John Health; *pg.* 1596, *pg.* 912
Scholl, Joanna, VP-Program Adv - Home Box Office, Inc.; *pg.* 290, *pg.* 1240
Scholl, Katie, Dir-Targeted Mktg & Customer Loyalty - Giant Eagle, Inc.; *pg.* 1020, *pg.* 1575
Scholl, Kevin, Dir-Digital Mktg - Red Roof Inns, Inc.; *pg.* 1110, *pg.* 1443
Scholl, Sandy, Analyst-Mktg - UBS Financial Services Inc.; *pg.* 812, *pg.* 1306
Scholtyssek, Nicole, Sr Dir-Sls Ops-NBC News Digital - NBC Universal, Inc.; *pg.* 300, *pg.* 1266
Scholz, Carol L., Sr Dir-Access Svcs - Johnson & Johnson; *pg.* 1549, *pg.* 1091
Scholz, Eric, Sr Dir-Comm - Marriott International, Inc.; *pg.* 1102, *pg.* 764
Scholz, Lori, Mgr-PR - Hyundai Motor America; *pg.* 179, *pg.* 89
Schomp, Mark, Exec VP-Sls & Mktg - TOR Minerals International Inc.; *pg.* 1184, *pg.* 1672
Schonauer, Ken, Mgr-Natl Sls Sys & Support - HAR Adhesive Technologies; *pg.* 1442, *pg.* 1405
Schonberg, Mischel, Mgr-PR - Clopay Building Products Company; *pg.* 76, *pg.* 1459
Schoneboom, Sallie, Sr VP-PR-IFC - AMC Networks Inc.; *pg.* 269, *pg.* 1189
Schonewald, Dawn, Brand Mgr-Lingerie, Legwear & Home - Nordstrom, Inc.; *pg.* 1779, *pg.* 1837
Schooley, Bob, Reg Mgr-Mktg - Bozzuto's Inc.; *pg.* 1016, *pg.* 342
Schooley, Donna, Coord-Mktg Team - SVB Financial Group; *pg.* 808, *pg.* 270
Schools, Tim, Chief Strategy Officer - United Community Banks, Inc.; *pg.* 814, *pg.* 526
Schoonover, David, Sr Mgr-CRM & Digital Mktg - Kia Motors America Inc.; *pg.* 181, *pg.* 112
Schoos, Janine, Brand Mgr - Labatt USA LLC; *pg.* 254, *pg.* 1149
Schopp, Keith, VP-Corp PR-North America - Nestle Purina PetCare Company; *pg.* 1479, *pg.* 1000
Schott, Alex, Mgr-Digital Comm & Media Strategy - Entergy Corporation; *pg.* 1941, *pg.* 746
Schott, Darren, Dir-ECommerce Mktg - Blair Corporation; *pg.* 1762, *pg.* 1590
Schott, Jamie, Dir-Corp Digital Mktg - Mary Kay Inc.; *pg.* 516, *pg.* 1657
Schouten, Hendrik, Head-Product Mktg - AT&T Mobility LLC; *pg.* 619, *pg.* 488
Schouvieller, Lori, Sr Mgr-Mktg - Donaldson Company, Inc.; *pg.* 1329, *pg.* 917
Schrader, Charles, Specialist-Mktg Product-Fendt & Challenger - AGCO Corporation; *pg.* 700, *pg.* 530
Schrader, Marc, Mgr-Mktg-Product Mgmt Integrated Shipping Solutions - FedEx Corporation; *pg.* 1907, *pg.* 1642
Schrader, Marcy, Mgr-Mktg, Comm & Bus Dev - Cisco

First page reference indicates Business Class Edition
Second page reference indicates Geographic Edition

Systems, Inc.; pg. 372, pg. 240
Schrag, David, Sr Mgr-Assoc Comm-Global - Wal-Mart Stores, Inc.; pg. 1790, pg. 29
Schrage, Lynne, Mgr-Event Mktg - FCA US LLC; pg. 170, pg. 868
Schram, Melissa, Mgr-Web Mktg - Lenovo Group Ltd; pg. 427, pg. 1384
Schramm, Mark, District Mgr-Sls - FMC Corporation; pg. 1163, pg. 1564
Schreck, Mary, Mgr-Mktg-US - Philips Respironics; pg. 1585, pg. 1555
Schreger, Charles, Pres-Programming Sls - Home Box Office, Inc.; pg. 290, pg. 1240
Schreiber, Alle, Project Mgr-Digital Creative - Sephora USA Inc; pg. 522, pg. 227
Schreiber, Amy, Coord-PR & Mktg - Six Flags Entertainment Corporation; pg. 583, pg. 1698
Schreiber, Brian T., Chief Strategy Officer & Exec VP - American International Group, Inc.; pg. 1190, pg. 1193
Schreiber, Edgar, Product Mgr-Genetic Sciences - Thermo Fisher Scientific Inc.; pg. 1431, pg. 854
Schreiber, Yoav, Mgr-Mktg-Svc Provider Video Solutions - Cisco Systems, Inc.; pg. 372, pg. 240
Schreiner Gates, Cathleen, Exec VP-Sls & Mktg - ELLIE MAE, INC.; pg. 1243, pg. 183
Schrenker, Eric, Sr Analyst-Platform & Digital Product Dev - Scottrade, Inc.; pg. 802, pg. 1003
Schreve, Joost, VP-Product-Mobile - TripAdvisor, Inc.; pg. 1926, pg. 835
Schreyer, Ray, Sr Mgr-Global Recruitment Tech & Enablement - IBM; pg. 410, pg. 1449
Schriber, David, VP-Brand Mktg-North America - NIKE, Inc.; pg. 1812, pg. 1492
Schrift, Gary, Pres-Country Sls Org-North America - GEA Refrigeration North America, Inc.; pg. 1072, pg. 1597
Schriver, Eric, Gen Mgr-V-S Products Div - NN, Inc.; pg. 1365, pg. 1635
Schriver, Terri, Sr VP-Enterprise Media - Bank of America Corporation; pg. 718, pg. 1362
Schroder, Matt, Sr Head-Corp Comm & Media Rels - Owens Corning; pg. 102, pg. 1476
Schroder, Michele, Sr Mgr-Event - Sun Life Financial Inc.; pg. 806, pg. 1944
Schroder, Ron, Sr Mgr-Brand-Grilling - Johnsonville Sausage, LLC; pg. 867, pg. 1894
Schroder, Sharon R., Dir-Community Dev & Direct Sls - DPL Inc.; pg. 1939, pg. 1445
Schroeder, Allison, Mgr-Internet Mktg - Roto-Rooter, Inc.; pg. 108, pg. 1425
Schroeder, Erich, Product Mgr - Nilfisk-Advance, Inc.; pg. 332, pg. 953
Schroeder, Jan, Mgr-Mktg-Consumer Mktg - American Greetings Corporation; pg. 1615, pg. 1428
Schroeder, Jenny, Dir-Bus Strategy-Natl Acct Sls - CareerBuilder, LLC; pg. 1234, pg. 568
Schroeder, John J., VP & Dir-Sls & Mktg - Milne Food Products, Inc.; pg. 877, pg. 1824
Schroeder, Michelle, Coord-Reg Mktg - Meritage Homes Corporation; pg. 97, pg. 23
Schroeder, Valeska, Sr VP-Product Mgmt - Vital Connect; pg. 686, pg. 58
Schroedl, Jason, Dir-Product & Solutions Mktg - Cisco Systems, Inc.; pg. 372, pg. 240
Schroer, Brett, Dir-Digital Mktg-Analog Bus - Texas Instruments Incorporated; pg. 679, pg. 1688
Schroeter, Bobby, VP-Consumer Mktg - Spirit Airlines, Inc.; pg. 234, pg. 449
Schroeter, Laura, Assoc Rep-Sls-Neuro, Spine & ENT - Stryker Corporation; pg. 1598, pg. 894
Schroll, Kevin, Sr Product Mgr-Mktg - Samsung Electronics America, Inc.; pg. 669, pg. 1115
Schrom, Ben, Product Mgr - Google Inc.; pg. 1249, pg. 153
Schubert, Max, Mgr-Retirement Plan Product Mktg - FRANKLIN RESOURCES, INC.; pg. 760, pg. 254
Schuchardt, Karen, VP-US Video Sls - ABC, Inc.; pg. 268, pg. 1185
Schue, John, Asst Mgr-Digital & Loyalty Mktg - Dunkin' Brands Group, Inc.; pg. 1727, pg. 810
Schuecking, Matthias, Head-Mktg-Asia-Pacific - Airbnb, Inc.; pg. 1226, pg. 211
Schuele, Craig, VP-Mktg & Bus Dev - Altra Holdings, Inc.; pg. 198, pg. 802
Schuele, Craig, VP-Mktg & Bus Dev - Altria Industrial Motion Corp.; pg. 1312, pg. 802
Schuele, Craig, VP-Mktg & Bus Dev - Boston Gear; pg. 201, pg. 802
Schueren, Clare, Dir-Mktg - Central Garden & Pet Company; pg. 1475, pg. 303
Schuerenberg, John, Sr Mgr-Mktg - Microsoft Corporation; pg. 435, pg. 1824
Schuessler, Todd, Dir-Mktg & Strategic Natl Accounts - Remy Cointreau USA Inc.; pg. 1969, pg. 1285
Schuette, Linda, Mgr-Convention Sls-Natl - St. Louis Convention & Visitors Commission; pg. 1006, pg. 1003
Schuetz, Ashley, Sr Mgr-Mktg - Massage Heights Corporate, LLC; pg. 561, pg. 1741
Schuh, Clarissa, Dir-Field Mktg - Infor; pg. 414, pg. 484
Schuh, Jennifer, Specialist-PR - Here; pg. 404, pg. 576
Schuh, Michele, Sr Dir-Media & Brand Engagement - Old Navy; pg. 45, pg. 224
Schuh, Rebecca, Analyst-Global Sls Enablement Platform & Process - Motorola Solutions, Inc.; pg. 657, pg. 659
Schuit, Sydney, Asst Mgr-ECommerce Mktg - Levi Strauss & Co.; pg. 43, pg. 220
Schukai, Bob, Head-Mobile Tech-Global & Advanced Product Innovation - Thomson Reuters Markets; pg. 810, pg. 1299
Schuldt, Elana, Dir-Digital Mktg - Rodan + Fields, LLC; pg. 522, pg. 225
Schule, Sally, Dir-Mktg - Saks Fifth Avenue, Inc.; pg. 1783, pg. 1287
Schulenberg, Janelle, Sr Dir-Enterprise Growth - Best Buy Co., Inc.; pg. 1761, pg. 954
Schuler, Neal, VP & Sr Dir-Creative - The Yankee Candle Company, Inc.; pg. 1792, pg. 843
Schuler, Steven, Sr Mgr-Mktg-B2B Mobile - Yahoo! Inc.; pg. 1289, pg. 289
Schuler, Tara, Assoc Mgr-Mktg-Shredded Cheese - Sargento Foods Inc.; pg. 894, pg. 1886
Schuler, Tricia, Dir-Strategic Mktg & Brand Mgmt - UniGroup, Inc.; pg. 1927, pg. 977
Schulman, Alice, Coord-Adv & Circulation - Institute of Management Accountants, Inc.; pg. 144, pg. 1086
Schulman, Andrew, Dir-Consumer Mktg - Bonnier Corporation; pg. 1622, pg. 480
Schulman, Scott, Dir-Mktg Commercialization - Orkin, Inc.; pg. 1798, pg. 517
Schulman, Stephanie, Sr Mgr-PR - Weight Watchers International, Inc.; pg. 1609, pg. 1313
Schulte, Alex, Dir-Partnership Sls - International Speedway Corporation; pg. 553, pg. 420
Schulte, John, Mgr-Global Mktg Comm-Oil & Mining Svcs - Clariant Corporation; pg. 1153, pg. 1365
Schulte, Matthew, Dir-Natl Sls-Wenner Media - US Weekly LLC; pg. 1698, pg. 1308
Schulte, Melissa, Product Dir-Customer Experience - Travelzoo Inc; pg. 1926, pg. 1304
Schulte, Steve, VP-Sls & Mktg - Mark Andy, Inc.; pg. 1359, pg. 975
Schulte, Tom, VP-Sys Sls - Intelligrated, Inc.; pg. 1349, pg. 1460
Schultz, Bethany, Exec VP-Products & Client Engagement - Miller Heiman Inc.; pg. 440, pg. 1031
Schultz, Chris, Dir-Mktg - GN Netcom Inc.; pg. 640, pg. 1037
Schultz, Christine, Mgr-Integrated Sls-All You, Cooking Light & Health - Time Inc.; pg. 1693, pg. 1300
Schultz, Dave, Sr Mgr-Mktg & Bus-Cloud Drive - Amazon.com, Inc.; pg. 1226, pg. 1831
Schultz, John, Mgr-Tourism Mktg - Explore Minnesota Tourism; pg. 992, pg. 960
Schultz, Joseph G., Sr VP & Head-Intermediary Sls - American Century Investments; pg. 711, pg. 980
Schultz, Kelley, Dir-PR-North America - CA Technologies; pg. 366, pg. 1168
Schultz, Leah, Mgr-Social Media - Papa John's International, Inc.; pg. 1743, pg. 737
Schultz, Mary Ann, Sr Mgr-Pub Affairs & Govt Rels - Blue Cross & Blue Shield Association; pg. 1195, pg. 566
Schultz, Michael, District Mgr-Mktg - H&R Block, Inc.; pg. 764, pg. 983
Schultz, Richard, Sr VP-Sls & Retention - Charter Communications, Inc.; pg. 274, pg. 372
Schultz, Sonya, Dir-Adv - The Grand Island Daily Independent; pg. 1646, pg. 1010
Schultz, Teri L., VP-Mktg - Protective Life Corporation; pg. 1215, pg. 4
Schultz, Thomas, Sr VP-Sls - HealthStream, Inc.; pg. 1649, pg. 1651
Schultz, Tom, Dir-Sls & Mktg - Siemens Process Industries and Drive; pg. 1376, pg. 1587
Schultz-Berns, Heidi, Mgr-eBusiness & Direct Mktg - The Allstate Corporation; pg. 1189, pg. 639
Schulz, Amy, Mgr-Customer Mktg & Sls - National Football League; pg. 567, pg. 1264
Schulz, Duane, VP-Mktg Tech & Brand - Xerox Corporation; pg. 494, pg. 365
Schulz, Karen, Mgr-PR-Carolinas & Tennessee - Verizon Communications Inc.; pg. 1875, pg. 1309
Schulz, Megan, Mgr-Mktg & Comm - Giumarra Vineyards Corporation; pg. 1964, pg. 45
Schulz, Svenja, Dir-Mktg-Global - Tyco International (US) Inc.; pg. 1891, pg. 1113
Schulze, Dave, Dir-Sls - Amkor Technology, Inc.; pg. 67, pg. 25
Schulze, George, Exec VP-Sls-Global - OpenText GXS; pg. 1272, pg. 770
Schulze, Greg, Head-SAP Process-Pricing & Sls Ops - 3M Company; pg. 1142, pg. 956
Schulze, Laura, Mgr-Sls & Support - Boise Cascade; pg. 1453, pg. 788
Schulze, Patrick, Sr Mgr-Digital Media Acctg - ESPN, Inc.; pg. 285, pg. 340
Schum, Trisha, Brand Mgr - PPG Industries, Inc.; pg. 1445, pg. 1579
Schumacher, Allison, Mgr-Mktg Ops - ASICS America Corporation; pg. 1826, pg. 106
Schumacher, George, Dir-eSSS Product Mgmt for Core & Application Infrastructure - Arrow Electronics, Inc.; pg. 619, pg. 325
Schumacher, Ginny, Mgr-Mktg - Diamond Jo, LLC; pg. 1089, pg. 707
Schumacher, John, Asst VP-Adv - Hobby Lobby Stores Inc.; pg. 927, pg. 1486
Schumacher, Katy, Brand Mgr-Kraft Mayo - The Kraft Heinz Company; pg. 871, pg. 641
Schumacher, Susan, Dir-Mktg Comm - Zoll Medical Corporation; pg. 1612, pg. 814
Schumacher, Tara, Dir-PR - Cardinal Health, Inc.; pg. 1512, pg. 1448
Schuman, Amy, VP-Media & Promos - Showtime Networks Inc.; pg. 308, pg. 1291
Schuman, Chip, VP-Mktg-Consumer Products - Sargento Foods Inc.; pg. 894, pg. 1886
Schuman, Peter, Sr Dir-IR - Atmel Corporation; pg. 621, pg. 238
Schunker, Pio, Sr VP & Head-Integrated Brand Mktg-Global - Samsung Electronics America, Inc.; pg. 669, pg. 1115
Schunter, Joel, Mgr-ECommerce Mdsg & Mktg - Cellco Partnership; pg. 1869, pg. 1042
Schurk, Gary, Dir-Sports Sls - St. Louis Convention & Visitors Commission; pg. 1006, pg. 1003
Schurz, Mackenzi, Dir-Mktg - J.E. Dunn Construction Group, Inc.; pg. 89, pg. 984
Schussel, Marjorie, Dir-Corp Mktg - Toyota Motor North America, Inc.; pg. 192, pg. 1303
Schuster, Amy, Mgr-Consumer Mktg - Oxygen Media LLC; pg. 303, pg. 1275
Schuster, David, Product Mgr - Motorola Solutions, Inc.; pg. 657, pg. 659
Schuster, Derek, Dir-Sls - The Phillies, L.P.; pg. 575, pg. 1569
Schuster, Frank, Sr VP-Sls - Snyder's-Lance, Inc.; pg. 896, pg. 1368
Schuster, Gavriella, Partner-Mktg & Programs & Gen Mgr-WW - Microsoft Corporation; pg. 435, pg. 1824
Schuster, Michael, VP-Strategic Mktg Control Tech - ABB Inc.; pg. 1309, pg. 1359
Schutt, Douglas W., COO-Mdse & Exec VP - Costco Wholesale Corporation; pg. 1765, pg. 1820
Schutte, Jort, Head-Creative - Google Inc.; pg. 1249, pg. 153
Schutz, Mike, Gen Mgr-Product Mktg, Server & Tools Div - Microsoft Corporation; pg. 435, pg. 1824
Schuurmans, Niels, Exec VP-Mktg & Creative Content Solutions - Viacom Inc.; pg. 316, pg. 1310
Schwab, Cynthia, Sr Dir-Fin & Admin - Greater Tampa Chamber of Commerce; pg. 994, pg. 473
Schwab, Eric, Dir-Mktg & Program Optimization - Choice Hotels International, Inc.; pg. 1086, pg. 775
Schwab, Eric B., Exec VP-Sls & Mktg & Gen Mgr-In Market - TEN: The Enthusiast Network; pg. 1691, pg. 1298
Schwab, Joe, Mgr-Plant Sls - Viking Yacht Company; pg. 1712, pg. 1094
Schwab, John N., Sr VP & Gen Mgr-Hefty Consumer Products - Pactiv Corporation; pg. 1466, pg. 624
Schwab, Karin, Product Mgr - Leica Microsystems, Inc.; pg. 1420, pg. 555

Schwab, Kathy, Sr Dir-Mktg - Milwaukee Brewers Baseball Club, Inc.; pg. 562, pg. 1878
Schwab, Pat, Sr VP-Consumer Product Sls - Hormel Foods Corporation; pg. 863, pg. 915
Schwab, Rich, VP-Sls-Intl - Gold Eagle Company; pg. 206, pg. 575
Schwab, Rosanne, Asst VP-PR - Peapack-Gladstone Bank; pg. 792, pg. 1071
Schwab-Dolson, Katherine, Assoc Dir-Product Mktg - McKesson Corporation; pg. 1560, pg. 222
Schwaba, Hana, Reg Mgr-Comml Sls - salesforce.com, inc.; pg. 1278, pg. 226
Schwabe, Cori, Mgr-Digital Mktg - L'Oreal USA; pg. 514, pg. 1252
Schwalbach, Christine Haas, VP-Sls - National Band & Tag Co.; pg. 1479, pg. 739
Schwalen, Mary, Sr Mgr-Learning & Dev - Genentech, Inc.; pg. 1533, pg. 279
Schwalm, Haley, Sr Mgr-Mktg - Discovery Communications, Inc.; pg. 282, pg. 777
Schwan, Axel, CMO-Global & Exec VP - Burger King Corporation; pg. 1719, pg. 440
Schwan, Brad, Assoc Dir-Mktg - The Procter & Gamble Company; pg. 1129, pg. 1418
Schwan, Camie, Sr Mgr-Mktg-Automotive - Nuance Communications, Inc.; pg. 447, pg. 806
Schwar, Bill, VP-Sls Ops-YRC Freight - YRC Worldwide Inc.; pg. 1931, pg. 720
Schwartz, Aime, Mgr-Digital Mktg - The King Arthur Flour Company, Inc.; pg. 833, pg. 1767
Schwartz, Andrea, Dir-External & PR - Macy's East; pg. 1777, pg. 1254
Schwartz, Andrea, VP-Media Rels & Cause Mktg, Dir-External & PR & Dir-Media Rels - Macy's, Inc.; pg. 1778, pg. 1417
Schwartz, Barbara, Dir-Product Dev - Schwartz & Benjamin, Inc.; pg. 1818, pg. 1290
Schwartz, Brittany, Head-Adv Ops-Global - Spotify; pg. 1282, pg. 1295
Schwartz, David, Sr Head-Bus-Global Mktg - Authorize.Net Holdings, Inc.; pg. 356, pg. 1751
Schwartz, David, Dir-Mktg & Head-New Platform Innovation & Base Bus - Johnson & Johnson; pg. 1549, pg. 1091
Schwartz, David, VP-Sls-Worldwide - Micrel, Inc.; pg. 654, pg. 247
Schwartz, David, Sr VP & Sr Mgr-Relationship - Sunwest Bank; pg. 807, pg. 116
Schwartz, David F., VP-Sls - Sinclair Broadcast Group, Inc.; pg. 308, pg. 773
Schwartz, Greg, Chief Revenue Officer - Zillow Group, Inc.; pg. 1292, pg. 1843
Schwartz, Jacquelyn, Assoc Mgr-Mktg - Godiva Chocolatier, Inc.; pg. 1854, pg. 1235
Schwartz, Jake, Brand Mgr - Schwartz & Benjamin, Inc.; pg. 1818, pg. 1290
Schwartz, Jamie, Mgr-Client Mktg - Sports Illustrated; pg. 1688, pg. 1295
Schwartz, Jennifer, Brand Mgr-ABSOLUT vodka - Pernod Ricard USA, Inc.; pg. 1968, pg. 1332
Schwartz, Jon, Mng Dir-Integrated Mktg & Comm - National Association for Stock Car Auto Racing; pg. 566, pg. 420
Schwartz, Loren, Exec VP-Genre Mktg & Creative Adv - Warner Bros. Entertainment Inc.; pg. 319, pg. 54
Schwartz, Marc, VP-Consumer & Brand Mktg - Wyndham Worldwide Corporation; pg. 1119, pg. 1107
Schwartz, Margaret, Dir-Mktg - CORT Business Services Corporation; pg. 921, pg. 1777
Schwartz, Matt, Specialist-Product Mktg - Honeywell International Inc.; pg. 407, pg. 1088
Schwartz, Melissa, Brand Mgr-Diet Coke - Coca-Cola North America; pg. 848, pg. 500
Schwartz, Michelle, Mgr-Mktg & Comm - Arizona State University; pg. 597, pg. 25
Schwartz, Nancy, Mgr-Mktg - E.I. du Pont de Nemours & Company; pg. 1159, pg. 390
Schwartz, Rachel, Sr Specialist-Mktg - Deloitte & Touche USA LLP; pg. 743, pg. 1222
Schwartz, Robert, VP-Digital Mktg-Global - IBM; pg. 410, pg. 1449
Schwartz, Tara Gutkowski, Sr Dir - National Basketball Association; pg. 566, pg. 1264
Schwartzberg, Joel, Sr Dir-Strategic & Exec Comm - American Society for the Prevention of Cruelty to Animals; pg. 131, pg. 1193
Schwartzman, Steven, Mgr-Procurement Mktg & Print - Sony Pictures Entertainment Inc.; pg. 309, pg. 72
Schwartzman, Todd, Sr VP-Sls - BBC Worldwide America Inc.; pg. 271, pg. 1201
Schwarz, Andy, Dir-Sls - CIRCOR Aerospace, Inc.; pg. 226, pg. 69
Schwarz, Christian, VP-Mktg-USA - Miele Inc.; pg. 59, pg. 1112
Schwarz, Corrina, Sr Product Mgr-Global Strategic Mktg - Kimberly-Clark Corporation; pg. 1461, pg. 1720
Schwarz, Greg, VP-Mktg - Dean Foods Company; pg. 852, pg. 1679
Schwarz, Holger, Exec VP & Head-Sls-Global - Liquidity Services, Inc.; pg. 1263, pg. 401
Schwarz, Jarrod, Sr Dir-Product Mgmt - ESPN, Inc.; pg. 285, pg. 340
Schwarz, Ralph, Sr Product Dir - Cincom Systems, Inc.; pg. 372, pg. 1411
Schwarz, Shira F., Sr Mgr-Mktg-Tropicana - PepsiCo, Inc.; pg. 259, pg. 1327
Schwegman, John, Exec Dir-US Product & Pricing-Chevy-CMC Trucks & Corvette - General Motors Company; pg. 175, pg. 881
Schwehm, David, Grp VP-Sls - CORT Business Services Corporation; pg. 921, pg. 1777
Schweickert, Christine, Mgr-Mktg - Ingram Micro Inc.; pg. 415, pg. 261
Schweikhard, Amanda, Brand Mgr-Mktg - AMN Healthcare Services, Inc.; pg. 1494, pg. 200
Schweitzberger, Nicole, Dir-Creative Svcs - Lee Enterprises, Incorporated; pg. 1658, pg. 704
Schweitzer, Deana, Mgr-KCRA & KQCA Digital Sls - KCRA-TV; pg. 293, pg. 196
Schweitzer, George, Pres-CBS Mktg Grp - CBS Broadcasting Inc.; pg. 273, pg. 1210
Schweitzer, George, Pres-CBS Mktg Grp - CBS Corporation; pg. 273, pg. 1210
Schweitzer, Jeff, Mgr-Pub Rels - American Crystal Sugar Company; pg. 837, pg. 951
Schweitzer, Matt, Sr Dir-Integrated Mktg - HarperCollins Publishers Inc.; pg. 1647, pg. 1237
Schweitzer, Stephanie, Designer-Media - Audi of America, Inc.; pg. 164, pg. 1784
Schweitzer, Ted, Sr VP-Mktg & ECommerce - La Quinta Corporation; pg. 1099, pg. 1722
Schweitzer, Ted, Sr VP-Mktg & ECommerce - La Quinta Inns, Inc.; pg. 1100, pg. 1722
Schweizer, Donna, Project Coord-Media - Movado Group, Inc.; pg. 10, pg. 1101
Schwend-Katcher, Nicole, VP-Sls Maybelline & essie - L'Oreal USA; pg. 514, pg. 1252
Schwendinger, Derek, Sr Dir - Post Holdings, Inc.; pg. 833, pg. 1002
Schwensohn, Scott, Specialist-Unified Comm Product Sls - Cisco Systems, Inc.; pg. 372, pg. 240
Schwepker, Christine, Sr Mgr-Email Mktg - Express Scripts, Inc.; pg. 1530, pg. 997
Schweppe, Erin, Dir-Product Mktg - OnMobile Live, Inc.; pg. 449, pg. 829
Schwerdtfeger, Kara, Sr Mgr-Mktg & Comm - TriZetto Corporation; pg. 485, pg. 327
Schwerin, Rich, Strategist-Digital Content-Digital Mktg - VMware, Inc.; pg. 490, pg. 179
Schwertley, Rob, Mgr-Local Sls - Seattle Times Company; pg. 1685, pg. 1840
Schwiebert, Kirk, Dir-Product Dev - Ohmite Manufacturing Company; pg. 660, pg. 553
Schwiebert, Mike, VP-Mktg - Weatherby, Inc.; pg. 1848, pg. 181
Schwieger, Doug, Dir-Central Reg Sls & Svcs-OptiFreight Logistics - Cardinal Health, Inc.; pg. 1512, pg. 1448
Schwieterman, Laura, Dir-Mktg - Bayer Healthcare Consumer Care Division; pg. 1500, pg. 1087
Schwinden, Brianna, Analyst-Interactive Mktg & Emerging Digital Channels - Ameriprise Financial, Inc.; pg. 715, pg. 930
Schwindt, Thorsten, Product Mgr-Broad Acre Fungicides - Bayer CropScience; pg. 1149, pg. 981
Schwinefus, Jay, VP & Dir-Mktg & Client Info - HMN Financial, Inc.; pg. 766, pg. 955
Schwing, Patrick, Brand Mgr-Global eBusiness - The Procter & Gamble Company; pg. 1129, pg. 1418
Schwinnen, Traci R., Mgr-Shopper Mktg - Abbott Laboratories; pg. 1484, pg. 551
Schwoerer, Roger, Dir-Adv - The New York Times Company; pg. 1668, pg. 1270
Schymanski, Ryan, Mgr-Sls - Lindenmeyr Munroe; pg. 1464, pg. 1325
Sciacca, Fabio, Dir-Sls-EMEA - FlightSafety International, Inc.; pg. 601, pg. 1160
Sciarillo, Allen, Acting CFO - Electro Rent Corporation; pg. 390, pg. 300
Sciarrotta, Christine, VP-Mktg - Toll Brothers, Inc.; pg. 115, pg. 1541
Sciascia, Guido, VP-Mktg - Barilla America, Inc.; pg. 839, pg. 555
Scibelli, Angela, Assoc Mktg Mgr-Digital & Social Innovation - The Gap, Inc.; pg. 1770, pg. 218
Scibelli, Marc, Chief Creative Officer - Infor; pg. 414, pg. 484
Scicchitano, Katilin, Specialist-PR & Social Media - Auntie Anne's Inc.; pg. 1715, pg. 1546
Scicluna, Lisa M., Head-Sls Comm - Hershey Canada, Inc.; pg. 1855, pg. 1926
Scizak, Michelle, Mgr-Mktg Strategies - Safeway Inc.; pg. 1032, pg. 184
Sclafani, Scott, Dir-IT-Mktg, Pricing & Comm - General Electric Company; pg. 1297, pg. 347
Scocimara, Peter, Sr Dir-Global Support, Google for Work - Google Inc.; pg. 1249, pg. 153
Scoon, Trevor, Reg Mgr-Chain Sls - Diageo North America Inc.; pg. 248, pg. 1223
Scopaz, Justin, Sr Dir-Worldwide Distr - Juniper Networks; pg. 424, pg. 809
Scopellito, Tony, Dir-Global Mktg-Smokers' Health - GlaxoSmithKline; pg. 1536, pg. 1565
Scotland, Brian, Media Planner - Ritchie Bros. Auctioneers Incorporated; pg. 1372, pg. 1907
Scott, Allie, Producer-Social Media & Branded Content - Carnival Corporation; pg. 1902, pg. 441
Scott, Allison, Corp VP-PR - New York Life Insurance Company; pg. 1211, pg. 1268
Scott, Alys Reynders, CMO & Sr VP-Mktg Comm - PeopleFluent; pg. 453, pg. 853
Scott, Ann, Dir-Sls & Retailer Rels - The South Carolina Education Lottery; pg. 1005, pg. 1614
Scott, Anna, Mgr-Digital Mktg - Rent-A-Center, Inc.; pg. 940, pg. 1734
Scott, Ariel, Mgr-Digital Mktg - Whole Foods Market, Inc.; pg. 1038, pg. 1667
Scott, Avis, Product Dir - Macy's East; pg. 1777, pg. 1254
Scott, Ben, VP-Mktg-Americas - Carlson Wagonlit Travel; pg. 1902, pg. 948
Scott, Bill, Dir-Sls & Mktg-Global - Acton Technologies, Inc.; pg. 1145, pg. 1582
Scott, Brian, Brand Mgr-Client-Corp Accts - Dell Inc.; pg. 383, pg. 1737
Scott, Cathy, Mgr-Mktg Comm - Lennox Hearth Products; pg. 93, pg. 1652
Scott, Chris, VP-Performance Mktg - SolarCity Corporation; pg. 111, pg. 256
Scott, Christian, Dir-Global Mktg-Optics - Oakley, Inc.; pg. 1840, pg. 86
Scott, Christie, Reg Mgr-PR - Ameristar Casinos, Inc.; pg. 528, pg. 1022
Scott, David, Dir-IT, Mktg & Process Improvement - Butler Machinery Company; pg. 1321, pg. 1397
Scott, David, Grp Product Mgr - Symantec Corporation; pg. 478, pg. 161
Scott, Debbie, Dir-Media Svcs - Sterling Jewelers Inc.; pg. 13, pg. 1402
Scott, Derek, Dir-Mktg - Kemps LLC; pg. 867, pg. 961
Scott, Diane, CMO, Chief Product Officer-Global & Exec VP - The Western Union Company; pg. 822, pg. 327
Scott, Donna, Sr VP-Mktg - Spok; pg. 1873, pg. 1807
Scott, Duncan, VP-External Products - New Balance Athletic Shoe, Inc.; pg. 1811, pg. 798
Scott, Emily, VP-Digital Mktg - Kayak; pg. 1260, pg. 363
Scott, Erica, Exec Dir-Consumer Mktg & Strategic Insights - Yurman Design, Inc.; pg. 15, pg. 1316
Scott, Everton, Sr Mgr-Pub Affairs - Public Service Enterprise Group Incorporated; pg. 1950, pg. 1097
Scott, Garry, VP-Mktg & Brand Dev - Moen Incorporated; pg. 1056, pg. 1468
Scott, Geoff, VP-Product - DraftKings, Inc.; pg. 545, pg. 793
Scott, Greg, Mgr-Mktg-Emerging Markets - Ford Motor Company; pg. 172, pg. 876
Scott, Jack, Sr VP-Sls & Mktg - Alto-Shaam Inc.; pg. 836, pg. 1869
Scott, Jaimee, Dir-Digital Experience & Product Mgmt - Belk, Inc.; pg. 1760, pg. 1364
Scott, Jeffrey, VP-Mktg & Alliances - Smart Software, Inc.; pg. 470, pg. 787

First page reference indicates Business Class Edition
Second page reference indicates Geographic Edition

Scott, Joe, Dir-Mktg - The Detroit Lions, Inc.; *pg.* 544, *pg.* 864
Scott, Joy, Product Mgr - Intertape Polymer Group Inc.; *pg.* 1885, *pg.* 1960
Scott, Keecia, Sr Mgr-Mktg Ops - Gilead Sciences, Inc.; *pg.* 1535, *pg.* 88
Scott, Lauren, Dir-Mktg-Global - Diageo North America Inc.; *pg.* 248, *pg.* 1223
Scott, Marcia, Dir-Corp Mktg & Customer Insight - Thomson Reuters Corporation; *pg.* 1693, *pg.* 1944
Scott, Norris, VP-Partnership Mktg - National Association for Stock Car Auto Racing; *pg.* 566, *pg.* 420
Scott, Olen, VP-Channel Sls - EarthLink Holdings Corp.; *pg.* 1240, *pg.* 504
Scott, Rachel, Mgr-Bus Unit Mktg-Gene Expression Div - Bio-Rad Laboratories, Inc.; *pg.* 1504, *pg.* 101
Scott, Rafael, Sr Writer-eMail Mktg - FRANKLIN RESOURCES, INC.; *pg.* 760, *pg.* 254
Scott, Ryan, Product Mgr-Digital - Activision Blizzard, Inc.; *pg.* 948, *pg.* 271
Scott, Shannon, Exec Dir-Mktg Comm - Applebee's International, Inc.; *pg.* 1715, *pg.* 980
Scott, Shannon, Sr Dir-Mktg Comm & Adv - ASICS America Corporation; *pg.* 1826, *pg.* 106
Scott, Shelly, Sr Mgr-Bus Dev - Intuit Inc.; *pg.* 769, *pg.* 158
Scott, Stefanie A., Mgr-Mktg-Global Education - CA Technologies; *pg.* 366, *pg.* 1168
Scott, Stephanie, Mgr-Event Mktg - Jelly Belly Candy Company; *pg.* 1857, *pg.* 86
Scott, Steve, VP-Sls - AGI-VR/Wesson Inc; *pg.* 1041, *pg.* 415
Scott, Teisha L., Mgr-Mktg Comm - American Medical Systems Holdings, Inc.; *pg.* 1493, *pg.* 947
Scott, Terrance, Mgr-Production - The Boeing Company; *pg.* 225, *pg.* 567
Scott, Terry, Sr VP-Sls & Mktg - Aviall, Inc.; *pg.* 224, *pg.* 1676
Scott, Tim, Dir-Direct Mktg & Ops - Bass Pro Shops, Inc.; *pg.* 1826, *pg.* 1006
Scott, Troy, Mgr-Product Mktg - Synopsys, Inc.; *pg.* 480, *pg.* 162
Scott, Victor, Dir-Mktg, Comm & Pub Affairs - Aviall, Inc.; *pg.* 224, *pg.* 1676
Scott, Walter , Jr., Sr Mgr-Vendor - Level 3 Communications, Inc.; *pg.* 1262, *pg.* 312
Scott, Wendell, Sr VP-Multimedia Sls - ESPN, Inc.; *pg.* 285, *pg.* 340
Scott-Davidson, Louise, Brand Mgr-Nutri-Grain and Innovation - Kellogg Company; *pg.* 831, *pg.* 870
Scotto, Meghan, Traffic Mgr-Creative Solutions - Schneider Electric; *pg.* 467, *pg.* 1609
Scourfield, Gwyn, Sr VP & Head-Mktg-Americas & EMEA-CIT Aerospace - CIT GROUP INC.; *pg.* 735, *pg.* 1212
Scouvart, Michael, VP-Mktg-Mylan Pharmaceuticals & Mylan Institutional - Mylan, Inc.; *pg.* 1570, *pg.* 1520
Scoville, Sarah, Specialist-Mktg Promos - Kayem Foods, Inc.; *pg.* 867, *pg.* 814
Scrivanich, Luke, Sr VP & Gen Mgr-Optical Security & Performance Products - Viavi Solutions Inc.; *pg.* 1435, *pg.* 148
Scroggins, Jackie, Sr Mgr-Corp Events - Capital One Financial Corporation; *pg.* 730, *pg.* 1789
Scroggy, David, VP-Product Dev - Dark Horse Comics, Inc.; *pg.* 1633, *pg.* 1500
Scruggs, Craig, Product Mgr-Specialty-Automotive Ceramics - KEMET Corporation; *pg.* 649, *pg.* 1621
Scruggs, Criss H., Sr Mgr-Product Mktg - BMC Software, Inc.; *pg.* 362, *pg.* 1701
Scruggs, Tommy, Mgr-Sls & Mktg - Steel Dynamics, Inc.; *pg.* 113, *pg.* 681
Scurlock, Annie, Mgr-Art Traffic & Production - Zumiez Inc.; *pg.* 16, *pg.* 1822
Scurry, Maria, VP-Global PR & Comm - Qlik Technologies Inc.; *pg.* 457, *pg.* 1583
Scutakes, Jamie, Mgr-Mktg - Gartner, Inc.; *pg.* 1248, *pg.* 374
Scutari, Robert, Gen Mgr-Sls - WJLA & TBD; *pg.* 322, *pg.* 1775
Seaberg, Katherine, Mgr-Mktg Comm - Freescale Semiconductor, Inc.; *pg.* 398, *pg.* 1662
Seabold, Kathy, VP & Sr Mgr-Mktg - JPMorgan Chase & Co.; *pg.* 772, *pg.* 1246
Seabold, Kathy, VP & Sr Mgr-Mktg - JPMorgan Chase - Midwest Regional Office; *pg.* 773, *pg.* 579
Seaboldt, Carl, Sr Product Mgr - ITW - Evercoat; *pg.* 1443, *pg.* 1415
Seaborg, Peter, VP-Sls-Mid-Atlantic Reg - The Muralo Company; *pg.* 1444, *pg.* 1042
Seaburg, David, Head-Sls Trading - Cowen Group, Inc.; *pg.* 742, *pg.* 1219
Seager, Steve, Sr Mgr-Mdsg - Nestle Waters North America Inc.; *pg.* 257, *pg.* 375
Seago, Justin, Specialist-Global Digital Mktg-Golf - NIKE, Inc.; *pg.* 1812, *pg.* 1492
Seahorn, Chris, Dir-Digital Mktg - eBags, Inc.; *pg.* 1240, *pg.* 331
Seal, Allison, Mgr-ECommerce Mktg - P.C. Richard & Son; *pg.* 59, *pg.* 1159
Seal, Paul, Brand Mgr - Nestle Purina PetCare Company; *pg.* 1479, *pg.* 1000
Seal, Stephanie, Brand Mgr - Uno Restaurant Holdings Corporation; *pg.* 1754, *pg.* 856
Seale, Don, Dir-Mktg - The Allstate Corporation; *pg.* 1189, *pg.* 639
Seals, Mike, Dir-Mktg Strategy & Bus Dev - Hussmann International, Inc.; *pg.* 1347, *pg.* 973
Seals, Robert A., Sr VP & Dir-Mktg Analytics - Hancock Bank; *pg.* 765, *pg.* 968
Seals, Robert A., Sr VP & Dir-Mktg Analytics - Hancock Holding Company; *pg.* 765, *pg.* 968
Searcy, Geoff, VP-Converting Sls-Atlantic Pkg Corp - Atlantic Corporation; *pg.* 1452, *pg.* 1392
Searcy, Haydee, Exec Dir-Retail Mktg-Global - Yurman Design, Inc.; *pg.* 15, *pg.* 1316
Searcy, Zach, Coord-Digital & Social Media - Books-A-Million, Inc.; *pg.* 1623, *pg.* 2
Searfus, Matthew, Sr Dir-Product Mktg - Getty Images, Inc.; *pg.* 1645, *pg.* 1836
Searight, Christine, Dir-Corp Mktg - Gannett Co., Inc.; *pg.* 1643, *pg.* 1790
Searing, Lisa, Sr Mgr-Local Mktg, Grand Openings & Formats - Wal-Mart Stores, Inc.; *pg.* 1790, *pg.* 29
Searle, Collin, Mgr-Social Media - Intermountain Health Care Inc.; *pg.* 1546, *pg.* 1759
Searle, Jon, Brand Mgr-Global - NIKE, Inc.; *pg.* 1812, *pg.* 1492
Searle, Jonathan, Mgr-Mktg - The WhiteWave Foods Company; *pg.* 1037, *pg.* 324
Searle, Kathleen C., Sr VP-Mktg - Textron Inc.; *pg.* 235, *pg.* 1607
Searle, Sarah, Sr Mgr-Internal Comm - USANA Health Sciences, Inc.; *pg.* 1605, *pg.* 1761
Sears, Rebecca, Dir-Brand Mktg-Beauty - CVS Health Corporation; *pg.* 1765, *pg.* 1610
Seawright, Victoria, Dir-Mktg - Hanesbrands Inc.; *pg.* 26, *pg.* 1394
Seay, Gail, Dir-Global Event Mktg-North America - Citigroup Inc.; *pg.* 735, *pg.* 1212
Seay, Katherine, Sr Mgr-Managed Markets Mktg - Salix Pharmaceuticals, Inc.; *pg.* 1591, *pg.* 1388
Sebaali, Marcelle, Coord-Mktg - Meritage Homes Corporation; *pg.* 97, *pg.* 23
Sebastian, Cliff, Coord-Social & Mobile Media - Foxwoods Resort Casino; *pg.* 549, *pg.* 353
Sebastianelli, David J., VP-Sls & Mktg - Edlund Company, Inc.; *pg.* 1123, *pg.* 1765
Sebbag, Jack, VP-Sls & Advanced Solutions - TRIPWIRE, INC.; *pg.* 485, *pg.* 1507
Sebold, Laura, Mgr-Mktg - Outfront Media; *pg.* 1465, *pg.* 1275
Seboldt, Thomas, VP-Mdse - O'Reilly Automotive, Inc.; *pg.* 214, *pg.* 1006
Sebring, Harrison, Mgr-Adv-Global - Campbell Soup Company; *pg.* 844, *pg.* 1048
Sebring, Harrison, Mgr-Global Media Innovations - Mondelez International; *pg.* 877, *pg.* 1344
Seccombe, Jane, Sr Mgr-Comm & Pub Affairs - Reynolds American Inc.; *pg.* 1894, *pg.* 1395
Sechrist, Jennifer, Sr Specialist-Mktg-Iams Brand - Mars Petcare; *pg.* 1478, *pg.* 1633
Sechrist, Paul, Exec VP-Sls & Svc-Worldwide - Coherent, Inc.; *pg.* 1406, *pg.* 265
Seckler, Caren Pasquale, VP-Social Commitment - The Coca-Cola Company; *pg.* 240, *pg.* 493
Seckler, Ellen, VP-Mktg - Citizen Watch Co. of America, Inc.; *pg.* 3, *pg.* 293
Secor, Kiko, Mgr-Field Mktg - Aruba Networks, Inc.; *pg.* 353, *pg.* 284
Seculi, Juan, Product Mgr-Global - Kennametal Inc.; *pg.* 1052, *pg.* 1547
Secunda, Tom, Vice Chm & Head-Fin Products & Svcs-Global - Bloomberg L.P.; *pg.* 725, *pg.* 1204
Seddon, William, Dir-Comm & Data Sls - Graybar Electric Company, Inc.; *pg.* 1299, *pg.* 997
Sedgwick, Christopher, Dir-Intl & Govt Sls - Sellstrom Manufacturing Co.; *pg.* 1428, *pg.* 659
Sedgwick, David, Specialist-Mktg Ops - American Family Mutual Insurance Company; *pg.* 1190, *pg.* 1864
Sediq, Julie, Sr Mgr-Mktg Comm - Toyo Tire (U.S.A.) Corporation; *pg.* 1890, *pg.* 76
Sedlacek, Christine, Dir-Internet & Customer Mktg - Canon U.S.A., Inc.; *pg.* 1404, *pg.* 1178
Sedlacek, Walt, Dir-Sls & Mktg - SK Hand Tool Corporation; *pg.* 1062, *pg.* 663
Sedov, Dmitri, Head-Digital Mktg-Global - Standard & Poor's Ratings Services; *pg.* 805, *pg.* 1296
Seebeck, John, Dir-Direct Mktg Bus - Crate & Barrel, Inc.; *pg.* 922, *pg.* 640
Seeberger-Shefrin, Elissa, Brand Mgr - LifeLock Inc.; *pg.* 776, *pg.* 26
Seebohm, Monica, Sr Dir-Programmatic Sls - Tremor Video; *pg.* 682, *pg.* 1305
Seebold, Lori, Mgr-Adv Svcs - The Daily Item; *pg.* 1632, *pg.* 829
Seebold, Lori, Mgr-Adv Svcs - The Daily Item; *pg.* 1632, *pg.* 1588
Seecharan, Sondra, Assoc Mgr-Mktg - Benjamin Moore & Co.; *pg.* 1440, *pg.* 1085
Seefeld, Bernhard, Dir-Product Mgmt - Google Inc.; *pg.* 1249, *pg.* 153
Seefeldt, Jennifer, Sr Strategist-Media - Life Time Fitness, Inc.; *pg.* 1556, *pg.* 920
Seejattan, Laura, Brand Mgr-Coffee - The J.M. Smucker Company; *pg.* 865, *pg.* 1468
Seek, Andrea, Dir-Mktg-Shopper Mktg - PepsiCo, Inc.; *pg.* 259, *pg.* 1327
Seekford, James, VP-Comml Sls - Nationwide Homes, Inc.; *pg.* 99, *pg.* 1788
Seelam, Raj, Dir-Mktg - Analog Devices, Inc.; *pg.* 617, *pg.* 839
Seeley, Dale, Sr Engr-PR Mech Design - Medtronic, Inc.; *pg.* 1564, *pg.* 939
Seeley, Lauren, Mgr-Mktg - Vonage Holdings Corp.; *pg.* 686, *pg.* 1074
Seeley, Tom, Sr VP-Digital Media - The Hollywood Reporter Inc.; *pg.* 1650, *pg.* 133
Seemann, Dana, Product Mgr - Canadian Imperial Bank of Commerce; *pg.* 729, *pg.* 1935
Seemann, Robert H., Exec VP-Sls & Svcs - Darling Ingredients, Inc.; *pg.* 852, *pg.* 1718
Seen, Beth A., Mgr-ES Mktg Comm - Northrop Grumman Corporation; *pg.* 231, *pg.* 1781
Seeto, Nigel, Sr Mgr-Mktg - Ancestry.com LLC; *pg.* 1228, *pg.* 1754
Seeton, Mark, Dir-North American Sls - PPG Industries, Inc.; *pg.* 1445, *pg.* 1579
Seevers, Garret, Dir-Mktg-QuickBooks Online - Intuit Inc.; *pg.* 769, *pg.* 158
Seewald, Brian, Sr Dir-Ops - DSW, Inc.; *pg.* 1807, *pg.* 1439
Segal, Alexandra, Mgr-Mktg - Colavita USA, Inc.; *pg.* 849, *pg.* 1056
Segal, Jack, VP-PR-Chicago Reg - Comcast Corporation; *pg.* 276, *pg.* 1560
Segal, Steven, VP-Mktg-Europe & Africa - Schlumberger Limited; *pg.* 801, *pg.* 1714
Segall, Katie, Sr Mgr-Mktg - PepsiCo, Inc.; *pg.* 259, *pg.* 1327
Segall, Rachel, Brand Mgr-Comm - T. Rowe Price Group Inc.; *pg.* 808, *pg.* 759
Segarra, Jeanette, Sr Mgr-Mktg - ESPN, Inc.; *pg.* 285, *pg.* 340
Segars, Jacquie, Sr Dir-Brand Strategy - Equifax Inc.; *pg.* 748, *pg.* 504
Segato, Tim, Sr Product Mgr-BlackBerry Security - BlackBerry Limited; *pg.* 625, *pg.* 1947
Seghposs, Diane, Sr Dir-Product Mktg - Oracle Corporation; *pg.* 450, *pg.* 191
Segnit, Brian J., Mgr-Mktg - Xerox Corporation; *pg.* 494, *pg.* 365
Segovia, Michelle, Mgr-Mktg - Veterinary Pet Insurance Co.; *pg.* 1222, *pg.* 49
Seguin, Dana, Sr Dir-Creative Svcs - Spanx Inc.; *pg.* 32, *pg.* 520
Seguin, Daniele, Dir-Natl Sls-Away from Home Products-Canada-Cascades Tissue Grp - Cascades, Inc.; *pg.* 73, *pg.* 1950
Segura, Gustavo, Dir-Mktg - Prospect Mortgage, LLC; *pg.* 796, *pg.* 278
Sehgal, Anu, Brand Mgr - Colgate-Palmolive Company; *pg.* 504, *pg.* 1215

Sehgal, Cassidy, VP & Counsel-Adv & Digital Media - L'Oreal USA; pg. 514, pg. 1252
Sehm, Sara, Mgr-Comml Mktg - FirstMerit Corporation; pg. 758, pg. 1400
Sehring, Jeff, Sr Mgr-Global Brand Mktg - The Walt Disney Company; pg. 317, pg. 52
Seibald, Ilana, Mgr-Mktg Promos - The Walt Disney Company; pg. 317, pg. 52
Seibert, Harry D., Head-Sls - Mettler-Toledo International Inc.; pg. 1423, pg. 1441
Seidel, Paul, Asst VP-Mktg - Zenith Marketing Group, Inc.; pg. 1224, pg. 1071
Seidelmann, Alan, VP-Sls-Pro Products Div - The Clorox Company; pg. 327, pg. 169
Seideman, Nancy, Assoc VP-Media Rels - Emory University; pg. 601, pg. 504
Seiden, Krista, Mgr-Product Mktg-Analytics & Optimization - Google Inc.; pg. 1249, pg. 153
Seiden, Paul, Dir-Sls - Communications Specialties, Inc.; pg. 377, pg. 1338
Seidensticker, Patrick, Dir-Rugged Mobility Mktg - Dell Inc.; pg. 383, pg. 1737
Seidl, Andrew, Sr Mgr-Relationship - LinkedIn Corporation; pg. 1262, pg. 160
Seidl, Michelle, Sr Mgr-Mktg Res - TD Ameritrade Holding Corporation; pg. 808, pg. 1018
Seidman, Pam, Exec VP-Mktg - Nine West Holdings, Inc.; pg. 1815, pg. 1272
Seidner, Christina, Sr Assoc Brand Mgr-SCOTT - Kimberly-Clark Corporation; pg. 1461, pg. 1720
Seifert, Charles, Sr Product Mgr - Ixia; pg. 422, pg. 56
Seigal, Jennifer, Mgr-Online Mktg - The Men's Wearhouse, Inc.; pg. 44, pg. 1711
Seigler, Chad, VP-Team Mktg Svcs - National Association for Stock Car Auto Racing; pg. 566, pg. 420
Seigler, Peggy, VP-Sls & Mktg - Augusta Metropolitan Convention & Visitors Bureau, Inc.; pg. 989, pg. 524
Seikkula, Luke, Sr Dir-Materials & Logistics - ALLOS THERAPEUTICS, INC.; pg. 1492, pg. 336
Seiler, Judy, Mgr-Database Mktg - CDW Corporation; pg. 370, pg. 663
Seim, Doug, Mgr-Mktg-Specialty Tape Products - 3M Company; pg. 1142, pg. 956
Seim, Stephen, Chief Strategy Officer - Amedisys, Inc.; pg. 1493, pg. 741
Seipert, Curt, Dir-Retail Adv & Mktg - Unified Grocers, Inc.; pg. 1036, pg. 1842
Seiple, Jim, Grp VP-Product Dev-Own Brands - Safeway Inc.; pg. 1032, pg. 184
Seitz, Don, Sr VP-Sls-Worldwide - Author Solutions, Inc.; pg. 1618, pg. 674
Seitz, Katie, VP-Product Strategy & Ops - Tremor Video; pg. 682, pg. 1305
Seitz, Michael, Brand Mgr - The Procter & Gamble Company; pg. 1129, pg. 1418
Seitz, Pat, Dir-Comm & Mktg Svcs - Regal Ware, Inc.; pg. 1137, pg. 1862
Seitzinger, Roger, Sr Dir-ECommerce - National Railroad Passenger Corporation; pg. 1916, pg. 403
Seiwert, Paul, Mgr-Product Dev - Cargill, Inc.; pg. 845, pg. 965
Sejba, Katie, VP-Mktg & Comm - Rochester Philharmonic Orchestra Inc.; pg. 579, pg. 1337
Sekandari, Amina, Sr Mgr-Mktg - MATTEL, INC.; pg. 962, pg. 81
Selby, Darin P., VP-Sls & Mktg - The Kansas City Southern Railway Company; pg. 1913, pg. 985
Selby, David, Dir-Interactive Mktg - Club Car, Inc.; pg. 1830, pg. 532
Selekman, Aryeh, Product Mgr - Facebook, Inc.; pg. 1245, pg. 143
Selestow, Beth, Specialist-Mktg - Gardner Denver Nash; pg. 1338, pg. 381
Seletz, Andrew, Sr Mgr-Creative Svcs - Zoll Medical Corporation; pg. 1612, pg. 814
Selfridge, Katie, Assoc Mgr-Mktg - Constellation Brands, Inc.; pg. 1960, pg. 1348
Selig, Cindy, Mgr-Mktg - Super Sky Products, Inc.; pg. 113, pg. 1871
Selig, Julie, VP-Media - FMR LLC (Fidelity Investments); pg. 759, pg. 794
Seligstein, Rebecca, Sr Specialist-Mktg - FedEx Corporation; pg. 1907, pg. 1642
Selko, Karyn, Sr Mgr-ECommerce Application Dev & Mgmt - Verizon Communications Inc.; pg. 1875, pg. 1309
Sell, Jim, Sr Dir-Mktg-Wholesome Snacks - Kellogg Company; pg. 831, pg. 870
Sell, Kerry, Brand Mgr - Promotion In Motion, Inc.; pg. 1861, pg. 1052
Sell, Robert, CEO-Comm, Media & Tech - Accenture; pg. 1392, pg. 1186
Sellars, John, Asst Gen Mgr-Production - The Metropolitan Opera; pg. 561, pg. 1260
Sellaway, Sheryl, Exec Dir-PR - Verizon Communications Inc.; pg. 1875, pg. 1309
Sellberg, Mike, Chief Product Officer & Exec VP - Workiva; pg. 493, pg. 701
Seller, Jack, Dir-Mktg & PR - PCTEL, Inc.; pg. 452, pg. 557
Sellers, Allyson, VP-Sls Force Comm & Creative Svcs - Mary Kay Inc.; pg. 516, pg. 1657
Sellers, Amy, Mgr-Mktg, Marketplace & Product Mgmt - Amazon.com, Inc.; pg. 1226, pg. 1831
Sellers, Bob, Sr VP-Sls - Power Service Products, Inc.; pg. 983, pg. 1749
Sellers, Kevin, Sr VP-Mktg & Comm - Unilife Corporation; pg. 1603, pg. 1597
Sellers, Lindsay, Asst Brand Mgr-Global Mktg Dev Program - Colgate-Palmolive Company; pg. 504, pg. 1215
Sellin, Derek, Dir-Mktg-Data Center Software - Intel Corporation; pg. 645, pg. 266
Sellman, Karissa, Dir-Donor Comm & Mktg - Sierra Club; pg. 156, pg. 227
Sells, Brian, Dir-Corp Sls, Mktg & Brdcst - Cincinnati Bengals, Inc.; pg. 540, pg. 1410
Sells, Terry, Gen Mgr-Sls - Joe Machens Ford Inc.; pg. 180, pg. 976
Selman, Ashley, Sr Dir-Mktg-Crafts & Imports - MillerCoors LLC; pg. 255, pg. 582
Seltzer, Jeffrey, Sr Mgr-Category Dev - Post Holdings, Inc.; pg. 833, pg. 1002
Selvaggi, Michael, VP-Sls-Intl - Cornell Dubilier Electronics; pg. 630, pg. 1620
Selzer, Ethan, VP-Retail & Reg Adv - The Washington Post; pg. 1701, pg. 407
Selzler, Robert W., VP-Ops-Global Brand Advocacy Mktg - Dassault Systems Enovia; pg. 382, pg. 851
Semel, John, Chief Strategy Officer & Exec VP - John Wiley & Sons, Inc.; pg. 1655, pg. 1073
Semerad, Jason J., Mgr-Mktg-Global - 3M Company; pg. 1142, pg. 956
Seminario, Lourdes, Dir-Mktg & Partnerships - PepsiCo, Inc.; pg. 259, pg. 1327
Seminario, Steve, Sr Dir-Product Mktg-Global - Planar Systems, Inc.; pg. 455, pg. 1495
Semmes, Ben, Exec VP-Sls & Market Strategy - Monotype Imaging Holdings, Inc.; pg. 656, pg. 861
Semsey, Rob, Sr Mgr-Xbox PR - Microsoft Corporation; pg. 435, pg. 1824
Sen, Arnab, Sr Mgr-Digital Analytics & Insights - FMR LLC (Fidelity Investments); pg. 759, pg. 794
Sen, Jerry, Dir-Master Brands, Digital & Shopper Mktg - Maple Leaf Foods Inc.; pg. 875, pg. 1927
Sen, Meena, Brand Mktg Dir-Juices, Snacking & Mixers - Dr Pepper Snapple Group, Inc.; pg. 250, pg. 1729
Sen, Radhika, Sr Mgr-Digital Strategy & Integration - American Express Company; pg. 712, pg. 1190
Sena, Daniel, Head-Strategic Mktg - Interscope Geffen & A&M Records; pg. 293, pg. 274
Sena, Deirdre M., Sr Mgr-PR - Symantec Corporation; pg. 478, pg. 161
Senackerib, Michael, Chief Strategy Officer & Sr VP - Campbell Soup Company; pg. 844, pg. 1048
Senatore, Gabrielle, Mgr-Ford & Lincoln Media Plng - Ford Motor Company; pg. 172, pg. 876
Senci, Scott, Mgr-Sls - Cigna Corporation; pg. 1197, pg. 338
Senderowitz, Katie, Dir-Mktg Comm - Comcast Cable Communications, Inc.; pg. 276, pg. 1560
Sendlak, Colin, Rep-Security Mktg - Anixter International Inc.; pg. 1313, pg. 614
Sendra, Stace, Mgr-Mktg-Bimbo - Bimbo Bakeries USA; pg. 840, pg. 151
Senese, Jodi, CMO - Outfront Media; pg. 1465, pg. 1275
Sengara, Andrea, Dir-Brand Mktg-Tequila - Diageo North America Inc.; pg. 248, pg. 1223
Sengewalt, Stacey, Dir-Mktg - Food Lion, LLC; pg. 1019, pg. 1390
Sengupta, Caesar, VP-Product Mgmt - Google Inc.; pg. 1249, pg. 153
Sengupta, Sagarika, Product Mgr-Google Access - Google Inc.; pg. 1249, pg. 153
Seniff, Liz, Dir-Addressable Media - Travelers Insurance; pg. 1220, pg. 963
Sensback, Karen, Strategist-Mktg - Indianapolis Star; pg. 1652, pg. 687
Senter, Mark, VP-Corp Mktg - Regions Financial Corporation; pg. 798, pg. 4
Sentlowitz, Shari L., Sr Mgr-Education Solutions EBD-Vertical Bus - Sony Corporation of America; pg. 675, pg. 1293
Senzon, Darren, Mgr-Email Mktg Automation-Global - Pitney Bowes Inc.; pg. 454, pg. 376
Seow, Pauline, Reg Dir-Sls - CNBC; pg. 275, pg. 1059
Seppi, Gina, Sr Mgr-Mktg Comm-Neuromodulation - Medtronic, Inc.; pg. 1564, pg. 939
Sepulveda, Nancy, Mgr-Digital Mktg - American Automobile Association; pg. 1190, pg. 429
Serafin, Robert, Sr Dir-Grocery - Rite Aid Corporation; pg. 1590, pg. 1519
Seraphim, Sally, VP-Sls - Anchor Bay Entertainment, Inc.; pg. 270, pg. 910
Serck, Alison, Media Buyer-Digital - Casey's General Stores, Inc.; pg. 1017, pg. 701
Serena, Nicole, Community Mgr-Social Media - Caterpillar, Inc.; pg. 1321, pg. 650
Serey, Rob, Dir-Mktg - WSAZ-TV; pg. 323, pg. 1850
Serfoss, Tama, Sr Mgr-Comm-Contract - Staples, Inc.; pg. 474, pg. 821
Sergent, Doak, Head-Brand Dev & Mktg & Assoc Publr - Conde Nast Publications, Inc.; pg. 1629, pg. 1217
Sergent, Doak, Assoc Publr & Head-Brand Dev & Mktg - Vogue Magazine; pg. 1700, pg. 1311
Sergot, Mark, Sr VP-Sls Org-Global - Fairmont Hotels & Resorts Inc.; pg. 1091, pg. 1938
Serianni, Deborah Hsu, Sr VP & Grp Head-Global Consumer Mktg - MasterCard International, Inc.; pg. 780, pg. 1326
Serina, Janice, Assoc Mgr-Brand Mktg & Demand Plng-Mark - Avon Products, Inc.; pg. 500, pg. 1198
Serino, Joe, VP-Mdsg-North America - NIKE, Inc.; pg. 1812, pg. 1492
Serio, Joe, Sr Mgr-Mktg - Abbott Laboratories; pg. 1484, pg. 551
Serkhoshian, Stephanie B., Head-Comm & PR - General Electric Company; pg. 1297, pg. 347
Serko, Jefferey, VP-Sls-Retail Grp - The Page Seed Co.; pg. 1798, pg. 1163
Serkosky, Michael, Project Mgr-Digital & Social Media - Dal-Tile Corporation; pg. 78, pg. 1678
Serna, Gaelle, Sr Mgr-Mktg - AT&T Mobility LLC; pg. 620, pg. 1152
Serna, Olga, Sr Mgr-Mktg - AT&T Communications Corp.; pg. 1866, pg. 1043
Serota, Alison, Dir-Mktg & Events - Ben & Jerry's Homemade, Inc.; pg. 1850, pg. 1767
Seroussi, Marina, Brand Mgr-Gerber - Gerber Life Insurance Company; pg. 1201, pg. 1352
Seroussi, Marina, Brand Mgr-Gerber - Nestle USA - Beverage Division, Inc.; pg. 883, pg. 96
Seroussi, Marina, Brand Mgr-Gerber - Nestle USA, Inc.; pg. 883, pg. 96
Seroussi, Marina, Brand Mgr-Gerber - Unilever United States, Inc.; pg. 904, pg. 1061
Seroy, Jeff, Sr VP-Publicity & Mktg - Farrar, Straus & Giroux, Inc.; pg. 1640, pg. 1231
Serra, Michelle, Mgr-Social Media - The Atlanta Journal-Constitution; pg. 1618, pg. 490
Serra, Reinier, Sr Bus Mgr-Cloud Platform & Engr-Portal Sls-LATAM - Citrix Systems, Inc.; pg. 375, pg. 424
Serrano, Alvaro, Product Mgr - Goya Foods, Inc.; pg. 859, pg. 1075
Serrano, Claudia E., Mgr-Mktg Dev - Intel Corporation; pg. 645, pg. 266
Serrano, Jennifer, Coord-Mktg & Promos - Univision Communications Inc.; pg. 683, pg. 1307
Serrano, John, Sr Mgr-CRM & Loyalty Mktg-Retail North America - Tommy Hilfiger USA; pg. 48, pg. 1302
Serrano, Marc, Sr Mgr-ECommerce Content - Office Depot, Inc.; pg. 448, pg. 412
Serrano, Monique, Assoc Mgr-Sls & Mktg Ops-Intl - Constellation Brands, Inc.; pg. 1960, pg. 1348
Serrault, Jayson, VP-Omni Channel Mktg & Analytics - Batteries Plus Bulbs LLC; pg. 360, pg. 1860
Serridge, Ben, Sr Product Mgr - Google Inc.; pg. 1249, pg. 153
Serughetti, Marc, Dir-Product Mktg & Bus Dev - Synopsys, Inc.; pg. 480, pg. 162
Serure, Lori, Sr Mgr-Interactive Mktg & Comm - Citrix Systems,

Inc.; pg. 375, pg. 424
Servello, Vinnie, Reg VP-Sls & Ops - Staples, Inc.; pg. 474, pg. 821
Servetah, Eric, Specialist-Sls, Mktg & Data Integration - The Dun & Bradstreet Corp.; pg. 1637, pg. 1120
Service, Alecia, Sr Mgr-SMB Loyalty - American Airlines Inc.; pg. 1898, pg. 1693
Sery, Lisa, Project Mgr-Mktg - Medifast, Inc.; pg. 1562, pg. 774
Seshadri, Simon, VP-Mktg-North America - The Cooper Companies, Inc.; pg. 1518, pg. 183
Sesona, Karen W., Sr Mgr-Mktg Automation - Tyler Technologies, Inc.; pg. 486, pg. 1690
Sessler, Leigh, Sr Mgr-Mdse Mktg - Lord & Taylor LLC; pg. 1777, pg. 1252
Sestito, Sandro, Mgr-Sls - Ingram Micro Inc.; pg. 415, pg. 261
Sestrick, Linda, Dir-Digital Mktg - HSN, Inc.; pg. 291, pg. 462
Setchell, Jenna, Brand Mgr-Identity Design - The Procter & Gamble Company; pg. 1129, pg. 1418
Setford, Alida, Dir-Adv & Promo - John Wiley & Sons, Inc.; pg. 1655, pg. 1073
Seth, Danielle, Sr Dir-Mktg Res & Plng - Comcast Cable Communications, Inc.; pg. 276, pg. 1560
Seth, Kiernan A., Exec Dir-Mktg - Lexicon Pharmaceuticals, Inc.; pg. 1555, pg. 1747
Sethi, Arjun, Sr Dir-Product Mgmt, Growth & Emerging Products - Yahoo! Inc.; pg. 1289, pg. 289
Sethi, Jay, Dir-Mktg-Covergirl & P&G Beauty Digital & Media Innovation - Cover Girl Cosmetics; pg. 506, pg. 772
Sethi, Jay, Assoc Dir-Mktg-COVERGIRL, P&G Beauty Digital & Media Innovation - The Procter & Gamble Company; pg. 1129, pg. 1418
Sethi, Puneet, Dir-Bus Dev & Product Mgmt - QUALCOMM Incorporated; pg. 1873, pg. 207
Sethi, Rakesh B., Head-Tech & Product Plng-System LSI Grp - Toshiba America, Inc.; pg. 681, pg. 1302
Sethi, Sonia, Assoc Dir-Mktg-Optic White Toothpaste & Mouthwash - Colgate-Palmolive Company; pg. 504, pg. 1215
Sethiadi, Ricky, Assoc Dir-Creative - DIRECTV Group Holdings, LLC; pg. 281, pg. 79
Seti, Bryan, Mgr-Mktg-Natl - Yamaha Motor Corporation USA; pg. 1713, pg. 76
Setlak, Dan, VP-Mktg - Tempur Sealy International, Inc.; pg. 944, pg. 731
Seto, Mike, Mgr-Mktg Client Svcs - Ingram Micro Inc.; pg. 415, pg. 261
Seto, Patti, Sr Dir-Strategic Mktg - Applied Materials, Inc.; pg. 618, pg. 264
Setoodeh, Mozhgan, Dir-Off-Air Mktg & Promos - NBC Universal, Inc.; pg. 300, pg. 1266
Setoodeh, Mozhgan, Dir-Off-Air Mktg & Promos - Syfy; pg. 311, pg. 1297
Setti, Luca, CMO & Chief Sls Officer - Florida Tile Industries, Inc.; pg. 82, pg. 730
Settimi, Joe, VP-Products, Pricing & Innovation - United States Cellular Corporation; pg. 1875, pg. 594
Settle, Wade, Assoc Mgr-Field Mktg-PRO Div - The Timberland Company; pg. 1821, pg. 1039
Setzer, Meghan, Dir-Product Mktg - The Ultimate Software Group, Inc.; pg. 486, pg. 479
Setzko, Karen, Dir-Mktg - Massachusetts Mutual Life Insurance Company; pg. 1207, pg. 845
Seuferling, Pam, Sr Dir-Mktg - NPC International, Inc.; pg. 1742, pg. 719
Seurkamp, Aaron, Sr VP-Life Sls - Protective Life Insurance Company; pg. 1215, pg. 4
Sevegrand, Isabelle, Sr Dir-Global Mktg & Comm-Gas - Itron Inc.; pg. 422, pg. 1822
Severance, Susan, Dir-Adv - AARP; pg. 124, pg. 393
Severin, Terri, Dir-Mktg - Anthem, Inc.; pg. 1192, pg. 683
Severson, Darci, Sr Mgr-Mktg - Tyson Foods, Inc.; pg. 902, pg. 35
Sevilla, Kristine, Sr Mgr-Mktg - Verizon Communications Inc.; pg. 1875, pg. 1309
Sewall, Martha, VP-Clinical Mktg & Scientific Affairs - Smiths Medical MD, Inc.; pg. 1594, pg. 963
Sewalson, Jeff, Mgr-Sls - United Continental Holdings, Inc.; pg. 1927, pg. 593
Seward, Eric, Mgr-Comml Mktg - PODS Enterprises, Inc.; pg. 1919, pg. 416
Seward, Phil, Sr VP-Relationship & Loyalty Mktg - Live Nation Entertainment, Inc.; pg. 558, pg. 47
Seward, Ricky, VP-Sls - Milwaukee Valve Company, Inc.; pg. 1361, pg. 1884
Sexsmith, Bill, VP-Sls-Canada Safeway Ltd - Safeway Inc.; pg. 1032, pg. 184
Sexton, Beth, Sr Dir-Comml Ops-Global - Eli Lilly and Company; pg. 1527, pg. 684
Sexton, Mike, VP-Product Mgmt & Mktg-B2B & Alliance - Targus Group International, Inc.; pg. 482, pg. 43
Sexton, Tanya, Sr Brand Mgr-Mktg - Bandai America Incorporated; pg. 950, pg. 75
Sexton, Tara, Brand Mgr - Dunkin' Brands Group, Inc.; pg. 1727, pg. 810
Seybert, Doug, Sr VP-Mktg - Discovery Communications, Inc.; pg. 282, pg. 777
Seybold, Patrick, VP-Global Comm & Mktg Partnerships - Tapjoy, Inc.; pg. 1396, pg. 228
Seydel, Dennis, Sr Dir-Global Entertainment Mktg - NIKE, Inc.; pg. 1812, pg. 1492
Seykora, Robyn, Mgr-Global Mktg Comm & Channel Mktg - Honeywell International Inc.; pg. 407, pg. 1088
Seyler, Tasha, Product Mgr - BB&T Corporation; pg. 723, pg. 1393
Seymer, Fabian, Product Mgr - Belden, Inc.; pg. 624, pg. 993
Seymour, Dan, Dir-North American Retail & Shopper Mktg - Dell Inc.; pg. 383, pg. 1737
Seymour, Heather, Assoc Dir-Mktg Res & Strategic Analysis - Salix Pharmaceuticals, Inc.; pg. 1591, pg. 1388
Seymour, Kimo, Sr VP-Media & Events - Life Time Fitness, Inc.; pg. 1556, pg. 920
Seymour, Laura, Mgr-Digital Mktg - The Vermont Teddy Bear Company; pg. 969, pg. 1767
Seymour, Luanne, Sr Mgr-Design - Adobe Systems Incorporated; pg. 342, pg. 235
Seymus, Ingrid, Sr Dir-Mktg-Epilepsy - LivaNova; pg. 1557, pg. 1710
Seys, Debora, Sr Product Mgr - eBay Inc.; pg. 1240, pg. 243
Shaby, David, Sr VP-Consumer Mktg - Bright Horizons Family Solutions Inc.; pg. 598, pg. 855
Shackleton, Lane, Sr Product Mgr - YouTube, LLC; pg. 1291, pg. 198
Shade, Michael, VP-Digital Sls & Mktg - BB&T Corporation; pg. 723, pg. 1393
Shadle, Joel T., Dir-PR - Comcast Corporation; pg. 276, pg. 1560
Shadle, Rick, Dir-Creative Svcs - Shop-Vac Corporation; pg. 1375, pg. 1595
Shadley, Scott, Sr Mgr-Product Line-Data Center Storage Products - Micron Technology, Inc.; pg. 435, pg. 547
Shadroui, George, Chief Strategy Officer - St. Jude Children's Research Hospital; pg. 1596, pg. 1646
Shaev, Hilary, VP-Mktg - National Basketball Association; pg. 566, pg. 1264
Shafer, Brandon, Mgr-Mktg-North America - General Electric Company; pg. 1297, pg. 347
Shafer, Brian, Mgr-Mktg - 3M Company; pg. 1142, pg. 956
Shafer, Holly Hart, Mgr-Comm, Brand & Consumer PR-Global - Starbucks Corporation; pg. 897, pg. 1840
Shafer, Kristi, Dir-Mktg - American Licorice Co. Inc.; pg. 1850, pg. 692
Shafer, Rich, VP-Sports Mktg - Web.com, Inc.; pg. 1288, pg. 524
Shaffer, Chris, Exec Dir-Digital Mktg - Cox Communications, Inc.; pg. 279, pg. 501
Shaffer, Jennifer, Mgr-Channel Mktg - Kimberly-Clark Corporation; pg. 1461, pg. 1720
Shaffer, Jennifer, Mgr-Corp Consumer Mktg - Mary Kay Inc.; pg. 516, pg. 1657
Shaffer, Jennifer, Mgr-Corp Consumer Mktg - Mary Kay Inc.; pg. 516, pg. 1657
Shaffer, Karen, Sr Dir-Mktg & Customer Relationship Mgmt - Rent-A-Center, Inc.; pg. 940, pg. 1734
Shaffer, Megan E., Mgr-PR - The Hershey Co.; pg. 1855, pg. 1538
Shaffer, Randy, Dir-Sls-West Reg - Microsoft Corporation; pg. 435, pg. 1824
Shaffer, Tiffany, Sr Mgr-Natl Clients & Svcs - Grant Thornton International Ltd.; pg. 763, pg. 575
Shaffer, Tina, Mgr-Mktg-Land & Sea - Sabre Holdings Corporation; pg. 1922, pg. 1745
Shafran, Gil, Sr Dir-Product Dev - F5 Networks, Inc.; pg. 396, pg. 1835
Shah, Amee, Brand Mgr-Creative - Motorola Mobility LLC; pg. 657, pg. 627
Shah, Amit, Sr VP-Online Mktg, Mobile & Social Media - 1-800-Flowers.com, Inc.; pg. 1758, pg. 1151
Shah, Amy, Sr VP-Mktg & Comm - TE Connectivity Ltd.; pg. 677, pg. 1515
Shah, Anuja, Specialist-Inside Sls-Sys & Tech Grp-Cross Brand - IBM Canada Limited; pg. 411, pg. 1923
Shah, Atish, Dir-Product Mgmt-Cloud Svcs - Cisco Systems, Inc.; pg. 372, pg. 240
Shah, Atish, Interim CFO & Sr VP - Hyatt Hotels Corporation; pg. 1096, pg. 577
Shah, Bhavya, Head-Brand Mktg-India - BSH Home Appliances Corporation; pg. 53, pg. 108
Shah, Bimal, Sr Product Mgr - Siemens Canada Ltd.; pg. 1306, pg. 1921
Shah, Bindu, VP-Digital Mktg - Sephora USA Inc; pg. 522, pg. 227
Shah, Gopal, Mgr-Product Mktg - Google Inc.; pg. 1249, pg. 153
Shah, Harshal, Sr Specialist-Mktg - FedEx Corporation; pg. 1907, pg. 1642
Shah, Kavita, Mgr-Mktg-Global Innovation - Godiva Chocolatier, Inc.; pg. 1854, pg. 1235
Shah, Keyur, Brand Mgr-Global - Disney Interactive Media Group; pg. 1239, pg. 95
Shah, Laura, Coord-Mktg-Global - Novartis Corporation; pg. 1574, pg. 1273
Shah, Mihir, Sr Mgr-Mktg - DISH Network Corporation; pg. 283, pg. 325
Shah, Neil, Sr Product Mgr-Unified Storage Platform - Hitachi Data Systems Corporation; pg. 407, pg. 265
Shah, Nilay, Dir-Digital & Social Media Strategy - The New York Giants; pg. 570, pg. 1055
Shah, Nirav, Sr Mgr-Demand Generation-NASD - Bio-Rad Laboratories, Inc.; pg. 1504, pg. 101
Shah, Nisarg, Mgr-Product Mgmt, Cloud Networking & Svcs Grp - Cisco Systems, Inc.; pg. 372, pg. 240
Shah, Nishit, Product Mgr-Google Security - Google Inc.; pg. 1249, pg. 153
Shah, Pallavi, Head-IP Sls - Hewlett-Packard Company; pg. 404, pg. 175
Shah, Pareen, Dir-Mktg-Tomatoes & Broth - Del Monte Foods, Inc.; pg. 852, pg. 304
Shah, Priti, VP-Leadership Product Strategy & Corp Dev - SkillSoft plc; pg. 470, pg. 1037
Shah, Raunaq, Product Mgr - Google Inc.; pg. 1249, pg. 153
Shah, Reshma, Brand Mgr-Innovation - PepsiCo, Inc.; pg. 259, pg. 1327
Shah, Smiti, Mgr-Worldwide Product Mktg-Enterprise Grp - Hewlett-Packard Company; pg. 404, pg. 175
Shah, Sweta, Mgr-Online Mktg - The Home Depot, Inc.; pg. 1050, pg. 510
Shah, Tapan D., Dir-Mktg & Product Mgmt - Cardinal Health, Inc.; pg. 1512, pg. 1448
Shah, Umang, Dir-Digital Mktg & Innovation-Global - Campbell Soup Company; pg. 844, pg. 1048
Shah, Vishal, VP-Digital Media Bus Dev - National Football League; pg. 567, pg. 1264
Shah, Yash, Sr VP-Product Mgmt - CA Technologies; pg. 366, pg. 1168
Shah-Mehta, Shilpa, Sr Dir-NET Mktg - Novartis Pharmaceuticals Corp.; pg. 1575, pg. 1054
Shahani, Vinay R., VP-Mktg - Volkswagen Group of America, Inc.; pg. 194, pg. 1785
Shaheen, Bill, Exec VP-Sls-Worldwide - SumTotal Systems, Inc.; pg. 477, pg. 429
Shaheen, Lou, VP-Sls & Mktg - Trans Ocean Products Inc.; pg. 901, pg. 1818
Shaifer, Brian, Dir-Mktg-Whisky - Bacardi USA, Inc.; pg. 1956, pg. 417
Shaikh, Aleem, Reg Mgr-Sls - Adams Rite Aerospace Inc.; pg. 1041, pg. 93
Shaikh, Nishat, Sr Mgr-IT - Capella Education Company; pg. 599, pg. 931
Shain, Ben, Dir-Logistics & Sr Mgr-NA Parts Transportation - Nissan North America, Inc.; pg. 186, pg. 1633
Shainock, Julie, Head-Worldwide T&T Indus Solutions Sls - IBM; pg. 410, pg. 1449
Shakarchi, Richard, Mng Dir-Mktg Performance & Measurement - TD Ameritrade Holding Corporation; pg. 808, pg. 1018
Shakeshaft, Brent, VP-Global Mktg Dove Cleansing - Unilever United States, Inc.; pg. 904, pg. 1061
Shakespeare, Justin, Head-Mktg-Global & Exec Dir - Amgen Inc.; pg. 1493, pg. 291
Shakked, Orr, Sr Dir-Global Traffic Acq - TripAdvisor, Inc.; pg. 1926, pg. 835
Shakoske, Karen, Sr VP & Head-Mktg & Corp Comm - Janney Montgomery Scott LLC; pg. 772, pg. 1566
Shalit, Steven, VP-Adv Products & Plng - The New York Times

Company; *pg.* 1668, *pg.* 1270
Shalley, Gabe, Sr Mgr-Airline Mktg & Sls - Vail Resorts, Inc.; *pg.* 1117, *pg.* 313
Shallow, Kurt, VP-Risk Product Distr - The Guardian Life Insurance Company of America; *pg.* 1202, *pg.* 1237
Shaltry, Mindy, Brand Mgr-Savory Innovation - Mondelez International, Inc.; *pg.* 878, *pg.* 601
Shamblott, Jay, VP-Adv Sls - Fox Sports Net; *pg.* 288, *pg.* 131
Shames, Irina, Sls Dir-North America - Turner Broadcasting System, Inc.; *pg.* 314, *pg.* 521
Shamis, Natasha, Head-Product-Global - Liquidnet Holdings, Inc.; *pg.* 776, *pg.* 1251
Shamitko, Courtney Clements, Dir-Global Media-Disney Destinations - The Walt Disney Company; *pg.* 317, *pg.* 52
Shamo, Darrin, Dir-Direct & Online Mktg - Zappos.com, Inc.; *pg.* 1291, *pg.* 1030
Shampeny, Renelle, Dir-Mktg - SUNY Empire State College; *pg.* 608, *pg.* 1340
Shamroth, Lori, Mgr-Mktg Comm - Liberty Mutual Insurance Group Inc.; *pg.* 1205, *pg.* 797
Shamshoian, Jennifer, Brand Mgr-Gaming-Global - Hasbro, Inc.; *pg.* 954, *pg.* 1603
Shamshoian, Peter, Sr Dir-Bus Dev - KLA-Tencor Corporation; *pg.* 1353, *pg.* 146
Shamus, Amy, Planner-Mktg Events - Google Inc.; *pg.* 1249, *pg.* 153
Shan, Carol, Mgr-Mktg-Asia Pacific & Latin America - Plantronics, Inc.; *pg.* 663, *pg.* 270
Shanahan, Cynthia, Sr Mgr-Mktg Comm - ASPEN TECHNOLOGY, INC.; *pg.* 354, *pg.* 804
Shanahan, Rory, Head-Mktg & B2B Social Products-Interactive - Scientific Games Corporation; *pg.* 468, *pg.* 1029
Shanaman, Brett, VP-Mktg - AutoZone, Inc.; *pg.* 200, *pg.* 1641
Shanas, Gary, VP-Media Strategy - ABC, Inc.; *pg.* 268, *pg.* 1185
Shandera, Rebecca, Mgr-Social Media & Internet Mktg - School Specialty, Inc.; *pg.* 467, *pg.* 1860
Shane, Shari, Sr Dir-Comm - Ascension Health Alliance; *pg.* 1496, *pg.* 992
Shaner, Bill, Mng Dir-Mktg & Media Solutions - Meredith Corporation; *pg.* 1663, *pg.* 705
Shanes, Robert, VP-Sls - Talk-A-Phone Co.; *pg.* 481, *pg.* 638
Shang, Sarah, Sr Mgr-Svc Segment Mktg - Hewlett-Packard Company; *pg.* 404, *pg.* 175
Shang, Sheila, Sr Mgr-Mktg & Comm - Microsoft Corporation; *pg.* 435, *pg.* 1824
Shank, Amanda, Sr Mgr-Licensing & Bus Dev - National Football League Players Incorporated; *pg.* 149, *pg.* 401
Shank, Ben, Mgr-Community Mktg - Dick's Sporting Goods, Inc.; *pg.* 1832, *pg.* 1524
Shank, Nancy, Sr Mgr-Enterprise Relationship - CenturyLink, Inc.; *pg.* 1870, *pg.* 746
Shank, Sarah, Sr Mgr-Comm - Truth Initiative; *pg.* 158, *pg.* 405
Shankar, Vijay, Product Mgr-Facebook Lite - Facebook, Inc.; *pg.* 1245, *pg.* 143
Shanks, David, Dir-Digital Mktg - Palm Springs Desert Resorts Convention & Visitors Authority; *pg.* 1003, *pg.* 187
Shanks, Ron, Product Mgr - Cisco Systems, Inc.; *pg.* 372, *pg.* 240
Shanley, Joe, Acct Exec-Intl & Domestic Sls - Diamond Comic Distributors, Inc.; *pg.* 1635, *pg.* 772
Shannon, Alara, Specialist-Internet Mktg - icruise.com corp.; *pg.* 1258, *pg.* 421
Shannon, Chelsea, Mgr-Mktg - Bloomingdale's, Inc.; *pg.* 1763, *pg.* 1204
Shannon, Jennifer, Mgr-Mktg Ops - DSW, Inc.; *pg.* 1807, *pg.* 1439
Shannon, Joslin, Mgr-Mktg & Fin Svcs - Best Buy Co., Inc.; *pg.* 1761, *pg.* 954
Shannon, Katherine, Mgr-Cross-Brand Mktg-HCP & Sls - Takeda Pharmaceuticals USA, Inc.; *pg.* 1600, *pg.* 605
Shannon, Liam, Exec Creative Dir - VistaPrint USA, Incorporated; *pg.* 1700, *pg.* 829
Shannon, Paula, Chief Sls Officer & Sr VP - Lionbridge Technologies Inc.; *pg.* 428, *pg.* 851
Shannon, Stephanie, Sr Mgr-Mktg - PepsiCo, Inc.; *pg.* 259, *pg.* 1327
Shanti, Marcy, Sr Mgr-Integrated Mktg Comm - McKesson Corporation; *pg.* 1560, *pg.* 222
Shantiyai, Saman, Mgr-Retail Mktg - Hyundai Motor America; *pg.* 179, *pg.* 89
Shantz, Michael, Brand Mgr - The WhiteWave Foods Company; *pg.* 1037, *pg.* 324
Shao, Min, VP-Analytics, Advertising & Data & Head-Trust & Safety - Yahoo! Inc.; *pg.* 1289, *pg.* 289
Shao, Xuhui, VP-Engrg, Adv & Data - Yahoo! Inc.; *pg.* 1289, *pg.* 289
Shap, John, Exec VP-Sls-Worldwide - Keynote Systems Incorporated; *pg.* 425, *pg.* 255
Shapero, Daniel, Grp Product Mgr-LinkedIn Careers - LinkedIn Corporation; *pg.* 1262, *pg.* 160
Shapira, Harel, Brand Mgr - Natrol, Inc.; *pg.* 1570, *pg.* 64
Shapiro, Aaron, Head-West Coast Digital Sls - TV Guide Magazine Group, Inc.; *pg.* 1697, *pg.* 1305
Shapiro, Alexandra, Sr Dir-Merchant Mktg & Partner Dev - PayPal Inc.; *pg.* 1274, *pg.* 248
Shapiro, Alexandra, Exec VP-Mktg & Digital - USA Networks; *pg.* 315, *pg.* 1308
Shapiro, Danny, Sr Dir-Automotive - NVIDIA Corporation; *pg.* 447, *pg.* 268
Shapiro, Dmitry, Grp Product Mgr - Google Inc.; *pg.* 1249, *pg.* 153
Shapiro, Doug, Chief Strategy Officer & Exec VP - Turner Broadcasting System, Inc.; *pg.* 314, *pg.* 521
Shapiro, Elizabeth A., Coord-Digital Mktg-Southeast - CB Richard Ellis, Inc.; *pg.* 1085, *pg.* 1210
Shapiro, John, Grp Product Mgr-QuickBooks Online - Intuit Inc.; *pg.* 769, *pg.* 158
Shapiro, Kevin, Assoc Dir-Mktg-Mitchum & Almay - Revlon, Inc.; *pg.* 521, *pg.* 1286
Shapiro, Lauren, Mgr-Adv - The Vanguard Group, Inc.; *pg.* 816, *pg.* 1550
Shapiro, Lori, Asst Mgr-Mktg - Breast Cancer Research Foundation; *pg.* 134, *pg.* 1206
Shapiro, Melissa, Mgr-Mktg-Leisure-Americas Reg - Air New Zealand Ltd. (U.S.A.); *pg.* 1897, *pg.* 78
Shapiro, Rachel, Dir-Mktg - Complex Media, Inc.; *pg.* 1628, *pg.* 1217
Shapiro, Risa, Sr Mgr-Mktg-PepsiCo Shopper Mktg-Target Team - PepsiCo, Inc.; *pg.* 259, *pg.* 1327
Shapiro, Scott, Counsel-Comml & Product - eBay Inc.; *pg.* 1240, *pg.* 243
Shapiro, Scott, Mgr-Product Mktg - Facebook, Inc.; *pg.* 1245, *pg.* 143
Shapiro, Stacy, Assoc Publr-Mktg-Meredith Special Interest Media - Meredith Corporation; *pg.* 1663, *pg.* 705
Shapiro, Susan, Brand Mktg Mgr-Pro Segments - Benjamin Moore & Co.; *pg.* 1440, *pg.* 1085
Shapiro, Terri J., Exec Dir-Brand & Media Rels - Deluxe Corporation; *pg.* 1634, *pg.* 964
Shapiro, Will, Sr Mgr-Sponsorship - Liberty Mutual Insurance Group Inc.; *pg.* 1205, *pg.* 797
Shaps, Simon, Mng Dir-Intl Content & Production - Core Media Group; *pg.* 1765, *pg.* 1218
Sharaf, Justin, Dir-Customer Mktg - LOGMEIN, INC.; *pg.* 428, *pg.* 861
Sharan, Amit, Head-Mktg - LiveRail; *pg.* 1264, *pg.* 145
Sharan, Nimesh, Sr Product Mgr - GE Energy; *pg.* 1338, *pg.* 506
Share, Hugh, Sr Dir-Beer & Better World-Global - Anheuser-Busch Companies, LLC; *pg.* 237, *pg.* 991
Sharek, Sarah, Mgr-Mktg-Integrated Mktg - Citrix Systems, Inc.; *pg.* 375, *pg.* 424
Sharif, Liya, Sr Dir-Mktg & Comm-Global - QUALCOMM Incorporated; *pg.* 1873, *pg.* 207
Sharipo, Josh, VP-Mktg - Promotion In Motion, Inc.; *pg.* 1861, *pg.* 1052
Sharkey, Malcolm, Sr Product Mgr - Bentley Systems, Inc.; *pg.* 361, *pg.* 1531
Sharkey, Stacy, Mgr-Media Adv - Nestle USA, Inc.; *pg.* 883, *pg.* 96
Sharma, Anu, Sr Mgr-Sls & Mktg-Worldwide Territories - Simulations Plus, Inc.; *pg.* 470, *pg.* 121
Sharma, Arvind, Sr Planner-Product - Microsoft Corporation; *pg.* 435, *pg.* 1824
Sharma, Dilli, Sr Mgr-Product, Digital & Entertainment - Dolby Laboratories, Inc.; *pg.* 284, *pg.* 217
Sharma, Dinesh, VP-Mktg-Internet of Things - SAP; *pg.* 465, *pg.* 78
Sharma, Mala, VP-Creative Pro, Education Bus & GTM - Adobe Systems Incorporated; *pg.* 342, *pg.* 235
Sharma, Naina, Assoc Mgr-Online Mktg-Consumer Mktg Dev & Ops - Penguin Random House; *pg.* 1675, *pg.* 1276
Sharma, Prnuv, Brand Mgr - Abbott Nutrition; *pg.* 1485, *pg.* 1437
Sharma, Vikas, Head-Product Mktg-Americas - NCR Corporation; *pg.* 443, *pg.* 531
Sharman, Daria, Exec Dir-Enterprise Strategy & Mktg - United Services Automobile Association; *pg.* 1221, *pg.* 1743
Sharoni, Erez, Mgr-Sls-Eastern Reg - Talk-A-Phone Co.; *pg.* 481, *pg.* 638
Sharp, Bryant, Gen Mgr-Sls - John Eagle Honda of Houston; *pg.* 180, *pg.* 1709
Sharp, Kevin, Mgr-Bus Dev & Third Party Sls - GlaxoSmithKline; *pg.* 1536, *pg.* 1565
Sharp, Laurie, Sr Dir-Experiential Mktg - Dolby Laboratories, Inc.; *pg.* 284, *pg.* 217
Sharp, Leslie, Dir-Mktg - Level 3 Communications, Inc.; *pg.* 1262, *pg.* 312
Sharp, Michael, Sr VP & Dir-Sls - Nielsen Audio; *pg.* 446, *pg.* 768
Sharp, Phil, Product Mgr-Inbox - Google Inc.; *pg.* 1249, *pg.* 153
Sharp, Randy, Sr Reg Mgr-Mktg - GlaxoSmithKline; *pg.* 1536, *pg.* 1565
Sharp, Richard, Mng Dir-Media & Mobile UK, DE & MENA - Conversant, Inc.; *pg.* 1393, *pg.* 306
Sharp, Sarah, VP-Mktg - Hibbett Sports, Inc.; *pg.* 1836, *pg.* 3
Sharp, Todd R., Dir-Mktg-Integrated Customer Experience - GlaxoSmithKline; *pg.* 1536, *pg.* 1565
Sharpe, Pippa, Brand Mgr-Global Nike SB - NIKE, Inc.; *pg.* 1812, *pg.* 1492
Sharpe, Sabrina, Grp Mgr-Mktg - GlaxoSmithKline; *pg.* 1536, *pg.* 1389
Sharpe, Steve, Sr Mgr-PR - Intuit Inc.; *pg.* 769, *pg.* 158
Sharrock, Todd, VP-PR - Columbus Blue Jackets; *pg.* 542, *pg.* 1439
Sharron-Albright, Kristen, Head-Mktg - Noven Pharmaceuticals, Inc.; *pg.* 1576, *pg.* 445
Shasha, Danuta, Sr VP-Media & Sponsorships - FMR LLC (Fidelity Investments); *pg.* 759, *pg.* 794
Shashaty, Tara, Mgr-Mktg-Integrated Digital & Video - MARTHA STEWART LIVING OMNIMEDIA, INC.; *pg.* 1661, *pg.* 1256
Shaskey-Platek, Holly, Sr VP-Mdsg & Global Sourcing - Family Dollar Stores, Inc.; *pg.* 1768, *pg.* 1382
Shatara, Chris, Mgr-Global Mktg Data - NetApp, Inc.; *pg.* 444, *pg.* 287
Shattan, Emily, Brand Mgr-W Hotels Worldwide-Global - Starwood Hotels & Resorts Worldwide, Inc.; *pg.* 1114, *pg.* 378
Shattuck, Steve, Dir-PR - Western Digital Corporation; *pg.* 492, *pg.* 118
Shatzen, Hannah, Mgr-Channel Mktg - NetApp, Inc.; *pg.* 444, *pg.* 287
Shaub, Linda, Sr VP-Mktg & Brand - Interim Healthcare Inc.; *pg.* 417, *pg.* 469
Shaud, Jim, Sr Dir-Mktg & Strategic Partnerships - Comcast Corporation; *pg.* 276, *pg.* 1560
Shaughnessy, Diane, Specialist-Mktg Comm - Setra Systems, Inc.; *pg.* 1428, *pg.* 802
Shaughnessy, Timothy S., Mgr-Worldwide Mktg-Networking - Lenovo Group Ltd; *pg.* 427, *pg.* 1384
Shaukat, Haseeb, Head-Mktg & Comm-Pakistan - Microsoft Corporation; *pg.* 435, *pg.* 1824
Shaukat, Tariq M., CMO & Exec VP - Caesars Entertainment Corporation; *pg.* 1083, *pg.* 1023
Shaults, Donna, Dir-Comm & PR - DeVry Education Group Inc.; *pg.* 600, *pg.* 607
Shave, David, VP-Sls-Global - TurboChef Technologies, Inc.; *pg.* 902, *pg.* 1670
Shaver, Teracia, Specialist-Adv - SpartanNash Co; *pg.* 1034, *pg.* 889
Shavey, Heather, Asst Gen Mgr-Mdse-Fresh Foods-Produce Global - Costco Wholesale Corporation; *pg.* 1765, *pg.* 1820
Shaw, Amanda, Dir-Mktg & Production - CBS Broadcasting Inc.; *pg.* 273, *pg.* 1210
Shaw, Antwaunn, Analyst-Mktg Budget - Lenovo Group Ltd; *pg.* 427, *pg.* 1384
Shaw, Bianca, Brand Mgr - Capital One Financial Corporation; *pg.* 730, *pg.* 1789
Shaw, Christine, Sr VP-Comm & Mktg - FremantleMedia North America Inc.; *pg.* 288, *pg.* 1233
Shaw, Cindy, Sr Dir-HR - Comcast Corporation; *pg.* 276, *pg.* 1560
Shaw, Greg S., Dir-Product & Market Dev - Swagelok Company; *pg.* 1064, *pg.* 1473
Shaw, GW, VP-U-Verse & Video Product Mktg - AT&T Communications Corp.; *pg.* 1866, *pg.* 1043
Shaw, GW, VP-U-Verse & Video Product Mktg - AT&T Inc.;

First page reference indicates Business Class Edition
Second page reference indicates Geographic Edition

pg. 1867, pg. 1674
Shaw, Hilary, Brand Mgr - Electronic Arts Inc.; pg. 951, pg. 189
Shaw, Jeff, Exec VP-Store Ops & Sls - O'Reilly Automotive, Inc.; pg. 214, pg. 1006
Shaw, Jeffrey, Dir-Mktg - Trade Commission of Spain; pg. 158, pg. 1304
Shaw, Jennifer, Analyst-Mktg Res-Brand Strategy & Comm - John Hancock Financial Services; pg. 1205, pg. 796
Shaw, Jenny, VP & Mgr-Mktg-Affinity Direct Mail - Bank of America Corporation; pg. 718, pg. 1362
Shaw, Jon, Mgr-Digital Mktg-Sports Style - adidas America Inc.; pg. 1803, pg. 1500
Shaw, Jon, Dir-Mktg Comm-Global - Carrier Corporation; pg. 1070, pg. 349
Shaw, Jon, Sr Mgr-Video Ops - Yahoo! Inc.; pg. 1289, pg. 289
Shaw, Katina, Sr Dir-Community Rels & Family Liaison - Milwaukee Brewers Baseball Club, Inc.; pg. 562, pg. 1878
Shaw, Kristi, Sr Mgr-Mdsg & Creative Svcs - Checkers Drive-In Restaurants, Inc.; pg. 1017, pg. 472
Shaw, Kurt, VP-Franchise Sls - The Coffee Beanery Ltd.; pg. 849, pg. 886
Shaw, Lars, VP-Mktg-Global - Analogic Corporation; pg. 1399, pg. 840
Shaw, Lynn, Sr Mgr-Mktg - The Dress Barn, Inc.; pg. 1767, pg. 1343
Shaw, Margie, Dir-Media-Global - Staples, Inc.; pg. 474, pg. 821
Shaw, Mike, VP-Brand & Adv Mgmt - Wells Fargo & Company; pg. 819, pg. 232
Shaw, Phyllis, Mgr-Mktg Comm - Parker Hannifin Corporation; pg. 1368, pg. 1434
Shaw, Rebecca, Dir-Adv & Production - The Partnership at Drugfree.org; pg. 153, pg. 1276
Shaw, Rochelle, Brand Mgr-Digital Mktg & CRM - Johnson & Johnson Inc.; pg. 1552, pg. 1923
Shaw, Sid, Dir-Product Mktg - Broadcom Corporation; pg. 364, pg. 108
Shaw, Stacy, CMO & Asst Dir-Sls, Mktg & Retail Svcs - Oregon State Lottery; pg. 1003, pg. 1508
Shaw, Steve, Dir-Svcs Provider Mktg - Juniper Networks, Inc.; pg. 1260, pg. 286
Shaw, Suzanne, VP-Mktg & Comm - Missouri State University; pg. 605, pg. 1006
Shaw, Tammy, Head-Mktg Svcs Procurement-North America - Unilever United States, Inc.; pg. 904, pg. 1061
Shaw, Whitney, Brand Mgr-Oscar Mayer Hot Dogs - The Kraft Heinz Company; pg. 871, pg. 641
Shea, Cecilia, Dir-Digital Mktg - Build-A-Bear Workshop, Inc.; pg. 950, pg. 993
Shea, Danny, VP-Bus Dev Digital Media - E! Online, Inc.; pg. 1239, pg. 129
Shea, Elizabeth, Sr Dir-IR - AbbVie Inc.; pg. 1486, pg. 638
Shea, Gabriel, Mgr-Mktg - Hewlett-Packard Company; pg. 404, pg. 175
Shea, John, Sr Dir-Gatorade Sports Mktg - The Gatorade Company; pg. 251, pg. 574
Shea, Megan Dunleavy, Mgr-Mktg-Innovation - Campbell Soup Company; pg. 844, pg. 1048
Shea, Nancy, VP-Global Innovation & Mktg - Ashland Inc.; pg. 972, pg. 726
Shead, Ray, Mgr-Mktg - NDC Technologies; pg. 1423, pg. 118
Sheaffer, Elizabeth, Mgr-Mktg - Zip-Pak; pg. 1473, pg. 631
Sheaffer, Timothy A., Global Product Mgr-Aerospace, Defense & Marine - TE Connectivity Ltd.; pg. 677, pg. 1515
Sheahan, Bree, VP-Brand, Adv, Media & Content Mktg - Ameriprise Financial, Inc.; pg. 715, pg. 930
Sheairs, Bob, Specialist-Dealer Web Mktg - Subaru of America, Inc.; pg. 191, pg. 1050
Sheap, Christopher, Sr Dir-Ticket Ops - Washington Capitals; pg. 591, pg. 1775
Sheard, Julian, Dir-Global Social Media Mktg - Sony Corporation of America; pg. 675, pg. 1293
Shearer, Steve, Sr Mgr-Global Corp Accounts - Butler Manufacturing Company; pg. 72, pg. 981
Shearman, Paula, Mgr-Customer Mktg-Wines - Diageo North America, Inc.; pg. 1961, pg. 361
Sheats, Brandon, Mgr-Digital Strategy & Production - Atlanta Symphony Orchestra; pg. 531, pg. 490
Shechter, David, Sr Mgr-Medical Comm - Amgen Inc.; pg. 1493, pg. 291
Sheckler, Larisa, Sr Dir-Global Revenue Ops - Allrecipes.com; pg. 1226, pg. 1831
Shecrallah, John, Sr Dir-Transportation & Resource Mgmt - Peter Pan Bus Lines, Inc.; pg. 1919, pg. 846
Shecterle, Robert, Head-Mktg - Agilysys, Inc.; pg. 614, pg. 1409
Shedd, Mark, Dir-Mktg - QUALCOMM Incorporated; pg. 1873, pg. 207
Shedlock, Daniel, Product Mgr & Specialist-Mktg-Emerging Tech - Varian Medical Systems, Inc.; pg. 1434, pg. 178
Sheedy, Caroline, Mgr-Mktg - DraftKings, Inc.; pg. 545, pg. 793
Sheedy, Deborah, Mgr-Outbound Product Mktg-Enterprise Solutions Grp - Dell Inc.; pg. 383, pg. 1737
Sheehan, Craig, VP-Mktg-Vitamins, Minerals & Supplements - Church & Dwight Co., Inc.; pg. 1153, pg. 1063
Sheehan, Daniel, Dir-Sls & Market Dev - Ingram Micro Inc.; pg. 415, pg. 261
Sheehan, Erica, Dir-Mktg-Demand Generation - Akamai Technologies, Inc.; pg. 1226, pg. 807
Sheehan, Jim, Sr Dir-Comm & Mktg - SeaChange International, Inc.; pg. 1279, pg. 781
Sheehan, Joanne, Mgr-Global Fixed Mktg - Ford Motor Company; pg. 172, pg. 876
Sheehan, Liz, VP-Product Mgmt - Affinion Group, Inc.; pg. 1225, pg. 372
Sheehan, Mary, Sr Dir-Media & Strategy - ESPN, Inc.; pg. 285, pg. 340
Sheehan, Megan, Sr Product Mgr - Hewlett-Packard Company; pg. 404, pg. 175
Sheehan, Rachel, Mgr-Digital Mktg - L'Oreal USA; pg. 514, pg. 1252
Sheehe, Frank, Mgr-Retail & Mdse-Global - The Hershey Co.; pg. 1855, pg. 1538
Sheehy, Patrick J., Asst Dir-Investment Products - The Northwestern Mutual Life Insurance Company; pg. 1212, pg. 1879
Sheekey, Kevin, Head-Comm, Pub Policy & Mktg-Global - Bloomberg L.P.; pg. 725, pg. 1204
Sheel, Nikhil, Assoc Mgr-Product Mktg - Google Inc.; pg. 1249, pg. 153
Sheely, Steve, Sr Mgr-Destination - Expedia, Inc.; pg. 1244, pg. 1814
Sheeren, Bob, Mgr-Mktg - Technic Incorporated; pg. 1183, pg. 1601
Sheerin, Erica, Acct Rep-Sls - The Walt Disney Company; pg. 317, pg. 52
Sheets, Ashley, Dir-Media - AT&T Mobility LLC; pg. 619, pg. 488
Shefa, Lori, Sr VP-On-Air Adv & Promo-CBS Television Network - CBS Corporation; pg. 273, pg. 1210
Shefelbine, Kelly, Dir-Sls - CSX Transportation, Inc.; pg. 1904, pg. 432
Shefer, Randy, Sr Dir-Film & TV - Sony Corporation of America; pg. 675, pg. 1293
Sheffey, Dave, VP-Eastern Sls - Napco Security Systems, Inc.; pg. 658, pg. 1138
Sheffield, Bryon, Sr Dir-Consumer Mktg - Fair Isaac Corporation; pg. 1247, pg. 955
Sheffield, Michael, Dir-Customer Mktg-Oncology Managed Markets - Novartis Corporation; pg. 1574, pg. 1273
Sheffler, Brent, Mng Dir-Knowledge Transfer - Virginia Economic Development Partnership; pg. 1010, pg. 1804
Sheffler, Chris, Specialist-Digital Mktg - Comerica Incorporated; pg. 740, pg. 1677
Sheflin, Laurie, Dir-Mktg, Small Bus Payments & QuickBooks Customer Mktg - Intuit Inc.; pg. 769, pg. 158
Shehadeh, Adel, Sr Product Mgr - Yahoo! Inc.; pg. 1289, pg. 289
Shehadeh, Michelle, Mgr-Global CRM Strategy Mktg - InterContinental Hotels Corporation; pg. 1097, pg. 511
Shehi, Sabina, Mgr-Field Mktg - Starwood Hotels & Resorts Worldwide, Inc.; pg. 1114, pg. 378
Shehorn, Michael, Brand Mgr-Mazola - ACH Food Companies, Inc.; pg. 835, pg. 1631
Sheibani, Shida, Mgr-Channel Mktg-Retail Products - SanDisk Corporation; pg. 465, pg. 147
Sheidler, Leslie, Sr Dir-Strategic Initiatives - Kelly Services, Inc.; pg. 424, pg. 911
Sheikh, Patricia, Sr Mgr-Sls Ops-Mktg Solutions - LinkedIn Corporation; pg. 1262, pg. 160
Sheiner, Marla, Sr Dir-Mktg Comm - The University of Phoenix, Inc.; pg. 610, pg. 27
Sheirr, Gretchen, VP-Ticket Sls & Svc - Houston Rockets; pg. 552, pg. 1707
Shekar, Sheila, Sr Dir-Brand Mktg - Athleta; pg. 19, pg. 181
Shekel, Tomer, Product Mgr-Google Cast - Google Inc.; pg. 1249, pg. 153
Shekell, Dustin, Sr Dir-Global Creative - Electronic Arts Inc.; pg. 951, pg. 189
Shelby, Chris, Mgr-Mktg Campaign - ViewSonic Corporation; pg. 489, pg. 303
Shelden, Chris, Mgr-Indus Sls - J.R. Simplot Company; pg. 867, pg. 547
Sheldon, Adam, Brand Mgr-Cleveland Golf - Roger Cleveland Golf Company, Inc.; pg. 1844, pg. 105
Sheldon, Amanda, Dir-PR & Social Comm-Medtronic Diabetes - Medtronic, Inc.; pg. 1564, pg. 939
Sheldon, Bernard, Product Mgr - Thermo Fisher Scientific Inc.; pg. 1431, pg. 854
Sheldon, David, Mgr-Mktg - Hewlett-Packard Company; pg. 404, pg. 175
Sheldon, Jessica, Sr Analyst-Sls Ops - PAREXEL International Corporation; pg. 1580, pg. 853
Sheldon, Kyle, Sr Mgr-Digital & Social Media Comm - National Association for Stock Car Auto Racing; pg. 566, pg. 420
Sheldon, Susan, Mgr-Sls Admin-Global - Harsco Rail; pg. 1345, pg. 1623
Shelek, Bob, Mgr-Mktg-AT-A-GLANCE & Mass Market Plng Products - ACCO Brands Corporation; pg. 340, pg. 626
Shell, Matthew, Product Mgr - Armitron Watch Division; pg. 1, pg. 1174
Shellebarger, Jeff, Pres-Chevron North America Exploration & Production - Chevron Corporation; pg. 974, pg. 259
Shellen, Jason, Product Mgr - Pinterest; pg. 1275, pg. 225
Shellenberger, Dave, VP-Mktg Plng - Sears Holdings Corporation; pg. 1784, pg. 618
Shelley, Beverly, Dir-Sls & Mktg - South Carolina Parks Recreation & Tourism; pg. 1005, pg. 1614
Shelley, Dave, Mgr-Retail Mktg-Natl - Tribune Media Company; pg. 1696, pg. 592
Shellhammer, Alex, Mgr-Product Mktg - Google Inc.; pg. 1249, pg. 153
Shellhorn, Kari, Sr Dir-Corp Comm - The Gap, Inc.; pg. 1770, pg. 218
Shelly, Anthony R., Mgr-Lockbox Product & Ops - Fulton Financial Corporation; pg. 760, pg. 1546
Shelton, Bryan, Mgr-Mktg Events-North America - Oakley, Inc.; pg. 1840, pg. 86
Shelton, Cynthia, Ares VP-Special Program Sls-Govt - CenturyLink, Inc.; pg. 1870, pg. 746
Shelton, Evelyn, Coord-Production-Mktg & Creative - The Walt Disney Company; pg. 317, pg. 52
Shelton, Joslyn, Mgr-Mktg Dev - Intel Corporation; pg. 645, pg. 266
Shelton, Kim, Product Mgr-Inline Apparel - ASICS America Corporation; pg. 1826, pg. 106
Shelton, Nadya, Specialist-Mktg-Schlumberger Employees Credit Union - Schlumberger Limited; pg. 801, pg. 1714
Shelton, Paul, Dir-Adv - Astec Industries, Inc.; pg. 69, pg. 1628
Shelton, Vickki, VP-Sls-WWWQ-FM - Cumulus Media Inc.; pg. 280, pg. 503
Shema, Alan, Product Mgr - MOCON, Inc.; pg. 1363, pg. 940
Shen, Cindy, Product Dir-US ECommerce & Global - Benefit Cosmetics LLC; pg. 501, pg. 213
Shen, Donghua, Brand Mgr - Amazon.com, Inc.; pg. 1226, pg. 1831
Shen, Jon, Sr Dir-Interactive Mktg & Consumer Promos - ConAgra Foods, Inc.; pg. 826, pg. 1014
Shen, Lori, Sr Mgr-Comm - Citrix Systems, Inc.; pg. 375, pg. 424
Shen, Shaun, Mgr-Online Adv Sls-Western Reg - Investors Business Daily, Inc.; pg. 1653, pg. 133
Shenai, Rashmi, Sr Mgr-Mktg Comm-Windows Mktg - Microsoft Corporation; pg. 435, pg. 1824
Shenoha, Sara, Brand Mgr - Hillshire Brands; pg. 862, pg. 576
Sheobaran, Alicia, Mgr-Shopper Mktg - Kimberly-Clark Inc.; pg. 1463, pg. 1927
Sheopory, Mukul, Head-Product Mktg-ECommerce Product - Go Daddy Inc.; pg. 1249, pg. 21
Shepard, Adam D., Co-Head-Media & Comm Investment Banking-Global - Morgan Stanley; pg. 783, pg. 1261
Shepard, Andrea, Sr Mgr-Pro Practices - Fifth Third Bancorp; pg. 752, pg. 1413
Shepard, Hiram, Specialist-Mktg - FedEx Corporation; pg. 1907, pg. 1642
Shepard, Julie, Sr Dir-Mktg - Purple Communications, Inc.; pg. 457, pg. 194
Shepard, Mark, Product Mgr - GE Consumer & Industrial; pg. 55, pg. 733

Shepard, Mark, Product Mgr - General Electric Company; *pg.* 1297, *pg.* 347
Shepherd, Emily, Mgr-Digital Media & Analyst - PulteGroup, Inc.; *pg.* 1109, *pg.* 873
Shepherd, Matthew M., Coord-Adv Sys - The Home Depot, Inc.; *pg.* 1050, *pg.* 510
Shepherd, Neala, Sr Mgr-Mktg & Retail Adv - Cabela's Incorporated; *pg.* 535, *pg.* 1019
Sheppard, Erika, Mgr-Mktg - OPI Products Inc.; *pg.* 518, *pg.* 167
Sheppard, Jane, Mgr-Sls Specialty & Event Sls - Worcester Telegram & Gazette Corp.; *pg.* 1702, *pg.* 863
Sheppard, Kirena, Sr Mgr-Category Mgmt & Insights WMT Inc - Big Heart Pet Brands; *pg.* 1474, *pg.* 213
Sheppard, Nancy, VP Mktg-Viking-Penguin Grp USA - Penguin Random House; *pg.* 1675, *pg.* 1276
Sheppard, Nancy, VP-Mktg-Viking-Penguin Grp USA - Penguin Random House; *pg.* 1675, *pg.* 1276
Sheppard, Scott, Sr Dir-Mktg Ops - Automatic Data Processing, Inc.; *pg.* 357, *pg.* 1117
Sheppard, Ted, Sr Mgr-Visual - The Donna Karan Company LLC; *pg.* 23, *pg.* 1225
Shepperd, Demetrius, Sr Mgr-Digital Activation - The Coca-Cola Company; *pg.* 240, *pg.* 493
Sher, Sarah, Brand Mgr - Colgate-Palmolive Company; *pg.* 504, *pg.* 1215
Sherbow, Bruce W., VP-Sls & Mktg - Asimov's Science Fiction Magazine; *pg.* 1618, *pg.* 1197
Sherburn, Joan, Mgr-Mktg Svcs - Essentra Components; *pg.* 1335, *pg.* 901
Sheremet, Sharon, Dir-Global Product Res & Insights - General Motors Company; *pg.* 175, *pg.* 881
Sherer, Stacie, VP-PR - Weight Watchers International, Inc.; *pg.* 1609, *pg.* 1313
Sheridan Labarge, Joan, Grp Publr-Working Mother Magazine & Integrated Sls - Working Mother Media, Inc.; *pg.* 1702, *pg.* 1315
Sheridan Powers, Laura, VP-Media Rels - HSBC Bank USA; *pg.* 767, *pg.* 1241
Sheridan, Amy, Dir-Media-North America - NIKE, Inc.; *pg.* 1812, *pg.* 1492
Sheridan, Azadi, Product Mgr-Intl - Blackbaud, Inc.; *pg.* 361, *pg.* 1613
Sheridan, Barry, VP-Mktg-The Americas - Treasury Wine Estates; *pg.* 1971, *pg.* 164
Sheridan, Bonnie, Mgr-Product Line - Cargill, Inc.; *pg.* 845, *pg.* 965
Sheridan, David, Dir-Local Sls - KJRH; *pg.* 294, *pg.* 1490
Sheridan, James, Product Mgr-Line-Flow Assurance - Baker Hughes Incorporated; *pg.* 1315, *pg.* 1700
Sheridan, Kelly, Brand Mgr-Shopper Mktg - Kimberly-Clark Corporation; *pg.* 1461, *pg.* 1720
Sheridan, Tom, Sr Dir-Ticket Sls & Premium Seating - Chicago White Sox Ltd.; *pg.* 539, *pg.* 570
Sherief, Marilyn, Sr Product Mgr - Monster Worldwide, Inc.; *pg.* 1268, *pg.* 859
Sherifdeen, Mo, Dir-Integrated Mktg-Global - Oregon Tourism Commission; *pg.* 1003, *pg.* 1508
Sherlock, Bryan, Mgr-Web Mktg - Cisco Systems, Inc.; *pg.* 372, *pg.* 240
Sherlock, Kevin, Dir-Mktg-Pet Care - Church & Dwight Co., Inc.; *pg.* 1153, *pg.* 1063
Sherman, Adam, Dir-Social Media - New York Life Insurance Company; *pg.* 1211, *pg.* 1268
Sherman, Amy, Sr Dir-Digital Mktg-Lifestyle Brands - Marriott International, Inc.; *pg.* 1102, *pg.* 764
Sherman, Belinda, Pres & Mgr-Sls-Natl-The Huntington Investment Company - Huntington Bancshares Incorporated; *pg.* 767, *pg.* 1440
Sherman, Beth, Mgr-Sls - Cox Communications, Inc.; *pg.* 279, *pg.* 501
Sherman, Caroline, Sr Mgr-External Affairs US - Wm. Wrigley Jr. Company; *pg.* 1863, *pg.* 596
Sherman, David, VP-Sls & New Bus Dev - Amscan Holdings, Inc.; *pg.* 1760, *pg.* 1158
Sherman, Gordon, Dir-Mktg - Earl May Seed & Nursery L.C.; *pg.* 1795, *pg.* 712
Sherman, Ian, Mgr-Mktg Analytics - G&K Services Inc.; *pg.* 693, *pg.* 949
Sherman, Jaynee, Product Mgr-SPAM Brand-Intl Div - Hormel Foods Corporation; *pg.* 863, *pg.* 915
Sherman, Keith, Sr Mgr-Community Rels - Alliant Energy Corporation; *pg.* 1933, *pg.* 1864
Sherman, Kyle, Mgr-Digital Media - Cars.com; *pg.* 1234, *pg.* 568
Sherman, Lori, Sr Mgr-Mktg - USG Corporation; *pg.* 118, *pg.* 594
Sherman, Matthew, Sr Dir-Mktg - Chobani LLC; *pg.* 847, *pg.* 1318
Sherman, Patrice, Mgr-PR & Intl Marcom - Burt's Bees Inc.; *pg.* 502, *pg.* 1370
Sherman, Robert, VP-Media Rels - HSBC Bank USA; *pg.* 767, *pg.* 1241
Sherman, Scott, Sr Mgr-Fin-Dunkin' Donuts - Dunkin' Brands Group, Inc.; *pg.* 1727, *pg.* 810
Sherman, Wade, VP & Counsel-Digital Mktg - Adobe Systems Incorporated; *pg.* 342, *pg.* 235
Shermer, Sandy, Head-US Mktg-SYLATRON & INTRON - Merck & Co., Inc.; *pg.* 1566, *pg.* 1077
Sheroke, Ted, Mgr-Adv - CIE Direct; *pg.* 599, *pg.* 1429
Sherr, Scott, Exec VP-Worldwide Theatrical Distr & Mktg - Sony Pictures Entertainment Inc.; *pg.* 309, *pg.* 72
Sherrill, Bridget, VP-Mdsg - Kentucky Derby Festival, Inc.; *pg.* 556, *pg.* 735
Sherrod, Tina, Brand Mgr - Capital One Financial Corporation; *pg.* 730, *pg.* 1789
Sherry, Colleen, Sr Mgr-Media & Mktg Effectiveness - Macy's, Inc.; *pg.* 1778, *pg.* 1417
Sherry, Dominic, Head-Sls-Asia Pacific - Hilton Worldwide, Inc.; *pg.* 1094, *pg.* 1791
Sherry, Sophia, Coord-Comm & PR - U.S. News & World Report, L.P.; *pg.* 1698, *pg.* 1308
Sherry, Stephanie, Dir-Mktg Comm - Olympus America Inc.; *pg.* 1425, *pg.* 1521
Shervheim, Lee, Sr Mgr-Product Dev - Medtronic, Inc.; *pg.* 1564, *pg.* 939
Sherwin, Kyle, Sr VP-Strategy, Accts & Media - Sony Music Entertainment; *pg.* 309, *pg.* 1294
Sherwin, Sarina, Dir-Mktg & Visual Mdsg - Reebok International Ltd.; *pg.* 1817, *pg.* 811
Sherwood, Dennis, Dir-Outside Reg Sls-Medium Bus-Preferred Accts - Dell Inc.; *pg.* 383, *pg.* 1737
Sherwood, Melinda, Mgr-Comm & Media - CB Richard Ellis, Inc.; *pg.* 1085, *pg.* 1210
Shet, Vinay, Product Mgr-reCaptcha - Google Inc.; *pg.* 1249, *pg.* 153
Sheth, Parthiv, Sr Dir-Mktg Tech & Ops - Adobe Systems Incorporated; *pg.* 342, *pg.* 235
Sheth, Rajen, Dir-Product Mgmt - Google Inc.; *pg.* 1249, *pg.* 153
Shetty, Ketan, Mgr-Mktg - Piaggio USA, Inc.; *pg.* 188, *pg.* 1282
Shetty, Nikita, Sr Dir-Wholesale Mktg - Ralph Lauren Corporation; *pg.* 46, *pg.* 1284
Shetty, Shivram, Dir-Customer Segmentation & Strategy-Loyalty Mktg - Sears Holdings Corporation; *pg.* 1784, *pg.* 618
Shetty, Suraj, VP-Mktg - Cisco Systems, Inc.; *pg.* 372, *pg.* 240
Shevell, Steve, Head-Product Mktg - Ericsson, Inc.; *pg.* 638, *pg.* 1730
Shew, Clyde A., VP-Medical Sls & Mktg - Span-America Medical Systems, Inc.; *pg.* 1595, *pg.* 1618
Shewfelt, Chris, Sr Dir-Partnerships-Global - Maple Leaf Sports & Entertainment Ltd.; *pg.* 560, *pg.* 1940
Shi, Stella, Coord-PR & Social Media - Williams-Sonoma, Inc.; *pg.* 1140, *pg.* 234
Shia, Lori, Sr Dir-Product Mgmt - Bankrate, Inc.; *pg.* 1231, *pg.* 451
Shibaeva, Maria, Sr Asst Brand Mgr - Procter & Gamble Inc.; *pg.* 333, *pg.* 1929
Shibata, Andy, VP-Brand Mktg - Royal Bank of Canada; *pg.* 800, *pg.* 1942
Shibata, Masaaki, Sr VP-Mktg Grp - American Appraisal Associates, Inc.; *pg.* 349, *pg.* 1872
Shideleff, Melissa, Sr Mgr-Xeljanz HCP Mktg - Pfizer Inc.; *pg.* 1581, *pg.* 1278
Shieh, Anita, Sr Mgr-New Indus Dev - American Express Company; *pg.* 712, *pg.* 1190
Shieh, Emily, Sr Assoc Mgr-Mktg - General Mills, Inc.; *pg.* 828, *pg.* 933
Shiel, Alicia, VP-Sls-Control East - Diageo North America, Inc.; *pg.* 1961, *pg.* 361
Shield, Cassidy, VP-Solutions Mktg-Global - Alcatel-Lucent; *pg.* 615, *pg.* 38
Shields, Bill, Sr Mgr-Mktg - Cisco Systems, Inc.; *pg.* 372, *pg.* 240
Shields, Bill, Sr VP-Sls & Bus Dev - HemCon Medical Technologies, Inc.; *pg.* 1541, *pg.* 1503
Shields, Brian, Dir-Comm & Mktg - The Johns Hopkins University; *pg.* 603, *pg.* 757
Shields, Kit, Asst Mgr-Produce & Floral Sls - Albertson's LLC; *pg.* 1013, *pg.* 546
Shields, Lina P., Product Dir-Brand-Autoimmune Consumer Mktg-Lilly USA - Eli Lilly and Company; *pg.* 1527, *pg.* 684
Shields, Lisa, VP-Comm & Media Rels-Global - Council on Foreign Relations; *pg.* 138, *pg.* 1219
Shields, Matthew, Dir-Sls-Global - Illinois Tool Works Inc.; *pg.* 1348, *pg.* 614
Shiffer, Sondra, Mgr-Publ & Mdsg - Subaru of America, Inc.; *pg.* 191, *pg.* 1050
Shiffman, David, Sr VP-Mktg Solutions - comScore, Inc; *pg.* 1236, *pg.* 1798
Shiffman, Denise, Corp VP-Switching & Security Products & Solutions - Juniper Networks, Inc.; *pg.* 1260, *pg.* 286
Shiffman, Steve, Sr Dir-Ticket Sls & Customer Svc - Kansas City Royals Baseball Corporation; *pg.* 555, *pg.* 985
Shiffrin, Craig, Dir-Online Mktg - 1-800-Flowers.com, Inc.; *pg.* 1758, *pg.* 1151
Shifrin, Kim, Sr Mgr-Mktg - The Kraft Heinz Company; *pg.* 871, *pg.* 641
Shifrin, Kim, Sr Mgr-Mktg - Mondelez International, Inc.; *pg.* 878, *pg.* 601
Shifrin, Michael, Grp Mgr-Mktg-Digital Product Mktg - Toyota Motor Sales, U.S.A., Inc.; *pg.* 193, *pg.* 296
Shilling, Charlie, Sr Product Mgr - Hewlett-Packard Company; *pg.* 404, *pg.* 175
Shim, Jay, Mgr-Mktg-Terex Svcs - Terex Corporation; *pg.* 1381, *pg.* 384
Shim, Seojie, Media Planner-Digital & Analyst - salesforce.com, inc.; *pg.* 1278, *pg.* 226
Shimabukuro, Jill, Dir-Design & Production - University of Chicago Press; *pg.* 1698, *pg.* 594
Shimada, Tak, Dir-Brand Mktg - Toms Shoe's Inc; *pg.* 1821, *pg.* 276
Shimahara, Mark, Mgr-Online Mktg - Patagonia; *pg.* 31, *pg.* 301
Shimala, Craig, Dir-Creative - skinnyCorp L.L.C.; *pg.* 1280, *pg.* 590
Shimanek, Wes, Sr Mgr - Intel Corporation; *pg.* 645, *pg.* 266
Shimarova, Irina, Mgr-Channel-Broker-Dealer Mktg - Legg Mason, Inc.; *pg.* 775, *pg.* 758
Shime, Angela, Head-Global Events & Mktg Programs & Sr Dir - Software AG, Inc.; *pg.* 471, *pg.* 1799
Shimizu, Akira, VP, Deputy Gen Mgr-Corp Sls & Mktg & Gen Mgr-Reg Strategies - Hitachi America, Ltd.; *pg.* 642, *pg.* 1344
Shimkin, Anthony, Sr Dir-Bus Dev - QUALCOMM Incorporated; *pg.* 1873, *pg.* 207
Shimm, Joey, Dir-Mktg - Outwater Plastic Industries, Inc.; *pg.* 1058, *pg.* 1044
Shimmel, Howard, Sr VP - Turner Broadcasting System, Inc.; *pg.* 314, *pg.* 521
Shimokura, Goh, Dir-Sls - Micron Technology, Inc.; *pg.* 435, *pg.* 547
Shimp, Ginger, Dir-Mktg - SAP America, Inc.; *pg.* 466, *pg.* 1557
Shimp, Mark, Reg Mgr-Sls-W - Summit Plastic Co.; *pg.* 1470, *pg.* 1403
Shin, Carrie, Mgr-Mktg Programs-APAC - Citrix Systems, Inc.; *pg.* 375, *pg.* 424
Shin, Charlie, Sr Dir-Strategic Plng - Major League Soccer LLC; *pg.* 560, *pg.* 1256
Shin, David, Sr Product Mgr-Capital Games - Electronic Arts Inc.; *pg.* 951, *pg.* 189
Shin, Jong, Dir-Customer Mktg - Intel Corporation; *pg.* 645, *pg.* 266
Shin, Julie, Mgr-Media - Sony Pictures Entertainment Inc.; *pg.* 309, *pg.* 72
Shindo, Toshi, Mgr-Mktg - Cisco Systems, Inc.; *pg.* 372, *pg.* 240
Shinn, Leslie, Sr Mgr-Mktg-Social Media - The Gap, Inc.; *pg.* 1770, *pg.* 218
Shinnick, Deborah, Sr VP-Network Sls & Strategy Res - Univision Communications Inc.; *pg.* 683, *pg.* 1307
Shiozaki, Teri, Sr Mgr-Digital Comm & Social Media - Hewlett-Packard Company; *pg.* 404, *pg.* 175
Shipley, Steve, Dir-Product Qualification - ADTRAN, Inc.; *pg.* 344, *pg.* 6
Shipman, Jeri, Sr Mgr-Bus Dev & Strategic Partnerships - St. Jude Children's Research Hospital; *pg.* 1596, *pg.* 1646
Shipp, Amber, Mgr-Local Store Mktg - PETCO Animal Supplies, Inc.; *pg.* 1480, *pg.* 206
Shipp, Julie, Mgr-PR - AutoTrader, Inc.; *pg.* 1230, *pg.* 490
Shippam, Megan, Strategist-Digital Mktg - E&J Gallo Winery;

First page reference indicates Business Class Edition
Second page reference indicates Geographic Edition

pg. 1962, *pg.* 149
Shipton, Christine, Chief Creative Officer & Sr VP - Shaw Media Inc.; *pg.* 308, *pg.* 1943
Shirer, Joyce, Sr VP-Audience Dev & E-Tail Mktg - Rodale, Inc.; *pg.* 1681, *pg.* 1530
Shires, Todd, Mgr-Vendor Mktg - Ingram Micro Inc.; *pg.* 415, *pg.* 261
Shirk, Cindy, Brand Mgr - Beer Nuts, Inc.; *pg.* 1850, *pg.* 557
Shirley, Dave, Dir-Mktg & Sls - Comcast Corporation; *pg.* 276, *pg.* 1560
Shirley, Hillary, Dir-Global Mktg Comm-Comml aerospace - Honeywell Aerospace Electronic Systems; *pg.* 228, *pg.* 17
Shirley, Kathy, Dir-Mktg-Artificial Lift - Baker Hughes Incorporated; *pg.* 1315, *pg.* 1700
Shirley, S., Sr Dir-Employee Comm & Engagement - The McGraw-Hill Companies Inc.; *pg.* 1663, *pg.* 1257
Shirley, Saxon, Sr Mgr-PR-Asia Pacific Reg - Fair Isaac Corporation; *pg.* 1247, *pg.* 955
Shirley, Scott, Dir & Sr Mgr-Mktg - Nissan North America, Inc.; *pg.* 186, *pg.* 1633
Shirley, Wes, Sr Mgr-Comm - Charter Communications, Inc.; *pg.* 274, *pg.* 372
Shirodkar, Shama, Dir-Digital Adv Ops - The Weather Channel LLC; *pg.* 320, *pg.* 523
Shirokov, Dennis, Dir-Interactive Mktg - FedEx Corporation; *pg.* 1907, *pg.* 1642
Shirtliff, Bryan, Sr VP-Mdsg - Rite Aid Corporation; *pg.* 1590, *pg.* 1519
Shirtz, Kristin, Mgr-Mktg Brand-Three Olives Vodka & Kraken Rum - Proximo Spirits, Inc.; *pg.* 1969, *pg.* 1076
Shivel, John, Sr VP-Adv, Mktg & Corp Comm - Fruit of the Loom, Inc.; *pg.* 41, *pg.* 725
Shiveley, Robert, Mgr-Data Center Solutions Mktg - Intel Corporation; *pg.* 645, *pg.* 266
Shively, Derrek, Mgr-Retail Mktg - Cabela's Incorporated; *pg.* 535, *pg.* 1019
Shiver, Jason, VP-Sls - SkinnyPop Popcorn LLC; *pg.* 895, *pg.* 661
Shiverick, Asa, Mgr-Media - The Home Depot, Inc.; *pg.* 1050, *pg.* 510
Shklyar, Jenna, Brand Mgr-Economy Reinvention - MillerCoors LLC; *pg.* 255, *pg.* 582
Shlepr, Julie, Dir-Global Mktg-Personal Care - The Lubrizol Corporation; *pg.* 1171, *pg.* 1481
Shlonsky, Lynne, Dir-Design-New Product Concepts - American Greetings Corporation; *pg.* 1615, *pg.* 1428
Shnider, Ron, Mgr-Sls Dev - The Blade Co.; *pg.* 1621, *pg.* 1476
Shockey, John, Sr Assoc-Mktg & Program - Abbott Laboratories; *pg.* 1484, *pg.* 551
Shockley, Cara, Mgr-Mktg Comm-Imaging & Printing Solutions - Hewlett-Packard Company; *pg.* 404, *pg.* 175
Shockley, Jason, Sr Dir-Corp Comm - The ADT Corporation; *pg.* 612, *pg.* 409
Shockley, Kerry, Sr Dir-America's Channel Mktg - Gartner, Inc.; *pg.* 1248, *pg.* 374
Shockley, Michael, Dir-Corp Partnership Sls - Sacramento Kings; *pg.* 579, *pg.* 197
Shodjai, Payam, Product Mgr - Google Inc.; *pg.* 1249, *pg.* 153
Shoemaker, Amy, Brand Mgr-Innovation - Del Monte Foods, Inc.; *pg.* 852, *pg.* 304
Shoemaker, Joel, Sr Dir-Integrated Adv - Here Media Inc.; *pg.* 290, *pg.* 132
Shoemaker, Jon, Dir-Creative Svcs - Chicago Professional Sports Limited Partnership; *pg.* 539, *pg.* 570
Shoffner, Saga, VP-Global Brand Mktg - Owens-Illinois, Inc.; *pg.* 1466, *pg.* 1470
Shoja, Sahar, Mgr-Sponsorship Mktg - Canadian Imperial Bank of Commerce; *pg.* 729, *pg.* 1935
Sholkovitz, Luisa, Brand Mktg Mgr - TripAdvisor, Inc.; *pg.* 1926, *pg.* 835
Shondel, Cathy, Dir-Mktg - La Rosa's, Inc.; *pg.* 1735, *pg.* 1416
Shone, Kate, VP-PR, Fragrance & Beauty - Chanel, Inc.; *pg.* 503, *pg.* 1211
Shong, Audrey De, Dir-Integrated Adv-Macy's Corporate - Macy's, Inc.; *pg.* 1778, *pg.* 1417
Shonoiki, Abayomi, Brand Mgr - Kellogg Company; *pg.* 831, *pg.* 870
Shook, Amy, Dir-Ops-Creative Svcs - DIRECTV Group Holdings, LLC; *pg.* 281, *pg.* 79
Shook, Nathan, Sls Mgr-US Distr - STEPAN COMPANY; *pg.* 1182, *pg.* 643
Shoop, Kyle, Mgr-Sls & Tech - Tenova; *pg.* 114, *pg.* 1525
Shopiro, Kerry, Mgr-Mktg - Hershey Canada, Inc.; *pg.* 1855, *pg.* 1926
Shopis, Vanessa, Mgr-Mktg - John Hancock Financial Services; *pg.* 1205, *pg.* 796
Shopoff, Bill, VP-Sls - Exactech, Inc.; *pg.* 1529, *pg.* 428
Shopp, Brandon, Sr Dir-Product Mgmt-MSP Bus Unit - SOLARWINDS, INC.; *pg.* 471, *pg.* 1666
Shorbaji, Omar, Engr-Sys-Enterprise Sls - Cisco Systems, Inc.; *pg.* 372, *pg.* 240
Shore, Angie, VP-Mdsg - Lowe's Companies, Inc.; *pg.* 1053, *pg.* 1383
Shore, Michael, Exec Dir-Fin Products - CME Group, Inc.; *pg.* 738, *pg.* 571
Shore, Mussie, Grp Product Mgr - Google Inc.; *pg.* 1249, *pg.* 153
Shore, Veronica, Mgr-Mktg Brand - BUFFALO WILD WINGS, INC.; *pg.* 1718, *pg.* 931
Shores, Tom, Mgr-Natl Sls-Mountain Hardwear & Montrail - Mountain Hardwear, Inc.; *pg.* 1839, *pg.* 193
Shorooghi, Ali, Sr Product Mgr - NuVasive, Inc.; *pg.* 1577, *pg.* 205
Short, Alexis, Specialist-Mktg - SYNNEX Corporation; *pg.* 480, *pg.* 92
Short, Allison L., Mgr-Mktg & PR - Gosh Enterprises, Inc.; *pg.* 1730, *pg.* 1440
Short, Jill, VP-Sls-Natl Acct Teams - Atkins Nutritionals, Inc.; *pg.* 1498, *pg.* 316
Short, Kate, Grp Mgr-North America Mktg Procurement - Nestle USA - Beverage Division, Inc.; *pg.* 883, *pg.* 96
Short, Kerry, Sr Mgr-Field Mktg-Ultrasound - Philips Electronics North America; *pg.* 662, *pg.* 782
Short, Larry, Product Mgr-Cloud Applications - AT&T; *pg.* 1865, *pg.* 258
Shortal, Luciana, Dir-Sponsorship Mktg & Worldwide Events - Gartner, Inc.; *pg.* 1248, *pg.* 374
Shortall, Tim, VP-Eastern Reg Sls-US - International Game Technology; *pg.* 957, *pg.* 1024
Shortall, Valerie, VP-Mktg-Intl - Cinemark Holdings, Inc.; *pg.* 540, *pg.* 1729
Shorter, Emily, Dir-Product Mktg-Mobile - MicroStrategy, Inc.; *pg.* 1266, *pg.* 1809
Shottan, Shmuel, Sr VP-Product Ops & Tech - Hitachi Data Systems Corporation; *pg.* 407, *pg.* 265
Shotwell, Andy, Mgr-Mass Media Mktg - The Progressive Corporation; *pg.* 1214, *pg.* 1463
Shouldis, Kathleen, VP-Analytics & Software Field Mktg-North America - International Business Machines Corporation; *pg.* 418, *pg.* 1138
Shoultz, Luther, Mgr-Local Market Sls - Avis Budget Group, Inc.; *pg.* 1900, *pg.* 1102
Shoup, Jill, Strategist-Mktg - Dell Inc.; *pg.* 383, *pg.* 1737
Shoup, Vic, Mgr-Web Mktg-Web Analytics - LexisNexis Group; *pg.* 1658, *pg.* 1446
Showalter, Chad, Sr Mgr-Mktg - Newport Aquarium; *pg.* 571, *pg.* 739
Showalter, John, Sr Acct Mgr-Multi Media - Cox Media Group; *pg.* 280, *pg.* 502
Showers, Bryan, Sr Mgr-Digital Mktg - Herman Miller, Inc.; *pg.* 926, *pg.* 913
Showers, Rick, VP-Mktg-Manitowoc Ice - Manitowoc Ice, Inc.; *pg.* 58, *pg.* 1868
Shrago, Shera, Dir-ECommerce Mktg - Carter's, Inc.; *pg.* 21, *pg.* 491
Shray, Kimber, Dir-Shopper Mktg - Georgia-Pacific LLC; *pg.* 1458, *pg.* 507
Shreffler, Stacy, Mgr-Tourism Sls - Greater Boston Convention & Visitors Bureau Inc.; *pg.* 993, *pg.* 795
Shreve, Robert, VP-Sls & Mktg - Morris Coupling Company; *pg.* 1057, *pg.* 1530
Shrewsberry, Katie, Sr Analyst-Mktg - Constellation Energy Resources, LLC; *pg.* 1938, *pg.* 756
Shrewsberry, Lindsy, Specialist-PR - Stihl, Inc.; *pg.* 1064, *pg.* 1810
Shribman, Leslie, VP-Media Rels - The Goldman Sachs Group, Inc.; *pg.* 762, *pg.* 1236
Shripka, Andrew, Assoc Brand Mktg Dir - Kellogg Company; *pg.* 831, *pg.* 870
Shrivastava, Akshay, Sr Dir-Tech - Cox Media Group; *pg.* 280, *pg.* 502
Shrivastava, Irma, VP-Mktg - American Cancer Society, Inc.; *pg.* 126, *pg.* 487
Shrivastava, Rajeev, Chief Strategy Officer & Sr VP - INCONTACT, INC.; *pg.* 413, *pg.* 1752
Shrivats, Anu, Sr Dir-Fin - Canadian Imperial Bank of Commerce; *pg.* 729, *pg.* 1935
Shriver, Amy, Sr Mgr-Mktg - CenturyLink, Inc.; *pg.* 1870, *pg.* 746
Shriver, Julie, Mgr-Mktg - Wells Fargo & Company; *pg.* 819, *pg.* 232
Shriver, Sarah, VP-Digital Ad Sls - A&E Television Networks, LLC; *pg.* 267, *pg.* 1185
Shrom, Lainey, Brand Mgr - Kraft Canada Inc.; *pg.* 869, *pg.* 1939
Shryock, Marlena H., Mgr-Mktg - General Electric Company; *pg.* 1297, *pg.* 347
Shu, Victor, Sr Dir-Mdsg & Retail Mktg - VIZIO, Inc.; *pg.* 686, *pg.* 118
Shubitz, Jeremy, Dir-Mktg - Bosley Inc.; *pg.* 1508, *pg.* 46
Shucklin, Jane, Mgr-Adv - Costco Wholesale Corporation; *pg.* 1765, *pg.* 1820
Shuff, Andrea, Dir-Mktg Comm - Jack in the Box Inc.; *pg.* 1732, *pg.* 204
Shuff, Van, Sr Mgr-Pur - L Brands, Inc.; *pg.* 1776, *pg.* 1441
Shuford, Helen, Mgr-Mktg Res & Customer Analytics - Southern Company; *pg.* 1952, *pg.* 520
Shukla, Pryia, VP-PR - Vera Wang Bridal House Ltd.; *pg.* 34, *pg.* 1309
Shukla, Shailesh, CMO-Canada & VP-Mktg & Trade Mktg - Reckitt Benckiser Inc.; *pg.* 1136, *pg.* 1105
Shull, Chris, Mgr-Publ & PR - Dallas Symphony Association Inc.; *pg.* 543, *pg.* 1679
Shull-Chandler, Laura, Dir-Product Mktg, Mobile Apps & Web - AOL Inc.; *pg.* 1229, *pg.* 1195
Shulman, Dara, Dir-Retail Mktg - McKesson Corporation; *pg.* 1560, *pg.* 222
Shulman, Simon, Sr Mgr-Digital Strategy & Analytics - TD Ameritrade Holding Corporation; *pg.* 808, *pg.* 1018
Shultz, Brian, Corp VP-Mktg - Boyd Gaming Corporation; *pg.* 1082, *pg.* 1022
Shum, Ida, Sr Mgr-Bus Dev - Samsung Electronics America, Inc.; *pg.* 669, *pg.* 1115
Shum, Ronda, Sr Mgr-Mktg-Intl Brand & Acq - Charles Schwab & Company, Inc.; *pg.* 734, *pg.* 215
Shum, Winifred, Dir-PR - Imperva, Inc.; *pg.* 413, *pg.* 193
Shumate, John, Dir-Mktg-Southeast Region - Pepsi Beverages Company; *pg.* 258, *pg.* 1342
Shupe, Sarah, Mgr-Mktg-Intl - Johnson & Johnson; *pg.* 1549, *pg.* 1091
Shurtliff, Alyson, Mgr-Social Media - Eastman Kodak Company; *pg.* 1408, *pg.* 1333
Shurtz, Blake, Product Mgr - ScanSource, Inc.; *pg.* 671, *pg.* 1618
Shuster, Craig, Sr Producer-Brand Creative Grp - Yahoo! Inc.; *pg.* 1289, *pg.* 289
Shuster, Judith, Sr Dir-Regulatory CMC - Johnson & Johnson; *pg.* 1549, *pg.* 1091
Shuster, Steve, Brand Mgr-Global - W.L. Gore & Associates, Inc.; *pg.* 122, *pg.* 388
Shute, Jillian, Dir-Brand Mktg - Newell Rubbermaid Inc.; *pg.* 1128, *pg.* 515
Shutt, Mai Kha, Sr Mgr-Mktg-CRM - 24 Hour Fitness Worldwide Inc.; *pg.* 526, *pg.* 258
Shy, Erin, Sr VP-Product Mgmt & Product Mktg - Abila, Inc.; *pg.* 340, *pg.* 1660
Si, Adrian, Mgr-Scion Interactive Mktg - Toyota Motor North America, Inc.; *pg.* 192, *pg.* 1303
Sia, Ailee, Sr Assoc Brand Mgr-Listerine - Johnson & Johnson; *pg.* 1549, *pg.* 1091
Siano, Salvatore, Dir-Mktg - FGX International, Inc.; *pg.* 5, *pg.* 1608
Siao, Richard, Sr VP-Sls Plng & Ops - Warner Home Video Inc.; *pg.* 319, *pg.* 55
Sias, Jim, Sr Mgr-Brand PR & Entertainment Influencer Mktg - Diageo North America Inc.; *pg.* 248, *pg.* 1223
Sibbach, Jack, Dir-Sls, Mktg & PR-Sun Valley Resort - Sun Valley Company; *pg.* 1115, *pg.* 550
Sibel, Jeff E., Rep-PR - The Progressive Corporation; *pg.* 1214, *pg.* 1463
Sibley, Jessica, VP-Ad Sls-Eastern Reg - Forbes, Inc.; *pg.* 1641, *pg.* 1232
Sibley, Michelle, VP-Entertainment Mktg - Citigroup Inc.; *pg.* 735, *pg.* 1212
Sibony, Yaniv, Dir-Product Mgmt - Harmonic, Inc.; *pg.* 402, *pg.* 246
Sibony, Yoav, VP-Sls-Global - Harvard Bioscience, Inc.; *pg.* 1539, *pg.* 824
Sichel, Samantha, Sr Dir-Digital Dev - Live Nation Worldwide - Times Square Office; *pg.* 558, *pg.* 1252
Siciliano, Mark, Dir-Mktg - Howard Miller Company; *pg.* 7, *pg.* 914
Sicular, Eric, Sr Mgr-Digital Mktg - CVS Health Corporation;

pg. 1765, *pg.* 1610
Sicuso, Sabina, VP-Mktg - Club Med Sales, Inc.; *pg.* 1903, *pg.* 441
Sidari, Barbara, Head-Svcs Web & Sls Enablement Comm - Avaya Inc.; *pg.* 621, *pg.* 264
Siddens, Jessica, Designer-Adv - Angie's List Inc; *pg.* 1228, *pg.* 682
Siddiqi, Naeem, Product Mgr-Banking Analytics Solutions-Global - SAS Institute (Canada), Inc.; *pg.* 466, *pg.* 1943
Siddiqui, Faryal, Mgr-Bear Brand Mktg - Build-A-Bear Workshop, Inc.; *pg.* 950, *pg.* 993
Siddiqui, Yalmaz, Sr Dir-Environmental Strategy - Office Depot, Inc.; *pg.* 448, *pg.* 412
Sidebottom, Alex, Mgr-Trade Mktg - Reckitt Benckiser Inc.; *pg.* 1136, *pg.* 1105
Sidell, Kevin, Sr Mgr-Digital Strategy - Kellogg Company; *pg.* 831, *pg.* 870
Sidhu, Navdeep, Sr Dir-Product Mktg - Software AG, Inc.; *pg.* 471, *pg.* 1799
Sidhu, Sheila K., Head-Worldwide Indus Mktg-IBM Global Bus Svcs & Sr Mgr-Mktg - IBM; *pg.* 410, *pg.* 1449
Sidi, Ariff, Sr VP-Digital Products & Platforms - Fox Broadcasting Company; *pg.* 287, *pg.* 130
Sidorova, Jenny, Category Mgr-Mktg-Apparel - Wal-Mart Stores, Inc.; *pg.* 1790, *pg.* 29
Siebels, Keith, Sr VP-Sls - Owen Industries, Inc.; *pg.* 102, *pg.* 702
Siebens, Nate, Sr Mgr-Comm-IMSA - National Association for Stock Car Auto Racing; *pg.* 566, *pg.* 420
Siebers, Michael L., Sr VP-Sls & Mktg-Midwest - Peabody Energy Corporation; *pg.* 1176, *pg.* 1001
Siebert, Eric, VP-Global Digital Mktg - Boston Scientific Corporation; *pg.* 1508, *pg.* 831
Siebert, Jeffrey, Dir-Mktg - Six Flags Entertainment Corporation; *pg.* 583, *pg.* 1698
Siebert, Laura, Dir-Creative - Career Education Corporation; *pg.* 599, *pg.* 658
Siebert, Monica, Sr Specialist-Product Mktg - FRANKLIN RESOURCES, INC.; *pg.* 760, *pg.* 254
Siebler, Duane, Sr Specialist-Mktg - Mutual of Omaha Insurance Company; *pg.* 1210, *pg.* 1016
Sieck, Alison, Mgr-Mktg - T. Rowe Price Group Inc.; *pg.* 808, *pg.* 759
Siedel, Cynthia, Dir-Mktg Comm & Digital Strategy - Jamba, Inc.; *pg.* 1024, *pg.* 84
Siefker, Eric, Analyst-Mktg - United Parcel Service, Inc.; *pg.* 1928, *pg.* 522
Siegal, Jonathan, VP-Product Mktg - EMC Corporation; *pg.* 391, *pg.* 825
Siegel, Andrea, Dir-Mktg - Cumulus Media Inc.; *pg.* 280, *pg.* 503
Siegel, Anne, Dir-PR - Constellation Brands, Inc.; *pg.* 1960, *pg.* 1348
Siegel, Barry W., Exec VP-Sls - Central Florida Investments Inc.; *pg.* 1085, *pg.* 452
Siegel, Bill, Sr Dir-News Strategy - The E.W. Scripps Company; *pg.* 1639, *pg.* 1412
Siegel, Brooke, Dir-Editorial Ops-Digital Media - Hearst Magazines; *pg.* 1649, *pg.* 1239
Siegel, Dmitri, VP-Global ECommerce & Exec Dir-Creative - Patagonia; *pg.* 31, *pg.* 301
Siegel, Evan, Sr VP-Sls & Mktg - Wells Fargo & Company; *pg.* 819, *pg.* 232
Siegel, Geri, Dir-Mktg Comm - Bright House Networks LLC; *pg.* 272, *pg.* 461
Siegel, Gregg L., VP-Sls-Natl - Sinclair Broadcast Group, Inc.; *pg.* 308, *pg.* 773
Siegel, Jonathan, Product Dir - RACKSPACE HOSTING, INC.; *pg.* 1277, *pg.* 1742
Siegel, Marc, Dir-Sls-Bloomberg Radio - Bloomberg L.P.; *pg.* 725, *pg.* 1204
Siegel, Mark, Exec Dir-Media Rels - AT&T Mobility LLC; *pg.* 620, *pg.* 1152
Siegel, Melissa, Coord-Mktg - Party City Corporation; *pg.* 1781, *pg.* 1116
Siegel, Teri, VP-Global Mktg, Fashion & Lifestyle Fragrances - Coty, Inc.; *pg.* 506, *pg.* 1219
Siegel, Todd, Exec VP-Intl Ad Sls & Partnerships US - Fox Entertainment Group, Inc.; *pg.* 288, *pg.* 131
Siegert, Chad, Sr Mgr-Integrated Mktg - GameStop Corp.; *pg.* 399, *pg.* 1699
Siegfried, Michelle, Mgr-Mktg-Americas Hygiene Adhesives - H.B. Fuller Company; *pg.* 1165, *pg.* 961
Siegle, Jeff, Dir-Sls Promos & Incentives - Select Comfort Corporation; *pg.* 942, *pg.* 942
Siegling, Kathryn, Mgr-Mktg Comm - The Mattress Firm, Inc.; *pg.* 934, *pg.* 1711
Siegworth, Lorraine, Chief Strategy Officer - State Automobile Mutual Insurance Company; *pg.* 1217, *pg.* 1444
Siek, Debbie, VP-Sls & Svc - Apple Inc.; *pg.* 350, *pg.* 73
Siekmann, Jackie, Mgr-Media & Govt Rels - The Kroger Co.; *pg.* 1025, *pg.* 1416
Siemienas, Mike, Brand Mgr-Media Rels - General Mills, Inc.; *pg.* 828, *pg.* 933
Sierak, Mark, VP-Mktg - Sotheby's International Realty, Inc.; *pg.* 1113, *pg.* 1294
Sieron, Geoff, Specialist-Product - Rockwell Automation, Inc.; *pg.* 668, *pg.* 1880
Sierra, Carmen, VP-Sls, Mktg & Design Studio - KB Home; *pg.* 90, *pg.* 134
Sierra, Cindy, Coord-Zone Mktg - Whataburger, Inc.; *pg.* 1755, *pg.* 1744
Sierra, Ibed, Mgr-Mktg-Pro & Medical Div - Pfizer Inc.; *pg.* 1581, *pg.* 1278
Sierra, Maribel, Dir-Social Media Svcs-Global - Dell Inc.; *pg.* 383, *pg.* 1737
Sieve, Erik, Sr Mgr-IT Audit - Fifth Third Bancorp; *pg.* 752, *pg.* 1413
Sieve, Justin, Mgr-Mktg & SEO - Macy's, Inc.; *pg.* 1778, *pg.* 1417
Siewert, Victoria, Mgr-Mktg-Global - Godiva Chocolatier, Inc.; *pg.* 1854, *pg.* 1235
Sifford, Tim, Sr Dir-Product Solutions-Brakes, Batteries & Engine Mgmt - Advance Auto Parts, Inc.; *pg.* 197, *pg.* 1805
Sifuentes, Debbie, Dir-Mktg - United Technologies Corporation; *pg.* 235, *pg.* 353
Sigal, Orly, Dir-Trade Mktg - Luxottica Group; *pg.* 8, *pg.* 1323
Sigala, Ricardo, Dir-Creative Svcs & Production - Univision Communications Inc.; *pg.* 683, *pg.* 1307
Sigel, Jeff, VP-Mktg - Ahold USA, Inc.; *pg.* 1013, *pg.* 1520
Sigillito, Michael, Dir-Sls & Mktg - Firestone Industrial Products Division; *pg.* 1882, *pg.* 686
Sigismondo, Vincent, Sr Mgr-Mktg Analytics - Gilt Groupe Inc.; *pg.* 24, *pg.* 1234
Sigler, Bill, Dir-North American Sls - Echo Incorporated; *pg.* 1046, *pg.* 626
Sigler, Mark, Sr Dir-Product Mgmt - CA Technologies; *pg.* 366, *pg.* 1168
Sigmon, Christopher, Specialist-Field Mktg - Yokohama Tire Corporation; *pg.* 1892, *pg.* 94
Sigsworth, Mitchell, Mgr-Local Sls - Cox Communications, Inc.; *pg.* 279, *pg.* 501
Sigurdson, Tannis, Dir-Sls-Canada - BioLase Technology, Inc.; *pg.* 1506, *pg.* 107
Sigurdsson, Tomas Mar, Pres-Alcoa European Reg & Alcoa Global Primary Products - Alcoa Inc.; *pg.* 65, *pg.* 1188
Sikes, Ani, VP & Sr Mgr-Media - TD Bank US Holding Company; *pg.* 809, *pg.* 1051
Sikes, Diana, Sr VP-Mktg - Art Van Furniture, Inc.; *pg.* 914, *pg.* 912
Sikes, Paul, Sr Dir-Store Sys & Ops - Ace Hardware Corporation; *pg.* 1040, *pg.* 644
Sikora, Justin, Dir-PR & Social Media - Darden Restaurants, Inc.; *pg.* 1724, *pg.* 453
Sikora, Kerry, Sr Mgr-Web Ops - T-Mobile US, Inc.; *pg.* 676, *pg.* 1816
Sikora, Ron, Editor & Designer-Page One - Cape Cod Times; *pg.* 1625, *pg.* 826
Sikorski, Courtney, Sr Assoc Brand Mgr-Cottonelle - Kimberly-Clark Corporation; *pg.* 1461, *pg.* 1720
Silacci, Gary, Mgr-Sls-Ocean Mist Farms - Ocean Mist Farms Corp.; *pg.* 887, *pg.* 64
Silanesu, Emmanuele, Mgr-Specialist Sls-Devices & Mobility - Microsoft Corporation; *pg.* 435, *pg.* 1824
Silbaugh, Steve, Head-Mktg-Ralph Lauren ECommerce-North America - Ralph Lauren Corporation; *pg.* 46, *pg.* 1284
Silberman, Michael, Gen Mgr-Digital Media - New York Magazine; *pg.* 1667, *pg.* 1269
Silbert, Glenn, VP-Global Product-Men's, Outdoor & Team Sports - Under Armour, Inc.; *pg.* 49, *pg.* 759
Silcott, Gary, Sr Mgr-Corp Comm - Advanced Micro Devices, Inc.; *pg.* 613, *pg.* 282
Silfies, Jason, VP-Mktg & Tech-Coldwell Banker Comml - Coldwell Banker Real Estate LLC; *pg.* 1087, *pg.* 1103
Siliski, Michael, Dir-Product Mgmt-Google Play & Android - Google Inc.; *pg.* 1249, *pg.* 153
Silk, Karin, Sr VP-Mktg - Rubio's Restaurants, Inc.; *pg.* 1748, *pg.* 60
Silk, Kathy, Mgr-Sls - WLUK-TV; *pg.* 322, *pg.* 1860
Silk, Tom, Sr VP-Mktg & Comm - KB Home; *pg.* 90, *pg.* 134
Silkowitz, Jeremy, Mgr-Mktg - Philips Healthcare; *pg.* 1585, *pg.* 783
Sillan, Amy S., VP-Mktg & Strategy-Global Media - Time Warner Inc.; *pg.* 312, *pg.* 1302
Sills, Robyn, Mgr-Brand Experience-Global PR - Fossil Group, Inc.; *pg.* 5, *pg.* 1735
Sillus, Angela, Dir-Specialty Sls Support - Anthem, Inc.; *pg.* 1192, *pg.* 683
Silsby, David V., Dir-Sls - Simpson Technologies Corporation; *pg.* 111, *pg.* 555
Silva, Ashley, Mgr-Digital Mktg - Constant Contact, Inc.; *pg.* 379, *pg.* 850
Silva, Brooke, Mgr-Creative - Target Corporation; *pg.* 1786, *pg.* 942
Silva, Carlos, Mgr-Adv-Intl - Graham Holdings Company; *pg.* 1645, *pg.* 1773
Silva, Diana, Head-Global eCommerce Mktg - WebEx Communications, Inc.; *pg.* 491, *pg.* 270
Silva, Ed, Dir-Product Ops - DraftKings, Inc.; *pg.* 545, *pg.* 793
Silva, Hannah, Mgr-Mktg-Amazon Locker - Amazon.com, Inc.; *pg.* 1226, *pg.* 1831
Silva, Ilya, Dir-Mktg - Perry Ellis International, Inc.; *pg.* 45, *pg.* 445
Silva, Jaime, Sr Dir-Consumer Mktg-North America - Rosetta Stone Inc.; *pg.* 462, *pg.* 1774
Silva, Judy, Mgr-Mktg Comm & eBusiness - Parker Hannifin Corporation; *pg.* 1368, *pg.* 1434
Silva, Marisol, Mgr-Integrated Media Comm - Bulgari Corporation of America; *pg.* 2, *pg.* 1208
Silva, Ofelia, Dir-Mktg - Jarden Consumer Solutions; *pg.* 57, *pg.* 412
Silva, Patricia, Mgr-Mktg & Loyalty - TAP Portugal; *pg.* 1925, *pg.* 1098
Silva, Percy, Mgr-Mdse - Arizona Cardinals Football Club, Inc.; *pg.* 529, *pg.* 25
Silva, Rachael, Dir-Creative Svcs - The New York Public Library; *pg.* 605, *pg.* 1269
Silva, Rachel, Asst VP-Mktg - The Pep Boys - Manny, Moe & Jack; *pg.* 215, *pg.* 1568
Silva, Stephen, VP & Gen Mgr-Mktg - Boulder Brands, Inc.; *pg.* 1016, *pg.* 310
Silva, Yvonne, Sr Dir-Mktg Comm & Dir-Ops - Chick-fil-A, Inc.; *pg.* 1721, *pg.* 492
Silver, Allison, VP-Mktg - American Express Company; *pg.* 712, *pg.* 1190
Silver, Amy, Mgr-Mktg-Global Adv - Banana Republic; *pg.* 1760, *pg.* 212
Silver, Bob, Mgr-Local Sls - WTVG 13abc; *pg.* 323, *pg.* 1477
Silver, Charlie, VP-Mktg - Bloomingdale's, Inc.; *pg.* 1763, *pg.* 1204
Silver, Dan, VP-Ops, Mktg & Electrical Components Grp Sls - Panasonic Corporation of North America; *pg.* 661, *pg.* 1120
Silver, Emily, Sr Dir-Media & Digital Solutions-North America Beverages - PepsiCo, Inc.; *pg.* 259, *pg.* 1327
Silver, Jenna, Dir-Adv Sls Mktg - Univision Communications Inc.; *pg.* 683, *pg.* 1307
Silver, Marie, Assoc Dir-Menveo Mktg - Novartis Vaccines & Diagnostics, Inc.; *pg.* 1575, *pg.* 809
Silver, Michelle C., Mgr-Sls Bus Dev - Intel Corporation; *pg.* 645, *pg.* 266
Silver, Rachel, Dir-Social Media - Birchbox; *pg.* 1762, *pg.* 1203
Silver, Scott, Specialist-Mobile Product - Twitter, Inc.; *pg.* 1285, *pg.* 228
Silvera, Juan, Mng Dir-Digital Mktg & Adv-MUFG Americas - Union Bank, N.A.; *pg.* 813, *pg.* 230
Silverboard, Lisa, Brand Mgr - Georgia-Pacific LLC; *pg.* 1458, *pg.* 507
Silverio, Lisa, Sr Mgr-Design - Colgate-Palmolive Company; *pg.* 504, *pg.* 1215
Silverio, Mark, VP-Sls-Americas - Fitbit Inc.; *pg.* 639, *pg.* 218
Silverman, Ami, VP-Retail Sls & Mktg-US - Microsoft Corporation; *pg.* 435, *pg.* 1824
Silverman, Andrew, Grp Product Mgr - Google Inc.; *pg.* 1249, *pg.* 153
Silverman, Ann, Dir-PR - Lenox Hill Hospital; *pg.* 1555, *pg.* 1251
Silverman, Chrissy, Reg Mgr-Mktg - Bank of America Corporation; *pg.* 718, *pg.* 1362
Silverman, Diane, Mgr-PR - The Goodyear Tire & Rubber Company; *pg.* 1883, *pg.* 1401
Silverman, Doug, VP-Mktg & Strategic Fin-Aon Integramark - Aon Risk Services Inc.; *pg.* 1193, *pg.* 564

First page reference indicates Business Class Edition
Second page reference indicates Geographic Edition

Silverman, Evan, Sr VP-Digital Media - A&E Television Networks, LLC; pg. 267, pg. 1185
Silverman, Greg, Pres-Creative Dev & Worldwide Production - Warner Bros. Entertainment Inc.; pg. 319, pg. 54
Silverman, Joe, Sr Dir-Mktg - The Quaker Oats Company; pg. 834, pg. 588
Silverman, Ken, Asst Mgr-Mktg - General Motors Company; pg. 175, pg. 881
Silverstein, Craig, Product Mgr - Paychex, Inc.; pg. 792, pg. 1336
Silverstein, Lauren J., Dir-Events, Retail Mktg & Client Rels - Parfums Christian Dior, Inc; pg. 519, pg. 1276
Silverstein, Martin, Chief Strategy Officer & Exec VP - Anthem, Inc.; pg. 1192, pg. 683
Silverstein, Scott, Sr Mgr-Channel Mktg - Infinera Corporation; pg. 644, pg. 286
Silverstein, Seth, Sr Dir-Digital Customer Acq - DIRECTV Group Holdings, LLC; pg. 281, pg. 79
Silverstein, Sharon, Sr VP-Sls-Entertainment Clients - Viacom Inc.; pg. 316, pg. 1310
Silvestri, Angie K., Dir-Comml Acq Mktg - DIRECTV Group Holdings, LLC; pg. 281, pg. 79
Silvestri, Heather, Mgr-Mktg Comm - Trimble Navigation Limited; pg. 1384, pg. 288
Silvestri, Steve, Sr Dir-TV Adv & Tech Sls - AOL Inc.; pg. 1229, pg. 1195
Silvestrini-Stauffer, Amy, Sr Mgr-HR Solutions - Tyco International (US) Inc.; pg. 1891, pg. 1113
Silviera, Jorge, Product Dir-Framing Tools - DeWALT Industrial Tool Company; pg. 1328, pg. 757
Sim, Greg, VP-Consumer Products - Major League Baseball; pg. 560, pg. 1255
Sim, Judith, CMO - Oracle Corporation; pg. 450, pg. 191
Simaan, Kyra, Mgr-ECommerce Mktg-Wrangler-VF Jeanswear - V.F. Corporation; pg. 34, pg. 1376
Siman, Sireenah, Sr Assoc Mgr-Mktg - General Mills, Inc.; pg. 828, pg. 933
Simao, Steven, VP-Travel Agency Sls - Windstar Cruises; pg. 1931, pg. 1843
Simard, Stephanie, VP-Digital Mktg-Ubisoft Motion Pictures - Ubisoft Inc.; pg. 589, pg. 229
Simas, John, Producer-iAd Creative Dev - Apple Inc.; pg. 350, pg. 73
Simblist, Lauren, Dir-Sls-Digital Media - Weight Watchers International, Inc.; pg. 1609, pg. 1313
Simco, Kim, Dir-Channel Mktg - MetLife, Inc.; pg. 1208, pg. 1258
Simecka, Jessica, Acct Exec-Adv - Garmin International, Inc.; pg. 1414, pg. 717
Simek, Rob, Exec Dir-Channel Mktg - Comcast Cable Communications, Inc.; pg. 276, pg. 1560
Simensen, Erling, Mgr-Product Mktg-Wireless Connectivity Solutions - Texas Instruments Incorporated; pg. 679, pg. 1688
Simensky, Scott, Gen Mgr-Sls - WABC-TV Inc.; pg. 317, pg. 1312
Simeon, Adam, Reg Dir-Sls - Union Pacific Corporation; pg. 1927, pg. 1018
Simeon, Adam, Reg Dir-Sls - Union Pacific Railroad Company; pg. 1927, pg. 1019
Simeone, Lucy, Specialist-Channel Mktg - Schneider Electric; pg. 467, pg. 1609
Simeone, Tom, Dir-Product Mgmt - Milwaukee Electric Tool Corp.; pg. 1056, pg. 1855
Simes, Nuno, Reg Dir-Sls-Western Europe - Heineken USA Inc.; pg. 252, pg. 1352
Simitchieva, Kremena, Head-Therapeutic Area Immunology Mktg - Boehringer Ingelheim Pharmaceuticals, Inc.; pg. 1507, pg. 368
Simkins, Rosalie, Specialist-Mktg - Zulily; pg. 1792, pg. 1843
Simko, Chris, Sr VP-CBS Sports Sls & Dir-Mktg - CBS Corporation; pg. 273, pg. 1210
Simm, Ed, Mgr-Mktg - Wells Fargo & Company; pg. 819, pg. 232
Simmers, Matt, Product Mgr - Saint-Gobain Abrasives, Inc. - Philadelphia; pg. 1180, pg. 1553
Simmons, Aaron, Reg Mgr-Sls-North East - David Clark Company Incorporated; pg. 633, pg. 862
Simmons, Amy, Specialist-Trade Mktg - Lindt & Sprungli (USA) Inc.; pg. 1857, pg. 1039
Simmons, Brian, Grp Product Mgr-Global - Nilfisk-Advance, Inc.; pg. 332, pg. 953
Simmons, Chandra, VP-Admin & Sr Mgr-IT Audit - M&T Bank Corporation; pg. 777, pg. 1149
Simmons, Chris, Specialist-Web Mktg - Brocade Communications Systems, Inc.; pg. 365, pg. 239
Simmons, Christopher, Dir-Product Mktg - New York Life Insurance Company; pg. 1211, pg. 1268
Simmons, Claire, Mgr-PR - Cree Inc.; pg. 631, pg. 1371
Simmons, Clarice, Sr Mgr-Notebook GPU Product Mktg & Div Mgr-Launch - Advanced Micro Devices, Inc.; pg. 613, pg. 282
Simmons, Denise, Mgr-Branding & Mktg Comm - Scottrade, Inc.; pg. 802, pg. 1003
Simmons, Diana, Sr Dir-Product Commercialization & Process & Sys Improvement - Clif Bar Inc.; pg. 848, pg. 83
Simmons, Edrice, Sr Dir-Mktg-US Immunology - AbbVie Inc.; pg. 1486, pg. 638
Simmons, Erica, Mgr-Global Mktg-Energy & Utilities-Digital Factory Div - Siemens Process Industries and Drives; pg. 673, pg. 485
Simmons, Grant, VP-Search Mktg - Dominion Enterprises; pg. 1636, pg. 1796
Simmons, Grant, VP-Search Mktg - Homes.com, Inc.; pg. 1256, pg. 203
Simmons, Jade, Mgr-Mktg-Barbie Global Brand Team - Mattel Games/Puzzles; pg. 962, pg. 80
Simmons, Jade, Mgr-Mktg-Barbie Global Brand Team - MATTEL, INC.; pg. 962, pg. 81
Simmons, John, Mgr-Product Strategy & Product Plng-Natl - Toyota Motor Sales, U.S.A., Inc.; pg. 193, pg. 296
Simmons, Kristine, Dir-Mktg Comm - NuVasive, Inc.; pg. 1577, pg. 205
Simmons, Lauren, Dir-MTV 360 Events Mktg - Viacom Inc.; pg. 316, pg. 1310
Simmons, Lee, Mgr-Mktg - The Dun & Bradstreet Corp.; pg. 1637, pg. 1120
Simmons, Lisa F., Mgr-Daily Pipeline Mktg - Atmos Energy Corporation; pg. 1935, pg. 1675
Simmons, Mark, VP-Mktg & ECommerce - Design Within Reach, Inc.; pg. 923, pg. 216
Simmons, Mike, Sr Mgr-HR-SSG-Site Svcs - The Boeing Company; pg. 225, pg. 567
Simmons, Rod, Brand Mgr - Shaw Ross International Importers; pg. 1970, pg. 449
Simmons, Russ, Reg Mgr-Sls-Midwest - Cooper Interconnect; pg. 630, pg. 1118
Simmons, Ryan, Dir-Mktg-Live Svcs-EA Sports - Electronic Arts Inc.; pg. 951, pg. 189
Simmons, Tim, Gen Mgr-Sls-North America Demand Chain Applications & Svcs - Teradata Corporation; pg. 483, pg. 1447
Simmons, Todd, Sr Mgr-Retail Mktg - Rosetta Stone Inc.; pg. 462, pg. 1774
Simms, Joni, Mgr-Partnership Mktg - FTD Group, Inc.; pg. 1795, pg. 608
Simms, Joni, Mgr-Partnership Mktg-FTD.com - FTD.com Inc.; pg. 1770, pg. 608
Simms, Steve, Sr Analyst-Mktg-Wal-Mart Inc. - PepsiCo, Inc.; pg. 259, pg. 1327
Simo, Fidji, Product Dir - Facebook, Inc.; pg. 1245, pg. 143
Simon, Bryan, Sr Mgr-Digital Mktg - QUALCOMM Incorporated; pg. 1873, pg. 207
Simon, Cathy, Dir-Mktg & Brands - FremantleMedia North America Inc.; pg. 288, pg. 1233
Simon, Chris, Exec VP-Sls-CBS Television Network - CBS Broadcasting Inc.; pg. 273, pg. 1210
Simon, Chris, Exec VP-Sls-CBS Television Network - CBS Corporation; pg. 273, pg. 1210
Simon, Dawn, Mgr-Mktg - The Macerich Company; pg. 1101, pg. 275
Simon, Don, VP-Mktg - North Shore-LIJ Health System; pg. 1573, pg. 1162
Simon, Gary, Exec VP-Sls - Bulova Corporation; pg. 2, pg. 1356
Simon, Heather, Specialist-Adv - Auto-Owners Insurance Group; pg. 1194, pg. 895
Simon, Jared, Sr Dir-Mktg - The Hain Celestial Group, Inc.; pg. 860, pg. 1172
Simon, Jeremy, Exec Dir-Advancement Mktg & Comm - University Of Colorado; pg. 608, pg. 323
Simon, Julia, Sr Editor-Social Media Strategy-Audience Dev - The New York Times; pg. 1668, pg. 1270
Simon, Juliana, Sr Mgr-Partner Mktg-Google HPA - Hotels.com, L.P.; pg. 1257, pg. 1682
Simon, Kenneth, Assoc Dir-Vaccine Sls - Merck & Co., Inc.; pg. 1566, pg. 1077
Simon, Kurt, Sr Dir-Brand Mktg - Kellogg Company; pg. 831, pg. 870
Simon, Mary Kay, Sr Mgr-Mktg Comm - Medtronic, Inc.; pg. 1564, pg. 939
Simon, Melissa, Mgr-Digital Mktg - The Great Atlantic & Pacific Tea Company, Inc.; pg. 1021, pg. 1086
Simon, Michael, VP-Mktg - Cooper Tire & Rubber Company; pg. 1881, pg. 1453
Simon, Rachel, Mgr-Sls Plng - Conde Nast Publications, Inc.; pg. 1629, pg. 1217
Simon, Shari, Sr VP-Corp Mktg - Simon Property Group, Inc.; pg. 1112, pg. 690
Simon, Todd, Sr Mgr-Strategy & Insights - The Boston Beer Company, Inc.; pg. 239, pg. 790
Simon, Walter, Mgr-Mktg - Six Flags Entertainment Corporation; pg. 583, pg. 1698
Simon, Wayne, Mgr-Mktg-Global Pro Rels & Strategic Mktg - Zoll Medical Corporation; pg. 1612, pg. 814
Simone, Daniella, Sr Mgr-Fin - Bacardi USA, Inc.; pg. 1956, pg. 417
Simone, Erica, Sr Product Mgr-New Products, Tiny Prints & Wedding Paper Divas - SHUTTERFLY, INC.; pg. 1280, pg. 192
Simonelli, Michelle, Supvr-Mktg - Canon U.S.A., Inc.; pg. 1404, pg. 1178
Simonelli, Richard, Sr Dir-IR - CoStar Group, Inc.; pg. 742, pg. 397
Simonet, Carla, VP-Mktg Sciences - Comcast Corporation; pg. 276, pg. 1560
Simonetta, Teresa, Campaign Mgr-North America Consumer Mktg - Dell Inc.; pg. 383, pg. 1737
Simoni, Jamie, Sr Mgr-Mktg-Social Media - American Eagle Outfitters, Inc.; pg. 37, pg. 1572
Simons, John, VP-Sls & Mktg - Robertet, Inc.; pg. 522, pg. 1100
Simons, John, Dir-Sls-Intl - Rust-Oleum Corporation; pg. 1447, pg. 664
Simons, Scott, Sr Dir-Mktg-Global - Whole Foods Market, Inc.; pg. 1038, pg. 1667
Simonsen, Janice, Specialist-Media - Ikea North America Services LLC; pg. 929, pg. 1523
Simonson, Megan, Assoc Brand Mgr & Product Mgr - Spectrum Brands Holdings, Inc.; pg. 60, pg. 1867
Simpkins, Cliff, Sr Product Mgr-Windows Platform Developer Mktg - Microsoft Corporation; pg. 435, pg. 1824
Simpkins, Tom, Dir-Sls & Mktg - Panavise Products, Inc.; pg. 1058, pg. 1032
Simpson, Alyssa, Sr Product Mgr-Mobile - International Business Machines Corporation; pg. 418, pg. 1138
Simpson, Annabel, Mgr-Mktg & Comm - Calico Corners; pg. 691, pg. 1543
Simpson, Ashley, Rep-Field Sls - Mike's Hard Lemonade Co.; pg. 1966, pg. 582
Simpson, Bryan, Dir-Media Rels - New Belgium Brewing Company, Inc.; pg. 258, pg. 328
Simpson, Carol, VP-Natl Customer Mktg - PepsiCo, Inc.; pg. 259, pg. 1327
Simpson, Claire, Dir-Mktg & Comm-Europe - eBay Inc.; pg. 1240, pg. 243
Simpson, Daniela, Mgr-Mktg-Wonka - Nestle USA, Inc.; pg. 883, pg. 96
Simpson, Doug, Dir-Sls - Facebook, Inc.; pg. 1245, pg. 143
Simpson, Emily, Mgr-Mktg Promos-OTC - Galderma Laboratories, L.P.; pg. 1532, pg. 1695
Simpson, George, Reg Mgr-Premium Offerings Sls - Yara N America, Inc.; pg. 1802, pg. 477
Simpson, Heather L., Sr Mgr-Mktg Comm - Computer Sciences Corporation; pg. 378, pg. 1780
Simpson, Jonathan, Dir-Comml Mktg - Heineken USA Inc.; pg. 252, pg. 1352
Simpson, Kelly, Mgr-Sports Brand Mktg - Royal Bank of Canada; pg. 800, pg. 1942
Simpson, Malcolm, Sr Brand Mgr-Pringles Global Mktg - Kellogg Company; pg. 831, pg. 870
Simpson, Mary K., Mgr-NA Mktg Events - Intel Corporation; pg. 645, pg. 266
Simpson, Matt, Dir-Media Svcs - PGA Tour, Inc.; pg. 574, pg. 460
Simpson, Michael, VP-Mktg - Fragrance Resources, Inc.; pg. 509, pg. 1052
Simpson, Neal, Assoc Dir-Oncology Mktg - Regeneron Pharmaceuticals, Inc.; pg. 1588, pg. 1345
Simpson, Paul, Dir-Sls - First Harrison Bank; pg. 755, pg. 676
Simpson, Peter, Dir-Online Mktg & Mktg Analysis - The ServiceMaster Company, LLC; pg. 335, pg. 1646
Simpson, Phil, Mgr-Product Mktg-Jboss - Red Hat, Inc.; pg. 460, pg. 1388
Simpson, Rich, Dir-US Sls Strategy-Skincare - Johnson &

Johnson; *pg.* 1549, *pg.* 1091
Simpson, Rob, Mgr-Mktg Programs & Dealer Comm - Volvo Trucks North America, Inc.; *pg.* 195, *pg.* 1377
Simpson, Roger, Assoc Dir-Creative - True Value Company; *pg.* 1065, *pg.* 592
Simpson, Sammy, VP-Mktg - Daily News, L.P.; *pg.* 1632, *pg.* 1221
Simpson, Shannon, Dir-Adv - The StarPhoenix; *pg.* 1689, *pg.* 1962
Simpson, Ted, Head-Mktg-North America - Philips Electronics North America; *pg.* 662, *pg.* 782
Simpson, Ted, Head-Mktg-North America - Philips Lighting; *pg.* 1303, *pg.* 806
Simpson, Tyler, Dir-Mktg-Michelob ULTRA, Michelob Golden & Select Bud Brands - Anheuser-Busch Companies, LLC; *pg.* 237, *pg.* 991
Sims, Aaron, Dir-Sls Mdsg - Ghirardelli Chocolate Company; *pg.* 1854, *pg.* 252
Sims, Chris, Co-Founder & Chief Strategy Officer - Answers Corporation; *pg.* 1220, *pg.* 1195
Sims, David, VP-Loyalty Mktg - La Quinta Inns, Inc.; *pg.* 1100, *pg.* 1722
Sims, Frank, Specialist-Digital Mktg - The Sherwin-Williams Company; *pg.* 1447, *pg.* 1435
Sims, Frank, Specialist-Digital Mktg - Sherwin Williams; *pg.* 1448, *pg.* 1436
Sims, Marshall, Dir-Global Mktg & Brand Building - Abbott Laboratories; *pg.* 1484, *pg.* 551
Sims, Mike, Sr VP-Sls & Mktg - Louisiana-Pacific Corporation; *pg.* 94, *pg.* 1652
Sims, Tara, Mgr-PR - QUALCOMM Incorporated; *pg.* 1873, *pg.* 207
Sims, Taryn, Mgr-Creative Comm - Duke Energy Corporation; *pg.* 1940, *pg.* 1366
Sims, Todd, Sr Dir-Comm - Omnicell Inc.; *pg.* 1578, *pg.* 161
Sims, Travis, VP-Sls - Makita U.S.A., Inc.; *pg.* 1358, *pg.* 120
Sims, Trisha, Mgr-Small Bus Mktg - Sprint Corporation; *pg.* 1874, *pg.* 719
Simutis, Michelle, Dir-Sls Ops - Noosa Yoghurt; *pg.* 886, *pg.* 310
Sinanagic, Amela, Sr Dir-Interactive Art - Nestle Purina PetCare Company; *pg.* 1479, *pg.* 1000
Sinanian, Mark A., Sr Dir-Solutions Mktg - Canon U.S.A., Inc.; *pg.* 1404, *pg.* 1178
Sinapi, Teresa, Brand Mgr - Allstar Products Group LLC; *pg.* 17, *pg.* 1166
Sinatra, Kelly, Mgr-PR - Benjamin Moore & Co.; *pg.* 1440, *pg.* 1085
Sinatra, Michael, Mgr-PR & Pub Affairs - Whole Foods Market, Inc.; *pg.* 1038, *pg.* 1667
Sinclair, Carrie, Dir-Digital Mktg - Honeywell International Inc.; *pg.* 407, *pg.* 1088
Sinclair, Ron, Sr VP-Mktg - AMERICAN TIRE DISTRIBUTORS HOLDINGS, INC.; *pg.* 199, *pg.* 1379
Sinclair, Ryan, Sr Mgr-Mktg-Amgen Digital Health - Amgen Inc.; *pg.* 1493, *pg.* 291
Sinclair, Ryan, VP-Local Mktg - Bloomin' Brands, Inc.; *pg.* 1716, *pg.* 471
Sinclair, Tracy, Dir-Mktg-Shopper Mktg-Walmart & Sam's Club - Kraft Foods Gevalia; *pg.* 253, *pg.* 387
Sinclair, Tracy, Dir-Mktg-Premium Coffee-Gevalia & Tassimo - The Kraft Heinz Company; *pg.* 871, *pg.* 641
Sine, Lindsey, Mgr-PR, Snowsports & Outdoor - The North Face, Inc.; *pg.* 1840, *pg.* 252
Sine, Paul, VP-Mktg - Timex Corporation; *pg.* 14, *pg.* 355
Singer, Dave, VP-Sls & Customer Dev - Ruiz Food Products, Inc.; *pg.* 893, *pg.* 77
Singer, Fanette, Sr VP-Mktg - COUNTRY Financial; *pg.* 1198, *pg.* 557
Singer, Jeff, Dir-Mktg-Global - Crestron Electronics Inc.; *pg.* 631, *pg.* 1116
Singer, Lisa, Sr Product Mgr - Elmer's Products, Inc.; *pg.* 1442, *pg.* 1479
Singer, Lori, Grp VP-Mktg-Marc Jacobs, Vera Wang & Kenneth Cole - Coty, Inc.; *pg.* 506, *pg.* 1219
Singer, Lorraine, Brand Mgr - Johnson & Johnson; *pg.* 1549, *pg.* 1091
Singer, Mark Chumley, Mgr-Events & Mktg-Eagles Youth Partnership - Philadelphia Eagles Football Club, Inc.; *pg.* 575, *pg.* 1569
Singer, Patricia Elwell, Gen Mgr-Global Brand & Media Partnerships - Shell Lubricants; *pg.* 217, *pg.* 1714
Singer, Paula R., Pres/CEO-Laureate Global Products & Svcs - Laureate Education, Inc.; *pg.* 603, *pg.* 757
Singer, Rebecca Goltzman, Grp Brand Dir - GlaxoSmithKline; *pg.* 1536, *pg.* 1389
Singer, Solomon, Mgr-Product Dev - Revlon Consumer Products Corporation; *pg.* 521, *pg.* 1286
Singer, Solomon, Mgr-Product Dev - Revlon, Inc.; *pg.* 521, *pg.* 1286
Singer, Tricia, Gen Mgr-Global Brand & Media Partnerships - Shell Oil Company; *pg.* 984, *pg.* 1714
Singery, Gary, Dir-Mktg - United Parcel Service, Inc.; *pg.* 1928, *pg.* 522
Singewald, Craig, Dir-Global Mktg-Xeljanz - Pfizer Inc.; *pg.* 1581, *pg.* 1278
Singh, Arun, Sr Mgr-Product Mktg - Oracle Corporation; *pg.* 1272, *pg.* 786
Singh, Baljeet, Head-TV & Video & Product Dir - Twitter, Inc.; *pg.* 1285, *pg.* 228
Singh, Devendra, VP-Product Mgmt - Oracle Corporation; *pg.* 1272, *pg.* 786
Singh, Gagandeep, Sr Mgr-Product-Prime - Amazon.com, Inc.; *pg.* 1226, *pg.* 1831
Singh, Gaitree, Mgr-Mktg - The Nielsen Company B.V.; *pg.* 1671, *pg.* 1272
Singh, Gurkirat, Mgr-Sls-Northern Territory - WatchGuard Technologies, Inc.; *pg.* 491, *pg.* 1842
Singh, Jesse, Sr VP-Sls & Mktg - 3M Company; *pg.* 1142, *pg.* 956
Singh, Mitu, Product Mgr - Facebook, Inc.; *pg.* 1245, *pg.* 143
Singh, Pooja, Sr Dir-Digital & Customer Experience - Wal-Mart.com; *pg.* 1287, *pg.* 50
Singh, Porush, VP-Product Dev - MasterCard International, Inc.; *pg.* 780, *pg.* 1326
Singh, Prabhjeet, Head-Education Mktg-APAC - Adobe Systems Incorporated; *pg.* 342, *pg.* 235
Singh, Prabhjot, VP-Global Bus Partners-Product Dev & Sourcing - Macy's East; *pg.* 1777, *pg.* 1254
Singh, Preeti, Dir-Mktg - Iconix Brand Group, Inc.; *pg.* 26, *pg.* 1243
Singh, Rajesh, VP-Sls, Svc & Mktg - General Motors Company; *pg.* 175, *pg.* 881
Singh, Richie, Mgr-Sls-Reo, Short Sls & Foreclosure - Country Wide Realty Inc.; *pg.* 1088, *pg.* 1144
Singh, Sachlene, Mgr-Technical Mktg - Autodesk Inc.; *pg.* 356, *pg.* 257
Singh, Shikhir, Sr Mgr-Enterprise Solutions - BlackBerry Limited; *pg.* 625, *pg.* 1947
Singh, Shiv, Sr VP & Head-Digital & Mktg Transformation-Global - Visa Inc.; *pg.* 816, *pg.* 230
Singh, Shiv, Sr VP-Global Brand & Mktg Transformation - Visa U.S.A., Inc.; *pg.* 817, *pg.* 231
Singh, Sonny, Dir-Mktg - Central Garden & Pet Company; *pg.* 1475, *pg.* 303
Singh, Vinay, Sr Product Mgr - Xilinx, Inc.; *pg.* 496, *pg.* 252
Singhi, Rishabh, Specialist-Product-User Acq - CareerBuilder, LLC; *pg.* 1234, *pg.* 568
Singleton, Deana, Sr Dir-Comml Adv - Microsoft Corporation; *pg.* 435, *pg.* 1824
Singleton, Denna, Dir-Mktg-Global - Elizabeth Arden, Inc.; *pg.* 507, *pg.* 448
Singley, Eric, VP-Consumer & Mobile Products - Yelp! Inc.; *pg.* 1291, *pg.* 235
Singraber, Molly, Coord-Social Media - Walgreen Co.; *pg.* 1608, *pg.* 605
Singson, Marguerite, Mgr-Field Mktg - Kind LLC; *pg.* 868, *pg.* 1249
Sinkoff, Martin, Dir-Mktg & Fine Wines - Frederick Wildman & Sons Ltd.; *pg.* 1963, *pg.* 1233
Sinks, David, Dir-Technical Mktg - CareFusion Corporation; *pg.* 1513, *pg.* 201
Sinner, Jerry, Mgr-Distributor Sls - IAC Industries, Inc.; *pg.* 929, *pg.* 48
Sinnott, Erica, Brand Mgr - Beachbody, LLC; *pg.* 271, *pg.* 272
Sinnott, John, Sr Dir-IR - QUALCOMM Incorporated; *pg.* 1873, *pg.* 207
Sinon, Jeremy, Dir-Digital Media - Hubbard Broadcasting, Inc.; *pg.* 291, *pg.* 961
Sintuvat, Connie, Brand Mgr-Milo's Kitchen - Big Heart Pet Brands; *pg.* 1474, *pg.* 213
Sintuvat, Connie, Brand Mgr-Milo's Kitchen Brand - Del Monte Foods, Inc.; *pg.* 852, *pg.* 304
Sioui, Daniel R., Sr Mgr-Strategic Mktg - Honeywell International Inc.; *pg.* 407, *pg.* 1088
Siovaila, Chad, Mgr-Mktg - Marsh Supermarkets, Inc.; *pg.* 1027, *pg.* 688
Sipos, Ellen, Sr Dir-Fin-US Immunology - Johnson & Johnson; *pg.* 1549, *pg.* 1091
Sippy, Brad, VP-Sls & Mktg - Sunovion Pharmaceuticals Inc.; *pg.* 1599, *pg.* 832
Sircar, Sanghamitra, Product Mgr-Rovings-Global - Owens Corning; *pg.* 102, *pg.* 1476
Sirgy, Peter, Exec VP-Sls & Mktg - Reser's Fine Foods Inc.; *pg.* 1032, *pg.* 1496
Siri, Mary, Exec Dir-Event Mktg - Conde Nast Publications, Inc.; *pg.* 1629, *pg.* 1217
Sirico, Drew, Sr Dir-Mktg & ECommerce - Edible Arrangements International, Inc.; *pg.* 1768, *pg.* 382
Sirigineedi, Ravi, Mgr-Digital Signage Mktg - Intel Corporation; *pg.* 645, *pg.* 266
Sirio, Mary Beth, VP-Product Mgmt - McKesson Corporation; *pg.* 1560, *pg.* 222
Sirjuesingh, Natalie, Sr VP-Mktg - Mission Pharmacal Company Inc.; *pg.* 1568, *pg.* 1742
Sironen, Joel F., Dir-Sls-Graphic Comm-Northwest Reg - Xerox Corporation; *pg.* 494, *pg.* 365
Siroty, David, VP-North American PR - Coldwell Banker Real Estate LLC; *pg.* 1087, *pg.* 1103
Sirstins, Max, Dir-Adv - Sanderson Ford Inc.; *pg.* 190, *pg.* 13
Sirvaitis, Ted, Planner-Integrated Sls - A&E Television Networks, LLC; *pg.* 267, *pg.* 1185
Sisco, David, Dir-New Product Concepts - United Parcel Service, Inc.; *pg.* 1928, *pg.* 522
Sisco, Matt, VP-Sls - Greenlee Textron Inc.; *pg.* 1048, *pg.* 655
Sisemore, Diane, Sr VP & Dir-Mktg - BancFirst Corporation; *pg.* 717, *pg.* 1484
Siskind, Steve, Pres-Domestic Mktg - Paramount Pictures Corporation; *pg.* 304, *pg.* 138
Siskind, Wendy, VP-Mktg - Burlington Coat Factory; *pg.* 1764, *pg.* 1047
Sisler, Bryan, Product Mgr-Global Customer Interfaces-LV Drives NAM - ABB Inc.; *pg.* 1309, *pg.* 1359
Sisler, Joe, Mgr-Email Mktg - Academy Sports & Outdoors, Ltd.; *pg.* 1824, *pg.* 1724
Sisombath, Terra, Specialist-Mktg Comm - Yokohama Tire Corporation; *pg.* 1892, *pg.* 94
Sisson, Graham, Coord-Mktg-Intl - American Eagle Outfitters, Inc.; *pg.* 37, *pg.* 1572
Sisson, Holly, Sr Mgr-Mktg - Chattem, Inc.; *pg.* 1515, *pg.* 1628
Sisson, Melanie, Mgr-Mktg - Fruit of the Loom, Inc.; *pg.* 41, *pg.* 725
Sisson, Rebecca, Sr Mgr-Database Mktg - Museum of Fine Arts of St. Petersburg Florida Inc.; *pg.* 565, *pg.* 463
Sistani, Sima, Head-Media - Tumblr, Inc.; *pg.* 1285, *pg.* 1305
Sistonen-Lonnroth, Jussi, Specialist-Mktg Comm-Design & Graphics - Corning Incorporated; *pg.* 1122, *pg.* 1154
Sit, Thomas, Sr Mgr-Global Comml Ops - Medtronic, Inc.; *pg.* 1564, *pg.* 939
Sitch, Allison, VP-PR-Global - The Ritz-Carlton Hotel Company LLC; *pg.* 1110, *pg.* 766
Sitrin, Todd, Sr VP-Mktg - Electronic Arts Inc.; *pg.* 951, *pg.* 189
Sitruk, Michel, Sr Dir-Mktg - Getty Images, Inc.; *pg.* 1645, *pg.* 1836
Sitzwohl, Robert, Dir-Mktg - Swagelok Company; *pg.* 1064, *pg.* 1473
Sivadasan, Ajit, VP & Gen Mgr-Global ECommerce, Digital Mktg & Tech-B2C & B2B - Lenovo Group Ltd; *pg.* 427, *pg.* 1384
Sivadasan, Babu, Exec VP-Product Dev - Envestnet, Inc.; *pg.* 748, *pg.* 573
Sivajee, Dhanusha, Exec VP-Mktg - XO Group Inc.; *pg.* 1289, *pg.* 1316
Sivak, Michael, Sr Mgr-Retail Mgmt Consulting Practice - Accenture; *pg.* 1392, *pg.* 1186
Sivak, Shannon, Mgr-Western USA Sls - Associated Research Inc.; *pg.* 1400, *pg.* 622
Sivalingam, Bala, Sr Dir-HR Analytics & Diversity Metrics - Wal-Mart Stores, Inc.; *pg.* 1790, *pg.* 29
Sivasamy, Dharaneedharan, Sr Mgr-Sls & Mktg - Donaldson Company, Inc.; *pg.* 1329, *pg.* 917
Sivera, Keith, Dir-Offline Mktg - BodyBuilding.com LLC; *pg.* 1232, *pg.* 549
Siverling, Curt, Pres-Specialty Products Div - Church & Dwight Co., Inc.; *pg.* 1153, *pg.* 1063
Sivetts, Michael G., III, Sr VP-Distr Sls - Microsemi Corporation; *pg.* 435, *pg.* 41
Sixberry, Bryan, Mgr-Mktg - General Electric Company; *pg.* 1297, *pg.* 347
Sizemore, Glenn, Engr-Technical Mktg - NetApp, Inc.; *pg.* 444, *pg.* 287
Sjoquist, Gary, Dir-Advocacy - Quality Bicycle Products; *pg.*

1710, *pg.* 918
Skaaden, Geir R., Sr VP-Corp Bus Dev, Digital Content & Media Solutions - DTS, Inc.; *pg.* 634, *pg.* 55
Skadan, Scott, Specialist-Brdcst Television, Mobile & Online Mktg-WJBF-TV - Media General, Inc.; *pg.* 297, *pg.* 1803
Skafidas, Mary, VP-Investor & PR - Loews Hotels Holding Corporation; *pg.* 1101, *pg.* 1252
Skaggs, Jaime, Mgr-Adv & Brand-Worldwide Franchise - Alimentation Couche-Tard Inc.; *pg.* 1013, *pg.* 1951
Skaggs, Jim, Gen Mgr-Sls - General Electric Company; *pg.* 1297, *pg.* 347
Skaggs, Kim, Mgr-Mktg - Morgan Foods, Inc.; *pg.* 881, *pg.* 673
Skahan, Kelly, Specialist-Fashion PR - Nordstrom, Inc.; *pg.* 1779, *pg.* 1837
Skahan, Mark, Sr Mgr-Technical Sls - Monadnock Paper Mills, Inc.; *pg.* 1464, *pg.* 1033
Skahen, Daniel, Dir-Mktg Svcs - Georgia Department of Economic Development; *pg.* 992, *pg.* 506
Skahen, Erin, Mgr-Sls Dev-Retail - Google Inc.; *pg.* 1249, *pg.* 153
Skala, Kasey, Head-Digital & Social - Solo Cup Company; *pg.* 1469, *pg.* 625
Skanderup, Josh, Product Mgr - Raven Industries, Inc.; *pg.* 1888, *pg.* 1625
Skapek, Gus, Reg Mgr-Sls-Intl - Campbell Wrapper Corporation; *pg.* 1454, *pg.* 1856
Skattum, T. J., Sr Dir-Fin - Chicago Blackhawk Hockey Team, Inc.; *pg.* 538, *pg.* 569
Skaug, Knut E., Assoc Dir-Global Product Strategy-Oncology - Novartis Corporation; *pg.* 1574, *pg.* 1273
Skaw, Jerry, Mgr-Sls & Mktg-Photogrammetry Products - Microsoft Corporation; *pg.* 435, *pg.* 1824
Skea, Bob, Head-Americas Sls - The Dun & Bradstreet Corp.; *pg.* 1637, *pg.* 1120
Skeba, Mark, Mgr-Mktg Excellence & Best Practices - General Mills, Inc.; *pg.* 828, *pg.* 933
Skelcher, Elizabeth, Sr Analyst-Social Media - State Farm Mutual Automobile Insurance Co.; *pg.* 1218, *pg.* 557
Skelly, James W., Dir-OE Sls-Americas - The Timken Company; *pg.* 218, *pg.* 1408
Skelly, Lance M., Dir-Comm-Media Rels - AT&T Communications Corp.; *pg.* 1866, *pg.* 1043
Skibinski, Mike, Dir-Mktg-Horizon Organic - The WhiteWave Foods Company; *pg.* 1037, *pg.* 324
Skibo, Jennifer, Head-Digital Media - United Natural Foods, Inc.; *pg.* 907, *pg.* 1608
Skidmore, Cary T., CMO & Exec VP - Glentel Inc.; *pg.* 1944, *pg.* 1907
Skildum, John, Bus Mgr-US - 3M Company; *pg.* 1142, *pg.* 956
Skiles, Mark, Acct Mgr-Sls-Natl - TODCO, Inc.; *pg.* 115, *pg.* 1459
Skiles, Todd, Sr VP-Sls & Solutions - Ryder System, Inc.; *pg.* 1922, *pg.* 446
Skillen, Andrew, Dir-Mktg - Equifax Inc.; *pg.* 748, *pg.* 504
Skinner, Dan, Mgr-PR & Social Media - ConAgra Foods, Inc.; *pg.* 826, *pg.* 1014
Skinner, Heather, Sr Mgr-PR - Western Digital Corporation; *pg.* 492, *pg.* 118
Skinner, Heidi, Mgr-Social Strategy-Global - Harley-Davidson, Inc.; *pg.* 178, *pg.* 1874
Skinner, Kelly, Dir-PR - The State Theatre; *pg.* 585, *pg.* 1094
Skinner, Lia, Mgr-Shopper Mktg - Reckitt Benckiser Inc.; *pg.* 1136, *pg.* 1105
Skinner, Lisa, Reg Mgr-Mktg - Aamco Transmissions, Inc.; *pg.* 197, *pg.* 1540
Skinner, Matt, Mgr-Mktg-Demand Generation-Global Levi.com eCommerce - Levi Strauss & Co.; *pg.* 43, *pg.* 220
Skinner, Philip J., Exec Dir-Reg Mktg Americas - PerkinElmer, Inc.; *pg.* 1426, *pg.* 853
Skipper, Greg, VP-Sls - AOL Inc.; *pg.* 1229, *pg.* 1195
Skipper, Monica, VP-Brand Experience Mktg-FedEx Svcs - FedEx Corporation; *pg.* 1907, *pg.* 1642
Skjold-Joergensen, Marie, Product Mgr-Media Sys - Veeder-Root Company; *pg.* 61, *pg.* 371
Skjonsby, Brooke, Mgr-Vail Mountain Mktg - Vail Resorts, Inc.; *pg.* 1117, *pg.* 313
Skladanek, Steve J., Dir-Mktg-Comml Launch Svcs - Lockheed Martin Corporation; *pg.* 229, *pg.* 762
Sklar, Remi, VP-PR-Warner Bros Interactive Entertainment - Warner Bros. Entertainment Inc.; *pg.* 319, *pg.* 54
Skobin, Jeff, Mgr-Mktg - Galpin Motors, Inc.; *pg.* 174, *pg.* 166
Skodol, Ted, Dir-Channel Mktg-North America - Unilever United States, Inc.; *pg.* 904, *pg.* 1061
Skogland, Elaine, Mgr-Antibacterial & Antifungal Mktg - Merck & Co., Inc.; *pg.* 1566, *pg.* 1077
Skoko, Goran, Sr VP & Dir-Product Dev - FactSet Research Systems Inc.; *pg.* 1247, *pg.* 361
Skoler, Liz, Head-Adv Strategy & Partnerships-MixRadio - Microsoft Corporation; *pg.* 435, *pg.* 1824
Skolfield, Emery, VP-Digital Strategy & Mktg - Office Depot, Inc.; *pg.* 448, *pg.* 412
Skollar, Adam L, Mgr-Mktg & Digital Programming - New York Rangers Hockey Club; *pg.* 570, *pg.* 1269
Skolones, Mike, Sr Mgr-PhysX - NVIDIA Corporation; *pg.* 447, *pg.* 268
Skomp, Jason, Mgr-Adv - The Bloomfield Manufacturing Co., Inc.; *pg.* 70, *pg.* 674
Skoog, Kari, Dir-Product, Tech & Consumer PR Grp - Intel Corporation; *pg.* 645, *pg.* 266
Skop, Francis Chip, Dir-Sls & Mktg - Rigidized Metals Corp.; *pg.* 108, *pg.* 1151
Skorjanec, Joe, Product Mgr - Eaton Corporation; *pg.* 1331, *pg.* 1429
Skoufalos, Ioannis, Officer-Global Product Supply - The Procter & Gamble Company; *pg.* 1129, *pg.* 1418
Skow, Kathi, VP-Brand & Product Mktg-Global - Ancestry.com LLC; *pg.* 1228, *pg.* 1754
Skrdlant, Lisa, Dir-Mktg-Australia & New Zealand - Rust-Oleum Corporation; *pg.* 1447, *pg.* 664
Skripic, Damir, Dir-Product Mgmt-Smart Home - NETGEAR, Inc.; *pg.* 444, *pg.* 247
Skripitsky, Lara, Dir-Digital Mktg - Johnson & Johnson Inc.; *pg.* 1552, *pg.* 1923
Skrubis, Steve, Dir-Product Mgmt - Pelican Products, Inc.; *pg.* 1842, *pg.* 295
Skrycki-Mohler, Ann, Brand Mgr-Champion - Federal-Mogul Holdings Corporation; *pg.* 205, *pg.* 907
Skul, Dave A., Sr Dir-US Enterprise Acct Org - Abbott Laboratories; *pg.* 1484, *pg.* 551
Skuller, Edward, Dir-Creative Svcs & Mktg - Wacoal America Inc.; *pg.* 35, *pg.* 1312
Skupien, Marek, Sr Mgr-Market - Cisco Systems, Inc.; *pg.* 372, *pg.* 240
Skupin, Michelle, Sr Mgr-Corp & B2B Comm - RetailMeNot Inc.; *pg.* 1782, *pg.* 1665
Skwara, Seona, Dir-Digital & Social Media - Nestle Waters North America Inc.; *pg.* 257, *pg.* 375
Slabaugh, Jordan, Dir-Strategy-Social Mktg, Digital & Content - LiveWorld, Inc.; *pg.* 1264, *pg.* 246
Slack, Amy, VP-Mktg - Lennar Homes, Inc.; *pg.* 1101, *pg.* 443
Slack, James, Dir-Mktg - Pernod Ricard USA, Inc.; *pg.* 1968, *pg.* 1332
Slack, Lindsey, Coord-Mktg - Polartec LLC; *pg.* 697, *pg.* 827
Slack, Mike, Mgr-Mktg - Leupold & Stevens, Inc.; *pg.* 1420, *pg.* 1492
Slade, Jennifer, Dir-Mktg - Koch Enterprises, Inc.; *pg.* 91, *pg.* 679
Slade, Rick, Sr Dir-Creative - Keurig Green Mountain, Inc.; *pg.* 868, *pg.* 1768
Sladek, Michael, Dir-Life Brokerage Sls - Mutual of Omaha Insurance Company; *pg.* 1210, *pg.* 1016
Sladich, Harry, Exec VP-Hotel Ops & Sls - Red Lion Hotels Corp.; *pg.* 1110, *pg.* 1844
Slafer, Rhonda, Sr Specialist-Mktg & Comm-Govt Healthcare Solutions - Xerox Corporation; *pg.* 494, *pg.* 365
Slagle, Scott, Head-Mktg & Brand-Consumer Trends & Motive Insights - FCA US LLC; *pg.* 170, *pg.* 868
Slanger, Breanne, Analyst-Mktg Intelligence - Valassis Communications, Inc.; *pg.* 1287, *pg.* 897
Slanoc, Cindy, Head-Dealer Mktg Programs - Harley-Davidson, Inc.; *pg.* 178, *pg.* 1874
Slater, Ken, Sr Mgr-Mktg Ops & Analytics - ASPEN TECHNOLOGY, INC.; *pg.* 354, *pg.* 804
Slater, Lisa, Sr Mgr-External Comm - Genentech, Inc.; *pg.* 1533, *pg.* 279
Slater, Nick, VP-Sls-Natl Sls Partner, Natl Retail, Mobile & RV - DISH Network Corporation; *pg.* 283, *pg.* 325
Slater, Peter, Reg Dir-Mktg - MetroPCS, Inc.; *pg.* 1872, *pg.* 1683
Slater, Summer, Dir-Digital Mktg - Palisades Media Group, Inc.; *pg.* 452, *pg.* 275
Slater, Tom, VP-Consumer Mktg - TEN: The Enthusiast Network; *pg.* 1691, *pg.* 1298
Slater-Kisla, Stacy, Sr Dir-Mktg - The Hartz Mountain Corp.; *pg.* 1476, *pg.* 1120
Slaton, Sandra, Sr Mgr-Meeting & Event - Honeywell International Inc.; *pg.* 407, *pg.* 1088
Slatter, Richard, Product Mgr - Twitter, Inc.; *pg.* 1285, *pg.* 228
Slatter, Robin, Dir-Product Dev-FMC Pro Solutions - FMC Corporation; *pg.* 1163, *pg.* 1564
Slattery, Joe, Sr VP-Global Sls & Mktg - Holland America Line Inc.; *pg.* 1911, *pg.* 1836
Slattery, Terry M., Pres-Dominion Homes Media - Dominion Enterprises; *pg.* 1636, *pg.* 1796
Slaughter, Shannon, Coord-Mktg Comm & Rep-Pkg Design - Eastman Chemical Company; *pg.* 1159, *pg.* 1636
Slaven, Drew, VP-Mktg - Mercedes-Benz USA, LLC; *pg.* 184, *pg.* 514
Slaven, Jeff, Dir-Media - Raymour & Flanigan Furniture Co.; *pg.* 940, *pg.* 1174
Slaven, Kay, Dir-Digital Mktg Student Loans - Discover Financial Services; *pg.* 744, *pg.* 653
Slavens, Jeremy, Dir-Mktg & Event Acq - Kansas City Chiefs Football Club, Inc.; *pg.* 555, *pg.* 984
Slavin, Irika, VP-Comm, PR & Talent Rels-Food Network & Cooking Channel - Food Network; *pg.* 287, *pg.* 1231
Slavin, Melissa, Mgr-Digital Mktg - Morgan Stanley; *pg.* 783, *pg.* 1261
Slavin, Nancy, Sr VP-Mktg-Macy's Mdsg Grp - Macy's East; *pg.* 1777, *pg.* 1254
Slavin, Rick, Dir-Sls - Virgin America Inc.; *pg.* 1930, *pg.* 55
Slayback, Kelli, Analyst-Mktg - Meggitt Safety Systems, Inc.; *pg.* 653, *pg.* 279
Slaydon, Nicole, Sr Coord-Mktg Comm - WestRock Company; *pg.* 1472, *pg.* 1805
Slayton, Derek, VP-Mktg - The Dun & Bradstreet Corp.; *pg.* 1637, *pg.* 1120
Slayton, Diane, VP-Consumer Mktg - UnitedHealth Group Incorporated; *pg.* 1221, *pg.* 950
Sleddens, Erin, Dir-Online & Target Mktg - Kansas City Royals Baseball Corporation; *pg.* 555, *pg.* 985
Sledzieski, Walt, Sr Dir-Corp Comm & Mktg - Micron Technology, Inc.; *pg.* 435, *pg.* 547
Slee, John, VP-Sls - Maverick Brands LLC; *pg.* 876, *pg.* 161
Sleete, Jeff, Corp Dir-Mktg - Sinclair Broadcast Group, Inc.; *pg.* 308, *pg.* 773
Sleeth, Carolyn, Dir-Mktg - Medtronic, Inc.; *pg.* 1564, *pg.* 939
Slek, Sebastien, Exec Dir-Global Category Mktg & Indirect - Warner Bros. Entertainment Inc.; *pg.* 319, *pg.* 54
Slepski, Joe, Mgr-Email Mktg - GameFly, Inc.; *pg.* 953, *pg.* 132
Slessareva, Leeza, Sr Dir-Strategy & Ops-Analytics - Visa Inc.; *pg.* 816, *pg.* 230
Slethaug, Kris, VP-Mktg Comm & Ops-New York - Merrill Corporation; *pg.* 1664, *pg.* 962
Slevin, Jim, Sr Dir-Global Sls & Customer Analytics - Equinix, Inc.; *pg.* 394, *pg.* 190
Slick, Adam C., Sr Mgr-Mktg - Jacobsen Textron; *pg.* 1708, *pg.* 1367
Sliefert, Paula, Sr Mgr-Mktg - The Toro Company; *pg.* 1065, *pg.* 918
Slifer, Jaclyn, Mgr-PR-Loews Hollywood Hotel - Loews Hotels Holding Corporation; *pg.* 1101, *pg.* 1252
Sliney, Keith, Dir-Creative - Boston Celtics Limited Partnership; *pg.* 533, *pg.* 790
Slinin, Alex, Sr Mgr-Broadband Strategy & Product Dev - Cox Communications, Inc.; *pg.* 279, *pg.* 501
Slinkman, Chris, District Mgr-Sls - Molex Incorporated; *pg.* 655, *pg.* 628
Sliter, David, VP & Gen Mgr-Comm, Media & Entertainment Solutions - Hewlett-Packard Company; *pg.* 404, *pg.* 175
Sliter, Rick, Sr VP-Marketing Svcs - Provide Commerce, Inc.; *pg.* 1276, *pg.* 206
Slitt, Mark, Mgr-PR - Cigna Corporation; *pg.* 1197, *pg.* 338
Slivensky, Jeannie, Brand Mgr-Europe & North America-Air Wick - Reckitt Benckiser Inc.; *pg.* 1136, *pg.* 1105
Slivers, Mike, Mgr-Sls - Heat Seal LLC; *pg.* 1345, *pg.* 1431
Slivinski, Larry, Sr Dir-Civil Programs - Orbital ATK; *pg.* 1425, *pg.* 1779
Slivko-Ament, Jane, Sr Mgr-Mktg - AT&T Mobility LLC; *pg.* 619, *pg.* 488
Slivon, Sara, Mgr-Mktg - Cumberland Packing Corp.; *pg.* 851, *pg.* 1146
Sloan, Adrienne, Sr Specialist-Mktg Comm - Medtronic, Inc.; *pg.* 1564, *pg.* 939
Sloan, Amanda, Sr Mgr-Shopper Mktg - Mondelez International; *pg.* 877, *pg.* 1344
Sloan, Gretchen, Sr Dir-Comm - SHUTTERFLY, INC.; *pg.* 1280, *pg.* 192
Sloan, Jacque, Mgr-Mktg & Creative - The New York Times Company; *pg.* 1668, *pg.* 1270
Sloan, Lea, VP-Comm & Mktg - American Forests; *pg.* 128, *pg.* 394

Sloan, Matt, VP-Mdsg - Trader Joe's Co.; *pg.* 1789, *pg.* 151
Sloan, Nikki, Mgr-Strategic Mktg-Life Science - VWR Funding, Inc.; *pg.* 1608, *pg.* 1583
Sloan, Rhonda, VP-Mktg Comm - Travel Guard Group, Inc.; *pg.* 1925, *pg.* 1895
Sloan, Scott, Mgr-Product Engrg - Titan International, Inc.; *pg.* 219, *pg.* 653
Sloan, Sharon, Sr Corp Mgr-Mktg Comm - Cameron International; *pg.* 1151, *pg.* 1702
Sloane, Maeve, Coord-Sports Mktg - The North Face, Inc.; *pg.* 1840, *pg.* 252
Sloane, Stacie, Sr Dir - VMware, Inc.; *pg.* 490, *pg.* 179
Sloane, Todd, Sr VP-Creative - Publishers Clearing House; *pg.* 1782, *pg.* 1324
Slobodien, Shannon, Mgr-Mktg - AECOM Technology Corporation; *pg.* 65, *pg.* 125
Slocum, Kathleen, Sr Specialist-PR - Liberty Mutual Insurance Group Inc.; *pg.* 1205, *pg.* 797
Sloka, Bill, Sr Product Mgr - Thomas & Betts Corporation; *pg.* 680, *pg.* 1040
Slominski, Sue, Exec Dir-Media Strategy - Comcast Cable Communications, Inc.; *pg.* 276, *pg.* 1560
Slomski, Caroline, Brand Mgr-Employment - Liberty Mutual Insurance Group Inc.; *pg.* 1205, *pg.* 797
Slonaker, Charlie, Dir-Consumer Ticket Sls - Pacers Basketball, LLC; *pg.* 573, *pg.* 689
Sloneker, Karen L., Dir-Customer Svcs & Mktg - AEP Ohio; *pg.* 1933, *pg.* 1454
Sloper, Gary, Area VP-Sls Engrg & Ops-Eastern US - CenturyLink, Inc.; *pg.* 1870, *pg.* 746
Sloser, Joshua, VP-Digital Product & Innovation - Hilton Worldwide, Inc.; *pg.* 1094, *pg.* 1791
Slotkin, Doug, VP-Local Adv Sls - Zillow Group, Inc.; *pg.* 1292, *pg.* 1843
Slotten, Dave, VP-Product Mktg - Trippe Manufacturing Company; *pg.* 220, *pg.* 592
Sluk, Sheila, Exec Dir-Digital Media - The Walt Disney Company; *pg.* 317, *pg.* 52
Slusher, John, Exec VP-Sports Mktg-Global - NIKE, Inc.; *pg.* 1812, *pg.* 1492
Sly, Paul, VP-Enterprise Adv Sls & Analytics-Spectrum Reach - Charter Communications, Inc.; *pg.* 274, *pg.* 372
Slye, Karen, Sr Dir-Mktg-Family Div - American Blue Ribbon Holdings; *pg.* 1714, *pg.* 1648
Slyker, Kate, VP-Consumer Mktg - General Communication, Inc.; *pg.* 1871, *pg.* 10
Slyter, Anthony, Sr Dir-Media & Adv Partnerships - NeuStar, Inc.; *pg.* 1872, *pg.* 1807
Smaciarz, Gene, Dir-Creative Svcs - Thrivent Financial for Lutherans; *pg.* 1219, *pg.* 944
Smagler, Alan, VP-Trade Sls - Scholastic Corporation; *pg.* 1683, *pg.* 1288
Smale, Patrick, Dir-US Mktg Science - Alcon; *pg.* 1399, *pg.* 530
Smalec, Andrea, VP-Comm & PR - John G. Shedd Aquarium; *pg.* 555, *pg.* 579
Smales, Alicia, CMO & VP - Snap-on Incorporated; *pg.* 1062, *pg.* 1862
Small, Andrew, VP-Sls - MORNINGSTAR, INC.; *pg.* 784, *pg.* 583
Small, David, Sr VP-Sls-Intl - Information Builders Inc.; *pg.* 415, *pg.* 1243
Small, David, VP-Channel Sls-EMEA - Juniper Networks, Inc.; *pg.* 1260, *pg.* 286
Small, Erik, Sr Mgr-Digital Media & Analytics - Meijer, Inc.; *pg.* 1779, *pg.* 888
Small, Jessica, Specialist-Brand & Field Mktg - NIKE Canada Ltd.; *pg.* 1840, *pg.* 1934
Small, Larry, Brand Mgr & Mgr-Adv - Georgia Lottery Corporation; *pg.* 993, *pg.* 506
Small, Rich, Mgr-Mktg Comm - Unilever United States, Inc.; *pg.* 904, *pg.* 1061
Small, Russ, Exec VP-Sls & Mktg - Theragenics Corporation; *pg.* 1431, *pg.* 527
Small, Tony, VP-Sls Strategy & Ops - Zillow Group, Inc.; *pg.* 1292, *pg.* 1843
Smalley, Andrew, Asst Dir-Mktg Brand & Adv - The Northwestern Mutual Life Insurance Company; *pg.* 1212, *pg.* 1879
Smalley, Dustin, Mgr-Premium Seating Sls - San Diego Chargers Football Co.; *pg.* 580, *pg.* 208
Smalley, Mark, Sr Mgr-Creative Svcs - BCBG Max Azria Group LLC; *pg.* 19, *pg.* 301
Smalley, Richard, Mgr-Mktg - Kansas Department of Commerce; *pg.* 996, *pg.* 722
Smallman-Tew, Peter, VP-Sls & Mktg - Yamaha Motor Canada Ltd.; *pg.* 1712, *pg.* 1947
Smalls, Mark, CMO & VP - JAMS, The Resolution Experts; *pg.* 423, *pg.* 111
Smalls-Worthington, Aleesha, Sr Dir-Interactive Mktg - Iconix Brand Group, Inc.; *pg.* 26, *pg.* 1243
Smallwood, Phillip, Dir-Mktg & Packaged Beverage - The Pantry, Inc.; *pg.* 1029, *pg.* 1360
Smalstig, Julie, Dir-Mktg Comm - AccuWeather, Inc.; *pg.* 268, *pg.* 1587
Smardo, Paul, Dir-Media & Print Promos - Meijer, Inc.; *pg.* 1779, *pg.* 888
Smark, Shawnn, Dir-Mktg-Global - Bio-Rad Laboratories, Inc.; *pg.* 1504, *pg.* 101
Smart, Bill, Mgr-Sls - Cenveo Inc.; *pg.* 1626, *pg.* 372
Smart, Chris, VP & Head-Global Sls Capability - MetLife, Inc.; *pg.* 1208, *pg.* 1258
Smart, Roland, VP-Social & Community Mktg - Oracle Corporation; *pg.* 450, *pg.* 191
Smartt, Jason, Brand Mgr - Tyson Foods, Inc.; *pg.* 902, *pg.* 35
Smayda, Michele, Mgr-Sls - Driver's Mart; *pg.* 169, *pg.* 480
Smedley, Megan, Sr Mgr-Strategic Mdsg & Targeting - Comcast Corporation; *pg.* 276, *pg.* 1560
Smedley, Michael, Coord-Fin & Mktg - Pepsi Beverages Company; *pg.* 258, *pg.* 1342
Smedstad, Ryan, Dir-Mktg-Creative Svcs - Penske Truck Leasing Company, L.P.; *pg.* 188, *pg.* 1585
Smejkal, Joel, Sr VP-Distr Sls-Global - Vishay Intertechnology, Inc.; *pg.* 1435, *pg.* 1551
Smela, Matthew, Mgr-Motorsports & Brand Mktg - Navistar International Corporation; *pg.* 186, *pg.* 630
Smerigan, Noah, Mgr-Application-Crown Media Family Networks - Crown Media Holdings Inc.; *pg.* 280, *pg.* 281
Smerigan, Ron, Dir-Mktg & Promos - Cumulus Media Inc.; *pg.* 280, *pg.* 503
Smette, Darryl G., Exec VP-Mktg, Midstream & Supply Chain - Devon Energy Corporation; *pg.* 976, *pg.* 1704
Smidebush, Dave, VP-Mktg-Direct Sls & Customer Svc - Escort, Inc.; *pg.* 1412, *pg.* 1479
Smilanich, Gayle, Assoc Dir-KNA Media COE - Kellogg Company; *pg.* 831, *pg.* 870
Smiley, Marybeth E., Dir-Mktg-Global - Aetna Inc.; *pg.* 1187, *pg.* 351
Smillie, Jill, Dir-Mktg - Victoria Symphony Society; *pg.* 590, *pg.* 1913
Smirles, William J., Dir-Mktg, Military & Air Medical - Zoll Medical Corporation; *pg.* 1612, *pg.* 814
Smit, Carl, VP-Retail Mktg - Under Armour, Inc.; *pg.* 49, *pg.* 759
Smit, Troels, Head-Demand Sls - LiveRail; *pg.* 1264, *pg.* 145
Smith, Aaron, VP & Mgr-ECommerce Sls - MACATAWA BANK CORPORATION; *pg.* 778, *pg.* 892
Smith, Abby, Sr Dir-Corp Comm - eBay Inc.; *pg.* 1240, *pg.* 243
Smith, Adam, Dir-Mktg - ACCO Brands Corporation; *pg.* 340, *pg.* 626
Smith, Adrien, Mgr-Mktg - Abbott Laboratories; *pg.* 1484, *pg.* 551
Smith, Alisa, Mgr-Mktg Comm - Sprint Corporation; *pg.* 1874, *pg.* 719
Smith, Allison, Mgr-Media & Mktg - NCL Corporation Ltd.; *pg.* 1916, *pg.* 444
Smith, Allison, Mgr-Content Mktg - Schneider Electric USA, Inc.; *pg.* 1306, *pg.* 650
Smith, Allison B., Brand Mgr-Oncology Global Mktg - Eli Lilly and Company; *pg.* 1527, *pg.* 684
Smith, Allison E., Sr Assoc Brand Mgr-HUGGIES - Kimberly-Clark Corporation; *pg.* 1461, *pg.* 1720
Smith, Amy, Mgr-Reg Sls & Inside Sls - Cars.com; *pg.* 1234, *pg.* 568
Smith, Amy, Specialist-Adv - TD Ameritrade Holding Corporation; *pg.* 808, *pg.* 1018
Smith, Andrea, Brand Mgr-Amana - Whirlpool Corporation; *pg.* 62, *pg.* 872
Smith, Andy, Dir-Mktg Res - The Hershey Co.; *pg.* 1855, *pg.* 1538
Smith, Angela, Sr Dir-Strategic Events - NetSuite, Inc.; *pg.* 1270, *pg.* 255
Smith, Angela P., Sr Brand Mgr-Brand Mktg & Comm - LG Electronics U.S.A., Inc.; *pg.* 651, *pg.* 1060
Smith, Angie, Mgr-Creative - The E.W. Scripps Company; *pg.* 1639, *pg.* 1412
Smith, Annette, Dir-Cross Vehicle Product & Pricing-US - General Motors Company; *pg.* 175, *pg.* 881
Smith, Arthur Russell, Assoc Dir-Cystic Fibrosis & HCV Mktg-Canada - Vertex Pharmaceuticals Incorporated; *pg.* 1606, *pg.* 801
Smith, Ashlee, Sr Mgr-Partner Mktg - Hotels.com, L.P.; *pg.* 1257, *pg.* 1682
Smith, Barry, Mgr-Mktg - The Great Atlantic & Pacific Tea Company, Inc.; *pg.* 1021, *pg.* 1086
Smith, Barry T., Dir-Sls & Mktg Comm - Anheuser-Busch Companies, LLC; *pg.* 237, *pg.* 991
Smith, Ben, Sr Mgr-Cox Bus Product Ops - Cox Communications, Inc.; *pg.* 279, *pg.* 501
Smith, Bhavana, Sr Mgr - Accenture; *pg.* 1392, *pg.* 1186
Smith, Bill, Dir-Newspaper Adv - The Free Lance-Star Publishing Co.; *pg.* 1643, *pg.* 1782
Smith, Bing, VP-Sls Trng & Nestle Pro Vitality - Nestle Professional Beverages; *pg.* 257, *pg.* 474
Smith, Bob, Mgr-Reg Sls-Africa, Process Sys & Solutions - Emerson Process Management Rosemount Inc.; *pg.* 1334, *pg.* 920
Smith, Bradley J., VP-Product Mgmt - ARI Network Services, Inc.; *pg.* 353, *pg.* 1873
Smith, Brian, Strategist-Product - DST Systems, Inc.; *pg.* 388, *pg.* 982
Smith, Brian, Dir-Mktg-US Cardiovascular - Eli Lilly and Company; *pg.* 1527, *pg.* 684
Smith, Brian, VP-Mktg - Lexus Division; *pg.* 182, *pg.* 294
Smith, Bridget, Sr VP-Digital Sls & Mktg - Bank of America Corporation; *pg.* 718, *pg.* 1362
Smith, Brittany, Brand Mgr-Licensing - Stanley Black & Decker, Inc.; *pg.* 1063, *pg.* 358
Smith, Bryan, Mgr-Trade Mktg Tech - Bumble Bee Foods LLC; *pg.* 842, *pg.* 201
Smith, Bryan O., Mgr-Channel Mktg - Tennant Company; *pg.* 1381, *pg.* 944
Smith, Candace, Asst VP-Media Rels - The George Washington University; *pg.* 602, *pg.* 400
Smith, Carly, Dir-Global Database Mktg & CRM - Levi Strauss & Co.; *pg.* 43, *pg.* 220
Smith, Carole, Mgr-Mktg - T. Rowe Price Group Inc.; *pg.* 808, *pg.* 759
Smith, Caty, District Mgr-Sls-Primary Care - AstraZeneca Pharmaceuticals LP; *pg.* 1497, *pg.* 389
Smith, Chad, Exec VP-Production & Direct Lending - loanDepot LLC; *pg.* 776, *pg.* 86
Smith, Chad, VP-Product Mgmt & Engrg - Thomas & Betts Corporation; *pg.* 680, *pg.* 1646
Smith, Charles, Dir-Product Engrg - Fisher-Price, Inc.; *pg.* 953, *pg.* 1156
Smith, Chelsea, Specialist-Comm & Social Media - Bridgestone Americas, Inc.; *pg.* 201, *pg.* 1649
Smith, Cheryl, Exec VP-Sls & Mktg-Cheese, Tablespreads & Yogurt - Parmalat Canada Inc.; *pg.* 888, *pg.* 1941
Smith, Cheryl, Dir-Mdsg - Stanfield's Limited; *pg.* 48, *pg.* 1917
Smith, Chris, Specialist-Mktg Analysis - UPS Ground Freight, Inc.; *pg.* 1929, *pg.* 1804
Smith, Christy, Mgr-Media Mktg - American Automobile Association; *pg.* 1190, *pg.* 429
Smith, Christy, Mgr-Email Mktg - Nordstrom, Inc.; *pg.* 1779, *pg.* 1837
Smith, Chuck, Mgr-Strategic Mktg, Drilling & Evaluation - Baker Hughes Incorporated; *pg.* 1315, *pg.* 1700
Smith, Cliff, VP-Sls-North America - Albany International Corp.; *pg.* 691, *pg.* 1038
Smith, Clint, Product Mgr - CarMax, Inc.; *pg.* 167, *pg.* 1800
Smith, Colin, Dir-Mac PR - Apple Inc.; *pg.* 350, *pg.* 73
Smith, Colin, VP-NASCAR Digital Media - National Association for Stock Car Auto Racing; *pg.* 566, *pg.* 420
Smith, Colleen, VP-Product Mktg - Progress Software Corporation; *pg.* 457, *pg.* 786
Smith, Courtney, Dir-Mktg - Beasley Broadcast Group, Inc.; *pg.* 271, *pg.* 450
Smith, Craig, Sr Dir-Mktg-People to People Ambassador Programs - Ambassadors Group, Inc.; *pg.* 1898, *pg.* 1843
Smith, Dan, Team Head-Earned & Social Media & Strategist-PR - Cerner Corporation; *pg.* 1514, *pg.* 981
Smith, Dan, Dir-Channel Mktg - Hewlett-Packard Company; *pg.* 404, *pg.* 175
Smith, Dave, Dir-Sls & Mktg - Summit Corporation of America; *pg.* 1182, *pg.* 380
Smith, David, Specialist-Product Mktg - Honeywell International Inc.; *pg.* 407, *pg.* 1088
Smith, David, Sr Mgr-Compliance - LEGO Systems, Inc.; *pg.* 961, *pg.* 346
Smith, David, Product Mgr - Virtek Vision International, Inc.;

First page reference indicates Business Class Edition
Second page reference indicates Geographic Edition

pg. 1435, *pg.* 1948
Smith, David Allen, Coord-DFMWR Mktg - United States Army; *pg.* 1008, *pg.* 405
Smith, Debbie, Specialist-Vendor Mktg - Academy Sports & Outdoors, Ltd.; *pg.* 1824, *pg.* 1724
Smith, Denis, VP-Mktg - Burlington Northern Santa Fe, LLC; *pg.* 1901, *pg.* 1694
Smith, Dennis, Brand Mgr-Right Guard - Henkel Corporation; *pg.* 1165, *pg.* 1535
Smith, Derek, VP-Sls & Mktg - ZAGG INCORPORATED; *pg.* 690, *pg.* 1762
Smith, Desmond, Sr Product Mgr - T-Mobile US, Inc.; *pg.* 676, *pg.* 1816
Smith, Diane, Sr Specialist-Mktg - TBC Corporation; *pg.* 1889, *pg.* 457
Smith, Donald, VP-Mktg - Family Dollar Stores, Inc.; *pg.* 1768, *pg.* 1382
Smith, Donna, VP-Mktg - Tasti D-Lite LLC; *pg.* 1753, *pg.* 1634
Smith, Dora, Dir-Online, Social Media & Partner Strategy - Siemens PLM Software; *pg.* 469, *pg.* 1734
Smith, Doug, Mgr-Product Mktg - Epicor Software Corporation; *pg.* 393, *pg.* 110
Smith, Doug, Dir-Mktg-Shared Svcs - Foot Locker, Inc.; *pg.* 1808, *pg.* 1231
Smith, Doug, VP-Sls & Mktg - Fossil Group, Inc.; *pg.* 5, *pg.* 1735
Smith, Doug, Sr VP-Sls & Acct Svcs - HealthPartners, Inc.; *pg.* 1203, *pg.* 918
Smith, Doug W., Mgr-Natl Sls-US Rep Travel Network - American Express Company; *pg.* 712, *pg.* 1190
Smith, Ed, Pres-Avnet Electronics Mktg-Americas - Avnet, Inc.; *pg.* 622, *pg.* 15
Smith, Ed, VP-Sls & Mktg - Bracco Diagnostics, Inc.; *pg.* 1509, *pg.* 1085
Smith, Elizabeth J., Coord-Media Rels-Natl - Whole Foods Market, Inc.; *pg.* 1038, *pg.* 1667
Smith, Emily, Mgr-Digital & Social Mktg - MillerCoors LLC; *pg.* 255, *pg.* 582
Smith, Emily, Supvr-Social Media - The Pep Boys - Manny, Moe & Jack; *pg.* 215, *pg.* 1568
Smith, Eric, VP-Sls & Mktg-Food, Pharma & Nutrition - Balchem Corporation; *pg.* 839, *pg.* 1183
Smith, Erica, Mgr-Social Media Mktg - Safeway Inc.; *pg.* 1032, *pg.* 184
Smith, Erin, Sr Specialist-Mktg - Lowe's Companies, Inc.; *pg.* 1053, *pg.* 1383
Smith, Eva, Head-Partner Mktg Comm & Insights - Pinterest; *pg.* 1275, *pg.* 225
Smith, Frank, Mgr-Product Sls & Corp Sls - American Airlines Inc.; *pg.* 1898, *pg.* 1693
Smith, Fred, Head-Reg Sls, Adometry - Google Inc.; *pg.* 1249, *pg.* 153
Smith, Gail, Sr Mgr-Comm - NRG Energy, Inc.; *pg.* 1948, *pg.* 1712
Smith, Gary L., VP-Product Design & Exploration - Herman Miller, Inc.; *pg.* 926, *pg.* 913
Smith, Gena, Sr VP-HR & Head-Global Exec & Creative Recruitment - LVMH Inc.; *pg.* 9, *pg.* 1254
Smith, Gordon, Dir & Mgr-Product-DPS - Visa Inc.; *pg.* 816, *pg.* 230
Smith, Greg, Mgr-Strategic Mktg - 3M Company; *pg.* 1142, *pg.* 956
Smith, Greg, Mgr-Mktg Comm - Allied Construction Products, LLC; *pg.* 1311, *pg.* 1427
Smith, Greg, Sr Mgr-Sys Engrg-South Comml Territory - Cisco Systems, Inc.; *pg.* 372, *pg.* 240
Smith, Greg, Rep-Experienced Tech Sls - Oracle Corporation; *pg.* 450, *pg.* 191
Smith, Gretchen, Mgr-Mktg-Root Sports-Directv Sports Networks - DIRECTV Group Holdings, LLC; *pg.* 281, *pg.* 79
Smith, Hallie, Dir-Mktg - Scientific Learning Corporation; *pg.* 607, *pg.* 172
Smith, Heather, Designer-Interactive - Highlights for Children, Inc.; *pg.* 1650, *pg.* 1440
Smith, Holly, Mgr-Social Media - Beall's, Inc.; *pg.* 1760, *pg.* 414
Smith, Houston, Dir-PR - Alabama Power Company; *pg.* 1933, *pg.* 1
Smith, Ian, Sr Mgr-Strategy & Product Dev - Aflac Incorporated; *pg.* 1188, *pg.* 527
Smith, James, Mgr-Future Offer Global Mktg - Schneider Electric USA, Inc.; *pg.* 1306, *pg.* 650
Smith, James, Sr VP & Head-Digital Sls, Crackle & PlayStation - Sony Pictures Entertainment Inc.; *pg.* 309, *pg.* 72
Smith, Janice, VP-Natl Media Sls - Rogers Media Inc.; *pg.* 1681, *pg.* 1942
Smith, Jason, Vp-Mdsg - Trunk Club; *pg.* 49, *pg.* 593
Smith, Jason, Sr Dir-Mdsg & Design-Footwear - Volcom, Inc.; *pg.* 1847, *pg.* 71
Smith, Jeanie, Sr Dir-Global Comml Mktg-Biologics & Insulins - Mylan, Inc.; *pg.* 1570, *pg.* 1520
Smith, Jeanne, Sr Strategist-Mktg - The Vanguard Group, Inc.; *pg.* 816, *pg.* 1550
Smith, Jeff, VP-Sls-North America - Blonder Tongue Laboratories, Inc.; *pg.* 625, *pg.* 1100
Smith, Jeff, Dir-Mktg & Global Ingredients Div - Blue Diamond Growers; *pg.* 840, *pg.* 195
Smith, Jeff, Product Mgr-Consumables & Pro Imaging Div - Epson America Inc.; *pg.* 394, *pg.* 122
Smith, Jeff, Mgr-Mdse-Event Sls - Hockey Western New York, LLC; *pg.* 552, *pg.* 1149
Smith, Jeffery, Reg Dir-Mktg - Wells Fargo & Company; *pg.* 819, *pg.* 232
Smith, Jeffrey W, Dir-Mktg-Bibles - Tyndale House Publishers, Inc.; *pg.* 1697, *pg.* 561
Smith, Jennifer, Sr Recruiter-Sls - Automatic Data Processing, Inc.; *pg.* 357, *pg.* 1117
Smith, Jennifer, Dir-Brand & Creative Strategy - Charter Communications, Inc.; *pg.* 274, *pg.* 372
Smith, Jennifer, Dir-Mktg - Direct Holdings Americas Inc.; *pg.* 1636, *pg.* 1780
Smith, Jennifer, Mgr-Digital Mktg - VeriFone Systems, Inc.; *pg.* 487, *pg.* 251
Smith, Jennifer Blanchard, Sr Dir - McDonald's Corporation; *pg.* 1737, *pg.* 645
Smith, Jenny, Sr Mgr-Segment - Wellmark, Inc; *pg.* 1223, *pg.* 707
Smith, Jeron, Mgr-Mktg-Jordan Brand - NIKE, Inc.; *pg.* 1812, *pg.* 1492
Smith, Jill, VP-Creative Svcs - Paul Fredrick Menstyle Inc.; *pg.* 45, *pg.* 1532
Smith, Jim, Sr VP-Sls & Mktg - Atlanta Falcons Football Club, LLC; *pg.* 530, *pg.* 532
Smith, Jim, VP-Segment Mktg - Ixia; *pg.* 422, *pg.* 56
Smith, Jodie E., Specialist-Sls & Mktg Solutions - The Dun & Bradstreet Corp.; *pg.* 1637, *pg.* 1120
Smith, Joe, VP-Sls & Dev-Global - Papa John's International, Inc.; *pg.* 1743, *pg.* 737
Smith, John A, Sr Mgr-Mktg - Honeywell International Inc.; *pg.* 407, *pg.* 1088
Smith, John G., Mgr-Mktg - Land O'Lakes, Inc.; *pg.* 873, *pg.* 915
Smith, Johnny, Dir-Media Rels - Ascension Health Alliance; *pg.* 1496, *pg.* 992
Smith, Jonathan, Sr Dir-Americas Channel Sls & Mktg - Western Digital Corporation; *pg.* 492, *pg.* 118
Smith, Julie, Mgr-PR - Fiserv, Inc.; *pg.* 397, *pg.* 1855
Smith, Justin, CEO-Bloomberg Media - Bloomberg L.P.; *pg.* 725, *pg.* 1204
Smith, Justin, Mgr-Mktg - PepsiCo, Inc.; *pg.* 259, *pg.* 1327
Smith, Kate, Assoc Product Mgr - CarMax, Inc.; *pg.* 167, *pg.* 1800
Smith, Kelly, Mgr-Mktg-New Store Openings - Ulta Salon, Cosmetics & Fragrance, Inc.; *pg.* 524, *pg.* 559
Smith, Kelly, Dir-Sls-Natl - United Online, Inc.; *pg.* 1286, *pg.* 308
Smith, Kelly Bednarchuk, Sr Mgr-Client Svcs - Chicago Blackhawk Hockey Team, Inc.; *pg.* 538, *pg.* 569
Smith, Ken, Mgr-Mktg - Ambac International Corporation; *pg.* 198, *pg.* 1615
Smith, Ken, Dir-Health Product Sls - Assurity Life Insurance Company; *pg.* 1194, *pg.* 1011
Smith, Ken, Dir-Mktg - Torcon, Inc.; *pg.* 116, *pg.* 1114
Smith, Kerry H., Sr Mgr-Global Mktg - Hewlett-Packard Company; *pg.* 404, *pg.* 175
Smith, Kevin, Dir-HIV Mktg - Gilead Sciences, Inc.; *pg.* 1535, *pg.* 88
Smith, Kevin, VP-Sls & Mktg - Lannett Company, Inc.; *pg.* 1555, *pg.* 1566
Smith, Kim, Asst Dir-Media-Corp Mktg - U.S. Bancorp; *pg.* 815, *pg.* 945
Smith, Kiran, VP-Mktg - The Stride Rite Corporation; *pg.* 1820, *pg.* 828
Smith, Kirk, Dir-Mktg & Sls - Six Flags Entertainment Corporation; *pg.* 583, *pg.* 1698
Smith, Kris, Exec VP-Refining & Mktg - Suncor Energy Inc.; *pg.* 985, *pg.* 1905
Smith, Kristi, Mgr-Mktg Solutions - Simplot Partners Inc.; *pg.* 1800, *pg.* 548
Smith, Larry, District Mgr-Sls - Mitsubishi Fuso Truck of America, Inc.; *pg.* 185, *pg.* 1045
Smith, Larry, Sr Product Mgr-Mktg Comm - Vishay Intertechnology, Inc.; *pg.* 1435, *pg.* 1551
Smith, Laura, Brand Mgr - Medtronic; *pg.* 1563, *pg.* 830
Smith, Laura, Brand Mgr - Medtronic; *pg.* 1563, *pg.* 183
Smith, LauraJ, Assoc Dir-Oncology Sls & Mktg Ops-US - Novartis Corporation; *pg.* 1574, *pg.* 1273
Smith, Laurel R., VP-Mktg - Warn Industries, Inc.; *pg.* 221, *pg.* 1497
Smith, Lee, Mgr-Adv - C.R. Daniels, Inc.; *pg.* 1456, *pg.* 769
Smith, Leland, Dir-Sls & Mktg - American Blue Ribbon Holdings; *pg.* 1714, *pg.* 1648
Smith, Leslie, Brand Mgr-Mktg-Intl - Blistex, Inc.; *pg.* 502, *pg.* 644
Smith, Lindsay, Sr Mgr-Corp Comm - Level 3 Communications, Inc.; *pg.* 1262, *pg.* 312
Smith, Lisa, Assoc Mgr-Shopper Mktg - Diamond Foods, Inc.; *pg.* 1851, *pg.* 216
Smith, Lisa, Sr Mgr-Consumer Promo & Shopper Mktg - Post Holdings, Inc.; *pg.* 833, *pg.* 1002
Smith, Lori, Mgr-Mktg-Energy & Chemicals - Fluor Corporation; *pg.* 82, *pg.* 1719
Smith, Lori, Mgr-Adv - The Kroger Co.; *pg.* 1025, *pg.* 1416
Smith, Lynn, Head-Mktg-US Vision Care - Alcon; *pg.* 1399, *pg.* 530
Smith, Mark, Sr Dir-Sls-Natl Accts - MATTEL, INC.; *pg.* 962, *pg.* 81
Smith, Mark, Dir-Mktg - Valeant Pharmaceuticals International; *pg.* 1605, *pg.* 1047
Smith, Marty, Mgr-Sls Academy - United Parcel Service, Inc.; *pg.* 1928, *pg.* 522
Smith, Mary, Dir-Mktg - Liberty Home Equity Solutions, Inc.; *pg.* 776, *pg.* 186
Smith, Matt, Brand Mgr - The Kraft Heinz Company; *pg.* 871, *pg.* 641
Smith, Matthew, Mgr-Programming Sls-Contract Mgmt & Reporting - Home Box Office, Inc.; *pg.* 290, *pg.* 1240
Smith, Maureen, Sr VP-Mktg - Hasbro, Inc.; *pg.* 954, *pg.* 1603
Smith, Meg, Mgr-Mktg-North America - Larson-Juhl US LLC; *pg.* 933, *pg.* 537
Smith, Meghan, Coord-Mktg & Events-Fox Hispanic Media - Fox Broadcasting Company; *pg.* 287, *pg.* 130
Smith, Meghan, Coord-Mktg & Events-Fox - FX Networks, LLC; *pg.* 288, *pg.* 131
Smith, Melanie, Dir-Mktg - Books-A-Million, Inc.; *pg.* 1623, *pg.* 2
Smith, Melissa, Mgr-PR & Comm - Carvel Corporation; *pg.* 846, *pg.* 492
Smith, Meredith Newbold, Dir-Mktg-Global - Elizabeth Arden, Inc.; *pg.* 507, *pg.* 448
Smith, Michael, Sr VP-Guest Experience & Product Dev - Holland America Line Inc.; *pg.* 1911, *pg.* 1836
Smith, Michael, Sr Dir-Store Ops - Luxottica Retail; *pg.* 8, *pg.* 1460
Smith, Michael, Mgr-Global Mktg Comm & Branding - Tecumseh Products Company; *pg.* 1381, *pg.* 866
Smith, Michael, VP-Convention Sls - Travel Portland; *pg.* 1008, *pg.* 1507
Smith, Michael, VP-Sls Corp Markets - Victorinox Swiss Army Inc.; *pg.* 1139, *pg.* 357
Smith, Michelle, Sr Dir-Product Mgmt - AppNexus; *pg.* 352, *pg.* 1196
Smith, Mieke, Sr Acct Mgr-Creative Svcs - DIRECTV Group Holdings, LLC; *pg.* 281, *pg.* 79
Smith, Mike, Interim CFO - Crocs, Inc.; *pg.* 1806, *pg.* 335
Smith, Mike, Sr VP-Sls - Mizkan Americas, Inc.; *pg.* 877, *pg.* 634
Smith, Mike, VP-Sls - Perry Ellis International, Inc.; *pg.* 45, *pg.* 445
Smith, Mike, Mgr-Digital Mktg - Rosebud Entertainment LLC; *pg.* 1681, *pg.* 759
Smith, Mindy, Mgr-North American Mktg-Comml Fleet - Shell Oil Company; *pg.* 984, *pg.* 1714
Smith, Nadine, Dir-Global Mktg & Comm-Pub Sector Practice - The Boston Consulting Group, Inc.; *pg.* 363, *pg.* 790
Smith, Nancy, COO & Bus Mgr - Credit Suisse Securities (USA) LLC; *pg.* 742, *pg.* 1220
Smith, Natalie, Brand Mktg Mgr - Eddie Bauer, Inc.; *pg.* 40, *pg.* 1814
Smith, Nate, Sr Mgr-Product Mktg-Adobe Analytics - Adobe Systems Incorporated; *pg.* 342, *pg.* 235
Smith, Nevada, Product Mgr-Horticulture - Bayer CropScience; *pg.* 1149, *pg.* 981

Smith, Nicole, Dir-Growth Segment Mktg - National Association for Stock Car Auto Racing; pg. 566, pg. 420
Smith, Nikole, Sr Dir-Brand Compliance Strategy - Choice Hotels International, Inc.; pg. 1086, pg. 775
Smith, Patrick, Editor-Media-UK - Buzzfeed; pg. 1233, pg. 1208
Smith, Patrick, Sr VP-Global Mktg - Deltek, Inc.; pg. 386, pg. 1784
Smith, Patrick, Program Mgr-Trader Mktg - TD Ameritrade Holding Corporation; pg. 808, pg. 1018
Smith, Paul Colman, Brand Mgr-Inchcape - Littelfuse, Inc.; pg. 1301, pg. 580
Smith, Randy, VP-Mktg - Sonics, Inc.; pg. 675, pg. 148
Smith, Ray, Mgr-Content Comm & Integrated Mktg Comm - National Association for Stock Car Auto Racing; pg. 566, pg. 420
Smith, Ray, District Mgr-Sls - Yamaha Motor Corporation USA; pg. 1713, pg. 76
Smith, Raymond, Sr Rep-Technical Sls - Bayer Corporation; pg. 1499, pg. 1573
Smith, Rebecca, VP-Mktg - Master Lock Company LLC; pg. 1055, pg. 1884
Smith, Rebecca, Dir-New Products & Bus Dev - Nestle Purina PetCare Company; pg. 1479, pg. 1000
Smith, Richard, VP-ICT Bus Div & Product Mktg - Komatsu America Corp.; pg. 92, pg. 655
Smith, Richard, Supvr-Sls - Rag & Bone; pg. 46, pg. 1284
Smith, Richard R., VP & Head-US Sls-Cardiovascular Franchise - Novartis Corporation; pg. 1574, pg. 1273
Smith, Rick, Product Mgr-Global - Applied Materials, Inc; pg. 618, pg. 1009
Smith, Robert, Mgr-Sls-Natl - All Star Carts and Vehicles Corp.; pg. 163, pg. 1141
Smith, Robert, Mgr-Mktg Res & Analytics - Bridgestone Americas, Inc.; pg. 201, pg. 1649
Smith, Robert, Engr-Product Reliability - Corning Incorporated; pg. 1122, pg. 1154
Smith, Robin, Sr Mgr-Internet Mktg Strategy & Programs - Thermo Fisher Scientific Inc.; pg. 1431, pg. 854
Smith, Rosemary, Dir-Mktg - Sony Electronics, Inc.; pg. 676, pg. 209
Smith, Royal, Sr VP-Reg Sls & Ops - Intelligrated, Inc.; pg. 1349, pg. 1460
Smith, Ryan, Mgr-Mktg - Veterinary Pet Insurance Co.; pg. 1222, pg. 49
Smith, Sally, Sr Mgr-Market - Expedia, Inc.; pg. 1244, pg. 1814
Smith, Sandy, Mgr-Sls-Natl - National Association of Convenience Stores; pg. 148, pg. 1771
Smith, Sarah, Acct Exec-Retail Sls - Comcast Corporation; pg. 276, pg. 1560
Smith, Scott, Sr Product Mgr - Adobe Systems Incorporated; pg. 342, pg. 235
Smith, Scott, Brand Mgr-Diet Dr Pepper & Dr Pepper Ten - Dr Pepper Snapple Group, Inc.; pg. 250, pg. 1729
Smith, Shane, Sr Dir-Product Dev - Chattem, Inc.; pg. 1515, pg. 1628
Smith, Shane, Sr VP-Mktg - TransCore Holdings Inc.; pg. 485, pg. 1541
Smith, Sheldon, Sr Product Mgr - XO Communications; pg. 497, pg. 1786
Smith, Sherina, Dir-Consumer Mktg - AbbVie Inc.; pg. 1486, pg. 638
Smith, Smitty, Coord-Technical Sls - Edelbrock Corporation; pg. 204, pg. 293
Smith, Stefanie, Reg Mgr-Mktg-Southeast - Ikea North America Services LLC; pg. 929, pg. 1523
Smith, Steve, VP-Global Sls-Americas - Japan Airlines Company, Ltd.; pg. 1913, pg. 1245
Smith, Steve, Sr Dir-Strategy & Mktg - Synopsys, Inc.; pg. 480, pg. 162
Smith, Steve C., Sr Mgr-Unified Comm - NetApp, Inc.; pg. 444, pg. 287
Smith, Steven, Pres-Digital Media - AccuWeather, Inc.; pg. 268, pg. 1587
Smith, Steven, Dir-Creative-Global - Mannatech, Incorporated; pg. 1558, pg. 1671
Smith, Summer, Graphic Designer-Corp Mktg - Stewart & Stevenson, LLC; pg. 985, pg. 1715
Smith, Susan E., Dir-Creative - The Priceline Group Inc.; pg. 1276, pg. 364
Smith, Suzanne, Dir-Mktg-Global - Medtronic, Inc.; pg. 1564, pg. 939
Smith, Tammi, Brand Mgr-Goody - Newell Rubbermaid Inc.; pg. 1128, pg. 515
Smith, Tara, VP & Product Mgr - Citigroup Inc.; pg. 735, pg. 1212
Smith, Taylor, Sr Mgr-Customer Insights - Lane Bryant; pg. 1776, pg. 1441
Smith, Taylor, Sr Dir-Xbox Global Mktg Comm - Microsoft Corporation; pg. 435, pg. 1824
Smith, Terri, Mgr-Channel Mktg - Autodesk Inc.; pg. 356, pg. 257
Smith, Terry, Sr Dir-Sls - Mary Kay Inc.; pg. 516, pg. 1657
Smith, Thao H., Sr Mgr-Comm & Data Tech - PayPal Inc.; pg. 1274, pg. 248
Smith, Theresa, Bus Mgr-Impact & Rheology Products - Instron Corporation; pg. 1349, pg. 839
Smith, Thomas F., Dir-Creative Svcs-ESPN - ESPN, Inc.; pg. 285, pg. 340
Smith, Tiffany, Analyst-Interactive Mktg - Xerox Corporation; pg. 494, pg. 365
Smith, Tim, Dir-Mktg Programs - Taco Incorporated; pg. 1077, pg. 1601
Smith, Todd, Exec Dir-Media Rels - Cox Communications, Inc.; pg. 279, pg. 501
Smith, Todd, Dir-Mktg-Frozen Veggie Foods - Kellogg Company; pg. 831, pg. 870
Smith, Todd, VP & Gen Mgr-Akro-Mils & Jamco Products - Myers Industries, Inc.; pg. 1887, pg. 1402
Smith, Todd, Dir-Product Strategy - SunGard Data Systems Inc.; pg. 477, pg. 1592
Smith, Tonya, Mgr-Strategic Sourcing-Global Mktg & Events - VMware, Inc.; pg. 490, pg. 179
Smith, Tracy, Mng Dir-Sls - Penton Media, Inc.; pg. 1676, pg. 719
Smith, Travis, Dir-Digital Mktg COE - Brown-Forman Corporation; pg. 1958, pg. 732
Smith, Tyler, Analyst-Mktg - Chattem, Inc.; pg. 1515, pg. 1628
Smith, Vicki W., Planner-Mktg & Strategist - Cisco Systems, Inc.; pg. 372, pg. 240
Smith, Wade, Mgr-Mktg & IT Engagement - Intuit Inc.; pg. 769, pg. 158
Smith, Ward, Product Mgr - DeWALT Industrial Tool Company; pg. 1328, pg. 757
Smith, Wendy, Mgr-Sls-Natl - Precision Frac; pg. 1427, pg. 1727
Smith, Whitney, Mgr-Enhancement Mktg - Alliance Data Systems Corporation; pg. 347, pg. 1729
Smith, Wynne, Mgr-Mktg Event - ScanSource, Inc.; pg. 671, pg. 1618
Smith, Zach, Mgr-Sls - John Eagle Honda of Houston; pg. 180, pg. 1709
Smith-Barrow, Rachel, Head-Annuity & Value Add Mktg & Dir - The Guardian Life Insurance Company of America; pg. 1202, pg. 1237
Smith-Palombit, Lynn, Dir-Adv - Acme Markets, Inc.; pg. 1012, pg. 1549
Smith-Reynolds, Kelly, Mgr-Mktg - Den-Mat Corporation; pg. 1522, pg. 271
Smith-Westbrook, Kristin, Dir-Creative - DIRECTV Group Holdings, LLC; pg. 281, pg. 79
Smith-Wood, Rosemarie, Head-Mktg Comm & Brand Mgmt - Coherent, Inc.; pg. 1406, pg. 265
Smithers, Kim, Sr Mgr-Sls & Mktg - BI-LO, LLC; pg. 1015, pg. 1617
Smithers, Leslie, Sr Dir-CRM & Email - Walgreen Co.; pg. 1608, pg. 605
Smits, John, Sr Dir-Data Science & Sls Ops - EMC Corporation; pg. 391, pg. 825
Smola, Earle, Dir-Brand Design & Sponsorships-Corp Mktg - Stanley Black & Decker, Inc.; pg. 1063, pg. 358
Smola, Jerry, VP & Mgr-Natl Sls - Pinnacle Foods Group LLC; pg. 889, pg. 1104
Smolarczyk, Monika, Dir-Mktg - UNITED INSURANCE HOLDINGS CORP.; pg. 1220, pg. 465
Smole, Jim, Mgr-Customer Svc & Inside Sls - Coleman Cable, Inc.; pg. 1324, pg. 665
Smolen, Riki, Mgr-Sls Strategy - U.S. News & World Report, L.P.; pg. 1698, pg. 1308
Smoley, Diana, Mgr-Mktg - Bonnier Corporation; pg. 1622, pg. 480
Smolinski, Chad, Chief Product Officer - U.S. News & World Report, L.P.; pg. 1698, pg. 1308
Smoller, Syndi, Sr Mgr-Integrated Mktg - Bauer Publishing USA; pg. 1620, pg. 1059
Smoot, Elizabeth Libby, Mgr-Mktg Comm - Trex Company, Inc.; pg. 116, pg. 1812
Smouha, Naomi, Sr Mgr-Community Rels - Capital One Financial Corporation; pg. 730, pg. 1789
Smucker, Mark A., Dir-Segment Mktg-McKesson Brands - McKesson Corporation; pg. 1560, pg. 222
Smyczek, Cris, Product Mgr - Master Lock Company LLC; pg. 1055, pg. 1884
Smyczek, Dan, Dir-PR - Milwaukee Bucks, Inc.; pg. 563, pg. 1878
Smyk, Paul, Engr-Sls - American Crane & Equipment Corporation; pg. 1312, pg. 1526
Smyth, Bill, Sr Mgr - 3M Company; pg. 1142, pg. 956
Smyth, Michelle, Dir-Social Media - Sun Life Financial Inc.; pg. 806, pg. 1944
Smyth, Patrick, Exec Dir-Media Rels - Denver Broncos Football Club; pg. 544, pg. 325
Smyth, Vincent, Sr VP-Sls-EMEA - Flexera Software Inc.; pg. 398, pg. 658
Snape, Alex, Mgr-Mktg-Thomson Reuters Eikon - Truven Health Analytics; pg. 486, pg. 331
Snare, Philippa, Dir-Bus Mktg-EMEA - Facebook, Inc.; pg. 1245, pg. 143
Snarski, Joe, Dir Creative & Sr Mgr-Marcom - Ecolab Inc.; pg. 329, pg. 960
Snavely, Heather, Sr Dir-Brand Mktg-Global - Brooks Sports Inc.; pg. 1805, pg. 1818
Snavely, Leslie, VP-Mktg - CHG Healthcare Services, Inc.; pg. 1515, pg. 1756
Snay, Kenneth, Mgr-Jaguar Sls - The Collection, Inc.; pg. 168, pg. 418
Snay, Michelle, Sr Specialist-Adv - Auto-Owners Insurance Group; pg. 1194, pg. 895
Snead, David, VP-Mktg - Philharmonic Symphony Society of New York Inc.; pg. 575, pg. 1282
Snead, Heather, Specialist-Mktg - United States Postal Service; pg. 1009, pg. 406
Snedeker, Melanie, Mgr-Mktg-Onboard Revenue - Holland America Line Inc.; pg. 1911, pg. 1836
Sneed, Colleen, Project Mgr-Print & Mktg - Protective Life Corporation; pg. 1215, pg. 4
Sneeden, Stephen, Mgr-Product Mktg - Sony Corporation of America; pg. 675, pg. 1293
Sneen, Alexander, Dir-Global Mktg-Vodka & Chambord - Brown-Forman Corporation; pg. 1958, pg. 732
Snehal Challa, Sairam, Mgr-Digital Mktg-Retail Mktg - SanDisk Corporation; pg. 465, pg. 147
Snell, Jillian, Strategist-Mktg - NBTY, Inc.; pg. 1572, pg. 1338
Sneyd, Andrew, VP-Global Mktg-Budweiser - Anheuser-Busch Companies, LLC; pg. 237, pg. 991
Snider, Brian, Sr Dir-Mktg-Thoracolumbar - NuVasive, Inc.; pg. 1577, pg. 205
Snider, Jennye, Sr Mgr-Sls - Baton Rouge Area Convention & Visitors Bureau; pg. 989, pg. 741
Snider, Lisa, Dir-Consumer Mktg - Baxter International Inc.; pg. 1499, pg. 599
Snider, Terry, Sr Dir-Sls & New Bus Dev - Evenflo Company, Inc.; pg. 924, pg. 1470
Snider-Young, Jennifer, Dir-Mktg Comm-Core Mobility & IRU - AT&T; pg. 1865, pg. 258
Sniegocki, Jodi, Sr Mgr-Strategic Event Mktg - Allscripts Healthcare Solutions, Inc.; pg. 1492, pg. 563
Sniezek, Andrew, Dir-Art & Supvr-Digital Mktg - Mercury Computer Systems, Inc.; pg. 434, pg. 813
Sniffen, Patrick, VP-Mktg - Signature Flight Support Corp.; pg. 234, pg. 456
Snipes, Kimberly, VP-Consumer Products & Ops Tech - Capital One Bank (USA), N.A.; pg. 730, pg. 1789
Snizek, Michael, Product Mgr-Advisory - Fiserv, Inc.; pg. 397, pg. 1855
Snoad, Nigel, Product Mgr-Crisis Response & Civic Innovation - Google Inc.; pg. 1249, pg. 153
Snoble, Diane, Office Mgr-Adv - East Valley Tribune; pg. 1638, pg. 25
Snodgrass, Bryan, Asst VP-Mktg - Caliber Home Loans, Inc.; pg. 728, pg. 1717
Snodgrass, G. Lynn, VP-Sls - Heska Corporation; pg. 1542, pg. 335
Snodgrass, Ken, VP-Mktg & Product Mgmt-Platforms - Honeywell Aerospace Electronic Systems; pg. 228, pg. 17
Snook, Amanda, Mgr-Mktg - Live Nation Entertainment, Inc.; pg. 558, pg. 47
Snook, David, Product Mgr - Zebra Technologies Corporation; pg. 690, pg. 628
Snorek, Doug, Mgr-Sls & Mktg - Gandy Company; pg. 703, pg. 952
Snow, Angela, Mgr-Corp Adv - Exxon Mobil Corporation; pg. 977, pg. 1718

First page reference indicates Business Class Edition
Second page reference indicates Geographic Edition

Snow, Jeff, Mgr-Digital Mktg - SmartWool; *pg.* 32, *pg.* 335
Snow, Lori, Mgr-Integrated Mktg - The Finish Line, Inc.; *pg.* 1769, *pg.* 686
Snowden, Tamara, Sr Mgr-Product Comm - Broadcom Corporation; *pg.* 364, *pg.* 108
Snowgold, Kelli, Mgr-Product Dev - American Greetings Corporation; *pg.* 1615, *pg.* 1428
Snuggs, Sue, Product Mgr - Weyerhaeuser Company; *pg.* 121, *pg.* 1820
Snyder, Allison, Sr Product Mgr - Crocs, Inc.; *pg.* 1806, *pg.* 335
Snyder, Amanda, Asst VP & Mgr-Social Media - First Niagara Bank; *pg.* 756, *pg.* 1174
Snyder, Amy, Sr Mgr-Compliance & Comm - Charles Schwab; *pg.* 1235, *pg.* 1661
Snyder, Andrew, VP-Sls - Yahoo! Inc.; *pg.* 1289, *pg.* 289
Snyder, Angie, VP-Mktg-Nordstrom Rack - Nordstrom, Inc.; *pg.* 1779, *pg.* 1837
Snyder, Annette, Program Mgr-Mktg - Salt River Project; *pg.* 707, *pg.* 26
Snyder, Brian, Mgr-Mktg Comm - Gannett Co., Inc.; *pg.* 1643, *pg.* 1790
Snyder, Ceci, VP-Domestic Mktg - National Pork Board; *pg.* 882, *pg.* 703
Snyder, Chris, Dir-Mktg - Ben E. Keith Company; *pg.* 840, *pg.* 1676
Snyder, Christine, Dir-Therapy Mktg-Global Nutrition - Baxter International Inc.; *pg.* 1499, *pg.* 599
Snyder, Clay, Sr Dir-Brand Performance-Full Svc Brands - Hilton Worldwide, Inc.; *pg.* 1094, *pg.* 1791
Snyder, Dan, Mgr-PR - Intel Corporation; *pg.* 645, *pg.* 266
Snyder, Darren, Sr Mgr-Project-City Bicycles - Trek Bicycle Corporation; *pg.* 1847, *pg.* 1896
Snyder, Dawnette, Mgr-Customer Mktg - Pepsi Beverages Company; *pg.* 258, *pg.* 1342
Snyder, Dee, Mgr-Mktg - General Growth Properties, Inc.; *pg.* 1093, *pg.* 574
Snyder, Eric, Dir-Bus Dev-High Speed Copper Products - TE Connectivity Ltd.; *pg.* 677, *pg.* 1515
Snyder, Erika, Mgr-Siebel Mktg - Starbucks Corporation; *pg.* 897, *pg.* 1840
Snyder, Gowon K., Sr Mgr-Mktg-Online Education - Career Education Corporation; *pg.* 599, *pg.* 658
Snyder, Greg, VP-Sls - Siemens Process Industries and Drive; *pg.* 1376, *pg.* 1587
Snyder, Jami, Brand Mgr-Dev - Unilever United States, Inc.; *pg.* 904, *pg.* 1061
Snyder, Jeanne, Dir-Product Mktg - Diebold, Incorporated; *pg.* 387, *pg.* 1407
Snyder, Jeannie, Asst Dir-Advising Svcs - Golden Gate University; *pg.* 602, *pg.* 219
Snyder, Jennifer, Mgr-Mktg - H&R Block, Inc.; *pg.* 764, *pg.* 983
Snyder, Judith, Grp Dir-Global Brand PR - The Coca-Cola Company; *pg.* 240, *pg.* 493
Snyder, Judith, Grp Dir-Brand PR-Global - Coca-Cola North America; *pg.* 848, *pg.* 500
Snyder, Laura, Dir-Mktg Tech-Global - Dell Inc.; *pg.* 383, *pg.* 1737
Snyder, Laurie, Grp Dir-Mktg-DePuy Synthes Advantage - DePuySynthes; *pg.* 1523, *pg.* 699
Snyder, Mark, Specialist-Social Media Programming - Red Bull North America, Inc.; *pg.* 264, *pg.* 275
Snyder, Matthew, Mgr-Social Media Adv - Zappos.com, Inc.; *pg.* 1291, *pg.* 1030
Snyder, Melissa, Sr Mgr-Mktg - Nobel Learning Communities, Inc.; *pg.* 605, *pg.* 1593
Snyder, Michael, Sr Mgr-Powersports Mktg - American Honda Motor Co., Inc.; *pg.* 163, *pg.* 292
Snyder, Molly, Grp Mgr-PR - Target Corporation; *pg.* 1786, *pg.* 942
Snyder, Paul, Product Mgr-Support - General Electric Company; *pg.* 1297, *pg.* 347
Snyder, Rob, Product Mgr-Network Infrastructure & Security - Rockwell Automation, Inc.; *pg.* 668, *pg.* 1880
Snyder, Robert, Mgr-Mktg - ADTRAN, Inc.; *pg.* 344, *pg.* 6
Snyder, Terri, Exec VP-Mktg - Checkers Drive-In Restaurants, Inc.; *pg.* 1017, *pg.* 472
Snyder, Tim, VP-Mktg - Mars, Incorporated; *pg.* 1858, *pg.* 1792
Snyder, Wayne, Sr Mgr-Mktg Analytics & Reporting - CIENA Corporation; *pg.* 628, *pg.* 771
So, Gary, Sr Dir-Mktg-Pepsi-Lipton North America - Pepsi Beverages Company; *pg.* 258, *pg.* 1342
So, Gary, Sr Dir-Mktg-Pepsi-Lipton North America - PepsiCo, Inc.; *pg.* 259, *pg.* 1327
So, Kevin, Engr-Product Mktg - PMC-Sierra, Inc.; *pg.* 664, *pg.* 287
So, Susie, Dir-Channel Mktg Strategies - New York Life Insurance Company; *pg.* 1211, *pg.* 1268
Soane, Daniel, VP-Affiliate Sls & Emerging Media - The Outdoor Channel; *pg.* 303, *pg.* 291
Soares, Jennifer, Specialist-Channel Mktg - Western Digital Corporation; *pg.* 492, *pg.* 118
Sobczak, Joseph, Mgr-Media & Adv Fin - The Kraft Heinz Company; *pg.* 871, *pg.* 641
Sobolewski, Natalie, Sr Mgr-Comm - Chamberlain College of Nursing, LLC; *pg.* 599, *pg.* 607
Sobolewski, Tara C., Dir-Event Mktg - Gartner, Inc.; *pg.* 1248, *pg.* 374
Sobota, Nancy, Dir-Strategic Mktg & Digital Transformation - Panasonic Corporation of North America; *pg.* 661, *pg.* 1120
Sobraske, John, Product Mgr - Paychex, Inc.; *pg.* 792, *pg.* 1336
Socha, Dennis, Acct Mgr-Adv Res - General Motors Company; *pg.* 175, *pg.* 881
Socha, Tori, Sr Dir-Programming & Dev - Spike TV; *pg.* 310, *pg.* 1295
Sochodolak, Marthina, Dir-Intl Trade Mktg - OPI Products Inc.; *pg.* 518, *pg.* 167
Socke, Amanda, Sr Mgr-Online Mktg - Crate & Barrel, Inc.; *pg.* 922, *pg.* 640
Socquet, Jorn, VP-Mktg - Anheuser-Busch Companies, LLC; *pg.* 237, *pg.* 991
Soder, Brian, Specialist-Motorsports Mktg - Lincoln Electric Holdings, Inc.; *pg.* 1355, *pg.* 1432
Soderlund, Laurie, Asst Mgr-Mktg - World's Finest Chocolate, Inc.; *pg.* 1864, *pg.* 597
Sodersten, Adam, Specialist-PR - Lands' End, Inc.; *pg.* 1776, *pg.* 1857
Soderstrom, Ryan, Sr Dir-Mktg & Corp Comm - Express Scripts, Inc.; *pg.* 1530, *pg.* 997
Sodos, Jonathon, Sr Mgr-Engrg - Apple Inc.; *pg.* 350, *pg.* 73
Soehl, Scott T., Sr VP-Sls - Elekta; *pg.* 391, *pg.* 284
Soehner, Cory, Mgr-Creative Svcs-Sun Life Global Investments - Sun Life Financial Inc.; *pg.* 806, *pg.* 1944
Sofen, Patrick, Assoc Mgr-Sports & Brand Mktg - ESPN, Inc.; *pg.* 285, *pg.* 340
Soffer, Sarah-Ann, Mgr-PR - InterContinental Hotels Corporation; *pg.* 1097, *pg.* 511
Sofko, Elana, VP-Digital Content Strategy & Ops & VP-Intl Digital Media - World Wrestling Entertainment, Inc.; *pg.* 595, *pg.* 380
Soh, Christina, Dir-Global Partner Mktg - QUALCOMM Incorporated; *pg.* 1873, *pg.* 207
Sohn, Adam, Head-Media Rels Team - Microsoft Corporation; *pg.* 435, *pg.* 1824
Sohn, Christine, Dir-Mktg-Global - Coach, Inc.; *pg.* 3, *pg.* 1214
Sohosky, Jamie, VP-US Mktg-Gen Mdse, Softlines & Apparel - Wal-Mart Stores, Inc.; *pg.* 1790, *pg.* 29
Soine, Jeremy, VP-Sls-U S - Rodan + Fields, LLC; *pg.* 522, *pg.* 225
Sokol, Bill, VP-Mktg - Arrow Fastener Company, Inc.; *pg.* 1042, *pg.* 1118
Sokol, Jason, Dir-Retail Mktg - Associated Food Stores, Inc.; *pg.* 1014, *pg.* 1756
Sokol, Tina, Dir & Category Mgr-Social, Digital Media & Production-Global - Novartis Pharmaceuticals Corp.; *pg.* 1575, *pg.* 1054
Sokolik, Dan, Mgr-Field Mktg - Subway Restaurants; *pg.* 1751, *pg.* 356
Sokoloff, Emma, Coord-Brand Mktg - Beats Electronics LLC; *pg.* 624, *pg.* 272
Sokoloff, Gregory, Sr Dir-Bus Dev & New Products-Comcast Wholesale - Comcast Corporation; *pg.* 276, *pg.* 1560
Sokolovsky, Karina, Sr Dir-Global Consumer Engagement - eBay Inc.; *pg.* 1240, *pg.* 243
Sokolowski, Jessica, VP-Corp Mktg & Adv - Frontier Communications Corporation; *pg.* 1871, *pg.* 362
Sokolyanskaya, Ksenia, Dir-Sls - MORNINGSTAR, INC.; *pg.* 784, *pg.* 583
Solano Vila, Susan, Exec VP-Mktg - Telemundo Network Inc.; *pg.* 311, *pg.* 430
Solarski, Audra, Mgr-Intl Mktg-Institutional Software - MORNINGSTAR, INC.; *pg.* 784, *pg.* 583
Solat, Bob, Sr Mgr-Sls - Intuit Inc.; *pg.* 769, *pg.* 158
Solazzo, Catherine, Dir-IBM Mktg Demand Programs - International Business Machines Corporation; *pg.* 418, *pg.* 1138
Solazzo, Nicole, Analyst-Mktg-Consulting - The New York Times Company; *pg.* 1668, *pg.* 1270
Solberg, Carrie, Specialist-Mktg Comm - Polaris Industries Inc.; *pg.* 1709, *pg.* 928
Solberg, Gina, Mgr-Mktg-Community & State - UnitedHealth Group Incorporated; *pg.* 1221, *pg.* 950
Soldano, Maggie, Mng Editor-Content & Sr Mgr - Kaiser Permanente; *pg.* 1552, *pg.* 171
Soldato, Fabiano Del, VP-Sls Center-South America - AT&T Inc.; *pg.* 1867, *pg.* 1674
Soldatos, Linda, Sr VP-Mktg - Wells Fargo & Company; *pg.* 819, *pg.* 232
Soldavini, Patti, Dir-Corp Mktg - SGK; *pg.* 1686, *pg.* 590
Sole, Lorrie, Sr Mgr-Social Media & Email Mktg - Kelly Services, Inc.; *pg.* 424, *pg.* 911
Solens, Laurie, Dir-Mktg Ops - Mercury Insurance Company; *pg.* 1208, *pg.* 136
Soli, Patrick, Dir-Sls & Mktg - Zebra Technologies Corporation; *pg.* 690, *pg.* 628
Soliani, Gail M., Dir-Direct to Consumer Creative - ACCO Brands Corporation; *pg.* 340, *pg.* 626
Solidon, Beverly, Dir-Adv - BCBG Max Azria Group LLC; *pg.* 19, *pg.* 301
Soliman, Adam, Grp VP-Residential Sls & Products - Generac Power Systems Inc.; *pg.* 1340, *pg.* 1898
Solis, Daniel, Mgr-Production - Circle Foods, LLC; *pg.* 848, *pg.* 201
Solis, Dominic, VP-Sls - Symmons Industries, Inc.; *pg.* 114, *pg.* 803
Solis, Henry, Supvr-Adv Dept - Fry's Electronics, Inc.; *pg.* 640, *pg.* 245
Solis, Marissa, VP-Mktg & Bus Dev - Frito-Lay North America, Inc.; *pg.* 1853, *pg.* 1730
Soller, Jennifer, VP-Intl Sls & Bus Dev - Bare Escentuals, Inc.; *pg.* 500, *pg.* 213
Solodar, Rita, VP-Partnership Mktg - American Express Company; *pg.* 712, *pg.* 1190
Soloff, Gary, Head-Sls & Mktg-Americas - Air New Zealand Ltd. (U.S.A.); *pg.* 1897, *pg.* 78
Solomito, James, Acct Exec-MLS Media Partnerships - Major League Soccer LLC; *pg.* 560, *pg.* 1256
Solomon, Angela, Mgr-PR & Corp Comm - Capital One Bank (USA), N.A.; *pg.* 730, *pg.* 1789
Solomon, Cindy, Mgr-Sls-Natl - KTVI-TV; *pg.* 295, *pg.* 999
Solomon, Cynthia J., Coord-Production & Distr-The Lamp - Exxon Mobil Corporation; *pg.* 977, *pg.* 1718
Solomon, Kelly, Head-Digital Mktg - Samsung Electronics America, Inc.; *pg.* 669, *pg.* 1115
Solomon, Lauren, Head-Google Creative Lab - Google Inc.; *pg.* 1249, *pg.* 153
Solomon, Lori, Sr Mgr-Mktg-Games - Dolby Laboratories, Inc.; *pg.* 284, *pg.* 217
Solomon, Michael, Dir-Retail Mktg & Sls - OnStar Corporation; *pg.* 214, *pg.* 884
Solomon, Nubia, Product Mgr-Category Brand Mgmt - Starbucks Corporation; *pg.* 897, *pg.* 1840
Solomon, Richard, Sr Mgr-Mktg - Yahoo! Inc.; *pg.* 1289, *pg.* 289
Solomon, Samantha, Brand Mgr-Info Svcs - The Boeing Company; *pg.* 225, *pg.* 567
Solomon, Samantha, Brand Mgr-Info Svcs - The Boeing Company - Helicopter Division; *pg.* 226, *pg.* 13
Solomon, Stephanie, VP-Consumer Mktg & Revenue-Customer Retention - Time Inc.; *pg.* 1693, *pg.* 1300
Solomonov, Mike, Sr Specialist-Digital Mktg - Champion Enterprises Holdings, LLC; *pg.* 75, *pg.* 910
Solone, Denise L., Mgr-Global Sls & Channel Mktg Comm - Micron Technology, Inc.; *pg.* 435, *pg.* 547
Solorzano, Raquel, Dir-LA&C Procurement Media & Adv Agencies - Diageo North America, Inc.; *pg.* 1961, *pg.* 361
Soltero, Eugenio, Sr Mgr-Mktg - Dell Inc.; *pg.* 383, *pg.* 1737
Soltoff, Charles C., Assoc VP-Mktg - Temple University Health System; *pg.* 1601, *pg.* 1571
Solvales, Dan, Dir-Mktg & Adv - Rogerson Aircraft Corporation; *pg.* 234, *pg.* 115
Som, Teresa, Mgr-Online Adv - Nordstrom, Inc.; *pg.* 1779, *pg.* 1837
Somaiya, Nikunj, Dir-Product Mgmt-Mobile Apps - Hotwire, Inc.; *pg.* 1912, *pg.* 219
Somanchi, Harsha, Product Mgr - Google Inc.; *pg.* 1249, *pg.* 153
Somani, Sanjeev, Dir-Sls Strategy-Platform - salesforce.com, inc.; *pg.* 1278, *pg.* 226
Somasundaram, Vivek, Specialist-Offer Mktg-Schneider

Electric - Schneider Canada, Inc.; *pg.* 1374, *pg.* 1928
Somboun, Sysounthone, Dir-Mktg Res & Analytics - Scholastic Corporation; *pg.* 1683, *pg.* 1288
Somers, Jeff, Chief Product Officer - Ticketmaster Entertainment LLC; *pg.* 1284, *pg.* 48
Somers, Kristin C., Mgr-Mktg Comm & Global Segments - Eaton Corporation; *pg.* 1331, *pg.* 1429
Somers, Pamela B., Sr VP-Corp Sls - Radio One, Inc.; *pg.* 305, *pg.* 778
Somers, Ron, VP-Sls & Mktg - Phantom Mfg. (Intl.) Ltd.; *pg.* 104, *pg.* 1907
Somes, Gary, VP-Adv - Smart & Final, Inc.; *pg.* 1034, *pg.* 66
Somma, Joe, VP-Corp Mktg - Caesars Entertainment Corporation; *pg.* 1083, *pg.* 1023
Sommer, Adoria, Mgr-Social Media - Nine West Holdings, Inc.; *pg.* 1815, *pg.* 1272
Sommer, Amy, Coord-Adv Special Projects Production - Macy's Florida; *pg.* 1777, *pg.* 444
Sommer, Erika, Brand Mgr-Digital - Brooks Sports Inc.; *pg.* 1806, *pg.* 1818
Sommer, Jeff, Mgr-Mktg & Sls - The Hershey Co.; *pg.* 1855, *pg.* 1538
Sommer, John E., Jr., VP-Sls - Kidron, Inc.; *pg.* 181, *pg.* 1457
Sommer, Meagan, Brand Mgr - Tweezerman International; *pg.* 524, *pg.* 1324
Sommer, Rolf-Dieter, Product Mgr - Belden, Inc.; *pg.* 624, *pg.* 993
Sommerfeld, Catherine, Mgr-Partner Mktg - Wyndham Worldwide Corporation; *pg.* 1119, *pg.* 1107
Sommers, Eric, Specialist-Product-Welding Helmets - Miller Electric Manufacturing Co.; *pg.* 1361, *pg.* 1852
Sommers, Scott, Grp Product Mgr - Molex Incorporated; *pg.* 655, *pg.* 628
Sommers, Steven, VP-Media - Under Armour, Inc.; *pg.* 49, *pg.* 759
Sommers, Sue, VP-Sls & Mktg - Atlantic Aviation Corporation; *pg.* 224, *pg.* 1729
Sommese, Regina, Dir-Media - Discovery Communications, Inc.; *pg.* 282, *pg.* 777
Somnolet, Marc, Dir-Global Mktg - Colgate-Palmolive Company; *pg.* 504, *pg.* 1215
Somo, David, VP-Corp Strategy & Mktg - ON Semiconductor Corporation; *pg.* 101, *pg.* 18
Somogyi, Stephan, Product Mgr-Safe Browsing - Google Inc.; *pg.* 1249, *pg.* 153
Son, Christopher M., Dir-IR, Corp Comm & Mktg - American Axle & Manufacturing Holdings, Inc.; *pg.* 198, *pg.* 879
Son, Melissa, Product Dev Mgr-Emerging Devices - AT&T Mobility LLC; *pg.* 619, *pg.* 488
Sondag, Rachel, Coord-Mktg Matls - Toll Brothers, Inc.; *pg.* 115, *pg.* 1541
Sondergaard, Brian, CIO & Sr VP-Global Product Dev-Fin & Risk Mgmt - Fiserv, Inc.; *pg.* 758, *pg.* 537
Sondergard, Rosemarie, Mgr-Intl Mktg-Hertz Rent a Car - The Hertz Corporation; *pg.* 1911, *pg.* 450
Sondgeroth, Jason, Sr Dir - Chattem, Inc.; *pg.* 1515, *pg.* 1628
Song, Andrew, Product Mgr - Facebook, Inc.; *pg.* 1245, *pg.* 143
Song, Christine, Exec Dir-Skincare Mktg-Global - The Estee Lauder Companies Inc.; *pg.* 508, *pg.* 1229
Song, Grace, Mgr-Mktg-Small & Medium Bus - Facebook, Inc.; *pg.* 1245, *pg.* 143
Song, Irene, Dir-Mktg & Bus Dev - Skyworks Solutions, Inc.; *pg.* 674, *pg.* 862
Song, Josie, Mgr-Media & Adv - Mitsubishi Motors North America, Inc.; *pg.* 185, *pg.* 75
Song, Keqing, Product Mgr - Autodesk Inc.; *pg.* 356, *pg.* 257
Song, Peter, Brand Mgr-Flonase - GlaxoSmithKline; *pg.* 1536, *pg.* 1389
Song, Steven, Mgr-Mktg - Cisco Systems, Inc.; *pg.* 372, *pg.* 240
Song, Susan, Head-Global Brand Mktg & Comm - Getty Images, Inc.; *pg.* 1645, *pg.* 1836
Song, Tony, VP-Sls & Partnerships - AMC Networks Inc.; *pg.* 269, *pg.* 1189
Soni, Duhita, Program Mgr-Digital Mktg - Abbott Laboratories; *pg.* 1484, *pg.* 551
Soni, Karan, Sr Mgr-Brand Partnership - Amazon.com, Inc.; *pg.* 1226, *pg.* 1831
Sonnek, Marcene, Brand Mgr-Digital - Hormel Foods Corporation; *pg.* 863, *pg.* 915
Sonnek, Marcene, Brand Mgr-Digital - Hormel Foods Corporation - Foodservice Division; *pg.* 864, *pg.* 916
Sonnemaker, Scott A., Sr VP-Sls - Sysco Corporation; *pg.* 1035, *pg.* 1716
Sonnenberg, Andy, Dir-Adv-WIRED-Natl - Conde Nast Publications, Inc.; *pg.* 1629, *pg.* 1217
Sonnenberg, Andy, Dir-Natl Adv-Wired - Vogue Magazine; *pg.* 1700, *pg.* 1311
Sonnenberg, Heather, VP-Strategic Mktg - Therma-Tru Corp.; *pg.* 115, *pg.* 1462
Sonnenberg, Scott, Sr Dir-Corp Partnerships - Chicago Professional Sports Limited Partnership; *pg.* 539, *pg.* 570
Sonnenfeld, Laura, VP-Adv - The New York Times Company; *pg.* 1668, *pg.* 1270
Sonnenfeld, Stephen, VP-Adv & Brand Integration - Thomson Reuters Markets; *pg.* 810, *pg.* 1299
Sonner, David, VP-Mktg-Liebert AC Power - Emerson Network Power; *pg.* 1071, *pg.* 1479
Sonner, David, VP-Mktg-Liebert AC Power - Emerson Network Power Liebert; *pg.* 1071, *pg.* 1439
Sontag, Janet, Mgr-Fin-Media Ops - The Kraft Heinz Company; *pg.* 871, *pg.* 641
Soo, Jeanette, Sr Mgr-Convention & Special Events - Canadian Marketing Association; *pg.* 136, *pg.* 1936
Soo, Katie, Head-Social Media Strategy - Hulu LLC; *pg.* 1257, *pg.* 274
Sood, Hema, Sr Specialist-Brand Mktg - United States Postal Service; *pg.* 1009, *pg.* 406
Sood, Nidhi, Sr Mgr-Mktg-Payer & Provider Solutions - IMS Health, Inc.; *pg.* 1544, *pg.* 344
Sood, Prateek, Sr Dir-Media, Creative Agencies PAB & Global Adv Production COE - PepsiCo, Inc.; *pg.* 259, *pg.* 1327
Soolman, Jan Velco, Mgr-Mktg-Growth Initiatives - The Gorton Group; *pg.* 859, *pg.* 823
Sooter, Jerry, Mgr-Mktg - Bruker Corporation; *pg.* 1511, *pg.* 788
Soper, Matt, Dir-Automotive Sls - The News-Times; *pg.* 1670, *pg.* 344
Sorber, Tiffany H., Head-Interactive Mktg Ops - Lenovo Group Ltd; *pg.* 427, *pg.* 1384
Sorce, Tom, Dir-Mktg-Customer Analytics - Nationwide Mutual Insurance Company; *pg.* 1210, *pg.* 1442
Sorckoff, Peter, Chief Creative Officer & Sr VP-Mktg - Hawks Basketball, Inc.; *pg.* 551, *pg.* 509
Sordi, Jason M., Reg Sls Mgr-Ontario-Grp Solutions - Royal Bank of Canada; *pg.* 800, *pg.* 1942
Sordillo, Nora, Sr Assoc Brand Mgr - Manischewitz Company; *pg.* 875, *pg.* 1097
Sordyl, Douglas J., Mng Dir-Mktg, Sls & Indus Rels - American Concrete Institute; *pg.* 127, *pg.* 885
Soreng, Katherine, Dir-Clinical & Scientific Mktg - Siemens Healthcare Diagnostics; *pg.* 673, *pg.* 604
Sorensen, Bryan, Dir-Digital Mktg - Navistar International Corporation; *pg.* 186, *pg.* 630
Sorensen, Chris, Head-Social Mktg - Microsoft Corporation; *pg.* 435, *pg.* 1824
Sorensen, Randy, VP-Sls-US, Canada & LATAM - CTI Group Holdings Inc.; *pg.* 381, *pg.* 684
Sorenson, Daren, Dir-Shopper Mktg Insights - The Coca-Cola Company; *pg.* 240, *pg.* 493
Sorenson, Melinda, Dir-Mktg, Ops & Trng - Lifetouch, Inc.; *pg.* 1420, *pg.* 922
Sorenson, Stephen, Sr Dir-Consumer & Support Experience-Global - Microsoft Corp.; *pg.* 440, *pg.* 321
Sorenson, Steven P., Exec VP-Product Ops - The Allstate Corporation; *pg.* 1189, *pg.* 639
Sorgen, Mike, VP-Digital Mktg & Analytics-ThankYou Rewards - Citigroup Inc.; *pg.* 735, *pg.* 1212
Sorger, Patrick, Mgr-Competitive Intelligence-Global & Mgr-Clinical Mktg-Global - Siemens Medical Solutions USA, Inc.; *pg.* 469, *pg.* 1550
Sorgie, Chris, Corp VP-Mktg, Prospecting & Dev - New York Life Insurance Company; *pg.* 1211, *pg.* 1268
Sorgini, Jillian, Coord-Social Media & PR - The Estee Lauder Companies Inc.; *pg.* 508, *pg.* 1229
Soriani, Andrea, Head-Mktg & Comm - Maserati North America, Inc.; *pg.* 183, *pg.* 1060
Soriano, Alicia, VP-Acq Mktg - Citigroup Inc.; *pg.* 735, *pg.* 1212
Soriano, Jamie, Brand Mgr-Champagnes Krug & Ruinart - Moet Hennessy; *pg.* 1966, *pg.* 1260
Soriano, John, Asst Mgr-PR-USA - Hong Kong Tourism Board - New York; *pg.* 1911, *pg.* 1241
Sorkin, Marc, Dir-Mktg-Verizon Wireless Bus Grp - LG Electronics U.S.A., Inc.; *pg.* 651, *pg.* 1060
Sorkin, Mark, Dir-Digital Mktg & Analytics - Orchard Brands Corporation; *pg.* 1780, *pg.* 1590
Sorkness, Bret, Brand Mgr-Digital-NBC News, TODAY, Meet the Press & Dateline - NBC News; *pg.* 300, *pg.* 1265
Soroka, Amy, Sr Mgr-Mktg-Strategy - Honeywell International Inc.; *pg.* 407, *pg.* 1088
Sorokko, Katya, VP-PR & Mktg - Restoration Hardware Holdings, Inc.; *pg.* 1060, *pg.* 70
Sorrano, David, Mgr-Mktg - Ziff Davis, LLC; *pg.* 1703, *pg.* 1316
Sorrel, Larry, Dir-Creative Svcs-Global - Newell Rubbermaid Inc.; *pg.* 1128, *pg.* 515
Sorrell, Megan, Dir-Mktg - S.C. Johnson & Son, Inc.; *pg.* 334, *pg.* 1889
Sorrells, Philip, VP-Strategic Mktg - CommScope, Inc.; *pg.* 278, *pg.* 1378
Sorrells, Steven, Head-Reg Comml & Sr Dir - Pfizer Inc.; *pg.* 1581, *pg.* 1278
Sorrels, Garrett, Assoc Mgr-Mktg - The Allstate Corporation; *pg.* 1189, *pg.* 639
Sorrentino, Christina Neil, Specialist-Mktg - American Tower Corporation; *pg.* 164, *pg.* 789
Sorrosa, Saskia, VP-Mktg - National Basketball Association; *pg.* 566, *pg.* 1264
Sortino, John, VP Sls, Mktg & Plng - LOGIKA Corporation; *pg.* 1264, *pg.* 581
Sosa, Leonard, Specialist-Food Svc Sls - GSC Enterprises, Inc.; *pg.* 1021, *pg.* 1746
Sosa, Wallys, Mgr-Adv - Dunkin' Brands Group, Inc.; *pg.* 1727, *pg.* 810
Sosa-Krall, Rafael, Sr Mgr-Mktg-Microsoft Mktg - Microsoft Corporation; *pg.* 435, *pg.* 1824
Sosalski, Rachel, Dir-Pharmacy Mktg - GlaxoSmithKline; *pg.* 1536, *pg.* 1565
Sosnoff, Kate, Mgr-Comm & Social Media - Discovery Communications, Inc.; *pg.* 282, *pg.* 777
Sosso, Greg, Dir-Product Dev - Airlite Plastics Company; *pg.* 1451, *pg.* 1013
Sotelo, Liza, Dir-Mdsg, Women's & Maternity-Online - Banana Republic; *pg.* 1760, *pg.* 212
Sotelo, Michael, Head-US Multicultural Mktg - Facebook, Inc.; *pg.* 1245, *pg.* 143
Soto, Aimee, Specialist-Mktg & PR - Kawasaki Motors Corp., U.S.A.; *pg.* 1708, *pg.* 111
Soto, Alekssandra, Coord-Sls - American Express Company; *pg.* 712, *pg.* 1190
Soto, Coco, Mgr-Strategic Event Mktg-Europe, Middle East, Africa & Russia - Cisco Systems, Inc.; *pg.* 372, *pg.* 240
Soto, Helen, Analyst-Digital Mktg Svcs Program Plng - Unilever United States, Inc.; *pg.* 904, *pg.* 1061
Soto, Joe, Sr Product Mgr - BSH Home Appliances Corporation; *pg.* 53, *pg.* 108
Soto, Juan, Mgr-Sls-Latin America - Waterous Company; *pg.* 1387, *pg.* 965
Soto, Roberto, Dir-Product Pricing - First Data Corporation; *pg.* 754, *pg.* 505
Soto, Vanessa, Mng Dir-Digital Adv - Charles Schwab; *pg.* 1235, *pg.* 1661
Soto, Vanessa, Mng Dir-Digital Adv - Charles Schwab & Company, Inc.; *pg.* 734, *pg.* 215
Sottosanti, Frank, CMO - Protective Life Corporation; *pg.* 1215, *pg.* 4
Soubrier, Alexandra, Sr Gen Mgr-Mktg - Unilever United States, Inc.; *pg.* 904, *pg.* 1061
Souchon, Eduardo, Sr Dir-Mktg Brand Strategy New Products - Office Depot, Inc.; *pg.* 448, *pg.* 412
Soucy, Alison, Mgr-Mktg Client Svcs-Apple - Ingram Micro Inc.; *pg.* 415, *pg.* 261
Soucy, Art, Pres-Products & Svcs-Global - Baker Petrolite Corporation; *pg.* 1148, *pg.* 1745
Soucy, Arthur L., Pres-Products & Svcs-Global - Baker Hughes Incorporated; *pg.* 1315, *pg.* 1700
Souder, Rick, Exec VP-Mdsg - Crutchfield Corporation; *pg.* 1237, *pg.* 1777
Soudodi, Ahmed, Reg Brand Mgr-Chevrolet & GMC-Middle East Reg - General Motors Company; *pg.* 175, *pg.* 881
Souers, Terry, VP-PR-US Mortgage Insurance - Genworth Financial, Inc.; *pg.* 761, *pg.* 1802
Soukas, Nick, Sr Dir-Mktg - Unilever United States, Inc.; *pg.* 904, *pg.* 1061
Soule, Dick, Head-Sls, Sponsorship & Media Programs - Google Inc.; *pg.* 1249, *pg.* 153
Soule, Erik, VP & Gen Mgr-Signal Conditioning Products - Linear Technology Corp.; *pg.* 652, *pg.* 147
Soule, Jennifer, Specialist-Creative Comm & Design - Manulife Financial Corporation; *pg.* 778, *pg.* 1939
Soule, Meghan, Sr Specialist-Digital Mktg - ACI Worldwide Inc.; *pg.* 341, *pg.* 1010
Sourini, Jodi, Mgr-Mktg Comm - Rockwell Automation, Inc.;

First page reference indicates Business Class Edition
Second page reference indicates Geographic Edition

pg. 668, pg. 1880
Soursos, Harry, Sr Mgr-Comm, Media & High Tech-Mgmt Consulting - Accenture; pg. 1392, pg. 1186
Sousa, Cristina, Mgr-Social Media - Philips Electronics North America; pg. 662, pg. 782
Sousa, Jessica, Mgr-Mktg & Demand Generation - Lionbridge Technologies Inc.; pg. 428, pg. 851
South, Garrett, Product Mgr - Deere & Company; pg. 703, pg. 632
South, Jill, Dir-Production - Trend Magazines, Inc.; pg. 1696, pg. 465
Southard, Bob, Reg Mgr-Sls-Southeast Reg - Dorner Manufacturing Corp.; pg. 1329, pg. 1861
Souther, Jason, Supvr-Digital Media & eMarketing - Zimmer Biomet Holdings, Inc.; pg. 1611, pg. 699
Southerland, Michelle, Product Mgr-ProServices - ADTRAN, Inc.; pg. 344, pg. 6
Southern Chickering, Melissa, Sr Dir-Mktg, Media Strategy & Analytics - Yahoo! Inc.; pg. 1289, pg. 289
Southwell, Jerry, Reg Mgr-Premium Offerings Sls - Yara N America, Inc.; pg. 1802, pg. 477
Souza, Emerson, Graphic Designer-Mktg - Solis Foods Corporation Inc.; pg. 897, pg. 1919
Souza, Vinda, Dir-Mktg Comm - Bullhorn, Inc.; pg. 1233, pg. 792
Sowards, Joshua, Brand Mgr-Activation - Tempur Sealy International, Inc.; pg. 944, pg. 731
Sowell, Audrey D., Specialist-Integrated Brand Mktg - Mary Kay Inc.; pg. 516, pg. 1657
Sowinski, Tim, Sr Mgr-Channel Mktg - Medline Industries, Inc.; pg. 1562, pg. 635
Sowry, Melissa, Mgr-Social Media, Digital Content & Digital Adv Global Mktg - Burt's Bees Inc.; pg. 502, pg. 1370
Soyao, Jesse, Sr Mgr-Asset Mgmt - Siemens Canada Ltd.; pg. 1306, pg. 1921
Sozzi, Gary, VP-Adv Ops - Daily News, L.P.; pg. 1632, pg. 1221
Spaar, Steve, Dir-Mktg-Americas - EnerSys Inc.; pg. 1334, pg. 1584
Spada, Fernando, VP-Product Mktg-Ta BG Global - KEMET Corporation; pg. 649, pg. 1621
Spadaccini, Chris, Sr VP-Brand Mktg - Home Box Office, Inc.; pg. 290, pg. 1240
Spadafora, Megan, Coord-Mktg - Pet Valu Canada, Inc.; pg. 1480, pg. 1924
Spadora, Dan, Asst Mgr-Social Media Mktg - Toys "R" Us, Inc.; pg. 968, pg. 1130
Spady, Rodney, Dir-Consumer & ECommerce Mktg - Sanofi Pasteur, Inc; pg. 1591, pg. 1588
Spaeth, Dana, VP & Gen Mgr-FoodSvc & Indus Sls - Boulder Brands, Inc.; pg. 1016, pg. 310
Spaeth, Jeff, VP-Sls & Mktg - Summit Brewing Co.; pg. 265, pg. 963
Spages, Antoinette, Dir-Mktg & Comm-Acrylic Polymers - Evonik Corporation; pg. 1162, pg. 1103
Spagle, Allison, Dir-NW Sls-Media - Complex Media, Inc.; pg. 1628, pg. 1217
Spagnualo, Joe, Acct Mgr-Social Media - Lithia Motors Inc; pg. 183, pg. 1499
Spagnuolo, Paulette, Mgr-Mktg & Comm - A123 Systems Inc.; pg. 1309, pg. 855
Spahr, Andrea B., Specialist-Wealth Advisory Mktg - Wilmington Trust Corporation; pg. 822, pg. 392
Spahr, Brad, VP-Product Dev-Global Digital Bus - Sony Music Entertainment; pg. 309, pg. 1294
Spahr, Eric, Sr Dir-Global Strategy & Innovation - Kao Brands Co. Inc.; pg. 513, pg. 1415
Spahr, Sarah, Coord-Mktg Comm Dept - Fender Musical Instruments Corporation; pg. 547, pg. 21
Spain, John, Mgr-Mktg-Coffee - The J.M. Smucker Company; pg. 865, pg. 1468
Spain, Peter, Reg Mgr-Sls - Anderson & Vreeland, Inc.; pg. 1616, pg. 1064
Spain, Steve, Head-Sls - Syngenta Professional Products; pg. 1183, pg. 1376
Spaine, Jennifer, Dir-Direct Response Mktg - American Diabetes Association; pg. 127, pg. 1770
Spalding, Jim, Dir-Mktg-Quaker Oats - PepsiCo, Inc.; pg. 259, pg. 1327
Spalding, Jim, Dir-Mktg - The Quaker Oats Company; pg. 834, pg. 588
Spalding, Kent, VP-Sls & Mktg - Oregon Cherry Growers, Inc.; pg. 1028, pg. 1508
Spall, Jennifer, Sr Dir-Political Programs - Wal-Mart Stores, Inc.; pg. 1790, pg. 29
Spande, Carl, Analyst-Mktg Bus - General Mills, Inc.; pg. 828, pg. 933
Spangenthal, Alissa, Coord-Mktg & PR - Hugo Boss Fashions Inc.; pg. 42, pg. 1242
Spangler, Gary, Head-Global Digital Mktg-Performance Polymers - E.I. du Pont de Nemours & Company; pg. 1159, pg. 390
Spangler, Richard, VP-Mktg - Chattem, Inc.; pg. 1515, pg. 1628
Spangler, Tom, Sr Dir-Bus Unit Controls - Allianz Life Insurance Company of North America; pg. 1188, pg. 929
Spangler, Tom, Mgr-Mktg - Siemens PLM Software; pg. 469, pg. 1734
Spanier, Joshua, Dir-Mktg-Global Media - Google Inc.; pg. 1249, pg. 153
Spanos, Jaimee, Mgr-Global Mktg-Optical & Sun Specialty - Oakley, Inc.; pg. 1840, pg. 86
Sparacino, Nikki, Brand Mgr-Restoratives - Dentsply International Inc.; pg. 1522, pg. 1596
Sparaga, Sherri, VP-Retail Sls-Natl - The Coca-Cola Company; pg. 240, pg. 493
Spare, David, VP-Mktg & Bus Dev - DOLE FOOD COMPANY, INC.; pg. 853, pg. 306
Sparkman, Worth, Mgr-PR - Tyson Foods, Inc.; pg. 902, pg. 35
Sparks, Darren, Dir-Strategic Mktg - Siemens Corporation; pg. 803, pg. 1291
Sparks, Doug, Sr Dir-Global Procurement-Indirect Sourcing - NIKE, Inc.; pg. 1812, pg. 1492
Sparks, Joan, Dir-Mktg, Copy & Print Depot - Office Depot, Inc.; pg. 448, pg. 412
Sparks, Peter, VP-Sls & Mktg - KB Home; pg. 90, pg. 134
Sparks, Stuart, Asst Mgr-Mktg - Wal-Mart Stores, Inc.; pg. 1790, pg. 29
Sparks, Vicky, Sr Mgr-Customer & Lead Mgmt - W.W. Grainger, Inc.; pg. 1390, pg. 625
Sparling, Deana, Planner-Segment & Product-LexisNexis Digital Library - LexisNexis Litigation Solutions; pg. 1659, pg. 1446
Sparre, Janet, Dir-Mktg-Fin Svcs - Accenture; pg. 1392, pg. 1186
Sparrow, Cindy, VP-Mktg & Product Mgmt - Lennox International Inc.; pg. 1073, pg. 1736
Spatara, Molly, Dir-Digital Mktg-Accenture Interactive, Analytics & Mobility - Accenture; pg. 1392, pg. 1186
Spaude, Jennifer M., Dir-IR & Mktg - Enventis; pg. 637, pg. 927
Spaulding, Kristen, Corp Mng Editor-Social Media - Neiman Marcus, Inc.; pg. 30, pg. 1684
Spaulding, Sean, VP & Dir-Investment Mktg - MFS Investment Management; pg. 782, pg. 798
Spaulding, Stephen, Sr Dir & Dir-Mktg-Intl-EMEA, Asia & Caribbean - ConAgra Foods, Inc.; pg. 826, pg. 1014
Speak, Chris, Dir-Sls-Natl - JanSport; pg. 1837, pg. 38
Speaks, Jonathan, VP-Sls-Natl - Makita U.S.A., Inc.; pg. 1358, pg. 120
Speal, Stephanie, Sr Dir-Talent Strategies - Canadian Imperial Bank of Commerce; pg. 729, pg. 1935
Spear, Ally, Brand Mktg Mgr - Capella Education Company; pg. 599, pg. 931
Spear, Jana, Key Acct Mgr-Mktg - Columbia Sportswear Company; pg. 1830, pg. 1501
Spear, Jonathan, Sr Planner-Integrated Mktg Comm - General Mills, Inc.; pg. 828, pg. 933
Spearman, Simeon, Mgr-Emerging Mktg - AT&T Mobility LLC; pg. 619, pg. 488
Spears, Candace, Product Mgr-Global - Brady Corporation; pg. 363, pg. 1873
Spears, Janice, Mgr-Feed Products Mktg - MFA Incorporated; pg. 1479, pg. 976
Spears, Rebecca, Mgr-Digital Mktg-Global - Starbucks Corporation; pg. 897, pg. 1840
Spears, Robert, Dir-Search & Display Mktg - Guitar Center, Inc.; pg. 1771, pg. 306
Spears, Sean, Sr Dir-Trade & Pharmacy Rels - Eisai Inc.; pg. 1526, pg. 1133
Spears, Stuart, VP-Bus Ops & Sls - Tennessee Football, Inc.; pg. 587, pg. 1654
Speciale, Donna, Pres-Ad Sls - Turner Broadcasting System, Inc.; pg. 314, pg. 521
Speciale, Kim, Sr Mgr-Mktg - Navistar International Corporation; pg. 186, pg. 630
Speciale, Phil, Dir-Sls - LANGUAGE LINE SERVICES HOLDINGS, INC.; pg. 426, pg. 151
Spector, Brandon, Brand Mgr-Digital Mktg - DISH Network Corporation; pg. 283, pg. 325
Spector, Josh, Mng Dir-Digital Media & Mktg - Academy of Motion Picture Arts & Sciences; pg. 526, pg. 46
Speed, Sarah, Mgr-Mktg Ops - Luxottica Retail; pg. 8, pg. 1460
Speer, Mark, VP & Dir-Adv & Promo - Simon & Schuster, Inc.; pg. 1687, pg. 1292
Spegman, Jonah, Dir-Digital Media & Database Mktg - Scripps Networks Interactive, Inc.; pg. 1279, pg. 1638
Speicher, Daniel, Pres, Mgr-Sls & Mgr-Adv - The Cyclone Mfg. Co.; pg. 78, pg. 698
Speigel, Donna, Dir-Creative-Brand Comm & Editorial - Crate & Barrel, Inc.; pg. 922, pg. 640
Speight, Bruce, Sr Dir-Media Rels - New York Jets Football Club, Inc.; pg. 570, pg. 1067
Speights, Kimberly, Coord-Recruiting-Retail Mktg - Bluegreen Corporation; pg. 1082, pg. 410
Speir, Jim, VP-Sls - SVM, LP; pg. 1786, pg. 606
Spelhaug, Annette, Bus Mgr-Mktg - Whataburger, Inc.; pg. 1755, pg. 1744
Spellen, Raymond, Producer-Creative & Graphic Design - AT&T Mobility LLC; pg. 619, pg. 488
Spellman, Dan, Sr Dir-Mktg - FTD Group, Inc.; pg. 1795, pg. 608
Spellman, Kirk J., Dir-Mktg Svcs - Assurity Life Insurance Company; pg. 1194, pg. 1011
Spellman, Leo, Sr Dir-Comm - Steinway & Sons; pg. 586, pg. 1176
Speltz, Bob, Sr Dir-Pub Affairs - Standard Insurance Company; pg. 1217, pg. 1506
Spence, Allen, VP-Worldwide Customer Success, Pro Svcs & Sls Engrg - Good Technology, Inc.; pg. 1249, pg. 285
Spence, Amanda, Specialist-Mktg - Merrill Corporation; pg. 1664, pg. 962
Spence, Betsy, VP-Integrated Mktg - Macy's, Inc.; pg. 1778, pg. 1417
Spence, Emily, Dir-Field Mktg - Arby's Restaurant Group, Inc.; pg. 1014, pg. 488
Spence, Greg, Sr Mgr-VDI Bus Dev - Samsung Electronics America, Inc.; pg. 669, pg. 1115
Spence, Linda, Mgr-Channel Mktg - Xerox Canada Inc.; pg. 494, pg. 1930
Spence, Margie, Mgr-Adv - Recreation Vehicle Industry Association; pg. 155, pg. 1799
Spence, Robert, VP-Sls & Product Mgmt - FRESH DEL MONTE PRODUCE INC.; pg. 856, pg. 418
Spence, Suzanne, Head-Media Solutions-B2B - Google Inc.; pg. 1249, pg. 153
Spence, Timothy, Chief Strategy Officer & Exec VP - Fifth Third Bancorp; pg. 752, pg. 1413
Spencer, Andrew, Brand Mgr-Prego Italian Sauce - Campbell Soup Company; pg. 844, pg. 1048
Spencer, Anita, Sr Mgr-Mktg - Hanesbrands Inc.; pg. 26, pg. 1394
Spencer, Bryan, Mgr-Sls-Southeast Reg - Unified Brands Inc.; pg. 1385, pg. 970
Spencer, Darin, Media Buyer - Raymour & Flanigan Furniture Co.; pg. 940, pg. 1174
Spencer, David, Dir-Brand Mktg - Wal-Mart Stores, Inc.; pg. 1790, pg. 29
Spencer, Eriana, Assoc Dir-Mktg - UBS Financial Services Inc.; pg. 812, pg. 1306
Spencer, Gaylord, VP-Mktg - National Automotive Parts Association; pg. 213, pg. 515
Spencer, Jennifer, Assoc VP-Mktg - Danier Leather, Inc.; pg. 22, pg. 1937
Spencer, Jesse, Dir-Social Media-Global - The Western Union Company; pg. 822, pg. 327
Spencer, Joanna, Media Planner & Media Buyer - Turner Broadcasting System, Inc.; pg. 314, pg. 521
Spencer, John E., VP-Distr Sls - Cree Inc.; pg. 631, pg. 1371
Spencer, Kathy, Brand Mgr-Global Licensing - Energizer Holdings, Inc.; pg. 637, pg. 996
Spencer, Kendra, Acct Mgr-Mktg Performance - Puma North America, Inc.; pg. 1816, pg. 858
Spencer, Lindsay, Program Mgr-Adv Ops - The Weather Channel LLC; pg. 320, pg. 523
Spencer, Lucy, Dir-Mktg-Victoria's Secret Beauty & Accessories - L Brands, Inc.; pg. 1776, pg. 1441
Spencer, Mark, Sr Mgr-Call Center Ops - Guthy-Renker LLC; pg. 289, pg. 273
Spencer, Scott, Dir-Product Mgmt - Google Inc.; pg. 1249, pg. 153
Spencer, Scott, Sr Dir-Sl Alliances - Oracle Corporation; pg. 450, pg. 191

Spencer, Stephen, Brand Mgr - Newell Rubbermaid Inc.; *pg.* 1128, *pg.* 515
Spencer, Tremaine, Dir-Product Mgmt - United Services Automobile Association; *pg.* 1221, *pg.* 1743
Spendiff, Stephen, Mgr-Product, Mktg & Ops - Rosco Laboratories, Inc.; *pg.* 1782, *pg.* 378
Speranza, Mark A., VP-Sls - Electric Eel Manufacturing Co., Inc.; *pg.* 80, *pg.* 1473
Speranza, Stephanie, Coord-Ad Sls Mktg - The Tennis Channel, Inc.; *pg.* 679, *pg.* 276
Sperber, Marie, Dir-Dev & Mktg - Visiting Nurse Association of Somerset Hills Inc.; *pg.* 1607, *pg.* 1042
Sperling, Allison, Mgr-Sports Mktg - Jewel-Osco; *pg.* 1024, *pg.* 620
Sperling, Matthew, Mgr-Email Mktg - Etsy, Inc.; *pg.* 1768, *pg.* 1230
Sperling, Meir, Chief Strategy Officer - VERINT SYSTEMS INC.; *pg.* 488, *pg.* 1182
Sperling, Michal, Sr VP & Head-Integrated Mktg - Cable News Network LP; *pg.* 1624, *pg.* 1208
Spero, Jason, VP-Global Brand Solutions & Innovations - Google Inc.; *pg.* 1249, *pg.* 153
Sperry, Sue, Sr Mgr-PR - AT&T; *pg.* 1865, *pg.* 258
Spexarth, Matt, Principal & Product Mgr-Embedded Sys - National Instruments Corporation; *pg.* 443, *pg.* 1664
Speyer, Rick, Mgr-Global Mktg-Enterprise Applications - Cisco Systems, Inc.; *pg.* 372, *pg.* 240
Spezialetti, Stephanie, Coord-Mktg-ROOT SPORTS Pittsburgh-DIRECTV Sports Networks - DIRECTV Group Holdings, LLC; *pg.* 281, *pg.* 79
Spiak, Jake, Coord-Corp Partnerships Sls - Boston Celtics Limited Partnership; *pg.* 533, *pg.* 790
Spicehandler, Nikki, Sr Mgr-Integrated Mktg - In Style Magazine; *pg.* 1652, *pg.* 1243
Spicer, Michael G., Pres-Sls & Global Svc-Americas - Cantel Medical Corp.; *pg.* 1405, *pg.* 1079
Spicher, Doug, Dir-Club Sites Product & Ops - National Football League; *pg.* 567, *pg.* 1264
Spidare, Todd, Dir-US Mktg-Biosurgery - Johnson & Johnson; *pg.* 1549, *pg.* 1091
Spiegel, Arielle, Specialist-Social Media & Brand Partnerships-Pink - Victoria's Secret Stores, LLC; *pg.* 1789, *pg.* 1471
Spiegel, Darren, VP-Sls & Mktg - AAR Corp.; *pg.* 223, *pg.* 671
Spiegel, Laura, Grp Mktg Mgr-Strategy & Innovation - Roche Diagnostics Corporation; *pg.* 1590, *pg.* 689
Spiegelberg, Kim, Sr Dir-Brand Partnerships - Pandora Media Inc.; *pg.* 1273, *pg.* 172
Spiegelman, Michael, Dir-Product Innovation - Netflix, Inc.; *pg.* 1269, *pg.* 141
Spiegelman, Traci, Dir-Global Brand Media-Aramis Designer Fragrances - The Estee Lauder Companies Inc.; *pg.* 508, *pg.* 1229
Spiegelthal, Karen, VP-Mktg - K12, Inc.; *pg.* 1260, *pg.* 1785
Spielfogel, Whitney, Dir-Field Mktg & PR - Popchips; *pg.* 890, *pg.* 182
Spielmaker, Sandy, VP-Global Sls - Amway Corporation; *pg.* 326, *pg.* 864
Spielvogel, Jurgen, Sr Product Mgr-Particle Instruments-Global - TSI Incorporated; *pg.* 1432, *pg.* 965
Spies, Jason, Coord-Mktg Database - Adobe Systems Incorporated; *pg.* 342, *pg.* 235
Spies, Joe, Sr Dir-Sls & Head-Segment - Converse Inc.; *pg.* 1831, *pg.* 793
Spiesman, Michael H., VP & Dir-Sls-Natl - Gray Television, Inc.; *pg.* 289, *pg.* 509
Spiess, Markus, VP-Sls & Mktg-Global - Koppers Holdings Inc.; *pg.* 1170, *pg.* 1577
Spiewak, Kristin, Sr Mgr-Brand Mktg AIU - Career Education Corporation; *pg.* 599, *pg.* 658
Spight, Jermaine, Sr Mgr-PR - AT&T Inc.; *pg.* 1867, *pg.* 1674
Spignese, John, VP-Sls - AWR Corporation; *pg.* 623, *pg.* 78
Spiliotopoulos, Antonis, Sr VP-Consumer Products Div-Americas - L'Oreal USA; *pg.* 514, *pg.* 1252
Spilker, Kim, Sr Mgr-Content Product - Microsoft Corporation; *pg.* 435, *pg.* 1824
Spilker, Robyn H., Reg Dir-Sls - Abbott Laboratories; *pg.* 1484, *pg.* 551
Spillane, Jeff, Sr Product Mgr - Benjamin Moore & Co.; *pg.* 1440, *pg.* 1085
Spillane, Kelley, Sr VP-US Sls - Castle Brands Inc.; *pg.* 239, *pg.* 1209
Spiller, Doug, Product Mgr-Heavy Duty-Vehicle Service Grp-A Dover Company - Rotary Lift; *pg.* 216, *pg.* 694
Spillman, Johnny, VP-Sls & Svc - Coventry Health Care, Inc.; *pg.* 1519, *pg.* 761
Spillner, Cassie, Sr Mgr-Direct Mktg - Best Western International, Inc.; *pg.* 1081, *pg.* 15
Spilseth, Karl, Sr Specialist-Digital Mktg & Analytics - Medtronic, Inc.; *pg.* 1564, *pg.* 939
Spina, Dario, Exec VP-Integrated Mktg - Viacom Inc.; *pg.* 316, *pg.* 1310
Spinale, Mike, Sr Dir-HR - DATATRAK International, Inc.; *pg.* 383, *pg.* 1462
Spindel, Jennifer, VP-Consumer Products - EarthLink Holdings Corp.; *pg.* 1240, *pg.* 504
Spindler, Ken, Coord-Media Rels - Milwaukee Brewers Baseball Club, Inc.; *pg.* 562, *pg.* 1878
Spinelli, Karen, Dir-Media & Partnerships - Apple Vacations Inc.; *pg.* 1899, *pg.* 1556
Spinelli, Vito, Dir-Product Mgmt - Stanley Access Technologies, LLC; *pg.* 112, *pg.* 349
Spinello, Laura, Sr Specialist-Digital Mktg - Liberty Mutual Insurance Group Inc.; *pg.* 1205, *pg.* 797
Spini, Mark, Dir-Indus Sls - Guittard Chocolate Company; *pg.* 1855, *pg.* 55
Spink, Jon, Mgr-Timber Mktg - Rayonier Inc.; *pg.* 1179, *pg.* 434
Spinner, Melissa E., Specialist-Digital & Creative Comm - FMC Corporation; *pg.* 1163, *pg.* 1564
Spinney, Susan, Sr Dir-Market Mgmt-Northeast & Canada - Expedia, Inc.; *pg.* 1244, *pg.* 1814
Spirito, Michael, VP-Bus Dev & Digital Media - Fox Sports Net; *pg.* 288, *pg.* 131
Spiro, Art, Exec VP-Mktg - Elizabeth Arden, Inc.; *pg.* 507, *pg.* 448
Spisak, Shannon, Dir-Mktg - Garden Fresh Restaurant Corp.; *pg.* 1729, *pg.* 203
Spitalieri, Victoria, Mgr-Intl Mktg-Sundance Global - AMC Networks Inc.; *pg.* 269, *pg.* 1189
Spithaler, Stacey, Program Mgr-Direct Mktg - Wells Fargo & Company; *pg.* 819, *pg.* 232
Spittle, Hilary R., Sr Mgr-External Comm-Global - Eaton Corporation; *pg.* 1331, *pg.* 1429
Spitz, Colleen, VP-Mktg & Comm - Sacramento Kings; *pg.* 579, *pg.* 197
Spitz, David, Project Mgr-Offline Mktg Strategy - Discover Financial Services; *pg.* 744, *pg.* 653
Spitz, Stephanie, Supvr-Adv Production - Meredith Corporation; *pg.* 1663, *pg.* 705
Spitzer, Christopher, Dir-PR - The Walt Disney Company; *pg.* 317, *pg.* 52
Spivock, Robert, Assoc Dir-HCV Mktg - Gilead Sciences, Inc.; *pg.* 1535, *pg.* 88
Splane, Terry, VP-Mktg - Ventura Foods, LLC; *pg.* 908, *pg.* 49
Splitstone, Anne Marie, Sr Dir-Category-Gum - Wm. Wrigley Jr. Company; *pg.* 1863, *pg.* 596
Spohn-O'brien, Jeanene D., VP-Mktg-Global - Insurance Auto Auctions, Inc.; *pg.* 180, *pg.* 669
Spokane, Steve, VP-Mktg & Customer Retention - McKesson Corporation; *pg.* 1560, *pg.* 222
Spon, Morgen, Mgr-Social Media Strategy - Big Lots, Inc.; *pg.* 1762, *pg.* 1438
Sponheim, Kathy, Sr Product Mgr-John Deere - Deere & Company; *pg.* 703, *pg.* 632
Spoon, Ryan, Sr VP-Product Dev - ESPN, Inc.; *pg.* 285, *pg.* 340
Spooner, Mary, Sr Mgr-Corp Reseller Partner Mktg - NetApp, Inc.; *pg.* 444, *pg.* 287
Spoonts, John, Reg Mgr-Sls - Texas Refinery Corp.; *pg.* 986, *pg.* 1696
Spotts, Lara, Sr VP-Dev-Bravo Media - NBC Universal, Inc.; *pg.* 300, *pg.* 1266
Spradlin, Dwight, Asst Dir-Media Rels - Tennessee Football, Inc.; *pg.* 587, *pg.* 1654
Spradlin, Phil, Mgr-Product Mktg - ACI Worldwide Inc.; *pg.* 341, *pg.* 1010
Sprague, Jennifer, VP-Mktg-Global - BCBG Max Azria Group LLC; *pg.* 19, *pg.* 301
Sprague, Joe, Sr VP-Comm & External Rels - Alaska Airlines, Inc.; *pg.* 1897, *pg.* 1830
Sprague, Joseph A., VP-Mktg - Alaska Air Group, Inc.; *pg.* 1897, *pg.* 1830
Sprague, Kerri, VP-Consumer Credit Card Mktg - Bank of America Corporation; *pg.* 718, *pg.* 1362
Sprague, Lauren, Sr Mgr-Mktg Vendor Mgmt - Wal-Mart Stores, Inc.; *pg.* 1790, *pg.* 29
Sprague, Shawn, Sr Dir & Mgr-Product Line-SiteMinder - CA Technologies; *pg.* 366, *pg.* 1168
Spraker, Ann, Brand Mgr - Capital One Financial Corporation; *pg.* 730, *pg.* 1789
Spralls, Dionne, Sr Mgr-Mktg Reinvestment-Global - The Coca-Cola Company; *pg.* 240, *pg.* 493
Sprangers, Amy, Mng Dir-Suite Sls & Svc - Seattle Seahawks; *pg.* 582, *pg.* 1830
Spratlen, Robert, VP-Digital Media, Data & Audience Dev - Viacom Inc.; *pg.* 316, *pg.* 1310
Spratt, Emily, Mgr-eMail Mktg - Belk, Inc.; *pg.* 1760, *pg.* 1364
Sprawka, Jason, Mgr-US Product Mktg - Ford Motor Company; *pg.* 172, *pg.* 876
Sprecher, Anne, Dir-Mktg - Sprecher Brewing Company; *pg.* 265, *pg.* 1858
Sprenger, Gina, Exec VP-Mdsg - Bluestem Brands, Inc.; *pg.* 1763, *pg.* 922
Sprenger, Randy, Mgr-Customer Lifecycle Mktg - Harley-Davidson, Inc.; *pg.* 178, *pg.* 1874
Sprick, Darrell, Dir-Paragon Product Quality - McKesson Corporation; *pg.* 1560, *pg.* 222
Spriggs, James, VP-Mktg & Dev - Almost Family, Inc.; *pg.* 1492, *pg.* 731
Spring, Andre B., Dir-Payer Mktg-Oncology - GlaxoSmithKline; *pg.* 1537, *pg.* 776
Spring, Heather, Mgr-Digital Mktg - Accenture; *pg.* 1392, *pg.* 1186
Springborn, Sharon, Sr Mgr-Mktg - PepsiCo, Inc.; *pg.* 259, *pg.* 1327
Springer, Cieja, Dir-Client Solutions & Integrated Mktg - Townsquare Media, Inc.; *pg.* 313, *pg.* 350
Springer, Jeff, VP-Mktg & Member Svcs - The American Gastroenterological Association; *pg.* 128, *pg.* 761
Springer, Scott J., Dir-Sls-Polymer Processing Sys-Americas - Nordson Corporation; *pg.* 1365, *pg.* 1480
Springsteen, Jeff, Mgr-Mktg-Selective Corn Herbicides - Bayer CropScience; *pg.* 1149, *pg.* 981
Springsteen, Michael, VP-Bus & Product Dev - Virginia Dare Extract Co., Inc.; *pg.* 908, *pg.* 1147
Sprinkel, Aimee, VP & Dir-Mktg & Comm - Asheville Savings Bank SSB; *pg.* 716, *pg.* 1358
Sprinkle, Connie, Sr VP-Direct & Digital Mktg - City National Bank; *pg.* 737, *pg.* 725
Sprinkle, Connie, Sr VP-Direct & Digital Mktg - City National Corporation; *pg.* 738, *pg.* 128
Sprinkle, Erin, Dir-MDU Sls - DIRECTV Group Holdings, LLC; *pg.* 281, *pg.* 79
Sprinkle, Meredith, Mgr-Mktg-Hospitality & Products - Colonial Williamsburg Foundation; *pg.* 541, *pg.* 1811
Sprinkles, Sara, Sr Mgr-Events - Electronic Arts Inc.; *pg.* 951, *pg.* 189
Spritzer, Shelly, Sr Mgr-Mktg - Sprint Corporation; *pg.* 1874, *pg.* 719
Sprogis, John K., Dir-Mktg - The Coca-Cola Company; *pg.* 240, *pg.* 493
Sprott, Judy, Mgr-Internet Mktg - Best Western International, Inc.; *pg.* 1081, *pg.* 15
Sproul, Dawn, Mgr-Local Sls - Cox Communications, Inc.; *pg.* 279, *pg.* 501
Spruck, Rebecca, Brand Mgr - Pinnacle Foods Group LLC; *pg.* 889, *pg.* 1104
Spudic, Ruth, Sr Mgr - PepsiCo, Inc.; *pg.* 259, *pg.* 1327
Spuller, Matthew, Product Mgr-Global - Applied Materials, Inc.; *pg.* 618, *pg.* 264
Spungin, Jessie, CMO & Chief Sls Officer - K&N Engineering Inc.; *pg.* 210, *pg.* 194
Spurgeon, Trent, Exec VP-Product Strategy & Support - U.S. Bancorp; *pg.* 815, *pg.* 945
Spurlin, Karen, Mgr-Brand Mktg - Make-A-Wish Foundation of Greater Los Angeles; *pg.* 146, *pg.* 136
Spurling, Erin, Dir-Mktg - Comcast Corporation; *pg.* 276, *pg.* 1560
Spurrier, Glen, VP-Creative-Global - Kao Brands Co. Inc.; *pg.* 513, *pg.* 1415
Spurrier, Kati, Coord-Global Mktg Comm - Alcon; *pg.* 1399, *pg.* 530
Squara, Gina, Dir-Digital Mktg - Big Heart Pet Brands; *pg.* 1474, *pg.* 213
Squire, Ryan, Sr Dir-Social Media - Kindred Healthcare, Inc.; *pg.* 1553, *pg.* 736
Squirell, Matt, Dir-Sls-Canada - Reliable Automatic Sprinkler Co., Inc.; *pg.* 1137, *pg.* 1158
Squyres, Tyri, VP-Mktg - Frontier Airlines, Inc.; *pg.* 1909, *pg.* 319
Sreter, Allison, Mgr-Mktg-Accountable Care Solutions - Aetna Inc.; *pg.* 1187, *pg.* 351
Sridharan, Srikanth, Mgr-Product Mktg - Skyworks Solutions,

First page reference indicates Business Class Edition
Second page reference indicates Geographic Edition

Inc.; pg. 674, pg. 862
Srikant, Kirti, Asst VP & Dir-Brand Mktg & Adv - OppenheimerFunds, Inc.; pg. 790, pg. 1274
Srikanth, Belwadi, Product Mgr - Google Inc.; pg. 1249, pg. 153
Srinivasan, Nikila, Product Mgr-Emerging Markets Monetisation - Facebook, Inc.; pg. 1245, pg. 143
Srinivasan, Paddy, VP-Customer Engagement Products - LOGMEIN, INC.; pg. 428, pg. 861
Srinivasan, Partha, Sr Mgr-Product Mktg - Microsoft Corporation; pg. 435, pg. 1824
Srinivasan, Ragavan, Product Mgr - Facebook, Inc.; pg. 1245, pg. 143
Srinivasan, Santosh, Sr Dir-Bus Ops - Cisco Systems, Inc.; pg. 372, pg. 240
Srinivasan, Siddharth, Assoc Product Mgr - Harsco Rail; pg. 1345, pg. 1623
Srisethnil, Arisara, Assoc Mgr-Integrated Mktg - The Hearst Corporation; pg. 1649, pg. 1239
Srivastava, Amitabh, Pres-Advanced Software Div - EMC Corporation; pg. 391, pg. 825
Srivastava, Pankaj , Sr., CMO & Sr VP-Mktg - White Sky, Inc.; pg. 492, pg. 256
Srivats, Ganesh, VP-Sls-North America - Tesla Motors, Inc.; pg. 191, pg. 178
Sroujian, Lori, Mgr-Digital Mktg - Glaxo Smith Kline Inc.; pg. 1536, pg. 1926
St Clair, Sean, Sr Mgr-Americas Alliance Mktg - VMware, Inc.; pg. 490, pg. 179
St Jacques, Michelle, VP-Mktg - H.J. Heinz Co. of Canada Ltd.; pg. 863, pg. 1929
St John, Jim, Sr Dir-Chocolate Product Dev - The Hershey Co.; pg. 1855, pg. 1538
St Louis, Stacy, Sr Mgr-PR - Citrix Systems, Inc.; pg. 375, pg. 424
St. Bernard, Carl J., VP-Mktg-North America - LifeCell Corporation; pg. 1556, pg. 1045
St. John, Russell, Sr VP-Mktg-Global - DataCard Corporation; pg. 382, pg. 948
St. John, Scott, Sr VP-Sls & Svc-Global - MRV Communications, Inc.; pg. 441, pg. 64
St. Mary, Julia, Sr Mgr-Web Analytics-Consumer Digital Analytics - AT&T Mobility LLC; pg. 619, pg. 488
St.Germain, Julia, VP-Mktg Ops - Unum Group; pg. 1222, pg. 1629
St.Germain, Scott, Dir-Managed Care & Mktg - Genentech, Inc.; pg. 1533, pg. 279
Staats, Cindy, Dir-Mktg - Jacmar Companies, Inc.; pg. 1733, pg. 67
Staats, Cindy, VP-Mktg - Shakey's USA, Inc.; pg. 1749, pg. 40
Stabile, Bill, Exec Dir-Branding, Adv & Sponsorships - Siemens Corporation; pg. 803, pg. 1291
Stabile, Nancy, Mgr-Mktg - Ingram Micro Inc.; pg. 415, pg. 261
Stables, LeeAnne, Exec VP-Mktg Partnerships-Worldwide - Paramount Pictures Corporation; pg. 304, pg. 138
Stacey, Craig, Dir-Content Mktg - Thrivent Financial for Lutherans; pg. 1219, pg. 944
Stacey, Jeff, VP-Sls & Corp Dev & Head-Analytics & Big Data - Ericsson, Inc.; pg. 638, pg. 1730
Stacey, Jessica, VP-PR & Store Mktg - Sephora USA Inc; pg. 522, pg. 227
Stack, Ann, Dir-Mktg - Dover Downs Gaming & Entertainment, Inc.; pg. 545, pg. 387
Stack, Mary, Dir-Media - Discovery Communications, Inc.; pg. 282, pg. 777
Stackle, Viktoryia, Mgr-Content & Media - Anheuser-Busch Companies, LLC; pg. 237, pg. 991
Stackman, Amanda, Brand Mgr-Absolut Elyx - The Absolut Spirits Company Inc.; pg. 1956, pg. 1325
Stacy, Dave, Sr Dir-Info Risk Mgmt & Security - Allianz Life Insurance Company of North America; pg. 1188, pg. 929
Stadd, Allison, Sr Mgr-Mktg & Comm - Shake Shack Inc.; pg. 1749, pg. 1291
Stadelman, Kurt, Mgr-Social Media - Electronic Arts Inc.; pg. 951, pg. 189
Stadler, Chris, Mgr-Product Mktg - Volvo Trucks North America, Inc.; pg. 195, pg. 1377
Stadnyuk, Olena, Assoc Dir-IHD Mktg - Gilead Sciences, Inc.; pg. 1535, pg. 88
Staebler, Douglas A., VP-Ops, Engrg & Mktg-Washington Gas - Washington Gas Light Co.; pg. 1954, pg. 407
Staehelin, Rolf, Dir-Mktg-Intl - Varian Medical Systems, Inc.; pg. 1434, pg. 178
Staehle, Angela, Brand Mgr-Concept Innovation & Global Refreshment - Starbucks Corporation; pg. 897, pg. 1840
Staffon, Carla, Acct Mgr-Sls - Brainerd Daily Dispatch; pg. 1623, pg. 919
Stafford, Charlie, VP-Sls - Chattem, Inc.; pg. 1515, pg. 1628
Stafford, Jennifer, Mgr-Social Media - HomeAway, Inc.; pg. 1911, pg. 1663
Stafford, John, Sr Dir-Digital Media Strategy - Stanford University; pg. 607, pg. 280
Stafford, Kristie, Mgr-Mktg - Lee Enterprises, Incorporated; pg. 1658, pg. 704
Stafford, Lauren, Brand Mgr-COVERGIRL North America Delivery - The Procter & Gamble Company; pg. 1129, pg. 1418
Stafford, Michelle, Mgr-Mktg - Millipore Corporation; pg. 1423, pg. 788
Stafford, Paul, VP-Global Channel Sls - Exar Corporation; pg. 395, pg. 91
Stafford, Sharon, Sr Mgr-Ops - The Bank of Nova Scotia; pg. 721, pg. 1935
Stafford, Shelli, Sr Mgr-Trade Mktg - Newell Rubbermaid Inc.; pg. 1128, pg. 515
Stafford, Sonny, Dir-Mktg-Opioids Portfolio-US Primary Care - Pfizer Inc.; pg. 1581, pg. 1278
Stager, Diana, Dir-Mktg & Comm - Bon Secours Health System, Inc.; pg. 1508, pg. 774
Staggs, Jennifer, Assoc Dir-Creative-Digital Media Grp - DIRECTV Group Holdings, LLC; pg. 281, pg. 79
Staggs, Lynn, Specialist-PR - Verizon Communications Inc.; pg. 1875, pg. 1309
Stahl, Eric, Sr VP-Product Mktg - salesforce.com, inc.; pg. 1278, pg. 226
Stahl, Jenny, Dir-Event Mktg - Univision Communications Inc.; pg. 683, pg. 1307
Stahl, Johannes, Dir-Product Mktg - Synopsys, Inc.; pg. 480, pg. 162
Stahl, Lesley, Assoc Mgr-Mktg Comm-Global - Mattel Games/Puzzles; pg. 962, pg. 80
Stahl, Linda S., VP-Strategic Products - COCC; pg. 376, pg. 337
Stahl, Megan, Mgr-Mktg Channel-STAINMASTER - INVISTA B.V.; pg. 1168, pg. 723
Stahley-Zuniga, Cynthia, Mgr-Mktg-Scotch Tape & Post it Notes - 3M Company; pg. 1142, pg. 956
Stahulak, Nancy, Mgr-Healthcare Programming & Mktg - GE Capital; pg. 761, pg. 362
Staib, Jill, Sr Dir-Brand Mktg - NBTY, Inc.; pg. 1572, pg. 1338
Stailey, Dawn, Specialist-Mktg - LEGOLAND California LLC; pg. 557, pg. 59
Staines, Reuben, Sr Mgr-Strategic Content-Samsung Bus - Samsung Electronics America, Inc.; pg. 669, pg. 1115
Stake, Jessica, Asst VP & Mgr-Content Mktg - JPMorgan Chase & Co.; pg. 772, pg. 1246
Staker, Alicia, Dir-Customer Mktg - Hillshire Brands; pg. 862, pg. 576
Stalcup, Jeff, VP-Mktg - McKesson Corporation; pg. 1560, pg. 222
Stalker, Chad, VP-OEM Sls - Acuity Brands, Inc.; pg. 1294, pg. 487
Stalker, Tim, Dir-Digital Mktg - Toys "R" Us, Inc.; pg. 968, pg. 1130
Stalling, Serra, Specialist-Interactive Mktg - InterContinental Hotels Corporation; pg. 1097, pg. 511
Stallings, Traci, Sr Mgr-Online Mktg - AT&T Mobility LLC; pg. 620, pg. 1824
Stallman, Bob, VP-Mktg & Innovation - Chiquita Brands International, Inc.; pg. 847, pg. 1365
Stallone, Tony, VP-Mdsg - Peapod, LLC; pg. 1029, pg. 661
Stallone, Trish, Sr Coord-Mktg Comm - QUALCOMM Incorporated; pg. 1873, pg. 207
Stallworth, Brandon, Specialist-Mktg - Endo Pharmaceuticals Holdings, Inc.; pg. 1528, pg. 1549
Stalnaker, Brett, Product Mgr - The Progressive Corporation; pg. 1214, pg. 1463
Stalnecker, Sarah, Mgr-Content & Media-Michelob ULTRA - Anheuser-Busch Companies, LLC; pg. 237, pg. 991
Stam, Nick, Sr Dir-Technical Mktg - NVIDIA Corporation; pg. 447, pg. 268
Stamas, Andrea, Mgr-Mktg Comm - Teradata Corporation; pg. 483, pg. 1447
Stamates, Jessica, Assoc Dir-Mktg-Digital, ECommerce & OmniChannel Innovation - The Procter & Gamble Company; pg. 1129, pg. 1418
Stambolis, Stamatina, Asst Mktg Mgr-Werther's Original - Storck USA, L.P.; pg. 1862, pg. 591
Stamm, Jennifer, Dir-Affiliate Mktg - BBC Worldwide America Inc.; pg. 271, pg. 1201
Stamm, Tracie, VP-Prepaid Debit Mktg - JPMorgan Chase & Co.; pg. 772, pg. 1246
Stammen, Brent, Rep-Mktg-Comm & PR - AGCO Corporation; pg. 700, pg. 530
Stamp, Donna, Dir-Mktg Procurement - Enterprise Holdings, Inc.; pg. 1906, pg. 996
Stamp, Elizabeth, Mgr-Sls Enablement - Honeywell International Inc.; pg. 407, pg. 1088
Stamulis, Brad, Gen Mgr-Digital Mktg - DISH Network Corporation; pg. 283, pg. 325
Stancil, Jennifer, Specialist-Mktg Comm - Alere Health Systems, Inc.; pg. 1488, pg. 535
Stanciu, Daniel, Dir-Mktg & Strategy-Romania, Bulgaria & Moldova - Monsanto Company; pg. 1173, pg. 999
Stanczyk, Gary, VP-Sls - Andis Company; pg. 498, pg. 1895
Standifer, Sheryl, Dir-Media-Consumer Insights & Partnerships - CEC Entertainment, Inc.; pg. 1721, pg. 1717
Stanec, Chuck, Mgr-Specialty Product - UniFirst Corporation; pg. 50, pg. 860
Stanfield, Amy, Dir-Sls & Mktg-Jeep Brand - FCA US LLC; pg. 170, pg. 868
Stanfield, Amy, Dir-Global Mktg-Live Cycling - Giant Bicycle Inc.; pg. 1707, pg. 164
Stanfield, Michael, Sr VP-Sls - New Orleans Saints L.P.; pg. 569, pg. 745
Stange, Joachim, Product Mgr-Transistors - NXP Semiconductors; pg. 660, pg. 248
Stangel, Lauren, Dir-Mktg Partnerships-Global - Starwood Hotels & Resorts Worldwide, Inc.; pg. 1114, pg. 378
Stangel, Tara, Sr Dir-Hotel Team-Global - Hotwire, Inc.; pg. 1912, pg. 219
Stangl-McGaughey, Joan M., Sr Specialist-Mktg Comm - Air Products and Chemicals, Inc.; pg. 1145, pg. 1513
Stangle, Derek, Mgr-Product Mktg - VistaPrint USA, Incorporated; pg. 1700, pg. 829
Stangler, Dan, Dir-Mktg-Annie's - General Mills, Inc.; pg. 828, pg. 933
Stanhope, Dave, Mgr-Mktg - Toshiba America, Inc.; pg. 681, pg. 1302
Stanhouse, Kameryn, Brand Mgr-Women's - Under Armour, Inc.; pg. 49, pg. 759
Stanichi, Roberto, Dir-Mktg - Mattel Games/Puzzles; pg. 962, pg. 80
Stanichi, Roberto, Dir-Mktg - MATTEL, INC.; pg. 962, pg. 81
Stankevich, Craig, Dir-Channel Mktg - The BLUE Buffalo Co.; pg. 1474, pg. 385
Stankevich, Santina, Specialist-Media Rels - ShopRite Supermarkets, Inc.; pg. 1033, pg. 1160
Stankey, John T., Chief Strategy Officer - AT&T Inc.; pg. 1867, pg. 1674
Stankiewicz, Amy, Mgr-Digital Mktg, Programmatic Display & Affiliate Mktg - The Allstate Corporation; pg. 1189, pg. 639
Stanko, Jim, Dir-Sls - Eaton Corporation; pg. 1331, pg. 1429
Stanko, Rachelle, Program Mgr-Loyalty Mktg - Recreational Equipment, Inc.; pg. 1843, pg. 1821
Stanley, Clay, Sr Dir-Info Mgt & Delivery - PayPal Inc.; pg. 1274, pg. 248
Stanley, Cody, Asst Mgr-Mktg - The Bradford Group; pg. 1763, pg. 637
Stanley, James, Sr Mgr-Sls & Acct Mgmt - Twitter, Inc.; pg. 1285, pg. 228
Stanley, Lauren, Mgr-US Mktg - Hasbro, Inc.; pg. 954, pg. 1603
Stanley, Lisa, VP-Mktg - Hot Topic, Inc.; pg. 42, pg. 67
Stanley, Lora, Dir-Convention Sls-Midwest Reg - Anaheim/Orange County Visitor & Convention Bureau; pg. 988, pg. 42
Stanley, Mila, Sr Mgr-Mktg - Verizon Communications Inc.; pg. 1875, pg. 1309
Stanley, Paul, Mgr-US Domestic Residential Products-FedEx Svcs - FedEx Corporation; pg. 1907, pg. 1642
Stanley, Rick, VP-Mktg - Brunswick Corporation; pg. 1828, pg. 623
Stanley, Russ, Mng VP-Ticket Sls & Svcs - San Francisco Giants Baseball Club; pg. 581, pg. 226
Stanley, Tamara, Dir-Media & Multicultural Mktg - SONIC Corp.; pg. 1750, pg. 1487
Stanley, Thomas, Global Partner-Sls & Alliances & Sr VP - NetApp, Inc.; pg. 444, pg. 287
Stann, Denita, VP-Investor & PR - Potash Corp.; pg. 1177, pg. 641
Stano, Karyn, Strategist-Mktg - Quicken Loans, Inc.; pg. 797, pg. 884

Stansberry, James, VP & Gen Mgr-Brdcst Products - Silicon Laboratories Inc.; pg. 674, pg. 1666
Stansberry, Joanne, Mgr-Global CGI, Digital Mktg & Corp Adv - General Motors Company; pg. 175, pg. 881
Stansberry, Sarah, VP-Product Mktg & Solutions Sls Trng - Equifax Inc.; pg. 748, pg. 504
Stanski, Jim, VP-Production - Corby Distilleries Ltd.; pg. 1961, pg. 1937
Stanski, Stan, Sr VP-Creative Svcs - World Wrestling Entertainment, Inc.; pg. 595, pg. 380
Stanton Cannarella, Ann, Asst VP & Mgr-Corp Mktg - AMERIS BANCORP; pg. 715, pg. 536
Stanton, Courtney, District Sls Mgr-Oncology - AstraZeneca Pharmaceuticals LP; pg. 1497, pg. 389
Stanton, Donald R, Sr Dir-Gas Delivery - CPS Energy; pg. 1939, pg. 1739
Stanton, Elizabeth, Coord-Mktg-Global - Diageo North America Inc.; pg. 248, pg. 1223
Stanton, Ellen, Sr Mgr-Mktg Comm - Medtronic, Inc.; pg. 1561, pg. 939
Stanton, Jill, Exec VP-Product Old Navy - The Gap, Inc.; pg. 1770, pg. 218
Stanton, John, Dir-Mktg - Merck & Co., Inc.; pg. 1566, pg. 1077
Stanton, Katie Jacobs, VP-Media-Global - Twitter, Inc.; pg. 1285, pg. 228
Stanton, Priscila, Sr Mgr-Mktg-Intl Brands - Nestle USA, Inc.; pg. 883, pg. 96
Stanton, Richard, Chief Product & Tech Officer - Penton Media, Inc.; pg. 1676, pg. 1277
Stanwick, George M., Gen Mgr-Comm Media & Entertainment - Hewlett-Packard Company; pg. 404, pg. 175
Stanziano, Don, Corp VP-Mktg & Comm - Scripps; pg. 1593, pg. 209
Stanziano, Joe, VP-Mktg-Peanut Butter - The J.M. Smucker Company; pg. 865, pg. 1468
Stapel, Harald, Mgr-Industrial & Process Sls - Xylem Inc.; pg. 1078, pg. 1339
Stapel, Karen, Dir-Targeted Mktg - Tractor Supply Company; pg. 708, pg. 1627
Stapler, John, Mgr-Sls & Channel - Verizon Communications Inc.; pg. 1875, pg. 1309
Staples, Doug, Sr VP-Strategic Mktg & Comm - March of Dimes Birth Defects Foundation; pg. 146, pg. 1354
Staples, Eric, Dir-Product Mgmt-Production Software - Ricoh Americas Corporation; pg. 461, pg. 1131
Staples, Francis, Dir-North American Sls - Institute of Electrical and Electronics Engineers, Inc.; pg. 144, pg. 1109
Stapleton, Christine, Coord-Sls - The Boston Globe; pg. 1623, pg. 790
Stapleton, Kim, Coord-Category & Brand Mktg-Young Men's, Team Sports & Juniors - Kohl's Corporation; pg. 1775, pg. 1870
Starace, Nicole, Product Mgr-Mktg-Farxiga - AstraZeneca Pharmaceuticals LP; pg. 1497, pg. 389
Starbuck, Chad, Sr Product Mgr-Mobile Svcs - Acxiom Corporation; pg. 342, pg. 607
Starbuck, Rick, Sr VP-Product & Experience Design - Emdeon, Inc.; pg. 747, pg. 1650
Staresinic, Daniel J., VP-Corp & Mktg Comm - Siemens Process Industries and Drives; pg. 673, pg. 485
Starford, Gina, Dir-Sls - Young Electric Sign Company; pg. 1308, pg. 1762
Stark, David, VP-Sls & Mktg-CNN Networks - Turner Broadcasting System, Inc.; pg. 314, pg. 521
Stark, Debbie, Product Mgr-Private Brands - Belk, Inc.; pg. 1760, pg. 1364
Stark, Efrat, Product Mgr - Autodesk Inc.; pg. 356, pg. 257
Stark, Greg, Sr Product Mgr-Internet of Things - TELUS CORPORATION; pg. 1952, pg. 1912
Stark, Loni Kao, Dir-Product, Solution & Indus Mktg - Adobe Systems Incorporated; pg. 342, pg. 235
Stark, Matt, Gen Mgr-Food Preparation & B2B Sls-China - Whirlpool Corporation; pg. 62, pg. 872
Stark, Mike, VP-Sls Plng & Admin - Southeast Toyota Distributors, LLC; pg. 190, pg. 421
Stark, Reva, Mgr-Media - Boy Scouts of America; pg. 134, pg. 1717
Stark, Richard, Dir-Product Data - Barnes & Noble, Inc.; pg. 1619, pg. 1201
Stark, Ronald J., Sr VP-Sls & Mktg - Airgas, Inc.; pg. 1146, pg. 1583
Stark, Rose, VP-Mktg-Strategy-TLC - Discovery Communications, Inc.; pg. 282, pg. 777
Stark-Flora, Marie-Pierre, Sr VP-Mktg-Global - The Estee Lauder Companies Inc.; pg. 508, pg. 1229
Starkey, Chris, Team Head & Sr Strategist-Mktg - Edward D. Jones & Co., LP; pg. 746, pg. 995
Starkey, Dan, Sr Dir-Ballpark Dev - Minnesota Twins, LLC; pg. 563, pg. 940
Starkey, Jennifer, Assoc Dir-PR - Webster University; pg. 610, pg. 1004
Starkey, Meredith, Sr Dir-Sponsorships, Entertainment & Events - T-Mobile US, Inc.; pg. 676, pg. 1816
Starkey, Steve, VP-Mktg-Global - Lenovo Group Ltd; pg. 427, pg. 1384
Starkey, Tiffany, Sr Partner-Talent Worldwide Field Ops-Sls - Adobe Systems Incorporated; pg. 342, pg. 235
Starkloff, Eric, Exec VP-Global Sls & Mktg - National Instruments Corporation; pg. 443, pg. 1664
Starks, Colin B., Dir-Sls-Natl - Federated Investors, Inc.; pg. 752, pg. 1575
Starks, Darlene, Coord-Convention Sls - Louisville Convention & Visitors Bureau; pg. 998, pg. 736
Starks, Kimberly, Mgr-Media Rels - Georgia Lottery Corporation; pg. 993, pg. 506
Starks, Renny, Project Mgr-Mktg & Media - Hunter Douglas, Inc.; pg. 928, pg. 1320
Starkweather, Brock, Mgr-Sls Plng & Integration - Ubisoft Inc.; pg. 589, pg. 229
Starkweather, Jeff, Dir-Sls Mktg - WHAM-TV; pg. 321, pg. 1338
Starkweather, John, Exec Dir-Digital Mktg, Mobile & Bus Solutions - AT&T Inc.; pg. 1867, pg. 1674
Starling, Kelly L., Sr Mgr-PR - AT&T; pg. 1865, pg. 258
Starling, Nicole, Brand Mgr-Sebastian & Nioxin - The Procter & Gamble Company; pg. 1129, pg. 1418
Starman, Kelly, Gen Mgr-Product Mktg-Clinical Bus Solutions - GE Healthcare; pg. 399, pg. 1765
Starmann, Molly, Sr Dir-PR, Brand Reputation & US Comm - McDonald's Corporation; pg. 1737, pg. 645
Starmer, Samantha, VP-Digital Product Mgmt - Ralph Lauren Corporation; pg. 46, pg. 1284
Starnes, Rodger, VP-Mktg & Customer Dev-Food Svc - Tyson Foods, Inc.; pg. 902, pg. 35
Starostka, Mary J., Mgr-Technical Mktg - Tyler Technologies, Inc.; pg. 486, pg. 1690
Starowitz, Todd, Dir-PR - Tyndale House Publishers, Inc.; pg. 1697, pg. 561
Starr, Barb, Dir-New Products & Pkg - Crown Imports LLC; pg. 248, pg. 572
Starr, Cindy, VP-Mktg - VistaPrint USA, Incorporated; pg. 1700, pg. 829
Starr, Gena, Assoc Dir-Makeup Mktg - Chanel, Inc.; pg. 503, pg. 1211
Starr, Jason, Sr Dir-Analyst Rels - Equinix, Inc.; pg. 394, pg. 190
Starr, John, VP-Sls Channels & Pro Svcs-Global - Websense, Inc.; pg. 491, pg. 210
Starr, Karen, Mgr-Consumer Mktg-Call of Duty Franchise - Activision Blizzard, Inc.; pg. 948, pg. 271
Starr, Wendy, Product Mgr - Cumberland Pharmaceuticals, Inc.; pg. 1521, pg. 1650
Starr-Culp, Kara, Specialist-Mktg - Comcast Cable Communications, Inc.; pg. 276, pg. 1560
Starrett, Ken, VP-Sls & Mktg - American Excelsior Company; pg. 1451, pg. 1659
Starrett, Mark, Mgr-Product Mktg - SanDisk Corporation; pg. 465, pg. 147
Stasi, Jo Di, Dir-Brand Mktg Comm-Global - The Gap, Inc.; pg. 1770, pg. 218
Stasik, Jim, Dir-Sls - Hypertension Diagnostics, Inc.; pg. 1543, pg. 921
Stasiowski, Eric, Sr Mgr-Comm - Swagelok Company; pg. 1064, pg. 1473
Staszak, Hilary, Dir-Mktg Comm - WellCare Health Plans Inc.; pg. 1223, pg. 476
Stathatos, James, Div VP-Creative Svcs - Coach, Inc.; pg. 3, pg. 1214
Statmore, Sarah H., Assoc Dir-Mktg Res - Johnson & Johnson; pg. 1549, pg. 1091
Staton, Brenda, Mgr-Mktg Asset - The Coca-Cola Company; pg. 240, pg. 493
Staton, Ed, Sr Project Mgr-Mktg Programs - FileMaker, Inc.; pg. 639, pg. 265
Staub, Christine, Specialist-Web Mktg-System - International Business Machines Corporation; pg. 418, pg. 1138
Staub, Diane, Dir-Sls Support & Ops - Novartis Pharmaceuticals Corp.; pg. 1575, pg. 1054
Staub, Francie, Dir-Digital Mktg - TD Ameritrade Holding Corporation; pg. 808, pg. 1018
Staub, Geoff, VP-Corp Mktg & Comm - Cross Country Healthcare, Inc.; pg. 1520, pg. 411
Staubach, Denise, Dir-Mktg Programs, Corp Mktg - ASPEN TECHNOLOGY, INC.; pg. 354, pg. 804
Stauber, Tim, Sr Dir-Corp & Sr Care Segment Mktg - GlaxoSmithKline; pg. 1536, pg. 1389
Staubly, John, Product Mgr-Premium & Emerging Formats - AARP; pg. 124, pg. 393
Staubs, Dwight, Reg Mgr-Sls - Impreso, Inc.; pg. 413, pg. 1671
Stauch, Sandra, Grp VP-Mktg - Nutraceutical International Corporation; pg. 1576, pg. 1753
Staudt, Grace, Program Mgr-Mktg - Benjamin Moore & Co.; pg. 1440, pg. 1085
Stauffenecker, Mary Ann, Sr Product Mgr-Mktg - Merrill Corporation; pg. 1664, pg. 962
Stauffer, Dan, VP-Mktg & Real Estate - McCoy's Building Supply Centers; pg. 1055, pg. 1744
Stauffer, Emily, Dir-Mktg - Genentech, Inc.; pg. 1533, pg. 279
Stauffer, Helen, Sr Mgr-Mdsg & Digital - Recreational Equipment, Inc.; pg. 1843, pg. 1821
Stauffer, Jeff, Exec VP & Mng Dir-Creative Studios - inVentiv Health Clinical; pg. 1547, pg. 1111
Stauffer, John, VP & Sr Dir-Interactive Media Grp - Apple Inc.; pg. 350, pg. 73
Stavast, Andy, Gen Mgr-Sls - KSTC-TV Channel 45; pg. 295, pg. 962
Staveley, Catheryn, Mgr-Mktg Comm-Drilling Grp - Schlumberger Limited; pg. 801, pg. 1714
Staves, Laura, Sr Dir & Head-Mktg-US - Dermalogica, Inc.; pg. 1523, pg. 63
Stavrakas, Scott, VP-Sls & Mktg - Miller Group Media; pg. 1665, pg. 621
Stavrou, Alex, Sr Mgr-Gaithersburg - McGladrey, LLP; pg. 781, pg. 938
Stawarz, Elise, Specialist-Mktg-PLG - Sony Music Entertainment; pg. 309, pg. 1294
Ste. Marie, Jordan, Sr Mgr-ECommerce Mktg Strategy - Dr Pepper Snapple Group, Inc.; pg. 250, pg. 1729
Steadman, Melissa, Head-Content & Community Mktg - Royal Bank of Canada; pg. 800, pg. 1942
Stealey, Carl, VP-Mktg - Mead Johnson Nutrition Company; pg. 1561, pg. 615
Stearns, Jeff, VP-Mktg - Fareway Stores, Inc.; pg. 1019, pg. 702
Stearns, Jeffrey W., VP-Sls & Mktg - Westinghouse Air Brake Technologies Corporation; pg. 1388, pg. 1595
Steber, John, Head-Enterprise Strategy & Mktg-Voluntary Segment - Cigna Corporation; pg. 1197, pg. 338
Stech, Brian, Exec VP-Sls & Mktg-Global - ZAGG INCORPORATED; pg. 690, pg. 1762
Stechmesser, Paul, Head-Creative & Design-Coca-Cola Studios - The Coca-Cola Company; pg. 240, pg. 493
Steck, Alex, Sr Assoc Brand Mgr - Campbell Soup Company; pg. 844, pg. 1048
Steck, Ronnie, VP-Mktg - Mr. Gatti's, LP; pg. 1741, pg. 1664
Steckler, Rebecca, Sr VP-Sls & Mktg - MICHIGAN.COM; pg. 1665, pg. 884
Stecklow, Rob, Gen Mgr-Sports Products & Mktg - DIRECTV Group Holdings, LLC; pg. 281, pg. 79
Steed, John, Dir-Mktg - Anheuser-Busch Companies, LLC; pg. 237, pg. 991
Steel, Brian, Sr VP-PR - CNBC; pg. 275, pg. 1059
Steel, Carol, Dir-Creative - The Street, Inc.; pg. 1283, pg. 1296
Steel, Sarah, Dir-Sls - Aon Hewitt; pg. 350, pg. 627
Steele Flippin, Candace, VP-PR & External Comm - St. Jude Medical, Inc.; pg. 1596, pg. 963
Steele, Amanda, Sr VP-Mktg - Annie's Inc.; pg. 1760, pg. 45
Steele, Audrey, Sr VP-Sls Res & Mktg - Fox Broadcasting Company; pg. 287, pg. 130
Steele, Audrey, Sr VP-Sls Res Insights & Strategy - Fox Entertainment Group, Inc.; pg. 288, pg. 131
Steele, Ben, Chief Creative Officer & Sr VP - Recreational Equipment, Inc.; pg. 1843, pg. 1821
Steele, Carla, Dir-Sls & Mktg - Capital Senior Living Corporation; pg. 1084, pg. 1677
Steele, Chad, VP-PR - Baltimore Ravens Limited Partnership; pg. 532, pg. 755
Steele, Charles, Sr VP-Sls - Assurant Health; pg. 1193, pg. 1873
Steele, David, Dir-PR - State of Florida Department of Citrus; pg. 1006, pg. 437
Steele, Delaney, Sr VP-Strategy & Mktg - Ross Stores, Inc.;

First page reference indicates Business Class Edition
Second page reference indicates Geographic Edition

pg. 1783, pg. 78
Steele, Duane, VP-Sls & Mktg - Dynex Technologies, Inc.; pg. 1408, pg. 1777
Steele, Jeff, Dir-Retail Mktg & Bus Dev - Washington State Dairy Products Commission; pg. 161, pg. 1822
Steele, Jennifer, Sr Mgr-Mktg - Microsoft Corporation; pg. 435, pg. 1824
Steele, Jennifer, VP-Product Mgmt-Global - The Walt Disney Company; pg. 317, pg. 52
Steele, Mark, VP-Global Sls & Mktg - Speed Commerce, Inc.; pg. 967, pg. 1737
Steele, Scott, Mgr-Mktg Comm-Social Media & Sponsorships - Avista Corporation; pg. 1935, pg. 1843
Steele, Tyler, Asst VP-US Mktg-La Roche-Posay - L'Oreal USA; pg. 514, pg. 1252
Steelman, Larry, VP-Sls Channels & Programs - Cox Communications, Inc.; pg. 279, pg. 501
Steen, Brett, Brand Mgr-Newcastle Brown Ale - Heineken USA Inc.; pg. 252, pg. 1352
Steen, Ed, Reg Mgr-Sls - Universal Lighting Technologies; pg. 1307, pg. 1655
Steen, Susan, Sr VP-Worldwide Mktg Svcs - Warner Bros. Entertainment Inc.; pg. 319, pg. 54
Steenhaut, Steven, Sr Dir-Mktg-EMEA - Nuance Communications, Inc.; pg. 447, pg. 806
Steenport, Allison, Mgr-Digital Mktg & Relationship Mktg - The Dun & Bradstreet Corp.; pg. 1637, pg. 1120
Steensland, Pamela, VP-Meeting & Event Mktg - Piper Jaffray Companies; pg. 794, pg. 941
Steenstra, Paula, Dir-Creative Dev - Tyson Foods, Inc.; pg. 902, pg. 35
Steever, Scott, Sr Dir-ECommerce Ops - Michael Kors (USA), Inc.; pg. 29, pg. 1260
Steeves, Jeff, VP-Mktg - Rue La La; pg. 1278, pg. 800
Stefanak, Josette, Specialist-Internet Mdsg Mktg - Canon U.S.A., Inc.; pg. 1404, pg. 1178
Stefanoni, Arianna M., Rep-PR - The Vanguard Group, Inc.; pg. 816, pg. 1550
Stefanski, Michael, VP-Brand & Mktg-US - MetLife, Inc.; pg. 1208, pg. 1258
Steffan, Carrie, Program Mgr-Adv - Xcel Energy Inc.; pg. 1955, pg. 946
Steffel, Lisa, Mgr-Natl Sls-Prepaid-Field Dev & Sls Strategy - ACE Cash Express, Inc.; pg. 710, pg. 1717
Steffen, Shane, Dir-Product Mgmt-Boat Div - Confluence Watersports Co. Inc.; pg. 1706, pg. 1617
Steffens, Brad, Mgr-Sls - Iowa Farmer Today; pg. 1653, pg. 702
Steffens, Carl, VP-Demand & Field Mktg - NeuStar, Inc.; pg. 1872, pg. 1807
Steffens, Neil, Sr VP-Market & Products - Humana, Inc.; pg. 1204, pg. 734
Steffensen, Venus, Sr Mgr-Bus Dev - G&K Services Inc.; pg. 693, pg. 949
Steffensen-Edenborough, Karla, Dir Mktg & Comm - Sun Life Financial Inc.; pg. 806, pg. 1944
Stegall, Stephanie, Dir-Event Booking & Sls - Houston Astros Baseball Club; pg. 552, pg. 1707
Stege, Susan, Sr Dir-Category & Shopper Insights - Dean Foods Company; pg. 852, pg. 1679
Stegemann, Jackie, Brand Mgr - The Scotts Miracle-Gro Company; pg. 1799, pg. 1459
Steger, Jennifer, Dir-Mktg - University of Michigan; pg. 609, pg. 867
Steger, John, Dir-Global Mktg Strategy-Building Efficiency - Johnson Controls, Inc.; pg. 209, pg. 1876
Stegman, Kara, Dir-Existing Customer Mktg - DISH Network Corporation; pg. 283, pg. 325
Stegner, Robert L., Sr VP-Mktg-North America - SYNNEX Corporation; pg. 480, pg. 92
Stegner, Vanya, Mgr-Channel Dev Mktg - Ingram Micro Inc.; pg. 415, pg. 261
Stehl, Mary, Product Mgr-Networking - CDW Corporation; pg. 370, pg. 663
Stehney, Denise, Dir-Adv - Merle Norman Cosmetics, Inc.; pg. 517, pg. 136
Stehney, Jane, Dir-PR - Kelly Services, Inc.; pg. 424, pg. 911
Steiber, Art, Dir-Mktg Strategy - Quicken Loans, Inc.; pg. 797, pg. 884
Steichen, Curtis J., CMO, Chief Sls Officer & Sr VP - Nortech Systems Incorporated; pg. 659, pg. 966
Steidl, Lindsay, Coord-Brand Mktg - Everlast Worldwide Inc.; pg. 1833, pg. 1230
Steidle, Brendan, Brand Mgr - Rust-Oleum Corporation; pg. 1447, pg. 664
Steifman, Marc, Global Co-Head-Tech, Media & Telecom Investment Banking Grp - Piper Jaffray Companies; pg. 794, pg. 941
Steiger, Brett, Sr Dir-Mktg - Travelocity, Inc.; pg. 1284, pg. 1745
Steiger, Jordan, Planner-Digital Sls - Pandora Media Inc.; pg. 1273, pg. 172
Steiger, Mimi, Mgr-Promos & Social Mktg - The Boppy Company, LLC; pg. 20, pg. 329
Steiger, Sarah, Sr Dir - Microsoft Corporation; pg. 435, pg. 1824
Steigerwald, Michael, Mgr-Integrated Mktg - GlaxoSmithKline; pg. 1536, pg. 1565
Steimel, Greg, Mgr-Sls Ops & Event - McKesson Corporation; pg. 1560, pg. 222
Stein, Andrea, Sr Mgr-Events & Mktg Partnerships-Strategy & Execution - General Mills, Inc.; pg. 828, pg. 933
Stein, Ari, Dir-Natl Sls-Programmatic & Performance Media Sls - Pandora Media Inc.; pg. 1273, pg. 172
Stein, Aviad, Sr Mgr-Global - Bloomberg L.P.; pg. 725, pg. 1204
Stein, Cody, Assoc-Mktg - The Bradford Group; pg. 1763, pg. 637
Stein, Debbie, Mgr-Retail Mktg - Birks & Mayors Inc.; pg. 1, pg. 1953
Stein, Doug, Product Mgr - Toyota Motor Sales, U.S.A., Inc.; pg. 193, pg. 296
Stein, Elizabeth, Designer-Web-Stores, Promos & Social Media - Saks Incorporated; pg. 1783, pg. 1288
Stein, Erica, Mgr-Digital Mktg - Omni Hotels & Resorts; pg. 1107, pg. 1685
Stein, Evan, VP-Mktg - SDI Technologies, Inc.; pg. 671, pg. 1113
Stein, Janet, Sr VP-Mdsg - MARTHA STEWART LIVING OMNIMEDIA, INC.; pg. 1661, pg. 1256
Stein, Joshua, Sr Mgr-Loyalty - Total Wine & More; pg. 1971, pg. 775
Stein, Lindsay, Assoc Dir-Global Creative - General Electric Company; pg. 1297, pg. 347
Stein, Mark, Chief Strategy Officer-IAC Search - IAC/InterActiveCorp; pg. 292, pg. 1242
Stein, Matt, Sr VP-Mktg, Promo & Creative Svcs - BBC Worldwide America Inc.; pg. 271, pg. 1201
Stein, Rasa, Dir-Media - Macy's, Inc.; pg. 1778, pg. 1417
Stein, Sarah, Mgr-Digital Mktg - Broan-NuTone LLC; pg. 1069, pg. 1860
Stein, Shari, VP-Corp Mktg & Branding - Standard & Poor's Ratings Services; pg. 805, pg. 1296
Stein, Sheryl, Mgr-Adv & PR - El Al Israel Airlines, Ltd.; pg. 1906, pg. 1226
Stein, Suzanne, Dir-Brand & Adv Effectiveness - Citigroup Inc.; pg. 735, pg. 1212
Stein, Wendy, Mgr-Product Dev-Interactive Channels - Zions Bancorporation; pg. 824, pg. 1762
Steinback, Jon, VP-Product Experience - FourSquare Labs, Inc; pg. 1248, pg. 1232
Steinbarger, Ann L., Sr VP-Sls & Mktg - Corgenix Medical Corporation; pg. 1519, pg. 312
Steinberg, Andrew, Dir-New Media Distr - Scripps Networks Interactive, Inc.; pg. 1279, pg. 1638
Steinberg, Brooke, Mgr-Mktg - ESPN, Inc.; pg. 285, pg. 340
Steinberg, Jed, VP-Mktg - AXA Equitable Life Insurance Company; pg. 1194, pg. 1199
Steinberg, Jeff, Mgr-Mktg - Cisco Systems, Inc.; pg. 372, pg. 240
Steinberg, Jeremy, Head-Sls - The Weather Channel LLC; pg. 320, pg. 523
Steinberg, Jill, Sr Dir-Media & Promotions - Ubisoft Inc.; pg. 589, pg. 229
Steinberg, Jon, Dir-Media Rels - Hawks Basketball, Inc.; pg. 551, pg. 509
Steinberg, Matthew, Dir-Creative Svcs - Buffalo Niagara Convention & Visitors Bureau, Inc.; pg. 1901, pg. 1147
Steinberg, Rose, Dir-Strategic Acct Svcs-Microsoft Adv - Microsoft Corporation; pg. 435, pg. 1824
Steinberg, Scott A., VP-Mktg-Platforms - LeapFrog Enterprises, Inc.; pg. 961, pg. 84
Steinbreder, Susan G., Dir-Adv-Atlanta NSO - The New York Times; pg. 1668, pg. 1270
Steinbring, Denise, Sr Dir-Mktg, Education & Field Svc-Perfusion & Blood Mgmt - Medtronic, Inc.; pg. 1564, pg. 939
Steinbruecker, Amy Jo, Mgr-Media Rels - American Cancer Society, Inc.; pg. 126, pg. 487
Steinbrunner, Steve, Mgr-Digital Mktg-Section - The Procter & Gamble Company; pg. 1129, pg. 1418
Steiner, Isabelle, VP-Mktg & Customer Retention - SHUTTERFLY, INC.; pg. 1280, pg. 192
Steiner, Jeremy, Project Mgr-Mktg-Intl - Beltone Electronics LLC; pg. 1503, pg. 614
Steiner, Paula A., Chief Strategy Officer & Exec VP-Mktg & Retail - Health Care Service Corporation; pg. 1203, pg. 576
Steiner, Stephanie, Dir-Sls & Mktg-Market Centre Natural & Signature Brands - Unified Grocers, Inc.; pg. 1036, pg. 1842
Steinert, Brian, Sr Dir-Product Mgmt - Automatic Data Processing, Inc.; pg. 357, pg. 1117
Steinerte, Inga, Mgr-Mktg Comm - Samsung Electronics America, Inc.; pg. 669, pg. 1115
Steingart, Adam, Sr VP-Integrated Mktg-Viacom Velocity-CMT - MTV Networks Company; pg. 298, pg. 1262
Steingraber, Alissa, Coord-Search Mktg - Kohl's Corporation; pg. 1775, pg. 1870
Steinhart, Alex, Dir-Mktg Ops - CyberSource Corporation; pg. 381, pg. 216
Steinhoff, Curtis, Sr Dir - Veterinary Pet Insurance Co.; pg. 1222, pg. 49
Steinhour, Jill, Exec Dir-Mktg & High Tech Industry Strategy - Adobe Systems Incorporated; pg. 342, pg. 235
Steinhouse, Eric, Exec VP & Corp Dir-Mktg - Commerce Bancshares, Inc.; pg. 740, pg. 982
Steinhubl, John, Sr Dir-Content Creation & Production - Anheuser-Busch Companies, LLC; pg. 237, pg. 991
Steinkamp, Mark, Dir-Mktg - Daktronics, Inc.; pg. 633, pg. 1624
Steinkrauss, Molly, Assoc Mgr-PR-Digital Strategy & Media Planner - The Clorox Company; pg. 327, pg. 169
Steinlauf, Jon, Pres-Natl Ad Sls & Mktg-New York - Scripps Networks Interactive, Inc.; pg. 1279, pg. 1638
Steinman, Axel, VP-Emerging Markets, Adv & Online Bus - Microsoft Corporation; pg. 435, pg. 1824
Steinman, Jeff, Dir-Product Dev - CQ Roll Call; pg. 1631, pg. 397
Steinmuller, Dave, VP-Sls - Hammons Products Company; pg. 1855, pg. 1007
Steinys, Leo, Product Mgr-Laundry-Kenmore - Sears Holdings Corporation; pg. 1784, pg. 618
Steldt, Ashley, Coord-Mktg - Briggs & Stratton Corporation; pg. 201, pg. 1899
Stelea, Kristin, Coord-Social Media - Guess?, Inc.; pg. 25, pg. 132
Stellberg, John, Dir-Mktg Comm - Coilcraft, Inc.; pg. 1324, pg. 562
Stelling, Bill, Mgr-OEM Mktg - Brocade Corporation; pg. 365, pg. 312
Stelling, Frederick, Dir-Mktg-Global - Siemens Healthcare Diagnostics; pg. 673, pg. 604
Stelling, Jennifer, Mgr-Strategic Mktg - American Airlines Inc.; pg. 1898, pg. 1693
Stellmach, Jim, VP-Sls - Cable News Network LP; pg. 1624, pg. 1208
Stellwag, Chris, Dir-Mktg Comm - CAE INC.; pg. 226, pg. 1959
Stellwag, Chris, Dir-Mktg Comm - CAE USA, Inc.; pg. 226, pg. 472
Stellwag, Maureen, Sr Dir-Mktg-GATTEX - NPS Pharmaceuticals, Inc.; pg. 1576, pg. 1043
Stelnik, Jeff, Sr VP-Strategy, Sls & Mktg - Anthem Blue Cross Blue Shield; pg. 1192, pg. 1886
Stelter, Steven, Mgr-Mktg - Tribune Media Company; pg. 1696, pg. 592
Stelzner, John, Sr Dir-Mktg - Playmates Toys Inc.; pg. 965, pg. 82
Stembridge, Garret, Coord-Interactive Mktg - Extra Space Storage, Inc.; pg. 1091, pg. 1757
Stemen, Vince, VP-Field Sls-West & Central US - Tech Data Corporation; pg. 482, pg. 416
Stemmermann, Scott, VP-Digital Mktg-Domestic Television Distr - NBC Universal, Inc.; pg. 300, pg. 1266
Stemmler, Jay, Mgr-Mktg & Comm - Airgas, Inc.; pg. 1146, pg. 1583
Stemple, Melissa, Dir-Mktg - MARTHA STEWART LIVING OMNIMEDIA, INC.; pg. 1661, pg. 1256
Stencel, Victoria, Sr Dir-Health, Wellness Mktg & Policy - The Kraft Heinz Company; pg. 871, pg. 641
Stencel, Victoria, Sr Dir-Health, Wellness Mktg & Policy - Mondelez International, Inc.; pg. 878, pg. 601
Stender, Jeff, Mgr-Social Media Strategy-Global - 3M Company; pg. 1142, pg. 956

Stengel, Catherine, Sr Mgr-PR - AT&T; *pg.* 1865, *pg.* 258
Stenger, Shawn, Assoc Mgr-Mktg - BCBG Max Azria Group LLC; *pg.* 19, *pg.* 301
Stengren, Lori, VP-Sls, Mdsg & Mktg - Darvin Furniture; *pg.* 922, *pg.* 649
Stening, Ed, Assoc Dir-Digital Strategy & MultiChannel Mktg - Zoetis Inc.; *pg.* 1611, *pg.* 1067
Stennet, Robin, Dir-Media & Experiential Mktg - The ADT Corporation; *pg.* 612, *pg.* 409
Stenson, Jennifer, Sr Mgr-Mktg-Pepsi Bottling Grp - PepsiCo, Inc.; *pg.* 259, *pg.* 1327
Stensrud, Steven J., Head-Svcs Sls-West - IBM; *pg.* 410, *pg.* 1449
Stenstrom, Scott, VP-Consumer Bank Mktg - Fifth Third Bancorp; *pg.* 752, *pg.* 1413
Stenz, Julie Taylor, Sr Dir-Partnership Mktg - World Wrestling Entertainment, Inc.; *pg.* 595, *pg.* 380
Stenzel, Kyle, VP-Sls - Beiersdorf North America Inc.; *pg.* 501, *pg.* 385
Stepan, Darnell, Analyst-Mktg - 3M Company; *pg.* 1142, *pg.* 956
Stepanek, Megan, Sr Mgr-Media - Charles Schwab; *pg.* 1235, *pg.* 1661
Stepansky, Ben, Associate-Mktg-Partnerships - DraftKings, Inc.; *pg.* 545, *pg.* 793
Stephan, Kevin, Brand Mgr - Abbott Nutrition; *pg.* 1485, *pg.* 1437
Stephan, Mike, Dir-Sls-Eastern Reg - Monterey Mushrooms, Inc.; *pg.* 881, *pg.* 305
Stephani, Bill, Sr Dir-Info Sys - Colorado Rockies Baseball Club, Ltd.; *pg.* 542, *pg.* 317
Stephany, Melissa, Mgr-Mktg - Phoenix Products Company; *pg.* 1304, *pg.* 1879
Stephen, Nancy, Coord-Mktg - Fastline Publications Inc.; *pg.* 1641, *pg.* 726
Stephens, Adam, Dir-Sls-Walmart - Reckitt Benckiser Inc.; *pg.* 1136, *pg.* 1105
Stephens, Brendan, Dir-Creative - ZIPCAR, INC.; *pg.* 1931, *pg.* 810
Stephens, Brooke, Mgr-Comml Brand Mktg - Advance Auto Parts, Inc.; *pg.* 197, *pg.* 1805
Stephens, Darin, Sr Product Mgr-Hunting Gear & Accessories - Bushnell Outdoor Products, Inc.; *pg.* 1403, *pg.* 718
Stephens, David, Mgr-Email Mktg - Camping World, Inc.; *pg.* 1830, *pg.* 725
Stephens, Donna, Sr VP-Adv Sls - Scripps Networks Interactive, Inc.; *pg.* 1279, *pg.* 1638
Stephens, Doug, Dir-Engrg-Firetrol Products - Emerson Network Power; *pg.* 1071, *pg.* 1479
Stephens, Greg, VP-Mktg - United Community Banks, Inc.; *pg.* 814, *pg.* 526
Stephens, Hardin, Reg Mgr-Sls-North West - Northwest Pipe Company; *pg.* 100, *pg.* 1846
Stephens, Heather, Sr Mgr-Creative Svcs Production - Big Heart Pet Brands; *pg.* 1474, *pg.* 213
Stephens, Joe, Dir-Native Adv Strategy - Yahoo! Inc.; *pg.* 1289, *pg.* 289
Stephens, John, Dir-Digital Mktg - Dolby Laboratories, Inc.; *pg.* 284, *pg.* 217
Stephens, John, Sr Dir-Strategic Sourcing - Microsoft Corporation; *pg.* 435, *pg.* 1824
Stephens, Jyoti, Sr Dir-HR & Sustainability - Nature's Path Foods Inc.; *pg.* 833, *pg.* 1908
Stephens, Lynne, VP-Media Plng & Partnerships - Discovery Communications, Inc.; *pg.* 282, *pg.* 777
Stephens, Marc, Brand Mgr - Pinnacle Foods Group LLC; *pg.* 889, *pg.* 1104
Stephens, Matt, Reg Mgr-Mktg - Atmos Energy Corporation; *pg.* 1935, *pg.* 1675
Stephens, Nathlie, Analyst-ECommerce Mktg - Kate Spade LLC; *pg.* 28, *pg.* 1248
Stephens, Stephanie, Asst Dir-Creative Services - Georgia Institute Of Technology; *pg.* 602, *pg.* 506
Stephens, Tom, Mgr-Creative Svc - Kansas City Chiefs Football Club, Inc.; *pg.* 555, *pg.* 984
Stephenson, Clay, Product Mgr - Honeywell International Inc.; *pg.* 407, *pg.* 1088
Stephenson, Dave, Mgr-Mktg - The Allstate Corporation; *pg.* 1189, *pg.* 639
Stephenson, Don, VP-Volkswagen After Sls - Volkswagen Group of America, Inc.; *pg.* 194, *pg.* 1785
Stephenson, Kassie, Dir-Email Mktg-Global - Groupon, Inc.; *pg.* 1255, *pg.* 575
Stephenson, Kathy, Dir-Mktg Comm - Pear Bureau Northwest; *pg.* 153, *pg.* 1500
Stephenson, Tom, Product Mgr & Sr Analyst - AccuWeather, Inc.; *pg.* 268, *pg.* 1587
Stephenson, Topher, Mgr-Bus & Mktg Strategy - Intuit Inc.; *pg.* 769, *pg.* 158
Stephensone, Jacqueline, Mgr-ECommerce Mktg - Carter's, Inc.; *pg.* 21, *pg.* 491
Stepka, Cynthia A., Specialist-Mktg Comm - Ceridian Corporation; *pg.* 371, *pg.* 932
Stepp, Dana, Sr Product Mgr - Hewlett-Packard Company; *pg.* 404, *pg.* 175
Stepp, Elizabeth, Asst VP-Mktg - BB&T Corporation; *pg.* 723, *pg.* 1393
Stepp, Sherry, Mgr-Mktg - Kyzen Corporation; *pg.* 331, *pg.* 1652
Stepper, Amber, VP-Mktg & Adv-Global - National Amusements, Inc.; *pg.* 299, *pg.* 840
Sterbentz, Mike, Mgr-OEM Sls - Waterous Company; *pg.* 1387, *pg.* 965
Sterett, Shawnita, Dir-Mfg Field & Named Accts Mktg - Autodesk Inc.; *pg.* 356, *pg.* 257
Sterling, Alex, Dir-Mdsg & Comm - Einstein Noah Restaurant Group, Inc.; *pg.* 1019, *pg.* 332
Sterling, Kyle, Sr Mgr-Mktg Creative-Branded Retail & Experience Dev - AT&T Mobility LLC; *pg.* 619, *pg.* 488
Sterling, Nancy, Mgr-Tech Adv - The New York Times Company; *pg.* 1668, *pg.* 1270
Sterman, Theresa, Sr Dir-Design & Product Dev Outlets - Chico's FAS, Inc.; *pg.* 21, *pg.* 427
Stern, Daniel, Sr Dir-Brand Digital-Global - NIKE, Inc.; *pg.* 1812, *pg.* 1492
Stern, Deena, VP-Brand Mktg - Comedy Partners; *pg.* 278, *pg.* 1216
Stern, Deena, Sr VP-Mktg - Esquire Network; *pg.* 286, *pg.* 1229
Stern, Erica, Dir-Adv - Tourneau Inc.; *pg.* 14, *pg.* 1303
Stern, Ilene H., Dir-Adv - The New York Times; *pg.* 1668, *pg.* 1270
Stern, Jeff, Dir-Brand Strategy & Enterprise Mktg - Humana, Inc.; *pg.* 1204, *pg.* 734
Stern, Jeffrey, Sr Mgr-Fin Plng & Analysis - PepsiCo, Inc.; *pg.* 259, *pg.* 1327
Stern, Jeffrey, Sr VP-Sls - Rocky Brands, Inc.; *pg.* 1818, *pg.* 1466
Stern, Jeffrey, Mgr-Digital Mktg - Sonic Automotive, Inc.; *pg.* 190, *pg.* 1369
Stern, Jonathan, Dir-Media Rels & IR - MillerCoors LLC; *pg.* 255, *pg.* 582
Stern, Joshua E., Sr Dir-Mktg & Adv - DIRECTV Group Holdings, LLC; *pg.* 281, *pg.* 79
Stern, Judy, VP-Online Mktg - Nordstrom, Inc.; *pg.* 1779, *pg.* 1837
Stern, Kristina, Mgr-Paid Mktg - Starbucks Corporation; *pg.* 897, *pg.* 1840
Stern, Margot, Assoc Mgr-Brand Mktg-Global - Mattel Games/Puzzles; *pg.* 962, *pg.* 80
Stern, Margot, Assoc Mgr-Brand Mktg-Global - MATTEL, INC.; *pg.* 962, *pg.* 81
Stern, Peter, Chief Strategy Officer, Chief Product Officer & Exec VP - Time Warner Cable Inc.; *pg.* 312, *pg.* 1301
Stern, Sharon, Mgr-Media - Pernod Ricard USA, Inc.; *pg.* 1968, *pg.* 1332
Stern, Stephanie, Sr Mgr-Mktg-Online Acq - Intuit Inc.; *pg.* 769, *pg.* 158
Sternberg, Jordan, Rep-Social Media-Cedar Point Amusement Park - Cedar Fair, L.P.; *pg.* 537, *pg.* 1471
Sternoff, Sarah, Mgr-Digital Mktg-Global - Starbucks Corporation; *pg.* 897, *pg.* 1840
Sternschein, Evan, Exec VP-Adv Sls-Natl - Travel Channel LLC; *pg.* 313, *pg.* 766
Stetkiewicz, Jill, Sr Mgr-Mktg Portfolio Optimization - Office Depot, Inc.; *pg.* 448, *pg.* 412
Stetson, Joseph, VP-Mktg & Comm - Red Bull North America, Inc.; *pg.* 264, *pg.* 275
Stettler, Amy, Gen Mgr-Media, Integrated Media Partnerships & Branded Content - Microsoft Corporation; *pg.* 435, *pg.* 1824
Stetzer, Alexandra, Mgr-Mktg-Lucky Magazine - Conde Nast Publications, Inc.; *pg.* 1629, *pg.* 1217
Stetzer, Alexandra, Assoc Dir-Mktg Res-Harper's BAZAAR - Hearst Magazines; *pg.* 1649, *pg.* 1239
Steube, Fred, Sr Dir-Emerging Tech - Valpak Direct Marketing Systems, Inc.; *pg.* 1699, *pg.* 438
Stevanus Troha, Kristie, Dir-Mktg & Corp Partnerships-Companion Animals - The Humane Society of the United States; *pg.* 143, *pg.* 400
Steven, James, Exec VP-Comm & Mktg - Warner Music Group Corp.; *pg.* 590, *pg.* 1313
Steven, Jim, Product Mgr - Robert Bosch Tool Corp; *pg.* 1060, *pg.* 634
Stevens, Angela K., Principal-Mktg & Content Strategy-FedEx Svcs - FedEx Corporation; *pg.* 1907, *pg.* 1642
Stevens, Brigid, Dir-Mktg - Toms Shoe's Inc; *pg.* 1821, *pg.* 276
Stevens, Chris, Sr Mgr-Reg Sls - TM Studios, Inc.; *pg.* 588, *pg.* 1689
Stevens, Clement, Sr VP-Mktg & Mdsg - Haggen, Inc.; *pg.* 1022, *pg.* 1817
Stevens, Dan, Reg Dir-Sls - Golfsmith International Holdings, Inc.; *pg.* 1835, *pg.* 1662
Stevens, Dana N., Rep-Sls-Graphic Comm - Xerox Canada Inc.; *pg.* 494, *pg.* 1930
Stevens, Edward, Mgr-Sls - Fort Wayne Philharmonic Orchestra; *pg.* 549, *pg.* 680
Stevens, Ellen, VP-Mktg - BrandsMart USA; *pg.* 627, *pg.* 430
Stevens, Jeremy, Dir-Creative - MetLife, Inc.; *pg.* 1208, *pg.* 1258
Stevens, Lindsay, VP-Mktg & Comm - Stevens Group, Inc.; *pg.* 1924, *pg.* 906
Stevens, Mark, Dir-Digital Mktg - LCA-Vision Inc.; *pg.* 1419, *pg.* 1416
Stevens, Mary, Sr VP-Mktg-Global - Herman Miller, Inc.; *pg.* 926, *pg.* 913
Stevens, Melanie, Sr Mgr-Internal & Exec Comm-Intel Svcs - Intel Corporation; *pg.* 645, *pg.* 266
Stevens, Melissa, VP-Sls - Mohawk Fine Papers, Inc.; *pg.* 1464, *pg.* 1153
Stevens, Neil Schambra, VP-Brand Mktg - Vans, Inc.; *pg.* 1821, *pg.* 76
Stevens, Pete, Mgr-Domestic Sls - Associated Research Inc.; *pg.* 1400, *pg.* 622
Stevens, Piper, Sr Dir-Brand Loyalty & Mktg Comm - Loews Hotels Holding Corporation; *pg.* 1101, *pg.* 1252
Stevens, Rick, Dir-Enterprise Mktg - J2 Global Communications, Inc.; *pg.* 1260, *pg.* 133
Stevens, Stacey M., Sr VP-Mktg & Strategy - iCad, Inc.; *pg.* 643, *pg.* 1037
Stevens, Tami, Mgr-Mktg - Golden Corral Corporation; *pg.* 1730, *pg.* 1387
Stevens, Terry, Sr Mgr-Sls-Central Reg - Ideal Industries, Inc.; *pg.* 1051, *pg.* 662
Stevens, Tiffany, Sr Mgr-Brand Partnership - Amazon.com, Inc.; *pg.* 1226, *pg.* 1831
Stevens, Tonie, Dir-Mktg, Events & Sponsorships - Style Weekly Inc.; *pg.* 1690, *pg.* 1804
Stevenson, Amy, Sr VP-Mktg - Victoria's Secret Stores, LLC; *pg.* 1789, *pg.* 1471
Stevenson, Anthony, VP-Mktg - Electronic Arts Inc.; *pg.* 951, *pg.* 189
Stevenson, Craig, VP-Sls & Mktg - Abbott Ball Company; *pg.* 1040, *pg.* 383
Stevenson, Damon S., Mgr-Sls-Global - Dover Chemical Corporation; *pg.* 1156, *pg.* 1447
Stevenson, Julia, Mgr-Contracts-Bus Dev & Adv - Amazon.com, Inc.; *pg.* 1226, *pg.* 1831
Stevenson, Keith, Mgr-Adv - Mendocino Brewing Company; *pg.* 254, *pg.* 298
Stevenson, Mark, Dir-Creative - Nature's Sunshine Products, Inc.; *pg.* 1571, *pg.* 1754
Stevenson, Matt, VP & Head-Sls - Xap Corporation; *pg.* 1289, *pg.* 73
Stevenson, Matthew, VP-Comml Mktg - Bridgestone Americas, Inc.; *pg.* 1879, *pg.* 1648
Stevenson, Pete, VP-Global Injectables-Established Products BU - Pfizer Inc.; *pg.* 1581, *pg.* 1278
Stevenson, Robin W., Specialist-Mktg Events - Allscripts Healthcare Solutions, Inc.; *pg.* 1492, *pg.* 563
Stevenson, Tim, Engr-Distinguished Technical Mktg - Cisco Systems, Inc.; *pg.* 372, *pg.* 240
Stevermer, Lori, Mgr-Swine Mktg - Hubbard Feeds Inc.; *pg.* 1477, *pg.* 928
Steward, Ralph, Mgr-Mktg-Natl - Freescale Semiconductor, Inc.; *pg.* 398, *pg.* 1662
Steward, Rob, VP-Product Dev - Progress Software Corporation; *pg.* 457, *pg.* 786
Stewart, Alison, Mgr-Integrated Mktg - DefyMedia; *pg.* 1237, *pg.* 1222
Stewart, Andrew, Dir-Global Brand Mktg-Young Athletes Category - NIKE, Inc.; *pg.* 1812, *pg.* 1492
Stewart, Ashton, Sr Product Mgr-Global Payments - Amazon.com, Inc.; *pg.* 1226, *pg.* 1831

First page reference indicates Business Class Edition
Second page reference indicates Geographic Edition

Stewart, Bobby, Brand Mgr-Draftmark & Home Draught - Anheuser-Busch Companies, LLC; *pg.* 237, *pg.* 991
Stewart, Carl L., Engr-GT Field Svc Mktg - Siemens Corporation; *pg.* 803, *pg.* 1291
Stewart, Dave, VP-Mktg - Dollar General Corporation; *pg.* 1767, *pg.* 1635
Stewart, Dave, Mgr-Application Sls-MDM & DQ - Oracle Corporation; *pg.* 1272, *pg.* 786
Stewart, Dawn A., Mgr-Mktg-The Work Number - Equifax Inc.; *pg.* 748, *pg.* 504
Stewart, Dick, VP-Property Mktg - Isle of Capri Casinos, Inc.; *pg.* 553, *pg.* 998
Stewart, Duncan, Sr Mgr-Mktg - Verizon Communications Inc.; *pg.* 1875, *pg.* 1309
Stewart, Earl K., Sr Acct Mgr-Creative Svcs - General Electric Company; *pg.* 1297, *pg.* 347
Stewart, Elizabeth, Dir-Mktg - Doctor's Associates Inc.; *pg.* 1726, *pg.* 356
Stewart, Farley, VP-Product Mgmt - Edgewave Inc; *pg.* 390, *pg.* 202
Stewart, Heather, Dir-Global Auto Shows & Exhibits & Experiential Mktg - General Motors Company; *pg.* 175, *pg.* 881
Stewart, Ian, VP-Mktg-Global - Converse Inc.; *pg.* 1831, *pg.* 793
Stewart, John, Dir-Sls-OTC - Bausch & Lomb Incorporated; *pg.* 1401, *pg.* 1045
Stewart, John J., Head-Mktg-Equities, Indices, Advisory, Investment Mgmt & Wealth - Thomson Reuters Markets; *pg.* 810, *pg.* 1299
Stewart, Josie, Mgr-Mktg Comm-Global - Hospira, Inc.; *pg.* 1542, *pg.* 623
Stewart, Julia A., Chm, Interim Pres & CEO - Applebee's International, Inc.; *pg.* 1715, *pg.* 980
Stewart, Kaci, Reg Supvr-Mktg - McDonald's Corporation; *pg.* 1737, *pg.* 645
Stewart, Kat, Sr Dir - Cable in the Classroom; *pg.* 272, *pg.* 397
Stewart, Keith, Mgr-Social Media - Tiffany & Co.; *pg.* 13, *pg.* 1299
Stewart, Kitty, Sr Mgr-Mktg-TIAA-CREF - Teachers Insurance & Annuity Association - College Retirement Equities Fund; *pg.* 1219, *pg.* 1297
Stewart, Lisa, VP-Design & Mdsg, Superior Uniform Grp & HPI Direct - Superior Uniform Group, Inc.; *pg.* 33, *pg.* 468
Stewart, Lyn, Mgr-Digital Comm & Social Media - Huntsman Corporation; *pg.* 1167, *pg.* 1758
Stewart, Maria A., Asst VP & Mgr-Mktg Svcs - F.N.B. Corporation; *pg.* 759, *pg.* 1575
Stewart, Mark, Chief Strategy Officer & Exec VP - Townsquare Media, Inc.; *pg.* 313, *pg.* 350
Stewart, Mary, Dir-Mktg Svcs - Waddell & Reed Financial, Inc.; *pg.* 818, *pg.* 721
Stewart, Meredith, Mktg Analyst-NA Mktg Center-Excellence - Oracle Corporation; *pg.* 450, *pg.* 191
Stewart, Mike, Mgr-Creative Dev & Production - Anheuser-Busch Companies, LLC; *pg.* 237, *pg.* 991
Stewart, Neal, VP-Mktg - Dogfish Head Craft Brewery, Inc.; *pg.* 249, *pg.* 388
Stewart, Reid, VP-Men's Mktg - Ralph Lauren Corporation; *pg.* 46, *pg.* 1284
Stewart, Reuben, Sr Product Mgr-Electronic Delivery Channel Risk Mgmt - BB&T Corporation; *pg.* 723, *pg.* 1393
Stibbard, Sherry, Sr Mgr-Brand Design & Pkg - The Kraft Heinz Company; *pg.* 870, *pg.* 1577
Sticco, Maureen, Dir-Mktg - Bimbo Bakeries USA Inc.; *pg.* 840, *pg.* 1540
Stice, Scott, CMO & Chief Sls Officer - Farm Bureau Bank FSB; *pg.* 750, *pg.* 1740
Stichweh, John, Dir-Digital, Social Shopper Mktg, CRM & ECommerce - ConAgra Foods, Inc.; *pg.* 826, *pg.* 1014
Stickells, Neil, Sr Dir-SEO-Expedia Worldwide - Expedia, Inc.; *pg.* 1244, *pg.* 1814
Stickelman, Laura, VP-Sls & Mktg - Lennar Corporation; *pg.* 1100, *pg.* 443
Stickelman, Laura, VP-Sls & Mktg - Lennar Homes, Inc.; *pg.* 1101, *pg.* 443
Stickels, Robert K., Dir-Creative - Valassis; *pg.* 1698, *pg.* 386
Stickles, Jennifer, Mgr-Mktg - Wegmans Food Markets, Inc.; *pg.* 1037, *pg.* 1337
Stickley, Lisa, Sr Mgr-Channel Mktg & Trng - Rheem Manufacturing Company; *pg.* 1075, *pg.* 519
Stickney, Robert, VP-Comml Sls - RGS Energy; *pg.* 1951, *pg.* 1322
Stidham, David, VP-Mktg - Culver Franchising System, Inc.; *pg.* 1724, *pg.* 1887
Stiebel, Jessica, Brand Mgr - ConAgra Foods, Inc.; *pg.* 826, *pg.* 1014
Stiehl, Rob, Specialist-Retail Sls-South Dakota & Nebraska - Remington Arms Company, LLC; *pg.* 1844, *pg.* 1382
Stier, Dean, VP-Multi-Channel Mktg - National Business Furniture Inc; *pg.* 1269, *pg.* 1879
Stierle, Chris, Sr Mgr-Network Svcs-Global - Red Hat, Inc.; *pg.* 460, *pg.* 1388
Stiers, Jonathan, Dir-Creative-Private Brand Pkg - Wal-Mart Stores, Inc.; *pg.* 1790, *pg.* 29
Stiff, Greg, Mgr-Sls-Natl - The J.M. Smucker Company; *pg.* 865, *pg.* 1468
Stiffler, Kathryn, Mgr-Retention Mktg - Deckers Outdoor Corporation; *pg.* 1807, *pg.* 100
Stigall, Roy, Sr Mgr-Lifestyle Mktg - Electronic Arts Inc.; *pg.* 951, *pg.* 189
Stigelman, Stacy, Acct Exec-Adv - Bank of America Corporation; *pg.* 718, *pg.* 1362
Stiglitz, Meredith, Mgr-Mktg-Dreyer's & Edy's - Nestle USA, Inc.; *pg.* 883, *pg.* 96
Stiles, Johnathan, Mgr-Mktg-North America - Datalogic; *pg.* 382, *pg.* 1588
Stiles, Linda, Sr Product Mgr-Spice Portfolio - La Cie McCormick Canada Co.; *pg.* 872, *pg.* 1922
Stiles, Linda, Sr Product Mgr-Spice Portfolio - McCormick & Company, Incorporated; *pg.* 1027, *pg.* 779
Stiles, Mike, Sr Mgr-Corp Events - Adobe Systems Incorporated; *pg.* 342, *pg.* 235
Still, Annie, Dir-Sls - Chattanooga Choo-Choo Holiday Inn; *pg.* 1086, *pg.* 1628
Still, Brian, Sr Product Mgr-Mktg - Go Daddy Inc.; *pg.* 1249, *pg.* 21
Still, Caroline, Asst Product Mgr-Accessories - AT&T Mobility LLC; *pg.* 619, *pg.* 488
Stiller, Valerie A., Grp Mgr-Branding & Channel Mktg - Abbott Laboratories; *pg.* 1484, *pg.* 551
Stillo, Lauren, Asst VP-Integrated Brand Mktg - Morgan Stanley; *pg.* 783, *pg.* 1261
Stillwell, G. R., Mgr-Internet Sls - Sanderson Ford Inc.; *pg.* 190, *pg.* 13
Stilmann, Linda, Sr Dir-Sls-USA, Canada & Emerging Markets - Greater Miami Convention & Visitors Bureau; *pg.* 993, *pg.* 442
Stilwell, Jay, Dir-Mktg - The Clorox Company; *pg.* 327, *pg.* 169
Stimac, Ryan, Mgr-Customer Mktg - Colgate-Palmolive Company; *pg.* 504, *pg.* 1215
Stines, Andrew, Sr Mgr - Ernst & Young Global Limited; *pg.* 748, *pg.* 1228
Stingelin, Tom, Assoc Mgr-Mktg - PepsiCo, Inc.; *pg.* 259, *pg.* 1327
Stingle, Jennifer, Brand Mgr-Neutrogena Cosmetics-Johnson & Johnson - Neutrogena Corporation; *pg.* 517, *pg.* 137
Stinson, Erika, Dir-Product Mgmt - Genworth Financial, Inc.; *pg.* 761, *pg.* 1802
Stinson, Sarah, Specialist-Mktg Res - Landstar System, Inc.; *pg.* 1914, *pg.* 434
Stinson, Sarah, Mgr-Mktg-Americas Field Mktg - NetApp, Inc.; *pg.* 444, *pg.* 287
Stipanovic, Art, Product Mgr-Custom Engineered Sys - GEA Refrigeration North America, Inc.; *pg.* 1072, *pg.* 1597
Stippich, Paul, Sr Mgr-Channel Mktg - Kellogg Company; *pg.* 831, *pg.* 870
Stirlacci, Joseph, VP-Sls - Monterey Gourmet Foods, Inc.; *pg.* 881, *pg.* 94
Stirling, Ruthi, VP-Conceptual Dev & Adv - OPI Products Inc.; *pg.* 518, *pg.* 167
Stites, Caroline E., Mgr-Mktg Comm - Verizon Communications Inc.; *pg.* 1875, *pg.* 1309
Stitt, Jeanne, VP-Mktg, Product & Innovation - UnitedHealth Group Incorporated; *pg.* 1221, *pg.* 950
Stitt, Roger, Dir-Mktg - Browning; *pg.* 1828, *pg.* 1752
Stitt, Ronald, Grp VP Digital Media - Fox Television Stations Inc.; *pg.* 288, *pg.* 131
Stivale, Melissa, Coord-Social Media - Bed Bath & Beyond Inc.; *pg.* 1121, *pg.* 1127
Stjernstrom, Marcus, Dir-Global Mktg-Eliquis - Pfizer Inc.; *pg.* 1581, *pg.* 1278
Stob, Neal, Mgr-North Central Reg Sls - NABCO Entrances, Inc.; *pg.* 99, *pg.* 1882
Stobaugh, Tracy, Dir-Sls - Charisma Brands, LLC; *pg.* 2, *pg.* 120
Stock, Jeremy, Mgr-Mktg Ops - Bristol-Myers Squibb Company; *pg.* 1509, *pg.* 1206
Stockard, Tracy, Sr Dir-Brand-US Retail Experience Mktg - McDonald's Corporation; *pg.* 1737, *pg.* 645
Stockbridge, Tania, Dir-Mktg Comm - PeopleFluent; *pg.* 453, *pg.* 853
Stocker, Meg, Sr Assoc Brand Mgr - Campbell Soup Company; *pg.* 844, *pg.* 1048
Stockholm, Zack, Sr Mgr-Market Dev - AT&T Inc.; *pg.* 1867, *pg.* 1674
Stockman, Ann, Brand Mgr-Cool Whip - The Kraft Heinz Company; *pg.* 871, *pg.* 641
Stockman, Troy, Mgr-Interactive Mktg & User Experience - SCANA Corporation; *pg.* 1951, *pg.* 1612
Stocks, Aileen, VP-Mktg-Nestle Infant Nutrition - Nestle USA, Inc.; *pg.* 883, *pg.* 96
Stocks, Kim, Dir-Corp PR - Microsoft Corporation; *pg.* 435, *pg.* 1824
Stockton, Jordan, Dir-Mktg-Enterprise Informatics - Illumina, Inc.; *pg.* 412, *pg.* 203
Stockwell, Sharon, VP-Consumer Mktg - The Travelers Companies, Inc.; *pg.* 1220, *pg.* 352
Stockwell, Tom, III, Dir-Sls-Global - Burgess-Norton Manufacturing Company; *pg.* 202, *pg.* 613
Stockwell, Will, Brand Mgr-Pringles Brand - Kellogg Company; *pg.* 831, *pg.* 870
Stoddard, Kate, Analyst-Product Mktg-Emerging Market Svcs - Ford Motor Company; *pg.* 172, *pg.* 876
Stoddard, Lauren, Product Mgr-Mktg - Cigna Corporation; *pg.* 1197, *pg.* 338
Stoddard, Zane, VP-Entertainment Mktg & Content Dev - National Association for Stock Car Auto Racing; *pg.* 566, *pg.* 420
Stoddart, Paul, VP-Mktg - Providence Health System; *pg.* 1587, *pg.* 1829
Stoddart, Stephanie, Sr Dir-Mktg - Wal-Mart Stores, Inc.; *pg.* 1790, *pg.* 29
Stoecker, Jessica, Sr Mgr-Adv-Global - Oracle Corporation; *pg.* 450, *pg.* 191
Stoehr, Tim, Mgr-Comml Truck Mktg - Ford Motor Company; *pg.* 172, *pg.* 876
Stoeppler, Jim, Asst VP-Enterprise Brand Mktg - Enterprise Holdings, Inc.; *pg.* 1906, *pg.* 996
Stoesz, Anna, Sr Mgr-Consumer Insights - General Mills, Inc.; *pg.* 828, *pg.* 933
Stoewahse, Martin, VP-Mktg - Ferrero U.S.A., Inc.; *pg.* 1852, *pg.* 1121
Stoffel, Scott, Head-Media Rels & Sr Dir - Abbott Laboratories; *pg.* 1484, *pg.* 551
Stoffer, Alan, Assoc Mgr-Mktg - General Mills, Inc.; *pg.* 828, *pg.* 933
Stofko, Rebecca, Mgr-Mktg - Morgan Foods, Inc.; *pg.* 881, *pg.* 673
Stohrer, Bob, Sr VP-Brand Creative - Yahoo! Inc.; *pg.* 1289, *pg.* 289
Stojka, Keith, Sr Mgr-Search Engine Mktg - NetApp, Inc.; *pg.* 444, *pg.* 287
Stoker, Melinda, Dir-Mktg Comm - Xerox Corporation; *pg.* 494, *pg.* 365
Stokes, Alan, VP-Film Mktg & Adv - Metropolitan Theatres Corporation; *pg.* 562, *pg.* 136
Stokes, Colleen, VP & Dir-Creative-New Media - Coach, Inc.; *pg.* 3, *pg.* 1214
Stokes, Kendra, Assoc VP-Mktg - Victoria's Secret Stores, LLC; *pg.* 1789, *pg.* 1471
Stokes, Nathan, Sr Engr-Mktg - Emerson Process Management; *pg.* 1334, *pg.* 1636
Stokes, Ron, Exec Dir-Online Adv Sls & Mktg - New York Magazine; *pg.* 1667, *pg.* 1269
Stokes, Stacy, Brand Mgr-Clorox 2 - The Clorox Company; *pg.* 327, *pg.* 169
Stokes, Tracy, Sr VP-Adv - Eastern Bank Corporation; *pg.* 745, *pg.* 793
Stokley, Deborah, Mgr-Mktg Support - Citgo Petroleum Corporation; *pg.* 974, *pg.* 1703
Stokoe, Brian, Mgr-Social Media - Caterpillar, Inc.; *pg.* 1321, *pg.* 650
Stolakis, Steve, Dir-Product Launch Ops - Samsung Electronics America, Inc.; *pg.* 669, *pg.* 1115
Stolarczyk, Lauri, Mgr-Mktg - Thermos L.L.C.; *pg.* 61, *pg.* 660
Stoll, Charles, Mgr-Mktg Segment - The Bank of New York Mellon Corporation; *pg.* 720, *pg.* 1200
Stoll, Darren, Grp VP-Interactive Mktg & Analytics - Macy's East; *pg.* 1777, *pg.* 1254
Stoll, Joe, Dir-Production - Indianapolis Colts, Inc.; *pg.* 553, *pg.* 687
Stoll, Kim, VP-Sls & Mktg - Badger Meter, Inc.; *pg.* 1401, *pg.*

1873
Stoll, Kristine, Sr Product Mgr - Eaton Corporation; *pg.* 1331, *pg.* 1429
Stoller, Lucia, Dir-Social Mktg - Marriott International, Inc.; *pg.* 1102, *pg.* 764
Stoller, Sandi, Dir-Brand Strategy & Mktg - Outerwall Inc.; *pg.* 1367, *pg.* 1816
Stolp, Jennifer, Sr Mgr-Field Comm - Charles Schwab; *pg.* 1235, *pg.* 1661
Stolpe, Bill, Dir-Worldwide Enterprise Mktg IBM Sls & Distr - International Business Machines Corporation; *pg.* 418, *pg.* 1138
Stolsky, Chris, Assoc Dir-Morning Foods Mktg - Kellogg Company; *pg.* 831, *pg.* 870
Stolte, Jennifer Rubinstein, Sr Dir-Mktg - The Hain Celestial Group, Inc.; *pg.* 860, *pg.* 1172
Stoltenow, Jenny, Mgr-Mktg Comm - 3M Company; *pg.* 1142, *pg.* 956
Stolz, Tom A., Reg Mgr-Sls-Merrell Footwear - Wolverine World Wide, Inc.; *pg.* 1822, *pg.* 905
Stolz, Udo, VP-Sls & Mktg-Worldwide - Gleason Corporation; *pg.* 1340, *pg.* 1335
Stolz, Udo, VP-Sls & Mktg-Worldwide - Gleason - M&M Precision Systems Corporation; *pg.* 1341, *pg.* 1479
Stomel, Bob, Dir-Sls - Huffy Corporation; *pg.* 1836, *pg.* 1409
Stone, Barbara, Sr Mgr-Comm & Admin - Pfizer Inc.; *pg.* 1581, *pg.* 1278
Stone, Cari, Sr Mgr-Mktg - Amgen Inc.; *pg.* 1493, *pg.* 291
Stone, Charlie, VP-Sls & Mktg - GIW Industries, Inc.; *pg.* 1340, *pg.* 533
Stone, Dan, Sr Product Mgr-User-centric Analytics & Audience Mktg - Google Inc.; *pg.* 1249, *pg.* 153
Stone, Dawn, Coord-Sls Svc - Unette Corporation; *pg.* 1184, *pg.* 1114
Stone, Ellen, Sr VP-Mktg-Bravo - NBC Universal, Inc.; *pg.* 300, *pg.* 1266
Stone, Ellen, Exec VP-Mktg - NBC Universal Television Networks Group; *pg.* 302, *pg.* 1267
Stone, Emily, Analyst-Mktg - Windstream Corporation; *pg.* 321, *pg.* 34
Stone, Jeff A., Sr Acct Exec-Charter Media - Charter Communications, Inc.; *pg.* 274, *pg.* 372
Stone, John, Assoc Gen Counsel & VP-Kindle & Digital Media - Amazon.com, Inc.; *pg.* 1226, *pg.* 1831
Stone, John, Exec VP-Sls & Mktg-Global - Amkor Technology, Inc.; *pg.* 67, *pg.* 25
Stone, Josh, Mgr-Digital Sls - Robb Report; *pg.* 1681, *pg.* 142
Stone, Kelsey, Asst Dir-Mktg & Recruiting - The University of Virginia; *pg.* 610, *pg.* 1778
Stone, Kevin, CMO, Chief Sls Officer & Exec VP - Cengage Learning; *pg.* 1626, *pg.* 215
Stone, Kris, Dir-Sports Mktg-Pro Basketball - Under Armour, Inc.; *pg.* 49, *pg.* 759
Stone, Leah, Brand Mgr - Kao Brands Co. Inc.; *pg.* 513, *pg.* 1415
Stone, Meagan, Specialist-Mktg - FedEx Corporation; *pg.* 1907, *pg.* 1642
Stone, Scott, Sr Dir-Digital & Print Media - Miami Dolphins, Ltd.; *pg.* 562, *pg.* 419
Stone, Scott A., Dir-Brand, Digital & Social Media - ConocoPhillips; *pg.* 975, *pg.* 1703
Stone, Thomas, Dir-Sls & Bus Dev - Farmers Pride, Inc.; *pg.* 855, *pg.* 1534
Stone, Todd, Brand Mgr-Pedigree & The Goodlife Recipe - Mars Petcare; *pg.* 1478, *pg.* 1633
Stone, Trevor, Mgr-Mktg - Potlatch Corporation; *pg.* 1467, *pg.* 1844
Stonebraker, Christopher, Dir-Mktg - CBS Interactive, Inc.; *pg.* 369, *pg.* 215
Stonebrook, Shannon, Sr Writer-Mktg - Ariba, Inc.; *pg.* 353, *pg.* 283
Stoneham, Shelagh, Sr VP-Mktg - Shoppers Drug Mart Corporation; *pg.* 1594, *pg.* 1943
Stoneley, Dean, VP-Sls-Asia Pacific - Ford Motor Company; *pg.* 172, *pg.* 876
Stoner, Tom, Mgr-Direct Mktg - Liberty Tax Service; *pg.* 776, *pg.* 1810
Stonkus, Andrew A., Sr VP-Mktg & Sls - Teck Resources Limited; *pg.* 1183, *pg.* 1912
Stooke, Megan, Gen Dir-Global Mktg - General Motors Company; *pg.* 175, *pg.* 881
Stoop, Dirk, Product Mgr - Facebook, Inc.; *pg.* 1245, *pg.* 143
Storbeck, Sonia, Mgr-Natl Sls-Corp Accounts - Atlanta Convention & Visitors Bureau; *pg.* 989, *pg.* 489
Storey Koch, Betsy, Mgr-Mktg-Yogurt Platform, Convenience & Foodservice - General Mills, Inc.; *pg.* 828, *pg.* 933
Storey, Katie, Mgr-Adv & Promos - Sally Beauty Holdings, Inc.; *pg.* 522, *pg.* 1691
Storino, Jenny, Sr Dir-Creative Direction & Activation - American Cancer Society, Inc.; *pg.* 126, *pg.* 487
Storm-Fallows, Kristin, Mgr-Wholesale Mktg & Tradeshow - Tommy Bahama; *pg.* 48, *pg.* 1842
Storms, Jennifer, Sr VP-Global Sports Mktg - PepsiCo, Inc.; *pg.* 259, *pg.* 1327
Storti, Denisse, Brand Mgr & Mgr-Adv - Norwegian Cruise Line; *pg.* 1917, *pg.* 444
Stortroen, Travis, Mgr-Internet Sls - Dave Syverson Inc.; *pg.* 168, *pg.* 915
Stortz, Erin, Coord-Mktg-Portable Power & Cleaning Sys - Briggs & Stratton Corporation; *pg.* 201, *pg.* 1899
Stortz, Pat, VP-PR - AT&T; *pg.* 1865, *pg.* 258
Story, Phillip, Mgr-Medium Duty Mktg-Natl - Rush Enterprises Inc.; *pg.* 189, *pg.* 1728
Story, Roger, VP-Mdsg - Brookshire Grocery Company; *pg.* 1016, *pg.* 1748
Storz, Fabiola, Product Dir-Cardiovascular - Janssen Pharmaceutica Products, L.P.; *pg.* 1548, *pg.* 1125
Stotko, Bryan, Dir-Mktg Strategy & Insights - Anthem, Inc.; *pg.* 1192, *pg.* 683
Stotsenburg, Rodreich, Mgr-Motorsports Mktg - Bridgestone Americas, Inc.; *pg.* 201, *pg.* 1649
Stouffer, Linda S., Mgr-Global Product Data - General Motors Company; *pg.* 175, *pg.* 881
Stouffs, Katie, Dir-Global Mktg & Bus Dev - National Association of Realtors; *pg.* 1666, *pg.* 584
Stout, Craig, VP-Product Dev - Ethan Allen Interiors Inc.; *pg.* 924, *pg.* 343
Stout, Dana, Mgr-Product Comm - Waddell & Reed Financial, Inc.; *pg.* 818, *pg.* 721
Stout, Jennifer, Mgr-Indus Mktg-Comm, Media & Entertainment - Hewlett-Packard Company; *pg.* 404, *pg.* 175
Stout, Jessica, Mgr-Mktg-Brand Content + Events - Virgin America Inc.; *pg.* 1930, *pg.* 55
Stout, Jill, Bus Mgr - Valley Morning Star; *pg.* 1699, *pg.* 1699
Stout, Kevin, Product Mgr-Mobile Apps & Social Media - UBM Advanstar; *pg.* 1697, *pg.* 1306
Stout, Margaret, Reg Mgr-Mktg-Midwest Reg - AECOM; *pg.* 64, *pg.* 173
Stout, Tim, Reg Mgr-Sls - The Gates Corporation; *pg.* 205, *pg.* 319
Stover, Brandon, Product Mgr-Accessories - Makita U.S.A., Inc.; *pg.* 1358, *pg.* 120
Stover, Marc, Dir-Mktg - Twinlab Corporation; *pg.* 1603, *pg.* 1306
Stowe, Bob, Dir-Mktg Ops & Admin - The Wendy's Company; *pg.* 1755, *pg.* 1450
Stowe, Bob, Dir-Mktg Ops & Admin - Wendy's International, Inc.; *pg.* 1755, *pg.* 1451
Stowell, Brian, Dir-Mktg-North America - Fluke Corporation; *pg.* 1413, *pg.* 1819
Stowell, Jennifer, Mgr-Bus Partner Mktg - IBM; *pg.* 410, *pg.* 1449
Stoy, Kelley A., Mgr-Info Mgmt Software Channel Mktg-North America - IBM; *pg.* 410, *pg.* 1449
Strachan, Christopher, Mgr- Brand Mgmt-Global - Reebok International Ltd.; *pg.* 1817, *pg.* 811
Strachan, Dougal, VP-Mktg - 20th Century Fox Film Corp.; *pg.* 267, *pg.* 124
Strachan, Marc, VP-On Premise Strategy & Multicultural Mktg - Diageo North America Inc.; *pg.* 248, *pg.* 1223
Strack, Allie, Brand Mgr-AXE & Lever2000 - Unilever United States, Inc.; *pg.* 904, *pg.* 1061
Strader, Erika V., Dir-Community Mktg - The Coca-Cola Company; *pg.* 240, *pg.* 493
Strader, Jennifer L., Specialist-Mktg - Fluor Corporation; *pg.* 82, *pg.* 1719
Strader, Kristin, Program Mgr-Paid Media - NetApp, Inc.; *pg.* 444, *pg.* 287
Stradnick, Melissa, Mgr-PR - The Hershey Co.; *pg.* 1855, *pg.* 1538
Straffon, Lisa, Mgr-Corp Mktg Events - Performance Food Group Company, LLC; *pg.* 1030, *pg.* 1803
Strage, Richard, VP-Sls - Scan-Optics, LLC; *pg.* 467, *pg.* 354
Strain, Charles H., VP-Mktg-US - United Parcel Service, Inc.; *pg.* 1928, *pg.* 522
Strain, Dan J, Sr Dir-IT Shared Svcs - Chick-fil-A, Inc.; *pg.* 1721, *pg.* 492
Strain, John, VP-Mktg - Unisys Corporation; *pg.* 487, *pg.* 1517
Strammiello, Chris, VP-Mktg & Product Strategy - Nuance Communications, Inc.; *pg.* 447, *pg.* 806
Strand, Steven A., Supvr-Adv Program - S&C Electric Company; *pg.* 1305, *pg.* 589
Stranz, Greg, Sr Mgr-Mktg - JPMorgan Chase & Co.; *pg.* 772, *pg.* 1246
Strasberg, Katie, Specialist-PR - The Home Depot, Inc.; *pg.* 1050, *pg.* 510
Strasbourg, Del, VP-Sls Dev - Jacuzzi Brands Corporation; *pg.* 554, *pg.* 65
Strasfeld, Lauren, Mgr-Engagement Mktg - AARP; *pg.* 124, *pg.* 393
Strassburger, Daniel, VP-Mktg-Ralph Lauren Home - Ralph Lauren Corporation; *pg.* 46, *pg.* 1284
Straszewski, Tom, VP-Interactive Sls - Comcast Corporation; *pg.* 276, *pg.* 1560
Stratton, Jim, Sr Dir - National Parks Conservation Association; *pg.* 150, *pg.* 403
Stratton, Kristy, Dir-Mktg & Exhibitor Rels - Imax Corporation; *pg.* 1417, *pg.* 1926
Stratton, Michael, Sr Dir-Natl Health Sys - AstraZeneca Pharmaceuticals LP; *pg.* 1497, *pg.* 389
Stratton, Mike, Reg VP-VIP Mktg - Caesars Entertainment Corporation; *pg.* 1083, *pg.* 1023
Stratton, Rhonda, Mgr-Global Mktg Comm - Littelfuse, Inc.; *pg.* 1301, *pg.* 580
Straub, Bill, VP-Engrg & Product Mgmt - Nordco, Inc.; *pg.* 1365, *pg.* 1884
Straub, Jennifer, Mgr-Social Strategy - Current USA, Inc.; *pg.* 1765, *pg.* 315
Straub, Sam, VP-Trade Sls - Delta Faucet Company; *pg.* 78, *pg.* 684
Strauch, Dan F., Dir-Mktg - General Electric Company; *pg.* 1297, *pg.* 347
Strausbaugh, Debbie, VP & Mgr-Mktg-Retail Channel Mktg - Huntington Bancshares Incorporated; *pg.* 767, *pg.* 1440
Strauss, Andrew, Asst Mgr-Mktg - Wizards of the Coast, Inc.; *pg.* 970, *pg.* 1830
Strauss, Brad, Mgr-PR - Illinois Bureau of Tourism; *pg.* 995, *pg.* 578
Strauss, Kathie, Mgr-Mktg - General Growth Properties, Inc.; *pg.* 1093, *pg.* 574
Strauss, Mark C., VP-Sls - Cenveo Inc.; *pg.* 1626, *pg.* 372
Strauss, Ricky, Pres-Mktg - The Walt Disney Company; *pg.* 317, *pg.* 52
Stravinsky, Amanda, Specialist-PR Media - Tennessee Department of Tourist Development; *pg.* 1007, *pg.* 1654
Strawbridge, Tammy, Mgr-Adv - South Carolina Parks Recreation & Tourism; *pg.* 1005, *pg.* 1614
Strawderman, Bill, Sr Dir-Digital Mktg & Social Media - Siemens Corporation; *pg.* 803, *pg.* 1291
Strawn, John, Mgr-Mktg Tech - ABB Inc.; *pg.* 1309, *pg.* 1359
Strawser, Kevin, Sr Mgr-Pub Affairs - Chesapeake Energy Corporation; *pg.* 1937, *pg.* 1485
Strazza, Matthew, Gen Mgr-Sls Ops-Global - CA Technologies; *pg.* 366, *pg.* 1168
Strechay, Kate, Dir-Events Mktg - Gartner, Inc.; *pg.* 1248, *pg.* 374
Streeter, Carol, Rep-Mktg - Electronics For Imaging, Inc.; *pg.* 390, *pg.* 88
Streets, Jenny, Sr Dir-Digital Strategy-Global - AstraZeneca Pharmaceuticals LP; *pg.* 1497, *pg.* 389
Streett, Kristin, Sr VP & Dir-Sls Process & CRM-Comml Div - BOK Financial Corporation; *pg.* 726, *pg.* 1489
Streisand, Blaine, Brand Mgr-Vitamins & Supplements-Global - Reckitt Benckiser Inc.; *pg.* 1136, *pg.* 1105
Streitmatter, Laurie, Sr Mgr-HR-North America Beauty - The Procter & Gamble Company; *pg.* 1129, *pg.* 1418
Strekal, Heather, VP-Brand Mktg & Comm & Head-US Sponsorships - Morgan Stanley; *pg.* 783, *pg.* 1261
Strelau, Tina, Sr Specialist-Mktg Comm - Ecolab Inc.; *pg.* 329, *pg.* 960
Strelzick, Paul, Pres-Sls-Worldwide & Exec VP - SOLARWINDS, INC.; *pg.* 471, *pg.* 1666
Strem, John, Dir-Mktg - Standard Motor Products, Inc.; *pg.* 218, *pg.* 1176
Streng, Joe, Sr Mgr-Employee Comm - eBay Inc.; *pg.* 1240, *pg.* 243
Streng, Kathy, VP-Sls & Mktg - Yenkin-Majestic Paint Corporation; *pg.* 1450, *pg.* 1445
Strenger, Carl, VP-Sls Ops & Compensation - United Parcel Service, Inc.; *pg.* 1928, *pg.* 522
Strenski, Robert O., VP & Div Mgr-Mdse - Big Lots, Inc.; *pg.* 1762, *pg.* 1438
Strezo, Dan, Product Mgr - J.C. Whitney & Co.; *pg.* 209, *pg.*

First page reference indicates Business Class Edition
Second page reference indicates Geographic Edition

621
Stricker, Ben, Sr Mgr-PR - Cisco Systems, Inc.; *pg.* 372, *pg.* 240
Strickhouser, Marsha, Mgr-PR - Valpak Direct Marketing Systems, Inc.; *pg.* 1699, *pg.* 438
Strickland, Amy T., Dir-Creative Ops - Sam's Club; *pg.* 1783, *pg.* 29
Strickland, Julie, Dir-Brand Adv - UnitedHealth Group Incorporated; *pg.* 1221, *pg.* 950
Strickland, Kristi, Dir-Mktg - Dunkin' Brands Group, Inc.; *pg.* 1727, *pg.* 810
Strickland, Shawn, VP & Head-Video Product - Cellco Partnership; *pg.* 1869, *pg.* 1042
Strickler, Kristen, Mgr-Social Media & PR - Charlotte Russe, Inc.; *pg.* 21, *pg.* 201
Strickler, Nelson, VP-Corp Mktg - California Bank & Trust; *pg.* 728, *pg.* 201
Stricklin, Lou, Dir-Mktg & Sls Support - Muratec America, Inc.; *pg.* 443, *pg.* 1733
Strimban, Katie, VP-Mktg & Dev - The Monarch Beverage Company, Inc.; *pg.* 257, *pg.* 514
Stringer, Matt, Sr VP-Mktg - The Men's Wearhouse, Inc.; *pg.* 44, *pg.* 1711
Stringer, Peter, Sr Dir-Interactive Media - Boston Celtics Limited Partnership; *pg.* 533, *pg.* 790
Striplin, Becky, Mgr-Classified Adv - Lee Enterprises, Incorporated; *pg.* 1658, *pg.* 704
Stripp, Laura, Sr Mgr-Mktg - Blue Nile, Inc.; *pg.* 2, *pg.* 1834
Strle, Danielle, Product Dir - Tumblr, Inc.; *pg.* 1285, *pg.* 1305
Strobel, Charlie, Product Mgr-Panasonic Electric Works of America - Panasonic Corporation of North America; *pg.* 661, *pg.* 1120
Strobel, Emily, Mgr-Mktg-5 Brand-Global - Wm. Wrigley Jr. Company; *pg.* 1863, *pg.* 596
Strobel, Marybeth, VP & Mgr-Sls - Cable News Network LP; *pg.* 1624, *pg.* 1208
Strobel, Rachel, Sr Mgr-Digital Mktg - LifeLock Inc.; *pg.* 776, *pg.* 26
Strober, Michael, Sr VP-Adv Sls - Turner Broadcasting System, Inc.; *pg.* 314, *pg.* 521
Strods, Sal, Sr Dir-Diagnostic & Enabling Solutions - Welch Allyn Inc.; *pg.* 1436, *pg.* 1342
Stroebel, Hettie A., Dir-Mktg-Global - Merck & Co., Inc.; *pg.* 1566, *pg.* 1077
Stroh, Joe, Mgr-Mktg - 3M Company; *pg.* 1142, *pg.* 956
Strohl, Jason, Asst Dir-Mktg & Comm - University of Pennsylvania; *pg.* 609, *pg.* 1571
Strohm, Joe, VP-Ticket Sls - Saint Louis Cardinals, L.P.; *pg.* 580, *pg.* 1002
Strohmeyer, David, Supvr-Program Mktg - Salt River Project; *pg.* 707, *pg.* 26
Strokovsky, Dana, Strategist-Social Mktg & Content - Discover Financial Services; *pg.* 744, *pg.* 653
Strom, Eric, Product Mgr-Safety & Maintenance-Fleet Svcs - GE Capital; *pg.* 761, *pg.* 362
Strom, John, Sr VP-Mktg - Georgia-Pacific LLC; *pg.* 1458, *pg.* 507
Strom, Suzanne, Key Acct Mgr-Mktg-Lowes Acct - 3M Company; *pg.* 1142, *pg.* 956
Strome, David, VP-Media Svcs-Americas - LVMH Inc.; *pg.* 9, *pg.* 1254
Stromer, Michael, VP-Digital, Loyalty & Customer Insights-Mktg - JetBlue Airways Corporation; *pg.* 1913, *pg.* 1174
Stromeyer, George, Sr VP-Worldwide Sls - Harmonic, Inc.; *pg.* 402, *pg.* 246
Stromswold, Amy, Reg Sls Mgr-Patient Care - Stryker Corporation; *pg.* 1598, *pg.* 894
Strong, Chas, Sr Mgr-Corp Comm - ABM Industries, Inc.; *pg.* 64, *pg.* 1186
Strong, Esco, Dir-ONE for Publishers Product Mgmt - AOL Inc.; *pg.* 1229, *pg.* 1195
Strong, Karan, Mgr-Mktg Execution - Hewlett-Packard Company; *pg.* 404, *pg.* 175
Strong, Narender, Asst Dir-Bus Dev-Brand Mktg & Comm - Ernst & Young Global Limited; *pg.* 748, *pg.* 1228
Strong, Whitney, Specialist-Social Media & PR - Nordstrom, Inc.; *pg.* 1779, *pg.* 1837
Strongin, Lauren, Sr Mgr-Integrated Promos-Kashi & Bear Naked - Kellogg Company; *pg.* 831, *pg.* 870
Stropoli, Mark, Bus Mgr-Worldwide Cable Infrastructure & Wireline Comm - Texas Instruments Incorporated; *pg.* 679, *pg.* 1688
Strother, E. J., VP-Mktg-Advanced Matls Grp - Materion Microelectronics & Services; *pg.* 1559, *pg.* 1149
Strotman, Ingrid D., Dir-Mktg - Hewlett-Packard Company; *pg.* 404, *pg.* 175
Stroud, Greg, VP-Creative Svcs-Programming Integration - Scripps Networks Interactive, Inc.; *pg.* 1279, *pg.* 1638
Stroud, Howard, Dir-Mdsg & Pur - GSC Enterprises, Inc.; *pg.* 1021, *pg.* 1746
Stroud, John, VP-Mktg - Chattem, Inc.; *pg.* 1515, *pg.* 1628
Stroud, Mickey, Dir-Creative - RBC Life Sciences, Inc.; *pg.* 1588, *pg.* 1723
Stroud, Rick, VP-Sls - Thomasville Furniture Industries, Inc.; *pg.* 945, *pg.* 1391
Stroud, Rick D., Reg Dir-Mktg-Texas - Meritage Homes Corporation; *pg.* 97, *pg.* 23
Stroud, Scott, VP-Mktg & Strategy - Rue La La; *pg.* 1278, *pg.* 800
Stroup, Katrina, Reg Mgr-Mktg - Beazer Homes USA, Inc.; *pg.* 1081, *pg.* 491
Stroup, Terry, VP-Dealer Sls - Neopost Canada Limited; *pg.* 1364, *pg.* 1924
Stroup, Will, Mgr-Sls - The Daily Item; *pg.* 1632, *pg.* 829
Strouse, Jackie, Specialist-Digital Mktg - Golf Channel; *pg.* 551, *pg.* 454
Strout, Heather, Dir-Product Mktg - Lithium Technologies; *pg.* 1263, *pg.* 221
Strowbridge, Christine, Asst Mgr-Loyalty Mktg - Toys "R" Us, Inc.; *pg.* 968, *pg.* 1130
Stroyan, Laura, Mgr-Digital Mktg - Ford Motor Company; *pg.* 172, *pg.* 876
Strub, Michelle, Sr Mgr-Mktg Comm - Microsoft Corporation; *pg.* 435, *pg.* 1824
Strubbe, Steve, Sr Mgr-Mktg - Sargento Foods Inc.; *pg.* 894, *pg.* 1886
Strubhar-Masick, Rachel, Product Mgr - Carbonite, Inc.; *pg.* 368, *pg.* 792
Struchen, Nikki, Dir-Mktg-Foodservice - ACH Food Companies, Inc.; *pg.* 835, *pg.* 1631
Strug, Elysa, Dir-Digital Mktg - Party City Corporation; *pg.* 1781, *pg.* 1116
Strughold, Jorg, VP-Sls-EMEA - Atmel Corporation; *pg.* 621, *pg.* 238
Strunk, Chris, Dir-Mktg Promos & Comm - The Scotts Miracle-Gro Company; *pg.* 1799, *pg.* 1459
Struthers, Dave, Dir-Promo Mktg - General Mills Canada Corp.; *pg.* 828, *pg.* 1926
Strykowski, Laura, Sr Mgr-Corp Rels - The Allstate Corporation; *pg.* 1189, *pg.* 639
Strzelecki, Kerry, Dir-Mktg - Newell Rubbermaid Inc.; *pg.* 1128, *pg.* 515
Stuart, Andy, Exec VP-Sls & Passenger Svcs-Global - NCL Corporation Ltd.; *pg.* 1916, *pg.* 444
Stuart, Becky, Sr Dir & Head-Bus Mgmt - Teachers Insurance & Annuity Association - College Retirement Equities Fund; *pg.* 1219, *pg.* 1297
Stuart, Danielle, Head-Product Comm Team - Monsanto Company; *pg.* 1173, *pg.* 999
Stuart, Jennifer, Sr Mgr-Consumer Insights - Electrolux Home Products North America; *pg.* 54, *pg.* 1366
Stuart, Lisa K., Sr Mgr-Mktg - AT&T Mobility LLC; *pg.* 620, *pg.* 1152
Stuart, Michelle, VP-Mktg - Bright House Networks LLC; *pg.* 272, *pg.* 461
Stuart, Peter, Dir-Mktg & Comm - National Association for Stock Car Auto Racing; *pg.* 566, *pg.* 420
Stuart, Renee, Specialist-Mktg - The Lubrizol Corporation; *pg.* 1171, *pg.* 1481
Stuart, Robert J., Exec VP-Sls & Mktg - The Hertz Corporation; *pg.* 1911, *pg.* 450
Stuart, Robert J., Exec VP-Sls & Mktg - Hertz Global Holdings, Inc.; *pg.* 179, *pg.* 450
Stuart, Stacy, Exec VP-Mktg & HR - Edison Properties, LLC; *pg.* 1906, *pg.* 1096
Stubbee, Melinda, Dir-Media, Global R&D & Pipeline News - GlaxoSmithKline; *pg.* 1536, *pg.* 1565
Stubblefield, Greg, Chief Strategy Officer & Exec VP-Sls & Mktg-Global - Enterprise Holdings, Inc.; *pg.* 1906, *pg.* 996
Stubbs, Ayumi, Sr Dir-Digital Mktg - American Society for the Prevention of Cruelty to Animals; *pg.* 131, *pg.* 1193
Stubbs, Chad, Sr Dir-Mountain Dew Brand Mktg - PepsiCo, Inc.; *pg.* 259, *pg.* 1327
Stubbs, Thomas, Sr Dir-Global IT-Bus & Tech Strategy - The Coca-Cola Company; *pg.* 240, *pg.* 493
Stubelt, Steve, VP-Sls-North America - Grass Valley, Inc.; *pg.* 641, *pg.* 164
Stuber, Billie, Mgr-Media Rels - Dippin' Dots LLC; *pg.* 853, *pg.* 739
Stubler, Heidi, Mgr-Digital Mktg-ECommerce - Athleta; *pg.* 19, *pg.* 181
Stucke, Todd, VP-Sls, Mktg & Product Support - Kubota Tractor Corporation; *pg.* 705, *pg.* 294
Studebaker, Dana, Sr Mgr-Promos - CheapCaribbean.com; *pg.* 1903, *pg.* 1526
Studer, Daniel, VP-Sls-USA - Lindt & Sprungli (USA) Inc.; *pg.* 1857, *pg.* 1039
Studer, Marcel R., Sr Rep-Mktg-CAN Surety - CNA Insurance Companies; *pg.* 1198, *pg.* 571
Stueckemann, Peter C., Dir-Comml Strategy-US Immunology Mktg - AbbVie Inc.; *pg.* 1486, *pg.* 638
Stueven, Mary, Specialist-Mktg Comm - Boston Scientific Corporation; *pg.* 1508, *pg.* 831
Stufflebean, Jocelyn M., Head-Americas Enterprise Customer Mktg - Adobe Systems Incorporated; *pg.* 342, *pg.* 235
Stukel, Michelle, Sr Mgr-Digital Mktg - The Allstate Corporation; *pg.* 1189, *pg.* 639
Stull, Michael, VP-Mktg-Global - MANPOWER INC.; *pg.* 430, *pg.* 1877
Stumo, Thomas, Sr Mgr-Procurement - Hillshire Brands; *pg.* 862, *pg.* 576
Stump, Eva, Sr Mgr-Market Res - Amgen Inc.; *pg.* 1493, *pg.* 291
Stump, Karen, Sr Dir-Consumer Insights - Country Music Association; *pg.* 138, *pg.* 1649
Stump, Leigh Ann, Mgr-Franchise Mktg Dev - Bojangles' Restaurants, Inc.; *pg.* 1717, *pg.* 1364
Stump, Sheri, Sr Dir-Mktg-Neuroscience Consumer - Shire; *pg.* 1593, *pg.* 1532
Stumpf, Allison, Reg Mgr-Mktg - CKE Restaurants Inc.; *pg.* 1723, *pg.* 63
Stumph, Megan, Product Mgr & Mgr-Mktg - CareerBuilder, LLC; *pg.* 1234, *pg.* 568
Stup, Steve, VP-Digital Adv - The Washington Post; *pg.* 1701, *pg.* 407
Stupak, Darren, Exec VP-Sls & Distr-US - Sony Music Entertainment; *pg.* 309, *pg.* 1294
Stupka, Andrea, Brand Mgr - Annie's Inc.; *pg.* 1760, *pg.* 45
Stupp, Joe, Mgr-New Media - Chipotle Mexican Grill, Inc.; *pg.* 1722, *pg.* 317
Sturchio, Donna, Sr Dir-Internal Comm - Standard & Poor's Ratings Services; *pg.* 805, *pg.* 1296
Sturdevant, Michael, Sr Mgr-Mktg Svcs-Global - Oregon Tourism Commission; *pg.* 1003, *pg.* 1508
Sturdivant, Lisa, Head-US West Creative Svcs & Dir - BlackRock, Inc.; *pg.* 724, *pg.* 1203
Sturdivant, Troy, Analyst-BIG O & Mdsg - TBC Corporation; *pg.* 1889, *pg.* 457
Sturgill, Bryan, Specialist-Sls Application - Federal Signal Corporation; *pg.* 638, *pg.* 645
Sturgis, Yvonne, Project Mgr-Mktg - Magellan Health Services, Inc.; *pg.* 1557, *pg.* 337
Sturm, Alexandra, Mgr-PR - Hearst Magazines; *pg.* 1649, *pg.* 1239
Sturtz, Stan, Dir-Mktg Comm - Pella Corporation; *pg.* 104, *pg.* 711
Sturznickel, Katie, Mgr-Mktg-Global Events - Diebold, Incorporated; *pg.* 387, *pg.* 1407
Stutz, Kristen, Brand Mgr-North America Tide Innovation - The Procter & Gamble Company; *pg.* 1129, *pg.* 1418
Stuyck, Jorge, Head-Customer Mktg - Diageo North America, Inc.; *pg.* 1961, *pg.* 361
Stydinger, Kevin, VP-Fuel Retail Sls & Pricing - The Pantry, Inc.; *pg.* 1029, *pg.* 1360
Styles, Destene, Sr Mgr-Content Mktg - TD Ameritrade Holding Corporation; *pg.* 808, *pg.* 1018
Stylides, Kim, VP-Mktg - Ralph Lauren Corporation; *pg.* 46, *pg.* 1284
Su, Cathy, Dir-Comml Strategy & Mktg Lead-Liver Disease-Global - Gilead Sciences, Inc.; *pg.* 1535, *pg.* 88
Su, Daisy, Sr Mgr-Mktg-Product & Solution Mktg - Alcatel-Lucent; *pg.* 615, *pg.* 38
Su, Tina, Sr Dir-Citrix SaaS Div - Citrix Systems, Inc.; *pg.* 375, *pg.* 424
Suarez, Aileen, Mgr-Adv & Mdsg - Pollo Tropical Inc.; *pg.* 1745, *pg.* 445
Suarez, David, Reg Dir-Mktg - Mercury Insurance Company; *pg.* 1208, *pg.* 136
Suarez, Jay G., Mgr-Digital Mktg - LG Electronics U.S.A., Inc.; *pg.* 651, *pg.* 1060
Suarez, Norbert, VP-Sls - H.S. Crocker Co., Inc.; *pg.* 1651, *pg.* 619
Suarez, Tony, Dir-Mktg-Multicultural Consumer Experience - Humana, Inc.; *pg.* 1204, *pg.* 734
Suarez, Yadira I., Tech & Integrated Mktg-Latin America & The

Caribbean Reg - Xerox Corporation; pg. 494, pg. 365
Suarez-Davis, AnneMarie, VP-Frozen Foods Mktg & Innovation - Kellogg Company; pg. 831, pg. 870
Suastegui, Teresa, Mgr-Mktg Sourcing - Intel Corporation; pg. 645, pg. 266
Subercaseaux, Ben, Mgr-Product Dev - Oracle Corporation; pg. 450, pg. 191
Sublette, Bill, Chief Sls Officer - TruGreen-ChemLawn; pg. 1801, pg. 1647
Subowicz, Pete, Sr Mgr-Digital Media Design - AutoTrader, Inc.; pg. 1230, pg. 490
Subramania, Jaishree, Dir-Internet of Things Mktg - Cisco Systems, Inc.; pg. 372, pg. 240
Subramaniam, Anand, VP-Mktg - eGain Communications Corporation; pg. 1242, pg. 284
Subramaniam, Nathan, Sr Head-Mktg & Innovation - MetLife, Inc.; pg. 1208, pg. 1258
Subramaniam, Rajesh, Exec VP-Global Mktg & Comm-FedEx Svcs - FedEx Corporation; pg. 1907, pg. 1642
Subramanian, Kartik, Dir Product Mgmt Mobile Commerce - Walgreen Co.; pg. 1608, pg. 605
Subramanian, Krishna, VP-Mktg-Cloud Platforms - Citrix Systems, Inc.; pg. 375, pg. 424
Subramanian, Ramesh, Sr Dir-Global Consumer Care-Global Mktg - Electrolux Home Products North America; pg. 54, pg. 1366
Subramanyam, Sriram, Mgr-Field Mktg-North America & Mid-Market - Motorola Solutions, Inc.; pg. 657, pg. 659
Subramoni, Raja, Head-Product Mktg - Sonos, Inc.; pg. 675, pg. 263
Such, John, Mgr-Strategic Mktg - SYNNEX Corporation; pg. 480, pg. 92
Such, Karen, Sr Dir-Brand Experience - Juniper Networks, Inc.; pg. 1260, pg. 286
Suchy, Sarah, Specialist-Mktg & Brand - The Lubrizol Corporation; pg. 1171, pg. 1481
Suda, Joan E., Mgr-Mktg Comm & Adv - Graybar Electric Company, Inc.; pg. 1299, pg. 997
Suddarth, Steven, Mgr-Mktg - Annie's; pg. 1617, pg. 673
Sudduth, David, Dir-Sls & Mktg-Breckenridge Hospitality - Vail Resorts, Inc.; pg. 1117, pg. 313
Suderman, Don, Product Mgr-Matl Handling - Bunting Magnetics Co.; pg. 1320, pg. 717
Suding, Mike, Sr Product Mgr-Technical - Citrix Systems, Inc.; pg. 375, pg. 424
Sudler, Bruce, Mgr-Sls & Ops-Midwest - Intelligrated, Inc.; pg. 1349, pg. 1460
Sudnik, Laura, Sr Mgr-Comm - Iron Mountain Incorporated; pg. 421, pg. 796
Sudol, Eric, Sr Dir-Corp Partnerships Sls & Svc - Dallas Cowboys Football Club, Ltd.; pg. 543, pg. 1718
Sudy, Carol, Specialist-Mktg - United States Air Force Recruiting Service; pg. 1008, pg. 1735
Sue-Kyung, Lee, Dir-Mktg-ASEAN, India, Australia, Japan & Korea - The Procter & Gamble Company; pg. 1129, pg. 1418
Suech, Michael, Sr Product Mgr - Kronos International, Inc.; pg. 980, pg. 1683
Suehle, Ruth, Mgr-Community Mktg-Open Source & Standards - Red Hat, Inc.; pg. 460, pg. 1388
Suen, Donna, Mgr-Mktg-ProAV, Physical Security & Peripherals - Ingram Micro Inc.; pg. 415, pg. 261
Suen-Spennato, Kitty, Dir-Creative - Theatre Communications Group, Inc.; pg. 587, pg. 1298
Sueper, Jeremy, Brand Mgr - JAKKS Pacific, Inc.; pg. 960, pg. 142
Suerth, Chris, Brand Mgr-Allied - Dr Pepper Snapple Group, Inc.; pg. 250, pg. 1729
Suetholz, Jim, Reg Mgr-Sls - Stedman Machine Company; pg. 1379, pg. 673
Sugaski-Salazar, Andrea, Coord-Mktg & Social Media - GEICO Corporation; pg. 1200, pg. 399
Sugden, Andrea, Sr VP-US Sls Adecco Staffing US & Adecco Grp North America - Adecco USA, Inc.; pg. 342, pg. 1178
Suggett, Paul, Dir-Creative-Digital - Starz Entertainment, LLC; pg. 310, pg. 327
Sugita-Hulme, Jill, Dir-Strategic Mktg Initiatives-Big Data & Analytics - Oracle Corporation; pg. 450, pg. 191
Suh, Ted, Sr Dir-Strategic Plng & Ops-Biomarkers & Personalized Medicine - Eisai Inc.; pg. 1526, pg. 1133
Sukhtankar, Nikhil, Mgr-Global Commerce Product Solutions - PayPal Inc.; pg. 1274, pg. 248
Suku, Orela, Specialist-Media-US - Ikea North America Services LLC; pg. 929, pg. 1523
Sulentic, Beth, Dir-Mktg Comm - IDEX Corporation; pg. 1347, pg. 623
Sulentic, Gary, Sr Mgr-Mktg - Autodesk Inc.; pg. 356, pg. 257
Suler, Dennis, Mgr-ECommerce Mktg - Verizon Communications Inc.; pg. 1875, pg. 1309
Sulgit, Kathleen, Sr Dir-Mktg Ops & Events - Plantronics, Inc.; pg. 663, pg. 270
Sulima, Marcin, Sr Mgr-Supply Chain - Unilever United States, Inc.; pg. 904, pg. 1061
Sulliva, Chris, VP-Sls-Americas - Elo Touch Solutions; pg. 635, pg. 145
Sullivan Moreno, Amanda Rae, Mgr-PR - United States Navy Recruiting Command; pg. 1009, pg. 1648
Sullivan, Amanda, Mgr-Social Media Bus Dev - National Hockey League; pg. 568, pg. 1265
Sullivan, Andy, Sr Dir-Mobile Adv Tech Strategy - Turner Broadcasting System, Inc.; pg. 314, pg. 521
Sullivan, Ann, Assoc Dir-Product Mktg-Mobile - WebMD Health Corporation; pg. 1288, pg. 1313
Sullivan, Ben, VP-Sls-Worldwide - ON24, Inc.; pg. 1272, pg. 224
Sullivan, Brendan, Mgr-Product Mktg - Facebook, Inc.; pg. 1245, pg. 143
Sullivan, Brian, Dir-Mktg - Boston Red Sox Baseball Club Limited Partnership; pg. 534, pg. 791
Sullivan, Brian, Sr Mgr-IR-North America - BP America Inc.; pg. 972, pg. 1702
Sullivan, Brian, Specialist-PR Sls - The NASDAQ OMX Group, Inc.; pg. 785, pg. 1263
Sullivan, Bryan, Chief Investment Officer, Chief Strategy Officer & Exec VP - loanDepot LLC; pg. 776, pg. 86
Sullivan, Bryant, Mgr-Global Sls & Ecommerce Bus Dev - BJ's Wholesale Club, Inc.; pg. 1762, pg. 857
Sullivan, Caeli, Sr Mgr-Mktg & Social Responsibility - Reebok International Ltd.; pg. 1817, pg. 811
Sullivan, Carl J., Dir-Technical & Mktg - StanChem, Inc.; pg. 1449, pg. 345
Sullivan, Chryste, Sr Mgr-Mktg - Intel Corporation; pg. 645, pg. 266
Sullivan, Chuck, CMO & Exec VP - K12, Inc.; pg. 1260, pg. 1785
Sullivan, Cindy, Product Mgr - Sprint Corporation; pg. 1874, pg. 719
Sullivan, Craig, Sr VP-Enterprise & Intl Products - NetSuite, Inc.; pg. 1270, pg. 255
Sullivan, Dave, Specialist-Mktg Comm - Airgas, Inc.; pg. 1146, pg. 1583
Sullivan, David, Mgr-Mktg Launch & Strategy - Subaru of America, Inc.; pg. 191, pg. 1050
Sullivan, Dawn, Dir-Mktg - PFIP, LLC; pg. 1842, pg. 1037
Sullivan, Desmond, Specialist-Product - EarthCam, Inc.; pg. 1239, pg. 1072
Sullivan, Dj, Mgr-Digital Mktg - Juniper Networks, Inc.; pg. 1260, pg. 286
Sullivan, Doreen, Sr Mgr-HR - TE Connectivity Ltd.; pg. 677, pg. 1515
Sullivan, Elaine, Dir-Retail Mktg - Eaton Vance Corp.; pg. 746, pg. 794
Sullivan, Ellie, VP-Mktg & Consulting-Weichert Workforce Mobility - Weichert Relocation Resources Inc.; pg. 1118, pg. 1087
Sullivan, Erin, Sr Dir-Fisher-Price Mktg - Mattel Games/Puzzles; pg. 962, pg. 80
Sullivan, Erin, Sr Dir-Fisher-Price Mktg - MATTEL, INC.; pg. 962, pg. 81
Sullivan, Francis, Brand Mgr-Gaming-Global - Hasbro, Inc.; pg. 954, pg. 1603
Sullivan, Frank, Exec Dir-Grp & Arena Sls - Brooklyn Nets; pg. 534, pg. 1145
Sullivan, Franklin, Sr VP-Product Mgmt & Mktg-Global - Thomas & Betts Corporation; pg. 680, pg. 1646
Sullivan, Greg, Sr Mgr-Mktg - Microsoft Corporation; pg. 435, pg. 1824
Sullivan, Heather, Sr Mgr-Digital Mktg - United States Cellular Corporation; pg. 1875, pg. 594
Sullivan, Jaime, Mgr-Channel Mktg - Intuit Inc.; pg. 769, pg. 158
Sullivan, Jana, Assoc Mgr-Mktg - Pacific Sunwear of California, Inc.; pg. 1781, pg. 43
Sullivan, Jay, Sr VP-Consumer Product-Palo Alto - Groupon, Inc.; pg. 1255, pg. 575
Sullivan, Jennifer, Mgr-Campaign - Culver Franchising System, Inc.; pg. 1724, pg. 1887
Sullivan, Jim, Pres-Sls-CBS Television Stations - CBS Corporation; pg. 273, pg. 1210
Sullivan, Joan, Dir-Mktg - PNM Resources, Inc.; pg. 1949, pg. 1135
Sullivan, John, Head-Data Center-Fin Product Dev-Global - Cisco Systems, Inc.; pg. 372, pg. 240
Sullivan, John, VP-US Sls - Kao Brands Co. Inc.; pg. 513, pg. 1415
Sullivan, Jon, Sr Mgr-Corp Comm - Aflac Incorporated; pg. 1188, pg. 527
Sullivan, Joseph P., Pres-Specialty Products - Airgas, Inc.; pg. 1146, pg. 1583
Sullivan, Julie, Mgr-Global GTM Mktg - Reebok International Ltd.; pg. 1817, pg. 811
Sullivan, Katherine, Sr Dir-Concur Travel Product Mgmt - Concur Technologies, Inc.; pg. 1236, pg. 1813
Sullivan, Kathleen, Brand Mgr - Zulily; pg. 1792, pg. 1843
Sullivan, Kerry, Grp Brand Dir - Neutrogena Corporation; pg. 517, pg. 137
Sullivan, Kevin, Sr Mgr-Corp Rels-Natl - Southwest Airlines Co.; pg. 1923, pg. 1687
Sullivan, Kristi, VP-Mktg - CERC; pg. 990, pg. 369
Sullivan, Laura, Sr Product Mgr-Lung & GI Cross-Tumor Mktg & Ops - Genentech, Inc.; pg. 1533, pg. 279
Sullivan, Lauren, Sr Dir-Global Mktg Partnerships - National Basketball Association; pg. 566, pg. 1264
Sullivan, Marc, Assoc Dir-Diabetes HCP Mktg - Boehringer Ingelheim Pharmaceuticals, Inc.; pg. 1507, pg. 368
Sullivan, Maria M., VP-Sls Capability - CDW Corporation; pg. 370, pg. 663
Sullivan, Mark, Product Dir-Digital Printing - Presstek, Inc.; pg. 456, pg. 606
Sullivan, Mary, Dir-Mktg - Mark Andy, Inc.; pg. 1359, pg. 975
Sullivan, MaryAnn, Mgr-OEM Mktg Programs - Brocade Communications Systems, Inc.; pg. 365, pg. 239
Sullivan, MaryAnn, Mgr-OEM Mktg Programs - Brocade Corporation; pg. 365, pg. 312
Sullivan, MaryJean, Sr Mgr-Comm - AT&T; pg. 1865, pg. 258
Sullivan, Matt, VP-Mktg - The Sportsman's Guide, Inc.; pg. 1846, pg. 965
Sullivan, Maureen, Chief Strategy Officer & Sr VP - Blue Cross & Blue Shield Association; pg. 1195, pg. 566
Sullivan, Michael, Sr Dir-Global Brand Mktg-Baby Toys - Fisher-Price, Inc.; pg. 953, pg. 1156
Sullivan, Mike, Brand Dir-Enbrel Rheumatology Mktg - Amgen Inc.; pg. 1493, pg. 291
Sullivan, Mike, Dir-Mktg - Amway Corporation; pg. 326, pg. 864
Sullivan, Peter, Sr Analyst-Mobile Sls Enablement - Staples, Inc.; pg. 474, pg. 821
Sullivan, Rob, Sr VP-Svc, Consumer & Premium Sls - New York Jets Football Club, Inc.; pg. 570, pg. 1067
Sullivan, Robert, Exec VP-Sls & Mktg - Cablevision Systems Corporation; pg. 272, pg. 1141
Sullivan, Ryan, VP-Product Engrg & Dev - Sprint Corporation; pg. 1874, pg. 719
Sullivan, Sarah Pfouts, Sr Mgr-Bus Mktg - Hyatt Hotels Corporation; pg. 1096, pg. 577
Sullivan, Sean, Sr Dir-Event Presentation - Boston Celtics Limited Partnership; pg. 533, pg. 790
Sullivan, Sean, Mgr-Product Mgmt-Global - Shure Incorporated; pg. 672, pg. 638
Sullivan, Suzanne, Sr VP-Adv Sls - Fox Broadcasting Company; pg. 287, pg. 130
Sullivan, Tara, Sr Mgr-Branded Products - Nathan's Famous Inc.; pg. 1741, pg. 1171
Sullivan, Ted, Sr VP-Bus Dev & Sls - Equifax Inc.; pg. 748, pg. 504
Sullivan, Tim, VP-Media - The Wendy's Company; pg. 1755, pg. 1450
Sullivan, Tim, VP-Media - Wendy's International, Inc.; pg. 1755, pg. 1451
Sullivan, Tom, Mgr-Adv Sls - The Phillies, L.P.; pg. 575, pg. 1569
Sullivan, William, Mgr-Search Mktg-SEO & PPC - Intuit Inc.; pg. 769, pg. 158
Sullivan-Cross, Lisa, VP-Growth & Retention Mktg - Pandora Media Inc.; pg. 1273, pg. 172
Sullivan-Stoesser, Kristin, VP-Advertiser Sls - Rentrak Corporation; pg. 306, pg. 1506
Sulser, Dan, Mgr-Internet Mktg - Texas Instruments Incorporated; pg. 679, pg. 1688
Sultan, Omar, Product Mgr-Network Operating Sys Tech Grp-Mktg & Architecture - Cisco Systems, Inc.; pg. 372, pg. 240
Sum, Karen, Strategist-Email Mktg-Brand experience - lululemon athletica inc.; pg. 44, pg. 1911
Sumal, Sharondeep, Sr Mgr-Corp Comm - Pfizer Inc.; pg.

First page reference indicates Business Class Edition
Second page reference indicates Geographic Edition

1581, *pg.* 1278
Sumaquial, Edith, Strategist-Digital Mktg - E&J Gallo Winery; *pg.* 1962, *pg.* 149
Sumar, Alicia, Brand Mgr-Barbie - MATTEL, INC.; *pg.* 962, *pg.* 81
Sumitra, Michael, Mgr-Product Mktg - ADTRAN, Inc.; *pg.* 344, *pg.* 6
Summer, Wes, VP Mktg & Comm - Florida Institute of Technology; *pg.* 601, *pg.* 439
Summerfield, Todd, Sr Dir-Leasing & Dev - Liberty Property Trust; *pg.* 1101, *pg.* 1550
Summers, Betsy, Dir-Retail Mktg-Durable Medical Equipment Div - Medline Industries, Inc.; *pg.* 1562, *pg.* 635
Summers, Daniel, Product Mgr-Arm & Hammer - Church & Dwight Co., Inc.; *pg.* 1153, *pg.* 1063
Summers, Jeff, Specialist-RAM Brand Adv - FCA US LLC; *pg.* 170, *pg.* 868
Summers, Scott, Dir-Mktg-Retail Chain Pharmacy - Cardinal Health, Inc.; *pg.* 1512, *pg.* 1448
Summers, Shannon, Dir-Corp Consumer Mktg, & PR - Mary Kay Inc.; *pg.* 516, *pg.* 1657
Summons, Chris, Dir-Mktg-Dailies Contact Lens Franchise - Alcon; *pg.* 1399, *pg.* 530
Sumner, Jamie, Mgr-Mktg - Intel Corporation; *pg.* 645, *pg.* 266
Sumner, Paul, Area Mgr-Sls - Terral Seed, Inc.; *pg.* 1801, *pg.* 748
Sumner, Rob, Mgr-Natl Sls & Reg Sls-Western Div - Philips Emergency Lighting; *pg.* 1303, *pg.* 1631
Sumoski, Dave, Exec VP-Engineered Bar Products - Nucor Corporation; *pg.* 101, *pg.* 1368
Sumrall, Rose, Sr Mgr-Mktg-Display - J.C. Penney Company, Inc.; *pg.* 1774, *pg.* 1732
Sun, Gordon, Dir-Strategic Mktg - Kellogg Company; *pg.* 831, *pg.* 870
Sun, Shirley, Specialist-Comm & Mktg - DIRECTV Group Holdings, LLC; *pg.* 281, *pg.* 79
Sun, Shirley, Product Mgr - Facebook, Inc.; *pg.* 1245, *pg.* 143
Sun, Will, Product Mgr - LinkedIn Corporation; *pg.* 1262, *pg.* 160
Sun, Yong, VP-Strategic Mktg, Bus Dev, R&D - Harvard Bioscience, Inc.; *pg.* 1539, *pg.* 824
Sundar, Seema, Brand Mgr-Skinny Cow - Nestle USA, Inc.; *pg.* 883, *pg.* 96
Sundaram, Mahesh, VP-Worldwide OEM Sls - Immersion Corporation; *pg.* 413, *pg.* 246
Sundaram, Suresh, Sr VP-Mktg - ASPEN TECHNOLOGY, INC.; *pg.* 354, *pg.* 804
Sunday, Deborah E., Dir-Healthcare Mktg - AT&T; *pg.* 1865, *pg.* 258
Sunderland, Tom, VP-Mktg & Comm - Ocean Beauty Seafoods, Inc.; *pg.* 1028, *pg.* 1838
Sundheim, Scott, Sr Dir-Brand Mktg - RetailMeNot Inc.; *pg.* 1782, *pg.* 1665
Sundt, Amanda, Dir-Mktg - Crate & Barrel, Inc.; *pg.* 922, *pg.* 640
Sung, Dominic W., Dir-Structured Products - BP America Inc.; *pg.* 972, *pg.* 1702
Sung, Henry, Head-Digital-Social Engagement, Brand Sys Mktg & Comm - IBM; *pg.* 410, *pg.* 1449
Sunnquist, Bryan, Reg Dir-Sls - Sanofi US; *pg.* 1592, *pg.* 1046
Sunset, David, Sr Dir-Shopper Mktg - Jarden Consumer Solutions; *pg.* 57, *pg.* 412
Suomi, Markku, Dir-Product & Portfolio Plng - Hewlett-Packard Company; *pg.* 404, *pg.* 175
Suortti, Miia, Mgr-Digital Mktg-Starbucks & Seattle's Best Coffee - Starbucks Corporation; *pg.* 897, *pg.* 1840
Superina, Kristen, Planner-Sls - Scripps Networks Interactive, Inc.; *pg.* 1279, *pg.* 1638
Supovitz, Bruce, VP & Dir-Sls-Natl Radio Svcs - Nielsen Audio; *pg.* 446, *pg.* 768
Suppelsa, Kristin, VP-Mktg - Hearts on Fire Company; *pg.* 6, *pg.* 796
Suraci, Anthony D., Jr., Dir-Sls & Mktg - Avanti Cigar Corporation; *pg.* 1894, *pg.* 1527
Suraci, Anthony F., Dir-Sls & Mktg - Avanti Cigar Corporation; *pg.* 1894, *pg.* 1527
Surane, John, Sr VP-Mdsg, Mktg & Sls - Ace Hardware Corporation; *pg.* 1040, *pg.* 644
Suratt, Dan, Exec VP-Digital Media & Bus Dev - A&E Television Networks, LLC; *pg.* 267, *pg.* 1185
Surber, Karen, Specialist-Application-Mktg Ops - International Game Technology; *pg.* 957, *pg.* 1024
Surdan, Ken, Sr VP-Product - Constant Contact, Inc.; *pg.* 379, *pg.* 850
Surdyka, Jill, Sr Mgr-Internal Com-Global - Avon Products, Inc.; *pg.* 500, *pg.* 1198
Surette, Dan, Reg VP-Sls & Mktg-South Reg - Starwood Hotels & Resorts Worldwide, Inc.; *pg.* 1114, *pg.* 378
Surgeoner, Gwen, Sr Mgr-Comm-Worldwide Alliances & Channels - Oracle Corporation; *pg.* 450, *pg.* 191
Suriel, Dinorah, Sr Specialist-Mfg Mktg Svcs - Cardinal Health, Inc.; *pg.* 1512, *pg.* 1448
Surman, Steve, Head-Digital & Social Strategy-Global - Mead Johnson Nutrition Company; *pg.* 1561, *pg.* 615
Surratt, Mollie, Sr Dir-PR & Content - Mohawk Industries, Inc.; *pg.* 935, *pg.* 527
Surrette, Deborah, VP-Sls-Smarter Commerce Solutions - IBM; *pg.* 410, *pg.* 1449
Suryo, Olivia, Principal-Mktg-Global Mktg & Customer Experience - FedEx Corporation; *pg.* 1907, *pg.* 1642
Susel, Joel I., Sr VP-Sls & Solution Dev - Eagle:XM; *pg.* 1239, *pg.* 319
Susen, Lee, Dir-Mktg - E&J Gallo Winery; *pg.* 1962, *pg.* 149
Suskey, Aelon, Coord-Intl Sls & Market Dev - Visit Florida Inc.; *pg.* 1010, *pg.* 470
Susnow, Ilana, VP-Mktg - NBC Universal, Inc.; *pg.* 300, *pg.* 1266
Susnow, Ilana, VP-Consumer Mktg & Brand Strategy - NBC Universal Television Networks Group; *pg.* 302, *pg.* 1267
Sussman, Bruce, Sr Mgr-Mktg Bus Analytics - DIRECTV Group Holdings, LLC; *pg.* 281, *pg.* 79
Sussman, Carl, Product Dir-Comml-Bloomberg Law - Bloomberg BNA; *pg.* 1621, *pg.* 1772
Sussman, Daniel, Product Mgr - Harmonix Music Systems, Inc.; *pg.* 1256, *pg.* 808
Sussman, Gary, VP-PR - Brooklyn Nets; *pg.* 534, *pg.* 1145
Sussman, Mark, Dir-Trade Show Sls - Atlanta Convention & Visitors Bureau; *pg.* 989, *pg.* 489
Sussna, Ben, Product Mgr-L'il Critters - Church & Dwight Co., Inc.; *pg.* 1153, *pg.* 1063
Sustak, Carole, Brand Mgr - American Automobile Association; *pg.* 1190, *pg.* 429
Susz, Mark, Sr Dir-Global Product Innovation - Krispy Kreme Doughnuts, Inc.; *pg.* 1734, *pg.* 1394
Susz, Samuel, Mgr-Brand Mktg-Global - Fisher-Price, Inc.; *pg.* 953, *pg.* 1156
Susz, Samuel, Mgr-Mktg - MATTEL, INC.; *pg.* 962, *pg.* 81
Sutaria, Kavita, Brand Mgr - Moet Hennessy; *pg.* 1966, *pg.* 1260
Sutch, Catherine, Supvr & Sr Specialist-Mktg - Canon U.S.A., Inc.; *pg.* 1404, *pg.* 1178
Sutcliffe, Jennifer, Mgr-Travel Indus Mktg - Arizona Office of Tourism; *pg.* 988, *pg.* 14
Suth, Michele, Sr Dir-Mktg, Mdsg & Studio Ops - KB Home; *pg.* 90, *pg.* 134
Sutherland, Andrew, Sr Product Mgr - Exactech, Inc.; *pg.* 1529, *pg.* 428
Sutherland, Ben, VP-Sls-Worldwide - Power Integrations, Inc.; *pg.* 1369, *pg.* 249
Sutherland, Brenda, Sr Product Mgr-Design, Customer Engagement & Feature Validation - Adobe Systems Incorporated; *pg.* 342, *pg.* 235
Sutherland, George, Mgr-Global Technical Sls & Mktg - Halliburton Company; *pg.* 978, *pg.* 1707
Sutherland, Maura, Sr Mgr-Corp Mktg - Akamai Technologies, Inc.; *pg.* 1226, *pg.* 807
Sutherland, Rachel, Mgr-Comm & Media Rels - Intel Corporation; *pg.* 645, *pg.* 266
Sutherland, Spencer, Mgr-PR & Social Media - CHG Healthcare Services, Inc.; *pg.* 1515, *pg.* 1756
Sutherland, Thomas, Dir-Sls & Mktg - Westerbeke Corporation; *pg.* 1388, *pg.* 847
Sutphen, Carolyn, Mgr-PR & Media Event - Ulta Salon, Cosmetics & Fragrance, Inc.; *pg.* 524, *pg.* 559
Sutter, Alexandra, Coord-Retail Mktg - Puma North America, Inc.; *pg.* 1816, *pg.* 858
Sutter, Carmen, Product Mgr-Social - Adobe Systems Incorporated; *pg.* 342, *pg.* 235
Sutter, Greg, Dir-Creative Svcs - State Farm Mutual Automobile Insurance Co.; *pg.* 1218, *pg.* 557
Sutterer, Mike, VP-Mktg & Brand Ops-North America - The Scotts Miracle-Gro Company; *pg.* 1799, *pg.* 1459
Suttle, Michael, VP-Sls - CommVault Systems, Inc.; *pg.* 377, *pg.* 1125
Suttle, Phil, Mgr-Shopper Mktg - ConAgra Foods, Inc.; *pg.* 826, *pg.* 1014
Sutton, Beth, VP-Advocacy Comm-Global - Peabody Energy Corporation; *pg.* 1176, *pg.* 1001
Sutton, Chip, Mgr-Mktg - The Nature Conservancy; *pg.* 151, *pg.* 1774
Sutton, Chris, VP-Media & Customer Insights - hhgregg, Inc.; *pg.* 56, *pg.* 686
Sutton, Cynthia, Mgr-PR - Sage Software, Inc.; *pg.* 464, *pg.* 116
Sutton, Dan, Sr VP-Sls & Mktg - Zim-American Israeli Shipping Co.; *pg.* 1931, *pg.* 1798
Sutton, David, Sr Mgr-Corp Comm - Altria Group, Inc.; *pg.* 1893, *pg.* 1800
Sutton, Doniel, Sr Dir-HR-PayPal - PayPal Inc.; *pg.* 1274, *pg.* 248
Sutton, Jean, Mgr-Special Projects Mktg - Bob's Stores Corp.; *pg.* 38, *pg.* 354
Sutton, Mike, VP-Sls - Miracle Recreation Equipment Company; *pg.* 1839, *pg.* 988
Sutton, Rob, Dir-Sls-Car Electronics - Kenwood USA Corporation; *pg.* 649, *pg.* 123
Sutton, Scott, Specialist-Media & Mktg-Mars Petcare - Mars, Incorporated; *pg.* 1858, *pg.* 1792
Sutton, Steve, VP-Sls & Reel Rack Div - Reel-O-Matic, Inc.; *pg.* 1371, *pg.* 1487
Suvak, Jack, Sr Dir-Consumer & Market Insights - Moen Incorporated; *pg.* 1056, *pg.* 1468
Suvarna, Sandeep, Head-Consumer Mktg-Asia Pacific - LinkedIn Corporation; *pg.* 1262, *pg.* 160
Suydan, Gretchen, Dir-Mktg - Weis Markets, Inc.; *pg.* 1037, *pg.* 1588
Suykens, Steve, Acct Mgr-Svcs Sls - Avaya Inc.; *pg.* 621, *pg.* 264
Svarney, Ashley, Dir-PR & Comm - Palm Beach County Convention & Visitors Bureau; *pg.* 1003, *pg.* 479
Svendsen, Joel, Mgr-Sls & Mktg Initiatives-Rosco U.S. - Rosco Laboratories, Inc.; *pg.* 1782, *pg.* 378
Svenson, Erik, VP-Sls - Hood River Distillers Inc.; *pg.* 1964, *pg.* 1498
Svensson, Elisabeth, VP-Strategic Mktg & Specialty Solutions - Cardinal Health, Inc.; *pg.* 1512, *pg.* 1448
Svirchevski, Julia, Dir-Mktg & Applications-KT Certified Div - KLA-Tencor Corporation; *pg.* 1353, *pg.* 146
Svoboda, Adam, VP-Digital Sls Ops - NBC Universal, Inc.; *pg.* 300, *pg.* 1266
Swaback, Ray, Pres-Sls - Medline Industries, Inc.; *pg.* 1562, *pg.* 635
Swade, Michael, Sr VP-Sls & Mktg-Worldwide - Sonus Networks Inc.; *pg.* 1281, *pg.* 858
Swafford, Leslie, Sr VP & Sr Mgr-Mktg - BOK Financial Corporation; *pg.* 726, *pg.* 1489
Swahn, Chris, VP-Solutions Sls NA - Avnet Technology Solutions; *pg.* 359, *pg.* 25
Swahn, Elizabeth, Specialist-Mktg - Time Warner Cable Inc.; *pg.* 312, *pg.* 1301
Swaigen, Rob, VP-Mktg-Global - Jelly Belly Candy Company; *pg.* 1857, *pg.* 86
Swaim, Dennis, Exec Dir-Adv & Promo-Penguin Publ Grp - Penguin Random House; *pg.* 1675, *pg.* 1276
Swaim, Ed, Product Mgr - Thomas Built Buses, Inc.; *pg.* 191, *pg.* 1379
Swain, Fred, Dir-Direct Mktg & ECommerce - W. Atlee Burpee & Co.; *pg.* 1801, *pg.* 1590
Swain, Jovie, Sr Mgr-Mktg - Tyson Foods, Inc.; *pg.* 902, *pg.* 35
Swain, Liz, Sr Analyst-eMail & Mobile Mktg - Tribune Media Company; *pg.* 1696, *pg.* 592
Swainson-Barreveld, Alexa, VP-Products & Solutions-Watson - IBM; *pg.* 410, *pg.* 1449
Swales, Whitney, Mgr-Fin Mktg Support - Einstein Noah Restaurant Group, Inc.; *pg.* 1019, *pg.* 332
Swan, Alex, VP-Corp Comm & Intl Mktg - Arris Group, Inc.; *pg.* 353, *pg.* 541
Swan, James, Dir-Sls - Active Electrical Supply Company; *pg.* 612, *pg.* 563
Swan, Jeffrey, VP-Client Mktg - Valassis; *pg.* 1698, *pg.* 386
Swanciger, Jennifer, Exec Dir-Mktg - The New Yorker Magazine, Inc.; *pg.* 1669, *pg.* 1271
Swank, Stacey, Mgr-Mktg & Comms - Pinellas County Economic Development; *pg.* 1004, *pg.* 416
Swann, Colby, Dir-Mktg - Dollar General Corporation; *pg.* 1767, *pg.* 1635
Swann, Lynn, Dir-Mktg & Comm - The Omni Homestead Resort; *pg.* 1106, *pg.* 1786
Swanson, Ben, Sr Mgr-Digital Mktg & Content Strategy - Ubisoft Inc.; *pg.* 589, *pg.* 229
Swanson, Brian, Mgr-Mktg - Aetna Inc.; *pg.* 1187, *pg.* 351
Swanson, Carrie E., Sr Mgr-Mktg-Global Nutrition Group -

PepsiCo, Inc.; *pg.* 259, *pg.* 1327
Swanson, Erik, Mgr-Creative Svcs - Bright House Networks LLC; *pg.* 272, *pg.* 461
Swanson, Hanna, Coord-Natl Event Mktg - Fifth Generation, Inc.; *pg.* 1963, *pg.* 1662
Swanson, John, Mgr-Mktg & Bus Dev - Synopsys, Inc.; *pg.* 480, *pg.* 162
Swanson, Joyce, Acct Exec-Charter Media - Charter Communications, Inc.; *pg.* 274, *pg.* 372
Swanson, Kristin, Mgr-Trade & Media Rels - Arizona Office of Tourism; *pg.* 988, *pg.* 14
Swanson, Michelle, Asst Dir-Adv - Principal Financial Group, Inc.; *pg.* 796, *pg.* 706
Swanson, Ruth, VP-Mktg - Dessange International, Inc.; *pg.* 506, *pg.* 787
Swanson, Sue, Specialist-Mktg Comm - 3M Company; *pg.* 1142, *pg.* 956
Swanson, Tami A., Sr Mgr-Sourcing Ops - The Standard Register Company; *pg.* 473, *pg.* 1446
Swanson, Todd, Exec VP-Sls & Mktg - Finisar Corporation; *pg.* 639, *pg.* 285
Swart, Hugo, Head-IoE-Consumer Electronics & Sr Dir - QUALCOMM Incorporated; *pg.* 1873, *pg.* 207
Swartz, Donna, Mgr-Adv & Creative Svcs - HealthPartners, Inc.; *pg.* 1203, *pg.* 918
Swartz, Erin, Mgr-Mktg-Branding & Digital Strategy - Minnesota Vikings Football Club, Inc.; *pg.* 563, *pg.* 923
Swartz, Ian, Sr Dir-Mktg & IT Fin Ops - AutoNation, Inc.; *pg.* 165, *pg.* 423
Swartz, J., VP & Gen Mgr-Creative & Digital - salesforce.com, inc.; *pg.* 1278, *pg.* 226
Swartz, Lisa, Dir-Digital Mktg - Eastman Kodak Company; *pg.* 1408, *pg.* 1333
Swartz, Rion, Sr Dir-Acq - LegalZoom.com, Inc.; *pg.* 1261, *pg.* 96
Swartz, Steven, Specialist-Product Dev - 3M Touch Systems, Inc.; *pg.* 339, *pg.* 833
Swasey, Lindsay, Mgr-eMail Mktg - Ann Inc.; *pg.* 18, *pg.* 1195
Swatt, Meghan, Dir-Mktg Howard Johnson & Super 8 - Wyndham Worldwide Corporation; *pg.* 1119, *pg.* 1107
Swearengin, Dana, Dir-Mktg - Range Kleen Manufacturing Inc.; *pg.* 60, *pg.* 1458
Swearengin, Jeremy, Sr Mgr-Mktg - Verizon Communications Inc.; *pg.* 1875, *pg.* 1309
Swearengin, Jessica, Coord-Mktg - La-Z-Boy Incorporated; *pg.* 932, *pg.* 901
Swearengin, Mike, Sr VP-Mdse - O'Reilly Automotive, Inc.; *pg.* 214, *pg.* 1006
Swearingen, Christine M., Exec VP-Plng, Mktg & Community Rels - MedStar Health Inc.; *pg.* 1563, *pg.* 767
Swearingen, Jeff, Sr VP-Portfolio Mktg & Analytics - Frito-Lay North America, Inc.; *pg.* 1853, *pg.* 1730
Swearingen, Joanie, Specialist-Americas Mktg - Fossil Group, Inc.; *pg.* 5, *pg.* 1735
Swearingen, Valerie, Specialist-Mktg & Ops - The Procter & Gamble Company; *pg.* 1129, *pg.* 1418
Sweasy, Leta, Sr Mgr-Adv Ops & Sls - RealNetworks, Inc.; *pg.* 460, *pg.* 1839
Sweatt, Hilary, Category Head-Gift Wrap & Natl Mktg - Hallmark Cards, Inc.; *pg.* 1646, *pg.* 983
Sweeney, Ann, Dir-Creative Svcs - Trek Bicycle Corporation; *pg.* 1847, *pg.* 1896
Sweeney, Ashley, Specialist-Affiliate Mktg - InterContinental Hotels Corporation; *pg.* 1097, *pg.* 511
Sweeney, Brian, Sr VP-Worldwide Sls & Customer Care - IHS Inc.; *pg.* 1652, *pg.* 326
Sweeney, CarolAnn, Sr Mgr-Bus Ops - Arris Group, Inc.; *pg.* 353, *pg.* 541
Sweeney, Debbie, VP-Natl Field & Team Mktg-USA - Domino's Pizza, Inc.; *pg.* 1726, *pg.* 865
Sweeney, Deena, Assoc Mgr-Customer Mktg - Mattel Games/Puzzles; *pg.* 962, *pg.* 80
Sweeney, Deena, Assoc Mgr-Customer Mktg - MATTEL, INC.; *pg.* 962, *pg.* 81
Sweeney, Dina, Sr VP-Mdsg - The Children's Place, Inc.; *pg.* 22, *pg.* 1119
Sweeney, Joseph Edward, Pres-Advice, Wealth Mgmt, Products & Svc Delivery - Ameriprise Financial, Inc.; *pg.* 715, *pg.* 930
Sweeney, Kelly, Mgr-Digital Mktg - The Kroger Co.; *pg.* 1025, *pg.* 1416
Sweeney, Kerry, Mgr-Mktg - The New York Times Company; *pg.* 1668, *pg.* 1270
Sweeney, Kevin M., Interim Pres & CEO - Hampton Roads Economic Development Alliance; *pg.* 994, *pg.* 1797
Sweeney, Krista, Dir-Mktg-Brand, Customer & Store Portfolio Strategy - Best Buy Co., Inc.; *pg.* 1761, *pg.* 954
Sweeney, Scott, Sr Mgr-ECommerce-Amazon - Unilever United States, Inc.; *pg.* 904, *pg.* 1061
Sweeny, Haifa, Sr Mgr-Mktg & Search - Travelzoo Inc; *pg.* 1926, *pg.* 1304
Sweers, Karl, Mgr-Technical Mktg - DIT-MCO International Corporation; *pg.* 634, *pg.* 982
Sweet Gardiner, Kimberley, Dir-Digital & Integrated Mktg Strategy - Toyota Motor Sales, U.S.A., Inc.; *pg.* 193, *pg.* 296
Sweet, Evan, Dir-Fin Reporting & Analysis-Viacom Media Networks - Viacom Inc.; *pg.* 316, *pg.* 1310
Sweeten, Jason, Mgr-Creative - Buzzfeed; *pg.* 1233, *pg.* 1208
Sweeten, Michael, Product Mgr - Browning; *pg.* 1828, *pg.* 1752
Sweeting, Nadia, Sr Specialist-Digital Mktg Projects - The ADT Corporation; *pg.* 612, *pg.* 409
Sweetser, Kimberly, Mgr-Retail Adv - The Grand Island Daily Independent; *pg.* 1646, *pg.* 1010
Sweitzer, Rick, VP-Sls - Dr Pepper Snapple Group, Inc.; *pg.* 250, *pg.* 1729
Swensen, Sam, Brand Mgr-Online - Suja Juice; *pg.* 265, *pg.* 210
Swenson, Damon, Mgr-Mktg Partnerships - Dr Pepper Snapple Group, Inc.; *pg.* 250, *pg.* 1729
Swenson, Eric, Sr Mgr-Solutions-Cloud & Security - F5 Networks, Inc.; *pg.* 396, *pg.* 1835
Swenson, Keith, Sr Specialist-Mktg & Media Rels - Pelican Products, Inc.; *pg.* 1842, *pg.* 295
Swenson, Kendall, Mgr-Mktg - J. Crew Group, Inc.; *pg.* 1773, *pg.* 1245
Swenson, Mason, Sr Product Mgr-High Density Storage - Imation Nexsan Solutions; *pg.* 413, *pg.* 292
Swenson, Todd M., VP-Special Markets & Product Dev - Columbian Mutual Life Insurance Company; *pg.* 1198, *pg.* 1142
Swick, Greg, Sr VP-Sls - The Ultimate Software Group, Inc.; *pg.* 486, *pg.* 479
Swiderski, Keith, Dir-Digital Mktg - Avis Rent A Car System, LLC; *pg.* 165, *pg.* 1102
Swiergol, Stefanie, Sr Mgr-Mktg Programs Dev - Bank of America Corporation; *pg.* 718, *pg.* 1362
Swierk, Jeff, VP-US Consumer Mktg - MasterCard Incorporated; *pg.* 779, *pg.* 1325
Swift, Andrea T., Analyst-Mktg - State Farm Mutual Automobile Insurance Co.; *pg.* 1218, *pg.* 557
Swift, Charles, VP-Strategy & Mktg Ops - The Hearst Corporation; *pg.* 1649, *pg.* 1239
Swift, Christopher, Analyst-IT Bus-Sls Comm - Kellogg Company; *pg.* 831, *pg.* 870
Swift, Dylan, Dir-Natl Mktg - Yelp! Inc.; *pg.* 1291, *pg.* 235
Swift, Eric, Gen Mgr-Worldwide Server & Cloud-Azure & Specialist-Sls - Microsoft Corporation; *pg.* 435, *pg.* 1824
Swift, Megan, Analyst-Mktg - Windstream Corporation; *pg.* 321, *pg.* 34
Swigart, Tommy, Product Mgr-COM Express-IPC's & Sys - GE Intelligent Platforms; *pg.* 400, *pg.* 1135
Swiger, Terrence C., Head-PM Product Ops Team - Liberty Mutual Insurance Group Inc.; *pg.* 1205, *pg.* 797
Swilley, Carrie, Product Mgr - Southern Company; *pg.* 1952, *pg.* 520
Swinarski, Ken, VP-Creative Svcs - King Koil Licensing Company Inc.; *pg.* 932, *pg.* 671
Swineford, Randy, Grp Product Mgr-Acrobat.com Svcs - Adobe Systems Incorporated; *pg.* 342, *pg.* 235
Swinehart, Buffy, Sr Mgr-Cause Mktg - Aflac Incorporated; *pg.* 1188, *pg.* 527
Swingos, Susannah, Brand Mgr-Kids Div - Guess?, Inc.; *pg.* 25, *pg.* 132
Swinimer, John, Mgr-PR-Pro Graphics - Advanced Micro Devices, Inc.-Markham; *pg.* 345, *pg.* 1922
Swint, Angie, Sr Dir-Brdcst Ops - Rangers Baseball LLC; *pg.* 578, *pg.* 1659
Swirbul, Paul M., Head-Private Wealth Mgmt Mktg-High Net Worth Bus - GAMCO Investors, Inc.; *pg.* 761, *pg.* 1339
Swire, Nora, Sr Dir-Mktg-Hotels & Casinos - Hard Rock Cafe International, Inc.; *pg.* 1730, *pg.* 454
Swissman, Josh, Sr VP-Loyalty Mktg - MGM Resorts International; *pg.* 1105, *pg.* 1028
Swittenberg, Lamont, VP-Strategy & Trade Mktg - USA Networks; *pg.* 315, *pg.* 1308
Switzer, Daniel, Brand Mgr - NIKE Canada Ltd.; *pg.* 1840, *pg.* 1934
Switzer, Don, Mgr-Mktg - Steel Dynamics, Inc.; *pg.* 113, *pg.* 681
Swope, Allison, Product Mgr - Facebook, Inc.; *pg.* 1245, *pg.* 143
Swope, Christopher, Sr VP-Strategic Alliances & Innovation-Media & Sponsorship - Live Nation Entertainment, Inc.; *pg.* 558, *pg.* 47
Swope, Christopher, Sr VP-Strategic Alliances & Innovation-Media & Sponsorship - Live Nation Worldwide - Times Square Office; *pg.* 558, *pg.* 1252
Sword, Emily, Dir-Cub Cadet Brand Mktg - MTD Products, Inc.; *pg.* 1057, *pg.* 1478
Swymer, Heidi, Mgr-Upromise Credit Card Mktg - Upromise, Inc.; *pg.* 815, *pg.* 837
Syed, Farhan, Sr Dir-Sls Ops-Global - LinkedIn Corporation; *pg.* 1262, *pg.* 160
Sykes, Danielle, VP-New Product Dev-OPEN - American Express Company; *pg.* 712, *pg.* 1190
Sykes, Leontyne Green, Mgr-Mktg-US - Ikea North America Services LLC; *pg.* 929, *pg.* 1523
Sylvain, Fromage, Dir-Market Strategy & Sls - Agropur Cooperative; *pg.* 836, *pg.* 1950
Sylvan, Nancy V., Mgr-Digital & Direct Mktg - ViaSat, Inc.; *pg.* 489, *pg.* 62
Sylvan, Zack, Community Mgr-Social Media - Regions Financial Corporation; *pg.* 798, *pg.* 4
Sylvester, Dan, Mgr-Sls-Intl - DHL Holdings (USA), Inc.; *pg.* 1906, *pg.* 459
Sylvia, Chris, Dir-Digital Mktg - Regal Entertainment Group; *pg.* 579, *pg.* 1638
Symes, Phil, VP-Sls & Mktg - Star Building Systems; *pg.* 112, *pg.* 1488
Symock, Joe, Program Mgr-Adv & Brand Comm - Recreational Equipment, Inc.; *pg.* 1843, *pg.* 1821
Symonds, Stacey, Sr Dir-Consumer Insights - Orbitz Worldwide, Inc.; *pg.* 1918, *pg.* 586
Symson, Sherri, Brand Mgr-Global Olay Skin Care - The Procter & Gamble Company; *pg.* 1129, *pg.* 1418
Syngal, Sonia, Exec VP-Global Supply Chain & Product Ops-Gap, Inc - The Gap, Inc.; *pg.* 1770, *pg.* 218
Synhorst, Ildiko, Mgr-Solar Mktg Comm - NRG Energy, Inc.; *pg.* 1948, *pg.* 1712
Syperek, Allyson, Assoc Mgr-Mktg-Workspace Mgmt - Fellowes, Inc.; *pg.* 397, *pg.* 620
Syposs, Dave, VP-Mktg & Partnerships - HealthTrio Inc.; *pg.* 403, *pg.* 320
Syring, Joseph, Mgr-Sls-Natl - Crosman Corporation; *pg.* 951, *pg.* 1143
Sytman, Dan, Sr Mgr-PR - Microsoft Corporation; *pg.* 435, *pg.* 1824
Syverson, Katryn, Product Mgr - Hill's Pet Nutrition, Inc.; *pg.* 1476, *pg.* 721
Syverson-Mercer, Cynthia, Dir-Mktg & Catalog Sls - Swift Optical Instruments, Inc.; *pg.* 1430, *pg.* 1744
Szabados, Sandra, Sr Mgr-Early Engagement Mktg - American Express Company; *pg.* 712, *pg.* 1190
Szabo, Adrienne, Dir-Channel Mktg - Sony Corporation of America; *pg.* 675, *pg.* 1293
Szabo, Kellie, Dir-Media - United States Cellular Corporation; *pg.* 1875, *pg.* 594
Szabo, Steve, VP-Mktg-Large Joints - Exactech, Inc.; *pg.* 1529, *pg.* 428
Szahun, David, Dir-Media-US - American Express Company; *pg.* 712, *pg.* 1190
Szanto, Peter, Mgr-Mktg - E.I. du Pont de Nemours & Company; *pg.* 1159, *pg.* 390
Szarkowski, Ted, Product Mgr-Global - Molex Incorporated; *pg.* 655, *pg.* 628
Szczepaniak, Agatha, Sr Mgr-Media Rels - National Audubon Society; *pg.* 148, *pg.* 1263
Szczepaniak, Bob, Mgr-Mktg-Email & Refer-a-Friend Channels - Vonage Holdings Corp.; *pg.* 686, *pg.* 1074
Szczepaniec, Jessica, Analyst-Mktg - Citigroup Inc.; *pg.* 735, *pg.* 1212
Szczsponik, John J., Jr., Sr VP & Mgr-Worldwide Sls - Texas Instruments Incorporated; *pg.* 679, *pg.* 1688
Szczupak, David, Exec VP-Global Product Organization - Whirlpool Corporation; *pg.* 62, *pg.* 872
Szeli, Trisha, VP-Creative Svcs - Calvin Klein, Inc.; *pg.* 20, *pg.* 1209
Szilagyi, Marie, Dir-Product Mgmt - AutoTrader, Inc.; *pg.* 1230, *pg.* 490
Szriftgiser, Sabrina, Mgr-Adv-Natl - DIRECTV Group Holdings, LLC; *pg.* 281, *pg.* 79
Szul, Michael, VP-Sls - Carta Mundi, Inc.; *pg.* 951, *pg.* 1677

First page reference indicates Business Class Edition
Second page reference indicates Geographic Edition

Szulinski, Andy, VP-Sls & Mktg - C.R. Daniels, Inc.; *pg.* 1456, *pg.* 769
Szumera, Michael, Dir-PR & Comm-US - Sanofi Pasteur, Inc; *pg.* 1591, *pg.* 1588
Szumylo, Debbie, Mgr-Adv Mktg & Branding - GE Capital; *pg.* 761, *pg.* 362
Szurley, Shawn, Specialist-Social Media - Lithium Technologies; *pg.* 1263, *pg.* 221
Szvoren, Ali, Dir-Mktg-Neiman Marcus Stores - Neiman Marcus, Inc.; *pg.* 30, *pg.* 1684
Szwast, Scott, Dir-Mktg-South Atlantic District - United Parcel Service, Inc.; *pg.* 1928, *pg.* 522
Szwiec, Chris, Sr Assoc Brand Mgr-Kraft Salad Dressings - The Kraft Heinz Company; *pg.* 871, *pg.* 641
Szych, Dave, Mgr-Adv Sls - Red Bull North America, Inc.; *pg.* 264, *pg.* 275
Szymanski, Lauri, Mgr-Comml Mktg-On Premise - Heineken USA Inc.; *pg.* 252, *pg.* 1352

T

Ta, Bernard, Sr Mgr-Pro A/V & Digital Signage Bus Unit - Ingram Micro Inc.; *pg.* 415, *pg.* 261
Ta, Cindy, Sr Dir-IR - Juniper Networks, Inc.; *pg.* 1260, *pg.* 286
Taback, Jason, Exec Dir-Creative Svcs - ABC Cable Networks Group; *pg.* 268, *pg.* 51
Tabaksblat, Israel, VP-Sls & Mktg - Allomatic Products Company; *pg.* 198, *pg.* 1160
Tabar, Greg, Mgr-Product Mktg-Cloud Collaboration - Cisco Systems, Inc.; *pg.* 372, *pg.* 240
Tabata, Dave, Mgr-Consumer Programs, Mktg & Customer Experience-AEP Ohio - American Electric Power Company, Inc.; *pg.* 1934, *pg.* 1437
Tabb, Sarah, Brand Mgr-Coke - The Coca-Cola Company; *pg.* 240, *pg.* 493
Tabb, Sean, Mgr-Mktg-Direct to Bus - L.L. Bean, Inc.; *pg.* 1777, *pg.* 750
Tabbush, Sarah, Dir-Global Social & Mobile Mktg - Toms Shoe's Inc; *pg.* 1821, *pg.* 276
Taber, Kristin, Dir-Digital & Social Media - House of Raeford Farms, Inc.; *pg.* 864, *pg.* 1386
Taber, Scott, Acct Mgr-Adv - Graham Holdings Company; *pg.* 1645, *pg.* 1773
Taberski, Kimberly, Mgr-Mktg Client Svcs - Ingram Micro Inc.; *pg.* 415, *pg.* 261
Tabor, Mark, Dir-Mktg - United Parcel Service, Inc.; *pg.* 1928, *pg.* 522
Tacey, Rob, VP & Mgr-PR - Chase Card Services, Inc.; *pg.* 734, *pg.* 215
Tack, Maria, Coord-Sls - The Boston Globe; *pg.* 1623, *pg.* 790
Tackett, Brent, Mgr-Sls-Natl - Cherry Central Cooperative, Inc.; *pg.* 847, *pg.* 909
Tackett, Lillian, Mgr-Adv Production - Six Flags Entertainment Corporation; *pg.* 583, *pg.* 1698
Tacorian, Paul, Pres-Sls & Mktg - Tacori Enterprises; *pg.* 13, *pg.* 99
Tadic, Natasha, Coord-Media - NEOC; *pg.* 1395, *pg.* 459
Tafaro, Devinn Kraut, Head-Vertical Mktg-Global Bus Mktg - Facebook, Inc.; *pg.* 1245, *pg.* 143
Tafese, Henok, Sr Dir-Bus Dev - EMCORE Corporation; *pg.* 636, *pg.* 39
Taffet, Stacy, Dir-Mktg-Global - PepsiCo, Inc.; *pg.* 259, *pg.* 1327
Taft, Adam, Planner-Sls - Pandora Media Inc.; *pg.* 1273, *pg.* 172
Taft, Russell S., Sr VP/Sr Mgr-Relationship-Salt Lake City Market - Sunwest Bank; *pg.* 807, *pg.* 116
Taggart, Tim, Dir-Sls - Nasco International, Inc.; *pg.* 1779, *pg.* 1858
Taggart, Tom, Dir-Global Fixed Income Product Mktg - FRANKLIN RESOURCES, INC.; *pg.* 760, *pg.* 254
Taggatz, Casey, Mgr-PR - Phoenix Suns; *pg.* 576, *pg.* 19
Taggett, Muffie, Mgr-Adv & Branding - General Mills, Inc.; *pg.* 828, *pg.* 933
Taglioni, Rocco, Sr VP-Distr, Mktg, Individual Insurance & Investments - Sun Life Financial Inc.; *pg.* 806, *pg.* 1944
Taguchi, Hajimu, Sr Dir - CB Richard Ellis Group, Inc.; *pg.* 1085, *pg.* 127
Tague, Brian, Dir-Mktg - Kelly Services, Inc.; *pg.* 424, *pg.* 911
Tahbaz, Aresh, Dir-Rare Disease Mktg-US Oncology - Novartis Pharmaceuticals Corp.; *pg.* 1575, *pg.* 1054
Tahnk, Jeff, VP-Retail Mktg - High Liner Foods (USA) Incorporated; *pg.* 862, *pg.* 816
Tai, Wei-Ai, Dir-Sls & Bus Dev - PMC-Sierra, Inc.; *pg.* 664, *pg.* 287
Tai, Wilson, Mgr-Mktg - Champion Motorsport; *pg.* 168, *pg.* 459
Taibi, Catherine, Deputy Editor-Media - TheHuffingtonPost.com, Inc.; *pg.* 1692, *pg.* 1298
Taillon, Martin, Gen Mgr-Sls - Cascades, Inc.; *pg.* 73, *pg.* 1950
Tait, Bill, VP-Corp Sls & Market Ops - Humana, Inc.; *pg.* 1204, *pg.* 734
Tait, Carlos M, Dir-Travel Indus Sls, Latin America & Caribbean - Greater Miami Convention & Visitors Bureau; *pg.* 993, *pg.* 442
Taite, Michelle, Sr Mgr-Global Brand Dev-Dove - Unilever United States, Inc.; *pg.* 904, *pg.* 1061
Taitz, Mike, Sr Mgr-Trade Mktg - Glaxo Smith Kline Inc.; *pg.* 1536, *pg.* 1926
Takac, Mike, Exec VP-Sls - Warner Bros. Entertainment Inc.; *pg.* 319, *pg.* 54
Takach, Michail, Dir-Digital Mktg-North America - Manpower Group; *pg.* 430, *pg.* 1710
Takach, Michail, Head-Digital Mktg - MANPOWER INC.; *pg.* 430, *pg.* 1877
Takacs, Julian, Mgr-Online Mktg-EMEA - Systemax, Inc.; *pg.* 481, *pg.* 1324
Takahara, Amy, Dir-Distr & TV Sls-Global - The Jim Henson Company; *pg.* 293, *pg.* 103
Takasumi, Kumi, Dir-Mktg - Dell Inc.; *pg.* 383, *pg.* 1737
Takayama, Chris, Dir-Strategic Pricing & Global Mktg - Johnson & Johnson; *pg.* 1549, *pg.* 1091
Takeda, Koji, Exec Mgr-2nd Mktg Div Global Sls & Mktg Unit - Renesas Electronics America Inc.; *pg.* 667, *pg.* 269
Taketa, Jaimie, Planner-Digital Sls - NBC Universal, Inc.; *pg.* 300, *pg.* 1266
Takeuchi, Mitzi, Asst VP-Mktg & Brand Mgmt - Transamerica Insurance & Investment Group; *pg.* 1219, *pg.* 141
Takeuchi, Suzanne, Dir-Strategic Mktg & Mktg Ops-Natl - American Diabetes Association; *pg.* 127, *pg.* 1770
Talan, Maria, VP-Sls - MORNINGSTAR, INC.; *pg.* 784, *pg.* 583
Talano, Pat, Mgr-Sls-Natl - Paslode; *pg.* 1059, *pg.* 664
Talati, Chintan, Sr Dir-PR - Kelley Blue Book Co., Inc.; *pg.* 1656, *pg.* 112
Talavera, Dominic, Sr Dir-Dev - The Johnny Rockets Group, Inc.; *pg.* 1733, *pg.* 41
Talbert, Ernie, Mgr-Brand Mktg-Global - Under Armour, Inc.; *pg.* 49, *pg.* 759
Talbert, Lauren, Brand Mgr-Jimmy Deans - Hillshire Brands; *pg.* 862, *pg.* 576
Talbot, Brian, VP-Mktg-Wet N Wild & Black Radiance - Markwins International Corp.; *pg.* 516, *pg.* 67
Talbot, Jackie, Sr Dir-CRM Products & Solutions - Hilton Worldwide, Inc.; *pg.* 1094, *pg.* 1791
Talbot, Jeanne M., Sr Mgr-Customer Comm - Lexmark International, Inc.; *pg.* 427, *pg.* 730
Talbot, Julie, Dir-Mktg - Mars, Incorporated; *pg.* 1858, *pg.* 1792
Talbot, Julie, Dir-Mktg - Mars North America; *pg.* 1859, *pg.* 1072
Talbot, Kimberley, Dir-Campaign Mktg - Adobe Systems Incorporated; *pg.* 342, *pg.* 235
Talbot, Kimberly, Mgr-PR - Boise Philharmonic Association, Inc.; *pg.* 533, *pg.* 546
Talbot, Trish, Dir-Promotional Pur Pro Products Div - L'Oreal USA; *pg.* 514, *pg.* 1252
Talbott, Mark, Product Mgr-Molecular Spectroscopy - Shimadzu Scientific Instruments, Inc.; *pg.* 1428, *pg.* 768
Talentti, Gabriel Estrella, Dir-Sls-Middle East & Africa - Alto-Shaam Inc.; *pg.* 836, *pg.* 1869
Taliaferro, Matt, Sr Dir-Mktg & Local Mktg - Wal-Mart Stores, Inc.; *pg.* 1790, *pg.* 29
Talierco, Maggie, Mgr-Internet Mktg - Olympus America Inc.; *pg.* 1425, *pg.* 1521
Talkad, Jyothsna, Sr Analyst-Fin-Mktg Effectiveness - The Gap, Inc.; *pg.* 1770, *pg.* 218
Talkar, Eric, Sr Designer-Digital Media Grp - DIRECTV Group Holdings, LLC; *pg.* 281, *pg.* 79
Tall, Brittany, Mgr-Media & Digital Strategy - MillerCoors LLC; *pg.* 255, *pg.* 582
Tall, James, Mgr-Bus & Mktg Ops - Adobe Systems Incorporated; *pg.* 342, *pg.* 235
Talla, Donna, Dir-Adv - The Walton Sun; *pg.* 1701, *pg.* 465
Tallent, Steve, Dir-Sls-West - Edlund Company, Inc.; *pg.* 1123, *pg.* 1765
Talley, Cheryl, Mgr-Mktg - Marnier-Lapostolle Inc.; *pg.* 1966, *pg.* 1256
Talley, Darren, VP-Mktg & Tech - Exxon Mobil Corporation; *pg.* 977, *pg.* 1718
Talley, Victoria, Sr Specialist-Mktg - FedEx Corporation; *pg.* 1907, *pg.* 1642
Talling-Smith, Simon, Pres-Products & Emerging Bus - Travelzoo Inc; *pg.* 1926, *pg.* 1304
Talluri, Raj, Sr VP-Product Mgmt - QUALCOMM Incorporated; *pg.* 1873, *pg.* 207
Talluto, Sal, Dir-Multi-Media Sls - ESPN, Inc.; *pg.* 285, *pg.* 340
Talmor, Calia, Sr Product Mgr - Etsy, Inc.; *pg.* 1768, *pg.* 1230
Talwar, Jay, CMO & Sr VP-Mktg - Hawaii Visitors & Convention Bureau; *pg.* 994, *pg.* 543
Talwar, Shilpi, Sr Mgr-Mktg-CRM & Loyalty - The Western Union Company; *pg.* 822, *pg.* 327
Talwar, Varun, Product Mgr-Cloud Platform - Google Inc.; *pg.* 1249, *pg.* 153
Tam, Benny, Dir-Category Mktg & Mdsg - Newegg Inc.; *pg.* 1271, *pg.* 67
Tam, Christopher, Dir-Customer Experience Mktg - Hilton Worldwide, Inc.; *pg.* 1094, *pg.* 1791
Tam, David, Mgr-Online Mktg - salesforce.com, inc.; *pg.* 1278, *pg.* 226
Tam, Henry, Mgr-Product Mktg - F5 Networks, Inc.; *pg.* 396, *pg.* 1835
Tam, Herman, VP-Mktg & Consumer Products Grp - Leggett & Platt, Incorporated; *pg.* 933, *pg.* 974
Tam, Joe, Mgr-Sls-North Asia - ShoreTel, Inc.; *pg.* 469, *pg.* 288
Tam, Lawrence, Dir-Sls & Mktg Ops - DIRECTV Group Holdings, LLC; *pg.* 281, *pg.* 79
Tamariz, Gabriela, Head-EM Rare Diseases Mktg Platform - Pfizer Inc.; *pg.* 1581, *pg.* 1278
Tamaro, Marisol, VP-Mktg - PepsiCo, Inc.; *pg.* 259, *pg.* 1327
Tamayo-Byun, Myra, Dir-Mktg-Consumer Respiratory Strategy - Boehringer Ingelheim Pharmaceuticals, Inc.; *pg.* 1507, *pg.* 368
Tamble, Joe, VP-Retail Sls-North America - Sun-Maid Growers of California; *pg.* 899, *pg.* 119
Tambosi, Fabio, Brand Mgr-Nike Women's-Global - NIKE, Inc.; *pg.* 1812, *pg.* 1492
Tamburino, Jennifer L., Dir-Mktg - Aetna Inc.; *pg.* 1187, *pg.* 351
Tamburro, Catherine A., Specialist-Mktg - Travelers Insurance; *pg.* 1220, *pg.* 963
Tamchyna, Radka, Mgr-Sls-Intl - Scintrex Ltd.; *pg.* 1374, *pg.* 1920
Tamer, Bernard, Brand Mktg Mgr - Samsung Electronics America, Inc.; *pg.* 669, *pg.* 1115
Tamoutselis, Philip, Brand Mgr-Ensure - Abbott Nutrition; *pg.* 1485, *pg.* 1437
Tamplin, Tiffany, Sr Dir-Data Strategy & Mktg Integration - The Kraft Heinz Company; *pg.* 871, *pg.* 641
Tan, Carlo, Dir-Sls - ASI Corporation; *pg.* 354, *pg.* 90
Tan, Cindy, VP-Display Adv-APAC - TripAdvisor, Inc.; *pg.* 1926, *pg.* 835
Tan, Dave, Head-Performance Media Agencies - Google Inc.; *pg.* 1249, *pg.* 153
Tan, Ebony, Sr Mgr-Product Mktg - Yahoo! Inc.; *pg.* 1289, *pg.* 289
Tan, Erol, Brand Mgr-Sweet Baby Ray's & Sticky Fingers - Ken's Foods, Inc.; *pg.* 867, *pg.* 832
Tan, Jennifer, Assoc Dir-Mktg - BCBG Max Azria Group LLC; *pg.* 19, *pg.* 301
Tan, Jennifer, Sr Dir-Performance Mktg - Experian Consumer Direct; *pg.* 1245, *pg.* 71
Tan, Jorge, Sr Mgr-Mktg - Intuit Inc.; *pg.* 769, *pg.* 158
Tan, Julian, Sr Mgr-Category & Shopper Solutions - Bayer Healthcare Consumer Care Division; *pg.* 1500, *pg.* 1087
Tan, Madeline, Dir-Adv Sls APAC - ESPN, Inc.; *pg.* 285, *pg.* 340
Tan, Melody, Sr VP-Content Distr & Mktg, Strategy & Bus Ops - MTV Networks Company; *pg.* 298, *pg.* 1262
Tan, Mimi, Sr VP-Bus Dev & Mktg - Universal Power Group, Inc.; *pg.* 683, *pg.* 1671
Tan, Naveen, Sls Mgr-North America Offshore & Well Svcs - Schlumberger Limited; *pg.* 801, *pg.* 1714
Tan, Randall, Brand Mgr-South Asia - Gruma Corporation; *pg.* 860, *pg.* 951
Tan, Thomas, VP-Integrated Mktg-Global - VMware, Inc.; *pg.* 490, *pg.* 179
Tanabe, Goji, Product Mgr - Molex Incorporated; *pg.* 655, *pg.* 628

Tanabe, Jennifer, Sr Mgr-Comm - Intuit Inc.; *pg.* 769, *pg.* 158
Tanagretta, Anthony, Rep-Sls - Les Trois Petits Cochons, Inc.; *pg.* 874, *pg.* 1146
Tanaka, Nancy, Sr Mgr-Mktg - Intuit Inc.; *pg.* 769, *pg.* 158
Tanaka, Tsubasa, Mgr-Mktg - General Mills, Inc.; *pg.* 828, *pg.* 933
Tandon, Mukta, Sr Mgr-Brand Comm - BP Corporation North America Inc.; *pg.* 973, *pg.* 665
Taneja, Anshuman, Head-Digital Product Mgmt & Sr Dir - ABERCROMBIE & FITCH CO.; *pg.* 37, *pg.* 1466
Tanem, Michelle, Dir-Comm, Products & Distr-North America - Johnson Controls, Inc.; *pg.* 1073, *pg.* 1597
Tanenbaum, Howard, VP-Call Center Sls & Ops - Club Med Sales, Inc.; *pg.* 1903, *pg.* 441
Tanenbaum, Jonas, VP-Sls & Mktg Hospitality TV - Samsung Electronics America, Inc.; *pg.* 669, *pg.* 1115
Tang, Angeline, Dir-Sls & Mktg-Asia - Avis Budget Group, Inc.; *pg.* 1900, *pg.* 1102
Tang, Francis, VP-Discrete Products-Worldwide - Diodes Incorporated; *pg.* 634, *pg.* 1729
Tang, Jeff, Assoc Mgr-Mktg - General Mills, Inc.; *pg.* 828, *pg.* 933
Tang, John, Sr Product Mgr-Mktg - Gilead Sciences, Inc.; *pg.* 1535, *pg.* 88
Tang, Katie, Coord-Social Media - Philadelphia Eagles Football Club, Inc.; *pg.* 575, *pg.* 1569
Tang, Laura, Reg Mgr-Sls-Canada - Annie's Inc.; *pg.* 1760, *pg.* 45
Tang, Pinky, Sr Asst Brand Mgr-Building -TRESemme - Unilever Canada Inc.; *pg.* 903, *pg.* 1946
Tang, Rock, Sr Dir-Corp Real Estate - Hawaiian Airlines, Inc.; *pg.* 1910, *pg.* 543
Tang, Sophia, Sr VP & Dir-Creative - Bloomingdale's, Inc.; *pg.* 1763, *pg.* 1204
Tangeman, Scott, Head-Sls - Arrow Electronics, Inc.; *pg.* 619, *pg.* 325
Tangen, Randy, Mgr-Production - Deco Products Co.; *pg.* 1045, *pg.* 704
Taniguchi, Ann, Dir-Media-Natl - Fox Broadcasting Company; *pg.* 287, *pg.* 130
Taniguchi, Yumi, Specialist-Product Mgmt - Molex Incorporated; *pg.* 655, *pg.* 628
Tanis, David, Dir-Strategic Mktg - CommScope, Inc.; *pg.* 278, *pg.* 1378
Tank, Jen, Dir-Creative-Floral Brands - Provide Commerce, Inc.; *pg.* 1276, *pg.* 206
Tank, Jitesh, Sr Dir-Strategy & Bus Dev-CRDM - Medtronic, Inc.; *pg.* 1564, *pg.* 939
Tank, Vikram, Mgr-Product Mktg - Google Inc.; *pg.* 1249, *pg.* 153
Tankersley, Lauren, Brand Mgr - The WhiteWave Foods Company; *pg.* 1037, *pg.* 324
Tanki, Frank, Exec VP-Brand Mktg & Creative - Spike TV; *pg.* 310, *pg.* 1295
Tanko, Diane, VP-Creative Grp - Henry Schein, Inc.; *pg.* 1541, *pg.* 1180
Tann, Daphne, Assoc Product Mgr - MicroStrategy, Inc.; *pg.* 1266, *pg.* 1809
Tanna, Naresh H., Brand Mgr-Oncology Mktg-Global - Eli Lilly and Company; *pg.* 1527, *pg.* 684
Tannenbaum, Hope R., Dir-Customer Engagement Mktg - American Express Company; *pg.* 712, *pg.* 1190
Tannenholtz, Jackelyn, Mgr-Adv - LVMH Inc.; *pg.* 9, *pg.* 1254
Tanner, Amy, Mgr-Mktg Comm - The Lubrizol Corporation; *pg.* 1171, *pg.* 1481
Tanner, Bill, Sr Dir-Strategic Res & Consumer Insights - The Dallas Morning News Co.; *pg.* 1633, *pg.* 1679
Tanner, Catherine, Sr Mgr-Shopper Mktg-Big Heart Pet Brands - Del Monte Foods, Inc.; *pg.* 852, *pg.* 304
Tanner, Christy, Sr VP & Gen Mgr-Media Grp - CBS Interactive, Inc.; *pg.* 369, *pg.* 215
Tanner, David, VP & Program Mgr-Mktg - Wells Fargo & Company; *pg.* 819, *pg.* 232
Tanner, Glenn E., CMO & Exec VP - ITT Educational Services, Inc.; *pg.* 603, *pg.* 675
Tanner, James, Head-Bus Dev & Sls-Global - MORNINGSTAR, INC.; *pg.* 784, *pg.* 583
Tanner, Scott, Corp VP-Sls - Cedar Fair, L.P.; *pg.* 537, *pg.* 1471
Tannous, Carol, Sr Mgr - Deloitte & Touche USA LLP; *pg.* 743, *pg.* 1222
Tannoux, Pierre, Dir-Mktg - Henkel Corporation; *pg.* 1049, *pg.* 369
Tannoux, Pierre, Dir-Mktg - Henkel Corporation; *pg.* 1165, *pg.* 1535
Tanov, Erica, Owner, Dir-Creative & Designer - Erica Tanov Inc.; *pg.* 24, *pg.* 46
Tansey, Hugh, Global Product Dir-Centrifugation - Thermo Fisher Scientific Inc.; *pg.* 1431, *pg.* 854
Tansey, Joe, Engr-Technical Mktg - Cisco Systems, Inc.; *pg.* 372, *pg.* 240
Tansor, Kimberly, Mgr-Adv - Aldi Food Inc.; *pg.* 1013, *pg.* 556
Tant, Kasey, Mgr-Field Mktg - Denny's, Inc.; *pg.* 1725, *pg.* 1622
Tanzer, Jeff, Sr Dir-Season Ticket Sls & Svc - Tampa Bay Rays Baseball, Ltd.; *pg.* 586, *pg.* 464
Tao Go, Nancy, VP-Brand Mktg - Wayfair LLC; *pg.* 1288, *pg.* 801
Tapangan, Kisha, Mgr-Social Media Strategy & Digital Mktg - Houghton Mifflin Harcourt Publishing Company; *pg.* 1651, *pg.* 796
Tapia, Claudia, VP-Corp Comm & PR - Delphi Automotive LLP; *pg.* 204, *pg.* 910
Tapia, Joe, Sr Mgr-Intl Compensation-Latin America - Wal-Mart Stores, Inc.; *pg.* 1790, *pg.* 29
Tapkas, Gabi, Coord-Corp Sls, Sponsors & Events - Baltimore Orioles, L.P.; *pg.* 532, *pg.* 755
Tapley, John, Sr Product Mgr-Innovations & New Ventures - eBay Inc.; *pg.* 1240, *pg.* 243
Tapp, Paul, Mgr-Global Mktg-Intel RealSense Tech - Intel Corporation; *pg.* 645, *pg.* 266
Tapp, Scott, Exec VP-Sls & Mktg - Premiere Global Services, Inc.; *pg.* 1275, *pg.* 518
Tappen, Henry, Product Mgr - DoubleClick, Inc.; *pg.* 1239, *pg.* 1225
Tapply, Donna, Specialist-Mktg-USIG Mktg - Massachusetts Mutual Life Insurance Company; *pg.* 1207, *pg.* 845
Tappy, Dawn, Mgr-Mktg-Healthcare Svcs - Humana, Inc.; *pg.* 1204, *pg.* 734
Tapscott, Claudia, Acct Mgr-Adv - Graham Holdings Company; *pg.* 1645, *pg.* 1773
Tapu, Dragos, Program Mgr-Mktg-Worldwide - Hewlett-Packard Company; *pg.* 404, *pg.* 175
Taradash, Randy, Dir-Sls & Strategic Partnerships - American Conservatory Theatre; *pg.* 528, *pg.* 212
Tarallo, Matthew, Sr Mgr-Channel Plng & Dev - The Coca-Cola Company; *pg.* 240, *pg.* 493
Tarantello, Nicole, Assoc Dir-Mktg Immunoscience - Bristol-Myers Squibb Company; *pg.* 1509, *pg.* 1206
Tarantik, Sven, Dir-Digital Brand Mktg-ECommerce - Kohl's Corporation; *pg.* 1775, *pg.* 1870
Tardio, David, Dir-Adv Sls - Discovery Communications, Inc.; *pg.* 282, *pg.* 777
Tare, Sandeep, Mgr-Mktg & Ops-Industrial Sys - Texas Instruments Incorporated; *pg.* 679, *pg.* 1688
Taricco, Terri, VP-Mktg - Helen of Troy L.P.; *pg.* 511, *pg.* 1692
Tarini, Pam, Sr Mgr-Mktg Ops - Software AG, Inc.; *pg.* 471, *pg.* 1799
Tariq, Musa, Dir-Digital Mktg-Apple Retail - Apple Inc.; *pg.* 350, *pg.* 73
Tarkey, Cathy A., Dir-Mktg Comm & Acct Mgr-Strategic - Sherwin Williams; *pg.* 1448, *pg.* 1436
Tarkington, Shawn, Exec Dir-Production - ABC Cable Networks Group; *pg.* 268, *pg.* 51
Tarkoff, Dan, VP-Sls - Middle Atlantic Products Inc.; *pg.* 1360, *pg.* 1065
Tarlowe, Erica, Mgr-Digital Mktg - Nestle USA, Inc.; *pg.* 883, *pg.* 96
Tarnai, Andreas, Dir-Global Mktg-Denture Care & Dry Mouth - GlaxoSmithKline Consumer Healthcare; *pg.* 510, *pg.* 1554
Tarnofsky, Laura L., Mgr-Product & Mktg - LexisNexis Corporate Affiliations; *pg.* 1658, *pg.* 1095
Tarpey, Erinn, VP-Mktg - iCIMS, Inc.; *pg.* 411, *pg.* 1083
Tarpy, Rachel, Sr Dir-Consumer Mktg - The Cartoon Network; *pg.* 273, *pg.* 492
Tarr, Kate, Mgr-Mktg - CACI International Inc.; *pg.* 367, *pg.* 1773
Tarrell, Ev, Dir-Mdsg - Cabela's Incorporated; *pg.* 535, *pg.* 1019
Tarricone, Dana, Sr Mgr-Mktg - Under Armour, Inc.; *pg.* 49, *pg.* 759
Tartabini, Dan, VP-Sls & Mktg - M/I Homes, Inc.; *pg.* 95, *pg.* 1441
Tartaglia, Gabriel, VP-Sls - Pandora Media Inc.; *pg.* 1273, *pg.* 172
Tarzian, Kelley C., Mgr-Media Rels - Macy's, Inc.; *pg.* 1778, *pg.* 1417
Tarzon, Karen, Sr Mgr-Integrated Mktg & Brand Dev - United States Cellular Corporation; *pg.* 1875, *pg.* 594
Tas, Robert, CMO - Pegasystems Inc.; *pg.* 453, *pg.* 809
Tash, Davi, Mgr-Mdsg & Display - Energizer Holdings, Inc.; *pg.* 637, *pg.* 996
Tash, Eric, Mgr-Social Media - Prestige Brands Holdings, Inc.; *pg.* 520, *pg.* 1345
Tasher, Christine, Dir-PR - GEICO Corporation; *pg.* 1200, *pg.* 399
Tashjian, David, VP-Sls & Mktg - Comcast Corporation; *pg.* 276, *pg.* 1560
Tasi, John, Product Mgr-Government & Military - David Clark Company Incorporated; *pg.* 633, *pg.* 862
Tassinari, Noreen P., Dir-Mktg - Eastern States Exposition; *pg.* 992, *pg.* 857
Tasso, Maria, Sr Mgr-Mktg-DACH - Expedia, Inc.; *pg.* 1244, *pg.* 1814
Tassone, Megan, Asst Mgr-Social Media - Boulder Brands, Inc.; *pg.* 1016, *pg.* 310
Tassos, Kelly, Assoc Dir-Adv - Cincinnati Business Courier; *pg.* 1627, *pg.* 1411
Tatarsky, Marc, Dir-Mktg-Life Sciences R&D, MedTech - Accenture; *pg.* 1392, *pg.* 1186
Tataseo, Frank, Exec VP-Pro Products, Mergers & Acq, Partnerships & IT - The Clorox Company; *pg.* 327, *pg.* 169
Tate, Andrew, Sr Mgr-Participant Svcs Mktg - Teachers Insurance & Annuity Association - College Retirement Equities Fund; *pg.* 1219, *pg.* 1297
Tate, Bill, Sr VP-Mktg - Transamerica Insurance & Investment Group; *pg.* 1219, *pg.* 141
Tate, Dina C., Head-B2B Global Digital Mktg - MasterCard Incorporated; *pg.* 779, *pg.* 1325
Tate, John, Dir-Sls & Mktg - Graco, Inc.; *pg.* 1342, *pg.* 935
Tate, Maureen, Mgr-Agent Channel Co-op Adv - United States Cellular Corporation; *pg.* 1875, *pg.* 594
Tate, Nick, Mgr-Brand Mktg - BROOKDALE SENIOR LIVING INC.; *pg.* 1511, *pg.* 1627
Tate, Patalia, VP-Creative Strategy &Mktg - Scripps Networks Interactive, Inc.; *pg.* 1279, *pg.* 1638
Tate, Stacey, VP & Mgr-Digital Mktg Channel - Bank of America Corporation; *pg.* 718, *pg.* 1362
Tatge, David, Head-Issuer Mktg-US Reg - MasterCard Incorporated; *pg.* 779, *pg.* 1325
Tatoris, Melissa, Sr Dir-Mktg - Ulta Salon, Cosmetics & Fragrance, Inc.; *pg.* 524, *pg.* 559
Tatro, Alicia, Dir-Regulatory Adv & Promo Policy - GlaxoSmithKline; *pg.* 1536, *pg.* 1389
Tatta, Ben, Pres-Sls-Cablevision Media - Cablevision Systems Corporation; *pg.* 272, *pg.* 1141
Tattersall, David, Product Mgr-Google Maps - Google Inc.; *pg.* 1249, *pg.* 153
Tatum, Steve, VP-Mktg - Baylor Health Care System; *pg.* 1500, *pg.* 1676
Tatum, Walt, Sr VP-North American Sls - PlayNetwork, Inc.; *pg.* 577, *pg.* 1829
Taub, Carla M., Sr Mgr-Employee Comm & Engagement - Hologic, Inc.; *pg.* 1416, *pg.* 784
Taub, Justin, Brand Mgr - Wm. Wrigley Jr. Company; *pg.* 1863, *pg.* 596
Tauber, Hayes, Sr VP-Mktg - National Geographic Channel; *pg.* 299, *pg.* 402
Tauer, Melissa, Mgr-Brand Mktg-Holiday - Target Corporation; *pg.* 1786, *pg.* 942
Tauer, Rich, VP-Bus Ops & Quality Bicycle Products - Quality Bicycle Products; *pg.* 1710, *pg.* 918
Taugner, Bill, Mgr-Mktg-North America - Vital Images, Inc.; *pg.* 1607, *pg.* 950
Tauvaa, Junior, Sr VP-Sls & Svcs - Anaheim/Orange County Visitor & Convention Bureau; *pg.* 988, *pg.* 42
Tavella, MinJung, Dir-Sls Strategy, Sls Plng, Sls Ops, Trade & Trng - The Kraft Heinz Company; *pg.* 871, *pg.* 641
Taveras, Ramil, Engr-Sls-Programmatic - Tremor Video; *pg.* 682, *pg.* 1305
Tawfall, Eric, Asst VP & Reg Product Mgr - Horace Mann Companies; *pg.* 1203, *pg.* 662
Tay, Michael, Product Mgr-Pavilion - Rockwell Automation, Inc.; *pg.* 668, *pg.* 1880
Tayler, Glenn, Mgr-Adv & Mktg - General Motors Company; *pg.* 175, *pg.* 881
Taylor Old, Dana, Brand Mgr-Product Mktg - Red Bull North America, Inc.; *pg.* 264, *pg.* 275
Taylor, Aaron, Sr VP-Mktg - ESPN, Inc.; *pg.* 285, *pg.* 340
Taylor, Adam, Mgr-Mktg - GlaxoSmithKline; *pg.* 1536, *pg.* 1389
Taylor, Alison, Sr VP-Sls - Starwood Hotels & Resorts Worldwide, Inc.; *pg.* 1114, *pg.* 378
Taylor, Amy, VP-Mktg - Red Bull North America, Inc.; *pg.* 264,

First page reference indicates Business Class Edition
Second page reference indicates Geographic Edition

pg. 275
Taylor, Andrew, VP-PR - Burberry Limited; pg. 20, pg. 1208
Taylor, Angela, Sr Mgr-Promos & Pkg - PepsiCo, Inc.; pg. 259, pg. 1327
Taylor, Bill, Sr Mgr-Engrg - Cisco Systems, Inc.; pg. 372, pg. 240
Taylor, Brandi, Mgr-Online Mktg - Hotels.com, L.P.; pg. 1257, pg. 1682
Taylor, Brendan, Dir-Mktg - Seventh Generation, Inc.; pg. 335, pg. 1765
Taylor, Brian, Analyst-Mktg Process & Specialist-Comm - The Progressive Corporation; pg. 1214, pg. 1463
Taylor, Carl, VP-US Channel Sls - Oki Data Americas, Inc.; pg. 449, pg. 1090
Taylor, Chad, Product Mgr-Computers, Tablets & Accessories - Abt Electronics, Inc.; pg. 612, pg. 614
Taylor, Chase, Sr Mgr-Digital Mktg - NIKE, Inc.; pg. 1812, pg. 1492
Taylor, Chris, Sr VP-Mktg - 1-800-Flowers.com, Inc.; pg. 1758, pg. 1151
Taylor, Chris, Sr Product Mgr - Entrust, Inc.; pg. 393, pg. 1680
Taylor, Chris, Mgr-Mktg Comm-MEP Div - Trimble Navigation Limited; pg. 1384, pg. 288
Taylor, Christina, Sr Dir-Brand Mgmt - Marriott International, Inc.; pg. 1102, pg. 764
Taylor, Cindy, Mgr-Mktg - Mitchell Gold & Bob Williams; pg. 935, pg. 1391
Taylor, Claire, Exec VP & Dir-Creative Strategy - Carpenter Co.; pg. 920, pg. 1801
Taylor, Colin, Dir-Sls - Legg Mason, Inc.; pg. 775, pg. 758
Taylor, Courtney, Sr Assoc Mgr-Mktg - Capital One Financial Corporation; pg. 730, pg. 1789
Taylor, David B., VP-Mktg-Global - Siemens PLM Software; pg. 469, pg. 1734
Taylor, Elena, Mgr-Customer Team Mktg - The Procter & Gamble Company; pg. 1129, pg. 1418
Taylor, Gail, Brand Mgr-Shopper Mktg - Energizer Holdings, Inc.; pg. 637, pg. 996
Taylor, Geoff, Specialist-Digital Mktg - Jo-Ann Stores LLC; pg. 696, pg. 1455
Taylor, Greg, Dir-Production - Los Angeles Dodgers Inc.; pg. 559, pg. 135
Taylor, Gregory, Mgr-Mktg Info - Armstrong World Industries, Inc.; pg. 914, pg. 1545
Taylor, James, Dir-Creative-Global - Chevron Corporation; pg. 974, pg. 259
Taylor, Jamie J., Sr VP-Product Mktg-The Home Depot - Citigroup Inc.; pg. 735, pg. 1212
Taylor, Janelle, Mgr-Mktg - Cellco Partnership; pg. 1869, pg. 1042
Taylor, Janelle, Mgr-Mktg - Verizon Communications Inc.; pg. 1875, pg. 1309
Taylor, Jason, Sr Product Mgr-Skylanders - Activision Blizzard, Inc.; pg. 948, pg. 271
Taylor, Jeff, VP-Sls & Customer Strategic Mktg - Hasbro, Inc.; pg. 954, pg. 1603
Taylor, Jeff, Acct Exec-Media Sls - National Football League; pg. 567, pg. 1264
Taylor, Jim, Sr VP-Product Dev & Innovation - Arby's Restaurant Group, Inc.; pg. 1014, pg. 488
Taylor, Jim, Sr VP-Product Dev & Innovation - Darden Restaurants, Inc.; pg. 1724, pg. 453
Taylor, Joan, Mgr-Internal Sls - T&S Brass & Bronze Works, Inc.; pg. 114, pg. 1623
Taylor, John, Corp VP-Global Corp Mktg - Advanced Micro Devices, Inc.; pg. 613, pg. 282
Taylor, John, VP-Mktg - Carowinds; pg. 537, pg. 1364
Taylor, John, Mgr-Creative Svcs - Cedar Fair, L.P.; pg. 537, pg. 1471
Taylor, John, Asst VP-Creative Strategy & Brand Mgmt - Georgia Institute Of Technology; pg. 602, pg. 506
Taylor, Joy, Sr Dir-Media Strategy & Ops - Electronic Arts Inc.; pg. 951, pg. 189
Taylor, Kari, VP-Territory Sls - W.W. Grainger, Inc.; pg. 1390, pg. 625
Taylor, Karin, Mgr-PR - Altera Corporation; pg. 348, pg. 237
Taylor, Kasey, Coord-Creative Mktg - AMERICAN TIRE DISTRIBUTORS HOLDINGS, INC.; pg. 199, pg. 1379
Taylor, Kate, Specialist-Search Mktg - MSC Industrial Direct Co., Inc.; pg. 1057, pg. 1181
Taylor, Kevin, VP-Mktg & Program Mgmt - Cardinal Health, Inc.; pg. 1512, pg. 1448
Taylor, Kristen, Brand Mgr-Mktg - NIKE, Inc.; pg. 1812, pg. 1492
Taylor, Kristin, Sr Dir-Internal Comm - Citrix Systems, Inc.; pg. 375, pg. 424
Taylor, Lauren, VP & Div Mgr-Mdse - Bergdorf Goodman, Inc.; pg. 1761, pg. 1202
Taylor, Lauren, Acct Mgr-Affiliate Mktg - Groupon, Inc.; pg. 1255, pg. 575
Taylor, Lisa, Sr Dir-PR-Global - Feld Entertainment, Inc.; pg. 547, pg. 458
Taylor, Lisa, Sr Mgr-Contract Mktg - Staples; pg. 474, pg. 313
Taylor, Liz, Mgr-Corp Mktg Comm - Rochester Midland Corporation; pg. 334, pg. 1337
Taylor, Mark, Mgr-Mktg-Gas Chromatography Products - Shimadzu Scientific Instruments, Inc.; pg. 1428, pg. 768
Taylor, Matthew, Product Mgr - American Automobile Association; pg. 1190, pg. 429
Taylor, Melissa, Media Planner & Media Buyer - Affinity Gaming LLC; pg. 526, pg. 1022
Taylor, Melissa, Analyst-Mktg - Six Flags Entertainment Corporation; pg. 583, pg. 1698
Taylor, Meryl, Sr Dir-Product Dev - C.R. Gibson, LLC; pg. 1631, pg. 1650
Taylor, Mick, Mgr-Sls - Reliable Automatic Sprinkler Co., Inc.; pg. 1137, pg. 1158
Taylor, Mike, VP-Sls-Muni Markets - Honeywell International Inc.; pg. 407, pg. 1088
Taylor, Mike, Dir-Mktg & Data Analytics - Roto-Rooter, Inc.; pg. 108, pg. 1425
Taylor, Milt, Dir-Sls-Dairy Portland-Seattle & North California - Unified Grocers, Inc.; pg. 1036, pg. 66
Taylor, Mitch, Sr Mgr-Solution Mktg & Portfolio Mgmt - Cisco Systems, Inc.; pg. 372, pg. 240
Taylor, Monique, Mgr-Product Mgmt - Canadian Imperial Bank of Commerce; pg. 729, pg. 1935
Taylor, Peter, Dir-Product Mgmt-WeMo - Belkin International, Inc.; pg. 361, pg. 182
Taylor, Preston, Sr Mgr-Comml Products-Lenovo Brazil - Lenovo Group Ltd; pg. 427, pg. 1384
Taylor, Rebecca, Creative Dir-Rebecca Taylor - Kellwood Company; pg. 28, pg. 975
Taylor, Rob, Dir-Loyalty Mktg - La Quinta Corporation; pg. 1099, pg. 1722
Taylor, Rob, Dir-Loyalty Mktg - La Quinta Inns, Inc.; pg. 1100, pg. 1722
Taylor, Robert L., Head-Sls & Mktg Integration-Global - Eaton Corporation; pg. 1331, pg. 1429
Taylor, Russell, VP-Corp Mktg-UK - Samsung Electronics America, Inc.; pg. 669, pg. 1115
Taylor, Ryan, Product Mgr - BASF Corporation; pg. 1149, pg. 1066
Taylor, Seckeita, Dir-Mktg - Frito-Lay North America, Inc.; pg. 1853, pg. 1730
Taylor, Silvia, Sr VP-IR, PR & Corp Comm - Sucampo Pharmaceuticals, Inc.; pg. 1599, pg. 765
Taylor, Stacey, Mgr-Digital Mktg - The J.M. Smucker Company; pg. 865, pg. 1468
Taylor, Stephanie, Dir-Digital Mktg-Global - CyberSource Corporation; pg. 381, pg. 216
Taylor, Steven J., VP-Foodservice Sls - J&J Snack Foods Corporation; pg. 865, pg. 1107
Taylor, Sydney, Dir-Mktg-Global - The Coca-Cola Company; pg. 240, pg. 493
Taylor, Tammy, Sr Mgr-Customer Experience & Mktg - Southwest Airlines Co.; pg. 1923, pg. 1687
Taylor, Tom, Sr VP-Sls & Mktg - O.F. Mossberg & Sons, Inc.; pg. 1842, pg. 360
Taylor, Tonya, Specialist-Mktg - BlueLinx Holdings, Inc.; pg. 70, pg. 491
Taylor, Van, Asst VP-Shopper Mktg, Plng & Dev - The Coca-Cola Company; pg. 240, pg. 493
Taylor, Whitney, Assoc-Mktg - Diageo North America Inc.; pg. 248, pg. 1223
Taylor, Zak, Specialist-Inside Sls - Southern Lumber & Millwork Corp.; pg. 112, pg. 1613
Tayur, Sushma, Specialist-Mktg - FedEx Corporation; pg. 1907, pg. 1642
Tchakarov, Svetlin, Dir-Sls-Catalyst Franchise-East - Diageo North America, Inc.; pg. 1961, pg. 361
Tchao, Michel, VP-Product Mktg - Apple Inc.; pg. 350, pg. 73
Teachey, Michael, VP-Mktg - House of Raeford Farms, Inc.; pg. 864, pg. 1386
Teague, Michele, Gen Mgr-Mktg - Kmart Corporation; pg. 1775, pg. 617
Teague, Shawn, VP-Sls & Mktg-US & Intl - Multi-Metals; pg. 1363, pg. 737
Teague, Tracy, VP & Category Dir-Creative-Basketball - NIKE, Inc.; pg. 1812, pg. 1492
Teal, Melissa, Analyst-Sls Ops & Mktg - Bridgestone Americas, Inc.; pg. 201, pg. 1649
Teare, Nick, Sr Dir-Brand & Field Mktg - The Ritz-Carlton Hotel Company LLC; pg. 1110, pg. 766
Teasdale, Esperanza, Sr Dir-Mktg - PepsiCo, Inc.; pg. 259, pg. 1327
Teasdale, Jenny, Sr Mgr-Mktg Engagement - Getty Images, Inc.; pg. 1645, pg. 1836
Teasley, John, Sr Mgr-Relationship-Natl Healthcare Grp - Fifth Third Bank, Indiana (Southern); pg. 753, pg. 678
Teaster, Michael, Sr VP-Sls-North America & Asia Pacific - Getty Images, Inc.; pg. 1645, pg. 1836
Teats, Aaron, CMO & VP - Anaheim Ducks Hockey Club, LLC; pg. 528, pg. 42
Tebbe, Allison, Sr Mgr-Mktg-Innovation - Safeway Inc.; pg. 1032, pg. 184
TeBockhorst, Teri Wood, VP-Mktg - Iowa Lottery; pg. 996, pg. 705
Techtmann, Lauren, Sr Specialist-Mktg - Epicor Software Corporation; pg. 393, pg. 110
Tedder, Stan, VP-Sls & Mktg - The Kenan Advantage Group, Inc.; pg. 1914, pg. 1408
Tedesco, Chris, Gen Mgr-Mktg - Reckitt Benckiser Inc.; pg. 1136, pg. 1105
Tedesco, Holly, VP-Mktg-Ann Taylor - Ann Inc.; pg. 18, pg. 1195
Tedesco, Kathleen, Dir-CRM & Channel Mktg - E*TRADE Financial Corporation; pg. 749, pg. 1230
Tedesco, Kristin, Mgr-Cinema Mktg - Dolby Laboratories, Inc.; pg. 284, pg. 217
Tedford, Thomas W., Pres-US Consumer & Office Products & Exec VP - ACCO Brands Corporation; pg. 340, pg. 626
Tedino, Joseph J., Sr Mgr-Employee Comm - The Boeing Company; pg. 225, pg. 567
Tedone, Michael, Exec VP-Natl Adv Sls & Direct Response Sls - Viacom Inc.; pg. 316, pg. 1310
Teehan, Geoff, Dir-Product Design - Facebook, Inc.; pg. 1245, pg. 143
Teele, Emily, Sr Planner-Mktg-West Elm - Williams-Sonoma, Inc.; pg. 1140, pg. 234
Teeluck, Tisha M., Dir-Geographic Recruitment Mktg-Global - Accenture; pg. 1392, pg. 1186
Teer, Linda, Mgr-Adv, Publ Production, Print & Digital - True Value Company; pg. 1065, pg. 592
Teeter, Daniel, Sr Mgr-Mktg-Amazon Periodicals - Amazon.com, Inc.; pg. 1226, pg. 1831
Teets O'Connor, Katie, Mgr-Digital Mktg - Sun Tan City, LLC; pg. 523, pg. 738
Teeven, Nancy, VP-Institutional Mktg - Teachers Insurance & Annuity Association - College Retirement Equities Fund; pg. 1219, pg. 1297
Tegeder, Kris, Product Mgr - Xtek, Inc.; pg. 1390, pg. 1427
Tegtmeier, Lindsay, Mgr-Sls & Mktg - State Farm Mutual Automobile Insurance Co.; pg. 1218, pg. 557
Tegtmeyer, Volker, Sr Mgr-Product & Solution Mktg - Cisco Systems, Inc.; pg. 372, pg. 240
Teh, Joanne, Brand Mgr-Michael Kors - Michael Kors (USA), Inc.; pg. 29, pg. 1260
Tehrani, Natalie, Sr Mgr-Bus Dev-Alliances & Mobile Applications - BlackBerry Limited; pg. 625, pg. 1947
Teiber, Todd, Sr VP-Specialty Sls - Craftmade International, Inc.; pg. 1295, pg. 1670
Teicher, Michael, Exec VP-Media Sls - Warner Bros. Entertainment Inc.; pg. 319, pg. 54
Teichman, Daniel, Sr Mgr-Product Mktg - Sonus Networks Inc.; pg. 1281, pg. 858
Teichmann, Susanne, Brand Mgr - Plantronics, Inc.; pg. 663, pg. 270
Teifeld, Tamar, VP-Interactive Mktg - Paramount Pictures Corporation; pg. 304, pg. 138
Teitt, Hannah, Sr Mgr-Mktg Automation - The McGraw-Hill Companies Inc.; pg. 1663, pg. 1257
Teixeira, Ana, Dir-Theater Mktg - Imax Corporation; pg. 1417, pg. 1926
Teixeira, Kathleen, Sr Dir-Govt Affairs - The American Gastroenterological Association; pg. 128, pg. 761
Teixeira, Paul, Dir-Mktg - Triad Speakers, Inc.; pg. 682, pg. 1507
Tejada, Luis, VP-Sls - Goya Foods, Inc.; pg. 859, pg. 1075
Tejada, Willie M., Sr VP & Gen Mgr-Emerging Products Bus Unit - Akamai Technologies, Inc.; pg. 1226, pg. 807
Tekle, Fenot, Head-Comm-Ads Monetization PR - LinkedIn Corporation; pg. 1262, pg. 160
Tekle, Kacie L., Mgr-Product & Market - Cardinal Health, Inc.;

pg. 1512, pg. 1448
Televik, Ian, Sr Mgr-Digital & Social Media - Kia Motors America Inc.; pg. 181, pg. 112
Telfer, Mark, Dir-Retirement Plan Investment Product Mktg - Teachers Insurance & Annuity Association - College Retirement Equities Fund; pg. 1219, pg. 1297
Tellache, Whitney, Mgr-Influencer Mktg - Toms Shoe's Inc; pg. 1821, pg. 276
Tellers, Alicia, Specialist-Mktg & Comm - Automation Devices, Inc.; pg. 1315, pg. 1532
Temenak, Amanda, Planner-Digital Media - AARP; pg. 124, pg. 393
Temes, Sam, Head-Global Product & Sls Strategy - Google Inc.; pg. 1249, pg. 153
Temistokle, Eddie, Sr Mgr-Corp Comm & CSR - Toshiba America, Inc.; pg. 681, pg. 1302
Temkin, Ashley, Program Mgr-Social Media - Citrix Systems, Inc.; pg. 375, pg. 424
Temkin, Judy, Dir-Multi-Platform Sls Res - BBC Worldwide America Inc.; pg. 271, pg. 1201
Tempesco, Larry, Sr VP-Sls & Mktg - Shop-Vac Corporation; pg. 1375, pg. 1595
Tempest, Andrew, Dir-Mktg - Calero Software, LLC; pg. 368, pg. 1333
Temple, Jeffery, Dir-Customer Insights Mktg & Mdsg - Fred Meyer Stores, Inc.; pg. 1769, pg. 1502
Temple, Thomas J., VP-Wood Products Div & Arkansas Resource - Potlatch Corporation; pg. 1467, pg. 1844
Templeton, Chantal, Dir-Sls Strategy - Mars Canada Inc.; pg. 1478, pg. 1918
Templin, Dan, Sr VP-Mediacom Bus - Mediacom Communications Corporation; pg. 653, pg. 1182
Temporale, Kendra, Mgr-Online Mktg - Royal Bank of Canada; pg. 800, pg. 1942
Ten Broek, Bryan, Sr VP-Resort Sls & Mktg - Interval Leisure Group, Inc.; pg. 1912, pg. 443
Ten Eyck, Linda, Sr VP-Sls Ops - Shiseido Cosmetics America of SAC; pg. 522, pg. 1291
Tencatie, Stephanie, Mgr-ECommerce Mktg - BJ's Wholesale Club, Inc.; pg. 1762, pg. 857
Tendam, Ronda, Brand Mgr-Div Sls - Marathon Petroleum Company LLC; pg. 981, pg. 1454
Tendick, Melissa, VP-Mktg - Barilla America, Inc.; pg. 839, pg. 555
Tenedini, Amanda, Mgr-Social Bus - International Business Machines Corporation; pg. 418, pg. 1138
Tener, Hampden, Product Dir-Cadillac - General Motors Company; pg. 175, pg. 881
Teng, Jean, Mgr-Offline Media - Hulu LLC; pg. 1257, pg. 274
Tenn, Peter, Mgr-Advanced Product Concept-Design - Subaru of America, Inc.; pg. 191, pg. 1050
Tennant, Matthew, Dir-Global Social-Global Brand Hub - McDonald's Corporation; pg. 1737, pg. 645
Tennesen, Zoe, Dir-Creative - Mannatech, Incorporated; pg. 1558, pg. 1671
Tenney, H. M., Program Mgr-Tech, Comm & Mktg Svcs Platform & Mgr-Dev-Global - Xerox Corporation; pg. 494, pg. 365
Tennison, Jerry, Reg Mgr-Sls - Campbell Wrapper Corporation; pg. 1454, pg. 1856
Tennison, Jon, Mgr-Mktg - Bluegreen Corporation; pg. 1082, pg. 410
Tennyson, Scott D., Sr Mgr-Regulatory CMC Compliance - Pfizer Inc.; pg. 1581, pg. 1278
Tenore, Brenna, Mgr-Sponsorship Mktg - Bose Corporation; pg. 626, pg. 820
Tenorio, Christie, Specialist-Hispanic Segment Mktg - The PNC Financial Services Group, Inc.; pg. 795, pg. 1579
Tenten, Geraldine, Dir-Mktg & Comm - IBM Canada Limited; pg. 411, pg. 1923
Tenuta, Alessandro, Brand Mgr - Johnson & Johnson Inc.; pg. 1552, pg. 1923
Tenzer, Marjorie C., VP-Mktg & Comm - International Business Machines Corporation; pg. 418, pg. 1138
Tepp, Tara, Specialist-Mktg Comm - Cytec Industries, Inc.; pg. 1155, pg. 1131
Tepper, Karen, VP-Mobile Product - The Priceline Group Inc.; pg. 1276, pg. 364
Terada, Amy, VP-Mktg - Pleasant Holidays LLC; pg. 1919, pg. 307
Tercek, Tom, VP-Digital Strategy & Products - Madison Square Garden Network; pg. 297, pg. 1255
Terentjev, Andy, Sr Dir-Enterprise West - comScore, Inc; pg. 1236, pg. 1798
Terfehr, Doug, Dir-PR, Comm & Corp Social Responsibility - Pizza Hut, Inc.; pg. 1744, pg. 1733
Terlep, Bob, VP-Automotive Grp & Mgr-Mktg - Flambeau, Inc.; pg. 1336, pg. 1854
Terlep, Jeff, VP-Mktg & Product Plng - Blue Bird Corporation; pg. 1705, pg. 532
Terlep, Joanne, Sr Mgr-Comm - General Dynamics Corporation; pg. 228, pg. 1781
Ternes, Peter, Strategist-Social Media & Corp Reputation - General Motors Company; pg. 175, pg. 881
Terr, Brian, VP-Sls & Bus Dev - Edmunds, Inc.; pg. 1241, pg. 273
Terranova, John M., VP-Sls-Americas - Gleason - M&M Precision Systems Corporation; pg. 1341, pg. 1479
Terrasas, Denise, Assoc Mgr-Direct Mktg - Intuit Inc.; pg. 769, pg. 158
Terrell Hernandez, Erica, Mgr-Ops-Channel Mktg - AliphCom, Inc.; pg. 616, pg. 212
Terrell, Jennifer, VP-Local Sls-North America - LivingSocial, Inc.; pg. 1264, pg. 401
Terrey, Karl, Product Mgr-Defense & Intelligence - Environmental Systems Research Institute Inc.; pg. 393, pg. 188
Terrick, Melissa, Sr Mgr-Mktg-Retail Mktg & Consumer Products - MATTEL, INC.; pg. 962, pg. 81
Terrill, John, Sr Mgr-Corp Comm - Red Hat, Inc.; pg. 460, pg. 1388
Terrill, Sacha, Program Mgr-Product Trng & Digital Mktg - Toyota Motor Sales, U.S.A., Inc.; pg. 193, pg. 296
Terry, Alicia, Mgr-Product Mktg-Sls Enablement - Cisco Systems, Inc.; pg. 372, pg. 240
Terry, Amanda, Specialist-Direct Response Mktg - Twitter, Inc.; pg. 1285, pg. 228
Terry, Bentina, VP-Customer Svc & Sls - Gulf Power Company; pg. 1944, pg. 458
Terry, Diana, VP-Brand Dev & Corp Mktg - Univision Communications Inc.; pg. 683, pg. 1307
Terry, Howard, Sr VP-Mktg - Golden Franchising Corporation; pg. 1730, pg. 1736
Terry, Myron K., Sr Dir - Pfizer Inc.; pg. 1581, pg. 1278
Terry, Psalm, Product Mgr-Mobile - Alaska Air Group, Inc.; pg. 1897, pg. 1830
Tersigni, Elena, Dir-Creative Comm & Design, Mktg Promo & Comm - Manulife Financial Corporation; pg. 778, pg. 1939
Tertel, Joe, Mgr-Mktg-E-Commerce - Rite Aid Corporation; pg. 1590, pg. 1519
Tervo, Sara, Sr VP-Mktg & Creative Svcs - Victoria's Secret Stores, LLC; pg. 1789, pg. 1471
Terwedow, Cathy, Mgr-Mktg Programs - Mentor Graphics Corporation; pg. 432, pg. 1510
Teryek, Mary, Dir-Mktg-Skincare Div - Valeant Pharmaceuticals International; pg. 1605, pg. 1047
Teshera, Matt, Sr Product Dev Mgr-Ad Targeting & Big Data - AT&T; pg. 1865, pg. 258
Teske, Kirk, VP-Fresh-cut Sls & Ops-North America - FRESH DEL MONTE PRODUCE INC.; pg. 856, pg. 418
Teske, Steve, Dir-Field Mktg - The Boeing Company; pg. 225, pg. 567
Teslenko, Olia, Coord-Sls Svc - Unette Corporation; pg. 1184, pg. 1114
Tessier, Jim, Product Mgr - Eaton Corporation; pg. 1331, pg. 1429
Testamark, Ayana, Mgr-Mktg Bus Analytics - DIRECTV Group Holdings, LLC; pg. 281, pg. 79
Testani, Melanie, Mgr-PR - Toyota Canada, Inc.; pg. 192, pg. 1934
Tester, Bill, Sr Dir-Centralized Supervision - Ameriprise Financial, Inc.; pg. 715, pg. 930
Tetrault, P. Jaime, Dir-Product Support & Asset Intelligence-Marine Power Sys - Caterpillar, Inc.; pg. 1321, pg. 650
Tetreault, Bruce, Dir-Mktg, Arm & Hammer Laundry Products - Church & Dwight Co., Inc.; pg. 1153, pg. 1063
Tetro, Brendan, Controller-Adv & Mktg Comm-Global - Ford Motor Company; pg. 172, pg. 876
Tetserawati, Tanya, Dir-Consumer Mktg - R.J. Reynolds Tobacco Co.; pg. 1895, pg. 1395
Tetuan, Michael, Sr Dir-Media Rels - Teachers Insurance & Annuity Association - College Retirement Equities Fund; pg. 1219, pg. 1297
Tevah, Harvey, Mgr-Sls - Robb & Stucky, Ltd.; pg. 941, pg. 428
Teves, Juliana, Brand Mgr-Ana Maria - Bimbo Bakeries USA; pg. 840, pg. 151
Tevlowitz, Janna, Sr Analyst-Sls Ops - WebMD Health Corporation; pg. 1288, pg. 1313
Tew, Ronald, Product Mgr-Line Mktg - Deere & Company; pg. 703, pg. 632
Texido, Lisa, Brand Mgr - Labatt USA LLC; pg. 254, pg. 1149
Tezanos, Millie, VP-Mktg-Univision Television Group - Univision Communications Inc.; pg. 683, pg. 1307
Thabet, Donna, Mgr-Sls Comm & Support - United States Postal Service; pg. 1009, pg. 406
Thach, Pat, Mgr-Production - Travel Industry Association of America; pg. 158, pg. 405
Thacher, Brad, Brand Mgr-Quality - General Motors Company; pg. 175, pg. 881
Thacker, Brad, Sr Dir-Parts Quality Engrg-North America - Nissan North America, Inc.; pg. 186, pg. 1633
Thacker, Carrie, Dir-Corp & Media Comm - American Heart Association Inc.; pg. 128, pg. 1673
Thacker, David, VP-Product - LinkedIn Corporation; pg. 1262, pg. 160
Thacker, Michael, Dir-Corp Media Rels - Hewlett-Packard Company; pg. 404, pg. 175
Thacker, Michael, Dir-Corp PR - VMware, Inc.; pg. 490, pg. 179
Thaens, Volker, Sr VP-Product & Brand Mgmt-North America - BSH Home Appliances Corporation; pg. 53, pg. 108
Thakkar, Deepak, Sr Dir-Strategic Mktg - Flextronics International Ltd.; pg. 81, pg. 245
Thakker, Kapil, Head-Global Digital IT-Mktg Analytics & Measurement - Johnson & Johnson; pg. 1549, pg. 1091
Thakurdesai, Shailesh, Mgr-Strategic Mktg - Texas Instruments Incorporated; pg. 679, pg. 1688
Thall, Barbara Ward, Sr VP-Brand Mktg-Global - Audible, Inc.; pg. 1230, pg. 1095
Thames, Dorothy, Specialist-Digital Mktg - Visit Florida Inc.; pg. 1010, pg. 470
Thaney, Robyn, Sr Specialist-Adv & Brand Comm - Cancer Treatment Centers of America; pg. 1511, pg. 410
Thankappan, Sharad, VP-Product Mgmt - Oracle Corporation; pg. 450, pg. 191
Thankaswamy, Chitra, Dir-Mktg - Dell Inc.; pg. 383, pg. 1737
Tharnstrom, Jonathan, Reg Mgr-Sls - Archer-Daniels-Midland Company; pg. 825, pg. 565
Tharp, Christina, Mgr-Mktg Comm-Global - The Timken Company; pg. 218, pg. 1408
Tharpe, Richard, Mgr-Mktg - Sunsetter Products, LP; pg. 113, pg. 830
Tharrington, Jeannie, Sr Mgr-Comm-North America Feminine Care - The Procter & Gamble Company; pg. 1129, pg. 1418
Thatcher, Jennifer B., Mgr-Channel Mktg - AT&T; pg. 1865, pg. 258
Thatt, Larry, Mgr-Mktg & Advisory Mktg Svcs - FRANKLIN RESOURCES, INC.; pg. 760, pg. 254
Thaut, Stephanie, Sr Dir-Mobile & In-App Global Sls Strategy - Microsoft Corporation; pg. 435, pg. 1824
Thavenet, Jenny, Brand Mgr - Rust-Oleum Corporation; pg. 1447, pg. 664
Thawley, Emily, Sr Mgr-Product Mktg - HomeAway, Inc.; pg. 1911, pg. 1663
Thayer, David, Coord-Sls - The Boston Globe; pg. 1623, pg. 790
Thayer, Matthew, Brand Mgr-Red Lobster - Olive Garden Italian Restaurant; pg. 1742, pg. 454
Thayer, Michael T., Bus Mgr - Dillard's, Inc.; pg. 1766, pg. 34
Thayer, Ron, Dir-Adv - Marin Independent Journal; pg. 1661, pg. 258
Thaysen, Jonas, Strategist-Creative Shop - Facebook, Inc.; pg. 1245, pg. 143
Theile, Lindsay E., Dir-Comm-Power Gen Products - General Electric Company; pg. 1297, pg. 347
Theiler, Abbey, Specialist-PR - Best Buy Co., Inc.; pg. 1761, pg. 954
Theiler, Matt, Sr VP-Sls - Boston Heart Diagnostics; pg. 1508, pg. 820
Theis, Daryl, Sr Mgr-Market-Specialty Crops - BASF Corporation; pg. 1149, pg. 1066
Theisen, Jeanne, Specialist-Principal Mktg Comm - Boston Scientific Corporation; pg. 1508, pg. 831
Theisen, Pete, VP-Mktg-Purina Animal Nutrition - Land O'Lakes, Inc.; pg. 873, pg. 915
Theiss, Kathleen N., Mgr-Mktg Svcs - Mylan, Inc.; pg. 1570, pg. 1520
Thelander, Michael A., Dir-Innovation & Strategic Mktg - Kinetic Concepts, Inc.; pg. 1553, pg. 1741
Thelen, Lauren, Mgr-Event Mktg - Adobe Systems Incorporated; pg. 342, pg. 235
Thelen, Leah, Dir-Interactive Mktg & ECommerce - L'Oreal USA; pg. 514, pg. 1252

Thelen, Peter, Mgr-Search & Tech Media - Cisco Systems, Inc.; pg. 372, pg. 240
Thell, Debbie, Sr Mgr-Mktg Comm - Medtronic, Inc.; pg. 1564, pg. 939
Thellen, Isabelle, Mgr-Pub Affairs & Media - Hydro-Quebec; pg. 1944, pg. 1955
Then, Maria, Sr Dir-Creative - Fossil Group, Inc.; pg. 5, pg. 1735
Theno, Meg, Sr Editor-Photo - Chicago Tribune Company; pg. 1627, pg. 570
Theobald, Stanley C., Sr Dir-Bus Dev - ASM International; pg. 132, pg. 1461
Theodore, Andrea, Head-Mktg - Naked Juice Company, Inc.; pg. 882, pg. 150
Theofila, Katerina, Sr Mgr-Creative Svcs - Glu Mobile Inc.; pg. 954, pg. 219
Theophilis, Mark, Sr Dir-Ad Products, Digital Ad Ops - A&E Television Networks, LLC; pg. 267, pg. 1185
Theos, James, VP-Mktg - Micron Corporation; pg. 654, pg. 840
Theran, Peter, VP-Global Consumer Products - 3D Systems Corporation; pg. 339, pg. 1621
Therios, Sofia, Sr Dir-Global Menu Strategy - McDonald's Corporation; pg. 1737, pg. 645
Therkalsen, Jim, Strategist-Creative-Facebook Creative Shop - Facebook, Inc.; pg. 1245, pg. 143
Theroff, Nicholas, Specialist-Gift Card Mktg - NIKE, Inc.; pg. 1812, pg. 1492
Therrien, Craig, Sr Product Mgr - Solidworks Corporation; pg. 472, pg. 815
Thesing, Christina, Mgr-Mktg - Evenflo Company, Inc.; pg. 924, pg. 1470
Thesing, Gina, Mgr-Brand & Digital Mktg - Cargill, Inc.; pg. 845, pg. 965
Thibaudeau, Elizabeth, VP-Mktg - Nu Skin Enterprises, Inc.; pg. 518, pg. 1755
Thibault, Bob, VP-Mktg - Palm Springs Desert Resorts Convention & Visitors Authority; pg. 1003, pg. 187
Thibault, Mary, Strategist-PR & Brand - IDEO, Inc.; pg. 411, pg. 178
Thiebaud, Allison, Mgr-Mktg Comm - Eaton Corporation; pg. 1331, pg. 1429
Thieken, Paul, Dir-Mktg - Cree Inc.; pg. 631, pg. 1371
Thiel, Andrew, Brand Mgr-Smart Ones - The Kraft Heinz Company; pg. 870, pg. 1577
Thiel, Dominic A., Dir-Mktg Svcs - Abbott Laboratories; pg. 1484, pg. 551
Thiel, Doug, Dir-Mktg-Wilson Golf - Wilson Sporting Goods Co.; pg. 1848, pg. 596
Thiel, Liz, Sr Dir-Assoc & Leadership Dev & Health Clinic Ops - Cerner Corporation; pg. 1514, pg. 981
Thiel, Mark, Mgr-Email & Social Media - Baker Knapp & Tubbs Inc.; pg. 916, pg. 566
Thiel, Ryan, Assoc Mgr-Online Mktg - Kohler Co.; pg. 91, pg. 1862
Thiel, Thorsten, Dir-Mktg Comm - Bruker Corporation; pg. 1511, pg. 788
Thiel, Wayne, Reg Mgr-Sls-N - Summit Plastic Co.; pg. 1470, pg. 1403
Thiele, Roger, VP-Mktg - BROOKDALE SENIOR LIVING INC.; pg. 1511, pg. 1627
Thielen, Jennifer, Asst Mgr-Mktg - Storck USA, L.P.; pg. 1862, pg. 591
Thielen, Maryellen, Sr Mgr-Fin Comm - The Allstate Corporation; pg. 1189, pg. 639
Thielman, Sarah, Sr Mgr-Design - The Procter & Gamble Company; pg. 1129, pg. 1418
Thieman, James, Product Mgr-Upstream Mktg - Olympus America Inc.; pg. 1425, pg. 1521
Thiemel, Jeanine, Sr Product Mgr-Leadership Bus Unit - SkillSoft plc; pg. 470, pg. 1037
Thien, Kelly, Mgr-Comm & Mktg - Ronald McDonald House Charities, Inc.; pg. 155, pg. 648
Thieneman, Kevin, Pres-Forest Products - Caterpillar, Inc.; pg. 1321, pg. 650
Thierer, Donn, Dir-Integrated Mktg - Advance Auto Parts, Inc.; pg. 197, pg. 1805
Thiffault, Thomas, Mgr-Mktg - The Carlyle Johnson Machine Company, L.L.C.; pg. 1321, pg. 339
Thirot, Olivier, Acting CFO & Sr VP - Kelly Services, Inc.; pg. 424, pg. 911
Thissen, Joanna, Mgr-Programmatic Adv - DISH Network Corporation; pg. 283, pg. 325
Thode, Glenn, Dir-Creative - Gartner, Inc.; pg. 1248, pg. 374
Thoen, Kristen K., Mgr-US Mktg-Acute Care & Acute Wound Care Products - 3M Company; pg. 1142, pg. 956
Thoman, Bobbi, Product Mgr & Mgr-Pur - Evaporated Metal Films Corp.; pg. 1412, pg. 1170
Thomas, Alan, Area Mgr-Sls - Community Coffee Company LLC; pg. 849, pg. 741
Thomas, Alyssa, Mgr-Multichannel Mktg - Wal-Mart Stores, Inc.; pg. 1790, pg. 29
Thomas, Amy E., Sr Mgr-Comm - Community Health Systems, Inc.; pg. 1516, pg. 1632
Thomas, Anne, Mgr-Mktg Comm-HumanaOne - Humana, Inc.; pg. 1204, pg. 734
Thomas, Aubyn, VP-Mktg & Consumer Intelligence - The ADT Corporation; pg. 612, pg. 409
Thomas, Barry, VP-Global Mktg & Innovation-Subway Global Team - The Coca-Cola Company; pg. 240, pg. 493
Thomas, Bill, Sr VP-Mktg - NTN Buzztime, Inc.; pg. 659, pg. 60
Thomas, Bill, Dir-Digital Mktg Dev - The Sun Products Corporation; pg. 336, pg. 385
Thomas, Brandi, Mgr-PR - Seventh Generation, Inc.; pg. 335, pg. 1765
Thomas, Brea, Sr Mgr-Mktg - Florida Panthers Hockey Club, Ltd.; pg. 548, pg. 469
Thomas, Brian, Mgr-Mktg Comm - Alcoa Inc.; pg. 65, pg. 1188
Thomas, Brian, Dir-Global Creative Content-Chevrolet Brand - General Motors Company; pg. 175, pg. 881
Thomas, Brittney, Mgr-Channel Partner Sls Americas-Bing Ads - Microsoft Corporation; pg. 435, pg. 1824
Thomas, Carol Ann, Mgr-Mktg - Alacra, Inc.; pg. 346, pg. 1188
Thomas, Chris, Dir-VCT Product Mgmt - BorgWarner Inc.; pg. 167, pg. 867
Thomas, Chuck, Dir-Creative - Cargill, Inc.; pg. 845, pg. 965
Thomas, Colleen, Mgr-Sls Ops - Oakhurst Dairy; pg. 887, pg. 752
Thomas, Colleen A., Assoc Planner-Mdse-Boy's - Macy's, Inc.; pg. 1778, pg. 1417
Thomas, Daniel, Sr Mgr-Program & Employee Dev-World Wide - Apple Inc.; pg. 350, pg. 73
Thomas, Danny, Gen Mgr-Sls - Nordco, Inc.; pg. 1365, pg. 1884
Thomas, Daryl, Sr VP-Sls & Mktg - Herr Foods Inc.; pg. 861, pg. 1557
Thomas, David, Sr Mgr-Customer Engagement - ASICS America Corporation; pg. 1826, pg. 106
Thomas, David, Sr Dir-Content & Engagement - salesforce.com, inc.; pg. 1278, pg. 226
Thomas, Deepak, Head-Mobile Product & Growth Strategy - SHUTTERFLY, INC.; pg. 1280, pg. 192
Thomas, Desirae, Mgr-Digital Mktg - Stewart & Stevenson, LLC; pg. 985, pg. 1715
Thomas, Elisa C., Exec Dir-Global Digital Mktg-Social & CRM - Clinique Laboratories LLC; pg. 503, pg. 1214
Thomas, Ellie, Dir-Interactive Mktg - Ameriprise Financial, Inc.; pg. 715, pg. 930
Thomas, Erik, Sr Mgr-Auto Shows & Events - Hyundai Motor America; pg. 179, pg. 89
Thomas, Floyd, Dir-Sls - Reliable Automatic Sprinkler Co., Inc.; pg. 1137, pg. 1158
Thomas, Frank, Dir-Sls - Comcast Corporation; pg. 276, pg. 1560
Thomas, Greg, Sr Dir - Cisco Systems, Inc.; pg. 372, pg. 240
Thomas, Hansley, Specialist-Community Mktg - Herr Foods Inc.; pg. 861, pg. 1557
Thomas, Heather M., Mgr-PR Event - Intel Corporation; pg. 645, pg. 266
Thomas, Henry, Dir-Brdcst & New Media - Panthers Football, LLC; pg. 573, pg. 1368
Thomas, Holly, Grp VP-Media Rels & Cause Mktg - Macy's East; pg. 1777, pg. 1254
Thomas, Jacob, Bus Dir-Sls-Crude, LPG & Petroleum Products - Union Pacific Corporation; pg. 1927, pg. 1018
Thomas, Jacob, Bus Dir-Sls-Crude, LPG & Petroleum Products - Union Pacific Railroad Company; pg. 1927, pg. 1019
Thomas, Jake, Dir-Product Mgmt-Residential - Generac Power Systems Inc.; pg. 1340, pg. 1898
Thomas, Jan, Mgr-Mktg-Chevy Racing - General Motors Company; pg. 175, pg. 881
Thomas, Jim, Sr Mgr-Market Intelligence & Res - Bayer CropScience; pg. 1149, pg. 981
Thomas, Jim, Mgr-Sls - ConsumerREVIEW, Inc.; pg. 1237, pg. 193
Thomas, Joey, Mgr-Media Rels - J.C. Penney Company, Inc.; pg. 1774, pg. 1732
Thomas, Jon, Mng Dir-Creative Svcs - Fruit of the Loom, Inc.; pg. 41, pg. 725
Thomas, Julian, Mgr-Mktg Comm - The Guild Inc.; pg. 1255, pg. 1866
Thomas, Kara, Sr Dir-Video Product Mgmt - Charter Communications, Inc.; pg. 274, pg. 372
Thomas, Katherine, Asst VP-Mktg Svcs - Protective Life Insurance Company; pg. 1215, pg. 4
Thomas, Kathy, VP & Div Mgr-Mdse - Belk, Inc.; pg. 1760, pg. 1364
Thomas, Kathy, Mgr-Sports Mktg - Cleveland Clinic; pg. 1516, pg. 1429
Thomas, Kathy Choe, Sr Mgr-Commodity & Supply Chain Mgmt - NetApp, Inc.; pg. 444, pg. 287
Thomas, Kelly, Mgr-Mktg-Centralized Mktg Dept - American Greetings Corporation; pg. 1615, pg. 1428
Thomas, Kelly, Chief Product Officer & Sr VP - JDA Software Group, Inc.; pg. 423, pg. 22
Thomas, Kevin D., Dir-Adv Sls - The New York Times; pg. 1668, pg. 1270
Thomas, Lanier, Sr Dir-Sls-Target Team - Georgia-Pacific LLC; pg. 1458, pg. 507
Thomas, Leslie, Mgr-Mktg - Rich Products Corporation; pg. 892, pg. 1150
Thomas, Linda, Dir-Digital & Social Media - Philadelphia Eagles Football Club, Inc.; pg. 575, pg. 1569
Thomas, Lou Ann, Exec Dir-Mktg - AMC, Inc.; pg. 1759, pg. 487
Thomas, Mary, Sr Mgr-Device Grp Partnerships & Events - Sony Corporation of America; pg. 675, pg. 1293
Thomas, Megan, Head-EIS Mktg - Owens Corning; pg. 102, pg. 1476
Thomas, Molly, Mgr-Mktg-Always & Tampax - The Procter & Gamble Company; pg. 1129, pg. 1418
Thomas, Nick, Sr Dir-Head-Gaming - Immersion Corporation; pg. 413, pg. 246
Thomas, Nikki, Sr Mgr-Adv - Microsoft Corporation; pg. 435, pg. 1824
Thomas, Paige, Exec VP & Gen Mgr-Mdse & Nordstrom Rack - Nordstrom, Inc.; pg. 1779, pg. 1837
Thomas, Patrick, Mgr-Product Mktg - Google Inc.; pg. 1249, pg. 153
Thomas, Peter, VP-US Sls - Linde Gas LLC; pg. 1356, pg. 1095
Thomas, Rachel Nyswander, VP-Govt Affairs & Exec Dir-Data-Driven Mktg Institute - The Direct Marketing Association Inc.; pg. 139, pg. 1224
Thomas, Randy, Reg Territory Mgr-Sls-Illinois - Flambeau, Inc.; pg. 1336, pg. 1854
Thomas, Rasheda, Dir-Adv Sls Mktg Bus Dev - Fox Sports Net; pg. 288, pg. 131
Thomas, Renee, VP-Mktg - Sonic Foundry, Inc.; pg. 472, pg. 1867
Thomas, Richard L., Sr VP-Sls & Mktg - Domtar Corporation; pg. 1456, pg. 1954
Thomas, Robert, Product Mgr-Men's Performance Apparel, Accessories & Socks - SmartWool; pg. 32, pg. 335
Thomas, Robin, Dir-Media-Chili's - Brinker International, Inc.; pg. 1718, pg. 1676
Thomas, Shaji, Dir-Sls & Mktg-Dubai - Hyatt Hotels Corporation; pg. 1096, pg. 577
Thomas, Todd, Specialist-Digital Mktg - Piaggio USA, Inc.; pg. 188, pg. 1282
Thomas, Tommy R, VP-Sls & Bus Dev - The H.T. Hackney Company; pg. 1023, pg. 1637
Thomas, Tracy, VP-Mktg - U.S. Premium Beef, LLC; pg. 907, pg. 987
Thomas, Vanessa, Head-Adv-Global Mktg Comm Grp - Bose Corporation; pg. 626, pg. 820
Thomas, Vince, Dir-Social Action Mktg - Intel Corporation; pg. 645, pg. 266
Thomas-Moore, Christopher, Sr Dir-ECommerce & Digital Mktg - Extended Stay Hotels LLC; pg. 1091, pg. 1622
Thomas-Reis, Kelley, Dir-Mktg - SMSC Enterprises; pg. 584, pg. 954
Thomason, Erskine, Mgr-Sls - Fairway Outdoor Advertising of the GSA; pg. 1640, pg. 1615
Thomassie, Brett, Dir-US Federal Civil Programs Sls - DigitalGlobe, Inc.; pg. 1408, pg. 333
Thomasson, Maxwell, Dir-Trading & Mktg-Global - CHS INC.; pg. 702, pg. 926
Thometz, Frank, Dir-Mktg - Tootsie Roll Industries, Inc.; pg. 1863, pg. 591
Thomlison, Lynn, VP-Mktg Comm & Creative - Anthem, Inc.;

pg. 1192, *pg.* 683
Thompsen, Sandra, Mgr-eMail Mktg-Enterprise Mktg - Farmers Group, Inc.; *pg.* 1199, *pg.* 130
Thompson, Aaron, Mgr-Sls-Natl - The Enkeboll Company; *pg.* 923, *pg.* 63
Thompson, Alex, VP & Mgr-Product & Intl Trade Svcs - Wells Fargo & Company; *pg.* 819, *pg.* 232
Thompson, Ann, Brand Mgr-Wood Care - Rust-Oleum Corporation; *pg.* 1447, *pg.* 664
Thompson, Ashley, Mgr-Mktg Comm - Blackbaud, Inc.; *pg.* 361, *pg.* 1613
Thompson, Ashley, Mgr-Online Mktg - Books-A-Million, Inc.; *pg.* 1623, *pg.* 2
Thompson, Bret, VP-Quality & Product Svcs - Lochinvar Corporation; *pg.* 1073, *pg.* 1640
Thompson, Brittany, Supvr-Preparation Program & Sls - GEICO Corporation; *pg.* 1200, *pg.* 399
Thompson, Bruce, Sr Product Mgr-M2M Solutions - AT&T Inc.; *pg.* 1867, *pg.* 1674
Thompson, Cedric, Mgr-Trade Mktg - Newell Rubbermaid Inc.; *pg.* 1128, *pg.* 515
Thompson, Chad, Sr Dir-Mktg & Product Mgmt-Global - Logitech Inc.; *pg.* 1264, *pg.* 164
Thompson, Chris, Sr Product Mgr - ADTRAN, Inc.; *pg.* 344, *pg.* 6
Thompson, Christian, Sr Dir-Shopper Insights - Kellogg Company; *pg.* 831, *pg.* 870
Thompson, Cindy, Sr Mgr-Event Mktg-Global Mktg & Comm - Ecolab Inc.; *pg.* 329, *pg.* 960
Thompson, Cindy, Dept Mgr-Licensing & Planner-Apparel Product - Yamaha Motor Corporation USA; *pg.* 1713, *pg.* 76
Thompson, Dan, Sr Mgr-Customer Care - United Airlines, Inc.; *pg.* 1927, *pg.* 593
Thompson, Darrell, Dir-Trailer Sls - SAF-Holland International, Inc.; *pg.* 217, *pg.* 902
Thompson, Dave, CIO & Exec VP-Digital Media Ops - American Media, Inc.; *pg.* 1615, *pg.* 410
Thompson, David, Dir-Creative Svcs - Memphis Grizzlies; *pg.* 561, *pg.* 1645
Thompson, David, Mgr-Trade Mktg - Reckitt Benckiser Inc.; *pg.* 1136, *pg.* 1105
Thompson, Elyse, Dir-Mktg - DIRECTV Group Holdings, LLC; *pg.* 281, *pg.* 79
Thompson, Emily, Product Mgr-Online Mktg - Southwest Airlines Co.; *pg.* 1923, *pg.* 1687
Thompson, Eric, Dir-Online Sls-Americas - Intel Corporation; *pg.* 645, *pg.* 266
Thompson, Erik, Dir-Adv - Mercury Insurance Company; *pg.* 1208, *pg.* 136
Thompson, Geoffrey, Mgr-Strategic Mktg - Cigna Corporation; *pg.* 1197, *pg.* 338
Thompson, Heather, Specialist-Media Rels - Siemens; *pg.* 1376, *pg.* 1466
Thompson, Jana S., Mgr-Mktg - Xerox Corporation; *pg.* 494, *pg.* 365
Thompson, Jaye, Dir-PR-Europe - Tiffany & Co.; *pg.* 13, *pg.* 1299
Thompson, Jeff, VP-Sls-Southern Div - DS Waters of America, Inc.; *pg.* 250, *pg.* 504
Thompson, Jeff, Brand Mgr-Beauty & Grooming - The Procter & Gamble Company; *pg.* 1129, *pg.* 1418
Thompson, Jeff, VP-Footwear Product Dev-Global - The Timberland Company; *pg.* 1821, *pg.* 1039
Thompson, Jennifer, Sr Mgr-Global Merchant Svcs - American Express Company; *pg.* 712, *pg.* 1190
Thompson, Jeremy, Engr-Product - Specialized Bicycle Components, Inc.; *pg.* 1711, *pg.* 152
Thompson, Jessica, Mgr-Mktg-Mobile Web - The New York Times; *pg.* 1668, *pg.* 1270
Thompson, John, Sr Project Mgr-Sls-Global - Baker Hughes Incorporated; *pg.* 1315, *pg.* 1700
Thompson, John, Brand Mgr - Johnson & Johnson Inc.; *pg.* 1552, *pg.* 1923
Thompson, John K., Sr VP-Sls & Mktg - AeroGrow International, Inc.; *pg.* 1393, *pg.* 310
Thompson, Julie, VP-Sls & Mktg - Sunburst Hospitality Corporation; *pg.* 1115, *pg.* 778
Thompson, Karen, Sr Mgr-Products Mktg - Humana, Inc.; *pg.* 1204, *pg.* 734
Thompson, Kari, Sr Dir-Internal Mktg & Enterprise Comm - Target Corporation; *pg.* 1786, *pg.* 942
Thompson, Kathleen, Mgr-Mktg Comm - Honeywell Aerospace; *pg.* 228, *pg.* 16
Thompson, Ken, Mgr-Mktg - Cornell Dubilier Electronics; *pg.* 630, *pg.* 1620
Thompson, Kevin, Mgr-Comml Fuel Sls - Speedway LLC; *pg.* 985, *pg.* 1452
Thompson, Kevin C., Brand Mgr-Global - Newell Rubbermaid Inc.; *pg.* 1128, *pg.* 515
Thompson, Kim, Sr Dir-Global Branding, PR & Strategic Comm - Whirlpool Corporation; *pg.* 62, *pg.* 872
Thompson, Kristen, Dir-Mktg-Wish-Bone & Western Salad Dressing Brands - Pinnacle Foods Group LLC; *pg.* 889, *pg.* 1104
Thompson, Kristine, Dir-Mktg Comm - CHS INC.; *pg.* 702, *pg.* 926
Thompson, Kyle, Mgr-Mktg Production - Pacific Sunwear of California, Inc.; *pg.* 1781, *pg.* 43
Thompson, Laresa, Mgr-PR & Comm - Carowinds; *pg.* 537, *pg.* 1364
Thompson, Linda, Mgr-Sls-Natl - Eastman Industries; *pg.* 1046, *pg.* 751
Thompson, Lisa, Sr Mgr Mktg Res - Mondelez International, Inc.; *pg.* 878, *pg.* 601
Thompson, Lori, VP-Engine Bus Mktg - Cummins Inc.; *pg.* 1326, *pg.* 676
Thompson, Marcy, VP-Mktg & Innovation - Sonoco Products Company; *pg.* 1469, *pg.* 1619
Thompson, Margot L., Dir-North American Sls - The Port Canvas Company; *pg.* 11, *pg.* 750
Thompson, Marisa, VP-Mktg Strategy & Plng - Meijer, Inc.; *pg.* 1779, *pg.* 888
Thompson, Mark, VP & Gen Mgr-Timing Products - Silicon Laboratories Inc.; *pg.* 674, *pg.* 1666
Thompson, Melissa, Head-Mktg - Cerora, Inc.; *pg.* 1405, *pg.* 1516
Thompson, Melissa, Dir-NBCU Digital Media - NBC Universal, Inc.; *pg.* 300, *pg.* 1266
Thompson, Michael, Mgr-Packages & Ancillary Products - Southwest Airlines Co.; *pg.* 1923, *pg.* 1687
Thompson, Michelle, Dir-Mktg - Comcast Corporation; *pg.* 276, *pg.* 1560
Thompson, Mike, Sr Mgr-Product Mktg - Synopsys, Inc.; *pg.* 480, *pg.* 162
Thompson, Newell, VP-Content Mktg & Strategies - Time Inc.; *pg.* 1693, *pg.* 1300
Thompson, Paige, Coord-Online Mktg - Ann Inc.; *pg.* 18, *pg.* 1195
Thompson, Pamela, Mgr-Field Mktg - Kind LLC; *pg.* 868, *pg.* 1249
Thompson, Patty, Dir-Global Mktg Programs - Informatica Corporation; *pg.* 414, *pg.* 190
Thompson, Reeve, Sr Mgr-Bus Dev - Twitter, Inc.; *pg.* 1285, *pg.* 228
Thompson, Robert, Sr VP-Mktg - Papa John's International, Inc.; *pg.* 1743, *pg.* 737
Thompson, Ron, Program Mgr-Integrated Mktg Comm - MSC Industrial Direct Co., Inc.; *pg.* 1057, *pg.* 1181
Thompson, Ryan, Sr VP-Sls - Lifevantage Corporation; *pg.* 1556, *pg.* 1762
Thompson, Sarah, Global Mktg Mgr - D.V.F. Studios; *pg.* 24, *pg.* 1226
Thompson, Sarah, Mgr-Mktg-Digital & Ecommerce - Seventh Generation, Inc.; *pg.* 335, *pg.* 1765
Thompson, Scott, Bus Mgr-Store Brands-Natl - Post Consumer Brands; *pg.* 833, *pg.* 927
Thompson, Shawn, Mgr-Multicultural Mktg - Ford Motor Company; *pg.* 172, *pg.* 876
Thompson, Sheila, Head-Consumer Brand Mktg Strategy - Facebook, Inc.; *pg.* 1245, *pg.* 143
Thompson, Skip H., Dir-Sls - The Boeing Company; *pg.* 225, *pg.* 567
Thompson, Steve, Sr Dir-Bus Dev & Mktg - Cumulus Media Inc.; *pg.* 280, *pg.* 503
Thompson, Thad, Mgr-Mktg & Comm & Brand Steward-Govt Healthcare Solutions - Xerox Corporation; *pg.* 494, *pg.* 365
Thompson, Thomas T., Reg Dir-Sls - Groendyke Transport, Inc.; *pg.* 1910, *pg.* 1484
Thompson, Tim, Product Mgr - FMC Corporation; *pg.* 1163, *pg.* 1564
Thompson, Tricia, Mgr-Field Mktg-Natl - Popchips; *pg.* 890, *pg.* 182
Thomsen, Brian, CEO-Bunge Product Lines & Mng Dir-Bunge Global Agribusiness - Bunge Limited; *pg.* 842, *pg.* 1351
Thomsen, Jim, CMO & Sr VP-Mktg, Products & Svc - Thrivent Financial for Lutherans; *pg.* 1219, *pg.* 944
Thomsen, Michael, Product Mgr - Google Inc.; *pg.* 1249, *pg.* 153
Thomsic, Tracy, Dir-Corp Digital Strategy & Mktg - McKesson Corporation; *pg.* 1560, *pg.* 222
Thomson, Clair, Brand Mgr-LG - CDW Corporation; *pg.* 370, *pg.* 663
Thomson, Nicola, Dir-Media - The Estee Lauder Companies Inc.; *pg.* 508, *pg.* 1229
Thomson, Stacy, Mgr-Digital Mktg-Display, Social & Mobile-TurboTax - Intuit Inc.; *pg.* 769, *pg.* 158
Thomson, Wendy, Mgr-Channel Mktg Comm - Xerox Canada Inc.; *pg.* 494, *pg.* 1930
Thomton, Mark, Mgr-Comm & Media - CB Richard Ellis Group, Inc.; *pg.* 1085, *pg.* 127
Thon, Scott, Acting Exec VCP-Power - SNC-Lavalin Group Inc.; *pg.* 111, *pg.* 1956
Thor, James E., Sr VP-Retail Sls - Rush Enterprises Inc.; *pg.* 189, *pg.* 1728
Thoreau, David, Mgr-PR - Verengo, Inc.; *pg.* 1954, *pg.* 297
Thoresen, Candy, Mgr-Sls & Customer Svc - Barker Creek Publishing Inc.; *pg.* 1619, *pg.* 1818
Thorgeson, Bob, Dir-Internet Mktg - CIGI Direct Insurance Services, Inc.; *pg.* 1197, *pg.* 335
Thorn George, Amanda, Sr Dir-Mktg Comm - National Basketball Association; *pg.* 566, *pg.* 1264
Thornblad, Kerri, Mgr-Ad Sls Mktg - DIRECTV Group Holdings, LLC; *pg.* 281, *pg.* 79
Thornburgh, Ron, Sr VP-Sls & Mktg - NIC Inc.; *pg.* 445, *pg.* 718
Thornbury, Thomas J., Assoc Dir-Sls - Keeneland Association Inc.; *pg.* 1477, *pg.* 730
Thorne, Malcolm, Chief Strategy Officer-Global - CDK Global, Inc.; *pg.* 370, *pg.* 617
Thorne, Sean, Dir-Bus Intelligence, Mktg, Mobile Dev & Delivery - T-Mobile US, Inc.; *pg.* 676, *pg.* 1816
Thornhill, Mary, Sr Specialist-Mktg & Tech Consulting - Deloitte & Touche USA LLP; *pg.* 743, *pg.* 1222
Thornsberry, Tracy, Brand Mgr-Sonoma-Cutrer - Brown-Forman Corporation; *pg.* 1958, *pg.* 732
Thornton, Aaron, Dir-Creative - Richardson Group Inc.; *pg.* 461, *pg.* 1570
Thornton, Dennette, Sr Mgr-Grp & Premium Sls - Atlanta National League Baseball Club, Inc.; *pg.* 530, *pg.* 490
Thornton, Greg, Sr VP-Media - Moody Publishers; *pg.* 1665, *pg.* 583
Thornton, Gregory R., Sr VP-Media - Moody Bible Institute; *pg.* 605, *pg.* 583
Thornton, Kalen, Dir-Brand Mktg-Nike Running-East - NIKE, Inc.; *pg.* 1812, *pg.* 1492
Thornton, Kara, Mgr-Digital Mktg-Deluxe Fin Svcs - Deluxe Corporation; *pg.* 1634, *pg.* 964
Thornton, Matthew, Sr Dir-Comm - Audible, Inc.; *pg.* 1230, *pg.* 1095
Thornton, Michael, Chief Revenue Officer-Colorado - Starz Entertainment, LLC; *pg.* 310, *pg.* 327
Thornton, Nicky, VP & Mgr-Comml Div Mktg - BOK Financial Corporation; *pg.* 726, *pg.* 1489
Thornton-Kilbride, Katie, Dir-Sls Alvina Valenta-Intl Sls - JLM Couture, Inc.; *pg.* 27, *pg.* 1246
Thorogood, Nick, Sr VP-Content & Mktg-UK & EMEA-Scripps Networks Interactive - Scripps Networks Interactive, Inc.; *pg.* 1279, *pg.* 1638
Thorpe, Christina, Dir-Product Mgmt-Customer Experience - The Gap, Inc.; *pg.* 1770, *pg.* 218
Thorpe, Steven, Sr Mgr-Media Rels - Capital One Bank (USA), N.A.; *pg.* 730, *pg.* 1789
Thorsen, Brian, Mgr-Mktg - NKK Switches; *pg.* 1302, *pg.* 23
Thorsen, Jennifer, Sr Acct Exec-Media Platforms - Google Inc.; *pg.* 1249, *pg.* 153
Thorsen, Jon, Sr Dir-Catalog & Database Mktg - Northern Tool + Equipment; *pg.* 1366, *pg.* 919
Thorsen, Steve, VP-Sls-WW - Micron Technology, Inc.; *pg.* 435, *pg.* 547
Thorsgaard, Claus, Exec VP & Gen Mgr-Enterprise, Intl & Channel Sls - Deltek, Inc.; *pg.* 386, *pg.* 1784
Thorson, Phil, Product Mgr - Farmers Group, Inc.; *pg.* 1199, *pg.* 130
Thoukis, Gerard, Sr Dir-Mktg-Spirits - E&J Gallo Winery; *pg.* 1962, *pg.* 149
Thouvenin, Mathieu, Product Mgr - Apple Inc.; *pg.* 350, *pg.* 73
Thouvenot, Ken, Sr Dir-Project Mgmt - Intelligrated Systems LLC; *pg.* 1350, *pg.* 998
Thrash, Elizabeth, Sr Planner-Digital Media - Palisades Media Group, Inc.; *pg.* 452, *pg.* 275
Thrasher, Kathy, Sr Mgr-Procurement - The Clorox Company; *pg.* 327, *pg.* 169
Thraves, Tim, Mgr-Strategic Product - Intel Corporation; *pg.* 645, *pg.* 266

First page reference indicates Business Class Edition
Second page reference indicates Geographic Edition

Threadgold, Damien, Dir-Sls-Intl - Amy's Kitchen, Inc.; *pg.* 837, *pg.* 276
Threde, Jill, Dir-Adv - The McClatchy Company; *pg.* 1662, *pg.* 196
Thricovil, Raghu, Product Mgr - Adobe Systems Incorporated; *pg.* 342, *pg.* 235
Throndson, Mark, Dir-Processor Mktg - Imagination Technologies; *pg.* 412, *pg.* 285
Throne, Craig, VP-Global Mktg Merrell - Wolverine World Wide, Inc.; *pg.* 1822, *pg.* 905
Throneburg, Derek, VP-Ticket Sls Strategy - Pacers Basketball, LLC; *pg.* 573, *pg.* 689
Throop, Stu, Product Mgr-FMC Agricultural Products North America - FMC Corporation; *pg.* 1163, *pg.* 1564
Thuente, Tom, Territory Mgr-Sls - Sirona Dental Systems, Inc.; *pg.* 1429, *pg.* 1175
Thumma, Cliff, Head-Market Analytics & Sr Dir - Pfizer Inc.; *pg.* 1581, *pg.* 1278
Thunstrom, Jason, VP-PR & Corp Comm - Life Time Fitness, Inc.; *pg.* 1556, *pg.* 920
Thurber, Alex, VP-Sls - WatchGuard Technologies, Inc.; *pg.* 491, *pg.* 1842
Thurber, Jessica, VP-Digital Mktg - Warner Bros. Entertainment Inc.; *pg.* 319, *pg.* 54
Thurgate, Maura, Sr Mgr-Mktg Activation - Del Monte Foods, Inc.; *pg.* 852, *pg.* 304
Thurmon, Melissa, Mgr-Integrity Mktg - Hewlett-Packard Company; *pg.* 404, *pg.* 175
Thurmond, Cassondra, Coord-Field Mktg - Publix Super Markets, Inc.; *pg.* 1031, *pg.* 437
Thurmond, Jenna, Dir-Partnership Mktg - The Weather Channel LLC; *pg.* 320, *pg.* 523
Thurmond, Mark, Exec VP-Worldwide Sls & Svcs - Qlik Technologies Inc.; *pg.* 457, *pg.* 1583
Thurmond, Matt, Sr Product Mgr - W.W. Grainger, Inc.; *pg.* 1390, *pg.* 625
Thurston, Jack, Dir-Digital & Mktg - William Blair & Company LLC; *pg.* 822, *pg.* 596
Thye, Lee-Lin, Sr Mgr-Product Mktg - Symantec Corporation; *pg.* 478, *pg.* 161
Thygesen, Mariana, Mgr-Email Mktg - Art.com; *pg.* 1229, *pg.* 83
Thygesen, Mikael, CMO & Pres Simon Brand Ventures - Simon Property Group, Inc.; *pg.* 1112, *pg.* 690
Thyregod, Kristian, Sr VP-Sls-EMEA - Riverbed Technology, Inc.; *pg.* 1277, *pg.* 225
Tiamsic, Gil, Mgr-Adv Sls - Rodale, Inc.; *pg.* 1681, *pg.* 1530
Tiano, Vincent J., VP-Sls-North America - Miller Industries, Inc.; *pg.* 185, *pg.* 1655
Tibb, Harpreet Singh, Dir-Mktg-India & South Asia - Kellogg Company; *pg.* 831, *pg.* 870
Tibbets, Carla, Asst Mgr-Mktg - Ghirardelli Chocolate Company; *pg.* 1854, *pg.* 252
Tiburzi, Joe, Sr Dir - AOL Inc.; *pg.* 1229, *pg.* 1195
Tice, Carrie, Sr Dir-Bus Convergence - Ubisoft Inc.; *pg.* 589, *pg.* 229
Tice, Robyn, Dir-Media Rels - Eaton Vance Corp.; *pg.* 746, *pg.* 794
Tichindelean, Teo, Global Product Mgr - Molex Incorporated; *pg.* 655, *pg.* 628
Tichy, Ross, VP-Product Dev - Thexton Manufacturing Company, Inc.; *pg.* 218, *pg.* 925
Ticzon, Nancy, Sr Mgr-Customer Mktg - Del Monte Foods, Inc.; *pg.* 852, *pg.* 304
Tidball, Cathie, Sr Specialist-Mktg Comm-Indian Motorcycle - Polaris Industries Inc.; *pg.* 1709, *pg.* 928
Tidd, Diana H., Head-Equity Index Products-Worldwide - MSCI Inc.; *pg.* 785, *pg.* 1262
Tidd, Jennifer, Mgr-Mktg - Hologic, Inc.; *pg.* 1416, *pg.* 784
Tidey, Scott, Sr VP-Sls & Mktg-North America - Hamilton Beach Brands, Inc.; *pg.* 56, *pg.* 1783
Tidman, Wil, Head-Production - GoPro; *pg.* 1414, *pg.* 255
Tidmarsh, Justin, Dir-Loyalty & Membership Mktg - Best Buy Co., Inc.; *pg.* 1761, *pg.* 954
Tidwell, Steve, Sr VP-Sls & Mdsg - Service Corporation International; *pg.* 1395, *pg.* 1714
Tiedje, Chris, Mgr-Digital & Creative Svcs - BBX Capital; *pg.* 723, *pg.* 423
Tiedt, Lisa, Dir-Digital Mktg - Xbox; *pg.* 970, *pg.* 1829
Tiefenbacher, Danyel, Brand Mgr - Pfister, Inc.; *pg.* 1059, *pg.* 88
Tielbur, Diane, Sr Dir-Consumer Insight & Strategy-Growth Cohorts & COE - The Kraft Heinz Company; *pg.* 871, *pg.* 641
Tien, Michael, Sr Mgr-Mktg - Intel Corporation; *pg.* 645, *pg.* 266
Tierney, Sean, Sr VP-Product Dev & Tech - TechTarget, Inc.; *pg.* 482, *pg.* 837
Tierney-Kanning, David, Sr Dir-Art - Garmin International, Inc.; *pg.* 1414, *pg.* 717
Tieszen, Leslie, Sr Mgr-Community Rels - Capital One Financial Corporation; *pg.* 730, *pg.* 1789
Tietbohl, Mark, Mgr-Bus Dev-Installed Sls - Lowe's Companies, Inc.; *pg.* 1053, *pg.* 1383
Tietjen, Carsten, VP-Mktg-Intl - Sun-Maid Growers of California; *pg.* 899, *pg.* 119
Tietjen, Tom, VP-Sls & Mktg - ZCL Composites Inc.; *pg.* 1892, *pg.* 1906
Tietjens, Jim, Sr Dir-Trade Channel Mktg - Anheuser-Busch Companies, LLC; *pg.* 237, *pg.* 991
Tieu, Dan, Dir-Product Mktg & Mgmt-Travel Ticker - Hotwire, Inc.; *pg.* 1912, *pg.* 219
Tieu, Stacey, Product Mgr - Epson America Inc.; *pg.* 394, *pg.* 122
Tifford, Gail, VP-Media & Digital Engagement - Unilever United States, Inc.; *pg.* 904, *pg.* 1061
Tifft, Daniel, Mgr-Mktg-US Comml - Keurig Green Mountain, Inc.; *pg.* 868, *pg.* 1768
Tigchelaar, Ian, Sr Dir-Bus & Mktg Ops - New Orleans Saints L.P.; *pg.* 569, *pg.* 745
Tiger, Michael, Sr Mgr-Product Mktg-LED TV - Samsung Electronics America, Inc.; *pg.* 669, *pg.* 1115
Tighe, John, Chief Merchant Officer & Exec VP - J.C. Penney Company, Inc.; *pg.* 1774, *pg.* 1732
Tighe, Leo, Mgr-Central Mktg - Intuit Inc.; *pg.* 769, *pg.* 158
Tighe, Mike, Dir-Mktg Comm - Plantronics, Inc.; *pg.* 663, *pg.* 270
Tikk, Laszlo, Sr Mgr-Innovation - The Kroger Co.; *pg.* 1025, *pg.* 1416
Tikku, Nirvana, Principal & Product Mgr-Technical-Platform - Nuance Communications, Inc.; *pg.* 447, *pg.* 806
Tilak, Dayanand, Product Mgr-Global - Molex Incorporated; *pg.* 655, *pg.* 628
Tilaro, Mike, VP-Mobile Payments & Debit Card Product Dev - Wells Fargo & Company; *pg.* 819, *pg.* 232
Tilden-Smith, Tessa, Dir-Creative - Open Sky Media; *pg.* 1673, *pg.* 451
Tilford, Doug, VP-Sls-North America ESS - Akamai Technologies, Inc.; *pg.* 1226, *pg.* 807
Tiliakos, Rose, Mgr-Product Mktg - VeriFone Systems, Inc.; *pg.* 487, *pg.* 251
Tilki, Sonja, Dir-Mktg Activation - Subway Restaurants; *pg.* 1751, *pg.* 356
Till, Gregory B., VP-Sls - Gibraltar Packaging Group, Inc.; *pg.* 1459, *pg.* 1011
Tiller, Jim, Sr Dir-Global Therapeutic Area Strategy-CVM - Takeda Pharmaceuticals USA, Inc.; *pg.* 1600, *pg.* 605
Tiller, Peter, Gen Mgr-Device Products - Murata Electronics North America, Inc.; *pg.* 658, *pg.* 540
Tillery, Adam, Grp Dir-Digital Sls & Strategy - Gannett Co., Inc.; *pg.* 1643, *pg.* 1790
Tillery, Lynda, Program Mgr & Mgr-Mktg Comm - Adobe Systems Incorporated; *pg.* 342, *pg.* 235
Tilley, Michael, Assoc Dir-Shopper Mktg & Strategic Partnerships - Mondelez International; *pg.* 877, *pg.* 1344
Tilley, Tana, Reg Dir-Sls - Takeda Pharmaceuticals USA, Inc.; *pg.* 1600, *pg.* 605
Tillman, David, Sr Mgr-Comm - Exelon Corporation; *pg.* 1942, *pg.* 573
Tillman, Denis, Specialist-Mktg Automation - Adobe Systems Incorporated; *pg.* 342, *pg.* 235
Tillman, Mac, VP-Mktg - Big Heart Pet Brands; *pg.* 1474, *pg.* 213
Tillman, Miguel V., Sr Dir-Consumer Retention Mktg - Travelers Insurance; *pg.* 1220, *pg.* 963
Tillmanns, Tara, Specialist-Adv - Regis Corporation; *pg.* 521, *pg.* 941
Tillotson, Joe, Sr Mgr-HUMIRA - Abbott Laboratories; *pg.* 1484, *pg.* 551
Tillson, Mary T, VP-Product & Field Support - Boston Mutual Life Insurance Company; *pg.* 1196, *pg.* 810
Tilson, Rose, Exec Dir-Integrated Mktg Cooking Light & MyRecipes - Time Inc.; *pg.* 1693, *pg.* 1300
Tilt, Linda, Sr Dir-ECommerce - Dollar General Corporation; *pg.* 1767, *pg.* 1635
Tilton, John, Exec Dir-Sls & Mktg Ops-Global - Alexion Pharmaceuticals, Inc.; *pg.* 1489, *pg.* 341
Timbo, Sue, Dir-Mktg - Exxel Outdoors LLC; *pg.* 1833, *pg.* 311
Timm, Aubrey, Assoc Mgr-Mktg-Snacks Division - General Mills, Inc.; *pg.* 828, *pg.* 933
Timm, Eric, VP-Mktg & Customer - Phonak LLC; *pg.* 1585, *pg.* 665
Timm, James, Dir-Mktg & Brand Mgmt - Ballet Theatre Foundation, Inc.; *pg.* 531, *pg.* 1200
Timmerman, Debbie, Mgr-Mktg - Intersil Corporation; *pg.* 647, *pg.* 146
Timmermann, Jonathan, Sr Mgr-Shopper Mktg - The Coca-Cola Company; *pg.* 240, *pg.* 493
Timmons, Jeff, Sr Mgr-Comm & Strategic Initiatives - Canadian Imperial Bank of Commerce; *pg.* 729, *pg.* 1935
Timol, Christian A., Mgr-Zone & Sls-SAAS HR BPO - Paychex, Inc.; *pg.* 792, *pg.* 1336
Timosaari, Maritta, Dir-Sls & Mktg - Pulse Electronics Corporation; *pg.* 666, *pg.* 206
Timothy, David, Mgr-Mktg Comm - Honeywell Aerospace; *pg.* 228, *pg.* 16
Timpano, Erin, Mgr-CRM Mktg-Babies"R"Us Div - Toys "R" Us, Inc.; *pg.* 968, *pg.* 1130
Tincher, David, Bus Mgr - Multi-Tech Systems Inc.; *pg.* 442, *pg.* 951
Tiner, Christina A., Dir-Cloud Servers Product Mgmt - Hewlett-Packard Company; *pg.* 404, *pg.* 175
Tingley, Stephen, VP-Sls & Mktg-Bioprocessing - Repligen Corporation; *pg.* 1589, *pg.* 854
Tinkham, Sasha, Reg Specialist-Mktg - Subaru of America, Inc.; *pg.* 191, *pg.* 1050
Tinkoff, Jay, Reg Mgr-Sls - Harodite Industries, Inc.; *pg.* 693, *pg.* 847
Tino, Amanda, Asst Mgr-Mktg - Godiva Chocolatier, Inc.; *pg.* 1854, *pg.* 1235
Tinseth, Randy, VP-Mktg - The Boeing Company - Helicopter Division; *pg.* 226, *pg.* 13
Tinseth, Randy J., VP-Mktg-Boeing Comml Airplanes - The Boeing Company; *pg.* 225, *pg.* 567
Tinucci, Stacie, Dir-Mktg, Website & Social Media - M/I Homes, Inc.; *pg.* 95, *pg.* 1441
Tipp, Jayson, Sr VP-Mktg, Strategy & Tech - Papa Murphy's International, LLC; *pg.* 1743, *pg.* 1846
Tipping, Emire, Sr Mgr-Consumer Analytics - Diageo North America Inc.; *pg.* 248, *pg.* 1223
Tipton, Cynthia, Mgr-Traits Mktg - Monsanto Company; *pg.* 1173, *pg.* 999
Tipton, Joan, Sr Dir-Category Advisory & Mktg - Coca-Cola Bottling Co. Consolidated; *pg.* 240, *pg.* 1365
Tiran, Nancy, Sr Dir-IT Procurement - Best Buy Co., Inc.; *pg.* 1761, *pg.* 954
Tiriolo, Juliette, Assoc Dir-Search Mktg - Starwood Hotels & Resorts Worldwide, Inc.; *pg.* 1114, *pg.* 378
Tirman, Kelly, VP-Social Strategy & Trends-Enterprise Social Media - Wells Fargo & Company; *pg.* 819, *pg.* 232
Tirol, Daniel, Sr Mgr-Global Mktg-Hershey Brand - The Hershey Co.; *pg.* 1855, *pg.* 1538
Tirpak, Cathy, Sr Dir-Bus Intelligence - University Of Denver; *pg.* 609, *pg.* 323
Tirre, Emelie, Sr VP-Sls-North America - Monster Beverage Corporation; *pg.* 257, *pg.* 69
Tirrell, Taryn, Brand Mgr-Craisins & Cranberry Sauce - Ocean Spray Cranberries, Inc.; *pg.* 887, *pg.* 827
Tirsch, Jadzia Zielinski, Sr VP-Comm & Media - Shiseido Cosmetics America of SAC; *pg.* 522, *pg.* 1291
Tischler, Russell, Mgr-Performance Media - Major League Baseball; *pg.* 560, *pg.* 1255
Tisdalle, Stephen, Sr VP & Head-Brand Mktg Grp - OppenheimerFunds, Inc.; *pg.* 790, *pg.* 1274
Tisera, Julie A., Mgr-Sls Analytics - General Electric Company; *pg.* 1297, *pg.* 347
Tishman, Eric, Mgr-Sls & Strategic Accounts - Rosco Laboratories, Inc.; *pg.* 1782, *pg.* 378
Titmuss, Caroline, VP-Brand Mktg & PR - British Airways; *pg.* 1901, *pg.* 1207
Titus, Dan, Reg Mgr-Sls - The Flexitallic Group; *pg.* 1337, *pg.* 1691
Titus, Etonya, Brand Mgr-Kids - The Gap, Inc.; *pg.* 1770, *pg.* 218
Tiwari, Anoop, Sr Dir-Strategy & Bus Dev - Cars.com; *pg.* 1234, *pg.* 568
Tiwari, Deepak, Product Mgr - Google Inc.; *pg.* 1249, *pg.* 153
Tiziano, Domenick, Dir-Mktg-First Aid, Skin, Ear & Loyalty Health Brands - Prestige Brands Holdings, Inc.; *pg.* 520, *pg.* 1345
Tjaden, Scott, Reg Mgr-Sls-Mid Central - ESAB Welding & Cutting Products; *pg.* 1335, *pg.* 1615
Tkach, Keith, Dir-Sls Vendor Mgmt & Bus Implementation - MetLife, Inc.; *pg.* 1208, *pg.* 1258

Tlucek, Karen, Brand Mgr-Global Skincare - Kao Brands Co. Inc.; *pg.* 513, *pg.* 1415
Toan, Agnes, Sr Mgr-Comm-Global - Atmel Corporation; *pg.* 621, *pg.* 238
Toaspern, John, VP-Mktg-Intl - National Potato Promotion Board; *pg.* 150, *pg.* 322
Tobecksen, Nate, Sr Dir-Global Comm - NIKE, Inc.; *pg.* 1812, *pg.* 1492
Tobey, Ken, Sr Mgr-Analytics - Sargento Foods Inc.; *pg.* 894, *pg.* 1886
Tobi, Ian, Engr-Mktg Support - Toshiba America, Inc.; *pg.* 681, *pg.* 1302
Tobias, Angela, Sr Coord-Mktg - Semonin Realtors; *pg.* 1112, *pg.* 738
Tobias, Chris, Dir-PC Client Customer Mktg - Intel Corporation; *pg.* 645, *pg.* 266
Tobias, Maura, Dir-PR, Comm & Community - Friendly Ice Cream, LLC; *pg.* 1853, *pg.* 859
Tobin, Alexis, Brand Mgr-Global Mktg - Coty, Inc.; *pg.* 506, *pg.* 1210
Tobin, James, Sr Mgr-Indirect Retail - Comcast Corporation; *pg.* 276, *pg.* 1560
Tobin, James J., Sr., Bus Mgr-Cosma Casting Michigan - Magna International Inc.; *pg.* 211, *pg.* 1918
Tobin, Rachel, Specialist-Mktg-Web Analytics - Whirlpool Corporation; *pg.* 62, *pg.* 872
Tobin, Scott, Mgr-iTunes Mktg Production - Apple Inc.; *pg.* 350, *pg.* 73
Tobin, Tom, Dir-Creative Innovation & Insights - Staples, Inc.; *pg.* 474, *pg.* 821
Tobin, Wendy, Mgr-Channel Mktg - Honeywell International Inc.; *pg.* 407, *pg.* 1088
Toca, Ann, VP-Integrated Mktg & Comm - Arizona State University; *pg.* 597, *pg.* 25
Tocatlian, Eric, VP-Sls-Americas-Identity Assurance - HID Global Corporation; *pg.* 1416, *pg.* 111
Tockman, Craig, VP-Sls & Mktg-North American Animal Health - Abaxis, Inc.; *pg.* 1483, *pg.* 298
Toda, Larry, Sr Mgr-Mktg Comm-Corp Mktg - Mentor Graphics Corporation; *pg.* 432, *pg.* 1510
Todd, Abby, Sr Mgr-Pub Affairs & Comm - The Coca-Cola Company; *pg.* 240, *pg.* 493
Todd, Angela, Dir-Category Mktg - Tyson Foods, Inc.; *pg.* 902, *pg.* 35
Todd, Charles T., Sr VP-Sls & Mktg - Bio-Reference Laboratories, Inc.; *pg.* 1402, *pg.* 1058
Todd, Erin, Brand Mgr - Zaxby's Franchising, Inc.; *pg.* 1756, *pg.* 486
Todd, Karen E., Dir-Mktg - Kyowa Hakko U.S.A., Inc.; *pg.* 1554, *pg.* 1249
Todd, Kenneth, Analyst-Mktg-Catalog & eData - Federal-Mogul Holdings Corporation; *pg.* 205, *pg.* 907
Todd, Leigh, Area Mgr-Mktg - Regions Financial Corporation; *pg.* 798, *pg.* 4
Todd, Lindsey, Specialist-Mktg - The ADT Corporation; *pg.* 612, *pg.* 409
Todd, Patrick, Dir-Retail Mktg-Nestle Health Science - Gerber Life Insurance Company; *pg.* 1201, *pg.* 1352
Todd, Patti, Head-Svcs Sls-Integrated Comm - IBM Canada Limited; *pg.* 411, *pg.* 1923
Todd, Phil, Dir-Sls Support - Haworth, Inc.; *pg.* 402, *pg.* 891
Todd, Sara, Specialist-Mktg Comm - Tyler Technologies, Inc.; *pg.* 486, *pg.* 1690
Todd, Scott, Exec Dir-Mktg & Comm - Indiana Wesleyan University; *pg.* 602, *pg.* 694
Todd, Timothy, Product Mgr-Comm-Fixed Income - Waddell & Reed Financial, Inc.; *pg.* 818, *pg.* 721
Todkar, Rahul, Head-Mktg Analytics & Optimization-Global - Intuit Inc.; *pg.* 769, *pg.* 158
Todorova, Anna, Mgr-Natl Media Strategy & Plng-Infiniti-Nissan Motor Corporation - Nissan North America, Inc.; *pg.* 186, *pg.* 1633
Tofano, Kathy, Mgr-Mktg - Gerber Life Insurance Company; *pg.* 1201, *pg.* 1352
Toffolo, Barbara Ann, Dir-Sls & Promotion - Long Island Rail Road; *pg.* 1914, *pg.* 1170
Toft, Don, Sr VP-Sls - Arris Group, Inc.; *pg.* 353, *pg.* 541
Tokatlian, Alex, Head-Program-New Product Mktg - Domino's Pizza, Inc.; *pg.* 1726, *pg.* 865
Tokie, Terry, Dir-Adv - Sun Journal; *pg.* 1690, *pg.* 1386
Tokos, Trent, Sr Dir-Reg Sls-Northwest & Hawaii - Craft Brewers Alliance, Inc; *pg.* 247, *pg.* 1502
Tolan, Brian, Reg Dir-Mktg-Southern Bus Unit - Wyndham Vacation Ownership; *pg.* 1119, *pg.* 457
Tolbert, Carol, Analyst-Mktg - West Marine, Inc.; *pg.* 1712, *pg.* 305
Tolbert, Toni, Mgr-Mktg & Mdsg - Bojangles' Restaurants, Inc.; *pg.* 1717, *pg.* 1364
Toldoya, Diana, Sr Mgr-Mktg - Rakuten.com Shopping; *pg.* 1277, *pg.* 41
Toledo, Alexandre, Dir-Trade Mktg-Colombia, Peru & Chile - The Procter & Gamble Company; *pg.* 1129, *pg.* 1418
Toledo, Reuben, Dir-Mktg-Demand Plng Enterprise Products - Dell Inc.; *pg.* 383, *pg.* 1737
Tolentino, Teresa, Sr Mgr-Mktg Comm & Corp Comm - Lam Research Corporation; *pg.* 1354, *pg.* 91
Toler, James, Dir-Client Mktg - Valassis; *pg.* 1698, *pg.* 386
Toler, Mark, Dir-Creative - PricewaterhouseCoopers LLP; *pg.* 795, *pg.* 1283
Toli, Kristin, Dir-Mktg, Brand & Sponsorship Mgmt - Liberty Mutual Insurance Group Inc.; *pg.* 1205, *pg.* 797
Tolle, Miki, Program Mgr & Specialist-Mktg Automation - Polycom, Inc.; *pg.* 664, *pg.* 249
Tolle, Sheila P., Sr Dir-ECommerce & Small Bus Mktg-Autodesk & AutoCAD - Autodesk Inc.; *pg.* 356, *pg.* 257
Tolliver, Howard R., Mgr-Mktg - 3M Company; *pg.* 1142, *pg.* 956
Tolliver, Nikki, Mgr-Mktg - Applied Industrial Technologies, Inc.; *pg.* 199, *pg.* 1428
Tolosa, Jose, COO-Viacom International Media Networks - Viacom Inc.; *pg.* 316, *pg.* 1310
Tolstunova, Julia, Brand Mgr-St. Regis, The Luxury Collection & W Hotels-Global - Starwood Hotels & Resorts Worldwide, Inc.; *pg.* 1114, *pg.* 378
Tom, Eric P., Exec VP-Sls-Global - International Game Technology; *pg.* 957, *pg.* 1024
Tom, Lydia L., Sr Mgr-Event - Autodesk Inc.; *pg.* 356, *pg.* 257
Toman, Justin, Dir-Sports Mktg - PepsiCo, Inc.; *pg.* 259, *pg.* 1327
Tomao, Victoria, Sr Mgr-Mktg - Penguin Random House; *pg.* 1675, *pg.* 1276
Tomao, Victoria, Sr Mgr-Mktg - Penguin Random House; *pg.* 1675, *pg.* 1276
Tomas, Steve, Dir-Product Branding - FLEXcon Corporation; *pg.* 1457, *pg.* 844
Tomas-Haarstick, Tori, Mgr-Mktg - Charter Communications, Inc.; *pg.* 274, *pg.* 372
Tomasch, Kenn, Sr Mgr-Mktg & Comm - Greater Phoenix Chamber of Commerce; *pg.* 994, *pg.* 16
Tomasek, Bethe, Mgr-Direct Field Mktg - Progress Software Corporation; *pg.* 457, *pg.* 786
Tomaselli, Deanna, Mgr-Media Rels - rue21, inc.; *pg.* 32, *pg.* 1591
Tomasetti, Elissa, Sr VP-Mktg-Scholastic Education - Scholastic Corporation; *pg.* 1683, *pg.* 1288
Tomasi, David, Dir-Mktg-Vicks North America - The Procter & Gamble Company; *pg.* 1129, *pg.* 1418
Tomasovic, Jennifer, Dir-PR - Apollo Education Group Inc.; *pg.* 597, *pg.* 14
Tomassen, Lisa, Mgr-Integrated Mktg Comm & Digital-Big G - General Mills, Inc.; *pg.* 828, *pg.* 933
Tomassetti, Diana, Brand Mgr - Bayer Healthcare Consumer Care Division; *pg.* 1500, *pg.* 1087
Tomassini, Joyce, Brand Mgr-Asset - AS America, Inc.; *pg.* 68, *pg.* 1108
Tomat, John, Mgr-Mktg - SCANA Corporation; *pg.* 1951, *pg.* 1612
Tomback, Jessica, Mgr-Programmatic & Product Innovation - Live Nation Entertainment, Inc.; *pg.* 558, *pg.* 47
Tombalakian, Celia, Sr Dir-Mktg-Global - Elizabeth Arden, Inc.; *pg.* 507, *pg.* 448
Tomblin, Art, Mgr-Digital & Mobile Mktg - Jo-Ann Stores LLC; *pg.* 696, *pg.* 1455
Tome, Julio, Mgr-Product Mktg-Generators - Atlas Copco Comptec LLC; *pg.* 1314, *pg.* 1349
Tomei, Robert I., Pres-Consumer & Shopper Mktg - IRI Group; *pg.* 421, *pg.* 579
Tomeo, Adam, Sr Mgr-Mktg-Pro & Trng Svcs - Ingram Micro Inc.; *pg.* 415, *pg.* 261
Tomeo, Charles, VP-Worldwide Channel & Technical Sls - Webroot Software, Inc.; *pg.* 1289, *pg.* 313
Tomich, Sebastian, Sr VP-Adv & Innovation - The New York Times Company; *pg.* 1668, *pg.* 1270
Tomins, John, VP-Sls & Mktg - AirBoss of America Corp.; *pg.* 1878, *pg.* 1929
Tomita-Oswald, Gayle, Sr Mgr-CRM & Blue Link - Hyundai Motor America; *pg.* 179, *pg.* 89
Tomkiewicz, Brittany, Mgr-PR & Partnerships - Birchbox; *pg.* 1762, *pg.* 1203
Tomkins, Jennifer, Head-Target Team & Sr Mgr-Bus - John B. Sanfilippo & Son, Inc.; *pg.* 1024, *pg.* 610
Tomko, Carole, Gen Mgr & Dir-Creative - Vulcan, Inc.; *pg.* 687, *pg.* 5
Tomlin, Alex, Sr VP Mktg, North America - Diageo North America, Inc.; *pg.* 1961, *pg.* 361
Tomlinson, Elizabeth, Mgr-Email Mktg - AT&T; *pg.* 1865, *pg.* 258
Tomlinson, John, Dir-Pur & Mdsg-C-Stores - Englefield Oil Company; *pg.* 976, *pg.* 1455
Tomlinson, Kristin, Exec Coord-Mktg - MetLife, Inc.; *pg.* 1208, *pg.* 1258
Tomlinson, Michael J., Sr VP & Dir-US Sls - Aflac Incorporated; *pg.* 1188, *pg.* 527
Tommervik, Laura, Sr Mgr-Brand Mktg-Dungeons & Dragons - Wizards of the Coast, Inc.; *pg.* 970, *pg.* 1830
Tomoda, Stacey, Head-Integrated Mktg Plng Ops - Kimberly-Clark Corporation; *pg.* 1461, *pg.* 1720
Tompkins, Brian, Dir-Mktg-Proxima Div - Medline Industries, Inc.; *pg.* 1562, *pg.* 635
Tompkins, Erich, Sr Product Mgr-Advanced Mobility Solutions - AT&T Mobility LLC; *pg.* 619, *pg.* 488
Tompkins, Mark, Dir-Domestic Sls - Sunkist Growers, Inc.; *pg.* 899, *pg.* 299
Tompkins, Trisha, Mgr-Mktg - Ujena Swimwear and Fashions; *pg.* 34, *pg.* 163
Tompkins, Wayne G., Sls Mgr-Power Control - Rockwell Automation, Inc.; *pg.* 668, *pg.* 1880
Tompoles, Brian, VP-Sls - Grain Processing Corporation; *pg.* 859, *pg.* 709
Toms, Janice M., Specialist-Software Sls-Cloud & Smarter Infrastructure Solutions - IBM; *pg.* 410, *pg.* 1449
Toms, Michael, Pres/CEO-New Dimensions Media - New Dimensions World Broadcasting Network; *pg.* 302, *pg.* 298
Tomsic, Tami, Mgr-Client Sls & Svc - The Baseball Club of Seattle, L.P.; *pg.* 532, *pg.* 1833
Tomulonis, John, Dir-Brand Mktg-Global - Hasbro, Inc.; *pg.* 954, *pg.* 1603
Tonar, Bill, VP-Applied Matls - Gentex Corporation; *pg.* 206, *pg.* 913
Tonarelli, Nathan, Sr VP-Sls - IHeartMedia Inc.; *pg.* 292, *pg.* 1741
Toner, Amy, Sr Dir-Mktg & Design - NATSO, Inc.; *pg.* 151, *pg.* 1771
Toner, Michael, Dir-Customer Mktg Innovation-Morning Foods - Kellogg Company; *pg.* 831, *pg.* 870
Tonetti, Susan, Sr Dir-Customer Acq - K12, Inc.; *pg.* 1260, *pg.* 1785
Tong, Cindy, Mgr-Mktg Programs - Time Inc.; *pg.* 1693, *pg.* 1300
Tong, Kathleen, Sr Mgr-Loyalty & Digital Mktg - Fresh & Easy Neighborhood Market Inc; *pg.* 1020, *pg.* 80
Tong, Louis, Mgr & Sr Strategist-Acq Media - Electronic Arts Inc.; *pg.* 951, *pg.* 189
Tong, Melody, Mgr-Mktg-Email & Promos-Gap Online Europe - The Gap, Inc.; *pg.* 1770, *pg.* 218
Tong, Vincent, Sr VP-New Product Introductions & Worldwide Quality - Xilinx, Inc.; *pg.* 496, *pg.* 252
Tongen, Ward, Strategist-Innovative Principal Digital Mktg - Medtronic, Inc.; *pg.* 1564, *pg.* 939
Tonne, Erik, Sr Mgr-Customer Mktg-Cereal - Kellogg Company; *pg.* 831, *pg.* 870
Tonsing, Mike, Dir-Brand & Product Mktg - SunPower Corporation; *pg.* 1952, *pg.* 250
Tontala, Frank, Sr Mgr-Software - Thermo Fisher Scientific Inc.; *pg.* 1431, *pg.* 854
Toohey, Erin, Specialist-Client Mktg - Valassis; *pg.* 1698, *pg.* 386
Toohey, Mike, Mgr-Sls & Mktg - The Bilco Company; *pg.* 70, *pg.* 383
Toohey, Robert, Pres-Digital Media Svcs - Verizon Communications Inc.; *pg.* 1875, *pg.* 1309
Toor, Stephen, Sr Dir-US Mktg & CTCL Sls, Immunology & Mature Brands Franchise - Valeant Pharmaceuticals International; *pg.* 1605, *pg.* 1047
Toosley, Amy, Dir-PR, Pub Affairs & Corp Rels - Provide Commerce, Inc.; *pg.* 1276, *pg.* 206
Toovell, Bethridge, Sr Dir-Comm - Rodale, Inc.; *pg.* 1681, *pg.* 1530
Topen, Andrew, VP & Head-Global Media Rels & Digital Comm - Pfizer Inc.; *pg.* 1581, *pg.* 1278
Topete, Olivia A., Mgr-Mktg-North America - W.R. Grace & Co.; *pg.* 123, *pg.* 810
Topf, Sarah, Editor & Designer-Comm & Mktg - Colorado Rockies Baseball Club, Ltd.; *pg.* 542, *pg.* 317
Topham, Traci, Sr VP-Interactive Ad Sls Mktg - Scripps

Networks Interactive, Inc.; pg. 1279, pg. 1638
Topinka, Tom, Coord-PR - Genworth Financial, Inc.; pg. 761, pg. 1802
Topkis, Karly, Specialist-Mktg - McKesson Corporation; pg. 1560, pg. 222
Tople, Ashley, Brand Mgr-Ore-Ida Frozen Potatoes - The Kraft Heinz Company; pg. 870, pg. 1577
Toporek, Dan, VP-PR & Corp Comm - Wal-Mart.com; pg. 1287, pg. 50
Topp, Michael W., Product Mgr-Technical - The Lubrizol Corporation; pg. 1171, pg. 1481
Topper, Natalie, Specialist-Graphics & Mktg Comm - Avemco Insurance Company; pg. 1194, pg. 769
Torch, Howard, Program Mgr-Residential Mktg - Alabama Power Company; pg. 1933, pg. 1
Torek, Dean, Mgr-Creative Team - RaceTrac Petroleum, Inc.; pg. 983, pg. 519
Torelli, Vicky, Sr Assoc Mgr-Mktg - General Mills, Inc.; pg. 828, pg. 933
Toren, Steve, Dir-North American Sls & Mktg - Waterous Company; pg. 1387, pg. 965
Torgerson, Kirsten, Sr Analyst-Mktg Ops - Expedia, Inc.; pg. 1244, pg. 1814
Torgerson, Sharon, Dir-PR - Blue Cross Blue Shield of Massachusetts; pg. 1507, pg. 789
Torggle, Chris, Sr VP-Sls - Precor, Inc.; pg. 1843, pg. 1847
Torman, Stacey, Sr Dir-Comm-EMEA - salesforce.com, inc.; pg. 1278, pg. 226
Tormey, Beth, VP-Sls & Mktg - Lonza Inc.; pg. 1171, pg. 1041
Tornaghi, Frank, Sr VP-Sls-Worldwide - Xilinx, Inc.; pg. 496, pg. 252
Tornblom, Julie, Brand Mgr - Zale Corporation; pg. 16, pg. 1724
Tornetta, Anthony, Mgr-Product Mktg-Healthcare & Mobile Preparedness - American Red Cross; pg. 130, pg. 395
Toro, Joanne Del, VP-Mktg & ECommerce - Web.com, Inc.; pg. 1288, pg. 524
Toro, Luis, Sr Mgr-Digital Design - Hilton Worldwide, Inc.; pg. 1094, pg. 1791
Torr, Graham, Mgr-Sls - Haviland Enterprises Inc.; pg. 1165, pg. 887
Torrado, Stephanie, Specialist-Mktg Comm - Schneider Electric; pg. 467, pg. 1609
Torralba, Sue, Mgr-Mktg - 180s, LLC; pg. 1824, pg. 754
Torrance, Jim, Head-Brand Mktg-RBC Wealth Mgmt - Royal Bank of Canada; pg. 800, pg. 1942
Torre, Javier Herrero de la, Project Engr-Product Dev & Tech - The Boeing Company; pg. 225, pg. 567
Torrell, Lesley, Dir-Internet Mktg & Web Dev - Memphis Grizzlies; pg. 561, pg. 1645
Torrent, Lynn, Exec VP-Sls & Guest Svcs - Carnival Cruise Lines; pg. 1902, pg. 441
Torres, Andrew, Project Mgr-Driving Programs & Reg Mgr-Mktg - Ferrari North America, Inc.; pg. 171, pg. 1060
Torres, Christine, Mgr-Mktg - GlaxoSmithKline; pg. 1536, pg. 1565
Torres, Christy, Brand Mgr-Barbie-Global - MATTEL, INC.; pg. 962, pg. 81
Torres, Elisa, Sr VP-Network Ops & Affiliate Sls - Spanish Broadcasting System Inc.; pg. 310, pg. 446
Torres, Fabiola, Sr Dir-Global Brand Mktg-Nike Sportswear - NIKE, Inc.; pg. 1812, pg. 1492
Torres, Isela, Mgr-Digital Mktg Mobile & Acq - Academy Sports & Outdoors, Ltd.; pg. 1824, pg. 1724
Torres, Jeff, Global Product Mgr - Molex Incorporated; pg. 655, pg. 628
Torres, Juan, Head-Multicultural Adv & Mktg - FCA US LLC; pg. 170, pg. 868
Torres, Karen, VP-Field Sls & Acct Mktg - HBG Books, Inc.; pg. 1648, pg. 1238
Torres, Kate, Head-Global Mktg-Dockers Brand - Levi Strauss & Co.; pg. 43, pg. 220
Torres, Katherine, Coord-PR - Cole-Haan LLC; pg. 1806, pg. 1034
Torres, Liliana, Dir-Mktg, Spec & Channel-Latin America - General Electric Company; pg. 1297, pg. 347
Torres, Marcos, Mng Dir-Media Investment Banking Grp - RBC Capital Markets; pg. 798, pg. 225
Torres, Maricelis, Brand Mgr-Whiskey - Diageo North America, Inc.; pg. 1961, pg. 361
Torres, Natalia, Dir-Corp Brand Mgmt, Adv Strategy & Ops - The Boeing Company - Helicopter Division; pg. 226, pg. 13
Torres, Ondria, Sr Dir-Events - NYC & Company, Inc.; pg. 1002, pg. 1274
Torres, Owen, Sr Mgr-PR - Office Depot, Inc.; pg. 448, pg. 412
Torres, Paola, Mgr-Media Rels - AARP; pg. 124, pg. 393
Torres, Patricia, Reg Mgr-Sls-Latin America - Butler Manufacturing Company; pg. 72, pg. 981
Torres, Patty, Sr Mgr-Sourcing-Global Ingredients - Mondelez International, Inc.; pg. 878, pg. 601
Torres, Rene, Dir-Mktg-Software Defined Networking Grp - Intel Corporation; pg. 645, pg. 266
Torres, Robin A., Dir-Customer Mktg - The Coca-Cola Company; pg. 240, pg. 493
Torres, Sergio, Dir-Creative - SGK; pg. 1686, pg. 590
Torres, Sherice, Dir-Mktg-Google Commerce - Google Inc.; pg. 1249, pg. 153
Torres, Veronica, Dir-Diversity Mktg - Dallas Convention & Visitors Bureau; pg. 991, pg. 1678
Torresan, Julia, Mgr-Mktg - Intel Corporation; pg. 645, pg. 266
Torrey, John, Chief Strategy Officer-SAP Business Network Grp - Concur Technologies, Inc.; pg. 1236, pg. 1813
Torrini, Megan, Program Mgr-Mktg - AutoZone, Inc.; pg. 200, pg. 1641
Torru, John, Sr VP-Sls & Market Dev Org - Del Monte Foods, Inc.; pg. 852, pg. 304
Torru, John E., Sr VP-Sls & Market Dev Org - Big Heart Pet Brands; pg. 1474, pg. 213
Torstenson, David, Head-Social Mktg - Yahoo! Inc.; pg. 1289, pg. 289
Torstrick, Kelly, Acct Exec-Inside Sls - Scripps Networks Interactive, Inc.; pg. 1279, pg. 1638
Tortorella, Bernadette, Sr Mgr-Media Mktg - Nestle USA, Inc.; pg. 883, pg. 96
Tortoreti, Sarah, Sr Mgr-Consumer Mktg - MTVN Video Hits Inc.; pg. 299, pg. 1263
Torvestad, Pat, Vice Chancellor-Comm & Mktg - University of Arkansas for Medical Sciences; pg. 608, pg. 34
Torzillo, Joseph, VP-Sls HMI Components - EAO Switch Corporation; pg. 1046, pg. 356
Toscano, Jill, VP-US Media - American Express Company; pg. 712, pg. 1190
Toscano, June, Sr Dir-Mktg - The Scotts Miracle-Gro Company; pg. 1799, pg. 1459
Tosch, Paul, VP-Sls-PTMD - One Lambda, Inc.; pg. 1578, pg. 58
Tosswill, Chris, Product Mgr - Facebook, Inc.; pg. 1245, pg. 143
Tosto, Lou, Sr VP-Sls - NBC News; pg. 300, pg. 1265
Tosto, Nick, Dir-Sls-Middle East & Africa - Harsco Rail; pg. 1345, pg. 1623
Totaro, Christine, Analyst-Mktg-South Jersey Energy Solutions - South Jersey Gas Company; pg. 1951, pg. 1067
Totaro, Gina, Specialist-Experiential Mktg - The TJX Companies, Inc.; pg. 1788, pg. 822
Toth, Aurora, VP-Mktg, Midscale Brands-The Americas - Carlson Companies Inc.; pg. 1084, pg. 947
Toth, Bill, Reg Mgr-Sls - Shuttleworth, Inc.; pg. 1375, pg. 682
Toth, Bob, VP-Mktg - Canson Inc.; pg. 1625, pg. 844
Toth, Bob, Dir-Products & Innovation - The Goodyear Tire & Rubber Company; pg. 1883, pg. 1401
Toth, Claudia M., Dir-Mktg - Microsoft Corporation; pg. 435, pg. 1824
Toth, Joseph, Sr Product Mgr - IHS Automotive Driven by Polk; pg. 1652, pg. 907
Toth, Keena, Brand Mgr-Global - Henkel Corporation; pg. 1166, pg. 897
Toth, Mark, VP-Mktg - Bellisio Foods, Inc.; pg. 840, pg. 931
Toth, Steve, Sr Mgr-CMC Regulatory Affairs - Gilead Sciences, Inc.; pg. 1535, pg. 88
Toth, Terry, Sr Project Mgr-Mktg - Juno Lighting Group; pg. 648, pg. 679
Toth, Wendy, Mgr-Mktg - Nestle USA, Inc.; pg. 883, pg. 96
Totman, Damian, Exec Dir-Creative - Bloomberg L.P.; pg. 725, pg. 1204
Totusek, Megan, Coord-Mktg - Ameristar Casinos, Inc.; pg. 528, pg. 1022
Tou, Alan, Product Mgr-Customer Implementation-LiveRamp - Acxiom Corporation; pg. 342, pg. 33
Tou, Joana, Mgr-Mktg - Philips Electronics North America; pg. 662, pg. 782
Touchette, Barbara S., Dir-Health-Care-Tech Mktg & PR - SunTrust Banks, Inc.; pg. 807, pg. 520
Touchton, Jill, Dir-ECommerce Mktg - Kate Spade LLC; pg. 28, pg. 1248
Touchton, Terry, VP-Sls & Mktg - Performance Food Group Company, LLC; pg. 1030, pg. 1803
Tougas, Sue, Dir-Events, Sponsorship & Promos Mktg - Cigna Corporation; pg. 1197, pg. 338
Touhey, Dan, VP-Mktg - Spalding; pg. 1845, pg. 846
Toumey, Shannon, Sr Dir-Partner Mktg, Data & Audience Dev - MTV Networks Company; pg. 298, pg. 1262
Tourangeau, Terrilyn, Sr Dir-Customer Relationship Mktg - Marriott International, Inc.; pg. 1102, pg. 764
Tourek, Beth, Mgr-Social Media - Cellco Partnership; pg. 1869, pg. 1042
Tous, Natasha, Sr Mgr-Mktg - MATTEL, INC.; pg. 962, pg. 81
Tovar, Jorge, Mgr-Digital Mktg Capabilities - Time Inc.; pg. 1693, pg. 1300
Towe, Jessica, Mgr-Corp Adv - Station Casinos, Inc.; pg. 585, pg. 1030
Towell, Jean, Asst Dir-Media & PR - The Northwestern Mutual Life Insurance Company; pg. 1212, pg. 1879
Towell, Patti, Dir-Citywide Sls - Dallas Convention & Visitors Bureau; pg. 991, pg. 1678
Towes, Kevin, Sr Product Mgr-Flash Media Server - Adobe Systems Incorporated; pg. 342, pg. 235
Towle, Geoffrey, Dir-Oncology Mktg - Astellas Pharma US, Inc.; pg. 1496, pg. 640
Towle, Jacquelyn, Sr Mgr-NCO Customer Experience - Comcast Corporation; pg. 276, pg. 1560
Towle, Kimberly, Mgr-Direct Mktg - Intuit Inc.; pg. 769, pg. 158
Townend, Stark, Dir-Online Sls & Advanced Media-Natl - Comcast Corporation; pg. 276, pg. 1560
Towner, Kay, Sr VP-Sls & Mktg - Centerplate, Inc.; pg. 1017, pg. 372
Towner, Steve, Dir-Product Design - Echo Incorporated; pg. 1046, pg. 626
Townes, Drew, Mgr-Sls - Bonnier Corporation; pg. 1622, pg. 480
Townes, Sarah, VP-Mktg - Gander Mountain Company; pg. 1834, pg. 960
Towns, Keenan, Dir-Mktg-Zacapa Rum - Diageo North America Inc.; pg. 248, pg. 1223
Towns, Shelly, VP-Product - Angie's List Inc; pg. 1228, pg. 682
Towns, Wes, Dir-North America ThinkPad Product Mktg - Lenovo Group Ltd; pg. 427, pg. 1384
Townsend, Brian, Designer-Visual Comm-Surface Team - Microsoft Corporation; pg. 435, pg. 1824
Townsend, Drue, Sr VP-Mktg - FASTSIGNS International, Inc.; pg. 81, pg. 1669
Townsend, Landy, Sr Product Mgr-Mktg - Salix Pharmaceuticals, Inc.; pg. 1591, pg. 1388
Townsend, Lois M., Dir-Social Media & Community - Autodesk Inc.; pg. 356, pg. 257
Townsend, Lourdes, Exec Dir-Mktg & Coord - Whole Foods Market, Inc.; pg. 1038, pg. 1667
Townsend, Rob, Sr Product Mgr-Virtual Contact Center - 8x8, Inc.; pg. 1865, pg. 282
Townsend, Tara, Dir-Channel Mktg - Zynga Inc.; pg. 1292, pg. 235
Towson, Lauren, Dir-Integrated Mktg - Viacom Inc.; pg. 316, pg. 1310
Towson, Matthew, Sr Mgr-Media Rels & Community Affairs - Discover Financial Services; pg. 744, pg. 653
Toynton, Aaron, Dir-Digital Mktg - Beall's, Inc.; pg. 1760, pg. 414
Toyota, Wayne, Sr Mgr-Adv & Press - American Honda Motor Co., Inc.; pg. 163, pg. 292
Tq, Pam, Coord-Mktg - Aetna Inc.; pg. 1187, pg. 351
Tracey, Derek, Coord-Production-Digital - David's Bridal, Inc.; pg. 23, pg. 1523
Tracey, Phillip, Product Dir - The TJX Companies, Inc.; pg. 1788, pg. 822
Tracey, Rachel, Strategist-Social Media - Generac Power Systems Inc.; pg. 1340, pg. 1898
Tracey, Susan, Assoc Mgr-Mktg - J&J Snack Foods Corporation; pg. 865, pg. 1107
Trach, Elisabeth, Mgr-Mktg - Wells Fargo & Company; pg. 819, pg. 232
Trackey, Ron, VP-Product Mgmt - Carbonite, Inc.; pg. 368, pg. 792
Tracy, Bill, Dir-Adv Sls - CoStar Group, Inc.; pg. 742, pg. 397
Tracy, Brin, Specialist-Mktg - Southwest Airlines Co.; pg. 1923, pg. 1687
Tracy, Carolyn, Dir-Direct Response Mktg - Sun Life Financial Inc.; pg. 806, pg. 1944
Tracy, Jennifer, Sr VP-Integrated Mktg - Nickelodeon Direct Inc.; pg. 303, pg. 1271

Tracy, Mark, Dir-Product & Bus Dev - Middle Atlantic Products Inc.; pg. 1360, pg. 1065
Tracy, Michelle, Dir-Mktg - Billings Symphony Society Inc.; pg. 533, pg. 1008
Trade, Robert, Specialist-PRC-Mktg Ops - Gilead Sciences, Inc.; pg. 1535, pg. 88
Trader, Blair, Mgr-PR - Valentino Home Entertainment; pg. 684, pg. 742
Traficanti, Pamela, Mgr-Sls-Natl - Metropolitan Tucson Convention & Visitors Bureau; pg. 998, pg. 27
Trager, Doreen, Dir-Creative Svcs - Congoleum Corporation; pg. 921, pg. 1084
Trager, Nicole, Dir-Mktg-US - Coty, Inc.; pg. 506, pg. 1219
Tragseiler, Cara, Brand Mgr-Global Digital Innovation - The Procter & Gamble Company; pg. 1129, pg. 1418
Traicoff, Andy, VP-Consumer Sls & Customer Dev - The Goodyear Tire & Rubber Company; pg. 1883, pg. 1401
Trailer, Jazz, Sr Mgr-Sls - Baton Rouge Area Convention & Visitors Bureau; pg. 989, pg. 741
Train, Lisa, Sr Mgr-Loyalty & Analytics - Safeway Inc.; pg. 1032, pg. 184
Trainor, Ed, VP-Fitness, Svcs & Product Dev - Town Sports International Holdings, Inc.; pg. 589, pg. 1303
Traisman, Frances, VP-Sls - The Baseball Club of Seattle, L.P.; pg. 532, pg. 1833
Trama, Anthony, Sr VP-Creative Svcs-IZOD, Van Heusen, Arrow, Warner's & Speedo - PVH Corp.; pg. 46, pg. 1283
Trames, Cindy, VP-Design & Mdsg-Nike Swim - Perry Ellis International, Inc.; pg. 45, pg. 445
Tramontano, Nicole, Sr Dir-Res-Young Adults Ad Sls - Turner Broadcasting System, Inc.; pg. 314, pg. 521
Trampota, Joe, Territory Mgr-Sls-Central - Engine Components, Inc.; pg. 227, pg. 1740
Tran, Aili J., Corp Mgr-Social Advocacy - Caterpillar, Inc.; pg. 1321, pg. 650
Tran, Andy, Head-Concept-Brand Solutions & Dir-Creative - Viacom Inc.; pg. 316, pg. 1310
Tran, Angela, Brand Mgr-Shopper Mktg - The Clorox Company; pg. 327, pg. 169
Tran, Bryan, Mgr-Product Mktg - Kelley Blue Book Co., Inc.; pg. 1656, pg. 112
Tran, Catherine, Coord-Admin-HIV Mktg-OLP - Gilead Sciences, Inc.; pg. 1535, pg. 88
Tran, Elizabeth, Brand Mgr-Hot Wheels - Mattel Games/Puzzles; pg. 962, pg. 80
Tran, Francis, VP-Mktg - loanDepot LLC; pg. 776, pg. 86
Tran, Jennifer, Assoc Mgr-Mktg-Wilson Jones - ACCO Brands Corporation; pg. 340, pg. 626
Tran, Linda, Mgr-Email Mktg - Oakley, Inc.; pg. 1840, pg. 86
Tran, Linda A., Dir-Media-Magazine Strategy - Macy's East; pg. 1777, pg. 1254
Tran, Lucinda, Category Mgr-Mktg - Newegg Inc.; pg. 1271, pg. 67
Tran, Lydia, Coord-Beltway Mktg Comm - Comcast Cable Communications, Inc.; pg. 276, pg. 1560
Tran, Minh, Brand Mgr-WB Interactive Entertainment - Warner Bros. Entertainment Inc.; pg. 319, pg. 54
Tran, Peter, Mgr-Natl Sls-NY & CHI - Univision Communications Inc.; pg. 683, pg. 1307
Tran, Phu, Acct Exec-MoPub Platform Sls - Twitter, Inc.; pg. 1285, pg. 228
Tran, Thai, Product Mgr - Facebook, Inc.; pg. 1245, pg. 143
Tran, Tuan, Sr Mgr-Bus Dev - Starbucks Corporation; pg. 897, pg. 1840
Tran, Vivan, Dir-Brand Mktg-Universal Studios Home Entertainment - Universal Studios, Inc.; pg. 315, pg. 298
Trancygier, Ann, Dir-Mktg-Licensed Bus - Sears Holdings Corporation; pg. 1784, pg. 618
Trani, Anthony, VP-Global Mktg-Bazooka Candy Brands - The Topps Company, Inc.; pg. 588, pg. 1302
Transit, Lisa Mcclain-Dart, Engr-Mktg - Dart Transit Company; pg. 1905, pg. 921
Traola, Nerissa R., Sr Mgr-Field Mktg-Security Bus Unit-North America - CA Technologies; pg. 366, pg. 1168
Trapani, Ed, VP-Sls Ops - L'Oreal USA; pg. 514, pg. 1252
Trapp, Erin, Dir-Mktg - The University of Alabama; pg. 608, pg. 9
Traquandi, Francesco, Product Mgr - General Electric Company; pg. 1297, pg. 347
Tratt, Noah, VP-Expedia Media Solutions-Global - Expedia, Inc.; pg. 1244, pg. 1814
Trattner, David, Asst Dir-Sls - Milwaukee Bucks, Inc.; pg. 563, pg. 1878
Trattner, Scott, Exec Dir-Creative - Facebook, Inc.; pg. 1245, pg. 143
Traub, Patty, Dir-Product Dev - New York & Company, Inc.; pg. 1779, pg. 1268
Traun, Steve, Dir-Sls - Bozzuto's Inc.; pg. 1016, pg. 342
Trautwein, Jason, Dir-Mktg & Creative - National Football League; pg. 567, pg. 1264
Travaglio, Sarah, Mgr-Media Acct Managers-North America - LinkedIn Corporation; pg. 1262, pg. 160
Traver, Hal, Mgr-Worldwide Channel Mktg - IBM; pg. 410, pg. 1449
Travers, John, VP-Mktg - Home Products International, Inc.; pg. 1125, pg. 577
Traverso, Nat, Mgr-Natl Mktg-Low Voltage Distr Canada - Siemens Canada Ltd.; pg. 1306, pg. 1921
Travieso, Karine, VP-Digital Mktg & Promos - Turner Broadcasting System, Inc.; pg. 314, pg. 521
Travieso, Lisa, Brand Mgr - Georgia-Pacific LLC; pg. 1458, pg. 507
Travis, Amanda R., Mgr-ICS Demand Programs Mktg - International Business Machines Corporation; pg. 418, pg. 1138
Travis, Jeff, Mgr-Bus Dev & Inside Sls - 3M Company; pg. 1142, pg. 956
Travis, Joe, Sr Product Mgr-Knowledge Platform - Autodesk Inc.; pg. 356, pg. 257
Travis, John, VP-Brand Mktg - Adobe Systems Incorporated; pg. 342, pg. 235
Travis, Richard, Sr Product Mgr-Enterprise - Genband, Inc.; pg. 640, pg. 1731
Travis, Ryan, Dir-Online Sls - Dorel Juvenile Group, Inc.; pg. 923, pg. 676
Travostino, Patti, Mgr-Mktg - SDI Technologies, Inc.; pg. 671, pg. 1113
Trawick, Buck, Dir-Mktg - Kubota Tractor Corporation; pg. 705, pg. 294
Trawick, Crystal, Project Mgr-Mktg - Carmike Cinemas, Inc.; pg. 273, pg. 528
Traylor, Alan, Bus Mgr-Food Safety Products - MOCON, Inc.; pg. 1363, pg. 940
Traylor, Andrea, VP & Sr Mgr-Mktg Program-Digital Owned Properties - Regions Financial Corporation; pg. 798, pg. 4
Traynor, Dennis, Mgr-Sls - Gleason - M&M Precision Systems Corporation; pg. 1341, pg. 1479
Traynor, John F.K., Sr VP-Products - BSQUARE Corporation; pg. 366, pg. 1813
Traynor, Peter, Product Mgr-Process Analytics - Thermo Fisher Scientific Inc.; pg. 1431, pg. 854
Trbovich, Ron, Dir-Products & Svcs - Stanley Steemer International, Inc.; pg. 944, pg. 1450
Treadway, Alicia, First VP & Product Mgr - Sun Trust Bank, Atlanta; pg. 806, pg. 520
Treadway, Alicia, First VP & Product Mgr - SunTrust Banks, Inc.; pg. 807, pg. 520
Treadway, Kristina, Mgr-Digital Mktg - Humana, Inc.; pg. 1204, pg. 734
Treadwell, Charlie, Dir-Social Mktg - Symantec Corporation; pg. 478, pg. 161
Treadwell, Priscilla, Dir-Digital Sls - Princeton University Press; pg. 1678, pg. 1112
Trebar, Jacqueline, Mgr-Digital Mktg - Baker Hughes Incorporated; pg. 1315, pg. 1700
Trebby, Kate, Analyst-Web Content-Digital Mktg - Bluegreen Corporation; pg. 1082, pg. 410
Trebilcock, Jim, Exec VP-Mktg - Dr Pepper Snapple Group, Inc.; pg. 250, pg. 1729
Trebino, Kathy, Mgr-Mktg Fin - Johnson & Johnson; pg. 1549, pg. 1091
Trees, Edward, Reg VP-Printed Products - Scientific Games Corporation; pg. 468, pg. 1029
Treese, Monica, Mgr-Sls Ops & Comm - Comcast Corporation; pg. 276, pg. 1560
Treffiletti, Cory, VP-Mktg-Oracle Data Cloud - Oracle Corporation; pg. 450, pg. 191
Trefgarne, Mark, Dir-Product Mgmt - Facebook, Inc.; pg. 1245, pg. 143
Trefgarne, Mark, Co-Founder & Dir-Product - LiveRail; pg. 1264, pg. 145
Tregear, Joshua, Mgr-Mktg Comm - Mitsubishi Fuso Truck of America, Inc.; pg. 185, pg. 1045
Tregurtha, Lindsey, Product Mgr-Aczone - Allergan, Inc.; pg. 1491, pg. 106
Trehub, Eric, Mgr-Headquarters Shopper Mktg - Dreyer's Grand Ice Cream Holdings, Inc.; pg. 1852, pg. 171
Treier, David, Dir-Mktg-Brand, Adv & Social Media - Anthem, Inc.; pg. 1192, pg. 683
Treinen, Danny, Coord-Adv & Brand Mgmt Client Mktg - TD Ameritrade Holding Corporation; pg. 808, pg. 1018
Treinen, Steve, VP-Sls - Fandango Media, LLC; pg. 1247, pg. 130
Trejo, Brian, Analyst-Email Mktg - GoPro; pg. 1414, pg. 255
Treleani, Kristy, Principal-Mktg - FedEx Corporation; pg. 1907, pg. 1642
Trelow, Sam, VP-Sls - Parkhurst Manufacturing Co., Inc.; pg. 214, pg. 1005
Tremayne, Lexine, Exec VP-Mktg-Worldwide - Sony Pictures Home Entertainment; pg. 310, pg. 72
Tremellen, Dustin, Dir-Natl Mktg Execution - Burger King Corporation; pg. 1719, pg. 440
Tremont, Natalia, Sr Mgr-Mktg - Puma North America, Inc.; pg. 1816, pg. 858
Tremont, Steve, Product Mgr - BASF Corporation; pg. 1149, pg. 1066
Trencher, Danielle, Dir-Digital Product Mktg - Meredith Corporation; pg. 1663, pg. 705
Trenholm, Angela, Sr Mgr & Store Mgr-Dev - Wal-Mart Canada Corp.; pg. 1790, pg. 1929
Trent, Emily, VP & Dir-Mktg-HomeGoods - The TJX Companies, Inc.; pg. 1788, pg. 822
Trent, Kara, Dir-Mdsg - Under Armour, Inc.; pg. 49, pg. 759
Trent, Kathy, Sr Dir-Pub Affairs - Waste Management, Inc.; pg. 1954, pg. 1716
Trent, Sydney, Sr Editor-Social Issues - The Washington Post; pg. 1701, pg. 407
Trepanier, Pierre-Paul, Sr Dir & Gen Mgr - Nintendo of America, Inc.; pg. 965, pg. 1829
Trepanier, Scott, Sr Mgr-PR, Promos & Social Media - Columbia Sportswear Company; pg. 1830, pg. 1501
Treptow, Erin, Sr Brand Mgr-Tea Promos & Mktg - Starbucks Corporation; pg. 897, pg. 1840
Trerotola, Khrista, Program Mgr-Consumer Mktg Social Media - Liberty Mutual Insurance Group Inc.; pg. 1205, pg. 797
Tresslar, Nick, Mgr-Mktg - BASF; pg. 1793, pg. 992
Tresslar, Nick, Mgr-Mktg - BASF Corporation; pg. 1149, pg. 1066
Tresslar, Tessa, Specialist-US Retail Mktg - Wolverine World Wide, Inc.; pg. 1822, pg. 905
Trettenero, Patrick, VP-Creative-USA Brandworks-USA Network - NBC Universal, Inc.; pg. 300, pg. 1266
Treurniet, Wim, Sr Mgr-Svc - Welch Allyn Inc.; pg. 1436, pg. 1342
Trevallion, Emily, Dir-Media Rels - The Hanover Insurance Company; pg. 1202, pg. 862
Trevathan, Scott, VP-Mktg & Online Acq - Match.Com, LLC; pg. 1265, pg. 1683
Trever, Natasha, Mgr-Mktg Insights - The Wall Street Journal; pg. 1700, pg. 1312
Treves, Pamela, Dir-Strategic Mktg - Educational Testing Service Inc.; pg. 1394, pg. 1111
Tribbett, Heather, Mgr-Product Mktg - Honeywell International Inc.; pg. 407, pg. 1088
Tribbey, Chris, Mgr-Svc Mktg & Retail Capabilities - Harley-Davidson, Inc.; pg. 178, pg. 1874
Tribick, Vicki, Sr Mgr-Creative Svcs - AutoTrader, Inc.; pg. 1230, pg. 490
Tribula, Dana, VP-Mktg & Applied Global Svcs - Applied Materials, Inc; pg. 618, pg. 1009
Tribula, Dana, VP-Mktg-Applied Global Svcs - Applied Materials, Inc.; pg. 618, pg. 264
Trice, Karen, Sr Mgr-Shopper Mktg - Kashi Company; pg. 830, pg. 119
Trickett, Lindsey, Dir-Strategic Mktg-Global - AstraZeneca Pharmaceuticals LP; pg. 1497, pg. 389
Triebes, Karl, CTO & Sr VP-Product Dev - F5 Networks, Inc.; pg. 396, pg. 1835
Triebwasser, Cameron, Sr Dir-PR & Mktg - I-5 Publishing LLC; pg. 1651, pg. 133
Trieu, Paul, Product Mgr - Google Inc.; pg. 1249, pg. 153
Trigg, Duncan, VP-Adv Effectiveness-London - comScore, Inc; pg. 1236, pg. 1798
Trigg, Kevin, Dir-Mktg Ops - Cable News Network LP; pg. 1624, pg. 1208
Trikha, Sameer, Dir-OEM Sls - WIKA Instrument Corporation; pg. 1437, pg. 534
Trilikis, Elizabeth, Mgr-Media - Dr Pepper Snapple Group, Inc.; pg. 250, pg. 1729
Trillos-Decarie, Jasmine, Dir-Mktg & Bus Dev-Boston - Foley Hoag LLP; pg. 398, pg. 794
Trimarchi, Meaghan, Mgr-Integrated Mktg - The Hearst Corporation; pg. 1649, pg. 1239
Trimble, Don, VP-WW Channel & Cloud Sls - MERU NETWORKS, INC.; pg. 434, pg. 286

First page reference indicates Business Class Edition
Second page reference indicates Geographic Edition

Trimble, John, Chief Revenue Officer - Pandora Media Inc.; pg. 1273, pg. 172
Trimble, Tammy, Brand Mgr - Amway Corporation; pg. 326, pg. 864
Trimble, Whitney, Mgr-Mktg - Acushnet Company; pg. 1824, pg. 818
Trimboli, Alexandria, Specialist-Mktg Comm - Krispy Kreme Doughnuts, Inc.; pg. 1734, pg. 1394
Trinen, Bill, Dir & Product Mgr-Mktg - Nintendo of America, Inc.; pg. 965, pg. 1829
Trinh, Huy, Mgr-Production, Intake & Reporting - Cigna Corporation; pg. 1197, pg. 338
Trinh, Jeanne, Sr Mgr-Seller Mktg & Comm - Ariba, Inc.; pg. 353, pg. 283
Trinh, Linda V., Dir-Mktg & Promos - Multimedia Games Inc.; pg. 442, pg. 1664
Trinh, Margie, Mgr-Mktg - Manulife Financial Corporation; pg. 778, pg. 1939
Trinidad-Bulla, Christina, Sr Dir-Art-Brand Mgmt - CVS Health Corporation; pg. 1765, pg. 1610
Triola, Margaret C., Sr Mgr-Global Mktg-Hematology - Siemens Healthcare Diagnostics; pg. 673, pg. 604
Triolo, Christopher, Brand Mgr-Sourcing - Reebok International Ltd.; pg. 1817, pg. 811
Triolo, Julie, Head-Global Mktg-Yahoo News & Yahoo Fin - Yahoo! Inc.; pg. 1289, pg. 289
Tripathi, Shweta, Mgr-Mktg-North America - Elizabeth Arden, Inc.; pg. 507, pg. 448
Tripathi, Vikram D., Sr Mgr-Intl Mktg IG & India Bus Dev - USG Corporation; pg. 118, pg. 594
Tripi, Alexander, Product Planner-Jaguar XE & XJ - Jaguar Land Rover North America LLC; pg. 180, pg. 1081
Triplett, Greg, VP-Sls & Mktg - Marlite, Inc.; pg. 95, pg. 1448
Tripp, Adam, Specialist-Mktg - Ledo Pizza System Inc.; pg. 874, pg. 754
Tripp, Brian, Mgr-Adv-Great Lakes Ace Hardware - ACO Hardware, Inc.; pg. 1040, pg. 885
Tripp, Justin, VP-LEGO Retail Dev & Shopper Mktg - LEGO Systems, Inc.; pg. 961, pg. 346
Tripp, Kevin, Sr Mgr-Channel Mktg - New Balance Athletic Shoe, Inc.; pg. 1811, pg. 798
Tripp, Patrick, Sr Product Mgr-Mktg-Campaign - Adobe Systems Incorporated; pg. 342, pg. 235
Trisatriya, Yasser, Mgr-Sls - Stanbee Company, Inc.; pg. 1819, pg. 1050
Tritschler, Carolyn, Dir-Mktg - Travelers Insurance; pg. 1220, pg. 963
Tritschler, Carolyn A., Dir-Mktg - The Travelers Companies, Inc.; pg. 1220, pg. 352
Tritton, Mark, Pres-Nordstrom Product Grp - Nordstrom, Inc.; pg. 1779, pg. 1837
Trivedi, Ritu, Head-Brand Mktg-US - Microsoft Corp.; pg. 440, pg. 321
Triverio, Jennifer, Sr Mgr-Comm-Worldwide R&D & Medical - Pfizer Inc.; pg. 1581, pg. 1278
Trivette, Marty, Mgr-Product Mktg-North America-GE Industrial Solutions - GE Energy; pg. 1338, pg. 506
Trlica, Cindy, Sr VP-Quality Mortgage Mktg - Bank of America Corporation; pg. 718, pg. 1362
Troast, Jennifer, Brand Mgr-Gas-X - Novartis Corporation; pg. 1574, pg. 1273
Troast, Tim, Dir-Product Mgmt - Middle Atlantic Products Inc.; pg. 1360, pg. 1065
Trocano, Lauren, Sr Mgr-Internal Engagement - GlaxoSmithKline; pg. 1537, pg. 776
Trocchia, Justine, Mgr-Integrated Mktg - Wenner Media LLC; pg. 1701, pg. 1314
Trochez, Nicole, Mgr-Mktg - Kingston Technology Company, Inc.; pg. 425, pg. 90
Trofholz, Kirk, Pres-US Bakery Products - Dawn Food Products, Inc.; pg. 1018, pg. 893
Troiano, Amy, Sr VP-Creative & Brand Strategy - NBC Universal, Inc.; pg. 300, pg. 1266
Troiano, Kimberly A., Specialist-Mktg - Canon U.S.A., Inc.; pg. 1404, pg. 1178
Troidl, Geoff, Mgr-Internet Mktg - GEICO Corporation; pg. 1200, pg. 399
Trojan, Jeffrey, VP-Mktg - Playmates Toys Inc.; pg. 965, pg. 82
Trojan, T. J., Sr VP-Product Mgmt - SYNNEX Corporation; pg. 480, pg. 92
Troka, Matthew A., Sr VP-Product & Partner Mgmt - CDW Corporation; pg. 370, pg. 663
Trombetta, Ian, VP-Consumer Mktg - Activision Blizzard, Inc.; pg. 948, pg. 271
Trombone, Lisa, Sr Mgr-CMI - Unilever United States, Inc.; pg. 904, pg. 1061
Troncale, Michael, Sr Mgr-PR - Experian Consumer Direct; pg. 1245, pg. 71
Tronco, Ana, Reg Mgr-Mktg-Latin America & the Caribbean - Wilson Sporting Goods Co.; pg. 1848, pg. 596
Trone, Rebecca, Sr VP-Digital Mktg - Bank of America Corporation; pg. 718, pg. 1362
Trone, Stephanie, Mgr-Mktg & Comm - NuSil Technology LLC; pg. 1887, pg. 63
Tropeano, Chris, Sr Mgr-Bus Comm - National Association for Stock Car Auto Racing; pg. 566, pg. 420
Tropeano, Mona, Sr VP-Adv Sls Ops & Admin - A&E Television Networks, LLC; pg. 267, pg. 1185
Trosin, Christopher M., VP-Sls & Mktg-Retail - High Liner Foods (USA) Incorporated; pg. 862, pg. 816
Trost, Karla, Sr Product Mgr-Global - G&W Electric Company; pg. 1338, pg. 558
Trotter, Carol, Dir-Sls-Admin - Ducommun Technologies, Inc.; pg. 634, pg. 63
Trotter, Carrie, Dir-Film & Theatre Mktg - AMC Entertainment Inc.; pg. 527, pg. 716
Trotter, Julie, Dir-Midwest Adv-People - Time Inc.; pg. 1693, pg. 1300
Trotter, Susan M., Reg Sr Mgr-PR - Macy's, Inc.; pg. 1778, pg. 1417
Trotz, Joey, VP-Adv, Data & Ad Product Tech Strategies - Turner Broadcasting System, Inc.; pg. 314, pg. 521
Trouard-Riolle, Marc, Sr Product Mgr-Mktg - Citrix Systems, Inc.; pg. 375, pg. 424
Trout, Megan, Assoc Product Mgr - Target Corporation; pg. 1786, pg. 942
Trout, Timothy, Sr Mgr-Digital Mktg - Veterinary Pet Insurance Co.; pg. 1222, pg. 49
Trovato, Lisa, Sr Mgr-Mktg-Online Strategy - Affinion Group, Inc.; pg. 1225, pg. 372
Trovinger, Nicci, Assoc Mgr-Mktg-Green Giant - General Mills, Inc.; pg. 828, pg. 933
Troxell, Shelby, Mgr-Product Mktg - Electronic Arts Inc.; pg. 951, pg. 189
Troy, David, Dir-Mktg-Americas - Branson Ultrasonics Corporation; pg. 1319, pg. 342
Troya, Marcela, Analyst-Mktg - Univision Communications Inc.; pg. 683, pg. 1307
Truax, Lauren, Specialist-Media Buying Support - The Tire Rack Inc.; pg. 1890, pg. 697
Truax, Todd, Sr Dir-Alliance Ops - JLG Industries, Inc.; pg. 1351, pg. 1551
Trubowitz, Jason, Sr Dir-Media Plng & Adv-Today Show, NBC News & MSNBC - NBC Universal, Inc.; pg. 300, pg. 1266
Trudel, Beau, Sr Strategist-Adv-Worldwide - Apple Inc.; pg. 350, pg. 73
True, Carmen, Sr Dir-Strategy & Capabilities-Digital User Experience - Hewlett-Packard Company; pg. 404, pg. 175
True, Colin, Dir-Sls-North America - Polartec LLC; pg. 697, pg. 827
Truelove, Anthony, Mgr-Global Truck Mktg Comm - Eaton Corporation; pg. 1331, pg. 1429
Truitt, Laurie, Dir-Intl Mktg & Digital Products - The New York Times; pg. 1668, pg. 1270
Trujillo, Amy, Dir-Mktg - Comcast Corporation; pg. 276, pg. 1560
Trujillo, Laura, Sr Mgr-Corp Comm - Fifth Third Bancorp; pg. 752, pg. 1413
Trujillo, Maria, Sr Mgr-Mktg - 7-Eleven, Inc.; pg. 1012, pg. 1672
Trumble, Jane, Sr VP-Product Dev - Leanin' Tree, Inc.; pg. 1658, pg. 311
Trumbo, Steve, Specialist-Mktg - USANA Health Sciences, Inc.; pg. 1605, pg. 1761
Trumbull, Joe, Mgr-Sls Ops - United Parcel Service, Inc.; pg. 1928, pg. 522
Trumbull, Kate, Dir-Engagement Mktg - Domino's Pizza, Inc.; pg. 1726, pg. 865
Trump, Jeff, Mgr-Mktg - Pactiv Corporation; pg. 1466, pg. 624
Trunk, Brian, Sr Mgr-Trade Mktg - Wizards of the Coast, Inc.; pg. 970, pg. 1830
Truong, Autumn, Sr Mgr-Global Social Media Mktg - Cisco Systems, Inc.; pg. 372, pg. 240
Truong, Thien, Sr VP-Sls & Bus Dev - GREEN DOT CORPORATION; pg. 763, pg. 180
Truss, Felicia, Sr Mgr-Mktg - Verizon Communications Inc.; pg. 1875, pg. 1309
Trusty, Brooke, Mgr-Digital & Social Mktg - Tempur Sealy International, Inc.; pg. 944, pg. 731
Truxal, Erin, Mgr-Global Media - FedEx Corporation; pg. 1907, pg. 1642
Truxal, Jeremy, Sr Assoc Brand Mgr - The Kraft Heinz Company; pg. 871, pg. 641
Truxillo, Wanda, VP-Global Sls Excellence - mBlox Inc.; pg. 1266, pg. 286
Tryon, William, Dir-Investor & PR - Rogers Corporation; pg. 1305, pg. 369
Trypus, Mary Beth, Exec VP-Sls & Mktg - Bulova Corporation; pg. 2, pg. 1356
Trzemzalski, Marisa, Project Mgr-Mktg - ScanSource, Inc.; pg. 671, pg. 1618
Tsai, Chanthana, Dir-Social Media Mktg-Sears Holdings Corporation - Kmart Corporation; pg. 1775, pg. 617
Tsai, Chanthana, Dir-Social Media Mktg - Sears Holdings Corporation; pg. 1784, pg. 618
Tsai, Jennifer, Principal & Product Mgr - Oracle Corporation; pg. 1272, pg. 786
Tsakeres, Alexandra, Brand Mgr-Oral Care Innovation - Colgate-Palmolive Company; pg. 504, pg. 1215
Tsalolikhin, Paul, Dir-Mktg - Hilti, Inc.; pg. 1346, pg. 1490
Tsang, Anne, Head-Mktg-US Consumer Mktg - MasterCard Incorporated; pg. 779, pg. 1325
Tsavaris, Penni, Sr Assoc Brand Mgr-Campbell's Homestyle Soup - Campbell Soup Company; pg. 844, pg. 1048
Tsay, Wei-Shin, Sr VP-Product & Bus Dev - Alliance Fiber Optic Products, Inc.; pg. 1399, pg. 283
Tschantz, Molly, Sr Mgr - AT&T Mobility LLC; pg. 619, pg. 488
Tschanz, Lee, VP-Sls-North America - Rockwell Automation, Inc.; pg. 668, pg. 1880
Tschetter, Nate, Mgr-Music Production Mktg-Pro Music Div - Yamaha Corporation of America; pg. 595, pg. 51
Tschida, Jamie, Assoc Mgr-Mktg-Innovation - Constellation Brands, Inc.; pg. 1960, pg. 1348
Tschopik, Harry, Dir-Product Mktg-Global - Accuray Incorporated; pg. 1486, pg. 282
Tschudy, Phil, Mgr-Media Rels - CUNA Mutual Insurance Society; pg. 743, pg. 1865
Tseng, Christine, Head-SMB Mktg & Mktg Ops - Twitter, Inc.; pg. 1285, pg. 228
Tseng, Richard, VP-Mktg & ECommerce - Rakuten.com Shopping; pg. 1277, pg. 41
Tseng, Robbie, Assoc Dir-Creative-Patterns & Design Solutions-Global - DIRECTV Group Holdings, LLC; pg. 281, pg. 79
Tsigrikes, Paul, VP-Mktg - The Washington Post; pg. 1701, pg. 407
Tsimpides, Sherry, Planner-Mdse - Books-A-Million, Inc.; pg. 1623, pg. 2
Tsonis, Tony, Mgr-Digital Media Ops - Bright House Networks LLC; pg. 272, pg. 461
Tsoutsas, Ariana, Assoc Mgr-Mktg-Trade & Strategic Retail Accounts - Transitions Optical, Inc.; pg. 1432, pg. 458
Tsuei, Janet, Sr Designer-Barbie Brand - MATTEL, INC.; pg. 962, pg. 81
Tsui, Lynn, VP-Global Product Dev & Sourcing-Women's - Levi Strauss & Co.; pg. 43, pg. 220
Tsukikawa, Yugo, Sr VP-Mktg & Brand Strategy - Mikimoto (America) Co. Ltd.; pg. 10, pg. 1260
Tsuruta, Jun, Sr Dir-Maintenance Procurement - Hawaiian Airlines, Inc.; pg. 1910, pg. 543
Tu, Jane, Project Mgr & Sr Engr-Staff Product - Power Integrations, Inc.; pg. 1369, pg. 249
Tu, Tuan, Dir-Mktg - Revlon, Inc.; pg. 521, pg. 1286
Tuason, Nico, Sr Product Mgr - Fluidigm Corporation; pg. 1413, pg. 279
Tubbini, Luca, Dir-Sls-Latin America - X-Rite, Incorporated; pg. 1437, pg. 891
Tubbs, Boyd, Brand Mgr - The Kraft Heinz Company; pg. 871, pg. 641
Tubekis, Ted, Dir-Digital Sls - Valassis; pg. 1698, pg. 386
Tuck, Jordan, Mgr-Adv Sls Ops - Weight Watchers International, Inc.; pg. 1609, pg. 1313
Tuck, Rob, Exec VP-Sls-Natl - The CW Television Network; pg. 632, pg. 52
Tucker, Amanda, Mgr-Social Media - Analog Devices, Inc.; pg. 617, pg. 839
Tucker, Ann C., VP-Mktg Comm & Institutional Div - Ecolab Inc.; pg. 329, pg. 960
Tucker, Bob, Reg Mgr-Sls - AAR Corp.; pg. 223, pg. 671
Tucker, Christine, VP-Mktg-Retirement Solutions Div - Pacific Life Insurance Company; pg. 1213, pg. 166
Tucker, David, Dir-Direct Mktg - The Progressive Corporation; pg. 1214, pg. 1463

Tucker, Diane, Sr Product Mgr - Verizon Communications Inc.; *pg.* 1875, *pg.* 1309
Tucker, James, Dir-Mktg, Invoice & Payment Solutions - Ariba, Inc.; *pg.* 353, *pg.* 283
Tucker, Jason, Sr Dir-Mktg - Kinetic Concepts, Inc.; *pg.* 1553, *pg.* 1741
Tucker, Jeff, VP-Sls - San Francisco Giants Baseball Club; *pg.* 581, *pg.* 226
Tucker, Jennie Vitello, Mgr-Mktg Automation Process - Adobe Systems Incorporated; *pg.* 342, *pg.* 235
Tucker, Jeremy, VP-Mktg Comm & Media - Nissan North America, Inc.; *pg.* 186, *pg.* 1633
Tucker, Lauren, Analyst-Southeastern Mktg - State Farm Mutual Automobile Insurance Co.; *pg.* 1218, *pg.* 557
Tucker, Mark, VP-Sls & Sls Plng - Blue Rhino Corporation; *pg.* 1318, *pg.* 1393
Tucker, Mark, VP-Mktg - New Horizons Worldwide, Inc.; *pg.* 445, *pg.* 43
Tucker, Michael, Sr Mgr-Product-Tealeaf - IBM; *pg.* 410, *pg.* 1140
Tucker, Nora, Sr Product Mgr-Small Bus Fin Solutions - Intuit Inc.; *pg.* 769, *pg.* 158
Tucker, Rachel, Product Mgr - Facebook, Inc.; *pg.* 1245, *pg.* 143
Tucker, Rick G., Bus Mgr-Global - Honeywell International Inc.; *pg.* 407, *pg.* 1088
Tucker, Ronnie, VP-Mktg & Digital - New York Road Runners Club, Inc.; *pg.* 152, *pg.* 1269
Tucker, T.J., Dir-Creative - Texas Monthly; *pg.* 1692, *pg.* 1666
Tucker, Tara, VP-Mktg Comm-Global - Spin Master Ltd.; *pg.* 967, *pg.* 1943
Tucker, Tom, Engr-Technical Mktg - Intel Corporation; *pg.* 645, *pg.* 266
Tudhope, John, Dir-Product Mktg - Sprint Corporation; *pg.* 1874, *pg.* 719
Tudisco, Aaron, Dir-Mktg - Big Lots, Inc.; *pg.* 1762, *pg.* 1438
Tuell, Sarah, Specialist-Mobile Product - Delta Air Lines, Inc.; *pg.* 1905, *pg.* 503
Tuerk, Andreas, Product Mgr - Google Inc.; *pg.* 1249, *pg.* 153
Tueros, Sheri, Sr Mgr-Mktg-Imports Portfolio - Trinchero Family Estates; *pg.* 1971, *pg.* 197
Tufenkjian, David, Sr Product Mgr - Welch Allyn Inc.; *pg.* 1436, *pg.* 1342
Tuffaha, Nadia, Specialist-Mktg Dev - The Telx Group, Inc.; *pg.* 483, *pg.* 1298
Tuffney, Rachel, Acct Dir-Global Multi Media - The Wall Street Journal; *pg.* 1700, *pg.* 1312
Tuggle, Nathan, Mgr-Mobile Channel Mktg - The Home Depot, Inc.; *pg.* 1050, *pg.* 510
Tuinman, Jaap, Sr Dir-Campaign Strategy & Media Plng - Electronic Arts Inc.; *pg.* 951, *pg.* 189
Tula, Marcia, Dir-Sls - Lexicon Marketing Corporation; *pg.* 604, *pg.* 134
Tull, Cathy, Sr VP-Mktg - Las Vegas Convention & Visitors Authority; *pg.* 997, *pg.* 1027
Tullio, Ian Di, Sr Dir-Customer Engagement & Partnership Mktg - Air Canada; *pg.* 1896, *pg.* 1902
Tullio, Mark, VP-Mktg-Worldwide - Lantronix, Inc.; *pg.* 426, *pg.* 112
Tully, Chad, Sr Mgr-Sls - Twitter, Inc.; *pg.* 1285, *pg.* 228
Tully, Chris, Exec VP-Media - Major League Baseball; *pg.* 560, *pg.* 1255
Tully, Merit, Dir-Media & Comm - Anaheim Ducks Hockey Club, LLC; *pg.* 528, *pg.* 42
Tully, Patricia, Mgr-Mktg-Intl - Trek Bicycle Corporation; *pg.* 1847, *pg.* 1896
Tully, Reagan, Sr Dir-Mktg-US Customer Strategy-Vaccines - GlaxoSmithKline; *pg.* 1536, *pg.* 1565
Tully, Sean, Sr Mng Dir-Interest Rate & OTC Products - CME Group Inc.; *pg.* 738, *pg.* 571
Tulsiani, Bobby, Dir-Mktg Plng & Analysis - Netflix, Inc.; *pg.* 1269, *pg.* 141
Tuma, Beth, VP-Sls & Mktg - HCA HOLDINGS, INC.; *pg.* 1539, *pg.* 1651
Tumacder, Jacint, Product Mgr-QuickBooks Accountant - Intuit Inc.; *pg.* 769, *pg.* 158
Tumaneng, Aimee, Mgr-Adv & Mktg Sls - Google Inc.; *pg.* 1249, *pg.* 153
Tumati, Prasad, Dir-Global Product-Clamping Tech - DE-STA-CO Industries; *pg.* 1045, *pg.* 867
Tumbarello, Jamie, Specialist-Mktg - The Timberland Company; *pg.* 1821, *pg.* 1039
Tumelty, Mark, Brand Mgr - Campbell Soup Company; *pg.* 844, *pg.* 1048
Tumler, Barbara, Sls Mgr-Large Format & Strategic Accounts - Johanna Foods Inc.; *pg.* 866, *pg.* 1066
Tummillo, Michael A., Sr VP & Gen Mgr-Mdsg-Building & Maintenance - Lowe's Companies, Inc.; *pg.* 1053, *pg.* 1383
Tummings, Monika, Coord-Mktg Events - Clean Harbors, Inc.; *pg.* 376, *pg.* 839
Tumtton, Susie, Gen Mgr-Sls - KTVE-TV; *pg.* 295, *pg.* 748
Tumula, Naveen, Dir-Product Mktg - Osram Sylvania, Inc.; *pg.* 1302, *pg.* 816
Tung, Emilia, Mgr-Mktg & Comm Ops - IBM Canada Limited; *pg.* 411, *pg.* 1923
Tung, Lillian, Sr Mgr-Mktg - Maybelline LLC; *pg.* 516, *pg.* 1257
Tung, Roger, Mgr-Mktg - Snapfish; *pg.* 1687, *pg.* 228
Tungler, Antal, Mgr-PR-AMD Graphics - Advanced Micro Devices, Inc.-Markham; *pg.* 345, *pg.* 1922
Tungseth, Lori, Dir-Product Mgmt & Usability - Academy Sports & Outdoors, Ltd.; *pg.* 1824, *pg.* 1724
Tunik, Gal, Mgr-Product Line - Hewlett-Packard Company; *pg.* 404, *pg.* 175
Tunn, Pat, Product Mgr-Global - Molex Incorporated; *pg.* 655, *pg.* 628
Tunney, Susan, Sr Dir-HR-Global - Edmund Industrial Optics Inc.; *pg.* 1411, *pg.* 1041
Tuohy, John, Mgr-Education Indus Mktg - Cisco Systems, Inc.; *pg.* 372, *pg.* 240
Turchin, Elizabeth, Assoc Dir-Mktg - University of Minnesota; *pg.* 609, *pg.* 945
Turchioe, Danielle, Sr Mgr-Vendor Mktg Partnerships - Toys "R" Us, Inc.; *pg.* 968, *pg.* 1130
Turcotte, Michael, VP-Mktg - JPMorgan Chase & Co.; *pg.* 772, *pg.* 1246
Tureman, Shawn, Dir-Intermodal Domestic Mktg - Norfolk Southern Corporation; *pg.* 1917, *pg.* 1797
Turetzky, Heather, Dir-Partnership Mktg, Events & PR - Burlington Coat Factory; *pg.* 1764, *pg.* 1047
Turevon, Lauri, VP-Svc & Sls - Emerson Network Power; *pg.* 1071, *pg.* 1479
Turfler, Troy, Sr Dir-Smokeless Product Dev - American Snuff Company; *pg.* 1893, *pg.* 1641
Turgeon, C. J., Sr Product Dir - Johnson & Johnson; *pg.* 1549, *pg.* 1091
Turim, Caroline, Sr Assoc Brand Mgr - The Kraft Heinz Company; *pg.* 871, *pg.* 641
Turk, Tim, VP-Sls-Worldwide - Cirrus Logic, Inc.; *pg.* 629, *pg.* 1661
Turke, Kathryn, VP-Sls - Lavelle Industries Inc.; *pg.* 1053, *pg.* 1856
Turkelson, Scott, Sr Product Mgr-Oncology & Hematology-US - GlaxoSmithKline; *pg.* 1536, *pg.* 1389
Turkelson, Scott, Sr Product Mgr-Oncology & Hematology-US - GlaxoSmithKline; *pg.* 1536, *pg.* 1565
Turkelson, Scott, Sr Product Mgr-Oncology & Hematology-US - GlaxoSmithKline Consumer Healthcare; *pg.* 510, *pg.* 1554
Turkowski, Rita, Mgr-Customer Product Mktg-Digital Gaming - Advanced Micro Devices, Inc.; *pg.* 613, *pg.* 282
Turley, Mark, Sr Dir-Media - Pittsburgh Penguins LLC; *pg.* 577, *pg.* 1578
Turli, Michelle, Mgr-Mktg & Brand Comm - Cole-Haan LLC; *pg.* 1806, *pg.* 1034
Turman, Marty, Sr Dir-CRM - Vail Resorts, Inc.; *pg.* 1117, *pg.* 313
Turnbow, Sheri, Sr Dir-Private Sector Engagement - World Wildlife Fund, Inc.; *pg.* 162, *pg.* 408
Turnbull, Laura, Dir-Mktg APAC-Rubbermaid Comml Products - Newell Rubbermaid Inc.; *pg.* 1128, *pg.* 515
Turnbull, Stephen, Dir-Mktg-Thin Client - Advanced Micro Devices, Inc.; *pg.* 613, *pg.* 282
Turner, Bart, VP-Mktg Strategy & Comm - Ameriprise Financial, Inc.; *pg.* 715, *pg.* 930
Turner, Brent, Mng Dir-Spatial Energy & Sr VP-Sls & Mktg - DigitalGlobe, Inc.; *pg.* 1408, *pg.* 333
Turner, Chase, Strategist-Creative - Tumblr, Inc.; *pg.* 1285, *pg.* 1305
Turner, Chris, VP-Pro Sls-Clarisonic - L'Oreal USA; *pg.* 514, *pg.* 1252
Turner, Cristel, Dir-Adv, Brand Strategy & Bus Mktg - United States Cellular Corporation; *pg.* 1875, *pg.* 594
Turner, Dan, Head-Media Rels-Global - E.I. du Pont de Nemours & Company; *pg.* 1159, *pg.* 390
Turner, Danny, Sr VP-Programming & Production-Global - Mood Media; *pg.* 298, *pg.* 1616
Turner, Dawn, Dir-Mktg & Brand Mgmt - Oklahoma City Thunder; *pg.* 571, *pg.* 1487
Turner, Eileen, Sr Mgr-Product Mktg-IBM Security - International Business Machines Corporation; *pg.* 418, *pg.* 1138
Turner, Erin, Assoc Mgr-Mktg-ACDelco Mdsg - General Motors Company; *pg.* 175, *pg.* 881
Turner, Fabian, Mgr-Mktg Dev - Coca-Cola Refreshments USA, Inc.; *pg.* 247, *pg.* 500
Turner, Gwynn, Mgr-Product & Social Media - Bloomberg L.P.; *pg.* 725, *pg.* 1204
Turner, Haley, Coord-Mktg - World Gold Council; *pg.* 162, *pg.* 1315
Turner, Heather Lau, Dir-Mktg - THE DOW CHEMICAL COMPANY; *pg.* 1157, *pg.* 898
Turner, Holly, Dir-Mktg-Global - GlaxoSmithKline; *pg.* 1536, *pg.* 1565
Turner, Ida, Coord-Mktg - The Northwestern Mutual Life Insurance Company; *pg.* 1212, *pg.* 1879
Turner, Janna, Sr VP-Digital Mktg & Mgr-Digital Media - Bank of America Corporation; *pg.* 718, *pg.* 1362
Turner, Jared, Dir-New Media - NewsChannel 5; *pg.* 303, *pg.* 1653
Turner, Jeffrey, Sr Dir-Ad Product & Monetization - TheHuffingtonPost.com, Inc.; *pg.* 1692, *pg.* 1298
Turner, Jordan, Sr Product Mgr-Global - Conmed Corporation; *pg.* 1517, *pg.* 1347
Turner, Julie, Sr Dir-Product Mktg-Maxis - Electronic Arts Inc.; *pg.* 951, *pg.* 189
Turner, Julie A., Dir-Creative Production & MIS - Plumbing-Heating-Cooling Contractors-National Association; *pg.* 154, *pg.* 1782
Turner, Keith, Sr Mgr-Comm & Govt Rels - Safeway Inc.; *pg.* 1032, *pg.* 184
Turner, Keith, Pres-Adv Sls & Mktg - Univision Communications Inc.; *pg.* 683, *pg.* 1307
Turner, Kelli, Dir-Mktg Comm - Zoll Medical Corporation; *pg.* 1612, *pg.* 814
Turner, Lowell, Dir-Mktg Procurement-Global - Kimberly-Clark Corporation; *pg.* 1461, *pg.* 1720
Turner, Lynne, Mgr-Mktg - Inverness Corporation; *pg.* 512, *pg.* 783
Turner, Mary, Exec VP-Mdsg - Hudson's Bay Company; *pg.* 1773, *pg.* 1938
Turner, Meg, Brand Mktg Mgr - Build-A-Bear Workshop, Inc.; *pg.* 950, *pg.* 993
Turner, Natalie, Specialist-PR - Lowe's Companies, Inc.; *pg.* 1053, *pg.* 1383
Turner, Nicole, Assoc Mgr-ECommerce Mktg - Spencer Gifts LLC; *pg.* 1786, *pg.* 1057
Turner, Paul, Dir-Creative - Gallery Model Homes, Inc.; *pg.* 926, *pg.* 1706
Turner, R. David, Sr Dir-West Reg - Chick-fil-A, Inc.; *pg.* 1721, *pg.* 492
Turner, Ryan, Dir-Social Media-Global - Starbucks Corporation; *pg.* 897, *pg.* 1840
Turner, Scott, Dir-Mktg-Global - Dell Inc.; *pg.* 383, *pg.* 1737
Turner, Shaundra, Sr Mgr-Field Corp Rels-Midwest Reg - The Allstate Corporation; *pg.* 1189, *pg.* 639
Turner, Shelley, Dir-California Sls - Stoli Group USA LLC; *pg.* 1970, *pg.* 1296
Turner, Sue, Dir-Mktg Svcs - Canon U.S.A., Inc.; *pg.* 1404, *pg.* 1178
Turner, Thomas A., Jr., VP-Sls & Customer Svc - Rogers Communications Inc.; *pg.* 668, *pg.* 1942
Turner, Ursula, Reg Product Mgr - Dell Inc.; *pg.* 383, *pg.* 1737
Turner, Victoria, Gen Mgr-Customer Relationship Mktg-Australia - News Corporation; *pg.* 1669, *pg.* 1271
Turner, Wayne, Mgr-Mktg Equipment-Southern California - PepsiCo, Inc.; *pg.* 259, *pg.* 1327
Turnier, Christine, Sr Mgr-Product Mktg-New Initiatives - TripAdvisor, Inc.; *pg.* 1926, *pg.* 835
Turpel, Gina, Dir-Women's Mktg - Volcom, Inc.; *pg.* 1847, *pg.* 71
Turpen, Carol, Sr Mgr-Corp Comm - Ingram Micro Inc.; *pg.* 415, *pg.* 261
Turpin, Fred, Head-Media & Telecom Banking-TMT - JPMorgan Chase & Co.; *pg.* 772, *pg.* 1246
Turpin, Lucile, Mgr-Mktg Comm - Cameron International; *pg.* 1151, *pg.* 1702
Turpin, Michael, Reg VP-MediaNews Grp Audience Solutions - San Jose Mercury News; *pg.* 1683, *pg.* 250
Turpin, Xavier, Dir-Multicultural Mktg - Dunkin' Brands Group, Inc.; *pg.* 1727, *pg.* 810
Turrentine, Kara, Strategist-Mktg Ops-Pricing - Nissan North America, Inc.; *pg.* 186, *pg.* 1633

First page reference indicates Business Class Edition
Second page reference indicates Geographic Edition

Tursi, Louis, Exec VP-Sls & Customer Mktg - Church & Dwight Co., Inc.; *pg.* 1153, *pg.* 1063
Tuscany-Warren, Pamela, VP & Gen Mgr-Production - Universal Studios, Inc.; *pg.* 315, *pg.* 298
Tushingham, Keith, Dir-Mktg Ops - Schlumberger Limited; *pg.* 801, *pg.* 1714
Tusiani, Michael, Sr VP-Corp Sls & Sponsorships - New York Yankees; *pg.* 570, *pg.* 1144
Tussy, Susan, Sr Mgr-Bus Dev - Adobe Systems Incorporated; *pg.* 342, *pg.* 235
Tutalo, Frank, Sr Mgr-Social Media - Pegasystems Inc.; *pg.* 453, *pg.* 74
Tuteleers, Jean, Mgr-Mktg-In store Presence - Nestle Canada Inc.; *pg.* 883, *pg.* 1929
Tuthill, Allen, Sr VP-Sls & Mktg-Global - Assurant, Inc.; *pg.* 1193, *pg.* 1198
Tuthill, Molly, Sr Specialist-Adv - Amica Mutual Insurance Co.; *pg.* 1192, *pg.* 1602
Tutkovics, Julie, CMO & Exec VP - FirstMerit Corporation; *pg.* 758, *pg.* 1400
Tutolo, John, Mgr-Sls-Food Svc & Retail-Natl - Kanan Enterprises, Inc.; *pg.* 1857, *pg.* 1473
Tutt, Troy, Sr Dir-Tournament Revenue - PGA Tour, Inc.; *pg.* 574, *pg.* 460
Tuttell, Wit, VP-Tourism & Mktg & Exec Dir-Visit NC - North Carolina Department of Commerce Division of Tourism, Film & Sports Development; *pg.* 1001, *pg.* 1388
Tuttle, John, Sr Mgr-EAP - American Airlines Inc.; *pg.* 1898, *pg.* 1693
Tuttle, Michelle, Mgr-Mktg - IBM; *pg.* 410, *pg.* 1449
Tuttle, Terry, VP-Sls & Mktg - HellermannTyton; *pg.* 642, *pg.* 1875
Tuza, Joe, Sr VP-Retail Mktg, Sls & Innovation - T. Marzetti Company; *pg.* 900, *pg.* 1444
Tweed, Jennifer, Sr Mgr-Experiential Mktg-Xbox - Microsoft Corporation; *pg.* 435, *pg.* 1824
Tweed, Lorna, Sr Product Mgr-EMEA - Jarden Consumer Solutions; *pg.* 57, *pg.* 412
Tweeten, Donna, Asst VP-Mktg & Comm - Hy-Vee, Inc.; *pg.* 1023, *pg.* 713
Twells, Katherine, Asst VP-Customer Mktg-Western US - The Coca-Cola Company; *pg.* 240, *pg.* 493
Twemlow, Jessica, Mgr-PR - EnCana Corp.; *pg.* 976, *pg.* 1903
Twining, Steve, Sr Mgr-Internet Product Merchant - National Business Furniture Inc; *pg.* 1269, *pg.* 1879
Twiss, Jeff, VP-Media Rels & Alumni Rels - Boston Celtics Limited Partnership; *pg.* 533, *pg.* 790
Twohig, Kelly, Specialist-Mktg-MassMutual Fin Grp - Massachusetts Mutual Life Insurance Company; *pg.* 1207, *pg.* 845
Twohill, Lorraine, Sr VP-Mktg-Global - Google Inc.; *pg.* 1249, *pg.* 153
Twomey, Amy, Dir-Mktg - Popeye's Chicken & Biscuits; *pg.* 1745, *pg.* 517
Twomey, Amy, Reg Dir-Mktg-East - Popeyes Louisiana Kitchen, Inc.; *pg.* 1745, *pg.* 517
Twomey, Bill, Brand Mgr-Tylenol PM & Simply Sleep - Johnson & Johnson; *pg.* 1549, *pg.* 1091
Twomey, Colin, Sr Dir-Strategy & Analytics - Sacramento Kings; *pg.* 579, *pg.* 197
Tworetzky, Brent, Exec VP-Product - XO Group Inc.; *pg.* 1289, *pg.* 1316
Twyman, Artis, Sr Dir-Comm - Saint Louis Rams Football Company; *pg.* 580, *pg.* 1002
Twyman, Brad, Product Mgr-Biology eMarketing - Sigma-Aldrich Corporation; *pg.* 1181, *pg.* 1003
Tyagi, Richard, Mgr-League Rels-Sports Mktg - Gannett Co., Inc.; *pg.* 1643, *pg.* 1790
Tyagi, Ritesh, VP-Mktg Unit - Renesas Electronics America Inc.; *pg.* 667, *pg.* 269
Tycienski, Paula, Dir-Adv - Mohegan Tribal Gaming Authority; *pg.* 564, *pg.* 381
Tye, Beverly J., Dir-Creative Svcs & Events - Magellan Health Services, Inc.; *pg.* 1557, *pg.* 337
Tye, Roger, Sr Dir-eBusiness & Consumer Engagement - The Allstate Corporation; *pg.* 1189, *pg.* 639
Tyioran, Paula, Sr Dir-Sls Ops & Svcs - AutoTrader, Inc.; *pg.* 1230, *pg.* 490
Tylec, Jennie D., Mgr-Mktg - Caterpillar, Inc.; *pg.* 1321, *pg.* 650
Tyler, Alexandra I., VP & Head-Digital Mktg - Teachers Insurance & Annuity Association - College Retirement Equities Fund; *pg.* 1219, *pg.* 1297
Tyler, Amanda, Specialist-Digital Mktg - Golf Channel; *pg.* 551, *pg.* 454
Tyler, Ashley, Assoc Mgr-Mktg Comm - Reebok International Ltd.; *pg.* 1817, *pg.* 811
Tyler, Brent, Brand Mgr-Global - Zippo Manufacturing Company, Inc.; *pg.* 1895, *pg.* 1518
Tyler, Caryn, Mgr-BioResearch Mktg - Molecular Devices Corporation; *pg.* 1568, *pg.* 287
Tyler, Christina, Mgr-PR - McDonald's Corporation; *pg.* 1737, *pg.* 645
Tyler, Clayton R., Dir-Acq Mktg-Consumer Electronics & Natl Strategic Partners - DIRECTV Group Holdings, LLC; *pg.* 281, *pg.* 79
Tyler, Johanna, Asst Mgr-Mktg - L'Oreal USA; *pg.* 514, *pg.* 1252
Tyler, Larry, VP-Sls Plng, Analytics & In-Store Execution - Moran Foods, Inc.; *pg.* 1028, *pg.* 976
Tyler, Mac, Designer-Product - Facebook, Inc.; *pg.* 1245, *pg.* 143
Tyler, Monica, Dir-Brand Mktg - Newell Rubbermaid Inc.; *pg.* 1128, *pg.* 515
Tyler, Shana, Sr Mgr-Site Mktg & Promos - Sally Beauty Holdings, Inc.; *pg.* 522, *pg.* 1691
Tyler, Stephen, Mgr-Product Mktg - Ford Motor Company; *pg.* 172, *pg.* 876
Tyler, Tim, Dir-Mktg - Viking Range Corporation; *pg.* 61, *pg.* 968
Tyler, Woody, VP-Sls & Mktg - Kadant Black Clawson Inc.; *pg.* 1352, *pg.* 1460
Tylka, Kathleen, Mgr-Field Mktg - Cisco Systems, Inc.; *pg.* 372, *pg.* 240
Tylman, Alina, Mgr-Social Media - World Kitchen LLC; *pg.* 1141, *pg.* 657
Tylski, Scott, Sr Dir-IT - ConAgra Foods, Inc.; *pg.* 826, *pg.* 1014
Tymon, Deborah, Sr VP-Mktg - New York Yankees; *pg.* 570, *pg.* 1144
Tynan, Angie, Assoc Mgr-Mktg-Hyatt Gold Passport - Hyatt Hotels Corporation; *pg.* 1096, *pg.* 577
Tyrholm, Laura, Head-US Institutional Mktg & Dir - BlackRock, Inc.; *pg.* 724, *pg.* 1203
Tyrrell, Kimberly, Assoc Brand Mgr-Baskin-Robbins Intl Mktg - Dunkin' Brands Group, Inc.; *pg.* 1727, *pg.* 810
Tyrrell, Rick, VP-Sls - Perfetti Van Melle USA, Inc.; *pg.* 1860, *pg.* 727
Tyrrell, Sarah, Gen Mgr-Sls - WMOR; *pg.* 322, *pg.* 476
Tyson, Charles, Exec VP-Mdsg, Mktg & Supply Chain - Advance Auto Parts, Inc.; *pg.* 197, *pg.* 1805
Tyson, Dan, Product Mgr - Johnson Controls, Inc.; *pg.* 1073, *pg.* 1597
Tyson, Dave, Sr Dir-Information Security - S.C. Johnson & Son, Inc.; *pg.* 334, *pg.* 1889
Tyson, Scott, Product Dir-Digital - Johnson & Johnson; *pg.* 1549, *pg.* 1091
Tyulpin, Vladimir, Product Mgr - Avery Dennison Corporation; *pg.* 1452, *pg.* 95
Tzou, Olivia, Sr Mgr-Mktg - Intuit Inc.; *pg.* 769, *pg.* 158
Tzoumas, Charlie, Sr Dir - Comcast Corporation; *pg.* 276, *pg.* 1560
Tzucker, Jeff, Dir-Digital Mktg - Pacers Basketball, LLC; *pg.* 573, *pg.* 689

U

Ua, Mai L., Sr Mgr-PR - Walgreen Co.; *pg.* 1608, *pg.* 605
Uaje, Eric, Assoc Product Mgr - Epson America Inc.; *pg.* 394, *pg.* 122
Ubaldo, Jose, Mgr-Comm & Media Rels - Los Angeles County Metropolitan Transportation Authority; *pg.* 1914, *pg.* 135
Uberoi, Sonal, Product Mgr - Converse Inc.; *pg.* 1831, *pg.* 793
Ubinas, Diana, Sr Product Mgr-Intl Programming Ops - Comcast Corporation; *pg.* 276, *pg.* 1560
Uchimura, Karalynn, Sr Mgr-Internal Audit - Alexander & Baldwin, Inc.; *pg.* 1079, *pg.* 543
Uchrin, Lauren, Sr Mgr-Global Consumer Mktg - Levi Strauss & Co.; *pg.* 43, *pg.* 220
Uddenberg, Erik, Reg Dir-Mktg - Diageo North America, Inc.; *pg.* 1961, *pg.* 361
Udeshi, Dharmen, Sr Mgr-Bus Dev - Time Warner Cable Inc.; *pg.* 312, *pg.* 1301
Udom, Charuma, Coord-Mktg Comm - QUALCOMM Incorporated; *pg.* 1873, *pg.* 207
Uebele, Tim, Sr Dir-Global Foods R&D - PepsiCo, Inc.; *pg.* 259, *pg.* 1327
Ueberle, Diane, Head-Mktg & Brand - Intuit Inc.; *pg.* 769, *pg.* 158
Ueberroth, Gail, Vice Chm & Chief Creative Officer - Preferred Hotel Group; *pg.* 1108, *pg.* 587
Uecker, Matt, Reg Mgr-Sls - Stedman Machine Company; *pg.* 1379, *pg.* 673
Uecker, Russell, Head-Promotional Mktg - Best Buy Co., Inc.; *pg.* 1761, *pg.* 954
Uetz, Carl, Sr VP & Head-Corp Mktg - Northern Trust Corporation; *pg.* 787, *pg.* 585
Uffelman, Brian, Dir-Product Mgmt, Enterprise Mobility Mgmt Mobile - Symantec Corporation; *pg.* 478, *pg.* 161
Uffelman, David, Sr Mgr-Amazon Prime - Amazon.com, Inc.; *pg.* 1226, *pg.* 1831
Uffindell, Colin, VP-Midwest Sls - R.J. Reynolds Tobacco Co.; *pg.* 1895, *pg.* 1395
Uffner, Brandon, Mgr-Mktg - The Weather Channel LLC; *pg.* 320, *pg.* 523
Ugarcovici, Mihaela, Assoc Dir-Mktg Sciences Hospital & Transplant - Astellas Pharma US, Inc.; *pg.* 1496, *pg.* 640
Ugarte, Cecil, Reg Mgr-Sls-Latin America - North Star Ice Equipment Corporation; *pg.* 1366, *pg.* 1838
Uhland, Melinda, Dir-Product Mgmt - Oracle Corporation; *pg.* 450, *pg.* 191
Uhler, Karen, Dir-Mktg-Sponsorships, Promos, Consumer PR & Affinity Solutions - The Allstate Corporation; *pg.* 1189, *pg.* 639
Uhrich, Marie, VP-Membership Mktg - Thrivent Financial for Lutherans; *pg.* 1219, *pg.* 944
Uhrich, Patricia, Sr Mgr-Mktg - AEGON USA, Inc.; *pg.* 1187, *pg.* 755
Ukani, Karim, Mgr-Mktg Optimization & Sys Strategy - United Airlines, Inc.; *pg.* 1927, *pg.* 593
Ukleja, Dan, Sr Mgr-Category Strategy & Insights - The WhiteWave Foods Company; *pg.* 1037, *pg.* 324
Uku, Leslie, Brand Mgr-Prestige Fragrance - Coty, Inc.; *pg.* 506, *pg.* 1219
Ulabarro, Carmen D., Mgr-Direct Mktg - Chevron Corporation; *pg.* 974, *pg.* 259
Ulakovich, Karen, Mgr-Sls - Mlive Media Group; *pg.* 1665, *pg.* 888
Ulatowski, Daniel, Chief Sls Officer - Credit Acceptance Corporation; *pg.* 742, *pg.* 906
Uldbjørg, Erika, Acct Exec-Digital Sls & Plng - Target Corporation; *pg.* 1786, *pg.* 942
Uli, Linda, Mgr-Sls Trng - Cisco Systems, Inc.; *pg.* 372, *pg.* 240
Ullah, Millie, Assoc Dir-Product & Market Mgmt - Repligen Corporation; *pg.* 1589, *pg.* 854
Ullery, Sheila, VP-Retail & Mdsg - Massage Envy Limited, LLC; *pg.* 516, *pg.* 23
Ullman, Lindsay, Mgr-Relationship Mktg - National Basketball Association; *pg.* 566, *pg.* 1264
Ullman, Ross, Exec Dir-Mktg-Consumer Healthcare - Boehringer Ingelheim Pharmaceuticals, Inc.; *pg.* 1507, *pg.* 368
Ullman, Tom, Sr VP-Solution Sls-Worldwide - Kofax Image Products, Inc.; *pg.* 1419, *pg.* 112
Ullmann, Brian, Asst VP-Mktg & Comm - University of Maryland; *pg.* 609, *pg.* 767
Ullrich, Katie, Mgr-Mktg - Sony Pictures Entertainment Inc.; *pg.* 309, *pg.* 72
Ullstrup, Mark, VP-Sls & Mktg - Superior Die Set Corp.; *pg.* 1379, *pg.* 1885
Ulrey, Lauren, Brand Mgr-Cape Cod, Tom's, Jay's, Okedoke & Krunchers - Snyder's-Lance, Inc.; *pg.* 896, *pg.* 1368
Ulrey, Sarah, Sr Mgr-Partner Mktg - Hotwire, Inc.; *pg.* 1912, *pg.* 219
Ulrich, Al, Assoc Dir-Mktg-Global - Merck & Co., Inc.; *pg.* 1566, *pg.* 1077
Ulrich, Brittany, Mgr-Global Mktg-Packaging - ITW Dynatec; *pg.* 1351, *pg.* 1635
Ulrich, Catherine, Chief Product Officer - Shutterstock, Inc.; *pg.* 1280, *pg.* 1291
Ulrich, Jeff, Sr Mgr-Emerging Tech & Mobile App - United Continental Holdings, Inc.; *pg.* 1927, *pg.* 593
Ulrich, Karl, Mgr-Svc & Parts Mktg-Natl - Kia Motors America Inc.; *pg.* 181, *pg.* 112
Ulrich, Robyn, Sr VP-Brand Mktg & Creative-DIY Network - Scripps Networks Interactive, Inc.; *pg.* 1279, *pg.* 1638
Ulrich-Sturmat, Yosha, VP-Product Mktg - NeuStar, Inc.; *pg.* 1872, *pg.* 1807
Ulsh, Sherry, Sr Dir-Ops & Mktg Fin - Church's Chicken, Inc.; *pg.* 1722, *pg.* 493
Ulysse, Dora, Sr Planner-Integrated Mktg Comm - General

Mills, Inc.; pg. 828, pg. 933
Umali, Angela, Mgr-Media - Enterprise Holdings, Inc.; pg. 1906, pg. 996
Umana, Kymber, Mgr-Hispanic Mktg - Sprint Corporation; pg. 1874, pg. 719
Umapathy, Vijay, Product Mgr - Google Inc.; pg. 1249, pg. 153
Umphry, Deborah, Assoc Dir-Energy Mktg - KPMG LLP; pg. 774, pg. 1086
Umscheid, Marc, Team Head-Bus Dev Platform & Sr Dir - The Clorox Company; pg. 327, pg. 169
Umur, Nesrin, Sr Mgr-CRM-GAP Inc - GE Capital; pg. 761, pg. 362
Unapanta, Lillian, Mgr-Mktg - Univision Communications Inc.; pg. 683, pg. 1307
Unbehagen, Chelsea, Mgr-Mktg Production - American National Insurance Company; pg. 1191, pg. 1697
Underhill, Elizabeth Swan, Dir-Mktg - HP Hood LLC; pg. 864, pg. 829
Underhill, Katie, Mgr-Mktg - Burberry Limited; pg. 20, pg. 1208
Underwood, Jerry, Exec Dir-Mktg - HOM Furniture, Inc.; pg. 927, pg. 938
Underwood, Judy, Product Mgr - Church & Dwight Co., Inc.; pg. 1153, pg. 1063
Underwood, Paddy, Product Mgr - Facebook, Inc.; pg. 1245, pg. 143
Underwood, Steve, Interim Pres - Tennessee Football, Inc.; pg. 587, pg. 1654
Underwood, Tracy, Mgr-Corp Contributions & Social Investments - Toyota Motor Sales, U.S.A., Inc.; pg. 193, pg. 296
Unell, Samantha, Specialist-Social Media-Social Care - Southwest Airlines Co.; pg. 1923, pg. 1687
Uner, Jason, Mgr-Digital Mktg - COUNTRY Financial; pg. 1198, pg. 557
Ungar, Jocelyn, Sr Product Mgr-Mktg - Amazon.com, Inc.; pg. 1226, pg. 1831
Ungar, Scott, Sr VP-Media, Creative & Interactive - National CineMedia, Inc.; pg. 567, pg. 314
Ungard, Todd, Dir-Mktg - Vertex Pharmaceuticals Incorporated; pg. 1606, pg. 801
Unger, Ann, Head-Consumer Mktg - Puma North America, Inc.; pg. 1816, pg. 858
Unger, Stephanie, Sr Product Mgr-Change - Post Holdings, Inc.; pg. 833, pg. 1002
Unger, Ted, Mgr-Mktg Ops - Sirius XM Holdings Inc.; pg. 308, pg. 1292
Unger-Moore, Wendy, Sr Dir-Mktg - Spalding; pg. 1845, pg. 846
Unuvar, Tora, Mgr-Product Mktg - Honeywell International Inc.; pg. 407, pg. 1088
Upalawanna, Nora, Sr Mgr-Campaign Mktg - Adobe Systems Incorporated; pg. 342, pg. 235
Updike, Jaci, Pres-Sls - Penguin Random House; pg. 1675, pg. 1276
Upham, Steve, VP-Sls - Crosman Corporation; pg. 951, pg. 1143
Uppal, Jack, VP-Mktg & Customer Experience-India - General Motors Company; pg. 175, pg. 881
Uppal, Sonja, Coord-Digital Mktg - Arby's Restaurant Group, Inc.; pg. 1014, pg. 488
Uppala, Lakshmi, Sr Mgr-Applications Engrg - Intel Corporation; pg. 645, pg. 266
Upperman, Sandy, Sr VP-Reg Mktg & Mgr-PR - Huntington Bancshares Incorporated; pg. 767, pg. 1440
Upshur, Erica, Sr Mgr-Mktg-Beachbody LIVE - Beachbody, LLC; pg. 271, pg. 272
Upson, Tommy, Dir-Creative - International Speedway Corporation; pg. 553, pg. 420
Upward, Liz, Sr Mgr-Bus Dev & Strategic Partnerships - New York Road Runners Club, Inc.; pg. 152, pg. 1269
Uram, Susan, Sr Mgr-Channel-Olympic Exterior Stain - PPG Industries, Inc.; pg. 1445, pg. 1579
Urbahns, Alaina, Specialist-Sls Rep-Salesforce1 Lightning Platform - salesforce.com, inc.; pg. 1278, pg. 226
Urbaitis, Jim, Mgr-Product Mktg-Xbox - Microsoft Corporation; pg. 435, pg. 1824
Urban, Andrew, Sr VP-Retail Sls - Perdue Farms Incorporated; pg. 889, pg. 777
Urban, Chris, Mgr-Core Customer Mktg - Harley-Davidson, Inc.; pg. 178, pg. 1874
Urban, Chris, Dir-Mktg-Kraft Natural Cheese - The Kraft Heinz Company; pg. 871, pg. 641
Urban, Colette, Dir-PR - NorthShore University HealthSystem; pg. 606, pg. 612
Urban, James M., Mgr-Creative & Delivery - First National Bank; pg. 756, pg. 1553
Urban, Pat, Mgr-Mktg - athenahealth, Inc.; pg. 1497, pg. 855
Urban, Stephanie, Mgr-eMail Mktg - Ann Inc.; pg. 18, pg. 1195
Urban, Tina, Dir-Print & Creative Svcs - The Phillies, L.P.; pg. 575, pg. 1569
Urbanek, Jon, Sr VP-Sls, Mktg & Employer Markets - Blue Cross & Blue Shield of Florida, Inc.; pg. 1507, pg. 432
Urbano-DesJardin, Gina, Mgr-Mktg - SKECHERS U.S.A., INC.; pg. 1819, pg. 143
Urbanske, Stan, Sr Dir-Sls - Peet's Coffee & Tea, Inc.; pg. 1029, pg. 85
Urbanski, Lana, Mgr-Events & Mktg - Tyco International (US) Inc.; pg. 1891, pg. 1113
Urbanski, Leisel, Brand Mgr Immunology-Global - Eli Lilly and Company; pg. 1527, pg. 684
Urbanski, Robin, Mgr-Media Relo - United Airlines, Inc.; pg. 1927, pg. 593
Urch, Jonathan, Dir-Customer Mktg-Guinness USA - Diageo North America Inc.; pg. 248, pg. 1223
Ure, Mariela, Sr VP-Segments Strategy & Enterprise Mktg - Wells Fargo & Company; pg. 819, pg. 232
Urena, David, Reg Mgr-Sls - Milton Roy Company; pg. 1361, pg. 1542
Uretsky, Karen, Sr Dir-Mktg, Gap Foundation & Global Sustainability - The Gap, Inc.; pg. 1770, pg. 218
Uri, Karl, Specialist-Food Service Mktg - Alaska Seafood Marketing Institute; pg. 125, pg. 10
Urian, Bill E., Mgr-Mktg Comm - Vapor Bus International; pg. 221, pg. 560
Uribarri, Mari, VP & Mgr-Retail Mktg - FirstMerit Corporation; pg. 758, pg. 1400
Uribe, Mary, Sr VP-Adv Sls & Reprints-North America, Europe & Asia - MORNINGSTAR, INC.; pg. 784, pg. 583
Urich, Gerald R., Sr Dir-External Reporting & Compliance - The Hershey Co.; pg. 1855, pg. 1538
Uricheck, Mike, Sr Dir-Partner Bus Dev-Enterprise Social Software - SAP America, Inc.; pg. 466, pg. 1557
Urintsev, Sonia, Brand Mgr-Coors Light Multicultural - MillerCoors LLC; pg. 255, pg. 582
Urmey, Wyatt, Program Dir-MobileFirst Svcs Strategy & Category Mktg - International Business Machines Corporation; pg. 418, pg. 1138
Urquhart, Loren, VP-Comml & Sls - ADM Milling; pg. 825, pg. 718
Urquhart, Matthew, Engr-Product Design - Specialized Bicycle Components, Inc.; pg. 1711, pg. 152
Urquia, Danny, Mgr-Partnership Mktg - Major League Soccer LLC; pg. 560, pg. 1256
Urquidez, Regina, Mgr-Special Events Sls - San Jose Convention/Visitors Bureau; pg. 1005, pg. 250
Urrea, Luis, Dir-Mktg-Latin America & Caribbean - Avis Budget Group, Inc.; pg. 1900, pg. 1102
Urrea, Luis, Dir-Mktg-Latin America & Caribbean - Avis Rent A Car System, LLC; pg. 165, pg. 1102
Urry, Cameron, Sr Mgr-Acq Interactive Mktg - Extra Space Storage, Inc.; pg. 1091, pg. 1757
Ursem, Terry, Reg Mgr-Sls - PepsiCo, Inc.; pg. 259, pg. 1327
Urso, Betsy, Coord-Mktg - Federal Agricultural Mortgage Corporation; pg. 751, pg. 399
Urvina, Gabriela, Dir-Mktg-OneStopPlus.com - FULLBEAUTY Brands; pg. 1770, pg. 1233
Uschak, Christopher, Assoc Dir-Product Quality Complaints Mgmt - Bristol-Myers Squibb Company; pg. 1509, pg. 1206
Usherwood, Dorian, Head-Creative Svcs & Exec Dir-Creative - Equifax Inc.; pg. 748, pg. 504
Ushman, John, Sr Dir-Global Media - Electronic Arts Inc.; pg. 951, pg. 189
Uskert, Daniel, Sr Mgr-Mktg - Tyson Foods, Inc.; pg. 902, pg. 35
Ussary, Josh, Dir-Media & Analytics - AMC Entertainment Inc.; pg. 527, pg. 716
Utay, Paul, Mgr-Scientific & Indus Sls - Continental Electronics Corporation; pg. 630, pg. 1678
Utay, Robin, Dir-Pkg Creative & Productions - Dr Pepper Snapple Group, Inc.; pg. 250, pg. 1729
Utenwoldt, Debra, Acct Exec-Adv - Cablevision Systems Corporation; pg. 272, pg. 1141
Uthman, Janet, VP-Inclusion & Multicultural Mktg-Northeast Div - Comcast Corporation; pg. 276, pg. 1560
Utlaut, Kim, Dir-Sports Mktg & Partnership Mgmt - Coca-Cola Refreshments USA, Inc.; pg. 247, pg. 500
Utley, Holland, Dir-Creative - Redbook; pg. 1680, pg. 1285
Utter, Lisa, Mgr-Mktg Svcs - John Morrell Food Group; pg. 866, pg. 628
Utterback, Duane, Dir-Channel Mktg - MTD Products, Inc.; pg. 1057, pg. 1478
Utz, Jennifer, VP-Buzz Mktg & Partnerships-Global Mktg - Marriott International, Inc.; pg. 1102, pg. 764
Uyeda, Mason, Sr Dir-Solutions Mktg, Mgmt & Technical Enablement - VMware, Inc.; pg. 490, pg. 179
Uyleman, Xander, Sr Mgr-Partner Mktg-Global - Cisco Systems, Inc.; pg. 372, pg. 240
Uzzell, David, Brand Mgr - Kashi Company; pg. 830, pg. 119

V

Vaccari, Andrea, Product Mgr - Facebook, Inc.; pg. 1245, pg. 143
Vaccari, Christopher, Dir Library Mktg - Sterling Publishing Co., Inc.; pg. 1689, pg. 1296
Vaccaro, Jim, Product Mgr - Rinnai America Corp.; pg. 1076, pg. 538
Vaccaro, Sue, Sr Dir-Govt Affairs-California - Comcast Corporation; pg. 276, pg. 1560
Vacha, Sara, Brand Mgr - The Goodyear Tire & Rubber Company; pg. 1883, pg. 1401
Vadillo, Jenine, Mgr-Digital Media - Apollo Education Group Inc.; pg. 597, pg. 14
Vadnere, Harshal, Product Mgr - Microsoft Corporation; pg. 435, pg. 1824
Vaghani, Ketan, Sr Assoc Brand Mgr - The Kraft Heinz Company; pg. 871, pg. 641
Vagher, Joseph, Sr Dir-Franchise Ops - Famous Dave's of America, Inc.; pg. 1728, pg. 926
Vaglio, Nick, VP-Comml Mktg - Wells Fargo & Company; pg. 819, pg. 232
Vagner, Nika, Editor-Social Media - AMC Networks Inc.; pg. 269, pg. 1189
Vagner, Nika, Sr Editor-Social Media & Partnerships - In Style Magazine; pg. 1652, pg. 1243
Vagnone, Lauren, Mgr-Solutions & Product Mktg - R.R. Donnelley & Sons Company; pg. 1682, pg. 589
Vahle, Paul, Dir-CRDM Mktg Comm - Medtronic, Inc.; pg. 1564, pg. 939
Vahora, Nilofar, Dir-Product Strategy-Tech Accessories - Kate Spade & Company; pg. 27, pg. 1248
Vaideeswaran, Shivram, Dir-Global Mktg & Digital - Taco Bell Corp.; pg. 1752, pg. 117
Vaidya, Anjali, Sr Mgr-Mobile Products - Yahoo! Inc.; pg. 1289, pg. 289
Vaidya, Avi, CTO & Exec VP-Product Dev - Shure Incorporated; pg. 672, pg. 638
Vaidyanathan, Suja, Sr Product Mgr - WhitePages.com Inc.; pg. 1289, pg. 1842
Vaile, John, Assoc Dir-Dermatology Mktg - Novartis Corporation; pg. 1574, pg. 1273
Vaile, John, Assoc Dir-Dermatology Mktg - Novartis Pharmaceuticals Corp.; pg. 1575, pg. 1054
Vainisi, Frank, Mgr-Sls - Rose Packing Company; pg. 892, pg. 556
Vaish, Parag, Dir-Mobile Product Mgmt - StubHub, Inc.; pg. 586, pg. 228
Vakil, Nishita, Brand Mgr-Innovation - The Clorox Company; pg. 327, pg. 169
Vakoutis, Evangelia, Sr Dir-Comm & Media-Global - adidas America Inc.; pg. 1803, pg. 1500
Vaky, Stephanie, Mgr-Product Mktg-Google Fiber - Google Inc.; pg. 1249, pg. 153
Valachos, Michael, Dir-Sls & Mktg - Conax Technologies LLC; pg. 1325, pg. 1148
Valade, Jessica, Brand Mktg Mgr - Hotwire, Inc.; pg. 1912, pg. 219
Valcarcel, Anthony, Sr Product Mgr-Live Svcs Mktg - Amazon.com, Inc.; pg. 1226, pg. 1831
Valdes, Eduardo, Sr Dir-Global Product Mktg-Girls Div - MATTEL, INC.; pg. 962, pg. 81
Valdes, Joe, Mgr-Sls - Frontera Foods, Inc.; pg. 857, pg. 574
Valdes, Katiana, Mgr-Mktg-Comm - FRESH DEL MONTE PRODUCE INC.; pg. 856, pg. 418
Valdes, Renae, Sr Mgr-Shopper Mktg-Multicultural & Head-Hispanic Channel - The Coca-Cola Company; pg. 240, pg. 493
Valdez, Augusto, Dir-Product Mktg-Windows Phone - Microsoft Corporation; pg. 435, pg. 1824
Valdez, Rachelle R., VP-Comm & Mktg-Delphi Electrical &

Electronic Architecture - Delphi Automotive LLP; *pg.* 204, *pg.* 910
Valdivia, Carlos, Brand Mgr-Brand Plng & Execution-Cottonelle - Kimberly-Clark Corporation; *pg.* 1461, *pg.* 1720
Valdov, Louise H., Dir-Mktg - Toll Brothers, Inc.; *pg.* 115, *pg.* 1541
Vale, Amy, Head-Global B2B Mktg & Brand Experience - Spotify; *pg.* 1282, *pg.* 1295
Valencia, Carolina V., Sr Dir-Corp Comm - Univision Communications Inc.; *pg.* 683, *pg.* 1307
Valencia, Raymond, Mgr-Digital Mktg - Intuit Inc.; *pg.* 769, *pg.* 158
Valencia, Venita, Mgr-Mktg - Cisco Systems, Inc.; *pg.* 372, *pg.* 240
Valencic Laudato, Silvana, Category Mgr-Mktg - The Goodyear Tire & Rubber Company; *pg.* 1883, *pg.* 1401
Valencourt, Jay, Mgr-Adv Sls Ops - Worcester Telegram & Gazette Corp.; *pg.* 1702, *pg.* 863
Valenta, Jodi, Dir-Mktg - Go Daddy Inc.; *pg.* 1249, *pg.* 21
Valenta, Michael J., Dir-Oncology Payer & Access Mktg-Tafinlar, Mekinist & Tykerb - GlaxoSmithKline; *pg.* 1536, *pg.* 1565
Valente, John, Sr Product Mgr-Seller Insights - eBay Inc.; *pg.* 1240, *pg.* 243
Valente, Nick, Assoc Dir-Social Media - Verizon Communications Inc.; *pg.* 1875, *pg.* 1309
Valenti, Lou, Dir-Sls - Flexbar Machine Corp.; *pg.* 1337, *pg.* 1169
Valenti, Sandra P., Dir-Mktg Ops - Comcast Cable Communications, Inc.; *pg.* 276, *pg.* 1560
Valentin, Amity, Sr Mgr-Mktg-QuickBooks Desktop - Intuit Inc.; *pg.* 769, *pg.* 158
Valentin, Ryan, Engr-Product Support - Disqus; *pg.* 1239, *pg.* 216
Valentine, Derek, Mgr-Inside Sls-Demand Generation - Dell Inc.; *pg.* 383, *pg.* 1737
Valentine, Meredith, Brand Mgr-Global - Johnson & Johnson; *pg.* 1549, *pg.* 1091
Valentine, Michael, VP-Content Media Ops - Gannett Co., Inc.; *pg.* 289, *pg.* 1681
Valentine, Shauna, Specialist-Clinical Mktg - Siemens Healthcare Diagnostics; *pg.* 673, *pg.* 604
Valentine, Stephanie, Mgr-Mktg & Strategist-Comm - Invesco Ltd.; *pg.* 771, *pg.* 513
Valentine, Tiffany, Dir-Mktg-Smucker's Fruit Spreads & Ice Cream Toppings - The J.M. Smucker Company; *pg.* 865, *pg.* 1468
Valentine, Will, VP & Head-Corp Comm & PR - Pandora Media Inc.; *pg.* 1273, *pg.* 172
Valentini, Giovanni, VP-Mktg-Giorgio Armani USA-New York - L'Oreal USA; *pg.* 514, *pg.* 1252
Valentino, Michael, VP-Comm & Mktg - Wyndham Worldwide Corporation; *pg.* 1119, *pg.* 1107
Valentino, Tara, Sr Mgr-Comm, Pub Affairs & Corp Events - TD Ameritrade Holding Corporation; *pg.* 808, *pg.* 1018
Valentzas, Anne, VP-Affluent Consumer Mktg - MasterCard Incorporated; *pg.* 779, *pg.* 1325
Valentzas, Anne, VP-Affluent Consumer Mktg - MasterCard Worldwide Inc.; *pg.* 780, *pg.* 988
Valeria, Todd, Exec Dir-Creative Mktg Svcs - Colony Brands Inc.; *pg.* 849, *pg.* 1881
Valette, Kristin, VP-Mktg & Comm - PADI Americas; *pg.* 573, *pg.* 188
Valiente, Alfredo, Brand Mgr - Benjamin Moore & Co.; *pg.* 1440, *pg.* 1085
Valiente, Federico, Sr Mgr-Mktg - Pollo Campero; *pg.* 1782, *pg.* 1685
Valim, Alexandre, Sr Product Mgr - Pfizer Inc.; *pg.* 1581, *pg.* 1278
Valitchka, Tom, Dir-Whirl-Pak Sls - Nasco International, Inc.; *pg.* 1779, *pg.* 1858
Valk, Maarten, Mgr-Mktg-Western Europe - Heineken USA Inc.; *pg.* 252, *pg.* 1352
Valle, Annie, Dir-Digital Mktg - Sony Pictures Home Entertainment; *pg.* 310, *pg.* 72
Valle, Ayan, Dir-Digital & Social Media Partnerships - Telemundo Network Inc.; *pg.* 311, *pg.* 430
Valle, Chris, Head-Indus-Media Sls - Google Inc.; *pg.* 1249, *pg.* 153
Valle, Christine, Sr Mgr-Mktg Programs-Global - Luminex Corporation; *pg.* 1421, *pg.* 1664
Valle, Fherlette Del, Mgr-Mktg Dev - Coca-Cola Refreshments USA, Inc.; *pg.* 247, *pg.* 500
Valle, Jose, Pres-Political & Advocacy Sls - Univision Communications Inc.; *pg.* 683, *pg.* 1307
Valle, Tamara Del, Sr Specialist-Social Media Plng & Strategy - J.C. Penney Company, Inc.; *pg.* 1774, *pg.* 1732
Vallejo, Delia, Sr Dir-ECommerce - Keurig Green Mountain, Inc.; *pg.* 868, *pg.* 1768
Vallejo, Hector, Mgr-Multicultural Mktg - Stanley Black & Decker, Inc.; *pg.* 1063, *pg.* 358
Vallejo-Bohnert, Rachel, Coord-Mktg-Latin America Reg - Brown-Forman Corporation; *pg.* 1958, *pg.* 732
Vallery, Melissa, Brand Mgr-Retail Dev - Ralph Lauren Corporation; *pg.* 46, *pg.* 1284
Vallett, Jeff, Product Mgr - Lochinvar Corporation; *pg.* 1073, *pg.* 1640
Valletta, David, Exec VP-Sls-Worldwide - Vishay Americas; *pg.* 686, *pg.* 371
Valletta, David, Exec VP-Sls-Worldwide - Vishay Intertechnology, Inc.; *pg.* 1435, *pg.* 1551
Valley, Amy W., Dir-Mktg Mgmt-VitalSource GPO - Cardinal Health, Inc.; *pg.* 1512, *pg.* 1448
Valley, Chris, Sr Mgr - Deloitte & Touche USA LLP; *pg.* 743, *pg.* 1222
Valli, Amy, Mgr-PR - McKesson Corporation; *pg.* 1560, *pg.* 222
Valli, Gail, Mgr-Classified Adv - The Canton Repository; *pg.* 1625, *pg.* 1407
Vallier, Michael, Mgr-Product Dev & Mktg-Drive Svcs - ABB Inc.; *pg.* 1309, *pg.* 1359
Vallo, Mia, Sr Dir-Mktg Analytics & Optimization - National Geographic Society; *pg.* 1667, *pg.* 402
Valosky, Chris, Reg Dir-Sls - Takeda Pharmaceuticals USA, Inc.; *pg.* 1600, *pg.* 605
Valtierra, Lisa, Assoc Dir-Cross Cultural Mktg - Boehringer Ingelheim Pharmaceuticals, Inc.; *pg.* 1507, *pg.* 368
Vamos, Frank, Mgr-Event Mktg - The Wendy's Company; *pg.* 1755, *pg.* 1450
Vamvakidou, Alexandra, Specialist-Field Mktg - PerkinElmer, Inc.; *pg.* 1426, *pg.* 853
Van Adelsberg, Janet, Sr Dir-Immunology & Inflammation - Regeneron Pharmaceuticals, Inc.; *pg.* 1588, *pg.* 1345
Van Allen, Rich, Dir-Mktg Data Svcs - CDS Global, Inc.; *pg.* 370, *pg.* 704
Van Ark, Andy, Brand Mgr-Nutro Innovation - Mars Petcare; *pg.* 1478, *pg.* 1633
Van Auker, Tracy M., Program Mgr-PR - Paychex, Inc.; *pg.* 792, *pg.* 1336
van Benten, Susan, Sr VP-Mdsg, Plng & Allocation - Hancock Fabrics, Inc.; *pg.* 693, *pg.* 968
Van Boerum, Robert, Dir-Mktg - BAZI INTERNATIONAL, INC.; *pg.* 1501, *pg.* 107
Van Breusegen, Thane, VP-Corp Mktg & Stadium Entertainment - Saint Louis Cardinals, L.P.; *pg.* 580, *pg.* 1002
Van Brocklin, Laurie, Sr Dir-Comm & Mktg Svcs - General Dynamics Corporation; *pg.* 228, *pg.* 1781
Van Buren, Justin, Mgr-Cloud & Data Center Mktg-North America - Intel Corporation; *pg.* 645, *pg.* 266
Van Buren, Liza, Assoc-Brand Mktg - Amway Corporation; *pg.* 326, *pg.* 864
Van Buren, Maggie, Mgr-Mktg - Briggs & Stratton Corporation; *pg.* 201, *pg.* 1899
Van Buskirk, Mark, Exec VP-Mdsg & Mktg - SUPERVALU, Inc.; *pg.* 1035, *pg.* 924
Van Cott, Kristen, Sr VP-Creative Dev - SKECHERS U.S.A., INC.; *pg.* 1819, *pg.* 143
van de Beek, Garen, Exec VP & Dir-Creative-CBS Mktg Grp-CBS Television Network - CBS Broadcasting Inc.; *pg.* 273, *pg.* 1210
van de Beek, Garen, Exec VP & Dir-Creative-CBS Mktg Grp - CBS Corporation; *pg.* 273, *pg.* 1210
Van De Hey, Michele, VP-Sls-Worldwide - Daegis Inc; *pg.* 381, *pg.* 195
Van De Veere, Theresa, Sr Mgr-Demand Generation Mktg - Blackbaud, Inc.; *pg.* 361, *pg.* 1613
Van de Vyvor, Erik, Dir-Sls-Europe - O'Brien Corporation; *pg.* 1366, *pg.* 1001
Van De Wal, Eric, VP-Mktg - Snyder's-Lance, Inc.; *pg.* 896, *pg.* 1368
Van De Water, Joe, Dir-Mktg - Intel Corporation; *pg.* 645, *pg.* 266
Van Dell, Andrea, Sls Mgr-Application & Manufacturing Vertical - Oracle Corporation; *pg.* 1272, *pg.* 786
Van Den Berg, Michael, VP-Mdsg, Mktg & Digital-Intl - GameStop Corp.; *pg.* 399, *pg.* 1699
Van Den Boom, Dirk, Interim Pres, Interim CEO & Chief Scientific & Strategy Officer - Sequenom, Inc.; *pg.* 1593, *pg.* 209
Van Den Bos, Katie, Sr VP-Digital Mktg-Ask com - IAC Search & Media, Inc.; *pg.* 1257, *pg.* 171
van den Brink, Ruud, Product Mgr-Power Interconnects - TE Connectivity Ltd.; *pg.* 677, *pg.* 1515
Van Den Goorbergh, Desiree, Dir-Product Mgmt - Expedia, Inc.; *pg.* 1244, *pg.* 1814
van der Kooi, Rik, Corp VP-Microsoft Adv - Microsoft Corporation; *pg.* 435, *pg.* 1824
van der Lugt, Pat, Dir-Integrated Mktg Comm-Purina Animal Nutrition - Land O'Lakes, Inc.; *pg.* 873, *pg.* 915
van der Meijden, Martin, Product Mgr-Ceilings - Hunter Douglas, Inc.; *pg.* 928, *pg.* 1320
Van Dillen, Rich, VP-Sls & Mktg - MEG; *pg.* 97, *pg.* 675
Van Dorselaer, Dave, Sr Dir-Bus Dev & Industrial-IoT Solutions - AT&T Communications Corp.; *pg.* 1866, *pg.* 1043
Van Dyck, Brandon, Sr Mgr-Global Brand Mktg - Honeywell International Inc.; *pg.* 407, *pg.* 1088
Van Dyck, Jeffery J., Dir-Creative-Boeing Comml Airplanes - The Boeing Company; *pg.* 225, *pg.* 567
Van Dyck, Rebecca, Head-Brand Mktg - Facebook, Inc.; *pg.* 1245, *pg.* 143
Van Dyke, Vicky, Dir-Mktg - Earnhardt's Auto Centers; *pg.* 169, *pg.* 12
Van Epps, David, Exec VP-Sls & Global Chief Product Officer - Mood Media; *pg.* 298, *pg.* 1616
van Es, Charles, Head-Mktg-Americas-Vita Coco - All Market, Inc.; *pg.* 237, *pg.* 1189
van Essen, Randy, Dir-Adv-Global - Reebok International Ltd.; *pg.* 1817, *pg.* 811
Van Fleet, Ryan, Sr Dir-Insights & Analytics - Tremor Video; *pg.* 682, *pg.* 1305
Van Gieson, Michael P., Sr VP-Product Mktg - SYNNEX Corporation; *pg.* 480, *pg.* 92
Van Gorp, Craig, Exec VP-Sls - Virgil Films & Entertainment; *pg.* 317, *pg.* 1311
Van Helvoirt, Michael, Mgr-Product Mktg - Ariens Company Inc.; *pg.* 700, *pg.* 1855
Van Hoffman, Jason, Dir-Mktg & Comm - Chesapeake Energy Corporation; *pg.* 1937, *pg.* 1485
Van Houten, Allison, Head-Mktg-Google Fiber, Brand, Adv & Content Partnerships - Google Inc.; *pg.* 1249, *pg.* 153
Van Huizen, Harvey, Dir-Customer Svc & Sls Support - Anchor Danly; *pg.* 67, *pg.* 1948
van Hummel, Monique, Dir-Mktg-Portfolio Brands - Fossil Group, Inc.; *pg.* 5, *pg.* 1735
Van Keuren, Carol, Dir-Adv - Theatre Communications Group, Inc.; *pg.* 587, *pg.* 1298
Van Kirk, Jim, VP-Mktg Comm - PulteGroup, Inc.; *pg.* 1109, *pg.* 873
Van Kirk, Tom, VP-Sls & Mktg - SFS intec, Inc.; *pg.* 1061, *pg.* 1596
Van Kooten, B. Chad, Dir-Sls - HSM Solutions; *pg.* 1884, *pg.* 1378
van Kooten, Lidwina, VP-Mktg-Hormel Foods-Farmer John - Clougherty Packing Company; *pg.* 848, *pg.* 128
Van Landingham, Stacey, Sr Mgr-Production - Texas Monthly; *pg.* 1692, *pg.* 1666
Van Laningham, Bill, Dir-Mktg - Los Angeles Daily News Publishing Company; *pg.* 1660, *pg.* 308
Van Leer, Jack, Sr Mgr-US Mktg-Hasbro Gaming - Hasbro, Inc.; *pg.* 954, *pg.* 1603
Van Leuvan, Nicole, Brand Mgr - Central Garden & Pet Company; *pg.* 1475, *pg.* 303
van Lingen, Dennis, Chief Product Officer - Forrester Research, Inc.; *pg.* 1642, *pg.* 807
Van Loon, Emily, Sr Mgr-Fin Svcs Mktg - Best Buy Co., Inc.; *pg.* 1761, *pg.* 954
van Maaren, Jan-Paul, VP-Mktg - Pall Corporation; *pg.* 232, *pg.* 1323
Van Malssen, Hannah, Asst Mgr-PR - Newell Rubbermaid Inc.; *pg.* 1128, *pg.* 515
Van Matre, Allison, Sr Mgr-Global Assoc Comm - Wal-Mart.com; *pg.* 1287, *pg.* 50
Van Meter, Joshua, Mgr-Mktg-Fats & Oils Sls - Archer-Daniels-Midland Company; *pg.* 825, *pg.* 565
Van Meter, Melissa, VP-Mktg & Adv - TV Guide Magazine Group, Inc.; *pg.* 1697, *pg.* 1305
Van Mierlo, Chris, CMO & Sr VP-Sls - Pacific Life Insurance Company; *pg.* 1213, *pg.* 166
Van Munching, Brennan, Mgr-Mktg - The New Yorker Magazine, Inc.; *pg.* 1669, *pg.* 1271
Van Nostran, Derek, VP-Digital Mktg - Cable News Network LP; *pg.* 1624, *pg.* 1208
Van Nostrand, Breanne, Mgr-Social Media - Hofstra University;

pg. 602, *pg.* 1166
Van Ongevalle, Alan, Sr VP-Mdsg - Hastings Entertainment, Inc.; *pg.* 1773, *pg.* 1659
Van Orman, Mark H., Sr Dir-Content Ops - R.R. Bowker LLC; *pg.* 1682, *pg.* 1095
van Pelt, Marten, Exec Dir-Advisory Mktg - KPMG LLP; *pg.* 774, *pg.* 1086
Van Plew, Daniel, Sr VP & Gen Mgr-Indus Ops & Product Supply - Regeneron Pharmaceuticals, Inc.; *pg.* 1588, *pg.* 1345
Van Put, Susan, Brand Mgr-Dior Eyewear-Americas Reg - Safilo USA Inc.; *pg.* 11, *pg.* 1106
Van Raalte, Hanno, Product Mgr-Moldflow - Autodesk Inc.; *pg.* 356, *pg.* 257
Van Ryan, Lori, Mgr-Mktg Alliances-NA - Shell Oil Company; *pg.* 984, *pg.* 1714
Van Ryne, Therese, Head-PR & Analyst Rels-Global - Zebra Technologies Corporation; *pg.* 690, *pg.* 628
Van Sach, Amy, Dir-Mktg-Global - Mallinckrodt Pharmaceuticals; *pg.* 1557, *pg.* 978
Van Sicklen, Nick, VP-Digital Sls - Time Inc.; *pg.* 1693, *pg.* 1300
van Steenberge, Cecile, Dir-Large Customer Sls - Google Inc.; *pg.* 1249, *pg.* 153
Van Stone, Jim, Sr VP-Ticket Sls & Svc - Washington Capitals; *pg.* 591, *pg.* 1775
Van Tieghem, Stephanie, Assoc-Social Media Mktg - The Bradford Group; *pg.* 1763, *pg.* 637
Van Til, Evelyn, Coord-Digital Media Mktg - Tween Brands Inc.; *pg.* 34, *pg.* 1467
Van Ullen, Julie, Sr Dir-Publr Bus Dev - OpenX Technologies, Inc.; *pg.* 1272, *pg.* 180
Van Valkenburgh, Deborah, Sr VP-Strategic Brand Mgmt & Corp Mktg-PNC Bank - The PNC Financial Services Group, Inc.; *pg.* 795, *pg.* 1579
Van Velsor, Lora, VP-Mktg-all - The Sun Products Corporation; *pg.* 336, *pg.* 385
Van Vleet, Matthew, Mgr-US Mktg-Laminating Adhesives - 3M Company; *pg.* 1142, *pg.* 956
Van Wieren, Michael, Head-Trade Mktg-BD Medical & Diabetes Care - Becton, Dickinson & Company; *pg.* 1501, *pg.* 1068
Van Winkel, Steef, Head-Product & Remarketing-Global - Google Inc.; *pg.* 1249, *pg.* 153
Van Winkle, Jon, VP-Product Mgmt - Omnitracs, LLC; *pg.* 449, *pg.* 1685
Van Woudenberg, Scott, Product Mgr-Cloud - Google Inc.; *pg.* 1249, *pg.* 153
Van Wylick, Bastien, Strategist-Creative & Digital - Deloitte & Touche USA LLP; *pg.* 743, *pg.* 1222
Van Wyngarden, Tim, VP-Sls - CIBER, Inc.; *pg.* 372, *pg.* 330
Van Zandt, Devin, Product Mgr-Software - GE Energy; *pg.* 1338, *pg.* 506
van Zwol, Roelof, Dir-Product Innovation, Search & Personalization Algorithms - Netflix, Inc.; *pg.* 1269, *pg.* 141
Vanacore, Chris, Bus Mgr-Domestic Intermodal - Union Pacific Corporation; *pg.* 1927, *pg.* 1018
VanAntwerp, Jay, Mgr-Strategic Initiatives & Additional Products - The Progressive Corporation; *pg.* 1214, *pg.* 1463
Vanasin, Vanessa, Mgr-PR - Blizzard Entertainment; *pg.* 950, *pg.* 107
VanBibber, Jim, Dir-Mdse - The Sharper Image; *pg.* 1785, *pg.* 886
VanBuren, Denise D., Corp Sec & VP-PR - Central Hudson Gas & Electric Corporation; *pg.* 1937, *pg.* 1324
VanBuren, Denise D., Corp Sec & VP-PR - CH Energy Group, Inc.; *pg.* 973, *pg.* 1324
VanBuskirk, Kathy, Acct Exec-Adv - The Daily Item; *pg.* 1632, *pg.* 829
Vance, Donia, Sr Dir-Mktg Comm - WebMD Health Services Group; *pg.* 1609, *pg.* 1508
Vance, Jessica, Specialist-Adv-Apparel - Academy Sports & Outdoors, Ltd.; *pg.* 1824, *pg.* 1724
Vance, Kristy, Dir-Media Insights-Global - Unilever United States, Inc.; *pg.* 904, *pg.* 1061
Vance, Oscar, Sr Dir-Mktg & Fulfillment Ops - UnitedHealth Group Incorporated; *pg.* 1221, *pg.* 950
Vance, Simon, Brand Mgr-Durables - Amway Corporation; *pg.* 326, *pg.* 864
Vance, Tim, Dir-Mktg - Kunzler & Company, Inc.; *pg.* 1026, *pg.* 1546
Vancura, Robin, Sr Mgr-Mktg-Social Small Bus Comm Strategy - Staples, Inc.; *pg.* 474, *pg.* 821
Vandal, Frances E., Brand Mgr & Strategist-Mktg Comm - Raytheon Company; *pg.* 233, *pg.* 854
Vandarakis, Nick, Sr Mgr-Product Mktg - Esurance, Inc.; *pg.* 1243, *pg.* 217
Vandegrift, Jim, Sr Dir-Creative Svcs - NVIDIA Corporation; *pg.* 447, *pg.* 268
Vandehey, Brad, Product Mgr - Cascade Corporation; *pg.* 1321, *pg.* 1497
Vandel, Michael, Mgr-Retail Mktg - FMC Corporation; *pg.* 1163, *pg.* 1564
Vandenberg, Neil, VP-Sls - LabelQuest, Inc.; *pg.* 1463, *pg.* 611
Vandenbergh, Jim, VP-Sls & Mktg - Rose Packing Company; *pg.* 892, *pg.* 556
Vandenberghe, Cory, Mgr-Digital Mktg - CARIBOU COFFEE COMPANY, INC.; *pg.* 1764, *pg.* 932
VanDenBerghe, Donald, Mgr-Northeast Reg Sls - Redco Foods, Inc.; *pg.* 891, *pg.* 1174
Vandenberghe, Heather, Exec VP-Mktg & Comm-The Americas - Tommy Hilfiger USA; *pg.* 48, *pg.* 1302
VandenBoom, Bob, Sr Mgr-Mktg - The Toro Company; *pg.* 1065, *pg.* 918
Vandenbrouck, Heidi A., Sr Mgr-Comm-New England - Charter Communications, Inc.; *pg.* 274, *pg.* 372
Vanderham, Gloria K., Head-Social & Digital Media-Global - Novartis Corporation; *pg.* 1574, *pg.* 1273
Vanderheyden, Don, Dir-Mktg - Hennessy Industries, Inc.; *pg.* 207, *pg.* 1639
Vanderheyden, Douglas, Sr Dir-Ticket Ops - Coyotes Hockey, LLC; *pg.* 542, *pg.* 13
Vanderhoof, Troy, Dir-Mktg - Siemens PLM Software; *pg.* 469, *pg.* 1734
VanderHorst, Kacy, Product Mgr-REV Brand - Hormel Foods Corporation; *pg.* 863, *pg.* 915
Vandermause, Katie, Mgr-PR - Constellation Brands, Inc.; *pg.* 1960, *pg.* 1348
Vandermeulen, Joel, Assoc Brand Mgr-Cardiovascular Mktg & Strategy - Eli Lilly and Company; *pg.* 1527, *pg.* 684
Vanderminden, Adam, Dir-Adv - Telescope Casual Furniture Inc.; *pg.* 944, *pg.* 1162
Vanderpool, Kimberly, Specialist-Mktg - CB Richard Ellis, Inc.; *pg.* 1085, *pg.* 1210
Vanderstelt, Marty, Assoc Dir-Mktg-Feminine Care-Central, Eastern, & Southern Europe - The Procter & Gamble Company; *pg.* 1129, *pg.* 1418
Vandervoet, Jeremy, Dir-Mktg - Nestle USA, Inc.; *pg.* 883, *pg.* 96
Vanderwaal, David, VP-Mktg - LG Electronics U.S.A., Inc.; *pg.* 651, *pg.* 1060
Vanderwel, Erin, Mgr-Mktg-Global Brand Loyalty - Starbucks Corporation; *pg.* 897, *pg.* 1840
Vanderzanden, Marty, Sr Dir - Allianz Life Insurance Company of North America; *pg.* 1188, *pg.* 929
VanDerzee, Jay, Head-Programmatic Media Platform Sls - Google Inc.; *pg.* 1249, *pg.* 153
VanDette, Joseph, VP-CRM, Analytics & Digital Mktg - Smart & Final, Inc.; *pg.* 1034, *pg.* 66
Vandiver, Gregory P., Sr VP-Sls & Mktg - Peabody Energy Corporation; *pg.* 1176, *pg.* 1001
Vandiver, Lauren, Coord-PR & Mktg & Copywriter - Fossil Group, Inc.; *pg.* 5, *pg.* 1735
Vando, Jacqueline M., Coord-Event Mktg - National Grid USA; *pg.* 1946, *pg.* 852
Vandor, Mollie, Product Mgr-Safety & Security - Twitter, Inc.; *pg.* 1285, *pg.* 228
Vandoros, Jerry, Product Mgr-Kadant Solutions - KADANT INC.; *pg.* 1352, *pg.* 858
VanDyke, Matt, Dir-Global Lincoln Mktg, Sls & Svc - Ford Motor Company; *pg.* 172, *pg.* 876
Vaneri, Gaston, VP-Mktg-Rubbermaid, Dymo & Licensing-Global - Newell Rubbermaid Inc.; *pg.* 1128, *pg.* 515
Vanes, Amber Stafford, VP & Mgr-Mdse-Apparel & Accessories - The Finish Line, Inc.; *pg.* 1769, *pg.* 686
Vanfossen, Don, Brand Mgr - The Procter & Gamble Company; *pg.* 1129, *pg.* 1418
Vangeli, Dominick, VP-Product Dev & iTV Production Svcs - Cablevision Systems Corporation; *pg.* 272, *pg.* 1141
VanHimbergen, David, Brand Mgr-Global Laundry Front-End Innovation - The Procter & Gamble Company; *pg.* 1129, *pg.* 1418
Vankomen, J. J., Brand Mgr-Natl Field Ops - Extra Space Storage, Inc.; *pg.* 1091, *pg.* 1757
VanLammeren, Patty, Sr VP-Sls & Reg Mktg - The Allstate Corporation; *pg.* 1189, *pg.* 639
Vanlerberghe, Marc, Sr Dir-Global Mktg-Android, Content & Devices - Google Inc.; *pg.* 1249, *pg.* 153
Vann, Gary, Sr VP-Sls & Mktg - Mighty Distributing System of America; *pg.* 213, *pg.* 538
Vann, Kate, Dir-Mktg - Lifetouch, Inc.; *pg.* 1420, *pg.* 922
Vannan, Shivanthi, Dir-Mktg-Healthcare - Reckitt Benckiser Inc.; *pg.* 1136, *pg.* 1105
Vannatter, Jay, Sr VP-Sls & Bus Dev - Nikon Inc.; *pg.* 1424, *pg.* 1181
Vannerson, Lance, Sr Mgr-Customer Mktg - PepsiCo, Inc.; *pg.* 259, *pg.* 1327
Vannicola, Tony, VP-Integrated Mktg - American Century Investments; *pg.* 711, *pg.* 980
Vannoy, Jeff, Sr Product Mgr - BASF; *pg.* 1793, *pg.* 992
VanOfferen, Andy, Dir-Mktg-Global - Kimberly-Clark Corporation; *pg.* 1461, *pg.* 1720
VanRoekel, Larry, Dir-Mktg-Animal Milk Products Company - Land O'Lakes, Inc.; *pg.* 873, *pg.* 915
VanSickle, Megan, Sr Mgr-Food Mktg - Wal-Mart Stores, Inc.; *pg.* 1790, *pg.* 29
VanSlyke, Heather, Mgr-Mktg-GE, Indus Solutions & Canada - GE Canada Company; *pg.* 1296, *pg.* 1926
VanSomeren, Barb, VP-Mktg - Beltone Electronics LLC; *pg.* 1503, *pg.* 614
VanWagoner, Erica, Brand Mgr - Newell Rubbermaid Inc.; *pg.* 1128, *pg.* 515
VanWetten, Ray, VP-Sls-Pacific Northwest - Unified Grocers, Inc.; *pg.* 1036, *pg.* 66
VanWyngarden, Diane, Asst Dir-Adv - Principal Financial Group, Inc.; *pg.* 796, *pg.* 706
Vanzant, Joshua, VP & Product Mgr-Bankcard - Fifth Third Bancorp; *pg.* 752, *pg.* 1413
Vanzini, Giorgio, Sr VP-Product Dev & Integration - DIRECTV Group Holdings, LLC; *pg.* 281, *pg.* 79
Vara, April, VP-Mktg-Intl - Discovery Communications, Inc.; *pg.* 282, *pg.* 777
Varadi, Ben, Chief Creative Officer & Exec VP - Spin Master Ltd.; *pg.* 967, *pg.* 1943
Varalli, Sharon, Mgr-Global Indus & Offering Mktg - Xerox Corporation; *pg.* 494, *pg.* 365
Varela, Jen, Mgr-Natl Customer Mktg - Wm. Wrigley Jr. Company; *pg.* 1863, *pg.* 596
Vargas, Carolyn, Mgr-Strategic Mktg Programs - Cisco Systems, Inc.; *pg.* 372, *pg.* 240
Vargas, David, Dir-Football Mktg - Stanford University; *pg.* 607, *pg.* 280
Vargas, Jessica, Mgr-Multicultural Mktg - Home Box Office, Inc.; *pg.* 290, *pg.* 1240
Vargas, Lauren, Sr Dir-Digital Mktg - Aetna Inc.; *pg.* 1187, *pg.* 351
Vargas, Lotty, Sr Mgr-Social Media & Community-Univision Interactive Media - Univision Communications Inc.; *pg.* 683, *pg.* 1307
Vargas, Myrdna, Assoc Product Mgr - Church & Dwight Co., Inc.; *pg.* 1153, *pg.* 1063
Vargas, Rick, Dir-Creative - Apple Inc.; *pg.* 350, *pg.* 73
Vargas, Stacy, Coord-New Media - PGA Tour, Inc.; *pg.* 574, *pg.* 460
Vargas, Valerie, VP-Adv & Mktg Comm - AT&T Communications Corp.; *pg.* 1866, *pg.* 1043
Vargas, Valerie, VP-Adv - AT&T Mobility LLC; *pg.* 619, *pg.* 488
Vargo, Natasha, Brand Mgr - Unilever United States, Inc.; *pg.* 904, *pg.* 1061
Varieur, Lauri, VP-Brand-Social Media, Visual Mdsg & Display - BCBG Max Azria Group LLC; *pg.* 19, *pg.* 301
Variola, Kristen, Dir-Social Media - Discovery Communications, Inc.; *pg.* 282, *pg.* 777
Varley, Chris, Exec Dir & Head-HCV Mktg-US - Bristol-Myers Squibb Company; *pg.* 1509, *pg.* 1206
Varma, Manju, Sr Mgr-Product Mgmt & Mktg - QUALCOMM Incorporated; *pg.* 1873, *pg.* 207
Varma, Manu, Sr Dir & Head-Mktg & Strategy - Philips Healthcare; *pg.* 1585, *pg.* 783
Varma, Ritu, Dir-Product Mgmt-Global Digital - McDonald's Corporation; *pg.* 1737, *pg.* 645
Varnadoe, Brian, Sr Dir-Premium Seating - Houston Texans, L.P.; *pg.* 553, *pg.* 1708
Varner, Brandt, Dir-Mktg-Kitchen Solutions - Samsung Electronics America, Inc.; *pg.* 669, *pg.* 1115
Varney, Claire, Specialist-Mktg - Servpro Industries, Inc.; *pg.* 335, *pg.* 1635
Varon, Connie, Brand Mgr - The Coca-Cola Company; *pg.* 240, *pg.* 493
Varon, Leslie F., Interim CFO - Xerox Corporation; *pg.* 494, *pg.* 365
Varones, Elizabeth, Sr Mgr-Digital Mktg - Pfizer Inc.; *pg.* 1581,

pg. 1278
Varrone, Joyce, Dir-Media Svcs - Conair Corporation; *pg.* 505, *pg.* 1055
Vartabedian, Allison, VP-Brand & Product Mktg-NOOK - Barnes & Noble, Inc.; *pg.* 1619, *pg.* 1201
Vasallo, Adam, Sr Mgr-New Bus Dev - HSN, Inc.; *pg.* 291, *pg.* 462
Vasaly, L. William, III, Chief Creative Officer & Exec VP - Oak Ridge Financial Services, Inc.; *pg.* 789, *pg.* 1386
Vasas, Ashley, Sr Specialist-Mktg - Vital Images, Inc.; *pg.* 1607, *pg.* 950
Vasbinder, Jessica, Sr Dir-Consumer Relationship Mktg - Warner Music Group Corp.; *pg.* 590, *pg.* 1313
Vasbinder, Leslie, Coord-Mktg & Special Projects - Trend Magazines, Inc.; *pg.* 1696, *pg.* 465
Vasco, Wendy, Mgr-Corp Brand & Mktg - Sun Life Financial Inc.; *pg.* 806, *pg.* 1944
Vasconez, Juan, Co-Founder & Product Mgr - Panjo; *pg.* 1274, *pg.* 275
Vasel, Todd E., Dir-Mktg & Adv - Dierbergs Markets Inc.; *pg.* 1018, *pg.* 974
Vasko, Michael, Dir-Admissions & Mktg - Bryant & Stratton College; *pg.* 599, *pg.* 1147
Vasquez, David, Mgr-Product Dev - United Airlines, Inc.; *pg.* 1927, *pg.* 593
Vasquez, Debbie, Sr Mgr-Shopper Mktg-Walmart & Sam's Club - Coca-Cola North America; *pg.* 848, *pg.* 500
Vasquez, Margie A., Coord-Mktg - Tetra Tech, Inc.; *pg.* 115, *pg.* 181
Vasquez, Mario, Sr Dir-QA - Electronic Arts Inc.; *pg.* 951, *pg.* 189
Vass, Barbara, Dir-Pharmacy Channel Mktg - Merck & Co., Inc.; *pg.* 1566, *pg.* 1077
Vassak, Rachel, Brand Mgr-Breyers - Unilever United States, Inc.; *pg.* 904, *pg.* 1061
Vassall, Jessica, Coord-Integrated Mktg - New Balance Athletic Shoe, Inc.; *pg.* 1811, *pg.* 798
Vassallo, Mark, VP-Sls-Global - Electronic Theatre Controls, Inc.; *pg.* 1296, *pg.* 1872
Vassallo, Mike, Dir-Media Rels - Milwaukee Brewers Baseball Club, Inc.; *pg.* 562, *pg.* 1878
Vassi, Bob, Reg Mgr-Sls - Draper Knitting Co., Inc.; *pg.* 692, *pg.* 810
Vasudevan, Jay, Sr Product Mgr - StubHub, Inc.; *pg.* 586, *pg.* 228
Vaszily, Michael, Dir-Mktg-Alternate Channels & Strategic Mdsg - Sargento Foods Inc.; *pg.* 894, *pg.* 1886
Vatsa, Saurabh, Dir-Mktg, CRM & Product Plng-India Ops - General Motors Company; *pg.* 175, *pg.* 881
Vatter, Holly, Mgr-Cloud Events Mktg - Hewlett-Packard Company; *pg.* 404, *pg.* 175
Vattimo, Fred, Dir-Corp Adv - Bradford-White Corporation; *pg.* 1069, *pg.* 1514
Vaughan, Delane, Dir-Mktg - R.J. Reynolds Tobacco Co.; *pg.* 1895, *pg.* 1395
Vaughan, Frederick H., Reg Mgr-Sls - Noshok Inc.; *pg.* 1366, *pg.* 1406
Vaughan, Jasmin, Mgr-Creative Mktg - General Electric Company; *pg.* 1297, *pg.* 347
Vaughan, Jennifer, Dir-Sls-US - The Spectranetics Corporation; *pg.* 1595, *pg.* 315
Vaughan, Jo, Mgr-Consumer Relationship Mktg - The Procter & Gamble Company; *pg.* 1129, *pg.* 1418
Vaughan, Koren, Dir-Interactive Sls & Mktg - Inner City Broadcasting Corporation; *pg.* 292, *pg.* 1243
Vaughan, Margot, Sr VP-Customized Mktg-Global - MasterCard Incorporated; *pg.* 779, *pg.* 1325
Vaughan, Margot, Sr VP-Customized Mktg-Global - MasterCard International, Inc.; *pg.* 780, *pg.* 1326
Vaughan, Mark, CMO, Chief Sls Officer & Exec VP - Atlanta Convention & Visitors Bureau; *pg.* 989, *pg.* 489
Vaughan, Mark, VP-Sls & Mktg - BE Aerospace, Inc.; *pg.* 224, *pg.* 478
Vaughan, Michelle, Sr Dir-Integrated Demand Mktg - Imperva, Inc.; *pg.* 413, *pg.* 193
Vaughan, Ryan, Sr VP-Home Loans & Insurance Mktg - Bank of America Corporation; *pg.* 718, *pg.* 1362
Vaughan-Edmunds, Llewellyn, Sr Mgr-Product Mktg-IGBT - International Rectifier Corporation; *pg.* 647, *pg.* 80
Vaughn, Chelsea, VP-Mktg Ops, Digital Channel & Mktg Dev - Penguin Random House; *pg.* 1675, *pg.* 1276
Vaughn, Chelsea, VP-Mktg Ops, Digital Channel & Mktg Dev - Penguin Random House; *pg.* 1675, *pg.* 1276
Vaughn, Chris, Dir-Clinical-Mktg - Erlanger Health System; *pg.* 1529, *pg.* 1629
Vaughn, Francesca, Mgr-Mktg Comm - CertainTeed Corporation; *pg.* 74, *pg.* 1589
Vaughn, Jeff, VP-Sls, Mktg & Customer Svc - Boston Whaler, Inc.; *pg.* 1705, *pg.* 422
Vaughn, Julie O., VP-Bus Dev & Mktg Svcs - Emerald Performance Materials, LLC; *pg.* 1161, *pg.* 1445
Vaughn, Kelly, Mgr-Field Mktg - Dunkin' Brands Group, Inc.; *pg.* 1727, *pg.* 810
Vaughn, Lyndsey, Mgr-LensCrafters Mktg - Luxottica Retail; *pg.* 8, *pg.* 1460
Vaughn, Maria, Mgr-Global Mktg-Intl Fin Institutions - CH2M HILL Companies, Ltd.; *pg.* 75, *pg.* 325
Vaughn, Percy, VP-Eastern Sls Operation - Kia Motors America Inc.; *pg.* 181, *pg.* 112
Vaughn, Peter, Sr VP-Intl Consumer Products & Mktg - American Express Company; *pg.* 712, *pg.* 1190
Vaughn, Steven, Mgr-Mktg-Cardiovascular Ultrasound - General Electric Company; *pg.* 1297, *pg.* 347
Vaughn, Tony D., Exec VP-Exploration & Production - Devon Energy Corporation; *pg.* 976, *pg.* 1704
Vaughn, Tony D., Exec VP-Exploration & Production - Devon Energy Corporation; *pg.* 975, *pg.* 1485
Vaught, Caryn, Mgr-Production - American Hereford Association; *pg.* 129, *pg.* 980
Vawter, Laura, Reg Mgr-Mktg - H&R Block, Inc.; *pg.* 764, *pg.* 983
Vaynberg, Victoria, Dir-Digital Mktg - CBS Sports Division; *pg.* 274, *pg.* 1211
Vaynerman, Marina, Planner-Digital Sls - Turner Broadcasting System, Inc.; *pg.* 314, *pg.* 521
Vazquez, Evelyn, Dir-Leisure Sls - St. Augustine, Ponte Vedra & The Beaches Visitors & Convention Bureau; *pg.* 1006, *pg.* 461
Vazquez, Julie, Sr Mgr-Content Mktg - SHUTTERFLY, INC.; *pg.* 1280, *pg.* 192
Vazquez, Martiza, Asst VP-Residential Lending Sls - Totalbank Corp.; *pg.* 811, *pg.* 447
Vazquez, Tony, Strategist-Creative - Facebook, Inc.; *pg.* 1245, *pg.* 143
Veal, Helen, Mgr-Plng & Effectiveness Mktg - British Airways; *pg.* 1901, *pg.* 1207
Veale, Dannette, Sr Mgr-Digital, Audience & Measurement Strategy - Cisco Systems, Inc.; *pg.* 372, *pg.* 240
Veaney, Simon, Dir-Social Media Comm - American Express Company; *pg.* 712, *pg.* 1190
Vecchio, Danilo Del, Sr Mgr-IT Field Market - Samsung Electronics America, Inc.; *pg.* 669, *pg.* 1115
Vecin, Manuel, VP & Sls Dir - Totalbank Corp.; *pg.* 811, *pg.* 447
Veeck, Lisa, Dir-Media Comm & Publ - ISSA; *pg.* 145, *pg.* 640
Veenstra, Dan, Product Mgr & Head-Huntsville Site - GE Intelligent Platforms; *pg.* 400, *pg.* 1135
Veerepalli, Praneeth, Sr Mgr-Digital & Mobile - CVS Health Corporation; *pg.* 1765, *pg.* 1610
Veevaert, Jim, VP-Product Mgmt-DoubleDown Interactive - International Game Technology; *pg.* 957, *pg.* 1024
Vega, Angelique, Dir-Media - Kaiser Permanente; *pg.* 1552, *pg.* 171
Vega, Laura I., Reg Mgr-Mktg & Comm - McDonald's Corporation; *pg.* 1737, *pg.* 645
Vega, Lily, Head-Multicultural Mktg - Cellco Partnership; *pg.* 1869, *pg.* 1042
Vega, Liz A., Sr Mgr-Pub Sector Indus Mktg - Xerox Corporation; *pg.* 494, *pg.* 365
Vega, Waleska, Mgr-Mktg-Texas Div - Toll Brothers, Inc.; *pg.* 115, *pg.* 1541
Vega, Willy, Mng Dir-Mktg-Americas - Citrix Systems, Inc.; *pg.* 375, *pg.* 424
Vegas, Ricardo E., Mgr-Diageo Europe Customer Mktg-Global Travel Western - Diageo North America, Inc.; *pg.* 1961, *pg.* 361
Vegas, Ricardo E., Mgr-Diageo Europe Customer Mktg-Global Travel Western - Diageo North America Inc.; *pg.* 248, *pg.* 1223
Veglio, Paola, Mgr-Mktg-Brand & Creative-Google Play - Google Inc.; *pg.* 1249, *pg.* 153
Vehlewald, John, Dir-Online Media - Quicken Loans, Inc.; *pg.* 797, *pg.* 884
Veilleux, Cara, Sr Mgr-Internal Comm - Vertex Pharmaceuticals Incorporated; *pg.* 1606, *pg.* 801
Veis, Jeff, VP & Head-Solutions Mktg-HP Autonomy - Autonomy, Inc.; *pg.* 358, *pg.* 212
Veit, Alan, Sr Mgr-Dealer Network Strategy - Volkswagen Group of America, Inc.; *pg.* 194, *pg.* 1785
Veith, Charlstie, VP-Media Rels - Cablevision Systems Corporation; *pg.* 272, *pg.* 1141
Veith, Stephen, VP-Sls - Penton Media, Inc.; *pg.* 1676, *pg.* 1277
Vejdani, Scott, Sr Dir-Media Mgmt - Catalina Marketing Corporation; *pg.* 369, *pg.* 462
Vejrostek, Erica, Sr Mgr-Digital Mktg - Grand Canyon Education, Inc.; *pg.* 602, *pg.* 16
Vela, Mark, Dir-Product Mgmt - Activision Blizzard, Inc.; *pg.* 948, *pg.* 271
Vela, Olivia, Dir-Multicultural Mktg - Dr Pepper Snapple Group, Inc.; *pg.* 250, *pg.* 1729
Velarde, Pamela, Sr Mgr-Barbie Global Mktg - Mattel Games/Puzzles; *pg.* 962, *pg.* 80
Velarde, Pamela, Sr Mgr-Barbie Global Mktg - MATTEL, INC.; *pg.* 962, *pg.* 81
Velasco, Adriana, Assoc Mgr-Mktg-Barbie - MATTEL, INC.; *pg.* 962, *pg.* 81
Velasco, Daniel, Sr Mgr-Mktg - Houston Texans, L.P.; *pg.* 553, *pg.* 1708
Velasco, Enrique Ruiz, Dir-Tech-Media & Entertainment Products - Verizon Communications Inc.; *pg.* 1875, *pg.* 1309
Velasco, Jose, Mgr-Mktg-Intl - Payless Shoesource, Inc.; *pg.* 31, *pg.* 722
Velasco-Aznar, Whitney, VP-Mktg - Galaxy Nutritional Foods, Inc.; *pg.* 857, *pg.* 1603
Velasquez, Camilla, Head-Product - Justworks, Inc.; *pg.* 424, *pg.* 1247
Velasquez, Diana, Mgr-Online Mktg - Simon & Schuster, Inc.; *pg.* 1687, *pg.* 1292
Velazquez, Esteban, Brand Mgr-SMB Desktop Virtualization Solutions - Dell Inc.; *pg.* 383, *pg.* 1737
Velez, Jill, Sr Mgr-Field Mktg - Best Western International, Inc.; *pg.* 1081, *pg.* 15
Velez, Luis, Project Mgr-Creative - ISSA; *pg.* 145, *pg.* 640
Velez, Maria A., Exec Dir-Corp Comm-Global PR, Media Rels & Branding - Laureate Education, Inc.; *pg.* 603, *pg.* 757
Velez, Sandra, Head-Digital Mktg Strategy-Intl Markets - Merck & Co., Inc.; *pg.* 1566, *pg.* 1077
Velez-Lopez, Emma, Dir-Adv US Hispanic - DIRECTV Group Holdings, LLC; *pg.* 281, *pg.* 79
Velez-Silva, Jose E., Exec Dir-Multicultural Mktg Comm - Comcast Corporation; *pg.* 276, *pg.* 1560
Velie, Erin, Mgr-Sls & Mktg Personnel - Schlumberger Limited; *pg.* 801, *pg.* 1714
Veling, Karen, VP-Mktg, Comm & Education Svcs - Fiserv, Inc.; *pg.* 397, *pg.* 1855
Velisek, Bruce, Head-Chrysler Brand Product Mktg - FCA US LLC; *pg.* 170, *pg.* 868
Vella, Ashley, Specialist-Mktg-Domino's Smart Slice Brand - Domino's Pizza, Inc.; *pg.* 1726, *pg.* 865
Vella, Kaitlyn, Editor-Social Media - MTV Networks Company; *pg.* 298, *pg.* 1262
Veloso, Silvio, Sr Mgr-IT Innovation & Bus Relationship - Diageo North America Inc.; *pg.* 248, *pg.* 1223
Velthoven, Aaron, VP-Mktg - MICHIGAN.COM; *pg.* 1665, *pg.* 884
Veltri, Joe, VP-Product Plng & Head-Jeep Brand Europe - FCA US LLC; *pg.* 170, *pg.* 868
Velutini, Ramon, Brand Mgr - The Procter & Gamble Company; *pg.* 1129, *pg.* 1418
Vemana, Prat, VP-ECommerce-Global Product Mgmt - Staples, Inc.; *pg.* 474, *pg.* 821
Vemuri, Sunil, Product Mgr - Google Inc.; *pg.* 1249, *pg.* 153
Vena, Gene, Sr Dir-Global Sys New Product Dev & R&D - Brady Corporation; *pg.* 363, *pg.* 1873
Venable, Leigh Ann, Dir-Mktg Comm-Atrium Windows & Doors - Atrium Companies, Inc.; *pg.* 69, *pg.* 1676
Venancio, Charles, VP & Exec Dir-Creative - FMR LLC (Fidelity Investments); *pg.* 759, *pg.* 794
Venderbush, Todd, Mgr-Tech Sls-Healthcare - Oracle Corporation; *pg.* 450, *pg.* 191
Venegas, Bob, Product Mgr-Bus Dev-Enterprise Svcs - Hewlett-Packard Company; *pg.* 404, *pg.* 175
Venekas, Lauren, Assoc Mgr-Brand Mktg-Femoral - Stryker Orthopaedics; *pg.* 1599, *pg.* 1082
Venen-Bock, Susan, Mgr-Media-US - Ford Motor Company; *pg.* 172, *pg.* 876
Venenga, Steven J., VP-Mktg Meat Products - Hormel Foods Corporation; *pg.* 863, *pg.* 915
Venenga, Steven J., VP-Mktg Meat Products - Hormel Foods Corporation - Foodservice Division; *pg.* 864, *pg.* 916
Vener, Marie, Dir-Inside Sls - Crescent/Stonco Supply Division; *pg.* 1295, *pg.* 1121

Veneri, Melissa, Mgr-Digital Mktg - The J.M. Smucker Company; *pg.* 865, *pg.* 1468
Veneski, David, Dir-Media-US - Intel Corporation; *pg.* 645, *pg.* 266
Venhoff, Hannah, Brand Mgr - Heaven Hill Distilleries, Inc.; *pg.* 1964, *pg.* 725
Venimadhavan, Ganesh, Sr Mgr-Mktg-Refining - Honeywell International Inc.; *pg.* 407, *pg.* 1088
Venkataraman, Shankar, Mgr-Consumer Mktg Analytics - PayPal Inc.; *pg.* 1274, *pg.* 248
Venn, Marcie, Sr Mgr-Mktg - Best Buy Co., Inc.; *pg.* 1761, *pg.* 954
Venn, Pam, Mgr-Shopper Mktg-Point of Sale - Nestle Waters North America Inc.; *pg.* 257, *pg.* 375
Vennard, Chris, Sr Head-Global Product-Mobile Call Adv - Google Inc.; *pg.* 1249, *pg.* 153
Venter, Liz, Mgr-Digital Mktg & User Experience - Ford Motor Company; *pg.* 172, *pg.* 876
Vento, Brenda, Mgr-Mktg-Mayfair, Fox River Mall & Oakwood Mall - General Growth Properties, Inc.; *pg.* 1093, *pg.* 574
Venton, Leon, Product Mgr - Arris Group, Inc.; *pg.* 353, *pg.* 541
Ventresca, Michelle, Assoc Mgr-Adv - Dunkin' Brands Group, Inc.; *pg.* 1727, *pg.* 810
Ventura, Elizabeth, Sr VP-Consumer Mktg - Sun Trust Bank, Atlanta; *pg.* 806, *pg.* 520
Ventura, Elizabeth, Sr VP-Consumer Mktg - SunTrust Banks, Inc.; *pg.* 807, *pg.* 520
Ventura, Ralph X., Mgr-Adv - SUPERVALU, Inc. - Eastern Region; *pg.* 1035, *pg.* 1795
Ventura, Tina E., Sr Dir-IR - Abbott Laboratories; *pg.* 1484, *pg.* 551
Venturella, Frank, VP-Sls & Mktg - Magna Visual, Inc.; *pg.* 429, *pg.* 999
Venturini, Patti, Sr Mgr-Mktg-The Bradford Exchange - The Bradford Group; *pg.* 1763, *pg.* 637
Venuto, Peter, Sr VP-Sls - AVX Corporation; *pg.* 623, *pg.* 1616
Verador, Grace, Program Mgr-Direct Mktg - Wells Fargo & Company; *pg.* 819, *pg.* 232
Veras, Orlando, Dir-Natl Media Rels - Macy's, Inc.; *pg.* 1778, *pg.* 1417
Verbus, Jeff, Editor-Copy & Designer - The Canton Repository; *pg.* 1625, *pg.* 1407
Vercelletto, Michael, Grp Product Mgr-OxiClean Stain Fighters - Church & Dwight Co., Inc.; *pg.* 1153, *pg.* 1063
Vercelli, Donald, Sr Sls Dir-US - Mad Catz Interactive Inc.; *pg.* 429, *pg.* 204
Vercollone, Shaye, Mng Dir-Brand Mktg Innovation Center - Theory; *pg.* 34, *pg.* 1299
Verdejo, Patricia, Mgr-Digital Mktg Svcs Plng - Unilever United States, Inc.; *pg.* 904, *pg.* 1061
Verdier, Courtney, Exec Dir-Integrated Mktg-The Food Innovation Grp - Conde Nast Publications, Inc.; *pg.* 1629, *pg.* 1217
Verdier, Nancy, Strategist-Mktg - Thrivent Financial for Lutherans; *pg.* 1219, *pg.* 944
Verdino, Vanessa, Dir-Intl Luxury-Integrated Sls - MAXIMUS, Inc.; *pg.* 780, *pg.* 1799
Verdon, John, VP-Mktg-East Side Mario's - Prime Restaurants Inc.; *pg.* 1746, *pg.* 1947
Verdone, Meredith, Head-Enterprise Mktg - Bank of America Corporation; *pg.* 718, *pg.* 1362
Verducci, Mary, Mgr-Campaign Plng-Mktg Comm - Symantec Corporation; *pg.* 478, *pg.* 161
Verdugo-Del Real, Susana, Coord-Social Media & Mktg - Lazare Kaplan International, Inc.; *pg.* 8, *pg.* 1250
Verellen, Helena, VP-Mktg & Comm-Intl - World Wrestling Entertainment, Inc.; *pg.* 595, *pg.* 380
Verellen, Jay, Dir-Mktg Operational Excellence - Kennametal Inc.; *pg.* 1052, *pg.* 1547
Verest, Tom, Product Mgr-CCTV - Bosch Security Systems, Inc.; *pg.* 626, *pg.* 1158
Verette, David, VP-Partner Sls - SPS COMMERCE, INC.; *pg.* 472, *pg.* 942
Verette, Molly, Sr Mgr-PR-Consumer Brands - Kohl's Corporation; *pg.* 1775, *pg.* 1870
Vergalito, Christie, Brand Mgr - GlaxoSmithKline; *pg.* 1536, *pg.* 1389
Vergin, Cathi, Sr Product Mgr - Ergotron, Inc.; *pg.* 395, *pg.* 960
Vergis, Asha, Specialist-Partner Mktg - Brocade Communications Systems, Inc.; *pg.* 365, *pg.* 239
Vergote, Josh, Dir-Retail Mktg-Global - The Donna Karan Company LLC; *pg.* 23, *pg.* 1225
Verhulst, Roger, Sr VP-Mdsg - Cabela's Incorporated; *pg.* 535, *pg.* 1019
Verhulst-Santos, An, Pres-Pro Product Div - L'Oreal USA; *pg.* 514, *pg.* 1252
Verissimo, Marc J., Chief Strategy Officer - SVB Financial Group; *pg.* 808, *pg.* 270
Verissimo, Victor, Dir-Mktg - Flowserve Corporation; *pg.* 82, *pg.* 1719
Verity, Lindsay, Dir-Digital Mktg-Online Consumer & Education Programs - Apple Inc.; *pg.* 350, *pg.* 73
Verlen, Jason, Dir-Product Mgmt, Predictive Analytics & Big Data - IBM; *pg.* 410, *pg.* 1449
Verma, Amit, VP-Mktg - AMAG Pharmaceuticals, Inc.; *pg.* 1492, *pg.* 827
Verma, Anu, Assoc-Mktg - Jet.com, Inc.; *pg.* 1260, *pg.* 1073
Verma, Rajnish, Exec VP-Sls-Worldwide - TIBCO Software Inc.; *pg.* 484, *pg.* 178
Verma, Sanjeev, Product Mgr - YouTube, LLC; *pg.* 1291, *pg.* 198
Vermeer, Kevin, Chief Strategy Officer, Exec VP & CEO-Accountable Care - UnityPoint Health; *pg.* 1604, *pg.* 706
Vermilion, Amy, Dir-Social Media & Mobile-Victoria's Secret - L Brands, Inc.; *pg.* 1776, *pg.* 1441
Vermilion, Amy, Dir-Social Media & Mobile-Lbrands - Victoria's Secret Stores, LLC; *pg.* 1789, *pg.* 1471
Vernier, Kristine M., Sr Mgr-Pub & Media Rels-Global - Whirlpool Corporation; *pg.* 62, *pg.* 872
Verniere, Peter, Dir-Creative-Sears Hometown & Outlet - Sears Holdings Corporation; *pg.* 1784, *pg.* 618
Vernola, Nicholas, Dir-Mktg-Private Brand - Henry Schein, Inc.; *pg.* 1541, *pg.* 1180
Vernon, Adrian, Mgr-Mktg Comm - Cisco Systems, Inc.; *pg.* 372, *pg.* 240
Vernon, Christina, Dir-Mktg-Channel Dev - Herman Miller, Inc.; *pg.* 926, *pg.* 913
Vernon, Richard, Mgr-Strategic Product - Thermo Fisher Scientific Inc.; *pg.* 1431, *pg.* 854
Vernon, William F., Specialist-Mktg & Product Dev - The Vernon Company; *pg.* 488, *pg.* 710
Veronie, Marci, VP-Sls & Mktg - Avemco Insurance Company; *pg.* 1194, *pg.* 769
Verrastro, Paul, VP-Global Mktg Strategy - Medtronic, Inc.; *pg.* 1564, *pg.* 939
Verratti, Mark, VP-Sls-Global - LivaNova; *pg.* 1557, *pg.* 1710
Verrelli, Sandro, VP-Sls & Mktg - Acklands-Grainger Inc.; *pg.* 197, *pg.* 1933
Verret, Ryan, Principal Product Mgr-FPGA Tech for Test & Embedded - National Instruments Corporation; *pg.* 443, *pg.* 1664
Verrey, Alex, Dir-PR & Comm-Global - Mad Catz Interactive Inc.; *pg.* 429, *pg.* 204
Verrill, Sam, Sr Product Mgr - American Express Company; *pg.* 712, *pg.* 1190
Verrone, Elaine, Mgr-Mktg - CherryRoad Technologies Inc.; *pg.* 1235, *pg.* 1087
Verrone, Michael, Sr Dir-Bus Dev - National Basketball Association; *pg.* 566, *pg.* 1264
Versaggi, Shannon, Dir-Mktg Plng & Media - Lowe's Companies, Inc.; *pg.* 1053, *pg.* 1383
Versak, Chris, VP-Sls & Svc-East - Emkay, Inc.; *pg.* 1906, *pg.* 619
Versen, Alex, Mgr-Mktg - Uber USA, LLC; *pg.* 1286, *pg.* 229
Verses, Jeff, Dir-Customer Mktg - Diageo North America, Inc.; *pg.* 1961, *pg.* 361
Versh, Ben, Dir-Media - Pfizer Inc.; *pg.* 1581, *pg.* 1278
Versichelli, Stephanie, Sr VP-Adv Sls-Crown Media Family Networks - Crown Media Holdings Inc.; *pg.* 280, *pg.* 281
Versteden, Margaret, Sr VP-Mktg-Bol com - Ahold USA, Inc.; *pg.* 1013, *pg.* 1520
Vertacnik, Lynn, Dir-Global Mktg Sls, Svc Bus Processes & Forecasting - Allison Transmission, Inc.; *pg.* 198, *pg.* 682
Verticchio, Lu, Dir-Adv - The Prince George Citizen; *pg.* 1678, *pg.* 1908
Verucchi, Michael, Specialist-Principal Mktg Comm - Medtronic, Inc.; *pg.* 1564, *pg.* 939
Vervaeke, Bill, VP-Mktg - Palm Beach County Convention & Visitors Bureau; *pg.* 1003, *pg.* 479
Verzal, Brandon, Mgr-Comml Sls - Advance Auto Parts, Inc.; *pg.* 197, *pg.* 1805
Vesik, Michael, Sr Mgr-Product Dev Comm-Global - Genentech, Inc.; *pg.* 1533, *pg.* 279
Vesnaver, Victor, Sr VP-Sls & Mktg - PAR Technology Corporation; *pg.* 452, *pg.* 1183
Vespa, Valerie, Mgr-Sls - Outfront Media; *pg.* 1465, *pg.* 1275
Vessa, Antoniette, Brand Mgr-Skincare - Prestige Brands Holdings, Inc.; *pg.* 520, *pg.* 1345
Vest, Dave, Sr Dir-News Content - Coyotes Hockey, LLC; *pg.* 542, *pg.* 13
Vestal, Anthony, Dir-Media Rels - National Hot Rod Association; *pg.* 149, *pg.* 99
Vesterheden, Jakob, Dir-Mktg-Corp Mktg Analytics - Dell Inc.; *pg.* 383, *pg.* 1737
Vestin, Chris, Dir-Mdsg-Seventh Avenue - Colony Brands Inc.; *pg.* 849, *pg.* 1881
Vesuna, Sarosh, VP-Product Mgmt & Mktg & Gen Mgr-Enterprise Networking Bus - MERU NETWORKS, INC.; *pg.* 434, *pg.* 286
Vethencourt, Adriana, Sr Dir-CRM - American Eagle Outfitters, Inc.; *pg.* 37, *pg.* 1572
Veto, Joanne, Dir-Media & Analyst Rels - Accenture; *pg.* 1392, *pg.* 1186
Vetrano, Anthony, Mgr-Trade Mktg - Luxottica Retail; *pg.* 8, *pg.* 1460
Vetter, Dana, Program Mgr-Music Mktg - Google Inc.; *pg.* 1249, *pg.* 153
Vetter, Danna, VP-Mktg & Consumer Insight - Aramark; *pg.* 1013, *pg.* 1558
Vetter, John P., Dir-Creative - DIRECTV Group Holdings, LLC; *pg.* 281, *pg.* 79
Vetter, Kristy R., Mgr-Co-Op Mktg & Comm - Waddell & Reed Financial, Inc.; *pg.* 818, *pg.* 721
Veverka, Tracy, Mgr-Digital Mktg - Intuit Inc.; *pg.* 769, *pg.* 158
Vevers, Stuart, Exec Dir-Creative - Coach, Inc.; *pg.* 3, *pg.* 1214
Veygman, Rita, Mktg Dir - Dolce & Gabbana USA, Inc.; *pg.* 23, *pg.* 1225
Vezmar, Danny, Sr Mgr-Market Dev-North America - Dentsply International Inc.; *pg.* 1522, *pg.* 1596
Via, Greg, Dir-Sports Mktg-Global - The Gillette Company; *pg.* 509, *pg.* 795
Via, Greg, Dir-Sports Mktg-Global - The Procter & Gamble Company; *pg.* 1129, *pg.* 1418
Via, Kelsey, Mgr-Mktg - American Equity Mortgage Inc.; *pg.* 712, *pg.* 991
Viali, Christine, Assoc Mgr-Email Mktg - The Children's Place, Inc.; *pg.* 22, *pg.* 1119
Viall, Dean, Sr Mgr-Partner Mktg-Natl Partner Org - Cisco Systems, Inc.; *pg.* 372, *pg.* 240
Vian, Paul, Dir-Sls - Internap Network Services Corporation; *pg.* 417, *pg.* 513
Viana, Diego, VP-New Product Accelerator Team & Global Emulsions Team - Rich Products Corporation; *pg.* 892, *pg.* 1150
Viane, Janet, CEO-Evoke Productions & VP-Mktg & Digital Ops - Sears Holdings Corporation; *pg.* 1784, *pg.* 618
Vibert, Sean, Coord-Mktg - Books-A-Million, Inc.; *pg.* 1623, *pg.* 2
Viberud, Annika, Dir-Strategic Brand & Mktg Comm - Volvo Trucks North America, Inc.; *pg.* 195, *pg.* 1377
Vicente, Gerard, Mgr-Integrated Mktg - Comedy Partners; *pg.* 278, *pg.* 1216
Vicente, Sisy, Head-Segment Mktg - JPMorgan Chase & Co.; *pg.* 772, *pg.* 1246
Vicioso, Peggy, VP-Mktg & Product Dev - Charisma Brands, LLC; *pg.* 2, *pg.* 120
Vick, James, Dir-Adv Bus-IEEE Spectrum - Institute of Electrical and Electronics Engineers, Inc.; *pg.* 144, *pg.* 1109
Vickers, Fred, Dir-Production - National Thoroughbred Racing Association; *pg.* 569, *pg.* 730
Vickery, Kathrin, Mgr-Mktg Comm-Low & Medium Voltage-Energy Mgmt Div - Siemens Process Industries and Drive; *pg.* 1376, *pg.* 1587
Vickery, Wendy, Mgr-Mktg - Pentel of America, Ltd.; *pg.* 453, *pg.* 295
Victor, Daniel, Editor-Social Media - The New York Times; *pg.* 1668, *pg.* 1270
Victor, Jolawn, Sr Mgr-Mktg - PepsiCo, Inc.; *pg.* 259, *pg.* 1327
Vidal, Xavier, Brand Mgr - Dell Inc.; *pg.* 383, *pg.* 1737
Vidalin, John, VP-Sls & Mktg - Houston Texans, L.P.; *pg.* 553, *pg.* 1708
Vides, Jennifer, Dir-Brand Mktg, Comm & Creative Svcs - Hot Topic, Inc.; *pg.* 42, *pg.* 67
Vides, Wanda, Mgr-Trade Brand Mktg-Latin America - Reckitt Benckiser Inc.; *pg.* 1136, *pg.* 1105
Vidoli, Michelle, Sr Mgr-Corp Comm - CUBIST PHARMACEUTICALS, INC.; *pg.* 1521, *pg.* 828
Vidyanandan, Premduth, Sr Engr-Product Mktg - Xilinx, Inc.; *pg.* 496, *pg.* 252

First page reference indicates Business Class Edition
Second page reference indicates Geographic Edition

Vieira, Michele, Brand Mgr-Perrier - Nestle Waters North America Inc.; *pg.* 257, *pg.* 375
Viele, Lisa, VP-Sls-Northeast - Zimmer Biomet Holdings, Inc.; *pg.* 1611, *pg.* 699
Viera, Joanna, Mgr-Mktg & Referral - Community Nurse & Hospice Care; *pg.* 1517, *pg.* 818
Vieregg, David, Dir-Sls & Mktg - Intuit Inc.; *pg.* 769, *pg.* 158
Vietmeier, Brett, Mng Dir-Client Dev & Sls-Proprietary Trading - CME Group Inc.; *pg.* 738, *pg.* 571
Vietti, Sean, Mgr-Sls - Chicago Tube & Iron Co.; *pg.* 1323, *pg.* 656
Vig, Michele, Sr VP-Mktg & Product - CARIBOU COFFEE COMPANY, INC.; *pg.* 1764, *pg.* 932
Vigier, Benjamin, Product Mgr-Mobile Commerce - Apple Inc.; *pg.* 350, *pg.* 73
Vigil, Kristy, Dir-Trade Mktg-Horizon - The WhiteWave Foods Company; *pg.* 1037, *pg.* 324
Vigliarolo, Frank, Dir-Adv - ABC Carpet & Home Inc.; *pg.* 912, *pg.* 1185
Vigna, John, Exec VP-Sls - Carl Buddig & Company; *pg.* 846, *pg.* 619
Vignali, Jaime, Dir-Global Digital Mktg Ops - Novartis Corporation; *pg.* 1574, *pg.* 1273
Vignolo, Andrew, Sr Dir-Shopper Insights - Levi Strauss & Co.; *pg.* 43, *pg.* 220
Vignon, Vanessa, Sr Dir-Mktg Analytics - Ubisoft Inc.; *pg.* 589, *pg.* 229
Vigo, Roberto, Dir-Sls & Mktg - CeramTec North America Electronic Applications, Inc.; *pg.* 628, *pg.* 1620
Vigon, Robert, Mgr-Creative Services - Florida Marlins, L.P.; *pg.* 548, *pg.* 442
Vigue, Doreen I., VP-PR - Comcast Corporation; *pg.* 276, *pg.* 1560
Vigue, Nicole, Brand Mgr - Prestige Brands Holdings, Inc.; *pg.* 520, *pg.* 1345
Viken, Mark, VP-Mktg - Sharp Electronics Corporation; *pg.* 672, *pg.* 1082
Vila, Adriana L., Dir-Experiential Mktg - Univision Communications Inc.; *pg.* 683, *pg.* 1307
Vilagi, Scott, Sr VP-Sls - Gorilla Glue Co.; *pg.* 1048, *pg.* 1414
Vilaret, Victoria, VP-Mktg Analytics - New York Life Insurance Company; *pg.* 1211, *pg.* 1268
Vilchez, Yolanda, Brand Mgr-Global - Tiffany & Co. International; *pg.* 14, *pg.* 1300
Vilk, Elina, Head-Mktg-Enterprise Solutions - PayPal Inc.; *pg.* 1274, *pg.* 248
Villa, Anthony, Sr Mgr-Mktg - Philips Electronics North America; *pg.* 662, *pg.* 782
Villa, Colby, Specialist-Social Advocacy - Go Daddy Inc.; *pg.* 1249, *pg.* 21
Villa, Elke, Assoc Dir-Mktg-Children's Div - Simon & Schuster Children's Publishing; *pg.* 1686, *pg.* 1292
Villa, Zhenia, Dir Mktg Ops-Global - Converse Inc.; *pg.* 1831, *pg.* 793
Villacis, Barbara, Mgr-Latin America Mktg - Harley-Davidson, Inc.; *pg.* 178, *pg.* 1874
Villacres, Luis, Brand Mgr - Hugo Boss Fashions Inc.; *pg.* 42, *pg.* 1242
Villadelgado, Sheila, Rep-PR - Varian Medical Systems, Inc.; *pg.* 1434, *pg.* 178
Villalobos, Claudia Pizarro, Specialist-Sls - D'Arrigo Bros. Company; *pg.* 852, *pg.* 197
Villalobos, Dianne, Specialist-Mktg - Jenny Craig Operations, Inc.; *pg.* 1548, *pg.* 59
Villamil, Gian Pablo, Product Mgr - Autodesk Inc.; *pg.* 356, *pg.* 257
Villanella, Megan, Dir-Global Brand & Mktg - MetLife, Inc.; *pg.* 1208, *pg.* 1258
Villano, Meredith, Specialist-Channel Mktg - Schneider Electric; *pg.* 467, *pg.* 1609
Villano, Mike, VP-Foodservice Sls & Mktg - Basic American Foods, Inc.; *pg.* 839, *pg.* 303
Villanova, Kaitlin, Dir-Digital Mktg - Burton Snowboard Company; *pg.* 1829, *pg.* 1765
Villanueva, Judy A., Acct Mgr-Mktg-VMWare Pub Sector - Ingram Micro Inc.; *pg.* 415, *pg.* 261
Villanueva, Mara Heras, VP-Corp Mktg - CertainTeed Corporation; *pg.* 74, *pg.* 1589
Villanueva, Michael, Sr Mgr-Search Mktg - Reply! Inc.; *pg.* 1277, *pg.* 260
Villanueva, Rebecca, Mgr-Media Svcs - Denver Broncos Football Club; *pg.* 544, *pg.* 325
Villanueva-Heras, Mara L., VP-Residential Mktg-Armstrong Floor Products - Armstrong World Industries, Inc.; *pg.* 914, *pg.* 1545
Villapudua, Brian, Mgr-Product & Principal-Amazon Instant Video - Amazon.com, Inc.; *pg.* 1226, *pg.* 1831
Villar, Cam, Dir-Integrated Mktg - L.M. Scofield Company; *pg.* 94, *pg.* 134
Villar, Patricia Del, Mgr-Mktg Ops - Safeway Inc.; *pg.* 1032, *pg.* 184
Villard, Philippe, Sr Dir-Comml Mktg-Global - Stereotaxis, Inc.; *pg.* 1597, *pg.* 1004
Villarreal, Chris, Dir-Branding & Mktg-Plenti - American Express Company; *pg.* 712, *pg.* 1190
Villarreal, Jenna, Mgr-Mktg - Encon Safety Products; *pg.* 1334, *pg.* 1705
Villarroel, Daniel, Asst VP-Integrated Mktg - Maybelline LLC; *pg.* 516, *pg.* 1257
Villars, Curtis, VP-Product & Innovation - MasterCard Worldwide Inc.; *pg.* 780, *pg.* 988
Villas, Huyenchau, Product Mgr-Cooper Industries Ltd - Eaton Corporation; *pg.* 1331, *pg.* 1429
Villasenor, Gilberto , II, VP-Mktg & Gen Mgr - V&V Supremo Foods, Inc.; *pg.* 907, *pg.* 595
Villasenor, Victor, Brand Mgr-Cracker Jack'D Brand - Frito-Lay North America, Inc.; *pg.* 1853, *pg.* 1730
Villasenor, Victor, Brand Mgr-Cracker Jack'D - PepsiCo, Inc.; *pg.* 259, *pg.* 1327
Villatoro, Claudia, Mgr-Mktg Strategies - Safeway Inc.; *pg.* 1032, *pg.* 184
Villegas, Ana, Dir-North America Comml Bus-Mktg Strategy - Dell Inc.; *pg.* 383, *pg.* 1737
Villegas, Isabel, Brand Mgr-Innovation Brands-Redds Family of Brands - MillerCoors LLC; *pg.* 255, *pg.* 582
Villegas, Marcel, Sr Mgr-District Parts & Svc - American Honda Motor Co., Inc.; *pg.* 163, *pg.* 292
Villegas, Robert, Sr Project Mgr-Media Rels - Southern California Edison Company; *pg.* 1952, *pg.* 194
Villiano, Joe, Dir-Mktg - B&G Foods, Inc.; *pg.* 838, *pg.* 1102
Villierme, Anna Cornell, Dir-Global Media & Bus Dev-Gap Factory - Banana Republic; *pg.* 1760, *pg.* 212
Villierme, Anna Cornell, Dir-Global Mktg-Gap Factory - The Gap, Inc.; *pg.* 1770, *pg.* 218
Vilminot, Nicole, Dir-Mktg - Biggby Coffee; *pg.* 1716, *pg.* 885
Viloria, Joshua, Sr Specialist-Mktg & Brand Alliance - Sony Computer Entertainment America LLC; *pg.* 966, *pg.* 256
Vilsack, Karlee, Sr Mgr-Mktg - Dermalogica, Inc.; *pg.* 1523, *pg.* 63
Vincelette, Scott, Sr Mgr-Sls - Ingram Micro Inc.; *pg.* 415, *pg.* 261
Vincent, Berkeley, Head-Mktg-Global - Johnson & Johnson; *pg.* 1549, *pg.* 1091
Vincent, Brian, Sr VP-Sls - Brother International Corporation - USA; *pg.* 53, *pg.* 1046
Vincent, Marilyn, Sr Mgr-Mktg - Hormel Foods Corporation; *pg.* 863, *pg.* 915
Vincent, Marilyn, Sr Mgr-Mktg - MegaMex Foods, LLC; *pg.* 833, *pg.* 66
Vincent, Meredith, Dir-Adv - AT&T Communications Corp.; *pg.* 1866, *pg.* 1043
Vincent, Molly, Dir-Adv - Adventure Lands of America, Inc.; *pg.* 526, *pg.* 701
Vincent, Sara P., Dir-Mktg - MetroPCS, Inc.; *pg.* 1872, *pg.* 1683
Vincent, Wayne, Dir-Product Comm - The McGraw-Hill Companies Inc.; *pg.* 1663, *pg.* 1257
Vincz, Tom, Mgr-PR - Horizon Blue Cross Blue Shield of New Jersey; *pg.* 1203, *pg.* 1096
Viner, Jacob, Mgr-Mktg - Turtle Wax, Inc.; *pg.* 220, *pg.* 671
Viner, Susan, Mgr-Creative Svcs - Manulife Financial Corporation; *pg.* 778, *pg.* 1939
Viner, Tonja, Sr Mgr-Comm - Avnet Technology Solutions; *pg.* 359, *pg.* 25
Viney, Peter, Mgr-Retail Mktg - Volkswagen Canada, Inc.; *pg.* 194, *pg.* 1918
Vinh, Dan, VP-Global Mktg-Renaissance Hotels - Marriott International, Inc.; *pg.* 1102, *pg.* 764
Vining, Richard, Sr Mgr-Product Mktg-Data Protection - Hitachi Data Systems Corporation; *pg.* 407, *pg.* 265
Viola, George, Sr Engr-Sls - Dynapower Corporation; *pg.* 1330, *pg.* 1768
Viola, Richard, VP-Sls & Mktg-Building Matls Distr - Boise Cascade; *pg.* 1453, *pg.* 788
Violante, Anthony, Mgr-Digital Mktg & Content - Bad Boy Worldwide Entertainment Group; *pg.* 270, *pg.* 1199
Violo, Antoniette, Dir-Sls & Svc-Oceania - PerkinElmer, Inc.; *pg.* 1426, *pg.* 853
Viramontes, Ricardo, Dir-Creative-Worldwide Mktg - Apple Inc.; *pg.* 350, *pg.* 73
Virani, Tariq, Assoc Mgr-ECommerce Mktg - StubHub, Inc.; *pg.* 586, *pg.* 228
Viray, Jon, Mgr-Product Mktg - Adobe Systems Incorporated; *pg.* 342, *pg.* 235
Virayodhin, Marisa, Mgr-Integrated Mktg - Johnson & Johnson; *pg.* 1549, *pg.* 1091
Virgo, Brian, Sr Mgr-Technical & Corp Events Tech - AOL Inc.; *pg.* 1229, *pg.* 1195
Virgo, Paul, Dir-Vertical Mktg - Emerson Network Power; *pg.* 1071, *pg.* 1479
Virji, Shazia, Mgr-Mktg-Mint.com - Intuit Inc.; *pg.* 769, *pg.* 158
Virtue, William, Mgr-Mktg Promos - Carowinds; *pg.* 537, *pg.* 1364
Viscarra, Alex, Sr Asst Brand Mgr - Altria Group, Inc.; *pg.* 1893, *pg.* 1800
Viscon, Susan, Sr VP-Mdsg & Private Brands - Recreational Equipment, Inc.; *pg.* 1843, *pg.* 1821
Visconti, Frank, Dir-Sls & Adv - New Jersey Monthly; *pg.* 1667, *pg.* 1089
Visconti, Mia L., Mgr-Comml Mktg-USCAN - General Electric Company; *pg.* 1297, *pg.* 347
Visconti, Todd, Product Mgr - ON Semiconductor Corporation; *pg.* 101, *pg.* 18
Viscusi, Mike, Sr Dir-Men's Design & Brands - Pacific Sunwear of California, Inc.; *pg.* 1781, *pg.* 43
Viserto, Neil, Sr Dir-Corp Sponsorships - Angels Baseball, L.P.; *pg.* 529, *pg.* 42
Visicaro, Greg, Mgr-Adv - Horizon Blue Cross Blue Shield of New Jersey; *pg.* 1203, *pg.* 1096
Visioli, Anna, VP-Digital Mktg - Coldwell Banker Real Estate LLC; *pg.* 1087, *pg.* 1103
Vismans, David, Chief Product Officer - The Priceline Group Inc.; *pg.* 1276, *pg.* 364
Visocchi, Michael J., Dir-Mktg & Sls Channel Enablement - Comcast Cable Communications, Inc.; *pg.* 276, *pg.* 1560
Visser, Rochelle, Specialist-Brand Adv - FCA US LLC; *pg.* 170, *pg.* 868
Visser, Rochelle, Specialist-Brand Adv - TD Auto Finance; *pg.* 809, *pg.* 886
Viswanatha, Naveen, Product Mgr - Google Inc.; *pg.* 1249, *pg.* 153
Vita, Jordan, Analyst-Product Intern-Web Analytics - The New York Times Company; *pg.* 1668, *pg.* 1270
Vitale, Chris, VP-Mktg - Slomin's Inc.; *pg.* 1076, *pg.* 1167
Vitale, Jillian, Sr Mgr-Strategic Mktg - Benefit Cosmetics LLC; *pg.* 501, *pg.* 213
Vitale, Maurizio, Sr VP-Mktg Networks - Sony Pictures Entertainment Inc.; *pg.* 309, *pg.* 72
Vitale, Sal, Category Head-Media Procurement - Johnson & Johnson; *pg.* 1549, *pg.* 1091
Vitalee, Andrew, Mgr-ECommerce Mktg - hhgregg, Inc.; *pg.* 56, *pg.* 686
Vitaliano, Sara, Dir-Sls Plng - Screenvision Cinema Network LLC; *pg.* 581, *pg.* 1290
Vitellas, Tina, Program Mgr-Mktg - Hewlett-Packard Company, *pg.* 404, *pg.* 175
Viteri, Sandy, VP-Mktg Ops-Global - comScore, Inc; *pg.* 1236, *pg.* 1798
Vitkus, April, Dir-Brand Mktg & Strategy-Global - Vans, Inc.; *pg.* 1821, *pg.* 76
Vito, Melanie De, Mgr-Conversion Mktg-The Art Institutes - Education Management Corporation; *pg.* 601, *pg.* 1575
Vitrano, Leslie, Dir-Channel Mktg & Comm - Schneider Electric; *pg.* 467, *pg.* 1609
Vittal, Rashmi, Sr Dir-Product Mktg-Product Solutions - NeuStar, Inc.; *pg.* 1872, *pg.* 1807
Vitters, Scott, Sr Dir-Environmental Mgmt & Innovation - NIKE, Inc.; *pg.* 1812, *pg.* 1492
Vittoria, Ed, VP-Loyalty Mktg & Innovation Partnerships - Simon Property Group, Inc.; *pg.* 1112, *pg.* 690
Vitucci, Michelle A., Sr Dir-Mktg Comm & Creative Svcs - Gartner, Inc.; *pg.* 1248, *pg.* 374
Vivaldelli, Melba, Reg Mgr-Mktg - The Allstate Corporation; *pg.* 1189, *pg.* 639
Vivanco, Fernando, Sr Dir-Corp Comm - Medtronic, Inc.; *pg.* 1564, *pg.* 939
Vivas, Francisco, Dir-Software Mktg - IBM; *pg.* 410, *pg.* 1449
Vives, Elina, Dir-Sls-Natl Accounts - MillerCoors LLC; *pg.* 255, *pg.* 582
Vivona, John, VP-Sls - Andrews McMeel Universal; *pg.* 1616, *pg.* 980
Vizcarra, Joseph, Sr Mgr-Shopper Mktg - Campbell Soup Company; *pg.* 844, *pg.* 1048
Vizioli, Tony, Mgr-Mktg - Nestle Waters North America Inc.; *pg.* 257, *pg.* 375

Vizl, Ralph, Head-Mktg & Bus Dev-Retail Div - Manulife Financial Corporation; pg. 778, pg. 1939
Vizon, Gilbert, Mgr-Creative Svcs - Goodwill Industries International, Inc.; pg. 1771, pg. 776
Vizon, Kay, Dir-Media - The Kroger Co.; pg. 1025, pg. 1416
Vleck, Christine, Brand Mgr-Experience Mktg - Clif Bar Inc.; pg. 848, pg. 83
Vo, Jamie, VP-Worldwide Mktg - Western Digital Corporation; pg. 492, pg. 118
Vo, Troy, Mgr-Direct Mktg - Autobytel Inc.; pg. 1230, pg. 107
Vo, Uyen, Mgr-Digital Mktg-Education - The New York Times Company; pg. 1668, pg. 1270
Voden, Heather, Mgr-In-Trial Web Mktg - Autodesk Inc.; pg. 356, pg. 257
Vodick, Tom, Dir-Creative-WGN-TV, CLTV, Antenna TV & THIS TV - Tribune Media Company; pg. 1696, pg. 592
Vodicka, Nancy, Dir-Global Mktg-Data Connectivity & Integration - Progress Software Corporation; pg. 457, pg. 786
Vodola, Catherine, Dir-Mktg-Global - Godiva Chocolatier, Inc.; pg. 1854, pg. 1235
Voeller, Scott, Sr VP-Partnership & Event Mktg - MGM Resorts International; pg. 1105, pg. 1028
Vogel, Amanda Cortese, Sr Dir-PR - FreshDirect, LLC; pg. 857, pg. 1174
Vogel, Brett, Product Mktg Mgr-Monetization - Facebook, Inc.; pg. 1245, pg. 143
Vogel, Dan, Sr Mgr-Mktg Ops - Destination Maternity Corporation; pg. 23, pg. 1563
Vogel, Jesse, Dir-Digital Mktg - Career Education Corporation; pg. 599, pg. 658
Vogel, Kristie, Mgr-Field Mktg-West - Del Taco Restaurants, Inc.; pg. 1725, pg. 121
Vogel, Laura, Dir-US Oral Care Mktg - Colgate-Palmolive Company; pg. 504, pg. 1215
Vogel, Mark, Dir-Sls Mktg - Diamond Vogel Paint, Inc.; pg. 1441, pg. 710
Vogel, Scott, Assoc Dir-Deep Cleaning Sys Mktg - Bissell Homecare, Inc.; pg. 52, pg. 887
Vogel, Trish, Mgr-Sls-Natl - WMF of America, Inc.; pg. 1140, pg. 1380
Vogelsong, Chad, Dir-Mktg - Monster Inc.; pg. 656, pg. 50
Vogenthaler, Alex, Grp Product Mgr - Google Inc.; pg. 1249, pg. 153
Vogl, Ron, Mgr-Technical Mktg - Honeywell International Inc.; pg. 407, pg. 1088
Vogrin, David, Dir-Mktg - Escalade Inc.; pg. 1833, pg. 678
Vogt, Ed, Gen Dir-Consumer Websites, CRM Mktg Ops & Dealer Sys - General Motors Company; pg. 175, pg. 881
Vogt, John, VP-Sls - E.V. Roberts & Associates, Inc.; pg. 1161, pg. 63
Vogt, Ole, Sr Product Mgr-Interactive Mktg - Phonak LLC; pg. 1585, pg. 665
Vohra, Navin, VP-Wireless Sls-APAC & India - CommScope, Inc.; pg. 278, pg. 1378
Vohra, Puja, Sr VP-Mktg & Digital - TruTV; pg. 314, pg. 1305
Voigt, Derek, Sr Product Mgr-Residential Plumbing - Elkay Manufacturing Company; pg. 80, pg. 645
Voigt, Kelly, Sr Mgr-Publicity & Media - Naxos of America Inc.; pg. 1779, pg. 1633
Voiles, John, VP-Bell Media Sls-Western Canada - Bell Canada; pg. 1936, pg. 1960
Voinigescu, Victoria, Sr Product Mgr & Mgr-HP Agile - Hewlett-Packard Company; pg. 404, pg. 175
Voionmaa, Mark, VP & Sr Product Mgr - The PNC Financial Services Group, Inc.; pg. 795, pg. 1579
Voisin, Julie, Product Mgr-Aerospace Coatings-Global - Sherwin Williams; pg. 1448, pg. 1436
Voitel, Jim, Product Mgr-Tech Insulation - CertainTeed Corporation; pg. 74, pg. 1589
Volante, Frank, Mgr-Mktg - Honest Tea; pg. 253, pg. 762
Volante, Rachel, Brand Mgr-St. Regis & The Luxury Collection - Starwood Hotels & Resorts Worldwide, Inc.; pg. 1114, pg. 378
Volborth, Veronica, Mgr-Creative Svcs-Design - Blackbaud, Inc.; pg. 361, pg. 1613
Volk, Alex, Dir-Search Mktg - Microsoft Corporation; pg. 435, pg. 1824
Volk, Jennifer, Sr Specialist-Product Mktg - FRANKLIN RESOURCES, INC.; pg. 760, pg. 254
Volk, Willy, Product Dir - TheHuffingtonPost.com, Inc.; pg. 1692, pg. 1298
Volkart, Liliana A., Sr Mgr-Search, Local & Affiliate Mktg - Safeway Inc.; pg. 1032, pg. 184
Volker, Cindy, Sr Dir-Mktg Comm & Product Mgmt - Broadridge Financial Solutions Inc.; pg. 727, pg. 1172
Volker, Daniel, VP-Product Mgmt - Swisher International, Inc.; pg. 1600, pg. 1369
Volker, Kathryn A., Assoc Dir-Mktg-Women's Health - Allergan; pg. 1490, pg. 1101
Volkman, Natalie, Sr Mgr-Mktg - Time Inc.; pg. 1693, pg. 1300
Vollero, Drew, Acting CFO & VP-Fin - Snapchat, Inc.; pg. 1281, pg. 301
Vollman Warwick, Stacy, Head-Content & Social Media - JPMorgan Chase & Co.; pg. 772, pg. 1246
Vollman, Andrea, Sr Dir-Mktg & Adv Effectiveness - comScore, Inc; pg. 1236, pg. 1798
Vollman, Emily, Mgr-Mktg Comm - Kirkland's Inc.; pg. 1126, pg. 1652
Vollmer, John, Engr-Inside Sls - The Cincinnati Gilbert Machine Tool Company, L.L.C.; pg. 1323, pg. 1411
Vollmert, Jennifer, Mgr-Brand Direct Mktg-Williams-Sonoma - Williams-Sonoma, Inc.; pg. 1140, pg. 231
Volmer, Tamara, Dir-Transaction & Adv Valorem Taxes - DISH Network Corporation; pg. 283, pg. 325
Voloshin, Carol, Mgr-Sls Strategy & Plng - Stonyfield Farm, Inc.; pg. 899, pg. 1035
Volosin, Pierre L., Dir-Flight Svcs Sls - The Boeing Company; pg. 225, pg. 567
Volpe, Bill, Sr Mgr-Digital Mktg & ECommerce - Charter Communications, Inc.; pg. 274, pg. 372
Volpe, Ken Z., Sr VP-Product Dev - Oracle Corporation; pg. 450, pg. 191
Vomacka, Tanya, VP-Experience & Mktg - MOSI (Museum of Science & Industry); pg. 564, pg. 474
Von Deylen, Larry, Sr VP-Sls & Bus Dev - Oregon Freeze Dry, Inc.; pg. 888, pg. 1492
Von Eschen, Arthur, Sr Dir-Game Analytics - Activision Blizzard, Inc.; pg. 948, pg. 271
von Essen, Craig, Mgr-Product Comm-Global - Ford Motor Company; pg. 172, pg. 876
Von Glinow, Kiki, Deputy Mng Editor-Audience Dev, Social Strategy & Newsroom Mgmt - TheHuffingtonPost.com, Inc.; pg. 1692, pg. 1298
Von Heiland Strader, Erika, Dir-Community Mktg - Coca-Cola North America; pg. 848, pg. 500
Von Hoene, William A., Jr., Chief Strategy Officer & Sr Exec VP - Exelon Corporation; pg. 1942, pg. 573
Von Iderstein, Casey, Mgr-Partnership Mktg - Rue La La; pg. 1278, pg. 800
Von Sehrwald, Alex, VP-Mktg - Gerland Corporation; pg. 1020, pg. 1706
von Stegmann, Stefan, VP-Sls-Europe, North Africa, Near & Middle East - Deere & Company; pg. 703, pg. 632
von Stein, Emily, Product Mgr - Elmer's Products, Inc.; pg. 1442, pg. 1479
von Wachter, Diana, Mgr-Mktg-FL, IN, KY - Diageo North America, Inc.; pg. 1961, pg. 361
Vonderhaar, George, Chief Sls Officer - Limelight Networks, Inc.; pg. 1262, pg. 26
Vonk, John, VP-Product Plng - Comcast Corporation; pg. 276, pg. 1560
Vono, Todd, Mgr-Production - Citigroup Inc.; pg. 735, pg. 1212
Vonwerssowetz, Dena, Mgr-Mktg-Doritos - PepsiCo, Inc.; pg. 259, pg. 1327
Voorhees, Alison, Mgr-Adv - Capital City Bank Group, Inc.; pg. 730, pg. 469
Voorhees, Lindsey, Specialist-Email Mktg - Overstock.com, Inc.; pg. 1273, pg. 1760
Voorhees, Shannon, Mgr-Mktg Sponsorship & Activation - Coca-Cola Bottling Co. Consolidated; pg. 240, pg. 1365
Voorhies, Michelle, Dir-Mktg Strategy - HSN, Inc.; pg. 291, pg. 462
Voorhis, Paul Van, Sr Mgr-Internal Comm - Intuit Inc.; pg. 769, pg. 158
Vootkur, Anil, Sr Dir-Strategic Mktg-Global - Allergan, Inc.; pg. 1491, pg. 106
Vora, Kenil, Sr Product Mgr-AWS Mobile Svcs - Amazon.com, Inc.; pg. 1226, pg. 1831
Vorhees Siripoke, Sarah, Mgr-Integrated Mktg - Xilinx, Inc.; pg. 496, pg. 252
Vorobiev, Mikhail, Global Product Mgr - Owens Corning; pg. 102, pg. 1476
Voron, Vince, VP & Exec Dir-Creative - Dolby Laboratories, Inc.; pg. 284, pg. 217
Vorpahl, Larry L., Pres-Consumer Products Sls & Grp VP - Hormel Foods Corporation; pg. 863, pg. 915
Vos, Emily, Brand Mgr-Frigidaire - Electrolux Home Products North America; pg. 54, pg. 1366
Vosik, Doug, Dir-Brand Strategy & Mktg Comm - Virgin Mobile USA, LP; pg. 685, pg. 1129
Voss, Briana, Sr Mgr-Sls Dev-Video - AOL Inc.; pg. 1229, pg. 1195
Voss, Donald W., Sr Mgr-Strategic Partnership Mktg - Coca-Cola Refreshments USA, Inc.; pg. 247, pg. 500
Voss, Shannon L., Reg Dir-Media - Coca-Cola Refreshments USA, Inc.; pg. 247, pg. 500
Vossen, Klaus, Sr Product Mgr-Technical Graphics - Corel Corporation; pg. 380, pg. 1931
Vostrejs, Phil, Exec VP-Mdse Plng, Allocation, Distr & Supply Chain - PetSmart, Inc.; pg. 1481, pg. 18
Votava, Caitlin, Sr Assoc Brand Mgr - Church & Dwight Co., Inc.; pg. 1153, pg. 1063
Votava, John, Sr Mgr-Corp Comm-4G, Global Wholesale & New Ventures - Sprint Corporation; pg. 1874, pg. 719
Vough, Leah, Specialist-Internal Mktg & Comm-Bayer Bus Svcs - Bayer Corporation; pg. 1499, pg. 1573
Voytovich, Thomas E., Exec VP-Intl, Production Tech, Offshore & Exploration - Apache Corporation; pg. 1934, pg. 1700
Vozar, David, Sr VP-Creative Svcs - Scholastic Inc.; pg. 1683, pg. 1288
Vrabely, Jon P., Pres & CEO - Huttig Building Products, Inc.; pg. 88, pg. 998
Vranakis, Steve, Exec Dir-Creative-Google Creative Lab - Google Inc.; pg. 1249, pg. 153
Vranek, Brian, Product Mgr-Laser Measuring - Robert Bosch Tool Corp; pg. 1060, pg. 634
Vranica, Suzanne, Editor-Adv - The Wall Street Journal; pg. 1700, pg. 1312
Vrankova, Martina, Dir-Mktg-Central Europe - NIKE, Inc.; pg. 1812, pg. 1492
Vrban, Michele, Sr Dir-Mktg Ops-Connected Vehicle Svcs - Sirius XM Holdings Inc.; pg. 308, pg. 1292
Vrcek, Caitlin, Sr Mgr-Mktg - Lone Star Steakhouse & Saloon, Inc.; pg. 1736, pg. 1733
Vredenburgh, Caren, Sr Dir-Creative Svcs - Caleres, Inc.; pg. 1805, pg. 993
Vreeland, Lynne A., Mgr-PR - Neiman Marcus, Inc.; pg. 30, pg. 1684
Vrees, Marybeth, Dir-Customer Comm & Mktg - Pepco Holdings, Inc.; pg. 1949, pg. 404
Vriezelaar, Brad, Dir-New Media - The Blade Co.; pg. 1621, pg. 1476
Vroman, Kendal, Sr Mng Dir-Commodity Products & OTC Solutions - CME Group Inc.; pg. 738, pg. 571
Vrsansky, Kristen, VP-Outdoor Products - totes Isotoner Corporation; pg. 14, pg. 1426
Vu, Ann, Brand Mgr-Quilted Northern - Georgia-Pacific LLC; pg. 1458, pg. 507
Vu, Don, Head-Media-North America-RBWM - HSBC Bank USA; pg. 767, pg. 1241
Vu, Lauren, Mgr-Consumer Mktg, Program Adv & Promos - Home Box Office, Inc.; pg. 290, pg. 1240
Vu, Maveric, Head-Internal Social Collaboration - Wells Fargo & Company; pg. 819, pg. 232
Vu, Phuong, Sr VP-Digital Mktg - Citigroup Inc.; pg. 735, pg. 1212
Vu, Theresa, Sr Mgr-Integrated Mktg - Ingram Micro Inc.; pg. 415, pg. 261
Vu, Tony, Brand Mktg Mgr - LinkedIn Corporation; pg. 1262, pg. 160
Vuadens, Vincent, Sr Mgr-Creative Strategy - Electronic Arts Inc.; pg. 951, pg. 189
Vukanovich, Patty, Mgr-Shopper Mktg - Del Monte Foods, Inc.; pg. 852, pg. 304
Vukelich, Vicki, Sr Specialist-Mktg - The Procter & Gamble Company; pg. 1129, pg. 1418
Vuncannon, Aleasha, Asst Mgr-PR-Honda Aircraft Company - American Honda Motor Co., Inc.; pg. 163, pg. 292
Vuong, Mary, Engr-Network & Sls Support - AT&T; pg. 1865, pg. 258
Vuturo, Chris, Mgr-External Rels & Influencer Mktg - The Procter & Gamble Company; pg. 1129, pg. 1418
Vyas, Ronak, VP-Engrg & Comm Products - Yahoo! Inc.; pg. 1289, pg. 289

W

Waard, Roelant de, Head-Sls & Mktg-Ford of Europe Div - Ford Motor Company; pg. 172, pg. 876
Waas, Amanda, Assoc Dir-Mktg - National Geographic

Society; *pg.* 1667, *pg.* 402
Waayers, Tom, Product Mgr - NXP Semiconductors; *pg.* 660, *pg.* 248
Wabel, David, Sr Dir-Mktg - Travelzoo Inc; *pg.* 1926, *pg.* 1304
Waber, Michele, Sr Mgr-Brand Identity - Dupont Pioneer; *pg.* 1795, *pg.* 708
Wabler, Theresa, Sr Dir-Mktg - Blackhawk Engagement Solutions, Inc.; *pg.* 1232, *pg.* 1725
Wachholz, Heidi, VP-Sls-Northeast - Allianz Life Insurance Company of North America; *pg.* 1188, *pg.* 929
Wachsman, Sean, Brand Mgr-Chambord Trademark - Brown-Forman Corporation; *pg.* 1958, *pg.* 732
Wachtel, Jennifer, Exec Dir-Digital Mktg & Strategy - CME Group Inc.; *pg.* 738, *pg.* 571
Wachtel, Jennifer, Exec Dir-Digital Mktg & Strategy - CME Group, Inc.; *pg.* 738, *pg.* 571
Wachtendonk, Dave, Sr Product Mgr - Constant Contact, Inc.; *pg.* 379, *pg.* 850
Wachter, Susan, Exec VP-Sls Pricing, Plng & Analysis - Fox Broadcasting Company; *pg.* 287, *pg.* 130
Wachtmeister, Rutger, Sr VP-Mktg & Sls - Dometic Corporation; *pg.* 1070, *pg.* 677
Wacksman, Jeremy, CMO - Zillow Group, Inc.; *pg.* 1292, *pg.* 1843
Waco, Dave, VP-Sls - MOC Products Company, Inc.; *pg.* 332, *pg.* 174
Waddell, Brice, Mgr-Interactive Mktg-Titleist Golf Clubs - Acushnet Company; *pg.* 1824, *pg.* 818
Waddell, Dave, Brand Mgr - Arrow Electronics, Inc.; *pg.* 619, *pg.* 325
Waddell, Grant, Dir-Sls & Mktg - Auto Driveaway Co.; *pg.* 1900, *pg.* 566
Waddell, Randy, Sr VP-Mktg-Northeast Div - Comcast Corporation; *pg.* 276, *pg.* 1560
Waddell, Tim, Dir-Product Mktg - Adobe Systems Incorporated; *pg.* 342, *pg.* 235
Wadden, Colleen, Sr Dir-External Comm - Providence Health System; *pg.* 1587, *pg.* 1829
Waddoups, Rand, Sr Dir-Electronics Accessories - Wal-Mart Stores, Inc.; *pg.* 1790, *pg.* 29
Wade, Gordon, Dir-Mktg - Nestle Purina PetCare Company; *pg.* 1479, *pg.* 1000
Wade, Julie, Head-Mktg-Roofing & Asphalt - Owens Corning; *pg.* 102, *pg.* 1476
Wade, Kelly, Mgr-Mktg - Florida's Natural Growers; *pg.* 855, *pg.* 437
Wade, Lindsay, Brand Mgr-Hair Care & Men's Skincare - Neutrogena Corporation; *pg.* 517, *pg.* 137
Wade, Ron, Dir-Mktg - Detroit Tigers Baseball Club, Inc.; *pg.* 545, *pg.* 880
Wade, Tom, CMO & Exec VP - PGA Tour, Inc.; *pg.* 574, *pg.* 460
Wade, Tom, Brand Mgr - William Grant & Sons, Inc.; *pg.* 1972, *pg.* 1057
Wade, Will, Dir-Product Mgmt-Pro Solutions Grp - NVIDIA Corporation; *pg.* 447, *pg.* 268
Wadel, Terry, Specialist-Mktg Graphics - Kimberly-Clark Corporation; *pg.* 1461, *pg.* 1720
Wadham, Kathy, Dir-Creative Programming - Los Angeles County Fair Association; *pg.* 559, *pg.* 185
Wadhawan, Smita, Dir-Product Mktg - PayPal Inc.; *pg.* 1274, *pg.* 248
Wadhwa, Bhuvan, Dir-Svcs Mktg-Global - SAP America, Inc.; *pg.* 466, *pg.* 1557
Wadhwa, Sunena, Assoc Dir-Mktg Ops - MedImmune LLC; *pg.* 1562, *pg.* 770
Wadhwani, Prita, Mgr-Mktg-Integrated Mktg Comm - Barilla America, Inc.; *pg.* 839, *pg.* 555
Wadlington, Mark, Corp VP-Sls-Worldwide - Lattice Semiconductor Corporation; *pg.* 651, *pg.* 1498
Wadsworth, Ann, Mgr-Corp Trng-Sls & Mktg - American Woodmark Corporation; *pg.* 913, *pg.* 1811
Wadzinski, Tricia, Project Mgr-Digital Revenue Mktg - GE Capital; *pg.* 761, *pg.* 362
Waecker, Jonathan, Sr Dir-Mktg Comm-Global Brand Mgmt - Yahoo! Inc.; *pg.* 1289, *pg.* 289
Waelchli, Christophe, Product Mgr - ON Semiconductor Corporation; *pg.* 101, *pg.* 18
Wafer, Deborah Y., Sr Mgr-HCV Mktg - Gilead Sciences, Inc.; *pg.* 1535, *pg.* 88
Wafford, Jeff, Supvr-PR-UPS - United Parcel Service, Inc.; *pg.* 1928, *pg.* 522
Wafler, Porter, Reg Mgr-Sls-Eastern Div - Philips Emergency Lighting; *pg.* 1303, *pg.* 1631
Wagasky, Mark, VP-Sls - Applied Software Technology, Inc.; *pg.* 352, *pg.* 488
Wagenbrenner-Hogan, Wendy, Mgr-Mktg Comm - Siemens Process Industries and Drives; *pg.* 673, *pg.* 485
Wagenheim, Marc, Product Dir-Personalization-Gold Crown - Hallmark Cards, Inc.; *pg.* 1646, *pg.* 983
Wager, Russell, VP-Mktg - Mazda North American Operations; *pg.* 183, *pg.* 113
Wagers, Gary W., Exec VP-Retail Products & Svcs - Banner Corporation; *pg.* 722, *pg.* 1846
Wages, Steve, Mgr-Email Mktg - Patagonia; *pg.* 31, *pg.* 301
Waggenheim, Dan, VP-Digital Media & Event Ops - TechTarget, Inc.; *pg.* 482, *pg.* 837
Waggoner, Bob, VP-Mktg & Sls - United States Pipe & Foundry Company, Inc.; *pg.* 117, *pg.* 5
Waggoner, Jason, Mgr-Mktg - King's Hawaiian Bakery West, Inc.; *pg.* 869, *pg.* 293
Waggoner, Mike, Strategist-Bus Markets Product Mktg - Cincinnati Bell Inc.; *pg.* 1871, *pg.* 1410
Wagman, Jonathan, Mgr-Indus Sls - Waste Management, Inc.; *pg.* 1954, *pg.* 1716
Wagner, Abbi, Brand Mgr-Adv-North America - Tiffany & Co.; *pg.* 13, *pg.* 1299
Wagner, Al, Mgr-Technical Mktg-Rational Mktg - IBM Canada Limited; *pg.* 411, *pg.* 1923
Wagner, Alexandra, Dir-Purpose Integration & Purpose Mktg - Sun Trust Bank, Atlanta; *pg.* 806, *pg.* 520
Wagner, Alexandra, Dir-Event Mktg - SunTrust Banks, Inc.; *pg.* 807, *pg.* 520
Wagner, Alexis, Dir-Digital Media - Gucci America Inc.; *pg.* 6, *pg.* 1237
Wagner, Amy, Dir-Retail Mktg - Walgreen Co.; *pg.* 1608, *pg.* 605
Wagner, Barbara, Specialist-PR - Beckman Coulter, Inc.; *pg.* 1402, *pg.* 48
Wagner, Brian, Dir-Mktg & Retail Sls - Greenlee Textron Inc.; *pg.* 1048, *pg.* 655
Wagner, Diane, Sr VP-Media Rels - Bank of America Corporation; *pg.* 718, *pg.* 1362
Wagner, Ellen, Specialist-Natl Accounts Product - Honeywell International Inc.; *pg.* 407, *pg.* 1088
Wagner, Elliot, VP-Intl Program Sls & North America Partnerships - Discovery Communications, Inc.; *pg.* 282, *pg.* 777
Wagner, Franziska, Sr Specialist-Mktg Comm - Siemens Corporation; *pg.* 803, *pg.* 1291
Wagner, Fritz J., Bus Mgr-Manufactured Products & Specialty Chemicals - Hawkins, Inc.; *pg.* 1165, *pg.* 937
Wagner, Gary A., Sr Mgr-Revenue & Bus Forecasting - Avago Technologies; *pg.* 358, *pg.* 238
Wagner, George Van, Copywriter-Adv - Guitar Center, Inc.; *pg.* 1771, *pg.* 306
Wagner, Gerry, VP-Merchant Sls - Discover Financial Services; *pg.* 744, *pg.* 653
Wagner, Greg, Mgr-Product Mktg - AT&T Mobility LLC; *pg.* 620, *pg.* 1152
Wagner, Heather, Mgr-Direct Mktg & Response - Beutlich Pharmaceuticals LP; *pg.* 1503, *pg.* 665
Wagner, Heather, Mgr-Mktg Sys & Promos - The McGraw-Hill Companies Inc.; *pg.* 1663, *pg.* 1257
Wagner, Helen, Mgr-PR - 3M Company; *pg.* 1142, *pg.* 956
Wagner, Jan, Dir-Fin Plng & Sls Support - The Northwestern Mutual Life Insurance Company; *pg.* 1212, *pg.* 1879
Wagner, Jeff, Sr Mgr-Pub Affairs - Fluor Corporation; *pg.* 82, *pg.* 1719
Wagner, Jim, VP & Head-Internal Sls - Protective Life Insurance Company; *pg.* 1215, *pg.* 4
Wagner, Joe, Head-Retail Mktg - Owens Corning; *pg.* 102, *pg.* 1476
Wagner, Kenneth, Mgr-Integrated Mktg - USG Corporation; *pg.* 118, *pg.* 594
Wagner, Lisa, Sr Product Mgr-Game Informer - GameStop Corp.; *pg.* 399, *pg.* 1699
Wagner, Maleeda, Mgr-Mktg Strategy - Nestle USA, Inc.; *pg.* 883, *pg.* 96
Wagner, Mandy, Mgr-Media Rels-Global - The Procter & Gamble Company; *pg.* 1129, *pg.* 1418
Wagner, Monica, Designer & Coord-Mktg - McKesson Corporation; *pg.* 1560, *pg.* 222
Wagner, Rachel, Sr Mgr-Walmart Leverage-ISD Comm - Wal-Mart Stores, Inc.; *pg.* 1790, *pg.* 29
Wagner, Rick, Mgr-Sls - Snyder Industries, Inc.; *pg.* 1377, *pg.* 1012
Wagner, Sandy, Mgr-Mktg Comm - PolyOne Corporation; *pg.* 1177, *pg.* 1404
Wagner, Shelley, Dir-Adv & Promos - Los Angeles Dodgers Inc.; *pg.* 559, *pg.* 135
Wagner, Timothy, Sr VP-Samsung Bus Sls - Samsung Electronics America, Inc.; *pg.* 669, *pg.* 1115
Wagstaff, Janelle, Coord-Mktg - MetLife, Inc.; *pg.* 1208, *pg.* 1258
Wagstaff, Robert, Sr Mgr - Deloitte & Touche USA LLP; *pg.* 743, *pg.* 1222
Wah, Evelyn, Dir-Mktg-Innovation-North America Premium Nutrition - PepsiCo, Inc.; *pg.* 259, *pg.* 1327
Wah, Loh Kin, Exec VP-Sls & Mktg - NXP Semiconductors; *pg.* 660, *pg.* 248
Wahl, Clay, Exec VP-Sls & Ops - Follett Higher Education Group; *pg.* 1769, *pg.* 669
Wahl, Debbie, VP-Mktg & Product Dev - Citigroup Inc.; *pg.* 735, *pg.* 1212
Wahl, Gretchen, Sr Dir-ECommerce Ops - Bare Necessities, Inc.; *pg.* 19, *pg.* 1056
Wahl, Kelsey, Mgr-Mktg & Generation - The Nielsen Company B.V.; *pg.* 1671, *pg.* 1272
Wahl, Martin, Principal & Program Mgr-Azure Media Svcs - Microsoft Corporation; *pg.* 435, *pg.* 1824
Wahl, Steve, VP-Mktg - Rug Doctor, LP; *pg.* 1373, *pg.* 1734
Wahl, Wendy, Head-Enterprise Mktg - Aetna Inc.; *pg.* 1187, *pg.* 351
Wahle, Aaron, Sr VP-Digital Mktg-Intl - Sony Pictures Entertainment Inc.; *pg.* 309, *pg.* 72
Wahlers, Jason, Dir-PR - Green Bay Packers, Inc.; *pg.* 551, *pg.* 1859
Wahtera, Megan, Sr VP-Interactive Mktg - Paramount Pictures Corporation; *pg.* 304, *pg.* 138
Wai-Poi, Clayton, Dir-Mktg & CRM - Mondelez International; *pg.* 877, *pg.* 1344
Wai-Poi, Clayton, Dir-Mktg-Enhancers - Mondelez International, Inc.; *pg.* 878, *pg.* 601
Waidelich, Kirk, VP-Mktg - J.C. Penney Company, Inc.; *pg.* 1774, *pg.* 1732
Waight, Steve, Sr Exec Dir-Corp Sls - Chicago Blackhawk Hockey Team, Inc.; *pg.* 538, *pg.* 569
Wainwright, Adrian, Head-Intl PR Strategy-Xbox - Microsoft Corporation; *pg.* 435, *pg.* 1824
Wainwright, Bill, Dir-Suite Sls & Svcs - Tennessee Football, Inc.; *pg.* 587, *pg.* 1654
Wainwright, Mary J., Dir-Mktg-Oncology Bus Unit - Amgen Inc.; *pg.* 1493, *pg.* 291
Wainwright, Tim, Head-Global Mktg-Cardiovascular - Amgen Inc.; *pg.* 1493, *pg.* 291
Wait, Greg, VP-Sls - The Salvajor Company; *pg.* 60, *pg.* 986
Waite, Leslie, Sr Dir-Info Svcs - The American Gastroenterological Association; *pg.* 128, *pg.* 761
Waite, Lisa, Dir-Creative - Oklahoma City Thunder; *pg.* 571, *pg.* 1487
Waite, Ryan, Sr VP-Products - Cray Inc.; *pg.* 380, *pg.* 1834
Waite, Shannon, Sr Dir-Contact Center-Ops Div - Allianz Life Insurance Company of North America; *pg.* 1188, *pg.* 929
Waits, Daniel, Sr Mgr-Global Strategic Mktg - Becton, Dickinson & Company; *pg.* 1501, *pg.* 1068
Waitt, Robert, Dir-Adv - Greater Media Newspapers, Inc.; *pg.* 1646, *pg.* 1071
Wake, Michael, Product Dir - Travelport Limited; *pg.* 1925, *pg.* 521
Wakefield, Todd, Mgr-Mktg Res - Nu Skin Enterprises, Inc.; *pg.* 518, *pg.* 1755
Wakeley, Meredith, Coord-Mktg - Orbital ATK; *pg.* 1425, *pg.* 1779
Wakely, Sheena, Head-Program & Strategist-Social Media - Wells Fargo & Company; *pg.* 819, *pg.* 232
Walach, Jackie, Mgr-Mktg Programs - Emulex Corporation; *pg.* 392, *pg.* 70
Walant, Leigh, Sr Mgr-Content Ops & Mktg - OnMobile Live, Inc.; *pg.* 449, *pg.* 829
Walcott, Sara, Asst VP-Client Experience-USIS Mktg - T. Rowe Price Group Inc.; *pg.* 808, *pg.* 759
Walczak, Heidi, Sr Mgr-Integrated Mktg-North America Demand Center - Motorola Solutions, Inc.; *pg.* 657, *pg.* 659
Walczyk, Radoslaw, Mgr-Enterprise PR-Europe, The Middle East & Africa - Intel Corporation; *pg.* 645, *pg.* 266
Wald, Karen, VP-Corp Mktg - Alliance Data Systems Corporation; *pg.* 347, *pg.* 1729
Walden, Mitch, Mgr-ECommerce Mktg - AutoZone, Inc.; *pg.* 200, *pg.* 1641
Walden, Nick, Sr VP-Sls-EMEA - Infinera Corporation; *pg.* 644, *pg.* 286
Walden, Wayne, VP-Production - Robinson Helicopter Company; *pg.* 234, *pg.* 295

Waldinger, Jamie, Sr Dir-Corp Strategy - Constant Contact, Inc.; *pg.* 379, *pg.* 850

Waldman, Andrea, Dir-Consumer Activation & Creative Svcs - Merck & Co., Inc.; *pg.* 1566, *pg.* 1077

Waldman, Dave, Brand Mktg Mgr - Conagra Foods; *pg.* 826, *pg.* 994

Waldo, Denise, Sr VP-Sls & Mktg - Leggett & Platt, Incorporated; *pg.* 933, *pg.* 974

Waldock, Chris, Dir-Mktg-Heineken Portfolio - Molson Coors Canada Inc.; *pg.* 256, *pg.* 1955

Waldren, Emily, Mgr-PR - The Field Museum; *pg.* 548, *pg.* 573

Waldron, Kimberly, Assoc Mgr-Mktg - McKesson Corporation; *pg.* 1560, *pg.* 222

Waldron, Laura, Dir-Mktg - University of Pennsylvania; *pg.* 609, *pg.* 1571

Waldron, Morgan, Specialist-Digital Mktg - Capriotti's Sandwich Shop Inc; *pg.* 1720, *pg.* 1023

Waldron, Theresa, Dir-Visitor Svcs & Mktg - Museum of Discovery & Science, Inc.; *pg.* 565, *pg.* 425

Waldron, William, III, VP-Intl & Security Sls - Holliston LLC; *pg.* 1460, *pg.* 1630

Waldrop, Brooke, Mgr-Pub Rels - Commonwealth Zoological Corp.; *pg.* 542, *pg.* 793

Waldt, Jobie, Sr Mgr-Stadium Ops - Baltimore Ravens Limited Partnership; *pg.* 532, *pg.* 755

Waldvogel, Nathan, Mgr-Mktg - University of Minnesota; *pg.* 609, *pg.* 945

Walega, Larisa, Dir-Mktg - Ziebart International Corporation; *pg.* 222, *pg.* 912

Waleke, Jessica, Strategist-Global Mktg Automation - Dell Inc.; *pg.* 383, *pg.* 1737

Walen, Brady, Brand Mgr-Widmer Brothers - Craft Brewers Alliance, Inc; *pg.* 247, *pg.* 1502

Walenz, Michelle, Sr VP-Mktg, Creative & Branding - ABC Family Channel; *pg.* 268, *pg.* 51

Walery, Debi, Dir-Adv-Natl & Majors - Oregonian Publishing Co.; *pg.* 1673, *pg.* 1504

Wales, Holly, Brand Mgr - Boulder Brands, Inc.; *pg.* 1016, *pg.* 310

Walhof, Kelley, Asst Mgr-Integrated Mktg Comm - General Mills, Inc.; *pg.* 828, *pg.* 933

Walhovd, Bryan, Sr Mgr-CMTS Ops - Charter Communications, Inc.; *pg.* 274, *pg.* 372

Walia, Vic, Sr Dir-Brand Mktg-Expedia com - Expedia, Inc.; *pg.* 1244, *pg.* 1814

Waligora, Rafal, Sr Mgr-Network Engrg - Twitter, Inc.; *pg.* 1285, *pg.* 228

Waligunda, Robert, Dir-Mktg - Knoll, Inc.; *pg.* 425, *pg.* 1527

Walker, Adam, Brand Mgr-BENYLIN - Johnson & Johnson; *pg.* 1549, *pg.* 1091

Walker, Adelle, Dir-Mktg-Juvederm & Voluma - Allergan, Inc.; *pg.* 1491, *pg.* 106

Walker, Albert, Dir-Sls Mktg & Client Svcs - The Northwestern Mutual Life Insurance Company; *pg.* 1212, *pg.* 1879

Walker, Amy, Acct Exec-Mktg-Global - Oregon Tourism Commission; *pg.* 1003, *pg.* 1508

Walker, Angela, Sr Mgr-Quality Control - American Snuff Company; *pg.* 1893, *pg.* 1641

Walker, Ashleigh, Specialist-Adv & Mktg - FLIR Systems, Inc.; *pg.* 1413, *pg.* 1510

Walker, Barbara, Sr VP-Consumer Mktg - Safeway Inc.; *pg.* 1032, *pg.* 184

Walker, Bettie, Exec Dir-Mktg Point of Sale - Chanel, Inc.; *pg.* 503, *pg.* 1211

Walker, Bob, VP-Sls-Global - Emerson Process Management; *pg.* 1334, *pg.* 1636

Walker, Bob, Mgr-Sls-Natl - Mulberry Metal Products, Inc.; *pg.* 1302, *pg.* 1127

Walker, Carole, Acct Exec-Adv - Dierbergs Markets Inc.; *pg.* 1018, *pg.* 974

Walker, Cathy, Sr Mgr-HR - Sigma-Aldrich Corporation; *pg.* 1181, *pg.* 1003

Walker, Chanel, Brand Mgr-Handbags - Calvin Klein, Inc.; *pg.* 20, *pg.* 1209

Walker, Christopher E., Asst Dir-Mktg - Georgia Institute Of Technology; *pg.* 602, *pg.* 506

Walker, Colby, Dir-Mktg, Promotional Plng & ECommerce - Lumber Liquidators Holdings, Inc.; *pg.* 94, *pg.* 1808

Walker, Dawn, Specialist-Registered Sls & Securities - BOK Financial Corporation; *pg.* 726, *pg.* 1489

Walker, Dee, Dir-Mktg - Raising Cane's USA; *pg.* 1746, *pg.* 742

Walker, Derek, Sr Mgr-Engrg Tech Support - T-Mobile US, Inc.; *pg.* 676, *pg.* 1816

Walker, Derrick, CMO & Sr VP-Mktg - Destination XL Group, Inc.; *pg.* 40, *pg.* 810

Walker, Donna McDade, Mgr-Product Mktg & Support - Agilent Technologies, Inc.; *pg.* 614, *pg.* 264

Walker, Earl, Sr Dir-Govt Affairs - Airbus Helicopters, Inc.; *pg.* 223, *pg.* 1698

Walker, Ed, Mgr-ECommerce Mktg-North America - Crucial Technology Div of Micron; *pg.* 1237, *pg.* 550

Walker, Fred, VP-Global Mktg Svcs - GlaxoSmithKline Consumer Healthcare; *pg.* 510, *pg.* 1554

Walker, Fred, Mgr-Mktg-Intl - North Dakota Department of Commerce Tourism Division; *pg.* 1002, *pg.* 1397

Walker, Heather, Sr Dir-PR - Boston Celtics Limited Partnership; *pg.* 533, *pg.* 790

Walker, Jean, Mgr-Mktg Comm - Samsung Electronics America, Inc.; *pg.* 669, *pg.* 1115

Walker, Jeff, Dir-Global Product Strategy & Program Mgmt - Eaton Corporation; *pg.* 1331, *pg.* 1429

Walker, Jeff, VP-Mktg - Renaissance Learning, Inc.; *pg.* 607, *pg.* 1899

Walker, Jennifer, Sr Mgr-Worksite Mktg & Product Mktg - Aflac Incorporated; *pg.* 1188, *pg.* 527

Walker, Jim, VP-Sls - Agilysys, Inc.; *pg.* 614, *pg.* 1409

Walker, John, VP-Global Mktg-Enterprise & Intelligence Solutions - Syniverse Holdings, Inc.; *pg.* 479, *pg.* 475

Walker, Julian, Mgr-Retail Mktg - adidas America Inc.; *pg.* 1803, *pg.* 1500

Walker, Justin, Sr Product Mgr - NVIDIA Corporation; *pg.* 447, *pg.* 268

Walker, Kenneth, Pres-Engineered Products Segment - EnPro Industries, Inc.; *pg.* 1334, *pg.* 1366

Walker, Kevin, Program Mgr-Channel Mktg - Lenovo Group Ltd; *pg.* 427, *pg.* 1384

Walker, Kyle, Dir-PR-Call of Duty - Activision Blizzard, Inc.; *pg.* 948, *pg.* 271

Walker, Kyle, Product Mgr-Aerospace - Milacron LLC; *pg.* 1361, *pg.* 1405

Walker, Laura, Sr Mgr-Product Mktg & Bus - Constant Contact, Inc.; *pg.* 379, *pg.* 850

Walker, Lee, Product Dir-Global - NIKE, Inc.; *pg.* 1812, *pg.* 1492

Walker, Lisa, VP-Product Mktg - Forrester Research, Inc.; *pg.* 1642, *pg.* 807

Walker, Lisa, Sr Mgr-Technical Mktg - NetApp, Inc.; *pg.* 444, *pg.* 287

Walker, Lisa M., Assoc Dir-Natl Mktg & Digital Omni-Channel - AT&T; *pg.* 1865, *pg.* 258

Walker, Liz, Dir-Product - NIKE, Inc.; *pg.* 1812, *pg.* 1492

Walker, Louise, Acct Mgr-Adv - Snowmass Village Sun; *pg.* 1687, *pg.* 335

Walker, Marjory L., Dir-Comm, Production & AV Svcs - National Cotton Council of America; *pg.* 148, *pg.* 1631

Walker, Mark, VP-Mktg & Media Rels - EnergySolutions Inc.; *pg.* 1941, *pg.* 1757

Walker, Mark L., Sr VP & Gen Mgr-Disney Interactive Media - Disney Interactive Media Group; *pg.* 1239, *pg.* 95

Walker, Mathew, Sr Analyst-Mktg - Liberty Mutual Insurance Group Inc.; *pg.* 1205, *pg.* 797

Walker, Matt, Designer-Digital - Time Inc.; *pg.* 1693, *pg.* 1300

Walker, Mica, Mgr-Vendor Mktg - Ingram Micro Inc.; *pg.* 415, *pg.* 261

Walker, Mike, Sr Product Mgr-Soccer & Major League Soccer - adidas America Inc.; *pg.* 1803, *pg.* 1500

Walker, Mike, Reg Mgr-Sls-Southeastern - Clark Material Handling Company; *pg.* 1323, *pg.* 729

Walker, Mike, VP-Sls - Lennox International Inc.; *pg.* 1073, *pg.* 1736

Walker, Nathan, VP-Sls-Natl Accts - Owens Corning; *pg.* 102, *pg.* 1476

Walker, Nathan, Sr Designer-Mktg - ProLogis; *pg.* 1108, *pg.* 322

Walker, Pamela, Sr Dir-Mktg & Comm - MultiPlan, Inc.; *pg.* 1570, *pg.* 852

Walker, Peter, Chief Strategy Officer & Exec VP - Assurant, Inc.; *pg.* 1193, *pg.* 1198

Walker, Piper, VP-Digital Ad Sls - The Weather Channel LLC; *pg.* 320, *pg.* 523

Walker, Rachel, Coord-Production-Penguin Random House Audio - Penguin Random House; *pg.* 1675, *pg.* 1276

Walker, Rachel, Coord-Production-Penguin Random House Audio-Penguin Grp USA - Penguin Random House; *pg.* 1675, *pg.* 1276

Walker, Rachel, Mgr-PR - Yelp! Inc.; *pg.* 1291, *pg.* 235

Walker, Ryan, Dir-Product Mgmt - Rand McNally & Company; *pg.* 1679, *pg.* 661

Walker, Scott, Dir-Sls-Tech Data Solutions - Tech Data Corporation; *pg.* 482, *pg.* 416

Walker, Shauna, Sr Dir-Natl Programs - Papa Murphy's International, LLC; *pg.* 1743, *pg.* 1846

Walker, Shawn, VP-Natl Ad Sls - A&E Television Networks, LLC; *pg.* 267, *pg.* 1185

Walker, Stephen, VP-Mktg-APL - GlaxoSmithKline Consumer Healthcare; *pg.* 510, *pg.* 1554

Walker, Stuart, Sr VP-Partnership Mktg - National CineMedia, Inc.; *pg.* 567, *pg.* 314

Walker, Susan, VP-Mktg - Sally Beauty Holdings, Inc.; *pg.* 522, *pg.* 1691

Walker, Tariq Muhammad, VP-Creative Dev - AOL Inc.; *pg.* 1229, *pg.* 1195

Walker, Todd, Sr Mgr-Brand & Product Mktg - Logitech Inc.; *pg.* 1264, *pg.* 164

Walker, Todd Anthony, VP-Mktg - Interleukin Genetics, Inc.; *pg.* 1546, *pg.* 851

Walker, Tom, Dir-Creative-Mktg & Adv Design - Hulu LLC; *pg.* 1257, *pg.* 274

Walker, Vanessa, Exec VP-Sls & Mktg-LaCroix Sparkling Water - National Beverage Corp.; *pg.* 257, *pg.* 425

Walker, Wendy, Sr Mgr-Sls & Relationship Mgmt-Health & Wellness - Caremark Pharmacy Services; *pg.* 1513, *pg.* 1649

Walker-Baptist, Frances, Brand Mgr & Mgr-Mktg Comm - Freescale Semiconductor, Inc.; *pg.* 398, *pg.* 1662

Walker-Heminway, April, Sr Dir-Mktg Ops - Gilead Sciences, Inc.; *pg.* 1535, *pg.* 88

Walker-Jones, Yvette, Product Mgr-US Renal Mktg - Sanofi US; *pg.* 1592, *pg.* 1046

Walker-Wright, Edwina, Mgr-Consumer Mktg - Volvo Cars of North America LLC; *pg.* 195, *pg.* 1117

Wall, Brian, Dir-Sls - Xilinx, Inc.; *pg.* 496, *pg.* 252

Wall, Emma, Asst VP-Mktg - North Carolina Symphony; *pg.* 571, *pg.* 1388

Wall, Erin, Specialist-Mktg Comm - SPX Thermal Product Solutions; *pg.* 1378, *pg.* 1555

Wall, Gary, Mgr-Crude Oil Mktg Ops - Occidental Petroleum Corporation; *pg.* 1175, *pg.* 137

Wall, Jason B., VP-Mdsg & Sls Strategy - Rent-A-Center, Inc.; *pg.* 940, *pg.* 1734

Wall, Jenny, Sr VP & Head-Mktg - Hulu LLC; *pg.* 1257, *pg.* 274

Wall, Justin, Dir-Sls - Ujena Swimwear and Fashions; *pg.* 34, *pg.* 163

Wall, Lorelei, Sr Dir-Integrated Media-Alli Sports - NBC Sports Network; *pg.* 300, *pg.* 375

Wall, Matthew, Mgr-Mktg - Philips Lighting; *pg.* 1303, *pg.* 806

Wall, Tony, Dir-VISR-Mktg Svcs - Hanesbrands Inc.; *pg.* 26, *pg.* 1394

Wall, Virginia L., Dir-Mktg - Pfizer Inc.; *pg.* 1581, *pg.* 1278

Wallace, Becky, Brand Mgr-Digital - Ghirardelli Chocolate Company; *pg.* 1854, *pg.* 252

Wallace, Bernie, Dir-Creative Svcs - Hanesbrands Inc.; *pg.* 26, *pg.* 1394

Wallace, Betsy, Sr VP & Mgr-Mktg Svcs-KeyBank - KeyCorp; *pg.* 774, *pg.* 1432

Wallace, Bridget, Mgr-Mktg Svcs - Atmos Energy Corporation; *pg.* 1935, *pg.* 1675

Wallace, Heather, VP-Retailer Brand Mktg - The Sun Products Corporation; *pg.* 336, *pg.* 385

Wallace, Liza, Product Mgr-Digital-Mobile Security - Capital One Financial Corporation; *pg.* 730, *pg.* 1789

Wallace, Megan, Specialist-PR & Social Media - Qdoba Mexican Grill Inc.; *pg.* 1031, *pg.* 336

Wallace, Michael, VP-Sls & Mktg - Loos & Company, Inc.; *pg.* 1356, *pg.* 368

Wallace, Michael, Sr Dir-Mktg - Ottawa Senators Hockey Club; *pg.* 573, *pg.* 1921

Wallace, Molly, Dir-Experiential Mktg - Wilson Sporting Goods Co.; *pg.* 1848, *pg.* 596

Wallace, Pat, Dir-Mktg - Leanin' Tree, Inc.; *pg.* 1658, *pg.* 311

Wallace, Shayn, VP-Consumer & Industrial Sls & Mktg - Morton Salt, Inc.; *pg.* 881, *pg.* 583

wallace, steve, VP-Sls, Mktg & Bus Dev - Medicool, Inc.; *pg.* 1562, *pg.* 294

Wallace, Tom, Sr Dir-Advocacy & Corp Affairs-Global - Eli Lilly and Company; *pg.* 1527, *pg.* 684

Wallan, Simon, VP-Agricultural Sls - Ritchie Bros. Auctioneers Incorporated; *pg.* 1372, *pg.* 1907

Walle, Jesse, Mgr-Mktg Comm - The Andersons Incorporated; *pg.* 1793, *pg.* 1461

Wallenhorst, Mike, Dir-Comml-Product Mgmt - Ashland Inc.; *pg.* 972, *pg.* 726

Waller, Leslie, Dir-Global Mktg-Trident Gum - Mondelez International, Inc.; pg. 878, pg. 601
Wallick, Beth, Sr Dir-Mktg Comm - The Sherwin-Williams Company; pg. 1447, pg. 1435
Wallin, Eric, Mgr-Mktg - Lexmark International, Inc.; pg. 427, pg. 730
Walling, Emily, Head-Bus Plng & Ops, B2B & Product Mktg - Yahoo! Inc.; pg. 1289, pg. 289
Walling, Leah, Dir-Mktg Comm & Product Mktg - CPP, Inc.; pg. 1631, pg. 153
Wallingford, Stacey, Dir-Sls - Hasbro, Inc.; pg. 954, pg. 1603
Wallis, Audrey, VP-Sls - Infogroup Inc.; pg. 1652, pg. 1016
Wallis, Jamie, Mgr-Mktg - Hanesbrands Inc.; pg. 26, pg. 1394
Wallis, Sarah, Brand Mgr-Retail Dev-Men's - Ralph Lauren Corporation; pg. 46, pg. 1284
Walls, Billie Jo, Dir-Mktg - Hoss's Steak & Sea House, Inc.; pg. 1731, pg. 1526
Walls, Brad W., Dir-Sls & Central Div - Tanknology Inc; pg. 114, pg. 1666
Walls, Brian, Dir-Access Mktg-Metabolics - Alexion Pharmaceuticals, Inc.; pg. 1489, pg. 341
Walls, Geoff, VP-Product Mktg & Comm - Verizon Communications Inc.; pg. 1875, pg. 1309
Walls, Kyp, Dir-Product Mgmt - Panasonic Corporation of North America; pg. 661, pg. 1120
Walls, Leigh, Dir-Exhibit Sls & Svcs - National Association of Convenience Stores; pg. 148, pg. 1771
Walmsley, Mark, Mgr-Global Strategic Mktg-Insecticides - FMC Corporation; pg. 1163, pg. 1564
Walpole, J. Carrie, Sr Dir-Digital & Integrated Mktg - Time Inc.; pg. 1693, pg. 1300
Walraven, Anne, Dir-Champagne Strategy & Dir-Mktg - Moet Hennessy; pg. 1966, pg. 1260
Walraven, Ben, Dir-Sls - PanAmerican Seed Co.; pg. 1798, pg. 668
Walroth, Chris, Mgr-Production - Toronto Symphony Orchestra; pg. 589, pg. 1946
Walser, James, Div Mgr-Mdse-Watches - Amazon.com, Inc.; pg. 1226, pg. 1831
Walsh, Andrea, CMO & Exec VP - HealthPartners, Inc.; pg. 1203, pg. 918
Walsh, Anne M., Sr Mgr-Environmental & Comm - Puget Energy, Inc.; pg. 1950, pg. 1816
Walsh, Barbara, Analyst-Digital Content Mktg-Enterprise Mktg - State Farm Mutual Automobile Insurance Co.; pg. 1218, pg. 557
Walsh, Brendan, Dir-Adv-Fin Svcs Digital - The New York Times Company; pg. 1668, pg. 1270
Walsh, Brian, Sr Dir-Shopper Insights - PepsiCo, Inc.; pg. 259, pg. 1327
Walsh, Brian, VP-Classified Adv & Ad Ops - St. Louis Post-Dispatch LLC; pg. 1688, pg. 1004
Walsh, Carmen, Dir-Brand & Corp Mktg-Global - AGCO Corporation; pg. 700, pg. 530
Walsh, Charlotte, Sr VP-Mktg - Susan G. Komen for the Cure; pg. 158, pg. 1688
Walsh, Chip, Product Mgr-Global - Molex Incorporated; pg. 655, pg. 628
Walsh, Chris, Sr VP-Sales-Americas - Bullhorn, Inc.; pg. 1233, pg. 792
Walsh, Dan, Asst VP, Sr Specialist-Mktg-ECommerce Mktg - Associated Banc-Corp; pg. 716, pg. 1859
Walsh, David L., Sr VP-Tech & Mktg - Goodway Technologies Corporation; pg. 1341, pg. 374
Walsh, Don, Sr VP-Mdsg & Product Dev - MDI Entertainment LLC; pg. 964, pg. 484
Walsh, Erin, Sr Mgr-Integrated Mktg-RSA - EMC Corporation; pg. 391, pg. 825
Walsh, Eva, Exec VP-Mktg & Leasing - Dallas Market Center Company; pg. 78, pg. 1678
Walsh, Gerard, Supvr-Sls Support - NRG Energy, Inc.; pg. 1948, pg. 1712
Walsh, James, VP-Product Mgmt - AS America, Inc.; pg. 68, pg. 1108
Walsh, James, Exec VP-Sls - HP Hood LLC; pg. 864, pg. 829
Walsh, Jay, Sr Dir-Comm - Wikimedia Foundation Inc.; pg. 161, pg. 234
Walsh, Jenna, Specialist-PR - Bose Corporation; pg. 626, pg. 820
Walsh, Jenna, Mgr-Membership Mktg - The Museum of Modern Art; pg. 565, pg. 1263
Walsh, John, VP-Mktg - Mack Trucks, Inc.; pg. 183, pg. 1375
Walsh, John L., Dir-Creative Svcs - Leggett & Platt, Incorporated; pg. 933, pg. 974
Walsh, Joseph M., Mgr-Customer Svc & Social Media - ESPN, Inc.; pg. 285, pg. 340
Walsh, Kaitlin, Sr Specialist-Mktg-Enterprise & Retail - Panasonic Corporation of North America; pg. 661, pg. 1120
Walsh, Kathy, Dir-Mktg - Scholastic Inc.; pg. 1683, pg. 1288
Walsh, Kelli, Dir-Product Dev - Travelpro International, Inc.; pg. 14, pg. 413
Walsh, Laura, Mgr-Mktg - Air Techniques, Inc.; pg. 1487, pg. 1178
Walsh, Lisa Pollack, Sr Mgr-Comm & Social Media-Foundation - The Home Depot, Inc.; pg. 1050, pg. 510
Walsh, Marti M., Sr Mgr-Brand Activation - The Coca-Cola Company; pg. 240, pg. 493
Walsh, Meg, VP-Product Delivery & Launch - Frontier Communications Corporation; pg. 1871, pg. 362
Walsh, Mike, Sr VP-Mktg-KILZ Paints & Primers - Masterchem Industries, LLC; pg. 1444, pg. 979
Walsh, Nancy, Dir-Digital Mktg-US - MasterCard Incorporated; pg. 779, pg. 1325
Walsh, Nathan, Mgr-APAC Search Mktg - Adobe Systems Incorporated; pg. 342, pg. 235
Walsh, Natosha, Dir-Sls-Safeway Team - Hormel Foods Corporation; pg. 863, pg. 915
Walsh, Patrick, Sls Mgr-Enterprise Networking - CDW Corporation; pg. 370, pg. 663
Walsh, Sabina, Dir-Creative - Lands' End, Inc.; pg. 1776, pg. 1857
Walsh, Stephanie, Sr Mgr-PR - Sprint Corporation; pg. 1874, pg. 719
Walsh, Susan, Sr Mgr-Mktg-CLM Northeast Reg - AT&T Mobility LLC; pg. 620, pg. 1152
Walsh, Thomas, VP-Sls & Tech - Tenova; pg. 114, pg. 1525
Walsh, Tina, Dir-Global Brand Strategy & Mktg-NERF - Hasbro, Inc.; pg. 954, pg. 1603
Walshak, Sherry, Dir-Pub Sector Indus Mktg-Worldwide - Hewlett-Packard Company; pg. 404, pg. 175
Walsingham, Jeff, Mgr-Mktg-Healthcare & Life Sciences - United Parcel Service, Inc.; pg. 1928, pg. 522
Walski, Jenny, Mgr-Media - Chanel, Inc.; pg. 503, pg. 1211
Walski, Thomas, Sr Product Mgr - Bentley Systems, Inc.; pg. 361, pg. 1531
Walstrom, Mike, Sr Dir-Info Svcs - Capella Education Company; pg. 599, pg. 931
Walstrom, Wally, Dir-Mktg Pipe, Valves & Fittings - Chicago Tube & Iron Co.; pg. 1323, pg. 656
Walsworth, Rick, Dir-Product Mktg - EMC Corporation; pg. 391, pg. 825
Walter, Aarron, Gen Mgr-New Products - The Rocket Science Group, LLC; pg. 1278, pg. 519
Walter, Carl, VP-Mktg Comm - United Van Lines, LLC; pg. 1929, pg. 978
Walter, Debi, Mgr-Corp Mktg Svcs - Epicor Software Corporation; pg. 393, pg. 110
Walter, Frank E., Exec VP-Comml Sls - Heartland Financial USA, Inc.; pg. 765, pg. 707
Walter, Gerri, Dir-Mktg & Comm - Special Olympics International, Inc.; pg. 157, pg. 405
Walter, Janelle, Dir-Distr Mktg - Allianz Life Insurance Company of North America; pg. 1188, pg. 929
Walter, Jennifer, Mgr-Product Comm & Pkg - Sprint Corporation; pg. 1874, pg. 719
Walter, Jim, Sr VP-Global Product Integrity - MATTEL, INC.; pg. 962, pg. 81
Walter, Kaitlin, Dir-Mktg - Califia Farms LLC; pg. 843, pg. 179
Walter, Kathleen, Project Mgr-Mktg - Penske Truck Leasing Company, L.P.; pg. 188, pg. 1585
Walter, Ken, Mgr-Mdse - Sierra Trading Post Inc.; pg. 1819, pg. 1901
Walter, Kerry, Asst VP-ECommerce & Mktg - The Cato Corporation; pg. 21, pg. 1364
Walter, Maria, Mng Dir-Product & Brand Strategy - United Airlines, Inc.; pg. 1927, pg. 593
Walters, Brad, Dir-Social Media & Content Strategy - Lowe's Companies, Inc.; pg. 1053, pg. 1383
Walters, Connie, Sr Dir-Mktg - Arris Group, Inc.; pg. 353, pg. 541
Walters, Edward, Sr Mgr - T. Rowe Price Group Inc.; pg. 808, pg. 759
Walters, Heidi, Mgr-Mktg-Intl - North Carolina Department of Commerce Division of Tourism, Film & Sports Development; pg. 1001, pg. 1388
Walters, Jamie, Exec VP-Sls - ClubCorp, Inc.; pg. 1086, pg. 1677
Walters, Jason, Brand Mgr - Wendy's International, Inc.; pg. 1755, pg. 1451
Walters, Jenn, Mgr-Database Mktg & Outbound Mktg - Expedia, Inc.; pg. 1244, pg. 1814
Walters, Julie, Mgr-Mktg Comm - Emerson Climate Technologies, Inc.; pg. 1333, pg. 1472
Walters, Kathleen A., Exec VP-Consumer Products Grp - Georgia-Pacific LLC; pg. 1458, pg. 507
Walters, Kayleen, VP-Mktg - Lucasfilm, Ltd.; pg. 297, pg. 222
Walters, Kevin, Project Mgr-Mktg Comm - Texas Instruments Incorporated; pg. 679, pg. 1688
Walters, Kira, Mgr-Mktg Comm - Matthews International Corporation; pg. 1662, pg. 1578
Walters, Kristin, Sr Mgr-Mktg Activation - PepsiCo, Inc.; pg. 259, pg. 1327
Walters, Leslie, Mgr-Trade Mktg - Treasury Wine Estates; pg. 1971, pg. 164
Walters, Mark, Bus Mgr-Lindenmeyr Envelope - Lindenmeyr Munroe; pg. 1464, pg. 1325
Walters, Marnie G., Mgr-Sls & Mktg - Brown-Forman Corporation; pg. 1958, pg. 732
Walters, Sahran, Brand Mgr-Baby & Child Care-Global - Kimberly-Clark Corporation; pg. 1461, pg. 1720
Walters, Scott, Product Mgr - Author Solutions, Inc.; pg. 1618, pg. 674
Walterson, Colin, Product Mgr-Printing & Pkg - Epicor Software Corporation; pg. 393, pg. 110
Walther, Eckart, Product Mgr-Gifts Feature - Twitter, Inc.; pg. 1285, pg. 228
Walther, Linda, Product Mgr - Medline Industries, Inc.; pg. 1562, pg. 635
Walther, Mike, VP-Mktg - Prometheus Laboratories, Inc.; pg. 1586, pg. 206
Walton, Akil, Sr Dir-HR - Apple Inc.; pg. 350, pg. 73
Walton, Jermaine, Mgr-Mktg - Phoenix Suns; pg. 576, pg. 19
Walton, Krista M., Specialist-Mktg Comm - Armstrong World Industries, Inc.; pg. 914, pg. 1545
Walton, Larry, VP-Sls, Mktg & Technical Svc - American Packaging Corporation; pg. 1451, pg. 1333
Walton, Laura, Acct Dir-Programmatic & Platform Sls - Yahoo! Inc.; pg. 1289, pg. 289
Walton, Thomas W.H., Sr VP-Sls & Mktg-Corrugated Products - Packaging Corporation of America; pg. 1466, pg. 624
Waluszko, Alex, VP-Sls & Mktg & Reg Mgr-North America - UVP, Inc.; pg. 1434, pg. 298
Walz, Quentin, VP-Digital Sls-Eastern Reg - Meredith Corporation; pg. 1663, pg. 705
Wammock, Gina L., Dir-Mktg - CH2M HILL Companies, Ltd.; pg. 75, pg. 325
Wamsley, Christine, Dir-Category Mktg - Cabela's Incorporated; pg. 535, pg. 1019
Wamsley, Jane, Coord-Mktg & Building Efficiency - Johnson Controls, Inc.; pg. 1073, pg. 1597
Wan, Jessie, Mgr-Mktg - Mattel Games/Puzzles; pg. 962, pg. 80
Wan, Jessie, Mgr-Mktg - MATTEL, INC.; pg. 962, pg. 81
Wander, Bill, Mgr-Field Mktg - Lionel LLC; pg. 961, pg. 875
Wandishin, John, VP-Mktg - Brother International Corporation - USA; pg. 53, pg. 1046
Wanetka, Scott, VP-Mktg - Cabela's Incorporated; pg. 535, pg. 1019
Wang, Alfred, Sr Dir-Brand Mktg - Apollo Education Group Inc.; pg. 597, pg. 14
Wang, Andi, Mgr-Comm & Digital Media - The Walt Disney Company; pg. 317, pg. 52
Wang, Anna Sansan, Product Mgr-Optics - Newport Corporation; pg. 1424, pg. 114
Wang, Bessie, Mgr-PR - Cisco Systems, Inc.; pg. 372, pg. 240
Wang, Carolyn, Dir-Consumer Mktg - Activision Blizzard, Inc.; pg. 948, pg. 271
Wang, Catherine, Dir-Mktg-Consumer Ecosystem Grp - Intuit Inc.; pg. 769, pg. 158
Wang, Cathy, VP-Product Mgmt - ASI Corporation; pg. 354, pg. 90
Wang, Connie Chan, Sr Mgr-Social Media - LinkedIn Corporation; pg. 1262, pg. 160
Wang, Daisy, Mgr-Channel Mktg - ASUSTeK Computer Inc; pg. 355, pg. 90
Wang, Danchen, Assoc Dir-Mktg Res - Bristol-Myers Squibb Company; pg. 1509, pg. 1206
Wang, Daniel, Dir-Global Product Mgmt-Electronics Bus Unit - Littelfuse, Inc.; pg. 1301, pg. 580
Wang, Diane, Mgr-Server & Tools Product Mktg - Microsoft Corporation; pg. 435, pg. 1824
Wang, Emmy, Sr Mgr-Corp Rels - Genentech, Inc.; pg. 1533, pg. 279

Wang, Evelyn, VP-Mktg-Wet N Wild Cosmetics - Markwins International Corp.; *pg.* 516, *pg.* 67
Wang, Geri, Pres-Sls - ABC, Inc.; *pg.* 268, *pg.* 1185
Wang, Jinyu, Sr Principal & Product Mgr - Oracle Corporation; *pg.* 450, *pg.* 191
Wang, Julia, Mgr-Digital Mktg & Analytics - Polycom, Inc.; *pg.* 664, *pg.* 249
Wang, Loretta, Mgr-Mktg - Hanesbrands Inc.; *pg.* 26, *pg.* 1394
Wang, Lucy, Sr Head-Product Mktg-Bing Ads Verticals - Microsoft Corporation; *pg.* 435, *pg.* 1824
Wang, Maria, Coord-Mktg-Intl - Aldo Group; *pg.* 1804, *pg.* 1959
Wang, Mark, Asst Mgr-Sls - Hilton Worldwide, Inc.; *pg.* 1094, *pg.* 1791
Wang, Phillip, Sr VP & Mgr-Brand & Adv - Wells Fargo & Company; *pg.* 819, *pg.* 232
Wang, Sally, Sr Dir-Product Mktg - ViewSonic Corporation; *pg.* 489, *pg.* 303
Wang, Tanya, Mgr Digital Marcom-One Consumer Global Adv - Microsoft Corporation; *pg.* 435, *pg.* 1824
Wang, Thomas, Acct Mgr-Sls - Amkor Technology, Inc.; *pg.* 67, *pg.* 25
Wang, Ying, Dir-Product Mgmt & Ads - Google Inc.; *pg.* 1249, *pg.* 153
Wanke, Randall, Sr Mgr-Indus Rels - Dupont Pioneer; *pg.* 1795, *pg.* 708
Wannenmacher, Carlye, VP & Dir-Mktg - Guaranty Bank; *pg.* 764, *pg.* 1006
Wanner, Erin, VP-Production - Animal Planet, LLC; *pg.* 270, *pg.* 777
Wansley, Jacquie, Grp Mgr-Mktg - The Coca-Cola Company; *pg.* 240, *pg.* 493
Wantt, Jenny, Coord-Sls Support - Sierra Nevada Brewing Co.; *pg.* 265, *pg.* 65
Wanzer, Eric, VP-Sls - Comcast Cable Communications, Inc.; *pg.* 276, *pg.* 1560
Wanzie, Mike, Sr Mgr-Mktg Comm - Brother International Corporation - USA; *pg.* 53, *pg.* 1046
Waple, Brian, Product Mgr - Church & Dwight Co., Inc.; *pg.* 1153, *pg.* 1063
Waplinger, Johann, VP-Sls-Intl - GEA Refrigeration North America, Inc.; *pg.* 1072, *pg.* 1597
Wappel, Paul, Asst VP-PR & Community Rels - Horace Mann Companies; *pg.* 1203, *pg.* 662
Warble, Brennan, Head-Sls-US - Liquidnet Holdings, Inc.; *pg.* 776, *pg.* 1251
Warburton, Michael, Brand Mgr - Zoological Society of San Diego; *pg.* 595, *pg.* 211
Warchalowski, Alexis, Asst VP-Digital Mktg-Global - L'Oreal USA; *pg.* 514, *pg.* 1252
Ward, Andrea, VP-Mktg - Oracle Corporation; *pg.* 450, *pg.* 191
Ward, Beth, Asst VP-Mktg - State Farm Mutual Automobile Insurance Co.; *pg.* 1218, *pg.* 557
Ward, Cecil J., VP-Sls - Don Bell Signs LLC; *pg.* 388, *pg.* 460
Ward, Chris, Engr-Technical Mktg - Cisco Systems, Inc.; *pg.* 372, *pg.* 240
Ward, Chris, Dir-Mktg & PR - Goodwill Industries-Suncoast, Inc.; *pg.* 142, *pg.* 462
Ward, Christina, Asst Product Mgr-Foodservice Mktg - The J.M. Smucker Company; *pg.* 865, *pg.* 1468
Ward, Christina, Brand Mgr-Balance Bar - NBTY, Inc.; *pg.* 1572, *pg.* 1338
Ward, Deborah, Dir-Mktg & Comm - Omaha Convention and Visitors Bureau; *pg.* 152, *pg.* 1017
Ward, Derek, Head-Global Svc Product-OEC Surgery - General Electric Company; *pg.* 1297, *pg.* 347
Ward, Jason A., Dir-Mktg Strategy - Sears Holdings Corporation; *pg.* 1784, *pg.* 618
Ward, Jay L., Sr VP-Indus Products - Donaldson Company, Inc.; *pg.* 1329, *pg.* 917
Ward, Jim, Sr Dir-Sls Support Svcs - Golden Flake Snack Foods, Inc.; *pg.* 1854, *pg.* 3
Ward, John, VP-Sls & Mktg - Arburg, Inc.; *pg.* 1314, *pg.* 359
Ward, Ken, Sr VP-Sls & Ops Plng - Summer Infant, Inc.; *pg.* 1139, *pg.* 1610
Ward, Kirsten, Sr Dir-Devices & Studios Mktg - Microsoft Corporation; *pg.* 435, *pg.* 1824
Ward, Mary, Dir-Mktg & Paint Brands - Sherwin Williams; *pg.* 1448, *pg.* 1436
Ward, Matt, Sr Mgr-Digital Mktg - LG Electronics U.S.A., Inc.; *pg.* 651, *pg.* 1060
Ward, Matt, Acct Exec-Enterprise-Mktg Solutions - LinkedIn Corporation; *pg.* 1262, *pg.* 160
Ward, Maureen, Product Mgr-Mktg Ops - Boston Scientific Corporation; *pg.* 1508, *pg.* 831
Ward, Paula, Sr Mgr-Mktg - Best Buy Co., Inc.; *pg.* 1761, *pg.* 954
Ward, Randy, VP-Sls - Moore Fans LLC; *pg.* 1363, *pg.* 987
Ward, Richard, Reg Mgr-Sls-Western - NABCO Entrances, Inc.; *pg.* 99, *pg.* 1882
Ward, Ryan, Product Mgr - Browning; *pg.* 1828, *pg.* 1752
Ward, S. Brandon, Sr Mgr-Mktg Partnerships & Brdcst - San Diego Chargers Football Co.; *pg.* 580, *pg.* 208
Ward, Sarah Calkin, Dir-Ad Effectiveness-Product Leadership - The Nielsen Company B.V.; *pg.* 1671, *pg.* 1272
Ward, Scott, Coord-Social Media - Denver Broncos Football Club; *pg.* 544, *pg.* 325
Ward, Sharon, Dir-Pub & Media Rels - Pelican Products, Inc.; *pg.* 1842, *pg.* 295
Ward, Ted, VP-Mktg - GEICO Corporation; *pg.* 1200, *pg.* 399
Ward, Ted, VP-Mktg - GEICO General Insurance Company; *pg.* 1201, *pg.* 766
Ward, Timothy, Mgr-Digital Mktg - ESPN, Inc.; *pg.* 285, *pg.* 340
Ward, Tom, Dir-Production - Dallas Mavericks; *pg.* 543, *pg.* 1678
Warda, Jim, Sr Mgr-Comm - Walgreen Co.; *pg.* 1608, *pg.* 605
Wardell-Smith, Sara, Exec VP & Head-Foreign Exchange & Intl Treasury-Sls & Trading - Wells Fargo & Company; *pg.* 819, *pg.* 232
Wardlaw, Beth, Mgr-Classified Sls - The Florida Times-Union; *pg.* 1641, *pg.* 433
Wardle, Bill, VP-Sls & Mktg-Global - Maxion Wheels; *pg.* 212, *pg.* 903
Wardle, Duncan, VP-Creative Inc - The Walt Disney Company; *pg.* 317, *pg.* 52
Wardle, Jay, Head-Fin Category-AOL Adv - AOL Inc.; *pg.* 1229, *pg.* 1195
Wardlow, Adam, Dir-SMB Brand & Mktg Comm - Symantec Corporation; *pg.* 478, *pg.* 161
Wardrup, Jamie, Asst VP-Mktg - Aflac Incorporated; *pg.* 1188, *pg.* 527
Wardwell, Kate, Sr Specialist-Mktg - FedEx Corporation; *pg.* 1907, *pg.* 1642
Wardzinski, Steve, Reg VP-Product Mgmt - 21st Century Insurance Group; *pg.* 1187, *pg.* 389
Ware, Dan, Exec VP-Sls-Worldwide - GemStone Systems, Inc.; *pg.* 400, *pg.* 1492
Ware, Jodi, Sr Mgr-Comm & Trng - Baldor Electric Company; *pg.* 1316, *pg.* 32
Ware, Kevin, Sr Mgr-Mktg-Global Digital Strategy - Assurant, Inc.; *pg.* 1193, *pg.* 1198
Ware, Marissa, Mgr-Social Media - Zale Corporation; *pg.* 16, *pg.* 1724
Ware, Molly, Analyst-Interactive Mktg Search - The Goodyear Tire & Rubber Company; *pg.* 1883, *pg.* 1401
Ware, Monique, VP-Digital Mktg-BET Shows & Web Originals - BET Holdings LLC; *pg.* 271, *pg.* 396
Ware, Tony, Sr VP-Product Dev - Eli Lilly and Company; *pg.* 1527, *pg.* 684
Wareham, Chris, Sr Dir-Product Mgmt-Adobe Analytics - Adobe Systems Incorporated; *pg.* 342, *pg.* 235
Warf, Doug, VP-Mktg & Exec Dir-Kids 'N Community Foundation - Carolina Hurricanes Hockey Club; *pg.* 537, *pg.* 1386
Warfel, Karolyn, Sr Mgr-Category Dev-TERRO Brand - The Woodstream Corporation; *pg.* 1801, *pg.* 1549
Warfield, Kristin, VP-Sls & Partnerships - Churchill Downs, Inc.; *pg.* 540, *pg.* 733
Warfield, Scott, Sr Dir-Social Media & Brdcst Comm - National Association for Stock Car Auto Racing; *pg.* 566, *pg.* 420
Wargo, Alex, Acct Coord-Mktg - Microsoft Corp.; *pg.* 440, *pg.* 321
Wargo, Shawn, Engr-Technical Mktg - Cisco Systems, Inc.; *pg.* 372, *pg.* 240
Warhaftig, Daniel, Mgr-Customer Mktg - MillerCoors; *pg.* 254, *pg.* 1877
Warheit, Kevin, Product Mgr - Evoqua; *pg.* 1336, *pg.* 1590
Wark, Lisa, Mgr-Brand Media - Arby's Restaurant Group, Inc.; *pg.* 1014, *pg.* 488
Wark, Scott, Dir-Product Dev & Mgmt - Cox Communications, Inc.; *pg.* 279, *pg.* 501
Warley, Nelson, Sr Mgr-Mktg-Sauce & Meals Strategy - Campbell Soup Company; *pg.* 844, *pg.* 1048
Warman, Bryan, Sr VP-Intl Interactive Mktg - Paramount Pictures Corporation; *pg.* 304, *pg.* 138
Warne, Kim, Dir-Mktg - Tyco International (US) Inc.; *pg.* 1891, *pg.* 1113
Warner, Andrew, VP-Mktg - Monster Worldwide, Inc.; *pg.* 1268, *pg.* 859
Warner, Bill, Mgr-Application Sls-Customer Experience - Oracle Corporation; *pg.* 450, *pg.* 191
Warner, Bonnie, Mgr-Mktg-Base Mktg - Sprint Corporation; *pg.* 1874, *pg.* 719
Warner, Christopher D., VP-Sls - Daw Technologies, Inc.; *pg.* 78, *pg.* 1756
Warner, Jason, Mgr-Retail Channel Mktg - Sony Electronics, Inc.; *pg.* 676, *pg.* 209
Warner, Karen, Dir-Mktg Ops - W.W. Grainger, Inc.; *pg.* 1390, *pg.* 625
Warner, Kerri, Dir-Mktg-US Merchant Svcs - American Express Company; *pg.* 712, *pg.* 1190
Warner, Kim, Mgr-Influencer Mktg - Audible, Inc.; *pg.* 1230, *pg.* 1095
Warner, Laura L., Engr-Technical Mktg - Intel Corporation; *pg.* 645, *pg.* 266
Warner, Melissa, Brand Mgr - The Western Union Company; *pg.* 822, *pg.* 327
Warner, Nathan, Sr Mgr-Mktg Comm - Microsoft Corporation; *pg.* 435, *pg.* 1824
Warner, Paul D., Specialist-Sls & Promo - SUPERVALU, Inc.; *pg.* 1035, *pg.* 924
Warner, Paula, Sr Mgr-PR & Corp Comm - Delta Faucet Company; *pg.* 78, *pg.* 684
Warner, Ralph G., Mgr-CM Product Support Dev - Caterpillar, Inc.; *pg.* 1321, *pg.* 650
Warner, Susan, Dir-Publ & Adv - New York Institute of Technology; *pg.* 605, *pg.* 1318
Warner, Todd, Mng Dir-US Mktg - Pfizer Inc.; *pg.* 1581, *pg.* 1278
Warnock, Craig, Product Mgr - Fiserv, Inc.; *pg.* 758, *pg.* 537
Warnock, Lisa, Assoc Mgr-Mktg - Naked Juice Company, Inc.; *pg.* 882, *pg.* 150
Warnock, Mariel, Sr Specialist-Mktg - School Specialty, Inc.; *pg.* 467, *pg.* 1860
Warras, Dean, Pres-Prince Agri Products - PhibroChem; *pg.* 1177, *pg.* 1124
Warren, Andrew, Mgr-Sls-Tech, Retail & CPG - AT&T Mobility LLC; *pg.* 619, *pg.* 488
Warren, Bill, Sr Dir-Bus Dev - Bzzagent, Inc.; *pg.* 1233, *pg.* 792
Warren, Chad, Sr Strategist-Social Media - Adobe Systems Incorporated; *pg.* 342, *pg.* 235
Warren, Charles, Sr Dir-Comml Segment Strategy - W.W. Grainger, Inc.; *pg.* 1390, *pg.* 625
Warren, David, VP-Digital Media - Pennwell Publishing Company Inc.; *pg.* 1676, *pg.* 1490
Warren, Fred, Dir-Creative - Microsoft Corporation; *pg.* 435, *pg.* 1824
Warren, Greg, VP-Creative - Wal-Mart Stores, Inc.; *pg.* 1790, *pg.* 29
Warren, Harris, Product Portfolio Mgr-Mobile, Automotive & Cloud Products - TELENAV, INC.; *pg.* 678, *pg.* 288
Warren, Jeff, VP-Mobile & Online Partner Mktg - Expedia, Inc.; *pg.* 1244, *pg.* 1814
Warren, Jessica, Brand Mgr-Mktg-Dairy Queen Canada Inc. - Dairy Queen Corporate Store; *pg.* 1724, *pg.* 932
Warren, Kelly, Sr Product Mgr-Insulation Grp - CertainTeed Corporation; *pg.* 74, *pg.* 1589
Warren, Ken, Dir-Adv - The Jacksonville Daily News Co.; *pg.* 1654, *pg.* 1380
Warren, Keri, Supvr-Mktg Comm - 3M Company; *pg.* 1142, *pg.* 956
Warren, Lisa, Mgr-Global Mktg-Post-it - 3M Company; *pg.* 1142, *pg.* 956
Warren, Matt, Mgr-Social Media - Panera Bread Company; *pg.* 1029, *pg.* 1001
Warren, Richard P., Jr., Sr VP-Sls, Mdsg & Sourcing - Croscill, Inc.; *pg.* 1122, *pg.* 1220
Warren, Scot E., Sr Mng Dir-Equity Index Products & Index Svcs - CME Group Inc.; *pg.* 738, *pg.* 571
Warren, Stacy, Dir-Private Client Grp Reg Mktg - American International Group, Inc.; *pg.* 1190, *pg.* 1193
Warrenfelt, Paul, Mng Dir-TSNA & Sr VP-Sls-Americas & APAC Reg - T-Systems North America Inc.; *pg.* 1875, *pg.* 630
Warrington, Adam, Sr Dir-High End Comm - Anheuser-Busch Companies, LLC; *pg.* 237, *pg.* 991
Warrington, Bob, Head-Bus & Mktg Strategy-Healthcare - Intuit Inc.; *pg.* 769, *pg.* 158
Warrington, Mark, Dir-New Product Dev - Prestige Brands Holdings, Inc.; *pg.* 520, *pg.* 1345
Warsaw, Harris, Sr VP-Sls-Global SMB Solutions - Pitney

Bowes Inc.; *pg.* 454, *pg.* 376
Wartchow, Troy, Brand Mgr-Entertainment Brands - Enesco, LLC; *pg.* 1124, *pg.* 620
Warter, Kaitlyn, Planner-Mktg - Nordstrom, Inc.; *pg.* 1779, *pg.* 1837
Warun, Ken, Dir-Creative-Brdcst Adv & Video - Amazon.com, Inc.; *pg.* 1226, *pg.* 1831
Warwick, Colin, Product Mgr-Power Electronics - Agilent Technologies, Inc.; *pg.* 614, *pg.* 264
Warwick, Jodee, Mgr-Pub Sector Mktg - Cisco Systems, Inc.; *pg.* 372, *pg.* 240
Wascavage, Mary, Dir-PR & Mktg - Crozer-Keystone Health System Inc.; *pg.* 1520, *pg.* 1587
Wasfi, Mohammed, VP-Sls & Bus Dev-Strategic Accts - NVIDIA Corporation; *pg.* 447, *pg.* 268
Washburn, Kate, Supvr-PR & Social Media - Amway Corporation; *pg.* 326, *pg.* 864
Washenik, Taryn, Brand Mgr-Global Licensing - The Donna Karan Company LLC; *pg.* 23, *pg.* 1225
Washer, Tim, Sr Mgr-Mktg-Social Media - Cisco Systems, Inc.; *pg.* 372, *pg.* 240
Washida, Kenji, VP-Entertainment Mktg - Bandai America Incorporated; *pg.* 950, *pg.* 75
Washington, Aisha, Mgr-Mktg - The New York Times Company; *pg.* 1668, *pg.* 1270
Washington, Alvis, Sr Dir-Mktg-Customer Experience-Propositions & Plng - Wal-Mart Stores, Inc.; *pg.* 1790, *pg.* 29
Washington, Charlae, Brand Mktg Mgr-Google for Work - Google Inc.; *pg.* 1249, *pg.* 153
Washington, Glenn, Analyst-Mktg - Xerox Corporation; *pg.* 494, *pg.* 365
Washington, Julia, Mgr-Mktg - JetBlue Airways Corporation; *pg.* 1913, *pg.* 1174
Washington, Kindel, Dir-Media & Mktg - T-Mobile US, Inc.; *pg.* 676, *pg.* 1816
Washington, Michelle Lynn, District Mgr-Sls - Essilor of America, Inc.; *pg.* 1412, *pg.* 1680
Washington, Mildred, Product Mgr - Aetna Inc.; *pg.* 1187, *pg.* 351
Washington, Patty, Mgr-Trade Mktg - Bacardi USA, Inc.; *pg.* 1956, *pg.* 417
Washington, Raquel, Mgr-Ad Sls Trng - Turner Broadcasting System, Inc.; *pg.* 314, *pg.* 521
Washington, Vincent, Mgr-Social Media - United Parcel Service, Inc.; *pg.* 1928, *pg.* 522
Wasielewski, Leah, VP-Mktg - HarperCollins Publishers Inc.; *pg.* 1647, *pg.* 1237
Wasielewski, Lynn, Sr Mgr-Mktg - General Electric Company; *pg.* 1297, *pg.* 347
Wasik, Jennifer, Sr Dir-CRM & Direct Mktg - dELiA's, Inc.; *pg.* 23, *pg.* 1222
Wasklewicz, Mark J., Head Vaccine Regulatory CMC & Takeda Vaccines-Global & Sr Dir - Takeda Pharmaceuticals USA, Inc.; *pg.* 1600, *pg.* 605
Wasser, Glenn, Sr VP-Mktg - Comcast Corporation; *pg.* 276, *pg.* 1560
Wasser, Hartley, Dir-Editorial & Content Mktg - New Orleans Tourism Marketing Corporation; *pg.* 1001, *pg.* 747
Wasserman, Bob, Sr VP-eBusiness & Direct Mktg - The Allstate Corporation; *pg.* 1189, *pg.* 639
Wasserman, Jodi, Dir-Mktg - The Upper Deck Company, LLC; *pg.* 969, *pg.* 62
Wasserman, Melissa, Sr VP-Client Solutions & Integrated Mktg - AMC Networks Inc.; *pg.* 269, *pg.* 1189
Wasserman, Todd, VP-Mktg - Myx Beverages LLC; *pg.* 257, *pg.* 1263
Wasson, Brian, Dir-Mktg & Comm-Global - SAP; *pg.* 465, *pg.* 78
Wasson, Holly, VP-Portfolio Media Mgmt & Partnership Dev - Turner Broadcasting System, Inc.; *pg.* 314, *pg.* 521
Waste, Linda, Sr Mgr-Recruiting-Marcom - Apple Inc.; *pg.* 350, *pg.* 73
Wastney, Tim, VP-Adv Sls-North America - BBC Worldwide America Inc.; *pg.* 271, *pg.* 1201
Wasvick, Lars, Mgr-Mktg - MORNINGSTAR, INC.; *pg.* 784, *pg.* 583
Waszczenko, Heather, Brand Mgr-ACDelco-Natl - General Motors Company; *pg.* 175, *pg.* 881
Waterbury, Todd, Chief Creative Officer - Target Corporation; *pg.* 1786, *pg.* 942
Waterfall, Charles, Head-Creative - NRG Energy, Inc.; *pg.* 1366, *pg.* 1112
Waterman, Matt, Dir-Mktg - Hanesbrands Inc.; *pg.* 26, *pg.* 1394
Waterman, Win, VP-Sls & Mktg - Peace Industries Inc.; *pg.* 1368, *pg.* 656
Waters, Alicia, Sr Dir-Mktg - Crate & Barrel, Inc.; *pg.* 922, *pg.* 640
Waters, Brian, Sr Dir-B2B Mktg & Integrated Insight - Hilton Worldwide, Inc.; *pg.* 1094, *pg.* 1791
Waters, Kerri, Product Dir-Matl Girl Juniors-Macy's Mdsg Grp - Macy's East; *pg.* 1777, *pg.* 1254
Waters, Melissa, VP-Brand & Product Mktg - Pandora Media Inc.; *pg.* 1273, *pg.* 172
Waters, Sharon, Reg Dir-Media & Commercialization - Coca-Cola Refreshments USA, Inc.; *pg.* 247, *pg.* 500
Waters-Brown, Laura, Coord-Digital Media - Cleveland Browns Football Company LLC; *pg.* 541, *pg.* 1406
Watford, Monique, Sr Mgr-Performance Metrics & Analytics - Cox Media Group; *pg.* 280, *pg.* 502
Wathen, Brian, Mgr-Product Mktg - Johnson Controls, Inc.; *pg.* 1073, *pg.* 1597
Wathen, Catherine, VP-Direct Mktg - Fifth Third Bancorp; *pg.* 752, *pg.* 1413
Watkins, Barbara, Dir-Event Mktg-Global - VeriFone Systems, Inc.; *pg.* 487, *pg.* 251
Watkins, Clif, VP-Video Product Mgmt - Charter Communications, Inc.; *pg.* 274, *pg.* 372
Watkins, Craig, Product Mgr-Rack & Cooling Solutions Tripp Lite - Trippe Manufacturing Company; *pg.* 220, *pg.* 592
Watkins, Ellen, Mgr-Global Mktg Ops & Trng - National Instruments Corporation; *pg.* 443, *pg.* 1664
Watkins, Ingrid, Sr Mgr-Global Supplier Diversity - The Coca-Cola Company; *pg.* 240, *pg.* 493
Watkins, Joy, Coord-Adv - The Home Depot, Inc.; *pg.* 1050, *pg.* 510
Watkins, Kelly, Brand Mgr - Kellogg Company; *pg.* 831, *pg.* 870
Watkins, Kimberly, Sr Mgr-Bus Dev-Programmatic & Display - Demand Media, Inc.; *pg.* 1238, *pg.* 273
Watkins, Rebecca, Mgr-Creative Svcs - WESCO International Inc.; *pg.* 687, *pg.* 1582
Watkins, Talitha, VP-Multicultural Mktg - Universal Studios, Inc.; *pg.* 315, *pg.* 298
Watret, John R., Interim Pres - Embry-Riddle Aeronautical University; *pg.* 601, *pg.* 420
Watrob, Emilie, Sr Coord-Mktg Events - Insight Enterprises, Inc.; *pg.* 415, *pg.* 26
Watson, Allison, Corp VP-Mktg & Ops-US - Microsoft Corporation; *pg.* 435, *pg.* 1824
Watson, Andrew, Brand Mgr-Tennessee Honey - Jack Daniel's Distillery; *pg.* 1964, *pg.* 1640
Watson, Beth, Dir-Mktg - Rib City Grill, Inc.; *pg.* 1748, *pg.* 428
Watson, Brandon, Head-Sls-Insurance Svcs - Insperity, Inc.; *pg.* 416, *pg.* 1725
Watson, Carl, Sr Dir-Art & Dir-Creative - Heritage Galleries & Auctioneer; *pg.* 143, *pg.* 1682
Watson, Chad, Dir-Sls & Bus Dev - Green Bay Packers, Inc.; *pg.* 551, *pg.* 1859
Watson, Claire, Mgr-Product Mktg - Ball Horticultural Company; *pg.* 1793, *pg.* 668
Watson, Eric, Brand Mgr-Pur-Apparel, Halloween, Collectibles & Novelties - Diamond Comic Distributors, Inc.; *pg.* 1635, *pg.* 772
Watson, Erika, Sr Mgr-Mktg - Tervis Tumbler Company; *pg.* 1890, *pg.* 477
Watson, Jim, Product Mgr-Cordless - DeWALT Industrial Tool Company; *pg.* 1328, *pg.* 757
Watson, Jim, Sr Mgr-Building Svcs - The Home Depot, Inc.; *pg.* 1050, *pg.* 510
Watson, John, Sr VP-Sls & Mktg-Amenities Div - Marietta Hospitality; *pg.* 1464, *pg.* 1155
Watson, Julia, Brand Mgr-Miller Lite Multicultural - MillerCoors LLC; *pg.* 255, *pg.* 582
Watson, Kate, Sr Brand Mgr-Cadbury Coco - Bayer CropScience; *pg.* 1149, *pg.* 981
Watson, Kathleen, Sr Mgr-Global Adv, Media & Sponsorships - Cisco Systems, Inc.; *pg.* 372, *pg.* 240
Watson, Kelly, Mgr-Digital Mktg - Cigna Corporation; *pg.* 1197, *pg.* 338
Watson, Mark, Mgr-Govt Mktg - Ricoh America; *pg.* 461, *pg.* 1550
Watson, Maureen, Sr VP-Mdsg - Sephora USA Inc; *pg.* 522, *pg.* 227
Watson, Mike, VP-Product Strategy - Cree Inc.; *pg.* 631, *pg.* 1371
Watson, Pat, VP-Mdsg - Hooker Furniture Corporation; *pg.* 928, *pg.* 1788
Watson, Peggy, Dir-Product & Partner Mktg - Wright Express Corporation; *pg.* 493, *pg.* 753
Watson, Peter, Sr Dir-Sls & Svcs - Harsco Rail; *pg.* 1345, *pg.* 1623
Watson, Ryan, Brand Mgr - Conagra Foods; *pg.* 826, *pg.* 994
Watson, Ryan, Brand Mgr - ConAgra Foods, Inc.; *pg.* 826, *pg.* 1014
Watson, Stacey, Sr Dir-Retail Dev & Customer Experience - Harley-Davidson, Inc.; *pg.* 178, *pg.* 1874
Watson, Terry, VP-Channel Mktg - Hubbell Power Systems, Inc.; *pg.* 643, *pg.* 1614
Watson, Tom, Sr Mgr-In-Store Mktg - Columbia Sportswear Company; *pg.* 1830, *pg.* 1501
Watson, Tom, Designer-Product - Pinterest; *pg.* 1275, *pg.* 225
Watson, Vance, Dir-Cheese Sls - Leprino Foods Company; *pg.* 874, *pg.* 320
Watt, Eugene, Mgr-Product Mktg - Zynga Inc.; *pg.* 1292, *pg.* 235
Wattelet, Kurt, Product Mgr - Bourns, Inc.; *pg.* 627, *pg.* 193
Watters, Lauren, Dir-Digital Content Products - Penton Media, Inc.; *pg.* 1676, *pg.* 1277
Watters, Margaret, Specialist-External Comm & Social Media - The Home Depot, Inc.; *pg.* 1050, *pg.* 510
Watterson, Alison, Mgr-Enterprise Svcs Social Media - Hewlett-Packard Company; *pg.* 404, *pg.* 175
Wattie, Gary, Sr VP-Sls - Centerplate, Inc.; *pg.* 1017, *pg.* 372
Watts, Aarti, Sr Mgr-Global IT Strategy, Comm & Performance Mgmt - Bunge Limited; *pg.* 842, *pg.* 1351
Watts, Aimee, Dir-Media - Stage Stores, Inc.; *pg.* 33, *pg.* 1715
Watts, Emma, Pres-Production - 20th Century Fox Film Corp.; *pg.* 267, *pg.* 124
Watts, Jeff, VP-HVAC Sls - Southwire Company; *pg.* 1063, *pg.* 527
Watts, John, Sr Mgr - American Honda Motor Co., Inc.; *pg.* 163, *pg.* 292
Watts, Jurgen, Mgr-Men's Digital Mktg - lululemon athletica inc.; *pg.* 44, *pg.* 1911
Watts, Keller, Sr VP-Bus Dev & Indus Sls - The Smithfield Packing Co., Inc.; *pg.* 896, *pg.* 1807
Watts, Megan, Mgr-Mktg Comm - E-Z-GO Textron; *pg.* 1706, *pg.* 525
Watts, Michelle, Mgr-Product Mktg-Ad Products - Kelley Blue Book Co., Inc.; *pg.* 1656, *pg.* 112
Waugh, Peter, Dir-Mktg - Dell Inc.; *pg.* 383, *pg.* 1737
Waurin, Ken, Mgr-Segment Mktg & Automotive Infotainment - Analog Devices, Inc.; *pg.* 617, *pg.* 839
Waxlax, Christina, Asst Mgr-Mktg-Women's Socks - Hanesbrands Inc.; *pg.* 26, *pg.* 1394
Waxman, Karen, Mgr-Mktg Ops - Keds LLC; *pg.* 1810, *pg.* 828
Waxman, Kate, Mgr-Digital & Mktg Comm-Global - LifeCell Corporation; *pg.* 1556, *pg.* 1045
Waxman, Mark M., CMO - CBIZ, INC.; *pg.* 733, *pg.* 1429
Way, Alyssa, Sr Mgr-Consumer Insights - Pernod Ricard USA, Inc.; *pg.* 1968, *pg.* 1332
Way, Lisa, Sr Mgr-Revenue Mgmt - FCA US LLC; *pg.* 170, *pg.* 868
Wayland, Dan, Dir-Mktg Tech - Broadcom Corporation; *pg.* 364, *pg.* 108
Wayne, Amy Jo, Sr VP-Ad Sls - The Hallmark Channel; *pg.* 290, *pg.* 281
Wayne, Arthur, VP-Global PR - Brooks Brothers Group, Inc.; *pg.* 39, *pg.* 1208
Wayne, Carlye, Assoc Mgr-Consumer Mktg - Home Box Office, Inc.; *pg.* 290, *pg.* 1240
Wayne, Joanne, VP & Dir-Media - Time Warner Cable Inc.; *pg.* 312, *pg.* 1301
Wayne, Michael J., Sr VP & Dir-Mktg - Chemung Financial Corporation; *pg.* 734, *pg.* 1157
Wayne, Tim, Dir-Field Sls - The J.M. Smucker Company; *pg.* 865, *pg.* 1468
Wayt, Dawn, Head-Social Media & Dir-Mktg - American Greetings Corporation; *pg.* 1615, *pg.* 1428
Waywood, Rick, Head-Xeljanz Psoriasis Global Mktg - Pfizer Inc.; *pg.* 1581, *pg.* 1278
Weadon, Mark, Sr Mgr-Product Mktg-Life Sciences - SAS Institute Inc.; *pg.* 466, *pg.* 1361
Weathers, Esther, Project Mgr-Mktg - ScanSource, Inc.; *pg.* 671, *pg.* 1618
Weathersby, Sharnell, Sr Assoc Brand Mgr-Ice Breakers - The Hershey Co.; *pg.* 1855, *pg.* 1538
Weaton, Jeff, Mgr-Digital Ad Sls Research - NBC Universal, Inc.; *pg.* 300, *pg.* 1266
Weaver, Annette, Sr Assoc Brand Mgr - The Hershey Co.; *pg.*

1855, *pg.* 1538
Weaver, Bill, Grp VP-MedLar Sls - CDW Corporation; *pg.* 370, *pg.* 663
Weaver, Brenda S., Exec Dir-Mktg - Acorda Therapeutics, Inc.; *pg.* 1486, *pg.* 1138
Weaver, Charlotte, Assoc Mgr-Mktg - The Toronto-Dominion Bank; *pg.* 810, *pg.* 1945
Weaver, Dave, Product Dir - Berry Plastics; *pg.* 1879, *pg.* 678
Weaver, David, Grp Dir-Creative - Bonnier Corporation; *pg.* 1622, *pg.* 480
Weaver, Eric, Sr Dir-Mktg-Case IH - CNH America LLC; *pg.* 702, *pg.* 560
Weaver, Jenny, Mgr-PR - Cellco Partnership; *pg.* 1869, *pg.* 1042
Weaver, John, Dir-Creative - Seattle Seahawks; *pg.* 582, *pg.* 1830
Weaver, John A., Dir-Mktg - Honeywell International Inc.; *pg.* 407, *pg.* 1088
Weaver, John D., Mgr-Generator Controls Sls - Flight Systems, Inc.; *pg.* 1007, *pg.* 1548
Weaver, Ken, Sr Acct Mgr & Mgr-Mktg - Case Paper Company Inc.; *pg.* 1455, *pg.* 1163
Weaver, Mallory, Specialist-PR - Bath & Body Works, LLC; *pg.* 500, *pg.* 1471
Weaver, Michael, Dir-Data Strategy & Precision Mktg - The Coca-Cola Company; *pg.* 240, *pg.* 493
Weaver, Mike, Mgr-Digital Mktg - Wilsonart International, Inc.; *pg.* 1450, *pg.* 1746
Weaver, Rob, Sr Mgr-Product Mktg - AT&T; *pg.* 1865, *pg.* 258
Weaver, Ross, Exec Dir-Mktg-Global - Amgen Inc.; *pg.* 1493, *pg.* 291
Weaver, Sandy, Mgr-Mktg - Nashville Predators, LLC; *pg.* 565, *pg.* 1652
Weaver, Sarah, Mgr-Mktg - Sentry Insurance Group; *pg.* 1217, *pg.* 1895
Weaver, Shannon, Brand Mktg Mgr - Publix Super Markets, Inc.; *pg.* 1031, *pg.* 437
Weaver, Tom, Product Mgr - FRANKLIN RESOURCES, INC.; *pg.* 760, *pg.* 254
Weaver-Ertley, Aimee, Sr Dir-PR - Sage Software, Inc.; *pg.* 464, *pg.* 116
Webb, Aga, Dir-IT-Mktg Sys Dev - General Motors Company; *pg.* 175, *pg.* 881
Webb, Andy, Product Mgr - Gardner Denver, Inc.; *pg.* 1338, *pg.* 1592
Webb, Betsy, Gen Mgr-Media & Mgmt - Microsoft Corp.; *pg.* 440, *pg.* 321
Webb, Brad, VP-Sls - Gerber Legendary Blades; *pg.* 1834, *pg.* 1503
Webb, Chris, Mgr-Sls - Anthony Forest Products Co., Inc.; *pg.* 67, *pg.* 31
Webb, Darin, Sr Dir-Global Hardlines Mktg - The Coleman Company, Inc.; *pg.* 1830, *pg.* 723
Webb, Denielle, VP-PR & Mktg-SundanceTV - AMC Networks Inc.; *pg.* 269, *pg.* 1189
Webb, Devin, Sr Mgr-Mktg-QuickBooks - Intuit Inc.; *pg.* 769, *pg.* 158
Webb, Graham, Dir-Product Mgmt - Singer Sewing Company; *pg.* 698, *pg.* 1639
Webb, Jennifer J., Dir-Mktg-Client Solutions - Dell Inc.; *pg.* 383, *pg.* 1737
Webb, Jill, Mgr-Digital Mktg - Hallmark Cards, Inc.; *pg.* 1646, *pg.* 983
Webb, John, Mgr-Graphics Mktg - Intel Corporation; *pg.* 645, *pg.* 266
Webb, John W., Sr Dir-Government Relations & Assoc Legal Counsel - Direct Selling Association; *pg.* 139, *pg.* 398
Webb, Julie M., Specialist-Mktg & Comm - American Concrete Institute; *pg.* 127, *pg.* 885
Webb, Katie, Brand Mgr - Dr Pepper Snapple Group, Inc.; *pg.* 250, *pg.* 1729
Webb, Lisa, Mgr-Field Mktg - MillerCoors; *pg.* 254, *pg.* 1877
Webb, Matt, VP-Mktg Strategy - AmerisourceBergen Corporation; *pg.* 1493, *pg.* 1522
Webb, Melissa, Dir-Product Mgmt - Determine, Inc.; *pg.* 386, *pg.* 254
Webb, Renee, Dir-Sls Plng, Mktg & Customer Svcs - Mohawk Finishing Products, Inc.; *pg.* 1173, *pg.* 1378
Webb, Richard, VP-Sls & Mktg - Keystone Steel & Wire Co.; *pg.* 91, *pg.* 651
Webb, Robert, Sr Dir-Pub Affairs & Corp Comm - Mohawk Industries, Inc.; *pg.* 935, *pg.* 527
Webb, Rochelle, Sr VP-Global Mktg Activation - Quiksilver, Inc.; *pg.* 31, *pg.* 104
Webb, Scott, Grp Acct Dir - Accenture; *pg.* 1392, *pg.* 1186
Webb, Stephen, Mgr-Global Mktg-Toothbrushes - Colgate-Palmolive Company; *pg.* 504, *pg.* 1215
Webb, Tia, Brand Mgr - Bacardi USA, Inc.; *pg.* 1956, *pg.* 417
Webb, Tracy, Sr Mgr-Mktg - QUALCOMM Incorporated; *pg.* 1873, *pg.* 207
Webber, Jill, Sr Mgr-PR-Consumer Products - Autodesk Inc.; *pg.* 356, *pg.* 257
Webby, Lauren, Coord-PR - JAKKS Pacific, Inc.; *pg.* 960, *pg.* 142
Weber, Adam, Sr VP-Mktg - Dollar Shave Club, Inc.; *pg.* 507, *pg.* 273
Weber, Alison, Exec VP-Strategy & Creative - Levy Restaurants, Inc.; *pg.* 1736, *pg.* 580
Weber, Alison, Specialist-Creative Mktg - Musicnotes, Inc.; *pg.* 1268, *pg.* 1866
Weber, Alyssa E., Dir-Mktg Ops - Juniper Networks; *pg.* 424, *pg.* 809
Weber, Angela, Dir-Mktg - OrthoSynetics, Inc.; *pg.* 791, *pg.* 1657
Weber, Betsy, Sr Mgr-Consumer Media Rels - Netflix, Inc.; *pg.* 1269, *pg.* 141
Weber, Bob, Mgr-Comml Vehicle Sls - Jefferson Chevrolet Co.; *pg.* 180, *pg.* 883
Weber, Bob, VP-Corp Mktg - Smithfield Foods, Inc.; *pg.* 896, *pg.* 1806
Weber, Chris, Corp VP-Mobile Device Sls - Microsoft Corporation; *pg.* 435, *pg.* 1824
Weber, Christine, Mgr-Product Mktg - Zebra Technologies Corporation; *pg.* 690, *pg.* 628
Weber, Colin, Sr Planner-Digital Sls-WIRED - Conde Nast Publications, Inc.; *pg.* 1629, *pg.* 1217
Weber, David, Dir-Ethanol Sls - Abengoa Bioenergy Corp.; *pg.* 971, *pg.* 974
Weber, David F., VP-Mktg-Foodsvc - Hormel Foods Corporation; *pg.* 863, *pg.* 915
Weber, Deb, Sr Mgr-Child Res - Fisher-Price, Inc.; *pg.* 953, *pg.* 1156
Weber, Donna, Sr VP-Mktg & Implementation - 1-800-Doctors; *pg.* 1392, *pg.* 1074
Weber, Ed, Mgr-Software Sls - International Business Machines Corporation; *pg.* 418, *pg.* 1138
Weber, Frank, VP-Product Dev - Norwegian Cruise Line; *pg.* 1917, *pg.* 444
Weber, Gabriele, Sr Mgr-Contracts - Chevron Corporation; *pg.* 974, *pg.* 259
Weber, Gus, Sr Product Dir - ESPN, Inc.; *pg.* 285, *pg.* 340
Weber, Harrison, Media Planner-Digital - WebMD Health Corporation; *pg.* 1288, *pg.* 1313
Weber, John, VP-Ticket Sls & Ops - The Phillies, L.P.; *pg.* 575, *pg.* 1569
Weber, Kathleen G., Sr VP & Gen Mgr-Consumer Products - OraSure Technologies Inc; *pg.* 1578, *pg.* 1516
Weber, Lauren, Asst Mgr-Mktg - Penguin Random House; *pg.* 1675, *pg.* 1276
Weber, Matt, Mgr-Advanced Product Mktg - Ford Motor Company; *pg.* 172, *pg.* 876
Weber, Monica, Analyst-Small Merchant Mktg - American Express Company; *pg.* 712, *pg.* 1190
Weber, Monica, Asst VP-Mktg - Dover Motorsports, Inc.; *pg.* 545, *pg.* 387
Weber, Natasha, Mgr-PR-Global - The Donna Karan Company LLC; *pg.* 23, *pg.* 1225
Weber, Paul, VP-Enterprise Sls-North America - Interactive Intelligence, Inc.; *pg.* 417, *pg.* 687
Weber, Sharon, Sr Mgr-Corp Comm - Wal-Mart Stores, Inc.; *pg.* 1790, *pg.* 29
Weber, Todd, Dir-Comm-Product PR - Kohler Co.; *pg.* 91, *pg.* 1862
Webster, Amy, VP-Mdsg - Hollander Sleep Products; *pg.* 927, *pg.* 411
Webster, David, Gen Mgr-Brand & Mktg Strategy - Microsoft Corporation; *pg.* 435, *pg.* 1824
Webster, Doug, VP-Svc Provider Mktg - Cisco Systems, Inc.; *pg.* 372, *pg.* 240
Webster, Elizabeth, Dir-Video Sls - AOL Inc.; *pg.* 1229, *pg.* 1195
Webster, Eric, VP-Mktg - State Farm Mutual Automobile Insurance Co.; *pg.* 1218, *pg.* 557
Webster, James, Mgr-Strategic Mktg & Innovations - Shell Oil Company; *pg.* 984, *pg.* 1714
Webster, Jim, Mgr-Strategic Mktg & Innovations - Shell Lubricants; *pg.* 217, *pg.* 1714
Webster, Kathy, Dir-Mktg - Miller Multiplex Display Fixture Co.; *pg.* 935, *pg.* 609
Webster, Mike, Dir-Sls-North America - Arctic Cat Inc.; *pg.* 1705, *pg.* 953
Wecera, Tom, Mng Dir-Print Products - Mergent, Inc.; *pg.* 1664, *pg.* 1616
Wechsler, Sharon E., Program Mgr-Mktg Comm-Global - Honeywell Aerospace Electronic Systems; *pg.* 228, *pg.* 17
Weck, Tom, CIO-OTC Bus, Product Innovation, Global Quality & VP - McNEIL-PPC, Inc.; *pg.* 1560, *pg.* 1533
Weckerle, Elena, Sr Assoc Brand Mgr - The Kraft Heinz Company; *pg.* 871, *pg.* 641
Weckerlin, Glenn, Dir-Brand & Product Line Mgmt-Global - Chevron Corporation; *pg.* 974, *pg.* 259
Weddle, Lynn A., Sr Dir-Global Brand Insights - McDonald's Corporation; *pg.* 1737, *pg.* 645
Wedel, Lisa, Mgr-Integrated Mktg - Scottrade, Inc.; *pg.* 802, *pg.* 1003
Weden, Brandi, Mgr-Field Mktg - Concur Technologies, Inc.; *pg.* 1236, *pg.* 1813
Wedeven, Kris, Sr Mgr-Enterprise Mktg - Comcast Corporation; *pg.* 276, *pg.* 1560
Wedge, David, Product Mgr - Draper Knitting Co., Inc.; *pg.* 692, *pg.* 810
Wedin, Rob, VP-Fresh Sls & Mktg - Calavo Growers, Inc.; *pg.* 843, *pg.* 276
Week, Ben, Mgr-Mktg Field - Harley-Davidson, Inc.; *pg.* 178, *pg.* 1874
Weeks, Eric, VP-Sls - Markwins International Corp.; *pg.* 516, *pg.* 67
Weeks, Jennifer, Sr Mgr-Brand Dev & Corp Mktg - Univision Communications Inc.; *pg.* 683, *pg.* 1307
Weeks, Robyn, Dir-Mobile Products - The Weather Channel LLC; *pg.* 320, *pg.* 523
Weeks, Sherri, Partner-Mktg Bus - HP Enterprise Services, LLC; *pg.* 409, *pg.* 1731
Weeks, Steve, Sr Mgr-Media Strategy & Plng - Adobe Systems Incorporated; *pg.* 342, *pg.* 235
Weeks, Tony, Sr Mgr-Electric Vehicle Mktg & Sls Strategy - Nissan North America, Inc.; *pg.* 186, *pg.* 1633
Weems, Walter, Dir-Sls & Bus Dev-Partner Mktg - American Airlines Inc.; *pg.* 1898, *pg.* 1693
Weerheim, Jennifer, VP-Mktg - Yard House USA, Inc.; *pg.* 1756, *pg.* 118
Weflen, Jill, Mgr-Mktg Comm - SurModics, Inc.; *pg.* 1600, *pg.* 924
Wegemer, Chris, VP-Mktg - Eternal World Television Network, Inc.; *pg.* 286, *pg.* 6
Weger, Mandy, Strategist-Digital Mktg - Campbell Soup Company; *pg.* 844, *pg.* 1048
Wegman, Jon, Dir-Global Bus Mktg - Twitter, Inc.; *pg.* 1285, *pg.* 228
Wegner, Christina Morris, Asst Dir-Field Mktg - The Northwestern Mutual Life Insurance Company; *pg.* 1212, *pg.* 1879
Wehr, Alexandra, VP & Sr Mgr-Relationship-First Niagara Bank - FIRST NIAGARA FINANCIAL GROUP, INC.; *pg.* 757, *pg.* 1148
Wehren, Vincent, Product Mgr - Microsoft Corporation; *pg.* 435, *pg.* 1824
Wehrenberg, Justin, Supvr-Mktg - Major League Baseball; *pg.* 560, *pg.* 1255
Wei, Albert, Sr Mgr-Client-B2B-Natl Client Grp - American Express Company; *pg.* 712, *pg.* 1190
Wei, Jenny, Brand Mgr - Del Monte Foods, Inc.; *pg.* 852, *pg.* 304
Wei, Maggie, Dir-Mktg - Lalique North America; *pg.* 1126, *pg.* 1054
Wei, Matthew, Mgr-Online Mktg - ACE Cash Express, Inc.; *pg.* 710, *pg.* 1717
Weick, Steven, Mgr-Channel Mktg - Honeywell International Inc.; *pg.* 407, *pg.* 1088
Weidick, Tania, VP-Event Mktg - Oracle Corporation; *pg.* 450, *pg.* 191
Weidner, Shelly, Dir-Mktg & Bus Dev-Town Center-Cobb - Simon Property Group, Inc.; *pg.* 1112, *pg.* 690
Weigand, Craig, Mgr-Adv & Credit Card - Marathon Petroleum Company LLC; *pg.* 981, *pg.* 1454
Weigand, Rachael, Assoc Mgr-Product Mktg - Diebold, Incorporated; *pg.* 387, *pg.* 1407
Weigel, Brenda, Mgr-Social Media - Aflac Incorporated; *pg.* 1188, *pg.* 527
Weigel, Joe, Dir-Mktg & Comm - Celadon Group, Inc.; *pg.* 1903, *pg.* 683
Weigel, Luke, Specialist-Mktg - Batteries Plus Bulbs LLC; *pg.* 360, *pg.* 1860
Weigel, Tim, VP-Mktg - CKE Restaurants Inc.; *pg.* 1723, *pg.*

First page reference indicates Business Class Edition
Second page reference indicates Geographic Edition

63
Weiger, Steven, Product Mgr-Events & Trade Shows - Sony Corporation of America; pg. 675, pg. 1293
Weikel, Frank, Dir-Corp Mktg & Comm - The Western & Southern Financial Group; pg. 1223, pg. 1427
Weiks, Darin, Mgr-Sls - Brickner Motors, Inc.; pg. 167, pg. 1869
Weil, Garry, Mgr-Technical Mktg - Intel Corporation; pg. 645, pg. 266
Weil, Jeff, Mgr-Digital Mktg - Nestle Waters North America Inc.; pg. 257, pg. 375
Weil, Ken, Sr VP-Mktg - The Priceline Group Inc.; pg. 1276, pg. 364
Weil, Kevin, Product Mgr - Twitter, Inc.; pg. 1285, pg. 228
Weil, Scott, Sr Mgr-Sls - CSPI Technology Solutions; pg. 381, pg. 421
Weil, Stella, Dir-Corp Sls - Time Inc.; pg. 1693, pg. 1300
Weiland, Doug, Dir-Adv & Bus Dev-East - Kelley Blue Book Co., Inc.; pg. 1656, pg. 112
Weiland, Jeffrey, Sr Mgr-Amex Offers Strategy - American Express Company; pg. 712, pg. 1190
Weiland, Kellie, Sr Mgr-Comm - Select Comfort Corporation; pg. 942, pg. 942
Weiland, Mark, Dir-Mktg-Specialty Components - Highfield Manufacturing Co.; pg. 1346, pg. 339
Weiland, Nicholas, Brand Mgr-Novelties - Wells Enterprises, Inc.; pg. 909, pg. 709
Weiler, Jane, Dir-Mktg Comm - Cincinnati Bell Inc.; pg. 1871, pg. 1410
Weiler, Kyle, Category Dir-Rain Products - totes Isotoner Corporation; pg. 14, pg. 1426
Weiler, Scott, VP-Mktg & Comm - Sonesta International Hotels Corporation; pg. 1113, pg. 836
Weiller, Andrew, Dir-Sls-EMEA & APAC - Purafil, Inc.; pg. 333, pg. 530
Wein, Garrett, VP-OEM Sls-Worldwide - Dot Hill Systems Corp.; pg. 388, pg. 333
Weinberg, Brett J., Sr VP-PR - LPL Financial Corporation; pg. 777, pg. 798
Weinberg, Mike, Product Mgr - Daktronics, Inc.; pg. 633, pg. 1624
Weinberg-Scalo, Sarah, Coord-PR - San Diego Convention & Visitors Bureau; pg. 1004, pg. 208
Weinberger, Eric, Brand Mgr-Starburst - Wm. Wrigley Jr. Company; pg. 1863, pg. 596
Weinberger, Keith, CMO & Exec VP-Sls - Empire Today, LLC; pg. 923, pg. 643
Weinberger, Lisa, Dir-SEO, Content & Social Media - VITACOST.COM, INC.; pg. 1607, pg. 414
Weindruch, Larry, Dir-PR - National Sporting Goods Association; pg. 151, pg. 634
Weine, Kenneth, VP-Comm & Mktg - The New York Public Library; pg. 605, pg. 1269
Weiner, Dan, VP-Sls-West Reg - Pandora Media Inc.; pg. 1273, pg. 172
Weiner, David, Dir-Creative & Editorial - Digg, Inc.; pg. 1238, pg. 1224
Weiner, Debbie, Sr Specialist-Mktg Comm - Boston Scientific Corporation; pg. 1508, pg. 831
Weiner, Faith S., Sr Dir-Community Rels - CVS Health Corporation; pg. 1765, pg. 1610
Weiner, Glen, Sr VP-Sls - Mole-Richardson Co.; pg. 1302, pg. 103
Weiner, Jonathan R., Sr VP-Mktg Strategy, Insights & Activation - Big Heart Pet Brands; pg. 1474, pg. 213
Weingarten, Jason, Product Mgr-Merchant Financing-Comml Bus Loans - American Express Company; pg. 712, pg. 1190
Weingarten, Liat, Dir-Mktg - Old Navy; pg. 45, pg. 224
Weinhold, Daniel, Mgr-Mktg - General Mills, Inc.; pg. 828, pg. 933
Weinkselbaum, Ian, Sr Dir-Integrated Mktg & Insights - The Hartz Mountain Corp.; pg. 1476, pg. 1120
Weinman, Samantha, Mgr-Fashion Media & Mktg - American Apparel, Inc.; pg. 18, pg. 126
Weinrauch, Danielle, Specialist-Sponsorship Mktg - Aon Risk Services Inc.; pg. 1193, pg. 564
Weinreich, Rebecca, Dir-Integrated Sls - Rodale, Inc.; pg. 1681, pg. 1530
Weinroth, David, VP-Sls-East Reg - Tapjoy, Inc.; pg. 1396, pg. 228
Weinstein, Barry, Sr Product Mgr - EMC Corporation; pg. 391, pg. 825
Weinstein, Brittany, Specialist-Mktg - Samsung Telecommunications America, LLC; pg. 670, pg. 1736
Weinstein, Jennifer, Assoc Dir-Mktg Svcs - Takeda Pharmaceuticals USA, Inc.; pg. 1600, pg. 605
Weinstein, Jessica, Sr Mgr-Consumer Plng - Diageo North America Inc.; pg. 248, pg. 1223
Weinstein, Jonathon, Mgr-Renewals Ops-Comm & Mktg Grp - AARP; pg. 124, pg. 393
Weinstein, Mary, Vp-Interactive Mktg - Citizens Financial Group, Inc.; pg. 737, pg. 1606
Weinstein, Miriam, Mgr-Comm & Media Rels - Johnson & Wales University; pg. 603, pg. 1606
Weinstein, Nola, VP-Consumer Style Brands-Mode Media & Editor-in-Chief-Glam.com - Mode Media; pg. 1267, pg. 50
Weinstein, Steve, Sr Dir-Global Supply Chain-Baby & Beauty GFOs - Johnson & Johnson; pg. 1549, pg. 1091
Weinstock, John, Sr VP-Mktg-North America - Electrolux Home Products North America; pg. 54, pg. 1366
Weinstock, Stephanie, Mgr-Mktg-North America Retail - Coach, Inc.; pg. 3, pg. 1214
Weintraub, Abbe, Dir-Specialty Mktg - U.S. News & World Report, L.P.; pg. 1698, pg. 1308
Weintraub, Gary, Brand Mgr - S.C. Johnson & Son, Inc.; pg. 334, pg. 1889
Weintraub, Nancy, Sr Dir-Mktg - Juniper Networks, Inc.; pg. 1260, pg. 286
Weintraub, Stefanie, Brand Mgr-Schick Intuition - Edgewell Personal Care; pg. 1526, pg. 995
Weintraub, Tova, Assoc Dir-Brand Mktg - 20th Century Fox Film Corp.; pg. 267, pg. 124
Weir, Charlie, Dir-Mktg-Digital & Partnerships - Cellco Partnership; pg. 1869, pg. 1042
Weir, Joe, VP-Digital Media Ops - Gannett Co., Inc.; pg. 289, pg. 1681
Weir, Mark, Sr Mgr-Tech - Sony Electronics, Inc.; pg. 676, pg. 209
Weir, Meredith, Sr Principal & Mgr-Digital Mktg & Strategist - Medtronic, Inc.; pg. 1564, pg. 939
Weir, Rob, Mgr-Motorsports Mktg - Subaru of America, Inc.; pg. 191, pg. 1050
Weir, Shannon, Mgr-Mktg-Architectural Specialties - Armstrong World Industries, Inc.; pg. 914, pg. 1545
Weirbach, Nate, Dir-Mktg & Bus Dev - Simon Property Group, Inc.; pg. 1112, pg. 690
Weis, Barry, Mgr-Mktg - Great Plains Manufacturing, Incorporated; pg. 704, pg. 721
Weis, Dan, Product Mgr - Digital Insight; pg. 744, pg. 189
Weis, Danielle, Analyst-Sls - Cardinal Health, Inc.; pg. 1512, pg. 1448
Weis, Janet, Dir-Mktg - Jacobsen Manufacturing, Inc.; pg. 1098, pg. 460
Weis, Mary, Coord-Adv - Mlive Media Group; pg. 1665, pg. 888
Weisbarth, Jenny, Sr Mgr-Media - Guthy-Renker LLC; pg. 289, pg. 273
Weisberg, Ken, Dir-Media - TracFone Wireless, Inc.; pg. 681, pg. 447
Weisberg, Leah, Mgr-Product Mktg - Twitter, Inc.; pg. 1285, pg. 228
Weisenbach, Amy, VP-Mktg - Wilson Sporting Goods Co.; pg. 1848, pg. 596
Weisenbeck, Scott, Dir-Integrated Mktg - Hormel Foods Corporation; pg. 863, pg. 915
Weisenberger, Stephanie, Dir-Mktg Ops - Astellas Pharma US, Inc.; pg. 1496, pg. 640
Weiser, Gabriella, Dir-Mktg - Steven Madden, Ltd.; pg. 1819, pg. 1176
Weiser, Wayne, Mgr-Mktg-Global - Motorola Solutions, Inc.; pg. 657, pg. 659
Weisgerber, Dennis W., VP-Sls - Stewart & Stevenson, LLC; pg. 985, pg. 1715
Weisgerber, Stacy, Asst Mgr-Mktg-Carnivor & Columbia Winery - E&J Gallo Winery; pg. 1962, pg. 149
Weisglass, Ivonne, Coord-Mktg - Pfizer Inc.; pg. 1581, pg. 1278
Weishaar, Jane, Coord-Admin, Mktg & Comm-Chicago Reg-McDonald's USA - McDonald's Corporation; pg. 1737, pg. 645
Weishaupt, Raphael, Dir-Global Mktg-Consumer - QUALCOMM Incorporated; pg. 1873, pg. 207
Weisiger, Jeff, Exec Dir-Sls - Amgen Inc.; pg. 1493, pg. 291
Weiskopf, David, VP-Corp PR - Charles Schwab & Company, Inc.; pg. 734, pg. 215
Weisman, Dale, Mgr-PR-Global - Silicon Laboratories Inc.; pg. 674, pg. 1666
Weisman, Lisa, Media Buyer - The Progressive Corporation; pg. 1214, pg. 1463
Weismiller, Margaret, Recruiter-Sls - Google Inc.; pg. 1249, pg. 153
Weispfenning, Ryan, Sr Dir-IR - Medtronic, Inc.; pg. 1564, pg. 939
Weiss, Amber, Mgr-Adv & Mktg Comm - Virbac Corporation; pg. 1606, pg. 1696
Weiss, Beth, Sr Mgr-Pub Affairs - Cox Communications, Inc.; pg. 279, pg. 501
Weiss, Brian, Program Mgr-Adv-CPG - Amazon.com, Inc.; pg. 1226, pg. 1831
Weiss, Bruce, VP-Mktg & Head-Strategic Bus Unit - Church & Dwight Co., Inc.; pg. 1153, pg. 1063
Weiss, Catherine, Assoc Mgr-Online Mktg - Tommy Hilfiger USA; pg. 48, pg. 1302
Weiss, Danielle, Brand Mgr-Digital - NIKE, Inc.; pg. 1812, pg. 1492
Weiss, Dave, Dir-Mktg & Promos - Fox Sports Net; pg. 288, pg. 131
Weiss, Eric, Sr VP-Mktg - Intermedia; pg. 417, pg. 1815
Weiss, Gregg, VP & Bus Head-Social Media-US Mktg - MasterCard Incorporated; pg. 779, pg. 1325
Weiss, Jill, Dir-Media - Royal Caribbean Cruises Ltd; pg. 1921, pg. 446
Weiss, John, Jr., Mgr-Digital Mktg - Pacers Basketball, LLC; pg. 573, pg. 689
Weiss, Jordan, Sr Dir-Mktg Program Strategy-Global - CA Technologies; pg. 366, pg. 1168
Weiss, Karen M., Sr Mgr-Indus Mktg-Civil Infrastructure - Autodesk Inc.; pg. 356, pg. 257
Weiss, Ken, Dir-Direct Mktg - Things Remembered, Inc.; pg. 1788, pg. 1455
Weiss, Lee, Head-New Product Ventures - Kaplan, Inc.; pg. 603, pg. 425
Weiss, Louis H., CMO & Sr VP - VITAMIN SHOPPE, INC.; pg. 1608, pg. 1098
Weiss, Mary Jo, Dir-Mktg - Comerica Incorporated; pg. 740, pg. 1677
Weiss, Melissa, Sr VP-Mktg - J. Crew Group, Inc.; pg. 1773, pg. 1245
Weiss, Michael, Sr Mgr-PR - Robert Half International Inc.; pg. 462, pg. 145
Weiss, Michelle, Mgr-Mktg & Comm - MORNINGSTAR, INC.; pg. 784, pg. 583
Weiss, Nicole, Mgr-Mktg-Social Media & Content Mktg - LexisNexis Group; pg. 1658, pg. 1446
Weiss, Noah, VP-Product Mgmt - FourSquare Labs, Inc; pg. 1248, pg. 1232
Weiss, Zurit, Dir-Mktg & Retail Div - SanDisk Corporation; pg. 465, pg. 147
Weisser, Will, VP, Assoc Publr & Dir-Mktg - Penguin Random House; pg. 1675, pg. 1276
Weissert, John, VP-Revenue Acctg & Claims - Wheaton Van Lines, Inc.; pg. 1930, pg. 691
Weist, Jennifer, Sr Mgr-Mktg - McKesson Corporation; pg. 1560, pg. 222
Weitzman, Ali, Sr Dir-Digital Ops - Gannett Co., Inc.; pg. 1643, pg. 1790
Weitzman, Stuart, Dir-Mktg-Americas - General Electric Company; pg. 1297, pg. 347
Weiwei, Vivian Zhuo, Sr Mgr-Mktg - QUALCOMM Incorporated; pg. 1873, pg. 207
Welborn, Heather, Exec VP-Sls-Natl - InterCall, Inc.; pg. 417, pg. 578
Welborn, Mandy, Sr Mgr-Internal Comm - PetSmart, Inc.; pg. 1481, pg. 18
Welch, Aimee, Specialist-Mktg - MetroPCS, Inc.; pg. 1872, pg. 1683
Welch, Beth, Mgr-PR & Social Engagement - Honeywell International Inc.; pg. 407, pg. 1088
Welch, Beth, Mgr-Media Rels - Notifier Co.; pg. 659, pg. 360
Welch, Brittany, Supvr-PR - The TJX Companies, Inc.; pg. 1788, pg. 822
Welch, Cedric, Sr Dir-Product Mgmt - Motorola Mobility LLC; pg. 657, pg. 627
Welch, David C., Sr Dir-LiveCycle - Adobe Systems Incorporated; pg. 342, pg. 235
Welch, Elissa, VP-Enterprise Mktg - Wells Fargo & Company; pg. 819, pg. 232
Welch, Jack, Dir-Social Collaboration Sls-Global - IBM; pg. 410, pg. 1449
Welch, James, Chief Product Officer & Sr VP - Kronos Incorporated; pg. 425, pg. 813
Welch, Janice, Rep-Sls - RSCC Aerospace & Defense; pg. 1373, pg. 1036
Welch, Jason, Mgr-Interactive Media - AARON'S, INC.; pg.

912, *pg.* 486
Welch, Kim, Brand Mgr - Safilo USA Inc.; *pg.* 11, *pg.* 1106
Welch, Mark, Asst VP-Product Realization - AT&T Inc.; *pg.* 1867, *pg.* 1674
Welch, Michael, Product Mgr-Rigid Film - Avery Dennison Corporation; *pg.* 1452, *pg.* 95
Welch, Michelle, VP-Mktg - WatchGuard Technologies, Inc.; *pg.* 491, *pg.* 1842
Welch, Mike, Dir-Partnership Sls - Minnesota Timberwolves Basketball Limited Partnership; *pg.* 563, *pg.* 940
Welch, Orren, Sr VP-Sls & Field Performance - Lifetouch, Inc.; *pg.* 1420, *pg.* 922
Welch, Patrick, Mgr-Digital Online Media - Verizon Communications Inc.; *pg.* 1875, *pg.* 1309
Welch, Richard, Head-Digital Sales & Programmatic - Conde Nast Publications, Inc.; *pg.* 1629, *pg.* 1217
Welch, Robert, VP-Multimedia Sls - The Wall Street Journal; *pg.* 1700, *pg.* 1312
Welch, Shawn, Dir-Svcs Mktg - Dell Inc.; *pg.* 383, *pg.* 1737
Welch, Terri, Mgr Mktg Comm - Nissan North America, Inc.; *pg.* 186, *pg.* 1633
Welden, Lisel, VP-Brand Mktg - Lyft; *pg.* 429, *pg.* 222
Weldon, Cherie, Sr Mgr-Affiliate & Partnership - Guitar Center, Inc.; *pg.* 1771, *pg.* 306
Weldon, Jim, Rep-Enterprise Sys Sls - IBM; *pg.* 410, *pg.* 1449
Weldon, Mj, VP-Mktg - Novartis Corporation; *pg.* 1574, *pg.* 1273
Weldon, Patrick, Product Mgr - Polaris Industries Inc.; *pg.* 1709, *pg.* 928
Welge, Tom, Gen Counsel & VP-Technical Sls - Gilster-Mary Lee Corporation; *pg.* 858, *pg.* 563
Welke, Breanna, Mgr-PR - Marvin Windows & Doors; *pg.* 934, *pg.* 965
Welkener, Wade, Mgr-Offshore Mktg-North America - Schlumberger Limited; *pg.* 801, *pg.* 1714
Wellard, Ronald G., Exec VP & Gen Mgr-Mitel Products & Solutions - Mitel Networks Corporation; *pg.* 654, *pg.* 1921
Wellborn, Julie, Product Dir - GlaxoSmithKline; *pg.* 1536, *pg.* 1389
Wellborn, Julie, Product Dir - GlaxoSmithKline Consumer Healthcare; *pg.* 510, *pg.* 1554
Wellen, Alex, Chief Product Officer - Cable News Network LP; *pg.* 1624, *pg.* 1208
Wellen, Jacqueline, Mgr-Digital Mktg - eHarmony.com, Inc.; *pg.* 1242, *pg.* 180
Weller, Jessica, Brand Mgr-Global - Unilever United States, Inc.; *pg.* 904, *pg.* 1061
Weller, Joey, VP-Sls - Grady-White Boats, Inc.; *pg.* 1707, *pg.* 1377
Weller, Ron, Sr Analyst-Database Mktg - T. Rowe Price Group Inc.; *pg.* 808, *pg.* 759
Weller, Susan, Mgr-Global Food Svc Mktg - National Potato Promotion Board; *pg.* 150, *pg.* 322
Welles, Peter, Sr Mgr-Mktg - IDEXX Laboratories, Inc.; *pg.* 1543, *pg.* 753
Wellington, Deborah M., Sr Mgr-Mktg - IBM; *pg.* 410, *pg.* 1449
Wellington, Lisa, Sr Mgr-Mktg Ops - Comcast Cable Communications, Inc.; *pg.* 276, *pg.* 1560
Wellman, Julie, Mgr-Natl Sls-Teva - Deckers Outdoor Corporation; *pg.* 1807, *pg.* 100
Wellman, Kim, Mktg Mgr-Residential & Landscape Parts - The Toro Company; *pg.* 1065, *pg.* 918
Wellman, Matt, Mgr-Graphic Design Mktg - Columbia Sportswear Company; *pg.* 1830, *pg.* 1501
Wellman, Steve, Specialist-Digital Mktg & ECommerce Acq - Wolverine World Wide, Inc.; *pg.* 1822, *pg.* 905
Wellmerling, Sondra L., Sr Dir-Affinity Mktg - DIRECTV Group Holdings, LLC; *pg.* 281, *pg.* 79
Wells, Angela, Dir-Outbound Product Mgmt-Social - Oracle Corporation; *pg.* 1272, *pg.* 786
Wells, Axel, Dir-Mktg - AT&T Mobility LLC; *pg.* 619, *pg.* 488
Wells, Brian, Dir-Mktg - J.R. Simplot Company; *pg.* 867, *pg.* 547
Wells, Brock, Head-Social Command Center & Sr Mgr-Mktg-US Central Mktg Org - Microsoft Corporation; *pg.* 435, *pg.* 1824
Wells, Charlotte, Dir-Mktg - Samson Rope Technologies; *pg.* 1468, *pg.* 1820
Wells, Chris, Sr Mgr-Product Mktg - Red Hat, Inc.; *pg.* 460, *pg.* 1388
Wells, Erika, Sr Mgr & Brand Strategist - Discovery Communications, Inc.; *pg.* 282, *pg.* 777
Wells, Esi, Mgr-Mktg Comm-Brand & Brdcst Adv - Verizon Communications Inc.; *pg.* 1875, *pg.* 1309
Wells, Jason M., Exec Dir-Publicity & Mktg - Abrams; *pg.* 1613, *pg.* 1186
Wells, Jessica, Specialist-Adv & Branding-Health Solutions - Arizona State University; *pg.* 597, *pg.* 25
Wells, Jessica, VP-Social Media Mktg - Chico's FAS, Inc.; *pg.* 21, *pg.* 427
Wells, Jessica, Sr Mgr-Digital Customer Ops - Penguin Random House; *pg.* 1675, *pg.* 1276
Wells, Julia, Brand Mgr-US Strategic New Brand - GlaxoSmithKline; *pg.* 1536, *pg.* 1389
Wells, Julia, Brand Mgr-US Strategic New Brand - GlaxoSmithKline Consumer Healthcare; *pg.* 510, *pg.* 1554
Wells, Kimberly, Dir-Interactive Mktg - Scottrade, Inc.; *pg.* 802, *pg.* 1003
Wells, Kristie, Dir-Social Media-Global & Customer Engagement - Ancestry.com LLC; *pg.* 1228, *pg.* 1754
Wells, Kristin, Head-Reg Sls - Owens Corning; *pg.* 102, *pg.* 1476
Wells, Linda, Dir-Adv - Conde Nast Publications, Inc.; *pg.* 1629, *pg.* 1217
Wells, Mary, VP-Software Mktg-Americas - Hewlett-Packard Company; *pg.* 404, *pg.* 175
Wells, Mary Kaye, Dir-Adv - Palatka Daily News; *pg.* 1674, *pg.* 457
Wells, Matt, Sr Mgr-Silicon Valley Ops - The Home Depot, Inc.; *pg.* 1050, *pg.* 510
Wells, Meredith, Assoc Product Mgr - McCormick & Company, Incorporated; *pg.* 1027, *pg.* 779
Wells, Randy, VP-Creative - Stanley Furniture Co., Inc.; *pg.* 943, *pg.* 1379
Wells, Renata, Mgr-Interactive Mktg - Six Flags Entertainment Corporation; *pg.* 583, *pg.* 1698
Wells, Rich, Sr VP & Mgr-Product Mgmt - Wells Fargo Advisors, LLC; *pg.* 819, *pg.* 1005
Wells, Stuart C., CTO, Chief Product Officer & Exec VP - Fair Isaac Corporation; *pg.* 1247, *pg.* 955
Wells, Tony, Sr VP-Mktg-North America - Schneider Electric USA, Inc.; *pg.* 1306, *pg.* 650
Wells, Travis, Mgr-Customer Mktg - Mead Johnson Nutrition Company; *pg.* 1561, *pg.* 615
Wellwood, David, Sr Dir-HP.com, Enterprise & Software - Hewlett-Packard Company; *pg.* 404, *pg.* 175
Welnack, Rochelle, Sr Mgr-Mktg Svcs - PetSmart, Inc.; *pg.* 1481, *pg.* 18
Welsch, Kurt, Mgr-Reg Mktg & Natl Events - Ferrari North America, Inc.; *pg.* 171, *pg.* 1060
Welsh, Bettina S., Mgr-Sls Trng - Pfizer Inc.; *pg.* 1581, *pg.* 1278
Welsh, Bob, VP-Brand Mktg & Indus Design-DEWALT - Stanley Black & Decker, Inc.; *pg.* 1063, *pg.* 358
Welsh, Colin, Product Mgr-FENN Products - SPX Precision Components - Fenn Division; *pg.* 1378, *pg.* 360
Welsh, Eric, Dir-Digital Sls & Mktg - Bayada Nurses Inc.; *pg.* 1499, *pg.* 1087
Welsh, Evan, Sr Dir-Corp Affairs - SAP America, Inc.; *pg.* 466, *pg.* 1557
Welsh, Gene, Sr VP-Sls & Mktg - Automotive Resources International (ARI); *pg.* 1900, *pg.* 1090
Welsh, Jim, Exec VP-Content Solutions & Worldwide Sls - Western Digital Corporation; *pg.* 492, *pg.* 118
Welsh, Maryann, Mgr-Mktg & Events - Alcatel-Lucent; *pg.* 615, *pg.* 38
Welsh, Natasha, Analyst-Mktg-Small Bus Banking - Citigroup Inc.; *pg.* 735, *pg.* 1212
Welter, Kathy, Specialist-Mktg & Support - The Western & Southern Financial Group; *pg.* 1223, *pg.* 1427
Weltken, Suzana, Product Mgr - Health Net, Inc.; *pg.* 1540, *pg.* 308
Weltner, Katie, Coord-Mktg - Tillamook County Creamery Association; *pg.* 901, *pg.* 1509
Welton, Lisa, Product Mgr - Tyson Foods, Inc.; *pg.* 902, *pg.* 35
Welton, Tracy, Product Mgr-eBusiness Site - Advance Auto Parts, Inc.; *pg.* 197, *pg.* 1805
Welty, Jodi, Mgr-Sls Support - Alliance Data Systems Corporation; *pg.* 347, *pg.* 1729
Welty, Pam, Brand Mgr - GIW Industries, Inc.; *pg.* 1340, *pg.* 533
Welty, Peg, Dir-Mktg - Barbara B. Mann Performing Arts Hall; *pg.* 532, *pg.* 427
Welu-Engel, Nicole, Bus Mgr-Mktg Comm - Lifetouch, Inc.; *pg.* 1420, *pg.* 922
Wen Parng, Kai, Dir-Product Mktg - ASUSTeK Computer Inc; *pg.* 355, *pg.* 90
Wenas, Lucy, Sr Mgr-Creative Svcs - Munchkin, Inc.; *pg.* 964, *pg.* 300
Wendelken, Roger, Sr VP-Sls-Worldwide - Intersil Corporation; *pg.* 647, *pg.* 146
Wendell, Dale, Sr VP-Global Bus Sls & Mktg - Blue Bird Corporation; *pg.* 1705, *pg.* 532
Wendell, Raymond, Sr Dir-Mktg Comm - Intrado Inc.; *pg.* 420, *pg.* 334
Wendling, Brenda, Dir-Product Ops-Annie's - Dynamic Resource Group; *pg.* 1637, *pg.* 674
Wendroff, Alessandra, Coord-Mktg-Comedy, Spike & TV Land - MTV Networks Company; *pg.* 298, *pg.* 1262
Wendroff, Alessandra, Coord-Mktg-Comedy, Spike & TV Land - Viacom Inc.; *pg.* 316, *pg.* 1310
Wendt, Eckard, Mgr-Die Attach Sls-Central Europe - Alpha; *pg.* 1146, *pg.* 1123
Wendt, Kristen, Sr VP-Mktg-Product Mgmt - Citigroup Inc.; *pg.* 735, *pg.* 1212
Wonger, Julie, Sr Dir-US Mktg - McDonald's Corporation; *pg.* 1737, *pg.* 645
Wengle, Nicole, VP-Sls & Country Mgr-Canada - F5 Networks, Inc.; *pg.* 396, *pg.* 1835
Wenk, James, VP-Sls & Mktg - American Casting & Manufacturing Corporation; *pg.* 1312, *pg.* 1321
Wenson, Jessica, Mgr-Mktg & PR - Giordano's Enterprises, Inc.; *pg.* 1729, *pg.* 575
Wentworth, Harold M., Sr VP-Retail Banking, Sls & Mktg - Community Bank, N.A.; *pg.* 741, *pg.* 1155
Wentworth, Harold M., Sr VP-Retail Banking, Sls & Mktg - Community Bank System, Inc.; *pg.* 741, *pg.* 1155
Wentworth, Timothy C., Pres-Sls & Acct Mgmt & Sr VP - Express Scripts; *pg.* 1530, *pg.* 1070
Wentz, Bradley, Sr Mgr-Customer Strategy & Dev - Del Monte Foods, Inc.; *pg.* 852, *pg.* 304
Wentz, Don, Dir-Mktg Art - The Dispatch Printing Company; *pg.* 1636, *pg.* 1439
Wentzel, Dave, Rep-Media - Brainerd Daily Dispatch; *pg.* 1623, *pg.* 919
Wenzel, Kevin, Assoc Dir-Mktg-P&G Pro Global - The Procter & Gamble Company; *pg.* 1129, *pg.* 1418
Weprin, Steve, Project Mgr-Mktg-Print & Digital - Amgen Inc.; *pg.* 1493, *pg.* 291
Werblin, Pat B., VP-Adv & PR - Parlux Fragrances, Inc.; *pg.* 519, *pg.* 426
Weredyk, Stephen, Exec Dir-Creative Svcs - Bauer Publishing USA; *pg.* 1620, *pg.* 1059
Werkheiser, Jeff, Mgr-Digital Mktg-Social Media & Mobile Messaging - The Sports Authority, Inc.; *pg.* 1846, *pg.* 326
Werlin, Harry, VP-Sls - Calumet Photographic, Inc.; *pg.* 1404, *pg.* 568
Werner, Amber, Mgr-Mktg Comm - The Schwan Food Company; *pg.* 894, *pg.* 928
Werner, Dean D., Dir-Mktg-Global - Merck & Co., Inc.; *pg.* 1566, *pg.* 1077
Werner, Eric, Mgr-Search Mktg - The Home Depot, Inc.; *pg.* 1050, *pg.* 510
Werner, Gary, Coord-Adv - Chief Industries, Inc.; *pg.* 1323, *pg.* 1010
Werner, George, VP-Retail Sls - BrassCraft Manufacturing Company; *pg.* 1043, *pg.* 902
Werner, Marlene, Mgr-Mktg & Comm - 3M Company; *pg.* 1142, *pg.* 956
Werner, Mike, Sr Dir-Global Tech Partner Programs - Red Hat, Inc.; *pg.* 460, *pg.* 1388
Werner, Scott, Dir-Shopper Mktg & In-Store Visibility - Newell Rubbermaid Inc.; *pg.* 1128, *pg.* 515
Werner, Teddy, Sr Dir-Bus Ops - Milwaukee Brewers Baseball Club, Inc.; *pg.* 562, *pg.* 1878
Werner, Wendy, Head-Digital Mktg - E.I. du Pont de Nemours & Company; *pg.* 1159, *pg.* 390
Wernke, Doug, Dir-Creative & Brand Mgr - Fifth Third Bancorp; *pg.* 752, *pg.* 1413
Wert, Larry, Pres-Brdcst Media - Tribune Media Company; *pg.* 1696, *pg.* 592
Wertheimer, Brian E., District Mgr-Sls - Gardner Publications, Inc.; *pg.* 1644, *pg.* 1413
Werther, Johanna Kirsch, Grp Product Mgr-Mktg, Search & Growth - Google Inc.; *pg.* 1249, *pg.* 153
Wertymer, Megan, Sr Mgr-Email Mktg - Crate & Barrel, Inc.; *pg.* 922, *pg.* 640
Werwie, Joe, Dir-Product Dev-Bikes-Global - Pacific Cycle Inc.; *pg.* 1709, *pg.* 1867
Wescott, Jim, Sr Strategist-Enterprise Solutions Mktg - Dell Inc.; *pg.* 383, *pg.* 1737
Weseley, Lisa, Sr Dir-North America Mktg - Align Technology,

Inc.; *pg.* 1489, *pg.* 237
Wesely, Brianna, Specialist-Credit Mktg - Kwik Trip Inc.; *pg.* 1026, *pg.* 1864
Weser, Lisa, Sr Dir-Mktg Comm-US Brands - Anheuser-Busch Companies, LLC; *pg.* 237, *pg.* 991
Weskamp, Trace, Dir-Product Dev-Global - Weber-Stephen Products LLC; *pg.* 62, *pg.* 650
Wesley, Gabrielle, Head-Experienced Brand Mktg - General Mills, Inc.; *pg.* 828, *pg.* 933
Wesley, Jessica, Mgr-Mktg - The Reader's Digest Association, Inc.; *pg.* 1679, *pg.* 1322
Wesley, Mike, Dir-Mktg-KFC-Yum! Brands - KFC Corporation; *pg.* 1733, *pg.* 735
Wesley, Mike, Dir-Mktg-KFC - YUM! Brands, Inc.; *pg.* 1756, *pg.* 738
Wesley, Rob, Dir-Sls - Virginia State Lottery Department; *pg.* 1010, *pg.* 1804
Wesolek, Doug, Brand Mgr - Brocade Communications Systems, Inc.; *pg.* 365, *pg.* 239
Wessel, Allison, Product Mgr-Digital - McDonald's Corporation; *pg.* 1737, *pg.* 645
Wessel, Teryn, Brand Mgr - Bob Evans Farms, LLC; *pg.* 841, *pg.* 1467
Wessel, Thomas, Sr VP-Sls & Mktg-Worldwide - Analog Devices, Inc.; *pg.* 617, *pg.* 839
Wessling, Joyce Cron, Mgr-Tours & Media Production - San Francisco Symphony; *pg.* 581, *pg.* 227
Wessner, Karen, Rep-Territory Sls - G&K Services Inc.; *pg.* 693, *pg.* 949
Wesson, Bob, VP-Mktg-Field Ops Support - U-Haul International, Inc.; *pg.* 1926, *pg.* 20
West Peterson, Jennifer, Asst Mgr-Acq Mktg, Onboard & Loyalty Mktg - NCL Corporation Ltd.; *pg.* 1916, *pg.* 444
West Peterson, Jennifer, Asst Mgr-Acq Mktg - Norwegian Cruise Line; *pg.* 1917, *pg.* 444
West, Aaron, Pres & Sr VP-Mktg - Investment Seminars, Inc.; *pg.* 420, *pg.* 466
West, Amy, Mgr-Channel Mktg - Generac Power Systems Inc.; *pg.* 1340, *pg.* 1898
West, Andy, Product Mgr-Software - GE Intelligent Platforms; *pg.* 400, *pg.* 1135
West, Betty, Project Mgr-Media & Partnerships - Discover Financial Services; *pg.* 744, *pg.* 653
West, Brian, Mgr-Media & Community Rels - Publix Super Markets, Inc.; *pg.* 1031, *pg.* 437
West, Cari, Mgr-Product Ops - Under Armour, Inc.; *pg.* 49, *pg.* 759
West, Cassie, Analyst-Sls-Just One You - Carter's, Inc.; *pg.* 21, *pg.* 491
West, Christopher J., Sr Mgr-Mktg - CVS Health Corporation; *pg.* 1765, *pg.* 1610
West, Craig, VP-Channel Sls - NetSuite, Inc.; *pg.* 1270, *pg.* 255
West, David, VP-Mktg & Engrg-Global - Arrow Electronics, Inc.; *pg.* 619, *pg.* 325
West, David, Sr Dir-Category Mgmt - Sysco Corporation; *pg.* 1035, *pg.* 1716
West, Dennis, Mgr-Product Design - Heckethorn Manufacturing Company, Inc.; *pg.* 207, *pg.* 1632
West, Erin, Analyst-Mktg Product - T&S Brass & Bronze Works, Inc.; *pg.* 114, *pg.* 1623
West, Gillis, VP-Sls & Svcs-Americas - Cincom Systems, Inc.; *pg.* 372, *pg.* 1411
West, Greg, VP-Product Dev - Bob Evans Farms, LLC; *pg.* 841, *pg.* 1467
West, Gretchen, Media Buyer - Caesars Entertainment Corporation; *pg.* 1083, *pg.* 1023
West, Jacob, Chief Architect-Security Products - NetSuite, Inc.; *pg.* 1270, *pg.* 255
West, Janet, VP-Mktg - Cox Communications, Inc.; *pg.* 279, *pg.* 501
West, Jennifer, Product Mgr-ColdFusion - The Boeing Company; *pg.* 225, *pg.* 567
West, Jerret, VP-Mktg-North America - Netflix, Inc.; *pg.* 1269, *pg.* 141
West, Jessica, Dir-Mktg & Comm-ENE & ES - Tetra Tech, Inc.; *pg.* 115, *pg.* 181
West, Kathryn, Coord-PR - Neiman Marcus, Inc.; *pg.* 30, *pg.* 1684
West, Kendall, Sr VP-Enterprise Digital Mktg - Bank of America Corporation; *pg.* 718, *pg.* 1362
West, Kevin, Mgr-Sls - Joe Machens Ford Inc.; *pg.* 180, *pg.* 976
West, Kimberly, Sr Assoc-Media & Industry Analyst Rels - Booz Allen Hamilton Inc; *pg.* 363, *pg.* 1788
West, Laura, Dir-Global Digital Brand Mktg - NIKE, Inc.; *pg.* 1812, *pg.* 1492
West, Linda, Sr VP-Mdsg, Design & Product Dev - Gaiam, Inc.; *pg.* 1532, *pg.* 334
West, Liz, Sr Dir-Individual Mktg - Teachers Insurance & Annuity Association - College Retirement Equities Fund; *pg.* 1219, *pg.* 1297
West, Mary Beth, Chief Customer & Mktg Officer & Exec VP - J.C. Penney Company, Inc.; *pg.* 1774, *pg.* 1732
West, Micah, Dir-Digital Mktg - The Dress Barn, Inc.; *pg.* 1767, *pg.* 1343
West, Mike, VP-Mktg-Intl - Broadridge Financial Solutions Inc.; *pg.* 727, *pg.* 1172
West, Natalie, Brand Mgr-Global - Fossil Group, Inc.; *pg.* 5, *pg.* 1735
West, Nick, Sr Mgr - Jet.com, Inc.; *pg.* 1260, *pg.* 1073
West, Peggy, Coord-Mktg Comm - MTD Products, Inc.; *pg.* 1057, *pg.* 1478
West, Phil, Sr VP-Mktg - William Grant & Sons, Inc.; *pg.* 1972, *pg.* 1057
West, Ron, Product Mgr-Solid End Mills-Global - Kennametal Inc.; *pg.* 1052, *pg.* 1547
West, Scott, Chief Strategy Officer - Oregon Tourism Commission; *pg.* 1003, *pg.* 1508
West, Starla, Mgr-Digital Media - Sprint Corporation; *pg.* 1874, *pg.* 719
West, Taylor, Sr Mgr-Mktg-Green Giant, Muir Glen & Cascadian Farm - General Mills, Inc.; *pg.* 828, *pg.* 933
West, Tim, Assoc-Mktg - Jet.com, Inc.; *pg.* 1260, *pg.* 1073
West, Todd, Sr Mgr-Global Mktg & Corp Comm IT - Cisco Systems, Inc.; *pg.* 372, *pg.* 240
Westbrook, Craig, VP-Sls Channel Dev & Customer Rels - BMW of North America, LLC; *pg.* 166, *pg.* 1133
Westcott-Pitt, Colin T., Head-Mktg, Global Brands & Innovation-Africa Middle East - Heineken USA Inc.; *pg.* 252, *pg.* 1352
Westdal, Anita, Mgr-Mktg & Adv - SpartanNash Co.; *pg.* 1034, *pg.* 925
Westdorp, Jim, Dir-Indus Mktg & Govt - CIENA Corporation; *pg.* 628, *pg.* 771
Westendorf, Liz, Acct Mgr-DIRECTV Creative Svcs - DIRECTV Group Holdings, LLC; *pg.* 281, *pg.* 79
Westendorf, Melanie, Mgr-Digital Mktg - The J.M. Smucker Company; *pg.* 865, *pg.* 1468
Westerfield, Blake A., VP-Product Mgmt - CNO Financial Group, Inc.; *pg.* 1198, *pg.* 675
Westerfield, Mark, Dir-Product Dev - Clopay Building Products Company; *pg.* 76, *pg.* 1459
Westergren, Andrew, Chief Dev Officer & Chief Strategy Officer - Intuit Inc.; *pg.* 769, *pg.* 158
Westerhout, Renee, Sr Mgr-Digital & Social Media - Pacific Sunwear of California, Inc.; *pg.* 1781, *pg.* 43
Westerlund, Jenna, Sr Planner-Mdse - Ulta Salon, Cosmetics & Fragrance, Inc.; *pg.* 524, *pg.* 559
Westerman, Jim, Head-Sls-Farmers Bus Insurance - Farmers Group, Inc.; *pg.* 1199, *pg.* 130
Westermark, Christine, Dir-Product & Mdsg - Helly-Hansen (US), Inc.; *pg.* 26, *pg.* 1813
Westfall, Elizabeth, Sr Dir-Interactive Mktg - Ameriprise Financial, Inc.; *pg.* 715, *pg.* 930
Westfall, Emily, Dir-Mktg Svcs Tech - Valassis; *pg.* 1698, *pg.* 386
Westfall, Jennie, Analyst-Email Mktg Bus - Alaska Air Group, Inc.; *pg.* 1897, *pg.* 1830
Westgaard, Heidi, VP-Brand Mktg - The Sports Authority, Inc.; *pg.* 1846, *pg.* 326
Westley, Jeff, VP-Sls - Fisher Manufacturing Company; *pg.* 81, *pg.* 297
Westlund, Rachelle, Mgr-Digital Media - Target Corporation; *pg.* 1786, *pg.* 942
Westman, Meredith, Specialist-Mktg Comm - Boston Scientific Corporation; *pg.* 1508, *pg.* 831
Westmoreland, Paula, Mgr-Sls Reg - Purafil, Inc.; *pg.* 333, *pg.* 530
Weston, Brooke, Mgr-Digital Mktg - LegalZoom.com, Inc.; *pg.* 1261, *pg.* 96
Weston, Cameron, Sr Mgr-Integrated Mktg - Del Monte Foods, Inc.; *pg.* 852, *pg.* 304
Weston, Jamie, VP-Brand Mgmt & Creative - National Football League; *pg.* 567, *pg.* 1264
Weston, Matt, Mgr-Mktg-Intl - Penguin Random House; *pg.* 1675, *pg.* 1276
Weston, Tim, Sr Product Mgr - GE Energy; *pg.* 1338, *pg.* 506
Weston, Todd, Product Mgr-Global Clinical - General Electric Company; *pg.* 1297, *pg.* 347
Westover, Christina, Mgr-Brand Mgmt & Creative Svcs - VeriSign, Inc.; *pg.* 488, *pg.* 1799
Westphal, Birgitta, Strategist-Digital Mktg - Nestle USA, Inc.; *pg.* 883, *pg.* 96
Westrick, Mark, Dir-Wholesale Branded Sls - Valero Energy Corporation; *pg.* 986, *pg.* 1743
Westrick, Phil, Sr Analyst-Mktg - Bridgestone Americas, Inc.; *pg.* 201, *pg.* 1649
Westrum, Barry, Exec VP-Mktg - American Dairy Queen Corporation; *pg.* 1714, *pg.* 930
Westrum, Barry, Exec VP-Mktg - International Dairy Queen, Inc.; *pg.* 1732, *pg.* 938
Westwood, Theresa, Sr Mgr-Mktg-Personal Advisor Svcs - The Vanguard Group, Inc.; *pg.* 816, *pg.* 1550
Westwood, Victoria, Mgr-PR-UK - Turner Broadcasting System, Inc.; *pg.* 314, *pg.* 521
Wetherbee, Robert S., Exec VP-Flat Rolled Products - Allegheny Technologies Incorporated; *pg.* 66, *pg.* 1572
Wethington, Drew, Product Mgr-Cotton Pickers - Deere & Company; *pg.* 703, *pg.* 632
Wettengel, Andrew, Sr Strategist-Creative - Yahoo! Inc.; *pg.* 1289, *pg.* 289
Wetzel, Dan, District Mgr-Sls - Philips Lighting; *pg.* 1303, *pg.* 806
Wetzel, Kate, Sr Mgr-Fin & Net Pricing - PepsiCo, Inc.; *pg.* 259, *pg.* 1327
Wetzel, Nikki, Mgr-Mktg - Arden Realty, Inc.; *pg.* 1080, *pg.* 126
Wetzel, Steve, Mgr-Sls-Natl - Interplastic Corporation; *pg.* 1168, *pg.* 961
Wetzonis, John, Sr VP-Sls - Polar Beverages; *pg.* 264, *pg.* 862
Wexelbaum, Joshua, Sr Mgr-Digital Mktg - MillerCoors; *pg.* 254, *pg.* 1877
Wexelbaum, Joshua, Brand Mgr-Miller Lite - MillerCoors LLC; *pg.* 255, *pg.* 582
Wexler, Ben, VP-Channel Sls - The WhiteWave Foods Company; *pg.* 1037, *pg.* 324
Wexler, Debbie, Mgr-Comm, PR & Events - GE Consumer & Industrial; *pg.* 55, *pg.* 733
Wexler, Deborah R., Mgr-Comm, PR & Events - General Electric Company; *pg.* 1297, *pg.* 347
Wexler, Eden, Dir-PR - Safilo USA Inc.; *pg.* 11, *pg.* 1106
Wexler, Jon, Dir-Entertainment & Influencer Mktg-Global - adidas America Inc.; *pg.* 1803, *pg.* 1500
Wexler, Lauren, Sr Dir-Global Media - Revlon, Inc.; *pg.* 521, *pg.* 1286
Wexler, Risa, Sr Dir-Media & US Digital Acceleration - Pfizer Inc.; *pg.* 1581, *pg.* 1278
Weyand, John, Dir-Digital Mktg - Pier 1 Imports, Inc.; *pg.* 940, *pg.* 1695
Weyenberg, Joeri, VP-Mktg - Kaplan, Inc.; *pg.* 603, *pg.* 425
Weyer, Laura, Specialist-Mktg Matls Compliance - The Northwestern Mutual Life Insurance Company; *pg.* 1212, *pg.* 1879
Weygandt, Irene, Specialist-Mktg-Denver & Anschutz Medical Campus - University Of Colorado; *pg.* 608, *pg.* 323
Weylman, Bill, Mgr-Search Mktg - Putnam Investments, LLC; *pg.* 797, *pg.* 800
Whah, Danielle, Dir-Product-NAR Front Load Laundry - Whirlpool Corporation; *pg.* 62, *pg.* 872
Whaite, Vanessa, Mgr-Mktg - TracFone Wireless, Inc.; *pg.* 681, *pg.* 447
Whalen, Billy, Mgr-Field Mktg-Midwest Reg - Kind LLC; *pg.* 868, *pg.* 1249
Whalen, Christopher, VP-Integrated Mktg - Kimberly-Clark Corporation; *pg.* 1461, *pg.* 1720
Whalen, DeAnna, Mgr-Mktg-Global - GlaxoSmithKline; *pg.* 1536, *pg.* 1389
Whalen, DeAnna, Mgr-Mktg-Global - GlaxoSmithKline Consumer Healthcare; *pg.* 510, *pg.* 1554
Whalen, Jim, Mgr-Technical Mktg - Plasti-Fab Ltd.; *pg.* 1888, *pg.* 1904
Whalen, Larry, Jr., Sr Mgr-Shopper Mktg - GlaxoSmithKline; *pg.* 1536, *pg.* 1389
Whalen, Patrick, VP-Mktg - Yetter Manufacturing Co., Inc.; *pg.* 708, *pg.* 598
Whaley, Jasmine, Rep-College Mktg - Warner Music Group Corp.; *pg.* 590, *pg.* 1313
Whaling, Jennifer, Product Mgr - Tyson Foods, Inc.; *pg.* 902, *pg.* 35
Wharton, Brian, Mgr-Retail Strategy & Product Mktg-FedEx Svcs Mktg - FedEx Corporation; *pg.* 1907, *pg.* 1642
Wharton, Donald, Pres-VYCOM & Scranton Products - CPG International, Inc.; *pg.* 1881, *pg.* 1586

Wharton, Sterling, COO-Global Media Solutions - Electronic Arts Inc.; *pg.* 951, *pg.* 189
Whatley, Kim, Project Mgr-Mktg-Global - Whole Foods Market, Inc.; *pg.* 1038, *pg.* 1667
Wheat, Tony, Sr Dir-Brand Mktg Analytics - Catalina Marketing Corporation; *pg.* 369, *pg.* 462
Wheatley, Brett, VP-Mktg, Sls & Svc-Asia Pacific - Ford Motor Company; *pg.* 172, *pg.* 876
Wheatley, Sean, Dir-Mktg - Old World Industries, Inc.; *pg.* 1175, *pg.* 641
Wheaton, Bill, Exec VP & Gen Mgr-Media - Akamai Technologies, Inc.; *pg.* 1226, *pg.* 807
Wheaton, Brant, Brand Mgr-Kraft Macaroni & Cheese-Meals Innovation - The Kraft Heinz Company; *pg.* 871, *pg.* 641
Wheaton, Tom, Dir-Brand & Digital Mktg - Florida Hospital Orlando; *pg.* 1531, *pg.* 453
Wheeler, Alexandra, VP-Digital Mktg-Global - Starbucks Corporation; *pg.* 897, *pg.* 1840
Wheeler, Angie, Mgr-Sls Comm - AT&T Inc.; *pg.* 1867, *pg.* 1674
Wheeler, Ashley, Area Dir-Mktg & Bus Dev - Simon Property Group, Inc.; *pg.* 1112, *pg.* 690
Wheeler, Colin, Sr Dir-Global External Comm - Molson Coors Brewing Company; *pg.* 256, *pg.* 321
Wheeler, Dan, VP-New Products & Innovation - Dunkin' Brands Group, Inc.; *pg.* 1727, *pg.* 810
Wheeler, Felicia, Supvr-Mktg Promos - Galderma Laboratories, L.P.; *pg.* 1532, *pg.* 1695
Wheeler, Jaime, Assoc Mgr-Mktg-Barbie - MATTEL, INC.; *pg.* 962, *pg.* 81
Wheeler, Jeremy, VP-Sls-Home Center & Hardware Channel - Newell Rubbermaid Inc.; *pg.* 1128, *pg.* 515
Wheeler, Jessica, Dir-Mktg Comm - Allegiant Travel Company; *pg.* 346, *pg.* 1022
Wheeler, Lara, Sr Mgr-Comm - Canadian Imperial Bank of Commerce; *pg.* 729, *pg.* 1935
Wheeler, Mark, Global Product Mgr-Sys & Svc - Chromalox, Inc.; *pg.* 1070, *pg.* 1574
Wheeler, Melissa, Mgr-Digital Mktg Channel - Bank of America Corporation; *pg.* 718, *pg.* 1362
Wheeler, Patrick, Sr Dir-Product Mgmt - Oracle Corporation; *pg.* 1272, *pg.* 786
Wheeler, Shana, Mgr-Mktg Events & Media Rels - Mettler-Toledo Inc.; *pg.* 1056, *pg.* 1441
Wheeler, T.J., VP-Product Mgmt - Friedrich Air Conditioning Co.; *pg.* 1072, *pg.* 1740
Whelan, Brandy, Dir-Search-Digital Mktg - FMR LLC (Fidelity Investments); *pg.* 759, *pg.* 794
Whelan, Jen, Dir-Partner Mktg - QUALCOMM Incorporated; *pg.* 1873, *pg.* 207
Whelan, Joseph, Acct Exec-Sponsorship Sls - Major League Baseball; *pg.* 560, *pg.* 1255
Whelan, Lisa, Assoc Dir-Mktg - Lippincott Williams & Wilkins; *pg.* 1659, *pg.* 1514
Whelan, Michael, Sr Mgr-Mktg Analytics - QUALCOMM Incorporated; *pg.* 1873, *pg.* 207
Whelan, Mike, Dir-Creative - The Fuller Brush Company; *pg.* 330, *pg.* 715
Whelan, Timothy, Dir-Brand Mktg - Hunter Fan Company; *pg.* 57, *pg.* 1631
Whelehon, Chuck, Mgr-Branded Sls - J.D. Streett & Co., Inc.; *pg.* 980, *pg.* 988
Whelley, Stacy, Mgr-Mktg & Comm - GE Capital; *pg.* 761, *pg.* 362
Whelpley, John, Pres/COO-Vector Marketing - CUTCO Corporation; *pg.* 1123, *pg.* 1318
Wherley, Susan, Mgr-Adv - Yetter Manufacturing Co., Inc.; *pg.* 708, *pg.* 598
Whetstone, Cicely, Specialist-Corp Mktg Comm - Philips Lighting; *pg.* 1303, *pg.* 806
Whickman, Graeme, VP-Mktg - Ford Motor Company of Canada, Limited; *pg.* 174, *pg.* 1930
Whidden, Christie, Dir-Bus Strategy & Plng-Intl Mktg - American Express Company; *pg.* 712, *pg.* 1190
Whidden, Holly, Exec Dir-PR - The Hearst Corporation; *pg.* 1649, *pg.* 1239
Whiddon, Bill, Dir-Creative - The Miami Herald; *pg.* 1665, *pg.* 444
Whipkey, Bill, Sr Mgr-Mktg - AT&T Inc.; *pg.* 1867, *pg.* 1674
Whipple, Glenn, Rep-Sls - Giant Bicycle Inc.; *pg.* 1707, *pg.* 164
Whipple, Grant, Dir-Sls & Bus Dev - Winegard Company; *pg.* 688, *pg.* 702
Whipple, Richard N., Mgr-Mktg Comm - Parker Hannifin Corporation; *pg.* 1368, *pg.* 1434
Whipple, Steve, VP-Sls & Mktg - Edelbrock Corporation; *pg.* 204, *pg.* 293
Whirley, Gregory A., Interim CFO - Lumber Liquidators Holdings, Inc.; *pg.* 94, *pg.* 1808
Whisler, Patricia K., Sr VP-Women's Mdsg - The Buckle, Inc.; *pg.* 1764, *pg.* 1011
Whitaker, Leroy M., Sr Dir-Compensation, Benefits & HRIS - Spirit Airlines, Inc.; *pg.* 234, *pg.* 449
Whitaker, Shelly, Dir-Adv & Compliance - Financial Brokerage Inc.; *pg.* 1200, *pg.* 1015
Whitaker, Stephanie, Mgr-Digital Mktg - Amazon.com, Inc.; *pg.* 1226, *pg.* 1831
Whitby, Kristen, Specialist-Mktg - Caterpillar, Inc.; *pg.* 1321, *pg.* 650
Whitcomb, John, Sr VP-Mktg & Distr Svcs - Genworth Financial, Inc.; *pg.* 761, *pg.* 1802
White, Adam, Sr VP-Sls-Global - International Rectifier Corporation; *pg.* 647, *pg.* 80
White, Aimee, VP-Sls & Ops - BBC Worldwide America Inc.; *pg.* 271, *pg.* 1201
White, Alan, VP-Sls Mktg & Delivery AP - Itron Inc.; *pg.* 422, *pg.* 1822
White, Albert G., III, Chief Strategy Officer & VP - The Cooper Companies, Inc.; *pg.* 1518, *pg.* 183
White, Amy, Sr Dir-Employee Comm & Engagement - Nortek, Inc.; *pg.* 100, *pg.* 1607
White, Aubrey, Specialist-Social Media - The WhiteWave Foods Company; *pg.* 1037, *pg.* 324
White, Barry V., VP-Mktg Svcs - Chick-fil-A, Inc.; *pg.* 1721, *pg.* 492
White, Ben, Sr Mgr-ECommerce - MetroPCS, Inc.; *pg.* 1872, *pg.* 1683
White, Brad, Sr Mgr-Mktg - Waterloo Industries, Inc.; *pg.* 946, *pg.* 1885
White, Brent, Mgr-Mktg-Structural Adhesives, Industrial Adhesives & Tapes - 3M Company; *pg.* 1142, *pg.* 956
White, Carol, Sr Assoc Brand Mgr - Mars, Incorporated; *pg.* 1858, *pg.* 1792
White, Cheryl, Sr Mgr-Mktg-New Bus Dev - Wal-Mart.com; *pg.* 1287, *pg.* 50
White, Chinissa, Dir-Mktg Health & Wellness - Wal-Mart Stores, Inc.; *pg.* 1790, *pg.* 29
White, Chris, Mgr-Digital Media Technical - Savannah Morning News; *pg.* 1683, *pg.* 540
White, Christopher M., Dir-Mktg & Refining IT - Hess Corporation; *pg.* 979, *pg.* 1240
White, Courtney, Mgr-Global PR - Spredfast; *pg.* 1282, *pg.* 1666
White, Dagan, Product Mgr-aerospace & Defense - Xilinx, Inc.; *pg.* 496, *pg.* 252
White, Dan, VP-Adv - Bliss Communications Inc.; *pg.* 1621, *pg.* 1861
White, Dana, Product Mgr-Client Experience - Raymond James Financial, Inc.; *pg.* 798, *pg.* 464
White, Daniel, Sr Mgr-Retail Sls - Charter Communications, Inc.; *pg.* 274, *pg.* 372
White, David, Sr Mgr-Project, Mfg & Quality, Processes & Sys Integration - The Boeing Company; *pg.* 225, *pg.* 567
White, David G., Mgr-Digital Mktg & Creative Svcs - F.A. Davis Publishing Company; *pg.* 1640, *pg.* 1564
White, Debbie, Sr Acct Exec-Adv - The New York Times Company; *pg.* 1668, *pg.* 1270
White, Debbie, Dir-Mktg - PepsiCo, Inc.; *pg.* 259, *pg.* 1327
White, Dena, Coord-Digital Mktg - LVMH Inc.; *pg.* 9, *pg.* 1254
White, Doug, Sr Dir-Programming & Acq - ESPN, Inc.; *pg.* 285, *pg.* 340
White, Elijah, VP-Mktg - Zoll Medical Corporation; *pg.* 1612, *pg.* 814
White, Ellen, Mgr-Mktg Operation - 3M Company; *pg.* 1142, *pg.* 956
White, Ilana, Sr Assoc Brand Mgr-US Retail - Campbell Soup Company; *pg.* 844, *pg.* 1048
White, J. Edward, Exec VP & Mgr-Client Advisory Grp-Nashville - Pinnacle Financial Partners, Inc.; *pg.* 794, *pg.* 1653
White, Jared, Coord-Mktg - Meredith Corporation; *pg.* 1663, *pg.* 705
White, Jay, Sr Engr-Technical Mktg - NetApp, Inc.; *pg.* 444, *pg.* 287
White, Julia, Product Mgr - Microsoft Corporation; *pg.* 435, *pg.* 1824
White, Kaleb, Mgr-Mktg - Cabela's Incorporated; *pg.* 535, *pg.* 1019
White, Karen, Mgr-Mktg Comm - Bolthouse Farms; *pg.* 841, *pg.* 44
White, Karen, Brand Mgr-Intl Delight Iced Coffee - The WhiteWave Foods Company; *pg.* 1037, *pg.* 324
White, Karen E., Sr Mgr-Mktg - Whirlpool Corporation; *pg.* 62, *pg.* 872
White, Kate, Brand Mgr-Kate Spade New York Watches - Fossil Group, Inc.; *pg.* 5, *pg.* 1735
White, Katherine, Brand Mgr-Chandon - Moet Hennessy; *pg.* 1966, *pg.* 1260
White, Kathy, Deputy Dir-Mktg & Admin - Salvador Dali Museum; *pg.* 580, *pg.* 464
White, Katie, Assoc Mgr-Adv & PR - Fruit of the Loom, Inc.; *pg.* 41, *pg.* 725
White, Kelly, Mgr-Online & Direct Channel Sls - Air New Zealand Ltd. (U.S.A.); *pg.* 1897, *pg.* 78
White, Kirsten, Sr Specialist-Mktg Comm-Brand & Commercialization Grp - Boston Scientific Corporation; *pg.* 1508, *pg.* 831
White, Kristina D., Sr Coord-Adv - Universal Health Services Inc.; *pg.* 1604, *pg.* 1544
White, Kyle, Mgr-Mktg & Comm - MARKETAXESS HOLDINGS INC.; *pg.* 778, *pg.* 1256
White, Leigh P., Sr Dir-Comm - Kindred Healthcare, Inc.; *pg.* 1553, *pg.* 736
White, Leslie, VP-Mktg Comm - McKesson Corporation; *pg.* 1560, *pg.* 222
White, Libby, Mgr-Digital Mktg - U.S. Bancorp; *pg.* 815, *pg.* 945
White, Lisa, Dir-Store Mktg - Tractor Supply Company; *pg.* 708, *pg.* 1627
White, Lydia, Product Designer - Tumblr, Inc.; *pg.* 1285, *pg.* 1305
White, Lynn, Specialist-Enterprise Mktg-Tier II - Windstream Corporation; *pg.* 321, *pg.* 34
White, Margaret, Mgr-Adv - Alabama Power Company; *pg.* 1933, *pg.* 1
White, Mark, Mgr-Interline Mktg - Union Pacific Corporation; *pg.* 1927, *pg.* 1018
White, Mark, Mgr-Interline Mktg - Union Pacific Railroad Company; *pg.* 1927, *pg.* 1019
White, Mark, VP-Mfg & Specialty Mktg - U.S. News & World Report, L.P.; *pg.* 1698, *pg.* 1308
White, Matthew, Grp Dir-Digital Sls - Time Inc.; *pg.* 1693, *pg.* 1300
White, Michael, CTO & Sr VP-Disney Interactive & Disney Consumer Products - The Walt Disney Company; *pg.* 317, *pg.* 52
White, Mike, Dir-Global Supplier Mktg - Arrow Electronics, Inc.; *pg.* 619, *pg.* 325
White, Mike, CMO & Dir-Mktg & Corp Comm - Raymond James Financial, Inc.; *pg.* 798, *pg.* 464
White, Molly, Brand Mgr-Heinz Heritage - The Kraft Heinz Company; *pg.* 870, *pg.* 1577
White, Monty, Mgr-Mktg - Irving Convention & Visitors Bureau; *pg.* 996, *pg.* 1720
White, Nicki, Assoc Mgr-Digital Mktg-Integrated Customer Experience Grp - GlaxoSmithKline; *pg.* 1536, *pg.* 1565
White, Nicki, Assoc Mgr-Digital Mktg-Integrated Customer Experience Grp - GlaxoSmithKline Consumer Healthcare; *pg.* 510, *pg.* 1554
White, Patricia, VP-PR-Global - Coty, Inc.; *pg.* 506, *pg.* 1219
White, Pepper W., Sr Dir-Promo & Integration - Golf Channel; *pg.* 551, *pg.* 454
White, Robert, Sr Mgr-Bus Ops - DISH Network Corporation; *pg.* 283, *pg.* 325
White, Robert, Mgr-Technical & Mktg Comm - Snap-on Incorporated; *pg.* 1062, *pg.* 1862
White, Robert RJ, Sr Analyst-Digital Mdsg-Mktg - Southwest Airlines Co.; *pg.* 1923, *pg.* 1687
White, Shannon, Sr Product Mgr - NuVasive, Inc.; *pg.* 1577, *pg.* 205
White, Shaun, VP-PR - RE/MAX International, Inc.; *pg.* 1109, *pg.* 322
White, Sloan, Brand Mgr-Retail Partnerships - Capital One Financial Corporation; *pg.* 730, *pg.* 1789
White, Steve, Product Mgr - MicroBilt Corporation; *pg.* 782, *pg.* 534
White, Steven, Sr Mgr-Product Engrg - Comcast Cable Communications, Inc.; *pg.* 276, *pg.* 1560
White, Stoney, Mgr-Value Channel Mktg - Xerox Corporation; *pg.* 494, *pg.* 365
White, Taigh, Dir-Digital Mktg - The Ultimate Software Group, Inc.; *pg.* 486, *pg.* 479
White, Tammy, Rep-Comm & Data Sls - Graybar Electric Company, Inc.; *pg.* 1299, *pg.* 997

First page reference indicates Business Class Edition
Second page reference indicates Geographic Edition

White, Taryn, Analyst-Sls Ops & Mktg - 3M Company; *pg.* 1142, *pg.* 956
White, Thomas E., Jr., Mng Dir-Sls - United Parcel Service, Inc.; *pg.* 1928, *pg.* 522
White, Tiffany, Assoc Mgr-Mktg-Yoplait Innovation - General Mills, Inc.; *pg.* 828, *pg.* 933
White, Tim, Dir-Sls & Mktg-AFTD - Graco, Inc.; *pg.* 1342, *pg.* 935
White, Tim, VP & Mgr-Sls - Purity Dairies, LLC; *pg.* 891, *pg.* 1653
White, Tina, Sr Mgr-Digital Mktg - Big Heart Pet Brands; *pg.* 1474, *pg.* 213
White, Todd R., Mgr-Sls - Educational Development Corporation; *pg.* 1638, *pg.* 1490
White, Tom, Exec VP-Ops & Product - PASSUR Aerospace, Inc.; *pg.* 233, *pg.* 376
White, Tracy, VP-Mktg - Bankrate, Inc.; *pg.* 1231, *pg.* 451
White, Tracy, Brand Mgr-Digital Retail-Tier 1 Brand Stories - NIKE, Inc.; *pg.* 1812, *pg.* 1492
White, Travis D., Sr Mgr-Mktg - Eli Lilly and Company; *pg.* 1527, *pg.* 684
White, William, VP-Mktg - Target Corporation; *pg.* 1786, *pg.* 942
White-Keating, Emily, VP-Mktg - Visionworks of America, Inc.; *pg.* 1436, *pg.* 1744
White-Randolph, Angela, Dir-Mktg-Hispanic - Eli Lilly and Company; *pg.* 1527, *pg.* 684
White-Swift, E. G., Brand Mgr - Equipment Depot Ltd.; *pg.* 1335, *pg.* 1749
Whited, Jeannie, Sr Mgr-Brand Mktg & Dealer Comm - Nissan North America, Inc.; *pg.* 186, *pg.* 1633
Whitehead, Jeff, Bus Dir-Club Sls & Mktg - McCormick & Company, Incorporated; *pg.* 1027, *pg.* 779
Whitehead, Jesse, VP-Mktg-Ecolab QSR - Ecolab Inc.; *pg.* 329, *pg.* 960
Whitehead, Justin, Brand Mgr-Digital Mktg - Raising Cane's USA; *pg.* 1746, *pg.* 742
Whitehead, Mark, Sr Dir-Digital Mktg - Reebok International Ltd.; *pg.* 1817, *pg.* 811
Whitehead, Michelle, Dir-Brand & Sports Mktg - Skullcandy, Inc.; *pg.* 674, *pg.* 1754
Whitehill, N. James, Dir-Production - Ballet Theatre Foundation, Inc.; *pg.* 531, *pg.* 1200
Whitehouse, Emily, Mgr-Mktg Insights & Program - Potbelly Sandwich Works LLC; *pg.* 1746, *pg.* 587
Whitehouse, Niles, Dir-Sls - Winnebago Industries, Inc.; *pg.* 1712, *pg.* 707
Whitehurst, Roslyn, Dir-PR - Experian Consumer Direct; *pg.* 1245, *pg.* 71
Whiteley, Kristen, Sr Brand Mktg Mgr - Zappos.com, Inc.; *pg.* 1291, *pg.* 1030
Whitelock, Jeremy R., Brand Dir-Diabetes Mktg - Eli Lilly and Company; *pg.* 1527, *pg.* 684
Whitesell, Ben, Supvr-Social Media - United Parcel Service, Inc.; *pg.* 1928, *pg.* 522
Whiteside, Darrell, VP-Sls & Bus Dev - National Fruit Product Company, Inc.; *pg.* 882, *pg.* 1811
Whiteside, Ewa, Head-Voluntary Strategy & Mktg - Cigna Corporation; *pg.* 1197, *pg.* 338
Whiteside, Frances, Brand Mgr - Georgia-Pacific LLC; *pg.* 1458, *pg.* 507
Whiteside, Tamara, Sr Mgr-Worldwide Adv - Apple Inc.; *pg.* 350, *pg.* 73
Whitford, Kim, Mgr-Mktg Admin - Sally Beauty Holdings, Inc.; *pg.* 522, *pg.* 1691
Whitford, Norma, Acct Mgr-Direct Sls - The Penn Companies; *pg.* 10, *pg.* 1568
Whitford, Richard, Mgr-Sls - ZCL Composites Inc.; *pg.* 1892, *pg.* 1906
Whiting, Jason, VP-Global Mktg & Clinical Ops - Zoll Medical Corporation; *pg.* 1612, *pg.* 814
Whiting, Katie, Mgr-Channel Mktg - The Valspar Corporation; *pg.* 1449, *pg.* 945
Whiting, Lawson, Chief Brands & Strategy Officer - Brown-Forman Corporation; *pg.* 1958, *pg.* 732
Whiting, Rick, Product Mgr - Cascade Corporation; *pg.* 1321, *pg.* 1497
Whiting, Shelley Woods, VP-Mktg - Avery Dennison Corporation; *pg.* 1452, *pg.* 95
Whiting, Todd, Sr VP-Television & New Media Distr - NBC Universal, Inc.; *pg.* 300, *pg.* 1266
Whiting, Wendy, Mgr-Mktg Production - Christopher & Banks Corporation; *pg.* 22, *pg.* 953
Whitlatch, Brian, Mng Dir-Energy Mktg - American Electric Power Company, Inc.; *pg.* 1934, *pg.* 1437
Whitley, Cara, CMO-Global - Century 21 Real Estate LLC; *pg.* 1085, *pg.* 1080
Whitlock, Bryan, Mgr-Local Mktg - Lowe's Companies, Inc.; *pg.* 1053, *pg.* 1383
Whitlock, Jenny, VP-Television Mktg-Global - Marvel Entertainment, LLC; *pg.* 1662, *pg.* 1257
Whitlow, Stephanie, Dir-Mktg & Comm - RED Development; *pg.* 1109, *pg.* 19
Whitman, Jake, Sr Asst Brand Mgr-Old Spice - The Procter & Gamble Company; *pg.* 1129, *pg.* 1418
Whitmer, Ben, Dir-Digital Mktg - Stage Stores, Inc.; *pg.* 33, *pg.* 1715
Whitmore, Rob, Mgr-Adv - Alaska Industrial Hardware Inc.; *pg.* 1041, *pg.* 10
Whitmore, Todd, Dir-Petroleum Sls-BNSF Railway - Burlington Northern Santa Fe, LLC; *pg.* 1901, *pg.* 1694
Whitney, Benjamin, Head-Sls Excellence-Innovation - E.I. du Pont de Nemours & Company; *pg.* 1159, *pg.* 390
Whitney, Jeff, Assoc Dir-Creative - Apple Inc.; *pg.* 350, *pg.* 73
Whitney, Joe, Dir-Sls & Mktg - Sierra Nevada Brewing Co.; *pg.* 265, *pg.* 65
Whitney, Josh, VP-Technical Product Solutions & Intl Svcs - Black Box Corporation; *pg.* 361, *pg.* 1547
Whitney, Lynn, Exec VP-Media - Warner Bros. Entertainment Inc.; *pg.* 319, *pg.* 54
Whitney, Shon, VP-Sls & Mktg - Morinda Holdings Inc.; *pg.* 1569, *pg.* 1754
Whitney, Susan, Mgr-Mktg - Intuit Inc.; *pg.* 769, *pg.* 158
Whitsett, Peter, Exec VP-Mdsg & Mktg - Meijer, Inc.; *pg.* 1779, *pg.* 888
Whitt, Nancy, Sr Dir-Institutional Mktg - Teachers Insurance & Annuity Association - College Retirement Equities Fund; *pg.* 1219, *pg.* 1297
Whittaker, Amanda, Sr Mgr-Shopper Mktg - The Coca-Cola Company; *pg.* 240, *pg.* 493
Whittaker, Cathy A., Dir-Mktg Comm & Channel Sls-Global - Littelfuse, Inc.; *pg.* 1301, *pg.* 580
Whittaker, Guy, VP-Global Mktg - CooperVision, Inc.; *pg.* 1407, *pg.* 1159
Whittaker, Lisa, Sr Mgr-ECommerce Mktg - Office Depot, Inc.; *pg.* 448, *pg.* 412
Whitten, Marc, Chief Product Officer - Sonos, Inc.; *pg.* 675, *pg.* 263
Whittier, Matt, Sr Mgr-Mktg - Naxos of America Inc.; *pg.* 1779, *pg.* 1633
Whittington, JD, Dir-Trade Mktg Brand Activation - Anheuser-Busch Companies, LLC; *pg.* 237, *pg.* 991
Whittle, Brad, VP-Sls-Global - SirsiDynix Corporation; *pg.* 470, *pg.* 1751
Whittle, Bridget, Assoc Dir-Consumer Mktg, Acq & Retention - AT&T Inc.; *pg.* 1867, *pg.* 1674
Whittle, Teresa, Dir-Svc Mgmt Mktg - IBM; *pg.* 410, *pg.* 1449
Whitton, Laura, Sr Dir-Govt Rels & Advocacy - Juvenile Diabetes Research Foundation International; *pg.* 145, *pg.* 1247
Whitworth, Brad, Sr Mgr-Mktg & Comm-Indus Solutions Grp-Ecosystems - Cisco Systems, Inc.; *pg.* 372, *pg.* 240
Whitworth, Monica, Mgr-Adv Ops - Gannett Co., Inc.; *pg.* 1643, *pg.* 1790
Whoriskey, John, Pres-U S Sls & Mktg - Keurig Green Mountain, Inc.; *pg.* 868, *pg.* 1768
Whyley, Bob, Sr VP-Production & Exec Producer - The Tennis Channel, Inc.; *pg.* 679, *pg.* 276
Whymark, Katherine, Sr Product Mgr-Mktg - Gerber Life Insurance Company; *pg.* 1201, *pg.* 1352
Whyte, Barry, VP-Comm & PR - St. Jude Children's Research Hospital; *pg.* 1596, *pg.* 1646
Whyte, Philip, VP-Supplier Bus Dev & Mktg-Global - Avnet Technology Solutions; *pg.* 359, *pg.* 25
Wiatroski, Lisa, Category Head-Media-Global & Dir-Procurement - Novartis Corporation; *pg.* 1574, *pg.* 1273
Wichers, Chris, Chief Sls Officer - Pegasus Solutions, Inc.; *pg.* 452, *pg.* 1685
Wicht, Michael, Dir-Mktg - Prochaska & Associates; *pg.* 105, *pg.* 1017
Wichter, Jennifer, Brand Mgr-Jim Beam & Alberta Rye - Beam Suntory Inc.; *pg.* 1957, *pg.* 599
Wicinski, Tom, VP-Digital Access Mktg - FedEx Corporation; *pg.* 1907, *pg.* 1642
Wick, Randall W., Sr VP-Mdsg - Office Depot, Inc.; *pg.* 448, *pg.* 412
Wicka, Garry, Sr Dir-Mktg - LG Electronics U.S.A., Inc.; *pg.* 651, *pg.* 1060
Wickenhauser, Autumn, Mgr-Mktg & Comm-Caterpillar Visitors Center - Caterpillar, Inc.; *pg.* 1321, *pg.* 650
Wicker, Sarah, Mgr-Mktg - Verizon Communications Inc.; *pg.* 1875, *pg.* 1309
Wickham, Joan, Mgr-Adv & PR - Sunkist Growers, Inc.; *pg.* 899, *pg.* 299
Wickham, Rene, VP-Product Quality - Mary Kay Inc.; *pg.* 516, *pg.* 1657
Wicks, Doug, Product Mgr-Off Grid Sys & Battery Based Inverters - Schneider Electric; *pg.* 467, *pg.* 1609
Wicks, Gary, Sr Mgr-Digital Strategy-Boeing Comml Airplanes - The Boeing Company; *pg.* 225, *pg.* 567
Widaman, Fritz, Dir-Sls & Bus Dev - Daily Racing Form, LLC; *pg.* 1632, *pg.* 1221
Widder, Dionna, VP-Ticket Sls & Svc - Cleveland Cavaliers/Quicken Loans Arena; *pg.* 541, *pg.* 1429
Widdows, Tiffany, Dir-Mktg & Adv - Golden Nugget Hotel; *pg.* 550, *pg.* 1024
Wideroe, David, VP-Mktg Solutions & Branded Entertainment - E! Online, Inc.; *pg.* 1239, *pg.* 129
Widhelm, Lizzie, Sr VP-Ad Product Sls & Strategy - Pandora Media Inc.; *pg.* 1273, *pg.* 172
Widman, Steve, Dir-Audience & Programmatic Sls - Yahoo! Inc.; *pg.* 1209, *pg.* 289
Widmann, Bill, VP-Sls & Mktg - Guardian Industries Corp.; *pg.* 85, *pg.* 869
Widmann, Sue, Sr Mgr-Mktg Svcs - PepsiCo, Inc.; *pg.* 259, *pg.* 1327
Widowski, Sonya, Dir-Field Mktg Enablement - State Farm Mutual Automobile Insurance Co.; *pg.* 1218, *pg.* 557
Widseth, Benjamin, Brand Mgr-Innovation - Anheuser-Busch Companies, LLC; *pg.* 237, *pg.* 991
Wieberg, Dan, Mgr-PR - Home Instead, Inc.; *pg.* 1542, *pg.* 1016
Wiebusch, Jon, VP-Sls - Carta Mundi, Inc.; *pg.* 951, *pg.* 1677
Wiecek, Debbie, Mgr-Product Mktg - Siemens Healthcare Diagnostics; *pg.* 673, *pg.* 604
Wiedemann, Jason, Brand Mgr-E&J Brandy & Viniq Liqueur - E&J Gallo Winery; *pg.* 1962, *pg.* 149
Wiedenmann, Marc, Sr Mgr-Digital Mktg-Customer Strategy & Shared Svcs - Sunovion Pharmaceuticals Inc.; *pg.* 1599, *pg.* 832
Wiegman, Tracy, Mgr-Mktg - 1st Franklin Financial Corporation; *pg.* 710, *pg.* 542
Wieland, Christie, Mgr-Mktg, Digital & LRM - Perkins & Marie Callender's Inc.; *pg.* 1744, *pg.* 1645
Wieland, Elizabeth, Mgr-Mktg Comm - Parker Hannifin Corporation; *pg.* 1368, *pg.* 1434
Wiener, Bill, Jr., Sr Dir-Bus Svcs - Tampa Bay Rays Baseball, Ltd.; *pg.* 586, *pg.* 464
Wiener, David, Sr VP-Sls - Loews Hotels Holding Corporation; *pg.* 1101, *pg.* 1252
Wiener, James, Sr Dir-Engrg & Facilities - Colorado Rockies Baseball Club, Ltd.; *pg.* 542, *pg.* 317
Wiener, Lauren, Pres-Sls & Mktg-Global - Tremor Video; *pg.* 682, *pg.* 1305
Wiener, Suzanne, Coord-Mktg - Mount Sinai Medical Center; *pg.* 1569, *pg.* 448
Wiens, Susan, Sr Asst Brand Mgr-Home Care - Procter & Gamble Inc.; *pg.* 333, *pg.* 1929
Wiernik, Karen, Dir-Brand Mktg-Cytosport - Hormel Foods Corporation; *pg.* 863, *pg.* 915
Wierzbicka, Kinga, Mgr-Online Mktg-5-hour ENERGY - Living Essentials, LLC; *pg.* 1026, *pg.* 886
Wiese, Carl, Pres-Global Sls - BlackBerry Limited; *pg.* 625, *pg.* 1947
Wiese, Tara, Product Mgr - McKee Foods Corporation; *pg.* 1860, *pg.* 1630
Wieseneck, Noah, Head-YouTube Partner Sls-Global - Google Inc.; *pg.* 1249, *pg.* 153
Wiesner, Karen, Dir-Mktg - Cincinnati Bell Inc.; *pg.* 1871, *pg.* 1410
Wiessinger, Gary, Exec VP-Products - NetSuite, Inc.; *pg.* 1270, *pg.* 255
Wieszeck, Paul, VP-Engrg & Technical Svcs Sensor Products - Vulcan Electric Company; *pg.* 1078, *pg.* 751
Wiezorek, Steve, Dir-Product Mktg - The Valspar Corporation; *pg.* 1449, *pg.* 945
Wigetman, Lisa, Specialist-Product Mktg - VistaPrint USA, Incorporated; *pg.* 1700, *pg.* 829
Wiggers, Monica M., Coord-Mktg - American Express Company; *pg.* 712, *pg.* 1190
Wiggin, Cindi, Mgr-Mktg Event-World Ahead Grp - Intel Corporation; *pg.* 645, *pg.* 266
Wiggins, Angela, Sr Dir-Workplace Comm - Marriott International, Inc.; *pg.* 1102, *pg.* 764
Wiggins, Chad, Dir-Networked Audio Sys-Global Product

Mgmt - Shure Incorporated; *pg.* 672, *pg.* 638
Wiggins, Charles, Sr VP & Grp Product Mgr - City National Bank; *pg.* 737, *pg.* 725
Wiggins, Rasheed, Assoc Mgr-Social Media - Darden Restaurants, Inc.; *pg.* 1724, *pg.* 453
Wiggins, Rasheed, Assoc Mgr-Social Media - Olive Garden Italian Restaurant; *pg.* 1742, *pg.* 454
Wiggins, Shaun, Exec Head-Global PR - General Electric Company; *pg.* 1297, *pg.* 347
Wiggins, Terry, Dir-Sls-South - The Libman Company; *pg.* 331, *pg.* 553
Wiggs, Steven B, CMO & Sr Exec VP - BB&T Corporation; *pg.* 723, *pg.* 1393
Wight, John, VP-Mktg - Cost Plus World Market; *pg.* 921, *pg.* 170
Wijangco, Genevieve, Mgr-Global Adv & Online - Oracle Corporation; *pg.* 450, *pg.* 191
Wik, Katherine, Sr VP-Brand Mktg - MGM Resorts International; *pg.* 1105, *pg.* 1028
Wiland, Ilka, Mgr & Specialist-Corp Events Mktg - NVIDIA Corporation; *pg.* 447, *pg.* 268
Wilander, Amanda, Mgr-Affinity Mktg Program - The American Dental Association; *pg.* 127, *pg.* 564
Wilbanks, Christopher, Mgr-Creative Svcs - FTD Group, Inc.; *pg.* 1795, *pg.* 608
Wilbanks, Dan, Sr VP-Bus Dev & Mktg - Team Health Holdings, Inc.; *pg.* 1601, *pg.* 1639
Wilber, Kimberly, Specialist-Mktg - Amazon.com, Inc.; *pg.* 1226, *pg.* 1831
Wilbourn, Micheal, Product Mgr - TE Connectivity Ltd.; *pg.* 677, *pg.* 1515
Wilbrink, Jacko, Dir-Product Mktg - Atmel Corporation; *pg.* 621, *pg.* 238
Wilbur, Brenda, Dir-Branding & Creative - St. Louis Blues Hockey Club, LLC; *pg.* 585, *pg.* 1003
Wilburn, Bobby, Dir-Sls & Mktg - Peco Foods Inc.; *pg.* 888, *pg.* 8
Wilburn, Brian, Sr Mgr-Publ Plng - Amgen Inc.; *pg.* 1493, *pg.* 291
Wilburn, Michael, Head-Enterprise Data Strategy & Sr Dir - Ancestry.com LLC; *pg.* 1228, *pg.* 1754
Wilco, Michelle, Specialist-Digital Mktg - Atlanta Convention & Visitors Bureau; *pg.* 989, *pg.* 489
Wilcox, Bob, Mgr-Mktg - Miller-Stephenson Chemical Company, Inc.; *pg.* 1172, *pg.* 344
Wilcox, Casey, Dir-Player & Media Rels - Arizona Diamondbacks; *pg.* 529, *pg.* 14
Wilcox, Cathy, VP-Adv - Simon Property Group, Inc.; *pg.* 1112, *pg.* 690
Wilcox, Crystal, Analyst-Field Mktg Enablement - State Farm Mutual Automobile Insurance Co.; *pg.* 1218, *pg.* 557
Wilcox, Don, VP-Digital Mktg & Svcs - Public Broadcasting Service; *pg.* 305, *pg.* 1774
Wilcox, Gina, Sr Dir-Mobile Product Mgmt - Bankrate, Inc.; *pg.* 1231, *pg.* 451
Wilcox, Heather, Dir-Channel Mktg-Global - Dell Inc.; *pg.* 383, *pg.* 1737
Wilcox, Jamie, Assoc Dir-Product Mktg - Bissell Homecare, Inc.; *pg.* 52, *pg.* 887
Wilcox, Justin, Mgr-Mktg-Global Search - The Gap, Inc.; *pg.* 1770, *pg.* 218
Wilcox, Matt, Sr VP-Mktg Strategy & Innovation - Fiserv, Inc.; *pg.* 397, *pg.* 1855
Wilcox, Matthew, Sr VP-Mktg Strategy & Innovation - Fiserv, Inc.; *pg.* 758, *pg.* 537
Wilcox, Steve, Mgr-Sports Mktg - Pacific Cycle Inc.; *pg.* 1709, *pg.* 1867
Wilcox, Steve, Brand Mgr - Robert Bosch Tool Corp; *pg.* 1060, *pg.* 634
Wilcox, Tony, Gen Mgr-Motorcycle New Product Delivery - Harley-Davidson, Inc.; *pg.* 178, *pg.* 1874
Wild, Andrew, Mgr-Segment Mktg-Music & Education - Avid Technology, Inc.; *pg.* 622, *pg.* 804
Wild, Andrew, Dir-Brokerage Sls - Zillow Group, Inc.; *pg.* 1292, *pg.* 1843
Wild, Colette, Dir-Creative Svcs - Banfi Vintners; *pg.* 1957, *pg.* 1161
Wild, Ed, Sr Dir-Analytics-Pepsi North America Beverages - PepsiCo, Inc.; *pg.* 259, *pg.* 1327
Wildasin, Annie, Sr Mgr-Mktg-Retail Assets - Bozzuto's Inc.; *pg.* 1016, *pg.* 342
Wilde, Anne, Brand Mgr - Einstein Noah Restaurant Group, Inc.; *pg.* 1019, *pg.* 332
Wilde, Frederic De, Sr VP-Mktg & Sls - Philip Morris International Inc.; *pg.* 1894, *pg.* 1282
Wilde, Jennie, Sr VP-Design & Mktg - The Robert Allen Group, Inc.; *pg.* 698, *pg.* 819
Wilde, Karen, VP-Product & Process Dev - IDG Enterprise; *pg.* 1258, *pg.* 821
Wildenauer, Michelle, Sr Dir-Strategic Mktg-Small Law Firm & Consumer - Truven Health Analytics; *pg.* 486, *pg.* 331
Wildenhaus, Mark, Dir-Mktg Creative - Learfield Communications, Inc.; *pg.* 296, *pg.* 979
Wilder, Jack, Mgr-Mktg-Global Chocolate Innovation - The Hershey Co.; *pg.* 1855, *pg.* 1538
Wilder, Jen, Sr Dir-Competitive Strategy - Kimberly-Clark Corporation; *pg.* 1461, *pg.* 1720
Wildhack, John, Exec VP-Programming & Production - ESPN, Inc.; *pg.* 285, *pg.* 340
Wiles, Amanda, Mgr-Digital Mktg - The Huntington National Bank; *pg.* 767, *pg.* 1440
Wiles, Erin, Mgr-Digital Mktg - Unum Group; *pg.* 1222, *pg.* 1629
Wiles, Sandy, VP & Product Mgr - Northern Trust Corporation; *pg.* 787, *pg.* 585
Wiles, Tommy, Sr Mgr-Mktg-Digital Media - Google Inc.; *pg.* 1249, *pg.* 153
Wiley, Hugh, Grp Publr-Bloomberg Media - Bloomberg BusinessWeek; *pg.* 1621, *pg.* 1204
Wiley, Melissa, Dir-Digital Products-Core Content & Adv - National Geographic Channel; *pg.* 299, *pg.* 402
Wiley, Tim, VP-Sls - Rinnai America Corp.; *pg.* 1076, *pg.* 538
Wiley, Tom, Exec VP-Sls - Digital First Media; *pg.* 1238, *pg.* 1224
Wiley, Zealous D., Sr Head-Digital Mktg - Hewlett-Packard Company; *pg.* 404, *pg.* 175
Wilf, Gonen, Head-Production - LivePerson, Inc.; *pg.* 1264, *pg.* 1252
Wilhelm, Christophe, Sr Mgr-Consumer Mktg-Strategy & Plng - PayPal Inc.; *pg.* 1274, *pg.* 248
Wilhelm, Frank, Mgr-Adv - Yamaha Motor Corporation USA; *pg.* 1713, *pg.* 76
Wilhelm, Harald, Mgr-Global Partner Mktg - Intel Corporation; *pg.* 645, *pg.* 266
Wilhelm, Selvan, Product Mgr-Global - Molex Incorporated; *pg.* 655, *pg.* 628
Wilhelmy, David B., VP-Sls & Mktg - International Baler Corp.; *pg.* 1350, *pg.* 433
Wilhite, Brian, Dir-Mktg - Kauffman Tire Inc.; *pg.* 1885, *pg.* 532
Wilk, Chuck A., Mgr-Product Dev - Victaulic Company; *pg.* 1066, *pg.* 1529
Wilk, Jeffrey, Mgr-Mktg - Cross Country Healthcare, Inc.; *pg.* 1520, *pg.* 411
Wilk, Jeffrey, Head-US Retail Wealth Mgmt-Sls, Product Mgmt & Mktg - MetLife, Inc.; *pg.* 1208, *pg.* 1258
Wilk, Rob, VP-Search Sls & Svc-North America - Microsoft Corporation; *pg.* 435, *pg.* 1824
Wilke, Douglas, VP-Mktg & Tech - Foremost Farms USA Cooperative; *pg.* 856, *pg.* 1854
Wilke, Fritz, Mgr-Mustang & Mondeo Product Mktg-Asia Pacific - Ford Motor Company; *pg.* 172, *pg.* 876
Wilke, Jeff, VP-Affiliate Mktg - Scripps Networks Interactive, Inc.; *pg.* 1279, *pg.* 1638
Wilken, Virginia, Sr Rep-District Sls-San Diego - Philips Lighting; *pg.* 1303, *pg.* 806
Wilkerson, John, Sr Mgr-Comm - ZF TRW; *pg.* 222, *pg.* 897
Wilkerson, Laura, Sr Mgr-Mktg Comm-Global - Freescale Semiconductor, Inc.; *pg.* 398, *pg.* 1662
Wilkes, David, VP-Sls - BizBash Media Inc.; *pg.* 1621, *pg.* 1203
Wilkes, Linnea M., Bus Mgr-Transformation - 3M Company; *pg.* 1142, *pg.* 956
Wilkie, Cary, Rep-Mktg - Auto-Owners Insurance Group; *pg.* 1194, *pg.* 895
Wilkie, Ronald, Territory Mgr-Sls - Honeywell International Inc.; *pg.* 407, *pg.* 1088
Wilkin, Beth, Mgr-Adv - The Kroger Co.; *pg.* 1025, *pg.* 1416
Wilkin, Patricia, Mgr-Interactive Mktg-Global Adv - Campbell Soup Company; *pg.* 844, *pg.* 1048
Wilkins, Amy, Grp Publr-Martha Stewart Media - Meredith Corporation; *pg.* 1663, *pg.* 705
Wilkins, Catherine, Specialist-Online & Relationship Mktg - Porsche Cars North America, Inc.; *pg.* 189, *pg.* 518
Wilkins, Glen, Sr Mgr-Pub Affairs & Govt Rels - Wal-Mart Stores, Inc.; *pg.* 1790, *pg.* 29
Wilkins, Jennifer, Sr Mgr-Mktg - Intuit Inc.; *pg.* 769, *pg.* 158
Wilkins, KeJuan, Sr Dir-Media Rels-North America - NIKE, Inc.; *pg.* 1812, *pg.* 1492
Wilkinson, Ana, Sr Mgr-DTC & HCP MCM Campaign Mgmt Ops - Amgen Inc.; *pg.* 1493, *pg.* 291
Wilkinson, Ashley, Brand Mktg Mgr - Popeye's Chicken & Biscuits; *pg.* 1745, *pg.* 517
Wilkinson, Cory, Dir-Mktg - MasterBrand Cabinets, Inc.; *pg.* 96, *pg.* 692
Wilkinson, Drew, Product Mgr-Online - The Home Depot, Inc.; *pg.* 1050, *pg.* 510
Wilkinson, Holly, Dir-Mktg & Innovation - Diageo North America Inc.; *pg.* 248, *pg.* 1223
Wilkinson, Joni, Brand Mgr-Jeep Cherokee - FCA US LLC; *pg.* 170, *pg.* 868
Wilkinson, Lee, VP-Strategy & Product Mgmt - Hearst Magazines; *pg.* 1649, *pg.* 1239
Wilkinson, Scott, Sr Dir-Technical Mktg - MRV Communications, Inc.; *pg.* 441, *pg.* 64
Wilkinson, Tom, Interim CFO - Xplore Technologies Corp.; *pg.* 497, *pg.* 1667
Wilkinson-Rae, Laura, Head-Consumer PR-UK & Ireland - eBay Inc.; *pg.* 1240, *pg.* 243
Will, Cait, Sr Mgr-Digital Mktg - athenahealth, Inc.; *pg.* 1497, *pg.* 855
Will, Edward E., VP-Mktg & Strategy - Cameron Drilling & Production Systems; *pg.* 1321, *pg.* 1702
Willaman, Joe, Mgr-Mktg Implementation - Cardinal Health, Inc.; *pg.* 1512, *pg.* 1448
Willard, Amanda, VP-Mktg & Comm - Lincoln Park Zoo; *pg.* 557, *pg.* 580
Willard, Jeff, Exec VP-Mktg - Simmons Company; *pg.* 943, *pg.* 520
Willardson, Bruce, Sr Dir-Clorox Creative Svcs & Dir-Creative - The Clorox Company; *pg.* 327, *pg.* 169
Wille, Dan, VP-Mktg, Product & Bus Dev - Brunswick Corporation; *pg.* 1828, *pg.* 623
Willebeek-LeMair, Jason, Engr-Sls - Avaya Inc.; *pg.* 621, *pg.* 264
Willems, Pieter, Sr Mgr-Consumer Insights-BeNeFraLux - Anheuser-Busch Companies, LLC; *pg.* 237, *pg.* 991
Willems, Sue, VP-Sls & Mktg - Sunrise Soya Foods; *pg.* 900, *pg.* 1912
Willemse, Norman, Pres-Metal Formed Products - American Axle & Manufacturing Holdings, Inc.; *pg.* 198, *pg.* 879
Willenborg, Jeremy, Mgr-Consulting Mktg-Americas - Hewlett-Packard Company; *pg.* 404, *pg.* 175
Willenborg, Mark, Dir-Mktg & Creative - KVUE-TV; *pg.* 295, *pg.* 1663
Willensky, Allison, Sr Dir-Worldwide Consumer Insights - Mattel Games/Puzzles; *pg.* 962, *pg.* 80
Willensky, Laura, Exec VP-Mdsg - J. Crew Group, Inc.; *pg.* 1773, *pg.* 1245
Willett, Alison, Mgr-Global Demand Generation Mktg - Bio-Rad Laboratories, Inc.; *pg.* 1504, *pg.* 101
Willett, Shannon Grimes, Mgr-Mktg - Netflix, Inc.; *pg.* 1269, *pg.* 141
Willette, Margaret, Sr Mgr-Paid Search Mktg - Intuit Inc.; *pg.* 769, *pg.* 158
Williams, Aaliyah, Mgr-Adv - MATTEL, INC.; *pg.* 962, *pg.* 81
Williams, Aaron, Brand Mgr - Nestle Purina PetCare Company; *pg.* 1479, *pg.* 1000
Williams, Alison, Mgr-Media Rels - Acer America Corporation; *pg.* 341, *pg.* 235
Williams, Amanda, Mgr-Social Media - Express, Inc.; *pg.* 24, *pg.* 1440
Williams, Amber, Dir-Mktg & Internet Sls - Lennar Homes, Inc.; *pg.* 1101, *pg.* 443
Williams, Amy, Sr Mgr-PR - Convergys Corporation; *pg.* 379, *pg.* 1412
Williams, Amy, VP-Mktg & Vendor Rels - Matrix Integration LLC; *pg.* 430, *pg.* 692
Williams, Andrew, VP-Media Rels - The Goldman Sachs Group, Inc.; *pg.* 762, *pg.* 1236
Williams, Anne, Brand Mgr - The Procter & Gamble Company; *pg.* 1129, *pg.* 1418
Williams, Antje, Dept Mgr-Mktg Svcs & Product Mgmt Vans - Mercedes-Benz USA, LLC; *pg.* 184, *pg.* 514
Williams, Aubrey, Mgr-Shopper Mktg-Mars Petcare - Mars, Incorporated; *pg.* 1858, *pg.* 1792
Williams, Becky, Dir-Catering, Sls & Mktg - MCCORMICK & SCHMICK'S SEAFOOD RESTAURANTS, INC.; *pg.* 1737, *pg.* 1711
Williams, Bianca, Mgr-Mktg & Promos Activations - NBC Universal, Inc.; *pg.* 300, *pg.* 1266
Williams, Bill, VP-Sls & Delivery Svcs - Piedmont Natural Gas Company, Inc.; *pg.* 1949, *pg.* 1368
Williams, Bill, Mgr-Relationship Mktg-Global - United Parcel Service, Inc.; *pg.* 1928, *pg.* 522

First page reference indicates Business Class Edition
Second page reference indicates Geographic Edition

Williams, Blake, Product Mgr - Facebook, Inc.; *pg.* 1245, *pg.* 143
Williams, Bob, Dir-Sls & Dev - Lee Enterprises, Incorporated; *pg.* 1658, *pg.* 704
Williams, Brandon, Mgr-Product Mktg - Saucony, Inc.; *pg.* 1818, *pg.* 828
Williams, Brandon, Mgr-Production - Wolverine World Wide, Inc.; *pg.* 1822, *pg.* 905
Williams, Brett, Acct Exec-Mktg Solutions - LinkedIn Corporation; *pg.* 1262, *pg.* 160
Williams, Britni, Sr Mgr-Acct Dev - San Angelo Standard, Inc.; *pg.* 1682, *pg.* 1739
Williams, Brucetta, VP-360 Consumer Mktg & Brand Strategy - BET Holdings LLC; *pg.* 271, *pg.* 396
Williams, Camille, Coord-Adv - TEN: The Enthusiast Network; *pg.* 1691, *pg.* 1298
Williams, Caroline, Sr Dir-Digital Art - Starwood Hotels & Resorts Worldwide, Inc.; *pg.* 1114, *pg.* 378
Williams, Chad E., Sr VP-Production - EPL Oil & Gas, Inc.; *pg.* 976, *pg.* 746
Williams, Cheryl, VP-Mktg - Wakefern Food Corporation; *pg.* 1037, *pg.* 1058
Williams, Chris, Chief Product Officer - IHeartMedia Inc.; *pg.* 292, *pg.* 1741
Williams, Christina, Sr Analyst-Media-Health Comm - Northrop Grumman Corporation; *pg.* 231, *pg.* 1781
Williams, Christine, Mgr-Consumer Mktg - AutoTrader, Inc.; *pg.* 1230, *pg.* 490
Williams, Christine, Mgr-Mktg & Sls Support - PRAHealth Sciences; *pg.* 1585, *pg.* 1388
Williams, Christopher, Head-Mktg-Global - Amdocs Inc.; *pg.* 348, *pg.* 974
Williams, Dan, Mgr-Technical Sls - Eureka Chemical Company; *pg.* 1161, *pg.* 279
Williams, Dan, Asst VP-Mktg - University Of Florida; *pg.* 609, *pg.* 429
Williams, Dana, Dir-Integrated Mktg & Comm - Southwest Airlines Co.; *pg.* 1923, *pg.* 1687
Williams, Danielle, Head-Mktg Program - Herman Miller, Inc.; *pg.* 926, *pg.* 913
Williams, Darryl, VP-Sls, Mktg & Design - Landau Uniforms Incorporated; *pg.* 28, *pg.* 971
Williams, David, VP-Product Mgmt & Strategy - Emulex Corporation; *pg.* 392, *pg.* 70
Williams, David, VP-Sls & Mktg - RLI Corp.; *pg.* 1216, *pg.* 652
Williams, David, Sr VP-Digital Mktg - Wells Fargo & Company; *pg.* 819, *pg.* 232
Williams, David W., Head-Design & Mktg - MORNINGSTAR, INC.; *pg.* 784, *pg.* 583
Williams, Deanna, Dir-Media Rels - Macy's, Inc.; *pg.* 1778, *pg.* 1417
Williams, Deborah M., Dir-Mktg-New Jersey - Lennar Corporation; *pg.* 1100, *pg.* 443
Williams, Deborah T., Sr Mgr-Mktg-Americas - Polycom, Inc.; *pg.* 664, *pg.* 249
Williams, Debra, Dir-Segment Mktg - McKesson Corporation; *pg.* 1560, *pg.* 222
Williams, Deidra R., VP & Gen Mgr-Western Sls & Ops - Xerox Corporation; *pg.* 494, *pg.* 365
Williams, Douglas, Mgr-Entertainment Mktg - Columbia Sportswear Company; *pg.* 1830, *pg.* 1501
Williams, Doyle, CMO - COUNTRY Financial; *pg.* 1198, *pg.* 557
Williams, Emily L., Dir-Consumer Mktg Insights - Newell Rubbermaid Inc.; *pg.* 1128, *pg.* 515
Williams, Eric, Dir-Sls-Natl - Electro Rent Corporation; *pg.* 390, *pg.* 300
Williams, Erin, Mgr-Mktg - Aeropostale, Inc.; *pg.* 17, *pg.* 1188
Williams, Esmee Huggard, VP-Brand Mktg - Allrecipes.com; *pg.* 1226, *pg.* 1831
Williams, Filippa, Assoc Mgr-Mktg-International - Home Box Office, Inc.; *pg.* 290, *pg.* 1240
Williams, Fiona, Dir-PR-EMEA - salesforce.com, inc.; *pg.* 1278, *pg.* 226
Williams, Fonda, Mgr-New Store Mktg - AARON'S, INC.; *pg.* 912, *pg.* 486
Williams, Gareth, Brand Mgr - Mars, Incorporated; *pg.* 1858, *pg.* 1792
Williams, Heidi, Dir-Creative-Global Mktg - The Scotts Miracle-Gro Company; *pg.* 1799, *pg.* 1459
Williams, Ian, Dir-Mktg - Chase Card Services, Inc.; *pg.* 734, *pg.* 215
Williams, Ian, Mgr-EMEA PR - Eaton Corporation; *pg.* 1331, *pg.* 1429
Williams, Isha Metz, Dir-Global Mktg-Smoking Reduction & Cessation - GlaxoSmithKline Consumer Healthcare; *pg.* 510, *pg.* 1554
Williams, JaeLynn, Sr VP-Sls, Mktg & Client Ops - 3M Company; *pg.* 1142, *pg.* 956
Williams, Jai Santiago, Mgr-Global Mobile SMS Mktg - InterContinental Hotels Corporation; *pg.* 1097, *pg.* 511
Williams, Jamie, Mgr-Mdsg - Furst-McNess Company; *pg.* 1476, *pg.* 613
Williams, Jason D., Sls Dir-Strategic Accounts-Aesthetic & Corrective BU - Galderma Laboratories, L.P.; *pg.* 1532, *pg.* 1695
Williams, Jay, Sr Asst Brand Mgr-Marlboro - Altria Group, Inc.; *pg.* 1893, *pg.* 1800
Williams, Jeff, VP-Sls & Mktg - General Bearing Corporation; *pg.* 205, *pg.* 1350
Williams, Jeff, Specialist-ExperienceOne Brand Sls - IBM; *pg.* 410, *pg.* 1449
Williams, Jeff R., VP-Sls, Mktg, Bus & Product Dev-Walco Intl - Animal Health International, Inc.; *pg.* 1474, *pg.* 1749
Williams, Jeremy, Mgr-Online & Mobile Sls - Bank of America Corporation; *pg.* 718, *pg.* 1362
Williams, Jerri, Dir-Media Rels - Southeastern Pennsylvania Transportation Authority; *pg.* 1923, *pg.* 1570
Williams, Jessica, Head-Global Innovation Mktg & Analytics - Visa Inc.; *pg.* 816, *pg.* 230
Williams, Jim, VP-Pur & Supplier Rels, Product Mgmt, Automation & Process Pumps - Motion Industries, Inc.; *pg.* 213, *pg.* 3
Williams, John, Engr-Outside Sls - Standard Wire & Cable Co.; *pg.* 1306, *pg.* 187
Williams, Jolorie, Asst VP-Mktg-Make-Up - L'Oreal USA; *pg.* 514, *pg.* 1252
Williams, Jon, Mgr-Reg Sls-Southwestern Div - American Airlines Inc.; *pg.* 1898, *pg.* 1693
Williams, Jordan, Dir-Mktg & Retail Div - Vail Resorts, Inc.; *pg.* 1117, *pg.* 313
Williams, Josh, Sr Mgr-Mktg Sponsorships - Dollar General Corporation; *pg.* 1767, *pg.* 1635
Williams, Judd, VP & Gen Mgr-Svc Sls - Young Electric Sign Company; *pg.* 1308, *pg.* 1762
Williams, Judy, Sr Dir-Bus Advisors & Practice Efficiencies - Allergan, Inc.; *pg.* 1491, *pg.* 106
Williams, Julie, Product Mgr - CRC Industries, Inc.; *pg.* 329, *pg.* 1590
Williams, Katie, Sr Dir-Mktg-Global Savory & Kid Wholesome - Mondelez International, Inc.; *pg.* 878, *pg.* 601
Williams, Katie, Sr Dir-Mktg-Global Savory & Kid Wholesome - Mondelez North America; *pg.* 881, *pg.* 1054
Williams, Katina, Mgr-Mktg-Intl - The Children's Place, Inc.; *pg.* 22, *pg.* 1119
Williams, Kay, VP & Product Line Mgr - ACI Worldwide Inc.; *pg.* 341, *pg.* 1010
Williams, Kelly, VP-Wireless Product Ops - Cox Communications, Inc.; *pg.* 279, *pg.* 501
Williams, Kelly, Mgr-Social Analytics & Customer Insights & Analytics-Global - Wal-Mart.com; *pg.* 1287, *pg.* 50
Williams, Kevin, Media Planner - AARP; *pg.* 124, *pg.* 393
Williams, Kevin M., Head-Multicultural Mktg - BMW of North America, LLC; *pg.* 166, *pg.* 1133
Williams, Kim, Dir-Mktg-East Reg - J.E. Dunn Construction Group, Inc.; *pg.* 89, *pg.* 984
Williams, Kristen, Brand Mgr-Mktg Ops - Borden Dairy Company; *pg.* 842, *pg.* 1676
Williams, Laura, Product Mgr-Residential Air Conditioning Sys - Carrier Corporation; *pg.* 1070, *pg.* 349
Williams, Lauren, Analyst-Mktg - The Priceline Group Inc.; *pg.* 1276, *pg.* 364
Williams, Leroy, VP-Mktg & Sls Ops-South Area - Cellco Partnership; *pg.* 1869, *pg.* 1042
Williams, Leroy, VP-Mktg & Sls Ops-South Area - Verizon Communications Inc.; *pg.* 1875, *pg.* 1309
Williams, Leslee, Sr Dir-Public & Professional Comm - The American Dental Association; *pg.* 127, *pg.* 564
Williams, Linda, Sr Dir-Educational - ideastream; *pg.* 292, *pg.* 1431
Williams, Lisa, Mgr-Mktg-All Family Ice Cream Snacks - Nestle USA, Inc.; *pg.* 883, *pg.* 96
Williams, Lisa, Chief Product Officer - Patagonia; *pg.* 31, *pg.* 301
Williams, Lizette, Head-Multicultural Mktg-North America - Kimberly-Clark Corporation; *pg.* 1461, *pg.* 1720
Williams, Maria, VP-Creative Godiva Worldwide - Godiva Chocolatier, Inc.; *pg.* 1854, *pg.* 1235
Williams, Marie, Sr Mgr-Global Product Line-Jordan Brand - NIKE, Inc.; *pg.* 1812, *pg.* 1492
Williams, Mark, Sr Product Mgr - Hobbico, Inc.; *pg.* 956, *pg.* 562
Williams, Mark R., Sr VP-Enterprise Sls-Americas Eastern Reg - Merrill Corporation; *pg.* 1664, *pg.* 962
Williams, Matthew, Dir-Mktg Ops - Hilton Worldwide, Inc.; *pg.* 1094, *pg.* 1791
Williams, Medgar, Dir-Immunology Mktg-Abbott - Abbott Laboratories; *pg.* 1484, *pg.* 551
Williams, Megan, Brand Mgr - Neutrogena Corporation; *pg.* 517, *pg.* 137
Williams, Melissa, Dir-Mktg & Advisor Solutions-Global - MORNINGSTAR, INC.; *pg.* 784, *pg.* 583
Williams, Nick, Sr Product Mgr-Data Centre IP-EMEA - Brocade Communications Systems, Inc.; *pg.* 365, *pg.* 239
Williams, Nikole, Program Mgr-Mktg - Intel Corporation; *pg.* 645, *pg.* 266
Williams, Page, Mgr-Social Media Mktg-Global Brand - LinkedIn Corporation; *pg.* 1262, *pg.* 160
Williams, Paul, Sr Product Mgr - Kubota Tractor Corporation; *pg.* 705, *pg.* 294
Williams, Penny, Sr Mgr-Mktg - Market Leader, Inc.; *pg.* 1102, *pg.* 1822
Williams, Penny, Sr Mgr-Product Mktg - Sprint Corporation; *pg.* 1874, *pg.* 719
Williams, Rachel, Acct Exec-Adv - Graham Holdings Company; *pg.* 1645, *pg.* 1773
Williams, Rhys, Dir-Production - Spoleto Festival USA; *pg.* 584, *pg.* 1613
Williams, Rusty, Sr Rep-Mktg - BP America Inc.; *pg.* 972, *pg.* 1702
Williams, Samantha, Dir-PR - GOJO Industries, Inc.; *pg.* 330, *pg.* 1401
Williams, Sara, Sr Mgr-Product-Toddler Grain & Bakery Snacks - Nestle Healthcare Nutrition; *pg.* 1572, *pg.* 941
Williams, Scott, Assoc VP-Uverse.com & Adv - AT&T Southeast; *pg.* 1868, *pg.* 489
Williams, Scott, Mgr-Product Dev - Digital River, Inc.; *pg.* 1238, *pg.* 948
Williams, Scott K., Mgr-Mktg - United Parcel Service, Inc.; *pg.* 1928, *pg.* 522
Williams, Shana, Mgr-Online & Mktg - D.R. Horton, Inc.; *pg.* 1090, *pg.* 1694
Williams, Shannon, Dir-Demand Generation, Mktg & Sls Ops - Blackbaud, Inc.; *pg.* 361, *pg.* 1613
Williams, Shelley, Dir-Sls-Eastern Reg - Caesars Entertainment Corporation; *pg.* 1083, *pg.* 1023
Williams, Shelly, Principal & Specialist-Sls Trng - Boston Scientific Corporation; *pg.* 1508, *pg.* 831
Williams, Stacy E., Mgr-Mktg Partnership Activation - The Coca-Cola Company; *pg.* 240, *pg.* 493
Williams, Stephanie, Mgr-Credit & Gift Card Mktg - Ann Inc.; *pg.* 18, *pg.* 1195
Williams, Steven, Mgr-Mktg Partnerships - Verizon Communications Inc.; *pg.* 1875, *pg.* 1309
Williams, Susan, Mgr-Mktg & Brand - American Airlines Inc.; *pg.* 1898, *pg.* 1693
Williams, Susan, Dir-Strategic Mktg-Resource & Sr Mgr-Mktg - Cardinal Health, Inc.; *pg.* 1512, *pg.* 1448
Williams, Susan, Mgr-Product Ops - H&R Block, Inc.; *pg.* 764, *pg.* 983
Williams, Thomas, VP-Mktg - Chamberlain College of Nursing, LLC; *pg.* 599, *pg.* 607
Williams, Tim, VP-Sls - Penda Corporation; *pg.* 214, *pg.* 1887
Williams, Todd, Supvr-Source Naturals Mktg - Source Naturals; *pg.* 1595, *pg.* 278
Williams, Tomeka, Mgr-Mktg - Comcast Cable Communications, Inc.; *pg.* 276, *pg.* 1560
Williams, Tracy, Asst Dir-Mktg - Harvard Business Review; *pg.* 1648, *pg.* 1238
Williams, Travis M., Mgr-Product Mktg - Advanced Micro Devices, Inc.; *pg.* 613, *pg.* 282
Williams, Tricia, Assoc Mgr-Mktg-IS - Kayem Foods, Inc.; *pg.* 867, *pg.* 814
Williams, Trisha, Dir-Integrated Mktg - Macy's East; *pg.* 1777, *pg.* 1254
Williams, Verla, Coord-Mktg - Schneller, Inc.; *pg.* 234, *pg.* 1456
Williams, Vikki, Dir-Mktg-Global - L'Oreal USA; *pg.* 514, *pg.* 1252
Williams, Wendy, Mgr-Mktg - Dell Inc.; *pg.* 383, *pg.* 1737
Williams, Wendy, Dir-Creative - Simmons-Boardman Publishing Corp.; *pg.* 1686, *pg.* 1292
Williamson, Dan, Mgr-Product Mktg - Microsoft Corporation; *pg.* 435, *pg.* 1824
Williamson, David, Exec VP & Gen Mgr-Office Products Grp -

MeadWestvaco Corp. - Office Products Group; pg. 431, pg. 1342
Williamson, Dawn, Sr VP-Adv Sls-North America - BBC Worldwide America Inc.; pg. 271, pg. 1201
Williamson, Eric, Mgr-Creative Svcs Production & Engr-Audio - DIRECTV Group Holdings, LLC; pg. 281, pg. 79
Williamson, James D., Reg Mgr-Sls-Northeast - Dover Chemical Corporation; pg. 1156, pg. 1447
Williamson, Kimberly, Dir-Mktg & Strategy, Parts & Accessories - Cessna Aircraft Company; pg. 226, pg. 723
Williamson, Kylie, Coord-Mktg Content - Gerber Legendary Blades; pg. 1834, pg. 1503
Williamson, Martine, Sr VP-Mktg-Global - Revlon Consumer Products Corporation; pg. 521, pg. 1286
Williamson, Martine, Sr VP-Mktg-Global - Revlon, Inc.; pg. 521, pg. 1286
Williamson, Melissa, Mgr-Mktg-Creative Svcs Banana Republic - The Gap, Inc.; pg. 1770, pg. 218
Williamson, Michael, VP-Sls-USA - Sirona Dental Systems, Inc.; pg. 1429, pg. 1175
Williamson, Norby, Exec VP-Production - ESPN, Inc.; pg. 285, pg. 340
Williamson, Russ, Product Mgr - Hobbico, Inc.; pg. 956, pg. 562
Williamson, Sally, Sr Product Mgr-Immunology - Janssen Pharmaceutica Products, L.P.; pg. 1548, pg. 1125
Williamson, Tom, VP-Sls & Mktg - Sportif USA Inc.; pg. 33, pg. 1032
Williford, Michelle, Dir-Product & Portfolio Strategy-Immuno-Oncology - Bristol-Myers Squibb Company; pg. 1509, pg. 1206
Willinger, Steve, Dir-Product Adv & QA - Guitar Center, Inc.; pg. 1771, pg. 306
Willingham, Brennen, Sr Mgr-Funding & Liquidity Risk Mgmt - Fifth Third Bancorp; pg. 752, pg. 1413
Willingham, Joe, Dir-Sls - South Dakota Lottery; pg. 1006, pg. 1624
Willingham, Mitchell, Dir-Digital Mktg-Performance Platforms & Products - Dex Media Inc; pg. 1635, pg. 1680
Willins, Bruce, Sr Dir-Tech Solutions Grp - Motorola Solutions, Inc.; pg. 657, pg. 659
Williquett, Danielle, Mgr-Global Grp Mktg - Boston Scientific Corporation; pg. 1508, pg. 831
Willis, Angela, Exec Dir-Access Mktg-US Value & Access - Amgen Inc.; pg. 1493, pg. 291
Willis, Anissa, VP-Sls - Miller and Smith Homes, Inc.; pg. 97, pg. 1794
Willis, Chris, Mgr-Mktg Ops - Elekta; pg. 391, pg. 284
Willis, Diana, Mgr-Media Rels - Jamaica Tourist Board; pg. 996, pg. 443
Willis, Erik, Sr Product Mgr-Global - TSI Incorporated; pg. 1432, pg. 965
Willis, Gene, Brand Mktg Dir-North America - Netflix, Inc.; pg. 1269, pg. 141
Willis, Heath, Dir-Intl Mktg & Insights-Global Wal-Mart Acct Team - The Coca-Cola Company; pg. 240, pg. 493
Willis, Heath, Dir-Intl Mktg & Insights-Global Wal-Mart Acct Team - Coca-Cola Refreshments USA, Inc.; pg. 247, pg. 500
Willis, Kelland, Sr Mgr - SAP America, Inc.; pg. 466, pg. 1557
Willis, Liz, Brand Mgr-Global - Starbucks Corporation; pg. 897, pg. 1840
Willis, Lynn, VP-PR - Chico's FAS, Inc.; pg. 21, pg. 427
Willis, Paul, Reg Mgr-Healthcare-Strategic Sls-Kelly Healthcare Resources - Kelly Services, Inc.; pg. 424, pg. 911
Willis, Susan, Dir-Mktg & Corp Accounts - Thermo Fisher Scientific Inc.; pg. 1431, pg. 854
Willison, Brett, Mgr-Adv - OGE Energy Corp.; pg. 1948, pg. 1486
Willison, Lynee, Mgr-Customer Mktg - AutoTrader, Inc.; pg. 1230, pg. 490
Willman, Elisa, Sr Mgr-Mktg Comm, Corp Citizenship & Pub Affairs - Microsoft Corporation; pg. 435, pg. 1824
Willms, Delia, Mgr-Long Term Suite Sls - Rangers Baseball LLC; pg. 578, pg. 1659
Willner, Jeff, Coord-Mktg & Comm-Law & Corp Affairs - Starbucks Corporation; pg. 897, pg. 1840
Willott, Peter, Editor-New Media - The St. Augustine Record; pg. 1688, pg. 461
Wills, Jennifer, Sr Mgr-Shopper Mktg-Walmart Global Group - The Hershey Co.; pg. 1855, pg. 1538
Wills, Lee, Sr Dir-Global Brand & Mktg Comm - Varian Medical Systems, Inc.; pg. 1434, pg. 178
Wills, Royce, Dir-Customer Mktg - MillerCoors LLC; pg. 255, pg. 582
Wills-Quam, Susan, Sr Mgr-Sl & SP Mktg - Riverbed Technology, Inc.; pg. 1277, pg. 225
Willson, Frank, VP-Mktg - American Electric Power Company, Inc.; pg. 1934, pg. 1437
Willson, Jim, Dir-Immersive Products & VR - Samsung Electronics America, Inc.; pg. 669, pg. 1115
Willyerd, Karie, VP-Learning & Social Adoption - SuccessFactors, Inc.; pg. 477, pg. 228
Wilmarth, Steve, Reg Mgr-Sls Ops-Northeast & North American Agent Ops - Xerox Corporation; pg. 494, pg. 365
Wilmes, Kathy, Dir-Convention Sls - Anaheim/Orange County Visitor & Convention Bureau; pg. 988, pg. 42
Wilmot, Suzanne, Dir-Mktg - Novartis Pharmaceuticals Corp.; pg. 1575, pg. 1054
Wilner, Stephanie, Sr Mgr-Vendor Mktg - Ingram Micro Inc.; pg. 415, pg. 261
Wilson, Aaron, Sr VP-Mktg - Live Nation Entertainment, Inc.; pg. 558, pg. 47
Wilson, Amanda, Dir-Mktg - Qvidian; pg. 458, pg. 829
Wilson, Andi, Specialist-External Comm & Social Media Project - ITT Educational Services, Inc.; pg. 603, pg. 675
Wilson, Ashley, Program Mgr-Mktg - Anixter International Inc.; pg. 1313, pg. 614
Wilson, Ashley, Assoc Mgr-Production-Banana Republic Factory Store Accessories - The Gap, Inc.; pg. 1770, pg. 218
Wilson, Blake, Sr Mgr-Mktg - CenturyLink, Inc.; pg. 1870, pg. 746
Wilson, Brandon, Dir-Mktg - Intuit Inc.; pg. 769, pg. 158
Wilson, Brian, Dir-Product Dev - Felt Racing LLC; pg. 1707, pg. 110
Wilson, Brian, Sr Planner-Product, Product Plng - Nissan North America, Inc.; pg. 186, pg. 1633
Wilson, Bryan, Rep-Pharmaceutical Sls - PDI, Inc.; pg. 1580, pg. 1104
Wilson, Charles, Dir-Mktg & New Bus Dev - Dunkin' Brands Group, Inc.; pg. 1727, pg. 810
Wilson, Chris, Mgr-Mktg - Diamond Chain Company; pg. 1328, pg. 684
Wilson, Chris, Sr Dir-Marine Svcs Sls - DigitalGlobe; pg. 227, pg. 1785
Wilson, Christopher, Mgr-Content Mktg & Custom Publ - BNP Media; pg. 1622, pg. 910
Wilson, Cindy, Mgr-Mktg Comm Program - Synopsys, Inc.; pg. 480, pg. 162
Wilson, Courtney, Dir-Mktg - KB Home; pg. 90, pg. 134
Wilson, Courtney, Mgr-Digital Mktg - LaCrosse Footwear, Inc.; pg. 1811, pg. 1503
Wilson, Crystal, VP-Enterprise Social Media - Wells Fargo & Company; pg. 819, pg. 232
Wilson, Dan R., Mgr-Mktg-Internet of Things NA - Intel Corporation; pg. 645, pg. 266
Wilson, David, Sr Mgr-Mktg - Kemps LLC; pg. 867, pg. 961
Wilson, De Juan, Sr VP-Strategy & Creative Mktg-MTV2, MTVu & Logo - Viacom Inc.; pg. 316, pg. 1310
Wilson, Demitra L., Sr Dir-PR - Equifax Inc.; pg. 748, pg. 504
Wilson, Donna, Sr Dir-Diversity, Inclusion & Consumer-Global - Johnson & Johnson; pg. 1549, pg. 1091
Wilson, Doug, VP-Mktg-TireBuyer.com - AMERICAN TIRE DISTRIBUTORS HOLDINGS, INC.; pg. 199, pg. 1379
Wilson, Doug, VP & CMO-Star Media - Gannett Co., Inc.; pg. 1643, pg. 1790
Wilson, Emily H., Dir-Solutions Mktg - SuccessFactors, Inc.; pg. 477, pg. 228
Wilson, Eric, Dir-Mktg - DRG Texas LP; pg. 1637, pg. 1668
Wilson, Erin, Sr Mgr-Mktg Promos - Disney Interactive Media Group; pg. 1239, pg. 95
Wilson, Garrett, Sr Product Mgr-Mktg & Integrity - Marvin Windows & Doors; pg. 934, pg. 965
Wilson, Greta, VP-Brand Strategy & Social Media - Pitney Bowes Inc.; pg. 454, pg. 376
Wilson, Heather, Sr Mgr-Brand Mktg - Landry's, Inc.; pg. 1735, pg. 1709
Wilson, Heather E., Mgr-Coode & Channel Mktg - General Electric Company; pg. 1297, pg. 347
Wilson, Jaime, Sr Dir-Web & Mobile Product Dev - Overstock.com, Inc.; pg. 1273, pg. 1760
Wilson, Jeff, Reg Mgr-Sls-Western - Broadcast Electronics, Inc.; pg. 627, pg. 653
Wilson, Jeff, VP-Innovation & Head-Creative Platform - Hallmark Cards, Inc.; pg. 1646, pg. 983
Wilson, Jennifer, Mgr-Solutions Mktg - Interactive Intelligence, Inc.; pg. 417, pg. 687
Wilson, Jennifer, Dir-Mdsg-Paint - Lowe's Companies, Inc.; pg. 1053, pg. 1383
Wilson, Jennifer, Dir-Sls - National Enzyme Company; pg. 882, pg. 978
Wilson, Jill, Asst Mgr-Mktg - Toll Brothers, Inc.; pg. 115, pg. 1541
Wilson, Joffrey, Mgr-Mktg-Global Corp Strategy - General Mills, Inc.; pg. 828, pg. 933
Wilson, John, Mgr-Global Mktg-Emerging Brands - AstraZeneca Pharmaceuticals LP; pg. 1497, pg. 389
Wilson, John, Sr Mgr-Sls Ops - Big Heart Pet Brands; pg. 1474, pg. 213
Wilson, John, Sr VP-Mktg & Indus Affairs - Dairy Farmers of America, Inc.; pg. 851, pg. 982
Wilson, John, Sr Mgr-Product Mktg - Reebok International Ltd.; pg. 1817, pg. 811
Wilson, Josh, Sr Mgr-Franchise Analytics-Global - Hilton Worldwide, Inc.; pg. 1094, pg. 1791
Wilson, Kacey L., Sr Product Mgr-Customer Loyalty - Cardinal Health, Inc.; pg. 1512, pg. 1448
Wilson, Kari, Sr Mgr-Accessories - Google Inc.; pg. 1249, pg. 153
Wilson, Katie, Dir-Mktg & Dev - Chattanooga Symphony & Opera Association; pg. 538, pg. 1628
Wilson, Katie, Sr Specialist-Integrated Mktg Comm - J.C. Penney Company, Inc.; pg. 1774, pg. 1732
Wilson, Katie Gaon, Dir-Mktg-The Reading Room - The Reader's Digest Association, Inc.; pg. 1679, pg. 1322
Wilson, Keith, Brand Mgr-Expedition - Ford Motor Company; pg. 172, pg. 876
Wilson, Kevin, Reg Mgr-Mktg - Home Properties Inc.; pg. 1096, pg. 1336
Wilson, Kinsey, Exec VP-Product & Tech & Editor-Innovation & Strategy - The New York Times Company; pg. 1668, pg. 1270
Wilson, Krisztina, Product Mgr - BrassCraft Manufacturing Company; pg. 1043, pg. 902
Wilson, Kyona M., Sr Mgr-Customer Mktg - American Express Company; pg. 712, pg. 1190
Wilson, Kyra, Sr Mgr-Media - Cracker Barrel Old Country Store, Inc.; pg. 1723, pg. 1639
Wilson, Laura, Dir-Mktg, Online Media & Adv Svcs - SAS Institute (Canada), Inc.; pg. 466, pg. 1943
Wilson, Laura, Reg Dir-Sls - Townsquare Media, Inc.; pg. 313, pg. 350
Wilson, Liz, Dir-Apparel Specialty Sls - Brooks Sports Inc.; pg. 1805, pg. 1818
Wilson, Mark, Sr Dir-People & Org Dev - Taco Bell Corp.; pg. 1752, pg. 117
Wilson, Martin, Mgr-Mktg - Hanesbrands Inc.; pg. 26, pg. 1394
Wilson, Mary, Dir-Channel Mktg-North America - Dell Inc.; pg. 383, pg. 1737
Wilson, Matt, Buyer-Natl Media - Fox Broadcasting Company; pg. 287, pg. 130
Wilson, Michael, VP-Digital Media - The Newark Advocate; pg. 1669, pg. 1467
Wilson, Michelle D., Chief Revenue & Mktg Officer - World Wrestling Entertainment, Inc.; pg. 595, pg. 380
Wilson, Monte, VP & Head-Americas Digital Media Field Ops - Adobe Systems Incorporated; pg. 342, pg. 235
Wilson, Paul, Sr VP-Olympic Sls - NBC Universal, Inc.; pg. 300, pg. 1266
Wilson, Phil, VP-Intl Digital Mktg - American Express Company; pg. 712, pg. 1190
Wilson, Quentin, Dir-Mktg - Capriotti's Sandwich Shop Inc; pg. 1720, pg. 1023
Wilson, Rachel, Dir-Mktg Ops - Pet Supplies Plus; pg. 1781, pg. 897
Wilson, Ramon, Interim Pres - Relativity Media, LLC; pg. 306, pg. 47
Wilson, Rebecca, Brand Mgr - Starbucks Corporation; pg. 897, pg. 1840
Wilson, Reid, Mgr-Mktg-Motorcycles - Polaris Industries Inc.; pg. 1709, pg. 928
Wilson, Risa, Dir-Creative Svcs - Acuity Brands, Inc.; pg. 1294, pg. 487
Wilson, Rob, Dir-Creative Solutions - BBC Worldwide America Inc.; pg. 271, pg. 1201
Wilson, Rudy, VP-Brand Mktg & Adv - AT&T Inc.; pg. 1867, pg. 1674
Wilson, Rudy, VP-Mktg-Doritos, Cheetos, SunChips & Fritos - Frito-Lay North America, Inc.; pg. 1853, pg. 1730
Wilson, Ryan, Dir-Product Mktg - Delta Faucet Company; pg. 78, pg. 684
Wilson, Ryan, Mgr-Fin-Developer Products Div-Software &

First page reference indicates Business Class Edition
Second page reference indicates Geographic Edition

Svcs Grp - Intel Corporation; *pg.* 645, *pg.* 266
Wilson, Sally, Dir-Mktg - Zimmer Biomet Holdings, Inc.; *pg.* 1611, *pg.* 699
Wilson, Scott, Sr Mgr-Ops Integration - Captain D's, LLC; *pg.* 1720, *pg.* 1649
Wilson, Scott, VP-ECommerce & Mdsg - United Airlines, Inc.; *pg.* 1927, *pg.* 593
Wilson, Scott, VP-ECommerce & Mdsg - United Continental Holdings, Inc.; *pg.* 1927, *pg.* 593
Wilson, Shannon, Mgr-Customer Channel Mktg - Honeywell International Inc.; *pg.* 407, *pg.* 1088
Wilson, Shauna, Mgr-Media & Film Production - Henry Ford Museum and Greenfield Village; *pg.* 552, *pg.* 878
Wilson, Shawn, Mgr-PR-Global - DST Systems, Inc.; *pg.* 388, *pg.* 982
Wilson, Stan, Sr VP & Head-EMEA Product - First Data Corporation; *pg.* 754, *pg.* 505
Wilson, Stephanie, Mgr-Mktg - Anthem, Inc.; *pg.* 1192, *pg.* 683
Wilson, Steve, Product Mgr - K-Tel International, Inc.; *pg.* 1052, *pg.* 953
Wilson, Terry, Dir-Sls & Mktg - Textile Rubber & Chemical Company; *pg.* 1890, *pg.* 530
Wilson, Thomas, VP-Mktg - Monsanto Company; *pg.* 1173, *pg.* 999
Wilson, Thomas, Mgr-Global Social, Brand & Content Mktg - Uber USA, LLC; *pg.* 1286, *pg.* 229
Wilson, Tiffany, Mgr-Brand PR-Hampton Hotels & Hilton Garden Inn - Hilton Worldwide, Inc.; *pg.* 1094, *pg.* 1791
Wilson, Tom, Head-Display Adv - Amazon.com, Inc.; *pg.* 1226, *pg.* 1831
Wilson, Tonia, Sr Mgr-Enterprise Messaging - The Western Union Company; *pg.* 822, *pg.* 327
Wilson, Valerie, Dir-Channel Mktg - Nationwide Mutual Insurance Company; *pg.* 1210, *pg.* 1442
Wilson, Wendy, VP-Program & Product Mgmt - Time Warner Cable Inc.; *pg.* 312, *pg.* 1301
Wilt, Mike, Mgr-Mobile Mktg - Rite Aid Corporation; *pg.* 1590, *pg.* 1519
Wilt, Robert, Pres-Global Primary Products & Exec VP - Alcoa Inc.; *pg.* 65, *pg.* 1188
Wilts, Ingo, Dir-Creative-Menswear - Tommy Hilfiger USA; *pg.* 48, *pg.* 1302
Wiltse, Monte, Sr VP-Sls & Mktg - Fujirebio Diagnostics Inc.; *pg.* 1531, *pg.* 1550
Wiltshire, Kimberly, VP-Ad Sls & Integrated Mktg - FUSE Networks LLC; *pg.* 288, *pg.* 1233
Wimsatt, John, VP-Mktg - Verizon Communications Inc.; *pg.* 1875, *pg.* 1309
Winans, Maria, VP-Industry Cloud Solutions & Social Bus Mktg - IBM; *pg.* 410, *pg.* 1449
Winborn, April, Product Mgr-Private Brand & Mgr-Global Sourcing - Michaels Stores, Inc.; *pg.* 1127, *pg.* 1722
Winburn, Bryn, Mgr-Pub & Media Rels - Family Dollar Stores, Inc.; *pg.* 1768, *pg.* 1382
Wincek, Christopher, Brand Mgr-Dodge - FCA US LLC; *pg.* 170, *pg.* 868
Winckler, Bradley, Mgr-Adv Ops - Tribune Media Company; *pg.* 1696, *pg.* 592
Wincko, Ken, Sr VP-Mktg - PR Newswire Association LLC; *pg.* 1678, *pg.* 1283
Winczewski, Chris, VP-Product Mktg - X-Rite, Incorporated; *pg.* 1437, *pg.* 891
Windett, Corey, Sr Mgr-Corp Comm & Sls - AstraZeneca Pharmaceuticals LP; *pg.* 1497, *pg.* 389
Windham, Chan, Dir-Commodity Sls - House of Raeford Farms, Inc.; *pg.* 864, *pg.* 1386
Windom, Kathy, Dir-Social Svcs - Intermountain Hospital; *pg.* 1546, *pg.* 547
Windram, Elizabeth, Mgr-Global Mktg-Content, Digital & CRM-Barefoot Wine & Bubbly - E&J Gallo Winery; *pg.* 1962, *pg.* 149
Windsor, Andrea, Product Mgr-Spinbrush & Tooth Tunes - Church & Dwight Co., Inc.; *pg.* 1153, *pg.* 1063
Windsor, Andrew, VP-Sls-Americas - Watts Water Technologies, Inc.; *pg.* 1078, *pg.* 837
Windsor, Angela, Brand Mgr - Mary Brown's, Inc.; *pg.* 1737, *pg.* 1924
Windsor, Bruce, VP-Sls & Dir-Natl Accounts - Hillyard, Inc.; *pg.* 331, *pg.* 990
Windsor, Tyler, Sr Dir-Supply Chain-North America - SI Group, Inc.; *pg.* 1181, *pg.* 1341
Windsperger, Greg, VP-Sls-Ellsworth & Cokato Factories & Mgr-Sls - Federal Foam Technologies Inc.; *pg.* 692, *pg.* 1884
Wine, Sean, Reg Mgr-Sls - Clean Energy Fuels Corp.; *pg.* 974, *pg.* 165
Wineberg, Matt, Dir-Partner Mktg - Brocade Communications Systems, Inc.; *pg.* 365, *pg.* 239
Winebrenner, Clinton, Head-Technical-Product Certifications - Cisco Systems, Inc.; *pg.* 372, *pg.* 240
Winer, John, Mgr-Digital Mktg - Hearts on Fire Company; *pg.* 6, *pg.* 796
Winet, Shari, VP-PR - Bridgepoint Education, Inc.; *pg.* 598, *pg.* 201
Winfrey, Sarah, Coord-Cause-Related Mktg - City of Hope National Medical Center; *pg.* 1516, *pg.* 77
Wing, Deborah, Dir-Mktg - Cigna Corporation; *pg.* 1197, *pg.* 338
Wing, Melanie, VP-Strategic Mktg - Equifax Inc.; *pg.* 748, *pg.* 504
Wing-Larson, Julia, Sr Mgr-Mktg - General Mills, Inc.; *pg.* 828, *pg.* 933
Wingate, Jennifer, Mgr-Mktg - Comcast Corporation; *pg.* 276, *pg.* 1560
Winger, Brock, Brand Mgr-Ford F-Series Trucks Super Duty - Ford Motor Company; *pg.* 172, *pg.* 876
Winger, Patti, Mgr-Mktg Comm - Ecolab Inc.; *pg.* 329, *pg.* 960
Wingert, Meaghan, Sr Mgr-Mktg Activation - Reebok International Ltd.; *pg.* 1817, *pg.* 811
Winglar, Samantha, Asst Product Mgr-Sebago Footwear - Wolverine World Wide, Inc.; *pg.* 1822, *pg.* 905
Wingo, Erica, Sr Dir-Mdsg - Bernhardt Design; *pg.* 918, *pg.* 1381
Winiarski, Tom, Exec VP-Adv Sls Plng & Monetization - NBC Universal, Inc.; *pg.* 300, *pg.* 1266
Winick, Andrew, Dir-Indus Mktg Fin Svcs - SAP America, Inc.; *pg.* 466, *pg* 1557
Wink, Jon, Dir-Creative - Abbott Nutrition; *pg.* 1485, *pg.* 1437
Winkel, Kevin, Sr Mgr-Mktg - Zumiez Inc.; *pg.* 16, *pg.* 1822
Winkelman, Taryn, VP-Consumer Mktg-Bravo TV - Bravo Media LLC; *pg.* 271, *pg.* 1206
Winkelmann, Adam, VP-EMEA Sls & Intl Ops - Emulex Corporation; *pg.* 392, *pg.* 70
Winking, Kim, Mgr-Mktg Svcs - Broadcast Electronics, Inc.; *pg.* 627, *pg.* 653
Winkler, Hartmut, Mgr-Sls - Reliable Automatic Sprinkler Co., Inc.; *pg.* 1137, *pg.* 1158
Winkler, Josh, VP-Partner Mktg Media Sls-Global - Orbitz Worldwide, Inc.; *pg.* 1918, *pg.* 586
Winkler, Julie M., Sr Mng Dir-Res & Product Dev - CME Group Inc.; *pg.* 738, *pg.* 571
Winkler, Lisa, Product Mgr-Global - E.I. du Pont de Nemours & Company; *pg.* 1159, *pg.* 390
Winkler, Lori, Mgr-Mktg Comm - NovAtel Inc.; *pg.* 1424, *pg.* 1904
Winkler, Shannon, Product Mgr - ITT Corporation; *pg.* 1351, *pg.* 1354
Winkler, Sonja, Sr Dir-Ops & Mgr-Orchestra - Nashville Symphony Association; *pg.* 565, *pg.* 1653
Winkles, Ken, Mgr-Reg Platform Investment Sls - Comerica Incorporated; *pg.* 740, *pg.* 1677
Winley, Jared, Sr Mgr-Pub & Media Rels - New York Jets Football Club, Inc.; *pg.* 570, *pg.* 1067
Winn, Kate, Sr VP-Consumer Products - The History Channel; *pg.* 290, *pg.* 1240
Winn, Peter, Dir-Plng, Dev & Consumer Mktg - Bonnier Corporation; *pg.* 1622, *pg.* 480
Winn, Wilson, Dir-Creative - Tyson Foods, Inc.; *pg.* 902, *pg.* 35
Winnecke, Lloyd, Sr VP & Dir-Mktg - Fifth Third Bank, Indiana (Southern); *pg.* 753, *pg.* 678
Winokur, Mara, Sr VP-Digital Media & Bus Dev - Starz Entertainment, LLC; *pg.* 310, *pg.* 327
Winschel, Daniel, Asst Mgr-Social Media Mktg - Giant Eagle, Inc.; *pg.* 1020, *pg.* 1575
Winscott, Alan, Mgr-Mktg - Intel Corporation; *pg.* 645, *pg.* 266
Winslow, Paul, VP & Gen Mgr-Mdsg - Toys "R" Us, Inc.; *pg.* 968, *pg.* 1130
Winston, Kevin, Sr Dir-Player Affairs - Atlanta Falcons Football Club, LLC; *pg.* 530, *pg.* 532
Winte, Jill, Dir-PR - Nestle Purina PetCare Company; *pg.* 1479, *pg.* 1000
Winter Stafford, Jessica, VP-Consumer Mktg - AutoTrader, Inc.; *pg.* 1230, *pg.* 490
Winter, Amy, Sr Mgr-Mktg Comm - AT&T Mobility LLC; *pg.* 619, *pg.* 488
Winter, Darryl, Dir-East Coast Sls Discovery Digital Networks - Discovery Communications, Inc.; *pg.* 282, *pg.* 777
Winter, Eric, Mgr-Retail Mktg-Trade Channel Mktg - Anheuser-Busch Companies, LLC; *pg.* 237, *pg.* 991
Winter, George, Product Mgr-Technical - Symantec Corporation; *pg.* 478, *pg.* 161
Winter, Jeff, Dir-Mktg & Residential Repaint - Sherwin Williams; *pg.* 1448, *pg.* 1436
Winter, Jeffrey, Sr VP-Sls & Mktg - IPC The Hospitalist Company, Inc.; *pg.* 1547, *pg.* 167
Winter, Jeremy, Product Mgr - Microsoft Corporation; *pg.* 435, *pg.* 1824
Winter, Kurt, VP-Reg Mktg & Program Mgmt - The Allstate Corporation; *pg.* 1189, *pg.* 639
Winter, Marlan, Mgr-Product & Bus-Tools Ecosystem - Freescale Semiconductor, Inc.; *pg.* 398, *pg.* 1662
Winter, Paige, Sr Acct Mgr-Digital Adv - Google Inc.; *pg.* 1249, *pg.* 153
Winter, Seth, Exec VP-Sls & Sls Mktg - NBC Universal, Inc.; *pg.* 300, *pg.* 1266
Winter, Valerie, Dir-Mktg & Bus Comm-Global - FMC Corporation; *pg.* 1163, *pg.* 1564
Winters, Barbara, Sr Strategist-Mktg - Intel Corporation; *pg.* 645, *pg.* 266
Winters, Christine, Mgr-Comm & Media Rels-Healthcare - The Standard Register Company; *pg.* 473, *pg.* 1446
Winters, Derek, VP-Sls - Willert Home Products, Inc.; *pg.* 1140, *pg.* 1005
Winters, Erin, VP-Mktg Strategy - Acxiom Corporation; *pg.* 342, *pg.* 33
Winters, Heather, Community Mgr-Specialty Restaurant Grp & Specialist-Social Media - Darden Restaurants, Inc.; *pg.* 1724, *pg.* 453
Winters, Keli, Dir-Tech Products - Evan-Moor Corporation; *pg.* 1639, *pg.* 151
Winters, Michelle, Mgr-Product Mktg-Chromecast - Google Inc.; *pg.* 1249, *pg.* 153
Winters, Michelle, Dir-Mktg - Louisville Orchestra, Inc.; *pg.* 559, *pg.* 736
Winterstein, Florian, Chief Strategy Officer-Vorstand - BravoSolution US; *pg.* 1233, *pg.* 1549
Wintriss, Marie, Sr Mgr-Mktg Ops - Overstock.com, Inc.; *pg.* 1273, *pg.* 1760
Wion, Rick, Sr Dir-Consumer Engagement - Kellogg Company; *pg.* 831, *pg.* 870
Wirkus, Karen, Sls Mgr - Multimedia Games Inc.; *pg.* 442, *pg.* 1664
Wirsbinski, Carol, Chief Sls Officer - Enventis; *pg.* 637, *pg.* 927
Wirth, Kim, Sr Mgr-Comm-P&C Papers & Sustainability - International Paper Company; *pg.* 1460, *pg.* 1644
Wirth, Kurt, Mgr-Social Media - GEICO Corporation; *pg.* 1200, *pg.* 399
Wisco, Ivy, Dir-Mktg-Multicultural & Banking Solutions - MoneyGram International, Inc.; *pg.* 783, *pg.* 1684
Wisdom, Dave, VP-Sls-Intl - Vital Pharmaceuticals, Inc.; *pg.* 1607, *pg.* 479
Wise, Abby, Dir-Mktg - Diageo North America Inc.; *pg.* 248, *pg.* 1223
Wise, Angela, VP-Mktg - Cosmopolitan; *pg.* 1630, *pg.* 1218
Wise, Kamal, Brand Mgr-Sharpie-Global - Newell Rubbermaid Inc.; *pg.* 1128, *pg.* 515
Wise, Melissa, Mgr-Adv - White's Electronics; *pg.* 688, *pg.* 1509
Wise, Penny H., Dir-3M Brand & Core Mktg-Global - 3M Company; *pg.* 1142, *pg.* 956
Wise, Peter, VP-Mktg - Marcos Pizza Inc.; *pg.* 1737, *pg.* 1476
Wise, Sarah, Mgr-Mktg Comm-Honeywell Process Solutions - Honeywell Aerospace Electronic Systems; *pg.* 228, *pg.* 17
Wise, Ted, VP & Gen Mgr-Mktg & Bus Dev - Premera Blue Cross; *pg.* 1214, *pg.* 1823
Wise, Vanessa, Sr Dir-New Product Introductions & Rx Lens Procurement - Luxottica Retail; *pg.* 8, *pg.* 1460
Wise, Wes, Dir-Sls & Mktg - O'Reilly Automotive, Inc.; *pg.* 214, *pg.* 1006
Wiseberg, Jason I., Exec VP-Sls & B2B Mktg - Value Line, Inc.; *pg.* 1699, *pg.* 1308
Wisecup, Elif, Dir-Mktg - Independent Insurance Agents & Brokers of America, Inc.; *pg.* 144, *pg.* 1770
Wiseley, Laura, Coord-Mktg - Villanova University; *pg.* 610, *pg.* 1589
Wiseman, Beth, Sr Mgr-HR - Thermal Industries, Inc.; *pg.* 115, *pg.* 1555
Wiseman, Christina, Product Mgr-Web Svcs & Mobile - Thomson Reuters Tax & Accounting; *pg.* 1693, *pg.* 1299
Wiseman, Jennifer Jo, VP-Consumer, Product Insights & Dev - E&J Gallo Winery; *pg.* 1962, *pg.* 149
Wiseman, Lindsay, Sr Specialist-Social Media - Darden

Restaurants, Inc.; *pg.* 1724, *pg.* 453
Wiser, Brian, Pres-Sls-North America - Bosch Security Systems, Inc.; *pg.* 626, *pg.* 1158
Wisher, Rick, Sr Product Mgr-Primetime - Adobe Systems Incorporated; *pg.* 342, *pg.* 235
Wishman, Lisa, Asst VP-Mktg - Merchants Group, Inc.; *pg.* 1208, *pg.* 1149
Wisler, Cristine, Specialist-Media Buying Support - The Tire Rack Inc.; *pg.* 1890, *pg.* 697
Wisler, Liz, VP-Production - Eileen Fisher, Inc.; *pg.* 24, *pg.* 1168
Wismer, Meghan, Sr Mgr-MDU Sls & Mktg - Comcast Cable Communications, Inc.; *pg.* 276, *pg.* 1560
Wismer, Rich, Mgr-Sls - Newage Testing Instruments, Inc.; *pg.* 1058, *pg.* 1532
Wisner, Candyce, Sr Mgr-Customer Insights & Competitive Intelligence - Ecolab Inc.; *pg.* 329, *pg.* 960
Wisner, Sabrina, Mgr-Mktg - Accenture; *pg.* 1392, *pg.* 1186
Wisnew, Kevin, Specialist-Digital Mktg - Life Time Fitness, Inc.; *pg.* 1556, *pg.* 920
Wisnewski, Nancy, Exec VP-Product Dev & Customer Svc - Heska Corporation; *pg.* 1542, *pg.* 335
Wisniakowski, Rebecca, Sr Mgr-Local Sls-West Coast - Hulu LLC; *pg.* 1257, *pg.* 274
Wisnoski, Kenneth P., Pres-Global Primary Products - Alcoa Inc.; *pg.* 65, *pg.* 1188
Wisot, Jeff, VP-Enterprise Digital Mktg - Guitar Center, Inc.; *pg.* 1771, *pg.* 306
Wissehr, Kate, Product Mgr-Tech - Enterprise Holdings, Inc.; *pg.* 1906, *pg.* 996
Witbeck, James Kai, Mgr-Experiential Mktg - LEGO Systems, Inc.; *pg.* 961, *pg.* 346
Withers, Keller, VP & Mgr-Sls - Turner Broadcasting System, Inc.; *pg.* 314, *pg.* 521
Withers, Travis, Brand Mgr-Bertolli Frozen Meals - ConAgra Foods, Inc.; *pg.* 826, *pg.* 1014
Witherspoon, Jennifer, Sr Buyer-Natl Media - CarMax, Inc.; *pg.* 167, *pg.* 1800
Withington, Matthew, Brand Mgr - Lindt & Sprungli (USA) Inc.; *pg.* 1857, *pg.* 1039
Withoft, Leslie, Dir-Sponsorships & Event Mktg - Farmers Group, Inc.; *pg.* 1199, *pg.* 130
Withrow, Wayne M., Exec VP-SEI Advisor Network - SEI Investments Company; *pg.* 802, *pg.* 1558
Witkemper, Todd, Dir-Consumer PR - eBay Inc.; *pg.* 1240, *pg.* 243
Witkop, Lois, Sr VP-Mktg Comm - American Diabetes Association; *pg.* 127, *pg.* 1770
Witman, David, Exec VP & Gen Mgr-Mdse-Men's Apparel - Nordstrom, Inc.; *pg.* 1779, *pg.* 1837
Witt, Debbie, Mgr-Adv & PR - Aladdin Temp-Rite, LLC; *pg.* 1013, *pg.* 1635
Witt, Larry, Sr VP-Sls & Mktg-OXO - Helen of Troy L.P.; *pg.* 511, *pg.* 1692
Witt, Larry, Sr VP-Sls & Mktg - OXO; *pg.* 1058, *pg.* 1275
Witt, Ronald L., VP & Gen Mgr-Sls & Mktg-Intl - Westinghouse Air Brake Technologies Corporation; *pg.* 1388, *pg.* 1595
Witt, Suzanne, Mgr-Mktg Dev - The Chubb Corporation; *pg.* 1196, *pg.* 1128
Witta, Andrea, Mgr-Mktg & Comm - Woodruff Arts Center; *pg.* 595, *pg.* 524
Witte, Michele, Mgr-Brand Mgmt & Mktg Design Svcs - COUNTRY Financial; *pg.* 1198, *pg.* 557
Wittel, Mark L., VP-Sls-Natl - The Medical Protective Company; *pg.* 1208, *pg.* 680
Witten, Matthew, Analyst-Mktg-Mainstream Coffee - The J.M. Smucker Company; *pg.* 865, *pg.* 1468
Witten, Steve B., Sr Dir - Marcus & Millichap Real Estate Investment Company; *pg.* 1102, *pg.* 56
Wittenberg, Christa, Dir-Retail Mktg - Nintendo of America, Inc.; *pg.* 965, *pg.* 1829
Wittenberger, Megan, Mgr-PR - Carbonite, Inc.; *pg.* 368, *pg.* 792
Wittliff, Sarah, Coord-Direct Mktg Strategy & Plng - Kohl's Corporation; *pg.* 1775, *pg.* 1870
Wittman, Laura, Dir-Global Mktg Capability - GlaxoSmithKline; *pg.* 1536, *pg.* 1389
Wittman, Laura, Dir-Global Mktg Capability - GlaxoSmithKline Consumer Healthcare; *pg.* 510, *pg.* 1554
Wittmann, Michael, Sr Dir-Mktg - Intel Corporation; *pg.* 645, *pg.* 266
Wittmeier, Jordan, Dir-Sls-Intl - Perseon Corporation; *pg.* 1581, *pg.* 1760
Witty, Cindy, Mng Dir-Subscription Mktg - The New York Times Company; *pg.* 1668, *pg.* 1270
Witzel, Kurt, Sr Mgr-Mktg Comm - Anheuser-Busch Companies, LLC; *pg.* 237, *pg.* 991
Witzig, Dave, Sr Dir-ECommerce Mktg - The Sportsman's Guide, Inc.; *pg.* 1846, *pg.* 965
Wlazlowski, Tiffany, Sr Dir-Comm & Pub Affairs - NATSO, Inc.; *pg.* 151, *pg.* 1771
Wo, Shiming, Dir-Strategic Mktg - Honeywell International Inc.; *pg.* 407, *pg.* 1088
Wobig, John, Sr Mgr-Technical Sls - Snyder Industries, Inc.; *pg.* 1377, *pg.* 1012
Wodarek, John, Mgr-Entertainment & Mktg - Pittsburgh Steelers Sports Inc.; *pg.* 577, *pg.* 1578
Wodarz, Sage, Assoc Dir-Content & Social Mktg - The Kraft Heinz Company; *pg.* 871, *pg.* 641
Woerner, Chris, Sr VP-Product Mgmt - Onvia, Inc.; *pg.* 1272, *pg.* 1838
Woerner, John Robert, Chief Strategy Officer & Pres-Insurance-Annuities - Ameriprise Financial, Inc.; *pg.* 715, *pg.* 930
Woerner, Sangita, VP-Mktg - Alaska Airlines, Inc.; *pg.* 1897, *pg.* 1830
Woeste, Ken, VP-Sls & Ops Plng - Boulder Brands, Inc.; *pg.* 1016, *pg.* 310
Woestenenk, Rik, Mgr-Sls & Mktg-Benelux - Whirlpool Corporation; *pg.* 62, *pg.* 872
Wofford, Becky, Sr Mgr-Mktg-Expedia Affiliate Network-Global - Expedia, Inc.; *pg.* 1244, *pg.* 1814
Wofford, Heather, Assoc Mgr-Customer Mktg - Revlon Consumer Products Corporation; *pg.* 521, *pg.* 1286
Wofford, Heather, Assoc Mgr-Customer Mktg - Revlon, Inc.; *pg.* 521, *pg.* 1286
Woginrich, Mike, Sr Dir-HR Retail - Sephora USA Inc; *pg.* 522, *pg.* 227
Wohl, Matthew, Sr VP-Mktg-Cheese & Dairy - The Kraft Heinz Company; *pg.* 871, *pg.* 641
Wohle, Crystal, Brand Mgr - Duraflame, Inc.; *pg.* 1123, *pg.* 280
Wohlrob, Ken, Sr Mgr-Product - WebMD Health Corporation; *pg.* 1288, *pg.* 1313
Wohltman, Lucy, VP-Sls - Zillow Group, Inc.; *pg.* 1292, *pg.* 1843
Wohlwend, Erica, Dir-Mktg - Redken Laboratories LLC; *pg.* 520, *pg.* 1285
Wojanis, Jessica, Sr Specialist-Mktg - Aon Risk Services Inc.; *pg.* 1193, *pg.* 564
Wojciechowski, David, VP-Sls - EMCORE Corporation; *pg.* 636, *pg.* 39
Wojciechowski, Orin, Dir-Mktg - MORNINGSTAR, INC.; *pg.* 784, *pg.* 583
Wojciehowski, Jim, Dir-Mktg & Product Mgmt-Americas - Hexcel Corporation; *pg.* 1884, *pg.* 375
Wojick, John, VP-Sls-Comml Airplanes - The Boeing Company; *pg.* 225, *pg.* 567
Wokosin, Michael, VP-Digital Mktg - Redbox Automated Retail, LLC; *pg.* 306, *pg.* 649
Wokoun, Linda, VP-Sls Strategy & Channel Dev - Bright House Networks LLC; *pg.* 272, *pg.* 461
Wolak, Jim, Mng Dir-Comm, Media & Tech - Accenture; *pg.* 1392, *pg.* 1186
Woland, Aaron T., Engr-Principal Technical Mktg - Cisco Systems, Inc.; *pg.* 372, *pg.* 240
Wolbert, Amy, Sr VP-Mktg - Kindel Furniture Company; *pg.* 931, *pg.* 887
Wolchock, Ilene, Dir-Voice & Data Product Mgmt - Cox Communications, Inc.; *pg.* 279, *pg.* 501
Wolcott, Bruce, VP-Mktg - Seneca Foods Corporation; *pg.* 895, *pg.* 1177
Wolcott, Pat, Planner-Social Media - Hewlett-Packard Company; *pg.* 404, *pg.* 175
Wolcott, Theresa, Corp VP-PR - New York Life Insurance Company; *pg.* 1211, *pg.* 1268
Wold, Aaron, Specialist-Sls Ops & Comm - Comcast Cable Communications, Inc.; *pg.* 276, *pg.* 1560
Wold, Jeremy, Sr Mgr-Interactive Mktg - CHG Healthcare Services, Inc.; *pg.* 1515, *pg.* 1756
Woldar, Daniel, Assoc Bus Dir-Media Svcs - Conde Nast Publications, Inc.; *pg.* 1629, *pg.* 1217
Woldt, Andre, Brand Mgr-Dos Equis - Heineken USA Inc.; *pg.* 252, *pg.* 1352
Woldum, Kari, VP-Mdsg - Design Within Reach, Inc.; *pg.* 923, *pg.* 216
Wolf, Ashley, Coord-Mktg Comm-DuPont Pioneer - Dupont Pioneer; *pg.* 1795, *pg.* 708
Wolf, Audra, Dir-Adv & PR - MetroPCS, Inc.; *pg.* 1872, *pg.* 1683
Wolf, Ben, Sr VP-Sls-Optical Channel - Marcolin USA Inc.; *pg.* 1421, *pg.* 23
Wolf, Brad, Sr Dir-Brand Innovation-LA Studio - Sonos, Inc.; *pg.* 675, *pg.* 263
Wolf, Carl, VP-Aviation Sls & Mktg - Garmin International, Inc.; *pg.* 1414, *pg.* 717
Wolf, Cindie, Specialist-Media - E&J Gallo Winery; *pg.* 1962, *pg.* 149
Wolf, David, VP-Global Product & Bus Dev - American Express Company; *pg.* 712, *pg.* 1190
Wolf, Hannah, Sr Mgr-Digital Ops - Ubisoft Inc.; *pg.* 589, *pg.* 229
Wolf, Jay D., First VP-Mktg & Customer Rels - DCB Financial Corp.; *pg.* 743, *pg.* 1457
Wolf, Jeffrey, Dir-Mktg-Fragrance & Personal Care - Coty, Inc.; *pg.* 506, *pg.* 1219
Wolf, John, VP-Brand PR-Global - Marriott International, Inc.; *pg.* 1102, *pg.* 764
Wolf, Karen, Mgr-Digital Mktg - American Express Company; *pg.* 712, *pg.* 1190
Wolf, Kathleen, Sr Mgr-Whirlpool Corp Brand Reputation & Global Interactive Comm - Whirlpool Corporation; *pg.* 62, *pg.* 872
Wolf, Rhonda J., VP-Mdsg - Haverty Furniture Companies, Inc.; *pg.* 926, *pg.* 509
Wolf, Robin, Sr Mgr-Cisco Sls Enablement - NetApp, Inc.; *pg.* 444, *pg.* 287
Wolf, Sarah, Dir-Special Sls - The Perseus Books Group; *pg.* 1676, *pg.* 1278
Wolf, Susie E., Sr Dir-Global Employee Comm & Exec Engagement - Eli Lilly and Company; *pg.* 1527, *pg.* 684
Wolfe, Amanda, Sr Dir-Digital - Meredith Corporation; *pg.* 1663, *pg.* 705
Wolfe, Dan, Exec VP-Creative Ops-Worldwide - NBC Universal, Inc.; *pg.* 300, *pg.* 1266
Wolfe, Dawn, Sr Mgr-Digital Mktg - Autodesk Inc.; *pg.* 356, *pg.* 257
Wolfe, Jenny, VP & Mgr-Adv & Media - Sun Trust Bank, Atlanta; *pg.* 806, *pg.* 520
Wolfe, Jenny, Mgr-Adv - SunTrust Banks, Inc.; *pg.* 807, *pg.* 520
Wolfe, Marc, VP-Mktg - Barracuda Networks, Inc.; *pg.* 360, *pg.* 58
Wolfe, Margie, Dir-Mktg Comm - Honeywell International Inc.; *pg.* 407, *pg.* 1088
Wolfe, Michael, VP-Consumer Mktg - Spike TV; *pg.* 310, *pg.* 1295
Wolfe, Mike, Sr Dir-Brand Mktg - Hotels.com, L.P.; *pg.* 1257, *pg.* 1682
Wolfe, Neera, Sr Mgr-Mktg-Quicken - Intuit Inc.; *pg.* 769, *pg.* 158
Wolfe, Royce, VP-Experiential Mktg & Sponsorship Strategy - Wells Fargo & Company; *pg.* 819, *pg.* 232
Wolfe, Sam, Mgr-Client Event-Event Mktg - Yahoo! Inc.; *pg.* 1289, *pg.* 289
Wolfe, Scott, Sr VP-Mdsg - Citizen Watch Co. of America, Inc.; *pg.* 3, *pg.* 293
Wolfe, Skip, Dir-Sls & Mktg - ASM International; *pg.* 132, *pg.* 1461
Wolfe, Stacie, Dir-Creative - OXO; *pg.* 1058, *pg.* 1275
Wolfel, Steve, Program Mgr & Mgr-Sls - Arrow Electronics, Inc.; *pg.* 619, *pg.* 325
Wolfenson, Barry J., Grp Pres-Advanced Wound Care & Pharmaceutical Dev - DERMA SCIENCES, INC.; *pg.* 1523, *pg.* 1111
Wolff, Andres, Assoc Dir-Mktg-US Latin - Sony Music Entertainment; *pg.* 309, *pg.* 1294
Wolff, David, Dir-Creative & Media - AARON'S, INC.; *pg.* 912, *pg.* 486
Wolff, Frank, Mgr-Natl Sls-Private Label - Cherry Central Cooperative, Inc.; *pg.* 847, *pg.* 909
Wolff, Rebecca, Mgr-Digital Mktg - Starbucks Corporation; *pg.* 897, *pg.* 1840
Wolff, Roland, VP-Mktg & Corp Retail - Leica Camera, Inc.; *pg.* 1420, *pg.* 1041
Wolford, Shelley, VP-Natl Mktg & Media - Golden Corral Corporation; *pg.* 1730, *pg.* 1387
Wolfson, Danielle, Sr Mgr-Digital & Social Media Mktg-Global - Activision Blizzard, Inc.; *pg.* 948, *pg.* 271
Wolfver, JP, Mgr-ECommerce & Channel Mktg - Loews Hotels Holding Corporation; *pg.* 1101, *pg.* 1252
Wolk, Janet, Product Mgr-Mktg-Medicare - Coventry Health Care, Inc.; *pg.* 1519, *pg.* 761
Wolken, Matt, Gen Mgr-Info Mgmt Products-Software Grp - Dell Inc.; *pg.* 383, *pg.* 1737

First page reference indicates Business Class Edition
Second page reference indicates Geographic Edition

Woll, Lynn, Dir-Digital Mktg - TrueBlue, Inc.; *pg.* 485, *pg.* 1845
Wolland, Jahn, Sr Dir-US Sls, Video & Skype Adv - Microsoft Corporation; *pg.* 435, *pg.* 1824
Wollin, Edee, VP-Mktg - TracFone Wireless, Inc.; *pg.* 681, *pg.* 447
Woloson, John, Mgr-Mktg - IBM; *pg.* 410, *pg.* 1449
Woloszczuk, Alex, VP-Sls - PepsiCo, Inc.; *pg.* 259, *pg.* 1327
Woloszynek, Kerry, Sr Mgr-Adv & Promos - Cleveland Cavaliers/Quicken Loans Arena; *pg.* 541, *pg.* 1429
Wolowic, Carol A., Sr Mgr-Media - Panera Bread Company; *pg.* 1029, *pg.* 1001
Wolpert, Maureen, Mgr-Grassroots Mktg - Seventh Generation, Inc.; *pg.* 335, *pg.* 1765
Wolpin, Matt, Sr Mgr-Content & Digital Strategy - Brocade Communications Systems, Inc.; *pg.* 365, *pg.* 239
Wolpin, Matt, Sr Mgr-Content & Digital Strategy - Brocade Corporation; *pg.* 365, *pg.* 312
Wolski, Jenny, Dir-Category Mktg & Mktg Ops - PETCO Animal Supplies, Inc.; *pg.* 1480, *pg.* 206
Wolstenholme, Mike, Mgr-Natl Tilt-Up Sls - Meadow Burke; *pg.* 96, *pg.* 474
Wolters, Lauren, Dir-Sls & Global Messaging - Sabre Holdings Corporation; *pg.* 1922, *pg.* 1745
Wolterstorff, Jason, Sr Mgr-Convention Sls - San Francisco Travel Association; *pg.* 1005, *pg.* 227
Wolverton, Nicole, Mgr-Mktg - Polaris Industries Inc.; *pg.* 1709, *pg.* 928
Womack, Brenda, Dir-Technical Product Mgmt - Cardinal Health, Inc.; *pg.* 1512, *pg.* 1448
Womack, Ciera, Asst Mgr-Mktg - Rich Products Corporation; *pg.* 892, *pg.* 1150
Won, Cathy, Sr Mgr-Product Mktg - Brocade Communications Systems, Inc.; *pg.* 365, *pg.* 239
Won, Gina, Brand Mgr-Nuts New Products - Diamond Foods, Inc.; *pg.* 1851, *pg.* 216
Wonder, Llora, Sr Dir-Market Dev-Fluid Sys - Baxter International Inc.; *pg.* 1499, *pg.* 599
Wonderlin, Beth, Asst VP-Creative & Gen Svcs, Sr Dir-Art & Dir-Creative & Gen Svcs - National Pork Board; *pg.* 882, *pg.* 703
Wong, Abe, CIO & Exec VP-Viacom Global Media Svcs - Paramount Pictures Corporation; *pg.* 304, *pg.* 138
Wong, Alice, Analyst-Personalized Digital Mktg - American Express Company; *pg.* 712, *pg.* 1190
Wong, Alyssa, Mgr-Growth Mktg-Consumer & 3D Printing - Autodesk Inc.; *pg.* 356, *pg.* 257
Wong, Calto, Dir-Technical Mktg - ESS Technology, Inc.; *pg.* 395, *pg.* 90
Wong, Candice, Sr Mgr-Digital Mktg - American Eagle Outfitters, Inc.; *pg.* 37, *pg.* 1572
Wong, Carmela, Head-Mktg Automation, Data & Analytics - Brocade Communications Systems, Inc.; *pg.* 365, *pg.* 239
Wong, Carol, Mgr-Creative Svcs - McKesson Corporation; *pg.* 1560, *pg.* 222
Wong, Chris, VP-Strategy & Product Mgmt - IBM; *pg.* 410, *pg.* 1449
Wong, Christina, Principal & Product Mgr-Mktg - Red Hat, Inc.; *pg.* 460, *pg.* 1388
Wong, Christina, Exec Dir & Sr Mgr-Sls-Wealth Mgmt - UBS Financial Services Inc.; *pg.* 812, *pg.* 1306
Wong, Connie, Dir-IR & Media Rels - Ross Stores, Inc.; *pg.* 1783, *pg.* 78
Wong, Craig, Mgr-Search Mktg - Esurance, Inc.; *pg.* 1243, *pg.* 217
Wong, David, Sr VP-Product Leadership - The Nielsen Company B.V.; *pg.* 1671, *pg.* 1272
Wong, Derrick, Mng Dir & Sr Mgr-Client-Comml Banking - Opus Bank; *pg.* 790, *pg.* 1819
Wong, Ealeen, Sr Asst Brand Mgr-North America Crest & Scope - Procter & Gamble Inc.; *pg.* 333, *pg.* 1929
Wong, Eddy, Mgr-Digital Mktg - Safeway Inc.; *pg.* 1032, *pg.* 184
Wong, Edwin, Sr Dir-B2B Insights - Yahoo! Inc.; *pg.* 1289, *pg.* 289
Wong, Erika, Dir-Mktg Automation - Intralinks Inc.; *pg.* 420, *pg.* 1244
Wong, Garrett, Product Mgr - Nordson Corporation; *pg.* 1365, *pg.* 1480
Wong, Gloria, Mgr-Media & PR - Trippe Manufacturing Company; *pg.* 220, *pg.* 592
Wong, Grace d, VP-Global Mktg-Gap brands - The Gap, Inc.; *pg.* 1770, *pg.* 218
Wong, Jimmy, Sr Mgr-Bus Analytics-B2B Mktg - LinkedIn Corporation; *pg.* 1262, *pg.* 160
Wong, Jimmy T., Sr VP & Sr Mgr-Cross Sell Relationship - Wells Fargo & Company; *pg.* 819, *pg.* 232
Wong, Jocelyn, Sr VP & Gen Mgr-Mdsg - Lowe's Companies, Inc.; *pg.* 1053, *pg.* 1383
Wong, Jody, Coord-Retail Sls & Mktg - National Hockey League; *pg.* 568, *pg.* 1265
Wong, Jonathan, Head-Media Acq Support Onsite - Microsoft Corporation; *pg.* 435, *pg.* 1824
Wong, K.K., Dir-FOG Product Line - EMCORE Corporation; *pg.* 636, *pg.* 39
Wong, Katie, Mgr-Integrated Mktg Comm - General Mills, Inc.; *pg.* 828, *pg.* 933
Wong, Lily, Sr Mgr-Channel Web Mktg & Community - Polycom, Inc.; *pg.* 664, *pg.* 249
Wong, Melissa, Sr Mgr-Corp Comm - The Gap, Inc.; *pg.* 1770, *pg.* 218
Wong, Pamela, Mgr-Email Mktg - Hulu LLC; *pg.* 1257, *pg.* 274
Wong, Patrick, Corp Dir-Field Mktg - MetroPCS, Inc.; *pg.* 1872, *pg.* 1683
Wong, Quinnie, Head-Learning Comm & Social Learning - Motorola Solutions, Inc.; *pg.* 657, *pg.* 659
Wong, Richard, Dir-Sls & Svcs - Houston Grand Opera Association; *pg.* 552, *pg.* 1707
Wong, Robert, VP-Google Creative Lab - Google Inc.; *pg.* 1249, *pg.* 153
Wong, Roberto, Dir-Digital Mktg Strategy - BI-LO, LLC; *pg.* 1015, *pg.* 1617
Wong, Roger, Sr Dir-Creative - TrueCar Inc.; *pg.* 1284, *pg.* 276
Wong, Stephanie, Mgr-Mktg & Publicity-Lifestyle - Chronicle Books; *pg.* 1627, *pg.* 216
Wong-Cairns, Stephanie, Brand Mgr-Cough & Cold Portfolio-Benylin - Johnson & Johnson; *pg.* 1549, *pg.* 1091
Wons, Derek, Mgr-Global Budget & PR - Volcom, Inc.; *pg.* 1847, *pg.* 71
Woo, Alison, Head-Corp Digital & Social Media Strategy - Bristol-Myers Squibb Company; *pg.* 1509, *pg.* 1206
Woo, Allison, Sr Mgr-Partner Mktg-Global Brand - LinkedIn Corporation; *pg.* 1262, *pg.* 160
Woo, Brian, Dir-Mktg - Abbott Nutrition; *pg.* 1485, *pg.* 1437
Woo, Christopher, Assoc Product Mgr-Intl - Ubisoft Inc.; *pg.* 589, *pg.* 229
Woo, Genevieve, Asst Product Mgr - La Cie McCormick Canada Co.; *pg.* 872, *pg.* 1922
Woo, George, Mgr-Event Mktg-Worldwide - Intel Corporation; *pg.* 645, *pg.* 266
Woo, Jooeun, Analyst-Digital Mktg - American Express Company; *pg.* 712, *pg.* 1190
Wood, Alison, Dir-Web & Social Mktg - Panasonic Corporation of North America; *pg.* 661, *pg.* 1120
Wood, Andrea, Sr Mgr-Community Rels - Best Buy Co., Inc.; *pg.* 1761, *pg.* 954
Wood, Andy, Sr Dir-IT Infrastructure - Meredith Corporation; *pg.* 1663, *pg.* 705
Wood, Becca, Specialist-Product - DISH Network Corporation; *pg.* 283, *pg.* 325
Wood, Brett, Sr Dir-Market Mgmt - Fireman's Fund Insurance Company; *pg.* 1200, *pg.* 168
Wood, Cara, Sr Mgr-Mktg Comm - McKesson Corporation; *pg.* 1560, *pg.* 222
Wood, Christie, Dir-Mktg - Seattle Symphony Orchestra; *pg.* 582, *pg.* 1840
Wood, Christopher E., VP-Sls - Griffith Laboratories, Inc.; *pg.* 860, *pg.* 552
Wood, Claire, Sr Mgr-Footwear Product & Performance Running - New Balance Athletic Shoe, Inc.; *pg.* 1811, *pg.* 798
Wood, Corey, Mgr-Digital Mktg - AliphCom, Inc.; *pg.* 616, *pg.* 212
Wood, Cynthia, Program Mgr-Mktg - Wells Fargo & Company; *pg.* 819, *pg.* 232
Wood, Debbie, Gen Mgr-Mktg & Indus Res - Jack Henry & Associates, Inc.; *pg.* 422, *pg.* 988
Wood, Derrick, VP & Dir-Creative-Global - Staples; *pg.* 474, *pg.* 313
Wood, Emmett, Exec VP-Mktg & Strategy - Telos Corporation; *pg.* 483, *pg.* 1776
Wood, Ethan, Dir-Enterprise Mktg-North America - Dell Inc.; *pg.* 383, *pg.* 1737
Wood, Frederick, Mgr-Brand Mktg - Community Coffee Company LLC; *pg.* 849, *pg.* 741
Wood, Greg, Sr Product Dir-Photo Editing - Corel Corporation; *pg.* 380, *pg.* 1931
Wood, Jeff T., Sls Dir-Power & Cooling Solutions-Natl - Anixter International Inc.; *pg.* 1313, *pg.* 614
Wood, Jessica, Assoc Mgr-Mktg - Burt's Bees Inc.; *pg.* 502, *pg.* 1370
Wood, Joe, VP-Mktg-Bus Intelligence - Roundy's Supermarkets Inc.; *pg.* 1032, *pg.* 1880
Wood, Kami, Mgr-Social Media & PR - Zaxby's Franchising, Inc.; *pg.* 1756, *pg.* 486
Wood, Lisa M., Mgr-Segment Mktg - CDW Corporation; *pg.* 370, *pg.* 663
Wood, Lori, Product Mgr - Xap Corporation; *pg.* 1289, *pg.* 73
Wood, Matthew, Producer-Digital Media - NBC Universal, Inc.; *pg.* 300, *pg.* 1266
Wood, Matthew, Exec Dir-Worldwide Technical Ops, Media Svcs, Ops & Distr - Paramount Pictures Corporation; *pg.* 304, *pg.* 138
Wood, Mike, Dir-Product Dev-Hallmark Gold Crown Retail - Hallmark Cards, Inc.; *pg.* 1646, *pg.* 983
Wood, Peter, Dir-Product Mktg-Global - EXACT SCIENCES CORPORATION; *pg.* 1529, *pg.* 1865
Wood, Peter, Mgr-Product Mktg - Key Technology, Inc.; *pg.* 868, *pg.* 1847
Wood, Roland, Sr Mgr - Apple Inc.; *pg.* 350, *pg.* 73
Wood, Ron, Exec VP-Sls-Global - Travelpro International, Inc.; *pg.* 14, *pg.* 413
Wood, Scott, Mgr-Sls - Lista International Corporation; *pg.* 934, *pg.* 825
Wood, Steve, VP-Foodservice Mktg - Mondelez International, Inc.; *pg.* 878, *pg.* 601
Wood, Sven, VP-Brand & Product Mktg - Edmunds, Inc.; *pg.* 1241, *pg.* 273
Wood, Thomas, Sr Product Mgr-Running Footwear - Reebok International Ltd.; *pg.* 1817, *pg.* 811
Wood, Tracy, Brand Mgr-Safeway Care - Safeway Inc.; *pg.* 1032, *pg.* 184
Wood, Tripp, Sr VP-Digital Sls & Distr - Paramount Pictures Corporation; *pg.* 304, *pg.* 138
Woodall, Dan, Product Mgr-Everyday Gift Solutions - Hallmark Cards, Inc.; *pg.* 1646, *pg.* 983
Woodall, Yanique, VP-PR & Comm - 1-800-Flowers.com, Inc.; *pg.* 1758, *pg.* 1151
Woodard, Allison, Reg Dir-Mktg - Aramark; *pg.* 1013, *pg.* 1558
Woodard, Kevin, Dir-Mktg - University of Michigan; *pg.* 609, *pg.* 867
Woodard, Ross L., CMO & Sr VP - Bridgepoint Education, Inc.; *pg.* 598, *pg.* 201
Woodard, Shannon, Dir-Mktg - The Coleman Company, Inc.; *pg.* 1830, *pg.* 723
Woodbridge, Stacey B., Dir-Mktg-Consumer Mktg - Anthem, Inc.; *pg.* 1192, *pg.* 683
Woodbury, Jessica, Sr Mgr-Social Media & Customer Engagement - Alex and Ani; *pg.* 1, *pg.* 1600
Woodcock, Chris, Dir-Mktg Comm - Tyco SimplexGrinnell LP; *pg.* 682, *pg.* 859
Wooden, Jason, Dir-Media - Academy Sports & Outdoors, Ltd.; *pg.* 1824, *pg.* 1724
Woodiel, Theresa, Sr Specialist-Mktg Comm - National Instruments Corporation; *pg.* 443, *pg.* 1664
Woodin, Deb, Sr Analyst-Mktg Res - Valassis; *pg.* 1698, *pg.* 386
Woodiwiss, Steven, Brand Mgr-Arrowhead Mills, Maranatha, DeBoles & SunSpire - The Hain Celestial Group, Inc.; *pg.* 860, *pg.* 1172
Woodland, Daniel D., VP-Mktg - Cabot Microelectronics Corporation; *pg.* 1151, *pg.* 554
Woodland, Mark, VP-Mktg - Chapman University; *pg.* 599, *pg.* 174
Woodlee, Jeremy, Dir-DoubleClick Media Platforms - Google Inc.; *pg.* 1249, *pg.* 153
Woodley, David, Exec VP-Sls & Mktg - Sheetz, Inc.; *pg.* 1033, *pg.* 1514
Woodlief, Meghan, Sr Dir-Mktg - FairPoint Communications, Inc.; *pg.* 1871, *pg.* 1366
Woodman, Sarah, Mgr-Partner Sls Contact Center - CDW Corporation; *pg.* 370, *pg.* 663
Woodmansee, Jason, Mgr-Digital Mktg - QUALCOMM Incorporated; *pg.* 1873, *pg.* 207
Woodring, Sue, Mgr-Mktg - LifeCell Corporation; *pg.* 1556, *pg.* 1045
Woodrow, Mallory, Asst Mgr-Chevrolet Digital & Social Adv - General Motors Company; *pg.* 175, *pg.* 881
Woods, Andrea, VP-Mktg-Sr Living & Healthcare - Morrison Management Specialists, Inc.; *pg.* 1028, *pg.* 515
Woods, Angela, Dir-Creative Design - Phoenix Suns; *pg.* 576, *pg.* 19

Woods, Donovan, Mgr-Strategic Sls Initiatives - National Association of Convenience Stores; *pg.* 148, *pg.* 1771
Woods, George, Dir-Mktg - Family First; *pg.* 140, *pg.* 472
Woods, Jacci, Dir-Pub Rel - Detroit Entertainment, LLC; *pg.* 1089, *pg.* 879
Woods, Jeff, Mgr-Mktg - Alliant Energy Corporation; *pg.* 1933, *pg.* 1864
Woods, Karen, Dir-PR - The Yankee Candle Company, Inc.; *pg.* 1792, *pg.* 843
Woods, Maria M., Mgr-Mktg-Gulf of Mexico Reg - Baker Hughes Incorporated; *pg.* 1315, *pg.* 1700
Woods, Melanie, Sr VP & Product Mgr-Digital - UMB Financial Corporation; *pg.* 812, *pg.* 987
Woods, Nicole, Mgr-Digital Creative - Focus Features; *pg.* 287, *pg.* 273
Woods, Phyllis, Sr Dir-Creative & Content Studio-Ops & Content Distr-Global - Marriott International, Inc.; *pg.* 1102, *pg.* 764
Woods, Roger, Sr Product Mgr-Mobile Solutions - Adobe Systems Incorporated; *pg.* 342, *pg.* 235
Woods, Sam, Sr VP-Sls & Ops - The Mattress Firm, Inc.; *pg.* 934, *pg.* 1711
Woodson, Laura, Exec Dir-Corp Digital Mktg-North America - The Estee Lauder Companies Inc.; *pg.* 508, *pg.* 1229
Woodward, Jackie, VP-Media-Global - General Mills, Inc.; *pg.* 828, *pg.* 933
Woodward, Jacqueline, Sr Mgr-Consumer Insights-Global - Expedia, Inc.; *pg.* 1244, *pg.* 1814
Woodward, Joel, Sr Product Mgr - Agilent Technologies, Inc.; *pg.* 614, *pg.* 264
Woodward, Josh, Sr Product Mgr - Google Inc.; *pg.* 1249, *pg.* 153
Woodward, Russell, Sr Mgr-Product Mktg - Texas Beef Council; *pg.* 158, *pg.* 1666
Woodwick, Kelli, Mgr-Mktg - Valent U.S.A. Corp.; *pg.* 708, *pg.* 305
Woodworth, Ben, VP-Sls - CCpress.net Inc.; *pg.* 1626, *pg.* 756
Woodworth, Christi, VP-PR - SONIC Corp.; *pg.* 1750, *pg.* 1487
Woodworth, Lisa, VP-Mktg - CORT Business Services Corporation; *pg.* 921, *pg.* 1777
Woodworth, Roger D., Chief Strategy Officer & VP - Avista Corporation; *pg.* 1935, *pg.* 1843
Woody, Kelly, Mgr-Mktg - HCA HOLDINGS, INC.; *pg.* 1539, *pg.* 1651
Wooldridge, Lisa, Dir-Mktg-Americas - Tourism Australia; *pg.* 1007, *pg.* 140
Woolen, Amy, Dir-Field & Franchise Mktg - Red Robin Gourmet Burgers, Inc.; *pg.* 1747, *pg.* 331
Wooler, John, Head-Media Svcs, Licensing & Label Rels - PlayNetwork, Inc.; *pg.* 577, *pg.* 1829
Woolff, Alan, VP-Mdsg - Diamond.com; *pg.* 1238, *pg.* 1954
Woolfolk, Brian T, Sr VP & Chief Actuary-Product-Retirement Solutions Div - Pacific Life Insurance Company; *pg.* 1213, *pg.* 166
Woolford, Brandy, Assoc Mgr-Global Brand PR & Consumer Engagement - The Hershey Co.; *pg.* 1855, *pg.* 1538
Woolley, Adrian, VP-Strategic Mktg - Cypress Semiconductor Corporation; *pg.* 1326, *pg.* 243
Woolley, Jay, Dir-Mktg - Harman International Industries, Incorporated; *pg.* 641, *pg.* 374
Woolley, Sharon, Mgr-Mktg - SpectorSoft Corporation; *pg.* 1281, *pg.* 478
Woon, Brianna, Sr Mgr-Corp Comm - Polycom, Inc.; *pg.* 664, *pg.* 249
Woonton, Ellen, Dir-Global Mktg & Physical Assessment - Welch Allyn Inc.; *pg.* 1436, *pg.* 1342
Wooster, Laura, VP-Mktg - John Hancock Financial Services; *pg.* 1205, *pg.* 796
Wooten, Kourtney, Mgr-Federal Field Mktg - Polycom, Inc.; *pg.* 664, *pg.* 249
Wootton, Sabrina, Mgr-New Product - Sunsweet Growers, Inc.; *pg.* 900, *pg.* 309
Worcester, Nicole, Acct Coord-Mktg - Pacific Life Insurance Company; *pg.* 1213, *pg.* 166
Word, Larry, Program Mgr-Creative - SHUTTERFLY, INC.; *pg.* 1280, *pg.* 192
Workman, Eric, Sr VP-Mktg - Altadis USA, Inc.; *pg.* 1893, *pg.* 423
Workman, Eric, Exec VP-Mktg & Bus Dev - Polynesian Cultural Center; *pg.* 577, *pg.* 545
Workman, John, Interim Chm - Universal Hospital Services, Inc.; *pg.* 1604, *pg.* 945
Workman, Royce, Dir-Digital Mktg - Nationwide Mutual Insurance Company; *pg.* 1210, *pg.* 1442
Workman, Trey, Dir-Corp Partnerships & Radio Sls - Atlanta National League Baseball Club, Inc.; *pg.* 530, *pg.* 490
Worlock, David, Dir-Media Coordination & Statistics - National Collegiate Athletic Association; *pg.* 567, *pg.* 688
Worman, Brad, VP-Sls & Mktg - Automated Packaging Systems Inc.; *pg.* 1452, *pg.* 1474
Worman, Charles, Mgr-Digital Media-North America - MANPOWER INC.; *pg.* 430, *pg.* 1877
Worne, Simon, Dir-Mktg-New Bus Dev-Europe & Australasia - General Mills, Inc.; *pg.* 828, *pg.* 933
Worob, Andrew, Mgr-Social Media - Bed Bath & Beyond Inc.; *pg.* 1121, *pg.* 1127
Woroch, David, VP-Sls & Mktg - Tucows, Inc.; *pg.* 1285, *pg.* 1946
Woronko, Kathy S., Mgr-Events Mktg & Channel Comm - Steelcase Inc.; *pg.* 475, *pg.* 889
Worple, Bill, Dir-Mktg Tech - Best Buy Co., Inc.; *pg.* 1761, *pg.* 954
Worrell, Andrew, Mgr-Fin Ops Sls & Mktg - DIRECTV Group Holdings, LLC; *pg.* 281, *pg.* 79
Worrick, Elizabeth, Sr VP & Mgr-Sls-Residential Lending - Boston Private; *pg.* 726, *pg.* 791
Worrilow, Georgia, Supvr-Mktg Media - The Pep Boys - Manny, Moe & Jack; *pg.* 215, *pg.* 1568
Worsell, Shawn, Dir-Product Mgmt - OCZ Storage Solutions; *pg.* 448, *pg.* 248
Worsley, Michael, Dir-Mdsg & Product Dev - Overton's Inc.; *pg.* 1781, *pg.* 1377
Worth, Brian, Sr Dir-Airport Customer Svc-Pacific Island Reg - Hawaiian Holdings, Inc.; *pg.* 1910, *pg.* 544
Worth, Sue, Sr Mgr-Customer Support-EMEA - TripAdvisor, Inc.; *pg.* 1926, *pg.* 835
Worthem, Crystal, Brand Mgr-Content & Alliances - Ford Motor Company; *pg.* 172, *pg.* 876
Worthey, Kate, Sr Mgr-Innovation - Anheuser-Busch Companies, LLC; *pg.* 237, *pg.* 991
Worthing, Al, VP-Sls & Mktg - Andersen Corporation; *pg.* 67, *pg.* 916
Worthing, Sadie, Acct Exec-Charter Media - Charter Communications, Inc.; *pg.* 274, *pg.* 372
Worthington, Karen, Dir-Mktg - Bank of America Corporation; *pg.* 718, *pg.* 1362
Wortley, Don, Sr Mgr-Mktg - Best Buy Co., Inc.; *pg.* 1761, *pg.* 954
Wortman, Danielle, Asst VP & Mgr-Digital Media - Bank of America Corporation; *pg.* 718, *pg.* 1362
Wortman, David, Brand Mgr-Intl - 3M Company; *pg.* 1142, *pg.* 956
Worwa, Susan, Sr Dir-Corp Comm & Community Engagement - Ameriprise Financial, Inc.; *pg.* 715, *pg.* 930
Woseth, Rob, Chief Strategy Officer & Exec VP - SUPERVALU, Inc.; *pg.* 1035, *pg.* 924
Wosilius, Jacquelyn, Dir-Digital Mktg - Bowlmor AMF; *pg.* 1828, *pg.* 1206
Wosiski, Ian, Dir-Sls-Global Solutions - Intermap Technologies Corporation; *pg.* 417, *pg.* 1903
Wotton, Megan, Dir-Mktg & Comm - The Northwestern Mutual Life Insurance Company; *pg.* 1212, *pg.* 1879
Wotus, Tara, Coord-Mktg-Intl - American Eagle Outfitters, Inc.; *pg.* 37, *pg.* 1572
Woulfe, Michael, VP-Sls - De'Longhi America Inc.; *pg.* 54, *pg.* 1118
Woychick, Jay F., VP-Inside Sls - Transcat, Inc.; *pg.* 682, *pg.* 1337
Woys, James E., CFO, COO & Interim Treas - Health Net, Inc.; *pg.* 1540, *pg.* 308
Wozinsky, Jessica, Editor-Social Media-Parade Media Grp - Parade Magazine; *pg.* 1674, *pg.* 1275
Wozniak, David, Head-Adv - Lincoln Financial Group; *pg.* 1206, *pg.* 1375
Wragg, Zack, Sr Mgr-ECommerce-South Asia & Thailand - Hilton Worldwide, Inc.; *pg.* 1094, *pg.* 1791
Wray, Arlene, Dir-Sls Western Canada-Natl - Atlific Inc.; *pg.* 1080, *pg.* 1953
Wray, Cindy Archer, Mgr-Product Mktg - ChildFund International; *pg.* 137, *pg.* 1801
Wray, Lea, VP-Mktg - T. Rowe Price Group Inc.; *pg.* 808, *pg.* 759
Wrazen, Frank , III, Sr Dir-Mfg-Topping, Icings & Donuts - Rich Products Corporation; *pg.* 892, *pg.* 1150
Wrede, Paul, Exec Dir-Mktg - Merck & Co., Inc.; *pg.* 1566, *pg.* 1077
Wreden, Kathy, Product Mgr - Intuit Inc.; *pg.* 769, *pg.* 158
Wreden, Merrell, VP-Mktg - AMF Bowling Centers, Inc.; *pg.* 528, *pg.* 1795
Wrenn, Cherie H., Sr Product Mgr - W.R. Grace & Co.; *pg.* 123, *pg.* 810
Wressell, Mary Beth, VP-Mktg Comm - Holland America Line Inc.; *pg.* 1911, *pg.* 1836
Wright, Adam, Interim CEO - Famous Dave's of America, Inc.; *pg.* 1728, *pg.* 926
Wright, Allison, Mgr-Mktg-Core Products - First Data Corporation; *pg.* 754, *pg.* 505
Wright, Andy, Publr-The New York Times Magazine & Sr VP-Adv - The New York Times Company; *pg.* 1668, *pg.* 1270
Wright, Brian, VP-Sls & Mktg - Elyria Foundry Company; *pg.* 1046, *pg.* 1451
Wright, Caroline, Dir-Mktg Svcs - Maple Leaf Sports & Entertainment Ltd.; *pg.* 560, *pg.* 1940
Wright, Cheresa, Sr Brand Mgr-Mktg - Intuit Inc.; *pg.* 769, *pg.* 158
Wright, Courtney, Brand Mgr-Digital - DISH Network Corporation; *pg.* 283, *pg.* 325
Wright, Craig, Sr Dir-Sls - Coach, Inc.; *pg.* 3, *pg.* 1214
Wright, Curtis, Mgr-Retail Mktg Comm - Publix Super Markets, Inc.; *pg.* 1031, *pg.* 437
Wright, Danisha, Mgr-Paid Social Mktg - Wells Fargo & Company; *pg.* 819, *pg.* 232
Wright, Dave, Dir-Sls & Mktg - Wet 'n Wild, Inc.; *pg.* 592, *pg.* 457
Wright, David, Sr Dir-Mktg-Worldwide - NVIDIA Corporation; *pg.* 447, *pg.* 268
Wright, Donna, Sr Mgr-Mktg - Siemens PLM Software; *pg.* 469, *pg.* 1734
Wright, Ed, VP-Mdsg-Div - Safeway Inc.; *pg.* 1032, *pg.* 184
Wright, Fritz, Rep-Mktg - Hooper Holmes, Inc.; *pg.* 1542, *pg.* 718
Wright, Haydn, Dir-Sls-Western Region - Essence Magazine; *pg.* 1639, *pg.* 1229
Wright, Howard, Dir-Sls-US - Axiall Corporation; *pg.* 69, *pg.* 491
Wright, Jacque'line, Coord-Mktg - LSI Industries Inc.; *pg.* 58, *pg.* 1416
Wright, Jamie, Product Mgr - Terex Corporation; *pg.* 1381, *pg.* 384
Wright, Jeff, Dir-Mktg Programs - Bentley University; *pg.* 598, *pg.* 850
Wright, Jill, Sr Mgr-HR - Honeywell Aerospace Electronic Systems; *pg.* 228, *pg.* 17
Wright, Julia, Sr Mgr - Fair Isaac Corporation; *pg.* 1247, *pg.* 955
Wright, Katherine, VP-Mktg & Comm - Wells Fargo & Company; *pg.* 819, *pg.* 232
Wright, Kathleen, Mgr-Sls - Q.E.P. CO., INC.; *pg.* 1371, *pg.* 413
Wright, Kathleen, Product Mgr-Handwriting-Natl - Zaner-Bloser, Inc.; *pg.* 970, *pg.* 1445
Wright, Kati, Mgr-Analog & Interface IP Mktg Programs - Synopsys, Inc.; *pg.* 480, *pg.* 162
Wright, Keisha, Sr Dir-Brand Mktg & Solutions - Brooklyn Nets; *pg.* 534, *pg.* 1145
Wright, Kelly, Exec VP-Sls - Tableau Software, Inc.; *pg.* 481, *pg.* 1841
Wright, Kevin, VP-Mktg-Global - Oregon Tourism Commission; *pg.* 1003, *pg.* 1508
Wright, Kristen, Assoc Mgr-Mktg Comm - Papa Ginos-Deangelo Holding Corporation, Inc.; *pg.* 1743, *pg.* 817
Wright, Lauren, Sr Mgr-Customer Engagement Mktg - Panera Bread Company; *pg.* 1029, *pg.* 1001
Wright, Mark, VP-Media Svcs & Sponsorships - AT&T Communications Corp.; *pg.* 1866, *pg.* 1043
Wright, Mark, VP-Media Svcs & Sponsorships - AT&T Inc.; *pg.* 1868, *pg.* 358
Wright, Mary, VP-Mktg & Brand Strategy - Hannaford Brothers Co.; *pg.* 1022, *pg.* 752
Wright, Matt, Sr VP-Mktg Partnerships - Phoenix Suns; *pg.* 576, *pg.* 19
Wright, Michelle, Sr Mgr-Digital Content - Levi Strauss & Co.; *pg.* 43, *pg.* 220
Wright, Michelle, VP-Sls - NBC Universal, Inc.; *pg.* 300, *pg.* 1266
Wright, Natasha, Sr Mgr-Mktg - Level 3 Communications, Inc.; *pg.* 1262, *pg.* 312
Wright, Nate, Mgr-Product Mktg-Commerce - Twitter, Inc.; *pg.* 1285, *pg.* 228
Wright, Nick B., VP-Sls-West Reg - United States Cellular Corporation; *pg.* 1875, *pg.* 594
Wright, Pat, Mgr-Mktg - Cisco Systems, Inc.; *pg.* 372, *pg.* 240
Wright, Paul, Dir-Local Media Dev - Comcast Corporation; *pg.*

First page reference indicates Business Class Edition
Second page reference indicates Geographic Edition

276, pg. 1560
Wright, Rachael, Sr Mgr-Field Events-America & Digital Mktg - Adobe Systems Incorporated; pg. 342, pg. 235
Wright, Renee, Mgr-Production - Bluegreen Corporation; pg. 1082, pg. 410
Wright, Rich, VP-Sls & Mktg - Dietz & Watson Inc.; pg. 853, pg. 1563
Wright, Richard, Sr Mgr-Shopper Mktg - Georgia-Pacific LLC; pg. 1458, pg. 507
Wright, Scott, Mgr-Product Mktg - Toshiba America, Inc.; pg. 681, pg. 1302
Wright, Sean, Reg Mgr-Sls - Riverbed Performance Management; pg. 462, pg. 765
Wright, Stanley A., Mgr-Sls - Noshok Inc.; pg. 1366, pg. 1406
Wright, Stephen, Sr VP-Sls & Mktg-Latin America & Asia Pacific - Avis Budget Group, Inc.; pg. 1900, pg. 1102
Wright, Steve, CMO & Chief Sls Officer - Jay Peak, Inc.; pg. 1098, pg. 1766
Wright, Sue, Product Mgr - General Motors Company; pg. 175, pg. 881
Wright, Tim, Mgr-Sls-North America - Tecumseh Products Company; pg. 1381, pg. 866
Wright, Timothy, Sr Mgr-Online Mktg-ECommerce - AT&T; pg. 1865, pg. 258
Wright, Tom, VP-Mktg - Turkey Hill Dairy, Inc.; pg. 902, pg. 1522
Wright, Wenmei, Sr Analyst-Strategic Project Mktg - FedEx Corporation; pg. 1907, pg. 1642
Wright, William J., Sr VP-Global Product Innovation - Tupperware Brands Corporation; pg. 1139, pg. 456
Wright-Ruiz, Kiera, Mgr-Mktg - Uber USA, LLC; pg. 1286, pg. 229
Wrigley, Joy, Sr Mgr-Product Line-Ultra Low Density Products - Lattice Semiconductor Corporation; pg. 651, pg. 1498
Write, Jo, Product Mgr - Bentley Systems, Inc.; pg. 361, pg. 1531
Wronski, Ed, Dir-Food & Beverage Product Dev - The Walt Disney Company; pg. 317, pg. 52
Wu, Annie, Head-Mktg-Small Bus Employee Mgmt Solutions - Intuit Inc.; pg. 769, pg. 158
Wu, Audrey, VP-Comml Strategy Mktg-Maternal Health Bus - AMAG Pharmaceuticals, Inc.; pg. 1492, pg. 827
Wu, Bibie, VP-Mktg - The Sun Products Corporation; pg. 336, pg. 385
Wu, Cheng, VP & Head-Technology Strategy-BUSS Media Platform - Ericsson, Inc.; pg. 638, pg. 1730
Wu, Christine, Mgr-Mktg-Global - Colgate-Palmolive Company; pg. 504, pg. 1215
Wu, David, Mgr-Digital Mktg - Jet.com, Inc.; pg. 1260, pg. 1073
Wu, Eddy, Dir-Product Innovation - Netflix, Inc.; pg. 1269, pg. 141
Wu, Eric, Sr Dir-Customer Acq - Edmunds, Inc.; pg. 1241, pg. 273
Wu, Helen, Mgr-Mktg Comm - Siemens Process Industries and Drives; pg. 673, pg. 485
Wu, Isabelle, Mgr-Search Mktg - SHUTTERFLY, INC.; pg. 1280, pg. 192
Wu, Jimmy, Dir-Mktg - Mondelez International; pg. 877, pg. 1344
Wu, Jimmy, Dir-Mktg - Mondelez International, Inc.; pg. 878, pg. 601
Wu, Natalie, Sr Mgr-Brand Strategy - Intel Corporation; pg. 645, pg. 266
Wu, Natalie I., Dir-Mktg & Emerging Markets - Eli Lilly and Company; pg. 1527, pg. 684
Wu, Phillip, VP-Mktg Emerging Markets - United Parcel Service, Inc.; pg. 1928, pg. 522
Wu, Rebecca, Mgr-Mktg-Toyota Trucks & Scion - Toyota Canada, Inc.; pg. 192, pg. 1934
Wu, Ted, Dir-Global Mktg-Hot Wheels - Mattel Games/Puzzles; pg. 962, pg. 80
Wu, Ted, Dir-Global Mktg-Hot Wheels - MATTEL, INC.; pg. 962, pg. 81
Wu, Ugil, Mgr-Mktg - GameFly, Inc.; pg. 953, pg. 132
Wu, Vince, Sr Product Mgr-Chromebook APAC Go-To-Market - Google Inc.; pg. 1249, pg. 153
Wu, Wendy, Dir-Loyalty Mktg - Omni Hotels & Resorts; pg. 1107, pg. 1685
Wu, William W., VP-Sls & Mktg - Synutra International, Inc.; pg. 1600, pg. 776
Wu, Xinjie, Mgr-Analytics-Mktg Science - Genentech, Inc.; pg. 1533, pg. 279
Wu, Yujunjie, Specialist-Mktg - HSBC Bank USA; pg. 767, pg. 1241
Wuebbling, Matt, Dir-Product Mktg-Tegra - NVIDIA Corporation; pg. 447, pg. 268
Wuelfing, Amy Yates, Asst VP-Mktg - Caliper Corporation; pg. 368, pg. 1111
Wuellner, Trond, Product Mgr - Google Inc.; pg. 1249, pg. 153
Wuerst, Jessie, Sr Mgr-Comm - Avista Corporation; pg. 1935, pg. 1843
Wuertz, Bill, Sr VP-Products & Solutions - Dot Hill Systems Corp.; pg. 388, pg. 333
Wuestenfeld, Kenneth R., VP-Sls & Technical Svcs - Fuchs North America.; pg. 857, pg. 774
Wujek, Cynthia, Asst VP-Mktg & Comm - Sun Life Financial Inc.; pg. 806, pg. 1944
Wulf, Christoph, Sr Dir-Global Mktg-Hemophilia - Baxter International Inc.; pg. 1499, pg. 599
Wulf, Michael, Dir-Product Mgmt - Kelley Blue Book Co., Inc.; pg. 1656, pg. 112
Wulff, Brenda, Dir-Product Design & Innovation - Choice Hotels International, Inc.; pg. 1086, pg. 775
Wulff, Carrie, Coord-Mktg - Drexel University; pg. 600, pg. 1564
Wulff, Kurt, VP-Mktg - Reliv International, Inc.; pg. 1589, pg. 975
Wulfow, Rachel, Sr Mgr-Client Svcs - U.S. News & World Report, L.P.; pg. 1698, pg. 1308
Wulfraat, Peter, VP-Sls - West Corporation; pg. 492, pg. 1019
Wun, Michelle, Sr Mgr-Mktg - Mattel Games/Puzzles; pg. 962, pg. 80
Wun, Michelle, Sr Mgr-Mktg - MATTEL, INC.; pg. 962, pg. 81
Wunderlich, Eileen, Mgr-Mktg Comm - FCA US LLC; pg. 170, pg. 868
Wundrock, Andy, Sr VP-Sls & Mktg - Wisconsin Pharmacal Company, LLC; pg. 1610, pg. 1861
Wung, Tina, Brand Mgr-Digital Strategy & Innovation - Anheuser-Busch Companies, LLC; pg. 237, pg. 991
Wunnenberg, Eric, Dir-Sls Talk Formats WIBC & WFNI & Gen Sls Mgr WFNI - 1070 WIBC; pg. 267, pg. 682
Wunrow, Tracy, Sr Specialist-Mktg Matls Compliance - The Northwestern Mutual Life Insurance Company; pg. 1212, pg. 1879
Wunsch, Casey, Planner-Adv Sls - NBC Universal, Inc.; pg. 300, pg. 1266
Wunstel, Linda, Dir-Mktg - Capital City Press; pg. 1625, pg. 741
Wurm, Mike, Sr Mgr-Technical - 3M Detection Solutions; pg. 1398, pg. 1885
Wurm, Sandy, Coord-Shopper Mktg - Kimberly-Clark Corporation; pg. 1461, pg. 1720
Wurster, David, Sr Product Mgr-Windows Embedded - Microsoft Corporation; pg. 435, pg. 1824
Wurster, Hal, Dir-Retail Mktg - FCA US LLC; pg. 170, pg. 868
Wurster, Karen, Sr Dir-Mktg - Eli Lilly and Company; pg. 1527, pg. 684
Wurster, Lea, Brand Mgr-Tory Burch, Burberry & DKNY - Luxottica Retail; pg. 8, pg. 1460
Wurth, Michael, Product Mgr-Mktg-Workware Tech - Haworth, Inc.; pg. 402, pg. 891
Wurtzel, Alan, Pres-Res & Media Dev - NBC Universal, Inc.; pg. 300, pg. 1266
Wuthrich, Kent, Exec VP-Mktg - ZAGG INCORPORATED; pg. 690, pg. 1762
Wutkewicz, Mirko, Dir-Bus Dev & Strategic Mktg - Siemens Corporation; pg. 803, pg. 1291
Wyant, Steve, VP-Sls & Mktg - Sazerac Company, Inc.; pg. 1969, pg. 745
Wyatt, John H.A., Pres-Sls & Mktg - Stanley Black & Decker, Inc.; pg. 1063, pg. 358
Wyatt, Mike, Dir-Customer Dev & Mktg - FIJI Water; pg. 251, pg. 130
Wyatt, Steve, VP-Mktg & Dir-Creative - Kenneth Cole Productions, Inc.; pg. 1810, pg. 1248
Wyckoff, Lily, Strategist-Creative - Facebook, Inc.; pg. 1245, pg. 143
Wydra, A.J., Strategist-Mktg - Quicken Loans, Inc.; pg. 797, pg. 884
Wyeth, Max, Sr Strategist-Digital Mktg-Social Media - DIRECTV Group Holdings, LLC; pg. 281, pg. 79
Wyld, Kelly, Mgr-Digital Mktg - MyWebGrocer.com Corp.; pg. 1269, pg. 1769
Wyler, Alyse, Sr Dir-HR - SAP America, Inc.; pg. 466, pg. 1557
Wyman, Bill, Head-Customer Mktg - Harman International Industries, Incorporated; pg. 641, pg. 374
Wyndowe, Matt, Head-Product Partnerships - Uber USA, LLC; pg. 1286, pg. 229
Wynn, Janet, Project Mgr-Digital Mktg - DeVry Education Group Inc.; pg. 600, pg. 607
Wynn, Jessica, Dir-Digital Mktg & Strategy-Global - Federal-Mogul Holdings Corporation; pg. 205, pg. 907
Wynne, Dan, Dir-B2B Channel Mktg & CRM - Sharp Electronics Corporation; pg. 672, pg. 1082
Wynne, Marcy, Sr Mgr-Res & Insights - C Spire Wireless; pg. 628, pg. 971
Wynne-Jones, Kenna, Mgr-Social Media - bebe stores, inc.; pg. 19, pg. 49
Wyrick, Christine, Dir-Digital Mktg strategy & Plng - Zurich Holding Company of America, Inc.; pg. 1224, pg. 660
Wyrwas, Anna, Sr Specialist-Creative - Ace Hardware Corporation; pg. 1040, pg. 644
Wyse, Kenneth L., Pres-Licensing & PR - PVH Corp.; pg. 46, pg. 1283
Wysocki, Kelly R., Mgr-GMC Product Comm - General Motors Company; pg. 175, pg. 881
Wyss, Lara, Dir-PR - NeuStar, Inc.; pg. 1872, pg. 1807
Wzorek, Andy, Dir-Media-North America - Tommy Hilfiger USA; pg. 48, pg. 1302

X

Xeller, Stephen, Exec VP-Sls-Intl - MicroStrategy, Inc.; pg. 1266, pg. 1809
Xenis, Samantha, Asst Mgr-PR - Toys "R" Us, Inc.; pg. 968, pg. 1130
Xi, Angela, Brand Mgr-China - Intel Corporation; pg. 645, pg. 266
Xiao, Xiangye, Product Mgr - Google Inc.; pg. 1249, pg. 153
Xie, Bing, VP & Deputy Mgr-World-Wide Sls & Mktg - Texas Instruments Incorporated; pg. 679, pg. 1688
Xu, Jason, Sr Mgr-Global Supply Chain Mgmt - Dolby Laboratories, Inc.; pg. 284, pg. 217
Xu, Linda, VP-Worldwide Product Mktg - Hitachi Data Systems Corporation; pg. 407, pg. 265
Xu, May, Product Mgr-Sls System & Ops - LinkedIn Corporation; pg. 1262, pg. 160
Xu, Nora, Sr Product Mktg Mgr - Zynga Inc.; pg. 1292, pg. 235

Y

Yacavone, Matt, VP-Sls & Chartering Crowley Petroleum Svcs - Crowley Maritime Corporation; pg. 1904, pg. 170
Yaccarino, Linda, Pres-NBC Universal Ad Sls - NBC Universal, Inc.; pg. 300, pg. 1266
Yacey, Daniel, Mgr-Trade Mktg-Healthcare - Reckitt Benckiser Inc.; pg. 1136, pg. 1105
Yacovone, Cheryl, Sr Mgr-Mktg Comm - Boston Scientific Corporation; pg. 1508, pg. 831
Yacovone, Kristy, Mgr-Mktg - Nestle Waters North America Inc.; pg. 257, pg. 375
Yacovone, Rose, Mgr-Mktg & Production Svcs - The Hibbert Group; pg. 407, pg. 1126
Yadav, Abhishek, Sr Mgr-Corp Strategy - Dell Inc.; pg. 383, pg. 1737
Yadav, Rani, Sr Dir-Mktg - Blue Apron, Inc.; pg. 1016, pg. 1205
Yaeger, Steve, VP-Mktg & PR - The Star Tribune Company; pg. 1689, pg. 942
Yagci, Ali, Mgr-Field Mktg - Morgan Stanley; pg. 783, pg. 1261
Yager, John, Sr VP-Sls - RealPage, Inc.; pg. 1277, pg. 1669
Yaggi, W. Timothy, Interim CEO - Tempur Sealy International, Inc.; pg. 944, pg. 731
Yaggie, Karen, Dir-Mktg - Universal Security Instruments, Inc.; pg. 683, pg. 775
Yaggy, Mark, Product Mgr-ECommerce-Testing & Personalization - Crate & Barrel, Inc.; pg. 922, pg. 640
Yagoda, Shayna, Brand Mgr-Beauty Owned Brands - Walgreen Co.; pg. 1608, pg. 605
Yahev, Alan, Mgr-Crude Oil Mktg - Newfield Exploration Company; pg. 45, pg. 1747
Yaklich, Bob, Sr Mgr-Mktg & Strategy - BASF Corporation; pg. 1149, pg. 1066
Yakoubyan, Yves, Sr Mgr-Mktg - CBS Interactive, Inc.; pg. 369, pg. 215
Yakubik, Kathy, Sr Mgr-Mktg-Americas Reg - Brocade Communications Systems, Inc.; pg. 365, pg. 239
Yalon, Dan, Exec VP-Bus Dev, Mktg & Vertical Solutions - Stratasys, Inc.; pg. 476, pg. 923

Yam, Serena, Mgr-Mobile Mktg - Toys "R" Us, Inc.; *pg.* 968, *pg.* 1130
Yamada, Chris, VP-Aerospace Products - Northrop Grumman Corporation; *pg.* 231, *pg.* 1781
Yamada, Kaori, Dir-Mktg - Best Buy Co., Inc.; *pg.* 1761, *pg.* 954
Yamada, Shannon, Brand Mgr - DOLE FOOD COMPANY, INC.; *pg.* 853, *pg.* 306
Yamada, Shannon, Brand Mgr - Dole Fresh Vegetables; *pg.* 854, *pg.* 198
Yamada, Takuji, Sr Dir-North America Area & Pres-Subsidiaries - American Honda Motor Co., Inc.; *pg.* 163, *pg.* 292
Yamagishi, Tomoko, Sr VP-Mktg - Shiseido Cosmetics America of SAC; *pg.* 522, *pg.* 1291
Yamamoto, Emily, Mgr-Digital Mktg - Mitsubishi Motors North America, Inc.; *pg.* 185, *pg.* 75
Yamamoto, Julie, Head-Comm & Strategist-Social Media - IBM; *pg.* 410, *pg.* 1449
Yamartino, Michael, Product Mgr - Pinterest; *pg.* 1275, *pg.* 225
Yamasaki, Mari, VP-Global Product Innovation-Artistry Brands - The Estee Lauder Companies Inc.; *pg.* 508, *pg.* 1229
Yampolsky, Hannah, Assoc Dir-Creative - Coach, Inc.; *pg.* 3, *pg.* 1214
Yanagisawa, Kenji, Product Mgr-Mgmt - DIRECTV Group Holdings, LLC; *pg.* 281, *pg.* 79
Yancey, Doug, Mgr-Adv - Varco Pruden Buildings, Inc.; *pg.* 118, *pg.* 1647
Yancey, W. Timothy, Sr Dir-Distr & Logistics - Chick-fil-A, Inc.; *pg.* 1721, *pg.* 492
Yanchunas, Marcy, Acting Head-ZYVOX Mktg - Pfizer Inc.; *pg.* 1581, *pg.* 1278
Yancy, Telisa, VP-Mktg - American Family Mutual Insurance Company; *pg.* 1190, *pg.* 1864
Yandrick, Rob, Product Mgr-Vibratory & Screening - Eriez Manufacturing Co. Inc.; *pg.* 1335, *pg.* 1530
Yanez, Guadalupe, Specialist-Bilingual Mktg - UnitedHealth Group Incorporated; *pg.* 1221, *pg.* 950
Yanez, Tomas, Dir-Enterprise Mktg - Comcast Cable Communications, Inc.; *pg.* 276, *pg.* 1560
Yang, Angela Yoonjeong, Sr Product Mgr - LinkedIn Corporation; *pg.* 1262, *pg.* 160
Yang, Annabel, Sr Mgr-Mktg Analytics - Sephora USA Inc; *pg.* 522, *pg.* 227
Yang, Calvin, Head-Product Mktg, Mobile & Desktop Product - Ancestry.com LLC; *pg.* 1228, *pg.* 1754
Yang, Eling, Brand Mgr-Nature's Recipe - Big Heart Pet Brands; *pg.* 1474, *pg.* 213
Yang, Eric, Sr Dir-TV Brand Mktg-Home Entertainment - NBC Universal, Inc.; *pg.* 300, *pg.* 1266
Yang, Gerald, Mgr-Strategic Mktg & Comml Dev-Specialty Matls - Honeywell International Inc.; *pg.* 407, *pg.* 1088
Yang, Gerald, Engr-Product Mktg - Pulse Electronics Corporation; *pg.* 666, *pg.* 206
Yang, Han, Mgr-Technical Mktg - Cisco Systems, Inc.; *pg.* 372, *pg.* 240
Yang, Jeni, Head-Brand & Consumer Mktg - Levi Strauss & Co.; *pg.* 43, *pg.* 220
Yang, Kelly, Sr Mgr-Mktg & Mgr-Pricing - SanDisk Corporation; *pg.* 465, *pg.* 147
Yang, Larry, Mgr-Lead Product - Google Inc.; *pg.* 1249, *pg.* 153
Yang, Mary C., Sr Strategist-Mktg-Federal - GovDelivery, Inc.; *pg.* 1255, *pg.* 961
Yang, Meryl, Specialist-Online Inventory & Coord-Mdse - The Gap, Inc.; *pg.* 1770, *pg.* 218
Yang, Michelle, Specialist-Loyalty Mktg - True Value Company; *pg.* 1065, *pg.* 592
Yang, Peter, Product Mgr - Facebook, Inc.; *pg.* 1245, *pg.* 143
Yang, Richard C., VP-Corp Sls & Connected Solutions - DexCom Inc; *pg.* 1524, *pg.* 202
Yang, Sai, Product Mgr - Agilent Technologies, Inc.; *pg.* 614, *pg.* 264
Yang, Shoen, Sr Dir-Global Bus Plng & Ops - Yahoo! Mobile; *pg.* 1291, *pg.* 290
Yang, Sunny, Dir-Creative Svcs - LifeLock Inc.; *pg.* 776, *pg.* 26
Yang, Wenge, VP-Mktg - ENTEGRIS, INC.; *pg.* 1882, *pg.* 788
Yannicelli, Caterina, Coord-Product Mgmt - Home Box Office, Inc.; *pg.* 290, *pg.* 1240
Yannucci, Douglas J., Sr VP-Sls-Footwear - R.G. Barry Corporation; *pg.* 1818, *pg.* 1470
Yanovick, Joanne, Mgr-Sls-Natl - Palm Springs Desert Resorts Convention & Visitors Authority; *pg.* 1003, *pg.* 187
Yantosca, Lou, Dir-Global Sls - Parker Chomerics; *pg.* 662, *pg.* 862
Yanulavich, Mark F., Dir-Mktg & Creative Comm - New York State Department of Health; *pg.* 1001, *pg.* 1137
Yanushpolsky, Shelly, Mgr-Mobile Products Strategy & Bus Dev - American Express Company; *pg.* 712, *pg.* 1190
Yao, Chen, Sr Mgr-Mktg Comm - Honeywell International Inc.; *pg.* 407, *pg.* 1088
Yao, Louie, Global Product Mgr - Kensington Technology Group; *pg.* 424, *pg.* 191
Yao, Renee, Specialist-Product Mktg - Cisco Systems, Inc.; *pg.* 372, *pg.* 240
Yao, Rose, Product Head - Facebook, Inc.; *pg.* 1245, *pg.* 143
Yap, Angela, Sr Product Mgr - Macy's East; *pg.* 1777, *pg.* 1254
Yap, Daniel, Exec Dir-Mktg Strategy & Innovation - Kaplan, Inc.; *pg.* 603, *pg.* 425
Yap, Teck, Mgr-Western Reg Sls-LPG - Corken, Inc.; *pg.* 1325, *pg.* 1485
Yarber, Danielle, Dir-Sls - xpedx; *pg.* 1472, *pg.* 1458
Yarbrough, Jenny, VP-Mktg-CFMP - MutualFirst Financial, Inc.; *pg.* 785, *pg.* 696
Yarmey, Jessica, Dir-Franchise Mktg - Gold's Gym; *pg.* 550, *pg.* 1681
Yarnall, Casey, VP & Mgr-Mktg - JPMorgan Chase & Co.; *pg.* 772, *pg.* 1246
Yarnell, Kimberly, VP-Digital Media - Macy's East; *pg.* 1777, *pg.* 1254
Yarnell, Kimberly, VP-Digital Media - Macy's, Inc.; *pg.* 1778, *pg.* 1417
Yarrington, Darci, Mgr-Customer Engagement Mktg - Hewlett-Packard Company; *pg.* 404, *pg.* 175
Yarroll, Marie, Sr Mgr-Comm - Medtronic, Inc.; *pg.* 1564, *pg.* 939
Yasenchak, Randy, Sr Mgr-Loyalty & Email - Toms Shoe's Inc; *pg.* 1821, *pg.* 276
Yashinsky, Joel, VP-Mktg - McDonald's Corporation; *pg.* 1737, *pg.* 645
Yasi, Daniel, Sr Dir-Comml Infrastructure Channels - LIGHTING SCIENCE GROUP CORPORATION; *pg.* 1301, *pg.* 467
Yaskanich, Marla, Head-Direct to Consumer Mktg-Individual & Family Plans - Cigna Corporation; *pg.* 1197, *pg.* 338
Yasutake, Leilani, Supvr-Adv - Fry's Electronics, Inc.; *pg.* 640, *pg.* 245
Yates, Aaron, Mgr-Mktg - Affinia Group Intermediate Holdings Inc.; *pg.* 197, *pg.* 1373
Yates, Ann L., Mgr-Mktg Comm - Trane Inc.; *pg.* 116, *pg.* 1109
Yates, Beth, Dir-Creative Mktg - Becton, Dickinson & Company; *pg.* 1501, *pg.* 1068
Yates, Casey, Sr Mgr-Interactive Adv - The Home Depot, Inc.; *pg.* 1050, *pg.* 510
Yates, David, Dir-Mktg-Svc Provider Video - Cisco Systems, Inc.; *pg.* 372, *pg.* 240
Yates, Gary, Mgr-Strategic Mktg - Air Products and Chemicals, Inc.; *pg.* 1145, *pg.* 1513
Yates, Gary W., Dir-Adv & Exhibit Sls - Alexander Graham Bell Association for the Deaf and Hard of Hearing; *pg.* 126, *pg.* 393
Yates, Justin, Head-Mktg-Media, Social Media & CRM - FCA US LLC; *pg.* 170, *pg.* 868
Yates, Kayleen, Sr Dir-Corp Comm - Bankrate, Inc.; *pg.* 1231, *pg.* 451
Yates, Kim, Sr VP-Mktg & Assoc Dir-Mktg-Prestige Beauty - The Procter & Gamble Company; *pg.* 1129, *pg.* 1418
Yates, Lisa, VP-Product Dev-Card Linked Offer Redemption - MasterCard Incorporated; *pg.* 779, *pg.* 1325
Yates, Lisa, VP-Global Product Dev-Merchant Value Proposition - MasterCard Worldwide Inc.; *pg.* 780, *pg.* 988
Yates, Mike, Sr Dir-Art - AutoZone, Inc.; *pg.* 200, *pg.* 1641
Yates, Norman, Dir-Sls-Asia - O'Brien Corporation; *pg.* 1366, *pg.* 1001
Yates, Oliver, Reg VP-Sls - Infor; *pg.* 414, *pg.* 484
Yates, Patricia, Reg Dir-Sls - NetSuite, Inc.; *pg.* 1270, *pg.* 255
Yates, Stacey S., VP-Mktg Comm - Louisville Convention & Visitors Bureau; *pg.* 998, *pg.* 736
Yates, Whitney, Specialist-Mktg - Brookshire Grocery Company; *pg.* 1016, *pg.* 1748
Yavil, Sabrina, Exec Dir-Global Skincare Mktg - Clinique Laboratories LLC; *pg.* 503, *pg.* 1214
Yavor, Suzanne, Mgr-Global Employer Brand & Mktg - Marriott International, Inc.; *pg.* 1102, *pg.* 764
Yaw, Theresa, Dir-Mktg - Baldwin Filters; *pg.* 1316, *pg.* 1011
Ybarra, Stacy, Sr Dir-IR & Corp Comm - Blucora; *pg.* 1232, *pg.* 1813
Yde, Steven, Dir-Mktg - Wahl Clipper Corporation; *pg.* 524, *pg.* 662
Ye, Donna, Coord-Mktg Ops - Time Warner Cable Inc.; *pg.* 312, *pg.* 1301
Yeadon, Gregory, Brand Mgr-Pet Health & Wellness - Central Garden & Pet Company; *pg.* 1475, *pg.* 303
Yeager, Amy, VP-Adv & Visual Display - W.S. Badcock Corporation; *pg.* 947, *pg.* 449
Yeager, Chuck, VP-Mktg & Mktg Ops - Central Garden & Pet Company; *pg.* 1475, *pg.* 303
Yeaman, Sterling, Dir-Production - The Record Searchlight; *pg.* 1680, *pg.* 188
Yeaney, Jacqueline, Exec VP-Strategy & Corp Mktg - Red Hat, Inc.; *pg.* 460, *pg.* 1388
Yearsley, Ryan, Sr Dir-Mktg & Education - Stryker Corporation; *pg.* 1598, *pg.* 894
Yearwood, Charles, Mgr-Brand Mktg - NIKE, Inc.; *pg.* 1812, *pg.* 1492
Yee, Brendan, Dir-Mktg-QuantiGene & Procarta Products - Affymetrix, Inc.; *pg.* 1487, *pg.* 263
Yee, Christina, Specialist-Mktg - Comcast Cable Communications, Inc.; *pg.* 276, *pg.* 1560
Yee, Dacy, Sr Dir-Emerging Media & Ecommerce - Experian Consumer Direct; *pg.* 1245, *pg.* 71
Yee, Dorothy, VP-Wholesale Mktg & Mgr-Creative Svcs & Mktg - Wells Fargo & Company; *pg.* 819, *pg.* 232
Yee, Lianne, Dir-Mktg - Pepsi Beverages Company; *pg.* 258, *pg.* 1342
Yee, Yang Chiah, VP-Sls-Worldwide - Atmel Corporation; *pg.* 621, *pg.* 238
Yee-Garcia, Allison, Sr Dir-Mktg - Sacramento Kings; *pg.* 579, *pg.* 197
Yeganeh, Jody, Sr Dir-ECommerce - Lawson Products, Inc.; *pg.* 1355, *pg.* 580
Yeh, Chantal, Bus Mgr-US Mobility - Acer America Corporation; *pg.* 341, *pg.* 235
Yeh, Chris, Sr VP-Product & Platform - Box Inc.; *pg.* 1232, *pg.* 124
Yeh, Deborah, Sr VP-Mktg & Brand - Sephora USA Inc; *pg.* 522, *pg.* 227
Yeh, Emily, Mgr-Mktg - Cinemark Holdings, Inc.; *pg.* 540, *pg.* 1729
Yeh, Linda, Brand Mgr-Small Bus - United States Cellular Corporation; *pg.* 1875, *pg.* 594
Yehoshua, Tamar, VP-Product Mgmt - Google Inc.; *pg.* 1249, *pg.* 153
Yelle, Sean, Dir-Comml & Customer Mktg-Smirnoff Global Brand - Diageo North America Inc.; *pg.* 248, *pg.* 1223
Yellin, Ezrie, Product Mgr-Work Opportunity Tax Credit - Equifax Workforce Solutions; *pg.* 394, *pg.* 997
Yellin, Todd, VP-Product Innovation - Netflix, Inc.; *pg.* 1269, *pg.* 141
Yelton, Jason, Mgr-North America Channel & SMB Mktg - Lenovo Group Ltd; *pg.* 427, *pg.* 1384
Yelton, Kristal, Mgr-Mktg - Cincinnati Sub-Zero Products, Inc.; *pg.* 1070, *pg.* 1411
Yelton, Scott, Dir-Product Dev - EarthLink Holdings Corp.; *pg.* 1240, *pg.* 504
Yembrick, John, Mgr-Social Media - National Aeronautics & Space Administration (NASA); *pg.* 1000, *pg.* 401
Yen, Bruce, Sr Dir-Bus Intelligence & Mobile - Guess?, Inc.; *pg.* 25, *pg.* 132
Yeomans, Elaine, Mgr-Mktg Comm - Nordson Corporation; *pg.* 1365, *pg.* 1480
Yeomans, Emily, VP-Comm-Bravo & Oxygen Media - Oxygen Media LLC; *pg.* 303, *pg.* 1275
Yeomans, Michael, Dir-Digital Mktg - Alcatel-Lucent; *pg.* 615, *pg.* 38
Yeray, Amber, Mgr-Digital Mktg - Express, Inc.; *pg.* 24, *pg.* 1440
Yerges, Sheri, Mgr-Mktg - School Specialty, Inc.; *pg.* 467, *pg.* 1860
Yering, Alison, Dir-Accts Comm & Sls-Natl - The Travelers Companies, Inc.; *pg.* 1220, *pg.* 352
Yeschick, Amanda Doble, Grp Mgr-Mktg-Global - Imation Corp.; *pg.* 413, *pg.* 952
Yeskel, Zach, Product Mgr - Google Inc.; *pg.* 1249, *pg.* 153
Yesville, Brenda, Brand Mgr - Nestle Purina PetCare Company; *pg.* 1479, *pg.* 1000
Yetman, Jill, Sr Mgr-Comm - TELUS CORPORATION; *pg.* 1952, *pg.* 1912
Yetta, Shea, Coord-Creative - Gibson Guitar Corp.; *pg.* 550, *pg.* 1650
Yetter, John, Assoc Dir-Oncology Payer Mktg - Bristol-Myers

First page reference indicates Business Class Edition
Second page reference indicates Geographic Edition

Squibb Company; pg. 1509, pg. 1206
Yeung, Ada, Mgr-Natl Adv - Burger King Corporation; pg. 1719, pg. 440
Yeung, Steve, Mgr-Sls - Reliable Automatic Sprinkler Co., Inc.; pg. 1137, pg. 1158
Yevin, Shira, Mgr-Field Mktg-New York City & Los Angeles - Pabst Brewing Company; pg. 258, pg. 137
Yi, Duke, Sr Mgr-Display Components & Materials Res - IHS Inc.; pg. 1652, pg. 326
Yi, Joanne, Coord-Digital Mktg - Netflix, Inc.; pg. 1269, pg. 141
Yick, David, Asst Mgr-Acura Interactive Mktg - American Honda Motor Co., Inc.; pg. 163, pg. 292
Yim, Gary, Writer-Mktg Comm - Anthem, Inc.; pg. 1192, pg. 683
Yim, Kwan, Dir-Media - Luxottica Retail; pg. 8, pg. 1460
Yin, Aaron, Sr Dir-Customer Acq - Newegg Inc.; pg. 1271, pg. 67
Yin, Nathalie, Dir-Mktg - The Hain Celestial Group, Inc.; pg. 860, pg. 1172
Ying Zeng, Anna, Mgr-Mobile Mktg - Starwood Hotels & Resorts Worldwide, Inc.; pg. 1114, pg. 378
Yingling, Loretta, Mgr-Sls-Natl - Greater Raleigh Convention & Visitors Bureau; pg. 994, pg. 1387
Yip, Darren, Sr Dir-Fin & IR - Zynga Inc.; pg. 1292, pg. 235
Yip, Janice, Brand Mgr - Bombardier Inc.; pg. 1318, pg. 1953
Ylipekkala, Kari, Product Mgr - Bombardier Recreational Products, Inc.; pg. 201, pg. 1960
Ylisastigui, Angel, Mgr-Mktg - Avid Technology, Inc.; pg. 622, pg. 804
Yoakum Queen, Molly, Dir-Interactive Mktg & Internal Agency - Abbott Nutrition; pg. 1485, pg. 1437
Yoakum, Marina, Sr Dir-Digital Mktg - Banana Republic; pg. 1760, pg. 212
Yob, Matt, Sr Mgr-Pub & Media Rels - Chicago Professional Sports Limited Partnership; pg. 539, pg. 570
Yocky, Stefani, Mgr-Mktg-Global - Mattel Games/Puzzles; pg. 962, pg. 80
Yocky, Stefani, Mgr-Mktg-Global - MATTEL, INC.; pg. 962, pg. 81
Yocum, Mark, Dir-Adv - Sandusky Newspapers Inc.; pg. 1683, pg. 1472
Yoder, Deb, Mgr-Creative Svcs - Meredith Corporation; pg. 1663, pg. 705
Yoder, Lisa M., Dir-Mktg - Candy Swick & Company; pg. 1084, pg. 465
Yoder, Shem, Sr Mgr-Fin - Johnson & Johnson; pg. 1549, pg. 1091
Yoegel, Rich, VP-Mdsg-Home - QVC Inc; pg. 305, pg. 1593
Yoffe, Scott, Asst Dir-PR - San Diego Chargers Football Co.; pg. 580, pg. 208
Yoffee, Ellen, Mgr-Digital Mktg - Dolby Laboratories, Inc.; pg. 284, pg. 217
Yohannan, Jonathan, Dir-PR - Panera Bread Company; pg. 1029, pg. 1001
Yohman, Kim, Brand Mgr - The Procter & Gamble Company; pg. 1129, pg. 1418
Yohn, Jeanne C., Sr Mgr-Comm - GlaxoSmithKline; pg. 1536, pg. 1565
Yoho, Michelle, Mgr-Mktg - Intuit Inc.; pg. 769, pg. 158
Yokota, David, Bus Mgr-Customer - Honeywell International Inc.; pg. 407, pg. 1088
Yomoah, Jen, Brand Mgr - Edgewell Personal Care; pg. 1526, pg. 995
Yong, Renee, Mgr-Enterprise Events Mktg-Worldwide - Microsoft Corporation; pg. 435, pg. 1824
Yonker, Seth, Sr Mgr-Performance Mktg-Global Store - NIKE, Inc.; pg. 1812, pg. 1492
Yoo, David, Sr VP-Mobile Products & Svcs-US - American Express Company; pg. 712, pg. 1190
Yoo, Sam, Dir-Digital Acq Mktg - FourSquare Labs, Inc; pg. 1248, pg. 1232
Yoon, Kristina, Mgr-Integrated Mktg - Hyundai Motor America; pg. 179, pg. 89
Yoon, Ted, Sr Mgr-Digital Servicing Comm - American Express Company; pg. 712, pg. 1190
Yoresen, Kirk, Mgr-Global Mktg-Construction & Indus Div - ESCO Corporation; pg. 1335, pg. 1502
York, Bethany, Sr Product Mgr-Global - Blount International, Inc.; pg. 1043, pg. 1501
York, Conrad, VP-Mktg - The Northwestern Mutual Life Insurance Company; pg. 1212, pg. 1879
York, Danette, Dir-Mktg - Georgia-Pacific LLC; pg. 1458, pg. 507
York, Kara, Producer-Adv - Apple Inc.; pg. 350, pg. 73
York, Mary, Analyst-Online Mktg - A Book Company, LLC; pg. 1225, pg. 729
York, Nicole, Dir-Mktg Comm - Jeld-Wen, Inc.; pg. 1051, pg. 1499
York, Reida, Dir-Mktg Comm - Theater League Inc.; pg. 587, pg. 986
Yoshida, Brian, Dir-Web Mktg - Brocade Communications Systems, Inc.; pg. 365, pg. 239
Yoshinaka, Brian, Mgr-Mktg Programs - Intel Corporation; pg. 645, pg. 266
Yosick, Lana, Mgr-Mktg Comm - Intel Corporation; pg. 645, pg. 266
Yost, Bill, VP-Natl Acct Sls - Landstar System, Inc.; pg. 1914, pg. 434
Yost, John, Engr-Technical Mktg-Collaboration Tech - Cisco Systems, Inc.; pg. 372, pg. 240
Yost, Kathryn, Coord-Social Media - The North Face, Inc.; pg. 1840, pg. 252
Yothers, Keith R., Dir-Customer Mktg, Pharmacy & Distr - Merck & Co., Inc.; pg. 1566, pg. 1077
Young, Aaron, Sr Dir-Bus Dev & Strategic Partnerships - Match.Com, LLC; pg. 1265, pg. 1683
Young, Abby, Dir-PR-Global - Burton Snowboard Company; pg. 1829, pg. 1765
Young, Allison, Head-Media Platform Sls-Programmatic - Google Inc.; pg. 1249, pg. 153
Young, Amy, Mgr-Accessories Mktg - Sprint Corporation; pg. 1874, pg. 719
Young, Andrea, Sr Dir-Mktg-Global - The Coca-Cola Company; pg. 240, pg. 493
Young, Andrew, VP-Product Mgmt - WatchGuard Technologies, Inc.; pg. 491, pg. 1842
Young, Andy, Dir-Adv - The ADT Corporation; pg. 612, pg. 409
Young, Annette, Dir-Mktg-Vlasic Franchise - Pinnacle Foods Group LLC; pg. 889, pg. 1104
Young, Barrie, Pres-Sls & Franchising - Snap-on Incorporated; pg. 1062, pg. 1862
Young, Bettina, Brand Mgr-Westin Hotels & Resorts North America - Starwood Hotels & Resorts Worldwide, Inc.; pg. 1114, pg. 378
Young, Brandon, Specialist-Interactive Mktg - Advent Software, Inc.; pg. 345, pg. 211
Young, Brian, Dir-Sls Admin-Trade Promo Analytics - L'Oreal USA; pg. 514, pg. 1252
Young, Bud, Dir-Solutions Mktg - Emerson Process Management; pg. 1334, pg. 1636
Young, Christopher, Dir-Mktg - Michaels Stores, Inc.; pg. 1127, pg. 1722
Young, Cliff, Mgr-Mktg-North America - IDEXX Laboratories, Inc.; pg. 1543, pg. 753
Young, Cole, Coord-Mktg & Promos - GameStop Corp.; pg. 399, pg. 1699
Young, Connie, Sr Dir-Mktg Acq - Sephora USA Inc; pg. 522, pg. 227
Young, Darrell, Mgr-Sls - Interplastic Corporation; pg. 1168, pg. 961
Young, Debbie, Dir-Product Mktg & Converged Sys - Hewlett-Packard Company; pg. 404, pg. 175
Young, Dennis, Exec VP-Sls & Mktg - Sanmina-SCI Corporation; pg. 671, pg. 250
Young, Diahann, Dir-Innovation & New Product Dev - PulteGroup, Inc.; pg. 1109, pg. 873
Young, Diane, VP-Customer Engagement Mktg - E*TRADE Financial Corporation; pg. 749, pg. 1230
Young, Don, VP-Mktg-MG Brands - LOUD Technologies Inc.; pg. 652, pg. 1847
Young, Emily, Brand Mgr - Nestle Purina PetCare Company; pg. 1479, pg. 1000
Young, Frank T., Sr VP-Global Product & Innovation - Global Payments Inc.; pg. 762, pg. 508
Young, Gabe, Exec Dir-Software Mktg - Dell Inc.; pg. 383, pg. 1737
Young, Grant, Dir-Mktg-Comml Div - The Toro Company; pg. 1065, pg. 918
Young, Ian, Product Mgr-Rigur - Poly Pak America, Inc.; pg. 1467, pg. 138
Young, Jamison, Sr Mgr-Mktg - The Allstate Corporation; pg. 1189, pg. 639
Young, Jason, VP-Production - 20th Century Fox Film Corp.; pg. 267, pg. 124
Young, Jaye, Brand Mgr-Segment-Michelin LT & SUV - Michelin North America Inc.; pg. 1886, pg. 1618
Young, Jayson, Product Mgr-Technical - KEMET Corporation; pg. 649, pg. 1621
Young, Jeff, Sr Dir - Akamai Technologies, Inc.; pg. 1226, pg. 807
Young, Jennifer, VP-Partnership Mktg - Oxygen Media LLC; pg. 303, pg. 1275
Young, Jennifer, Sr Dir-Adv & Consumer Res - Robert Half International Inc.; pg. 462, pg. 145
Young, John, Sr VP & Gen Mgr-Mdse-Home - Boscov's Department Store, LLC; pg. 1763, pg. 1583
Young, John, VP-Customer Mktg Comm - Comcast Cable Communications, Inc.; pg. 276, pg. 1560
Young, John P., Sr VP-Sls-Intl - Cybex International, Inc.; pg. 1521, pg. 832
Young, Jovina, Sr Mgr-Mktg-Channel Solutions, Liquor & Large Format - MillerCoors; pg. 254, pg. 1877
Young, Jovina, Brand Mgr-Blue Moon Brewing Company - MillerCoors LLC; pg. 255, pg. 582
Young, Julie, Sr Mgr-Mktg-Mgmt - Charles Schwab & Company, Inc.; pg. 734, pg. 215
Young, Kathy, VP-Mktg Svcs - Shaw Industries Group, Inc.; pg. 942, pg. 530
Young, Kevin, Dir-Digital Mktg - 24 Hour Fitness Worldwide Inc.; pg. 526, pg. 258
Young, Kimberly, Sr Mgr-Mktg - The Allstate Corporation; pg. 1189, pg. 639
Young, Kristine, Dir-Mktg Ops-Global - Levi Strauss & Co.; pg. 43, pg. 220
Young, Mary, Mgr-Event Mktg - Ecolab Inc.; pg. 329, pg. 960
Young, Matthew, Sr VP-Sls - Genworth Financial, Inc.; pg. 761, pg. 1802
Young, Megan, Gen Mgr-Brand Mktg - DISH Network Corporation; pg. 283, pg. 325
Young, Melody Lai, Mgr-Product Dev - Sephora USA Inc; pg. 522, pg. 227
Young, Michelle, Mgr-Sls-Eastern Reg - OptoSigma Corp.; pg. 1425, pg. 262
Young, Oliver, Sr Product Mgr - Twitter, Inc.; pg. 1285, pg. 228
Young, Robyn, Dir-Mktg - Annie's Inc.; pg. 1760, pg. 45
Young, Ryan, Mgr-Sls - Young Electric Sign Company; pg. 1308, pg. 1762
Young, Sandy, Dir-Mktg - Denver Broncos Football Club; pg. 544, pg. 325
Young, Sarah, Dir-Mktg - DS Waters of America, Inc.; pg. 250, pg. 504
Young, Scott, Sr VP-Product & Bus Dev - Staples; pg. 474, pg. 313
Young, Shawn D., Dir-Investment Comm & Mktg - The Guardian Life Insurance Company of America; pg. 1202, pg. 1237
Young, Steven F., Sr VP-Mktg Comm - Eastern Bank Corporation; pg. 745, pg. 793
Young, Tracy, Product Mgr-Comml - Rinnai America Corp.; pg. 1076, pg. 538
Young, Tracy, VP-Mktg & Comm - Team Health, Inc.; pg. 482, pg. 1639
Young, Veronica, Sr Dir-Sls Tech Ops - Pandora Media Inc.; pg. 1273, pg. 172
Young, Wallace, Mgr-Mktg - AMC, Inc.; pg. 1759, pg. 487
Young, Wanda, VP-Media & Digital Mktg - Wal-Mart Stores, Inc.; pg. 1790, pg. 29
Young, William, Planner-Digital Sls - Major League Soccer LLC; pg. 560, pg. 1256
Young-Krauss, Marjorie, Head-Audience & Segment Mktg - VMware, Inc.; pg. 490, pg. 179
Youngbauer, Mary, Mgr-Americas Mktg-Gen Imaging Ultrasound - GE Healthcare; pg. 399, pg. 1765
Youngbauer, Sarah, Head-PR - Advanced Micro Devices, Inc.; pg. 613, pg. 282
Youngblade, Stephen, Coord-Brand Mktg - The North Face, Inc.; pg. 1840, pg. 252
Youngblood, Chaney, Mgr-Shopper Mktg - General Mills, Inc.; pg. 828, pg. 933
Youngblood, Dave, VP-Internet Mktg - Texas Instruments Incorporated; pg. 679, pg. 1688
Youngdale, Eric, Mgr-Mktg-Global - E.I. du Pont de Nemours & Company; pg. 1159, pg. 390
Younggren, Maggie, Dir-Mktg Comm - Fiskars Brands, Inc.; pg. 1124, pg. 1866
Youngless, Chris, Mgr-Mktg - The D.S. Brown Company; pg. 79, pg. 1468
Youngman, Kevin, Dir-Online Mktg - CME Group Inc.; pg. 738, pg. 571
Youngman, Kevin, Dir-Online Mktg - CME Group, Inc.; pg. 738, pg. 571
Youngquist, Erin, Reg Dir-Recruitment Adv - The News-Times;

pg. 1670, pg. 344
Youngren, Lisa, Mgr-Corp Mktg Ops - Land O'Lakes, Inc.; pg. 873, pg. 915
Youngworth, Mark, Brand Dir-Mktg - Dunkin' Brands Group, Inc.; pg. 1727, pg. 810
Younker, Jared A., Mgr-Interactive Mktg - UnitedHealth Group Incorporated; pg. 1221, pg. 950
Yount, Kathy, Asst Dir-Mktg & Comm - Kentucky Department of Tourism; pg. 996, pg. 728
Yousef, Moheb, Mgr-Mktg-Internal Comm & Events - Xerox Canada Inc.; pg. 494, pg. 1930
Youssef, Nadine, Dir-Media Rels - MORNINGSTAR, INC.; pg. 784, pg. 583
Youtsey, Phil, Dir-Ticket Sls - Panthers Football, LLC; pg. 573, pg. 1368
Yovan, Kendra, Sr Assoc Mgr-Brand Mktg - Taco Bell Corp.; pg. 1752, pg. 117
Yovanovich, Jack, Dir-West Reg Mktg - Frontier Communications of New York, Inc.; pg. 398, pg. 1335
Ysseldyke, Lauren, Specialist-Digital Mktg - Yokohama Tire Corporation; pg. 1892, pg. 94
Yturri, Robert, Sr VP-Global Sls, Product & Brand Mgmt - Sport Obermeyer Ltd.; pg. 1846, pg. 310
Yu, Annie, Sr Mgr-Forecasting & Analytics-Global Mktg - Takeda Pharmaceuticals USA, Inc.; pg. 1600, pg. 605
Yu, Carly, Mktg, Women's Apparel & Classics - Vans, Inc.; pg. 1821, pg. 76
Yu, Cherie, Partner-Product Mktg - Pinterest; pg. 1275, pg. 225
Yu, Edison, Partner & VP-Mktg, Value & Premium Light Brands - Anheuser-Busch Companies, LLC; pg. 237, pg. 991
Yu, Ellen, Sr Mgr-Media Rels - Verizon Communications Inc.; pg. 1875, pg. 1309
Yu, Jacqueline, Sr Mgr-CRM Digital Mktg - LG Electronics U.S.A., Inc.; pg. 651, pg. 1060
Yu, Jessica, Project Mgr-Creative Svcs - DIRECTV Group Holdings, LLC; pg. 281, pg. 79
Yu, Karen, Dir-Product Mgmt & Corp Solutions - The NASDAQ OMX Group, Inc.; pg. 785, pg. 1263
Yu, Katie, Mgr-Global Brand Strategic Mktg - Levi Strauss & Co.; pg. 43, pg. 220
Yu, May, Sr Asst Brand Mgr - Procter & Gamble Inc.; pg. 333, pg. 1929
Yu, Songtao, Sr Analyst-Strategic Project Mktg - FedEx Corporation; pg. 1907, pg. 1642
Yu, Sunny, Dir-PR & Community Projects - Molina Healthcare, Inc.; pg. 1569, pg. 123
Yu, Tom, Head-Programmatic Ad Tech Mktg & Dir - Yahoo! Inc.; pg. 1289, pg. 289
Yu, Victor, Sr Mgr-Audience Operation-Programmatic Media Buying - The Hearst Corporation; pg. 1649, pg. 1239
Yu, Wainwright, Mgr-Product Mgmt-Kindle - Amazon.com, Inc.; pg. 1226, pg. 1831
Yuanis, Mark, Coord-Social Media & Branded Content - Carnival Corporation; pg. 1902, pg. 441
Yucht, Nicole, Dir-Mktg - University Of Florida; pg. 609, pg. 429
Yue, Franklin, Sr Mgr-Technical Mktg - F5 Networks, Inc.; pg. 396, pg. 1835
Yuen, Jennifer, Head-Mktg-North America - Airbnb, Inc.; pg. 1226, pg. 211
Yuen, Mike, Mgr-Digital Mktg - Verizon Communications Inc.; pg. 1875, pg. 1309
Yuen, Stephanie, Specialist-Media - QuikTrip Corporation; pg. 1031, pg. 1490
Yuen, Warner, Engr-Sls - Apple Inc.; pg. 350, pg. 73
Yule, Kris, Gen Mgr-Sls - News Corporation; pg. 1669, pg. 1271
Yum, Clara, Sr Mgr-Mobile Conversion Mktg - Audible, Inc.; pg. 1230, pg. 1095
Yurchich, Jessica, Brand Mgr - Seura, Inc.; pg. 672, pg. 1860
Yurcisin, John, Dir-Social - Amazon.com, Inc.; pg. 1226, pg. 1831
Yurtin, John, Product Mgr - Delphi Automotive LLP; pg. 204, pg. 910
Yuzva, Aubrey, Sr Assoc Brand Mgr - The WhiteWave Foods Company; pg. 1037, pg. 324

Z

Zabaglo, Kristen, Brand Mgr - Starbucks Corporation; pg. 897, pg. 1840
Zaballos, Peter, VP-Mktg & Product - SPS COMMERCE, INC.; pg. 472, pg. 942
Zabalua, Gabriela, VP-Multicultural Mktg - Frontier Communications Corporation; pg. 1871, pg. 362
Zabel, Deanna, Sr Mgr-Corp Comm - Briggs & Stratton Corporation; pg. 201, pg. 1899
Zabik, Kathryn, Sr Assoc Brand Mgr-Cheese Snacking - The Kraft Heinz Company; pg. 871, pg. 641
Zabita, Nicole, Dir-Ad Sls - Al Jazeera America, LLC; pg. 269, pg. 1188
Zabloski, Jill, Brand Mgr - Capital One Financial Corporation; pg. 730, pg. 1789
Zablud, Jo, Dir-Social Media - Audible, Inc.; pg. 1230, pg. 1095
Zabransky, Don, VP-Sls & Mktg-Pettit Marine Paint - Pettit Paint Company; pg. 1444, pg. 1116
Zabritski, Melinda, Sr Dir-Product, Mktg, Thought Leadership & Automotive Fin - Experian Consumer Direct; pg. 1245, pg. 71
Zabrouski, Amanda, Mgr-Mktg Res - TEN: The Enthusiast Network; pg. 1091, pg. 1298
Zaccone, Deidre, Dir-Mktg - Duane Reade, Inc.; pg. 1525, pg. 1226
Zacek, Kevin, Mgr-Production - Gazette Communications, Inc.; pg. 1644, pg. 702
Zachary, Jordan, Chief Strategy Officer - Live Nation Entertainment, Inc.; pg. 558, pg. 47
Zachos, Chris, Sr Product Mgr-StubHub Music - StubHub, Inc.; pg. 586, pg. 228
Zack, Marla, Mgr-Digital Mktg - Sheplers, Inc.; pg. 1785, pg. 724
Zadeh, Joe, Chief Product Officer - Airbnb, Inc.; pg. 1226, pg. 211
Zaffrann, Kathy, Mgr-Mktg Field - Harley-Davidson, Inc.; pg. 178, pg. 1874
Zagorski, Alexandra, Mgr-Mktg & Sls - Medieval Times Inc.; pg. 561, pg. 51
Zagorski, Maria E., Sr Mgr-Indus Mktg-Comm & Media - salesforce.com, inc.; pg. 1278, pg. 226
Zaheer, Asim, Sr VP-Mktg-Worldwide - Hitachi Data Systems Corporation; pg. 407, pg. 265
Zaher, Paul, VP-IT Mktg Sys - Dunkin' Brands Group, Inc.; pg. 1727, pg. 810
Zahery, Renee, Sr Dir-Corp Affairs-North America - The Kraft Heinz Company; pg. 871, pg. 641
Zahm, Deborah, Mgr-Field Mktg & Residential - SunPower Corporation; pg. 1952, pg. 250
Zahn, Andrea, Sr Dir-Fan Experience - Milwaukee Bucks, Inc.; pg. 563, pg. 1878
Zahn, Victoria, Acct Exec-Programmatic-Google Mktg - Google Inc.; pg. 1249, pg. 153
Zahner, Tracy, Specialist-Mktg Trng - The Procter & Gamble Company; pg. 1129, pg. 1418
Zaiontz, Patrick, Mgr-Acct Sls - Singer Sewing Company; pg. 698, pg. 1639
Zajdel, Bob, Mgr-North Central Reg Sls - David Clark Company Incorporated; pg. 633, pg. 862
Zakin, Charlie, VP-Corp Media - Hasbro, Inc.; pg. 954, pg. 1603
Zaky, Amanda, Sr Mgr-Interactive - Mars, Incorporated; pg. 1858, pg. 1792
Zaky, Amanda, Sr Mgr-Interactive - Mars North America; pg. 1859, pg. 1072
Zalazar, Cecilia, Sr Dir-Creative - Orchard Brands Corporation; pg. 1780, pg. 1590
Zale, Jillian, Mgr-Mktg - MANPOWER INC.; pg. 430, pg. 1877
Zaleski, Joe, Sr Mgr-Mktg-Suprane Global Team - Baxter International Inc.; pg. 1499, pg. 599
Zalka, Amanda, Sr Mgr-Digital Creative Svcs - Michael Kors (USA), Inc.; pg. 29, pg. 1260
Zamanski, Thomas, VP-Sls - Tenova; pg. 114, pg. 1525
Zamansky, Merle, Mgr-Mktg & Creative Svcs - Big Y Foods, Inc.; pg. 1015, pg. 845
Zamarripa, Henry, Dir-Sls-Latin America, Caribbean & Yahoo Colombia - Yahoo! Inc.; pg. 1289, pg. 289
Zambanini, Adam, VP-Mktg - Trex Company, Inc.; pg. 116, pg. 1812
Zambito, Kathryn, Dir-PR - Wyndham Worldwide Corporation; pg. 1119, pg. 1107
Zamichow, Steve, VP-Mktg - Bimbo Bakeries USA; pg. 840, pg. 151
Zamir, Kim, Dir-Mktg - Rubio's Restaurants, Inc.; pg. 1748, pg. 60
Zammit, Elizabeth, Sr Dir-Res & Analytics - Sony Music Entertainment; pg. 309, pg. 1294
Zammit, Kristin, Exec Dir-Sls - Institutional Investor, Inc.; pg. 1653, pg. 1244
Zamoiski Halprin, Caki, Dir-Mktg - Pret A Manger; pg. 1746, pg. 1283
Zamora, Carlos, Dir-Creative - Express Scripts, Inc.; pg. 1530, pg. 997
Zamora, Carmen, Mng Dir-Intl Market Dev US Export-Product Mgmt & Go-To-Market - FedEx Corporation; pg. 1907, pg. 1642
Zamore, Neal, VP-Consumer Mktg - Avis Budget Group, Inc.; pg. 1900, pg. 1102
Zampogna, Sharon, VP-Sls - McCourt Label Company; pg. 1464, pg. 1548
Zamzow, Nash, Sr Mgr-Channel Mktg - PG&E Corporation; pg. 1949, pg. 224
Zanardi, Jeff, VP-Bus Dev & Global Mktg - Curvature; pg. 381, pg. 263
Zanca, Nelie, Sr Assoc Brand Mgr-Dixie Ultra Plates - Georgia-Pacific LLC; pg. 1458, pg. 507
Zanchettin, Adrian, Mgr-Media-Americas - Burberry Limited; pg. 20, pg. 1208
Zanchettin, Valerie, Sr Brand Mgr-New Product Commercialization & Activation - Johnsonville Sausage, LLC; pg. 867, pg. 1894
Zander, Matthew, Acct Mgr-Tech Adv - The New York Times Company; pg. 1668, pg. 1270
Zandri, Justin, VP-Creative & Brand Strategy-Global - Subway Restaurants; pg. 1751, pg. 356
Zane, David, Dir-Brand Mktg - National Association for Stock Car Auto Racing; pg. 566, pg. 420
Zane, Michael, Sr Dir-Online Mktg - Publishers Clearing House; pg. 1782, pg. 1324
Zanelli, Jeff, Dir-Mktg & Outreach-North America - The Nature Conservancy; pg. 151, pg. 1774
Zanet, Joia, Dir-Mktg-Travel Retail Worldwide - M.A.C. Cosmetics; pg. 516, pg. 1924
Zanettos, Zoe, Sr Mgr-Comm Retail Distr & Channel Strategy-Corp & Pub Affairs - Canadian Imperial Bank of Commerce; pg. 729, pg. 1935
Zank, Elicia, Sr Mgr-Community & Content - Michael Kors (USA), Inc.; pg. 29, pg. 1260
Zankowski, Corey, VP-Product Mgmt-Global - Varian Medical Systems, Inc.; pg. 1434, pg. 178
Zantout, Jade, Mgr-Product Mktg - Maserati North America, Inc.; pg. 183, pg. 1060
Zanzucchi, Kathy, Sr Dir-Brand & PPM Single Use Gloves - Ansell; pg. 1495, pg. 1114
Zapala, Megan, Dir-Mdsg-Old Navy Women's Online - The Gap, Inc.; pg. 1770, pg. 218
Zapanta, David, Mgr-Adv - Barnes & Noble, Inc.; pg. 1619, pg. 1201
Zapantiotis, Stamatis, Mgr-Mktg - The Dun & Bradstreet Corp.; pg. 1637, pg. 1120
Zapata, Brooke, VP-Sls Dev - Gannett Co., Inc.; pg. 1643, pg. 1790
Zapata, David, Head-Ops & Asst Brand Mgr-Programmatic, Mobile Media & Strategy - The Procter & Gamble Company; pg. 1129, pg. 1418
Zapata, Jay, Analyst-Mktg Res - Honeywell International Inc.; pg. 407, pg. 1088
Zapata, Katie, Sr Dir-Brand Partnerships - FreshDirect, LLC; pg. 857, pg. 1174
Zapin, Ross, VP-Promos & Event Mktg - Sirius XM Holdings Inc.; pg. 308, pg. 1292
Zappala, Mark, VP-Adv - Haverhill Gazette; pg. 1648, pg. 837
Zappala, Peter, VP-Specialty Sls - New Balance Athletic Shoe, Inc.; pg. 1811, pg. 798
Zappasodi, Rosie, Brand Mgr - The Kroger Co.; pg. 1025, pg. 1416
Zaragoza, Enrique, VP-Indus, Foodservice & Export Sls - Riviana Foods Inc.; pg. 892, pg. 1713
Zaralidis, George, Dir-Network Program Publicity & Social Media - The Hallmark Channel; pg. 290, pg. 281
Zaraszczak, Petrina Z., Dir-Global Product Line - Honeywell International Inc.; pg. 407, pg. 1088
Zarate-Bayani, Ronalee, Head-Global Digital Mktg - The Hershey Co.; pg. 1855, pg. 1538
Zaremba, Thomais, Mgr-Ford & Lincoln Digital Mktg - Ford Motor Company; pg. 172, pg. 876
Zaretsky, Andrea, VP-Global Mktg-Digital Partnerships & Dev - American Express Company; pg. 712, pg. 1190
Zaring, Donna, VP & Sr Mgr-Mktg - Fifth Third Bancorp; pg. 752, pg. 1413
Zarkin, Douglas, VP & Head-Mktg & Visual Mdsg-Pearle Vision - Luxottica Retail; pg. 8, pg. 1460
Zarlenga, Joy E., Sr Mgr-Medical Comm - Amgen Inc.; pg.

First page reference indicates Business Class Edition
Second page reference indicates Geographic Edition

1493, *pg.* 291
Zarlingo, Ben, Product Mgr-Comm Test - Agilent Technologies, Inc.; *pg.* 614, *pg.* 264
Zaro, Dave, Sr Mgr-Field Mktg - Oracle Corporation; *pg.* 1272, *pg.* 786
Zarraga, David, Product Mgr-Core Knowledge - TripAdvisor, Inc.; *pg.* 1926, *pg.* 835
Zarrello, Michael V., Dir-Adv Sls - Information Today Inc.; *pg.* 1653, *pg.* 1084
Zarrouk, Monty, Sr Mgr-Mktg-Health & Wealth - NetApp, Inc.; *pg.* 444, *pg.* 287
Zaslavski, Severine, Dir-Mktg - Manpower Group; *pg.* 430, *pg.* 1710
Zaspel, Rusty, Brand Mgr - Kimberly-Clark Corporation; *pg.* 1461, *pg.* 1720
Zastrow, Gregg, Sr Product Mgr-Mktg - Multi-Tech Systems Inc.; *pg.* 442, *pg.* 951
Zastrow, Teri, Dir-Sls & Mktg - Ikegami Electronics (U.S.A.), Inc.; *pg.* 644, *pg.* 1083
Zatulovskaya, Asya, Assoc Dir-Mktg - AVANIR Pharmaceuticals; *pg.* 1498, *pg.* 40
Zaucha, Shannon, Mgr-Mktg Svcs - Alva/Amco Pharmacal Companies, Inc.; *pg.* 1492, *pg.* 637
Zavodsky, Mike, Sr VP-Corp Sls - Brooklyn Nets; *pg.* 534, *pg.* 1145
Zavoral, Jeremy, Brand Mgr - Hormel Foods Corporation; *pg.* 863, *pg.* 915
Zayas, Hector, Sr Mgr-Product Dev - Cox Communications, Inc.; *pg.* 279, *pg.* 501
Zbikowski, Kathryn, Mgr-Media & Analyst Rels - Accenture; *pg.* 1392, *pg.* 1186
Zdanowicz, Danielle, Brand Mgr-Men's Wholesale-Polo Ralph Lauren - Ralph Lauren Corporation; *pg.* 46, *pg.* 1284
Ze'evi, Shahar, Dir-Product Mgmt-Integration Platforms - Tyco International (US) Inc.; *pg.* 1891, *pg.* 1113
Zebryk, Monica, Reg Dir-Sls - The Dannon Company, Inc.; *pg.* 851, *pg.* 1351
Zech, Jenifer, Sr Mgr-Internal Comm - Ingram Micro Inc.; *pg.* 415, *pg.* 261
Zecha, Alysse, Mgr-Mktg-Brand Strategy - Toys "R" Us, Inc.; *pg.* 968, *pg.* 1130
Zecha, Robert, Chief Product Officer & Exec VP - FalconStor Software, Inc.; *pg.* 396, *pg.* 1179
Zedan, Karima, Sr Dir-Internet Essentials - Comcast Corporation; *pg.* 276, *pg.* 1560
Zedayko, Tara, Brand Mgr-US Mktg-AVEENO Baby & Sun - Johnson & Johnson; *pg.* 1549, *pg.* 1091
Zeff, Stanton D., Mgr-Technical Mktg - Mitel Networks, Inc.; *pg.* 1872, *pg.* 13
Zefkeles, Erin, Mgr-Global Online Mktg-Bing Ads - Microsoft Corporation; *pg.* 435, *pg.* 1824
Zefting, Dana, Mgr-Interactive Sls - WJBF-TV; *pg.* 321, *pg.* 525
Zegal, Christian, VP-Mktg - Wausau Financial Systems Inc.; *pg.* 819, *pg.* 1882
Zegarelli, Chris, Sr Dir-Fin Plng & Analysis - Broadcom Corporation; *pg.* 364, *pg.* 108
Zegarelli, Judy, Founder & Dir-Creative - The Color Factory, Inc.; *pg.* 505, *pg.* 281
Zehnder, Aaron, Assoc-Sls - Semonin Realtors; *pg.* 1112, *pg.* 738
Zehnder, Guido, Product Mgr - Bourns, Inc.; *pg.* 627, *pg.* 193
Zehringer, Rob, Grp VP-Utility Coal Mktg - Norfolk Southern Corporation; *pg.* 1917, *pg.* 1797
Zeidler, Donald, Dir-Direct Mktg - W. Atlee Burpee & Co.; *pg.* 1801, *pg.* 1590
Zeifman, Jesse, Dir-Creative - Apple Inc.; *pg.* 350, *pg.* 73
Zeigler, Eric, Sr Analyst-Sls & Adv Compliance - Eaton Vance Corp.; *pg.* 746, *pg.* 794
Zeiler, Jeffrey, VP-Product Innovation-Global - Briggs & Stratton Corporation; *pg.* 201, *pg.* 1899
Zeilinger, Steve, Product Mgr-Global - Molex Incorporated; *pg.* 655, *pg.* 628
Zeilstra, Scott, Reg Mgr-Sls - Ritchie Bros. Auctioneers Incorporated; *pg.* 1372, *pg.* 1907
Zeimetz, Terry, Mgr-Comml Mktg - Pella Corporation; *pg.* 104, *pg.* 711
Zeinert, Paul, Product Mgr - Anderson & Vreeland, Inc.; *pg.* 1616, *pg.* 1064
Zeise, Danica, Product Mgr-United States & Canada - The Sherwin-Williams Company; *pg.* 1447, *pg.* 1435
Zeise, Danica, Product Mgr-North America - Sherwin Williams; *pg.* 1448, *pg.* 1436
Zeiss, Michele, Asst Mgr-Mktg & Adv-Buick - General Motors Company; *pg.* 175, *pg.* 881
Zeitlin, Monica, Dir-Mktg-Animal Planet - Discovery Communications, Inc.; *pg.* 282, *pg.* 777
Zeituni, Michal, Sr Assoc Brand Mgr - Del Monte Foods, Inc.; *pg.* 852, *pg.* 304
Zejnati, Elona, Sr Mgr-Digital Mktg - Bonnier Corporation; *pg.* 1622, *pg.* 480
Zekoski, Joe, Product Mgr-Appliances - General Electric Company; *pg.* 1297, *pg.* 347
Zeledon, Analorena, Mgr-Social Media - NCL Corporation Ltd.; *pg.* 1916, *pg.* 444
Zelek, Anne, Mgr-Digital Mktg-The Wall Street Journal - Dow Jones & Company, Inc.; *pg.* 1637, *pg.* 1225
Zelesko, Matthew, Sr VP-Tech & Product - Comcast Corporation; *pg.* 276, *pg.* 1560
Zeljak, Maureen, Dir-Partner Mktg - TiVo Inc.; *pg.* 313, *pg.* 251
Zell, Kathryn, Mgr-US Advisor Mktg - FRANKLIN RESOURCES, INC.; *pg.* 760, *pg.* 254
Zell, Krystal, Sr VP-Field Mktg - Simon Property Group, Inc.; *pg.* 1112, *pg.* 690
Zellen, David, Dir-Mktg-SunnyD - Sunny Delight Beverages Co.; *pg.* 899, *pg.* 1426
Zeller, Adam, VP-Social Media-Bravo & Oxygen Media - NBC Universal, Inc.; *pg.* 300, *pg.* 1266
Zeller, Jason, Assoc Dir-Digital Media - Publishers Clearing House; *pg.* 1782, *pg.* 1324
Zeller, Jessica, Sr Mgr-Brand Mktg-Fragrance - Sephora USA Inc; *pg.* 522, *pg.* 227
Zellers, Dana, Sr Mgr-Demand Mktg - Adobe Systems Incorporated; *pg.* 342, *pg.* 235
Zellmer, Karl, VP-Air Conditioning Sls - Emerson Climate Technologies, Inc.; *pg.* 1333, *pg.* 1472
Zellmer, Liz, Coord-Digital Mktg - Briggs & Stratton Corporation; *pg.* 201, *pg.* 1899
Zellner, Brittaney, Product Mgr-Mobile - InterContinental Hotels Corporation; *pg.* 1097, *pg.* 511
Zeltser, Amanda Jackson, Brand Mgr - Colgate-Palmolive Company; *pg.* 504, *pg.* 1215
Zeluf, Sarah, Sr Mgr-Mktg Acq Analytics - TD Ameritrade Holding Corporation; *pg.* 808, *pg.* 1018
Zeman, Mike, Dir-Programmatic & Digital Mktg-Global - Netflix, Inc.; *pg.* 1269, *pg.* 141
Zeman, Patricia, Reg Mgr-Mktg - Cabela's Incorporated; *pg.* 535, *pg.* 1019
Zemba, Emma, Specialist-Digital Media - Valassis Communications, Inc.; *pg.* 1287, *pg.* 897
Zembrowski, Lauren, Specialist-Global Inbound Mktg - Rockwell Automation, Inc.; *pg.* 668, *pg.* 1880
Zemljak, Renee, Exec VP-Midstream, Mktg & Fundamentals - EnCana Corp.; *pg.* 976, *pg.* 1903
Zemmin, Ryan, Mgr-Adv, CRM, Digital & Social-GM Fleet & Comml - General Motors Company; *pg.* 175, *pg.* 881
Zemon, Rebecca, Sr Mgr-Partnership Acq OPEN Co-Brand - American Express Company; *pg.* 712, *pg.* 1190
Zendel, Rachel, Brand Mgr - Capital One Financial Corporation; *pg.* 730, *pg.* 1789
Zender, Bob, Mgr-Mktg-PEANUT CHEWS - Just Born, Inc.; *pg.* 1857, *pg.* 1516
Zendrian, Alexandra, Dir-PR-Eastern Region - North Shore-LIJ Health System; *pg.* 1573, *pg.* 1162
Zeng, Felix, Dir-Bus Dev-Programmatic Sls - The Weather Channel LLC; *pg.* 320, *pg.* 523
Zeng, Henry, Product Mgr-Comml Genset Bus - Cummins Inc.; *pg.* 1326, *pg.* 676
Zeng, Henry, Product Mgr-Comml Genset Bus - Cummins Power Generation; *pg.* 1326, *pg.* 932
Zenkel, Meredith, Dir-Mktg & PR - Poppin; *pg.* 1782, *pg.* 1282
Zenker, Amanda, Mgr-Mktg - NBC News; *pg.* 300, *pg.* 1265
Zenn, Amy, VP-Premium, Proprietary & Diversified Sls - Penguin Random House; *pg.* 1675, *pg.* 1276
Zens, Steven, VP-Sls, Mktg & Product Dev - Royal Adhesives & Sealants LLC; *pg.* 1179, *pg.* 697
Zentz, John, VP-Sls - Hunter Engineering Company; *pg.* 208, *pg.* 973
Zepernick, Ashley, Mgr-Social Media - Raley's Inc.; *pg.* 1031, *pg.* 305
Zepp, Pamela, Dir-Adv - Physicians Weight Loss Centers, Inc.; *pg.* 1585, *pg.* 1402
Zerber, Pamela, VP-Mktg & Reg Dev - European Wax Center; *pg.* 1529, *pg.* 409
Zerbonia, Jeanne, Mgr-Sls - Hannibal Courier-Post; *pg.* 1647, *pg.* 978
Zerhusen, Vicky, VP-Retail Mktg - U.S. Bancorp; *pg.* 815, *pg.* 945
Zeringue, Ellen, VP-Mktg - Detroit Tigers Baseball Club, Inc.; *pg.* 545, *pg.* 880
Zernell, James T., VP-Production - Newfield Exploration Company; *pg.* 45, *pg.* 1747
Zeroual, Bachir, Dir-Mktg Ventures-Global - The Coca-Cola Company; *pg.* 240, *pg.* 493
Zerwer, Jennifer, Mgr-Product Mktg-Outdoor Departments - True Value Company; *pg.* 1065, *pg.* 592
Zettl, Paul, Head-Integrated Mktg - T. Rowe Price Group Inc.; *pg.* 808, *pg.* 759
Zeuli, Aaron, Asst Mgr-Experiential Mktg - Hyundai Motor America; *pg.* 179, *pg.* 89
Zeuschner, Peter, Dir-AARP Digital Media Sls - AARP; *pg.* 124, *pg.* 393
Zevallos, Lora, Mgr-Mktg Admin - Toyota Motor Sales, U.S.A., Inc.; *pg.* 193, *pg.* 296
Zevallos, Suzie, Planner-Ad Sls-Content Partnerships - Comcast Interactive Media, LLC; *pg.* 1236, *pg.* 1562
Zezzo, Tony, Exec VP-Mktg & Sls - OraSure Technologies Inc; *pg.* 1578, *pg.* 1516
Zgola, Michele, Dir-Mktg Comm - Johnson Controls, Inc.; *pg.* 209, *pg.* 1876
Zhai, Lance, Mgr-Sls - INVISTA B.V.; *pg.* 1168, *pg.* 723
Zhang, Casey, Mgr-Brand Mktg - Urban Outfitters, Inc.; *pg.* 1789, *pg.* 1571
Zhang, Janice, Dir-Digital Mktg-Global - RACKSPACE HOSTING, INC.; *pg.* 1277, *pg.* 1742
Zhang, Katherine, Dir-Mktg - General Motors Company; *pg.* 175, *pg.* 881
Zhang, Laurel, Specialist-Mktg - ASUSTeK Computer Inc; *pg.* 355, *pg.* 90
Zhang, Shirley, Mgr-Mktg-Haagen-Dazs - General Mills, Inc.; *pg.* 828, *pg.* 933
Zhang, Weiran, Sr Mgr-Dev - Oracle Corporation; *pg.* 450, *pg.* 191
Zhang, Yi-Bing, Mgr-Performance Media Mktg - Google Inc.; *pg.* 1249, *pg.* 153
Zhang, Zarah, Sr Asst Brand Mgr-POND'S-North America - Unilever United States, Inc.; *pg.* 904, *pg.* 1061
Zhao, Brittany, Mgr-Mktg-B2B - Showtime Networks Inc.; *pg.* 308, *pg.* 1291
Zhao, Kenneth, Mgr-Mktg - W.R. Grace & Co.; *pg.* 123, *pg.* 810
Zhao, Ning, Principal-Mktg - FedEx Corporation; *pg.* 1907, *pg.* 1642
Zhaunerchyk, Julia, Sr Asst Brand Mgr - DISH Network Corporation; *pg.* 283, *pg.* 325
Zheng, Ben, Global Product Mgr-835 Series - Littelfuse, Inc.; *pg.* 1301, *pg.* 580
Zheng, Yi, Product Mgr - QNX Software Systems Ltd; *pg.* 458, *pg.* 1932
Zhivkovich, Ilya, Dir-Global Mktg-Nutrition - Lonza Inc.; *pg.* 1171, *pg.* 1041
Zhiwei, Yu, VP-Mktg - LinkedIn Corporation; *pg.* 1262, *pg.* 160
Zhong, John, Sr Dir - Apple Inc.; *pg.* 350, *pg.* 73
Zhou, Irene, Mgr-Mktg-Global - Honeywell International Inc.; *pg.* 407, *pg.* 1088
Zhou, Jennifer, Mgr-Alcohol Segment & Reg Mgr-Mktg - International Flavors & Fragrances Inc.; *pg.* 512, *pg.* 1244
Zhou, Jessie, Sr Mgr-Loyalty Programs - Expedia, Inc.; *pg.* 1244, *pg.* 1814
Zhou, Wenda, Specialist-Technical Sls - AOL Inc.; *pg.* 1229, *pg.* 1195
Zhu, Gene J., Sr Dir-Regulatory Affairs - Regeneron Pharmaceuticals, Inc.; *pg.* 1588, *pg.* 1345
Zhu, Laura A., Sr Dir-Brand Bus Dev & Licensing - IMPAX Laboratories, Inc.; *pg.* 1544, *pg.* 101
Zhu, Yilan, Mgr-Search Engine Mktg - Amazon.com, Inc.; *pg.* 1226, *pg.* 1831
Zhuang, Julie, Product Mgr-TurboTax - Intuit Inc.; *pg.* 769, *pg.* 158
Zhuo, Julie, Dir-Product Design - Facebook, Inc.; *pg.* 1245, *pg.* 143
Zhupleva, Marianna, Dir-Product Mktg - Farmer Brothers Company; *pg.* 855, *pg.* 293
Zialcita, Susana, Deputy Dir-Mktg - Penguin Random House; *pg.* 1675, *pg.* 1276
Zialcita, Susana, Deputy Dir-Digital Mktg - Penguin Random House; *pg.* 1675, *pg.* 1276
Zibelli, Sue, Mgr-Media Svcs - Novartis Pharmaceuticals Corp.; *pg.* 1575, *pg.* 1054
Zibenberg, Claudio, Mgr-Media - International Business Machines Corporation; *pg.* 418, *pg.* 1138
Zick, Cameron, Mgr-Mktg - Uber USA, LLC; *pg.* 1286, *pg.* 229

Zick, John, Reg Mgr-Sls - Babcox Media; *pg.* 1619, *pg.* 1400
Zickefoose, Brandy, Mgr-Corp Ops Mktg - PODS Enterprises, Inc.; *pg.* 1919, *pg.* 416
Zickert, Adam, Dir-Channel Mktg - Cooper Tire & Rubber Company; *pg.* 1881, *pg.* 1453
Zidar, Owen M., VP-Sls & Mktg - The Kansas City Southern Railway Company; *pg.* 1913, *pg.* 985
Ziegenfuss, Audra, Product Mgr-Technical - Thermo Fisher Scientific Inc.; *pg.* 1431, *pg.* 854
Ziegler, Elizabeth, Mgr-Mktg Sourcing - NBC Universal, Inc.; *pg.* 300, *pg.* 1266
Ziegler, Jackie, CEO-E-Alternative Solutions & VP-Sls & Mktg - Swisher International, Inc.; *pg.* 1895, *pg.* 345
Ziegler, Jeana, Sr Planner-Media Strategy - Target Corporation; *pg.* 1786, *pg.* 942
Ziegler, Michael, Dir-Global IBM MobileFirst Software Sls - IBM; *pg.* 410, *pg.* 1449
Ziegler, Patti, VP-Mktg & Comm-Global - The Scotts Miracle-Gro Company; *pg.* 1799, *pg.* 1459
Ziehe, Jennifer, Sr Dir-Client Dev & Sls - CME Group Inc.; *pg.* 738, *pg.* 571
Zielinski, Jen, Dir-Mktg - Alva/Amco Pharmacal Companies, Inc.; *pg.* 1492, *pg.* 637
Zielinski, William J., VP-Mktg - Chicago Tube & Iron Co.; *pg.* 1323, *pg.* 656
Zielke, William, VP-Mktg & Intl Dev - Do It Best Corp.; *pg.* 1045, *pg.* 680
Ziemba, Joe, Mgr-Global Mktg-Novec & 1230 Fluid - 3M Company; *pg.* 1142, *pg.* 956
Zieminski, Kristen, Sr Assoc Brand Mgr-Pull-Ups Brand - Kimberly-Clark Corporation; *pg.* 1461, *pg.* 1720
Zierten, Lisa, Dir-Mktg, Svcs & Segment - Cardinal Health, Inc.; *pg.* 1512, *pg.* 1448
Zieses, David, Dir-The Walmart Media Exchange - Wal-Mart.com; *pg.* 1287, *pg.* 50
Zietlow, Debbie, Product Mgr-Pratt & Lambert Paints - Pratt & Lambert Paints; *pg.* 1446, *pg.* 1434
Zietlow, Debbie, Product Mgr-Pratt & Lambert Paints - Sherwin Williams; *pg.* 1448, *pg.* 1436
Ziewacz, Doug, Head-North America Digital Media & Adv - Under Armour, Inc.; *pg.* 49, *pg.* 759
Ziff, Steve, VP-Mktg - Jacksonville Jaguars, Ltd.; *pg.* 554, *pg.* 433
Zigman, Sherri L., Dir-Adv - The New York Times; *pg.* 1668, *pg.* 1270
Zigulich, Dan, VP-Creative Mktg-Global - Payless Shoesource, Inc.; *pg.* 31, *pg.* 722
Zik, Jim, VP-Product Mgmt & Mktg - PCTEL, Inc.; *pg.* 452, *pg.* 557
Ziller, Jason, Dir-Thunderbolt Mktg & Plng - Intel Corporation; *pg.* 645, *pg.* 266
Zillo, Jason, Dir-Media - New York Yankees; *pg.* 570, *pg.* 1144
Zim, Jake, Sr VP-Digital Mktg - Sony Pictures Entertainment Inc.; *pg.* 309, *pg.* 72
Zima, Susan M., Dir-Brand & Creative Svcs - Thrivent Financial for Lutherans; *pg.* 1219, *pg.* 944
Zima, Valerie, Coord-Mktg - Grant Thornton International Ltd.; *pg.* 763, *pg.* 575
Ziman, Eric, Sr Mgr-Creative Svcs - Bulova Corporation; *pg.* 2, *pg.* 1356
Zimbalist, Michael, Sr VP-Adv Products-R&D - The New York Times; *pg.* 1668, *pg.* 1270
Zimbalist, Michael, Sr VP-Adv Products, R&D - The New York Times Company; *pg.* 1668, *pg.* 1270
Zimbelman, Rob, Dir-Adv & eBusiness - Lennox International Inc.; *pg.* 1073, *pg.* 1736
Zimdar, Travis, Product Mgr - Steelcase Inc.; *pg.* 475, *pg.* 889
Zimet, David, Specialist-Digital Mktg - Domino's Pizza, Inc.; *pg.* 1726, *pg.* 865
Zimlichman, Jacob, Mgr-Mktg Res - Merck & Co., Inc.; *pg.* 1566, *pg.* 1077
Zimmer, Jeremiah, Sr Mgr-Community Mktg - Dick's Sporting Goods, Inc.; *pg.* 1832, *pg.* 1524
Zimmer, Michele, Dir-Digital-Global Brand Mktg - Fisher-Price, Inc.; *pg.* 953, *pg.* 1156
Zimmer, Paula, Mgr-Sls-Natl - San Jose Convention/Visitors Bureau; *pg.* 1005, *pg.* 250
Zimmer, Stephanie, Dept Head-Brand Experience Mktg - Mercedes-Benz USA, LLC; *pg.* 184, *pg.* 514
Zimmer, Tom, Sr Product Mgr-High Efficiency Water Heating - General Electric Company; *pg.* 1297, *pg.* 347
Zimmer, Tony, Mgr-Media & PR - William Blair & Company LLC; *pg.* 822, *pg.* 596
Zimmerman, Andrew, Sr Analyst-Compliance-Adv & Mktg Matls Review - Genworth Financial, Inc.; *pg.* 761, *pg.* 1802
Zimmerman, Courtney, Dir-Mktg - Dallas Symphony Association Inc.; *pg.* 543, *pg.* 1679
Zimmerman, Derek, Pres-Product Support - Gulfstream Aerospace Corporation; *pg.* 228, *pg.* 540
Zimmerman, Eric, Product Mgr-Flights - Google Inc.; *pg.* 1249, *pg.* 153
Zimmerman, Jeremy, Dir-Adv Ops - American Media, Inc.; *pg.* 1615, *pg.* 410
Zimmerman, Jeremy, Mgr-Mktg Comm - Starz Entertainment, LLC; *pg.* 310, *pg.* 327
Zimmerman, Joost, Dir-Digital Mktg - Subway Restaurants; *pg.* 1751, *pg.* 356
Zimmerman, Jordan, Mgr-Mktg & Comm - Shake Shack Inc.; *pg.* 1749, *pg.* 1291
Zimmerman, Katherine, Dir-Pro Mktg-Afrezza - Sanofi US; *pg.* 1592, *pg.* 1046
Zimmerman, Michelle, Dir-CRM & Digital Mktg - Bon Ton Stores, Inc.; *pg.* 1763, *pg.* 1596
Zimmerman, Rob, Sr Mgr-Channel-Sustainability - Kohler Co.; *pg.* 91, *pg.* 1862
Zimmerman, Shannan, Product Specialist-Govt Contracting - Deltek, Inc.; *pg.* 386, *pg.* 1784
Zimmerman, Tegan, Mgr-Social & Content - Walgreen Co.; *pg.* 1608, *pg.* 605
Zimmerman-Smith, Melinda, Mgr-Mktg Comm-Terex AWP & Genie branded products - Terex Corporation; *pg.* 1381, *pg.* 384
Zimmermann, Eric, Dir-Parts Sls & Pipe Tech - Putzmeister America; *pg.* 1371, *pg.* 1896
Zimmermann, Fred, Mgr-Mktg-Central Area - March Manufacturing Inc.; *pg.* 1359, *pg.* 615
Zincke, Jessica, Mgr-Product Mktg - Ancestry.com LLC; *pg.* 1228, *pg.* 1754
Zingle, Maddy, Brand Mgr - S.C. Johnson & Son, Inc.; *pg.* 334, *pg.* 1889
Zingler, Jeff, Sr Dir-Bus Dev - Charter Communications, Inc.; *pg.* 274, *pg.* 372
Zinke, Adam, Dir-Digital Mktg & Video Promos - Warner Music Group Corp.; *pg.* 590, *pg.* 1313
Zinsley, Chris, Coord-Reg Sls Program - New York State Lottery; *pg.* 1001, *pg.* 1340
Zintl, Cristina, Assoc Mgr-Mktg-Americas - Tennant Company; *pg.* 1381, *pg.* 944
Ziobro, Monika, Dir-North America Mktg-Estee Lauder Fragrances & AERIN BEAUTY - The Estee Lauder Companies Inc.; *pg.* 508, *pg.* 1229
Ziperovich, Pablo, Sr Dir-Flash Channel Dev - HGST; *pg.* 406, *pg.* 260
Zipfel, Karen M., Dir-Mktg - Alcoa Inc.; *pg.* 65, *pg.* 1188
Zipkin, David, Principal & Product Mgr-New Initiative - Amazon.com, Inc.; *pg.* 1226, *pg.* 1831
Zipp, Carly, Dir-PR - XO Group Inc.; *pg.* 1289, *pg.* 1316
Ziring, Steve, Mgr-Adv Tech - Comcast Interactive Media, LLC; *pg.* 1236, *pg.* 1562
Zirkle, Susan, Sr Media Planner - CarMax, Inc.; *pg.* 167, *pg.* 1800
Zitek, Joe, Mgr-Sls-Indus Products - InterSystems; *pg.* 1350, *pg.* 1016
Zitney, Adam, VP-Mktg - Smucker Foods Of Canada Co.; *pg.* 896, *pg.* 1924
Zito, Alex, Analyst-Digital Mktg-Global - Kimberly-Clark Corporation; *pg.* 1461, *pg.* 1720
Zito, Calvin, Strategist-Social Media - Hewlett-Packard Company; *pg.* 404, *pg.* 175
Zito, Chris, Coord-Production - The Boston Globe; *pg.* 1623, *pg.* 790
Zito, Rosemarie, Dir-EMEA Aftermarket Sls - Printronix, Inc.; *pg.* 456, *pg.* 115
Zitta, Steve, Sr Dir - R.J. Reynolds Tobacco Co.; *pg.* 1895, *pg.* 1395
Zizak, Dani, VP-Mktg-Global - Wolverine World Wide, Inc.; *pg.* 1822, *pg.* 905
Zlotnick, Leslie, Mgr-Adv-Watercraft Grp - Yamaha Motor Corporation USA; *pg.* 1713, *pg.* 76
Zlotnik, David, Dir-Mktg-Global - McDonald's Corporation; *pg.* 1737, *pg.* 645
Zlotsky, Tatyana, VP-Digital Mktg & Innovation - American Express Company; *pg.* 712, *pg.* 1190
Zmrhal, Jennifer, Dir-Mktg - John Morrell Food Group; *pg.* 866, *pg.* 628
Zmuda, Natalie, Mng Editor - Advertising Age; *pg.* 1613, *pg.* 1187
Zobal, Casandra, Dir-Field Mktg - Forrester Research, Inc.; *pg.* 1642, *pg.* 807
Zoberi, Asad, Product Mgr - Radio Frequency Systems, Inc.; *pg.* 666, *pg.* 354
Zoblotsky, Toni, Dir-B2B Mktg - Hilton Worldwide, Inc.; *pg.* 1094, *pg.* 1791
Zoccola, Matthew, Specialist-Dynamics Mktg Solution - Microsoft Corporation; *pg.* 435, *pg.* 1824
Zochert, John, Dir-Mktg & Product Dev - Wells Manufacturing, L.P.; *pg.* 222, *pg.* 1858
Zoellner, Mike, VP-Mktg Svcs - Mohawk Industries, Inc.; *pg.* 935, *pg.* 527
Zoellner, Sushma, Dir-Product - RetailMeNot Inc.; *pg.* 1782, *pg.* 1665
Zoetmulder, Eric, VP-Product Mgmt-SciQuest - SCIQUEST, INC.; *pg.* 468, *pg.* 1361
Zogas, Peter, Sr VP-Sls - National Instruments Corporation; *pg.* 443, *pg.* 1664
Zoglin, John, Head-Enterprise Mktg Mgmt-Digital Mktg Svcs Practice - International Business Machines Corporation; *pg.* 418, *pg.* 1138
Zohar, Yossi, Head-Product Mktg-Clarify - Amdocs Inc.; *pg.* 348, *pg.* 974
Zola, Nathaniel, Sr Dir-Product Mgmt & Design - MapQuest, Inc.; *pg.* 1265, *pg.* 321
Zolla, Leslie, Mgr-Channel Mktg - Zoll Medical Corporation; *pg.* 1612, *pg.* 814
Zollar, Natalie, Mgr-Sls Support - Naples Daily News; *pg.* 1666, *pg.* 451
Zoller, Chris, Dir-Mktg - Everlast Worldwide Inc.; *pg.* 1833, *pg.* 1230
Zolten, Amanda, Dir-Global Brand Mktg-Hot Wheels - Mattel Games/Puzzles; *pg.* 962, *pg.* 80
Zonder, Howard, Sr VP-Mktg & Audience Dev - United Business Media LLC; *pg.* 1697, *pg.* 1177
Zongker, Brett, Sr Assoc Dir-Media Rels - The George Washington University; *pg.* 602, *pg.* 400
Zongker, Dan, Owner, VP & Designer-Furniture - Zongkers Custom Furniture, Inc.; *pg.* 947, *pg.* 1019
Zopff, Jeff, Mgr-Mktg - Universal Instruments Corporation; *pg.* 683, *pg.* 1154
Zoppel, Lori, Dir-Mktg-Global-Unilever Brand - Unilever United States, Inc.; *pg.* 904, *pg.* 1061
Zorn, Jeremy, VP-Product - MeetMe, Inc.; *pg.* 1266, *pg.* 1556
Zorr, Bill, Head-Digital Mktg-Global - Fossil Group, Inc.; *pg.* 5, *pg.* 1735
Zorrilla, Paul, Dir-Latino Sls - AutoTrader, Inc.; *pg.* 1230, *pg.* 490
Zou, Harrison, Dir-Product Mktg - Broadcom Corporation; *pg.* 364, *pg.* 108
Zoucha, Janice A., Reg Mgr-Sls-West Coast - Assurity Life Insurance Company; *pg.* 1194, *pg.* 1011
Zrike, Andrew, Sr Mgr-Mktg-Innovation & New Bus Dev-Quaker - PepsiCo, Inc.; *pg.* 259, *pg.* 1327
Zrimsek, Brian, Chief Product Officer - MRI Software, LLC; *pg.* 1106, *pg.* 1473
Zsigray, Lauren, Brand Mgr-Spreads - Unilever United States, Inc.; *pg.* 904, *pg.* 1061
Zuber, Kim, Assoc Mgr-Mktg - Robert Mondavi Winery; *pg.* 1969, *pg.* 173
Zuber, Lisa, Assoc Mgr-Mktg-Mobile Accessories - Fellowes, Inc.; *pg.* 397, *pg.* 620
Zubrod, Ronald, Acct Exec-Charter Media - Charter Communications, Inc.; *pg.* 274, *pg.* 372
Zuby, Matt, Assoc Product Mgr-X-ACTO & Krazy Glue - Elmer's Products, Inc.; *pg.* 1442, *pg.* 1479
Zucca, Erika, Assoc Mgr-Firm Mktg - FRANKLIN RESOURCES, INC.; *pg.* 760, *pg.* 254
Zuccala, Karen, Dir-Brand Comm, Digital & Media - NIKE Canada Ltd.; *pg.* 1840, *pg.* 1934
Zuccarino, Scott, Product Mgr - Google Inc.; *pg.* 1249, *pg.* 153
Zucht, Mia, Sr Mgr-Field Mktg - EMC Corporation; *pg.* 391, *pg.* 825
Zucker, Daniel, Sr Mgr-Social Media - Autodesk Inc.; *pg.* 356, *pg.* 257
Zucker, Michael, VP-Mdsg & Mktg - Samsonite Corporation; *pg.* 11, *pg.* 830
Zuckerman, Kelly, Assoc Dir-Mktg - UCLA; *pg.* 608, *pg.* 141
Zuckerman, Leora, Sr Mgr-Print Production - Coach, Inc.; *pg.* 3, *pg.* 1214
Zuehlk, Andrea, Mgr-Car Digital Mktg - Ford Motor Company; *pg.* 172, *pg.* 876
Zuehlk, Matt, Mgr-Truck/SUV Digital Mktg - Ford Motor Company; *pg.* 172, *pg.* 876
Zugno, Joanna, Dir-Customer Mktg & Sr Mgr - Maybelline LLC; *pg.* 516, *pg.* 1257

First page reference indicates Business Class Edition
Second page reference indicates Geographic Edition

Zukauskas, Lisa, Sr Dir-Procurement-Global - Merck & Co., Inc.; *pg.* 1566, *pg.* 1077
Zukoski, Nadine, VP-Digital Mktg Strategy - JPMorgan Chase & Co.; *pg.* 772, *pg.* 1246
Zukowski, Cheryl, Sr Dir-Consumer Mktg-VUSE - R.J. Reynolds Tobacco Co.; *pg.* 1895, *pg.* 1395
Zukowski, Paul A., Sr VP-Production - The Hibbert Group; *pg.* 407, *pg.* 1126
Zulawski, Timothy, VP-Sponsorship Sls & Svc - Atlanta Falcons Football Club, LLC; *pg.* 530, *pg.* 532
Zuloaga, Rodrigo, VP-New Product Dev - Kind LLC; *pg.* 868, *pg.* 1249
Zumerova, Inna, Specialist-Mktg - McKesson Corporation; *pg.* 1560, *pg.* 222
Zumstein, Gary, VP-Product Dev - Glen Raven, Inc.; *pg.* 693, *pg.* 1373
Zuna, Michael W., Chief Mktg & Digital Officer & Sr VP - PETCO Animal Supplies, Inc.; *pg.* 1480, *pg.* 206
Zung, Elvin, Sr Dir-Strategic Sourcing - The Gap, Inc.; *pg.* 1770, *pg.* 218
Zuniga, Lizz, Assoc Mgr Partnership Mktg - Southwest Airlines Co.; *pg.* 1923, *pg.* 1687
Zuparko, Kate, Dir-Digital Mktg - Major League Soccer LLC; *pg.* 560, *pg.* 1256
Zupnik, Sarah, Mgr-Mktg-Customer Base Education & Engagement - Rogers Communications Inc.; *pg.* 668, *pg.* 1942
Zurawka, Julie, Sr Dir-Mktg - Big Boy Restaurants International, LLC; *pg.* 1716, *pg.* 912
Zurfluh, Mark, Mgr-Media-North American - Kimberly-Clark Corporation; *pg.* 1461, *pg.* 1720
Zuri, Jaime, Brand Mgr-Innovation Sys - Keurig Green Mountain, Inc.; *pg.* 868, *pg.* 1768
Zurich, Amy, Analyst-Sls Strategy - Briggs & Stratton Corporation; *pg.* 201, *pg.* 1899
Zurlini, Paul, Dir-Mktg Comm - Stryker Orthopaedics; *pg.* 1599, *pg.* 1082
Zurzolo, Pablo, VP-Mktg - Tech Data Corporation; *pg.* 482, *pg.* 416
Zurzuski, Ed, Specialist-Gravity Conveyor Sls - Unex Manufacturing, Inc.; *pg.* 1385, *pg.* 1075
Zusman, Josh, Brand Mgr-Hockey - The Upper Deck Company, LLC; *pg.* 969, *pg.* 62
Zussman, Molly, Adv Acct Exec-Sparknotes.com - Barnes & Noble, Inc.; *pg.* 1619, *pg.* 1201
Zuzenak, Carrie, Coord-Production - Avatar Studios; *pg.* 270, *pg.* 992
Zveibil, Michel, Dir-Creative-Brazil - Apple Inc.; *pg.* 350, *pg.* 73
Zweber, Aimee, Mgr-Mktg - Winmark Corporation; *pg.* 1792, *pg.* 946
Zweifler, Jonathan, Dir-Creative-Mobile Product Innovation - American Express Company; *pg.* 712, *pg.* 1190
Zweig, Julia, Mgr-Media & PR - The Hartford Financial Services Group, Inc.; *pg.* 1202, *pg.* 352
Zweig, Steve, Dir-Natl Sls-US Stores Grp - PPG Industries, Inc.; *pg.* 1445, *pg.* 1579
Zwicky, Sarah L., Mgr-Comm & PR-Global - Johnson Controls, Inc.; *pg.* 209, *pg.* 1876
Zwiebel, Marcey, VP & Sr Mgr - The PNC Financial Services Group, Inc.; *pg.* 795, *pg.* 1579
Zwiener, Jill A., Brand Mgr - Valmont Industries, Inc.; *pg.* 1387, *pg.* 1019
Zwit, Grace Guerrero, Sr Dir-Minor League Ops - Chicago White Sox Ltd.; *pg.* 539, *pg.* 570
Zwolen, Jennifer, Mgr-Mktg Comm & Branding - Allegheny Technologies Incorporated; *pg.* 66, *pg.* 1572
Zygmont, Fran, Asst Dir-Digital Mktg - The Hartford Financial Services Group, Inc.; *pg.* 1202, *pg.* 352
Zyla, Julie, Reg Head-Segment Mktg Comm - Cigna Corporation; *pg.* 1197, *pg.* 338
Zylber, Jenna, Brand Mgr - Kraft Canada Inc.; *pg.* 869, *pg.* 1939
Zylick, Justin, VP-Sls - Diageo North America, Inc.; *pg.* 1961, *pg.* 361
Zymet, Matt, Exec Dir-Digital Media - National Geographic Channel; *pg.* 299, *pg.* 402

ALPHABETICAL COMPENDIUM OF N.A.I.C.S. CODES

North American Industry Classification System Manual, 2002, U.S. Government Office of Management and Budget; All codes for manufacturing unless otherwise stated.

N.A.I.C.S.	*Description*
A	
Abrasive Product Manufacturing	327910
Adhesive Manufacturing	325520
Administration of Air and Water Resource and Solid Waste Management Programs	924110
Administration of Conservation Programs	924120
Administration of Education Programs	923110
Administration of General Economic Programs	926110
Administration of Housing Programs	925110
Administration of Human Resource Programs (except Education, Public Health, and Veterans' Affairs Programs)	923130
Administration of Public Health Programs	923120
Administration of Urban Planning and Community and Rural Development	925120
Administration of Veterans' Affairs	923140
Administrative Management and General Management Consulting Services	541611
Advertising Agencies	541810
Advertising Material Distribution Services	541870
Agents and Managers for Artists, Athletes, Entertainers, and Other Public Figures	711410
Air and Gas Compressor Manufacturing	333912
Air Purification Equipment Manufacturing	333411
Air Traffic Control	488111
Air-Conditioning and Warm Air Heating Equipment and Commercial and Industrial Refrigeration Equipment Manufacturing	333415
Aircraft Engine and Engine Parts Manufacturing	336412
Aircraft Manufacturing	336411
Alkalies and Chlorine Manufacturing	325181
All Other Amusement and Recreation Industries	713990
All Other Animal Production	112990
All Other Automotive Repair and Maintenance	811198
All Other Basic Inorganic Chemical Manufacturing	325188
All Other Basic Organic Chemical Manufacturing	325199
All Other Business Support Services	561499
All Other Consumer Goods Rental	532299
All Other Converted Paper Product Manufacturing	322299
All Other Cut and Sew Apparel Manufacturing	315299
All Other General Merchandise Stores	452990
All Other Grain Farming	111199
All Other Health and Personal Care Stores	446199
All Other Home Furnishings Stores	442299
All Other Industrial Machinery Manufacturing	333298
All Other Information Services	519190
All Other Insurance Related Activities	524298
All Other Leather Good Manufacturing	316999
All Other Legal Services	541199
All Other Metal Ore Mining	212299
All Other Miscellaneous Ambulatory Health Care Services	621999
All Other Miscellaneous Chemical Product and Preparation Manufacturing	325998
All Other Miscellaneous Crop Farming	111998
All Other Miscellaneous Electrical Equipment and Component Manufacturing	335999
All Other Miscellaneous Fabricated Metal Product Manufacturing	332999
All Other Miscellaneous Food Manufacturing	311999
All Other Miscellaneous General Purpose Machinery Manufacturing	333999
All Other Miscellaneous Manufacturing	339999
All Other Miscellaneous Nonmetallic Mineral Product Manufacturing	327999
All Other Miscellaneous Schools and Instruction	611699
All Other Miscellaneous Store Retailers (except Tobacco Stores)	453998
All Other Miscellaneous Textile Product Mills	314999
All Other Miscellaneous Waste Management Services	562998
All Other Miscellaneous Wood Product Manufacturing	321999
All Other Motor Vehicle Dealers	441229
All Other Motor Vehicle Parts Manufacturing	336399
All Other Nondepository Credit Intermediation	522298
All Other Nonmetallic Mineral Mining	212399
All Other Outpatient Care Centers	621498
All Other Personal Services	812990
All Other Petroleum and Coal Products Manufacturing	324199
All Other Pipeline Transportation	486990
All Other Plastics Product Manufacturing	326199
All Other Professional, Scientific, and Technical Services	541990
All Other Publishers	511199
All Other Rubber Product Manufacturing	326299
All Other Special Trade Contractors	235990
All Other Specialty Food Stores	445299
All Other Specialty Trade Contractors	238990
All Other Support Activities for Transportation	488999

N.A.I.C.S.	*Description*
All Other Support Services	561990
All Other Transit and Ground Passenger Transportation	485999
All Other Transportation Equipment Manufacturing	336999
All Other Travel Arrangement and Reservation Services	561599
All Other Traveler Accommodation	721199
Alumina Refining	331311
Aluminum Die-Casting Foundries	331521
Aluminum Extruded Product Manufacturing	331316
Aluminum Foundries (except Die-Casting)	331524
Aluminum Sheet, Plate, and Foil Manufacturing	331315
Ambulance Services	621910
American Indian and Alaska Native Tribal Governments	921150
Ammunition (except Small Arms) Manufacturing	332993
Amusement and Theme Parks	713110
Amusement Arcades	713120
Analytical Laboratory Instrument Manufacturing	334516
Animal (except Poultry) Slaughtering	311611
Anthracite Mining	212113
Apiculture	112910
Apple Orchards	111331
Appliance Repair and Maintenance	811412
Apprenticeship Training	611513
Architectural Services	541310
Armored Car Services	561613
Art Dealers	453920
Asphalt Paving Mixture and Block Manufacturing	324121
Asphalt Shingle and Coating Materials Manufacturing	324122
Audio and Video Equipment Manufacturing	334310
Automatic Environmental Control Manufacturing for Residential, Commercial, and Appliance Use	334512
Automatic Vending Machine Manufacturing	333311
Automobile and Other Motor Vehicle Merchant Wholesalers	423110
Automobile and Other Motor Vehicle Wholesalers	421110
Automobile Driving Schools	611692
Automobile Manufacturing	336111
Automotive Body, Paint, and Interior Repair and Maintenance	811121
Automotive Exhaust System Repair	811112
Automotive Glass Replacement Shops	811122
Automotive Oil Change and Lubrication Shops	811191
Automotive Parts and Accessories Stores	441310
Automotive Transmission Repair	811113
B	
Baked Goods Stores	445291
Ball and Roller Bearing Manufacturing	332991
Barber Shops	812111
Bare Printed Circuit Board Manufacturing	334412
Beauty Salons	812112
Bed-and-Breakfast Inns	721191
Beef Cattle Ranching and Farming	112111
Beer and Ale Merchant Wholesalers	424810
Beer and Ale Wholesalers	422810
Beer, Wine, and Liquor Stores	445310
Beet Sugar Manufacturing	311313
Berry (except Strawberry) Farming	111334
Biological Product (except Diagnostic) Manufacturing	325414
Bituminous Coal and Lignite Surface Mining	212111
Bituminous Coal Underground Mining	212112
Blankbook, Looseleaf Binders, and Devices Manufacturing	323118
Blind and Shade Manufacturing	337920
Blood and Organ Banks	621991
Boat Building	336612
Boat Dealers	441222
Bolt, Nut, Screw, Rivet, and Washer Manufacturing	332722
Book Publishers	511130
Book Stores	451211
Book, Periodical, and Newspaper Merchant Wholesalers	424920
Book, Periodical, and Newspaper Wholesalers	422920
Books Printing	323117
Bottled Water Manufacturing	312112
Bowling Centers	713950
Breakfast Cereal Manufacturing	311230
Breweries	312120
Brick and Structural Clay Tile Manufacturing	327121
Brick, Stone, and Related Construction Material Merchant Wholesalers	423320
Brick, Stone, and Related Construction Material Wholesalers	421320
Bridge and Tunnel Construction	234120
Broadwoven Fabric Finishing Mills	313311
Broadwoven Fabric Mills	313210
Broilers and Other Meat Type Chicken Production	112320

Description	*N.A.I.C.S.*
Broom, Brush, and Mop Manufacturing	339994
Building Equipment and Other Machinery Installation Contractors	235950
Building Inspection Services	541350
Burial Casket Manufacturing	339995
Bus and Other Motor Vehicle Transit Systems	485113
Business and Secretarial Schools	611410
Business Associations	813910
Business to Business Electronic Markets	425110
C	
Cable and Other Program Distribution	517510
Cable and Other Subscription Programming	515210
Cable Networks	513210
Cafeterias	722212
Camera and Photographic Supplies Stores	443130
Cane Sugar Refining	311312
Canvas and Related Product Mills	314912
Car Washes	811192
Carbon and Graphite Product Manufacturing	335991
Carbon Black Manufacturing	325182
Carbon Paper and Inked Ribbon Manufacturing	339944
Carburetor, Piston, Piston Ring, and Valve Manufacturing	336311
Carpentry Contractors	235510
Carpet and Rug Mills	314110
Carpet and Upholstery Cleaning Services	561740
Casino Hotels	721120
Casinos (except Casino Hotels)	713210
Caterers	722320
Cattle Feedlots	112112
Cellular and Other Wireless Telecommunications	513322
Cellulosic Organic Fiber Manufacturing	325221
Cement Manufacturing	327310
Cemeteries and Crematories	812220
Ceramic Wall and Floor Tile Manufacturing	327122
Charter Bus Industry	485510
Cheese Manufacturing	311513
Chicken Egg Production	112310
Child and Youth Services	624110
Child Day Care Services	624410
Children's and Infants' Clothing Stores	448130
Chocolate and Confectionery Manufacturing from Cacao Beans	311320
Cigarette Manufacturing	312221
Citrus (except Orange) Groves	111320
Civic and Social Organizations	813410
Claims Adjusting	524291
Clay and Ceramic and Refractory Minerals Mining	212325
Clay Refractory Manufacturing	327124
Clothing Accessories Stores	448150
Coal and Other Mineral and Ore Merchant Wholesalers	423520
Coal and Other Mineral and Ore Wholesalers	421520
Coastal and Great Lakes Freight Transportation	483113
Coastal and Great Lakes Passenger Transportation	483114
Coated and Laminated Packaging Paper and Plastics Film Manufacturing	322221
Coated and Laminated Paper Manufacturing	322222
Coffee and Tea Manufacturing	311920
Coin-Operated Laundries and Drycleaners	812310
Collection Agencies	561440
Colleges, Universities, and Professional Schools	611310
Commercial Air, Rail, and Water Transportation Equipment Rental and Leasing	532411
Commercial and Industrial Machinery and Equipment (except Automotive and Electronic) Repair and Maintenance	811310
Commercial and Institutional Building Construction	236220
Commercial Bakeries	311812
Commercial Banking	522110
Commercial Flexographic Printing	323112
Commercial Gravure Printing	323111
Commercial Laundry, Drycleaning, and Pressing Machine Manufacturing	333312
Commercial Lithographic Printing	323110
Commercial Photography	541922
Commercial Screen Printing	323113
Commercial, Industrial, and Institutional Electric Lighting Fixture Manufacturing	335122
Commodity Contracts Brokerage	523140
Commodity Contracts Dealing	523130
Communication Equipment Repair and Maintenance	811213
Community Food Services	624210
Commuter Rail Systems	485112
Computer and Computer Peripheral Equipment and Software Merchant Wholesalers	423430

Description	*N.A.I.C.S.*
Computer and Computer Peripheral Equipment and Software Wholesalers	421430
Computer and Office Machine Repair and Maintenance	811212
Computer and Software Stores	443120
Computer Facilities Management Services	541513
Computer Storage Device Manufacturing	334112
Computer Systems Design Services	541512
Computer Terminal Manufacturing	334113
Computer Training	611420
Concrete Block and Brick Manufacturing	327331
Concrete Contractors	235710
Concrete Pipe Manufacturing	327332
Confectionery and Nut Stores	445292
Confectionery Manufacturing from Purchased Chocolate	311330
Confectionery Merchant Wholesalers	424450
Confectionery Wholesalers	422450
Construction and Mining (except Oil Well) Machinery and Equipment Merchant Wholesalers	423810
Construction and Mining (except Oil Well) Machinery and Equipment Wholesalers	421810
Construction Machinery Manufacturing	333120
Construction Sand and Gravel Mining	212321
Construction, Mining, and Forestry Machinery and Equipment Rental and Leasing	532412
Consumer Electronics and Appliances Rental	532210
Consumer Electronics Repair and Maintenance	811211
Consumer Lending	522291
Continuing Care Retirement Communities	623311
Convenience Stores	445120
Convention and Trade Show Organizers	561920
Convention and Visitors Bureaus	561591
Conveyor and Conveying Equipment Manufacturing	333922
Cookie and Cracker Manufacturing	311821
Copper Foundries (except Die-Casting)	331525
Copper Ore and Nickel Ore Mining	212234
Copper Rolling, Drawing, and Extruding	331421
Copper Wire (except Mechanical) Drawing	331422
Corn Farming	111150
Corporate, Subsidiary, and Regional Managing Offices	551114
Correctional Institutions	922140
Corrugated and Solid Fiber Box Manufacturing	322211
Cosmetics, Beauty Supplies, and Perfume Stores	446120
Cosmetology and Barber Schools	611511
Costume Jewelry and Novelty Manufacturing	339914
Cotton Farming	111920
Cotton Ginning	115111
Couriers	492110
Court Reporting and Stenotype Services	561492
Courts	922110
Creamery Butter Manufacturing	311512
Credit Bureaus	561450
Credit Card Issuing	522210
Credit Unions	522130
Crop Harvesting, Primarily by Machine	115113
Crown and Closure Manufacturing	332115
Crude Petroleum and Natural Gas Extraction	211111
Crushed and Broken Granite Mining and Quarrying	212313
Crushed and Broken Limestone Mining and Quarrying	212312
Current-Carrying Wiring Device Manufacturing	335931
Curtain and Drapery Mills	314121
Custom Architectural Woodwork and Millwork Manufacturing	337212
Custom Compounding of Purchased Resins	325991
Custom Computer Programming Services	541511
Custom Roll Forming	332114
Cut Stock, Resawing Lumber, and Planing	321912
Cut Stone and Stone Product Manufacturing	327991
Cutlery and Flatware (except Precious) Manufacturing	332211
Cutting Tool and Machine Tool Accessory Manufacturing	333515
Cyclic Crude and Intermediate Manufacturing	325192
D	
Dairy Cattle and Milk Production	112120
Dairy Product (except Dried or Canned) Merchant Wholesalers	424430
Dairy Product (except Dried or Canned) Wholesalers	422430
Dance Companies	711120
Data Processing Services	514210
Data Processing, Hosting, and Related Services	518210
Database and Directory Publishers	511140
Deep Sea Freight Transportation	483111
Deep Sea Passenger Transportation	483112
Dental Equipment and Supplies Manufacturing	339114

Description	*N.A.I.C.S.*
Dental Laboratories	339116
Department Stores	452110
Department Stores (except Discount Department Stores)	452111
Diagnostic Imaging Centers	621512
Die-Cut Paper and Paperboard Office Supplies Manufacturing	322231
Diet and Weight Reducing Centers	812191
Digital Printing	323115
Dimension Stone Mining and Quarrying	212311
Direct Health and Medical Insurance Carriers	524114
Direct Life Insurance Carriers	524113
Direct Mail Advertising	541860
Direct Property and Casualty Insurance Carriers	524126
Direct Title Insurance Carriers	524127
Discount Department Stores	452112
Display Advertising	541850
Distilleries	312140
Document Preparation Services	561410
Dog and Cat Food Manufacturing	311111
Doll and Stuffed Toy Manufacturing	339931
Drafting Services	541340
Dried and Dehydrated Food Manufacturing	311423
Drilling Oil and Gas Wells	213111
Drinking Places (Alcoholic Beverages)	722410
Drive-In Motion Picture Theaters	512132
Drugs and Druggists' Sundries Wholesalers	422210
Drugs and Druggists' Sundries Merchant Wholesalers	424210
Dry Pasta Manufacturing	311823
Dry Pea and Bean Farming	111130
Dry, Condensed, and Evaporated Dairy Product Manufacturing	311514
Drycleaning and Laundry Services (except Coin-Operated)	812320
Drywall and Insulation Contractors	238310
Drywall, Plastering, Acoustical, and Insulation Contractors	235420
Dual Purpose Cattle Ranching and Farming	112130
E	
Educational Support Services	611710
Electric Bulk Power Transmission and Control	221121
Electric Housewares and Household Fan Manufacturing	335211
Electric Lamp Bulb and Part Manufacturing	335110
Electric Power Distribution	221122
Electrical and Electronic Appliance, Television, and Radio Set Merchant Wholesalers	423620
Electrical Apparatus and Equipment, Wiring Supplies, and Construction Material Wholesalers	421610
Electrical Apparatus and Equipment, Wiring Supplies, and Related Equipment Merchant Wholesalers	423610
Electrical Appliance, Television, and Radio Set Wholesalers	421620
Electrical Contractors	238210
Electromedical and Electrotherapeutic Apparatus Manufacturing	334510
Electrometallurgical Ferroalloy Product Manufacturing	331112
Electron Tube Manufacturing	334411
Electronic Auctions	454112
Electronic Capacitor Manufacturing	334414
Electronic Coil, Transformer, and Other Inductor Manufacturing	334416
Electronic Computer Manufacturing	334111
Electronic Connector Manufacturing	334417
Electronic Resistor Manufacturing	334415
Electronic Shopping	454111
Electronic Shopping and Mail-Order Houses	454110
Electroplating, Plating, Polishing, Anodizing, and Coloring	332813
Elementary and Secondary Schools	611110
Elevator and Moving Stairway Manufacturing	333921
Emergency and Other Relief Services	624230
Employee Leasing Services	561330
Employment Placement Agencies	561310
Enameled Iron and Metal Sanitary Ware Manufacturing	332998
Engineered Wood Member (except Truss) Manufacturing	321213
Engineering Services	541330
Envelope Manufacturing	322232
Environment, Conservation and Wildlife Organizations	813312
Environmental Consulting Services	541620
Ethyl Alcohol Manufacturing	325193
Exam Preparation and Tutoring	611691
Excavation Contractors	235930
Executive and Legislative Offices, Combined	921140
Executive Offices	921110
Explosives Manufacturing	325920
Exterminating and Pest Control Services	561710

Description	*N.A.I.C.S.*
F	
Fabric Coating Mills	313320
Fabricated Pipe and Pipe Fitting Manufacturing	332996
Fabricated Structural Metal Manufacturing	332312
Facilities Support Services	561210
Family Clothing Stores	448140
Family Planning Centers	621410
Farm and Garden Machinery and Equipment Merchant Wholesalers	423820
Farm and Garden Machinery and Equipment Wholesalers	421820
Farm Labor Contractors and Crew Leaders	115115
Farm Machinery and Equipment Manufacturing	333111
Farm Management Services	115116
Farm Product Warehousing and Storage	493130
Farm Supplies Merchant Wholesalers	424910
Farm Supplies Wholesalers	422910
Fast Food Restaurants	722211
Fastener, Button, Needle, and Pin Manufacturing	339993
Fats and Oils Refining and Blending	311225
Fertilizer (Mixing Only) Manufacturing	325314
Fiber Can, Tube, Drum, and Similar Products Manufacturing	322214
Fiber Optic Cable Manufacturing	335921
Financial Transactions Processing, Reserve, and Clearinghouse Activities	522320
Fine Arts Schools	611610
Finfish Farming and Fish Hatcheries	112511
Finfish Fishing	114111
Finish Carpentry Contractors	238350
Fire Protection	922160
Fish and Seafood Markets	445220
Fish and Seafood Merchant Wholesalers	424460
Fish and Seafood Wholesalers	422460
Fitness and Recreational Sports Centers	713940
Flat Glass Manufacturing	327211
Flavoring Syrup and Concentrate Manufacturing	311930
Flight Training	611512
Floor Covering Stores	442210
Floor Laying and Other Floor Contractors	235520
Flooring Contractors	238330
Floriculture Production	111422
Florists	453110
Flour Milling	311211
Flour Mixes and Dough Manufacturing from Purchased Flour	311822
Flower, Nursery Stock, and Florists' Supplies Wholesalers	422930
Flower, Nursery Stock, and Florists' Supplies Merchant Wholesalers	424930
Fluid Milk Manufacturing	311511
Fluid Power Cylinder and Actuator Manufacturing	333995
Fluid Power Pump and Motor Manufacturing	333996
Fluid Power Valve and Hose Fitting Manufacturing	332912
Folding Paperboard Box Manufacturing	322212
Food (Health) Supplement Stores	446191
Food Product Machinery Manufacturing	333294
Food Service Contractors	722310
Footwear and Leather Goods Repair	811430
Footwear Merchant Wholesalers	424340
Footwear Wholesalers	422340
Forest Nurseries and Gathering of Forest Products	113210
Formal Wear and Costume Rental	532220
Fossil Fuel Electric Power Generation	221112
Framing Contractors	238130
Freestanding Ambulatory Surgical and Emergency Centers	621493
Freight Transportation Arrangement	488510
Fresh and Frozen Seafood Processing	311712
Fresh Fruit and Vegetable Merchant Wholesalers	424480
Fresh Fruit and Vegetable Wholesalers	422480
Frozen Cakes, Pies, and Other Pastries Manufacturing	311813
Frozen Fruit, Juice, and Vegetable Manufacturing	311411
Frozen Specialty Food Manufacturing	311412
Fruit and Tree Nut Combination Farming	111336
Fruit and Vegetable Canning	311421
Fruit and Vegetable Markets	445230
Full-Service Restaurants	722110
Funeral Homes and Funeral Services	812210
Fur and Leather Apparel Manufacturing	315292
Fur-Bearing Animal and Rabbit Production	112930
Furniture Merchant Wholesalers	423210
Furniture Stores	442110
Furniture Wholesalers	421210

Description	N.A.I.C.S.
G	
Game, Toy, and Children's Vehicle Manufacturing	339932
Gasket, Packing, and Sealing Device Manufacturing	339991
Gasoline Engine and Engine Parts Manufacturing	336312
Gasoline Stations with Convenience Stores	447110
General Automotive Repair	811111
General Freight Trucking, Local	484110
General Freight Trucking, Long-Distance, Less Than Truckload	484122
General Freight Trucking, Long-Distance, Truckload	484121
General Line Grocery Merchant Wholesalers	424410
General Line Grocery Wholesalers	422410
General Medical and Surgical Hospitals	622110
General Rental Centers	532310
General Warehousing and Storage	493110
Geophysical Surveying and Mapping Services	541360
Gift, Novelty, and Souvenir Stores	453220
Glass and Glazing Contractors	238150
Glass Container Manufacturing	327213
Glass Product Manufacturing Made of Purchased Glass	327215
Glove and Mitten Manufacturing	315992
Goat Farming	112420
Gold Ore Mining	212221
Golf Courses and Country Clubs	713910
Grain and Field Bean Merchant Wholesalers	424510
Grain and Field Bean Wholesalers	422510
Grantmaking Foundations	813211
Grape Vineyards	111332
Graphic Design Services	541430
Greeting Card Publishers	511191
Ground or Treated Mineral and Earth Manufacturing	327992
Guided Missile and Space Vehicle Manufacturing	336414
Guided Missile and Space Vehicle Propulsion Unit and Propulsion Unit Parts Manufacturing	336415
Gum and Wood Chemical Manufacturing	325191
Gypsum Product Manufacturing	327420
H	
Hand and Edge Tool Manufacturing	332212
Hardware Manufacturing	332510
Hardware Merchant Wholesalers	423710
Hardware Stores	444130
Hardware Wholesalers	421710
Hardwood Veneer and Plywood Manufacturing	321211
Hat, Cap, and Millinery Manufacturing	315991
Hay Farming	111940
Hazardous Waste Collection	562112
Hazardous Waste Treatment and Disposal	562211
Health and Welfare Funds	525120
Heating Equipment (except Warm Air Furnaces) Manufacturing	333414
Heating Oil Dealers	454311
Heavy Duty Truck Manufacturing	336120
Highway and Street Construction	234110
Highway, Street, and Bridge Construction	237310
Historical Sites	712120
HMO Medical Centers	621491
Hobby, Toy, and Game Stores	451120
Hog and Pig Farming	112210
Home and Garden Equipment Repair and Maintenance	811411
Home Centers	444110
Home Furnishing Merchant Wholesalers	423220
Home Furnishing Wholesalers	421220
Home Health Care Services	621610
Home Health Equipment Rental	532291
Homes for the Elderly	623312
Horse and Other Equine Production	112920
Hotels (except Casino Hotels) and Motels	721110
House Slipper Manufacturing	316212
Household Appliance Stores	443111
Household Cooking Appliance Manufacturing	335221
Household Furniture (except Wood and Metal) Manufacturing	337125
Household Laundry Equipment Manufacturing	335224
Household Refrigerator and Home Freezer Manufacturing	335222
Household Vacuum Cleaner Manufacturing	335212
Human Resources and Executive Search Consulting Services	541612
Human Rights Organizations	813311
Hunting and Trapping	114210
Hydroelectric Power Generation	221111
I	
Ice Cream and Frozen Dessert Manufacturing	311520
Ice Manufacturing	312113
Independent Artists, Writers, and Performers	711510
Industrial and Commercial Fan and Blower Manufacturing	333412
Industrial and Personal Service Paper Merchant Wholesalers	424130
Industrial and Personal Service Paper Wholesalers	422130
Industrial Building Construction	236210
Industrial Design Services	541420
Industrial Gas Manufacturing	325120
Industrial Launderers	812332
Industrial Machinery and Equipment Merchant Wholesalers	423830
Industrial Machinery and Equipment Wholesalers	421830
Industrial Mold Manufacturing	333511
Industrial Nonbuilding Structure Construction	234930
Industrial Pattern Manufacturing	332997
Industrial Process Furnace and Oven Manufacturing	333994
Industrial Sand Mining	212322
Industrial Supplies Merchant Wholesalers	423840
Industrial Supplies Wholesalers	421840
Industrial Truck, Tractor, Trailer, and Stacker Machinery Manufacturing	333924
Industrial Valve Manufacturing	332911
Infants' Cut and Sew Apparel Manufacturing	315291
Inland Water Freight Transportation	483211
Inland Water Passenger Transportation	483212
Inorganic Dye and Pigment Manufacturing	325131
Institutional Furniture Manufacturing	337127
Instrument Manufacturing for Measuring and Testing Electricity and Electrical Signals	334515
Instruments and Related Products Manufacturing for Measuring, Displaying, and Controlling Industrial Process Variables	334513
Insurance Agencies and Brokerages	524210
Integrated Record Production/Distribution	512220
Interior Design Services	541410
International Affairs	928120
International Trade Financing	522293
Internet Publishing and Broadcasting	516110
Internet Service Providers	518111
Interurban and Rural Bus Transportation	485210
Investigation Services	561611
Investment Advice	523930
Investment Banking and Securities Dealing	523110
In-Vitro Diagnostic Substance Manufacturing	325413
Iron and Steel Forging	332111
Iron and Steel Mills	331111
Iron and Steel Pipe and Tube Manufacturing from Purchased Steel	331210
Iron Foundries	331511
Iron Ore Mining	212210
Irradiation Apparatus Manufacturing	334517
J	
Janitorial Services	561720
Jewelers' Material and Lapidary Work Manufacturing	339913
Jewelry (except Costume) Manufacturing	339911
Jewelry Stores	448310
Jewelry, Watch, Precious Stone, and Precious Metal Merchant Wholesalers	423940
Jewelry, Watch, Precious Stone, and Precious Metal Wholesalers	421940
Junior Colleges	611210
K	
Kaolin and Ball Clay Mining	212324
Kidney Dialysis Centers	621492
Kitchen Utensil, Pot, and Pan Manufacturing	332214
L	
Labor Unions and Similar Labor Organizations	813930
Laboratory Apparatus and Furniture Manufacturing	339111
Laminated Aluminum Foil Manufacturing for Flexible Packaging Uses	322225
Laminated Plastics Plate, Sheet, and Shape Manufacturing	326130
Land Subdivision	237210
Landscape Architectural Services	541320
Landscaping Services	561730
Language Schools	611630
Lawn and Garden Tractor and Home Lawn and Garden Equipment Manufacturing	333112
Lead Ore and Zinc Ore Mining	212231
Lead Pencil and Art Good Manufacturing	339942
Leather and Hide Tanning and Finishing	316110

Description	*N.A.I.C.S.*
Legal Counsel and Prosecution	922130
Legislative Bodies	921120
Lessors of Miniwarehouses and Self-Storage Units	531130
Lessors of Nonfinancial Intangible Assets (except Copyrighted Works)	533110
Lessors of Nonresidential Buildings (except Miniwarehouses)	531120
Lessors of Other Real Estate Property	531190
Lessors of Residential Buildings and Dwellings	531110
Libraries and Archives	519120
Light Truck and Utility Vehicle Manufacturing	336112
Lime Manufacturing	327410
Limousine Service	485320
Line-Haul Railroads	482111
Linen Supply	812331
Liquefied Petroleum Gas (Bottled Gas) Dealers	454312
Livestock Merchant Wholesalers	424520
Livestock Wholesalers	422520
Local Messengers and Local Delivery	492210
Locksmiths	561622
Logging	113310
Luggage and Leather Goods Stores	448320
Luggage Manufacturing	316991
Lumber, Plywood, Millwork, and Wood Panel Merchant Wholesalers	423310
Lumber, Plywood, Millwork, and Wood Panel Wholesalers	421310
M	
Machine Shops	332710
Machine Tool (Metal Cutting Types) Manufacturing	333512
Machine Tool (Metal Forming Types) Manufacturing	333513
Magnetic and Optical Recording Media Manufacturing	334613
Mail-Order Houses	454113
Malt Manufacturing	311213
Manifold Business Forms Printing	323116
Manufactured (Mobile) Home Dealers	453930
Manufactured Home (Mobile Home) Manufacturing	321991
Manufacturing and Industrial Building Construction	233310
Marinas	713930
Marine Cargo Handling	488320
Marketing Consulting Services	541613
Marketing Research and Public Opinion Polling	541910
Marking Device Manufacturing	339943
Masonry and Stone Contractors	235410
Masonry Contractors	238140
Materials Recovery Facilities	562920
Mattress Manufacturing	337910
Mayonnaise, Dressing, and Other Prepared Sauce Manufacturing	311941
Measuring and Dispensing Pump Manufacturing	333913
Meat and Meat Product Merchant Wholesalers	424470
Meat and Meat Product Wholesalers	422470
Meat Markets	445210
Meat Processed from Carcasses	311612
Mechanical Power Transmission Equipment Manufacturing	333613
Media Buying Agencies	541830
Media Representatives	541840
Medical Laboratories	621511
Medical, Dental, and Hospital Equipment and Supplies Merchant Wholesalers	423450
Medical, Dental, and Hospital Equipment and Supplies Wholesalers	421450
Medicinal and Botanical Manufacturing	325411
Men's and Boys' Clothing and Furnishings Merchant Wholesalers	424320
Men's and Boys' Clothing and Furnishings Wholesalers	422320
Men's and Boys' Cut and Sew Apparel Contractors	315211
Men's and Boys' Cut and Sew Other Outerwear Manufacturing	315228
Men's and Boys' Cut and Sew Shirt (except Work Shirt) Manufacturing	315223
Men's and Boys' Cut and Sew Suit, Coat, and Overcoat Manufacturing	315222
Men's and Boys' Cut and Sew Trouser, Slack, and Jean Manufacturing	315224
Men's and Boys' Cut and Sew Underwear and Nightwear Manufacturing	315221
Men's and Boys' Cut and Sew Work Clothing Manufacturing	315225
Men's and Boys' Neckwear Manufacturing	315993
Men's Clothing Stores	448110
Men's Footwear (except Athletic) Manufacturing	316213
Metal Can Manufacturing	332431
Metal Coating, Engraving (except Jewelry and Silverware), and Allied Services to Manufacturers	332812
Metal Heat Treating	332811
Metal Household Furniture Manufacturing	337124
Metal Service Centers and Offices	421510
Metal Service Centers and Other Metal Merchant Wholesalers	423510
Metal Stamping	332116
Metal Tank (Heavy Gauge) Manufacturing	332420
Metal Window and Door Manufacturing	332321
Military Armored Vehicle, Tank, and Tank Component Manufacturing	336992
Mineral Wool Manufacturing	327993
Mining Machinery and Equipment Manufacturing	333131
Miscellaneous Financial Investment Activities	523999
Miscellaneous Intermediation	523910
Mixed Mode Transit Systems	485111
Mobile Food Services	722330
Monetary Authorities - Central Bank	521110
Mortgage and Nonmortgage Loan Brokers	522310
Motion Picture and Video Distribution	512120
Motion Picture and Video Production	512110
Motion Picture Theaters (except Drive-Ins)	512131
Motor and Generator Manufacturing	335312
Motor Home Manufacturing	336213
Motor Vehicle Air-Conditioning Manufacturing	336391
Motor Vehicle Body Manufacturing	336211
Motor Vehicle Brake System Manufacturing	336340
Motor Vehicle Metal Stamping	336370
Motor Vehicle Parts (Used) Merchant Wholesalers	423140
Motor Vehicle Parts (Used) Wholesalers	421140
Motor Vehicle Seating and Interior Trim Manufacturing	336360
Motor Vehicle Steering and Suspension Components (except Spring) Manufacturing	336330
Motor Vehicle Supplies and New Parts Merchant Wholesalers	423120
Motor Vehicle Supplies and New Parts Wholesalers	421120
Motor Vehicle Towing	488410
Motor Vehicle Transmission and Power Train Parts Manufacturing	336350
Motorcycle Dealers	441221
Motorcycle, Bicycle, and Parts Manufacturing	336991
Multifamily Housing Construction	233220
Museums	712110
Mushroom Production	111411
Music Publishers	512230
Musical Groups and Artists	711130
Musical Instrument and Supplies Stores	451140
Musical Instrument Manufacturing	339992
N	
Nail Salons	812113
Narrow Fabric Mills	313221
National Security	928110
Natural Gas Distribution	221210
Natural Gas Liquid Extraction	211112
Nature Parks and Other Similar Institutions	712190
Navigational Services to Shipping	488330
New Car Dealers	441110
New Housing Operative Builders	236117
New Multifamily Housing Construction (except Operative Builders)	236116
New Single-Family Housing Construction (except Operative Builders)	236115
News Dealers and Newsstands	451212
News Syndicates	519110
Newspaper Publishers	511110
Newsprint Mills	322122
Nitrogenous Fertilizer Manufacturing	325311
Noncellulosic Organic Fiber Manufacturing	325222
Nonchocolate Confectionery Manufacturing	311340
Nonclay Refractory Manufacturing	327125
Noncurrent-Carrying Wiring Device Manufacturing	335932
Nonferrous (except Aluminum) Die-Casting Foundries	331522
Nonferrous Forging	332112
Nonferrous Metal (except Copper and Aluminum) Rolling, Drawing, and Extruding	331491
Nonfolding Sanitary Food Container Manufacturing	322215
Nonresidential Property Managers	531312
Nonscheduled Chartered Freight Air Transportation	481212
Nonscheduled Chartered Passenger Air Transportation	481211
Nonupholstered Wood Household Furniture Manufacturing	337122
Nonwoven Fabric Mills	313230
Nuclear Electric Power Generation	221113
Nursery and Garden Centers	444220
Nursery and Tree Production	111421
Nursing Care Facilities	623110
O	
Office Administrative Services	561110
Office Equipment Merchant Wholesalers	423420
Office Equipment Wholesalers	421420
Office Furniture (except Wood) Manufacturing	337214
Office Machinery and Equipment Rental and Leasing	532420
Office Machinery Manufacturing	333313

Description	*N.A.I.C.S.*
Office Supplies and Stationery Stores	453210
Offices of All Other Miscellaneous Health Practitioners	621399
Offices of Bank Holding Companies	551111
Offices of Certified Public Accountants	541211
Offices of Chiropractors	621310
Offices of Dentists	621210
Offices of Lawyers	541110
Offices of Mental Health Practitioners (except Physicians)	621330
Offices of Notaries	541120
Offices of Optometrists	621320
Offices of Other Holding Companies	551112
Offices of Physical, Occupational and Speech Therapists, and Audiologists	621340
Offices of Physicians (except Mental Health Specialists)	621111
Offices of Physicians, Mental Health Specialists	621112
Offices of Podiatrists	621391
Offices of Real Estate Agents and Brokers	531210
Offices of Real Estate Appraisers	531320
Oil and Gas Field Machinery and Equipment Manufacturing	333132
Oil and Gas Pipeline and Related Structures Construction	237120
Oilseed (except Soybean) Farming	111120
Oilseed and Grain Combination Farming	111191
One-Hour Photofinishing	812922
On-Line Information Services	514191
Open-End Investment Funds	525910
Ophthalmic Goods Manufacturing	339115
Ophthalmic Goods Merchant Wholesalers	423460
Ophthalmic Goods Wholesalers	421460
Optical Goods Stores	446130
Optical Instrument and Lens Manufacturing	333314
Other Fabricated Wire Product Manufacturing	332618
Other Farm Product Raw Material Merchant Wholesalers	424590
Other Farm Product Raw Material Wholesalers	422590
Other Financial Vehicles	525990
Other Food Crops Grown Under Cover	111419
Other Footwear Manufacturing	316219
Other Foundation, Structure, and Building Exterior Contractors	238190
Other Fuel Dealers	454319
Other Gambling Industries	713290
Other Gasoline Stations	447190
Other General Government Support	921190
Other Grantmaking and Giving Services	813219
Other Grocery and Related Products Merchant Wholesalers	424490
Other Grocery and Related Products Wholesalers	422490
Other Guided Missile and Space Vehicle Parts and Auxiliary Equipment Manufacturing	336419
Other Heavy and Civil Engineering Construction	237990
Other Hosiery and Sock Mills	315119
Other Household Textile Product Mills	314129
Other Individual and Family Services	624190
Other Insurance Funds	525190
Other Justice, Public Order, and Safety Activities	922190
Other Knit Fabric and Lace Mills	313249
Other Lighting Equipment Manufacturing	335129
Other Major Household Appliance Manufacturing	335228
Other Management Consulting Services	541618
Other Marine Fishing	114119
Other Measuring and Controlling Device Manufacturing	334519
Other Metal Container Manufacturing	332439
Other Metal Valve and Pipe Fitting Manufacturing	332919
Other Metalworking Machinery Manufacturing	333518
Other Millwork (including Flooring)	321918
Other Miscellaneous Durable Goods Merchant Wholesalers	423990
Other Miscellaneous Durable Goods Wholesalers	421990
Other Miscellaneous Nondurable Goods Wholesalers	422990
Other Motion Picture and Video Industries	512199
Other Motor Vehicle Electrical and Electronic Equipment Manufacturing	336322
Other Noncitrus Fruit Farming	111339
Other Nonferrous Foundries (except Die-Casting)	331528
Other Nonhazardous Waste Treatment and Disposal	562219
Other Nonscheduled Air Transportation	481219
Other Oilseed Processing	311223
Other Ordnance and Accessories Manufacturing	332995
Other Performing Arts Companies	711190
Other Personal and Household Goods Repair and Maintenance	811490
Other Personal Care Services	812199
Other Poultry Production	112390
Other Pressed and Blown Glass and Glassware Manufacturing	327212
Other Professional Equipment and Supplies Merchant Wholesalers	423490
Other Professional Equipment and Supplies Wholesalers	421490

Description	*N.A.I.C.S.*
Other Residential Care Facilities	623990
Other Scientific and Technical Consulting Services	541690
Other Services Related to Advertising	541890
Other Services to Buildings and Dwellings	561790
Other Similar Organizations (except Business, Professional, Labor, and Political Organizations)	813990
Other Snack Food Manufacturing	311919
Other Social Advocacy Organizations	813319
Other Sound Recording Industries	512290
Other Specialized Design Services	541490
Other Spectator Sports	711219
Other Structural Clay Product Manufacturing	327123
Other Support Activities for Air Transportation	400190
Other Support Activities for Road Transportation	488490
Other Support Activities for Water Transportation	488390
Other Technical and Trade Schools	611519
Other Telecommunications	517910
Other Tobacco Product Manufacturing	312229
Other Urban Transit Systems	485119
Other Vegetable (except Potato) and Melon Farming	111219
Other Warehousing and Storage	493190
Other Waste Collection	562119
Outdoor Power Equipment Stores	444210
Outerwear Knitting Mills	315191
Outpatient Mental Health and Substance Abuse Centers	621420
Overhead Traveling Crane, Hoist, and Monorail System Manufacturing	333923

P

Description	*N.A.I.C.S.*
Packaged Frozen Food Merchant Wholesalers	424420
Packaged Frozen Food Wholesalers	422420
Packaging and Labeling Services	561910
Packaging Machinery Manufacturing	333993
Packing and Crating	488991
Paging	517211
Paint and Coating Manufacturing	325510
Paint and Wallpaper Stores	444120
Paint, Varnish, and Supplies Merchant Wholesalers	424950
Paint, Varnish, and Supplies Wholesalers	422950
Painting and Wall Covering Contractors	238320
Paper (except Newsprint) Mills	322121
Paper Industry Machinery Manufacturing	333291
Paperboard Mills	322130
Parking Lots and Garages	812930
Parole Offices and Probation Offices	922150
Passenger Car Leasing	532112
Passenger Car Rental	532111
Payroll Services	541214
Peanut Farming	111992
Pen and Mechanical Pencil Manufacturing	339941
Pension Funds	525110
Periodical Publishers	511120
Perishable Prepared Food Manufacturing	311991
Personal Leather Good (except Women's Handbag and Purse) Manufacturing	316993
Pesticide and Other Agricultural Chemical Manufacturing	325320
Pet and Pet Supplies Stores	453910
Pet Care (except Veterinary) Services	812910
Petrochemical Manufacturing	325110
Petroleum and Petroleum Products Merchant Wholesalers (except Bulk Stations and Terminals)	424720
Petroleum and Petroleum Products Wholesalers (except Bulk Stations and Terminals)	422720
Petroleum Bulk Stations and Terminals	424710
Petroleum Lubricating Oil and Grease Manufacturing	324191
Petroleum Refineries	324110
Pharmaceutical Preparation Manufacturing	325412
Pharmacies and Drug Stores	446110
Phosphate Rock Mining	212392
Phosphatic Fertilizer Manufacturing	325312
Photofinishing Laboratories (except One-Hour)	812921
Photographic and Photocopying Equipment Manufacturing	333315
Photographic Equipment and Supplies Merchant Wholesalers	423410
Photographic Equipment and Supplies Wholesalers	421410
Photographic Film, Paper, Plate, and Chemical Manufacturing	325992
Photography Studios, Portrait	541921
Piece Goods, Notions, and Other Dry Goods Merchant Wholesalers	424310
Piece Goods, Notions, and Other Dry Goods Wholesalers	422310
Pipeline Transportation of Crude Oil	486110
Pipeline Transportation of Natural Gas	486210
Pipeline Transportation of Refined Petroleum Products	486910

Description	*N.A.I.C.S.*
Plastics and Rubber Industry Machinery Manufacturing	333220
Plastics Bottle Manufacturing	326160
Plastics Material and Resin Manufacturing	325211
Plastics Materials and Basic Forms and Shapes Merchant Wholesalers	424610
Plastics Materials and Basic Forms and Shapes Wholesalers	422610
Plastics Pipe and Pipe Fitting Manufacturing	326122
Plastics Plumbing Fixture Manufacturing	326191
Plastics, Foil, and Coated Paper Bag Manufacturing	322223
Plate Work Manufacturing	332313
Plumbing and Heating Equipment and Supplies (Hydronics) Merchant Wholesalers	423720
Plumbing and Heating Equipment and Supplies (Hydronics) Wholesalers	421720
Plumbing Fixture Fitting and Trim Manufacturing	332913
Plumbing, Heating, and Air-Conditioning Contractors	235110
Police Protection	922120
Polish and Other Sanitation Good Manufacturing	325612
Political Organizations	813940
Polystyrene Foam Product Manufacturing	326140
Porcelain Electrical Supply Manufacturing	327113
Port and Harbor Operations	488310
Portfolio Management	523920
Postal Service	491110
Postharvest Crop Activities (except Cotton Ginning)	115114
Potash, Soda, and Borate Mineral Mining	212391
Potato Farming	111211
Poultry and Poultry Product Merchant Wholesalers	424440
Poultry and Poultry Product Wholesalers	422440
Poultry Hatcheries	112340
Poultry Processing	311615
Poured Concrete Foundation and Structure Contractors	238110
Powder Metallurgy Part Manufacturing	332117
Power and Communication Line and Related Structures Construction	237130
Power and Communication Transmission Line Construction	234920
Power Boiler and Heat Exchanger Manufacturing	332410
Power, Distribution, and Specialty Transformer Manufacturing	335311
Power-Driven Handtool Manufacturing	333991
Precision Turned Product Manufacturing	332721
Prefabricated Metal Building and Component Manufacturing	332311
Prefabricated Wood Building Manufacturing	321992
Prepress Services	323122
Prerecorded Compact Disc (except Software), Tape, and Record Reproducing	334612
Prerecorded Tape, Compact Disc, and Record Stores	451220
Primary Aluminum Production	331312
Primary Battery Manufacturing	335912
Primary Smelting and Refining of Copper	331411
Primary Smelting and Refining of Nonferrous Metal (except Copper and Aluminum)	331419
Printed Circuit Assembly (Electronic Assembly) Manufacturing	334418
Printing and Writing Paper Merchant Wholesalers	424110
Printing and Writing Paper Wholesalers	422110
Printing Ink Manufacturing	325910
Printing Machinery and Equipment Manufacturing	333293
Private Households	814110
Private Mail Centers	561431
Process, Physical Distribution, and Logistics Consulting Services	541614
Professional and Management Development Training	611430
Professional Organizations	813920
Promoters of Performing Arts, Sports, and Similar Events with Facilities	711310
Promoters of Performing Arts, Sports, and Similar Events without Facilities	711320
Psychiatric and Substance Abuse Hospitals	622210
Public Finance Activities	921130
Public Relations Agencies	541820
Pulp Mills	322110
Pump and Pumping Equipment Manufacturing	333911
Q	
Quick Printing	323114
R	
Racetracks	711212
Radio and Television Broadcasting and Wireless Communications Equipment Manufacturing	334220
Radio Networks	515111
Radio Stations	515112
Radio, Television, and Other Electronics Stores	443112
Railroad Rolling Stock Manufacturing	336510
Ready-Mix Concrete Manufacturing	327320
Real Estate Credit	522292
Real Estate Investment Trusts	525930
Reconstituted Wood Product Manufacturing	321219
Record Production	512210
Recreational and Vacation Camps (except Campgrounds)	721214
Recreational Goods Rental	532292
Recreational Vehicle Dealers	441210
Recyclable Material Merchant Wholesalers	423930
Recyclable Material Wholesalers	421930
Refrigerated Warehousing and Storage	493120
Refrigeration Equipment and Supplies Merchant Wholesalers	423740
Refrigeration Equipment and Supplies Wholesalers	421740
Regulation and Administration of Communications, Electric, Gas, and Other Utilities	926130
Regulation and Administration of Transportation Programs	926120
Regulation of Agricultural Marketing and Commodities	926140
Regulation, Licensing, and Inspection of Miscellaneous Commercial Sectors	926150
Reinsurance Carriers	524130
Relay and Industrial Control Manufacturing	335314
Religious Organizations	813110
Remediation Services	562910
Rendering and Meat Byproduct Processing	311613
Repossession Services	561491
Research and Development in the Physical, Engineering, and Life Sciences	541710
Research and Development in the Social Sciences and Humanities	541720
Residential Electric Lighting Fixture Manufacturing	335121
Residential Mental Health and Substance Abuse Facilities	623220
Residential Mental Retardation Facilities	623210
Residential Property Managers	531311
Residential Remodelers	236118
Resilient Floor Covering Manufacturing	326192
Retail Bakeries	311811
Reupholstery and Furniture Repair	811420
Rice Farming	111160
Rice Milling	311212
Roasted Nuts and Peanut Butter Manufacturing	311911
Rolled Steel Shape Manufacturing	331221
Rolling Mill Machinery and Equipment Manufacturing	333516
Roofing Contractors	238160
Roofing, Siding, and Insulation Material Merchant Wholesalers	423330
Roofing, Siding, and Insulation Material Wholesalers	421330
Roofing, Siding, and Sheet Metal Contractors	235610
Rooming and Boarding Houses	721310
Rope, Cordage, and Twine Mills	314991
Rubber and Plastics Footwear Manufacturing	316211
Rubber and Plastics Hoses and Belting Manufacturing	326220
Rubber Product Manufacturing for Mechanical Use	326291
RV (Recreational Vehicle) Parks and Campgrounds	721211
S	
Sales Financing	522220
Sanitary Paper Product Manufacturing	322291
Satellite Telecommunications	517410
Savings Institutions	522120
Saw Blade and Handsaw Manufacturing	332213
Sawmill and Woodworking Machinery Manufacturing	333210
Sawmills	321113
Scale and Balance (except Laboratory) Manufacturing	333997
Scenic and Sightseeing Transportation, Land	487110
Scenic and Sightseeing Transportation, Other	487990
Scenic and Sightseeing Transportation, Water	487210
Scheduled Freight Air Transportation	481112
Scheduled Passenger Air Transportation	481111
Schiffli Machine Embroidery	313222
School and Employee Bus Transportation	485410
Seafood Canning	311711
Search, Detection, Navigation, Guidance, Aeronautical, and Nautical System and Instrument Manufacturing	334511
Secondary Market Financing	522294
Secondary Smelting and Alloying of Aluminum	331314
Secondary Smelting, Refining, and Alloying of Copper	331423
Secondary Smelting, Refining, and Alloying of Nonferrous Metal (except Copper and Aluminum)	331492
Securities and Commodity Exchanges	523210
Securities Brokerage	523120
Security Guards and Patrol Services	561612
Security Systems Services (except Locksmiths)	561621
Semiconductor and Related Device Manufacturing	334413
Semiconductor Machinery Manufacturing	333295

Description	N.A.I.C.S.
Septic Tank and Related Services	562991
Service Establishment Equipment and Supplies Merchant Wholesalers	423850
Service Establishment Equipment and Supplies Wholesalers	421850
Services for the Elderly and Persons with Disabilities	624120
Setup Paperboard Box Manufacturing	322213
Sewage Treatment Facilities	221320
Sewing, Needlework, and Piece Goods Stores	451130
Sheep Farming	112410
Sheer Hosiery Mills	315111
Sheet Metal Work Manufacturing	332322
Shellfish Farming	112512
Shellfish Fishing	114112
Ship Building and Repairing	336611
Shoe Stores	448210
Short Line Railroads	482112
Showcase, Partition, Shelving, and Locker Manufacturing	337215
Siding Contractors	238170
Sign Manufacturing	339950
Silver Ore Mining	212222
Silverware and Hollowware Manufacturing	339912
Single Family Housing Construction	233210
Site Preparation Contractors	238910
Skiing Facilities	713920
Small Arms Ammunition Manufacturing	332992
Small Arms Manufacturing	332994
Snack and Nonalcoholic Beverage Bars	722213
Soap and Other Detergent Manufacturing	325611
Soft Drink Manufacturing	312111
Software Publishers	511210
Software Reproducing	334611
Softwood Veneer and Plywood Manufacturing	321212
Soil Preparation, Planting, and Cultivating	115112
Solid Waste Collection	562111
Solid Waste Combustors and Incinerators	562213
Solid Waste Landfill	562212
Sound Recording Studios	512240
Soybean Farming	111110
Soybean Processing	311222
Space Research and Technology	927110
Special Die and Tool, Die Set, Jig, and Fixture Manufacturing	333514
Special Needs Transportation	485991
Specialized Freight (except Used Goods) Trucking, Local	484220
Specialized Freight (except Used Goods) Trucking, Long-Distance	484230
Specialty (except Psychiatric and Substance Abuse) Hospitals	622310
Specialty Canning	311422
Speed Changer, Industrial High-Speed Drive, and Gear Manufacturing	333612
Spice and Extract Manufacturing	311942
Sporting and Athletic Goods Manufacturing	339920
Sporting and Recreational Goods and Supplies Merchant Wholesalers	423910
Sporting and Recreational Goods and Supplies Wholesalers	421910
Sporting Goods Stores	451110
Sports and Recreation Instruction	611620
Sports Teams and Clubs	711211
Spring (Heavy Gauge) Manufacturing	332611
Spring (Light Gauge) Manufacturing	332612
Stationery and Office Supplies Merchant Wholesalers	424120
Stationery and Office Supplies Wholesalers	422120
Stationery, Tablet, and Related Product Manufacturing	322233
Steam and Air-Conditioning Supply	221330
Steel Foundries (except Investment)	331513
Steel Investment Foundries	331512
Steel Wire Drawing	331222
Storage Battery Manufacturing	335911
Strawberry Farming	111333
Structural Steel and Precast Concrete Contractors	238120
Structural Steel Erection Contractors	235910
Sugar Beet Farming	111991
Sugarcane Farming	111930
Sugarcane Mills	311311
Supermarkets and Other Grocery (except Convenience) Stores	445110
Support Activities for Animal Production	115210
Support Activities for Coal Mining	213113
Support Activities for Forestry	115310
Support Activities for Metal Mining	213114
Support Activities for Nonmetallic Minerals (except Fuels)	213115
Support Activities for Oil and Gas Operations	213112
Support Activities for Rail Transportation	488210
Surface Active Agent Manufacturing	325613
Surface-Coated Paperboard Manufacturing	322226
Surgical and Medical Instrument Manufacturing	339112
Surgical Appliance and Supplies Manufacturing	339113
Surveying and Mapping (except Geophysical) Services	541370
Switchgear and Switchboard Apparatus Manufacturing	335313
Synthetic Organic Dye and Pigment Manufacturing	325132
Synthetic Rubber Manufacturing	325212
T	
Tax Preparation Services	541213
Taxi Service	485310
Telecommunications Resellers	517310
Telemarketing Bureaus	561422
Telephone Answering Services	561421
Telephone Apparatus Manufacturing	334210
Teleproduction and Other Postproduction Services	512191
Television Broadcasting	515120
Temporary Help Services	561320
Temporary Shelters	624221
Testing Laboratories	541380
Textile and Fabric Finishing (except Broadwoven Fabric) Mills	313312
Textile Bag Mills	314911
Textile Machinery Manufacturing	333292
Theater Companies and Dinner Theaters	711110
Third Party Administration of Insurance and Pension Funds	524292
Thread Mills	313113
Tile and Terrazzo Contractors	238340
Tile, Marble, Terrazzo, and Mosaic Contractors	235430
Timber Tract Operations	113110
Tire and Tube Merchant Wholesalers	423130
Tire and Tube Wholesalers	421130
Tire Cord and Tire Fabric Mills	314992
Tire Dealers	441320
Tire Manufacturing (except Retreading)	326211
Tire Retreading	326212
Title Abstract and Settlement Offices	541191
Tobacco and Tobacco Product Merchant Wholesalers	424940
Tobacco and Tobacco Product Wholesalers	422940
Tobacco Farming	111910
Tobacco Stemming and Redrying	312210
Tobacco Stores	453991
Toilet Preparation Manufacturing	325620
Tortilla Manufacturing	311830
Totalizing Fluid Meter and Counting Device Manufacturing	334514
Tour Operators	561520
Toy and Hobby Goods and Supplies Merchant Wholesalers	423920
Toy and Hobby Goods and Supplies Wholesalers	421920
Tradebinding and Related Work	323121
Translation and Interpretation Services	541930
Transportation Equipment and Supplies (except Motor Vehicle) Merchant Wholesalers	423860
Transportation Equipment and Supplies (except Motor Vehicle) Wholesalers	421860
Travel Agencies	561510
Travel Trailer and Camper Manufacturing	336214
Tree Nut Farming	111335
Truck Trailer Manufacturing	336212
Truck, Utility Trailer, and RV (Recreational Vehicle) Rental and Leasing	532120
Truss Manufacturing	321214
Trust, Fiduciary, and Custody Activities	523991
Trusts, Estates, and Agency Accounts	525920
Turbine and Turbine Generator Set Units Manufacturing	333611
Turkey Production	112330
U	
Unclassified Establishments	999990
Uncoated Paper and Multiwall Bag Manufacturing	322224
Underwear and Nightwear Knitting Mills	315192
Unsupported Plastics Bag Manufacturing	326111
Unsupported Plastics Film and Sheet (except Packaging) Manufacturing	326113
Unsupported Plastics Packaging Film and Sheet Manufacturing	326112
Unsupported Plastics Profile Shape Manufacturing	326121
Upholstered Household Furniture Manufacturing	337121
Uranium-Radium-Vanadium Ore Mining	212291
Urethane and Other Foam Product (except Polystyrene) Manufacturing	326150
Used Car Dealers	441120
Used Household and Office Goods Moving	484210
Used Merchandise Stores	453310
V	
Vehicular Lighting Equipment Manufacturing	336321

Description	*N.A.I.C.S.*
Vending Machine Operators	454210
Veterinary Services	541940
Video Tape and Disc Rental	532230
Vitreous China Plumbing Fixture and China and Earthenware Bathroom Accessories Manufacturing	327111
Vitreous China, Fine Earthenware, and Other Pottery Product Manufacturing	327112
Vocational Rehabilitation Services	624310
Voluntary Health Organizations	813212
W	
Warehouse Clubs and Superstores	452910
Warm Air Heating and Air-Conditioning Equipment and Supplies Merchant Wholesalers	423730
Warm Air Heating and Air-Conditioning Equipment and Supplies Wholesalers	421730
Watch, Clock, and Part Manufacturing	334518
Water and Sewer Line and Related Structures Construction	237110
Water Supply and Irrigation Systems	221310
Water Well Drilling Contractors	235810
Water, Sewer, and Pipeline Construction	234910
Web Search Portals	518112
Weft Knit Fabric Mills	313241
Welding and Soldering Equipment Manufacturing	333992
Wet Corn Milling	311221
Wheat Farming	111140
Wholesale Trade Agents and Brokers	425120
Window Treatment Stores	442291
Wine and Distilled Alcoholic Beverage Merchant Wholesalers	424820
Wine and Distilled Alcoholic Beverage Wholesalers	422820

Description	*N.A.I.C.S.*
Wineries	312130
Wired Telecommunications Carriers	517110
Women's, Children's, and Infants' Clothing and Accessories Merchant Wholesalers	424330
Women's and Girls' Cut and Sew Blouse and Shirt Manufacturing	315232
Women's and Girls' Cut and Sew Dress Manufacturing	315233
Women's and Girls' Cut and Sew Lingerie, Loungewear, and Nightwear Manufacturing	315231
Women's and Girls' Cut and Sew Other Outerwear Manufacturing	315239
Women's and Girls' Cut and Sew Suit, Coat, Tailored Jacket, and Skirt Manufacturing	315234
Women's Clothing Stores	448120
Women's Footwear (except Athletic) Manufacturing	316214
Women's Handbag and Purse Manufacturing	316992
Women's, Children's, and Infants' Clothing and Accessories Wholesalers	422330
Women's, Girls', and Infants' Cut and Sew Apparel Contractors	315212
Wood Container and Pallet Manufacturing	321920
Wood Kitchen Cabinet and Countertop Manufacturing	337110
Wood Office Furniture Manufacturing	337211
Wood Preservation	321114
Wood Television, Radio, and Sewing Machine Cabinet Manufacturing	337129
Wood Window and Door Manufacturing	321911
Wrecking and Demolition Contractors	235940
Y	
Yarn Spinning Mills	313111
Yarn Texturizing, Throwing, and Twisting Mills	313112
Z	
Zoos and Botanical Gardens	712130

NUMERICAL COMPENDIUM OF N.A.I.C.S. CODES

North American Industry Classification System Manual, 2002, U.S. Government Office of Management and Budget; All codes for manufacturing unless otherwise stated.

N.A.I.C.S.	*Description*
111120	Oilseed (except Soybean) Farming
111130	Dry Pea and Bean Farming
111110	Soybean Farming
111140	Wheat Farming
111150	Corn Farming
111160	Rice Farming
111191	Oilseed and Grain Combination Farming
111199	All Other Grain Farming
111211	Potato Farming
111219	Other Vegetable (except Potato) and Melon Farming
111310	Orange Groves
111320	Citrus (except Orange) Groves
111331	Apple Orchards
111332	Grape Vineyards
111333	Strawberry Farming
111334	Berry (except Strawberry) Farming
111335	Tree Nut Farming
111336	Fruit and Tree Nut Combination Farming
111339	Other Noncitrus Fruit Farming
111411	Mushroom Production
111419	Other Food Crops Grown Under Cover
111421	Nursery and Tree Production
111422	Floriculture Production
111910	Tobacco Farming
111920	Cotton Farming
111930	Sugarcane Farming
111940	Hay Farming
111991	Sugar Beet Farming
111992	Peanut Farming
111998	All Other Miscellaneous Crop Farming
112111	Beef Cattle Ranching and Farming
112112	Cattle Feedlots
112120	Dairy Cattle and Milk Production
112130	Dual Purpose Cattle Ranching and Farming
112210	Hog and Pig Farming
112310	Chicken Egg Production
112320	Broilers and Other Meat Type Chicken Production
112330	Turkey Production
112390	Other Poultry Production
112420	Goat Farming
112512	Shellfish Farming
112519	Other Animal Aquaculture
112930	Fur-Bearing Animal and Rabbit Production
112990	All Other Animal Production
113210	Forest Nurseries and Gathering of Forest Products
113310	Logging
114112	Shellfish Fishing
114210	Hunting and Trapping
115112	Soil Preparation, Planting, and Cultivating
115114	Postharvest Crop Activities (except Cotton Ginning)
115115	Farm Labor Contractors and Crew Leaders
115210	Support Activities for Animal Production
211111	Crude Petroleum and Natural Gas Extraction
211112	Natural Gas Liquid Extraction
212112	Bituminous Coal Underground Mining
212113	Anthracite Mining
212221	Gold Ore Mining
212231	Lead Ore and Zinc Ore Mining
212291	Uranium-Radium-Vanadium Ore Mining
212299	All Other Metal Ore Mining
212312	Crushed and Broken Limestone Mining and Quarrying
212313	Crushed and Broken Granite Mining and Quarrying
212321	Construction Sand and Gravel Mining
212322	Industrial Sand Mining
212324	Kaolin and Ball Clay Mining
212391	Potash, Soda, and Borate Mineral Mining
212392	Phosphate Rock Mining
212393	Other Chemical and Fertilizer Mineral Mining
213111	Drilling Oil and Gas Wells
213112	Support Activities for Oil and Gas Operations
213114	Support Activities for Metal Mining
213115	Support Activities for Nonmetallic Minerals (except Fuels)
221112	Fossil Fuel Electric Power Generation
221113	Nuclear Electric Power Generation
221121	Electric Bulk Power Transmission and Control
221122	Electric Power Distribution
221310	Water Supply and Irrigation Systems
221330	Steam and Air-Conditioning Supply
233210	Single Family Housing Construction
233220	Multifamily Housing Construction
233310	Manufacturing and Industrial Building Construction
234110	Highway and Street Construction
234120	Bridge and Tunnel Construction
234910	Water, Sewer, and Pipeline Construction
234920	Power and Communication Transmission Line Construction
234930	Industrial Nonbuilding Structure Construction
235110	Plumbing, Heating, and Air-Conditioning Contractors
235410	Masonry and Stone Contractors
235420	Drywall, Plastering, Acoustical, and Insulation Contractors
235430	Tile, Marble, Terrazzo, and Mosaic Contractors
235510	Carpentry Contractors
235520	Floor Laying and Other Floor Contractors
235610	Roofing, Siding, and Sheet Metal Contractors
235710	Concrete Contractors
235810	Water Well Drilling Contractors
235910	Structural Steel Erection Contractors
235930	Excavation Contractors
235940	Wrecking and Demolition Contractors
235950	Building Equipment and Other Machinery Installation Contractors
235990	All Other Special Trade Contractors
311111	Dog and Cat Food Manufacturing
311119	Other Animal Food Manufacturing
311211	Flour Milling
311212	Rice Milling
311213	Malt Manufacturing
311221	Wet Corn Milling
311222	Soybean Processing
311223	Other Oilseed Processing
311225	Fats and Oils Refining and Blending
311230	Breakfast Cereal Manufacturing
311311	Sugarcane Mills
311312	Cane Sugar Refining
311320	Chocolate and Confectionery Manufacturing from Cacao Beans
311340	Nonchocolate Confectionery Manufacturing
311411	Frozen Fruit, Juice, and Vegetable Manufacturing
311412	Frozen Specialty Food Manufacturing
311422	Specialty Canning
311423	Dried and Dehydrated Food Manufacturing
311512	Creamery Butter Manufacturing
311514	Dry, Condensed, and Evaporated Dairy Product Manufacturing
311611	Animal (except Poultry) Slaughtering
311612	Meat Processed from Carcasses
311613	Rendering and Meat Byproduct Processing
311711	Seafood Canning
311811	Retail Bakeries
311812	Commercial Bakeries
311821	Cookie and Cracker Manufacturing
311822	Flour Mixes and Dough Manufacturing from Purchased Flour
311823	Dry Pasta Manufacturing
311911	Roasted Nuts and Peanut Butter Manufacturing
311920	Coffee and Tea Manufacturing
311930	Flavoring Syrup and Concentrate Manufacturing
311942	Spice and Extract Manufacturing
311991	Perishable Prepared Food Manufacturing
311999	All Other Miscellaneous Food Manufacturing
312111	Soft Drink Manufacturing
312112	Bottled Water Manufacturing
312120	Breweries
312210	Tobacco Stemming and Redrying
312229	Other Tobacco Product Manufacturing
313112	Yarn Texturizing, Throwing, and Twisting Mills
313210	Broadwoven Fabric Mills
313222	Schiffli Machine Embroidery
313241	Weft Knit Fabric Mills
313311	Broadwoven Fabric Finishing Mills
313312	Textile and Fabric Finishing (except Broadwoven Fabric) Mills
314110	Carpet and Rug Mills
314129	Other Household Textile Product Mills
314911	Textile Bag Mills
314991	Rope, Cordage, and Twine Mills
314992	Tire Cord and Tire Fabric Mills
315111	Sheer Hosiery Mills
315119	Other Hosiery and Sock Mills
315192	Underwear and Nightwear Knitting Mills
315211	Men's and Boys' Cut and Sew Apparel Contractors
315221	Men's and Boys' Cut and Sew Underwear and Nightwear Manufacturing
315222	Men's and Boys' Cut and Sew Suit, Coat, and Overcoat Manufacturing
315223	Men's and Boys' Cut and Sew Shirt (except Work Shirt)

N.A.I.C.S.	Description
	Manufacturing
315225	Men's and Boys' Cut and Sew Work Clothing Manufacturing
315228	Men's and Boys' Cut and Sew Other Outerwear Manufacturing
315231	Women's and Girls' Cut and Sew Lingerie, Loungewear, and Nightwear Manufacturing
315232	Women's and Girls' Cut and Sew Blouse and Shirt Manufacturing
315234	Women's and Girls' Cut and Sew Suit, Coat, Tailored Jacket, and Skirt Manufacturing
315239	Women's and Girls' Cut and Sew Other Outerwear Manufacturing
315291	Infants' Cut and Sew Apparel Manufacturing
315299	All Other Cut and Sew Apparel Manufacturing
315991	Hat, Cap, and Millinery Manufacturing
315993	Men's and Boys' Neckwear Manufacturing
315999	Other Apparel Accessories and Other Apparel Manufacturing
316211	Rubber and Plastics Footwear Manufacturing
316212	House Slipper Manufacturing
316214	Women's Footwear (except Athletic) Manufacturing
316219	Other Footwear Manufacturing
316991	Luggage Manufacturing
316993	Personal Leather Good (except Women's Handbag and Purse) Manufacturing
316999	All Other Leather Good Manufacturing
321114	Wood Preservation
321212	Softwood Veneer and Plywood Manufacturing
321213	Engineered Wood Member (except Truss) Manufacturing
321219	Reconstituted Wood Product Manufacturing
321912	Cut Stock, Resawing Lumber, and Planing
321918	Other Millwork (including Flooring)
321991	Manufactured Home (Mobile Home) Manufacturing
321992	Prefabricated Wood Building Manufacturing
321999	All Other Miscellaneous Wood Product Manufacturing
322122	Newsprint Mills
322130	Paperboard Mills
322212	Folding Paperboard Box Manufacturing
322213	Setup Paperboard Box Manufacturing
322214	Fiber Can, Tube, Drum, and Similar Products Manufacturing
322221	Coated and Laminated Packaging Paper and Plastics Film Manufacturing
322222	Coated and Laminated Paper Manufacturing
322224	Uncoated Paper and Multiwall Bag Manufacturing
322225	Laminated Aluminum Foil Manufacturing for Flexible Packaging Uses
322226	Surface-Coated Paperboard Manufacturing
322232	Envelope Manufacturing
322233	Stationery, Tablet, and Related Product Manufacturing
322291	Sanitary Paper Product Manufacturing
322299	All Other Converted Paper Product Manufacturing
323111	Commercial Gravure Printing
323112	Commercial Flexographic Printing
323114	Quick Printing
323116	Manifold Business Forms Printing
323118	Blankbook, Looseleaf Binders, and Devices Manufacturing
323121	Tradebinding and Related Work
324110	Petroleum Refineries
324122	Asphalt Shingle and Coating Materials Manufacturing
324191	Petroleum Lubricating Oil and Grease Manufacturing
324199	All Other Petroleum and Coal Products Manufacturing
325120	Industrial Gas Manufacturing
325131	Inorganic Dye and Pigment Manufacturing
325181	Alkalies and Chlorine Manufacturing
325182	Carbon Black Manufacturing
325188	All Other Basic Inorganic Chemical Manufacturing
325192	Cyclic Crude and Intermediate Manufacturing
325193	Ethyl Alcohol Manufacturing
325211	Plastics Material and Resin Manufacturing
325212	Synthetic Rubber Manufacturing
325222	Noncellulosic Organic Fiber Manufacturing
325311	Nitrogenous Fertilizer Manufacturing
325312	Phosphatic Fertilizer Manufacturing
325320	Pesticide and Other Agricultural Chemical Manufacturing
325411	Medicinal and Botanical Manufacturing
325413	In-Vitro Diagnostic Substance Manufacturing
325414	Biological Product (except Diagnostic) Manufacturing
325520	Adhesive Manufacturing
325611	Soap and Other Detergent Manufacturing
325613	Surface Active Agent Manufacturing
325620	Toilet Preparation Manufacturing
325910	Printing Ink Manufacturing
325991	Custom Compounding of Purchased Resins
325998	All Other Miscellaneous Chemical Product and Preparation Manufacturing
326111	Unsupported Plastics Bag Manufacturing
326112	Unsupported Plastics Packaging Film and Sheet Manufacturing
326113	Unsupported Plastics Film and Sheet (except Packaging) Manufacturing
326122	Plastics Pipe and Pipe Fitting Manufacturing
326130	Laminated Plastics Plate, Sheet, and Shape Manufacturing
326150	Urethane and Other Foam Product (except Polystyrene) Manufacturing
326160	Plastics Bottle Manufacturing
326191	Plastics Plumbing Fixture Manufacturing
326199	All Other Plastics Product Manufacturing
326211	Tire Manufacturing (except Retreading)
326220	Rubber and Plastics Hoses and Belting Manufacturing
326299	All Other Rubber Product Manufacturing
327111	Vitreous China Plumbing Fixture and China and Earthenware Bathroom Accessories Manufacturing
327112	Vitreous China, Fine Earthenware, and Other Pottery Product Manufacturing
327113	Porcelain Electrical Supply Manufacturing
327121	Brick and Structural Clay Tile Manufacturing
327122	Ceramic Wall and Floor Tile Manufacturing
327123	Other Structural Clay Product Manufacturing
327124	Clay Refractory Manufacturing
327125	Nonclay Refractory Manufacturing
327211	Flat Glass Manufacturing
327212	Other Pressed and Blown Glass and Glassware Manufacturing
327213	Glass Container Manufacturing
327215	Glass Product Manufacturing Made of Purchased Glass
327310	Cement Manufacturing
327320	Ready-Mix Concrete Manufacturing
327331	Concrete Block and Brick Manufacturing
327332	Concrete Pipe Manufacturing
327390	Other Concrete Product Manufacturing
327410	Lime Manufacturing
327420	Gypsum Product Manufacturing
327910	Abrasive Product Manufacturing
327991	Cut Stone and Stone Product Manufacturing
327992	Ground or Treated Mineral and Earth Manufacturing
327993	Mineral Wool Manufacturing
327999	All Other Miscellaneous Nonmetallic Mineral Product Manufacturing
331111	Iron and Steel Mills
331112	Electrometallurgical Ferroalloy Product Manufacturing
331210	Iron and Steel Pipe and Tube Manufacturing from Purchased Steel
331221	Rolled Steel Shape Manufacturing
331222	Steel Wire Drawing
331311	Alumina Refining
331312	Primary Aluminum Production
331314	Secondary Smelting and Alloying of Aluminum
331315	Aluminum Sheet, Plate, and Foil Manufacturing
331316	Aluminum Extruded Product Manufacturing
331319	Other Aluminum Rolling and Drawing
331411	Primary Smelting and Refining of Copper
331419	Primary Smelting and Refining of Nonferrous Metal (except Copper and Aluminum)
331421	Copper Rolling, Drawing, and Extruding
331422	Copper Wire (except Mechanical) Drawing
331423	Secondary Smelting, Refining, and Alloying of Copper
331491	Nonferrous Metal (except Copper and Aluminum) Rolling, Drawing, and Extruding
331492	Secondary Smelting, Refining, and Alloying of Nonferrous Metal (except Copper and Aluminum)
331511	Iron Foundries
331512	Steel Investment Foundries
331513	Steel Foundries (except Investment)
331521	Aluminum Die-Casting Foundries
331522	Nonferrous (except Aluminum) Die-Casting Foundries
331524	Aluminum Foundries (except Die-Casting)
331528	Other Nonferrous Foundries (except Die-Casting)
332111	Iron and Steel Forging
332114	Custom Roll Forming
332116	Metal Stamping
332117	Powder Metallurgy Part Manufacturing
332212	Hand and Edge Tool Manufacturing
332213	Saw Blade and Handsaw Manufacturing
332214	Kitchen Utensil, Pot, and Pan Manufacturing
332312	Fabricated Structural Metal Manufacturing
332313	Plate Work Manufacturing
332321	Metal Window and Door Manufacturing
332323	Ornamental and Architectural Metal Work Manufacturing
332410	Power Boiler and Heat Exchanger Manufacturing

N.A.I.C.S.	Description
332431	Metal Can Manufacturing
332439	Other Metal Container Manufacturing
332510	Hardware Manufacturing
332612	Spring (Light Gauge) Manufacturing
332618	Other Fabricated Wire Product Manufacturing
332721	Precision Turned Product Manufacturing
332811	Metal Heat Treating
332812	Metal Coating, Engraving (except Jewelry and Silverware), and Allied Services to Manufacturers
332813	Electroplating, Plating, Polishing, Anodizing, and Coloring
332912	Fluid Power Valve and Hose Fitting Manufacturing
332913	Plumbing Fixture Fitting and Trim Manufacturing
332991	Ball and Roller Bearing Manufacturing
332992	Small Arms Ammunition Manufacturing
332993	Ammunition (except Small Arms) Manufacturing
332995	Other Ordnance and Accessories Manufacturing
332997	Industrial Pattern Manufacturing
332998	Enameled Iron and Metal Sanitary Ware Manufacturing
332999	All Other Miscellaneous Fabricated Metal Product Manufacturing
333112	Lawn and Garden Tractor and Home Lawn and Garden Equipment Manufacturing
333120	Construction Machinery Manufacturing
333132	Oil and Gas Field Machinery and Equipment Manufacturing
333210	Sawmill and Woodworking Machinery Manufacturing
333220	Plastics and Rubber Industry Machinery Manufacturing
333292	Textile Machinery Manufacturing
333293	Printing Machinery and Equipment Manufacturing
333295	Semiconductor Machinery Manufacturing
333298	All Other Industrial Machinery Manufacturing
333312	Commercial Laundry, Drycleaning, and Pressing Machine Manufacturing
333313	Office Machinery Manufacturing
333315	Photographic and Photocopying Equipment Manufacturing
333319	Other Commercial and Service Industry Machinery Manufacturing
333411	Air Purification Equipment Manufacturing
333414	Heating Equipment (except Warm Air Furnaces) Manufacturing
333415	Air-Conditioning and Warm Air Heating Equipment and Commercial and Industrial Refrigeration Equipment Manufacturing
333511	Industrial Mold Manufacturing
333513	Machine Tool (Metal Forming Types) Manufacturing
333514	Special Die and Tool, Die Set, Jig, and Fixture Manufacturing
333515	Cutting Tool and Machine Tool Accessory Manufacturing
333518	Other Metalworking Machinery Manufacturing
333611	Turbine and Turbine Generator Set Units Manufacturing
333612	Speed Changer, Industrial High-Speed Drive, and Gear Manufacturing
333618	Other Engine Equipment Manufacturing
333911	Pump and Pumping Equipment Manufacturing
333912	Air and Gas Compressor Manufacturing
333921	Elevator and Moving Stairway Manufacturing
333922	Conveyor and Conveying Equipment Manufacturing
333924	Industrial Truck, Tractor, Trailer, and Stacker Machinery Manufacturing
333991	Power-Driven Handtool Manufacturing
333992	Welding and Soldering Equipment Manufacturing
333993	Packaging Machinery Manufacturing
333995	Fluid Power Cylinder and Actuator Manufacturing
333996	Fluid Power Pump and Motor Manufacturing
333997	Scale and Balance (except Laboratory) Manufacturing
334111	Electronic Computer Manufacturing
334112	Computer Storage Device Manufacturing
334113	Computer Terminal Manufacturing
334119	Other Computer Peripheral Equipment Manufacturing
334220	Radio and Television Broadcasting and Wireless Communications Equipment Manufacturing
334290	Other Communications Equipment Manufacturing
334411	Electron Tube Manufacturing
334412	Bare Printed Circuit Board Manufacturing
334414	Electronic Capacitor Manufacturing
334415	Electronic Resistor Manufacturing
334416	Electronic Coil, Transformer, and Other Inductor Manufacturing
334418	Printed Circuit Assembly (Electronic Assembly) Manufacturing
334419	Other Electronic Component Manufacturing
334511	Search, Detection, Navigation, Guidance, Aeronautical, and Nautical System and Instrument Manufacturing
334512	Automatic Environmental Control Manufacturing for Residential, Commercial, and Appliance Use
334513	Instruments and Related Products Manufacturing for Measuring, Displaying, and Controlling Industrial Process Variables
334515	Instrument Manufacturing for Measuring and Testing Electricity and Electrical Signals
334516	Analytical Laboratory Instrument Manufacturing
334517	Irradiation Apparatus Manufacturing
334518	Watch, Clock, and Part Manufacturing
334611	Software Reproducing
334612	Prerecorded Compact Disc (except Software), Tape, and Record Reproducing
334613	Magnetic and Optical Recording Media Manufacturing
335121	Residential Electric Lighting Fixture Manufacturing
335122	Commercial, Industrial, and Institutional Electric Lighting Fixture Manufacturing
335211	Electric Housewares and Household Fan Manufacturing
335212	Household Vacuum Cleaner Manufacturing
335222	Household Refrigerator and Home Freezer Manufacturing
335224	Household Laundry Equipment Manufacturing
335228	Other Major Household Appliance Manufacturing
335312	Motor and Generator Manufacturing
335313	Switchgear and Switchboard Apparatus Manufacturing
335314	Relay and Industrial Control Manufacturing
335912	Primary Battery Manufacturing
335921	Fiber Optic Cable Manufacturing
335931	Current-Carrying Wiring Device Manufacturing
335932	Noncurrent-Carrying Wiring Device Manufacturing
335991	Carbon and Graphite Product Manufacturing
336111	Automobile Manufacturing
336112	Light Truck and Utility Vehicle Manufacturing
336120	Heavy Duty Truck Manufacturing
336211	Motor Vehicle Body Manufacturing
336213	Motor Home Manufacturing
336214	Travel Trailer and Camper Manufacturing
336312	Gasoline Engine and Engine Parts Manufacturing
336321	Vehicular Lighting Equipment Manufacturing
336322	Other Motor Vehicle Electrical and Electronic Equipment Manufacturing
336330	Motor Vehicle Steering and Suspension Components (except Spring) Manufacturing
336350	Motor Vehicle Transmission and Power Train Parts Manufacturing
336360	Motor Vehicle Seating and Interior Trim Manufacturing
336391	Motor Vehicle Air-Conditioning Manufacturing
336399	All Other Motor Vehicle Parts Manufacturing
336411	Aircraft Manufacturing
336413	Other Aircraft Parts and Auxiliary Equipment Manufacturing
336414	Guided Missile and Space Vehicle Manufacturing
336415	Guided Missile and Space Vehicle Propulsion Unit and Propulsion Unit Parts Manufacturing
336510	Railroad Rolling Stock Manufacturing
336611	Ship Building and Repairing
336612	Boat Building
336991	Motorcycle, Bicycle, and Parts Manufacturing
336992	Military Armored Vehicle, Tank, and Tank Component Manufacturing
337110	Wood Kitchen Cabinet and Countertop Manufacturing
337121	Upholstered Household Furniture Manufacturing
337124	Metal Household Furniture Manufacturing
337125	Household Furniture (except Wood and Metal) Manufacturing
337127	Institutional Furniture Manufacturing
337129	Wood Television, Radio, and Sewing Machine Cabinet Manufacturing
337212	Custom Architectural Woodwork and Millwork Manufacturing
337214	Office Furniture (except Wood) Manufacturing
337910	Mattress Manufacturing
337920	Blind and Shade Manufacturing
339111	Laboratory Apparatus and Furniture Manufacturing
339113	Surgical Appliance and Supplies Manufacturing
339114	Dental Equipment and Supplies Manufacturing
339115	Ophthalmic Goods Manufacturing
339911	Jewelry (except Costume) Manufacturing
339913	Jewelers' Material and Lapidary Work Manufacturing
339914	Costume Jewelry and Novelty Manufacturing
339931	Doll and Stuffed Toy Manufacturing
339932	Game, Toy, and Children's Vehicle Manufacturing
339942	Lead Pencil and Art Good Manufacturing
339943	Marking Device Manufacturing
339944	Carbon Paper and Inked Ribbon Manufacturing
339991	Gasket, Packing, and Sealing Device Manufacturing
339993	Fastener, Button, Needle, and Pin Manufacturing
339994	Broom, Brush, and Mop Manufacturing
339999	All Other Miscellaneous Manufacturing
421110	Automobile and Other Motor Vehicle Wholesalers
421120	Motor Vehicle Supplies and New Parts Wholesalers
421130	Tire and Tube Wholesalers
421140	Motor Vehicle Parts (Used) Wholesalers

N.A.I.C.S.	Description
421210	Furniture Wholesalers
421220	Home Furnishing Wholesalers
421310	Lumber, Plywood, Millwork, and Wood Panel Wholesalers
421320	Brick, Stone, and Related Construction Material Wholesalers
421330	Roofing, Siding, and Insulation Material Wholesalers
421390	Other Construction Material Wholesalers
421410	Photographic Equipment and Supplies Wholesalers
421420	Office Equipment Wholesalers
421430	Computer and Computer Peripheral Equipment and Software Wholesalers
421440	Other Commercial Equipment Wholesalers
421450	Medical, Dental, and Hospital Equipment and Supplies Wholesalers
421460	Ophthalmic Goods Wholesalers
421490	Other Professional Equipment and Supplies Wholesalers
421510	Metal Service Centers and Offices
421520	Coal and Other Mineral and Ore Wholesalers
421610	Electrical Apparatus and Equipment, Wiring Supplies, and Construction Material Wholesalers
421620	Electrical Appliance, Television, and Radio Set Wholesalers
421690	Other Electronic Parts and Equipment Wholesalers
421710	Hardware Wholesalers
421720	Plumbing and Heating Equipment and Supplies (Hydronics) Wholesalers
421730	Warm Air Heating and Air-Conditioning Equipment and Supplies Wholesalers
421740	Refrigeration Equipment and Supplies Wholesalers
421810	Construction and Mining (except Oil Well) Machinery and Equipment Wholesalers
421820	Farm and Garden Machinery and Equipment Wholesalers
421830	Industrial Machinery and Equipment Wholesalers
421840	Industrial Supplies Wholesalers
421850	Service Establishment Equipment and Supplies Wholesalers
421860	Transportation Equipment and Supplies (except Motor Vehicle) Wholesalers
421910	Sporting and Recreational Goods and Supplies Wholesalers
421920	Toy and Hobby Goods and Supplies Wholesalers
421930	Recyclable Material Wholesalers
421940	Jewelry, Watch, Precious Stone, and Precious Metal Wholesalers
421990	Other Miscellaneous Durable Goods Wholesalers
422110	Printing and Writing Paper Wholesalers
422120	Stationery and Office Supplies Wholesalers
422130	Industrial and Personal Service Paper Wholesalers
422210	Drugs and Druggists' Sundries Wholesalers
422310	Piece Goods, Notions, and Other Dry Goods Wholesalers
422320	Men's and Boys' Clothing and Furnishings Wholesalers
422330	Women's, Children's, and Infants' Clothing and Accessories Wholesalers
422340	Footwear Wholesalers
422410	General Line Grocery Wholesalers
422420	Packaged Frozen Food Wholesalers
422430	Dairy Product (except Dried or Canned) Wholesalers
422440	Poultry and Poultry Product Wholesalers
422450	Confectionery Wholesalers
422460	Fish and Seafood Wholesalers
422470	Meat and Meat Product Wholesalers
422480	Fresh Fruit and Vegetable Wholesalers
422490	Other Grocery and Related Products Wholesalers
422510	Grain and Field Bean Wholesalers
422520	Livestock Wholesalers
422590	Other Farm Product Raw Material Wholesalers
422610	Plastics Materials and Basic Forms and Shapes Wholesalers
422720	Petroleum and Petroleum Products Wholesalers (except Bulk Stations and Terminals)
422810	Beer and Ale Wholesalers
422820	Wine and Distilled Alcoholic Beverage Wholesalers
422910	Farm Supplies Wholesalers
422920	Book, Periodical, and Newspaper Wholesalers
422930	Flower, Nursery Stock, and Florists' Supplies Wholesalers
422940	Tobacco and Tobacco Product Wholesalers
422950	Paint, Varnish, and Supplies Wholesalers
422990	Other Miscellaneous Nondurable Goods Wholesalers
441110	New Car Dealers
441120	Used Car Dealers
441221	Motorcycle Dealers
441222	Boat Dealers
441310	Automotive Parts and Accessories Stores
441320	Tire Dealers
442210	Floor Covering Stores
442299	All Other Home Furnishings Stores
443112	Radio, Television, and Other Electronics Stores

N.A.I.C.S.	Description
443120	Computer and Software Stores
444110	Home Centers
444120	Paint and Wallpaper Stores
444190	Other Building Material Dealers
444220	Nursery and Garden Centers
445110	Supermarkets and Other Grocery (except Convenience) Stores
445210	Meat Markets
445230	Fruit and Vegetable Markets
445292	Confectionery and Nut Stores
445310	Beer, Wine, and Liquor Stores
446110	Pharmacies and Drug Stores
446130	Optical Goods Stores
446191	Food (Health) Supplement Stores
446199	All Other Health and Personal Care Stores
447190	Other Gasoline Stations
448110	Men's Clothing Stores
448130	Children's and Infants' Clothing Stores
448150	Clothing Accessories Stores
448190	Other Clothing Stores
448320	Luggage and Leather Goods Stores
451120	Hobby, Toy, and Game Stores
451140	Musical Instrument and Supplies Stores
451211	Book Stores
451212	News Dealers and Newsstands
452110	Department Stores
452910	Warehouse Clubs and Superstores
452990	All Other General Merchandise Stores
453110	Florists
453220	Gift, Novelty, and Souvenir Stores
453310	Used Merchandise Stores
453920	Art Dealers
453930	Manufactured (Mobile) Home Dealers
454110	Electronic Shopping and Mail-Order Houses
454210	Vending Machine Operators
454311	Heating Oil Dealers
454312	Liquefied Petroleum Gas (Bottled Gas) Dealers
454319	Other Fuel Dealers
481111	Scheduled Passenger Air Transportation
481112	Scheduled Freight Air Transportation
481212	Nonscheduled Chartered Freight Air Transportation
481219	Other Nonscheduled Air Transportation
482111	Line-Haul Railroads
483111	Deep Sea Freight Transportation
483113	Coastal and Great Lakes Freight Transportation
483114	Coastal and Great Lakes Passenger Transportation
483212	Inland Water Passenger Transportation
484110	General Freight Trucking, Local
484122	General Freight Trucking, Long-Distance, Less Than Truckload
484210	Used Household and Office Goods Moving
484220	Specialized Freight (except Used Goods) Trucking, Local
485111	Mixed Mode Transit Systems
485112	Commuter Rail Systems
485113	Bus and Other Motor Vehicle Transit Systems
485119	Other Urban Transit Systems
485310	Taxi Service
485320	Limousine Service
485510	Charter Bus Industry
485999	All Other Transit and Ground Passenger Transportation
486110	Pipeline Transportation of Crude Oil
486210	Pipeline Transportation of Natural Gas
486910	Pipeline Transportation of Refined Petroleum Products
487110	Scenic and Sightseeing Transportation, Land
487210	Scenic and Sightseeing Transportation, Water
488111	Air Traffic Control
488119	Other Airport Operations
488210	Support Activities for Rail Transportation
488310	Port and Harbor Operations
488320	Marine Cargo Handling
488390	Other Support Activities for Water Transportation
488410	Motor Vehicle Towing
488510	Freight Transportation Arrangement
488991	Packing and Crating
488999	All Other Support Activities for Transportation
492110	Couriers
493110	General Warehousing and Storage
493120	Refrigerated Warehousing and Storage
493190	Other Warehousing and Storage
511110	Newspaper Publishers
511130	Book Publishers
511191	Greeting Card Publishers

N.A.I.C.S.	Description
511199	All Other Publishers
512110	Motion Picture and Video Production
512120	Motion Picture and Video Distribution
512132	Drive-In Motion Picture Theaters
512191	Teleproduction and Other Postproduction Services
512199	Other Motion Picture and Video Industries
512220	Integrated Record Production/Distribution
512240	Sound Recording Studios
513210	Cable Networks
513322	Cellular and Other Wireless Telecommunications
514191	On-Line Information Services
514210	Data Processing Services
521110	Monetary Authorities - Central Bank
522110	Commercial Banking
522130	Credit Unions
522210	Credit Card Issuing
522220	Sales Financing
522292	Real Estate Credit
522294	Secondary Market Financing
522298	All Other Nondepository Credit Intermediation
522320	Financial Transactions Processing, Reserve, and Clearinghouse Activities
522390	Other Activities Related to Credit Intermediation
523120	Securities Brokerage
523130	Commodity Contracts Dealing
523210	Securities and Commodity Exchanges
523910	Miscellaneous Intermediation
523930	Investment Advice
523999	Miscellaneous Financial Investment Activities
524113	Direct Life Insurance Carriers
524126	Direct Property and Casualty Insurance Carriers
524127	Direct Title Insurance Carriers
524128	Other Direct Insurance (except Life, Health, and Medical) Carriers
524210	Insurance Agencies and Brokerages
524292	Third Party Administration of Insurance and Pension Funds
525110	Pension Funds
525120	Health and Welfare Funds
525910	Open-End Investment Funds
525920	Trusts, Estates, and Agency Accounts
525990	Other Financial Vehicles
531120	Lessors of Nonresidential Buildings (except Miniwarehouses)
531130	Lessors of Miniwarehouses and Self-Storage Units
531190	Lessors of Other Real Estate Property
531311	Residential Property Managers
531312	Nonresidential Property Managers
531390	Other Activities Related to Real Estate
532111	Passenger Car Rental
532120	Truck, Utility Trailer, and RV (Recreational Vehicle) Rental and Leasing
532210	Consumer Electronics and Appliances Rental
532230	Video Tape and Disc Rental
532292	Recreational Goods Rental
532299	All Other Consumer Goods Rental
532310	General Rental Centers
532412	Construction, Mining, and Forestry Machinery and Equipment Rental and Leasing
532420	Office Machinery and Equipment Rental and Leasing
532490	Other Commercial and Industrial Machinery and Equipment Rental and Leasing
533110	Lessors of Nonfinancial Intangible Assets (except Copyrighted Works)
541110	Offices of Lawyers
541120	Offices of Notaries
541191	Title Abstract and Settlement Offices
541199	All Other Legal Services
541211	Offices of Certified Public Accountants
541213	Tax Preparation Services
541214	Payroll Services
541219	Other Accounting Services
541310	Architectural Services
541320	Landscape Architectural Services
541330	Engineering Services
541340	Drafting Services
541350	Building Inspection Services
541360	Geophysical Surveying and Mapping Services
541370	Surveying and Mapping (except Geophysical) Services
541380	Testing Laboratories
541410	Interior Design Services
541420	Industrial Design Services
541430	Graphic Design Services

N.A.I.C.S.	Description
541490	Other Specialized Design Services
541511	Custom Computer Programming Services
541512	Computer Systems Design Services
541513	Computer Facilities Management Services
541519	Other Computer Related Services
541611	Administrative Management and General Management Consulting Services
541612	Human Resources and Executive Search Consulting Services
541613	Marketing Consulting Services
541614	Process, Physical Distribution, and Logistics Consulting Services
541618	Other Management Consulting Services
541620	Environmental Consulting Services
541690	Other Scientific and Technical Consulting Services
541710	Research and Development in the Physical, Engineering, and Life Sciences
541720	Research and Development in the Social Sciences and Humanities
541810	Advertising Agencies
541820	Public Relations Agencies
541830	Media Buying Agencies
541840	Media Representatives
541850	Display Advertising
541860	Direct Mail Advertising
541870	Advertising Material Distribution Services
541890	Other Services Related to Advertising
541910	Marketing Research and Public Opinion Polling
541921	Photography Studios, Portrait
541922	Commercial Photography
541930	Translation and Interpretation Services
541940	Veterinary Services
551111	Offices of Bank Holding Companies
551112	Offices of Other Holding Companies
551114	Corporate, Subsidiary, and Regional Managing Offices
561210	Facilities Support Services
561310	Employment Placement Agencies
561330	Employee Leasing Services
561421	Telephone Answering Services
561422	Telemarketing Bureaus
561439	Other Business Service Centers (including Copy Shops)
561450	Credit Bureaus
561492	Court Reporting and Stenotype Services
561510	Travel Agencies
561520	Tour Operators
561599	All Other Travel Arrangement and Reservation Services
561611	Investigation Services
561612	Security Guards and Patrol Services
561613	Armored Car Services
561621	Security Systems Services (except Locksmiths)
561622	Locksmiths
561710	Exterminating and Pest Control Services
561720	Janitorial Services
561730	Landscaping Services
561740	Carpet and Upholstery Cleaning Services
561790	Other Services to Buildings and Dwellings
561910	Packaging and Labeling Services
561920	Convention and Trade Show Organizers
561990	All Other Support Services
562111	Solid Waste Collection
562112	Hazardous Waste Collection
562119	Other Waste Collection
562211	Hazardous Waste Treatment and Disposal
562212	Solid Waste Landfill
562213	Solid Waste Combustors and Incinerators
562219	Other Nonhazardous Waste Treatment and Disposal
562910	Remediation Services
562920	Materials Recovery Facilities
562991	Septic Tank and Related Services
562998	All Other Miscellaneous Waste Management Services
611110	Elementary and Secondary Schools
611210	Junior Colleges
611310	Colleges, Universities, and Professional Schools
611410	Business and Secretarial Schools
611420	Computer Training
611430	Professional and Management Development Training
611511	Cosmetology and Barber Schools
611512	Flight Training
611513	Apprenticeship Training
611519	Other Technical and Trade Schools
611610	Fine Arts Schools
611620	Sports and Recreation Instruction
611630	Language Schools

N.A.I.C.S.	*Description*
611691	Exam Preparation and Tutoring
611692	Automobile Driving Schools
611699	All Other Miscellaneous Schools and Instruction
611710	Educational Support Services
621111	Offices of Physicians (except Mental Health Specialists)
621210	Offices of Dentists
621310	Offices of Chiropractors
621320	Offices of Optometrists
621340	Offices of Physical, Occupational and Speech Therapists, and Audiologists
621391	Offices of Podiatrists
621399	Offices of All Other Miscellaneous Health Practitioners
621420	Outpatient Mental Health and Substance Abuse Centers
621492	Kidney Dialysis Centers
621498	All Other Outpatient Care Centers
621511	Medical Laboratories
621512	Diagnostic Imaging Centers
621610	Home Health Care Services
621910	Ambulance Services
621991	Blood and Organ Banks
621999	All Other Miscellaneous Ambulatory Health Care Services
622110	General Medical and Surgical Hospitals
622210	Psychiatric and Substance Abuse Hospitals
622310	Specialty (except Psychiatric and Substance Abuse) Hospitals
623110	Nursing Care Facilities
623210	Residential Mental Retardation Facilities
623220	Residential Mental Health and Substance Abuse Facilities
623311	Continuing Care Retirement Communities
623312	Homes for the Elderly
623990	Other Residential Care Facilities
624110	Child and Youth Services
624120	Services for the Elderly and Persons with Disabilities
624190	Other Individual and Family Services
624210	Community Food Services
624221	Temporary Shelters
624229	Other Community Housing Services
624230	Emergency and Other Relief Services
624310	Vocational Rehabilitation Services
624410	Child Day Care Services
711110	Theater Companies and Dinner Theaters
711120	Dance Companies
711130	Musical Groups and Artists
711190	Other Performing Arts Companies
711211	Sports Teams and Clubs
711212	Racetracks
711219	Other Spectator Sports
711310	Promoters of Performing Arts, Sports, and Similar Events with Facilities
711320	Promoters of Performing Arts, Sports, and Similar Events without Facilities
711410	Agents and Managers for Artists, Athletes, Entertainers, and Other Public Figures
711510	Independent Artists, Writers, and Performers
712110	Museums
712120	Historical Sites
712130	Zoos and Botanical Gardens
712190	Nature Parks and Other Similar Institutions
713110	Amusement and Theme Parks
713120	Amusement Arcades
713210	Casinos (except Casino Hotels)
713290	Other Gambling Industries
713910	Golf Courses and Country Clubs
713920	Skiing Facilities
713930	Marinas
713940	Fitness and Recreational Sports Centers
713950	Bowling Centers
713990	All Other Amusement and Recreation Industries
721110	Hotels (except Casino Hotels) and Motels
721120	Casino Hotels
721191	Bed-and-Breakfast Inns
721199	All Other Traveler Accommodation
721211	RV (Recreational Vehicle) Parks and Campgrounds
721214	Recreational and Vacation Camps (except Campgrounds)
721310	Rooming and Boarding Houses
722110	Full-Service Restaurants
722211	Fast Food Restaurants
722212	Cafeterias
722213	Snack and Nonalcoholic Beverage Bars
722310	Food Service Contractors
722320	Caterers

N.A.I.C.S.	*Description*
722330	Mobile Food Services
722410	Drinking Places (Alcoholic Beverages)
811111	General Automotive Repair
811112	Automotive Exhaust System Repair
811113	Automotive Transmission Repair
811118	Other Automotive Mechanical and Electrical Repair and Maintenance
811121	Automotive Body, Paint, and Interior Repair and Maintenance
811122	Automotive Glass Replacement Shops
811191	Automotive Oil Change and Lubrication Shops
811192	Car Washes
811198	All Other Automotive Repair and Maintenance
811211	Consumer Electronics Repair and Maintenance
811212	Computer and Office Machine Repair and Maintenance
811213	Communication Equipment Repair and Maintenance
811219	Other Electronic and Precision Equipment Repair and Maintenance
811310	Commercial and Industrial Machinery and Equipment (except Automotive and Electronic) Repair and Maintenance
811411	Home and Garden Equipment Repair and Maintenance
811412	Appliance Repair and Maintenance
811420	Reupholstery and Furniture Repair
811430	Footwear and Leather Goods Repair
811490	Other Personal and Household Goods Repair and Maintenance
812111	Barber Shops
812112	Beauty Salons
812113	Nail Salons
812191	Diet and Weight Reducing Centers
812199	Other Personal Care Services
812210	Funeral Homes and Funeral Services
812220	Cemeteries and Crematories
812310	Coin-Operated Laundries and Drycleaners
812320	Drycleaning and Laundry Services (except Coin-Operated)
812331	Linen Supply
812332	Industrial Launderers
812910	Pet Care (except Veterinary) Services
812921	Photofinishing Laboratories (except One-Hour)
812922	One-Hour Photofinishing
812930	Parking Lots and Garages
812990	All Other Personal Services
813110	Religious Organizations
813211	Grantmaking Foundations
813212	Voluntary Health Organizations
813219	Other Grantmaking and Giving Services
813311	Human Rights Organizations
813312	Environment, Conservation and Wildlife Organizations
813319	Other Social Advocacy Organizations
813410	Civic and Social Organizations
813910	Business Associations
813920	Professional Organizations
813930	Labor Unions and Similar Labor Organizations
813940	Political Organizations
813990	Other Similar Organizations (except Business, Professional, Labor, and Political Organizations)
814110	Private Households
921110	Executive Offices
921120	Legislative Bodies
921130	Public Finance Activities
921140	Executive and Legislative Offices, Combined
921150	American Indian and Alaska Native Tribal Governments
921190	Other General Government Support
922110	Courts
922120	Police Protection
922130	Legal Counsel and Prosecution
922140	Correctional Institutions
922150	Parole Offices and Probation Offices
922160	Fire Protection
922190	Other Justice, Public Order, and Safety Activities
923110	Administration of Education Programs
923120	Administration of Public Health Programs
923130	Administration of Human Resource Programs (except Education, Public Health, and Veterans' Affairs Programs)
923140	Administration of Veterans' Affairs
924110	Administration of Air and Water Resource and Solid Waste Management Programs
924120	Administration of Conservation Programs
925110	Administration of Housing Programs
925120	Administration of Urban Planning and Community and Rural Development
926110	Administration of General Economic Programs
926120	Regulation and Administration of Transportation Programs
926130	Regulation and Administration of Communications, Electric, Gas, and

N.A.I.C.S.	Description
	Other Utilities
926140	Regulation of Agricultural Marketing and Commodities
926150	Regulation, Licensing, and Inspection of Miscellaneous Commercial Sectors
927110	Space Research and Technology
928110	National Security
928120	International Affairs
999990	Unclassified Establishments
238910	Site Preparation Contractors
236115	New Single-Family Housing Construction (except Operative Builders)
236220	Commercial and Institutional Building Construction
236116	New Multifamily Housing Construction (except Operative Builders)
236117	New Housing Operative Builders
236210	Industrial Building Construction
237310	Highway, Street, and Bridge Construction
237990	Other Heavy and Civil Engineering Construction
237130	Power and Communication Line and Related Structures Construction
237110	Water and Sewer Line and Related Structures Construction
238210	Electrical Contractors
238320	Painting and Wall Covering Contractors
238310	Drywall and Insulation Contractors
238340	Tile and Terrazzo Contractors
238130	Framing Contractors
238330	Flooring Contractors
238390	Other Building Finishing Contractors
238160	Roofing Contractors
238990	All Other Specialty Trade Contractors
238110	Poured Concrete Foundation and Structure Contractors
238140	Masonry Contractors
238120	Structural Steel and Precast Concrete Contractors
238190	Other Foundation, Structure, and Building Exterior Contractors
238290	Other Building Equipment Contractors
517310	Telecommunications Resellers
517110	Wired Telecommunications Carriers
515112	Radio Stations
515111	Radio Networks
515120	Television Broadcasting
515210	Cable and Other Subscription Programming
425120	Wholesale Trade Agents and Brokers
423110	Automobile and Other Motor Vehicle Merchant Wholesalers
425110	Business to Business Electronic Markets
423410	Photographic Equipment and Supplies Merchant Wholesalers
423440	Other Commercial Equipment Merchant Wholesalers
423460	Ophthalmic Goods Merchant Wholesalers
423520	Coal and Other Mineral and Ore Merchant Wholesalers
423730	Warm Air Heating and Air-Conditioning Equipment and Supplies Merchant Wholesalers
423740	Refrigeration Equipment and Supplies Merchant Wholesalers
423810	Construction and Mining (except Oil Well) Machinery and Equipment Merchant Wholesalers
423830	Industrial Machinery and Equipment Merchant Wholesalers
423840	Industrial Supplies Merchant Wholesalers
423860	Transportation Equipment and Supplies (except Motor Vehicle) Merchant Wholesalers
424130	Industrial and Personal Service Paper Merchant Wholesalers
424420	Packaged Frozen Food Merchant Wholesalers
424520	Livestock Merchant Wholesalers
424690	Other Chemical and Allied Products Merchant Wholesalers
424720	Petroleum and Petroleum Products Merchant Wholesalers (except Bulk Stations and Terminals)
424950	Paint, Varnish, and Supplies Merchant Wholesalers
452112	Discount Department Stores
452111	Department Stores (except Discount Department Stores)
454111	Electronic Shopping
454113	Mail-Order Houses
237210	Land Subdivision
518210	Data Processing, Hosting, and Related Services
518111	Internet Service Providers
519120	Libraries and Archives
541990	All Other Professional, Scientific, and Technical Services
561110	Office Administrative Services
561320	Temporary Help Services
561410	Document Preparation Services
561431	Private Mail Centers
561440	Collection Agencies
561491	Repossession Services
561499	All Other Business Support Services
561591	Convention and Visitors Bureaus
621112	Offices of Physicians, Mental Health Specialists
621330	Offices of Mental Health Practitioners (except Physicians)

N.A.I.C.S.	Description
621410	Family Planning Centers
621491	HMO Medical Centers
621493	Freestanding Ambulatory Surgical and Emergency Centers
485991	Special Needs Transportation
486990	All Other Pipeline Transportation
487990	Scenic and Sightseeing Transportation, Other
488190	Other Support Activities for Air Transportation
488330	Navigational Services to Shipping
488490	Other Support Activities for Road Transportation
491110	Postal Service
492210	Local Messengers and Local Delivery
493130	Farm Product Warehousing and Storage
511120	Periodical Publishers
511140	Database and Directory Publishers
511210	Software Publishers
512131	Motion Picture Theaters (except Drive-Ins)
512210	Record Production
512230	Music Publishers
512290	Other Sound Recording Industries
517211	Paging
517510	Cable and Other Program Distribution
522120	Savings Institutions
522190	Other Depository Credit Intermediation
522291	Consumer Lending
522293	International Trade Financing
522310	Mortgage and Nonmortgage Loan Brokers
523110	Investment Banking and Securities Dealing
523140	Commodity Contracts Brokerage
523920	Portfolio Management
523991	Trust, Fiduciary, and Custody Activities
524114	Direct Health and Medical Insurance Carriers
524130	Reinsurance Carriers
524291	Claims Adjusting
524298	All Other Insurance Related Activities
525190	Other Insurance Funds
525930	Real Estate Investment Trusts
531110	Lessors of Residential Buildings and Dwellings
531210	Offices of Real Estate Agents and Brokers
531320	Offices of Real Estate Appraisers
532112	Passenger Car Leasing
532220	Formal Wear and Costume Rental
532291	Home Health Equipment Rental
532411	Commercial Air, Rail, and Water Transportation Equipment Rental and Leasing
424610	Plastics Materials and Basic Forms and Shapes Merchant Wholesalers
441210	Recreational Vehicle Dealers
441229	All Other Motor Vehicle Dealers
442110	Furniture Stores
442291	Window Treatment Stores
443111	Household Appliance Stores
443130	Camera and Photographic Supplies Stores
444130	Hardware Stores
444210	Outdoor Power Equipment Stores
445120	Convenience Stores
445220	Fish and Seafood Markets
445291	Baked Goods Stores
445299	All Other Specialty Food Stores
446120	Cosmetics, Beauty Supplies, and Perfume Stores
447110	Gasoline Stations with Convenience Stores
448120	Women's Clothing Stores
448140	Family Clothing Stores
448210	Shoe Stores
448310	Jewelry Stores
451110	Sporting Goods Stores
451130	Sewing, Needlework, and Piece Goods Stores
451220	Prerecorded Tape, Compact Disc, and Record Stores
453210	Office Supplies and Stationery Stores
453910	Pet and Pet Supplies Stores
453991	Tobacco Stores
453998	All Other Miscellaneous Store Retailers (except Tobacco Stores)
454112	Electronic Auctions
454390	Other Direct Selling Establishments
481211	Nonscheduled Chartered Passenger Air Transportation
482112	Short Line Railroads
483112	Deep Sea Passenger Transportation
483211	Inland Water Freight Transportation
484121	General Freight Trucking, Long-Distance, Truckload
484230	Specialized Freight (except Used Goods) Trucking, Long-Distance
485210	Interurban and Rural Bus Transportation

N.A.I.C.S.	Description
485410	School and Employee Bus Transportation
238350	Finish Carpentry Contractors
112340	Poultry Hatcheries
112410	Sheep Farming
112511	Finfish Farming and Fish Hatcheries
112910	Apiculture
112920	Horse and Other Equine Production
113110	Timber Tract Operations
114111	Finfish Fishing
114119	Other Marine Fishing
115111	Cotton Ginning
115113	Crop Harvesting, Primarily by Machine
115116	Farm Management Services
115310	Support Activities for Forestry
212111	Bituminous Coal and Lignite Surface Mining
212210	Iron Ore Mining
212222	Silver Ore Mining
212234	Copper Ore and Nickel Ore Mining
212311	Dimension Stone Mining and Quarrying
212319	Other Crushed and Broken Stone Mining and Quarrying
212325	Clay and Ceramic and Refractory Minerals Mining
212399	All Other Nonmetallic Mineral Mining
213113	Support Activities for Coal Mining
221111	Hydroelectric Power Generation
221119	Other Electric Power Generation
221210	Natural Gas Distribution
221320	Sewage Treatment Facilities
236118	Residential Remodelers
237120	Oil and Gas Pipeline and Related Structures Construction
238170	Siding Contractors
311313	Beet Sugar Manufacturing
311330	Confectionery Manufacturing from Purchased Chocolate
311421	Fruit and Vegetable Canning
311511	Fluid Milk Manufacturing
311513	Cheese Manufacturing
311520	Ice Cream and Frozen Dessert Manufacturing
311615	Poultry Processing
311712	Fresh and Frozen Seafood Processing
311813	Frozen Cakes, Pies, and Other Pastries Manufacturing
311830	Tortilla Manufacturing
311919	Other Snack Food Manufacturing
311941	Mayonnaise, Dressing, and Other Prepared Sauce Manufacturing
312113	Ice Manufacturing
312130	Wineries
312140	Distilleries
312221	Cigarette Manufacturing
313111	Yarn Spinning Mills
313113	Thread Mills
313221	Narrow Fabric Mills
313230	Nonwoven Fabric Mills
313249	Other Knit Fabric and Lace Mills
313320	Fabric Coating Mills
314121	Curtain and Drapery Mills
314912	Canvas and Related Product Mills
314999	All Other Miscellaneous Textile Product Mills
315191	Outerwear Knitting Mills
315212	Women's, Girls', and Infants' Cut and Sew Apparel Contractors
315224	Men's and Boys' Cut and Sew Trouser, Slack, and Jean Manufacturing
315233	Women's and Girls' Cut and Sew Dress Manufacturing
315292	Fur and Leather Apparel Manufacturing
315992	Glove and Mitten Manufacturing
316110	Leather and Hide Tanning and Finishing
316213	Men's Footwear (except Athletic) Manufacturing
316992	Women's Handbag and Purse Manufacturing
321113	Sawmills
321211	Hardwood Veneer and Plywood Manufacturing
321214	Truss Manufacturing
321911	Wood Window and Door Manufacturing
321920	Wood Container and Pallet Manufacturing
322110	Pulp Mills
322121	Paper (except Newsprint) Mills
322211	Corrugated and Solid Fiber Box Manufacturing
322215	Nonfolding Sanitary Food Container Manufacturing
322223	Plastics, Foil, and Coated Paper Bag Manufacturing
322231	Die-Cut Paper and Paperboard Office Supplies Manufacturing
323110	Commercial Lithographic Printing
323113	Commercial Screen Printing
323115	Digital Printing
323117	Books Printing
323119	Other Commercial Printing
323122	Prepress Services
324121	Asphalt Paving Mixture and Block Manufacturing
325110	Petrochemical Manufacturing
325132	Synthetic Organic Dye and Pigment Manufacturing
325191	Gum and Wood Chemical Manufacturing
325199	All Other Basic Organic Chemical Manufacturing
325221	Cellulosic Organic Fiber Manufacturing
325314	Fertilizer (Mixing Only) Manufacturing
325412	Pharmaceutical Preparation Manufacturing
325510	Paint and Coating Manufacturing
325612	Polish and Other Sanitation Good Manufacturing
325920	Explosives Manufacturing
325992	Photographic Film, Paper, Plate, and Chemical Manufacturing
326121	Unsupported Plastics Profile Shape Manufacturing
326140	Polystyrene Foam Product Manufacturing
326192	Resilient Floor Covering Manufacturing
326212	Tire Retreading
326291	Rubber Product Manufacturing for Mechanical Use
331525	Copper Foundries (except Die-Casting)
332112	Nonferrous Forging
332115	Crown and Closure Manufacturing
332211	Cutlery and Flatware (except Precious) Manufacturing
332311	Prefabricated Metal Building and Component Manufacturing
332322	Sheet Metal Work Manufacturing
332420	Metal Tank (Heavy Gauge) Manufacturing
332611	Spring (Heavy Gauge) Manufacturing
332710	Machine Shops
332722	Bolt, Nut, Screw, Rivet, and Washer Manufacturing
332911	Industrial Valve Manufacturing
332919	Other Metal Valve and Pipe Fitting Manufacturing
332994	Small Arms Manufacturing
332996	Fabricated Pipe and Pipe Fitting Manufacturing
333111	Farm Machinery and Equipment Manufacturing
333131	Mining Machinery and Equipment Manufacturing
333291	Paper Industry Machinery Manufacturing
333294	Food Product Machinery Manufacturing
333311	Automatic Vending Machine Manufacturing
333314	Optical Instrument and Lens Manufacturing
333412	Industrial and Commercial Fan and Blower Manufacturing
333512	Machine Tool (Metal Cutting Types) Manufacturing
333516	Rolling Mill Machinery and Equipment Manufacturing
333613	Mechanical Power Transmission Equipment Manufacturing
333913	Measuring and Dispensing Pump Manufacturing
333923	Overhead Traveling Crane, Hoist, and Monorail System Manufacturing
333994	Industrial Process Furnace and Oven Manufacturing
333999	All Other Miscellaneous General Purpose Machinery Manufacturing
334210	Telephone Apparatus Manufacturing
334310	Audio and Video Equipment Manufacturing
334413	Semiconductor and Related Device Manufacturing
334417	Electronic Connector Manufacturing
334510	Electromedical and Electrotherapeutic Apparatus Manufacturing
334514	Totalizing Fluid Meter and Counting Device Manufacturing
334519	Other Measuring and Controlling Device Manufacturing
335110	Electric Lamp Bulb and Part Manufacturing
335129	Other Lighting Equipment Manufacturing
335221	Household Cooking Appliance Manufacturing
335311	Power, Distribution, and Specialty Transformer Manufacturing
335911	Storage Battery Manufacturing
335929	Other Communication and Energy Wire Manufacturing
335999	All Other Miscellaneous Electrical Equipment and Component Manufacturing
336212	Truck Trailer Manufacturing
336311	Carburetor, Piston, Piston Ring, and Valve Manufacturing
336340	Motor Vehicle Brake System Manufacturing
336370	Motor Vehicle Metal Stamping
336412	Aircraft Engine and Engine Parts Manufacturing
336419	Other Guided Missile and Space Vehicle Parts and Auxiliary Equipment Manufacturing
336999	All Other Transportation Equipment Manufacturing
337122	Nonupholstered Wood Household Furniture Manufacturing
337211	Wood Office Furniture Manufacturing
337215	Showcase, Partition, Shelving, and Locker Manufacturing
339112	Surgical and Medical Instrument Manufacturing
339116	Dental Laboratories
339912	Silverware and Hollowware Manufacturing
339920	Sporting and Athletic Goods Manufacturing
339941	Pen and Mechanical Pencil Manufacturing
339950	Sign Manufacturing

N.A.I.C.S.	Description
339992	Musical Instrument Manufacturing
339995	Burial Casket Manufacturing
423510	Metal Service Centers and Other Metal Merchant Wholesalers
423930	Recyclable Material Merchant Wholesalers
516110	Internet Publishing and Broadcasting
517410	Satellite Telecommunications
517910	Other Telecommunications
518112	Web Search Portals
519110	News Syndicates
519190	All Other Information Services
424330	Women's, Children's, and Infants' Clothing and Accessories Merchant Wholesalers
424340	Footwear Merchant Wholesalers
424410	General Line Grocery Merchant Wholesalers
424430	Dairy Product (except Dried or Canned) Merchant Wholesalers
424440	Poultry and Poultry Product Merchant Wholesalers
424450	Confectionery Merchant Wholesalers
424460	Fish and Seafood Merchant Wholesalers
424470	Meat and Meat Product Merchant Wholesalers
424480	Fresh Fruit and Vegetable Merchant Wholesalers
424490	Other Grocery and Related Products Merchant Wholesalers
424510	Grain and Field Bean Merchant Wholesalers
424590	Other Farm Product Raw Material Merchant Wholesalers
424710	Petroleum Bulk Stations and Terminals
424810	Beer and Ale Merchant Wholesalers
424820	Wine and Distilled Alcoholic Beverage Merchant Wholesalers
424910	Farm Supplies Merchant Wholesalers
424920	Book, Periodical, and Newspaper Merchant Wholesalers
424930	Flower, Nursery Stock, and Florists' Supplies Merchant Wholesalers
424940	Tobacco and Tobacco Product Merchant Wholesalers
238150	Glass and Glazing Contractors
423120	Motor Vehicle Supplies and New Parts Merchant Wholesalers
423130	Tire and Tube Merchant Wholesalers
423140	Motor Vehicle Parts (Used) Merchant Wholesalers
423210	Furniture Merchant Wholesalers

N.A.I.C.S.	Description
423220	Home Furnishing Merchant Wholesalers
423310	Lumber, Plywood, Millwork, and Wood Panel Merchant Wholesalers
423320	Brick, Stone, and Related Construction Material Merchant Wholesalers
423330	Roofing, Siding, and Insulation Material Merchant Wholesalers
423390	Other Construction Material Merchant Wholesalers
423420	Office Equipment Merchant Wholesalers
423430	Computer and Computer Peripheral Equipment and Software Merchant Wholesalers
423450	Medical, Dental, and Hospital Equipment and Supplies Merchant Wholesalers
423490	Other Professional Equipment and Supplies Merchant Wholesalers
423610	Electrical Apparatus and Equipment, Wiring Supplies, and Related Equipment Merchant Wholesalers
423620	Electrical and Electronic Appliance, Television, and Radio Set Merchant Wholesalers
423690	Other Electronic Parts and Equipment Merchant Wholesalers
423710	Hardware Merchant Wholesalers
423720	Plumbing and Heating Equipment and Supplies (Hydronics) Merchant Wholesalers
423820	Farm and Garden Machinery and Equipment Merchant Wholesalers
423850	Service Establishment Equipment and Supplies Merchant Wholesalers
423910	Sporting and Recreational Goods and Supplies Merchant Wholesalers
423920	Toy and Hobby Goods and Supplies Merchant Wholesalers
423940	Jewelry, Watch, Precious Stone, and Precious Metal Merchant Wholesalers
423990	Other Miscellaneous Durable Goods Merchant Wholesalers
424110	Printing and Writing Paper Merchant Wholesalers
424120	Stationery and Office Supplies Merchant Wholesalers
424210	Drugs and Druggists' Sundries Merchant Wholesalers
424310	Piece Goods, Notions, and Other Dry Goods Merchant Wholesalers
424320	Men's and Boys' Clothing and Furnishings Merchant Wholesalers

ALPHABETICAL COMPENDIUM OF S.I.C. CODES

Standard Industrial Classification Manual, 1987, U.S. Government Office of Management and Budget; All codes for manufacturing unless otherwise stated.

Description	*SIC Code*
A	
Abrasive Products	3291
Accessory & Specialty Stores, Women's	5632
Accident & Health Insurance	6321
Accounting Services	8721
Acetate, Cellulose	2821
Acetate, Synthetic	2869
Acetate Fibers	2823
Acids, Cool Tar	2865
Acids, Fatty	2899
Acids, Inorganic, Except Nitric & Phosphoric	2899
Acids, Organic	2869
Acids, Wholesale	5169
Acoustical Tile & Board	3296
Adhesive Tape, Cellophane	2672
Adhesives	2891
Advertising, NEC	7319
Advertising Agencies	7311
Advertising Representatives, Radio, Television & Publishers	7313
Advertising Services, Outdoor	7312
Agricultural Chemicals	2879
Air Conditioners	3585
Air Conditioning Contractors	1711
Air Conditioning Equipment & Supplies, Wholesale	5075
Air Courier Services	4513
Air Purification Equipment	3564
Air Purifiers, Portable	3634
Air & Water Resource & Solid Waste Management	9511
Aircraft	3721
Aircraft Lighting Fixtures	3647
Aircraft Parts & Equipment	3728
Aircraft Repair & Service	4581
Airplane Models, Toys & Hobby	3944
Airplane Rental & Leasing	7359
Airports	4581
Alarms, Security	3669
Alcohol, Non-Beverage	2869
Alcoholism, Residential Rehabilitation Centers	8361
Alcoholism, Residential Hospitals	8069
Alfalfa, Wholesale	5191
Alfalfa Farms	0139
Alfalfa Prepared as Feed	2048
Alkalies	2812
Alkaline Storage Batteries	3691
Alternators & Generator Testers	3825
Alternators, Motor Vehicle	3694
Alumina	2819
Aluminum Castings, Except Dye Casting	3365
Aluminum Dye Casting	3363
Aluminum Ingots, Primary Production	3334
Aluminum Ore Mining	1099
Aluminum Products Wholesale	5051
Aluminum Rolling & Drawing, NEC	3355
Aluminum Smelting & Refining, Secondary	3341
Ambulance Services, Air	4522
Ambulance Services, Road	4119
Amines	2869
Ammonia, Anhydrous	2873
Ammonium Compounds	2819
Ammonium Phosphate	2874
Ammunition & Component Parts, More Than 30mm	3483
Ammunition & Component Parts, Small Arms	3482
Amplifiers	3651
Amusement Centers & Parks	7996
Amusement Rides & Concessions Services	7999
Amusement Rides for Carnivals	3599
Analog Converters, Electronic	3825
Animal Shelters	0752

Description	*SIC Code*
Animal Specialties	0279
Antennas, Communication	3663
Antennas, Receiving	3679
Antibiotics, Bulk	2833
Antibiotics, Packaged	2834
Apparel & Accessories, NEC	2389
Apparel & Accessory Stores, Misc.	5699
Appliance Cords	3699
Appliances, Electric Televisions & Radio Sets, Wholesale	5064
Appliances, Household, NEC	3639
Aquaculture	0273
Architectural Services	8712
Armature Rewinding Shops	7694
Armored Car Services	7381
Asbestos Products	3292
Asphalt Paving Mixtures & Blocks	2951
Associations, Civic, Social & Fraternal	8641
Atom Smashers	3699
Audio Equipment	3651
Automatic Merchandising Machine Operators	5962
Automobile & Home Supply Stores	5531
Automobile Services, Except Repair & Car Washes	7549
Automobiles, Dealers, New & Used	5511
Automobiles, Manufacturing	3711
Automotive Dealers, NEC	5599
Automotive Lighting	3447
Automotive Trimmings	2396
B	
Baby Foods, Canned	2032
Baby Formula	2023
Badminton Equipment	3949
Bag & Envelope Making Machinery	3554
Bagel Stores, Retail	5461
Bags, Plastic, Foil & Coated Paper	2673
Bags, Paper	2674
Bags, Textile	2393
Bags, Uncoated Paper & Multiwall	2674
Bakeries	5461
Bakery Products, Fresh	2051
Bakery Products, Frozen	2053
Bakery Products, Frozen, Wholesale	5142
Bakery Products, Wholesale	5149
Balances, Except Laboratory	3596
Balances, Except Laboratory, Wholesale	5046
Balances, Laboratory	3821
Balances, Wholesale	5049
Ball Bearings & Parts	3562
Ballpoint Pens	3951
Balls, Sports	3949
Banana Farms	0179
Bandages & Dressings	3842
Bandages, Wholesale	5122
Bands, Orchestras, Actors & Other Entertainers & Entertainment Groups	7929
Banjos & Parts	3931
Bank Holding Cos.	6712
Banks, National	6021
Banks, State	6022
Barbecue Sauce	2033
Barbecues, Grills	3631
Barber Shops	7231
Barite Mining	1479
Barium Compounds	2819
Barium Diagnostic Agents	2835
Barley Farms	0119
Barley, Wholesale	5153
Barometers	3829
Barrels, Stripping, Steel & Other Metal	3412
Barrels, Wood	2449
Bathing Suits, Girls', Children's & Infants'	2369

Description	*SIC Code*
Bathing Suits, Men's & Boys'	2329
Bathing Suits, Women's, Misses' & Juniors'	2329
Bathroom Accessories, Vitreous China & Earthenware	3261
Bathroom Fixtures, Enameled Iron	3431
Bathroom Fixtures, Plastics	3088
Bathroom Scales	3596
Batteries, Primary Dry & Wet	3692
Batteries, Storage	3691
Battery Cable Wiring Sets	3694
Bauxite Mining	1099
Bauxite, Refined	2819
Beans, Grain & Field, Buying & Marketing	5153
Bearings, Ball and Roller	3562
Bearings, Motor Vehicle	3714
Beauty Shops	7231
Beauticians	7231
Beds & Springs, Retail	5712
Beds, Household, Metal	2514
Beds, Household, Wood	2511
Bedspreads	2392
Bedspreads, Wholesale	5023
Bedsprings, Assembled	2515
Bedsprings, Wholesale	5021
Beef Cattle, Except Feedlots	0212
Beef Cattle, Feedlots	0211
Beeper Communications Service	4812
Beer & Ale, Wholesale	5181
Beets (Sugar)	0133
Belting, Rubber & Plastics	3052
Belts	2387
Berry Farms	0171
Bicycles & Parts	3751
Bicycles & Parts, Retail	5941
Bicycles & Parts, Wholesale	5091
Billboard Advertising	7312
Billiard Equipment	3949
Billiards Equipment & Supplies, Wholesale	5091
Binoculars	3827
Biological Products, Except Diagnostic Substances	2836
Bird Food	2048
Biscuits	2051
Bits, Rock, Oil & Gas Fields	3533
Bituminous Coal Mining	1221
Bituminous Coal Strip Mining	1221
Blacktop Work, Contractors	1771
Blades, Knife & Razor	3421
Blades, Saw	3425
Blast Furnaces	3212
Bleaches, Hair	2844
Bleaches, Household	2842
Bleaches, Industrial	2819
Blenders, Electric	3634
Blinds, Venetian & Vertical	2591
Blood Banks	8099
Blood Pressure Apparatus	3841
Blouses, Girls', Children's & Infants'	2361
Blouses, Wholesale	5137
Blouses & Shirts, Women's, Misses' & Juniors'	2331
Blow Torches	3423
Blueprint, Paper & Equipment	3861
Blueprinting Equipment, Wholesale	5044
Blueprinting Service	7334
Boat Dealers	5551
Boats, Fiberglass	3732
Body Shops, Automotive	7532
Boilers, Industrial	3443
Boilers, Steam & Hot Water	3433
Boilers, Wholesale	5074
Bolts, Metal	3452
Bolts, Nuts, Rivets & Screws, Wholesale	5072

Description	*SIC Code*
Bond & Mortgage Cos.	6162
Bone China	3262
Book Clubs, Not Publishing	5961
Book Printing	2732
Book Publishing	2731
Book Stores, New Publications	5942
Book Stores, Used Publications	5932
Bookbinding	2789
Bookcases, Household, Metal	2514
Bookcases, Household, Wood	2511
Bookcases, Office, Except Wood	2522
Bookcases, Office, Wood	2521
Bookkeeping & Billing Services	8721
Books, Blank	2782
Books, Wholesale	5192
Boot & Shoe Cut Stock & Findings	3131
Boots, Dress & Casual, Men's	3143
Boots, Plastic or Rubber	3021
Boots, Women's	3144
Borax Mining	1474
Botanical Products	2833
Bottle Caps & Tops, Metal	3466
Bottle Caps & Tops, Plastic	3089
Bottle Corks and Covers	2499
Bottles, Glass	3221
Bottles, Plastic	3085
Bottles, Rubber	3069
Bottles, Vacuum	3429
Bottling Machinery	3565
Bow Ties, Men's & Boys'	2323
Bowling Alleys & Accessories	3949
Box Making Machines for Plastic Boxes	3554
Box Making Machines for Wooden Boxes	3553
Boxes, Corrugated & Solid Fiber	2653
Boxes, Folding Paperboard	2657
Boxes, Set-up Paperboard	2652
Boxes, Nailed & Lock Corner Wooden	2441
Boxes, Paperboard, Wholesale	5113
Boxes, Plastic	3089
Boxes, Wood, Wirebound	2449
Boxing Equipment	3949
Brackets, Iron & Steel	3429
Brackets, Wood	2431
Brads, Steel	3429
Brads, Wholesale	5072
Brake Drums	3714
Brake Fluid, Hydraulic	2992
Brake Lining, Pads, Asbestos	3292
Brake Lining, Rubber	3069
Brakes, Aircraft	3728
Brakes & Brake Parts, Automotive	3714
Bran, Except Rice	2041
Bran, Rice	2044
Brandy & Brandy Spirits	2084
Brandy & Spirits, Wholesale	5182
Brass Die Castings	3364
Brass Foundries	3366
Brass Goods, Plumbers	3432
Brass Goods, Plumbers, Wholesale	5074
Brass, Rolling & Drawing	3351
Brass Smelting & Refining, Secondary	3341
Brassieres, Girdles, etc.	2342
Breakfast Cereals	2043
Breakfast Cereals, Wholesale	5149
Breathing Systems	3829
Breweries	2082
Brewers Machinery	3556
Brick & Tile Dealers, Retail	5211
Brick, Common, Face	3251
Brick, Refractory	3297
Brick, Stone & Related Construction Materials, Wholesale	5032
Bricklaying Contractors	1741
Bridge Construction	1622
Briefcases	3161

Description	*SIC Code*
Briquettes, Fuel	2999
Broadcast Equipment	3663
Broadcasting Stations, Radio	4832
Broadcasting Stations, Television	4833
Broiler, Fryer, & Roaster Chickens	0251
Brokers, Commodity	6221
Brokers, Insurance	6411
Brokers, Real Estate	6531
Brokers, Security	6211
Brokers, Shipping	4731
Bronze, Rolling & Drawing	3351
Bronze, Smelting & Refining, Secondary	3341
Brooms, Hand & Machine	3991
Broth, Except Seafood, Canned	2032
Brushes	3991
Building Equipment, Installation or Erection, NEC	1796
Business Associations	8611
Business Consulting Services, NEC	8748
Bulbs, Growing of	0181
Bulbs, Seeds, Nursery Stock, Retail	5261
Bulbs, Seeds, Nursery Stock, Wholesale	5191
Bulldozers, Construction	3531
Bulletin Boards	2499
Bullion, Precious Metals, Wholesale	5094
Buns, Bread	2051
Burglar Alarms	3669
Burlap, Jute	2299
Burlap, Wholesale	5199
Bus Charter Services, Local	4141
Bus Services, NEC	7389
Buses, Motor	3711
Buses, Wholesale	5012
Business Forms, Manifold	2761
Business Forms, Wholesale	5112
Business Management Services	8741
Butane Gas, Bottled, Retail	5984
Butane Gas, Natural, Production	1321
Butane Gas, Wholesale	5172
Butter	2021
Butter, Wholesale	5143
Buttons	3965

C

Description	*SIC Code*
Cabinets, Wood, for Televisions, Radios, Phonographs & Sewing Machines	2517
Cable, Fiber	2298
Cable, Steel, Insulated	3315
Cable, Uninsulated Wire	3496
Cable Television Equipment	3663
Cable Television Services	4841
Cafeterias	5812
Cake Mixes	2045
Calcium Carbide, Chloride & Hydrochloride	2819
Camera & Photographic Supply Stores	5946
Cameras, Still & Motion Picture	3861
Cameras, Television	3663
Campers, For Mounting on Trucks	3792
Campgrounds	7033
Camping Equipment, Retail	5941
Camping Equipment, Wholesale	5091
Camping Trailers	3792
Camshafts, Motor Vehicle	3714
Can Openers, Electric	3634
Can Openers, Except Electric	3423
Cane Sugar Refining	2062
Cans, Aluminum, Metal	3411
Canvas	2211
Canvas Bags	2393
Canvas Products, Except Bags	2394
Capacitors, Electronic	3675
Capacitors, Electronic, Wholesale	5065
Caps & Plugs, Attachment, Electric	3643
Capsules, Gelatin, Empty	2899
Car Leasing, Passenger	7515
Car Phones	3663
Car Washes	7542
Carbide	2819
Carbon Black	2895
Carbon Paper	3955
Carbon Products	3624
Cardboard	2631
Cardboard, Die-Cut, Coated	2675
Cardboard, Wholesale	5113
Cards, Greeting	2771
Cards, Index	2675
Carnival & Amusement Park Equipment, Wholesale	5087
Carnival Amusement Rides	3599
Carpentry Work	1751
Carpet Laying & Removal Service	1752
Carpet Stores, Retail	5713
Carpet Sweepers, Except Vacuum Cleaners	3589
Carpet & Upholstery Cleaning	7217
Carpet Yarn	2281
Carpets, Textile Fiber	2273
Carpets, Wholesale	5023
Carry-Out Restaurants	5812
Carts, Golf, Hand	3949
Carts, Grocery	3496
Carts, Restaurant	2599
Cash Grains	0119
Cash Registers	3578
Cash Registers, Wholesale	5044
Casino Hotels	7011
Caskets, Burial	3995
Caskets, Burial, Wholesale	5087
Cassette Tapes, Blank	3695
Catalog, Order Taking	5961
Catalog Showrooms	5399
Catalogs, Printing of Only	2759
Catalogs, Publishing	2741
Catfish Farms	0273
Cathode Ray Tubes	3671
Catsup	2033
Caulking Compounds	2891
Caulking Guns, Tool, Hand	3423
Caustic Soda, Potash	2812
Caustic Soda, Wholesale	5119
Ceilings, Acoustical	3296
Ceilings, Acoustical Installation	1742
Cellophane Adhesive Tape	2672
Cellos & Parts	3931
Cellular Radio Telephone	3663
Cellular Telephone Services	4812
Cellulose, Man-Made Fibers	2823
Cellulose Fibers	2821
Cement, Hydraulic, Portland	3241
Cemeteries	6553
Centrifuges, Industrial	3569
Centrifuges, Laboratory	3821
Ceramic Kilns	3567
Ceramic Tile	3253
Ceramic Tile, Wholesale	5032
Cesspool Cleaning	7699
Chainsaw Blades	3425
Chainsaws	3546
Chainsaws, Retail	5251
Chainsaws, Wholesale	5084
Chairs, Household, Not Upholstered	2511
Chairs, Office, Except Wood	2522
Chairs, Office, Wood	2521
Chairs, Upholstered	2512
Chairs, Wholesale	5021
Chamois Leather	3111
Chamois Leather, Wholesale	5199
Chandeliers, Commercial	3646
Chandeliers, Residential	3645
Change-Making Machines	3578
Charcoal, Activated	2819

Description	SIC Code
Charcoal, Except Activated	2861
Charcoal, Wholesale	5199
Chart & Graph Design Services	7336
Chart & Graph Paper, Ruled	2782
Checkbooks	2782
Check-Writing Machines	3579
Cheese, Mail-Order, Retail	5961
Cheese Curls & Puffs	2096
Cheese Products	2022
Cheese Stores, Retail	5451
Cheesecloth	2211
Cheesecloth, Wholesale	5131
Cheese-Making Machines	3556
Chemical Bulk Stations & Terminals	5169
Chemicals, NEC	2899
Chewing Gum	2067
Chewing Gum, Wholesale	5145
Chewing Tobacco	2131
Chewing Tobacco, Wholesale	5194
Chicken Production	0251
Child Care Centers	8351
Children's & Infants' Wear Stores	5641
Chili Con Carne, Canned	2032
Chili Pepper or Powder	2099
Chili Sauce	2033
Chimes, Electric	3699
Chimney Cleaning Service	7349
Chimney Construction & Maintenance	1741
China Closets	2511
China Tableware	3262
China, Wholesale	5023
Chisels	3423
Chlorine	2812
Chlorine, Compressed or Liquefied	2812
Chlorine, Wholesale	5169
Chocolate, Sweetened or Unsweetened	2066
Chlorine Bleach	2842
Chocolate Bars	2066
Chocolate Candy, Except Bars	2064
Chocolate Syrup	2066
Chow Mein, Chop Suey, Canned	2032
Chowders, Fish & Seafood, Canned	2091
Chowders, Fish & Seafood, Frozen	2092
Christmas Tree Growing	0811
Christmas Tree Lighting Sets	3699
Christmas Trees, Artificial	3999
Christmas Trees, Natural, Retail	5261
Christmas Trees, Wholesale	5199
Chromium Compounds	2819
Chromium Ore Mining	1061
Chromium Plating of Metals	3471
Chromium Refining	3339
Cider, Nonalcoholic	2099
Cider Presses	3556
Cigar Stores & Stands	5993
Cigarettes	2111
Cigarettes, Wholesale	5194
Cigars	2121
Cigars, Wholesale	5194
Circuit Boards	3672
Citizen's Band (CB) Radios	3663
Citric Acid	2869
Citrus Fruits	0174
Citrus Groves	0724
Clay Refractories	3255
Clays, Common, Quarrying	1459
Cleaning & Dying Plants, Except Rug	7216
Cleaning Preparations	2842
Cleansing Tissues	2676
Clock Radios	3651
Clock Repair	7631
Clocks, Except Timeclocks	3873
Clocks, Wholesale	5094
Clothes Dryers, Electric, Commercial	3582
Clothes Dryers, Electric, Household	3633

Description	SIC Code
Clothes Dryers, Wood	2499
Clothing, Men's, Boys' NEC	2329
Clothing & Accessories, Women's, Children's, Infants', Wholesale	5137
Clothing & Accessory Stores, Men's & Boys'	5611
Clothing & Furnishings, Men's & Boys', Wholesale	5136
Clothing Stores, Women's	5621
Coal Mining, Anthracite	1231
Coal Mining, Bituminous, Surface	1221
Coal Mining, Bituminous, Underground	1222
Coal Mining Services	1241
Coal Products, NEC	2999
Coal Tar	2865
Coal Tar Products	5169
Coal, Wholesale	5052
Coating, Engraving & Allied Services, NEC	3479
Coating of Metals	3479
Coats, Girls', Children's, Infants'	2369
Coats, Women's, Misses', Juniors'	2339
Coats, Men's, Boys'	2311
Coaxial Cable, Nonferrous	3357
Coaxial Cable, Wholesale	5063
Cobalt Ore Mining	1061
Cocktails, Alcoholic	2085
Cocktails, Alcoholic, Premixed, Retail	5182
Cocoa, Powdered & Mix	2066
Codfish, Smoked, Dried, etc.	2091
Coffee, Instant	2095
Coffee Farms	0179
Coffee Makers, Electric	3634
Coffee Roasting	2095
Coffee Roasting & Grinding Machines	3556
Coffee Shops	5812
Coffee Stores, Retail	5499
Coils, Electronics	3677
Coils, Ignition	3694
Coils for Motors & Generators	3621
Coin-Operated Game Machines, Wholesale	5099
Coin-Operated Laundries	7215
Coin-Operated Machines, Selling Merchandise	5962
Coke Ovens	3212
Coke, Petroleum	2911
Cold Storage Locker Rental	4222
Cold Storage Warehousing	4222
Collection Agencies, Accounts	7322
Colognes	2844
Combination Utilities, NEC	4939
Combs, Plastics	3089
Comic Books Publishing	2721
Commercial Art & Graphic Design	7336
Commercial Equipment, Wholesale	5046
Communication Services, NEC	4899
Communications Equipment, Mobile & Microwave	3663
Communications Equipment, NEC	3669
Communications Equipment, Telephone & Telegraph	3661
Communications Equipment, Wholesale	5065
Communications Equipment Installation	1731
Compact Disc Players	3651
Compact Discs, Prerecorded, Except Video	3652
Compasses, Except Portable	3812
Compasses, Portable	3829
Compressors, Air & Gas, Industrial	3563
Compressors, Refrigeration	3585
Computer & Computer Software Stores	5734
Computer Consultants	7379
Computer Facilities Management Services	7376
Computer Forms	2761
Computer Hardware Rental	7377
Computer Logic Modules	3674
Computer Paper, Wholesale	5112

Description	SIC Code
Computer Peripherals	3577
Computer Peripherals, Rental	7377
Computer Peripherals, Wholesale	5045
Computer Repair & Maintenance	7378
Computer Software	7372
Computer Software, Stores	5734
Computer Software, Tape & Disks, Blank	3685
Computer Software, Wholesale	5045
Computer Storage Units	3572
Computer Stores, Retail	5734
Computer Terminals	3575
Computer Terminals, Wholesale	5045
Computers, Electronic	3571
Concrete Block & Brick	3271
Concrete Block Laying	1741
Concrete & Cinder Block, Retail	5211
Concrete & Cinder Block, Wholesale	5032
Concrete Curing Compounds	2899
Concrete Mixers, Plants	3531
Concrete Products, Precast, Except Block & Brick	3272
Concrete, Ready-Mix	3273
Concrete Reinforcement Mesh	3496
Concrete Reinforcement Steel Bars	3449
Concrete Work, Except Paving	1771
Concrete Work, Paving	1611
Condensed Milk	2032
Condensers, Electronic	3675
Condensers, Electronic, Wholesale	5065
Condensers, Refrigeration	3585
Condensers, Steam	3443
Condensers for Motors & Generators	3629
Condensing Units, Air-Conditioning, Wholesale	5075
Condensing Units, Refrigeration, Wholesale	5078
Condominium Developers	1531
Conduits & Fittings, Electrical	3644
Conduits, Concrete	3272
Confectionery	2064
Confectionery Stores	5441
Confectionery, Wholesale	5145
Connectors, Electric Cord	3643
Connectors, Electronic	3678
Connectors, Electronic Wholesale	5065
Construction, Bridges, Tunnels	1622
Construction, Sand & Gravel	1442
Construction, Water, Sewer, Pipeline, Power Line	1623
Construction Equipment, Heavy Rental	7353
Construction Machinery, Except Mining	3531
Construction Material, Wholesale	5039
Construction Paper	2651
Consumer Finance Companies	6141
Contact Lenses	3851
Contact Lenses, Wholesale	5048
Containers, Wood, Nec	2449
Contractors, Family Houses	1521
Contractors, Industrial Buildings & Warehouses	1541
Contractors, Non-Residential Buildings	1542
Contractors, Residential Buildings	1522
Contractors, Special Trade	1799
Control Panels	3613
Control Transformers	3612
Control Valves	3492
Controls, Industrial	3625
Controls, Industrial, Wholesale	5084
Controls & Timing Devices	3824
Convection Ovens	3631
Convenience Food Stores	5411
Conveyor Belts	3496
Conveyor Systems, Industrial	3535
Conveyor Systems, Wholesale	5084
Cookie Stores	5461
Cookies	2052

Description	SIC Code
Cookies, Wholesale	5149
Cooking Appliances	3634
Cooking Oils, Vegetable	2079
Cooking Oils, Wholesale	5149
Coolers, Drinking Fountain	3431
Copiers	3579
Copper Alloy Foundries	3366
Copper Chloride, Sulfate	2819
Copper Die-Castings	3364
Copper Ingots	3331
Copper Ore, Wholesale	5052
Copper Ore Mining	1021
Copper Rolling, Drawing, Extruding	3351
Copper Smelting	3331
Cord, Braided	2298
Cord Connectors, Electric	3643
Cord for Reinforcing Rubber Tires	2296
Cord Sets, Flexible	3357
Cordage & Twine	2298
Corduroys, Cotton	2211
Core Drills	3532
Cork, Wholesale	5085
Cork Products	2499
Corn, Wholesale	5153
Corn Chips, Wholesale	5145
Corn Chips & Snacks	2096
Corn Flakes	2043
Corn Oil	2046
Corn Pickers & Shellers	3523
Corn Popping Machines	3589
Corn Production	0115
Corn Starch	2046
Correctional Facilities, Private	8744
Correspondence Schools	8249
Cosmetics	2844
Cosmetics, Wholesale	5122
Costume Jewelry	3961
Cottage Cheese	2026
Cotton, Finishers of Broad Woven Fabrics	2261
Cotton, Raw, Wholesale	5159
Cotton & Cottonseed Production	0131
Cotton Balers & Presses	3523
Cotton Fabric	2211
Cotton Ginning	0724
Cotton Ginning Machinery	3559
Cotton Piece Goods, Wholesale	5131
Cotton Thread	2284
Cotton Yarn	2281
Cotton Yarns, Wholesale	5199
Cottonseed Oil	2074
Cough Drops	2064
Cough Medicines	2834
Couplings, Hose	3429
Couplings, Pipe	3494
Courier Services, Air	4513
Courier Services, Except Air	4215
Crackers	2052
Crackers, Wholesale	5149
Craft & Hobby Sets	3944
Craft & Hobby Shops	5945
Craft Kits, Wholesale	5092
Cranes, Construction	3531
Cranes, Wholesale	5084
Crankshaft Assemblies	3714
Crowns & Closures, Metal	3466
Crayons	3952
Cream Substitutes	2023
Credit Card Service	7389
Credit Clearinghouses	7323
Credit Institutions, Misc. Business	6159
Credit Institutions, Short-Term Business, Except Agriculture	6153
Credit Unions, Federal	6061
Credit Unions, State	6062
Crepe Paper	2679

Description	SIC Code
Crop Driers	3523
Crop Dusting	0721
Crop Planting, Cultivation & Protection Services	0721
Crop Preparation Services for Market, Except Cotton Ginning	0723
Crops, Food, Grown Under Cover	0182
Crucibles, Fire Clay	3255
Crucibles, Non-Clay	3297
Crude Oil, Wholesale	5172
Crude Oil Production	1311
Crude Petroleum Pipe Lines	4612
Crystals & Crystal Assemblies	3679
Cultured Pearl Production	0919
Cups, Foamed Plastic	3086
Cups, Paper	2656
Cups, Plastic, Except Foam	3089
Cured Meats	2011
Curio Shops	5947
Curlers, Hair	3965
Curling Irons, Electrical	3634
Current-Carrying Wiring Devices	3643
Curtains & Draperies, NEC	2391
Curtains & Fabrics, Lace	2258
Curtains, Wholesale	5023
Cylinders, Pump	3561

D

Description	SIC Code
Dairy Farms	0241
Dairy Product Stores	5451
Dairy Products, Except Dried or Canned, Wholesale	5143
Dairy Products Machinery & Equipment	3556
Dairy Products Machinery, Wholesale	5084
Data Base Information Retrieval Services	7375
Data Entry Services	7374
Data Processing Services	7374
Deciduous Tree Fruits Production	0175
Decoders, Computer	3577
Deep Sea Foreign Freight Transportation	4412
Deep Sea Foreign Passenger Transportation	4481
Dehumidifiers, Not Portable, Electric	3585
Dehumidifiers, Portable, Electric	3634
Dehydrated Fruits, Vegetables, Soups	2034
Dehydrating Equipment, Food	3556
Denims	2211
Dental Equipment	3843
Dental Equipment, Wholesale	5047
Deodorants, Non Personal	2842
Deodorants, Personal	2844
Department Stores, Retail	5311
Deposit Insurance	6399
Desalination Equipment	3559
Desalter Kits, Sea Water	2899
Desserts, Frozen, Except Bakery	2024
Desserts, Ready-to-Mix	2099
Detection Systems & Instruments	3812
Detective Agencies	7381
Detergents	2841
Detergents, Wholesale	5169
Developing & Printing, Commercial Motion Picture Film	7819
Developing & Printing, Home Movies	7384
Diamond Cutting & Polishing	3915
Diamond Mining, Industrial	1499
Diamonds, Gems, Wholesale	5094
Diamonds, Industrial & Natural, Wholesale	5085
Diapers, Cotton	2399
Diapers, Disposable	2676
Diapers, Wholesale	5137
Die-Casting Machines	3542
Die-Castings, Aluminum	3363
Die-Castings, Nonferrous, Except Aluminum	3634
Dies, Metalworking, Except Threading	3544
Dies, Thread Cutting	3545

Description	SIC Code
Diesel Engines & Parts	3519
Diesel Engines & Parts, Wholesale	5084
Diet Workshops	7299
Dietary Supplements	2023
Digital Encoders	3663
Digital Test Equipment	3825
Dimension Stone	1411
Dining Room Furniture, Wood	2511
Dinners, Frozen & Packaged	2038
Dinners, Frozen, Wholesale	5142
Dinnerware, Plastic	3089
Diodes, Solid-State	3074
Diodes, Wholesale	5065
Direct Mail Advertising	7331
Direct Selling Establishments	5963
Directories, Printed, Not Published	2759
Directories, Publishing	2741
Dishes, Fine & Earthenware	3263
Dishes, Paper	2656
Dishes, Paper & Plastics, Wholesale	5113
Dishwashers, Commercial, Electric	3589
Dishwashers, Electric, Wholesale	5064
Dishwashers, Household, Electric	3639
Disinfecting & Pest Control Services	7342
Disk & Diskette Conversion Services	7379
Disk Drives, Computer	3572
Disk Drives, Wholesale	5045
Diskettes, Wholesale	5065
Dog & Cat Food	2047
Dog & Cat Food, Wholesale	5149
Dogs, Rental of, Protective	7381
Dolls	3942
Dolls, Wholesale	5092
Door Frames & Sash, Metal	3442
Door Frames & Sash, Wood	2431
Door Frames, Wholesale	5031
Door Locks & Lock Sets	3429
Door Opening & Closing Devices, Electrical	3699
Doors, Metal	3442
Doors, Wood	2431
Doughnut Shops, Retail	5461
Drafting Instruments	3829
Drafting Instruments, Wholesale	5049
Drafting Service	7389
Draperies & Fabrics, Cotton	2211
Draperies, Plastic	2391
Draperies, Silk & Man-made Fibers	2221
Draperies, Wholesale	5023
Drapery Rods, Fixture	2591
Dresses, Girls', Children's & Infants'	2361
Dresses, Womens', Misses' & Juniors'	2335
Dressing Tables	2511
Dressings, Surgical	3842
Dried Fruits & Vegetables	2034
Driers, Hand, Face & Hair, Electric	3634
Drill Bits, Metalworking	3545
Drill Bits, Wholesale	5084
Drill Bits, Woodworking	3423
Drilling Mud	2899
Drilling Mud, Wholesale	5169
Drinking Places (Alcoholic Beverages)	5813
Drug Stores, Retail	5912
Drugs, Wholesale	5122
Dry Cell Batteries	3692
Dry Cleaning	7215
Dry Ice	2813
Dry Ice, Wholesale	5169
Dryers, Laboratory	3821
Dryers, Laundry	3633
Drywall	1742
Duplicating Ink	2893
Duplicating Machines	3579
Duplicating Machines, Wholesale	5044
Durable Goods, NEC, Wholesale	5099
Dyes, Hair	2844

Description	SIC Code
Dyes, Household	2899
Dyes, Synthetic	2865
Dyestuffs, Natural	2861
Dyestuffs, Wholesale	5169
Dynamite	2892
E	
Earth Moving Equipment Rental & Leasing	7353
Earth Moving, Contractors	1794
Earthenware	3263
Edge Act Corporations	6082
Editing Equipment, Motion Picture	3861
Egg Production	0252
Egg Substitutes	2015
Eggs, Wholesale	5144
Elastomers	2822
Electric Lamp Bulbs & Tubes	3641
Electric & Other Services Combined	4931
Electric Services	4911
Electric Wiring, Construction Wholesale	5063
Electrical Industrial Apparatus, NEC	3629
Electrical Work Contractors	1731
Electromedical & Electrotherapeutic Apparatus	3845
Electrometallurgical Products, Except Steel	3213
Electron Tubes	3671
Electronic Parts & Equipment, Wholesale	5065
Electronic Stores, Consumer, Radio & Television	5731
Elevator Installation	1796
Elevators, Grain Storage	4221
Elevators, Passenger & Freight	3534
Elevators, Wholesale	5084
Emergency Medical Centers, Freestanding	8011
Employment Agencies, General	7361
Enamel Tile	3253
Enamels	2851
Enamels, Wholesale	5198
Energy Measuring Equipment, Electrical	3825
Engine Repair, Automotive	7538
Engine Repair, Except Automotive	7699
Engineering Services	8711
Engines & Engine Parts, Aircraft	3724
Engines & Engine Parts, Automotive	3714
Engines, Internal Combustion, Except Aircraft & Non-Diesel Automotive	3519
Enlargers, Photographic	3861
Envelopes	2677
Envelopes, Wholesale	5112
Epoxy Adhesives	2891
Epoxy Resins	2821
Equipment Rental & Leasing, NEC	7359
Erasers, Rubber	3069
Escalators	3534
Escrow Agents	6531
Esters	2869
Ethanol Industrial	2869
Ether	2869
Ethyl Acetate	2869
Ethyl Chloride	2869
Evaporated Milk	2023
Excavation & Foundation Work	1794
Exercise Cycles	3949
Exercising Machines	3949
Exhaust Systems & Parts, Aircraft	3724
Exhaust Systems & Parts, Motor Vehicle	3714
Explosives	2892
Extruded Shapes, Aluminum	3354
Extruded Shapes, Copper	3351
Extruded Shapes, Nonferrous, Except Copper & Aluminum	3356
Eyeglass Cases	3172
Eyeglasses, Lenses & Frames	3851
F	
Fabric, Nonwoven	2297
Fabric Shops, Retail	5949
Fabric Softeners	2842
Fabricated Metal Products, NEC	3499
Fabricated Pipe & Fabricated Pipe Fittings	3498
Fabricated Wire Products, Misc.	3469
Facial Tissues	2676
Facilities Support Management Services	8744
Facsimile Equipment	3661
Facsimile Transmission Services	4822
Factors of Commercial Paper	6153
Family Clothing Stores	5651
Family Services	8322
Fans, Electric, Household	3634
Fans, Except Household	3564
Fans, Industrial, Wholesale	5084
Farm Labor Contractors	0761
Farm Machinery & Equipment	3523
Farm Machinery & Equipment, Wholesale	5083
Farm Management Services	0762
Farm Production Warehousing & Storage	4221
Farm Supplies, Wholesale	5191
Farms, Primarily Crop	0191
Farms, Primarily Livestock	0291
Fasteners	3965
Fats & Oils, Animal & Marine	2077
Feed Grinders	3523
Feed Pre-mixes & Supplements	2048
Felt Tip Markers	3951
Fencing, Wire	3496
Fencing, Wood	2499
Ferries	4482
Fertilizers, Mixing Only	2875
Fertilizers, Nitrogenous	2873
Fertilizers, Phosphatic	2874
Fiber Cans, Tubes, Drums & Similar Products	2655
Fiber Optics Cable	3357
Fiber Optics Strands	3229
Fibers, Synthetic	2284
Field Crops, Except Cash Grains, Nec	0139
Filing Boxes, Paperboard	2652
Filing Folders	2675
Film, Movie, X-Ray, Still Camera	3861
Filters, Air for Furnaces	3564
Filters, Fluid, General	3569
Finance Leasing of Automobiles, Trucks, Machinery	6159
Financial Advice	6282
Financing of Automobiles, Furniture, Appliances	6141
Finfish, Catching	0912
Fire Alarm Apparatus	3669
Fire Extinguishers, Portable	3999
Fire Extinguishers, Wholesale	5099
First Aid Kits	3842
Fish, Canned	2091
Fish, Cured, Dried, Smoked	2091
Fish, Cured, Fresh, Wholesale	5146
Fish, Fresh & Frozen, Prepared	2092
Fish Food	2048
Fish Hatcheries	0921
Fish Sticks	2092
Fishing Lines, Nets	2298
Flags, Fabric	2399
Flagstones	3281
Flannels, Wool, Mohair	2231
Flares	2899
Flashlights	3648
Flashlights, Wholesale	5063
Flatware, Table	3914
Flavoring Concentrates, Extracts	2087
Flight Simulators	3699
Float Glass	3211
Floodlights	3648
Floor Coverings, Asphalted-Feltbase	3996
Floor Laying & Other Floor Work	1752
Floor Tile, Asphalt	3292
Floor Tile, Ceramic	3253
Floor Tile Stores	5713
Floor Waxes	2842
Floor Waxes & Polishes, Electric	3639
Florists, Retail	5992
Florists, Wholesale	5193
Flour, Blended	2041
Flour, Wholesale	5149
Flowers, Artificial Except Glass	3999
Flowers, Artificial Glass	3231
Flowers, Artificial, Retail	5999
Flowers, Artificial, Wholesale	5193
Flowers, Growing of	0181
Fluid Power Motors	3593
Fluid Power Pumps	3594
Fluid Power Valves & Fittings	3492
Fluorescent Lamps	3641
Fluorescent Lighting Fixtures, Commercial	3646
Fluorescent Lighting Fixtures, Residential	3645
Flush Valves	3432
Flying Instruction	8299
Foam Rubber	3069
Foam Rubber, Wholesale	5199
Foil, Aluminum	3353
Food Brokers	5141
Food, Mail-Order Retail	5961
Food Mixers, Household, Electric	3634
Food Preparation, NEC	2099
Food Processing Machinery	3556
Food Service, Institutional	5812
Food Stores, Misc.	5499
Food Warming Equipment, Commercial	3589
Food Warming Equipment, Commercial, Wholesale	5046
Foods, Frozen, Packaged, Wholesale	5142
Footwear, Men's	3143
Footwear, Women's	3144
Foreign Banks, Branches & Agencies	6081
Foreign Trade & International Banking Institutions	6082
Forest Nurseries & Forest Products	0831
Forestry Services	0851
Forgings, Iron & Steel	3462
Forgings, Nonferrous	3463
Forklift Trucks	3537
Forks, Garden	3423
Foundries, Gray & Ductile Iron	3321
Foundries, Malleable Iron	3322
Foundries, Nonferrous, Except Aluminum & Copper	3369
Foundries, Steel	3325
Foundries, Steel Investment	3324
Fountain Pens & Sets	3951
Flour Mill Machinery	3556
Flour Mills	2041
Freezers	3632
Freezers, Ice Cream, Commercial	3556
Freezers, Ice Cream, Household	3499
Freight Cars & Equipment	3743
Freight Forwarding	4731
Freight Packing & Crating	4783
Freight Trucking Terminals	4231
Frosting, Prepared	2099
Frozen Dinners, Packaged	2038
Frozen Fish, Packaged	2092
Frozen Fruits, Juices, Vegetables	2037
Frozen Vegetables, Juices, Fruits, Wholesale	5142

Description	*SIC Code*
Fruit Stores	5431
Fruit Tree Production	0175
Fruits, Fresh, Wholesale	5148
Fuel Oil Dealers	5983
Fuel Pumps, Automotive	3714
Funeral Homes, Parlors	7261
Fur Goods	2371
Fur-Bearing Animals	0271
Furnaces, Industrial	3567
Furnaces, Warm Air	3585
Furnaces, Warm Air, Wholesale	5075
Furniture & Fixtures	2599
Furniture Rental & Leasing	7359
Furniture, Household, Glass & Plastic	2519
Furniture, Household, Metal	2514
Furniture, Household, Rattan, Wicker	2519
Furniture, Household, Upholstered	2512
Furniture, Household, Wood	2511
Furniture, Laboratory	3821
Furniture, Office, Metal	2522
Furniture, Office, Wood	2521
Furniture, Public Building & Related	2531
Furniture, Wholesale	5021
Furniture Stores	5712
Fuses	3613
Futures Dealers & Brokers	6221
G	
Games, Coin-Operated	3999
Games, Computer Software	7372
Games, Puzzles	3944
Garage Doors, Overhead, Metal	3442
Garage Doors, Overhead, Wood	2431
Garages, Automobile Parking	7521
Garages, Automotive Repair	7538
Garages, Prefabricated, Metal	3448
Garbage Collecting, Not Disposal	4212
Garbage Collecting & Disposal	4953
Garbage Containers, Metal	3469
Garbage Containers, Plastic	3089
Garbage Disposers, Commercial	3589
Garbage Disposers, Electric, Household	3639
Garden Handtools	3423
Garden Hose	3052
Garden Supplies & Tools, Retail	5261
Gas, Natural, Compressed	1623
Gas, Natural, Distribution	4924
Gas, Natural, Production	1311
Gas, Natural, Transmission & Distribution	4923
Gas, Natural, Transmission Only	4922
Gas & Other Services Combined	4932
Gas Masks	3842
Gas Turbines	3511
Gases, Industrial	2813
Gaskets	3053
Gaskets, Wholesale	5085
Gasoline, Natural, Production	1321
Gasoline & Oil, Retail	5541
Gauges, Machine Tool	3545
Gauges, Pressure, Temperature	3824
Gear Motors	3566
Gears, Motor Vehicle	3714
Gears, Motorcycle & Bicycle	3751
Gears, Steel	3462
Gears, Wholesale	5085
Geiger Counters	3829
Gelatin Dessert Preparations	2099
Gem Stone Mining	1499
Gems, Preparation of for Setting	3915
General Stores, Retail	5399
Generators	3621
Generators, Aircraft & Motor Vehicle	3694
Gift Shops	5947
Gift Wrap Paper	2679
Gin, Alcoholic Beverage	2085

Description	*SIC Code*
Ginger Ale, Bottled, Canned	2086
Glass, Flat, Colored	3211
Glass & Glazing Work	1793
Glass & Glassware, Pressed & Blown	3229
Glass Products, Made of Purchased Glass	3231
Globes, Geographical	3999
Gloves, Dress & Work	2381
Gloves, Leather	3151
Gloves, Rubber	3069
Goggles, Underwater, Safety	3851
Gold Ores Mining	1041
Government, General, NEC	9199
Granite, Crushed & Broken	1423
Grape Production	0172
Graphite Products	3624
Grave Markers, Vaults, Concrete	3272
Greeting Cards	2771
Grills for Outdoor Cooking	3631
Groceries, General Line, Wholesale	5141
Groceries & Related Products, Wholesale, NEC	5149
Guided Missle Propulsion Units & Propulsion Unit Parts	3764
Gum, Chemicals	2861
Guns, 30mm or Less	3484
Guns, More Than 30mm	3489
Guns, BB and Pellet	3484
Guns, Toy	3944
Gypsum Building Board	3275
H	
Hair Goods	3999
Hammers	3423
Handbags, Retail	5632
Handbags, Wholesale	5137
Handbags, Women's	3171
Handtools	3423
Handtools, Power Driven	3546
Hang Gliders	3721
Hardboard	2493
Hardboard, Wholesale	5031
Hardware, Wholesale	5072
Hardware Stores	5251
Harness Assemblies, Electronic	3679
Harvesting Machines	3523
Hatcheries, Fish	0921
Hatcheries, Poultry	0254
Hats	2353
Hazardous Waste Disposal Sites	4953
Headlights, Vehicular	3647
Headphones, Radio	3679
Health Food Stores	5499
Health Foods, Wholesale	5149
Health Insurance	6321
Health Lamps	3641
Health Practitioners, Offices & Clinics, NEC	8049
Health Programs, Public, Administration of	9431
Hearing Aids	3842
Hearing Aids, Retail	5999
Hearing Aids, Wholesale	5047
Heat Exchangers	3443
Heat Exchangers, Wholesale	5084
Heating & Air Conditioning Units, Combined	3585
Heating Units, Electric	3634
Heavy Construction, NEC	1629
Heavy Water	2819
Helicopters	3721
Helium	2813
Helmets, Athletic	3949
Help Supply Service	7363
Herbicides	2879
High Fidelity Equipment	3651
High Fidelity Equipment, Retail	5731
High Fidelity Equipment, Wholesale	5064
Highway & Street Construction	1611

Description	*SIC Code*
Hinges	3429
Hobby Kits	3944
Hobby Stores	5945
Hog Production	0213
Hoists	3536
Hoists, Wholesale	5084
Holding Companies, Bank	6712
Holding Companies, Except Bank	6719
Home Construction, Single-Family	1521
Home Furnishing Stores, Misc.	5719
Home Furnishings, Wholesale	5023
Home Healthcare Services	8082
Horses & Other Equines Farms	0272
Hose Fittings & Assemblies	3492
Hose, Plastic or Rubber	3052
Hosiery, Ankle-Length	2252
Hosiery, Men's & Boys' Wholesale	5136
Hosiery, Women's & Children's Wholesale	5137
Hosiery, Women's Full Length & Knee High	2251
Hospital & Medical Service Plans	6324
Hospitals, Children's	8069
Hospitals, General	8062
Hospitals, Psychiatric	8063
Hospitals, Specialty	8069
Hospitals for Mentally Retarded	8051
Hot Tubs	2449
Hot Tubs, Retail	5999
Hot Tubs, Wholesale	5091
Hotels	7011
House Furnishings, Except Curtains & Draperies	2392
House-to-House Sales	5963
Household Appliance Stores	5722
Humidifiers, Dehumidifiers, Not Portable	3585
Humidifiers, Dehumidifiers, Portable	3634
Hunting, Trapping & Game	0971
Hydraulic Hose	3492
Hydraulic Pumps, Aircraft	3594
Hydraulic Turbines	3511
Hydraulic Valves	3492
Hydrochloric Acid	2819
Hydrogen	2813
I	
IV Transfusion Equipment	3841
Ice	2097
Ice Chests or Coolers, Except Insulated Foam Plastic	3429
Ice Chests or Coolers, Foam Plastics	3086
Ice Chests or Coolers, Plastics, not Insulated or Foam Plastic	3089
Ice Cream	2024
Ice Cream Stores	5451
Ice Cream, Wholesale	5143
Ice Skates	3949
Iced Tea, Bottled or Canned	2086
Ignition Apparatus	3694
Ignition Testing Equipment	3825
In Vitro & In Vivo Diagnostics	2835
Incinerator Operation	4953
Incinerators, Metal	3567
Industrial Chemicals, Wholesale	5169
Industrial Controls	3625
Industrial Machinery & Equipment, Wholesale	5084
Industrial Molds	3544
Industrial Patterns	3543
Industrial Supplies, Wholesale	5085
Ink	2893
Inner Tubes	3011
Inorganic Chemicals, NEC	2819
Insecticides	2879
Insecticides, Wholesale	5191
Inspection & Weighing Services for Motor Vehicle Transportation	4785

Description	SIC Code
Instant Coffee	2095
Instruments & Apparatus, Medical Except Electromedical	3841
Instruments, Electrical Measurement	3825
Instruments, Musical	3931
Insulated Wire & Cable, Nonferrous	3357
Insulation Asbestos	3292
Insulation Materials, Plastic Foam	3086
Insulation Siding Board	2493
Insulation Work	1742
Insulin	2834
Insurance, Accident	6321
Insurance, Casualty	6331
Insurance, Health	6321
Insurance, Life	6311
Insurance, Surety	6351
Insurance, Title	6361
Insurance Brokers, Agents	6411
Insurance Carriers, NEC	6399
Investment Counselors	6282
Investment Firm	6211
Investment Funds, Closed-End	6726
Investment Funds, Open-End	6722
Investors, NEC	6799
Iron, Pig	3312
Iron, Pig, Wholesale	5051
Iron & Steel Scrap	5093
Iron Ore Mining	1011
Iron Ore Wholesale	5052
Irons, Electric, Household	3634
Irrigation Systems	4971

J

Description	SIC Code
Jackets, Girls', Children's, Infants'	2369
Jackets, Leather	2386
Jackets, Men's & Boys' Sport	2329
Jackets, Men's & Boys' Work	2326
Jackets, Not Tailored	2339
Jacks, Hydraulic	3569
Janitorial Service	7349
Jeans, Girls, Children's, Infants'	2369
Jeans, Men's & Boys'	2325
Jeans, Women's, Misses', Juniors'	2339
Jellies, Jams, Edible	2033
Jet Engines	3724
Jewelry	3911
Jewelry Findings & Materials	3915
Jewelry Repair	7631
Jewelry Stores, Costume	5632
Jewelry Stores, Not Costume	5944
Jewelry, Wholesale	5094
Job Counseling	8331
Juices, Fruit & Vegetable	2033

K

Description	SIC Code
Kaolin, Ground Treated	3295
Kaolin Mining	1455
Karate Instruction	7999
Kennels	0752
Ketone	2869
Ketchup	2033
Keys	3429
Kilns, Cement	3559
Kilns, Except Cement	3567
Kitchen Utensils, Metal Stamped/Pressed	3469
Kitchen Woodenware	2499
Kitchenware, Cast Aluminum	3365
Kitchenware, China	3262
Kitchenware, Earthenware	3263
Kitchenware, Plastic	3089
Kitchenware Stores	5719
Knit Fabrics, Warp	2258
Knit Fabrics, Weft	2257
Knit Fabrics, Wholesale	5131
Knit Outerwear Mills	2253
Knit Underwear & Nightwear Mills	2254
Knitting Machines	3552
Knitting Mills, NEC	2259
Knitting Yarn	2281
Knitting Yarn Shops	5949
Knives, Kitchen & Table	3421
Knives, Surgical	3841
Kraft Liner Board	2631

L

Description	SIC Code
LP Gas Distribution, Retail	5984
LP Gas Production	1321
Labels, Cotton, Printed	2269
Labels, Printed	2759
Labels, Woven	2241
Laboratories, Commercial	8731
Laboratories, Medical & X-Ray	8071
Laboratories, Testing	8734
Laboratory Apparatus	3821
Lacquers	2851
Lacquers, Wholesale	5198
Ladders, Metal, Portable	3499
Ladders, Wood	2499
Laminated Cardboard	2675
Laminated Glass	3211
Laminated Plastics	3083
Lamp Light Bulbs	3641
Lamp Light Bulbs, Wholesale	5063
Lamps, Residential	3645
Landfill Sanitary	4953
Landscape Counseling & Planning	0781
Language Schools	8299
Lapidary Work	3915
Laser Diodes	3674
Laser Systems, Medical	3845
Laser Welding Equipment	3699
Launderers, Industrial	7218
Launderettes, Laundromats	7215
Laundry Equipment, Commercial	3582
Laundry Equipment, Household	3633
Laundry & Garment Services, NEC	7219
Laundry Services	7211
Law Offices	8111
Lawn & Garden Services	0782
Lawnmowers	3524
Laxatives	2834
Lead Ore Mining	1031
Lead Smelting & Refining, Primary	3339
Lead Smelting & Refining, Secondary	3341
Lead, Wholesale	5051
Leather Dyes & Stains	2865
Leather Finishing Agents	2843
Leather Goods, NEC	3199
Leather Goods, Personal Except Handbags & Purses	3172
Leather Tanning & Finishing	3111
Legal Services	8111
Lemonade	2086
Lenses, Ophthalmic	3851
Lenses, Optical	3827
Leotards, Girls', Children's & Infants'	2369
Leotards, Womens', Misses' & Juniors'	2339
Lessors of Railroad Property	6517
Lessors of Real Property, NEC	6519
Lettuce Farms	0161
Levels, Carpenters	3423
Libraries & Information Centers	8231
Licensing & Inspection of Misc. Commercial Sectors	9651
Lift Trucks	3537
Lift Trucks, Wholesale	5084
Lifts, Elevator	3534
Lighting Equipment	3648
Lighting Fixtures, Commercial	3646
Lighting Fixtures, Residential	3645
Lighting Fixtures, Vehicular	3647
Lignite Mining	1221
Limbs, Artificial	3842
Lime	3274
Lime Groves	0174
Limestone, Crushed & Broken	1422
Limestone, Wholesale	5032
Linen Fabrics	2299
Linoleum	3996
Liquor, Packaged, Retail	5921
Liquors, Distilled & Blended	2085
Liquors, Wholesale	5182
Lithium	2819
Lithographic Plates	2796
Lithographic Printing	2752
Livestock, Buying & Marketing	5154
Livestock Services, Except Veterinary	0751
Loan Agents, Brokers	6163
Loan Companies, Small	6141
Loan Institutions	6159
Locker Rental, Except Cold Storage	7299
Lockers, Not Refrigerated	2542
Lockers, Refrigerated	3585
Locomotives	3743
Lodging Houses on Membership Basis	7041
Log Cabins, Prefabricated	2452
Logging Camps & Contractors	2411
Logs, Fireplace, Electric	3699
Logs, Fireplace, Gas	3433
Looseleaf Binders	2782
Looseleaf Binders, Wholesale	5112
Lotteries	7999
Lubricating Oils & Leases	2992
Lubricating Oils & Leases, Wholesale	5172
Lubrication Equipment	3569
Lubrication Systems, Aircraft	3724
Lubrication Systems & Parts, Automotive	3714
Lubrication Systems, Locomotive	3743
Luggage	3161
Luggage, Wholesale	5099
Lumber & Building Material Dealers, Retail	5211
Lumber, Frying, Stacking, Rough	2421
Lumber, Retail	5211
Lumber, Wholesale	5031
Luncheon Meat, Except Poultry	2011
Luncheon Meat, Poultry	2015
Lye, Household	2842

M

Description	SIC Code
Machinery, Electrical Equipment & Supplies, NEC	3699
Machinery, Special Industry	3559
Machines & Equipment, General Industry, NEC	3569
Magazine Publishing & Printing	2721
Magazines, Wholesale	5192
Magnesium & Alloys Bars, Rods, Shapes	3356
Magnesium Compounds	2819
Magnetic Recording Tape, Blank	3695
Magnetic Recording Tape, Prerecorded	3625
Magnetic Recording Tape, Wholesale	5065
Magnetic Storage Devices, Computer	3572
Magnets, Permanent, Ceramic or Ferrite	3264
Magnets, Permanent, Metal	3499
Mail Advertising Services	7331
Mail Order Houses	5961
Mailgram Services	4822
Mainframe Computers	3571
Malt, Barley, Rye, Wheat, etc.	2083
Malt, Wholesale	5149
Management Consulting Services	8742
Manifold Business Forms	2761
Manifold Business Forms, Wholesale	5112
Manila Folders	2675
Manufacturing Industries, NEC	3999

Description	SIC Code
Maps, Publishing & Printing	2741
Margarine	2079
Margarine, Wholesale	5149
Marinas	4493
Marine Cargo Handling	4491
Marine Engines	3519
Marine Paints	2851
Marine Products Production, Misc.	0919
Marketing Consultants	8742
Marking Devices	3953
Marshmallows	2064
Masking Tape	2672
Masonry, Stone Work	1741
Matches & Match Books	3999
Matches, Wholesale	5199
Materials Handling Equipment	3537
Materials Handling Equipment, Wholesale	5084
Mattresses, Innerspring, Box Spring, etc.	2515
Mattresses, Wholesale	5021
Mayonnaise	2035
Meat Markets	5421
Meat & Meat Products, Wholesale	5147
Meat Packing Plants	2011
Meat Products, Cooked, Cured	2013
Meat Products, Prepared	2013
Mechanical Power Transmission Equipment, NEC	3568
Medical Equipment, Renting, Leasing	7352
Medical Services Plans	6324
Medicinal Chemicals	2833
Melon Farms	0161
Membership Organizations, Professional	8621
Mental Hospitals	8063
Merchandising Stores, Misc. General	5399
Mercury Compounds, Medical	2833
Mercury Ore Mining	1099
Mercury Oxides, Inorganic	2819
Metal, Structural, Fabricated	3441
Metal Buildings	3448
Metal Buildings, Wholesale	5039
Metal Fasteners	3429
Metal Foil & Leaf	3497
Metal Heat Treating	3398
Metal Mining Services	1081
Metal Products, Primary, NEC	3399
Metal Stampings	3469
Metal Waste & Scrap, Wholesale	5093
Metal Work, Architectural & Ornamental	3446
Metal Work, Structural, NEC	3449
Metals Service Centers & Offices	5051
Metalworking Machinery, NEC	3549
Metalworking Tools & Machinery	3545
Metalworking Tools & Machinery, Wholesale	5084
Meters, Electric	3825
Meters, Gas, Liquid	3824
Methanol, Natural	2861
Methanol, Synthetic	2869
Methyl Alcohol	2861
Methyl Chloride	2869
Mexican Foods, Canned	2032
Mica Mining	1499
Mica Products	3299
Microcircuits Integrated	3674
Microcomputers	3571
Microfiche Readers	3861
Microscopes, Electron & Proton	3826
Microscopes, Except Electron & Proton	3827
Microwave Communication Equipment	3663
Microwave Components	3679
Microwave Ovens, Household	3631
Microwave Ovens Wholesale	5064
Milk, Bottled	2026
Milk, Concentrated & Condensed, Dried, Evaporated	2023
Milking Machines	3523
Mills, Hardwood Dimension & Flooring	2426
Millwork Products	2431
Millwork, Wholesale	5031
Mineral Products, Nonmetallic, NEC	3299
Mineral Water	2086
Minerals & Earths, Ground or Otherwise Treated	3295
Minerals, Nonmetallic, Except Fuels, Misc., NEC	1499
Minerals, Nonmetallic, Except Fuels, Services	1481
Mining, Chemical & Fertilizer Mineral, NEC	1479
Mining, Gold Ores	1041
Mining Machinery & Equipment	3532
Mining Machinery & Equipment, Wholesale	5082
Mirrors	3231
Mirrors, Optical	3827
Missile Guidance Systems	3812
Missile Warheads	3483
Mixers, Concrete	3531
Mixers, Electric, Food	3556
Mobile Communications Equipment	3663
Mobile Homes, Except Recreational	2451
Mobile Homes, Recreational	3792
Mobile Homes, Retail	5271
Mobile Homes, Wholesale	5039
Modems	3661
Modems, Wholesale	5065
Moldings & Trim, Stamped, Metal Automotive	3465
Moldings & Trim, Stamped, Metal, Except Automotive	3442
Moldings, Plastic	3089
Moldings, Wood	2431
Monorail Systems	3536
Mortgage Brokers & Companies	6162
Mortgage Guarantee Insurance	6351
Morticians	7261
Motels	7011
Motion Picture Distribution	7822
Motion Picture Equipment	3861
Motion Picture Equipment, Wholesale	5043
Motion Picture Distribution, Services Allied	7829
Motion Picture Production, Services Allied	7819
Motion Picture Production & Distribution	7812
Motor Homes, Self-Contained	3711
Motor Vehicle Dealers, Used	5521
Motor Vehicle Distribution, Wholesale	5012
Motor Vehicle Parts	3714
Motor Vehicle Parts, Used Wholesale & Retail	5015
Motor Vehicle Supplies & New Parts, Wholesale	5013
Motorcycle Dealers	5571
Motorcycles & Parts	3751
Motorcycles & Parts, Wholesale	5012
Mufflers, Exhaust, Motor Vehicle	3714
Mufflers, Installation, Repair	7533
Museums & Art Galleries	8412
Music Sheet, Publishing	2741
Music Video Production	7812
Musical Instrument Stores	5736
Musical Instruments & Accessories	3931
Musical Instruments & Accessories, Wholesale	5099
Mutual Funds	6722
Mutual Funds, Agents	6211

N

Description	SIC Code
Nails	3315
Nails, Wholesale	5051
Napkins, Fabric	2392
Napkins, Paper & Sanitary	2676
Natural Gas, Liquid Production	1321
Natural Gas, Production	1311
Natural Gas Storage & Transmission	4922
Navigation Systems & Instruments	3812
Neckwear, Men's & Boys'	2323
Needles, Hand, Machine	3965
Needles, Hypodermic, Suture	3841
Needlework	2395
Needlework Stores	5949
Neon	2813
Neon Signs	3993
Neon Signs, Wholesale	5046
News Dealers & Newsstands	5994
News Ticker Services	7383
Newspaper Publishing	2711
Newspapers, Wholesale	5192
Newsprint	2621
Nickel & Alloy Products	3356
Nickel Ore Mining	1061
Nickel Refining, Primary	3339
Nitric Acid	2873
Nitrogen	2813
Nonclassifiable Establishments	9999
Nondurable Goods, Wholesale	5199
Nuclear Reactors	3443
Nursery Schools	8351
Nursery Stock, Production	0181
Nursery Stock, Retail	5261
Nursery Stock, Wholesale	5193
Nursing Homes, Intermediate Care	8052
Nursing Homes, Skilled Care	8051
Nuts, Candy Covered	2064
Nuts, Dehydrated, Dried, Salted, Roasted	2068
Nuts, Metal	3452
Nuts, Plastic	3089
Nylon Fabrics, Resins	2221
Nylon Fibers, Bristles, Threads	2824
Nylon Yarn, Spinning	2281
Nylon Yarn, Throwing	2282

O

Description	SIC Code
Oats, Oatmeal	2043
Oats, Wholesale	5153
Off-Highway Machinery	3536
Office Equipment, Wholesale	5049
Office Supplies, Wholesale	5112
Offset Printing	2752
Oil & Gas Field Exploration Services	1382
Oil & Gas Field Machinery & Equipment	3533
Oil & Gas Field Services, NEC	1389
Oil Royalty Traders	6792
Oil, Corn	2046
Oil, Cottonseed	2074
Oil Refining Machinery, Equipment, Wholesale	5084
Oil, Vegetable, Except Corn Oil	2079
Oils, Lubricating	2911
Oils, Sulfonated	2843
Oleo	2079
On-Line Database Information Retrieval	7375
Operators of Apartment Buildings	6513
Operators of Nonresidential Buildings	6512
Ophthalmic Goods	3851
Ophthalmic Goods, Wholesale	5048
Ophthalmic Instruments & Apparatus	3841
Optical Goods, Retail	5995
Optical Lens Machinery	3559
Optical Readers & Scanners	3577
Optical Test & Inspection Equipment	3827
Optometrists, Offices & Clinics	8042
Ordnance & Accessories, NEC	3489
Ore Crushing Machinery	3532
Organic Chemicals	2869
Organic Fibers	2824
Organic Pigments	2865
Ornamental Shrub & Tree Services	0783
Outboard Motors, Electric	3699

Description	*SIC Code*
Outboard Motors, Except Electric	3519
Outboard Motors, Wholesale	5091
Oxygen, Compressed & Liquefied	2813
P	
Pacemakers	3845
Packaging Machinery	3565
Packing & Scaling Devices	3053
Padlocks	3429
Painting & Paper Hanging	1721
Paints	2851
Paints, Wholesale	5198
Pallets, Wooden	2653
Paper, Coated & Laminated, NEC	2672
Paper, Industrial & Personal Service, Wholesale	5113
Paper, Printing & Writing, Wholesale	5111
Paper & Paperboard, Die-cut	2675
Paper & Paperboard Products, Converted, NEC	2679
Paper Mills	2621
Paperboard Mills	2631
Parcel Delivery, Air	4513
Parcel Delivery, Except Air	4215
Parking Lots	7521
Parquet Flooring, Wood	2426
Particleboard	2493
Particleboard, Wholesale	5031
Partitians, Wood	2541
Pasta, Dry	2098
Patent Owners & Lessors	6794
Payroll Accounting Service	8721
Peanut Butter	2099
Pencils, Mechanical	3951
Pencils, Not Mechanical	3952
Pencils & Pens Wholesale	5112
Pens & Pen Parts	3951
Pension, Health & Welfare Funds	6371
Percale	2211
Perfumes	2844
Perfumes, Wholesale	5122
Periodicals, Publishing & Printing	2721
Periodicals, Wholesale	5192
Peripheral Equipment	3577
Peripheral Equipment, Wholesale	5045
Personal Services, NEC	7299
Pesticides	2879
Pesticides, Wholesale	5191
Pet Food, Dog & Cat	2047
Pet Food, Except Dog & Cat	2048
Pet Food Stores	5999
Pet Food, Wholesale	5149
Petroleum Brokers	5172
Petroleum Bulk Stations & Terminals, Wholesale	5171
Petroleum Gas Products &/or Distribution, Mixed or Liquified	4925
Petroleum Products, NEC	2999
Petroleum Refining	2911
Pharmaceuticals	2834
Pharmaceuticals, Wholesale	5122
Phonographs	3651
Phonographs, Wholesale	5046
Phosphate Rock	1475
Phosphates	2874
Phosphoric Acid	2874
Photocopy Machine	3861
Photocopy Machines, Wholesale	5044
Photocopy Service	7334
Photofinishing Laboratories	7384
Photographers & Photographic Studios	7221
Photographic Equipments & Supplies, Wholesale	5043
Physical Fitness Centers	7991
Pianos	3931
Pickles & Relishes	2035
Pigments, Inorganic	2816
Pigments, Organic	2865
Pins	3965
Pipe, Non-Ferrous	3356
Pipe, Sewer, Clay	3259
Pipe, Stainless Steel	3317
Pipe Lines, NEC	4619
Pipeline Construction	1623
Pizza, Frozen	2038
Pizzerias	5812
Plastering	1742
Plastic Coating of Metals	3479
Plastics, Bottle	3085
Plastics, Film, Coated, Laminated for Packaging	2671
Plastics, Film & Sheet Unsupported	3081
Plastics, Foam	3086
Plastics, Laminated, Except Packaging	3083
Plastics Materials, Wholesale	5162
Plastics, Pipe	3084
Plastics, Plumbing Fixtures	3088
Plastics Products, NEC	3089
Plastics, Resins	2821
Plastics, Resins Wholesale	5162
Plate Glass	3211
Plate Glass, Wholesale	5039
Platinum Ore Mining	1099
Plumbing Contractors	1711
Plumbing Fixture Fittings & Trim	3432
Plumbing Fixtures, Vitreous China	3261
Plywood, Hardwood	2435
Plywood, Softwood	2436
Plywood, Wholesale	5031
Pneumatic Valves	3492
Polishes	2842
Polishes, Wholesale	5169
Polyester, Polypropylene, Polyvinyl Fabrics	2221
Polyester, Polypropylene, Polyvinyl Resins	2821
Polyester, Polypropylene, Polyvinyl Yarn	2281
Polyester Fibers, Threads	2284
Popcorn Farms	0119
Popcorn, Packaged, Except Popped	2099
Popcorn, Popped	2096
Popcorn, Wholesale	5145
Porcelain Cement, Household	2891
Porcelain Parts for Electrical & Electronic Use	3264
Portland Cement	3241
Potash Mining	1474
Potassium Chloride, Chlorate	2819
Potato Farms	0134
Potatoes, Fresh, Wholesale	5148
Pottery Products	3269
Poultry Feeds & Supplements	2048
Poultry, Processed	2015
Poultry Production	0259
Poultry Products, Wholesale	5144
Pre-Mixed Concrete, Wholesale	5032
Precious Metals & Stones, Wholesale	5094
Prefabricated Buildings, Metal	3448
Prefabricated Buildings, Wholesale	5039
Prefabricated Buildings, Wood	2452
Preschool Centers	8351
Presses, Hydraulic & Pneumatic	3542
Pressure Control Valves	3492
Pressure Gauges	3823
Pressure Sensitive Tape	2672
Pressure Sensitive Tape Wholesale	5113
Printed Circuit Boards	3672
Printing, Commercial, NEC	2759
Printers, Computer	3577
Printing, Lithographic & Off-Set	2752
Printing Gravure	2754
Printing Ink	2893
Printing Presses	3555
Printing Trade Machinery & Equipment, Wholesale	5084
Propane Production	1321
Protective Service, Guard	7381
Psychiatric Hospitals	8063
Public Finance, Taxation & Monetary Policy	9311
Public Relations Services	8743
Publishing, Book	2731
Publishing, Directory	2741
Publishing & Printing, Magazines	2721
Pulp Mills	2611
Pumps	3561
Pumps, Measuring & Dispensing	3586
R	
Racing, Including Track Operation	7948
Radar Systems	3812
Radio Stations	4832
Radioactive Waste, Disposal of	4953
Radios	3651
Railroad Cars & Locomotives, Equipment	3743
Railroad Equipment & Supplies, Wholesale	5088
Railroad Switching & Terminal Establishments	4013
Railroads, Commuter, Suburban	4111
Railroads, Line-Haul	4011
Rain Coats & Waterproof Outwear	2385
Ramie Fabrics	2299
Razor Blades	3421
Razors, Non-Electric	3421
Ready-Mix Concrete	3273
Real Estate Agents	6531
Real Estate Development	6552
Real Estate Investment Trusts	6798
Record & Prerecorded Tape Stores	5735
Records, Phonograph	3652
Rectifiers, Electronic Wholesale	5065
Rectifiers, Except Solid-State	3679
Rectifiers, Solid-State	3674
Refined Petroleum Pipe Lines	4613
Refineries, Petroleum	2911
Refractories, Clay	3255
Refractories, Non-Clay	3297
Refractory Material, Wholesale	5085
Refrigerated Warehouses	4222
Refrigeration Controls	3822
Refrigeration Machinery	3585
Refrigerators, Commercial, Wholesale	5078
Refrigerators, Household	3632
Refrigerators, Household, Wholesale	5064
Refuse Systems	4953
Regulation & Administration of Communication, Electric, Gas & Other Utilities	9631
Regulation of Agricultural Marketing & Commodities	9641
Relays	3625
Relays, Wholesale	5063
Rental of Automobiles	7514
Rental of Computers	7377
Rental of Equipment	7359
Rental of Motion Picture Films	7819
Rental of Railroad Cars	4741
Repair of Equipment	7699
Repair Shops, Air Conditioning	7623
Repair Shops, Automobile, NEC	7539
Repair Shops, Automotive Exhaust System	7533
Repair Shops, Automotive Transmission	7537
Repair Shops, Electrical & Electronic, NEC	7631
Repair Shops, Radio & Television	7622
Repair Shops, Refrigeration	7623
Research, Commercial Economic, Sociological & Educational	8732
Research & Development	8731

Description	SIC Code
Research Organizations, Noncommercial	8733
Residential Care	8361
Resins	2821
Resins, Custom Compounding of Purchased Plastic	3087
Resistors, Electronic	3676
Resistors, Electronic, Wholesale	5065
Restaurants	5812
Retail Stores, Misc., NEC	5999
Ribbons, Inked	3955
Ribbons, Inked, Wholesale	5112
Rice Cleaning & Polishing	2044
Rice Production	0112
Rifles	3484
Rivets, Metal	3452
Road Construction	1611
Robes & Dressing Gowns	2384
Robots	3569
Rockets, Guided Missiles	3761
Rockets, Pyrotechnic	2899
Rolling Mill Machinery	3547
Rolling Mills	3212
Roofing Contractor, Siding, Sheet Metal Work	1761
Roofing Fabrics	2952
Roofing, Siding & Installation Materials, Wholesale	5033
Rooming & Boarding Houses	7021
Rotogravure Printing	2754
Rubber & Plastic Hose	3052
Rubber Goods, Molded, Extruded	3061
Rubber Goods, NEC	3069
Rubber, Synthetic	2822
Rugs	2273
Rugs, Wholesale	5023
Rust Removers	2842

S

Description	SIC Code
Saccharin	2869
Saddles & Parts	3199
Saddles, Motorcycle, Bicycle	3751
Safes & Vaults	3499
Safes & Vaults, Wholesale	5044
Safety Glass	3231
Safety Gloves	3842
Safety Pins	3965
Sailboats	3732
Sailboats, Wholesale	5091
Salad Dressings, Dry Mixes	2099
Salad Dressings, Except Dry Mixes	2035
Salad Oils	2079
Salads, Fresh	2099
Salmon, Smoked, etc.	2091
Salt	2899
Salt Mining	1479
Salt, Wholesale	5149
Sand, Industrial	1446
Sand & Gravel Dealers	5211
Sandpaper	3291
Sanitary Napkins	2676
Sanitary Services, NEC	4959
Sanitary Paper Food Containers	2656
Satellite Home Antennas	3679
Satellites, Communications	3663
Sauces, Tomato-Based	2033
Sauces, Vegetable Meat	2035
Sauces, Wholesale	5149
Sausages	2013
Savings & Loan, Federal	6035
Savings & Loan, State	6036
Saw Blades	3425
Saw Blades, Wholesale	5072
Sawmills	2421
Sawmills, Special Product, NEC	2429
Saws, Hand	3425
Saws, Power, Metal Cutting	3541
Saws, Power Woodworking	3553
Scaffolds, Metal	3446
Scaffolds, Wholesale	5082
Scaffolds, Wood	2499
Scales, Except Laboratory	3596
Scales, Except Laboratory, Wholesale	5046
Scales, Laboratory	3821
Schiffli Machine Embroideries	2397
School Buses	4151
School Photographers	7221
Schools & Camps, Sports	7999
Schools & Educational Services, NEC	8299
Schools for Handicapped	8211
Schools, Business & Secretarial	8244
Schools, Colleges, Universities & Professional	8221
Schools, Correspondence	8249
Schools, Dance	7911
Schools, Data Processing	8243
Schools, Elementary & Secondary	8211
Schools, Junior Colleges & Technical Institutes	8222
Schools, Riding	7999
Schools, Vocational & Correspondence	8249
Scissors, Electric	3634
Scissors, Hand	3421
Scotch Whiskey	2085
Scrap & Waste Materials, Wholesale	5093
Screening, Window, Plastic	3089
Screening, Window, Wire	3496
Screens, Door & Window, Metal Frame	3442
Screw Drivers	3423
Screw Machine Products	3451
Screws, Metal	3452
Seafood Products, Canned & Cured	2091
Seafood Products, Fresh & Frozen	2092
Sealants, Wholesale	5169
Sealing Compounds	2891
Search Systems & Instruments	3812
Seasonings	2035
Seatbelts, Automotive & Aircraft	2399
Seatbelts, Automotive, Wholesale	5013
Seats, Automobile, Aircraft	2531
Security Dealers, Brokers	6211
Security Systems Services	7382
Semiconductor Devices	3674
Semiconductor Devices, Wholesale	5065
Service Establishment Equipment & Supplies, Except Motor Vehicle, Wholesale	5087
Service Stations, Gasoline	5541
Services, NEC	8999
Services Allied With Exchange of Securities or Commodities, NEC	6289
Servomotors	3621
Sewage Systems	4959
Sewing Machines, Household	3639
Sewing Machines, Household, Wholesale	5064
Sewing Machines, Industrial	3559
Sewing Machines, Industrial, Wholesale	5084
Sewing Thread	2284
Shampoos, Hair	2844
Sheet Metal Work	3444
Shellfish	0913
Shelving, Not Wood	2542
Shelving, Wholesale	5046
Shelving, Wood	2541
Shingles, Asphalt, Tar	2952
Shingles, Wood	2429
Ship Building & Repairing	3731
Shirts, Men's & Boys', Except Work Shirts	2321
Shirts, Women's, Misses' & Juniors'	2337
Shoe Stores	5661
Shoes, Children's & Infants'	3149
Shoes, Men's	3143
Shoes, Wholesale	5139
Shoes, Women's	3144
Siding, Plastic	3089
Siding, Sheet Metal	3444
Signs & Advertising Displays	3993
Silver Mining	1044
Ski Wear	2329
Skids, Wooden	2448
Skis & Skiing Equipment	3949
Simulators, Training	3699
Slacks, Girls' & Children's	2369
Slacks, Men's & Boys'	2325
Slacks, Women's, Misses' & Juniors'	2339
Slippers, House	3142
Slot Machines	3999
Smoke Detectors	3669
Soaps & Cleaners	2841
Soft Drinks, Bottled or Canned	2086
Soft Drinks, Wholesale	5149
Software, Prepackaged	7372
Software, Systems Analysis, Custom	7371
Software, Wholesale	5045
Soil Preparation Services	0711
Solar Cells	3674
Solar Energy Collectors, Heaters	3433
Soldering Guns & Tools, Hand, Electric	3423
Solenoid Switches	3625
Solenoid Valves	3492
Solvents, Degreasing	2842
Solvents, Organic	2869
Sonar Systems	3812
Sound Recording Equipment	3861
Soup Mixes	2034
Soups, Canned, Except Fish & Seafood	2032
Soups, Canned, Fish & Seafood	2091
Soups, Frozen, Except Seafood	2038
Soups, Frozen, Fish & Seafood	2092
Sour Cream	2026
Soy Sauce	2035
Soybean Oil Mills	2075
Soybean Production	0116
Soybeans, Wholesale	5153
Space Capsules	3769
Space Vehicle Propulsion Units & Propulsion Unit Parts	3764
Space Vehicles	3761
Spaghetti Sauce	2033
Spaghetti, Dry	2098
Spectrometers	3829
Speed Changers, Industrial High Speed Drives	3566
Spices	2099
Spices, Wholesale	5149
Sponge Gathering	0919
Sporting Goods	3949
Sporting Goods, Retail	5941
Sporting & Recreational Goods & Supplies, Wholesale	5091
Sports Clubs & Promoters, Professional	7941
Sports & Recreation Clubs, Membership	7997
Stainless Steel	3312
Stamp Pads, Stamping Devices	3953
Staples, Steel	3315
Staples, Wire	3496
State Banks	6022
Stationery	2678
Stationery Stores	5943
Steam & Air-Conditioning Supply	4961
Steam Fittings	3494
Steam Fittings, Wholesale	5074
Steam Turbines	3511
Steel Bars, Sheet, Strip	3316
Steel Foundries	3312
Steel, Wholesale	5051

Description	*SIC Code*
Sterilizers, Dental	3843
Sterilizers, Laboratory	3821
Sterilizers, Medical	3842
Stevedoring	4491
Stitching & Tucking, Pleating, Decorative & Novelty	2395
Stone, Crushed & Broken, NEC	1429
Stone Quarrying	3281
Storage Batteries	3691
Stoves, Commercial	3589
Stoves, Household, Cooking	3631
Stoves, Household Heating	3433
Strip Mining, Anthracite	1231
Strip Mining, Bituminous	1221
Structural Steel Erection	1791
Sugar, Granulated, Beet	2063
Sugar, Granulated, Cane	2061
Sugar, Wholesale	5149
Sugar Beet Production	0133
Sugar Cane Production	0133
Suitcases	3161
Suits & Overcoats, Men's & Boys'	2311
Sulfuric Acid	2819
Sunflower Farms	0119
Sunflower Seed Oil	2076
Sunglasses	3851
Supermarkets	5411
Surface Active Agents	2843
Surfboards	3949
Surgical Equipment, Wholesale	5047
Surgical Instruments	3841
Surveying Instruments	3829
Surveying Services	8713
Sweeteners, Synthetic	2869
Switchboard Apparatus	3613
Switches, Electric	3643
Switches, Electronic	3679
Switchgear	3613
Switchgear, Wholesale	5063
Synthesizers, Music	3931
Synthetic Fibers	2284
Systems Analysis & Design	7371
Systems Engineering	8748

T

Description	*SIC Code*
Tablets, Writing	2678
Tanks & Tank Components	3795
Tape, Audio Magnetic, Prerecorded	3652
Tape, Magnetic, Blank	3695
Tape, Masking	2672
Tape, Pressure Sensitive	2672
Tape, Pressure Sensitive, Wholesale	5113
Tape Distribution for Television	7822
Tape Recorders	3651
Tape Storage Units, Computer	3572
Tapes, Audio & Video Recording, Wholesale	5065
Tax Return Preparation	7291
Tea, Wholesale	5149
Tea Blending	2099
Telegraph Services	4822
Telephone Answering Machines	3661
Telephone Communication, Except Radio	4813
Telephone Equipment, Wholesale	5065
Telephones	3661
Telephones, Cellular, Radio	3663
Television Sets	3651
Television Stations	4833
Temperature Controls, Automatic	3822
Terminals, Computer	3575
Textile Goods, NEC	2299
Textile Machinery	3552
Textile Mills, Broadwoven	2211
Textile Mills, Narrow Woven	2241
Textile Products, Fabricated, NEC	2399
Textiles, Wholesale	5131
Theaters, Movie, Drive-In	7833
Theaters, Moving Picture	7832
Theatrical Producers & Services, Except Motion Picture	7922
Theme Parks	7996
Thermostats	3822
Tile, Acoustical	3296
Tile, Asphalt	3292
Tile, Ceramic & Clay	3253
Tile, Concrete	3272
Tile, Gypsum	3275
Tile, Terrazzo, Marble, Mosaic Contractors	1743
Tile, Vinyl Asbestos	3292
Timber Tracts	0811
Timeclocks, Time-stamps	3579
Timing Devices	3625
Tin Cans	3411
Tin Compounds	2819
Tin Ore Mining	1099
Tin Smelting & Refining	3341
Tire Retreading & Repair Shop	7534
Tires & Tubes, Wholesale	5014
Tires, Cushion or Solid Rubber	3011
Title Insurance	6361
Title Search Companies	6541
Tobacco Production	0132
Tobacco Stemming & Redrying	2141
Tobacco Stores & Stands	5993
Toilet Fixtures, Iron	3431
Toilet Fixtures, Plastics	3088
Toilet Fixtures, Vitreous China	3261
Toilet Tissue	2621
Toiletries	2844
Toiletries, Wholesale	5122
Tool Rental	7359
Tools, Cutting, NEC	3545
Tools, Drilling, Oil Wells, etc.	3533
Tools, Hand, Except Power Driven	3423
Tools, Hand, Power Driven	3546
Tools, Machine, Metal Cutting	3541
Tools, Machine, Metal Forming	3542
Tools, Power Driven & Hand, Wholesale	5251
Tour Operators	4725
Towing & Tugboat Services	4492
Toy Stores	5945
Toys, Except Dolls	3944
Toys, Dolls	3942
Toys, Stuffed	3942
Toys & Hobby Goods & Supplies, Wholesale	5092
Tractors, Industrial	3537
Tractors, Lawn & Garden	3524
Trading Companies	6799
Trailer & Recreational Vehicle Utility Rental	7519
Trailers, Boat	3799
Trailers, Farm	3523
Trailers, Industrial	3537
Trailers, Mobile Home, Recreational	3792
Trailers, Travel, Camping	3792
Trains, Toy, & Equipment	3944
Transformers, Electric	3612
Transformers, Electric, Wholesale	5063
Transformers, Electronic	3677
Transformers, Electronic, Wholesale	5065
Transistors	3674
Transistors, Wholesale	5065
Translation Service	7389
Transmission Equipment, Motor Vehicle	3714
Transportation, Air, Nonscheduled	4522
Transportation, Air, Services, NEC	4512
Transportation, Arrangement of Freight & Cargo	4731
Transportation, Arrangement of Passenger	4729
Transportation, Deep Sea Freight, Domestic	4424
Transportation, Equipment & Supplies, Except Motor Vehicle, Wholesale	5088
Transportation, Great Lakes Freight	4432
Transportation, Intercity & Rural Bus	4131
Transportation, Local Passenger, NEC	4119
Transportation Equipment, NEC	3799
Transportation Services, NEC	4789
Travel Agencies	4724
Trophies, Metal	3499
Trophies, Silver, Nickel Silver, Pewter, Plated	3914
Trophies, Wholesale	5094
Trousers, Men's & Boys'	2325
Truck Beds & Bodies	3713
Truck Leasing	7513
Truck Trailers	3715
Truck Trailers, Wholesale	5012
Trucking, Except Local	4213
Trucking, Local	4212
Trucking, Local, with Storage	4214
Trucks, Off-Highway	3531
Trucks, Wholesale	5012
Trust Facilities, Nondeposit	6091
Trusts, Personal Investment, Management	6733
Tubes, Aluminum	3353
Tubes, Plastics	3082
Tubes, Seamless Steel	3317
Tubing, Glass	3229
Tubing, Metal	3317
Tubing, Metal, Wholesale	5051
Tuna Fish, Canned	2091
Tunnel Construction	1622
Turbine Generator Sets	3511
Turbines, Aircraft	3724
Turkeys, Processed	2015
Turkeys & Turkey Egg Products	0251
Turnstiles	3829
Turtles, Catching of	0919
Typesetting	2791
Typewriter Ribbons	3955
Typewriters	3579
Typewriters, Wholesale	5044

U

Description	*SIC Code*
Underwear, Men's & Boys'	2322
Ultraviolet Lamps	3641
Ultraviolet Sensors	3674
Umbrellas	3999
Underwear, Men's and Boys'	2322
Underwear, Men's and Boys', Wholesale	5136
Underwear, Women's, Misses', Children's, Infants'	2341
Underwear, Women's, Misses', Children's, Infants', Wholesale	5137
Uniform Supply Service	7213
Uranium Ore Mining	1094

V

Description	*SIC Code*
Vacuum Bottles	3429
Vacuum Brakes, Motor Vehicle	3714
Vacuum Brakes, Railway	3743
Vacuum Cleaner Hose	3052
Vacuum Cleaners, Electric, Household	3635
Vacuum Cleaners, Electric, Household, Wholesale	5064
Vacuum Cleaners, Electric, Industrial & Commercial	3589
Vacuum Cleaning Systems, Wholesale	5087
Vacuum Pumps, Except Laboratory	3563
Vacuum Pumps, Laboratory	3821
Vacuum Tubes	3671
Vacuum Tunnels	3443
Valves, Air Ventilating	3491
Valves, Automatic Control, Fluid Power	3492
Valves, Hard Rubber	3069
Valves, Hydraulic & Pneumatic	3492
Valves, PCV	3714

Description	*SIC Code*
Valves, Plumbing & Heating	3494
Valves, Plumbing & Heating Wholesale	5074
Van Conversions	7532
Vanadium Ore Mining	1094
Vaporizers, Electric, Household	3634
Variety Stores	5331
Varnish Removers & Stains	2851
Varnishes	2851
Varnishes, Wholesale	5198
Veal	2011
Vegetable Farms	0161
Vegetable Juices	2033
Vegetable Oil Mills, Except Corn, Cottonseed & Soybean	2070
Vegetable Oils	2899
Vegetables, Canned	2033
Vegetables, Frozen	2037
Vegetables, Wholesale	5148
Vending Machines, Coin Operated	3581
Vending Machines, Rental	7359
Vending Machines, Wholesale	5046
Veneer, Hardwood Including Plywood	2435
Veneer, Softwood, Not Including Plywood	2436
Venetian Blinds	2591
Ventilating Fans, Electric, Household	3634
Veterinary Pharmaceutical Preparations	2834
Video Cameras	3651
Video Cassette Recorders, Players	3651
Video Game Machines	3944
Video Remote Control Devices	3651
Video Tape Production	7812
Video Tape Rental	7841
Vinegar	2099
Vineyards	0172
Vinyl Acetate	2869
Vinyl Asbestos Tile	3292
Vinyl Coated Fabrics	2295
Vinyl Fibers	2824
Vinyl Resins	2821
Vinyl Sheet & Film	3081
Vitamin Preparation	2834
Vitamins, Natural	2833
Vitamins, Wholesale	5122
Vocational Schools	8249
Voltage Regulators, Motor Vehicle	3694
Voltage Regulators, Transmission, Transformers	3612
Voltmeters	3825

W

Description	*SIC Code*
Wallboard, Gypsum	3275
Wallboard, Wholesale	5031
Wallboard, Wood Fiber	2493
Wallpaper	2679
Wallpaper, Wholesale	5198
Warehousing, Cold Storage	4222
Warehousing, General	4225
Warehousing & Storage, Special, NEC	4226
Warm Air Heating Equipment & Supplies, Wholesale	5075
Washers, Metal	3452
Washers, Plastics	3089
Washing Machines, Household, Electric	3633
Washing Machines, Household, Electric, Wholesale	5064
Waste Treatment Plants	4953
Wastepaper, Recycling, Wholesale	5093
Watch Crystals	3231
Watch Jewels	3915
Watches & Parts	3873
Watches & Parts, Wholesale	5094
Water Coolers, Electric	3585
Water Filters & Softeners	3589
Water Heaters, Electric, Wholesale	5064
Water Heaters, Except Electric, Wholesale	5074
Water Heaters, Household	3639
Water Purification & Softening Equipment, Household	3589
Water Quality Controls	3823
Water, Sewer Construction	1623
Water Softening Service	7389
Water Supply	4941
Water Transportation, Passenger, NEC	4489
Water Transporation Services, NEC	4499
Water Well Drilling	1781
Welding & Cutting Tools	3548
Welding & Cutting Tools, Wholesale	5084
Welding Repair	7692
Well Drilling, Oil Gas	1381
Well Drilling, Water	1781
Well Servicing Oil & Gas	1389
Wet Corn Milling	2041
Wet Corn Milling Products	5149
Wheat Production	0111
Wheat Products	2041
Wheat, Wholesale	5153
Wheel Balancing Equipment	3559
Wheel Chairs	3842
Wheelbarrows	3799
Wheels, Abrasive	3843
Wheels, Aircraft	3728
Wheels, Grinding, Abrasive	3291
Wheels, Motor Vehicle	3714
Wheels, Stamped Metal	3499
Whiskey, Scotch Whiskey	2085
Wicker Furniture	2519
Wigs	3999
Wigs, Wholesale	5199
Wind Tunnels	3443
Window Frames & Sash, Metal	3442
Window Frames & Sash, Wood	3431
Window Units	2431
Window Glass	3211
Window Glass, Wholesale	5039
Window Screens, Metal Frame	3442
Window Screens, Wood Frame	2331
Window Shades	2591
Windows & Doors, Wholesale	5031
Wines	2084
Wines, Wholesale	5182
Wire, Nonferrous	3357
Wire, Steel	3315
Wood Alcohol	2861
Wood Chips	2421
Wood Chips, Wholesale	5099
Wood Kitchen Cabinets	2434
Wood Members, Structural, NEC	2439
Wood Panels, Wholesale	5031
Wood Preserving	2491
Wood Production	0214
Wood Products	0214
Wood Products, Reconstituted	2493
Wood Stains	2851
Wooden Pallets	2448
Woodworking Machinery, Wholesale	5084
Woodworking Machines	3553
Wool Fabrics, Broad Woven	2231
Wool Fabrics, Narrow Woven	2241
Wool, Mineral	3296
Wool, Raw, Wholesale	5159
Wool Yarn	2282
Work Clothing, Men's & Boys'	2326
Wrecker Service	7549
Wrecking of Buildings	1795
Wrenches	3423

X

Description	*SIC Code*
X-Ray Apparatus	3844
X-Ray Film	3861
X-Ray Machines & Parts, Wholesale	5047

Y

Description	*SIC Code*
Yard Goods, Stores	5949
Yard Goods, Wholesale	5131
Yarn, Spun	2281
Yarns, Wholesale	5199
Yeast	2099
Yeast, Wholesale	5149
Yogurt	2026
Yogurt, Frozen	2024
Yogurt, Wholesale	5143

Z

Description	*SIC Code*
Zinc Ore, Wholesale	5052
Zinc Ore Mining	1031
Zinc Pigments	2816
Zinc, Rolling, Drawing, Extruding	3341
Zippers	3965
Zippers, Wholesale	5131
Zirconium Bars, Strips, etc.	3356
Zirconium Ore Mining	1099

NUMERICAL COMPENDIUM OF S.I.C. CODES

*** NEC Denotes a Business or Service Not Elsewhere Classified**

Code	Title
01	**AGRICULTURAL PRODUCTION-CROPS**
0111	Wheat Production
0112	Rice Production
0115	Corn Production
0116	Soybean Production
0119	Cash Grains, NEC
0131	Cotton & Cottonseed Production
0132	Tobacco Production
0133	Sugarcane & Sugar Beet Production
0134	Irish Potato Production
0139	Field Crops, Except Cash Grains, NEC
0161	Vegetable & Melon Production
0171	Berry Farms
0172	Production of Grapes
0173	Production of Tree Nuts
0174	Citrus Fruits Production
0175	Deciduous Tree Fruits Production
0179	Production of Fruits & Tree Nuts, NEC
0181	Ornamental Floraculture & Nursery Products Production
0182	Food Crops Grown Under Cover
0191	General Farms, Primarily Crop
02	**AGRICULTURAL PRODUCTION-LIVESTOCK**
0211	Beef Cattle Feedlots
0212	Beef Cattle, Except Feedlots
0213	Hog Production
0214	Sheep & Goats Production
0219	General Livestock, Except Dairy & Poultry
0241	Dairy Farms
0251	Broiler, Fryer & Roaster Chickens
0252	Chicken Eggs Production
0253	Turkeys & Turkey Eggs Production
0254	Poultry Hatcheries Production
0259	Poultry & Eggs Production, NEC
0271	Fur-Bearing Animals & Rabbits
0272	Horses & Other Equines Farms
0273	Animal Aquaculture
0279	Animal Specialties, NEC
0291	General Farms, Primarily Livestock & Animal
07	**AGRICULTURAL SERVICES**
0711	Soil Preparation Services
0721	Crop Planting, Cultivating & Protection Services
0722	Crop Harvesting, Primarily by Machine
0723	Crop Preparation Services for Market
0724	Cotton Ginning
0751	Livestock Services, Except Veterinary
0752	Animal Specialty Services, Except Veterinary
0761	Farm Labor Contractors & Crew Leaders
0762	Farm Management Services
0781	Landscape Counseling & Planning
0782	Lawn & Garden Services
0783	Ornamental Shrub & Tree Services
08	**FORESTRY & FOREST PRODUCTS**
0811	Timber Tracts
0831	Forest Nurseries & Forest Products
0851	Forestry Services
09	**FISHING & HUNTING**
0912	Catching of Finfish
0913	Catching or Taking of Shellfish
0919	Miscellaneous Marine Products Production
0921	Fish Hatcheries & Preserves
0971	Hunting, Trapping & Game Propagation
1791	Structural Steel Erection
1793	Glass & Glazing Work
1794	Excavating & Foundation Work
1796	Installation or Erection of Building Equipment, NEC
10	**METAL MINING & RELATED SERVICES**
1011	Iron Ores Mining
1021	Copper Ores Mining
1031	Lead & Zinc Ores Mining
1041	Gold Ores Mining
1044	Silver Ores Mining
1061	Ferroalloy Ores Mining, Except Vanadium
1081	Metal Mining Services
1094	Uranium-Radium-Vanadium Ores
1099	Miscellaneous Metal Ores Mining, NEC
12	**COAL MINING**
1221	Surface Mining-Bituminous Coal & Lignite
1222	Underground Mining-Bituminous Coal
1231	Anthracite Mining
1241	Coal Mining Services
13	**OIL & GAS PRODUCTION**
1311	Crude Petroleum & Natural Gas
1321	Natural Gas Liquids
1381	Drilling Oil & Gas Wells
1382	Oil & Gas Field Exploration Services
1389	Oil & Gas Field Services, NEC
14	**NONMETALLIC MINERALS**
1411	Dimension Stone
1422	Crushed & Broken Limestone
1423	Crushed & Broken Granite
1429	Crushed & Broken Stone, NEC
1442	Construction Sand & Gravel
1446	Industrial Sand
1455	Kaolin & Ball Clay
1459	Clay, Ceramic & Refractory Minerals, NEC
1474	Potash, Soda & Borate Minerals
1475	Phosphate Rock
1479	Chemical & Fertilizer Mineral Mining, NEC
1481	Nonmetallic Minerals (Except Fuel) Services
1499	Miscellaneous Nonmetallic Minerals, Except Fuels
15	**BUILDING CONTRACTORS**
1521	General Contractors, Single-Family Houses
1522	General Contractors, Other Than Single-Family Houses
1531	Operative Builders
1541	General Contractors, Industrial Buildings & Warehouses
1542	General Contractors, Non-Residential Buildings
16	**HEAVY CONSTRUCTION**
1611	Highway & Street Construction, Except Elevated Hwy.
1622	Bridge, Tunnel & Elevated Highway Construction
1623	Water, Sewer, Power Line, Pipeline & Communications Construction
1629	Heavy Construction, NEC
17	**SPECIAL TRADE CONTRACTORS**
1711	Plumbing, Heating & Air Conditioning Contractors
1721	Painting & Paper Hanging Contractors
1731	Electrical Work Contractors
1741	Masonry, Stone Setting & Other Stone Work
1742	Plastering, Drywall & Insulation Work Contractors
1743	Terrazzo, Tile, Marble & Mosaic Work Contractors
1751	Carpentry Work
1752	Floor Laying & Other Floor Work, NEC
1761	Roofing, Siding & Sheet Metal Work

Code	Title
1771	Concrete Work
1781	Water Well Drilling
20	**FOOD & RELATED PRODUCTS**
2011	Meat Packing Plants
2013	Sausage & Other Prepared Meats
2015	Poultry Slaughtering & Processing
2021	Creamery Butter
2022	Natural, Processed & Imitation Cheese
2023	Dry, Condensed & Evaporated Dairy Products
2024	Ice Cream & Frozen Desserts
2026	Fluid Milk
2032	Canned Specialties
2033	Canned Fruits, Vegetables, Preserves, Jams & Jellies
2034	Dried & Dehydrated Fruits, Vegetables & Soup Mixes
2035	Pickled Fruits & Vegetables, Salad Dressings, Vegetable Sauces & Seasonings
2037	Frozen Fruits, Fruit Juices & Vegetables
2038	Frozen Specialties, NEC
2041	Flour & Other Grain Mill Products
2043	Cereal Breakfast Foods
2044	Rice Milling
2045	Prepared Flour Mixes & Doughs
2046	Wet Corn Milling
2047	Dog & Cat Food
2048	Prepared Feeds for Livestock
2051	Bread & Bakery Products, Except Cookies & Crackers
2052	Cookies & Crackers
2053	Frozen Baking Products, Except Bread
2061	Cane Sugar, Except Refining
2062	Cane Sugar Refining
2063	Beet Sugar Manufacturing
2064	Candy & Confectionery Products
2066	Chocolate & Cocoa Products
2067	Chewing Gum
2068	Salted & Roasted Nuts & Seeds
2074	Cottonseed Oil Mills
2075	Soybean Oil Mills
2076	Vegetable Oil Mills, Except Corn, Cottonseed & Soybean
2077	Animal & Marine Fats & Oils
2079	Shortening, Margarine, Fats & Oils, NEC
2082	Malt Beverages
2083	Malt
2084	Wines, Brandy & Brandy Spirits
2085	Distilled & Blended Liquors
2086	Bottled & Canned Soft Drinks & Carbonated Waters
2087	Flavoring Extracts & Flavoring Syrups, NEC
2091	Canned & Cured Fish & Seafoods
2092	Prepared Fresh or Frozen Fish & Seafoods
2095	Roasted Coffee
2096	Potato Chips, Corn Chips & Similar Snacks
2097	Manufactured Ice
2098	Macaroni, Spaghetti, Vermicelli & Noodles
2099	Food Preparations, NEC
21	**TOBACCO PRODUCTS**
2111	Cigarettes
2121	Cigars
2131	Tobacco (Chewing & Smoking) & Snuff
2141	Tobacco Stemming & Redrying
22	**TEXTILES**
2211	Broad Woven Fabric Mills, Cotton
2221	Broad Woven Fabric Mills, Man-Made Fiber & Silk
2231	Broad Woven Fabric Mills, Wool
2241	Narrow Fabrics & Other Smallwares Mills
2251	Women's Full-Length & Knee-Length Hosiery
2252	Hosiery, NEC
2253	Knit Outerwear Mills
2254	Knit Underwear & Nightwear Mills
2257	Circular Knit Fabric Mills
2258	Lace & Warp Knit Fabric Mills
2259	Knitting Mills, NEC
2261	Finishers of Broad Woven Fabrics of Cotton
2262	Finishers of Broad Woven Fabrics, Man-Made Fiber & Silk
2269	Finishers of Textiles, NEC
2273	Carpets & Rugs
2281	Yarn Spinning Mills
2282	Yarn Throwing, Twisting & Winding Mills
2284	Thread Mills
2295	Coated Fabrics, Not Rubberized
2296	Tire Cord & Fabric
2297	Nonwoven Fabrics
2298	Cordage & Twine
2299	Textile Goods, NEC
23	**APPAREL & OTHER TEXTILE PRODUCTS**
2311	Men's & Boys' Suits, Coats & Overcoats
2321	Men's & Boys' Shirts, Except Work Shirts
2322	Men's & Boys' Underwear & Nightwear
2323	Men's & Boys' Neckwear
2325	Men's & Boys' Trousers & Slacks
2326	Men's & Boys' Work Clothing
2329	Men's & Boys' Clothing, NEC
2331	Women's, Misses' & Juniors' Blouses & Shirts
2335	Women's, Misses' & Juniors' Dresses
2337	Women's, Misses' & Juniors' Suits, Skirts & Coats
2339	Women's, Misses' & Juniors' Outerwear, NEC
2341	Women's, Misses', Children's & Infants' Underwear & Nightwear
2342	Brassieres, Girdles & Allied Garments
2353	Hats, Caps & Millinery
2361	Girls', Children's & Infants' Dresses, Blouses & Shirts
2369	Girls', Children's & Infants' Outerwear, NEC
2371	Fur Goods
2381	Dress & Work Gloves, Except Knit & Leather
2384	Robes & Dressing Gowns
2385	Raincoats & Waterproof Outerwear
2386	Leather & Sheep-Lined Clothing
2387	Apparel Belts
2389	Apparel & Accessories, NEC
2391	Curtains & Draperies, NEC
2392	Housefurnishings, Except Curtains & Draperies
2393	Textile Bags
2394	Canvas & Related Products
2395	Pleating, Tucking for the Trade, Decorative & Novelty Stitching
2396	Automotive Trimmings, Apparel Findings & Related Prods.
2397	Schiffli Machine Embroideries
2399	Fabricated Textile Products, NEC
24	**LUMBER & WOOD PRODUCTS**
2411	Logging Camps & Logging Contractors
2421	Sawmills & Planing Mills, General
2426	Hardwood Dimension & Flooring Mills
2429	Special Product Sawmills, NEC
2431	Millwork
2434	Wood Kitchen Cabinets
2435	Hardwood Veneer & Plywood
2436	Softwood Veneer & Plywood
2439	Structural Wood Members, NEC

Code	Title
2441	Nailed & Lock Corner Wooden Boxes & Shook
2448	Wood Pallets & Skids
2449	Wood Containers, NEC
2451	Mobile Homes
2452	Prefabricated Wood Buildings & Components
2491	Wood Preserving
2493	Reconstituted Wood Products
2499	Wood Products, NEC
25	**FURNITURE & FIXTURES**
2511	Wood Household Furniture, Except Upholstered
2512	Wood Household Furniture, Upholstered
2514	Metal Household Furniture
2515	Mattresses, Foundations & Convertible Beds
2517	Wood Television, Radio, Phonograph & Sewing Machine Cabinets
2519	Household Furniture, NEC
2521	Wood Office Furniture
2522	Metal Office Furniture
2531	Public Building & Related Furniture
2541	Wood Partitions, Shelving & Fixtures
2542	Office & Store Fixtures & Shelving, Except Wood
2591	Drapery Hardward & Window Blinds & Shades
2599	Furniture & Fixtures, NEC
26	**PAPER & RELATED PRODUCTS**
2611	Pulp Mills
2621	Paper Mills
2631	Paperboard Mills
2652	Set-Up Paperboard Boxes
2653	Corrugated & Solid Fiber Boxes
2655	Fiber Cans, Tubes, Drums & Similar Products
2656	Sanitary Food Containers, Except Folding
2657	Folding Paperboard Boxes, Including Sanitary
2671	Coated & Laminated Paper & Plastic Film
2673	Plastics, Foil & Coated Paper Bags
2674	Uncoated Paper & Multiwall Bags
2675	Die-Cut Paper, Paperboard & Cardboard
2676	Sanitary Paper Products
2677	Envelopes
2678	Stationery, Tablets & Related Products
2679	Converted Paper & Paperboard Products, NEC
27	**PRINTING & PUBLISHING**
2711	Newspapers: Publishing, or Publishing & Printing
2721	Periodicals: Publishing, or Publishing & Printing
2731	Books: Publishing, or Publishing & Printing
2732	Book Printing
2741	Miscellaneous Publishing
2752	Commercial Printing, Lithographic
2754	Commercial Printing, Gravure
2759	Commercial Printing, NEC
2761	Manifold Business Forms
2771	Greeting Card Publishing & Printing
2782	Blankbooks, Loose Leaf Binders & Devices
2789	Bookbinding & Related Work
2791	Typesetting
2796	Platemaking & Related Services
28	**CHEMICALS & RELATED PRODUCTS**
2812	Alkalies & Chlorine
2813	Industrial Gases
2816	Inorganic Pigments
2819	Industrial Inorganic Chemicals, NEC
2821	Plastics Materials, Nonvulcanizable Elastomers & Synthetic Resins

Code	Title
2822	Synthetic Rubber (Vulcanizable Elastomers)
2823	Cellulosic Man-Made Fibers
2824	Synthetic Organic Fibers Exept Cellulosic
2833	Medicinal Chemical & Botanical Products
2834	Pharmaceutical Preparations
2835	In Vitro & In Vivo Diagnostic Substances
2836	Biological Products, Except Diagnostic Substances
2841	Soap & Other Detergents, Except Specialty Cleaners
2842	Specialty Cleaning, Polishing & Sanitation Preparations
2843	Surface Active Agents, Finishing Agents & Sulfonated Oils & Assistants
2844	Perfumes, Cosmetics & Other Toilet Preparations
2851	Paints, Varnishes, Lacquers, Enamels & Allied Products
2861	Gum & Wood Chemicals
2865	Cyclic Organic Crudes & Intermediates, Organic Dyes & Pigments
2869	Industrial Organic Chemicals, NEC
2873	Nitrogenous Fertilizers
2874	Phosphatic Fertilizers
2875	Fertilizers, Mixing Only
2879	Pesticides & Agricultural Chemicals, NEC
2891	Adhesives & Sealants
2892	Explosives
2893	Printing Ink
2895	Carbon Black
2899	Chemicals & Chemical Preparations, NEC
29	**PETROLEUM & COAL PRODUCTS**
2911	Petroleum Refining
2951	Asphalt Paving Mixtures & Blocks
2952	Asphalt Felts & Coatings
2992	Lubricating Oils & Greases
2999	Products of Petroleum & Coal, NEC
30	**RUBBER & MISCELLANEOUS PLASTICS**
3011	Tires & Inner Tubes
3021	Rubber & Plastics Footwear
3052	Rubber & Plastics Hose & Belting
3053	Gaskets, Packing & Sealing Devices
3061	Molded, Extruded & Lathe-Cut Rubber Goods
3069	Fabricated Rubber Products, NEC
3081	Unsupported Plastics Film & Sheet
3082	Unsupported Plastics Profile Shapes
3083	Laminated Plastics, Plate, Sheet & Profile Shapes
3084	Plastic Pipe
3085	Plastic Bottles
3086	Plastic Foam Products
3087	Custom Compounding of Purchased Plastic Resins
3088	Plastic Plumbing Fixtures
3089	Plastic Products, NEC
31	**LEATHER & LEATHER PRODUCTS**
3111	Leather Tanning & Finishing
3131	Boot & Shoe Cut Stock & Findings
3142	House Slippers
3143	Men's Footwear, Except Athletic
3144	Women's Footwear, Except Athletic
3149	Footwear, Except Rubber, NEC
3151	Leather Gloves & Mittens
3161	Luggage
3171	Women's Handbags & Purses
3172	Personal Leather Goods, Except Women's Handbags & Purses
3199	Leather Goods, NEC

Code	Title
32	**STONE, CLAY & GLASS PRODUCTS**
3211	Flat Glass
3221	Glass Containers
3229	Pressed & Blown Glass & Glassware, NEC
3231	Glass Products, Made of Purchased Glass
3241	Cement, Hydraulic
3251	Brick & Structural Clay Tile
3253	Ceramic Wall & Floor Tile
3255	Clay Refractories
3259	Structural Clay Products, NEC
3261	Vitreous China Plumbing Fixtures, China & Earthenware Fittings & Bathroom Accessories
3262	Vitreous China Table & Kitchen Articles
3263	Fine Earthenware (Whiteware) Table & Kitchen Articles
3264	Porcelain Electrical Supplies
3269	Pottery Products, NEC
3271	Concrete Block & Brick
3272	Concrete Products, Except Block & Brick
3273	Ready-Mix Concrete
3275	Gypsum Products
3281	Cut Stone & Stone Products
3291	Abrasive Products
3292	Asbestos Products
3299	Nonmetallic Mineral Products, NEC
33	**PRIMARY METAL INDUSTRIES**
3312	Steel Works & Blast Furnaces
3313	Electrometalurgic Products, Except Steel
3315	Steel Wiredrawing, Steel Nails & Spikes
3316	Cold Rolled Steel Sheet, Strip & Bars
3317	Steel Pipe & Tubes
3321	Gray & Ductile Iron Foundries
3322	Malleable Iron Foundries
3324	Steel Investment Foundries
3325	Steel Foundries, NEC
3331	Primary Smelting & Refining of Copper
3334	Primary Production of Aluminum
3339	Primary Smelting & Refining of Nonferrous Metals, Except Copper & Aluminum
3341	Secondary Smelting & Refining of Nonferrous Metals
3351	Rolling, Drawing & Extruding of Copper
3353	Aluminum Sheet, Plate & Foil
3354	Aluminum Extruded Products
3355	Aluminum Rolling & Drawing, NEC
3356	Rolling, Drawing & Extruding of Nonferrous Metals, Except Copper & Aluminum
3357	Drawing & Insulating of Nonferrous Wire
3363	Aluminum Die-Castings
3364	Nonferrous Die-Castings, Except Aluminum
3365	Aluminum Foundries
3366	Copper Foundries
3369	Nonferrous Foundries, Except Aluminum & Copper
3398	Metal Heat Treating
3399	Primary Metal Products, NEC
34	**FABRICATED METAL PRODUCTS**
3411	Metal Cans
3412	Metal Shipping Barrels, Drums, Kegs & Pails
3421	Cutlery
3423	Hand & Edge Tools, Except Machine Tools & Hand Saws
3425	Hand Saws & Blades
3429	Hardware, NEC
3431	Enameled Iron & Metal Sanitary Ware
3432	Plumbing Fixture Fittings & Trim
3433	Heating Equipment, Except Electrical & Warm Air Furnaces
3441	Fabricated Structural Metal
3442	Metal Doors, Sash, Frames, Molding & Trim
3443	Fabricated Plate Work (Boiler Shops)
3444	Sheet Metal Work
3446	Architectural & Ornamental Metal Work
3448	Prefabricated Metal Buildings & Components
3449	Miscellaneous Structural Metal Work
3451	Screw Machine Products
3452	Bolts, Nuts, Screws, Rivets & Washers
3462	Iron & Steel Forgings
3463	Nonferrous Forgings
3465	Automotive Stampings
3466	Metal Crowns & Closures
3469	Metal Stampings, NEC
3471	Electroplating, Plating, Polishing, Anodizing & Coloring
3479	Coating, Engraving & Allied Services, NEC
3482	Small Arms Ammunition
3483	Ammunition, Except Small Arms, NEC
3484	Small Arms
3489	Ordnance & Accessories, NEC
3491	Industrial Valves
3492	Fluid Power Valves & Hose Fittings
3493	Steel Springs, Except Wire
3494	Valves & Pipe Fittings, NEC
3495	Wire Springs
3496	Miscellaneous Fabricated Wire Products
3497	Metal Foil & Leaf
3498	Fabricated Pipe & Fabricated Pipe Fittings
3499	Fabricated Metal Products, NEC
35	**INDUSTRIAL EQUIPMENT & MACHINERY**
3511	Steam, Gas & Hydraulic Turbines
3519	Internal Combustion Engines, NEC
3523	Farm Machinery & Equipment
3524	Lawn & Garden Tractors, Home Lawn & Garden Equipment
3531	Construction Machinery & Equipment
3532	Mining Machinery & Equipment, Except Oil & Gas Field Machinery Equipment
3533	Oil & Gas Field Machinery & Equipment
3534	Elevators & Moving Stairways
3535	Conveyors & Conveying Equipment
3536	Overhead Traveling Cranes, Hoists & Monorail Systems
3537	Industrial Trucks, Tractors, Trailers & Stackers
3541	Machine Tools, Metal Cutting Types
3542	Machine Tools, Metal Forming Types
3543	Industrial Patterns
3544	Special Dies, Tools, Die Sets, Jigs, Fixtures, Industrial Molds
3545	Cutting Tools, Machine Tool Accessories & Machinists Precision Measuring Devices
3546	Power Driven Hand Tools
3547	Rolling Mill Machinery & Equipment
3548	Electric & Gas Welding & Soldering Equipment
3549	Metalworking Machinery, NEC
3552	Textile Machinery
3553	Woodworking Machinery
3554	Paper Industries Machinery
3555	Printing Trades Machinery & Equipment
3556	Food Products Machinery
3559	Special Industry Machinery, NEC
3561	Pumps & Pumping Equipment
3562	Ball & Roller Bearings
3563	Air & Gas Compressors
3564	Industrial & Commercial Fans, Blowers & Air Purification Equipment
3565	Packaging Machinery

Code	Title
3566	Speed Changers, Industrial High Speed Drives & Gears
3567	Industrial Process Furnaces & Ovens
3568	Mechanical Power Transmission Equipment, NEC
3569	General Industrial Machinery & Equipment, NEC
3571	Electronic Computers
3572	Computer Storage Devices
3575	Computer Terminals
3577	Computer Peripheral Equipment, NEC
3578	Calculating & Accounting Machines, Except Electronic Computers
3579	Office Machines, NEC
3581	Automatic Vending Machines
3582	Commercial Laundry, Dry Cleaning & Pressing Machines
3585	Air Conditioning, Warm Air Heating Equipment & Commercial & Industrial Refrigeration Equipment
3586	Measuring & Dispensing Pumps
3589	Service Industry Machines, NEC
3592	Carburetors, Pistons, Piston Rings & Valves
3593	Fluid Power Cylinders & Actuators
3594	Fluid Power Pumps & Motors
3596	Scales & Balances, Except Laboratory
3599	Industrial & Commercial Machinery & Equipment, NEC
36	**ELECTRONIC & ELECTRIC EQUIPMENT**
3612	Power, Distribution & Specialty Transformers
3613	Switchgear & Switchboard Apparatus
3621	Motors & Generators
3624	Carbon & Graphite Products
3625	Relays & Industrial Controls
3629	Electrical Industrial Apparatus, NEC
3631	Household Cooking Equipment
3632	Household Refrigerators & Home & Farm Freezers
3633	Household Laundry Equipment
3634	Electric Housewares & Fans
3635	Household Vacuum Cleaners
3639	Household Appliances, NEC
3641	Electric Lamp Bulbs & Tubes
3643	Current-Carrying Wiring Devices
3644	Noncurrent-Carrying Wiring Devices
3645	Residential Electric Lighting Fixtures
3646	Commercial, Industrial & Institutional Electric Lighting Fixtures
3647	Vehicular Lighting Equipment
3648	Lighting Equipment, NEC
3651	Household Audio & Video Equipment
3652	Phonograph Records & Pre-Recorded Audio Tapes & Discs
3661	Telephone & Telegraph Apparatus
3663	Radio & TV Broadcasting & Communications Equipment
3669	Communications Equipment, NEC
3671	Electron Tubes
3672	Printed Circuit Boards
3674	Semiconductors & Related Devices
3675	Electronic Capacitors
3676	Electronic Resistors
3677	Electronic Coils, Transformers & Other Inductors
3678	Electronic Connectors
3679	Electronic Components, NEC
3691	Storage Batteries
3692	Primary Batteries, Dry & Wet
3694	Electrical Equipment for Internal Combustion Engines
3695	Magnetic & Optical Recording Media
3699	Electrical Machinery, Equipment & Supplies, NEC
37	**TRANSPORTATION EQUIPMENT**
3711	Motor Vehicles & Passenger Car Bodies
3713	Truck & Bus Bodies
3714	Motor Vehicle Parts & Accessories
3715	Truck Trailers
3716	Motor Homes
3721	Aircraft
3724	Aircraft Engines & Engine Parts
3728	Aircraft Parts & Auxiliary Equipment, NEC
3731	Ship Building & Repairing
3732	Boat Building & Repairing
3743	Railroad Equipment
3751	Motorcycles, Bicycles & Parts
3761	Guided Missiles & Space Vehicles
3764	Guided Missile & Space Vehicle Propulsion Units & Propulsion Unit Parts
3769	Guided Missile & Space Vehicle Parts & Auxiliary Equipment, NEC
3792	Travel Trailers & Campers
3795	Tanks & Tank Components
3799	Transportation Equipment, NEC
38	**INSTRUMENTS & RELATED PRODUCTS**
3812	Navigation, Guidance, Search & Detection Systems & Instruments
3821	Laboratory Apparatus & Furniture
3822	Automatic Controls for Regulating Residential & Commercial Environments & Appliances
3823	Industrial Instruments for Measurement, Display & Control of Process Variables & Related Products
3824	Totalizing Fluid Meters & Counting Devices
3825	Instruments for Measuring & Testing of Electricity & Electrical Signals
3826	Laboratory Analytical Instruments
3827	Optical Instruments & Lenses
3829	Measuring & Controlling Devices, NEC
3841	Surgical & Medical Instruments & Apparatus
3842	Orthopedic, Prosthetic & Surgical Supplies
3843	Dental Equipment & Supplies
3844	X-Ray Apparatus, Tubes & Equipment
3845	Electromedical & Electrotherapeutic Apparatus
3851	Ophthalmic Goods
3861	Photographic Equipment & Supplies
3873	Watches, Clocks, & Clockwork Operated Devices & Parts
39	**MISCELLANEOUS MANUFACTURING**
3912	Jewelry, Precious Metal
3914	Silverware, Plated Ware & Stainless Steel Ware
3915	Jewelers Findings & Materials & Lapidary Work
3925	Minerals & Earths, Ground or Otherwise Treated
3926	Mineral Wool
3927	Nonclay Refractories
3931	Musical Instruments
3942	Dolls & Stuffed Toys
3944	Games, Toys & Children's Vehicles, Except Dolls & Bicycles
3951	Pens, Mechanical Pencils & Parts
3952	Lead Pencils, Crayons & Artists' Materials
3953	Marking Devices
3955	Carbon Paper & Inked Ribbons
3961	Costume Jewelry & Costume Novelties, Except Precious Metal
3965	Fasteners, Buttons, Needles & Pins
3991	Brooms & Brushes
3993	Signs & Advertising Displays
3995	Burial Caskets
3996	Linoleum, Asphalt-Feltbase & Other Hard Surface Floor Coverings, NEC

Code	Title
3999	Manufacturing Industries, NEC
40	**RAILROAD TRANSPORTATION**
4011	Railroads, Line-Haul Operating
4013	Railroad Switching & Terminal Establishments
41	**LOCAL & INTERURBAN PASSENGER TRANSIT**
4111	Local & Suburban Transit
4119	Local Passenger Transportation, NEC
4121	Taxicabs
4131	Intercity & Rural Bus Transportation
4141	Local Bus Charter Service
4142	Bus Charter Service, Except Local
4151	School Buses
4173	Terminal & Passenger Transportation Service Facilities for Motor Vehicles
42	**TRUCKING & WAREHOUSING**
4212	Local Trucking Without Storage
4213	Trucking, Except Local
4214	Local Trucking With Storage
4215	Courier Services, Except by Air
4221	Farm Product Warehousing & Storage
4222	Refrigerated Warehousing & Storage
4225	General Warehousing & Storage
4226	Special Warehousing & Storage, NEC
4231	Terminal & Joint Terminal Maintenance Facilities for Motor Freight Transportation
43	**U.S. POSTAL SERVICE**
4311	U.S. Postal Service
44	**WATER TRANSPORTATION**
4412	Deep Sea Freight Transportation-Foreign
4424	Deep Sea Freight Transportation-Domestic
4432	Great Lakes Freight Transportation
4449	Freight Transportation-Water, NEC
4481	Passenger Transportation-Deep Sea
4482	Ferries
4489	Water Transportation-Passenger, NEC
4491	Marine Cargo Handling
4492	Towing & Tugboat Services
4493	Marinas
4499	Water Transportation Services, NEC
45	**AIR TRANSPORTATION**
4512	Air Transportation, Scheduled
4513	Air Courier Services
4522	Air Transportation, Non-Scheduled
4581	Airports, Flying Fields & Airport Terminal Services
46	**PIPELINES, EXCEPT GAS**
4612	Crude Petroleum Pipe Lines
4613	Refined Petroleum Pipe Lines
4619	Pipe Lines, NEC
47	**TRANSPORTATION SERVICES**
4724	Travel Agencies
4725	Tour Operators
4729	Arrangement of Passenger Transportation, NEC
4731	Arrangement of Transportation of Freight & Cargo
4741	Rental of Railroad Cars
4783	Packing & Crating
4785	Inspection & Weighing Services for Motor Vehicle Transportation
4789	Transportation Services, NEC

Code	Title
48	**COMMUNICATIONS**
4812	Radio Telephone Communications
4813	Telephone Communications, Except Radio Telephone
4822	Telegraph & Other Message Communications
4832	Radio Broadcasting Stations
4833	Television Broadcasting Stations
4841	Cable & Other Pay Television Services
4899	Communication Services, NEC
49	**ELECTRIC, GAS & SANITARY SERVICES**
4911	Electric Services
4922	Natural Gas Transmission
4923	Natural Gas Transmission & Distribution
4924	Natural Gas Distribution
4925	Mixed, Manufactured or Liquefied Petroleum Gas Production and/or Distribution
4931	Electric & Other Services Combined
4932	Gas & Other Services Combined
4939	Combination Utilities, NEC
4941	Water Supply
4952	Sewage Systems
4953	Refuse Systems
4959	Sanitary Services, NEC
4961	Steam & Air-Conditioning Supply
4971	Irrigation Systems
50	**DURABLE WHOLESALE TRADE**
5012	Distribution of Automobiles & Other Motor Vehicles
5013	Motor Vehicle Supplies & New Parts
5014	Tires & Tubes
5015	Motor Vehicle Parts, Used
5021	Furniture
5023	Home Furnishings
5031	Lumber, Plywood, Millwork & Wood Panels
5033	Roofing, Siding & Insulation Materials
5039	Construction Materials, NEC
5043	Photographic Equipment & Supplies
5044	Office Equipment
5045	Computers & Computer Peripheral Equipment & Software
5046	Commercial Equipment
5047	Medical, Dental & Hospital Equipment & Supplies
5048	Ophthalmic Goods
5049	Professional Equipment & Supplies
5051	Metals Service Centers & Offices
5052	Coal & Other Minerals & Ores
5063	Electrical Apparatus & Equipment
5064	Electrical Appliances, Television & Radio Sets
5065	Electronic Parts & Equipment
5072	Hardware
5074	Plumbing & Heating Equipment & Supplies
5075	Warm Air Heating & Air Conditioning Equipment
5078	Refrigeration Equipment & Supplies
5082	Construction & Mining Machinery & Equipment, Except Petroleum, Wholesale
5083	Farm & Garden Machinery & Equipment
5084	Industrial Machinery & Equipment
5085	Industrial Supplies
5087	Service Establishment Equipment & Supplies
5088	Transportation Equipment & Supplies, Except Motor Vehicles
5091	Sporting & Recreational Goods & Supplies
5092	Toys & Hobby Goods & Supplies
5093	Scrap & Waste Materials
5094	Jewelry, Watches, Precious Stones & Precious Metals, Wholesale
5099	Wholesale Durable Goods, NEC

Code	Title
51	**NONDURABLE WHOLESALE TRADE**
5111	Printing & Writing Paper
5112	Stationery & Office Supplies
5113	Industrial & Personal Service Paper
5122	Drugs, Drug Proprietaries & Sundries
5131	Piece Goods, Notions & Other Dry Goods
5136	Men's & Boys' Clothing & Furnishings
5137	Women's, Children's & Infants' Clothing & Accessories
5139	Footwear
5141	Groceries, General Line
5142	Packaged Frozen Foods
5143	Dairy Products, Except Dried or Canned
5144	Poultry & Poultry Products
5145	Confectionery
5146	Fish & Seafoods
5147	Meats & Meat Products
5148	Fresh Fruits & Vegetables
5149	Grocers & Related Products, NEC
5153	Grains & Field Beans-Buying & Marketing
5154	Livestock Buying & Marketing
5159	Farm Product Raw Materials Buying & Marketing, NEC
5162	Plastics Materials & Basic Forms & Shapes
5169	Chemicals & Allied Products, NEC
5171	Petroleum Bulk Stations & Terminals
5172	Petroleum & Petroleum Products, NEC-Except Bulk Stations & Terminals-Wholesale
5181	Beer & Ale
5182	Wines & Distilled Alcoholic Beverages
5191	Farm Supplies
5192	Books, Periodicals & Newspapers
5193	Flowers, Nursery Stock & Florists' Supplies-Wholesale
5194	Tobacco & Tobacco Products
5198	Paints, Varnishes & Supplies
5199	Nondurable Goods, NEC
52	**RETAIL BUILDING MATERIALS & GARDEN SUPPLIES**
5211	Lumber & Other Building Materials Dealers
5231	Paint, Glass & Wallpaper Stores
5251	Hardware Stores
5261	Retail Nurseries, Lawn & Garden Supply Stores
5271	Mobile Home Dealers
53	**RETAIL GENERAL MERCHANDISE STORES**
5311	Department Stores
5331	Variety Stores
5399	Miscellaneous General Merchandise Stores
54	**RETAIL FOOD STORES**
5411	Grocery Stores
5421	Meat & Fish Markets, Including Freezer Provisions
5441	Candy, Nut & Confectionary Stores
5451	Dairy Products Stores
5461	Retail Bakeries
5499	Miscellaneous Food Stores
55	**RETAIL AUTOMOTIVE DEALERS & SERVICE STATIONS**
5511	Motor Vehicle Dealers (New & Used Cars)
5521	Motor Vehicle Dealers (Used Cars Only)
5531	Auto & Home Supply Stores
5541	Gasoline Service Stations
5551	Boat Dealers
5561	Recreational Vehicle Dealers
5571	Motorcycle Dealers
5599	Automotive Dealers, NEC

Code	Title
56	**RETAIL APPAREL STORES**
5611	Men's & Boys' Clothing & Accessory Stores
5621	Women's Clothing Stores
5632	Women's Accessory & Specialty Stores
5641	Children's & Infants' Wear Stores
5651	Family Clothing Stores
5661	Shoe Stores
5699	Miscellaneous Apparel & Accessory Stores
57	**RETAIL FURNITURE & HOME FURNISHINGS**
5712	Furniture Stores
5713	Floor Covering Stores
5714	Drapery, Curtain & Upholstery Stores
5719	Miscellaneous Home Furnishing Stores
5722	Household Appliance Stores
5731	Radio, Television & Consumer Electronic Stores
5734	Computer & Computer Software Stores
5735	Record & Prerecorded Tape Stores
5736	Musical Instrument Stores
58	**DINING & DRINKING PLACES**
5812	Eating Places
5813	Drinking Places (Alcoholic Beverages)
59	**MISCELLANEOUS RETAIL**
5912	Drug Stores & Proprietary Stores
5921	Liquor Stores
5932	Used Merchandise Stores
5941	Sporting Goods & Bicycle Shops
5942	Book Stores
5943	Stationery Stores
5944	Jewelry Stores
5945	Hobby, Toy & Game Shops
5946	Camera & Photographic Supply Stores
5947	Gift, Novelty & Souvenir Shops
5948	Luggage & Leather Goods Stores
5949	Sewing, Needlework & Piece Goods Stores
5961	Catalog, Mail Order Houses
5962	Automatic Merchandising Machine Operators
5963	Direct Selling Establishments
5983	Fuel Oil Dealers
5984	Bottled or Bulk Liquefied Petroleum (LP) Gas Dealers
5989	Fuel Dealers, NEC
5992	Tobacco Stores & Stands
5994	News Dealers & Newsstands
5995	Optical Goods Stores
5999	Miscellaneous Retail Stores, NEC
60	**BANKS & BANKING SERVICES**
6011	Federal Reserve Banks
6019	Central Reserve Depository Institutions, NEC
6021	National Commercial Banks
6022	State Commercial Banks & Trust Companies
6029	Commercial Banks, NEC
6035	Savings Institutions, Federally Chartered
6036	Savings Institutions, Not Federally Chartered
6061	Credit Unions, Federally Chartered
6062	Credit Unions, Not Federally Chartered
6081	Branches & Agencies of Foreign Banks
6082	Foreign Trade & International Banking Institutions
6091	Nondeposit Trust Facilities
6099	Functions Related to Depository Banking, NEC
61	**NONDEPOSITORY FINANCIAL INSTITUTIONS**
6111	Federal & Federally Sponsored Credit Agencies

Code	Title
6141	Personal Credit Institutions
6153	Short-Term Business Credit Institutions, Except Agricultural
6159	Miscellaneous Business Credit Institutions
6162	Mortgage Bankers & Loan Correspondents
6163	Loan Brokers
62	**SECURITY & COMMODITY BROKERS**
6211	Security Brokers, Dealers & Flotation Companies
6221	Commodity Contracts Brokers & Dealers
6231	Security & Commodity Exchanges
6282	Investment Advice
6289	Services Allied With Exchange of Securities or Commodities, NEC
63	**INSURANCE CARRIERS**
6311	Life Insurance
6321	Accident & Health Insurance
6324	Hospital & Medical Service Plans
6331	Fire, Marine & Casualty Insurance
6351	Surety Insurance
6361	Title Insurance
6371	Pension, Health & Welfare Funds
6399	Insurance Carriers, NEC
64	**INSURANCE AGENTS, BROKERS & SERVICES**
6411	Insurance Agents, Brokers & Services
65	**REAL ESTATE**
6512	Operators of Nonresidential Buildings
6513	Operators of Apartment Buildings
6514	Operators of Dwellings Other Than Apartment Buildings
6515	Operators of Residential Mobile Home Sites
6517	Lessors of Railroad Property
6519	Lessors of Real Property, NEC
6531	Real Estate Agents & Managers
6541	Title Abstract Offices
6552	Land Subdividers & Developers, Except Cemeteries
6553	Cemetery Subdividers & Developers
67	**HOLDING & INVESTMENT OFFICES**
6712	Offices of Bank Holding Companies
6719	Offices of Holding Companies, NEC
6722	Management Investment Companies, Open-End
6726	Unit Investment Trusts, Face-Amount Certificate Offices, Closed-End Management Investment Offices
6732	Educational Religious & Charitable Trusts
6733	Trusts, Except Educational, Religious & Charitable
6792	Oil Royalty Traders
6794	Patent Owners & Lessors
6798	Real Estate Investment Trusts
6799	Investors, NEC
70	**HOTELS & LODGING PLACES**
7011	Hotels & Motels
7021	Rooming & Boarding Houses
7032	Sporting & Recreational Camps
7033	Recreational Vehicle Parks & Campsites
7041	Organization Hotels & Lodging Houses, Membership Basis
72	**PERSONAL SERVICES**
7211	Power Laundries, Family & Commercial
7212	Garment Pressing & Agents for Laundries & Dry Cleaners
7213	Linen Supply Services
7215	Coin-Operated Laundries & Dry Cleaning
7216	Dry Cleaning Plants, Except Rug Cleaning
7217	Carpet & Upholstery Cleaning
7218	Industrial Launderers
7219	Laundry & Garment Services, NEC
7221	Photographic Studios, Portrait
7231	Beauty Shops
7241	Barber Shops
7251	Shoe Repair Shops & Shoe Shine Parlors
7261	Funeral Service & Crematories
7291	Tax Return Preparation Services
7299	Miscellaneous Personal Services, NEC
73	**BUSINESS SERVICES**
7311	Advertising Agencies
7312	Outdoor Advertising Services
7313	Radio, Television & Publishers' Advertising Representatives
7319	Advertising, NEC
7322	Adjustment & Collection Services
7323	Credit Reporting Services
7331	Direct Mail Advertising Services
7334	Photocopy & Duplicating Service
7335	Commercial Photography
7336	Commercial Art & Graphic Design
7338	Secretarial & Court Reporting Services
7342	Disinfecting & Pest Control Services
7349	Building Cleaning & Maintenance Services, NEC
7352	Medical Equipment Rental & Leasing
7353	Heavy Construction Equipment Rental & Leasing
7359	Equipment Rental & Leasing, NEC
7361	Computer Programming Services
7372	Prepackaged Software
7373	Computer Integrated Systems Design
7374	Computer Processing & Processing & Data Preparation Services
7375	Information Retrieval Services
7376	Computer Facilities Management Services
7377	Computer Rental & Leasing
7378	Computer Maintenance & Repair
7379	Computer Related Services, NEC
7381	Detective, Guard & Armored Car Services
7382	Security Systems Services
7383	News Syndicates
7384	Photofinishing Laboratories
7389	Business Services, NEC
75	**AUTO REPAIR, SERVICES & PARKING**
7513	Truck Rental & Leasing, Without Drivers
7514	Passenger Car Rental
7515	Passenger Car Leasing
7519	Utility Trailer & Recreational Vehicle Rental
7521	Automobile Parking
7532	Top, Body, Upholstery Repair & Paint Shops
7533	Automotive Exhaust System Repair Shops
7534	Tire Retreading & Repair Shops
7536	Automotive Glass Replacement Shops
7537	Automotive Transmission Repair Shops
7538	General Automotive Repair Shops
76	**MISCELLANEOUS REPAIR SERVICES**
7622	Radio & Television Repair Shops
7623	Refrigeration & Air Conditioning Service & Repair Shops
7629	Electrical & Electronic Repair Shops, NEC
7631	Watch, Clock & Jewelry Repair
7641	Reupholstery & Furniture Repair
7692	Welding Repair
7694	Armature Rewinding Shops
7699	Repair Shops & Related Services, NEC

Code	Title
78	**MOTION PICTURES**
7812	Motion Picture & Video Tape Production
7819	Services Allied to Motion Picture Production
7822	Motion Picture & Video Tape Distribution
7829	Services Allied to Motion Picture Distribution
7832	Motion Picture Theaters, Except Drive-In
7833	Drive-In Motion Picture Theaters
7841	Video Tape Rental
79	**AMUSEMENT & RECREATION**
7911	Dance Halls, Studios & Schools
7922	Theatrical Producers (Except Motion Picture) & Miscellaneous Theatrical Services
7929	Bands, Orchestras, Actors & Other Entertainers & Entertainment Groups
7933	Bowling Alleys
7941	Professional Sports Clubs & Promoters
7948	Racing, Including Track Operation
7991	Physical Fitness Facilities
7992	Public Golf Courses
7993	Coin-Operated Amusement Devices
7996	Amusement Parks
7997	Membership Sports & Recreation Clubs
7999	Amusement & Recreation Services, NEC
80	**HEALTH SERVICES**
8011	Offices & Clinics of Doctors of Medicine
8021	Offices & Clinics of Dentists
8031	Offices & Clinics of Doctors of Osteopathy
8041	Offices & Clinics of Chiropractors
8042	Offices & Clinics of Optometrists
8043	Offices & Clinics of Podiatrists
8049	Offices & Clinics of Health Practitioners, NEC
8051	Skilled Nursing Care Facilities
8052	Intermediate Care Facilities
8059	Nursing & Personal Care Facilities, NEC
8062	General Medical & Surgical Hospitals
8063	Psychiatric Hospitals
8069	Specialty Hospitals, Except Psychiatric
8071	Medical Laboratories
8072	Dental Laboratories
8082	Home Health Care Services
8092	Kidney Dialysis Centers
8093	Specialty Outpatient Facilities, NEC
8099	Health & Allied Services, NEC
81	**LEGAL SERVICES**
8111	Legal Services
82	**EDUCATIONAL SERVICES**
8211	Elementary & Secondary Schools
8221	Colleges, Universities & Professional Schools
8222	Junior Colleges & Technical Institutes
8231	Libraries & Information Centers
8243	Data Processing Schools
8244	Business & Secretarial Schools
8249	Vocational Schools, NEC
8299	Schools & Educational Services, NEC
83	**SOCIAL SERVICES**
8322	Individual & Family Social Services
8331	Job Training & Vocational Rehabilitation Services
8351	Child Day Care Services
8361	Residential Care
8399	Social Services, NEC

Code	Title
84	**MUSEUMS & BOTANICAL OR ZOOLOGICAL GARDENS**
8412	Museums & Art Galleries
8422	Arboreta & Botanical or Zoological Gardens
86	**MEMBERSHIP ORGANIZATIONS**
8611	Business Associations
8621	Professional Membership Organizations
8631	Labor Unions & Similar Labor Organizations
8641	Civic, Social & Fraternal Associations
8651	Political Organizations
8661	Religious Organizations
8699	Membership Organizations, NEC
87	**ENGINEERING & MANAGEMENT SERVICES**
8711	Engineering Services
8712	Architectural Services
8713	Surveying Services
8721	Accounting, Auditing & Bookkeeping Services
8731	Commercial, Physical & Biological Research
8732	Commercial, Economic, Sociological & Educational Research
8733	Noncommercial Research Organizations
8734	Testing Laboratories
8741	Management Services
8742	Management Consulting Services
8743	Public Relations Services
8744	Facilities Support Management Services
8748	Business Consulting Services, NEC
88	**PRIVATE HOUSEHOLDS**
8811	Private Households
89	**SERVICES, NEC**
8999	Services, NEC
91	**EXECUTIVE, LEGISLATIVE & GENERAL GOVERNMENT**
9111	Executive Offices
9121	Legislative Bodies
9131	Executive & Legislative Offices Combined
9199	General Government, NEC
92	**JUSTICE, PUBLIC ORDER & SAFETY**
9211	Courts
9221	Police Protection
9222	Legal Counsel & Prosecution
9223	Correctional Institutions
9224	Fire Protection
9229	Public Order & Safety, NEC
93	**PUBLIC FINANCE ADMINISTRATION**
9311	Public Finance, Taxation & Monetary Policy
7539	Automobile Repair Shops, NEC
7542	Car Washes
7549	Automobile Services, Except Repair & Washes
94	**HUMAN RESOURCES ADMINISTRATION**
9411	Administration of Educational Programs
9431	Administration of Public Health Programs
9441	Administration of Social Manpower Programs
9451	Administration of Veterans' Affairs
95	**ENVIRONMENTAL QUALITY & HOUSING**
9511	Air & Water Resource & Solid Waste Management
9512	Land, Mineral, Wildlife & Forest Conservation
9531	Administration of Housing Programs
9532	Administration of Urban Planning & Community & Rural Development

Code	Title
96	**ECONOMIC PROGRAM ADMINISTRATION**
9611	Administration of General Economic Programs
9621	Regulation & Administration of Transportation Programs
9631	Regulation & Administration of Communication, Electric, Gas & Other Utilities
9641	Regulation of Agricultural Marketing & Commodities
9651	Regulation, Licensing & Inspection of Miscellaneous Commercial Sectors
9661	Space Research & Technology
97	**NATIONAL SECURITY & INTERNATIONAL AFFAIRS**
9711	National Security
9721	International Affairs
99	**NONCLASSIFIABLE ESTABLISHMENTS**
9999	Nonclassifiable Establishments